2014 Higher Education Directory®

Published by

Higher Education Publications, Inc.

Edited by

Mary Pat Rodenhouse

Editor Emerita

Jeanne M. Burke

Reston, Virginia

2014

2014 Edition

Higher Education Publications, Inc.
1801 Robert Fulton Drive, Suite 555
Reston, VA 20191-4387
(888) 349-7715
(571) 313-0478
FAX (571) 313-0526
Email: info@hepinc.com
Internet address: www.hepinc.com

Carnegie classification codes with permission from
The Carnegie Foundation for the Advancement of Teaching.

Internet addresses (URL's) were originally drawn from lists maintained by Washington and Lee University and the University of North Carolina-Chapel Hill and through the annual survey sent out by Higher Education Publications, Inc.

Printed in the United States of America

ISBN-10: 0-914927-71-X; ISBN-13: 978-0-914927-71-6
ISSN 0736-0797
Library of Congress Catalogue Card Number: 83-641119
Library of Congress Cataloging-in Publication Data

HEP. . . Higher Education Directory®
Reston, VA; Higher Education Publications.
V.: 28cm
Annual
Began with issue for 1983.

A directory of accredited postsecondary, degree-granting institutions in the U.S., its possessions and territories accredited by regional, national, professional and specialized agencies recognized as accrediting bodies by the U.S. Secretary of Education and the Council for Higher Education Accreditation (CHEA) which honors recognition provided by the former Council on Postsecondary Accreditation (COPA)/Commission on Recognition of Postsecondary Accreditation (CORPA)
Description based on 2014.
Cover title: 2014 Higher Education Directory®
Spine title: 2014 Higher Education Directory® Thirty-second Edition

ISSN 0736-0797 = The Higher Education Directory®.

1. Education, Higher—United States—Directories.
2. Recognized accrediting agencies and associations—United States—Directories.
3. Acronyms, explanatory notes and symbols—United States—Directories.
4. Institution changes (additions, deletions, mergers and name changes)—United States—Directories.
5. Administrative officers, titles and title codes—United States—Directories.
6. United States Department of Education offices, statewide agencies for higher education and educational associations (and consortia)—United States—Directories.
7. Religious affiliation by denomination.
8. Carnegie classification codes.
9. Statistics.
10. Universities and colleges—United States—Directories.
11. College administrators alphabetical listing, phone numbers—United States—Directories.
12. Regional, national, professional and specialized accreditation alphabetical listing—United States—Directories.
13. Institutional FICE & Unit ID Number listing—United States—Directories.
14. Institutional alphabetical listing—United States—Directories.

I. Higher Education Publications, Inc.
II. Title: Higher Education Directory®.

L901.E34 378.73-dc19 83-641119 AACR 2 MARC-S

Table of Contents

Acknowledgments iv

Foreword v

Accrediting Agencies vi

Abbreviations, Explanatory Notes and Symbols xv

Institution Changes xix

Codes and Descriptions of Administrative Officers xxvi

Statewide Agencies of Higher Education xxvii

Higher Education Associations xxxi

Consortia of Institutions of Higher Education xl

Association Name Index xliii

Institutions by Religious Affiliation xliv

Carnegie Classification Code Definitions xlvii

Statistics xlviii

Reclassified Branch Campuses xlix

Universities, Colleges and Schools 1

Index of Key Administrators 557

Accreditation Index of Institutions by Regional, National, Professional and Specialized Agencies 977

Index of FICE Numbers 1029

Index of Universities, Colleges and Schools 1043

Acknowledgments

Thirty-one years ago, Higher Education Publications, Inc. was formed to produce a directory to succeed the Department of Education's *Education Directory: Colleges and Universities.*

When we undertook the *Higher Education Directory* project, we worked toward three main goals: To publish accurate data, to make the directory more usable, and to have the directory ready for distribution much earlier in the academic year.

We continue to meet these objectives and more, while keeping the changing landscape of reference publishing in mind. This year we modified our definition of branch campuses to conform to the definition used by the United States Department of Education (34 CFR §600.2). As a result, we have added or reclassified over 1,400 institutional listings. Due to space limitations in the printed directory, we list limited information on these additional branch campuses, but more detailed information is available online with HED-Connect.

Our thanks to the thousands of people who have supplied us the necessary data contained in the directory. We had a response/update rate of 99.5%—truly outstanding! We are most appreciative of the many subscribers who have supported us in our efforts to bring you the most accurate and current information available. And, a special thanks to all of you who suggest improvements to our directory.

We continue to work on a tight schedule starting in mid-June to distribution in November—especially when you consider the complexity and increase in the size of the database.

The accuracy and completeness of the contents of the 2014 edition was assured by a group of editors, updating and proofing specialists including Mary Pat Rodenhouse, Jodi Mondragon, Emmy Brown, Jackie Hafner, Doris Jean, Pat Parks and Phil Hafner. Barbara Herrman handled our typesetting. Mark Schreiber managed the HED-Connect update system and the database.

You may be familiar with our Website, but if you have not yet visited it, I encourage you to go to www.hepinc.com. The site features the latest news on higher education, accreditations and administrative changes along with many helpful resources. Also, please visit our new LinkedIn and Facebook pages. We feel that our increased Internet and social media presence will help us to continue to meet the goals we established for ourselves thirty-one years ago—to provide you with the most authoritative, timely and accurate information on the higher education community.

Frederick F. Hafner
Publisher

Reston, Virginia

Foreword

The 2014 edition of the *Higher Education Directory®* contains listings of accredited, degree-granting institutions of postsecondary education in the United States and its territories.

Criteria for Listing in this Directory

To be listed in this Directory, an institution must meet the following guidelines:

(1) They are degree-granting (legally authorized to offer and are offering a program of college-level studies leading toward a degree[1]);
(2) They have submitted the information required for listing; and
(3) They meet one of the following criteria for listing:
   A. The institution is accredited at the college level by an accrediting agency that is recognized by the U.S. Secretary of Education;
   B. The institution holds pre-accredited status with an accrediting agency recognized by the U.S. Secretary of Education whose recognition includes the pre-accreditation status;
   C. The institution is accredited at the college level by an accrediting agency recognized by the Council for Higher Education Accreditation (CHEA).

"College level" means a postsecondary associate, baccalaureate, post-baccalaureate, or rabbinical education program.

Verification of Accreditations

Verification of each accreditation for all institutions was done by comparing the accreditation against the current Directory (and updated lists) for each respective regional, national, professional and specialized association or agency, along with telephone calls to numerous accrediting associations whenever there was a question of accuracy. Over 19,000 accreditations were verified through September 2013.

The reader is reminded that many institutions have programs which may not be recognized by a professional or specialized association, but are considered fine programs. The institutions may or may not have sought such recognition.

General Organization of the Directory

Our approach to the organization of the material is to make the desired information readable and easy to find. There are four indexes which are cross-referenced to the main institutional listing.

A. Prologue
   1. Accrediting agencies with addresses. Regional accrediting commissions are listed alphabetically while national, professional and specialized bodies are listed alphabetically under headings showing their specialties.
   2. Acronyms used in the Directory for accrediting bodies are listed alphabetically.
   3. Explanatory notes and symbols.
   4. U.S. postal abbreviations of states.
   5. Institution changes.
   6. Administrative officers' description and job codes.
   7. U.S. Department of Education offices.
   8. Statewide agencies of higher education.
   9. Higher education associations.
   10. Consortia of institutions of higher education.
   11. Association name index.
   12. Religious affiliation by denomination.
   13. Carnegie classification codes.
   14. Statistical data.

B. College and university listings by state with institutional characteristics and administrative officers.
   1. Institution Name. If an * appears before the institution's name, it is a part of a system. A line between institutions separates two systems.
   2. Alpha Code. The first institution listed on a page is coded (A), the second (B), etc. The Administrators' index is also coded to enable the reader to locate the desired institution quickly.
   3. Address.
   4. County.
   5. FICE Identification. This was the Federal Interagency Commission on Education number originally assigned by the Department of Education. We continue to use the term FICE. However, the Department of Education in their Office of Student Financial Assistance uses OPEID, Office of Postsecondary Education Identification. OPEID consists of the first six digits of the FICE plus two more digits indicating branch campuses. Numbers beginning with 66 are for accredited institutions for which we cannot locate a FICE or OPEID number. These are identification numbers only.
   6. Telephone Number.
   7. Unit ID Number. A unique number developed by the National Center for Education Statistics (NCES) for the Education Department's IPEDS Reports.
   8. Carnegie Classification Code. (see page **xlvii**)
   9. Main FAX Number.
   10. School Calendar.
   11. URL (Universal Resource Locator).
   12. Date Established.
   13. Annual Tuition & Fees for 2013-14 school year.
   14. Fall 2012 Enrollment. Head count (not FTE) in degree programs as reported on the latest IPEDS survey.
   15. Type of Student Body.
   16. Affiliation or Control.
   17. IRS Status.
   18. Highest Degree Offered.
   19. Program. This is the general type of education offered.
   20. Accreditation (see page **vi**). **N.B. Institutional accreditation is in bold face.**
   21. Administrative and academic officers with job classification code (see page **xxvi** for descriptions).
   22. **New for 2014:** Non-system branch campuses. The names of these campuses are in italic type and their listings are shortened. Non-system branch campuses are listed if they are identified by the parent institutions' accrediting organization as a branch campus.

C. Index of administrators is an alphabetical listing of all the administrators with their most direct phone number and E-mail address. The page and reference letter indicate the page on which the administrator's institution listing begins.

D. Index of regional, national, professional and specialized accreditation alphabetically by state. This index standardizes and simplifies reviewing of the 139 accrediting classifications.

E. FICE number index. Numeric listing of FICE number and school.

F. Alphabetic index of institutions.

[1]The *Higher Education Directory®* lists degree-granting institutions approved by regional, national, professional or specialized accrediting agencies.

Accrediting Agencies

The following regional, national, professional and specialized accrediting agencies are recognized by the U.S. Secretary of Education or the Council for Higher Education Accreditation (CHEA). The U.S. Department of Education (USDE) dates specified are the date of initial listing as a U.S. Department of Education recognized agency, the date of the U.S. Secretary's most recent grant of renewed recognition based on the last full review of the agency by the National Advisory Committee on Institutional Quality and Integrity, and the date of the agency's next scheduled review for renewal of recognition.[1] The Council for Higher Education (CHEA) date reflects initial or continued recognition by CHEA.

Regional Accrediting Bodies

Delaware, District of Columbia, Maryland, New Jersey, New York, Pennsylvania, Puerto Rico, Virgin Islands

Middle States Commission on Higher Education M
USDE: 1952/2012/2014 CHEA: 2013
3624 Market Street, Second Floor West
Philadelphia, PA 19104
(267) 284-5000 Fax (215) 662-5501
Elizabeth H. Sibolski, President
E-mail: info@msche.org
URL: www.msche.org

Connecticut, Maine, Massachusetts, New Hampshire, Rhode Island, Vermont

Commission on Institutions of Higher Education
New England Association of Schools and Colleges EH
USDE: 1952/2008/2013 CHEA: 2013
3 Burlington Woods Drive, Suite 100
Burlington, MA 01803-4531
(781) 425-7700 Fax (781) 425-1001
Barbara E. Brittingham, Director
E-mail: cihe@neasc.org
URL: http://cihe.neasc.org

Arizona, Arkansas, Colorado, Illinois, Indiana, Iowa, Kansas, Michigan, Minnesota, Missouri, Nebraska, New Mexico, North Dakota, Ohio, Oklahoma, South Dakota, West Virginia, Wisconsin, Wyoming

Higher Learning Commission
North Central Association NH
USDE: 1952/2008/2013 CHEA: 2003
230 South LaSalle Street, Suite 7-500
Chicago, IL 60604-1411
(800) 621-7440 Fax (312) 263-7462
Sylvia Manning, President
E-mail: info@hlcommission.org
URL: www.ncahlc.org

Alaska, Idaho, Montana, Nevada, Oregon, Utah, Washington

Northwest Commission on Colleges and Universities NW
USDE: 1952/2008/2013
8060 165th Avenue, NE, Suite 100
Redmond, WA 98052
(425) 558-4224 Fax (425) 376-0596
Sandra E. Elman, President
E-mail: selman@nwccu.org
URL: www.nwccu.org

Alabama, Florida, Georgia, Kentucky, Louisiana, Mississippi, North Carolina, South Carolina, Tennessee, Texas, Virginia

Commission on Colleges
Southern Association of Colleges and Schools SC
USDE: 1952/2012/2014 CHEA: 2003
1866 Southern Lane
Decatur, GA 30033-4097
(404) 679-4500 Fax (404) 679-4558
Belle S. Wheelan, President
E-mail: questions@sacscoc.org
URL: www.sacscoc.org

California, Hawaii, American Samoa, Guam, Commonwealth of the Northern Marianas, Federated States of Micronesia, Republic of the Marshall Islands, Republic of Palau

Accrediting Commission for Senior Colleges and Universities
Western Association of Schools and Colleges WC
USDE: 1952/2012/2014 CHEA: 2003
985 Atlantic Avenue, Suite 100
Alameda, CA 94501
(510) 748-9001 Fax (510) 748-9797
Mary Ellen Petrisko, President
E-mail: wascsr@wascsenior.org
URL: www.wascsenior.org

Accrediting Commission for Community and Junior Colleges
Western Association of Schools and Colleges WJ
USDE: 1952/2008/2013 CHEA: 2003
10 Commercial Boulevard, Suite 204
Novato, CA 94949
(415) 506-0234 Fax (415) 506-0238
Barbara A. Beno, President
E-mail: accjc@accjc.org
URL: www.accjc.org

[1]U.S. Department of Education, Nationally Recognized Accrediting Agencies, www2.ed.gov/admins/finaid/accred/accreditation.html.

National, Professional and Specialized Accrediting Bodies

Acupuncture

Accreditation Commission for Acupuncture and Oriental Medicine (ACAOM)
USDE: 1988/2013/2016
8941 Aztec Drive
Eden Praire, MN 55347
(952) 212-2434 Fax (301) 313-0912
Mark S. McKenzie, Executive Director
E-mail: coordinator@acaom.org
URL: www.acaom.org

First-professional master's degree, professional master's level certificate and diploma programs and professional post-graduate doctoral programs in acupuncture and Oriental medicine, and free-standing institutions that offer such programs **ACUP**

Allied Health

Accrediting Bureau of Health Education Schools (ABHES)
USDE: 1969/2011/2016
7777 Leesburg Pike, Suite 314N
Falls Church, VA 22043
(703) 917-9503 Fax (703) 917-4109
Carol Moneymaker, Executive Director
E-mail: info@abhes.org
URL: www.abhes.org

Institutions specializing in allied health education **ABHES**
Specialized programs for
Medical laboratory technician **MLTAB**
Medical assistant **MAAB**
Surgical technologist **SURTEC**

Commission on Accreditation of Allied Health Education Programs (CAAHEP)
CHEA: 2011
1361 Park Street
Clearwater, FL 33756
(727) 210-2350 Fax (727) 210-2354
Kathleen Megivern, Executive Director
E-mail: mail@caahep.org
URL: www.caahep.org

The Commission on Accreditation of Allied Health Education Programs (CAAHEP) is recognized as an accrediting agency for accreditation of education for the allied health occupations. In carrying out its accreditation activities, CAAHEP cooperates with the Committees on Accreditation sponsored by various allied health and medical specialty organizations. CAAHEP is the coordinating agency for accreditation of education for the following allied health occupations:
Anesthesiologist assistant **AA**
Blood bank technology **BBT**
Cardiovascular technologist **CVT**
Cytotechnologist **CYTO**
Diagnostic medical sonographer **DMS**
Emergency medical technician-paramedic **EMT**
Exercise science **EXSC**
Kinesiotherapy **KIN**
Medical assistant **MAC**
Medical illustrator **MIL**
Neurodiagnostic technologist **NDT**
Orthotist/prosthetist **OPE**
Perfusionist **PERF**
Polysomnographic technologist **POLYT**
Surgical assistant **SURGA**
Surgical technologist **SURGT**

Anesthesiologist Assistant

Commission on Accreditation of Allied Health Education Programs (see listing under Allied Health)
Accreditation Review Committee for the Anesthesiologist Assistant
N84 W33137 Becker Lane
Merton, WI 53066
(612) 836-3311
Jennifer Anderson Warwick, Executive Director
E-mail: jennifer@arc-aa.org
URL: www.caahep.org/arc-aa

Post-baccalaureate programs for anesthesiologist assistant **AA**

Art

Commission on Accreditation
National Association of Schools of Art and Design (NASAD)
USDE: 1966/2013/2014
11250 Roger Bacon Drive, Suite 21
Reston, VA 20190
(703) 437-0700 Fax (703) 437-6312
Samuel Hope, Executive Director
E-mail: info@arts-accredit.org
URL: www.arts-accredit.org

Institutions and departments within institutions offering degree and non-degree granting programs in art/design and art/design-related programs **ART**

Audiology

Accreditation Commission for Audiology Education
CHEA: 2012
1718 M Street, NW #297
Washington, DC 20036-4504
(202) 986-9500 Fax (202) 986-9550
Doris Gordon, Executive Director
E-mail: info@acaeaccred.org
URL: www.acaeaccred.org

Programs leading to the Doctor of Audiology degree **ACAE**

Council on Academic Accreditation in Audiology and Speech Language Pathology
American Speech-Language-Hearing Association (ASHA)
USDE: 1967/2010/2015 CHEA: 2003
2200 Research Boulevard
Rockville, MD 20850-3289
(301) 296-5700 Fax (301) 296-8570
Patrima L. Tice, Director of Accreditation
E-mail: accreditation@asha.org
URL: www.asha.org

Doctoral degree programs in audiology **AUD**

Aviation

Aviation Accreditation Board International
CHEA: 2013
3410 Skyway Drive
Auburn, AL 36830
(334) 844-2431 Fax (334) 844-2432
Gary W. Kiteley, President
E-mail: bavenva@auburn.edu
URL: www.aabi.aero

Non-engineering programs for aviation **AAB**

Bible College Education

Commission on Accreditation
Association for Biblical Higher Education (ABHE)
USDE: 1952/2012/2014 CHEA: 2011
5850 T. G. Lee Boulevard, Suite 130
Orlando, FL 32822
(407) 207-0808 Fax (407) 207-0840
Ron Kroll, Director
E-mail: info@abhe.org
URL: www.abhe.org

Bible colleges and programs offering undergraduate and graduate programs **BI**

Blood Bank Technology

Commission on Accreditation of Allied Health Education Programs (see listing under Allied Health)
American Association of Blood Banks (AABB) Committee on Accreditation of Specialists in Blood Bank Technology Schools
8101 Glenbrook Road
Bethesda, MD 20814-2749
(301) 907-6977 Fax (301) 907-6895
Anne Chenoweth, Manager Accreditation Programs
E-mail: aabb@aabb.org
URL: www.aabb.org

Programs for blood bank technologist **BBT**

Business

AACSB International-The Association to Advance Collegiate Schools of Business
CHEA: 2002
777 South Harbour Island Boulevard, Suite 750
Tampa, FL 33602
(813) 769-6500 Fax (813) 769-6559
Robert Reid, Executive Vice President and Chief Accreditation Officer
E-mail: accreditation@aacsb.edu
URL: www.aacsb.edu

Programs for:
Business administration education **BUS**
Accounting **BUSA**

Accrediting Council for Independent Colleges and Schools (ACICS)
USDE: 1956/2013/2016 CHEA: 2012
750 First Street NE, Suite 980
Washington, DC 20002-4223
(202) 336-6780 Fax (202) 842-2593
Albert C. Gray, Executive Director
E-mail: agray@acics.org
URL: www.acics.org

Institutions offering certificates/diplomas, associate, baccalaureate and master's degree programs to educate students for professional, technical, or occupational careers **ACICS**

Accreditation Council for Business Schools and Programs (ACBSP)
CHEA: 2011
11520 West 119th Street
Overland Park, KS 66213
(913) 339-9356 Fax (913) 339-6226
Douglas Viehland, Executive Director
E-mail: info@acbsp.org
URL: www.acbsp.org

Business administration, management, ac-counting and related business fields **ACBSP**

International Assembly for Collegiate Business Education
CHEA: 2011
11374 Strang Line Rd
Lenexa, KS 66215
(913) 631-3009 Fax (913) 631-9154
Dennis N. Gash, President
E-mail: iacbe@iacbe.org
URL: www.iacbe.org

Undergraduate and graduate level business programs in institutions that grant bachelor's and/or graduate degrees **IACBE**

Cardiovascular Technology

Commission on Accreditation of Allied Health Education Programs (see listing under Allied Health)
Joint Review Committee on Education in Cardiovascular Technology (JRC-CVT)
1449 Hill Street
Whitinsville, MA 01588-1032
(978) 456-5594
William W. Goding, Executive Director
E-mail: office@jrccvt.org
URL: www.jrccvt.org

Programs for cardiovascular technology **CVT**

Chiropractic

The Council on Chiropractic Education (CCE)
USDE: 1974/2011/2013 CHEA: 2005
8049 North 85th Way
Scottsdale, AZ 85258-4321
(480) 443-8877 Fax (480) 483-7333
S. Ray Bennett, Vice President for Accreditation and Operations
E-mail: cce@cce-usa.org
URL: www.cce-usa.org

Programs leading to and institutions offering the Doctorate of Chiropractic (D.C.) degree **CHIRO**

Christian Studies Education

Accreditation Commission
Transnational Association of Christian Colleges and Schools (TRACS)
USDE: 1991/2013/2016 CHEA: 2011
15935 Forest Road
Forest, VA 24551
(434) 525-9539 Fax (434) 525-9538
T. Paul Boatner, President
E-mail: info@tracs.org
URL: www.tracs.org

Christian liberal arts institutions which offer certificates/diplomas and associate, baccalaureate and graduate degrees **TRACS**

Clinical Laboratory Sciences

National Accrediting Agency for Clinical Laboratory Sciences (NAACLS)
CHEA: 2013
5600 North River Road, Suite 720
Rosemont, IL 60018
(773) 714-8880 Fax (773) 714-8886
Dianne M. Cearlock, Chief Executive Officer
E-mail: info@naacls.org
URL: www.naacls.org

Programs for:
- clinical assistant **CA**
- cytogenetic technologist **CGTECH**
- diagnostic molecular scientist **DMOLS**
- histologic technician/technologist **HT**
- medical laboratory technician **MLTAD**
- medical technologist/laboratory scientist **MT**
- pathologists' assistant **PA**
- phlebotomy **PHLEB**

Clinical Pastoral Education

Accreditation Commission
Association for Clinical Pastoral Education, Inc. (ACPEI)
USDE: 1969/2012/2013
1549 Clairmont Road, Suite 103
Decatur, GA 30033-4635
(404) 320-1472 Fax (404) 320-0849
Trace Haythorn, Executive Director
E-mail: acpe@acpe.edu
URL: www.acpe.edu

Basic, advanced and supervisory clinical pastoral education programs **PAST**

Construction Education

American Council for Construction Education (ACCE)
CHEA: 2011
1717 North Loop 1604 East, Suite 320
San Antonio, TX 78232-1570
(210) 495-6161 Fax (210) 495-6168
Michael Holland, Executive Vice President
E-mail: mholland@acce-hq.org
URL: www.acce-hq.org

Associate and baccalaureate degree programs **CONST**

Continuing Education

Accrediting Council for Continuing Education and Training (ACCET)
USDE: 1978/2013/2018
1722 N Street NW
Washington, DC 20036
(202) 955-1113 Fax (202) 955-1118
William V. Larkin, Executive Director
E-mail: wvlarkin@accet.org
URL: www.accet.org

Institutions offering noncollegiate continuing education and institutions offering occupational associate degree programs **CNCE**

Cosmetology

National Accrediting Commission of Career Arts and Sciences (NACCAS)
USDE: 1970/2010/2015
4401 Ford Avenue, Suite 1300
Alexandria, VA 22302-1432
(703) 600-7600 Fax (703) 379-2200
Anthony Mirando, Executive Director
E-mail: naccas@naccas.org
URL: www.naccas.org

Postsecondary schools and departments of cosmetology arts and sciences and massage therapy **COSME**

Counseling and Related Educational Programs

Council for Accreditation of Counseling and Related Educational Programs (CACREP)
CHEA: 2002
1001 North Fairfax Street, Suite 510
Alexandria, VA 22314
(703) 535-5990 Fax (703) 739-6209
Carol L. Bobby, Executive Director
E-mail: cacrep@cacrep.org
URL: www.cacrep.org

Master's degree programs in addiction counseling, career counseling, marriage, couple and family counseling, mental health counseling, school counseling, student affairs and college counseling and doctorate degree programs in counselor education and supervision **CACREP**

Culinary Arts

Accrediting Commission
American Culinary Federation
CHEA: 2004
180 Center Place Way
St. Augustine, FL 32095
(904) 824-4468 Fax (904) 825-4758
Candice Childers, Director of Accreditation
E-mail: acf@acfchefs.net
URL: www.acfchefs.org

Programs in culinary arts which award certificates, diplomas or associate degrees and bachelor degree programs in culinary management **ACFEI**

Cytotechnology

Commission on Accreditation of Allied Health Education Programs (see listing under Allied Health)
Cytotechnology Programs Review Committee
American Society of Cytopathology
100 West 10th Street, Suite 605
Wilmington, DE 19801
(302) 543-6583 Fax (302) 543-6597
Elizabeth Jenkins, Executive Director
E-mail: asc@cytopathology.org
URL: www.cytopathology.org

Programs for the cytotechnologist **CYTO**

Dance

Commission on Accreditation
National Association of Schools of Dance (NASD)
USDE: 1983/2008/2014
11250 Roger Bacon Drive, Suite 21
Reston, VA 20190
(703) 437-0700 Fax (703) 437-6312
Samuel Hope, Executive Director
E-mail: info@arts-accredit.org
URL: www.arts-accredit.org

Institutions and departments within institutions offering degree and non-degree-granting programs in dance and dance-related disciplines **DANCE**

Dental and Dental Auxiliary Programs

Commission on Dental Accreditation
American Dental Association (ADA)
USDE: 1952/2013/2017
211 East Chicago Avenue
Chicago, IL 60611
(800) 621-8099 Fax (312) 440-2915
Sherin Tooks, Director
E-mail: tookss@ada.org
URL: www.ada.org

Programs leading to:
- D.D.S. or D.M.D. degree, advanced general dentistry and specialty programs **DENT**
- Dental hygiene **DH**
- Dental assisting **DA**
- Dental laboratory technology **DT**

Diagnostic Medical Sonography

Commission on Accreditation of Allied Health Education Programs (see listing under Allied Health)
Joint Review Committee on Education in Diagnostic Medical Sonography
6021 University Boulevard, Suite 500
Ellicot City, MD 21043-6090
(443) 973-3251 Fax (866) 738-3444
Cindy Weiland, Executive Director
E-mail: mail@jrcdms.org
URL: www.jrcdms.org

Programs for the diagnostic medical sonographer **DMS**

Dietetics

Accreditation Council for Education in Nutrition and Dietetics
Academy of Nutrition and Dietetics
USDE: 1974/2012/2014
120 South Riverside Plaza, Suite 2000
Chicago, IL 60606-6995
(312) 899-0040 Fax (312) 899-4817
Mary Ann Taconna, Interim Executive Director
E-mail: acend@eatright.org
URL: www.eatright.org/cade

Coordinated programs in dietetics **DIETC**
Didactic programs **DIETD**
Post-baccalaureate internships **DIETI**
Dietetic technician programs **DIETT**

Distance Education and Training

Accrediting Commission
Distance Education and Training Council (DETC)
USDE: 1959/2012/2017 CHEA: 2013
1601 18th Street NW, Suite 2
Washington, DC 20009
(202) 234-5100 Fax (202) 332-1386
Leah K. Matthews, Executive Director
E-mail: info@detc.org
URL: www.detc.org

Distance education institutions including associate, baccalaureate, master's, and doctoral degree-granting programs primarily through the distance learning method **DETC**

Emergency Medical Services

Commission on Accreditation for Allied Health Programs (see listing under Allied Health)
Committee on Accreditation of Educational Programs for the Emergency Medical Services Professions
8301 Lakeview Parkway, Suite 111-312
Rowlett, TX 75088
(214) 703-8445 Fax (214) 703-8992
George Hatch, Executive Director
E-mail: george@coaemsp.org
URL: www.coaemsp.org

Programs for the emergency medical technician-paramedic **EMT**

Engineering

ABET, Inc.
CHEA: 2003
111 Market Place, Suite 1050
Baltimore, MD 21202
(410) 347-7700 Fax (410) 625-2238
Michael Milligan, Executive Director
E-mail: accreditation@abet.org
URL: www.abet.org

Baccalaureate programs in computer science **CS**
Basic (baccalaureate) and advanced (master's) level programs in engineering **ENG**
Applied science programs at the associate, baccalaureate and master's level **ENGR**
Associate and baccalaureate degree programs in engineering technology **ENGT**

English Language

Commission on English Language Program Accreditation (CEA)
USDE: 2003/2011/2013
801 North Fairfax Drive, Suite 402A
Alexandria, VA 22314
(703) 665-3400 Fax (703) 519-2071
Teresa D. O'Donnell, Executive Director
E-mail: info@cea-accredit.org
URL: www.cea-accredit.org

English language programs **CEA**

Exercise Sciences

Commission on Accreditation of Allied Health Education Programs (see listing under Allied Health)
Committee on Accreditation for the Exercise Sciences
401 West Michigan Street
Indianapolis, IN 46202
(317) 637-9200 Fax (317) 634-7817
Traci Sue Rush, Executive Director
E-mail: trush@acsm.org
URL: www.coaes.org

Programs for exercise science and related departments **EXSC**

Family and Consumer Sciences

Council for Accreditation
American Association of Family and Consumer Sciences (AAFCS)
CHEA: 2001
400 North Columbus Street, Suite 202
Alexandria, VA 22314
(703) 706-4600 Fax (703) 706-4663
Carolyn W. Jackson, Executive Director
E-mail: accreditation@aafcs.org
URL: www.aafcs.org

Baccalaureate programs in family and consumer sciences **AAFCS**

Fire and Emergency

International Fire Service Accreditation Congress Degree Assembly
CHEA: 2011
1700 West Tyler
Oklahoma State University
Stillwater, OK 74078
(405) 744-8303 Fax (405) 744-8802
Clayton Moorman, Manager
E-mail: cmoorman@ifsac.org
URL: www.ifsac.org

Undergraduate fire and emergency related programs **IFSAC**

Forensic Science

Forensic Science Educational Program Accreditation Commission
American Academy of Forensic Sciences (AAFS)
CHEA: 2012
410 North 21st Street
Colorado Springs, CO 80904
(719) 636-1100 Fax (719) 636-1993
Nancy J. Jackson, Director of Development and Accreditation
Email: njackson@aafs.org
URL: www.aafs.org/fepac

Bachelor or master's degree programs in forensic science **FEPAC**

Forestry

Society of American Foresters (SAF)
CHEA: 2001
5400 Grosvenor Lane
Bethesda, MD 20814-2198
(301) 897-8720 Fax (301) 897-3690
Carol Redelsheimer, Director of Science and Education
E-mail: redelsheimerc@safnet.org
URL: www.safnet.org

Programs leading to a bachelor's or higher first-professional degree in forestry **FOR**

Funeral Service Education

Committee on Accreditation
American Board of Funeral Service Education (ABFSE)
USDE: 1972/2010/2015 CHEA: 2012
3414 Ashland Avenue, Suite G
St. Joseph, MO 64506
(816) 233-3747 Fax (816) 233-3793
Michael Smith, Executive Director
E-mail: exdir@abfse.org
URL: www.abfse.org

Institutions and programs awarding diplomas, associate and bachelor's degrees in funeral service or mortuary science **FUSER**

Health Informatics and Information Management

Commission on Accreditation for Health Informatics and Information Management Education (CAHIIM)
CHEA: 2012
233 North Michigan Avenue, 21st Floor
Chicago, IL 60601-5800
(312) 233-1100 Fax (312) 233-1948
Claire Dixon-Lee, Executive Director
Email: info@cahiim.org
URL: www.cahiim.org

Associate and baccalaureate degree programs in health information management and master's degree programs in health informatics and health information management **CAHIIM**

Healthcare Management

Commission on Accreditation of Healthcare Management Education (CAHME)
USDE: 1970/2007/2013 CHEA: 2003
1700 Rockville Pike, Suite 400
Rockville, MD 20852
(301) 998-6101
Margaret Schulte, JD, President and CEO
E-mail: info@cahme.org
URL: www.cahme.org

Graduate programs in healthcare management **HSA**

Histologic Technology

See Clinical Laboratory Sciences

Home Study Education

See Distance Education and Training

Industrial Technology

The Association of Technology, Management, and Applied Engineering
CHEA: 2013
1390 Eisenhower Place
Ann Arbor, MI 48108
(734) 677-0720 Fax (734) 677-0046
Rick Coscarelli, Director of Accreditation
E-mail: atmae@atmae.org
URL: www.atmae.org

Technology, applied technology, engineering technology and technology-related programs at the associate, baccalaureate and master's degree level **NAIT**

Interior Design

Council for Interior Design Accreditation (CIDA)
CHEA: 2013
206 Grandville Avenue, Suite 350
Grand Rapids, MI 49503
(616) 458-0400 Fax (616) 458-0460
Holly Mattson, Executive Director
E-mail: info@accredit-id.org
URL: www.accredit-id.org

First professional degree level programs (master's and baccalaureate degrees) **CIDA**

Journalism and Mass Communications

Accrediting Committee
Accrediting Council on Education in Journalism and Mass Communications (ACEJMC)
CHEA: 2002
University of Kansas School of Journalism
Stauffer-Flint Hall
1435 Jayhawk Boulevard
Lawrence, KS 66045-7575
(785) 864-3973 Fax (785) 864-5225
Susanne Shaw, Executive Director
E-mail: sshaw@ku.edu
URL: www2.ku.edu/~acejmc

Units within institutions offering professional baccalaureate and master's degree programs in journalism and mass communications **JOUR**

Kinesiotherapy

Commission on Accreditation of Allied Health Education Programs (see listing under Allied Health)
Committee on Accreditation of Education Programs for Kinesiotherapy

118 College Drive #5142
Hattiesburg, MS 39406-0002
(601) 266-5371 Fax (601) 266-4445
Jerry W. Purvis, Executive Director
E-mail: jerry.purvis@usm.edu
URL: www.akta.org

Kinesiotherapy programs **KIN**

Landscape Architecture

Landscape Architectural Accreditation Board
American Society of Landscape Architects (ASLA)
CHEA: 2003
636 Eye Street, NW
Washington, DC 20001-3736
(202) 898-2444 Fax (202) 898-1185
Ron Leighton, Executive Director
E-mail: rleighton@asla.org
URL: www.asla.org

Baccalaureate and master's programs leading to the first professional degree **LSAR**

Law

Council of the Section of Legal Education and Admissions to the Bar
American Bar Association (ABA)
USDE: 1952/2013/2016
321 North Clark Street, 21st Fl
Chicago, IL 60654-7598
(312) 988-6738 Fax (312) 988-5681
Barry A. Currier, Managing Director of Accreditation and Legal Education
E-mail: legaled@americanbar.org
URL: www.americanbar.org/groups/legal_education.html

Programs in legal education; professional schools of law **LAW**

Librarianship

Committee on Accreditation
American Library Association (ALA)
CHEA: 2013
50 East Huron Street
Chicago, IL 60611-2729
(312) 280-2432 Fax (312) 280-2433
Karen O'Brien, Director of Accreditation
E-mail: accred@ala.org
URL: www.ala.org/accreditation

Master's programs in library and information studies **LIB**

Marriage and Family Therapy

Commission on Accreditation for Marriage and Family Therapy Education
American Association for Marriage and Family Therapy (AAMFT)
CHEA: 2003
112 South Alfred Street
Alexandria, VA 22314-3061
(703) 838-9808 Fax (703) 838-9805
Tanya A. Tamarkin, Director of Educational Affairs
E-mail: coa@aamft.org
URL: www.aamft.org

Clinical training programs at the master's, doctorate and post-graduate levels **MFCD**

Massage Therapy

Commission on Massage Therapy Accreditation
USDE: 2002/2010/2015
5335 Wisconsin Avenue NW, Suite 440
Washington, DC 20015
(202) 895-1518 Fax (202) 895-1519
Kate Zulaski, Executive Director
E-mail: kzulaski@comta.org
URL: www.comta.org

Institutions that award postsecondary certificates, diplomas, and associate degrees in the practice of massage therapy, bodywork, aesthetics/esthetics and skin care **COMTA**

Medical Assistant Education

(see listing under Allied Health)
Accrediting Bureau of Health Education Schools (ABHES)

Medical assistant programs **MAAB**

Commission on Accreditation of Allied Health Education Programs (see listing under Allied Health)
Medical Assisting Education Review Board
20 North Wacker Drive, Suite 1575
Chicago, IL 60606-2963
(312) 899-1500 Fax (312) 899-1259
Judy Jondahl, Executive Director of Accreditation
E-mail: jjondahl@maerb.org
URL: www.maerb.org

One and two year medical assistant programs **MAC**

Medical Illustrator Education

Commission on Accreditation of Allied Health Education Programs (see listing under Allied Health)
Accreditation Review Committee for the Medical Illustrator
Saint Luke's Hospital Instructional Resources
32531 Meadowlark Way
Pepper Pike, OH 44124
(216) 595-9363 Fax (216) 595-9360
Kathy Jung, Chair, ARC-MI
E-mail: kijung@aol.com
URL: www.ami.org

Programs for medical illustrator **MIL**

Medical Laboratory Technician Education

(see listing under Allied Health)
Accrediting Bureau of Health Education Schools (ABHES)

Schools and programs for the medical laboratory technician **MLTAB**

(see listing under Clinical Laboratory Sciences)
National Accrediting Agency for Clinical Laboratory Sciences (NAACLS)

Programs for medical laboratory technician **MLTAD**

Medical Technology

(see listing under Clinical Laboratory Sciences)
National Accrediting Agency for Clinical Laboratory Sciences (NAACLS)

Programs for medical technologist/laboratory scientist **MT**

Medicine

Liaison Committee on Medical Education (LCME) of the Council on Medical Education of the American Medical Association and the Association of American Medical Colleges
USDE: 1952/2012/2014
The LCME is administered in odd-numbered years, beginning each July 1, by:
Council on Medical Education of the American Medical Association (AMA)
515 North State Street
Chicago, IL 60610
(312) 464-4690 Fax (312) 464-5830
Barbara Barzansky, LCME Co-Secretary
E-mail: barbara.barzansky@ama-assn.org
URL: www.ama-assn.org

The LCME is administered in even-numbered years, beginning each July 1, by:
Association of American Medical Colleges (AAMC)
2450 N Street NW
Washington, DC 20037-1127
(202) 828-0596 Fax (202) 828-1125
Dan Hunt, LCME Co-Secretary
E-mail: dhunt@aamc.org
URL: www.aamc.org

Programs leading to the M.D. degree **MED**

Midwifery Education

Midwifery Education Accreditation Council (MEAC)
USDE: 2001/2012/2015
1935 Pauline Boulevard, Suite 100B
Ann Arbor, MI 48103
(360) 466-2080 Fax (480) 907-2936
Sandra Bitonti Stewart, Executive Director
E-mail: info@meacschools.org
URL: www.meacschools.org

Accreditation of direct-entry midwifery educational institutions and programs conferring degrees and certificates **MEAC**

Montessori Teacher Education

Montessori Accreditation Council for Teacher Education (MACTE)
USDE: 1995/2010/2013
313 Second Street, SE, Suite 112
Charlottesville, VA 22902
(434) 202-7793 Fax (888) 525-8838
Rebecca Pelton, Executive Director
E-mail: rebecca@macte.org
URL: www.macte.org

Montessori teacher-education programs and institutions **MACTE**

Music

Commission on Accreditation
National Association of Schools of Music (NASM)
USDE: 1952/2008/2014
11250 Roger Bacon Drive, Suite 21
Reston, VA 20190
(703) 437-0700 Fax (703) 437-6312
Samuel Hope, Executive Director
E-mail: info@arts-accredit.org
URL: www.arts-accredit.org

Institutions and departments within institutions offering degree and non-degree-granting programs in music and music-related disciplines **MUS**

Naturopathic Medical Education

Council on Naturopathic Medical Education (CNME)
USDE: 2003/2010/2015
PO Box 178
Great Barrington, MA 01230
(413) 528-8877 Fax (413) 528-8880
Daniel Seitz, Executive Director
E-mail: council@cnme.org
URL: www.cnme.org

Graduate-level, four-year naturopathic medical education programs **NATUR**

Neurodiagnostic Technology

Commission on Accreditation of Allied Health Education Programs (see listing under Allied Health)
Committee on Accreditation for Education in Neurodiagnostic Technology

22 Railroad Avenue, Suite 3
Beverly, MA 01915
(978) 338-6300 Fax (978) 832-2638
Jackie Long-Goding, Executive Director
E-mail: office@coa-ndt.org
URL: http://coa-ndt.org

Programs for the electroneurodiagnostic technologist **NDT**

Nuclear Medicine Technology

Joint Review Committee on Educational Programs in Nuclear Medicine Technology
CHEA: 2013
2000 West Danforth Road, Suite 130 #203
Edmund, OK 73003
(405) 285-0546 Fax (405) 285-0579
Jan M. Winn, Executive Director
E-mail: jrcnmt@coxinet.net
URL: www.jrcnmt.org

Programs for the nuclear medicine technologist **NMT**

Nurse Anesthetists

Council on Accreditation of Nurse Anesthesia Educational Programs
USDE: 1955/2007/2013 CHEA: 2011
222 South Prospect Avenue, Suite 304
Park Ridge, IL 60068-4001
(847) 655-1160 Fax (847) 692-7137
Francis Gerbasi, Executive Director
E-mail: accreditation@coa.us.com
URL: home.coa.us.com

Nurse anesthesia educational institutions and programs at the post-master's certificate, master's and doctoral degree levels **ANEST**

Nurse-Midwifery

Accreditation Commission for Midwifery Education
USDE: 1982/2012/2014
8403 Colesville Road, Suite 1550
Silver Spring, MD 20910
(240) 485-1802 Fax (240) 485-1818
Susan E. Stone, Chair, Accreditation Commission
E-mail: susan.stone@frontierschool.edu
URL: www.midwife.org/accreditation

Pre-certification, basic certificate and master's degree nurse-midwifery educational programs **MIDWF**

Nursing

Commission on Collegiate Nursing Education (CCNE)
USDE: 2000/2012/2014
One Dupont Circle NW, Suite 530
Washington, DC 20036-1120
(202) 887-6791 Fax (202) 887-8476
Jennifer Butlin, Executive Director
E-mail: info@aacn.nche.edu
URL: www.aacn.nche.edu/accreditation

Baccalaureate and higher degree nursing education **NURSE**

Accreditation Commission for Education in Nursing
USDE: 1952/2012/2014 CHEA: 2011
3343 Peachtree Road NE, Suite 850
Atlanta, GA 30326
(404) 975-5000 Fax (404) 975-5020
Sharon J. Tanner, CEO
E-mail: info@nlnac.org
URL: www.nlnac.org

Programs in:
- Practical nursing (certificate) **PNUR**
- Diploma nurse education **DNUR**
- Associate degree **ADNUR**
- Baccalaureate and higher degree nurse education **NUR**

Occupational Education

Council on Occupational Education (COE)
USDE: 1969/2013/2016
7840 Roswell Road, Bldg 300, Suite 325
Atlanta, GA 30350
(770) 396-3898 Fax (770) 396-3790
Gary Puckett, Executive Director
E-mail: info@council.org
URL: www.council.org

Occupational/vocational institutions that grant certificates or diplomas and the applied associate degree in specific career and technical education **COE**

Occupational Therapy

Accreditation Council for Occupational Therapy Education
American Occupational Therapy Association
USDE: 1952/2012/2017 CHEA: 2013
4720 Montgomery Lane, Suite 200
Bethesda, MD 20814-3449
(301) 652-6611 Fax (301) 652-7711
Neil Harvison, Director of Accreditation
E-mail: accred@aota.org
URL: www.aota.org

Occupational therapy programs **OT**
Occupational therapy assistant programs **OTA**

Opticianry

Commission on Opticianry Accreditation
CHEA: 2010
PO Box 592
Canton, NY 13617
(703) 468-0566
Debra White, Director of Accreditation
E-mail: director@COAccreditation.com
URL: www.coaccreditation.com

Two-year opticianry degree programs **OPD**
One year programs for opthalmic laboratory technician **OPLT**

Optometry

Accreditation Council on Optometric Education
American Optometric Association (AOA)
USDE: 1952/2008/2013 CHEA: 2012
243 North Lindbergh Boulevard
St. Louis, MO 63141
(314) 991-4100 Fax (314) 991-4101
Joyce L. Urbeck, Administrative Director
E-mail: accredit@aoa.org
URL: www.theacoe.org

Programs in:
- First professional **OPT**
- Optometric residency **OPTR**
- Optometric technology **OPTT**

Orthotic and Prosthetic Education

Commission on Accreditation of Allied Health Education Programs (see listing under Allied Health)
National Commission on Orthotic and Prosthetic Education (NCOPE)
330 John Carlyle Street, Suite 200
Alexandria, VA 22314
(703) 836-7114 Fax (703) 836-0838
Robin C. Seabrook, Executive Director
E-mail: info@ncope.org
URL: www.ncope.org

Programs for orthotic and prosthetic education **OPE**

Osteopathic Medicine

Commission on Osteopathic College Accreditation
American Osteopathic Association
USDE: 1952/2011/2016
Department of Education
142 East Ontario Street
Chicago, IL 60611-2864
(312) 202-8048 Fax (312) 202-8202
Konrad C. Miskowicz-Retz, Director
E-mail: predoc@osteopathic.org
URL: www.osteopathic.org

Programs leading to and institutions offering the D.O. (Doctor of Osteopathy/Osteopathic Medicine) degree **OSTEO**

Perfusion

Commission on Accreditation of Allied Health Education Programs (see listing under Allied Health)
Accreditation Committee - Perfusion Education
6654 South Sycamore Street
Littleton, CO 80120
(303) 738-0770 Fax (303) 738-3223
Theresa Sisneros, Executive Director
E-mail: ac-pe@msn.com
URL: www.ac-pe.org

Programs for the perfusionist **PERF**

Pharmacy

Accreditation Council for Pharmacy Education (ACPE)
USDE: 1952/2012/2014 CHEA: 2004
135 South LaSalle Street, Suite 4100
Chicago, IL 60603
(312) 664-3575 Fax (312) 664-4652
Peter H. Vlasses, Executive Director
E-mail: csinfo@acpe-accredit.org
URL: www.acpe-accredit.org

Professional degree programs in pharmacy **PHAR**

Physical Therapy

Commission on Accreditation in Physical Therapy Education
American Physical Therapy Association (APTA)
USDE: 1977/2012/2014 CHEA: 2012
Trans Potomac Plaza
1111 North Fairfax Street
Alexandria, VA 22314
(703) 706-3245 Fax (703) 684-7343
Mary Jane Harris, Director
E-mail: accreditation@apta.org
URL: www.apta.org

Professional programs for the physical therapist **PTA**
Programs for the physical therapist assistant **PTAA**

Physician Assistant

Accreditation Review Commission on Education for the Physician Assistant (ARC-PA)
CHEA: 2004
12000 Findley Road, Suite 150
John's Creek, GA 30097
(770) 476-1224 Fax (770) 476-1738
John McCarty, Executive Director
E-mail: arc-pa@arc-pa.org
URL: www.arc-pa.org

Programs for the physician assistant **ARCPA**

Planning (City and Regional)

Planning Accreditation Board
CHEA: 2013
53 West Jackson Boulevard, Suite 1315
Chicago, IL 60604
(312) 662-1440 Fax (312) 662-1460
Shonagh Merits, Executive Director
E-mail: smerits@planningaccreditationboard.org
URL: www.planningaccreditationboard.org

Bachelor and master's level programs in planning **PLNG**

Podiatry

Council on Podiatric Medical Education
American Podiatric Medical Association (APMA)
USDE: 1952/2011/2013 CHEA: 2004
9312 Old Georgetown Road
Bethesda, MD 20814-1621
(301) 581-9200 Fax (301) 571-4903
Alan R. Tinkleman, Director
E-mail: artinkleman@apma.org
URL: www.cpme.org

Colleges and programs of podiatric medicine, including first professional and doctorate degree programs **POD**

Polysomnographic Technology

Commission on Accreditation of Allied Health Education Programs (see listing under Allied Health)
Committee on Accreditation for Polysomnographic Technologists Education
1711 Frank Avenue
New Bern, NC 28560
(252) 626-3238
Karen Monarchy Rowe, Executive Director
E-mail: office@coapsg.org
URL: www.coapsg.org

Programs for polysomnographic technology **POLYT**

Psychology

Psychological Clinical Science Accreditation System (PCSAS)
CHEA: 2012
1101 East Tenth Street
IU Psychology Building
Bloomington, IN 47405-7007
(812) 856-2570 Fax (812) 322-5545
Richard M. McFall, Executive Director
Email: rmmcfall@pcsas.org
URL: www.pcsas.org

Psychological clinical science doctoral training programs **PCSAS**

Commission on Accreditation
American Psychological Association (APA)
USDE: 1970/2013/2016 CHEA: 2013
750 First Street NE
Washington, DC 20002-4242
(202) 336-5979 Fax (202) 336-5978
Susan F. Zlotlow, Director Program Consultation and Accreditation
E-mail: apaaccred@apa.org
URL: www.apa.org/ed/accred.html

Doctoral programs in:
- Clinical psychology **CLPSY**
- Counseling psychology **COPSY**
- Combined professional-scientific psychology **PSPSY**
- School psychology **SCPSY**
- Pre-doctoral internship program in professional psychology **IPSY**
- Post-doctoral residency in professional psychology **PDPSY**

Public Affairs and Administration

Commission on Peer Review and Accreditation
Network of Schools of Public Policy, Affairs and Administration (NASPAA)
CHEA: 2004
1029 Vermont Avenue, NW, Suite 1100
Washington, DC 20005
(202) 628-8965 Fax (202) 626-4978
Crystal Calarusse, Chief Accreditation Officer
E-mail: copra@naspaa.org
URL: www.naspaa.org

Master's degree programs in public affairs, public policy and administration **SPAA**

Public Health

Council on Education for Public Health (CEPH)
USDE: 1974/2007/2013
1010 Wayne Avenue, Suite 220
Silver Spring, MD 20910-5600
(202) 789-1050 Fax (202) 789-1895
Laura Rasar King, Executive Director
E-mail: lking@ceph.org
URL: www.ceph.org

Baccalaureate and graduate level programs in schools of public health and public health programs outside of schools of public health **PH**

Rabbinical and Talmudic Education

Accreditation Commission
Association of Advanced Rabbinical and Talmudic Schools (AARTS)
USDE: 1974/2007/2013 CHEA: 2011
11 Broadway, Suite 405
New York, NY 10004
(212) 363-1991 Fax (212) 533-5335
Bernard Fryshman, Executive Vice President
E-mail: BFryshma@nyit.edu

Advanced rabbinical and Talmudic schools **RABN**

Radiologic Technology

Joint Review Committee on Education in Radiologic Technology
USDE: 1957/2011/2013 CHEA: 2004
20 North Wacker Drive, Suite 2850
Chicago, IL 60606-3182
(312) 704-5300 Fax (312) 704-5304
Leslie F. Winter, Chief Executive Officer
E-mail: mail@jrcert.org
URL: www.jrcert.org

Programs for:
- Magnetic resonance **RADMAG**
- Medical dosimetry **RADDOS**
- Radiographer **RAD**
- Radiation therapist technologist **RTT**

Recreation, Park and Leisure Studies

Council on Accreditation of Parks, Recreation, Tourism and Related Professions
National Recreation and Park Association
CHEA: 2003
22377 Belmont Ridge Road
Ashburn, VA 20148-4501
(703) 858-2195 Fax (703) 858-0794
Danielle Price, Education and Accreditation Manager
E-mail: coaprt@nrpa.org
URL: www.nrpa.org

Baccalaureate degree programs in recreation, park resources and leisure studies **NRPA**

Rehabilitation Education

Commission on Standards and Accreditation
Council on Rehabilitation Education (CORE)
CHEA: 2012
1699 Woodfield Road, Suite 300
Schaumburg, IL 60173
(847) 944-1345 Fax (847) 944-1346
Frank Lane, Executive Director
E-mail: lane@iit.edu
URL: www.core-rehab.org

Rehabilitation counselor education programs at the master's level and rehabilitation services at the bachelor's level **CORE**

Respiratory Care

Commission on Accreditation for Respiratory Care (CoARC)
CHEA: 2012
1248 Harwood Road
Bedford, TX 76021-4244
(817) 283-2835 Fax (817) 354-8519
Thomas Smalling, Executive Director
Email: tom@coarc.com
URL: www.coarc.com
- Degree programs in respiratory care **COARC**
- Certificate programs in polysomnography **COARCP**

Social Work

Commission on Accreditation
Council on Social Work Education (CSWE)
CHEA: 2003
1701 Duke Street, Suite 200
Alexandria, VA 22314-3457
(703) 683-8080 Fax (703) 683-8099
Jo Ann Regan, Director, Office of Social Work Accreditation
E-mail: info@cswe.org
URL: www.cswe.org

Master's and baccalaureate degree programs **SW**

Speech-Language Pathology

Council on Academic Accreditation in Audiology and Speech Language Pathology
American Speech-Language-Hearing Association (ASHA)
USDE: 1967/2010/2015 CHEA: 2003
2200 Research Boulevard
Rockville, MD 20850-3289
(301) 296-5700 Fax (301) 296-8570
Patrima L. Tice, Director of Accreditation
E-mail: accreditation@asha.org
URL: www.asha.org

Master's in speech-language pathology **SP**

Surgical Assisting and Technology

(see listing under Allied Health)
Accrediting Bureau of Health Education Schools (ABHES)

Surgical technologist programs **SURTEC**

Commission on Accreditation of Allied Health Education Programs (see listing under Allied Health)
Accreditation Review Council On Education in Surgical Technology and Surgical Assisting
6 West Dry Creek Circle, Suite 110
Littleton, CO 80120
(303) 694-9262 Fax (303) 741-3655
Keith Orloff, Executive Director
E-mail: info@arcstsa.org
URL: www.arcst.org

Programs for the surgical technologist **SURGT**
Programs for the surgical assistant **SURGA**

Teacher Education

Council for the Accreditation of Educator Preparation*

2010 Massachusetts Avenue, NW, Suite 500
Washington, DC 20036
(202) 223-0077
James G. Cibulka, President
Email: caep@caepnet.org
URL: caepnet.org

*On July 1 2013, the National Council for Accreditation of Teacher Education (NCATE) and the Teacher Education Accreditation Council (TEAC) consolidated, making the Council for the Accreditation of Educator Preparation (CAEP) the new, sole specialized accreditor for educator preparation. Under the consolidation, NCATE and TEAC are subsidiaries of CAEP, maintaining their recognition by the U.S. Department of Education and the Council for Higher Education Accreditation for the purpose of maintaining the accreditation of educator preparation providers until such time as said providers come up for accreditation under CAEP.

National Council for Accreditation of Teacher Education (NCATE)
USDE: 1952/2006/2014 CHEA: 2013
2010 Massachusetts Avenue NW, Suite 500
Washington, DC 20036-1023
(202) 466-7496 Fax (202) 296-6620
James G. Cibulka, President
E-mail: ncate@ncate.org
URL: www.ncate.org

Baccalaureate and graduate programs for the preparation of teachers and other professional personnel for elementary and secondary schools **TED**

Accreditation Committee
Teacher Education Accreditation Council (TEAC)
USDE: 2003/2005/2014 CHEA: 2012
One Dupont Circle NW, Suite 320
Washington, DC 20036
(202) 466-7236 Fax (202) 466-7238
Mark LaCelle-Peterson, President
E-mail: teac@teac.org
URL: www.teac.org

Professional teacher education programs in institutions offering baccalaureate and graduate degrees for the preparation of K-12 teachers **TEAC**

Theatre

Commission on Accreditation
National Association of Schools of Theatre (NAST)
USDE: 1982/2008/2014
11250 Roger Bacon Drive, Suite 21
Reston, VA 20190
(703) 437-0700 Fax (703) 437-6312
Samuel Hope, Executive Director
E-mail: info@arts-accredit.org
URL: www.arts-accredit.org

Institutions and departments within institutions offering degree granting and non-degree-granting programs in theatre and theatre-related disciplines **THEA**

Theology

Commission on Accrediting
Association of Theological Schools (ATS)
USDE: 1952/2013/2016 CHEA: 2012
10 Summit Park Drive
Pittsburgh, PA 15275-1103
(412) 788-6505 Fax (412) 788-6510
Daniel O. Aleshire, Executive Director
E-mail: ats@ats.edu
URL: www.ats.edu

Freestanding schools, as well as schools or programs affiliated with larger institutions, offering graduate professional education for ministry and graduate study of theology **THEOL**

Trade and Technical Education

Accrediting Commission of Career Schools and Colleges (ACCSC)
USDE: 1967/2011/2016
2101 Wilson Boulevard, Suite 302
Arlington, VA 22201
(703) 247-4212 Fax (703) 247-4533
Michale McComis, Executive Director
E-mail: info@accsc.org
URL: www.accsc.org

Private, postsecondary degree-granting and non-degree-granting institutions that are predominantly organized to educate students for trade, occupational or technical careers **ACCSC**

Veterinary Medicine

Council on Education
American Veterinary Medical Association (AVMA)
USDE: 1952/2012/2014 CHEA: 2012
1931 North Meacham Road, Suite 100
Schaumburg, IL 60173
(800) 248-2862 Fax (847) 925-1329
David E. Granstrom, Director Education and Research
E-mail: avmainfo@avma.org
URL: www.avma.org

Colleges of veterinary medicine offering programs leading to a D.V.M./D.M.V. professional degree **VET**

Other

New York State Board of Regents Commission of Education
USDE: 1952/2012/2014
State Education Department
The University of the State of New York
89 Washington Avenue, Room 1106B
Albany, NY 12234
(518) 474-5844 Fax (518) 473-4909
John B. King, Jr., Commissioner of Education
E-mail: jking@mail.nysed.gov
URL: www.nysed.gov

Degree-granting institutions of higher education in New York that designate the agency as their sole or primary nationally recognized accrediting agency for purposes of establishing elibility to participate in Higher Education Act programs **NY**

Accrediting Agencies Recognized for their Pre-accreditation Categories[1]

Under the terms of the Higher Education Act and other Federal legislation providing funding assistance to postsecondary education, an institution or program is eligible to apply for participation in certain Federal programs if, in addition to meeting other statutory requirements, it is accredited by a nationally recognized accrediting agency—or if it is an institution with respect to which the U.S. Secretary of Education has determined that there is satisfactory assurance the institution or program will meet the accreditation standards of such agency or association within a reasonable time. An institution or program may establish satisfactory assurance of accreditation by acquiring pre-accreditation status with a nationally recognized accrediting agency which has been recognized by the U.S. Secretary of Education for the award of such status. According to the Criteria for Nationally Recognized Accrediting Agencies, if an accrediting agency has developed a pre-accreditation status, it must demonstrate that it applies criteria and follows procedures that are appropriately related to those used to award accreditation status. The criteria for recognition also requires an agency's standards for pre-accreditation to permit an institution or program to hold pre-accreditation no more than five years.

The following is a list of accrediting agencies recognized by the U.S. Secretary of Education for their pre-accreditation categories and the categories which are recognized.

Regional Institution Accrediting Bodies

Middle States Commission on Higher Education:
Candidate for Accreditation

New England Association of Schools and Colleges:
Commission on Institutions of Higher Education: *Candidate for Accreditation*

Higher Learning Commission
North Central Association: *Candidate for Accreditation*

Northwest Commission on Colleges and Universities:
Candidate for Accreditation

Southern Association of Colleges and Schools
Commission on Colleges: *Candidate for Accreditation*

Western Association of Schools and Colleges
Accrediting Commission for Community and Junior Colleges: *Candidate for Accreditation*

Western Association of Schools and Colleges
Accrediting Commission for Senior Colleges and Universities: *Candidate for Accreditation*

National, Institutional and Specialized Accrediting Bodies

Academy of Nutrition and Dietetics
Accreditation Council for Education in Nutrition and Dietetics: *Pre-accreditation*

Accreditation Commission for Acupuncture and Oriental Medicine: *Candidate for Accreditation*

Accreditation Commission for Midwifery Education: *Pre-accreditation*

Accreditation Council for Pharmacy Education: *Candidate, Pre-candidate*

American Optometric Association
Accreditation Council on Optometric Education: *Preliminary Approval* (for professional degree programs); *Candidacy Pending* (for optometric residency programs in Veterans Administration facilities)

American Osteopathic Association
Commission on Osteopathic College Accreditation: *Provisional Accreditation*

American Physical Therapy Association
Commission on Accreditation in Physical Therapy Education: *Candidate for Accreditation*

American Podiatric Medical Association
Council on Podiatric Medical Education: *Candidate for Accreditation*

American Speech-Language-Hearing Association
Council on Academic Accreditation: *Candidate for Accreditation*

American Veterinary Medical Association
Council on Education: *Reasonable Assurance of Accreditation*

Association for Biblical Higher Education
Commission on Accreditation: *Candidate for Accreditation*

Association of Advanced Rabbinical and Talmudic Schools
Accreditation Commission: *Correspondent, Candidate for Accreditation*

Association of Theological Schools
Commission on Accrediting: *Candidate for Accredited Membership*

Council on Education for Public Health: *Pre-accreditation*

Council on Naturopathic Medical Education: *Pre-accreditation*

Council on Occupational Education: *Candidate for Accreditation*

Midwifery Education Accreditation Council: *Pre-accreditation*

Teacher Education Accreditation Council Accreditation Committee: *Pre-accreditation*

Transnational Association of Christian Colleges and Schools
Accreditation Commission: *Candidate for Accreditation*

[1]U.S. Department of Education, Nationally Recognized Accrediting Agencies and Associations, www2.ed.gov/admins/finaid/accred/accreditation_pg8.html.

Abbreviations, Explanatory Notes and Symbols

Abbreviations

Listed below are the abbreviations used in this Directory for the recognized regional accrediting commissions and the recognized national, professional and specialized accrediting bodies. Addresses for these associations can be found under our listing of Accrediting Agencies beginning on page viii.

The recognized regional accrediting commissions are indicated throughout this Directory by the following abbreviations:

EH New England Association of Schools and Colleges, Commission on Institutions of Higher Education

M Middle States Commission on Higher Education

NH Higher Learning Commission, North Central Association

NW Northwest Commission on Colleges and Universities

SC Southern Association of Colleges and Schools, Commission on Colleges

WC Western Association of Schools and Colleges, Accrediting Commission for Senior Colleges and Universities

WJ Western Association of Schools and Colleges, Accrediting Commission for Community and Junior Colleges

National, professional and specialized accrediting agencies and associations are listed below. Wherever possible, degree levels are shown by the following symbols: (C) diploma/certificate; (A) associate; (B) baccalaureate; (M) master's; (S) beyond master's but less than doctorate; (FP) first professional; (D) doctorate.

AA Commission on Accreditation of Allied Health Education Programs: anesthesiologist assistant (M)

AAB Aviation Accreditation Board International: aviation (A,B,M)

AAFCS American Association of Family and Consumer Sciences: family and consumer sciences (B)

ABHES Accrediting Bureau of Health Education Schools: allied health (C,A,B)

ACAE Accreditation Commission for Audiology Education: audiology (D)

ACBSP Accreditation Council for Business Schools and Programs: business administration, management, accounting and related business fields (A,B,M,D)

ACCSC Accrediting Commission of Career Schools and Colleges: occupational, trade and technical education (C,A,B,M)

ACFEI American Culinary Federation, Inc.: culinary arts and culinary management (C,A,B)

ACICS Accrediting Council for Independent Colleges and Schools: business and business-related programs (C,A,B,M)

ACUP Accreditation Commission for Acupuncture and Oriental Medicine: acupuncture (C,M,D)

ADNUR Accreditation Commission for Education in Nursing: nursing (A)

ANEST Council on Accreditation of Nurse Anesthesia Educational Programs: nurse anesthesia (C,M,D)

ARCPA Accreditation Review Commission on Education for the Physician Assistant: physician assisting programs (C,A,B,M)

ART National Association of Schools of Art and Design: art and design (C,A,B,M,D)

AUD American Speech-Language-Hearing Association: audiology (D)

BBT Commission on Accreditation of Allied Health Education Programs: blood bank technology (C,M)

BI Association for Biblical Higher Education: bible college education (C,A,B,M,FP,D)

BUS AACSB-The Association to Advance Collegiate Schools of Business: business and management (B,M,D)

BUSA AACSB-The Association to Advance Collegiate Schools of Business: accounting (B,M,D)

CA National Accrediting Agency for Clinical Laboratory Sciences: clinical assistant (C)

CACREP Council for Accreditation of Counseling & Related Education programs: addiction counseling, career counseling, marriage, couple and family counseling, mental health counseling, school counseling, student affairs and college counseling (M) and counselor education and supervision (D)

CAHIIM Commission on Accreditation for Health Informatics and Information Management Education: health information management and health informatics (A,B,M)

CEA Commission on English Language Program Accreditation: english language (C)

CGTECH National Accrediting Agency for Clinical Laboratory Sciences: cytogenetic technologist (B)

CHIRO Council on Chiropractic Education: chiropractic education (FP,D)

CIDA Council for Interior Design Accreditation: interior design (B,M)

CLPSY American Psychological Association: clinical psychology (D)

CNCE Accrediting Council for Continuing Education and Training: continuing education (C,A)

COARC Commission on Accreditation for Respiratory Care: respiratory care (A,B,M)

COARCP Commission on Accreditation for Respiratory Care: polysomnography (C)

COE Council on Occupational Education: occupational, trade, and technical education (C,A)

COMTA Commission on Massage Therapy Accreditation: massage therapy, bodywork, aesthetics/esthetics and skin care (C,A)

CONST American Council for Construction Education: construction education (A,B)

COPSY American Psychological Association: counseling psychology (D)

CORE Council on Rehabilitation Education: rehabilitation counseling and rehabilitation services (B,M)

COSME National Accrediting Commission of Career Arts and Sciences: cosmetology and massage therapy (C)

CS ABET, Inc.: computer science (B)

CVT Commission on Accreditation of Allied Health Education Programs: cardiovascular technology (C,A,B)

CYTO Commission on Accreditation of Allied Health Education Programs: cytotechnology (C,B,M)

DA American Dental Association: dental assisting (C,A)

DANCE National Association of Schools of Dance: dance (C,A,B,M,D)

DENT American Dental Association: dentistry (FP,D)

DETC Distance Education and Training Council: home study schools (A,B,M,D)

DH American Dental Association: dental hygiene (C,A,B,M)

DIETC Academy of Nutrition and Dietetics: coordinated dietetics programs (B,M)

DIETD Academy of Nutrition and Dietetics: didactic dietetics programs (B,M)

DIETI Academy of Nutrition and Dietetics: dietetic post-baccalaureate internships

DIETT Academy of Nutrition and Dietetics: dietetic technician (A)

DMOLS National Accrediting Agency for Clinical Laboratory Sciences: diagnostic molecular scientist (C,B,M)

DMS Commission on Accreditation of Allied Health Education Programs: diagnostic medical sonography (C,A,B,M)

DNUR Accreditation Commission for Education in Nursing: nursing (C)

DT American Dental Association: dental laboratory technology (C,A)

EMT Commission on Accreditation of Allied Health Education Programs: emergency medical technician-paramedic (C,A,B)

ENG ABET, Inc.: engineering (B,M)

ENGR ABET, Inc.: applied science (A,B,M)

ENGT ABET, Inc.: engineering technology (A,B)

EXSC Commission on Accreditation of Allied Health Education Programs: exercise science (C,B,M)

FEPAC American Academy of Forensic Sciences: forensic science (B,M)

FOR Society of American Foresters: forestry (B,M)

FUSER American Board of Funeral Service Education: funeral service education (C,A,B)

HSA Commission on Accreditation of Healthcare Management Education: healthcare management (B,M)

HT National Accrediting Agency for Clinical Laboratory Sciences: histologic technology (C,A,B)

IACBE International Assembly for Collegiate Business Education: business programs in institutions that grant bachelor/graduate degrees (A,B,M,D)

IFSAC International Fire Service Accreditation Congress Degree Assembly: fire and emergency related degree (A,B)

IPSY American Psychological Association: pre-doctoral internships in professional psychology

JOUR Accrediting Council on Education for Journalism and Mass Communications: journalism and mass communications (B,M)

KIN Commission on Accreditation of Allied Health Education Programs: kinesiotherapy (B)

LAW American Bar Association: law (FP,D)

LIB American Library Association: librarianship (M)

LSAR American Society for Landscape Architects: landscape architecture (B,M)

MAAB Accrediting Bureau of Health Education Schools: medical assisting (C,A)

MAC Commission on Accreditation of Allied Health Education Programs: medical assisting (C,A)

MACTE Montessori Accreditation Council for Teacher Education: Montessori teacher education (C)

MEAC Midwifery Education Accreditation Council: midwifery education (C,A,B,M,D)

MED Liaison Committee on Medical Education: medicine (FP,D)

MFCD American Association for Marriage and Family Therapy: marriage and family therapy (M,D)

MIDWF Accreditation Commission for Midwifery Education: nurse midwifery (C,M,D)

MIL Commission on Accreditation of Allied Health Education Programs: medical illustrator (M)

MLTAB Accrediting Bureau of Health Education Schools: medical laboratory technician (C,A)

MLTAD National Accrediting Agency for Clinical Laboratory Sciences: medical laboratory technician (C,A)

MT National Accrediting Agency for Clinical Laboratory Sciences: medical technology/laboratory scientist (C,B)

MUS National Association of Schools of Music: music (C,A,B,M,D)

NAIT The Association of Technology, Management, and Applied Engineering: technology, applied technology, engineering technology and technology-related programs (A,B,M)

NATUR Council on Naturopathic Medical Education: naturopathic medical education (FP,D)

NDT Commission on Accreditation of Allied Health Education Programs: neurodiagnostic technology (C,A)

NMT Joint Review Committee on Educational Programs in Nuclear Medicine Technology: nuclear medicine technology (C,A,B)

NRPA National Recreation and Park Association: recreation, park resources, and leisure studies (B)

NUR Accreditation Commission for Education in Nursing: nursing (B, M,D)

NURSE Commission on Collegiate Nursing Education: nursing (B,M,D)

NY New York State Board of Regents:
Degree-granting institutions of higher education in New York that designate the agency as their sole or primary nationally recognized accrediting agency for purposes of establishing elibility to participate in Higher Education Act programs

OPD Commission on Opticianry Accreditation: opticianry (A)

OPE Commission on Accreditation of Allied Health Education Programs: orthotics and prosthetics (C,B,M)

OPLT Commission on Opticianry Accreditation: opthalmic laboratory technician (C)

OPT American Optometric Association: optometry (FP,D)

OPTR American Optometric Association: optometric residency programs

OPTT American Optometric Association: optometric technician (C,A)

OSTEO American Osteopathic Association, Office of Osteopathic Education: osteopathic medicine (FP,D)

OT American Occupational Therapy Association: occupational therapy (M,D)

OTA American Occupational Therapy Association: occupational therapy assistant (C,A)

PA National Accrediting Agency for Clinical Laboratory Sciences: pathologist's assistant (C,M)

PAST Association for Clinical Pastoral Education: clinical pastoral education

PCSAS Psychological Clinical Science Accreditation System: psychological clinical science (D)

PDPSY American Psychological Association: post-doctorate residency in professional psychology

PERF Commission on Accreditation of Allied Health Education Programs: perfusionist (C,B,M)

PH Council on Education for Public Health: public health (B,M,D)

PHAR Accreditation Council for Pharmaceutical Education: pharmacy (FP,D)

PHLEB National Accrediting Agency for Clinical Laboratory Sciences: phlebotomist (C)

PLNG Planning Accreditation Board: certified planning (B,M)

PNUR Accreditation Commission for Education in Nursing: practical nursing (C)

POD American Podiatric Medical Association: podiatry (FP,D)

POLYT Commission on Accreditation of Allied Health Education Programs: polysomnographic technologist education (C,A)

PSPSY American Psychological Association: combined professional-scientific psychology (D)

PTA American Physical Therapy Association: physical therapy (M,D)

PTAA American Physical Therapy Association: physical therapy assistant (A)

RABN Association of Advanced Rabbinical and Talmudic Schools: rabbinical and Talmudic education (B,M,D)

RAD Joint Review Committee on Education in Radiologic Technology: radiography (C,A,B)

RADDOS Joint Review Committee on Education in Radiologic Technology: medical dosimetry (C,B,M)

RADMAG Joint Review Committee on Education in Radiologic Technology: magnetic resonance (C,B)

RTT Joint Review Committee on Education in Radiologic Technology: radiation therapist/technologist (C,A,B)

SCPSY American Psychological Association: school psychology (D)

SP American Speech-Language-Hearing Association: speech-language pathology (M)

SPAA Network of Schools of Public Policy, Affairs and Administration: public affairs and administration (M)

SURGA Commission on Accreditation of Allied Health Education Programs: surgical assistant (C,A)

SURGT Commission on Accreditation of Allied Health Education Programs: surgical technology (C,A)

SURTEC Accrediting Bureau of Health Education Schools: surgical technologist (C,A)

SW Council on Social Work Education: social work (B,M)

TEAC Teacher Education Accreditation Council: teacher education (B, M,D)

TED National Council for Accreditation of Teacher Education: teacher education (B,M,S,D)

THEA National Association of Schools of Theatre: theatre (C,A,B,M,D)

THEOL Association of Theological Schools: theology (M,FP,D)

TRACS Transnational Association of Christian Colleges and Schools: christian studies education (C,A,B,M,D)

VET American Veterinary Medical Association: veterinary medicine (FP,D)

Explanatory Notes and Symbols

Associate degree: includes junior colleges, community colleges, technical institutes, and schools offering at least a two-year program of college-level studies, either leading to an associate degree wholly or principally creditable toward a baccalaureate degree.

Baccalaureate: includes those institutions offering programs of studies leading to the customary bachelor of arts or bachelor of science degrees.

First professional degree: includes those institutions that offer the academic requirements for selected professions based on programs that require at least two academic years of previous college work for entrance and a total of at least six years of college work for completion.

Master's: includes those institutions offering the customary first graduate degree, master of arts or master of science degree in the liberal arts and sciences, or the next degree in the same field after the first professional degree.

Beyond master's but less than doctorate: includes those institutions offering "postgraduate pre-doctoral degrees".

Graduate non-degree granting: includes institutions offering work beyond the bachelor's level but not conferring degrees. In some instances the degrees are conferred by cooperating institutions.

Doctorate: includes those institutions offering a Ph.D. or its equivalent in any field.

Postdoctoral research only: includes institutions operating solely for the purpose of research at the postdoctoral level.

First Talmudic degree: undergraduate degree granted by accredited Rabbinical schools. The schools in New York "using this designation do not imply that the 'First Talmudic Degree' is equivalent to any secular academic degree recognized by the Board of Regents".*

Second Talmudic degree: graduate degree granted by accredited Rabbinical schools. The schools in New York "using this designation do not imply that the 'Second Talmudic Degree' is equivalent to any secular academic degree recognized by the Board of Regents".*

---

*The University of the State of New York, The State Education Department, Albany, New York, letter August 17, 1983.

Type of Program

Occupational: refers to programs beyond high school designed to provide students with knowledge and skills necessary for immediate employment.

Two-year principally bachelor's creditable: refers to the first two years of college work.

Liberal arts and general: refers to four or five year baccalaureate or postbaccalaureate degree programs in the liberal arts and sciences.

Teacher preparatory programs: refers to programs of at least four years duration.

Professional programs: refers to separate programs of at least four years beyond high school and organized around a professionally oriented academic discipline.

Business, fine arts, music, nursing, religious, or technical emphasis: refers to programs that are organized around a specific discipline.

Symbols

* The institution is part of a system.

Used preceding any of the acronyms for the accrediting agencies the following symbols indicate that:

The accrediting agency has stated publicly that the institution or program is preliminary or provisionally accredited, accredited with some reservations, or approved on probation.

@ The institution or program has attained a pre-accredited status.

& The institution is covered under the regional accreditation of the parent institution.

U.S. Postal Abbreviation of States and Territories

Alabama .... AL
Alaska .... AK
American Samoa .... AS
Arizona .... AZ
Arkansas .... AR
California .... CA
Colorado .... CO
Connecticut .... CT
Delaware .... DE
District of Columbia .... DC
Florida .... FL
Georgia .... GA
Guam .... GU
Hawaii .... HI
Idaho .... ID
Illinois IL
Indiana .... IN
Iowa .... IA
Kansas .... KS
Kentucky .... KY
Louisiana .... LA
Maine .... ME
Maryland .... MD
Marshall Islands .... MH
Massachusetts .... MA
Michigan .... MI
Micronesia .... FM
Minnesota .... MN
Mississippi .... MS
Missouri .... MO
Montana .... MT
Nebraska .... NE
Nevada .... NV
New Hampshire .... NH
New Jersey .... NJ
New Mexico .... NM
New York .... NY
North Carolina .... NC
North Dakota .... ND
Northern Marianas .... MP
Ohio .... OH
Oklahoma .... OK
Oregon .... OR
Palau .... PW
Pennsylvania .... PA
Puerto Rico .... PR
Rhode Island .... RI
South Carolina .... SC
South Dakota .... SD
Tennessee .... TN
Texas .... TX
Utah .... UT
Vermont .... VT
Virgin Islands VI
Virginia .... VA
Washington .... WA
West Virginia .... WV
Wisconsin .... WI
Wyoming .... WY

Institution Changes

Institutions and Offices Added

	FICE/ID Number
Alabama	
Alabama College of Osteopathic Medicine	667138
California	
Advanced Computing Institute	667142
Angeles College	041604
Charter College-Canyon Country	032783
CNI College	032423
East San Gabriel Valley Regional Occupational Program and Technical Center	031166
Gurnick Academy of Medical Arts	041698
International Professional School of Bodywork	041347
International Reformed University and Seminary	667132
Kaiser Permanente School of Allied Health Sciences	667152
Los Angeles Pacific College	667143
Mayfield College	041156
Methodist Theological Seminary in America	667133
National Career College	041460
Presidio Graduate School	667150
Valley College of Medical Careers	041145
Willow International Community College Center	667125
Colorado	
Academy of Natural Therapy	040933
Pima Medical Institute	041771
Delaware	
Irish American University	667120
District of Columbia	
Graduate School USA	667121
Florida	
Allied Health Institute	041359
American Medical Academy	041921
Institute of Technical Arts	036183
Orlando Medical Institute	667127
Saber College	036964
San Ignacio College	667130
The Praxis Institute	031147
Unilatina International College	667155
WyoTech	023462
Georgia	
Medtech College	038044
SAE Institute Atlanta	042066

	FICE/ID Number
Illinois	
Ambria College of Nursing	041247
Chamberlain College of Nursing	667149
Indiana	
Radiological Technologies University-VT	667156
Kansas	
Kansas City College and Bible School	667134
Wichita Technical Institute	010503
Louisiana	
Blue Cliff College	034225
Maine	
New England Bible College	667135
Michigan	
Manthano Christian College	667140
MIAT College of Technology	020603
Minnesota	
Bethany College of Missions	667136
Missouri	
Brookes Bible Institute	667137
Midwest University	035283
Rockbridge Seminary	667151
Nevada	
Northwest Career College	038385
New Jersey	
Eastwick College	667131
New York	
Bet Medrash Gadol Ateret Torah	667146
City University of New York Stella and Charles Guttman Community College	667126
Dorothea Hopfer School of Nursing at Mount Vernon Hospital	022178
Finger Lakes Health College of Nursing	667154
Rabbinical College Ohr Yisroel	667145
Yeshiva Sholom Shachna	667147
Oklahoma	
College of the Muscogee Nation	667122
Comanche Nation College	667123

Institution Changes

	FICE/ID Number
Oregon	
National College of Technical Instruction-College of Emergency Services	667128
Sumner College	021049
Pennsylvania	
Great Lakes Institute of Technology	021122
Lancaster County Career and Technology Center	023108
Tennessee	
SAE Institute of Technology Nashville	038303
The Crown College of the Bible	667141
Texas	
Baptist Hospitals of Southeast Texas School of Radiologic Technology	667153
Concorde Career Institute	035423
Dallas Nursing Institute	034165
Quest College	034003
University of North Texas at Dallas	667124
Utah	
Nightingale College	038383
Virginia	
Centra College of Nursing	021758
Riverside School of Health Careers	021400
Standard Healthcare Services College of Nursing	667129
Virginia Tech Carilion School of Medicine	667148
Washington	
Perry Technical Institute	009387
Tacoma Bible College	667139
Wisconsin	
Milwaukee Career College	041174

Institutions and Offices Dropped

	FICE/ID Number
Arizona	
DeVry University - Northeast Phoenix Center *(Closed)*	666191
Lamson College *(Closed)*	025215
California	
Carrington College California - Antioch *(Closed)*	666041
Carrington College California - Emeryville *(Closed)*	666372
Fashion Careers College *(Closed)*	022343
ICDC College *(Closed)*	033953
Infotech Career College *(No longer degree granting)*	041327
ITT Technical Institute *(Closed)*	022916
Kaplan College *(Closed)*	025654
LA College International *(Closed)*	023124
North-West College *(No longer degree ganting)*	011707
Samra University of Oriental Medicine *(Closed)*	026193
Colorado	
Boulder College of Massage Therapy *(Closed)*	030131
ITT Technical Institute *(Closed)*	023217
Kaplan College *(Closed)*	021676
National Theatre Conservatory *(Closed)*	025179
District of Columbia	
Washington Theological Union *(Closed)*	010065
Florida	
Aerosim Flight Academy *(No longer degree granting)*	041571
ATI Career Training Center *(No longer accredited by ACCSC)*	022159
ATI Career Training Center *(No longer accredited by ACCSC)*	030355
ATI Career Training Center *(No longer accredited by ACCSC)*	022932
Florida Medical Training Institute-Coral Springs *(No longer accredited by ABHES)*	666612
Kaplan College *(Closed)*	666752
Stenotype Institute of Jacksonville *(No longer degree granting)*	008417
Teacher Education University *(Withdrew from DETC)*	666342
Georgia	
DeVry University - Atlanta Buckhead Center *(Closed)*	666200
Everest Institute *(Closed)*	666285

	FICE/ID Number
University of Atlanta *(No longer accredited)*	666399

Illinois

The College of Office Technology *(No longer accredited by ACICS)*	023378

Indiana

Harrison College - Muncie Campus *(Closed)*	030097

Louisiana

Baton Rouge College *(No longer accredited by CNCE)*	026171

Maryland

Washington Bible College/Capital Bible Seminary *(Closed)*	001462

Minnesota

College of Visual Arts *(Closed)*	007462
Globe University Northwest Technical Institute *(Closed)*	008267

Missouri

IHM Academy of EMS *(No longer degree granting)*	667021
Sanford-Brown College *(Closed)*	666456

New Jersey

University of Medicine and Dentistry of New Jersey *(Closed)*	010394

New York

Long Island College Hospital School of Nursing *(Closed)*	021187
Olean Business Institute *(Closed)*	009003
Seminary of the Immaculate Conception *(Closed)*	002683
Simmons Institute of Funeral Service, Inc. *(Closed)*	010837

Ohio

ATS Institute of Technology *(No longer degree granting)*	034685
Chancellor University *(Closed)*	003043
Kaplan College *(Closed)*	011005
Lincoln College *(Closed)*	666472

	FICE/ID Number
Lincoln College of Technology *(Closed)*	666473
Lincoln College of Technology *(Closed)*	012128
Lincoln College of Technology *(Closed)*	666471

Oregon

Carrington College - Portland *(Closed)*	030425

Pennsylvania

ITT Technical Institute *(Closed)*	666320
ITT Technical Institute *(Closed)*	666322

Texas

ATI Career Training Center *(No longer accredited by ACCSC)*	025966
Lon Morris College *(Closed)*	003585
Westwood College-Dallas *(Closed)*	666427
Westwood College-Fort Worth *(Closed)*	666434
Westwood College-Houston South *(Closed)*	666309

Virginia

Aviation Institute of Maintenance *(No longer degree granting)*	031263
Saint Paul's College *(Closed)*	003739

West Virginia

Mountain State University *(Closed)*	003807

Wisconsin

Sanford-Brown College-Milwaukee *(Closed)*	666306

Merged Institutions

California

Fresno Pacific Biblical Seminary *into*	010368
Fresno Pacific University	001253

Florida

Everest Institute *into*	666271
Everest Institute	021218

Institution Changes

FICE/ID Number

Georgia

Augusta State University *into*	001552
Merged with Georgia Health Science *to become*	
Georgia Regents University	001579
Gainesville State College *into*	001567
North Georgia College & State University *to become*	
The University of North Georgia	001585
Middle Georgia College *into*	001581
Merged with Macon State College *to become*	
Middle Georgia State College	007728
Waycross College *into*	020550
South Georgia State College	001592

Louisiana

Northeast Louisiana Technical College Bastrop Campus *into*	667030
Louisiana Delta Community College	041301
Northeast Louisiana Technical College Delta-Ouachita Campus *into*	005471
Louisiana Delta Community College	041301
Northeast Louisiana Technical College Farmerville Campus *into*	005476
Louisiana Delta Community College	041301
Northeast Louisiana Technical College Northeast Campus *into*	005475
Louisiana Delta Community College	041301
Northeast Louisiana Technicial College Ruston Campus *into*	023404
Louisiana Delta Community College	041301

Missouri

Assemblies of God Theological Seminary *into*	012120
Evangel University	002463
Central Bible College *into*	002452
Evangel University	002463

New Jersey

UMDNJ-School of Osteopathic Medicine *into*	024540
Rowan University	002609

Ohio

Laura and Alvin Siegal College of Judaic Studies *into*	012838
Case Western Reserve University	003024

Texas

Hallmark College of Aeronautics *into*	666623
Hallmark College of Technology	010509

FICE/ID Number

Name Changes

Arizona

from: Arizona College of Allied Health *to:* Arizona College	031150
from: Asian Institute of Medical Studies *to:* Han University of Traditional Medicine	041193
from: Pima County Community College District *to:* Pima Community College	007266

Arkansas

from: Bryan College *to:* Bryan University	666252

California

from: Alliant International University-Fresno & Sacramento *to:* Alliant International University-Fresno	001158
from: Applied Professional Training, Inc. *to:* APT College	666245
from: California Culinary Academy *to:* Le Cordon Bleu College of Culinary Arts	022202
from: Chicago School of Professional Psychology *to:* Chicago School of Professional Psychology Los Angeles Campus	021553
from: Everest College-LA Wilshire *to:* Bryman College-LA Wilshire	007606
from: Hands-on Medical Massage School *to:* Ashdown College of Health Sciences	041789
from: Horizon College of San Diego *to:* Horizon University	041405
from: LA Music Academy *to:* LAMA	038684
from: Marymount College *to:* Marymount California University	010474
from: National Test Pilot Institute *to:* National Test Pilot School	667009
from: San Joaquin Valley College, Inc. *to:* San Joaquin Valley College, Inc. - Visalia	021207
from: San Joaquin Valley College-Hesperia *to:* San Joaquin Valley College-Victor Valley (Hesperia)	667044

Colorado

from: Memorial Hospital/Memorial Health System School of Radiologic Technology *to:* UCH Memorial Hospital School Of Radiologic Technology	667097

District of Columbia

from: Potomac College *to:* University of the Potomac	032183

	FICE/ID Number

Florida

from: Academy for Practical Nursing and Health Occupations — 033463
to: Academy for Nursing and Health Occupations

from: Brevard Community College — 001470
to: Eastern Florida State College

from: Centura Institute — 039394
to: Centura College

from: Florida Christian College — 021567
to: Johnson University Florida

from: Lake-Sumter Community College — 001502
to: Lake-Sumter State College

from: Southern Career College — 025982
to: University of Southernmost Florida

from: University of South Florida Manatee-Sarasota — 667058
to: University of South Florida Sarasota-Manatee

Georgia

from: Darton College — 001543
to: Darton State College

from: Georgia Health Sciences University — 001579
to: Georgia Regents University

from: Macon State College — 007728
to: Middle Georgia State College

from: Middle Georgia Technical College — 025086
to: Central Georgia Technical College

from: North Georgia College & State University — 001585
to: University of North Georgia

from: South Georgia College — 001592
to: South Georgia State College

Illinois

from: Ellis University — 041433
to: John Hancock University

from: Rockford College — 001748
to: Rockford University

from: Seabury-Western Theological Seminary — 001754
to: Bexley Seabury

from: Spertus College — 001663
to: Spertus Institute for Jewish Learning and Leadership

Kansas

from: Bryan College — 030662
to: Bryan University

Kentucky

from: Bowling Green Technical College — 005271
to: Southcentral Kentucky Community and Technical College

FICE/ID Number

Louisiana

from: Capital Area Technical College Baton Rouge Campus — 005488
to: Baton Rouge Community College, Acadian Branch

from: Capital Area Technical College Folkes Campus — 025099
to: Baton Rouge Community College, Jackson Branch

from: Capital Area Technical College Jumonville Campus — 005478
to: Baton Rouge Community College, New Roads Branch

from: MedVance Institute-Baton Rouge — 034803
to: Fortis College

Maryland

from: Tai Sophia Institute — 025784
to: Maryland University of Integrative Health

Massachusetts

from: Massachusetts College of Pharmacy and Health Sciences — 002165
to: MCPHS University

from: Zion Bible College — 035705
to: Northpoint Bible College

Michigan

from: Jackson Community College — 002274
to: Jackson College

Minnesota

from: Globe University/Minnesota School of Business — 666453
to: Minnesota School of Business

from: Rasmussen College - Lake Elmo/Woodbury — 667034
to: Rasmussen College Corporate Office

Missouri

from: Bryan College — 030663
to: Bryan University

from: Chamberlain College of Nursing - St. Louis — 006385
to: Chamberlain College of Nursing - Addison

from: Vatterott College-O'Fallon — 666584
to: Vatterott College-St. Charles

Montana

from: The University of Montana - College of Technology — 007561
to: The University of Montana - Missoula College

Nebraska

from: Bryan LGH College of Health Sciences — 006399
to: Bryan College of Health Sciences

Institution Changes

FICE/ID Number

Nevada

from: Morrison University — 010098
to: Neumont University

New Hampshire

from: Hesser College — 004729
to: Mount Washington College

from: Rivier College — 002586
to: Rivier University

New Jersey

from: Saint Peter's College — 002638
to: Saint Peter's University

from: Somerset Christian College — 036663
to: Pillar College

from: UMDNJ-Graduate School of Biomedical Sciences — 011174
to: Rutgers Graduate School of Biomedical Sciences

from: UMDNJ-New Jersey Dental School — 024635
to: Rutgers School of Dental Medicine

from: UMDNJ-New Jersey Medical School — 002620
to: Rutgers-New Jersey Medical School

from: UMDNJ-Robert Wood Johnson Medical School — 024549
to: Rutgers - Robert Wood Johnson Medical School

from: UMDNJ-School of Health Related Professions — 020668
to: Rutgers School of Health Related Professions

from: UMDNJ-School of Nursing — 666970
to: Rutgers School of Nursing

from: UMDNJ-School of Public Health — 666991
to: Rutgers-School of Public Health

New York

from: Ellis School of Nursing — 006448
to: The Belanger School of Nursing

from: Long Island University C.W. Post Campus — 002754
to: Long Island University - Post Campus

from: Mount Sinai School of Medicine — 007026
to: Icahn School of Medicine at Mount Sinai

from: Salvation Army School for Officer Training — 666020
to: Salvation Army College for Officer Training

from: Yeshiva Zidvon Aryeh — 667110
to: Yeshiva Zichron Aryeh

North Carolina

from: Carolina Bible College — 041542
to: Carolina College of Biblical Studies

from: Piedmont Baptist College and Graduate School — 002956
to: Piedmont International University

from: South College — 010264
to: South College-Asheville

FICE/ID Number

North Dakota

from: Jamestown College — 002990
to: University of Jamestown

from: Medcenter One College of Nursing — 009354
to: Sanford College of Nursing

Ohio

from: Akron Institute of Herzing University — 020695
to: Herzing University-Akron

from: Bexley Hall Seminary — 037473
to: Bexley Seabury

from: Kent State University at Stark — 003054
to: Kent State University Stark Campus

from: Kettering College of Medical Arts — 007035
to: Kettering College

from: University of Cincinnati-Raymond Walters College — 004868
to: University of Cincinnati-Blue Ash College

Pennsylvania

from: CHI Institute/Broomall Campus — 007781
to: Kaplan Career Institute/Broomall Campus

from: Clarion University-Venango Campus — 003319
to: Venango College of Clarion University

from: Gwynedd-Mercy College — 003270
to: Gwynedd-Mercy University

from: Philadelphia Biblical University — 003351
to: Cairn University

Puerto Rico

from: Colegio de las Ciencias Artes y Television — 031576
to: Colegio de Cinematografia, Artes y Television

from: EDP College of Puerto Rico — 666488
to: EDP University of Puerto Rico

from: EDP College of Puerto Rico — 021651
to: EDP University of Puerto Rico

from: University of Puerto Rico-Carolina University College — 030160
to: University of Puerto Rico-Carolina

South Carolina

from: Clinton Junior College — 004923
to: Clinton College

Tennessee

from: Baptist Memorial College of Health Sciences — 034403
to: Baptist College of Health Sciences

from: Carson-Newman College — 003481
to: Carson-Newman University

from: Free Will Baptist Bible College — 030018
to: Welch College

from: King College — 003496
to: King University

from: Nashville Auto-Diesel College — 007440
to: Lincoln College of Technology Nashville

	FICE/ID Number
Texas	
from: Computer Career Center *to:* Vista College	025720
from: Franklin College *to:* International Business College	009082
from: Grayson County College *to:* Grayson College	003570
from: Southwest Career College *to:* Southwest University at El Paso	041317
from: Texas A & M Health Science Center Baylor College of Dentistry *to:* Texas A & M University Baylor College of Dentistry	666240
from: Texas College of Traditional Chinese Medicine *to:* Texas Health and Science University	031795
from: Virginia College at Austin *to:* Virginia College Austin	666074
Utah	
from: Utah State University-College of Eastern Utah *to:* Utah State University Eastern	003676
Virginia	
from: National College *to:* American National University	003726
from: Potomac College *to:* University of the Potomac	666178
West Virginia	
from: Alderson Broaddus College *to:* Alderson Broaddus University	003806
from: Martinsburg Institute *to:* Martinsburg College	667035
Wisconsin	
from: Mount Mary College *to:* Mount Mary University	003869

Codes and Descriptions of Administrative Officers

(01) **Chief Executive Officer (President/Chancellor)** - Directs all affairs and operations of a higher education institution.

(02) **Chief Executive Officer Within a System (President/Chancellor)** - Directs all affairs and operations of a campus or an institution which is part of a university-wide system.

(03) **Executive Vice President** - Responsible for all or most functions and operations of an institution under the direction of the Chief Executive Officer.

(04) **Administrative Assistant to the President** - Senior administrative assistant to the Chief Executive Officer.

(05) **Chief Academic Officer** - Directs the academic program of the institution. Typically includes academic planning, teaching, research, extensions and coordination of interdepartmental affairs.

(06) **Registrar** - Responsible for student registration, scheduling of classes, examinations and classroom facilities, student records and related matters.

(07) **Director of Admissions** - Responsible for the recruitment, selection and admission of students.

(08) **Head Librarian** - Directs the activities of all institutional libraries.

(09) **Director of Institutional Research** - Conducts research and studies on the institution including design of studies, data collection, analysis and reporting.

(10) **Chief Financial/Business Officer** - Directs business and financial affairs including accounting, purchasing, investments, auxiliary enterprises and related business matters.

(11) **Chief of Operations/Administration** - Responsible for administrative functions that are generally non-academic and non-financial.

(12) **Director of Branch Campus** - Official who is in charge of a branch campus.

(13) **Director, Computing and Information Management** - Coordinates computing systems and the flow of information to and from computing operations.

(14) **Director, Computer Center** - Directs the institution's major data processing facilities and services.

(15) **Director, Personnel Services** - Administers the institution's personnel policies and programs for staff or faculty and staff.

(16) **Chief, Personnel** - Responsible for establishing and directing personnel policies including government related requirements.

(17) **Chief, Health Care Professions** - Senior administrator of academic health care programs, hospitals, clinic or affiliated healthcare programs.

(18) **Chief, Facilities/Physical Plant** - Responsible for the construction, rehabilitation and maintenance of buildings and grounds.

(19) **Director, Security/Safety** - Manages campus police. Responsible for security programs, training, traffic and parking regulations.

(20) **Associate Academic Officer** - Responsible for many of the functions and operations under the direction of the Chief Academic Officer.

(21) **Associate Business Officer** - Assists and reports to the Chief Business Officer.

(22) **Director, Affirmative Action/Equal Opportunity** - Responsible for the institution's program relating to affirmative action and equal opportunity.

(23) **Director, Health Services** - Directs the operation of clinics, medical staff and other programs which provide institutional health services.

(24) **Director, Educational Media** - Responsible for audio-visual services and multimedia learning devices.

(25) **Contract Administrator** - Conducts administrative activities in connection with contracts and grants.

(26) **Chief Public Relations Officer** - Directs public relations program. May include alumni relations, publication, marketing and development.

(27) **Chief Information Officer** - Provides information about the institution to students, faculty, staff and the public.

(28) **Director of Diversity** - Responsible for the institution's programs relating to diversity.

(29) **Director, Alumni Relations** - Coordinates alumni activities between the institution and the alumni.

(30) **Chief, Development** - Organizes and directs programs connected with the fund raising activities of the institution.

(31) **Chief Community Relations Officer** - Directs the educational (usually non-credit), cultural and recreational services to the community.

(32) **Chief Student Life Officer** - Responsible for the direction of student life programs including counseling and testing, housing, placement, student union, relationships with student organizations and related functions.

(33) **Dean of Men** - Directs student life activities solely concerned with male students.

(34) **Dean of Women** - Directs student life activities solely concerned with female students.

(35) **Director, Student Affairs** - Assists Chief Student Life Officer in the non-academic student life activities.

(36) **Director, Student Placement** - Directs the operation of the student placement office to provide career counseling and job placement services to undergraduates, graduates and alumni.

(37) **Director, Student Financial Aid** - Directs the administration of all forms of student aid.

(38) **Director, Student Counseling** - Directs non-academic counseling and testing for students including referral to outside agencies.

(39) **Director, Student Housing** - Manages student housing operations.

(40) **Director, Bookstore** - Responsible for the operation of the bookstore including purchasing, advertising, sales, employment, inventory and related functions.

(41) **Athletic Director** - Manages intramural and intercollegiate programs including employment, scheduling, promotion, maintenance and related functions.

(42) **Chaplain, Director Campus Ministry** - Plans, directs the pastoral ministry and religious activities.

(43) **Director, Legal Services (General Counsel)** - Salaried staff person responsible for advising on legal rights, obligations and related matters.

(44) **Director, Annual or Planned Giving** - Operates the annual giving from all supporters of the institutions.

(45) **Chief Planning Officer** - Directs the long-range planning and the allocation of the institution's resources.

(46) **Chief, Research and Development (not fundraising)** - Initiates and directs research in using the facilities and personnel in new areas of academic and scientific exploration.

Dean or Director. Serves as the principal administrator for the institutional program indicated:

(47) **Agriculture**
(48) **Architecture**
(49) **Art and Sciences**
(50) **Business**
(51) **Continuing Education**
(52) **Dentistry**
(53) **Education**
(54) **Engineering**
(55) **Evening Division**
(56) **Extension**
(57) **Fine Arts**
(58) **Graduate Programs**
(59) **Home Economics**
(60) **Journalism/Communications**
(61) **Law**
(62) **Library Services**
(63) **Medicine**
(64) **Music**
(65) **Natural Resources**
(66) **Nursing**
(67) **Pharmacy**
(68) **Physical Education**
(69) **Public Health**
(70) **Social Work**
(71) **Special Session**
(72) **Technology**
(73) **Theology**
(74) **Veterinary Medicine**
(75) **Vocational/Occupational Education**
(76) **Allied Health Sciences**
(77) **Computer Science**
(78) **Cooperative Education**
(79) **Humanities**
(80) **Government/Public Affairs**
(81) **Mathematics/Sciences**
(82) **Political Science/International Affairs**
(83) **Social and Behavioral Sciences**
(87) **Summer School/Session**
(89) **Freshmen Studies**
(92) **Honors Program**
(93) **Minority Students**
(94) **Women's Studies**
(97) **General Studies**
(106) **Online Education/E-learning**
(107) **Professional Studies**

(84) **Director, Enrollment Management** - Plans, develops, and implements strategies to sustain enrollment. Supervises administration of all admissions and financial aid operations.

(85) **Director, Foreign Students** - Directs student life activities solely concerned with foreign students.

(86) **Director, Government Relations** - Coordinates institution's relations with local, state, and federal government.

(90) **Director, Academic Computing** - Responsible for operation and coordination of the institution's various academic computer facilities and labs.

(91) **Director, Administrative Computing** - Responsible for operation of the institution's administrative computing facility.

(96) **Director of Purchasing** - Coordinates purchasing of goods and services.

(100) **Chief of Staff** - Senior non-secretarial staff assistant to the President/Chancellor. Manages administration and operations of The Office of the President.

(101) **Secretary of the Institution/Board of Governors** - Responsible for liaison between the Board and the institution. Maintains governance and official Board records.

(102) **Director, Foundation/Corporate Relations** - Directs institution's efforts in the area of soliciting grants and gifts from foundations and corporations.

(103) **Director, Workforce Development** - Directs the institution's efforts in course development and instruction for students and the community in skills necessary to gain employment.

(104) **Director, Study Abroad** - Coordinates and advises students and faculty on academic studies conducted internationally.

(105) **Director, Web Services** - Directs the development, operations and content of the institution's web sites.

(108) **Director, Institutional Assessment** - Facilitates and directs institution-wide assessment activities for academic programs and non-academic departments.

(88) Use this code for those titles that do not fit the above positions.

(00) **President Emeritus**

United States Department of Education Offices

Arne Duncan (A)
Secretary of Education
United States Department of Education
400 Maryland Avenue, SW
Washington, DC 20202
(202) 401-3000
FAX: (202) 260-7867
URL: www.ed.gov

Martha J. Kanter Ed.D. (B)
Under Secretary of Education
United States Department of Education
400 Maryland Avenue, SW
Washington, DC 20202
(202) 401-0264
FAX: (202) 205-0063
E-MAIL: martha.kanter@ed.gov
URL: www.ed.gov

Brenda Dann-Messier (C)
Acting Assistant Secretary
Office of Postsecondary Education
United States Department of Education
1990 K Street, NW
Washington, DC 20006
(202) 502-7750
FAX: (202) 502-7677
E-MAIL: brenda.dann-messier@ed.gov
URL: www2.ed.gov/about/offices/list/ope/index.html

Ms. Carol Griffiths (D)
Executive Director
National Advisory Committee on Institutional Quality & Integrity
Office of Postsecondary Education
United States Department of Education
1990 K Street, NW
Room 8073
Washington, DC 20006
(202) 219-7009
FAX: (202) 219-7005
E-MAIL: carol.griffiths@ed.gov
URL: www.ed.gov/about/bdscomm/list/naciqi.html

Ms. Kay Gilcher (E)
Director
Accreditation Division
Office of Postsecondary Education
U.S. Department of Education
1990 K Street, NW
Room 8027
Washington, DC 20006-8509
(202) 502-7693
URL: www.ed.gov/admins/finaid/accred/index.html

Mr. Jack Buckley (F)
Commissioner
National Center for Education Statistics
1990 K Street, NW
Room 9049
Washington, DC 20006
(202) 502-7300
FAX: (202) 502-7466
E-MAIL: jack.buckley@ed.gov
URL: www.nces.ed.gov

Ms. Carol Griffiths (G)
Executive Director
National Committee on Foreign Medical Education
and Accreditation (NCFMEA)
U.S. Department of Education
1990 K Street, NW
Room 8073
Washington, DC 20006
(202) 219-7009
FAX: (202) 219-7005
E-MAIL: carol.griffiths@ed.gov
URL: www2.ed.gov/about/bdscomm/list/ncfmea.html

Statewide Agencies of Higher Education

ALABAMA

Alabama Commission on Higher Education (H)
PO Box 302000
Montgomery, AL 36130-2000
(334) 242-1998
FAX: (334) 242-0268
Dr. Gregory G. Fitch
Executive Director
E-MAIL: gregory.fitch@ache.alabama.gov
URL: www.ache.alabama.gov

State of Alabama Department of Postsecondary Education (I)
135 South Union Street
PO Box 302130
Montgomery, AL 36130
(334) 293-4524
FAX: (334) 293-4526
Mark A. Heinrich Ph.D.
Chancellor
E-MAIL: mark.heinrich@dpe.edu
URL: www.accs.cc

ALASKA

Alaska Commission on Postsecondary Education (J)
PO Box 110505
Juneau, AK 99811-0505
(907) 465-6740
FAX: (907) 465-3293
Ms. Diane Barrans
Executive Director
E-MAIL: ACPE.execdirector@alaska.gov
URL: www.acpe.alaska.gov

ARIZONA

Arizona Board of Regents (K)
2020 North Central Avenue
Suite 230
Phoenix, AZ 85004-4593
(602) 229-2500
FAX: (602) 229-2555
Eileen Klein
President
E-MAIL: eileen.klein@azregents.edu
URL: www.azregents.edu

Arizona Commission for Postsecondary Education (L)
2020 North Central Avenue
Suite 650
Phoenix, AZ 85004-4503
(602) 258-2435
FAX: (602) 258-2483
Dr. April L. Osborn
Executive Director
E-MAIL: acpe@azhighered.gov
URL: www.azhighered.gov

ARKANSAS

Arkansas Department of Higher Education (M)
423 Main Street
Suite 400
Little Rock, AR 72106
(501) 371-2030
FAX: (501) 371-2003
Mr. Shane Broadway
Interim Director of Higher Education
E-MAIL: shane.broadway@adhe.edu
URL: www.adhe.edu

CALIFORNIA

California Community Colleges Chancellor's Office (N)
1102 Q Street
4th Floor
Sacramento, CA 95811
(916) 322-4005
FAX: (916) 322-4783
Dr. Brice W. Harris
Chancellor
E-MAIL: bharris@cccco.edu
URL: www.cccco.edu

COLORADO

Colorado Department of Higher Education (O)
1560 Broadway
Suite 1600
Denver, CO 80202
(303) 866-2723
FAX: (303) 866-4266
Lt.Gov. Joseph Garcia
Executive Director
E-MAIL: josephgarcia.executivedirector@dhe.state.co.us
URL: highered.colorado.gov

Colorado Community College System (P)
9101 East Lowry Boulevard
Denver, CO 80230-6011
(303) 595-1552
FAX: (303) 620-4043
Dr. Nancy J. McCallin
President
E-MAIL: president@cccs.edu
URL: www.cccs.edu

CONNECTICUT

Board of Regents for Higher Education (Q)
Connecticut State Colleges & Universities
39 Woodland Street
Hartford, CT 06105
(860) 493-0011
Dr. Gregory W. Gray
President
E-MAIL: grayg@ct.edu
URL: www.ct.edu

Office of Higher Education (R)
61 Woodland Street
Hartford, CT 06105-2326
(860) 947-1801
FAX: (860) 947-1310
Jane A. Ciarleglio
Executive Director
E-MAIL: jciarleglio@ctohe.org
URL: www.ctohe.org

DELAWARE

Delaware Higher Education Office (S)
Townsend Building
401 Federal Street
Suite 2
Dover, DE 19901
(302) 735-4120
FAX: (302) 739-5894
Director
E-MAIL: dheo@doe.k12.de.us
URL: www.doe.k12.de.us/dheo

Delaware Technical Community College (T)
PO Box 897
Dover, DE 19903
(302) 739-4053
FAX: (302) 739-6225
Dr. Orlando J. George Jr.
President
E-MAIL: pres@dtcc.edu
URL: www.dtcc.edu

DISTRICT OF COLUMBIA

Office of the State Superintendent of Education Government of the District of Columbia (U)
810 First Street, NE
9th Floor
Washington, DC 20002
(202) 727-6436
FAX: (202) 727-2019
Hosanna Mahaley-Jones
State Superintendent of Education
E-MAIL: osse@dc.gov
URL: www.osse.dc.gov

District of Columbia Education Licensure Commission (V)
810 First Street, NE
2nd Floor
Washington, DC 20002
(202) 724-2095
FAX: (202) 741-0229
Ms. Robin Y. Jenkins
Executive Director
E-MAIL: robin.jenkins@dc.gov
URL: www.osse.dc.gov

FLORIDA

Board of Governors State University System of Florida (W)
325 West Gaines Street
Suite 1614
Tallahassee, FL 32399-0400
(850) 245-0466
FAX: (850) 245-9685
Frank T. Brogan
Chancellor
E-MAIL: chancellor@flbog.edu
URL: www.flbog.edu

State of Florida Department of Education Division of Florida Colleges (X)
325 West Gaines Street
1544 Turlington Building
Tallahassee, FL 32399-0400
(850) 245-9449
FAX: (850) 245-9525
Mr. Randall W. Hanna
Chancellor
E-MAIL: randy.hanna@fldoe.org
URL: www.fldoe.org/cc

GEORGIA

Board of Regents of the University System of Georgia (Y)
270 Washington Street, SW
Atlanta, GA 30334
(404) 962-3000
FAX: (404) 962-3013
Mr. Henry Huckaby
Chancellor
E-MAIL: chancellor@usg.edu
URL: www.usg.edu

University System of Georgia (Z)
270 Washington Street, SW
Atlanta, GA 30334
(404) 962-3069
FAX: (404) 962-3093
Dr. Susan Campbell Lounsbury
Asst Vice Chanc for Research & Policy Analysis
E-MAIL: susan.campbell@usg.edu
URL: www.usg.edu

HAWAII

State Post-Secondary Education Commission Department of Commerce and Consumer Affairs Professional and Vocational Licensing (a)
HI
(808) 586-3000
URL: www.hawaii.edu/offices/bor/

Statewide Agencies of Higher Education

IDAHO

Idaho State Board of Education (A)
PO Box 83720
Boise, ID 83720-0037
(208) 334-2270
FAX: (208) 334-2632
Dr. Mike Rush
Executive Director
E-MAIL: mike.rush@osbe.idaho.gov
URL: boardofed.idaho.gov

ILLINOIS

Illinois Board of Higher Education (B)
431 East Adams
2nd Floor
Springfield, IL 62701-1404
(217) 782-2551
FAX: (217) 782-8548
Dr. Harry J. Berman
Executive Director
E-MAIL: berman@ibhe.org
URL: www.ibhe.org

Illinois Community College Board (C)
401 East Capitol Avenue
Springfield, IL 62701-1874
(217) 785-0123
FAX: (217) 785-7495
Dr. Karen Hunter Anderson
Executive Director
E-MAIL: karen.h.anderson@illinois.gov
URL: www.iccb.org

INDIANA

Indiana Commission for Higher Education (D)
101 West Ohio Street
Suite 550
Indianapolis, IN 46204
(317) 464-4400
FAX: (317) 464-4410
Mrs. Teresa Lubbers
Commissioner for Higher Education
E-MAIL: Teresal@che.in.gov
URL: www.che.in.gov

IOWA

Board of Regents, State of Iowa (E)
11260 Aurora Avenue
Urbandale, IA 50322-7905
(515) 281-3934
FAX: (515) 281-6420
Mr. Robert Donley
Executive Director
E-MAIL: bdonley@iastate.edu
URL: www.regents.iowa.gov

Iowa College Student Aid Commission (F)
430 East Grand Avenue
3rd Floor
Des Moines, IA 50309
(515) 725-3410
FAX: (515) 725-3401
Ms. Karen Misjak
Executive Director
E-MAIL: karen.misjak@iowa.gov
URL: www.iowacollegeaid.org

Iowa Department of Education Division of Community Colleges (G)
400 East 14th Street
Grimes State Office Building
Des Moines, IA 50319-0146
(515) 281-8260
FAX: (515) 242-5988
Jeremy Varner
Administrator
E-MAIL: jeremy.varner@iowa.gov
URL: www.educateiowa.gov

KANSAS

Kansas Board of Regents (H)
1000 SW Jackson
Suite 520
Topeka, KS 66612-1368
(785) 296-3421
FAX: (785) 296-0983
Dr. Andy Tompkins
President and CEO
E-MAIL: atompkins@ksbor.org
URL: www.kansasregents.org

Kansas Legislative Research Department (I)
Room 68 West, State Capitol Building
300 SW 10th Avenue
Topeka, KS 66612-1504
(785) 296-3181
FAX: (785) 296-3824
Mr. Raney L. Gilliland
Director
E-MAIL: kslegres@klrd.ks.gov
URL: www.kslegislature.org/klrd

KENTUCKY

Kentucky Council on Postsecondary Education (J)
1024 Capital Center Drive
Suite 320
Frankfort, KY 40601
(502) 573-1555
FAX: (502) 573-1535
Mr. Robert L. King
President
E-MAIL: mary.morse@ky.gov
URL: cpe.ky.gov

Kentucky Community & Technical College System (K)
300 North Main Street
Versailles, KY 40383
(859) 256-3132
FAX: (859) 256-3116
Dr. Michael B. McCall
President
E-MAIL: president@kctcs.edu
URL: www.kctcs.edu

LOUISIANA

Board of Regents (L)
PO Box 3677
Baton Rouge, LA 70821-3677
(225) 342-4253
FAX: (225) 342-9318
Dr. James E. Purcell
Commissioner of Higher Education
E-MAIL: jim.purcell@la.gov
URL: regents.la.gov

Louisiana Department of Education (M)
PO Box 94064
Baton Rouge, LA 70804-9064
(225) 342-3607
FAX: (225) 342-7316
Mr. John White
State Superintendent of Education
URL: www.louisianabelieves.com

MAINE

Maine Department of Education Office of Higher Education (N)
23 State House Station
Augusta, ME 04333-0023
(207) 624-6600
FAX: (207) 624-6700
Mr. Stephen Bowen
Commissioner
URL: www.maine.gov/doe/

MARYLAND

Maryland Higher Education Commission (O)
6 North Liberty Street
Baltimore, MD 21201
(410) 767-3301
FAX: (410) 332-0270
Dr. Danette G. Howard
Secretary of Higher Education
E-MAIL: dhoward@mhec.state.md.us
URL: www.mhec.state.md.us

MASSACHUSETTS

Massachusetts Department of Higher Education (P)
1 Ashburton Place
Room 1401
McCormack Building
Boston, MA 02108
(617) 994-6901
FAX: (617) 727-6656
Richard M. Freeland Ph.D.
Commissioner
URL: www.mass.edu

MICHIGAN

Department of Licensing and Regulatory Affairs Corporations, Securities & Commercial Licensing Bureau Licensing Division (Q)
PO Box 30714
Lansing, MI 48909-8214
(517) 241-1017
FAX: (517) 373-3085
Mr. Michael Beamish
Manager
E-MAIL: beamishm@michigan.gov
URL: www.michigan.gov/cscl

Workforce Development Agency, State of Michigan Division of Education and Career Success (R)
201 North Washington Square
Victor Building, 2nd Floor
Lansing, MI 48013
(517) 373-3430
FAX: (517) 373-2759
Ms. Dianne Duthie
Director
E-MAIL: duthied@michigan.gov
URL: www.michigan.gov/adulteducation

MINNESOTA

Minnesota Office of Higher Education (S)
1450 Energy Park Drive
Suite 350
St. Paul, MN 55108-5227
(651) 642-0567
FAX: (651) 642-0597
Mr. Larry Pogemiller
Commissioner
E-MAIL: info.ohe@state.mn.us
URL: www.ohe.state.mn.us

Minnesota State Colleges and Universities (T)
30 7th Street East
Suite 350
St. Paul, MN 55101
(651) 201-1696
FAX: (651) 297-7465
Dr. Steven J. Rosenstone
Chancellor
E-MAIL: steven.rosenstone@so.mnscu.edu
URL: www.mnscu.edu

MISSISSIPPI

Board of Trustees of State Institutions of Higher Learning (U)
3825 Ridgewood Road
Jackson, MS 39211
(601) 432-6623
FAX: (601) 432-6972
Dr. Hank Bounds
Commissioner of Higher Education
URL: www.mississippi.edu

Mississippi Community College Board (V)
3825 Ridgewood Drive
Jackson, MS 39211
(601) 432-6084
FAX: (601) 432-6480
Dr. Eric Clark
Executive Director
E-MAIL: info@mccb.edu
URL: www.mccb.edu

MISSOURI

Coordinating Board for Higher Education Department of Higher Education (W)
205 Jefferson Street, 11th Floor
PO Box 1469
Jefferson City, MO 65102-1469
(573) 751-2361
FAX: (573) 751-6635
Dr. David R. Russell
Commissioner of Higher Education
E-MAIL: david.russell@dhe.mo.gov
URL: www.dhe.mo.gov

MONTANA

Office of the Commissioner of Higher Education (X)
PO Box 203201
Academic, Research & Student Affairs
Helena, MT 59620-3201
(406) 444-0312
FAX: (406) 444-1469
Neil Moisey
Deputy Commissioner
E-MAIL: nmoisey@montana.edu
URL: www.mus.edu/che

NEBRASKA

Coordinating Commission for Postsecondary Education (Y)
PO Box 95005
Lincoln, NE 68509-5005
(402) 471-2847
FAX: (402) 471-2886
Dr. Marshall A. Hill
Executive Director
E-MAIL: marshall.hill@nebraska.gov
URL: www.ccpe.state.ne.us

NEVADA

Nevada System of Higher Education (Z)
2601 Enterprise Road
Reno, NV 89512
(775) 784-4901
FAX: (775) 784-1127
Mr. Daniel J. Klaich
Chancellor
E-MAIL: chancellor@nevada.edu
URL: www.nevada.edu

NEW HAMPSHIRE

New Hampshire Department of Education Division of Higher Education Higher Education Commission (a)
101 Pleasant Street
Concord, NH 03301
(603) 271-0256
FAX: (603) 271-1953
Dr. Richard A. Gustafson
Director
E-MAIL: patricia.edes@doe.nh.gov
URL: www.education.nh.gov/highered

Community College System of New Hampshire (b)
26 College Drive
Concord, NH 03301-7407
(603) 230-3501
FAX: (603) 271-2725
Dr. Ross Gittell
Chancellor
E-MAIL: rgittell@ccsnh.edu
URL: www.ccsnh.edu

NEW JERSEY

New Jersey Higher Education Office of the Secretary (c)
20 West State Street, 4th Floor
PO Box 542
Trenton, NJ 08625-0542
(609) 292-4310
FAX: (609) 292-7225
E-MAIL: njhe@njhe.state.nj.us
URL: www.state.nj.us/highereducation

NEW MEXICO

New Mexico Higher Education Department (d)
2048 Galisteo Street
Santa Fe, NM 87505
(505) 476-8404
FAX: (505) 476-8454
Dr. Jose Garcia
Cabinet Secretary
E-MAIL: jose.garcia@state.nm.us
URL: www.hed.state.nm.us

NEW YORK

New York State Education Department (A)
89 Washington Avenue
Room 111
Albany, NY 12234
(518) 474-5844
FAX: (518) 473-4909
John B. King Jr.
Commissioner
E-MAIL: commissioner@mail.nysed.gov

State University of New York (B)
Room S411A
SUNY Plaza
353 Broadway
Albany, NY 12246
(518) 320-1276 or (518) 320-1303
FAX: (518) 320-1570
Ms. Johanna Duncan-Poitier
Sr Vice Chanc, Community Colleges & Educ Pipeline
E-MAIL: johanna.duncan-poitier@suny.edu
URL: www.suny.edu

New York State Education Department (C)
Education Building Annex
Room 977
Albany, NY 12234
(518) 486-3633
FAX: (518) 486-2254
Mr. John D'Agati
Deputy Commissioner
E-MAIL: jdagati@mail.nysed.gov
URL: www.highered.nysed.gov

NORTH CAROLINA

The University of North Carolina (D)
910 Raleigh Road
Chapel Hill, NC 27514
(919) 962-9000
FAX: (919) 843-9695
Mr. Thomas W. Ross
President
E-MAIL: tomross@northcarolina.edu
URL: www.northcarolina.edu

North Carolina Community College System (E)
200 West Jones Street
Raleigh, NC 27603
(919) 807-6950
FAX: (919) 807-7166
Dr. Scott Ralls
President
E-MAIL: ralls@nccommunitycolleges.edu
URL: www.nccommunitycolleges.edu

NORTH DAKOTA

North Dakota State Board of Higher Education (F)
600 East Boulevard Avenue
State Capitol
10th Floor
Bismarck, ND 58505-0230
(701) 328-2960
FAX: (701) 328-2961
Dr. Kirsten Diederich
President
URL: www.ndus.edu/board

OHIO

Ohio Board of Regents (G)
25 South Front Street
Columbus, OH 43215
(614) 466-6000
FAX: (614) 466-5866
Mr. John Carey
Chancellor
E-MAIL: regents@regents.state.oh.us
URL: www.regents.ohio.gov

OKLAHOMA

Oklahoma State Regents for Higher Education (H)
655 Research Parkway
Suite 200
Oklahoma City, OK 73104
(405) 225-9100
FAX: (405) 225-9230
Dr. Glen D. Johnson
Chancellor
E-MAIL: gjohnson@osrhe.edu
URL: www.okhighered.org

OREGON

Oregon State Board of Higher Education (I)
PO Box 751
Portland, OR 97207-0751
(503) 725-5717
FAX: (503) 725-5709
Mr. Charles L. Triplett III
Chief of Staff and Board Secretary
E-MAIL: charles_triplett@ous.edu
URL: www.ous.edu/dept/board

Department of Community Colleges and Workforce Development (J)
255 Capitol Street, NE
Salem, OR 97310
(503) 947-2433
FAX: (503) 378-8434
Mr. Gerald Hamilton
Interim Executive Director
E-MAIL: gerald.hamilton@state.or.us
URL: www.oregon.gov/ccwd

PENNSYLVANIA

Pennsylvania Department of Education Liaison to Postsecondary and Higher Education Institutions (K)
333 Market Street
12th Floor
Harrisburg, PA 17126-0333
(717) 736-7710
FAX: (717) 772-3622
L. Jill Hans
Deputy Secretary, Ofc Postsecondary & Higher Educ
E-MAIL: jhans@pa.gov
URL: www.education.state.pa.us

Pennsylvania Department of Education Liaison to Postsecondary and Higher Education Institutions (L)
333 Market Street
12th Floor
Harrisburg, PA 17126-0333
(717) 783-8228
FAX: (717) 772-3622
Ms. Patricia Landis
Division Chief - Higher and Career Education
E-MAIL: plandis@state.pa.us
URL: www.education.state.pa.us

RHODE ISLAND

Rhode Island Board of Education (M)
80 Washington Street
Suite 524
Providence, RI 02903
(401) 456-6000
FAX: (401) 456-6028
Commissioner of Higher Education
URL: www.ribghe.org

Community College of Rhode Island (N)
400 East Avenue
Warwick, RI 02886
(401) 825-2188
FAX: (401) 825-2166
Mr. Ray M. Di Pasquale
President
E-MAIL: rmdipasquale@ccri.edu
URL: www.ccri.edu

SOUTH CAROLINA

South Carolina Commission on Higher Education (O)
1122 Lady Street
Suite 300
Columbia, SC 29201
(803) 737-2275
FAX: (803) 737-2297
Dr. Richard C. Sutton
Executive Director
E-MAIL: rsutton@che.sc.gov
URL: www.che.sc.gov

South Carolina State Board for Technical and Comprehensive Education (P)
111 Executive Center Drive
Columbia, SC 29210
(803) 896-5280
FAX: (803) 896-5281
Dr. Darrel Staat
System President
E-MAIL: staatd@sctechsystem.edu
URL: www.sctechsystem.edu

SOUTH DAKOTA

South Dakota Board of Regents (Q)
306 East Capitol Avenue
Suite 200
Pierre, SD 57501-2545
(605) 773-3455
FAX: (605) 773-5320
Dr. Jack R. Warner
Executive Director and Chief Executive Officer
E-MAIL: jack.warner@sdbor.edu
URL: www.sdbor.edu

South Dakota Department of Education (R)
Office of the Secretary
800 Governors Drive
Pierre, SD 57501-2291
(605) 773-5669
FAX: (605) 773-6139
Dr. Melody Schopp
Secretary
E-MAIL: melody.schopp@state.sd.us
URL: www.doe.sd.gov

TENNESSEE

Tennessee Higher Education Commission (S)
404 James Robertson Parkway
Parkway Towers
Suite 1900
Nashville, TN 37243-0830
(615) 741-3605
FAX: (615) 741-6230
Dr. Richard G. Rhoda
Executive Director
E-MAIL: richard.rhoda@tn.gov

Tennessee Board of Regents (T)
1415 Murfreesboro Road
Suite 324
Nashville, TN 37217
(615) 366-4482
FAX: (615) 366-3903
Dr. Kay Clark
Interim Vice Chancellor for Academic Affairs
E-MAIL: kay.clark@tbr.edu
URL: www.tbr.edu

University of Tennessee Board of Trustees (U)
719 Andy Holt Tower
Knoxville, TN 37996-0170
(865) 974-3245
FAX: (865) 974-3074
Ms. Catherine S. Mizell
General Counsel and Secretary
E-MAIL: cmizell@tennessee.edu
URL: www.tennessee.edu/system/

TEXAS

Texas Higher Education Coordinating Board (V)
PO Box 12788
Austin, TX 78711
(512) 427-6101
FAX: (512) 427-6127
Dr. Raymund A. Paredes
Commissioner of Higher Education
E-MAIL: raymund.paredes@thecb.state.tx.us
URL: www.thecb.state.tx.us

Texas Higher Education Coordinating Board P-16 Initiatives (W)
PO Box 12788
Austin, TX 78711-2788
(512) 427-6545
FAX: (512) 427-6444
Dr. Judith Loredo
Assistant Commissioner
E-MAIL: judy.loredo@thecb.state.tx.us
URL: www.thecb.state.tx.us

UTAH

Utah System of Higher Education State Board of Regents (X)
60 South 400 West
Salt Lake City, UT 84101-1284
(801) 321-7101
FAX: (801) 321-7156
David L. Buhler
Commissioner of Higher Education
E-MAIL: dbuhler@utahsbr.edu
URL: www.utahsbr.edu

VERMONT

Vermont Agency of Education School Finance Team (Y)
120 State Street
Montpelier, VT 05620-2501
(802) 828-3135
FAX: (802) 828-1631
URL: www.education.vermont.gov

VIRGINIA

State Council of Higher Education for Virginia (Z)
101 North Fourteenth Street
James Monroe Building
9th Floor
Richmond, VA 23219
(804) 225-2600
FAX: (804) 371-7911
Mr. Peter Blake
Director
E-MAIL: peterblake@schev.edu
URL: www.schev.edu

Virginia Community College System (a)
101 North Fourteenth Street
James Monroe Building
Richmond, VA 23219
(804) 819-4903
FAX: (804) 819-4760
Dr. Glenn DuBois
Chancellor
E-MAIL: gdubois@vccs.edu
URL: www.vccs.edu

WASHINGTON

Washington Student Achievement Council (b)
917 Lakeridge Way, SW
PO Box 43430
Olympia, WA 98504-3430
(360) 753-7810
FAX: (360) 753-7808
Dr. Gene Sharratt Ph.D.
Executive Director
E-MAIL: info@wsac.wa.gov
URL: www.wsac.wa.gov

Washington State Board for Community and Technical Colleges (c)
PO Box 42495
1300 Quince Street, SE
Olympia, WA 98504-2495
(360) 704-4355
FAX: (360) 704-4415
Mr. Marty Brown
Executive Director
URL: www.sbctc.edu

WEST VIRGINIA

West Virginia Higher Education Policy Commission (d)
1018 Kanawha Boulevard, East
Suite 700
Charleston, WV 25301-2800
(304) 558-0699
FAX: (304) 558-1011
Dr. Paul L. Hill
Chancellor
E-MAIL: paul.hill@hepc.wvnet.edu
URL: wvhepcnew.wvnet.edu

WISCONSIN

Higher Educational Aids Board (e)
PO Box 7885
Madison, WI 53707-7885
(608) 267-2206
FAX: (608) 267-2808
E-MAIL: heabmail@wisconsin.gov
URL: heab.wi.gov

Wisconsin Technical College System (f)
PO Box 7874
Madison, WI 53707-7874
(608) 267-9066
FAX: (608) 266-1285
Ms. Morna K. Foy
President
E-MAIL: president@wtcsystem.edu
URL: www.wtcsystem.edu

Statewide Agencies of Higher Education

WYOMING

Wyoming Community College Commission (A)
2300 Capital Avenue
5th Floor, Suite B
Cheyenne, WY 82002
(307) 777-7763
FAX: (307) 777-6567
Dr. Jim Rose
Executive Director
E-MAIL: jim.rose@wyo.gov
URL: www.communitycolleges.wy.edu

AMERICAN SAMOA

Board of Higher Education (American Samoa) American Samoa Community College (B)
PO Box 2609
Pago Pago, AS 96799
(684) 699-9155
FAX: (684) 699-6259
URL: www.amsamoa.edu

FEDERATED STATES OF MICRONESIA

Board of Regents College of Micronesia-FSM (C)
PO Box 159
Kolonia Pohnpei, FM 96941
(691) 320-2480
FAX: (691) 320-2479
E-MAIL: national@comfsm.fm
URL: www.comfsm.fm

PUERTO RICO

Puerto Rico Council on Education (D)
PO Box 19900
San Juan, PR 00910-1900
(787) 641-7100, ext. 2047
FAX: (787) 641-2573
Ms. Carmen Luz Berrios Rivera
Executive Director
E-MAIL: cberrios@ce.pr.gov
URL: www.ce.pr.gov

Higher Education Associations

AACSB International-The Association to Advance Collegiate Schools of Business (A)
777 South Harbour Island Boulevard
Suite 750
Tampa, FL 33602-5730
(813) 769-6500
Fax: (813) 769-6559
Mr. John J. Fernandes
President and Chief Executive Officer
E-mail: mediarelations@aacsb.edu
URL: www.aacsb.edu

AAUW (B)
1111 Sixteenth Street, NW
Washington, DC 20036
(202) 785-7700
Fax: (202) 872-1425
Linda D. Hallman CAE
Executive Director
E-mail: connect@aauw.org
URL: www.aauw.org

ABET (C)
415 North Charles Street
Baltimore, MD 21201
(410) 347-7700
Fax: (410) 625-2238
Michael K. J. Milligan Ph.D., PE
Executive Director
E-mail: info@abet.org
URL: www.abet.org

Academy of Legal Studies in Business (D)
Miami University
Department of Finance
3111 FSB
Oxford, OH 45056
(513) 529-1574
Fax: (513) 523-8180
Dr. Daniel J. Herron
Executive Secretary
E-mail: herrondj@muohio.edu
URL: www.alsb.org

Academy of Nutrition and Dietetics Accreditation Council for Education in Nutrition and Dietetics (ACEND) (E)
120 South Riverside Plaza
Suite 2000
Chicago, IL 60606-6995
(312) 899-0040, ext. 5400
Fax: (312) 899-4817
Dr. Ulric Chung
Executive Director
E-mail: uchung@eatright.org
URL: www.eatright.org/acend

Accreditation Commission for Acupuncture and Oriental Medicine (ACAOM) (F)
8941 Aztec Drive
Eden Prairie, MN 55347
(952) 212-2434
Fax: (301) 313-0912
Mr. Mark McKenzie
Executive Director
E-mail: mark.mckenzie@acaom.org
URL: www.acaom.org

Accreditation Commission for Education in Nursing (ACEN) (G)
3343 Peachtree Road, NE
Suite 850
Atlanta, GA 30326
(404) 975-5000
Fax: (404) 975-5020
Dr. Sharon J. Tanner
CEO
E-mail: sjtanner@acenursing.org
URL: www.acenursing.org

Accreditation Commission for Midwifery Education (H)
8403 Colesville Road
Suite 1550
Silver Spring, MD 20910
(240) 485-1802
Fax: (240) 485-1818
Susan E. Stone
Chair ACME
E-mail: jburke@acnm.org
URL: www.midwife.org/Accreditation

Accreditation Committee - Perfusion Education (I)
6663 South Sycamore Street
Littleton, CO 80120
(303) 794-6283
Fax: (303) 738-3223
Ms. Theresa Sisneros
Executive Director
E-mail: office@ac-pe.org
URL: www.ac-pe.org

Accreditation Council for Business Schools and Programs (J)
11520 West 119th Street
Overland Park, KS 66213
(913) 339-9356
Fax: (913) 339-6226
Mr. Douglas Viehland CAE
Executive Director
E-mail: info@acbsp.org
URL: www.acbsp.org

Accreditation Council for Pharmacy Education (K)
135 South LaSalle Street
Suite 4100
Chicago, IL 60603
(312) 664-3575
Fax: (312) 664-4652
Peter H. Vlasses, PharmD BCPS
Executive Director
E-mail: pvlasses@acpe-accredit.org
URL: www.acpe-accredit.org

Accreditation Review Commission on Education for the Physician Assistant (ARC-PA) (L)
12000 Findley Road
Suite 150
John's Creek, GA 30097
(770) 476-1224
Fax: (770) 476-1738
Mr. John McCarty
Executive Director
E-mail: arc-pa@arc-pa.org
URL: www.arc-pa.org

Accreditation Review Committee for the Anesthesiologist's Assistant (M)
N84W33137 Becker Lane
Merton, WI 53066
(612) 836-3311
Ms. Jennifer Anderson Warwick
Executive Director
E-mail: jennifer@arc-aa.org
URL: www.caahep.org/arc-aa

Accreditation Review Committee for the Medical Illustrator (N)
32531 Meadowlark Way
Pepper Pike, OH 44124
(216) 595-9363
Fax: (216) 595-9360
E-mail: kijung@aol.com
URL: www.caahep.org/arc-mi

Accreditation Review Council on Education in Surgical Technology and Surgical Assisting (O)
6 West Dry Creek Circle
Suite 110
Littleton, CO 80120
(303) 694-9262
Fax: (303) 741-3655
Mr. Keith Orloff
Executive Director
E-mail: info@arcstsa.org
URL: www.arcstsa.org

Accrediting Bureau of Health Education Schools (P)
7777 Leesburg Pike
Suite 314 N
Falls Church, VA 22043
(703) 917-9503
Fax: (703) 917-4109
Ms. Carol Moneymaker
Executive Director
E-mail: info@abhes.org
URL: www.abhes.org

Accrediting Commission for Community and Junior Colleges Western Association of Schools and Colleges (Q)
10 Commercial Boulevard
Suite 204
Novato, CA 94949
(415) 506-0234
Fax: (415) 506-0238
Dr. Barbara A. Beno
President
E-mail: accjc@accjc.org
URL: www.accjc.org

Accrediting Commission of Career Schools and Colleges (R)
2101 Wilson Boulevard
Suite 302
Arlington, VA 22201
(703) 247-4212
Fax: (703) 247-4533
Dr. Michale McComis
Executive Director
E-mail: info@accsc.org
URL: www.accsc.org

Accrediting Council for Continuing Education & Training (ACCET) (S)
1722 N Street, NW
Washington, DC 20036
(202) 955-1113
Fax: (202) 955-1118
Mr. Bill Larkin
Executive Director
URL: www.accet.org

Accrediting Council for Independent Colleges and Schools (T)
750 First Street, NE
Suite 980
Washington, DC 20002-4223
(202) 336-6780
Fax: (202) 464-5621
Dr. Albert Gray
President & CEO
E-mail: agray@acics.org
URL: www.acics.org

Accrediting Council on Education in Journalism and Mass Communications (U)
University of Kansas, School of Journalism
1435 Jayhawk Boulevard
Stauffer-Flint Hall
Lawrence, KS 66045-7575
(785) 864-3986
Fax: (785) 864-5225
Prof. Susanne Shaw
Executive Director
E-mail: sshaw@ku.edu
URL: www.ku.edu/~acejmc

ACT, Inc. (V)
500 ACT Drive
Box 168
Iowa City, IA 52243-0168
(319) 337-1079
Fax: (319) 337-1059
Dr. Jon S. Whitmore
CEO
URL: www.act.org

ACUTA: Connecting Campus IT Professionals with Ideas and Solutions (W)
152 West Zandale Drive
Suite 200
Lexington, KY 40503-2486
(859) 278-3338
Fax: (859) 278-3268
Ms. Corinne Hoch
CEO
E-mail: choch@acuta.org
URL: www.acuta.org

American Academy for Liberal Education (AALE) (X)
127 S. Peyton Street
Suite 210
Alexandria, VA 22314
(703) 717-9719
Prof. Charles Butterworth
President
E-mail: aaleinfo@aale.org
URL: www.aale.org

American Anthropological Association (Y)
2300 Clarendon Boulevard
Suite 1301
Arlington, VA 22201
(703) 528-1902
Fax: (703) 528-3546
Mr. Edward Liebow
Executive Director
E-mail: eliebow@aaanet.org
URL: www.aaanet.org

American Association for Adult and Continuing Education (AAACE) (Z)
10111 Martin Luther King, Jr. Highway
Suite 200C
Bowie, MD 20720
(301) 459-6261
Fax: (301) 459-6241
Dr. Linda Morris
President
E-mail: aaace10@aol.com
URL: www.aaace.org

American Association for Employment in Education (a)
947 East Johnstown Road
#170
Gahanna, OH 43230
(614) 485-1111
Fax: (360) 244-7802
Mr. Doug Peden
Executive Director
E-mail: execdir@aaee.org
URL: www.aaee.org

American Association for Marriage and Family Therapy Commission on Accreditation for Marriage & Family Therapy Education (b)
112 South Alfred Street
Alexandria, VA 22314-3061
(703) 253-0457
Fax: (703) 253-0508
Ms. Tatiana A. Tamarkin
Director of Educational Affairs
E-mail: ttamarkin@aamft.org
URL: www.aamft.org

American Association for Vocational Instructional Materials (c)
220 Smithonia Road
Winterville, GA 30683
(706) 742-5355
Fax: (706) 742-7005
Mr. Gary Farmer
Director
E-mail: gary@aavim.com
URL: www.aavim.com

American Association for Women in Community Colleges (AAWCC) (d)
PO Box 3098
Gaithersburg, MD 20855
(301) 442-3374
Dr. Allatia Harris
President
E-mail: info@aawccnatl.org
URL: www.aawccnatl.org

American Association of Blood Banks Committee on Accreditation of Specialist in Blood Banking Technology Schools (e)
8101 Glenbrook Road
Bethesda, MD 20814-2749
(301) 215-6586
Fax: (301) 657-0957
Anne Chenoweth
Deputy Director Accreditation and Quality
E-mail: accreditation@aabb.org
URL: www.aabb.org

American Association of Colleges for Teacher Education (f)
1307 New York Avenue, NW
Suite 300
Washington, DC 20005-4701
(202) 293-2450
Fax: (202) 457-8095
Dr. Sharon P. Robinson
President & Chief Executive Officer
E-mail: aacte@aacte.org
URL: www.aacte.org

American Association of Colleges of Nursing (g)
1 Dupont Circle, NW
Suite 530
Washington, DC 20036-1120
(202) 463-6930
Fax: (202) 785-8320
Dr. Geraldine Bednash
CEO and Executive Director
E-mail: pbednash@aacn.nche.edu
URL: www.aacn.nche.edu

American Association of Colleges of Osteopathic Medicine (h)
5550 Friendship Boulevard
Suite 310
Chevy Chase, MD 20815-7231
(301) 968-4142
Fax: (301) 968-4101
Stephen C. Shannon DO, MPH
President and CEO
E-mail: president@aacom.org
URL: www.aacom.org

Higher Education Associations

American Association of Collegiate Registrars and Admissions Officers (AACRAO) (A)
1 Dupont Circle, NW
Suite 520
Washington, DC 20036-1135
(202) 293-9161
FAX: (202) 872-8857
Mr. Michael Reilly
Executive Director
E-MAIL: reillym@aacrao.org
URL: www.aacrao.org

American Association of Community Colleges (B)
1 Dupont Circle, NW
Suite 410
Washington, DC 20036
(202) 728-0200, ext. 235
FAX: (202) 452-1461
Dr. Walter G. Bumphus
President/CEO
E-MAIL: wbumphus@aacc.nche.edu
URL: www.aacc.nche.edu

American Association of Family and Consumer Sciences (AAFCS) (C)
400 North Columbus Street
Suite 202
Alexandria, VA 22314
(703) 706-4600
FAX: (703) 706-4663
Ms. Carolyn W. Jackson
Executive Director
E-MAIL: accreditation@aafcs.org
URL: www.aafcs.org

American Association of Medical Assistants (D)
20 North Wacker Drive
Suite 1575
Chicago, IL 60606
(312) 899-1500
FAX: (312) 899-1259
Mr. Donald A. Balasa J.D., MBA
Executive Director
E-MAIL: dbalasa@aama-ntl.org
URL: www.aama-ntl.org

American Association of Physics Teachers (E)
One Physics Ellipse
College Park, MD 20740-3845
(301) 209-3311
FAX: (301) 209-0845
Dr. Beth A. Cunningham
Executive Officer
E-MAIL: eo@aapt.org
URL: www.aapt.org

American Association of Presidents of Independent Colleges and Universities (F)
Box 7070
Provo, UT 84602-7070
(801) 422-5625
FAX: (801) 422-0617
Mr. John B. Stohlton
Executive Director
E-MAIL: john_stohlton@byu.edu
URL: www.aapicu.org

American Association of School Administrators (G)
1615 Duke Street
Alexandria, VA 22314
(703) 528-0700
FAX: (703) 841-1543
Dr. Daniel A. Domenech
Executive Director
E-MAIL: ddomenech@aasa.org
URL: www.aasa.org

American Association of State Colleges and Universities (H)
1307 New York Avenue, NW
5th Floor
Washington, DC 20005-4701
(202) 293-7070
FAX: (202) 296-5819
Dr. Muriel A. Howard
President
E-MAIL: howardm@aascu.org
URL: www.aascu.org

American Association of Teachers of Slavic and East European Languages (I)
University of Southern California
3501 Trousdale Parkway
THH 255L
Los Angeles, CA 90089-4353
(213) 740-2734
FAX: (213) 740-8550
Dr. Elizabeth Durst
Executive Director
E-MAIL: aatseel@usc.edu
URL: www.aatseel.org

American Association of University Professors (J)
1133 19th Street, NW
Suite 200
Washington, DC 20036
(202) 737-5900
FAX: (202) 737-5526
Dr. Julie Schmid
Senior Associate General Secretary
E-MAIL: aaup@aaup.org
URL: www.aaup.org

American Bar Association Section of Legal Education and Admissions to the Bar (K)
321 North Clark Street
21st Floor
Chicago, IL 60654
(312) 988-6738
FAX: (312) 988-5681
Mr. Barry A. Currier
Managing Director Accreditation & Legal Education
E-MAIL: legaled@americanbar.org
URL: www.americanbar.org/groups/legal_education

American Board of Funeral Service Education Committee on Accreditation (L)
3414 Ashland Avenue
Suite G
St. Joseph, MO 64506
(816) 233-3747
FAX: (816) 233-3793
Dr. Michael Smith
Executive Director
E-MAIL: exdir@abfse.org
URL: www.abfse.org

American Catholic Philosophical Association (M)
University of St. Thomas
3800 Montrose Boulevard
Houston, TX 77006
(713) 525-3596
FAX: (713) 942-3464
Dr. R. E. Houser
National Secretary
E-MAIL: acpa@stthom.edu
URL: www.acpaweb.org

American Chemical Society Committee on Professional Training (N)
1155 Sixteenth Street, NW
Washington, DC 20036
(202) 872-4589
FAX: (202) 872-6066
Ms. Cathy A. Nelson
Assistant Director
E-MAIL: cpt@acs.org
URL: www.acs.org/cpt

American College of Microbiology Committee on Postgraduate Educational Programs (O)
1752 N Street, NW
Washington, DC 20036-2804
(202) 942-9225
FAX: (202) 942-9353
Ms. Peggy McNult
Assistant Director
E-MAIL: college@asmusa.org
URL: www.asm.org/cpep

American College of Nurse-Midwives (P)
8403 Colesville Road
Suite 1550
Silver Spring, MD 20910
(240) 485-1800
FAX: (240) 485-1818
Ms. Lorrie Kaplan
Executive Director
E-MAIL: info@acnm.org
URL: www.midwife.org

American College Personnel Association (ACPA) (Q)
1 Dupont Circle, NW
Suite 300
Washington, DC 20036-1188
(202) 835-2272
FAX: (202) 296-3286
Mr. Gregory Roberts
Executive Director
E-MAIL: info@acpa.nche.edu
URL: www.myacpa.org

American Collegiate Retailing Association (R)
Hofstra University
Department of Marketing & International Business
Weller Hall 144
Hempstead, NY 11549-1000
Dr. Barry Berman
President
URL: www.acraretail.org

American Conference of Academic Deans (ACAD) (S)
1818 R Street, NW
Washington, DC 20009
(202) 884-7419
FAX: (202) 265-9532
Mrs. Laura A. Rzepka
Executive Director
E-MAIL: info@acad-edu.org
URL: www.acad-edu.org

American Council for Construction Education (T)
1717 North Loop 1604 East
Suite 320
San Antonio, TX 78232-1570
(210) 495-6161
FAX: (210) 495-6168
Mr. Michael Holland
Executive Vice President
E-MAIL: acce@acce-hq.org
URL: www.acce-hq.org

American Council of Trustees and Alumni (U)
1726 M Street, NW
Suite 802
Washington, DC 20036-4525
(202) 467-6787
FAX: (202) 467-6784
Ms. Anne D. Neal
President
E-MAIL: info@goacta.org
URL: www.goacta.org

American Council on Education (V)
1 Dupont Circle, NW
Washington, DC 20036
(202) 939-9300
FAX: (202) 659-2122
Molly Corbett Broad
President
E-MAIL: acepresident@acenet.edu
URL: www.acenet.edu

American Council on Education Center for Education Attainment and Innovation (W)
1 Dupont Circle, NW
Suite 250
Washington, DC 20036
(202) 939-9710
FAX: (202) 833-3005
Cathy Sandeen
Vice President
E-MAIL: credit@ace.nche.edu
URL: www.acenet.edu

American Council on Education Division of Leadership and Lifelong Learning (X)
1 Dupont Circle, NW
Suite 250-73A
Washington, DC 20036
(202) 939-9389
FAX: (202) 939-9302
Dr. Claire Van Ummersen
Senior Adviser
E-MAIL: cvanummersen@acenet.edu
URL: www.acenet.edu

American Counseling Association (Y)
5999 Stevenson Avenue
Alexandria, VA 22304
(800) 347-6647
FAX: (800) 473-2329
Mr. Richard Yep
Executive Director
E-MAIL: ryep@counseling.org
URL: www.counseling.org

American Culinary Federation Education Foundation Accrediting Commission (Z)
180 Center Place Way
St. Augustine, FL 32095
(904) 824-4468
FAX: (904) 825-4758
E-MAIL: cchilders@acfchefs.net
URL: www.acfchefs.org

American Educational Research Association (a)
1430 K Street, NW
Suite 1200
Washington, DC 20005
(202) 238-3200
FAX: (202) 238-3250
Dr. Felice J. Levine
Executive Director
E-MAIL: flevine@aera.net
URL: www.aera.net

American Forensic Association (b)
Box 256
River Falls, WI 54022-0256
(800) 228-5424
FAX: (715) 425-9533
Dr. James W. Pratt
Executive Secretary
E-MAIL: amforensicassoc@aol.com
URL: www.americanforensics.org

American Institute of Architecture Students (c)
1735 New York Avenue, NW
Washington, DC 20006-5209
(202) 626-7472
FAX: (202) 626-7414
Mr. Joshua Caulfield
Executive Director
E-MAIL: mailbox@aias.org
URL: www.aias.org

American Library Association Office for Accreditation (d)
50 East Huron Street
Chicago, IL 60611-2729
(312) 280-2432
FAX: (312) 280-2433
Karen O'Brien
Director, Office for Accreditation
E-MAIL: accred@ala.org
URL: www.ala.org/accreditation

American Mathematical Association of Two Year Colleges (e)
Southwest Tennessee Community College
5983 Macon Cove
Memphis, TN 38134
(901) 333-6243
FAX: (901) 333-6251
Dr. Cheryl Cleaves
Interim Executive Director
E-MAIL: amatyc@amatyc.org
URL: www.amatyc.org

American Occupational Therapy Association (f)
4720 Montgomery Lane
Suite 200
Bethesda, MD 20814-3449
(301) 652-6611 Ext. 2202
FAX: (301) 652-1417
Dr. Neil Harvison
Chief Academic and Scientific Affairs Officer
E-MAIL: accred@aota.org
URL: www.aota.org

American Optometric Association Accreditation Council on Optometric Education (g)
243 North Lindbergh Boulevard
St. Louis, MO 63141
(314) 991-4100
FAX: (314) 991-4101
Ms. Joyce L. Urbeck
Administrative Director
E-MAIL: jlurbeck@aoa.org
URL: www.theacoe.org

American Osteopathic Association (h)
Commission on Osteopathic College Accreditation
142 East Ontario Street
Chicago, IL 60611-2864
(312) 202-8048
FAX: (312) 202-8348
Konrad C. Miskowicz-Retz Ph.D.
Secretary
E-MAIL: kretz@osteopathic.org
URL: www.aoacoca.org

American Physical Therapy Association (A)
1111 North Fairfax Street
Alexandria, VA 22314
(703) 684-2782
FAX: (703) 684-7343
Ms. Bonnie Polvinali
Interim Chief Executive Officer
E-MAIL: dorisellmore@apta.org
URL: www.apta.org

American Political Science Association (B)
1527 New Hampshire Avenue, NW
Washington, DC 20036
(202) 483-2512
FAX: (202) 483-2657
Dr. Steven Rathgeb Smith
Executive Director
E-MAIL: apsa@apsanet.org
URL: www.apsanet.org

American Psychological Association Commission on Accreditation (C)
750 First Street, NE
Washington, DC 20002-4242
(202) 336-5979
FAX: (202) 336-5978
Dr. Susan F. Zlotlow
Dir. Program Consultation & Accred
E-MAIL: apaaccred@apa.org
URL: www.apa.org/ed/accreditation.html

American Real Estate and Urban Economics Association (D)
PO Box 3061110
Tallahassee, FL 32306-1110
(850) 644-7898
FAX: (850) 644-4077
E-MAIL: elaffitte@fsu.edu
URL: www.areuea.org

American Society for Engineering Education (E)
1818 N Street, NW
Suite 600
Washington, DC 20036
(202) 331-3545
FAX: (202) 265-8504
Mr. Norman L. Fortenberry
Executive Director
E-MAIL: n.fortenberry@asee.org
URL: www.asee.org

American Society for Microbiology (F)
1752 N Street, NW
Washington, DC 20036
(202) 942-9264
FAX: (202) 942-9329
Ms. Amy Chang
Director, Education Department
E-MAIL: education@asmusa.org
URL: www.asm.org

American Society of Cytopathology Cytotechnology Programs Review Committee (CPRC) (G)
100 West 10th Street
Suite 605
Wilmington, DE 19801
(302) 543-6583
FAX: (302) 543-6597
Deborah M. Sheldon
Coordinator, CPRC
E-MAIL: asc@cytopathology.org
URL: www.cytopathology.org

American Society of Landscape Architects Landscape Architectural Accreditation Board (H)
636 Eye Street, NW
Washington, DC 20001-3736
(202) 898-2444
FAX: (202) 898-1185
Mr. Ron Leighton
LAAB Administrator
E-MAIL: rleighton@asla.org
URL: www.asla.org

American Student Government Association (I)
412 NW 16th Avenue
Gainesville, FL 32601-4203
(352) 373-6907
FAX: (352) 373-8120
Mr. W. H. Oxendine Jr.
Executive Director
E-MAIL: info@asgaonline.com
URL: www.asgaonline.com

American Veterinary Medical Association (J)
1931 North Meacham Road
Suite 100
Schaumburg, IL 60173
(800) 248-2862
FAX: (847) 925-1329
Dr. Karen Brandt
Interim Director Education and Research
E-MAIL: kbrandt@avma.org
URL: www.avma.org

APPA (K)
1643 Prince Street
Alexandria, VA 22314-2818
(703) 684-1446, ext. 229
FAX: (703) 549-2772
E. Lander Medlin
Executive Vice President
E-MAIL: lander@appa.org
URL: www.appa.org

Association for Asian Studies (L)
825 Victors Way
Suite 310
Ann Arbor, MI 48108
(734) 665-2490
FAX: (734) 665-3801
Mr. Michael Paschal
Executive Director
E-MAIL: mpaschal@asian-studies.org
URL: www.asian-studies.org

Association for Biblical Higher Education Commission on Accreditation (M)
5850 T.G. Lee Boulevard
Suite 130
Orlando, FL 32822
(407) 207-0808
FAX: (407) 207-0840
Dr. Ronald C. Kroll
Director, Commission on Accreditation
E-MAIL: coa@abhe.org
URL: www.abhe.org

Association for Business Communication (N)
355 Shanks Hall (0112)
180 Turner Street, NW
Blacksburg, VA 24061
(540) 231-8460
FAX: (540) 231-1452
Dr. James Dubinsky
Executive Director
E-MAIL: exec_director@businesscommunication.org
URL: www.businesscommunication.org

Association for Business Simulation and Experiential Learning (O)
c/o School of Global Business
Arcadia University
450 South Easton Road
Glenside, PA 19038
(215) 572-2849
FAX: (215) 572-4489
Dr. Annette Halpin
VP/Executive Director
E-MAIL: absel@email.com
URL: www.absel.org

The Association for Canadian Studies in the United States (ACSUS) (P)
Johns Hopkins, SAIS
1740 Massachusetts Avenue NW
Nitze 516
Washington, DC 20036
(202) 670-1424
FAX: (202) 663-5717
Myrna Delson-Karan
President
URL: www.acsus.org

Association for Clinical Pastoral Education, Inc. (Q)
1549 Clairmont Road
Suite 103
Decatur, GA 30033-4635
(404) 320-1472
FAX: (404) 320-0849
Robin Brown-Haithco
President
E-MAIL: acpe@acpe.edu
URL: www.acpe.edu

Association for Consortium Leadership (R)
101 South Mills Avenue
Claremont, CA 91711-3978
(909) 607-9870
FAX: (909) 607-9837
Adele Vuong
Association Administrator
E-MAIL: adelev@cuc.claremont.edu
URL: www.national-acl.com

Association for Continuing Higher Education (S)
University of Oklahoma Outreach
OCCE Administration Building
1700 Asp Avenue
Norman, OK 73072-6400
(800) 807-2243
FAX: (405) 325-4888
Ynez Walske
Executive Secretary
E-MAIL: admin@acheinc.org
URL: www.acheinc.org

Association for Education in Journalism and Mass Communication (T)
234 Outlet Pointe Boulevard
Suite A
Columbia, SC 29210-5667
(803) 798-0271
FAX: (803) 772-3509
Ms. Jennifer H. McGill
Executive Director
E-MAIL: aejmchq@aol.com
URL: www.aejmc.org

Association for General and Liberal Studies (U)
445 Fifth Street
Suite A
Columbus, IN 47201
(812) 376-7468
Ms. Joyce Lucke
Executive Director
E-MAIL: execdir@agls.org
URL: www.agls.org

Association for Institutional Research (V)
1435 East Piedmont Drive
Suite 211
Tallahassee, FL 32308
(850) 385-4155
FAX: (850) 385-5180
Dr. Randy L. Swing
Executive Director
E-MAIL: executivedirector@airweb.org
URL: www.airweb.org

Association for Library and Information Science Education (ALISE) (W)
65 East Wacker Place
Suite 1900
Chicago, IL 60601
(312) 795-0996
FAX: (312) 419-8950
Ms. Kathleen Combs
Executive Director
E-MAIL: contact@alise.org
URL: www.alise.org

Association for Prevention Teaching and Research (X)
1001 Connecticut Avenue, NW
Suite 610
Washington, DC 20036
(202) 463-0550
FAX: (202) 463-0555
E-MAIL: info@aptrweb.org
URL: www.aptrweb.org

Association for the Study of Higher Education (ASHE) (Y)
UNLV
4505 South Maryland Parkway
Box 3068
Las Vegas, NV 89154-3068
(702) 895-2737
FAX: (702) 895-4269
Dr. Kimberly Nehls
Executive Director
E-MAIL: ASHE@unlv.edu
URL: www.ashe.ws

Association for Theatre in Higher Education (ATHE) (Z)
PO Box 1290
Boulder, CO 80306-1290
(888) 284-3737
FAX: (303) 530-2168
Ms. Nancy Erickson
Executive Director
E-MAIL: executivedirector@athe.org
URL: www.athe.org

Association of Advanced Rabbinical and Talmudic Schools Accreditation Commission (a)
11 Broadway
Suite 405
New York, NY 10004
(212) 363-1991
FAX: (212) 533-5335
Dr. Bernard Fryshman
Executive Vice President

Association of American Colleges and Universities (b)
1818 R Street, NW
Washington, DC 20009
(202) 387-3760
FAX: (202) 265-9532
Dr. Carol G. Schneider
President
E-MAIL: info@aacu.org
URL: www.aacu.org

Association of American Law Schools (c)
1201 Connecticut Avenue, NW
Suite 800
Washington, DC 20036-2605
(202) 296-8851
FAX: (202) 296-8869
Ms. Susan Westerberg Prager
Executive Director
E-MAIL: aals@aals.org
URL: www.aals.org

Association of American Medical Colleges (d)
2450 N Street, NW
Washington, DC 20037-1127
(202) 828-0400
FAX: (202) 828-1125
Dr. Darrell G. Kirch
President/CEO
E-MAIL: aamcpresident@aamc.org
URL: www.aamc.org

Association of American Universities (e)
1200 New York Avenue, NW
Suite 550
Washington, DC 20005
(202) 408-7500
FAX: (202) 408-8184
Dr. Hunter R. Rawlings III
President
URL: www.aau.edu

Association of American University Presses (f)
28 West 36th Street
Suite 602
New York, NY 10018
(212) 989-1010
FAX: (212) 989-0275
Peter M. Berkery Jr.
Executive Director
E-MAIL: info@aaupnet.org
URL: www.aaupnet.org

Association of Catholic Colleges and Universities (g)
1 Dupont Circle, NW
Suite 650
Washington, DC 20036
(202) 457-0650
FAX: (202) 728-0977
Michael Galligan-Stierle Ph.D.
President/CEO
E-MAIL: accu@accunet.org
URL: www.accunet.org

Association of College and University Housing Officers-International (h)
1445 Summit Street
Columbus, OH 43201
(614) 292-0099
FAX: (614) 292-3205
Ms. Sallie Traxler
Executive Director
E-MAIL: office@acuho-i.org
URL: www.acuho-i.org

Higher Education Associations

Association of College and University Religious Affairs (A)
Macalester College
1600 Grand Avenue
St. Paul, MN 55105
(651) 696-6293
RevDr. Lucy Forster-Smith
President
E-MAIL: forstersmith@macalester.edu
URL: www.site.acuraonline.net

Association of College Unions International (B)
One City Centre
Suite 200
120 West Seventh Street
Bloomington, IN 47404-3925
(812) 245-2284
FAX: (812) 245-6710
Ms. Marsha Herman-Betzen
Executive Director
E-MAIL: acui@acui.org
URL: www.acui.org

Association of Collegiate Conference and Events Directors-International (C)
2900 South College Avenue
Suite 3B
Fort Collins, CO 80525
(970) 449-4960
FAX: (970) 449-4965
Ms. Monica Nesbit Schultz
Director of Sales & Marketing
E-MAIL: monica@acced-i.org
URL: www.acced-i.org

Association of Collegiate Schools of Architecture (D)
1735 New York Avenue, NW
Washington, DC 20006
(202) 785-2324
FAX: (202) 628-0448
Michael Monti Ph.D.
Executive Director
E-MAIL: info@acsa-arch.org
URL: www.acsa-arch.org

Association of Collegiate Schools of Planning (E)
c/o Donna Dodd, Association Manager
6311 Mallard Trace Drive
Tallahassee, FL 32312
(850) 385-2054
FAX: (850) 385-2084
Dr. Charles Connerly
President
E-MAIL: president@acsp.org
URL: www.acsp.org

Association of Community College Trustees (F)
1233 20th Street, NW
Suite 301
Washington, DC 20036
(202) 775-4667
FAX: (202) 223-1297
Mr. J. Noah Brown
President and CEO
E-MAIL: nbrown@acct.org
URL: www.acct.org

Association of Departments of English (G)
26 Broadway
3rd Floor
New York, NY 10004-1789
(646) 576-5130
FAX: (646) 458-0033
Dr. David Laurence
Director
E-MAIL: ade@mla.org
URL: www.ade.org

Association of Departments of Foreign Languages (H)
26 Broadway
3rd Floor
New York, NY 10004-1789
(646) 576-5140
FAX: (646) 458-0033
Dr. Nelly Furman
Director
E-MAIL: adfl@mla.org
URL: www.adfl.org

Association of Governing Boards of Universities and Colleges (I)
1133 20th Street, NW
Suite 300
Washington, DC 20036
(202) 296-8400
FAX: (202) 223-7053
Mr. Richard Legon
President
E-MAIL: rickl@agb.org
URL: www.agb.org

Association of Graduate Liberal Studies Programs (J)
c/o Duke University
Box 90095
Durham, NC 27708-0095
(919) 684-1987
FAX: (919) 681-8905
Ms. Ellen Levine
Administrative Manager
E-MAIL: info@aglsp.org
URL: www.aglsp.org

Association of International Education Administrators (K)
Campus Box 90404
Duke University
Durham, NC 27708-0404
(919) 668-1928
FAX: (919) 684-8749
Dr. Darla K. Deardorff
Executive Director
E-MAIL: aiea@duke.edu
URL: www.aieaworld.org

Association of Jesuit Colleges and Universities (L)
1 Dupont Circle, NW
Suite 405
Washington, DC 20036
(202) 862-9893
FAX: (202) 862-8523
Rev. Michael J. Sheeran S.J.
President
E-MAIL: msheeran@ajcunet.edu
URL: www.ajcunet.edu

Association of Military Colleges and Schools of the United States (M)
12332 Washington Brice Road
Fairfax, VA 22033
(703) 272-8406
Ray Rottman
Executive Director
E-MAIL: amcsus@cox.net
URL: www.amcsus.org

Association of Performing Arts Presenters (N)
1211 Connecticut Avenue, NW
Suite 200
Washington, DC 20036
(202) 833-2787
FAX: (202) 833-1543
E-MAIL: info@artspresenters.org
URL: www.apap365.org

Association of Practical Theology (O)
Princeton Theological Seminary
Tennent Hall
108 Stockton Street
Princeton, NJ 08540
(609) 497-7739
FAX: (609) 279-9014
Mr. Gordon Mikoski
President
E-MAIL: gordon.mikoski@ptsem.edu
URL: www.practicaltheology.org

Association of Presbyterian Colleges and Universities (P)
100 Witherspoon Street
Louisville, KY 40202-1396
(502) 569-5509
FAX: (502) 569-8077
Mr. Gary Luhr
Executive Director
E-MAIL: gary.luhr@pcusa.org
URL: www.presbyteriancolleges.org

Association of Private Sector Colleges and Universities (APSCU) (Q)
1101 Connecticut Avenue, NW
Suite 900
Washington, DC 20036
(202) 336-6700
FAX: (202) 336-6828
Mr. Brian Moran
Executive Vice President of Government Relations
E-MAIL: brian.moran@apscu.org
URL: www.apscu.org

Association of Public and Land-Grant Universities (R)
1307 New York Avenue, NW
Suite 400
Washington, DC 20005-4722
(202) 478-6040
FAX: (202) 478-6046
M. Peter McPherson
President
E-MAIL: pmcpherson@aplu.org
URL: www.aplu.org

Association of Research Libraries (S)
21 Dupont Circle, NW
Suite 800
Washington, DC 20036
(202) 296-2296
FAX: (202) 872-0884
Dr. Elliott Shore
Executive Director
E-MAIL: elliott@arl.org
URL: www.arl.org

Association of Schools of Allied Health Professions (T)
122 C Street, NW
Suite 650
Washington, DC 20001-2151
(202) 237-6481
FAX: (202) 237-6485
Mr. John Colbert
Executive Director
E-MAIL: john@asahp.org
URL: www.asahp.org

Association of Specialized and Professional Accreditors (U)
3304 North Broadway Street
#214
Chicago, IL 60657
(773) 857-7900
FAX: (773) 857-7901
Mr. Joseph Vibert
Executive Director
E-MAIL: aspa@aspa-usa.org
URL: www.aspa-usa.org

Association of Teacher Educators (V)
PO Box 793
Manassas, VA 20113
(703) 659-1708
FAX: (703) 595-4324
Dr. David Ritchey
Executive Director
E-MAIL: dritchey@ate1.org
URL: www.ate1.org

Association of Teachers of Technical Writing (W)
University of North Texas
Dept. of Linguistics & Technical Communication
1155 Union Circle, #305298
Denton, TX 76203-5017
(940) 565-4458
Dr. Brenda R. Sims
Executive Secretary
E-MAIL: sims@unt.edu
URL: www.attw.org

The Association of Technology, Management, and Applied Engineering (ATMAE) (X)
1390 Eisenhower Place
Ann Arbor, MI 48108
(734) 677-0720
FAX: (734) 677-0046
Mr. Rick Coscarelli
Executive Director
E-MAIL: rcoscarelli@atmae.org
URL: atmae.org

Association of Theological Schools in the United States and Canada The Commission on Accrediting (Y)
10 Summit Park Drive
Pittsburgh, PA 15275-1103
(412) 788-6505
FAX: (412) 788-6510
Dr. Daniel O. Aleshire
Executive Director
E-MAIL: ats@ats.edu
URL: www.ats.edu

Association of University Programs in Health Administration (Z)
2000 14th Street North
Suite 780
Arlington, VA 22201-2543
(703) 894-0940
FAX: (703) 894-0941
Gerald L. Glandon Ph.D.
President & CEO
E-MAIL: gglandon@aupha.org
URL: www.aupha.org

Association of University Research Parks (a)
6262 North Swan Road
Suite 100
Tucson, AZ 85718
(520) 529-2521
FAX: (520) 529-2499
Ms. Eileen Walker
CEO
E-MAIL: info@aurp.net
URL: www.aurp.net

Aviation Accreditation Board International (b)
3410 Skyway Drive
Auburn, AL 36830
(334) 844-2431
FAX: (334) 844-2432
Mr. Gary W. Kiteley
President
E-MAIL: kitelgw@auburn.edu
URL: www.aabi.aero

Broadcast Education Association (c)
1771 N Street, NW
Washington, DC 20036-2891
(202) 429-5355
FAX: (202) 775-2981
Ms. Heather Birks
Executive Director
E-MAIL: hbirks@nab.org
URL: www.beaweb.org

The Carnegie Foundation for the Advancement of Teaching (d)
51 Vista Lane
Stanford, CA 94305
(650) 566-5100
FAX: (650) 326-0278
Dr. Anthony S. Bryk
President
E-MAIL: milligan@carnegiefoundation.org
URL: www.carnegiefoundation.org

Center for Women Policy Studies (e)
4620 North Park Avenue
Suite 302W
Chevy Chase, MD 20815
(202) 872-1770
Leslie R. Wolfe
President
E-MAIL: lwolfe@centerwomenpolicy.org
URL: www.centerwomenpolicy.org

CETE (Center on Education and Training for Employment) (f)
The Ohio State University
1900 Kenny Road
Columbus, OH 43210-1016
(614) 292-9072
Mr. Robert A. Mahlman
Director
E-MAIL: mahlman.1@osu.edu
URL: www.cete.org

College and University Professional Association for Human Resources (CUPA-HR) (g)
1811 Commons Point Drive
Knoxville, TN 37932
(877) 287-2474
FAX: (865) 637-7674
Mr. Andy Brantley
President and Chief Executive Officer
E-MAIL: memberservice@cupahr.org
URL: www.cupahr.org

College Art Association (h)
50 Broadway
Floor 21
New York, NY 10004
(212) 691-1051
FAX: (212) 627-2381
Ms. Linda Downs
Executive Director
E-MAIL: nyoffice@collegeart.org
URL: www.collegeart.org

The College Board (A)
45 Columbus Avenue
New York, NY 10023
(212) 713-8000
David Coleman
President
URL: www.collegeboard.org

College English Association (B)
Borough of Manhattan Community College
English Department
199 Chambers Street
New York, NY 10007
(212) 220-1406
FAX: (718) 783-3317
Dr. Juliet Emanuel
Executive Director
E-MAIL: jaemanuel@cs.com
URL: cea-web.org

College Media Association (C)
2301 Vanderbilt Place
VU Station B351669
Nashville, TN 37235-1669
(615) 322-6610
Mr. Christopher Carroll
Interim Executive Director
E-MAIL: chris.carroll@vanderbilt.edu
URL: www.cma.cloverpad.org

Columbia Scholastic Press Association (D)
Columbia University
Mail Code 5711
New York, NY 10027-6902
(212) 854-9400
FAX: (212) 854-9401
Mr. Edmund J. Sullivan
Executive Director
E-MAIL: cspa@columbia.edu
URL: www.columbia.edu/cu/cspa

Commission on Accreditation for Health Informatics and Information Management Education (CAHIIM) (E)
233 North Michigan Avenue
21st Floor
Chicago, IL 60601-5800
(312) 233-1100
FAX: (312) 233-1483
Dr. Claire Dixon-Lee
Executive Director CAHIIM
E-MAIL: info@cahiim.org
URL: www.cahiim.org

Commission on Accreditation of Allied Health Education Programs (F)
1361 Park Street
Clearwater, FL 33756
(727) 210-2350
FAX: (727) 210-2354
Dr. Kathleen Megivern J.D., CAE
Executive Director
E-MAIL: megivern@caahep.org
URL: www.caahep.org

Commission on Accreditation of Healthcare Management Education (CAHME) (G)
1700 Rockville Pike
Suite 400
Rockville, MD 20852
(301) 998-6101
Margaret Schulte
Interim CEO
E-MAIL: mschulte@cahme.org
URL: www.cahme.org

Commission on Collegiate Nursing Education (CCNE) (H)
One Dupont Circle, NW
Suite 530
Washington, DC 20036-1120
(202) 887-6791
FAX: (202) 887-8476
Dr. Jennifer Butlin
Executive Director
E-MAIL: jbutlin@aacn.nche.edu
URL: www.aacn.nche.edu/ccne-accreditation

Commission on Dental Accreditation (I)
211 East Chicago Avenue
Chicago, IL 60611
(312) 440-4653
FAX: (312) 440-2915
Dr. Sherin Tooks
Director
E-MAIL: tookss@ada.org
URL: www.ada.org/100.aspx

Commission on English Language Program Accreditation (CEA) (J)
801 North Fairfax Street
Suite 402A
Alexandria, VA 22314
(703) 665-3400, x101
Ms. Teresa D. O'Donnell
Executive Director
E-MAIL: todonnell@cea-accredit.org
URL: www.cea-accredit.org

Commission on Independent Colleges and Universities (CICU) (K)
17 Elk Street
PO Box 7289
Albany, NY 12224
(518) 436-4781
FAX: (518) 436-0417
Ms. Laura L. Anglin
President
E-MAIL: mail@cicu.org
URL: www.cicu.org, www.nycolleges.org

Commission on Massage Therapy Accreditation (L)
5335 Wisconsin Avenue, NW
Suite 440
Washington, DC 20015
(202) 895-1518
FAX: (202) 895-1519
Ms. Kate Ivane Henri Zulaski
Executive Director
E-MAIL: kzulaski@comta.org
URL: www.comta.org

Commission on Opticianry Accreditation (M)
PO Box 592
Canton, NY 13617
(703) 468-0566
Mrs. Debra White
Director of Accreditation
E-MAIL: director@coaccreditation.com
URL: www.coaccreditation.com

Committee on Accreditation for Education in Neurodiagnostic Technology (N)
1449 Hill Street
Whitinsville, MA 01588
(978) 338-6300
FAX: (978) 832-2638
Dr. Jackie Long-Goding RRT-NPS
Executive Director
E-MAIL: office@coa-ndt.org
URL: www.coa-ndt.org

Committee on Accreditation for Polysomnographic Technologist Education (O)
1711 Frank Avenue
New Bern, NC 28560
(252) 626-3238
Ms. Karen Monarchy Rowe
Executive Director
E-MAIL: office@coapsg.org
URL: www.coapsg.org

Committee on Accreditation for the Exercise Sciences (P)
401 West Michigan Street
Indianapolis, IN 46202
(317) 637-9200
FAX: (317) 634-7817
E-MAIL: trush@acsm.org
URL: www.coaes.org

Committee on Accreditation of Education Programs for Kinesiotherapy (Q)
University of Southern Mississippi
118 College Drive
#5142
Hattiesburg, MS 39406-0002
(601) 266-5371
FAX: (601) 266-4445
Jerry W. Purvis
E-MAIL: jerry.purvis@usm.edu
URL: www.akta.org

Committee on Accreditation of Educational Programs for the Emergency Medical Services Professions (R)
8301 Lakeview Parkway
Suite 111-312
Rowlett, TX 75088
(214) 703-8445
FAX: (214) 703-8992
Dr. George Hatch
Executive Director
E-MAIL: george@coaemsp.org
URL: www.coaemsp.org

Committee on Institutional Cooperation (S)
1819 South Neil Street
Suite D
Champaign, IL 61820
(217) 333-8475
FAX: (217) 244-7127
Ms. Barbara McFadden Allen
Director
E-MAIL: cic@staff.cic.net
URL: www.cic.net

Conference on College Composition and Communication (T)
1111 West Kenyon Road
Urbana, IL 61801-1096
(800) 369-6283
FAX: (217) 328-0977
Mr. Kent Williamson
Executive Secretary-Treasurer
E-MAIL: kwilliamson@ncte.org
URL: www.ncte.org/cccc

Council for Accreditation of Counseling and Related Educational Programs (CACREP) (U)
1001 North Fairfax Street
Suite 510
Alexandria, VA 22314
(703) 535-5990
FAX: (703) 739-6209
Dr. Carol L. Bobby
President and CEO
E-MAIL: cacrep@cacrep.org
URL: www.cacrep.org

Council for Adult and Experiential Learning (V)
55 East Monroe
Suite 2710
Chicago, IL 60603
(312) 499-2600
FAX: (312) 499-2601
Ms. Pamela Tate
President
E-MAIL: ptate@cael.org
URL: www.cael.org

Council for Advancement and Support of Education (W)
1307 New York Avenue, NW
Suite 1000
Washington, DC 20005-4701
(202) 328-2273
FAX: (202) 387-4973
Mr. John Lippincott
President
E-MAIL: lippincott@case.org
URL: www.case.org

Council for Agricultural Science and Technology (CAST) (X)
4420 West Lincoln Way
Ames, IA 50014-3447
(515) 292-2125
FAX: (515) 292-4512
Linda M. Chimenti
Executive Vice President
E-MAIL: cast@cast-science.org
URL: www.cast-science.org

Council for Aid to Education (Y)
215 Lexington Avenue
New York, NY 10016-6023
(212) 661-5800, x808
FAX: (212) 661-9766
Dr. Roger Benjamin
President & CEO
E-MAIL: rbenjamin@cae.org
URL: www.cae.org

Council for Christian Colleges & Universities (Z)
321 8th Street, NE
Washington, DC 20002-6158
(202) 546-8713
FAX: (202) 546-8913
Dr. Edward O. Blews Jr.
President
E-MAIL: council@cccu.org
URL: www.cccu.org

Council for Economic Education (a)
122 East 42nd Street
Suite 2600
New York, NY 10168
(212) 730-7007 or (800) 338-1192
FAX: (212) 730-1793
Ms. Nan Morrison
President and CEO
E-MAIL: njmorrison@councilforeconed.org
URL: www.councilforeconed.org

Council for Higher Education Accreditation (b)
1 Dupont Circle, NW
Suite 510
Washington, DC 20036-1135
(202) 955-6126
FAX: (202) 955-6129
Dr. Judith Eaton
President
E-MAIL: chea@chea.org
URL: www.chea.org

Council for Interior Design Accreditation (CIDA) (formerly FIDER) (c)
206 Grandville Avenue
Suite 350
Grand Rapids, MI 49503
(616) 458-0400
FAX: (616) 458-0460
Ms. Holly Mattson
Executive Director
E-MAIL: info@accredit-id.org
URL: www.accredit-id.org

Council for Research in Music Education (d)
University of Illinois at Urbana-Champaign
1114 West Nevada
Urbana, IL 61801
(217) 333-1027
Dr. Eve Harwood
Editor
E-MAIL: crme@illinois.edu
URL: bcrme.press.illinois.edu

Council for the Accreditation of Educator Preparation (e)
2010 Massachusetts Avenue, NW
Suite 500
Washington, DC 20036
(202) 223-0077
FAX: (202) 296-6620
Dr. James G. Cibulka
President
E-MAIL: caep@caepnet.org
URL: www.caepnet.org

Council for the Advancement of Standards in Higher Education (f)
One Dupont Circle, NW
Suite 300
Washington, DC 20036-1188
(202) 862-1400
FAX: (202) 296-3286
Dr. Marybeth Drechsler Sharp
Executive Director
E-MAIL: executive_director@cas.edu
URL: www.cas.edu

Council of Colleges of Acupuncture and Oriental Medicine (CCAOM) (g)
600 Wyndhurst Avenue
Suite 112
Baltimore, MD 21210
(410) 464-6041
FAX: (410) 464-6042
Mr. David M. Sale
Executive Director
E-MAIL: executivedirector@ccaom.comcastbiz.net
URL: www.ccaom.org

Council of Colleges of Arts and Sciences (h)
c/o The College of William and Mary
PO Box 8795
Williamsburg, VA 23187-8795
(757) 221-1784
FAX: (757) 221-1776
Dr. Anne-Marie McCartan
Executive Director
E-MAIL: ccas@wm.edu
URL: www.ccas.net

Council of Graduate Schools (i)
1 Dupont Circle, NW
Suite 230
Washington, DC 20036
(202) 223-3791
FAX: (202) 331-7157
Dr. Debra W. Stewart
President
E-MAIL: president@cgs.nche.edu
URL: www.cgsnet.org

Council of Independent Colleges (A)
1 Dupont Circle, NW
Suite 320
Washington, DC 20036-1142
(202) 466-7230
FAX: (202) 466-7238
Dr. Richard Ekman
President
E-MAIL: cic@cic.nche.edu
URL: www.cic.edu

The Council of Writing Program Administrators (B)
Grand Valley State University
Department of Writing
326 Lake Ontario Hall
Allendale, MI 49401
(616) 331-8147
Dr. Keith Rhodes
Secretary
E-MAIL: rhodekei@gvsu.edu
URL: www.wpacouncil.org

Council on Academic Accreditation in Audiology and Speech-Language Pathology (C)
2200 Research Boulevard
Rockville, MD 20850
(301) 296-5700
FAX: (301) 296-8570
Patrima L. Tice
Director of Accreditation
E-MAIL: accreditation@asha.org
URL: www.asha.org

Council on Accreditation of Nurse Anesthesia Educational Programs (COA) (D)
222 South Prospect Avenue
Park Ridge, IL 60068-4001
(847) 655-1154
FAX: (847) 692-7137
Francis Gerbasi CRNA,Ph.D.
Executive Director
E-MAIL: fgerbasi@coa.us.com
URL: www.home.coa.us.com

Council on Chiropractic Education (E)
8049 North 85th Way
Scottsdale, AZ 85258-4321
(480) 443-8877
FAX: (480) 483-7333
Tom Benberg
President
E-MAIL: cce@cce-usa.org
URL: www.cce-usa.org

Council on Education for Public Health (F)
1010 Wayne Avenue
Suite 220
Silver Spring, MD 20910-5660
(202) 789-1050
FAX: (202) 789-1895
Ms. Laura Rasar King
Executive Director
E-MAIL: lking@ceph.org
URL: www.ceph.org

Council on Governmental Relations (G)
1200 New York Avenue, NW
Suite 750
Washington, DC 20005
(202) 289-6655
FAX: (202) 289-6698
Mr. Anthony DeCrappeo
President
E-MAIL: tdecrappeo@cogr.edu
URL: www.cogr.edu

Council on Higher Education Solutions for Adults (H)
104 Johnson Street
Marshall, TX 75670
(903) 472-2762
FAX: (903) 935-3890
Dr. Tracy Andrus
President/CEO
E-MAIL: chesa1962@gmail.com
URL: www.chesa1.com

Council on Law in Higher Education (I)
9386 Via Classico West
Wellington, FL 33411
(561) 792-4440
FAX: (561) 792-4441
Mr. Daren Bakst
President
E-MAIL: moss@clhe.org
URL: www.clhe.org

Council on Naturopathic Medical Education (J)
PO Box 178
Great Barrington, MA 01230
(413) 528-8877
Dr. Daniel Seitz J.D., Ed.D
Executive Director
E-MAIL: danseitz@cnme.org
URL: www.cnme.org

Council on Occupational Education (K)
7840 Roswell Road
Building 300
Suite 325
Atlanta, GA 30350
(800) 917-2081
FAX: (770) 396-3790
Dr. Gary Puckett
President
E-MAIL: puckettg@council.org
URL: www.council.org

Council on Podiatric Medical Education (L)
9312 Old Georgetown Road
Bethesda, MD 20814
(301) 581-9200
FAX: (301) 571-4903
Mr. Alan R. Tinkleman
Director
E-MAIL: artinkleman@apma.org
URL: www.cpme.org

Council on Rehabilitation Education (CORE) (M)
1699 Woodfield Road
Suite 300
Schaumburg, IL 60173
(847) 944-1345
FAX: (847) 944-1346
Dr. Frank Lane
Executive Director
E-MAIL: flane@core-rehab.org
URL: www.core-rehab.org

Council on Social Work Education (N)
1701 Duke Street
Suite 200
Alexandria, VA 22314-3457
(703) 519-2048
FAX: (703) 683-8099
Dr. JoAnn Regan
Director, Office of Social Work Accreditation
E-MAIL: jregan@cswe.org
URL: www.cswe.org

Council on Undergraduate Research (O)
734 15th Street, NW
Suite 550
Washington, DC 20005
(202) 783-4810
FAX: (202) 783-4811
Dr. Elizabeth L. Ambos
Executive Officer
E-MAIL: cur@cur.org
URL: www.cur.org

CSAB, Inc. (P)
417 Terrace Way
Towson, MD 21204-3725
(410) 339-5456
Ms. Liz Glazer
Executive Director
E-MAIL: csab@csab.org
URL: www.csab.org

Cultural Vistas (Q)
440 Park Avenue South
2nd Floor
New York, NY 10016
(212) 497-3500
FAX: (212) 497-3535
Mr. Robert Fenstermacher
President & CEO
E-MAIL: info@culturalvistas.org
URL: www.culturalvistas.org

Decision Sciences Institute (R)
75 Piedmont Road
Suite 340
Atlanta, GA 30303
(404) 413-7711
FAX: (404) 413-7714
Executive Director
E-MAIL: dsi@gsu.edu
URL: www.decisionsciences.org

Direct Marketing Association, Inc. (S)
1120 Avenue of the Americas
13th Floor
New York, NY 10036-6700
(212) 768-7277
FAX: (212) 302-6714
Ms. Linda M. Wolley Esq.
CEO & President
E-MAIL: info@the-dma.org
URL: www.thedma.org

Distance Education and Training Council (T)
1601 Eighteenth Street, NW
Suite 2
Washington, DC 20009
(202) 234-5100
FAX: (202) 332-1386
Dr. Leah K. Matthews
Executive Director
E-MAIL: info@detc.org
URL: www.detc.org

Education Commission of the States (U)
700 Broadway
Suite 810
Denver, CO 80203-3442
(303) 299-3600
FAX: (303) 296-8332
Mr. Jeremy Anderson
President
E-MAIL: ecs@ecs.org
URL: www.ecs.org

Education Development Center, Inc. (V)
43 Foundry Avenue
Waltham, MA 02453
(617) 969-7100
FAX: (617) 969-5979
Mr. Luther S. Luedtke
President
E-MAIL: comment@edc.org
URL: www.edc.org

EDUCAUSE (W)
1150 18th Street, NW
Suite 900
Washington, DC 20036-3816
(202) 872-4200
FAX: (202) 872-4318
Diana Oblinger Ph.D.
President
E-MAIL: doblinger@educause.edu
URL: www.educause.edu

FHI360 (X)
1825 Connecticut Avenue, NW
Washington, DC 20009-5721
(202) 884-8000
FAX: (202) 884-8400
Dr. Albert J. Siemens
Chief Executive Officer
E-MAIL: contact@fhi.org
URL: www.fhi360.org

Financial Management Association International (Y)
University of South Florida
College of Business Administration
4202 East Fowler Avenue, BSN 3331
Tampa, FL 33620-5500
(813) 974-2084
FAX: (813) 974-3318
Mr. Jack S. Rader
Executive Director
E-MAIL: fma@coba.usf.edu
URL: www.fma.org

Friends Association for Higher Education (Z)
1501 Cherry Street
Philadelphia, PA 19102
(215) 241-7116
FAX: (215) 241-7028
Ms. Kimberley Haas
FAHE Coordinator
E-MAIL: fahe@quaker.org
URL: www.quakerfahe.com

The George Washington University HEATH Resource Center at the National Youth Transitions Center Graduate School of Education & Human Development (a)
2134 G Street, NW
Washington, DC 20052-0001
E-MAIL: askheath@gwu.edu
URL: www.heath.gwu.edu

The Gerontological Society of America (b)
1220 L Street, NW
Suite 901
Washington, DC 20005-4018
(202) 587-2821
FAX: (202) 587-2850
Mr. James Appleby
Executive Director
E-MAIL: geron@geron.org
URL: www.geron.org

Graduate Record Examinations Board (c)
Educational Testing Service
Mail Stop 57L
660 Rosedale Road
Princeton, NJ 08541
(609) 683-2014
FAX: (609) 683-2040
Dr. David G. Payne
Vice President & COO of Higher Education Division
E-MAIL: dpayne@ets.org
URL: www.ets.org/highered

H. Wiley Hitchcock Institute for Studies in American Music (d)
Brooklyn College/CUNY
2900 Bedford Avenue
Brooklyn, NY 11210-2889
(718) 951-5655
Dr. Jeffrey Taylor
Director
E-MAIL: hisam@brooklyn.cuny.edu
URL: www.hisam.org

Higher Education Resource Services (HERS) (e)
University of Denver
1901 East Asbury Avenue
Denver, CO 80208
(303) 871-6866
FAX: (303) 871-6766
Dr. Judith White
President/Executive Director
E-MAIL: judith.white@du.edu
URL: www.hersnet.org

Higher Learning Commission North Central Association (f)
230 South LaSalle Street
Suite 7-500
Chicago, IL 60604-1413
(312) 263-0456 / (800) 621-7440
FAX: (312) 263-7462
Ms. Sylvia Manning
President
E-MAIL: info@hlcommission.org
URL: www.ncahlc.org

Hispanic Association of Colleges and Universities (g)
8415 Datapoint Drive
Suite 400
San Antonio, TX 78229
(210) 692-3805
FAX: (210) 692-0823
Dr. Antonio R. Flores
President and CEO
E-MAIL: hacu@hacu.net
URL: www.hacu.net

IACLEA (International Association of Campus Law Enforcement Administrators) (h)
342 North Main Street
West Hartford, CT 06117-2507
(860) 586-7517, x565
FAX: (860) 586-7550
Mr. Christopher Blake CAE
Chief Staff Officer
E-MAIL: cblake@iaclea.org
URL: www.iaclea.org

The Institute for Higher Education Policy (i)
1825 K Street, NW
Suite 720
Washington, DC 20006
(202) 861-8223
FAX: (202) 861-9307
Michelle A. Cooper Ph.D.
President
E-MAIL: institute@ihep.org
URL: www.ihep.org

Institute of International Education (A)
809 United Nations Plaza
New York, NY 10017-3580
(212) 883-8200
FAX: (212) 984-5496
E-MAIL: info@iie.org
URL: www.iie.org

Institute of International Education Council for International Exchange of Scholars (B)
1400 K Street, NW
Suite 700
Washington, DC 20005
(202) 686-4000
FAX: (202) 686-4029
Jamie Bellis
Deputy Executive Director
E-MAIL: scholars@iie.org
URL: www.cies.org

Intercollegiate Broadcasting System, Inc. (C)
367 Windsor Highway
New Windsor, NY 12553-7900
(845) 565-0003
FAX: (845) 565-7446
Mr. Fritz Kass
Director-Operations
E-MAIL: ibshq@aol.com
URL: www.collegeradio.tv

International Assembly for Collegiate Business Education (D)
11374 Strang Line Road
Lenexa, KS 66215
(913) 631-3009
FAX: (913) 631-9154
Mr. Dennis N. Gash
President
E-MAIL: iacbe@iacbe.org
URL: www.iacbe.org

International Association of Baptist Colleges and Universities (E)
8120 Sawyer Brown Road
Suite 108
Nashville, TN 37221-1410
(615) 673-1896
Dr. Michael Arrington
Executive Director
E-MAIL: marrington@baptistschools.org
URL: www.baptistschools.org

International Communication Association (F)
1500 21st Street, NW
Washington, DC 20036
(202) 955-1444
FAX: (202) 955-1448
Dr. Michael Haley
Executive Director
E-MAIL: mhaley@icahdq.org
URL: www.icahdq.org

International Council on Education for Teaching (G)
National-Louis University
1000 Capitol Drive
Wheeling, IL 60090
(847) 947-5622
James O'Meara
President
E-MAIL: ICET_Secretariat@nl.edu
URL: www.icet4u.org

International Fire Service Accreditation Congress (H)
1700 West Tyler
Stillwater, OK 74078
(405) 744-8303
FAX: (405) 744-8802
Mr. Clayton Moorman
Manager
E-MAIL: cmoorman@ifsac.org
URL: www.ifsac.org

Joint Review Committee on Education in Cardiovascular Technology (JRC-CVT) (I)
1449 Hill Street
Whitinsville, MA 01588-1032
(978) 456-5594
Mr. William W. Goding
Executive Director
E-MAIL: office@jrccvt.org
URL: www.jrccvt.org

Joint Review Committee on Education in Diagnostic Medical Sonography (J)
6021 University Boulevard
Suite 500
Ellicott City, MD 21043-6090
(443) 973-3251
FAX: (866) 738-3444
Mr. Gerry Magat
Accreditation Specialist
E-MAIL: mail@jrcdms.org
URL: www.jrcdms.org

Joint Review Committee on Education in Radiologic Technology (K)
20 North Wacker Drive
Suite 2850
Chicago, IL 60606-3182
(312) 704-5300
FAX: (312) 704-5304
Leslie F. Winter
Chief Executive Officer
E-MAIL: mail@jrcert.org
URL: www.jrcert.org

Joint Review Committee on Educational Programs in Nuclear Medicine Technology (L)
2000 West Danforth Road
Suite 130, #203
Edmond, OK 73003
(405) 285-0546
FAX: (405) 285-0579
Ms. Jan M. Winn
Executive Director
E-MAIL: jrcnmt@coxinet.net
URL: www.jrcnmt.org

Journalism Association of Community Colleges (M)
PO Box 163509
Sacramento, CA 95816
(562) 860-2451, ext 2619
FAX: (562) 467-5044
Mr. Rich Cameron
Communications Director
E-MAIL: rich@rcameron.com
URL: www.jacconline.org

LASPAU: Academic and Professional Programs for the Americas (N)
25 Mount Auburn Street
Suite 300
Cambridge, MA 02138-6095
(617) 495-5255
FAX: (617) 495-8990
Dr. Peter DeShazo
Executive Director
E-MAIL: laspau-info@calists.harvard.edu
URL: www.laspau.harvard.edu

Law School Admission Council (O)
662 Penn Street
Newtown, PA 18940
(215) 968-1001
FAX: (215) 968-1119
Mr. Daniel Bernstine
President
URL: www.lsac.org

Liaison Committee on Medical Education (LCME) American Medical Association (P)
330 North Wabash
Suite 39300
Chicago, IL 60611-5885
(312) 464-4933
FAX: (312) 464-5830
Barbara Barzansky Ph.D.,MHPE
LCME Co-Secretary
E-MAIL: barbara.barzansky@ama-assn.org
URL: www.lcme.org

Linguistic Society of America (Q)
1325 Eighteenth Street, NW
Archibald A. Hill
Suite #211
Washington, DC 20036-6501
(202) 835-1714
FAX: (202) 835-1717
Ms. Alyson Reed
Executive Director
E-MAIL: lsa@lsadc.org
URL: www.linguisticsociety.org

Literacy Research Association, Inc. (R)
222 South Westmonte Drive
#101
Altamonte Springs, FL 32714
(407) 774-7880
FAX: (407) 774-6440
Lynn Hupp
Executive Director
E-MAIL: lhupp@kmgnet.com
URL: www.LiteracyResearchAssociation.org

Lutheran Educational Conference of North America (S)
PMB #377
2601 South Minnesota Avenue
Suite 105
Sioux Falls, SD 57105-4750
(605) 271-9894
FAX: (605) 271-9895
Mr. William E. Hamm
President
E-MAIL: hamm@lutherancolleges.org
URL: www.lutherancolleges.org

Marketing EDGE (T)
1120 Avenue of the Americas
13th Floor
New York, NY 10036-6700
(212) 768-7277
FAX: (212) 790-1561
Terri L. Bartlett
President
E-MAIL: admin@marketingedge.org
URL: www.marketingedge.org

Medical Assisting Education Review Board (U)
20 North Wacker Drive
Suite 1575
Chicago, IL 60606-2963
(312) 899-1500
FAX: (312) 899-1259
Director of Accreditation
URL: www.maerb.org

Middle States Commission on Higher Education (V)
3624 Market Street
2nd Floor West
Philadelphia, PA 19104-2680
(267) 284-5000
FAX: (215) 662-5501
E-MAIL: info@msche.org
URL: www.msche.org

Midwest Association of Colleges and Employers (W)
3601 East Joppa Road
Baltimore, MD 21234
(410) 931-8100
FAX: (410) 931-8111
E-MAIL: admin@mwace.org
URL: www.mwace.org

Midwestern Higher Education Compact (MHEC) (X)
105 Fifth Avenue South
Suite 450
Minneapolis, MN 55401
(612) 677-2777
FAX: (612) 767-3353
Mr. Larry A. Isaak
President
E-MAIL: mhec@mhec.org
URL: www.mhec.org

Midwifery Education Accreditation Council (MEAC) (Y)
1935 Pauline Boulevard
Suite 100B
Ann Arbor, MI 48103
(360) 466-2080
FAX: (480) 907-2936
Ms. Sandra Stewart
Executive Director
E-MAIL: executivedirector@meacschools.org
URL: www.meacschools.org

Modern Language Association (Z)
26 Broadway
3rd Floor
New York, NY 10004-1789
(646) 576-5000
FAX: (646) 458-0030
Dr. Rosemary G. Feal
Executive Director
URL: www.mla.org

Montessori Accreditation Council for Teacher Education (MACTE) (a)
313 Second Street, SE
Suite 112
Charlottesville, VA 22902
(434) 202-7793
FAX: (888) 525-8838
Dr. Rebecca Pelton
Executive Director/President
E-MAIL: rebecca@macte.org
URL: www.macte.org

NACAS (b)
3 Boar's Head Lane
Suite B
Charlottesville, VA 22903-4610
(434) 245-8425
FAX: (434) 245-8453
Ron Campbell
CEO
E-MAIL: info@nacas.org
URL: www.nacas.org

NASH (c)
1250 H Street, NW
Suite 880
Washington, DC 20005
(202) 478-3453
FAX: (202) 513-8065
Rebecca Martin
Executive Director
E-MAIL: rebecca@nash-dc.org
URL: www.nashonline.org

NASPA-Student Affairs Administrators in Higher Education (d)
111 K Street, NE
10th Floor
Washington, DC 20002-4409
(202) 265-7500
FAX: (202) 898-5737
Dr. Kevin Kruger
President
E-MAIL: office@naspa.org
URL: www.naspa.org

National Academic Advising Association (e)
2323 Anderson Avenue
Suite 225
Manhattan, KS 66502-2912
(785) 532-5717
FAX: (785) 532-7732
Dr. Charlie L. Nutt
Executive Director
E-MAIL: nacada@ksu.edu
URL: www.nacada.ksu.edu

The National Academy of Education (f)
500 5th Street, NW
Suite 307
Washington, DC 20001
(202) 334-2341
FAX: (202) 334-2350
E-MAIL: info@naeducation.org
URL: www.naeducation.org

National Academy of Kinesiology (g)
1607 North Market Street
Champaign, IL 61820
(217) 403-7545
FAX: (217) 351-2674
Ms. Kim Scott
Business Manager
E-MAIL: kims@hkusa.com
URL: www.nationalacademyofkinesiology.org

National Accreditation Council for Blind and Low Vision Services (h)
PO Box 15368
Chattanooga, TN 37415
(423) 875-2033
Mr. William A. Robinson III
Executive Director
E-MAIL: bill@nacblvs.org
URL: www.nacblvs.org

National Accrediting Agency for Clinical Laboratory Sciences (i)
5600 North River Road
Suite 720
Rosemont, IL 60018
(773) 714-8880
FAX: (773) 714-8886
Dr. Dianne M. Cearlock Ph.D.
CEO
E-MAIL: dcearlock@naacls.org
URL: www.naacls.org

Higher Education Associations

National Accrediting Commission of Career Arts & Sciences (A)
4401 Ford Avenue
Suite 1300
Alexandria, VA 22302-1432
(703) 600-7600
Fax: (703) 379-2200
Tony Mirando M.S., D.C.
Executive Director
E-mail: naccas@naccas.org
URL: www.naccas.org

National Association for College Admission Counseling (B)
1050 North Highland Street
Suite 400
Arlington, VA 22201
(703) 836-2222
Fax: (703) 836-8015
Ms. Joyce E. Smith
Chief Executive Officer
E-mail: jsmith@nacacnet.org
URL: www.nacacnet.org

National Association for Equal Opportunity in Higher Education (C)
209 Third Street, SE
Washington, DC 20003
(202) 552-3300
Fax: (202) 552-3330
Lezli Baskerville Esquire
President & CEO
E-mail: presidentsoffice@nafeo.org
URL: www.nafeo.org

National Association for Ethnic Studies, Inc. (D)
Mississippi State University
Department of Ethnic Studies
PO Box PC
Mississippi State, MS 39762
(662) 325-7862
Fax: (662) 325-2716
E-mail: naes@ethnicstudies.org
URL: www.ethnicstudies.org

National Association for Legal Support of Alternative Schools (E)
PO Box 66758 CRZ
Moffat, CO 81143
(719) 429-2672
Mr. Ed Nagel
Coordinator
E-mail: nalsas@msn.com

National Association for Practical Nurse Education and Service, Inc. (F)
1940 Duke Street
Suite 200
Alexandria, VA 22314
(703) 933-1003
Fax: (703) 940-4089
Ann Bauer LPN
President
E-mail: president@napnes.org
URL: www.napnes.org

National Association of Agricultural Educators (G)
300 Garrigus Building
University of Kentucky
Lexington, KY 40546-0215
(859) 257-2224
Fax: (859) 323-3919
Dr. Wm. Jay Jackman
Executive Director
E-mail: jjackman.naae@uky.edu
URL: www.naae.org

National Association of College and University Attorneys (H)
1 Dupont Circle, NW
Suite 620
Washington, DC 20036
(202) 833-8390
Fax: (202) 296-8379
Ms. Kathleen Curry Santora Esq.
President & Chief Executive Officer
E-mail: ksantora@nacua.org
URL: www.nacua.org

National Association of College and University Business Officers (I)
1110 Vermont Avenue, NW
Suite 800
Washington, DC 20005
(202) 861-2500
Fax: (202) 861-2583
Mr. John Walda
President
E-mail: john.walda@nacubo.org
URL: www.nacubo.org

The National Association of College & University Food Services (J)
2525 Jolly Road
Suite 280
Okemos, MI 48864
(517) 332-2494
Fax: (517) 332-8144
Gretchen Couraud CAE, CFRE
Executive Director
E-mail: gcouraud@nacufs.org
URL: www.nacufs.org

National Association of College Stores (K)
500 East Lorain Street
Oberlin, OH 44074-1294
(440) 775-7777
Fax: (440) 775-4769
Mr. Brian E. Cartier CAE
Chief Executive Officer
E-mail: info@nacs.org
URL: www.nacs.org

National Association of College Wind and Percussion Instructors (L)
Division of Fine Arts
Truman State University
Kirksville, MO 63501
(660) 665-2558
Dr. Richard Weerts
Executive Secretary-Treasurer
URL: www.nacwpi.org

National Association of Colleges and Employers (M)
62 Highland Avenue
Bethlehem, PA 18017-9085
(610) 868-1421
Fax: (610) 868-0208
Dr. Marilyn Mackes
Executive Director
E-mail: cnader@naceweb.org
URL: www.naceweb.org

National Association of Educational Procurement (N)
5523 Research Park Drive
Suite 340
Baltimore, MD 21228
(443) 543-5540
Fax: (443) 543-5550
Mrs. Doreen Murner
CEO
E-mail: dmurner@naepnet.org
URL: www.naepnet.org

National Association of Independent Colleges and Universities (O)
1025 Connecticut Avenue, NW
Suite 700
Washington, DC 20036-5405
(202) 785-8866
Fax: (202) 835-0003
Dr. David L. Warren
President
E-mail: geninfo@naicu.edu
URL: www.naicu.edu

National Association of Schools of Art and Design (P)
11250 Roger Bacon Drive
Suite 21
Reston, VA 20190
(703) 437-0700
Fax: (703) 437-6312
Samuel Hope
Executive Director
E-mail: info@arts-accredit.org
URL: www.arts-accredit.org

National Association of Schools of Dance (Q)
11250 Roger Bacon Drive
Suite 21
Reston, VA 20190
(703) 437-0700
Fax: (703) 437-6312
Samuel Hope
Executive Director
E-mail: info@arts-accredit.org
URL: www.arts-accredit.org

National Association of Schools of Music (R)
11250 Roger Bacon Drive
Suite 21
Reston, VA 20190
(703) 437-0700
Fax: (703) 437-6312
Samuel Hope
Executive Director
E-mail: info@arts-accredit.org
URL: www.arts-accredit.org

National Association of Schools of Theatre (S)
11250 Roger Bacon Drive
Suite 21
Reston, VA 20190
(703) 437-0700
Fax: (703) 437-6312
Samuel Hope
Executive Director
E-mail: info@arts-accredit.org
URL: www.arts-accredit.org

National Association of State Directors of Teacher Education and Certification (T)
1629 K Street, NW
Suite 300
Washington, DC 20006
(202) 204-2208
Fax: (202) 204-2210
Dr. Phillip Rogers
Executive Director
E-mail: philrogers@nasdtec.com
URL: www.nasdtec.net

National Association of Student Financial Aid Administrators (U)
1101 Connecticut Avenue, NW
Suite 1100
Washington, DC 20036-4303
(202) 785-0453
Fax: (202) 785-1487
Mr. Justin Draeger
President
E-mail: web@nasfaa.org
URL: www.nasfaa.org

National Catholic Educational Association (V)
1005 North Glebe Road
Suite 525
Arlington, VA 22201-5792
(571) 257-0010
Fax: (703) 243-0025
Br. Robert R. Bimonte FSC
President
E-mail: rbimonte@ncea.org
URL: www.ncea.org

National Coalition for Campus Childrens Centers (W)
2036 Larkhall Circle
Folsom, CA 95630
(916) 790-8261
Fax: (916) 790-8261
Ms. Tonya Palla
Executive Director
E-mail: info@campuschildren.org
URL: www.campuschildren.org

National Collegiate Athletic Association (X)
PO Box 6222
Indianapolis, IN 46206
(317) 917-6222
Fax: (317) 917-6364
Mr. Todd Petr
Managing Director of Research
E-mail: tpetr@ncaa.org
URL: www.ncaa.org

National Commission on Orthotic and Prosthetic Education (NCOPE) (Y)
330 John Carlyle Street
Suite 200
Alexandria, VA 22314
(703) 836-7114
Fax: (703) 836-0838
Ms. Robin C. Seabrook
Executive Director
E-mail: rseabrook@ncope.org
URL: www.ncope.org

National Communication Association (Z)
1765 N Street, NW
Washington, DC 20036
(202) 464-4622
Fax: (202) 464-4600
Nancy Kidd Ph.D.
Executive Director
E-mail: inbox@natcom.org
URL: www.natcom.org

National Council for Continuing Education and Training (a)
PO Box 2916
Columbus, OH 43216-2916
(888) 771-0179
Fax: (888) 853-2213
Kirk White RN, MSN
President
E-mail: nccet@nccet.org
URL: www.nccet.org

National Council of Instructional Administrators (NCIA) Dept of Educational Administration (b)
141 Teachers College Hall
PO Box 880360
University of Nebraska - Lincoln
Lincoln, NE 68588-0360
(402) 472-8958
Fax: (402) 472-4300
Katherine Wesley
Executive Director
E-mail: ncia@unl.edu
URL: ncia.unl.edu

National Council of University Research Administrators (c)
1015 18th Street, NW
Suite 901
Washington, DC 20036
(202) 466-3894
Fax: (202) 223-5573
Mrs. Kathleen M. Larmett
Executive Director
E-mail: info@ncura.edu
URL: www.ncura.edu

National Education Association (d)
1201 Sixteenth Street, NW
Suite 310
Washington, DC 20036
(202) 822-7110
Fax: (202) 822-7624
Ms. Valerie Wilk
Higher Education Organizer
E-mail: vwilk@nea.org
URL: www.nea.org/he

National Forensic Association (e)
Illinois State University
School of Communication
Campus Box 4480
Normal, IL 61790-4480
(309) 438-8447
Fax: (309) 438-3048
Prof. Megan Koch
National Secretary-Treasurer
E-mail: mkoch@ilstu.edu
URL: www.nationalforensics.org

National League for Nursing (f)
The Watergate Buliding
2600 Virginia Avenue
8th Floor
Washington, DC 20037
(800) 669-1656
Dr. Beverly L. Malone
Chief Executive Officer
E-mail: oceo@nln.org
URL: www.nln.org

National Recreation and Park Association Council on Accreditation for Parks, Recreation, Tourism and Related Professions (COAPRT) (g)
22377 Belmont Ridge Road
Ashburn, VA 20148-4501
(703) 858-2195
Fax: (703) 858-0794
Ms. Danielle Price
Accreditation Manager
E-mail: coaprt@nrpa.org
URL: www.nrpa.org

National Rural Education Association (h)
Purdue University
Beering Hall of Liberal Arts & Education
100 North University Street
West Lafayette, IN 47907
(765) 494-0086
Fax: (765) 496-1228
Dr. John Hill
Executive Director
E-mail: jehill@purdue.edu
URL: www.nrea.net

National Safety Council College and University Initiative (A)
1121 Spring Lake Drive
Itasca, IL 60143
(630) 775-2358
FAX: (630) 285-1139
Mr. Tony Randall
Volunteer Pgm Mgr, (College/University Oversight)
E-MAIL: tony.randall@nsc.org
URL: www.nsc.org

National Society for Experiential Education (B)
c/o Talley Management Group, Inc.
19 Mantua Road
Mt. Royal, NJ 08061
(856) 423-3427
FAX: (856) 423-3420
Haley Brust
Executive Director
E-MAIL: nsee@talley.com
URL: www.nsee.org

National Writing Project (C)
2105 Bancroft Way
#1042
University of California
Berkeley, CA 94720-1042
(510) 642-0963
FAX: (510) 642-4545
Dr. Sharon J. Washington
Executive Director
E-MAIL: nwp@nwp.org
URL: www.nwp.org

Network of Schools of Public Policy, Affairs, and Administration (D)
1029 Vermont Avenue, NW
Suite 1100
Washington, DC 20005
(202) 628-8965
Laurel McFarland
Executive Director
E-MAIL: naspaa@naspaa.org
URL: www.naspaa.org

New England Association of Schools and Colleges, Inc. Commission on Institutions of Higher Education (E)
3 Burlington Woods Drive
#100
Burlington, MA 01803
(781) 425-7747
FAX: (781) 425-1001
Dr. Barbara Brittingham
Director of the Commission
E-MAIL: cihe@neasc.org
URL: cihe.neasc.org

New England Board of Higher Education (F)
45 Temple Place
Boston, MA 02111
(617) 357-9620, ext. 128
FAX: (617) 338-1577
Dr. Michael K. Thomas
President and CEO
E-MAIL: mthomas@nebhe.org
URL: www.nebhe.org

North American Association of Summer Sessions (G)
1501 West Bradley Avenue
Peoria, IL 61625
(866) 880-9607
FAX: (309) 677-3321
Ms. Janet Lange
Executive Secretary
E-MAIL: lange@bradley.edu
URL: www.naass.org

North Central Association Commission on Accreditation and School Improvement (H)
9115 Westside Parkway
Alpharetta, GA 30009
(678) 392-2285, ext. 5595
Mr. Mark A. Elgart
President/CEO
E-MAIL: contactus@advanc-ed.org
URL: www.advanc-ed.org

North Central Conference on Summer Sessions (I)
Bradley University
Peoria, IL 61625
(309) 677-2374
FAX: (309) 677-3321
Mr. Jon C. Neidy
Director of Summer and Interim Sessions
E-MAIL: neidy@bradley.edu

Northwest Commission on Colleges and Universities (J)
8060 165th Avenue, NE
Suite 100
Redmond, WA 98052
(425) 558-4224
FAX: (425) 376-0596
Dr. Sandra E. Elman
President
E-MAIL: ruthb@nwccu.org
URL: www.nwccu.org

Organizational Systems Research Association (K)
Morehead State University
Department of Information Systems
150 University Boulevard, Box 2478
Morehead, KY 40351-1689
(606) 783-2718
FAX: (606) 783-5025
Dr. Donna R. Everett
Executive Director
E-MAIL: d.everett@moreheadstate.edu
URL: www.osra.org

Planning Accreditation Board (L)
53 West Jackson Boulevard
Suite 1315
Chicago, IL 60604
(312) 662-1440
Shonagh Merits
Executive Director
URL: www.planningaccreditationboard.org

Quality Education for Minorities (QEM) Network (M)
1818 N Street, NW
Suite 350
Washington, DC 20036
(202) 659-1818
FAX: (202) 659-5408
Dr. Shirley M. McBay
President
E-MAIL: qemnetwork@qem.org
URL: qemnetwork.qem.org

Society for College and University Planning (N)
1330 Eisenhower Place
Ann Arbor, MI 48108
(734) 669-3270
FAX: (734) 661-0157
Ms. Jolene Knapp, CAE
Executive Director
E-MAIL: info@scup.org
URL: www.scup.org

Society for Slovene Studies (O)
Suzzallo Library
Box 352900
University of Washington
Seattle, WA 98195
(206) 543-5588
Mr. Michael Biggins
Secretary
E-MAIL: mbiggins@uw.edu
URL: www.slovenestudies.com

Society for the Advancement of Scandinavian Study (P)
Department of Scandanavian Studies
University of Wisconsin
1220 Linden Drive
Madison, WI 53706
(608) 262-2090
Ms. Susan Brantley
Managing Editor
E-MAIL: sass.subscriptions@gmail.com
URL: www.scandinavianstudy.org

Society for Values in Higher Education (Q)
c/o Western Kentucky University
1906 College Heights Boulevard
#8020
Bowling Green, KY 42101
(270) 745-2907
FAX: (270) 745-5347
Mrs. Sandy McAllister
Director
E-MAIL: society@svhe.org
URL: www.svhe.org

Society of American Foresters (R)
5400 Grosvenor Lane
Bethesda, MD 20814-2198
(866) 897-8720
FAX: (301) 897-3690
Mr. Michael T. Goergen Jr.
Executive Vice President & CEO
E-MAIL: goergenm@safnet.org
URL: www.safnet.org

Society of Professors of Education (S)
University of West Georgia
Department of L & I
1600 Maple Street
Carrollton, GA 30118-5160
(678) 839-6132
FAX: (678) 839-6097
Dr. Robert C. Morris
Secretary-Treasurer
E-MAIL: rmorris@westga.edu

Southeastern Universities Research Association (T)
1201 New York Avenue, NW
Suite 430
Washington, DC 20005
(202) 408-7872
FAX: (202) 408-8250
Dr. Jerry Draayer
President & CEO
E-MAIL: draayer@sura.org
URL: www.sura.org

Southern Association for College Student Affairs (U)
Armstrong Atlantic State University
11935 Abercorn Street
Savannah, GA 31419
(912) 344-2510
FAX: (912) 344-3468
Dr. Joe Buck
Executive Director
E-MAIL: joe.buck@armstrong.edu
URL: www.sacsa.org

Southern Association of Colleges and Schools Commission on Colleges (V)
1866 Southern Lane
Decatur, GA 30033-4097
(404) 679-4500
FAX: (404) 679-4528
Dr. Belle S. Wheelan
President
E-MAIL: bwheelan@sacscoc.org
URL: www.sacscoc.org

Southern States Communication Association (W)
Valdosta State University
Communication Arts
1500 North Patterson
Valdosta, GA 31698
(229) 333-5820
FAX: (229) 293-6182
Dr. Carl M. Cates
Executive Director
E-MAIL: director@ssca.net
URL: www.ssca.net

State Higher Education Executive Officers (X)
3035 Center Green Drive
Suite 100
Boulder, CO 80301-2205
(303) 541-1600
FAX: (303) 541-1639
Dr. Paul E. Lingenfelter
President
E-MAIL: sheeo@sheeo.org
URL: www.sheeo.org

Tennessee Independent Colleges and Universities Association (Y)
1031 17th Avenue South
Nashville, TN 37212
(615) 242-6400
FAX: (615) 242-8033
Dr. Claude O. Pressnell Jr.
President
E-MAIL: pressnell@ticua.org
URL: www.ticua.org

Transnational Association of Christian Colleges and Schools (TRACS) (Z)
15935 Forest Road
Forest, VA 24551
(434) 525-9539
FAX: (434) 525-9538
Dr. T. Paul Boatner
President
E-MAIL: info@tracs.org
URL: www.tracs.org

The Tuition Exchange, Inc. (a)
3 Bethesda Metro Center
Suite 700
Bethesda, MD 20814
(301) 941-1827
FAX: (301) 657-9776
Mr. Robert D. Shorb
Executive Director/CEO
E-MAIL: rshorb@tuitionexchange.org
URL: www.tuitionexchange.org

UNCF (b)
1805 7th Street NW
Washington, DC 20001
(202) 810-0220
FAX: (202) 234-0222
Dr. Michael Lomax
President & CEO
URL: www.uncf.org

University Aviation Association (c)
2415 Moore's Mill Road
Suite 265-216
Auburn, AL 36830-6444
(334) 528-0300
Ms. Carolyn Williamson
Executive Director
E-MAIL: uaamail@uaa.aero
URL: www.uaa.aero

University Film and Video Association (d)
University of Southern California
School of Cinematic Arts
900 West 34th Street, SCA 428
Los Angeles, CA 90089-2211
(866) 647-8382
Mr. Norman Hollyn
E-MAIL: ufvahome@gmail.com
URL: www.ufva.org

University Photographers' Association of America (e)
Moraine Valley Community College
9000 West College Parkway
Palos Hills, IL 60465
(708) 974-5495
FAX: (708) 974-0681
Mr. Glenn Carpenter
UPAA President
E-MAIL: carpenter@morainevalley.edu
URL: www.upaa.org

University Professional & Continuing Education Association (UPCEA) (f)
1 Dupont Circle, NW
Suite 615
Washington, DC 20036
(202) 659-3130
FAX: (202) 785-0374
Dr. Robert J. Hansen
CEO
E-MAIL: rhansen@upcea.edu
URL: www.upcea.edu

Urban Affairs Association (g)
University of Wisconsin-Milwaukee
PO Box 413
Milwaukee, WI 53201-0413
(414) 229-3025
E-MAIL: info@uaamail.org
URL: www.urbanaffairsassociation.org

WASC Senior College and University Commission (h)
985 Atlantic Avenue
Suite 100
Alameda, CA 94501
(510) 748-9001
FAX: (510) 748-9797
Mary Ellen Petrisko
President
URL: www.wascsenior.org

Western Interstate Commission for Higher Education (i)
3035 Center Green Drive
Suite 200
Boulder, CO 80301-2204
(303) 541-0201
FAX: (303) 541-0245
Dr. David A. Longanecker
President
E-MAIL: dlonganecker@wiche.edu
URL: www.wiche.edu

Women in Higher Education (j)
5376 Farmco Drive
Madison, WI 53704
(608) 251-3232
FAX: (608) 284-0601
Ms. Mary Dee Wenniger
E-MAIL: women@wihe.com
URL: www.wihe.com

Consortia of Institutions of Higher Education

Alabama Association of Independent Colleges and Universities (A)
5950 Carmichael Place
Suite 213
Montgomery, AL 36117
(334) 356-2220
FAX: (334) 356-2202
Gen. Paul M. Hankins
President
E-MAIL: hankinsp@knology.net
URL: www.aaicu.net

Alliance for Higher Education (B)
PO Box 836696
Richardson, TX 75083-6696
(972) 883-4920
Maria Smith
Executive Director
E-MAIL: marias@ntxrcic.org
URL: www.ntxrcic.org

Arkansas' Independent Colleges and Universities (C)
One Riverfront Place
Suite 610
US Bank Building
North Little Rock, AR 72114
(501) 378-0843
FAX: (501) 374-1523
Mr. Rex Nelson
President
E-MAIL: rnelson@arkindcolleges.org
URL: www.arkindcolleges.org

Associated Colleges of Central Kansas (D)
210 South Main Street
McPherson, KS 67460
(620) 241-5150
FAX: (620) 241-5153
URL: www.acck.edu

Associated Colleges of the Midwest (E)
11 East Adams Street
Suite 800
Chicago, IL 60603
(312) 263-5000
FAX: (312) 263-5879
Dr. Christopher Welna
President
E-MAIL: acm@acm.edu
URL: www.acm.edu

Associated Colleges of the Twin Cities (ACTC) (F)
570 Asbury Street
Suite 109
St. Paul, MN 55104
(651) 556-1863
FAX: (651) 294-8959
Dr. Carole Chabries
Executive Director
E-MAIL: info@actc-mn.org
URL: www.actc-mn.org

Association of Independent California Colleges and Universities (G)
1100 Eleventh Street
Suite 10
Sacramento, CA 95814
(916) 446-7626
FAX: (916) 446-7948
Ms. Kristen Soares
President
E-MAIL: aiccu@aiccu.edu
URL: www.aiccu.edu

Association of Independent Colleges and Universities in Massachusetts (H)
11 Beacon Street
Suite 1224
Boston, MA 02108-3093
(617) 742-5147
FAX: (617) 742-3089
Mr. Richard Doherty
President
E-MAIL: richard.doherty@bc.edu
URL: www.masscolleges.org -or- www.aicum.org

Association of Independent Colleges and Universities in New Jersey (I)
797 Springfield Avenue
Summit, NJ 07901-1107
(908) 277-3738
FAX: (908) 277-0851
Mr. John B. Wilson
President and CEO
E-MAIL: jbwilson@njcolleges.org
URL: www.njcolleges.org

Association of Independent Colleges and Universities of Michigan (J)
124 West Allegan Street
Suite 650
Lansing, MI 48933-1707
(517) 372-9160
FAX: (517) 372-9165
Robert LeFevre
E-MAIL: rlefevre@goaicum.org
URL: aicum.org

Association of Independent Colleges and Universities of Nebraska (K)
635 South 14th Street
Suite 310
Lincoln, NE 68508
(402) 434-2818
FAX: (402) 434-2825
Mr. Thomas O'Neill
President
E-MAIL: tiponeill2@aol.com

Association of Independent Colleges and Universities of Ohio (L)
41 South High Street
Suite 2424
Columbus, OH 43215
(614) 228-2196
FAX: (614) 228-8406
Mr. C. Todd Jones
President & General Counsel
E-MAIL: tjones@aicuo.edu
URL: www.aicuo.edu

Association of Independent Colleges and Universities of Pennsylvania (M)
101 North Front Street
Harrisburg, PA 17101-1405
(717) 232-8649
FAX: (717) 233-8574
Dr. Don L. Francis
President
E-MAIL: francis@aicup.org
URL: www.aicup.org

Association of Independent Colleges and Universities of Rhode Island (N)
30 Exchange Terrace
Providence, RI 02903
(401) 272-8270
FAX: (401) 272-9194
Mr. Daniel Egan
President
E-MAIL: pmulcahey@aicuri.org
URL: www.aicuri.org

Association of Independent Colleges of Art & Design (O)
236 Hope Street
Providence, RI 02906
(401) 270-5991
FAX: (401) 270-5993
Ms. Deborah Obalil
Executive Director
URL: www.aicad.org

Association of Independent Kentucky Colleges and Universities (P)
484 Chenault Road
Frankfort, KY 40601
(502) 695-5007
FAX: (502) 695-5057
Dr. Gary S. Cox
President
E-MAIL: gary.cox@aikcu.org
URL: www.aikcu.org

Association of Vermont Independent Colleges (Q)
PO Box 254
Montpelier, VT 05601
(802) 828-8826
Susan Stitely
President
E-MAIL: sstitely@vermont-icolleges.org
URL: www.vermont-icolleges.org

Atlanta Regional Council for Higher Education (R)
133 Peachtree Street, NE
Suite 4925
Atlanta, GA 30303-2923
(404) 651-2668
FAX: (404) 880-9816
Ms. Jackie Smith
E-MAIL: arche@atlantahighered.org
URL: www.atlantahighered.org

Boston Theological Institute (S)
210 Herrick Road
Newton Centre, MA 02459
(617) 527-4880
FAX: (617) 527-1073
Dr. Rodney Petersen
Executive Director
E-MAIL: btioffice@bostontheological.org
URL: www.bostontheological.org

Central Pennsylvania Consortium (T)
c/o Franklin & Marshall College
PO Box 3003
Lancaster, PA 17604-3003
(717) 291-4282
FAX: (717) 358-4455
Ms. Kathryn Missildine
Executive Assistant
E-MAIL: kathy.missildine@fandm.edu
URL: www.centralpennsylvaniaconsortium.org

CHESLA (U)
10 Columbus Boulevard
Hartford, CT 06106-1978
(860) 761-8453
Ms. Jeanette W. Weldon
Executive Director
E-MAIL: jweldon@chefa.com
URL: www.chesla.org

Christian College Consortium (V)
255 Grapevine Road
Wenham, MA 01984-1813
(978) 867-4755
FAX: (978) 867-4650
Dr. Stan Gaede
President
E-MAIL: stan.gaede@gordon.edu
URL: www.ccconsortium.org

Community College Leadership Consortium & Futures Assembly (W)
University of Florida, College of Education
Box 117049
229 Norman Hall
Gainesville, FL 32611-7049
(352) 273-4300
FAX: (352) 846-2697
Dr. Dale F. Campbell
Director
E-MAIL: dfc@coe.ufl.edu
URL: futures.education.ufl.edu/index.html

The Consortium for Graduate Study in Management (X)
229 Chesterfield Business Parkway
Chesterfield, MO 63005
(636) 681-5553
FAX: (636) 681-5499
Mr. Peter J. Aranda III
Executive Director and CEO
E-MAIL: recruiting@cgsm.org
URL: www.cgsm.org

Consortium for the Advancement of Adult Higher Education (Y)
4025 South Riverpoint Parkway
Mail Stop CF-K601
Phoenix, AZ 85040
(602) 557-1153
Dr. Sue Salter Dietrich
Executive Director
E-MAIL: sue.dietrich@ipd.org
URL: www.caahe.org

Consortium of College & University Media Centers (Z)
Indiana University
601 East Kirkwood Avenue
Franklin Hall 0009
Bloomington, IN 47405-1223
(812) 855-6049
FAX: (812) 855-2103
Aileen Scales
Executive Director
E-MAIL: ccumc@ccumc.org
URL: www.ccumc.org

Consortium of Universities of the Washington Metropolitan Area (a)
1100 H Street, NW
Suite 500
Washington, DC 20005
(202) 331-8080
FAX: (202) 331-7925
Dr. John Cavanaugh
President & CEO
E-MAIL: jcavanaugh@consortium.org
URL: www.consortium.org

Consortium on Financing Higher Education (b)
238 Main Street
Suite 402
Cambridge, MA 02142-1046
(617) 253-5030
FAX: (617) 258-8280
Dr. Kristine E. Dillon
President
E-MAIL: kedillon@mit.edu
URL: www.cofhe.org

Cooperating Raleigh Colleges (c)
Meredith College
3800 Hillsborough Street
Raleigh, NC 27607-5298
(919) 760-8538
Ms. Jenny Spiker
Director
E-MAIL: crc@meredith.edu
URL: www.crcraleighcolleges.org

Council of Independent Colleges in Virginia (d)
PO Box 1005
Bedford, VA 24523
(540) 586-0606
FAX: (540) 586-2630
Mr. Robert B. Lambeth Jr.
President
E-MAIL: lambeth@cicv.org
URL: www.cicv.org

Council of North Central Two Year Colleges (e)
200 South 14th Street
Parsons, KS 67357
(620) 820-1223
FAX: (620) 421-0921
Dr. George Knox
Executive Director
E-MAIL: cnctyc@labette.edu
URL: www.labette.edu/cnctyc

Council of Presidents (f)
410 Eleventh Avenue, SE
Suite 101
Olympia, WA 98501
(360) 292-4100
FAX: (360) 292-4110
Mr. Paul Francis
Executive Director
E-MAIL: pfrancis@cop.wsu.edu
URL: www.councilofpresidents.org

Federation of Independent Illinois Colleges and Universities (g)
1123 South Second Street
Springfield, IL 62704
(217) 789-1400
FAX: (217) 789-6259
Mr. David W. Tretter
President
E-MAIL: davetretter@federationedu.org
URL: www.federationedu.org

Five Colleges, Incorporated (h)
97 Spring Street
Amherst, MA 01002
(413) 542-4009
FAX: (413) 542-4029
Dr. Neal B. Abraham
Executive Director
E-MAIL: nabraham@fivecolleges.edu
URL: www.fivecolleges.edu

Georgia Independent College Association (i)
600 West Peachtree Street, NW
Suite 1510
Atlanta, GA 30308
(404) 233-5433
FAX: (404) 233-6309
Dr. Susanna Baxter
President
E-MAIL: sbaxter@georgiacolleges.org
URL: www.georgiacolleges.org

Graduate Theological Foundation Oxford/Rome/Indiana Consortia (j)
Dodge House
415 Lincoln Way East
Mishawaka, IN 46544-2213
(800) 423-5983
FAX: (574) 255-7520
Bethany Morgan MBA
Registrar
E-MAIL: information@gtfeducation.org
URL: www.gtfeducation.org

Great Lakes Colleges Association (A)
535 West William
Suite 301
Ann Arbor, MI 48103
(734) 661-2350
FAX: (734) 661-2349
Dr. Richard A. Detweiler
President
E-MAIL: detweiler@glca.org
URL: www.glca.org

Greater Cincinnati Consortium of Colleges and Universities (B)
Northern Kentucky University
241 Campbell Hall
Highland Heights, KY 41099
(859) 392-2428
FAX: (859) 392-2416
Ms. Janet Piccirillo
Executive Director
E-MAIL: gcccu@nku.edu
URL: www.gcccu.org

Hartford Consortium for Higher Education (C)
31 Pratt Street
4th Floor
Hartford, CT 06103
(860) 702-3801
FAX: (860) 241-1130
Dr. Martin Estey
Executive Director
E-MAIL: mestey@metrohartford.com
URL: www.hartfordconsortium.org

Higher Education Consortium for Urban Affairs, Inc. (HECUA) (D)
2233 University Avenue West
Suite 210
St. Paul, MN 55114
(651) 287-3300
FAX: (651) 659-9421
Dr. Jenny Keyser
Executive Director
E-MAIL: hecua@hecua.org
URL: www.hecua.org

Higher Education Consortium of Metropolitan St. Louis (E)
8420 Delmar Boulevard
Suite 504
St. Louis, MO 63124
(314) 991-2700
FAX: (314) 991-2874
URL: www.heccstl.com

Higher Education Data Sharing (HEDS) Consortium (F)
Wabash College
PO Box 352
Crawfordsville, IN 47933
(765) 361-6331
FAX: (717) 361-6475
Charles Blaich
Director
E-MAIL: charles.blaich@gmail.com
URL: www.hedsconsortium.org

Independent Colleges and Universities of Missouri (G)
PO Box 1865
Jefferson City, MO 65102-1865
(573) 635-9160
FAX: (573) 635-6258
Dr. Ronald A. Slepitza
President
E-MAIL: bill@molobby.com
URL: www.icum.org

Independent Colleges and Universities of Texas, Inc. (H)
PO Box 13105
Austin, TX 78701-3105
(512) 472-9522
FAX: (512) 472-2371
Dr. Carol McDonald
President
E-MAIL: carol.mcdonald@icut.org
URL: www.icut.org

Independent Colleges of Indiana Inc. (I)
3135 North Meridian Street
Indianapolis, IN 46208
(317) 236-6090
FAX: (317) 236-6086
Dr. Richard Ludwick
President and CEO
E-MAIL: rludwick@icindiana.org
URL: www.icindiana.org

Independent Colleges of Washington (J)
600 Stewart Street
Suite 600
Seattle, WA 98101
(206) 623-4494
FAX: (206) 625-9621
Ms. Violet A. Boyer
President & CEO
E-MAIL: violet@icwashington.org
URL: www.icwashington.org

Inter-University Consortium for Political and Social Research (K)
The University of Michigan
Institute for Social Research
PO Box 1248
Ann Arbor, MI 48106-1248
(734) 615-8400
FAX: (734) 647-8200
Dr. George Alter
Director
E-MAIL: netmail@icpsr.umich.edu
URL: www.icpsr.umich.edu

Iowa Association of Community College Trustees (L)
855 East Court Avenue
Des Moines, IA 50309
(515) 282-4692
FAX: (515) 282-3743
M. J. Dolan J.D.
Executive Director
E-MAIL: mjdolan@iacct.com
URL: www.iacct.com

Iowa Association of Independent Colleges and Universities (M)
505 Fifth Avenue
Suite 1030
Des Moines, IA 50309
(515) 282-3175
FAX: (515) 282-8177
Mr. Gary W. Steinke
President
E-MAIL: president@iaicu.org
URL: www.iowaprivatecolleges.org

Kansas Independent College Association (N)
700 South Kansas Avenue
Suite 622 A
Topeka, KS 66603
(785) 235-9877
FAX: (785) 235-1437
Mr. Matthew Lindsey
President
E-MAIL: matt@kscolleges.org
URL: www.kscolleges.org

Kentuckiana Metroversity (O)
109 East Broadway
Louisville, KY 40202
(502) 213-4562
Kathleen Mandlehr Ed.D.
Executive Director
E-MAIL: kathleen.mandlehr@kctcs.edu
URL: www.metroversity.org

Lehigh Valley Association of Independent Colleges (P)
130 West Greenwich Street
Bethlehem, PA 18018
(610) 625-7888
FAX: (610) 625-7891
Diane Dimitroff
Executive Director
E-MAIL: dimitroffd@lvaic.org
URL: www.lvaic.org

Louisiana Association of Independent Colleges and Universities (Q)
320 Third Street
Suite 104
Baton Rouge, LA 70801
(225) 389-9885
FAX: (225) 389-0149
Ms. Mary Ann Coleman
President
E-MAIL: maryann@laicu.org
URL: www.laicu.org

Maine Independent Colleges Association (R)
c/o Preti Flaherty
PO Box 1058
Augusta, ME 04332-0158
(207) 623-5300
FAX: (207) 623-2914
Dr. Daniel Walker
Legal Counsel
E-MAIL: dwalker@preti.com

Maryland Independent College and University Association (S)
60 West Street
Suite 201
Annapolis, MD 21401
(410) 269-0306
FAX: (410) 269-5905
Ms. Tina M. Bjarekull
President
E-MAIL: lstrayer@micua.org
URL: www.micua.org

Massachusetts Education & Career Opportunities (T)
484 Main Street
Suite 500
Worcester, MA 01608
(508) 754-6829
FAX: (508) 797-0069
Ms. Pamela Boisvert
CEO
URL: www.massedco.org

Midwest Universities Consortium for International Activities, Inc. (U)
4700 South Hagadorn Road
Suite 150
East Lansing, MI 48823-6808
(517) 432-0661
FAX: (517) 432-4457
Dr. Philip R. Smith
President & Executive Director
E-MAIL: mucia@msu.edu
URL: www.muciainc.org

Minnesota Private College Council, Inc. (V)
445 Minnesota Street
Suite 500
St. Paul, MN 55101
(651) 228-9061
FAX: (651) 228-0379
E-MAIL: colleges@mnprivatecolleges.org
URL: www.mnprivatecolleges.org

Mississippi Association of Independent Colleges and Universities (W)
PO Box 2933
Ridgeland, MS 39158-2933
(601) 957-2052
FAX: (601) 977-0233
Dr. E. Harold Fisher
Executive Director
E-MAIL: ehfisher@bellsouth.net

National Student Exchange (X)
4656 West Jefferson
Suite 140
Fort Wayne, IN 46804
(260) 436-2634
FAX: (260) 436-5676
Ms. Bette Worley
President
E-MAIL: bworley@nse2.org
URL: www.nse.org

New England Faculty Development Consortium (Y)
New England Institute of Technology
1408 Division Road
East Greenwich, RI 02818
(401) 739-5000
Dr. Richard Gouse
President
URL: www.nefdc.org

New Hampshire College & University Council (Z)
3 Barrell Court
Suite 100
Concord, NH 03301-8543
(603) 225-4199
FAX: (603) 225-8108
Thomas R. Horgan
President and CEO
E-MAIL: horgan@nhcuc.org
URL: www.nhcuc.org

New Jersey Association of State Colleges and Universities (a)
150 West State Street
Trenton, NJ 08608
(609) 989-1100
FAX: (609) 989-7017
Dr. Michael W. Klein
CEO
E-MAIL: njascu@njascu.org
URL: www.njascu.org

New Jersey Council of County Colleges (b)
330 West State Street
Trenton, NJ 08618
(609) 392-3434
FAX: (609) 392-8158
Dr. Lawrence A. Nespoli
President
E-MAIL: info@njccc.org
URL: www.njccc.org

New Mexico Independent College Fund (c)
c/o St. John's College
Office of the President
1160 Camino Cruz Blanca
Santa Fe, NM 87505
(505) 984-6098
FAX: (505) 984-6031
E-MAIL: president@sjcsf.edu
URL: www.sjcsf.edu

New Orleans Educational Telecommunications Consortium, Inc. (d)
5000 West Esplanade Avenue
#290
Metairie, LA 70006
(504) 524-0350
E-MAIL: noetc@noetc.org
URL: www.noetc.com

North Carolina Independent Colleges and Universities (e)
530 North Blount Street
Raleigh, NC 27604
(919) 832-5817
FAX: (919) 833-0794
Dr. A. Hope Williams
President
E-MAIL: williams@ncicu.org
URL: www.ncicu.org

North Dakota Independent College Fund (f)
University of Mary
7500 University Drive
Bismarck, ND 58504-9652
(701) 355-8222
FAX: (701) 255-7687
Mr. Neal Kalberer
Executive Director
E-MAIL: kalberer@umary.edu

Northeast Consortium of Colleges and Universities in Massachusetts (NECCUM) (g)
North Shore Community College
1 Ferncroft Road
PO Box 3340
Danvers, MA 01923
(781) 477-2143
FAX: (781) 477-2144
Ms. Donna L. Richemond
Vice President for Student and Enrollment Services
E-MAIL: drichemo@northshore.edu
URL: www.northshore.edu

Northeast Ohio Council on Higher Education (h)
1422 Euclid Avenue
Suite 840
Cleveland, OH 44115
(216) 420-9200
FAX: (216) 420-9292
Ms. Ann Womer Benjamin J.D.
Executive Director
E-MAIL: awomerbenjamin@noche.org
URL: www.noche.org

Oak Ridge Associated Universities (i)
MC-100-22
PO Box 117
Oak Ridge, TN 37831-0117
(865) 576-3300
FAX: (865) 576-3816
Mr. Harry A. Page
President and CEO
E-MAIL: andy.page@orau.org
URL: www.orau.org

The Ohio College Association, Inc. (j)
10 West Broad Street
Suite 450
Columbus, OH 43215
(614) 464-1266
FAX: (614) 464-9281
Ms. Cindy McQuade
URL: www.ohiocollege.org

Consortia of Institutions of Higher Education

Oklahoma Independent Colleges and Universities (A)
PO Box 57148
Oklahoma City, OK 73157-7148
(405) 501-2885
Lesa Smaligo
Executive Director
E-MAIL: lesa@oicu.org
URL: www.oicu.org

Oregon Alliance of Independent Colleges & Universities (B)
16101 SW 72nd Avenue
Suite 100
Portland, OR 97224
(503) 639-4541
FAX: (503) 639-4851
Dr. Larry D. Large
President
E-MAIL: larry@oaicu.org
URL: www.oaicu.org

Pennsylvania Association of Colleges and Universities (C)
950 Walnut Bottom Road
Suite 15-214
Carlisle, PA 17015
(800) 687-9010
FAX: (717) 240-0673
URL: www.pacu.org

Pennsylvania State System of Higher Education Foundation, Inc. (D)
2986 North Second Street
Harrisburg, PA 17110
(717) 720-4056
FAX: (717) 720-7082
Ms. Jennifer S. Scipioni
President/CEO
E-MAIL: jscipioni@thepafoundation.org
URL: www.thepafoundation.org

Pittsburgh Council on Higher Education (E)
201 Wood Street
Pittsburgh, PA 15222-1912
(412) 392-4217
FAX: (412) 392-4218
Executive Director
URL: www.pchepa.org

Quad-Cities Graduate Study Center (F)
WIU - QC Campus
3561 60th Street
Moline, IL 61265
(309) 762-9481
Shirley Moore
Administrative Assistant
E-MAIL: shirley@gradcenter.org
URL: www.gradcenter.org

South Carolina Independent Colleges & Universities, Inc. (G)
PO Box 12007
Columbia, SC 29211
(803) 799-7122
FAX: (803) 254-7504
Mr. Michael G. LeFever
President & CEO
E-MAIL: mike@scicu.org
URL: www.scicu.org

South Metropolitan Higher Education Consortium (H)
One University Parkway
University Park, IL 60484
(708) 534-4984
FAX: (708) 534-8458
Ms. Genevieve Boesen
Executive Director
E-MAIL: gboesen@govst.edu
URL: www.southmetroed.org

Southern Regional Education Board (I)
592 Tenth Street, NW
Atlanta, GA 30318-5776
(404) 875-9211
FAX: (404) 872-1477
Dr. David S. Spence
President
E-MAIL: dave.spence@sreb.org
URL: www.sreb.org

Southwestern Ohio Council for Higher Education (SOCHE) (J)
3155 Research Boulevard
Suite 204
Dayton, OH 45420-4015
(937) 258-8890
FAX: (937) 258-8899
Dr. Sean Creighton
Executive Director
E-MAIL: soche@soche.org
URL: www.soche.org

Texas International Education Consortium (K)
1103 West 24th Street
Austin, TX 78705
(512) 477-9283, ext. 114
FAX: (512) 322-0592
Dr. Ronald Aqua
President & CEO
E-MAIL: ron.aqua@tiec.org
URL: www.tiec.org

Tuition Plan Consortium (L)
7425 Forsyth Boulevard
St. Louis, MO 63105
(314) 727-0900
FAX: (314) 727-0930
Ms. Nancy Farmer
President
E-MAIL: nancy@pc529.com
URL: www.tomorrowstuitiontoday.org

University City Science Center (M)
3711 Market Street
8th Floor
Philadelphia, PA 19104
(215) 966-6000
FAX: (215) 966-6002
Dr. Stephen Tang
President & CEO
E-MAIL: info@sciencecenter.org
URL: www.sciencecenter.org

The Virginia College Fund (N)
4900 Augusta Avenue
Suite 101
Richmond, VA 23230
(804) 355-3271
FAX: (804) 359-5765
Mr. James K. Dill
President
E-MAIL: jkdill@thevcf.org
URL: www.thevcf.org

Virginia Tidewater Consortium for Higher Education (O)
4900 Powhatan Avenue
Norfolk, VA 23508-1836
(757) 683-3183
FAX: (757) 683-4515
Dr. Lawrence G. Dotolo
President
E-MAIL: lgdotolo@aol.com
URL: www.vtc.odu.edu

Washington Theological Consortium (P)
3025 4th Street, NE
Suite 120
Washington, DC 20017-1103
(202) 832-2675
Dr. Larry Golemon
Executive Director
E-MAIL: wtc@washtheocon.org
URL: washtheocon.org

West Virginia Independent Colleges & Universities, Inc. (Q)
900 Lee Street
Suite 910
Charleston, WV 25301
(304) 345-5525
FAX: (304) 345-5526
Mr. Ben Exley IV
Executive Director
E-MAIL: benexley@wvicu.org
URL: www.wvicu.org

Wisconsin Association of Independent Colleges and Universities (R)
122 West Washington Avenue
Suite 700
Madison, WI 53703-2723
(608) 256-7761
FAX: (608) 256-7065
Dr. Rolf Wegenke
President
E-MAIL: mail@waicu.org
URL: www.waicu.org

NAME INDEX

US Department of Education Offices, Statewide Agencies of Higher Education, Higher Education Associations, Consortia of Institutions of Higher Education

A

Abraham, Neal, B. .... xl h
Aleshire, Daniel, O .... xxxiv Y
Alter, George .... xli K
Ambos, Elizabeth, L .... xxxvi O
Anderson, Jeremy .... xxxvi U
Anderson, Karen Hunter .... xxviii C
Andrus, Tracy .... xxxvi H
Anglin, Laura, L .... xxxv K
Appleby, James .... xxxvi b
Aqua, Ronald .... xlii K
Aranda, Peter, J .... xl X
Arrington, Michael .... xxxvii E

B

Bakst, Daren .... xxxvi I
Balasa, Donald, A .... xxxii D
Barrans, Diane .... xxvii J
Bartlett, Terri, L .... xxxvii T
Barzansky, Barbara .... xxxvii P
Baskerville, Lezli .... xxxvii C
Bauer, Ann .... xxxvii F
Baxter, Susanna .... xl i
Beamish, Michael .... xxviii Q
Bednash, Geraldine .... xxxi g
Bellis, Jamie .... xxxvii B
Benberg, Tom .... xxxvi E
Benjamin, Ann Womer .... xli h
Benjamin, Roger .... xxxv Y
Beno, Barbara, A .... xxxi Q
Berkery, Peter, M .... xxxiii f
Berman, Barry .... xxxii R
Berman, Harry, J .... xxviii B
Bernstine, Daniel .... xxxvii O
Biggins, Michael .... xxxix O
Bimonte, Robert, R .... xxxvii V
Birks, Heather .... xxxiv c
Bjarekull, Tina, M .... xli S
Blaich, Charles .... xli F
Blake, Christopher .... xxxvi h
Blake, Peter .... xxix Z
Blews, Edward, O .... xxxv Z
Boatner, T. Paul .... xxxix Z
Bobby, Carol, L .... xxxv U
Boesen, Genevieve .... xlii H
Boisvert, Pamela .... xli T
Bounds, Hank .... xxviii U
Bowen, Stephen .... xxviii N
Boyer, Violet, A .... xli J
Brandt, Karen .... xxxiii J
Brantley, Andy .... xxxiv g
Brantley, Susan .... xxxix P
Brittingham, Barbara .... xxxix E
Broad, Molly Corbett .... xxxiv V
Broadway, Shane .... xxvii M
Brogan, Frank, T .... xxvii W
Brown, J. Noah .... xxxiv F
Brown, Marty .... xxix c
Brown-Haithco, Robin .... xxxiii Q
Brust, Haley .... xxxix B
Bryk, Anthony, S .... xxxiv d
Buck, Joe .... xxxix U
Buckley, Jack .... xxvii F
Buhler, David, L .... xxix X
Bumphus, Walter, G .... xxxii B
Butlin, Jennifer .... xxxv H
Butterworth, Charles .... xxxi X

C

Cameron, Rich .... xxxvii M
Campbell, Dale, F .... xl W
Campbell, Ron .... xxxvii b
Campbell Lounsbury,
Susan .... xxvii Z
Carey, John .... xxix G
Carpenter, Glenn .... xxxix e
Carroll, Christopher .... xxxv C
Cartier, Brian, E .... xxxvii K
Cates, Carl, M .... xxxix W
Caulfield, Joshua .... xxxii c
Cavanaugh, John .... xl a
Cearlock, Dianne, M .... xxxvii i
Chabries, Carole .... xl F
Chang, Amy .... xxxiii F
Chenoweth, Anne .... xxxi e
Chimenti, Linda, M .... xxxv X
Chung, Ulric .... xxxi E
Ciarleglio, Jane, A .... xxvii R
Cibulka, James, G .... xxxv e
Clark, Eric .... xxviii V
Clark, Kay .... xxix T
Cleaves, Cheryl .... xxxii e
Colbert, John .... xxxiv T
Coleman, David .... xxxv A
Coleman, Mary Ann .... xli Q
Combs, Kathleen .... xxxiii W
Connerly, Charles .... xxxiv E
Cooper, Michelle, A .... xxxvi i
Coscarelli, Rick .... xxxiv X
Couraud, Gretchen .... xxxvii J
Cox, Gary, S .... xl P
Creighton, Sean .... xlii J
Cunningham, Beth, A .... xxxii E
Currier, Barry, A .... xxxii K

D

D'Agati, John .... xxix C
Dann-Messier, Brenda .... xxvii C
Deardorff, Darla, K .... xxxiv K
DeCrappeo, Anthony .... xxxvi G
Delson-Karan, Myrna .... xxxiii P
DeShazo, Peter .... xxxvii N
Detweiler, Richard, A .... xli A
Di Pasquale, Ray, M .... xxix N
Diederich, Kirsten .... xxix F
Dill, James, K .... xlii N
Dillon, Kristine, E .... xl b
Dimitroff, Diane .... xli P
Dixon-Lee, Claire .... xxxv E
Doherty, Richard .... xl H
Dolan, M., J .... xli L
Domenech, Daniel, A .... xxxii G
Donley, Robert .... xxviii E
Dotolo, Lawrence, G .... xlii O
Downs, Linda .... xxxiv h
Draayer, Jerry .... xxxv T
Draeger, Justin .... xxxvii U
Dubinsky, James .... xxxiii N
DuBois, Glenn .... xxix a
Duncan, Arne .... xxvii A
Duncan-Poitier, Johanna .... xxix B
Durst, Elizabeth .... xxxii I
Duthie, Dianne .... xxviii R

E

Eaton, Judith .... xxxv b
Egan, Daniel .... xl N
Ekman, Richard .... xxxvi A
Elgart, Mark, A .... xxxix H
Elman, Sandra, E .... xxxix J
Emanuel, Juliet .... xxxv B
Erickson, Nancy .... xxxiii Z
Estey, Martin .... xli C
Everett, Donna, R .... xxxix K
Exley, Ben .... xlii Q

F

Farmer, Gary .... xxxi c
Farmer, Nancy .... xlii L
Feal, Rosemary, G .... xxxvii Z
Fenstermacher, Robert .... xxxvi Q
Fernandes, John, J .... xxxi A
Fisher, E. Harold .... xli W
Fitch, Gregory, G .... xxvii H
Flores, Antonio, R .... xxxvi g
Forster-Smith, Lucy .... xxxiv A
Fortenberry, Norman, L .... xxxiii E
Foy, Morna, K .... xxix f
Francis, Don, L .... xl M
Francis, Paul .... xl f
Freeland, Richard, M .... xxviii P
Fryshman, Bernard .... xxxiii a
Furman, Nelly .... xxxiv H

G

Gaede, Stan .... xl V
Galligan-Stierle, Michael .... xxxiii g
Garcia, Jose .... xxviii d
Garcia, Joseph .... xxvii O
Gash, Dennis, N .... xxxvii D
George, Orlando, J .... xxxvi T
Gerbasi, Francis .... xxxvi D
Gilcher, Kay .... xxxvii E
Gilliland, Raney, L .... xxviii I
Gittell, Ross .... xxviii b
Glandon, Gerald, L .... xxxiv Z
Glazer, Liz .... xxxvi P
Goding, William, W .... xxxvii I
Goergen, Michael, T .... xxxix R
Golemon, Larry .... xlii P
Gouse, Richard .... xli Y
Gray, Albert .... xxxi T
Gray, Gregory, W .... xxxvi Q
Griffiths, Carol .... xxvii D
Griffiths, Carol .... xxvii G
Gustafson, Richard, A .... xxviii a

H

Haas, Kimberley .... xxxvi Z
Haley, Michael .... xxxvii F
Hallman, Linda, D .... xxxi B
Halpin, Annette .... xxxiii O
Hamilton, Gerald .... xxix J
Hamm, William, E .... xxxvii S
Hankins, Paul, M .... xl A
Hanna, Randall, W .... xxvii X
Hans, L. Jill .... xxix K
Hansen, Robert, J .... xxxix f
Harris, Allatia .... xxxi d
Harris, Brice, W .... xxvii N
Harvison, Neil .... xxxii f
Harwood, Eve .... xxxv d
Hatch, George .... xxxv R
Heinrich, Mark, A .... xxvii I
Henri Zulaski, Kate Ivane .... xxxv L
Herman-Betzen, Marsha .... xxxiv B
Herron, Daniel, J .... xxxi D
Hill, John .... xxxvii h
Hill, Marshall, A .... xxviii Y
Hill, Paul, L .... xxix d
Hoch, Corinne .... xxxi W
Holland, Michael .... xxxii T
Hollyn, Norman .... xxxix d
Hope, Samuel .... xxxvii P
Hope, Samuel .... xxxvii Q
Hope, Samuel .... xxxvii R
Hope, Samuel .... xxxvii S
Horgan, Thomas, R .... xli Z
Houser, R., E .... xxxii M
Howard, Danette, G .... xxviii O
Howard, Muriel, A .... xxxii H
Huckaby, Henry .... xxvii Y
Hupp, Lynn .... xxxvii R

I

Isaak, Larry, A .... xxxvii X

J

Jackman, Wm. Jay .... xxxvii G
Jackson, Carolyn, W .... xxxii C
Jenkins, Robin, Y .... xxxii V
Johnson, Glen, D .... xxix H
Jones, C. Todd .... xl L

K

Kalberer, Neal .... xli f
Kanter, Martha, J .... xxvii B
Kaplan, Lorrie .... xxxII P
Kass, Fritz .... xxxvii C
Keyser, Jenny .... xli D
Kidd, Nancy .... xxxvii Z
King, John, B .... xxix A
King, Laura Rasar .... xxxvi F
King, Robert, L .... xxviii J
Kirch, Darrell, G .... xxxiii d
Kiteley, Gary, W .... xxxiv b
Klaich, Daniel, J .... xxviii Z
Klein, Eileen .... xxvii K
Klein, Michael, W .... xli a
Knapp,, Jolene .... xxxix N
Knox, George .... xl e
Koch, Megan .... xxxvii e
Kroll, Ronald, C .... xxxiii M
Kruger, Kevin .... xxxvii d

L

Lambeth, Robert, B .... xl d
Landis, Patricia .... xxix L
Lane, Frank .... xxxvi M
Lange, Janet .... xxxix G
Large, Larry, D .... xlii B
Larkin, Bill .... xxxi S
Larmett, Kathleen, M .... xxxvii c
Laurence, David .... xxxiv G
LeFever, Michael, G .... xlii G
LeFevre, Robert .... xl J
Legon, Richard .... xxxiv I
Leighton, Ron .... xxxiii H
Levine, Ellen .... xxxiv J
Levine, Felice, J .... xxxii a
Liebow, Edward .... xxxi Y
Lindsey, Matthew .... xli N
Lingenfelter, Paul, E .... xxxix X
Lippincott, John .... xxxv W
Lomax, Michael .... xxxix b
Long-Goding, Jackie .... xxxv N
Longanecker, David, A .... xxxix i
Loredo, Judith .... xxix W
Lubbers, Teresa .... xxviii D
Lucke, Joyce .... xxxiii U
Ludwick, Richard .... xli I
Luedtke, Luther, S .... xxxvi V
Luhr, Gary .... xxxiv P

M

Mackes, Marilyn .... xxxvii M
Magat, Gerry .... xxxvii J
Mahaley-Jones, Hosanna .... xxvii U
Mahlman, Robert, A .... xxxiv f
Malone, Beverly, L .... xxxvii f
Mandlehr, Kathleen .... xli O
Manning, Sylvia .... xxxvi f
Martin, Rebecca .... xxxvii c
Matthews, Leah, K .... xxxvi T
Mattson, Holly .... xxxv c
McAllister, Sandy .... xxxix Q
McBay, Shirley, M .... xxxix M
McCall, Michael, B .... xxviii K
McCallin, Nancy, J .... xxvii P
McCartan, Anne-Marie .... xxxv h
McCarty, John .... xxxi L
McComis, Michale .... xxxi R
McDonald, Carol .... xli H
McFadden Allen,
Barbara .... xxxv S
McFarland, Laurel .... xxxix D
McGill, Jennifer, H .... xxxiii T
McKenzie, Mark .... xxxi F
McNult, Peggy .... xxxii O
McPherson, M. Peter .... xxxiv R
McQuade, Cindy .... xli j
Medlin, E. Lander .... xxxiii K
Megivern, Kathleen .... xxxv F
Merits, Shonagh .... xxxix L
Mikoski, Gordon .... xxxiv O
Milligan, Michael K., J .... xxxi C
Mirando, Tony .... xxxvii A
Misjak, Karen .... xxxvii F
Miskowicz-Retz,
Konrad, C .... xxxii h
Missildine, Kathryn .... xl T
Mizell, Catherine, S .... xxix U
Moisey, Neil .... xxviii X
Moneymaker, Carol .... xxxi P
Monti, Michael .... xxxiv D
Moore, Shirley .... xlii F
Moorman, Clayton .... xxxvii H
Moran, Brian .... xxxiv Q
Morgan, Bethany .... xl j
Morris, Linda .... xxxi Z
Morris, Robert, C .... xxxix S
Morrison, Nan .... xxxv a
Murner, Doreen .... xxxvii N

N

Nagel, Ed .... xxxvii E
Neal, Anne, D .... xxxii U
Nehls, Kimberly .... xxxiii Y
Neidy, Jon, C .... xxxix I
Nelson, Cathy, A .... xxxii N
Nelson, Rex .... xl C
Nesbit Schultz, Monica .... xxxiv C
Nespoli, Lawrence, A .... xli b
Nutt, Charlie, L .... xxxvii e

O

O'Brien, Karen .... xxxii d
O'Donnell, Teresa, D .... xxxv J
O'Meara, James .... xxxvii G
O'Neill, Thomas .... xl K
Obalil, Deborah .... xl O
Oblinger, Diana .... xxxvi W
Orloff, Keith .... xxxi O
Osborn, April, L .... xxvii L
Oxendine, W. H .... xxxiii I

P

Page, Harry, A .... xli i
Palla, Tonya .... xxxvii W
Paredes, Raymund, A .... xxix V
Paschal, Michael .... xxxiii L
Payne, David, G .... xxxvi c
Peden, Doug .... xxxi a
Pelton, Rebecca .... xxxvii a
Petersen, Rodney .... xl S
Petr, Todd .... xxxvii X
Petrisko, Mary Ellen .... xxxix h
Piccirillo, Janet .... xli B
Pogemiller, Larry .... xxviii S
Polvinali, Bonnie .... xxxiii A
Pratt, James, W .... xxxii b
Pressnell, Claude, O .... xxxix Y
Price, Danielle .... xxxvii g
Puckett, Gary .... xxxvi K
Purcell, James, E .... xxviii L
Purvis, Jerry, W .... xxxv Q

R

Rader, Jack, S .... xxxvi Y
Ralls, Scott .... xxix E
Randall, Tony .... xxxix A
Rawlings, Hunter, R .... xxxiii e
Reed, Alyson .... xxxvii Q
Regan, JoAnn .... xxxvi N
Reilly, Michael .... xxxii A
Rhoda, Richard, G .... xxix S
Rhodes, Keith .... xxxvi B
Richemond, Donna, L .... xli g
Ritchey, David .... xxxiv V
Rivera,
Carmen Luz Berrios .... xxx D
Roberts, Gregory .... xxxii Q
Robinson, Sharon, P .... xxxi f
Robinson, William, A .... xxxvii h
Rogers, Phillip .... xxxvii T
Rose, Jim .... xxx A
Rosenstone, Steven, J .... xxviii T
Ross, Thomas, W .... xxix D
Rottman, Ray .... xxxiv M
Rowe, Karen Monarchy .... xxxv O
Rush, Mike .... xxviii A
Russell, David, R .... xxviii W
Rzepka, Laura, A .... xxxii S

S

Sale, David, M .... xxxv g
Salter Dietrich, Sue .... xl Y
Sandeen, Cathy .... xxxii W
Santora, Kathleen Curry .... xxxvii H
Scales, Aileen .... xl Z
Schmid, Julie .... xxxii J
Schneider, Carol, G .... xxxiii b
Schopp, Melody .... xxix R
Schulte, Margaret .... xxxv G
Scipioni, Jennifer, S .... xli D
Scott, Kim .... xxxvii g
Seabrook, Robin, C .... xxxvii Y
Seitz, Daniel .... xxxvi J
Shannon, Stephen, C .... xxxi h
Sharp,
Marybeth Drechsler .... xxxv f
Sharratt, Gene .... xxix b
Shaw, Susanne .... xxxi U
Sheeran, Michael, J .... xxxiv L
Sheldon, Deborah, M .... xxxiii G
Shorb, Robert, D .... xxxix a
Shore, Elliott .... xxxiv S
Siemens, Albert, J .... xxxvi X
Sims, Brenda, R .... xxxiv W
Sisneros, Theresa .... xxxi I
Slepitza, Ronald, A .... xli G
Smaligo, Lesa .... xlii A
Smith, Jackie .... xl R
Smith, Joyce, E .... xxxvii B
Smith, Maria .... xl B
Smith, Michael .... xxxii L
Smith, Philip, R .... xli U
Smith, Steven Rathgeb .... xxxiii B
Soares, Kristen .... xl G
Spence, David, S .... xlii I
Spiker, Jenny .... xl c
Staat, Darrel .... xxix P
Steinke, Gary, W .... xli M
Stewart, Debra, W .... xxxv i
Stewart, Sandra .... xxxvii Y
Stitely, Susan .... xl Q
Stohlton, John, B .... xxxii F
Stone, Susan, E .... xxxi H
Sullivan, Edmund, J .... xxxv D
Sutton, Richard, C .... xxix O
Swing, Randy, L .... xxxiii V

T

Tamarkin, Tatiana, A .... xxxi b
Tang, Stephen .... xlii M
Tanner, Sharon, J .... xxxi G
Tate, Pamela .... xxxv V
Taylor, Jeffrey .... xxxvi d
Thomas, Michael, K .... xxxix F
Tice, Patrima, L .... xxxvi C
Tinkleman, Alan, R .... xxxvi L
Tompkins, Andy .... xxviii H
Tooks, Sherin .... xxxv I
Traxler, Sallie .... xxxiii h
Tretter, David, W .... xl g
Triplett, Charles, L .... xxix I

U

Urbeck, Joyce, L .... xxxii g

V

Van Ummersen, Claire .... xxxii X
Varner, Jeremy .... xxviii G
Vibert, Joseph .... xxxiv U
Viehland, Douglas .... xxxi J
Vlasses, PharmD,
Peter, H .... xxxi K
Vuong, Adele .... xxxiii R

W

Walda, John .... xxxvii I
Walker, Daniel .... xli R
Walker, Eileen .... xxxiv a
Walske, Ynez .... xxxiii S
Warner, Jack, R .... xxix Q
Warren, David, L .... xxxvii O
Warwick,
Jennifer Anderson .... xxxi M
Washington, Sharon, J .... xxxix C
Weerts, Richard .... xxxvii L
Wegenke, Rolf .... xlii R
Weldon, Jeanette, W .... xl U
Welna, Christopher .... xl E
Wenniger, Mary Dee .... xxxix j
Wesley, Katherine .... xxxvii b
Westerberg Prager,
Susan .... xxxiii c
Wheelan, Belle, S .... xxxix V
White, Debra .... xxxv M
White, John .... xxviii M
White, Judith .... xxxvi e
White, Kirk .... xxxvii a
Whitmore, Jon, S .... xxxi V
Wilk, Valerie .... xxxvii d
Williams, A. Hope .... xli e
Williamson, Carolyn .... xxxix c
Williamson, Kent .... xxxv T
Wilson, John, B .... xl I
Winn, Jan, M .... xxxvii L
Winter, Leslie, F .... xxxvii K
Wolfe, Leslie, R .... xxxiv e
Wolley, Linda, M .... xxxvi S
Worley, Bette .... xli X

Y

Yep, Richard .... xxxii Y

Z

Zlotlow, Susan, F .... xxxiii C

Institutions By Religious Affiliation

African Methodist Episcopal
Allen University ..... SC
Edward Waters College ..... FL
Paul Quinn College ..... TX
Payne Theological Seminary ..... OH
Shorter College ..... AR
Wilberforce University ..... OH

African Methodist Episcopal Zion Church
Clinton College ..... SC
Hood Theological Seminary ..... NC
Livingstone College ..... NC

Alabama Baptist State Convention
Judson College ..... AL

American Baptist
Alderson Broaddus University ..... WV
American Baptist Seminary of the West .. CA
Bacone College ..... OK
Eastern University ..... PA
Franklin College of Indiana ..... IN
Judson University IL
Linfield College ..... OR
Northern Seminary IL
Ottawa University ..... KS
Palmer Theological Seminary of Eastern University ..... PA
University of Sioux Falls ..... SD

Assemblies Of God Church
American Indian College of the Assemblies of God ..... AZ
Bethel College ..... VA
Evangel University ..... MO
Global University ..... MO
Native American Bible College ..... NC
North Central University ..... MN
Northpoint Bible College ..... MA
Northwest University ..... WA
Southeastern University ..... FL
Southwestern Assemblies of God University ..... TX
Trinity Bible College ..... ND
Valley Forge Christian College ..... PA
Vanguard University of Southern California ..... CA

Baptist
American Baptist College ..... TN
Arkansas Baptist College ..... AR
Arlington Baptist College ..... TX
Baptist Bible College ..... MO
Baptist Bible College and Seminary ..... PA
Baptist Missionary Association Theological Seminary ..... TX
Baptist University of the Americas ..... TX
Baylor University ..... TX
Bethel University ..... MN
Bluefield College ..... VA
Boston Baptist College ..... MA
Brewton-Parker College ..... GA
Campbell University ..... NC
Campbellsville University ..... KY
Cedarville University ..... OH
Central Baptist College ..... AR
Central Baptist Theological Seminary ..... KS
Central Baptist Theological Seminary ..... VA
Central Baptist Theological Seminary of Minneapolis ..... MN
Chowan University ..... NC
Dallas Baptist University ..... TX
Gardner-Webb University ..... NC
Georgetown College ..... KY
Hardin-Simmons University ..... TX
Howard Payne University ..... TX
Huntsville Bible College ..... AL
International Baptist College ..... AZ
Jacksonville College ..... TX
Maple Springs Baptist Bible College & Seminary ..... MD
Missouri Baptist University ..... MO
Morris College ..... SC
Northland International University ..... WI
Oakland City University ..... IN
Ohio Mid-Western College (Formerly Temple Baptist College) ..... OH
Selma University ..... AL
Shaw University ..... NC
Shorter University ..... GA
Simmons College of Kentucky ..... KY
Southeastern Baptist College ..... MS
Tennessee Temple University ..... TN
The Crown College of the Bible ..... TN
The John Leland Center for Theological Studies ..... VA
Trinity Baptist College ..... FL
Truett McConnell College ..... GA
University of the Cumberlands ..... KY
Virginia Baptist College ..... VA
Virginia Intermont College ..... VA
Virginia Union University ..... VA
Washington Baptist University ..... VA

Brethren Church
Ashland University ..... OH

Christian Church (Disciples Of Christ)
Barton College ..... NC
Bethany College ..... WV
Chapman University ..... CA
Christian Theological Seminary ..... IN
Columbia College ..... MO
Culver-Stockton College ..... MO
Eureka College IL
Jarvis Christian College ..... TX
Lexington Theological Seminary ..... KY
Lynchburg College ..... VA
Midway College ..... KY
Northwest Christian University ..... OR
Phillips Theological Seminary ..... OK
Texas Christian University ..... TX
Transylvania University ..... KY
William Woods University ..... MO

Christian Churches And Churches of Christ
Belmont University ..... TN
Boise Bible College ..... ID
Central Christian College of the Bible ..... MO
Cincinnati Christian University ..... OH
Crossroads College ..... MN
Dallas Christian College ..... TX
Emmanuel Christian Seminary ..... TN
Great Lakes Christian College ..... MI
Johnson University ..... TN
Kentucky Christian University ..... KY
Lincoln Christian University IL
Manhattan Christian College ..... KS
Nebraska Christian College ..... NE
Piedmont College ..... GA
Point University ..... GA

Christian Methodist Episcopal
Lane College ..... TN
Miles College ..... AL
Texas College ..... TX

Christian Reformed Church
Calvin College ..... MI
Calvin Theological Seminary ..... MI
Dordt College ..... IA

Church Of Christ
Pepperdine University ..... CA

Church Of God
Anderson University ..... IN
Lee University ..... TN
Mid-America Christian University ..... OK
Pentecostal Theological Seminary ..... TN
The University of Findlay ..... OH
Universidad Teologica Del Caribe ..... PR
Warner Pacific College ..... OR
Warner University ..... FL

Church of God in Christ
All Saints Bible College ..... TN

Church of New Jerusalem
Bryn Athyn College of the New Church ... PA

Church Of The Brethren
Bethany Theological Seminary ..... IN
Bridgewater College ..... VA
Elizabethtown College ..... PA
Manchester University ..... IN
McPherson College ..... KS

Church Of The Nazarene
Eastern Nazarene College ..... MA
MidAmerica Nazarene University ..... KS
Mount Vernon Nazarene University ..... OH
Nazarene Bible College ..... CO
Nazarene Theological Seminary ..... MO
Northwest Nazarene University ..... ID
Olivet Nazarene University IL
Point Loma Nazarene University ..... CA
Southern Nazarene University ..... OK
Trevecca Nazarene University ..... TN

Churches Of Christ
Abilene Christian University ..... TX
Amridge University ..... AL
Crowley's Ridge College ..... AR
Faulkner University ..... AL
Freed-Hardeman University ..... TN
Harding University Main Campus ..... AR
Heritage Christian University ..... AL
Lipscomb University ..... TN
Lubbock Christian University ..... TX
Mid-Atlantic Christian University ..... NC
Ohio Valley University ..... WV
Southwestern Christian College ..... TX
York College ..... NE

Cumberland Presbyterian
Bethel University ..... TN
Memphis Theological Seminary ..... TN

Evangelical Congregational Church
Evangelical Theological Seminary ..... PA

Evangelical Covenant Church Of America
North Park University IL

Evangelical Free Church Of America
Trinity International University IL

Evangelical Lutheran Church In America
Augsburg College ..... MN
Augustana College IL
Augustana College ..... SD
Bethany College ..... KS
California Lutheran University ..... CA
Capital University ..... OH
Carthage College ..... WI
Concordia College ..... MN
Finlandia University ..... MI
Gettysburg College ..... PA
Grand View University ..... IA
Gustavus Adolphus College ..... MN
Lenoir-Rhyne University ..... NC
Luther College ..... IA
Luther Seminary ..... MN
Lutheran School of Theology at Chicago IL
Lutheran Theological Seminary at Gettysburg ..... PA
Lutheran Theological Seminary at Philadelphia ..... PA
Lutheran Theological Southern Seminary of Lenoir-Rhyne University ..... SC
Midland University ..... NE
Muhlenberg College ..... PA
Newberry College ..... SC
Pacific Lutheran Theological Seminary .... CA
Pacific Lutheran University ..... WA
Roanoke College ..... VA
St. Olaf College ..... MN
Susquehanna University ..... PA
Texas Lutheran University ..... TX
Thiel College ..... PA
Trinity Lutheran Seminary ..... OH
Wartburg College ..... IA
Wartburg Theological Seminary ..... IA
Wittenberg University ..... OH

Evangelical Lutheran Synod
Bethany Lutheran College ..... MN

Fellowship Of Grace Brethren Churches
Grace College and Seminary ..... IN

Free Methodist
Central Christian College of Kansas ..... KS
Greenville College IL
Seattle Pacific University ..... WA
Spring Arbor University ..... MI

Free Will Baptist
California Christian College ..... CA
Hillsdale Free Will Baptist College ..... OK
Welch College ..... TN

Friends
Earlham College and Earlham School of Religion ..... IN
George Fox University ..... OR
Guilford College ..... NC
Malone University ..... OH
William Penn University ..... IA
Wilmington College ..... OH

Greek Orthodox
Hellenic College-Holy Cross Greek Orthodox School of Theology ..... MA

Interdenominational
Bethany College of Missions ..... MN
Carolina Graduate School of Divinity ..... NC
Denver Seminary ..... CO
Evangelical Seminary of Puerto Rico ..... PR
Faith Evangelical College & Seminary ..... WA
God's Bible School and College ..... OH
Inste Bible College ..... IA
Interdenominational Theological Center .. GA
Messiah College ..... PA
Oak Hills Christian College ..... MN
Palm Beach Atlantic University ..... FL
Phoenix Seminary ..... AZ
Rocky Mountain College ..... MT
Shepherd University School of Theology . CA
South Florida Bible College ..... FL
Wesley Biblical Seminary ..... MS

Jewish
Academy for Jewish Religion ..... CA
Hebrew Union College-Jewish Institute of Religion ..... NY
New York Medical College ..... NY
Rabbi Isaac Elchanan Theological Seminary ..... NY
Reconstructionist Rabbinical College ..... PA

Latter-day Saints
Brigham Young University ..... UT
Brigham Young University Hawaii ..... HI
Brigham Young University-Idaho ..... ID
LDS Business College ..... UT

Lutheran
Valparaiso University ..... IN

Lutheran Church - Missouri Synod
Concordia College ..... NY
Concordia College Alabama ..... AL
Concordia Seminary ..... MO
Concordia Theological Seminary ..... IN
Concordia University ..... CA
Concordia University ..... MI
Concordia University ..... NE
Concordia University ..... OR
Concordia University Chicago IL
Concordia University Texas ..... TX
Concordia University Wisconsin ..... WI
Concordia University, St. Paul ..... MN

Mennonite Brethren Church
Fresno Pacific University ..... CA
Tabor College ..... KS

Mennonite Church
Anabaptist Mennonite Biblical Seminary .. IN
Bethel College ..... KS
Bluffton University ..... OH
Eastern Mennonite University ..... VA
Goshen College ..... IN
Hesston College ..... KS
Rosedale Bible College ..... OH

Missionary Church
Bethel College ..... IN

Moravian Church
Moravian College ..... PA
Salem College ..... NC

Multiple Protestant Denominations
Huston-Tillotson University ..... TX
LeMoyne-Owen College ..... TN
Paine College ..... GA

Non-denominational
Carolina College of Biblical Studies ..... NC
Cedar Crest College ..... PA
Clearwater Christian College ..... FL
Faith Theological Seminary ..... MD
Heartland Christian College ..... MO
Manthano Christian College ..... MI
Midwest University ..... MO
Montreat College ..... NC
North American College ..... TX
Providence Christian College ..... CA
University of Fort Lauderdale ..... FL
Williamson Christian College ..... TN

North American Baptist
Sioux Falls Seminary ... SD

Original Free Will Baptist Church
Mount Olive College ... NC

Other Protestant
Beulah Heights University ... GA
Grace College of Divinity ... NC
Ohio Christian University ... OH
Saint Louis Christian College ... MO
Urshan Graduate School of Theology ... MO

Pentecostal Church of God
Messenger College ... TX
Universidad Pentecostal Mizpa ... PR

Pentecostal Holiness Church
Emmanuel College ... GA
Southwestern Christian University ... OK

Pentecostal/Charismatic Non-Denominational
Christian Life College ... IL

Presbyterian
Whitworth University ... WA

Presbyterian Church (U.S.A.)
Agnes Scott College ... GA
Austin College ... TX
Austin Presbyterian Theological Seminary ... TX
Belhaven University ... MS
Blackburn College ... IL
Bloomfield College ... NJ
Buena Vista University ... IA
Carroll University ... WI
Columbia Theological Seminary ... GA
Davidson College ... NC
Davis & Elkins College ... WV
Eckerd College ... FL
Grove City College ... PA
Hampden-Sydney College ... VA
Hanover College ... IN
Hastings College ... NE
King University ... TN
Lees-McRae College ... NC
Louisville Presbyterian Theological Seminary ... KY
Lyon College ... AR
Macalester College ... MN
Mary Baldwin College ... VA
Maryville College ... TN
McCormick Theological Seminary ... IL
Millikin University ... IL
Missouri Valley College ... MO
Monmouth College ... IL
Muskingum University ... OH
Pittsburgh Theological Seminary ... PA
Presbyterian College ... SC
Princeton Theological Seminary ... NJ
Queens University of Charlotte ... NC
Rhodes College ... TN
San Francisco Theological Seminary ... CA
Schreiner University ... TX
Sterling College ... KS
Stillman College ... AL
Tusculum College ... TN
Union Presbyterian Seminary ... VA
University of Dubuque ... IA
University of Jamestown ... ND
University of Pikeville ... KY
University of the Ozarks ... AR
Warren Wilson College ... NC
Waynesburg University ... PA
Westminster College ... PA
William Peace University (formerly Peace College) ... NC
Wilson College ... PA

Presbyterian Church In America
Covenant College ... GA
Covenant Theological Seminary ... MO
Grace Mission University ... CA
Presbyterian Theological Seminary in America ... CA

Protestant Episcopal
Bexley Seabury ... IL
Church Divinity School of the Pacific ... CA
Episcopal Divinity School ... MA
General Theological Seminary ... NY
Nashotah House ... WI
Protestant Episcopal Theological Seminary in Virginia ... VA
Saint Augustine's University ... NC
Seminary of the Southwest ... TX
Sewanee: The University of the South ... TN
Trinity Episcopal School for Ministry ... PA
Voorhees College ... SC

Reformed Church In America
Central College ... IA
Hope College ... MI
New Brunswick Theological Seminary ... NJ
Northwestern College ... IA
Western Theological Seminary ... MI

Reformed Episcopal Church
Reformed Episcopal Seminary ... PA

Reformed Presbyterian Church
Evangelia University ... CA
Geneva College ... PA
Reformed Presbyterian Theological Seminary ... PA

Roman Catholic
Alvernia University ... PA
Ancilla College ... IN
Anna Maria College ... MA
Aquinas College ... MI
Aquinas College ... TN
Aquinas Institute of Theology ... MO
Assumption College ... MA
Assumption College for Sisters ... NJ
Athenaeum of Ohio ... OH
Ave Maria School of Law ... FL
Avila University ... MO
Barry University ... FL
Bayamon Central University ... PR
Belmont Abbey College ... NC
Benedictine College ... KS
Benedictine University ... IL
Blessed John XXIII National Seminary ... MA
Boston College ... MA
Brescia University ... KY
Briar Cliff University ... IA
Cabrini College ... PA
Caldwell College ... NJ
Calumet College of Saint Joseph ... IN
Canisius College ... NY
Cardinal Stritch University ... WI
Carlow University ... PA
Carroll College ... MT
Catholic Theological Union ... IL
Chestnut Hill College ... PA
Christ the King Seminary ... NY
Christendom College ... VA
Christian Brothers University ... TN
Clarke University ... IA
College of Mount St. Joseph ... OH
College of Our Lady of the Elms ... MA
College of Saint Benedict ... MN
College of Saint Elizabeth ... NJ
College of Saint Mary ... NE
College of St. Joseph ... VT
College of the Holy Cross ... MA
Conception Seminary College ... MO
Creighton University ... NE
DePaul University ... IL
DeSales University ... PA
Divine Word College ... IA
Dominican School of Philosophy and Theology ... CA
Dominican University ... IL
Donnelly College ... KS
Duquesne University ... PA
Edgewood College ... WI
Emmanuel College ... MA
Fairfield University ... CT
Felician College ... NJ
Fontbonne University ... MO
Franciscan University of Steubenville ... OH
Gannon University ... PA
Georgetown University ... DC
Georgian Court University ... NJ
Gonzaga University ... WA
Gwynedd-Mercy University ... PA
Holy Apostles College and Seminary ... CT
Holy Cross College ... IN
Holy Family University ... PA
Immaculata University ... PA
John Carroll University ... OH
Kenrick-Glennon Seminary-Kenrick School of Theology ... MO
King's College ... PA
La Roche College ... PA
La Salle University ... PA
Laboure College ... MA
Lewis University ... IL
Loras College ... IA
Lourdes University ... OH
Loyola Marymount University ... CA
Loyola University Chicago ... IL
Loyola University Maryland ... MD
Loyola University New Orleans ... LA
Madonna University ... MI
Marian Court College ... MA
Marian University ... IN
Marian University ... WI
Marquette University ... WI
Marygrove College ... MI
Marymount California University ... CA
Marymount University ... VA
Marywood University ... PA
Mercy College of Health Sciences ... IA
Mercy College of Ohio ... OH
Mercyhurst University ... PA
Merrimack College ... MA
Misericordia University ... PA
Mount Angel Seminary ... OR
Mount Carmel College of Nursing ... OH
Mount Marty College ... SD
Mount Mary University ... WI
Mount Mercy University ... IA
Mount St. Mary's College ... CA
Mount St. Mary's University ... MD
Neumann University ... PA
Newman University ... KS
Notre Dame College ... OH
Notre Dame of Maryland University ... MD
Notre Dame Seminary, Graduate School of Theology ... LA
Oblate School of Theology ... TX
Ohio Dominican University ... OH
Our Lady of Holy Cross College ... LA
Our Lady of the Lake College ... LA
Our Lady of the Lake University ... TX
Pontifical College Josephinum ... OH
Pontifical Faculty of the Immaculate Conception at the Dominican House of Studies ... DC
Pontifical John Paul II Institute for Studies on Marriage and Family ... DC
Presentation College ... SD
Providence College ... RI
Quincy University ... IL
Regis University ... CO
Rivier University ... NH
Rockhurst University ... MO
Rosemont College ... PA
Sacred Heart Major Seminary ... MI
Sacred Heart School of Theology ... WI
Saint Anselm College ... NH
Saint Anthony College of Nursing ... IL
Saint Bernard's School of Theology & Ministry ... NY
Saint Charles Borromeo Seminary ... PA
Saint Francis Medical Center College of Nursing ... IL
Saint Francis University ... PA
Saint Gregory the Great Seminary ... NE
Saint John's Seminary ... CA
Saint John's Seminary ... MA
Saint John's University ... MN
Saint Joseph Seminary College ... LA
Saint Joseph's College ... IN
Saint Joseph's College of Maine ... ME
Saint Joseph's Seminary ... NY
Saint Joseph's University ... PA
Saint Leo University ... FL
Saint Louis University ... MO
Saint Martin's University ... WA
Saint Mary Seminary and Graduate School of Theology ... OH
Saint Mary's College ... IN
Saint Mary's College of California ... CA
Saint Mary's Seminary and University ... MD
Saint Mary's University of Minnesota ... MN
Saint Mary-of-the-Woods College ... IN
Saint Meinrad School of Theology ... IN
Saint Michael's College ... VT
Saint Norbert College ... WI
Saint Patrick's Seminary & University ... CA
Saint Peter's University ... NJ
Saint Vincent College ... PA
Saint Vincent Seminary ... PA
Saint Xavier University ... IL
Salve Regina University ... RI
Seattle University ... WA
Seton Hall University ... NJ
Seton Hall University School of Law ... NJ
Seton Hill University ... PA
Siena Heights University ... MI
Silver Lake College of the Holy Family ... WI
Spring Hill College ... AL
SS. Cyril and Methodius Seminary ... MI
St. Ambrose University ... IA
St. Bonaventure University ... NY
St. Catharine College ... KY
St. Catherine University ... MN
St. Gregory's University ... OK
St. John Vianney College Seminary ... FL
St. John Vianney Theological Seminary ... CO
St. John's University ... NY
St. Mary's University ... TX
St. Thomas University ... FL
St. Vincent De Paul Regional Seminary ... FL
Stonehill College ... MA
The Catholic University of America ... DC
The College of Saint Scholastica ... MN
The College of Saints John Fisher & Thomas More ... TX
The Pontifical Catholic University of Puerto Rico ... PR
The University of Scranton ... PA
Thomas More College ... KY
Trinity Washington University ... DC
University of Dallas ... TX
University of Dayton ... OH
University of Detroit Mercy ... MI
University of Great Falls ... MT
University of Mary ... ND
University of Notre Dame ... IN
University of Saint Francis ... IN
University of Saint Joseph ... CT
University of Saint Mary ... KS
University of Saint Mary of the Lake-Mundelein Seminary ... IL
University of Saint Thomas ... MN
University of San Diego ... CA
University of San Francisco ... CA
University of St. Francis ... IL
University of St. Thomas ... TX
University of the Incarnate Word ... TX
University of the Sacred Heart ... PR
Ursuline College ... OH
Villanova University ... PA
Viterbo University ... WI
Walsh University ... OH
Wheeling Jesuit University ... WV
Xavier University ... OH
Xavier University of Louisiana ... LA

Russian Orthodox
Holy Trinity Orthodox Seminary ... NY

Seventh-day Adventist
Adventist University of Health Sciences ... FL
Andrews University ... MI
Griggs University ... MI
Kettering College ... OH
La Sierra University ... CA
Loma Linda University ... CA
Oakwood University ... AL
Pacific Union College ... CA
Southern Adventist University ... TN
Southwestern Adventist University ... TX
Union College ... NE
Universidad Adventista de las Antillas ... PR
Walla Walla University ... WA
Washington Adventist University ... MD

Southern Baptist
B.H. Carroll Theological Institute ... TX
Blue Mountain College ... MS
California Baptist University ... CA
Carson-Newman University ... TN
Charleston Southern University ... SC
Clear Creek Baptist Bible College ... KY
East Texas Baptist University ... TX
Golden Gate Baptist Theological Seminary ... CA
Hannibal-La Grange University ... MO
Houston Baptist University ... TX
Louisiana College ... LA
Mid-Continent University ... KY
Midwestern Baptist Theological Seminary MO
Mississippi College ... MS
New Orleans Baptist Theological Seminary ... LA
North Greenville University ... SC
Oklahoma Baptist University ... OK
Ouachita Baptist University ... AR
Samford University ... AL
Southeastern Baptist Theological Seminary ... NC
Southwest Baptist University ... MO
Southwestern Baptist Theological Seminary ... TX
The Baptist College of Florida ... FL
The Southern Baptist Theological Seminary ... KY
Union University ... TN
University of Mary Hardin-Baylor ... TX
University of Mobile ... AL
Wayland Baptist University ... TX
William Carey University ... MS
Williams Baptist College ... AR
Wingate University ... NC

The Christian And Missionary Alliance
Crown College ... MN
Nyack College ... NY
Simpson University ... CA

Unification Church
Unification Theological Seminary ... NY

Unitarian Universalist

Meadville Lombard Theological School ... IL
Starr King School for the Ministry .... CA

United Brethren Church

Huntington University .... IN

United Church Of Christ

Bangor Theological Seminary .... ME
Catawba College .... NC
Chicago Theological Seminary IL
Doane College .... NE
Eden Theological Seminary .... MO
Elmhurst College IL
Heidelberg University .... OH
Lakeland College .... WI
Lancaster Theological Seminary .... PA
Northland College .... WI
The Defiance College .... OH
Tougaloo College .... MS
United Theological Seminary of the Twin Cities .... MN

United Methodist

Adrian College .... MI
Albion College .... MI
Albright College .... PA
American University .... DC
Andrew College .... GA
Baker University .... KS
Baldwin Wallace University .... OH
Bennett College .... NC
Bethune Cookman University .... FL
Birmingham-Southern College .... AL
Brevard College .... NC
Centenary College of Louisiana .... LA
Central Methodist University .... MO
Claflin University .... SC
Claremont School of Theology .... CA
Clark Atlanta University .... GA
Columbia College .... SC
Cornell College .... IA
Dakota Wesleyan University .... SD
DePauw University .... IN
Dillard University .... LA
Emory & Henry College .... VA
Emory University .... GA
Ferrum College .... VA
Florida Southern College .... FL
Garrett-Evangelical Theological Seminary IL
Greensboro College .... NC
Hamline University .... MN
Hendrix College .... AR
High Point University .... NC
Hiwassee College .... TN
Huntingdon College .... AL
Iliff School of Theology .... CO
Iowa Wesleyan College .... IA
Kansas Wesleyan University .... KS
Kentucky Wesleyan College .... KY
LaGrange College .... GA
Lebanon Valley College .... PA
Lindsey Wilson College .... KY
Louisburg College .... NC
Lycoming College .... PA
MacMurray College IL
Martin Methodist College .... TN
McKendree University IL
McMurry University .... TX
Methodist Theological School in Ohio ..... OH
Methodist University .... NC
Millsaps College .... MS
Morningside College .... IA
Nebraska Wesleyan University .... NE
North Carolina Wesleyan College .... NC
North Central College IL
Ohio Northern University .... OH
Ohio Wesleyan University .... OH
Oklahoma City University .... OK
Otterbein University .... OH
Pfeiffer University .... NC
Philander Smith College .... AR
Randolph College .... VA
Randolph-Macon College .... VA
Reinhardt University .... GA
Rust College .... MS
Saint Paul School of Theology .... KS
Shenandoah University .... VA
Simpson College .... IA
Southern Methodist University .... TX
Southwestern College .... KS
Southwestern University .... TX
Spartanburg Methodist College .... SC
Tennessee Wesleyan College .... TN
Texas Wesleyan University .... TX
Union College .... KY
United Theological Seminary .... OH
University of Evansville .... IN
University of Indianapolis .... IN
University of Mount Union .... OH
Virginia Wesleyan College .... VA
Wesley College .... DE
Wesley Theological Seminary .... DC
Wesleyan College .... GA
West Virginia Wesleyan College .... WV
Wiley College .... TX
Wofford College .... SC
Young Harris College .... GA

Wesleyan Church

Allegheny Wesleyan College .... OH
Houghton College .... NY
Indiana Wesleyan University .... IN
Oklahoma Wesleyan University .... OK
Pillar College .... NJ
Southern Wesleyan University .... SC

Wisconsin Evangelical Lutheran Synod

Martin Luther College .... MN

Carnegie Classification Code Definitions*

This year, the Higher Education Directory lists the updated 2010 Carnegie Classifications. The 2010 Classification update retains the same structure of classifications initially adopted in 2005. Due to space limitation, the *Higher Education Directory*® only lists the original classification framework—now called the basic classification—which was substantially revised in 2005. These new codes are listed below:

Associate's Colleges: Includes institutions where all degrees are at the associate's level, or where bachelor's degrees account for less than 10 percent of all undergraduate degrees. Excludes institutions eligible for classification as Tribal Colleges or Special Focus Institutions.

Assoc/Pub-R-S: Associate's — Public Rural-serving Small
Assoc/Pub-R-M: Associate's — Public Rural-serving Medium
Assoc/Pub-R-L: Associate's — Public Rural-serving Large
Assoc/Pub-S-SC: Associate's — Public Suburban-serving Single Campus
Assoc/Pub-S-MC: Associate's — Public Suburban-serving Multicampus
Assoc/Pub-U-SC: Associate's — Public Urban-serving Single Campus
Assoc/Pub-U-MC: Associate's — Public Urban-serving Multicampus
Assoc/Pub-Spec: Associate's — Public Special Use
Assoc/PrivNFP: Associate's — Private Not-for-profit
Assoc/PrivFP: Associate's — Private For-profit
Assoc/Pub2in4: Associate's — Public 2-year Colleges under Universities
Assoc/Pub4: Associate's — Public 4-year, Primarily Associate's
Assoc/PrivNFP4: Associate's — Private Not-for-profit 4-year, Primarily Associate's
Assoc/PrivFP4: Associate's — Private For-profit 4-year, Primarily Associate's

Doctorate-granting Universities. Includes institutions that award at least 20 doctoral degrees per year (excluding doctoral-level degrees that qualify recipients for entry into professional practice, such as the JD, MD, PharmD, DPT, etc.). Excludes Special Focus Institutions and Tribal Colleges.

RU/VH: Research Universities (very high research activity)
RU/H: Research Universities (high research activity)
DRU: Doctoral/Research Universities

Master's Colleges and Universities. Includes institutions that award at least 50 master's degrees per year. Excludes Special Focus Institutions and Tribal Colleges.

Master's/L: Master's Colleges and Universities (larger programs)
Master's/M: Master's Colleges and Universities (medium programs)
Master's/S: Master's Colleges and Universities (smaller programs)

Baccalaureate Colleges. Includes institutions where baccalaureate degrees represent at least 10 percent of all undergraduate degrees and that award fewer than 50 master's degrees or fewer than 20 doctoral degrees per year. Excludes Special Focus Institutions and Tribal Colleges.

Bac/A&S: Baccalaureate Colleges — Arts & Sciences
Bac/Diverse: Baccalaureate Colleges — Diverse Fields
Bac/Assoc: Baccalaureate/Associate's Colleges

Special Focus Institutions. Institutions awarding baccalaureate or higher-level degrees where a high concentration of degrees is in a single field or set of related fields. Excludes Tribal Colleges.

Spec/Faith: Theological seminaries, Bible colleges, and other faith-related institutions
Spec/Medical: Medical schools and medical centers
Spec/Health: Other health profession schools
Spec/Engg: Schools of engineering
Spec/Tech: Other technology-related schools
Spec/Bus: Schools of business and management
Spec/Arts: Schools of art, music, and design
Spec/Law: Schools of law
Spec/Other: Other special-focus institutions

Tribal Colleges. Colleges and universities that are members of the American Indian Higher Education Consortium, as identified in IPEDS Institutional Characteristics.

Tribal: Tribal Colleges

*All data provided by The Carnegie Foundation for the Advancement of Teaching. For more detailed information on the revised Carnegie Codes, please visit http://classifications.carnegiefoundation.org/

Statistics

Institutions of Higher Education by Control, Level and State

STATE	TWO YEAR		FOUR YEAR		TOTAL		SYSTEM	GRAND
	PRIVATE	PUBLIC	PRIVATE	PUBLIC	PRIVATE	PUBLIC	OFFICE	TOTAL
AL	3	26	22	15	25	41	2	68
AK	2	1	3	3	5	4	1	10
AZ	12	19	30	4	42	23	1	66
AR	1	22	12	11	13	33	2	48
CA	62	116	222	36	284	152	29	465
CO	21	14	28	15	49	29	3	81
CT	1	12	22	7	23	19	1	43
DE	1	3	4	2	5	5	1	11
DC	2	0	14	3	16	3	0	19
FL	41	5	77	36	118	41	1	160
GA	9	27	37	30	46	57	1	104
HI	1	6	7	4	8	10	2	20
ID	1	4	5	4	6	8	0	14
IL	16	47	94	12	110	59	6	175
IN	8	1	44	15	52	16	2	70
IA	1	18	41	3	42	21	3	66
KS	4	25	24	9	28	34	0	62
KY	3	16	35	8	38	24	1	63
LA	11	23	12	17	23	40	4	67
ME	3	7	14	8	17	15	2	34
MD	4	16	23	15	27	31	1	59
MA	4	16	84	14	88	30	2	120
MI	4	29	45	15	49	44	1	94
MN	4	30	45	11	49	41	3	93
MS	1	15	10	9	11	24	0	35
MO	12	18	63	13	75	31	3	109
MT	6	5	5	6	11	11	1	23
NE	7	7	17	7	24	14	2	40
NV	4	1	2	6	6	7	1	14
NH	2	7	12	4	14	11	2	27
NJ	4	19	29	13	33	32	1	66
NM	0	13	7	8	7	21	0	28
NY	33	36	189	44	222	80	5	307
NC	2	59	53	16	55	75	2	132
ND	1	4	8	7	9	11	1	21
OH	29	24	72	17	101	41	1	143
OK	5	12	16	15	21	27	0	48
OR	5	16	26	8	31	24	1	56
PA	65	16	114	20	179	36	1	216
RI	0	1	9	3	9	4	0	13
SC	3	19	24	14	27	33	0	60
SD	1	5	9	6	10	11	1	22
TN	10	13	56	9	66	22	2	90
TX	29	64	72	46	101	110	8	219
UT	4	4	12	6	16	10	1	27
VT	0	1	17	5	17	6	1	24
VA	16	24	57	18	73	42	1	116
WA	5	26	28	13	33	39	2	74
WV	9	9	11	11	20	20	2	42
WI	2	16	32	14	34	30	2	66
WY	1	7	0	1	1	8	0	9
AS	0	0	0	1	0	1	0	1
GU	0	1	1	1	1	2	0	3
MH	0	1	0	0	0	1	0	1
MP	0	0	0	1	0	1	0	1
PR	7	0	39	14	46	14	3	63
FM	0	1	0	0	0	1	0	1
PW	0	1	0	0	0	1	0	1
VI	0	0	0	1	0	1	0	1
Total	**482**	**928**	**1934**	**654**	**2416**	**1582**	**113**	**4111**

Figures do not include the 868 new additional branch campus listings nor the 616 reclassified listings.

50 Largest Universities by Fall 2012 Enrollment

Institution	Enrollment
1. Ashford University	77734
2. Liberty University	74372
3. Arizona State University	73378
4. University of Central Florida	59212
5. The Ohio State University Main Campus	56387
6. Air University	54754
7. Texas A & M University	53187
8. University of Texas at Austin	52186
9. University of Minnesota-Twin Cities	51853
10. American Public University System	50838
11. Walden University	50208
12. University of Florida	49913
13. Michigan State University	48906
14. Kaplan University	48865
15. Grand Canyon University	48650
16. Ohio University (all campuses)	47415
17. Florida International University	46261
18. Penn State University Park	44679
19. New York University	44516
20. University of Michigan-Ann Arbor	43426
21. University of Wisconsin-Madison	42820
22. University of Washington	42446
23. University of Maryland University College	42268
24. Indiana University Bloomington	42133
25. University of Cincinnati Main Campus	41970
26. University of South Florida	41212
27. University of Houston	40747
28. Florida State University	40695
29. Rutgers the State University of New Jersey New Brunswick Campus	40434
30. University of Arizona	40223
31. University of Southern California	39958
32. University of California-Los Angeles	39945
33. Purdue University Main Campus	39256
34. Western Governors University	39000
35. California State University-Fullerton	37677
36. University of Maryland College Park	37200
37. Temple University	36744
38. Capella University	36375
39. California State University-Long Beach	36279
40. California State University-Northridge	36164
41. University of North Texas	35778
42. University of Missouri - Columbia	34748
43. University of Georgia	34519
44. Brigham Young University	34409
45. North Carolina State University	34340
46. Texas State University-San Marcos	34225
47. The University of Alabama	33602
48. University of California-Davis	33300
49. The University of Texas at Arlington	33239
50. Boston University	33226

Institutions by Control and Tuition Range

Tuition	Public*	Private	Total
0 - 1,000	39	110	149
1,001 - 2,000	193	10	203
2,001 - 4,000	548	43	591
4,001 - 6,000	309	92	401
6,001 - 8,000	245	95	340
8,001 - 10,000	125	119	244
Over 10,000	123	1946	2069
Total	**1582**	**2415**	**3997**

* Figures for Public Institutions are In-State Tuitions

Reclassified Branch Campuses

In order to conform to the definition of branch campuses used by the United States Department of Education (34 CFR §600.2), we have changed the way branch campuses are listed in the *Higher Education Directory*. A branch campus is defined as a site that is geographically apart from and independent of the main campus of the institution. The location is independent if it:

- offers courses in educational programs leading to a degree, certificate, or other recognized educational credential
- has its own faculty and administrative or supervisory organization; AND
- has its own budgetary and hiring authority

We have added 868 new branch campus listings and reclassified 616 institutional listings...this information has come from the regional, national or specialized accrediting agencies. Due to space limitations in the printed directory, we list limited information on these additional branch campuses. More detailed information is available in our online directory, HED-Connect.

The following is a list of the branch campuses that have been reclassified:

	FICE/ID Number
Alabama	
Community College of the Air Force (Maxwell AFB, Gunter Annex)	12308
Fortis Institute (Birmingham)	666683
Herzing University (Birmingham)	10193
ITT Technical Institute (Bessemer)	666530
ITT Technical Institute (Madison)	666695
ITT Technical Institute (Mobile)	666165
School of Advanced Air and Space Studies (Maxwell AFB)	666746
South University (Montgomery)	4463
Virginia College (Huntsville)	666400
Virginia College (Mobile)	666069
Virginia College (Montgomery)	666408
Arizona	
Argosy University, Phoenix (Phoenix)	666790
The Art Institute of Tucson (Tucson)	37405
Brookline College (Tempe)	666403
Brookline College (Tucson)	666402
Brown Mackie College-Phoenix (Phoenix)	666782
Brown Mackie College-Tucson (Tucson)	9451
Carrington College - Mesa (Mesa)	23352
Carrington College - Tucson (Tucson)	30898
Carrington College - Westside (Phoenix)	666248
CollegeAmerica-Phoenix (Phoenix)	666017
DeVry University - Phoenix Campus (Phoenix)	8322
Embry-Riddle Aeronautical University-Prescott Campus (Prescott)	21047
Fortis College, Phoenix (Phoenix)	666761
Golf Academy of America (Chandler)	666023
ITT Technical Institute (Phoenix)	666696
ITT Technical Institute (Tempe)	20652
ITT Technical Institute (Tucson)	23611
Midwestern University (Glendale)	666001
Ottawa University Arizona (Phoenix)	666066
Pima Medical Institute-Mesa (Mesa)	11570
Sanford-Brown College (Phoenix)	666739
Arkansas	
Bryan University (Rogers)	666252
ITT Technical Institute (Little Rock)	666531
Remington College-Little Rock (Little Rock)	666286
California	
Alliant International University-Fresno	1158
Alliant International University-Irvine	666157
Alliant International University-Los Angeles	10113
Alliant International University-San Francisco	11881
American Academy of Dramatic Arts, Los Angeles Campus (Hollywood)	21069
American Career College-Orange County (Anaheim)	667073
Antioch University Los Angeles (Culver City)	666236

	FICE/ID Number
Antioch University Santa Barbara (Santa Barbara)	666231
Argosy University, Inland Empire (Ontario)	666007
Argosy University, Los Angeles (Los Angeles)	666011
Argosy University, San Diego (San Diego)	666034
Argosy University, San Francisco Bay Area (Alameda)	666081
The Art Institute of California, A College of Argosy University - Hollywood (North Hollywood)	31254
The Art Institute of California, A College of Argosy University - Inland Empire (San Bernardino)	16471
The Art Institute of California, A College of Argosy University - Los Angeles (Santa Monica)	666045
The Art Institute of California, A College of Argosy University - Orange County (Santa Ana)	666182
The Art Institute of California, A College of Argosy University - Sacramento (Sacramento)	666619
The Art Institute of California, A College of Argosy University - San Diego (San Diego)	23276
The Art Institute of California, A College of Argosy University - San Francisco (San Francisco)	7236
The Art Institute of California, A College of Argosy University - Sunnyvale (Sunnyvale)	666620
Brooks Institute (Ventura)	666250
Carrington College California - Citrus Heights (Citrus Heights)	667042
Carrington College California - Pleasant Hill (Pleasant Hill)	666043
Carrington College California - San Jose (San Jose)	666042
Carrington College California - San Leandro (San Leandro)	666751
Carrington College California - Stockton (Stockton)	666140
Charter College-Oxnard (Oxnard)	666675
Coleman University (San Marcos)	666259
Concord Law School of Kaplan University (Los Angeles)	41259
The Culinary Institute of America at Greystone (Saint Helena)	666260
DeVry University - Pomona Campus (Pomona)	23329
El Camino College Compton Center (Compton)	1188
Everest College-Ontario Metro (Ontario)	666621
Everest College-West LA (Los Angeles)	666749
Fashion Institute of Design and Merchandising-Orange County (Irvine)	666004
Fashion Institute of Design and Merchandising-San Diego (San Diego)	666005
Fashion Institute of Design and Merchandising-San Francisco (San Francisco)	13041
Golf Academy of America (Carlsbad)	15609
Heald College, Modesto (Salida)	667043
International Academy of Design and Technology (Sacramento)	666740
ITT Technical Institute (Clovis)	666144
ITT Technical Institute (Concord)	666697
ITT Technical Institute (Lathrop)	666533
ITT Technical Institute (Orange)	23219
ITT Technical Institute (Oxnard)	666534
ITT Technical Institute (Rancho Cordova)	21209
ITT Technical Institute (San Bernardino)	30704
ITT Technical Institute (San Dimas)	22915
ITT Technical Institute (Sylmar)	23218
ITT Technical Institute (Torrance)	30874
Kaplan College (Bakersfield)	666291
Monterey Institute of International Studies (Monterey)	1241
Palmer College of Chiropractic, West Campus (San Jose)	21849

	FICE/ID Number
Pima Medical Institute-Chula Vista (Chula Vista)	666272
Platt College (Ontario)	666056
Sage College (San Diego)	666304
San Joaquin Valley College-Bakersfield (Bakersfield)	23135
San Joaquin Valley College-Fresno (Fresno)	666008
San Joaquin Valley College-Fresno Aviation Campus (Fresno)	666009
San Joaquin Valley College-Modesto (Salida)	666128
San Joaquin Valley College-Rancho Cordova (Rancho Cordova)	666133
San Joaquin Valley College-Rancho Cucamonga (Rancho Cucamonga)	666096
San Joaquin Valley College-Victor Valley (Hesperia) (Hesperia)	667044
Santa Barbara Business College (Rancho Mirage)	666582
Santa Barbara Business College (Santa Barbara)	666099
Western State University College of Law (Fullerton)	10832
Westwood College-Anaheim (Anaheim)	666047
Westwood College-Inland Empire (Upland)	666104
WyoTech-Sacramento (West Sacramento)	666292

Colorado

Anthem College (Aurora)	666510
Argosy University, Denver (Denver)	666654
CollegeAmerica Colorado Springs (Colorado Springs)	666293
CollegeAmerica Fort Collins (Fort Collins)	666362
Colorado Technical University (Aurora)	666732
DeVry University - Westminster Campus (Westminster)	666227
Everest College (Aurora)	666412
IntelliTec College (Pueblo)	666366
Johnson & Wales University - Denver Campus (Denver)	666411
Pima Medical Institute-Denver (Westminster)	666171
Southwest Acupuncture College (Boulder)	666618
Westwood College-Denver South (Denver)	666512

Connecticut

Rensselaer at Hartford (Hartford)	2804
University of Connecticut Health Center (Farmington)	9867

Delaware

Widener University School of Law (Wilmington)	12962

District of Columbia

Medtech College (Washington)	666591

Florida

American InterContinental University (Weston)	666336
Argosy University, Sarasota (Sarasota)	25906
Argosy University, Tampa (Tampa)	666082
Brown Mackie College-Miami (Miramar)	666110
Carlos Albizu University Miami Campus (Miami)	666814
Central Florida Institute (Orlando)	667022
City College (Gainesville)	666413
City College (Miami)	666414
DeVry University - Miramar Campus (Miramar)	666196
DeVry University - Orlando Campus (Orlando)	666112
Embry-Riddle Aeronautical University-Worldwide (Daytona Beach)	666089
Everest University-Brandon Campus (Tampa)	666416
Everest University-Jacksonville Campus (Jacksonville)	666994
Everest University-Lakeland Campus (Lakeland)	666415
Everest University-Melbourne Campus (Melbourne)	666417
Everest University-Orange Park (Orange Park)	666590
Everest University-South Orlando Campus (Orlando)	666418
Florida Career College (Clearwater)	25862
Florida Career College (Hialeah)	666624
Florida Career College (Lauderdale Lakes)	666622
Florida Career College (Pembroke Pines)	666025
Florida College of Natural Health (Bradenton)	666830
Florida College of Natural Health (Maitland)	666513
Florida College of Natural Health (Miami)	666514
Florida National University South Campus (Miami)	666691
Florida National University Training Center (Hialeah)	666690
Florida Technical College (Deland)	666419
Florida Technical College (Lakeland)	25981
Golf Academy of America (Apopka)	666186
Herzing University (Winter Park)	666422
ITT Technical Institute (Fort Lauderdale)	666536
ITT Technical Institute (Fort Myers)	666669
ITT Technical Institute (Jacksonville)	666537
ITT Technical Institute (Lake Mary)	30876
ITT Technical Institute (Miami)	666026
ITT Technical Institute (St. Petersburg)	666163
ITT Technical Institute (Tampa)	22865
Johnson & Wales University (North Miami)	666423
Johnson University Florida (Kissimmee)	21567
Keiser University (Port Saint Lucie)	666289
Keiser University (West Palm Beach)	667032
Le Cordon Bleu College of Culinary Arts in Miami (Miramar)	666369
Le Cordon Bleu College of Culinary Arts in Orlando (Orlando)	666064
MedVance Institute of Fort Lauderdale (Lauderdale Lakes)	666269
Palmer College of Chiropractic, Florida Campus (Port Orange)	666330
Polytechnic University of Puerto Rico (Miami)	666238
Professional Golfers Career College (Winter Garden)	666300
Rasmussen College - Fort Myers (Fort Myers)	667062
Rasmussen College - New Port Richey (New Port Richey)	666425
Rasmussen College - Ocala (Ocala)	8501
Rasmussen College - Tampa/Brandon (Tampa)	667067
Reformed Theological Seminary (Oviedo)	666628
Sanford-Brown Institute (Fort Lauderdale)	667031
Sanford-Brown Institute (Tampa)	666027
South University (Royal Palm Beach)	666117
Southeastern College (Miami Lakes)	666290
Southeastern College (St. Petersburg)	666758
Trinity International University, Florida Regional Center (Davie)	12314
Virginia College (Pensacola)	31005

Georgia

American InterContinental University (Atlanta)	666723
Argosy University, Atlanta (Atlanta)	666735
Brown Mackie College-Atlanta (Atlanta)	26214
DeVry University - Decatur Campus (Decatur)	9224
Herzing University (Atlanta)	20897
ITT Technical Institute (Atlanta)	666595
ITT Technical Institute (Duluth)	666325
ITT Technical Institute (Kennesaw)	666378
Le Cordon Bleu College of Culinary Arts in Atlanta (Tucker)	666298
Westwood College-Atlanta Midtown (Atlanta)	666421
Westwood College-Atlanta Northlake (Atlanta)	666597

Hawaii

Argosy University, Hawaii (Honolulu)	666787
Heald College, Honolulu (Honolulu)	4546
New Hope Christian College-Hawaii (Honolulu)	667010
Remington College-Honolulu Campus (Honolulu)	666028

Idaho

Brown Mackie College-Boise (Boise)	666780
ITT Technical Institute (Boise)	4553
Stevens-Henager College-Boise (Boise)	666329

Illinois

Argosy University, Chicago (Chicago)	666736
Argosy University, Schaumburg (Schaumburg)	666789
Chicago School of Professional Psychology-Chicago (Chicago)	770349
International Academy of Design and Technology-Schaumburg (Schaumburg)	666141
ITT Technical Institute (Mount Prospect)	666538
ITT Technical Institute (Oak Brook)	666118
ITT Technical Institute (Orland Park)	666539
Midwest College of Oriental Medicine (Chicago)	666090
Pacific College of Oriental Medicine (Chicago)	666615
Rasmussen College - Aurora (Aurora)	667060
Rasmussen College - Mokena/Tinley Park (Mokena)	667064
Rasmussen College - Rockford (Rockford)	667065
Rasmussen College - Romeoville/Joliet (Romeoville)	667066
Sanford-Brown College (Collinsville)	666753
Westwood College-Chicago Loop (Chicago)	666424
Westwood College-River Oaks (Calumet City)	666440

Indiana

The Art Institute of Indianapolis (Indianapolis)	666247
Brown Mackie College-Fort Wayne (Fort Wayne)	666435
Brown Mackie College-Indianapolis (Indianapolis)	666394
Brown Mackie College-Merrillville (Merrillville)	21032
Brown Mackie College-Michigan City (Michigan City)	666426
Brown Mackie College-South Bend (South Bend)	4583
Harrison College - Anderson Campus (Anderson)	666030

	FICE/ID Number
Harrison College - Columbus Indiana Campus (Columbus)	666428
Harrison College - Elkhart Campus (Elkhart)	666143
Harrison College - Evansville Campus (Evansville)	666429
Harrison College - Fort Wayne Campus (Fort Wayne)	666029
Harrison College - Indianapolis East Campus (Indianapolis)	666430
Harrison College - Indianapolis Northwest Campus (Indianapolis)	666388
Harrison College - Lafayette Campus (Lafayette)	666431
Harrison College - Terre Haute Campus (Terre Haute)	666433
International Business College (Indianapolis)	666929
ITT Technical Institute (Fort Wayne)	8329
ITT Technical Institute (Newburgh)	7327
ITT Technical Institute (South Bend)	666700
Ivy Tech Community College of Indiana- North Central (South Bend)	8423
Ivy Tech Community College of Indiana-Bloomington (Bloomington)	35213
Ivy Tech Community College of Indiana-Columbus (Columbus)	10038
Ivy Tech Community College of Indiana-East Central (Muncie)	9924
Ivy Tech Community College of Indiana-Kokomo (Kokomo)	10041
Ivy Tech Community College of Indiana-Lafayette (Lafayette)	10039
Ivy Tech Community College of Indiana-Northeast (Fort Wayne)	9926
Ivy Tech Community College of Indiana-Northwest (Gary)	10040
Ivy Tech Community College of Indiana-Richmond (Richmond)	10037
Ivy Tech Community College of Indiana-Southeast (Madison)	9923
Ivy Tech Community College of Indiana-Southern Indiana (Sellersburg)	10109
Ivy Tech Community College of Indiana-Southwest (Evansville)	9925
Ivy Tech Community College of Indiana-Wabash Valley (Terre Haute)	8547
MedTech College (Fort Wayne)	666677
MedTech College (Greenwood)	666678
Ottawa University Jeffersonville (Jeffersonville)	666088

Iowa

Brown Mackie College-Quad Cities (Bettendorf)	666792
ITT Technical Institute (Clive)	666596
Kaplan University (Cedar Rapids)	4220
Kaplan University (Mason City)	666438
Kaplan University (Urbandale)	666437

Kansas

The Art Institutes International - Kansas City (Lenexa)	666765
Brown Mackie College-Kansas City (Lenexa)	666091
ITT Technical Institute (Wichita)	666168
Kansas State University-Salina, College of Technology and Aviation (Salina)	4611
Ottawa University Kansas City (Overland Park)	666083
University of Kansas Medical Center (Kansas City)	24579
Vatterott College - Wichita (Wichita)	666583

Kentucky

Brown Mackie College-Hopkinsville (Hopkinsville)	666516
Brown Mackie College-Louisville (Louisville)	21082
Brown Mackie College-Northern Kentucky (Fort Mitchell)	666446
Daymar College-Bellevue (Bellevue)	666390
Daymar College-Bowling Green (Bowling Green)	666439
Daymar College-Louisville (Louisville)	666391
Daymar College-Louisville East (Louisville)	667081
Daymar College-Madisonville (Madisonville)	667079
Daymar College-Scottsville (Scottsville)	667080
ITT Technical Institute (Lexington)	666158
ITT Technical Institute (Louisville)	666540
National College (Danville)	666441
National College (Florence)	666442
National College (Louisville)	666443
National College (Pikeville)	666444
National College (Richmond)	666445
Spencerian College (Lexington)	666448

Louisiana

	FICE/ID Number
Baton Rouge Community College, Acadian Branch (Baton Rouge)	5488
Baton Rouge Community College, Jackson Branch (Jackson)	25099
Baton Rouge Community College, New Roads Branch (New Roads)	5478
Herzing University (Kenner)	666450
ITT Technical Institute (Baton Rouge)	666164
ITT Technical Institute (Saint Rose)	666031
Northwest Louisiana Technical College Natchitoches Campus (Natchitoches)	21602
Northwest Louisiana Technical College Shreveport Campus (Shreveport)	5469
Remington College-Baton Rouge Campus (Baton Rouge)	666449
Remington College-Lafayette Campus (Lafayette)	5203
Remington College-Shreveport (Shreveport)	666302
South Central Louisiana Technical College Lafourche Campus (Thibodaux)	30091
South Central Louisiana Technical College River Parishes Campus (Reserve)	23334

Maine

Kaplan University-Maine (South Portland)	9292

Maryland

ITT Technical Institute (Owings Mills)	666377
Kaplan University (Hagerstown)	7946

Massachusetts

ITT Technical Institute (Norwood)	666541
ITT Technical Institute (Wilmington)	666119

Michigan

The Art Institute of Michigan (Novi)	666692
Baker College of Allen Park (Allen Park)	666996
Baker College of Auburn Hills (Auburn Hills)	666940
Baker College of Cadillac (Cadillac)	666941
Baker College of Clinton Township (Clinton Township)	666942
Baker College of Jackson (Jackson)	4680
Baker College of Muskegon (Muskegon)	2296
Baker College of Owosso (Owosso)	666937
Baker College of Port Huron (Port Huron)	666943
International Academy of Design and Technology (Troy)	666632
ITT Technical Institute (Canton)	666323
ITT Technical Institute (Swartz Creek)	666146
ITT Technical Institute (Troy)	666542
ITT Technical Institute (Wyoming)	10627
Moody Theological Seminary-Michigan (Plymouth)	31353

Minnesota

Argosy University, Twin Cities (Eagan)	7619
Herzing University (Minneapolis)	11017
ITT Technical Institute (Eden Prairie)	666319
Le Cordon Bleu College of Culinary Arts in Minneapolis/St Paul (Mendota Heights)	666370
Mayo Clinic College of Medicine-Mayo Graduate School (Rochester)	11516
Mayo School of Health Sciences (Rochester)	8182
Minnesota School of Business (Brooklyn Center)	666453
Rasmussen College - Blaine (Blaine)	667061
Rasmussen College - Bloomington (Bloomington)	11686
Rasmussen College - Brooklyn Park (Brooklyn Park)	666769
Rasmussen College - Eagan (Eagan)	4648
Rasmussen College - Mankato (Mankato)	25033

Mississippi

Antonelli College (Hattiesburg)	666517
Antonelli College (Jackson)	666518
ITT Technical Institute (Madison)	666701
Virginia College (Biloxi)	666073
Virginia College (Jackson)	666032

Missouri

Bolivar Technical College (Bolivar)	667033
Brown Mackie College-St. Louis (Fenton)	666793
Colorado Technical University, Kansas City (North Kansas City)	666457
DeVry University - Kansas City Campus (Kansas City)	2455
Graceland University (Independence)	666262
Heritage College (Kansas City)	666155
ITT Technical Institute (Arnold)	666033
ITT Technical Institute (Earth City)	7557

	FICE/ID Number
ITT Technical Institute (Kansas City)	666380
ITT Technical Institute (Springfield)	666702
L'Ecole Culinaire (Saint Louis)	666275
Metro Business College (Jefferson City)	666454
Metro Business College (Rolla)	666455
Saint Louis College of Health Careers-Fenton Campus (Fenton)	666274
Saint Louis Community College at Florissant Valley (Saint Louis)	2470
Saint Louis Community College at Meramec (Kirkwood)	2472
Saint Louis Community College at Wildwood (Wildwood)	667084
Sanford-Brown College (Saint Peters)	666458
Vatterott College-Joplin (Joplin)	666060
Vatterott College-Kansas City (Kansas City)	666519
Vatterott College-Saint Joseph (Saint Joseph)	666520
Vatterott College-Springfield (Springfield)	666521
Vatterott College-St. Charles (St. Charles)	666584
Vatterott College-Sunset Hills (Sunset Hills)	666522

Montana

City College at Montana State University Billings (Billings)	10166
Highlands College of Montana Tech (Butte)	9282

Nebraska

ITT Technical Institute (Omaha)	666543
Kaplan University (Lincoln)	4721
Kaplan University (Omaha)	8491
The University of Montana - Missoula College (Missoula)	7561

Nevada

The Art Institute of Las Vegas (Henderson)	30846
ITT Technical Institute (Henderson)	666544
Le Cordon Bleu College of Culinary Arts in Las Vegas (Las Vegas)	666303
Pima Medical Institute-Las Vegas (Las Vegas)	666273

New Hampshire

Antioch University New England (Keene)	666992
University of New Hampshire at Manchester (Manchester)	9009

New Jersey

DeVry University - North Brunswick Campus (North Brunswick)	9228
Rutgers - Robert Wood Johnson Medical School (Piscataway)	24549

New Jersey

Rutgers Graduate School of Biomedical Sciences (Newark)	11174
Rutgers School of Dental Medicine (Newark)	24635
Rutgers School of Health Related Professions (Newark)	20668
Rutgers School of Nursing (Newark)	666970
Rutgers-New Jersey Medical School (Newark)	2620
Rutgers-School of Public Health (Piscataway)	666991

New Mexico

Brookline College (Albuquerque)	666724
Carrington College - Albuquerque (Albuquerque)	666014
ITT Technical Institute (Albuquerque)	666545
New Mexico State University Grants (Grants)	8854
Pima Medical Institute-Albuquerque (Albuquerque)	36783
Southwest Acupuncture College-Albuquerque (Albuquerque)	666666
Southwest University of Visual Arts (Albuquerque)	666524
University of New Mexico-Gallup (Gallup)	6881
University of New Mexico-Los Alamos (Los Alamos)	666742
University of New Mexico-Taos (Ranchos de Taos)	666743
University of New Mexico-Valencia (Los Lunas)	666741

New York

	FICE/ID Number
Bryant & Stratton College (Albany)	4749
Bryant & Stratton College (Rochester)	12470
Bryant & Stratton College (Syracuse)	8276
Erie Community College North Campus (Williamsville)	2865
Erie Community College-South Campus (Orchard Park)	12427
ITT Technical Institute (Albany)	666138
ITT Technical Institute (Getzville)	666609
ITT Technical Institute (Liverpool)	666137
LIU Riverhead	666174
Long Island University Brentwood Campus (Brentwood)	666076
Long Island University Brooklyn Campus (Brooklyn)	4779
Long Island University Hudson Graduate Center at Rockland (Orangeburg)	666077
Long Island University Hudson Graduate Center at Westchester (Purchase)	666078
Pacific College of Oriental Medicine (New York)	666139
Saint Joseph's College, New York - Suffolk Campus (Patchogue)	29081
Suffolk County Community College Eastern Campus (Riverhead)	4816
Suffolk County Community College Grant Campus (Brentwood)	13204
Weill Cornell Medical College (New York)	4762

North Carolina

The Art Institute of Charlotte (Charlotte)	21105
ITT Technical Institute (Cary)	666704
ITT Technical Institute (Charlotte)	666705
ITT Technical Institute (Charlotte)	666161
ITT Technical Institute (High Point)	666703
Johnson & Wales University-Charlotte (Charlotte)	666375
Miller-Motte Technical College (Wilmington)	30632
Reformed Theological Seminary (Charlotte)	666785
St. Andrews University (Laurinburg)	2967

North Dakota

Rasmussen College - Bismarck (Bismarck)	666301
Rasmussen College - Fargo/Moorhead (Fargo)	4846

Ohio

The Art Institute of Ohio-Cincinnati (Cincinnati)	666693
Beckfield College (Cincinnati)	666673
Bowling Green State University Firelands College (Huron)	7856
Brown Mackie College-Akron (Akron)	666470
Brown Mackie College-Cincinnati (Cincinnati)	5127
Brown Mackie College-Findlay (Findlay)	26162
Brown Mackie College-North Canton (Canton)	30778
Bryant & Stratton College (Parma)	22744
Daymar College-Jackson (Jackson)	666468
Daymar College-Lancaster (Lancaster)	666469
Daymar College-New Boston (New Boston)	667082
DeVry University - Columbus Campus (Columbus)	3099
Fortis College (Ravenna)	23036
Herzing University-Akron (Akron)	20695
ITT Technical Institute (Columbus)	666706
ITT Technical Institute (Dayton)	9088
ITT Technical Institute (Hilliard)	666318
ITT Technical Institute (Maumee)	666160
ITT Technical Institute (Norwood)	666546
ITT Technical Institute (Strongsville)	666547
ITT Technical Institute (Warrensville Heights)	666379
ITT Technical Institute (Youngstown)	9837
Kent State University at Ashtabula (Ashtabula)	3052
Kent State University at Stark (North Canton)	3054
Kent State University East Liverpool Campus (East Liverpool)	3056
Kent State University Geauga Campus (Burton Township)	3059
Kent State University Salem Campus (Salem)	3061
Kent State University Trumbull Campus (Warren)	3064
Kent State University Tuscarawas Campus (New Philadelphia)	3062
Miami University Hamilton Campus (Hamilton)	3079
Miami University Middletown (Middletown)	3080
Miami-Jacobs Career College (Columbus)	666465
Miami-Jacobs Career College (Dayton)	3076
Miami-Jacobs Career College (Independence)	21521
Ohio Business College (Hillard)	30658
Ohio Business College (Sandusky)	666467
The Ohio State University at Lima Campus (Lima)	3092
The Ohio State University at Marion (Marion)	3094
The Ohio State University Mansfield Campus (Mansfield)	3093
The Ohio State University Newark Campus (Newark)	3095
Ohio University Chillicothe Campus (Chillicothe)	3102
Ohio University Eastern Campus (Saint Clairsville)	3101
Ohio University Lancaster Campus (Lancaster)	3104
Ohio University Southern Campus (Ironton)	666000
Ohio University Zanesville Branch (Zanesville)	3108

	FICE/ID Number
Vatterott College-Cleveland (Broadview Heights)	666156
Wright State University Lake Campus (Celina)	9169

Oklahoma

Brown Mackie College-Tulsa (Tulsa)	666783
Clary Sage College (Tulsa)	666368
ITT Technical Institute (Oklahoma City)	666159
ITT Technical Institute (Tulsa)	666147
Oklahoma State University - Tulsa (Tulsa)	666053
Oklahoma State University Center for Health Sciences College of Osteopathic Medicine (Tulsa)	11282
Oklahoma Technical College (Tulsa)	666718
Platt College-OKC Central (Oklahoma City)	666341
University of Oklahoma Health Sciences Center (Oklahoma City)	5889
Vatterott College-Oklahoma City (Warr Acres)	666061
Vatterott College-Tulsa (Tulsa)	666102

Oregon

Heald College, Portland (Portland)	37454
ITT Technical Institute (Portland)	11852
Oregon Culinary Institute (Portland)	666177

Pennsylvania

Cambria-Rowe Business College (Indiana)	666476
Career Training Academy (Monroeville)	666051
Career Training Academy (Pittsburgh)	666100
DeVry University - Fort Washington Campus (Fort Washington)	666218
DuBois Business College (Huntingdon)	666479
DuBois Business College (Oil City)	666480
Erie Business Center South (New Castle)	3305
ITT Technical Institute (Dunmore)	666150
ITT Technical Institute (Harrisburg)	666548
ITT Technical Institute (Pittsburgh)	666483
ITT Technical Institute (Tarentum)	666482
McCann School of Business & Technology (Hazleton)	666484
McCann School of Business & Technology (Sunbury)	666485
Penn State Abington (Abington)	3342
Penn State Altoona (Altoona)	3331
Penn State Beaver (Monaca)	3332
Penn State Berks (Reading)	3334
Penn State Brandywine (Media)	6922
Penn State DuBois (DuBois)	3335
Penn State Erie, The Behrend College (Erie)	3333
Penn State Fayette, The Eberly Campus (Lemont Furnace)	3336
Penn State Great Valley School of Graduate Professional Studies (Malvern)	3348
Penn State Greater Allegheny (McKeesport)	3339
Penn State Harrisburg (Middletown)	6814
Penn State Hazleton (Hazleton)	3338
Penn State Lehigh Valley (Center Valley)	3330
Penn State Milton S. Hershey Medical Center College of Medicine (Hershey)	6813
Penn State Mont Alto (Mont Alto)	3340
Penn State New Kensington (New Kensington)	3341
Penn State Schuylkill (Schuylkill Haven)	3343
Penn State Shenango (Sharon)	3345
Penn State Wilkes-Barre (Lehman)	3346
Penn State Worthington-Scranton (Dunmore)	3344
Penn State York (York)	3347
Pennsylvania Institute of Health and Technology (Mount Braddock)	666035
Sanford-Brown Institute-Wilkins Township (Pittsburgh)	666526
The Penn State Dickinson School of Law (University Park)	3254
University of Pittsburgh at Bradford (Bradford)	3380
University of Pittsburgh at Greensburg (Greensburg)	3381
University of Pittsburgh at Johnstown (Johnstown)	3382
University of Pittsburgh at Titusville (Titusville)	3383
Venango College of Clarion University (Oil City)	3319
WyoTech-Blairsville (Blairsville)	666305

Puerto Rico

	FICE/ID Number
Columbia Centro Universitario (Yauco)	666036
EDP University of Puerto Rico (San Sebastian)	666488
National University College (Arecibo)	666489
Pontifical Catholic University of Puerto Rico-Arecibo Campus (Arecibo)	666603
Pontifical Catholic University of Puerto Rico-Mayaguez Campus (Mayaguez)	666605

South Carolina

Brown Mackie College-Greenville (Greenville)	666781
Golf Academy of America (Myrtle Beach)	666490
ITT Technical Institute (Columbia)	666162
ITT Technical Institute (Greenville)	666549
Miller-Motte Technical College (North Charleston)	666256
South University Columbia Campus (Columbia)	4922
University of South Carolina Lancaster (Lancaster)	3453

South Dakota

Colorado Technical University (Sioux Falls)	666731

Tennessee

Argosy University, Nashville (Nashville)	666668
Daymar Institute (Clarksville)	666492
Daymar Institute (Murfreesboro)	666392
Harding School of Theology (Memphis)	4081
International Academy of Design and Technology (Nashville)	666347
ITT Technical Institute (Chattanooga)	666708
ITT Technical Institute (Cordova)	666550
ITT Technical Institute (Knoxville)	30734
ITT Technical Institute (Nashville)	23598
National College of Business and Technology (Bristol)	666500
Remington College (Memphis)	666062
Remington College (Nashville)	666307
University of Tennessee Health Science Center (Memphis)	6725
Vatterott College-Memphis (Memphis)	666308
Virginia College School of Business and Health (Chattanooga)	666136

Texas

American InterContinental University-Houston Campus (Houston)	666335
Argosy University, Dallas (Farmers Branch)	666181
Art Institute of Dallas (Dallas)	25396
DeVry University - Houston Campus (Houston)	666219
DeVry University - Irving Campus (Irving)	10139
Everest College (Dallas)	666254
International Academy of Design and Technology (San Antonio)	666733
ITT Technical Institute (Arlington)	23286
ITT Technical Institute (Austin)	666551
ITT Technical Institute (Houston)	23287
ITT Technical Institute (Houston)	666554
ITT Technical Institute (Richardson)	666327
ITT Technical Institute (San Antonio)	30714
ITT Technical Institute (Webster)	666552
Le Cordon Bleu College of Culinary Arts in Dallas (Dallas)	666728
Remington College-Dallas Campus (Garland)	666037
Remington College-Fort Worth Campus (Fort Worth)	666063
Sanford-Brown College-Houston (Houston)	666382
Texas A & M University at Galveston (Galveston)	10298
Texas A & M University Baylor College of Dentistry (Dallas)	666240
Texas A & M University-San Antonio (San Antonio)	666689
Texas School of Business-Friendswood (Friendswood)	667051
Virginia College Austin (Austin)	666074
Western Technical College (El Paso)	666103

Utah

Argosy University, Salt Lake City (Draper)	666655
The Art Institute of Salt Lake City (Draper)	666694
Fortis College (Salt Lake City)	666762
ITT Technical Institute (Murray)	23610
Stevens-Henager College (Orem)	30030
Stevens-Henager College (Salt Lake City)	666038
Utah State University Eastern (Price)	3676

Virginia

Argosy University, Washington DC (Arlington)	666788
Bryant & Stratton College (North Chesterfield)	666496
Bryant & Stratton College (Virginia Beach)	10061
California University of Management and Sciences Virginia (Falls Church)	666734

	FICE/ID Number
DeVry University - Arlington Campus (Arlington)	666220
ITT Technical Institute (Chantilly)	666324
ITT Technical Institute (Norfolk)	666555
ITT Technical Institute (Richmond)	666040
ITT Technical Institute (Springfield)	666321
Medical Careers Institute (Newport News)	22472
Medical Careers Institute (Richmond)	667038
National College (Charlottesville)	666501
National College (Danville)	666502
National College (Harrisonburg)	666503
National College (Lynchburg)	666504
National College (Martinsville)	666505
Reformed Theological Seminary (McLean)	666079
University of the Potomac (Vienna)	666178
Westwood College-Annandale (Annandale)	666599
Westwood College-Arlington Ballston (Arlington)	666660

Washington

Antioch University Seattle (Seattle)	666812
Argosy University, Seattle (Seattle)	666080
DeVry University - Federal Way Campus (Federal Way)	666224
Everest College (Vancouver)	666737
International Academy of Design and Technology (Seattle)	666265
ITT Technical Institute (Everett)	666326
ITT Technical Institute (Seattle)	8443
Pima Medical Institute-Seattle (Seattle)	666172

West Virginia

ITT Technical Institute (Huntington)	666709
National College (Princeton)	666499
Potomac State College of West Virginia University (Keyser)	3829
West Virginia Business College (Nutter Fort)	666507
West Virginia University Institute of Technology (Montgomery)	3825

Wisconsin

Anthem College-Milwaukee (Brookfield)	666613
Bryant & Stratton College (Milwaukee)	5009
ITT Technical Institute (Green Bay)	666317
ITT Technical Institute (Greenfield)	30875
Ottawa University Wisconsin (Brookfield)	666084
Rasmussen College - Appleton (Appleton)	667059
Rasmussen College - Green Bay (Green Bay)	667063
Rasmussen College - Wausau (Wausau)	667068

Wyoming

Institute of Business and Medical Careers (Cheyenne)	666738

The following schools were listed in the *2013 Higher Education Directory* but do not meet the criteria for a branch campus by the regional, national or specialized accrediting agency and therefore are not listed in the 2014 edition:

Arizona

DeVry University - Mesa Center (Mesa)	666190

California

DeVry University - Bakersfield (Bakersfield)	666486
DeVry University - Colton (Colton)	666487
DeVry University - Daly City (Daly City)	666493
DeVry University - Fremont Campus (Fremont)	666829
DeVry University - Fresno (Fresno)	666494
DeVry University - Long Beach Campus (Long Beach)	666988
DeVry University - Oakland Center (Oakland)	666194
DeVry University - Palmdale (Palmdale)	666495
DeVry University - Sacramento (Sacramento)	666497
DeVry University - San Diego Campus (San Diego)	666193
DeVry University - San Jose (San Jose)	666523
DeVry University - Sherman Oaks Campus (Sherman Oaks)	666065

Colorado

DeVry University - Colorado Springs Center (Colorado Springs)	666511
DeVry University - Denver South Center (Greenwood Village)	7648

Florida

DeVry University - Fort Lauderdale (Ft. Lauderdale)	666525
DeVry University - Jacksonville (Jacksonville)	666527
DeVry University - Miami Center (Miami)	666197
DeVry University - Orlando North Center (Orlando)	666198
DeVry University - Tampa Bay Campus (Tampa)	666199
DeVry University - Tampa East (Tampa)	666528

Georgia

DeVry University - Alpharetta Campus (Alpharetta)	666989
DeVry University - Atlanta Cobb/Galleria Center (Atlanta)	666257
DeVry University - Atlanta/Perimeter Center (Atlanta)	666201
DeVry University - Gwinnett Center (Duluth)	666202
DeVry University - Henry County (Stockbridge)	666532
Lincoln College of Technology (Marietta)	666282

Illinois

DeVry University - Addison Campus (Addison)	22966
DeVry University - Chicago Loop Center (Chicago)	666203
DeVry University - Chicago O'Hare Center (Chicago)	666204
DeVry University - Downers Grove (Downers Grove)	666791
DeVry University - Elgin Center (Elgin)	666205
DeVry University - Gurnee (Gurnee)	666535
DeVry University - Naperville Center (Naperville)	666207
DeVry University - Schaumburg Center (Schaumburg)	666208
DeVry University - Tinley Park Campus (Tinley Park)	666113

Indiana

DeVry University - Indianapolis (Indianapolis)	666556
DeVry University - Merrillville Center (Merrillville)	666209

Kansas

Highland Community College-Technical Center (Atchison)	5266

Kentucky

DeVry University - Louisville (Louisville)	666588
Lincoln College of Technology (Florence)	666447

Maryland

DeVry University - Bethesda Center (Bethesda)	666210
Peabody Institute of Johns Hopkins University (Baltimore)	2088

Michigan

DeVry University - Southfield (Southfield)	666557

Minnesota

DeVry University - Edina (Edina)	666558

Missouri

DeVry University - Kansas City Downtown Center (Kansas City)	666211
DeVry University - St. Louis (Saint Louis)	666214

	FICE/ID Number
Nevada	
DeVry University - Henderson (Henderson)	666560
New Jersey	
DeVry University - Paramus (Paramus)	666561
Immaculate Conception Seminary of Seton Hall University (South Orange)	2611
New York	
Bryant & Stratton College (Liverpool)	666115
Bryant & Stratton College (Orchard Park)	666460
Bryant & Stratton College (Getzville)	666114
Bryant & Stratton College (Rochester)	666116
DeVry College of New York (New York)	666979
Keller Graduate School of Management (New York)	666258
North Carolina	
DeVry University - Charlotte Center (Charlotte)	666215
DeVry University - Raleigh/Durham (Morrisville)	666562
Ohio	
Bryant & Stratton College (Eastlake)	666466
Bryant & Stratton College (Cleveland)	9343
DeVry University - Cincinnati (Cincinnati)	666563
DeVry University - Columbus North Center (Columbus)	666217
DeVry University - Dayton (Dayton)	666564
DeVry University - Seven Hills (Seven Hills)	666565
Kent State University College of Podiatric Medicine (Independence)	3088
Oklahoma	
DeVry University - Oklahoma City (Oklahoma City)	666566

	FICE/ID Number
Oregon	
DeVry University - Portland (Portland)	666567
Pennsylvania	
DeVry University - King of Prussia (King of Prussia)	666570
DeVry University - Philadelphia (Philadelphia)	666568
DeVry University - Pittsburgh (Pittsburgh)	666569
Tennessee	
DeVry University - Memphis (Memphis)	666571
DeVry University - Nashville (Nashville)	666589
Texas	
DeVry University - Austin (Austin)	666573
DeVry University - Fort Worth (Fort Worth)	666574
DeVry University - Richardson (Richardson)	666575
Utah	
DeVry University - Sandy (Sandy)	666576
Virginia	
DeVry University - Chesapeake (Chesapeake)	666577
DeVry University - Manassas (Manassas)	666222
Washington	
DeVry University - Bellevue Center (Bellevue)	666223
Wisconsin	
DeVry University - Milwaukee Center (Milwaukee)	666225
DeVry University - Waukesha Center (Waukesha)	666226

Universities, Colleges and Schools

by State*

*Includes the District of Columbia and, separately, U.S. Service Schools, American Samoa, Federated States of Micronesia, Guam, Marshall Islands, Northern Marianas, Palau, Puerto Rico, and Virgin Islands.

ALABAMA

Alabama Agricultural and Mechanical University (A)

4900 Meridian Street, Normal AL 35762-1357
County: Madison FICE Identification: 001002
Unit ID: 100654
Telephone: (256) 372-5230 Carnegie Class: Master's L
FAX Number: (256) 372-5244 Calendar System: Semester
URL: www.aamu.edu
Established: 1875 Annual Undergrad Tuition & Fees (In-State): $9,186
Enrollment: 4,945 Coed
Affiliation or Control: State IRS Status: 501(c)3
Highest Offering: Doctorate
Program: Liberal Arts And General; Teacher Preparatory; Professional
Accreditation: SC, AAFCS, CORE, CS, DIETD, ENG, ENGT, FOR, PLNG, SP, SW, TED

01 President ....Dr. Andrew HUGINE, JR.
03 Executive VP/COO ....Dr. Kevin A. ROLLE
05 Vice Pres Academic Affairs ....Dr. Daniel K. WIMS
10 Interim VP of Business & Finance ....Mr. Clayton GIBSON
26 Vice Pres Mktg/Commun/Advancement ....Ms. Wendy KOBLER
32 VP Student Affairs ....Dr. Jeffery BURGIN
41 Director of Athletics ....Mr. Bryan HICKS
46 Interim VP Inst Rsrch/Spons Pgms ....Dr. Vann NEWKIRK
22 AVP Budget & Planning ....Mr. Gregory JACKSON
21 Comptroller ....Mr. Norman JONES
15 Director Human Resources ....Ms. Cassandra TARVER-ROSS
18 Director Physical Facilities ....Mr. Walter ALEXANDER
06 Registrar ....Ms. Brenda K. WILLIAMS
30 Director of Development ....Mr. Archie TUCKER
84 AVP of Enrollment Management ....Ms. Venita KING
35 Director of Career Student Activities ....Ms. Jasmine BUXTON
37 Director of Financial Aid ....Mr. Darryl JACKSON
88 Director of Emergency Management ....Ms. Monica RAY
23 Dir Student Health & Counseling ....Dr. Jennifer PARKER-AYERS
36 Dir Career Development Services ....Ms. Yvette CLAYTON
09 Dir Institutional Research ....Dr. Thomas COAXUM
88 Director Marketing & PR ....Mr. Jerome SAINTJONES
39 Dir of Residential Housing ....Mr. Kenneth MADDOX
27 Chief Information Officer ....Vacant
19 Chief of Police ....Ms. Monica RAY
08 Dean Learn Resources Center ....Dr. Annie PAYTON
96 Director of Purchasing ....Mr. Jeffrey ROBINSON
58 Dean Graduate School ....Dr. Vann NEWKIRK
47 Dean College Agricultural ....Dr. Lloyd WALKER
53 Dean College of Education ....Dr. Curtis MARTIN
54 Dean College of Engineering ....Dr. Chance GLENN
50 Dean College of Business ....Dr. Amin SARKAR
88 Interim Dean University College ....Dr. Juarine STEWART

Alabama College of Osteopathic Medicine (B)

445 Health Sciences Blvd., Dothan AL 36303
County: Houston Identification: 667138
Telephone: (334) 699-2266 Carnegie Class: Not Classified
FAX Number: N/A Calendar System: Semester
URL: www.acomedu.org
Established: 2011 Annual Graduate Tuition & Fees: $40,945
Enrollment: N/A Coed
Affiliation or Control: Independent Non-Profit IRS Status: 501(c)3
Highest Offering: First Professional Degree; No Undergraduates
Program: Professional
Accreditation: @OSTEO

01 President ....Ronald S. OWEN
05 Dean/Senior Vice President ....Craig J. LENZ

Alabama Southern Community College (C)

PO Box 2000, Monroeville AL 36461-2000
County: Monroe FICE Identification: 001034
Unit ID: 101949
Telephone: (251) 575-3156 Carnegie Class: Assoc/Pub-R-S
FAX Number: (251) 575-5356 Calendar System: Semester
URL: www.ascc.edu
Established: 1965 Annual Undergrad Tuition & Fees (In-State): $4,808
Enrollment: 1,312 Coed
Affiliation or Control: State IRS Status: 501(c)3
Highest Offering: Associate Degree
Program: Occupational; 2-Year Principally Bachelor's Creditable
Accreditation: SC, ADNUR

01 President ....Dr. Reginald SYKES
10 VP Finance/Administrative Services ....Mr. Roger CHANDLER
05 Dean of Instruction ....Mrs. Ann CLANTON
08 Dean of Library Services ....Ms. LaShannon HOLLINGER
06 Registrar ....Ms. Jana HORTON
37 Director of Financial Aid ....Ms. Amy ROWELL
26 Director of Public Information ....Ms. Maconica SAWYER
18 Chief Facilities/Physical Plant ....Mr. Tom REED

Alabama State University (D)

915 S Jackson Street, Montgomery AL 36101-0271
County: Montgomery FICE Identification: 001005
Unit ID: 100724
Telephone: (334) 229-4200 Carnegie Class: Master's L
FAX Number: (334) 834-6861 Calendar System: Semester
URL: www.alasu.edu
Established: 1867 Annual Undergrad Tuition & Fees (In-State): $6,799
Enrollment: 5,816 Coed
Affiliation or Control: State IRS Status: 501(c)3
Highest Offering: Doctorate
Program: Liberal Arts And General; Teacher Preparatory
Accreditation: SC, ACBSP, ART, CACREP, CAHIIM, CORE, MUS, OT, PTA, SW, TED, THEA

01 Interim President ....Dr. William H. HARRIS
03 Chief Operating Ofcr/Exec Vice Pres ....Dr. John F. KNIGHT, JR.
05 Int Provost/Vice Pres Academic Affs ....Dr. Leon C. WILSON
10 Vice President Business & Finance ..Mr. Freddie C. GALLOT, JR.
90 Vice President Information Tech ....Dr. Kenley OBAS
26 Vice Pres Marketing/Communications ....Ms. Danielle KENNEDY
18 Int Vice Pres Buildings & Grounds ....Mr. Brian THORNTON
15 Vice Pres Human Resources ....Mrs. Carmen DOUGLAS
88 Assoc Exec Vice President ....Dr. Bernadette CHAPPLE
32 Assoc Provost/VP Student Affairs ....Dr. William P. HYTCHE
84 Assoc Provost/Dir Enrollment Mgmt ....Mrs. Cherise PETERS
20 Int Assoc Provost Academic Affairs ....Dr. Sharron HERRON-WILLIAMS
35 Asst Vice Pres Student Affairs ....Mr. Ricky DRAKE
21 Int Comt/Asst VP Business & Finance ....Mrs. Alondrea J. PRITCHETT
20 Asst VP Acad Advisement & Supp Svc ....Dr. Ronald BROWN
108 Dir Acad Planning & Evaluation ....Dr. Christine C. THOMAS
09 Int Director Institutional Research ....Dr. Yiyun JIE
88 Dir Quality Enhancement Plng ....Dr. Tanjula PETTY
08 Dean Libraries/Learning Resource ....Dr. Janice FRANKLIN
07 Director Admissions/Recruitment ....Mr. Freddie WILLIAMS, JR.
13 Interim IT Director ....Mr. Willie CARLISLE
37 Acting Financial Aid Director ....Ms. Patricia COTTON
36 Dir Placement Svcs/Cooperative Educ ....Ms. Ella TUCKER
26 Director University Relations ....Mr. Kenneth MULLINAX
50 Dean College Business Admin ....Dr. LaQuita BOOTH
89 Dean University College ....Dr. Evelyn HODGE
53 Int Dean College of Education ....Dr. Charlie GIBBONS
64 Dean Visual & Performing Arts ....Dr. Tommie T. STEWART
58 Dean Graduate Studies ....Dr. William PERSON
81 Dean College of Sci Math & Tech ....Dr. Cajetan AKAJUOBI
49 Inter Dean Liberal Arts/Social Sci ....Dr. Anthony T. ADAMS
76 Dean Colle Health Sciences ....Dr. Steven B. CHESBRO
51 Director Cmty Svcs/Cont Education ....Mr. Olan L. WESLEY
30 Assoc Vice President of Development ....Ms. Zillah FLUKER
29 Director Alumni Relations ....Mr. Cromwell HANDY
23 Director Student Health Services ....Ms. Gwendolyn MANN
19 Exec Dir Police & Campus Security ....Mr. Henry C. DAVIS
38 Dir Counseling & Development Svcs ....Mrs. Jessyca M. DARRINGTON
39 Acting Dir Housing/Residential Life ....Mr. Keith RAY
41 Acting Director of Athletics ....Mr. Melvin HINES
25 Director Grants & Contracts ....Mrs. Valerie T. PITTMAN
96 Director of Purchasing ....Ms. Ann SMITH

Amridge University (E)

1200 Taylor Road, Montgomery AL 36117-3553
County: Montgomery FICE Identification: 025034
Unit ID: 100690
Telephone: (800) 351-4040 Carnegie Class: Bac/A&S
FAX Number: (334) 387-3878 Calendar System: Semester
URL: www.amridgeuniversity.edu
Established: 1967 Annual Undergrad Tuition & Fees: $6,870
Enrollment: 712 Coed
Affiliation or Control: Churches Of Christ IRS Status: 501(c)3
Highest Offering: Doctorate
Program: Liberal Arts And General; Professional; Religious Emphasis
Accreditation: SC

01 President ....Dr. Michael C. TURNER
05 Academic Vice President/Dean ....Dr. Stanley PATTERSON
30 VP of Student Affairs ....Mrs. Laina T. COSTANZA
20 Asst VP of Academic Affairs ....Dr. Lee TAYLOR
06 Registry Officer ....Mrs. Elaine P. TARENCE
07 Admissions ....Mrs. Ora DAVIS
08 Director of Library ....Ms. Kay S. NEWMAN
10 Chief Business Officer ....Mrs. B. P. TURNER
88 Chief Accountant ....Mrs. Anita L. CROSBY
13 Director of Computing/Information ....Mr. Clayton F. SCHMIDT
37 Financial Aid Director ....Ms. Starr FAIN
42 Director of Church Relations ....Mr. Curtis SAMPLEY
88 Director of World Missions ....Mr. Demar ELAM
29 Director of Alumni Relations ....Vacant
91 Network and Web Admin ....Vacant
14 Director of Computer Center ....Mr. Jack TEMPLE
18 Chief Facilities/Physical Plant ....Mr. Robert SHIRLEY
24 Coordinator of Network Opers ....Mr. Thomas PATTERSON
38 Director of Student Counseling ....Vacant
26 Chief Public Relations Officer ....Mrs. Laina COSTANZA
42 Chaplain/Director Campus Ministry ....Dr. Leon F. ESTEP
44 Director Annual/Planned Giving ....Vacant
73 Dean of School of Theology ....Dr. Rodney CLOUD
50 Dean of Col of Business & Ldrshp ....Dr. Kenyetta MCCURTY
97 Dean of College of General Studies ....Dr. Roger SHEPHERD
88 Dean of Sch of Human Svcs ....Dr. Jerry MARTIN
90 Director Academic Computing ....Mr. Donnie E. CROSBY
15 Director Personnel Services ....Vacant
08 Head Librarian ....Mr. Terence SHERIDAN
35 Student Affairs Coordinator ....Mr. Carl BYRD

Athens State University (F)

300 N Beaty Street, Athens AL 35611-1902
County: Limestone FICE Identification: 001008
Unit ID: 100812
Telephone: (256) 233-8100 Carnegie Class: Bac/Diverse
FAX Number: (256) 216-3324 Calendar System: Semester
URL: www.athens.edu
Established: 1822 Annual Undergrad Tuition & Fees (In-State): $5,340
Enrollment: 3,415 Coed
Affiliation or Control: State IRS Status: 501(c)3
Highest Offering: Baccalaureate
Program: Liberal Arts And General; Teacher Preparatory
Accreditation: SC, ACBSP, TED

01 President ....Dr. Robert K. GLENN
05 Provost & VP for Academic Affs ....Dr. Ronald CROMWELL
20 Associate VP for Academic Affairs ....Ms. Belinda KRIGEL
20 Asst VP for Academic Affairs ....Dr. Jackie SMITH
32 Vice Pres for Enroll & Student Supp ....Vacant
35 Asst VP for Enrollment & Stdnt Svcs ....Ms. Sarah MCABEE
10 Vice President for Financial Aff ....Mr. Mike MCCOY
21 Associate Business Officer ....Mr. Evan THORNTON
26 Vice Pres for University Advance ....Mr. Richard MOULD
08 Director of Libraries ....Dr. Robert BURKHARDT
50 Dean College of Business ....Vacant
53 Dean College of Education ....Vacant
49 Dean College of Arts & Sciences ....Dr. Ronald FRITZE
36 Dir of Career Services ....Ms. Saralyn MITCHELL
37 Dir of Student Financial Services ....Vacant
06 Registrar ....Ms. Teresa SUIT
07 Director of Admissions & Records ....Ms. Necedah HENDERSON
35 Director of Student Activities ....Ms. Tena BULLINGTON
29 Director of Alumni Affairs/Ann Giv ....Ms. Trish DI LULLO
30 Director of Development ....Mr. Ronnie KNOX
88 Director of Printing & Public Rels ....Mr. Guy MCCLURE
09 Director of Institutional Research ....Ms. Sylvia CORREA
18 Director of Physical Plant ....Mr. Jerry BRADFORD
15 Director of Human Resources ....Ms. Suzanne SIMS
102 Director of Gov Corp & Found Rel ....Vacant
36 Director of Student Recruitment ....Ms. Deborah SCHAUS
51 Director of Ctr for Lifelong Lrng ....Dr. Diane SAUERS
88 Director of Transfer Advising Ctr ....Ms. Lisa PAYNE

Auburn University (G)

Auburn AL 36849
County: Lee FICE Identification: 001009
Unit ID: 100858
Telephone: (334) 844-4000 Carnegie Class: RU/H
FAX Number: N/A Calendar System: Semester
URL: www.auburn.edu
Established: 1856 Annual Undergrad Tuition & Fees (In-State): $9,852
Enrollment: 25,134 Coed
Affiliation or Control: State IRS Status: 501(c)3
Highest Offering: Doctorate
Program: Liberal Arts And General; Teacher Preparatory; Professional
Accreditation: SC, AAB, ART, #AUD, BUS, BUSA, CACREP, CIDA, CLPSY, CONST, COPSY, CORE, CS, DIETD, ENG, FOR, #JOUR, LSAR, MFCD, MUS, NURSE, PHAR, #PLNG, SP, SPAA, SW, TED, THEA, VET

01 President ....Dr. Jay GOGUE
03 Executive Vice President ....Dr. Donald L. LARGE
05 Provost/VP Acad Affairs ....Dr. Timothy R. BOOSINGER
29 Vice President Alumni Affairs ....Dr. Deborah L. SHAW
30 Vice President Development ....Ms. Jane DIFOLCO PARKER
32 Int Vice President Student Affairs ....Mr. Jon WAGGONER
46 Assoc Provost/VP Research ....Dr. John M. MASON
20 Associate Provost ....Dr. Emmett WINN
56 Assistant Vice President Outreach ....Dr. Royrickers COOK
84 Dean of Enrollment Services ....Dr. Charles W. ALDERMAN
11 Asst Vice Pres Auxiliary Services ....Mr. Robert C. RITENBAUGH
18 Assistant Vice Pres Facilities ....Mr. Daniel P. KING
15 Asst Vice Pres Human Resources ....Ms. Lynne B. HAMMOND
26 Acting Exec Dir Comm/Marketing ....Ms. Camille BARKLEY
28 Assoc Provost Multicultural Affs ....Dr. Overtoun JENDA
20 Assoc Provost Undergrad Studies ....Dr. Constance C. RELIHAN
21 Assoc Vice Pres Business & Finance ....Ms. Marcie SMITH
43 General Counsel ....Mr. Lee F. ARMSTRONG
101 Secretary to Board of Trustees ....Mr. C. Grant DAVIS
14 Exec Dir Information Technology ....Mr. Bliss BAILEY
37 Exec Dir Student Financial Services ....Mr. Michael C. REYNOLDS
96 Exec Dir Procurement & Payment Svcs ....Ms. Shawn C. ASMUTH
11 Director Public Affairs ....Mr. Brian C. KEETER
22 Director Affirmative Action/EEO ....Ms. Kelley G. TAYLOR
86 Director Governmental Affairs ....Ms. Sherri FULFORD
09 Director Inst Research & Assessment ....Dr. James A. CLARK
41 Director of Athletics ....Mr. John O. JACOBS, JR.
06 Registrar ....Ms. Laura Ann FOREST
40 Director University Bookstore ....Ms. Catherine LEE
88 Director JCS Museum of Art ....Dr. Marilyn LAUFER
56 Dir AL Cooperative Extension Syst ....Dr. Gary D. LEMME
39 Director Housing & Residence Life ....Ms. Kim L. TRUPP
10 Chief Business Officer ....Dr. Donald L. LARGE
36 Director Career Center ....Mrs. Nancy M. BERNARD
13 Associate Executive Director IT ..Dr. Nickolas A. BACKSCHEIDER
108 Assoc Dir for Assessment ....Dr. Iryna Y. JOHNSON
47 Dean of Agriculture ....Dr. William D. BATCHELOR
48 Dean Architecture/Design/Construct ....Dr. Vini NATHAN
49 Dean of Liberal Arts ....Dr. Anne-Katrin GRAMBERG
50 Dean of Business ....Dr. Bill HARDGRAVE
53 Dean of Education ....Dr. Betty Lou WHITFORD

54 Dean of Engineering .... Dr. Christopher B. ROBERTS
65 Dean of Forestry/Wildlife Sciences .... Dr. James P. SHEPARD
59 Dean of Human Sciences .... Dr. June M. HENTON
66 Dean of Nursing .... Dr. Gregg NEWSCHWANDER
67 Dean of Pharmacy .... Dr. R. Lee EVANS, JR.
81 Dean Sciences & Mathematics .... Dr. Nicholas J. GIORDANO
74 Dean Veterinary Medicine .... Dr. Calvin M. JOHNSON
58 Dean Graduate School .... Dr. George FLOWERS
08 Dean University Libraries .... Dr. Bonnie MACEWAN
92 Asst Provost & Dir Honors College ...... Dr. Melissa J. BAUMANN

Auburn University at Montgomery (A)

PO Box 244023, Montgomery AL 36124-4023
County: Montgomery FICE Identification: 008310
Unit ID: 100830
Telephone: (334) 244-3000 Carnegie Class: Master's L
FAX Number: (334) 244-3762 Calendar System: Semester
URL: www.aum.edu
Established: 1967 Annual Undergrad Tuition & Fees (In-State): $8,750
Enrollment: 4,981 Coed
Affiliation or Control: State IRS Status: 501(c)3
Highest Offering: Doctorate
Program: Teacher Preparatory; Professional
Accreditation: SC, BUS, BUSA, CACREP, MT, NURSE, SPAA, TED

01 Chancellor .... Dr. John G. VERES, III
05 Provost .... Dr. Joe KING
30 Vice Chancellor Advancement .... Ms. Carolyn GOLDEN
10 Vice Chancellor Finance .... Ms. Wanda MEADOWS
88 Vice Chanc University Outreach .... Dr. Katherine JACKSON
20 Assoc Provost Undergraduate Studies .... Dr. Joy CLARK
58 Assoc Provost Research/Grad Studies .... Dr. Matthew RAGLAND
28 Assoc Prov Diversity/MultiCultural .... Mr. Timothy SPRAGGINS
85 Asst Provost International Affairs .... Vacant
15 Senior Human Resources Director ... Ms. Jeanine BODDIE-LAVAN
18 Sr Director of Facilities .... Mr. Dorsey SMITH
19 Sr Director of Public Safety .... Mr. Ricky ADAMS
08 Dean of Library .... Ms. Barbara HIGHTOWER
07 Director of Admissions/Recruiting .... Mr. Olivier CHARLES
32 Vice Chancellor of Student Affairs .... Ms. Janice LYN
84 Assoc Prov of Enrollment Management .... Mr. Tyler PETERSON
41 Athletic Director .... Mr. Steve CROTZ
37 Sr Director of Financial Aid .... Mr. Anthony RICHEY
07 Director of Admissions Processing ..... Ms. Valerie S. CRAWFORD
39 Dir Housing & Residence Life .... Mr. Daryl MORRIS
27 Chief Information Officer .... Dr. Jeffery ANDERSON
35 Associate Dean of Student Affairs .... Dr. Yulanda TYRE
88 Dir Writing Across the Curriculum .... Vacant
19 Chief Campus Police .... Ms. Nell ROBINSON
13 Asst Chief Information Officer .... Ms. Carolyn D. RAWL
13 Asst Chief Information Officer .... Mr. Jon FISHER
21 Chief Accounting Officer .... Ms. Kim DECKER
36 Assoc Director Career Development .... Mr. Keith CULLEN
40 Director of Bookstore .... Mr. Jeffrey P. VINZANT
06 Registrar .... Vacant
25 Director of Sponsored Programs .... Ms. Fariba S. DERAVI
35 Director Student Affairs .... Mrs. Lakecia HARRIS
26 Communications Manager .... Mr. Frank MILES
85 Coord Intl Student Admissions .... Mr. Ron BLAESING
49 Dean of Liberal Arts .... Dr. Michael BURGER
50 Dean of Business .... Dr. Wanda Rhea INGRAM
53 Dean of Education .... Dr. Samuel FLYNT
66 Dean of Nursing .... Dr. Gregg NEWSCHWANDER
81 Dean of Sciences .... Dr. Karen STINE
51 Sr Director of Continuing Education .... Ms. Kathy GUNTER
06 Associate Registrar .... Ms. Holly BENSON

Bevill State Community College (B)

1411 Indiana Avenue, Jasper AL 35501
County: Walker FICE Identification: 005733
Unit ID: 102429
Telephone: (205) 387-0511 Carnegie Class: Assoc/Pub-R-M
FAX Number: (205) 387-5192 Calendar System: Semester
URL: www.bscc.edu
Established: 1965 Annual Undergrad Tuition & Fees (In-State): $4,230
Enrollment: 3,734 Coed
Affiliation or Control: State IRS Status: 501(c)3
Highest Offering: Associate Degree
Program: Occupational; 2-Year Principally Bachelor's Creditable
Accreditation: SC, ADNUR, EMT, PNUR, SURGT

01 President .... Dr. Anne MCNUTT
03 Executive Vice President .... Mr. Mark ELLARD
05 Interim Dean of Instruction .... Dr. Leslie CUMMINGS
32 Dean of Students .... Dr. Kim ENNIS

Birmingham-Southern College (C)

900 Arkadelphia Road, Birmingham AL 35254-0001
County: Jefferson FICE Identification: 001012
Unit ID: 100937
Telephone: (205) 226-4600 Carnegie Class: Bac/A&S
FAX Number: (205) 226-4627 Calendar System: 4/1/4
URL: www.bsc.edu
Established: 1856 Annual Undergrad Tuition & Fees: $29,600
Enrollment: 1,231 Coed
Affiliation or Control: United Methodist IRS Status: 501(c)3
Highest Offering: Baccalaureate
Program: Liberal Arts And General; Teacher Preparatory; Professional
Accreditation: SC, MUS, TED

01 President .... Gen. Charles C. KRULAK
05 Provost .... Dr. Mark SCHANTZ
10 Vice President of Finance .... Mr. Eli H. PHILLIPS
11 Vice President Administration .... Mr. Lane ESTES
30 VP Institutional Advancement .... Vacant
27 Vice President Communications .... Vacant
13 Vice Pres Information Technology .... Mr. Anthony HAMBEY
84 Vice Pres of Enrollment Management ... Ms. Kathleen ROSSMANN
32 Vice Pres Student Development .... Dr. David EBERHARDT
07 Assoc Vice President of Admissions .... Ms. Sheri SALMON
04 Assistant to the President .... Mrs. Terri L. HICKS
20 Associate Provost .... Dr. Susan HAGEN
20 Assistant Provost .... Ms. Martha A. STEVENSON
06 Dean of Records .... Mr. Danny K. BROOKS
42 Chaplain .... Rev. Jack HINNEN
29 Director of Alumni Affairs .... Ms. Lisa HARRISON
23 Director of Health Services .... Ms. Yvette SPENCER
04 Exec Asst to the President .... Ms. Katie GLENN
08 Director of the Library .... Ms. Charlotte FORD
18 Director of Facilities & Events .... Ms. Anne CURRY
37 Director of Financial Aid .... Mr. Brian QUISENBERRY
15 Director of Human Resources .... Ms. Susan E. KINNEY
26 Director of Church Relations .... Ms. Laura SISSON
38 Director Personal Counseling .... Ms. Sara HOOVER
41 Athletic Director .... Mr. Joe DEAN, JR.
19 Chief of Campus Police .... Mr. Randy YOUNGBLOOD
36 Director of Career Counseling .... Mr. Michael LEBEAU
30 Director Advancement Services .... Mr. Jeff SHERRELL
88 Dir of Interim & Contract Learning .... Dr. Katy LEONARD
28 Director of Multi-Cultural Affairs .... Ms. Erica BROWN
68 Dir Physical Fitness & Recreation .... Mr. Mike ROBINSON
88 Director of Leadership Studies .... Mr. Kent ANDERSEN
88 Director of Service Learning .... Ms. Kristin HARPER
88 Sports Information Director .... Ms. Sarah ERRECA
27 Communications Specialist .... Ms. Patricia COLE
27 Assoc Dir of Comm Publications .... Ms. Tracy THOMAS
88 Assc Dir Communications-New Media .... Mr. Mike HAMILTON
88 Assoc Dir of International Programs .... Ms. Anne LEDVINA
88 Manager of Printing Services .... Mr. Jerome DAVIS
40 Manager of the Bookstore .... Mr. William ALEXANDER
96 Coordinator of Purchasing .... Ms. Cassandra BROWN
100 Chief of Staff .... Mr. Russ APPLETON
27 Director of Communications .... Mrs. Hannah WOLFSON
108 Director of Inst Effective/Assess .... Dr. Noreen GAUBATZ

Bishop State Community College (D)

351 N Broad Street, Mobile AL 36603-5898
County: Mobile FICE Identification: 001030
Unit ID: 102030
Telephone: (251) 405-7000 Carnegie Class: Assoc/Pub-U-MC
FAX Number: (251) 438-3249 Calendar System: Semester
URL: www.bishop.edu
Established: 1965 Annual Undergrad Tuition & Fees (In-State): $3,312
Enrollment: 3,748 Coed
Affiliation or Control: State IRS Status: 501(c)3
Highest Offering: Associate Degree
Program: Occupational; 2-Year Principally Bachelor's Creditable
Accreditation: SC, ACBSP, ACFEI, ADNUR, CAHIIM, FUSER, PNUR, PTAA

01 President .... Dr. James LOWE, JR.
05 Dean of Instructional Services .... Dr. Latitia MCCANE
12 Director of Carver Campus .... Dr. Betty LESLIE
12 Director of Central Campus .... Mrs. Madeline STOKES
05 Dean of Technical School .... Vacant
32 Dean of Students .... Dr. Terry HAZZARD
10 Dean of Business/Finance .... Mrs. Bonita ALLEN
35 Assistant to the Dean of Students .... Mrs. Wanda DANIELS
09 Coordinator Institutional Planning .... Ms. Aundrea WHEELER-DUNNER
15 Director of Human Resources .... Mrs. Marcella SIMS
18 Director of Physical Plant .... Mr. Lorenzo GRAYSON
26 Director of Public Relations .... Mr. Herb JORDAN
12 SW Campus Dir/Tech Faculty Spvr .... Mr. Roderick MCSWAIN
103 Coordinator Workforce Development .... Mr. Jim KELLEN
37 Mgr Student Fin Aid/Veterans Svcs .... Dr. Samuel CHUKS

Brown Mackie College (E)

105 Vulcan Road, Birmingham AL 35209
Telephone: (205) 909-1500 Identification: 770625
Accreditation: ACICS, OTA, SURTEC

† Main campus is The Art Institute of Phoenix in Phoenix, AZ.

Calhoun Community College (F)

PO Box 2216, Decatur AL 35609-2216
County: Limestone FICE Identification: 001013
Unit ID: 101514
Telephone: (256) 306-2500 Carnegie Class: Assoc/Pub-R-L
FAX Number: (256) 306-2877 Calendar System: Semester
URL: www.calhoun.edu
Established: 1963 Annual Undergrad Tuition & Fees (In-State): $3,312
Enrollment: 11,177 Coed
Affiliation or Control: State IRS Status: 501(c)3
Highest Offering: Associate Degree
Program: Occupational; 2-Year Principally Bachelor's Creditable
Accreditation: SC, ACBSP, ADNUR, DA, EMT, MLTAD, PNUR, PTAA, SURGT

01 President .... Dr. Marilyn C. BECK
05 Vice Pres Instruction/Student Succ .... Ms. Alicia TAYLOR
32 Dean of Student Affairs .... Dr. Kermit CARTER
10 Vice Pres for Finance & Admin Svcs .... Mr. James B. HELMS
07 Dir Admissions & Records/Registrar .... Ms. Pauletta BURNS
08 Head Librarian .... Ms. Lucinda BEDDOW
13 Int Director Information Systems .... Mr. Nathan TYLER
102 Executive Director Foundation .... Ms. Terri BRYSON
12 Dean Research Park Campus .... Ms. Terri BRYSON
55 Director Evening Program .... Dr. Vinetta WESLEY
29 Director of Alumni Relations .. Ms. Janet KINCHERLOW-MARTIN
18 Director of Physical Plant .... Mr. Bruce CAUSEY
09 Dean Planning/Research & Grants .... Dr. Debra HENDERSHOT
103 Dean Workforce Development .... Ms. Bethany SHOCKNEY
84 Coord Enrollment Management .... Ms. Samantha NELSON
26 Chief Public Relations Officer .... Ms. Janet KINCHERLOW-MARTIN
76 Dean Health Sciences .... Mr. Bret MCGILL
81 Dean Mathematics & Natural Science .... Mr. Jimmy DUKE
79 Dean Humanities & Social Sciences .... Dr. Donna ESTILL

Central Alabama Community College (G)

1675 Cherokee Road, Alexander City AL 35010
County: Tallapoosa FICE Identification: 001007
Unit ID: 100760
Telephone: (256) 234-6346 Carnegie Class: Assoc/Pub-R-M
FAX Number: (256) 234-0384 Calendar System: Semester
URL: www.cacc.edu
Established: 1963 Annual Undergrad Tuition & Fees (In-State): $3,780
Enrollment: 2,512 Coed
Affiliation or Control: State IRS Status: 501(c)3
Highest Offering: Associate Degree
Program: Occupational; 2-Year Principally Bachelor's Creditable
Accreditation: SC, ADNUR

01 Acting President .... Dr. Susan BORROW
03 Executive Vice President .... Mr. Richard HAWKSHEAD
05 Provost/CAO/Dean of Instruction .... Dr. Amelia PEARSON
32 Provost/Dean of Students .... Ms. Amanda HARKINS
35 Associate Dean of Student Services .... Ms. Glenda BLAND
09 Asc Dean Instruction/Instl Effectiv .... Ms. Sherie FLEMING
66 Director of Nursing .... Ms. Melanie BOLTON
08 Librarian .... Ms. Denita OLIVER
06 Registrar .... Ms. Janice STEPHENS
26 Chief Public Relations Officer .... Mr. Brett PRITCHARD
37 Director Student Financial Aid .... Ms. Cindy ENTREKIN
30 Advancement Officer .... Mr. Michael LOVETT

Chattahoochee Valley Community College (H)

2602 College Drive, Phenix City AL 36869-7960
County: Russell FICE Identification: 012182
Unit ID: 101028
Telephone: (334) 291-4900 Carnegie Class: Assoc/Pub-R-M
FAX Number: (334) 291-4944 Calendar System: Semester
URL: www.cv.edu
Established: 1973 Annual Undergrad Tuition & Fees (In-State): $5,112
Enrollment: 1,733 Coed
Affiliation or Control: State IRS Status: 501(c)3
Highest Offering: Associate Degree
Program: Occupational; 2-Year Principally Bachelor's Creditable
Accreditation: SC, ADNUR, PNUR

01 President .... Dr. Donald G. CANNON
05 Vice President/Dean of the College .... Dr. David HODGE
05 Dean of Instruction .... Vacant
32 Dean of Student Services .... Dr. Joy HAMM
103 Assoc Dean of Workforce Development .... Dr. Robert PIERCE
81 Chair of Mathematics & Science .... Mr. Earl COOK
57 Chair of Humanities .... Mr. Andy SCALES
76 Chair of Health Sciences .... Ms. Resa LORD
88 Program Dir Public Safety Academy .... Mr. Kenneth HARRISON
50 Chair Business & Information Tech .... Ms. Debra PLOTTS
08 Director Learning Resources Center .... Ms. Xueying CHEN
37 Director of Financial Aid .... Mrs. Joan WATERS
18 Director Facilities & Maintenance .... Mr. Johann WELLS
30 Dean of Advancement/Inst Effect .... Dr. Joree JONES
26 Director of Marketing .... Vacant
41 Director of Athletics .... Mr. Adam THOMAS
38 Director of Counseling & Advising .... Ms. Cynthia FLOYD
27 Director of Information Systems .... Mr. Jody NOLES
88 Director of Student Development .... Mrs. Vickie WILLIAMS
51 Director of Adult Education .... Ms. Darlene THOMPSON
15 Director of Human Resources .... Ms. Debbie BOONE
44 Director of Development .... Ms. Karen KELLY
10 Chief Financial Officer .... Ms. Brenda KELLEY
55 Evening Coordinator .... Mr. Reggie GORDY
07 Director of Admissions/Registrar .... Ms. Sanquita ALEXANDER

Columbia Southern University (I)

21982 University Lane, Orange Beach AL 36561-3845
County: Baldwin FICE Identification: 041215
Unit ID: 450933
Telephone: (251) 981-3771 Carnegie Class: Master's L
FAX Number: (251) 981-3815 Calendar System: Other
URL: www.columbiasouthern.edu
Established: 1993 Annual Undergrad Tuition & Fees: $4,895
Enrollment: 19,933 Coed
Affiliation or Control: Proprietary IRS Status: Proprietary
Highest Offering: Doctorate

Program: Occupational; 2-Year Principally Bachelor's Creditable; Liberal Arts And General; Professional; Business Emphasis
Accreditation: DETC

01 President ..... Mr. Robert G. MAYES, JR.
03 Provost ..... Dr. Terry DIXON
09 VP IR/Ext Compliance/Accreditation ..... Dr. Karen J. SMITH
27 VP of Marketing and Outreach ..... Mr. Billy HAYES
13 Chief Information Officer ..... Mr. Ken STYRON
88 VP of Business Development ..... Mr. Rick COOPER
07 Associate VP of Admissions ..... Ms. Kathy COLE
10 Associate VP of Business Affairs ..... Mr. Pat TROUP
24 Dean of Instructional Design ..... Dr. Jon CRISPIN
16 Associate VP of Human Resources ..... Ms. Sue BUTTS
05 Dean of Academic Services ..... Mr. Elwin JONES
97 Dean of Undergraduate Programs ..... Ms. Nichole GOTSCHALL
32 Dean of Students ..... Mr. F. Poche WAGUESPACK
58 Dean of Graduate Programs ..... Dr. Mark PANTALEO
09 Director of Institutional Research ..... Dr. Katherine ODOM
06 Registrar ..... Ms. Rachel FARRIS
37 Director of Financial Aid ..... Mr. Aaron COLLINS
45 Director of Quality Assurance ..... Ms. Tina SHIPP
08 Director of Learning Resources ..... Ms. Marsha HINNEN
108 Director of Outcomes Assessment ..... Dr. Michael DANIEL
26 Director of Marketing ..... Mr. Beau VIGNES

Concordia College Alabama (A)

1712 Broad Street, Selma AL 36701
County: Dallas FICE Identification: 010554
Unit ID: 101073
Telephone: (334) 874-5700 Carnegie Class: Bac/Diverse
FAX Number: (334) 874-5755 Calendar System: Semester
URL: www.ccal.edu
Established: 1922 Annual Undergrad Tuition & Fees: $8,090
Enrollment: 611 Coed
Affiliation or Control: Lutheran Church - Missouri Synod
IRS Status: 501(c)3
Highest Offering: Baccalaureate
Program: 2-Year Principally Bachelor's Creditable; Liberal Arts And General; Teacher Preparatory; Business Emphasis
Accreditation: SC

01 President/Chief Executive Officer ..... Dr. Tilahun M. MENDEDO
05 Vice Pres Academic Affs ..... Dr. Cheryl WASHINGTON
32 VP of Student Services ..... Dr. Eric JACKSON
30 Int VP Advancement and Development ..... Mr. Daniel JENKINS
10 Chief Financial Officer ..... Mr. Dexter JACKSON
37 Director Financial Aid ..... Mrs. Tharsteen BRIDGES
09 Effectiveness/Research and Plng ..... Mrs. Ruthie J. ORSBORN
64 Director of Music ..... Mr. Bobby MCKENZIE
08 Librarian ..... Mr. Scott WHITING
06 Registrar ..... Mrs. Chinester GRAYSON
29 Director Alumni Affairs/Development ..... Mrs. Minnie MCMILLAN
26 Public Relations ..... Vacant
36 Dir Student Placement/Counseling ..... Ms. Sadie JARETT
15 Director of Human Respources ..... Ms. Xaviere J. IRBY
27 Chief Information Officer ..... Mr. Wayne GREEN
41 Director of Athletics ..... Mr. Donald LEE
85 Director of International Students ..... Mr. Katiso ALEMU
42 Chaplain ..... Rev. Lavaugn WIGGINS
21 Controller ..... Mr. Aron EZAZ
07 Dean of Enrollment ..... Mr. Larry JONES

*Education Corporation of America (B)

3660 Grandview Parkway Suite 300,
Birmingham AL 35243
County: Jefferson Identification: 666006
Telephone: (205) 329-7900 Carnegie Class: N/A
FAX Number: (205) 329-7906
URL: www.ecacolleges.com

00 Chief Executive Officer ..... Mr. Tom A. MOORE, JR.
01 President & Chief Operating Officer ..... Mrs. Deborah LENART
05 Exec VP/Chf Compl Ofcr/Gen Counsel ..... Mr. Roger L. SWARTZWELDER
26 Exec VP/Chief Marketing Officer ..... Mr. Charles S. TRIERWEILER
10 Exec VP/Chief Financial Officer ..... Mr. Christopher BOEHM
88 Exec VP Campus Support ..... Mr. William R. OWENS
16 Exec VP/Human Resource & People Dev ..... Mr. Michael C. WILLIAMS
05 Exec VP Academic Affairs ..... Dr. Sara LAWHORNE
20 SVP Academic Compliance Curriculum ..... Ms. Judy E. LIMA
36 SVP Career Services ..... Mr. Scot STAPLETON
37 SVP Student Finance ..... Ms. Kathy CHEATHAM
21 SVP Financial Ops & Controller ..... Mr. Ryan BREWER
26 SVP of Marketing ..... Mr. Jason MANN
18 SVP Facilities & Interior Design ..... Ms. Celeste PRESTENBACH
84 SVP of Student Enrollment ..... Mr. Dean MAHAFFEY
88 Regional VP & Operations Mgr ..... Mr. Wayne S. BANKS, III
88 Regional VP & Operations Mgr ..... Mr. Jack CLARK
88 Regional VP & Operations Mgr ..... Mr. Michael LARGENT

*Virginia College (C)

488 Palisades Boulevard, Birmingham AL 35209
County: Jefferson FICE Identification: 030106
Unit ID: 420307
Telephone: (205) 802-1200 Carnegie Class: Master's S
FAX Number: (205) 271-8225 Calendar System: Quarter
URL: www.vc.edu
Established: 1993 Annual Undergrad Tuition & Fees: $14,000
Enrollment: 1,900 Coed
Affiliation or Control: Proprietary IRS Status: Proprietary
Highest Offering: Master's
Program: Occupational; 2-Year Principally Bachelor's Creditable
Accreditation: ACICS, ACFEI, CIDA, COARC, DMS, SURGT

02 Campus President ..... Mr. Chris MOORE
05 VP Academics ..... Vacant
07 Vice President of Enrollment ..... Mr. Karl S. COOPER
20 Associate Academic Dean ..... Ms. Adriane M. WHEAT

*Virginia College (D)

2021 Drake Avenue SW, Huntsville AL 35801
Telephone: (256) 533-7387 Identification: 666400
Accreditation: ACICS, MAAB

† Main campus is Virginia College in Birmingham, AL.

*Virginia College (E)

3725 Airport Boulevard, Suite 165, Mobile AL 36608
Telephone: (251) 343-7227 Identification: 666069
Accreditation: ACICS, MAAB, SURGT

† Main campus is Virginia College in Birmingham, AL.

*Virginia College (F)

6200 Atlanta Highway, Montgomery AL 36117-2802
Telephone: (334) 277-3390 Identification: 666408
Accreditation: ACICS, MAAB, SURGT

† Main campus is Virginia College in Birmingham, AL.

Enterprise State Community College (G)

PO Box 1300, Enterprise AL 36331-1300
County: Coffee FICE Identification: 001015
Unit ID: 101143
Telephone: (334) 347-2623 Carnegie Class: Assoc/Pub-R-M
FAX Number: (334) 393-6223 Calendar System: Semester
URL: www.escc.edu
Established: 1963 Annual Undergrad Tuition & Fees (In-State): $4,050
Enrollment: 2,487 Coed
Affiliation or Control: State IRS Status: 501(c)3
Highest Offering: Associate Degree
Program: Occupational; 2-Year Principally Bachelor's Creditable
Accreditation: SC

01 President ..... Dr. Nancy W. CHANDLER
05 Dean of Instruction ..... Dr. Matthew HUGHES
32 Dean of Students ..... Dr. Jeffrey COATS
10 Dean Administration & Finance ..... Ms. Alonzetta LANDRUM-SIMS
45 Dn Plng/Info Svcs/Inst Effective ..... Ms. Veronica CROCK
35 Associate Dean of Students ..... Mr. Kevin AMMONS
26 Dir Marketing & Media Relations ..... Vacant
37 Director Student Financial Aid ..... Dr. Henry L. QUISENBERRY, JR.
13 Director Information Technology ..... Vacant
55 Director Evening Division ..... Mr. Carl HOLBROOK
15 Director Personnel Services ..... Vacant
06 Registrar ..... Mr. Kevin AMMONS

Faulkner University (H)

5345 Atlanta Highway, Montgomery AL 36109-3398
County: Montgomery FICE Identification: 001003
Unit ID: 101189
Telephone: (334) 272-5820 Carnegie Class: Bac/Diverse
FAX Number: (334) 386-7107 Calendar System: Semester
URL: www.faulkner.edu
Established: 1942 Annual Undergrad Tuition & Fees: $18,230
Enrollment: 3,327 Coed
Affiliation or Control: Churches Of Christ IRS Status: 501(c)3
Highest Offering: Doctorate
Program: Liberal Arts And General; Teacher Preparatory; Professional
Accreditation: SC, LAW, TED

01 President ..... Dr. Billy D. HILYER
05 Vice President Academic Affairs ..... Dr. Marci JOHNS
10 Vice President Financial Services ..... Mrs. Wilma D. PHILLIPS
30 Vice President for Advancement ..... Dr. Ben BRUCE
18 Vice Pres Facilities & Risk Mgmt ..... Mr. Jim SPRATLIN
32 Vice President Student Services ..... Dr. Jean-Noel THOMPSON
84 Vice President Enrollment ..... Mr. Keith MOCK
61 Dean Jones School of Law ..... Mr. Charles NELSON
49 Dean College Arts & Sciences ..... Dr. Dave RAMPERSAD
50 Dean College Business/Exec Educ ..... Dr. Dave KHADANGA
73 Dean College of Biblical Studies ..... Dr. Scott GLEAVES
53 Dean College of Education ..... Dr. Tammy BROWN
88 Assoc Dean Acad/Dir of Law Library ..... Mr. Tim CHINARIS
43 General Counsel/Assoc Dean Business ..... Mr. Gerald JONES
21 Associate Vice President of Finance ..... Mr. Jamie HORN
88 Assoc Vice President Development ..... Mr. Billy CAMP
88 Assoc Vice Pres Exec & Prof Enroll ..... Mr. Mark HUNT
16 Asst VP Human Resources/Diversity ..... Mrs. Renee DAVIS
06 Registrar ..... Mr. Don REYNOLDS
35 Dean of Students ..... Mr. Faires AUSTIN
37 Director Student Financial Aid ..... Mr. Buddy JACKSON
12 Director Mobile Center ..... Mrs. Diane NEWELL
12 Director Birmingham Center ..... Mr. Tim PARKER
12 Director Huntsville Center ..... Ms. Barbara GAMBLE
41 Athletic Director ..... Mr. Brent BARKER
08 Director of Libraries ..... Mrs. Barbara KELLY
09 Director of Institutional Research ..... Dr. Brenda TURNER
104 Director of International Studies ..... Dr. Ed HICKS
26 Director of Public Relations ..... Mr. Dave HOGAN
07 Director of Admissions ..... Mr. Neil SCOTT
88 Director Student Success ..... Mrs. Michelle OTWELL
29 Director of Alumni Relations ..... Mr. Adam DONALDSON
88 Director Quality Enhancement Plng ..... Dr. Cindy WALKER
92 Director of Honors Program ..... Dr. Matthew SOKOLOSKI
36 Director Career Services ..... Mrs. Marie OTTINGER
38 Counselor ..... Mrs. Michelle BOND
04 Exec Assistant to the President ..... Mrs. Darlene GREGORY

Fortis College (I)

3590 Pleasant Valley Road, Mobile AL 36609
County: Mobile FICE Identification: 023410
Unit ID: 371052
Telephone: (251) 344-1203 Carnegie Class: Assoc/PrivFP
FAX Number: (251) 344-1299 Calendar System: Other
URL: www.fortiscollege.edu
Established: 1978 Annual Undergrad Tuition & Fees: N/A
Enrollment: 309 Coed
Affiliation or Control: Proprietary IRS Status: Proprietary
Highest Offering: Associate Degree
Program: Occupational; 2-Year Principally Bachelor's Creditable; Technical Emphasis
Accreditation: ABHES, DA

01 Campus President ..... Joseph DALTO

Fortis College-Montgomery (Atlanta Highway) (J)

3736 Atlanta Highway, Montgomery AL 36109
Telephone: (334) 272-3857 Identification: 770511
Accreditation: ABHES

† Main campus is Fortis College in Mobile, AL.

Fortis College-Montgomery (Eastdale Circle) (K)

3470 Eastdale Circle, Montgomery AL 36117
Telephone: (334) 244-1827 Identification: 770512
Accreditation: ABHES

† Main campus is Fortis College in Mobile, AL.

Fortis Institute (L)

100 London Parkway Suite 150, Birmingham AL 35211
Telephone: (205) 940-7800 Identification: 666683
Accreditation: ACICS, DH

† Main campus is Fortis Institute in Erie, PA.

Gadsden State Community College (M)

1001 Geo Wallace Drive, PO Box 227,
Gadsden AL 35902-0227
County: Etowah FICE Identification: 001017
Unit ID: 101240
Telephone: (256) 549-8200 Carnegie Class: Assoc/Pub-R-L
FAX Number: (256) 549-8288 Calendar System: Semester
URL: www.gadsdenstate.edu
Established: 1925 Annual Undergrad Tuition & Fees (In-State): $3,900
Enrollment: 5,882 Coed
Affiliation or Control: State IRS Status: 501(c)3
Highest Offering: Associate Degree
Program: Occupational; 2-Year Principally Bachelor's Creditable
Accreditation: SC, ACBSP, ADNUR, EMT, MLTAD, PNUR, RAD

01 Interim President ..... Dr. William BLOW
03 Vice President ..... Dr. Valerie RICHARDSON
05 Dean of Instructional Services ..... Dr. Jim L. JOLLY
10 Dean Financial/Administrative Svcs ..... Dr. James R. PRUCNAL
72 Dean Tech Educ/Workforce Develop ..... Mr. Tim GREEN
30 Assoc Dean Instnl Advance/Cmty Svc ..... Ms. Pam JOHNSON
20 Assoc Dean Instructional Services ..... Dr. Karen BLYTHE-SMITH
56 Assoc Dean for Distance Education ..... Ms. Sara POOVEY
32 Asc Dean Stdnt Svcs/Instl Effective ..... Dr. Teresa C. RHEA
26 Director Public Relations/Marketing ..... Ms. Kay S. FOSTER
19 Director Physical Plant ..... Mr. Stewart DAVIS
21 Director of Financial Services ..... Ms. Jacqueline CLARK
28 Director of Diversity & Compliance ..... Ms. Michele BRADFORD
13 Director of Computer Services ..... Mr. Jeff W. GREEN
16 Director Human Resources ..... Ms. Kim S. COBB
41 Athletic Director ..... Mr. Mike CANCILLA
38 Assoc Dean Stdnt Svcs & Counse Svcs ..... Dr. Cheryl C. VICKERS
51 Director Adult Education ..... Mr. Johnny BAKER
37 Director of Financial Aid ..... Ms. Kelly D'EATH
06 Assistant to President/Registrar ..... Mrs. Jennie P. DOBSON

George C. Wallace Community College - Dothan (N)

1141 Wallace Drive, Dothan AL 36303-9234
County: Dale FICE Identification: 001018
Unit ID: 101286
Telephone: (334) 983-3521 Carnegie Class: Assoc/Pub-R-M
FAX Number: (334) 983-6066 Calendar System: Semester

URL: www.wallace.edu
Established: 1947 Annual Undergrad Tuition & Fees (In-State): $3,120
Enrollment: 4,583 Coed
Affiliation or Control: State IRS Status: 501(c)3
Highest Offering: Associate Degree
Program: Occupational; 2-Year Principally Bachelor's Creditable; Business Emphasis
Accreditation: SC, ADNUR, COARC, EMT, MAC, PNUR, PTAA, RAD

01 President ....Dr. Linda C. YOUNG
32 Dean of Student Affs/Sparks Campus .Ms. Jacqueline B. SCREWS
05 Dean of Instructional Affairs ....Mr. Tony HOLLAND
10 Dean of Business Affairs ....Mr. Lynn BELL
07 Director Enroll Svcs/Registrar ....Mr. Keith SAULSBERRY
08 Dir Learning Resources Ctrs System ....Mr. A. P. HOFFMAN
37 Director of Financial Aid ....Ms. Erma PERRY
14 AS-400 Progm/Sys Admin ....Mr. Gordon FREE
15 Director of Human Resources ....Ms. Brooke STRICKLAND
09 Dir Institutional Effectiveness ....Mr. Frank BAREFIELD
40 Bookstore Manager ....Mr. Jeremy JAMES
38 Director Student Counseling ....Ms. Jean DAGOSTIN
21 Director of Accounting & Finance ....Ms. Kay GAMBLE
26 Dir Public Relations & Marketing ....Ms. Barbara THOMPSON
30 Dean Institutional Svcs/Com Dev ....Dr. Ashli BOUTWELL

George Corley Wallace State Community College - Selma (A)

PO Box 2530, 3000 Earl Goodwin Pkwy, Selma AL 36702-2530
County: Dallas FICE Identification: 005699
Unit ID: 101301
Telephone: (334) 876-9227 Carnegie Class: Assoc/Pub-R-M
FAX Number: (334) 876-9250 Calendar System: Semester
URL: www.wccs.edu
Established: 1963 Annual Undergrad Tuition & Fees (In-State): $3,840
Enrollment: 1,790 Coed
Affiliation or Control: State IRS Status: 501(c)3
Highest Offering: Associate Degree
Program: Occupational; 2-Year Principally Bachelor's Creditable
Accreditation: SC, ADNUR, PNUR

01 President ....Dr. James M. MITCHELL
05 Vice President for Instruction ....Dr. Robert MCCONNELL
20 Instructional Administrator ....Mr. Raji GOURDINE
10 Dean of Business & Finance ....Mrs. Jacqueline SMITH
32 Dean of Students/Exec to President ....Mrs. Donitha GRIFFIN
08 Librarian ....Ms. Minnie CARSTARPHEN
66 Director Associate Degree Nursing ....Ms. Becky CASEY
37 Director of Financial Aid/Cmty Educ ....Mrs. Chenetta LEE
38 Counselor College Division ....Mr. Lonzy CLIFTON
09 Director of Institutional Research ....Mrs. Earlene LARKIN
26 Coord College Rels/Instl Research ....Mrs. Rita LETT
19 Director Security/Safety ....Mr. Ray MOORE
41 Athletic Director ....Mr. Marcus HANNAH
18 Act Chief Facilities/Physical Plant ....Mr. Jimmie GOLDSBY
28 Director of Diversity ....Vacant
40 Bookstore Manager ....Ms. Chezra HALL
15 Human Resource Generalist ....Mrs. Daphne CHARLEY

Heritage Christian University (B)

PO Box HCU, Florence AL 35630-0050
County: Lauderdale FICE Identification: 021997
Unit ID: 101453
Telephone: (256) 766-6610 Carnegie Class: Spec/Faith
FAX Number: N/A Calendar System: Semester
URL: www.hcu.edu
Established: 1971 Annual Undergrad Tuition & Fees: $12,030
Enrollment: 85 Coed
Affiliation or Control: Churches Of Christ IRS Status: 501(c)3
Highest Offering: Master's
Program: Religious Emphasis
Accreditation: BI

01 President ....Mr. Dennis H. JONES
05 Vice President of Academic Affairs ....Dr. Bill BAGENTS
10 VP Business/Finance/Operations ....Mr. Freddie P. MOON
30 Vice Pres University ....Mr. Philip GOAD
32 Dean of Students ....Mr. Brad MCKINNON
33 Dean of Men ....Dr. Ed GALLAGHER
34 Dean of Women ....Dr. Rosemary SNODGRASS
58 Director of Graduate Studies ....Dr. Jeremy BARRIER
06 Registrar ....Mrs. Charlotte ORR
08 Librarian ....Miss Jamie S. COX
42 Director of Christian Service ....Mr. Brad MCKINNON
84 Dir Enrollment Svcs/Stdnt Fin Aid ....Mr. Jim COLLINS

Herzing University (C)

280 W Valley Avenue, Birmingham AL 35209-4816
Telephone: (205) 916-2800 FICE Identification: 010193
Accreditation: &NH

† Main campus is Herzing University in Madison, WI.

Huntingdon College (D)

1500 East Fairview Avenue, Montgomery AL 36106-2148
County: Montgomery FICE Identification: 001019
Unit ID: 101435
Telephone: (334) 833-4222 Carnegie Class: Bac/Diverse
FAX Number: (334) 833-4486 Calendar System: Semester
URL: www.huntingdon.edu
Established: 1854 Annual Undergrad Tuition & Fees: $23,500
Enrollment: 1,118 Coed
Affiliation or Control: United Methodist IRS Status: 501(c)3
Highest Offering: Baccalaureate
Program: Liberal Arts And General
Accreditation: SC, MUS

01 President ....Rev. J. Cameron WEST
10 Treasurer & Sr VP for Plng & Admin ....Mr. Jay A. DORMAN
30 VP for College & Alumni Relations ....Mr. Anthony J. LEIGH
84 VP for Enrollment Management ....Ms. Laura H. DUNCAN
05 Provost & Dean of the College ....Dr. Sidney J. STUBBS
32 VP Student Life & Dean of Students .Dr. Frank R. PARSONS, JR.
20 Associate Provost ....Dr. Frank W. BUCKNER, JR.
108 Associate Provost for Assessment ....Dr. Cinzia BALIT-MOUSSALLI
50 Dean School for Bus & Prof Stds ....Dr. Samir R. MOUSSALLI
88 Dir Adult Degree Completion Program ....Dr. Renee CULVERHOUSE
27 Assoc VP for Comm and Marketing ....Ms. Suellen S. OFE
35 Coordinator of Student Activities ....Ms. Sara Beth TERRY
06 Registrar ....Ms. Maryann M. BECK
13 Dir of Institutional Technology ....Mr. Frank O. GRIER
36 Dir of the Center for Career & Voc ....Ms. Francis H. TAYLOR
37 Dir Student Financial Services ....Mr. Tommy G. DISMUKES, JR.
37 Dir of Student Financial Aid ....Ms. Belinda G. DUETT
18 Director of Facilities and Grounds ....Mr. T. Michael DUNN
40 Manager Follett Bookstore ....Ms. Pam BELL
23 Director of Student Health ....Ms. Camilla IRVIN
04 Exec Asst to President/Corp Secy ....Ms. Sandra B. KELSER
08 Director Houghton Memorial Library ....Mr. Eric A. KIDWELL
21 Comptroller ....Ms. Tina S. NIXON
39 Director of Residence Life ....Ms. Sandra Betts HALL
41 Director of Athletics ....Mr. Mike TURK
42 Chaplain and Dir of Community Svcs ....Rev. Brian L. SMITH
19 Chief of Security ....Mr. Michael S. WARD
104 Coordinator Travel & Event Planning ....Ms. Tricia S. GRIER

Huntsville Bible College (E)

904 Oakwood Avenue NW, Huntsville AL 35811-1632
County: Madison FICE Identification: 038943
Unit ID: 449348
Telephone: (256) 539-0834 Carnegie Class: Assoc/PrivNFP4
FAX Number: (256) 542-2900 Calendar System: Semester
URL: www.hbc1.edu
Established: 1986 Annual Undergrad Tuition & Fees: $4,605
Enrollment: 121 Coed
Affiliation or Control: Baptist IRS Status: 501(c)3
Highest Offering: Master's
Program: Liberal Arts And General; Religious Emphasis
Accreditation: BI

01 President ....Dr. John L. CLAY
05 Dean of Academic/Instruction ....Rev. David L. FAYLOR
06 Registrar ....Ms. Belinda F. HARDIN

ITT Technical Institute (F)

6270 Park South Drive, Bessemer AL 35022-5655
Telephone: (205) 497-5700 Identification: 666530
Accreditation: ACICS

† Main campus is ITT Technical Institute in Indianapolis, IN.

ITT Technical Institute (G)

9238 Madison Boulevard, Suite 500, Madison AL 35758
Telephone: (256) 542-2900 Identification: 666695
Accreditation: ACICS

† Main campus is ITT Technical Institute in Indianapolis, IN.

ITT Technical Institute (H)

3100 Cottage Hill Road, Bldg 3, Mobile AL 36606-2913
Telephone: (251) 472-4760 Identification: 666165
Accreditation: ACICS

† Main campus is ITT Technical Institute in Indianapolis, IN.

J.F. Drake State Technical College (I)

3421 Meridian Street N, Huntsville AL 35811-1584
County: Madison FICE Identification: 005260
Unit ID: 101462
Telephone: (256) 539-8161 Carnegie Class: Assoc/Pub-R-S
FAX Number: (256) 539-6439 Calendar System: Semester
URL: www.drakestate.edu
Established: 1961 Annual Undergrad Tuition & Fees (In-State): $3,336
Enrollment: 1,239 Coed
Affiliation or Control: State IRS Status: 501(c)3
Highest Offering: Associate Degree
Program: Occupational; 2-Year Principally Bachelor's Creditable; Technical Emphasis
Accreditation: SC

01 President ....Dr. Helen T. MCALPINE
05 Dean of Instruction ....Dr. Patricia SIMS
10 Business Manager/Treasurer ....Mr. Horace FRANKLIN
103 Director of Workforce Development ....Mrs. Beth WESTER
45 Dir of Planning & Research Dev ....Dr. John REUTTER
20 Associate Dean of Instruction ....Dr. Kemba CHAMBERS
15 Human Resource Specialist ....Mrs. Katie CHANCE
14 Director Computer Services ....Vacant
08 Director of Library Services ....Ms. Carla CLIFT
07 Director of Admissions/Registrar ....Mr. Cedric ARRINGTON
37 Director Student Financial Aid ....Ms. Jennifer O'LINGER
26 Director of Public Relations ....Mrs. Yibeli GALINDO-BAIRD
36 College Counselor ....Ms. Denise GAYMON
09 Dir of Institutional Effectiveness ....Dr. Alice RAYMOND
32 Student Services Management Dir ....Dr. Nicole BARNETT
51 Director of Adult Education ....Mrs. Wendy ROBERTS
18 Director of Operations ....Mr. Bruce BULLUCK

J.F. Ingram State Technical College (J)

PO Box 220350, Deatsville AL 36022-0350
County: Elmore FICE Identification: 030025
Unit ID: 101471
Telephone: (334) 285-5177 Carnegie Class: Assoc/Pub-R-S
FAX Number: (334) 285-5328 Calendar System: Semester
URL: www.ingram.edu
Established: 1965 Annual Undergrad Tuition & Fees (In-State): $12,288
Enrollment: 1,409 Coed
Affiliation or Control: State IRS Status: 501(c)3
Highest Offering: Associate Degree
Program: Occupational; Technical Emphasis
Accreditation: COE

01 President ....Dr. Hank DASINGER
11 Dean of Administration ....Mr. Jon KLAAREN
05 Interim Dean of Instruction ....Mr. William GRISWOLD
32 Int Dean Students/Support Services ....Mrs. Rosie EDWARDS
45 Dean of Strategic Planning and Eval ....Vacant
15 Human Resources Coordinator ....Ms. Erica PORTIS-TURNER
07 Director of Admissions & Registrar ....Vacant
36 Asst Transition Specialist ....Mrs. Mary KING

Jacksonville State University (K)

700 Pelham Road N, Jacksonville AL 36265-1602
County: Calhoun FICE Identification: 001020
Unit ID: 101480
Telephone: (256) 782-5781 Carnegie Class: Master's L
FAX Number: (256) 782-5291 Calendar System: Semester
URL: www.jsu.edu
Established: 1883 Annual Undergrad Tuition & Fees (In-State): $6,792
Enrollment: 9,161 Coed
Affiliation or Control: State IRS Status: 501(c)3
Highest Offering: Doctorate
Program: Liberal Arts And General; Teacher Preparatory; Professional
Accreditation: SC, AAFCS, ART, BUS, CACREP, CS, DIETD, JOUR, MUS, NAIT, NURSE, SPAA, SW, TED, THEA

01 President ....Dr. William A. MEEHAN
05 Provost/VP Academic/Student Affairs ....Dr. Rebecca O. TURNER
10 Actg Vice Pres Admin/Business Affs ....Ms. Allyson BARKER
30 Vice Pres University Advancement ....Dr. Charles R. LEWIS
13 Vice Pres Information Technology ....Mr. Vinson HOUSTON
20 Assoc Vice Pres Academic Affairs ....Dr. Joe DELAP
84 Assoc VP Enrol Mgmt/Student Affairs ....Dr. Tim KING
08 Dean of Library Services ....Mr. John-Bauer GRAHAM
58 Actg Dean College Graduate Studies ....Dr. Joe DELAP
49 Dean College Arts & Sciences ....Dr. James E. WADE
66 Acting Dean College Nursing ....Dr. Christie SHELTON
53 Dean College Education/Prof Studies ....Dr. John HAMMETT
50 Dean Col Commerce/Business Admin ....Dr. William FIELDING
21 University Controller ....Ms. Allyson BARKER
07 Director of Enrollment Management ....Mr. Andy GREEN
45 Dir Institutional Support Services ....Mr. Joe WHITMORE
44 Director University Development ....Mr. Earl WARREN
39 Dir Univ Housing/Residence Life ....Mr. Kevin HOULT
88 Dir International House/Programs ....Dr. John J. KETTERER
29 Director of Alumni Relations ....Ms. Kaci OGLE
15 Director of Human Resources ....Ms. Rosalynn MARTIN
37 Dir Student Financial Services ....Ms. Vickie ADAMS
72 Director Department of Technology ....Mr. Terry MARBUT
41 Director Athletics ....Mr. Warren KOEGEL
09 Exec Dir Planning & Research ....Dr. Alicia SIMMONS
06 Acting Registrar ....Dr. Tim KING
18 Director Physical Plant ....Mr. George F. LORD
36 Director Career Placement Services ....Ms. Rebecca E. TURNER
38 Dir Counseling/Disability Sppt Svcs ....Ms. Julie NIX
35 Director Student Life ....Mr. Terry CASEY
96 Director of Purchasing ....Ms. Pamela L. FINDLEY
26 Dir of Marketing/Communications ....Mr. Tim GARNER

James H. Faulkner State Community College (L)

1900 Highway 31 S, Bay Minette AL 36507-2698
County: Baldwin FICE Identification: 001060
Unit ID: 101161
Telephone: (251) 580-2100 Carnegie Class: Assoc/Pub-S-MC
FAX Number: (251) 580-2253 Calendar System: Semester
URL: www.faulknerstate.edu
Established: 1965 Annual Undergrad Tuition & Fees (In-State): $4,200
Enrollment: 4,029 Coed
Affiliation or Control: State IRS Status: 501(c)3
Highest Offering: Associate Degree
Program: Occupational; 2-Year Principally Bachelor's Creditable

Accreditation: SC, ACFEI, ADNUR, DA, EMT, PNUR, SURGT

01 President Dr. Gary L. BRANCH
32 VP of Inst Adv & Student Dev Dr. Brenda J. KENNEDY
05 Dean of Instruction Ms. Emily MARTIN
35 Dean of Student Services Mr. Michael NIKOLAKIS
86 Dean of Federal Programs Mrs. Lena DEXTER
11 Dean Administrative Services Mr. Jim FITZ-GERALD
103 Dean of Workforce Development Ms. Patty HUGHSTON
26 Director College Relations Vacant
06 Registrar Mrs. Elaine GORDON
08 Dir Learning Resource Ms. Rheena ELMORE
37 Financial Aid Director Dr. Jim THEEUWES
88 Director High School Relations Ms. Carmelita MIKKELSEN
18 Director of Buildings & Ground Mr. Jim FITZ-GERALD
51 Director of Cont and Distance Educ Mrs. Joli JONES
19 Chief of Police Vacant
15 Director Human Resources Mrs. Laura BURKS
39 Dir of Housing and Special Events Ms. Linda CALDWELL
66 Director Nursing & Allied Health Ms. Jean GRAHAM
13 Coordinator Technology Services Mr. Brian STRICKLAND

Jefferson Davis Community College (A)

PO Box 958, Brewton AL 36427-0958

County: Escambia FICE Identification: 001021
Unit ID: 101499
Telephone: (251) 867-4832 Carnegie Class: Assoc/Pub-R-S
FAX Number: (251) 867-7399 Calendar System: Semester
URL: www.jdcc.edu
Established: 1965 Annual Undergrad Tuition & Fees (In-State): $3,128
Enrollment: 1,034 Coed
Affiliation or Control: State IRS Status: 501(c)3
Highest Offering: Associate Degree
Program: Occupational; 2-Year Principally Bachelor's Creditable
Accreditation: SC, ADNUR

01 President Dr. Daniel BAIN
05 Dean of Instruction Ms. Catherine PACKER-WILLIAMS
10 Dean of Business Affairs Mr. Brad PENDERGRASS
32 Dean of Student Affairs Mr. David JONES
20 Associate Dean of Instruction Vacant
15 Director of Human Resources Ms. Veronica MCKINNEY
06 Registrar Ms. Robin SESSIONS
13 Director of MIS Mr. Anthony HARDY
26 Director Mktg & Community Relations Vacant
08 Librarian Mr. Jeffrey FAUST
37 Financial Aid Director Ms. Vanessa M. KYLES
09 Dir Institutional Research/Testing Mr. Randal BARNETT
18 Chief Facilities/Physical Plant Mr. Richard LYNN
88 Dir Stdnt Support Svcs/Development Dr. Beth BILLY

Jefferson State Community College (B)

2601 Carson Road, Birmingham AL 35215-3098

County: Jefferson FICE Identification: 001022
Unit ID: 101505
Telephone: (205) 853-1200 Carnegie Class: Assoc/Pub-U-MC
FAX Number: (205) 983-5918 Calendar System: Semester
URL: www.jeffstateonline.com
Established: 1963 Annual Undergrad Tuition & Fees (In-State): $4,200
Enrollment: 8,887 Coed
Affiliation or Control: State IRS Status: 501(c)3
Highest Offering: Associate Degree
Program: Occupational; 2-Year Principally Bachelor's Creditable
Accreditation: SC, ACBSP, ACFEI, ADNUR, CONST, EMT, FUSER, MLTAD, PTAA, RAD

01 President Dr. Judy M. MERRITT
03 Vice President Dr. Joe E. MORRIS
05 Dean of Instruction Ms. Danielle COBURN
75 Dean Career & Technical Education Ms. Norma G. BELL
30 Dean Campus Development/Campus Svcs Mr. Keith A. BROWN
10 Director Financial Services Ms. Mary WATSON
32 Director of Student Services Dr. Linda J. HOOTON
97 Assoc Dean Transf Gen Stds Shelby Ms. Jeanette ROGERS
97 Assoc Dean Transf Gen Stds Jeffrsn Dr. Aliakbar R. YAZDI
106 Associate Dean Distance Education Mr. Alan B. DAVIS
51 Director College/Cmty/Corp Educ Ms. Kay C. POTTER
13 Director Information Technology Mr. Nader ZANDI
37 Director Financial Aid Ms. Tracy R. ADAMS
84 Dean of Enrollment Services Dr. Phillip M. HOBBS
18 Director Maintenance Mr. Bill MIXON
08 Director of Learning Resources Ms. Barbara GOSS
36 Director Career/Job Resource Center Dr. Tamara PAYNE
07 Director Admissions and Retention Ms. Lillian OWENS
15 Director Human Resources Ms. Ruby RUSSELL
26 Director Media Relations Mr. David BOBO
96 Purchasing Coordinator Ms. Ann CIMALORE
19 Director Safety & Security Mr. Mark BAILEY

Judson College (C)

302 Bibb Street, Marion AL 36756-2504

County: Perry FICE Identification: 001023
Unit ID: 101541
Telephone: (334) 683-5100 Carnegie Class: Bac/A&S
FAX Number: (334) 683-5147 Calendar System: Semester
URL: www.judson.edu
Established: 1838 Annual Undergrad Tuition & Fees: $14,620
Enrollment: 381 Female
Affiliation or Control: Alabama Baptist State Convention
IRS Status: 501(c)3
Highest Offering: Baccalaureate
Program: Liberal Arts And General; Teacher Preparatory
Accreditation: SC, MUS, @SW

01 President Dr. David E. POTTS
05 Interim Vice Pres & Academic Dean Dr. Scott W. BULLARD
32 Vice Pres & Dean of Students Vacant
07 Exec Dir for Enrollment Services Ms. Layne CALHOUN
10 Vice President Business Affairs Vacant
30 VP Institutional Advancement Dr. Terry SMITH MORGAN
43 VP and General Counsel Mr. Bill MATHEWS

Lawson State Community College (D)

3060 Wilson Road, SW, Birmingham AL 35221-1798

County: Jefferson FICE Identification: 001059
Unit ID: 101569
Telephone: (205) 925-2515 Carnegie Class: Assoc/Pub-U-MC
FAX Number: (205) 925-8526 Calendar System: Semester
URL: www.lawsonstate.edu
Established: 1949 Annual Undergrad Tuition & Fees (In-State): $4,206
Enrollment: 3,420 Coed
Affiliation or Control: State IRS Status: 501(c)3
Highest Offering: Associate Degree
Program: Occupational; 2-Year Principally Bachelor's Creditable
Accreditation: SC, ACBSP, ADNUR, DA, PNUR

01 President Dr. Perry W. WARD
05 Vice Pres Instructional Services Dr. Bruce CRAWFORD
11 Vice President of Administration Mrs. Sharon CREWS
35 Dean of Students Dr. Cynthia ANTHONY
09 Director of Institutional Research Dr. Randy GLAZE
20 Academic Dean Dr. Sherri DAVIS
75 Asc Dean Business/Information Tech Dr. Alice MILTON
49 Asc Dn Liberal Arts/Coll Trans Pgms Dr. Karl PRUITT
76 Assoc Dean of Health Occupations Dr. Shelia MARABLE
75 Asst Dean Career Technical Programs Mr. Donald SLEDGE
84 Asst Dean of Admissions/Records Mr. Darren ALLEN
07 Director of Admissions Mr. Jeff SHELLEY
08 Librarian Ms. Sandra HENDERSON
37 Director Student Financial Aid Ms. Cassandra MATTHEWS
15 Director of Personnel Services Mrs. Janice MCGEE
30 Chief Development Dr. Myrtes GREEN
26 Chief Public Relations Officer Mrs. Geri ALBRIGHT
18 Chief Facilities/Physical Plant Mr. Chad YANCY
19 Director Safety/Security Mr. Walter WILLIAMS
13 Dir Computing and Information Mgmt Mr. James MANKOWICH
40 Director Bookstore Mr. Al YOUNG
31 Director Auxiliary Services Dr. Craig LAWRENCE
41 Athletic Director Mrs. Eleanor PITTS
06 Registrar Ms. Lori CHISEM
91 Director of Academic Computing Dr. Alice MILTON
24 Director Educational Media Ms. Sandra HENDERSON
39 Director Student Housing Mr. Robert SMITH
29 Coordinator Alumni Relations Ms. Philana SUGGS
35 Coordinator Student Affairs Mrs. Sandra HOWARD
38 Coordinator Student Counseling Ms. Philana SUGGS
84 Coordinator Enrollment Management Mr. Jeff SHELLEY

Lurleen B. Wallace Community College (E)

PO Drawer 1418, 1000 Dannelly Blvd, Andalusia AL 36420-1224

County: Covington FICE Identification: 008988
Unit ID: 101602
Telephone: (334) 222-6591 Carnegie Class: Assoc/Pub-R-S
FAX Number: (334) 881-2300 Calendar System: Semester
URL: www.lbwcc.edu
Established: 1969 Annual Undergrad Tuition & Fees (In-State): $4,170
Enrollment: 1,645 Coed
Affiliation or Control: State IRS Status: 501(c)3
Highest Offering: Associate Degree
Program: Occupational; 2-Year Principally Bachelor's Creditable; Technical Emphasis
Accreditation: SC, ADNUR, DMS, EMT, SURGT

01 President Dr. Herbert H. RIEDEL
05 Dean of Instruction Ms. Peggy LINTON
32 Dean of Student Affairs Ms. Judy H. HALL
10 Chief Financial Officer Mrs. Linda A. HARTIN
12 Vice Pres/Greenville Campus Direct Dr. James D. KRUDOP
103 Assoc Dean Adult Educ/Workforce Dev Mr. Jimmy HUTTO
14 Assoc Dean Instr/Info Technology Mr. Greg APLIN
15 Director of Human Resources Ms. Peige JOSEY
09 Dir Inst Effectiveness & Quality Mr. Larry JONES
18 Dir College Facilities/Maintenance Mr. Tim JONES
07 Director Admissions & Records Ms. Jan RILEY
41 Athletic Director Mr. Steve HELMS
08 Director of Learning Resources Ms. Mary Beth GREEN
88 Director Student Support Services Ms. Patricia POWELL
88 Dir Upward Bound/Andalusia Camp Dir Mr. Bridges ANDERSON
21 Comptroller Ms. Lynne DAYTON
37 Dir Financial Aid MacArthur/Luverne Ms. Wanda S. BASS
37 Dir Fin Aid Andalusia/Greenville Ms. Donna BASS
26 Public Info Officer/Dir Mktg & Dev Ms. Renee LEMAIRE

Marion Military Institute (F)

1101 Washington Street, Marion AL 36756-3213

County: Perry FICE Identification: 001026
Unit ID: 101648
Telephone: (800) 664-1842 Carnegie Class: Assoc/Pub-R-S
FAX Number: (334) 683-2380 Calendar System: Semester
URL: www.marionmilitary.edu
Established: 1842 Annual Undergrad Tuition & Fees (In-State): $6,700
Enrollment: 385 Coed
Affiliation or Control: State IRS Status: 501(c)3
Highest Offering: Associate Degree
Program: 2-Year Principally Bachelor's Creditable
Accreditation: SC

01 President Col. David J. MOLLAHAN
03 Executive Vice President Dr. Susan G. STEVENSON
10 Int VP for Finance & Business Affs Mrs. Jennifer C. BARNETTE
05 Academic Dean Mr. David TIPMORE
32 VP for Student Affairs & Commandant Col. Thomas L. TATE
30 VP for Institutional Advancement Mrs. Suzanne MCKEE
84 VP for Enrollment Mgmt LtCol. James G. LAKE
41 Director of Athletics Dr. Michelle IVEY
29 Director of Alumni Affairs Mr. Brandon TAYLOR
88 ROTC Professor of Military Science Maj. Gregory WALL
09 Director of Institutional Research Mrs. Donna LEEMON
06 Registrar Mrs. Wanda CALAME
38 Director of Guidance Ms. Brenda A. COOK
37 Director of Financial Aid Ms. Jacqueline WILSON
08 Library Director Ms. Glenda LAMMERS
18 Supt of Buildings & Grounds Mr. Brian HALE
17 Director of Health Services Mrs. Sue HAZEWINKEL

Miles College (G)

5500 Myron Massey Boulevard, Fairfield AL 35064-2621

County: Jefferson FICE Identification: 001028
Unit ID: 101675
Telephone: (205) 929-1000 Carnegie Class: Bac/Diverse
FAX Number: (205) 929-1453 Calendar System: Semester
URL: www.miles.edu
Established: 1898 Annual Undergrad Tuition & Fees: $11,454
Enrollment: 1,691 Coed
Affiliation or Control: Christian Methodist Episcopal IRS Status: 501(c)3
Highest Offering: Baccalaureate
Program: Liberal Arts And General; Teacher Preparatory
Accreditation: SC, SW, TED

01 President Dr. George T. FRENCH, JR.
05 Dean Academic Affairs Dr. Emmanuel CHEKWA
100 Special Asst/Chief of Staff Mr. Kenneth COACHMAN
10 Chief Financial Ofcr/Business Affs Mrs. Diana W. KNIGHTON
07 Director Admissions & Recruitment Mr. Christopher ROBERTSON
06 Registrar Ms. Jennifer WYCOFF
08 Librarian Dr. Geraldine BELL
30 Director Institutional Development Mr. W. Frank TOPPING
32 Dean Student Affairs Ms. Griena KNIGHT
36 Director Career Planning/Placement Dr. Glenda BROWN-WADE
26 Director College Relations Vacant
09 Dir Institutional Effective/Rsrch Dr. Ba-Shen WELCH
37 Director Financial Aid Mr. Percy LANIER
18 Director Physical Plant Mr. Edward JENKINS
25 Director Sponsored Programs Vacant
38 Dir Counseling/Advising/Testing Ms. Keisha LEWIS
29 Director Alumni Affairs Mr. Charles CROCKROM, SR.
15 Director Personnel Services Mrs. Verlanda TATE
42 Chaplain Rev. Larry BATIE
14 Manager of Data Processing Ms. Jackie HUDSON

Northeast Alabama Community College (H)

PO Box 159, 138 Alabama Highway 35, Rainsville AL 35986-0159

County: DeKalb/Jackson FICE Identification: 001031
Unit ID: 101897
Telephone: (256) 638-4418 Carnegie Class: Assoc/Pub-R-M
FAX Number: (256) 638-3052 Calendar System: Semester
URL: www.nacc.edu
Established: 1963 Annual Undergrad Tuition & Fees (In-State): $4,200
Enrollment: 3,144 Coed
Affiliation or Control: State IRS Status: 501(c)3
Highest Offering: Associate Degree
Program: Occupational; 2-Year Principally Bachelor's Creditable; Business Emphasis
Accreditation: SC, ADNUR, EMT, PNUR

01 President Dr. J. David CAMPBELL
05 Dean of Instruction Dr. Joseph D. BURKE
56 Dean of Extended Day Program Ms. Marilyn REECE
32 Dean of Student Services Ms. Tonie M. NIBLETT
11 Dean of Admin Services/Registrar Mr. Larry D. GUFFEY
37 Director of Financial Aid Mr. Nixon WILLMON
103 Dir Workforce Devel/Skills Training Mr. Mike KENNAMER
26 Chief Public Relations Officer Mrs. Debra A. BARRENTINE
07 Dir Admissions & Student Services Mrs. Tonie M. NIBLETT
09 Dir Instl Planning & Assessment Mr. Brad FRICKS
18 Chief Facilities/Physical Plant Mr. Kent JONES
06 Registrar/Chief Bus Ofcr/Dir Purchg Mr. Larry D. GUFFEY
30 Development Director Ms. Heather RICE
19 Director of Security Mr. Norman SMITH

Northwest - Shoals Community College (A)

800 George Wallace Boulevard,
Muscle Shoals AL 35661-3205
County: Colbert FICE Identification: 005697
Unit ID: 101736
Telephone: (256) 331-5200 Carnegie Class: Assoc/Pub-R-M
FAX Number: (256) 331-5222 Calendar System: Semester
URL: www.nwscc.edu
Established: 1963 Annual Undergrad Tuition & Fees (In-State): $3,312
Enrollment: 3,728 Coed
Affiliation or Control: State IRS Status: 501(c)3
Highest Offering: Associate Degree
Program: Occupational; 2-Year Principally Bachelor's Creditable
Accreditation: SC, ADNUR, EMT

01 President ....Dr. Humphrey LEE
05 Vice President ....Dr. Glenda COLAGROSS
10 Chief Fiscal Officer ....Mr. Paul MERRILL
35 Assoc Dean Students/Athletic Admin ....Mr. Charles TAYLOR
09 Assoc Dean Inst Effect/Dist Ed/Dev ....Mr. John MCINTOSH
20 Assoc Dean Instructional Programs ....Dr. Timmy JAMES
30 Director of Foundation/Advancement ....Vacant
37 Director of Financial Aid ....Ms. Shauna JAMES
07 Asst Dean Recruit/Adm/FA ....Mr. Tom CARTER
15 Dir of HR/Senior Personnel Officer ....Ms. Pam TOWNSEND
29 Director of Alumni Relations ....Vacant
36 Director/Counselor ETS/YSP ....Ms. Lanetta PHILLIPS
14 Director of Management Info Systems ....Mr. Alan MITCHELL
19 Director of Safety and Security ....Mr. Doug HARGETT
07 Coordinator Admissions ....Vacant
103 Assoc Dean of Workforce Develop ....Ms. Rose JONES
21 Comptroller ....Ms. Janet JONES
88 Director of Adult Education ....Mr. Donnie SWEENEY
88 Dir College and Career Readiness ....Mr. Ed CARTER
88 Coordinator/Advisor RTW ....Ms. Tara BRANSCOME

Oakwood University (B)

7000 Adventist Boulevard, NW, Huntsville AL 35896-0003
County: Madison FICE Identification: 001033
Unit ID: 101912
Telephone: (256) 726-7000 Carnegie Class: Bac/Diverse
FAX Number: (256) 726-8335 Calendar System: Semester
URL: www.oakwood.edu
Established: 1896 Annual Undergrad Tuition & Fees: $16,184
Enrollment: 2,019 Coed
Affiliation or Control: Seventh-day Adventist IRS Status: 501(c)3
Highest Offering: Master's
Program: Occupational; Liberal Arts And General; Teacher Preparatory
Accreditation: SC, ACBSP, DIETD, DIETI, NUR, SW, TED

01 President ....Dr. Leslie POLLARD
05 Provost & Sr Vice President ....Dr. Tim MCDONALD
20 Vice President Academic Affairs ....Dr. Garland DULAN
10 Vice President Financial Affairs ....Ms. Sabrina COTTON
32 Vice President Student Services ....Mr. David KNIGHT
30 Executive Director Advancement/Dev ....Ms. Kisha NORRIS
20 Asst Vice Pres Academic Affairs ....Dr. George ASHLEY
21 Asst VP Financial Affs/Controller ....Mrs. Gail CALDWELL
35 Asst Vice Pres Student Services ....Mr. Ryan SMITH
16 Director Human Resources ....Mrs. Sylvia GERMANY
25 Director Sponsored Programs ....Mrs. Ivy STARKS
26 Director Public Relations ....Mr. Tim ALLSTON
07 Director Enrollment Management ....Ms. Nikki LAWSON
37 Interim Director Financial Aid ....Mrs. Lynda BARTHOLOMEW
06 Interim Registrar ....Mr. John HILL
39 Residence Life Coordinator-Men ....Mr. Woodrow VAUGHN
88 Resident Life Coordinator-Women ....Ms. Leah CALDWELL
08 Director Library Services ....Mrs. Paulette JOHNSON
09 Director Inst Effectiveness ....Mrs. Janis NEWBORN
18 Director Physical Plant ....Mr. Colins ALEXANDER
19 Director Security ....Mr. Lewis EAKINS
29 Director Alumni Relations ....Vacant
36 Director Career Services & Testing ....Mrs. Sonia PAUL
38 Dir Counseling & Health Services ....Dr. Janice LEWIS-THOMAS
51 Dir Adult & Continuing Education ....Dr. Rachel WILLIAMS
42 Chaplain ....Dr. Howard WEEMS
46 Dir Research & Faculty Dev ....Dr. Prudence L. POLLARD
89 Director Freshmen Studies ....Mr. James HUTCHINSON
50 Chair Business & Info Systems ....Mrs. Hyacinth BURTON
53 Chair Education ....Dr. James MBYIRUKIRA
76 Chair Allied Health ....Dr. Maxine GARVEY
60 Chair English & Foreign Languages ....Dr. Benson PRIGG
64 Chair Music ....Dr. Wayne BUCKNOR
65 Chair Biological Sciences ....Dr. Safawo GULLO
65 Chair Chemistry ....Dr. Kenneth LAI HING
66 Chair Nursing ....Dr. Flora FLOOD
68 Chair Health & Physical Education ....Dr. Howard SHAW
70 Chair Social Work ....Dr. Octavio RAMIREZ
73 Chair Religion & Theology ....Dr. M.A WARREN
81 Chair Math & Computer Science ....Mrs. Kathleen DOBBINS
82 Chair History ....Dr. Samuel LONDON
83 Chair Psychology ....Dr. Cherryl GALLEY
60 Chair Communication ....Dr. Rennae ELLIOTT
96 Director Purchasing ....Mrs. Belita NEWBY

Prince Institute - Southeast (C)

7735 Atlanta Highway, Montgomery AL 36117-4231
County: Montgomery FICE Identification: 022960
Unit ID: 101958
Telephone: (334) 271-1670 Carnegie Class: Assoc/PrivFP
FAX Number: (334) 271-1671 Calendar System: Quarter
URL: www.princeinstitute.edu
Established: 1976 Annual Undergrad Tuition & Fees: $12,600
Enrollment: 122 Coed
Affiliation or Control: Proprietary IRS Status: Proprietary
Highest Offering: Associate Degree
Program: Occupational
Accreditation: ACICS

01 Director ....Mrs. Patricia L. HILL
05 Dean of Academic Affairs ....Ms. Candace H. SHEPHERD
10 Business Manager ....Mr. Reginald JAMES
11 Director Campus Operations ....Mr. Keith WEROSH
07 Admissions Representative ....Mrs. Sherry A. HILL

Reid State Technical College (D)

PO Box 588, Evergreen AL 36401-0588
County: Conecuh FICE Identification: 005692
Unit ID: 101994
Telephone: (251) 578-1313 Carnegie Class: Assoc/Pub-R-S
FAX Number: (251) 578-5355 Calendar System: Semester
URL: www.rstc.edu
Established: 1966 Annual Undergrad Tuition & Fees (In-State): $3,360
Enrollment: 495 Coed
Affiliation or Control: State IRS Status: 501(c)3
Highest Offering: Associate Degree
Program: Occupational; Technical Emphasis
Accreditation: COE

01 President ....Dr. Douglas M. LITTLES
05 Dean of Students & Instruction ....Dr. Tangela PURIFOY
103 Assoc Dean Workforce Development ....Dr. Alesia K. STUART
09 Assoc Dean for Institutional Effect ....Ms. Coretta BOYKIN
37 Director Financial Aid ....Ms. Christy GOODWIN
07 Dir of Recruiting/Retention/Plcmt ....Vacant
38 Director of Counseling ....Ms. Monica ROBINSON
21 Business Manager ....Mr. David J. RHODES
06 Registrar/Enrollment Management ....Ms. Vickie NICHOLSON

Remington College, Mobile Campus (E)

828 Downtowner Loop W, Mobile AL 36609-5404
County: Mobile FICE Identification: 026055
Unit ID: 366535
Telephone: (251) 343-8200 Carnegie Class: Assoc/PrivFP4
FAX Number: (251) 343-0577 Calendar System: Quarter
URL: www.remingtoncollege.edu
Established: 1986 Annual Undergrad Tuition & Fees: $33,900
Enrollment: 450 Coed
Affiliation or Control: Independent Non-Profit IRS Status: 501(c)3
Highest Offering: Associate Degree
Program: Occupational; 2-Year Principally Bachelor's Creditable; Technical Emphasis
Accreditation: ACCSC

01 President ....Mr. Stephen M. BACKMAN
05 Director of Education ....Ms. Cindy MCMILLAN
07 Director of Admissions ....Mr. Jason STANLEY
36 Dir of Career Services & Placement ....Ms. Kristy KING
06 Registrar ....Mr. Donald SCHERMERHORN
15 Director Personnel Services ....Ms. Pamela EVANS
26 Chief Public Relations Officer ....Ms. Pamela EVANS
35 Director Student Affairs ....Ms. Bonnie LEDBETTER

Samford University (F)

800 Lakeshore Drive, Birmingham AL 35229-0001
County: Jefferson FICE Identification: 001036
Unit ID: 102049
Telephone: (205) 726-2011 Carnegie Class: Master's M
FAX Number: (205) 726-2171 Calendar System: 4/1/4
URL: www.samford.edu
Established: 1841 Annual Undergrad Tuition & Fees: $25,528
Enrollment: 4,758 Coed
Affiliation or Control: Southern Baptist IRS Status: 501(c)3
Highest Offering: Doctorate
Program: Liberal Arts And General; Teacher Preparatory; Professional
Accreditation: SC, ANEST, BUS, CIDA, DIETD, LAW, MUS, NURSE, PHAR, TED, THEOL

01 President ....Dr. T. Andrew WESTMORELAND
03 Provost/Exec Vice President ....Dr. J. Bradley CREED
32 Vice President for Student Affairs ....Dr. Phil KIMREY
30 Vice President of Advancement ....Mr. W. Randall PITTMAN
10 Vice President Business Affairs ....Mr. Harry B. BROCK, III
05 Associate Provost ....Dr. Mary Sue BALDWIN
20 Assistant Provost ....Dr. Nancy BIGGIO
04 Assistant to the President ....Dr. Michael D. MORGAN
13 Interim Chief Information Officer ....Mrs. Debi WHITCOMB
21 Controller ....Mr. Mike DARWIN
41 Athletic Director ....Mr. Martin NEWTON
88 Dir of Ethics & Leadership ....Mr. John C. KNAPP
88 Director of Advancement Services ....Mrs. Judi F. AUCOIN
29 Director of Alumni ....Mr. David GOODWIN
45 Director of Planning and Giving ....Mr. Stan DAVIS
88 Dir Orientation/Parent Prgm ....Ms. Kelia FURR
21 Director of Business Services ....Mr. Mike MCCORMACK
88 Director of Capital Planning & Imp ....Mr. David T. WHITT
88 Dir Venue & Event Management ....Mr. Sean WRIGHT
18 Director of Facilities Management ....Mr. Mark FULLER
37 Director of Student Financial Svcs ....Mr. Lane M. SMITH
15 Director of Human Resources ....Mr. Fred R. ROGAN
09 Director Inst Effectiveness ....Mrs. Karen G. HAMBY
104 Director of International Studies ....Dr. David SHIPLEY
43 Director Investments and Legal Svcs ....Ms. Lisa IMBRAGULIO
08 Dean of University Library ....Dr. Kimmetha D. HERNDON
30 Director of Univ Advancement ....Mr. Douglas WILSON
19 Director of Pub Safety & Emer Mgmt ....Mr. Wayne PITTMAN
39 Director Residence Life & Univ Svcs ....Ms. Lauren M. TAYLOR
88 Director of Risk Mmgt & Insurance ....Mr. James A. CLEMENT
10 Director of Budget & Financial Plng ....Mr. Matt DEFORE
102 Dir of Advancement/Legacy League ....Ms. Sharon SMITH
07 Dean of Admissions ....Mr. Jason BLACK
42 Assistant Dean for Spritual Life ....Dr. Matthew S. KERLIN
35 Assistant Dean of Student Services ....Mr. Garry L. ATKINS
35 Assistant Dean for Campus Life ....Ms. Renie MOSS
26 Dir Marketing & Communications ....Mr. Philip POOLE
88 Dir of University Fellows ....Mr. Bryan M. JOHNSON
53 Dean Education/Professional Studies ....Dr. Jean A. BOX
49 Dean Howard College Arts/Sciences ....Dr. David W. CHAPMAN
67 Interim Dean School of Pharmacy ....Dr. Michael HOGUE
73 Dean Beeson School of Divinity ....Dr. Timothy F. GEORGE
50 Dean Brock School of Business ....Dr. J. Howard FINCH
61 Dean Cumberland School of Law ....Dr. John L. CARROLL
66 Dean Ida Moffett School of Nursing ....Dr. Nena F. SANDERS
57 Dean School of the Arts ....Dr. Joseph HOPKINS
06 Registrar ....Mr. John FLYNN
44 Director of Annual Giving ....Ms. Kimberly CRIPPS
44 Director Gift and Estate Planning ....Mr. Stan DAVIS
28 Dir Diversity & Intercultural Ed ....Dr. Denise GREGORY
104 Director of International Education ....Dr. Angela FERGUSON

Selma University (G)

1501 Lapsley Street, Selma AL 36701-5232
County: Dallas FICE Identification: 001037
Unit ID: 102058
Telephone: (334) 872-2533 Carnegie Class: Spec/Faith
FAX Number: (334) 872-7746 Calendar System: Semester
URL: www.selmauniversity.org
Established: 1878 Annual Undergrad Tuition & Fees: $5,840
Enrollment: 643 Coed
Affiliation or Control: Baptist IRS Status: 501(c)3
Highest Offering: Master's
Program: Liberal Arts And General; Religious Emphasis
Accreditation: BI

01 President ....Dr. Alvin A. CLEVELAND, SR.
05 Dean ....Dr. Kayarda LOWE
06 Registrar ....Ms. Gloria ANDERSON

Shelton State Community College (H)

9500 Old Greensboro Road, Tuscaloosa AL 35405-8522
County: Tuscaloosa FICE Identification: 005691
Unit ID: 102067
Telephone: (205) 391-2211 Carnegie Class: Assoc/Pub-R-L
FAX Number: (205) 391-2426 Calendar System: Semester
URL: www.sheltonstate.edu
Established: 1953 Annual Undergrad Tuition & Fees (In-State): $4,680
Enrollment: 5,104 Coed
Affiliation or Control: State IRS Status: 501(c)3
Highest Offering: Associate Degree
Program: Occupational; 2-Year Principally Bachelor's Creditable
Accreditation: SC, ADNUR, #COARC, PNUR

01 Interim President ....Ms. Joan Y. DAVIS
05 Dean of Academic Services ....Dr. Peggy Shaddock PALOMBI
10 Comptroller ....Mrs. Ann BRACKNELL
32 Dean of Student Services ....Dr. Thomas HUEBNER
13 Dean Technology/Instl Rsrch ....Dr. Michelle JARRELL
12 Director Fredd Campus/Title III ....Mr. Ronald RANGE
20 Assoc Dn Trng Existing Bus/Industry ....Mr. Jason MOORE
06 Asst Dean Student Svcs/Registrar ....Mr. Byron ABSTON
76 Assistant Dean for Health Services ....Ms. Gladys HILL
37 Asst Dean Financial Aid ....Ms. Amanda HARBISON
84 Asst Dean Stdnt Support & Retention ....Dr. Fran TURNER
15 Director of Personnel Services ....Vacant
88 Director Special Projects ....Ms. Channing HOWINGTON
08 Director Library Services ....Mr. Glen JOHNSON
30 Director Institutional Advancement ....Vacant
103 Director Workforce Development ....Mr. Lew DRUMMOND
25 Director Grant/Resource Development ....Vacant
88 Director Adult Education ....Mr. Phillip JOHNSON
38 Counseling Center Coordinator ....Ms. Holly ELLIOTT
88 Dean of Technical Services ....Mr. Steve FAIR
88 Dean of Auxiliary Services ....Dr. Thomas TAYLOR

Snead State Community College (I)

PO Box 734, Boaz AL 35957-0734
County: Marshall FICE Identification: 001038
Unit ID: 102076
Telephone: (256) 593-5120 Carnegie Class: Assoc/Pub-R-M
FAX Number: (256) 593-7180 Calendar System: Semester
URL: www.snead.edu
Established: 1898 Annual Undergrad Tuition & Fees (In-State): $4,544
Enrollment: 2,436 Coed
Affiliation or Control: State IRS Status: Exempt
Highest Offering: Associate Degree

Program: Occupational; 2-Year Principally Bachelor's Creditable
Accreditation: SC, ADNUR

01 President ... Dr. Robert EXLEY
32 Vice President for Student Services ... Mr. Jason CANNON
10 Chief Financial Officer ... Mr. Mark RICHARD
05 Chief Academic Officer ... Dr. Jason WATTS
13 Chief IT Officer ... Mr. Randy MALTBIE
26 Director of PR/Marketing ... Ms. Shelley SMITH
38 Director of Testing ... Ms. Jessamine HUFFMAN
09 Assoc Dean Acad Planning/Research ... Dr. Annette CEDERHOLM
81 Science Division Director ... Ms. Deborah RHODEN
79 Humanities Division Director ... Dr. Cynthia DENHAM
83 Social Science Division Director ... Mr. Alan BATES
81 Mathematics Division Director ... Mr. Blake LEETH
50 Business Division Director ... Mr. Vann SCOTT
75 Technology Division Director ... Mr. Greg RANDALL
103 Director Community Education ... Ms. Teresa WALKER
76 Director Health Sciences ... Ms. Amy LANGLEY
41 Athletic Director ... Mr. Mark RICHARD
08 Head Librarian ... Mr. John MILLER
15 Director of Human Resources ... Ms. Arlene BROWN
18 Director of Physical Plant ... Mr. Steve WILLIAMS

South University (A)

5355 Vaughn Road, Montgomery AL 36116-1120
Telephone: (334) 395-8800 FICE Identification: 004463
Accreditation: &SC, MAC, NURSE, PTAA

† Main campus is South University in Savannah, GA.

Southeastern Bible College (B)

2545 Valleydale Road, Birmingham AL 35244-2083
County: Shelby FICE Identification: 022704
Unit ID: 102261
Telephone: (205) 970-9200 Carnegie Class: Spec/Faith
FAX Number: (205) 970-9207 Calendar System: Semester
URL: www.sebc.edu
Established: 1935 Annual Undergrad Tuition & Fees: $12,930
Enrollment: 179 Coed
Affiliation or Control: Independent Non-Profit IRS Status: 501(c)3
Highest Offering: Baccalaureate
Program: Liberal Arts And General; Religious Emphasis
Accreditation: BI

01 President ... Dr. Don HAWKINS
05 Provost ... Dr. Vicki WOLFE
32 Dean of Students ... Ms. Kristie HARRICK
42 Campus Pastor ... Mr. Micah SIMPSON
49 Chair Dept of Arts & Sciences ... Dr. Dwain WALDREP
53 Chair Dept of Education ... Dr. Lynn GANNETT-MALICK
73 Chair Dept of Biblical Studies ... Dr. Jason SNYDER
10 Business Manager ... Mrs. Carme PHILLIPS
04 Admin Asst to the President ... Mrs. Anita SCROGGINS
06 Registrar ... Mr. Joel WOLFE
08 Director of Library Services ... Mr. Paul ROBERTS
09 Coordinator of Inst Effectiveness ... Mrs. Michelle HOWER
18 Director of Facilities ... Mr. David POWLESS
37 Director of Financial Aid ... Mrs. Joanne BELIN
55 Director of ACHIEVE Adult Educ ... Mr. Steven CLECKLER

Southern Union State Community College (C)

PO Box 1000, Wadley AL 36276-1000
County: Randolph FICE Identification: 001040
Unit ID: 251260
Telephone: (256) 395-2211 Carnegie Class: Assoc/Pub-R-M
FAX Number: (256) 395-2215 Calendar System: Semester
URL: www.suscc.edu
Established: 1922 Annual Undergrad Tuition & Fees (In-State): $3,900
Enrollment: 4,978 Coed
Affiliation or Control: State IRS Status: 501(c)3
Highest Offering: Associate Degree
Program: Occupational; 2-Year Principally Bachelor's Creditable
Accreditation: SC, ADNUR, EMT, RAD, SURGT

01 Interim President ... Dr. Glenda COLAROSS
05 Dean of Academics ... Dr. Linda NORTH
32 Dean of Students ... Ms. Tiffany SANDERS
97 Assoc Dean of Instructional Pgms ... Mr. Steve SPRATLIN
72 Dean of Technology/Educ/Wrkfce Dev ... Mr. Darin BALDWIN
20 Dean Student Development ... Mr. Gary BRANCH
13 Director Management Info Systems ... Ms. Cheryl JORDAN
41 Director Athletics ... Mr. Ron RADFORD
30 Director Institutional Advancement ... Vacant
06 Registrar ... Ms. Catherine STRINGFELLOW
26 Chief Public Relations Officer ... Ms. Shondae BROWN
10 Chief Business Officer ... Mr. Ben JORDAN
35 Coordinator of Student Life ... Ms. Lori DANIEL

Spring Hill College (D)

4000 Dauphin Street, Mobile AL 36608-1791
County: Mobile FICE Identification: 001041
Unit ID: 102234
Telephone: (251) 380-4000 Carnegie Class: Master's S
FAX Number: (251) 460-2182 Calendar System: Semester
URL: www.shc.edu
Established: 1830 Annual Undergrad Tuition & Fees: $30,924
Enrollment: 1,328 Coed
Affiliation or Control: Roman Catholic IRS Status: 501(c)3
Highest Offering: Master's
Program: Liberal Arts And General; Teacher Preparatory
Accreditation: SC, NURSE

01 President ... Rev. Richard P. SALMI, SJ
05 Provost/Vice Pres Academic Affairs ... Dr. George E. SIMS
10 Vice President Business & Finance ... Ms. Rhonda SHIRAZI
30 Vice President Advancement ... Mr. Jeffrey HILPERTS
32 Vice Pres Student Affs/Dn Stdnts ... Mr. Joe DEIGHTON
07 Vice Pres Admissions/Financial Aid ... Mr. Robert STEWART
20 Assistant VP for Academic Affairs ... Vacant
20 Associate Provost ... Ms. Jennifer GOOD
35 Associate Dean of Students ... Ms. Margarita PEREZ
21 Controller ... Ms. Wendy BOUTWELL
37 Director of Financial Aid ... Mrs. Ellen FOSTER
06 Registrar ... Mr. Stuart MOORE
88 Director Student Development Center ... Ms. Josetta MULLOY
29 Director of Alumni & Parents ... Mrs. Monde DONALDSON
91 Director Administrative Computing ... Mr. Mac HORTON
90 Dir Information Technology Services ... Mr. Glenn R. BELL
15 Director of Personnel ... Ms. Patricia A. DAVIS
19 Director of Public Safety/Security ... Mr. Todd WARREN
23 Director of Health Services ... Mrs. Melissa MELTON
42 Director of Campus Ministry ... Ms. Maureen BERGAN
41 Director Athletics & Recreation ... Mr. James HALL
31 Dir Foley CommunityService Center ... Dr. Kathleen ORANGE
26 Dir Communications/Instl Mktng ... Vacant
40 Bookstore Manager ... Ms. Genevieve MORRIS
36 Coordinator of Career Services ... Ms. Elizabeth DEXTER-WILSON
38 Counselor ... Ms. Lynda OLEN

Stillman College (E)

3601 Stillman Boulevard, POB 1430,
Tuscaloosa AL 35403-1430
County: Tuscaloosa FICE Identification: 001044
Unit ID: 102270
Telephone: (205) 349-4240 Carnegie Class: Bac/A&S
FAX Number: (205) 366-8996 Calendar System: Semester
URL: www.stillman.edu
Established: 1876 Annual Undergrad Tuition & Fees: $15,865
Enrollment: 1,019 Coed
Affiliation or Control: Presbyterian Church (U.S.A.) IRS Status: 501(c)3
Highest Offering: Baccalaureate
Program: Liberal Arts And General; Teacher Preparatory
Accreditation: SC, IACBE, MUS, TED

01 President ... Dr. Ernest MCNEALEY
05 Provost/VP Academic Affairs ... Dr. Peter MILLET
10 Vice President Fiscal Affairs ... Mr. Sama MONDEH
84 Vice President Retention ... Dr. Charlotte CARTER
30 VP Institutional Advancement ... Mr. Anthony HOLLOMAN
32 Vice President for Students Affairs ... Dr. Sharon WHITTAKER-DAVIS
31 Vice Pres External Affairs ... Dr. Eddie B. THOMAS
44 Associate VP for Development ... Mr. Adrian SCOTT
26 Assoc Vice President/Marketing & PR ... Mrs. Veronica CLARK-HOLLAND
21 Asst Vice Pres/Business Manager ... Vacant
29 Asst Vice Pres Alumni Affairs ... Vacant
18 Asst VP Logistics/Plant Operations ... Mr. Mason BONNER
53 Dean of Professional Educ/Asst VP ... Dr. Linda BRADFORD
49 Dean of Arts & Sciences/Asst VP ... Dr. Mary Jane KROTZER
08 Dean of Library ... Mr. Robert HEATH
09 Director of Institutional Research ... Ms. Cynthia D. LEATHERWOOD
06 Registrar ... Mrs. Barbara SMITH
37 Director of Financial Aid ... Mrs. Jacqueline MORRIS
38 Director of Student Development ... Ms. Jacqueline CURRIE
13 Director of Info Tech ... Mr. Dominic MURUAKO
07 Director of Admissions ... Mrs. Victoria BOMAN
19 Chief of Campus Police ... Mr. James TAGGART
41 Athletic Director ... Mr. Paul BRYANT
15 Human Resources Director ... Mrs. Patricia WILSON
42 College Chaplain ... Dr. Mark MCCORMICK

Talladega College (F)

627 W Battle Street, Talladega AL 35160-2354
County: Talladega FICE Identification: 001046
Unit ID: 102298
Telephone: (256) 362-0206 Carnegie Class: Bac/A&S
FAX Number: (256) 761-9206 Calendar System: Semester
URL: www.talladega.edu
Established: 1867 Annual Undergrad Tuition & Fees: $17,996
Enrollment: 1,202 Coed
Affiliation or Control: Independent Non-Profit IRS Status: 501(c)3
Highest Offering: Baccalaureate
Program: Liberal Arts And General; Teacher Preparatory; Professional; Business Emphasis
Accreditation: SC, SW

01 President ... Dr. Billy C. HAWKINS
05 Provost/Vice Pres Academic Affairs ... Dr. Evelyn M. WHITE
10 Vice President of Finance and Admin ... Dr. Gerald WILLIAMS
32 Vice President Student Affairs ... Mrs. Jacqueline PADDIO
30 Vice Pres Institutional Advancement ... Ms. Tysus JACKSON
18 Director Facilities Management ... Mr. Gary LAWSON
26 Director of Public Relations ... Vacant
37 Director Financial Aid ... Mrs. Russelle KEESE
07 Director of Admissions ... Mr. Kola AREMU
09 Director of Institutional Research ... Vacant
32 Director of Student Activities ... Mr. Anthony JONES
41 Athletic Director ... Mr. Wilberto RAMOS
08 Librarian ... Dr. Joseph MCDONALD
14 Information Technology Director ... Mrs. LaRita BREWSTER
36 Director of Career Placement ... Ms. Delores TRAYLOR
40 Materials Management/Convenience St ... Ms. Regina ALLEN
15 Director of Human Resources ... Mrs. Brenda RHODEN
19 Chief Campus Police ... Mr. Jefferson WALKER
50 Dean Div Administration & Business ... Mr. Eric HELVY
79 Dean Div Humanities/Fine Arts ... Vacant
81 Dean Div of Natural Sci/Math ... Dr. Charlie STINSON
83 Dean Div EWJ Social Sciences/Educ ... Dr. Lisa LONG
23 Health Services on Campus ... Mrs. Valarie ALFRED
25 Title III Coor/Grants Administrator ... Mrs. Nicola LAWLER
29 Director Alumni Relations ... Vacant
06 Registrar ... Mrs. Shametra MILLER
38 Director Student Counseling ... Ms. Delores TRAYLOR

Trenholm State Technical College (G)

PO Box 10048, Montgomery AL 36108
County: Montgomery FICE Identification: 005734
Unit ID: 102313
Telephone: (334) 420-4200 Carnegie Class: Assoc/Pub-R-S
FAX Number: (334) 420-4206 Calendar System: Semester
URL: www.trenholmstate.edu
Established: 1963 Annual Undergrad Tuition & Fees (In-State): $2,055
Enrollment: 1,445 Coed
Affiliation or Control: State IRS Status: 501(c)3
Highest Offering: Associate Degree
Program: Occupational; 2-Year Principally Bachelor's Creditable; Technical Emphasis
Accreditation: @SC, ACFEI, COE, DA, DMS, EMT, MAC, PNUR, RAD

01 President ... Mr. Samuel MUNNERLYN
10 Interim Dean of Finance/Admin Svcs ... Ms. Cathy WRIGHT
05 Dean of Instruction ... Ms. Barbara A. SPEARS
30 Dean of Development ... Dr. Suresh C. KAUSHIK
32 Dean of Students ... Ms. Beverly ROSS
103 Dean of Workforce Development ... Mr. Wilford HOLT
13 Assoc Dean of IT ... Mr. Charles HARRIS
09 Director of Institutional Research ... Dr. Mimi JOHNSON
18 Director Physical Facilities ... Mr. Dennis MONROE
37 Director Student Financial Aid ... Ms. Betty EDWARDS
07 Director of Admissions/Registrar ... Mrs. Tennie S. MCBRYDE
27 Public Information Officer ... Mr. Michael EVANS
15 Director of Human Resources ... Ms. Pam ROLLINS
51 Dir Title III/Marketing/Cont Educ ... Ms. Arlinda KNIGHT
36 Coordinator Job Placement ... Vacant

Troy University (H)

University Avenue, Troy AL 36082-0001
County: Pike FICE Identification: 001047
Unit ID: 102368
Telephone: (334) 670-3100 Carnegie Class: Master's L
FAX Number: (334) 670-3774 Calendar System: Semester
URL: www.troy.edu
Established: 1887 Annual Undergrad Tuition & Fees (In-State): $7,920
Enrollment: 22,554 Coed
Affiliation or Control: State IRS Status: 501(c)3
Highest Offering: Doctorate
Program: Liberal Arts And General; Teacher Preparatory; Professional
Accreditation: SC, ACBSP, ADNUR, CACREP, CORE, ENGR, MUS, NUR, SPAA, SW, TED

01 Chancellor ... Dr. Jack HAWKINS, JR.
05 Sr Vice Chanc for Academic Affairs ... Dr. Earl INGRAM
32 Sr Vice Chanc Student Svcs/Admin ... Dr. John R. DEW
30 Sr Vice Chanc Advance/External Affs ... Dr. John SCHMIDT
10 Sr VC for Finance & Business Affs ... Dr. James BOOKOUT
12 Vice Chancellor Troy Global Campus ... Dr. Lance TATUM
12 Vice Chancellor Troy Dothan ... Dr. Don JEFFREY
12 Vice Chancellor Troy Phenix City ... Dr. David WHITE
35 Dean of Student Svcs Troy Dothan ... Mr. Bob WILLIS
49 Assoc Dean Col Arts/Sci Troy Dothan ... Dr. Robert SAUNDERS
50 Assoc Dean Col Bus Troy Dothan ... Dr. Orrin AMES
53 Assoc Dean Col of Educ Troy Dothan ... Dr. Robin BYNUM
12 Vice Chanc Troy Montgomery ... Mr. Ray WHITE
49 Assoc Dean Arts/Sci Troy Montgomery ... Dr. Robert SANDERS
53 Assoc Dean Col Educ Troy Montgomery ... Dr. Pamela ARRINGTON
30 Assoc Vice Chanc for Development ... Dr. Jean LALIBERTE
37 Assoc Vice Chanc for Financial Aid ... Ms. Carol BALLARD
20 Associate Provost for Academics ... Dr. Lee VARDAMAN
27 Assoc VC for Mktg/Communication ... Mrs. Donna SCHUBERT
06 Registrar ... Mrs. Vickie MILES
84 Dean Enrollment Services ... Mr. Buddy STARLING
08 Dean Library Services ... Dr. Henry STEWART
15 Senior Director Human Resources ... Dr. Toni TAYLOR
13 Chief Technology Officer ... Mr. Greg PRICE
26 Director University Relations ... Mr. Tom DAVIS
29 Director Alumni Affairs ... Ms. Faith W. WARD
36 Coordinator Career Services ... Ms. Lauren COLE
18 Director Facilities/Physical Plant ... Mr. Mark SALMON
60 Director of Journalism ... Dr. Steven PADGETT
04 Exec Assistant to the Chancellor ... Mr. Dave BARRON
38 Director Student Counseling ... Ms. Teresa P. RODGERS
07 Director of Graduate Admissions ... Mrs. Brenda CAMPBELL
88 Dir Not for Profit/Assoc Controller ... Mrs. Lauri DORRILL
106 eTROY Dir Educational Technology ... Mr. Ronnie CREEL

86 Director of Federal/State Govt Rels .... Mr. Marcus PARAMORE
86 Dir of Local Governmental Relations .... Mr. Alan BOOTHE
44 Director of Annual Giving .... Mrs. Bronda DENISON
25 Director Sponsored Programs .... Mrs. Judy FULMER
62 Dir of Library Svcs Troy Dothan .... Mr. Chris SHAFFER
62 Dir of Library Svcs Troy Montgomery .... Mr. Kent SNOWDEN
20 Dean Undergrad Pgms/Assoc Provost .... Dr. Hal FULMER
35 Dean of Student Svcs Troy Campus .... Mr. Herbert REEVES
49 Dean Arts & Sciences .... Dr. James RINEHART
50 Dean Business .... Dr. Judson EDWARDS
53 Dean Education .... Dr. Kathryn HILDEBRAND
58 Dean Graduate Pgms/Assoc Provost .... Dr. Dianne BARRON
76 Dean Health/Human Services .... Dr. Damon ANDREW
57 Dean Communication/Fine Arts .... Dr. Maryjo COCHRAN
35 Assoc Dean Student Svcs Troy Mont .... Dr. James SMITH
35 Assoc Dean Student Svcs Troy Phenix .... Mr. Jack MILLER

Tuskegee University (A)

Tuskegee AL 36088
County: Macon FICE Identification: 001050
Unit ID: 102377
Telephone: (334) 727-8011 Carnegie Class: Bac/Diverse
FAX Number: (334) 727-5276 Calendar System: Semester
URL: www.tuskegee.edu
Established: 1881 Annual Undergrad Tuition & Fees: $18,900
Enrollment: 3,117 Coed
Affiliation or Control: Independent Non-Profit IRS Status: 501(c)3
Highest Offering: Doctorate
Program: Liberal Arts And General; Teacher Preparatory; Professional
Accreditation: SC, BUS, DIETD, ENG, MT, NUR, #OT, SW, TED, VET

01 President .... Dr. Gilbert L. ROCHON
05 Provost .... Dr. Luther S. WILLIAMS
10 Vice President Finance/CFO .... Mr. Cecil LUCY
09 VP Inst Research/Assessment/Plng .... Dr. John A. WILLIAMS
46 Vice Pres Research/Sponsored Pgms .... Dr. Shaik JEELANI
30 Vice Pres for Development .... Vacant
84 VP Student Affairs/Enrollment Mgmt .... Dr. Cynthia D. SELLERS
26 VP Communications/Public Rels/Mktg .... Mr. Kevin J. MCLIN, SR.
101 Exec Asst to Pres/Secy to the Board .... Mrs. Verna S. LITTLE
100 Chief of Staff .... Ms. Shamima AMIN
13 Chief Information Officer .... Mr. Fred JUDKINS
45 Asst VP & Dir Budget & Planning .... Ms. Belinda HOGUE
20 Assoc Provost & Director Intl Pgms .... Dr. Eloise CARTER
47 Vice Provost/Dean of CAENS .... Dr. Walter A. HILL
49 Dean School of Education .... Dr. Carlton E. MORRIS
50 Dean Col Business/Information Sci .... Dr. Tejnder SARA
54 Dean College of Engineering .... Dr. Legand L. BURGE
74 Dean Col Vet Med/Nurs/Allied Health .... Dr. Tsegaye HABTEMARIAM
32 Dean of Students .... Mr. Peter J. SPEARS, SR.
42 Dean of the Chapel .... Dr. Gregory S. GRAY
08 Director of Library Services .... Mrs. Juanita ROBERTS
29 Alumni Affairs Director .... Ms. Kimberly WOODARD
86 Director Federal Relations .... Mrs. Willa HALL SMITH
51 Int Assoc Prov Cont Educ/Extension .... Dr. Ntam BAHARANYI
36 Assoc Dir Career Devel/Placement .... Ms. Sarah STRINGER
21 Bursar .... Ms. Barbara CHISHOLM
37 Director of Financial Aid .... Mr. A. D. JAMES
09 Assoc Dir Inst Analysis/Evaluation .... Mr. Willie J. JACKSON
15 Director Personnel Services .... Ms. Kathy WEBB
18 Project Mgr Sodexho/Physical Plant .... Mr. Tony WARD
91 Director of Applications Support .... Mr. James E. COOPER
06 Registrar .... Mrs. Edrice LEFTWICH
38 Director Student Counseling .... Dr. Joyce RHODEN
96 Director of Purchasing .... Vacant

United States Sports Academy (B)

One Academy Drive, Daphne AL 36526-7055
County: Baldwin FICE Identification: 021706
Unit ID: 102395
Telephone: (251) 626-3303 Carnegie Class: Spec/Other
FAX Number: (251) 626-3874 Calendar System: Semester
URL: www.ussa.edu
Established: 1972 Annual Undergrad Tuition & Fees: $4,600
Enrollment: 915 Coed
Affiliation or Control: Independent Non-Profit IRS Status: 501(c)3
Highest Offering: Doctorate
Program: Professional
Accreditation: SC

01 President .... Dr. Thomas P. ROSANDICH
11 Vice President & COO .... Dr. Thomas J. ROSANDICH
05 Dean of Academic Affairs .... Dr. Stephen L. BUTLER
10 Dean of Admin & Finance .... Ms. Holly H. MCLELLAN
51 Assoc Dn Cont Ed/Distance Learning .... Ms. Betsy R. SMITH
32 Director of Student Services .... Dr. Timothy FOLEY
27 Director of Communications .... Mr. Duwayne ESCOBEDO
06 Registrar .... Ms. Sarah COLE
08 Director of Library/Archivist .... Mr. Greg TYLER
37 Director of Financial Aid .... Vacant
18 Building and Grounds .... Mr. Matthew COPE

*University of Alabama System Office (C)

401 Queen City Avenue, Tuscaloosa AL 35401-1551
County: Tuscaloosa FICE Identification: 008004
Unit ID: 100733
Telephone: (205) 348-5861 Carnegie Class: N/A
FAX Number: (205) 348-9788
URL: www.uasystem.ua.edu

01 Chancellor .... Dr. Robert E. WITT
101 Sec Board & Exec Asst to Chanc .... Mr. Michael A. BOWNES
05 Vice Chancellor Academic Affairs .... Dr. Charles R. NASH
10 Exec Vice Chanc Financial Affairs .... Mr. Ray HAYES
26 Vice Chancellor System Relations .... Mrs. Kellee C. REINHART
86 Vice Chanc Govt Rels/Economic Devel .... Mr. Jo BONNER
43 General Counsel .... Mr. R. Cooper SHATTUCK
21 General Auditor .... Ms. Sabrina B. HEARN

*The University of Alabama (D)

Tuscaloosa AL 35487-0100
County: Tuscaloosa FICE Identification: 001051
Unit ID: 100751
Telephone: (205) 348-6010 Carnegie Class: RU/H
FAX Number: (205) 348-9046 Calendar System: Semester
URL: www.ua.edu
Established: 1831 Annual Undergrad Tuition & Fees (In-State): $9,200
Enrollment: 33,602 Coed
Affiliation or Control: State IRS Status: 501(c)3
Highest Offering: Doctorate
Program: Liberal Arts And General; Teacher Preparatory; Professional
Accreditation: SC, AAFCS, ART, BUS, BUSA, CACREP, CEA, CIDA, CLPSY, CORE, CS, DANCE, DIETC, DIETD, ENG, JOUR, LAW, LIB, MUS, NURSE, SP, SW, TED, THEA

02 President .... Dr. Judy L. BONNER
05 Interim Provost .... Dr. Joe BENSON
10 Vice Pres for Financial Affairs .... Dr. Lynda GILBERT
30 Vice Pres for Advancement .... Dr. Karen BALDWIN
46 Vice President for Research .... Dr. Joe BENSON
32 Vice Pres for Student Affairs .... Dr. Mark NELSON
31 Vice Pres for Community Affairs .... Dr. Samory T. PRUITT
13 Vice Provost/Chief Information Ofcr .... Dr. John MCGOWAN
18 Assistant VP University Facilities .... Mr. Duane LAMB
18 Ast VP Univ Facilities/Construction .... Mr. Tim LEOPARD
19 Asst Vice Pres Public Safety .... Mr. W. Steven TUCKER
20 Vice Provost Academic Affairs .... Dr. Mark NELSON
11 Asst Provost for Administration .... Ms. Dorothy J. MARTIN
15 Assoc Vice Pres Human Resources .... Ms. Charlotte M. HARRIS
21 Assoc Vice President for Finance .... Ms. Reba J. ESSARY
21 Assoc Vice Pres Financial Affairs .... Ms. Dana S. KEITH
26 Asst VP University Relations .... Ms. Deborah LANE
29 Asst VP for Alumni Affs/Annual Fund .... Mr. Calvin BROWN
85 Asst VP Internatl Ed/Global Affairs .... Dr. Teresa WISE
06 University Registrar .... Mr. W. Michael GEORGE
09 Director Inst Research/Assessment .... Dr. Lorne KUFFELL
36 Exec Director of Career Center .... Mr. Travis RAILSBACK
07 Dir of Undergraduate Admissions .... Ms. Mary K. SPIEGEL
22 Dir & University Compliance Officer .... Ms. Gwendolyn D. HOOD
11 Chief Admin Officer CCHS/RSHC .... Mr. John B. MAXWELL, JR.
37 Director of Student Financial Aid .... Ms. Helen ALLEN
84 Director Enrollment Management .... Mrs. Terri TERRY
39 Director Dept of Housing/Res Cmty .... Dr. Steven HOOD
40 Director of University Supply Store .... Ms. Teresa SHREVE
41 Athletic Director .... Mr. Bill BATTLE
43 University Counsel .... Mr. Mike SPEARING
08 Dean of University Libraries .... Dr. Louis A. PITSCHMANN
49 Dean of Arts & Sciences .... Dr. Robert F. OLIN
50 Dean Col Commerce & Business Admin .... Dr. J. Michael HARDIN
51 Dean College of Continuing Studies .... Dr. Carolyn C. DAHL
53 Dean College of Education .... Dr. Peter HLEBOWITSH
54 Dean College of Engineering .... Dr. Charles L. KARR
58 Dean Graduate School/Asst Acad VP .... Dr. David A. FRANCKO
59 Dean Human Environmental Sciences .... Dr. Milla BOSCHUNG
60 Dean Col of Communication/Info Sci .... Dr. Loy SINGLETON
61 Dean School of Law .... Mr. Kenneth C. RANDALL
62 Dir Sch of Library/Info Studies .... Dr. Heidi JULIEN
38 Manager Stdnt Support Svcs-Trio Pgm .... Ms. Wendy L. COGBURN
96 Asc Purchasing Mgr Genl Procurement .... Ms. Pollye HARDY
96 Asc Purchas Mgr Facil Procurement .... Mr. Lane COX
76 Dean Cmty Health Sciences .... Dr. Rick STREIFFER
66 Dean Capstone College of Nursing .... Dr. Suzanne S. PREVOST
70 Interim Dean School of Social Work .... Dr. Lucinda L. ROFF
92 Dean of Honors College .... Dr. Shane SHARPE
94 Chair of Women's Studies .... Ms. Elle SHAABAN-MAGANA

*University of Alabama at Birmingham (E)

1720 2nd Avenue South, Birmingham AL 35294-0001
County: Jefferson FICE Identification: 001052
Unit ID: 100663
Telephone: (205) 934-4011 Carnegie Class: RU/VH
FAX Number: N/A Calendar System: Semester
URL: www.uab.edu
Established: 1969 Annual Undergrad Tuition & Fees (In-State): $7,206
Enrollment: 17,999 Coed
Affiliation or Control: State IRS Status: 501(c)3
Highest Offering: Doctorate
Program: Liberal Arts And General; Teacher Preparatory; Professional
Accreditation: SC, ANEST, ARCPA, ART, BUS, BUSA, CACREP, CAHIIM, CLPSY, COARC, CS, CYTO, DENT, DIETI, ENG, FEPAC, HSA, IPSY, MED, MT, MUS, NMT, NURSE, OPT, OPTR, OT, PH, PTA, SPAA, SW, TED, THEA

02 President .... Dr. Ray L. WATTS
05 Provost .... Dr. Linda C. LUCAS
10 Vice Pres Financial Affairs/Admin .... Mr. Richard L. MARGISON
17 CEO UAB Health System .... Dr. Will FERNIANY
30 Vice Pres Dev/Alumni/External Rels .... Dr. Shirley S. KAHN
13 Int Vice Pres Info Technology .... Dr. Doug RIGNEY
28 Vice Pres for Equity and Diversity .... Dr. Louis DALE
46 Vice Pres for Research/Economic Dev .... Dr. Richard B. MARCHASE
63 Int VP/Dean School of Medicine .... Dr. Anupam AGARWAL
11 Vice Prov Admin/Quality Improvement .... Mr. Harlan M. SANDS
20 Vice Prov Student/Faculty Success .... Dr. Suzanne E. AUSTIN
43 University Counsel .... Mr. W. John DANIEL
49 Dean College of Arts & Sciences .... Dr. Robert PALAZZO
50 Dean School of Business .... Dr. Eric JACK
52 Dean School of Dentistry .... Dr. Michael S. REDDY
53 Dean School of Education .... Dr. Deborah L. VOLTZ
54 Interim Dean School of Engineering .... Dr. Melinda M. LALOR
76 Dean School of Health Professions .... Dr. Harold P. JONES
66 Dean School of Nursing .... Dr. Doreen C. HARPER
88 Dean School of Optometry .... Dr. Rodney NOWAKOWSKI
69 Dean School of Public Health .... Dr. Max MICHAEL, III
58 Dean Graduate School .... Dr. Bryan D. NOE
18 Assoc Vice President Facilities .... Mr. Robert E. MCMAINS, III
21 Assoc VP Business/Auxiliary Svcs .... Mr. Christopher CLIFFORD
29 Assoc VP Alumni/Annual Giving .... Ms. Rebecca WATSON
44 Asst Vice Pres Development .... Mr. Thomas I. BRANNAN
26 Assoc VP Public Relations & Mktg .... Ms. Dale TURNBOUGH
84 Assoc Provost Enrollment Management .... Dr. Brent GAGE
21 Assoc Vice Pres Financial Affairs .... Ms. Patricia A. RACZYNSKI
35 Asst Vice Pres for Student Life .... Mr. Andrew J. MARSCH, III
08 Director Mervyn Sterne Library .... Dr. Jerry W. STEPHENS
08 Director Lister Hill Library .... Mr. Scott PLUTCHAK
41 Athletic Director .... Mr. Brian W. MACKIN
15 Chief Human Resources Officer .... Ms. Alesia M. JONES
09 Exec Dir Inst Effect & Analysis .... Mr. Lee SMITH
19 Assistant VP & Chief of Police .... Mr. Anthony B. PURCELL
07 Director Undergraduate Admissions .... Mr. Kirk KLUVER
37 Director of Financial Aid .... Ms. Janet B. MAY
06 University Registrar .... Ms. Tina COLLINS
39 Interim Director Student Housing .... Ms. Amy OWENS
36 Executive Director Career Services .... Ms. Suzanne SCOTT-TRAMMELL
38 Dir Student Counseling & Wellness .... Ms. Susan L. HART

*University of Alabama in Huntsville (F)

301 Sparkman Drive, Huntsville AL 35899-1911
County: Madison FICE Identification: 001055
Unit ID: 100706
Telephone: (256) 824-1000 Carnegie Class: RU/VH
FAX Number: (256) 824-6073 Calendar System: Semester
URL: www.uah.edu
Established: 1950 Annual Undergrad Tuition & Fees (In-State): $9,192
Enrollment: 7,636 Coed
Affiliation or Control: State IRS Status: 501(c)3
Highest Offering: Doctorate
Program: Liberal Arts And General; Teacher Preparatory; Professional
Accreditation: SC, ART, BUS, CS, ENG, MUS, NURSE, TED

02 President .... Dr. Robert A. ALTENKIRCH
05 Provost & Exec VP Academic Affairs .... Vacant
10 VP Finance & Administration .... Mr. Ray PINNER
41 Director Intercollegiate Athletics .... Dr. William E. BROPHY, JR.
43 University Counsel .... Mr. Robert W. RIEDER, JR.
46 VP Research .... Dr. Ray VAUGHN
30 VP University Advancement .... Mr. Robert LYON
28 VP Diversity .... Ms. Delois SMITH
86 Dir Govt Relations & Public Affairs .... Mr. Ray GARNER
30 Asst VP for Development .... Ms. Brenda WALKER
84 Asst Provost Enrollment Services .... Ms. Ingrid HAYES
46 Assoc VP Research .... Dr. Thomas M. KOSHUT
35 Assc VP Stdnt Affs/Dean of Students .... Dr. Regina G. HYATT
39 Assoc VP Auxiliary Services .... Mr. John MAXON
11 Assoc VP Finance & Business Svcs .... Mr. Robert LEONARD
27 CIO/Assoc Provost .... Ms. Dee CHILDS
18 Assoc VP Facilities & Operations .... Mr. Michael S. FINNEGAN
20 Assoc Provost UG Studies/Inst Effec .... Dr. Brent M. WREN
21 Associate VP Budgets & Fin Planning .... Mr. Chih LOO
29 Assoc VP for Advancement-Alumni Rel .... Mr. Joel C. LONERGAN
16 Assoc VP Human Resources .... Ms. Laurel LONG
30 Assoc VP Advancement .... Ms. April HARRIS
09 Director Institutional Research .... Ms. Deborah STOWERS
88 Director Internal Audit .... Ms. Tharanee M. RAVINDRAN
85 Dir International Engagement .... Dr. Susan STEEN
36 Exec Dir Student Success Center .... Mr. Alan CONSTANT
25 Director Sponsored Programs .... Ms. Gloria GREENE
88 Director Institute for Science Educ .... Dr. James A. MILLER
08 Director Library .... Dr. David P. MOORE
79 Dean College of Liberal Arts .... Mr. Glenn DASHER
81 Dean College of Science .... Dr. John FIX
50 Dean College Business Admin .... Dr. Caron ST. JOHN
51 Director Div Continuing Education .... Dr. Karen CLANTON
54 Dean College of Engineering .... Dr. Shankar MAHALINGAM
58 Dean Graduate Studies .... Dr. David BERKOWITZ
66 Dean College of Nursing .... Dr. C. Fay RAINES
88 Dir Ctr for Mgmt of Science & Tech .... Dr. John P. BALLENGER
40 Bookstore Manager .... Ms. Amber YOUNG
37 Director Financial Aid .... Mr. Andrew M. WEAVER
38 Dir Student Counseling Svcs .... Vacant
23 Dir Faculty & Staff Clinic .... Ms. Louise O'KEEFE
19 Director Public Safety .... Mr. Michael R. SNELLGROVE
06 Registrar .... Ms. Janet WALLER
07 Director Admissions .... Ms. Sandra BARINOWSKI
29 Director Alumni Relations .... Ms. Rachel V. OSBY
88 Director Advancement Services .... Ms. Marcie T. EPPLING
23 Director Student Health Services .... Ms. Kathleen S. RHODES
88 Director ITSC .... Dr. Sara J. GRAVES
88 Dir Small Business Develop Center .... Mr. Foster PERRY

102 Asst Director Corporate Relations .... Ms. Katie S. THURSTON
14 Director Networks & Infrastructure .... Mr. David DIONNE
88 Director Library Info Technology .... Mr. Jack DROST
90 Dir Academic Tech & e-Learning .... Mr. Chad HYATT
88 Director Cust Rels/Svc & Support .... Ms. Pam TEJES
88 Director Research Institute .... Dr. Steven MESSERVY
88 Director CMSA .... Dr. Mikel D. PETTY
88 Director SMAP Center .... Dr. Gary MADDUX
88 Acting Director Rotocraft Center .... Ms. Susan O'BRIEN
88 Interim Director CAO .... Dr. Pat REARDON
88 Int Dir Ctr Mgmt & Econ Research .... Mr. Jeff S. THOMPSON
88 Director Propulsion Research Center .... Dr. Robert FREDERICK
88 Dir Center Space Plsm & Aeron Res .... Dr. Gary ZANK
88 Director Earth Systems Science Ctr .... Dr. John R. CHRISTY
88 Director University Center .... Mr. William M. HALL
91 Director Enterprise Apps & IAM .... Mr. Malcolm RICE
104 Director Global Studies Program .... Dr. David JOHNSON
92 Director Honors Program .... Dr. Harry S. DELUGACH

University of Mobile (A)

5735 College Parkway, Mobile AL 36613-2842

County: Mobile FICE Identification: 001029
Unit ID: 101693
Telephone: (251) 675-5990 Carnegie Class: Bac/Diverse
FAX Number: (251) 675-6293 Calendar System: Semester
URL: www.umobile.edu
Established: 1961 Annual Undergrad Tuition & Fees: $18,540
Enrollment: 1,719 Coed
Affiliation or Control: Southern Baptist IRS Status: 501(c)3
Highest Offering: Master's
Program: 2-Year Principally Bachelor's Creditable; Liberal Arts And General; Teacher Preparatory; Professional
Accreditation: SC, ACBSP, ADNUR, MUS, NURSE

01 President .... Dr. Mark R. FOLEY
05 Vice Pres for Academic Affairs .... Dr. Audrey C. EUBANKS
10 Vice President for Business Affairs .... Mr. J. Steve LEE
30 VP Institutional Advancement .... Mr. Brian BOYLE
84 VP Enrollment/Campus Life/Athletics .... Mrs. Kim LEOUSIS
44 Dir of Development for Major Gifts .... Mrs. Hali GIVENS
20 Associate VP for Academic Affairs .... Dr. Anne B. LOWERY
21 Associate VP for Business Affairs .... Mrs. Carol CAMP
20 Assoc VP Academic Svcs/Registrar .... Dr. Donald K. BERRY
84 Assoc VP for Enrollment Services .... Ms. Marie BATSON
04 Assistant to the President .... Dr. Fred G. LACKEY
26 Executive Director of Marketing .... Ms. Lesa MOORE
41 Athletic Director .... Mr. Joe NILAND
07 Director of Enrollment Services .... Mrs. Charity WITTNER
08 Director of Library Services .... Mr. Jeffrey D. CALAMETTI
27 Director of Media Relations .... Mrs. Kathy L. DEAN
09 Director of Inst Effectiveness .... Dr. Anne B. LOWERY
50 Dean School of Business .... Dr. Jane FINLEY
49 Dean College of Arts & Sciences .... Dr. Dwight STEEDLEY
53 Dean School of Education .... Dr. Peter KINGSFORD
66 Dean School of Nursing .... Dr. Jan WOOD
64 Dean School of Music .... Dr. Al MILLER
88 Dean Sch of Worship Leadership .... Dr. Al MILLER
88 Exec Dean Sch of Christian Ministry .... Dr. Joe SAVAGE
51 Dean Center for Adult Programs .... Dr. Pam BUCHANAN
73 Dean School of Christian Ministries .... Dr. Doug WILSON
58 Dean of Graduate Programs .... Dr. Anne B. LOWERY
39 Director of Residential Life .... Mr. Kris NELSON
29 Director Annual Giving/Alum Rels .... Mrs. Tonya GOLLETTE
44 Senior Development Officer .... Mr. Bill HART
102 Dev Officer for Corp/Govt Relations .... Mr. Claude BUMPERS
90 Director Academic Computing Lab .... Mr. Mitch DAVIS
42 Director of Campus Ministries .... Mr. Neal LEDBETTER
15 Director of Human Resources .... Mrs. Diane BLACK
13 Director of Information Technology .... Mr. Buck NORRED
18 Director of Campus Operations .... Mrs. Vicki BURGIN
38 Director Student Retention .... Mrs. Shirley SUTTERFIELD
88 Exec Dir Col of Christian Leadershp .... Dr. Roger BRELAND

University of Montevallo (B)

Station 6001, Montevallo AL 35115-6001

County: Shelby FICE Identification: 001004
Unit ID: 101709
Telephone: (205) 665-6000 Carnegie Class: Master's M
FAX Number: (205) 665-6003 Calendar System: Semester
URL: www.montevallo.edu
Established: 1896 Annual Undergrad Tuition & Fees (In-State): $9,780
Enrollment: 3,047 Coed
Affiliation or Control: State IRS Status: 501(c)3
Highest Offering: Beyond Master's But Less Than Doctorate
Program: Liberal Arts And General; Teacher Preparatory; Professional
Accreditation: SC, AAFCS, ART, BUS, CACREP, DIETD, MUS, SP, SW, TED

01 President .... Dr. John W. STEWART, III
05 Provost and VP Academic Affairs .... Dr. Suzanne OZMENT
32 Dean of Students .... Dr. Tammi DAHLE
30 VP for Enrollment Management .... Dr. Rick BARTH
10 VP Business Affairs .... Ms. DeAnna M. SMITH
11 Sr VP for Administratiave Affairs .... Dr. Michelle JOHNSTON
18 Director Physical Plant .... Mr. Billy HUGHES
35 Director Student Life .... Ms. Jenny BELL
06 Assoc Registrar .... Ms. Amanda T. FOX
08 Director Libraries .... Ms. Kathy LOWE
07 Director Admissions .... Mr. Greg EMBRY
29 Dir Development/Alumni Relations .... Vacant
14 Chief Information Officer .... Mr. Bob STACK

26 Director of University Relations .... Mr. Jamie BESSETTE
37 Dir of Student Financial Services .... Ms. Maria D. PARKER
38 Director Counseling Services .... Mr. Joshua MILLER
19 Chief of Police .... Mr. Chadd ADAMS
39 Dir Housing & Residence Life .... Mr. John DENSON
41 Director Athletics .... Mr. James E. HERLIHY
15 Director of HR and Risk Management .... Ms. Barbara FORREST
51 Dir of Regional Inservice Center .... Mr. Dwight JINRIGHT
58 Dir Graduate Admissions & Records . Mr. Kevin THORNTHWAITE
49 Dean College Arts & Sciences .... Dr. Mary Beth ARMSTRONG
50 Dean College of Business .... Dr. Stephen CRAFT
53 Dean College of Education .... Dr. Anna E. MCEWAN
57 Interim Dean College of Fine Arts .... Dr. Scott STEPHENS

University of North Alabama (C)

One Harrison Plaza, Florence AL 35632-0001

County: Lauderdale FICE Identification: 001016
Unit ID: 101879
Telephone: (256) 765-4100 Carnegie Class: Master's L
FAX Number: (256) 765-4644 Calendar System: Semester
URL: www.una.edu
Established: 1830 Annual Undergrad Tuition & Fees (In-State): $7,068
Enrollment: 7,032 Coed
Affiliation or Control: State IRS Status: 501(c)3
Highest Offering: Beyond Master's But Less Than Doctorate
Program: Liberal Arts And General; Teacher Preparatory; Professional
Accreditation: SC, ACBSP, ART, CACREP, CS, ENGR, MUS, NURSE, SW, TED

01 President .... Dr. William G. CALE, JR.
05 Vice Pres Acad Affairs & Provost .... Dr. John THORNELL
88 Vice Provost for Intl Affairs .... Dr. Chunsheng ZHANG
10 VP for Business/Financial Affairs .... Dr. Steve SMITH
32 Vice President Student Affairs .... Mr. David P. SHIELDS, JR.
30 Vice President Advancement .... Dr. Daniel L. HENDRICKS
84 Vice Pres Enrollment Management .... Dr. Thomas C. CALHOUN, JR.
44 Assoc VP Advancement Services .... Dr. Judy T. JACKSON
49 Dean College of Arts & Sciences .... Dr. Vagn K. HANSEN
50 Dean College of Business .... Dr. Gregory A. CARNES
53 Dean Col Education/Human Sciences .... Dr. Donna P. LEFORT
66 Dean College Nursing/Allied Health .... Dr. Birdie I. BAILEY
31 Director University Events .... Mr. Bret JENNINGS
41 Director of Athletics .... Mr. Mark LINDER
21 Controller .... Ms. Donna F. TIPPS
39 Director of Housing .... Ms. Audrey MITCHELL
37 Director Student Financial Services .... Mr. Ben J. BAKER
15 Dir Human Resources/Affirm Action .... Ms. Catherine D. WHITE
26 Int Dir University Communications .... Mr. Terry G. PACE
24 Dir Educational Technology Services .... Ms. Debbie CHAFFIN
18 Director Facilities Admin/Planning .... Mr. Michael B. GAUTNEY
19 Director of University Police .... Mr. Robert G. PASTULA
51 Dir Continuing Studies and Outreach .... Ms. Lavonne GATLIN
23 Director University Health Services .... Dr. Kyrel L. BUCHANAN
35 Dir Judicial Affairs/Stdnt Aff Plng .... Dr. Kimberly GREENWAY
91 Director Information Tech Services .... Mr. Stephen J. PUTMAN
07 Director of Admissions .... Ms. Kim MAULDIN
09 Dir Inst Rsrch/Plng & Assessment .... Dr. Andrew L. LUNA
29 Director Alumni Relations .... Ms. Carol S. LYLES
96 Director of Procurement .... Ms. Cindy H. CONLON
28 Dir Diversity/Institutional Equity .... Ms. Joan J. WILLIAMS
36 Dir Career Planning & Development .... Ms. Melissa T. MEDLIN
06 Interim Registrar .... Ms. Lisa E. BURTON
38 Director University Advising .... Dr. Amy CREWS
86 Governmental Relations Specialist .... Ms. Rita F. FOSTER
40 Manager University Bookstore .... Mr. Griffin HITE

University of Phoenix Birmingham Campus (D)

100 Corporate Parkway, Suite 250,
Birmingham AL 35242-2982

Telephone: (205) 747-1001 Identification: 770187
Accreditation: &NH, ACBSP

† Main campus is University of Phoenix in Tempe, AZ.

University of South Alabama (E)

307 University Boulevard, N, Mobile AL 36688-0002

County: Mobile FICE Identification: 001057
Unit ID: 102094
Telephone: (251) 460-6101 Carnegie Class: RU/H
FAX Number: (251) 461-1537 Calendar System: Semester
URL: www.southalabama.edu
Established: 1963 Annual Undergrad Tuition & Fees (In-State): $8,310
Enrollment: 14,883 Coed
Affiliation or Control: State IRS Status: 501(c)3
Highest Offering: Doctorate
Program: Liberal Arts And General; Teacher Preparatory; Professional
Accreditation: SC, ARCPA, AUD, BUS, BUSA, COARC, CS, EMT, ENG, MED, MUS, NURSE, OT, PTA, RAD, RTT, SP, SW, TED

01 Acting President .... Dr. John SMITH
05 Sr Vice Pres Academic Affairs .... Dr. G. David JOHNSON
30 Vice Pres Developmental/Alumni Rels .... Dr. Joseph F. BUSTA
10 Vice President Financial Affairs .... Mr. Steve SIMMONS
23 Vice President Health Sciences .... Dr. Ronald FRANKS
32 Vice President for Student Affairs .... Dr. John SMITH
46 Vice President for Research .... Dr. Lynne CHRONISTER
84 Interim Dir Enrollment Services .... Mr. Christopher LYNCH
58 Assoc VP Acad Affs/Dean Grad Sch .... Dr. B. Keith HARRISON
13 Exec Director of Information Tech .... Mr. Chris CANNON

46 Interim Assoc VP IRPA .... Dr. Charles GUEST
15 Asst Vice President Human Resources . Ms. Pamela HENDERSON
17 Dean College of Medicine .... Dr. Samuel J. STRADA
86 Exec Dir Government Relations .... Mr. William J. FULFORD
88 Dir Student Acad Success/Retention .... Dr. Nicole T. CARR
88 Director of Assessment .... Ms. Cecelia MARTIN
26 Director of Public Relations .... Mr. Keith AYERS
41 Director of Athletics .... Dr. Joel ERDMANN
07 Director of Admissions .... Ms. Norma J. TANNER
85 Director Intl Student Services .... Ms. Donna PIGG
07 Director New Student Recruitment .... Mr. Christopher LYNCH
09 Dir Inst Research/Plng & Analysis .... Dr. Gordon E. MILLS, JR.
06 Registrar .... Ms. Kelly OSTERBIND
29 Director Alumni Relations .... Ms. Karen EDWARDS
19 Chief of Police .... Mr. Zeke AULL, JR.
37 Director of Financial Aid .... Ms. Emily JOHNSTON
36 Director Career Services .... Ms. Bevley W. GREEN
12 Director USA Baldwin County .... Ms. Cynthia WILSON
18 Director Facilities Management .... Mr. Randy MOON
38 Int Dir Student Counseling/Test .... Dr. Robert HANKS
88 Manager New Student Orientation .... Mr. Scott R. SMITH
28 Director Multicultural Student Affs .... Dr. Carl G. CUNNINGHAM
96 Purchasing Agent .... Mr. Robert M. BROWN
54 Dean College of Engineering .... Dr. John STEADMAN
51 Dean Continuing Educ/Spec Pgms .... Dr. Vaughn S. MILLNER
49 Dean of Arts and Sciences .... Dr. Andrzej WIERZBICKI
08 Dean of University Libraries .... Dr. Richard J. WOOD
50 Dean Mitchell College of Business .... Dr. Carl C. MOORE
53 Dean of Education .... Dr. Richard L. HAYES
66 Dean of College of Nursing .... Dr. Debra C. DAVIS
76 Dean of Allied Health Professions .... Dr. Richard TALBOTT
77 Dean Computer & Information Science .... Dr. Alec YASINSAC

The University of West Alabama (F)

205 N Washington Street, Livingston AL 35470-2099

County: Sumter FICE Identification: 001024
Unit ID: 101587
Telephone: (205) 652-3400 Carnegie Class: Master's L
FAX Number: (205) 652-3718 Calendar System: Semester
URL: www.uwa.edu
Established: 1835 Annual Undergrad Tuition & Fees (In-State): $7,312
Enrollment: 4,943 Coed
Affiliation or Control: State IRS Status: 501(c)3
Highest Offering: Beyond Master's But Less Than Doctorate
Program: Liberal Arts And General; Teacher Preparatory; Professional
Accreditation: SC, ACBSP, ADNUR, TED

01 President .... Dr. Richard D. HOLLAND
05 Provost .... Dr. David M. TAYLOR
10 Vice President Financial Affairs .... Mr. T. Raiford NOLAND
30 Vice Pres Institutional Advancement .... Mr. Clemit W. SPRUIELL
32 Vice President for Student Affairs ...... Mr. Thomas D. BUCKALEW
49 Dean of Liberal Arts .... Dr. Tim EDWARDS
50 Dean of Business .... Dr. Ken TUCKER
53 Dean of Teacher Education .... Dr. Kathy CHANDLER
81 Dean of Natural Science/Math .... Mr. Sammy CULPEPPER
58 Dean of Graduate Studies .... Dr. Kathy CHANDLER
51 Dean Continuing Education .... Dr. Tina N. JONES
106 Dean Online Programs .... Dr. Martha HOCUTT
66 Chairperson of Nursing .... Mrs. Marsha CANNON
08 Director of Library .... Dr. Neil SNIDER
09 Dir Institutional Effectiveness .... Mrs. Angel JOWERS
41 Athletic Director .... Mr. Stan WILLIAMSON
35 Director of Student Life & Housing .... Mr. Luther GREMMELS
06 Registrar .... Mrs. Susan SPARKMAN
37 Director Student Financial Aid .... Mr. Don RAINER
13 Director Information Systems .... Mr. Michael PRATT
18 Director of Physical Plant .... Mr. Robert L. HOLYCROSS
40 Director of Auxiliary Services .... Ms. Mamie REED
36 Director Career Services/Placement .... Ms. Tammy S. WHITE
29 Director Alumni Relations .... Mrs. Tyanne S. STONE
38 Director Student Success Center .... Dr. Vicki P. SPRUIELL
86 Director Government Relations .... Mr. Clemit W. SPRUIELL
07 Dir of Admissions/Enrollment Mgmt .... Mr. Bill WAGNON
96 Director of Purchasing .... Mr. Lawson C. EDMONDS
89 Director Freshmen Studies .... Dr. James GENTSCH
92 Director Honors Program .... Dr. Lesa SHAUL
15 Director Personnel Services .... Mrs. Jessie W. EGBERT
30 Director of Development .... Mr. Tom TARTT
20 Associate Academic Officer .... Mrs. Angel JOWERS
26 Chief Public Relations Officer .... Ms. Betsy COMPTON
19 Director of Security/Safety .... Mr. Jeff MANUEL
103 Director Workforce Development .... Mr. Kenneth WALKER
105 Director of Web Services .... Mrs. Christi GEORGE
101 Secretary Board of Trustees .... Mrs. Earlene LINDSEY
28 Director of Diversity .... Dr. David M. TAYLOR
85 Director of Foreign Students .... Mr. John KEY

Wallace State Community College - Hanceville (G)

PO Box 2000, 801 Main Street, NW,
Hanceville AL 35077-2000

County: Cullman FICE Identification: 007871
Unit ID: 101295
Telephone: (256) 352-8000 Carnegie Class: Assoc/Pub-R-M
FAX Number: (256) 352-8228 Calendar System: Semester
URL: www.wallacestate.edu
Established: 1966 Annual Undergrad Tuition & Fees (In-State): $3,360
Enrollment: 5,399 Coed
Affiliation or Control: State IRS Status: 501(c)3
Highest Offering: Associate Degree
Program: Occupational; 2-Year Principally Bachelor's Creditable

Accreditation: SC, ACBSP, ACFEI, ADNUR, CAHIIM, COARC, DA, DH, DMS, EMT, MAC, MLTAD, OTA, PNUR, POLYT, PTAA, RAD

01 President .... Dr. Vicki HAWSEY
03 Executive Vice President .... Dr. Tomesa SMITH
10 Dean of Finance & Admin Svcs .... Jason MORGAN
05 College Dean .... Johnny MCMOY
20 Dean of Applied Technologies .... Jimmy HODGES
26 Dean of Institutional Outreach .... Melinda EDWARDS
76 Dean of Health Sciences .... Lisa GERMAN
84 Asst Dean Enrollment Management .... Jennifer HILL
88 Auxiliary Director .... Mark BOLIN
08 Librarian .... Lisa HULLETT
07 Director Admissions & Registrar .... Vacant
37 Director of Financial Aid .... Becky GRAVES
56 Extended Day Program Director .... Wayne MANORD
15 Director of Human Resources .... Alyce FLANAGAN
30 Director of Advancement .... Suzanne HARBIN
18 Director of Plant Operations .... Phil STUDDARD
26 Director of Communication/Marketing .... Kristen HOLMES

ALASKA

Alaska Bible College (A)

Box 289, 200 College Road, Glennallen AK 99588-0289

FICE Identification: 008843
Unit ID: 102580

Telephone: (907) 822-3201 Carnegie Class: Not Classified
FAX Number: (907) 822-5027 Calendar System: Semester
URL: www.akbible.edu
Established: 1966 Annual Undergrad Tuition & Fees: $10,000
Enrollment: 55 Coed
Affiliation or Control: Independent Non-Profit IRS Status: 501(c)3
Highest Offering: Baccalaureate
Program: Religious Emphasis
Accreditation: BI

01 President .... Mr. Nick RINGGER
05 Vice Pres Academic Affs/Dist Lrng .... Mr. John FERCH
32 Vice Pres Student Development .... Mr. Hal GIVENS
88 Vice Pres of Broadcasting .... Mr. Scott YAHR
06 Registrar/Bookkeeper .... Miss Carol REIMER
08 Librarian .... Mrs. Pamela HORST
07 Director Admissions/Recruiting .... Mrs. Nikki PALMER
27 Director of Communications .... Ms. Michelle EASTTY

Alaska Career College (B)

1415 E. Tudor Road, Anchorage AK 99507-1033

County: Anchorage FICE Identification: 025410
Unit ID: 103501

Telephone: (907) 563-7575 Carnegie Class: Not Classified
FAX Number: (907) 563-8330 Calendar System: Other
URL: www.alaskacareercollege.edu
Established: Annual Undergrad Tuition & Fees: $13,493
Enrollment: 600 Coed
Affiliation or Control: Proprietary IRS Status: Proprietary
Highest Offering: Associate Degree
Program: Occupational; 2-Year Principally Bachelor's Creditable; Technical Emphasis
Accreditation: ACCSC

01 Director .... Ms. Linda STURE

Alaska Pacific University (C)

4101 University Drive, Anchorage AK 99508-4672

County: Anchorage FICE Identification: 001061
Unit ID: 102669

Telephone: (907) 561-1266 Carnegie Class: Master's S
FAX Number: (907) 562-4276 Calendar System: Semester
URL: www.alaskapacific.edu
Established: 1957 Annual Undergrad Tuition & Fees: $29,700
Enrollment: 616 Coed
Affiliation or Control: Independent Non-Profit IRS Status: 501(c)3
Highest Offering: Master's
Program: Liberal Arts And General; Teacher Preparatory
Accreditation: NW, TED

01 President .... Dr. Don BANTZ
04 Assistant to the President .... Ms. Debbie ROLL
05 Academic Dean .... Ms. Tracy STEWART
10 Chief Financial Officer .... Ms. Deborah JOHNSTON
32 Dean of Students .... Mr. Kelly SMITH
06 Registrar .... Ms. Michelle WHEELER
07 Director of Admissions .... Mr. Carter CAYWOOD
37 Director of Financial Aid .... Mr. Phong MOUA
18 Director Facilities Management .... Ms. Kathy MINCKS
13 Director Information Technology .... Mr. Michael BAKER
30 Chief Development Officer .... Ms. Stephanie HAYDN
42 Chaplain .... Vacant
15 Director Human Resources .... Ms. Kathleen WYRICK
40 Assistant Campus Store Manager .... Ms. Lydia HARVEY
29 Alumni Relations Coord .... Ms. Heather HANSEN

† Granted candidacy at the Doctorate level.

Charter College (D)

2221 E Northern Lights Blvd, #120,
Anchorage AK 99508-4157

County: Anchorage FICE Identification: 025769
Unit ID: 102845

Telephone: (907) 277-1000 Carnegie Class: Bac/Assoc
FAX Number: (907) 274-3342 Calendar System: Quarter
URL: www.chartercollege.edu
Established: 1985 Annual Undergrad Tuition & Fees: $18,000
Enrollment: 1,259 Coed
Affiliation or Control: Proprietary IRS Status: Proprietary
Highest Offering: Baccalaureate
Program: Occupational; 2-Year Principally Bachelor's Creditable
Accreditation: ACICS

01 President .... Dr. Larry CAPPS
36 Director of Career Services .... Ms. Wendy NOVAK
08 Corporate Librarian .... Ms. Angela WATSON
07 Director of Admission .... Ms. Callie EASTMAN
32 Director of Student Success .... Ms. Lynn PAULSON

Charter College (E)

721 W Parks Highway, Suite 5, Wasilla AK 99654

Telephone: (907) 952-1000 Identification: 770626
Accreditation: ACICS

† Main campus is Charter College in Anchorage, AK.

Ilisagvik College (F)

PO Box 749, Barrow AK 99723

County: North Slope Borough FICE Identification: 034613
Unit ID: 434584

Telephone: (907) 852-3333 Carnegie Class: Tribal
FAX Number: (907) 862-2729 Calendar System: Semester
URL: www.ilisagvik.edu
Established: 1996 Annual Undergrad Tuition & Fees: $6,270
Enrollment: 621 Coed
Affiliation or Control: Independent Non-Profit IRS Status: 501(c)3
Highest Offering: Associate Degree
Program: Occupational; 2-Year Principally Bachelor's Creditable
Accreditation: NW

01 President .... Ms. Pearl K. BROWER
06 Registrar .... Ms. Amm CAHOON
05 Chief Academic Officer .... Ms. Birgit MEANY
15 Director Human Resources .... Mrs. Linda STANFORD
18 Chief Facilities/Physical Plant .... Mr. David ONGLEY
26 Chief Public Relations Officer .... Mrs. Sarah MARTINSEN
32 Chief Student Life Officer .... Mrs. Gloria BURNETT
36 Director Student Placement .... Ms. Debora GOLDIZEN
37 Director Student Financial Aid .... Mr. Fred MILLER

*University of Alaska System (G)

910 Yukon Drive, Suite 202, Fairbanks AK 99775-5000

County: Fairbanks FICE Identification: 008005
Unit ID: 103529

Telephone: (907) 450-8000 Carnegie Class: N/A
FAX Number: (907) 450-8012
URL: www.alaska.edu

01 President .... Mr. Patrick K. GAMBLE
26 Vice President for Univ Relations .... Ms. Carla BEAM
05 Vice Pres for Academic Affairs .... Dr. Dana L. THOMAS
10 Vice Pres for Finance .... Dr. Ashok ROY
46 Associate Vice President Budget .... Ms. Michelle RIZK
09 AVP Institutional Research/Analysis .... Ms. Gwen GRUENIG
43 General Counsel .... Mr. Michael HOSTINA
15 Interim Chief HR Officer .... Ms. Michelle RIZK
102 President of Foundation .... Ms. Carla BEAM
13 Chief Info Technology Officer .... Mr. Karl KOWALSKI
26 Director of Public Affairs .... Ms. Kate RIPLEY
16 Director Labor & Employee Relations .... Mr. Donald SMITH
88 Chief Risk Officer .... Ms. Nancy SPINK

*University of Alaska Anchorage (H)

3211 Providence Drive, Anchorage AK 99508-8000

County: Anchorage FICE Identification: 011462
Unit ID: 102553

Telephone: (907) 786-1800 Carnegie Class: Master's L
FAX Number: (907) 786-4888 Calendar System: Semester
URL: www.uaa.alaska.edu
Established: 1954 Annual Undergrad Tuition & Fees (In-State): $6,806
Enrollment: 18,898 Coed
Affiliation or Control: State IRS Status: 501(c)3
Highest Offering: Master's
Program: Occupational; 2-Year Principally Bachelor's Creditable; Liberal Arts And General; Teacher Preparatory; Professional
Accreditation: NW, ADNUR, ART, BUS, CLPSY, CONST, DA, DH, @DIETD, DIETI, ENG, ENGR, JOUR, MAC, MT, MUS, NUR, PH, SW, TED

02 Chancellor .... Gen. Tom CASE
05 Provost .... Dr. Elisha (Bear) BAKER
11 Vice Chancellor Administrative Svcs .... Dr. William SPINDLE
09 Sr Vice Provst Inst Effectiveness .... Ms. Renee M. CARTER-CHAPMAN
84 Assoc Vice Chanc Enrollment Mgmt .... Mr. Eric R. PEDERSEN
30 Vice Chancellor Univ Advancement .... Ms. Megan OLSON
32 Vice Chancellor Student Affairs .... Dr. Bruce SCHULTZ
26 Asst Vice Chanc University Rels .... Ms. Kristin DESMITH
91 Assoc Vice Chanc Information Tech .... Mr. Pat SHIER
09 Assoc VP of Institutional Research .... Dr. Erin HOLMES
18 Assoc Vice Chanc Facilities .... Mr. Christopher TURLETES
96 Assoc VC Financial Services .... Ms. Sandi CULVER
44 Assoc VC of Development .... Vacant
29 Asst Vice Chanc Alumni Relations .... Ms. Rachel MORSE
88 AVC Student Access/Advis/Transition .... Dr. Lacy KARPILO
20 Int Exec Dir Acad/Multic Stdnt Suc .... Ms. Theresa LYONS
35 Dean of Students .... Dr. Dewain LEE
37 Dir Student Financial Assistance .... Ms. Sonya STEIN
85 Director Multicultural Center .... Mr. Andre THORN
35 Director Student Life & Leadership .... Ms. Annie ROUTE
07 Director of Admissions .... Vacant
28 Dir Campus Diversity & Compliance .... Ms. Marva WATSON
41 Acting Director Athletics .... Mr. Tim MCDIFFETT
06 University Registrar .... Ms. Lora VOLDEN
36 Director Career Services Center .... Ms. Diane KOZAK
15 Director Human Resources .... Mr. Ron KAMAHELE
08 Dean Consortium Library .... Mr. Stephen J. ROLLINS
63 Director Biomedical Program .... Dr. Jane SHELBY
88 Director Native Student Services .... Mr. William TEMPLETON
38 Int Dir Student Health/Counseling .... Ms. Georgia DEKEYSER
50 Dean Col Business/Public Policy .... Dr. Rashmi PRASAD
51 Dean Community/Tech College .... Dr. Karen R. SCHMITT
83 Dean College of Health .... Mr. William HOGAN
54 Dean School of Engineering .... Dr. Tien-Chien JEN
49 Dean Arts & Sciences College .... Dr. John STALVEY
53 Dean College of Education .... Dr. Heather RYAN
92 Dean Honors College .... Mr. Ronald SPATZ

† Granted candidacy at the Doctorate level.

*University of Alaska Fairbanks (I)

215 Signers' Hall, Admissions, Fairbanks AK 99775-7480

County: Fairbanks North Star Borough FICE Identification: 001063
Unit ID: 102614

Telephone: (907) 474-7500 Carnegie Class: RU/H
FAX Number: (907) 474-5379 Calendar System: Semester
URL: www.uaf.edu
Established: 1917 Annual Undergrad Tuition & Fees (In-State): $6,443
Enrollment: 10,799 Coed
Affiliation or Control: State IRS Status: 501(c)3
Highest Offering: Doctorate
Program: Occupational; 2-Year Principally Bachelor's Creditable; Liberal Arts And General; Teacher Preparatory; Professional
Accreditation: NW, BUS, BUSA, CLPSY, CS, DH, EMT, ENG, FOR, JOUR, MAC, MUS, SW, TED

02 Chancellor .... Mr. Brian D. ROGERS
05 Provost .... Dr. Susan M. HENRICHS
11 Vice Chancellor Administrative Svcs .... Ms. Pat PITNEY
18 Assoc Vice Chancellor Facilities .... Mr. Scott BELL
32 VC University & Student Advancement .... Dr. Mike SFRAGA
45 Vice Chancellor Research .... Dr. Mark MYERS
21 Assoc VC for Financial Services .... Mr. Raaj KURAPATI
44 Director of Development .... Ms. Emily DRYGAS
58 Dean Graduate School .... Dr. John EICHELBERGER
81 Dean Col of Natural Science/Math .... Dr. Paul LAYER
35 Assoc Vice Chanc for Student Life .... Mr. Don FOLEY
31 VC Rural/Cmty & Native Educ .... Vacant
12 Dean UAF Comm & Tech College .... Ms. Michele STALDER
47 Dean Sch of Natural Res/Ag Sciences .... Dr. Carol E. LEWIS
88 Dean Sch Fisheries & Ocean Sciences .... Dr. Mike CASTELLINI
50 Dean School of Management .... Dr. Mark HERRMANN
54 Dean Col of Engineering & Mines .... Dr. Doug GOERING
88 Dir Intl Arctic Research Center .... Dr. Larry HINZMAN
88 Dir Institute of Arctic Biology .... Dr. Brian M. BARNES
54 Director Inst Northern Engineering .... Dr. Daniel WHITE
15 Interim Director Human Resources .... Mr. Brad LOBLAND
19 Chief of Police .... Mr. Sean MCGEE
37 Director Financial Aid .... Ms. Deanna L. DIERINGER
26 Director of Community Advocacy .... Ms. Ann RINGSTAD
41 Director Athletics .... Dr. Gary GRAY
39 Director Residence Life .... Ms. Laura L. MCCOLLOUGH
56 Vice Provost for Extension/Outreach .... Mr. Fred SCHLUTT
40 Director of Aux/Recharge/Cntrct Ops .... Vacant
85 Director International Programs .... Ms. Donna ANGER
88 Fire Chief .... Mr. Doug SCHRAGE
88 Dir Institute of Marine Science .... Dr. Terry WHITLEDGE
49 Dean College of Liberal Arts .... Mr. Todd SHERMAN
53 Dean School of Education .... Dr. Allan MOROTTI
12 Director Bristol Bay Campus .... Dr. Deborah MCLEAN
12 Director Chukchi Campus .... Ms. Pauline HARVEY
12 Director Interior Aleutians Campus .... Ms. Teisha SIMMONS
12 Director Kuskokwim Campus .... Ms. Mary C. PETE
12 Director Northwest Campus .... Mr. Robert METCALF
28 Dir Diversity & Equal Opportunity .... Ms. Mae MARSH
23 Director Health and Counseling .... Dr. B.J ALDRICH
29 Exec Director Alumni Association .... Mr. Joe HAYES
07 Interim Registrar & Dir Admissions .... Ms. Libby EDDY
88 Director Geophysical Institute .... Mr. Robert MCCOY
21 Director Business Operations .... Ms. Amanda WALL
36 Director Career Services .... Ms. Patti PICHA
38 Director Academic Advising Center .... Ms. Linda M. HAPSMITH
92 Director Honors Program .... Vacant
94 Coordinator Women's Studies .... Dr. Sine ANAHITA
09 Dir Planning/Analysis/Inst Research .... Mr. Ian OLSON
26 Director Marketing/Communications .... Ms. Michelle RENFREW
08 Dean of Libraries .... Dr. Bella GERLICH

88 Interim Dir UA Museum of the North .... Dr. Aldona JONAITIS
14 Dir Arctic Reg Supercomputing Ctr .... Dr. Greg NEWBY
13 Chief Info Technology Officer ....Mr. Karl KOWALSKI
88 Director for Disability Services ....Ms. Mary MATTHEWS
96 Dir of Procurement & Contract Svcs ....Mr. John HEBARD
88 Director Wood Center Student Union ....Mrs. Lydia ANDERSON
46 AVC Research ....Dr. John BLAKE
46 AVC Research ....Dr. Nettie LABELLE-HAMER
30 AVC for Univ & Student Advancement ....Ms. Kris RACINA
97 Vice Provost/Dean Gen Studies ....Dr. Alex FITTS

*University of Alaska Southeast (A)

11120 Glacier Highway, Juneau AK 99801-8681
County: Juneau FICE Identification: 001065
Unit ID: 102632
Telephone: (907) 796-6000 Carnegie Class: Master's S
FAX Number: N/A Calendar System: Semester
URL: www.uas.alaska.edu
Established: 1956 Annual Undergrad Tuition & Fees (In-State): $5,470
Enrollment: 3,117 Coed
Affiliation or Control: State IRS Status: 501(c)3
Highest Offering: Master's
Program: Occupational; 2-Year Principally Bachelor's Creditable; Liberal Arts And General; Teacher Preparatory; Professional
Accreditation: NW, CAHIIM, TED

02 Chancellor ....Mr. John PUGH
05 Provost & Executive Dean SCE ....Dr. Richard CAULFIELD
75 Associate Dean Sch of Career Educ ....Mr. Pete TRAXLER
46 Vice Provost for Research ....Dr. Marsha SOUSA
20 Vice Provost for Academic Affairs ....Ms. Carol HEDLIN
11 Vice Chanc & Director Admin Svcs ....Mr. Michael CIRI
12 Sitka Campus Director ....Dr. Jeffrey JOHNSTON
12 Ketchikan Campus Director ....Dr. Priscilla SCHULTE
49 Dean of Arts & Sciences ....Dr. Marsha SOUSA
88 Dean of School of Management ....Mr. John BLANCHARD
88 Director UAS Ctr for Mine Training ....Mr. Mike BELL
53 Dean Education & Graduate Studies ....Dr. Deborah LO
37 Financial Aid Officer ....Ms. Corinne SOLTIS
26 Dir of Marketing/Public Relations ....Ms. Katie BAUSLER
06 Registrar ....Ms. Barbara HEGEL
84 VC Enrollment Mgmt & Stdnt Affs ....Mr. Joseph NELSON
09 Institutional Effectiveness Manager ....Ms. Diane MEADOR
10 Director Business Services ....Mr. Tom DIENST
15 Director Personnel Services ....Mr. Kirk MCALLISTER
18 Director Facilities Services ....Mr. Keith GERKEN
08 Director Library Services ....Ms. Elise TOMLINSON
13 Director Information/Technology ....Mr. Michael CIRI
30 Dir Development/Alumni Relations ....Ms. Lynne JOHNSON
29 Annual Fund Alumni Manager ....Ms. Keni CAMPBELL
21 Chief Budget Officer ....Ms. Barbara HYDE
88 Director Learning Center ....Ms. Hildegard SELLNER
32 Director Stdnt Resource Services ....Ms. Lori KLEIN

*Prince William Sound Community College (B)

PO Box 97, Valdez AK 99686-0097
County: Valdez-Cordova-Glennallen Identification: 666659
Unit ID: 103361
Telephone: (907) 834-1600 Carnegie Class: Assoc/Pub-R-M
FAX Number: (907) 834-1611 Calendar System: Semester
URL: www.pwscc.edu
Established: 1978 Annual Undergrad Tuition & Fees (In-State): $4,100
Enrollment: 1,000 Coed
Affiliation or Control: State IRS Status: 501(c)3
Highest Offering: Associate Degree
Program: Occupational; 2-Year Principally Bachelor's Creditable; Fine Arts Emphasis
Accreditation: NW

02 President ....Mr. Jacob NG
05 Dean of Instruction ....Vacant
10 Business Manager ....Mr. Steve SHIELL
06 Registrar ....Ms. Shannon FOSTER
07 Dir Admissions/Finan Aid/Stdnt Svc ....Mr. Chris WASHKO
15 Director Personnel Services ....Ms. Ana HINKLE
26 Chief Public Relations Officer .... Ms. Wendy GOLDSTEIN
38 Director Student Counseling ....Vacant
88 Director of Training ....Mr. BJ WILLIAMS

ARIZONA

Acacia University (C)

7665 South Research Drive, Tempe AZ 85284-1812
County: Maricopa Identification: 667017
Telephone: (480) 428-6034 Carnegie Class: Not Classified
FAX Number: (480) 428-6033 Calendar System: Other
URL: www.acacia.edu
Established: 2003 Annual Undergrad Tuition & Fees: $7,500
Enrollment: 200 Coed
Affiliation or Control: Proprietary IRS Status: Proprietary
Highest Offering: Master's
Program: Occupational; 2-Year Principally Bachelor's Creditable; Teacher Preparatory; Professional; Technical Emphasis
Accreditation: DETC

01 President ....Mr. Michael TURICO
106 Exec VP Trainining/Online Learning ....Dr. Marilynn D. HENLEY
32 Exec VP Student Affairs ....Mr. Tim MOMAN

American Indian College of the Assemblies of God (D)

10020 N 15th Avenue, Phoenix AZ 85021-2199
County: Maricopa FICE Identification: 021999
Unit ID: 103787
Telephone: (602) 944-3335 Carnegie Class: Bac/Diverse
FAX Number: (602) 943-8299 Calendar System: Semester
URL: www.aicag.edu
Established: 1957 Annual Undergrad Tuition & Fees: $11,700
Enrollment: 73 Coed
Affiliation or Control: Assemblies Of God Church IRS Status: 501(c)3
Highest Offering: Baccalaureate
Program: 2-Year Principally Bachelor's Creditable; Liberal Arts And General; Teacher Preparatory; Professional; Religious Emphasis
Accreditation: NH

01 President & CFO ....Dr. David J. MOORE
03 Executive Vice Pres & Campus Pastor ....Rev. Jim H. LOPEZ
05 Vice President for Academic Affairs ....Dr. Joseph J. SAGGIO
09 Director of Institutional Research ....Dr. Lori P. KUBA
07 Director Enrollment Mgmt/ Admissions ....Ms. Sandra M. GONZALES
37 Director of Student Financial Aid ....Ms. Nadine WALDROP
38 Director of Student Counseling ...... Rev. Vincent R. ROUBIDEAUX
06 Registrar ....Ms. Jennifer ROUBIDEAUX
08 Library Director ....Rev. John S. ROSE
50 Business Chairperson ....Dr. Barry SHENNUM
73 Christian Min Chairperson ....Rev. Ron CLOUSE
53 Education Chairperson ....Dr. Lori P. KUBA
97 General Education Chairperson ....Ms. Karen BRAMBLE

Anthem College (E)

1515 East Indian School Road, Phoenix AZ 85014
County: Maricopa FICE Identification: 022631
Unit ID: 104805
Telephone: (602) 279-9700 Carnegie Class: Assoc/PrivFP4
FAX Number: N/A Calendar System: Other
URL: www.anthem.edu
Established: 1982 Annual Undergrad Tuition & Fees: $28,200
Enrollment: 1,856 Coed
Affiliation or Control: Proprietary IRS Status: Proprietary
Highest Offering: Baccalaureate
Program: Occupational
Accreditation: ACICS

01 Interim Campus President ....Ms. Sara MAYER

Argosy University, Phoenix (F)

2233 W Dunlap Avenue, Phoenix AZ 85021
Telephone: (602) 216-2600 Identification: 666790
Accreditation: &WC, CLPSY

† Main campus is Argosy University, Orange County in Orange, CA.

Arizona Christian University (formerly Southwestern College) (G)

2625 E Cactus Road, Phoenix AZ 85032-7042
County: Maricopa FICE Identification: 007113
Unit ID: 105899
Telephone: (602) 489-5300 Carnegie Class: Bac/Diverse
FAX Number: (602) 404-2159 Calendar System: Semester
URL: www.arizonachristian.edu
Established: 1960 Annual Undergrad Tuition & Fees: $20,880
Enrollment: 684 Coed
Affiliation or Control: Independent Non-Profit IRS Status: 501(c)3
Highest Offering: Baccalaureate
Program: Liberal Arts And General; Teacher Preparatory
Accreditation: NH

01 President ....Mr. Len MUNSIL
05 Senior Vice President and Provost ....Dr. Gary P. DAMORE
10 Senior VP & Chief Financial Officer ....Ms. Diane CATLIN
11 Vice Pres for Operations/Athletics ....Mr. Don MITCHELL
84 Vice Pres Enrollment & Marketing ....Ms. Heather KIM
07 Director of Admissions ....Mr. Brant NYHART
04 Executive Assistant to President ....Mrs. Tiffani RICKEY
30 Director of Advancement ....Mr. Shawn BOSKIE
20 Academic Dean ....Dr. William P. BAKER
32 Dean of Student Services ....Ms. Karen SUMNER
21 Controller ....Ms. June TAYLOR
06 Registrar & Asst Dir of Enroll Mgmt ....Mr. Lambert CRUZ
37 Director Financial Aid ....Mr. Steve YOUNG
34 Dean of Women ....Vacant
08 Director of Library Services ....Mr. Sean J. MCNULTY
39 Director of Residence Life ....Mr. Anthony SUAREZ
13 Information Technology Director ....Mr. Joel HAYS

Arizona College (H)

4425 W Olive Avenue, Suite 300, Glendale AZ 85302-3851
County: Maricopa FICE Identification: 031150
Unit ID: 421708
Telephone: (602) 222-9300 Carnegie Class: Assoc/PrivFP
FAX Number: (602) 200-8726 Calendar System: Other
URL: www.arizonacollege.edu
Established: 1991 Annual Undergrad Tuition & Fees: $14,935
Enrollment: 573 Coed
Affiliation or Control: Proprietary IRS Status: Proprietary
Highest Offering: Associate Degree
Program: 2-Year Principally Bachelor's Creditable; Nursing Emphasis
Accreditation: ABHES

01 President ....Mr. Nick MANSOUR
11 Regional Vice Pres of Operations ....Mr. Kevin LAMOUNTAIN
37 Financial Aid Director ....Mr. Matthew CALHOUN

Arizona College-Mesa (I)

163 N. Dobson Road, Mesa AZ 85201
Telephone: (480) 265-3600 Identification: 770514
Accreditation: ABHES

† Main campus is Arizona College in Glendale, AZ.

Arizona School of Acupuncture and Oriental Medicine (J)

4646 E Fort Lowell Road, Suite 103, Tucson AZ 85712-1100
County: Pima FICE Identification: 036955
Unit ID: 446039
Telephone: (520) 795-0787 Carnegie Class: Spec/Health
FAX Number: (877) 222-4606 Calendar System: Quarter
URL: www.asaom.edu
Established: 1996 Annual Graduate Tuition & Fees: $50,336
Enrollment: 20 Coed
Affiliation or Control: Proprietary IRS Status: Proprietary
Highest Offering: Master's; No Undergraduates
Program: Professional; Fine Arts Emphasis
Accreditation: ACUP

01 CEO/Founder ....Dr. David EPLEY
37 Financial Aid Advisor ....Ms. Susan WAGNER
07 Admissions Director ....Mr. Bob CHASAN

Arizona State University (K)

300 E. University Drive, Tempe AZ 85281
County: Maricopa FICE Identification: 001081
Unit ID: 104151
Telephone: (480) 965-2100 Carnegie Class: RU/VH
FAX Number: N/A Calendar System: Semester
URL: www.asu.edu
Established: 1885 Annual Undergrad Tuition & Fees (In-State): $10,002
Enrollment: 73,378 Coed
Affiliation or Control: State IRS Status: 501(c)3
Highest Offering: Doctorate
Program: Liberal Arts And General; Professional
Accreditation: NH, AAB, ART, AUD, BUS, BUSA, CACREP, CIDA, CLPSY, CONST, COPSY, CS, DIETD, DIETI, ENG, ENGT, IPSY, JOUR, LAW, LSAR, MT, MUS, NRPA, NURSE, PCSAS, PLNG, SCPSY, SP, SPAA, SW

01 President ....Dr. Michael M. CROW
05 Exec Vice President and Provost ....Dr. Elizabeth D. PHILLIPS
10 Exec Vice President/Treasurer & CFO ....Dr. Morgan R. OLSEN
03 Sr Vice Pres/Sec of the University ...Dr. Christine K. WILKINSON
102 CEO ASU Foundation ....Mr. Rick SHANGRAW
43 Sr Vice President & General Counsel ......Mr. Jose A. CARDENAS
32 Sr VP Educ Outreach & Student Svcs ....Dr. James A. RUND
41 Vice Pres of University Athletics ....Mr. Stephen PATTERSON
13 Chief Information Officer ....Mr. Gordon D. WISHON
26 Vice President for Public Affairs ....Mr. Virgil N. RENZULLI
46 Univ Chief Research Officer ..... Dr. Sethuraman PANCHANATHEN
16 Asst VP & Chief Human Resources Ofc ......Mr. Kevin J. SALCIDO
100 VP/Chief of Staff ....Mr. Jim O'BRIEN
106 Exec Vice Provost/Dean ASU Online ....Dr. Philip R. REGIER
88 VProv/Dean Liberal Arts & Sciences ....Dr. Robert E. PAGE
50 Dean WP Carey School of Business ....Dr. Amy HILLMAN
54 Dean Ira A Fulton Schls of Engr ....Dr. Paul C. JOHNSON
53 Dean Mary Lou Fulton Teachers Col ....Dr. Mari E. KOERNER
58 Exec Vice Prov/Dean Graduate Col ....Dr. Maria T. ALLISON
92 Dean of Barrett Honors College ....Dr. Mark JACOBS
12 VP of West Campus/Dean New College . Dr. Elizabeth LANGLAND
57 Dean Herberger Inst for Design/Arts .... Dr. Kwang-Wu KIM
60 Dean Cronkite Sch Journal/Mass Comm ....Mr. Christopher CALLAHAN
61 Dean College of Law ....Mr. Douglas SYLVESTER
66 Dean College of Nursing & Health In ....Dr. Teri BRITT PIPE
88 Dean School of Sustainability ....Dr. Sander VAN DER LEEUW
72 Vice Prov/Dean College Tech & Innov .....Dr. Mitzi M. MONTOYA
88 Vice Prov/Dean University College ....Dr. Frederick C. COREY
88 Dean College of Health Solutions ....Dr. Keith D. LINDER
88 Dean College of Public Programs ....Jonathan KOPPELL
49 Dean of Liberal Arts & Sciences ....Dr. Patrick KENNEY
88 Dir Nutrition and Health Promotion .... Dr. Linda VAUGHAN

Arizona Western College (L)

2020 Avenue 8E, Yuma AZ 85365
County: Yuma FICE Identification: 001071
Unit ID: 104160
Telephone: (928) 317-6000 Carnegie Class: Assoc/Pub-R-L
FAX Number: (928) 344-7730 Calendar System: Semester
URL: www.azwestern.edu
Established: 1963 Annual Undergrad Tuition & Fees (In-District): $2,420
Enrollment: 7,877 Coed

Affiliation or Control: State/Local IRS Status: 501(c)3
Highest Offering: Associate Degree
Program: Occupational; 2-Year Principally Bachelor's Creditable
Accreditation: NH, ADNUR, RAD

01 President ... Dr. Glenn MAYLE
10 Vice Pres Finance/Administration ... Mrs. Carole T. COLEMAN
26 Dean Public Relations & Marketing ... Mrs. Lori STOFFT
09 Dean Instnl Effect/Rsrch/Grants ... Dr. Mary SCHAAL
20 Dean of Instruction ... Mrs. Linda ELLIOTT-NELSON
103 Dean of Business & Workforce Devel ... Mrs. Lynn LABRIE
07 Dean Admission/Enrollment Services ... Mr. Bryan DOAK
75 Dean of Career & Technical Educ ... Mr. Daniel BARAJAS
102 Executive Director AWC Foundation ... Mrs. Christina HAWKEY
06 Registrar ... Ms. Amy PIGNATORE
29 Director Alumni Relations ... Ms. Christina HAWKEY
21 Director of Financial Services ... Ms. Diana G. DOUCETTE
15 Director of Human Resources ... Dr. Ruth WHISLER
96 Director of Purchasing & Aux Svcs ... Ms. Margaret HAYES
18 Director of District Operations ... Mr. Steve ECKERT
14 Co-Dir Tech & Network Services ... Mr. Chad COLEMAN
14 Co-Dir Tech & Network Services ... Ms. Brenda WARNOCK
08 Director of Library Services ... Ms. Angie CREEL
41 Director of Athletics ... Mr. Jerry SMITH
19 Chief of Police ... Mr. John EDMUNDSON
35 Dean for Campus Life ... Ms. Mary Kay HARTON
12 Associate Dean La Paz County Svcs ... Mr. Rich TOZER
12 Assoc Dean for South Yuma County ... Mr. Everardo MARTINEZ
37 Director of Financial Aid ... Ms. Lisa SEALE
85 Coordinator of Intl Student Program ... Mr. Ken KUNTZELMAN
07 Director of Admissions/Registrar ... Ms. Amy PIGNATORE
106 Associate Dean for Distance Educ ... Mrs. Jana MOORE
88 Director of Testing Services ... Mrs. Leticia MARTINEZ
105 Webmaster II ... Mr. Damien BATES

The Art Institute of Phoenix (A)

2233 W Dunlap Avenue, Phoenix AZ 85021-2859
County: Maricopa FICE Identification: 040513
Unit ID: 428444
Telephone: (602) 331-7500 Carnegie Class: Spec/Arts
FAX Number: (602) 331-5301 Calendar System: Quarter
URL: www.artinstitutes.edu/phoenix
Established: 1995 Annual Undergrad Tuition & Fees: $28,860
Enrollment: 1,018 Coed
Affiliation or Control: Proprietary IRS Status: Proprietary
Highest Offering: Baccalaureate
Program: 2-Year Principally Bachelor's Creditable; Professional; Fine Arts Emphasis
Accreditation: ACICS, ACFEI, CIDA

01 President ... Mr. Chad WILLIAMS
05 Dean of Academic Affairs ... Dr. Meryl EPSTEIN
07 Senior Director of Admissions ... Ms. Terri SPENCER
32 Dean of Student Affairs ... Ms. Tanisha WASHINGTON
36 Director of Career Services ... Ms. Kristin FRANK
10 Director of Admin & Fin Svcs ... Ms. Lori RYAN
15 Human Resources Generalist ... Ms. Jennifer BOHNSACK
09 Dir of Institutional Effectiveness ... Vacant
13 Technology Support Supervisor ... Mr. Nate YOUNG
37 Director of Student Financial Svcs ... Ms. Abigail GARCIA
06 Registrar ... Ms. Bonnie BOWERS

The Art Institute of Tucson (B)

5099 East Grant Road, Suite 100, Tucson AZ 85712-2733
Telephone: (520) 318-2700 FICE Identification: 037405
Accreditation: ACICS

† Main campus is The Art Institute of Phoenix in Phoenix, AZ.

Benedictine University at Mesa (C)

51 E Main Street, Suite 105, Mesa AZ 85201
Telephone: (602) 888-5000 Identification: 770068
Accreditation: &NH

† Main campus is Benedictine University in Lisle, IL.

Brighton College (D)

7332 E Butherus Drive, Suite 102, Scottsdale AZ 85260
County: Maricopa Identification: 666710
Telephone: (800) 231-3803 Carnegie Class: Not Classified
FAX Number: (602) 212-0502 Calendar System: Other
URL: www.brightoncollege.edu
Established: 1961 Annual Undergrad Tuition & Fees: $7,800
Enrollment: 500 Coed
Affiliation or Control: Proprietary IRS Status: Proprietary
Highest Offering: Associate Degree
Program: Occupational; 2-Year Principally Bachelor's Creditable; Technical Emphasis
Accreditation: DETC

01 President ... Kathleen MIRABILE

Brookline College (E)

2445 West Dunlap Avenue, Suite 100, Phoenix AZ 85021
County: Maricopa FICE Identification: 022188
Unit ID: 104090
Telephone: (602) 242-6265 Carnegie Class: Bac/Assoc
FAX Number: (602) 973-2572 Calendar System: Other
URL: www.brooklinecollege.edu
Established: 1979 Annual Undergrad Tuition & Fees: $19,975
Enrollment: 1,186 Coed
Affiliation or Control: Proprietary IRS Status: Proprietary
Highest Offering: Baccalaureate
Program: Occupational
Accreditation: ACICS, MLTAD, NUR, PTAA

01 Director ... Mr. Louis ARMENDARIZ

Brookline College (F)

1140 South Priest Drive, Tempe AZ 85281
Telephone: (480) 545-8755 Identification: 666403
Accreditation: ACICS, SURTEC

† Main campus is Brookline College in Phoenix, AZ.

Brookline College (G)

5441 E 22nd Street, Suite 125, Tucson AZ 85711-5444
Telephone: (520) 748-9799 Identification: 666402
Accreditation: ACICS

† Main campus is Brookline College in Phoenix, AZ.

Brown Mackie College-Phoenix (H)

13430 North Black Canyon Highway, Phoenix AZ 85029
Telephone: (602) 337-3044 Identification: 666782
Accreditation: ACICS, OTA, SURTEC

† Main campus is The Art Institute of Phoenix in Phoenix, AZ.

Brown Mackie College-Tucson (I)

4585 E Speedway Boulevard, Tucson AZ 85712-5300
Telephone: (520) 319-3300 FICE Identification: 009451
Accreditation: ACICS, OTA, SURTEC

† Main campus is The Art Institute of Phoenix in Phoenix, AZ.

Bryan University Online (J)

350 West Washington Street, Ste 100, Tempe AZ 85281
Telephone: (602) 384-2555 Identification: 770627
Accreditation: ACICS

† Main campus is Bryan University in Springfield, MO.

The Bryman School (K)

2250 W Peoria Avenue, Suite A100,
Phoenix AZ 85029-4923
County: Maricopa FICE Identification: 030764
Unit ID: 384209
Telephone: (602) 274-4300 Carnegie Class: Assoc/PrivFP
FAX Number: (602) 248-9087 Calendar System: Other
URL: www.brymanschool.edu
Established: Annual Undergrad Tuition & Fees: $14,657
Enrollment: 604 Coed
Affiliation or Control: Proprietary IRS Status: Proprietary
Highest Offering: Associate Degree
Program: Occupational; 2-Year Principally Bachelor's Creditable; Technical Emphasis
Accreditation: ACICS, MAAB

01 Executive Director ... Ms. Lisa RAMIREZ
05 Dean of Education ... Ms. Sue WHITE
37 Director of Financial Aid ... Mrs. Patricia SIMON
07 Director of Admissions ... Ms. Melissa CAIRNS
36 Career Service Director ... Mr. Ernest WATSON
11 Office Manager ... Ms. Sarah ROSE

Carrington College - Mesa (L)

1001 W Southern Avenue, Suite 130, Mesa AZ 85210
Telephone: (480) 212-1600 FICE Identification: 023352
Accreditation: ACICS, COARC, DH, MAAB, PTAA

† Main campus is Carrington College - Phoenix in Phoenix, AZ.

Carrington College - Phoenix (M)

8503 N 27th Avenue, Phoenix AZ 85051-4096
County: Maricopa FICE Identification: 021006
Unit ID: 103893
Telephone: (602) 393-5900 Carnegie Class: Assoc/PrivFP
FAX Number: N/A Calendar System: Other
URL: www.carrington.edu
Established: 1976 Annual Undergrad Tuition & Fees: $14,212
Enrollment: 785 Coed
Affiliation or Control: Proprietary IRS Status: Proprietary
Highest Offering: Associate Degree
Program: Occupational; 2-Year Principally Bachelor's Creditable
Accreditation: ACICS, ADNUR, MAAB

01 Executive Campus Director ... Ms. Val COLMONE
05 Dean Academic Affairs ... Ms. Susan OPALKA

Carrington College - Tucson (N)

3550 N Oracle Road, Tucson AZ 85705-3591
Telephone: (520) 888-5885 FICE Identification: 030898
Accreditation: ACICS, MAAB

† Main campus is Carrington College - Phoenix in Phoenix, AZ.

Carrington College - Westside (O)

2701 W Bethany Home Road, Phoenix AZ 85017-1705
Telephone: (602) 433-1333 Identification: 666248
Accreditation: ACICS, COARC, RAD

† Main campus is Carrington College - Phoenix in Phoenix, AZ.

Central Arizona College (P)

8470 N Overfield Road, Coolidge AZ 85128-9779
County: Pinal FICE Identification: 007283
Unit ID: 104346
Telephone: (520) 494-5444 Carnegie Class: Assoc/Pub-S-MC
FAX Number: (520) 494-5008 Calendar System: Semester
URL: www.centralaz.edu
Established: 1962 Annual Undergrad Tuition & Fees (In-District): $2,310
Enrollment: 7,018 Coed
Affiliation or Control: Local IRS Status: 501(c)3
Highest Offering: Associate Degree
Program: Occupational; 2-Year Principally Bachelor's Creditable
Accreditation: NH, ADNUR, CAHIIM, DIETT, DMS, MAC, RAD

01 President ... Dr. Doris HELMICH
05 Acting VP Learning Servcies ... Dr. James MOORE
20 Acting Assoc VP Academic Affairs ... Dr. Steven GONZALES
32 Acting Assoc VP Student Affairs ... Dr. Philip TOMPKINS
76 Dean of Health Careers & Sciences ... Mr. Julian EASTER
107 Acting Asst Dean Prof & Tech Educ ... Dr. Janice PRATT
49 Dean of Arts & Social Sciences ... Ms. Terri ACKLAND
35 Acting Asst Dean Student Affairs ... Ms. Jenni GONZALES
10 Vice President Financial & Admn Svc ... Mr. Chris WODKA
13 Associate VP Technology Svcs ... Mr. Richard KING
16 Vice President Human Resources ... Mr. James KIMSEY
15 Director III-Human Reources ... Mr. T.J FERRER
09 Exec Dir II Institutional Research ... Mr. William BROWN
08 Director Library Services ... Ms. Adrianna SAAVEDRA
26 Exec Dir I PR & Foundation ... Mr. Thomas DICAMILLO
37 Director of Financial Aid ... Ms. Elisa JUAREZ
41 Acting Athletic Director ... Mr. Chuck SCHNOOR
39 Director of Residence Life ... Mr. Nev KRAGULJEVIC
19 Chief Campus Police Officer ... Mr. Luis MARTINEZ
18 Exec Director of Facilities ... Mr. Ernesto VALENZUELA
96 Director of Purchasing ... Mr. Mark SALAZ
06 Registrar ... Ms. Veronica DURAN
07 Director of Recruitment ... Mr. Luis SANCHEZ
21 Exec Dir Accounting Svc/Comptroller ... Ms. Luisa OTT

Chamberlain College of Nursing-Phoenix Campus (Q)

2149 West Dunlap Avenue, Phoenix AZ 85021
Telephone: (602) 331-2720 Identification: 770502
Accreditation: &NH, NURSE

† Main campus is Chamberlain College of Nursing - Addison in Addison, IL.

Cochise College (R)

4190 W Highway 80, Douglas AZ 85607-6190
County: Cochise FICE Identification: 001072
Unit ID: 104425
Telephone: (800) 966-7943 Carnegie Class: Assoc/Pub-R-L
FAX Number: (520) 417-4006 Calendar System: Semester
URL: www.cochise.edu
Established: 1961 Annual Undergrad Tuition & Fees (In-District): $2,190
Enrollment: 4,618 Coed
Affiliation or Control: Local IRS Status: 170(c)1
Highest Offering: Associate Degree
Program: Occupational; 2-Year Principally Bachelor's Creditable
Accreditation: NH, ADNUR, EMT

01 President ... Dr. J. D. ROTTWEILER
05 Vice Pres for Instruction/Provost ... Dr. Verlyn FICK
13 Vice Pres Information Technology ... Mr. Carlos CARTAGENA
15 Vice Pres Human Resources ... Ms. Wendy DAVIS
49 Dean of Liberal Arts ... Mr. Chuck HOYACK
56 Dean of Extended Learning ... Ms. Sheila DEVOE HEIDMAN
32 Dean of Student Services ... Dr. James (Bo) HALL
09 Director of Institutional Research ... Dr. Jerome V. WARD
06 Director Admissions & Rec/Registrar ... Ms. Debbie QUICK
08 Director of College Libraries ... Ms. Pat HOTCHKISS
10 Interim VP for Administration ... Ms. Sandy BRYAN
18 Dir Facilities Mgmt & Planning ... Mr. Frank DYKSTRA
29 Director Office of External Affairs ... Ms. Denise HOYOS
106 Director of Online Campus ... Mr. George SELF
37 Director of Financial Aid ... Ms. Karen BENNETT
39 Dir of Residental & Student Life ... Ms. Marisol ARENIVAS
88 Director Ctr for Economic Research ... Dr. Robert CARREIRA
51 Director Ctr for Lifelong Learning ... Ms. Sharon GILMAN
26 Dir Marketing & Creative Services ... Mr. Ed ROSKOWSKI
72 Dean of Business & Technology ... Mr. Bruce RICHARDSON
81 Dean of Math/Science & Health Sci ... Dr. Richard (Bubba) HALL
35 Asst Dean of Student Services ... Mr. Mark BOGGIE

Cochise College Sierra Vista Campus (A)
901 North Colombo Avenue, Sierra Vista AZ 85635
Telephone: (520) 515-0500 Identification: 770004
Accreditation: &NH

† Main campus is Cochise College in Douglas, AZ.

Coconino Community College (B)
2800 S Lone Tree Road, Flagstaff AZ 86005
County: Coconino FICE Identification: 031004
Unit ID: 404426
Telephone: (928) 527-1222 Carnegie Class: Assoc/Pub-R-M
FAX Number: (928) 226-4106 Calendar System: Semester
URL: www.coconino.edu
Established: 1991 Annual Undergrad Tuition & Fees (In-State): $2,760
Enrollment: 31,004 Coed
Affiliation or Control: State IRS Status: 501(c)3
Highest Offering: Associate Degree
Program: 2-Year Principally Bachelor's Creditable
Accreditation: NH

01 President .... Dr. Leah L. BORNSTEIN
05 Vice President for Academic Affairs .... Dr. Russ ROTHAMER
10 VP for Business & Administration .... Ms. Jami VAN ESS
32 Director of Student Services .... Ms. Veronica HIPOLITO
12 Page Campus Director .... Mr. Jim HUNTER
51 Exec Dir of Cmty & Corp Learning .... Mr. John CARDANI
49 Dean of Art & Sciences .... Dr. Ingrid LEE
15 Director for Human Resources .... Ms. Gayle BENTON
09 Dir Institutional Research/Assess .... Mr. Michael MERICA
37 Director for Financial Aid .... Mr. Robert VOYTEK
06 Registrar/Dir Enrollment Services .... Ms. Kimmi GRULKE
88 Dean of Occupational/Profess Tech .... Dr. Monica BAKER
18 Director Facilities .... Mr. Mark EASTON
13 Chief Technical Officer .... Mr. Joe TRAINO
96 Director Purchasing/Auxiliary Svcs .... Mr. Robert SEDILLO
21 Director of Accounting & Finance .... Ms. Siri MULLANEY
30 Director Institutional Advancement .... Mr. Scott TALBOOM
04 Exec Assistant to the President .... Ms. Joan WHITE

Coconino County Community College Flagstaff Fourth Street Campus (C)
3000 N Fourth Street, Flagstaff AZ 86004
Telephone: (928) 526-7600 Identification: 770005
Accreditation: &NH

† Main campus is Coconino Community College in Flagstaff, AZ.

Coconino County Community College Page/ Lake Powell Campus (D)
475 S Lake Powell Blvd., PO Box 728,
Page AZ 86040-0728
Telephone: (928) 645-3987 Identification: 770006
Accreditation: &NH

† Main campus is Coconino Community College in Flagstaff, AZ.

CollegeAmerica-Flagstaff (E)
3012 East Route 66, Flagstaff AZ 86004-6323
County: Coconino FICE Identification: 031203
Unit ID: 103945
Telephone: (928) 213-6060 Carnegie Class: Assoc/PrivFP
FAX Number: (928) 526-3468 Calendar System: Other
URL: www.collegeamerica.edu
Established: 1964 Annual Undergrad Tuition & Fees: $16,558
Enrollment: 200 Coed
Affiliation or Control: Proprietary IRS Status: Proprietary
Highest Offering: Baccalaureate
Program: Occupational
Accreditation: ACCSC

01 Executive Director .... Ms. Suzanne SCALES

CollegeAmerica-Phoenix (F)
9801 N. Metro Parkway East, Phoenix AZ 85051
Telephone: (602) 257-7522 Identification: 666017
Accreditation: ACCSC

† Main campus is CollegeAmerica-Flagstaff in Flagstaff, AZ.

DeVry University - Phoenix Campus (G)
2149 W Dunlap Avenue, Phoenix AZ 85021-2995
Telephone: (602) 870-9222 FICE Identification: 008322
Accreditation: &NH, ENGT, MT

† Main campus is DeVry University - Chicago Campus in Chicago, IL.

Diné College (H)
One Circle Drive, Tsaile AZ 86556-9998
County: Apache FICE Identification: 008246
Unit ID: 105297
Telephone: (928) 724-6671 Carnegie Class: Tribal
FAX Number: (928) 724-3327 Calendar System: Semester
URL: www.dinecollege.edu
Established: 1968 Annual Undergrad Tuition & Fees (In-District): $850
Enrollment: 1,970 Coed
Affiliation or Control: Local IRS Status: 501(c)3
Highest Offering: Baccalaureate
Program: Occupational; 2-Year Principally Bachelor's Creditable
Accreditation: NH

01 President .... Dr. Maggie GEORGE
05 Vice President of Academics .... Ms. Rebecca M. BENALLY
11 Vice President for Admin & Finance .... Mr. Ronald BELLOLI
32 Vice Pres of Student Success .... Ms. Glennita HASKEY
30 Director of Development .... Mr. Darryl R. BEGAY
06 Registrar .... Ms. Louise LITZIN
20 Interim Dean .... Mr. Abraham BITOK
37 Director Student Financial Aid .... Mr. Gary SEGAY
15 Dir Department of Human Resources .... Mrs. Derphelia FOWLER
18 Supt Maintenance Operations .... Mr. Delbert PAQUIN
21 Controller .... Vacant
26 Public Relations Director .... Mr. Ed MCCOMBS
09 Director of Institutional Research .... Vacant

Dunlap-Stone University (I)
19820 North 7th Street, Suite 100, Phoenix AZ 85024
County: Maricopa Identification: 666315
Telephone: (602) 648-5750 Carnegie Class: Not Classified
FAX Number: (602) 648-5755 Calendar System: Other
URL: www.dunlap-stone.edu
Established: 1995 Annual Undergrad Tuition & Fees: $8,290
Enrollment: 492 Coed
Affiliation or Control: Proprietary IRS Status: Proprietary
Highest Offering: Baccalaureate
Program: Professional; Business Emphasis
Accreditation: DETC

01 President .... Dr. Donald N. BURTON
106 Vice Pres Online Programs/Registrar .... Mrs. Caulyne BARRON

Eastern Arizona College (J)
615 N Stadium Avenue, Thatcher AZ 85552-0769
County: Graham FICE Identification: 001073
Unit ID: 104577
Telephone: (928) 428-8233 Carnegie Class: Assoc/Pub-R-L
FAX Number: (928) 428-2578 Calendar System: Semester
URL: www.eac.edu
Established: 1888 Annual Undergrad Tuition & Fees (In-District): $1,920
Enrollment: 6,435 Coed
Affiliation or Control: State/Local IRS Status: 501(c)3
Highest Offering: Associate Degree
Program: Occupational; 2-Year Principally Bachelor's Creditable
Accreditation: NH

01 President .... Mr. Mark BRYCE
03 Executive Vice President .... Mr. Brent MCEUEN
10 Chief Business Officer .... Mr. Timothy CURTIS
05 Provost .... Mrs. Jeanne BRYCE
20 Dean of Instruction .... Mr. Michael CROCKETT
20 Dean of Instruction .... Dr. Phil MCBRIDE
20 Dean of Curriculum and Instruction .... Dr. Janice LAWHORN
32 Dean of Students .... Dr. Gary SORENSEN
06 Associate Dean/Registrar .... Dr. Randall SKINNER
38 Assistant Dean of Counseling .... Ms. Sharon ALLEN
12 Director of Discovery Park Campus .... Mr. Paul ANGER
21 Director Fiscal Control/Controller .... Mr. Darwin WEECH
37 Director of Financial Aid .... Mr. William OSBORN
14 Director of Information Resources .... Mr. Thomas THOMPSON
09 Director of Institutional Research .... Mr. Glen SNIDER
08 Director of Library Services .... Mrs. Karen JAGGERS
26 Director of Marketing & Public Rels .... Mr. Todd HAYNIE
18 Director of Physical Resources .... Mr. Dan WELKER
30 Executive Director EAC Foundation .... Mr. David UDALL
35 Director of Student Life .... Mr. Danny BATTRAW
41 Athletic Director .... Mr. James BAGNALL
15 Assoc Director Admin Support EEO Co .... Ms. Lauri AVILA
04 Exec Asst to the President and DGB .... Mrs. Laurie PENNINGTON

Eastern Arizona College Gila Pueblo Campus (K)
8274 Six Shooter Canyon PO Box 2656, Globe AZ 85502
Telephone: (928) 425-8481 Identification: 770008
Accreditation: &NH

† Main campus is Eastern Arizona College in Thatcher, AZ.

Eastern Arizona College Payson Campus (L)
201 N Mud Springs Rd., PO Box 359, Payson AZ 85547
Telephone: (928) 468-8039 Identification: 770009
Accreditation: &NH

† Main campus is Eastern Arizona College in Thatcher, AZ.

Embry-Riddle Aeronautical University-Prescott Campus (M)
3200 Willow Creek Road, Prescott AZ 86301-3270
Telephone: (800) 888-3728 FICE Identification: 021047
Accreditation: &SC, AAB, ENG

† Main campus is Embry-Riddle Aeronautical University in Daytona Beach, FL.

Everest College Phoenix (N)
10400 N 25th Avenue, Suite 190, Phoenix AZ 85021-1610
County: Maricopa FICE Identification: 022950
Unit ID: 103644
Telephone: (602) 942-4141 Carnegie Class: Assoc/PrivFP4
FAX Number: (602) 943-0960 Calendar System: Other
URL: www.everest-college.com
Established: 1982 Annual Undergrad Tuition & Fees: $12,420
Enrollment: 1,578 Coed
Affiliation or Control: Proprietary IRS Status: Proprietary
Highest Offering: Baccalaureate
Program: Occupational; 2-Year Principally Bachelor's Creditable
Accreditation: NH

01 Campus President .... Ms. Maria WALTERS
07 Director of Admissions .... Ms. Hamsa WILSON

Everest College Phoenix-Mesa (O)
5416 E Baseline Road, Suite 200, Mesa AZ 85206
Telephone: (480) 830-5151 Identification: 770010
Accreditation: &NH

† Main campus is Everest College Phoenix in Phoenix, AZ.

Fortis College, Phoenix (P)
555 N 18th Street, Suite 110, Phoenix AZ 85006
Telephone: (602) 254-3099 Identification: 666761
Accreditation: ACCSC, DH

† Main campus is Fortis College in Centerville, OH.

Frank Lloyd Wright School of Architecture (Q)
PO Box 4430, Scottsdale AZ 85261-4430
County: Maricopa FICE Identification: 025332
Unit ID: 104665
Telephone: (480) 860-2700 Carnegie Class: Spec/Arts
FAX Number: N/A Calendar System: Other
URL: www.taliesin.edu
Established: 1932 Annual Undergrad Tuition & Fees: $30,000
Enrollment: 17 Coed
Affiliation or Control: Independent Non-Profit IRS Status: 501(c)3
Highest Offering: Master's
Program: Professional; Music Emphasis
Accreditation: NH

01 Head of School and Dean .... Mr. Victor SIDY
05 Director of Academic Affairs .... Dr. Stephanie Grace SCHULL
08 Dean of Libraries .... Ms. Elizabeth AL-HAZZAM DAWASARI
07 Dir Admissions/Student Services .... Mr. Nick DEPORTER
10 COO and Vice President Finance .... Ms. Lisa MURPHY
30 Vice President of Development .... Ms. Dottie O'ÇARROLL

Golf Academy of America (R)
2031 N. Arizona Ave Suite 2, Chandler AZ 85225
Telephone: (800) 342-7342 Identification: 666023
Accreditation: ACICS

† Main campus is Virginia College in Birmingham, AL.

Grand Canyon University (S)
3300 W Camelback Road, Phoenix AZ 85017-3030
County: Maricopa FICE Identification: 001074
Unit ID: 104717
Telephone: (602) 639-7500 Carnegie Class: Master's L
FAX Number: N/A Calendar System: Semester
URL: www.gcu.edu
Established: 1949 Annual Undergrad Tuition & Fees: $16,900
Enrollment: 48,650 Coed
Affiliation or Control: Proprietary IRS Status: Proprietary
Highest Offering: Doctorate
Program: Liberal Arts And General; Teacher Preparatory; Professional
Accreditation: NH, ACBSP, NURSE

01 President/Chief Executive Officer .... Mr. Brian MUELLER
05 Provost .... Dr. Hank RADDA
11 Chief Operations Officer .... Mr. Stan MEYER
15 Vice President Human Resources .... Mr. Scott RALEIGH
26 Vice Pres of Marketing .... Ms. Christel MOSBY
50 Int Dean Ken Blanchard Col Business .... Dr. Kevin MCCLEAN
53 Dean College of Education .... Dr. Kimberly LAPRADE
66 Dean College of Nursing .... Dr. Anne MCNAMARA
49 Dean of College of Arts and Science .... Dr. Mark WOODEN
58 Dean Graduate Studies .... Dr. Hank RAADA
57 Dean of Fine Arts and Production .... Mr. Claude PENSIS
73 Dean College of Theology .... Dr. Jason HILES

Han University of Traditional Medicine (T)
2856 E. Fort Lowell Road, Tucson AZ 85716
County: Pima FICE Identification: 041193
Telephone: (520) 322-6330 Carnegie Class: Not Classified
FAX Number: (520) 322-5661 Calendar System: Quarter
URL: www.hanuniversity.edu
Established: 2000 Annual Undergrad Tuition & Fees: $49,998

Enrollment: 12 Coed
Affiliation or Control: Proprietary IRS Status: Proprietary
Highest Offering: Master's
Program: Professional
Accreditation: **ACUP**

01 President Mr. Alex HOLLAND
07 Admissions Director Ms. Sonia TORRES
06 Registrar Ms. Linda STONE

Harrison Middleton University (A)

1105 East Broadway Road, Tempe AZ 85282-1505
County: Maricopa Identification: 666169
Telephone: (877) 248-6724 Carnegie Class: Not Classified
FAX Number: (800) 762-1622 Calendar System: Other
URL: www.hmu.edu
Established: 1998 Annual Undergrad Tuition & Fees: $7,900
Enrollment: 400 Coed
Affiliation or Control: Proprietary IRS Status: Proprietary
Highest Offering: Doctorate
Program: Liberal Arts And General
Accreditation: **DETC**

01 President Mr. David CURD
05 Director of Education Mr. Michael CURD
06 Registrar Ms. Lauren GUTHRIE
10 Director of Finance Mr. Walter MILLER

International Baptist College (B)

2211 W Germann Road, Chandler AZ 85286
County: Maricopa FICE Identification: 033473
Unit ID: 436614
Telephone: (480) 245-7903 Carnegie Class: Spec/Faith
FAX Number: (480) 245-7909 Calendar System: Semester
URL: www.ibcs.edu
Established: 1980 Annual Undergrad Tuition & Fees: $11,566
Enrollment: 68 Coed
Affiliation or Control: Baptist IRS Status: 501(c)3
Highest Offering: Doctorate
Program: Occupational; 2-Year Principally Bachelor's Creditable; Teacher Preparatory; Religious Emphasis
Accreditation: **TRACS**

00 Chancellor Dr. Jerry C. TETREAU
01 President Rev. Larry P. BALL
32 Dean of Students Mr. Nathan MESTLER
05 Academic Dean Mr. Jeffrey G. CAUPP
10 Chief Financial Officer Mr. Matt EBERLE
08 Media Center Director Mr. Lee WILL
33 Dean of Men Mr. Nathan MESTLER
34 Dean of Women Ms. Marcia GAMMON
06 Registrar Mr. Stephen PENA
37 Financial Aid Administrator Mrs. Jane BUSHEY
07 Director of PR and Enrollment Mr. Jason MCDONNELL

ITT Technical Institute (C)

10220 North 25th Avenue, Suite 100, Phoenix AZ 85021
Telephone: (602) 749-7900 Identification: 666696
Accreditation: **ACICS**

† Main campus is ITT Technical Institute in Indianapolis, IN.

ITT Technical Institute (D)

1840 N 95th Avenue, Suite 132, Phoenix AZ 85037
Telephone: (623) 474-7900 Identification: 667190
Accreditation: **ACICS**

† Main campus is ITT Technical Institute in Indianapolis, IN.

ITT Technical Institute (E)

5005 S Wendler Drive, Tempe AZ 85282-6321
Telephone: (602) 437-7500 FICE Identification: 020652
Accreditation: **ACICS**

† Main campus is ITT Technical Institute in Indianapolis, IN.

ITT Technical Institute (F)

1455 W River Road, Tucson AZ 85704-5829
Telephone: (520) 408-7488 FICE Identification: 023611
Accreditation: **ACICS**

† Main campus is ITT Technical Institute in Indianapolis, IN.

Kaplan College (G)

13610 N Black Canyon Highway, #104,
Phoenix AZ 85029-6323
County: Maricopa FICE Identification: 020712
Unit ID: 105118
Telephone: (602) 548-1955 Carnegie Class: Assoc/PrivFP
FAX Number: (602) 548-1956 Calendar System: Semester
URL: www.kaplancollege.com
Established: 1972 Annual Undergrad Tuition & Fees: $13,125
Enrollment: 419 Coed
Affiliation or Control: Proprietary IRS Status: Proprietary
Highest Offering: Associate Degree
Program: Occupational
Accreditation: **ACCSC**, COARC

01 Campus President Ms. Jackie RUPE

Le Cordon Bleu College of Culinary Arts in Scottsdale (H)

8100 E Camelback Road, Ste 1001,
Scottsdale AZ 85251-3940
County: Maricopa FICE Identification: 026167
Unit ID: 262332
Telephone: (480) 990-3773 Carnegie Class: Spec/Other
FAX Number: (480) 990-0351 Calendar System: Other
URL: www.chefs.edu/scottsdale
Established: 1986 Annual Undergrad Tuition & Fees: $12,912
Enrollment: 1,498 Coed
Affiliation or Control: Proprietary IRS Status: Proprietary
Highest Offering: Baccalaureate
Program: Occupational
Accreditation: **ACCSC**, ACFEI, ACICS

01 President Mr. Lloyd KIRSCH
37 Vice Pres/Director of Financial Aid Ms. Yvonne MARTINEZ
11 Director Administration Ms. Shannon FERRER
36 Director Career Services Ms. Kathleen DOELLER
06 Registrar Ms. Polly GIBSON
07 Director of Admission Ms. Shannon FERRER

*Maricopa County Community College District Office (I)

2411 W 14th Street, Tempe AZ 85281-6941
County: Maricopa FICE Identification: 001075
Unit ID: 105136
Telephone: (480) 731-8000 Carnegie Class: N/A
FAX Number: (480) 731-8850
URL: www.maricopa.edu

01 Chancellor Dr. Rufus GLASPER
05 Executive Vice Chancellor/Provost Dr. Maria HARPER-MARINICK
26 VC Resource Devel/Community Rels Dr. Steven HELFGOT
10 Vice Chanc Business Services Ms. Debra THOMPSON
16 Vice Chancellor Human Resources Vacant
13 Vice Chanc Information Technologies Mr. George KAHKEDJIAN
21 Assoc Vice Chanc Business Services Ms. Gaye MURPHY
103 Dir Center Workforce Development Mr. Randy KIMMENS
30 Exec Director Resource Development Ms. Mary O'CONNOR
09 Assoc VC Inst Strategy/Rsrch/Effect Dr. Sherri ONDRUS
18 Assoc Vice Chanc Cap Plng/Spec Proj Vacant
88 Special Assistant to the Chancellor Dr. Sue KATER

*Chandler-Gilbert Community College (J)

2626 E Pecos Road, Chandler AZ 85225-2499
County: Maricopa FICE Identification: 030722
Unit ID: 364025
Telephone: (480) 732-7000 Carnegie Class: Assoc/Pub-U-MC
FAX Number: (480) 732-7090 Calendar System: Semester
URL: www.cgc.maricopa.edu
Established: 1992 Annual Undergrad Tuition & Fees (In-District): $1,974
Enrollment: 14,653 Coed
Affiliation or Control: State/Local IRS Status: 501(c)3
Highest Offering: Associate Degree
Program: 2-Year Principally Bachelor's Creditable
Accreditation: **NH**, ADNUR, DIETT

02 President Dr. Linda LUJAN
05 Vice President Academic Affairs Dr. William GUERRIERO
32 Vice President Student Affairs Dr. William H. CRAWFORD, III
11 Vice Pres Administrative Services Dr. Jacalyn A. ASKIN
12 Provost Williams Campus Vacant
49 Dean of Arts and Sciences Dr. Maria WISE
31 Dean of Community Affairs Dr. Cindy BARNES PHARR
32 Dean of Student Affairs Mr. Daniel HERBST
10 Assoc Dean Finance/Business Svcs Mr. Bradley KENDREX
07 Dir Admissions/Registr & Records Ms. Linda SHAW
13 Director Information Technology Mr. Victor NAVARRO
09 Dir Research/Planning/Development Vacant
24 Dir Instructional Tech & Media Svcs Mr. Tim KEEFE
36 Dir Career/Education Planning Svcs Mrs. Mary FREDERICK
85 Director International Education Ms. Annie JIMENEZ
32 Director College Student Services Ms. Dawn GRUICHICH
18 Director Buildings and Grounds Mr. Charles POURE
35 Director Student Life Mr. Mike GREENE
41 Director Athletics Mr. Ed YEAGER
19 Director Public Safety Mr. Robert EVERETT
37 Director Financial Aid Ms. Donna PISANO
26 Director Marketing/Public Relations Ms. Cathleen CHLARSON
21 Manager College Cashier Services Mr. Anthony LITTLE
15 Manager College Employee Services Ms. Lynda ANDERSON
27 Coordinator of Marketing Ms. Carol CRANE
28 Coordinator of Diversity Vacant
28 Coordinator of Diversity Ms. Caryl TERRELL-BAMIRO
25 Project Coordinator Admin Svcs Ms. Trina LARSON

*Estrella Mountain Community College (K)

3000 N Dysart Road, Avondale AZ 85392
County: Maricopa FICE Identification: 031563
Unit ID: 384333
Telephone: (623) 935-8000 Carnegie Class: Assoc/Pub-U-MC
FAX Number: (623) 935-8008 Calendar System: Semester
URL: www.estrellamountain.edu
Established: 1990 Annual Undergrad Tuition & Fees (In-District): $2,460
Enrollment: 8,361 Coed
Affiliation or Control: State/Local IRS Status: 501(c)3
Highest Offering: Associate Degree
Program: Occupational; 2-Year Principally Bachelor's Creditable
Accreditation: **NH**, ADNUR

02 President Dr. Ernest LARA
05 Vice President of Academic Affairs Dr. Bryan TIPPETT
32 Vice President Student Affairs Dr. Debbie KUSHIBAB
11 Vice President Admin Services Ms. Sue TAVAKOLI
75 Vice President Occupational Educ Dr. Clay GOODMAN
20 Dean of Academic Affairs Ms. Joyce M. JACKSON
20 Dean of Academic Affairs Dr. Sylvia ORR
13 Director Information Technology Mr. Richard MARMON
35 Interim Dean of Student Services Ms. Laura DULGAR
08 Division Chair Information Resource Ms. Nikol PRICE
09 Dean Planning/Rsrch/Effectiveness Dr. Rene G. WILLEKENS
18 Director Facilities Planning/Devel Mr. Randy NAUGHTON
07 Director of Enrollment Services Mr. Frank AMPARO
10 Manager College Fiscal Services Ms. Leda JOHNSON
26 Chief Public Relations Officer Mr. Ralph CAMPBELL
37 Director Student Financial Aid Ms. Rosanna SHORT
21 Manager College Budget Ms. Maggie CASTILLO

*Gateway Community College (L)

108 N 40th Street, Phoenix AZ 85034-1795
County: Maricopa FICE Identification: 008303
Unit ID: 105145
Telephone: (602) 286-8000 Carnegie Class: Assoc/Pub-U-MC
FAX Number: (602) 286-8072 Calendar System: Semester
URL: www.gatewaycc.edu/
Established: 1968 Annual Undergrad Tuition & Fees (In-District): $1,944
Enrollment: 6,800 Coed
Affiliation or Control: State/Local IRS Status: 501(c)3
Highest Offering: Associate Degree
Program: Occupational; 2-Year Principally Bachelor's Creditable
Accreditation: **NH**, ADNUR, COARC, DMS, NDT, NMT, POLYT, PTAA, RAD, RTT, SURGT

02 President Dr. Steven GONZALEZ
05 Vice President Academic Affairs Dr. Paula NORBY
32 Vice President Student Affairs Dr. Diana MUNIZ
11 Vice President Administrative Svcs Vacant
35 Dean Student Services Vacant
20 Associate Dean Academic Affairs Vacant
07 Supervisor Admissions/Reg & Rec Ms. Brenda STARCK
09 Dir Research Planning & Development Ms. Cathy HERNANDEZ
88 College Budget Analyst Mr. Mark VELARDE
10 Manager College Fiscal Services Mr. Sidney DIETZ
18 Chief Facilities/Physical Plant Vacant
26 Director Marketing/Public Relations Ms. Christine LAMBRAKIS
30 Director Inst Advance & Entrep Pgm Ms. Susie PULIDO
37 Director Student Financial Aid Ms. Suzanne RINGLE
84 Coordinator Enrollment Services Ms. Kelly MCPHEE
16 Manager College Employee Services Ms. Alice CORNELIUS

*Glendale Community College (M)

6000 W Olive Avenue, Glendale AZ 85302-3006
County: Maricopa FICE Identification: 001076
Unit ID: 104708
Telephone: (623) 845-3000 Carnegie Class: Assoc/Pub-U-MC
FAX Number: (623) 845-3329 Calendar System: Semester
URL: www.gc.maricopa.edu
Established: 1965 Annual Undergrad Tuition & Fees (In-District): $2,280
Enrollment: 21,356 Coed
Affiliation or Control: State/Local IRS Status: 170(c)1
Highest Offering: Associate Degree
Program: Occupational; 2-Year Principally Bachelor's Creditable
Accreditation: **NH**, ADNUR, EMT

02 President Dr. Irene KOVALA
05 Int VP Academic & Student Affairs Dr. Janet LANGLEY
11 VP Admin Services & Planning Mr. Greg ROGERS
20 Dean of Academic Affairs Dr. Fernando CAMOU
20 Interim Dean of Academic Affairs Mr. Scott SCHULZ
20 Dean of Academic Affairs Mr. Eric LESHINSKIE
84 Dean Enrollment Services Ms. Mary D. BLACKWELL
32 Dean Student Life Dr. Patricia CARDENAS-ADAME
12 Dean GCC North Site Mr. Charles F. JEFFERY
37 Director Financial Aid Ms. Ellen NEEL
18 Director Facilities Mr. Al GONZALES
21 Director College Business Services Mr. Herman GONZALEZ
26 Dir Sales Mktg & Public Rels Ms. Tressa JUMPS
09 Dean of Strat/Planning & Acctbility Dr. Alka ARORA SINGH
15 Manager College Employee Svcs Ms. June S. FESSENDEN
30 Asst Director of Development Ms. Judy SANCHEZ
38 Dept Chair Counseling Mr. David GERKIN
08 Dept Chair Librarian Mr. Frank TORRES
19 Director College Safety Ms. Debra PALOK

04 Admin Assistant I to College Pres .... Ms. Esmeralda ACOSTA
04 Admin Assistant II to College Pres .... Ms. Jennifer MEANS

*Mesa Community College (A)

1833 W Southern Avenue, Mesa AZ 85202-4866
County: Maricopa FICE Identification: 001077
Unit ID: 105154
Telephone: (480) 461-7000 Carnegie Class: Assoc/Pub-U-MC
FAX Number: (480) 461-7805 Calendar System: Semester
URL: www.mesacc.edu/
Established: 1965 Annual Undergrad Tuition & Fees (In-District): $1,824
Enrollment: 25,024 Coed
Affiliation or Control: State/Local IRS Status: 501(c)3
Highest Offering: Associate Degree
Program: Occupational; 2-Year Principally Bachelor's Creditable
Accreditation: NH, ADNUR, DH, FUSER

02 President .... Dr. Shouan PAN
05 Vice Pres Academic Affairs .... Dr. James MABRY
32 Vice Pres Student Affairs .... Dr. Sonya PEARSON
11 Vice Pres Admin Services .... Mr. Jeff DARBUT
13 Vice Pres Information Technology ...... Mr. Sasan POUREETEZADI
12 Provost Red Mountain/Downtown Ctr ...... Mr. Patrick BURKHART
09 Dean of Inst Planning & Analysis .... Mr. Matthew ASHCRAFT
35 Dean of Student Affairs .... Dr. Barbara BOROS
20 Dean Instruction .... Dr. Rodney HOLMES
20 Dean Instruction .... Ms. Phebe BLITZ
20 Dean Instruction .... Ms. Carol ACHS
20 Dean Instruction .... Mr. Roger YOHE
06 Registrar .... Dr. Barbara BOROS
15 Associate Dean Human Resources .... Dr. Emily WEINACKER
18 Director Facilities .... Mr. Richard CLUFF
21 Dean Administrative Services .... Mr. John MOLL
26 Director of Institutional Advance .... Ms. Sonia FILAN
30 Director of Development .... Mr. Jared LANGKILDE
37 Dir Fin Aid/Scholarships .... Ms. Patricia PEPPIN
38 Dept Chair Counseling .... Dr. Karen HARDIN

*Paradise Valley Community College (B)

18401 N 32nd Street, Phoenix AZ 85032-1210
County: Maricopa FICE Identification: 026236
Unit ID: 364016
Telephone: (602) 787-6500 Carnegie Class: Assoc/Pub-U-MC
FAX Number: (602) 787-6625 Calendar System: Semester
URL: www.pvc.maricopa.edu/
Established: 1985 Annual Undergrad Tuition & Fees (In-District): $2,460
Enrollment: 9,555 Coed
Affiliation or Control: State/Local IRS Status: 501(c)3
Highest Offering: Associate Degree
Program: Occupational; 2-Year Principally Bachelor's Creditable
Accreditation: NH, ADNUR, DIETT

02 President .... Dr. Paul DALE
05 Vice President of Academic Affairs .... Dr. Mary Lou MOSLEY
11 VP Administrative Services .... Mr. Herman GONZALEZ
20 Dean of Academic Affairs .... Dr. Denise DIGIANFILIPPO
32 Vice President of Student Affairs .... Dr. Sandra MILLER HOLST
35 Dean of Students .... Dr. Shirley GREEN
13 Dean of Information Technology .... Mr. Paul GOLISCH
07 Supervisor of Admissions .... Ms. Stella NAPOLES
10 Dean of Fiscal/Enrollment Services .... Ms. Sandy MCDILL
15 Director Personnel Services .... Ms. Lori LINDSETH
18 Chief Facilities/Physical Plant .... Mr. David MATUS
37 Director Student Financial Aid .... Vacant
38 Director Student Counseling .... Dr. James RUBIN
06 Registrar .... Ms. Stella NAPOLES
36 Director Student Placement .... Ms. Norma CHANDLER
26 Chief Public Relations Officer .... Ms. Candace OEHLER
09 Director of Institutional Research .... Mr. John SNELLING
19 Director Security/Safety .... Mr. Scott MEEK
41 Athletic Director .... Mr. Greg SILCOX

*Phoenix College (C)

1202 W Thomas Road, Phoenix AZ 85013-4234
County: Maricopa FICE Identification: 001078
Unit ID: 105428
Telephone: (602) 285-7800 Carnegie Class: Assoc/Pub-U-MC
FAX Number: (602) 285-7700 Calendar System: Semester
URL: www.pc.maricopa.edu
Established: 1920 Annual Undergrad Tuition & Fees (In-District): $2,460
Enrollment: 12,324 Coed
Affiliation or Control: State/Local IRS Status: 501(c)3
Highest Offering: Associate Degree
Program: Occupational; 2-Year Principally Bachelor's Creditable; Technical Emphasis
Accreditation: NH, ADNUR, CAHIIM, DA, DH, HT, MAAB, MLTAD

02 President .... Dr. Anna SOLLEY
05 VP of Academic Affairs .... Dr. Casandra KAKAR
11 VP Administrative Services .... Mr. Paul DEROSE
32 Vice Pres Student Affairs .... Ms. Yira BRIMAGE
35 Dean of Student Affairs .... Ms. Chris HAINES
20 Dean of Academic Affairs .... Mr. Wilbert NELSON
103 Dean of Workforce Development .... Dr. Sharon HALFORD
14 Dean of Technology .... Mr. Mark KOAN
08 Department Chair Library .... Ms. Linda SOLAND
38 Department Chair Counseling .... Ms. Nancy NAVARRETE
06 Dir Admissions/Registration/Records .... Ms. Brenda STARCK
07 Director of Enrollment Services .... Ms. Carmen NEWLAND
41 Athletic Director .... Ms. Samantha EZELL
37 Director Financial Aid .... Ms. Cynthia RAMOS
88 Director Student Leadership .... Ms. Genesis TOOLE
84 Director Advisement Enrollment .... Ms. Julie VOLLER
09 Dir Instl Plng/Rsrch/Effectiveness .... Ms. Jan BINDER
19 Director of College Safety .... Mr. Doug SPARKS
30 Director Institutional Advancement .... Ms. Eileen ARCHIBALD
18 Director of Facilities .... Mr. Douglas MCCARTHY
10 Manager Business Services .... Ms. Angela GENNA
15 Supv College Employee Services .... Ms. Martha ANDERSON
29 Coord Alumni/Cmty Relations .... Vacant
04 Assistant to the President .... Ms. Renee PERRY

*Rio Salado College (D)

2323 W 14th Street, Tempe AZ 85281-6950
County: Maricopa FICE Identification: 021775
Unit ID: 105668
Telephone: (480) 517-8000 Carnegie Class: Assoc/Pub-U-MC
FAX Number: (480) 377-4719 Calendar System: Semester
URL: www.riosalado.edu
Established: 1978 Annual Undergrad Tuition & Fees (In-District): $2,310
Enrollment: 29,216 Coed
Affiliation or Control: State/Local IRS Status: 501(c)3
Highest Offering: Associate Degree
Program: Occupational; 2-Year Principally Bachelor's Creditable; Business Emphasis
Accreditation: NH, DA, DH

02 President .... Dr. Chris BUSTAMANTE
05 Vice President Teaching & Learning .... Dr. Dana OFFERMAN
10 Vice Pres Business & Employee Svcs .... Mr. Todd SIMMONS
32 Vice President Student Services .... Ms. Kishia BROCK
13 Vice President Information Services .... Mr. Edward KELTY
20 Dean of Instruction .... Mr. Rick KEMP
105 Dean of Instruction .... Ms. Dana REID
20 Dean of Instruction .... Dr. Jo JORGENSON
84 Dean Student Enrollment Services .... Vacant
26 Director Inst Advancement .... Mr. Kevin BILDER
07 Assoc Dean of Enrollment Services .... Ms. Ruby MILLER
37 Director of Financial Aid .... Mr. Ryan CHASE
09 Dir Research Planning & Development .... Mr. Daniel HUSTON
18 Director of Facilities .... Mr. Ernest ADKINS
19 Director College Safety .... Ms. Margaret TURNER-SAMPLE
21 Director College Business Services .... Ms. Devi BALA
15 Manager College Employee Services .... Ms. Anna FLORES
28 Director of Diversity .... Dr. Sharon KOBERNA
08 Faculty Chair Library .... Ms. Hazel DAVIS
25 Assoc Dir Grants/Corp Development .... Vacant
85 Director International Education .... Vacant

*Scottsdale Community College (E)

9000 E Chaparral, Scottsdale AZ 85256-2626
County: Maricopa FICE Identification: 008304
Unit ID: 105747
Telephone: (480) 423-6000 Carnegie Class: Assoc/Pub-U-SC
FAX Number: (480) 423-6200 Calendar System: Semester
URL: www.scottsdalecc.edu
Established: 1969 Annual Undergrad Tuition & Fees (In-District): $1,854
Enrollment: 10,895 Coed
Affiliation or Control: State/Local IRS Status: 501(c)3
Highest Offering: Associate Degree
Program: Occupational; 2-Year Principally Bachelor's Creditable
Accreditation: NH, ACFEI, ADNUR

02 President .... Dr. Jan L. GEHLER
05 Vice Pres Academic/Student Affairs .... Dr. Daniel P. CORR
11 Vice Pres Administrative Services .... Mr. Carl COUCH
20 Dean of Instruction .... Dr. Stephanie FUJI
32 Dean of Student Affairs .... Dr. Donna YOUNG
84 Dean of Student Enrollment .... Ms. Gia TAYLOR
07 Director of Admissions .... Ms. Fran VITALE
09 Director of Institutional Research .... Dr. Laurie COHEN
30 Director of Development .... Mr. Charles SILVER
08 Director of Library Services .... Dr. Pat LOKEY
37 Director Financial Aid/Placement .... Ms. Stacie BECK
18 Director Buildings/Grounds .... Mr. Samuel J. VAN CLEAVE
19 Director of College Safety .... Mr. Les STRICKLAND
26 Dir of Marketing/Public Relations .... Vacant
51 Director Continuing Education .... Vacant
41 Athletic Director .... Mr. Vernon MUMMERT
88 Dir of Southwest Studies Program .... Mr. Marshall TRIMBLE
38 Director Student Advisement .... Mr. Michael CORNELIUS

*South Mountain Community College (F)

7050 S 24th Street, Phoenix AZ 85042-5806
County: Maricopa FICE Identification: 021466
Unit ID: 105792
Telephone: (602) 243-8000 Carnegie Class: Assoc/Pub-U-MC
FAX Number: (602) 243-8329 Calendar System: Semester
URL: www.southmountaincc.edu
Established: 1979 Annual Undergrad Tuition & Fees (In-District): $2,460
Enrollment: 4,843 Coed
Affiliation or Control: State/Local IRS Status: 501(c)3
Highest Offering: Associate Degree
Program: Occupational; 2-Year Principally Bachelor's Creditable
Accreditation: NH, MACTE

02 President .... Dr. Shari L. OLSON
05 Vice Pres Academic Affairs .... Dr. Rey RIVERA
11 Vice Pres Administrative Svcs .... Ms. Janet ORTEGA
32 Vice Pres Student Affairs .... Dr. Osaro IGHODARO
09 Dean Research/Plng & Development .... Ms. Damita KALOOSTIAN
75 Assc Dean Career Tech Educ/Ext Camp .... Ms. Cindy ODGERS
84 Assoc Dan Enrollment Services .... Vacant
35 Assoc Dean Student Development .... Vacant
102 Assoc Dean of Foundation Rels .... Dr. Cheryl CRUTCHER
37 Director Financial Aid .... Ms. Inez MORENO-WEINERT
07 Director of Admission & Records .... Ms. Della GARCIA
10 Director College Business Services .... Ms. Cecilia SOTO
18 Director of Facilities .... Mr. Robert HOLMES
26 Director Marketing/Public Relations .... Vacant
21 Manager Fiscal Services .... Mr. Thomas NICOL
15 Coordinator Human Resources .... Vacant
07 Coordinator Advisement/Recruitment .... Ms. Christine NEILL
36 Coordinator Job Placement .... Ms. Suzanne HIPPS

*Chandler-Gilbert Community College-Williams Campus (G)

7360 E Tahoe Avenue, Mesa AZ 85212-0908
Telephone: (480) 988-8000 Identification: 770178
Accreditation: &NH

† Main campus is Chandler-Gilbert Community College in Chandler, AZ.

*Glendale Community College North (H)

5727 W Happy Valley Road, Phoenix AZ 85310
Telephone: (623) 845-4000 Identification: 770179
Accreditation: &NH

† Main campus is Glendale Community College in Glendale, AZ.

*Mesa Community College at Red Mountain (I)

7110 East McKellips Road, Mesa AZ 85207
Telephone: (480) 654-7200 Identification: 770180
Accreditation: &NH

† Main campus is Mesa Community College in Mesa, AZ.

Mesa Center for Higher Education (J)

238 West 2nd Street, Mesa AZ 85201
Telephone: (800) 888-9266 Identification: 770330
Accreditation: &NH

† Main campus is Westminster College in Fulton, MO.

Midwestern University (K)

19555 N 59th Avenue, Glendale AZ 85308
Telephone: (623) 572-3215 Identification: 666001
Accreditation: &NH, ANEST, ARCPA, CLPSY, DENT, OPT, OSTEO, OT, PERF, PHAR, POD, PTA, @VET

† Main campus is Midwestern University in Downers Grove, IL.

Mohave Community College (L)

1971 E. Jagerson Avenue, Kingman AZ 86409-1238
County: Mohave FICE Identification: 011864
Unit ID: 105206
Telephone: (928) 757-0879 Carnegie Class: Assoc/Pub-S-MC
FAX Number: (928) 757-0836 Calendar System: Semester
URL: www.mohave.edu
Established: 1971 Annual Undergrad Tuition & Fees (In-District): $2,340
Enrollment: 10,453 Coed
Affiliation or Control: State/Local IRS Status: 501(c)3
Highest Offering: Associate Degree
Program: Occupational; 2-Year Principally Bachelor's Creditable; Technical Emphasis
Accreditation: NH, ADNUR, DH, EMT, #PTAA, SURGT

01 President .... Dr. Michael KEARNS
03 Vice President for Administration .... Dr. H. Lynn CUNDIFF
05 Dean of Instruction .... Dr. Jill LOVELESS
32 Dean of Student Services .... Ms. Ana MASTERSON
10 Dean of Business Services .... Mr. Dick MACDONALD
30 Assoc Vice Pres College Advancement .... Dr. Alan KLAAS
27 Chief Information Officer .... Mr. Ted MCKEVER
106 Campus Dean Distance Education .... Ms. Diana STITHEM
12 Campus Dean Bullhead City .... Mr. Shawn BRISTLE
12 Campus Dean Lake Havasu .... Dr. Nicolas SANCHEZ
12 Campus Dean Neal Kingman .... Dr. Fred GILBERT
12 Campus Dean North Mohave .... Ms. Carolyn HAMBLIN
06 Registrar .... Ms. Lynne PETERSEN
21 Bursar .... Ms. Camille HOLDEN
37 Director Student Financial Aid .... Ms. Shannon SHEAFF
09 Dir of Institutional Research .... Mr. Bob FAUBERT
26 Chief Public Relations Officer .... Ms. Charlotte KELLER
07 Director of Recruitment/Admissions .... Ms. Brandi COLBERT
35 Dir Student Services Distance Educ .... Mr. John WILSON
35 Dir Stdnt Svcs Neal Campus Kingman .... Ms. Shirley JOHNSON-CRAFT
35 Dir Student Svcs Lake Havasu Campus .... Ms. Bree KARLIN
35 Dir Stdnt Svcs Bullhead Cty Campus .... Vacant
15 Director Personnel Services .... Ms. Jenny DIXON

National Paralegal College (A)

717 East Maryland Avenue, Phoenix AZ 85014-1561
County: Maricopa FICE Identification: 041574
Unit ID: 461023
Telephone: (800) 371-6105 Carnegie Class: Not Classified
FAX Number: (866) 347-2744 Calendar System: Other
URL: nationalparalegal.edu
Established: 2003 Annual Undergrad Tuition & Fees: $6,829
Enrollment: 720 Coed
Affiliation or Control: Proprietary IRS Status: Proprietary
Highest Offering: Master's
Program: Occupational; 2-Year Principally Bachelor's Creditable; Professional; Business Emphasis
Accreditation: DETC

01 President .... Avi KATZ
05 Dean/Director .... Mark GELLER
88 Technical Director .... David COHEN
20 Educational Director .... Stephen HAAS

Northcentral University (B)

10000 E University Drive, Prescott Valley AZ 86314-2336
County: Yavapai FICE Identification: 038133
Unit ID: 444130
Telephone: (928) 541-7777 Carnegie Class: DRU
FAX Number: (928) 541-7817 Calendar System: Other
URL: www.ncu.edu
Established: 1996 Annual Undergrad Tuition & Fees: $8,800
Enrollment: 9,252 Coed
Affiliation or Control: Proprietary IRS Status: Proprietary
Highest Offering: Doctorate
Program: Teacher Preparatory; Professional; Business Emphasis
Accreditation: NH, ACBSP, MFCD, @TEAC

01 President .... Dr. Clinton D. GARDNER
05 Provost/Chief Academic Officer .... Dr. Scott BURRUS
10 Executive VP & Chief Financial Ofcr .... Mr. Christopher LYNNE
11 Vice President Operations .... Mr. Eric STODDARD
04 Director Office of the President .... Ms. Stephnie HOPPLE
50 Dean School of Business & Tech Mgmt .... Dr. Lee SMITH
53 Dean School of Education .... Dr. Cindy GUILLAUME
83 Dean School of Psychology .... Dr. Robert HAUSSMANN
83 Dean Sch of Marriage & Family Ther .... Dr. Branden H. HENLINE
97 Chair of General Education .... Ms. Melinda LYONS
21 Controller .... Ms. Shannyn STERN
06 Registrar .... Ms. Barbara HICKS
27 Chief Information Officer .... Mr. Patrick PENDLETON
37 Dir of Learner Financial Services .... Ms. Valerie STEINBOCK
08 Director of Library Services .... Mr. Ed SALAZAR
15 Director of Human Resources .... Mr. Rodd RUSSOW
26 Director of Marketing .... Mr. Kevin LUSTIG
50 Director of Strategic Business Know .... Vacant
84 Enrollment Manager .... Mr. Bob HANKS

Northern Arizona University (C)

South San Francisco Street, Flagstaff AZ 86011-0001
County: Coconino FICE Identification: 001082
Unit ID: 105330
Telephone: (928) 523-9011 Carnegie Class: RU/H
FAX Number: (928) 523-1848 Calendar System: Semester
URL: www.nau.edu
Established: 1899 Annual Undergrad Tuition & Fees (In-State): $9,738
Enrollment: 26,002 Coed
Affiliation or Control: State IRS Status: 501(c)3
Highest Offering: Doctorate
Program: Liberal Arts And General; Teacher Preparatory; Professional
Accreditation: NH, ACBSP, #ARCPA, BUS, CACREP, CONST, CS, DH, ENG, FOR, MUS, NRPA, NURSE, PTA, SP, SW, TED

01 President .... Dr. John D. HAEGER
03 Vice President and Chief of Staff .... Dr. Sarah BICKEL
05 Provost and VP for Academic Affairs .... Dr. Laura HUENNEKE
30 VP University Advancement .... Dr. Mason GERETY
84 Sr VP Enrollment Mgmt/Student Affs .... Mr. David BOUSQUET
09 VP Planning/Budget/Inst Research .... Dr. Patricia N. HAEUSER
10 VP Finance and Administration .... Dr. Jennus L. BURTON
46 Vice President Research .... Dr. William GRABE
56 Sr VP Extended Campuses .... Mr. Fred HURST
86 VP Govt Affairs/Business Ptnr .... Ms. Christy FARLEY
41 VP Intercollegiate Athletics .... Ms. Lisa CAMPOS
43 VP and General Counsel .... Mr. Mark NEUMAYR
14 Chief Information Tech Officer .... Mr. Fred ESTRELLA
35 Associate VP Student Affairs .... Vacant
28 Associate VP of Diversity .... Dr. David E. CAMACHO
88 Director Enrollment Services .... Mr. James CASEBEER
12 Assoc VP/Campus Executive Officer .... Mr. Larry GOULD
15 Associate VP Human Resources .... Ms. Diane VERKEST
84 Assoc VP Enroll Mgmt/Sutdent Affs .... Ms. Jane KUHN
84 Assoc VP Enroll Mgmt/Student Affs .... Ms. Cynthia KOSSO
18 Assoc VP Facility Services .... Mr. John MORRIS
21 Assoc VP Financial Services .... Mr. Robert NORTON
20 Vice Provost Academic Affairs .... Dr. Karen L. PUGLIESI
85 Vice Provost Center Intl Education .... Mr. Harvey CHARLES
08 Dean/University Librarian .... Ms. Cynthia A. CHILDREY
53 Dean College of Education .... Mr. Michael SAMPSON
58 Dean Graduate College .... Dr. Ramona N. MELLOTT
54 Dean College Eng/Forestry/Nat Sci .... Dr. Paul JAGODZINSKI
50 Dean W.A. Franke Col of Business .... Dr. Craig VAN SLYKE
49 Dean College of Arts & Letters .... Dr. Michael VINCENT
83 Dean Col Social/Behavioral Sciences .... Dr. Stephen WRIGHT
17 Exec Dean Col of Health/Human Svcs .... Dr. Leslie SCHULZ
06 University Registrar .... Ms. Pamela L. ANASTASSIOU
19 Director University Police .... Mr. Gregory T. FOWLER
22 Director Affirmative Action .... Ms. Priscilla L. MILLS
23 Exec Director Campus Health Svcs .... Ms. Elizabeth M. APPLEBEE
39 Exec Dir Housing/Residence Life .... Mr. Rich PAYNE
29 Director Alumni Relations .... Ms. Georgette VIGIL
36 Dir Gateway Student Success Center .... Ms. Tamara HARRISON
07 Director of Admissions .... Ms. Anika OLSEN
26 Director of Public Affairs .... Mr. Thomas BAUER
35 Dean of Students .... Dr. Rick L. BRANDEL
38 Dir Counseling & Testing Center .... Ms. Carol O'SABEN
96 Director of Purchasing .... Ms. Becky E. MCGAUGH

Northern Arizona University Yuma Branch Campus (D)

2020 S Avenue 8E, Yuma AZ 85365
Telephone: (928) 317-6400 Identification: 770011
Accreditation: &NH

† Main campus is Northern Arizona University in Flagstaff, AZ.

Northland Pioneer College (E)

PO Box 610, Holbrook AZ 86025-0610
County: Navajo FICE Identification: 011862
Unit ID: 105349
Telephone: (928) 524-7311 Carnegie Class: Assoc/Pub-R-L
FAX Number: (928) 524-7312 Calendar System: Semester
URL: www.npc.edu
Established: 1973 Annual Undergrad Tuition & Fees (In-State): $1,736
Enrollment: 3,718 Coed
Affiliation or Control: State IRS Status: 501(c)3
Highest Offering: Associate Degree
Program: Occupational; 2-Year Principally Bachelor's Creditable
Accreditation: NH, ADNUR

01 President .... Dr. Jeanne SWARTHOUT
05 Vice Pres Learning/Student Services .... Mr. Mark H. VEST
11 Vice Pres Administrative Services .... Mr. Blaine HATCH
13 Director of Information Services .... Mr. Eric BISHOP
06 Registrar/Dir Enrollment Mgmt .... Mr. Jake HINTON-RIVERA
04 Assistant to the President .... Ms. Lisa JAYNE
10 Director of Financial Services .... Ms. Maderia ELLISON
21 Comptroller .... Mr. John H. BREMER
15 Director of Human Resources .... Ms. Sharon HOKANSON
37 Financial Aid Coordinator .... Ms. Beaulah BOB-PENNYPACKER
88 Director of Developmental Services .... Mr. Rickey JACKSON
50 Dean of Career & Technical Educ .... Ms. Peggy BELKNAP
49 Dean of Arts & Sciences .... Dr. Eric HENDERSON
66 Dean of Nursing .... Ms. Peg ERDMAN
18 Chief Facilities/Physical Plant .... Mr. David HUISH
26 Dir of Marketing/Public Relations .... Ms. Ann HESS
09 Director of Institutional Effective .... Dr. Leslie WASSON
88 Network and Systems Administrator .... Vacant
88 Director Small Business Development .... Ms. Tracy MANCUSO
08 Head Librarian .... Ms. Trudy BENDER

Northland Pioneer College Little Colorado Campus (F)

1400 E Third Street, Winslow AZ 86047
Telephone: (928) 289-6511 Identification: 770015
Accreditation: &NH

† Main campus is Northland Pioneer College in Holbrook, AZ.

Northland Pioneer College Painted Desert Campus (G)

2251 E Navajo Boulevard, Holbrook AZ 86025
Telephone: (928) 524-7311 Identification: 770012
Accreditation: &NH

† Main campus is Northland Pioneer College in Holbrook, AZ.

Northland Pioneer College Silver Creek Campus (H)

1611 S Main Street, Snowflake AZ 85937
Telephone: (928) 536-6211 Identification: 770014
Accreditation: &NH

† Main campus is Northland Pioneer College in Holbrook, AZ.

Northland Pioneer College White Mountain Campus (I)

1001 W Deuce of Clubs, Show Low AZ 85901
Telephone: (928) 532-6111 Identification: 770013
Accreditation: &NH

† Main campus is Northland Pioneer College in Holbrook, AZ.

Ottawa University Arizona (J)

10020 N 25th Avenue, Phoenix AZ 85021-1660
Telephone: (602) 371-1188 Identification: 666066
Accreditation: &NH

† Main campus is Ottawa University in Ottawa, KS.

The Paralegal Institute (K)

7332 E Butherus Drive, Scottsdale AZ 85260
County: Maricopa FICE Identification: 030737
Unit ID: 105385
Telephone: (800) 354-1254 Carnegie Class: Not Classified
FAX Number: (602) 212-0502 Calendar System: Other
URL: www.theparalegalinstitute.edu
Established: 1974 Annual Undergrad Tuition & Fees: $9,000
Enrollment: 360 Coed
Affiliation or Control: Proprietary IRS Status: Proprietary
Highest Offering: Associate Degree
Program: Occupational; 2-Year Principally Bachelor's Creditable; Business Emphasis
Accreditation: DETC

01 President .... Kathleen MIRABILE
26 Vice President Marketing .... Chris CARAWAY

Penn Foster College (L)

14300 N Northsight Blvd, Suite 120, Scottsdale AZ 85260-3673
County: Maricopa FICE Identification: 004049
Unit ID: 211486
Telephone: (480) 947-6644 Carnegie Class: Not Classified
FAX Number: (480) 951-6030 Calendar System: Other
URL: www.pennfostercollege.edu
Established: 1974 Annual Undergrad Tuition & Fees: $2,200
Enrollment: 31,450 Coed
Affiliation or Control: Proprietary IRS Status: Proprietary
Highest Offering: Baccalaureate
Program: 2-Year Principally Bachelor's Creditable
Accreditation: DETC, MAAB

01 President .... Mr. Joseph GAGNON
05 Chief Learning Officer .... Mr. Ray MCNULTY
88 Chief Certification/Licensing Ofcr .... Ms. Connie DEMPSEY

Phoenix Institute of Herbal Medicine and Acupuncture (M)

301 E Bethany Home Road, Ste A-100, Phoenix AZ 85012-1275
County: Maricopa FICE Identification: 036175
Unit ID: 447698
Telephone: (602) 274-1885 Carnegie Class: Spec/Health
FAX Number: (602) 274-1895 Calendar System: Semester
URL: www.pihma.edu
Established: 1996 Annual Graduate Tuition & Fees: $13,574
Enrollment: 111 Coed
Affiliation or Control: Proprietary IRS Status: Proprietary
Highest Offering: Master's; No Undergraduates
Program: Professional
Accreditation: ACUP

01 President .... Ms. Catherine NIEMIEC
06 Admissions .... Ms. Yvette MORAN

Phoenix School of Law (N)

One North Central 14th Floor, Phoenix AZ 85004
County: Maricopa FICE Identification: 041314
Unit ID: 450942
Telephone: (602) 682-6800 Carnegie Class: Spec/Law
FAX Number: (602) 682-6999 Calendar System: Semester
URL: www.phoenixlaw.edu
Established: Annual Graduate Tuition & Fees: $41,114
Enrollment: 1,097 Coed
Affiliation or Control: Proprietary IRS Status: Proprietary
Highest Offering: First Professional Degree; No Undergraduates
Program: Professional
Accreditation: LAW

01 Dean .... Ms. Shirley L. MAYS
05 Assoc Dean of Academic Affairs .... Ms. Penny L. WILLRICH

Phoenix Seminary (O)

4222 E Thomas Road, Suite 400, Phoenix AZ 85018-7607
County: Maricopa FICE Identification: 034784
Unit ID: 381459
Telephone: (602) 850-8000 Carnegie Class: Spec/Faith
FAX Number: (602) 850-8080 Calendar System: Semester
URL: www.phoenixseminary.edu
Established: 1988 Annual Graduate Tuition & Fees: $10,740
Enrollment: 193 Coed
Affiliation or Control: Interdenominational IRS Status: 501(c)3
Highest Offering: Doctorate; No Undergraduates
Program: Religious Emphasis
Accreditation: NH, THEOL

01 President .... Dr. Darryl L. DELHOUSAYE
03 Executive Vice President/Provost .... Dr. W. B. HUNTER
11 Vice President of Administration .... Mr. Grant GASSON
32 Vice President Student Development .... Dr. Chip MOODY
30 Vice President of Advancement/Mktg .... Ms. Patti SELLERS
20 Dir Acad Services/Admiss/Assess .... Ms. Roma ROYER
06 Registrar .... Mr. Lee P. RICHARDS

84 Director of Enrollment .... Mr. Nate BRADLEY
08 Director of Library Services .... Mr. Doug OLBERT
10 Director of Finance .... Mr. Dave HESTON
37 Financial Aid Officer .... Mrs. Lynn GORDON

Pima Community College (A)

4905 C East Broadway Boulevard, Tucson AZ 85709-1005
County: Pima FICE Identification: 007266
Unit ID: 105525
Telephone: (520) 206-4500 Carnegie Class: Assoc/Pub-U-MC
FAX Number: (520) 206-4535 Calendar System: Semester
URL: www.pima.edu
Established: 1966 Annual Undergrad Tuition & Fees (In-District): $2,150
Enrollment: 30,011 Coed
Affiliation or Control: State/Local IRS Status: 501(c)3
Highest Offering: Associate Degree
Program: Occupational; 2-Year Principally Bachelor's Creditable
Accreditation: #NH, ADNUR, COARC, DA, DH, DT, EMT, MAC, MLTAD, RAD, SURGT

01 Chancellor .... Mr. Lee D. LAMBERT
05 Provost/Exec Vice Chancellor .... Dr. Jerome MIGLER
10 Exec Vice Chanc for Administration .... Dr. David BEA
16 Vice Chanc for Human Resources .... Ms. Janet MAY
13 Vice Chanc Information Tech .... Mr. Keith MCINTOSH
26 Vice Chanc Public Info & Govt Rels .... Mr. C.J KARAMARGIN
18 Vice Chancellor Facilities .... Mr. Bill WARD
12 Actg President Northwest Campus .... Dr. Darla ZIRBES
12 President East Campus .... Ms. Charlotte A. FUGETT
12 President Downtown Campus .... Dr. Luba CHLIWNIAK
12 President Community Campus .... Vacant
12 President West Campus .... Dr. Louis ALBERT
12 President Desert Vista Campus .... Dr. Johnson BIA
43 College General Counsel .... Mr. Jeffrey SILVYN
88 Assistant Vice Chancellor .... Ms. Deborah YOKLIC
21 Asst Vice Chanc for Finance .... Ms. Diane GROOVER
21 Asst VC for Business Services .... Mr. William HOWARD
20 Vice Provost Academic Svcs .... Dr. Mary Ann MARTINEZ-SANCHEZ
91 Asst VC Information Technology .... Vacant
15 Asst VC for Employee Services .... Vacant
32 Asst Vice Chanc for Student Dev .... Ms. Leticia MENCHACA
09 Exec Dir Planning & Inst Research .... Dr. Heather L. TILSON
37 Executive Director Financial Aid .... Ms. Anna REESE
102 Executive Director Foundation .... Ms. Cheryl HOUSE
41 Executive Director of Athletics .... Mr. Edgar SOTO
19 Exec Director Dept of Public Safety .... Vacant
66 Dean Nursing/Health Rel Prof .... Ms. Marty MAYHEW
06 Director Admissions/Registrar .... Ms. Terra BENSON
96 Director of Purchasing .... Mr. Thomas HARRINGTON

Pima Community College Community Campus (B)

401 North Bonita Avenue, Tucson AZ 85709
Telephone: (520) 206-3933 Identification: 770016
Accreditation: &NH

† Main campus is Pima Community College in Tucson, AZ.

Pima Community College Desert Vista Campus (C)

5901 South Calle Santa Cruz, Tucson AZ 85709
Telephone: (520) 206-5000 Identification: 770017
Accreditation: &NH

† Main campus is Pima Community College in Tucson, AZ.

Pima Community College Downtown Campus (D)

1255 North Stone Avenue, Tucson AZ 85709-3000
Telephone: (520) 206-7171 Identification: 770018
Accreditation: &NH

† Main campus is Pima Community College in Tucson, AZ.

Pima Community College East Campus (E)

8181 East Arrington Road, Tucson AZ 85709-4000
Telephone: (520) 206-7000 Identification: 770019
Accreditation: &NH

† Main campus is Pima Community College in Tucson, AZ.

Pima Community College Northwest Campus (F)

7600 North Shannon Road, Tucson AZ 85709-7200
Telephone: (520) 206-2200 Identification: 770020
Accreditation: &NH

† Main campus is Pima Community College in Tucson, AZ.

Pima Community College West Campus (G)

2202 West Alklam Road, Tucson AZ 85709-0001
Telephone: (520) 206-3210 Identification: 770021
Accreditation: &NH

† Main campus is Pima Community College in Tucson, AZ.

Pima Medical Institute-East Valley (H)

2160 S Power Road, Mesa AZ 85209
Telephone: (480) 898-9898 Identification: 770515
Accreditation: ABHES

† Main campus is Pima Medical Institute-Tucson in Tucson, AZ.

Pima Medical Institute-Mesa (I)

957 S Dobson Road, Mesa AZ 85202-2903
Telephone: (480) 644-0267 FICE Identification: 011570
Accreditation: ABHES, COARC, OTA, PTAA, RAD

† Main campus is Pima Medical Institute-Tucson in Tucson, AZ.

Pima Medical Institute-Tucson (J)

3350 E Grant Road, Suite 200, Tucson AZ 85716-2932
County: Pima FICE Identification: 022171
Unit ID: 105534
Telephone: (520) 326-1600 Carnegie Class: Assoc/PrivFP
FAX Number: (520) 326-4125 Calendar System: Other
URL: www.pmi.edu
Established: 1972 Annual Undergrad Tuition & Fees: N/A
Enrollment: 1,811 Coed
Affiliation or Control: Proprietary IRS Status: Proprietary
Highest Offering: Baccalaureate
Program: Occupational
Accreditation: ABHES, COARC, OTA, PTAA, RAD

01 Director .... Mr. Dale BERG

Prescott College (K)

220 Grove Avenue, Prescott AZ 86301-2912
County: Yavapai FICE Identification: 020653
Unit ID: 105589
Telephone: (928) 350-2100 Carnegie Class: Master's S
FAX Number: (928) 776-5137 Calendar System: Semester
URL: www.prescott.edu
Established: 1966 Annual Undergrad Tuition & Fees: $28,320
Enrollment: 1,065 Coed
Affiliation or Control: Independent Non-Profit IRS Status: 501(c)3
Highest Offering: Doctorate
Program: Liberal Arts And General; Teacher Preparatory
Accreditation: NH

01 President .... Dr. Kristin R. WOOLEVER
05 Exec VP of Academic Affairs/Provost .... Dr. Paul BURKHARDT
10 Vice President of Financial Affairs .... Ms. Catherine BOLAND
07 Dean of Enrollment Services .... Dr. Brian SAJKO
30 VP for Insitutional Advancement .... Ms. Marjory SENTE
32 Director of Student Life .... Ms. Sophia ANDALI
84 Director Enrollment Services .... Ms. Jerri BROWN
06 Acting Registrar .... Ms. Peggy BAIR
37 Financial Aid Director .... Ms. Mary Frances CAUSEY
04 Executive Assistant .... Ms. Cathy CHURCH
88 Dean On-Campus Delivery/Research .... Dr. Jack HERRING
106 Dean Distance Learning and Acad Aff .... Dr. Jan KEMPSTER
20 Director of Academic Operations .... Vacant
18 Director of Facilities .... Mr. Greg LAZZELL
08 Director of Library .... Mr. Richard LEWIS
09 Director of Institutional Research .... Ms. Peggy BAIR
90 Director of Instructional Tech .... Vacant
91 Manager of Information Technology .... Mr. Jonah VAN TUYL
21 Director of Financial Services .... Ms. Anne LABRUZZO

The Refrigeration School (L)

4210 E Washington Street, Phoenix AZ 85034-1816
County: Maricopa FICE Identification: 011689
Unit ID: 105659
Telephone: (602) 275-7133 Carnegie Class: Assoc/PrivFP
FAX Number: (602) 267-4805 Calendar System: Other
URL: www.refrigerationschool.com
Established: 1965 Annual Undergrad Tuition & Fees: $31,074
Enrollment: 782 Coed
Affiliation or Control: Proprietary IRS Status: Proprietary
Highest Offering: Associate Degree
Program: Occupational; Technical Emphasis
Accreditation: ACCSC

01 Campus President .... Mr. Stephen M. MALUTICH
37 Assistant Director of Financial Aid .... Ms. Angela CROSSLEY
07 Admissions Director .... Mr. Michael ADKINS

Sanford-Brown College (M)

9630 North 25th Avenue, Phoenix AZ 85021
Telephone: (480) 444-1112 Identification: 666739
Accreditation: ACICS, DMS

† Main campus is Le Cordon Bleu College of Culinary Arts in Los Angeles in Pasadena, CA.

Sessions College for Professional Design (N)

350 S. Mill Avenue, Suite B-104, Tempe AZ 85281-2863
County: Maricopa FICE Identification: 042176
Unit ID: 475839
Telephone: (480) 212-1704 Carnegie Class: Not Classified
FAX Number: (480) 212-1705 Calendar System: Semester
URL: www.sessions.edu
Established: 1997 Annual Undergrad Tuition & Fees: $6,650
Enrollment: 39 Coed
Affiliation or Control: Proprietary IRS Status: Proprietary
Highest Offering: Associate Degree
Program: Occupational; 2-Year Principally Bachelor's Creditable
Accreditation: DETC

00 CEO .... Ms. Doris GRANATOWSKI
01 President .... Mr. Gordon DRUMMOND
03 Executive Vice President .... Mr. Louis J. SCHILT
05 Chief Academic Officer .... Ms. Tara MACKAY
10 Chief Financial Officer/Bursar .... Ms. Carole Anne BAILO
32 Director of Student Services .... Ms. Nomi ALTABEF

Sonoran Desert Institute (O)

10245 East Via Linda, Ste 110, Scottsdale AZ 85258-5316
County: Maricopa Identification: 667057
Telephone: (480) 314-2102 Carnegie Class: Not Classified
FAX Number: (480) 314-2138 Calendar System: Semester
URL: www.sdi.edu
Established: 2000 Annual Undergrad Tuition & Fees: $10,200
Enrollment: 175 Coed
Affiliation or Control: Proprietary IRS Status: Proprietary
Highest Offering: Associate Degree
Program: Occupational
Accreditation: DETC

01 President .... Paul L. ZAGNONI

Southwest College of Naturopathic Medicine & Health Sciences (P)

2140 E Broadway Road, Tempe AZ 85282-1751
County: Maricopa FICE Identification: 031070
Unit ID: 420246
Telephone: (480) 858-9100 Carnegie Class: Spec/Health
FAX Number: (480) 858-9116 Calendar System: Quarter
URL: www.scnm.edu
Established: 1993 Annual Graduate Tuition & Fees: $27,249
Enrollment: 411 Coed
Affiliation or Control: Independent Non-Profit IRS Status: 501(c)3
Highest Offering: First Professional Degree; No Undergraduates
Program: Professional
Accreditation: NH, NATUR

01 President/Chief Executive Officer .... Paul A. MITTMAN
03 Executive Vice President .... Christine L. GIRARD
10 Vice Pres Finance & Administration .... Dawn RECTOR
32 Vice President Student Affairs .... Melissa WINQUIST
05 Chief Academic Officer .... Becky CLARK

Southwest Institute of Healing Arts (Q)

1100 E Apache Boulevard, Tempe AZ 85281-5822
County: Maricopa FICE Identification: 035933
Unit ID: 442879
Telephone: (480) 994-9244 Carnegie Class: Assoc/PrivFP
FAX Number: (480) 994-3228 Calendar System: Other
URL: www.swiha.edu
Established: 1992 Annual Undergrad Tuition & Fees: $18,500
Enrollment: 1,171 Coed
Affiliation or Control: Proprietary IRS Status: Proprietary
Highest Offering: Associate Degree
Program: Occupational
Accreditation: CNCE

01 President/Owner .... Mrs. K. C. MILLER
05 Director of Education .... Mr. Michael DYE
32 Director Student Support/Analytics .... Mr. Matt BILACH
35 Director Student Services .... Ms. Maria HUNTER
106 Director Online Curriculum .... Ms. Angela RYAN
37 Financial Aid Manager .... Ms. Joy KLEIN

Southwest University of Visual Arts (R)

2525 N Country Club Road, Tucson AZ 85716-2505
County: Pima FICE Identification: 024915
Unit ID: 104188
Telephone: (520) 325-0123 Carnegie Class: Spec/Arts
FAX Number: (520) 325-5535 Calendar System: Semester
URL: www.suva.edu
Established: 1983 Annual Undergrad Tuition & Fees: $27,665
Enrollment: 500 Coed
Affiliation or Control: Proprietary IRS Status: Proprietary
Highest Offering: Master's
Program: Fine Arts Emphasis
Accreditation: NH, CIDA

01 President .... Mrs. Sharmon WOODS
07 Director of Admissions .... Mr. Steve DIETZMAN
32 Director of Student Services .... Vacant
12 Director of Albuquerue Campus .... Ms. Cindy WHITAKER
06 Registrar .... Ms. Stephanie GASSER

Thunderbird School of Global Management (A)

1 Global Place, Glendale AZ 85306-3236
County: Maricopa FICE Identification: 001070
Unit ID: 103778
Telephone: (602) 978-7011 Carnegie Class: Spec/Bus
FAX Number: (602) 978-8238 Calendar System: Trimester
URL: www.thunderbird.edu
Established: 1946 Annual Graduate Tuition & Fees: $44,080
Enrollment: 1,190 Coed
Affiliation or Control: Independent Non-Profit IRS Status: 501(c)3
Highest Offering: Master's; No Undergraduates
Program: Professional; Business Emphasis
Accreditation: NH, BUS

01 President .... Dr. Larry PENLEY
05 Int Chief Acad Officer/Provost .... Dr. Dale DAVISON
88 SVP Executive Education .... Dr. Dennis BALTZLEY
10 Int Chief Financial Officer .... Mr. Daniel KUSTER
30 Vice Pres & Chief Development Ofcr .... Vacant
84 VP of Enrollment Mgmt/Student Svcs ... Ms. Rebecca HENRIKSEN
08 Chief Information Services .... Mr. Jim HERNDON
07 Assoc VP Admissions & Recruiting .... Mr. Jay BRYANT
27 Int VP Marketing/Communication .... Ms. Carol SUNNUCKS
36 Assoc VP for Prof Career Devel .... Vacant
20 Dean of Faculty .... Dr. Dale DAVISON
13 Director IT Operations .... Mr. Jim HERNDON
06 Registrar/Assoc VP Acad Operations .... Mr. James SCOTT
37 Director Student Financial Aid .... Mrs. Catherine KING-TODD
20 Assoc Dir Acad/International Svcs .... Ms. Felicia WELCH
04 Exec Assistant to the President .... Ms. Stacia SHELTON

Tohono O'odham Community College (B)

PO Box 3129, Sells AZ 85634-3129
County: Pima FICE Identification: 037844
Unit ID: 442781
Telephone: (520) 383-8401 Carnegie Class: Tribal
FAX Number: (520) 383-0029 Calendar System: Semester
URL: www.tocc.cc.az.us
Established: 1998 Annual Undergrad Tuition & Fees: $1,354
Enrollment: 214 Coed
Affiliation or Control: Tribal Control IRS Status: 501(c)3
Highest Offering: Associate Degree
Program: Occupational; 2-Year Principally Bachelor's Creditable
Accreditation: NH

01 President .... Mr. James VANDER HOOVEN
05 Vice President for Education .... Ms. Juana Clare JOSE
32 Vice Pres of Student Services .... Ms. Sylvia HENDRICKS
10 Vice Pres Admin Services/Finance .... Dr. Robert LEDMAN
46 Vice Pres Inst Research/Development .... Ms. Jane LATANE
75 Dept Chair Occupational Pgms .... Mr. George MIGUEL
07 Director of Admissions/Records .... Mr. Leslie LUNA
25 Sponsored Projects .... Mr. Samuel OROZCO
97 Dept Chair for General Education .... Dr. Paul ROBERTSON
08 Librarian .... Ms. Elaine CUBBINS
37 Director of Financial Aid .... Mr. Al RIVERA
88 Director Project NATIVE .... Ms. Camille MARTINEZ-YADEN
88 Director Project NATIVE .... Dr. Sandra LUCAS
30 Director of Fundraising .... Ms. Andrea AHMED
15 Human Resources Director .... Ms. Stacy OWSLEY

Tohono O'odham Community College West Campus (C)

PO Box 3129, Sells AZ 85634-3129
Telephone: (520) 383-8401 Identification: 770022
Accreditation: &NH

† Main campus is Tohono O'odham Community College in Sells, AZ.

Universal Technical Institute (D)

10695 W Pierce Street, Avondale AZ 85323-7946
County: Maricopa FICE Identification: 008221
Unit ID: 106041
Telephone: (623) 245-4600 Carnegie Class: Assoc/PrivFP
FAX Number: (623) 245-4601 Calendar System: Other
URL: www.uti.edu
Established: 1965 Annual Undergrad Tuition & Fees: $31,212
Enrollment: 2,529 Coed
Affiliation or Control: Proprietary IRS Status: Proprietary
Highest Offering: Associate Degree
Program: Occupational
Accreditation: ACCSC

01 Campus President .... Mr. Michael ROMANO
05 Director of Education .... Mr. Gary STARK
32 Director of Student Services .... Mrs. Heather GONZALES
10 Director of Campus Accounting .... Mr. Dale KENNEDY
07 Admissions Director .... Mr. Adam HELLER
36 Director of Graduate Employment .... Ms. Cheryl RADKE
37 Director of Financial Aid .... Ms. Terri MEIXSEL-CORDERO
18 Maintenance Director .... Mr. George MICKENS

University of Advancing Technology (E)

2625 W Baseline Road, Tempe AZ 85283-1056
County: Maricopa FICE Identification: 025590
Unit ID: 363934
Telephone: (602) 383-8228 Carnegie Class: Bac/Diverse
FAX Number: (602) 383-8250 Calendar System: Other
URL: www.uat.edu
Established: 1983 Annual Undergrad Tuition & Fees: $21,000
Enrollment: 958 Coed
Affiliation or Control: Proprietary IRS Status: Proprietary
Highest Offering: Master's
Program: Technical Emphasis
Accreditation: NH

01 President .... Mr. Jason PISTILLO
05 Provost/Dean & Secretary .... Mr. Dave BOLMAN
11 Chief Administrative Officer .... Ms. Traci LEE
10 Vice President of Finance .... Mr. Marc PROCHELLO
07 Vice President Admissions .... Ms. Shawn ALEXANDER

University of Arizona (F)

1401 E University Blvd, Tucson AZ 85721-0001
County: Pima FICE Identification: 001083
Unit ID: 104179
Telephone: (520) 621-2211 Carnegie Class: RU/VH
FAX Number: (520) 621-9323 Calendar System: Semester
URL: www.arizona.edu
Established: 1885 Annual Undergrad Tuition & Fees (In-State): $10,391
Enrollment: 40,223 Coed
Affiliation or Control: State IRS Status: 501(c)3
Highest Offering: Doctorate
Program: Liberal Arts And General; Teacher Preparatory; Professional
Accreditation: NH, ART, AUD, BUS, BUSA, CEA, CLPSY, CORE, DANCE, DIETD, DIETI, ENG, IPSY, JOUR, LAW, LIB, LSAR, MED, MUS, NURSE, PCSAS, PERF, PH, PHAR, PLNG, SCPSY, SP, SPAA, THEA

01 President .... Dr. Ann WEAVER HART
05 Sr VP for Acad Affairs & Provost .... Mr. Andrew C. COMRIE
10 Sr VP and CFO/Business Affairs .... Mr. James A. HYATT
88 Sr VP University Relations .... Ms. Teresa THOMPSON
46 VP for Research .... Dr. Jennifer K. BARTON
17 Sr VP Health Sciences .... Vacant
41 VP and Director Athletics .... Mr. Gregory K. BYRNE
43 VP Legal Affs/General Counsel .... Ms. Laura T. JOHNSON
03 Executive Director/Vice President .... Mr. Jack C. MUTCHLER
13 CIO/Exec Director UITS .... Ms. Michele L. NORIN
88 VP Reg Devel Outreach Global Init .... Mr. Michael A. PROCTOR
49 VP Innovation & Strategy .... Dr. Joaquin RUIZ
21 VP Business Affairs .... Mr. Robert R. SMITH
16 Vice Pres Human Resources .... Ms. Allison M. VAILLANCOURT
32 Vice President Student Affairs .... Ms. Melissa VITO
20 Vice Provost Academic Affairs .... Dr. Gail D. BURD
86 Assoc VP State Relations .... Mr. Timothy S. BEE
88 Assoc VP External Relations-Phoenix .... Ms. Judith A. BERNAS
35 Assoc VP Student Affairs .... Mr. Frank FARIAS
88 Assoc VP Finance & Admin .... Ms. Karen S. FILIPPELLI
88 Asst VP Institutional Analysis .... Mr. James S. FLORIAN
45 Assoc VP Academic Res/Plng/Mgmt .... Mr. Edward G. FRISCH
88 Assoc VP Research .... Ms. Caroline M. GARCIA
26 Assoc VP Community Relations .... Mr. Jaime P. GUTIERREZ
21 Assoc VP/Comptroller/Financial Svc .... Mr. Mark A. MCGURK
86 Assoc VP Federal Relations .... Mr. Shay D. STAUTZ
07 Asst VP Dean of Admissions .... Ms. Kasandra K. URQUIDEZ
88 Assoc VP Univ Research Parks .... Mr. Bruce A. WRIGHT
09 Assoc Vice Provost Inst Research .... Dr. Richard J. KROC
88 Assoc Provost Faculty Affairs .... Mr. Thomas P. MILLER
88 Sr Asst VP Student Affairs .... Mr. Jeffrey M. ORGERA
39 Sr Asst VP Stdnt Aff & Univ Housing .... Mr. James D. VAN ARSDEL
88 Asst VP Tribal Relations .... Ms. Karen F. BEGAY
18 Asst VP Plng/Design & Construction .... Mr. Peter DOURLEIN
88 Asst VP Student Affairs/Fin & Admin .... Mr. Joel S. HAUFF
19 Asst VP Risk Management/Safety .... Mr. Steven C. HOLLAND
88 Asst VP Health Sciences/Pub Affairs .. Mr. George D. HUMPHREY
88 Asst VP Marketing .... Ms. Kathleen M. JENSEN
18 Asst VP Facilities Management .... Mr. Christopher M. KOPACH
88 Asst VP Financial Services .... Mr. Duc D. MA
28 Asst VP Chief Diversity Officer .... Mr. Raji A. RHYS WIETECHA
88 Asst VP Finance Administration .... Ms. Marilyn TAYLOR
88 Asst VProvost Ofc of Instruc/Assess .... Ms. Debra J. TOMANEK
88 Asst VP Budget .... Ms. Kathryn E. WHISMAN
06 Registrar/Enrollment Management .... Dr. Elizabeth A. ACREE
67 Dean Pharmacy .... Mr. J. L. BOOTMAN
47 V Provost/Dean Col Agri/Life Sci .... Mr. Shane C. BURGESS
58 Dean Graduate College .... Mr. Andrew H. CARNIE
48 Dean Col Arch & Landscape Arch .... Dr. Janice A. CERVELLI
63 Dean College of Med-Phoenix Campus .... Mr. Stuart D. FLYNN
54 Dean College of Engineering .... Dr. Jeffrey B. GOLDBERG
63 Dean College of Medicine .... Dr. Steven GOLDSCHMID
69 Dean Zuckerman AZ Col Public Hlth .... Dr. Iman A. HAKIM
57 Dean College of Fine Arts .... Dr. Jory L. HANCOCK
50 Dean Eller College of Management .... Dr. Leonard M. JESSUP
83 Dean Col of Social/Behav Science .... Dr. John P. JONES
81 Dean College of Optical Sciences .... Mr. Thomas L. KOCH
92 Dean Honors College .... Dr. Patricia MACCORQUODALE
53 Dean College of Education .... Dr. Ronald W. MARX
61 Dean College of Law .... Mr. Marc L. MILLER
66 Dean College of Nursing .... Dr. Joan L. SHAVER
12 Dean UA South .... Dr. James W. SHOCKEY
08 Dean of Libr/Ctr for Creative Photo .... Ms. Carla J. STOFFLE
79 Dean College of Humanities ..... Dr. Mary E. WILDNER-BASSETT
88 Exec Director/VP Tech Launch AZ .... Mr. David N. ALLEN
85 Director International Admissions .... Ms. Rachel A. BEECH
29 Exec Director Alumni Office .... Ms. Melinda W. BURKE
25 Director Sponsored Proj/Services .... Ms. Sherry L. ESHAM
27 Director External Communications .... Ms. Jennifer M. FITZENBERGER
23 Exec Director Campus Health .... Dr. Harry MCDERMOTT
36 Director Career Services .... Ms. Eileen M. MCGARRY
37 Exec Director Student Financial Aid .... Mr. John NAMETZ
96 Director Procurement & Contract Svs .... Mr. Edward D. NASSER
40 Director Univ of Arizona Bookstores .... Ms. Debby L. SHIVELY
22 Dir Office of Institutional Equity .... Ms. Mary E. TUCKER
102 President UA Foundation .... Mr. Jim H. MOORE

University of Arizona Phoenix Biomedical Campus (G)

550 E Van Buren Street, Phoenix AZ 85004
Telephone: (602) 827-2001 Identification: 770023
Accreditation: &NH

† Main campus is University of Arizona in Tucson, AZ.

University of Arizona South (H)

1140 N Colombo Avenue, Sierra Vista AZ 85635
Telephone: (520) 458-8278 Identification: 770024
Accreditation: &NH

† Main campus is University of Arizona in Tucson, AZ.

University of Phoenix (I)

1625 W. Fountainhead Parkway, Tempe AZ 85282
County: Maricopa FICE Identification: 020988
Unit ID: 105516
Telephone: (480) 557-2000 Carnegie Class: Master's L
FAX Number: N/A Calendar System: Other
URL: www.phoenix.edu
Established: 1976 Annual Undergrad Tuition & Fees: N/A
Enrollment: 287,500 Coed
Affiliation or Control: Proprietary IRS Status: Proprietary
Highest Offering: Doctorate
Program: Liberal Arts And General; Teacher Preparatory; Professional
Accreditation: NH, ACBSP, CACREP, NURSE, TEAC

01 President University of Phoenix .... Dr. William PEPICELLO
04 Executive Administrator .... Ms. Sandy MEYER
05 Provost/VP Academic Affairs .... Vacant
20 Interim Provost/SVP .... Dr. Dawn IWAMOTO
03 EVP Chief Business Operating Ofcr .... Mr. Barry FEIERSTEIN
03 EVP Chief Std & Campus Ops Officer .... Mr. Jerrad TAUSZ
37 EVP Student Admin Svcs & FA .... Mr. Jeff SONNENBERG
10 SVP/Chief Financial Officer .... Mr. Byron JONES
100 SVP/Chief of Staff .... Ms. Nina MUNSON
11 SVP Operations .... Mr. Randy LICHTENFELD
45 SVP University Strategy .... Mr. Thomas MCCARTY
84 SVP Enrollment .... Ms. Trish ELLIOTT
32 SVP Student Services .... Ms. Nancy CERVASIO
20 SVP Academic Operations .... Dr. Russ PADEN
88 SVP Campus Operations Admin .... Mr. Vince GRELL
88 SVP East Territory .... Mr. Brent FITCH
88 SVP West Territory .... Ms. Jennifer CISNA
15 SVP Human Resources .... Ms. Cheryl NAUMANN
88 SVP Student Experience .... Ms. Ruth VELORIA
65 Assoc Provost/VP Acad Affairs .... Dr. Hinrich EYLERS
07 VP Office of Admissions & Records .... Ms. Evelyn GASKIN
100 VP Academic Administration .... Mr. Lee FINKEL
88 VP Operations .... Ms. Lori SANTIAGO
29 VP Alumni Relations .... Ms. Kathleen FERN
46 VP Academic Affairs/Library .... Mr. David BICKFORD
09 Assoc VP Academic Research .... Dr. Jay KLAGGE
88 Exec Dir/Dean Sch Advanced Studies .... Dr. Jeremy MORELAND
50 Exec Dir/Dean Sch Advanced Studies .... Dr. Freda HARTMAN
83 Exec Dir/Dean College Social Sci .... Dr. Lynn HALL
88 Exec Dir/Dean College of IS&T .... Dr. Blair SMITH
79 Exec Dir/Dean College of Humanities .... Dr. Robert RIDEL
53 Exec Dir/Dean of Education .... Dr. Meredith CURLEY
88 Exec Dir/Dean Criminal Justice/Sec .... Dr. James NESS
29 Exec Director Alumni Relations .... Ms. Nikki SANDOVAL
07 Sr Director of Admissions .... Mr. Marc BOOKER
108 Sr Director Institutional Assess .... Mr. Wayne FORAKER
06 Registrar .... Ms. Audra MCQUARIE
28 Diversity Officer .... Mr. Javier FELICIANO
12 Campus Director Central Florida .... Mr. Tony ABRUSCATO
12 Acting Campus Director Cincinnati .... Mr. Stephen FLATT
12 Campus Director Cleveland .... Ms. Gina CUFFARI
12 Campus Director Columbus OH .... Ms. Heather LOUGHLEY
12 Campus Director Connecticut .... Mr. Robert ORLANDO
12 Acting Campus Director Delaware .... Mr. Stephen FLATT
12 Actg Campus Director Harrisburg PA .... Mr. Stephen FLATT
12 Campus Director Knoxville .... Mr. Mark AMREIN
12 Acting Campus Director Madison .... Ms. Lori SANTIAGO
12 Campus Director Northern Virginia .... Mr. Erik GREENBERG
12 Campus Director Philadelphia .... Vacant
12 Campus Director Phoenix .... Mr. David FITZGERALD
12 Campus Director Pittsburgh .... Mr. Ernie FULLERTON
12 Campus Director Puerto Rico .... Mr. Jorge A. RIVERA
12 Campus Director Raleigh NC .... Ms. Candice MORGAN
12 Campus Director Reno .... Dr. Bob LARKIN
12 Campus Dir Shreveport/Bossier City .... Ms. Julie MARBLE

12 Campus Director South Florida ..... Ms. Leslie KRISTOF
12 Acting Campus Director Springfield ..... Ms. Lori SANTIAGO
12 Campus Director West Michigan ..... Mr. Brian GLEASON

University of Phoenix Southern Arizona Campus (A)

300 S Craycroft Road, Tucson AZ 85711-4574
Telephone: (520) 881-6512 Identification: 770236
Accreditation: &NH

† Main campus is University of Phoenix in Tempe, AZ.

West Coast Ultrasound Institute (B)

4250 E Camelback Road, #K158, Phoenix AZ 85018
Telephone: (602) 954-3834 Identification: 770550
Accreditation: ACCSC

† Main campus is West Coast Ultrasound Institute in Beverly Hills, CA.

Western International University (C)

1601 W. Fountainhead Parkway, Tempe AZ 85282
County: Maricopa FICE Identification: 021715
Unit ID: 106102
Telephone: (602) 943-2311 Carnegie Class: Master's M
FAX Number: (602) 371-8637 Calendar System: Other
URL: www.west.edu
Established: 1978 Annual Undergrad Tuition & Fees: $11,040
Enrollment: 2,926 Coed
Affiliation or Control: Proprietary IRS Status: Proprietary
Highest Offering: Master's
Program: Professional; Business Emphasis
Accreditation: NH

01 President ..... Ms. Tracy LORENZ
05 Provost/Sr VP ..... Dr. Barbara BADERMAN
06 Registrar/Sr Dir of University ..... Ms. Hue HASLIM
45 VP Strategy & Development ..... Ms. Allison POOLEY
13 VP InformationTechnology ..... Ms. Stephanie LEACH
11 VP of Administration ..... Mr. Kris MCCALL
26 VP of Marketing ..... Ms. Debbie MCKEAN
10 Regional Director of Finance ..... Ms. Heidi PHHIPPS
21 Sr Dir Student Administrative Svcs ..... Ms. Beth CARLISLE
88 Director of Student Advisement ..... Ms. Melilssa MACHUCA

Western International University East Valley Campus (D)

55 North Arizona Place, Suite 101, Chandler AZ 85225
Telephone: (602) 943-2311 Identification: 770025
Accreditation: &NH

† Main campus is Western International University in Tempe, AZ.

Western International University Ft. Huachuca Campus (E)

Bldg #52104, ATZS HRH-E, Fort Huachuca AZ 85670
Telephone: (602) 943-2311 Identification: 770026
Accreditation: &NH

† Main campus is Western International University in Tempe, AZ.

Western International University Peoria Campus (F)

14100 N 83rd Avenue, #100, Peoria AZ 85381
Telephone: (602) 943-2311 Identification: 770027
Accreditation: &NH

† Main campus is Western International University in Tempe, AZ.

Western International University Scottsdale Campus (G)

8860 East Chaparral Road, Suite 120,
Scottsdale AZ 85250
Telephone: (602) 943-2311 Identification: 770028
Accreditation: &NH

† Main campus is Western International University in Tempe, AZ.

Yavapai College (H)

1100 E Sheldon Street, Prescott AZ 86301-3297
County: Yavapai FICE Identification: 001079
Unit ID: 106148
Telephone: (928) 445-7300 Carnegie Class: Assoc/Pub-R-L
FAX Number: (928) 776-2119 Calendar System: Semester
URL: www.yc.edu
Established: 1966 Annual Undergrad Tuition & Fees (In-District): $1,888
Enrollment: 8,274 Coed
Affiliation or Control: Local IRS Status: 501(c)3
Highest Offering: Associate Degree
Program: Occupational; 2-Year Principally Bachelor's Creditable
Accreditation: NH, ADNUR, EMT, IFSAC, RAD

01 President ..... Dr. Penelope WILLS
05 Vice Pres Instruction/Student Affs ..... Dr. Stuart BLACKLAW
10 Vice Pres Finance/Admin Svcs ..... Dr. Clint EWELL
30 VP College Development/Foundation ..... Mr. Steve WALKER
20 Dean Instruct Support & Improvement ..... Ms. Stacey HILTON
12 Dean Verde Valley Campus ..... Mr. James PEREY
75 Dean Career Technical Education ..... Mr. John MORGAN
66 Dn Sci/Nursing/Allied Hlth ..... Mr. Scott FARNSWORTH
32 Dean Student Services ..... Ms. Sandy GARBER
26 Director of Marketing/Public Info ..... Mr. Mike LANGE
37 Director of Financial Aid ..... Ms. Terri ECKEL
09 Dir Inst Planning/Research/Assess ..... Mr. Tom HUGHES
15 Director for Human Resources ..... Ms. Rose HURLEY
19 Director of Campus Safety ..... Mr. Joe CAPELLI
21 Dir of Business Svcs & Controller ..... Mr. Frank D'ANGELO
07 Recruitment Officer ..... Ms. Kornelia MARKOV
18 Director for Facilities ..... Mr. David LAURENCE
13 Chief Information Officer ..... Mr. Patrick BURNS
88 Paralegal Director ..... Ms. Ruth HARRISON
06 Registrar ..... Ms. Sheila JARRELL
29 Director Alumni Relations ..... Vacant
96 Director of Purchasing ..... Ms. Phyllis LEWELLEN
88 Custom Training Coordinator ..... Vacant
36 Coordinator Career Services ..... Vacant

Yavapai College Verde Valley Campus (I)

601 Black Hills Drive, Clarkdale AZ 86324
Telephone: (928) 634-7501 Identification: 770029
Accreditation: &NH

† Main campus is Yavapai College in Prescott, AZ.

ARKANSAS

Arkansas Baptist College (J)

1621 Martin Luther King Drive, Little Rock AR 72202-6099
County: Pulaski FICE Identification: 001087
Unit ID: 106306
Telephone: (501) 370-4000 Carnegie Class: Bac/Assoc
FAX Number: (501) 372-7992 Calendar System: Semester
URL: www.arkansasbaptist.edu
Established: 1884 Annual Undergrad Tuition & Fees: $8,040
Enrollment: 1,082 Coed
Affiliation or Control: Baptist IRS Status: 501(c)3
Highest Offering: Baccalaureate
Program: 2-Year Principally Bachelor's Creditable; Liberal Arts And General
Accreditation: NH

01 President ..... Dr. Fitz HILL
04 President's Executive Assistant ..... Ms. Patsy DIGGS
10 Exec VP/Chief Financial Officer ..... Mr. Billy OWENS
100 Chief of Staff ..... Mrs. LaCresha NEWTON
05 VP of Academic Affairs ..... Dr. Joyce O. JENKINS
32 Vice President Student Affairs ..... Dr. Vicki WILLIAMS
09 Director of Institutional Research ..... Mrs. Jerelyn L. DUNCAN
103 Dir of Adult Ed & Workforce Dev ..... Vacant
07 Director of Admissions/Recruitment ..... Mr. Willie HICKS
84 Dean of Enrollment Management ..... Vacant
06 Registar ..... Ms. Delores VOLIBER
37 Director of Financial Aid ..... Ms. Eva ALEXANDER
08 Director of Library/Media Services ..... Vacant
26 College Relations/Marketing ..... Mrs. Linda GILLAM WEIR
21 Business Manager ..... Vacant
34 Dean of Women ..... Vacant
35 Asst Dean of Student Affairs ..... Mr. Brian MILLER
33 Dean of Men ..... Mr. Donald NORTHCROSS
19 Chief of Campus Safety ..... Mr. Curtis JOHNSON
18 Facilities Director ..... Mr. Bryan RUSHER

Arkansas Northeastern College (K)

2501 S Division Street, Blytheville AR 72315-5111
County: Mississippi FICE Identification: 012860
Unit ID: 107327
Telephone: (870) 762-1020 Carnegie Class: Assoc/Pub-R-M
FAX Number: (870) 763-3704 Calendar System: Semester
URL: www.anc.edu
Established: 1974 Annual Undergrad Tuition & Fees (In-District): $1,045
Enrollment: 1,672 Coed
Affiliation or Control: State/Local IRS Status: 501(c)3
Highest Offering: Associate Degree
Program: Occupational; 2-Year Principally Bachelor's Creditable
Accreditation: NH, ADNUR, DA, EMT

01 President ..... Dr. James SHEMWELL
03 Executive Vice President ..... Mrs. June WALTERS
05 Vice President of Instruction ..... Ms. Mary DEMENT
10 Vice President for Finance ..... Ms. Pacey BOWENS
32 Vice Pres Student Svcs/Registrar ..... Mrs. Laura YARBROUGH
30 Vice President for Advancement ..... Mrs. Sherri BENNETT
09 Vice President MITS/Human Resources ..... Mr. James W. MCCLAIN
26 Assoc VP for Dev/College Relations ..... Ms. Rachel GIFFORD
72 Dean Tech Programs & Training ..... Mrs. Robin SINGLETON
49 Dean Arts & Sciences ..... Mrs. Deborah PARKER
12 Dean for Economic Development ..... Mr. Gene BENNETT
66 Dean Nursing/Allied Hlth/PE/Rec ..... Mrs. Brenda HOLIFIELD
83 Chair Communications/Humanities ..... Mrs. Deanita HICKS
88 Coordinator University Center ..... Mrs. Candice BLANKENSHIP
31 Community Education Specialist ..... Ms. Mary Ann GARREN
08 Director of College Library ..... Mrs. Bronwyn MORGAN
07 Director of Admissions ..... Vacant
36 Coordinator of Placement Services ..... Dr. Bridget SHEMWELL
37 Director Financial Aid ..... Vacant
72 Dean MITS ..... Mrs. Ruby MEADOR
21 Controller ..... Vacant
15 Human Resources & ADA Coordinator ..... Mrs. Carol WILF
90 Director Academic Tech Services ..... Mr. James ODOM
18 Director Physical Plant and Grounds ..... Mr. Ralph HILL
88 Director Talent Search/Educ Opp Ctr ..... Mrs. Tonya HARRIS
88 Director Student Support Services ..... Ms. Lisa MCGHEE
04 Assistant to Board/President ..... Mrs. Courtney FISHER

*Arkansas State University System (L)

501 Woodlane Drive, Suite 301N, Little Rock AR 72201
County: Pulaski Identification: 666187
Telephone: (501) 660-1000 Carnegie Class: N/A
FAX Number: (501) 660-1010
URL: www.asusystem.edu

01 President ..... Dr. Charles L. WELCH
04 Exec Assistant to the President ..... Ms. Pam KAIL
10 Vice President for Finance ..... Ms. Julie BATES
86 Vice Pres Governmental Relations ..... Mr. Robert EVANS
102 System VP/President ASU Foundation ..... Mr. Steve OWENS
43 Legal Counsel ..... Ms. Lucinda MCDANIEL
88 Internal Auditor ..... Ms. Jo LUNBECK
45 Vice Pres Strategic Com/Econ Dev ..... Mr. Jeff HANKINS

*Arkansas State University-Beebe (M)

PO Box 1000, Beebe AR 72012-1000
County: White FICE Identification: 001091
Unit ID: 106449
Telephone: (501) 882-3600 Carnegie Class: Assoc/Pub2in4
FAX Number: (501) 882-8970 Calendar System: Semester
URL: www.asub.edu
Established: 1927 Annual Undergrad Tuition & Fees (In-State): $3,030
Enrollment: 4,643 Coed
Affiliation or Control: State IRS Status: 501(c)3
Highest Offering: Associate Degree
Program: Occupational; 2-Year Principally Bachelor's Creditable
Accreditation: NH, EMT, MLTAD

02 Chancellor ..... Dr. Eugene MCKAY
100 Executive Assistant to Chancellor ..... Mr. Joe BERRY
03 Vice Chancellor ASU-Heber Springs ..... Dr. James C. BOYETT
03 Vice Chancellor of ASU-Searcy ..... Mr. Don HARLAN
05 Vice Chanc External/Advanced Pgms ..... Mr. Barry N. FARRIS
05 Vice Chancellor Academic Affairs ..... Dr. Theodore J. KALTHOFF
32 Vice Chancellor Student Services ..... Dr. Deborah A. GARRETT
10 Vice Chanc Finance & Administration ..... Mr. Jerry H. CARLISLE
30 Vice Chanc Inst Advancement ..... Dr. Keith PINCHBACK
26 Director of Public Information ..... Ms. Frances MERRELL
06 Registrar ..... Ms. Amy J. MAHAN
08 Head Librarian ..... Ms. Tracy D. SMITH
15 Director of Human Resources ..... Ms. Susan A. COLLIE
19 Chief of Police ..... Mr. James J. MARTIN
18 Director of Physical Plant ..... Mr. Jerry L. THOMPSON
37 Director Student Financial Aid ..... Ms. Louise DRIVER
09 Director of Institutional Research ..... Ms. Bonnie SMYTH-MCGAHA
14 Director of Computer Service ..... Mr. Wade FINCHER
21 Business Manager ..... Ms. Charlette MOORE
21 Controller ..... Ms. Sharon A. BEEN
84 Director of Enrollment Management ..... Mr. David M. MAYES
38 Dir Student Success and Retention ..... Mr. Roger MOORE
36 Career Service/Transfer Coord ..... Ms. Heather GARCIA
39 Director of Student Life ..... Mr. Chad GRAY
24 Director of Learning Center ..... Ms. Rebecca E. WOLF
72 Director Advanced Tech/Allied Hlth ..... Dr. Keith MCCLANAHAN
106 Director of Distance Learning ..... Ms. Rhonda DURHAM
96 Dir Administrative Support Services ..... Ms. Robin LANCASTER
12 Dir ASU-Beebe Degree Ctr at LRAFB . Ms. Nancy A. SHEFFLETTE
07 Director of Admissions ..... Ms. Robin A. HAYES
35 Coordinator of Campus Life ..... Mr. Andy ISOM
105 Website Coordinator ..... Mr. Rikky L. FREE
31 Coord Marketing/Community Relations ..... Mrs. Rose Mary JACKSON

*Arkansas State University-Jonesboro (N)

PO Box 600, State University AR 72467
County: Craighead FICE Identification: 001090
Unit ID: 106458
Telephone: (870) 972-2100 Carnegie Class: Master's L
FAX Number: (870) 972-3465 Calendar System: Semester
URL: www.astate.edu
Established: 1909 Annual Undergrad Tuition & Fees (In-State): $7,510
Enrollment: 13,877 Coed
Affiliation or Control: State IRS Status: 501(c)3
Highest Offering: Doctorate
Program: Liberal Arts And General; Teacher Preparatory; Professional
Accreditation: NH, ADNUR, ANEST, ART, BUS, CACREP, CEA, CORE, @DIETC, DMS, ENG, JOUR, MLTAD, MT, MUS, NUR, PTA, PTAA, RAD, RADMAG, RTT, SP, SPAA, SW, TED

02 Chancellor ..... Dr. Tim HUDSON
100 Chief of Staff ..... Dr. Jason PENRY
05 Provost & VC Acad Affairs & Research ..... Dr. Lynita COOKSEY
10 VC Finance & Administration ..... Dr. Len T. FREY
32 Vice Chancellor Student Affairs ..... Dr. William R. STRIPLING
30 Interim VC Univ Advancement ..... Dr. Jason PENRY

41 Director of Athletics .... Mr. Terry MOHAJIR
20 Assoc Vice Chanc Academic Svcs .... Dr. Gina HOGUE
21 Assoc Vice Chancellor Finance .... Dr. Russ HANNAH
21 Asst Vice Chanc Budget .... Ms. Donna MCMILLIN
15 Asst VC Human Resources .... Ms. Lori WINN
35 Assoc Vice Chanc Student Affairs .... Dr. Lonnie R. WILLIAMS
46 Vice Provost Resrch & Grad Studies .... Dr. Andrew SUSTICH
35 Asst Vice Chanc Student Affairs .... Dr. Craig JOHNSON
13 Interim CIO .... Mr. Henry TORRES
18 Asst Vice Chancellor Facilities .... Mr. Al STOVERINK
51 Dean Continuing Educ/Cmty Outreach .... Dr. Beverly BOALS-GILBERT
88 Interim Executive Director of ABI .... Dr. Andrew SUSTICH
37 Dir of Financial Aid & Scholarship .... Mr. Terry FINNEY
09 Dir Inst Research/Plng/Assessment .... Dr. Kathryn C. JONES
06 Dir Admissions/Records/Registration .... Ms. Tracy FINCH
07 Director of Recruitment .... Dr. Tammy L. FOWLER
39 Director of Residence Life .... Mr. Patrick DIXON
38 Dean of Student Development .... Mr. Randall TATE
19 Chief University Police .... Mr. Randy MARTIN
28 Director of Disability Services .... Dr. Jenifer R. MASON
36 Director Career Management Center .... Dr. Markel QUARLES
38 Director Student Counseling .... Dr. Phil HESTAND
23 Director Student Health Center .... Ms. Victoria WILLIAMS
29 Exec Dir Alumni Relations .... Ms. Beth SMITH
26 Exec Dir Marketing .... Vacant
27 Director of Media Relations .... Ms. Gina BOWMAN
88 Director Pub & Creative Services .... Mr. Mark REEVES
96 Dir Procurement & Travel Svcs .... Ms. Carol BARNHILL
62 Dir Library .... Mr. Jeff BAILEY
47 Dean College Agri/Technology .... Dr. Timothy BURCHAM
81 Dean College Sciences & Math .... Dr. John PRATTE
50 Interim Dean College of Business .... Dr. Jim WASHAM
53 Dean College of Education .... Dr. Thillainatarajan SIVAKUMARAN
60 Dean College of Communications .... Dr. Brad RAWLINS
66 Dean College of Nursing Health Prof .... Dr. Susan N. HANRAHAN
88 Executive Dir University College .... Dr. Jill SIMONS
57 Dean Fine Arts .... Dr. Donald BOWYER
79 Dean College Humanities/Social Sci .... Dr. Lauri UMANSKY
92 Director of The Honors College .... Ms. Rebecca OLIVER
54 Dean College of Engineering .... Dr. David BEASLEY

*Arkansas State University-Mountain Home (A)

1600 S College Street, Mountain Home AR 72653-5326
County: Baxter Identification: 666311
Unit ID: 420538
Telephone: (870) 508-6100 Carnegie Class: Assoc/Pub2in4
FAX Number: (870) 508-6287 Calendar System: Semester
URL: www.asumh.edu
Established: 1995 Annual Undergrad Tuition & Fees (In-District): $3,192
Enrollment: 1,413 Coed
Affiliation or Control: State/Local IRS Status: 501(c)3
Highest Offering: Associate Degree
Program: Occupational; Business Emphasis
Accreditation: NH, COARC, EMT

02 Chancellor .... Dr. Robin MYERS
05 Vice Chanc Academic Affairs .... Dr. Martin EGGENSPERGER
11 Vice Chanc Administrative Affairs .... Mr. John DAVIDSON
32 Vice Chancellor for Student Affairs .... Mrs. Rosalyn BLAGG
30 Vice Chancellor Development .... Vacant
46 Assoc VC Special Projects .... Mrs. Karen S. HOPPER
06 Registrar .... Vacant
18 Chief Facilities/Physical Plant .... Mr. Nickey L. ROBBINS
26 Director of Communications .... Mrs. Christy C. KEIRN
35 Director Student Affairs .... Mr. Mason CAMPBELL
37 Director Student Financial Aid .... Mr. Clay BERRY

*Arkansas State University-Newport (B)

7648 Victory Boulevard, Newport AR 72112-8912
County: Jackson Identification: 666153
Unit ID: 440402
Telephone: (870) 512-7800 Carnegie Class: Assoc/Pub2in4
FAX Number: (870) 512-7807 Calendar System: Semester
URL: www.asun.edu
Established: 1991 Annual Undergrad Tuition & Fees (In-State): $3,000
Enrollment: 2,043 Coed
Affiliation or Control: State IRS Status: 501(c)3
Highest Offering: Associate Degree
Program: Occupational; 2-Year Principally Bachelor's Creditable
Accreditation: NH, SURGT

02 Chancellor .... Dr. Larry N. WILLIAMS
04 Assistant to the Chancellor .... Ms. Laura KING
05 Vice Chancellor Academic Affairs .... Dr. Sandra MASSEY
10 Vice Chancellor Fiscal Affairs .... Mr. Adam ADAIR
32 Vice Chancellor Student Affairs .... Dr. Mary ROBERTSON
12 Vice Chancellor Jonesboro Campus .... Mr. Charley APPLEBY
12 Vice Chancellor Marked Tree Campus .... Mr. Jeff BOOKOUT
88 Division Chair .... Mr. Ike WHEELER
88 Division Chair .... Dr. Allen MOONEYHAN
88 Division Chair .... Mr. Robert SUMMERS
88 Division Chair .... Mr. Joeseph CAMPBELL
06 Registrar/Director of Admissions .... Ms. Candace GROSS
13 Director of Computer Services .... Ms. Tamya STALLINGS
15 Director Human Resources .... Mr. Charles WALKER
18 Director of Physical Plant .... Mr. David WINSTON
21 Controller .... Ms. Melissa WATSON
25 Director of Grants Management .... Ms. Monika PHILLIPS
37 Director Student Financial Aid .... Ms. Deana TIMS
32 Director Student Services .... Ms. Ashley BUCHMAN
38 Counselor .... Ms. Amber GRADY
08 Librarian .... Ms. Jennifer BALLARD
24 Director of Learning Resource Ctr .... Ms. Christy MANN
19 Public Safety Officer .... Mr. Jeff GRIZZLE
96 Director of Procurement .... Ms. Lee WEBB
17 Director of Nursing .... Vacant
108 Director of Career Pathways .... Ms. Kimberly LONG
75 Adult Education Coordinator .... Ms. Martha TAUSSIG

*Arkansas State University-Heber Springs (C)

101 River Crest Drive, Heber Springs AR 72543
Telephone: (501) 362-1100 Identification: 770001
Accreditation: &NH

† Main campus is Arkansas State University-Beebe in Beebe, AR.

*Arkansas State University-Searcy (D)

1800 East Monroe Avenue, Searcy AR 72143
Telephone: (501) 207-6200 Identification: 770002
Accreditation: &NH

† Main campus is Arkansas State University-Beebe in Beebe, AR.

Arkansas Tech University (E)

1509 North Boulder Avenue, Russellville AR 72801-2222
County: Pope FICE Identification: 001089
Unit ID: 106467
Telephone: (479) 968-0389 Carnegie Class: Master's L
FAX Number: (479) 964-0522 Calendar System: Semester
URL: www.atu.edu
Established: 1909 Annual Undergrad Tuition & Fees (In-State): $5,598
Enrollment: 10,950 Coed
Affiliation or Control: State IRS Status: 501(c)3
Highest Offering: Beyond Master's But Less Than Doctorate
Program: Liberal Arts And General; Teacher Preparatory; Professional
Accreditation: NH, BUS, CAHIIM, CORE, CS, EMT, ENG, MAC, MUS, NRPA, NUR, PTAA, TED

01 President .... Dr. Robert C. BROWN
11 Sr Vice Pres Administration/Finance .... Mr. David MOSELEY
05 Vice President Academic Affairs .... Dr. John WATSON
32 VP Student Services/Univ Rels .... Ms. Susie S. NICHOLSON
30 Vice President for Development .... Ms. Jayne W. JONES
86 Vice President Government Relations .... Mr. Phillip JACOBS
20 Assoc Vice Pres Academic Affairs .... Dr. David UNDERWOOD
43 Associate VP & Counsel to President . Mr. Thomas PENNINGTON
88 Assistant VP for Academic Affairs .... Dr. Hanna NORTON
84 Assistant VP Enrollment Management ... Ms. Shauna H. DONNELL
06 Registrar .... Ms. Tammy WEAVER
09 Director of Institutional Research .... Mr. Wyatt WATSON
08 Librarian .... Mr. William PARTON
21 Controller .... Ms. Donna RANKIN
14 Director Information Systems .... Mr. Ken WESTER
37 Director of Student Accounts .... Ms. Marilyn JOHNSON
15 Director Human Resources .... Ms. Angela REYNOLDS
37 Director Student Financial Aid .... Ms. Shirley M. GOINES
29 Director Alumni Relations .... Mr. Kelly DAVIS
85 Director of International Students .... Mr. Yasushi ONODERA
18 Director of Physical Plant Services .... Mr. Brian LASEY
96 Director of Purchasing .... Ms. Jessica HOLLOWAY
92 Director of Honors Program .... Dr. Jan JENKINS
22 Director of Affirmative Action .... Ms. Jennifer FLEMING
58 Dean of Graduate College .... Dr. Mary GUNTER
53 Dean of College of Education .... Dr. Sherry FIELD
49 Dean College of Arts & Humanities .... Dr. Micheal TARVER
50 Dean of College of Business .... Dr. Edward BASHAW
77 Dn Col Engineering & Applied Sci .... Dr. William HOEFLER
81 Dean College of Natural & Health Sc .... Dr. Jeff ROBERTSON
51 Dn Col Prof Studies Cmty Outreach .... Dr. Mary Ann ROLLANS

Arkansas Tech University-Ozark Campus (F)

1700 Helberg Lane, Ozark AR 72949
Telephone: (866) 225-2884 Identification: 770003
Accreditation: &NH

† Main campus is Arkansas Tech University in Russellville, AR.

Black River Technical College (G)

PO Box 468, Pocahantas AR 72455-0468
County: Randolph FICE Identification: 020522
Unit ID: 106625
Telephone: (870) 248-4000 Carnegie Class: Assoc/Pub-R-M
FAX Number: (870) 248-4100 Calendar System: Semester
URL: www.blackrivertech.org
Established: 1991 Annual Undergrad Tuition & Fees (In-State): $2,850
Enrollment: 2,408 Coed
Affiliation or Control: State IRS Status: 501(c)3
Highest Offering: Associate Degree
Program: Occupational; 2-Year Principally Bachelor's Creditable
Accreditation: NH, COARC, DIETT, EMT

01 President .... Dr. Wayne HATCHER
05 Vice President General Education .... Dr. Roger JOHNSON
72 Vice President Technical Education .... Mrs. Angela CALDWELL
10 Vice President of Finance .... Mrs. Loretta WILLIAMS
32 Vice President Student Affairs .... Vacant
30 Vice President of Development .... Dr. Jan ZIEGLER
37 Director Student Financial Aid .... Mrs. Brandi CHESTER
06 Registrar .... Mrs. Kimberly BIGGER

Bryan University (H)

3704 West Walnut, Rogers AR 72756-1825
Telephone: (479) 899-6644 Identification: 666252
Accreditation: ACICS

† Main campus is Bryan University in Springfield, MO.

Central Baptist College (I)

1501 College Avenue, Conway AR 72034-6470
County: Faulkner FICE Identification: 001093
Unit ID: 106713
Telephone: (501) 329-6872 Carnegie Class: Bac/Diverse
FAX Number: (501) 329-2941 Calendar System: Semester
URL: www.cbc.edu
Established: 1952 Annual Undergrad Tuition & Fees: $13,350
Enrollment: 832 Coed
Affiliation or Control: Baptist IRS Status: 501(c)3
Highest Offering: Baccalaureate
Program: Liberal Arts And General; Teacher Preparatory
Accreditation: NH

01 President .... Mr. Terry KIMBROW
05 Vice President Academic Affairs .... Dr. Gary MCALLISTER
10 Vice President for Finance .... Mrs. Donna GRAY
30 VP for Advancement .... Mrs. Sancy FAULK
04 Admin Asst to President .... Ms. Peggy CANTRELL
84 Assoc VP for Enrollment .... Mr. Ryan JOHNSON
07 Director of Admissions .... Mr. Jonathan WILSON
06 Registrar .... Mrs. Phylis HOFFMANN
19 Dean of Students/Campus Security .... Mr. Chris MITCHELL
08 Library Director .... Mrs. Rachel WHITTINGHAM
26 Director of Public Relations .... Mrs. Deanna OTT
44 Director of Annual Fund Giving .... Mr. Michael MAYO
37 Director of Financial Aid .... Mrs. Tonya HAMMONTREE
88 Director of Special Events .... Ms. Jessica FAULKNER
13 Director of Information Technology .... Mr. Doug BIBLE
41 Athletic Director .... Mr. Lyle MIDDLETON
32 Director of Student Services .... Ms. Rachel WAYMIRE
39 Director of Student Housing .... Ms. Sarah HEADLEY
15 Director of Human Resources .... Mrs. Pam TEAGUE
29 Alumni & Communications Officer .... Miss Jessica MYRICK
88 Director of Military Relations .... Ms. Robin STEPHENS

College of the Ouachitas (J)

One College Circle, Malvern AR 72104-0816
County: Hot Spring FICE Identification: 009976
Unit ID: 107521
Telephone: (501) 337-5000 Carnegie Class: Assoc/Pub-R-S
FAX Number: (501) 337-9382 Calendar System: Semester
URL: www.coto.edu
Established: 1991 Annual Undergrad Tuition & Fees (In-State): $3,182
Enrollment: 1,412 Coed
Affiliation or Control: State IRS Status: 501(c)3
Highest Offering: Associate Degree
Program: Occupational; 2-Year Principally Bachelor's Creditable; Technical Emphasis
Accreditation: NH

01 President .... Dr. Stephen SCHOONMAKER
10 Vice Pres Admin & Operations .... Mr. David SEE
05 Vice President of Instruction .... Vacant
32 Vice President Student Affairs .... Ms. Donna HILL
09 Exec Dir Planning & Assessment .... Ms. Carla CRUTCHFIELD
30 Exec Dir College Advancement .... Ms. Amber CHILDERS
88 Exec Dir to President .... Mr. Mike KOLB
49 Dean Liberal Arts .... Mr. Pat SIMMS
75 Dean Career & Technical Studies .... Mr. Ruben KEISLER
76 Dean Allied Health Sciences .... Mr. Gerald SONGER
08 Dean Learning Resources .... Ms. Mary Ann HARPER
06 Registrar .... Ms. Keesha JOHNSON
21 Controller .... Ms. Jackie HOLLOWAY
37 Director of Financial Aid .... Ms. Jayna WINIECKI
35 Director Student Success .... Ms. Shanea MORRISON
88 Dir TRIO Student Support Services .... Ms. Vergina SMITH
103 Director Adult Education .... Dr. Blake ROBERTSON
36 Director Career Pathways .... Mr. Billy FRANCIS

Crowley's Ridge College (K)

100 College Drive, Paragould AR 72450-9775
County: Greene FICE Identification: 001095
Unit ID: 106810
Telephone: (870) 236-6901 Carnegie Class: Assoc/PrivNFP4
FAX Number: (870) 236-7748 Calendar System: Semester
URL: www.crc.edu
Established: 1964 Annual Undergrad Tuition & Fees: $10,350
Enrollment: 207 Coed
Affiliation or Control: Churches Of Christ IRS Status: 501(c)3
Highest Offering: Baccalaureate
Program: Liberal Arts And General
Accreditation: NH

01 President .... Mr. Ken HOPPE
05 Vice President for Academic Affairs .... Mr. Phil WILKERSON
32 Vice President for Student Affairs .... Mr. Art SMITH
30 Vice President for Advancement .... Mr. Richard JOHNSON
06 Registrar .... Mr. Paul MCFADDEN
37 Director Student Financial Services .... Mr. David W. GOFF
26 Director Public Information .... Mrs. Andrea JOHNSON
07 Director Admissions/Student Life .... Mrs. Nancy JONESHILL
41 Athletic Director/Campus Minister .... Mr. Paul MCFADDEN
08 Director Learning Center .... Mr. Mark WARNICK
21 Business Office Manager .... Mrs. Sonia JOHNSON
27 Director of Information Services .... Mr. Larry JOHNSON

East Arkansas Community College (A)

1700 Newcastle Road, Forrest City AR 72335-2204
County: Saint Francis　FICE Identification: 012260
Unit ID: 106883
Telephone: (870) 633-4480　Carnegie Class: Assoc/Pub-R-S
FAX Number: (870) 633-7222　Calendar System: Semester
URL: www.eacc.edu
Established: 1974　Annual Undergrad Tuition & Fees (In-District): $2,520
Enrollment: 1,463　Coed
Affiliation or Control: State/Local　IRS Status: 501(c)3
Highest Offering: Associate Degree
Program: Occupational; 2-Year Principally Bachelor's Creditable
Accreditation: NH, ADNUR, EMT

01 President .... Dr. Coy F. GRACE
05 Vice President Academic Affairs .... Mrs. Janie BAILEY
10 Vice President Business Affairs .... Mr. Vernie MEADOR
32 Vice President Student Affairs .... Mrs. Catherine T. COLEMAN
37 Director Student Financial Aid .... Mr. Alvin COLEMAN
88 Assoc VP for Applied Sciences .... Mrs. Joanne LAWSON
88 AVP for Community/Business Outreach .... Mrs. Tiffany BILLINGSLEY
97 Assoc VP for General Studies .... Dr. Cathie CLINE
08 Director Library Services .... Mrs. Paige LAWS
84 Director Enrollment Mgmt/Registrar .... Mrs. Sharon COLLIER
26 Director of Public Relations/Mktg .... Mrs. Lindsay MIDKIFF
15 Director Personnel Management .... Mrs. Yvonne RUCKER-FRANKLIN
18 Director Physical Plant .... Mr. Glenn FORD
35 Assoc VP for Student Affairs .... Mrs. Michelle WILSON
96 Director of Purchasing .... Ms. Tracy MATHEWS
11 Director of Administrative Services .... Mr. Christopher A. HEIGLE
51 Director of Continuing Education .... Mrs. Jessica HIGGINBOTHOM

Ecclesia College (B)

9653 Nations Drive, Springdale AR 72762-8159
County: Benton　FICE Identification: 038553
Unit ID: 446233
Telephone: (479) 248-7236　Carnegie Class: Spec/Faith
FAX Number: (479) 248-1455　Calendar System: Semester
URL: www.ecollege.edu
Established: 1975　Annual Undergrad Tuition & Fees: $15,140
Enrollment: 171　Coed
Affiliation or Control: Independent Non-Profit　IRS Status: 501(c)3
Highest Offering: Baccalaureate
Program: Liberal Arts And General; Religious Emphasis
Accreditation: BI

01 President .... Mr. Oren PARIS, III
05 Academic Dean .... Dr. Robert HEADRICK
10 Director of Business & Finance .... Mr. Shannon WORTHEN
32 Dean of Students .... Mr. Jesse E. WADKINS
30 Director of Financial Development .... Mr. Mike NOVAK
26 Director of Communications .... Ms. Angie P. SNYDER
37 Director Student Financial Aid .... Mr. Josh MCGUIRE
41 Athletic Director .... Mr. Dean SKINNER
06 Registrar .... Mrs. Donna BROWN
08 Head Librarian .... Mrs. Joanne CAMPBELL
103 Director Work/Learning/Service Pgms .... Mr. Nic STICE
84 Director of Enrollment .... Mr. Jesse E. WADKINS

Harding University Main Campus (C)

915 E. Market Avenue, Searcy AR 72149-5615
County: White　FICE Identification: 001097
Unit ID: 107044
Telephone: (501) 279-4000　Carnegie Class: Master's L
FAX Number: (501) 279-4600　Calendar System: Semester
URL: www.harding.edu
Established: 1924　Annual Undergrad Tuition & Fees: $16,690
Enrollment: 6,815　Coed
Affiliation or Control: Churches Of Christ　IRS Status: 501(c)3
Highest Offering: Doctorate
Program: Occupational; Liberal Arts And General; Teacher Preparatory; Professional
Accreditation: NH, PA, ACBSP, ARCPA, CIDA, DIETD, ENG, MUS, NUR, PHAR, @PTA, SP, SW, TED

01 President .... Dr. Bruce D. MCLARTY
03 Executive Vice President .... Dr. David COLLINS
88 Senior Vice President .... Dr. James W. CARR
05 Provost .... Dr. Larry LONG
30 Sr Vice President for Development .... Mr. Floyd DANIEL
10 Vice President Finance .... Mr. Mel SANSOM
44 Vice President Advancement .... Dr. Mike WILLAMS
42 Vice President of Church Relations .... Dr. Dan WILLIAMS
07 Assistant Vice President Admissions .... Mr. Glenn DILLARD
32 Asst VP Student Life/Dean Students .... Mr. Zeal NEAL
06 Registrar .... Mrs. Janice HURD
38 Director of Counseling .... Dr. Lew MOORE
26 Director of Public Relations .... Mr. David CROUCH
37 Director Student Financial Aid .... Mr. Jon ROBERTS
58 Director of Graduate Studies .... Mr. Pat BASHAW
08 Librarian .... Mrs. Ann DIXON
09 Director of Institutional Research .... Dr. Marty SPEARS
18 Chief Facilities/Physical Plant .... Mr. Danny DERAMUS
29 Director Alumni Relations .... Mrs. Liz HOWELL
93 Director of Minority Students .... Dr. Butch GARDNER
15 Director Personnel Services .... Mr. David ROSS
36 Director Student Placement .... Mr. Butch GARDNER
96 Director of Purchasing .... Vacant
33 Assistant Dean of Students .... Mr. Stu VARNER
35 Asst Dean of Students .... Mrs. Kara ABSTON
34 Assistant Dean of Students .... Mrs. Ranan HESTER
92 Dean of Honors College .... Dr. Warren CASEY
50 Dean School of Business .... Dr. Bryan BURKS
53 Dean School of Education .... Dr. Tony FINLEY
66 Dean School of Nursing .... Dr. Cathleen M. SHULTZ
79 Dean College of Arts & Humanities .... Dr. Warren CASEY
81 Dean College of Sciences .... Dr. Travis THOMPSON
04 Assistant to the President .... Vacant

Henderson State University (D)

1100 Henderson Street, Arkadelphia AR 71999-0001
County: Clark　FICE Identification: 001098
Unit ID: 107071
Telephone: (870) 230-5000　Carnegie Class: Master's M
FAX Number: (870) 230-5144　Calendar System: Semester
URL: www.hsu.edu
Established: 1890　Annual Undergrad Tuition & Fees (In-State): $7,284
Enrollment: 3,773　Coed
Affiliation or Control: State　IRS Status: 501(c)3
Highest Offering: Beyond Master's But Less Than Doctorate
Program: Liberal Arts And General; Teacher Preparatory; Professional
Accreditation: NH, BUS, CACREP, DIETD, MUS, NURSE, TED

01 President .... Dr. Glendell JONES
05 Provost/VPAA .... Dr. Maralyn SOMMER
10 Vice Pres Finance & Administration .... Mr. Bobby G. JONES
32 VP Student Services/External Affair .... Dr. Lewis SHEPHERD
43 General Counsel .... Ms. Elaine KNEEBONE
35 Asst VP/Dean of Students .... Mr. Chad FIELDING
39 Asst VP/Director of Residence Life .... Mr. Dam MABERY
13 Director Computer/Communication Svc .... Mr. David H. EPPERHART
30 Director of University Advancement .... Ms. Carrie ROBERSON
41 Director Athletics .... Mr. T. Kale GOBER
26 Director of Public Relations .... Vacant
49 Int Dean Ellis Col Arts/Sciences .... Dr. John HARDEE
50 Dean of School of Business .... Dr. Barbara PONSFORD
53 Dean Teachers College Henderson .... Dr. Judy HARRISON
58 Interim Dean of Graduate School .... Dr. Kenneth TAYLOR
06 Registrar .... Mr. Tom GATTIN
08 Director Huie Library .... Mr. Robert F. YEHL
18 Director Physical Plant .... Mr. John C. CORLEY
15 Director of Human Resources .... Ms. Kathy TAYLOR
19 Director of University Police .... Mr. Jonathan CAMPBELL
38 Director of Counseling .... Ms. Deborah COLLINS
07 Director Univ Relations/Admissions .... Ms. Vikita B. HARDWRICK
37 Director of Financial Aid .... Ms. Vicki TAYLOR
92 Director of Honors College .... Dr. David T. THOMSON
88 Director of Student Research .... Dr. Martin CAMPBELL
96 Director of Purchasing .... Mr. Tim JONES
24 Dir Multi Media Learning Center .... Ms. Jennifer HOLBROOK
85 Director International Students .... Dr. Drew SMITH
29 Coordinator of Alumni Services .... Ms. Sherry WRIGHT

Hendrix College (E)

1600 Washington Avenue, Conway AR 72032-3080
County: Faulkner　FICE Identification: 001099
Unit ID: 107080
Telephone: (501) 329-6811　Carnegie Class: Bac/A&S
FAX Number: (501) 450-1200　Calendar System: Semester
URL: www.hendrix.edu
Established: 1876　Annual Undergrad Tuition & Fees: $48,436
Enrollment: 1,376　Coed
Affiliation or Control: United Methodist　IRS Status: 501(c)3
Highest Offering: Master's
Program: Liberal Arts And General
Accreditation: NH, MUS, TED

01 Acting President .... Mr. W. Ellis ARNOLD, III
04 Executive Assistant to President .... Ms. Donna PLEMMONS
30 Exec Vice Pres/Dean Inst Advance .... Mr. W. Ellis ARNOLD, III
05 Provost .... Dr. Robert L. ENTZMINGER
27 Exec Vice Pres & Chief Communicat .... Mr. Frank COX
10 Executive Vice President and CFO .... Mr. Tom SIEBENMORGEN
45 Exec Vice Pres and Strategic Plng .... Ms. Karen R. FOUST
18 Assoc VP Operations & Facilities .... Mr. Loyd RYAN
32 VP Student Affairs/Dean Students .... Mr. Jim WILTGEN, JR.
26 Exec Director of Communications .... Ms. Helen S. PLOTKIN
06 Registrar .... Ms. Xinying WANG
08 Director of Libraries .... Ms. Britt Anne MURPHY
13 Exec Vice Pres & Chief Info Office .... Mr. David J. HINSON
29 Director Alumni Relations .... Ms. Pamela OWEN
37 Director of Financial Aid .... Ms. Kristina BURFORD
40 Bookstore Manager .... Ms. Dee Dee ALLEN
79 Area Head/Humanities .... Dr. Alex VERNONE
81 Area Head/Natural Sciences .... Dr. Carl BURCH
83 Area Head/Social Sciences .... Dr. Leslie TEMPLETON
42 Chaplain .... Rev. Wayne CLARK
07 Director of Admission .... Mr. Fred BAKER
15 Director Personnel Services .... Ms. Vicki LYNN
20 Associate Academic Officer .... Dr. David SUTHERLAND
21 Associate Business Officer .... Mr. Shawn MATHIS
36 Director Career Services .... Mr. Danny POWELL
38 Director Student Counseling .... Ms. Mary Anne SIEBERT

ITT Technical Institute (F)

12200 Westhaven Drive, Little Rock AR 72211
Telephone: (501) 565-5550　Identification: 666531
Accreditation: ACICS

† Main campus is ITT Technical Institute in Indianapolis, IN.

John Brown University (G)

2000 W University Street, Siloam Springs AR 72761-2121
County: Benton　FICE Identification: 001100
Unit ID: 107141
Telephone: (479) 524-9500　Carnegie Class: Bac/Diverse
FAX Number: (479) 524-9548　Calendar System: Semester
URL: www.jbu.edu
Established: 1919　Annual Undergrad Tuition & Fees: $22,734
Enrollment: 2,215　Coed
Affiliation or Control: Independent Non-Profit　IRS Status: 501(c)3
Highest Offering: Master's
Program: Liberal Arts And General; Teacher Preparatory
Accreditation: NH, ACBSP, CONST, ENG, IACBE, TED

01 President .... Dr. Charles POLLARD
03 Executive Vice President .... Vacant
10 Vice Pres Finance & Administration .... Mrs. Kim HADLEY
84 Vice Pres Enrollment Management .... Mr. Donald W. CRANDALL
30 Vice Pres of University Advancement .... Dr. Jim KRALL
32 Vice Pres for Student Development .... Dr. Stephen T. BEERS
05 VP Academic Affairs/Dean of Faculty .... Dr. Ed ERICSON, III
88 Dean Degree Completion Program .... Mrs. Susan DEWOODY
42 Campus Pastor/Assoc Dean of Stdnts .... Mr. Rod REED
06 Registrar .... Mrs. Rebecca LAMBERT
21 Controller .... Mr. Tom PERRY
13 Chief Information Systems Ofcr .... Mr. Paul NAST
18 Director of Facilities Services .... Mr. Steve BRANKLE
44 Director of Planned Giving .... Mr. Eric GREENHAW
08 Director of Library .... Mrs. Mary HABERMAS
85 Director International Programs .... Mr. Bill STEVENSON
29 Director of Alumni/Parent Relations .... Mr. Jerry ROLLENE
37 Director of Financial Aid .... Mr. Kim ELDRIDGE
41 Athletic Director .... Ms. Robyn DAUGHERTY
38 Director of Counseling .... Dr. Tim DINGER

Lyon College (H)

PO Box 2317, Batesville AR 72503-2317
County: Independence　FICE Identification: 001088
Unit ID: 106342
Telephone: (870) 307-7000　Carnegie Class: Bac/A&S
FAX Number: (870) 307-7001　Calendar System: Semester
URL: www.lyon.edu
Established: 1872　Annual Undergrad Tuition & Fees: $31,154
Enrollment: 602　Coed
Affiliation or Control: Presbyterian Church (U.S.A.)　IRS Status: 501(c)3
Highest Offering: Baccalaureate
Program: Liberal Arts And General; Teacher Preparatory; Fine Arts Emphasis
Accreditation: NH, TED

01 President .... Dr. Donald V. WEATHERMAN
05 VP Academic Svcs/Dean of Faculty .... Dr. Virginia F. WRAY
10 Vice President Business & Finance .... Mr. Kenneth J. RUETER
11 Vice Pres for Administration .... Mr. David L. HERINGER
32 Vice President Student Life .... Dr. F. Bruce JOHNSTON
30 VP Institutional Advancement .... Mr. Jon VESTAL
06 Registrar/Dir Inst Research/Comm .... Mr. Donald R. TAYLOR
08 Director Library .... Mr. Dean COVINGTON
26 Director Public Relations .... Vacant
29 Dir Alumni Services & Development .... Ms. Gina GARRETT
15 Director Personnel .... Mrs. Clarinda L. FOOTE
37 Director of Financial Assistance .... Mr. Tommy TUCKER
36 Director Career Development .... Ms. Vicki WEBB
13 Director Information Services .... Mr. Karl KEMP
41 Director of Athletics .... Mr. Kevin JENKINS
42 Chaplain .... Vacant
104 Director Nichols Intl Studies Pgm .... Dr. Virginia F. WRAY
53 Int Director of Teacher Education .... Ms. Kim CROSBY
07 Director of Admissions .... Mr. Josh MANNING
09 Director of Institutional Research .... Mr. Donald R. TAYLOR
38 Director Student Counseling .... Ms. Diane ELLIS
18 Director Security .... Mr. Gene DAVIS
40 Director Bookstore .... Mrs. Lana FUGETT
08 Head Librarian .... Ms. Kathy WHITTENTON
23 Director of Health Services .... Mrs. LuAnn BAKER
18 Chief Facilities/Physical Plant .... Mr. Jade ANDERSON

Mid-South Community College (I)

2000 W Broadway, West Memphis AR 72301-3829
County: Crittenden　FICE Identification: 023482
Unit ID: 107318

Telephone: (870) 733-6722 Carnegie Class: Assoc/Pub-S-SC
FAX Number: (870) 733-6799 Calendar System: Semester
URL: www.midsouthcc.edu
Established: 1992 Annual Undergrad Tuition & Fees (In-District): $3,060
Enrollment: 1,980 Coed
Affiliation or Control: State/Local IRS Status: 501(c)3
Highest Offering: Associate Degree
Program: Occupational; 2-Year Principally Bachelor's Creditable
Accreditation: NH, #COARC

01 President .... Dr. Glen F. FENTER
03 Executive Vice President .... Dr. Barbara C. BAXTER
05 Vice Pres Learning and Instruction .... Dr. Cliff JONES
10 Vice Pres Finance & Administration .... Mrs. Susan MARSHALL
32 Assoc Vice Pres Student Life .... Mr. Gheric BRUCE
84 Assoc Vice Pres Enrollment Services .... Mr. Jeremy REECE
103 Associate VP Workforce Programs .... Mr. Pete SELDEN
09 Assoc VP Instnl Effectiveness .... Dr. Topeka SMALL
21 Associate Vice Pres Finance .... Ms. Karyn WEAVER
20 VP Learning and Instruction .... Ms. Roshell COLEMAN
26 Director Marketing/Public Relations .... Mr. Todd PENDERGRASS
37 Director of Financial Aid .... Ms. Amy CABLE
08 Director of Library Media Center .... Ms. Rene JONES
06 Registrar .... Ms. Leslie ANDERSON
15 Director of Human Resources .... Ms. Jackie BRUBAKER
18 Director Facilities/Physical Plant .... Mr. Randy WEBB

National Park Community College (A)

101 College Drive,
Hot Springs National Park AR 71913-9174
County: Garland FICE Identification: 012105
Unit ID: 106980
Telephone: (501) 760-4222 Carnegie Class: Assoc/Pub-R-M
FAX Number: (501) 760-4100 Calendar System: Semester
URL: www.npcc.edu
Established: 1973 Annual Undergrad Tuition & Fees (In-District): $2,870
Enrollment: 3,559 Coed
Affiliation or Control: State/Local IRS Status: 501(c)3
Highest Offering: Associate Degree
Program: Occupational; 2-Year Principally Bachelor's Creditable; Technical Emphasis
Accreditation: NH, ADNUR, CAHIIM, #COARC, COE, EMT, MLTAD, RAD

01 President .... Dr. Sally CARDER
05 Exec Vice Pres for Instruction .... Dr. Gordon WATTS
10 Vice President for Business Affairs .... Ms. Janis SAWYER
32 Vice President Student Services .... Ms. Margaret PICKING
72 Assoc Vice Pres Technical Education .... Mr. David HUGHES
04 Assistant to the President .... Dr. Susan ALDRIDGE
20 Assoc Dean for Academic Affairs .... Dr. Brad MOODY
35 Director of Student Affairs .... Ms. Holly GARRETT-MILLER
15 Director of Human Resources .... Ms. Janet BREWER
08 Director of the Library .... Ms. Sara SEAMAN
37 Director of Financial Aid .... Ms. Lisa HOPPER
26 Chief Public Relations Officer .... Ms. Jill JOHNSON
30 Chief Development .... Vacant
38 Director Student Counseling .... Mr. Ron CHESSER
06 Registrar .... Dr. Brad MOODY

North Arkansas College (B)

1515 Pioneer Drive, Harrison AR 72601-5599
County: Boone FICE Identification: 012261
Unit ID: 107460
Telephone: (870) 743-3000 Carnegie Class: Assoc/Pub-R-M
FAX Number: (870) 391-3250 Calendar System: Semester
URL: www.northark.edu
Established: 1974 Annual Undergrad Tuition & Fees (In-District): $2,370
Enrollment: 2,315 Coed
Affiliation or Control: State/Local IRS Status: 501(c)3
Highest Offering: Associate Degree
Program: Occupational; 2-Year Principally Bachelor's Creditable; Nursing Emphasis
Accreditation: NH, ACBSP, ADNUR, EMT, MLTAD, RAD, SURGT

01 President .... Dr. Jacquelyn ELLIOTT
05 Exec Vice President of Learning .... Dr. Michael WIGGINS
10 Vice Pres Finance & Administration .... Mr. Donald SUGG
30 Vice Pres Institutional Advancement .... Dr. Rodney ARNOLD
04 Executive Assistant to President .... Mrs. Trish VILLINES
49 Dean Arts & Science/Business & IT .... Dr. Laura BERRY
66 Dean Nursing/Allied Hlth/Tech Pgms .... Mrs. Cindy MAYO
31 Dean of Outreach .... Mrs. Nell BONDS
08 Director of Libraries .... Mr. Jim ROBB
44 Dir Institutional Effectiveness .... Mrs. Katherine VAUGHN
32 Director of Student Success .... Mrs. Tavonda BROWN
41 Athletic Director .... Vacant
15 Director Human Resources .... Mrs. Kris GREENING
18 Chief Facilities/Physical Plant .... Mr. Kevin SOMERS
96 Director of Purchasing .... Mrs. Shari HOLT
37 Director Student Financial Aid .... Mrs. Jennifer HADDOCK
06 Registrar .... Mrs. Charla JENNINGS
07 Director of Admissions .... Mr. Randy SCAGGS
26 Director of Public Relations .... Mrs. Micki SOMERS
90 Director Academic Computing .... Mr. Rick WILLIAMS
91 Director Administrative Computing .... Mr. Glenn COLMAN
31 Director of Community Education .... Mrs. Amy BELL

NorthWest Arkansas Community College (C)

1 College Drive, Bentonville AR 72712-5091
County: Benton FICE Identification: 030633
Unit ID: 367459
Telephone: (479) 636-9222 Carnegie Class: Assoc/Pub-R-L
FAX Number: (479) 619-4335 Calendar System: Semester
URL: www.nwacc.edu
Established: 1989 Annual Undergrad Tuition & Fees (In-District): $2,998
Enrollment: 8,341 Coed
Affiliation or Control: State/Local IRS Status: 501(c)3
Highest Offering: Associate Degree
Program: Occupational; 2-Year Principally Bachelor's Creditable
Accreditation: NH, COARC, EMT, IFSAC, PTAA

01 President .... Dr. Evelyn JORGENSON
05 Sr Vice Pres Learning/Provost .... Dr. Steve GATES
10 Sr VP Admin Svcs/Chief Fin Ofcr .... Ms. Debi BUCKLEY
20 Interim Vice Pres for Learning .... Dr. Ricky TOMPKINS
26 VP Public Relations & Development .... Mr. Wyley ELLIOTT
32 Vice Pres Learner Services .... Dr. Todd KITCHEN
21 VP Finance & Treasury Services .... Mr. Chuck RAMSEYER
88 VP for Learning GB/HP/External Pgms .... Mr. Tim CORNELIUS
103 AVP Corporate Learning .... Ms. Susan PIKE
91 Assoc VP Information Technology Svc .... Ms. Paige FRANCIS
88 AVP Retail & Supplier Education .... Ms. Renee CAMPBELL
11 Executive Director of Operations .... Mr. Jack THOMPSON
51 Dean of Adult Education .... Mr. Ben ALDAMA
32 Int Dean Learner Administrative Svc .... Mr. Dale MONTGOMERY
88 Dean of Learner Success .... Ms. Brooke HOLT
102 Executive Director of Foundation .... Dr. Meredith BRUNEN
88 Exec Director of Public Relations .... Mr. Steven HINDS
86 Exec Dir Community/Government Rels .... Mr. Jim HALL
21 Accountant/General Ledger .... Mr. John HIXSON
21 Dir Budget/Fin Analysis/Reporting .... Ms. Gulizar BAGGSON
26 Director of Marketing .... Mr. Rob HANLON
15 Director of Human Resources .... Ms. Wendi CADLE
56 Director of Distance Learning .... Dr. Kate BURKES
50 Exec Dir of Business Development .... Ms. Teresa WHITMIRE
88 Director of Building Sciences .... Mr. Rick MAYES
88 Exec Dir for High School Rels .... Dr. Diana JOHNSON
88 Director of Learning Resources .... Ms. Gwen DOBBS
25 Exec Dir Grants and Effectiveness .... Dr. Shauna STERLING
06 Director Student Records .... Ms. Taysha CARTER
07 Director of Admissions .... Ms. Michelle WALLACE
37 Director Student Financial Aid .... Ms. Michelle CORDELL
35 Director of Learner Success .... Mr. Eric VEST
28 Director of Diversity & Inclusion .... Ms. Kathryn BIRKHEAD
88 Dir Food Services/Event Management .... Ms. Diane BOSS
09 Director of Institutional Research .... Dr. Lisa ANDERSON
18 Director of Physical Plant .... Mr. Jim NELSON
29 Director Alumni Relations .... Ms. Jasmine POPE
51 Business Manager & Continuing Educ .... Vacant
88 Coordinator Culinary & Hospitality .... Ms. Dede HAMM

Ouachita Baptist University (D)

410 Ouachita Street, Arkadelphia AR 71998-0001
County: Clark FICE Identification: 001102
Unit ID: 107512
Telephone: (870) 245-5000 Carnegie Class: Bac/A&S
FAX Number: (870) 245-5500 Calendar System: Semester
URL: www.obu.edu
Established: 1886 Annual Undergrad Tuition & Fees: $22,340
Enrollment: 1,532 Coed
Affiliation or Control: Southern Baptist IRS Status: 501(c)3
Highest Offering: Baccalaureate
Program: Liberal Arts And General; Teacher Preparatory
Accreditation: NH, BUS, DIETD, MUS, TED

01 President .... Dr. Rex M. HORNE, JR.
44 Vice Pres Institutional Advancement .... Dr. Keldon HENLEY
05 Vice President Academic Affairs .... Dr. Stan POOLE
11 Vice President for Admin Services .... Dr. Brett POWELL
32 Vice President for Student Services .... Dr. Wesley KLUCK
30 Vice President for Development .... Mrs. Terry G. PEEPLES
27 Vice Pres for Communications .... Mr. Trennis HENDERSON
04 Asst to President/Administration .... Mr. Philip W. HARDIN
07 Director of Admissions Counseling .... Mrs. Lori MOTL
09 Director of Institutional Research .... Mr. Phil HARDIN
15 Director of Human Resources .... Mrs. Sherri PHELPS
18 Chief Facilities/Physical Plant .... Mr. John HARDMAN
29 Director of Alumni Relations .... Mr. Jon MERRYMAN
35 Dean of Students .... Dr. Scott HAYNES
20 Assoc Vice Pres Academic Affairs .... Dr. Doug REED
26 Vice Pres for Communications .... Mr. Trennis HENDERSON
36 Director of Career Services .... Mrs. Lauren LAND
38 University Counselor .... Mr. Dan JARBOE
08 Librarian .... Dr. Ray GRANADE
06 Registrar/Director of Admissions .... Mrs. Judy JONES
37 Director Student Financial Svcs .... Mrs. Susan HURST
96 Director of Purchasing .... Mrs. Kim HUNTER
92 Director Honors Program .... Dr. Barbara PEMBERTON
13 Dir Information Technology Services .... Mr. Bill PHELPS
39 Director of Housing .... Ms. Margaret FRAZIER
41 Athletic Director .... Mr. David SHARP
43 General Counsel .... Mr. Bryan MCKINNEY
21 Director of Financial Services .... Mrs. Kim HUNTER
40 Bookstore Manager .... Mrs. Yvonne CLOUD
57 Dean of School of Fine Arts .... Dr. Scott HOLSCLAW
50 Dean of the School of Business .... Mr. Bryan MCKINNEY
53 Dean Sch of Interdisciplinary Stds .... Dr. Stan POOLE
73 Dean School of Christian Studies .... Dr. Danny HAYS
53 Dean School of Education .... Dr. Merribeth BRUNING
79 Dean School of Humanities .... Dr. Jeff ROOT
81 Dean School of Natural Sciences .... Dr. Tim KNIGHT
83 Dean School of Social Sciences .... Dr. Randall WIGHT

Ozarka College (E)

PO Box 10, Melbourne AR 72556-0010
County: Izard FICE Identification: 020870
Unit ID: 107549
Telephone: (870) 368-7371 Carnegie Class: Assoc/Pub-R-S
FAX Number: (870) 368-2091 Calendar System: Semester
URL: www.ozarka.edu
Established: 1991 Annual Undergrad Tuition & Fees (In-State): $2,930
Enrollment: 1,556 Coed
Affiliation or Control: State IRS Status: 501(c)3
Highest Offering: Associate Degree
Program: Occupational; 2-Year Principally Bachelor's Creditable
Accreditation: NH

01 President .... Dr. Richard L. DAWE
05 Vice President of Academic Affairs .... Dr. Dennis RITTLE
10 Vice President of Finance .... Ms. Tina WHEELIS
11 Vice President of Administration .... Mr. Jason LAWRENCE
32 Vice President of Student Services .... Mr. Ron C. HELM
45 Vice President of Planning/IR .... Mrs. Joan R. STIRLING
13 Chief Information Officer .... Mr. Scott PINKSTON
04 Executive Asst to the President .... Ms. Carol LANGSTON
30 Director of College Advancement .... Ms. Suellen DAVIDSON
29 Development Officer/Dir Alumni Rels .... Ms. Carol LANGSTON
37 Director of Financial Aid .... Ms. Laura LAWRENCE
07 Director of Admissions .... Mr. Dylan MOWERY
06 Registrar .... Mrs. Zeda WILKERSON
26 Dir Public Relations/Marketing .... Ms. Molly CARPENTER
21 Business Manager .... Ms. Amber RUSH

Philander Smith College (F)

900 W. Daisy L. Gatson Bates Drive,
Little Rock AR 72202-3799
County: Pulaski FICE Identification: 001103
Unit ID: 107600
Telephone: (501) 375-9845 Carnegie Class: Bac/Diverse
FAX Number: (501) 370-5277 Calendar System: Semester
URL: www.philander.edu
Established: 1877 Annual Undergrad Tuition & Fees: $11,804
Enrollment: 667 Coed
Affiliation or Control: United Methodist IRS Status: 501(c)3
Highest Offering: Baccalaureate
Program: Liberal Arts And General; Teacher Preparatory; Business Emphasis
Accreditation: NH, ACBSP, SW, TED

01 President .... Dr. Johnny M. MOORE
04 Assistant to the President .... Mrs. Anita HATLEY
05 Interim VP of Academic Affairs .... Dr. Jesse HARGROVE
10 Vice President for Fiscal Affairs .... Mr. Terry WALLACE
32 Interim VP of Student Affairs .... Mr. Kevin HAMILTON
30 Vice Pres Inst Advancement .... Vacant
43 General Counsel .... Vacant
06 Registrar .... Ms. Bertha OWENS
42 Chaplain/Dir Ofc Religious Life .... Rev. Ronnie MILLER-YOW
20 Associate Dean of Instruction .... Dr. Jesse HARGROVE
35 Dean of Students/Residential Life .... Vacant
15 Director of Human Resources .... Mr. Christopher NEWTON
37 Director of Financial Aid .... Mr. Damien WILLIAMS
18 Supervisor .... Mr. Robert YOUNG
26 Director Marketing/Public Relations .... Vacant
08 Director of the Library .... Ms. Theresa OJEZUA
07 Dir of Admissions/Recruitment .... Mr. Al DORSEY
29 Director of Alumni Relations .... Ms. Yvonne ALEXANDER
41 Athletic Director .... Mr. Sam WEAVER
13 Director Computer Information Sys .... Mr. Cedric KONYAOLE
09 Director of Institutional Research .... Ms. Beverly RICHARDSON
19 Chief of Security .... Mr. Jack MATLOCK
51 Director of Continuing Education .... Mr. Bruce JAMES
88 Mission Center Director .... Dr. Cynthia BURROUGHS
38 Director Student Counseling .... Vacant
40 Bookstore Manager .... Ms. Veda MAXWELL
17 Nurse .... Vacant
88 Director Integrated Campus Center .... Ms. Rhonda LOVELACE
49 Division Chair Natural Sciences .... Dr. Samar SWAID
50 Division Chair of Business .... Dr. Adrian PRICE
53 Division Chair of Education .... Dr. Llyod HERVEY
70 Director of Social Work .... Ms. Angela SANDERS
79 Int Chair Division of Humanities .... Dr. Lia STEELE
83 Chair Division of Social Sciences .... Dr. Daniel EGBE

Pulaski Technical College (G)

3000 W Scenic Drive, North Little Rock AR 72118-3399
County: Pulaski FICE Identification: 020753
Unit ID: 107664
Telephone: (501) 812-2200 Carnegie Class: Assoc/Pub-U-SC
FAX Number: (501) 771-2844 Calendar System: Semester
URL: www.pulaskitech.edu
Established: 1991 Annual Undergrad Tuition & Fees (In-State): $3,200
Enrollment: 11,938 Coed
Affiliation or Control: State IRS Status: 501(c)3
Highest Offering: Associate Degree
Program: Occupational; 2-Year Principally Bachelor's Creditable; Technical Emphasis

Accreditation: NH, ACFEI, COARC, DA, OTA

01 President .... Dr. Margaret ELLIBEE
05 Executive Vice President/Provost .... Mr. Michael DELONG
20 Vice President for Learning .... Ms. Mary Ann SHOPE
32 Vice President for Student Services .... Ms. Cindy HARKEY
10 Vice President for Finance .... Ms. Patricia PALMER
30 VP for Economic Development .... Mr. Bentley WALLACE
44 Chief Development Officer .... Ms. Joyce TAYLOR
84 Dean Enrollment Svcs .... Ms. Beth TRAFFORD
07 Director of Admissions .... Mr. Clark ATKINS
08 Library Director .... Ms. Wendy DAVIS
18 Director of Physical Plant .... Mr. Stuart SMITH
09 Assoc VP for Institutional Research .... Ms. Jasmine RAY
96 Director of Purchasing .... Mr. Tim WALBERT
13 Assoc VP for Information Services .... Mr. David GLOVER
15 Assoc VP of Human Resources .... Ms. Mickey QUATTLEBAUM
04 Assistant to the President .... Ms. Tena CARRIGAN
37 Director of Financial Aid .... Ms. Lavonne JUHL
26 Assoc VP Public Relations/Marketing .... Mr. Tim JONES
72 Dean Technical Education Division .... Mr. Mike SNEED
81 Dean Mathematics/Nat Social Scis .... Mr. Ben RAINS
50 Dean Business/IT Division .... Ms. Christy SHERRILL
57 Dean Fine Arts & Humanities .... Mr. Joey COLE
06 Registrar .... Ms. Catherine DIVITO
76 Dean Allied Health/Human Services .... Ms. Pam CICIRELLO

Remington College-Little Rock (A)

19 Remington Drive, Little Rock AR 72204-8202
Telephone: (501) 312-0007 Identification: 666286
Accreditation: ACCSC

† Main campus is Remington College, Mobile Campus in Mobile, AL.

Rich Mountain Community College (B)

1100 College Drive, Mena AR 71953-2500
County: Polk FICE Identification: 021111
Unit ID: 107743
Telephone: (479) 394-7622 Carnegie Class: Assoc/Pub-R-S
FAX Number: (479) 394-7295 Calendar System: Semester
URL: www.rmcc.edu
Established: 1983 Annual Undergrad Tuition & Fees (In-District): $2,760
Enrollment: 1,051 Coed
Affiliation or Control: State/Local IRS Status: 501(c)3
Highest Offering: Associate Degree
Program: Occupational; 2-Year Principally Bachelor's Creditable; Liberal Arts And General
Accreditation: NH

01 President .... Dr. Phillip WILSON
05 Vice Pres Academic Affairs .... Dr. Steve ROOK
32 Vice Pres Student Affairs/Registrar .... Dr. Steve ROOK
10 VP Administration/CFO .... Mr. Morris BOYDSTUN
13 Dir of Information Technology .... Mr. J. Mark BARTON
08 Director Library Services .... Ms. Mary SHEAHAN
37 Financial Aid Director .... Ms. Mary STANDERFER
30 Director of Development .... Ms. Tammy YOUNG
18 Director of Physical Plant .... Mr. Dennis HILL
53 Director of Adult Basic Education .... Ms. Shannon ROGERS
15 Director of Human Resources .... Ms. Amy LUDWIG
07 Director of Admissions .... Mr. Brandon BURK
21 Controller .... Ms. Patricia HALL
26 Chief Public Relations Officer .... Ms. Tammy YOUNG
40 Bookstore Manager .... Mr. Jason WOOD
09 Coordinator Institutional Research .... Ms. Tammy ODOM
21 Fiscal Project Coordinator .... Ms. Amy LUDWIG

Shorter College (C)

604 Locust Street, North Little Rock AR 72114
County: Pulaski FICE Identification: 001105
Unit ID: 107840
Telephone: (501) 374-6305 Carnegie Class: Not Classified
FAX Number: (501) 374-9333 Calendar System: Semester
URL: www.shortercollege.org
Established: 1886 Annual Undergrad Tuition & Fees: $1,800
Enrollment: 236 Coed
Affiliation or Control: African Methodist Episcopal IRS Status: 501(c)3
Highest Offering: Associate Degree
Program: 2-Year Principally Bachelor's Creditable
Accreditation: @TRACS

01 President .... Dr. O. Jerome GREEN

South Arkansas Community College (D)

300 S West Avenue, PO Box 7010,
El Dorado AR 71731-7010
County: Union FICE Identification: 020746
Unit ID: 107974
Telephone: (870) 862-8131 Carnegie Class: Assoc/Pub-R-S
FAX Number: (870) 864-7190 Calendar System: Semester
URL: www.southark.edu
Established: 1992 Annual Undergrad Tuition & Fees (In-State): $2,108
Enrollment: 1,757 Coed
Affiliation or Control: State IRS Status: 501(c)3
Highest Offering: Associate Degree
Program: Occupational; 2-Year Principally Bachelor's Creditable
Accreditation: NH, COARC, EMT, MLTAD, OTA, PHLEB, PTAA, RAD, SURGT

01 President .... Dr. Barbara JONES
05 VP of Academic Learning .... Dr. Valeriano CANTU
10 Vice President for Fiscal Affairs .... Mr. Lathan HAIRSTON
32 Vice Pres of Student Services .... Vacant
84 Dean of Enrollment Services .... Mr. Dean INMAN
08 Director Library Media Center .... Mrs. Francis KUYKENDALL
31 Dean of Community Education .... Ms. Jamie MCCONATHY
37 Director of Financial Aid .... Ms. Veronda TATUM
04 Executive Asst to the President .... Ms. Susan JORDAN
26 Chief Information Officer .... Dr. Tim KIRK
27 Public Information Officer .... Mr. Heath WALDROP
15 Director Personnel Services .... Mrs. Becky RIGGS
18 Director of Physical Plant .... Mr. Graham PETERSON
30 Dir of Foundation/External Funding .... Ms. Cynthia REYNA
09 CIEAO .... Dr. Stephanie TULLY-DARTEZ
96 Director of Purchasing .... Ms. Ann SOUTHALL
07 Student Recruitment & Activities .... Vacant
49 Dean of Liberal Arts .... Mr. Phillip BALLARD
76 Dean Health/Natural Sciences .... Mr. Arthur BROWN
50 Dean Business/Technical Education .... Mr. Jim ROOMSBURG

Southeast Arkansas College (E)

1900 Hazel Street, Pine Bluff AR 71603-3900
County: Jefferson FICE Identification: 005707
Unit ID: 107637
Telephone: (870) 543-5900 Carnegie Class: Assoc/Pub-R-M
FAX Number: (870) 850-8636 Calendar System: Semester
URL: www.seark.edu
Established: 1991 Annual Undergrad Tuition & Fees (In-State): $2,892
Enrollment: 3,130 Coed
Affiliation or Control: State IRS Status: 501(c)3
Highest Offering: Associate Degree
Program: Occupational; 2-Year Principally Bachelor's Creditable; Technical Emphasis
Accreditation: NH, ADNUR, COARC, EMT, PHLEB, RAD, SURGT

01 President .... Dr. Stephen HILTERBRAN
05 Vice President Academic Affairs .... Ms. Kaleybra MOREHEAD
32 Vice President Student Affairs .... Dr. Michael GUNTER
10 Vice President Financial Affairs .... Ms. Debbie WALLACE
76 VP Assessment/Nursing/Allied Health .... Ms. Diann W. WILLIAMS
30 VP College Affairs/Advancement .... Dr. Kaleybra M. MOREHEAD
21 Controller .... Mr. Steve BALLARD
13 Director of Technology Services .... Ms. JoAnn DUPRA
06 Assistant Registrar .... Ms. Laqueta HILL
07 Director of Admissions .... Ms. Barbara DUNN
15 Director of Personnel Services .... Ms. Dena CHILDS
18 Chief Facilities/Physical Plant .... Mr. Joel BARBAREE
28 Director of Diversity .... Dr. Kaleybra MOREHEAD
29 Dir Alumni Relations/Development .... Dr. Kaleybra MOREHEAD
37 Director Student Financial Aid .... Ms. Donna COX

Southern Arkansas University (F)

100 E University Street, Magnolia AR 71753-5000
County: Columbia FICE Identification: 001107
Unit ID: 107983
Telephone: (870) 235-4000 Carnegie Class: Master's M
FAX Number: (870) 235-5005 Calendar System: Semester
URL: www.saumag.edu
Established: 1909 Annual Undergrad Tuition & Fees (In-State): $6,324
Enrollment: 3,330 Coed
Affiliation or Control: State IRS Status: 501(c)3
Highest Offering: Master's
Program: Liberal Arts And General; Teacher Preparatory; Professional
Accreditation: NH, ADNUR, BUS, MUS, NUR, SW, TED

01 President .... Dr. David F. RANKIN
05 Vice President Academic Affairs .... Dr. Trey BERRY
11 VP Administration/General Counsel .... Mr. Roger W. GILES
32 Vice President Student Affairs .... Dr. Donna Y. ALLEN
18 Vice President of Facilities .... Mr. C. Jasper LEWIS
10 Vice President for Finance .... Mr. Paul MCLENDON
49 Dean Col Liberal/Perform Arts .... Dr. Helmut LANGERBEIN
50 Dean College of Business .... Dr. Lisa C. TOMS
53 Dean College of Education .... Dr. Zaidy MOHDZAIN
72 Dean College of Sci & Technology .... Dr. Scott MCKAY
58 Dean School of Graduate Studies .... Dr. Kim K. BLOSS
06 Registrar .... Dr. G. Edward NIPPER
84 Dean Enrollment Services .... Ms. Sarah E. JENNINGS
08 Interim Director of Library .... Mr. Del G. DUKE
14 Director Info Technology Services .... Mr. Mike A. ARGO
38 Director Counsel/Testing Center .... Ms. Paula WASHINGTON-WOODS
35 Dean of Students .... Ms. Sandra E. HUGHES
29 Director of Alumni Affairs .... Ms. Ceil L. BRIDGES
30 Director of Development .... Ms. Jeanie BISMARK
37 Director of Financial Aid .... Ms. Bronwyn C. SNEED
51 Director of Continuing Education .... Vacant
41 Director of Athletics .... Mr. Steve BROWNING
88 Director Student Support Services .... Ms. Eunice E. WALKER
36 Director of Placement Services .... Vacant
27 Asst Dean Integrated Marketing .... Mr. Aaron J. STREET
28 Assoc Dean Multicultural Affairs .... Mr. Cledis D. STUART
21 Coordinator of Fringe Benefits .... Mr. Alan DAVIS

Southern Arkansas University Tech (G)

Post Office Box 3349, Camden AR 71711
County: Calhoun FICE Identification: 007738
Unit ID: 107992
Telephone: (870) 574-4500 Carnegie Class: Assoc/Pub2in4
FAX Number: (870) 574-4520 Calendar System: Semester
URL: www.sautech.edu
Established: 1967 Annual Undergrad Tuition & Fees (In-State): $3,990
Enrollment: 1,856 Coed
Affiliation or Control: State IRS Status: 501(c)3
Highest Offering: Associate Degree
Program: Occupational; 2-Year Principally Bachelor's Creditable
Accreditation: NH

01 Chancellor .... Dr. Corbet J. LAMKIN
10 VC for Finance & Administration .... Mrs. Gaye MANNING
05 VC for Academics .... Mr. Robert GUNNELS
32 VC for Student Services .... Dr. Reginald COOPER
13 VC for Information Technology .... Mrs. Valerie WILSON
26 Director of Communications .... Mrs. Kim COKER
09 Director of Research .... Mr. Lee SANDERS
84 Director of Enrollment Services .... Mrs. Patricia SINDLE
103 Director of Career Pathways .... Ms. LaTonya REED
31 Director of Special Programs .... Mr. Robert WHITE
75 Director of B & I Training .... Mr. Mike BASHFORD
88 Director of Career Academy .... Mr. Terry STARKEY
88 Director of AETA .... Mr. Randy HARPER
88 Director of AFTA .... Mrs. Rachel NIX
14 Director of ITS .... Mrs. Laura JOHNSON
37 Director of Financial Aid .... Vacant
18 Director of Physical Plant .... Mr. Gerald MANNING
35 Director of Student Life .... Mr. David MCLEANE
06 Registrar .... Mr. Wayne BANKS
08 Director of LRC .... Ms. Allison MALONE
04 Assistant to the Chancellor .... Mrs. Paula BERGSTROM
15 Human Resources Director .... Mrs. Olivia CLACK
21 Controller .... Mr. Dale TOMMEY
45 Vice Chancellor for PAD .... Dr. Diane BETTS
39 Residential Advisor .... Mrs. LaDonna FUSILIER
96 Buyer .... Mrs. Angela FRY
43 Legal Counsel .... Mrs. Mary THOMASON
51 Director of Adult Education .... Mrs. Barbara HAMILTON

*University of Arkansas System Office (H)

2404 N University Avenue, Little Rock AR 72207-3608
County: Pulaski FICE Identification: 008008
Unit ID: 108056
Telephone: (501) 686-2500 Carnegie Class: N/A
FAX Number: (501) 686-2507
URL: www.uasys.edu

01 President .... Dr. Donald R. BOBBITT
04 Assistant to the President .... Ms. Angela HUDSON
05 Vice President Academic Affairs .... Dr. Michael K. MOORE
88 Vice President for Learning Tech .... Dr. Daniel E. FERRITOR
10 Vice President for Finance .... Ms. Barbara GOSWICK
11 Vice President for Administration .... Ms. Ann KEMP
26 Vice President University Relations .... Ms. Melissa RUST
47 Vice President Agriculture .... Dr. Mark J. COCHRAN
43 General Counsel .... Mr. Fred H. HARRISON
88 Director Internal Audit .... Mr. Jacob W. FLOURNOY
21 Assoc Vice President for Finance .... Ms. Rita FLEMING

*University of Arkansas Main Campus (I)

Fayetteville AR 72701-1201
County: Washington FICE Identification: 001108
Unit ID: 106397
Telephone: (479) 575-2000 Carnegie Class: RU/VH
FAX Number: (479) 575-2361 Calendar System: Semester
URL: www.uark.edu
Established: 1871 Annual Undergrad Tuition & Fees (In-State): $7,818
Enrollment: 24,537 Coed
Affiliation or Control: State IRS Status: 501(c)3
Highest Offering: Doctorate
Program: Liberal Arts And General; Teacher Preparatory; Professional
Accreditation: NH, AAFCS, BUS, BUSA, CACREP, CIDA, CLPSY, CORE, CS, DIETD, ENG, JOUR, LAW, LSAR, MUS, NURSE, SP, SW, TED

02 Chancellor .... Dr. G. David GEARHART
04 Executive Asst to the Chancellor .... Ms. Gloria SUTHERLAND
05 Provost & Vice Chanc Academic Affs .... Dr. Sharon GABER
10 Vice Chanc Finance & Administration .... Dr. Donald O. PEDERSON
30 Vice Chanc University Advancement .... Mr. Chris WYRICK
86 Vice Chanc Govt & Cmty Relations .... Mr. Richard B. HUDSON
09 Vice Provost Planning/Dir Inst Res .... Dr. Kathy M. VAN LANINGHAM
46 Vice Provost Research/Econ Dev .... Dr. James M. RANKIN
35 Vice Prov Stdnt Affs/Dean Students .... Dr. Daniel PUGH
28 Vice Provost for Diversity .... Mr. Charles ROBINSON
84 Vice Prov Enrol Mgt/Dean Admissions .... Dr. Suzanne MCCRAY
26 Assoc Vice Chanc Univ Relations .... Mr. John N. DIAMOND
15 Assoc Vice Chanc Human Resources .... Ms. Barbara A. ABERCROMBIE
18 Assoc Vice Chanc Facilities Mgmt .... Mr. Mike JOHNSON
21 Assoc Vice Chanc Business Affairs .... Mr. David O. MARTINSON
08 Dean of Libraries .... Ms. Carolyn H. ALLEN
49 Interim Dean of Arts & Sciences .... Mr. Todd G. SHIELDS
50 Dean Sam Walton College of Business .... Mr. Eli JONES
47 Dean of Agriculture .... Dr. Michael E. VAYDA
53 Dean Education/Health Professions .... Dr. Tom SMITH
48 Dean of Architecture .... Mr. Jeff SHANNON

51 Interim Dean of Graduate School ... Dr. Todd SHIELDS
54 Dean of Engineering ... Dr. Ashok SAXENA
92 Dean Honors College ... Dr. Robert MCMATH
61 Dean of the Law School ... Ms. Stacy LEEDS
29 Assoc Vice Chanc for Alumni ... Mr. Graham G. STEWART
22 Director of Equal Opportunity ... Ms. Danielle L. WOOD
37 Exec Director Financial Aid ... Ms. Wendy D. STOUFFER
38 Dir of Counseling/Psych Services ... Dr. Jonathan C. PERRY
25 Director Research & Sponsored Pgms ... Ms. Rosemary H. RUFF
19 Director University Police ... Mr. Steve GAHAGANS
36 Dir of Career Development Center ... Ms. Barbara BATSON
14 Director of Computing Services ... Mr. Robert E. ZIMMERMAN
06 Registrar ... Mr. Dave DAWSON
96 Director of Purchasing ... Ms. Linda FAST
58 Director Graduate & Intl Admissions ... Ms. Lynn MOSESSO

*University of Arkansas at Fort Smith (A)

PO Box 3649, Fort Smith AR 72913-3649

County: Sebastian — FICE Identification: 001110
Unit ID: 108092
Telephone: (479) 788-7000 — Carnegie Class: Bac/Assoc
FAX Number: (479) 788-7003 — Calendar System: Semester
URL: www.uafs.edu
Established: 1928 — Annual Undergrad Tuition & Fees (In-District): $5,624
Enrollment: 7,337 — Coed
Affiliation or Control: State/Local — IRS Status: 501(c)3
Highest Offering: Baccalaureate
Program: Occupational; Liberal Arts And General; Teacher Preparatory
Accreditation: NH, ADNUR, BUS, DH, DMS, MUS, NAIT, NUR, RAD, SURGT, TED

02 Chancellor ... Dr. Paul B. BERAN
05 Provost and Sr Vice Chancellor ... Dr. Ray WALLACE
04 Vice Chancellor Univ Relations ... Mr. Mark HORN
30 Vice Chancellor Univ Advancement ... Dr. Marta LOYD
10 Vice Chanc Finance & Administration ... Mr. Darrell MORRISON
32 Vice Chancellor Student Affairs ... Dr. Lee KREHBIEL
20 Assoc Provost Academic Affairs ... Dr. Brenda MITCHELL
31 Assoc Vice Chanc Campus/Cmty Events ... Mr. Stacey JONES
79 Dean Col Humanities/Social Sci ... Dr. Henry RINNE
76 Dean College of Health Sciences ... Dr. Carolyn MOSLEY
53 Dean College of Education ... Dr. John R. JONES
50 Dean College of Business ... Dr. Steve WILLIAMS
72 Dean Col Applied Science/Technology ... Dr. Georgia HALE
72 Dean Col Sci/Tech/Engineering/Math ... Dr. Mark ARANT
60 Dean Col of Languages/Communication ... Dr. Joe HARDIN
88 Dean Student Success ... Ms. Diana ROWDEN
84 Dean of Enrollment Management ... Ms. Penny PENDLETON
16 Dir Human Resources/EEO Officer ... Ms. Bev MCCLENDON
51 Director of Lifelong Learning ... Mr. Jeff ADAMS
12 Dir Western Arkansas Tech Ctr ... Mr. Darrel C. RINK
45 Dir Institutional Effectiveness ... Vacant
36 Exec Director Career Services ... Mr. Pat WIDDERS
88 Exec Dir of International Relations ... Mr. Takeo SUZUKI
88 Director of Instructional Support ... Dr. Tara MISHRA
06 Registrar ... Mr. Wayne WOMACK
08 Director of Library Services ... Mr. Robert FRIZZELL
39 Director of Student Housing ... Ms. Beth EPPINGER
37 Director Student Financial Aid ... Mr. Alan PIXLEY
38 Director of Advisement ... Ms. Julie MOSLEY
36 Dir of Student Professional Dev Ctr ... Mr. Ron ORICK
86 Government Relations ... Dr. Elizabeth UNDERWOOD
07 Director of Admissions ... Vacant
26 Director Marketing & Communications ... Mr. Jeff HARMON
41 Director of Athletics ... Dr. Dustin SMITH
27 Director of Public Information ... Ms. Sondra LAMAR
18 Director of Plant Operations ... Mr. Bill PIERCE
21 Controller ... Vacant
96 Associate Controller ... Ms. Debbie BREEDLOVE

*University of Arkansas at Little Rock (B)

2801 S University Avenue, Little Rock AR 72204-1099

County: Pulaski — FICE Identification: 001101
Unit ID: 106245
Telephone: (501) 569-3000 — Carnegie Class: DRU
FAX Number: (501) 569-8915 — Calendar System: Semester
URL: www.ualr.edu
Established: 1927 — Annual Undergrad Tuition & Fees (In-State): $7,601
Enrollment: 12,958 — Coed
Affiliation or Control: State — IRS Status: 501(c)3
Highest Offering: Doctorate
Program: Occupational; Liberal Arts And General; Teacher Preparatory; Professional
Accreditation: NH, ADNUR, ART, AUD, BUS, CONST, CORE, CS, ENG, ENGT, LAW, MUS, NUR, RADDOS, SP, SPAA, SW, TED, THEA

02 Chancellor ... Dr. Joel E. ANDERSON
05 Executive Vice Chancellor & Provost ... Dr. Zulma R. TORO
32 Int Vice Chanc Educ Student Svcs ... Dr. Logan C. HAMPTON
10 Vice Chanc Finance & Administration ... Dr. Robert H. ADAMS
30 Interim Vice Chanc Univ Advance ... Ms. Joni C. LEE
58 Vice Prov Rsrch/Dn Grad School ... Ms. Paula J. CASEY
13 Interim Vice Chanc IT Services ... Mr. Nathan NOLEN
84 Vice Chanc Enrollment Management ... Dr. Dean R. KAHLER
45 Director of Budget Planning ... Dr. Sandra L. ROBERTSON
11 Assoc Vice Chanc Facilities Mgt ... Mr. David MILLAY
21 Associate Vice Chancellor Finance ... Mr. Steven J. MCCLELLAN

44 Vice Chancellor Development ... Mr. Bob G. DENMAN
88 Assoc Vice Chanc for Advancement ... Vacant
35 Div Chief Student Dev/Dean Students ... Vacant
06 Registrar Records & Registration ... Ms. Joyce HAIL
15 Director of Human Resource Devel ... Ms. Annette MURDOCK-TANGYE
21 Director of Financial Services ... Ms. Stacey L. HOGUE
18 Director of Physical Plant ... Mr. David L. MILLAY
80 Director Arkansas Institute of Govt ... Dr. Hunter BACOT
88 Director Ark Institute Econ Advance ... Mr. Jim L. YOUNGQUIST
27 Director of Communications ... Ms. Judy G. WILLIAMS
09 Interim Director Inst Research ... Ms. Sonia H. HAZELWOOD
08 Director of the Library ... Vacant
19 Dir Public Safety/Chief of Police ... Mr. Edward L. SMITH
40 Director of Bookstore ... Ms. Brenda R. THOMAS
46 Director of Research/Sponsored Pgms ... Mr. Allen D. STANLEY
37 Director Financial Aid ... Ms. Tammy HARRISON
41 Director of Athletics ... Mr. Chris PETERSON
29 Director of Alumni Relations ... Mr. Christian O'NEAL
36 Director of Student Placement ... Vacant
07 Director of Admissions ... Ms. Katie YOUNG
38 Director Student Counseling ... Vacant
96 Director of Purchasing ... Ms. Deborah HANKINS
20 Associate Academic Officer ... Dr. Christina S. DRALE
20 Associate Academic Officer ... Dr. Karen J. WHEELER
50 Dean of Business ... Dr. Jane P. WAYLAND
53 Interim Dean of Education ... Dr. Gail D. HUGHES
79 Dean Arts/Human/Social Science ... Dr. Deborah J. BALDWIN
54 Dean of Eng & Information Technolog ... Dr. Eric SANDGREN
81 Dean of Science ... Vacant
61 Dean of Bowen School of Law ... Mr. Micheal H. SCHWARTZ
107 Int Dean of Professional Studies ... Dr. Jamie M. BYRNE

*University of Arkansas for Medical Sciences (C)

4301 W Markham, Little Rock AR 72205-7199

County: Pulaski — FICE Identification: 001109
Unit ID: 106263
Telephone: (501) 686-7000 — Carnegie Class: Spec/Med
FAX Number: (501) 686-5905 — Calendar System: Semester
URL: www.uams.edu
Established: 1879 — Annual Undergrad Tuition & Fees (In-State): $7,717
Enrollment: 2,809 — Coed
Affiliation or Control: State — IRS Status: 501(c)3
Highest Offering: Doctorate
Program: Occupational; 2-Year Principally Bachelor's Creditable; Liberal Arts And General; Professional
Accreditation: NH, #ARCPA, CAHIIM, COARC, CYTO, DH, DIETI, DMS, EMT, HSA, IPSY, MED, MT, NMT, NURSE, PH, PHAR, RAD, SURGT

02 Chancellor ... Dr. Daniel RAHN
05 Vice Chancellor Academic Affairs ... Dr. Jeanne K. HEARD
10 Vice Chancellor Finance & CEO ... Mr. David O. WILCOX
26 Vice Chancellor Communications ... Ms. Leslie W. TAYLOR
30 Vice Chancellor Development ... Mr. Lance E. BURCHETT
11 Vice Chancellor Campus Operations ... Mr. Mark A. KENNEDAY
08 Director of Library ... Ms. Mary L. RYAN
27 Chief Information Officer ... Mr. David L. MILLER
15 Director Human Resources ... Mr. Hosea LONG
37 Director Financial Services ... Ms. Gloria KEMP
63 Dean College of Medicine ... Dr. G. Richard H. SMITH
76 Dean Col Health Related Professions ... Dr. Douglas L. MURPHY
66 Dean College of Nursing ... Dr. Lorraine FRAZIER
67 Dean College of Pharmacy ... Dr. Stephanie F. GARDNER
58 Dean of the Graduate School ... Dr. Robert E. MCGEHEE, JR.
88 Dean College of Public Health ... Dr. James M. RACZYNSKI

† Tuition figure is for Medical School. Other school's tuitions vary widely.

*University of Arkansas at Monticello (D)

346 University Drive, Monticello AR 71656-3596

County: Drew — FICE Identification: 001085
Unit ID: 106485
Telephone: (870) 367-1020 — Carnegie Class: Master's S
FAX Number: (870) 460-1321 — Calendar System: Semester
URL: www.uamont.edu
Established: 1909 — Annual Undergrad Tuition & Fees (In-State): $5,793
Enrollment: 3,945 — Coed
Affiliation or Control: State — IRS Status: 501(c)3
Highest Offering: Master's
Program: Occupational; 2-Year Principally Bachelor's Creditable; Liberal Arts And General; Teacher Preparatory
Accreditation: NH, EMT, FOR, MUS, NUR, SW, TED

02 Chancellor ... Dr. Jack LASSITER
05 Provost/VC for Acad Affairs ... Dr. Jimmie YEISER
10 Vice Chanc Finance & Administration ... Mr. Jay JONES
30 Vice Chanc Advancement/Univ Rels ... Vacant
32 Vice Chanc Student Affairs ... Mr. Jay HUGHES
12 Vice Chanc UAM Col of Tech Crossett ... Ms. Linda RUSHING
12 Vice Chanc UAM Col of Tech McGehee ... Mr. Bob WARE
21 Assoc VC for Finance ... Ms. Debbie GASAWAY
06 Registrar ... Ms. Carol DOLBERRY
21 Business Manager ... Ms. Melodie COLWELL
07 Director of Admissions ... Ms. Mary WHITING
84 Director of Enrollment Mgmt ... Ms. Mary WHITING
41 Director of Athletics ... Mr. Chris RATCLIFF
35 Dean of Students/Dir Govt Relations ... Mr. Scott KUTTENKULER

13 Director Information Technology ... Mr. Bobby HOYLE
08 Director of Library ... Ms. Sandra CAMPBELL
26 Director of Media Services ... Mr. Jim L. BREWER
37 Director of Financial Aid ... Ms. Susan BREWER
09 Director of Institutional Research ... Ms. Linda YEISER
18 Chief Facilities/Physical Plant ... Mr. Jim HUDGINS
38 Dir Counseling/Testing Services ... Ms. Laura HUGHES
96 Director of Purchasing ... Ms. Gay PACE
29 Director of Alumni Affairs ... Ms. Julie BARNES

*University of Arkansas at Pine Bluff (E)

1200 N University Drive, Pine Bluff AR 71601-2799

County: Jefferson — FICE Identification: 001086
Unit ID: 106412
Telephone: (870) 575-8000 — Carnegie Class: Bac/Diverse
FAX Number: (870) 543-8009 — Calendar System: Semester
URL: www.uapb.edu
Established: 1873 — Annual Undergrad Tuition & Fees (In-State): $5,754
Enrollment: 2,828 — Coed
Affiliation or Control: State — IRS Status: 501(c)3
Highest Offering: Doctorate
Program: Liberal Arts And General; Teacher Preparatory; Professional
Accreditation: NH, AAFCS, ART, @DIETD, MUS, NAIT, SW, TED

02 Interim Chancellor ... Dr. Calvin JOHNSON
04 Assistant to the Chancellor ... Mrs. Liz F. STRICKLAND
05 Vice Chancellor Academic Affairs ... Dr. Mary E. BENJAMIN
10 Vice Chanc Finance & Admin ... Ms. Pauline THOMAS
30 Director of Development ... Mrs. Margaret MARTIN-HALL
20 Associate Academic Officer ... Dr. Verma JONES
08 Librarian ... Mr. Edward J. FONTENETTE
91 Director of Technical Services ... Mrs. Willette TOTTEN
37 Director of Financial Aid ... Mrs. Janice KEARNEY
09 Director of Institutional Research ... Mrs. Margaret TAYLOR
15 Director Human Resources ... Ms. Gladys BENFORD
36 Director Career Services/Admissions ... Mrs. Mary JONES
26 Director Public Relations/Info ... Mrs. Tisha ARNOLD
35 Dir Student Life/Enrollment Mgmt ... Mr. Leon CRUMBLIN
38 Director Student Counseling ... Ms. Joyce VAUGHN
06 Registrar ... Mrs. Erica FULTON
19 Chief of Police ... Mr. Maxcie THOMAS
18 Chief Facilities/Physical Plant ... Mr. Robert WALL
29 Director of Alumni Affairs ... Mr. John KUYKENDALL
96 Director of Purchasing ... Mrs. A. Kay TURNER
32 Admin Coordinator Student Affairs ... Mr. Elbert BENNETT
47 Dean Agricult/Fisheries/Hum Sci ... Dr. James GARNER
49 Interim Dean Arts & Sciences ... Dr. Andrea STEWART
53 Interim Dean School of Education ... Dr. Fredda CARROLL
51 Interim Dean Continuing Education ... Dr. George HERTS
50 Dean School of Business/Management ... Dr. Carla MARTIN
92 Dean Honors College ... Dr. Jewell WALKER
41 Director of Athletics ... Mr. Lonza HARDY, JR.

*Cossatot Community College of the University of Arkansas (F)

183 College Drive, PO Box 960,
De Queen AR 71832-0960

County: Sevier — FICE Identification: 022209
Unit ID: 106795
Telephone: (870) 584-4471 — Carnegie Class: Assoc/Pub2in4
FAX Number: (870) 642-3320 — Calendar System: Semester
URL: cccua.edu
Established: 1991 — Annual Undergrad Tuition & Fees (In-District): $2,042
Enrollment: 1,442 — Coed
Affiliation or Control: State/Local — IRS Status: 501(c)3
Highest Offering: Associate Degree
Program: Occupational; 2-Year Principally Bachelor's Creditable
Accreditation: NH, ACBSP

02 Chancellor ... Dr. Steve COLE
05 Vice Chancellor of Academics ... Dr. Maria PARKER
45 VC of Planning and Facilities ... Mr. Mike KINKADE
10 Vice Chancellor Business/Finance ... Mrs. Charlotte JOHNSON
32 Director of Student Services ... Mr. Justin WHITE
37 Director Student Financial Aid ... Mrs. Denise HAMMOND
26 Director of Marketing ... Ms. Alisha LEWIS
09 Director of Inst Research/Registrar ... Mrs. Brenda MORRIS
103 Dir of Public Svc/Workforce Dev ... Mrs. Tammy COLEMAN
12 Director of Ashdown Campus ... Mr. Barrett REED
15 Director of Human Resources ... Ms. Kelly PLUNK
13 Information Manager ... Mr. David BLACKWELL
102 Executive Director of Foundation ... Mr. Dustin ROBERTS

*Phillips Community College of the University of Arkansas (G)

PO Box 785, Helena AR 72342-0785

County: Phillips — FICE Identification: 001104
Unit ID: 107619
Telephone: (870) 338-6474 — Carnegie Class: Assoc/Pub2in4
FAX Number: (870) 338-7542 — Calendar System: Semester
URL: www.pccua.edu
Established: 1965 — Annual Undergrad Tuition & Fees (In-District): $2,420
Enrollment: 2,063 — Coed
Affiliation or Control: State/Local — IRS Status: 501(c)3
Highest Offering: Associate Degree
Program: Occupational; 2-Year Principally Bachelor's Creditable

Accreditation: NH, ACBSP, ADNUR, MLTAD, PHLEB

02 Chancellor ... Dr. Steven MURRAY
05 Vice Chancellor for Instruction ... Dr. Deborah KING
10 Vice Chanc Finance & Administration ... Mr. Stan SULLIVANT
32 Vice Chanc Student Svcs/Registrar ... Mr. Scott POST
30 Vice Chanc Col Advancement/Bus Dev ... Mrs. Rhonda ST. COLUMBIA
12 Vice Chancellor Stuttgart Campus ... Dr. Susan LUEBKE
12 Vice Chancellor DeWitt Campus ... Mrs. Carolyn TURNER

*University of Arkansas Community College at Batesville (A)

2005 White Drive, PO Box 3350,
Batesville AR 72503-3350

County: Independence FICE Identification: 020735
Unit ID: 106999
Telephone: (870) 612-2000 Carnegie Class: Assoc/Pub2in4
FAX Number: (870) 793-4988 Calendar System: Semester
URL: www.uaccb.edu
Established: 1975 Annual Undergrad Tuition & Fees (In-District): $2,540
Enrollment: 1,443 Coed
Affiliation or Control: State/Local IRS Status: 501(c)3
Highest Offering: Associate Degree
Program: Occupational; 2-Year Principally Bachelor's Creditable
Accreditation: NH, ADNUR, EMT

02 Chancellor ... Ms. Deborah J. FRAZIER
04 Assistant to the Chancellor ... Ms. Jan W. RORIE
05 Vice Chancellor for Academics ... Dr. Brian SHONK
32 VC Enrollment Mgmt/Student Services ... Mr. Brian BERRY
10 Vice Chancellor Finance and Admin ... Mr. Gayle COOPER
09 VC Research/Planning/Assessment ... Dr. Anne AUSTIN
49 Chair Div of Arts & Humanities ... Ms. Susan TRIPP
50 Chair Div Business/Tech/Public Svc ... Ms. Tamara GRIFFIN
76 Chair Div Nursing/Allied Health ... Ms. Rebecca KING
81 Chair Div of Math and Science ... Mr. Douglas MUSE
51 Chair Div Community and Tech Educ ... Ms. Kathleen MCNAMEE
09 Dir of Institutional Research ... Mr. Blake CANNON
84 Director of Enrollment Management ... Mr. Christopher DICKIE
106 Director of Distance Learning ... Ms. Tammy JOLLEY
13 Director Information Services ... Mr. Steve COLLINS
06 Dir Student Information/Registrar ... Ms. Shelly MOSER
37 Director of Financial Aid ... Ms. Kristen CROSS
30 Director of Development ... Ms. Tina PAUL
18 Director of Maintenance ... Mr. Heath WOOLDRIDGE
36 Director Student Development ... Ms. Louise HUGHES
38 Career & Counseling Services Coord ... Vacant
08 Director Library ... Ms. Linda BENNETT
21 Controller ... Ms. Waynna DOCKINS
15 Personnel Officer ... Ms. Alexa SMITH
96 Purchasing Agent ... Ms. Peggy JACKSON
40 Bookstore Manager ... Ms. Luanne BARBER

*University of Arkansas Community College at Hope (B)

PO Box 140, 2500 S Main Street, Hope AR 71802-0140

County: Hempstead FICE Identification: 005732
Unit ID: 107725
Telephone: (870) 777-5722 Carnegie Class: Assoc/Pub2in4
FAX Number: (870) 777-5957 Calendar System: Semester
URL: www.uacch.edu
Established: 1991 Annual Undergrad Tuition & Fees (In-State): $2,415
Enrollment: 1,513 Coed
Affiliation or Control: State IRS Status: 501(c)3
Highest Offering: Associate Degree
Program: Occupational; 2-Year Principally Bachelor's Creditable
Accreditation: NH, COARC, EMT, #FUSER

02 Chancellor ... Mr. Chris THOMASON
05 Vice Chancellor for Academics ... Dr. Jennifer METHVIN
32 Vice Chancellor Student Services ... Mr. Bobby JAMES
10 Vice Chancellor for Finance ... Mr. Jerald BARBER
08 Librarian ... Ms. Marielle MCFARLAND
51 Director of Cont Educ/Ind Relations ... Mr. Shaun CLARK
26 Communications Coordinator ... Mr. Brent TALLEY
24 Director of Telecommunications ... Mr. Dave PHILLIPS
15 Human Resources Officer ... Ms. Kathryn HOPKINS
06 Registrar ... Ms. Diana SYATA
12 Texarkana Campus Director ... Ms. Jolane COOK

*University of Arkansas Community College at Morrilton (C)

1537 University Boulevard, Morrilton AR 72110-9601

County: Conway FICE Identification: 005245
Unit ID: 107585
Telephone: (501) 354-2465 Carnegie Class: Assoc/Pub2in4
FAX Number: (501) 977-2134 Calendar System: Semester
URL: www.uaccm.edu
Established: 1961 Annual Undergrad Tuition & Fees (In-State): $3,500
Enrollment: 2,139 Coed
Affiliation or Control: State IRS Status: 501(c)3
Highest Offering: Associate Degree
Program: Occupational; 2-Year Principally Bachelor's Creditable
Accreditation: NH

02 Chancellor ... Dr. Larry D. DAVIS
05 Vice Chancellor Academic Services ... Ms. Diana ARN
10 Vice Chancellor for Finance ... Ms. Lisa GUNDERMAN
11 Vice Chancellor for Administration ... Dr. Linda M. BIRKNER
32 Vice Chancellor Student Services ... Mr. Darren JONES
09 Director of Institutional Research ... Ms. Wanda F. HENSLEY
08 Librarian ... Mr. Vincent TINERELLA
06 Registrar ... Ms. Linda HOLLAND
37 Financial Aid Director ... Mrs. Teresa Y. CASH
13 Director of Computer Services ... Mr. Richard O. GROWNS
18 Director of the Physical Plant ... Mr. C. Allen HOLLOWAY
27 Chief Information Officer ... Ms. Mary CLARK
07 Director of Admissions ... Ms. Susan DEWEY
103 Coord Workforce Develop/Cmty Educ ... Ms. Stephanie ELLIS
15 Director Personnel Services ... Ms. Judy SANDERS
26 Chief Public Relations Officer ... Ms. Mary CLARK
30 Chief Development ... Ms. Morgan ZIMMERMAN
38 Director Student Counseling ... Ms. Staci DUVALL
96 Director of Purchasing ... Ms. Kimberly BULL

*Phillips Community College of the University of Arkansas-DeWitt (D)

1210 Rice Belt Avenue, DeWitt AR 72042

Telephone: (870) 946-3506 Identification: 770174
Accreditation: &NH

† Main campus is Phillips Community College of the University of Arkansas in Helena, AR.

*Phillips Community College of the University of Arkansas-Stuttgart (E)

2807 Hwy 165 South, Stuttgart AR 72160-2408

Telephone: (870) 673-4201 Identification: 770175
Accreditation: &NH

† Main campus is Phillips Community College of the University of Arkansas in Helena, AR.

*University of Arkansas at Monticello College of Technology-Crussett (F)

1326 Highway 52 W, Crussett AR 71635

Telephone: (870) 364-6414 Identification: 770176
Accreditation: &NH

† Main campus is University of Arkansas at Monticello in Monticello, AR.

*University of Arkansas at Monticello College of Technology-McGehee (G)

PO Box 747, McGehee AR 71654

Telephone: (870) 222-5360 Identification: 770177
Accreditation: &NH

† Main campus is University of Arkansas at Monticello in Monticello, AR.

University of Central Arkansas (H)

201 Donaghey Avenue, Conway AR 72035-0001

County: Faulkner FICE Identification: 001092
Unit ID: 106704
Telephone: (501) 450-5000 Carnegie Class: Master's L
FAX Number: (501) 450-5003 Calendar System: Semester
URL: www.uca.edu
Established: 1907 Annual Undergrad Tuition & Fees (In-State): $7,595
Enrollment: 11,107 Coed
Affiliation or Control: State IRS Status: 501(c)3
Highest Offering: Doctorate
Program: Occupational; Liberal Arts And General; Teacher Preparatory; Professional
Accreditation: NH, ART, BUS, #CIDA, CS, DIETD, DIETI, MUS, NURSE, OT, PTA, SCPSY, SP, TED, THEA

01 President ... Mr. Tom COURTWAY
05 Provost/VP Academic Affairs ... Dr. Steve RUNGE
10 VP Finance/Administration ... Ms. Diane D. NEWTON
32 VP Student Services/Inst Diversity ... Mr. Ronnie D. WILLIAMS
43 Interim General Counsel ... Ms. Katie HENRY
26 VP for University & Govt Relations ... Mr. Jeffery L. PITCHFORD
30 VP for UCA Advancement ... Ms. Shelley MEHL
41 Athletics Director ... Dr. Brad TEAGUE
15 Assoc Vice Pres for Human Resources ... Dr. Graham GILLIS
85 Asst Provost/Dir Intl Engagement ... Dr. Jane Ann WILLIAMS
20 Associate Provost ... Ms. Laura YOUNG
21 Controller ... Mr. Jeremy BRUNER
58 Int Dean of Graduate School ... Dr. Gary MCCOLLOUGH
51 Academic Outreach/Extended Pgm ... Mr. Gilbert BAKER
50 Interim Dean of Col Business Admin ... Dr. Michael HARGIS
53 Dean of College of Education ... Dr. Diana G. POUNDER
76 Int Dean Col Health/Applied Science ... Dr. Art GILLASPY
49 Dean of Liberal Arts ... Dr. Maurice A. LEE
81 Interim Dean Col Natural Sci/Math ... Dr. Steve ADDISON
57 Int Dean Fine Arts & Communication ... Mr. Terry WRIGHT
35 Dean of Students ... Dr. Gary A. ROBERTS
92 Dean of Honors College ... Dr. Richard I. SCOTT
07 Director Admissions ... Mr. Ron PATTERSON
08 Library Director ... Mr. Art LICHTENSTEIN
06 Int Registrar ... Ms. Becky D. RASNICK
09 Dir Institutional Research ... Ms. Amber L. HALL
13 Chief Information Officer ... Dr. Jonathan A. GLENN
37 Director Student Financial Aid ... Ms. Cheryl C. LYONS
36 Dir Career Svcs/Cooperative Educ ... Dr. Kathy RICE-CLAYBORN
19 Chief University Police ... Mr. Larry K. JAMES
38 Director Counseling Center ... Dr. Maurice E. NESS
39 Asst VP for Housing & Contract Svcs ... Mr. Rick L. MCCOLLUM
29 Director of Alumni Services ... Mrs. Jan A. NEWCOMER
21 Director Internal Audits ... Ms. Pamela L. MASSEY
18 Director Physical Plant ... Mr. Larry D. LAWRENCE
27 Dir Publications/Creative Services ... Mr. Richard R. HANCOCK
96 Director of Purchasing ... Ms. Cassandra MCCUIEN-SMITH
21 Director Student Accounts ... Mr. Jason A. RANKIN

University of Phoenix Little Rock Campus (I)

10800 Financial Ctr Pkwy, Suite 125,
Little Rock AR 72211-3552

Telephone: (501) 225-9337 Identification: 770188
Accreditation: &NH, ACBSP

† Main campus is University of Phoenix in Tempe, AZ.

University of the Ozarks (J)

415 College Avenue, Clarksville AR 72830-2880

County: Johnson FICE Identification: 001094
Unit ID: 107558
Telephone: (479) 979-1000 Carnegie Class: Bac/Diverse
FAX Number: (479) 979-1355 Calendar System: Semester
URL: www.ozarks.edu
Established: 1834 Annual Undergrad Tuition & Fees: $31,340
Enrollment: 576 Coed
Affiliation or Control: Presbyterian Church (U.S.A.) IRS Status: 501(c)3
Highest Offering: Baccalaureate
Program: Liberal Arts And General; Teacher Preparatory; Professional
Accreditation: NH, IACBE, TED

01 President ... Mr. Richard L. DUNSWORTH
05 Provost ... Dr. Daniel L. TADDIE
10 Chief Financial Officer ... Mr. Jeff SCACCIA
84 Director of Admission ... Mr. Brian HULL
07 Dean of Admissions & Financial Aid ... Ms. Jana D. HART
42 Chaplain ... Rev. Elizabeth GABBARD
35 Dean of Students ... Mr. Joe W. HOING
39 Dean of Residential & Campus Life ... Ms. Sherrie AREY
06 Registrar ... Ms. Wilma K. HARRIS
08 Librarian ... Mr. Stuart P. STELZER
27 Director of Public Information ... Mr. Larry A. ISCH
36 Director Student Placement ... Ms. Kim A. SPICER
29 Director Alumni Affairs ... Ms. Lori A. MCBEE
41 Athletic Director ... Mr. Jimmy CLARK
26 Chief Public Relations Officer ... Mr. Larry A. ISCH
30 Director of Development ... Ms. Lori A. MCBEE
18 Chief Facilities/Physical Plant ... Mr. Mike QUALLS
88 Director Jones Learning Center ... Ms. Julia H. FROST
90 Director Academic Computing ... Mr. Nathan SAIN
09 Director of Institutional Research ... Mr. Randolph L. PETERSON
96 Director of Purchasing ... Mr. Darrell W. WILLIAMS
89 Director of Freshmen Studies ... Dr. Elissa HEIL
14 Director Computer Services ... Mr. Rick OTTO
32 Chief Student Life Officer ... Ms. Sherrie AREY
20 Associate Academic Dean ... Dr. Elissa HEIL
21 Business Manager ... Mr. Darrell W. WILLIAMS
81 Chair Division Sciences/Mathematics ... Mr. Stacy KEY
50 Chair Division of Business ... Dr. Robert C. HILTON
53 Chair Division of Education ... Dr. Glenda EZELL
79 Chair Division Humanities/Fine Arts ... Dr. David M. STRAIN
37 Student Financial Aid Counselor ... Ms. Melody JOHNSON

Williams Baptist College (K)

56 McClellan Drive, Walnut Ridge AR 72476

County: Lawrence FICE Identification: 001106
Unit ID: 107877
Telephone: (870) 886-6741 Carnegie Class: Bac/Diverse
FAX Number: (870) 886-3924 Calendar System: Semester
URL: www.wbcoll.edu
Established: 1941 Annual Undergrad Tuition & Fees: $19,100
Enrollment: 566 Coed
Affiliation or Control: Southern Baptist IRS Status: 501(c)3
Highest Offering: Baccalaureate
Program: Liberal Arts And General; Religious Emphasis
Accreditation: NH, TED

01 President ... Dr. Tom O. JONES
05 Vice Pres Academic Affairs ... Dr. Kenneth M. STARTUP
10 Vice President for Business Affairs ... Mr. Dale LEATHERMAN
30 Vice Pres Institutional Advancement ... Dr. Brett COOPER
84 VP for Enrollment Mgmt/Student Svcs ... Mrs. Angela D. FLIPPO
32 Dean of Students ... Mrs. Susan M. WATSON
06 Registrar ... Mrs. Tonya D. BOLTON
04 Administrative Asst to President ... Mrs. Jo C. PHILLIPS
08 Librarian ... Mrs. Pamela MERIDITH
37 Director Student Financial Aid ... Mrs. Barbara J. TURNER
38 Director Student Counseling ... Ms. Aneita COOPER
42 Director Campus Ministry ... Mr. Josh MCCARTY
18 Chief Facilities/Physical Plant ... Vacant
36 Director Student Placement ... Ms. Aneita COOPER
44 Director of Annual Giving & Alumni ... Mr. Aaron ANDREWS
13 Director Information Technology ... Mr. Blake MCGINNIS
41 Athletic Director ... Mr. Jeff RIDER
106 Dean of Adult Education ... Dr. Eric TURNER
88 Director of International Programs ... Mr. Adam ADAMS
07 Director of Admissions ... Mr. Andrew WATSON

CALIFORNIA

Abraham Lincoln University (A)

3530 Wilshire Blvd, Ste 1430, Los Angeles CA 90010
County: Los Angeles Identification: 667049
Unit ID: 480444
Telephone: (213) 252-5100 Carnegie Class: Not Classified
FAX Number: (213) 252-5112 Calendar System: Other
URL: www.alu.edu
Established: 1996 Annual Undergrad Tuition & Fees: $8,000
Enrollment: 157 Coed
Affiliation or Control: Proprietary IRS Status: Proprietary
Highest Offering: First Professional Degree
Program: 2-Year Principally Bachelor's Creditable; Liberal Arts And General; Professional
Accreditation: DETC

01 President & CEO .... Mr. Hyung PARK
27 Chief Information Officer .... Ms. Jessica PARK
61 Dean School of Law & CAO .... Ms. Carole BUCKNER
11 Chief Administrative Officer .... Dr. Daryl FISHER-OGDEN
07 Manager of Admissions .... Mr. Angelo LIOUDAKIS
06 Registrar .... Ms. Elizabeth GOMEZ
32 Student Services Coordinator .... Ms. Jin CHUNG
13 Technology Manager .... Mr. Myeong KIM

Academy for Jewish Religion (B)

574 Hilgard Avenue, Los Angeles CA 90024-3234
County: Los Angeles FICE Identification: 041555
Unit ID: 457271
Telephone: (310) 824-1586 Carnegie Class: Not Classified
FAX Number: (310) 824-1614 Calendar System: Trimester
URL: www.ajrca.org
Established: 2001 Annual Graduate Tuition & Fees: $22,550
Enrollment: 63 Coed
Affiliation or Control: Jewish IRS Status: 501(c)3
Highest Offering: Master's; No Undergraduates
Program: Professional; Religious Emphasis
Accreditation: WC

01 President .... Dr. Tamar FRANKIEL
37 Director Student Financial Aid .... Ms. Lauren GOLDNER
06 Registrar .... Ms. Reesa ROTMAN
07 Director of Admissions .... Ms. Robin FEDERMAN
26 Chief Public Relations Officer .... Ms. Cheryl AZAIR
88 Dean of Cantorial School .... Cantor Nathan LAM
73 Dean of Rabbinical School .... Rabbi Michael MENITOFF
88 Associate Dean of Cantorial School .... Cantor Perryne ANKER

Academy of Art University (C)

79 New Montgomery Street,
San Francisco CA 94105-3410
County: San Francisco FICE Identification: 007531
Unit ID: 108232
Telephone: (415) 274-2200 Carnegie Class: Spec/Arts
FAX Number: (415) 274-8665 Calendar System: Semester
URL: www.academyart.edu
Established: 1929 Annual Undergrad Tuition & Fees: $23,550
Enrollment: 17,871 Coed
Affiliation or Control: Proprietary IRS Status: Proprietary
Highest Offering: Master's
Program: Fine Arts Emphasis
Accreditation: WC, ART, CIDA

01 President .... Ms. Elisa STEPHENS

Academy of Chinese Culture and Health Sciences (D)

1601 Clay Street, Oakland CA 94612-1540
County: Alameda FICE Identification: 032883
Unit ID: 108269
Telephone: (510) 763-7787 Carnegie Class: Spec/Health
FAX Number: (510) 834-8646 Calendar System: Other
URL: www.acchs.edu
Established: 1982 Annual Undergrad Tuition & Fees: $16,900
Enrollment: 111 Coed
Affiliation or Control: Independent Non-Profit IRS Status: 501(c)3
Highest Offering: Master's; No Lower Division
Program: Professional
Accreditation: ACUP

01 President .... Mr. John NIETERS
03 Vice President .... Mr. Phillip TOU
11 Dean of Administration .... Ms. Jane ZHANG

Academy of Couture Art (E)

8484 Wilshire Boulevard, Suite 730,
Beverly Hills CA 90211-3235
County: Los Angeles FICE Identification: 041855
Unit ID: 475635
Telephone: (310) 360-8888 Carnegie Class: Not Classified
FAX Number: (310) 857-6974 Calendar System: Quarter
URL: www.academyofcoutureart.edu
Established: 2005 Annual Undergrad Tuition & Fees: $19,998
Enrollment: 48 Coed
Affiliation or Control: Proprietary IRS Status: Proprietary
Highest Offering: Baccalaureate
Program: Occupational; 2-Year Principally Bachelor's Creditable; Professional; Fine Arts Emphasis
Accreditation: ACICS

01 CEO .... Sonia ETE

Acupuncture and Integrative Medicine College-Berkeley (F)

2550 Shattuck Avenue, Berkeley CA 94704-2724
County: Alameda FICE Identification: 033274
Unit ID: 384306
Telephone: (510) 666-8248 Carnegie Class: Spec/Health
FAX Number: (510) 666-0111 Calendar System: Quarter
URL: www.aimc.edu
Established: 1990 Annual Undergrad Tuition & Fees: $15,500
Enrollment: 142 Coed
Affiliation or Control: Independent Non-Profit IRS Status: 501(c)3
Highest Offering: Master's; No Lower Division
Program: Professional
Accreditation: ACUP

01 President .... Mr. Yasuo TANAKA
05 Academic Dean .... Ms. Megan HAUNGS
05 Clinic Dean .... Mr. Mike MORGAN
06 Registrar .... Ms. Katherine FORST
20 Student Advisor .... Ms. Vim OSATHANUGRAH
07 Director of Admissions .... Ms. Erin OLINICK

Advanced College (G)

13180 Paramount Boulevard, South Gate CA 90280-7956
County: Los Angeles FICE Identification: 037863
Unit ID: 444343
Telephone: (562) 408-6969 Carnegie Class: Assoc/PrivFP
FAX Number: (562) 408-0471 Calendar System: Other
URL: www.advancedcollege.edu
Established: 1999 Annual Undergrad Tuition & Fees: $28,595
Enrollment: 134 Coed
Affiliation or Control: Proprietary IRS Status: Proprietary
Highest Offering: Associate Degree
Program: Occupational
Accreditation: COE

01 Chief Executive Officer .... Dr. Mehdi KARIMPOR
66 Director Vocational Nursing .... Dr. Minnie L. DOUGLAS
11 Director of Operations .... Dr. Mehdi KARIMPOUR

Advanced Computing Institute (H)

3470 Wilshire Blvd #1100, Los Angeles CA 90010
County: Los Angeles Identification: 667142
Telephone: (213) 383-8999 Carnegie Class: Not Classified
FAX Number: (213) 383-5765 Calendar System: Semester
URL: www.advancedcomputinginstitute.com
Established: 1992 Annual Undergrad Tuition & Fees: N/A
Enrollment: N/A Coed
Affiliation or Control: Proprietary IRS Status: Proprietary
Highest Offering: Associate Degree
Program: Occupational
Accreditation: COE

01 School Director/CEO .... Mr. Daniel MAINCA
05 Exec Vice Pres/Academic Dean .... Dr. Michael RAHNI

Advanced Training Associates (I)

1810 Gillespie Way, Suite 104, El Cajon CA 92020-1234
County: San Diego FICE Identification: 035324
Unit ID: 444361
Telephone: (619) 596-2766 Carnegie Class: Not Classified
FAX Number: (619) 596-4526 Calendar System: Other
URL: www.advancedtraining.edu
Established: 2000 Annual Undergrad Tuition & Fees: $11,990
Enrollment: 86 Coed
Affiliation or Control: Proprietary IRS Status: Proprietary
Highest Offering: Associate Degree
Program: Occupational; Technical Emphasis
Accreditation: COE

01 President .... Joann ZAKARIN
11 School Operations Director .... Valerie PHILLIPS

Alhambra Medical University (J)

25 S. Raymond Ave., Suite 201, Alhambra CA 91801
County: Los Angeles Identification: 667052
Telephone: (626) 289-7719 Carnegie Class: Not Classified
FAX Number: (626) 289-8641 Calendar System: Quarter
URL: www.amuedu.com
Established: 2005 Annual Graduate Tuition & Fees: $13,282
Enrollment: N/A Coed
Affiliation or Control: Proprietary IRS Status: Proprietary
Highest Offering: Master's; No Undergraduates
Program: Professional
Accreditation: @ACUP

01 President .... Dr. Jonathan WU
05 Academic Dean .... Jerome JIANG
23 Director of University Clinic .... Anyork LEE
07 Director of Admissions .... Qing MA
06 Registrar .... Alan LIU
08 Librarian .... Yue LU

Allan Hancock College (K)

800 S College Drive, Santa Maria CA 93454-6399
County: Santa Barbara FICE Identification: 001111
Unit ID: 108807
Telephone: (805) 922-6966 Carnegie Class: Assoc/Pub-R-L
FAX Number: (805) 928-7905 Calendar System: Semester
URL: www.hancockcollege.edu
Established: 1920 Annual Undergrad Tuition & Fees (In-District): $1,152
Enrollment: 10,142 Coed
Affiliation or Control: State/Local IRS Status: 501(c)3
Highest Offering: Associate Degree
Program: Occupational; 2-Year Principally Bachelor's Creditable
Accreditation: WJ

01 Superintendent/President .... Dr. Kevin G. WALTHERS
10 Assoc Supt/VP Administrative Svcs .... Dr. Elizabeth MILLER
05 Assoc Supt/VP Academic Affairs .... Mr. Luiz P. SANCHEZ
32 VP Student Services .... Vacant
18 Vice Pres Facilities & Operations .... Mr. Felix HERNANDEZ
35 Dean Student Services .... Mr. Rob PARISI
88 Dean Counseling & Matriculation .... Vacant
20 Dean Academic Affairs .... Ms. Roanna BENNIE
20 Dean Academic Affairs .... Ms. Nancy MEDDINGS
20 Dean Acad Afrs/Dir HSI STEM .... Dr. Paul MURPHY
20 Dean Academic Affairs .... Ms. Ardis NEILSEN
12 Dean The Extended Campus .... Mr. Rick RANTZ
41 Assoc Dean Athletics/Kinesiology .... Ms. Kim ENSING
102 Executive Director AHC Foundation .... Mr. Jeff COTTER
88 Artistic Director PCPA .... Mr. Mark BOOHER
13 Director Information Technology .... Ms. Carol MOORE
15 Director Human Resources .... Ms. Cyndi MESAROS
21 Director Business Services .... Mr. Richard CARMODY
07 Int Director Admissions & Records .... Ms. Marian QUAID-MALTAGLIATI
37 Director Student Financial Aid .... Mr. Robert PARISI
26 Dir Public Affairs & Publications .... Mrs. Rebecca ALARCIO
40 Director Bookstore Services .... Mr. William HOCKENSMITH
88 Director EOPS & Special Outreach .... Mr. Will BRUCE
18 Director Plant Services .... Mr. Rex VAN DEN BERG
09 Director Inst Research & Planning .... Dr. Laurie PEMBERTON
19 Dir Public Safety/Chief of Police .... Wesley MARONEY
88 Director College Achvmt Now (CAN) .... Mr. Francisco DORAME
88 Director Cal-SOAP .... Ms. Diana PEREZ
25 Director Institutional Grants .... Dr. Suzanne VALERY
81 Counselor/Coordinator MESA .... Ms. Christine REED
88 Managing Director PCPA .... Mr. Michael BLACK

*Alliant International University President's Office (L)

One Beach Street, Suite 200,
San Francisco CA 94133-1221
County: San Francisco Identification: 666132
Unit ID: 110431
Telephone: (415) 955-2000 Carnegie Class: N/A
FAX Number: (414) 955-2062
URL: www.alliant.edu

01 President .... Dr. Geoffrey COX
05 Provost/Vice Pres Academic Affairs .... Dr. Russ NEWMAN
11 VP Administration .... Vacant
10 Vice Pres Finance & CFO .... Ms. Jeanine HAWK
09 Assoc Provost Inst Research .... Ms. Patty MULLEN
53 Dean Grad School of Education .... Dr. Karen Schuster WEBB
88 Systemwide Dean CSPP .... Dr. Morgan SAMMONS
15 Chief Human Resources Officer .... Ms. Lesa HAMMOND
88 Controller .... Ms. Marina SHEVYAKOVA
96 Purchasing Manager .... Mr. Malvin AGNO

*Alliant International University-San Diego (M)

10455 Pomerado Road, San Diego CA 92131-1799
County: San Diego FICE Identification: 011117
Unit ID: 110468
Telephone: (858) 635-4000 Carnegie Class: DRU
FAX Number: (858) 693-8562 Calendar System: Semester
URL: www.alliant.edu
Established: 1952 Annual Undergrad Tuition & Fees: $15,190
Enrollment: 3,489 Coed
Affiliation or Control: Independent Non-Profit IRS Status: 501(c)3
Highest Offering: Doctorate
Program: Liberal Arts And General; Teacher Preparatory; Professional
Accreditation: WC, CLPSY, MFCD

02 President .... Dr. Geoffrey COX
05 Provost/Vice Pres Academic Affairs .... Dr. Russ NEWMAN
43 Vice President and Univ Counsel .... Ms. Jennifer WILSON
32 Assoc Vice Pres for Student Life .... Dr. Mike PITTENGER
09 Assoc Provost for Rsrch & Scholar .... Dr. Sharon FOSTER
11 Assoc Provost for Administration .... Dr. Tracy HELLER
26 Chief Marketing Officer .... Mrs. Madeleine WIENER
06 University Registrar .... Mr. Paul WELCH

37 Director of Financial Aid .... Ms. Deborah SPINDLER
08 University Librarian .... Mr. Scott ZIMMER

* *Alliant International University-Fresno* (A)

5130 E Clinton Way, Fresno CA 93727-2014
Telephone: (559) 456-2777 FICE Identification: 001158
Accreditation: WC, CLPSY, MFCD

† Main campus is Alliant International University-San Diego in San Diego, CA.

* *Alliant International University-Irvine* (B)

2855 Michelle Drive, Suite 300, Irvine CA 92606
Telephone: (949) 812-7440 Identification: 666157
Accreditation: WC, MFCD

† Main campus is Alliant International University-San Diego in San Diego, CA.

* *Alliant International University-Los Angeles* (C)

1000 S Fremont Avenue, Unit 5,
Alhambra CA 91803-1360
Telephone: (626) 284-2777 FICE Identification: 010013
Accreditation: WC, CLPSY, MFCD

† Main campus is Alliant International University-San Diego in San Diego, CA.

* *Alliant International University-San Francisco* (D)

One Beach Street, San Francisco CA 94133-1221
Telephone: (415) 955-2100 FICE Identification: 011881
Accreditation: WC, CLPSY

† Main campus is Alliant International University-San Diego in San Diego, CA.

Allied American University (E)

22952 Alcalde Drive, Laguna Hills CA 92653-1337
County: Orange FICE Identification: 041893
Telephone: (888) 384-0849 Carnegie Class: Not Classified
FAX Number: (949) 707-2978 Calendar System: Other
URL: www.allied.edu
Established: 2008 Annual Undergrad Tuition & Fees: $11,160
Enrollment: 3,061 Coed
Affiliation or Control: Proprietary IRS Status: Proprietary
Highest Offering: Baccalaureate
Program: Liberal Arts And General
Accreditation: @WC, DETC

01 President .... Charli HISLOP
05 Provost .... Dr. Bonny NICKLE
20 Director of Education .... Eric SHARKEY
09 Institutional Research .... Christopher BISHOP
06 Registrar .... Abby DOLAN
07 Director of Admissions .... Lindsay OGLESBY
32 Manager of Student Affairs .... Sasha HEARD
11 Director of Operations .... Frank VAZQUEZ

AMDA College and Conservatory of the Performing Arts (F)

6305 Yucca Street, Los Angeles CA 90028
Identification: 666721
Telephone: (323) 469-3300 Carnegie Class: Not Classified
FAX Number: (323) 469-5246 Calendar System: Semester
URL: www.amda.edu
Established: 1964 Annual Undergrad Tuition & Fees: $31,820
Enrollment: 1,258 Coed
Affiliation or Control: Independent Non-Profit IRS Status: 501(c)3
Highest Offering: Baccalaureate
Program: Liberal Arts And General; Fine Arts Emphasis
Accreditation: THEA

01 Artistic Director/President .... David MARTIN
05 Executive Director/Vice President .... Jan MARTIN
07 Sr Director of Admissions .... Karen JACKSON

American Academy of Dramatic Arts, Los Angeles Campus (G)

1336 N La Brea Avenue, Hollywood CA 90028-7504
Telephone: (323) 464-2777 FICE Identification: 021069
Accreditation: &M, THEA

† Main campus is American Academy of Dramatic Arts in New York, NY.

American Baptist Seminary of the West (H)

2606 Dwight Way, Berkeley CA 94704-3097
County: Alameda FICE Identification: 001120
Unit ID: 108861
Telephone: (510) 841-1905 Carnegie Class: Spec/Faith
FAX Number: (510) 841-2446 Calendar System: Semester
URL: www.absw.edu
Established: 1871 Annual Undergrad Tuition & Fees: $17,030
Enrollment: 96 Coed
Affiliation or Control: American Baptist IRS Status: 501(c)3
Highest Offering: Doctorate
Program: Professional; Religious Emphasis
Accreditation: THEOL

01 President .... Dr. Paul MARTIN
03 Vice President .... Rev. Michelle M. HOLMES
05 Academic Dean .... Dr. LeAnn SNOW FLESHER
10 Chief Financial Officer .... Rev. Michelle M. HOLMES
06 Registrar/Dir Academic Admin .... Ms. Nancy SVENSSON
07 Director of Admissions .... Ms. Marie ONWUBUARIRI

American Career College-Los Angeles (I)

4021 Rosewood Avenue, Los Angeles CA 90004
County: Los Angeles FICE Identification: 022418
Unit ID: 109040
Telephone: (323) 668-7555 Carnegie Class: Assoc/PrivFP
FAX Number: (322) 953-3654 Calendar System: Other
URL: www.americancareercollege.edu
Established: 1978 Annual Undergrad Tuition & Fees: $34,110
Enrollment: 1,743 Coed
Affiliation or Control: Proprietary IRS Status: Proprietary
Highest Offering: Associate Degree
Program: Occupational
Accreditation: ABHES, SURGT, SURTEC

01 Director .... Ms. Lani TOWNSEND

American Career College-Ontario (J)

3130 East Sedona Court, Ontario CA 91764
County: San Bernardino FICE Identification: 039713
Unit ID: 447768
Telephone: (909) 218-3253 Carnegie Class: Assoc/PrivFP
FAX Number: N/A Calendar System: Other
URL: www.americancareercollege.edu
Established: 2006 Annual Undergrad Tuition & Fees: $34,110
Enrollment: 1,574 Coed
Affiliation or Control: Proprietary IRS Status: Proprietary
Highest Offering: Associate Degree
Program: Occupational
Accreditation: ABHES, COARC, SURTEC

01 Campus President .... Mr. Scott WARDALL

American Career College-Orange County (K)

1200 North Magnolia Avenue, Anaheim CA 92801-2607
Telephone: (714) 952-9066 Identification: 667073
Accreditation: ABHES, CAHIIM, COARC, SURGT, SURTEC

† Main campus is American Career College-Los Angeles in Los Angeles, CA.

American College of Traditional Chinese Medicine (L)

455 Arkansas Street, San Francisco CA 94107-2813
County: San Francisco FICE Identification: 030782
Unit ID: 430591
Telephone: (415) 282-7600 Carnegie Class: Spec/Health
FAX Number: (415) 282-0856 Calendar System: Quarter
URL: www.actcm.edu
Established: 1980 Annual Undergrad Tuition & Fees: $15,404
Enrollment: 283 Coed
Affiliation or Control: Independent Non-Profit IRS Status: 501(c)3
Highest Offering: Doctorate; No Lower Division
Program: Professional; Technical Emphasis
Accreditation: ACUP

01 President .... Lixin HUANG
05 VP Academic Affairs/Dean of Faculty .... Bingzeng ZOU
17 Dean Clinical Educ/Dir Acad Assess .... Steve GIVEN
20 Chief Academic & Clinic Adviser .... Stanley LEUNG
06 Registrar .... Jim HABLE
32 Dir Student Affairs/Alumni Rels .... Michael SANO
84 Dir of Recruitment/Enrollment Mgmt .... Yuwen CHIU
10 Controller .... Reno GOLEZ
63 Dean of DAOM Program .... Carla WILSON
20 Asst Dean of Clinical Education .... Jung KIM
20 Asst to the Dean of Master's Pgm .... Richard ALBERTA
24 Director of Learning Resources .... Aileen HUANG
27 Director of Communications .... Cameron GILES
37 Financial Aid Director .... Daryl CULLEN
14 Network Administrator .... Yan LI
08 Library Administrator .... Sara WANG
07 Admissions Counselor .... Yuwen CHIU
88 Academic Advisor .... Andrea NATTA
04 Admn Asst/Asst to President .... Lena LIU
30 Development Officer .... Gigi HU
18 Facilities Manager .... Michael BLOSSOM

American Conservatory Theater (M)

30 Grant Avenue, 6th floor, San Francisco CA 94108-5800
County: San Francisco FICE Identification: 020992
Unit ID: 109086
Telephone: (415) 439-2350 Carnegie Class: Spec/Arts
FAX Number: (415) 834-3210 Calendar System: Semester
URL: www.act-sf.org
Established: 1969 Annual Graduate Tuition & Fees: $20,500
Enrollment: 28 Coed
Affiliation or Control: Independent Non-Profit IRS Status: 501(c)3
Highest Offering: Master's; No Undergraduates
Program: Professional; Fine Arts Emphasis
Accreditation: WC

01 Executive Director .... Ellen RICHARD
88 Artistic Director .... Carey PERLOFF
05 Conservatory Director .... Melissa SMITH
20 Director of Academic Affairs .... Jack SHARRAR
30 Senior Director Development .... Amory SHARPE
37 Director of Financial Aid .... Jerry LOPEZ

American Evangelical University (N)

1818 S. Western Ave #409, Los Angeles CA 90006
County: Los Angeles Identification: 667090
Telephone: (323) 643-0301 Carnegie Class: Not Classified
FAX Number: (323) 643-0302 Calendar System: Semester
URL: www.aeui.org
Established: 2001 Annual Undergrad Tuition & Fees: $4,400
Enrollment: N/A Coed
Affiliation or Control: Independent Non-Profit IRS Status: 501(c)3
Highest Offering: Master's
Program: Technical Emphasis
Accreditation: @BI

01 President .... Dr. Jong KIL RYU
05 Academic Dean .... Dr. Mark SUKKIL YOON
32 Dean of Student Affairs .... Rev. Jason SUNG CHOI
10 CFO .... Rev. Timothy LEE
30 Chief Development Officer .... Dr. Eui JUNG WHANG
08 Director of Library .... Dr. Duk YOUNG WON

American Film Institute Conservatory (O)

2021 N Western Avenue, Los Angeles CA 90027-1657
County: Los Angeles FICE Identification: 022220
Unit ID: 108870
Telephone: (323) 856-7600 Carnegie Class: Spec/Arts
FAX Number: (323) 467-4578 Calendar System: Semester
URL: www.afi.com
Established: 1969 Annual Graduate Tuition & Fees: $43,904
Enrollment: 357 Coed
Affiliation or Control: Independent Non-Profit IRS Status: 501(c)3
Highest Offering: Master's; No Undergraduates
Program: Professional; Fine Arts Emphasis
Accreditation: WC, ART

01 Director American Film Institute .... Mr. Bob GAZZALE
11 Chief Operating Officer .... Ms. Nancy HARRIS
05 Exec Vice Dean of Conservatory .... Mr. Joe PETRICCA
20 Vice Dean for Production/Post Prod .... Mr. Phil LINSON
20 Dean of Conservatory .... Mr. Robert MANDEL
32 Vice Dean Fellow Affairs .... Ms. Carolyn BROOKS
57 Artistic Director .... Mr. Roger BIRNBAUM
06 Registrar .... Ms. Sheryl REINSCHMIDT
15 Manager Human Resources .... Ms. Roschoune FRANKLIN
37 Financial Aid Director .... Ms. Trina RODLER
07 Admissions Manager .... Ms. Karin T. TUCKER
30 Sr Vice President Advancement .... Mr. Tom WEST
08 Librarian .... Mr. Robert VAUGHN
13 Chief Information Officer .... Mr. Paul JACQUES

American Graduate University (P)

733 N Dodsworth Avenue, Covina CA 91724-2408
County: Los Angeles Identification: 666982
Unit ID: 109095
Telephone: (626) 966-4576 Carnegie Class: Not Classified
FAX Number: (626) 915-1709 Calendar System: Other
URL: www.agu.edu
Established: 1969 Annual Graduate Tuition & Fees: $2,475
Enrollment: 1,130 Coed
Affiliation or Control: Proprietary IRS Status: Proprietary
Highest Offering: Master's; No Undergraduates
Program: Professional; Business Emphasis
Accreditation: DETC

01 President/Dir Academic Affairs .... Mr. Paul R. MCDONALD
11 Vice President Administration .... Ms. Marie SIRNEY
32 Director of Student Services .... Ms. Sherrie ANGSTER
06 Registrar .... Ms. Debbie MCDONALD

American Jewish University (Q)

15600 Mulholland Drive, Los Angeles CA 90077-1599
County: Los Angeles FICE Identification: 002741
Unit ID: 116846
Telephone: (310) 476-9777 Carnegie Class: Bac/A&S
FAX Number: (310) 471-1278 Calendar System: Semester
URL: www.ajula.edu
Established: 1947 Annual Undergrad Tuition & Fees: $27,080
Enrollment: 246 Coed
Affiliation or Control: Independent Non-Profit IRS Status: 501(c)3
Highest Offering: Master's
Program: Liberal Arts And General; Teacher Preparatory; Professional
Accreditation: WC

American University of Armenia (A)

300 Lakeside Drive, 12th Floor, Oakland CA 94612

County: Alameda — Identification: 666013
Telephone: (510) 987-9452 — Carnegie Class: Not Classified
FAX Number: (510) 208-3576 — Calendar System: Semester
URL: www.aua.am
Established: 1991 — Annual Graduate Tuition & Fees: $6,400
Enrollment: 302 — Coed
Affiliation or Control: Independent Non-Profit — IRS Status: 501(c)3
Highest Offering: Master's; No Undergraduates
Program: Professional
Accreditation: WC

01 President .... Dr. Bruce M. BOGHOSIAN
06 Associate Registrar .... Chaghig ARZROUNI-CHAHINIAN

American University of Health Sciences (B)

1600 E Hill St Building #1, Signal Hill CA 90755

County: Los Angeles — FICE Identification: 032253
Unit ID: 433004
Telephone: (562) 988-2278 — Carnegie Class: Assoc/PrivFP4
FAX Number: (562) 988-1791 — Calendar System: Quarter
URL: www.auhs.edu
Established: 1994 — Annual Undergrad Tuition & Fees: $32,000
Enrollment: 252 — Coed
Affiliation or Control: Proprietary — IRS Status: Proprietary
Highest Offering: Master's
Program: Professional
Accreditation: ACICS, NURSE

01 President .... Mr. Philip G. WOLFSON
11 Chief Operating Officer .... Pastor Gregory A. JOHNSON

Anaheim University (C)

1240 S State College Blvd, Ste 110,
Anaheim CA 92806-5152

County: Orange — Identification: 666651
Telephone: (714) 772-3330 — Carnegie Class: Not Classified
FAX Number: (714) 772-3331 — Calendar System: Other
URL: www.anaheim.edu
Established: 1996 — Annual Graduate Tuition & Fees: N/A
Enrollment: 350 — Coed
Affiliation or Control: Proprietary — IRS Status: Proprietary
Highest Offering: Doctorate; No Undergraduates
Program: Professional
Accreditation: DETC

07 Director of Admissions .... Ms. Kate STRAUSS

Angeles College (D)

3440 Wilshire Blvd, Ste 310, Los Angeles CA 90010

County: Los Angeles — FICE Identification: 041604
Unit ID: 457299
Telephone: (213) 487-2211 — Carnegie Class: Not Classified
FAX Number: (213) 487-2299 — Calendar System: Semester
URL: www.angelescollege.edu
Established: — Annual Undergrad Tuition & Fees: $26,720
Enrollment: 97 — Coed
Affiliation or Control: Proprietary — IRS Status: Proprietary
Highest Offering: Baccalaureate
Program: Occupational; 2-Year Principally Bachelor's Creditable
Accreditation: ABHES

01 Chief Operating Officer .... Ms. Teresa KRAUSE

Angeles College-Garden Grove (E)

9618 Garden Grove Blvd, Suite 220,
Garden Grove CA 92844

Telephone: (714) 636-2211 — Identification: 770518
Accreditation: ABHES

† Main campus is Angeles College in Los Angeles, CA.

Antelope Valley College (F)

3041 W Avenue K, Lancaster CA 93536-5426

County: Los Angeles — FICE Identification: 001113
Unit ID: 109350
Telephone: (661) 722-6300 — Carnegie Class: Assoc/Pub-S-SC
FAX Number: (661) 722-6333 — Calendar System: Semester
URL: www.avc.edu
Established: 1929 — Annual Undergrad Tuition & Fees (In-District): $1,144
Enrollment: 13,941 — Coed
Affiliation or Control: State/Local — IRS Status: 501(c)3
Highest Offering: Associate Degree
Program: Occupational; 2-Year Principally Bachelor's Creditable
Accreditation: WJ, COARC, RAD

01 President/Superintendent .... Mr. Edward T. KNUDSON
05 VP Academic Affairs .... Ms. Sharon LOWRY
32 VP Student Services .... Dr. Erin E. VINES
10 Vice Pres Administrative Services .... Ms. Mazie BREWINGTON
15 Vice President Human Resources .... Mr. Mark BRYANT
07 Dean Enrollment Svcs & Counseling .... Ms. LaDonna TRIMBLE
88 Director Disabled Students .... Dr. Louis LUCERO
26 Director Public Relations .... Mr. Steve STANDERFER
18 Dir Facilities Services .... Mr. Doug JENSEN
13 Director Information Technology .... Mr. Rick SHAW
30 Dir Inst Advancement & Foundation .... Ms. Bridget RAZO
46 Director Inst Research & Planning .... Vacant
96 Buyer .... Ms. Angela MUSIAL
37 Director Financial Aid .... Ms. Sherrie PADILLA
68 Dean PE/Athlet/Visual and Perf Arts .... Mr. Newton CHELETTE
79 Dean of Inst Res/Language Arts .... Dr. Charlotte FORTE-PARNELL
83 Dean Soc & Beh Sci/Bus/Comp Stds .... Dr. Tom O'NEIL
38 Dean Counseling & Matriculation .... Vacant
76 Dean Health Sciences/Tech Ed .... Dr. Karen COWELL
35 Dean of Student Develop & Services .... Dr. Jill ZIMMERMAN
75 Dean of Technical Education .... Vacant
81 Dean of Math/Science & Engineering .... Dr. Les UHAZY

Antioch University Los Angeles (G)

400 Corporate Pointe, Culver City CA 90230

Telephone: (310) 578-1080 — Identification: 666236
Accreditation: &NH

† Main campus is Antioch University in Yellow Springs, OH.

Antioch University Santa Barbara (H)

602 Anacapa Street, Santa Barbara CA 93101

Telephone: (805) 962-8179 — Identification: 666231
Accreditation: &NH

† Main campus is Antioch University in Yellow Springs, OH.

Apollos University (I)

17011 Beach Blvd, Ste 900, Huntington Beach CA 92647

County: Orange — Identification: 667096
Telephone: (714) 841-6252 — Carnegie Class: Not Classified
FAX Number: (866) 287-1938 — Calendar System: Quarter
URL: www.apollos-university.edu
Established: 2005 — Annual Undergrad Tuition & Fees: $5,570
Enrollment: N/A — Coed
Affiliation or Control: Proprietary — IRS Status: Proprietary
Highest Offering: Doctorate
Program: Liberal Arts And General; Business Emphasis
Accreditation: DETC

01 President & CEO .... Dr. Paul EIDSON

APT College (J)

1939 Palomar Oaks Way, Suite A,
Carlsbad CA 92011-1311

County: San Diego — Identification: 666245
Telephone: (800) 431-8488 — Carnegie Class: Not Classified
FAX Number: (888) 431-8588 — Calendar System: Semester
URL: www.aptc.edu
Established: 1993 — Annual Undergrad Tuition & Fees: $5,500
Enrollment: 1,500 — Coed
Affiliation or Control: Proprietary — IRS Status: Proprietary
Highest Offering: Associate Degree
Program: Occupational; 2-Year Principally Bachelor's Creditable
Accreditation: DETC

01 President/Chief Executive Officer .... Mr. Steven W. BLUME

Argosy University, Inland Empire (K)

3401 Centre Lake Drive, Suite 200, Ontario CA 91761

Telephone: (909) 472-0800 — Identification: 666007
Accreditation: &WC

† Main campus is Argosy University, Orange County in Orange, CA.

Argosy University, Los Angeles (L)

5230 Pacific Concourse Drive, Los Angeles CA 90045

Telephone: (310) 531-9700 — Identification: 666011
Accreditation: &WC

† Main campus is Argosy University, Orange County in Orange, CA.

Argosy University, Orange County (M)

601 South Lewis Street, Orange CA 92868

County: Orange — FICE Identification: 021799
Unit ID: 436438
Telephone: (714) 620-3700 — Carnegie Class: DRU
FAX Number: (714) 620-3802 — Calendar System: Semester
URL: www.argosy.edu/orangecounty
Established: 1999 — Annual Undergrad Tuition & Fees: $13,488
Enrollment: 742 — Coed
Affiliation or Control: Proprietary — IRS Status: Proprietary
Highest Offering: Doctorate
Program: Professional
Accreditation: WC, CLPSY

01 University President .... Dr. Craig D. SWENSON
05 Vice President of Academic Affairs .... Vacant
32 GVP West .... Mr. Michael FALOTICO
32 GVP East .... Dr. William BROWN
03 Executive Vice President .... Mr. Eric EVENSON
07 VP Admissions .... Mr. Jeff CROSS
26 VP of Marketing .... Mr. Daron RODRIGUEZ
15 Vice President Human Resources .... Ms. Sherl NESHIEM
32 VP Academic Ops & Student Services .... Ms. Julie JOHNSON
106 VP for Online & Distance Learning .... Ms. Kate NOONE
10 Vice President of Finance .... Mr. Ken STEVENS
50 Dean College of Business .... Ms. Cynthia LARSON
83 Dean Psychology and Behav Sciences .... Vacant
76 Dean College of Health Sciences .... Ms. Kristin BENSON
53 Dean College of Education .... Vacant
97 Dean Undergraduate Studies .... Ms. Ruki JAYARAMAN
12 Campus President Twin Cities .... Mr. Scott TJADEN
12 Campus President Atlanta .... Dr. Ronald SWANSON
12 Campus President Dallas .... Mr. Ronald HYSON
12 Campus President Hawaii .... Dr. Warren EVANS
12 Campus President Washington D.C. .... Mr. David EREKSON
12 Campus President Seattle .... Mr. Tom DYER
12 Campus President Sarasota .... Vacant
12 Campus President Orange County .... Dr. James COX
12 Campus President Schaumburg .... Mr. James CHITWOOD
12 Campus President Tampa .... Dr. Patricia MEREDITH
12 Campus President Phoenix .... Mr. Bart LERNER
12 Campus Pres San Francisco Bay Area .... Dr. Lucille SANSING
12 Campus President Inland Empire .... Dr. James COX
12 Campus President Nashville .... Dr. Sandra WISE
12 Int Campus President San Diego .... Dr. James COX
12 Campus President Los Angeles .... Dr. James COX
12 Campus President Salt Lake City .... Vacant
12 Campus President Denver .... Dr. Marcia BANKIRER

† Main Campus and HQ moved from Chicago, IL to Orange, CA

Argosy University, San Diego (N)

1615 Murray Canyon Rd, Suite 100,
San Diego CA 92108-4423

Telephone: (619) 321-3000 — Identification: 666034
Accreditation: &WC

† Main campus is Argosy University, Orange County in Orange, CA.

Argosy University, San Francisco Bay Area (O)

1005 Atlantic Avenue, Alameda CA 94501-1148

Telephone: (510) 217-4700 — Identification: 666081
Accreditation: &WC, #CLPSY

† Main campus is Argosy University, Orange County in Orange, CA.

Art Center College of Design (P)

1700 Lida Street, Pasadena CA 91103-1999

County: Los Angeles — FICE Identification: 001116
Unit ID: 109651
Telephone: (626) 396-2200 — Carnegie Class: Spec/Arts
FAX Number: N/A — Calendar System: Semester
URL: www.artcenter.edu
Established: 1930 — Annual Undergrad Tuition & Fees: $36,480
Enrollment: 1,720 — Coed
Affiliation or Control: Independent Non-Profit — IRS Status: 501(c)3
Highest Offering: Master's
Program: Professional
Accreditation: WC, ART

01 President .... Dr. Lorne M. BUCHMAN
10 Sr VP/Chief Financial Officer .... Mr. Rich HALUSCHAK
05 Provost .... Mr. Fred FEHLAU
30 Sr VP Development/External Affairs .... Ms. Arwen DUFFY
18 Senior Vice President Operations .... Mr. George FALARDEAU
07 VP Admissions/Enrollment Mgmt .... Ms. Kit BARON
32 Dean of Students .... Mr. Jeffrey HOFFMAN
88 VP Exhibitions .... Mr. Steve NOWLIN
08 VP Library Director .... Vacant
13 VP Information Technology .... Ms. Theresa ZIX
26 Assoc VP Marketing & Communication .... Ms. Wendy SHATTUCK
15 Executive Director Human Resources .... Ms. Nancy TORRES DUGGAN
21 Controller .... Ms. Diane WITTENBERG
37 Managing Director Financial Aid .... Ms. Victoria AMEZCUA
29 Director of Alumni Affairs .... Ms. Kristine BOWNE
06 Director of Enrollment & Registrar .... Mr. William GARTRELL
09 Director of Institutional Research .... Ms. Esmeralda NAVA
19 Dir Environmental Health & Safety .... Ms. Vicky MCCORMICK
102 Director Foundation Relations .... Mr. Darryl MORI
36 Director of Career Development .... Ms. Cathy KARRY
18 Director of Facilities .... Mr. Jess RIVAS
96 Director of Purchasing .... Ms. Monica MATSUO

The Art Institute of California, A College of Argosy University - Hollywood (Q)

5250 Lankershim Boulevard, North Hollywood CA 91601

Telephone: (213) 251-3636 — FICE Identification: 031254
Accreditation: &WC

† Main campus is Argosy University, Orange County in Orange, CA.

The Art Institute of California, A College of Argosy University - Inland Empire (R)

674 East Brier Drive, San Bernardino CA 92408-2800

Telephone: (909) 915-2100 — FICE Identification: 016471
Accreditation: &WC

† Main campus is Argosy University, Orange County in Orange, CA.

The Art Institute of California, A College of Argosy University - Los Angeles (A)

2900 31st Street, Santa Monica CA 90405-3035
Telephone: (310) 752-4700 Identification: 666045
Accreditation: &WC, ACFEI, CIDA

† Main campus is Argosy University, Orange County in Orange, CA.

The Art Institute of California, A College of Argosy University - Orange County (B)

3601 W Sunflower Avenue, Santa Ana CA 92704-7931
Telephone: (714) 830-0200 Identification: 666182
Accreditation: &WC, CIDA

† Main campus is Argosy University, Orange County in Orange, CA.

The Art Institute of California, A College of Argosy University - Sacramento (C)

2850 Gateway Oaks Drive, Suite 100,
Sacramento CA 95833-4348
Telephone: (916) 830-6320 Identification: 666619
Accreditation: &WC, ACFEI

† Main campus is Argosy University, Orange County in Orange, CA.

The Art Institute of California, A College of Argosy University - San Diego (D)

7650 Mission Valley Road, San Diego CA 92108-4423
Telephone: (858) 598-1200 FICE Identification: 023276
Accreditation: &WC, ACFEI, CIDA

† Main campus is Argosy University, Orange County in Orange, CA.

The Art Institute of California, A College of Argosy University - San Francisco (E)

1170 Market Street, San Francisco CA 94102-4908
Telephone: (888) 493-3261 FICE Identification: 007236
Accreditation: &WC

† Main campus is Argosy University, Orange County in Orange, CA.

The Art Institute of California, A College of Argosy University - Sunnyvale (F)

1120 Kifer Road, Sunnyvale CA 94086-5303
Telephone: (408) 962-6400 Identification: 666620
Accreditation: &WC

† Main campus is Argosy University, Orange County in Orange, CA.

Ashdown College of Health Sciences (G)

101 E. Redlands Boulevard, Ste 285, Redlands CA 92373
County: San Bernardino FICE Identification: 041789
Unit ID: 461777
Telephone: (909) 793-4263 Carnegie Class: Not Classified
FAX Number: (909) 793-5763 Calendar System: Semester
URL: www.ashdowncollege.edu
Established: 2003 Annual Undergrad Tuition & Fees: $9,750
Enrollment: 16 Coed
Affiliation or Control: Proprietary IRS Status: Proprietary
Highest Offering: Associate Degree
Program: Occupational
Accreditation: COE

01 CEO/Director .... Mr. William HERKELRATH

Azusa Pacific University (H)

901 E Alosta Avenue, Azusa CA 91702-7000
County: Los Angeles FICE Identification: 001117
Unit ID: 109785
Telephone: (626) 969-3434 Carnegie Class: DRU
FAX Number: (626) 969-7180 Calendar System: Semester
URL: www.apu.edu
Established: 1899 Annual Undergrad Tuition & Fees: $39,946
Enrollment: 10,221 Coed
Affiliation or Control: Independent Non-Profit IRS Status: 501(c)3
Highest Offering: Doctorate
Program: Liberal Arts And General; Teacher Preparatory; Professional
Accreditation: WC, ART, CLPSY, IACBE, MUS, NURSE, PTA, SW, TED, THEOL

01 President .... Dr. Jon R. WALLACE
05 Provost .... Dr. Mark STANTON
26 Exec Vice Pres External Affairs .... Mr. David E. BIXBY
11 Exec Vice President Administration .... Mr. John C. REYNOLDS
32 Senior Vice Pres for Student Life .... Dr. Terry FRANSON
10 Vice President Business Affairs/CFO .... Mr. Bob L. JOHANSEN
43 VP Legal Affs/Cmty Rels/Gen Counsel .... Mr. Mark DICKERSON
13 Vice President/CIO .... Mr. Don DAVIS
84 VP Grad/Nontrdtnl Enroll/Stdnt Svc .... Mrs. Heather PETRIDIS
84 VP for Enrollment Mangement .... Mr. David DUFAULT-HUNTER
58 Vice Provost Graduate Programs .... Dr. Diane GUIDO
20 Vice Provost Undergraduate Programs .... Dr. Vicky BOWDEN
35 AVP Student Life/Chief Judicial Ofc .... Mr. Willie HAMLETT
88 Assoc VP University Services .... Mr. Roger HODSDON
26 VP University Relations .... Mr. David PECK
49 Int Dean College Liberal Arts/Sci .... Dr. Don ISAAK
83 Dean School Behav/Applied Sciences .... Dr. Robert WELSH
50 Int Dean School of Business Mgmt .... Dr. Rose LIEGLER
53 Dean School of Education .... Dr. Anita HENCK
73 Dean Haggard School of Theology .... Dr. Scott DANIELS
64 Dean College of Music and the Arts .... Dr. Stephen JOHNSON
66 Dean School of Nursing .... Dr. Aja LESH
51 Dean Ctr Adult/Professional Studies .... Dr. Fred GARLETT
88 Dean Honors College .... Dr. David WEEKS
35 Assoc Dean Students/Dir Student Act .... Mrs. Shino SIMONS
15 Exec Director Human Resources .... Mr. John BAUGUS
30 Assoc VP University Advancement .... Mrs. Louise FURROW
21 Executive Director Finance .... Mrs. Joyce WILLIAMS
42 Campus Pastor .... Mr. Woody MOORWOOD
37 Dir Graduate Student Financial Svcs .... Mrs. Michelle JOHNSON
06 Registrar-Graduate .... Mrs. Norma MOCABEE
06 Associate Registrar-Undergraduate .... Ms. Mona MIKHAIL
29 Director Alumni Relations .... Mr. Craig WALLACE
09 Director Acad Info Mgmt Analysis .... Vacant
41 Director Athletics .... Mr. Gary PINE
38 Director Counseling Center .... Dr. Bill FIALA
37 Director UG/APS Student Finan Svcs .... Mr. Todd ROSS
18 Director Facilities Management .... Mr. Dennis ROBBINS
07 Director Undergraduate Admissions .... Mr. David BURKE
36 Director Career Services .... Ms. Lynn PEARSON
28 Exec Dir Diversity Planning/Assess .... Mr. Richard MARTINEZ
96 Purchasing Manager .... Mrs. Jo Ann BENGEL

Barstow Community College District (I)

2700 Barstow Road, Barstow CA 92311-6699
County: San Bernardino FICE Identification: 001119
Unit ID: 109907
Telephone: (760) 252-2411 Carnegie Class: Assoc/Pub-S-SC
FAX Number: (760) 252-1875 Calendar System: Semester
URL: www.barstow.edu
Established: 1959 Annual Undergrad Tuition & Fees (In-District): $1,104
Enrollment: 3,274 Coed
Affiliation or Control: State/Local IRS Status: 501(c)3
Highest Offering: Associate Degree
Program: Occupational; 2-Year Principally Bachelor's Creditable
Accreditation: WJ

01 Superintendent/President .... Dr. Deborah DITHOMAS
04 Exec Assistant to the President .... Mrs. Michelle HENDERSON
10 Vice President Administrative Svcs .... Mr. Virgil STANFORD
05 Vice President Academic Affairs .... Mr. Stephen B. EATON
32 Vice President Student Services .... Mr. James DANIELS
16 Vice President Human Resources .... Ms. Trinda BEST
09 Dean Research Dev & Planning .... Vacant
103 Dean Workforce & Economic Dev .... Mr. Ken EAVES
49 Interim Dean of Instruction .... Ms. Penny SHREVE
27 Director Public Information .... Ms. Maureen O. STOKES
18 Interim Director M&O .... Mr. Richard HERNANDEZ
21 Director Fiscal Services .... Ms. Shawna L. ROBBINS
84 Director Enrollment Services .... Ms. Heather CALDON
41 Interim Athletic Director .... Dr. Michael KARPEL
35 Director Student Dev & Outreach .... Mrs. Joann GARCIA
88 Director CTE Grants .... Ms. Sandra THOMAS
88 Director Military Programs .... Mr. Jerry PETERS
88 Dir Special Pgms & Svcs .... Vacant
40 Bookstore Manager .... Mrs. Kimberly YOUNG
21 Budget Analyst .... Mrs. Debbie WYNNE

Bergin University of Canine Studies (J)

5860 Labath Avenue, Rohnert Park CA 94928
County: Sonoma FICE Identification: 041763
Unit ID: 461643
Telephone: (707) 545-3647 Carnegie Class: Not Classified
FAX Number: (707) 545-0800 Calendar System: Semester
URL: www.berginu.edu
Established: 1991 Annual Undergrad Tuition & Fees: $7,911
Enrollment: 38 Coed
Affiliation or Control: Independent Non-Profit IRS Status: 501(c)3
Highest Offering: Master's
Program: Occupational
Accreditation: ACICS

01 President .... Dr. Bonita M. BERGIN

Bethesda University of California (K)

730 N Euclid Street, Anaheim CA 92801-4115
County: Orange FICE Identification: 032663
Unit ID: 110060
Telephone: (714) 517-1945 Carnegie Class: Spec/Faith
FAX Number: (714) 683-1440 Calendar System: Semester
URL: www.buc.edu
Established: 1976 Annual Undergrad Tuition & Fees: $7,005
Enrollment: 355 Coed
Affiliation or Control: Independent Non-Profit IRS Status: 501(c)3
Highest Offering: Doctorate
Program: Religious Emphasis
Accreditation: BI, TRACS

01 Vice President .... Pastor Dong Hwan LIM
05 Chief Academic Officer .... Dr. Hyo In KIM
10 Chief Financial Officer .... Dr. Young Joon KIM
08 Head Librarian .... Ms. Ho K. WOO
07 Director of Admissions .... Ms. Jee Won HA
06 Registrar .... Rev. Sung Keun PARK

Biola University (L)

13800 Biola Avenue, La Mirada CA 90639-0001
County: Los Angeles FICE Identification: 001122
Unit ID: 110097
Telephone: (562) 903-6000 Carnegie Class: DRU
FAX Number: (562) 903-4748 Calendar System: 4/1/4
URL: www.biola.edu
Established: 1908 Annual Undergrad Tuition & Fees: $31,004
Enrollment: 6,302 Coed
Affiliation or Control: Independent Non-Profit IRS Status: 501(c)3
Highest Offering: Doctorate
Program: Liberal Arts And General; Teacher Preparatory; Professional
Accreditation: WC, ACBSP, ART, CLPSY, MUS, NURSE, THEOL

01 President .... Dr. Barry H. COREY
05 Provost/Sr Vice President .... Dr. David P. NYSTROM
10 Vice Pres Business/Financial Affs .... Mr. Michael PIERCE
30 Vice President Advancement .... Dr. Adam MORRIS
11 Vice President University Services .... Mr. Gregory R. BALSANO
32 Vice Pres Student Dev/Univ Plng/IT .... Dr. Chris GRACE
84 Vice Pres Enrollment Management .... Mr. Greg VAUGHAN
26 Vice Pres University Comm & Mktg .... Mrs. Irene NELLER
20 Vice Provost/Undergraduate Educ .... Dr. Patricia PIKE
20 Vice Provost/Fac Dev & Univ Assess .... Vacant
28 Vice Provost/Multi-Eth & Cross Cult .... Dr. Doretha O'QUINN
73 Dean Talbot School Theology .... Dr. Clinton E. ARNOLD
83 Dean Rosemead School Psychology .... Dr. Clark D. CAMPBELL
88 Dean Cook Sch Intercultural Studies .... Dr. Douglas PENNOYER
53 Dean School of Education .... Dr. June HETZEL
08 Dean of the Library .... Dr. Rodney M. VLIET
42 Dean of Spiritual Development .... Dr. Todd PICKETT
35 Dean of Students .... Mr. Danny PASCHALL
06 Dean Academic Records/Inst Research .... Mr. Ken GILSON
87 Director Summer Session & Interterm .... Dr. Pete MENJARES
15 Sr Director Human Resources .... Mr. Ronald G. MOORADIAN
46 Sr Dir Financial Planning/Opers .... Ms. Sandie WEAVER
13 Sr Director Information Technology .... Mr. Gary WYTCHERLEY
29 Sr Director Alumni & Friends .... Mr. Richard BEE
37 Director Financial Aid .... Mr. Jonathan CHOY
21 Director Financial Mgmt/Reporting .... Mr. David KOONTZ
19 Director Campus Safety .... Mr. John O. OJEISEKHOBA
90 Director Technology Services .... Mr. Steven R. EARLE
36 Director Career Services .... Ms. Jeanie JANG
41 Athletic Director .... Dr. David HOLMQUIST
40 Manager Bookstore .... Mr. Harry EDWARDS
24 Supervisor Media Center .... Ms. Jill WATSON
18 Sr Director Facilities Services .... Mr. Brian PHILLIPS
38 Director Student Counseling .... Dr. Melanie TAYLOR
96 Director of Purchasing .... Mr. Jim SAMPLES
09 Dean of University Assessment .... Dr. Deborah TAYLOR

Brandman University (M)

16355 Laguna Canyon Road, Irvine CA 92618
County: Orange FICE Identification: 041618
Unit ID: 262086
Telephone: (949) 753-4774 Carnegie Class: Master's L
FAX Number: (714) 753-7875 Calendar System: Other
URL: www.brandman.edu
Established: 1958 Annual Undergrad Tuition & Fees: $15,000
Enrollment: 6,785 Coed
Affiliation or Control: Independent Non-Profit IRS Status: 501(c)3
Highest Offering: Doctorate
Program: Liberal Arts And General
Accreditation: WC, NURSE

01 Chancellor .... Dr. Gary BRAHM
12 Campus Director .... Ms. Jan HARTZ
05 Associate Dean of Education .... Ms. Patricia CLARK-WHITE
07 Director of Admissions .... Ms. Leticia ESPINOZA

† A member of the Chapman University System.

Bristol University (N)

2390 E Orangewood Avenue, Suite 485,
Anaheim CA 92806
County: Orange FICE Identification: 033083
Unit ID: 397270
Telephone: (714) 542-8086 Carnegie Class: Not Classified
FAX Number: (714) 245-2425 Calendar System: Semester
URL: www.bristoluniversity.edu
Established: 1991 Annual Undergrad Tuition & Fees: $6,800
Enrollment: 37 Coed
Affiliation or Control: Proprietary IRS Status: Proprietary
Highest Offering: Master's
Program: Occupational; 2-Year Principally Bachelor's Creditable; Business Emphasis
Accreditation: ACICS

01 President .... Dr. Paul MCGURR
03 Vice President Compliance .... Mr. Luke MARTIN
05 Chief Academic Officer .... Vacant
37 Financial Aid Director .... Mr. Bobby PEPITO

Brooks Institute (A)

27 Cota, Santa Barbara CA 93101
County: Santa Barbara FICE Identification: 001123
Unit ID: 110185
Telephone: (888) 304-3456 Carnegie Class: Spec/Arts
FAX Number: (805) 585-8001 Calendar System: Semester
URL: www.brooks.edu
Established: 1945 Annual Undergrad Tuition & Fees: $20,181
Enrollment: 650 Coed
Affiliation or Control: Proprietary IRS Status: Proprietary
Highest Offering: Master's
Program: Professional; Technical Emphasis
Accreditation: @WC, ACICS

01 President ... Susan KIRKMAN
05 Director of Academic Affairs ... Amanda BREY
10 Director of Finance and Operations ... Steve HAMAKER
07 Vice President Admissions ... Maggie BALDERAS
88 Dept Chair for Film & Communication ... Gail FISHER
36 Dir Career Services ... Laura NIELSEN
06 Registrar ... April REYES
31 Community Outreach ... Mark STANLEY
91 Director of Information Technology ... Greg LAWLER
08 Librarian ... Donna BURR

Brooks Institute (B)

5301 North Ventura Avenue, Ventura CA 93001-1023
Telephone: (805) 585-8000 Identification: 666250
Accreditation: @WC, ACICS

† Main campus is Brooks Institute in Santa Barbara, CA.

Bryan College (C)

2317 Gold Meadow Way, Gold River CA 95670-4443
County: Sacramento FICE Identification: 033993
Unit ID: 439826
Telephone: (916) 649-2400 Carnegie Class: Assoc/PrivFP
FAX Number: (916) 641-8649 Calendar System: Quarter
URL: www.bryancollege.edu
Established: 1996 Annual Undergrad Tuition & Fees: $51,788
Enrollment: 544 Coed
Affiliation or Control: Proprietary IRS Status: Proprietary
Highest Offering: Associate Degree
Program: Occupational; 2-Year Principally Bachelor's Creditable; Technical Emphasis
Accreditation: ACCSC

01 President ... Vacant
05 Director of Education ... Ms. Christine ZMIJEWSKI
29 Dir of Student & Alumni Outreach ... Mr. Jeff HORTON
07 Director of Admissions ... Ms. Orquedia CHAVEZ
37 Director Student Financial Aid ... Mr. Ramiro ONTIVEROS
06 Registrar ... Ms. Heather GARAT

Bryan College (D)

3580 Wilshire Boulevard, Suite 400,
Los Angeles CA 90010
County: Los Angeles FICE Identification: 007164
Unit ID: 110219
Telephone: (213) 484-8850 Carnegie Class: Assoc/PrivFP
FAX Number: (213) 483-3936 Calendar System: Semester
URL: www.bryancollege.edu
Established: 1940 Annual Undergrad Tuition & Fees: $11,695
Enrollment: 1,391 Coed
Affiliation or Control: Proprietary IRS Status: Proprietary
Highest Offering: Master's
Program: Occupational; 2-Year Principally Bachelor's Creditable
Accreditation: ACICS

01 President ... Mr. John KOLACINSKI

Bryman College-LA Wilshire (E)

3460 Wilshire Blvd, Ste 500, Los Angeles CA 90010
County: Los Angeles FICE Identification: 007606
Unit ID: 119368
Telephone: (213) 388-9950 Carnegie Class: Assoc/PrivFP
FAX Number: (213) 388-9907 Calendar System: Quarter
URL: bryman.edu
Established: 1960 Annual Undergrad Tuition & Fees: $14,994
Enrollment: 279 Coed
Affiliation or Control: Proprietary IRS Status: Proprietary
Highest Offering: Associate Degree
Program: Occupational
Accreditation: ACCSC

01 President ... Mr. Rob LADENDECKER

Butte College (F)

3536 Butte Campus Drive, Oroville CA 95965-8399
County: Butte FICE Identification: 008073
Unit ID: 110246
Telephone: (530) 895-2511 Carnegie Class: Assoc/Pub-R-L
FAX Number: (530) 895-2345 Calendar System: Semester
URL: www.butte.edu
Established: 1966 Annual Undergrad Tuition & Fees (In-District): $1,334
Enrollment: 12,290 Coed
Affiliation or Control: State/Local IRS Status: 501(c)3
Highest Offering: Associate Degree
Program: Occupational; 2-Year Principally Bachelor's Creditable
Accreditation: WJ, COARC, EMT

01 Superintendent/President ... Dr. Kimberly PERRY
05 Vice Pres Student Learning ... Dr. Samia YAQUB
10 VP Administrative Service/CBO ... Mr. Andrew SULESKI
45 Vice President Planning & Info ... Mr. Les JAURON
32 Vice President Student Services ... Mr. Allen RENVILLE
20 Dean Student Learning ... Mr. David DANIELSON
20 Dean Student Learning ... Ms. Kam BULL
20 Dean Student Learning ... Ms. Denise ADAMS
20 Dean Student Learning ... Dr. Luozhu CEN
37 Director Financial Aid/Vet Svcs ... Ms. Carolyn STEPHEN
15 Director Human Resources ... Vacant
18 Dir Facilities Planning/Management ... Mr. Ken ALBRIGHT
09 Director of Institutional Research ... Dr. Baba ADAM
07 Director Admissions/Records ... Mr. Clinton SLAUGHTER
12 Director Chico/Glenn Centers ... Mr. Rudy FLORES
103 Exec Dir Econ Workforce Development ... Ms. Linda ZORN
30 Director Institutional Advancement ... Ms. Lisa DELABY
41 Dir Physical Education/Athletics ... Mr. Craig RIGSBEE
13 Director Information Services ... Vacant
21 Director Business Services ... Mr. Trevor STEWART
38 Coordinator of Counseling ... Ms. Susan CAREY

Cabrillo College (G)

6500 Soquel Drive, Aptos CA 95003-3194
County: Santa Cruz FICE Identification: 001124
Unit ID: 110334
Telephone: (831) 479-6100 Carnegie Class: Assoc/Pub-R-L
FAX Number: (831) 479-6425 Calendar System: Semester
URL: www.cabrillo.edu
Established: 1959 Annual Undergrad Tuition & Fees (In-District): $1,148
Enrollment: 13,600 Coed
Affiliation or Control: State/Local IRS Status: 501(c)3
Highest Offering: Associate Degree
Program: Occupational; 2-Year Principally Bachelor's Creditable; Business Emphasis
Accreditation: WJ, DH, MAC, RAD

01 Superintendent/President ... Dr. Laurel JONES
05 Asst Supt/Vice Pres Instruction ... Dr. Kathleen WELCH
10 Asst Supt/VP Administrative Svcs ... Ms. Victoria LEWIS
32 Asst Supt/Vice Pres Student Svcs ... Dr. Dennis BAILEY-FOUGNIER
35 Dean Student Services ... Mr. Sesario ESCOTO
13 Information Technology Director ... Dr. Dan BORGES
08 Librarian ... Mr. Georg ROMERO
26 Director Marketing & Communications ... Ms. Kristin FABOS
15 Director Personnel/Human Resources ... Ms. Loree MCCAWLEY
21 Director Business Services ... Mr. Graciano MENDOZA
07 Director of Enrollment Services ... Ms. Tama BOLTON
09 Dir Planning/Research/Knowledge Sys ... Mr. Terrence WILLETT
18 Dir Facilities Planning/Plant Ops ... Mr. Joe NUGENT
40 Bookstore Manager ... Ms. Linda CULLENS
102 Executive Director Foundation ... Ms. Melinda SILVERSTEIN
37 Asst Dir Financial Aid/Scholarships ... Ms. Tootie TZIMBAL
38 Dn Stdnt Counseling/Educ Spprt Svcs ... Ms. Margery REGALADO RODRIGUEZ
96 Dir Purchasing/Contracts/Risk Mgmt ... Mr. Michael ROBINS

California Baptist University (H)

8432 Magnolia Avenue, Riverside CA 92504-3297
County: Riverside FICE Identification: 001125
Unit ID: 110361
Telephone: (951) 689-5771 Carnegie Class: Master's L
FAX Number: (951) 351-1808 Calendar System: Semester
URL: www.calbaptist.edu
Established: 1950 Annual Undergrad Tuition & Fees: $28,122
Enrollment: 6,031 Coed
Affiliation or Control: Southern Baptist IRS Status: 501(c)3
Highest Offering: Master's
Program: Liberal Arts And General; Teacher Preparatory; Professional
Accreditation: WC, ACBSP, ENG, MUS, NURSE

01 President ... Dr. Ronald L. ELLIS
04 Admin Asst to the President ... Ms. Ann CRAMER
10 Vice President for Finance & Admin ... Mr. Mark HOWE
21 Director of Financial Services ... Mr. Calvin SPARKMAN
21 Director of Accounting ... Ms. Jackie GONZALES
15 Director of Human Resources ... Ms. Julie FRESQUEZ
32 VP Enrollment & Student Services ... Mr. Kent DACUS
35 Dean of Students ... Mr. Anthony LAMMONS
39 Director of Residence Life ... Mr. Daron HUBBERT
85 Director of International Students ... Mr. Bryan DAVIS
36 Director Career Services ... Mrs. Kushi JONES
19 Director of Public Safety ... Mr. Jim WALTERS
84 Assoc Dean Graduate Enrollment ... Ms. Gail RONVEAUX
84 Assoc Dean Enrollment Services ... Mr. Allen JOHNSON
27 Vice Pres Marketing & Communication ... Dr. Mark A. WYATT
88 Director of Conferences & Events ... Mr. Coreylon POLK
26 Director of Marketing ... Mr. Jeremy ZIMMERMAN
26 Director of Communications ... Dr. Katherine CHUTE
30 Vice Pres Institution Advancement ... Dr. Arthur CLEVELAND
44 Director of Annual Giving ... Mr. Brian BUNNELL
102 Grants Administrator ... Vacant
29 Director Alumni & Parent Relations ... Vacant
106 Vice Pres for Online & Prof Studies ... Dr. David POOLE
13 Assoc Vice Pres of Technology ... Dr. Tran HONG
05 Provost ... Dr. Jonathan K. PARKER
45 Assoc Provost Institution Planning ... Dr. Neal MCBRIDE
20 Assoc Provost Administration ... Dr. Tracy WARD
108 Director of Assessment ... Mr. Phil MARTINEZ
24 Dir of Instructional Technology ... Mr. Keith CASTILLO
20 Dean of Academic Services ... Mr. Jeffrey BARNES
20 Vice Provost & Accreditation Liason ... Dr. Dawn Ellen JACOBS
43 Vice Pres and General Council ... Mr. Adam BURTON
88 Vice Pres for Global Initiatives ... Dr. Larry LINAMEN
06 Registrar ... Ms. Shawnn KONING
08 Director of Library ... Mr. Steve EMERSON
18 Director Facilities/Physical Plant ... Mr. Steve SMITH
37 Director Financial Aid ... Ms. Rebecca SANCHEZ
41 Athletic Director ... Dr. Micah PARKER
105 Web Site Manager ... Mr. Waylon BAUMGARDNER
40 Director of University Bookstore ... Ms. Carol BRACEY
42 Dean Spiritual Life/Campus Minister ... Mr. John MONTGOMERY
53 Dean School of Education ... Dr. John SHOUP
54 Dean College of Engineering ... Dr. Anthony DONALDSON
64 Dean School of Music ... Dr. Judd BONNER
66 Dean School of Nursing ... Dr. Geneva OAKS
73 Dean School of Christian Ministries ... Dr. Chris MORGAN
83 Interim Dean School Behav Sciences ... Dr. Gary COLLINS
49 Dean College of Arts & Sciences ... Dr. Gayne ANACKER
48 Dean Architecture ... Mr. Mark A. ROBERSON
50 Dean School of Business ... Dr. Franco GANDOLFI
106 Dean for Online and Prof Studies ... Dr. Dirk DAVIS
76 Dean of College of Allied Health ... Dr. Charles SANDS

California Christian College (I)

4881 E University Avenue, Fresno CA 93703-3599
County: Fresno FICE Identification: 008844
Unit ID: 110918
Telephone: (559) 251-4215 Carnegie Class: Spec/Faith
FAX Number: (559) 251-4231 Calendar System: Semester
URL: www.calchristiancollege.edu
Established: 1955 Annual Undergrad Tuition & Fees: $8,210
Enrollment: 35 Coed
Affiliation or Control: Free Will Baptist IRS Status: 501(c)3
Highest Offering: Baccalaureate
Program: 2-Year Principally Bachelor's Creditable; Liberal Arts And General; Religious Emphasis
Accreditation: TRACS

01 President ... Mr. Wendell L. WALLEY
05 VP of Academic Affairs ... Dr. Timothy M. POWELL
06 Registrar ... Mrs. Makenzie ZUERCHER
10 Chief Business Officer ... Mrs. Anna-Jean WALLEY
09 Dir Institutional Effectiveness ... Ms. Ingrid VOSS
08 Head Librarian ... Mrs. Nancy SINGH
37 Coordinator Financial Aid ... Ms. Melinda SCROGGINS
07 Director of Admissions ... Mr. Trent WALLEY
39 Director Student Housing ... Ms. Jennifer WALLEY

California Coast University (J)

925 N. Spurgeon Street, Santa Ana CA 92701-3515
County: Orange FICE Identification: 041276
Unit ID: 110936
Telephone: (714) 547-9625 Carnegie Class: Not Classified
FAX Number: (714) 547-5777 Calendar System: Other
URL: www.calcoast.edu
Established: 1973 Annual Undergrad Tuition & Fees: $9,500
Enrollment: 7,500 Coed
Affiliation or Control: Proprietary IRS Status: Proprietary
Highest Offering: Doctorate
Program: Professional; Business Emphasis
Accreditation: DETC

01 President ... Dr. Thomas M. NEAL
03 Executive Vice President ... Ms. Shelly MARQUARDT
32 Vice President of Student Relations ... Dr. Murl TUCKER
05 Chief Academic Officer ... Dr. Cynthia TEEPLE
20 Director of Academic Affairs ... Mr. Douglas PETRIKAT

California College of the Arts (K)

1111 Eighth Street, San Francisco CA 94107-2247
County: San Francisco FICE Identification: 001127
Unit ID: 110370
Telephone: (415) 703-9500 Carnegie Class: Spec/Arts
FAX Number: (510) 655-3541 Calendar System: Semester
URL: www.cca.edu
Established: 1907 Annual Undergrad Tuition & Fees: $40,334
Enrollment: 1,917 Coed
Affiliation or Control: Independent Non-Profit IRS Status: 501(c)3
Highest Offering: Master's
Program: Professional
Accreditation: WC, ART, CIDA

01 President ... Mr. Stephen BEAL
05 Provost ... Ms. Melanie CORN
10 Sr VP Finance & Administration ... Mrs. Laura HAZLETT
30 Sr Vice President of Advancement ... Ms. Susan AVILA
11 Vice President of Operations ... Ms. Jennifer STEIN
84 Vice Pres of Enrollment Management ... Ms. Sheri MCKENZIE
26 Vice President for Communications ... Ms. Chris BLISS
35 Vice President Student Affairs ... Mr. George SEDANO
15 Assoc Vice Pres Human Resources ... Vacant

21 Assoc Vice Pres Financial Services .... Mr. Ken TANZER
20 Associate Provost .... Vacant
36 Director Career Development .... Ms. Kate DEY
06 Registrar .... Mr. Jerry ALLEN
37 Director Financial Aid .... Mr. Scott CLINE
29 Director Alumni Relations .... Ms. Jessica RUSSELL
27 Chief Information Officer .... Ms. Mara HANCOCK
07 Director Undergrad Admissions .... Ms. Robynne ROYSTER
38 Director Student Counseling .... Dr. Tara RECH
45 Director Research and Planning .... Mr. David MECKEL
18 Chief Facilities/Physical Plant .... Ms. Deborah FELDMANN
07 Director Graduate Admissions .... Mr. Noel DAHL
09 Director of Institutional Research .... Ms. Brianna MOORE
96 Manager of Purchasing .... Ms. Jackie CRADDOCK

California College San Diego (A)

6602 Convoy Court Suite 100, San Diego CA 92111
County: San Diego FICE Identification: 021108
Unit ID: 110945
Telephone: (619) 680-4430 Carnegie Class: Spec/Health
FAX Number: (619) 295-5985 Calendar System: Other
URL: www.cc-sd.edu
Established: 1978 Annual Undergrad Tuition & Fees: $18,866
Enrollment: 921 Coed
Affiliation or Control: Proprietary IRS Status: 501(c)3
Highest Offering: Baccalaureate
Program: Occupational; 2-Year Principally Bachelor's Creditable; Business Emphasis
Accreditation: ACCSC, COARC

01 Executive Director .... Dr. Ken WEBB

California College San Diego (B)

277 Rancheros Drive, Suite 200, San Marcus CA 92069
Telephone: (619) 680-4430 Identification: 770551
Accreditation: ACCSC, #COARC

† Main campus is California College San Diego in San Diego, CA.

California Institute of the Arts (C)

24700 McBean Parkway, Valencia CA 91355-2397
County: Los Angeles FICE Identification: 001132
Unit ID: 111081
Telephone: (661) 255-1050 Carnegie Class: Spec/Arts
FAX Number: (661) 254-8352 Calendar System: Semester
URL: www.calarts.edu
Established: 1961 Annual Undergrad Tuition & Fees: $39,976
Enrollment: 1,441 Coed
Affiliation or Control: Independent Non-Profit IRS Status: 501(c)3
Highest Offering: Doctorate
Program: Professional; Fine Arts Emphasis
Accreditation: WC, ART, DANCE, MUS, THEA

01 President .... Dr. Steven D. LAVINE
05 Provost .... Dr. Jeannene PRZYBLYSKI
88 Vice Pres for Special Projects .... Lynn R. ROSENFELD
10 Vice Pres/Chief Financial Officer .... Donald MATTHEWSON
13 Vice President and CIO .... Michael CARTER
30 Vice Pres/Chief Advancement Officer .... Bianca ROBERTS
09 Assoc Provost Inst Rsrch/Effectiv .... Brian HARLAN
20 Associate Provost Academic Affairs .... Kim RUSSO
21 Assoc Vice President and Controller .... Karla TALAVERA
18 Assoc Vice Pres Facilities .... Jesse SMITH
84 Assoc Provost Enrollment Management .... Audrey TANNER
28 Asst Provost Equity and Diversity .... Vacant
08 Dean Div of Library & Info Resource .... Jeffrey GATTEN
88 Dean School of Critical Studies .... Amanda BEECH
88 Dean Sharon D. Lund School of Dance .... Stephan KOPLOWITZ
88 Dean School Film & Video .... Steve ANKER
88 Dean School of Theater .... Travis PRESTON
32 Dean of Students .... Vacant
57 Dean School of Art .... Thomas LAWSON
64 Dean Herb Alpert School of Music .... David ROSENBOOM
26 Executive Director Public Affairs .... Vacant
88 Director Community Arts Partnership .... Glenna AVILA
37 Director of Financial Aid .... Robin BAILEY-CHEN
29 Director Alumni Relations .... Nicole STARK LANE
15 Director of Human Resources .... Charmagne SHEARRILL
06 Registrar .... Nancy WHITTEMORE
07 Director of Admissions .... Molly RYAN

California Institute of Integral Studies (D)

1453 Mission Street, 4th Floor,
San Francisco CA 94103-2557
County: San Francisco FICE Identification: 012154
Unit ID: 110316
Telephone: (415) 575-6100 Carnegie Class: DRU
FAX Number: (415) 575-1264 Calendar System: Semester
URL: www.ciis.edu
Established: 1968 Annual Undergrad Tuition & Fees: $19,585
Enrollment: 1,350 Coed
Affiliation or Control: Independent Non-Profit IRS Status: 501(c)3
Highest Offering: Doctorate
Program: Professional
Accreditation: WC

01 President .... Mr. Joseph L. SUBBIONDO
05 Academic Vice President .... Dr. Judie WEXLER
32 Dean of Students/Director Diversity .... Ms. Shirley STRONG
29 Dean of Alumni/Dir of Travel Pgms .... Dr. Richard BUGGS
20 Dean Academic Plng/Administration .... Mr. Chip B. GOLDSTEIN
10 Controller/Director Finance .... Mr. Ken ABIKO
30 Director of Development .... Ms. Dorotea REYNA
15 Director of Human Resources .... Ms. S. Michelle COLEMAN
07 Dean Admissions & Financial Aid .... Mr. Michael GRIFFIN
13 Director of Info Systems Technology .... Mr. Scott CILIBERTI
08 Library Director .... Ms. Lise DYCKMAN
06 Registrar .... Mr. Dan GURLER
26 Director of Communications .... Mr. Jim David MARTIN
37 Director of Financial Aid .... Ms. Marisol NEALON
51 Director of Public Programs .... Mr. Karim BAER
18 Director Facilities & Operations .... Mr. Jonathan MILLS
40 Bookstore Manager .... Mr. Steven SWANSON
85 International Student Advisor .... Ms. Jody O'CONNOR

California Institute of Technology (E)

1200 E California Boulevard, Pasadena CA 91125-0001
County: Los Angeles FICE Identification: 001131
Unit ID: 110404
Telephone: (626) 395-6811 Carnegie Class: RU/VH
FAX Number: (626) 795-1547 Calendar System: Trimester
URL: www.caltech.edu
Established: 1891 Annual Undergrad Tuition & Fees: $41,538
Enrollment: 2,280 Coed
Affiliation or Control: Independent Non-Profit IRS Status: 501(c)3
Highest Offering: Doctorate
Program: Liberal Arts And General; Professional
Accreditation: WC, ENG

01 Interim President .... Dr. Edward M. STOLPER
04 Executive Assistant to President .... Mrs. Mary L. WEBSTER
05 Provost .... Dr. Edward M. STOLPER
88 Vice President/Director JPL .... Dr. Charles ELACHI
10 Vice President Business & Finance .... Mr. Dean W. CURRIE
30 Vice Pres Dev/Institute Relations .... Mr. Brian K. LEE
88 Assoc VP Advancement Svcs & COO ...... Ms. Donna GASTEVICH
32 Vice President Student Affairs .... Dr. Anneila I. SARGENT
43 General Counsel .... Ms. Victoria D. STRATMAN
20 Vice Provost .... Dr. Melany L. HUNT
20 Vice Provost .... Dr. Morteza GHARIB
15 Assoc Vice Pres HR/Campus Svcs .... Ms. Julia M. MCCALLIN
44 Asst Vice President Development .... Ms. Valerie A. OTTEN
31 Asst VP Campus & Cmty Relations ... Ms. Denise NELSON NASH
86 Director Govt Rels .... Mr. Hall P. DAILY
35 Senior Dir for Student Activities .... Mr. Tom N. MANNION
26 Asst VP Marketing & Communications .... Ms. Kristen BROWN
81 Chair Biology Division .... Dr. Stephen L. MAYO
81 Chair Chemistry & Chemical Engr Div . Dr. Jacqueline K. BARTON
54 Chair Engr & Applied Science Div .... Dr. Ares J. ROSAKIS
65 Chair Geology/Planet Science Div .... Dr. Kenneth FARLEY
79 Chair Humanities/Social Science Div .... Dr. Jonathan N. KATZ
81 Chair Physics/Math/Astro Division .... Dr. B. T. SOIFER
06 Registrar .... Mrs. Mary N. MORLEY
07 Director of Admissions .... Mr. Jarrid WHITNEY
08 University Librarian .... Ms. Kimberly DOUGLAS
14 Chief Information Officer .... Mr. Rich E. FAGEN
18 Assoc Vice Pres for Facilities .... Mr. James W. COWELL, JR.
18 Sr Director Facilities Management .... Mr. William R. TAYLOR
19 Manager Security Office .... Mr. Gregg HENDERSON
22 Director Employee Affirm Act/ Rels .... Ms. April WHITE CASTENADA
23 Director Health Services .... Dr. Stuart C. MILLER
25 Director Sponsored Research .... Dr. Richard P. SELIGMAN
29 Executive Director Alumni Assoc .... Ms. Alexandra C. TOBEK
37 Director Financial Aid .... Mr. Don CREWELL
36 Director Career Development .... Ms. Lauren B. STOLPER
40 Manager Bookstore .... Ms. Karyn SEIXAS
41 Director Athletics & Physical Ed .... Ms. Betsy MITCHELL
58 Dean of Graduate Studies .... Dr. Joseph E. SHEPHERD
88 Dean of Students .... Dr. D. R. KIEWIET
88 Associate Dean of Students .... Dr. Barbara C. GREEN
85 Assoc Dir International Student Pgm ...... Ms. Laura FLOWER KIM
96 Dir of Purchasing & Payment Svcs .... Ms. Tina LOWENTHAL

California Intercontinental University (F)

1470 Valley Vista Drive, Suite 150,
Diamond Bar CA 91765-3954
County: Los Angeles Identification: 666670
Telephone: (909) 396-6090 Carnegie Class: Not Classified
FAX Number: (909) 804-5151 Calendar System: Other
URL: www.caluniversity.edu
Established: 2003 Annual Undergrad Tuition & Fees: $18,000
Enrollment: 215 Coed
Affiliation or Control: Proprietary IRS Status: Proprietary
Highest Offering: Doctorate
Program: Professional; Business Emphasis
Accreditation: DETC

01 Executive Chairman .... Dr. Finian TAN
05 Chief Academic Ofcr/Dean Acad Affs .... Dr. Troy ROLAND
32 Dean of Student Success .... Dr. Fathiah INSERTO

California International Business University (G)

520 West Ash Street 3rd Floor, San Diego CA 92101
County: San Diego Identification: 666711
Telephone: (619) 702-9400 Carnegie Class: Not Classified
FAX Number: (619) 702-9476 Calendar System: Quarter
URL: www.cibu.edu
Established: 1994 Annual Undergrad Tuition & Fees: $13,800
Enrollment: 250 Coed
Affiliation or Control: Independent Non-Profit IRS Status: 501(c)3
Highest Offering: Master's
Program: Professional; Business Emphasis
Accreditation: ACICS

01 President .... Dr. Phillip BABB

California Lutheran University (H)

60 W Olsen Road, Thousand Oaks CA 91360-2787
County: Ventura FICE Identification: 001133
Unit ID: 110413
Telephone: (805) 492-2411 Carnegie Class: Master's L
FAX Number: (805) 493-3513 Calendar System: Semester
URL: www.clunet.edu
Established: 1959 Annual Undergrad Tuition & Fees: $53,598
Enrollment: 4,205 Coed
Affiliation or Control: Evangelical Lutheran Church In America
IRS Status: 501(c)3
Highest Offering: Doctorate
Program: Liberal Arts And General; Teacher Preparatory; Professional
Accreditation: WC, TED

01 President .... Dr. Christopher KIMBALL
05 Provost/Vice Pres Academic Affairs .... Dr. Leanne NEILSON
30 Vice Pres University Advancement .... Mr. Stephen WHEATLY
10 Vice Pres Admin/Finance/Treasurer .... Ms. Karen DAVIS
32 Vice Pres Stdnt Life/Dean of Stdnts .... Mr. William ROSSER
84 VP Enrollment Mgmt & Marketing .... Dr. Matthew WARD
08 Assoc Provost for Information Svcs .... Mr. Julius BIANCHI
18 Assoc Vice Pres Facilities .... Mr. Ryan VAN OMMEREN
26 Assc Vice Pres University Relations .... Ms. Lynda FULFORD
49 Dean College Arts & Sciences .... Dr. Joan GRIFFIN
53 Dean of School of Education .... Dr. George PETERSEN
50 Dean of School of Management .... Dr. Gerhard APFELTHALER
88 Director Church Relations .... Rev. Arne BERGLAND
15 Director of Human Resources .... Ms. Patricia PARHAM
06 Director Academic Svcs/Registrar .... Ms. Maria KOHNKE
42 University Pastor .... Rev. Scott MAXWELL-DOHERTY
42 University Pastor .... Rev. Melissa MAXWELL-DOHERTY
44 Director Estate & Gift .... Ms. Shannon YASMAN
41 Director Athletics .... Mr. Daniel KUNTZ
55 Director Adult Degree Program .... Dr. Lisa BUONO
36 Director of Career Services .... Ms. Cindy LEWIS
35 Director Multicultural/Intl Pgm .... Dr. Juanita HALL
21 Dir of Budget/Management Analysis .... Ms. Barbara REX
29 Director Alumni Relations .... Ms. Rachel RONNING LINDGREN
38 Director Counseling Services .... Dr. Alan GOODWIN
19 Director Security/Safety .... Mr. Frederick MILLER
07 Director of Undergrad Admissions .... Mr. Michael ELGARICO
09 Director of Institutional Research .... Dr. Rodney REYNOLDS
37 Director of Financial Aid .... Ms. Susan ARIAS

California Maritime Academy (I)

200 Maritime Academy Drive, Vallejo CA 94590-0644
County: Solano FICE Identification: 001134
Unit ID: 111188
Telephone: (707) 654-1000 Carnegie Class: Bac/Diverse
FAX Number: (707) 654-1001 Calendar System: Semester
URL: www.csum.edu
Established: 1929 Annual Undergrad Tuition & Fees (In-State): $7,956
Enrollment: 976 Coed
Affiliation or Control: State IRS Status: 501(c)3
Highest Offering: Master's
Program: Occupational; Liberal Arts And General; Technical Emphasis
Accreditation: WC, ENG, ENGT, IACBE

01 President .... RADM. Thomas A. CROPPER, USMS
05 Provost/VP Academic Affairs .... Dr. Gerald JAKUBOWSKI
10 Vice Pres Administration/Finance .... Mr. Kurt D. LOHIDE
102 VP Univ Advancement/Exec Dir Found .... Ms. Beverly BYL
32 VP Student Affairs .... Mr. Steve KRETA
20 Academic Dean .... Dr. Nael ALY
32 Dean of Students .... Dr. Deborrah HEBERT
88 Master of Training Ship .... Capt. Harry BOLTON
30 Director Developmen .... Ms. Sylvia REGALADO
21 Budget Officer .... Mr. Steve MASTRO
06 Registrar .... Ms. Evelyn ANDREWS
08 Director of Library .... Mr. Richard ROBISON
07 Dir Admissions/Enrollment Services .... Mr. Marc MCGEE
37 Director of Financial Aid .... Ms. Nicole HILL
88 Executive Director CMA Services .... Ms. Diane RAWICZ
88 Director Ctr Excellence & Learning ..... Dr. Vivienne MCCLENDON
36 Director Career Development .... Mr. James DALSKE
18 Director Facilities Planning .... Mr. Roger JAECKEL
19 Chief Security Officer .... Chief Roseann RICHARD
15 Director of Human Resources .... Ms. Ingrid WILLIAMS
41 Director of Athletics .... Mr. Marv CHRISTOPHER
26 Director Public Relations .... Mr. Bobby KING
40 Bookstore Manager .... Ms. Beth AYERS
96 Purchasing Manager .... Ms. Vineeta DHILLON

California Miramar University (A)

9750 Miramar Road Suite 180, San Diego CA 92126-7501

County: San Diego Identification: 666713
Telephone: (858) 653-3000 Carnegie Class: Not Classified
FAX Number: (858) 653-6786 Calendar System: Other
URL: www.calmu.edu
Established: 2005 Annual Undergrad Tuition & Fees: $7,740
Enrollment: N/A Coed
Affiliation or Control: Proprietary IRS Status: Proprietary
Highest Offering: Doctorate
Program: Professional
Accreditation: ACICS, DETC

01 President .... Dr. Janathin MILLER
07 Admissions Director .... Ms. Jeanie FOSTER

California National University for Advanced Studies (B)

8550 Balboa Boulevard, Suite 210,
Northridge CA 91325-3576

County: Los Angeles Identification: 666786
Telephone: (800) 782-2422 Carnegie Class: Not Classified
FAX Number: (818) 830-2418 Calendar System: Trimester
URL: www.cnuas.edu
Established: 1993 Annual Undergrad Tuition & Fees: $5,400
Enrollment: 311 Coed
Affiliation or Control: Proprietary IRS Status: Proprietary
Highest Offering: Master's
Program: Professional
Accreditation: DETC

01 President .... Mr. Carlton G. BRYANT
32 Vice Pres Student Affs/Registrar .... Ms. Stephanie M. SMITH
05 Director of Instruction .... Dr. Carol BACKER
50 Dean Business Administration .... Dr. Philip CHONG
54 Associate CNU Col of Engineering .... Dr. Robert RYAN
14 MIS Director .... Mr. Charles NG

California Northstate College of Pharmacy (C)

10811 International Drive, Rancho Cordova CA 95670

County: Sacramento Identification: 667020
Telephone: (916) 631-8108 Carnegie Class: Not Classified
FAX Number: (916) 631-8127 Calendar System: Semester
URL: www.californiacollegeofpharmacy.org
Established: 2008 Annual Graduate Tuition & Fees: $45,100
Enrollment: N/A Coed
Affiliation or Control: Independent Non-Profit IRS Status: 501(c)3
Highest Offering: Doctorate; No Undergraduates
Program: Professional
Accreditation: WC, PHAR

01 President .... Dr. Alvin CHEUNG
05 Dean .... Dr. Shane DESSELLE
11 Vice President of Operations .... Mr. Norman FONG
20 Assoc Dean Academic Affs/Research .... Dr. John MARTIN
32 Asst Dean Student Affs/Admissions .... Ms. Cyndi PORTER
08 Director of Library Resources .... Mr. Scott MINOR
06 Registrar .... Ms. Lisa ERCK
09 Dir of Inst Effect/Assessment .... Ms. Karen MCCLENDON

California Southern University (D)

930 Roosevelt, Irvine CA 92620

County: Orange Identification: 666770
Telephone: (714) 882-7800 Carnegie Class: Not Classified
FAX Number: (714) 480-0834 Calendar System: Semester
URL: www.calsouthern.edu
Established: 1978 Annual Undergrad Tuition & Fees: $6,000
Enrollment: N/A Coed
Affiliation or Control: Independent Non-Profit IRS Status: 501(c)3
Highest Offering: Doctorate
Program: Liberal Arts And General; Professional
Accreditation: DETC

01 President .... Dr. Caroll RYAN

*The California State University System Office (E)

401 Golden Shore, Long Beach CA 90802-4210

County: Los Angeles FICE Identification: 001136
Unit ID: 110501
Telephone: (562) 951-4000 Carnegie Class: N/A
FAX Number: (562) 951-4986
URL: www.calstate.edu

01 Chancellor .... Dr. Timothy P. WHITE
03 Executive Vice Chancellor & CAO .... Dr. Ephraim P. SMITH
10 Executive Vice Chancellor & CFO .... Dr. Benjamin F. QUILLIAN
15 Vice Chancellor Human Resources .... Ms. Gail BROOKS
30 Vice Chanc Univ Rels/Advancement .... Mr. Garrett P. ASHLEY
43 Interim General Counsel .... Mr. Andy JONES
88 University Auditor .... Mr. Larry MANDEL
100 Chief of Staff .... Dr. Lars WALTON
88 Deputy Chief of Staff .... Ms. Jessica DARIN

*California Polytechnic State University-San Luis Obispo (F)

1 Grand Avenue, San Luis Obispo CA 93407-9000

County: San Luis Obispo FICE Identification: 001143
Unit ID: 110422
Telephone: (805) 756-1111 Carnegie Class: Master's L
FAX Number: (805) 756-5400 Calendar System: Quarter
URL: www.calpoly.edu
Established: 1901 Annual Undergrad Tuition & Fees (In-State): $8,724
Enrollment: 18,679 Coed
Affiliation or Control: State IRS Status: 501(c)3
Highest Offering: Master's
Program: Liberal Arts And General; Teacher Preparatory; Professional; Technical Emphasis
Accreditation: WC, ART, BUS, CONST, CS, DIETD, DIETI, ENG, FOR, LSAR, MUS, NAIT, NRPA, PLNG, TED

02 President .... Dr. Jeffrey D. ARMSTRONG
100 Chief of Staff .... Ms. Betsy KINSLEY
05 Provost .... Dr. Kathleen ENZ FINKEN
32 Vice President Student Affairs .... Dr. Keith HUMPHREY
30 Vice Pres Univ Advance/CEO Found .... Ms. Deborah READ
10 Int Vice Pres Admin & Finance .... Mr. Stan NOSEK
20 Vice Provost Intl/Grad & Ext Educ .... Dr. Brian TIETJE
41 Athletic Director .... Mr. Don OBERHELMAN
11 Vice Provost Info Services/CIO .... Dr. Michael D. MILLER
88 Exec Dir CalPoly Corporation .... Ms. Bonnie D. MURPHY
46 Int VP Res & Industry Relations .... Bradford ANDERSON, ESQ
21 Associate Vice Pres Admin & Finance .... Ms. Karen WEBB
44 Assoc Vice Pres Advancement .... Mr. Grant TREXLER
44 Interim Assoc VP Development .... Ms. Tanya KIANI
26 Assoc VP Strategic Communications .... Mr. Chip VISCI
18 Associate Vice Pres Facilities .... Mr. Mark A. HUNTER
39 Dir Univ Housing & Assoc VP/SA .... Mr. Preston C. ALLEN
15 Assoc Vice Prov Academic Personnel .... Dr. Al LIDDICOAT
20 Assoc Vice Prov Acad Pgms/Planning .... Dr. Mary E. PEDERSEN
46 Assoc Vice Provost Systems/Res Mgmt .... Ms. Kimi M. IKEDA
07 Asst VP Admiss/Recruitment/Fin Aid .... Mr. James L. MARAVIGLIA
29 Int Asst Vice Pres Alumni Relations .... Ms. Ellen COHUNE
19 University Police Department .... Chief George HUGHES
06 Registrar/Dir of Academic Records .... Mr. Cem SUNATA
28 Director Diversity & Inclusivity .... Dr. Annie HOLMES
22 Dir Employment Equity .... Ms. Martha CODY
88 Dir Facil Planning/Capital Projects .... Mr. Joel NEEL
23 Director Health/Counseling Services .... Dr. Martin E. BRAGG
38 Head of Counseling Services .... Dr. Bruce MEYER
32 Interim ASI Executive Director .... Ms. Marcy MALONEY
35 Director Student Life & Leadership .... Vacant
40 Director University Bookstore .... Mr. Phillip DAVIS
35 Dean of Students .... Dr. Jean DECOSTA
102 Int Dean Research & Sponsored Pgm .... Dr. Dean WENDT
47 Dean Agriculture/Food & Env Sci .... Dr. Andrew THULIN
48 Dean Architect/Environmental Design .... Ms. Christine THEODOROPOULOS
50 Dean Orfalea College of Business .... Vacant
54 Dean College of Engineering .... Dr. Debra LARSON
49 Dean College of Liberal Arts .... Dr. Douglas EPPERSON
81 Dean Science & Mathematics .... Dr. Philip S. BAILEY, JR.
53 Int Dean School of Education .... Dr. Bob DETWEILER
15 Director Human Resources .... Ms. Beth E. GALLAGHER
96 Dir Contract Procrurement Risk Mgmt .... Mr. Dru ZACHMEYER
37 Director Financial Aid .... Ms. Lois M. KELLY
36 Director Career Services .... Mr. Martin C. SHIBATA
09 Int Director Inst Plng & Research .... Mr. Charlie CRABB
104 Director of International Center .... Ms. Caroline MOORE
92 Director University Honors Program .... Vacant

*California State Polytechnic University-Pomona (G)

3801 W Temple Avenue, Pomona CA 91768-2557

County: Los Angeles FICE Identification: 001144
Unit ID: 110529
Telephone: (909) 869-7659 Carnegie Class: Master's L
FAX Number: (909) 869-4535 Calendar System: Quarter
URL: www.csupomona.edu
Established: 1938 Annual Undergrad Tuition & Fees (In-State): $8,498
Enrollment: 22,104 Coed
Affiliation or Control: State IRS Status: 501(c)3
Highest Offering: Master's
Program: Liberal Arts And General; Teacher Preparatory; Professional
Accreditation: WC, ART, BUS, CIDA, CS, DIETD, DIETI, ENG, ENGT, LSAR, MUS, PLNG, SPAA

02 President .... Dr. J. Michael ORTIZ
05 Provost/VP Academic Affairs .... Dr. Marten DENBOER
32 Vice President Student Affairs .... Dr. Douglas R. FREER
11 Vice Pres Administrative Affairs .... Dr. Edwin A. BARNES
30 Vice Pres University Advancement .... Mr. Scott C. WARRINGTON
20 Assoc Provost Academic Affairs .... Dr. Claudia L. PINTER-LUCKE
18 Assoc VP Facilities Planning & Mgmt .... Vacant
35 Assoc VP & Dean of Students .... Dr. Rebecca L. GUTIERREZ-KEETON
84 Assoc VP Enroll Management & Svcs .... Ms. Kathleen A. STREET
20 Spec Asst to the VP Faculty Affairs .... Mr. Gary HAMILTON
46 Assoc VP Research Research .... Dr. Frank W. EWERS
26 Assoc Vice Pres for Univ Relations .... Vacant
10 Assoc VP Finance/Admin Svcs .... Mr. Darwin LABORDO
35 Assoc VP Student Services .... Dr. Kevin T. COLANER
35 Assoc VP Student Affairs .... Ms. Christi R. CHISLER
13 Chief Information Officer .... Mr. John W. MCGUTHRY
28 Admin in Charge D/HR/Employee Svcs .... Ms. Sharon L. REITER
04 Exec Assistant to the President .... Ms. Sandra L. DAVIS
47 Dean College of Agriculture .... Dr. Lester C. YOUNG
49 Int Dean Col Letters/Arts/Soc Sci .... Dr. Sharon HILLES
50 Dean Col of Business Admin .... Dr. Richard S. LAPIDUS
54 Dean College of Engineering .... Dr. Mahyar AMOUZEGAR
48 Dean Col Environmental Design .... Mr. Michael WOO
88 Dean Collins Sch of Hosp Mgmt .... Mr. Ed MERRITT
81 Dean College of Science .... Dr. Brian JERSKY
53 Dean College Educ/Integrat Stds .... Dr. Peggy KELLY
56 Dean Extended University .... Dr. Howard EVANS
44 Assoc VP for Development .... Ms. Michelle L. MOYER
08 Dean University Library .... Mr. Ray WANG
41 Director of Athletics .... Mr. Brian R. SWANSON
86 Dir of Government/External Affairs .... Mr. Doug P. GLAESER
19 Interim Chief of Police .... Mr. W. Bruce WILSON
102 Exec Dir Cal Poly Pomona Found Inc .... Mr. G. Paul STOREY
37 Director Student Financial Aid .... Ms. Diana Y. MINOR
06 Registrar/Academic Records Svcs .... Ms. Maria L. MARTINEZ
96 Director of Procurement .... Ms. Kathleen A. PRUNTY
84 Exec Dir Admissions and Outreach .... Ms. Deborah L. BRANDON
30 Exec Director Capital Campaign .... Vacant

*California State University-Bakersfield (H)

9001 Stockdale Highway, Bakersfield CA 93311-1022

County: Kern FICE Identification: 007993
Unit ID: 110486
Telephone: (661) 654-2011 Carnegie Class: Master's L
FAX Number: (661) 654-3194 Calendar System: Quarter
URL: www.csub.edu
Established: 1965 Annual Undergrad Tuition & Fees (In-State): $6,682
Enrollment: 8,520 Coed
Affiliation or Control: State IRS Status: 501(c)3
Highest Offering: Master's
Program: Occupational; Liberal Arts And General; Teacher Preparatory; Professional; Nursing Emphasis
Accreditation: WC, BUS, NURSE, SPAA, SW, TED

02 President .... Dr. Horace MITCHELL
100 Executive Asst to the President .... Ms. Evelyn YOUNG
04 Presidential Aide .... Ms. Tina GIBLIN
05 Provost/Vice Pres Academic Affairs .... Dr. Soraya COLEY
10 Vice Pres Business/Admin Services .... Mr. Michael A. NEAL
32 Vice President Student Affairs .... Dr. Thomas WALLACE
84 Assoc VP for Enrollment Management .... Dr. Jacqueline MIMMS
12 Int Assoc VP Antelope Valley Center .... Dr. Craig KELSEY
20 Assoc VP for Academic Programs .... Dr. Carl KEMNITZ
20 Interim Assoc VP Faculty Affairs .... Dr. Michael SUESS
15 AVP Human Res/Administrative Svcs .... Ms. Kellie GARCIA
88 Int AVP Information Tech Services .... Mr. Kallya SHENOY
88 Spec Asst to Provost Academic Aff .... Vacant
21 Asst Vice Pres Fiscal Services .... Mr. Douglas WADE
13 Asst Vice Pres Info Technology Svcs .... Mr. Kallya SHENOY
18 Asst VP Facilities Management/Dev .... Mr. Pat JACOBS
09 Asst VP Inst Rsrch/Planning/Assess .... Dr. Laura HECHT
25 Assoc Provost for Grants & Research .... Vacant
50 Dean Business/Public Administration .... Dr. John EMERY
53 Dean Social Sciences and Education .... Dr. Kathleen KNUTZEN
79 Dean Arts & Humanities .... Dr. Richard COLLINS
81 Dean Natural Sciences/Math/Eng .... Dr. Anne HOUTMAN
56 Dean Extended University Division .... Dr. Craig KELSEY
58 Dir of Academic Operation & Support .... Dr. John DIRKSE
08 Interim Dean University Library .... Dr. Curt ASHER
35 Dean Student Life .... Vacant
86 Int Exec Dir Government/Found Rels .... Mr. David MELENDEZ
06 Registrar .... Ms. Rita GUSTAFSON
88 Director Academic Advising .... Mr. Vikash LAKHANI
91 Dir Admn Computing Svcs/CMS Pgm Dir .... Mr. Kallya SHENOY
07 Asst Director Admissions & Records .... Mrs. Debbie BLOWERS
29 Director Alumni Relations .... Ms. Roopa DAVE-LAKHANI
41 Director Athletics .... Mr. Jeffrey KONYA
36 Dir for Cmty Engagement/Career Edu .... Ms. Jane EVARIAN
88 Director Children's Center .... Ms. Gladys GARCIA
96 Dir Contract Services/Procurement .... Mr. Michael CHAVEZ
38 Admin Supervisor Counseling Center .... Dr. Janet MILLAR
106 Director E-Learning Services .... Vacant
37 Director Financial Aid/Scholarships .... Dr. Ron RADNEY
92 Director CSUB Honors Program .... Dr. Michael FLACHMANN
39 Director Housing & Residential Life .... Ms. Crystal BECKS
26 Dir Public Affairs & Communications .... Ms. Colleen DILLAWAY
88 Director Safety & Risk Management .... Vacant
88 Dir Svcs Students w/Disabilities .... Ms. Janice CLAUSEN
17 Director Student Health Services .... Dr. Oscar RICO
30 Director of Development .... Mr. Victor MARTIN
88 Director Student Recreation Center .... Mr. Mark HARRIMAN
88 Director Student Union .... Mr. Emile CALLAHAN
88 Director Telecommunications .... Vacant
88 Director Outreach Services .... Mr. Steve WATKIN
19 Chief University Police .... Chief Marty WILLIAMSON
88 Director of Food Services .... Vacant
18 Manager Facilities Operations .... Mr. Tom VELASQUEZ
40 Bookstore Manager .... Ms. Lori FULLER

*California State University-Channel Islands (I)

One University Drive, Camarillo CA 93012-8599

County: Ventura FICE Identification: 039803
Unit ID: 441937
Telephone: (805) 437-8400 Carnegie Class: Master's S
FAX Number: (805) 437-8414 Calendar System: Semester

URL: www.csuci.edu
Established: 2002 Annual Undergrad Tuition & Fees (In-District): $3,538
Enrollment: 4,920 Coed
Affiliation or Control: State/Local IRS Status: 501(c)3
Highest Offering: Master's
Program: Liberal Arts And General
Accreditation: WC, NURSE

02 President ... Dr. Richard R. RUSH
05 Provost/Vice Pres Academic Affairs ... Dr. Gayle HUTCHINSON
10 Vice Pres Finance/Administration ... Ms. Ysabel TRINIDAD
32 Vice President for Student Affairs ... Dr. Wm. Gregory SAWYER
13 Vice Pres Tech & Communication ... Dr. Michael BERMAN
100 Chief of Staff ... Dr. Therese EYERMANN
20 Associate Provost ... Dr. Renny CHRISTOPHER
88 Assistant Provost ... Dr. Dan WAKELEE
08 AVP University Library ... Ms. Amy WALLACE
56 AVP Extended University ... Dr. Gary BERG
50 AVP MVS School Business/Economics ... Dr. William CORDEIRO
53 AVP School of Education ... Dr. Gary KINSEY
49 AVP Arts & Sciences ... Dr. Karen CAREY
30 AVP for Univ Development ... Ms. Nichole IPACH
25 AVP Research/Sponsored Programs ... Vacant
18 AVP Ops/Planning/Construction ... Mr. Dave CHAKRABORTY
21 AVP Finance & Budget ... Ms. Missy JARNAGIN
19 AVP Police & Parking ... Mr. John REID
15 AVP for Human Resources ... Ms. Anna PAVIN
88 AVP Resources & Auxiliaries ... Mr. Ed LEBIODA
35 AVP Dean of Students ... Mr. Damien PENA
108 Dir Assessment/Research/Staff Dev ... Dr. Jennifer MILLER
104 Dir Intl Pgms/AD Ctr Intl Affs ... Ms. Mayumi KOWTA
86 Director/Community/Govt Relations ... Ms. Celina ZACARIAS
29 Dir Development/Alumni Rels ... Ms. Tania GARCIA
88 Director Special Projects for F&A ... Ms. Caroline DOLL
07 Director Admissions & Recruitment ... Ms. Ginger REYES
37 Dir of Financial Aid & Scholarships ... Ms. Sunshine GARCIA
39 Dir Housing & Residential Education ... Ms. Cindy DERRICO
96 Dir Procurement/Contract Services ... Ms. Valerie PATSCHECK
27 Dir of Communication/Marketing ... Ms. Nancy GILL
06 Assoc Dir Records & Registration ... Ms. Gina R. FARRAR

*California State University-Chico (A)

400 W First Street, Chico CA 95929-0001
County: Butte FICE Identification: 001146
Unit ID: 110538
Telephone: (530) 898-6116 Carnegie Class: Master's L
FAX Number: (530) 898-6824 Calendar System: Semester
URL: www.csuchico.edu
Established: 1887 Annual Undergrad Tuition & Fees (In-State): $6,972
Enrollment: 16,470 Coed
Affiliation or Control: State IRS Status: 501(c)3
Highest Offering: Master's
Program: Liberal Arts And General; Teacher Preparatory; Professional
Accreditation: WC, ART, BUS, CONST, CS, DIETD, DIETI, ENG, JOUR, MUS, NAIT, NRPA, NURSE, SP, SPAA, SW, TED, THEA

02 President ... Dr. Paul J. ZINGG
100 Chief of Staff/Dir of Govt Rels ... Ms. Karla J. ZIMMERLEE
05 Provost/Vice Pres Academic Affairs ... Dr. Belle WEI
10 Vice President Business/Finance ... Ms. Lorraine B. HOFFMAN
32 Vice President Student Affairs ... Mr. Drew CALANDRELLA
30 Vice Pres University Advancement ... Mr. Richard ELLISON
45 Vice Prov Planning/Res Allocation ... Dr. Arno RETHANS
46 Vice Provost for Reseach ... Dr. E.K. (Eun) PARK
84 Vice Provost Enrollment Management ... Ms. Barbara FORTIN
13 Vice Prov Information Resources/CIO ... Mr. Michael SCHILLING
21 Assoc VP Financial Svcs/Univ Budget ... Ms. Stacie CORONA
15 Asst Vice Pres Faculty Affairs ... Vacant
47 Dean College of Agriculture ... Dr. Jennifer RYDER-FOX
51 Dean Continuing Education ... Ms. Debra E. BARGER
72 Dean Col Engr/Comp Sci/Const Mgmt ... Dr. Ben JULIANO
83 Dean Col Behavior & Social Sci ... Dr. Eddie VELA
50 Interim Dean College of Business ... Dr. Julie INDVIK
79 Dean College Humanities/Fine Arts ... Dr. Robert KNIGHT
81 Dean College Natural Sciences ... Dr. Frederika (Fraka) HARMSEN
60 Int Dean Coll Communication & Educ ... Ms. Maggie PAYNE
26 Director Public Affairs ... Mr. Joe WILLS
29 Director Alumni Relations ... Ms. Susan M. ANDERSON
09 Director Institutional Research ... Mr. William R. ALLEN
06 Registrar ... Ms. Jean H. IRVING
07 Director of Admissions ... Mr. Allan C. BEE
36 Interim Director Student Placement ... Ms. Megan ODOM
37 Director Financial Aid/Scholarships ... Mr. Dan REED
18 Director Facilities Management Svcs ... Mr. Luis CARABALLO
96 Director of Procurement ... Ms. Sara RUMIANO
92 Director Univ Honors Program ... Mr. John MAHONEY
35 Director Student Judicial Affairs ... Ms. Lisa ROOT
28 Director of Diversity and Inclusion ... Mr. Tray ROBINSON

*California State University-Dominguez Hills (B)

1000 E Victoria Street, Carson CA 90747-0005
County: Los Angeles FICE Identification: 001141
Unit ID: 110547
Telephone: (310) 243-3300 Carnegie Class: Master's L
FAX Number: N/A Calendar System: Semester
URL: www.csudh.edu
Established: 1960 Annual Undergrad Tuition & Fees (In-State): $6,104
Enrollment: 10,884 Coed
Affiliation or Control: State IRS Status: 501(c)3
Highest Offering: Master's
Program: Liberal Arts And General; Teacher Preparatory; Professional
Accreditation: WC, CS, MT, MUS, NURSE, OPE, OT, SPAA, SW, TED, THEA

02 President ... Dr. Willie J. HAGAN
05 Provost/Vice Pres Academic Affs ... Dr. Ramon S. TORRECILHA
10 Vice Pres Administration/Finance ... Ms. Mary Ann RODRIGUEZ
84 Vice Pres Enroll Mgmt/Stdnt Affairs ... Dr. Susan E. BORREGO
30 Interim VP Univ Advancement ... Mr. Jeff POLTORAK
20 Assoc VP Faculty Affairs ... Dr. Rene CASTRO
11 Assoc VP Administration/Finance ... Ms. Karen J. WALL
44 Assoc Vice President Development ... Mr. Jeff POLTORAK
13 Chief IT Officer ... Mr. Chris MANRIQUEZ
35 Assoc VP Student Life/Dean Students ... Dr. Daniels SONJA
21 Assoc VP Resource Management ... Dr. Janna BERSI
88 Assoc VP Student Success Services ... Dr. William FRANKLIN
15 Asst Vice Pres Human Resources/Mgmt ... Vacant
100 Chief of Staff ... Ms. Naomi GOODWIN
41 Director of Athletics ... Mr. Patrick GUILLEN
86 Dir Govt & Community Relations ... Mr. David GAMBOA
26 Dir Communications/Public Relations ... Ms. Brenda KNEPPER
37 Director of Financial Aid ... Ms. Delores LEE
06 Dir Stdnt Rec/Info Svcs/Registrar ... Ms. Brandy MCLELLAND
38 Dir Student Health & Psych Services ... Dr. Janie MACHARG
09 Assoc Director Institutional Rsrch ... Mr. Pete VAN HAMERSVELD
19 Chief of Police ... Mr. Carlos VELEZ
25 Director of Research/Funded Project ... Dr. Laura ROBLES
49 Dean College of Arts & Humanities ... Dr. Munashe FURUSA
107 Actg Dean Health/Human Svcs/Nursing ... Dr. Anupama JOSHI
53 Acting Dean College of Education ... Dr. Ann CHLEBICKI
50 Dean Col of Bus Admin/Public Plcy ... Dr. H. Joseph WEN
56 Actg Dean College of Ext & Intl Ed ... Dr. Joanne ZITELLI
83 Dean Col of Natural & Behav Sci ... Dr. Rod HAY
08 Dean of the Library ... Ms. Sandra PARHAM
18 Director of Physical Plant ... Mr. Jonathan C. SCHEFFLER
21 Accounting Director ... Ms. Cecilia PATZ
96 Director of Procurement & Contracts ... Vacant
07 Director Enrollment Services ... Dr. Sammuel KIM
29 Director Alumni & Family Programs ... Dr. Gayle BALL-PARKER

*California State University-East Bay (C)

25800 Carlos Bee Boulevard, Hayward CA 94542-3001
County: Alameda FICE Identification: 001138
Unit ID: 110574
Telephone: (510) 885-3000 Carnegie Class: Master's L
FAX Number: (510) 885-3808 Calendar System: Quarter
URL: www.csueastbay.edu
Established: 1957 Annual Undergrad Tuition & Fees (In-State): $6,549
Enrollment: 13,052 Coed
Affiliation or Control: State IRS Status: 501(c)3
Highest Offering: Doctorate
Program: Liberal Arts And General; Teacher Preparatory; Professional
Accreditation: WC, BUS, ENG, MUS, NURSE, SP, SW, TED

02 President ... Dr. Leroy M. MORISHITA
05 Provost/VP Academic Affairs ... Dr. James HOUPIS
10 Vice Pres Administration & Finance ... Mr. Brad WELLS
30 Vice President Univ Advancement ... Mr. Ara SERJOIE
84 VP Plng/Enroll Mgmt/Student Affs ... Dr. Linda DALTON
49 Dean Col of Ltrs/Arts/Soc Sci ... Dr. Kathleen ROUNTREE
50 Dean Col of Business/Economics ... Dr. Jagdish AGRAWAL
53 Dean Col of Educ/Allied Studies ... Dr. Carolyn NELSON
81 Dean College of Science ... Dr. Michael LEUNG
08 University Librarian ... Mr. John WENZLER

*California State University-Fresno (D)

5200 N. Barton Avenue, Fresno CA 93740-8027
County: Fresno FICE Identification: 001147
Unit ID: 110556
Telephone: (559) 278-4240 Carnegie Class: Master's L
FAX Number: (559) 278-4715 Calendar System: Semester
URL: www.csufresno.edu
Established: 1911 Annual Undergrad Tuition & Fees (In-State): $6,287
Enrollment: 22,565 Coed
Affiliation or Control: State IRS Status: 501(c)3
Highest Offering: Doctorate
Program: Liberal Arts And General; Teacher Preparatory; Professional
Accreditation: WC, BUS, CACREP, CIDA, CONST, CORE, DIETD, DIETI, ENG, MUS, NRPA, NURSE, #PH, PTA, SP, SPAA, SW, TED, THEA

02 President ... Dr. Joseph I. CASTRO
05 Int Provost/Vice Pres Academic Affs ... Dr. Andrew HOFF
10 VP Administration/Chief Fin Ofcr ... Dr. Cynthia TENIENTE-MATSON
30 Vice Pres University Advancement ... Dr. Peter N. SMITS
32 Vice Pres Student Affairs ... Dr. Paul M. OLIARO
15 Assoc VP Academic Personnel ... Dr. Michael CALDWELL
26 Assoc VP University Communications ... Ms. Shirley ARMBRUSTER
20 Associate Provost ... Dr. Lynnette ZELEZNY
20 Assoc VP/Dean Undergrad Students ... Dr. Dennis L. NEF
45 Assoc Vice President Research ... Dr. Thomas H. MCCLANAHAN
44 Assoc Vice Pres Univ Development ... Vacant
21 Assoc VP for Financial Services ... Mr. Clinton MOFFITT
18 Associate Vice President Facilities ... Mr. Robert BOYD
84 Assoc Vice Pres Enrollment Services ... Mr. Bernie VINOVRSKI
51 Dean/Assoc VP Continuing/Global Ed ... Dr. Lynnette ZELEZNY
47 Dean Agricultural Science/Tech ... Dr. Charles D. BOYER
79 Dean of Arts & Humanities ... Dr. Vida SAMIIAN
50 Dean Craig School of Business ... Dr. Robert HARPER
53 Dean of Kremen School of Education ... Dr. Paul BEARE
54 Dean of Engineering ... Dr. Ramakrishna NUNNA
76 Int Dean of Health/Human Services ... Dr. Jody HIRONAKA-JUTEAU
83 Dean of Social Sciences ... Dr. Luz GONZALEZ
81 Dean of Science & Mathematics ... Dr. Susan ELROD
08 Dean of Library Services ... Mr. Peter MCDONALD
58 Dean of Graduate Studies ... Dr. Sharon BROWN-WELTY
23 Dir Univ Health/Psyc Svcs Oper ... Ms. Catherine FELIX
19 Director of Public Safety ... Mr. David HUERTA
41 Director of Athletics ... Mr. Thomas BOEH
16 Director of Human Resources ... Ms. Janice PARTEN
13 Exec Director Technology Services ... Mr. Jim MICHAEL
09 Dir of Inst Research/Assessment ... Dr. Angel SANCHEZ
37 Director of Financial Aid ... Mr. Bernie OGDEN
06 Registrar ... Ms. Tina BEDDALL
27 Director of Publications ... Mr. Bruce WHITWORTH
29 Executive Director Alumni Relations ... Ms. Jacquelyn GLASENER
36 Director of Career Services ... Ms. Rita BOCCHINFUSO-COHEN
39 Director Univ Courtyard (Housing) ... Ms. Erin BOELE
96 Dir Procurement & Support Services ... Mr. Brian COTHAM
07 Director of Admissions ... Ms. Tina BEDDALL
35 Director of Student Involvement ... Ms. Melissa GINOTTI
40 Bookstore Manager ... Mr. Curt PARKINSON

*California State University-Fullerton (E)

PO Box 34080, 800 N State Col Blvd,
Fullerton CA 92831-3547
County: Orange FICE Identification: 001137
Unit ID: 110565
Telephone: (657) 278-2011 Carnegie Class: Master's L
FAX Number: (657) 278-2649 Calendar System: Semester
URL: www.fullerton.edu
Established: 1957 Annual Undergrad Tuition & Fees (In-State): $6,186
Enrollment: 37,677 Coed
Affiliation or Control: State IRS Status: 501(c)3
Highest Offering: Doctorate
Program: Liberal Arts And General; Teacher Preparatory; Professional
Accreditation: WC, ANEST, ART, BUS, BUSA, CACREP, CS, DANCE, ENG, JOUR, MIDWF, MUS, NURSE, PH, SP, SPAA, SW, TED, THEA

02 President ... Dr. Mildred GARCIA
100 Chief of Staff ... Ms. Ann CAMP
05 Provost & VP Academic Affairs ... Dr. Jose CRUZ
10 Interim VP Admin & Finance/CFO ... Mr. Stephan GARCIA
32 Vice President of Student Affairs ... Dr. Berenecea J. EANES
30 VP University Advancement ... Mr. Greg SAKS
13 VP Info Tech/Chief Info Ofcr ... Mr. Amir DABIRIAN
15 VP of Hum Res/Diversity & Inclusion ... Ms. Lori GENTLES
102 Int AVP Operations/CFO Foundation ... Ms. Tara GARCIA
44 Assoc VP University Advancement ... Mrs. Michele CESCA
58 AVP Graduate Studies/Research ... Dr. Dorota HUIZINGA
26 Assoc VP Strategic Communications ... Mr. Jeffrey COOK
20 Assoc Vice Pres Academic Affairs ... Dr. Jennifer FAUST
32 Assoc VP of Student Affairs ... Ms. Kandy MINK-SALAS
21 Associate VP of Financial Services ... Mr. Brian JENKINS
86 Assc VP Public Affs/Government Rels ... Mr. Owen HOLMES
45 Assoc VP Budget Planning & Admin ... Mrs. Sarah SONG
35 Assoc VP of Student Affairs ... Dr. Lea JARNAGIN
11 Int Associate VP Administration ... Ms. Paulette BLUMBERG
18 AVP Facilities Planning/Management ... Mr. Jay BOND
84 Asst Vice Pres Enrollment Services ... Ms. Nancy DORITY
09 Asst VP Inst Res/Analytical Stds ... Dr. Edward SULLIVAN
29 Exec Director Alumni Relations ... Ms. Dianna L. FISHER
88 Exec Director/CEO Aux Services Corp ... Mr. Frank MUMFORD
06 Registrar ... Ms. Melissa WHATLEY
08 Interim University Librarian ... Dr. Susan TSCHABRUN
07 Director of Admissions ... Ms. Jessica WAGONER
36 Director Career Development Center ... Mr. Jim CASE
40 Director Titan Shops ... Ms. Kimberly BALL
23 Director Health Center ... Ms. Kathy SPOFFORD
18 Director Physical Plant ... Mr. Willem VAN DER POL
19 Director University Police ... Mr. Dennis DEMAIO
28 Director Diversity/Equity Programs ... Vacant
37 Director Financial Aid ... Ms. Cecilia SCHOUWE
41 Director of Athletics ... Mr. James DONOVAN
85 Director International Programs ... Ms. Lay Tuan TAN
96 Director of Contracts & Procurement ... Mr. Don GREEN
38 Dir Counseling/Psychological Svcs ... Dr. Leticia GUTIERREZ-LOPEZ
51 Dean University Extended Educ ... Dr. Harry NORMAN
79 Int Dean Humanities/Social Science ... Dr. Sheryl FONTAINE
81 Int Dean Natural Sciences & Math ... Dr. Robert KOCH
50 Dean Mihaylo Col Business/Economics ... Dr. Anil PURI
83 Dean Col Health/Human Development ... Dr. Shari MCMAHAN
57 Dean Collge of the Arts ... Dr. Joseph ARNOLD
53 Dean College of Education ... Dr. Claire CAVALLARO
54 Dean Col Engineering & Computer Sci ... Dr. Raman UNNIKRISHNAN
60 Dean College of Communications ... Dr. William BRIGGS
12 Dean Irvine Campus ... Dr. Susan COOPER

*California State University-Long Beach (F)

1250 Bellflower Boulevard, Long Beach CA 90840-0119
County: Los Angeles FICE Identification: 001139
Unit ID: 110583
Telephone: (562) 985-4111 Carnegie Class: Master's L
FAX Number: (562) 985-5419 Calendar System: Semester
URL: www.csulb.edu

Established: 1949 Annual Undergrad Tuition & Fees (In-State): $6,738
Enrollment: 36,279 Coed
Affiliation or Control: State IRS Status: 501(c)3
Highest Offering: Doctorate
Program: Liberal Arts And General; Teacher Preparatory; Professional
Accreditation: WC, AAFCS, ART, BUS, CEA, CONST, CS, DANCE, DIETD, DIETI, ENG, HSA, IPSY, KIN, MUS, NRPA, NURSE, PH, PTA, SP, SPAA, SW, TED, THEA

02 Interim President ... Dr. Donald PARA
05 Provost/Sr Vice Pres Academic Affs ... Dr. David DOWELL
11 Vice Pres Administration/Finance ... Ms. Mary E. STEPHENS
32 Vice President Student Services ... Dr. Mary Ann TAKEMOTO
30 Vice Pres University Rels/Devel ... Ms. Andrea TAYLOR
04 Exec Assistant to the President ... Dr. Karen NAKAI
10 Assoc VP Financial Management ... Ms. Sharon TAYLOR
20 Assoc Academic Officer/Vice Provost ... Vacant
35 Assoc Vice Pres Student Services ... Vacant
82 Assoc VP Intl Educ/Global Engagemnt ... Dr. Jeet JOSHEE
18 Assoc Vice Pres Phys Plng/Facil Mgt ... Mr. David SALAZAR
58 Assoc VP/Grad & Undergrad Programs ... Dr. Cecile LINDSAY
46 Assoc Vice Pres University Research ... Dr. Zed MASON
16 Assoc VP Budget/Human Resource Mgmt ... Mr. Scott APEL
91 Int Assoc VP Academic Technology ... Mr. Roman KOCHAN
27 Asst Vice Pres Public Affairs ... Ms. Terri CARBAUGH
29 Asst Vice Pres Alumni Rel/Spec Proj ... Ms. Janice HATANAKA
09 Asst VP Institutional Research ... Dr. Van NOVACK
84 Asst Vice Pres Enrollment Services ... Mr. Thomas ENDERS
13 Asst VP Information Technology ... Ms. Janet FOSTER
76 Dean College Health/Human Svcs ... Dr. Kenneth MILLAR
50 Dean College of Business Admin ... Dr. Michael SOLT
53 Dean College of Education ... Dr. Marquita GRENOT-SCHEYER
54 Dean College of Engineering ... Dr. Forouzan GOLSHANI
57 Dean College of the Arts ... Mr. Chris MILES
81 Dean Col Natural Science/Math ... Dr. Laura KINGSFORD
49 Dean College of Liberal Arts ... Dr. David WALLACE
51 Dean Col Continuing & Profess Educ ... Dr. Jeet JOSHEE
08 Dean Library/Learning Resources ... Mr. Roman KOCHAN
39 Director Housing Administration ... Ms. Carol ROBERTS-CORB
15 Director Staff Personnel Services ... Ms. Nancy TORRES
41 Director Athletics ... Mr. Victor CEGLES
88 Dir Student Rels/Academic Support ... Ms. Donna GREEN
07 Director of Admissions ... Ms. Marie ALFORD
36 Director Career Plng & Placement ... Mr. Manuel PEREZ
23 Director Health Services ... Dr. Michael CARBUTO
19 Director Public Safety ... Mr. Fernando SOLORZANO
38 Director Counseling/Psych Services ... Dr. Brad COMPLIMENT
37 Director Financial Aid/Admissions ... Mr. Nicolas VALDIVIA
25 Director Found Grants/Contracts ... Ms. Sandra SHEREMAN
102 Executive Director Foundation ... Dr. Brian NOWLIN
28 Director of Equity & Diversity ... Ms. Larisa HAMADA
26 Chief Public Relations Officer ... Vacant
96 Director of Purchasing ... Ms. Laurinda FULLER
40 General Manager/49'er Shops ... Mr. Donald PENROD

*California State University-Los Angeles (A)

5151 State University Drive, Los Angeles CA 90032-8530
County: Los Angeles FICE Identification: 001140
Unit ID: 110592
Telephone: (323) 343-3000 Carnegie Class: Master's L
FAX Number: (323) 343-2670 Calendar System: Quarter
URL: www.calstatela.edu
Established: 1947 Annual Undergrad Tuition & Fees (In-State): $8,443
Enrollment: 21,755 Coed
Affiliation or Control: State IRS Status: 501(c)3
Highest Offering: Doctorate
Program: Liberal Arts And General; Teacher Preparatory; Professional
Accreditation: WC, ART, BUS, CACREP, CORE, CS, DIETC, DIETD, ENG, FEPAC, MUS, NURSE, SP, SPAA, SW, TED

02 President ... Dr. William A. COVINO
05 Provost/Vice Pres Academic Affairs ... Dr. Ashish VAIDYA
32 Vice President Student Affairs ... Dr. Anthony R. ROSS
13 Vice Pres/Chief Technology Officer ... Mr. Peter QUAN
10 VP Administration & CFO ... Ms. Lisa M. CHAVEZ
44 Vice Pres Institutional Advancement ... Mr. Kyle C. BUTTON
20 Assoc VP Academic Affairs ... Dr. Cheryl L. NEY
11 Assoc VP Admin & Finance ... Mr. Jose GOMEZ
21 Asst VP Admin & Finance/Budget ... Ms. Mae SANTOS
35 Asst VP Student Affs/Student Svcs ... Ms. Nancy WADA-MCKEE
30 Asst VP University Development ... Ms. Collette G. ROCHA
20 Asst VP Acad Affs/Acad Personnel ... Dr. Philip LAPOLT
29 Exec Director Alumni Relations ... Ms. Maria UBAGO
26 Exec Director Public Affairs ... Vacant
41 Director Intercollegiate Athletics ... Dr. Daniel BRIDGES
83 Dean Natural & Social Sciences ... Dr. James P. HENDERSON
08 University Librarian ... Ms. Alice K. KAWAKAMI
06 Univ Registrar & Dir of Enrollment ... Vacant
58 Dean Grad Studies/Research ... Dr. Lawrence M. FRITZ
88 Assoc Dean Graduate Studies ... Dr. Karin A. ELLIOT BROWN
09 Director Institutional Research ... Dr. Mark PAVELCHAK
36 Director Career Placement & Plng ... Mr. Christopher LENZ
37 Director Student Financial Services ... Ms. Tamie NGUYEN
23 Director Health Center ... Dr. Monica JAZZABI
39 Director Housing Svc/Residence Life ... Mr. Stephen FLEISCHER
22 Director Equal Opportunity Pgm ... Ms. Becky HOPKINS
18 Director Facilities/Physical Plant ... Mr. Carlos PORTILLO
19 Director Public Safety ... Mr. Joseph CURRERI
15 Asst VP Human Resources Management ... Ms. Lisa SANCHEZ
85 Director Intl Programs & Services ... Ms. Amy WANG
43 University Counsel ... Mr. Victor I. KING
07 Director Admissions & Recruitment ... Mr. Vince LOPEZ
96 Director Procurement & Contracts ... Mr. Thomas JOHNSON
09 Asst Dir Institutional Research ... Ms. Vivien KO
28 Director Equity & Diversity ... Ms. Mariel MULET
40 Manager Bookstore ... Mr. Todd MURPHY
88 Assoc Dean Undergraduate Studies ... Dr. Steven JONES
49 Dean Arts & Letters ... Dr. Peter MCALLISTER
54 Int Dean Engr/Computer Science/Tech ... Dr. Ethan LIPTON
51 Int Dean Extended Stds/Intl Pgms ... Mr. Justin CASSITY
76 Dean Health & Human Services ... Dr. Beatrice YORKER
53 Dean Charter College of Education ... Dr. Eunsook HYUN
50 Dean Business & Economics ... Dr. James A. GOODRICH
97 Dean Undergraduate Studies ... Dr. Jun XING
92 Director Honors College ... Dr. Michelle HAWLEY

† Grants Joint Doctoral degree in cooperation with the University of California-Los Angeles.

*California State University-Monterey Bay (B)

100 Campus Center, Seaside CA 93955-8000
County: Monterey FICE Identification: 032603
Unit ID: 409698
Telephone: (831) 582-3000 Carnegie Class: Master's S
FAX Number: (831) 582-3783 Calendar System: Semester
URL: www.csumb.edu
Established: 1994 Annual Undergrad Tuition & Fees (In-State): $5,718
Enrollment: 5,609 Coed
Affiliation or Control: State IRS Status: 501(c)3
Highest Offering: Master's
Program: Liberal Arts And General
Accreditation: WC, @SW, TED

02 President ... Dr. Eduardo M. OCHOA
05 Provost ... Dr. Julio R. BLANCO
10 Vice Pres Admin & Finance/CFO ... Mr. Kevin SAUNDERS
30 Vice Pres University Development ... Ms. Barbara ZAPPAS
32 VP Student Affairs & Enroll Service ... Dr. Ronnie HIGGS
26 Assoc VP for University Affairs ... Mr. Andre LEWIS
35 Dean of Student Life ... Dr. Christine ERICKSON
10 Assoc Vice President for Finance ... Mr. John FITZGIBBON
28 Assoc VP Inclusive Excellence ... Dr. Patti HIRAMOTO
06 Registrar ... Ms. Sheila HERNANDEZ
22 Director Employee Rels/EEO & ADA ... Ms. Tamberly PETROVICH
37 Director Financial Aid ... Ms. Angeles FUENTES
15 Assoc VP for Human Resources ... Ms. Mary ROBERTS
19 Chief of Police ... Chief Earl LAWSON
18 Chief Facilities/Physical Plant ... Mr. John MARKER
21 Associate Business Officer ... Mr. John FITZGIBBON
07 Dir for Admissions & Recruitment ... Mr. David LINNEVERS
29 Director Alumni Relations ... Ms. Pilar GOSE
41 Interim Athletic Director ... Mr. Kirby GARRY
20 Interim Associate Academic Officer ... Dr. David REICHARD
96 Director of Purchasing ... Mr. Art EVJEN

*California State University-Northridge (C)

18111 Nordhoff Street, Northridge CA 91330-0001
County: Los Angeles FICE Identification: 001153
Unit ID: 110608
Telephone: (818) 677-1200 Carnegie Class: Master's L
FAX Number: N/A Calendar System: Semester
URL: www.csun.edu
Established: 1958 Annual Undergrad Tuition & Fees (In-State): $6,520
Enrollment: 36,164 Coed
Affiliation or Control: State IRS Status: 501(c)3
Highest Offering: Doctorate
Program: Liberal Arts And General; Teacher Preparatory; Professional
Accreditation: WC, AAFCS, ART, BUS, CACREP, CIDA, CONST, CS, DIETD, DIETI, ENG, IPSY, JOUR, MUS, NURSE, PH, PTA, RAD, SP, SW, TED, THEA

02 President ... Dr. Dianne F. HARRISON
05 Provost/Vice Pres Academic Affairs ... Dr. Harry HELLENBRAND
10 Vice President Admin/Finance ... Mr. Colin DONAHUE
32 VP Student Affairs/Dean of Students ... Dr. William WATKINS
44 Vice Pres University Advancement ... Dr. Robert GUNSALUS
13 Vice President IT/CIO ... Ms. Hilary BAKER
88 Exec Director University Corp ... Mr. Rick EVANS
20 Vice Provost Academic Affairs ... Dr. Michael NEUBAUER
100 Chief of Staff ... Dr. Barbara L. GROSS
18 Assoc VP Facilities Dev/Operations ... Mr. Ken ROSENTHAL
58 Assoc VP Grad Studies/Intl Pgms ... Dr. Crist KHACHIKIAN
30 Assoc Vice Pres Development ... Ms. Maureen F. FITZGERALD
21 Associate VP Financial Services ... Ms. Deborah WALLACE
15 Assoc VP of Human Resources ... Ms. Jill A. SMITH
29 Asst Vice Pres Alumni Relations ... Mr. D. G. (Gray) MOUNGER
26 Interim Assoc VP of Mktg/Comm ... Mr. Robert RAWITCH
20 Senior Dir Undergraduate Studies ... Dr. Elizabeth T. ADAMS
91 Assoc VP of Academic Resources ... Ms. Diane S. STEPHENS
07 Director of Admissions and Records ... Ms. Patty R. LORD
08 Dean University Library ... Dr. Mark STOVER
51 Dean College of Extended Learning ... Dr. Joyce A. FEUCHT-HAVIAR
79 Dean College of Humanities ... Dr. Elizabeth A. SAY
50 Dean College Business/Economics ... Dr. Kenneth R. LORD
53 Dean College of Education ... Dr. Michael E. SPAGNA
57 Dean College Arts/Media/Commun ... Vacant
83 Dean Col Social/Behavioral Sci ... Dr. Stella Z. THEODOULOU
76 Dean Col Health/Human Development ... Dr. Sylvia A. ALVA
81 Dean College Science & Math ... Dr. Jerry STINNER
54 Dean College Engr/Computer Science ... Dr. S. K. RAMESH
09 Director Institutional Research ... Dr. Bettina HUBER
37 Director Financial Aid/Scholarships ... Mrs. Lili C. VIDAL
38 Director Univ Counseling Services ... Dr. Mark STEVENS
36 Director Career Center ... Ms. Ann N. MOREY
25 Dir Research/Sponsored Projects ... Mr. Scott L. PEREZ
18 Senior Dir Physical Plant Mgmt ... Mr. Jason WANG
19 Director of Police Services ... Ms. Anne P. GLAVIN
28 Director of Equity and Diversity ... Ms. Susan HUA
86 Dir Government/Community Relations ... Ms. Francesca VEGA
23 Director Student Health Center ... Dr. Linda REID-CHASSIAKOS
39 Dir Student Housing/Conf Services ... Mr. Timothy J. TREVAN
40 Director Matador Bookstore ... Ms. Amy C. BERGER
41 Director of Athletics ... Dr. Brandon MARTIN
85 Dir Student Devel/Intl Programs ... Mr. Thomas E. PIERNIK
92 Dir General Education Honors Pgm ... Dr. Beth A. WIGHTMAN
96 Manager Purchasing ... Ms. Deborah FLUGUM
84 Director Enrollment Management ... Dr. William WATKINS
06 Registrar ... Mr. Todd WOLFE

*California State University-Sacramento (D)

6000 J Street, Sacramento CA 95819-2694
County: Sacramento FICE Identification: 001150
Unit ID: 110617
Telephone: (916) 278-6011 Carnegie Class: Master's L
FAX Number: (916) 278-6664 Calendar System: Semester
URL: www.csus.edu
Established: 1947 Annual Undergrad Tuition & Fees (In-State): $6,602
Enrollment: 28,539 Coed
Affiliation or Control: State IRS Status: 501(c)3
Highest Offering: Doctorate
Program: Liberal Arts And General; Teacher Preparatory; Professional
Accreditation: WC, ART, BUS, CACREP, CIDA, CONST, CORE, CS, DIETD, DIETI, EMT, ENG, MUS, NRPA, NURSE, PTA, SP, SW

02 President ... Dr. Alexander GONZALEZ
05 Provost/Vice Pres Academic Affairs ... Dr. Charles GOSSETT
11 Vice President Administration & CFO .. Dr. Ming-Tung "Mike" LEE
30 Vice Pres University Advancement ... Mr. Vince SALES
32 Vice President Student Affairs ... Dr. Lori VARLOTTA
13 VP & Chief Information Officer ... Dr. Larry GILBERT
15 Vice President for Human Resources ... Ms. Christine D. LOVELY
26 Vice Pres Public Affairs/Advocacy ... Dr. Phil GARCIA
25 Asst VP Research/Contract Admin ... Mr. David EARWICKER
20 Vice Provost ... Vacant
45 Assoc VP Academic Affs/Planning ... Vacant
18 Assoc Vice Pres Facilities Mgmt ... Dr. Ali IZADIAN
27 Assoc VP University Communications ... Ms. Jeannie WONG
84 AVP Enrollment Mgmt/Student Support ... Mr. Edward MILLS
35 AVP Student Affairs/Campus Life ... Mr. Michael SPEROS
21 Interim Assoc VP Financial Svcs ... Ms. Justine HEARTT
36 Int Asst VP Student Engage/Success ... Dr. Dave EVANS
43 University Counsel ... Ms. Jill PETERSON
09 Director Institutional Research ... Dr. Jing WANG
07 Director Outreach & Admissions ... Mr. Emiliano DIAZ
08 Dean University Library ... Ms. Tabzeera DOSU
29 Director Alumni Relations ... Ms. Jennifer BARBER
19 Director Public Safety ... Mr. Mark IWASA
39 Dir Housing and Residential Life ... Mr. Michael SPEROS
41 Director Intercollegiate Athletics ... Dr. Terry WANLESS
37 Director Financial Aid ... Ms. Anita KERMES
22 Director of Employment Equity ... Mr. William BISHOP
40 Bookstore Director ... Ms. Julia MILARDOVICH
100 Chief of Staff ... Ms. Carol ENSLEY
06 University Registrar ... Mr. Dennis GEYER
85 Director Global Education ... Dr. Jack GODWIN
23 Dir Student Health Ctr & Psych Svcs .Dr. Joy STEWART-JAMES
96 Mgr Procurement/Contract Services ... Mr. John GUION
49 Dean College of Arts & Letters ... Dr. Edward INCH
50 Dean College of Business Admin ... Dr. Sanjay VARSHNEY
53 Dean College of Education ... Dr. Vanessa SHEARED
54 Dean College of Engr/Computer Sci ... Dr. Emir J. MACARI
76 Dean College of Health/Human Svcs ... Dr. Fred BALDINI
81 Dean College of Natural Sci/Math ... Dr. Jill TRAINER
51 Dean College Continuing Education ... Mr. Guido KRICKX
83 Dean College Soc Sci/Interdisc Stds ... Dr. Ted LASCHER
58 Dean Graduate Studies ... Dr. Chevelle NEWSOME

*California State University-San Bernardino (E)

5500 University Parkway, San Bernardino CA 92407-2393
County: San Bernardino FICE Identification: 001142
Unit ID: 110510
Telephone: (909) 537-5000 Carnegie Class: Master's L
FAX Number: N/A Calendar System: Quarter
URL: www.csusb.edu
Established: 1960 Annual Undergrad Tuition & Fees (In-State): $6,549
Enrollment: 18,234 Coed
Affiliation or Control: State IRS Status: 501(c)3
Highest Offering: Doctorate
Program: Liberal Arts And General; Teacher Preparatory; Professional
Accreditation: WC, ART, BUS, CORE, CS, DIETD, MUS, NURSE, SPAA, SW, TED, THEA

02 President ... Dr. Tomas MORALES
05 Provost/Vice Pres Academic Affairs ... Dr. Andrew R. BODMAN
10 Vice Pres Administration/Finance ... Mr. Robert GARDNER
32 Vice President Student Affairs ... Dr. Brian L. HAYNES

30 Vice Pres University Advancement ... Dr. Ronald FREMONT
13 Vice President IT/CIO ... Mr. Samuel SUDHAKAR
28 Chief Diversity Officer ... Dr. J. Milton CLARK
88 Director Executive Affairs ... Ms. Pamela LANGFORD
20 Assoc Provost Academic Programs ... Dr. Jenny ZORN
88 Assoc Provost Research ... Dr. Jeffrey M. THOMPSON
16 Assoc Provost Academic Personnel ... Dr. Jacqueline HUGHES
21 Assoc VP Finance ... Mr. M. Monir AHMED
15 Assoc VP Human Resources ... Mr. Cesar PORTILLO
84 Assoc VP Enrollment Mgmt ... Ms. Olivia ROSAS
35 Assoc VP Student Development ... Ms. Helga KRAY
88 Assoc VP IT ... Ms. Lorraine FROST
88 Associate VP Development ... Vacant
26 Associate VP Public Affairs ... Mr. Sid ROBINSON
09 Director Institutional Research ... Ms. Muriel LOPEZ-WAGNER
36 Director Career Development Center ... Mr. Larry BURNS
06 Dir Student Recs/Regis/Eval ... Ms. Grace DEMPSEY
07 Director Admissions ... Ms. Arlene REED
23 Director Health & Counseling Center ... Dr. Patricia SMITH
08 University Librarian ... Mr. Cesar CABALLERO
37 Director Financial Aid ... Ms. Roseanna RUIZ
39 Director Housing & Residential Life ... Ms. Lovellie ALMOGELA
45 Director Plng Design/Construction ... Mr. Hamid U. AZHAND
18 Sr Director Facilities Services ... Mr. Tony SIMPSON
41 Director Athletics ... Dr. Kevin L. HATCHER
29 Director Alumni Affairs ... Vacant
96 Director Purchasing ... Ms. Kathy HANSEN
22 Director Diversity (faculty) ... Dr. Jacqueline HUGHES
22 Director Diversity (staff) ... Mr. Cesar PORTILLO
40 Director Bookstore ... Ms. Lyly BIRD
94 Dir Gender & Sexuality Studies ... Dr. Todd JENNINGS
92 Director University Honors Program ... Dr. J. Milton CLARK
56 Dean Col of Extended Learning ... Dr. Tatiana KARMANOVA
49 Dean College of Arts & Letters ... Dr. Terry BALLMAN
81 Dean Col Natural Sciences ... Dr. Kirsten FLEMING
83 Dean Col Social/Behavioral Sciences ... Dr. Jamal R. NASSAR
53 Dean College of Education ... Dr. Jay FIENE
50 Dean College of Business ... Dr. Lawrence D. ROSE
58 Dean Graduate Studies ... Dr. Jeffrey M. THOMPSON
12 Dean CSUSB Palm Desert ... Dr. Fred E. JANDT
88 Dean Undergraduate Studies ... Dr. J. Milton CLARK

*California State University-San Marcos (A)

333 S Twin Oaks Valley Road,
San Marcos CA 92096-0001

County: San Diego — FICE Identification: 030113
Unit ID: 366711
Telephone: (760) 750-4000 — Carnegie Class: Master's M
FAX Number: (760) 750-4030 — Calendar System: Semester
URL: www.csusm.edu
Established: 1989 — Annual Undergrad Tuition & Fees (In-State): $6,800
Enrollment: 10,610 — Coed
Affiliation or Control: State — IRS Status: 501(c)3
Highest Offering: Doctorate
Program: Liberal Arts And General; Teacher Preparatory
Accreditation: WC, NURSE, @SP, TED

02 President ... Dr. Karen S. HAYNES
04 Executive Assistant ... Ms. Caroline TANNER
10 Vice President Finance/Admin Svcs ... Dr. Linda HAWK
05 Vice President Academic Affairs ... Dr. Graham OBEREM
32 Vice President of Student Affairs ... Dr. Lorena MEZA
30 Vice Pres University Advancement ... Mr. Neal HOSS
20 Assoc Vice Pres Academic Affairs ... Dr. Regina EISENBACH
20 Assoc VP Planning/Acad Resources ... Vacant
84 Assoc Vice Pres Enrollment Mgmt ... Mr. Scott HAGG
15 Assoc VP Human Resource/Equal Oppty ... Ms. Joanne SHYDIAN
22 Assoc VP Diversity & Educ Equity ... Mr. Arturo OCAMPO
49 Dean Col Hum Arts/Behav & Soc Sci ... Dr. Adam SHAPIRO
50 Dean Col Business Administration ... Dr. Sharon LIGHTNER
53 Dean Col Educ/Health & Human Svcs ... Dr. Janet POWELL
08 Dean of Library Services ... Mr. Wayne VERES
81 Dean Col of Science & Mathematics ... Dr. Katherine KANTARDJIEFF
56 Dean of Extended Studies ... Mr. Michael SCHRODER
88 Dean Instructional/Info Technology ... Mr. Wayne VERES
37 Director Financial Aid ... Ms. Vonda GARCIA
06 Registrar ... Mr. Thomas SWANGER
07 Dir of Admissions & Recruitment ... Ms. Carol MCALLISTER
09 Chief of Staff/Dir Inst Plng & Anal ... Mr. Matthew CEPPI
18 Director Facility Services ... Mr. Gary CINNAMON
21 Associate Business Officer ... Vacant
29 Director Alumni/Parent Relations ... Ms. Lori BROCKETT
96 Director Procurment/Support Svcs ... Ms. Bella NEWBERG
38 Director Undergraduate Advising ... Mr. Andres FAVELA

† Grants Joint Doctoral degree in cooperation with the University of California-San Diego.

*California State University-Stanislaus (B)

1 University Circle, Turlock CA 95382-0299

County: Stanislaus — FICE Identification: 001157
Unit ID: 110495
Telephone: (209) 667-3122 — Carnegie Class: Master's L
FAX Number: (209) 667-3206 — Calendar System: Semester
URL: www.csustan.edu
Established: 1957 — Annual Undergrad Tuition & Fees (In-State): $6,664
Enrollment: 8,882 — Coed
Affiliation or Control: State — IRS Status: 501(c)3
Highest Offering: Doctorate
Program: Liberal Arts And General; Teacher Preparatory; Professional
Accreditation: WC, ART, BUS, MUS, NURSE, SPAA, SW, TED, THEA

02 President ... Dr. Joseph F. SHELEY
05 Provost/VP Academic Affairs ... Dr. James T. STRONG
10 VP Business/Finance ... Mr. Russell GIAMBELLUCA
32 VP Enrollment/Student Affairs ... Dr. Suzanne M. ESPINOZA
30 VP University Advancement ... Ms. Shirley M. POK
15 Interim VP Faculty Affairs/HR ... Mr. Dennis W. SHIMEK
100 Executive Assistant to President ... Ms. Carrie M. RASMUSSEN
35 AVP Student Affairs/Dean of Student ... Mr. Ronald J. NOBLE
13 Assoc VP Information Technology ... Mr. Carl E. WHITMAN
27 Assoc VP Communication/Public Aff ... Mr. David L. TONELLI
18 Int Assoc VP Facilities Services ... Ms. Melody MAFFEI
21 Assoc VP Financial Services ... Ms. Julie K. BENEVEDES
30 Int Asst VP University Advanc ... Ms. Michele LAHTI
20 Int AVP Academic Planning/Analysis ... Dr. Marjorie A. JAASMA
79 Dean College Arts/Humanities & SS ... Dr. James A. TUEDIO
50 Dean College of Business Admin ... Dr. Linda I. NOWAK
65 Dean College of Science ... Dr. Reza KAMALI
53 Interim Dean College of Education ... Dr. Oddmund R. MYHRE
106 Interim Dean Stockton Center ... Dr. Ashour BADAL
51 Interim Dean Extended Education ... Mr. Chuck GONZALEZ
08 Interim Dean Library Services ... Ms. Annie Y. HOR
06 Registrar ... Ms. Lisa M. BERNARDO
37 Director Admissions & Financial Aid ... Ms. Noelia GONZALEZ
19 Dir of Public Safety/Police Chief ... Mr. Steven P. JAUREGUY
15 Senior Manager HR & Compliance ... Ms. Gina B. LEGURIA
22 Campus Compliance Officer ... Ms. Julie A. JOHNSON
85 Director of International Education ... Mr. Mahmoud LAMADANIE
41 Director Athletics ... Mr. Michael MATOSO
88 Director Retention & Advising ... Dr. J. Martyn GUNN
09 Director of Institutional Research ... Dr. John P. TILLMAN
38 Director Psychological Counseling ... Dr. Daniel BERKOW
29 Int Dir Alumni Rels/Annual Giving ... Ms. Shannon NICHOLS
23 Int Director Health Services ... Dr. David B. CANTON

*Humboldt State University (C)

1 Harpst Street, Arcata CA 95521-8222

County: Humboldt — FICE Identification: 001149
Unit ID: 115755
Telephone: (707) 826-3011 — Carnegie Class: Master's M
FAX Number: (707) 826-5555 — Calendar System: Semester
URL: www.humboldt.edu
Established: 1913 — Annual Undergrad Tuition & Fees (In-State): $7,130
Enrollment: 8,116 — Coed
Affiliation or Control: State — IRS Status: 501(c)3
Highest Offering: Master's
Program: Liberal Arts And General; Teacher Preparatory; Professional
Accreditation: WC, ART, ENG, FOR, MUS, SW

02 President ... Dr. Rollin C. RICHMOND
04 Special Assistant to the President ... Ms. Denice HELWIG
05 Provost/Vice Pres Academic Affairs ... Dr. Robert A. SNYDER
20 Vice Prov Acad Pgms/Undergrad Stds ... Dr. Jena BURGES
32 VP Student Affairs & Enroll Mgmt ... Dr. Peg BLAKE
11 Vice Pres Administrative Affairs ... Ms. Joyce LOPES
30 Vice President of Advancement ... Mr. Craig WRUCK
88 Assoc Vice President Faculty Affs ... Dr. Colleen MULLERY
10 Assoc Vice Pres Business Services ... Ms. Carol LORENTZEN
84 Assoc VP Enrollment Management ... Mr. Vikash LAKHANI
29 Assoc VP Development & Alumni Rels ... Vacant
106 Assoc VP eLearning & Ext Educ ... Dr. Alex HWU
26 Assoc VP for Mktg & Communications ... Mr. Frank WHITLATCH
18 Assoc Vice President Facilities ... Ms. Traci FERDOLAGE
88 Director University Budget Office ... Vacant
88 Director of Academic Resources ... Mr. Volga KOVAL
06 Registrar ... Mr. Clint REBIK
07 Director of Admissions ... Mr. Steven LADWIG
16 Associate VP for Human Resources ... Mr. David BUGBEE
08 Dean of Library ... Ms. Teresa GRENOT
44 Director Planned Giving ... Vacant
19 Chief of University Police ... Chief Lynn SODERBERG
41 Athletic Director ... Mr. Dan COLLEN
39 Director of Housing ... Mr. John CAPACCIO
40 Asst Director Bookstore ... Ms. Roberta DUGGAN
13 Chief Information Officer ... Ms. Anna KIRCHER
36 Director Career Devel Center ... Ms. Annie BOLICK-FLOSS
28 Director Diversity & Inclusion ... Ms. Radha WEBLEY
46 Dean of Research & Sponsored Prgms ... Dr. Rhea WILLIAMSON
85 Director International Programs ... Ms. Rebecca BROWN
104 Study Abroad Advisor ... Ms. Penelope SHAW
35 Dean Student Affairs ... Ms. Randi DARNALL BURKE
37 Director Student Financial Aid ... Ms. Peggy METZGER
09 Dir Institutional Research & Plng ... Dr. Jacqueline HONDA
96 Director of Contracts & Procurement ... Mr. Michael BURGHART
90 Director ITS User Support ... Mr. Steve DARNALL
14 Director ITS Enterprise Tech ... Mr. Josh CALLAHAN
23 Dir Health/Counseling/Psych Svcs ... Ms. Mary Grooms VANCOTT
38 Director Counseling & Psy Svc ... Dr. Jennifer SANFORD
56 Director Extended Education ... Mr. Carl F. HANSEN
79 Dean Col Arts/Humanities/Soc Sci ... Dr. Kenneth AYOOB
107 Dean College Professional Studies ... Dr. John LEE
81 Dean Col Natural Resources/Science ... Dr. Steven SMITH
21 Director Financial Services ... Ms. Lynne SANDSTROM
06 Registrar eLearning & Ext Educ ... Ms. Terri GEORGOPOULOS
105 Web Manager ... Mr. Matt HODGSON

*San Diego State University (D)

5500 Campanile Drive, San Diego CA 92182-8000

County: San Diego — FICE Identification: 001151
Unit ID: 122409
Telephone: (619) 594-5200 — Carnegie Class: RU/H
FAX Number: (619) 594-8894 — Calendar System: Semester
URL: www.sdsu.edu
Established: 1897 — Annual Undergrad Tuition & Fees (In-State): $6,766
Enrollment: 31,600 — Coed
Affiliation or Control: State — IRS Status: 501(c)3
Highest Offering: Doctorate
Program: Teacher Preparatory; Professional
Accreditation: WC, ART, AUD, BUS, BUSA, CIDA, CLPSY, CORE, DIETD, ENG, HSA, JOUR, MFCD, MIDWF, NURSE, PH, @PTA, SP, SPAA, SW, TED, THEA

02 President ... Dr. Elliot HIRSHMAN
05 Provost ... Dr. Nancy A. MARLIN
10 Vice President Business Affairs ... Mr. Tom MCCARRON
32 Acting VP for Student Affairs ... Mr. Eric RIVERA
30 VP University Relations/Development ... Ms. Mary Ruth CARLETON
46 Vice President for Research ... Dr. Stephen WELTER
20 Assoc Vice Pres Academic Affairs ... Dr. Ethan A. SINGER
11 Assoc Vice President Operations ... Mr. Robert SCHULZ
88 Assoc Vice Pres Faculty Affairs ... Dr. Edith BENKOV
21 Assoc VP for Financial Operations ... Ms. Lorretta LEAVITT
15 Associate VP Administration ... Ms. Jessica RENTTO
85 Asst Vice President Intl Programs ... Dr. Alan R. SWEEDLER
27 Acting Chief Communications Officer ... Mr. Greg BLOCK
35 Associate VP Student Services ... Mr. Reginald BLAYLOCK
88 Associate VP Campus Life ... Dr. Timothy QUINNAN
29 Assistant VP for Alumni Engagement ... Mr. James S. HERRICK
23 Director Student Health Svcs ... Mr. Russell KLINKENBERG
100 Chief of Staff President's Office ... Dr. Andrea ROLLINS
23 Med Dir Student Health Services ... Dr. Gregg LICHTENSTEIN
88 Asst Vice Pres Academic Affairs ... Dr. Sandra COOK
38 Director Counseling/Psych Services ... Dr. Sandy JORGENSEN-FUNK
08 Dean Library/Information Access ... Dr. Gale ETSCHMAIER
88 Associate VP of Development ... Ms. Joanne FERCHLAND-PARELLA
45 Exec Dir Research Foundation ... Mr. Bob E. WOLFSON
51 Dean of Extended Studies ... Dr. Joe SHAPIRO
58 Assoc Dean of Graduate Affairs ... Dr. Radmilla PRISLIN
49 Dean of Div Undergraduate Studies ... Dr. Geoffrey W. CHASE
79 Dean of College Arts & Letters ... Dr. Paul WONG
81 Dean College of Sciences ... Dr. Stanley MALOY
54 Dean of College of Engineering ... Dr. David T. HAYHURST
50 Int Dean College of Business Admin ... Dr. Gangaram SINGH
76 Dean of Col Health/Human Services ... Dr. Marilyn NEWHOFF
53 Int Dean of College of Education ... Dr. Joseph JOHNSON, JR.
12 Dean Imperial Valley Campus ... Dr. David PEARSON
57 Dean of Profess Studies/Fine Arts ... Dr. Joyce M. GATTAS
84 Assoc Exec Dir Enrollment Services ... Ms. Rita GAJOLI
19 Interim Director Public Safety ... Mr. Lamine SECKA
28 Chief Diversity Officer ... Dr. Aaron I. BRUCE
06 Registrar ... Ms. Rayanne WILLIAMS
07 Director of Admissions ... Ms. Beverly ARATA
36 Director Career Services ... Dr. James TARBOX
39 Director Housing Administration ... Dr. Eric HANSEN
40 CEO Aztec Shops ... Mrs. Donna TUSACK
41 Director Intercollegiate Athletics ... Mr. Jim STERK
85 Dir International Student Center ... Dr. Negar DAVIS
88 Director Environ Health & Safety ... Mr. Terry GEE
13 Sr Director Information & Tech/CIO ... Mr. Rich PICKETT
09 Dir Univ Analytic Stds/Instnl Rsrch ... Ms. Jeanne STRONACH
31 Dir Government/Community Relations ... Ms. Megan COLLINS
96 Mgr Contract/Procurement Mgmt ... Ms. Cathy GARCIA
21 Interim Controller ... Mr. Chris BRONSDON
18 Director of Facilities Services ... Mr. John FERRIS
21 Acting Asst VP/Budget & Admin ... Ms. Linda LEWISTON
88 Director of Communications ... Ms. Kimberly CALDERON
22 Acting Dir Educ Opportunity Pgms ... Dr. Beverly WARREN
37 Actg Dir Fin Aid & Scholarships ... Ms. Rose PASENELLI
88 Ombudsman ... Ms. Marit BESSESEN
88 Director of Residential Education ... Ms. Christy SAMARKOS
88 Director Student Disability Svcs ... Dr. Donald KIRSON

*San Francisco State University (E)

1600 Holloway Avenue, San Francisco CA 94132-1740

County: San Francisco — FICE Identification: 001154
Unit ID: 122597
Telephone: (415) 338-1111 — Carnegie Class: Master's L
FAX Number: (415) 338-2514 — Calendar System: Semester
URL: www.sfsu.edu
Established: 1899 — Annual Undergrad Tuition & Fees (In-State): $6,450
Enrollment: 30,500 — Coed
Affiliation or Control: State — IRS Status: 501(c)3
Highest Offering: Doctorate
Program: Liberal Arts And General
Accreditation: WC, AAFCS, ART, BUS, CACREP, CORE, CS, DIETD, DIETI, ENG, JOUR, MT, MUS, NRPA, NURSE, PH, PTA, SP, SPAA, SW, THEA

02 President ... Dr. Leslie E. WONG
05 Provost & VP Academic Affairs ... Dr. Sue V. ROSSER
30 Vice Pres University Advancement ... Mr. Robert J. NAVA
10 VP & CFO Administration and Finance ... Mr. Ronald S. CORTEZ
32 Int VP Student Affairs/Enroll Mgmt ... Dr. Jo VOLKERT
43 University Counsel ... Ms. Patricia B. BARTSCHER
45 AVP Academic Planning/Development ... Dr. Linda BUCKLEY
20 Assoc VP Academic Resources ... Dr. John J. KIM
46 Assoc VP Research Sponsored Pgms ... Dr. Jaylan TURKKAN
20 Assoc VP Academic Affairs Operation ... Dr. Brian BEATTY
85 Assoc VP International Education ... Dr. Yenbo WU
18 Assoc VP Capital Plan Design Const ... Mr. Simon Y. LAM
13 AVP Division Info Tech ... Ms. Phoebe KWAN
84 Senior AVP Enrollment Management ... Dr. Jo VOLKERT
18 Sr Assoc VP Physical Plng & Develop ... Ms. Marilyn LANIER

21 Assoc VP Fiscal Affairs .... Ms. Agnes WONG-NICKERSON
16 Assoc VP HR/Safety & Risk Mgt ....Vacant
45 AVP Strategic Plng/Univ Compliance ....Mr. Gene CHELBERG
100 Chief of Staff ....Mr. Shawn WHALEN
50 Dean College Business ....Ms. Linda OUBRE
53 Interim Dean College Education ....Dr. Betsy KEAN
88 Dean College Ethnic Studies ....Dr. Kenneth P. MONTEIRO
51 AVP/Dean College Extended Learning ....Dr. Jose L. GALVAN
69 Dean Col Health & Social Science ....Dr. Don TAYLOR
79 Dean Col Liberal & Creative Arts ....Dr. Paul SHERWIN
81 Dean College Science & Engineering ....Dr. Sheldon AXLER
15 Dean Faculty Affairs & Prof Dev ....Dr. Sacha BUNGE
58 Dean Graduate Studies ....Dr. Ann HALLUM
88 Interim Dean Undergraduate Studies ....Dr. Helen GOLDSMITH
102 SF State President Foundation ....Mr. Robert J. NAVA
08 University Librarian ....Ms. Deborah C. MASTERS
24 Director Academic Technology ....Dr. Maggie BEERS
85 Director International Programs ....Ms. Hildy HEATH
30 Associate Vice Pres Development ....Vacant
86 Director Government & Community Rel ..... Ms. Lisbet SUNSHINE
27 AVP University Communications ....Ms. Ellen GRIFFIN
88 Exec Dir Univ Property Management ....Mr. Mark GOODRICH
88 Director EHOS ....Mr. Aaron NEVATT
39 Dir Resident Life/Assc Dean of Stdn ....Dr. Mary Ann BEGLEY
37 Director Student Financial Aid ....Ms. Barbara HUBLER
88 Director Student Outreach Services ....Dr. Frieda LEE
07 Director Undergraduate Admissions ....Mr. John PLISKA
21 Director Univ Budget Planning ....Mr. Andrew SOM
06 Interim Registrar ....Ms. Renee MONTE
41 Director Athletics ....Dr. Michael J. SIMPSON
38 Director Counseling & Psych Svcs ....Dr. Derethia DUVAL
88 Director Disability Pgms/Res Ctr ....Ms. Nicole BOHN
88 Dir Education Opportunity Program ....Mr. Oscar M. GARDEA
19 Chf of Police/Dir of Public Safety ....Chief Patrick WASLEY
23 Medical Dir Student Health Svcs ....Dr. Alastair SMITH
35 Dean of Students ....Mr. Joseph D. GREENWELL
96 Director Procurement Department ....Mr. Stephen C. SMITH
29 Director Alumni Relations ....Mr. Doug HUPKE
88 Budget Officer ....Mr. Franz LOZANO
88 Sr Dir Facilities Svcs Enterprise ....Mr. Chuck MEYER
36 Dir Student Involv & Career Ctr ....Ms. Sarah BAUER
44 Chief of Operations Advancement .... Ms. Venesia THOMPSON
102 Secretary/Treasurer SF State Found .... Ms. Venesia THOMPSON

† Grants additional Doctoral degrees in cooperation with the UC-Berkeley and UC-San Francisco.

*San Jose State University (A)

One Washington Square, San Jose CA 95192-0001
County: Santa Clara FICE Identification: 001155
Unit ID: 122755
Telephone: (408) 924-1000 Carnegie Class: Master's L
FAX Number: (408) 924-1018 Calendar System: Semester
URL: www.sjsu.edu
Established: 1857 Annual Undergrad Tuition & Fees (In-State): $7,303
Enrollment: 30,000 Coed
Affiliation or Control: State IRS Status: 501(c)3
Highest Offering: Master's
Program: Liberal Arts And General; Teacher Preparatory; Professional; Business Emphasis
Accreditation: WC, ART, BUS, CEA, CS, DANCE, DIETD, DIETI, ENG, IPSY, JOUR, LIB, MT, MUS, NAIT, NRPA, NURSE, OT, PH, PLNG, SP, SPAA, SW, TED, THEA

02 President ....Dr. Mohammed QAYOUMI
11 Vice Pres Administration & Finance ....Mr. Shawn BIBB
32 Vice President Student Affairs ....Mr. William NANCE
30 VP University Advancement ....Ms. Rebecca DUKES
13 Deputy CIO ....Ms. Terry VAHEY
45 Vice Provost Academic Budgets/Plng ....Mr. Andy FEINSTEIN
14 Int Assoc VP Univ Computing/Telecom ....Mr. Don BAKER
09 Assoc VP Institutional Research .... Dr. Sutee SUJITPARAPITAYA
05 Provost/Vice Pres Acad Affairs ....Dr. Ellen JUNN
100 Chief of Staff ....Ms. Dorothy POOLE
20 Associate Vice Pres Faculty Affairs ....Dr. Elna GREEN
58 Assoc VP Graduate Studies/Research .... Dr. Pamela STACKS
20 Assoc VP Undergrad Studies .... Dr. Dennis JAEHNE
21 VP Admin Systems/Finance ....Ms. Josee LAROCHELLE
18 Assoc VP for Facilities/Operations ....Mr. Chris BROWN
15 Associate VP Human Resources ....Ms. Beth PUGLIESE
26 Assoc VP Public Affairs ....Vacant
44 Director Devel/Alumni Rels ....Mr. Brian BATES
51 Assoc VP/Dean Intl/Extended Stds ....Dr. Mark NOVAK
84 Int Assoc VP Enroll/Academic Svcs ....Ms. Sharon WILLEY
08 Dean of the University Library ....Dr. Ruth KIFER
28 Equal Opportunity Manager ....Ms. Julie PAISANT
27 Director Communications/Public Affs ....Mr. Barry SHILLER
29 Director Alumni Relations ....Ms. Janikke KLEM
06 Registrar ....Ms. Marion SOFISH
41 Director Intercollegiate Athletics ....Mr. Gene BLEYMAIER
96 Director Procurement Services ....Vacant
40 Director Spartan Bookstore .... Mr. Ryland METZINGER
19 Chief of Police ....Mr. Peter DECENA
36 Interim Director Career Center ....Ms. Susan ROCKWELL
38 Director Counseling Services ....Ms. Ellen LIN
37 Director Fin Aid/Schlarship Ofc .... Ms. Coleetta MCELROY
39 Dir University Housing Svcs ....Mr. Victor CULATTA
23 Dir Student Health Center ....Dr. Roger ELROD
49 Dean College of Applied Sci & Art .... Dr. Charles BULLOCK
50 Dean College of Business ....Dr. David STEELE
53 Dean College of Education ....Dr. Elaine CHIN
54 Dean College of Engineering ....Dr. Andrew HSU
79 Dean College of Humanities/Arts ....Dr. Lisa VOLLENDORF
81 Dean College of Science ....Dr. J. Michael PARRISH
83 Dean College Social Sciences ....Dr. Shella BIENENFELD

*Sonoma State University (B)

1801 E Cotati Avenue, Rohnert Park CA 94928-3609
County: Sonoma FICE Identification: 001156
Unit ID: 123572
Telephone: (707) 664-2880 Carnegie Class: Master's L
FAX Number: (707) 664-2505 Calendar System: Semester
URL: www.sonoma.edu
Established: 1960 Annual Undergrad Tuition & Fees (In-State): $7,162
Enrollment: 9,021 Coed
Affiliation or Control: State IRS Status: 501(c)3
Highest Offering: Master's
Program: Liberal Arts And General; Teacher Preparatory; Professional
Accreditation: WC, ART, BUS, CACREP, MUS, NUR, TED

02 President ....Dr. Ruben ARMINANA
05 Provost & Vice Pres Academic Affs ....Dr. Andrew ROGERSON
10 Vice Pres Administration & Finance .... Mr. Laurence FURUKAWA-SCHLERETH
26 Vice President University Affairs ....Mr. Dan CONDRON
30 Interim Vice President Development ....Mr. Erik GREENY
32 Chief Student Affairs Officer ....Mr. Matthew LOPEZ-PHILLIPS
20 Assoc VP for Faculty Affairs .... Dr. Melinda BARNARD
21 Assoc VP for Admin & Finance ....Ms. Letitia COATE
09 Director Institutional Research ....Mr. Sean JOHNSON
14 Acting CIO/Sr Dir Common Mgmt Sys ....Mr. Jason WENRICK
08 Library Director ....Mr. Brandon DUDLEY
79 Dean School of Arts & Humanities ....Dr. Thaine STEARNS
50 Dean Sch of Business/Economic .... Dr. William SILVER
53 Dean School of Education .... Dr. Carlos AYALA
81 Interim Dean School Science & Tech .... Dr. Lynn STAUFFER
83 Dean School of Social Sciences ....Dr. Elaine A. LEEDER
56 Dean School of Extended Education .... Dr. Mark MERICKEL
38 Dir of Counseling/Psych Services ....Dr. Lisa WYATT
37 Director of Financial Aid .... Mrs. Susan GUTIERREZ
18 Sr Dir Facilities Services/CPDC .... Mr. Christopher DINNO
27 Assoc VP for Communications & Mktg ....Ms. Susan KASHACK
41 Director Athletics ....Mr. William J. FUSCO
19 Interim Chief Police Services ....Ms. Sally MILLER
21 Director Seawolf Services ....Ms. Elizabeth O'BRIEN
88 Sr Director Entrepreneurial Srvcs .... Mr. Neil MARKLEY
06 Registrar ....Ms. Lisa NOTO
07 Director of Admissions ....Mr. Gustavo FLORES
29 Dir Alumni Relations/Annual Giving ....Ms. Laurie OGG
28 Mg Dir Employee Rel/Comp Svcs .... Ms. Joyce SUZUKI

California University of Management and Sciences (C)

721 North Euclid Street, Anaheim CA 92801
County: Orange FICE Identification: 041331
Telephone: (714) 533-3946 Carnegie Class: Not Classified
FAX Number: (714) 533-7778 Calendar System: Quarter
URL: www.calums.edu
Established: 1998 Annual Undergrad Tuition & Fees: $12,000
Enrollment: 450 Coed
Affiliation or Control: Independent Non-Profit IRS Status: 501(c)3
Highest Offering: Master's
Program: 2-Year Principally Bachelor's Creditable; Professional; Business Emphasis
Accreditation: ACICS

01 President ....David PARK
03 Vice President ....Jason SHIN
05 Academic Dean .... Mohammad SAFARZADEH
20 Program Director ....Woo Jin HAN
11 Director Administration ....Eunjoo LIM
07 Admissions Officer ....Lisa LEE
32 Director of Student Services .... Janet LAURIN
08 Library Director ....Edwin FOLLICK
90 Academic Computing/Network Support ....James KIM
88 Chair Dept of Sports Management ....Anthony CHOI
88 Taekwondo Instructor & Dept Chair ....Andrew CHOI

California Western School of Law (D)

225 Cedar Street, San Diego CA 92101-3090
County: San Diego FICE Identification: 013103
Unit ID: 111391
Telephone: (619) 239-0391 Carnegie Class: Spec/Law
FAX Number: (619) 525-7092 Calendar System: Trimester
URL: www.cwsl.edu
Established: 1928 Annual Graduate Tuition & Fees: $44,800
Enrollment: 850 Coed
Affiliation or Control: Independent Non-Profit IRS Status: 501(c)3
Highest Offering: First Professional Degree; No Undergraduates
Program: Professional
Accreditation: LAW

01 President & Dean .... Dean Neils SCHAUMANN
05 Associate Dean Academic Affairs ....Prof. William C. ACEVES
11 Associate Dean Administration ....Vacant
30 VP Institutional Advancement ....Mr. Richard S. PODGORSKI
32 Asst Dean Students/Diversity Svcs ....Ms. Kathleen SEIBEL
36 Assistant Dean Career Services .... Ms. Courtney MIKLUSAK
88 Asst Dean Mission Development ....Mr. James M. COOPER
37 Exec Director Financial Aid ....Mr. William KAHLER
40 Exec Dir Swortwood Bookstore ....Ms. Crystal L. HENGEL
13 Exec Director Computer Services ....Ms. Mary Lou MITCHELL
18 Exec Dir Facilities Management ....Ms. Jolie L. CARTIER
88 Ex Dir Inst for Criminal Def Advoc ....Prof. Justin P. BROOKS
88 Exec Dir Inst of Health Law Studies ....Prof. Bryan A. LIANG
08 Assoc Dean Law Library/Info Res ....Prof. Phyllis C. MARION
10 Chief Financial Officer ....Ms. Pamela A. DUFFY
07 Assistant Dean Admissions ....Ms. Traci D. HOWARD
06 Registrar ....Ms. Sandra E. MOREAU
88 Director MCL/LLM Program ....Prof. Jacquelyn H. SLOTKIN
26 Chief Public Relations Officer ....Ms. Pamela HARDY
29 Director Alumni Relations ....Ms. Lori BOYLE
15 VP Human Resources ....Ms. Rikklyn S. UEDA
28 Director Diversity ....Ms. Marion E. CLOETE
21 Director Business Office ....Ms. Ruth GOULDING
35 Asst Dean Student Affairs ....Ms. Kathleen SEIBEL

Cambridge Junior College (E)

990-A Klamath Lane, Yuba City CA 95993-8978
County: Sutter FICE Identification: 038743
Unit ID: 446093
Telephone: (530) 674-9199 Carnegie Class: Assoc/PrivFP
FAX Number: (530) 671-7319 Calendar System: Other
URL: www.cambridge.edu
Established: Annual Undergrad Tuition & Fees: $14,826
Enrollment: 129 Coed
Affiliation or Control: Proprietary IRS Status: Proprietary
Highest Offering: Associate Degree
Program: Occupational
Accreditation: ACICS

01 Director ....Ms. Sandy FOWLER

Carnegie Mellon University Silicon Valley Campus (F)

NASA Research Pk, BLdg 23 MS 23-11,
Moffett Field CA 94035
Telephone: (650) 335-2810 Identification: 770149
Accreditation: &M

† Main campus is Carnegie Mellon University in Pittsburgh, PA.

*Carrington College California - Administrative Office (G)

7801 Folsom Boulevard, Suite 210,
Sacramento CA 95826-2620
County: Sacramento Identification: 666086
Telephone: (916) 388-2800 Carnegie Class: N/A
FAX Number: (916) 381-1609
URL: www.carrington.edu

01 President ....Dr. Jeff AKENS

*Carrington College California - Sacramento (H)

8909 Folsom Boulevard, Sacramento CA 95826-9823
County: Sacramento FICE Identification: 009748
Unit ID: 125532
Telephone: (916) 361-1660 Carnegie Class: Assoc/PrivFP
FAX Number: (916) 361-6666 Calendar System: Other
URL: www.carrington.edu
Established: 1983 Annual Undergrad Tuition & Fees: $17,596
Enrollment: 1,392 Coed
Affiliation or Control: Proprietary IRS Status: Proprietary
Highest Offering: Associate Degree
Program: Occupational; 2-Year Principally Bachelor's Creditable
Accreditation: WJ, DH, MAC

02 Executive Director ....Ms. Sue SMITH
06 Registrar ....Ms. Ryanne GREEN-QUARLES
07 Director Enrollment Services ....Mr. Vance KLINKE
05 Dean of Academic Affairs ....Mr. James CRAIG

Carrington College California - Citrus Heights (I)

7301 Greenback Lane, Suite A, Citrus Heights CA 95621
Telephone: (916) 722-8200 Identification: 667042
Accreditation: &WJ, MAC, SURGT

† Main campus is Carrington College California - Sacramento in Sacramento, CA.

Carrington College California - Pleasant Hill (J)

380 Civic Drive, Suite 300, Pleasant Hill CA 94523-1984
Telephone: (925) 609-6650 Identification: 666043
Accreditation: &WJ, COARC, MAC, PTAA

† Main campus is Carrington College California - Sacramento in Sacramento, CA.

Carrington College California - Pomona (K)

901 Corporate Center Drive, #300, Pomona CA 91768
Telephone: (909) 868-5800 Identification: 770506
Accreditation: &WJ

† Main campus is Carrington College California - Sacramento in Sacramento, CA.

*Carrington College California - San Jose (A)
6201 San Ignacio Avenue, San Jose CA 95119-1325
Telephone: (408) 360-0840 Identification: 666042
Accreditation: &WJ, DH, MAC, SURGT

† Main campus is Carrington College California - Sacramento in Sacramento, CA.

*Carrington College California - San Leandro (B)
15555 E 14th Street, Suite 500,
San Leandro CA 94578-9930
Telephone: (510) 276-3888 Identification: 666751
Accreditation: &WJ, MAC

† Main campus is Carrington College California - Sacramento in Sacramento, CA.

*Carrington College California - Stockton (C)
1313 W Robinhood Drive, Suite B,
Stockton CA 95207-5509
Telephone: (209) 956-1240 Identification: 666140
Accreditation: &WJ, MAC

† Main campus is Carrington College California - Sacramento in Sacramento, CA.

Casa Loma College-Anaheim (D)
2641 W LaPalma Avenue, Anaheim CA 92801
Telephone: (818) 785-2726 Identification: 770519
Accreditation: ABHES

† Main campus is Casa Loma College-Van Nuys in Van Nuys, CA.

Casa Loma College-Hawthorne (E)
12540 S Crenshaw Boulevard, Hawthorne CA 90250
Telephone: (323) 290-6440 Identification: 770520
Accreditation: ABHES

† Main campus is Casa Loma College-Van Nuys in Van Nuys, CA.

Casa Loma College-Van Nuys (F)
6725 Kester Avenue, Van Nuys CA 91405
County: Los Angeles FICE Identification: 006731
Unit ID: 111638
Telephone: (818) 785-2726 Carnegie Class: Assoc/PrivNFP
FAX Number: (818) 785-2191 Calendar System: Other
URL: www.casalomacollege.edu
Established: 1966 Annual Undergrad Tuition & Fees: $38,020
Enrollment: 500 Coed
Affiliation or Control: Independent Non-Profit IRS Status: 501(c)3
Highest Offering: Associate Degree
Program: Occupational; Nursing Emphasis
Accreditation: ABHES, @PTAA

01 Campus Director/Controller ... Ms. Veronica PANTOJA
66 Director of Nursing ... Mr. Bill HUTCHISON
06 Registrar ... Ms. Lindsay ANTENUCCI
07 Director of Admissions ... Ms. Deanna BERNAL
26 Director Public Relations ... Vacant
36 Director Career Services ... Ms. Sharon DUGAN
37 Director Studend Financial Aid ... Ms. Rosleen AURORA

CBD College (G)
3699 Wilshire Boulevard, 4th Floor,
Los Angeles CA 90010
County: Los Angeles FICE Identification: 032503
Unit ID: 439367
Telephone: (213) 427-2200 Carnegie Class: Assoc/PrivNFP
FAX Number: (213) 427-9278 Calendar System: Other
URL: www.cbd.edu
Established: 1982 Annual Undergrad Tuition & Fees: $21,973
Enrollment: 227 Coed
Affiliation or Control: Independent Non-Profit IRS Status: 501(c)3
Highest Offering: Associate Degree
Program: Occupational
Accreditation: CNCE, SURTEC

01 President ... Mr. Alan HESHEL

Cedars-Sinai Medical Center Graduate Program in Biomedical Sciences and Translational Medicine (H)
8700 Beverly Blvd Atrium Bld 2nd Fl,
Los Angeles CA 90048
County: Los Angeles Identification: 667071
Telephone: (310) 423-6252 Carnegie Class: Not Classified
FAX Number: (310) 423-0120 Calendar System: Trimester
URL: www.cedars-sinai.edu
Established: Annual Graduate Tuition & Fees: N/A
Enrollment: 10 Coed
Affiliation or Control: Independent Non-Profit IRS Status: 501(c)3
Highest Offering: Doctorate; No Undergraduates
Program: Professional
Accreditation: WC

01 President ... Mr. Thomas PRISELAC
05 Sr Vice President Academic Affairs ... Dr. Shlomo MELMED

Cerritos College (I)
11110 Alondra Boulevard, Norwalk CA 90650-6298
County: Los Angeles FICE Identification: 001161
Unit ID: 111887
Telephone: (562) 860-2451 Carnegie Class: Assoc/Pub-S-SC
FAX Number: (562) 467-5005 Calendar System: Semester
URL: www.cerritos.edu
Established: 1955 Annual Undergrad Tuition & Fees (In-District): $1,172
Enrollment: 21,302 Coed
Affiliation or Control: State/Local IRS Status: 501(c)3
Highest Offering: Associate Degree
Program: Occupational; 2-Year Principally Bachelor's Creditable
Accreditation: WJ, ADNUR, DA, DH, PTAA

01 President ... Dr. Linda L. LACY
05 Vice President Academic Affairs ... Dr. JoAnna SCHILLING
10 Vice President Business Services ... Mr. David EL FATTAL
32 Vice President Student Services ... Dr. Stephen JOHNSON
16 Vice President Human Resources ... Dr. Mary Anne GULARTE
20 Dean of Academic Affairs ... Mr. Edmund (Rick) MIRANDA
07 Dean of Admissions/Records & Svcs ... Ms. Stephanie MURGUIA
38 Dean of Counseling Services ... Dr. Renee DeLong CHOMIAK
08 Dean of Library & Educational Tech ... Mr. Carl BENGSTON
88 Dean Disabled Student Pgms & Svcs ... Dr. Lucinda ABORN
88 Dean of Student Support Services ... Ms. Kim WESTBY
50 Instr Dean Business/Humanities/SS ... Ms. Rachel MASON
57 Instr Dean Fine Arts/Communications ... Dr. Gary PRITCHARD
76 Instr Dean Health Occupations ... Ms. Sandra MARKS
83 Dean Academic Success ... Vacant
49 Instr Dean Liberal Arts ... Mr. David FABISH
68 Instr Dean Health/PE/Dance/Athletic ... Dr. Daniel SMITH
54 Instr Dean Science/Engineering/Math ... Dr. Carolyn CHAMBERS
73 Instr Dean Technology ... Dr. Yannick REAL
14 Director of Information Technology ... Ms. Lee KRICHMAR
21 Director of Fiscal Services ... Mr. Noorali DELAWALLA
35 Acting Director Student Activities ... Ms. Amna JARA
36 Dir of Career/Assessment Services ... Ms. Theresa LOPEZ
18 Director Physical Plant & Const Svc ... Mr. David C. MOORE
44 Executive Director Foundation ... Mr. Steven RICHARDSON
88 Director Community Advancement ... Ms. Bellegran GOMEZ
96 Director of Purchasing ... Mr. Mark LOGAN
15 Director Human Resources/Risk Mgmt ... Dr. Adriana FLORES-CHURCH
104 Web Administrator ... Mr. Ty BOWMAN
19 Chief of Campus Police ... Mr. Richard BUKOWIECKI
28 Dir Adult Edu/Diversity Programs ... Ms. Graciela VASQUEZ
31 Director Community Education ... Dr. Patricia ROBBINS SMITH
88 Director Child Development Center ... Ms. Debra WARD
88 Operations Manager ... Mr. Arcadio AVILA
18 Facilities Manager ... Mr. Thomas RICHEY
88 Payroll Manager ... Ms. Deanna HART
21 Accounting Manager ... Vacant
21 Budget Manager ... Vacant
13 Manager Information Technology ... Mr. Patrick O'DONNELL
23 Assoc Dean Student Health Wellness . Ms. Nancy MONTGOMERY
88 Director of Student Program Svcs ... Ms. Norma RODRIGUEZ
09 Dir of Research & Planning ... Ms. Kay NGUYEN
88 Director Adv Trans Tech Proj ... Ms. Jannet MALIG
88 PeopleSoft Database Administrator ... Ms. Maria MENDEZ
88 PeopleSoft Database Administrator ... Mr. Michael SALAZAR
88 Director of Pathway Programs ... Ms. Maggie CORDERO
22 Director Emp/Diversity ... Vacant
88 EOPS Assistant Director ... Ms. Yvette TAFOYA

*Chabot-Las Positas Community College District (J)
7600 Dublin Blvd., 3rd Flr., Dublin CA 94568
County: Alameda Identification: 666925
Telephone: (925) 485-5208 Carnegie Class: N/A
FAX Number: (925) 485-5256
URL: www.clpccd.org

01 Interim Chancellor ... Dr. Judy E. WALTERS
10 Vice Chanc Business Svcs ... Mr. Lorenzo LEGASPI
05 Vice Chanc Educ Svc/Plng/Facilities ... Mr. Jeffrey KINGSTON
16 Vice Chanc HR Svcs ... Mr. Wyman FONG

*Chabot College (K)
25555 Hesperian Boulevard, Hayward CA 94545-2400
County: Alameda FICE Identification: 001162
Unit ID: 111920
Telephone: (510) 723-6600 Carnegie Class: Assoc/Pub-S-MC
FAX Number: (510) 782-9315 Calendar System: Semester
URL: www.chabotcollege.edu
Established: 1961 Annual Undergrad Tuition & Fees (In-District): $622
Enrollment: 15,148 Coed
Affiliation or Control: State/Local IRS Status: 501(c)3
Highest Offering: Associate Degree
Program: Occupational; 2-Year Principally Bachelor's Creditable
Accreditation: WJ, DH, MAC

02 President ... Dr. Susan S. SPERLING
05 Vice President Academic Services ... Mr. Dale WAGONER
32 Vice President Student Services ... Mr. Gerald SHIMADA
10 Int Vice President Business Svcs ... Ms. Connie WILLIS
04 Exec Asst to the College President ... Ms. Karen L. SILVA
08 Dean Instr-Learning Resource ... Vacant
38 Dean Counseling/Guidance ... Dr. Matt KRITSCHER
41 Dean Health/PE/Athletics ... Mr. Jeff DROUIN
07 Dir Admissions & Records/Registrar ... Mrs. Paulette LINO
37 Director of Financial Aid ... Ms. Kathryn LINZMEYER
19 Director Safety & Security ... Sgt. Bobbie KOLLER
09 Director of Institutional Research ... Dr. Carolyn ARNOLD
15 Director Human Resources ... Dr. Wyman FONG
18 Chief Facilities/Physical Plant ... Mr. Tim NELSON
26 Chief Public Relations Officer ... Vacant
35 Director Student Life ... Vacant
96 Manager Purchasing/Warehouse Svcs ... Ms. Victoria LAMICA

*Las Positas College (L)
3000 Campus Hill Drive, Livermore CA 94551-7623
County: Alameda FICE Identification: 030357
Unit ID: 366401
Telephone: (925) 424-1000 Carnegie Class: Assoc/Pub-S-MC
FAX Number: (925) 443-0742 Calendar System: Semester
URL: www.laspositascollege.edu
Established: 1975 Annual Undergrad Tuition & Fees (In-District): $1,784
Enrollment: 8,500 Coed
Affiliation or Control: State/Local IRS Status: 501(c)3
Highest Offering: Associate Degree
Program: Occupational; 2-Year Principally Bachelor's Creditable
Accreditation: WJ, SURGT

02 President ... Vacant
05 Vice President Academic Svcs ... Dr. Janice NOBLE
32 Vice President Student Svcs ... Ms. Diana RODRIGUEZ
10 Vice Pres Business Services ... Vacant
04 Admin Assistant to the President ... Ms. Sharon GACH
35 Dean of Student Services ... Vacant
49 Dean Arts/Letters/Social Sciences ... Ms. Marilyn FLORES
81 Dean Sci/Tech/Engr/Math/Pub Safety ... Dr. Lisa EVERETT
83 Dean Behav Sci/Business/Athletics ... Ms. Dyan MILLER
07 Dean of Admissions/Records ... Ms. Sylvia RODRIQUEZ
45 Director of Research & Planning ... Mr. Rajinder SAMRA
37 Financial Aid/Veterans Assistance ... Ms. Andi SCHREIBMAN
19 Campus Safety Supervisor ... Mr. Sean PRATHER
26 Exec Dir Public Info & Marketing ... Vacant
08 Head Librarian ... Ms. Cheryl WARREN
102 LPC Foundation Executive Director ... Dr. Ted KAYE
41 Athletic Director ... Ms. Dyan MILLER
21 Associate Business Officer ... Ms. Natasha LANG
18 Project Planner/Manager Facilities ... Mr. Jeffrey KINGSTON
06 Registrar ... Ms. Sylvia RODRIGUEZ

Chaffey College (M)
5885 Haven Avenue, Rancho Cucamonga CA 91737-3002
County: San Bernardino FICE Identification: 001163
Unit ID: 111939
Telephone: (909) 652-6000 Carnegie Class: Assoc/Pub-S-MC
FAX Number: (909) 652-6006 Calendar System: Semester
URL: www.chaffey.edu
Established: 1883 Annual Undergrad Tuition & Fees (In-District): $1,153
Enrollment: 18,420 Coed
Affiliation or Control: State/Local IRS Status: 501(c)3
Highest Offering: Associate Degree
Program: Occupational; 2-Year Principally Bachelor's Creditable
Accreditation: WJ, ADNUR, DA, RAD

01 Superintendent/President ... Dr. Henry D. SHANNON
11 Vice Pres Administrative Services ... Ms. Lisa BAILEY
11 VP/Chief Admin Officer Chino Campus ... Vacant
05 Assoc Supt Instruction/Student Svcs ... Dr. Sherrie L. GUERRERO
10 Assoc Supt Business Svcs/Econ Devel ... Dr. Ciriaco PINEDO
09 Int Dean Inst Research/Research Dev ... Mr. Jim FILLPOT
21 Exec Director Administrative Svcs ... Ms. Melanie SIDDIQI
29 Director Alumni Relations ... Mr. Nick NAZARIAN
85 Director Transfer Center/Intl Pgms ... Ms. Jenny DANNELLEY
32 Director Student Activities ... Ms. Susan STEWART
07 Administrator Admissions/Records ... Ms. Kathy LUCERO
19 Dir Public Safety/Chief of Police ... Mr. David RAMIREZ
96 Int Exec Director Business Services ... Ms. Kim ERICKSON
06 Registrar ... Vacant
88 Director Technical Services ... Mr. Michael FINK
88 Director Childrens Center ... Ms. Birgit MONKS
23 Director Student Health Services ... Ms. Katherine PEEK
75 Dean DD/PD/Vocation ... Vacant
18 Dir Maintenance and Central Plant ... Vacant
37 Director Financial Aid ... Ms. Patricia BOPKO
31 Director Auxiliary Services ... Mr. Jared CEJA
26 Director Marketing/Public Relations ... Ms. Peggy CARTWRIGHT
21 Int Exec Dir Budgeting & Fiscal Svc ... Ms. Anita UNDERCOFFER
88 Director Museum Gallery ... Ms. Rebecca TRAWICK
18 Manager Facilities Development ... Ms. Sarah RILEY
12 Dean Chino Campus & Health Sciences ... Dr. Teresa HULL
88 Dean Visual Perf Arts/Language Arts ... Mr. Michael DINIELLI
50 Interim Dean Bus & Applied Tech ... Ms. Joy HAERENS
81 Dean Mathematics & Science ... Mr. Theodore YOUNGLOVE
83 Dean Social & Behav Sci & PE ... Dr. Corene SCHWARTZ
38 Interim Dean Counseling & Matricula ... Ms. Amy NEVAREZ
12 Dean Fontana Campus ... Dr. Eric BISHOP
08 Dean Instructional Support ... Ms. Laura HOPE
04 Exec Assistant Supt/Pres Office ... Ms. Kathy NAPOLI

Chapman University (A)

One University Drive, Orange CA 92866-1099
County: Orange FICE Identification: 001164
Unit ID: 111948
Telephone: (714) 997-6815 Carnegie Class: Master's L
FAX Number: (714) 997-6713 Calendar System: 4/1/4
URL: www.chapman.edu
Established: 1861 Annual Undergrad Tuition & Fees: $43,573
Enrollment: 7,566 Coed
Affiliation or Control: Christian Church (Disciples Of Christ)
IRS Status: 501(c)3
Highest Offering: Doctorate
Program: Liberal Arts And General; Teacher Preparatory; Professional
Accreditation: WC, BUS, DANCE, LAW, MFCD, MUS, PTA, SP, TEAC, THEA

01 President .... Dr. James L. DOTI
05 Chancellor .... Dr. Daniele C. STRUPPA
03 Executive Vice President & COO .... Mr. Harold W. HEWITT, JR.
30 Exec VP University Advancement .... Ms. Sheryl BOURGEOIS
32 Vice Chancellor & Dean of Students .... Dr. Jerry PRICE
84 Vice Chancellor/Dean Enrollment Mgt .... Mr. Michael PELLY
20 Vice Chancellor for Academic Admin .... Dr. Raymond SFEIR
09 Vice Chan Inst Eff & Fac Affairs .... Mr. Joseph SLOWENSKY
49 Dean Wilkinson Col Hum/Soc Sci .... Dr. Patrick FUERY
61 Dean School of Law .... Dr. Tom CAMPBELL
50 Dean School Business/Economics .... Mr. Reginald GILYARD
67 Dean School of Pharmacy .... Dr. Ronald JORDAN
53 Dean College of Educational Studies .... Dr. Donald CARDINAL
88 Dean College of Film & Media Arts .... Mr. Robert BASSETT
88 Dean College of Performing Arts .... Mr. Dale MERRILL
81 Interim Dean Col of Science/Tech .... Dr. Janeen HILL
88 Dean/Artistic Dir Center for Arts .... Dr. William HALL
88 Director Ctr for Global Education .... Dr. James COYLE
97 Vice Chancellor Undergrad Education .... Dr. Jeanne GUNNER
45 Vice President Campus Planning .... Mr. Kris OLSEN
16 Vice President of Human Resources .... Ms. Becky CAMPOS
43 Assoc Vice Pres of Legal Affairs .... Ms. Janine DUMONTELLE
21 Assoc Vice President & Controller .... Mr. Behzad BINESH
07 Asst VC/Chief Admissions Officer .... Mr. Michael DRUMMY
88 Assistant Chancellor .... Ms. Iris GERBASI
18 Director of Facilities .... Mr. Alan SMITH
26 Director Public Relations .... Ms. Mary PLATT
08 Dean of Library .... Ms. Charlene BALDWIN
29 Sr Dir Strategic Engagement/Dev .... Ms. Delite TRAVIS
13 Chief Information Officer .... Ms. Shari WATERS
09 Director of Institutional Research .... Dr. Marisol ARREDONDO
06 Registrar .... Ms. Jan MCCUEN
46 Director Sponsored Research .... Ms. Yolanda UZZELL
37 Director Financial Aid .... Mr. Jack MILLIS
85 Director Intl Student Services .... Ms. Susan SAMS
19 Chief of Public Safety .... Mr. Randy BURBA
39 Assoc Dean/Director Residence Life .... Ms. Deborah MILLER
41 Athletic Director .... Mr. David CURREY
42 Dean of the Chapel .... Dr. Gail STEARNS
04 Associate to the President .... Ms. Ann CAMERON
88 Exec Assistant to the Chancellor .... Ms. Christina ZERMENO
22 Equal Opportunity Officer .... Mr. Eduardo MONGE
23 Director Student Health Services .... Ms. Jacqueline DEATS
35 Director of Student Engagement .... Mr. Chris HUTCHISON
36 Assoc Dean Career Development .... Mr. Ramon KNOX
38 Assoc Dean/Dir Student Psych Couns .... Ms. Jeannie WALKER
96 Director of Purchasing .... Ms. Pam AMES
04 Assistant to the President .... Ms. Dorothy FAROL
58 Vice Chancellor for Graduate Educ .... Dr. Richard REDDING

Charles R. Drew University of Medicine & Science (B)

1730 E 118th Street, Los Angeles CA 90059-3025
County: Los Angeles FICE Identification: 010365
Unit ID: 111966
Telephone: (323) 563-4800 Carnegie Class: Spec/Health
FAX Number: (323) 563-5987 Calendar System: Semester
URL: www.cdrewu.edu
Established: 1966 Annual Undergrad Tuition & Fees: $14,820
Enrollment: 504 Coed
Affiliation or Control: Independent Non-Profit IRS Status: 501(c)3
Highest Offering: Master's
Program: Occupational; 2-Year Principally Bachelor's Creditable; Liberal Arts And General; Professional
Accreditation: WC, CAHIIM, NUR, NURSE, PH, RAD

01 President & CEO .... Dr. David M. CARLISLE
05 Interim Provost .... Dr. Mary BOYCE
100 Chief of Staff .... Ms. Edna YOHANNES
10 Chief Operating Officer .... Mr. Jim E. MAIN
45 Interim EVP Research & Health Affs .... Dr. Jadutt VADGAMA
30 VP for Strategic Advancement .... Ms. Angela L. MINNIEFIELD
15 Chief Human Resources Officer .... Dr. Toni C. ELBOUSHI
11 University Auditor .... Mr. Nathaniel CLARK
63 Interim Dean College of Medicine .... Dr. Daphne CALMES
66 Interim Dean School of Nursing .... Dr. Shirley EVERS-MANLY
76 Dean College of Science & Health .... Dr. Gail ORUM-ALEXANDER
32 Chief Student Services Officer .... Dr. Rita GLORIA SAWYER
58 Interim Assoc Dean GME .... Dr. Jimmy HARA
20 Sr Assoc Dean Academic Affairs .... Dr. Ronald A. EDELSTEIN
09 Director Inst Research & Effectiv .... Mr. Richard W. LINDSTROM
27 Director Information Systems .... Mr. Matt CULLEN
08 Director Health Sciences Library .... Ms. Darlene PARKER-KELLY
37 Director Student Financial Aid .... Mr. Pierre FLOOD
06 Registrar .... Mr. Damon A. BLUE

Charter College-Canyon Country (C)

27125 Sierra Hwy Suite 329, Canyon Country CA 91351
FICE Identification: 032783
Unit ID: 434317
Telephone: (661) 252-1864 Carnegie Class: Not Classified
FAX Number: N/A Calendar System: Other
URL: chartercollege.edu
Established: Annual Undergrad Tuition & Fees: N/A
Enrollment: 658 Coed
Affiliation or Control: Proprietary IRS Status: Proprietary
Highest Offering: Associate Degree
Program: Occupational
Accreditation: ACICS

Charter College-Lancaster Campus (D)

43141 Business Center Pkwy, Ste 102, Lancaster CA 93535
Telephone: (661) 341-3500 Identification: 770846
Accreditation: ACICS

† Main campus is Charter College-Canyon Country in Canyon Country, CA.

Charter College-Long Beach (E)

100 West Broadway, Suite 3000, Long Beach CA 90802
Telephone: (562) 216-7500 Identification: 770847
Accreditation: ACICS

† Main campus is Charter College-Canyon Country in Canyon Country, CA.

Charter College-Oxnard (F)

2000 Outlet Center Drive, Suite 150, Oxnard CA 93036
Telephone: (805) 973-1240 Identification: 666675
Accreditation: ACICS

† Main campus is Charter College in Anchorage, AK.

Chicago School of Professional Psychology Los Angeles Campus (G)

617 West 7th Street, Los Angeles CA 90017
County: Los Angeles FICE Identification: 021553
Unit ID: 455664
Telephone: (213) 627-2580 Carnegie Class: Not Classified
FAX Number: (213) 615-7274 Calendar System: Semester
URL: www.the chicagoschool.edu
Established: 1979 Annual Graduate Tuition & Fees: $23,054
Enrollment: 4,188 Coed
Affiliation or Control: Independent Non-Profit IRS Status: 501(c)3
Highest Offering: Doctorate; No Undergraduates
Program: Professional
Accreditation: WC

01 President .... Dr. Michele NEALON-WOODS
05 Int Vice Pres Academic Affairs .... Dr. Patricia ARREDONDO
10 Vice Pres Finance & Administration .... Ms. Carole ROBERTSON
32 Vice Pres Student Affairs .... Ms. Jennifer STRIPE PORTILLO
106 Vice Pres Blended/Online Learning .... Dr. Gino NATALICCHIO
07 Assoc Vice Pres Admissions .... Ms. Heather LA BELLE
100 Chief of Staff .... Mr. Matt NEHMER
30 Chief Development Officer .... Dr. Orlando TAYLOR

Chicago School of Professional Psychology-Irvine Campus (H)

4199 Campus Drive, Irvine CA 92612
Telephone: (949) 737-5460 Identification: 770492
Accreditation: &WC

† Main campus is Chicago School of Professional Psychology Los Angeles Campus in Los Angeles, CA.

Chicago School of Professional Psychology-Westwood Campus (I)

1145 Gayley Avenue, Suite 322, Los Angeles CA 90024
Telephone: (310) 208-4240 Identification: 770491
Accreditation: &WC

† Main campus is Chicago School of Professional Psychology Los Angeles Campus in Los Angeles, CA.

Church Divinity School of the Pacific (J)

2451 Ridge Road, Berkeley CA 94709-1217
County: Alameda FICE Identification: 001165
Unit ID: 112127
Telephone: (510) 204-0700 Carnegie Class: Spec/Faith
FAX Number: (510) 644-0712 Calendar System: Semester
URL: www.cdsp.edu
Established: 1893 Annual Graduate Tuition & Fees: $16,800
Enrollment: 85 Coed
Affiliation or Control: Protestant Episcopal IRS Status: 501(c)3
Highest Offering: Doctorate; No Undergraduates
Program: Professional; Religious Emphasis
Accreditation: THEOL

01 President & Dean .... Dr. W. Mark RICHARDSON
05 Dean Academic Affairs .... Dr. Ruth MEYERS
10 Vice President Finance & Operations .... Ms. Amy VOGELSANG
30 Dir of Institutional Advancement .... Ms. Dolly PATTERSON
32 Dean of Students .... Rev. L. Ann HALLISEY
06 Registrar .... Vacant
07 Director of Recruitment .... Ms. Dianne SMITH
88 Program Manager .... Ms. Alissa FENCSIK
37 Director of Financial Aid .... Ms. Kathleen ANTOKHIN

Citrus College (K)

1000 W Foothill Boulevard, Glendora CA 91741-1899
County: Los Angeles FICE Identification: 001166
Unit ID: 112172
Telephone: (626) 963-0323 Carnegie Class: Assoc/Pub-S-SC
FAX Number: (626) 914-8618 Calendar System: Semester
URL: www.citruscollege.edu
Established: 1915 Annual Undergrad Tuition & Fees (In-District): $1,168
Enrollment: 11,876 Coed
Affiliation or Control: State/Local IRS Status: 501(c)3
Highest Offering: Associate Degree
Program: Occupational; 2-Year Principally Bachelor's Creditable; Business Emphasis
Accreditation: WJ, DA

01 Superintendent/President .... Dr. Geraldine M. PERRI
05 Vice President Academic Affairs .... Vacant
32 Vice President Student Services .... Dr. Arvid SPOR
10 Vice Pres Finance/Admin Services .... Mrs. Carol R. HORTON
07 Dean Admissions & Records .... Dr. Gerald SEQUEIRA
51 Dean Career/Technical/Continuing Ed .... Mr. James LANCASTER
38 Dean of Counseling .... Dr. Lucinda OVER
16 Director Human Resources .... Dr. Robert SAMMIS
102 Director Foundation .... Ms. Christina GARCIA
35 Dean of Students .... Dr. Martha MCDONALD
18 Director Facilities & Construction .... Mr. Fred DIAMOND
09 Director of Institutional Research .... Dr. Lan HAO
06 Registrar .... Ms. Kristina SPALDING
37 Director Financial Aid .... Ms. Carol THOMAS
96 Director of Purchasing .... Mr. Robert IVERSON
21 Director of Fiscal Services .... Ms. Rosalinda BUCHWALD
26 Director of Communication .... Ms. Paula GREEN
23 Director of Health Sciences .... Dr. Maureen RENAGHAN
28 Staff Diversity Officer .... Mrs. Brenda FINK
13 Chief Information Services Officer .... Ms. Linda WELZ
19 Int Campus Security Supervisor .... Mr. Benjamin MACIAS
83 Dean Social/Behavioral Sciences/DE .... Dr. Dana HESTER
41 Dean of Kinesiology & Athletics .... Ms. Jody WISE
79 Dean of Lang Arts & Enrollment Mgt .... Dr. Samuel LEE
65 Dean Library/Natural & Physical Sci .... Dr. Eric RABITOY
57 Dean of Fine & Performing Arts .... Mr. Robert SLACK
81 Dean Math/Business/Health Sciences .... Mr. James MCCLAIN
15 Director of Human Resources .... Dr. Robert SAMMIS
88 Dir EOPS CARE CalWORKS .... Ms. Sarah GONZALES-TAPIA
88 Project Dir RACE to STEM .... Ms. Marianne SMITH

City College of San Francisco (L)

33 Gough Street, San Francisco CA 94103-1292
County: San Francisco FICE Identification: 001167
Unit ID: 112190
Telephone: (415) 239-3000 Carnegie Class: Assoc/Pub-U-MC
FAX Number: (415) 239-3919 Calendar System: Semester
URL: www.ccsf.edu
Established: 1935 Annual Undergrad Tuition & Fees (In-District): $720
Enrollment: 31,529 Coed
Affiliation or Control: State/Local IRS Status: 501(c)3
Highest Offering: Associate Degree
Program: Occupational; 2-Year Principally Bachelor's Creditable
Accreditation: WJ, ACFEI, CAHIIM, DA, EMT, MAC, RAD, RTT

01 Interim Chancellor .... Dr. Thelma SCOTT-SKILLMAN
10 Vice Chanc Finance/Administration .... Mr. Peter A. GOLDSTEIN
05 Vice Chancellor Academic Affairs .... Ms. Joanne LOW
32 Vice Chanc Student Development .... Dr. Fabienne NAPLES
46 Dean of Institutional Effectiveness .... Dr. Pam MERY
12 Dean Civic Center Campus .... Mr. Carl JEW
12 Dean Southeast Campus .... Mr. Torrance BYNUM
12 Dean Mission Campus .... Vacant
12 Dean Downtown/Business School .... Dr. Geisce LY
26 Dean of Marketing/Public Relations .... Vacant
35 Interim Dean Student Affairs .... Mr. Samuel SANTOS
37 Dean Financial Aid & Scholarships .... Mr. Jorge BELL
07 Dean Admissions & Records .... Ms. Marylou LEYBA
20 Assoc Vice Chanc of Instruction .... Mr. Tom BOEGEL
20 Assoc Vice Chanc of Instruction .... Dr. Nicholas AKINKUOYE
16 Dean Human Resources .... Ms. Clara STARR
38 Dean/Dir Counseling/Student Support .... Vacant
108 Dean Matriculation/Assessment .... Ms. Margaret SANCHEZ
51 Dean Contract Educ/Voc Educ .... Vacant
85 Dean Chinatown/Intl Educ/ESL .... Dr. Minh-Hoa TA
88 Dean School of Visual & Performing .... Mr. Douglas BISH
83 Dean Behavioral/Social Sciences .... Mr. Raymond GAMBA
81 Dean Science & Math .... Mr. David YEE
68 Dean J Adams Campus/Sch Hlth Educ .... Mr. Terry HALL
30 Dean College Development .... Dr. Kathleen SULLIVAN ALIOTO
88 Assoc Dean (Non-Credit) Admiss/Recs .... Vacant
13 Director Information Services .... Mr. Doug RE
15 Director Employee Relations .... Mr. Mickey BRANCA
18 Superintendent Buildings/Grounds .... Mr. Scott CLINE

103 Assoc Vice Chanc of Instr/Workforce .... Ms. Darlene SPOOR
27 Chief Information Technology Office ....Vacant
96 Director of Purchasing .... Ms. Kathy HENNIG
19 Chief of Police .... Mr. Andre BARNES
88 ADA Compliance Officer .... Dr. Leilani BATTISTE
21 Assoc Vice Chanc/CFO .... Mr. John BILMONT
25 Dean Grants & Resource Dev ....Ms. Kristin CHARLES
06 Assoc Dean Admission & Records ....Ms. Monika LIU
88 Dean Faculty Support Svcs .... Dr. Minh-Hoa TA
23 Assoc Dean Student Health Svcs ....Ms. Sunny CLARK

City of Hope (A)

1500 East Duarte Road, Duarte CA 91010-3000
County: Los Angeles FICE Identification: 035924
Unit ID: 441238
Telephone: (626) 256-4673 Carnegie Class: Spec/Med
FAX Number: (626) 301-8105 Calendar System: Semester
URL: cityofhope.org
Established: 1994 Annual Graduate Tuition & Fees: N/A
Enrollment: 85 Coed
Affiliation or Control: Independent Non-Profit IRS Status: 501(c)3
Highest Offering: Doctorate; No Undergraduates
Program: Professional
Accreditation: WC

01 Dean .... John J. ROSSI
05 Director/Associate Dean Prof Educ ....Steven NORVAC

*Claremont University Consortium (B)

101 South Mills Avenue, Claremont CA 91711-5053
County: Los Angeles Identification: 666003
Telephone: (909) 621-8026 Carnegie Class: N/A
FAX Number: (909) 621-8517
URL: www.cuc.claremont.edu

01 Chief Executive Officer ....Mr. Robert WALTON
03 Executive VP/COO ....Mr. M.L. (Mel) DINKEL
10 Vice President/Treasurer .... Mr. Ken PIFER
32 Vice President of Student Affairs .... Dr. Denise HAYES
18 VP Facilities Management/Planning .... Mr. Tim MORRISON
101 Sec to Brd of Overseers/Asst to CEO ....Dr. Bonnie CLEMENS

*Claremont Graduate University (C)

150 E 10th Street, Claremont CA 91711-5909
County: Los Angeles FICE Identification: 001169
Unit ID: 112251
Telephone: (909) 621-8000 Carnegie Class: RU/H
FAX Number: (909) 621-8390 Calendar System: Semester
URL: www.cgu.edu
Established: 1925 Annual Graduate Tuition & Fees: $41,110
Enrollment: 2,261 Coed
Affiliation or Control: Independent Non-Profit IRS Status: 501(c)3
Highest Offering: Doctorate; No Undergraduates
Program: Liberal Arts And General; Teacher Preparatory; Professional
Accreditation: WC, BUS, CAHIIM, PH

02 President ....Dr. Deborah A. FREUND
04 Exec Asst to the President .... Ms. Donna STANDLEA
05 Exec Vice President and Provost ....Dr. Jacob ADAMS
10 Senior VP for Finance and Admin ....Dr. Steven N. GARCIA
30 Vice President for Advancement .... Mr. Bedford MCINTOSH
84 Vice Prov Enroll Svc/Dean of Stdnts ....Mr. Fred SIEGEL
46 Vice Provost/Research .... Dr. Dean GERSTEIN
88 Vice Provost/Transdisciplin Studies .... Dr. Wendy MARTIN
108 Director Institutional Effectivenes .... Ms. Alana OLSCHWANG
16 Assoc VP for Human Resources .... Ms. Brenda LESWICK
47 Botany Center .... Dr. Lucinda MCDADE
50 Drucker-Ito Grad School of Mgt .... Dr. Larry CROSBY
83 Behavioral & Organizational Sci .... Dr. Stewart DONALDSON
69 Community & Global Health ....Vacant
53 Educational Studies .... Dr. Scott THOMAS
77 Center for Information Science .... Dr. Thomas HORAN
81 Institute for Math Sciences .... Dr. Allon PERCUS
82 Politics & Economics .... Dr. Stewart DONALDSON
73 Arts and Humanities .... Dr. Tammi SCHNEIDER
09 Institutional Research Officer .... Ms. Jeannette GURROLA
44 Senior Director of Development .... Mr. Mike AVILA
21 Asst VP/Asst Treasurer .... Mr. Dean CALVO
29 Director Alumnae /Alumni Relations ....Vacant
26 Director University Communications ....Ms. Esther WILEY
06 Registrar .... Mr. Cliff RAMIREZ
37 Director Student Financial Aid .... Ms. Susie GUILBAULT
85 International Student Coordinator .... Ms. Sujata SHETH
07 Director of Admissions ....Ms. Julia EVANS
32 Assoc Dean of Student Services ....Vacant
18 Director of Facilities .... Mr. DeWayne HURST
39 Housing Manager .... Mr. Chris BASS
13 Exec Dir Office Information Tech ....Mr. Travis WYNBERRY
91 Application Services Director .... Mr. Manoj CHITRE
101 Secretary to the Board ....Ms. Louise WEBBER

*Claremont McKenna College (D)

500 E 9th Street, Claremont CA 91711-6400
County: Los Angeles FICE Identification: 001170
Unit ID: 112260
Telephone: (909) 621-8000 Carnegie Class: Bac/A&S
FAX Number: (909) 621-8790 Calendar System: Semester
URL: www.claremontmckenna.edu
Established: 1946 Annual Undergrad Tuition & Fees: $45,625
Enrollment: 1,295 Coed
Affiliation or Control: Independent Non-Profit IRS Status: 501(c)3
Highest Offering: Master's
Program: Liberal Arts And General
Accreditation: WC

02 President and CEO ....Hiram E. CHODOSH
05 Int VP Academic Affs/Dean Faculty .... Nicholas WARNER
30 Vice President for Development ....Ernie ISEMINGER
10 Vice Pres Business Admin/Treasurer ....Robin J. ASPINALL
11 VP for Planning and Administration .... Matthew G. BIBBENS
32 VP Student Affs/Admiss/Fin Aid ....Jefferson HUANG
21 VP and Chief Investment Officer ....James J. FLOYD
29 Vice President for Alumni Relations ....John P. FARANDA
32 Dean of Students .... Mary SPELLMAN
07 AVP & Dean Admission/Financial Aid ....Georgette DEVERES
26 Assoc VP Public Affs/Communications .... Max BENAVIDEZ
13 Assoc VP/Chief Technology Officer .... Cynthia HUMES
36 Assoc Dean/Dir Career Services .... Diana SEDER
18 Dir Facilities and Campus Services .... Brian WORLEY
06 Registrar/Dir Institutional Rsrch ....Elizabeth MORGAN
15 Director of Human Resources .... Andrea GALE
104 Director of Off-Campus Study .... Kristen MALLORY
41 Athletic Director .... Michael SUTTON
04 Special Assistant to the President .... Cheryl M. AGUILAR

*Claremont School of Theology (E)

1325 N College Avenue, Claremont CA 91711-3199
County: Los Angeles FICE Identification: 001288
Unit ID: 124283
Telephone: (909) 447-2500 Carnegie Class: Spec/Faith
FAX Number: (909) 626-7062 Calendar System: Semester
URL: www.cst.edu
Established: 1885 Annual Graduate Tuition & Fees: $16,080
Enrollment: 242 Coed
Affiliation or Control: United Methodist IRS Status: 501(c)3
Highest Offering: Doctorate; No Undergraduates
Program: Professional
Accreditation: WC, THEOL

02 President .... Dr. Jeffrey KUAN
05 Vice President Academic Affs & Dean .... Dr. Mark PARSONS
10 VP for Administration & Finance/ CFO .... Dr. Lynn O'LEARY-ARCHER
30 Vice President of Development .... Ms. Wendy LEE
21 Assoc VP for Finance & Planning .... Mr. Gamward QUAN
27 Director of Communications .... Mr. Jon HOOTEN
06 Registrar .... Ms. Jennie ALLEN
07 Director of Admission ....Ms. Jennifer HOOTEN
08 Dir of Library/Technological Svcs ....Mr. John DICKASON
42 Dir Church Rels & Ministry Resource .... Dr. Karen DALTON
37 Director of Financial Aid ....Ms. Jennifer HOOTEN
22 Affirmative Action Officer ....Ms. Elaine WALKER

*Keck Graduate Institute (F)

535 Watson Drive, Claremont CA 91711-4817
County: Los Angeles FICE Identification: 038533
Unit ID: 440031
Telephone: (909) 607-7855 Carnegie Class: Assoc/PrivNFP4
FAX Number: (909) 607-8086 Calendar System: Semester
URL: www.kgi.edu
Established: 1997 Annual Graduate Tuition & Fees: $38,550
Enrollment: 177 Coed
Affiliation or Control: Independent Non-Profit IRS Status: 501(c)3
Highest Offering: Doctorate; No Undergraduates
Program: Professional; Technical Emphasis
Accreditation: WC

02 President ....Dr. Sheldon M. SCHUSTER
06 Registrar .... Adam D. PAVE

CNI College (G)

702 West Town and Country Road, Orange CA 92868
County: Orange FICE Identification: 032423
Unit ID: 433013
Telephone: (714) 437-9697 Carnegie Class: Not Classified
FAX Number: (714) 437-9356 Calendar System: Other
URL: www.cnicollege.edu
Established: 1994 Annual Undergrad Tuition & Fees: N/A
Enrollment: 576 Coed
Affiliation or Control: Proprietary IRS Status: Proprietary
Highest Offering: Associate Degree
Program: Occupational
Accreditation: ABHES, SURGT, SURTEC

01 President .... Mr. James BUFFINGTON

*Coast Community College District Administration Offices (H)

1370 Adams Avenue, Costa Mesa CA 92626-5429
County: Orange FICE Identification: 008711
Unit ID: 112376
Telephone: (714) 438-4600 Carnegie Class: N/A
FAX Number: (714) 438-4882
URL: www.cccd.edu

01 Chancellor ....Dr. Andrew C. JONES
10 Vice Chancellor Finance & Adm Svcs .... Mr. Andrew DUNN
16 Vice Chancellor Human Resources ....Dr. Deborah D. HIRSH
05 Vice Chanc Educ Svcs & Technology ....Dr. Andreea SERBAN
26 Dir Public Affairs/Mktg & Govt Rels .... Dr. Martha PARHAM
96 Director of Purchasing ....Mr. John ERIKSEN

*Coastline Community College (I)

11460 Warner Avenue, Fountain Valley CA 92708-2597
County: Orange FICE Identification: 020635
Unit ID: 112385
Telephone: (714) 546-7600 Carnegie Class: Assoc/Pub-S-MC
FAX Number: (714) 241-6277 Calendar System: Semester
URL: www.coastline.edu
Established: 1976 Annual Undergrad Tuition & Fees (In-District): $1,136
Enrollment: 8,439 Coed
Affiliation or Control: State/Local IRS Status: 501(c)3
Highest Offering: Associate Degree
Program: Occupational; 2-Year Principally Bachelor's Creditable
Accreditation: WJ

02 President ....Dr. Loretta P. ADRIAN
05 VP of Instruction/Student Services .... Mr. Vince RODRIGUEZ
11 VP of Administrative Services .... Ms. Christine NGUYEN
84 Dean of Enrollment Services ....Ms. Lois WILKERSON
46 Admin Dean Instr Systems Devel ....Vacant
38 Int Dean Counseling/Matriculation ....Dr. John COLSON
106 Assoc Dean of Distance Learning .... Mr. Bob NASH
12 Dean of Instruction Newport Beach ....Vacant
12 Dean Instruction Garden Grove ....Ms. Nancy JONES
12 Dean Instruction Westminster ....Dr. Vinicio LOPEZ
88 Dean Military Programs/Contract Ed ....Ms. Joycelyn GROOT
72 Dean of Lrng Tech Innovation & Supp ....Vacant
26 Director of Mktg/PR & Govt Affairs ....Mrs. Michelle MA
06 Registrar/Director of Admissions .... Ms. Jennifer MCDONALD
37 Dir Student Financial Aid & EOPS ...... Ms. Cynthia PIENKOWSKI
18 Director Maintenance & Operations .... Mr. David CANT
21 Director Fiscal Services .... Ms. Helen ROTHGEB
102 Executive Director Foundation ....Ms. Mariam KHOSRAVANI
40 Director Bookstore ....Mr. Matthew IRBY
14 Director Computer Services ....Vacant
09 Director Research/Planning/Develop ....Dr. Jorge R. SANCHEZ
88 Manager Contract Education Programs .... Mr. Peter MAHARAJ
24 Director of Electronic Media ....Ms. Judy GARVEY
15 Int Director of Personnel Services .... Ms. Helen ROTHGEB
88 Director of EBUS program ....Ms. Laurie MELBY
88 Director of eLearning Rsrch and Dev .... Mr. Dave THOMPSON
103 Interim Dir Workforce & Econ Dev .... Ms. Sallie SALINAS

*Golden West College (J)

15744 Golden West Street,
Huntington Beach CA 92647-2748
County: Orange FICE Identification: 001206
Unit ID: 115126
Telephone: (714) 892-7711 Carnegie Class: Assoc/Pub-S-MC
FAX Number: (714) 895-8243 Calendar System: Semester
URL: www.gwc.info
Established: 1966 Annual Undergrad Tuition & Fees (In-District): $1,172
Enrollment: 12,333 Coed
Affiliation or Control: State/Local IRS Status: Exempt
Highest Offering: Associate Degree
Program: Occupational; 2-Year Principally Bachelor's Creditable
Accreditation: WJ, ADNUR

02 President .... Mr. Wes BRYAN
05 Vice Pres Instruc & Stdnt Learning ....Vacant
11 Vice Pres Student & Admin Support ......Ms. Janet M. HOULIHAN
38 Dean Counseling ....Dr. David L. BAIRD
08 Assoc Dean Learning Res/Online Inst .... Mr. Jorge ASCENCIO
72 Acting Dean Career & Tech Education ..Dr. Claudia LEE-SADDUL
81 Dean Business/Soc Sci/Math & Sci ....Mr. Jeff COURCHAINE
49 Dean Arts & Letters ....Dr. David D. HUDSON
23 Assoc Dean/Dir Student Health Svcs ....Mr. Robin BACHMANN
09 Admin Dir Research/Plan/Inst Effect ....Vacant
88 Dean Criminal Justice & Health Prof ....Mr. Ron LOWENBERG
35 Administrative Director Stdnt Svcs .....Ms. Shirley A. DONNELLY
15 Director Personnel Services ....Mrs. Crystal D. CRANE
21 Director Fiscal Services ....Mr. Paul WISNER
102 Director Foundation/Community Rels ....Vacant
88 Director Scholarships & Spec Events ......Ms. Valerie A. VENEGAS
07 Director of Admissions ....Ms. Jennifer L. ORTBERG
37 Director of Financial Aid .... Mr. Steve SKILLE
18 Chief Facilities/Physical Plant ....Mr. Joseph B. DOWLING
68 Dean Health PE & Athleics ....Mr. Albert GASPARIAN

*Orange Coast College (K)

2701 Fairview Road, POB 5005,
Costa Mesa CA 92628-5005
County: Orange FICE Identification: 001250
Unit ID: 120342
Telephone: (714) 432-0202 Carnegie Class: Assoc/Pub-S-MC
FAX Number: (714) 432-5609 Calendar System: Semester
URL: www.orangecoastcollege.edu
Established: 1947 Annual Undergrad Tuition & Fees (In-District): $1,450
Enrollment: 21,411 Coed
Affiliation or Control: State/Local IRS Status: 501(c)3
Highest Offering: Associate Degree
Program: Occupational; 2-Year Principally Bachelor's Creditable
Accreditation: WJ, ACFEI, COARC, CVT, DA, DIETT, DMS, MAC, NDT, POLYT, RAD

02 President .... Dr. Dennis HARKINS
05 Vice President Instruction .... Dr. John G. WEISPFENNING
32 Vice President Student Services .... Dr. Kristin CLARK
11 Vice Pres Administrative Services .... Dr. Richard PAGEL
84 Dean Enrollment Services .... Mr. Madjid NIROUMAND
38 Dean of Counseling .... Dr. Hue PHAM
35 Interim Dean Student Services .... Ms. Carla MARTINEZ
26 Director Community Relations .... Vacant
30 Executive Dir College Advancement .... Mr. Douglas BENNETT
09 Director of IR/Planning and IE .... Ms. Sheri STERNER
07 Director Admiss/Records/Enroll Tech .... Mr. Efren GALVAN
15 Director Personnel Services .... Vacant
18 Director M & O .... Mr. Mark GOODE
37 Director Student Financial Aid .... Ms. Melissa MOSER
13 Director Infomration Technology .... Mr. Craig OBERLIN
23 Associate Dean Health Services .... Ms. Sylvia WORDEN
88 Manager Child Care Center .... Ms. Sue BIERLICH
35 Associate Dean Student Services .... Vacant
40 Manager Bookstore .... Ms. Elizabeth BIRENBAUM
41 Athletic Director .... Dr. Michael SUTLIFF
88 Dean of Consumer & Health Sciences .... Mr. Kevin BALLINGER
68 Dean of Kiniseology & Athletics .... Dr. Michael SUTLIFF
72 Dean of Technology .... Dr. Doug BENOIT
50 Dean of Business & Computer Science .... Dr. Doug BENOIT
83 Dean of Social & Behavioral Science .... Dr. Paul ASIM
88 Dean of Literature & Languages .... Dr. Michael MANDELKERN
81 Dean of Math & Sciences .... Dr. Robert MENDOZA
57 Dean of Visual & Performing Arts .... Mr. Joe POSHEK
62 Dean of Library and Media Services .... Mr. Joe POSHEK
103 Director Career & Cmty Education .... Ms. Raine HAMBLY
105 Director Web Services .... Mr. Glen PROFETA

Cogswell Polytechnical College (A)

1175 Bordeaux Drive, Sunnyvale CA 94089-1299
County: Santa Clara FICE Identification: 001177
Unit ID: 112394
Telephone: (408) 541-0100 Carnegie Class: Bac/Diverse
FAX Number: (408) 747-0764 Calendar System: Semester
URL: www.cogswell.edu
Established: 1887 Annual Undergrad Tuition & Fees: $24,540
Enrollment: 331 Coed
Affiliation or Control: Independent Non-Profit IRS Status: 501(c)3
Highest Offering: Baccalaureate
Program: Liberal Arts And General; Professional; Technical Emphasis
Accreditation: WC

01 Chancellor/President .... Mr. Charles (Chuck) HOUSE
05 Dean of the College .... Mr. Michael MARTIN
10 Vice President Finance .... Mr. Rejino CASTANEDA
07 Executive Director of Admissions .... Mr. Abraham CHACKO
06 Registrar .... Ms. Milla ZLATANOV
08 Librarian .... Ms. Vivian KOBAYASHI
04 Executive Assistant .... Ms. Debbie PAVAO

The Colburn School (B)

200 S Grand Avenue, Los Angeles CA 90012-3007
County: Los Angeles Identification: 666233
Telephone: (213) 621-2200 Carnegie Class: Not Classified
FAX Number: (213) 621-2110 Calendar System: Semester
URL: www.colburnschool.edu
Established: 2003 Annual Undergrad Tuition & Fees: N/A
Enrollment: 114 Coed
Affiliation or Control: Independent Non-Profit IRS Status: 501(c)3
Highest Offering: Baccalaureate
Program: Music Emphasis
Accreditation: MUS

01 President & CEO .... Mr. Sel KARDAN
30 Senior Vice President Advancement .... Ms. Allison SAMPSON
10 Chief Financial Officer .... Mr. Seth WEINTRAUB
06 Registrar .... Ms. Jennifer LEE

† Full room, board, and tuition are provided to accepted students through the school's endowment.

Coleman University (C)

8888 Balboa Avenue, San Diego CA 92123-1506
County: San Diego FICE Identification: 007296
Unit ID: 112446
Telephone: (858) 499-0202 Carnegie Class: Bac/Assoc
FAX Number: (858) 499-0233 Calendar System: Quarter
URL: www.coleman.edu
Established: 1963 Annual Undergrad Tuition & Fees: $35,200
Enrollment: 814 Coed
Affiliation or Control: Independent Non-Profit IRS Status: 501(c)3
Highest Offering: Master's
Program: Occupational; Professional; Technical Emphasis
Accreditation: ACICS

01 President .... Mr. Paul S. PANESAR
03 Vice President/Branch Manager .... Ms. Sheryl L. RIDENS
07 Director of Admissions .... Ms. Bobbie A. STROHM
10 Chief Financial Officer .... Mr. Ron D. KLINGENSMITH
13 Director of Computer Services .... Mr. Keith R. WISSWELL
05 Dean of Academics .... Mr. Jason T. ABEL
09 Director of Institutional Research .... Mr. Bruce F. GILDEN
15 Human Resource Coordinator .... Ms. Maria HAMZAVI
06 Registrar .... Ms. Elaine A. RICHARDS
37 Director of Financial Aid .... Mr. Axel N. HERNANDEZ
36 Director Career Services .... Mr. John D. BULLOCK
21 Business Manager .... Ms. Elizabeth A. GALINDO
08 Librarian .... Mr. Manuel A. BERNAD
29 Director of Alumni Relations .... Ms. Ariana V. MARRON
14 Network Administrator .... Mr. Brian J. MORGAN
105 Web Master .... Mr. Chris J. CAREY
30 Chief Development Officer .... Mr. Rod P. WEISS
27 Data Analysist .... Ms. Rinat NAHUM
18 Facilities Manager .... Mr. Terry S. GLYNN

Coleman University (D)

1284 West San Marcos Boulevard,
San Marcos CA 92078-4073
Telephone: (760) 747-3990 Identification: 666259
Accreditation: ACICS

† Main campus is Coleman University in San Diego, CA.

College of the Canyons (E)

26455 Rockwell Canyon Road,
Santa Clarita CA 91355-1899
County: Los Angeles FICE Identification: 008903
Unit ID: 111461
Telephone: (661) 259-7800 Carnegie Class: Assoc/Pub-S-SC
FAX Number: (661) 259-8302 Calendar System: Semester
URL: www.canyons.edu
Established: 1967 Annual Undergrad Tuition & Fees (In-District): $1,152
Enrollment: 17,240 Coed
Affiliation or Control: State/Local IRS Status: 501(c)3
Highest Offering: Associate Degree
Program: Occupational; 2-Year Principally Bachelor's Creditable
Accreditation: WJ, ADNUR

01 Chancellor SCCCD & President COC .... Dr. Dianne G. VAN HOOK
10 Asst Supt/VP Business Services .... Ms. Sharlene COLEAL
15 Asst Supt/Vice Pres Human Resources .... Dr. Diane FIERO
46 Asst Supt/VP Inst Dev/Tech/Online .... Dr. Barry GRIBBONS
18 Asst Supt/VP Facil Plan Op/Const .... Mr. Jim SCHRAGE
32 Asst Superintendent/VP Student Svcs .... Dr. Michael WILDING
05 Int Asst Supt/Vice Pres Instruction .... Mr. Joe GERDA
27 VP Public Info/Advoc/Ext Relations .... Vacant
20 Assoc Vice Pres Academic Affairs .... Ms. Audrey GREEN
13 Assoc VP Information Technology .... Dr. Jim TEMPLE
57 Div Dean Fine & Performing Arts .... Dr. Carmen DOMINGUEZ
76 Div Dean Allied Health & Pub Safety .... Ms. Cynthia DORROH
79 Division Dean Humanities .... Dr. Jennifer BREZINA
41 Division Dean PE/Athletic Director .... Mr. Len MOHNEY
83 Div Dean Social Sci & Business .... Dr. Patricia ROBINSON
81 Div Dean Math/Science & Engineering .... Mr. Omar TORRES
106 Dean Educ Tech/Lrng Resrc/Dist Educ .... Mr. James GLAPA-GROSSKLAG
75 Dean Career Technical Education .... Ms. Kristin HOUSER
35 Dean Student Services .... Mr. Mike JOSLIN
88 Dean Instr Support & Student Succ .... Vacant
06 Dean Enrollment Services .... Ms. Deborah RIO
88 Dean ECE/TeachTraining/CommEd/Noncr .... Ms. Diane STEWART
35 Dean of Students CCC .... Mr. Ryan THEULE
103 Dean Economic Development .... Mr. Peter BELLAS
21 Controller .... Ms. Cindy GRANDGEORGE
102 COO COC Foundation/Int Dir UC .... Ms. Cathy RITZ
30 Chief Devel Officer COC Foundation .... Mr. Murray WOOD
86 Spec Asst Chan/Int Man Dir Gov Rels .... Mr. Eric HARNISH
26 Int Managing Director PR/Marketing .... Mr. Bruce BATTLE
96 Director Contracts Proc & Risk Mgmt .... Mr. Jon AASTED
88 Director Student Business Office .... Ms. Kathleen BENZ
37 Director Financial Aid .... Mr. Tom BILBRUCK
88 Director Professional Development .... Ms. Leslie CARR
19 Director Campus Safety .... Ms. Tammy CASTOR
88 Director MESA .... Ms. Susan CROWTHER
35 Director Student Development .... Ms. Allison DEVLIN
30 Director Development .... Ms. Michele EDMONSON
105 Dir Distance & Accelerated Learning .... Mr. John MAKEVICH
09 Director of Institutional Research .... Dr. Daylene MEUSCHKE
36 Director Career Services .... Mr. Anthony MICHAELIDES
06 Dir Admissions/Records/Online Svcs .... Dr. Jasmine RUYS
88 Dir Outreach & School Relations .... Ms. Kari SOFFA
88 Exec Dir Small Business Dev Ctr .... Mr. Steven TANNEHILL
88 Dir Reentry Pgm & Veterans Affair .... Mr. Renard THOMAS
16 Director Human Resources .... Ms. Christina CHUNG
25 Director Grants Development .... Ms. Theresa ZUZEVICH
23 Director Student Health & Wellness .... Ms. Colleen REEVES

College of the Desert (F)

43-500 Monterey Avenue, Palm Desert CA 92260-9399
County: Riverside FICE Identification: 001182
Unit ID: 113573
Telephone: (760) 346-8041 Carnegie Class: Assoc/Pub-S-MC
FAX Number: (760) 341-8678 Calendar System: Semester
URL: www.collegeofthedesert.edu
Established: 1958 Annual Undergrad Tuition & Fees (In-District): $1,316
Enrollment: 9,075 Coed
Affiliation or Control: State/Local IRS Status: 501(c)3
Highest Offering: Associate Degree
Program: Occupational; 2-Year Principally Bachelor's Creditable
Accreditation: WJ

01 Superintendent/President .... Dr. Joel L. KINNAMON
05 Interim Vice Pres Academic Affairs .... Dr. Joel L. KINNAMON
11 Vice President Business Affairs .... Dr. Edwin DEAS
32 Interim Vice Pres Student Affairs .... Mr. Adrian GONZALES
15 Interim Exec Dir Human Res .... Mr. Stan DUPREE
30 Instnl Advance & Title V Director .... Ms. Pam HUNTER
84 Dean of Enrollment Services .... Dr. Annebelle NERY
38 Dean Student Support Programs .... Mr. Adrian GONZALES
102 Exec Dir of Foundation .... Mr. Jim HUMMER
09 Dean Info Tech & Inst Research .... Ms. Bina ISAAC
18 Director of Maintenance/Operations .... Mr. Steve RENEW
29 Director Alumni Relations .... Mr. Gene MARCHU
37 Director Financial Aid .... Mr. Ken LIRA
96 Director of Fiscal Services .... Mr. Wade ELLIS
06 Registrar/Director of Admissions .... Ms. Sally TIAGA

College of Marin (G)

835 College Avenue, Kentfield CA 94904-2590
County: Marin FICE Identification: 001178
Unit ID: 118347
Telephone: (415) 457-8811 Carnegie Class: Assoc/Pub-S-MC
FAX Number: (415) 456-6017 Calendar System: Semester
URL: www.marin.edu
Established: 1926 Annual Undergrad Tuition & Fees (In-District): $1,380
Enrollment: 7,050 Coed
Affiliation or Control: State/Local IRS Status: 501(c)3
Highest Offering: Associate Degree
Program: Occupational; 2-Year Principally Bachelor's Creditable
Accreditation: WJ, ADNUR, DA

01 Superintendent/President .... Dr. David W. COON
05 Vice President Student Learning .... Vacant
20 Interim Dean of Instruction .... Ms. Cari TORRES
32 Vice President Student Services .... Mr. Jonathan ELDRIDGE
10 Vice President Operations .... Vacant
16 Exec Dir Human Res/Labor Relations .... Ms. Kristina A. COMBS
84 Int Dean Enrollment Services .... Ms. Patricia GANT
49 Dean Arts & Humanities .... Dr. David SNYDER
103 Exec Dean IVC/Work-Econ Dev .... Ms. Nanda SCHORSKE
81 Dean Math/Sciences .... Mr. Jim ARNOLD
21 Director Fiscal Services .... Ms. Peggy ISOZAKI
09 Dir Plng/Rsch/Inst Effectiveness .... Dr. Chialin HSIEH
37 Director Financial Aid/Career Pgms .... Mr. David COOK
18 Int Dir Maintenance & Operation .... Mr. Donald FLOWERS
13 Director Information Technology .... Mr. Marshall NORTHCOTT
35 Dir Student Affairs/Health Center .... Dr. Arnulfo CEDILLO
19 Chief of Police/Director of Safety .... Mr. Mitch LEMAY
68 Dir Physical Educ/Athletics .... Mr. Matt MARKOVICH
76 Interim Dean Health Sci/CDC .... Ms. Terry GESULGA
31 Dir Cmty Svc/Lifelong Lrng .... Dr. Jason LAU
30 Exec Dir Comm Rel/Advancement .... Ms. Cathy SUMMA-WOLFE
08 Director of Learning Resources .... Vacant
88 Dir of Academic Svcs/Articulation .... Ms. Cari TORRES

College of the Redwoods Community College District (H)

7351 Tompkins Hill Road, Eureka CA 95501-9300
County: Humboldt FICE Identification: 001185
Unit ID: 121707
Telephone: (707) 476-4100 Carnegie Class: Assoc/Pub-R-L
FAX Number: (707) 476-4400 Calendar System: Semester
URL: www.redwoods.edu
Established: 1964 Annual Undergrad Tuition & Fees (In-District): $1,140
Enrollment: 4,827 Coed
Affiliation or Control: State/Local IRS Status: 501(c)3
Highest Offering: Associate Degree
Program: Occupational; 2-Year Principally Bachelor's Creditable
Accreditation: #WJ, DA, EMT, NAIT

01 President/Superintendent .... Ms. Kathryn G. LEHNER
04 Assistant to the President .... Ms. Michelle ANDERSON
10 VP Administrative Services .... Mr. Lee LINDSEY
32 VP Student Success .... Dr. Keith SNOW-FLAMER
05 Executive Dean Instruction .... Mr. Jeff CUMMINGS
15 Director Human Resources .... Ms. Ahn FIELDING
12 Director Del Norte Campus .... Ms. Anita JANIS
12 Manager Mendocino Coast Campus .... Ms. Linda TURNER
17 Director Occupations .... Vacant
41 Athletic Director .... Mr. Joseph HASH
37 Director Financial Aid .... Ms. Lynn THIESEN
22 Director EOPS .... Ms. Cheryl TUCKER
88 Director Disabled Student Pgm Svcs .... Vacant
19 Director Maintenance & Operations .... Mr. Garry PATRICK
26 Public Information Officer .... Mr. Paul DEMARK
08 Director Learning Resource Center .. Ms. Mary Grace MCGOVERN
09 Director of Institutional Research .... Dr. Angeline HILL
07 Registrar/Mgr Admissions/Records .... Ms. Kathy GOODLIVE
88 Coord Basic Law Enforcement Academy .... Mr. Ron WATERS

College of the Sequoias (I)

915 S Mooney Boulevard, Visalia CA 93277-2234
County: Tulare FICE Identification: 001186
Unit ID: 123217
Telephone: (559) 730-3700 Carnegie Class: Assoc/Pub-R-L
FAX Number: (559) 730-3894 Calendar System: Semester
URL: www.cos.edu
Established: 1925 Annual Undergrad Tuition & Fees (In-District): $1,362
Enrollment: 10,947 Coed
Affiliation or Control: State/Local IRS Status: 501(c)3
Highest Offering: Associate Degree
Program: Occupational; 2-Year Principally Bachelor's Creditable
Accreditation: WJ, PTAA

01 Superintendent/President ....Mr. Stan A. CARRIZOSA
05 Vice President Academic Services ....Dr. Jennifer LA SERNA
11 Vice President Administrative Svcs ....Ms. Christine STATTON
10 Dean Fiscal Services ....Ms. Leangela MILLER-HERNANDEZ
32 Vice President Student Services ....Mr. Brent CALVIN
37 Dean Student Svcs/Financial Aid ....Ms. Jessica FAGILLO
75 Dean Academic Svcs/Voc Educ ....Dr. Larry DUTTO
81 Dean Science/Math/Eng ....Dr. Robert URTECHO
76 Dean Allied Health/Phys Education ....Mrs. Cindy DELAIN
49 Dean Arts & Letters ....Vacant
15 Dean Human Resources/Legal Affairs ....Mr. John BRATSCH
18 Dean Facilities/Facilities Plng ....Mr. Eric MITTLESTEAD
35 Dean Student Services ....Ms. Stephanie COLLIER
30 Exec Dir Found/Inst Advancement ....Mr. Tim FOSTER
66 Director Nursing & Allied Health ....Mrs. Karen ROBERTS
08 Dir Library/Instructional Tech ....Ms. Mary-Catherine OXFORD
09 Director of Research ....Dr. Mehmet OZTURK
06 Registrar/Record Technician ....Ms. Velia RODRIGUEZ
41 Associate Dean/Athletic Director ....Mr. Brent DAVIS
19 Chief Campus Police ....Mr. Robert MASTERSON
38 Div Chr Stdt Counsel/Hlth Std/Wk Ex ....Ms. Hunter CHURCH-GONZALES
40 Bookstore Manager ....Ms. Dorianna MENDIETTA
23 Head Nurse/Health Center ....Ms. Patricia ALVAREZ
32 Student Activities Coordinator ....Mrs. Debbie DOUGLASS
103 Program Coord Workforce Development ....Ms. Louann WALDNER
36 Coord Career/Placement Center ....Vacant

College of the Siskiyous (A)

800 College Avenue, Weed CA 96094-2899
County: Siskiyou FICE Identification: 001187
Unit ID: 123484
Telephone: (530) 938-5200 Carnegie Class: Assoc/Pub-R-M
FAX Number: (530) 938-5506 Calendar System: Semester
URL: www.siskiyous.edu
Established: 1957 Annual Undergrad Tuition & Fees (In-District): $1,410
Enrollment: 2,314 Coed
Affiliation or Control: State/Local IRS Status: 501(c)3
Highest Offering: Associate Degree
Program: Occupational; 2-Year Principally Bachelor's Creditable
Accreditation: WJ

01 Interim Superintendent/President ....Dr. Robert A. FROST
04 Exec Assistant to the President ....Ms. Kathy GASSAWAY
11 Interim VP Administrative Svcs ....Mr. Scotty THOMASON
08 Assistant Dean Learning Resources ....Ms. Nancy SHEPARD
32 Director Student Life ....Mr. Doug HAUGEN
09 Director Planning Assess & Research ....Ms. Kristy ANDERSON
41 Director Athletics ....Mr. Dennis ROBERTS
20 Dean Student Learning ....Dr. Gregory SOUTH
12 Director Yreka Campus ....Ms. Sarah WHITIS
07 Director of Enrollment Services ....Ms. Meghan WITHERELL
15 Director Personnel ....Ms. Nancy MILLER
37 Supervisor Financial Aid ....Ms. Meghan WITHERELL
18 Interim Asst Dir MOT ....Mr. Phil ALVARADO
30 Director of Institutional Advancemt ....Ms. Sonia WRIGHT
28 Director of Diversity ....Ms. Nancy MILLER

Columbia College Hollywood (B)

18618 Oxnard Street, Tarzana CA 91356-1411
County: Los Angeles FICE Identification: 021102
Unit ID: 112570
Telephone: (800) 785-0585 Carnegie Class: Spec/Arts
FAX Number: (818) 345-9053 Calendar System: Quarter
URL: www.columbiacollege.edu
Established: 1952 Annual Undergrad Tuition & Fees: $18,350
Enrollment: 348 Coed
Affiliation or Control: Independent Non-Profit IRS Status: 501(c)3
Highest Offering: Baccalaureate
Program: Liberal Arts And General; Fine Arts Emphasis
Accreditation: @WC, ART

01 President/CEO ....Mr. Richard KOBRITZ
05 Dean of the College ....Mr. Alan L. GANSBERG
10 Treasurer ....Mr. Theodore O'KARMA
22 Sr Compliance/Accreditation Manager ....Ms. Debra MONTOYA
21 Sr Director of Finance/New Ventures ....Mr. Richard CROWE
32 Dean of Student Services ....Dr. Yolanda DAWSON
13 Director of IT and Production Svcs ....Mr. Ronald REEVES
07 Director of Admissions ....Ms. Carmen MUNOZ
37 Financial Aid Manager ....Mr. Jan HASTINGS
36 Student Placement ....Ms. Kate MCARDLE
06 Registrar ....Ms. Carmela CHANEY

Community Christian College (C)

251 Tennessee Street, Redlands CA 92373-4438
County: San Bernardino FICE Identification: 038744
Unit ID: 446163
Telephone: (909) 335-8863 Carnegie Class: Assoc/PrivNFP
FAX Number: (909) 335-9101 Calendar System: Quarter
URL: www.cccollege.edu
Established: 1995 Annual Undergrad Tuition & Fees: $11,088
Enrollment: 110 Coed
Affiliation or Control: Independent Non-Profit IRS Status: 501(c)3
Highest Offering: Associate Degree
Program: 2-Year Principally Bachelor's Creditable
Accreditation: TRACS

01 President ....Mr. Troy VUGTEVEEN
05 Vice Pres Academic Affs/Registrar ....Dr. John HARBISON
27 Director Information Services ....Ms. Marilyn HOPE

Concord Law School of Kaplan University (D)

10866 Wilshire Blvd, Suite 1200,
Los Angeles CA 90024-4356
Telephone: (310) 689-3200 FICE Identification: 041259
Accreditation: &NH, DETC

† Main campus is Kaplan University in Davenport, IA.

Concorde Career College (E)

12951 Euclid Street, Suite 101,
Garden Grove CA 92840-1451
County: Orange FICE Identification: 008071
Unit ID: 123679
Telephone: (714) 703-1900 Carnegie Class: Assoc/PrivFP
FAX Number: (714) 530-8421 Calendar System: Semester
URL: www.concorde.edu
Established: 1960 Annual Undergrad Tuition & Fees: N/A
Enrollment: 1,006 Coed
Affiliation or Control: Proprietary IRS Status: Proprietary
Highest Offering: Associate Degree
Program: Occupational; Nursing Emphasis
Accreditation: ACCSC, COARC, DH, PTAA

01 Campus President ....Colleen MCDERMOTT

Concorde Career College (F)

12412 Victory Boulevard, North Hollywood CA 91606-3134
County: Los Angeles FICE Identification: 007607
Unit ID: 124937
Telephone: (818) 766-8151 Carnegie Class: Assoc/PrivFP
FAX Number: (818) 766-1587 Calendar System: Quarter
URL: www.concordecareercolleges.com
Established: 1955 Annual Undergrad Tuition & Fees: $29,383
Enrollment: 1,050 Coed
Affiliation or Control: Proprietary IRS Status: Proprietary
Highest Offering: Associate Degree
Program: Occupational
Accreditation: ACCSC, COARC, #PTAA, SURGT

01 Campus President ....Carmen BOWEN

Concorde Career College (G)

201 E Airport Drive, Suite A, San Bernadino CA 92408
FICE Identification: 008537
Unit ID: 124706
Telephone: (909) 884-8891 Carnegie Class: Assoc/PrivFP
FAX Number: (909) 884-1831 Calendar System: Semester
URL: www.concorde.edu
Established: 1970 Annual Undergrad Tuition & Fees: $28,806
Enrollment: 911 Coed
Affiliation or Control: Proprietary IRS Status: Proprietary
Highest Offering: Associate Degree
Program: Occupational
Accreditation: ACCSC, COARC, DH, SURGT

01 Campus President ....Fred FARIDIAN

Concorde Career College (H)

4393 Imperial Avenue, Suite 100,
San Diego CA 92113-1962
County: San Diego FICE Identification: 007930
Unit ID: 120661
Telephone: (619) 688-0800 Carnegie Class: Assoc/PrivFP
FAX Number: (619) 220-4177 Calendar System: Semester
URL: www.concorde.edu
Established: Annual Undergrad Tuition & Fees: N/A
Enrollment: 649 Coed
Affiliation or Control: Proprietary IRS Status: Proprietary
Highest Offering: Associate Degree
Program: Occupational
Accreditation: ACCSC, COARC, DH, PTAA, SURGT

01 Campus President ....Mr. Mike COOLING

Concordia University (I)

1530 Concordia W, Irvine CA 92612-3299
County: Orange FICE Identification: 020705
Unit ID: 112075
Telephone: (949) 854-8002 Carnegie Class: Master's L
FAX Number: (949) 214-3520 Calendar System: Semester
URL: www.cui.edu
Established: 1972 Annual Undergrad Tuition & Fees: $29,000
Enrollment: 3,519 Coed
Affiliation or Control: Lutheran Church - Missouri Synod
IRS Status: 501(c)3
Highest Offering: Doctorate
Program: Liberal Arts And General; Teacher Preparatory
Accreditation: WC, NURSE

01 President ....Dr. Kurt J. KRUEGER
05 Provost/Exec VP ....Dr. Mary K. SCOTT
03 Exec VP Student & Enroll Services ....Dr. Gary R. MCDANIEL
30 Exec VP Advancement ....Mr. Timothy J. JAEGER
10 Exec VP/Chief Finance Officer ....Mr. Kevin TILDEN
26 Exec VP External Relations ....Mr. Stephen CHRISTENSEN
20 Assoc Provost/VP Acad Affs ....Dr. Peter SENKBEIL
20 Asst Provost Adult/Grad/Online ....Dr. Doug GROVE
49 Dean School of Arts and Sciences ....Dr. Timothy PREUSS
107 Dean School of Professional Studies ....Dr. Timothy C. PETERS
50 Dean School of Business ....Prof. George WRIGHT
53 Dean School of Education ....Dr. Janice NELSON
73 Dean Christ College ....Dr. Steven P. MUELLER
06 Dean of Academic Records/Registrar ....Prof. Kenneth R. CLAVIR
32 Dean of Students ....Dr. Gilbert FUGITT
07 Director of Undergrad Admissions ....Mr. Doug WIBLE
07 Director of Graduate Admissions ....Mrs. Rina CAMPBELL
37 Director of Financial Aid ....Ms. Lori MCDONALD
21 Bursar ....Mr. Edgar LOPEZ
43 General Counsel ....Mr. Ronald VAN BLARCOM
15 Director of Human Resources ....Mrs. Pamela CLAVIR
08 Director of Library Services ....Prof. Carolina BARTON
41 Athletic Director ....Prof. David BIRELINE
39 Director Residence Life ....Mr. Scott KEITH
19 Director Security/Safety ....Mr. Steven RODRIGUEZ
29 Director of Alumni Relations ....Mr. Michael BERGLER
24 Director Educational Media ....Prof. John RANDALL
36 Director of Career Services ....Mrs. Victoria JAFFEE
44 Director Major Gift Planning ....Mr. Dennis COX
85 Exec Director Global Programs ....Dr. Dan WAITE
13 Director of IT Services ....Mr. Chris HARRIS

*Contra Costa Community College District Office (J)

500 Court Street, Martinez CA 94553-1278
County: Contra Costa FICE Identification: 001189
Unit ID: 112817
Telephone: (925) 229-1000 Carnegie Class: N/A
FAX Number: (925) 370-2019
URL: www.4cd.edu

01 Chancellor ....Dr. Helen BENJAMIN
05 VC Education and Technology ....Mr. Mojden MEHDIZADEH
11 Vice Chanc Admin Services ....Dr. John AL-AMIN
15 VC Human Resources/Chief Negotiator ....Mr. Eugene C. HUFF

*Contra Costa College (K)

2600 Mission Bell Drive, San Pablo CA 94806-3195
County: Contra Costa FICE Identification: 001190
Unit ID: 112826
Telephone: (510) 235-7800 Carnegie Class: Assoc/Pub-S-MC
FAX Number: (510) 236-6768 Calendar System: Semester
URL: www.contracosta.edu
Established: 1948 Annual Undergrad Tuition & Fees (In-District): $1,104
Enrollment: 7,263 Coed
Affiliation or Control: State/Local IRS Status: 501(c)3
Highest Offering: Associate Degree
Program: Occupational; 2-Year Principally Bachelor's Creditable
Accreditation: WJ, DA

02 President ....Dr. Denise NOLDON
03 Vice President ....Ms. Tammeil GILKERSON
05 Senior Dean of Instruction ....Dr. Donna FLOYD
32 Interim Sr Dean of Student Services ....Ms. Vicki FERGUSON
75 Dean Economic Development ....Ms. Priscilla LEADON
07 Director Admissions & Records ....Ms. Catherine FITES
10 Director Business Services ....Ms. Mariles MAGALONG
09 Director of Institutional Research ....Vacant
37 Interim Financial Aid Supervisor ....Ms. Jennifer MA
18 Chief Facilities/Physical Plant ....Mr. Bruce KING

*Diablo Valley College (L)

321 Golf Club Road, Pleasant Hill CA 94523-1544
County: Contra Costa FICE Identification: 001191
Unit ID: 113634
Telephone: (925) 685-1230 Carnegie Class: Assoc/Pub-S-MC
FAX Number: (925) 685-1551 Calendar System: Semester
URL: www.dvc.edu
Established: 1949 Annual Undergrad Tuition & Fees (In-District): $1,104
Enrollment: 19,069 Coed
Affiliation or Control: State/Local IRS Status: 501(c)3
Highest Offering: Associate Degree
Program: Occupational; 2-Year Principally Bachelor's Creditable
Accreditation: WJ, ACFEI, CEA, DA, DH

02 President ....Mr. Peter GARCIA
05 Vice President Instruction ....Ms. Susan E. LAMB
32 Vice President Student Services ....Dr. Newin ORANTE
10 Vice President Finance and Admin ....Mr. Chris LEIVAS
20 Senior Dean of Curriculum & Instr ....Ms. Kimberely SCHENK
84 Dean Outreach/Enroll Mgt/ Matric ....Ms. Elizabeth HAUSCARRIAGUE
12 Dean San Ramon Campus ....Ms. Kathleen COSTA
41 Dean of PE/Athl/Dance/Athletic Dir ....Ms. Christina WORSLEY
62 Director of the Library Services ....Mr. Andy KIVEL
26 Director of Media & Communications ....Ms. Chrisanne KNOX
57 Dean Applied & Fine Arts ....Mr. Michael ALMAGUER
54 Dean Physical Sci/Engr/Bio Sci ....Dr. Patricia YOUNG
50 Dean English & Social Science ....Mr. Obed VAZQUEZ

81 Dean Math/Computer Science & Bus ... Ms. Rachel WESTLAKE
06 Registrar ... Ms. Stephanie ALVES
35 Dean Student Support Services ... Ms. Emily STONE

*Los Medanos College (A)

2700 E Leland Road, Pittsburg CA 94565-5197
County: Contra Costa FICE Identification: 010340
Unit ID: 117894
Telephone: (925) 439-2181 Carnegie Class: Assoc/Pub-S-MC
FAX Number: (925) 427-1599 Calendar System: Semester
URL: www.losmedanos.edu
Established: 1973 Annual Undergrad Tuition & Fees (In-District): $1,124
Enrollment: 8,556 Coed
Affiliation or Control: State/Local IRS Status: 501(c)3
Highest Offering: Associate Degree
Program: Occupational; 2-Year Principally Bachelor's Creditable
Accreditation: WJ

02 President ... Mr. Bob KRATOCHVIL
05 Vice Pres Instruction/Student Svcs ... Dr. Kevin HORAN
10 Director Business Services ... Ms. Aderonke OLATUNJI
04 Senior Executive Assistant ... Ms. Jennifer ADAMS
26 Director Marketing & Media Design ... Ms. Barbara CELLA
102 Senior Foundation Director ... Ms. Ruth GOODIN
32 Senior Dean Student Services ... Ms. Gail NEWMAN
45 Sr Dean Plng & Inst Effectiveness ... Ms. Kiran KAMATH
81 Dean Math & Sciences ... Dr. A'kilah MOORE
83 Dean Career Tech Ed/Social Sci ... Ms. Natalie HANNUM
49 Dean Liberal Arts ... Ms. Nancy YBARRA
88 Interim Dean Student Success ... Mr. David BELMAN
38 Dean Counseling & EOPS ... Mr. Jeffrey BENFORD
07 Director Admissions ... Ms. Robin ARMOUR
37 Director Financial Aid ... Ms. Loretta CANTO-WILLIAMS
14 Supervisor Computer & Network Svcs ... Mr. Mike BECKER
18 Manager Buildings & Grounds ... Mr. Russ HOLT
103 Program Mgr Workforce Dev Projects ... Mr. David WAHL
20 Supervisor Office of Instruction ... Ms. Eileen VALENZUELA

Copper Mountain College (B)

6162 Rotary Way, Box 1398, Joshua Tree CA 92252-6102
County: San Bernardino FICE Identification: 035424
Unit ID: 395362
Telephone: (760) 366-3791 Carnegie Class: Assoc/Pub-S-SC
FAX Number: (760) 366-5255 Calendar System: Semester
URL: www.cmccd.edu
Established: 1999 Annual Undergrad Tuition & Fees (In-District): $1,380
Enrollment: 2,142 Coed
Affiliation or Control: State/Local IRS Status: 501(c)3
Highest Offering: Associate Degree
Program: Occupational; 2-Year Principally Bachelor's Creditable
Accreditation: WJ

01 Superintendent/President ... Dr. Roger WAGNER
05 Vice Pres for Academic Affairs ... Dr. Wei ZHOU
32 Vice President of Student Services ... Mr. Greg BROWN
15 Manager of Human Resources ... Ms. Andrea RIESGO
18 Chief of Facilities ... Vacant
12 Coordinator of Base Programs ... Vacant
102 Executive Director of Foundation ... Ms. Sandy SMITH
10 Chief Business Officer ... Ms. Meredith PLUMMER
37 Director of Financial Aid ... Mr. Brian HEINEMANN
76 Dir Hlth Science-Registered Nursing ... Ms. Christi BLAUWKAMP
91 Director of Information Systems ... Mr. Steve KEMP
26 Dir Marketing & Community Relations ... Vacant

Cuesta College (C)

PO Box 8106, San Luis Obispo CA 93403-8106
County: San Luis Obispo FICE Identification: 001192
Unit ID: 113193
Telephone: (805) 546-3100 Carnegie Class: Assoc/Pub-R-L
FAX Number: (805) 546-3904 Calendar System: Semester
URL: www.cuesta.edu
Established: 1963 Annual Undergrad Tuition & Fees (In-District): $1,400
Enrollment: 9,834 Coed
Affiliation or Control: State/Local IRS Status: 501(c)3
Highest Offering: Associate Degree
Program: Occupational; 2-Year Principally Bachelor's Creditable
Accreditation: WJ, EMT

01 Superintendent/President ... Dr. Gilbert H. STORK
05 VP/Asst Supt Academic Affairs ... Ms. Deborah WULFF
10 VP/Asst Supt Administrative Svcs ... Ms. Toni SOMMER
32 VP/Asst Supt Student Services ... Ms. Sandee MCLAUGHLIN
12 Exec Dean North Co Campus/S Co Ctr ... Gary J. RUBIN, JD
35 Dean of Students ... Ms. Nohemy ORNELAS
30 Exec Dir Foundation/Inst Adv ... Ms. Shannon HILL
08 Director Library/Lrng Resources/DE ... Mr. Mark STENGEL
35 Coordinator Student Life/Leadership ... Mr. Anthony GUTIERREZ
13 Director of Computer Services ... Ms. Janice M. HOUSE
66 Director of Nursing ... Ms. Marcia SCOTT
15 Exec Dir Human Res Labor Relations ... Mr. William BENJAMIN
19 Director of Public Safety ... Mr. Joseph ARTEAGA
40 Director of Bookstore ... Ms. Trudy BELL
41 Director of Athletics ... Mr. Robert MARIUCCI
18 Dir Maintenance/Operations/Grounds ... Mr. Terry REECE
38 Director Counseling Services ... Mr. Candelario MUNOZ
103 Dir Workforce Econ Devel Cmty Pgm ... Dr. Matthew GREEN
23 Coordinator of Health Services ... Ms. Vicki SAWZAK

81 Int Dean Ac Aff Sci/Math/Nursing/PE ... Mr. Bret CLARK
79 Dean Ac Aff Arts/Humanities/Soc Sci ... Dr. Pamela RALSTON
103 Dean Ac Aff Workforce Econ Dev ... Mr. John CASCAMO
76 Associate Director of Allied Health ... Ms. Lisa WEARDA
07 Director of Admissions & Records ... Ms. Kristin PIMENTEL
09 Director of Institutional Research ... Dr. Ryan CARTNAL
21 Director Fiscal Services ... Mr. Christopher GREEN
102 Director Foundation Programs ... Ms. Karen TACKET

The Culinary Institute of America at Greystone (D)

2555 Main Street, Saint Helena CA 94574-9504
Telephone: (707) 967-1100 Identification: 666260
Accreditation: &M

† Main campus is Culinary Institute of America in Hyde Park, NY.

Deep Springs College (E)

HC 72 Box 45001, Via Dyer, NV 89010-9803
County: Inyo FICE Identification: 001194
Unit ID: 113528
Telephone: (760) 872-2000 Carnegie Class: Not Classified
FAX Number: (760) 874-7077 Calendar System: Other
URL: www.deepsprings.edu
Established: 1917 Annual Undergrad Tuition & Fees: $0
Enrollment: 27 Male
Affiliation or Control: Independent Non-Profit IRS Status: 501(c)3
Highest Offering: Associate Degree
Program: 2-Year Principally Bachelor's Creditable
Accreditation: WJ

01 President ... Mr. David NEIDORF
05 Dean of College ... Mr. Kenneth CARDWELL
88 Ranch Manager ... Ms. Janice HUNTER
11 VP Operations ... Ms. Jill LAWRENCE
21 Office Manager ... Ms. Iris POPE
18 Mechanic & Plant Manager ... Mr. Padraic MACLEISH
88 Chef ... Ms. Donna BLAGDAN
88 Farm Manager ... Mr. Adam NYBORG
06 Registrar ... Ms. Jill BREWER

Dell'Arte International School of Physical Theatre (F)

P.O. Box 816, 131 H Street, Blue Lake CA 95525
County: Humboldt FICE Identification: 030256
Unit ID: 113537
Telephone: (707) 668-5663 Carnegie Class: Spec/Arts
FAX Number: (707) 668-5665 Calendar System: Other
URL: www.dellarte.com
Established: 1975 Annual Graduate Tuition & Fees: $12,350
Enrollment: 55 Coed
Affiliation or Control: Independent Non-Profit IRS Status: 501(c)3
Highest Offering: Master's; No Undergraduates
Program: Professional; Fine Arts Emphasis
Accreditation: THEA

01 Producing Artistic Director ... Mr. Michael FIELDS
10 Financial Officer ... Ms. Stephanie WITZEL
26 Marketing Director/Development ... Ms. Meghan FRANK
06 School Administrator/Registrar ... Ms. Nicholette ROUTHIER

Design Institute of San Diego (G)

8555 Commerce Avenue, San Diego CA 92121-2685
County: San Diego FICE Identification: 022980
Unit ID: 113582
Telephone: (858) 566-1200 Carnegie Class: Spec/Arts
FAX Number: (858) 566-2711 Calendar System: Semester
URL: www.disd.edu
Established: 1977 Annual Undergrad Tuition & Fees: $18,600
Enrollment: 320 Coed
Affiliation or Control: Proprietary IRS Status: Proprietary
Highest Offering: Baccalaureate
Program: Professional
Accreditation: ACICS, CIDA

01 President ... Mr. Arthur ROSENSTEIN
05 Vice President ... Ms. Gloria ROSENSTEIN
12 Campus Director ... Ms. Margot BLANK DOUCETTE
07 Director of Admissions ... Ms. Paula PARRISH
37 Director Financial Aid ... Ms. Jackie GLORIA
32 Director of Student Services ... Ms. Tena MOIOLA
08 Librarian ... Ms. Lisa SCHATTMAN
06 Registrar ... Ms. Tracy GULINO
07 Outreach & Admissions ... Ms. Liz BARRY

DeVry University - Pomona Campus (H)

901 Corporate Center Drive, Pomona CA 91768-2642
Telephone: (909) 622-8866 FICE Identification: 023329
Accreditation: &NH, CAHIIM, ENGT

† Main campus is DeVry University - Chicago Campus in Chicago, IL.

Dominican School of Philosophy and Theology (I)

2301 Vine Street, Berkeley CA 94708-1816
County: Alameda FICE Identification: 001296
Unit ID: 113704
Telephone: (510) 849-2030 Carnegie Class: Spec/Faith
FAX Number: (510) 849-1372 Calendar System: Semester
URL: www.dspt.edu
Established: 1932 Annual Undergrad Tuition & Fees: $15,700
Enrollment: 99 Coed
Affiliation or Control: Roman Catholic IRS Status: 501(c)3
Highest Offering: Master's
Program: Professional; Religious Emphasis
Accreditation: WC, THEOL

01 President ... Rev. Michael SWEENEY
05 Academic Dean ... Rev. Christopher M. RENZ
11 COO/CFO ... Mr. Ian BROOKS
30 Director Advancement/Donor Rels ... Mr. Michael CHINNAVASO
07 Director of Admissions ... Mr. John D. KNUTSEN
06 Registrar ... Sr. Francis Marie SEALE
21 Office Manager/Dir Student Services ... Ms. Colleen POWER
26 Director of Communications ... Ms. Heidi MCKENNA
84 Recruitment/Development Officer ... Ms. Justyna KRUKOWSKA

Dominican University of California (J)

50 Acacia Avenue, San Rafael CA 94901-2298
County: Marin FICE Identification: 001196
Unit ID: 113698
Telephone: (415) 457-4440 Carnegie Class: Master's M
FAX Number: (415) 485-3205 Calendar System: Semester
URL: www.dominican.edu
Established: 1890 Annual Undergrad Tuition & Fees: $39,050
Enrollment: 2,207 Coed
Affiliation or Control: Independent Non-Profit IRS Status: 501(c)3
Highest Offering: Master's
Program: Occupational; Liberal Arts And General; Teacher Preparatory; Professional
Accreditation: WC, NURSE, OT

01 President ... Dr. Mary B. MARCY
05 Provost ... Dr. Steven E. WEISLER
10 Vice President Business & Finance ... Ms. Michele HINKEN
26 Vice Pres External Relations ... Vacant
32 VP Student Life/Dean of Students ... Dr. John F. KENNEDY
84 Vice Pres of Enrollment Management ... Vacant
20 Associate VP Academic Affairs ... Ms. Martha NELSON
27 Director of Marketing ... Ms. Nancy BULETTE
04 Assistant to the President ... Mrs. Sarita PURECE
100 Asst Spec Projects/Trustee Liaison ... Dr. Francoise LEPAGE
79 Dean Sch Arts/Humanities/Social Sci ... Dr. Nicola PITCHFORD
76 Dean of School Health/Natural Sci ... Dr. Ching-Hua WANG
53 Dean School of Educ/Counsel Psych ... Dr. Edward KUJAWA
50 Dean School of Business/Leadership ... Vacant
88 Asc Dean Sch of Health/Natural Sci ... Vacant
35 Associate Dean of Students ... Mr. Paul RACCANELLO
18 Exec Dir Facilities/Physical Plant ... Mr. Jacques CHARTON
08 Executive Director Library Services ... Mr. Gary GORKA
09 Exec Dir of Institutional Research ... Mr. Scott CLARK
37 Director of Financial Aid ... Ms. Shanon LITTLE
07 Asst VP of Undergrad Admissions ... Ms. Rebecca FINN KENNEY
13 Chief Technology Officer ... Mr. Jackson RATCLIFFE
06 Registrar ... Ms. Marianne STICKEL
29 Director of Alumni Relations ... Ms. Tracy HOGAN
88 President Alumni Association ... Mr. James SALTER
15 Director of Human Resources ... Ms. Wendy LEE
36 Director Student Placement ... Ms. Susan FYLES
28 Director Diversity ... Dr. Suresh APPAVOO
92 Director Honors Program ... Dr. Diara SPAIN
38 Director Student Counseling ... Dr. Chuck BILLINGS
26 Public Relations Officer ... Mr. David ALBEE
85 Exec Director Intl & Global Educ ... Dr. Jayati GHOSH
30 VP Advancement/Alumni Engagement ... Ms. Kathleen KRUEGER PARK

Dongguk University (K)

440 Shatto Place, Los Angeles CA 90020-1704
County: Los Angeles FICE Identification: 031095
Unit ID: 122117
Telephone: (213) 487-0110 Carnegie Class: Spec/Health
FAX Number: (213) 487-0527 Calendar System: Quarter
URL: www.dula.edu
Established: 1979 Annual Undergrad Tuition & Fees: $11,900
Enrollment: 197 Coed
Affiliation or Control: Independent Non-Profit IRS Status: 501(c)3
Highest Offering: Master's; No Lower Division
Program: Professional
Accreditation: ACUP

01 President ... Dr. Un Kyo SEO
05 Office of the Provost/Admissions ... Mr. Seok Joo AUM
10 Director of Finance ... Mr. Albert KIM
37 Financial Aid Officer ... Ms. Julia PARK
06 Registrar ... Mr. Hoon SEO
63 Director of Oriental Medical Center ... Ms. Kay JOO
18 Director of Facilities ... Mr. Arturo AGUIRRE
21 Office Manager ... Ms. Bo Yoon CHOI
85 International Student Advisor ... Mr. Phillip YEW

East San Gabriel Valley Regional Occupational Program and Technical Center (A)

1501 W. Del Norte Street, West Covina CA 91790
County: Los Angeles FICE Identification: 031166
Unit ID: 413802
Telephone: (626) 472-5121 Carnegie Class: Not Classified
FAX Number: (626) 472-5125 Calendar System: Semester
URL: www.esgvrop.org
Established: Annual Undergrad Tuition & Fees (In-District): $5,650
Enrollment: 324 Coed
Affiliation or Control: State/Local IRS Status: 501(c)3
Highest Offering: Associate Degree
Program: Occupational
Accreditation: COE, MAC

El Camino College (B)

16007 Crenshaw Boulevard, Torrance CA 90506-0002
County: Los Angeles FICE Identification: 001197
Unit ID: 113980
Telephone: (310) 660-3670 Carnegie Class: Assoc/Pub-S-SC
FAX Number: (310) 660-7798 Calendar System: Semester
URL: www.elcamino.edu
Established: 1947 Annual Undergrad Tuition & Fees (In-District): $1,140
Enrollment: 24,224 Coed
Affiliation or Control: State/Local IRS Status: 501(c)3
Highest Offering: Associate Degree
Program: Occupational; 2-Year Principally Bachelor's Creditable
Accreditation: WJ, ADNUR, COARC, RAD

01 President .... Dr. Thomas M. FALLO
05 Vice President Academic Affairs .... Dr. Francisco M. ARCE
11 Vice Pres Administrative Services .... Ms. Jo Ann HIGDON
32 Vice Pres Student/Community Advance .... Dr. Jeanie NISHIME
15 Vice Pres of Human Resources .... Ms. Linda BEAM
30 Dean Community Advancement .... Mr. Jose ANAYA
45 Dean Planning/Research/Development .... Vacant
72 Dean Industry & Technology .... Dr. Stephanie RODRIGUEZ
81 Dean Math/Physical Sciences .... Dr. Donald GOLDBERG
50 Dean of Business .... Dr. Virginia RAPP
83 Dean Behavioral & Social Science .... Dr. Gloria MIRANDA
68 Dean Health/Exer/Science/Sport .... Mr. Rory NATIVIDAD
57 Dean Fine Arts .... Dr. Connie FITZSIMONS
76 Dean Natural Sciences .... Dr. Jean SHANKWEILER
79 Dean Humanities .... Mr. Tom LEW
38 Dean Counseling Matriculation Svcs .... Dr. Regina SMITH
84 Dean of Enrollment Services .... Vacant
27 Director of Information Systems .... Mr. John WAGSTAFF
31 Director of Community Relations .... Ms. Ann GARTEN
66 Director of Nursing .... Ms. Theresa KYLE
07 Dir Admissions/Records/Registrar .... Mr. Bill MULROONEY
10 Chief Business Officer .... Dr. Jo Ann HIGDON
20 Associate Academic Officer .... Vacant
26 Chief Public Relations Officer .... Ms. Ann M. GARTEN
102 Executive Director Foundation .... Ms. Katie GLEASON
36 Director Student Placement .... Dr. Regina SMITH
96 Acting Director of Purchasing .... Mr. Rocky BONURA
40 Director of Bookstore .... Ms. Julie BOURLIER
19 Chief of Campus Police .... Mr. Michael TREVIS
18 Director of Facilities Plng/Svcs .... Mr. Robert GANN
35 Director of Student Affairs .... Mr. Harold TYLER
37 Director Student Financial Aid .... Ms. Hortense COOPER
06 Registrar .... Mr. Bill MULROONEY
29 Director Alumni Relations .... Ms. Katie GLEASON
09 Director Institutional Research .... Ms. Irene GRAFF
28 Director of Diversity .... Ms. Leisa BIGGERS
21 Business Manager .... Ms. Janice ELY
25 Resource Devel/Grants Coordinator .... Ms. Katie GLEASON

El Camino College Compton Center (C)

1111 E Artesia Boulevard, Compton CA 90221-5393
Telephone: (310) 900-1600 FICE Identification: 001188
Accreditation: &WJ

† Main campus is El Camino College in Torrance, CA.

Emperor's College of Traditional Oriental Medicine (D)

1807-B Wilshire Boulevard, Santa Monica CA 90403-5678
County: Los Angeles FICE Identification: 026090
Unit ID: 114114
Telephone: (310) 453-8300 Carnegie Class: Spec/Health
FAX Number: (310) 829-3838 Calendar System: Quarter
URL: www.emperors.edu
Established: 1983 Annual Undergrad Tuition & Fees: $15,000
Enrollment: 256 Coed
Affiliation or Control: Proprietary IRS Status: Proprietary
Highest Offering: Doctorate
Program: Professional
Accreditation: ACUP

01 Chief Executive Officer .... Yun KIM
05 Academic Dean .... Jacques MORAMARCO
07 Director of Admissions .... Lisa ROCCHETTI
37 Financial Aid Officer .... Farida LUGEMBE
11 COO/Administrator .... George PARK
58 Dean Doctoral Programs .... John FANG

Empire College School of Business (E)

3035 Cleveland Avenue, Santa Rosa CA 95403-2100
County: Sonoma FICE Identification: 009032
Unit ID: 114123
Telephone: (707) 546-4000 Carnegie Class: Assoc/PrivFP
FAX Number: (707) 546-4058 Calendar System: Other
URL: www.empcol.edu
Established: 1961 Annual Undergrad Tuition & Fees: $16,775
Enrollment: 398 Coed
Affiliation or Control: Proprietary IRS Status: Proprietary
Highest Offering: Associate Degree
Program: Occupational; Technical Emphasis
Accreditation: ACICS

01 President .... Mr. Roy HURD
26 Vice Pres Marketing/Administration .... Mrs. Sherie HURD
05 Director of Education .... Mrs. Mary Ellen PASTORINO
07 Director of Admissions .... Ms. Dahnja STRAUB
37 Director Student Financial Aid .... Mrs. Mary O'BRIEN
11 Director of Administrative Svcs .... Ms. Eleanor NORIEL
10 Director of Accounting .... Mr. David YARBROUGH
36 Director Student Placement .... Vacant
40 Bookstore Manager .... Ms. Kass VON DER MEHDEN
06 Registrar .... Ms. Margareta CAMPBELL
38 Student Success Advisor .... Ms. Debbie BENDETTI
38 Student Success Advisor .... Ms. Nora SONGSTER

Epic Bible College (F)

4330 Auburn Blvd., Sacramento CA 95841
County: Sacramento FICE Identification: 034033
Unit ID: 124487
Telephone: (916) 348-4689 Carnegie Class: Spec/Faith
FAX Number: (916) 334-2315 Calendar System: Trimester
URL: www.EPIC.edu
Established: 1974 Annual Undergrad Tuition & Fees: $9,166
Enrollment: 300 Coed
Affiliation or Control: Independent Non-Profit IRS Status: 501(c)3
Highest Offering: Baccalaureate
Program: Liberal Arts And General; Religious Emphasis
Accreditation: TRACS

01 President .... Dr. Ronald W. HARDEN
05 Vice President of Academics .... Dr. Greg L. HARTLEY
108 Director of Assessment .... Mrs. Rosemarie HOWELL
08 Director Learning Resource .... Ms. Carol SIMON
10 Chief Financial Officer .... Mr. C. Steven CHANEY
37 Director of Financial Services .... Mr. David PINESCHI
06 Director of Records .... Ms. Kathy CLARKE
106 Director of Online Program .... Rev. John GALLEGOS

Eternity Bible College (G)

2136 Winifred Street, Simi Valley CA 93063
County: Ventura Identification: 667045
Telephone: (805) 581-1233 Carnegie Class: Not Classified
FAX Number: (805) 581-1245 Calendar System: Semester
URL: www.eternitybiblecollege.com
Established: 2004 Annual Undergrad Tuition & Fees: $5,000
Enrollment: 183 Coed
Affiliation or Control: Independent Non-Profit IRS Status: 501(c)3
Highest Offering: Baccalaureate
Program: Religious Emphasis
Accreditation: @BI

01 President .... Joshua WALKER
05 Academic Dean .... Spencer MACCUISH
07 Director of Admissions .... Nicole MCGLADDERY
06 Assistant Registrar .... Kristen AZBELL

Evangelia University (H)

2660 West Woodland Drive, Suite 200, Anaheim CA 92801-2650
County: Orange Identification: 666640
Telephone: (714) 527-0691 Carnegie Class: Not Classified
FAX Number: (714) 527-0693 Calendar System: Other
URL: www.evangelia.edu
Established: 1999 Annual Undergrad Tuition & Fees: $3,650
Enrollment: 50 Coed
Affiliation or Control: Reformed Presbyterian Church IRS Status: 501(c)3
Highest Offering: Doctorate
Program: Liberal Arts And General; Religious Emphasis
Accreditation: TRACS

01 President .... Dr. David H. SHIN
05 Academic Dean .... Dr. Soonhae KANG
11 Dean Admin/Chief Operating Officer .... Vacant
06 Registrar/Foreign Student Advisor .... Charley LEE
57 Chair Masters of Arts Program .... Cha Hi WON
32 Dean of Students .... Ki Won HAN
20 Associate Academic Dean .... Vacant

Everest College-Anaheim (I)

511 N. Brookhurst, Ste 300, Anaheim CA 92801
County: Orange FICE Identification: 011107
Unit ID: 371982
Telephone: (714) 953-6500 Carnegie Class: Not Classified
FAX Number: (714) 953-4163 Calendar System: Quarter
URL: www.everest.edu/campus/anaheim
Established: 1969 Annual Undergrad Tuition & Fees: $13,896
Enrollment: 718 Coed
Affiliation or Control: Proprietary IRS Status: Proprietary
Highest Offering: Associate Degree
Program: Occupational
Accreditation: ACCSC, MAC

01 President .... Ms. Connie ANTENORCRUC

Everest College-City of Industry (J)

12801 Crossroads Parkway S, City of Industry CA 91746-3412
County: Los Angeles FICE Identification: 030426
Unit ID: 372037
Telephone: (562) 908-2500 Carnegie Class: Assoc/PrivFP
FAX Number: (562) 908-7656 Calendar System: Quarter
URL: www.everest-college.com
Established: 1989 Annual Undergrad Tuition & Fees: $14,500
Enrollment: 995 Coed
Affiliation or Control: Proprietary IRS Status: Proprietary
Highest Offering: Associate Degree
Program: Occupational; Music Emphasis
Accreditation: ACCSC, MAAB

01 President .... Ms. Sherry TOMAN

Everest College-Gardena (K)

1045 W. Redondo Beach Blvd, Ste 275, Gardena CA 90247
County: Los Angeles FICE Identification: 011123
Unit ID: 119456
Telephone: (310) 527-7105 Carnegie Class: Not Classified
FAX Number: (310) 527-7985 Calendar System: Quarter
URL: www.everest.edu/campus/gardena
Established: Annual Undergrad Tuition & Fees: $21,700
Enrollment: 533 Coed
Affiliation or Control: Proprietary IRS Status: Proprietary
Highest Offering: Associate Degree
Program: Occupational
Accreditation: ACCSC, MAC

01 President .... Mr. JC RIVAS
07 Director of Admissions .... Mr. Victor ARIOLA

Everest College-Ontario Metro (L)

1819 South Excise Avenue, Ontario CA 91761-8525
Telephone: (909) 484-4311 Identification: 666621
Accreditation: ACICS

† Main campus is Everest College in Springfield, MO.

Everest College-Reseda (M)

18040 Sherman Way, Ste 400, Reseda CA 91335-4631
County: Los Angeles FICE Identification: 011109
Unit ID: 119359
Telephone: (818) 774-0550 Carnegie Class: Not Classified
FAX Number: (818) 774-1577 Calendar System: Quarter
URL: www.everest.edu/campus/reseda
Established: 1969 Annual Undergrad Tuition & Fees: $14,364
Enrollment: 699 Coed
Affiliation or Control: Proprietary IRS Status: Proprietary
Highest Offering: Associate Degree
Program: Occupational
Accreditation: ACCSC, SURGT

01 President .... Ms. Dorit SOLTANOVICH

Everest College-San Bernardino (N)

217 Club Center Drive, Suite A, San Bernardino CA 92408
County: San Bernardino FICE Identification: 004494
Unit ID: 119508
Telephone: (909) 777-3300 Carnegie Class: Assoc/PrivFP
FAX Number: (909) 777-3550 Calendar System: Other
URL: www.everest.edu/campus/san_bernardino
Established: 1969 Annual Undergrad Tuition & Fees: N/A
Enrollment: 820 Coed
Affiliation or Control: Proprietary IRS Status: Proprietary
Highest Offering: Associate Degree
Program: Occupational
Accreditation: ACICS, MAC

01 President .... Ms. Ruth DARTON

† Tuition varies by degree program.

Everest College-Santa Ana (O)

500 W Santa Ana Boulevard, Santa Ana CA 92701
Telephone: (714) 656-1000 Identification: 770610
Accreditation: ACICS

† Main campus is Everest College in Colorado Springs, CO.

Everest College-West LA (A)

3000 S Robertson Boulevard, Ste 300,
Los Angeles CA 90034-3158
Telephone: (310) 840-5777 Identification: 666749
Accreditation: ACCSC, MAAB

† Main campus is WyoTech-Long Beach in Long Beach, CA.

Ex'pression College for Digital Arts (B)

6601 Shellmound Street, Emeryville CA 94608-1021
County: Alameda FICE Identification: 039733
Unit ID: 447458
Telephone: (510) 654-2934 Carnegie Class: Spec/Arts
FAX Number: (510) 658-3414 Calendar System: Quarter
URL: www.expression.edu
Established: 1999 Annual Undergrad Tuition & Fees: $23,302
Enrollment: 690 Coed
Affiliation or Control: Proprietary IRS Status: Proprietary
Highest Offering: Baccalaureate
Program: Professional
Accreditation: ACCSC

01 Executive Director & CEO .... Mr. Dan LEVISON
88 Chief Creative Officer .... Vacant

Ex'pression College for Digital Arts-San Jose (C)

1751 Fox Drive, San Jose CA 95131
Telephone: (408) 620-3300 Identification: 770552
Accreditation: ACCSC

† Main campus is Ex'pression College for Digital Arts in Emeryville, CA.

Fashion Institute of Design and Merchandising-Los Angeles (D)

919 S Grand Avenue, Los Angeles CA 90015-1421
County: Los Angeles FICE Identification: 011112
Unit ID: 114354
Telephone: (213) 624-1200 Carnegie Class: Spec/Arts
FAX Number: (213) 624-9354 Calendar System: Quarter
URL: www.fidm.edu
Established: 1969 Annual Undergrad Tuition & Fees: $26,660
Enrollment: 4,967 Coed
Affiliation or Control: Proprietary IRS Status: Proprietary
Highest Offering: Baccalaureate
Program: Occupational; 2-Year Principally Bachelor's Creditable; Business Emphasis
Accreditation: WC, WJ, ART

01 President .... Mrs. Tonian HOHBERG
10 Vice President Finance .... Ms. Annie JOHNSON
45 Vice President Planning .... Mrs. Vivien LOWY
05 Vice President Education .... Mrs. Barbara BUNDY
20 Dean of Academic Development .... Dr. Carol ROOKSTOOL
12 Director Orange County Campus .... Ms. Dorothy METCALFE
12 Director San Francisco Campus .... Ms. Barbara CUPPER
27 Exec Director Industry Relations .... Ms. Sharon RYAN
08 Director Library .... Ms. Kathy BAILON
06 Registrar .... Mr. Michael GILBERT
37 Director Financial Aid .... Ms. Norine FULLER
26 Director Public Relations .... Ms. Shirley WILSON
88 Director Adv Fashion Design .... Ms. Mary STEPHENS
09 Director Institutional Research .... Dr. Andrea HELEKAR
38 Articulation Officer .... Mr. Ben WEINBERG
21 Director Student Financial Services .... Mr. Chris JENNINGS
96 Director of Purchasing .... Mrs. Darlene LATINVILLE
97 Chair General Educ/Dean Education .... Ms. Sheryl RABINOVICH
72 Chair Apparel Manufacturing Mgmt .... Ms. Roni MILLER START

Fashion Institute of Design and Merchandising-Orange County (E)

17590 Gillette Avenue, Irvine CA 92614-5610
Telephone: (888) 974-3436 Identification: 666004
Accreditation: &WC, &WJ, ART

† Main campus is Fashion Institute of Design and Merchandising-Los Angeles in Los Angeles, CA.

Fashion Institute of Design and Merchandising-San Diego (F)

350 10th Avenue, 3rd Floor, San Diego CA 92101
Telephone: (619) 235-2049 Identification: 666005
Accreditation: &WC, &WJ, ART

† Main campus is Fashion Institute of Design and Merchandising-Los Angeles in Los Angeles, CA.

Fashion Institute of Design and Merchandising-San Francisco (G)

55 Stockton Street, San Francisco CA 94108-5829
Telephone: (415) 675-5200 FICE Identification: 013041
Accreditation: &WC, &WJ, ART

† Main campus is Fashion Institute of Design and Merchandising-Los Angeles in Los Angeles, CA.

Feather River College (H)

570 Golden Eagle Avenue, Quincy CA 95971-9124
County: Plumas FICE Identification: 008597
Unit ID: 114433
Telephone: (530) 283-0202 Carnegie Class: Assoc/Pub-R-M
FAX Number: (530) 283-3757 Calendar System: Semester
URL: www.frc.edu
Established: 1968 Annual Undergrad Tuition & Fees (In-District): $1,446
Enrollment: 1,527 Coed
Affiliation or Control: State/Local IRS Status: 501(c)3
Highest Offering: Associate Degree
Program: 2-Year Principally Bachelor's Creditable
Accreditation: WJ

01 Interim Superintendent/President .... Dr. Kevin TRUTNA
10 Chief Financial Officer .... Mr. Jim SCOUBES
05 Chief Instructional Officer .... Dr. Derek LERCH
32 Chief Student Services Officer .... Dr. Karen PIERSON
15 Director Human Resources/EEO .... Mr. David BURRIS
18 Director of Facilities/CTO .... Mr. Nick BOYD
06 Registrar/Dir of Admissions .... Ms. Leslie MIKESELL
37 Director Student Financial Aid .... Ms. Barbara CORMACK
96 Purchasing Agent .... Ms. Tamara CLINE

Fielding Graduate University (I)

2020 De La Vina Street, Santa Barbara CA 93105-3538
County: Santa Barbara FICE Identification: 020961
Unit ID: 114549
Telephone: (805) 687-1099 Carnegie Class: DRU
FAX Number: (805) 687-4590 Calendar System: Trimester
URL: www.fielding.edu
Established: 1974 Annual Graduate Tuition & Fees: $24,900
Enrollment: 1,265 Coed
Affiliation or Control: Independent Non-Profit IRS Status: 501(c)3
Highest Offering: Doctorate; No Undergraduates
Program: Professional
Accreditation: WC, CLPSY

01 President & Provost .... Dr. Katrina ROGERS
101 Exec Asst to President & Provost .... Ms. Maisee THAO
05 Provost .... Dr. Katrina ROGERS
10 VP and Chief Financial Officer .... Ms. Lisa LEWIS
15 VP Administration & Human Resources .... Vacant
30 VP Advancement & Development .... Mr. David EDELMAN
84 Assoc Provost Acad/Enrollment Mgmt .... Dr. Monique L. SNOWDEN
58 Graduate Dean .... Dr. Mario R. BORUNDA
88 Assoc Dean School Human & Org Dev .... Vacant
83 Interim Dean School of Psychology .... Dr. Kristine JACQUIN
06 Registrar .... Ms. Bridget BRADY

Five Branches University, Graduate School of Traditional Chinese Medicine (J)

3031 Tisch Way, Ste 507, San Jose CA 95128
County: Santa Clara Identification: 667008
Telephone: (408) 260-0208 Carnegie Class: Not Classified
FAX Number: (408) 261-3166 Calendar System: Semester
URL: www.fivebranches.edu
Established: 2005 Annual Undergrad Tuition & Fees: $14,500
Enrollment: 300 Coed
Affiliation or Control: Proprietary IRS Status: Proprietary
Highest Offering: Doctorate; No Lower Division
Program: Professional
Accreditation: ACUP

01 President/CEO .... Ron ZAIDMAN
05 VP Academic Affairs .... Joanna ZHAO
06 Registrar .... Gina HUANG
07 Associate Director of Admissions .... Nancy BURNS
10 Chief Financial Officer .... Liana CHEN
88 Associate Director Doctoral .... Nan WANG
88 Associate Director Doctoral .... E-Sing HONG
88 Director Chinese Masters of TCM .... Jasmine HUANG
88 Director Korean Masters of TCM .... Heerei PARK
56 Director of Extension Program .... Phan GOH
88 Clinic Manager .... Joyce HE
88 Director of Mind-Body Center .... Laury RAPAPPORT

Five Branches University, Graduate School of Traditional Chinese Medicine (K)

200 7th Avenue, Santa Cruz CA 95062-4669
County: Santa Cruz FICE Identification: 031313
Unit ID: 114585
Telephone: (831) 476-9424 Carnegie Class: Spec/Health
FAX Number: (831) 476-8928 Calendar System: Semester
URL: www.fivebranches.edu
Established: 1984 Annual Undergrad Tuition & Fees: $14,500
Enrollment: 295 Coed
Affiliation or Control: Proprietary IRS Status: Proprietary
Highest Offering: Master's; No Lower Division
Program: Professional
Accreditation: ACUP

01 President .... Ron ZAIDMAN
05 Academic Dean .... Joanna ZHAO
07 Admissions Director .... Eleonor MENDELSON
32 Director of Student Services .... Ana LOBATO
37 Director Student Financial Aid .... Mecca MATILDA
08 Librarian .... Jim EMDY
17 Clinic Director .... Joanna ZHAO
84 Director of Enrollment Management .... Ali POLK

*Foothill-De Anza Community College District System Office (L)

12345 El Monte Road, Los Altos Hills CA 94022-4597
County: Santa Clara FICE Identification: 009020
Unit ID: 114831
Telephone: (650) 949-6100 Carnegie Class: N/A
FAX Number: (650) 941-1638
URL: www.fhda.edu

01 Chancellor .... Dr. Linda M. THOR
10 Vice Chancellor Business Services .... Mr. Kevin MCELROY
16 Vice Chancellor Human Resources .... Ms. Dorene NOVOTNY
13 Vice Chancellor Technology .... Mr. Joseph MOREAU
18 Exec Dir Facility Oper/Constr Mgmt .... Mr. Charles ALLEN

*De Anza College (M)

21250 Stevens Creek Boulevard,
Cupertino CA 95014-5793
County: Santa Clara FICE Identification: 004480
Unit ID: 113333
Telephone: (408) 864-5678 Carnegie Class: Assoc/Pub-S-MC
FAX Number: (408) 864-5698 Calendar System: Quarter
URL: www.deanza.edu
Established: 1967 Annual Undergrad Tuition & Fees (In-District): $1,494
Enrollment: 23,976 Coed
Affiliation or Control: State/Local IRS Status: 501(c)3
Highest Offering: Associate Degree
Program: Occupational; 2-Year Principally Bachelor's Creditable
Accreditation: WJ, MLTAD

02 President .... Dr. Brian MURPHY
05 Vice Pres of Instruction .... Dr. Christina ESPINOSA-PIEB
32 Vice Pres of Student Services .... Ms. Stacy A. COOK
10 Vice Pres Finance/Educ Resources .... Ms. Letha JEANPIERRE
20 Associate VP Academic Services .... Ms. Rowena TOMANENG
35 Dean Student Development/EOPS .... Ms. Michele LEBLEU BURNS
38 Dean Counseling & Matriculation .... Ms. Angela CABALLERO DE CORDERO
07 Dean Admissions & Records .... Ms. Kathleen MOBERG
37 Director Student Financial Aid .... Ms. Lisa MANDY
15 Director Personnel Services .... Mr. Bret WATSON
18 Director Facilities/Physical Plant .... Vacant
21 Director Budget .... Mr. Bret WATSON
26 Director Marketing/Communications .... Ms. Marisa SPATAFORE
30 Chief Development .... Ms. Sheryl ALEXANDER
84 Director Enrollment Management .. Ms. Christina ESPINOSA PIEB
28 Director of Diversity .... Dr. Veronica NEAL
96 Director of Purchasing .... Ms. Linda MAHI
36 Director Student Placement .... Mr. Stephen FLETCHER
09 Institutional Research Specialist .... Dr. Mallory NEWELL
06 Supervisor Admissions and Records .... Mr. Barry JOHNSON

*Foothill College (N)

12345 El Monte Road, Los Altos Hills CA 94022-4599
County: Santa Clara FICE Identification: 001199
Unit ID: 114716
Telephone: (650) 949-7777 Carnegie Class: Assoc/Pub-S-MC
FAX Number: (650) 949-7375 Calendar System: Quarter
URL: www.foothill.edu
Established: 1957 Annual Undergrad Tuition & Fees (In-District): $1,116
Enrollment: 14,228 Coed
Affiliation or Control: State/Local IRS Status: 501(c)3
Highest Offering: Associate Degree
Program: Occupational; 2-Year Principally Bachelor's Creditable
Accreditation: WJ, COARC, DA, DH, DMS, EMT, RAD

02 President .... Dr. Judy C. MINER
04 Executive Asst to the President .... Ms. Casie WHEAT
45 VP Institutional Resources .... Ms. Bernata SLATER
05 VP Instruc & Institutional Research .... Dr. Kimberlee MESSINA
32 VP Student Services .... Dr. Denise SWETT
103 VP Workforce Dev & Instr Advc .... Mr. John MUMMERT
26 Assoc VP of External Relations .... Vacant
35 Dean Student Affairs & Activities .... Ms. Patricia HYLAND
85 Dean Intl Education .... Mr. George S. BEERS
38 Dean Counseling & Special Programs .... Ms. Laureen BALDUCCI
12 Dean FHDA Education Center .... Vacant
88 Dir Disb Student Svcs & Vet Pgms .... Ms. Teresa ONG
88 Dir EOPS & Community Programs .... Ms. Alexandra DURAN
35 Dir Student Activities & Affairs .... Ms. Daphne SMALL
08 Librarian .... Ms. Pamela WILKES
40 Director Bookstore .... Mr. Romeo PAULE
84 Dean Enrollment Services .... Ms. Nazy GALOYAN
37 Director Financial Aid .... Mr. Kevin HARRAL
23 Coordinator Student Health Services .... Ms. Lorraine N. KITAJIMA
76 Dean Biology/Health Science .... Dr. Nanette SOLVASON
50 Dean Business/Social Science .... Mr. Kurt HUEG
88 Dean Foothill Global Access .... Dr. Judy BAKER
57 Dean Fine Arts/Communications .... Mr. Mark ANDERSON

88 Dean Language Arts & LRC .... Mr. Paul STARER
68 Dean Kinesiology & Athletics .... Ms. Susan GUTKIND
81 Dean Physical Science/Math/Engr .... Mr. Peter MURRAY

Franciscan School of Theology (A)

1712 Euclid Avenue, Berkeley CA 94709-1294
County: Alameda FICE Identification: 011792
Unit ID: 114734
Telephone: (510) 848-5232 Carnegie Class: Spec/Faith
FAX Number: (510) 549-9466 Calendar System: Semester
URL: www.fst.edu
Established: 1968 Annual Graduate Tuition & Fees: $17,500
Enrollment: 42 Coed
Affiliation or Control: Independent Non-Profit IRS Status: 501(c)3
Highest Offering: Master's; No Undergraduates
Program: Professional; Religious Emphasis
Accreditation: WC, THEOL

01 President .... Fr. Joseph CHINNICI, OFM
05 Dean .... Br. William SHORT, OFM
06 Registrar .... Ms. Jenna NIELSEN
07 Director of Admissions .... Mr. Vince NIMS
30 Associate Development Director .... Ms. Randi QUAID
10 Chief Financial Officer .... Ms. Carolyn RODKIN

Fremont College (B)

18000 Studebaker Rd 9th Floor, Cerritos CA 90703
County: Los Angeles FICE Identification: 030399
Unit ID: 372073
Telephone: (562) 809-5100 Carnegie Class: Assoc/PrivFP
FAX Number: (562) 809-7100 Calendar System: Other
URL: www.fremont.edu
Established: 1985 Annual Undergrad Tuition & Fees: N/A
Enrollment: 350 Coed
Affiliation or Control: Proprietary IRS Status: Proprietary
Highest Offering: Baccalaureate
Program: Occupational; 2-Year Principally Bachelor's Creditable
Accreditation: ACCSC

01 Chairman/CEO .... Dr. Sabrina KAY

Fremont College (C)

3440 Wilshire Blvd, 6th Floor, Los Angeles CA 90010
Telephone: (213) 355-7777 Identification: 770553
Accreditation: ACCSC

† Main campus is Fremont College in Cerritos, CA.

Fresno Pacific University (D)

1717 S Chestnut Avenue, Fresno CA 93702-4798
County: Fresno FICE Identification: 001253
Unit ID: 114813
Telephone: (559) 453-2000 Carnegie Class: Master's M
FAX Number: (559) 453-2007 Calendar System: Semester
URL: www.fresno.edu
Established: 1944 Annual Undergrad Tuition & Fees: $25,716
Enrollment: 3,768 Coed
Affiliation or Control: Mennonite Brethren Church IRS Status: 501(c)3
Highest Offering: Master's
Program: Liberal Arts And General; Teacher Preparatory
Accreditation: WC, NURSE, THEOL

01 President .... Dr. Pete C. MENJARES
05 Provost .... Dr. Stephen VARVIS
10 Int Vice Pres Business Affairs .... Mr. Dick HERRINTON
30 Vice President for Advancement .... Vacant
13 Vice Pres of Information Services .... Mr. Alan OURS
84 Interim Vice Pres Enroll Mgmt .... Mr. Jon ENDICOTT
50 Dean School of Business .... Dr. John KILROY
79 Int Dean Sch of Human/Rel/Soc Sci .... Dr. Rod JANZEN
53 Dean School of Education .... Dr. Gary GRAMENZ
78 Dean School of Natural Sciences .... Dr. Karen CIANCI
42 Dean of Spiritual Formation .... Rev. Angulus WILSON
32 Dean of Student Life .... Dr. Randy WORDEN
06 Registrar .... Ms. Linda PRYCE-SHEEHAN
08 Director of Library .... Mr. Kevin ENNS-REMPEL
36 Director of Career Resource Center .... Ms. Alicia ANDRADE
15 Human Resources Director .... Mrs. Marylou MILLER
25 Director of Grants & Research .... Vacant
27 Publications Director .... Mr. Wayne STEFFEN
29 Alumni Director .... Mrs. Charity BROWN
37 Director of Financial Aid .... Ms. April POWELL
41 Athletic Director .... Mr. Dennis JANZEN
19 Director of Security .... Mr. Gary MEJIA
26 Chief Public Relations Officer .... Ms. Diana MOCK
28 Director of Diversity .... Vacant
07 Director of Admissions .... Ms. Rina CAMPBELL
18 Facilities Manager .... Mr. Barry LOCKTON
40 Bookstore Manager .... Ms. Erin NOEL
38 Counseling Coordinator .... Vacant

Fuller Theological Seminary (E)

135 N Oakland, Pasadena CA 91182-1780
County: Los Angeles FICE Identification: 001200
Unit ID: 114840
Telephone: (626) 584-5200 Carnegie Class: Spec/Faith
FAX Number: (626) 584-5672 Calendar System: Quarter
URL: www.fuller.edu
Established: 1947 Annual Graduate Tuition & Fees: $17,595
Enrollment: 2,828 Coed
Affiliation or Control: Independent Non-Profit IRS Status: 501(c)3
Highest Offering: Doctorate; No Undergraduates
Program: Professional
Accreditation: WC, CLPSY, THEOL

01 President .... Dr. Mark A. LABBERTON
05 Provost & Sr Vice President .... Dr. C. Douglas MCCONNELL
10 Vice President for Finance .... Mr. John WARD
30 Vice President Seminary Advancement .... Mr. Joe B. WEBB
84 VP for Enrollment & Student Affairs .... Dr. Wendy WAKEMAN
73 Dean School of Theology .... Dr. Howard J. LOEWEN
88 Dean School of Psychology .... Dr. Winston E. GOODEN
88 Dean School Intercultural Studies .... Dr. Scott W. SUNQUIST
56 Assoc Provost Cont/Extended Educ .... Vacant
13 Assoc Provost Information Svc/CIO .... Mr. Kevin OSBORN
08 Asst Provost Library/IT & CIO .... Mr. Michael D. MURRAY
26 Assoc Vice Pres for Public Affairs .... Mr. Fred MESSICK
29 Assoc VP Alumni & Church Rels .... Mrs. Mary HUBBARD GIVEN
73 Assoc Dean/Advanced Theol Studies .... Dr. Joel GREEN
88 Assoc Dean Doctor of Ministry Pgm .... Dr. Kurt FREDRICKSON
88 Assoc Dean School of Psychology .... Vacant
06 Registrar .... Mr. David E. KIEFER
15 Director of Human Resources .... Mrs. Bernadette (BJ) BARBER
32 Director of Student Affairs .... Mr. Sam BANG
21 Director of Budget .... Dr. David R. ADAMS
39 Director of Student Housing .... Mr. David SMITH
04 Exec Asst to President & Trustees .... Ms. Wendy WALKER
18 Director of Campus Facilities .... Mr. Randall R. SMITH
31 Director of Auxiliary Services .... Mrs. Jeanne HANDOJO
24 Director of Academic Tech Center .... Vacant
43 General Counsel .... Ms. Rita K. ROWLAND
96 Director of Purchasing .... Ms. Silvia GUTIERREZ
85 Dir Student Affs/International Svcs .... Mr. Sam BANG
37 Director Student Financial Services .... Mr. David RICHARDS
07 Assoc Director of Admissions .... Mr. Chad CAIN

Gavilan College (F)

5055 Santa Teresa Boulevard, Gilroy CA 95020-9599
County: Santa Clara FICE Identification: 001202
Unit ID: 114938
Telephone: (408) 848-4800 Carnegie Class: Assoc/Pub-S-SC
FAX Number: (408) 848-4801 Calendar System: Semester
URL: www.gavilan.edu
Established: 1919 Annual Undergrad Tuition & Fees (In-District): $1,166
Enrollment: 5,659 Coed
Affiliation or Control: State/Local IRS Status: 501(c)3
Highest Offering: Associate Degree
Program: Occupational; 2-Year Principally Bachelor's Creditable
Accreditation: WJ

01 Superintendent/President .... Dr. Steven M. KINSELLA
05 Exec Vice Pres Instructional Svcs .... Dr. Kathleen A. ROSE
11 Vice Pres Administrative Services .... Vacant
32 Vice President Student Services .... Mr. John PRUITT
06 Registrar .... Ms. Candice WHITNEY
08 Head Librarian .... Dr. Douglas ACHTERMAN
37 Director Student Financial Aid .... Ms. Veronica MARTINEZ
09 Director of Institutional Research .... Dr. Randy BROWN
15 Director Personnel Services .... Mr. Eric RAMONES
18 Chief Facilities/Physical Plant .... Mr. Jeff GOPP
13 Dir Computing & Information Mgmt .... Ms. Mimi ARVIZU
19 Director Security/Safety .... Ms. Ana HIPOL
26 Director Public Information .... Ms. Jan CHARGIN
23 Director Health Services .... Ms. Alice DUFRESNE-REYES
41 Athletic Director .... Mr. Ron HANNON
40 Director Bookstore .... Ms. Alexis BOLIN
49 Dean Liberal Arts/Sci/Dir Cont Educ .... Ms. Fran LOZANO
72 Dean Career Technical Education .... Ms. Sherrean CARR
07 Director of Admissions .... Ms. Candice WHITNEY
10 Chief Business Officer .... Ms. Susan CHEU
96 Director of Purchasing .... Ms. Connie CAMPOS

Glendale Community College (G)

1500 N Verdugo Road, Glendale CA 91208-2894
County: Los Angeles FICE Identification: 001203
Unit ID: 115001
Telephone: (818) 240-1000 Carnegie Class: Assoc/Pub-S-SC
FAX Number: (818) 549-9436 Calendar System: Semester
URL: www.glendale.edu
Established: 1927 Annual Undergrad Tuition & Fees (In-District): $1,175
Enrollment: 16,196 Coed
Affiliation or Control: State/Local IRS Status: 501(c)3
Highest Offering: Associate Degree
Program: Occupational; 2-Year Principally Bachelor's Creditable
Accreditation: WJ

01 Superintendent/President .... Dr. David VIAR
11 Exec Vice Pres Administrative Svcs .... Mr. Ron NAKASONE
05 Vice Pres Instructional Services .... Dr. Mary MIRCH
32 Vice President Student Services .... Dr. Ricardo PEREZ
51 Admn Dn Workforce Dev Cont/Cmty Ed .... Mr. Alfred RAMIREZ
15 Administrative Dean Human Resources .... Ms. Donna VOOGT
45 Dean Research/Planning/Grants .... Dr. Edward KARPP
07 Director Admissions & Records .... Ms. Michelle MORA
20 Dean Instructional Services .... Mr. Michael RITTERBROWN
103 Dean Workforce Development .... Ms. Jan SWINTON
32 Dean Student Affairs .... Dr. Paul SCHLOSSMAN
35 Dean of Student Services .... Dr. Jewel A. PRICE

37 Associate Dean Financial Aid .... Dr. Patricia HURLEY
10 Int Director Business Services .... Ms. Susan COURTEY

Golden Gate Baptist Theological Seminary (H)

201 Seminary Drive, Mill Valley CA 94941-3197
County: Marin FICE Identification: 001204
Unit ID: 115047
Telephone: (415) 380-1300 Carnegie Class: Not Classified
FAX Number: (415) 383-1302 Calendar System: Semester
URL: www.ggbts.edu
Established: 1944 Annual Graduate Tuition & Fees: $5,800
Enrollment: 1,542 Coed
Affiliation or Control: Southern Baptist IRS Status: 501(c)3
Highest Offering: Doctorate; No Undergraduates
Program: Professional; Religious Emphasis
Accreditation: WC, THEOL

00 President Emeritus .... Dr. William O. CREWS
01 President/Chairman of the Faculty .... Dr. Jeff IORG
30 Vice Pres Institutional Advancement .... Dr. Ben SKAUG
10 Vice President Business & Finance .... Mr. Gary GROAT
05 Vice President Academic Affairs .... Dr. D. Michael MARTIN
84 VP Enrollment/Student Svcs/Dn Stdts .... Dr. Adam GROZA
21 Controller .... Mr. Harrison WEAVER
06 Registrar .... Ms. Jennifer PEACH
08 Director of Library Services .... Vacant
12 Director SC Campus .... Dr. Earl WAGGONER
12 Director PNW Campus .... Dr. Mark BRADLEY
12 Director Arizona Campus .... Vacant
12 Director Rocky Mountain Campus .... Dr. Steve VETETO
13 Director Information Technology .... Mr. Jeff COLBERT
15 Director Personnel Services .... Vacant
18 Chief Facilities/Physical Plant .... Mr. Robert DVORAK
40 Director Bookstore .... Mr. Darren DRAEGER
07 Director Admissions .... Ms. Karen ROBINSON
44 Director of Development .... Vacant
84 Director Enrollment Management .... Ms. Karen ROBINSON
39 Resident Life Manager .... Mr. Shane TANIGAWA

Golden Gate University (I)

536 Mission Street, San Francisco CA 94105-2968
County: San Francisco FICE Identification: 001205
Unit ID: 115083
Telephone: (415) 442-7000 Carnegie Class: Master's L
FAX Number: (415) 495-2671 Calendar System: Trimester
URL: www.ggu.edu
Established: 1901 Annual Undergrad Tuition & Fees: $18,000
Enrollment: 3,531 Coed
Affiliation or Control: Independent Non-Profit IRS Status: 501(c)3
Highest Offering: Doctorate
Program: Professional; Business Emphasis
Accreditation: WC, LAW

01 President .... Dr. Daniel D. ANGEL
05 VP of Academic Affairs .... Ms. Barbara H. KARLIN
10 VP of Business Affairs & CFO .... Mr. Robert D. HITE
30 VP of University Advancement .... Ms. Tasia NEEVE
61 Dean School of Law .... Ms. Rachel VAN CLEAVE
50 Dean Ageno School of Business .... Dr. Paul FOUTS
88 Dean School of Taxation & Acctng .... Ms. Mary CANNING
49 Dean Undergraduate Programs .... Dr. Cherron HOPPES
100 Executive Director Ofc of President .... Dr. John FYFE
12 Dean Cyber Campus .... Mr. Marvin WEINBAUM
32 Dean of Students & Student Affairs .... Ms. Janine MIXON
08 Director University Library .... Mr. James KRUSLING
08 Associate Dean Law Library .... Mr. Michael DAW
15 Director Human Resources/EEO .... Ms. Terri SHULTIS
84 Director Enrollment Services .... Mr. Louis D. RICCARDI, JR.
06 University Registrar .... Mr. Steven LIND
27 Chief Information Officer .... Mr. Scott CILIBERTI
26 Director Marketing & Communications .... Vacant
88 Director PLUS Program .... Dr. Karen MCROBIE
09 Dir Planning/Resources/Analysis .... Dr. Mercy LIM
18 Director Business Svcs/Facilities .... Mr. Mike KOPERSKI
21 Controller .... Ms. Suzanne GREVA
37 Director Student Financial Aid .... Mr. Steven LIND
38 Clinical Director/Counseling Svcs .... Ms. Michael Anne CONLEY

Golf Academy of America (J)

1950 Camino Vida Roble, Suite 125, Carlsbad CA 92008
Telephone: (800) 342-7342 FICE Identification: 015609
Accreditation: ACICS

† Main campus is Virginia College in Birmingham, AL.

Grace Communion Seminary (K)

2011 E. Financial Way, PO Box 5005,
Glendora CA 91740-0730
County: Los Angeles Identification: 667115
Telephone: (626) 650-2306 Carnegie Class: Not Classified
FAX Number: (626) 650-2307 Calendar System: Semester
URL: www.gcs.edu
Established: 2008 Annual Graduate Tuition & Fees: $600
Enrollment: 55 Coed
Affiliation or Control: Independent Non-Profit IRS Status: 501(c)3
Highest Offering: Master's; No Undergraduates
Program: Religious Emphasis

Accreditation: DETC

01 President/CEO ..... Dr. Russell DUKE
05 Dean of Faculty ..... Dr. Michael MORRISON
06 Registrar ..... Ms. Susan EARLE

Grace Mission University (A)

1645 West Valencia Drive, Fullerton CA 92833-3860
County: Orange Identification: 666642
Telephone: (714) 525-0088 Carnegie Class: Not Classified
FAX Number: (714) 525-0089 Calendar System: Semester
URL: www.gm.edu
Established: 1995 Annual Undergrad Tuition & Fees: $6,680
Enrollment: 206 Coed
Affiliation or Control: Presbyterian Church In America IRS Status: 501(c)3
Highest Offering: Master's
Program: Professional; Religious Emphasis
Accreditation: BI, TRACS

01 President ..... Kwangsin KIM
03 Executive Vice President & CEO ..... Dr. Kyunam CHOI
05 Academic Dean ..... Dr. Hyun Wan KIM
11 Dir Administration/Financial Aid ..... Mr. James KOO
06 Registrar ..... Ms. JungMo YOOK

Graduate Theological Union (B)

2400 Ridge Road, Berkeley CA 94709-1212
County: Alameda FICE Identification: 001207
Unit ID: 115214
Telephone: (510) 649-2400 Carnegie Class: Spec/Faith
FAX Number: (510) 649-1417 Calendar System: Semester
URL: www.gtu.edu
Established: 1962 Annual Graduate Tuition & Fees: $28,680
Enrollment: 213 Coed
Affiliation or Control: Independent Non-Profit IRS Status: 501(c)3
Highest Offering: Doctorate; No Undergraduates
Program: Professional; Religious Emphasis
Accreditation: WC, THEOL

01 President ..... Dr. Riess POTTERVELD
05 Dean/Vice Pres Academic Affairs ..... Dr. Arthur HOLDER
10 Vice Pres Administration/Finance ..... Mr. Steven G. ARGYRIS
30 Vice President for Advancement ..... Mr. Alan KELCHNER
32 VP Student Affairs/Dean Students ..... Dr. Kathleen KOOK
07 Director of Admissions ..... Dr. Andrea SHEAFFER
37 Director of Financial Aid ..... Ms. Kathleen ANTOKHIN
08 Library Director ..... Mr. Robert BENEDETTO
06 Consortial Registrar ..... Mr. John SEAL
13 Chief Information Officer ..... Mr. Jeffrey DIGREORIO
26 Director of Marketing & Comm ..... Mr. Jake STAFFORD
18 Building & Grounds Engineer ..... Mr. Curtis OSBORNE
15 Personnel Officer ..... Ms. Debi WALKER
04 Executive Assistant to President ..... Ms. Teresa JOYE

*Grossmont-Cuyamaca Community College District (C)

8800 Grossmont College Drive, El Cajon CA 92020-1799
County: San Diego FICE Identification: 007006
Unit ID: 115287
Telephone: (619) 644-7010 Carnegie Class: N/A
FAX Number: (619) 644-7936
URL: www.gcccd.edu

01 Chancellor ..... Dr. Cindy MILES
10 Vice Chanc Business Services ..... Ms. Sue REARIC
15 Int Vice Chanc Human Resources ..... Mr. Tim CORCORAN

*Cuyamaca College (D)

900 Rancho San Diego Parkway, El Cajon CA 92019-4304
County: San Diego FICE Identification: 021113
Unit ID: 113218
Telephone: (619) 660-4000 Carnegie Class: Assoc/Pub-S-MC
FAX Number: (619) 660-4399 Calendar System: Quarter
URL: www.cuyamaca.edu
Established: 1978 Annual Undergrad Tuition & Fees (In-District): $1,145
Enrollment: 8,280 Coed
Affiliation or Control: State/Local IRS Status: 501(c)3
Highest Offering: Associate Degree
Program: Occupational; 2-Year Principally Bachelor's Creditable
Accreditation: WJ

02 President ..... Dr. Mark J. ZACOVIC
05 Vice President Instruction ..... Dr. Wei ZHOU
32 Int Vice Pres Student Services ..... Dr. Teresa MCNEIL
11 Vice Pres Administrative Services ..... Dr. Arleen SATELE
20 Interim Dean of Instruction Div I ..... Dr. Scott HERRIN
20 Int Dean of Instruction Div II ..... Mr. Pat SETZER
51 Dean Cont Educ/Workforce Training ..... Ms. Jennifer LEWIS
08 Dean Learning/Technology Resources ..... Ms. Kerry KILBER REBMAN
88 Assistant Dean EOPS ..... Ms. Wendy CRAIG
41 Interim Athletic Director ..... Dr. Patrick THISS
35 Assoc Dean Student Affairs ..... Dr. Lauren VAKNIN
38 Dean Counseling & Enrollment Svc ..... Dr. Marsha GABLE
37 Director of Financial Aid ..... Mr. Ray REYES
07 Supervisor Admissions & Records ..... Mr. Victor DEVORE
18 Facilities Director ..... Mr. Bruce FARNHAM

*Grossmont College (E)

8800 Grossmont College Drive, El Cajon CA 92020-1799
County: San Diego FICE Identification: 001208
Unit ID: 115296
Telephone: (619) 644-7000 Carnegie Class: Assoc/Pub-S-MC
FAX Number: (619) 644-7922 Calendar System: Semester
URL: www.grossmont.edu
Established: 1961 Annual Undergrad Tuition & Fees (In-District): $1,110
Enrollment: 17,948 Coed
Affiliation or Control: State/Local IRS Status: 501(c)3
Highest Offering: Associate Degree
Program: Occupational; 2-Year Principally Bachelor's Creditable
Accreditation: WJ, ADNUR, COARC, CVT, OTA

02 President ..... Dr. Sunita COOKE
05 Vice Pres of Academic Affairs ..... Dr. Katrina VANDERWOUDE
32 Vice President of Student Services ..... Mr. Jeff BAKER
38 Dean Counseling Svcs ..... Vacant
72 Dean Career & Technical Workforce ..... Dr. Christina TAFOYA
81 Dean Math/Natural Sci/Phys Educ ..... Dr. Mike REESE
60 Dean Arts/Languages/Communication ..... Mr. Steve BAKER
79 Dean English/Social & Behav Sci ..... Mr. Agustin ALBARRAN
08 Dean of Learning Resources ..... Vacant
35 Associate Dean Student Affairs ..... Ms. Sara GLASGOW
09 Director of Institutional Research ..... Mr. Christopher TARMAN
10 Chief Business Officer ..... Mr. Tim FLOOD
15 Director Personnel Services ..... Vacant
18 Chief Facilities/Physical Plant ..... Mr. Ken EMMONS
26 Chief Public Relations Officer ..... Vacant
36 Director Student Placement ..... Ms. Nancy DAVIS
37 Director Student Financial Aid ..... Mr. Michael COPENHAVER
96 Director of Purchasing ..... Ms. Linda BERTOLUCCI

Gurnick Academy of Medical Arts (F)

2121 S. El Camino Real Bldg C200, San Mateo CA 94403
County: San Mateo FICE Identification: 041698
Unit ID: 459213
Telephone: (650) 685-6616 Carnegie Class: Not Classified
FAX Number: (650) 685-6640 Calendar System: Other
URL: www.gurnick.edu
Established: 2004 Annual Undergrad Tuition & Fees: $28,294
Enrollment: 611 Coed
Affiliation or Control: Proprietary IRS Status: Proprietary
Highest Offering: Associate Degree
Program: Occupational
Accreditation: ABHES, @PTAA

01 CEO ..... Konstantin GOURJI
12 Campus Director ..... Burke MALIN

Hartnell College (G)

411 Central Avenue, Salinas CA 93901-1697
County: Monterey FICE Identification: 001209
Unit ID: 115393
Telephone: (831) 755-6700 Carnegie Class: Assoc/Pub-R-L
FAX Number: (831) 755-6751 Calendar System: Semester
URL: www.hartnell.edu
Established: 1920 Annual Undergrad Tuition & Fees (In-District): $562
Enrollment: 20,140 Coed
Affiliation or Control: State/Local IRS Status: 501(c)3
Highest Offering: Associate Degree
Program: Occupational; 2-Year Principally Bachelor's Creditable
Accreditation: #WJ, #COARC

01 Superintendent/President ..... Dr. Willard LEWALLEN
32 VP Student Affairs ..... Dr. Romero JALOMO
11 VP Administrative Services ..... Mr. Al MUNOZ
13 VP Information & Tech Systems ..... Mr. Matt COOMBS
05 VP Academic Affairs ..... Ms. Lori KILDAL
30 Exec Dir of Advancement ..... Ms. Jackie CRUZ
41 Director Athletics ..... Mr. Daniel TERESA
15 Assoc VP Human Resources/EEO ..... Ms. Terri PYER
21 Controller ..... Ms. Tracey RICHARDSON
07 Dean of Enrollment Services ..... Ms. Mary DOMINGUEZ
35 Dean of Student Affairs ..... Dr. Mark SANCHEZ
18 Director of Facilities ..... Mr. Joseph REYES
20 Dean Academic Aff Programs/Support .. Ms. Kathy MENDELSOHN
81 Dean Academic Affs Math/Science ..... Ms. Shannon BLISS
35 Director of Student Life ..... Mr. Augustine NEVAREZ
27 Director of Communications ..... Ms. Esmeralda OWENS
88 Dir of Student Affairs EOPS/DSPS ..... Mr. Paul CASEY
66 Dean Academic Affairs/Nursing ..... Ms. Debra KACZMAR
72 Dean Academic Affs Adv Tech ..... Dr. Zahi ATALLAH
83 Dean Acad Affs Soc/Fine Lang Arts ..... Ms. Stephanie LOW
88 Dean South County Educ Programs ..... Ms. Renata FUNKE

Harvey Mudd College (H)

301 Platt Boulevard, Claremont CA 91711-5990
County: Los Angeles FICE Identification: 001171
Unit ID: 115409
Telephone: (909) 621-8000 Carnegie Class: Bac/A&S
FAX Number: (909) 621-8360 Calendar System: Semester
URL: www.hmc.edu
Established: 1955 Annual Undergrad Tuition & Fees: $46,509
Enrollment: 777 Coed
Affiliation or Control: Independent Non-Profit IRS Status: 501(c)3
Highest Offering: Baccalaureate
Program: Liberal Arts And General; Professional; Technical Emphasis
Accreditation: WC, ENG

01 President ..... Dr. Maria M. KLAWE
30 Vice President Advancement ..... Mr. Daniel MACALUSO
10 Vice President/Treasurer ..... Mr. Andrew R. DORANTES
05 Dean of the Faculty ..... Dr. Jeffrey GROVES
07 Vice Pres/Dean of Admissions ..... Ms. Thyra BRIGGS
32 Vice Pres/Dean of Students ..... Dr. Marguerite BROWNING
13 VP/CIO ..... Mr. Joseph VAUGHAN
09 Asst VP Institutional Research ..... Vacant
15 AVP of Human Resources ..... Ms. Cynthia A. BECKWITH
18 AVP Facilities/Physical Plant ..... Ms. Theresa LAUER
28 Assoc Dean Institutional Diversity ..... Ms. Sumun (Sumi) PENDAKUR
06 Registrar ..... Mr. Mark ASHLEY
26 Director of College Relations ..... Ms. Stephanie GRAHAM
29 Director of Alumni Relations ..... Ms. Jennifer GREEN
37 Director of Student Financial Aid ..... Ms. Gilma LOPEZ
20 Associate Academic Officer ..... Vacant
101 Exec Asst to the Pres/Secy to Board ..... Ms. Karen ANGEMI

*Heald College, Central Office (I)

601 Montgomery Street, 14th Floor, San Francisco CA 94111-2618
County: San Francisco Identification: 666712
Telephone: (415) 808-1400 Carnegie Class: N/A
FAX Number: (415) 808-1598
URL: www.heald.edu

01 President/CEO ..... Ms. Eeva DESHON
05 Sr VP/Chief Academic Officer ..... Dr. Jon PERSAVICH

*Heald College, Concord (J)

5130 Commercial Circle, Concord CA 94520-5617
County: Contra Costa FICE Identification: 020798
Unit ID: 115533
Telephone: (925) 288-5800 Carnegie Class: Assoc/PrivFP
FAX Number: (925) 288-5896 Calendar System: Quarter
URL: www.heald.edu
Established: 1863 Annual Undergrad Tuition & Fees: $13,020
Enrollment: 1,657 Coed
Affiliation or Control: Proprietary IRS Status: Proprietary
Highest Offering: Associate Degree
Program: Occupational
Accreditation: &WC, DA, MAC

02 Campus President ..... Mr. Timothy HANSEN
05 Dean of Educational Programs ..... Mr. Jerry DOTY
07 Director of Admissions ..... Vacant
36 Director of Career Services ..... Mr. Ryan SCHIEBER
10 Business Office Manager ..... Ms. Amalia COTA

† Regional accreditation is carried under the parent institution Heald College, Central Office in San Francisco, CA

*Heald College, Fresno (K)

255 W Bullard Avenue, Fresno CA 93704-1706
County: Fresno FICE Identification: 008093
Unit ID: 115472
Telephone: (559) 438-4222 Carnegie Class: Assoc/PrivFP
FAX Number: (559) 438-6368 Calendar System: Quarter
URL: www.heald.edu
Established: 1863 Annual Undergrad Tuition & Fees: $13,020
Enrollment: 1,993 Coed
Affiliation or Control: Proprietary IRS Status: Proprietary
Highest Offering: Associate Degree
Program: Occupational
Accreditation: &WC, MAC

02 Campus President ..... Ms. Carolyn PIERCE
07 Senior Director of Admissions ..... Ms. Tina MATHIS
05 Director of Academic Affairs ..... Ms. Jenny SAECHAO
36 Director of Career Services ..... Ms. Stephanie HAUSLADEN
37 Director of Student Finances ..... Ms. Tracy ZAVALA
32 Director of Student Services ..... Vacant
50 Business Program Director ..... Ms. Meredith BULNISKI
97 General Education Program Director ..... Ms. Krista HALL
61 Criminal Justice Program Director ..... Mr. Mike ROBISON
88 Paralegal Program Director ..... Ms. Joanne ALLEN
72 Technology Program Director ..... Mr. Michael BLACKSTON
76 Healthcare Program Director ..... Vacant
88 Med Insurance Billing/Codng Pgm Dir ..... Vacant
67 Pharmacy Technology Program Dir ..... Ms. Denise WALSH

† Regional accreditation is carried under the parent institution Heald College, Central Office in San Francisco, CA

*Heald College, Hayward (L)

25500 Industrial Boulevard, Hayward CA 94545-2349
County: Alameda FICE Identification: 025929
Unit ID: 371779
Telephone: (510) 783-2100 Carnegie Class: Assoc/PrivFP
FAX Number: (510) 783-3287 Calendar System: Quarter
URL: www.heald.edu
Established: 1967 Annual Undergrad Tuition & Fees: $18,000
Enrollment: 1,153 Coed
Affiliation or Control: Proprietary IRS Status: Proprietary
Highest Offering: Associate Degree
Program: Occupational

Accreditation: &WC, DA, MAC

02 Campus President .... Mr. Douglas M. DEN HARTOG, SR.
05 Director of Academic Affairs .... Mr. Kevin KENNY
36 Director of Career Services .... Ms. Christina JOHNSON
07 Director of Admissions .... Ms. Kenneshia DOWNING

† Regional accreditation is carried under the parent institution Heald College, Central Office in San Francisco, CA

*Heald College, Milpitas (A)

341 Great Mall Parkway, Milpitas CA 95035-8008
County: Santa Clara FICE Identification: 025932
Unit ID: 115490
Telephone: (408) 934-4900 Carnegie Class: Assoc/PrivFP
FAX Number: (408) 934-7777 Calendar System: Quarter
URL: www.heald.edu
Established: 1863 Annual Undergrad Tuition & Fees: $13,020
Enrollment: 1,738 Coed
Affiliation or Control: Proprietary IRS Status: Proprietary
Highest Offering: Associate Degree
Program: Occupational
Accreditation: &WC, MAC

02 Campus President .... Mr. Elmo FRAZER
05 Dean of Educational Programs .... Dr. Nelly MANGRO
07 Senior Director of Admissions .... Mr. Allen REYES
36 Director of Career Services .... Ms. Joellen SUTTERFIELD
10 Business Office Manager .... Ms. Merrynoll BARRERA

† Regional accreditation is carried under the parent institution Heald College, Central Office in San Francisco, CA

*Heald College, Rancho Cordova (B)

2910 Prospect Park Drive,
Rancho Cordova CA 95670-6005
County: Sacramento FICE Identification: 007477
Unit ID: 115454
Telephone: (916) 638-1616 Carnegie Class: Assoc/PrivFP
FAX Number: (916) 638-1580 Calendar System: Quarter
URL: www.heald.edu
Established: 1863 Annual Undergrad Tuition & Fees: $13,020
Enrollment: 1,329 Coed
Affiliation or Control: Proprietary IRS Status: Proprietary
Highest Offering: Associate Degree
Program: Occupational; 2-Year Principally Bachelor's Creditable
Accreditation: &WC, MAC

02 Campus President .... Ms. Ada GERARD
07 Director of Admissions .... Vacant
05 Director of Academic Affairs .... Ms. Nancy PLUNKETT
36 Director of Career Services .... Ms. Jessica HUNT-WEST
10 Director of Financial Services .... Ms. Jennifer RICARDI

† Regional accreditation is carried under the parent institution Heald College, Central Office in San Francisco, CA

*Heald College, Roseville (C)

7 Sierra Gate Plaza, Roseville CA 95678-6602
County: Sacramento FICE Identification: 025931
Unit ID: 363387
Telephone: (916) 789-8600 Carnegie Class: Assoc/PrivFP
FAX Number: (916) 896-8616 Calendar System: Quarter
URL: www.heald.edu
Established: 1863 Annual Undergrad Tuition & Fees: N/A
Enrollment: 1,340 Coed
Affiliation or Control: Proprietary IRS Status: Proprietary
Highest Offering: Associate Degree
Program: Occupational
Accreditation: &WC, MAC

02 Campus President .... Mr. Guy ADAMS
05 Director Academic Affairs .... Mr. John ROTH
10 Business Manager .... Vacant
36 Director Career Services .... Ms. Michelle DAVIDSON

† Regional accreditation is carried under the parent institution Heald College, Central Office in San Francisco, CA

*Heald College, Salinas (D)

1450 N Main Street, Salinas CA 93906-5100
County: Salinas FICE Identification: 030340
Unit ID: 409874
Telephone: (831) 443-1700 Carnegie Class: Assoc/PrivFP
FAX Number: (831) 443-1050 Calendar System: Quarter
URL: www.heald.edu
Established: 1863 Annual Undergrad Tuition & Fees: $13,020
Enrollment: 1,261 Coed
Affiliation or Control: Proprietary IRS Status: Proprietary
Highest Offering: Associate Degree
Program: Occupational
Accreditation: &WC, MAC

02 Campus President .... Mr. Richard A. COX
07 Director of Admissions .... Mr. David CASTILLO
37 Director of Student Finance .... Ms. Heloise MATA
05 Director of Academic Affairs .... Mr. Herbert CORTEZ
36 Director of Career Services .... Ms. Belyn WILSON

† Regional accreditation is carried under the parent institution Heald College, Central Office in San Francisco, CA

*Heald College, San Francisco (E)

875 Howard Street, Suite 100,
San Francisco CA 94105-2206
County: San Francisco FICE Identification: 007234
Unit ID: 115515
Telephone: (415) 808-3000 Carnegie Class: Assoc/PrivFP
FAX Number: (415) 808-3005 Calendar System: Quarter
URL: www.heald.edu
Established: 1863 Annual Undergrad Tuition & Fees: $13,020
Enrollment: 1,228 Coed
Affiliation or Control: Proprietary IRS Status: Proprietary
Highest Offering: Associate Degree
Program: Occupational
Accreditation: &WC, MAC

02 Acting Campus President .... Dr. Robb ERSKINE
05 Director of Academic Affairs .... Dr. Robb ERSKINE
36 Director of Career Services .... Vacant
07 Director of Admissions .... Mr. Daniel ALONSO
10 Business Manager .... Mr. Mike SUEOKA

† Regional accreditation is carried under the parent institution Heald College, Central Office in San Francisco, CA

*Heald College, Stockton (F)

1605 E March Lane, Stockton CA 95210-6632
County: San Joaquin FICE Identification: 025933
Unit ID: 371760
Telephone: (209) 473-5200 Carnegie Class: Assoc/PrivFP
FAX Number: (209) 477-2739 Calendar System: Quarter
URL: www.heald.edu
Established: 1863 Annual Undergrad Tuition & Fees: $13,020
Enrollment: 1,665 Coed
Affiliation or Control: Proprietary IRS Status: Proprietary
Highest Offering: Associate Degree
Program: Occupational
Accreditation: &WC, DA, MAC

02 Campus President .... Mr. Sandy LAMBA
05 Director of Academic Affairs .... Ms. Pamela CURTIS
06 Registrar .... Mr. John WHATLEY
07 Director of Admission .... Mrs. Hola MOTOUAPUAKA
10 Director of Financial Services .... Ms. Bobbie MCCORMICK
36 Director of Career Services .... Ms. Monique GRIFFIN

† Regional accreditation is carried under the parent institution Heald College, Central Office in San Francisco, CA

**Heald College, Modesto* (G)

5260 Pirrone Court, Salida CA 95368
Telephone: (209) 416-3700 Identification: 667043
Accreditation: &WC

† Main campus is Heald College, Hayward in Hayward, CA.

Henley-Putnam University (H)

2804 Mission College Blvd #240, Santa Clara CA 95054
County: Santa Clara Identification: 666120
Telephone: (408) 453-9900 Carnegie Class: Not Classified
FAX Number: (408) 453-9700 Calendar System: Quarter
URL: www.henley-putnam.edu
Established: 2001 Annual Undergrad Tuition & Fees: $11,880
Enrollment: N/A Coed
Affiliation or Control: Proprietary IRS Status: Proprietary
Highest Offering: Doctorate
Program: Professional; Technical Emphasis
Accreditation: DETC

01 Chief Executive Officer .... Jim P. KILLIN
05 Provost of Academics .... Dr. Amy DIMAIO
88 Provost of Co-Curricular Activites .... Amanda MORROW-JENSEN
10 Director of Finance .... Marlys YOSHIMURA
07 Director of Admissions .... Nancy REGGIO

High Tech High Graduate School of Education (I)

2861 Womble Road, San Diego CA 92106-6025
Identification: 667118
Telephone: (619) 398-4902 Carnegie Class: Not Classified
FAX Number: (619) 758-1960 Calendar System: Other
URL: gse.hightechhigh.org
Established: 2007 Annual Graduate Tuition & Fees: $12,500
Enrollment: N/A Coed
Affiliation or Control: Independent Non-Profit IRS Status: 501(c)3
Highest Offering: Master's; No Undergraduates
Program: Teacher Preparatory
Accreditation: @WC

01 President .... Rob RIORDAN
05 Dean .... Larry ROSENSTOCK
10 Chief Financial Officer .... Kay MCELRATH
12 Director of Clinical Sites .... Ben DALEY

Holy Names University (J)

3500 Mountain Boulevard, Oakland CA 94619-1699
County: Alameda FICE Identification: 001183
Unit ID: 115728
Telephone: (510) 436-1000 Carnegie Class: Master's M
FAX Number: (510) 436-1199 Calendar System: Semester
URL: www.hnu.edu
Established: 1868 Annual Undergrad Tuition & Fees: $32,590
Enrollment: 1,352 Coed
Affiliation or Control: Independent Non-Profit IRS Status: 501(c)3
Highest Offering: Master's
Program: Liberal Arts And General; Teacher Preparatory; Professional
Accreditation: WC, NURSE

01 President .... Dr. William J. HYNES
05 Vice President for Academic Affairs .... Dr. Lizbeth J. MARTIN
10 Vice President for Finance/Admin .... Mr. Stuart KOOP
32 Vice President for Student Affairs .... Mr. Michael S. MILLER
30 Vice President University Advance .... Mr. Richard ORTEGA
84 Asst VP Enrollment Management .... Mr. Cary KAPLAN
58 Director of ABD Program .... Ms. Nancy FLINN
06 Associate Registrar .... Ms. Jeanette CALIXTO
08 Director of Library Services .... Ms. Karen SCHNEIDER
37 Dir Student Financial Assistance .... Mr. Jeff HARDIE
31 Director Campus Services .... Mr. Luis GUERRA
42 Director of Campus Ministry .... Ms. Carrie REHAK
41 Director of Athletics .... Mr. Dennis JONES
26 Director Marketing/Communications .... Ms. Lesley SIMS
29 Director of Alumni Relations .... Vacant
13 Director Information Technology .... Ms. Elena OLKHOVSKAYA
19 Director Campus Safety .... Ms. Dana KIRKPATRICK
15 Director Human Resources .... Ms. Patricia BARTON

Hope International University (K)

2500 E Nutwood Avenue, Fullerton CA 92831-3104
County: Orange FICE Identification: 001252
Unit ID: 120537
Telephone: (714) 879-3901 Carnegie Class: Bac/Diverse
FAX Number: (714) 681-7451 Calendar System: 4/1/4
URL: www.hiu.edu
Established: 1928 Annual Undergrad Tuition & Fees: $25,550
Enrollment: 1,671 Coed
Affiliation or Control: Independent Non-Profit IRS Status: 501(c)3
Highest Offering: Master's
Program: 2-Year Principally Bachelor's Creditable; Liberal Arts And General; Teacher Preparatory; Professional; Religious Emphasis
Accreditation: WC, BI, MFCD

01 President .... Dr. John L. DERRY
04 Exec Asst to the President .... Mrs. Sharon L. CARTER
05 Vice President for Academic Affairs .... Dr. Paul H. ALEXANDER
49 Dean College of Arts and Sciences .... Dr. Steve EDGINGTON
50 Dean College of Business & Mgmt .... Dr. James WOEST
53 Dean College of Education .... Dr. George E. WEST
88 Dean College of Ministry & Bib Stds .... Dr. Joe GRANA
83 Dean College of Psych & Counseling .... Dr. Laura L. STEELE
09 Assc VP for Education Effectiveness .... Dr. Tamsen MURRAY
08 Librarian .... Mrs. Robin HARTMAN
06 Registrar .... Mr. Ron ARCHER
10 Vice President for Business/Finance .... Mr. Frank SCOTTI
37 Director Student Financial Services .... Mrs. Shannon O'SHIELDS
16 Director of Human Resources .... Mrs. Wende HOLTZEN
13 Director of Information Systems .... Mr. Mike CARTER
18 Director of Campus Facilities .... Mr. Steve MULLINS
30 Vice Pres Institutional Advancement .... Mr. Michael MULRYAN
26 Chief Public Relations Officer .... Mr. Michael MULRYAN
32 Vice President for Student Affairs .... Dr. Mark COMEAUX
36 Dean of Students .... Mr. Reid W. MCCORMICK
41 Athletic Director .... Mr. John G. TUREK
42 Chaplain/Director Campus Ministry .... Mr. Bryan A. SANDS
85 Director of International Students .... Vacant
38 Director Student Counseling .... Dr. Laura L. STEELE
36 Dir Student Career Services .... Mrs. Kirsten M. MCCORMICK
84 Vice Pres for Enrollment Management .... Mrs. Teresa L. SMITH
07 Director Undergraduate Admissions .... Ms. Dionne K. BUTLER

Horizon University (L)

5331 Mt Alifan Drive, San Diego CA 92111
County: San Diego FICE Identification: 041405
Unit ID: 457226
Telephone: (858) 695-8587 Carnegie Class: Not Classified
FAX Number: (858) 695-9527 Calendar System: Semester
URL: www.horizonuniversity.edu
Established: 1993 Annual Undergrad Tuition & Fees: $18,900
Enrollment: 110 Coed
Affiliation or Control: Independent Non-Profit IRS Status: 501(c)3
Highest Offering: Baccalaureate
Program: Liberal Arts And General; Religious Emphasis
Accreditation: #BI

01 President .... Mr. John LAUDADIO
05 Dean of Academics .... Mr. Wayne KINDE

Humphreys College (M)

6650 Inglewood Street, Stockton CA 95207-3896
County: San Joaquin FICE Identification: 001212
Unit ID: 115773
Telephone: (209) 478-0800 Carnegie Class: Bac/Diverse
FAX Number: (209) 478-8721 Calendar System: Quarter

URL: www.humphreys.edu
Established: 1896 Annual Undergrad Tuition & Fees: $13,506
Enrollment: 1,061 Coed
Affiliation or Control: Independent Non-Profit IRS Status: 501(c)3
Highest Offering: First Professional Degree
Program: Liberal Arts And General; Professional
Accreditation: WC

01 President .... Dr. Robert G. HUMPHREYS
05 Dn Instruction/Dir Arts & Sciences .... Dr. Robert G. HUMPHREYS, JR.
11 Dean Administration/Ofc Admin Pgm .... Ms. Wilma OKAMOTO-VAUGHN
09 Dean of Institutional Research .... Dr. Jess BONDS
61 Dean Law School .... Mr. Patrick L. PIGGOTT
20 Associate Dean of Instruction .... Ms. Cynthia BECERRA
06 Registrar .... Ms. Maria GARCIA-MILLER
07 Dir Admission/Placement/Public Rels .... Ms. Santa LOPEZ
26 Chief Public Relations Officer .... Vacant
08 Head Librarian .... Dr. Stanislav PERKNER
88 Director Paralegal Studies .... Mr. Stephen CHOI
88 Director Court Reporting Program .... Mrs. Kay REINDL
10 Chief Business Officer .... Ms. Carol KRAMLICH
37 Director Student Financial Aid .... Ms. Rita FRANCO
13 Director of Information Services .... Mr. Fabian ECHEVARRIA

Imperial Valley College (A)

380 E Aten Road, Imperial CA 92251-0158
County: Imperial FICE Identification: 001214
Unit ID: 115861
Telephone: (760) 352-8320 Carnegie Class: Assoc/Pub-R-L
FAX Number: (760) 355-2663 Calendar System: Semester
URL: www.imperial.edu
Established: 1922 Annual Undergrad Tuition & Fees (In-District): $1,326
Enrollment: 7,856 Coed
Affiliation or Control: Local IRS Status: 501(c)3
Highest Offering: Associate Degree
Program: Occupational; 2-Year Principally Bachelor's Creditable
Accreditation: WJ, EMT

01 Superintendent/President .... Dr. Victor JAIME
05 Vice President Academic Services .... Mrs. Kathy BERRY
32 VP Stdnt Svcs/Info Tech/Research .... Mr. Todd FINNELL
10 Vice President Business Services .... Mr. John LAU
15 Administrative Dean Human Services .... Mr. Travis GREGORY
103 Dean Economic & Worforce Develop .... Mr. Efrain SILVA
76 Dean of Health & Sciences .... Mrs. Tina AGUIRRE
62 Dean Arts/Letters/Learning Services .... Mr. Brian MCNEECE
38 Dean of Counseling .... Mr. Ted CEASAR
35 Dean Student Affs/Enrollment Svcs .... Mr. Sergio LOPEZ
07 Director of Admissions and Records .... Ms. Gloria HOISINGTON
37 Director of Financial Aid .... Ms. Lisa SEALS
09 Dir Research/Planning/Grant Admin .... Vacant
59 Dir Child/Family/Consumer Sciences .... Ms. Rebecca GREEN
26 Chief Public Relations Officer .... Mr. Bill GAY

Institute of Technology (B)

6249 Sunrose Boulevard, Citrus Heights CA 95610
Telephone: (916) 797-6337 Identification: 770557
Accreditation: ACCSC, ACFEI

† Main campus is Institute of Technology in Clovis, CA.

Institute of Technology (C)

564 West Herndon Avenue, Clovis CA 93612
County: Fresno FICE Identification: 030675
Unit ID: 431141
Telephone: (559) 297-4500 Carnegie Class: Assoc/PrivFP
FAX Number: (559) 297-5822 Calendar System: Semester
URL: www.iot.edu/
Established: Annual Undergrad Tuition & Fees: N/A
Enrollment: 2,763 Coed
Affiliation or Control: Proprietary IRS Status: Proprietary
Highest Offering: Associate Degree
Program: Occupational; Technical Emphasis
Accreditation: ACCSC, ACFEI

01 Acting President .... Rick WOOD

Institute of Technology (D)

5737 Stoddard Road, Modesto CA 95356
Telephone: (209) 545-3100 Identification: 770554
Accreditation: ACCSC, ACFEI

† Main campus is Institute of Technology in Clovis, CA.

Institute of Technology (E)

1755 Hilltop Drive, Redding CA 96002
Telephone: (530) 224-1000 Identification: 770555
Accreditation: ACCSC

† Main campus is Institute of Technology in Clovis, CA.

Institute of Technology (F)

1777 East Hammer Lane, Stockton CA 95210
Telephone: (209) 473-9000 Identification: 770556
Accreditation: ACCSC

† Main campus is Institute of Technology in Clovis, CA.

Interior Designers Institute (G)

1061 Camelback Road, Newport Beach CA 92660-3228
County: Orange FICE Identification: 025203
Unit ID: 116226
Telephone: (949) 675-4451 Carnegie Class: Spec/Arts
FAX Number: (949) 759-0667 Calendar System: Quarter
URL: www.idi.edu
Established: 1984 Annual Undergrad Tuition & Fees: $17,950
Enrollment: 310 Coed
Affiliation or Control: Proprietary IRS Status: Proprietary
Highest Offering: Master's
Program: Professional
Accreditation: ACCSC, CIDA

01 Executive Director .... Ms. Judy DEATON
37 Financial Aid Director .... Ms. Sharon DEATON

International Academy of Design and Technology (H)

2450 Del Paso Road, Sacramento CA 95834
Telephone: (916) 285-9468 Identification: 666740
Accreditation: ACICS

† Main campus is International Academy of Design and Technology in Tampa, FL.

International Professional School of Bodywork (I)

9025 Balboa Avenue, Suite 130, San Diego CA 92123
County: San Diego FICE Identification: 041347
Unit ID: 454740
Telephone: (858) 505-1100 Carnegie Class: Not Classified
FAX Number: (858) 565-4118 Calendar System: Quarter
URL: www.ipsb.edu
Established: 1977 Annual Undergrad Tuition & Fees: $6,714
Enrollment: 233 Coed
Affiliation or Control: Proprietary IRS Status: Proprietary
Highest Offering: Associate Degree
Program: Occupational
Accreditation: COMTA

International Reformed University and Seminary (J)

125 S. Vermont Avenue, Los Angeles CA 90004
County: Los Angeles Identification: 667132
Telephone: (213) 381-0081 Carnegie Class: Not Classified
FAX Number: (213) 381-0010 Calendar System: Semester
URL: www.irus.edu
Established: Annual Undergrad Tuition & Fees: N/A
Enrollment: N/A Coed
Affiliation or Control: Independent Non-Profit IRS Status: 501(c)3
Highest Offering: Master's
Program: Religious Emphasis
Accreditation: BI

International Technological University (K)

355 W. San Fernando Street, San Jose CA 95113
County: Santa Clara Identification: 667070
Unit ID: 443128
Telephone: (888) 488-4968 Carnegie Class: Not Classified
FAX Number: (408) 331-1026 Calendar System: Semester
URL: www.itu.edu
Established: 1994 Annual Graduate Tuition & Fees: $14,295
Enrollment: 900 Coed
Affiliation or Control: Independent Non-Profit IRS Status: 501(c)3
Highest Offering: Doctorate; No Undergraduates
Program: Professional
Accreditation: WC

01 President and CEO .... Yau-Gene CHAN
05 CAO .... Dr. Liz LI
10 CFO .... Edward LAM
11 COO .... Rebecca CHOI

International Theological Seminary (L)

3225 Tyler Avenue, El Monte CA 91731-3355
County: Los Angeles Identification: 666360
Unit ID: 396985
Telephone: (626) 448-0023 Carnegie Class: Not Classified
FAX Number: (626) 350-6343 Calendar System: Quarter
URL: www.itsla.edu
Established: 1982 Annual Undergrad Tuition & Fees: $11,280
Enrollment: 73 Coed
Affiliation or Control: Independent Non-Profit IRS Status: 501(c)3
Highest Offering: Doctorate
Program: Religious Emphasis
Accreditation: THEOL

01 President .... Dr. C. Melvin LOUCKS
05 Vice President for Academics .... Dr. Joy Jimena J. PALMER
11 Vice President for Administration .... Ms. Monica KAO
30 Vice Pres Seminary Advancement .... Dr. Edmund RHEE
06 Registrar .... Mrs. Zenda Gay P. EUSEBIO

ITT Technical Institute (M)

362 N Clovis Avenue, Clovis CA 93612-0300
Telephone: (559) 325-5400 Identification: 666144
Accreditation: ACICS

† Main campus is ITT Technical Institute in Indianapolis, IN.

ITT Technical Institute (N)

1140 Galaxy Way, Suite 400, Concord CA 94520
Telephone: (925) 674-8200 Identification: 666697
Accreditation: ACICS

† Main campus is ITT Technical Institute in Indianapolis, IN.

ITT Technical Institute (O)

4160 Temescal Canyon Rd, Suite 100, Corona CA 92883
Telephone: (951) 277-5400 Identification: 667194
Accreditation: ACICS

† Main campus is ITT Technical Institute in Indianapolis, IN.

ITT Technical Institute (P)

6101 West Centinela Avenue, Culver City CA 90230
Telephone: (310) 417-5800 Identification: 667192
Accreditation: ACICS

† Main campus is ITT Technical Institute in Indianapolis, IN.

ITT Technical Institute (Q)

16916 S Harlan Road, Lathrop CA 95330-8737
Telephone: (209) 858-0077 Identification: 666533
Accreditation: ACICS

† Main campus is ITT Technical Institute in Indianapolis, IN.

ITT Technical Institute (R)

401 Mile of Cars Way, Suite 100, National City CA 91950
Telephone: (619) 327-1800 Identification: 667193
Accreditation: ACICS

† Main campus is ITT Technical Institute in Indianapolis, IN.

ITT Technical Institute (S)

7901 Oakport Street, Suite 3000, Oakland CA 94621
Telephone: (510) 553-2800 Identification: 667195
Accreditation: ACICS

† Main campus is ITT Technical Institute in Indianapolis, IN.

ITT Technical Institute (T)

4000 West Metropolitan Dr, Ste. 100, Orange CA 92868
Telephone: (714) 941-2400 FICE Identification: 023219
Accreditation: ACICS, CAHIIM

† Main campus is ITT Technical Institute in Indianapolis, IN.

ITT Technical Institute (U)

2051 Solar Drive, Suite 150, Oxnard CA 93036-0641
Telephone: (805) 988-0143 Identification: 666534
Accreditation: ACICS

† Main campus is ITT Technical Institute in Indianapolis, IN.

ITT Technical Institute (V)

10863 Gold Center Drive,
Rancho Cordova CA 95670-6034
Telephone: (916) 851-3900 FICE Identification: 021209
Accreditation: ACICS

† Main campus is ITT Technical Institute in Indianapolis, IN.

ITT Technical Institute (W)

670 E Carnegie Drive, San Bernardino CA 92408-3519
Telephone: (909) 806-4600 FICE Identification: 030704
Accreditation: ACICS, CAHIIM

† Main campus is ITT Technical Institute in Indianapolis, IN.

ITT Technical Institute (X)

650 W Cienega Avenue, San Dimas CA 91773-2933
Telephone: (909) 971-2300 FICE Identification: 022915
Accreditation: ACICS, CAHIIM

† Main campus is ITT Technical Institute in Indianapolis, IN.

ITT Technical Institute (Y)

12669 Encinitas Avenue, Sylmar CA 91342-3664
Telephone: (818) 364-5151 FICE Identification: 023218
Accreditation: ACICS, CAHIIM

† Main campus is ITT Technical Institute in Indianapolis, IN.

ITT Technical Institute (A)
2555 West 190th Street, Suite 125, Torrance CA 90504
Telephone: (310) 965-5900 FICE Identification: 030874
Accreditation: ACICS

† Main campus is ITT Technical Institute in Indianapolis, IN.

John F. Kennedy University (B)
100 Ellinwood Way, Pleasant Hill CA 94523-4817
County: Contra Costa FICE Identification: 004484
Unit ID: 116712
Telephone: (925) 969-3300 Carnegie Class: Master's M
FAX Number: (925) 969-3399 Calendar System: Quarter
URL: www.jfku.edu
Established: 1964 Annual Undergrad Tuition & Fees: $19,853
Enrollment: 1,420 Coed
Affiliation or Control: Independent Non-Profit IRS Status: 501(c)3
Highest Offering: Doctorate
Program: Liberal Arts And General; Professional
Accreditation: WC, #CLPSY, IACBE

01 President .... Dr. Mac POWELL
10 VP of Business & Administration .... Mr. Aaron CHRISTOPHER
05 Int Vice President Academic Affairs .... Mr. Dean BARBIERI
30 Vice President of Advancement .... Mrs. Anne Marie TAYLOR
09 Vice Pres of Institutional Research .... Vacant
26 Assoc VP Marketing/Admissions .... Ms. Cathy SANTINI
07 Assistant Director of Admissions .... Ms. Wendy CAMPBELL-PARCO
28 Director of Diversity .... Mr. Jess DELEGENCIA
35 Director Student Services .... Ms. Eleanor ARMSTRONG
13 Director of Information Technology .... Ms. Mary HUNTER
15 Director of Human Resources .... Ms. Pamela FOSTER
61 College of Law Dean .... Mr. Dean BARBIERI
97 College of Undergraduate Studies .... Dr. Michael GRANEY-MULHOLLAND
58 College of Professional Studies .... Dr. Ruth FASSINGER
37 Director Financial Aid .... Ms. Mindy BERGERON
06 Registrar .... Mr. Stephen STICKA
08 Acting University Librarian .... Mrs. Claudia CHESTER
18 Director of Facilities .... Mr. David L. SADLER

John Paul the Great Catholic University (C)
10174 Old Grove Road, Ste 200, San Diego CA 92131
County: San Diego FICE Identification: 041937
Unit ID: 462354
Telephone: (858) 653-6740 Carnegie Class: Not Classified
FAX Number: (858) 653-3791 Calendar System: Quarter
URL: www.jpcatholic.com
Established: 2006 Annual Undergrad Tuition & Fees: N/A
Enrollment: 192 Coed
Affiliation or Control: Independent Non-Profit IRS Status: 501(c)3
Highest Offering: Master's
Program: Professional; Religious Emphasis
Accreditation: @WC

01 President .... Derry CONNOLLY
05 Provost & Academic Dean .... Michael BARBER
10 CFO/COO .... Greg BREEN
11 Sr VP for Administration .... Lidy CONNOLLY
07 Vice Pres Admissions .... Martin HAROLD
32 Dean of Students .... Vacant
13 Director Logistics & Technology .... Kevin MEZIERE
37 Director of Financial Aid .... Lisa WILLIAMS
06 Registrar .... Nick HEYE
42 Chaplain .... Fr. Richard HUSTON

Kaiser Permanente School of Allied Health Sciences (D)
938 Marina Way South, Richmond CA 94804
County: Contra Costa Identification: 667152
Telephone: (510) 231-5000 Carnegie Class: Not Classified
FAX Number: (510) 231-5001 Calendar System: Quarter
URL: www.kpsahs.org
Established: 1989 Annual Undergrad Tuition & Fees: $7,590
Enrollment: N/A Coed
Affiliation or Control: Proprietary IRS Status: Proprietary
Highest Offering: Baccalaureate
Program: Occupational
Accreditation: DMS, NMT, RAD, RTT

01 Medical Director .... Dr. Darryl JONES
05 Director of Academic Affairs .... Gregory WHEELER
10 Assoc Director of Finance .... Mary MCDONALD
11 Regional School Administrator .... James FITZGIBBONS
32 Student Services Administrator .... Candra RAYNOR

Kaplan College (E)
1914 Wible Road, Bakersfield CA 93304
Telephone: (661) 836-6300 Identification: 666291
Accreditation: ACICS

† Main campus is Kaplan College in Sacramento, CA.

Kaplan College (F)
555 Broadway, Suite 144, Chula Vista CA 91910-5342
Telephone: (619) 498-4100 Identification: 770560
Accreditation: ACCSC, ACICS

† Main campus is Kaplan College in San Diego, CA.

Kaplan College (G)
44 Shaw Avenue, Clovis CA 93612
Telephone: (559) 325-5100 Identification: 770559
Accreditation: ACCSC, ACICS

† Main campus is Kaplan College in Salida, CA.

Kaplan College (H)
2475 E Tahquitz Canyon Way, Palm Springs CA 92262
Telephone: (760) 778-3540 Identification: 770558
Accreditation: ACCSC, ACICS

† Main campus is Kaplan College in Vista, CA.

Kaplan College (I)
4330 Watt Avenue, Suite 400, Sacramento CA 95821-7000
County: Sacramento FICE Identification: 023519
Unit ID: 118259
Telephone: (916) 649-8168 Carnegie Class: Assoc/PrivFP
FAX Number: (916) 649-8344 Calendar System: Quarter
URL: www.kaplancollege.edu
Established: 1982 Annual Undergrad Tuition & Fees: $14,268
Enrollment: 558 Coed
Affiliation or Control: Proprietary IRS Status: Proprietary
Highest Offering: Associate Degree
Program: Occupational
Accreditation: ACICS

01 Executive Director .... Rob DILLMAN
05 Director of Education .... Hany NASRALLAH
37 Director of Student Financial Aid .... Ryan SMITH
07 Director of Admissions .... Heidi WINGO
36 Director of Career .... Julie MUIR

Kaplan College (J)
5172 Kiernan Court, Salida CA 95368
County: Stanislaus FICE Identification: 023063
Unit ID: 366960
Telephone: (209) 543-7000 Carnegie Class: Assoc/PrivFP
FAX Number: (209) 543-1755 Calendar System: Other
URL: www.kaplancollege.com
Established: 2005 Annual Undergrad Tuition & Fees: $13,246
Enrollment: 450 Coed
Affiliation or Control: Proprietary IRS Status: Proprietary
Highest Offering: Associate Degree
Program: Occupational
Accreditation: ACCSC, ACICS, COARC

01 Executive Director .... Mr. Bill JONES

Kaplan College (K)
9055 Balboa Avenue, San Diego CA 92123-1509
County: San Diego FICE Identification: 020917
Unit ID: 118277
Telephone: (858) 279-4500 Carnegie Class: Assoc/PrivFP
FAX Number: (858) 279-4885 Calendar System: Other
URL: www.kaplancollege.com
Established: 1976 Annual Undergrad Tuition & Fees: $32,922
Enrollment: 1,075 Coed
Affiliation or Control: Proprietary IRS Status: Proprietary
Highest Offering: Associate Degree
Program: Occupational
Accreditation: ACCSC, ACICS, CAHIIM, MAAB

01 Market President .... Mr. Kevin PREHN
01 Director of Education .... Mr. Alex POYUZINA
11 Executive Director .... Mr. David MOVSESIAN

Kaplan College (L)
2022 University Drive, Vista CA 92083-7736
County: San Diego FICE Identification: 025490
Unit ID: 118286
Telephone: (760) 630-1555 Carnegie Class: Assoc/PrivFP
FAX Number: (760) 630-1656 Calendar System: Other
URL: www.kaplancollege.com
Established: 1976 Annual Undergrad Tuition & Fees: $15,019
Enrollment: 800 Coed
Affiliation or Control: Proprietary IRS Status: Proprietary
Highest Offering: Associate Degree
Program: Occupational; Technical Emphasis
Accreditation: ACCSC, ACICS, MAAB

01 Executive Director .... Ms. Laura STINSON
05 Director of Education .... Mr. Alex POYUZINA
07 Director of Admissions .... Ms. Renee CODNER
36 Director of Career Services .... Ms. Maria BASCHSHI

37 Director of Financial Aid .... Ms. Elizabeth ALLEN
66 Director of Nursing .... Ms. Beth BUNYI

*Kern Community College District (M)
2100 Chester Avenue, Bakersfield CA 93301-4099
County: Kern FICE Identification: 006994
Unit ID: 436313
Telephone: (661) 336-5100 Carnegie Class: N/A
FAX Number: (661) 336-5134
URL: www.kccd.edu

01 Chancellor .... Ms. Sandra V. SERRANO
05 Vice Chanc Educational Services .... Vacant
11 Vice Chanc Operations Management .... Mr. Sean P. JAMES
16 Vice Chanc Human Resources .... Mr. Abe ALI
30 Assoc Vice Chanc Govt/External Rels .... Ms. Michele BRESSO
10 Chief Financial Officer .... Mr. Tom J. BURKE
13 Asst Dir Information Technology .... Mr. David W. PALINSKY
91 Asst Dir Information Technology .... Mr. Eddie D. ALVARADO
43 General Counsel .... Mr. Christopher HINE

*Bakersfield College (N)
1801 Panorama Drive, Bakersfield CA 93305-1299
County: Kern FICE Identification: 001118
Unit ID: 109819
Telephone: (661) 395-4011 Carnegie Class: Assoc/Pub-U-MC
FAX Number: (661) 395-4241 Calendar System: Semester
URL: www.bakersfieldcollege.edu
Established: 1913 Annual Undergrad Tuition & Fees (In-District): $902
Enrollment: 17,792 Coed
Affiliation or Control: State/Local IRS Status: 501(c)3
Highest Offering: Associate Degree
Program: Occupational; 2-Year Principally Bachelor's Creditable
Accreditation: WJ, EMT, RAD

02 President .... Dr. Sonya CHRISTIAN
05 Exec VP Academic Affairs/Stdnt Svcs .... Ms. Nan GOMEZ-HEITZEBERG
09 Dir Institutional Research/Planning .... Vacant
32 Vice Pres Student Services .... Dr. Zavareh DADABHOY
90 Dean Learning Resources/Info Tech .... Dr. Bonnie SUDERMAN
88 Dean Learning Support Services .... Vacant
30 Director Foundation & Development .. Mr. Michael STEPANOVICH
11 Exec Dir Administrative Services .... Mr. Sean JAMES
12 Director Delano Center .... Mr. Rich MCCROW
37 Director Financial Aid .... Ms. Primavera ARVIZU
07 Director Enrollment Services .... Mrs. Suzanne A. VAUGHN
26 Director Marketing & Public Info .... Mrs. Amber CHIANG
04 Admin Assistant to the President .... Ms. Debborah SPOHN
13 Director Information Services .... Mr. Todd COSTON
20 Dean of Student Learning .... Vacant
66 Dean of Nursing & Allied Health .... Ms. Cindy COLLIER
41 Director of Athletics .... Mr. Ryan BECKWITH
20 Dean of Instruction .... Ms. Leah CARTER
20 Dean of Instruction .... Ms. Liz ROZELL
20 Dean of Instruction .... Dr. Emmanuel MOURTZANOS

*Cerro Coso Community College (O)
College Heights Boulevard, Ridgecrest CA 93555-7777
County: Kern FICE Identification: 010111
Unit ID: 111896
Telephone: (760) 384-6100 Carnegie Class: Assoc/Pub-U-MC
FAX Number: (760) 375-4776 Calendar System: Semester
URL: www.cerrocoso.edu
Established: 1973 Annual Undergrad Tuition & Fees (In-District): $1,106
Enrollment: 4,737 Coed
Affiliation or Control: State/Local IRS Status: 501(c)3
Highest Offering: Associate Degree
Program: Occupational; 2-Year Principally Bachelor's Creditable
Accreditation: WJ

02 President .... Ms. A. Jill BOARD
05 Vice President Academic Affairs .... Dr. Corey MARVIN
32 Vice President of Student Services .... Ms. Heather OSTASH
12 Dir Eastern Sierra College Center .... Ms. Deanna CAMPBELL
12 Campus Manager Kern River Valley .... Ms. Lisa STEPHENS
75 Dean Career Technical Education .... Ms. Valerie KARNES
21 Director of Admin Services .... Ms. Gale LEBSOCK
38 Dir of Students & Counseling Svcs .... Ms. Paula SUOREZ
07 Dir Admiss/Records/VA/Fin Aid .... Ms. Jennifer SAN NICOLAS
10 Accounting Manager .... Ms. Lisa COUCH
15 Human Resources Manager .... Mr. Clint DOUGHERTY
88 Child Development Coordinator .... Vacant
26 Public Rel/Marketing & Dev Mgr .... Ms. Natalie DORRELL
13 Information Technology Manager .... Mr. Michael CAMPBELL
41 Dir Student Programs & Athletics .... Mr. John MERCER
106 Director Distance Education .... Mr. Charles OSTEEN

*Porterville College (P)
100 E College Avenue, Porterville CA 93257-6058
County: Tulare FICE Identification: 001268
Unit ID: 121363
Telephone: (559) 791-2200 Carnegie Class: Assoc/Pub-U-MC
FAX Number: (559) 784-4779 Calendar System: Semester
URL: www.portervillecollege.edu
Established: 1927 Annual Undergrad Tuition & Fees (In-District): $1,178
Enrollment: 3,887 Coed
Affiliation or Control: State/Local IRS Status: 501(c)3
Highest Offering: Associate Degree

Program: Occupational; 2-Year Principally Bachelor's Creditable
Accreditation: WJ

02 President .... Dr. Rosa F. CARLSON
05 Vice President Academic Affairs .... Mr. Bill HENRY
32 Vice President Student Services .... Mr. Steven SCHULTZ
04 Administrative Asst to President .... Ms. Carol BROWN
20 Dean Academic Affairs .... Dr. Antonia ECUNG
75 Dean Academic Affairs .... Mr. Val GARCIA
23 Assoc Dean Health Careers .... Ms. Kim BEHRENS
18 Maintenance & Operations Manager .... Mr. John WORD
07 Director Admissions/Records .... Ms. Erin CRUZ
10 Director Finance & Admin Services .... Ms. Arlitha WILLIAMS-HARMON
15 Human Resources Manager .... Ms. Resa HESS
37 Director Financial Aid .... Ms. Erin CRUZ
09 Institutional Researcher .... Mr. Michael CARLEY
13 Director Information Technology .... Mr. Chris CRAIG
88 Director CalWorks/EOPS .... Ms. Maria ROMAN
21 Accounting Manager .... Ms. Sonia HUCKABAY
88 Program Manager Child Dev Center .... Ms. Karen BALL
08 Interim Director Library .... Ms. Lorie BARKER
35 Student Programs/Athletics .... Mr. Eric MENDOZA
27 Pub Relations/Mkting/Outreach Mgr .... Ms. Maureen MONTGOMERY
105 Website Coordinator .... Ms. Randy MORGAN

The King's University (A)

14800 Sherman Way, Los Angeles CA 91405-2233
County: Los Angeles FICE Identification: 035163
Unit ID: 439701
Telephone: (818) 779-8040 Carnegie Class: Spec/Faith
FAX Number: (818) 779-8241 Calendar System: Quarter
URL: www.kingsuniversity.edu
Established: 1997 Annual Undergrad Tuition & Fees: $10,755
Enrollment: 519 Coed
Affiliation or Control: Independent Non-Profit IRS Status: 501(c)3
Highest Offering: Doctorate
Program: Professional; Religious Emphasis
Accreditation: BI, TRACS

01 President .... Dr. Steve E. RIGGLE
05 Exec VP & Chief Academic Officer .... Dr. John SPURLING
10 Director of Finance .... Mr. Dan J. DEHART
106 Dean/Administrator Online Education .... Prof. Donald C. BRUBAKER
09 Dir Inst Rsrch/Dean Doctoral Pgms .... Dr. Wesley M. PINKHAM
32 Chief Student Life Officer .... Dr. Michael J. GREGG
07 Director of Admissions .... Mr. Michael CLEMENS
06 Registrar .... Mrs. Martha S. BRANTLEY
37 Director Student Financial Aid ... Mr. Norman V. STOPPENBRINK
08 Head Librarian .... Prof. Barbara L. TARR
30 Chief Development .... Mr. Lee S. MIMMS
13 Director Computing & Info Mgmt ... Mr. Edmond M. MUGWANYA
21 Student Accounts Officer .... Ms. June M. HADLEY
90 Dir Acad Computing/Dir Student Affs .... Prof. Donald C. BRUBAKER
29 Director Alumni Relations .... Ms. Maureen A. BRODERSON
96 Director of Purchasing .... Mr. Bob CARON
28 Director of Diversity .... Dr. Michael J. GREGG
102 Dir Foundation/Corporate Relations .... Mr. Lee S. MIMMS
26 Chief Public Relations Officer .... Mrs. Janis A. GORAIEB

La Sierra University (B)

4500 Riverwalk Parkway, Riverside CA 92515-8247
County: Riverside FICE Identification: 001215
Unit ID: 117627
Telephone: (951) 785-2000 Carnegie Class: Master's M
FAX Number: (951) 785-2901 Calendar System: Quarter
URL: www.lasierra.edu
Established: 1922 Annual Undergrad Tuition & Fees: $29,103
Enrollment: 2,393 Coed
Affiliation or Control: Seventh-day Adventist IRS Status: 501(c)3
Highest Offering: Doctorate
Program: Liberal Arts And General; Teacher Preparatory; Professional; Business Emphasis
Accreditation: WC, MUS, SW, THEOL

01 President .... Dr. Randal R. WISBEY
05 Provost .... Dr. Steve PAWLUK
10 Vice President for Finance .... Mr. David GERIGUIS
32 Vice President for Student Life .... Ms. Yamilet BAZAN
30 Vice President Development .... Mr. Norman YERGEN
84 Vice Pres Enrollment Services .... Mr. David R. LOFTHOUSE
26 VP Communication/Integrated Mktg .... Dr. Marilyn THOMSEN
21 Associate Vice President Finance .... Ms. Pamela CHRISPENS
20 Associate Provost .... Dr. Barbara FAVORITO
49 Int Dean College Arts/Sciences .... Dr. Adeny SCHMIDT
50 Dean School of Business .... Dr. John THOMAS
53 Dean School of Education .... Dr. Ginger KETTING-WELLER
73 Dean School of Religion .... Dr. John W. WEBSTER
35 Dean of Students .... Ms. Marjorie ROBINSON
26 Exec Dir University Relations .... Mr. Larry BECKER
55 Director Adult Evening Program .... Ms. Nancy DITTEMORE
29 Director Alumni Relations .... Ms. Julie NARDUCCI
15 Director Human Resources .... Ms. Dell Jean VAN FOSSEN
08 Director Library .... Ms. Kitty SIMMONS
37 Director Student Financial Services .... Ms. Esther KINZER
42 Director Campus Ministries .... Mr. Samuel E. LEONOR, JR.
13 Director Information Technology .... Mr. Geoff INGRAM
09 Director of Institutional Research .... Mr. Guru UPPALA
18 Director Physical Plant .... Mr. Al VALDEZ
38 Director Counseling Center .... Ms. Debra WRIGHT
92 Director Honors Program .... Dr. Douglas R. CLARK
07 Director of Admissions/Registrar .... Mr. Issmael NZAMUTUNA
36 Director Career Services .... Mr. Natan VIGNA
41 Athletic Director .... Mr. Javier KRUMM

Laguna College of Art & Design (C)

2222 Laguna Canyon Road,
Laguna Beach CA 92651-1136
County: Orange FICE Identification: 023305
Unit ID: 117168
Telephone: (949) 376-6000 Carnegie Class: Spec/Arts
FAX Number: (949) 376-6009 Calendar System: Semester
URL: www.lcad.edu
Established: 1961 Annual Undergrad Tuition & Fees: $25,000
Enrollment: 488 Coed
Affiliation or Control: Independent Non-Profit IRS Status: 501(c)3
Highest Offering: Master's
Program: Professional
Accreditation: WC, ART

01 President .... Dr. Jonathan BURKE
05 Vice President Academic Affairs .... Dr. Helene GARRISON
30 Vice Pres of Development .... Mr. Domenick IETTO
07 Dean of Admissions .... Mr. Christopher BROWN
10 Chief Financial Officer .... Mr. Jim GODEK
06 Registrar .... Ms. Laura PATRICK
08 Library Director .... Ms. Jennifer WORMSER
04 Assistant to the President .... Ms. Jennifer DANIELS
37 Dir Financial Aid/Student Services .... Mr. Christopher BROWN

Lake Tahoe Community College (D)

1 College Drive, South Lake Tahoe CA 96150-4524
County: El Dorado FICE Identification: 012907
Unit ID: 117195
Telephone: (530) 541-4660 Carnegie Class: Assoc/Pub-S-SC
FAX Number: (530) 541-7852 Calendar System: Quarter
URL: www.ltcc.edu
Established: 1975 Annual Undergrad Tuition & Fees (In-District): $1,128
Enrollment: 2,668 Coed
Affiliation or Control: State/Local IRS Status: 501(c)3
Highest Offering: Associate Degree
Program: Occupational; 2-Year Principally Bachelor's Creditable; Business Emphasis
Accreditation: WJ

01 Superintendent/President .... Dr. Kindred MURILLO
04 Admin Assistant to President .... Ms. Julie BOOTH
05 VP Academic Affairs/Student Svcs .... Dr. Thomas GREENE
10 Vice President Administrative Svcs .... Mr. Jeff DEFRANCO
20 Dean of Instruction & CTE .... Dr. Virginia BOYAR
20 Interim Dean of Instruction .... Mr. Kurt GREEN
08 Director of Library .... Ms. Lisa FOLEY
13 Director Tech & Education Svcs .... Mr. Dave BURBA
84 Director Enrollment Services .... Ms. Cheri JONES
21 Director of Administrative Services .... Mr. Marc SABELLA
15 Director of Human Resources .... Ms. Susan WALTER
18 Director of Maintenance .... Vacant
88 Director Child Development Center .... Ms. Michelle SOWER
37 Director Financial Aid .... Ms. Julie CATHIE
09 Director of Institutional Research .... Mr. Aaron MCVEAN
26 Public Information Officer .... Mr. Peter BOSTIC
102 Foundation Director .... Mr. Peter BOSTIC
40 Bookstore Manager .... Mr. Lor COLLIN
96 Purchasing Agent .... Ms. Christinia AZEVEDO

LAMA (E)

370 South Fair Oaks Avenue, Pasadena CA 91105
County: Los Angeles FICE Identification: 038684
Unit ID: 446385
Telephone: (626) 568-8850 Carnegie Class: Assoc/PrivFP
FAX Number: (626) 568-8854 Calendar System: Quarter
URL: www.lamusicacademy.edu
Established: 1996 Annual Undergrad Tuition & Fees: $22,275
Enrollment: 180 Coed
Affiliation or Control: Proprietary IRS Status: Proprietary
Highest Offering: Associate Degree
Program: Occupational; 2-Year Principally Bachelor's Creditable; Music Emphasis
Accreditation: MUS

01 President .... Tom AYLESBURY
05 Dean .... Dave POZZI
11 Director of Administration .... Miranda TALBOT
07 Director of Admissions .... Ashley ROBERTS

Lassen Community College (F)

PO Box 3000, 478-200 Highway 139,
Susanville CA 96130-3000
County: Lassen FICE Identification: 001217
Unit ID: 117274
Telephone: (530) 257-6181 Carnegie Class: Assoc/Pub-R-M
FAX Number: (530) 251-8872 Calendar System: Semester
URL: www.lassencollege.edu
Established: 1925 Annual Undergrad Tuition & Fees (In-District): $647
Enrollment: 2,102 Coed
Affiliation or Control: State/Local IRS Status: 501(c)3
Highest Offering: Associate Degree
Program: Occupational; 2-Year Principally Bachelor's Creditable
Accreditation: WJ

01 District Superintendent/President .... Dr. Marlon R. HALL
04 Assistant to President .... Ms. Julie L. JOHNSTON
05 Exec Vice Pres of Academic Services .... Dr. Beatriz J. VASQUEZ
11 Vice Pres Administrative Services .... Mr. Dave CLAUSEN
20 Dean Instructional Services .... Dr. Tammy R. ROBINSON
32 Dean of Student Services .... Mr. Patrick WALTON
08 Librarian .... Ms. Marita DIMOND
09 Director Institutional Effectivenes .... Mr. Aeron ZENTNER
37 Director Financial Aid .... Mr. Matt LEVINE
35 Director Student Life .... Mr. Francis BEAUJON
41 Assistant Athletic Director .... Mr. Glen YONAN
18 Chief Facilities/Physical Plant .... Mr. Eric RULOFSON
15 Director Human Resources .... Ms. Vickie RAMSEY
13 Director of Information Technology .... Mr. David CORLEY
40 Director of Auxiliary Services .... Ms. Marlane MORSE

Le Cordon Bleu College of Culinary Arts (G)

350 Rhode Island Street, San Francisco CA 94103
County: San Francisco FICE Identification: 022202
Unit ID: 111009
Telephone: (888) 897-3222 Carnegie Class: Assoc/PrivFP
FAX Number: (415) 771-2194 Calendar System: Other
URL: www.chefs.edu/san-francisco
Established: 1977 Annual Undergrad Tuition & Fees: N/A
Enrollment: 749 Coed
Affiliation or Control: Proprietary IRS Status: Proprietary
Highest Offering: Associate Degree
Program: Occupational
Accreditation: ACCSC, ACICS, ACFEI

01 President .... Peter LEE
10 Vice Pres of Finance & Accounting .... Judy JIACOMETTI
07 Director of Admissions .... Brian ROSSITER
36 Director of Career Services .... Lisa WILSON

Le Cordon Bleu College of Culinary Arts in Los Angeles (H)

530 East Colorado Boulevard, Pasadena CA 91101
County: Los Angeles FICE Identification: 032103
Unit ID: 423980
Telephone: (626) 229-1300 Carnegie Class: Assoc/PrivFP
FAX Number: (626) 204-3907 Calendar System: Quarter
URL: www.chefs.edu/los-angeles
Established: 1994 Annual Undergrad Tuition & Fees: $12,912
Enrollment: 2,436 Coed
Affiliation or Control: Proprietary IRS Status: Proprietary
Highest Offering: Associate Degree
Program: Occupational
Accreditation: ACICS, ACFEI

01 President .... Mr. Tony BONDI

Life Chiropractic College West (I)

25001 Industrial Boulevard, Hayward CA 94545-2801
County: Alameda FICE Identification: 022285
Unit ID: 117520
Telephone: (510) 780-4500 Carnegie Class: Spec/Health
FAX Number: (510) 780-4525 Calendar System: Quarter
URL: www.lifewest.edu
Established: 1976 Annual Undergrad Tuition & Fees: $25,140
Enrollment: 323 Coed
Affiliation or Control: Independent Non-Profit IRS Status: 501(c)3
Highest Offering: First Professional Degree; No Lower Division
Program: Professional
Accreditation: CHIRO

01 President .... Dr. Brian KELLY
03 Executive Vice President .... Dr. Anatole BOGATSKI
05 Dean of Students .... Dr. Deborah LINDEMANN
23 Dean of the Health Center .... Dr. Kathy KINNEY
10 Director of Finance .... Ms. Susan DEVINE
17 Vice President of Academic Affairs .... Dr. Scott DONALDSON
51 Dean Postgraduate & Cont Education .... Dr. Kendra HOLLOWAY
32 Director of Student Services .... Mrs. Jackie BIRON
30 Director Institutional Advancement .... Mr. Drew BOSTER
88 Director of Special Projects .... Dr. George C. CASEY
46 Research Coordinator .... Dr. Dale JOHNSON
08 Library Director .... Ms. Annette OSENGA
07 Director of Admissions & Recruiting .... Ms. Mary FLANNERY
16 Human Resources Director .... Ms. Christie FARRON
40 Bookstore Director .... Mr. Robert BISHOP
37 Director Financial Aid .... Ms. Brenda R. JOHNSON
108 Director of Institutional Effective .... Dr. Kuan YANG
18 Facilities Manager .... Mr. George AMARAL
06 Registrar .... Ms. Cindy TAYAG
38 Academic Counselor .... Ms. Lori PINO

Life Pacific College (J)

1100 Covina Boulevard, San Dimas CA 91773-3298
County: Los Angeles FICE Identification: 022706
Unit ID: 117104
Telephone: (909) 599-5433 Carnegie Class: Spec/Faith
FAX Number: (909) 599-6690 Calendar System: Semester

URL: www.lifepacific.edu
Established: 1923 Annual Undergrad Tuition & Fees: $12,600
Enrollment: 652 Coed
Affiliation or Control: Other IRS Status: 501(c)3
Highest Offering: Master's
Program: Teacher Preparatory; Religious Emphasis
Accreditation: #WC, BI

01 President ... Dr. James J. ADAMS
04 Exec Assistant to the President ... Mrs. Karli ALBANESE
05 Vice President Academic Affairs ... Mr. Michael SALMEIER
32 Director Student Development ... Mr. Joshua ARNOLD
10 Chief Financial Officer ... Rev. Jarrod KULA
08 Librarian ... Mr. Gary MERRIMAN
06 Registrar ... Mrs. Brittany ADAMS
18 Director of Campus Operations ... Mr. Scott MARTZ
37 Director of Financial Aid ... Mrs. Becky HUYCK
20 Assoc Acad Dean NonTrad Pgms ... Rev. Brian TOMHAVE
30 Advancement Director ... Ms. Lynnette LOZOYA
40 Bookstore Director ... Mr. Jared BJUR
09 Director of Institutional Research ... Vacant
13 Director Information Technology ... Mr. Lawrence LIU
07 Director of Admissions ... Rev. Angie RICHEY
15 Director Personnel Services ... Mr. Todd ESKES

Lincoln University (A)

401 15th Street, Oakland CA 94612-2801
County: Alameda FICE Identification: 006975
Unit ID: 117557
Telephone: (510) 628-8010 Carnegie Class: Master's S
FAX Number: (510) 628-8012 Calendar System: Semester
URL: www.lincolnuca.edu
Established: 1919 Annual Undergrad Tuition & Fees: $12,550
Enrollment: 436 Coed
Affiliation or Control: Independent Non-Profit IRS Status: 501(c)3
Highest Offering: Master's
Program: Professional; Business Emphasis
Accreditation: ACICS

01 President/Rector ... Dr. Mikhail BRODSKY
05 Dean of Faculty ... Dr. Michael GUERRA
32 Dean of Students ... Mr. William HESS
07 Director of Admissions & Records ... Ms. Peggy AU
58 Director of Graduate Programs ... Dr. Marshall J. BURAK
08 Head Librarian ... Ms. Nicole Y. MARSH
32 Director of Student Services ... Ms. Annique DALLEY
37 Chief Financial Aid Director ... Mr. James PETERSON
06 Registrar ... Ms. Maggie HUA
10 Controller ... Ms. Sherry LIANG
20 Assistant Dean of Academic Affairs ... Ms. Mariya ORSHANSKY

Logos Evangelical Seminary (B)

9358 Telstar Avenue, El Monte CA 91731-2816
County: Los Angeles FICE Identification: 039454
Unit ID: 397553
Telephone: (626) 571-5110 Carnegie Class: Not Classified
FAX Number: (626) 571-5119 Calendar System: Semester
URL: www.logos-seminary.edu
Established: 1989 Annual Graduate Tuition & Fees: $9,120
Enrollment: 170 Coed
Affiliation or Control: Other IRS Status: 501(c)3
Highest Offering: Doctorate; No Undergraduates
Program: Religious Emphasis
Accreditation: WC, THEOL

01 President ... Dr. Felix LIU
05 Academic Dean ... Dr. Ekron CHEN
10 Director of Business Affairs ... Mr. Sonny GAN
32 Associate Dean of Students ... Mr. Godwin NGAI
30 Director of Advancement ... Dr. Kuoliang LIN

Loma Linda University (C)

Loma Linda CA 92350-0001
County: San Bernardino FICE Identification: 001218
Unit ID: 117636
Telephone: (909) 558-1000 Carnegie Class: Spec/Med
FAX Number: (909) 558-0242 Calendar System: Quarter
URL: www.llu.edu
Established: 1905 Annual Undergrad Tuition & Fees: $21,060
Enrollment: 4,652 Coed
Affiliation or Control: Seventh-day Adventist IRS Status: 501(c)3
Highest Offering: Doctorate
Program: Occupational; Liberal Arts And General; Professional
Accreditation: WC, ANEST, ARCPA, CAHIIM, CLPSY, COARC, CYTO, DENT, DH, DIETC, DMS, IPSY, MED, MFCD, MT, NURSE, OT, PH, PHAR, PTA, PTAA, RAD, RADDOS, RTT, SP, SW

01 President ... Dr. Richard H. HART
05 Provost ... Dr. Ronald L. CARTER
10 Sr Vice President Financial Affairs ... Mr. Rodney NEAL
30 Sr Vice President Advancement ... Mrs. Rachelle BUSSELL
27 Vice President Information Systems ... Dr. David P. HARRIS
84 VP Enrollment Mgmt/Student Services ... Dr. Rick E. WILLIAMS
63 Dean of Medicine ... Dr. H. Roger HADLEY
52 Dean of Dentistry ... Dr. Ronald DAILEY
69 Dean of Public Health ... Dr. Tricia Y. PENNIECOOK
66 Dean of Nursing ... Dr. Marilyn M. HERRMANN
76 Dean of Allied Health Professions ... Dr. Craig R. JACKSON
67 Dean School of Pharmacy ... Dr. W. William HUGHES
83 Dean School of Behavioral Health ... Dr. Beverly J. BUCKLES
73 Dean of School of Religion ... Dr. Jon PAULIEN
58 Dean Faculty of Graduate Studies ... Dr. Anthony J. ZUCCARELLI
06 Director of Records ... Ms. Erin SEHEULT
08 Director of University Libraries ... Ms. Carlene DRAKE
38 Director of Counseling ... Dr. William G. MURDOCH
43 General Legal Counsel ... Mr. Kent A. HANSEN
33 Dean of Men ... Mr. John NAFIE
34 Dean of Women ... Ms. Lynette BATES
37 Director Student Financial Aid ... Ms. Verdell SCHAEFER
09 Dir Educational Effectiveness ... Dr. Marilyn EGGERS
15 Exec Director Human Services ... Ms. Charlene WILSON
18 Director Campus Engineering ... Mr. Randy STEVENS
96 Director of Purchasing ... Mr. Tim HICKMAN
40 Campus Bookstore Manager ... Ms. Dionne LATTA
42 Campus Chaplain ... Pastor Terry SWENSON

Long Beach City College (D)

4901 E Carson Street, Long Beach CA 90808-1780
County: Los Angeles FICE Identification: 001219
Unit ID: 117645
Telephone: (562) 938-4111 Carnegie Class: Assoc/Pub-U-MC
FAX Number: (562) 938-4118 Calendar System: Other
URL: www.lbcc.edu
Established: 1927 Annual Undergrad Tuition & Fees (In-District): $1,182
Enrollment: 24,496 Coed
Affiliation or Control: State/Local IRS Status: 501(c)3
Highest Offering: Associate Degree
Program: Occupational; 2-Year Principally Bachelor's Creditable
Accreditation: WJ, ADNUR

01 Superintendent-President ... Mr. Eloy OAKLEY
25 Executive Vice Pres Econ & Res Dev ... Ms. Lou Anne BYNUM
05 Interim Vice Pres Academic Affairs ... Dr. Marilyn BROCK
10 Vice Pres Administrative Services ... Ms. Ann-Marie GABEL
16 Vice President Human Resources ... Ms. Rose DELGAUDIO
32 Vice Pres Student Support Services ... Dr. Greg PETERSON
12 Assoc Vice President PCC Campus ... Dr. Meena SINGHAL
15 Assoc VP Human Resources ... Ms. Cindy VYSKOCIL
13 Assoc VP Instruct & Info Tech ... Mr. Jay FIELD
07 Dean Admissions/Records ... Mr. Ross MIYASHIRO
09 Dean Academic Services ... Vacant
38 Dean Counseling/Stdt Support Svcs ... Dr. Kaneesha TARRANT
57 Dean Creative Arts/Applied Sciences ... Mrs. Dina HUMBLE
88 Dean of Language Arts ... Dr. Jose Ramon NUNEZ
32 Dean Student Affairs ... Ms. Connie SEARS
76 Dean School Health & Science ... Mr. Paul CREASON
45 Assoc Dean Inst Effectiveness ... Dr. Eva BAGG
26 Exec Dir Communications/College Adv ... Mr. Mark TAYLOR
102 Exec Director Foundation ... Dr. Ginny BAXTER
96 Director Business Support Services ... Mrs. Margie PADRON
18 Director of Facilities ... Mr. Tim WOOTTON
21 Director Fiscal Services & Payroll ... Mr. John THOMPSON
37 Director Financial Aid Programs ... Vacant

*Los Angeles Community College District Office (E)

770 Wilshire Boulevard, Los Angeles CA 90017
County: Los Angeles FICE Identification: 001221
Unit ID: 117681
Telephone: (213) 891-2000 Carnegie Class: N/A
FAX Number: N/A
URL: www.laccd.edu

01 Chancellor ... Dr. Adriana D. BARRERA
43 General Counsel ... Ms. Camille A. GOULET
03 Deputy Chancellor ... Vacant
05 VC Educational Pgms/Inst Effective . Dr. Yasmin DELAHOUSSAYE
103 Vice Chanc Econ Workforce Devel ... Dr. Felicito CAJAYON

*East Los Angeles College (F)

1301 Avenida Cesar Chavez,
Monterey Park CA 91754-6001
County: Los Angeles FICE Identification: 022260
Unit ID: 113856
Telephone: (323) 265-8650 Carnegie Class: Assoc/Pub-U-MC
FAX Number: (323) 265-8763 Calendar System: Semester
URL: www.elac.edu
Established: 1945 Annual Undergrad Tuition & Fees (In-District): $1,710
Enrollment: 38,065 Coed
Affiliation or Control: State/Local IRS Status: 501(c)3
Highest Offering: Associate Degree
Program: Occupational; 2-Year Principally Bachelor's Creditable
Accreditation: WJ, CAHIIM, COARC

02 President ... Mr. Marvin MARTINEZ
05 VP Academic Affairs ... Dr. Richard MOYER
103 Interim VP Workforce & Econ Devel ... Ms. Laura M. RAMIREZ
32 VP Student Services/Special Pgms ... Mr. Oscar VALERIANO
11 VP Administrative Services ... Mr. Tom FURUKAWA
88 Assoc VP Administrative Services ... Ms. Erlinda DE OCAMPO
75 Dean Acad Affs/Career & Tech Educ ... Mr. Laureano FLORES
49 Interim Dean Acad Affs/Liberal Arts ... Ms. Carol KOZERACKI
49 Dean Academic Affairs Liberal Arts ... Ms. Kerrin MCMAHAN
49 Dean Academic Affairs Liberal Arts ... Ms. Vi LY
07 Dean Admissions & Records ... Mr. Jeremy P. ALLRED
12 Dean Academic Affairs Southgate Ctr ... Mr. Alfonso RIOS
30 Dean Resource & Inst Development ... Ms. Selina CHI
09 Dean Institutional Effectiveness ... Dr. Ryan CORNNER
51 Dean Continuing Education ... Ms. Adrienne A. MULLEN
35 Dean Student Activities ... Ms. Sonia LOPEZ
88 Dean EOP&S/CARE ... Ms. Danelle FALLERT
88 Dean CFES ... Ms. Angelica TOLEDO
25 Assoc Dean Resource Development ... Dr. John RUDE
25 Assistant Dean Grants Management ... Ms. Martha ERMIAS
26 Chief Public Relations Officer ... Vacant
22 Affirmative Action Officer ... Ms. Maria E. YEPES
37 Financial Aid Manager ... Ms. Lindy FONG
40 Director Student Store ... Ms. Joyce GARCIA
41 Athletic Director (Men/Women) ... Mr. Allen J. CONE
28 Director of Diversity ... Ms. Maria Elena YEPES
88 Child Development Director ... Ms. Marcia CAGIGAS
38 Department Chair Counseling ... Mr. Daniel ORNELAS
21 College Fiscal Administrator ... Ms. Erlinda N. DEOCAMPO
08 Library Coordinator ... Ms. Choonhee L. RHIM
85 Foreign Student Advisement ... Ms. Nancy C. WONG
88 Director Vincent Price Art Museum ... Ms. Karen RAPP

*Los Angeles City College (G)

855 N Vermont Avenue, Los Angeles CA 90029-9990
County: Los Angeles FICE Identification: 001223
Unit ID: 117788
Telephone: (323) 953-4000 Carnegie Class: Assoc/Pub-U-MC
FAX Number: (323) 953-4013 Calendar System: Semester
URL: www.lacitycollege.edu
Established: 1929 Annual Undergrad Tuition & Fees (In-District): $959
Enrollment: 21,937 Coed
Affiliation or Control: Local IRS Status: 501(c)3
Highest Offering: Associate Degree
Program: Occupational; 2-Year Principally Bachelor's Creditable
Accreditation: WJ, DIETT, DT, #RAD

02 President ... Mrs. Renee D. MARTINEZ
05 Vice President Academic Affairs ... Dr. Dan WALDEN
10 Vice President Administrative Svcs ... Mr. Paul CARLSON
32 Vice President of Student Services ... Dr. Lawrence BRADFORD
21 Asst Vice Pres Administrative Svcs ... Mr. Anil JAIN
20 Dean of Academic Affairs ... Dr. Thelma DAY
20 Dean of Academic Affairs ... Ms. Allison JONES
20 Dean of Academic Affairs ... Dr. Todd SCOTT
103 Dean Workforce Development ... Dr. A. Alex DAVIS
09 Dean of Institutional Effectiveness ... Dr. Edward PAI
84 Dean of Enrollment Services ... Mr. William MARMOLEJO
35 Dean Student Svcs Special Programs ... Dr. Randy ANDERSON
35 Assoc Dean Student Svcs Access ... Mr. Jeremy VILLAR
37 Assoc Dean Financial Aid ... Mr. Jeremy VILLAR
35 Assoc Dean Office of Student Life ... Mr. Earic PETERS
40 Bookstore Manager ... Ms. Christi O'CONNOR
85 Director International Students ... Dr. Reginald BRADY
15 Human Resources Manager ... Ms. Lenore SAUNDERS
66 Nursing Department Chair ... Vacant
38 Counseling Chairperson ... Ms. Reri PUMPHREY
18 Facilities Director ... Mr. Bob GARCIA

*Los Angeles Harbor College (H)

1111 Figueroa Place, Wilmington CA 90744-2397
County: Los Angeles FICE Identification: 001224
Unit ID: 117690
Telephone: (310) 233-4000 Carnegie Class: Assoc/Pub-U-MC
FAX Number: (310) 233-4223 Calendar System: Semester
URL: www.lahc.edu
Established: 1949 Annual Undergrad Tuition & Fees (In-District): $1,162
Enrollment: 10,205 Coed
Affiliation or Control: State/Local IRS Status: 501(c)3
Highest Offering: Associate Degree
Program: Occupational; 2-Year Principally Bachelor's Creditable
Accreditation: WJ, ADNUR

02 President ... Mr. Farley HERZEK
04 Executive Assistant to President ... Ms. Danielle JACK
05 Vice President Academic Affairs ... Mr. Luis M. ROSAS
11 Vice Pres Administrative Services ... Dr. Ann W. TOMLINSON
32 Vice President Student Services ... Ms. Abbie L. PATTERSON
21 Assoc Vice Pres Administrative Svcs ... Mr. Nestor TAN
09 Dean of Institutional Effectiveness ... Dr. Kristi V. BLACKBURN
20 Dean of Academic Affairs ... Dr. Bobbi VILLALOBOS
07 Dean Admissions/Records/Eve Ops ... Mr. David M. CHING
35 Dean of Student Services ... Ms. Mercedes YANEZ
20 Dean of Academic Affairs ... Dr. Stephanie ATKINSON-ALSTON
25 Assoc Dean Grants Mgmt ... Ms. Susan RHI-KLEINERT
103 Dean of Economic/Workforce Devel ... Ms. Sandra SANCHEZ
83 Div Chair Behavioral/Social Sci ... Mr. Bradley J. YOUNG
50 Division Chairperson Business ... Mr. Stanley C. SANDELL
60 Div Chairperson Communications ... Ms. Carmen CARRILLO
57 Div Chair Humanities/Fine Arts ... Ms. Kate CAMPBELL
81 Div Chairperson Math/Phys Science ... Ms. Farah SADDIGH
76 Div Chairperson Health Sciences ... Mrs. Lynn YAMAKAWA
68 Div Chairperson Physical Education ... Mr. Nabeel M. BARAKAT
88 Div Chrp Sci & Fam/Consum Stds ... Mrs. Joyce E. PARKER
08 Division Chairperson Library ... Mr. Jonathan LEE
38 Division Chairperson Counseling ... Ms. Elizabeth COLOCHO
41 Athletic Director ... Mr. Nabeel BARAKAT
37 Director Student Financial Aid ... Mrs. Sheila U. MILLMAN
18 Facilities Manager ... Mr. William C. ENGLERT
31 Community Services Manager .. Ms. Carla R. MUSSA-MULDOON
40 College Enterprise Manager ... Mr. Mark A. ZANKICH
85 Foreign Student Advisor ... Vacant

*Los Angeles Mission College (A)

13356 Eldridge Avenue, Sylmar CA 91342-3244
County: Los Angeles FICE Identification: 012550
Unit ID: 117867
Telephone: (818) 364-7600 Carnegie Class: Assoc/Pub-U-MC
FAX Number: (818) 364-7826 Calendar System: Semester
URL: www.lamission.edu
Established: 1975 Annual Undergrad Tuition & Fees (In-District): $1,220
Enrollment: 9,674 Coed
Affiliation or Control: State/Local IRS Status: 501(c)3
Highest Offering: Associate Degree
Program: Occupational; 2-Year Principally Bachelor's Creditable
Accreditation: WJ

02 President .... Dr. Monte E. PEREZ
05 Vice President Academic Affairs .... Mr. Michael K. ALLEN
11 Vice President Administrative Svcs .... Mr. Daniel G. VILLANUEVA
32 Vice President of Student Services .... Mr. Joe RAMIREZ
20 Dean of Academic Affairs ...... Ms. Stephanie ATKINSON-ALSTON
35 Dean of Student Services .... Ms. Ludi VILLEGAS-VIDAL
88 Associate Dean of Academic Affairs .... Ms. Cathy BRINKMAN
88 Assistant Dean of Title V HSI .... Mrs. Susan RHI-KLEINERT
09 Dean of Institutional Effectiveness .... Dr. Sarah L. MASTERS
26 Chief Public Relations Officer .... Ms. Darlene MONTES
88 Director Child Development Center .... Ms. Monica MORENO
41 Athletic Director .... Mr. John KLITSNER
08 Head Librarian .... Ms. Sandy THOMSEN
38 Counseling Chairperson .... Ms. Diana BONILLA
37 Financial Aid Manager .... Mr. Dennis J. SCHROEDER
31 Community Services Manager .... Vacant
18 Facilities/Physical Plant Manager .... Mr. Walter J. BORTMAN
88 EOP & S/Care Director .... Ms. Ludi VILLEGAS-VIDAL
06 Sr Admissions & Records Supervisor ...... Ms. Rosalie S. TORRES

*Los Angeles Pierce College (B)

6201 Winnetka Avenue, Woodland Hills CA 91371-0001
County: Los Angeles FICE Identification: 001226
Unit ID: 117706
Telephone: (818) 347-0551 Carnegie Class: Assoc/Pub-U-MC
FAX Number: (818) 710-9844 Calendar System: Semester
URL: www.piercecollege.edu
Established: 1947 Annual Undergrad Tuition & Fees (In-District): $958
Enrollment: 19,951 Coed
Affiliation or Control: State/Local IRS Status: 501(c)3
Highest Offering: Associate Degree
Program: Occupational; 2-Year Principally Bachelor's Creditable
Accreditation: WJ, ADNUR

02 President .... Dr. Kathleen BURKE-KELLY
05 Vice President Academic Affairs .... Ms. Anna DAVIES
11 Vice President Administration .... Mr. Rolf SCHLEICHER
32 Vice President Student Services .Ms. Alma JOHNSON-HAWKINS
10 Assoc Vice President Admin Services .... Mr. Bruce ROSKY
10 Assoc Vice President Admin Services .... Mr. Larry KRAUS
08 Chairman Library Services .... Ms. Paula PAGGI
38 Chair Student Counseling .... Mr. Rudy DOMPE
20 Interim Dean of Academic Affairs .... Vacant
20 Dean of Academic Affairs .... Dr. Donna Mae VILLANUEVA
07 Dean Admissions/Records .... Mr. Marco DE LA GARZA
35 Dean Student Services .... Vacant
35 Dean Student Services .... Mr. David FOLLOSCO
37 Director of Financial Aid .... Ms. Anafe ROBINSON
09 Director Institutional Research .... Vacant
26 Public Information Officer .... Ms. Doreen CLAY
31 Director Community Services .... Ms. Cindy CHANG
102 Director of Foundation .... Vacant
36 Director Student Placement .... Vacant
22 Compliance Officer .... Vacant
18 Director of College Facilities .... Mr. Paul NIEMAN

*Los Angeles Southwest College (C)

1600 W Imperial Highway, Los Angeles CA 90047-4899
County: Los Angeles FICE Identification: 007047
Unit ID: 117715
Telephone: (323) 241-5225 Carnegie Class: Assoc/Pub-U-MC
FAX Number: (323) 241-5220 Calendar System: Semester
URL: www.lasc.edu
Established: 1967 Annual Undergrad Tuition & Fees (In-District): $1,220
Enrollment: 9,743 Coed
Affiliation or Control: State/Local IRS Status: 501(c)3
Highest Offering: Associate Degree
Program: Occupational; 2-Year Principally Bachelor's Creditable
Accreditation: WJ

02 President .... Dr. Yasmin DELAHOUSSAYE
05 Vice President Academic Affairs .... Dr. Patrick JEFFERSON
32 Vice President Student Services .... Ms. Trudy J. WALTON
10 Vice President Admin Services .... Mr. Ferris E. TRIMBLE
46 Dean Resource Development .... Ms. Felicia DUENAS
09 Dean Institutional Effectiveness .... Vacant
103 Dean Workforce Development .... Vacant
20 Dean Academic Affairs .... Dr. Tangelia ALFRED
20 Dean Academic Affairs .... Ms. Stephanie L. BRASLEY
38 Chairperson Counseling .... Mr. Reggie MORRIS
08 Chairperson Library .... Ms. Shelley WERTS
07 Sr Admissions & Records Supervisor . Ms. Kimberly CARPENTER
18 Director of College Facilities .... Mr. Randy CRAIG
37 Manager Student Financial Aid .... Ms. Kathleen STIGER
35 Dean Student Services .... Dr. Oscar COBIAN

*Los Angeles Trade-Technical College (D)

400 W Washington Boulevard,
Los Angeles CA 90015-4108
County: Los Angeles FICE Identification: 001227
Unit ID: 117724
Telephone: (213) 763-7000 Carnegie Class: Assoc/Pub-U-MC
FAX Number: (213) 763-5393 Calendar System: Semester
URL: www.lattc.edu
Established: 1925 Annual Undergrad Tuition & Fees (In-District): $1,273
Enrollment: 13,998 Coed
Affiliation or Control: State/Local IRS Status: 501(c)3
Highest Offering: Associate Degree
Program: Occupational; 2-Year Principally Bachelor's Creditable
Accreditation: WJ, ACFEI

02 President .... Mr. Larry FRANK
09 VP Inst Effectiveness & Innov .... Vacant
11 VP Administrative Services .... Dr. Mary GALLAGHER
05 VP Academic Affs & Workforce Devel .... Ms. Leticia BARAJAS
32 Vice President Student Services .... Vacant
21 Assoc Vice Pres Administrative Svcs .... Mr. William GASPER
35 Dean Student Services .... Vacant
20 Dean of Academic Affairs .... Mr. Vincent JACKSON
20 Dean Academic Affairs .... Ms. Cynthia MORLEY-MOWER
20 Dean Academic Affairs .... Mr. Joe GUERRIERI
84 Dean Enrollment Management .... Vacant
37 Manager Financial Aid/EOP&S .... Ms. Cecilia KWAN
88 Dean Inst Effective & Innovation .... Ms. Anna BADALYAN
88 Dean Matriculation/Student Success .... Ms. Dorothy SMITH
35 Dean Student Services .... Mr. Luis DORADO
18 Chief Facilities/Physical Plant .... Mr. Bill SMITH
06 Registrar .... Vacant
10 Chief Business Officer .... Mr. Marcus ANGLIN
38 Chair Student Counseling .... Mr. Thomas DAWKINS
96 Director of Purchasing .... Mr. Galen BULLOCK
102 Director Foundation/Corporate Rels .... Vacant
26 Public Relations Manager .... Mr. David YSAIS

*Los Angeles Valley College (E)

5800 Fulton Avenue, Valley Glen CA 91401-4096
County: Los Angeles FICE Identification: 001228
Unit ID: 117733
Telephone: (818) 947-2600 Carnegie Class: Assoc/Pub-U-MC
FAX Number: (818) 947-2602 Calendar System: Semester
URL: www.lavc.edu
Established: 1949 Annual Undergrad Tuition & Fees (In-District): $1,148
Enrollment: 18,000 Coed
Affiliation or Control: State/Local IRS Status: 501(c)3
Highest Offering: Associate Degree
Program: Occupational; 2-Year Principally Bachelor's Creditable
Accreditation: WJ, ADNUR, COARC

02 President .... Dr. A. Susan CARLEO
05 Vice President Academic Affairs .... Ms. Karen DAAR
10 Vice Pres Administrative Services .... Mr. Christopher M. BONVENUTO
32 Vice Pres Student Services .... Mr. Florentino MANZANO
11 Assoc Vice Pres Administrative Svcs .... Mr. Raul D. GONZALEZ
21 Financial Analyst .... Vacant
45 Chief Financial Anaylist .... Ms. Violet AMRIKHAS
20 Dean Academic Affairs .... Dr. Laurie NALEPA
20 Dean Academic Affairs .... Mr. Rudolph J. BESIKOF
20 Dean of Academic Affairs .... Dr. Deborah A. DICESARE
20 Dean of Academic Affairs .... Ms. Sheri L. BERGER
08 Chairperson of Library Service .... Ms. Dora E. ESTEN
37 Financial Aid Manager .... Mr. Vernon D. BRIDGES
09 Dean Research & Planning .... Ms. Michelle R. FOWLES
35 Associate Dean Student Services .... Ms. Elizabeth ORTIZ
88 Associate Dean of EOPS .... Dr. Sherri RODRIGUEZ
88 Associate Dean DSPS .... Mr. David M. GREEN
35 Assoc Dean of Student Services .... Ms. Annie G. REED
102 Director Foundation/Alumni Rels .... Mr. Raul V. CASTILLO
26 Public Relations Manager .... Ms. Jennifer C. FONG
18 Director of College Facilities .... Mr. Tom LOPEZ
40 Bookstore Manager .... Vacant
13 Manager College Info Svcs .... Mr. Aaron WEATHERSBY
31 Community Services Manager .... Mr. Michael B. ATKIN
38 Director Student Counseling .... Ms. Barbara GOLDBERG
41 Athletic Director .... Mr. Jim FENWICK
06 Registrar .... Ms. Ashley DUNN

*West Los Angeles College (F)

9000 Overland Avenue, Culver City CA 90230-5002
County: Los Angeles FICE Identification: 008596
Unit ID: 125471
Telephone: (310) 287-4200 Carnegie Class: Assoc/Pub-U-MC
FAX Number: (310) 841-0396 Calendar System: Semester
URL: www.wlac.edu
Established: 1969 Annual Undergrad Tuition & Fees (In-District): $1,030
Enrollment: 9,954 Coed
Affiliation or Control: State/Local IRS Status: 501(c)3
Highest Offering: Associate Degree
Program: Occupational; 2-Year Principally Bachelor's Creditable
Accreditation: WJ, DH

02 President .... Mr. Nabil S. ABU-GHAZALEH
11 Vice President Administrative Svcs .... Mr. Kenneth B. TAKEDA
05 Vice President Academic Affairs .... Mr. Robert L. SPRAGUE
32 Vice President Student Services .... Ms. Phyllis BRAXTON
84 Dean Student Svcs Enrollment .... Mr. John M. GOLTERMANN
97 Dean General Education/Transfer .... Dr. Colena ALCALA
20 Dean Advance Program Development .... Mr. Mark PRACHER
75 Dean Career/Technology Education .... Ms. Aracely AGUIAR
35 Dean of Student Support Services .... Dr. Shalamon DUKE
09 Dean of Research and Planning .... Ms. Rebecca TILLBERG
56 Dean Distance Learning/Inst Tech .... Mr. Eric ICHON
20 Dean of Academic Affairs .... Ms. Kathy S. WALTON
11 Associate Dean Contract Ed .... Mr. Barry SLOAN
35 Assoc Dean Student Svcs Activities .... Vacant
88 Academic Senate President .... Dr. Adrienne FOSTER
21 Chief Financial Administrator .... Ms. Maureen O'BRIEN
102 Actg Exec Director WLAC Foundation ...... Mr. Kenneth B. TAKEDA
26 Dir Advtg/Marketing/Public Rels .... Ms. Michelle LONG-COFFEE
41 Athletic Director .... Mr. Steve AGGERS
18 Facilities Manager .... Mr. Allan HANSEN
19 Sheriff/Deputy .... Mr. Nick GUSKOS
37 Financial Aid Manager .... Mr. Glenn SCHENK
40 College Enterprise Manager .... Mr. Larry PACKHAM
88 Operations Manager .... Mr. Bruce HICKS
22 Compliance Officer .... Vacant

Los Angeles County College of Nursing and Allied Health (G)

1237 N Mission Road, Los Angeles CA 90033-1083
County: Los Angeles FICE Identification: 006165
Unit ID: 117803
Telephone: (323) 226-4911 Carnegie Class: Assoc/Pub-Spec
FAX Number: (323) 226-6343 Calendar System: Semester
URL: www.ladhs.org/wps/portal/CollegeOfNursing/
Established: 1895 Annual Undergrad Tuition & Fees (In-District): $4,925
Enrollment: 211 Coed
Affiliation or Control: Local IRS Status: 501(c)3
Highest Offering: Associate Degree
Program: Occupational; 2-Year Principally Bachelor's Creditable
Accreditation: WJ

01 Provost .... Ms. Nancy W. MILLER
05 Dean of Nursing Programs .... Ms. Barbara COLLIER
32 Dean Administrative/Student Svcs .... Ms. Maria C. CABALLERO
53 Dean Education/Consulting Services .... Ms. Tammy BLASS

Los Angeles Film School (H)

6353 Sunset Boulevard, Hollywood CA 90028
County: Los Angeles FICE Identification: 040373
Unit ID: 436429
Telephone: (323) 464-5200 Carnegie Class: Assoc/PrivFP
FAX Number: (323) 646-0770 Calendar System: Other
URL: www.lafilm.edu
Established: 1999 Annual Undergrad Tuition & Fees: $29,500
Enrollment: 2,464 Coed
Affiliation or Control: Proprietary IRS Status: Proprietary
Highest Offering: Baccalaureate
Program: 2-Year Principally Bachelor's Creditable; Fine Arts Emphasis
Accreditation: ACCSC

01 President/CEO .... Ms. Diana DERYCZ-KESSLER

Los Angeles ORT College (I)

6435 Wilshire Blvd, Los Angeles CA 90048
County: Los Angeles FICE Identification: 025703
Unit ID: 368780
Telephone: (323) 966-5444 Carnegie Class: Assoc/PrivNFP
FAX Number: (323) 966-5455 Calendar System: Other
URL: www.laort.edu
Established: 1985 Annual Undergrad Tuition & Fees: $11,950
Enrollment: 363 Coed
Affiliation or Control: Independent Non-Profit IRS Status: 501(c)3
Highest Offering: Associate Degree
Program: Occupational; Technical Emphasis
Accreditation: CNCE

Los Angeles Pacific College (J)

3350 Wilshire Blvd, Ste 460, Los Angeles CA 90010
County: Los Angeles Identification: 667143
Telephone: (213) 384-2318 Carnegie Class: Not Classified
FAX Number: (213) 384-0419 Calendar System: Semester
URL: www.lapacific.net
Established: 1989 Annual Undergrad Tuition & Fees: $13,200
Enrollment: N/A Coed
Affiliation or Control: Proprietary IRS Status: Proprietary
Highest Offering: Associate Degree
Program: Occupational; 2-Year Principally Bachelor's Creditable
Accreditation: COE

*Los Rios Community College District Office (K)

1919 Spanos Court, Sacramento CA 95825-3981
County: Sacramento FICE Identification: 001231
Unit ID: 117900
Telephone: (916) 568-3021 Carnegie Class: N/A
FAX Number: (916) 568-3023
URL: www.losrios.edu

01 Chancellor ..... Dr. Brian KING
04 Chancellor's Executive Assistant ..... Ms. Jennifer DELUCCHI
10 Deputy Chancellor ..... Mr. Jon SHARPE
05 Vice Chancellor Education/Tech ..... Dr. Susan L. LORIMER
30 Vice Chanc Resource/Economic Dev ..... Dr. Beverly A. SANDEEN
26 Assoc Vice Chanc Comm/Media Rels ..... Mr. Mitchel BENSON
18 Assoc Vice Chanc Facilities Mgmt ..... Mr. Pablo MANZO
21 Assoc Vice Chancellor Finance ..... Ms. Theresa MATISTA
15 Assoc Vice Chanc Human Resouces ..... Mr. Ryan COX
13 Assoc Vice Chanc Information Tech ..... Mr. Mick HOLSCLAW
32 Assoc Vice Chanc Student Services ..... Dr. Victoria ROSARIO
103 Assoc Vice Chanc Workforce/Econ Dev ..... Dr. Daniel THROGMORTON
43 General Counsel ..... Mr. J.P SHERRY
37 Director Financial Aid ..... Mr. Roy BECKHORN
96 Director General Services ..... Mr. O.D BURR
09 Director Institutional Research ..... Ms. Flora B. YEN

*American River College (A)

4700 College Oak Drive, Sacramento CA 95841-4286
County: Sacramento FICE Identification: 001232
Unit ID: 109208
Telephone: (916) 484-8011 Carnegie Class: Assoc/Pub-U-MC
FAX Number: (916) 484-8674 Calendar System: Semester
URL: www.arc.losrios.edu
Established: 1955 Annual Undergrad Tuition & Fees (In-District): $1,200
Enrollment: 32,868 Coed
Affiliation or Control: State/Local IRS Status: 501(c)3
Highest Offering: Associate Degree
Program: Occupational; 2-Year Principally Bachelor's Creditable
Accreditation: WJ, COARC, EMT, FUSER

02 Interim President ..... Ms. Marie SMITH
05 Vice President of Instruction ..... Ms. Colleen H. OWINGS
32 Vice President of Student Services ..... Dr. Pamela D. WALKER
10 Vice President of Admin Services ..... Mr. Raymond DI GUILIO
20 Assoc Vice President of Instruction ..... Dr. Lisa LAWRENSON
62 Assoc VP of Instruction/Lrng Res ..... Dr. David REDFIELD
103 Assoc VP Workforce Development ..... Mr. Jerome COUNTEE
09 Dean Planning/Rsch/Tech/Prof Dev ..... Dr. Jane DE LEON
27 Interim Public Information Officer ..... Mr. Scott CROW
30 Director of College Advancement ..... Ms. Kirsten DUBRAY
37 Financial Aid Supervisor ..... Mr. Chad FUNK
07 Dean of Enrollment Services ..... Dr. Robin NEAL
57 Dean Fine & Applied Arts ..... Dr. Adam KARP
83 Dean Behavioral Social/Science ..... Mr. Carlos REYES
79 Dean Humanities ..... Ms. Kate JAQUES
38 Dean Counseling & Student Svcs ..... Mr. Jeffrey STEPHENSON
88 Dean of English ..... Dr. Tammy MONTGOMERY
81 Dean of Mathematics ..... Vacant
68 Dean of Kinesiology/Athletics ..... Mr. Greg WARZECKA
81 Dean Science/Engineering ..... Dr. Rina ROY
75 Dean of Technical/Vocational Educ ..... Ms. Gabriel M. MEEHAN
56 Dean McClellan Center ..... Mr. Steve SEGURA
38 Dean Student Support Services ..... Vacant
66 Dean Health & Education ..... Dr. Steven BOYD
56 Dean Natomas Center ..... Mr. Frank KOBAYASHI
35 Dean Student Development ..... Mr. Manuel PEREZ
50 Dean Business/Computer Science ..... Dr. Derrick BOOTH

*Cosumnes River College (B)

8401 Center Parkway, Sacramento CA 95823-5799
County: Sacramento FICE Identification: 007536
Unit ID: 113096
Telephone: (916) 691-7344 Carnegie Class: Assoc/Pub-U-MC
FAX Number: (916) 691-7375 Calendar System: Semester
URL: www.crc.losrios.edu
Established: 1970 Annual Undergrad Tuition & Fees (In-District): $1,104
Enrollment: 14,593 Coed
Affiliation or Control: State/Local IRS Status: 501(c)3
Highest Offering: Associate Degree
Program: Occupational; 2-Year Principally Bachelor's Creditable
Accreditation: WJ, CAHIIM, MAC

02 President ..... Dr. Deborah J. TRAVIS
05 VP Instruction & Student Learning ..... Mr. Whitney YAMAMURA
11 VP Admin Svcs & Student Support ..... Dr. Donald WALLACE
32 VP Student Svcs/Enrollment Mgmt ..... Ms. Celia ESPOSITO-NOY
84 Dean Student Svcs/Enrollment Mgmt ..... Ms. Christine THOMAS
20 Dean Instruction/Student Learning ..... Dr. Judith BEACHLER
08 Dean Learning Res/College Tech ..... Mr. Stephen MCGLOUGHLIN
38 Dean Counseling & Student Services ..... Dr. Michael MARION
50 Dean Business & Family Science ..... Mr. Jamey NYE
79 Dean Humanities & Social Science ..... Ms. Virginia REYNOLDS
41 Dean Kinesiology & Athletics ..... Ms. Elizabeth BELYEA
81 Dean Science/Math/Engineering ..... Dr. Robert MONTANEZ
72 Dean Careers & Technology ..... Mr. Robert JOHNSON
60 Dean Comm/Visual/Performing Arts ..... Mr. Torence POWELL
45 Dean of College Planning & Research ..... Ms. Katherine MCLAIN
06 Registrar/Admissions & Records ..... Mr. Richard ANDREWS
18 Chief Facilities/Physical Plant ..... Mr. Cory WATHEN
26 Public Information Officer ..... Ms. Kristie WEST

*Folsom Lake College (C)

10 College Parkway, Folsom CA 95630-6798
County: Sacramento FICE Identification: 038713
Unit ID: 444219
Telephone: (916) 608-6500 Carnegie Class: Assoc/Pub-U-MC
FAX Number: (916) 608-6584 Calendar System: Semester
URL: www.flc.losrios.edu
Established: 2004 Annual Undergrad Tuition & Fees (In-District): $1,318
Enrollment: 8,761 Coed
Affiliation or Control: State/Local IRS Status: 501(c)3
Highest Offering: Associate Degree
Program: 2-Year Principally Bachelor's Creditable
Accreditation: WJ

02 President ..... Dr. Rachel ROSENTHAL
11 Vice President Administration ..... Kathleen KIRKLIN
05 Vice President Instruction ..... Dr. David NEWNHAM
32 Vice President Student Services ..... Bryon BELL
88 Executive Director VAPAC ..... David PIER
30 Director College Advancement ..... Sally HOWARD
20 Dean of Instruction ..... Dr. Monica PACTOL
20 Dean of Instruction & Technology ..... Gary HARTLEY
20 Dean of Career & Tech Educ ..... Dr. Stu VAN HORN
20 Dean of Instruction/EDC ..... Dale VAN DAM
20 Dean of Instruction/OIR & VAPA ..... David WILLIAMS
35 Dean of Student Services ..... Aiden ELY
07 Admissions & Records Supervisor ..... Christine WURZER
40 Bookstore Manager ..... Rob MULLIGAN
10 Business Services Supervisor ..... Joany HARMAN
18 Campus Operations Supervisor ..... Colleen JOHNSON
12 Educational Center Supervisor ..... Adrienne ANDREWS
37 Financial Aid Supervisor ..... Ali PADASH
26 Interim Public Information Officer ..... Kristy HART
04 Assistant to the President ..... Beth SPRINKEL
09 Research Analyst ..... Chris OLSON

*Sacramento City College (D)

3835 Freeport Boulevard, Sacramento CA 95822-1386
County: Sacramento FICE Identification: 001233
Unit ID: 122180
Telephone: (916) 558-2111 Carnegie Class: Assoc/Pub-U-MC
FAX Number: (916) 558-2449 Calendar System: Semester
URL: www.scc.losrios.edu
Established: 1916 Annual Undergrad Tuition & Fees (In-State): $1,412
Enrollment: 24,828 Coed
Affiliation or Control: State Related IRS Status: 501(c)3
Highest Offering: Associate Degree
Program: Occupational; 2-Year Principally Bachelor's Creditable
Accreditation: WJ, DA, DH, OTA, PTAA

02 President ..... Dr. Kathryn JEFFERY
05 Vice Pres Instructional Services ..... Dr. Mary TURNER
10 Vice Pres Administrative Services ..... Mr. Robert J. MARTINELLI
32 Vice President Student Services ..... Mr. Michael C. POINTDEXTER
20 Associate Vice Pres Instruction ..... Mr. Rick IDA
20 Associate Vice Pres Instruction ..... Mrs. Julia A. JOLLY
35 Associate Vice Pres Student Svcs ..... Dr. Debra LUFF
13 Dean Information Technology ..... Dr. Elaine ADER
07 Dean Financial Aid/Enrollment ..... Ms. Christine HERNANDEZ
46 Dean Planning/Research/Development ..... Dr. Marybeth BUECHNER
08 Dean Learning Resources ..... Ms. Rhonda RIOS-KRAVITZ
36 Dean Counseling/Student Success ..... Dr. Kimberly MCDANIEL
40 Director College Store ..... Mr. Randy CLEM
66 Director Nursing ..... Ms. Dale S. COHEN
18 Director College Operations ..... Mr. Gregory HAYMAN
26 Director College Advancement ..... Mrs. Mary LELAND
27 Public Information Officer ..... Ms. Amanda DAVIS
76 Dean Science & Allied Health ..... Mr. James COLLINS
50 Dean Business ..... Dr. Deborah SAKS
79 Dean Humanities/Fine Arts ..... Mr. Chris IWATA
88 Dean Languages/Literature ..... Mr. Albert GARCIA
72 Dean Advanced Technology ..... Mrs. Donnetta WEBB
41 Dean PE/Health/Athletics ..... Mr. Mitchell L. CAMPBELL
81 Dean Statistics/Math/Engineering ..... Mrs. Anne LICCIARDI
83 Dean Behavioral & Social Science ..... Dr. Frank MALARET
56 Dean Davis Center Center ..... Mr. Don PALM
56 Interim Dean West Sacramento Ctr ..... Mr. Don PALM

Loyola Marymount University (E)

1 LMU Drive, Los Angeles CA 90045-2659
County: Los Angeles FICE Identification: 011649
Unit ID: 117946
Telephone: (310) 338-2700 Carnegie Class: Master's L
FAX Number: N/A Calendar System: Semester
URL: www.lmu.edu
Established: 1911 Annual Undergrad Tuition & Fees: $40,040
Enrollment: 9,492 Coed
Affiliation or Control: Roman Catholic IRS Status: 501(c)3
Highest Offering: Doctorate
Program: Liberal Arts And General; Teacher Preparatory; Professional
Accreditation: WC, ART, BUS, DANCE, ENG, LAW, MUS, TED, THEA, THEOL

01 President ..... Mr. David W. BURCHAM
00 Chancellor ..... Rev. Patrick J. CAHALAN, SJ
03 Exec Vice President & Provost ..... Dr. Joseph HELLIGE
04 Special Assistant to the President ..... Dr. Joseph LABRIE
05 Vice Provost for Academic Affairs ..... Dr. Michael J. O'SULLIVAN
10 Sr Vice Pres/Chief Financial Ofcr ..... Mr. Tom O. FLEMING
26 Sr Vice Pres University Relations ..... Mr. Dennis SLON
32 Sr Vice Pres for Student Affairs ..... Dr. Elena M. BOVE
11 Sr Vice Pres for Administration ..... Ms. Lynne B. SCARBORO
85 Vice President Intercultural Affs ..... Dr. Abbie ROBINSON-ARMSTRONG
15 Vice President for Human Resources ..... Ms. Rebecca CHANDLER
86 VP for Comm/Government Relations ..... Ms. Kathleen FLANAGAN
84 Vice Provost Enrollment Management ..... Dr. Maureen WEATHERALL
18 Vice Pres Facilities Management ..... Mr. Rick GARCIA
20 Asso Provost Undergraduate Studies ..... Dr. Rae Linda BROWN
21 Vice Pres for Finance/Controller ..... Ms. Lori A. HUSEIN
35 Assoc VP Student Affairs ..... Mr. Marshall SAUCEDA
21 AVP Auxiliary Mgmt & Business Affs ..... Mr. Raymond A. DENNIS
39 Assoc Vice Pres of Student Life ..... Mr. Richard ROCHELEAU
09 Assoc Provost Inst Effectiveness ..... Ms. Margaret KASIMATIS
35 Dean of Students ..... Dr. Linda MCMURDOCK
08 Dean of University Libraries ..... Ms. Kristine BRANCOLINI
06 University Registrar ..... Ms. Kathy REED
61 Dean Loyola Law School/Sr VP ..... Mr. Victor J. GOLD
50 Dean Business Administration ..... Dr. Dennis DRAPER
57 Dean Communication/Fine Arts ..... Dr. Bryant K. ALEXANDER
88 Dean School of Film & TV ..... Prof. Stephen G. UJLAKI
49 Dean Liberal Arts ..... Vacant
54 Dean Science & Engineering ..... Dr. Richard PLUMB
53 Dean School of Education ..... Dr. Shane MARTIN
30 Ex Dir Dev Plnd Gvng/Princpal Gifts ..... Ms. Joanie POHAS
29 Exec Dir Alumni Rels/Annual Giving ..... Ms. Lisa PIUMETTI FARLAND
102 Exec Dir Corporate/Foundation Rels ..... Mr. David A. TILLIPMAN
42 Director of Campus Ministry ..... Rev. James D. ERPS, SJ
07 Director of Admissions ..... Mr. Matthew X. FISSINGER
37 Director of Financial Aid ..... Ms. Catherine GRAHAM
36 Int Dir Career Devel/Placement Svcs ..... Ms. Jade SMITH
23 Medical Director ..... Dr. Daniel HYSLOP
41 Athletic Director ..... Dr. William HUSAK
19 Chief of Public Safety ..... Mr. Hampton CANTRELL
44 Director of Annual Giving ..... Mr. Kevin J. DELANEY
92 Director of Honors Program ..... Dr. John PARRISH
94 Director of Women's Studies ..... Dr. Tracy TIEMEIER
88 Dir Real Estate/Faculty Housing ..... Ms. Kirsten ANDRESEN
38 Dir of Student Counseling ..... Ms. Cassandra L. BAILEY

Marymount California University (F)

30800 Palos Verdes Drive E,
Rancho Palos Verdes CA 90275-6299
County: Los Angeles FICE Identification: 010474
Unit ID: 118541
Telephone: (310) 377-5501 Carnegie Class: Assoc/PrivNFP
FAX Number: (310) 377-6223 Calendar System: Semester
URL: www.marymountcalifornia.edu
Established: 1932 Annual Undergrad Tuition & Fees: $30,694
Enrollment: 1,001 Coed
Affiliation or Control: Roman Catholic IRS Status: 501(c)3
Highest Offering: Baccalaureate
Program: 2-Year Principally Bachelor's Creditable; Liberal Arts And General; Business Emphasis
Accreditation: WC

01 President ..... Dr. Michael S. BROPHY
10 Vice President of Finance ..... Mr. James REEVES
05 Dean of Academic Affairs ..... Dr. Ariane SCHAUER
30 Dean Institutional Advancement ..... Dr. Brenda SOLOMON
84 Vice President Enrollment Mgmt ..... Mr. Barry WARD
07 Asst VP Enr Mgmt/Dir Admissions ..... Mr. Eddie ARTEAGA
32 Dean of Students ..... Ms. Shane ARMSTRONG
20 Associate Academic Officer ..... Ms. Susie MARTIN
08 Librarian ..... Ms. Mary MCMILLAN
37 Director Student Financial Aid ..... Ms. Caterina D'ADAMO
15 Director Personnel Services ..... Ms. Karen THORDARSON
18 Chief Facilities/Physical Plant ..... Mr. Richard SCHULT
26 Chief Public Relations Officer ..... Ms. Kelly CURTIS
29 Director Alumni Relations ..... Ms. Megan MCCORMICK
36 Director Student Placement ..... Dr. Virginia WADE
38 Director Student Counseling ..... Dr. David DRAPER
96 Director of Purchasing ..... Ms. Denise FESSENBECKER
06 Registrar ..... Ms. Paula AVERY
35 Dir Student Life & Engagement ..... Ms. Kelly KRUSEE
09 Director of Institutional Research ..... Mr. Michael SEMENOFF
21 Associate Business Officer ..... Ms. Kathleen RUIZ

The Master's College and Seminary (G)

21726 Placerita Canyon Road,
Santa Clarita CA 91321-1200
County: Los Angeles FICE Identification: 001220
Unit ID: 117751
Telephone: (661) 259-3540 Carnegie Class: Bac/Diverse
FAX Number: N/A Calendar System: Semester
URL: www.masters.edu
Established: 1927 Annual Undergrad Tuition & Fees: $28,880
Enrollment: 1,153 Coed
Affiliation or Control: Independent Non-Profit IRS Status: 501(c)3
Highest Offering: Doctorate
Program: Liberal Arts And General; Teacher Preparatory
Accreditation: WC, MUS

01 President ..... Dr. John MACARTHUR
03 Exec Vice President and Provost ..... Dr. Mark TATLOCK
05 Vice President Academic Affairs ..... Dr. Alex GRANADOS
32 Dean of Student Life ..... Mr. Joe KELLER
58 Vice President Graduate School ..... Dr. Richard L. MAYHUE
11 Vice President of Operations ..... Mr. Bob HOTTON
30 Int Vice President for Development ..... Dr. Mark TATLOCK
46 Vice Pres Institutional Research ..... Dr. John HUGHES
88 Director of Educational Partnership ..... Vacant
10 Chief Financial Officer ..... Mr. Jason HARTUNG
18 Chief of Operations ..... Mr. Jason HARTUNG
06 Registrar ..... Mr. Don GILMORE

08 Director Library Services ..... Mr. John STONE
20 Associate Dean of Students ..... Vacant
07 Director Enrollment ..... Mrs. Hollie JACKSON
41 Athletic Director ..... Mr. Steve WALDECK
37 Director Financial Aid ..... Mr. Gary EDWARDS
35 Director Campus Activities ..... Mr. Peter BARGAS
29 Director Alumni Affairs ..... Mr. Steve CRAWFORD
09 Director of Institutional Research ..... Mr. John M. WALTER
36 Director Student Placement ..... Miss Elise AYDELOTTE
85 International Students Advisor ..... Miss Lisa LAGEORGE

† The Master's Seminary is located at 13248 Roscoe Boulevard, Sun Valley, CA 91352.

Mayfield College (A)

35-325 Date Palm Drive, Suite 101,
Cathedral City CA 92234

County: Riverside
FICE Identification: 041156
Unit ID: 454698
Telephone: (760) 328-5554
Carnegie Class: Not Classified
FAX Number: (760) 328-5357
Calendar System: Semester
URL: mayfieldcollege.org
Established: 1997
Annual Undergrad Tuition & Fees: $12,800
Enrollment: 291
Coed
Affiliation or Control: Proprietary
IRS Status: Proprietary
Highest Offering: Associate Degree
Program: Occupational
Accreditation: COE

01 Campus President ..... Kevin HA

Mendocino College (B)

1000 Hensley Creek Road, Ukiah CA 95482-7821

County: Mendocino
FICE Identification: 011672
Unit ID: 118684
Telephone: (707) 468-3000
Carnegie Class: Assoc/Pub-R-L
FAX Number: (707) 468-3120
Calendar System: Semester
URL: www.mendocino.edu
Established: 1973
Annual Undergrad Tuition & Fees (In-District): $850
Enrollment: 3,790
Coed
Affiliation or Control: State/Local
IRS Status: 501(c)3
Highest Offering: Associate Degree
Program: Occupational; 2-Year Principally Bachelor's Creditable
Accreditation: WJ

01 Superintendent/President ..... Mr. Arturo REYES
05 VP of Education & Student Services ..... Ms. Virginia GULEFF
11 Vice Pres Administrative Services ..... Dr. Larry PERRYMAN
08 Head Librarian ..... Mr. John KOETZNER
20 Dean of Instruction ..... Vacant
35 Dean of Student Services ..... Mr. Cary TEMPLETON
75 Dean Career and Technical Education ..... Ms. Susan GOFF
15 Director Human Resources ..... Ms. Karen CHATY
18 Director Maintenance and Operations ..... Mr. Steve OLIVERIA
26 Director Public Info & Marketing ..... Vacant
32 Director Student Life & Athletics ..... Mr. Mike MARI
21 Director Fiscal Services ..... Ms. Eileen CICHOCKI
14 Director Information Technology .. Ms. Karen CHRISTOPHERSON
09 Director of Institutional Research ..... Vacant
07 Director Admissions/Registrar ..... Ms. Anastasia SIMPSON-LOGG
37 Asst Dean Stdnt Financial Aid/EOPS ..... Ms. Jacquline BRADLEY

Menlo College (C)

1000 El Camino Real, Atherton CA 94027-4301

County: San Mateo
FICE Identification: 001236
Unit ID: 118693
Telephone: (800) 556-3656
Carnegie Class: Bac/Diverse
FAX Number: (650) 543-4085
Calendar System: Semester
URL: www.menlo.edu
Established: 1927
Annual Undergrad Tuition & Fees: $37,100
Enrollment: 681
Coed
Affiliation or Control: Independent Non-Profit
IRS Status: 501(c)3
Highest Offering: Baccalaureate
Program: Liberal Arts And General; Business Emphasis
Accreditation: WC

01 President ..... Dr. James KELLY
05 Provost ..... Dr. James WOOLEVER
03 Executive Vice President ..... Mr. Steven WEINER
84 VP Enrollment Mgmt & Planning ..... Vacant
30 VP for Institutional Advancement ..... Mr. Bill HOPKINS
10 Chief Financial Officer ..... Mr. Nilo VENTURA
20 Dean for Academic Affairs ..... Dr. Dale HOCKSTRA
15 Director of Human Resources ..... Mr. Jay NAIDU
107 Dean of Professional Studies Pgm ..... Dr. James WOOLEVER
18 Director Facilities & Operations ..... Mr. Robert TALBOTT
08 Dean Library Services ..... Dr. William WALTERS
41 Director of Athletics ..... Mr. Keith SPATARO
35 Associate Dean of Student Affairs ..... Ms. Sharyn MOORE
37 Director Office of Financial Aid ..... Ms. Anne HEATON-DUNLAP
36 Director of Career Services ..... Ms. Mary ROBINS
108 Assessment Coordinator ..... Ms. Ivana IZVONAR
21 Controller ..... Ms. Raagini ALI
26 Director of Commun/PR & Marketing ..... Ms. Darcy BLAKE
32 Dean of Student Affairs ..... Ms. Yasmin LAMBIE-SIMPSON
39 Director of Housing ..... Mr. Jessie GUILLIOT
07 Director Office of Admissions ..... Ms. Priscila DE SOUZA
06 Registrar ..... Ms. Cristine RABAGO
29 Director of Alumni Relations ..... Ms. Tina FAIRBAIRN

Merced College (D)

3600 M Street, Merced CA 95348-2898

County: Merced
FICE Identification: 001237
Unit ID: 118718
Telephone: (209) 384-6000
Carnegie Class: Assoc/Pub-R-L
FAX Number: (209) 384-6043
Calendar System: Semester
URL: www.mccd.edu
Established: 1962
Annual Undergrad Tuition & Fees (In-District): $901
Enrollment: 8,534
Coed
Affiliation or Control: State/Local
IRS Status: 501(c)3
Highest Offering: Associate Degree
Program: Occupational; 2-Year Principally Bachelor's Creditable; Business Emphasis
Accreditation: WJ, RAD

01 President ..... Dr. Ron TAYLOR
04 Executive Assistant to President ..... Mrs. Stacey HICKS
05 Interim Vice President Instruction ..... Dr. Kevin KISTLER
32 Interim VP Student Personnel Svcs ..... Dr. Everett LOVELACE
12 Dean Los Banos Campus ..... Dr. Brenda LATHAM
81 Dean Instructional Services ..... Dr. Douglas KAIN
71 Interim Dean Instructional Services ..... Dr. Mike MCCANDLESS
47 Dean Instructional Services ..... Mr. Jim ANDERSEN
50 Dean Instructional Services ..... Dr. Bobby ANDERSON
83 Dean Instructional Services ..... Mr. John ALBANO
103 Dean Instructional Services ..... Mrs. Karyn DOWER
35 Dean of Student Services ..... Dr. Everett LOVELACE
26 Chief Public Relations Officer ..... Mr. Robin SHEPARD
14 Director Info Technology Services ..... Mr. Don PETERSON
18 Dir Maint/Transport/Facilities ..... Mr. Rick SOUHRADA
06 Registrar & Dir Financial Aid ..... Mrs. Sharon REINHARDT
08 Director Learning Resources Center ..... Dr. Susan WALSH
09 Director of Institutional Research ..... Ms. Cherie DAVIS
15 Director of Human Resources ..... Ms. Christina TORRES-PETERS

Methodist Theological Seminary in America (E)

2525 James M Wood Blvd, Los Angeles CA 90006

County: Los Angeles
Identification: 667133
Telephone: (213) 386-0080
Carnegie Class: Not Classified
FAX Number: (213) 386-5229
Calendar System: Semester
URL: www.mtsamerica.com
Established: 1880
Annual Undergrad Tuition & Fees: N/A
Enrollment: N/A
Coed
Affiliation or Control: Independent Non-Profit
IRS Status: 501(c)3
Highest Offering: Master's
Program: Religious Emphasis
Accreditation: @BI

01 President ..... Dr. Ki Hyung HAN

Mills College (F)

5000 MacArthur Boulevard, Oakland CA 94613-1301

County: Alameda
FICE Identification: 001238
Unit ID: 118888
Telephone: (510) 430-2255
Carnegie Class: Master's M
FAX Number: (510) 430-3314
Calendar System: Semester
URL: www.mills.edu
Established: 1852
Annual Undergrad Tuition & Fees: $41,458
Enrollment: 1,546
Female
Affiliation or Control: Independent Non-Profit
IRS Status: 501(c)3
Highest Offering: Doctorate
Program: Liberal Arts And General; Teacher Preparatory
Accreditation: WC

01 President ..... Ms. Alecia A. DECOUDREAUX
05 Provost & Dean of the Faculty ..... Dr. Kimberley L. PHILLIPS
10 VP Finance & Administration ..... Dr. Tammi JACKSON
26 VP for Opers/Chief Public Rels Ofcr ..... Ms. Renee JADUSHLEVER
30 VP for Institutional Advancement ... Dr. Cynthia BRANDT STOVER
43 Vice President & General Counsel ..... Vacant
20 Associate Provost ..... Dr. David DONAHUE
16 Chief HR Officer & Career Svcs Dir ..... Dr. Lesa HAMMOND
84 VP for Enrollment Management ..... Mr. Brian O'ROURKE
32 VP Student Life/Dean of Students ..... Dr. Eloise STIGLITZ
21 Assoc VP for Student Fin/Admin Svcs ..... Vacant
07 Director of Undergraduate Admission ..... Vacant
09 Dir Acad Assess/Inst Research/Plng ..... Dr. Alice B. KNUDSEN
101 Secretary of Board of Trustees ..... Dr. Marianne SHELDON
06 Registrar ..... Ms. Jennifer FULLER
18 Associate VP of Operations ..... Ms. Linda ZITZNER
38 Assoc Dean/Dir Counsel/Psych Svcs ..... Ms. Dorian NEWTON
41 Director of Athletics ..... Ms. Themy ADACHI
29 Exec Director of Alumnae Relations ..... Ms. Laura GOBBI

MiraCosta Community College District (G)

One Barnard Drive, Oceanside CA 92056-3899

County: San Diego
FICE Identification: 001239
Unit ID: 118912
Telephone: (760) 757-2121
Carnegie Class: Assoc/Pub-S-MC
FAX Number: (760) 795-6609
Calendar System: Semester
URL: www.miracosta.edu
Established: 1934
Annual Undergrad Tuition & Fees (In-District): $1,336
Enrollment: 14,732
Coed
Affiliation or Control: State/Local
IRS Status: 501(c)3
Highest Offering: Associate Degree
Program: Occupational; 2-Year Principally Bachelor's Creditable
Accreditation: WJ, SURGT

01 Superintendent/President ..... Dr. Francisco RODRIGUEZ
04 Exec Assistant to Supt/President ..... Ms. Evelyn DALBY
04 Exec Assistant to Supt/President ..... Ms. Jeanne SWANSON
05 Vice President Instructional Svcs ..... Ms. Mary BENARD
32 Vice President Student Services ..... Dr. Richard J. ROBERTSON
10 Vice President Business/Admin Svcs ..... Mr. Charles NG
12 Dean San Elijo Campus-Letters/Comm ..... Ms. Dana SMITH
20 Dean Academic Information Svcs ..... Mr. Mario VALENTE
38 Dean Counseling/Student Develop ..... Ms. Wendy STEWART
07 Dean Admissions/Student Support ..... Mr. Gilbert HERMOSILLO
88 Associate Dean San Elijo Campus ..... Ms. Nikki SCHAPER
51 Interim Dean Community Education ..... Dr. Alketa WOJCIK
49 Dean Arts/Intl Languages ..... Mr. Jonathan FOHRMAN
81 Dean Math/Sciences ..... Mr. Carlos LOPEZ
75 Dean Career/Technical Education ..... Dr. Al TACCONE
88 Director Small Business Dev Ctr ..... Mr. Sudershan SHAUNAK
31 Director Community Services ..... Ms. Linda KUROKAWA
06 Registrar ..... Ms. Alicia TERRY
09 Director Institutional Research ..... Ms. Kimberly COUTTS
26 Director Marketing/Communications ..... Ms. Cheryl BROOM
102 Director Foundation/Fund Devel ..... Ms. Linda FOGERSON
18 Director Facilities ..... Mr. Tom MACIAS
37 Interim Director Financial Aid ..... Ms. Cindy SILBERBERGER
88 Director Risk Management ..... Mr. Joseph MAZZA
88 Director Cashiering Services ..... Ms. Jo FERRIS
15 Director Human Resources ..... Ms. Sheri WRIGHT
36 Director Career Center ..... Ms. Donna DAVIS
88 Director Transfer Center ..... Ms. Lise FLOCKEN
96 Director Purchasing/Material Mgmt ..... Ms. Susan ASATO
88 Director Retention Services ..... Dr. Edward POEHLERT
21 Director Fiscal Services ..... Ms. Myeisha ARMSTRONG
19 Director Campus Police ..... Chief Robert NORCROSS
106 Director Online Education ..... Dr. James JULIUS

Monterey Institute of International Studies (H)

460 Pierce Street, Monterey CA 93940-2691

Telephone: (831) 647-4100
FICE Identification: 001241
Accreditation: &EH, BUS, CEA

† Main campus is Middlebury College in Middlebury, VT.

Monterey Peninsula College (I)

980 Fremont Street, Monterey CA 93940-4799

County: Monterey
FICE Identification: 001242
Unit ID: 119067
Telephone: (831) 646-4000
Carnegie Class: Assoc/Pub-R-L
FAX Number: (831) 655-2627
Calendar System: Semester
URL: www.mpc.edu
Established: 1947
Annual Undergrad Tuition & Fees (In-District): $1,264
Enrollment: 4,778
Coed
Affiliation or Control: State/Local
IRS Status: 501(c)3
Highest Offering: Associate Degree
Program: Occupational; 2-Year Principally Bachelor's Creditable
Accreditation: WJ, ADNUR

01 Superintendent/President ..... Dr. Walter TRIBLEY
05 Vice President Academic Affairs ..... Dr. Celine PINET
11 Vice Pres Administrative Services ..... Mr. Stephen MA
32 Interim Vice Pres Student Services ..... Mr. Marty JOHNSON
20 Dean Instruction ..... Ms. Laura FRANKLIN
45 Dean Instructional Planning ..... Mr. Michael GILMARTIN
15 Associate Dean of Human Resources ..... Ms. Barbara LEE
35 Dean of Student Services ..... Mr. Larry WALKER
09 Director of Institutional Research ..... Dr. Rosaleen RYAN
06 Director of Admissions & Records ..... Ms. Nicole DUNNE
08 Librarian ..... Ms. Deborah RUIZ
37 Financial Aid Officer ..... Vacant
41 Athletic Director ..... Mr. Lyndon SCHUTZLER
18 Facilities Operations Supervisor ..... Mr. Pete OLSEN
26 Public Relations Officer ..... Vacant
96 Purchasing Agent ..... Ms. Mary WEBER

Mount St. Mary's College (J)

12001 Chalon Road, Los Angeles CA 90049-1599

County: Los Angeles
FICE Identification: 001243
Unit ID: 119173
Telephone: (310) 954-4000
Carnegie Class: Master's S
FAX Number: (310) 954-4379
Calendar System: Semester
URL: www.msmc.la.edu
Established: 1925
Annual Undergrad Tuition & Fees: $32,882
Enrollment: 3,166
Female
Affiliation or Control: Roman Catholic
IRS Status: 501(c)3
Highest Offering: Doctorate
Program: Occupational; 2-Year Principally Bachelor's Creditable; Liberal Arts And General; Teacher Preparatory; Professional
Accreditation: WC, NURSE, PTA

01 President ..... Dr. Ann MCELANEY-JOHNSON
05 Provost ..... Dr. Wendy MCCREDIE
30 Vice Pres Institutional Advancement ..... Dr. Stephanie CUBBA
10 Vice Pres Administration & Finance ..... Mr. Chris MCALARY
13 VP Info Support Svcs/Enroll Mgmt ..... Mr. Larry SMITH
32 Vice President Student Affairs ..... Dr. Jane LINGUA
20 Assistant Provost ..... Vacant
09 Asst VP Inst Planning & Research ..... Dr. Heather BROWN
35 Asst VP Student Affairs ..... Ms. Bernadette ROBERT
58 Graduate Dean ..... Dr. Linda MOODY
55 Dean of Weekend College ..... Mr. Merrill RODIN

84 Director Enrollment Management ....Mr. Dean KILGOUR
06 Registrar ....Ms. Rocio DELEON
26 Director of Public Relations ....Ms. Debbie REAM
15 Director of Human Resources ....Ms. Susan LUSK
18 Director of Facilities Mgmt ....Ms. Barbara TELL
37 Director of Student Financing ....Ms. La Royce HOUSLEY
08 Director of MSMC Libraries ....Ms. Claudia REED
28 Director of Diversity ....Dr. Pam HALDEMAN
29 Director Alumni Relations ....Ms. Elizabeth ROBLES
38 Director Student Counseling ....Dr. Susan SALEM
07 Director of Admissions ....Vacant
36 Director Career Services ....Ms. Marlene SIMON

Mt. San Antonio College (A)

1100 N Grand, Walnut CA 91789-1399
County: Los Angeles FICE Identification: 001245
Unit ID: 119164
Telephone: (909) 594-5611 Carnegie Class: Assoc/Pub-S-SC
FAX Number: (909) 598-2303 Calendar System: Semester
URL: www.mtsac.edu
Established: 1946 Annual Undergrad Tuition & Fees (In-District): $1,346
Enrollment: 34,351 Coed
Affiliation or Control: State/Local IRS Status: 501(c)3
Highest Offering: Associate Degree
Program: Occupational; 2-Year Principally Bachelor's Creditable
Accreditation: WJ, COARC, EMT, HT, RAD

01 President/CEO ....Dr. William T. SCROGGINS
05 Vice President Instruction ....Dr. Irene MALMGREN
11 Vice President Administrative Svcs ....Mr. Michael D. GREGORYK
32 Vice President Student Services ....Dr. Audrey YAMAGATA-NOJI
15 Vice President Human Resources ....Mr. James CZAJA
20 Dean Instructional Services ....Ms. Terri LONG
35 Dean Student Services ....Ms. Carolyn KEYS
08 Dean Library/Learning Resources ....Ms. Meghan CHEN
38 Dean Counseling ....Mr. Tom MAUCH
13 Chief Technology Officer/Info Tech ....Mr. Victor BELINSKI
84 Dean Enrollment Management ....Dr. George BRADSHAW
21 Assoc Vice Pres Fiscal Services ....Ms. Rosa ROYCE
102 Executive Director of Foundation ....Mr. Bill LAMBERT
37 Director Financial Aid ....Ms. Chau DAO
46 Director Grants ....Ms. Adrienne PRICE
26 Director Marketing & Public Affairs ....Mr. Clarence BROWN
09 Dir Research & Inst Effectiveness ....Ms. Barbara MCNEICE-STALLARD
18 Director Facilities Planning & Mgmt ....Mr. Gary NELLESEN
35 Director Student Life ....Dr. Maryann TOLANO-LEVEQUE
36 Director Career & Transfer Services ....Ms. Heidi LOCKHART
96 Int Purchasing Manager ....Ms. Teresa PATTERSON
50 Dean Business Division ....Dr. Joumana MCGOWAN
68 Dean Physical Education ....Mr. Joe JENNUM
79 Dean Humanities & Social Science ....Mr. Jim JENKINS
72 Dean Tech/Health Science ....Dr. Sarah DAUM
65 Int Dean Natural Sciences ....Mr. Matthew JUDD
57 Dean Arts ....Dr. Susan LONG
51 Dean Continuing Education ....Ms. Donna BURNS

Mt. San Jacinto College (B)

1499 N State Street, San Jacinto CA 92583-2399
County: Riverside FICE Identification: 001246
Unit ID: 119216
Telephone: (951) 487-6752 Carnegie Class: Assoc/Pub-S-MC
FAX Number: (951) 654-9712 Calendar System: Semester
URL: www.msjc.edu
Established: 1962 Annual Undergrad Tuition & Fees (In-District): $1,100
Enrollment: 13,165 Coed
Affiliation or Control: State/Local IRS Status: 501(c)3
Highest Offering: Associate Degree
Program: Occupational; 2-Year Principally Bachelor's Creditable
Accreditation: WJ

01 Superintendent/President ....Dr. Roger W. SCHULTZ
100 Director President's Office ....Ms. Kathy S. DONNELL
05 Int Vice Pres Instructional Svcs ....Dr. Patrick SCHWERDTFEGER
32 Vice President Student Services ....Dr. William K. VINCENT
35 Dean Student Services ....Ms. JoAnna QUEJADA
10 Vice President Business Svcs ....Ms. Becky ELAM
16 Vice President of Human Resources ....Ms. Irma RAMOS
18 Supervisor Maint & Operations ....Mr. Brian TWITTY
19 Chief of Police ....Vacant
20 Dean of Academic Programs ....Dr. Richard ROWLEY
20 Dean of Academic Programs - SJC ....Dr. Carlos TOVARES
21 Interim Dean of Business Services ....Mr. Wade ELLIS
72 Dean Instruct Acad Success/Tech ....Ms. Patricia JAMES
13 Interim Dean of Information Tech ....Mr. Brian ORLAUSKI
41 Dean of Athletics ....Mr. Patrick SPRINGER
38 Dean Counseling/Stdnt Sppt Svcs ....Mr. Tom SPILLMAN
56 Dean of Off-Site Programs ....Mrs. Laurie MCLAUGHLIN
103 Dean Career Education ....Ms. Joyce JOHNSON
27 Public Information Officer ....Ms. Karin MARRIOTT
09 Associate Dean of Research ....Mr. Charles HAWKINS
37 Supervisor Financial Aid ....Ms. Shanae WILLIAMS
84 Assoc Dean Enrollment Mgmt ....Ms. Susan LOOMIS
88 Assoc Dean Institutional Planning ....Ms. Rebecca TEAGUE
102 Foundation Director ....Vacant
66 Dean of Nursing and Allied Health ....Dr. Kathleen WINSTON
96 Assoc Dean Purchasing ....Ms. Teri SISCO

Mount Sierra College (C)

101 E Huntington Drive, Monrovia CA 91016-3414
County: Los Angeles FICE Identification: 031287
Unit ID: 398130
Telephone: (626) 873-2144 Carnegie Class: Bac/Diverse
FAX Number: (626) 359-5961 Calendar System: Quarter
URL: www.mtsierra.edu
Established: 1991 Annual Undergrad Tuition & Fees: $21,000
Enrollment: 548 Coed
Affiliation or Control: Proprietary IRS Status: Proprietary
Highest Offering: Baccalaureate
Program: Occupational; Professional
Accreditation: ACCSC

01 Campus Director ....Ms. Kristin STABB
03 Vice President ....Mr. John DAVIS
11 Chief Operating Officer ....Mr. Z. Greg KAHWAJIAN
07 Director of Admissions ....Mr. Patrick AZADIAN
37 Director of Student Accounts ....Ms. Joyce BOYLAN
06 Registrar ....Ms. Jeanette ANDERSON

MTI College (D)

5221 Madison Avenue, Sacramento CA 95841-3037
County: Sacramento FICE Identification: 012912
Unit ID: 118198
Telephone: (916) 339-1500 Carnegie Class: Assoc/PrivFP
FAX Number: (916) 339-0305 Calendar System: Quarter
URL: www.mticollege.edu
Established: 1965 Annual Undergrad Tuition & Fees: $24,125
Enrollment: 864 Coed
Affiliation or Control: Proprietary IRS Status: Proprietary
Highest Offering: Associate Degree
Program: Occupational
Accreditation: WJ

01 President ....Mr. John A. ZIMMERMAN
10 Vice Pres/Chief Financial Officer ....Mr. David W. ALLEN

Musicians Institute (E)

6752 Hollywood Boulevard, Hollywood CA 90028
County: Los Angeles FICE Identification: 021618
Unit ID: 119270
Telephone: (323) 462-1384 Carnegie Class: Spec/Arts
FAX Number: (323) 462-6978 Calendar System: Quarter
URL: www.mi.edu
Established: 1977 Annual Undergrad Tuition & Fees: $23,175
Enrollment: 1,259 Coed
Affiliation or Control: Proprietary IRS Status: Proprietary
Highest Offering: Baccalaureate
Program: Occupational; 2-Year Principally Bachelor's Creditable; Professional; Music Emphasis
Accreditation: MUS

01 President ....Mr. Hisatake SHIBUYA
03 Executive Vice President ....Mr. Jose FERRO
05 VP Instruction & Curricular Dev ....Mr. Donny GRUENDLER
05 VP Academic Affairs ....Mr. Jon CLAYDEN
06 Dean Compliance and Articulation ....Mr. Tom ENGFER

Napa Valley College (F)

2277 Napa-Vallejo Highway, Napa CA 94558-6236
County: Napa FICE Identification: 001247
Unit ID: 119331
Telephone: (707) 256-7000 Carnegie Class: Assoc/Pub-U-MC
FAX Number: (707) 253-3015 Calendar System: Semester
URL: www.napavalley.edu
Established: 1942 Annual Undergrad Tuition & Fees (In-District): $1,177
Enrollment: 6,287 Coed
Affiliation or Control: State/Local IRS Status: 501(c)3
Highest Offering: Associate Degree
Program: Occupational; 2-Year Principally Bachelor's Creditable
Accreditation: WJ, COARC, EMT

01 Superintendent/President ....Dr. Ronald D. KRAFT
10 Vice President Business & Finance ....Vacant
05 Int Vice President Instruction ....Ms. Faye SMYLE
32 Vice President Student Services ....Mr. Oscar DE HARO
15 Dean Human Resources ....Ms. Laura ECKLIN
103 Interim Dean of Instruction ....Mr. Jerry SOMERVILLE
08 Dean Library/Learning Resource Ctr ....Ms. Rebecca SCOTT
37 Dean Fin Aid/EOPS/Pre-Col TRIO Pgms ....Ms. Patricia MORGAN
103 Dean Workforce Devel/Career ....Mr. Gregory MIRAGLIA
13 Dean Institutional Technology ....Mr. Robert BUTLER
12 Assoc Dean Upper Valley Campus ....Ms. Judi WATKINS
07 Assoc Dean Admissions/Records ....Ms. Jessica MILLIKAN
18 Dir Camp Plng/Constr/Risk Mgmt Svcs ....Mr. Daniel J. TERAVEST
102 Exec Director NVC Foundation ....Ms. Melissa GIBBS
38 Division Chair Counseling ....Mr. Jose HURTADO
26 Director Community Relations ....Ms. Betty M. MALMGREN
19 Director College Police ....Mr. Kenneth L. ARNOLD
18 Director Facilities ....Mr. Matt CHRISTENSEN
09 Director Institutional Research ....Ms. Robyn WORNALL
29 Assoc Dir Alumni & Annual Fund Dev ....Ms. Kathy BAIRD
40 Bookstore Manager ....Vacant
96 Business Services Assistant ....Ms. Solange KADA
84 Enrollment Management ....Ms. Sue NELSON
88 Counselor/Coord Trans Center ....Ms. Gwen KELL
36 Counselor/Coordinator WA III ....Ms. Natalie BRADLEY

National Career College (G)

6850 Van Nuys Blvd Ste 300, Van Nuys CA 91405
County: Los Angeles FICE Identification: 041460
Unit ID: 455868
Telephone: (818) 988-2300 Carnegie Class: Not Classified
FAX Number: (818) 988-9944 Calendar System: Semester
URL: www.nccusa.edu
Established: 2005 Annual Undergrad Tuition & Fees: $19,680
Enrollment: 65 Coed
Affiliation or Control: Proprietary IRS Status: Proprietary
Highest Offering: Associate Degree
Program: Occupational
Accreditation: ABHES

01 President ....Gayane KHANOYAN

The National Hispanic University (H)

14271 Story Road, San Jose CA 95127-3823
County: Santa Clara FICE Identification: 025184
Unit ID: 119544
Telephone: (408) 254-6900 Carnegie Class: Bac/A&S
FAX Number: (408) 254-1369 Calendar System: 4/1/4
URL: www.nhu.edu
Established: 1981 Annual Undergrad Tuition & Fees: $9,870
Enrollment: 787 Coed
Affiliation or Control: Proprietary IRS Status: Proprietary
Highest Offering: Master's
Program: 2-Year Principally Bachelor's Creditable; Liberal Arts And General; Teacher Preparatory; Business Emphasis
Accreditation: WC

01 President ....Dr. David P. LOPEZ
05 Provost ....Dr. Gladys ATO
03 Vice President Campus Operations ....Mr. Jorge ESCOBAR
10 Vice President/Gen Mgr/Bus Operat ....Dr. Gary BURKHOLDER
06 Registrar ....Ms. Pamela BUSTILLO
84 Director of Enrollment ....Mr. Augustin CERVANTES
77 Director Computer Science ....Dr. Julio GARCIA
09 Director Institutional Research ....Dr. Isabel VALLEJO
37 Director Student Financial Aid ....Mr. Diondrae COLLIER
07 Manager Admissions ....Mr. Jesus MORALES
81 Int Pgm Dir Mathematics & Science ....Ms. Cynthia WAMBSGANS
88 Int Chair Childhood Development ....Dr. Gladys ATO
97 Chair Liberal Studies ....Dr. Carlos NAVARRO
53 Chair of Teacher Education ....Ms. Neva HOFEMANN
50 Chair of Business Administration ....Dr. George GUIM

National Test Pilot School (I)

PO Box 658, Mojave CA 93502-0658
County: Kern Identification: 667009
Telephone: (661) 824-2977 Carnegie Class: Not Classified
FAX Number: (661) 824-2943 Calendar System: Semester
URL: www.ntps.edu
Established: 1981 Annual Graduate Tuition & Fees: $915,000
Enrollment: N/A Coed
Affiliation or Control: Independent Non-Profit IRS Status: 501(c)3
Highest Offering: Master's; No Undergraduates
Program: Professional; Technical Emphasis
Accreditation: ENG

01 President/CEO ....Dr. Al L. PETERSON
05 Director NTPS ....Mr. Gregory V. LEWIS
10 Director of Business Operations ....Mike HILL
54 Director NFTI ....Dr. Lester A. INGHAM
107 Deputy Director Systems ....Mr. Bob MC SHEA
107 Deputy Director P&FQ ....Mr. Ed SOLSKI
11 Chief of Operations ....Mr. Nicola PECILE

National University (J)

11255 N Torrey Pines Road, La Jolla CA 92037-1011
County: San Diego FICE Identification: 011460
Unit ID: 119605
Telephone: (858) 642-8000 Carnegie Class: Master's L
FAX Number: (858) 642-8714 Calendar System: Other
URL: www.nu.edu
Established: 1971 Annual Undergrad Tuition & Fees: $18,144
Enrollment: 17,898 Coed
Affiliation or Control: Independent Non-Profit IRS Status: 501(c)3
Highest Offering: Master's
Program: 2-Year Principally Bachelor's Creditable; Liberal Arts And General; Teacher Preparatory; Professional
Accreditation: WC, ANEST, IACBE, NURSE, PH

01 University President ....Dr. Michael R. CUNNINGHAM
05 Interim Provost ....Ms. Debra BEAN
11 Vice Chancellor Business & Admin ....Mr. Randy C. FRISCH
20 Interim Associate Provost ....Dr. Dee FABRY
32 Vice President for Student Services ....Dr. Joseph ZAVALA
13 Vice President of Info Technology ....Mr. Christopher KRUG
07 Vice Chancellor of Marketing ....Ms. Ginny BENEKE
30 VP of Dev & Alumni Relations ....Vacant
09 Director Inst Research & Assess ....Mr. Jonathon CHILLAS
12 VP Regional Operations ....Mr. Daren UPHAM
12 AVP Regional Oper LAX Region ....Dr. Mahvash YADEGAR
15 AVP Human Resources ....Dr. Alan HONEYCUTT
12 AVP Regional Oper Northern Region ....Mr. Brandon JOUGANATOS
12 AVP Military and VA Programs ....Mr. Vernon TAYLOR

50 Dean School Business & Management .... Dr. Ronald UHLIG
53 Dean School of Education .... Dr. Don CHU
54 Dean School Engineer/Tech & Media .... Dr. John CICERO
49 Dean College of Letters & Sciences .... Dr. Carol RICHARDSON
76 Dean Health and Human Services .... Dr. Gloria J. MCNEAL
06 Registrar .... Ms. Veronica GARCIA
27 Director Communications .... Mr. Michael BURGOS
08 Director Library Services .... Ms. Anne-Marie SECORD
37 Director Financial Aid .... Ms. Valerie RYAN
26 Dir Information/Community Relations .... Mr. David NEVILLE
18 Director of Facilities .... Mr. Craig CROSBY
88 Director of Credentials .... Mr. Brad DAMON

New Charter University (A)

543 Howard Street, 5th Floor, San Francisco CA 94105
FICE Identification: 041292
Unit ID: 420361
Telephone: (415) 813-5970 Carnegie Class: Not Classified
FAX Number: (415) 813-5980 Calendar System: Trimester
URL: www.new.edu
Established: 1994 Annual Undergrad Tuition & Fees: $2,632
Enrollment: 510 Coed
Affiliation or Control: Proprietary IRS Status: Proprietary
Highest Offering: Master's
Program: Liberal Arts And General; Business Emphasis
Accreditation: DETC

00 CEO .... Dr. Salvatore MONACO
01 President .... Dr. Karen BALDESCHWIELER
05 Academic Dean .... Ms. Diane JOHNSON
06 Senior Registrar .... Ms. Tamica WARD
53 Dean General Education/Liberal Arts .... Dr. Trevor BELCHER

New York Film Academy, Los Angeles (B)

4444 Lakeside Drive, Burbank CA 91505
County: Burbank FICE Identification: 041188
Unit ID: 470269
Telephone: (818) 295-2020 Carnegie Class: Not Classified
FAX Number: (818) 295-2049 Calendar System: Semester
URL: www.nyfa.edu
Established: 2006 Annual Undergrad Tuition & Fees: $42,000
Enrollment: 874 Coed
Affiliation or Control: Proprietary IRS Status: Proprietary
Highest Offering: Master's
Program: Fine Arts Emphasis
Accreditation: ART

05 Provost .... Mr. Michael YOUNG
20 Academic Dean .... Mr. Sonny CALDERON
11 Senior Director .... Ms. Jean SHERLOCK

NewSchool of Architecture and Design (C)

1249 F Street, San Diego CA 92101-6634
County: San Diego FICE Identification: 030439
Unit ID: 119775
Telephone: (619) 684-8800 Carnegie Class: Spec/Arts
FAX Number: (619) 684-8880 Calendar System: Quarter
URL: www.newschoolarch.edu
Established: 1980 Annual Undergrad Tuition & Fees: $24,411
Enrollment: 570 Coed
Affiliation or Control: Proprietary IRS Status: Proprietary
Highest Offering: Master's
Program: Professional
Accreditation: @WC, ACICS

01 President .... Vacant
05 Provost .... Mr. Henri DE HAHN
10 Dean of Academic & Student Affairs .... Dr. Linda THOMAS-MOBLEY
32 Director of Domus Academy at NSAD .... Dr. Elena PACENTI
58 Director of Graduate Programs .... Mr. Kurt HUNKER
48 Chair Undergraduate Architecture .... Mr. Len ZEGARSKI
88 Chair Construction Management .... Mr. George WELCH
88 Chair Digital Media Arts .... Ms. Linda SELLHEIM
97 Director General Education Programs .... Mr. Bruce MATTHES
09 Director of Institutional Research .... Ms. Nga PHAN
21 Finance Manager .... Mr. Minh NGUYEN
06 Registrar .... Ms. Maureen QUINLAN
07 Director Field Enrollment .... Mr. John KIM
07 Director Enrollment .... Ms. Dahlia NAJOR
37 Director Financial Aid .... Mr. Mike NELSON
38 Director Advising .... Ms. Laura WILSON
36 Director Career Services .... Ms. Ellyn LESTER
07 Admissions Manager .... Ms. La'Shea ENGLISH
21 Business Services Manager .... Ms. Terre CORTEZ-FARAH
35 Student Life Manager .... Ms. Ashley WAGNER
08 Librarian .... Ms. Lucy CAMPBELL
04 Faculty Coordinator .... Mr. Robin BRISEBOIS
27 Marketing Manager .... Ms. Lisa APOLINSKI
26 Public Relations Manager .... Ms. Anna CEARLEY
35 Student Success Manager .... Ms. Virginia PHILLIPS
18 Facilities Manager .... Mr. Ba LE
88 Materials Lab Manager .... Mr. Erik LUHTALA

*North Orange County Community College District (D)

1830 W Romneya Drive, Anaheim CA 92801-1819
County: Orange FICE Identification: 009742
Unit ID: 120023
Telephone: (714) 808-4500 Carnegie Class: N/A
FAX Number: (714) 808-4791
URL: www.nocccd.edu

01 Chancellor .... Dr. Ned DOFFONEY
10 Vice Chancellor Finance/Facilities .... Mr. Fred WILLIAMS
15 Vice Chancellor Human Resources .... Mr. Jeff O. HORSLEY
05 Vice Chancellor of Instruction .... Vacant
13 District Director Information Svcs .... Ms. Deborah LUDFORD
04 Exec Admin Aide to Chancellor .... Ms. Violet R. AYON
26 District Dir Public & Govt Affairs .... Ms. Kai STEARNS MOORE
22 Dist Director Equity & Diversity .... Mr. Kenneth I. ROBINSON

*Cypress College (E)

9200 Valley View, Cypress CA 90630-5897
County: Orange FICE Identification: 001193
Unit ID: 113236
Telephone: (714) 484-7000 Carnegie Class: Assoc/Pub-S-MC
FAX Number: (714) 527-8238 Calendar System: Semester
URL: www.cypresscollege.edu
Established: 1966 Annual Undergrad Tuition & Fees (In-District): $1,136
Enrollment: 15,144 Coed
Affiliation or Control: State/Local IRS Status: 501(c)3
Highest Offering: Associate Degree
Program: Occupational; 2-Year Principally Bachelor's Creditable
Accreditation: WJ, ADNUR, CAHIIM, DA, DH, DMS, FUSER, RAD

02 President .... Dr. Robert G. SIMPSON
03 Executive Vice President .... Dr. Santanu BANDYOPADHYAY
11 Vice Pres of Administrative Svcs .... Ms. Karen CANT
08 Dean Language Arts/Lib/Lrng Res Ctr .... Mr. Eldon YOUNG
38 Dean Cnslg/Stdnt Dev/Admiss/Records .... Mr. Paul DEDIOS
06 Registrar .... Ms. Regina FORD
26 Public Relations Officer .... Mr. Marc POSNER
102 Exec Dir Foundation/Community Devel .... Mr. Raul ALVAREZ
32 Dean Student Support Services .... Dr. Richard RAMS
88 Director Disabled Student Services .... Vacant
90 Manager Systems Technology Svcs .... Mr. Michael KAVANAUGH
37 Manager Financial Aid .... Mr. Keith COBB
84 Matriculation Manager .... Vacant
09 Dir Institutional Research/Planning .... Vacant
18 Director Physical Plant/Facilities .... Mr. Albert MIRANDA
19 Director Campus Security .... Ms. Shirley SMITH
04 Executive Assistant to President .... Ms. Patricia HUMPRES
68 Interim Dean Physical Education .... Dr. Richard RAMS
57 Dean Fine Arts .... Ms. Joyce CARRIGAN
50 Dean Business/CIS .... Mr. Dave WASSENAAR
83 Dean Social Sciences .... Ms. Nina DEMARKEY
53 Dean Science Engineering & Math .... Dr. Richard FEE

*Fullerton College (F)

321 E Chapman Avenue, Fullerton CA 92832-2095
County: Orange FICE Identification: 001201
Unit ID: 114859
Telephone: (714) 992-7000 Carnegie Class: Assoc/Pub-S-MC
FAX Number: (714) 992-9930 Calendar System: Semester
URL: www.fullcoll.edu
Established: 1913 Annual Undergrad Tuition & Fees (In-District): $1,138
Enrollment: 20,885 Coed
Affiliation or Control: State/Local IRS Status: 501(c)3
Highest Offering: Associate Degree
Program: Occupational; 2-Year Principally Bachelor's Creditable; Liberal Arts And General
Accreditation: WJ

02 President .... Dr. Rajen VURDIEN
05 Vice President Instruction .... Dr. Terry GIUGNI
32 Vice President Student Services .... Dr. Toni DUBOIS
11 Vice President Administrative Svcs .... Ms. Claudette DAIN
50 Dean Business & CIS .... Dr. Ann HOVEY
57 Dean Fine Arts .... Mr. Robert JENSEN
79 Dean Humanities .... Mr. Dan WILLOUGHBY
81 Dean Math/Computer Science .... Mr. Mark GREENHALGH
88 Interim Dean Natural Sciences .... Mr. Mark GREENHALGH
68 Dean Physical Education .... Mr. David GROSSMAN
83 Dean Social Sciences .... Mr. Daniel TESAR
72 Dean Technology & Engr .... Mr. Scott MCKENZIE
37 Director of Financial Aid .... Mr. Greg RYAN
23 Director Health Services .... Vacant
18 Dir Facilities/Physical Plant .... Vacant
40 Director of Bookstore .... Mr. Nick KARVIA
88 Dean Student Support Services .... Mr. Robert MIRANDA
35 Director Student Affairs .... Ms. Darlene JENSEN
06 Registrar .... Ms. Rena MARTINEZ STLUKA
19 Director Campus Safety .... Mr. Steve SELBY
38 Dean Counseling/Student Development .... Ms. Lisa CAMPBELL
08 Interim Dean Library Services .... Mr. Dan TESAR
07 Dean Admissions & Records .... Mr. Albert ABUTIN
90 Academic Computing Technologies .... Mr. Co HO
09 Director of Institutional Research .... Dr. Jamail CARTER
88 Director Transfer Center .... Ms. Cecilia ARRIAZA
26 Public Information Officer .... Ms. Andrea HANSTEIN
04 Exec Assistant to the President .... Ms. Shannon BOWMAN

Northwestern Polytechnic University (G)

47671 Westinghouse Drive, Fremont CA 94539-7474
County: Alameda Identification: 666759
Unit ID: 120166
Telephone: (510) 592-9688 Carnegie Class: Spec/Engg
FAX Number: (510) 657-8975 Calendar System: Trimester
URL: www.npu.edu
Established: 1984 Annual Undergrad Tuition & Fees: $12,600
Enrollment: 708 Coed
Affiliation or Control: Independent Non-Profit IRS Status: 501(c)3
Highest Offering: Master's
Program: Technical Emphasis
Accreditation: ACICS

01 President .... Dr. George HSIEH
05 Dean of Academic Affairs .... Dr. Pochang HSU
07 Director of Admissions .... Ms. Monica SINHA
06 Registrar .... Ms. Lily HSIAO
10 Director of Business Affairs .... Dr. Bill WU
46 Director of Institutional Research .... Dr. Tai HSU
15 Director Personnel Services .... Ms. Linda REN
18 Chief Facilities/Physical Plant .... Mr. Dennis YU
32 Director Student Affairs .... Ms. Wen HSIEH
38 Director Student Counseling .... Dr. Mariam GHAZVINI

Notre Dame de Namur University (H)

1500 Ralston Avenue, Belmont CA 94002-1908
County: San Mateo FICE Identification: 001179
Unit ID: 120184
Telephone: (650) 508-3500 Carnegie Class: Master's M
FAX Number: (650) 508-3660 Calendar System: Semester
URL: www.ndnu.edu
Established: 1851 Annual Undergrad Tuition & Fees: $30,806
Enrollment: 2,065 Coed
Affiliation or Control: Independent Non-Profit IRS Status: 501(c)3
Highest Offering: Master's
Program: Liberal Arts And General; Teacher Preparatory; Professional
Accreditation: WC, ACBSP

01 President .... Dr. Judith M. GREIG
05 Provost .... Dr. Paul EWALD
10 Vice Pres Finance & Administration .... Mr. Henry ROTH
20 Dean of Students .... Ms. Jean CONDE
84 Vice President of Enrollment .... Mr. Hernan BUCHELI
04 Exec Assistant to the President .... Ms. Alison LYON
49 Dean Arts & Sciences .... Dr. John LEMMON
50 Interim Dean Business & Management .... Mr. Craig BREWER
53 Dean Education & Leadership .... Dr. Joanne ROSSI
06 Registrar .... Ms. Sandra LEE
36 Director Career Development .... Ms. Carrie MCKNIGHT
37 Director Financial Aid .... Mr. Wilbert LLESES
38 Director Student Counseling .... Ms. Karin SPONHOLZ
41 Athletic Director .... Mr. Josh DOODY
42 Director Spirituality .... Ms. Amy JOBIN
19 Chief Public Safety .... Mr. James SAUNDERS
23 Health Services Coordinator .... Ms. Abigail ORTIZ
29 Director Events/Alumni Relations .... Vacant
26 Director Communication .... Mr. Richard ROSSI
15 Director Human Resources .... Ms. Mary HAESLOOP

Occidental College (I)

1600 Campus Road, Los Angeles CA 90041-3314
County: Los Angeles FICE Identification: 001249
Unit ID: 120254
Telephone: (323) 259-2500 Carnegie Class: Bac/A&S
FAX Number: (323) 259-2958 Calendar System: Semester
URL: www.oxy.edu
Established: 1887 Annual Undergrad Tuition & Fees: $45,190
Enrollment: 2,123 Coed
Affiliation or Control: Independent Non-Profit IRS Status: 501(c)3
Highest Offering: Master's
Program: Liberal Arts And General
Accreditation: WC

01 President .... Dr. Jonathan VEITCH
05 Dean of the College/VP Acad Affs .... Dr. Jorge GONZALEZ
11 Vice President Administration .... Mr. Michael GROENER
30 Vice Pres Institutional Advancement .... Ms. Shelby RADCLIFFE
32 Vice Pres Stdnt Life/Dean of Stdnts .... Ms. Barbara AVERY
07 Vice Pres Admission & Financial Aid .... Mr. Vincent CUSEO
43 General Counsel .... Mr. Carl BOTTERUD
13 VP for Information Technology Svcs .... Dr. Pamela MCQUESTEN
10 Vice Pres for Finance & Planning .... Mr. Amos HIMMELSTEIN
41 Assoc Vice Pres/Dir Athletics .... Ms. Jaime HOFFMAN
18 Assoc VP for Facilities Management .... Mr. Michael STEPHENS
04 Exec Assistant to the President .... Ms. Rebecca STOLZ
06 Registrar .... Mr. Victor T. EGITTO
08 Librarian .... Dr. Robert KIEFT
37 Director of Financial Aid .... Ms. Maureen MCRAE
29 Director of Alumni Relations .... Ms. Dana VALK
36 Director Career Development Center .... Ms. Valerie SAVIOR
15 Director of Human Resources .... Mr. Richard LEDWIN
26 Director of Communications .... Mr. Jim TRANQUADA
09 Director Institutional Research .... Mr. Michael D. TAMADA
44 Int Dir Advance Svc Operations .... Ms. Regan REMULLA
39 Ast Dn Stdnts Resid Life/Hsng Svc .... Mr. Tim CHANG
19 Director of Campus Safety .... Ms. Hollis B. NIETO

Ohlone College (A)

43600 Mission Boulevard, Fremont CA 94539-0390

County: Alameda FICE Identification: 004481
Unit ID: 120290
Telephone: (510) 659-6000 Carnegie Class: Assoc/Pub-S-SC
FAX Number: N/A Calendar System: Semester
URL: www.ohlone.edu
Established: 1966 Annual Undergrad Tuition & Fees (In-District): $1,508
Enrollment: 10,270 Coed
Affiliation or Control: State/Local IRS Status: 501(c)3
Highest Offering: Associate Degree
Program: Occupational; 2-Year Principally Bachelor's Creditable
Accreditation: WJ, ADNUR, COARC, #PTAA

01 President/Superintendent .... Dr. Gari BROWNING
10 Vice Pres Administrative Services .... Mr. Ron LITTLE, II
05 Vice President Academic Affairs .... Dr. Leta STAGNARO
32 Vice President Student Services .... Dr. Ron TRAVENICK
13 Assoc Vice Pres Information Tech .... Mr. Bruce GRIFFIN
15 Assoc Vice Pres Human Resources .... Ms. Shairon ZINGSHEIM
08 Dean Learning Resource/Instruc Tech .... Ms. Lesley BUEHLER
38 Dean Counseling .... Vacant
09 Dean Institutional Research .... Mr. Michael BOWMAN
57 Dean Arts and Social Science .... Mr. Walter BIRKEDAHL
76 Dean Health Sciences & Env Studies .... Ms. Gale CARLI
83 Dean Language & Communication .... Mr. Mark LIEU
81 Dean Science/Engineering & Math .... Dr. Mike HOLTZCLAW
88 Dean Deaf Studies .... Vacant
102 Executive Director Foundation .... Ms. Susan HOUGHTON
35 Director EOPS/Student Services .... Ms. Debra TRIGG
21 Director Business Services .... Mr. Farhad SABIT
30 Director College Advancement .... Ms. Patrice BIRKEDAHL
19 Chief Safety & Security .... Mr. Steve OSAWA
18 Director Facilities/Physical Plant .... Mr. Thomas MOORE
37 Director Financial Aid .... Ms. Deborah GRIFFIN
96 Director of Purchasing .... Mr. Alex LEBEDEFF
104 Director International Programs .... Mr. Bill SHARAR
84 Director Enrollment Mgmt .... Ms. Kimberly ROBBIE

Olivet University (B)

250 Fourth Street, San Francisco CA 94103-3117

County: San Francisco Identification: 666176
Telephone: (415) 371-0002 Carnegie Class: Not Classified
FAX Number: (415) 371-0003 Calendar System: Quarter
URL: www.olivetuniversity.edu
Established: 1992 Annual Undergrad Tuition & Fees: $12,888
Enrollment: 1,079 Coed
Affiliation or Control: Independent Non-Profit IRS Status: 501(c)3
Highest Offering: Doctorate
Program: Liberal Arts And General; Professional; Religious Emphasis
Accreditation: BI

01 University President .... Dr. Tracy DAVIS
03 Vice President .... Mr. Nathanael TRAN
05 Academic Dean .... Dr. Christy TRAN
32 Dean of Students .... Dr. Julia TZENG
10 Chief Financial Officer .... Mr. Barnabas JUNG
11 Chief Operating Officer .... Dr. Walker TZENG

Otis College of Art and Design (C)

9045 Lincoln Boulevard, Westchester CA 90045-3550

County: Los Angeles FICE Identification: 001251
Unit ID: 120403
Telephone: (310) 665-6800 Carnegie Class: Spec/Arts
FAX Number: (310) 665-6805 Calendar System: Semester
URL: www.otis.edu
Established: 1918 Annual Undergrad Tuition & Fees: $38,300
Enrollment: 1,165 Coed
Affiliation or Control: Independent Non-Profit IRS Status: 501(c)3
Highest Offering: Master's
Program: Professional
Accreditation: WC, ART

01 President .... Mr. Samuel HOI
05 Chief Academic Officer/Provost .... Dr. Kerry WALK
10 VP of Administration & Finance Svcs .... Mr. William SCHAEFFER
84 VP Enrollment Management .... Mr. Marc MEREDITH
30 VP Institutional Advancement .... Ms. Carrie STEWART
15 Vice Pres Human Resources/Devel .... Ms. Dana LOPEZ
32 Dean of Students .... Dr. Laura KIRALLA
51 Dean of Continuing Education .... Ms. Amy GANTMAN
07 Dean of Admissions .... Ms. Yvette SOBKY-SHAFFER
06 Registrar .... Ms. Anna MANZANO
08 Director of Library .... Ms. Sue MABERRY
37 Assoc Director of Financial Aid .... Ms. Jessika VASQUEZ-HUERTA
88 Director of Galleries & Exhibitions .... Ms. Meg LINTON
36 Career Services Specialist .... Ms. Denise GIANOUSSOPOULOS
13 Chief Information Officer .... Mr. Robert WALTERS
18 Chief Facilities/Operation Ofcr .... Mr. Claude NICA
26 Director Communications .... Ms. Margi REEVE
29 Director Alumni Relations .... Ms. Laura DAROCA
96 Director of Purchasing .... Ms. Barbara TECLE
38 Director Student Counseling .... Dr. Fred BARNES

Pacific College (D)

3160 Redhill Avenue, Costa Mesa CA 92626-3402

County: Orange FICE Identification: 032993
Unit ID: 422695
Telephone: (800) 867-2243 Carnegie Class: Assoc/PrivFP
FAX Number: (714) 662-1702 Calendar System: Semester
URL: www.pacific-college.edu
Established: 1993 Annual Undergrad Tuition & Fees: $28,500
Enrollment: 257 Coed
Affiliation or Control: Proprietary IRS Status: Proprietary
Highest Offering: Baccalaureate
Program: Occupational; 2-Year Principally Bachelor's Creditable; Nursing Emphasis
Accreditation: ACCSC

01 President .... Mr. William L. NELSON

Pacific College of Oriental Medicine (E)

7445 Mission Valley Road, #105,
San Diego CA 92108-4408

County: San Diego FICE Identification: 030277
Unit ID: 378576
Telephone: (619) 574-6909 Carnegie Class: Spec/Health
FAX Number: (619) 574-6641 Calendar System: Trimester
URL: www.pacificcollege.edu
Established: 1986 Annual Undergrad Tuition & Fees: $11,585
Enrollment: 564 Coed
Affiliation or Control: Proprietary IRS Status: Proprietary
Highest Offering: Doctorate
Program: Professional; Business Emphasis
Accreditation: @WC, ACCSC, ACUP

01 President .... Mr. Jack MILLER
11 Vice President Operations .... Ms. Elaine GATES-MILINER
07 Vice Pres of Admissions/Marketing .... Ms. Suzanne KARSTEN
12 Campus Director NY Campus .... Mr. Malcolm YOUNGREN
12 Campus Director CH Campus .... Mr. Edward LAMADRID
05 Director of Academic Affairs .... Ms. Stacy GOMES
06 Registrar .... Mr. Nayeli CORONA
20 Academic Dean .... Mr. Bob DAMONE
37 Financial Aid Director .... Ms. Kyle POSTON
26 Director of Adv and Marketing .... Ms. Gail VOGT
23 Director of Clinical Services .... Mr. Greg LANE
08 Head Librarian .... Ms. Naomi BROERING
13 Director of Information Technology .... Mr. Roland ZAKARIA
88 Office Manager .... Ms. Cindy FLOYD
40 Bookstore Manager .... Ms. Patti HINES
21 Bursar .... Ms. Patti HINES
27 Pacific Symposium & Events Coord .... Ms. Tiffany HANSEN

Pacific Lutheran Theological Seminary (F)

2770 Marin Avenue, Berkeley CA 94708-1597

County: Alameda FICE Identification: 001254
Unit ID: 120740
Telephone: (510) 559-5264 Carnegie Class: Spec/Faith
FAX Number: (510) 559-2408 Calendar System: Semester
URL: www.plts.edu
Established: 1950 Annual Graduate Tuition & Fees: $14,445
Enrollment: 71 Coed
Affiliation or Control: Evangelical Lutheran Church In America
IRS Status: 501(c)3
Highest Offering: Master's; No Undergraduates
Program: Professional; Religious Emphasis
Accreditation: THEOL

01 President .... Dr. Phyllis ANDERSON
05 Dean of the Faculty .... Dr. Alicia VARGAS
10 VP for Finance and Operations .... Ms. Debora OW
30 Director of Development .... Mr. Brian STEIN-WEBBER
07 Director of Admissions .... Dr. Steve CHURCHILL
08 Library Director .... Mr. Robert BENEDETTO

Pacific Oaks College (G)

55 Eureka Street, Pasadena CA 91103

County: Los Angeles FICE Identification: 001255
Unit ID: 120768
Telephone: (877) 314-2380 Carnegie Class: Spec/Other
FAX Number: N/A Calendar System: Semester
URL: www.pacificoaks.edu
Established: 1945 Annual Undergrad Tuition & Fees: $24,679
Enrollment: 959 Coed
Affiliation or Control: Independent Non-Profit IRS Status: 501(c)3
Highest Offering: Master's
Program: Teacher Preparatory; Professional
Accreditation: WC

01 President .... Dr. Ezat PARNIA
05 Dean of the College .... Dr. Ellie KAUCHER
07 Associate Vice Pres Admissions .... Ms. Crystal CZUBERNAT
32 Assoc Vice Pres Student Services .... Mr. Frank FRIAS
88 Exec Director Children's School .... Ms. Jayanti TAMBE
15 Director of Human Resources .... Ms. Carolyn MATHIS
10 Director of Finance .... Ms. Yug Fon CHIQUITO
08 Campus Librarian .... Ms. Kelsey VUKIC
35 Dir Ctr Stdnt Achievmt/Res/Enrich .... Ms. Pat MEDA
06 Registrar .... Ms. Brooke JUDKINS
13 IT Director .... Mr. Bao LE
04 Executive Assistant to President .... Ms. Amy SEYERLE
88 Dir School of Human Development .... Dr. Joseph T. SUNDEEN
37 Director of Financial Aid .... Mr. Seph RODRIGUEZ
88 Dir Northern CA Instructional Site .... Dr. Marian BROWNING
88 Dir School of Cultural & Fmly Psy .... Ms. Connie DESTITO
21 Dir Alumni & External Relations .... Ms. Toni ARELLANES-MILLER

Pacific School of Religion (H)

1798 Scenic Avenue, Berkeley CA 94709-1323

County: Alameda FICE Identification: 001256
Unit ID: 120795
Telephone: (510) 849-8200 Carnegie Class: Spec/Faith
FAX Number: (510) 845-8948 Calendar System: Semester
URL: www.psr.edu
Established: 1866 Annual Graduate Tuition & Fees: $16,320
Enrollment: 218 Coed
Affiliation or Control: Independent Non-Profit IRS Status: 501(c)3
Highest Offering: Doctorate; No Undergraduates
Program: Professional; Religious Emphasis
Accreditation: WC, THEOL

01 President .... Dr. Riess POTTERVELD
05 Vice President & Academic Dean .... Dr. Bernard SCHLAGER
10 Chief Financial Officer .... Mr. Frank TSAI
30 VP for Institutional Advancement .... Vacant
20 Asst Dean Academic Pgms/Registrar .... Ms. Delphine HWANG
32 Asst Dean of Students & Cmty Life .... Vacant
08 Library Director GTU .... Mr. Robert BENEDETTO
07 Dir of Recruitment & Admissions .... Ms. Nicole NAFFAA
15 Personnel Director .... Ms. Deborah WALKER
04 Executive Asst to President .... Ms. Jen GALL

Pacific States University (I)

3450 Wilshire Boulevard, 5th Floor,
Los Angeles CA 90010

County: Los Angeles FICE Identification: 031633
Unit ID: 120838
Telephone: (323) 731-2383 Carnegie Class: Spec/Bus
FAX Number: (323) 731-7276 Calendar System: Quarter
URL: www.psuca.edu
Established: 1928 Annual Undergrad Tuition & Fees: $19,340
Enrollment: 175 Coed
Affiliation or Control: Independent Non-Profit IRS Status: 501(c)3
Highest Offering: Master's
Program: Liberal Arts And General; Professional; Business Emphasis
Accreditation: ACICS

01 President .... Mr. Hee Young AHN
04 Special Assistant to President .... Mr. Jin Song KIM
100 Chief Secretary .... Mr. Jae Young CHUNG
82 Actg Vice Pres/Dean Intl Affairs .... Dr. Zukweon KIM
05 University Dean Emeritus .... Mr. Meyer POLLACK
88 Assoc Dean General Affairs .... Dr. Joan B. WILSON
10 Assoc Dean Strategy/Finance .... Mr. Keith K. KIM
20 Associate Dean Academic Affairs .... Dr. Min Sang KIM
32 Associate Dean Student Affairs .... Mr. Moonsik KIM
50 Director College of Business .... Dr. Kamol SOMVICHIAN
72 Dir General & Technology Services .... Mr. Kuang Kai LU
88 Director ESL Program .... Ms. Karen CHEN
08 University Librarian .... Ms. Deborah HULL
06 Registrar/Student Financial Aid .... Ms. Namyoung CHAH

Pacific Union College (J)

One Angwin Avenue, Angwin CA 94508-9797

County: Napa FICE Identification: 001258
Unit ID: 120865
Telephone: (707) 965-6311 Carnegie Class: Bac/A&S
FAX Number: (707) 965-6390 Calendar System: Quarter
URL: www.puc.edu
Established: 1882 Annual Undergrad Tuition & Fees: $34,965
Enrollment: 1,564 Coed
Affiliation or Control: Seventh-day Adventist IRS Status: 501(c)3
Highest Offering: Master's
Program: 2-Year Principally Bachelor's Creditable; Liberal Arts And General; Teacher Preparatory; Professional
Accreditation: WC, ADNUR, IACBE, MUS, NUR, SW

01 President .... Dr. Heather J. KNIGHT
05 Vice Pres Admin & Academic Dean .... Dr. Nancy LECOURT
10 VP Financial Administration/CFO .... Dr. Dave LAWRENCE
32 Vice President Student Life .... Dr. Lisa BISSELL PAULSON
30 Vice President Advancement .... Mr. Walter COLLINS
84 Vice Pres Enrollment Mgt/Pub Rels .... Ms. Jennifer TYNER
33 Dean of Men .... Mr. James I. BOYD, JR.
34 Dean of Women .... Miss Janice R. WOOD
08 Director Library Services .... Mr. Adu WORKU
37 Director Student Financial Services .... Ms. Laurie WHEELER
13 Director Information Technology .... Mrs. Maria VANCE
06 Director Registration & Records .... Mrs. Marlo WATERS
15 Director Human Resources .... Mr. Gayln K. BOWERS
21 Director Budgets & Fiscal Services .... Mrs. Joy L. HIRDLER
38 Director Counseling Center .... Mr. Michael JEFFERSON
18 Chief Facilities/Facil Management .... Mr. Dale WITHERS
20 Associate Academic Officer .... Mr. Edwin MOORE

Pacifica Graduate Institute (K)

249 Lambert Road, Carpinteria CA 93013-3019

County: Carpinteria FICE Identification: 031268
Unit ID: 115746
Telephone: (805) 969-3626 Carnegie Class: DRU
FAX Number: (805) 565-1932 Calendar System: Quarter
URL: www.pacifica.edu

Established: 1974 Annual Graduate Tuition & Fees: $27,014
Enrollment: 1,097 Coed
Affiliation or Control: Proprietary IRS Status: Proprietary
Highest Offering: Doctorate; No Undergraduates
Program: Professional
Accreditation: WC

01 Chancellor/Chief Executive Officer ... Dr. Stephen AIZENSTAT
05 Vice President/Provost ... Dr. Patricia KATSKY
10 Vice President/CFO ... Mr. David HENKEL
07 Director of Admissions ... Ms. Wendy OVEREND
37 Director of Financial Aid ... Ms. Tracie TEAGUE

Palmer College of Chiropractic, West Campus (A)

90 E Tasman Drive, San Jose CA 95134-1617
Telephone: (408) 944-6000 FICE Identification: 021849
Accreditation: &NH, &CHIRO

† Main campus is Palmer College of Chiropractic in Davenport, IA.

Palo Alto University (B)

1791 Arastradero Road, Palo Alto CA 94304
County: San Mateo FICE Identification: 021383
Unit ID: 120698
Telephone: (800) 818-6136 Carnegie Class: Spec/Health
FAX Number: (650) 433-3888 Calendar System: Quarter
URL: www.paloaltou.edu
Established: 1975 Annual Undergrad Tuition & Fees: $19,548
Enrollment: 876 Coed
Affiliation or Control: Independent Non-Profit IRS Status: 501(c)3
Highest Offering: Doctorate
Program: Professional
Accreditation: WC, CLPSY

01 President ... Dr. Allen CALVIN
05 Academic Vice President ... Dr. William FROMING
32 Vice President Student Services ... Ms. Elizabeth HILT
88 Vice President for Prof Development ... Dr. Luli EMMONS
10 Vice Pres Business Affairs/CFO ... Ms. June KLEIN
84 VP of Enrollment Management ... Mr. Dacien SIMS
20 Dean Academic Admin/Operations ... Dr. Jim BRECKENRIDGE
17 Dir of Clinical Training-Ph.D. Pgm ... Dr. Robert RUSSELL
17 Dir of Clinical Training-Psy.D. Pgm ... Dr. Shelly HOWELL
23 Director of Clinic ... Dr. Sandy MACIAS
06 Registrar ... Ms. Nora MARQUEZ
37 Financial Aid Director ... Ms. America BRYANT
42 Chaplain ... Rev. Byron BLAND
08 University Librarian ... Mr. Scott HINES
30 Director of Advancement ... Ms. Megan O'MAHONEY
07 Director of Admissions ... Ms. Eirian WILLIAMS
13 Director Information Technology ... Mr. David LEAVITT
29 Director of Alumni Relations ... Ms. Kemper MITCHELL
09 Institutional Research Admin ... Ms. Kristen GUY

Palo Verde College (C)

One College Drive, Blythe CA 92225-9561
County: Riverside FICE Identification: 001259
Unit ID: 120953
Telephone: (760) 921-5500 Carnegie Class: Assoc/Pub-S-MC
FAX Number: (760) 921-5590 Calendar System: Semester
URL: www.paloverde.edu
Established: 1947 Annual Undergrad Tuition & Fees (In-District): $1,380
Enrollment: 3,367 Coed
Affiliation or Control: State/Local IRS Status: 501(c)3
Highest Offering: Associate Degree
Program: Occupational; 2-Year Principally Bachelor's Creditable
Accreditation: WJ

01 Superintendent/President ... Dr. Donald WALLACE
05 Int Vice Pres Instructional Svcs ... Ms. Sharon JONES
32 Int Vice President of Student Svcs ... Ms. Sharon JONES
04 Admin Asst to Supt/President ... Ms. Denise HUNT
66 Nursing & Allied Health Coord ... Ms. Sharron BURGESON
08 Librarian ... Ms. June TURNER
06 Registrar ... Ms. Shelley HAMILTON
88 Site Supervsr Child Dev/Teacher Ctr ... Ms. Maria KEHL
09 Institutional Research/Professor ... Mr. Brian THIEBAUX
18 Facilities & Operations Manager ... Mr. Albert BRAMBILA
13 Director of Information Technology ... Mr. Adam HOUSTON
26 Outreach & Events Coordinator ... Dr. Donald WALLACE
36 Transfer & Career Ctr Dir/Counselor ... Vacant
45 Dir Econ Dev Center/Inst Research ... Vacant
15 Director of Human Resources ... Ms. Debbie MITCHELL
10 Chief Business Officer ... Ms. Russi EGAN
20 Instructional Service Manager ... Ms. Naomi SMITH
07 Director of Admissions ... Ms. Shelley HAMILTON
37 Director Student Financial Aid ... Ms. Suzy WOODS
04 Admin Asst to Supt/President/Board ... Ms. Carrie MULLION

Palomar College (D)

1140 W Mission Road, San Marcos CA 92069-1487
County: San Diego FICE Identification: 001260
Unit ID: 120971
Telephone: (760) 744-1150 Carnegie Class: Assoc/Pub-S-MC
FAX Number: (760) 744-8123 Calendar System: Semester
URL: www.palomar.edu
Established: 1946 Annual Undergrad Tuition & Fees (In-District): $1,380
Enrollment: 24,668 Coed
Affiliation or Control: State/Local IRS Status: 501(c)3
Highest Offering: Associate Degree
Program: Occupational; 2-Year Principally Bachelor's Creditable
Accreditation: WJ, ADNUR, DA, EMT

01 Superintendent/President ... Mr. Robert P. DEEGAN
05 Asst Supt/Vice Pres Instruction ... Ms. Berta CUARON
32 Asst Supt/VP Student Services ... Mr. Adrian GONZALES
10 Asst Supt/VP Finance/Admin Svcs ... Mr. Ron PEREZ
16 Asst Supt/VP Human Resources ... Mr. John TORTAROLO
04 Assistant to the President ... Ms. Cheryl ASHOUR
79 Int Dean Languages & Literature ... Ms. Shayla SIVERT
81 Dean Math/Natural & Health Sciences ... Mr. Dan SOURBEER
38 Dean Counseling Services ... Vacant
75 Dean Career/Tech/Extended Educ Div ... Ms. Wilma G. OWENS
50 Dean Arts/Media/Bus & Computer Sci ... Ms. Norma MIYAMOTO
83 Int Dean Social/Behavioral Sciences ... Mr. Jack HAHN
13 Director Info Systems & Services ... Mr. Jose VARGAS
84 Director Enrollment Svcs/Admissions ... Mr. Kendyl MAGNUSON
09 Director Institutional Research ... Ms. Michelle BARTON
18 Int Director of Facilities ... Mr. Chris MILLER
35 Director Student Affairs ... Ms. Sherry TITUS
37 Director Student Financial Aid ... Ms. Mary SANAGUSTIN
21 Associate Business Officer ... Vacant
26 Chief Public Relations Officer ... Ms. Laura GROPEN
30 Chief of Development ... Mr. Richard TALMO
51 Director Extended Education ... Vacant
19 Interim Chief of Police ... Mr. Tony CRUZ
23 Director Health Services ... Ms. Jayne CONWAY
41 Director Athletics ... Mr. Scott CATHCART
24 Supervisor Media Equipment ... Vacant

Pardee RAND Graduate School of Policy Studies (E)

1776 Main Street, Santa Monica CA 90407-2138
County: Los Angeles FICE Identification: 010441
Unit ID: 121628
Telephone: (310) 393-0411 Carnegie Class: Spec/Other
FAX Number: (310) 451-6978 Calendar System: Quarter
URL: www.prgs.edu
Established: 1970 Annual Graduate Tuition & Fees: $25,000
Enrollment: 105 Coed
Affiliation or Control: Independent Non-Profit IRS Status: 501(c)3
Highest Offering: Doctorate; No Undergraduates
Program: Professional
Accreditation: WC

01 Dean ... Dr. Susan MARQUIS
05 Associate Dean ... Ms. Rachel SWANGER
06 Registrar ... Ms. Mary PARKER

Pasadena City College (F)

1570 E Colorado Boulevard, Pasadena CA 91106-2041
County: Los Angeles FICE Identification: 001261
Unit ID: 121044
Telephone: (626) 585-7123 Carnegie Class: Assoc/Pub-S-SC
FAX Number: (626) 585-7910 Calendar System: Semester
URL: www.pasadena.edu
Established: 1924 Annual Undergrad Tuition & Fees (In-District): $1,152
Enrollment: 26,195 Coed
Affiliation or Control: State/Local IRS Status: 501(c)3
Highest Offering: Associate Degree
Program: Occupational; 2-Year Principally Bachelor's Creditable
Accreditation: WJ, DA, DH, DT, MAC, RAD

01 Superintendent/President ... Dr. Mark W. ROCHA
05 Senior VP Academic & Student Affs ... Dr. Robert H. BELL
10 Senior VP Business & College Svcs ... Mr. Robert B. MILLER
21 Asst Supt Business & College Affs ... Mr. Robert B. MILLER
15 Exec Dir Human Resources ... Ms. Terri HAMPTON
43 General Counsel ... Ms. Gail S. COOPER
30 Interim Dean External Relations ... Mrs. Elaine F. CHAPMAN
09 Int Dir Inst Planning/Research ... Ms. Crystal KOLLROSS
35 Asst Dean Student Affairs ... Dr. Scott W. THAYER
31 Director Extension ... Ms. Elaine CHAPMAN
38 Assoc Dean Counseling/Curr Liaison ... Dr. Cynthia D. OLIVO
88 Assistant Dean Special Services ... Dr. Kent YAMAUCHI
07 Assoc Dean Admissions/Records ... Ms. Dina CHASE
37 Assistant Dean Financial Aid ... Ms. Kim MILES
91 Dir Mgmt Info Svcs/Admin Comp Svcs ... Mr. Dale PITTMAN
26 Director of Public Relations ... Mr. Juan F. GUTIERREZ
18 Exec Dir Facilities/Physical Plant ... Mr. Rueben SMITH

Patten University (G)

2433 Coolidge Avenue, Oakland CA 94601-2699
County: Alameda FICE Identification: 004490
Unit ID: 121071
Telephone: (510) 261-8500 Carnegie Class: Bac/Diverse
FAX Number: (510) 534-4344 Calendar System: Semester
URL: www.patten.edu
Established: 1944 Annual Undergrad Tuition & Fees: $8,036
Enrollment: 963 Coed
Affiliation or Control: Proprietary IRS Status: Proprietary
Highest Offering: Master's
Program: 2-Year Principally Bachelor's Creditable; Liberal Arts And General; Teacher Preparatory; Religious Emphasis
Accreditation: WC

01 President ... Dr. Terry RAWLS
05 Vice Pres for Academic Affairs ... Dr. Tana MONACO
32 Vice Pres for Student Services ... Ms. Darla CUADRA
26 Vice Pres of Communications ... Ms. Deborah DALLINGER
21 Chief Business Officer ... Mr. Andy GANES
06 Registrar ... Ms. Cindi HOGEBOOM
10 Director Finance/Administration ... Mr. Don GEDEON
07 Director of Admissions ... Ms. Sharon BARTA
08 Library Director ... Mr. Joshua ADARKWA
84 Dean Enrollment Services ... Mr. Robert OLIVERA
19 Director Security/Safety ... Mr. Richard SWANSON
32 Dean of Students ... Ms. Tatiana GUADAMUZ
37 Financial Aid Director ... Ms. Karen SHEPHERD
39 Director Student Housing ... Vacant
41 Athletic Director ... Mr. Robert OLIVERA
20 Associate Academic Officer ... Ms. Darlene WILLIAMS
26 Chief Public Relations Officer ... Dr. Glenn KUNKEL

Pepperdine University (H)

24255 Pacific Coast Highway, Malibu CA 90263-0001
County: Los Angeles FICE Identification: 010149
Unit ID: 121150
Telephone: (310) 506-4000 Carnegie Class: DRU
FAX Number: (310) 506-4861 Calendar System: Semester
URL: www.pepperdine.edu
Established: 1937 Annual Undergrad Tuition & Fees: $44,902
Enrollment: 7,319 Coed
Affiliation or Control: Church Of Christ IRS Status: 501(c)3
Highest Offering: Doctorate
Program: Liberal Arts And General; Teacher Preparatory; Professional
Accreditation: WC, BUS, CLPSY, DIETD, LAW, MUS

01 President ... Dr. Andrew K. BENTON
100 Chief of Staff ... Ms. Marne D. MITZE
03 Executive Vice President ... Mr. Gary A. HANSON
04 Exec Assistant to the President ... Ms. Beverly GANDY
05 Provost ... Dr. Darryl TIPPENS
00 Chancellor Emeritus ... Dr. Charles B. RUNNELS
30 Sr VP Advancement & Public Affairs ... Mr. Keith HINKLE
10 Senior Vice President Investments ... Mr. Jeff PIPPIN
43 General Counsel ... Mr. Marc P. GOODMAN
11 Chief Administrative Officer ... Mr. Phil E. PHILLIPS
10 Chief Business Officer ... Mrs. Edna POWELL
27 Chief Information Officer ... Mr. Jonathan SEE
26 Assoc Vice Pres for Public Affairs ... Mr. Rick GIBSON
10 Chief Financial Officer ... Mr. Paul B. LASITER
21 Assoc VP Campus Ops/Business Svcs ... Mr. Alex PANG
06 Assoc VP & University Registrar ... Mr. Hung V. LE
104 Dean of International Programs ... Dr. Charles F. HALL
84 Dean of Admission/Enrollment Mgmt ... Mr. Michael E. TRUSCHKE
32 Dean of Student Affairs ... Dr. Mark DAVIS
08 Dean of Libraries ... Mr. Mark S. ROOSA
61 Dean of the School of Law ... Dr. Deanell TACHA
50 Dean of School of Business/Mgmt ... Dr. Linda LIVINGSTON
53 Dean of Graduate School Educ/Psych ... Dr. Margaret J. WEBER
49 Dean of Seaver College ... Dr. Rick R. MARRS
80 Dean School of Public Policy ... Dr. James R. WILBURN
42 University Chaplain ... Mr. David LEMLEY
46 Vice Provost for Research and Strat ... Dr. Lee KATS
108 Asst Provost Inst Effectiveness ... Dr. Lisa BORTMAN
29 Exec Director for Alumni Affairs ... Mr. Bob CLARK
16 Assoc VP Center for Human Resources ... Mrs. Lauren COSENTINO
10 University Controller ... Mr. Brian THOMASON
10 Assistant Controller ... Mr. David BRANT
88 Director for Church Relations ... Vacant
46 Director Research & Sponsored Pgm ... Mrs. Alexandra ROOSA
39 Assoc Dean of Students/Housing ... Mr. Brian DAWSON
88 Managing Dir Center for the Arts ... Ms. Rebecca CARSON
88 Director of Special Programs ... Ms. Kanet THOMAS
85 Director Intl Student Services ... Mr. Rich DAWSON
26 Dir Public Relations and News ... Vacant
23 Director of Student Health Services ... Ms. Nancy SAFINICK
36 Assoc Dean of Students/Career Ctr ... Mr. Brad D. DUDLEY
41 Director of Athletics ... Dr. Steven POTTS
19 Assoc VP & Dir of Public Safety ... Mr. Earl CARPENTER
18 Managing Dir Fac/Physical Plant ... Vacant
86 Assoc VP Govt & Regulatory Affairs ... Ms. Rhiannon BAILARD
37 Director Student Financial Aid ... Mrs. Janet LOCKHART
38 Director Student Counseling ... Ms. Connie HORTON
09 Director of Institutional Research ... Ms. Lily PANG
88 Director of Educational Research ... Vacant
44 Director Estate & Gift Planning ... Ms. Stephanie BUCKLEY
88 Director Disability Services ... Mrs. Tammy SELBY
88 Director of Auditing Services ... Ms. Norma IADEVAIA

*Peralta Community Colleges District Office (I)

333 E Eighth Street, Oakland CA 94606-2889
County: Alameda FICE Identification: 001265
Unit ID: 121178
Telephone: (510) 466-7200 Carnegie Class: N/A
FAX Number: (510) 835-4078
URL: www.peralta.edu

01 Chancellor ... Dr. Jose M. ORTIZ
27 Assoc VC Information Technology ... Mr. Calvin MADLUCK
26 Exec Dir Public Info/Commun & Media ... Mr. Jeffrey HEYMAN

*Berkeley City College (A)

2050 Center Street, Berkeley CA 94704-1183
County: Alameda FICE Identification: 022427
Unit ID: 125170
Telephone: (510) 981-2800 Carnegie Class: Assoc/Pub-U-MC
FAX Number: (510) 841-7333 Calendar System: Semester
URL: www.berkeleycitycollege.edu
Established: 1974 Annual Undergrad Tuition & Fees (In-District): $1,288
Enrollment: 6,725 Coed
Affiliation or Control: State/Local IRS Status: 501(c)3
Highest Offering: Associate Degree
Program: 2-Year Principally Bachelor's Creditable
Accreditation: WJ

02 President ..... Dr. Deborah BUDD
05 Interim Vice President Instruction ..... Dr. Kerry COMPTON
32 Vice President Student Services ..... Dr. May K. CHEN
103 Dean Workforce Development ..... Ms. Lilia CELHAY
88 Dean Student Support Services ..... Ms. Brenda JOHNSON
10 Business Services Manager ..... Ms. Shirley SLAUGHTER
51 Dir Program Adult College Education ..... Dr. Linda MCALLISTER
88 Director of Special Projects ..... Ms. Maeve Katherine BERGMAN
27 Public Information Officer ..... Ms. Shirley FOGARINO
06 Registrar ..... Ms. Adela ESQUIVEL-SWINSON
07 Director of Admissions ..... Ms. Adela ESQUIVEL-SWINSON
09 Director of Institutional Research ..... Dr. Mike ORKIN
15 Director Personnel Services ..... Ms. Trudy LARGENT
18 Chief Facilities/Physical Plant ..... Dr. Sadiq IKHARO
20 Associate Academic Officer ..... Ms. Lilia CELHAY
21 Associate Business Officer ..... Mr. John PANG
26 Chief Public Relations Officer ..... Mr. Jeffrey HEYMAN
28 Director of Diversity ..... Ms. Trudy LARGENT
29 Director Alumni Relations ..... Mr. Romeo GARCIA
30 Chief Development ..... Ms. Cynthia REESE
36 Director Student Placement ..... Ms. Gail PENDLETON
37 Director Student Financial Aid ..... Ms. Loan NGUYEN
38 Director Student Counseling ..... Ms. Allene YOUNG
84 Director Enrollment Management ..... Dr. May CHEN
96 Director of Purchasing ..... Mr. John PANG

*College of Alameda (B)

555 Ralph Appezzato Memorial Pkwy,
Alameda CA 94501-2109
County: Alameda FICE Identification: 006720
Unit ID: 108667
Telephone: (510) 522-7221 Carnegie Class: Assoc/Pub-U-MC
FAX Number: (510) 337-0619 Calendar System: Semester
URL: www.peralta.edu
Established: 1968 Annual Undergrad Tuition & Fees (In-District): $1,380
Enrollment: 5,682 Coed
Affiliation or Control: State/Local IRS Status: 501(c)3
Highest Offering: Associate Degree
Program: Occupational; 2-Year Principally Bachelor's Creditable
Accreditation: WJ, DA

02 Interim President ..... Dr. Eric GRAVENBERG
05 Vice President of Instruction ..... Vacant
32 Int Vice President of Student Svcs ..... Mr. Alexis MONTEVIRGEN
88 Dean Special Programs ..... Ms. Toni COOK
26 Chief Public Relations Officer ..... Vacant
84 Dean Enrollment Services ..... Ms. Amy LEE
10 Business & Administrative Svcs Mgr ..... Ms. Mary Beth BENVENUTTI
88 Dean Acad Pathways/Student Success ..... Mr. Maurice JONES

*Laney College (C)

900 Fallon Street, Oakland CA 94607-4893
County: Alameda FICE Identification: 001266
Unit ID: 117247
Telephone: (510) 834-5740 Carnegie Class: Assoc/Pub-U-MC
FAX Number: (510) 464-3528 Calendar System: Semester
URL: www.laney.edu
Established: 1953 Annual Undergrad Tuition & Fees (In-District): $1,144
Enrollment: 11,387 Coed
Affiliation or Control: State/Local IRS Status: 501(c)3
Highest Offering: Associate Degree
Program: Occupational; 2-Year Principally Bachelor's Creditable
Accreditation: WJ

02 President ..... Dr. Elnora T. WEBB
05 Vice President ..... Dr. Steven COHEN
10 Business/Admin Services Manager ..... Ms. Connie WILLIS
49 Div Dean Liberal Arts ..... Mr. Marco MENENDEZ
81 Div Dean Mathematics and Science ..... Dr. Inger STARK
75 Div Dean Career & Technical Educ ..... Mr. Peter CRABTREE
20 Dean Student Wellness & Development ..... Dr. Tina VASCONCELLOS
31 Dean Cmty Leadership & Civic Engag ..... Mr. Newin P. ORANTE
04 Executive Assistant to President ..... Ms. Maisha JAMESON
37 Int Director Student Financial Aid ..... Mr. Gary NICHOLES
41 Director Athletics ..... Mr. John BEAM
88 Director APASS Program ..... Ms. Lilia CELHAY
88 Director Gateway to College Pgm ..... Mr. Anthony FLORES
88 Director TRIO Supp Services Pgm ..... Dr. Amy H. LEE
88 Director Green Jobs Program ..... Vacant

*Merritt College (D)

12500 Campus Drive, Oakland CA 94619-3196
County: Alameda FICE Identification: 001267
Unit ID: 118772
Telephone: (510) 531-4911 Carnegie Class: Assoc/Pub-U-MC
FAX Number: (510) 436-2405 Calendar System: Semester
URL: www.merritt.edu
Established: 1953 Annual Undergrad Tuition & Fees (In-District): $1,656
Enrollment: 6,982 Coed
Affiliation or Control: State/Local IRS Status: 501(c)3
Highest Offering: Associate Degree
Program: Occupational; 2-Year Principally Bachelor's Creditable
Accreditation: WJ, DIETT, RAD

02 President ..... Dr. Norma AMBRIZ-GALAVIZ
05 Vice President of Instruction ..... Dr. Elmer BUGG
32 Vice President of Student Services ..... Dr. Bill CORDERO
96 Vice Chancellor of General Services ..... Dr. Sadiq IKHARO
35 Vice Chancellor Student Services ..... Dr. Adela ESQUIVEL-SWINSON
15 Vice Chancellor for Human Resources ..... Ms. Trudy LARGENT
20 Vice Chanc Educational Services ..... Dr. Michael ORKIN
26 Exec Dir Marketing/Public Rels/Comm ..... Mr. Jeffrey HEYMAN
08 Head Librarian ..... Mr. Timothy HACKETT
06 Registrar ..... Ms. Susana DE LA TORRE
10 Business/Admin Service Mgr ..... Ms. Dativa DEL ROSARIO

Phillips Graduate Institute (E)

19900 Plummer Street, Chatsworth CA 91311
County: Los Angeles FICE Identification: 022372
Unit ID: 110307
Telephone: (818) 386-5600 Carnegie Class: Spec/Health
FAX Number: (818) 386-5636 Calendar System: Semester
URL: www.pgi.edu
Established: 1971 Annual Graduate Tuition & Fees: $22,206
Enrollment: 210 Coed
Affiliation or Control: Independent Non-Profit IRS Status: 501(c)3
Highest Offering: Doctorate; No Undergraduates
Program: Professional
Accreditation: WC

01 President ..... Dr. Yolanda J. GORMAN
05 Vice President Academic Affairs ..... Vacant
10 Vice President Finance - CFO ..... Ms. Tanya PONTEP
45 Vice Pres Strategic Initiatives ..... Ms. Josie YOUNG
07 Director of Admissions ..... Dr. Melinda VALENTE
08 Director Library ..... Ms. Caroline SISNEROS
37 Financial Aid Director ..... Ms. Cristina LOMELI
13 IT/Operations Director ..... Mr. Ed NILA
06 Registrar ..... Ms. Kacey GUILFOIL
09 Dir Institutional Rsrch/Assess/Plng ..... Dr. Elizabeth TREBOW
15 Director Human Resources ..... Ms. Theresa WRAY
51 Coordinator Continuing Education ..... Ms. Jocceline HERNANDEZ

Pima Medical Institute-Chula Vista (F)

780 Bay Boulevard, Suite 101,
Chula Vista CA 91910-5261
Telephone: (619) 425-3200 Identification: 666272
Accreditation: ABHES, COARC, RAD

† Main campus is Pima Medical Institute-Tucson in Tucson, AZ.

Pitzer College (G)

1050 N Mills Avenue, Claremont CA 91711-6110
County: Los Angeles FICE Identification: 001172
Unit ID: 121257
Telephone: (909) 621-8129 Carnegie Class: Bac/A&S
FAX Number: (909) 621-8770 Calendar System: Semester
URL: www.pitzer.edu
Established: 1963 Annual Undergrad Tuition & Fees: $45,018
Enrollment: 1,084 Coed
Affiliation or Control: Independent Non-Profit IRS Status: 501(c)3
Highest Offering: Baccalaureate
Program: Liberal Arts And General
Accreditation: WC

01 President ..... Dr. Laura SKANDERA TROMBLEY
05 Vice Pres Acad Affs/Dean of Faculty ..... Dr. Muriel POSTON
10 Treasurer/Vice Pres Administration ..... Mr. Yuet LEE
30 Vice Pres College Advancement ..... Dr. Adrian STEVENS
07 Vice Pres Admissions/Financial Aid ..... Mr. Angel PEREZ
32 Vice Pres Student Affairs ..... Mr. Brian CARLISLE
26 VP Marketing/Public Relations ..... Mr. Mark BAILEY
44 Associate Vice Pres of Development ..... Ms. Holly PREBLE
20 Associate Dean of Faculty ..... Mr. Kathleen PURVIS-ROBERTS
88 Assistant Dean of Faculty ..... Mrs. Barbara JUNISBAI
06 Registrar ..... Ms. Eva PETERS
37 Director Financial Aid ..... Ms. Robin THOMPSON
07 Director Admission ..... Ms. Jamila EVERETT
09 Director of Institutional Research ..... Mr. Jason RIVERA
15 Director Human Resources ..... Ms. Marni BOBICH
18 Director Facilities ..... Mr. Larry BURIK
21 Associate Treasurer ..... Ms. Lori YOSHINO
36 Director Career Services ..... Mr. Matt DONATO
29 Director Alumni Relations ..... Ms. Brooke HENDRICKSON
38 Director Student Counseling ..... Dr. Rebecca KORNBLUH

Platt College (H)

1000 S Fremont Avenue, Building A9W,
Alhambra CA 91803-8845
County: Los Angeles FICE Identification: 030627
Unit ID: 260789
Telephone: (626) 300-5444 Carnegie Class: Bac/Assoc
FAX Number: (626) 457-8295 Calendar System: Other
URL: www.plattcollege.edu
Established: 1987 Annual Undergrad Tuition & Fees: $19,258
Enrollment: 161 Coed
Affiliation or Control: Proprietary IRS Status: Proprietary
Highest Offering: Baccalaureate
Program: Occupational
Accreditation: ACCSC, COARC, DMS

01 President ..... Mr. Nicholas EWELL

Platt College (I)

3700 Inland Empire Blvd, Ste 400, Ontario CA 91764-4906
Telephone: (909) 941-9410 Identification: 666056
Accreditation: ACCSC, COARC

† Main campus is Platt College in Alhambra, CA.

Platt College (J)

6465 Sycamore Canyon Boulevard, Riverside CA 95207
Telephone: (626) 300-5444 Identification: 770561
Accreditation: ACCSC

† Main campus is Platt College in Alhambra, CA.

Platt College (K)

6250 El Cajon Boulevard, San Diego CA 92115-3919
County: San Diego FICE Identification: 023043
Unit ID: 121275
Telephone: (619) 265-0107 Carnegie Class: Spec/Arts
FAX Number: (619) 265-8655 Calendar System: Semester
URL: www.platt.edu
Established: 1980 Annual Undergrad Tuition & Fees: $27,957
Enrollment: 370 Coed
Affiliation or Control: Proprietary IRS Status: Proprietary
Highest Offering: Baccalaureate
Program: Occupational; Professional; Technical Emphasis
Accreditation: ACCSC

00 Chairman ..... Mr. Robert D. LEIKER
01 President ..... Mrs. Meg LEIKER
03 Vice President ..... Mr. Alfred MEDRO
05 Dean of Education ..... Ms. Marketa HANCOVA

Point Loma Nazarene University (L)

3900 Lomaland Drive, San Diego CA 92106-2899
County: San Diego FICE Identification: 001262
Unit ID: 121309
Telephone: (619) 849-2200 Carnegie Class: Master's L
FAX Number: (619) 849-2579 Calendar System: Semester
URL: www.pointloma.edu
Established: 1902 Annual Undergrad Tuition & Fees: $30,350
Enrollment: 3,192 Coed
Affiliation or Control: Church Of The Nazarene IRS Status: 501(c)3
Highest Offering: Beyond Master's But Less Than Doctorate
Program: Liberal Arts And General; Teacher Preparatory; Professional
Accreditation: WC, ACBSP, DIETD, EMT, MUS, NURSE, SW, TED

01 President ..... Dr. Bob BROWER
05 Provost/Chief Academic Officer ..... Dr. Kerry FULCHER
10 VP Finance/Administrative Svcs ..... Mr. George LATTER
26 Vice President External Relations ..... Dr. Joe WATKINS
32 Vice Pres for Student Development ..... Dr. Caye SMITH
88 Vice Pres Spiritual Development ..... Dr. Mary PAUL
15 Assoc VP for Human Resources ..... Mrs. Joyce FALK
37 Assoc Vice President for Finance ..... Mrs. Cindy CHAPPELL
35 Assc VP Stdnt Dev/Chf Diversity Ofc ..... Dr. Jeffrey CARR
30 Assoc VP University Advancement ..... Mr. David MCCURRY
21 Assoc VP for Budget/Accounting ..... Ms. Sonia CHIN
84 Assoc VP Enrollment ..... Dr. Scott SHOEMAKER
20 Vice Prov Academic Administration ..... Dr. Mark PITTS
88 Vice Prov Program Dev and Accred ..... Dr. Maggie BAILEY
35 Dean of Students ..... Dr. Jeff BOLSTER
13 Chief Information Officer ..... Mr. Corey FLING
09 Dir Institutional Effectiveness ..... Mr. Brent GOODMAN
12 Director of Wesleyan Center ..... Dr. Mark MANN
18 Director of Campus Facilities ..... Mr. Bruce KUNKEL
36 Executive Dir Strengths & Vocation ..... Ms. Reyna SUND
107 Exec Dir of External Pgm Develop ..... Ms. Jeanne COCHRAN
86 Dir Cmty Outreach/Government Rels ..... Ms. Jill MONROE
88 Director Center Pastoral Leadship ..... Dr. Norm SHOEMAKER
42 Director of Church Relations ..... Rev. Ron FAY
88 Director of Outreach Ministries ..... Ms. Dana HOJSACK
88 Director of Worship Ministries ..... Mr. George WILLIAMSON
49 Dean College of Arts & Sciences ..... Dr. Kathy MCCONNELL
83 Dean College of Social Sciences ..... Dr. Holly IRWIN
07 Director Graduate Admissions ..... Ms. Laura LEINWEBER
07 Director Undergraduate Admissions ..... Mr. Eric GROVES
08 Director of Ryan Library ..... Dr. Frank QUINN
31 Director Community Life ..... Ms. Melissa BURT-GRACIK

06 Dir Records/Institutional Research .... Ms. Cheryl GAUGHAN
26 Director Marketing/Creative Svcs .... Ms. Michele CORBETT
88 Assoc Dean Stdnt Success/Wellness .... Dr. Kim BOGAN
19 Director of Public Safety .... Mr. Mark GALBRAITH
29 Director of Alumni Relations .... Ms. Sheryl SMEE
40 Bookstore Manager .... Ms. Jillian RICHMOND
28 Dir Multicultural/Intnl Stdnt Svcs .... Ms. Lily DAVIS
41 Athletic Director .... Mr. Ethan HAMILTON
88 Director of Nicholson Commons .... Mr. Milton KARAHADIAN
94 Dir Stevenson Ctr for Women's Stds .... Dr. Linda BEAIL
104 Director Study Abroad .... Mr. Frank SERNA
88 Dir of Programs & Operations .... Mr. Nick WOLF

Pomona College (A)

550 N College Avenue, #206, Claremont CA 91711-6301
County: Los Angeles FICE Identification: 001173
Unit ID: 121345
Telephone: (909) 621-8000 Carnegie Class: Bac/A&S
FAX Number: (909) 621-8403 Calendar System: Semester
URL: www.pomona.edu
Established: 1887 Annual Undergrad Tuition & Fees: $43,580
Enrollment: 1,585 Coed
Affiliation or Control: Independent Non-Profit IRS Status: 501(c)3
Highest Offering: Baccalaureate
Program: Liberal Arts And General
Accreditation: WC

01 President .... Dr. David W. OXTOBY
05 Vice President/Dean of College .... Dr. Janice HUDGINGS
45 Vice President Planning .... Dr. Richard A. FASS
10 Vice President/Treasurer .... Dr. Karen SISSON
30 VP for Institutional Advancement .... Ms. Pamela BESNARD
32 Vice President/Dean of Students .... Mrs. Miriam FELDBLUM
07 VP of Admissions & Financial Aid .... Mr. Seth ALLEN
04 Special Assistant to President .... Dr. Teresa SHAW
06 Registrar .... Ms. Margaret ADORNO
26 Director Public Relations .... Mr. Mark WOOD
29 Director Alumni Relations .... Ms. Nancy J. TRESER-OSGOOD
37 Director Financial Aid .... Ms. Mary BOOKER
36 Director Career Development .... Ms. Mary RAYMOND
15 Director Human Resources .... Ms. Brenda RUSHFORTH
41 Director Physical Education .... Mr. Charles KATSIAFICAS
44 Director Annual Giving .... Mr. Michael SPICER
21 Assoc Treasurer/Controller .... Ms. Mary Lou WOODS
09 Director of Institutional Research .... Dr. Jennifer RACHFORD
18 Chief Facilities/Physical Plant .... Mr. Robert ROBINSON

Presbyterian Theological Seminary in America (B)

15605 Carmenita Rd., Santa Fe Springs CA 90670
County: Los Angeles FICE Identification: 041228
Telephone: (562) 926-1023 Carnegie Class: Not Classified
FAX Number: (562) 926-1025 Calendar System: Semester
URL: www.ptsa.edu
Established: 1977 Annual Undergrad Tuition & Fees: $5,760
Enrollment: 214 Coed
Affiliation or Control: Presbyterian Church In America IRS Status: 501(c)3
Highest Offering: First Professional Degree
Program: Professional; Religious Emphasis
Accreditation: BI

01 President .... Dr. Sang Meyng LEE
05 Academic Dean .... Dr. James S. LEE
11 Dean of Administration .... Vacant
32 Dean of Students/Student Ministry .... Rev. Choong Gi PARK
85 Dean/Director of Intl Students .... Mr. Mankyung SUNG
08 Head Librarian .... Mrs. Ruth CHO
06 Registrar .... Mrs. Mi PARK
88 Administrator .... Mrs. Michelle YOON

Presidio Graduate School (C)

36 Lincoln Blvd, Ste 120, San Francisco CA 94129
County: San Francisco Identification: 667150
Telephone: (415) 561-6555 Carnegie Class: Not Classified
FAX Number: (415) 561-6483 Calendar System: Semester
URL: www.presidioedu.org
Established: 2003 Annual Graduate Tuition & Fees: $31,200
Enrollment: N/A Coed
Affiliation or Control: Independent Non-Profit IRS Status: 501(c)3
Highest Offering: Master's; No Undergraduates
Program: Professional
Accreditation: @WC

01 President .... William SHUTKIN
05 Associate Dean .... Ryan CABINTE
05 Associate Dean .... Dwight COLLINS
10 CFO .... Santhi PERUMAL
32 Assoc Dean Stdnt Svds/Career Devel .... Mitchell FRIEDMAN

Professional Golfers Career College (D)

26109 Ynez Road, Temecula CA 92591-6013
County: Riverside FICE Identification: 033673
Unit ID: 437750
Telephone: (951) 719-2994 Carnegie Class: Assoc/PrivFP
FAX Number: (951) 719-1643 Calendar System: Semester
URL: www.golfcollege.edu
Established: 1990 Annual Undergrad Tuition & Fees: $14,400
Enrollment: 366 Coed
Affiliation or Control: Proprietary IRS Status: Proprietary
Highest Offering: Associate Degree
Program: Occupational; 2-Year Principally Bachelor's Creditable; Business Emphasis
Accreditation: ACICS

01 President .... Dr. Tim SOMERVILLE

Providence Christian College (E)

1539 E. Howard Street, Pasadena CA 91104
County: Los Angeles FICE Identification: 041539
Unit ID: 455770
Telephone: (866) 323-0233 Carnegie Class: Bac/A&S
FAX Number: (626) 696-4040 Calendar System: Semester
URL: www.providencecc.edu
Established: 2002 Annual Undergrad Tuition & Fees: $24,422
Enrollment: 64 Coed
Affiliation or Control: Non-denominational IRS Status: 501(c)3
Highest Offering: Baccalaureate
Program: Liberal Arts And General
Accreditation: WC

01 President .... Dr. Dominic AQUILA
05 VP Academic & Student Affairs .... Dr. Russ REEVES
10 VP Finance & Operations .... Dawn DIRKSEN
30 VP Advancement .... Michael KILEDJIAN
06 Registrar .... Patty TSAI
84 Director of Enrollment Management .... Larissa KAMPS
32 Director of Student Life .... Justin BLEEKER

*Rancho Santiago Community College District (F)

2323 N. Broadway, Santa Ana CA 92706-1640
County: Orange FICE Identification: 006991
Unit ID: 438665
Telephone: (714) 480-7300 Carnegie Class: N/A
FAX Number: (714) 796-3915
URL: www.rsccd.edu

01 Chancellor .... Dr. Raul RODRIGUEZ
16 Exec Vice Chanc Human Resources .... Mr. John DIDION
10 Vice Chanc Business & Fiscal Svcs .... Mr. Peter HARDASH
05 Asst Vice Chanc Education Svcs .... Mr. Enrique PEREZ
04 Exec Asst to the Chancellor .... Ms. Debra GERARD

*Santa Ana College (G)

1530 W 17th Street, Santa Ana CA 92706-3398
County: Orange FICE Identification: 001284
Unit ID: 121619
Telephone: (714) 564-6000 Carnegie Class: Assoc/Pub-S-MC
FAX Number: (714) 564-6379 Calendar System: Semester
URL: www.sac.edu
Established: 1915 Annual Undergrad Tuition & Fees (In-District): $1,434
Enrollment: 25,200 Coed
Affiliation or Control: State/Local IRS Status: 501(c)3
Highest Offering: Associate Degree
Program: Occupational; 2-Year Principally Bachelor's Creditable
Accreditation: WJ, ADNUR, OTA

02 President .... Dr. Erlinda J. MARTINEZ
05 Vice President Academic Affairs .... Dr. Linda ROSE
32 Vice President Student Services .... Dr. Sara LUNDQUIST
51 Int Vice President Continuing Educ .... James KENNEDY
35 Dean Student Affairs .... Dr. Lilia TANAKEYOWMA
11 Vice Pres Administrative Svcs .... Dr. Michael COLLINS
07 Director Admissions & Records .... Mark LIANG
06 Registrar .... Chris TRUONG
50 Dean Business Division .... Dr. Allen DOOLEY
35 Assoc Dean Student Development .... Dr. Loy NASHUA
38 Dean Counseling .... Dr. Micki BRYANT
37 Director of Financial Aid .... Robert MANSON
41 Dean KinesiologyAthletics .... Avie BRIDGES
57 Dean Fine & Performing Arts .... Vacant
30 Director College Advancement .... Christina ROMERO
18 Facilities Manager .... Mark WHEELER
79 Dean Humanities & Social Siences .... Shelly JAFFRAY
81 Interim Dean Sci/Math/Hlth Sci .... Cheryl CARRERA
72 Dean Career Educ/Workforce Develop .... Bart HOFFMAN
56 Associate Dean EOPS .... Christine LEON
88 Associate Dean DSPS .... Vacant

*Santiago Canyon College (H)

8045 E Chapman Avenue, Orange CA 92869-4512
County: Orange FICE Identification: 036957
Unit ID: 399212
Telephone: (714) 628-4900 Carnegie Class: Assoc/Pub-S-MC
FAX Number: (714) 628-4723 Calendar System: Semester
URL: www.sccollege.edu
Established: 1997 Annual Undergrad Tuition & Fees (In-District): $1,380
Enrollment: 11,579 Coed
Affiliation or Control: State/Local IRS Status: 501(c)3
Highest Offering: Associate Degree
Program: Occupational; 2-Year Principally Bachelor's Creditable
Accreditation: WJ

02 President .... Mr. Juan A. VAZQUEZ
04 Assistant to the President .... Ms. Lynn MANZANO
32 Vice President Student Services .... Dr. John HERNANDEZ
05 Vice President Academic Affairs .... Dr. Aracely MORA
51 Vice President Continuing Educ .... Mr. Jose VARGAS
11 Vice Pres Administrative Services .... Mr. Steve KAWA
38 Dean Counseling .... Ms. Ruth BABESHOFF
41 Dean Math and Sciences .... Mr. Martin STRINGER
79 Dean Arts/Hum/Soc Sci/Library .... Ms. Marilyn FLORES
36 Dean Business/Career Tech Education ..... Ms. Corinne DOUGHTY
20 Dean Instruction/Student Services .... Ms. Lori FASBINDER
20 Dean Instruction/Student Services .... Vacant
35 Assoc Dean Student Development .... Ms. Lorrie JORDAN
07 Assoc Dean of Admissions & Records .... Ms. Linda MISKOVIC
37 Assoc Dean Student Support Svcs .... Mr. Syed RIZVI
06 Registrar .... Mr. Tuyen NGUYEN
18 Physical Plant Manager .... Vacant

Rio Hondo College (I)

3600 Workman Mill Road, Whittier CA 90601-1699
County: Los Angeles FICE Identification: 001269
Unit ID: 121886
Telephone: (562) 692-0921 Carnegie Class: Assoc/Pub-S-SC
FAX Number: (562) 699-7386 Calendar System: Semester
URL: www.riohondo.edu
Established: 1960 Annual Undergrad Tuition & Fees (In-District): $1,104
Enrollment: 18,684 Coed
Affiliation or Control: State/Local IRS Status: 501(c)3
Highest Offering: Associate Degree
Program: Occupational; 2-Year Principally Bachelor's Creditable
Accreditation: WJ

01 Superintendent/President .... Ms. Teresa DREYFUSS
05 Vice President Academic Svcs .... Mr. Kenn PIERSON
10 Vice President Finance/Business .... Ms. Teresa DREYFUSS
32 Vice President Student Services .... Mr. Henry GEE
86 Dir Govt & Community Relations .... Mr. Russell CASTANEDA-CALLEROS
16 Director Human Resources .... Ms. Yolanda EMERSON
26 Director Mktg & Communications .... Ms. Susan HERNEY
35 Director Student Activities .... Vacant
07 Dir Admissions & Records/Registrar .... Ms. Judy G. PEARSON
38 Dean Counseling & Student Dev .... Dr. Walter JONES
30 Int Exec Director RHC Foundation ...... Mr. Howard KUMMERMAN
37 Director Financial Aid & Veteran's .... Ms. Elizabeth CORIA
18 Dir Facilities Services .... Mr. James POPER
96 Director of Purchasing .... Mr. Timothy CONNELL

*Riverside Community College District (J)

450 E Alessandro Blvd, Riverside CA 92508
County: Riverside Identification: 667039
Telephone: (951) 222-8000 Carnegie Class: N/A
FAX Number: (951) 222-8036
URL: www.rccd.edu

01 Interim Chancellor .... Dr. Cynthia E. AZARI
05 Vice Chancellor Academic Affairs .... Dr. Ray MAGHROORI
10 Vice Chanc Business & Financial .... Mr. Aaron BROWN
28 Vice Chanc Diversity/Human Resource .... Ms. Melissa KANE
100 Chief of Staff & Facilities Develop .... Ms. Chris CARLSON
12 President Moreno Valley College .... Dr. Sandra MAYO
12 President Norco College .... Dr. Paul PARNELL
12 Actg President Riverside City Col .... Dr. Wolde-Ab ISAAC
09 Dean Institutional Research .... Mr. David TORRES

*Moreno Valley College (K)

16130 Lasselle Street, Moreno Valley CA 92551
County: Riverside FICE Identification: 041735
Unit ID: 460394
Telephone: (951) 571-6100 Carnegie Class: Not Classified
FAX Number: N/A Calendar System: Semester
URL: www.mvc.edu
Established: 2010 Annual Undergrad Tuition & Fees (In-District): $1,117
Enrollment: 8,936 Coed
Affiliation or Control: State/Local IRS Status: 501(c)3
Highest Offering: Associate Degree
Program: Occupational; 2-Year Principally Bachelor's Creditable
Accreditation: WJ, DA, DH, EMT

02 President .... Dr. Sandra MAYO
05 Vice President Academic Affairs .... Dr. Robin STEINBACK
10 Vice Pres Business Services .... Mr. Norm GODIN
32 Vice President Student Services .... Dr. Greg SANDOVAL
20 Dean of Instruction .... Mr. David VAKIL
35 Dean of Student Services .... Ms. Eugenia VINCENT
06 Director Enrollment Services .... Ms. Jamie CLIFTON
37 Director Student Financial Services .... Ms. Linda PRATT

*Norco College (L)

2001 Third Street, Norco CA 92860
County: Riverside FICE Identification: 041761
Unit ID: 460464
Telephone: (951) 372-7000 Carnegie Class: Not Classified
FAX Number: N/A Calendar System: Semester
URL: www.norcocollege.edu
Established: 2010 Annual Undergrad Tuition & Fees (In-District): $1,380
Enrollment: 9,664 Coed
Affiliation or Control: State/Local IRS Status: 501(c)3
Highest Offering: Associate Degree

Program: 2-Year Principally Bachelor's Creditable
Accreditation: WJ

02 President ... Dr. Paul PARNELL
05 Vice President Academic Affairs ... Dr. Diane DIECKMEYER
32 Vice President Student Services ... Dr. Monica GREEN
10 Vice Pres Business Services ... Ms. Beth GOMEZ
20 Dean Instruction ... Dr. Carol FARRAR
35 Dean Student Services ... Dr. Monica GREEN
88 Dean Student Success ... Dr. Greg AYCOCK
08 Dean Technology Learning Resources ... Mr. Damon NANCE
75 Assoc Dean Career & Technical Educ ... Mr. Kevin FLEMING

*Riverside City College (A)

4800 Magnolia Avenue, Riverside CA 92506
County: Riverside FICE Identification: 001270
Unit ID: 121901
Telephone: (951) 222-8000 Carnegie Class: Assoc/Pub-U-MC
FAX Number: (951) 222-8036 Calendar System: Semester
URL: www.rcc.edu
Established: 1916 Annual Undergrad Tuition & Fees (In-District): $35,000
Enrollment: 35,225 Coed
Affiliation or Control: State/Local IRS Status: 501(c)3
Highest Offering: Associate Degree
Program: Occupational; 2-Year Principally Bachelor's Creditable
Accreditation: WJ, ADNUR, #ARCPA

00 Interim Chancellor ... Dr. Cynthia AZARI
02 Acting President ... Dr. Wolde-Ab ISAAC
10 Int Vice Pres Business Services ... Mr. Charles WYCKOFF
103 VP Workforce & Resource Development ... Dr. Shelagh CAMAK
05 Int Vice Pres Academic Affairs ... Ms. Susan MILLS
32 Vice President Student Services ... Dr. Edward BUSH
28 VC Diversity/Human Resources ... Ms. Melissa KANE
20 Dean of Instruction ... Mrs. Virginia MCKEE-LEONE
105 Director Distance Ed/Open Campus ... Mr. Glen BRADY
66 Dean School of Nursing ... Dr. Sandy BAKER
08 Dean Instruction Library/Lrng Res ... Dr. Bernard FRADKIN
57 Dean of Instr Fine & Perform Arts ... Vacant
75 Dean Instruction Career/Tech Educ ... Ms. Patricia AVILA
88 Assoc Dean Academic Support ... Ms. Debbie WHITAKER
24 Prod/Artistic Dir Perform Riverside ... Mr. Matthew NEVES
07 Dean Enrollment Services ... Ms. Joy CHAMBERS
35 Dean Student Services ... Ms. Cecilia ALVARADO
41 Director Athletics ... Mr. Derrick JOHNSON
09 Assoc Dean Institutional Research ... Mr. Daniel MARTINEZ
23 Director Health Services ... Ms. Deborah CLOAN
19 Sergeant Safety & Police ... Mr. Richard HENRY

Rudolf Steiner College (B)

9200 Fair Oaks Boulevard, Fair Oaks CA 95628
County: Sacramento Identification: 667088
Telephone: (916) 961-8727 Carnegie Class: Not Classified
FAX Number: (916) 961-8731 Calendar System: Other
URL: www.steinercollege.edu
Established: 1976 Annual Graduate Tuition & Fees: $13,050
Enrollment: N/A Coed
Affiliation or Control: Independent Non-Profit IRS Status: 501(c)3
Highest Offering: Master's; No Undergraduates
Program: Teacher Preparatory
Accreditation: @WC

01 Interim President ... Ms. Betty STALEY
03 Interim Executive Director ... Ms. Lauren HICKMAN

Sage College (C)

12125 Day Street, Building L,
Moreno Valley CA 92557-6720
FICE Identification: 030695
Unit ID: 410520
Telephone: (951) 781-2727 Carnegie Class: Assoc/PrivFP
FAX Number: (951) 781-0570 Calendar System: Semester
URL: www.sagecollege.edu
Established: 1973 Annual Undergrad Tuition & Fees: $12,460
Enrollment: 584 Coed
Affiliation or Control: Proprietary IRS Status: Proprietary
Highest Offering: Associate Degree
Program: Occupational; 2-Year Principally Bachelor's Creditable
Accreditation: ACICS

01 Executive Director ... Ms. Lauren SOMMA
03 Assistant Director ... Ms. Sharon GOUPIL

Sage College (D)

2820 Camino Del Rio South Ste 100,
San Diego CA 92108-3821
Telephone: (619) 683-2727 Identification: 666304
Accreditation: ACICS

† Main campus is Sage College in Moreno Valley, CA.

Saint John's Seminary (E)

5012 Seminary Road, Camarillo CA 93012-2500
County: Ventura FICE Identification: 001299
Unit ID: 123855
Telephone: (805) 482-2755 Carnegie Class: Spec/Faith
FAX Number: (805) 482-3470 Calendar System: Semester
URL: www.stjohnsem.edu
Established: 1939 Annual Graduate Tuition & Fees: $16,675
Enrollment: 104 Male
Affiliation or Control: Roman Catholic IRS Status: 501(c)3
Highest Offering: Master's; No Undergraduates
Program: Professional; Religious Emphasis
Accreditation: WC, THEOL

01 Rector ... RevMgr. Craig A. COX
05 Academic Dean ... Rev. Joel HENSON
07 Director of Admissions ... Dr. Mark FISCHER
06 Registrar ... Ms. Esme TAKAHASHI

Saint Mary's College of California (F)

1928 Saint Mary's Road, Moraga CA 94556-2744
County: Contra Costa FICE Identification: 001302
Unit ID: 123554
Telephone: (925) 631-4000 Carnegie Class: Master's L
FAX Number: (925) 376-8497 Calendar System: 4/1/4
URL: www.stmarys-ca.edu
Established: 1863 Annual Undergrad Tuition & Fees: $39,890
Enrollment: 4,228 Coed
Affiliation or Control: Roman Catholic IRS Status: 501(c)3
Highest Offering: Doctorate
Program: Liberal Arts And General; Teacher Preparatory; Professional
Accreditation: WC, MACTE

01 President ... Dr. James A. DONAHUE
05 Provost/Vice President Acad Affairs ... Dr. Bethami DOBKIN
32 Vice Provost Student Affairs ... Dr. Jane CAMARILLO
20 Vice Provost Undergrad Academics ... Dr. Richard M. CARP
10 Vice President for Finance/CFO ... Mr. Peter MICHELL
30 Vice President Development ... Dr. Keith E. BRANT
26 Interim Vice Pres College Communica ... Ms. Elizabeth SMITH
88 Vice President for Mission ... Dr. Carole SWAIN
84 Vice Provost Enrollment Services ... Vacant
107 Vice Prov Graduate/Professnl Stds ... Dr. Christopher SINDT
27 Asst Vice Pres of Communications ... Ms. Elizabeth SMITH
30 Asst Vice President of Development ... Ms. Lisa MOORE
43 General Counsel ... Mr. Larry NUTI
53 Interim Dean School of Education ... Dr. Christopher SINDT
50 Dean School Econ & Business Admin ... Dr. Zhan LI
81 Dean School of Science ... Dr. Roy WENSLEY
49 Dean School Liberal Arts ... Dr. Steve WOOLPERT
35 Dean of Students ... Vacant
08 Dean Academic Resources ... Ms. Patricia KREITZ
42 Director Mission & Ministry ... Br. Michael MURPHY
07 Dean of Admissions ... Mr. Michael MCKEON
15 Director Human Resources ... Mr. Eduardo SALAZ
58 Interim Assoc Dean Graduate Pgms ... Dr. Yung Jae LEE
06 Registrar ... Ms. Julia ODOM
20 Assistant Dean of Students ... Mr. Jim SCIUTO
37 Director of Financial Aid ... Ms. Priscilla MUHA
88 Director of Kinesiology ... Dr. Stephen MILLER
57 Director MFA in Creative Writing ... Ms. Brenda HILLMAN
29 Director Alumni/Volunteer Engagemnt ... Mr. Chris CARTER
14 Director of Information Technology ... Mr. Dennis RICE
13 Chief Technology Officer ... Mr. Peter GRECO
19 Director of Public Safety ... Mr. Adan TEJADA
38 Director of Counseling Center ... Ms. Dai L. TO
41 Dir of Athletic & Recreation Sports ... Mr. Mark C. ORR
88 Director Saint Mary's Art Museum ... Ms. Carrie BREWSTER
71 Director of January Term Program ... Dr. Sue FALLIS
18 Exec Director of Physical Plant ... Mr. Joseph KEHOE
102 Director of Foundation & Corp Rels ... Ms. Elizabeth GALLAGHER
30 Director of Development ... Mr. Daniel G. LEWIS
36 Director of Career Devel Center ... Ms. Patty BISHOP
23 Director Health & Wellness Center ... Ms. Sue PETERS
26 Media Relations Officer ... Mr. Michael MCALPIN
86 Director Community & Govt Relations ... Mr. Tim FARLEY
94 Director Women's Resource Ctr ... Ms. Sharon SOBOTTA
88 Director of CILSA ... Mr. Marshall WELCH
88 Associate Director of CILSA ... Ms. Jennifer PIGZA
21 Director of Finance/Controller ... Ms. Jeanne DEMATTEO
88 Director Ctr International Programs ... Ms. M. Susan MILLER-REID
88 Director of Food Services ... Mr. Matt CARROLL
39 Director Conferences & Housing ... Ms. Marie LUCERO
92 Director High Potential Program ... Ms. Tracy PASCUA DEA
28 Dir of Delphine Intercultural Ctr ... Ms. Joan CUBE
09 Director of Institutional Research ... Mr. Gregg THOMSON
88 Dir New Student/Family Programs ... Ms. Jennifer HERZOG
96 Purchasing/Buyer ... Ms. Janie KLEIN

Saint Patrick's Seminary & University (G)

320 Middlefield Road, Menlo Park CA 94025-3596
County: San Mateo FICE Identification: 010074
Unit ID: 122250
Telephone: (650) 325-5621 Carnegie Class: Not Classified
FAX Number: (650) 322-0997 Calendar System: Semester
URL: www.stpatricksseminary.org
Established: 1894 Annual Undergrad Tuition & Fees: $15,382
Enrollment: 93 Male
Affiliation or Control: Roman Catholic IRS Status: 501(c)3
Highest Offering: Master's
Program: Professional; Religious Emphasis
Accreditation: WC, THEOL

01 President/Rector & Vice Chancellor ... Rev. James L. MCKEARNEY
05 Vice Rector/Academic Dean ... Rev. Gladstone H. STEVENS
10 Vice Pres of Business & Finance ... Ms. Jennifer M. MORRIS
26 Vice President for External Affairs ... Rev. James MYERS
32 Dean of Students ... Rev. Vincent BUI
08 Library Manager ... Mr. David KRIEGH
06 Registrar ... Ms. Nuria ORTIZ

The Salvation Army College for Officer Training at Crestmont (H)

30840 Hawthorne Boulevard,
Rancho Palos Verdes CA 90275-5301
County: Los Angeles FICE Identification: 036954
Unit ID: 122269
Telephone: (310) 377-0481 Carnegie Class: Not Classified
FAX Number: (310) 541-1697 Calendar System: Quarter
URL: www.crestmont.edu
Established: 1878 Annual Undergrad Tuition & Fees: $7,335
Enrollment: 125 Coed
Affiliation or Control: Other IRS Status: 501(c)3
Highest Offering: Associate Degree
Program: 2-Year Principally Bachelor's Creditable; Religious Emphasis
Accreditation: WJ

01 CEO/Principal Col for Officer Trng ... Major Tim FOLEY
03 Assistant Principal ... Major Brian SAUNDERS
05 Director of Curriculum ... Major Brian JONES
10 Director of Business Administration ... Capt. Kelly NOLAN
32 Director of Campus Services ... Major Cindy FOLEY

Samuel Merritt University (I)

370 Hawthorne Avenue, Oakland CA 94609-3108
County: Alameda FICE Identification: 007012
Unit ID: 122296
Telephone: (510) 869-6511 Carnegie Class: Spec/Health
FAX Number: (510) 869-6525 Calendar System: Semester
URL: www.samuelmerritt.edu
Established: 1909 Annual Undergrad Tuition & Fees: $41,330
Enrollment: 1,530 Coed
Affiliation or Control: Independent Non-Profit IRS Status: 501(c)3
Highest Offering: Doctorate
Program: Professional
Accreditation: WC, ANEST, ARCPA, NURSE, OT, POD, PTA

01 President ... Dr. Sharon C. DIAZ
05 Academic Vice President/Provost ... Dr. Scot FOSTER
10 Vice President Business Affairs/CFO ... Mr. Gregory GINGRAS
84 Vice President Enrollment Services ... Mr. John GARTEN-SHUMAN
20 Assistant Academic Vice President ... Dr. Penny BAMFORD
20 Asst Academic Vice President ... Dr. Terry NORDSTROM
32 Asst Vice President Student Affairs ... Mr. Craig ELLIOTT
21 Asst VP Finance & Admin/Controller ... Vacant
04 Assistant to the President ... Ms. Margrette PETERSON
66 Dean & Professor of Nursing ... Dr. Audrey BERMAN
63 Dean Podiatric Medicine ... Dr. John VENSON
88 Chair Dept Physical Therapy ... Vacant
88 Chair Dept Occupational Therapy ... Dr. Kate HAYNER
66 Chair ABSN ... Dr. Nancy HAUGEN
66 Chairperson Undergraduate Nursing ... Dr. Margaret EARLY
07 Dean Admission ... Mr. Timothy CRANFORD
15 Exec Director Human Resources ... Ms. Elaine LEMAY
100 Exec Director Ofc of the President ... Ms. Stephanie BANGERT
30 Exec Director of Development ... Ms. Susan VALENCIA
09 Director Institutional Research ... Ms. Nandini DASGUPTA
06 Registrar ... Ms. Anne SCHER
08 Library Director ... Mr. Marcus BANKS
37 Director Financial Aid ... Ms. Tanya GRIGGS
88 Dir Family Nurse Practitioner Pgm ... Ms. Suzanne AUGUST-SCHWARTZ
29 Director of Alumni Relations ... Ms. Carla ROSS
18 Director Facilities Management ... Ms. Lillian HARVIN
88 Director Physician Assistant Pgm ... Dr. Michael DEROSA
12 Site Manager Sacramento ... Ms. Rene ENGELHART
12 Site Manager San Mateo ... Dr. Mileva LEWIS SAULO
13 Dir of Information Technology Svcs ... Mr. Blair SIMMONS
26 Assoc Dir Media Rels/Publication ... Ms. Elizabeth VALENTE

*San Bernardino Community College District (J)

114 S. Del Rosa Drive, San Bernardino CA 92401
County: San Bernardino Identification: 667040
Telephone: (909) 382-4091 Carnegie Class: N/A
FAX Number: (909) 382-0153
URL: www.sbccd.edu

01 Chancellor ... Bruce BARON
10 Int Vice Chancellor Fiscal Services ... Timothy OLIVER
15 Vice Chancellor Human Resources ... Tanya ROGERS

*Crafton Hills College (K)

11711 Sand Canyon Road, Yucaipa CA 92399-1799
County: San Bernardino FICE Identification: 009272
Unit ID: 113111
Telephone: (909) 794-2161 Carnegie Class: Assoc/Pub-U-MC
FAX Number: (909) 794-0423 Calendar System: Semester
URL: www.craftonhills.edu
Established: 1972 Annual Undergrad Tuition & Fees (In-District): $1,134
Enrollment: 5,280 Coed
Affiliation or Control: State/Local IRS Status: 501(c)3
Highest Offering: Associate Degree
Program: Occupational; 2-Year Principally Bachelor's Creditable

Accreditation: WJ, COARC, EMT

02 President .... Dr. Cheryl A. MARSHALL
05 Vice President of Instruction .... Dr. Bryan REECE
11 Vice President Administrative Svcs .... Mr. Mike STRONG
32 Vice President Student Services .... Ms. Rebeccah WARREN-MARLATT
88 Dean Stdnt Svcs/Stdnt Development .... Mr. Joe CABRALES
49 Dean of Arts & Sciences .... Mr. Richard HOGREFE
81 Dean Math/English/Reading/Inst Supp .... Mr. Raju HEGDE
36 Dean Career Educ & Human Devel .... Ms. June Y. YAMAMOTO
35 Dean Student Services/Counseling .... Ms. Kirsten S. COLVEY
09 Dean Instl Effect/Research/Planning .... Mr. Keith WURTZ
30 Dir Resource Development/Grants .... Ms. Karen CHILDERS
40 Director Bookstore .... Ms. Gloriann CHAVEZ
88 Director EOPS/CARE .... Ms. Rejoice CHAVIRA
25 Director Grant Mgt & Development .... Ms. Karen CHILDERS
37 Director Financial Aid .... Mr. John W. MUSKAVITCH
32 Director Student Life .... Ms. Ericka PADDOCK
18 Director Facilities .... Mr. Larry COOK
13 Director Technology Services .... Mr. Wayne BOGH
26 Director Marketing/Public Relations .... Ms. Donna HOFFMAN
08 Librarian .... Ms. Laura WINNINGHAM
06 Admissions and Records Coordinator .... Mr. Larry K. AYCOCK

*San Bernardino Valley College (A)

701 S Mt. Vernon Avenue,
San Bernardino CA 92410-2798

County: San Bernardino FICE Identification: 001272
Unit ID: 123527

Telephone: (909) 384-4400 Carnegie Class: Assoc/Pub-U-MC
FAX Number: N/A Calendar System: Semester
URL: www.valleycollege.edu
Established: 1926 Annual Undergrad Tuition & Fees (In-District): $1,554
Enrollment: 11,781 Coed
Affiliation or Control: State/Local IRS Status: 501(c)3
Highest Offering: Associate Degree
Program: Occupational; 2-Year Principally Bachelor's Creditable
Accreditation: WJ, ADNUR

02 Interim President .... Dr. Gloria M. FISHER
05 Vice President Instruction .... Dr. Haragewen KINDE
11 Interim VP Administrative Services .... Mr. Scott STARK
32 Interim VP Student Services .... Mr. Joe CABRALES
72 Dean AT/TRANS/CULA .... Dr. Achala CHATTERJEE
79 Dean Arts & Humanities .... Dr. Kay WEISS
38 Dean Counseling/Matriculation .... Mr. Marco COTA
50 Int Dean Math/Bus/Computer Tech .... Dr. Odette MCGINNIS
09 Dean Research/Planning/Inst Effect .... Dr. James SMITH
81 Dean Sciences .... Dr. Susan BANGASSER
83 Int Dean SS/Human Development & PE .... Dr. Edward MILLICAN
07 Director Admissions/Records .... Vacant
40 Director Bookstores .... Ms. Gloriann CHAVEZ
88 Director Child Development Ctr .... Mr. Mark MERJIL
31 Dir Community Relations/Resourc Dev .... Vacant
88 Director EOP&S/CalWORKs/STAR/DSP&S .... Vacant
37 Director Financial Aid .... Vacant
25 Dir Grant Development/Management .... Dr. Kathleen ROWLEY
08 Dir Library/Learning Support Svcs .... Vacant
26 Director Marketing/Public Relations .... Mr. Craig PETINAK
35 Director Student Life .... Ms. Carolyn LINDSEY
13 Director Technology Services .... Mr. Rick HRDLICKA
88 Manager Cafeteria .... Ms. Tracy MORRISON

San Diego Christian College (B)

2100 Greenfield Drive, El Cajon CA 92019-1157

County: San Diego FICE Identification: 012031
Unit ID: 112084

Telephone: (619) 201-8700 Carnegie Class: Bac/A&S
FAX Number: (619) 201-8749 Calendar System: Semester
URL: www.sdcc.edu
Established: 1970 Annual Undergrad Tuition & Fees: $25,888
Enrollment: 443 Coed
Affiliation or Control: Independent Non-Profit IRS Status: 501(c)3
Highest Offering: Baccalaureate
Program: Liberal Arts And General; Teacher Preparatory
Accreditation: WC

01 President .... Dr. Paul E. AGUE
04 Exec Assistant to the President .... Mrs. Kelly BUCHANAN
10 Dean for Administration and Finance .... Mr. Robert JENSEN
05 VP for Academic Affairs .... Dr. Jon DEPRIEST
32 VP for Student Services .... Mr. David MADDOX
07 Director of Enrollment Services .... Mrs. Susie M. PARKS
37 Director of Financial Aid .... Vacant
07 Director of Admissions .... Ms. Candice DELGIUDICE
42 Director of Spiritual Life .... Mr. Steve JENKINS
30 Director of Advancement .... Vacant
15 Director of Human Resources .... Mr. Robert JENSEN
08 Director of Library Services .... Ms. Ruth MARTIN
29 Manager of Alumni/Donor Relations .... Ms. Amanda GRAHAM
09 Dean of Assessment and Planning .... Mrs. Lundie CARSTENSEN
41 Athletic Director .... Mr. Chris BANDO
23 Director of Health Services .... Mrs. Malia JENKINS
28 Director of Diversity .... Mr. Carl CALDERSON

*San Diego Community College District Administrative Offices (C)

3375 Camino Del Rio South, San Diego CA 92108-3883

County: San Diego FICE Identification: 008895
Unit ID: 122339

Telephone: (619) 388-6500 Carnegie Class: N/A
FAX Number: (619) 388-6913
URL: www.sdccd.edu

01 Chancellor .... Dr. Constance M. CARROLL
05 Vice Chanc Instructional Svcs .... Dr. Otto LEE
10 Exec Vice Chanc Business Services .... Dr. Bonnie Ann DOWD
15 Vice Chancellor Human Resources .... Mr. Will SURBROOK
18 Vice Chanc Facilities Management .... Vacant
32 Vice Chancellor Student Services .... Ms. Lynn C. NEAULT
26 Director Comm & Public Relations .... Mr. Jack BERESFORD
43 Director Legal Services & EEO .... Ms. Mary ROGERS

*San Diego City College (D)

1313 Park Boulevard, San Diego CA 92101-4787

County: San Diego FICE Identification: 001273
Unit ID: 122320

Telephone: (619) 388-3400 Carnegie Class: Not Classified
FAX Number: (619) 388-3063 Calendar System: Semester
URL: www.sdcity.edu
Established: 1914 Annual Undergrad Tuition & Fees (In-District): $2,794
Enrollment: 16,923 Coed
Affiliation or Control: State/Local IRS Status: 501(c)3
Highest Offering: Associate Degree
Program: Occupational; 2-Year Principally Bachelor's Creditable
Accreditation: WJ, ADNUR

02 Interim President .... Dr. Lynn NEAULT
05 Vice President Instruction .... Dr. Randall BARNES
32 Vice President Student Services .... Mrs. Denise WHISENHUNT
11 Vice President of Admin Services .... Ms. Jacquelin BELL
35 Interim Dean of Student Affairs .... Mr. Larry MAXEY
08 Dean Information/Learning Tech .... Mr. Robbi EWELL
79 Dean School of Arts/Humanities .... Ms. Trudy GERALD
50 Interim Dean Sch Business/Info Tech .... Ms. Rose LAMURAGLIA
88 Dean Student Develop/Matriculation .... Ms. Helen ELIAS
88 Dean Engr & Tech/Math/Sci/Nurs .... Dr. Minou SPRADLEY
56 Director Off-Campus Programs .... Ms. Jeanie TYLER
18 Chief Facilities/Physical Plant .... Mr. Derrall CHANDLER
92 Director Honors Program .... Dr. Kelly MAYHEW
07 Admissions & Records Supervisor .... Ms. Lou HUMPHRIES
22 Affirmative Action Officer .... Mr. Edwin HIEL
40 Bookstore Supervisor .... Ms. DeeDee PORTER
26 Public Information Officer .... Ms. Heidi BUNKOWSKE
88 PgmMgr Disabled Student Services .... Ms. Debra WRIGHT-HOWARD
37 Financial Aid Supervisor .... Mr. Gregory SANCHEZ
88 Director EOPS .... Dr. Star RIVERA-LACEY
83 Dean Behav & Soc Sci/Consumer Stds .... Ms. Lori ERRECA
68 Dean Health/Exercise Sci/Athletics .... Ms. Kathy MCGINNIS

*San Diego Mesa College (E)

7250 Mesa College Drive, San Diego CA 92111-4998

County: San Diego FICE Identification: 001275
Unit ID: 122375

Telephone: (619) 388-2721 Carnegie Class: Assoc/Pub-U-MC
FAX Number: (619) 388-2929 Calendar System: Semester
URL: www.sdmesa.edu
Established: 1962 Annual Undergrad Tuition & Fees (In-District): $1,104
Enrollment: 25,468 Coed
Affiliation or Control: State/Local IRS Status: 501(c)3
Highest Offering: Associate Degree
Program: Occupational; 2-Year Principally Bachelor's Creditable
Accreditation: WJ, CAHIIM, DA, PTAA, RAD

02 President .... Dr. Pamela T. LUSTER
05 Vice President Instruction .... Dr. Tim MCGRATH
32 Vice Pres Student Services .... Dr. Juiliana BARNES
11 Actg VP Administrative Services .... Mr. Robert GARBER
88 Dean Student Development .... Ms. Susan TOPHAM
79 Acting Dean Arts & Languages .... Ms. Leslie SHIMAZAKI
76 Dean Health Sciences/Public Svc .... Ms. Margie FRITCH
81 Dean School Math/Natural Sciences .... Dr. Saeid EIDGAHY
50 Dean Sch Business Technology .... Dr. Danene BROWN
62 Actg Dean Lrng Res/Educational Tech .... Mr. Kevin BRANSON
68 Dean PE/Health Educ & Athletics .... Mr. Dave EVANS
79 Dean of Humanities .... Mr. Andrew J. MACNEILL
83 Dean Social/Behav Sci/Mult Stds .... Dr. Charles ZAPPIA
35 Dean Student Affairs .... Ms. Ashanti HANDS
09 Dean Institutional Effectiveness .... Dr. Jill BAKER
27 Public Information Officer .... Ms. Lina HEIL
37 Financial Aid Officer .... Ms. Gilda MALDONADO
07 Student Svcs Supervisor Admission .... Ms. Ivonne ALVAREZ
04 Exec Asst to the President .... Ms. Sara Beth CAIN

*San Diego Miramar College (F)

10440 Black Mountain Road, San Diego CA 92126-2999

County: San Diego FICE Identification: 011820
Unit ID: 122384

Telephone: (619) 388-7800 Carnegie Class: Assoc/Pub-U-MC
FAX Number: (619) 388-7901 Calendar System: Semester
URL: www.sdmiramar.edu
Established: 1969 Annual Undergrad Tuition & Fees (In-District): $1,104
Enrollment: 11,487 Coed
Affiliation or Control: State/Local IRS Status: 501(c)3
Highest Offering: Associate Degree
Program: 2-Year Principally Bachelor's Creditable
Accreditation: WJ

02 President .... Dr. Patricia HSIEH
05 Vice President Instruction .... Dr. Jerry BUCKLEY
32 Vice President Student Services .... Mr. Gerald RAMSEY
10 Vice President Admin Services .... Mr. Brett BELL
49 Dean of Liberal Arts .... Dr. Lou ASCIONE
50 Dean Business/Tech/Workforce Init .... Ms. Lynne ORNELAS
81 Dean Math and Science .... Dr. Paulette HOPKINS
88 Dean of Public Safety .... Mr. George BEITEY
88 Chair Physical Sciences .... Dr. Linda WOODS
26 Public Info Ofcr/Dir Alumni Rels .... Ms. Sandi TREVISAN
37 Financial Aid Officer .... Ms. Teresa VILABOY
18 Chief Facilities/Physical Plant .... Mr. Dane LINDSAY
88 Child Development .... Ms. Dawn BURGESS
35 Dean of Student Affairs .... Ms. Adela JACOBSON
08 Library Chair .... Ms. Mary HART
07 Admissions Supervisor .... Ms. Dana STACK
88 Chair Admin Justice/Police Acad .... Mr. Steve LICKISS
50 Chair Business .... Mr. Wahid HAMIDY
72 Chair Fire Science .... Ms. Mary KJARTANSON
79 Chair Arts & Humanities .... Mr. Robert FRITSCH
81 Chair Math .... Mr. Francois BEREAUD
83 Chair Social Sciences .... Mr. Thomas SCHILZ
88 Chair Trade/Ind/Aviation Mtn Tech .... Mr. Larry PINK
88 Associate Dean ATTE Center Director .... Mr. Greg NEWHOUSE
88 Chair Diesel Technology .... Mr. Dan WILLKIE
38 Chair Counseling .... Mr. David NAVARRO
76 Chair Dept of Natural Sciences .... Dr. Marie MCMAHON
68 Chair Exercise Science .... Mr. Nick GEHLER
60 Chair Comm/English & World Language .... Ms. Sheryl GOBBLE
88 Co-Chair Automotive .... Mr. Joseph YOUNG

San Francisco Art Institute (G)

800 Chestnut Street, San Francisco CA 94133-2206

County: San Francisco FICE Identification: 003948
Unit ID: 122454

Telephone: (415) 771-7020 Carnegie Class: Spec/Arts
FAX Number: (415) 749-4590 Calendar System: Semester
URL: www.sfai.edu
Established: 1871 Annual Undergrad Tuition & Fees: $37,536
Enrollment: 670 Coed
Affiliation or Control: Independent Non-Profit IRS Status: 501(c)3
Highest Offering: Master's
Program: Professional; Fine Arts Emphasis
Accreditation: WC, ART

01 President .... Charles DESMARAIS
05 Acting VP and Dean Academic Affairs .... Jennifer RISSLER
88 VP Exhibitions and Public Programs .... Hesse MCGRAW
84 Vice President for Enrollment .... Elizabeth O'BRIEN
30 VP of Institutional Advancement .... Cynthia COLEBROOK
10 Chief Operating Officer .... Espi SANJANA
04 Administrative Assistant .... Tamara LOWENSTEIN
32 Dean of Students .... Megann SEPT
25 Director of Academic Administration .... Sarah EWICK
06 Registrar .... Thomas CHAMPION
88 Administrative Dir of Studio Prac .... Sherry KNUTSON
88 Dir Dgtl Studies & Trans-Disc Tech .... Paul KLEIN
20 Asst Dean for Academic Success .... Susan MARTIN
58 Director of Graduate Administration .... Zeina BARAKEH
58 Director of MA Programs .... Claire DAIGLE
58 Director of MFA Programs .... Tony LABAT
08 Head Librarian .... Jeff GUNDERSON
88 Director of City Studio .... JD BELTRAN
51 Director of Community Education .... Barbara GARBER
35 Assistant Dean of Students .... Anthony MOLINAR
38 Director of Counseling Services .... Vacant
26 Marketing & Communications Director .... Janette ANDRAWES
37 Director of Financial Aid .... Larry BLAIR
13 Director of Information Technology .... Andrew SIMAS
21 Interim Controller .... Rachel DULAY
18 Director of Operations .... Heather HICKMAN
09 Inst Research & Acad Planning Assoc .... Jose DE LOS REYES
88 Director of Graduate Operations .... Ian KIMMERLY
104 Global Programs Advisor .... Jill TOLFA
07 Director of Admissions .... Jana RUMBERGER
88 Director of Admissions Operations .... Jeremy SIMMONS
102 Manager Foundations & Corp Rel .... Polly SPRINGHORN
29 Manager of Alumni Relations .... Julie WEINBERG
15 Human Resources Administrator .... Joanie PACHECO
90 Academic Computing Manager .... Jeremy HOBBS

San Francisco Conservatory of Music (H)

50 Oak Street, San Francisco CA 94102-6011

County: San Francisco FICE Identification: 001278
Unit ID: 122506

Telephone: (415) 864-7326 Carnegie Class: Spec/Arts
FAX Number: (415) 503-6299 Calendar System: Semester
URL: www.sfcm.edu
Established: 1917 Annual Undergrad Tuition & Fees: $39,823
Enrollment: 414 Coed
Affiliation or Control: Independent Non-Profit IRS Status: 501(c)3
Highest Offering: Beyond Master's But Less Than Doctorate
Program: Professional; Music Emphasis
Accreditation: WC, MUS

01 President .... David STULL
05 Dean .... Mary Ellen POOLE
32 Associate Dean of Student Life .... Jason SMITH
10 Vice Pres Finance & Administration .... Kathryn WITTENMYER

30 Vice President of Advancement ..... Elizabeth TOUMA
07 Director of Admission ..... Melissa COCCO-MITTEN
56 Director Preparatory/Extension ..... Joan GORDON
26 Director of Communications ..... Sam SMITH
30 Director of Development ..... Murrey NELSON
04 Executive Assistant to President ..... Jennifer SEAMAN
31 Performance Outreach Manager ..... Elisabeth LOWRY
20 Assistant to the Dean ..... Alice BECKETT
15 Human Resources Manager ..... Michael PATTERSON
37 Director of Financial Aid ..... Doris HOWARD
18 Chief Facilities Engineer ..... David MITCHELL
06 Registrar ..... Jonas WRIGHT
08 Head Librarian ..... Kevin MCLAUGHLIN

San Francisco Theological Seminary (A)

105 Seminary Road, San Anselmo CA 94960-2997
County: Marin FICE Identification: 001279
Unit ID: 122603
Telephone: (415) 451-2800 Carnegie Class: Spec/Faith
FAX Number: (415) 451-2852 Calendar System: Semester
URL: www.sfts.edu
Established: 1871 Annual Graduate Tuition & Fees: $12,100
Enrollment: 197 Coed
Affiliation or Control: Presbyterian Church (U.S.A.) IRS Status: 501(c)3
Highest Offering: Doctorate; No Undergraduates
Program: Professional; Religious Emphasis
Accreditation: WC, THEOL

01 President ..... Dr. James L. MCDONALD
05 Dean of the Seminary ..... Dr. Elizabeth LIEBERT
30 VP Inst Advancement ..... Ms. Cecilia TONSING
10 Vice Pres Administration/ Finance ..... Ms. Barbara BRENNER-BUDER
26 Vice Pres Communications ..... Dr. Kay CARNEY
84 Director of Enrollment ..... Ms. Elizabeth MCCORD
04 Exec Administrator to President ..... Ms. Bonnie JOHNSTON
32 Assoc Dean Student Svcs/Chaplain ..... Mr. Scott CLARK
36 Dir Vocational Formation/Placement ..... Rev. Leslie VEEN
06 Registrar ..... Ms. Susan LAWLOR
21 Controller ..... Ms. Susan BURNNETT
18 Chief of Physical Plant ..... Mr. Gary MILLER
91 Director of IT ..... Mr. Larry PICKARD
39 Director Student Housing ..... Ms. Gail LU
15 Dir Human Resources ..... Ms. Bonnie BLANK
44 Director of Annual Gifts ..... Ms. Sarah CAMPBELL

San Joaquin College of Law (B)

901 Fifth Street, Clovis CA 93612-1312
County: Fresno FICE Identification: 025000
Unit ID: 122649
Telephone: (559) 323-2100 Carnegie Class: Spec/Law
FAX Number: (559) 323-5566 Calendar System: Semester
URL: www.sjcl.edu
Established: 1969 Annual Graduate Tuition & Fees: $19,113
Enrollment: 202 Coed
Affiliation or Control: Independent Non-Profit IRS Status: 501(c)3
Highest Offering: Doctorate; No Undergraduates
Program: Professional
Accreditation: WC

01 Dean ..... Janice L. PEARSON
05 Dean Academic Affairs ..... Sally A. PERRING
11 Director of Operations ..... Joan K. LASSLEY
10 Chief Financial Officer ..... Jill A. RANDLES
32 Director of Student Services ..... Joyce K. MORODOMI
37 Financial Aid Administrator ..... Jeannie M. LEWIS
08 Library Director ..... Peter K. ROONEY
26 Public Relations Director ..... Missy M. CARTIER
15 Chief of Personnel ..... Beth PITCOCK
30 Chief Development ..... Janice L. PEARSON
84 Director Enrollment Management ..... Diane M. STEEL
61 Law Program Coordinator ..... Pat A. SMITH

San Joaquin Delta College (C)

5151 Pacific Avenue, Stockton CA 95207-6370
County: San Joaquin FICE Identification: 001280
Unit ID: 122658
Telephone: (209) 954-5151 Carnegie Class: Assoc/Pub-U-MC
FAX Number: (209) 954-5644 Calendar System: Semester
URL: www.deltacollege.edu
Established: 1935 Annual Undergrad Tuition & Fees (In-District): $1,104
Enrollment: 18,968 Coed
Affiliation or Control: State/Local IRS Status: 501(c)3
Highest Offering: Associate Degree
Program: Occupational; 2-Year Principally Bachelor's Creditable
Accreditation: WJ, ACFEI, ADNUR

01 Superintendent/President ..... Dr. Kathleen HART
05 Asst Supt/VP of Instruction ..... Dr. Matt WETSTEIN
32 Asst Supt/VP of Student Svc ..... Mr. Michael KERNS
11 Vice Pres of Administrative Svcs ..... Vacant
15 Director of Human Resources ..... Ms. Dianna GONZALES
13 Vice Pres Information Technology ..... Vacant
38 Dean Counseling & Special Svcs ..... Mrs. Delecia NUNNALLY
09 Dean Plng Research/Regional Educ ..... Vacant
103 Dean Workforce/Economic Development ..... Vacant
108 Dean Student Learning & Assessment ..... Dr. Charles JENNINGS

08 Div Dean Library/Learning Res/Lang ..... Mr. Joe GONZALES
12 Associate Dean of Tracy Center ..... Dr. Jessie GARZA-RODERICK
27 Dir Public Information/Marketing ..... Vacant
21 Director of Finance ..... Vacant
18 Director Facilities Management ..... Mr. Michael GARR
07 Director of Admissions ..... Vacant
37 Director of Financial Aid/Vet Svcs ..... Ms. Denise C. DONN
96 Director of Purchasing ..... Ms. Maria BERNARDINO
06 Registrar ..... Ms. Karen SEA

San Joaquin Valley College, Inc. - Visalia (D)

8344 West Mineral King Avenue, Visalia CA 93291-9283
County: Tulare FICE Identification: 021207
Unit ID: 122685
Telephone: (559) 651-2500 Carnegie Class: Assoc/PrivFP
FAX Number: (559) 651-0574 Calendar System: Quarter
URL: www.sjvc.edu/visalia
Established: 1977 Annual Undergrad Tuition & Fees: $15,500
Enrollment: 1,000 Coed
Affiliation or Control: Proprietary IRS Status: Proprietary
Highest Offering: Associate Degree
Program: Occupational; 2-Year Principally Bachelor's Creditable
Accreditation: WJ, #ARCPA, COARC, DH

01 President ..... Mr. Mark PERRY
00 Chief Executive Officer ..... Mr. Michael PERRY
05 College Director ..... Mr. Don WRIGHT
11 Vice President of Administration ..... Ms. Wendy MENDES
84 Vice Pres of Enrollment Services ..... Mr. Joseph HOLT
10 Chief Financial Officer ..... Mr. Russ LEBO
37 Vice Pres of Student Financial Aid ..... Mr. Kevin ROBINSON
96 Director of Purchasing ..... Mr. Ralph ORTIZ

San Joaquin Valley College-Bakersfield (E)

201 New Stine Road, Bakersfield CA 93309-2668
Telephone: (661) 834-0126 FICE Identification: 023135
Accreditation: &WJ, COARC, SURGT

† Main campus is San Joaquin Valley College, Inc. - Visalia in Visalia, CA.

San Joaquin Valley College-Fresno (F)

295 East Sierra Avenue, Fresno CA 93710-3616
Telephone: (559) 448-8282 Identification: 666008
Accreditation: &WJ, SURGT

† Main campus is San Joaquin Valley College, Inc. - Visalia in Visalia, CA.

San Joaquin Valley College-Fresno Aviation Campus (G)

4985 East Andersen Avenue, Fresno CA 93727
Telephone: (559) 453-0123 Identification: 666009
Accreditation: &WJ

† Main campus is San Joaquin Valley College, Inc. - Visalia in Visalia, CA.

San Joaquin Valley College-Hanford (H)

215 West 7th Street, Hanford CA 93230-4523
Telephone: (559) 584-8840 Identification: 770508
Accreditation: &WJ

† Main campus is San Joaquin Valley College, Inc. - Visalia in Visalia, CA.

San Joaquin Valley College-Modesto (I)

5380 Pirrone Road, Salida CA 95368-9090
Telephone: (209) 543-8800 Identification: 666128
Accreditation: &WJ

† Main campus is San Joaquin Valley College, Inc. - Visalia in Visalia, CA.

San Joaquin Valley College-Rancho Cordova (J)

11050 Olson Drive, Suite 210,
Rancho Cordova CA 95670-5600
Telephone: (916) 638-7582 Identification: 666133
Accreditation: &WJ, COARC

† Main campus is San Joaquin Valley College, Inc. - Visalia in Visalia, CA.

San Joaquin Valley College-Rancho Cucamonga (K)

10641 Church Street, Rancho Cucamonga CA 91730-6862
Telephone: (909) 948-7582 Identification: 666096
Accreditation: &WJ

† Main campus is San Joaquin Valley College, Inc. - Visalia in Visalia, CA.

San Joaquin Valley College-Temecula (L)

27270 Madison Avenue, Suite 305, Temecula CA 92590
Telephone: (951) 296-6015 Identification: 770507
Accreditation: &WJ, #COARC

† Main campus is San Joaquin Valley College, Inc. - Visalia in Visalia, CA.

San Joaquin Valley College-Victor Valley (Hesperia) (M)

9331 Mariposa Road, Hesperia CA 92344-8000
Telephone: (760) 948-1947 Identification: 667044
Accreditation: &WJ

† Main campus is San Joaquin Valley College, Inc. - Visalia in Visalia, CA.

*San Jose/Evergreen Community College District (N)

4750 San Felipe Road, San Jose CA 95135-1599
County: Santa Clara FICE Identification: 029042
Unit ID: 122737
Telephone: (408) 274-6700 Carnegie Class: N/A
FAX Number: (408) 531-8722
URL: www.sjeccd.edu

01 Chancellor ..... Dr. Rita CEPEDA
11 Vice Chanc Administrative Services ..... Mr. Douglas SMITH
15 Vice Chanc Human Resources ..... Ms. Kim L. GARCIA
09 Exec Dir Research & Instnl Effect ..... Ms. Tamela HAWLEY
18 Dir Facilities/Const Mgmt/Operation ..... Mr. Robert DIAS
07 Director Admiss/Records San Jose ..... Mr. Carlo SANTOS
10 Director of Fiscal Services ..... Mr. Peter FITZSIMMONS
13 Dir Information Technology Sys Svc ..... Mr. Thomas ONWILER
28 Dir of Employment Svcs/Diversity ..... Mr. Sam HO

*Evergreen Valley College (O)

3095 Yerba Buena Road, San Jose CA 95135-1598
County: Santa Clara FICE Identification: 012452
Unit ID: 114266
Telephone: (408) 274-7900 Carnegie Class: Assoc/Pub-U-MC
FAX Number: (408) 238-3179 Calendar System: Semester
URL: www.evc.edu
Established: 1975 Annual Undergrad Tuition & Fees (In-District): $1,162
Enrollment: 9,300 Coed
Affiliation or Control: State/Local IRS Status: 501(c)3
Highest Offering: Associate Degree
Program: Occupational; 2-Year Principally Bachelor's Creditable
Accreditation: WJ, ADNUR

02 President ..... Mr. Henry C. YONG
05 VP Academic Affairs ..... Mr. Keith AYTCH
32 Vice Pres Student Services ..... Ms. Irma ARCHULETA
10 VP Administrarive Services ..... Mr. Henry GEE
50 Dean Business & Workforce ..... Vacant
66 Dean Nursing & Allied Health ..... Dr. Antoinette HERRERA
62 Dean Library/Lrng Res ..... Dr. Merryl KRAVITZ
81 Dean Math/Science/Engineering ..... Mr. Michael HIGHERS
83 Dean Soc Sci/PE/Arts/Humanities ..... Mr. Mark GONZALES
84 Dean Enrollment Services ..... Mr. Octavio CRUZ
38 Dean of Counseling ..... Vacant
35 Director Student Life ..... Mr. Victor GARZA, JR.
37 Director Financial Aid ..... Ms. Alma TANON
88 Director Student Services Pgm ..... Mr. Savander PARKER
88 Director CalWorks/WIN ..... Ms. Elizabeth TYRRELL
11 Supervisor Administrative Services ..... Ms. Lauren MCKEE
19 District Police Chief ..... Mr. Ray AGUIRRE
88 Dean Language Arts ..... Dr. Merryl KRAVITZ
14 Supervisor Campus Tech Svcs ..... Mr. Eugenio CANOY

*San Jose City College (P)

2100 Moorpark Avenue, San Jose CA 95128-2799
County: Santa Clara FICE Identification: 001282
Unit ID: 122746
Telephone: (408) 298-2181 Carnegie Class: Assoc/Pub-U-MC
FAX Number: (408) 298-1935 Calendar System: Semester
URL: www.sjcc.edu
Established: 1921 Annual Undergrad Tuition & Fees (In-District): $1,334
Enrollment: 10,140 Coed
Affiliation or Control: State/Local IRS Status: 501(c)3
Highest Offering: Associate Degree
Program: Occupational; 2-Year Principally Bachelor's Creditable
Accreditation: WJ, DA

02 President ..... Dr. Byron BRELAND
11 Vice President Administrative Svcs ..... Mr. Greg NELSON
32 Vice President Student Services ..... Dr. Marie-Elaine BURNS
84 Dean of Enrollment Services ..... Mr. Takeo KUBO
88 Executive Director WIN Program ..... Ms. Marilyn BRODIE
92 Director Honors Program ..... Vacant
41 Director of Athletics & Kinesiology ..... Mr. Lamel HARRIS
04 Assistant to the President ..... Vacant
50 Dean Business/Workforce Development ..... Vacant
79 Dean Humanities/Social Science ..... Mr. Sean ABEL
38 Dean Couns/Retention/Spec Pgms ..... Vacant
88 Dean Language Arts ..... Dr. Keiko KIMURA

81 Dean Mathematics/Sciences Division .... Vacant

*San Mateo County Community College District Office (A)

3401 CSM Drive, San Mateo CA 94402-3651
County: San Mateo FICE Identification: 004697
Unit ID: 122782
Telephone: (650) 574-6500 Carnegie Class: N/A
FAX Number: (650) 574-6566
URL: www.smccd.edu

01 Chancellor .... Mr. Ron D. GALATOLO
03 Executive Vice Chancellor .... Ms. Kathy BLACKWOOD
03 Executive Vice Chancellor .... Mr. James W. KELLER
16 Vice Chanc Employee Rels/Human Res .... Mr. Harry JOEL
05 Vice Chanc Educational Svcs/Plng .... Dr. Jing LUAN
18 Vice Chanc Facil Plng/Maint/Oper .... Mr. Jose NUNEZ
88 Vice Chanc Auxilliary Services .... Mr. Tom BAUER
31 Director of Community/Govt Rels .... Ms. Barbara W. CHRISTENSEN
10 Chief Financial Officer .... Mr. Raymond CHOW
14 Chief Technology Officer .... Mr. Frank M. VASKELIS

*Cañada College (B)

4200 Farm Hill Boulevard, Redwood City CA 94061-1099
County: San Mateo FICE Identification: 006973
Unit ID: 111434
Telephone: (650) 306-3100 Carnegie Class: Assoc/Pub-S-MC
FAX Number: (650) 306-3457 Calendar System: Semester
URL: www.canadacollege.edu
Established: 1968 Annual Undergrad Tuition & Fees (In-District): $1,150
Enrollment: 6,783 Coed
Affiliation or Control: State/Local IRS Status: 501(c)3
Highest Offering: Associate Degree
Program: Occupational; 2-Year Principally Bachelor's Creditable
Accreditation: WJ, RAD

02 President .... Dr. Lawrence BUCKLEY
32 Vice President of Student Services .... Ms. Robin RICHARDS
05 Vice President of Instruction .... Mr. Gregory ANDERSON
38 Dean Counseling Services .... Ms. Kim LOPEZ
06 Registrar .... Ms. Ruth MILLER
10 Chief Business Officer .... Ms. Victoria NUNES
26 Director of Marketing .... Mr. Robert HOOD
45 Dir Plng/Research/Student Success .... Vacant
37 Director Financial Aid .... Ms. Margie CARRINGTON
18 Facilities Manager .... Mr. John HASHIZUME
103 Dean Business/Workforce/Athletics .... Ms. Linda HAYES
79 Dean of Humanities & Social Science .... Mr. David JOHNSON
81 Dean Science & Technology .... Dr. Janet STRINGER

*College of San Mateo (C)

1700 W Hillsdale Boulevard, San Mateo CA 94402-3795
County: San Mateo FICE Identification: 001181
Unit ID: 122791
Telephone: (650) 574-6161 Carnegie Class: Assoc/Pub-S-MC
FAX Number: (650) 574-6680 Calendar System: Semester
URL: www.collegeofsanmateo.edu
Established: 1922 Annual Undergrad Tuition & Fees (In-District): $1,418
Enrollment: 9,548 Coed
Affiliation or Control: State/Local IRS Status: 501(c)3
Highest Offering: Associate Degree
Program: Occupational; 2-Year Principally Bachelor's Creditable
Accreditation: WJ, DA

02 President .... Mr. Michael CLAIRE
05 Vice President Instruction .... Dr. Susan ESTES
32 Vice President Student Services .... Ms. Jennifer HUGHES
07 Dean Admissions & Records .... Dr. Henry VILLAREAL
38 Dean Counsel/Advis/Matriculation .... Ms. Marsha RAMEZANE
46 Dean Articulation & Research .... Dr. John J. SEWART
35 Dean Student Services/Counseling .... Ms. Marsha RAMEZANE
88 Dean Language Arts Division .Dr. Sandra STEFANI COMERFORD
08 Dean Kinesiology/Athletics Division .... Mr. Andreas WOLF
81 Dean Math/Science Division .... Dr. Charlene FRONTIERA
83 Dean Creative Arts/Social Sci Div .... Dr. Kevin HENSON
50 Dean Business & Technology Division .... Ms. Kathleen ROSS
06 Registrar .... Ms. Arlene FAJARDO
37 Director Financial Aid Services .... Ms. Claudia I. MENJIVAR
30 Dir College Development & Marketing .... Ms. Beverly MADDEN
18 Director Maintenance & Operations .... Ms. Karen POWELL

*Skyline College (D)

3300 College Drive, San Bruno CA 94066-1698
County: San Mateo FICE Identification: 007713
Unit ID: 123509
Telephone: (650) 738-4100 Carnegie Class: Assoc/Pub-S-MC
FAX Number: (650) 738-4338 Calendar System: Semester
URL: www.SkylineCollege.edu
Established: 1969 Annual Undergrad Tuition & Fees (In-District): $1,200
Enrollment: 10,411 Coed
Affiliation or Control: State/Local IRS Status: 501(c)3
Highest Offering: Associate Degree
Program: Occupational; 2-Year Principally Bachelor's Creditable
Accreditation: WJ, ACBSP, COARC, SURGT

02 President .... Dr. Regina STANBACK STROUD
05 Vice President Instruction .... Dr. Sarah F. PERKINS
32 Vice President Student Services .... Dr. Joi Lin BLAKE
84 Dean Enrollment Svcs/Financial Aid .... Dr. John MOSBY
09 Dean Plng/Rsrch/Instl Effective .... Dr. David D. ULATE
10 Director Business Service .... Ms. Eloisa M. BRIONES
83 Dean Social Science/Creative Arts .... Ms. Donna J. BESTOCK
50 Dean Business/Education/Prof Pgm .... Mr. Don CARLSON
60 Dean Language Arts/Learning Res .... Ms. Mary GUTIERREZ
68 Dean Kinesiology/Athletics/Dance .... Mr. Joseph MORELLO
81 Dean Science/Math/Technology .... Mr. Raymond HERNANDEZ
38 Interim Dean Counsel/Advis/Matric .... Mr. Nohel CORRAL
103 Director SparkPoint at Skyline Col .... Dr. William WATSON
26 Director Marketing/Comm/PR .... Ms. Cherie M. NAPIER
08 Director Library Services .... Mr. Thomas HEWITT
25 Workforce Devl Grants/Services .... Ms. Anjana RICHARDS
88 Director Bay Area Cntr Intnl Trade .... Mr. Richard SOYOMBO

Sanford-Burnham Graduate School of Biomedical Sciences (E)

10901 North Torrey Pines Road, La Jolla CA 92037
County: San Diego Identification: 667069
Telephone: (858) 646-3100 Carnegie Class: Not Classified
FAX Number: (858) 646-3199 Calendar System: Quarter
URL: sanfordburnham.org
Established: 2005 Annual Graduate Tuition & Fees: N/A
Enrollment: N/A Coed
Affiliation or Control: Independent Non-Profit IRS Status: 501(c)3
Highest Offering: Doctorate; No Undergraduates
Program: Professional
Accreditation: @WC

01 President/Interim CEO .... Dr. Kristiina VUORI
10 Exec VP/Chief Admin Officer/CFO .... Dr. Gary RAISL
05 Dean .... Dr. Guy SALVESEN
15 Vice Pres Human Res/Org Effect .... Ms. Beth ALTON
26 Sr Vice Pres External Relations .... Ms. Blair BLUM
30 Vice President Inst Advancement .... Mr. Philip GRAHAM
21 Vice President Finance/Controller .... Ms. Robin RYAN

Santa Barbara Business College (F)

5300 California Ave, Bakersfield CA 93309-2139
County: Kern FICE Identification: 025779
Unit ID: 122834
Telephone: (661) 835-1100 Carnegie Class: Assoc/PrivFP
FAX Number: (661) 835-0242 Calendar System: Semester
URL: www.sbbcollege.edu
Established: 1982 Annual Undergrad Tuition & Fees: N/A
Enrollment: 93 Coed
Affiliation or Control: Proprietary IRS Status: Proprietary
Highest Offering: Baccalaureate
Program: Occupational; 2-Year Principally Bachelor's Creditable
Accreditation: ACICS

01 President .... Matthew JOHNSTON
26 Marketing Coordinator .... Monica RAYMOND

Santa Barbara Business College (G)

34275 Monterey Ave, Rancho Mirage CA 92270
Telephone: (760) 341-7602 Identification: 666582
Accreditation: ACICS

† Main campus is Santa Barbara Business College in Bakersfield, CA.

Santa Barbara Business College (H)

506 Chapala Street, Santa Barbara CA 93101-3412
Telephone: (805) 967-9677 Identification: 666099
Accreditation: ACICS

† Main campus is Santa Barbara Business College in Ventura, CA.

Santa Barbara Business College (I)

303 E Plaza Drive, Santa Maria CA 93454
County: Santa Barbara FICE Identification: 025780
Unit ID: 122852
Telephone: (805) 922-8256 Carnegie Class: Assoc/PrivFP
FAX Number: (805) 346-1857 Calendar System: Semester
URL: www.sbbcollege.edu
Established: 1980 Annual Undergrad Tuition & Fees: N/A
Enrollment: 89 Coed
Affiliation or Control: Proprietary IRS Status: Proprietary
Highest Offering: Baccalaureate
Program: Occupational; 2-Year Principally Bachelor's Creditable
Accreditation: ACICS

01 President .... Matthew JOHNSTON
26 Marketing Coordinator .... Monica RAYMOND

Santa Barbara Business College (J)

4839 Market Street, Ventura CA 93003
County: Ventura FICE Identification: 009989
Unit ID: 433420
Telephone: (805) 339-2999 Carnegie Class: Assoc/PrivFP
FAX Number: (805) 339-2994 Calendar System: Other
URL: www.sbbcollege.edu
Established: 2003 Annual Undergrad Tuition & Fees: N/A
Enrollment: 29 Coed
Affiliation or Control: Proprietary IRS Status: Proprietary
Highest Offering: Baccalaureate
Program: Occupational; 2-Year Principally Bachelor's Creditable
Accreditation: ACICS

01 President .... Matthew JOHNSTON
26 Marketing Coordinator .... Monica RAYMOND

Santa Barbara Business College-Online (K)

1834 Palma Drive, Suite D, Ventura CA 93003
Telephone: (877) 305-7222 Identification: 770628
Accreditation: ACICS

† Main campus is Santa Barbara Business College in Ventura, CA.

Santa Barbara City College (L)

721 Cliff Drive, Santa Barbara CA 93109-2394
County: Santa Barbara FICE Identification: 001285
Unit ID: 122889
Telephone: (805) 965-0581 Carnegie Class: Assoc/Pub-R-L
FAX Number: (805) 963-7222 Calendar System: Semester
URL: www.sbcc.edu
Established: 1909 Annual Undergrad Tuition & Fees (In-District): $1,378
Enrollment: 19,790 Coed
Affiliation or Control: State/Local IRS Status: 501(c)3
Highest Offering: Associate Degree
Program: Occupational; 2-Year Principally Bachelor's Creditable
Accreditation: WJ, ACFEI, ADNUR, CAHIIM, DMS, RAD

01 Superintendent/President .... Dr. Lori GASKIN
05 Exec Vice Pres Educational Programs .... Dr. Jack FRIEDLANDER
10 Vice President Business Services .... Mr. Joseph SULLIVAN
15 Int Vice Pres Human Resources .... Ms. Patricia ENGLISH
14 Vice President Info Technology .... Dr. Paul BISHOP
72 Dean Educational Programs .... Dr. Ben PARTEE
76 Interim Dean Educational Programs .... Dr. Dean NEVINS
81 Dean Educational Programs .... Ms. Marilynn SPAVENTA
57 Dean Educational Programs .... Dr. Alice SCHARPER
53 Dean Educational Programs .... Dr. Diane HOLLEMS
72 Dean Educational Programs .... Dr. Doug HERSH
07 Associate Dean Admissions .... Ms. Allison CURTIS
08 Librarian .... Mr. Kenley NEUFELD
102 Exec Dir Foundation for SBCC .... Ms. Vanessa PATTERSON
09 Sr Director Institutional Research .... Mr. Robert ELSE
27 College Information Officer .... Ms. Joan GALVAN
37 Director of Student Financial Aid .... Mr. Brad HARDISON
18 Director of Facilities & Operations .... Ms. Julie HENDRICKS
85 Director International Students .... Ms. Carola SMITH
96 Manager of Purchasing .... Mr. Robert MORALES

Santa Clara University (M)

500 El Camino Real, Santa Clara CA 95053-0001
County: Santa Clara FICE Identification: 001326
Unit ID: 122931
Telephone: (408) 554-4000 Carnegie Class: Master's L
FAX Number: (408) 554-2700 Calendar System: Quarter
URL: www.scu.edu
Established: 1851 Annual Undergrad Tuition & Fees: $42,156
Enrollment: 8,519 Coed
Affiliation or Control: Independent Non-Profit IRS Status: 501(c)3
Highest Offering: Doctorate
Program: Liberal Arts And General; Teacher Preparatory; Professional
Accreditation: WC, BUS, BUSA, CS, ENG, LAW, THEOL

01 President .... Rev. Michael E. ENGH, SJ
05 Provost .... Mr. Dennis JACOBS
10 Vice President Admin & Finance .... Mr. Robert D. WARREN
43 General Counsel .... Mr. John OTTOBONI
26 Vice President University Relations .... Mr. James LYONS
04 Exec Assistant to the President .... Ms. Molly MC DONALD
49 Dean of Arts & Sciences .... Dr. Atom YEE
50 Dean of Business .... Dr. S. Andrew STARBIRD
53 Dean Educ & Counseling Psychology .... Dr. Nicholas LADANY
54 Dean of Engineering .... Dr. Godfrey MUNGAL
61 Dean of Law .... Ms. Lisa KLOPPENBERG
73 Dean Jesuit School of Theology .... Rev. Thomas MASSARO, SJ
88 Dean Academic Support Services .... Ms. Kathryn PALMIERI
20 Special Assistant to the President .... Dr. Don C. DODSON
20 Vice Provost Academic Affairs .... Dr. Diane E. JONTE-PACE
32 Vice Provost for Student Life .... Ms. Jeanne ROSENBERGER
84 Vice President for Enrollment Mgmt .... Mr. Mike B. SEXTON
20 Vice Provost Planning/Admin .... Dr. Charles F. EREKSON
27 Vice Provost Info Services/CIO .... Dr. Ronald L. DANIELSON
88 Assoc Provost Undergraduate Studies .... Dr. Philip R. KESTEN
88 Assoc Provost Research Initiatives .... Dr. Amy M. SHACHTER
88 Assoc Provost Faculty Development .... Dr. Eileen R. ELROD
07 Dean Undergraduate Admission .... Ms. Sandra L. HAYES
84 Assoc Vice Provost Enrollment Mgt .... Dr. Richard TOOMEY
27 Assoc Vice President Mktg/Comm .... Mr. Richard GIACCHETTI
21 Assoc Vice President Finance .... Mr. Harry M. FONG
15 Asst Vice President Human Resources .... Ms. Maria Elena DE GUEVARA
88 Asst Vice President University Oper .... Mr. Joe SUGG
30 Asst Vice President Development .... Mr. Mike J. WALLACE
31 Asst Vice Pres Auxiliary Services .... Ms. Jane BARRANTES
35 Assoc Dean for Student Life .... Mr. Matthew DUNCAN
06 University Registrar .... Ms. Monica L. AUGUSTIN
29 Asst Vice President Alumni Rels .... Ms. Kathy KALE

41 Director Athletics and Recreation ... Dr. Daniel COONAN
08 University Librarian ... Ms. Jennifer NUTEFALL
08 Law Librarian ... Dr. Mary D. HOOD
14 Director of Information Technology ... Mr. Carl FUSSELL
24 Director Media Services ... Ms. Nancy CUTLER
36 Director Career Center ... Ms. Elspeth ROSSETTI
09 Director Institutional Research ... Ms. Barbara A. STEWART
25 Director Sponsored Projects ... Ms. Mary-Ellen FORTINI
38 Director Health & Counseling Svcs ... Ms. Jill ROVARIS
85 Int Exec Dir International Programs ... Ms. Susan POPKO
21 Director Budget ... Ms. Robin REYNOLDS
88 Chief Investment Officer ... Mr. John E. KERRIGAN
21 Controller ... Ms. Suzanne GAUMONT
18 Director of Facilities ... Mr. Jeffrey R. CHARLES
96 Director University Support Service ... Mr. Ed MERRYMAN
19 Director Campus Safety Services ... Mr. Philip BELTRAN
40 General Manager Bookstore ... Ms. Deborah KENDALL
42 Director of Campus Ministry ... Rev. Jack R. TREACY, SJ
22 Director of Affirmative Action ... Ms. Deborah HIRSCH
88 Director de Saisset Museum ... Ms. Rebecca M. SCHAPP
88 Exec Dir Ignatian Ctr Jesuit Educ ... Rev. Michael MCCARTHY, SJ
88 Executive Dir Ctr Sci/Tech/Society ... Mr. Thane KREINER
88 Exec Dir Markkula Ctr Applied Ethic ... Mr. Kirk O. HANSON
30 Asst Vice President Development ... Ms. Nancy T. CALDERON
102 Asst Vice Pres Fndn Corp & Govt Rel ... Vacant
28 Assoc Provost Diversity & Inclusion ... Mr. Aldo BILLINGSLEA
30 Asst Vice President Ops & Campaigns ... Ms. Caroline CHANG
92 Director Univ Honors Program ... Dr. Leilani M. MILLER
94 Director Womens & Gender Studies ... Dr. Laura L. ELLINGSTON
93 Director Ethnic Studies ... Dr. James S. LAI

Santa Monica College (A)

1900 Pico Boulevard, Santa Monica CA 90405-1628
County: Los Angeles　FICE Identification: 001286
Unit ID: 122977
Telephone: (310) 434-4000　Carnegie Class: Assoc/Pub-S-MC
FAX Number: (310) 434-4386　Calendar System: Semester
URL: www.smc.edu
Established: 1929　Annual Undergrad Tuition & Fees (In-District): $1,205
Enrollment: 34,165　Coed
Affiliation or Control: State/Local　IRS Status: 501(c)3
Highest Offering: Associate Degree
Program: Occupational; 2-Year Principally Bachelor's Creditable
Accreditation: WJ, ADNUR

01 Superintendent/President ... Dr. Chui L. TSANG
03 Executive Vice President ... Mr. Randal R. LAWSON
10 Vice President Business/Admin ... Mr. Robert G. ISOMOTO
16 Vice President Human Resources ... Ms. Marcia WADE
05 Vice President Academic Affairs ... Mr. Jeffery SHIMIZU
45 Vice Pres Planning & Development ... Vacant
84 Vice Pres Enrollment Development ... Ms. Teresita RODRIGUEZ
32 Vice President Student Affairs ... Mr. Michael TUITASI
20 Dean Academic Affairs ... Ms. Erica LEBLANC
46 Dean Institutional Effectiveness ... Vacant
15 Dean Human Resources ... Ms. Sherri LEE-LEWIS
08 Dean Learning Resources ... Ms. Mona MARTIN
85 Dean International Education ... Ms. Kelley BRAYTON
56 Dean External Programs ... Ms. Katharine MULLER
38 Dean Counseling/Retention ... Ms. Brenda BENSON
14 Dean Information Technology ... Ms. Jocelyn CHONG
43 Campus Counsel ... Mr. Robert MYERS
106 Director Online Services & Support ... Ms. Julie YARRISH
51 Associate Dean Emeritus College ... Mr. Ron FURUYAMA
35 Dean Student Life ... Ms. Deyna HEARN
20 Dean Instructional Services ... Dr. Georgia LORENZ
17 Associate Dean of Health Sciences ... Dr. Ida DANZEY
07 Dean Enrollment Services ... Ms. Kiersten ELLIOTT
86 Sr Director Government Relations ... Mr. Don GIRARD
37 Assoc Dean Financial Aid/Scholarshp ... Mr. Steve MYROW
18 Chief Dir Facilities Management ... Ms. J.C SAUNDERS-KEURJIAN
21 Director Fiscal Services ... Vacant
09 Director Institutional Research ... Ms. Hannah LAWLER
104 Assoc Dean International Education ... Ms. Denise KINSELLA
41 Project Manager Athletics ... Mr. Joe CASCIO
88 Dean of Special Programs ... Vacant
102 Director of Grants ... Ms. Laurel MCQUAY-PENINGER
88 Director Performing Arts Center ... Ms. Dale FRANZEN
30 Sr Dir Institutional Advancement ... Ms. Vanessa BUTLER
31 Director Community Relations ... Ms. Judy NEVEAU
88 Director of Classified Personnel ... Vacant
88 Director Network Services ... Mr. Bob DAMMER
25 Director of Contracts ... Mr. Charlie YEN
96 Director of Purchasing ... Ms. Cynthia MOORE
19 Dean Camp Security Stdnt Hlth/Safe ... Dr. Albert VASQUEZ
27 Public Information Officer ... Vacant
04 Admin Asst to the President ... Ms. Lin D. CALDWELL
13 Director Management Info Systems ... Vacant
24 Mgr Media & Reprographic Services ... Mr. Albert DESALLES
40 Bookstore Manager ... Mr. David DEVER
103 Dean Workforce Development ... Dr. Patricia RAMOS
101 Coordinator Board of Trustees ... Ms. Lisa ROSE
88 Assoc Dean Outreach & Recruitment ... Ms. Sonali PERERA-BRIDGES
88 Director Radio Station (KCRW) ... Ms. Jennifer FERRO
88 Director Facilities Programming ... Ms. Linda SULLIVAN
30 Dean Institutional Development ... Vacant
88 Assoc Dean Stdnt Success Initiative ... Mr. Roberto GONZALEZ
88 Dir Sustainability Coordination ... Ms. Genevieve BERTONE
75 Dir Career & Contract Education ... Ms. Michelle KING
88 Assoc Dir Dual Enroll/Instr Svcs ... Ms. Maral HYELER
06 Registrar ... Vacant

Santa Rosa Junior College (B)

1501 Mendocino Avenue, Santa Rosa CA 95401-4395
County: Sonoma　FICE Identification: 001287
Unit ID: 123013
Telephone: (707) 527-4011　Carnegie Class: Assoc/Pub-R-L
FAX Number: (707) 527-4816　Calendar System: Semester
URL: www.santarosa.edu
Established: 1918　Annual Undergrad Tuition & Fees (In-District): $1,278
Enrollment: 25,381　Coed
Affiliation or Control: State/Local　IRS Status: 501(c)3
Highest Offering: Associate Degree
Program: Occupational; 2-Year Principally Bachelor's Creditable
Accreditation: WJ, DA, DH, DIETT, EMT, RAD

01 Superintendent/President ... Dr. Frank CHONG
12 Vice President Petaluma Campus ... Dr. Jane SALDANA-TALLEY
05 VP Acad Affs/Asst Superintendent ... Dr. Mary Kay RUDOLPH
10 Vice President Business Services ... Mr. Doug ROBERTS
32 VP Student Svcs/Asst Superintendent ... Mr. Ricardo D. NAVARRETTE
16 VP Human Resources ... Ms. Karen FURUKAWA
04 Executive Assistant to CEO/BOT ... Ms. Maria GAITAN
75 Dean Career/Tech Ed/Economic Dev ... Ms. Lorraine WILSON
11 Dean Facilities Planning/Operations ... Mr. Tony ICHSAN
88 Dean Curriculum/Education Support ... Dr. Abraham FARKAS
49 Dean Liberal Arts & Sciences ... Dr. Kris ABRAHAMSON
08 Dean Learning Res/Educ Tech ... Ms. Cherry LI-BUGG
88 Dean Counseling/Support Services ... Mr. Marty LEE
88 Dean Public Safety ... Ms. April CHAPMAN
81 Dean Sci/Tech/Engr/Math ... Ms. Karen FRINDELL TEUSCHER
17 Dean Health Sciences ... Dr. Ezbon JEN
50 Dean Business/Professional Studies ... Mr. Steve COHEN
83 Dean Arts/Comm/Behav & Soc Sci ... Dr. Tyra BENOIT
79 Dean Language Arts/Acad Foundation ... Mr. Victor CUMMINGS
41 Dean Kinesiology/Dance/Athletic Dir ... Mr. James FORKUM
88 Dean Disabled Students Pgm & Svcs ... Ms. Patie WEGMAN
72 Dean Instruction & Technical Svcs ... Mr. Robert CHUDNOFSKY
35 Dean Student Services Petaluma ... Ms. Lauralyn LARSEN
88 Dean Early Childhood Education ... Mr. Joel GORDON
88 Dean Student Success & Retention ... Ms. Ruth MCMULLEN
47 Dean Agriculture/Natural Resources ... Mr. Ganesan SRINIVASAN
19 Interim Chief of Police ... Mr. Joe PALLA
13 Director Information Technology ... Mr. Scott CONRAD
103 Director Economic/Workforce Dev ... Mr. Charles ROBBINS
21 Director of Fiscal Services ... Ms. Kate JOLLEY
37 Director Student Financial Services ... Ms. Kris SHEAR
18 Director Facilities Operations ... Mr. Paul BIELEN
23 Director Student Health Services ... Ms. Susan QUINN
09 Director Institutional Research ... Dr. KC GREANEY
35 Dir Student Affs/New Student Pgm ... Mr. Robert ETHINGTON
96 Director Purchasing & Graphics ... Mr. Tim BOSMA
40 Director Bookstore ... Ms. Lorraine FAZZOLARE
44 Director Alumni Rels & Foundation ... Ms. Kate MCCLINTOCK
66 Interim Director Nursing Program ... Ms. Anna VALDEZ
06 Dir Acad Records/Intl Admissions ... Ms. Freyja PEREIRA
07 Director Admissions/Enrollment Svcs ... Ms. Diane TRAVERSI
31 Director Community Education ... Ms. Betsy ROBERTS
15 Assistant Director Human Resources ... Ms. Sabrina MEYER
26 Interim Public Relations Manager ... Ms. Janet PARMER
90 Manager Instructional Computing ... Mr. Josh ADAMS
36 Manager Career Development Svcs ... Ms. Catherine WILSON
24 Manager Media Services ... Mr. Russ BOWDEN
24 Manager Media Services Petaluma ... Mr. Matt PEARSON

Saybrook University (C)

747 Front Street, 3rd Floor, San Francisco CA 94111-1920
County: San Francisco　FICE Identification: 021206
Unit ID: 123095
Telephone: (800) 825-4480　Carnegie Class: Spec/Health
FAX Number: (415) 433-9271　Calendar System: Semester
URL: www.saybrook.edu
Established: 1971　Annual Graduate Tuition & Fees: $24,760
Enrollment: 553　Coed
Affiliation or Control: Independent Non-Profit　IRS Status: 501(c)3
Highest Offering: Doctorate; No Undergraduates
Program: Professional
Accreditation: WC

01 President ... Dr. Mark SCHULMAN
05 Provost and Executive VP ... Dr. Daniel R. SEWELL
11 VP for Finance and Administration ... Mr. Michael CAIRNS
26 VP Communications/External Affairs ... Ms. Sigrid BADINELLI
06 Registrar ... Mr. Aaron HIATT
08 Director of Library Services ... Mr. Noah LOWENSTEIN
37 Director Student Financial Aid ... Ms. Shandel ROBERTS
04 Exec Assistant to the President ... Ms. Ann LUCKIESH
07 Director of Admissions ... Vacant
16 Human Resources Manager ... Ms. Julie LLOYD
13 Director IT and Network Resource ... Mr. Laurens DEHAAN
29 Director Alumni Relations ... Dr. George AIKEN
09 Director of Institutional Research ... Mr. Scott KERLIN
84 Enrollment Manager ... Mr. Russ (Lynn) WATJEN

Scripps College (D)

1030 Columbia, Claremont CA 91711-3948
County: Los Angeles　FICE Identification: 001174
Unit ID: 123165
Telephone: (909) 621-8000　Carnegie Class: Bac/A&S
FAX Number: (909) 621-8323　Calendar System: Semester
URL: www.scrippscollege.edu
Established: 1926　Annual Undergrad Tuition & Fees: $45,564
Enrollment: 950　Female
Affiliation or Control: Independent Non-Profit　IRS Status: 501(c)3
Highest Offering: Baccalaureate
Program: Liberal Arts And General
Accreditation: WC

01 President ... Dr. Lori BETTISON-VARGA
05 Vice Pres/Dean of the Faculty ... Dr. Amy MARCUS-NEWHALL
30 VP for Institutional Advancement ... Mr. Michael ARCHIBALD
10 Vice President for Business Affairs ... Ms. Joanne COVILLE
32 Vice President of Student Affairs ... Ms. Rebecca LEE
07 Vice President for Enrollment ... Ms. Victoria ROMERO
26 VP for Communications & Marketing ... Ms. MaryLou J. FERRY
29 Asst VP Alumnae & Parent Engagement ... Ms. Nikki KHURANA
100 Chief of Staff/Secy to Bd of Trust ... Vacant
04 Executive Asst to the President ... Ms. Claire BRIDGE
20 Associate Dean of Faculty ... Dr. Gretchen EDWALDS-GILBERT
15 Director of Human Resources ... Ms. Jennifer L. BERKLAS
09 Director of Assessment & Research ... Ms. Junelyn PEEPLES
08 Librarian ... Ms. Judy B. HARVEY-SAHAK
06 Registrar ... Ms. Kelly HOGENCAMP
37 Director of Financial Aid ... Vacant
36 Director of Career Planning ... Ms. Vicki P. KLOPSCH
13 Director of Information Technology ... Mr. Jeff SESSLER
18 Director of Facilities ... Mr. Niel ERRICKSON
104 Director of Off-Campus Study ... Ms. Neva BARKER

The Scripps Research Institute (E)

10550 N Torrey Pines Road, TPC19, La Jolla CA 92037-1000
County: San Diego　FICE Identification: 033213
Unit ID: 435338
Telephone: (858) 784-8469　Carnegie Class: Not Classified
FAX Number: (858) 784-2802　Calendar System: Quarter
URL: www.scripps.edu
Established: 1989　Annual Graduate Tuition & Fees: $5,000
Enrollment: 241　Coed
Affiliation or Control: Independent Non-Profit　IRS Status: 501(c)3
Highest Offering: Doctorate; No Undergraduates
Program: Professional
Accreditation: WC

01 Director ... Ms. Marylyn RINALDI
05 Dean Graduate Studies ... Dr. James R. WILLIAMSON

Shasta Bible College and Graduate School (F)

2951 Goodwater Avenue, Redding CA 96002-1544
County: Shasta　FICE Identification: 023593
Unit ID: 123280
Telephone: (530) 221-4275　Carnegie Class: Spec/Faith
FAX Number: (530) 221-6929　Calendar System: Semester
URL: www.shasta.edu
Established: 1972　Annual Undergrad Tuition & Fees: $10,370
Enrollment: 63　Coed
Affiliation or Control: Independent Non-Profit　IRS Status: 501(c)3
Highest Offering: Master's
Program: Religious Emphasis
Accreditation: TRACS

01 President ... Dr. David R. NICHOLAS
04 Exec Assistant to the President ... Ms. Lanell E. WREN
05 Academic Dean ... Dr. Stephen G. BROWN
32 Vice President for Student Life ... Dr. Keith H. STONE
07 Dean of Admissions & Records ... Mr. George A. GUNN
18 Coordinator Grounds & Maintenance ... Mr. Gary KELLOGG
06 Registrar ... Mrs. Faith MCCARTHY
10 Asst Dir Business Affs/Controller ... Mrs. Mary MCENTIRE
37 Financial Aid Officer ... Ms. Linda ILES
56 Director External Studies ... Mrs. Faith MCCARTHY

Shasta College (G)

PO Box 496006, 11555 Old Oregon Tr, Redding CA 96049-6006
County: Shasta　FICE Identification: 001289
Unit ID: 123299
Telephone: (530) 242-7500　Carnegie Class: Assoc/Pub-R-L
FAX Number: (530) 225-4990　Calendar System: Semester
URL: www.shastacollege.edu
Established: 1950　Annual Undergrad Tuition & Fees (In-District): $1,231
Enrollment: 9,401　Coed
Affiliation or Control: State/Local　IRS Status: Exempt
Highest Offering: Associate Degree
Program: Occupational; 2-Year Principally Bachelor's Creditable
Accreditation: WJ, DH

01 Superintendent/President ... Mr. Joe WYSE
04 Asst to the Superintendent/Pres ... Ms. Theresa MARKWORD
05 VP Academic Affairs ... Ms. Meridith RANDALL
10 VP Administrative Services ... Mr. Morris RODRIGUE
32 VP of Student Services ... Dr. Kevin O'RORKE
15 Assoc VP of Human Resources ... Ms. Laura CYPHERS BENSON
14 Assoc VP Info Services/Technology ... Mr. Doug MELINE
13 Supv Info Services Technology ... Mr. James CRANDALL
45 Director of Research & Planning ... Mr. Marc BEAM
21 Comptroller ... Ms. Nancy FUNK
84 Dean of Enrollment Services ... Mr. Timothy JOHNSTON
57 Dean Arts/Communications/Soc Sci ... Dr. Ralph PERRIN

50 Dean Bus/Ag/Industry/Technology/EWD Ms. Eva JIMENEZ
67 Dean Health Sciences Ms. Kathy ROYCE
41 Dean Safety/PE/Con Sci/Athletic Dir Mr. Gary HOUSER
81 Dean Science/Language Arts/Math Dr. Frank NIGRO
56 Dean Extended Education Mr. Thomas ORR, II
62 Dean Library Services/Educ Tech Mr. William BREITBACH
37 Financial Aid Director Ms. Connie BARTON
88 Director DSPS-EOPS/CARE Ms. Sandra HAMILTON SLANE
06 Chief Records Technician Ms. Sheree WHALEY
18 Director Physical Plant Mr. George ESTRADA
88 Director Food Services Ms. Denise AXTELL
19 Director of Campus Safety Mr. Craig CARMENA
88 Supervisor HazMat Compliance Pgm Mr. Dave FREEMAN
102 Executive Director SC Foundation Mr. Scott THOMPSON
40 Bookstore Manager Ms. Josee GENDRON

Shepherd University School of Theology (A)

3200 N. Fernando Rd, Los Angeles CA 90065
County: Los Angeles Identification: 667056
Telephone: (323) 550-8888 Carnegie Class: Not Classified
FAX Number: N/A Calendar System: Semester
URL: shepherduniversity.edu
Established: 1999 Annual Undergrad Tuition & Fees: $8,200
Enrollment: 51 Coed
Affiliation or Control: Interdenominational IRS Status: 501(c)3
Highest Offering: Doctorate
Program: Religious Emphasis
Accreditation: @THEOL

05 Vice Pres & Academic Dean Shalom Y. KIM

Sierra College (B)

5000 Rocklin Road, Rocklin CA 95677-3397
County: Placer FICE Identification: 001290
Unit ID: 123341
Telephone: (916) 624-3333 Carnegie Class: Assoc/Pub-S-MC
FAX Number: (916) 630-4530 Calendar System: Semester
URL: www.sierracollege.edu
Established: 1914 Annual Undergrad Tuition & Fees (In-District): $1,380
Enrollment: 18,800 Coed
Affiliation or Control: State/Local IRS Status: 501(c)3
Highest Offering: Associate Degree
Program: Occupational; 2-Year Principally Bachelor's Creditable
Accreditation: WJ

01 Superintendent/President Mr. William H. DUNCAN
05 Vice President Instruction Dr. Debra SUTPHEN
10 Vice Pres Finance & Administration Mr. Chris YATOOMA
32 Vice Pres Student Services Ms. Mandy DAVIES
15 Vice Pres Human Resources Vacant
04 Exec Assistant Presidents Office Ms. Jeannette BISCHOFF
08 Dean Library/Learning Resource Ctr Mr. Brian HALEY
50 Dean Business & Technology Ms. Sonja LOLLAND
81 Dean Science & Mathematics Ms. Heather ROBERTS
49 Interim Dean Liberal Arts Dr. Rebecca BOCCHICCHIO
68 Dean PE & Athletics Vacant
66 Associate Dean Nursing Ms. Nancy SCHWAB
21 Director of Finance Ms. Kerri HESTER
18 Dir of Facilities & Construction Ms. Laura DOTY
88 Director Economic Development Vacant
37 Financial Svcs Program Manager Ms. Linda WILLIAMS
31 Community Education Pgm Manager Ms. Adele HAMLETT
22 EEO Program Manager Mr. Cameron ABBOTT
26 Marketing/PR Supervisor Ms. Sue MICHAELS
39 Residence Life Supervisor Mr. Jon HAMBLEN

Silicon Valley University (C)

2160 Lundy Avenue, Suite 110, San Jose CA 95131
County: Santa Clara FICE Identification: 038103
Unit ID: 444848
Telephone: (408) 435-8989 Carnegie Class: Master's S
FAX Number: (408) 955-0887 Calendar System: Trimester
URL: www.svuca.edu
Established: 1997 Annual Undergrad Tuition & Fees: $11,700
Enrollment: 582 Coed
Affiliation or Control: Independent Non-Profit IRS Status: 501(c)3
Highest Offering: Master's
Program: Professional
Accreditation: ACICS

01 President Mr. Jerry SHIAO

Simpson University (D)

2211 College View Drive, Redding CA 96003-8606
County: Shasta FICE Identification: 001291
Unit ID: 123457
Telephone: (530) 224-5600 Carnegie Class: Bac/A&S
FAX Number: (530) 226-4860 Calendar System: Other
URL: www.simpsonu.edu
Established: 1921 Annual Undergrad Tuition & Fees: $23,300
Enrollment: 1,297 Coed
Affiliation or Control: The Christian And Missionary Alliance
IRS Status: 501(c)3
Highest Offering: Master's
Program: Liberal Arts And General; Teacher Preparatory
Accreditation: WC

01 Interim President Dr. Robin K. DUMMER
03 Executive Vice President Mr. Bradley E. WILLIAMS
05 Provost Dr. Deborah Gayle COPELAND
32 Vice President Student Development Dr. Richard W. BROWN
102 VP Marketing & Dev/Foundation Mr. Gordon B. FLINN
84 VP Enrollment Management Dr. Herb TOLBERT
10 Controller Mrs. Jill K. AULT
20 Associate Provost Dr. Ann S. MILLER
18 Director of Facilities Mr. Merlin D. WEBER
04 Exec Assistant to the President Mrs. Regina ERICKSON
08 Dir Lib Svcs/Ast Prof Librarianship Mr. Larry L. HAIGHT
06 Registrar Ms. Sarah E. TURNBLOM
88 Assoc Registrar/VA Certifying Offcl Mrs. Dannielle N. STAHLY
84 Director of Undergraduate Admission Mrs. Kendell M. KLUTTZ
13 Director of IT Mr. S. Curtis DODDS
41 Director of Athletics Mr. Joseph E. GRIFFIN
35 Director of Student Life Mr. Joe C. SLAVENS
44 Director of Advancement Services Mrs. Elizabeth A. SPENCER
38 Director of Wellness Center Dr. Michael C. SCHILL
09 Director Institutional Rsrch/Assess Mrs. Brooks CLARK
39 Bookstore Manager Mrs. Emma M. ASHBEE
15 Director of Human Resources Mrs. Kori D. OECHSLI
19 Director of Auxiliary Services Mr. Edward D. SCHNEIDER
39 Residence Life Supervisor Vacant
26 Director of Marketing Mr. Mark U. WOOD
29 Director of University Relations Mr. Matthew B. KLUTTZ
42 Director of Spiritual Formation Mr. Travis G. OSBORNE
13 Database Administrator Mr. Richard L. ARCHIBALD
23 Health Center Coordinator Mrs. Connie C. ECHOLS
36 Career Services Counselor Mrs. Pamela A. SCHALO
51 Dean of Continuing Studies Mr. Perry M. GEE
73 Dean AW Tozer Seminary Dr. Patrick A. BLEWETT
54 Dean Educ/Assoc Prof Education Dr. Glee R. BROOKS
37 Director Student Financial Services Mrs. Melissa A. HUDSON
66 Dean School of Nursing Mrs. Georgianne DINKEL
88 Dean MA in Counseling Dr. Addie R. JACKSON

Sofia University (formerly Institute of Transpersonal Psychology) (E)

1069 E Meadow Circle, Palo Alto CA 94303-4231
County: Santa Clara FICE Identification: 022676
Unit ID: 110778
Telephone: (650) 493-4430 Carnegie Class: Spec/Health
FAX Number: (650) 493-6835 Calendar System: Quarter
URL: www.sofia.edu
Established: 1975 Annual Graduate Tuition & Fees: $31,025
Enrollment: 545 Coed
Affiliation or Control: Independent Non-Profit IRS Status: 501(c)3
Highest Offering: Doctorate; No Undergraduates
Program: Professional
Accreditation: WC

01 President & CEO Dr. Neal KING
05 Provost/VP for Academic Affairs Dr. Paul ROY
10 Chief Financial Officer Ms. Maria PERRY
07 Vice President/Dean of Admissions Ms. Cheryl HOKE
30 Vice President for Advancement Ms. Tracy BYARS
06 Registrar Mr. Brian LIESKE
09 Director of Institutional Research Dr. John HOFMANN
32 Dean Student Services Ms. Rosalie COOK
15 Director of Human Resources Mr. Mark DUNAWAY
37 Director Student Financial Aid Ms. Eufemia AQUINO
18 Facilities Manager Mr. Jorge ALEMAN

Soka University of America (F)

1 University Drive, Aliso Viejo CA 92656-8081
County: Orange FICE Identification: 038144
Unit ID: 399911
Telephone: (949) 480-4000 Carnegie Class: Bac/A&S
FAX Number: (949) 480-4001 Calendar System: Semester
URL: www.soka.edu
Established: 2001 Annual Undergrad Tuition & Fees: $28,146
Enrollment: 437 Coed
Affiliation or Control: Independent Non-Profit IRS Status: 501(c)3
Highest Offering: Master's
Program: Liberal Arts And General
Accreditation: WC

01 President/Professor of Economics Dr. Daniel Y. HABUKI
04 Exec Asst to the President Mr. Hiro SAKAI
05 Provost/Vice Pres Academic Affairs Dr. Tomoko TAKAHASHI
10 Vice President Finance & Admin/CFO Mr. Archibald E. ASAWA
20 Dean of Faculty/Prof of Economics Dr. Edward M. FEASEL
58 Dean of Graduate School Dr. Tomoko TAKAHASHI
07 Dean of Enrollment Svcs/Records Mr. Andrew WOOLSEY
32 Dean of Students Dr. Jay HEFFRON
88 Dir Envir Hlth/Sfty/Security/Event Mr. Cliff MOSHER
31 Director of Community Relations Ms. Wendy WETZEL HARDER
41 Director of Athletics & Recreation Mr. Mike MOORE
35 Director of Student Services Dr. Hyon MOON
39 Dir Stdt Activities/Resident Life Ms. Michelle HOBBY-MEARS
30 Director of Philanthropy Ms. Linda KENNEDY
13 Director Information Technology Mr. Saeed FAKHRI RAVARI
44 Dir of International Development Mr. Hideki ABERA
15 Director of Human Resources Ms. Katherine KING
104 Dir Study Abroad & Intl Internships Mr. Alex H. OKUDA
06 Registrar Ms. Nancy YOSHIMURA
18 Chief of Operations Mr. Tom HARKENRIDER
84 Mgr Student Recruitment Programs Ms. Marilyn GOVE
08 Director of Library Mr. Hiroko TONONO

Solano Community College (G)

4000 Suisun Valley Road, Fairfield CA 94534-3197
County: Solano FICE Identification: 001292
Unit ID: 123563
Telephone: (707) 864-7000 Carnegie Class: Assoc/Pub-S-SC
FAX Number: (707) 864-0361 Calendar System: Semester
URL: www.solano.edu
Established: 1945 Annual Undergrad Tuition & Fees (In-District): $1,380
Enrollment: 9,830 Coed
Affiliation or Control: State/Local IRS Status: 501(c)3
Highest Offering: Associate Degree
Program: Occupational; 2-Year Principally Bachelor's Creditable
Accreditation: WJ

01 Superintendent/President Dr. Jowel C. LAGUERRE
05 Interim Exec VP Academic Affairs Ms. Diane M. WHITE
10 Vice President Finance & Admin Mr. Yulian LIGIOSO
13 Chief Technology Officer Mr. Roger CLAGUE
32 Dean Student Services Dr. Shirley LEWIS
38 Interim Dean Counseling Ms. Barbara PAVAO
37 Dean Financial Aid Ms. Robin DARCANGELO
09 Dean Research and Planning Mr. Peter CAMMISH
21 Director of Fiscal Services Mr. Patrick KILLINGSWORTH
07 Director of Admissions/Records Ms. Barbara FOUNTAIN
84 Director Enrollment Management Vacant
16 Interim Director Human Resources Ms. Charo ALBARRAN
18 Director Facilities Mr. Dwight CALLOWAY
35 Dir Student Development/Mesa Mr. Mostafa GHOUS
06 Registrar Ms. Barbara FOUNTAIN
30 Exec Dir of Institutional Advancmnt Vacant
13 Director Technology Services Mr. Kimo CALILAN
88 Director Children's Programs Ms. Christie SPECK
88 Director Small Bus Development Ctr Mr. Charles EASON
88 Director Theater Operations Vacant
26 Outreach/Public Relations Manager Ms. Shemila JOHNSON
96 Purchasing Tech/Buyer Ms. Laura SCOTT
36 Career & Job Placement Coordinator Ms. Patricia YOUNG
49 Dean School of Liberal Arts Dr. John FREEMAN
88 Dean School Human Performance/Devel Ms. Lily ESPINOZA
81 Dean of Math/Science Dr. John YU
76 Dn Sch Career Tech Ed/Bus/Vcvl/TAFB Mrs. Maire MORINEC
12 Center Dean Vallejo Dr. Jerry KEA

South Baylo University (H)

1126 N Brookhurst Street, Anaheim CA 92801-1702
County: Orange FICE Identification: 025973
Unit ID: 123633
Telephone: (714) 533-1495 Carnegie Class: Spec/Health
FAX Number: (714) 533-6040 Calendar System: Quarter
URL: www.southbaylo.edu
Established: 1977 Annual Undergrad Tuition & Fees: $12,104
Enrollment: 636 Coed
Affiliation or Control: Independent Non-Profit IRS Status: 501(c)3
Highest Offering: Doctorate
Program: Professional
Accreditation: ACUP

01 President Dr. Jason SHIN
05 Academic Dean Dr. Pia MELEN
11 Vice President Administration Dr. David KWON
07 Director of Admission Dr. Young Jin AHN
06 Registrar Ms. Michelle PARK
10 Director of Finance Ms. Michelle JANG
15 Operations/Personnel Director Dr. Sohila MOHIYEDDINI
36 Program Student Advisor Dr. Henry CHOI
08 Director of Libraries Dr. Edwin FOLLICK
13 Dir Computer Information System Mr. James KIM
88 Director of Clinics Dr. Sang Jo KIM
37 Financial Aid Officer Ms. Mimi PARK
35 Stdnt/Alumni/English LG Coordinator Ms. Rocio SALAS-BELTRAN
85 International Student Advisor Ms. Rachel SON
88 Doctoral Clerkship Coordinator Dr. Sheng LI
88 Doctoral Program Director Dr. Wayne CHENG
88 Master Program Director Dr. Hanjik KIM
18 Chief Facilities/Physical Plant Mr. Yong Hee PARK

South Baylo University (I)

2727 West 6th Street, Los Angeles CA 90057
Telephone: (213) 738-0712 Identification: 770911
Accreditation: ACUP

† Main campus is South Baylo University in Anaheim, CA.

South Coast College (J)

2011 W Chapman Avenue, Orange CA 92868-2609
County: Orange FICE Identification: 022774
Unit ID: 123642
Telephone: (714) 867-5009 Carnegie Class: Assoc/PrivFP
FAX Number: (714) 867-5026 Calendar System: Quarter
URL: www.southcoastcollege.com
Established: 1961 Annual Undergrad Tuition & Fees: $39,382
Enrollment: 392 Coed
Affiliation or Control: Proprietary IRS Status: Proprietary
Highest Offering: Associate Degree
Program: Occupational
Accreditation: ACICS

01 President .... Ms. Jean GONZALEZ
03 Vice President .... Ms. Lonnie SKELTON
11 Director of Operations .... Mr. Kevin MAGNER
37 Director of Financial Aid .... Vacant

*South Orange County Community College District (A)

28000 Marguerite Parkway, Mission Viejo CA 92692-3697
County: Orange FICE Identification: 033433
Unit ID: 432144
Telephone: (949) 582-4500 Carnegie Class: N/A
FAX Number: (949) 364-2726
URL: www.socccd.edu

01 Chancellor .... Mr. Gary POERTNER
05 Vice Chanc Technology/Learning Svcs .. Dr. Robert S. BRAMUCCI
16 Vice Chancellor Human Resources .... Dr. David P. BUGAY
10 Vice Chancellor Business Services .... Ms. Debra FITZSIMONS
26 Dir Public Affairs/Government Rels .... Ms. Tere FLUEGEMAN

*Irvine Valley College (B)

5500 Irvine Center Drive, Irvine CA 92618-4399
County: Orange FICE Identification: 025395
Unit ID: 116439
Telephone: (949) 451-5100 Carnegie Class: Assoc/Pub-S-MC
FAX Number: (949) 451-5270 Calendar System: Semester
URL: www.ivc.edu
Established: 1979 Annual Undergrad Tuition & Fees (In-District): $1,487
Enrollment: 13,208 Coed
Affiliation or Control: State/Local IRS Status: 501(c)3
Highest Offering: Associate Degree
Program: Occupational; 2-Year Principally Bachelor's Creditable
Accreditation: WJ

02 President .... Dr. Glenn R. ROQUEMORE
05 Vice President Instruction .... Dr. Stephen C. JUSTICE
32 Vice President Student Services .... Dr. Linda FONTANILLA
20 Dean of Academic Programs .... Dr. Kathy WERLE
38 Dean Sch Guidance/Counseling .... Dr. Elizabeth CIPRES
49 Dean Sch Humanities/Languages .... Dr. Karima FELDHUS
54 Dean Sch Math/Computer Sci/Engrng .... Dr. Lianna ZHAO
106 Dean Online Educ/Learning Resources .... Dr. Roger OWENS
76 Dn Kinesiology/Health/Athletics Dir .... Mr. Keith SHACKLEFORD
72 Dean Life Sciences/Technologies .... Dr. Lianna ZHAO
57 Dean Fine Arts/Business Services .... Dr. David GATEWOOD
84 Dean of Enrollment Services .... Ms. Arleen ELSEROAD
102 Exec Director IVC Foundation .... Mr. Richard H. MORLEY
10 Director Fiscal Services .... Mr. Davit KHACHATRYAN
07 Director Admiss/Records/Enroll Svcs .... Ms. Arleen ELSEROAD
18 Dir Facilities & Maintenance .... Mr. John EDWARDS
19 Chief of Police .... Mr. Will GLEN
37 Director Financial Aid .... Mr. Darryl COX
35 Director Student Development .... Ms. Helen LOCKE
13 Director Technology Services .... Mr. Bruce HAGAN
51 Int Director Extended Education .... Ms. Sharon LOUIE
09 Dir Research/Planning/Accreditation .... Mr. Craig HAYWARD
26 Director of Public Info & Marketing .... Ms. Diane G. OAKS
88 Child Development Center Manager .... Ms. Becky THOMAS
06 Registrar/Admissions/Records .... Mr. Ruben GUZMAN

*Saddleback College (C)

28000 Marguerite Parkway, Mission Viejo CA 92692-3635
County: Orange FICE Identification: 008918
Unit ID: 122205
Telephone: (949) 582-4500 Carnegie Class: Assoc/Pub-S-MC
FAX Number: (949) 347-0438 Calendar System: Semester
URL: www.saddleback.edu
Established: 1968 Annual Undergrad Tuition & Fees (In-District): $1,324
Enrollment: 27,289 Coed
Affiliation or Control: State/Local IRS Status: 501(c)3
Highest Offering: Associate Degree
Program: Occupational; 2-Year Principally Bachelor's Creditable
Accreditation: WJ, ADNUR, EMT

02 President .... Dr. Tod A. BURNETT
05 Vice President of Instruction .... Dr. Kathy WERLE
32 Vice President of Student Services .... Dr. Juan AVALOS
07 Director Admissions & Records .... Ms. Jane ROSENKRANS
45 Director Planning/Research/Grants .... Dr. Caroline DURDELLA
06 Registrar .... Ms. Joyce SEMANIK
19 Acting Director Security/Safety .... Mr. James PYLE
26 Director Public Information .... Ms. Jennie MCCUE
102 Director College Foundation .... Mr. Donald RICKNER
35 Director Student Development .... Ms. Audra DIPADOVA
31 Director of Community Education .... Ms. Estella GARRISON
88 Director Emeritus Institute .... Mr. David ANDERSON
66 Director of Nursing .... Ms. Tammy RICE
10 VP College Administrative Services .... Ms. Carol HILTON
15 Director Human Resources .... Ms. Teddi LORCH
18 Dir Facilities/Maint/Operation .... Mr. John OZUROVICH
37 Director Financial Assistance .... Mr. Christian ALVARADO
96 Director of Purchasing .... Ms. Brandye D'LENA
85 Intl Student Program Specialist .... Ms. Monika CONNOLLY
92 Honors Program .... Ms. Alannah ROSENBERG
38 Dean Counseling Svcs/Special Pgms .... Ms. Jerilyn CHUMAN
57 Dean Fine Arts .... Mr. Bart MCHENRY
75 Dean Bus Sci/Voc Educ/Econ Devel .... Mr. Rocky CIFONE
76 Dean Hlth Sci/Human Svcs & Emeritus .... Dr. Donna RANE-SZOSTAK
81 Dean Math/Science & Engineering ... Dr. Christopher MCDONALD
79 Dean Liberal Arts/Learning Res .... Dr. Kevin O'CONNOR
106 Dean Online Education/Learning Res .... Dr. Patricia FLANIGAN
72 Dean Advance Tech Appl Science .... Mr. Don TAYLOR
68 Dean Kinesiology/Athletic Director .... Mr. Tony LIPOLD
83 Dean Social & Behavioral Sciences .... Dr. Cadence WYNTER
35 Asst Dean Couns Svcs/Spec Pgms .... Mr. Terence NELSON
84 Chair Enrollment Management .... Vacant

Southern California College of Optometry (D)

2575 Yorba Linda Boulevard, Fullerton CA 92831-1699
County: Orange FICE Identification: 001230
Unit ID: 123943
Telephone: (714) 870-7226 Carnegie Class: Spec/Health
FAX Number: (714) 879-9834 Calendar System: Quarter
URL: www.scco.edu
Established: 1904 Annual Undergrad Tuition & Fees: $29,100
Enrollment: 399 Coed
Affiliation or Control: Independent Non-Profit IRS Status: 501(c)3
Highest Offering: Doctorate
Program: Professional
Accreditation: WC, OPT, OPTR

01 President .... Dr. Kevin L. ALEXANDER
05 Sr Vice Pres/Dean Academic Affairs .... Dr. Morris S. BERMAN
30 Vice Pres University Advancement .... Mr. Paul A. STOVER
88 VP/Dean Interprofessional Hlth Stds .... Dr. John H. NISHIMOTO
17 Vice Pres & Dean Clinical Affairs .... Dr. Julie A. SCHORNACK
32 Vice President of Student Affairs .... Dr. Lorraine I. VOORHEES
15 Vice Pres Human Resources .... Ms. Gail S. DEUTSCH
04 Special Assistant to President .... Mr. William HEATON, JR.
10 Controller .... Mr. Bill W. TOLMASOFF
46 Associate Dean for Research .... Dr. Jerry PAUGH
18 Director Campus Operations .... Mr. Gregory SMITH
51 Director Continuing Education .... Ms. Susan J. ATKINSON
25 Director Invest & Restricted Funds .... Mr. Glenn Y. KOJIMA
15 Director Human Resources .... Mr. Dennis GABY
27 Director of Communications .... Ms. Debra J. MARKS
13 Director of Information Technology .... Mr. Gary W. GRAY
37 Director Financial Aid .... Ms. Tami A. SATO
07 Director of Admissions .... Dr. Jane Ann MUNROE
30 Dir Development/Alumni Affairs .... Ms. Frances ROZNER
08 Director of Library Services .... Ms. Donnajean MATTHEWS
23 Dir Special Clinic Programs .... Ms. Michele WHITECAVAGE
26 Director of Marketing .... Ms. Arlene E. KAYE
40 Manager Campus Store .... Ms. Debra WOODS

Southern California Institute of Architecture (E)

960 E 3rd Street, Los Angeles CA 90013-1822
County: Los Angeles FICE Identification: 020758
Unit ID: 123952
Telephone: (213) 613-2200 Carnegie Class: Spec/Arts
FAX Number: (213) 613-2260 Calendar System: Semester
URL: www.sciarc.edu
Established: 1972 Annual Undergrad Tuition & Fees: $37,300
Enrollment: 514 Coed
Affiliation or Control: Independent Non-Profit IRS Status: 501(c)3
Highest Offering: Master's
Program: Professional
Accreditation: WC

01 Director .... Mr. Eric O. MOSS
04 Director's Assistant .... Ms. Jessica WHEELER
05 Director Academic Affairs .... Ms. Hsin-Ming FUNG
11 Chief Operating Officer .... Mr. Jamie BENNETT
30 Chief Development Officer .... Ms. Sarah SULLIVAN
58 Graduate Program Director .... Mr. Hernan DIAZ-ALONSO
88 Undergraduate Program Director .... Mr. John ENRIGHT
05 Academic Affairs Manager .... Mr. Paul HOLLIDAY
20 Academic Affairs Assistant .... Ms. Andrea YOUNG
10 Finance Director .... Mr. Christopher BANKS
15 Human Resources Director .... Ms. Marilyn SHERMAN
07 Admissions Director .... Ms. Sandy FRIGO
37 Financial Aid Director .... Ms. Helen LARA
90 Director of IT .... Mr. Vic JABRASSIAN
08 Library Manager .... Mr. Kevin MCMAHON
88 Wood & Metal Shopmaster .... Mr. Rodney ROJAS
88 Wood & Metal Shopmaster .... Mr. Katsumi MOROI
20 Academic Counselor .... Mr. Peter DUNG
06 Registrar/Chf of Staff/Intl Advisor .... Ms. Lisa RUSSO

Southern California Institute of Technology (F)

525 North Muller Street, Anaheim CA 92805-3758
County: Orange FICE Identification: 031136
Unit ID: 399869
Telephone: (714) 300-0300 Carnegie Class: Bac/Diverse
FAX Number: (714) 300-0311 Calendar System: Quarter
URL: www.scitech.edu
Established: 1987 Annual Undergrad Tuition & Fees: $16,000
Enrollment: 421 Coed
Affiliation or Control: Proprietary IRS Status: Proprietary
Highest Offering: Baccalaureate
Program: Technical Emphasis
Accreditation: ACCSC

01 President .... Dr. Parviz SHAMS
03 Vice President .... Mrs. Nazila SHAMS
05 Dean of Education .... Mr. Saravana RAMAN
13 MIS .... Mr. Arian SHAMS

Southern California Seminary (G)

2075 E Madison Avenue, El Cajon CA 92019-1108
County: San Diego FICE Identification: 033323
Unit ID: 117575
Telephone: (619) 201-8999 Carnegie Class: Spec/Faith
FAX Number: (619) 201-8975 Calendar System: Trimester
URL: www.socalsem.edu
Established: 1946 Annual Undergrad Tuition & Fees: $13,692
Enrollment: 189 Coed
Affiliation or Control: Independent Non-Profit IRS Status: 501(c)3
Highest Offering: Doctorate
Program: Religious Emphasis
Accreditation: TRACS

00 Chancellor .... Dr. George W. HARE
01 President .... Dr. Gary F. COOMBS
05 Vice President for Academics .... Dr. Edward J. HERRELKO, III
03 Executive Vice President .... Vacant
32 Vice President of Student Services .... Dr. Gino PASQUARIELLO
58 Int Dean Graduate Biblical Studies . Dr. Edward J. HERRELKO, III
83 Dean of Behavioral Science .... Dr. Julie M. HAYDEN
73 Dean of Undergrad Biblical Studies .... Mr. James I. FAZIO
06 Registrar .... Mrs. Cheryl OBST
37 Director of Financial Aid .... Mrs. Yuli MARTINEZ
08 Seminary Librarian .... Miss Jennifer EWING

Southern California University of Health Sciences (H)

16200 E Amber Valley Drive, Whittier CA 90604-4051
County: Los Angeles FICE Identification: 001229
Unit ID: 117672
Telephone: (562) 947-8755 Carnegie Class: Spec/Health
FAX Number: (562) 947-5724 Calendar System: Trimester
URL: www.scuhs.edu
Established: 1911 Annual Undergrad Tuition & Fees: $30,939
Enrollment: 1,006 Coed
Affiliation or Control: Independent Non-Profit IRS Status: 501(c)3
Highest Offering: First Professional Degree
Program: Professional
Accreditation: WC, ACUP, CHIRO

01 President .... Dr. John SCARINGE
05 Vice President of Academic Affs .... Dr. J. Todd KNUDSEN
30 AVP of Institutional Advancement .... Mrs. Debra BENAVENTE
11 VP Admin & Finance/CFO .... Mr. Thomas K. ARENDT
84 VP Enroll Mgmt/Stdnt Affs .... Dr. David BEHRS
06 Registrar .... Dr. David BEHRS
20 AVPAA New Programs/SPS Dean .... Dr. Marty HARRIS
17 AVP of SCU Health Systems .... Dr. Melissa KIMURA
20 AVPAA Teaching/Learning/Leadership .... Dr. Noni THREINEN
88 Dean of Chiropractic .... Dr. Mike SACKETT
88 Dean Acupuncture/Oriental Medicine .... Dr. Greg SPERBER
13 Executive Director IT .... Ms. Theresa EGGLESTON
21 Controller .... Mrs. Kelly GALLO
10 Directory of Auxillary Services .... Mr. Joseph EGGLESTON
09 Dean Supportive/Inst Research .... Dr. Melea FIELDS
07 Exec Director of Enrollment Svcs .... Dr. Peter HANNA
32 Director of Student Affairs .... Dr. Steven JAFFE
30 Exec Director of Inst Mktg/Advance .... Dr. Hubert CHANG
29 Director of Alumni .... Mrs. Babette TENO
08 Exec Dir of Seabury Learning Center .... Ms. Kathleen E. SMITH
96 Accounts Payable/Purchasing Coord .... Mrs. Catherine MCBRIDE
37 Financial Aid Counselor .... Ms. Nida LABAO

Southern California University School of Oriental Medicine and Acupuncture (I)

1541 Wilshire Boulevard, 3rd Floor,
Los Angeles CA 90017-2211
County: Los Angeles FICE Identification: 041720
Unit ID: 459222
Telephone: (213) 413-9500 Carnegie Class: Spec/Health
FAX Number: (213) 413-5400 Calendar System: Quarter
URL: www.scusoma.edu
Established: Annual Undergrad Tuition & Fees: $12,000
Enrollment: 255 Coed
Affiliation or Control: Proprietary IRS Status: Proprietary
Highest Offering: Master's
Program: Professional
Accreditation: ACUP

01 President .... Brian H. KIM
05 Academic Dean .... Dr. Katherine H S. CHO

Southern States University (J)

1601 Dove Street, Suite 105, Newport Beach CA 92660
Telephone: (949) 833-8868 Identification: 770629
Accreditation: ACICS

† Main campus is Southern States University in San Diego, CA.

Southern States University (A)

123 Camino de la Reina Ste 100 East,
San Diego CA 92108

County: San Diego Identification: 667108
Telephone: (619) 298-1829 Carnegie Class: Not Classified
FAX Number: (619) 704-0175 Calendar System: Quarter
URL: www.ssu.edu
Established: 1985 Annual Undergrad Tuition & Fees: N/A
Enrollment: N/A Coed
Affiliation or Control: Proprietary IRS Status: Proprietary
Highest Offering: Master's
Program: Business Emphasis
Accreditation: ACICS

00 Chancellor .... John D. TUCKER
01 President/PDSO .... Danny HSING
05 Int Vice Chanc Academic Affairs/CAO .... Dr. Claudia ARAIZA
06 University Registrar .... Sean SELL
32 Dean of Students & Acad Advis .... William AMOKE
08 University Librarian .... Svetlana KONDRATENKO

Southwestern College (B)

900 Otay Lakes Road, Chula Vista CA 91910-7299

County: San Diego FICE Identification: 001294
Unit ID: 123800
Telephone: (619) 421-6700 Carnegie Class: Assoc/Pub-S-SC
FAX Number: (619) 482-6413 Calendar System: Semester
URL: www.swccd.edu
Established: 1961 Annual Undergrad Tuition & Fees (In-District): $1,104
Enrollment: 19,992 Coed
Affiliation or Control: State/Local IRS Status: 501(c)3
Highest Offering: Associate Degree
Program: Occupational; 2-Year Principally Bachelor's Creditable
Accreditation: WJ, ADNUR, DH, EMT, MLTAD, SURGT

01 Superintendent/President .... Dr. Melinda NISH
05 Vice President Academic Affairs .... Ms. Kathy TYNER
10 VP Business & Financial Affairs .... Mr. Steven CROW
32 Vice President Student Affairs .... Dr. Angelica SUAREZ
16 Vice Pres Human Resources .... Dr. Albert J. ROMAN
12 Dn High Ed Ctr Otay Mesa/San Ysidro .... Ms. Silvia CORNEJO-DARCY
12 Dean HEC Natl City/Crown Cove .... Ms. Christine PERRI
79 Dean Language & Literature .... Dr. Joel LEVINE
81 Dean Math/Science Engineering .... Ms. Janet MAZZARELLA
30 Dean Inst Effect/Dir of Foundation .... Ms. Linda GILSTRAP
35 Dean Student Services .... Ms. Mia C. MCCLELLAN
83 Dean Social Sci/Business/Humanities .... Dr. Mark MEADOWS
38 Dean Counseling/Personal Develop .... Ms. Beatrice ZAMORA-AGUILAR
68 Dean Hlth/Exer Sci/Athltc/App Tech .... Mr. Terry DAVIS
60 Dean Arts & Communication .... Ms. Donna C. ARNOLD
88 Dean Instructional Support Services .... Dr. Mink STAVENGA
26 Chief Comm Cmty & Gov Rels Officer .... Ms. Lillian LEOPOLD
15 Director Human Resources .... Vacant
09 Dir Inst Rsrch Grants & Planning .... Ms. Linda HENSLEY
18 Dir Facilities Ops & Planning .... Mr. John BROWN
13 Director Computer Systems & Svcs .... Dr. Ben SEABERRY
40 Director Food Services/Bookstore .... Mr. Joe FIGHERA
88 Dir Center Ops San Ysidro .... Ms. Cynthia K. NAGURA
37 Director Financial Aid .... Ms. Patti LARKIN
96 Dir Procurement/Cntrl Svc/Risk Mgt .... Ms. Priya JEROME
54 Dir Math/Engr/Sci Achieve/Mesa Pgm .... Ms. Raga BAKHIET
88 Director Police Academy .... Mr. James DAVIS
88 Director Disability Support Svcs .... Dr. Malia FLOOD
52 Director Dental Hygiene Program .... Ms. Vickie KIMBROUGH-WALLS
66 Director Nursing & Health Occup .... Ms. Cathy MCJANNET
88 Director EOPS .... Ms. Arlie RICASA
88 Director Student Development .... Mr. Aaron STARCK
51 Director Cont Educ/Special Projects .... Mr. Steve TADLOCK
21 Director of Finance .... Mr. Wayne YANDA
88 Director Child Development Center .... Ms. Patricia BARTOW
04 Exec Asst to Supt & President .... Ms. Mary GANIO

Southwestern Law School (C)

3050 Wilshire Boulevard, Los Angeles CA 90010-1106

County: Los Angeles FICE Identification: 001295
Unit ID: 123970
Telephone: (213) 738-6700 Carnegie Class: Spec/Law
FAX Number: (213) 383-1688 Calendar System: Semester
URL: www.swlaw.edu
Established: 1911 Annual Graduate Tuition & Fees: $45,180
Enrollment: 1,086 Coed
Affiliation or Control: Independent Non-Profit IRS Status: 501(c)3
Highest Offering: Master's; No Undergraduates
Program: Professional
Accreditation: DETC, LAW

01 Interim Dean/Chief Exec Officer .... Mr. Austen L. PARRISH
03 Chief Operating Officer .... Ms. Janice A. MANIS
10 Chief Financial Officer .... Mr. Paul KALUSH
04 Corporate Secretary .... Ms. Janis K. YOKOYAMA
05 Vice Dean for Academic Affairs .... Ms. Anahid GHARAKHANIAN
46 Associate Dean of Research .... Mr. Arthur F. MCEVOY
08 Associate Dean of Library Services .... Ms. Linda A. WHISMAN
32 Assoc Dean/Dean of Stdnts & Div Aff .... Ms. Nyree GRAY
20 Associate Dean for Academic Admin .... Ms. Doreen E. HEYER
36 Sr Assoc Dean Career/Admiss/Fin Aid .... Mr. Gary J. GREENER
43 Associate Dean/General Counsel .... Mr. Patrick PYLE
30 Assoc Dean for Institutional Advanc .... Ms. Debra L. LEATHERS
27 Associate Dean for Public Affairs .... Ms. Leslie R. STEINBERG
07 Asst Dean of Admissions .... Ms. Lisa L. GEAR
06 Asst Dean Regist/Academic Records .... Ms. Carolyn HAITH
35 Asst Dean of Student Affairs .... Dr. Robert MENA
104 Asst Dean for Gen LLM/Intl Pgms .... Ms. Anne WILSON
37 Asst Dean for Financial Aid .... Mr. Wayne MAHONEY
13 Chief Information Systems Officer .... Ms. Bo SUZOW
88 Associate Dean of Special Projects .... Dr. Jane POWELL
88 Assoc Dean Interdisciplinary Pgms .... Ms. Molly SELVIN
88 Asst Dean Prop Admin/Development .... Mr. James C. CAMP
88 Dean Emeritus/Prof of Law .... Mr. Bryant G. GARTH

Stanbridge College (D)

2041 Business Center Drive, Irvine CA 92612

County: Orange FICE Identification: 038893
Unit ID: 446561
Telephone: (949) 794-9090 Carnegie Class: Assoc/PrivFP
FAX Number: (949) 794-9098 Calendar System: Other
URL: www.stanbridge.edu
Established: 1996 Annual Undergrad Tuition & Fees: $33,995
Enrollment: 950 Coed
Affiliation or Control: Proprietary IRS Status: Proprietary
Highest Offering: Master's
Program: Occupational; 2-Year Principally Bachelor's Creditable; Professional; Nursing Emphasis
Accreditation: ACCSC, OTA, @PTAA

01 Chief Executive Officer .... Yasith WEERASURIYA
10 Chief Financial Officer .... Nazi MASOUM
37 Director of Financial Aid .... Brian SILVANO
07 Director of Admissions .... Edward RIEPMA
05 VP of Instruction .... Dr. Everett PROCTER
66 Director of Nursing .... Kim MARTIN
75 Director of Occupational Therapy .... Satch PURCELL
88 Director of Physical Therapy .... Dr. Scott BENNIE
106 Director of Online Programs .... Dr. Jon INOUYE
20 Dean of Instruction .... Tim POWERS
32 Dean of Students .... Susan DUNN
11 Dean of Administrative Affairs .... John WALKER
105 VP of Internet and Media Technology .... Monir BOKTOR

Stanford University (E)

Stanford CA 94305-1684

County: Santa Clara FICE Identification: 001305
Unit ID: 243744
Telephone: (650) 723-2300 Carnegie Class: RU/VH
FAX Number: (650) 725-6847 Calendar System: Quarter
URL: www.stanford.edu
Established: 1885 Annual Undergrad Tuition & Fees: $42,690
Enrollment: 15,870 Coed
Affiliation or Control: Independent Non-Profit IRS Status: 501(c)3
Highest Offering: Doctorate
Program: Liberal Arts And General; Professional
Accreditation: WC, ARCPA, BUS, ENG, IPSY, LAW, MED, PDPSY, TED

01 President .... Mr. John L. HENNESSY
43 Vice President & General Counsel .... Ms. Debra L. ZUMWALT
05 Provost .... Mr. John W. ETCHEMENDY
30 Vice President for Development .... Mr. Martin SHELL
10 Vice President Business Affairs/CFO .... Mr. Randy LIVINGSTON
26 Vice President for Public Affairs .... Mr. David F. DEMAREST
15 Vice President of Human Resources .... Mr. David JONES
29 President of Alumni Associaton .... Mr. Howard E. WOLF
46 Vice Provost/Dean of Research .... Dr. Ann ARVIN
20 Vice Provost for Academic Affairs .... Dr. Stephanie KALFAYAN
88 Vice Provost Faculty Development .... Ms. Karen COOK
20 Vice Provost Undergrad Education .... Mr. Harry J. ELAM
18 Vice Provost for Land & Buildings .... Mr. Robert C. REIDY
21 Vice Provost Budget & Auxiliaries .... Mr. Timothy R. WARNER
32 Vice Provost Student Affairs .... Mr. Gregory E. BOARDMAN
04 Sr Assistant to the President .... Mr. Jeffrey H. WACHTEL
63 Dean School of Medicine .... Dr. Lloyd MINOR
50 Dean Graduate School Business .... Dr. Garth SALONER
65 Dean School of Earth Sciences .... Dr. Pamela A. MATSON
53 Dean School of Education .... Dr. Claude STEELE
54 Dean School of Engineering .... Dr. James D. PLUMMER
49 Dean School Humanities & Sciences .... Mr. Richard P. SALLER
61 Dean School of Law .... Ms. M. Elizabeth MAGILL
87 Dean Summer Session/Cont Stds .... Dr. Charles L. JUNKERMAN
42 Dean for Religious Life .... Rev. William L. MCLENNAN
88 Director Hoover Institution .... Dr. John RAISIAN
88 Director Stanford Lin Accelerator .... Mr. Chi-Chang KAO
13 Executive Director IT Services .... Mr. Bill CLEBSCH
86 Director Government Relations .... Mr. Larry N. HORTON
08 University Librarian .... Mr. Michael A. KELLER
41 Athletic Director .... Mr. Bernard MUIR
07 Director of Admission .... Ms. Colleen LIM
88 CEO Stanford Management Company .... Mr. John POWERS
16 Director of Compensation .... Ms. Linda S. LEE
21 Director of Business Development .... Ms. Susan L. WEINSTEIN
06 Registrar .... Mr. Thomas BLACK
36 Director Career Development Center .... Mr. Farouk DEY
09 Director of Institutional Research .... Ms. Kathleen DETTMAN
37 Director of Student Financial Aid .... Ms. Karen S. COOPER
27 Director Stanford News Service .... Mr. Dan STOBER
19 Director Public Safety .... Ms. Laura L. WILSON
96 Chief Procurement Officer .... Mr. Stuart DAVIS
35 Director of Student Activities .... Ms. Nanci HOWE
28 Director of Diversity .... Mr. Tommy Lee WOO
38 Director Student Counseling .... Dr. Ronald ALBURCHER

Stanton University (F)

12666 Brookhurst Street, Garden Grove CA 92840

County: Orange Identification: 667053
Telephone: (714) 539-6561 Carnegie Class: Not Classified
FAX Number: (714) 539-6542 Calendar System: Quarter
URL: www.stantonuniversity.com
Established: Annual Undergrad Tuition & Fees: N/A
Enrollment: N/A Coed
Affiliation or Control: Proprietary IRS Status: Proprietary
Highest Offering: Master's
Program: Professional
Accreditation: @ACUP

01 President .... Dr. Franklin R. TURNER

Starr King School for the Ministry (G)

2441 Le Conte Avenue, Berkeley CA 94709-1299

County: Alameda FICE Identification: 004080
Unit ID: 123916
Telephone: (510) 845-6232 Carnegie Class: Spec/Faith
FAX Number: (510) 845-6273 Calendar System: Semester
URL: www.sksm.edu
Established: 1904 Annual Graduate Tuition & Fees: $20,058
Enrollment: 74 Coed
Affiliation or Control: Unitarian Universalist IRS Status: 501(c)3
Highest Offering: Master's; No Undergraduates
Program: Professional
Accreditation: THEOL

01 President .... Dr. Rebecca PARKER
05 Dean of the Faculty .... Dr. Gabriella LETTINI
06 Registrar .... Ms. Katrina CROSWELL
07 Director of Admissions .... Ms. Becky LEYSER
30 Advancement Director .... Mr. Federico PACHECO
10 Finance Director .... Mrs. Anita NARANG

*State Center Community College District (H)

1525 E Weldon Avenue, Fresno CA 93704-6398

County: Fresno FICE Identification: 001306
Unit ID: 123925
Telephone: (559) 226-0720 Carnegie Class: N/A
FAX Number: (559) 229-7039
URL: www.scccd.edu

01 Chancellor .... Dr. Deborah G. BLUE
10 Vice Chancellor Finance & Admin .... Mr. Edwin ENG
16 Assoc Vice Chanc Human Resources .... Ms. Diane CLEROU
20 Vice Chanc Educ Svcs/Instl Effect .... Dr. George RAILEY
11 Assc Vice Chanc Business/Operations .... Mr. Brian SPEECE
07 Dist Dean Admiss/Records/Enroll Mgt .... Mr. Pedro AVILA
15 Int District Dir Human Resources .... Ms. Samerah CAMPBELL
26 Exec Dir Public & Legislative Rels .... Dr. Teresa PATTERSON
102 Executive Director of Foundation .... Ms. Gurdeep SIHOTA HE'BERT
25 Director Grants/External Funding .... Dr. Shelly CONNER
96 Director of Purchasing .... Mr. Randy VOGT
21 Director of Finance .... Mr. Wil SCHOFIELD
13 Director of Information Systems .... Mr. John BENGTSON
88 Director of Classified Personnel .... Ms. Elba GOMEZ
18 Director Maintenance/Operations .... Mr. Carl SIMMS
43 General Counsel .... Mr. Gregory TAYLOR
19 Chief of Police .... Chief Bruce HARTMAN

*Fresno City College (I)

1101 E University Avenue, Fresno CA 93741-0002

County: Fresno FICE Identification: 001307
Unit ID: 114789
Telephone: (559) 442-4600 Carnegie Class: Assoc/Pub-U-MC
FAX Number: (559) 237-4232 Calendar System: Semester
URL: www.fresnocitycollege.edu
Established: 1910 Annual Undergrad Tuition & Fees (In-District): $1,104
Enrollment: 22,067 Coed
Affiliation or Control: State/Local IRS Status: 501(c)3
Highest Offering: Associate Degree
Program: Occupational; 2-Year Principally Bachelor's Creditable
Accreditation: WJ, CAHIIM, COARC, DH, EMT, RAD, SURGT

02 President .... Mr. Tony CANTU
05 Vice President of Instruction .... Dr. Timothy WOODS
32 Vice President of Student Services .... Dr. Christopher M. VILLA
10 Vice Pres Administrative Services .... Ms. Cheryl SULLIVAN
07 Dist Dean Admissions/Records .... Mr. Pedro AVILA
08 Dean Library/Stdnt Lrng Support Svc .... Vacant
50 Dean Business Division .... Dr. Rick SANTOS
57 Dean Fine Perform Commun Arts .... Dr. Jothany L. BLACKWOOD
79 Dean Humanities Division .... Dr. Jennifer JOHNSON
54 Dean Math/Science/Engineering Div .... Dr. Ashok V. NAIMPALLY
83 Dean Social Sciences Division .... Dr. Margaret E. MERICLE
76 Dean Health Sciences Division .... Dr. Carolyn C. DRAKE
72 Dean Applied Technology Div .... Mr. Christopher WHITESIDE
38 Dean Counseling-Guidance .... Dr. Mark SANCHEZ
88 Dean of Students/EOPS .... Dr. Lee FARLEY
103 Dean Workforce Dev & CalWorks .... Dr. Natalie C. DOCKINS

75 Director FCC Training Institute ... Mr. Charles FRANCIS
88 Director Disabled Stdnt Pgms & Svcs ... Dr. Janice EMERZIAN
09 Director Institutional Research ... Dr. Lijuan ZHAI
88 Director Police Academy ... Mr. Richard LINDSTROM
35 Director of Student Activities ... Mr. Sean HENDERSON
26 Director Marketing/Communications ... Ms. Cris M. BREMER
37 Director Financial Aid ... Ms. Kira TIPPINS
27 Public Information Officer ... Ms. Kathleen BONILLA
41 Athletic Director ... Ms. Susan YATES
38 Director Student Support Svcs & ETS ... Vacant
72 Director of Technology ... Mr. Don LOPEZ
36 Director Career Advancement ... Vacant
66 Director of Nursing ... Ms. Stephanie R. ROBINSON
88 Director CalWORKs Program ... Ms. Anne WATTS
06 Admissions & Records Manager ... Ms. Frances LIPPMANN

*Reedley College (A)

995 N Reed Avenue, Reedley CA 93654-2099

County: Fresno — FICE Identification: 001308 — Unit ID: 117052
Telephone: (559) 638-3641 — Carnegie Class: Assoc/Pub-U-MC
FAX Number: (559) 638-5040 — Calendar System: Semester
URL: www.reedleycollege.edu
Established: 1926 — Annual Undergrad Tuition & Fees (In-District): $1,180
Enrollment: 13,737 — Coed
Affiliation or Control: State/Local — IRS Status: 501(c)3
Highest Offering: Associate Degree
Program: Occupational; 2-Year Principally Bachelor's Creditable
Accreditation: WJ

02 President ... Dr. Sandra CALDWELL
05 Int Vice President of Instruction ... Mr. David CLARK
11 Vice Pres Administrative Svcs ... Ms. Donna BERRY
32 Vice President of Student Services ... Mr. Michael WHITE
75 Dean of Instruction/Vocational Educ ... Dr. Claudia HABIB
79 Dean of Instruction/Humanities ... Dr. John FIRZER
81 Dean Instruct/Math/Sci/Tech/PE/Hlth ... Mr. Jan DEKKER
88 Dean Instruct/Madera/Oakhurst Ctrs ... Dr. Jim CHIN
27 Public Information Officer ... Ms. Lucy RUIZ
88 Director Disabled Stdnt Prgms/Svcs ... Dr. Janice EMERZIAN
22 Director EOPS ... Mr. Mario GONZALES
13 Director of Technology ... Mr. Gary SAKAGUCHI
37 Financial Aid Manager ... Ms. Chris CORTES
07 Admissions & Records Mgr/Registrar ... Ms. Leticia ALVAREZ

*Willow International Community College Center (B)

10309 North Willow Avenue, Fresno CA 93730

County: Fresno — Identification: 667125
Telephone: (559) 325-5200 — Carnegie Class: Not Classified
FAX Number: (559) 325-5380 — Calendar System: Semester
URL: www.willowinternationalcenter.com
Established: 2007 — Annual Undergrad Tuition & Fees (In-District): N/A
Enrollment: N/A — Coed
Affiliation or Control: State/Local — IRS Status: 501(c)3
Highest Offering: Associate Degree
Program: Occupational; 2-Year Principally Bachelor's Creditable
Accreditation: @WJ

02 President ... Deborah IKEDA

SUM Bible College and Theological Seminary (C)

735 105th Avenue, Oakland CA 94603-3603

County: Alameda — FICE Identification: 037524 — Unit ID: 447953
Telephone: (510) 567-6174 — Carnegie Class: Spec/Faith
FAX Number: (510) 568-1024 — Calendar System: Trimester
URL: www.sum.edu
Established: 1999 — Annual Undergrad Tuition & Fees: $8,320
Enrollment: 327 — Coed
Affiliation or Control: Independent Non-Profit — IRS Status: 501(c)3
Highest Offering: Master's
Program: Occupational; Liberal Arts And General; Professional; Religious Emphasis
Accreditation: BI

01 President/Chancellor ... Rev. George NEAU
05 Chief Academic Officer ... Dr. Elsie COOK
10 Vice President Finance ... Mr. Robert HORNICK
30 Marketing and Recruitment Director ... Mr. Isaac STOKES
42 Dean of Student Ministry ... Rev. Rondale TERRY
08 Director of the Library ... Vacant
32 Dean of Student Life ... Ms. Sharon JIMENEZ
06 Institutional Research/Registrar ... Ms. D'Lonika JENKINS-CARTER
37 Director of Financial Aid ... Mrs. Kathryn MANGAN
88 US Cohort Director ... Rev. Dave WALLACE

† Affiliated with School of Urban Missions-New Orleans, Gretna, LA.

Taft College (D)

29 Emmons Park Drive, Taft CA 93268-1437

County: Kern — FICE Identification: 001309 — Unit ID: 124113
Telephone: (661) 763-7700 — Carnegie Class: Assoc/Pub-S-SC
FAX Number: (661) 763-7705 — Calendar System: Semester
URL: www.taftcollege.edu
Established: 1922 — Annual Undergrad Tuition & Fees (In-District): $1,380
Enrollment: 5,261 — Coed
Affiliation or Control: State/Local — IRS Status: 501(c)3
Highest Offering: Associate Degree
Program: Occupational; 2-Year Principally Bachelor's Creditable; Liberal Arts And General
Accreditation: WJ, DH

01 Superintendent/President ... Dr. Dena MALONEY
11 Exec Vice Pres/Administrative Svcs ... Mr. Brock MCMURRAY
05 Vice President of Instruction ... Mr. Mark WILLIAMS
32 Int Vice Pres of Student Services ... Ms. Darcy BOGLE
04 Assistant to the President ... Ms. Shelley KLEIN
30 Director Foundation & Development ... Ms. Sheri HORN BUNK
13 Director Information Services ... Mr. Adrian AGUNDEZ
20 Associate Dean of Instruction ... Vacant
38 Lead Counselor ... Vacant
08 Research and Instruction Librarian ... Ms. Terri SMITH
46 Coord Inst Research/Assessment/Plng ... Dr. Eric BERUBE
41 Director Athletics ... Ms. Kanoe BANDY
15 Director Human Resources ... Ms. Jana PETERS
21 Director of Business Services ... Mr. Jim NICHOLAS
06 Registrar/Director of Admissions ... Ms. Michelle HINES
18 Supervisor Maintenance/Operations ... Mr. Michael CAPELA
37 Director Student Financial Aid ... Ms. Barbara AMERIO

Taft Law School (E)

3700 South Susan Street, Office 200, Santa Ana CA 92704-6954

County: Orange — Identification: 666398 — Unit ID: 454689
Telephone: (714) 850-4800 — Carnegie Class: Spec/Law
FAX Number: (714) 708-2082 — Calendar System: Other
URL: www.taftu.edu
Established: 1976 — Annual Undergrad Tuition & Fees: $7,400
Enrollment: 666 — Coed
Affiliation or Control: Proprietary — IRS Status: Proprietary
Highest Offering: Doctorate
Program: Professional
Accreditation: DETC

01 Chancellor ... Mr. David L. BOYD
05 Dean ... Mr. Robert K. STROUSE
86 VP of Governmental Relations ... Ms. Joan L. SLAVIN
20 Associate Dean ... Ms. Melody JOLLY

Teachers College of San Joaquin (F)

2857 Transworld Dr, Stockton CA 95206

County: San Joaquin — Identification: 667087
Telephone: (209) 468-9155 — Carnegie Class: Not Classified
FAX Number: (209) 468-9124 — Calendar System: Semester
URL: teacherscollegesj.edu
Established: 2009 — Annual Graduate Tuition & Fees: $12,550
Enrollment: 350 — Coed
Affiliation or Control: State — IRS Status: 501(c)3
Highest Offering: Master's; No Undergraduates
Program: Teacher Preparatory
Accreditation: WC

01 CEO ... Dr. Gary DEI ROSSI
05 Chief Academic Officer ... Dr. Catherine KEARNEY
06 Registrar ... Ms. Louise GAMMON

Theatre of Arts (G)

6755 Hollywood Blvd, Ste 200, Hollywood CA 90028

County: Los Angeles — Identification: 667098
Telephone: (323) 463-2500 — Carnegie Class: Not Classified
FAX Number: (323) 463-2645 — Calendar System: Trimester
URL: www.toa.edu
Established: 1927 — Annual Undergrad Tuition & Fees: $19,800
Enrollment: 23 — Coed
Affiliation or Control: Proprietary — IRS Status: Proprietary
Highest Offering: Associate Degree
Program: Occupational
Accreditation: THEA

01 President ... James WARWICK

Thomas Aquinas College (H)

10,000 Ojai Road, Santa Paula CA 93060-9621

County: Ventura — FICE Identification: 023580 — Unit ID: 124292
Telephone: (805) 525-4417 — Carnegie Class: Bac/A&S
FAX Number: (805) 525-9342 — Calendar System: Semester
URL: www.thomasaquinas.edu
Established: 1971 — Annual Undergrad Tuition & Fees: $24,500
Enrollment: 370 — Coed
Affiliation or Control: Independent Non-Profit — IRS Status: 501(c)3
Highest Offering: Baccalaureate
Program: Liberal Arts And General
Accreditation: WC

01 President ... Dr. Michael F. MCLEAN
04 Secretary to the President ... Mrs. Kelly BAILEY
26 Asst to Pres/Dir College Relations ... Mrs. Anne S. FORSYTH
30 Vice President for Development ... Dr. Paul J. O'REILLY
43 General Counsel ... Mr. John Q. MASTELLER
10 Vice President for Admn & Finance ... Mr. Peter L. DELUCA
05 Academic Dean ... Dr. Brian KELLY
46 Director of Development ... Mr. Robert A. BAGDAZIAN
44 Director of Gift Planning ... Mr. Thomas J. SUSANKA
07 Director of Admissions ... Mr. Jonathan P. DALY
21 Supervisor Business/Finance ... Mr. Michael COLLINS
37 Director of Financial Aid ... Mr. Gregory J. BECHER
32 Asst Dean for Student Affairs ... Mr. Steven R. CAIN
06 Registrar ... Mr. Mark KRETSCHMER
36 Director of Student Placement ... Mr. Mark R. KRETSCHMER
08 Librarian ... Mrs. Viltis A. JATULIS
42 Chaplain ... Fr. Joseph ILLO
27 Communications Manager ... Mr. Christopher WEINKOPF
13 Development Database Manager ... Mr. Aaron DUNKEL

Thomas Jefferson School of Law (I)

1155 Island Avenue, San Diego CA 92101

County: San Diego — FICE Identification: 010854 — Unit ID: 126049
Telephone: (619) 297-9700 — Carnegie Class: Spec/Law
FAX Number: (619) 961-4370 — Calendar System: Semester
URL: www.tjsl.edu
Established: 1969 — Annual Graduate Tuition & Fees: $44,000
Enrollment: 1,032 — Coed
Affiliation or Control: Independent Non-Profit — IRS Status: 501(c)3
Highest Offering: Doctorate; No Undergraduates
Program: Professional
Accreditation: LAW

01 President and Dean ... Thomas F. GUERNSEY
05 Assoc Dean Academic Affairs ... Linda KELLER
32 Assoc Dean for Student Affairs ... M. Elizabeth (Beth) KRANSBERGER
26 Asst Dean Communications/Admin ... Lori WULFEMEYER
18 Asst Dean Facilities Services ... Lisa BRUCE
36 Director for Career Services ... Beverly BRACKER
08 Interim Library Director ... Leigh INMAN
10 Chief Financial Officer ... Nancy VU
37 Director Financial Assistance ... Marc BERMAN
06 Registrar ... Kim GRENNAN
35 Student Services Director ... Lisa FERREIRA
21 Director of Business Office ... Christine MOORE
88 Dir Clin/Judicial Educ & Acad Cnslr ... Judybeth TROPP
07 Director of Admissions ... Tim SPEARMAN
15 Director of Personnel Services ... Lisa CHIGOS

Touro College Los Angeles (J)

1317 N Crescent Heights Boulevard, West Hollywood CA 90046-4506

County: Los Angeles — FICE Identification: 041425 — Unit ID: 459727
Telephone: (323) 822-9700 — Carnegie Class: Not Classified
FAX Number: (310) 654-2086 — Calendar System: Semester
URL: www.touro.edu/losangeles/
Established: 2005 — Annual Undergrad Tuition & Fees: $15,900
Enrollment: 175 — Coed
Affiliation or Control: Independent Non-Profit — IRS Status: 501(c)3
Highest Offering: Master's
Program: Liberal Arts And General
Accreditation: WC

01 President ... Dr. Alan KADISH
05 Founding Dean/Chief Academic Ofcr ... Dr. Esther LOWY
07 Director of Admissions ... Mrs. Samira MILLER
09 Dir Inst Research/Assessment ... Ms. Shana ROBINSON
10 Chief Business Officer/Bursar ... Mr. Kamran MANUEL
37 Dir Student Fin Aid/Registrar ... Ms. Rivka WEINBERG

Touro University California (K)

1310 Club Drive, Vallejo CA 94592

County: Solano — FICE Identification: 041426 — Unit ID: 459736
Telephone: (707) 638-5200 — Carnegie Class: Not Classified
FAX Number: (707) 638-5255 — Calendar System: Trimester
URL: www.tu.edu
Established: 1997 — Annual Undergrad Tuition & Fees: $45,000
Enrollment: 1,387 — Coed
Affiliation or Control: Independent Non-Profit — IRS Status: 501(c)3
Highest Offering: Doctorate
Program: Teacher Preparatory; Professional
Accreditation: WC, ARCPA, OSTEO, PH, PHAR

01 President & CEO ... Dr. Alan KADISH
05 Provost & COO ... Dr. Marilyn HOPKINS
32 Dean of Students ... Dr. Lisa WAITS
35 Associate Dean of Students ... Dr. James BINKERD
06 Registrar ... Dr. Harold BORRERO
07 Director of Admissions ... Mr. Steven DAVIS
09 Director of Institutional Research ... Dr. Meiling TANG
10 Director of Fiscal Affairs and Acct ... Ms. Jonalee ADRIANO
15 Director Human Resources ... Ms. Kathy LOWE
11 Associate VP of Administration ... Mr. Jay RITCHIE
08 Director University Library ... Ms. Tamara TRUJILLO
63 Dean College of Osteopathic Med ... Dr. Michael CLEARFIELD
67 Dean College of Pharmacy ... Dr. Katherine KNAPP
53 Dean Col of Education & Health Sci ... Dr. Jim O'CONNOR
13 Director of Information Technology ... Ms. Julia WELCH
26 Director of External Relations ... Ms. Andrea GARCIA

37 Director of Student Financial Aid ... Ms. Lynne MOSELEY
30 Chief Officer of Advancement ... Mr. James SOTIROS
35 Director of Student Activities ... Rabbi Elchonon TENENBAUM
23 Director of Student Health Center ... Ms. Jalynne SOUSA

Trident University International (A)

5757 Plaza Drive, Suite 100, Cypress CA 90630
County: Orange FICE Identification: 041279
Unit ID: 450979
Telephone: (714) 816-0366 Carnegie Class: DRU
FAX Number: (714) 816-0367 Calendar System: Semester
URL: www.trident.edu
Established: 1998 Annual Undergrad Tuition & Fees: $10,400
Enrollment: 6,985 Coed
Affiliation or Control: Proprietary IRS Status: Proprietary
Highest Offering: Doctorate
Program: Liberal Arts And General; Professional; Business Emphasis
Accreditation: WC

01 President/COO ... Mr. Andy VAUGHN
10 Exec Vice President Finance/CFO ... Ms. Lisa KEMP
05 Exec Vice President/Provost ... Dr. Michael MAHONEY
13 Exec Vice President/CIO ... Mr. Vahid SHARIAT
86 VP/Chief Compliance Officer ... Dr. Afshin AFROOKHTEH
30 Vice Pres Student Engagement ... Dr. Steven J. GOLD
88 Sr VP Outreach/Partnerships/Admiss ... Mr. Brett SHIVELY
20 Associate Provost ... Dr. Scott AMUNDSEN
50 Dean Business/Information Systems ... Dr. Simcha POLLARD
04 Executive Assistant ... Ms. Patricia PARKS
15 Sr Director Human Resources ... Ms. Brenda DUNBAR
06 Registrar ... Ms. Nimala SHARMA
37 Director Student Financial Aid ... Ms. Taisha AZLIN WRIGHT
09 Director of Institutional Research ... Dr. Heidi SATO
08 Librarian ... Ms. Leslie ANDERSEN
21 Director of Financial Operation ... Mr. Scott PAK
76 Dean Educ/Health Sciences ... Dr. Holly OROZCO

Trinity Law School (B)

2200 N Grand Avenue, Santa Ana CA 92705
Telephone: (714) 836-7500 Identification: 770098
Accreditation: &NH

† Main campus is Trinity International University in Deerfield, IL.

United Education Institute (C)

6055 Pacific Blvd, Huntington Park CA 90255
County: Los Angeles FICE Identification: 025593
Unit ID: 124681
Telephone: (323) 319-9500 Carnegie Class: Not Classified
FAX Number: (949) 788-2505 Calendar System: Other
URL: www.uei.edu
Established: 1986 Annual Undergrad Tuition & Fees: $16,650
Enrollment: 3,104 Coed
Affiliation or Control: Proprietary IRS Status: Proprietary
Highest Offering: Associate Degree
Program: Occupational
Accreditation: CNCE

01 Executive Area President ... Mr. John ESPRIO

United States University (D)

830 Bay Boulevard, Chula Vista CA 91911
County: San Diego FICE Identification: 040053
Unit ID: 447050
Telephone: (619) 477-6310 Carnegie Class: Bac/A&S
FAX Number: (619) 477-7340 Calendar System: Semester
URL: www.usuniversity.edu
Established: 1997 Annual Undergrad Tuition & Fees: $6,500
Enrollment: 266 Coed
Affiliation or Control: Proprietary IRS Status: Proprietary
Highest Offering: Master's
Program: Liberal Arts And General; Teacher Preparatory; Professional; Technical Emphasis
Accreditation: #WC

01 President and CEO ... Timothy P. COLE
05 Provost/Chief Academic Officer ... Dr. Steven A. STARGARDTER
11 Vice President Operations ... Lisa DEFARIA
10 Chief Financial Officer ... Douglas JENSON
27 Chief Information Officer ... Roy FINALY
25 Vice Pres Compliance/Regulatory Aff ... Robyn BURRELL
06 Registrar ... Maria Raquel CHANG
76 Director School of Health Science ... Dr. Rosalinda MILLA
97 Director School of Liberal Studies ... Vacant
53 Director School of Education ... Roberta MASO-FLEISHMAN
66 Director School of Nursing ... Pilar DE LA CRUZ-REYES

United States University (E)

6251 Katella Avenue, Cypress CA 90630
Telephone: (714) 252-8592 Identification: 770925
Accreditation: #WC

† Main campus is United States University in Chula Vista, CA.

Unitek College (F)

4670 Auto Mall Parkway, Fremont CA 94538
County: Alameda FICE Identification: 041697
Unit ID: 459204
Telephone: (888) 735-4355 Carnegie Class: Not Classified
FAX Number: (510) 249-9125 Calendar System: Other
URL: www.unitekcollege.edu
Established: 1992 Annual Undergrad Tuition & Fees: $14,567
Enrollment: 680 Coed
Affiliation or Control: Proprietary IRS Status: Proprietary
Highest Offering: Baccalaureate
Program: Occupational; 2-Year Principally Bachelor's Creditable; Nursing Emphasis
Accreditation: ACCSC

University of Antelope Valley (G)

44055 Sierra Hwy, Lancaster CA 93534
County: Los Angeles FICE Identification: 034275
Unit ID: 442930
Telephone: (661) 726-1911 Carnegie Class: Assoc/PrivFP
FAX Number: (661) 726-5158 Calendar System: Other
URL: www.uav.edu
Established: Annual Undergrad Tuition & Fees: N/A
Enrollment: 801 Coed
Affiliation or Control: Proprietary IRS Status: Proprietary
Highest Offering: Master's
Program: Occupational; 2-Year Principally Bachelor's Creditable
Accreditation: ACICS, EMT

01 President ... Mr. Marco JOHNSON
03 Vice President/CEO ... Ms. Sandra JOHNSON
32 Dean of Student Affairs ... Mr. Ronald FELTS
06 Dean of Records ... Mrs. Jaime MYERS
37 Financial Aid Officer ... Mr. Araceli JIMENEZ
10 Director of Operations ... Ms. Crystal STEPHENS

*University of California Office of the President (H)

1111 Franklin Street, Oakland CA 94607-5200
County: Alameda FICE Identification: 001311
Unit ID: 124557
Telephone: (510) 987-0700 Carnegie Class: N/A
FAX Number: (510) 987-0328
URL: www.ucop.edu

01 President ... Janet G. NAPOLITANO
05 Provost/Exec Vice Pres Acad Affairs ... Aimee DORR
10 Exec Vice President/CFO ... Paul WEISS
11 Exec Vice Pres Business Operations ... Nathan E. BROSTROM
88 Exec Vice Pres Laboratory Mgmt ... Glenn L. MARA
26 Sr Vice Pres External Relations ... Daniel M. DOOLEY
17 Sr Vice Pres Health Sciences & Svcs ... John D. STOBO
25 Sr Vice Pres Compliance/Audit ... Sheryl S. VACCA
43 General Counsel/VP Legal Affairs ... Charles F. ROBINSON
47 Vice Pres Agriculture/Nat Resources ... Barbara H. ALLEN-DIAZ
32 Vice President Student Affairs ... Judy K. SAKAKI
27 CIO/Vice Pres for Investments ... Marie N. BERGGREN
15 Vice Pres Human Resources ... Dwaine B. DUCKETT
46 Vice Pres Research/Graduate Studies ... Steven V W. BECKWITH
21 VP Budget & Capital Resources ... Patrick J. LENZ

*University of California-Berkeley (I)

Berkeley CA 94720-0001
County: Alameda FICE Identification: 001312
Unit ID: 110635
Telephone: (510) 642-6000 Carnegie Class: RU/VH
FAX Number: (510) 643-5499 Calendar System: Semester
URL: www.berkeley.edu
Established: 1868 Annual Undergrad Tuition & Fees (In-State): $12,874
Enrollment: 25,774 Coed
Affiliation or Control: State IRS Status: 501(c)3
Highest Offering: Doctorate
Program: Liberal Arts And General; Professional
Accreditation: WC, BUS, CLPSY, CS, DIETD, ENG, FOR, IPSY, JOUR, LAW, LSAR, OPT, OPTR, PCSAS, PH, PLNG, SCPSY, SW

02 Chancellor ... Nicholas B. DIRKS
05 Exec Vice Chancellor & Provost ... George W. BRESLAUER
11 Vice Chanc Administration & Finance ... John WILTON
32 Vice Chancellor Student Affairs ... Harry LE GRANDE
26 Vice Chanc University Relations ... Scott BIDDY
46 Vice Chancellor for Research ... Graham R. FLEMING
18 Vice Chancellor Facilities Services ... Edward DENTON
88 Vice Chanc Equity & Inclusion ... Gibor BASRI
100 Assoc Chancellor/Chief of Staff ... Beata FITZPATRICK
31 Assc Chanc Govt/Cmty Campus Liaison ... Linda M. WILLIAMS
25 Assc VC Research Admin & Compliance ... Patrick SCHLESINGER
13 Int Assc Vice Chanc Info Technology ... Lyle NEVELS
10 Assc Vice Chancellor/CFO ... Erin S. GORE
84 Assc Vice Chanc Admiss & Enrollment ... Anne DE LUCA
43 Chief Campus Counsel ... Christopher M. PATTI
26 Assoc Vice Chanc Public Affairs ... Claire HOLMES
21 Assoc VC Business & Admin Svcs ... Ron T. COLEY
88 Asst Vice Chanc Finance/Controller ... Delphine REGALIA
07 Asst VV & Dir Undergrad Admissions ... Amy JARICH
35 Asst Vice Chanc/Dean of Students ... Jonathan POULLARD
37 Asst VC & Dir Fin Aid & Scholarship ... Rachelle FELDMAN
08 University Librarian ... Thomas C. LEONARD
06 Registrar ... Walter WONG
88 Assoicate Registrar ... Johanna METZGAR
38 Dir Counseling & Psychological Svcs ... Jeff PRINCE
36 Director Career Center ... Thomas C. DEVLIN
87 Dean Sum Sess/Study Abr/Life Lrng ... Richard RUSSO
41 Director of Athletics ... Sandy BARBOUR
58 Dean of the Graduate Division ... Andrew J. SZERI
61 Dean of Law ... Christopher EDLEY, JR.
88 Dean of Optometry ... Dennis M. LEVI
54 Dean School of Engineering ... S. Shankar SASTRY
88 Dean of Environmental Design ... Jennifer WOLCH
65 Dean of Natural Resources ... J. Keith GILLESS
50 Dean of Haas School of Business ... Richard K. LYONS
70 Dean of Social Welfare ... Jeffrey EDELSON
88 Dean School of Information ... AnnaLee SAXENIAN
69 Dean of Public Health ... Stephen M. SHORTELL
53 Dean of Education ... Judith W. LITTLE
60 Dean of Journalism ... Ed WASSERMAN
88 Dean of Chemistry ... Richard MATHIES
80 Dean Goldman School/Public Pol ... Henry BRADY
79 Dean of Arts and Humanities ... Anthony CASCARDI
88 Interim Dean of Biological Sciences ... G. Steven MARTIN
81 Dean Mathematical/Physical Sciences ... Mark RICHARDS
83 Dean of Social Sciences ... Carla HESSE
97 Dean of the Undergraduate Division ... Tyler STOVALL
56 Dean of University Extension ... Diana WU

*University of California-Davis (J)

One Shields Avenue, Davis CA 95616-5270
County: Yolo FICE Identification: 001313
Unit ID: 110644
Telephone: (530) 752-1011 Carnegie Class: RU/VH
FAX Number: N/A Calendar System: Quarter
URL: www.ucdavis.edu
Established: 1905 Annual Undergrad Tuition & Fees (In-State): $13,896
Enrollment: 33,300 Coed
Affiliation or Control: State IRS Status: 501(c)3
Highest Offering: Doctorate
Program: Liberal Arts And General; Teacher Preparatory; Professional
Accreditation: WC, ARCPA, BUS, CS, DIETD, DIETI, ENG, FEPAC, IPSY, LAW, LSAR, MED, MT, NURSE, PH, VET

02 Chancellor ... Dr. Linda P. KATEHI
05 Provost & Exec Vice Chancellor ... Dr. Ralph J. HEXTER
100 Associate Chancellor ... Mr. Karl M. ENGELBACH
27 Assoc Chanc Strategic Commun ... Ms. Luanne M. LAWRENCE
46 Vice Chancellor Research ... Dr. Harris A. LEWIN
30 Vice Chanc Dev/Alumni Relations ... Dr. Shaun B. KEISTER
32 Int Vice Chancellor Student Affairs ... Dr. Adela I. DE LATORRE
45 VC Administrative & Resource Mgmt ... Mr. John A. MEYER
76 Int VC Human Health Sciences ... Dr. Tom NESBITT
17 CEO UCD Medical Center ... Ms. Ann M. RICE
66 Assoc VC/Dean Sch of Nursing ... Dr. Heather M. YOUNG
31 Assoc Exec VC Campus Cmty Relations ... Mr. Rahim REED
88 Exec Assoc VC Research ... Dr. Cindy M. KIEL
88 Assoc VC Research ... Dr. Paul DODD
88 Assoc VC Research ... Dr. Dushyant PATHAK
15 Assoc VC Human Resources ... Ms. Susan M. GILBERT
10 Assoc VC Accounting/Financial Svcs ... Mr. J. Michael ALLRED
88 Assoc VC Development ... Mr. Jason L. WOHLMAN
88 Assoc VC Development ... Mr. Paul PROKOP
88 Assoc VC Development Health Sci ... Ms. Chong U. PORTER
35 Assoc VC Student Affairs ... Ms. Emily GALINDO
35 Assoc VC Student Affairs ... Ms. Lora J. BOSSIO
35 Int Assoc VC Student Affairs ... Dr. Rich SHINTAKU
21 Assoc VC Budget ... Ms. Kelly M. RATLIFF
18 Assoc VC Safety Services ... Ms. Jill PARKER
88 Asst Executive Vice Chancellor ... Mr. Karl F. MOHR
45 Asst VC Campus Planning ... Mr. Robert B. SEGAR
88 Asst VC Environmental Stewardship ... Dr. Sid ENGLAND
88 Asst VC Design & Construction ... Mr. Clayton HALLIDAY
18 Asst VC Facilities Management ... Mr. Allen TOLLEFSON
86 Asst VC Govt & Community Relations ... Ms. Marjorie M. DICKINSON
29 AVC/Exec Director Alumni Relations ... Mr. Richard R. ENGEL
13 Vice Provost Info/Educ Tech ... Mr. Peter M. SIEGEL
53 Int Vice Provost Undergraduate Educ ... Dr. Carolyn DE LA PENA
85 Vice Prov Univ Outreach/Intl Pgm ... Dr. William B. LACY
20 Vice Provost Academic Affairs ... Dr. Maureen L. STANTON
88 Assoc Vice Provost Internatl Pgm ... Dr. Adrienne MARTIN
88 Assoc Vice Provost Univ Outreach ... Dr. Marc SCHENKER
43 Int Chief Campus Counsel ... Mr. Michael F. SWEENEY
06 Registrar ... Dr. Elias S. LOPEZ
08 University Librarian ... Ms. MacKenzie SMITH
58 VP Grad Education/Dean Grad Studies ... Dr. Jeffery C. GIBELING
47 Int Dean Agricultural/Environ Sci ... Dr. Mary E. DELANY
81 Dean Biological Sciences ... Dr. James E. HILDRETH
54 Dean Engineering ... Dr. Enrique J. LAVERNIA
83 Dean Social Sciences ... Dr. George R. MANGUN
81 Int Dean Math & Physical Sciences ... Dr. Alexandra NAVROTSKY
79 Dean Humanities/Arts & Culture ... Dr. Jessie A. OWENS
61 Dean School of Law ... Dr. Kevin R. JOHNSON
50 Dean Graduate School of Management ... Dr. Steven C. CURRALL
63 Dean School of Medicine ... Dr. Tom S. NESBITT
74 Dean Veterinary Medicine ... Dr. Michael D. LAIRMORE
53 Dean School of Education ... Dr. Harold G. LEVINE
56 Dean University Extension ... Mr. Dennis F. PENDLETON
88 Exec Director Mondavi Center ... Dr. Don F. ROTH
23 Exec Dir Student Health Services ... Dr. Michelle S. FAMULA
07 Exec Director Admissions ... Mr. Walter A. ROBINSON

37 Director Financial Aid ... Ms. Kathryn A. MALONEY
09 Director Institutional Analysis ... Mr. Robert J. LOESSBERG-ZAHL
38 Director Counseling & Psych Srvcs ... Dr. Sarah HAHN
36 Director Internship & Career Center ... Dr. Subhash H. RISBUD
40 Director Bookstore ... Mr. Jason LORGAN
41 Director Intercollegiate Athletics ... Mr. Terrance J. TUMEY
96 Director Materiel Management ... Ms. Janice KING
88 Director Internal Audit Services ... Mr. Jeremiah J. MAHER
19 Chief of Police ... Chief Matt CARMICHAEL

*University of California-Hastings College of the Law (A)

200 McAllister Street, San Francisco CA 94102-4978
County: San Francisco FICE Identification: 003947
Unit ID: 110398
Telephone: (415) 565-4600 Carnegie Class: Spec/Law
FAX Number: (415) 565-4865 Calendar System: Semester
URL: www.uchastings.edu
Established: 1878 Annual Graduate Tuition & Fees: $47,634
Enrollment: 1,159 Coed
Affiliation or Control: State IRS Status: 501(c)3
Highest Offering: First Professional Degree; No Undergraduates
Program: Professional
Accreditation: WC, LAW

02 Chancellor and Dean ... Mr. Frank H. WU
05 Provost & Academic Dean ... Ms. Elizabeth L. HILLMAN
43 General Counsel ... Ms. Elise TRAYNUM
10 Chief Financial Officer ... Mr. David SEWARD
20 Associate Academic Dean ... Ms. Heather M. FIELD
08 Director Law Library ... Ms. Jenni PARRISH
15 Executive Director Human Resources ... Ms. Marie HAIRSTON
19 Chief Public Safety ... Mr. Bill PALMINI
06 Registrar ... Ms. Gina BARNETT
07 Assistant Dean Admissions ... Mr. Greg CANADA
32 Director Student Services ... Ms. Rupa BHANDARI
27 Chief Information Officer ... Mr. Jacob HORNSBY
36 Asst Dean Career & Profess Devel ... Ms. Sari ZIMMERMAN
26 Assistant Dean Communications ... Vacant
22 Director LEOP ... Ms. Jan JEMISON
23 Student Health Manager/Admin Nurse ... Ms. Laurie BROOKNER
21 Controller ... Ms. Deborah TRAN
37 Assistant Dean Financial Aid ... Ms. Linda BISESI
40 Bookstore Manager ... Vacant
18 Property Manager ... Ms. Pansy MAR
96 Director of Purchasing ... Mr. Darryl SWEET
30 Asst Dean Institutional Advance ... Ms. Shino NOMIYA

*University of California-Irvine (B)

Campus Drive, Irvine CA 92697-0001
County: Orange FICE Identification: 001314
Unit ID: 110653
Telephone: (949) 824-5011 Carnegie Class: RU/VH
FAX Number: (949) 824-5451 Calendar System: Quarter
URL: www.uci.edu
Established: 1965 Annual Undergrad Tuition & Fees (In-State): $14,046
Enrollment: 28,184 Coed
Affiliation or Control: State IRS Status: 501(c)3
Highest Offering: Doctorate
Program: Liberal Arts And General; Teacher Preparatory; Professional
Accreditation: WC, BUS, CEA, CS, ENG, IPSY, #LAW, MED, MT, NURSE, PH, PLNG

02 Chancellor ... Michael V. DRAKE
05 Provost & Exec Vice Chancellor ... Howard GILLMAN
10 Vice Chanc Admin/Business Services ... Wendell C. BRASE
46 Vice Chancellor for Research ... John C. HEMMINGER
32 Vice Chanc Student Affairs ... Thomas A. PARHAM
30 Vice Chanc Univ Advancement ... Gregory R. LEET
45 Vice Chanc Planning & Budget ... Meredith MICHAELS
20 Senior Vice Provost for Acad Plng ... Michael P. CLARK
16 Vice Provost for Academic Personnel ... Herbert KILLACKEY
21 Assoc Vice Chanc Admin/Business Svc ... Paige L. MACIAS
29 Asst Vice Chanc Alumni Relations ... Vacant
35 Assoc Vice Chancellor Stdnt Affairs ... Daniel J. DOOROS
22 Asst Executive Vice Chancellor OEOD ... Kirsten K. QUANBECK
100 Associate Chancellor ... Ramona AGRELA
20 Associate Exec Vice Chancellor ... Michael R. ARIAS
35 Asst Vice Chanc/Dean of Students ... Rameen A. TALESH
84 Asst Vice Chanc Enrollment Services ... Brent W. YUNEK
06 University Registrar ... Elizabeth C. BENNETT
43 Chief Campus Counsel ... Diane F. GEOCARIS
51 Dean Continuing Educ/Summer Session ... Gary W. MATKIN
08 University Librarian ... Lorelei A. TANJI
37 Director Financial Aid ... Christopher SHULTZ
36 Interim Director Career Center ... Robert GOMEZ
41 Director Intercollegiate Athletics ... Michael A. IZZI
09 Asst Vice Chanc Inst Research ... Ryan M. CHERLAND
58 Dean Graduate Division ... Frances M. LESLIE
20 Dean Undergraduate Education ... Sharon V. SALINGER
63 Dean School of Medicine ... Ralph V. CLAYMAN
61 Dean of Law School ... Erwin CHEMERINSKY
81 Dean Biological Sciences ... Albert F. BENNETT
81 Dean Physical Sciences ... Kenneth C. JANDA
83 Dean School of Social Sciences ... William M. MAURER
50 Dean Paul Merage School of Business ... Vacant
79 Dean Humanities ... Georges VAN DEN ABBEELE
49 Dean Arts ... Joseph S. LEWIS
83 Dean Social Ecology ... Valerie JENNESS
54 Dean School of Engineering ... Gregory WASHINGTON

77 Dean Bren Sch of Info & Comp Sci ... Hal S. STERN
88 Chair Academic Senate ... Peter KRAPP
53 Dean School of Education ... Deborah L. VANDELL
13 CIO and Asst Vice Chancellor IT ... Dana F. ROODE
96 Director Materiel & Risk Management ... Richard COULON
26 Assoc Vice Chanc Communications ... Ria M. CARLSON
28 Director ADVANCE Program ... Douglas M. HAYNES

*University of California-Los Angeles (C)

405 Hilgard Avenue, Los Angeles CA 90095-1405
County: Los Angeles FICE Identification: 001315
Unit ID: 110662
Telephone: (310) 825-4321 Carnegie Class: RU/VH
FAX Number: N/A Calendar System: Quarter
URL: www.ucla.edu
Established: 1919 Annual Undergrad Tuition & Fees (In-State): $12,692
Enrollment: 39,945 Coed
Affiliation or Control: State IRS Status: 501(c)3
Highest Offering: Doctorate
Program: Liberal Arts And General; Professional
Accreditation: WC, BUS, CLPSY, CS, CYTO, DENT, EMT, ENG, ENGR, HSA, IPSY, LAW, LIB, MED, NURSE, PCSAS, PDPSY, PH, PLNG, RAD, SW, THEA

02 Chancellor ... Gene D. BLOCK
03 Exec Vice Chancellor/Provost ... Scott WAUGH
11 Administrative Vice Chancellor ... Jack J. POWAZEK
32 Vice Chancellor Student Affairs ... Janina MONTERO
26 Vice Chancellor External Affairs ... Rhea TURTELTAUB
10 Vice Chanc/Chief Financial Officer ... Steven A. OLSEN
23 Vice Chancellor Health Sciences ... A. Eugene WASHINGTON
46 Vice Chancellor Research ... James S. ECONOMOU
58 VC Grad Education/Dean Grad Div ... Robin L. GARRELL
16 Vice Chanc Academic Personnel ... Carole E. GOLDBERG
43 Vice Chancellor Legal Affairs ... Kevin REED
82 Int Vice Prov International Studies ... C. Cindy FAN
97 Vice Provost/Dean Undergrad Educ ... Patricia A. TURNER
28 Vice Prov Faculty Diversity/Develop ... Christine A. LITTLETON
13 Vice Provost Information Technology ... James DAVIS
88 Vice Prov New Collaborative Initiat ... Kathryn ATCHISON
17 Assoc VC and CEO Hospital Systems ... David T. FEINBERG
24 AVP Instructional Development ... Larry L. LOEHER
20 Asst Provost ... Margaret LEAL-SOTELO
20 Assistant Provost ... Maryann J. GRAY
88 Assoc Vice Chanc Acad Plng/Budget ... Glyn DAVIES
27 Assoc Vice Chanc Univ Communication ... Lawrence H. LOKMAN
18 Assoc Vice Chanc General Services ... Jack POWAZEK
30 Assoc Vice Chancellor Development ... Tracie CHRISTENSEN
21 Assoc Vice Chancellor/Controller ... Susan K. ABELES
15 Assoc Vice Chanc Campus Human Res ... Lubbe LEVIN
35 Assoc VC Dean Student & Campus Life ... Robert J. NAPLES
29 Asst Vice Chanc/Exec Dir Alumni Rel ... Ralph AMOS
86 Asst Vice Chanc Govt/Cmty Rels ... Keith S. PARKER
91 Asst Vice Chanc Adm Info Systems ... Andrew WISSMILLER
39 Asst VC Housing & Hospitality Svcs ... Peter ANGELIS
88 Executive Director Volunteer Center ... Antoinette MONGELLI
84 Assoc Vice Chanc Enrollment Mgmt ... Youlonda COPELAND-MORGAN
25 Asst VC Res Policy & Compliance ... Ann M. POLLACK
88 Asst VC Student Development/Health ... Vacant
06 Registrar ... Anita COTTER
87 Asst Prov Academic Program Dev ... David UNRUH
09 Dir Analysis/Information Management ... Caroline S. WEST
08 University Librarian ... Virginia STEEL
19 Chief of Police ... James HERREN
07 Dir Undergrad Admiss/Rels w/Schools ... Vu TRAN
36 Director Career Center ... Kathy L. SIMS
37 Director Financial Aid Office ... Ronald W. JOHNSON
38 Dir Student Psychological Services ... Elizabeth GONG-GUY
85 Dir Ctr for Intl Students/Scholars ... Robert B. ERICKSEN
41 Director Intercollegiate Athletics ... Daniel G. GUERRERO
22 Director Staff Affirmative Action ... Linda C. AVILA
96 Director of Purchasing ... William S. PROPST
88 Executive Director ASUCLA ... Robert WILLIAMS
51 Int Dean Cont Educ/UCLA Extension ... Cathy SANDEEN
53 Dean Grad Sch Educ/Info Studies ... Marcelo M. SUAREZ-OROZCO
54 Dean Sch of Engr & Applied Sci ... Vijay K. DHIR
61 Dean School of Law ... Rachel MORAN
50 Dean Anderson Grad Sch Management ... Judy D. OLIAN
52 Dean School of Dentistry ... No Hee PARK
66 Dean School of Nursing ... Courtney LYDER
48 Dean Sch of the Arts/Architecture ... Christopher WATERMAN
88 Dean School of Theater/Film/TV ... Teri SCHWARTZ
69 Dean School of Public Health ... Jody HEYMANN
63 Dean D Geffen School of Medicine ... A. Eugene WASHINGTON
80 Dean School of Public Affairs ... Franklin D. GILLIAM, JR.
79 Dean Division of Humanities ... David SCHABERG
88 Dean of Life Sciences ... Victoria SORK
88 Dean of Physical Sciences ... Joseph RUDNICK
83 Dean of Social Sciences ... Alessandro DURANTI
90 Director Academic Tech Svcs ... William LABATE
40 Divisional Manager Textbooks ... Anne COLLUM

*University of California-Merced (D)

5200 North Lake Road, Merced CA 95343
County: Merced FICE Identification: 041271
Unit ID: 445188
Telephone: (209) 228-4400 Carnegie Class: Not Classified
FAX Number: (209) 228-4424 Calendar System: Semester
URL: www.ucmerced.edu
Established: 1868 Annual Undergrad Tuition & Fees (In-District): $13,070
Enrollment: 5,198 Coed
Affiliation or Control: State/Local IRS Status: 501(c)3
Highest Offering: Doctorate
Program: Liberal Arts And General; Teacher Preparatory; Professional
Accreditation: WC

02 Chancellor ... Dr. Dorothy LELAND
05 Provost & Exec Vice Chancellor ... Dr. Tom PETERSON
11 Int Vice Chancellor Admin Svcs ... Michael REESE
30 Vice Chancellor Develop/Alumni Rels ... Kyle D. HOFFMAN
10 Vice Chancellor Budget/Planning ... Daniel FEITELBERG
32 Vice Chancellor Student Affairs ... Dr. Jane F. LAWRENCE
46 Vice Chancellor Research ... Dr. Samuel TRAINA
04 Associate Chancellor ... Janet YOUNG
35 Associate Vice Chancellor Students ... Dr. Charles NIES
84 Assoc Vice Chanc Enrollment Mgmt ... J. Michael THOMPSON
23 Assoc Vice Chanc Health & Wellness ... Dr. Fuji COLLINS
27 Asst Vice Chanc Univ Communications ... Patti W. WAID
06 University Registrar ... Dr. Laurie HERBRAND
07 Director of Admissions ... Encarnacion RUIZ
08 Int University Librarian ... Donald A. BARCLAY
37 Director of Financial Aid ... Diana RALLS
85 Director of International Programs ... Rebecca SWEELEY
56 Director of Extension & Summer Pgms ... Kevin M. BROWNE
19 Chief of Police ... Rita SPAUR
41 Director of Campus Athletics & Rec ... David DUNHAM
39 Director of Student Housing ... Leslie SANTOS
58 Dean Graduate Studies ... Dr. Christopher KELLO
65 Dean Natural Sciences ... Dr. Juan MEZA
54 Dean Engineering ... Dr. E. Daniel HIRLEMAN
79 Dean School of SSHA ... Dr. Mark S. ALDENDERFER

*University of California-Riverside (E)

900 University Avenue, Riverside CA 92521
County: Riverside FICE Identification: 001316
Unit ID: 110671
Telephone: (951) 827-1012 Carnegie Class: RU/VH
FAX Number: (951) 827-3800 Calendar System: Quarter
URL: www.ucr.edu
Established: 1954 Annual Undergrad Tuition & Fees (In-State): $12,960
Enrollment: 21,005 Coed
Affiliation or Control: State IRS Status: 501(c)3
Highest Offering: Doctorate
Program: Liberal Arts And General; Teacher Preparatory; Professional
Accreditation: WC, BUS, CS, ENG, #MED, SCPSY

02 Interim Chancellor ... Dr. Jane CLOSE CONOLEY
100 Associate Chancellor ... Ms. Cynthia R. GIORGIO
05 Exec Vice Chancellor/Provost ... Dr. Dallas RABENSTEIN
11 Vice Chanc Finance/Business Opers ... Mr. Charles J. ROWLEY
32 Vice Chancellor Student Affairs ... Mr. James W. SANDOVAL
26 Vice Chanc University Advancement ... Mr. Peter A. HAYASHIDA
46 Vice Chancellor Research ... Dr. Michael J. PAZZANI
17 VC Hlth Affs/Dean School of Med ... Dr. G. Richard OLDS
20 Vice Provost Academic Personnel ... Dr. David F. BOCIAN
18 Assoc Vice Chanc Facil Plant Admin ... Mr. Mike MILLER
84 Assoc Vice Chanc Enrollment ... Ms. LaRae LUNDGREN
30 Int Assoc Vice Chanc Development ... Mr. Zach SMITH
09 Asst Vice Chanc Strat Acad Rsrch An ... Mr. Robert F. DALY
28 Asst Vice Chanc Affirm Action ... Ms. Gladys BROWN
58 Dean Graduate Division ... Dr. Joseph CHILDERS
50 Int Dean School of Business Admin ... Dr. Yungzeng WANG
53 Interim Dean Grad School of Educ ... Dr. Douglas MITCHELL
54 Dean Bourns College of Engineering ... Dr. Reza ABBASCHIAN
79 Dean College of Humanities Arts SS ... Dr. Steven CULLENBERG
81 Dean Col of Nat and Agr Sciences ... Dr. Marylynn YATES
06 Registrar ... Ms. Bracken J. DAILEY
80 Dean School of Public Policy ... Dr. Anil DEOLALIKAR
36 Director Career Center ... Mr. Sean GILL
37 Director Financial Aid ... Mr. Jose A. AGUILAR
38 Director Counseling Center ... Ms. Laura HAMMOND
07 Director of Admissions ... Ms. Emily D. ENGELSCHALL
96 Director Material Management ... Mr. Russ LEWIS

*University of California-San Diego (F)

9500 Gilman Drive, La Jolla CA 92093-0014
County: San Diego FICE Identification: 001317
Unit ID: 110680
Telephone: (858) 534-2230 Carnegie Class: RU/VH
FAX Number: (858) 534-6523 Calendar System: Quarter
URL: www.ucsd.edu
Established: 1960 Annual Undergrad Tuition & Fees (In-State): $13,302
Enrollment: 28,037 Coed
Affiliation or Control: State IRS Status: 501(c)3
Highest Offering: Doctorate
Program: Liberal Arts And General; Professional
Accreditation: WC, AUD, BUS, CEA, CLPSY, @DIETI, DMS, ENG, IPSY, MED, MT, PDPSY, #PHAR

02 Chancellor ... Dr. Pradeep K. KHOSLA
05 Executive VC Academic Affairs ... Dr. Suresh SUBRAMANI
30 VC External and Business Affairs ... Mr. Steven W. RELYEA
32 Interim VC Student Affairs ... Dr. Alan HOUSTON
11 Vice Chanc Resource Mgmt/Planning ... Mr. Gary C. MATTHEWS
65 Vice Chancellor Marine Sciences ... Dr. Catherine CONSTABLE
63 VC Health Science/Dean Sch Med ... Dr. David A. BRENNER
46 Vice Chancellor Research ... Dr. Sandra BROWN
28 VC for Equity Diversity & Inclusion ... Dr. Linda S. GREENE
100 Associate Chancellor/Chief of Staff ... Ms. Clare M. KRISTOFCO
56 Assoc VC Public Pgms/Dean Univ Ext ... Dr. Mary L. WALSHOK

43 Chief Campus Counsel .... Mr. Daniel W. PARK
21 AVC Business Fin Svcs/Controller .... Mr. Don A. LARSON
88 Director Policy Admin .... Ms. Paula J. JOHNSON, CRM
23 AVC Student Health/Wellness .... Ms. Karen J. CALFAS
26 University Communications .... Ms. Clare M. KRISTOFCO
20 Asst Vice Chanc Academic Affairs .... Ms. Kristina L. LARSEN
35 Assoc Vice Chanc Student Affairs .... Mr. Edward J. SPRIGGS
16 Asst Vice Chanc Human Resources .... Mr. Thomas R. LEET
88 Associate Vice Chancellor Research .... Dr. Miroslav KRSTIC
84 Asst Vice Chanc Admiss/Enroll Svcs .... Ms. Mae W. BROWN
14 Asst VC Admin Computing/Teleco .... Mr. Min YAO
08 University Librarian .... Mr. Brian E C. SCHOTTLAENDER
06 University Registrar .... Mr. William R. HAID
23 CEO UCSD Medical Center .... Mr. Paul VIVIANO
29 Assistant Vice Chancellor .... Mr. Armin AFSAHI
96 Senior Director Purchasing .... Mr. Ted JOHNSON
54 Dean Jacobs Sch of Engineering .... Dr. Frieder SEIBLE
49 Dean Arts & Humanities .... Dr. Seth LERER
81 Dean Div of Biological Sciences .... Dr. Steve A. KAY
83 Dean of Social Sciences .... Dr. Jeffrey ELMAN
88 Dean Rady School of Management .... Mr. Robert S. SULLIVAN
81 Dean Physical Science .... Dr. Mark H. THIEMENS
82 Dean Sch Intl Rels/Pacific Stds .... Dr. Peter F. COWHEY
58 Dean Graduate Studies .... Dr. Kim E. BARRETT
12 Provost John Muir College .... Dr. Susan SMITH
12 Prov Thurgood Marshall Coll .... Mr. Allan HAVIS
12 Provost Earl Warren College .... Mr. Steven ADLER
12 Provost Revelle College .... Dr. Don WAYNE
12 Provost Eleanor Roosevelt College .... Dr. Alan C. HOUSTON
12 Provost Sixth College .... Dr. Daniel J. DONOGHUE
38 Director Stdt Psych/Counseling Svcs .... Dr. Reina JUAREZ

*University of California-San Francisco (A)

513 Parnassus Avenue, Room S-126,
San Francisco CA 94143-0402

County: San Francisco FICE Identification: 001319
Unit ID: 110699
Telephone: (415) 476-9000 Carnegie Class: Spec/Med
FAX Number: (415) 476-9634 Calendar System: Quarter
URL: www.ucsf.edu
Established: 1864 Annual Graduate Tuition & Fees: N/A
Enrollment: 2,932 Coed
Affiliation or Control: State IRS Status: 501(c)3
Highest Offering: Doctorate; No Undergraduates
Program: Professional
Accreditation: WC, DENT, DIETI, IPSY, MED, MIDWF, NURSE, PHAR, PTA

02 Chancellor .... Dr. Susan DESMOND-HELLMANN
03 Executive Vice Chancellor & Provost .. Dr. Jeffrey A. BLUESTONE
100 Assistant Chancellor .... Ms. Leigh MORGAN
10 Sr Vice Chanc Finance & Admin .... Mr. John E. PLOTTS
05 Actg Vice Provost Academic Affairs .... Dr. Renee NAVARRO
17 Dean School of Medicine/VC Med Affs .... Dr. Samuel HAWGOOD
20 Vice Chanc Student Academic Affairs .... Dr. Elizabeth WATKINS
21 Vice Chancellor Finance .... Vacant
30 Vice Chanc Univ Develop & Alum Rels .... Mr. John FORD
26 VC Strat Communications & Univ Rels .... Ms. Barbara FRENCH
91 Actg VC & Chief Info Officer - ITS .... Ms. Jane WONG
28 VC Diversity & Outreach .... Dr. Renee NAVARRO
32 Assoc VC Camp Life Svcs & FM .... Ms. Angela HAWKINS
15 Assoc VC Human Resources .... Mr. David ODATO
18 Asst VC Cap Pgms/Camp Architect .... Mr. Michael BADE
20 Vice Dean Acad Affairs/Faculty Dev . Dr. Elena FUENTES-AFFLICK
06 Associate Registrar .... Ms. Jina SHAMIM
37 Director Student Financial Services .... Ms. Carrie STEERE-SALAZAR
43 Chief Campus Counsel .... Ms. Greta SCHNETZLER
08 University Librarian/AVC .... Ms. Karen BUTTER
19 Chief of Police .... Ms. Pamela ROSKOWSKI
22 Dir Affirm Action/Equal Oppty/Diver .... Vacant
66 Dean School of Nursing .... Dr. David VLAHOV
52 Dean School of Dentistry .... Dr. John FEATHERSTONE
67 Dean School of Pharmacy .... Dr. B. Joseph GUGLIELMO
35 Director Student Life .... Mr. Eric KOENIG
39 Assoc Director of Housing Services .... Mr. Gary FORMAN
96 Exec Dir Camp Procurmt/Bus Contract .... Mr. James HINE
07 Registrar .... Mr. Douglas CARLSON
36 Dir Career/Professional Development ... Mr. William LINDSTAEDT
23 Director Student Health Services .... Mr. Henry KAHN
09 Director Institutional Research .... Mr. Chris CULLANDER

*University of California-Santa Barbara (B)

552 University Road, Santa Barbara CA 93106-0001

County: Santa Barbara FICE Identification: 001320
Unit ID: 110705
Telephone: (805) 893-8000 Carnegie Class: RU/VH
FAX Number: N/A Calendar System: Quarter
URL: www.ucsb.edu
Established: 1909 Annual Undergrad Tuition & Fees (In-State): $13,746
Enrollment: 21,927 Coed
Affiliation or Control: State IRS Status: 501(c)3
Highest Offering: Doctorate
Program: Liberal Arts And General; Teacher Preparatory
Accreditation: WC, CS, DANCE, ENG, IPSY, PSPSY

02 Chancellor .... Dr. Henry T. YANG
04 Exec Assistant to the Chancellor .... Mr. Kevin R. MCCAULEY
05 Exec Vice Chanc/Chief Academic Ofcr .... Dr. Glenn E. LUCAS
46 Vice Chancellor Research .... Dr. Michael S. WITHERELL
11 Sr Assoc Vice Chancellor Admin Svcs .... Mr. Marc FISHER
88 Acting AVC Admin Svcs .... Ms. Pam LOMBARDO
26 Vice Chanc Inst Advancement .... Vacant
32 Vice Chancellor Student Affairs .... Dr. Michael D. YOUNG
45 Assistant Chanc Budget & Planning .... Mr. Todd G. LEE
16 Assoc Vice Chanc Acad Personnel .... Dr. John E. TALBOTT
28 AVC Diversity/Equity/Acad Policy .... Dr. Anna EVERETT
20 Acting AVC Academic Programs .... Vacant
30 Assoc Vice Chancellor Development .... Ms. Beverly COLGATE
27 Assoc Vice Chanc Public Affairs .... Vacant
84 Asst Vice Chanc Enrollment Svcs/ Mgt .... Ms. Christine N. VAN GIESON
88 Exec Dir Student Acad Support Svc .... Dr. Mary JACOB
29 Asst Vice Chanc Alumni Affairs .... Mr. George THURLOW, III
88 Dean College Creative Studies .... Dr. Bruce H. TIFFNEY
54 Dean College of Engineering .... Dr. Rod ALFERNESS
58 Dean Graduate Division .... Dr. Carol GENETTI
53 Dean Gevirtz Graduate Sch Educ .... Dr. Gale MORRISON
65 Dean Bren School of Env Sci & Mgmt .... Dr. Steven D. GAINES
56 Dean UC Santa Barbara Extension .... Dr. Michael T. BROWN
35 Dean of Students .... Dr. Yonie HARRIS
79 Dean Humanities/Fine Arts .... Dr. David B. MARSHALL
81 Dean Math/Life & Physical Sciences .... Dr. Pierre WILTZIUS
87 Dean Summer Sessions .... Dr. Carol BRAUN PASTERNACK
83 Dean Social Sciences .... Dr. Melvin L. OLIVER
85 Director Intl Students/Scholars .... Dr. Mary J. JACOB
06 Registrar .... Ms. Leesa BECK
15 Interim Director Human Resources .... Ms. Tricia HIEMSTRA
21 Director Accounting Svcs & Controls .... Mr. Jim R. CORKILL
37 Director Financial Aid .... Mr. Michael MILLER
88 Acting Dir Audit & Advisory Service .... Mr. Robert TARSIA
07 Director Admissions & Outreach ... Ms. Christine N. VAN GIESON
09 Director Institutional Research .... Dr. Steven C. VELASCO
23 Director Student Health Svcs .... Dr. Mary FERRIS
39 Exec Dir Housing Residential Svcs .... Mr. Wilfred E. BROWN
40 Director of UCSB Bookstore .... Mr. Mark BEISECKER
19 Chief of Police .... Mr. Dustin OLSON
41 Director Intercollegiate Athletics .... Mr. Mark MASSARI
86 Dir Governmental Relations .... Ms. Kirsten DESHLER
88 Director Finance/Administration .... Mr. Eric J. SONQUIST
08 University Librarian .... Ms. Denise STEPHENS
88 Director Orientation Programs .... Ms. Tricia RASCON
44 Dir Capital Development .... Mr. Chuck HAINES
46 Acting Dir Campus Planning & Design .... Ms. Alissa HUMMER
44 Assoc Vice Chancellor Development .... Ms. Beverly COLGATE
31 Director Arts & Lectures .... Ms. Celesta BILLECI
88 Director Disabled Students Pgm .... Mr. Gary R. WHITE
104 Campus Dir Education Abroad Program .... Dr. Juan E. CAMPO
88 Director Env Health & Safety .... Ms. Pam LOMBARDO
88 Director MultiCultural Center .... Ms. Zaveeni KHAN-MARCUS
38 Director Counseling Services .... Dr. Jeanne STANFORD
94 Acting Director Women's Center .... Ms. Kim EQUINOA
88 Ombudsperson .... Ms. Kirsi AULIN
88 Exec Dir Instructional Devel .... Mr. George H. MICHAELS
36 Acting Director Career Services .... Mr. Ignacio GALLARDO
13 Acting AVC for IT and CIO .... Ms. Elise MEYER
43 UCSB Legal Counsel .... Ms. Nancy G. HAMILL
88 Equal Opport Sexual Harras/Title IX .... Mr. Ricardo ALCAINO
18 Director Design & Construction .... Mr. Jack WOLEVER
88 Director Univ Center/Events Center .... Mr. Gary LAWRENCE
68 Director of Recreation .... Mr. Jon SPAVENTA
24 Director Instructional Computing .... Mr. William KOSELUK
92 Honors Coord/Academic Advisor .... Ms. Rocio ANGELES
92 Honors Coord/Academic Advisor .... Mr. Scott KASSNER
96 Strategic Sourcing Specialist .... Mr. Chris CURLESS

*University of California-Santa Cruz (C)

1156 High Street, Santa Cruz CA 95064-1077

County: Santa Cruz FICE Identification: 001321
Unit ID: 110714
Telephone: (831) 459-0111 Carnegie Class: RU/VH
FAX Number: (831) 459-0146 Calendar System: Quarter
URL: www.ucsc.edu
Established: 1962 Annual Undergrad Tuition & Fees (In-State): $13,416
Enrollment: 17,404 Coed
Affiliation or Control: State IRS Status: 501(c)3
Highest Offering: Doctorate
Program: Liberal Arts And General; Professional
Accreditation: WC, ENG, IPSY

02 Chancellor .... Dr. George R. BLUMENTHAL
05 Campus Provost/Exec Vice Chancellor .... Dr. Alison GALLOWAY
10 Vice Chanc Business/Admin Services .... Dr. Sarah LATHAM
45 Vice Chancellor Planning/Budget .... Dr. Peggy DELANEY
46 Vice Chancellor Research .... Dr. Scott BRANDT
30 Vice Chanc of University Relations .... Ms. Donna M. MURPHY
13 Vice Provost Information Technology .... Dr. Mary DOYLE
20 V Prov/Dean Undergrad Educ .... Dr. Richard HUGHEY
20 Vice Provost Academic Affairs .... Dr. Herbert LEE
88 Sr Dir Silicon Valley Initiative .... Dr. Gordon RINGOLD
16 Asst VC Academic Personnel .... Dr. Pamela PETERSON
08 University Librarian .... Ms. Virginia STEEL
07 Assoc VC Enrollment Mgmt .... Ms. Michelle WHITTINGHAM
49 Dean of Humanities .... Dr. William LADUSAW
81 Dean Physical & Biological Sci .... Dr. Paul KOCH
49 Dean of the Arts .... Dr. David YAGER
83 Dean of Social Sciences .... Dr. Sheldon KAMIENIECKI
54 Dean of Engineering .... Dr. Arthur RAMIREZ
58 Vice Prov/Dean of Graduate Studies .... Dr. Tyrus MILLER
65 Director Institute Marine Sciences .... Dr. Gary B. GRIGGS
81 Director Institute Particle Physics .... Dr. Steven RITZ
88 Director UCO/Lick Observatory .... Dr. Michael BOLTE
12 Provost Stevenson College .... Dr. Alice YANG
12 Provost Cowell College .... Dr. Faye CROSBY
12 Provost Crown College .... Dr. F. Joel FERGUSON
12 Provost Merrill College .... Dr. Elizabeth ABRAMS
12 Provost Porter College .... Dr. David E. JONES
12 Provost Kresge College .... Dr. Juan POBLETE
12 Provost Oakes College .... Dr. Kimberly LAU
12 Provost College Eight .... Dr. Ronnie LIPSCHUTZ
12 Provost College Nine & Ten .... Dr. Helen SHAPIRO
06 Registrar .... Ms. Pamela HUNT-CARTER
09 Director Institutional Research .... Dr. Julian L. FERNALD
15 Assoc VC Staff Human Resources .... Ms. Jo PACKHAM
18 Int Assoc VC & Campus Arthitect .... Mr. John BARNES
29 Exec Director of Alumni Relations .... Ms. Carolyn CHRISTOPHERSON
37 Staff Director Financial Aid .... Vacant
22 Staff Dir EEO/Affirmative Action .... Mr. Ashish SAHNI
86 Director Government Relations .... Ms. Donna M. BLITZER
38 Interim Director Student Counseling .... Dr. Maryjan MURPHY
96 Director of Purchasing .... Mr. John BONO
35 Asst Vice Chanc Student Affairs .... Ms. Alma SIFUENTES

University of East-West Medicine (D)

595 Lawrence Expressway, Sunnyvale CA 94085

County: Santa Clara FICE Identification: 039953
Unit ID: 447801
Telephone: (408) 733-1878 Carnegie Class: Spec/Health
FAX Number: (408) 636-7705 Calendar System: Trimester
URL: www.uewm.edu
Established: 1997 Annual Undergrad Tuition & Fees: $33,660
Enrollment: 300 Coed
Affiliation or Control: Proprietary IRS Status: Proprietary
Highest Offering: Master's
Program: Professional
Accreditation: ACUP

01 President .... Dr. Ying Qiu WANG
11 COO .... Doreen SIMMONS

† Granted candidacy at the Doctorate level.

University of LaVerne (E)

1950 Third Street, La Verne CA 91750-4443

County: Los Angeles FICE Identification: 001216
Unit ID: 117140
Telephone: (909) 593-3511 Carnegie Class: DRU
FAX Number: (909) 593-0965 Calendar System: Semester
URL: www.laverne.edu
Established: 1891 Annual Undergrad Tuition & Fees: $35,000
Enrollment: 8,628 Coed
Affiliation or Control: Independent Non-Profit IRS Status: 501(c)3
Highest Offering: Doctorate
Program: Liberal Arts And General; Teacher Preparatory; Professional
Accreditation: WC, CLPSY, #LAW, SPAA, TED

01 President .... Dr. Devorah A. LIEBERMAN
05 Provost .... Dr. Gregory DEWEY
88 Special Assistant to the President .... Mr. Philip A. HAWKEY
10 Vice Pres for Finance & Treasurer .... Mr. Avedis (Avo) KECHICHIAN
30 Vice President Univ Advancement .... Ms. Myra GARCIA
20 Vice Provost .... Dr. Homa SHABAHANG
49 Dean College Arts & Sciences .... Dr. Jonathan REED
50 Dean College Business/Public Mgmt .... Dr. Ibrahim (Abe) HELOU
53 Dean College of Educ/Org Leadership .... Dr. Mark GOOR
61 Dean College of Law .... Mr. Gilbert HOLMES
32 Dean Student Affairs .... Dr. Loretta RAHMANI
12 Dean Regional Campus Admin .... Dr. Stephen L. LESNIAK
07 Dean of Admissions .... Mr. Chris KRZAK
88 Assoc VP Academic Sppt/Retent Svcs .... Ms. Adeline CARDENAS-CLAGUE
21 Associate Vice President of Finance . Ms. Lori K. GORDIEN CASE
20 Assoc VP Academic Affairs/Faculty .... Dr. Alfred P. CLARK
108 Assoc VP University Assessment/ Prof .... Dr. Aghop DER-KARABETIAN
16 Chief Human Resources Officer .... Ms. Jody L. BOMBA
13 Assoc VP Facil & Tech Svcs/ CIO .... Dr. Clive K. HOUSTON-BROWN
35 Associate Dean Student Affairs .... Mrs. Ruby S. MONTANO-CORDOVA
88 Asst Dean Grad Acad Supp/Ret Svcs .... Ms. Jo Nell BAKER
84 Assoc VP for Enrollment Management .... Mr. Fred A. CHYR
85 Director International Student Svcs .... Dr. Jeffrey NONEMAKER
18 Dir Physical Plant Operations/Svs .... Mr. Robert D. BEEBE
37 Associate Director of Financial Aid .... Mr. Jason NEAL
26 Int Director of Public Relations .... Mrs. Alisha ROSAS
29 Director Alumni Relations .... Ms. Bianca ROMERO
38 Director Student Counseling .... Dr. Richard R. ROGERS
88 Director Student Accounts .... Ms. Xochitl E. MARTINEZ
104 Int Director Intl/Study Aboard Ctr .... Dr. Alfred CLARK
96 Director Purchasing & Procurement .... Mrs. Deborah S. DEACY
28 Director Multicultural Affairs .... Dr. Daniel L. LOERA
23 Dir Health Svcs/Svcs for Stds-Disab .... Ms. Cynthia K. DENNE
39 Asst Dean/Dir Housing/Res Life Ed .... Mr. Juan REGALADO
36 Director Career Services .... Mrs. Paula E. VERDUGO
88 Dir Center for Adv/Teaching & Lrng .... Dr. Sammy ELZARKA
88 Director Graduate Success Center .... Dr. Lisa RODRIGUEZ
19 Dir Campus Safety & Transportation . Mr. Stanley T. SKIPWORTH
41 Athletic Director .... Ms. Julie KLINE

06 Registrar ... Ms. Marilyn S. DAVIES
08 University Librarian ... Dr. Vinaya L. TRIPURANENI
28 Chief Diversity/Inclusivity Officer ... Dr. Joy LEI
09 Director of Institutional Research ... Dr. Leeshawn MOORE
42 Chaplain/Dir of Campus Ministry ... Dr. Zandra L. WAGONER
88 Director of La Verne Experience ... Dr. Margaret D. REDMAN
88 Director Student Information Tech ... Mrs. Loreto D'MONTE
88 Director Pgm Outreach/Student Recr ... Dr. Todd ECKEL
88 Director International Admission ... Mr. Adam WU
20 Associate Provost ... Dr. Beatriz GONZALEZ
88 Director of Civic Engagement ... Ms. Marisol MORALES

University of the Pacific (A)

3601 Pacific Avenue, Stockton CA 95211-0197
County: San Joaquin FICE Identification: 001329
Unit ID: 120883
Telephone: (209) 946-2011 Carnegie Class: DRU
FAX Number: (209) 946-2845 Calendar System: Semester
URL: www.pacific.edu
Established: 1851 Annual Undergrad Tuition & Fees: $39,810
Enrollment: 6,652 Coed
Affiliation or Control: Independent Non-Profit IRS Status: 501(c)3
Highest Offering: Doctorate
Program: Liberal Arts And General; Teacher Preparatory; Professional
Accreditation: WC, ART, BUS, CS, DENT, DH, ENG, IPSY, LAW, MUS, PHAR, PTA, SP, TED

01 President ... Pamela A. EIBECK
05 Provost ... Maria G. PALLAVICINI
10 Vice President Business & Finance ... Patrick D. CAVANAUGH
32 Vice President Student Life ... Patrick DAY
30 VP Development & Alumni Relations ... G. Burnham "Burnie" ATTERBURY
26 Vice Pres External Relations ... Ted LELAND
101 VP & Secretary to Board of Regents ... Mary Lou LACKEY
21 Associate VP Business/Finance ... Ken MULLEN
84 Assoc Provost for Enrollment Svcs ... Vacant
26 Assoc VP Marketing/Univ Relations ... Richard ROJO
51 Asst Provost Ctr Prof & Cont Educ ... Barbara L. SHAW
08 Dean of the Library ... C. Brigid WELCH
58 Dean Research/Graduate Studies ... Vacant
25 Sponsored Pgms Administrator ... Carol BRODIE
29 Dir of Alumni Relations ... Kelli PAGE
37 Director of Financial Aid ... Lynn FOX
07 Director of Admissions ... Rich TOLEDO
06 Registrar ... Ann GILLEN
09 Director Institutional Research ... Mike ROGERS
35 Director Student Activities ... Jason VELO
96 Director of Purchasing ... Ronda MARR
92 Director Honors Program ... George RANDELS
93 Director Multicultural Affairs ... Ines RUIZ-HUSTON
94 Director Gender Studies ... Traci ROBERTS-CAMPS
38 Director of Counseling Services ... Stacie TURKS
39 Director of Housing ... Steven JACOBSON
36 Director of Career Resource Center ... Vacant
41 Director of Athletics ... Ted LELAND
42 University Chaplain ... Joel LOHR
13 Chief Information Officer ... Malik RAHMAN
15 Director of Human Resources ... Jane L. LEWIS
40 Director of Bookstore ... Nicole CASTILLO
19 Director of Public Safety ... Michael BELCHER
18 Director of Physical Plant ... Scott HEATON
28 Dir of Div/Asst to Prov for Acad ... Vacant
61 Dean McGeorge School of Law ... Jay MOOTZ
54 Dean Sch of Eng/Comp Science ... Steven HOWELL
67 Dean Sch of Pharm/Hlth Sciences ... Phillip R. OPPENHEIMER
64 Dean Conservatory of Music ... Giulio ONGARO
52 Dean School of Dentistry ... Patrick FERRILLO
53 Dean School of Education ... Lynn BECK
49 Dean College of the Pacific ... Rena FRADEN
50 Dean School Business/Public Admin ... Lewis GALE
82 Director Sch International Studies ... William HERRIN

University of Philosophical Research (B)

3910 Los Feliz Boulevard, Los Angeles CA 90027
County: Los Angeles Identification: 666373
Telephone: (323) 663-2167 Carnegie Class: Not Classified
FAX Number: (323) 663-9443 Calendar System: Quarter
URL: www.uprs.edu
Established: 1998 Annual Graduate Tuition & Fees: $5,900
Enrollment: 205 Coed
Affiliation or Control: Independent Non-Profit IRS Status: 501(c)3
Highest Offering: Master's; No Undergraduates
Program: Liberal Arts And General
Accreditation: DETC

01 President/Chief Executive Officer ... Dr. Obadiah HARRIS
05 Dean of Academic Affairs ... Dr. Debashish BANERJI
06 Registrar ... Mr. John CHASE

University of Phoenix Bay Area Campus (C)

3590 N First Street, San Jose CA 95134-1805
Telephone: (800) 266-2107 Identification: 770193
Accreditation: &NH, ACBSP

† Main campus is University of Phoenix in Tempe, AZ.

University of Phoenix Central Valley Campus (D)

45 River Park Place West, Fresno CA 93720-1552
Telephone: (800) 266-2107 Identification: 770190
Accreditation: &NH, ACBSP

† Main campus is University of Phoenix in Tempe, AZ.

University of Phoenix Sacramento Valley Campus (E)

2860 Gateway Oaks Drive, Sacramento CA 95833-4334
Telephone: (800) 266-2107 Identification: 770191
Accreditation: &NH, ACBSP

† Main campus is University of Phoenix in Tempe, AZ.

University of Phoenix San Diego Campus (F)

9645 Granite Ridge Dr, Suite 200,
San Diego CA 92123-2658
Telephone: (800) 473-4346 Identification: 770192
Accreditation: &NH

† Main campus is University of Phoenix in Tempe, AZ.

University of Phoenix Southern California Campus (G)

3100 Bristol Street, Costa Mesa CA 92626-3099
Telephone: (800) 888-1968 Identification: 770189
Accreditation: &NH, ACBSP

† Main campus is University of Phoenix in Tempe, AZ.

University of Redlands (H)

PO Box 3080, Redlands CA 92373-0999
County: San Bernardino FICE Identification: 001322
Unit ID: 121691
Telephone: (909) 793-2121 Carnegie Class: Master's L
FAX Number: (909) 793-2029 Calendar System: Semester
URL: www.redlands.edu
Established: 1907 Annual Undergrad Tuition & Fees: $39,338
Enrollment: 4,956 Coed
Affiliation or Control: Independent Non-Profit IRS Status: 501(c)3
Highest Offering: Doctorate
Program: Liberal Arts And General; Teacher Preparatory; Professional
Accreditation: WC, MUS, SP

01 President ... Dr. Ralph W. KUNCL
03 Executive Vice President/COO ... Mr. Phillip L. DOOLITTLE
05 Vice President Academic Affairs ... Dr. David FITE
10 Vice Pres Finance/Administration ... Mr. Cory NOMURA
26 Vice President University Relations ... Mr. Neil A. MACREADY
32 Vice President/Dean Student Life ... Ms. Charlotte G. BURGESS
84 Vice Pres of Enrollment Management ... Mr. Kevin DYERLY
30 Vice Pres for Advancement ... Ms. Anita WEST
27 Asc VP Mktg/Strategic Communication ... Ms. Kimberli MUNKRES
44 Assoc Vice Pres Development ... Mr. Ray WATTS
91 Assoc VP Integrated Tech Sys/CIO ... Mr. Hamid ETESAMNIA
21 Director Financial Ops & Controller ... Ms. Patricia M. CAUDLE
58 Dean School of Business ... Dr. Stuart NOBLE-GOODMAN
53 Dean School of Education ... Dr. James VALADEZ
49 Dean Arts & Sciences ... Dr. Kathy OGREN
64 Dean School of Music ... Dr. Andrew GLENDENING
28 Asc Dean Campus Diversity/Inclusion ... Ms. Leela MADHAVARAU
42 Chaplain ... Rev. John T. WALSH
06 Associate Registrar ... Ms. Laura VALLE
104 Director Study Abroad ... Ms. Sarah N. FALKENSTIEN
37 Director of Financial Aid ... Ms. Alisha AGUILAR
90 Director Academic Computing ... Mr. Shariq AHMED
81 Director Center of Sciences & Math ... Dr. Barbara M. MURRAY
88 Director of Environmental Programs ... Dr. Lamont C. HEMPEL
08 Director of Library Services ... Ms. Gabriela SONNTAG
15 Director of Human Resources ... Ms. Roberta G. DELLHIME
22 EEO & Employee Relations Manager ... Vacant
09 Director of Institutional Research ... Ms. Wendy MCEWEN
19 Director of Public Safety ... Mr. Jeffrey TALBOTT
18 Director of Facilities Management ... Mr. Roger CELLINI
29 Director of Alumni Relations ... Mr. John G. SERBEIN
20 Asst Dean of Acad Support Services ... Ms. Amy WILMS
38 Director Student Counseling ... Mr. Ruben ROBLES
41 Director of Athletics ... Mr. Jeffrey MARTINEZ
96 Director of Purchasing ... Ms. Sandi TAYLOR
36 Director Student Placement ... Ms. Kathryn WOOD

University of San Diego (I)

5998 Alcala Park, San Diego CA 92110-2492
County: San Diego FICE Identification: 010395
Unit ID: 122436
Telephone: (619) 260-4600 Carnegie Class: DRU
FAX Number: (619) 260-6833 Calendar System: 4/1/4
URL: www.sandiego.edu
Established: 1949 Annual Undergrad Tuition & Fees: $41,392
Enrollment: 8,105 Coed
Affiliation or Control: Roman Catholic IRS Status: 501(c)3
Highest Offering: Doctorate
Program: Liberal Arts And General; Teacher Preparatory; Professional
Accreditation: WC, BUS, BUSA, CACREP, ENG, IPSY, LAW, MFCD, NURSE, TED

01 President ... Dr. Mary E. LYONS
04 Special Assistant to the President ... Ms. Elaine ATENCIO
05 Interim Vice President & Provost ... Dr. Andrew T. ALLEN
10 Vice Pres Business & Admin ... Mr. Russell C. THACKSTON
42 Vice President Mission & Ministry ... Msgr. Daniel J. DILLABOUGH
32 Vice President Student Affairs ... Ms. Carmen M. VAZQUEZ
30 Vice President Univ Relations ... Dr. Timothy L. O'MALLEY
49 Dean College of Arts & Sciences ... Dr. Noelle NORTON
50 Dean School of Business Admin ... Dr. David F. PYKE
61 Dean School of Law ... Mr. Stephen C. FERRUOLO
53 Dean Sch Leadership/Educ Sciences ... Dr. Paula A. CORDEIRO
66 Dean School Nursing/Health Science ... Dr. Sally B. HARDIN
88 Dean School of Peace Studies ... Dr. Edward C. LUCK
51 Dean Prof & Continuing Education ... Dr. Jason LEMON
08 Dean University Library ... Dr. Theresa BYRD
35 Asst VP & Dean of Students ... Dr. Donald R. GODWIN
20 Vice Provost ... Dr. Thomas R. HERRINTON
20 Associate Provost ... Vacant
20 Assoc Provost International Affairs ... Dr. Denise DIMON
28 Assoc Provost for Incl & Diversity ... Dr. Esteban DEL RIO
13 Vice Provost & Chief Info Officer ... Mr. Christopher W. WESSELLS
41 Executive Director Athletics ... Mr. Ky L. SNYDER
21 Assoc Vice Pres Business Admin ... Ms. Patricia T. OLIVER PUTNAM
16 Interim Human Resources Officer ... Ms. Karen BRIGGS
18 Asst VP Facilities Management ... Mr. Mark NORITA
26 Asst Vice Pres Public Affairs ... Ms. Pamela GRAY PAYTON
19 Asst Vice President Public Safety ... Mr. Larry E. BARNETT
43 General Counsel ... Ms. Kelly C. DOUGLAS
06 University Registrar ... Ms. Susan H. BUGBEE
84 Asst VP Enrollment Management ... Mr. Stephen F. PULTZ
07 Director of Admissions ... Ms. Minh-Ha HOANG
09 Dir Inst Research & Planning ... Dr. Paula S. KRIST
54 Director Engineering Programs ... Dr. Kathleen A. KRAMER
90 Sr Director Academic Tech Services ... Ms. Shahra MESHKATY
91 Interim Director EASS ... Mr. Avi BADWAL
102 Sr Director Foundation Relations ... Ms. Annette KETNER
86 Sr Dir Community/Govt Relations ... Mr. Thomas R. CLEARY
44 Senior Director Planned Giving ... Mr. John A. PHILLIPS
29 Director Alumni Relations ... Mr. Charles BASS
44 Director Annual Giving ... Mr. Philip GARLAND
40 Director Bookstore ... Ms. Katherine MISSELL
36 Director Career Services ... Vacant
38 Director Counseling Center ... Dr. Stephen D. SPRINKLE
37 Director Financial Aid Services ... Ms. Judith LEWIS LOGUE
92 Director Honors Program ... Dr. Roger C. PACE
39 Director Housing ... Mr. Rick HAGAN
85 Dir International Students/Scholars ... Ms. Yvette M. FONTAINE
104 Dir International Studies Abroad ... Ms. Kira A. ESPIRITU
93 Director Multicultural Center ... Dr. Mayte PEREZ-FRANCO
27 Senior Director Media Relations ... Ms. Elizabeth HARMAN
96 Director Procurement Services ... Ms. Dawn L. ANDERSON
25 Director Sponsored Programs ... Ms. Kim EUDY
23 Director Student Health Center ... Ms. Pamela J. SIKES

University of San Francisco (J)

2130 Fulton Street, San Francisco CA 94117-1080
County: San Francisco FICE Identification: 001325
Unit ID: 122612
Telephone: (415) 422-5555 Carnegie Class: DRU
FAX Number: (415) 422-2303 Calendar System: 4/1/4
URL: www.usfca.edu
Established: 1855 Annual Undergrad Tuition & Fees: $40,294
Enrollment: 10,040 Coed
Affiliation or Control: Roman Catholic IRS Status: 501(c)3
Highest Offering: Doctorate
Program: Liberal Arts And General; Teacher Preparatory; Professional
Accreditation: WC, BUS, LAW, NURSE, SPAA

01 President ... Rev. Stephen A. PRIVETT, SJ
05 Provost/Vice Pres Academic Affairs ... Dr. Jennifer E. TURPIN
00 Chancellor ... Rev. John J. LO SCHIAVO, SJ
10 Vice President Business & Finance ... Mr. Charles E. CROSS
26 Vice Pres Communication & Marketing ... Mr. David F. MACMILLAN
88 Vice Pres International Relations ... Dr. Stanley D. NEL
30 Vice President Development ... Mr. Peter J. WILCH
32 Vice Provost Student Life ... Dr. Peter J. NOVAK
43 University Counsel ... Ms. Donna J. DAVIS
13 Acting CIO/Assoc VP Application Svc ... Mr. Way LEON
20 Senior Vice Provost Acad Affairs ... Dr. Gerardo MARIN
45 Vice Prov Ctr Inst Planning/Effect ... Dr. Ana KARAMAN
84 Vice Provost/Dean Acad & Enroll Svc ... Dr. Elizabeth J. JOHNSON
88 Assoc Vice Prov Planning and Budget ... Mr. Michael J. HARRINGTON
12 Vice Prov Branch Camp & Online Pgms ... Dr. Carol J. BATKER
16 Asst Vice Pres Human Resources ... Ms. Martha A. PEUGH-WADE
21 Assoc Vice Pres Financial Reporting ... Ms. Kimberly L. KVAAL
26 Assoc VP Public Affairs/Univ Comm ... Mr. Gary MCDONALD
18 Asst Vice Pres Facilities Mgmt ... Mr. Michael LONDON
28 Assoc Vice Prov Diversity/ Community ... Dr. Mary J. WARDELL-GHIRARDUZZI
88 Assoc Vice Prov Acad Affs/Historian ... Dr. Alan L. ZIAJKA
61 Dean of the School of Law ... Mr. John D. TRASVINA
49 Dean College Arts & Sciences ... Dr. Marcelo F. CAMPERI
08 Dean of Libraries ... Dr. Tyrone H. CANNON
53 Dean School of Education ... Dr. Kevin K. KUMASHIRO

50 Dean School of Management ... Dr. Mike WEBBER
66 Dean School of Nursing ... Dr. Judith KARSHMER
04 Exec Asst to President/Sec BOT ... Ms. Jaci E. NEESAM
37 Senior Assoc Dean Acad/Dir Fin Aid ... Ms. Susan L. MURPHY
07 Assoc Dean & Director of Admissions ... Mr. Michael HUGHES
06 Asst Dean University Registrar ... Mr. Robert L. BROMFIELD
96 Exec Dir Purchasing & Ancillary Svc ... Ms. Janet L. TEYMOURTASH
38 Senior Director Counseling Center ... Dr. Barbara J. THOMAS
36 Senior Dir of Career Services ... Mr. James CATIGGAY
19 Senior Director of Public Safety ... Dr. Daniel LAWSON
42 Director University Ministry ... Ms. Julia A. DOWD
85 Director Ctr for Global Education ... Ms. Sharon F. LI
85 Dir International Student Services ... Ms. Laura GERTH
41 Director of Athletics ... Mr. Scott A. SIDWELL
09 Director Institution Data Analysis ... Mr. Theodore M. LYDON, JR.
29 Asst VP Alumni Engage/Annual Giving ... Ms. Jessica JORDAN
15 Dir Employment & Employee Relations ... Ms. Diane L. NELSON
39 Int Dir Student Housing/Res Educ ... Mr. Golden T. VENTERS, III
24 Dir Ctr Learning Tech & Instruct ... Dr. John BANSAVICH

University of Southern California (A)

University Park, Los Angeles CA 90089-0012
County: Los Angeles — FICE Identification: 001328
Unit ID: 123961
Telephone: (213) 740-2311 — Carnegie Class: RU/VH
FAX Number: (213) 740-8502 — Calendar System: Semester
URL: www.usc.edu
Established: 1880 — Annual Undergrad Tuition & Fees: $46,363
Enrollment: 39,958 — Coed
Affiliation or Control: Independent Non-Profit — IRS Status: 501(c)3
Highest Offering: Doctorate
Program: Occupational; Liberal Arts And General; Teacher Preparatory; Professional
Accreditation: **WC**, ANEST, ARCPA, BUS, BUSA, CEA, CLPSY, CS, DENT, DH, DIETI, ENG, HSA, IPSY, JOUR, LAW, LSAR, MED, MUS, OT, PCSAS, PDPSY, PH, PHAR, PLNG, PTA, SPAA, SW

01 President ... Dr. C. L. M. NIKIAS
05 Provost and Sr VP Academic Affairs ... Prof. Elizabeth GARRETT
11 Sr Vice Pres Administration ... Mr. Todd R. DICKEY
10 Sr Vice President & CFO ... Mr. Robert ABELES
26 Sr Vice Pres University Relations ... Mr. Thomas SAYLES
30 Sr VP University Advancement ... Mr. Albert R. CHECCIO
23 Sr Vice Pres & CEO for USC Health ... Mr. Thomas E. JACKIEWICZ
88 Chief Investment Officer ... Ms. Lisa MAZZOCCO
43 General Counsel/Secretary of Univ ... Ms. Carol MAUCH AMIR
32 Vice President Student Affairs ... Vacant
07 VP Admissions and Planning ... Dr. L. Katharine HARRINGTON
46 VP for Research ... Dr. Randolph W. HALL
88 VP for Real Estate Dev & Asset ... Vacant
88 VP for Athletic Compliance ... Mr. David M. ROBERTS
88 VP Capital Construction/Facilities ... Mr. Thomas S. LEARY, JR.
21 VP for Finance ... Ms. Margo STEURBAUT
88 VP for Health Sciences Development ... Mr. William WATSON
26 VP Public Relations & Marketing ... Ms. Brenda K. MACEO
41 Athletic Director ... Mr. Patrick C. HADEN
100 Chief of Staff/Dir of Protocol ... Mr. Dennis CORNELL
00 President Emeritus ... Dr. Steven B. SAMPLE
88 Dean Leventhal School of Accounting ... Dr. William W. HOLDER
60 Dean Annenberg School Communication ... Dr. Ernest J. WILSON, III
48 Dean School of Architecture ... Mr. Qingyun MA
50 Dean Marshall School of Business ... Mr. James G. ELLIS
88 Dean School of Cinematic Arts ... Dr. Elizabeth M. DALEY
66 Dean Kaufman School of Dance ... Dr. Robert A. CUTIETTA
52 Dean Ostrow School of Dentistry ... Dr. Avishai SADAN
53 Dean Rossier School of Education ... Dr. Karen S. GALLAGHER
54 Dean Viterbi School of Engineering ... Dr. Yannis C. YORTSOS
57 Dean Roski School of Fine Arts ... Dr. Erica MUHL
88 Dean Davis School of Gerontology ... Dr. Pinchas COHEN
61 Dean Gould School of Law ... Mr. Robert K. RASMUSSEN
63 Dean Keck School of Medicine ... Dr. Carmen A. PULIAFITO
64 Dean Thornton School of Music ... Dr. Robert A. CUTIETTA
67 Dean School of Pharmacy ... Dr. R. Pete L. VANDERVEEN
70 Dean School of Social Work ... Dr. Marilyn L. FLYNN
88 Dean School of Dramatic Arts ... Ms. Madeline PUZO
88 Dean Price School of Public Policy ... Dr. Jack H. KNOTT
49 Dean Dornsife Col Ltrs Arts & Sci ... Dr. Steve A. KAY
42 Dean Religious Life ... Mr. Varun SONI
06 Dean Academic Records & Registrar ... Dr. Douglas SHOOK
08 Dean University Libraries ... Ms. Catherine QUINLAN
07 Dean of Admission ... Mr. Timothy BRUNOLD
37 Dean of Financial Aid ... Mr. Thomas MCWHORTER
36 Assoc Sr VP Career/Protective Svcs ... Dr. Charles E. LANE
29 Assoc Sr VP and CEO Alumni Assn ... Mr. Scott M. MORY
36 Asst VP Career Services ... Dr. Mary K. CAMPBELL
51 Exec Dir Cont Ed & Summer Programs ... Ms. Eileen B. KOHAN
28 Exec Dir Office of Equity/Diversity ... Ms. Jody SHIPPER
38 Director Student Counseling Service ... Dr. Ilene ROSENSTEIN
20 Executive Vice Provost ... Dr. Michael W. QUICK
88 Vice Provost and Senior Advisor ... Dr. Martin L. LEVINE
20 Vice Prov for Graduate Programs ... Dr. Sarah PRATT
20 Vice Prov for Undergraduate Program ... Dr. Eugene N. BICKERS
27 Vice Prov for Info Tech Svcs/CIO ... Mr. Peter SIEGEL
88 Vice Prov Acad Operations & Strate ... Mr. Robert A. COOPER
88 Vice Prov for Innovation ... Ms. Jennifer DYER
88 Int Vice Prov Global Initiatives ... Dr. Anthony BAILEY
20 Vice Provost for Faculty Affairs ... Dr. Beth E. MEYEROWITZ

University of the West (B)

1409 Walnut Grove Avenue, Rosemead CA 91770-3709
County: Los Angeles — FICE Identification: 036963
Unit ID: 449870
Telephone: (626) 571-8811 — Carnegie Class: Bac/Diverse
FAX Number: (626) 571-1413 — Calendar System: Semester
URL: www.uwest.edu
Established: 1991 — Annual Undergrad Tuition & Fees: $9,436
Enrollment: 310 — Coed
Affiliation or Control: Independent Non-Profit — IRS Status: 501(c)3
Highest Offering: Doctorate
Program: Liberal Arts And General
Accreditation: **WC**

01 President ... Dr. Stephen MORGAN
05 Dean of Academic Affairs ... Dr. William HOWE
32 Dean of Student Affairs ... Ms. Vanessa KARAM
10 Chief Financial Officer ... Dr. Bill CHEN
08 Director of Library ... Ms. Ling Ling KUO
06 Registrar ... Ms. Jeanette ANDERSON
07 Admissions Officer ... Ms. Grace HSIAO
35 Student Life Coordinator ... Mr. Eddie ESCALANTE
73 Chair Dept of Religious Studies ... Dr. Jane IWAMURA
50 Chair Dept of Business Admin ... Dr. Chi SHEH

† 2012-2013 tuition figure included room & board.

Valley College of Medical Careers (C)

8399 Topanga Canyon Blvd Ste 200, West Hills CA 91304
County: Los Angeles — FICE Identification: 041145
Unit ID: 449445
Telephone: (818) 883-9002 — Carnegie Class: Not Classified
FAX Number: (818) 883-9003 — Calendar System: Semester
URL: www.vcmc.edu
Established: — Annual Undergrad Tuition & Fees: $29,100
Enrollment: 63 — Coed
Affiliation or Control: Proprietary — IRS Status: Proprietary
Highest Offering: Associate Degree
Program: Occupational
Accreditation: **ABHES**

Vanguard University of Southern California (D)

55 Fair Drive, Costa Mesa CA 92626-6597
County: Orange — FICE Identification: 001293
Unit ID: 123651
Telephone: (714) 556-3610 — Carnegie Class: Bac/Diverse
FAX Number: (714) 957-9317 — Calendar System: Semester
URL: www.vanguard.edu
Established: 1920 — Annual Undergrad Tuition & Fees: $29,250
Enrollment: 2,213 — Coed
Affiliation or Control: Assemblies Of God Church — IRS Status: 501(c)3
Highest Offering: Master's
Program: Liberal Arts And General; Teacher Preparatory; Professional
Accreditation: **WC**, NURSE, THEA

01 President ... Dr. David W. CLARK
04 Exec Assistant to the President ... Ms. Shree CARTER
05 Provost/Vice President Acad Affairs ... Dr. Jeff HITTENBERGER
20 Assoc Provost/Dean Col Arts & Sci ... Dr. Michael D. WILSON
58 Dean Grad and Professional Studies ... Dr. Andrew STENHOUSE
73 Director for Graduate Religion ... Dr. Richard ISRAEL
53 Director for Graduate Education ... Vacant
83 Director for Graduate Psychology ... Dr. Jerre WHITE
06 Registrar ... Ms. Judy HAMILTON
09 Director of Institutional Research ... Dr. Ludmilla PRASLOVA
08 Head Librarian ... Ms. Alison ENGLISH
41 Athletic Director ... Mr. Bob WILSON
10 Vice President Business/Finance ... Ms. Lettie COWIE
21 Director of Fiscal Management ... Ms. Jill ROBINSON
21 Director of Accounting Operations ... Ms. Beverly MOORE
96 Director of Purchasing ... Ms. Jennifer PAUL
19 Director of Campus Safety Services ... Mr. Paul TURGEON
27 Chief Information Officer ... Mr. Derek DENSBERGER
15 Director of Human Resources ... Mr. Joe BAFFA
18 Director of Facility Services ... Mr. Bruce CROUCH
40 Bookstore Manager ... Mr. Matt ACUNA
101 Board of Trustees Liaison ... Ms. Shree CARTER
42 University Campus Pastor ... Dr. Michael J. BEALS
32 Dean of Student Life ... Dr. Tim YOUNG
39 Student Housing Coordinator ... Ms. Allison HESSE
24 Director of Learning Skills ... Ms. Barbi ROUSE
38 Director of Counseling Services ... Dr. Beth LORANCE
36 Career Planning Coordinator ... Ms. Kimberly GREENE
28 Director of Diversity ... Vacant
84 VP for Enrollment Management ... Ms. Kim JOHNSON
07 Director of Undergrad Admissions ... Vacant
07 Director of Graduate Admissions ... Mr. Drake LEVASHEFF
37 Director of Student Financial Aid ... Ms. Denise PENA
30 VP University Advancement ... Ms. Kelly KANNWISCHER
44 Director of Annual Fund ... Ms. Jennifer J. SMITH
29 Director of Alumni Relations ... Mr. Joel GACKLE
26 Chief Communications Officer ... Ms. Shana MARTIN
86 Director of Veteran/Government Rels ... Mr. Brent THEOBALD

*Ventura County Community College District (E)

255 W Stanley Avenue, Suite 150, Ventura CA 93001-1348
County: Ventura — FICE Identification: 006863
Unit ID: 125019
Telephone: (805) 652-5500 — Carnegie Class: N/A
FAX Number: (805) 652-7700
URL: www.vcccd.edu

01 Chancellor ... Dr. Jamillah MOORE
10 Vice Chanc Business Svcs/Fin Mgmt ... Mr. Brian FAHNESTOCK
15 Vice Chanc of Human Resources ... Vacant
13 Assoc Vice Chanc of IT ... Mr. Dave FUHRMANN
11 Director of Admin Relations ... Ms. Clare GEISEN
96 Director of Purchasing/Admin Svc ... Ms. Terry COBOS
21 Director of Fiscal Services ... Ms. Mary Anne MCNEIL
88 District Budget Officer ... Ms. Deborah LATEER

*Moorpark College (F)

7075 Campus Road, Moorpark CA 93021-1695
County: Ventura — FICE Identification: 007115
Unit ID: 119137
Telephone: (805) 378-1400 — Carnegie Class: Assoc/Pub-U-MC
FAX Number: (805) 378-1499 — Calendar System: Semester
URL: www.moorparkcollege.edu
Established: 1967 — Annual Undergrad Tuition & Fees (In-State): $1,338
Enrollment: 14,576 — Coed
Affiliation or Control: State — IRS Status: 501(c)3
Highest Offering: Associate Degree
Program: Occupational; 2-Year Principally Bachelor's Creditable
Accreditation: **WJ**, ADNUR, RAD

02 Acting President ... Ms. Iris INGRAM
03 Executive Vice President ... Dr. Lori BENNETT
10 Vice President Business Services ... Ms. Iris INGRAM
04 Executive Assistant to President ... Ms. Andrea RAMBO
66 Dean Student Learning ... Ms. Lisa PUTNAM
57 Dean Student Learning ... Ms. Patricia EWINS
50 Dean Student Learning ... Dr. Kim HOFFMANS
88 Dean Student Learning ... Dr. Amanuel GEBRU
79 Dean Student Learning ... Ms. Inajane NICKLAS
49 Dean Student Learning ... Dr. Julius SOKENU
18 Director Maintainence/Operations ... Mr. John SINUTKO
88 College Business Services Manager ... Ms. Darlene MELBY
41 Athletic Director ... Mr. Howard DAVIS
06 Registrar ... Mr. David ANTER
37 Student Financial Aid Officer ... Ms. Kim KORINKE

*Oxnard College (G)

4000 S Rose Avenue, Oxnard CA 93033-6699
County: Ventura — FICE Identification: 012842
Unit ID: 120421
Telephone: (805) 986-5800 — Carnegie Class: Assoc/Pub-U-MC
FAX Number: (805) 986-5908 — Calendar System: Semester
URL: www.oxnardcollege.edu
Established: 1975 — Annual Undergrad Tuition & Fees (In-District): $1,336
Enrollment: 7,126 — Coed
Affiliation or Control: State/Local — IRS Status: 501(c)3
Highest Offering: Associate Degree
Program: Occupational; 2-Year Principally Bachelor's Creditable
Accreditation: **WJ**, DH

02 President ... Dr. Richard DURAN
05 Exec Vice Pres of Student Learning ... Dr. Erika ENDRIJONAS
10 Vice President of Business Services ... Dr. Michael BUSH
32 Dean of Student Services ... Dr. Karen ENGELSEN
79 Dean Liberal Studies ... Mr. Kenneth SHERWOOD
41 Director of Athletics ... Mr. Jonas CRAWFORD
88 Dean Career & Technical Education ... Ms. Carmen GUERRERO
81 Dean Math Science/Health ... Dr. Carolyn INOUYE
18 Director Maintenance/Operations ... Mr. Will DEITS
06 Registrar ... Mr. Joel DIAZ
88 Director STEM ... Dr. Cynthia HERRERA
40 Bookstore Manager ... Mr. Christopher RENBARGER

*Ventura College (H)

4667 Telegraph Road, Ventura CA 93003-3899
County: Ventura — FICE Identification: 001334
Unit ID: 125028
Telephone: (805) 654-6400 — Carnegie Class: Assoc/Pub-U-MC
FAX Number: (805) 654-6466 — Calendar System: Semester
URL: www.venturacollege.edu
Established: 1925 — Annual Undergrad Tuition & Fees (In-District): $1,104
Enrollment: 12,130 — Coed
Affiliation or Control: State/Local — IRS Status: 501(c)3
Highest Offering: Associate Degree
Program: Occupational; 2-Year Principally Bachelor's Creditable
Accreditation: **WJ**, ADNUR, EMT

02 President ... Dr. Greg GILLESPIE
05 Exec Vice Pres Student Learning ... Dr. Ramiro SANCHEZ
10 Vice President Business Services ... Mr. David KEEBLER
04 Exec Assistant to the President ... Ms. Laura BROWER
75 Dean Career & Tech Education ... Dr. Kathleen SCHRADER
88 Dean Inst Effec/Eng/Learn Res Ctr ... Ms. Kathleen SCOTT
81 Dean Mathematics & Sciences ... Mr. Dan KUMPF

60 Dean Comm/Kinesiology/Athl/OS Pgm .... Mr. Tim HARRISON
83 Dean Dist Ed/Prof Dev/Soc Sci/Hum ..... Ms. Gwen HUDDLESTON
32 Dean Student Services .... Ms. Victoria LUGO
106 Asst Dean Distance Education .... Vacant
35 Asst Dean Student Services .... Mr. David BRANSKY
102 Executive Director Foundation .... Mr. Norbert N. TAN
30 Director Development Foundation .... Ms. Diana DUNBAR
06 Registrar .... Ms. Susan BRICKER
18 Director Maintenance/Operations .... Mr. Jay MOORE
35 Coordinator Student Activities .... Mr. Rick TREVINO
37 Financial Aid Officer .... Ms. Alma RODRIGUEZ
09 Institutional Research .... Mr. Michael CALLAHAN
85 International Students .... Ms. Rosie STUTTS
12 Coordinator Off Campus Programs .... Dr. Art SANDFORD
25 Coordinator Resource Development .... Vacant
103 Dir Center of Excellence .... Ms. Sharon DWYER
84 Enrollment Management .... Ms. Connie BAKER
23 Director Student Health Center .... Ms. Mary JONES
19 Campus Police .... Sgt. Mike PALLOTO

Veritas Evangelical Seminary (A)

39407 Murrieta Hot Springs Rd, Murrieta CA 92563
County: Riverside Identification: 667103
Telephone: (951) 698-6389 Carnegie Class: Not Classified
FAX Number: (951) 677-7017 Calendar System: Semester
URL: www.veritasseminary.com
Established: 2008 Annual Graduate Tuition & Fees: $7,740
Enrollment: 100 Coed
Affiliation or Control: Independent Non-Profit IRS Status: 501(c)3
Highest Offering: Master's; No Undergraduates
Program: Religious Emphasis
Accreditation: @TRACS

00 Chancellor .... Dr. Norman L. GEISLER
01 President .... Joseph M. HOLDEN
06 Registrar .... Ms. Wendy BONILLA

Victor Valley College (B)

18422 Bear Valley Road, Victorville CA 92395-5850
County: San Bernardino FICE Identification: 001335
Unit ID: 125091
Telephone: (760) 245-4271 Carnegie Class: Assoc/Pub-S-SC
FAX Number: (760) 245-9019 Calendar System: Semester
URL: www.vvc.edu
Established: 1961 Annual Undergrad Tuition & Fees (In-District): $1,114
Enrollment: 12,127 Coed
Affiliation or Control: State/Local IRS Status: 501(c)3
Highest Offering: Associate Degree
Program: Occupational; 2-Year Principally Bachelor's Creditable
Accreditation: #WJ, COARC, EMT

01 Acting Superintendent/President .... Mr. Peter ALLAN
05 Exec VP Instruction/Stdnt Svcs .... Dr. Peter MAPHUMULO
11 Vice President Admin Services .... Dr. G. H. JAVAHERIPOUR
15 Vice President Human Resources .... Ms. Fusako YOKOTOBI
76 Dean Health Science & Public Safety .... Dr. Patricia LUTHER
20 Dean Academic Programs .... Vacant
79 Dean Acad Pgms Humanities/Soc Sci .... Dr. Paul WILLIAMS
75 Dean Vocational Education .... Vacant
21 Director Fiscal Services .... Ms. Karen HARDY
07 Director of Admissions .... Mrs. Greta MOON
26 Director Public Info & Marketing .... Mr. William GREULICH
41 Director Athletics/Athletic Trainer .... Mrs. Jaye TASHIMA
18 Director Maintenance/Operations .... Vacant
37 Interim Director Financial Aid .... Mr. Arthur LOPEZ
13 Director MIS .... Mr. Sergio OKLANDER
40 Director Auxiliary Services/ASB Adv .... Mr. Robert SEWELL
35 Dean Student Services .... Dr. Tim JOHNSTON
18 Director Facilities Construction .... Mr. Steve GARCIA
19 Chief Campus Police .... Mr. Leonard KNIGHT
72 Exec Dean Technology/Info Resource .... Mr. Frank SMITH
22 Dir Disabled Student/ADA Compl Ofcr .... Vacant
88 Director Child Development Center .... Ms. Kelley JOHNSON
88 Dir Extended Optnty Pgms/Svcs/CARE .... Mr. Carl SMITH
09 Exec Dean Inst Effectiveness .... Mrs. Virginia MORAN
55 Dir Evening Opers/Inst Support Pgm .... Mr. Rolando REGINO

West Coast Ultrasound Institute (C)

291 S. La Cienega Blvd, Ste 500, Beverly Hills CA 90211
County: Los Angeles FICE Identification: 036393
Unit ID: 441229
Telephone: (310) 289-5123 Carnegie Class: Not Classified
FAX Number: (310) 289-5136 Calendar System: Quarter
URL: www.wcui.edu
Established: 1998 Annual Undergrad Tuition & Fees: $33,350
Enrollment: 783 Coed
Affiliation or Control: Proprietary IRS Status: Proprietary
Highest Offering: Associate Degree
Program: Occupational
Accreditation: ACCSC

01 Campus Director .... Ms. Myra CHASON

West Coast University (D)

1477 South Manchester Avenue, Anaheim CA 92802
Telephone: (949) 783-4841 Identification: 770480
Accreditation: &WC, DH

† Main campus is West Coast University in North Hollywood, CA.

West Coast University (E)

12215 Victory Boulevard, North Hollywood CA 91606-3206
County: Los Angeles FICE Identification: 036983
Unit ID: 443331
Telephone: (818) 299-5500 Carnegie Class: Spec/Health
FAX Number: (818) 299-5545 Calendar System: Semester
URL: www.westcoastuniversity.edu
Established: 1909 Annual Undergrad Tuition & Fees: $31,519
Enrollment: 1,371 Coed
Affiliation or Control: Proprietary IRS Status: Proprietary
Highest Offering: Master's
Program: Professional; Nursing Emphasis
Accreditation: WC, DH, NURSE

01 President .... Dr. Barry T. RYAN
03 Executive Director .... Mr. Ladd GRAHAM
05 Provost .... Dr. Jeb EGBERT
66 Dean of Nursing Los Angeles Campus . Dr. Rosanne SILBERLING
20 Academic Dean .... Dr. Miriam KAHAN
76 Founding Dean Occupational Therapy .... Dr. Nicolaas VAN DEN HEEVER
67 Interim Dean School of Pharmacy .... Dr. Reza TAHERI
07 Director of Admissions .... Ms. Julie CHIN
37 Director of Financial Aid .... Ms. Tracy CABUCO
76 Founding Dean of Physical Therapy .... Dr. Stan HARTGRAVES

West Coast University (F)

2855 E Guasti Road, Ontario CA 91761
Telephone: (909) 467-6100 Identification: 770484
Accreditation: &WC

† Main campus is West Coast University in North Hollywood, CA.

*West Hills Community College District (G)

9900 Cody Street, Coalinga CA 93210
County: Fresno Identification: 667041
Telephone: (559) 934-2180 Carnegie Class: N/A
FAX Number: (559) 934-2810
URL: www.westhillscollege.com

01 Chancellor .... Dr. Frank P. GORNICK
10 Deputy Chancellor .... Mr. Ken STOPPENBRINK
05 VC Educ Svcs/Workforce Development .... Dr. Stuart VAN HORN
13 Assoc VC Educ Svcs/Info Technology . Ms. Michelle KOZLOWSKI
90 Assoc VC Academic & Info Systems .... Mr. Keith STEARNS
21 Assoc VC of Business Services .... Ms. Tammy WEATHERMAN
102 Exec Director WHCC Foundation .... Ms. Frances SQUIRE
15 Director of Human Resources .... Ms. Rebecca CAZARES
26 Director of Marketing/PIO .... Mr. Tom WIXON
25 Interim Director of Grants .... Ms. Anita WRIGHT
103 Director of C6 Project .... Mr. Robert PIMENTEL
25 Director of Special Grant Programs .... Ms. Angela ALLISON
66 District Director of Health Careers .... Mr. Charles FREEMAN
88 Director of Child Dev Centers .... Ms. Kathy WATTS

*West Hills College Coalinga (H)

300 Cherry Lane, Coalinga CA 93210-1399
County: Fresno FICE Identification: 001176
Unit ID: 125462
Telephone: (559) 934-2000 Carnegie Class: Assoc/Pub-S-MC
FAX Number: N/A Calendar System: Semester
URL: www.westhillscollege.com/coalinga
Established: 1932 Annual Undergrad Tuition & Fees (In-District): $1,380
Enrollment: 1,754 Coed
Affiliation or Control: State/Local IRS Status: 501(c)3
Highest Offering: Associate Degree
Program: Occupational; 2-Year Principally Bachelor's Creditable; Business Emphasis
Accreditation: WJ

02 President .... Dr. Carole GOLDSMITH
05 Vice President of Educ Services .... Ms. Stephanie DROKER
32 Interim Vice Pres of Student Svcs .... Ms. Sandy MCGLOTHLIN
35 Assoc Dean of Student Services .... Mr. Mark GRITTON
20 Assoc Dean of Student Learning .... Ms. Raquel RODRIGUEZ
47 Interim Dir of Farm of the Future .... Mr. David CASTILLO
85 Dir of International Student Svcs .... Mr. Daniel TAMAYO
88 Director of Title IV Projects .... Ms. Bertha FELIX-MATA
12 Director of North District Center .... Dr. Marcel HETU
37 Director of Financial Aid .... Dr. Joseph KOROMA

*West Hills College Lemoore (I)

555 College Avenue, Lemoore CA 93245-9248
County: Kings FICE Identification: 041113
Unit ID: 448594
Telephone: (559) 925-3000 Carnegie Class: Assoc/Pub-R-M
FAX Number: (559) 924-1243 Calendar System: Semester
URL: www.westhillscollege.com/lemoore
Established: 2002 Annual Undergrad Tuition & Fees (In-District): $1,380
Enrollment: 3,105 Coed
Affiliation or Control: State/Local IRS Status: 501(c)3
Highest Offering: Associate Degree
Program: Occupational; 2-Year Principally Bachelor's Creditable; Business Emphasis
Accreditation: WJ

02 President .... Mr. Don WARKENTIN
05 Vice President of Educational Svcs .... Mr. Dave BOLT
32 Vice President of Student Services .... Ms. Sylvia DORSEY-ROBINSON
20 Dean of Educational Svcs .... Mr. James PRESTON
35 Dean of Student Services .... Mr. Joel RUBLE
88 Director of Upward Bound .... Mr. Jose LOPEZ
37 Director of Financial Aid .... Ms. Deborah SORIA
88 Director of DSPS .... Ms. Lataria HALL

*West Valley-Mission Community College District (J)

14000 Fruitvale Avenue, Saratoga CA 95070-5698
County: Santa Clara FICE Identification: 029139
Unit ID: 125222
Telephone: (408) 741-2011 Carnegie Class: N/A
FAX Number: (408) 867-8273
URL: www.wvm.edu

01 Chancellor .... Dr. Patrick SCHMITT
11 Vice Chancellor Admin Services .... Mr. Ed MADULI
30 Dean Advancement .... Ms. Cynthia SCHELCHER
15 Human Resources Director .... Mr. Albert MOORE
13 Director Information Systems .... Mr. Ron SMITH
18 Director of Facilities .... Mr. Javier CASTRUITA
19 Chief of Police .... Mr. Kenneth TANAKA

*Mission College (K)

3000 Mission College Boulevard,
Santa Clara CA 95054-1897
County: Santa Clara FICE Identification: 021191
Unit ID: 118930
Telephone: (408) 988-2200 Carnegie Class: Assoc/Pub-S-MC
FAX Number: (408) 496-0462 Calendar System: Semester
URL: www.missioncollege.org
Established: 1976 Annual Undergrad Tuition & Fees (In-District): $1,354
Enrollment: 9,686 Coed
Affiliation or Control: State/Local IRS Status: 501(c)3
Highest Offering: Associate Degree
Program: Occupational; 2-Year Principally Bachelor's Creditable
Accreditation: WJ

02 Interim President .... Mr. Daniel A. PECK
05 Vice Pres of Instruction .... Dr. Leandra MARTIN
32 Vice President Student Services .... Dr. Penny JOHNSON
11 Vice Pres Administrative Services .... Mr. Rick BENNETT
35 Dean of Student Support Services .... Mr. Daniel SANIDAD
103 Dean of Workforce Dev & Cmty Educ .... Mr. Danny NGUYEN
27 Dir of Public Info & Graphic Design .... Mr. Peter ANNING
20 Dean of Instruction .... Mr. Tim KARAS
24 Dean Instructional Technology .... Ms. Mina JAHAN
19 Chief of Police .... Lt. Kenneth TANAKA
18 Manager of Facilities .... Mr. Don HOUSTON
07 Assistant Director of Admissions .... Mr. Ed GREEN
37 Director of Financial Aid .... Ms. Rita GROGAN
04 Exec Assistant to the President .... Ms. Linda ANGELOTTI
81 Applied Science Division .... Mr. Rod PAVAO
88 Language Arts Division .... Ms. Kathy HENDERSON
60 Communications Division .... Mr. Rob DEWIS
81 Mathematics and Science Division .... Mr. Clement LAM
83 Liberal Studies Division .... Mr. Keith JOHNSON
35 Student Services Division .... Ms. Thuy TRANG

*West Valley College (L)

14000 Fruitvale Avenue, Saratoga CA 95070-5698
County: Santa Clara FICE Identification: 001338
Unit ID: 125499
Telephone: (408) 867-2200 Carnegie Class: Assoc/Pub-S-MC
FAX Number: (408) 867-5033 Calendar System: Semester
URL: www.westvalley.edu
Established: 1963 Annual Undergrad Tuition & Fees (In-District): $936
Enrollment: 10,288 Coed
Affiliation or Control: State/Local IRS Status: 501(c)3
Highest Offering: Associate Degree
Program: Occupational; 2-Year Principally Bachelor's Creditable
Accreditation: WJ

02 President .... Mr. Bradley DAVIS
05 Vice President Instruction .... Ms. Kuni HAY
32 Vice President Student Services .... Dr. Victoria HINDES
11 Interim VP Administrative Services .... Mr. Patrick FENTON
20 Dean Instruction & Student Success .... Ms. Stephanie KASHIMA
30 Dean Advancement .... Ms. Cindy SCHELCHER
36 Int Dean Career Pgm/Wrkforce Dev .... Ms. Lin MARELICK
72 Dean Info Technology & Services .... Mr. Fred CHOW
32 Dean of Student Services .... Vacant
100 Interim Associate Vice Chancellor .... Mr. Albert MOORE
07 Director of Admissions .... Ms. Herlisa HAMP
18 Chief Facilities/Physical Plant .... Mr. Bill TAYLOR
26 Chief Public Relations Officer .... Mr. Albert MOORE
37 Director Student Financial Aid .... Ms. Maritza CANTARERO
09 Dir Resrch/Planning/Inst Effectiv .... Ms. Inge BOND
35 Director Student Development .... Dr. Michelle DONOHUE-MENDOZA
29 Director Alumni Relations .... Ms. Cindy SCHELCHER
56 Coord Instruct Tech/Distance Lrng .... Ms. Lisa KAAZ

Western State University College of Law (A)

1111 N State College Boulevard, Fullerton CA 92831-3014
Telephone: (714) 459-1000 FICE Identification: 010832
Accreditation: &WC, LAW

† Main campus is Argosy University, Orange County in Orange, CA.

Western University of Health Sciences (B)

309 E 2nd Street, Pomona CA 91766-1854
County: Los Angeles FICE Identification: 024827
Unit ID: 112525
Telephone: (909) 623-6116 Carnegie Class: Spec/Med
FAX Number: N/A Calendar System: Semester
URL: www.westernu.edu
Established: 1977 Annual Graduate Tuition & Fees: N/A
Enrollment: 3,572 Coed
Affiliation or Control: Independent Non-Profit IRS Status: 501(c)3
Highest Offering: Doctorate; No Undergraduates
Program: Professional
Accreditation: WC, ARCPA, DENT, NURSE, OPT, OSTEO, PHAR, POD, PTA, VET

01 President .... Dr. Philip PUMERANTZ
05 Provost/COO .... Dr. Gary GUGELCHUK
10 Treasurer/Chief Financial Officer .... Mr. Kevin SHAW
46 Exec Vice Provost for Academic Dev .... Dr. Elizabeth REGA
03 Senior Vice President .... Dr. Thomas FOX
20 Vice Provost .... Dr. Sheree ASTON
32 Vice Pres Student Affs/Enroll Mgt .... Dr. Beverly SANKS GUIDRY
25 Asst VP Spnsrd Pgms/Contract Mgt .... Mr. Matthew KATZ
84 AVP Enroll Mgmt/Registrar .... Ms. Kimberly DEKRUIF
15 Executive Director Human Resources .... Ms. Linda EMILIO
18 Exec Dir Facilities/Physical Plant .... Mr. Todd CLARK
07 Director Admiss COP/CGN .... Ms. Kathy FORD
07 Director Admissions COMP/MSHS .... Ms. Susan HANSON
07 Director Admissions CO/CPM/CDM .... Ms. Marie ANDERSON
07 Director Admissions CVM/PT/PA ...... Ms. Karen HUTTON-LOPEZ
23 Medical Director .... Dr. David CONNETT
08 Director of University Library .... Ms. Patricia VADER
37 Director Financial Aid .... Mr. Otto REYER
88 Dir Ctr Disability Issues/Hlth Prof .... Ms. Brenda PREMO
13 Exec Director Information Tech .... Ms. Denise WILCOX
96 Sr Dir Business Services/Purchasing .... Mr. Michael BUTLER
26 Exec Director of Public Affs/Mrktg .... Mr. Jeff KEATING
88 Dir Learning Enhancement/Acad Devel .... Mr. David HACKER
09 Director of Institutional Research .... Dr. Juan RAMIREZ
40 Bookstore Director .... Ms. Elizabeth GUERRA
52 Dean College of Dental Medicine ..Dr. Steven W. FRIEDRICHSEN
67 Dean College of Pharmacy .... Dr. Daniel ROBINSON
88 Founding Dean College of Optometry .... Dr. Elizabeth HOPPE
88 Founding Dean College of Podiatry .... Dr. Lawrence HARKLESS
76 Dean College Allied Health Profess .... Dr. Stephanie BOWLIN
66 Dean College of Graduate Nursing .... Dr. Karen HANFORD
58 Dean Grad Col Biomedical Sciences .... Dr. Michel BAUDRY
74 Dean College of Veterinary Medicine .... Dr. Phil NELSON
63 Chr Dept Osteopath Manipulative Med .....Dr. Michael SEFFINGER
88 Chair Dept of Physical Therapy .... Dr. Denise SCHILLING
76 Chair Dept of Health Sciences .... Dr. Tina MEYER
88 Chair Physician Assistant Program .... Mr. Roy GUIZADO
63 Chair Department Family Medicine .... Dr. Alan CUNDARI

Westminster Theological Seminary in California (C)

1725 Bear Valley Parkway, Escondido CA 92027-4128
County: San Diego FICE Identification: 022768
Unit ID: 125718
Telephone: (760) 480-8474 Carnegie Class: Spec/Faith
FAX Number: (760) 480-0252 Calendar System: Semester
URL: www.wscal.edu
Established: 1979 Annual Graduate Tuition & Fees: $13,500
Enrollment: 150 Coed
Affiliation or Control: Independent Non-Profit IRS Status: 501(c)3
Highest Offering: Master's; No Undergraduates
Program: Professional
Accreditation: WC, THEOL

01 President .... Dr. W. Robert GODFREY
05 Academic Dean .... Dr. John FESKO
84 Director Enrollment Management .... Mr. Mark MACVEY
10 Business Manager .... Mr. Dan TERHORST
08 Library Director .... Mr. James LUND
32 Dean of Students .... Dr. Julius KIM
06 Registrar .... Ms. Heather GIDEON

Westmont College (D)

955 La Paz Road, Santa Barbara CA 93108-1089
County: Santa Barbara FICE Identification: 001341
Unit ID: 125727
Telephone: (805) 565-6000 Carnegie Class: Bac/A&S
FAX Number: (805) 565-7006 Calendar System: Semester
URL: www.westmont.edu
Established: 1937 Annual Undergrad Tuition & Fees: $50,670
Enrollment: 1,351 Coed
Affiliation or Control: Independent Non-Profit IRS Status: 501(c)3
Highest Offering: Baccalaureate
Program: Liberal Arts And General; Teacher Preparatory
Accreditation: WC, MUS

01 President .... Dr. Gayle D. BEEBE
05 Provost .... Dr. Mark L. SARGENT
10 Vice President Finance .... Mr. Douglas W. JONES
11 Vice President for Administration .... Mr. Christopher D. CALL
32 Vice President & Dean of Students .... Mrs. Jane H. HIGA
30 Vice President for Advancement .... Dr. Reed SHEARD
88 Vice President External Relations .... Mr. Cliff LUNDBERG
07 Dean of Admissions .... Mr. Silvio VAZQUEZ
35 Associate Dean of Students .... Mr. Timothy B. WILSON
88 Assoc Dean of Students for Res Life .... Mr. Stu CLEEK
06 Registrar .... Mrs. Michelle HARDLEY
08 Director Library/Information Svcs .... Mrs. Debra QUAST
09 Assoc Provost/Dir of Inst Research .... Dr. William A. WRIGHT
13 VP Information Technology & CIO .... Dr. Reed SHEARD
15 Director of Human Resources .... Ms. Beth CAUWELS
18 Director of Physical Plant .... Mr. Thomas BEVERIDGE
21 Controller .... Mr. Paul V. LARSON
23 Director of Student Health Services .... Dr. David HERNANDEZ
19 Manager Security & Public Safety .... Mr. Thomas G. BAUER
26 Director of Public Affairs .... Mrs. Nancy L. PHINNEY
29 Exec Director Alumni & Parent Rels .... Mrs. Teri BRADFORD ROUSE
36 Director of Career/Life Planning .... Mr. Dana C. ALEXANDER
88 Director of Campus Life .... Ms. Angela L. D'AMOUR
88 Director of Internships/Practica .... Mrs. Jennifer TAYLOR
37 Director of Financial Aid .... Mr. Sean SMITH
38 Director Counseling Services .... Mrs. Marcy O'HARA
39 Director of Housing .... Mr. David W. KING
40 Bookstore Manager .... Mrs. Joanne GISH
41 Athletic Director .... Mr. David ODELL
42 Campus Pastor .... Rev. Ben PATTERSON
44 Senior Director of Planned Giving .... Mrs. Kati BUEHLER
45 Director of Campus Planning .... Mr. Randy JONES
96 Director Procurement/Auxiliary Svcs .... Mr. Troy HARRIS
28 Director of Intercultural Programs .... Mr. Jason CHA
43 College Counsel .... Ms. Toya COOPER
20 Associate Academic Officer .... Dr. Tatiana NAZARENKO
24 Coord Media Services/Asst Librarian .... Ms. Mary LOGUE

Westwood College-Anaheim (E)

1551 S Douglass Road, Anaheim CA 92806-5949
Telephone: (714) 704-2720 Identification: 666047
Accreditation: ACICS

† Main campus is Westwood College-Denver North in Denver, CO.

Westwood College-Inland Empire (F)

20 W Seventh Street, Upland CA 91786-7148
Telephone: (909) 931-7550 Identification: 666104
Accreditation: ACICS

† Main campus is Westwood College-Denver North in Denver, CO.

Westwood College - Los Angeles Campus (G)

3250 Wilshire Boulevard, Suite 400,
Los Angeles CA 90010-1437
County: Los Angeles FICE Identification: 030727
Unit ID: 122843
Telephone: (213) 739-9999 Carnegie Class: Bac/Diverse
FAX Number: (213) 382-2468 Calendar System: Quarter
URL: www.westwood.edu
Established: 1997 Annual Undergrad Tuition & Fees: $5,480
Enrollment: 5,321 Coed
Affiliation or Control: Proprietary IRS Status: Proprietary
Highest Offering: Master's
Program: Occupational
Accreditation: ACICS

01 Campus President .... Mr. DeWayne JOHNSON
07 Director of Admissions .... Mr. Fred POLK

Westwood College-South Bay (H)

19700 S Vermont Avenue, #100, Torrance CA 90502-1148
County: Los Angeles FICE Identification: 011626
Unit ID: 121381
Telephone: (310) 965-0888 Carnegie Class: Bac/Diverse
FAX Number: (310) 516-8232 Calendar System: Other
URL: www.westwood.edu
Established: 2002 Annual Undergrad Tuition & Fees: $24,900
Enrollment: 662 Coed
Affiliation or Control: Proprietary IRS Status: Proprietary
Highest Offering: Baccalaureate
Program: Occupational; Technical Emphasis
Accreditation: ACICS

01 Campus President .... Mr. Christopher TUREN

Whittier College (I)

13406 E Philadelphia St, PO Box 634,
Whittier CA 90608-4413
County: Los Angeles FICE Identification: 001342
Unit ID: 125763
Telephone: (562) 907-4200 Carnegie Class: Bac/A&S
FAX Number: (562) 907-4242 Calendar System: 4/1/4
URL: www.whittier.edu
Established: 1887 Annual Undergrad Tuition & Fees: $53,560
Enrollment: 1,779 Coed
Affiliation or Control: Independent Non-Profit IRS Status: 501(c)3
Highest Offering: Doctorate
Program: Liberal Arts And General; Teacher Preparatory; Professional
Accreditation: WC, LAW, SW

01 President .... Dr. Sharon D. HERZBERGER
10 Vice Pres Finance & Administration .... Mr. James DUNKELMAN
05 VP Academic Affs/Dean of Faculty .... Dr. Charlotte BORST
61 VP Legal Education/Dean Sch of Law .... Ms. Penelope BRYAN
30 VP Advanc/Strategic Initiatives ...Ms. Elizabeth POWER ROBISON
84 Vice President Dean of Enrollment .... Mr. Fred PFURSICH
32 Dean of Students .... Dr. Jeanne ORTIZ
37 Director of Student Financial Aid .... Mr. David CARNEVALE
06 Registrar .... Mr. Christopher COBB
08 Librarian .... Vacant
20 Dir Whtr Scholar Pgm/Assc Acad Dean .... Ms. Doreen O'CONNOR-GOMEZ
29 Director of Alumni Relations .... Vacant
27 Director of Communications .... Ms. Dana RAKOCZY
14 Director of Computing Services .... Mr. Troy GREENUP
09 Director of Institutional Research .... Mr. Fritz SMITH
39 Director for Resident Life .... Mrs. Delaphine HUDSON
41 Director of Athletics .... Mr. Rob COLEMAN
53 Dir Lib Educ Pgm/Assoc Acad Dean .... Dr. Fritz SMITH
07 Director of Admissions .... Mr. Kieron MILLER
15 Director of Human Resources .... Vacant
21 Exec Director Finance/Business Svcs .... Ms. Hoang HAU
35 Director Student Activies .... Ms. Shauna YOUNG
18 Director Facilities/Physical Plant .... Mr. Ken BOHAN
26 Director Public Relations .... Mrs. Dana RAKOCZY
19 Director of Campus Safety .... Mr. Timm BROWNE

William Jessup University (J)

333 Sunset Boulevard, Rocklin CA 95765-3707
County: Placer FICE Identification: 001281
Unit ID: 122728
Telephone: (916) 577-2200 Carnegie Class: Spec/Faith
FAX Number: (916) 577-2203 Calendar System: Semester
URL: www.jessup.edu
Established: 1939 Annual Undergrad Tuition & Fees: $24,040
Enrollment: 1,016 Coed
Affiliation or Control: Independent Non-Profit IRS Status: 501(c)3
Highest Offering: Master's
Program: 2-Year Principally Bachelor's Creditable; Liberal Arts And General; Teacher Preparatory
Accreditation: WC, BI

01 President .... Dr. John JACKSON
05 Provost/Chief Academic Officer .... Dr. Dennis JAMESON
11 Chief Financial Officer .... Vacant
30 Chief Development Officer .... Mr. Eric HOGUE
27 Chief Information Officer .... Mrs. Judy RENTZ
88 Accreditation Liason Officer .... Dr. Kay LLOVIO
107 School of Professional Studies Dir .... Mr. Sam HEINRICH
15 Director of Human Resources .... Ms. DeDe HUDAK
10 Controller .... Ms. Diane KIM
08 Library Director .... Mr. Kevin PISCHKE
88 Director of Church Relations .... Mr. Jim JESSUP
32 Dean of Students .... Mr. Ezra JOHNSON
06 Registrar .... Mrs. Tina PETERSEN
07 Director of Admission .... Mr. Vance PASCUA
37 Financial Aid Director .... Mr. Korey COMPAAN
09 Institutional Research Director .... Mrs. Karen LAMBRECHTSEN
42 Director of Campus Ministries .... Mr. Daniel GLUCK
41 Athletic Director .... Mr. Mitch PLEIS
18 Facilities Director .... Vacant
84 Associate Provost Enrollment Mgmt .... Dr. Todd ERICKSON
45 Associate Provost Strategic Mgmt .... Mrs. Rhonda CAPRON
12 Academic Director Bay Area Center .... Dr. Daniel ALBRECHT

Woodbury University (K)

7500 N. Glenoaks Boulevard, Burbank CA 91504-7520
County: Los Angeles FICE Identification: 001343
Unit ID: 125897
Telephone: (818) 767-0888 Carnegie Class: Master's M
FAX Number: (818) 767-7520 Calendar System: Semester
URL: www.woodbury.edu
Established: 1884 Annual Undergrad Tuition & Fees: $33,150
Enrollment: 1,347 Coed
Affiliation or Control: Independent Non-Profit IRS Status: 501(c)3
Highest Offering: Master's
Program: Professional; Business Emphasis
Accreditation: WC, ACBSP, ART, CIDA

01 President .... Luis CALINGO
03 Provost & Exec Vice President .... David P. DAUWALDER
05 Asst VP Academic Affairs Relations .... M. Victoria LIPTAK
10 Vice Pres Finance & Administration .... Ken JONES
84 VP Enrollment Management .... Don E. ST. CLAIR
30 Vice Pres University Advancement .... Richard M. NORDIN
13 VP Information Technology .... Steve DYER
32 Vice Pres Student Development .... Phyllis A. CREMER
04 Exec Assistant to the President .... Seta JAVOR
35 Dean of Students .... Anne R. EHRLICH
50 Dean School of Business .... Andre VAN NIEKERK
48 Dean School of Architecture .... Norman MILLAR
88 Dean School of Media/Culture/Design .... Edward CLIFT
88 Ex Dir Inst for Exclnce Teach/Lrng .... Paul W. DECKER

06 Assistant Registrar ... Tamara L. BLOK
07 Director of Enrollment Services ... Celeastia WILLIAMS
20 Dean of Faculty ... Nedra PETERSON
15 Director of Human Resources ... Natalie AVALOS
36 Director of Career Services ... Liana JINDARYAN
18 Director of Physical Plant ... Jerry W. TRACY
38 Director of Student Counseling ... Tania ROSELLO
07 Director of Admissions ... Ruth G. LORENZANA
88 Dean Institute of Transdisciplinary ... Douglas CREMER
26 Chief Marketing Officer ... Shari GIBBONS
09 Director of Institutional Research ... Bruce FEINSTEIN
29 Director of Alumni Relations ... James MORSE

World Mission University (A)

500 Shatto Place, Suite 600, Los Angeles CA 90020-1789
County: Los Angeles FICE Identification: 038683
Unit ID: 401223
Telephone: (213) 385-2322 Carnegie Class: Spec/Faith
FAX Number: (213) 385-2332 Calendar System: Semester
URL: www.wmu.edu
Established: 1989 Annual Undergrad Tuition & Fees: $5,120
Enrollment: 296 Coed
Affiliation or Control: Independent Non-Profit IRS Status: 501(c)3
Highest Offering: First Professional Degree
Program: Religious Emphasis
Accreditation: BI, @THEOL, TRACS

01 President ... Dr. John M. SONG
05 Exec Vice Pres/Chief Acad Officer ... Dr. Sung Jin LIM
42 Vice President of Church Relations ... Vacant
32 Dean of Student Svcs/Financial Aid ... Mrs. Karen AHN
30 Director of Development ... Ms. Keum Hee LEE
10 Director of Business ... Mr. Paul LIM
06 Registrar ... Mrs. Jin Joo NAM

The Wright Institute (B)

2728 Durant Avenue, Berkeley CA 94704-1796
County: Alameda FICE Identification: 008846
Unit ID: 126012
Telephone: (510) 841-9230 Carnegie Class: Spec/Health
FAX Number: (510) 841-0167 Calendar System: Trimester
URL: www.wi.edu
Established: 1969 Annual Graduate Tuition & Fees: $29,500
Enrollment: 429 Coed
Affiliation or Control: Independent Non-Profit IRS Status: 501(c)3
Highest Offering: Doctorate; No Undergraduates
Program: Professional
Accreditation: WC, CLPSY

01 President ... Mr. Peter DYBWAD
05 Dean ... Dr. Chuck ALEXANDER
10 VP of Finance & Administrative Affs ... Ms. Tricia O'REILLY
07 Dir of Admissions/Student Services ... Ms. Melissa DELANEY
08 Librarian ... Mr. Jason STRAUSS
06 Registrar ... Ms. Ginny MORGAN

WyoTech-Fremont (C)

420 Whitney Place, Fremont CA 94539-7663
County: Alameda FICE Identification: 007190
Unit ID: 123208
Telephone: (510) 490-6900 Carnegie Class: Assoc/PrivFP
FAX Number: (510) 490-8599 Calendar System: Quarter
URL: www.wyotech.com
Established: 1965 Annual Undergrad Tuition & Fees: $28,140
Enrollment: 2,016 Coed
Affiliation or Control: Proprietary IRS Status: Proprietary
Highest Offering: Associate Degree
Program: Occupational; Technical Emphasis
Accreditation: ACCSC

01 President ... Vacant
07 Director of Admissions ... Ms. Hope ARROYO
05 Director of Education ... Ms. Joan LYONS
36 Director of Career Services ... Mr. Bijan SHAHMIRZA
37 Director of Financial Aid ... Ms. Lorena ANAYA
06 Registrar ... Ms. Liz GUSTAFSON
11 Dir Compliance/Administrative Svcs ... Mrs. Lisa-Marie CUSPARD

WyoTech-Long Beach (D)

2161 Technology Place, Long Beach CA 90810-3800
County: Los Angeles FICE Identification: 012873
Unit ID: 398574
Telephone: (562) 624-9530 Carnegie Class: Assoc/PrivFP
FAX Number: (562) 437-8111 Calendar System: Quarter
URL: www.wyotech.edu
Established: 1969 Annual Undergrad Tuition & Fees: $26,322
Enrollment: 1,500 Coed
Affiliation or Control: Proprietary IRS Status: Proprietary
Highest Offering: Associate Degree
Program: Occupational; Technical Emphasis
Accreditation: ACCSC, MAAB

01 President ... Mr. Brad JANIS

WyoTech-Sacramento (E)

980 Riverside Parkway, West Sacramento CA 95605-1507
Telephone: (916) 376-8888 Identification: 666292
Accreditation: ACCSC

† Main campus is WyoTech in Laramie, WY.

Yeshiva Ohr Elchonon Chabad/ West Coast Talmudical Seminary (F)

7215 Waring Avenue, Los Angeles CA 90046-7660
County: Los Angeles FICE Identification: 022624
Unit ID: 126076
Telephone: (323) 937-3763 Carnegie Class: Spec/Faith
FAX Number: (323) 937-9456 Calendar System: Semester
URL: www.yoec.edu
Established: 1953 Annual Undergrad Tuition & Fees: $13,300
Enrollment: 148 Male
Affiliation or Control: Independent Non-Profit IRS Status: 501(c)3
Highest Offering: Baccalaureate
Program: Professional
Accreditation: RABN

01 Chief Executive Officer ... Rabbi Ezra B. SCHOCHET
03 Executive Vice President ... Rabbi Mendel SPALTER
05 Curriculum Suprv/Education Counsel ... Rabbi Shimon RAICHIK
37 Director Student Financial Aid ... Mrs. Hendy TAUBER
06 Registrar ... Rabbi Chaim CITRON
38 Director Student Counseling ... Rabbi Mendel SCHAPIRO
08 Head Librarian ... Rabbi Ben Zion OSTER

Yo San University of Traditional Chinese Medicine (G)

13315 W Washington Boulevard, Los Angeles CA 90066
County: Los Angeles FICE Identification: 030982
Unit ID: 401250
Telephone: (310) 577-3000 Carnegie Class: Spec/Health
FAX Number: (310) 577-3033 Calendar System: Trimester
URL: www.yosan.edu
Established: 1989 Annual Undergrad Tuition & Fees: $13,607
Enrollment: 207 Coed
Affiliation or Control: Independent Non-Profit IRS Status: 501(c)3
Highest Offering: Doctorate; No Lower Division
Program: Professional
Accreditation: ACUP

01 President ... Lawrence RYAN
05 Dean of Academic & Clinical Educ ... Lawrence LAU
06 Registrar ... Tora FLINT
10 Chief Financial Officer ... Tracy WANG
20 Assistant Academic Dean ... Megan O'CONNOR
20 Assistant Academic Dean ... Alison DOHERTY
07 Director of Enrollment ... Joslyn WILLIAMS
37 Financial Aid & Student Services ... Ed MERVINE
21 Controller ... Mariani MAY

*Yosemite Community College District (H)

PO Box 4065, Modesto CA 95352-4065
County: Stanislaus FICE Identification: 009146
Unit ID: 126100
Telephone: (209) 575-6509 Carnegie Class: N/A
FAX Number: (209) 575-6565
URL: www.yosemite.edu

01 Chancellor ... Dr. Joan E. SMITH
03 Executive Vice Chancellor ... Ms. Teresa M. SCOTT
13 Assistant Vice Chancellor Info Tech ... Mr. Martin GANG
16 Vice Chancellor Human Resources ... Ms. Victoria SIMMONS

*Columbia College (I)

11600 Columbia College Drive, Sonora CA 95370-8580
County: Tuolumne FICE Identification: 007707
Unit ID: 112561
Telephone: (209) 588-5100 Carnegie Class: Assoc/Pub-R-M
FAX Number: (209) 588-5104 Calendar System: Semester
URL: www.columbia.yosemite.cc.ca.us
Established: 1968 Annual Undergrad Tuition & Fees (In-District): $1,162
Enrollment: 3,073 Coed
Affiliation or Control: State/Local IRS Status: 501(c)3
Highest Offering: Associate Degree
Program: Occupational; 2-Year Principally Bachelor's Creditable
Accreditation: WJ, ACFEI

02 Acting President ... Dr. Leslie BUCKALEW
05 Acting Vice Pres Student Learning ... Dr. Chris VITELLI
11 VP College & Administrative Svcs ... Mr. Gary WHITFIELD
20 Dean Instructional Svcs/Voc Educ ... Mr. Chris VITELLI
49 Dean of Instruction/Arts & Sciences ... Mr. Michael TOROK
24 Director of Info Tech & Media Svcs ... Mr. Brian DEMOSS
41 Athletic Director ... Mr. Michael TOROK
37 Financial Aid Manager ... Ms. Marnie SHIVELY
27 Public Information Officer ... Vacant
31 Director Community Services ... Vacant
30 Director of Development ... Ms. Colette SUCH
40 Bookstore Manager ... Mr. Jeff WHALEN
18 Manager Facilities/Operations ... Ms. Judy LANCHESTER

*Modesto Junior College (J)

435 College Avenue, Modesto CA 95350-9977
County: Stanislaus FICE Identification: 001240
Unit ID: 118976
Telephone: (209) 575-6498 Carnegie Class: Assoc/Pub-R-L
FAX Number: (209) 575-6630 Calendar System: Semester
URL: www.mjc.edu
Established: 1921 Annual Undergrad Tuition & Fees (In-District): $1,004
Enrollment: 17,362 Coed
Affiliation or Control: State/Local IRS Status: 501(c)3
Highest Offering: Associate Degree
Program: Occupational; 2-Year Principally Bachelor's Creditable
Accreditation: #WJ, COARC, MAC

02 President ... Ms. Jill STEARNS
05 Int Vice President for Instruction ... Ms. Susan KINCADE
32 Vice Pres for Student Services ... Ms. Brenda THAMES
11 Vice President Administrative Svcs ... Mr. Michael GUERRA
57 Div Dean Arts/Humanit & Communicat ... Mr. Mike SUNDQUIST
83 Div Dean Busi/Behav/Social Sci ... Ms. Cece HUDELSON-PUTNAM
76 Div Dean Inst/All Hlth/Fam/Con Sci ... Mr. Patrick BETTENCOURT
79 Int Div Dean Literature/Lang Arts ... Mr. Steve COLLINS
54 Div Dean Science/Math/Engineering ... Mr. Brian SANDERS
47 Dean Agri/Envir Science/Tech Ed ... Mr. Mark ANGLIN
31 Dean of Community & Economic Devel ... Mr. Pedro MENDEZ
68 Dean Phys/Rec/Health Educ/Athl Dir ... Dr. William KAISER
84 Director Matriculation/Enroll Svcs ... Vacant
09 Director of Institutional Research ... Vacant
37 Director Student Financial Aid ... Ms. Peggy FIKSE
40 Manager College Bookstore ... Ms. Rhonda T. GREEN

*Yuba Community College District (K)

2088 North Beale Road, Marysville CA 95901
County: Yuba Identification: 666478
Telephone: (530) 741-6700 Carnegie Class: N/A
FAX Number: (530) 634-7704
URL: www.yccd.edu

01 Chancellor ... Dr. Douglas B. HOUSTON
05 VC Educ Planning & Services ... Dr. Kayleigh CARABUJAL
13 Director Information Technologies ... Karen TRIMBLE
102 Ex Dir Foundation/Grants/Instnl Dev ... Dr. Phil KREBS
15 Chief Human Resources Officer ... Mr. Jacques WHITFIELD
10 Chief Business Officer ... Kuldeep KAUR
18 Director Facilities Planning ... George PARKER

*Woodland Community College (L)

2300 East Gibson Road, Woodland CA 95776-5156
County: Yolo FICE Identification: 041438
Unit ID: 455512
Telephone: (530) 661-5711 Carnegie Class: Assoc/Pub-R-M
FAX Number: (530) 666-9028 Calendar System: Semester
URL: www.yccd.edu/woodland/
Established: 2008 Annual Undergrad Tuition & Fees (In-District): $1,124
Enrollment: 4,270 Coed
Affiliation or Control: State/Local IRS Status: 501(c)3
Highest Offering: Associate Degree
Program: Occupational; 2-Year Principally Bachelor's Creditable
Accreditation: WJ

02 President ... Dr. Angela R. FAIRCHILDS
03 Vice President ... Dr. Alfred B. KONUWA

*Yuba College (M)

2088 N Beale Road, Marysville CA 95901-7699
County: Yuba FICE Identification: 001344
Unit ID: 126119
Telephone: (530) 741-6700 Carnegie Class: Assoc/Pub-R-L
FAX Number: (530) 741-3541 Calendar System: Semester
URL: www.yccd.edu
Established: 1927 Annual Undergrad Tuition & Fees (In-District): $1,144
Enrollment: 8,790 Coed
Affiliation or Control: State/Local IRS Status: 501(c)3
Highest Offering: Associate Degree
Program: Occupational; 2-Year Principally Bachelor's Creditable
Accreditation: #WJ, #RAD

02 Interim President ... Mr. Rodney BEILBY
05 Act Vice Pres Academic/Student Svcs ... Ms. Lisa JENSEN-MARTIN
07 Dir Admissions & Enrollment Svcs ... Ms. Sonia HORN
88 Director Disabled Students/Pgm/Svcs ... Ms. Jan PONTICELLI
37 Dean Financial Aid/EOPS/TRIO ... Dr. Marisela ARCE
50 Dean Bus/Soc Sci/Cosmetology ... Dr. Ed DAVIS
88 Dir Child Dev Ctr/AmeriCorps ... Ms. Laurie SCHEUERMANN
106 Dean Distributive Ed & Media Svcs ... Ms. Martha MILLS
88 Dir ETS/Upward Bound/SSS ... Ms. Delmy SPENCER
57 Dean Fine Arts/Language Arts ... Mr. Walter MASUDA
68 Dn Hlth/PE/Rec/Ath/Pub Safety ... Mr. Rod BEILBY
81 Dn Math/Engr/Sci/Hlth/Applied Tech ... Vacant
09 Dir Plng/Rsrch & Student Success ... Vacant
26 Pub Info Ofcr/Dir Cmty Ed/Camp Life ... Ms. Miriam ROOT
66 Dir Nursing/Allied Health ... Vacant

COLORADO

Academy of Natural Therapy (A)

625 8th Avenue, Greeley CO 80631

County: Weld FICE Identification: 040933
Unit ID: 449454
Telephone: (970) 352-1181 Carnegie Class: Not Classified
FAX Number: (970) 352-1906 Calendar System: Quarter
URL: www.natural-therapy.com
Established: 1989 Annual Undergrad Tuition & Fees: $17,500
Enrollment: 70 Coed
Affiliation or Control: Proprietary IRS Status: Proprietary
Highest Offering: Associate Degree
Program: Occupational
Accreditation: COMTA

01 President .... Mr. Jeremiah James MONGAN

Adams State University (B)

208 Edgemont Boulevard, Alamosa CO 81101-2320

County: Alamosa FICE Identification: 001345
Unit ID: 126182
Telephone: (719) 587-7011 Carnegie Class: Master's M
FAX Number: (719) 587-7522 Calendar System: Semester
URL: www.adams.edu
Established: 1921 Annual Undergrad Tuition & Fees (In-State): $7,448
Enrollment: 3,290 Coed
Affiliation or Control: State IRS Status: 501(c)3
Highest Offering: Master's
Program: 2-Year Principally Bachelor's Creditable; Liberal Arts And General; Teacher Preparatory
Accreditation: NH, CACREP, MUS, NURSE, TEAC

01 President .... Dr. David P. SVALDI
05 Vice President for Academic Affairs .... Dr. Frank J. NOVOTNY
10 VP Finance/Governmental Relations .... Mr. Bill MANSHEIM
84 Sr VP Enrollment Mgmt/Program Devel .... Dr. Michael MUMPER
30 Vice President Inst Advancement .... Vacant
18 AVP Facil Plng/Design/Construction .... Vacant
56 Asst VP Extended Campus - Academics .... Mr. Walter ROYBAL
21 Asst Vice Pres Budget & Technology .... Ms. Heather HEERSINK
20 Vice President for Academic Affairs .... Ms. Margaret DOELL
32 Dean Student Affairs .... Mr. Kenneth L. MARQUEZ
09 Senior Analyst Inst Research .... Mrs. Andrea BENTON-MESTAS
08 Director Library .... Ms. Carol SMITH
37 Director Student Financial Aid .... Mr. Philip SCHROEDER
07 Director of Admissions .... Mr. Eric CARPIO
06 Registrar .... Ms. Belen MAESTAS
31 Exec Dir Community Partnerships .... Ms. Mary HOFFMAN
13 Chief Information Officer .... Mr. Kevin S. DANIEL
41 Athletic Director .... Mr. Larry MORTENSEN
27 Asst to President Communications .... Ms. Julie WAECHTER
31 Director of Auxiliary Services .... Mr. Bruce DEL TONDO
38 Director Counseling/Career Services .... Mr. Gregg ELLIOTT
15 Director Human Resources .... Ms. Tracy ROGERS
102 Executive Director ASU Foundation .... Ms. Tammy L. LOPEZ
29 Director Alumni Relations .... Ms. Lori L. LASKE
96 Director of Purchasing .... Ms. Renee VIGIL
19 Dir Adams State Univ Police Dept .... Mr. Joel SHULTS
40 Director Bookstore .... Mr. Darrell MEIS
27 Interim Director of Communications .... Mr. Mark SCHOENECKER
88 Chair English/Theatre/Communication .... Dr. David MAZEL
50 Chair Business & Economics .... Dr. Michael TOMLIN
53 Chair Education .... Dr. Edward CROWTHER
81 Chair Chemistry/Computer Sci/Math .... Dr. Matthew S. NEHRING
81 Chair Biology/Earth Science .... Dr. Benita BRINK

Aims Community College (C)

Box 69, Greeley CO 80632-0069

County: Weld FICE Identification: 007582
Unit ID: 126207
Telephone: (970) 330-8008 Carnegie Class: Assoc/Pub-R-M
FAX Number: (970) 330-5705 Calendar System: Semester
URL: www.aims.edu
Established: 1967 Annual Undergrad Tuition & Fees (In-District): $2,280
Enrollment: 4,983 Coed
Affiliation or Control: Local IRS Status: 501(c)3
Highest Offering: Associate Degree
Program: Occupational; 2-Year Principally Bachelor's Creditable
Accreditation: NH, ADNUR, EMT, IFSAC, SURGT

01 President .... Dr. Marilynn LIDDELL
10 Chief Administrative Officer .... Mr. Bob COX
27 Chief Information Officer .... Mr. Bill WAGGONER
05 Chief Academic Officer .... Ms. Donna NORWOOD
20 Academic Dean .... Mr. Jeff REYNOLDS
20 Academic Dean .... Dr. Dan DOHERTY
32 Dean for Student Services .... Dr. Patricia MATIJEVIC
20 Academic Dean .... Dr. Albert BUYOK
43 Chief Legal Counsel .... Ms. Sandra OWENS
30 Dir Inst Advancement/Foundation .... Ms. Julie BUDERUS
15 Director Human Resources .... Mr. Damion CORDOVA
21 Budget Director .... Mr. Daniel ERBERT
21 Controller .... Vacant
18 Chief Facilities Management Officer .... Mr. Michael MILLSAPPS
37 Director Student Financial Assist .... Ms. Nancy GRAY
06 Registrar/Director Admissions .... Mr. Stuart THOMAS
38 Director Student Success Center .... Ms. Paula YANISH
09 Dir Inst Effectiveness & Assessment .... Ms. Lee Ann SAPPINGTON
13 Director Information Technology .... Ms. Andria ROGERS
31 Chief College/Community Relations .... Ms. Jenna OLIVER
35 Director Student Life .... Mr. Ron FAY
12 Director Loveland Campus .... Ms. Heather LELCHOOK
88 Director Windsor Auto/Tech Ctr .... Mr. Fred BROWN
96 Director of Purchasing .... Ms. Dorene BOYD
12 Assoc Dean Ft Lupton Campus .... Ms. Brenda RASK
75 Associate Dean Career & Tech Ed .... Ms. Brenda RASK
08 Assoc Dean Learning/Org Dev .... Mr. Rob UMBAUGH
66 Associate Dean Nursing .... Ms. Nina KIRK

American Sentinel University (D)

2260 South Xanadu Way, Ste 310, Aurora CO 80014

County: Arapahoe FICE Identification: 041277
Unit ID: 41277
Telephone: (303) 991-1575 Carnegie Class: Not Classified
FAX Number: (303) 991-1577 Calendar System: Other
URL: www.americansentinel.edu
Established: 2000 Annual Undergrad Tuition & Fees: $11,850
Enrollment: 2,817 Coed
Affiliation or Control: Proprietary IRS Status: Proprietary
Highest Offering: Doctorate
Program: Professional; Nursing Emphasis
Accreditation: DETC, NURSE

01 President .... Ms. Mary A. ADAMS
05 Chief Academic Officer .... Dr. John BOURNE
03 Provost .... Dr. Kurt LINBURG
66 Dean .... Dr. Judy BURCKHARDT

Anthem College (E)

350 Blackhawk Street, Aurora CO 80011-8754

Telephone: (720) 859-7900 Identification: 666510
Accreditation: ACICS, MAAB, SURTEC

† Main campus is The Bryman School in Phoenix, AZ.

Arapahoe Community College (F)

5900 S Santa Fe Drive, PO Box 9002,
Littleton CO 80160-9002

County: Arapahoe FICE Identification: 001346
Unit ID: 126289
Telephone: (303) 797-4222 Carnegie Class: Assoc/Pub-S-MC
FAX Number: (303) 797-5935 Calendar System: Semester
URL: www.arapahoe.edu
Established: 1965 Annual Undergrad Tuition & Fees (In-State): $4,599
Enrollment: 9,819 Coed
Affiliation or Control: State IRS Status: 501(c)3
Highest Offering: Associate Degree
Program: Occupational; 2-Year Principally Bachelor's Creditable
Accreditation: NH, ADNUR, EMT, FUSER, MLTAD, PTAA

01 President .... Dr. Diana DOYLE
11 Vice President Admin Services .... Dr. Cindy SOMERS
05 Vice President Instruction .... Dr. Diane HEGEMAN
10 Chief Financial Officer .... Mr. Joseph LORENZO, JR.
103 Dean Community/Workforce Partnershp .... Mr. Matt MCKEEVER
32 Dean of Student Services .... Ms. Connie SIMPSON
38 Director of Advising and Retention .... Mr. Michael MCMANUS
07 Director Admissions & Records .... Ms. Darcy BRIGGS
37 Dir of Student Financial Services .... Ms. Dorothy SHALLCROSS
31 Exec Dir of Community/Workforce Pgm .... Ms. Kim LARSON-COONEY
79 Dean Liberal Arts & Prof Programs .... Dr. Vanessa ANDERSON
76 Dean Health/Sciences & Engineering .... Ms. Linda COMEAUX
50 Dean Math/Business & Technology .... Dr. Cindy SOMERS
49 Dean Arts/Design/Social/Behav Sci .... Ms. Rebecca WOULFE
102 Executive Director Foundation .... Ms. Courtney LOEHFELM
21 Controller .... Ms. Xochil QUIJANO
19 Interim Chief of Police .... Mr. Joseph MORRIS
09 Director Institutional Research .... Mr. Jon PROCTOR
08 Director Learning Resource Center .... Dr. Thomas PHILLIPS
26 Dir of Marketing/Public Relations .... Mr. Murry UNELL
35 Assoc Dean of Student Affairs .... Ms. Heather WILCOX
96 Purchasing Coordinator .... Ms. Amy DEMROVSKY
18 Facilities Manager .... Mr. David CRAWFORD

Argosy University, Denver (G)

7600 East Eastman Avenue, Denver CO 80231

Telephone: (303) 923-4110 Identification: 666654
Accreditation: &WC, CACREP

† Main campus is Argosy University, Orange County in Orange, CA.

The Art Institute of Colorado (H)

1200 Lincoln Street, Denver CO 80203-2172

County: Denver FICE Identification: 020789
Unit ID: 126702
Telephone: (303) 837-0825 Carnegie Class: Spec/Arts
FAX Number: (303) 860-8520 Calendar System: Quarter
URL: www.artinstitutes.edu/denver
Established: 1952 Annual Undergrad Tuition & Fees: $17,832
Enrollment: 1,972 Coed
Affiliation or Control: Proprietary IRS Status: Proprietary
Highest Offering: Baccalaureate
Program: Occupational
Accreditation: NH, ACFEI, CIDA

01 President .... Mr. David C. ZORN
05 Vice President/Dean Academic Affs .... Dr. Benjamin VALDEZ
07 Senior Director of Admissions .... Ms. Sarah JOHNSON
32 Director of Student Services .... Mr. John RICHARDSON
10 Director Admin & Financial Services .... Ms. Wendy BUTLER
37 Director of Financial Aid .... Ms. Sophia LEUTH
06 Registrar .... Ms. Angel BLACK

Aspen University (I)

720 S Colorado Blvd, Suite 1150N, Denver CO 80246

County: Denver FICE Identification: 040803
Unit ID: 454829
Telephone: (800) 441-4746 Carnegie Class: Master's M
FAX Number: (303) 336-1144 Calendar System: Other
URL: www.aspen.edu
Established: 1987 Annual Undergrad Tuition & Fees: $12,000
Enrollment: 1,061 Coed
Affiliation or Control: Proprietary IRS Status: Proprietary
Highest Offering: Doctorate
Program: Business Emphasis
Accreditation: DETC, NURSE

01 President .... Dr. Gerry WILLIAMS
11 Vice Pres of Operations .... Ms. Barbara MAX
06 Registrar .... Ms. Tracy CRAVEN

Bel-Rea Institute of Animal Technology (J)

1681 S Dayton Street, Denver CO 80247-3048

County: Arapahoe FICE Identification: 012670
Unit ID: 126359
Telephone: (800) 950-8001 Carnegie Class: Assoc/PrivFP
FAX Number: (303) 751-9969 Calendar System: Quarter
URL: www.bel-rea.com
Established: 1971 Annual Undergrad Tuition & Fees: $10,550
Enrollment: 682 Coed
Affiliation or Control: Proprietary IRS Status: Proprietary
Highest Offering: Associate Degree
Program: Occupational
Accreditation: ACCSC

01 Director .... Paulette KAUFMAN
37 Director Student Financial Aid .... Stasi BONTINELLI
32 Director Student Services .... Cynthia MEDINA

College for Financial Planning (K)

9000 E. Nichols Avenue #200, Centennial CO 80112

County: Denver Identification: 666809
Unit ID: 126526
Telephone: (303) 220-1200 Carnegie Class: Not Classified
FAX Number: (303) 220-4940 Calendar System: Other
URL: www.cffp.edu
Established: 1972 Annual Graduate Tuition & Fees: $5,700
Enrollment: 8,000 Coed
Affiliation or Control: Proprietary IRS Status: Proprietary
Highest Offering: Master's; No Undergraduates
Program: Professional
Accreditation: NH

01 President .... Mr. John SEARS
05 Vice President Academic Affairs .... Mr. Jim PASZTOR
10 Vice President Business Development .... Mr. Dirk PANTONE
07 Sr Dir Enrollment & Student Svcs .... Mr. Brett SANBORN
06 Registrar .... Ms. Viviane PRICE
38 Director Student Service Center .... Ms. Alicia MEAD

CollegeAmerica Colorado Springs (L)

3645 Citadel Drive S, Colorado Springs CO 80909-5320

Telephone: (719) 637-0600 Identification: 666293
Accreditation: ACCSC

† Main campus is CollegeAmerica Denver in Denver, CO.

CollegeAmerica Denver (M)

1385 S Colorado Blvd, 5th Floor, Denver CO 80222

County: Denver FICE Identification: 025943
Unit ID: 126872
Telephone: (303) 300-8740 Carnegie Class: Bac/Assoc
FAX Number: (303) 692-9156 Calendar System: Other
URL: www.collegeamerica.edu
Established: 1964 Annual Undergrad Tuition & Fees: $23,062
Enrollment: 502 Coed
Affiliation or Control: Proprietary IRS Status: Proprietary
Highest Offering: Baccalaureate
Program: Occupational
Accreditation: ACCSC

01 Executive Director .... Mr. Nathan LARSON
05 Academic Director .... Ms. Kacey JECHURA
37 Director of Financial Aid .... Ms. Sonia MARTINEZ
07 Director of Admissions .... Ms. Jaclyn MILLER
06 Registrar .... Ms. Gwen ESTRIDGE

CollegeAmerica Fort Collins (A)

4601 S Mason, Fort Collins CO 80525-3740
Telephone: (970) 225-4860 Identification: 666362
Accreditation: ACCSC

† Main campus is CollegeAmerica Denver in Denver, CO.

Colorado Academy of Veterinary Technology (B)

2766 Janitell Road, Colorado Springs CO 80906
County: El Paso FICE Identification: 041850
Unit ID: 461953
Telephone: (719) 219-9636 Carnegie Class: Not Classified
FAX Number: (719) 302-5577 Calendar System: Quarter
URL: www.cavt.edu
Established: 2007 Annual Undergrad Tuition & Fees: $16,200
Enrollment: 71 Coed
Affiliation or Control: Proprietary IRS Status: Proprietary
Highest Offering: Associate Degree
Program: Occupational
Accreditation: COE

01 Site Director/Admissions .... Dr. Steve RUBIN
05 Chief Academic Officer .... Mrs. Ramona CRANE
38 Dir Student Counseling/Fin Aid .... Mrs. Traci THOMPSON

Colorado Christian University (C)

8787 W Alameda Avenue, Lakewood CO 80226-7499
County: Jefferson FICE Identification: 009401
Unit ID: 126669
Telephone: (303) 963-3000 Carnegie Class: Master's M
FAX Number: (303) 963-3001 Calendar System: Semester
URL: www.ccu.edu
Established: 1914 Annual Undergrad Tuition & Fees: $25,046
Enrollment: 3,542 Coed
Affiliation or Control: Independent Non-Profit IRS Status: 501(c)3
Highest Offering: Master's
Program: 2-Year Principally Bachelor's Creditable; Liberal Arts And General; Teacher Preparatory; Professional
Accreditation: NH, CACREP, MUS, NURSE

01 President .... Mr. William L. ARMSTRONG
10 VP for Business Affairs & CFO .... Mr. Daniel COHRS
05 VP Acad Affairs College UG Studies .... Dr. Cherri S. PARKS
30 VP for Development .... Mr. Paul ELDRIDGE
32 VP for Student Development .... Mr. Jim S. MCCORMICK
05 Asst VP of Acad Affairs/Dean CAGS .... Mrs. Sarah SCHERLING
11 Asst VP for Administrative Services .... Mr. Ronald W. BENTON
35 Asst VP Stdnt Pgm/Dean of Students .... Mrs. Sharon M. FELKER
42 Asst VP of Student Life/Ministry .... Mr. Joe WALTERS
07 Asst VP Enrollment & Marketing .... Mr. Chuck KLIJEWSKI
88 Asst VP of Student Success .... Mr. Roger CHANDLER
50 Dean School of Business .... Dr. Gary EWEN
72 Dean of Business and Technology .... Dr. Mellani J. DAY
53 Dean School of Education .... Dr. Sara E. DALLMAN
53 Dean of Ed/Curriculum & Instruction .... Dr. Wendy WENDOVER
79 Dean Sch Humanities & Sciences .... Dr. William R. SAXBY
64 Dean School of Music .... Mr. Steven T. TAYLOR
73 Dean School of Theology .... Dr. Sidney S. BUZZELL
66 Dean of Nursing & Sciences .... Dr. Barbara WHITE
73 Dean of Biblical Studies & Theology .... Dr. Richard V. YOHN
07 Dean of Admissions .... Mr. Derry EBERT
43 University Counsel .... Mr. Steven MILLER
21 Controller .... Mr. Wendell GEARY
06 Registrar .... Mrs. Linda K. PERCIANTE
41 Athletic Director .... Mr. Darren A. RICHIE
38 Director of Counseling Services .... Dr. Joannie L. DEBRITO
44 Director of Development .... Mr. David J. NYE
18 Director of Facilities .... Mr. Mathew J. GOTHARD
37 Director of Financial Aid .... Mr. Steve M. WOODBURN
23 Director of Health Services .... Ms. Mandy WILLIAMS
15 Director of Human Resources .... Mr. Rick GARRIS
13 Sr Dir of Information Systems/Tech .... Mr. Bryan SHOLTEN
08 Library Director .... Mrs. Gayle C. GUNDERSON
36 Director of Life Directions Center .... Mrs. Joy STRICKLAND
39 Director of Residence Life .... Mr. Joseph BROOKS
19 Director of Security .... Mr. Harry G. CAROTHERS
26 Dir of University Communications .... Mrs. Lisa L. ZELLER
29 Director Alumni Relations .... Vacant
105 Director of Web Development .... Mrs. Chris FRANZ

Colorado College (D)

14 E La Cache Poudre St.,
Colorado Springs CO 80903-3294
County: El Paso FICE Identification: 001347
Unit ID: 126678
Telephone: (719) 389-6000 Carnegie Class: Bac/A&S
FAX Number: (719) 634-4180 Calendar System: Other
URL: www.coloradocollege.edu
Established: 1874 Annual Undergrad Tuition & Fees: $43,812
Enrollment: 2,026 Coed
Affiliation or Control: Independent Non-Profit IRS Status: 501(c)3
Highest Offering: Master's
Program: Liberal Arts And General; Teacher Preparatory
Accreditation: NH

01 President .... Dr. Jill TIEFENTHALER
05 Dean of College & Faculty .... Dr. Sandra WONG
100 Chief of Staff .... Mr. Jermyn DAVIS
84 Vice Pres Enrollment Management .... Mr. Mark HATCH
30 Vice Pres for College Advancement .... Mr. Sean PIERI
10 Vice Pres Business/Finance & Treas .... Mr. Robert G. MOORE
32 VP Student Life/Dean of Students .... Mr. Mike EDMONDS
13 VP for Information Management .... Mr. Dave ARMSTRONG
45 Asst VP for Institutional Planning .... Ms. Lyrae WILLIAMS
87 Dean of Summer Programs .... Mr. Eric POPKIN
44 Asst VP Advancement Operations .... Ms. Molly BODNAR
39 Sr Assc Dn Stdnts/Dir Resident Life .... Mr. John LAUER
20 Associate Dean of the College .... Dr. Regula M. EVITT
20 Associate Dean of the Faculty .... Dr. Jeffrey NOBLETT
35 Associate Dean of Students .... Ms. Rochelle MASON
07 Director of Admissions .... Mr. Roberto GARCIA
37 Director of Financial Aid .... Mr. Jim M. SWANSON
06 Registrar .... Mr. Phillip C. APODACA
26 Director of Communications .... Ms. Jane TURNIS
41 Director of Athletics .... Mr. Ken RALPH
104 Director International Programs .... Dr. Inger BULL
15 Director Human Resources .... Ms. Barbara WILSON
18 Director of Facilities .... Mr. Chris COULTER
19 Director Campus Safety .... Mr. Pat CUNNINGHAM
08 Library Director .... Mr. Ivan GAETZ
96 Director of Purchasing .... Vacant
36 Director Career Center .... Ms. Megan NICKLAUS
85 Dir Minority/Internatl Students .... Mr. Roger SMITH
29 Director Alumni & Parent Relations .... Ms. Anita PARISEAU
91 Director Enterprise Info Svcs .... Mr. Vishvas PARADKAR
09 Dir Assessment/Program Review .... Ms. Amanda UDIS-KESSLER
88 Controller/Asst Treasurer .... Ms. Stacy LUTZ-DAVIDSON
24 Director of Media Services .... Mr. Randy BABB
105 Director Web Communications .... Ms. Karen TO
21 Senior Budget Analyst .... Ms. Enid RUIZMATTEI
88 Director Internal Audit .... Ms. Yolanda LYONS
38 Counseling Sup/Clin Psychologist .... Mr. Bill DOVE
38 Dir Disability Services .... Ms. Jan EDWARDS
27 College News Director .... Ms. Leslie WEDDELL
90 Director Educational Tech Svcs .... Mr. Chad SCHOENWILL
88 Director of Network & Systems .... Vacant
88 Dir Collab Cmty Engagement .... Vacant
46 College Research Professor .... Dr. Kevin RASK
42 Chaplain .... Dr. Bruce CORIELL

Colorado Heights University (E)

3001 S Federal Boulevard, Denver CO 80236-2711
County: Denver FICE Identification: 032893
Unit ID: 367839
Telephone: (303) 937-4225 Carnegie Class: Spec/Bus
FAX Number: (303) 937-4224 Calendar System: Semester
URL: www.chu.edu
Established: 1990 Annual Undergrad Tuition & Fees: $5,610
Enrollment: 230 Coed
Affiliation or Control: Independent Non-Profit IRS Status: 501(c)3
Highest Offering: Master's
Program: Professional; Business Emphasis
Accreditation: ACICS

01 Chief Operating Officer .... Mr. Douglas BJERKAAS
05 Dean of Academic Affairs .... Vacant
10 Chief Financial Officer .... Ms. Erin ONSAGER
50 Dir of MBA and BA Intl Business .... Vacant
06 Registrar .... Ms. Jennifer JOLY
08 Librarian .... Vacant
15 Director of Human Resources .... Ms. Debra POWELL
37 Director of Financial Aid .... Ms. Beba PREDIC
32 Exec Director of Student Affairs .... Vacant
39 Director of Public Safety .... Mr. Daniil YUSUFOV
07 Exec Dir of Mktg & Admissions .... Ms. Pam SMITH
13 Director Information Technology .... Vacant
18 Director of Facilities .... Mr. Jose GALLEGOS

Colorado Mesa University (F)

1100 North Avenue, Grand Junction CO 81501-3122
County: Mesa FICE Identification: 001358
Unit ID: 127556
Telephone: (970) 248-1020 Carnegie Class: Bac/A&S
FAX Number: (970) 248-1076 Calendar System: Semester
URL: www.coloradomesa.edu
Established: 1925 Annual Undergrad Tuition & Fees (In-State): $5,765
Enrollment: 9,482 Coed
Affiliation or Control: State IRS Status: 501(c)3
Highest Offering: Doctorate
Program: Occupational; 2-Year Principally Bachelor's Creditable; Liberal Arts And General; Teacher Preparatory; Professional
Accreditation: NH, ADNUR, EMT, MUS, NURSE, RAD

01 President .... Mr. Tim FOSTER
05 Vice Pres Academic/Student Affairs .... Dr. Carol FUTHEY
10 Vice President Financial/Admin Svcs .... Mr. Patrick DOYLE
31 Vice Pres Community College Affairs .... Mrs. Brigitte SUNDERMANN
96 Asst Vice Pres Auxiliary Services .... Mr. Andy RODRIGUEZ
32 Vice Pres Student Services .... Mr. John MARSHALL
13 Director Information Technology .... Mr. Jeremy BROWN
09 Director Institutional Research .... Ms. Sonia BRANDON
08 Library Director .... Ms. Sarah CRON
25 Director Sponsored Programs .... Ms. Cindy LUEB
20 Assistant Academic Officer .... Mr. Steve WERMAN
21 Controller .... Mr. Joe TAYLOR
21 Director Budget .... Ms. Whitney SUTTON
30 Director of Development .... Ms. Peggy LAMM
37 Director Financial Aid .... Mr. Curt MARTIN
18 Director of Facilities Services .... Mr. Kent MARSH
29 Director of Alumni Association .... Mr. Rick ADLEMAN
41 Athletic Director .... Mr. Tom SPICER
26 Director of Media Relations .... Ms. Dana NUNN
39 Director Housing & Residence Life .... Mr. Troy SEPPELT
06 Registrar .... Ms. Holly TEAL
07 Director of Admissions .... Mr. Jared MEIER
15 Director of Human Resources .... Ms. Barbara CASE-KING
20 Interim Director Academic Services .... Ms. Millie MOLAND
40 Bookstore Manager .... Ms. Tracy BRODRICK

Colorado Mountain College (G)

802 Grand Avenue, Glenwood Springs CO 81602-3961
County: Garfield FICE Identification: 004506
Unit ID: 126711
Telephone: (970) 945-8691 Carnegie Class: Assoc/Pub-R-L
FAX Number: (970) 947-8385 Calendar System: Semester
URL: www.coloradomtn.edu
Established: 1965 Annual Undergrad Tuition & Fees (In-District): $1,680
Enrollment: 5,847 Coed
Affiliation or Control: Local IRS Status: 501(c)3
Highest Offering: Baccalaureate
Program: Occupational; 2-Year Principally Bachelor's Creditable
Accreditation: NH, ADNUR, EMT

01 Interim President .... Dr. Charles DASSANCE
03 Senior Vice President .... Dr. Jill BOYLE
05 Sr Vice President Academic Affairs .... Dr. Brad TYNDALL
12 VP CMC/Aspen Campus .... Mr. Joseph MAESTAS
10 CFO .... Ms. Linda ENGLISH
09 VP Institutional Effectiveness .... Dr. Meeta GOEL
32 VP Student Affairs .... Vacant
15 Vice President of Human Resources .... Ms. Jan ASPELUND
26 Public Relations Officer .... Ms. Debbie CRAWFORD
13 Chief Information Officer .... Vacant
07 Dir Pre-Enrollment Svcs/Registrar .... Mr. Bill SOMMERS
37 Director of Financial Aid .... Ms. Rita BAYLESS
18 Director of College Facilities .... Mr. Peter WALLER
27 Director of Marketing/Publications .... Mr. Doug STEWART
96 Director of Purchasing .... Mr. Steve BOYD
20 Developmental Education Coordinator .... Vacant

Colorado Mountain College Alpine Campus (H)

1275 Crawford Avenue, Steamboat Springs CO 80487
Telephone: (970) 870-4444 Identification: 770038
Accreditation: &NH

† Main campus is Colorado Mountain College in Glenwood Springs, CO.

Colorado Mountain College Aspen Campus (I)

0255 Sage Way, Aspen CO 81611
Telephone: (970) 925-7740 Identification: 770032
Accreditation: &NH

† Main campus is Colorado Mountain College in Glenwood Springs, CO.

Colorado Mountain College Roaring Fork Campus-Spring Valley (J)

690 Colorado Avenue, Carbondale CO 81623
Telephone: (970) 963-2172 Identification: 770035
Accreditation: &NH

† Main campus is Colorado Mountain College in Glenwood Springs, CO.

Colorado Mountain College Summit Campus-Breckinridge Campus (K)

107 Denison Placer Road, Breckinridge CO 80424
Telephone: (970) 453-6757 Identification: 770033
Accreditation: &NH

† Main campus is Colorado Mountain College in Glenwood Springs, CO.

Colorado Mountain College-Timberline Campus (L)

27900 County Road 319, PO Box 897,
Buena Vista CO 81211
Telephone: (719) 395-8419 Identification: 770036
Accreditation: &NH

† Main campus is Colorado Mountain College in Glenwood Springs, CO.

Colorado Mountain College Vail/Eagle Valley Campus (M)

150 Miller Ranch Road, Edwards CO 81632
Telephone: (970) 569-2900 Identification: 770034
Accreditation: &NH

† Main campus is Colorado Mountain College in Glenwood Springs, CO.

Colorado Mountain College West Garfield Campus (A)

3695 Airport Road, Rifle CO 81650
Telephone: (970) 625-1871 Identification: 770037
Accreditation: &NH

† Main campus is Colorado Mountain College in Glenwood Springs, CO.

Colorado Northwestern Community College (B)

500 Kennedy Drive, Rangely CO 81648-3598
County: Rio Blanco FICE Identification: 001359
Unit ID: 126748
Telephone: (970) 675-2261 Carnegie Class: Assoc/Pub-R-M
FAX Number: (970) 675-5046 Calendar System: Semester
URL: www.cncc.edu
Established: 1962 Annual Undergrad Tuition & Fees (In-District): $3,994
Enrollment: 1,353 Coed
Affiliation or Control: State/Local IRS Status: 170(c)1
Highest Offering: Associate Degree
Program: Occupational; 2-Year Principally Bachelor's Creditable
Accreditation: NH, ADNUR, DH

01 President .... Mr. Russell GEORGE
12 Vice Pres Craig Campus .... Mr. Gene BILODEAU
05 Vice Pres Instruction/Student Svcs .... Mr. David SMITH
10 Vice Pres Business/Administration .... Mr. Christopher BISHOP
84 Dean of Enrollment Svcs/Registrar .... Ms. Tresa ENGLAND
08 Library Director .... Ms. Leana COX
15 Human Resource Specialist .... Ms. Kim TUCKER
26 Marketing Director .... Ms. Tresa ENGLAND
18 Facilities Director .... Mr. John BOTTELBERGHE
09 Director of Institutional Research .... Ms. Mindy SHUE
38 Director Student Counseling .... Ms. Charity STOLWORTHY
96 Director of Purchasing .... Mr. Roger HANNA
37 Financial Aid Technician .... Ms. Merrie BYERS
20 Dean of Instruction in Rangely .... Ms. Judy ALLRED
20 Dean of Instruction in Craig .... Ms. Donna THEIMER

Colorado Northwestern Community College Craig (C)

2801 W 9th Street, Craig CO 81625
Telephone: (970) 824-1101 Identification: 770039
Accreditation: &NH

† Main campus is Colorado Northwestern Community College in Rangely, CO.

Colorado School of Healing Arts (D)

7655 W Mississippi, Suite 100, Lakewood CO 80226-4332
County: Jefferson FICE Identification: 035844
Unit ID: 381732
Telephone: (303) 986-2320 Carnegie Class: Assoc/PrivFP
FAX Number: (303) 980-6594 Calendar System: Quarter
URL: www.csha.net
Established: 1986 Annual Undergrad Tuition & Fees: $12,600
Enrollment: 151 Coed
Affiliation or Control: Proprietary IRS Status: Proprietary
Highest Offering: Associate Degree
Program: Occupational; 2-Year Principally Bachelor's Creditable; Technical Emphasis
Accreditation: ACCSC

01 Executive Director & Owner .... Mr. Dennis SIMPSON
03 Director .... Ms. Gina SIMPSON
05 Director of Education Deg Pgm .... Mr. Dan GOLDEN
06 Registrar .... Ms. Bryn HERSHBERGER
53 Director of Education Cert Pgm .... Ms. Chris SMITH
08 Head Librarian .... Ms. Kris WILL
11 Office Manager .... Ms. Tiffany LAYNE
40 Bookstore Manager .... Mr. Greg SENICH
36 Career Advisor/Placement .... Ms. Sandra COOK
37 Financial Aid Advisor .... Ms. Andrea NIECE
07 Admissions Representative .... Ms. Rosa TORRES

Colorado School of Mines (E)

1500 Illinois Street, Golden CO 80401-1843
County: Jefferson FICE Identification: 001348
Unit ID: 126775
Telephone: (303) 273-3000 Carnegie Class: RU/H
FAX Number: (303) 273-3278 Calendar System: Semester
URL: www.mines.edu
Established: 1874 Annual Undergrad Tuition & Fees (In-State): $16,485
Enrollment: 5,549 Coed
Affiliation or Control: State IRS Status: 501(c)3
Highest Offering: Doctorate
Program: Professional; Technical Emphasis
Accreditation: NH, ENG

01 President .... Dr. M. W. SCOGGINS
05 Provost .... Dr. Terry PARKER
10 Executive Vice Pres Finance & Admin .... Ms. Kirsten VOLPI
88 Sr Vice Pres Strat Enterprises .... Dr. Nigel T. MIDDLETON
32 Vice Pres Student Life .... Dr. Dan FOX
30 VP for Institutional Advancement .... Mr. Brian WINKELBAUER
100 Chief of Staff .... Mr. Peter HAN
06 Registrar .... Ms. Lara MEDLEY
07 Director of Admissions .... Mr. Bruce P. GOETZ
08 Librarian .... Ms. Joanne V. LERUD-HECK
14 Director of Computer Center .... Mr. Derek J. WILSON
26 Director Integrated Marketing Comm .... Ms. Karen GILBERT
37 Director of Financial Aid .... Ms. Jill ROBERTSON
51 Director of Special Programs .... Dr. Barry MARTIN
58 Dean Graduate Studies/Research .... Dr. Thomas BOYD
18 Director of Plant Facilities .... Mr. Gary BOWERSOCK
22 Affirmative Action Officer .... Mr. Michael DOUGHERTY
39 Director of Student Housing .... Ms. Rebecca FLINTOFT
38 Director Student Development .... Mr. Ronald L. BRUMMETT
41 Athletic Director .... Mr. Thomas SPICER
04 Spec Assistant to the President .... Ms. Kristi GITKIND
09 Director of Institutional Research .... Ms. Tricia DOUTHIT
15 Director Personnel Services .... Mr. Michael DOUGHERTY
84 Director Enrollment Management .... Ms. Heather BOYD
35 Director Student Affairs .... Mr. Derek MORGAN
36 Director Student Placement .... Mr. Ronald L. BRUMMETT
19 Director Public Safety .... Mr. Keith TURNEY
94 Exec Dir Women in Sci Eng & Math .... Ms. Deb LASICH
92 Director Honors Program .... Dr. Ken OSGOOD
45 Dir Financial Planning & Budget .... Ms. Vicki NICHOL
93 Director Minority Engineering Pgm .... Mr. Fernando GUZMAN
91 Director Enterprise Systems .... Mr. David LEE
29 Director Alumni Relations .... Ms. Serena BRUZGO

Colorado School of Trades (F)

1575 Hoyt Street, Lakewood CO 80215-2996
County: Jefferson FICE Identification: 011572
Unit ID: 126784
Telephone: (800) 234-4594 Carnegie Class: Assoc/PrivFP
FAX Number: (303) 233-4723 Calendar System: Other
URL: www.schooloftrades.edu
Established: 1947 Annual Undergrad Tuition & Fees: $19,800
Enrollment: 162 Coed
Affiliation or Control: Proprietary IRS Status: Proprietary
Highest Offering: Associate Degree
Program: Occupational
Accreditation: ACCSC

01 President .... Mr. Robert E. MARTIN

Colorado School of Traditional Chinese Medicine (G)

1441 York Street, Suite 202, Denver CO 80206-2127
County: Denver FICE Identification: 036863
Unit ID: 381352
Telephone: (303) 329-6355 Carnegie Class: Spec/Health
FAX Number: (303) 388-8165 Calendar System: Trimester
URL: www.cstcm.edu
Established: 1989 Annual Undergrad Tuition & Fees: $16,170
Enrollment: 134 Coed
Affiliation or Control: Proprietary IRS Status: Proprietary
Highest Offering: Master's
Program: Occupational; Professional
Accreditation: ACUP

01 Administrative Director .... Vladimir DIBRIGIDA

*Colorado State University System Office (H)

410 17th Street, Suite 2440, Denver CO 80202-4426
County: Denver FICE Identification: 033437
Telephone: (303) 534-6290 Carnegie Class: N/A
FAX Number: (303) 534-6298
URL: www.csusystem.edu

01 Chancellor .... Dr. Michaeld MARTIN
05 Chief Academic Officer .... Dr. Rick MIRANDA
43 General Counsel .... Mr. Michael NOLSER
10 Chief Financial Officer .... Mr. Rich SCHWEIGERT
26 Director of Public Relations .... Mr. Kyle HENLEY
86 Government Relations Coordinator .... Mr. Rich SCHWEIGERT
04 Executive Asst to Chancellor .... Ms. Melanie GEARY

*Colorado State University (I)

Fort Collins CO 80523-0015
County: Larimer FICE Identification: 001350
Unit ID: 126818
Telephone: (970) 491-1101 Carnegie Class: RU/VH
FAX Number: (970) 491-0501 Calendar System: Semester
URL: www.colostate.edu
Established: 1870 Annual Undergrad Tuition & Fees (In-State): $9,313
Enrollment: 26,769 Coed
Affiliation or Control: State IRS Status: 501(c)3
Highest Offering: Doctorate
Program: Liberal Arts And General; Teacher Preparatory; Professional
Accreditation: NH, BUS, CACREP, CIDA, CONST, COPSY, DIETC, DIETD, ENG, ENGR, FOR, IPSY, JOUR, LSAR, MFCD, MUS, OT, PH, SW, TEAC, VET

02 President .... Dr. Anthony A. FRANK
05 Senior Executive VP/Provost .... Dr. Rick MIRANDA
46 Vice President for Research .... Dr. William H. FARLAND
10 Assoc VP for Finance and Budgets .... Ms. Lynn JOHNSON
11 VP for University Operations .... Ms. Amy PARSONS
30 VP Advancement/Strategic Initiative .... Mr. Brett B. ANDERSON
84 Vice Pres for Enrollment/Access .... Mr. Robin C. BROWN
20 Vice Prov for Undergraduate Affairs .... Dr. Kathleen A. SHERMAN
58 Dean Graduate School .... Dr. Jodie R. HANZLIK
27 VP for External Relations .... Mr. Tom MILLIGAN
90 VP for IT/Dean of Libraries .... Dr. Patrick BURNS
91 Director of Acad Comp/Network Svc .... Mr. Scott BAILY
15 Dir Human Resource Svcs .... Mr. Tony DECROSTA
36 Director Career Services .... Mr. Jeremy PODANY
08 Exec Assoc Dean of Libraries .... Vacant
07 Assoc VP Enroll/VP for Diversity .... Ms. Mary R. ONTIVEROS
29 Exec Director Alumni Relations .... Ms. Colleen D. MEYER
41 Athletic Director .... Mr. Jack GRAHAM
43 Deputy General Counsel .... Mr. Jason L. JOHNSON
47 Dean Agriculture Sciences .... Dr. Craig BEYROUTY
88 Dean Applied Human Sciences .... Dr. Jeff MCCUBBIN
50 Dean of Business .... Dr. Ajay MENON
54 Dean of Engineering .... Dr. David MCLEAN
49 Dean of Liberal Arts .... Dr. Ann M. GILL
62 VP for IT/Dean of Libraries .... Dr. Patrick BURNS
65 Dean of Natural Resources .... Dr. Joyce BERRY
81 Dean of Natural Sciences .... Dr. Janice L. NERGER
74 Dean of Veterinary Med & Biomed Sci .... Dr. Mark STETTER
56 Director Cooperative Extension Svcs .... Dr. Lou SWANSON
06 Registrar .... Mr. Chris SENG
18 Chief Facilities/Physical Plant .... Mr. Steve R. HULTIN
22 Dir of Equal Opportunity .... Ms. Diana PRIETO
37 Director of Student Financial Aid .... Mr. Thomas BIEDSCHEID
39 Exec Dir Housing & Dining Services .... Dr. James DOLAK
40 Director of Bookstore .... Mr. John PARRY
96 Director of Purchasing .... Mr. Frank KRAPPES
92 Director University Honors Program .... Dr. Donald MYKLES
94 Dir Women & Gender Advocacy Center .... Ms. Kathy SISNEROS
09 Director of Institutional Research .... Dr. Laura JENSEN

*Colorado State University-Global Campus (J)

8000 E Maplewood Ave, Bld 5 Ste 250,
Greenwood Village CO 80111-4766
County: Arapahoe FICE Identification: 042087
Unit ID: 476975
Telephone: (720) 279-0159 Carnegie Class: Not Classified
FAX Number: N/A Calendar System: Semester
URL: www.csuglobal.edu
Established: 2008 Annual Undergrad Tuition & Fees (In-State): $10,008
Enrollment: 5,258 Coed
Affiliation or Control: State IRS Status: 501(c)3
Highest Offering: Master's
Program: Professional; Business Emphasis
Accreditation: NH

02 President & CEO .... Dr. Becky TAKEDA-TINKER

*Colorado State University-Pueblo (K)

2200 Bonforte Boulevard, Pueblo CO 81001-4901
County: Pueblo FICE Identification: 001365
Unit ID: 128106
Telephone: (719) 549-2100 Carnegie Class: Master's S
FAX Number: (719) 549-2650 Calendar System: Semester
URL: www.colostate-pueblo.edu
Established: 1933 Annual Undergrad Tuition & Fees (In-State): $7,327
Enrollment: 6,805 Coed
Affiliation or Control: State IRS Status: 501(c)3
Highest Offering: Master's
Program: Liberal Arts And General; Teacher Preparatory; Professional
Accreditation: NH, BUS, ENG, ENGT, MUS, NUR, SW, TEAC

02 President .... Dr. Lesley DI MARE
05 Provost/VP for Academic Affairs .... Dr. Carl WRIGHT
10 VP Finance & Administration .... Mr. Martin HANIFIN
84 VP Student Svcs and Enrollment Mgmt .... Dr. Paul ORSCHELN
20 Asst Provost Assess/Student Lrng .... Dr. Erin FREW
08 Dean Library .... Ms. Rhonda GONZALES
51 Dean Continuing Education .... Dr. James MALM
50 Dean Hasan School of Business .... Dr. Bruce RAYMOND
79 Dean Col of Humanities/Soc Sci .... Dr. Roy SONNEMA
54 Dean Engr/Educ/Profess Studies .... Dr. Hector CARRASCO
81 Dean Science/Math .... Dr. Rick KREMINSKI
102 Executive Director Foundation .... Mr. Todd KELLY
26 Exec Director External Affairs .... Ms. Cora ZALETEL
09 Interim Dir Inst Research/Analysis .... Dr. Rick KREMINSKI
21 Controller .... Mr. Robert GONZALES
37 Director Student Financial Services .... Mr. Sean MCGIVNEY
06 Registrar .... Ms. Amy ROBERTSHAW
36 Director Career Center .... Mrs. Michelle B. GJERDE
14 Dir Info Tech Svcs/Chief Tech Ofcr .... Mr. Erich MATOLA
41 Director Athletics .... Mr. Joe FOLDA
18 Dir Facilities/Construction/Plng .... Mr. Craig CASON
15 Director Human Resources .... Mr. Ralph JACOBS
39 Int Dir Residence Life & Housing .... Mr. Jack KRIDER
31 Director Auxiliary Services .... Mr. Chris FENDRICH
23 Student Health Services Nurse .... Ms. Carolyn DAUGHERTY
29 Director Alumni Relations .... Ms. Tracy SAMORA
38 Director Student Counseling .... Vacant
89 Director First Year Programs .... Dr. Derek LOPEZ
22 Director Affirmative Action .... Vacant
85 Assoc Dir International Programs .... Ms. Annie WILLIAMS
04 Executive Asst to the President .... Ms. Trisha MACIAS

Colorado Technical University (A)

3151 South Vaughn Way, Suite 400, Aurora CO 80014
Telephone: (303) 632-2300 Identification: 666732
Accreditation: &NH

† Main campus is Colorado Technical University in Colorado Springs, CO.

Colorado Technical University (B)

4435 N Chestnut Street, Colorado Springs CO 80907-3896
County: El Paso FICE Identification: 010148
Unit ID: 126827
Telephone: (719) 598-0200 Carnegie Class: DRU
FAX Number: (719) 598-3740 Calendar System: Quarter
URL: www.coloradotech.edu
Established: 1965 Annual Undergrad Tuition & Fees: $11,517
Enrollment: 2,408 Coed
Affiliation or Control: Proprietary IRS Status: Proprietary
Highest Offering: Doctorate
Program: Occupational; 2-Year Principally Bachelor's Creditable; Professional; Technical Emphasis
Accreditation: NH, ENG

00 Interim CEO .... Mr. Jack KOEHN
01 Campus President .... Mr. Tim GRAMLING
07 Vice President of Admissions .... Ms. Beth BRAATEN
10 Regional Director of Operations .... Mr. Jeremy WALKER
08 Dir of University Libraries .... Ms. Joanna PRIMUS
37 Dir of Student Account Services .... Vacant
36 Director of Career Services .... Mr. Jason RAMSEY
13 Manager of Information Systems .... Mr. Thomas LEIGH
54 Dean Engineering/Computer Science .... Dr. Bruce HARMON

Community College of Aurora (C)

16000 E Centre Tech Parkway, Aurora CO 80011-9036
County: Arapahoe FICE Identification: 022769
Unit ID: 126863
Telephone: (303) 360-4700 Carnegie Class: Assoc/Pub-S-MC
FAX Number: (303) 360-4761 Calendar System: Semester
URL: www.ccaurora.edu
Established: 1983 Annual Undergrad Tuition & Fees (In-State): $4,318
Enrollment: 8,403 Coed
Affiliation or Control: State IRS Status: 501(c)3
Highest Offering: Associate Degree
Program: Occupational; 2-Year Principally Bachelor's Creditable
Accreditation: NH, EMT

01 President .... Mr. Alton D. SCALES
05 Vice President Instruction .... Ms. Xeturah WOODLEY
11 Vice Pres Administrative Services .... Mr. Richard MAESTAS
84 VP Enrollment Mgmt/Student Services .... Dr. Elizabeth OUDENHOVEN
07 Director Admissions & Registrar .... Ms. Kristen CUSACK
21 Controller .... Ms. Mercy ABRAHAM
15 Director of Human Resources .... Ms. Cindy HESSE
08 Director Library Services .... Ms. Megan KINNEY
13 Director Information Technology .... Ms. Sandra TOMPKINS
37 Director Financial Aid and Advising .... Mr. John YOUNG
32 Director Student Life .... Ms. Angie TIEDEMAN
27 Director College Communications .... Ms. Liz VANLANDINGHAM
09 Director of Institutional Research .... Dr. David BAILEY
18 Facilities Manager .... Mr. Jim MARSHALL
25 Coordinator of Grants & Funding .... Dr. Chris WARD

Community College of Denver (D)

Campus Box 250 P.O. Box 173363,
Denver CO 80217-3363
County: Denver FICE Identification: 009542
Unit ID: 126942
Telephone: (303) 556-2400 Carnegie Class: Assoc/Pub-U-MC
FAX Number: (303) 556-8555 Calendar System: Semester
URL: www.ccd.edu
Established: 1967 Annual Undergrad Tuition & Fees (In-State): $5,941
Enrollment: 5,211 Coed
Affiliation or Control: State IRS Status: 501(c)3
Highest Offering: Associate Degree
Program: Occupational; 2-Year Principally Bachelor's Creditable
Accreditation: NH, DH, RAD

01 Interim President .... Mr. Cliff RICHARDSON
05 Provost/Vice Pres Learning .... Dr. Bernice HARRIS
10 Vice Pres Finance & Admin/CFO .... Mr. Duane RISSE
32 Vice Pres Student Development .... Ms. Leslie MCCLELLON
102 Vice Pres Economic/Resource Devel .... Vacant
75 Dean Career/Technical Education .... Dr. Chris BUDDEN
49 Dean Language/Arts/Behavioral Sci .... Ms. Ruthanne ORIHUELA
88 Dean Educational Advancement .... Ms. Nancy STORY
35 Dean of Students/Ed Plng/Advising .... Dr. Ryan ROSS
84 Dean of Enrollment Svcs/Registrar .... Ms. Lori KESTER
35 Dean of Student Life .... Ms. Meloni RUDOLPH
37 Director Financial Aid .... Mr. Thad SPAULDING
07 Director Recruit/Student Outreach .... Vacant
15 Director Human Resources .... Ms. Rhonda PYLICAN
13 Executive Director IT Services .... Mr. Andy CORBETT
09 Exec Dir Inst Research & Planning .... Ms. Margaret PURYEAR

Concorde Career College (E)

111 N Havana Street, Aurora CO 80010-4314
County: Arapahoe FICE Identification: 008871
Unit ID: 126687
Telephone: (303) 861-1151 Carnegie Class: Assoc/PrivFP
FAX Number: (303) 839-5478 Calendar System: Other
URL: www.concorde.edu
Established: 1969 Annual Undergrad Tuition & Fees: $14,686
Enrollment: 764 Coed
Affiliation or Control: Proprietary IRS Status: Proprietary
Highest Offering: Associate Degree
Program: Occupational
Accreditation: ACCSC, COARC, DH, PTAA, RAD, SURGT

01 Campus President .... Ms. Staci HEGERTY
05 Academic Dean .... Ms. Cindy COBB
37 Director of Financial Aid .... Ms. Nancy DISATE
07 Director of Admissions .... Mr. Shebon KELIN

Denver School of Nursing (F)

1401 19th Street, Denver CO 80202
County: Denver FICE Identification: 041483
Unit ID: 454856
Telephone: (303) 292-0015 Carnegie Class: Spec/Health
FAX Number: (720) 974-0290 Calendar System: Quarter
URL: www.denverschoolofnursing.edu
Established: 2003 Annual Undergrad Tuition & Fees: $51,254
Enrollment: 564 Coed
Affiliation or Control: Proprietary IRS Status: Proprietary
Highest Offering: Baccalaureate
Program: Nursing Emphasis
Accreditation: @NH, ACCSC, ADNUR, NUR

01 President .... Dr. Marcia BANKIRER
05 Director of Business Operations .... Ms. Renee MCMILLIN
32 Director of Student Services .... Mr. Michael RUSCHIVAL
66 Dean/Dir of Nursing Education Pgms .... Dr. Shelley MORISTON

Denver Seminary (G)

6399 S Santa Fe Drive, Littleton CO 80120-2912
County: Arapahoe FICE Identification: 001352
Unit ID: 126979
Telephone: (303) 761-2482 Carnegie Class: Spec/Faith
FAX Number: (303) 761-8060 Calendar System: Semester
URL: www.denverseminary.edu
Established: 1950 Annual Graduate Tuition & Fees: $14,900
Enrollment: 1,005 Coed
Affiliation or Control: Interdenominational IRS Status: 501(c)3
Highest Offering: Doctorate; No Undergraduates
Program: Professional; Religious Emphasis
Accreditation: NH, CACREP, THEOL

01 President .... Dr. Mark S. YOUNG
00 Chancellor .... Dr. Gordon MACDONALD
05 Provost/Dean .... Dr. Randolph M. MACFARLAND
10 Vice President of Finance .... Ms. Deborah KELLAR
30 Vice President of Advancement .... Mr. Ron GASCHO
32 Vice President of Student Services .... Mr. Robert JONES
20 Associate Academic Dean .... Dr. W. David BUSCHART
06 Registrar/Dir Educ Services .... Ms. Pam BETKER
35 Dean of Student Services .... Mr. John WOOD
07 Director of Admissions .... Ms. Christine MULLER
44 Director of Development .... Mr. Chris JOHNSON
40 Director of Auxiliary Services .... Mr. Kent B. QUACKENBUSH
13 Director of Information Systems .... Mr. Jason ADAMS
27 Director of Communications .... Ms. Katie BREWERTON
88 Dir Educational Technology .... Mr. Aaron JOHNSON
88 Dir Educational Projects .... Mrs. Lisa LINHART
18 Director of Physical Plant .... Mr. Rob BACHMAN
37 Director of Financial Aid .... Mr. Joel LAOS
08 Director of Library .... Dr. Keith P. WELLS
73 Director of DMin Program .... Dr. Tim DOLAN
21 Director of Financial Services .... Mrs. Kristy EDLUND
15 Director of Human Resources .... Ms. Zandy WENNERSTROM

DeVry University - Westminster Campus (H)

1870 W 122nd Avenue, Westminster CO 80234-2010
Telephone: (303) 280-7400 Identification: 666227
Accreditation: &NH, ENGT

† Main campus is DeVry University - Chicago Campus in Chicago, IL.

Ecotech Institute (I)

1400 South Abilene Street, Aurora CO 80012
Telephone: (303) 586-5290 Identification: 770840
Accreditation: ACICS

† Main campus is Virginia College in Birmingham, AL.

Everest College (J)

14280 E Jewell Avenue, Suite 100, Aurora CO 80012
Telephone: (303) 745-6244 Identification: 666412
Accreditation: ACICS, MAC

† Main campus is Everest College in Denver, CO.

Everest College (K)

1815 Jet Wing Drive, Colorado Springs CO 80916
County: El Paso FICE Identification: 004503
Unit ID: 126401
Telephone: (719) 638-6580 Carnegie Class: Assoc/PrivFP
FAX Number: (719) 638-6818 Calendar System: Quarter
URL: www.everest.edu
Established: 1897 Annual Undergrad Tuition & Fees: $14,780
Enrollment: 435 Coed
Affiliation or Control: Proprietary IRS Status: Proprietary
Highest Offering: Associate Degree
Program: Occupational; 2-Year Principally Bachelor's Creditable
Accreditation: ACICS, MAC

01 President .... Mr. Robert LANTZY
05 Dean of Education .... Ms. Heidi GODBOLD
07 Director Admissions .... Mr. Dan NOEL
37 Director Student Finance .... Ms. Carrie IVERSON
36 Director Career Services .... Mr. Michael CAPPELLA

Everest College (L)

9065 Grant Street, Denver CO 80229-4339
County: Adams FICE Identification: 004507
Unit ID: 127787
Telephone: (303) 457-2757 Carnegie Class: Assoc/PrivFP
FAX Number: (303) 457-4030 Calendar System: Quarter
URL: www.cci.edu
Established: 1895 Annual Undergrad Tuition & Fees: $16,272
Enrollment: 298 Coed
Affiliation or Control: Proprietary IRS Status: Proprietary
Highest Offering: Associate Degree
Program: Occupational
Accreditation: ACICS, MAC, SURGT

01 President .... Ms. Pat SCHLOTTER
05 Academic Dean .... Mr. Raines GUINN
07 Director of Admissions .... Ms. Jennifer HEDRICK
37 Director of Student Finance .... Ms. Kim MARTINEZ
36 Director of Career Services .... Ms. Diane BOOREN
06 Registrar .... Mr. Bruce DOUGHTY

Fort Lewis College (M)

1000 Rim Drive, Durango CO 81301-3999
County: La Plata FICE Identification: 001353
Unit ID: 127185
Telephone: (970) 247-7010 Carnegie Class: Bac/A&S
FAX Number: (970) 247-7175 Calendar System: Semester
URL: www.fortlewis.edu
Established: 1911 Annual Undergrad Tuition & Fees (In-State): $6,923
Enrollment: 3,891 Coed
Affiliation or Control: State IRS Status: 170(c)1
Highest Offering: Master's
Program: Liberal Arts And General; Teacher Preparatory
Accreditation: NH, BUS, ENG, MUS, TEAC

01 President .... Dr. Dene Kay THOMAS
05 Provost/Vice Pres Academic Affairs .... Dr. Barbara MORRIS
10 Vice Pres Finance & Administration .... Mr. Steven J. SCHWARTZ
84 Assoc Vice Pres Enrollment Mgmt .... Dr. Carol SMITH
32 Vice President Student Affairs .... Dr. Glenna W. SEXTON
20 Assoc Vice Pres Academic Affairs .... Dr. Kenneth PEPION
09 Exec Dir of Institutional Research .... Mr. Richard A. MILLER
21 Director Budget .... Ms. Michele PETERSON
06 Registrar .... Ms. Kathy KENDALL
21 Controller .... Ms. Cheryl WIESCAMP
25 Director of Grants Management .... Ms. Angela ROCHAT
37 Director Financial Aid .... Ms. Tracey PICCOLI
07 Director of Admission .... Mr. Andrew BURNS
38 Int Dir Counseling/Student Dev Ctr .... Ms. Karen NAKAYAMA
08 Director of the Library .... Ms. Astrid OLIVER
18 Dir Physical Plant/College Engr .... Mr. Wayne KJONAAS
15 Dir Human Resources/Equal Opptnty .... Mr. Darren MATHEWS
39 Dir Stdnt Housing/Conferences Svcs .... Ms. Julie N. LOVE
41 Athletic Director .... Mr. Gary HUNTER
13 Director Computing & Telecomm .... Mr. Matt MCGLAMERY
29 Director Alumni Relations .... Mr. David KERNS
96 Director of Purchasing .... Mr. Wayne J. HERMES
26 Chief Public Relations Officer .... Mr. Mitch DAVIS
40 Bookstore Manager .... Ms. Brooke INGLE
28 Coord Equal Opport/Judicial Affs .... Dr. Haeryon KIM
83 Dean Sch Natural & Behavioral Sci .... Dr. Maureen BRANDON
50 Dean School of Business Admin .... Dr. Doug LYON
49 Ast Dean School Arts/Hum/Social Sci .... Ms. Bridget IRISH

Front Range Community College (N)

3645 W 112th Avenue, Westminster CO 80031-2105
County: Adams FICE Identification: 007933
Unit ID: 127200
Telephone: (303) 404-5000 Carnegie Class: Assoc/Pub-S-MC
FAX Number: (303) 466-1623 Calendar System: Semester
URL: www.frontrange.edu
Established: 1968 Annual Undergrad Tuition & Fees (In-State): $3,224
Enrollment: 21,155 Coed
Affiliation or Control: State IRS Status: 501(c)3
Highest Offering: Associate Degree
Program: Occupational; 2-Year Principally Bachelor's Creditable
Accreditation: NH, ADNUR, DA, MAC, PNUR

01 President Mr. Andrew R. DORSEY
04 Asst to the President Ms. Kimberly STEFANSKI
10 Vice Pres Finance & Administration Ms. Jennifer SOBANET
05 Chief Academic Officer Dr. Sandra VELTRI
12 Vice Pres Westminster Camp Ms. Therese BROWN
12 Vice Pres Larimer Campus Mr. Bruce WALTHERS
12 Vice Pres Boulder County Campus Dr. Linda CURRAN
84 Assoc VP Enroll Mgmt & Student Svcs Dr. Kris BINARD
72 Dean of Career Technical Ed Vacant
106 Dean of OnLine Learning Ms. Tammy VERCAUTEREN
88 Dean of Transfer Education Ms. Lisa DONALDSON
20 Dean of Instruction Larimer Dr. Kim DALE
20 Dean of Instruction Boulder County Mr. Matt JAMISON
20 Dean of Instruction Westminster Ms. Catherine PELLISH
32 Dean of Student Svcs Boulder County Ms. Carla STEIN
32 Dean of Student Svcs Westminister Ms. Renee TASTAD
88 Dean/Exec Dir of Secondary Programs Dr. Phyllis ABT
16 Exec Director of Human Resources Mr. Paul MEESE
09 Director of Institutional Research Ms. Kim WALLACE
21 Controller Mr. Paul SQUILLACE
21 Director of Budget & Contracts Vacant
06 Registrar Ms. Yolanda ESPINOZA
37 Dir of Financial Aid Campus Wide Ms. Carolee GOLDSMITH
08 Director of Library Services Vacant
18 Director of Facilities Westminster Mr. Patrick O'NEILL
18 Director of Facilities Larimer Mr. Scott MCKELVEY
35 Director Student Life Westminister Ms. Amy ROSDIL
35 Director Student Life Larimer Ms. Mary BRANTON-HOUSLEY
35 Dir Student Life Boulder County Ms. Amanda CLANCY
102 Director of Foundation Mr. Chuck CROWE
26 Dir of Marketing & Communications Ms. Marian MAHARAS
27 Public Information Officer Mr. John FEELEY
13 Director of Information Technology Ms. Jeannine MENEFEE
40 Director of Auxiliary Services Mr. Wes GEARY

Front Range Community College Boulder County Campus (A)

2190 Miller Drive, Longmont CO 80501
Telephone: (303) 678-3722 Identification: 770041
Accreditation: &NH

† Main campus is Front Range Community College in Westminster, CO.

Front Range Community College Larimer Campus (B)

4616 S Shields Street, Fort Collins CO 80526
Telephone: (970) 226-2500 Identification: 770040
Accreditation: &NH, PHLEB

† Main campus is Front Range Community College in Westminster, CO.

Heritage College (C)

12 Lakeside Lane, Denver CO 80212-7413
County: Jefferson FICE Identification: 026110
Unit ID: 262509
Telephone: (303) 477-7240 Carnegie Class: Assoc/PrivFP
FAX Number: (303) 477-7276 Calendar System: Other
URL: www.heritage-education.com
Established: 1986 Annual Undergrad Tuition & Fees: $24,875
Enrollment: 616 Coed
Affiliation or Control: Proprietary IRS Status: Proprietary
Highest Offering: Associate Degree
Program: Occupational
Accreditation: ABHES

01 College Director Denver Austin MORTON
88 President of Residential Schools Richard K. SHEPARD
03 Senior Vice President Shannon BEELER
05 Director of Education Kai STONE
07 Director of Admissions Reba ELDER
06 Registrar Julia WILLIAMS
36 Director of Career Services Michelle TYMOCZKO
37 Director of Financial Aid Amanda MASELBAS
22 Director of Compliance Bill PASCHALL

Holmes Institute of Consciousness Studies (D)

573 Park Point Drive, Golden CO 80401
County: Jefferson Identification: 666255
Telephone: (720) 496-1370 Carnegie Class: Not Classified
FAX Number: (303) 526-0913 Calendar System: Quarter
URL: www.holmesinstitute.org
Established: 1972 Annual Graduate Tuition & Fees: $22,000
Enrollment: 95 Coed
Affiliation or Control: Other IRS Status: 501(c)3
Highest Offering: Master's; No Undergraduates
Program: Religious Emphasis
Accreditation: DETC

01 Dir of HICS/Dir of Education Rev Dr. Lynn CONNOLLY
06 Registrar Ms. Maureen THURSTON

Iliff School of Theology (E)

2201 S University Boulevard, Denver CO 80210-4798
County: Denver FICE Identification: 001354
Unit ID: 127273
Telephone: (303) 744-1287 Carnegie Class: Spec/Faith
FAX Number: (303) 777-3387 Calendar System: Quarter
URL: www.iliff.edu
Established: 1892 Annual Graduate Tuition & Fees: $17,976
Enrollment: 374 Coed
Affiliation or Control: United Methodist IRS Status: 501(c)3
Highest Offering: Doctorate; No Undergraduates
Program: Professional; Religious Emphasis
Accreditation: NH, THEOL

01 President Dr. Thomas V. WOLFE
05 Vice Pres/Dean Academic Affairs Dr. Albert HERNANDEZ
10 Vice President for Business Affairs Ms. Kelly L. MCCORMICK
30 VP of Institutional Advancement Vacant
26 VP of Marketing Communications Ms. Greta GLOVEN
32 Dean Enrollment & Student Services Mr. David WORLEY
06 Registrar Ms. Carmen E. BACA-DOSTER
08 Director Library & Information Svcs Ms. Alice RUNIS
07 Director Admission/Financial Aid Ms. Peggy J. BLOCKER
28 Associate Dean of Diversities Dr. Edward ANTONIO

Institute of Business and Medical Careers (F)

3842 South Mason Street, Fort Collins CO 80526
County: Larimer FICE Identification: 030063
Unit ID: 372329
Telephone: (970) 223-2669 Carnegie Class: Assoc/PrivFP
FAX Number: (970) 223-2796 Calendar System: Quarter
URL: www.ibmc.edu
Established: 1987 Annual Undergrad Tuition & Fees: $11,340
Enrollment: 260 Coed
Affiliation or Control: Proprietary IRS Status: Proprietary
Highest Offering: Associate Degree
Program: Occupational
Accreditation: ACICS

00 CEO Mr. Steven STEELE
01 President Mr. Eric THOMPSON

Institute of Business and Medical Careers (G)

5400 West 11th Street, Greeley CO 80634
Telephone: (970) 356-4733 Identification: 770631
Accreditation: ACICS

† Main campus is Institute of Business and Medical Careers in Fort Collins, CO.

Institute of Business and Medical Careers (H)

2315 North Main Street, Longmont CO 80501
Telephone: (303) 651-6819 Identification: 770630
Accreditation: ACICS

† Main campus is Institute of Business and Medical Careers in Fort Collins, CO.

Institute of Taoist Education and Acupuncture (I)

325 West South Boulder Road, Ste 2, Louisville CO 80027
County: Boulder FICE Identification: 041212
Unit ID: 454838
Telephone: (720) 890-8922 Carnegie Class: Spec/Health
FAX Number: (720) 890-7719 Calendar System: Other
URL: www.itea.edu
Established: 1996 Annual Graduate Tuition & Fees: $18,500
Enrollment: 36 Coed
Affiliation or Control: Independent Non-Profit IRS Status: 501(c)3
Highest Offering: Master's; No Undergraduates
Program: Professional
Accreditation: ACUP

01 President Sandra LILLIE
05 Director Hilary SKELLON
06 Registrar Claudia O'NIELL
10 Financial Administrator Angela SMITH

IntelliTec College (J)

2315 E Pikes Peak Avenue,
Colorado Springs CO 80909-6096
County: El Paso FICE Identification: 022537
Unit ID: 128179
Telephone: (719) 632-7626 Carnegie Class: Assoc/PrivFP
FAX Number: (719) 632-7451 Calendar System: Quarter
URL: www.intellitec.edu
Established: 1965 Annual Undergrad Tuition & Fees: $19,700
Enrollment: 580 Coed
Affiliation or Control: Proprietary IRS Status: Proprietary
Highest Offering: Associate Degree
Program: Occupational; Technical Emphasis
Accreditation: ACCSC

01 COO/Executive Director Mr. Edwin KRAUS
06 Registrar Ms. Tammy ALESH

IntelliTec College (K)

772 Horizon Drive, Grand Junction CO 81506-3994
County: Mesa FICE Identification: 030669
Unit ID: 128188
Telephone: (970) 245-8101 Carnegie Class: Assoc/PrivFP
FAX Number: (970) 243-8074 Calendar System: Quarter
URL: www.intelliteccollege.com/
Established: 1984 Annual Undergrad Tuition & Fees: $24,191
Enrollment: 678 Coed
Affiliation or Control: Proprietary IRS Status: Proprietary
Highest Offering: Associate Degree
Program: Occupational
Accreditation: ACCSC

01 President Mr. Michael SCHRANZ
05 Director Dr. Dave SCOTT

IntelliTec College (L)

3673 Parker Boulevard, Suite 250, Pueblo CO 81008-2211
Telephone: (719) 542-3181 Identification: 666366
Accreditation: ACCSC

† Main campus is IntelliTec College in Grand Junction, CO.

IntelliTec Medical Institute (M)

6805 Corporate Drive, Suite 100,
Colorado Springs CO 80919
County: El Paso FICE Identification: 008635
Unit ID: 127839
Telephone: (719) 596-7400 Carnegie Class: Assoc/PrivFP
FAX Number: (719) 596-2464 Calendar System: Other
URL: www.intellitecmedical.edu
Established: 1966 Annual Undergrad Tuition & Fees: $21,984
Enrollment: 380 Coed
Affiliation or Control: Proprietary IRS Status: Proprietary
Highest Offering: Associate Degree
Program: Occupational
Accreditation: ABHES, DA

01 Campus Director Mr. Todd MATTHEWS

ITT Technical Institute (N)

12500 E Iliff Avenue, Suite 100, Aurora CO 80014
Telephone: (303) 695-6317 Identification: 770636
Accreditation: ACICS

† Main campus is ITT Technical Institute in Indianapolis, IN.

ITT Technical Institute (O)

8620 Wolff Court, Suite 100, Westminster CO 80031
Telephone: (303) 288-4488 Identification: 667189
Accreditation: ACICS

† Main campus is ITT Technical Institute in Indianapolis, IN.

Johnson & Wales University - Denver Campus (P)

7150 Montview Boulevard, Denver CO 80220-1866
Telephone: (303) 256-9300 Identification: 666411
Accreditation: &EH, DIETD

† Main campus is Johnson & Wales University in Providence, RI.

Jones International University (Q)

9697 E Mineral Avenue, Centennial CO 80112-3408
County: Arapahoe FICE Identification: 035343
Unit ID: 444723
Telephone: (800) 811-5663 Carnegie Class: Master's L
FAX Number: (303) 799-0966 Calendar System: Other
URL: www.jiu.edu
Established: 1993 Annual Undergrad Tuition & Fees: $12,720
Enrollment: 3,196 Coed
Affiliation or Control: Proprietary IRS Status: Proprietary
Highest Offering: Doctorate
Program: Teacher Preparatory; Professional; Business Emphasis
Accreditation: NH

01 Chancellor Dr. Milton GOLDBERG
05 Chief Academic Officer Vacant
10 Chief Financial Officer Ms. Christine SPATH
11 Chief Operating Officer Mr. Bryan WALLACE

Lamar Community College (R)

2401 S Main, Lamar CO 81052-3999
County: Prowers FICE Identification: 001355
Unit ID: 127389
Telephone: (719) 336-2248 Carnegie Class: Assoc/Pub-R-S
FAX Number: (719) 336-2448 Calendar System: Semester
URL: www.lamarcc.edu
Established: 1937 Annual Undergrad Tuition & Fees (In-State): $4,757
Enrollment: 916 Coed
Affiliation or Control: State IRS Status: 501(c)3
Highest Offering: Associate Degree
Program: Occupational; 2-Year Principally Bachelor's Creditable
Accreditation: NH, ADNUR

01 President Mr. John MARRIN
05 VP Academic Services/Student Svcs Mrs. Cheryl SANCHEZ
11 VP Admin Svcs/Institutional Rsrch Mr. Chad DE BONO

20 Dean of Academic Services Mr. Curtis TURNER
26 Director of Communication Mrs. Anne-Marie CRAMPTON
06 Registrar Mrs. Amber THOMPSON
08 Library Tech Ms. Ellen LOVELL
18 Director of Facilities Mr. Sean LIRLEY
15 Director Personnel Services Ms. Nichole EASTIN
39 Director Student Housing Mr. Chad DEBONO
38 Director Student Counseling Ms. Deanna SIEMSEN
96 Director of Purchasing Mrs. Ava BAIR
40 Director Bookstore Mrs. Sheila DIETERLE
41 Athletic Director Mr. Craig BROOKS
37 Director Financial Aid Mrs. Teale HEMPHILL
07 Director of Admissions Mrs. Jenna DAVIS
09 Coordinator Institutional Research Mrs. Kim WALLACE

Lincoln College of Technology (A)

11194 East 45th Avenue, Denver CO 80239
County: Denver FICE Identification: 007547
Unit ID: 126951
Telephone: (303) 722-5724 Carnegie Class: Assoc/PrivFP
FAX Number: (303) 778-8264 Calendar System: Other
URL: www.lincolnedu.com
Established: 1963 Annual Undergrad Tuition & Fees: N/A
Enrollment: 1,436 Coed
Affiliation or Control: Proprietary IRS Status: Proprietary
Highest Offering: Associate Degree
Program: Occupational
Accreditation: ACCSC

01 Executive Director Mr. Al SHORT
07 Director Admissions Ms. Jennifer HASH
05 Director of Education Mr. Randy BOBZIEN

McKinley College (B)

2001 Lowe Street, Fort Collins CO 80525-3474
County: Larimer Identification: 666237
Telephone: (970) 207-4550 Carnegie Class: Not Classified
FAX Number: (877) 599-5863 Calendar System: Other
URL: www.mckinleycollege.edu
Established: 2004 Annual Undergrad Tuition & Fees: $5,000
Enrollment: N/A Coed
Affiliation or Control: Proprietary IRS Status: Proprietary
Highest Offering: Associate Degree
Program: Occupational; 2-Year Principally Bachelor's Creditable
Accreditation: DETC

01 President Ann ROHR
32 Vice President of Student Affairs Joyce LINDQUIST
05 Director of Education Janet PERRY

Mesa State College-Montrose Campus (C)

234 South Cascade Avenue, Montrose CO 81401
Telephone: (970) 249-7009 Identification: 770031
Accreditation: &NH

† Main campus is Colorado Mesa University in Grand Junction, CO.

Metropolitan State University of Denver (D)

PO Box 173362, Denver CO 80217-3362
County: Denver FICE Identification: 001360
Unit ID: 127565
Telephone: (303) 556-3022 Carnegie Class: Bac/Diverse
FAX Number: (303) 556-3912 Calendar System: Semester
URL: www.msudenver.edu
Established: 1963 Annual Undergrad Tuition & Fees (In-State): $5,744
Enrollment: 23,550 Coed
Affiliation or Control: State IRS Status: 501(c)3
Highest Offering: Master's
Program: Liberal Arts And General; Teacher Preparatory; Professional
Accreditation: NH, ART, CS, DIETD, ENGT, EXSC, FEPAC, MT, MUS, NRPA, NUR, SW, TED, THEA

01 President Dr. Stephen M. JORDAN
05 Vice President Academic Affairs Dr. Vicki GOLICH
10 Vice Pres Administration Finance Mr. Steve KRIEDLER
30 Vice Pres Advancement/External Rela Dr. Erin TRAPP
20 Deputy Provost Academic Affairs Dr. Luis TORRES
43 Gen Counsel/Sec to Board Ms. Loretta P. MARTINEZ
102 Assoc VP External Relations/Advanc Mr. Gregory J. GEISSLER
27 Assoc VP/CIO Dr. James LYALL
20 Assoc VP for Academic Affairs Dr. Sheila THOMPSON
15 Assoc VP & Director Human Resources Ms. Judith L. ZEWE
84 Assoc VP for Enrollment Services Mrs. Judi DIAZ-BONACQUISTI
21 Assoc VP Admin & Finance Mr. George M. MIDDLEMIST
26 Chief of Staff/Marketing & Comm Ms. Catherine LUCAS
29 Director of Alumni Relations Mr. Mark JASTORFF
50 Dean School Business Dr. Ann B. MURPHY
107 Dean School Professional Studies Dr. Sandra HAYNES
49 Dean School Letters/Arts/Science Dr. Joan L. FOSTER
35 Dean Student Life Ms. Emilia PAUL
22 Exec Director EEO/Asst to President Dr. Percy A. MOREHOUSE, JR.
09 Dir Sponsored Research/Programs Ms. Gwendolyn MAMI
56 Director of Extended Education Ms. Carol SVENDSEN
06 Registrar Ms. Paula MARTINEZ
37 Director Financial Aid Ms. Cindy HEJL
38 Director Counseling Center Dr. Gail BRUCE-SANFORD
41 Athletic Director Ms. Joan MCDERMOTT
35 Director Student Activities Ms. Angela LEVALLEY
36 Director Career Services Ms. Bridgette COBLE
28 Assoc to Pres Inst Diversity Dr. Myron ANDERSON

Morgan Community College (E)

920 Barlow Road, Fort Morgan CO 80701-4399
County: Morgan FICE Identification: 009981
Unit ID: 127617
Telephone: (970) 542-3100 Carnegie Class: Assoc/Pub-R-M
FAX Number: (970) 542-3115 Calendar System: Semester
URL: www.morgancc.edu
Established: 1967 Annual Undergrad Tuition & Fees (In-State): $3,200
Enrollment: 1,839 Coed
Affiliation or Control: State IRS Status: Exempt
Highest Offering: Associate Degree
Program: Occupational; 2-Year Principally Bachelor's Creditable
Accreditation: NH, ADNUR, PTAA

01 President Dr. Kerry HART
10 Vice Pres Finance/Admin Services Ms. Susan CLOUGH
05 Vice President of Instruction Ms. Betty MCKIE
84 Vice President of Student Success Mr. Kent BAUER
04 Assistant to the President Ms. Jane FRIES
12 Center Director Ms. Mary ANDERSEN
12 Center Director Ms. Nancy BARDEN
12 Center Director Ms. Kellie OVERTURF
12 Center Director Ms. Valerie RHOADES
09 Dir of Institutional Effectiveness Mr. Derek GRUBB
26 Dir of Communications & Marketing Ms. Katie BARRON
30 Dir Community Relations/Development Vacant
37 Director of Financial Aid Ms. Sally NESTOR
07 Director of Admissions Ms. Kim MAXWELL
15 Director of Personnel Services Vacant
08 Director of Learning Resources Ms. April AMACK
96 Director of Purchasing Ms. Julie BEYDLER
40 Director of Bookstore Ms. Anita ERTLE
18 Coordinator of M & O Mr. Seth NOBLE
36 Voc Guidance/Placement Counselor Mr. Dan MARLER
14 Director Information Technology Mr. Michael SHRIVER
66 Div Chr Hlth Occup/Dir Nursing Educ Ms. Kathy FRISBIE
49 Division Chair Arts & Sciences Mr. Todd SCHNEIDER
50 Division Chair Business Ms. Jaylene EVANS

Naropa University (F)

2130 Arapahoe Avenue, Boulder CO 80302-6697
County: Boulder FICE Identification: 021175
Unit ID: 127653
Telephone: (303) 444-0202 Carnegie Class: Master's L
FAX Number: (303) 444-0410 Calendar System: Semester
URL: www.naropa.edu
Established: 1974 Annual Undergrad Tuition & Fees: $28,970
Enrollment: 1,019 Coed
Affiliation or Control: Independent Non-Profit IRS Status: 501(c)3
Highest Offering: Master's
Program: Liberal Arts And General
Accreditation: NH

01 President Mr. Charles G. LIEF
04 Assistant to the President Ms. Cathy CHEN-ORTEGA
10 Vice President Business Affs/CFO Mr. Todd KILBURN
05 Provost/Vice Pres Academic Affs Dr. Janet CRAMER
11 Chief Administrative Officer Mr. Todd KILBURN
30 Vice Pres Development/Ext Relations Ms. Andrea AUGUISTE
84 VP Student Affairs/Enrollment Mgmt Ms. Cheryl BARBOUR
13 Assistant Vice President for IT Mr. Harvey NICHOLS
07 Dean of Admissions Ms. Janet ERICKSON
97 Associate Dean Undergrad Educ Mr. Mark A. MILLER
35 Dean of Students Mr. Robert CILLO
39 Director of Student Housing Ms. Lisa CONSTANTINO
06 Registrar Vacant
08 Director of Library Mr. Nicolas WEISS
18 Director of Facilities Mr. Aaron COOK
37 Dir Student Financial Services Ms. Nancy MORRELL
15 Director of Human Resources Ms. Angie GOSSETT
106 Director of Online Curriculum Devel Mr. Jirka HLADIS
29 Alumni Relations Officer Ms. Melissa HOLLAND
14 Assistant Director Technical Mr. Mike PAXTON
19 Safety & Security Manager Mr. Steve JEWELL

National American University-Centennial (G)

8242 S University Blvd, Suite 100, Centennial CO 80122
Telephone: (303) 542-7000 Identification: 770389
Accreditation: &NH

† Main campus is National American University in Rapid City, SD.

National American University-Colorado Springs (H)

1915 Jamboree Drive, Suite 185,
Colorado Springs CO 80920
Telephone: (719) 590-8300 Identification: 770390
Accreditation: &NH, MAC

† Main campus is National American University in Rapid City, SD.

National American University-Colorado Springs South (I)

1079 Space Center Drive, Unit 140,
Colorado Springs CO 80915
Telephone: (719) 208-3800 Identification: 770391
Accreditation: &NH

† Main campus is National American University in Rapid City, SD.

National American University-Denver (J)

1325 South Colorado Blvd, Suite 100, Denver CO 80222
Telephone: (303) 876-7100 Identification: 770392
Accreditation: &NH, MAC

† Main campus is National American University in Rapid City, SD.

Nazarene Bible College (K)

1111 Academy Park Loop,
Colorado Springs CO 80910-3704
County: El Paso FICE Identification: 013007
Unit ID: 127714
Telephone: (719) 884-5000 Carnegie Class: Spec/Faith
FAX Number: (719) 884-5199 Calendar System: Trimester
URL: www.nbc.edu
Established: 1964 Annual Undergrad Tuition & Fees: $12,825
Enrollment: 881 Coed
Affiliation or Control: Church Of The Nazarene IRS Status: 501(c)3
Highest Offering: Baccalaureate
Program: Professional; Religious Emphasis
Accreditation: NH, BI

01 President Dr. Harold B. GRAVES
05 Vice President for Academic Affairs Dr. Alan D. LYKE
32 VP for Student Development Prof. Laurel L. MATSON
10 Vice President for Finance Mrs. Shirley A. CADLE
84 VP for Enrollment Management Prof. Laurel L. MATSON
08 Library Director Prof. Ann M. ATTIG
37 Financial Aid Officer Mr. Malcolm E. BRITTON
09 Director of Institutional Research Vacant
06 Registrar Dr. Jay W. OTT

Northeastern Junior College (L)

100 College Drive, Sterling CO 80751-2399
County: Logan FICE Identification: 001361
Unit ID: 127732
Telephone: (970) 521-6600 Carnegie Class: Assoc/Pub-R-M
FAX Number: (970) 522-4945 Calendar System: Semester
URL: www.njc.edu
Established: 1941 Annual Undergrad Tuition & Fees (In-State): $3,443
Enrollment: 1,971 Coed
Affiliation or Control: State IRS Status: 501(c)3
Highest Offering: Associate Degree
Program: Occupational; 2-Year Principally Bachelor's Creditable
Accreditation: NH, ADNUR, PNUR

01 President Mr. Jay LEE
05 Vice President Academic Services Mr. Stanton GARTIN
10 Vice Pres Finance & Administration Mr. Tyler KELSCH
32 Dean of Student Success Mr. Steve SMITH
84 Dean New Student Enroll/Admissions Vacant
29 Alumni Director Mr. Jack ANNAN
102 Executive Director NJC Foundation Ms. Gail LAFORCE
06 Director Records/Admission Process Ms. Angela ANDERSON
37 Director of Financial Aid Ms. Alice WEINGARDT
35 Dir Resident Life & Student Activit Mr. David MCNABB
18 Physical Plant Director Mr. Tracey KNOX
15 Human Resources Director Ms. Tammy KALLSEN
41 Athletic Director Ms. Marci HENRY
96 Director of Purchasing/AR Ms. Annie SHALLA
09 Dir of Inst Research/Plng/Devel Mr. Derek HERBERT
26 Director of Marketing Ms. Barbara BAKER
21 Controller Ms. Judy MCFADDEN
13 Director Information Technology Ms. Cherie BRUNGARDT
40 Bookstore Director Ms. Heather BRUNGARDT

Otero Junior College (M)

1802 Colorado Avenue, La Junta CO 81050-3346
County: Otero FICE Identification: 001362
Unit ID: 127778
Telephone: (719) 384-6831 Carnegie Class: Assoc/Pub-R-S
FAX Number: (719) 384-6933 Calendar System: Semester
URL: www.ojc.edu
Established: 1941 Annual Undergrad Tuition & Fees (In-State): $3,864
Enrollment: 1,440 Coed
Affiliation or Control: State IRS Status: 501(c)3
Highest Offering: Associate Degree
Program: Occupational; 2-Year Principally Bachelor's Creditable
Accreditation: NH, ADNUR

01 President Mr. James T. RIZZUTO
11 Vice Pres Administrative Services Mr. Pat MALOTT
05 Vice Pres Instructional Services Mr. Brad FRANZ
32 Vice President Student Services Mr. Jeff PAOLUCCI
20 Assoc VP Instructional Services Dr. David COCKRELL
08 Director Learning Resources Ms. Sue KEEFER
38 Assoc VP of Students & Advising Mr. Brad SMITH

41 Athletic Director .... Mr. Gary ADDINGTON
15 Director of Human Resources .... Mrs. Marlene F. BOETTCHER
18 Director of Physical Plant .... Mr. John CANADAY
40 Bookstore Manager .... Mrs. Debra NICHOLSON
37 Director of Financial Aid .... Ms. Angela BENFATTI
88 Director of Auxilliary Services .... Ms. Genia SHORT
26 Director of Communications and PR .... Mrs. Sue SAMANIEGO
14 Director of Computer Services .... Mr. Mark ALLEN
09 Director of Institutional Research .... Mr. Gary ASHIDA
30 Resource Development & Director .... Dr. Teri ERICKSON
84 Assoc VP Enrollment Management .... Mrs. Almabeth KAESS

Pikes Peak Community College (A)

5675 S Academy Boulevard,
Colorado Springs CO 80906-5498
County: El Paso FICE Identification: 008896
Unit ID: 127820
Telephone: (719) 502-2000 Carnegie Class: Assoc/Pub-U-MC
FAX Number: (719) 502-2201 Calendar System: Semester
URL: www.ppcc.edu
Established: 1968 Annual Undergrad Tuition & Fees (In-State): $6,448
Enrollment: 15,149 Coed
Affiliation or Control: State IRS Status: 501(c)3
Highest Offering: Associate Degree
Program: Occupational; 2-Year Principally Bachelor's Creditable
Accreditation: NH, ACFEI, ADNUR, DA, EMT

01 President .... Dr. Lance BOLTON
04 Exec Assistant to the President .... Ms. Kimberly BARNETT
05 Vice Pres Instructional Services .... Ms. Cindy BUCKLEY
88 Vice President Student Success .... Mr. Felix M. LOPEZ
10 Vice Pres Administrative Services .... Ms. Brenda LAUER
32 Vice Pres Enrollment Services .... Dr. Randy WEBER
20 Asst to VP Instructional Services .... Ms. Julie HAZEL
84 Director Enrollment Services .... Mr. Jeff HORNER
37 Director of Financial Aid .... Mr. Ronald SWARTWOOD
08 Director of Libraries .... Ms. Carole OLDS
16 Exec Dir of Human Resource Services .... Mr. Carlton BROOKS
26 Exec Dir Marketing/Communications .... Ms. Allison SWICKARD
21 Director of Business Svcs .... Ms. Eileen HOGUE
06 Registrar .... Ms. Twila HUMPHREY
102 Exec Dir Found/Res/Cmty Development .... Ms. Sue FENSKE
18 Dir Facilities/Maintenance/Opers .... Mr. Bob LUND
13 Director Information Technology .... Mr. Cyrille PARENT
19 Director Public Safety .... Mr. Jim BARRENTINE
88 Director Student Support Services .... Mr. Edmond QUESADA
88 Dir Military & Veteran Programs .... Ms. Cheri ARFSTEN
76 Dean Health and Science .... Ms. Mary NIFONG
81 Dean Mathematics & English .... Ms. Carol JONAS-MORRISON
50 Dean Business//Public Service/SS .... Ms. Bree LANGEMO
60 Dean Comm/Humanities/Tech Studies .... Ms. Fran HETRICK
36 Dir of Career Planning & Advising .... Mr. Lincoln WULF
35 Dean of Students .... Ms. Jennifer SENGENBERGER
96 Director of Purchasing .... Ms. Rockie HURRELL
38 Director Student Counseling .... Ms. Yolanda HARRIS
88 Dean of High School Programs .... Ms. Chelsy HARRIS
09 Director of Institutional Research .... Dr. Patrica DIWARA

Pima Medical Institute (B)

13750 E. Mississippi Ave, Aurora CO 80012
County: Arapahoe FICE Identification: 041771
Unit ID: 461689
Telephone: (303) 368-7462 Carnegie Class: Not Classified
FAX Number: N/A Calendar System: Other
URL: pmi.edu
Established: 2012 Annual Undergrad Tuition & Fees: $17,467
Enrollment: 17 Coed
Affiliation or Control: Proprietary IRS Status: Proprietary
Highest Offering: Associate Degree
Program: Occupational
Accreditation: ABHES

01 Campus Director .... Mr. Michael BEATY

Pima Medical Institute-Colorado Springs (C)

3770 Citadel Drive North, Colorado Springs CO 80909
Telephone: (719) 482-7462 Identification: 770516
Accreditation: ABHES

† Main campus is Pima Medical Institute-Tucson in Tucson, AZ.

Pima Medical Institute-Denver (D)

7475 Dakin Street, Westminster CO 80221
Telephone: (303) 426-1800 Identification: 666171
Accreditation: ABHES, COARC, OTA, PTAA, RAD

† Main campus is Pima Medical Institute-Tucson in Tucson, AZ.

Platt College (E)

3100 S Parker Road, Suite 200, Aurora CO 80014-3141
County: Arapahoe FICE Identification: 030149
Unit ID: 260813
Telephone: (303) 369-5151 Carnegie Class: Bac/Diverse
FAX Number: (303) 745-1433 Calendar System: Quarter
URL: www.plattcolorado.edu
Established: 1986 Annual Undergrad Tuition & Fees: $19,320
Enrollment: 205 Coed
Affiliation or Control: Proprietary IRS Status: Proprietary
Highest Offering: Baccalaureate
Program: Nursing Emphasis
Accreditation: ACCSC, NUR

01 President/CEO .... Mr. Jerald B. SIRBU
05 Vice President of Academic Affairs .... Dr. Julie BASLER
10 Director of Financial Services .... Mr. Robert CRAVER
37 Director of Financial Aid/Registrar .... Ms. Margie ROSE
08 Head Librarian .... Ms. Laura CULLERTON
66 Dean College of Nursing .... Mr. Glenn RAUP
66 Dean of Nursing Program .... Ms. Hollie CALDWELL

Prince Institute-Rocky Mountains (F)

9051 Harlan Street, Suite 20, Westminster CO 80030-2901
County: Jefferson FICE Identification: 021887
Unit ID: 126924
Telephone: (303) 427-5292 Carnegie Class: Assoc/PrivFP
FAX Number: (303) 427-5383 Calendar System: Quarter
URL: www.princeinstitute.edu
Established: 1976 Annual Undergrad Tuition & Fees: $9,285
Enrollment: 35 Coed
Affiliation or Control: Proprietary IRS Status: Proprietary
Highest Offering: Associate Degree
Program: Occupational; Technical Emphasis
Accreditation: ACICS

01 Acting Campus Director .... Mr. Bale MEYER

Pueblo Community College (G)

900 W Orman Avenue, Pueblo CO 81004-1499
County: Pueblo FICE Identification: 021163
Unit ID: 127884
Telephone: (719) 549-3200 Carnegie Class: Assoc/Pub-R-L
FAX Number: (719) 544-1179 Calendar System: Semester
URL: www.pueblocc.edu
Established: 1933 Annual Undergrad Tuition & Fees (In-State): $3,910
Enrollment: 7,432 Coed
Affiliation or Control: State IRS Status: 501(c)3
Highest Offering: Associate Degree
Program: Occupational; 2-Year Principally Bachelor's Creditable; Business Emphasis
Accreditation: NH, ACFEI, ADNUR, COARC, DA, DH, EMT, OTA, PNUR, POLYT, #PTAA

01 President .... Ms. Patricia ERJAVEC
10 Vice Pres Administration & Finance .... Ms. Colleen ARMSTRONG
05 Vice Pres of Learning .... Ms. Laura SOLANO
32 Dean of Student Services .... Ms. Carriann MARTINEZ
12 Dean SWCCC Campus .... Mr. Norm JONES
12 Dean Fremont Campus .... Mr. Sterling JENKINS
12 Dean of SCCC East Campus .... Dr. Lynn URBAN
12 Dean of SCCC West Campus .... Ms. Shannon SOUTH
76 Dean Health & Public Safety .... Ms. Mary CHAVEZ
49 Exec Dean/Dean of Arts & Science .... Dr. Lana CARTER
50 Dean of Business & Technology .... Dr. Jennifer SHERMAN
31 Dean of Community Educ & Training .... Ms. Juanita FUENTES
102 Exec Dir of PCC Foundation .... Ms. Diane PORTER
07 Director Admissions & Records .... Ms. Maija KURTZ
21 Controller .... Ms. Gayle PETTINARI
37 Director Financial Aid .... Mr. Ron SWARTWOOD
15 Director Human Resources .... Mr. Ken NUFER
13 Director of Computer Services .... Mr. Bryan CRAWFORD
18 Director Facility Svcs/Capital Plng .... Mr. Clifford KITCHEN
35 Director Student Activities/Col Ctr .... Mr. Joel ZARR
38 Director Learning Center .... Mr. Ross BARNHART
08 Director Library Services .... Ms. Jeanne W. GARDNER
27 Dir Communications/Community Rels .... Ms. Erin HERGERT
36 Director of Career & Counseling .... Mr. Dennis JOHNSON
84 Director of Recruitment .... Ms. Carriann MARTINEZ
06 Registrar .... Ms. Maija KURTZ
09 Dir Institutional Research/Accred .... Dr. Patricia DIAWARA
96 Purchasing Agent .... Ms. Leanne CORSENTINO
26 Director Marketing/Communications .... Ms. Erin HERGERT
103 Exec Dir Economic & Workforce Devel .... Mr. John VUKICH
88 Director of Academic Advising .... Mr. Gage MICHAEL

Pueblo Community College Fremont Campus (H)

51320 W Highway 50, Canon City CO 81212
Telephone: (719) 296-6100 Identification: 770042
Accreditation: &NH

† Main campus is Pueblo Community College in Pueblo, CO.

Red Rocks Community College (I)

13300 W Sixth Avenue, Lakewood CO 80228-1255
County: Jefferson FICE Identification: 009543
Unit ID: 127909
Telephone: (303) 914-6600 Carnegie Class: Assoc/Pub-S-MC
FAX Number: (303) 914-6666 Calendar System: Semester
URL: www.rrcc.edu
Established: 1969 Annual Undergrad Tuition & Fees (In-State): $3,446
Enrollment: 9,028 Coed
Affiliation or Control: State IRS Status: 501(c)3
Highest Offering: Associate Degree
Program: Occupational; 2-Year Principally Bachelor's Creditable
Accreditation: NH, ARCPA, MAC, RAD

01 President .... Dr. Michele HANEY
04 Assistant to the President .... Ms. Kathy SCHISSLER
11 Vice Pres Administrative Services .... Ms. Peggy MORGAN
05 Vice President Instruction .... Mr. Bob RIZZUTO
32 Vice Pres Stdnt Svc/Enrollment Mgt .... Vacant
35 Vice Pres Student Success .... Dr. Lisa FOWLER
103 Vice Pres Workforce/Community Devel .... Ms. Colleen JORGENSEN
20 Dean Support Learning Svcs .... Ms. Marilyn SMITH
20 Dean .... Mr. Rick REEVES
13 Dean Technology CTE .... Mr. Bill MCGREEVY
88 Dean of Instruct/Exec Dir RMEC-OSHA .... Ms. Joan SMITH
85 Director International Education .... Ms. Linda YAZDANI
07 Dir Student Recruit/Advising/Admiss .... Ms. Nancy CARLSON
21 Controller .... Ms. Kathy KAOUDIS
37 Director Financial Aid .... Ms. Linda CROOK
06 Registrar Enrollment Services .... Dr. Dean RATHE
18 Director Facilities .... Mr. Mark BANA
15 Director Human Resources .... Mr. Bill DIAL
102 Exec Director RRCC Foundation .... Mr. Ron SLINGER
27 Director Marketing/Communications .... Ms. Kim REIN
35 Director Student Activities .... Ms. Carolyn MATTERN
88 Dir Childhood Ed & Support Svcs .... Vacant
09 Director Institutional Research .... Mr. Andrew STEVENS
28 Director of Diversity & Inclusion .... Ms. Jennifer MACKEN
96 Coordinator Purchasing .... Ms. Renee ARCHULETA

Red Rocks Community College Arvada Campus (J)

5420 Miller Street, Arvada CO 80002
Telephone: (303) 914-6010 Identification: 770045
Accreditation: &NH

† Main campus is Red Rocks Community College in Lakewood, CO.

Redstone College (K)

10851 W 120th Avenue, Broomfield CO 80021-3401
County: Broomfield FICE Identification: 007297
Unit ID: 126605
Telephone: (303) 466-1714 Carnegie Class: Assoc/PrivFP
FAX Number: (303) 469-3797 Calendar System: Other
URL: www.redstone.edu
Established: 1965 Annual Undergrad Tuition & Fees: $14,094
Enrollment: 651 Coed
Affiliation or Control: Proprietary IRS Status: Proprietary
Highest Offering: Associate Degree
Program: Occupational
Accreditation: ACICS

01 Campus President .... Mr. Glen WILSON
05 Campus Academic Dean .... Mr. Tim GUERRERO
07 Senior Director of Admissions .... Ms. Cate CLARK
11 Director of Campus Operations .... Ms. Kim STROMIRE
06 Senior Registrar .... Ms. Vicki MIDDEKER

Redstone College-Denver East (L)

7350 N Broadway, Denver CO 80221
Telephone: (303) 426-7000 Identification: 770611
Accreditation: ACICS

† Main campus is Redstone College in Broomfield, CO.

Regis University (M)

3333 Regis Boulevard, Denver CO 80221-1099
County: Denver FICE Identification: 001363
Unit ID: 127918
Telephone: (303) 458-4100 Carnegie Class: Master's L
FAX Number: (303) 458-4921 Calendar System: Semester
URL: www.regis.edu
Established: 1877 Annual Undergrad Tuition & Fees: $32,424
Enrollment: 10,683 Coed
Affiliation or Control: Roman Catholic IRS Status: 501(c)3
Highest Offering: Doctorate
Program: Liberal Arts And General; Teacher Preparatory; Professional
Accreditation: NH, CACREP, CS, MFCD, NURSE, PHAR, PTA, TEAC

01 President .... Rev. John FITZGIBBONS
43 Legal Counsel .... Ms. Karen WEBBER
05 Provost .... Dr. Patricia A. LADEWIG
30 Vice President University Relations .... Ms. Julie A. CROCKETT
11 Vice President Administration .... Ms. Karen B. WEBBER
32 Vice President Mission .... Dr. Thomas E. REYNOLDS
10 Vice President/CFO .... Mr. Chuck DAHLMAN
26 Chief Marketing Officer/Assoc VP .... Dr. Soon Beng YEAP
84 Assoc VP Enrollment Services .... Mr. Bill HATHAWAY-CLARK
88 Assoc VP University Services .... Ms. Susan LAYTON
15 Assoc VP Human Resources .... Mr. Tony L. CROW
18 Assoc VP Physical Plant .... Mr. Michael J. REDMOND
20 Asst VP Academic Affairs .... Mr. Steve JACOBS
28 Asst VP for Diversity .... Ms. Sandra L. MITCHELL
26 Asst VP University Relations .... Ms. Marycate LUMPP
29 Exec Asst VP Alumni Engagement Pgms .... Ms. Sarah BEHUNEK
27 Interim Chief Information Officer .... Mr. Jaganmohan GUDUR
107 Dean Professional Studies .... Dr. Roxanne GONZALES
76 Dean Health Professions .... Dr. Janet HOUSER
49 Dean of Regis College .... Dr. Paul D. EWALD
08 Dean of Libraries .... Dr. Janet LEE
35 Dean of Students .... Ms. Diane M. MCSHEEHY
07 Director of Admissions .... Ms. Kathy RANK

88 Dir RHCHP/RC Admiss & Stdnt Op .... Ms. Kim FRISCH
37 Director Financial Aid .... Ms. Elinor MILLER
06 Director Registration .... Ms. Cathy GORRELL
06 Director Academic Records .... Ms. Terry GAURMER
38 Director Personal Counseling .... Dr. Chaney GIVENS
19 Director of Campus Safety .... Mr. William T. WILLIAMS
25 Director Academic Grants .... Mr. Donald BRIDGER
42 Director of University Ministry . Ms. Kristi GONSALVES-MCCABE
36 Director of Career Services .... Mr. Richard DELLIVENERI
41 Director Athletics .... Ms. Ann MARTIN

Remington College-Colorado Springs (A)

6050 Erin Park Drive, Suite 250,
Colorado Springs CO 80918
County: El Paso FICE Identification: 030121
Unit ID: 381741
Telephone: (719) 532-1234 Carnegie Class: Bac/Assoc
FAX Number: (719) 264-1234 Calendar System: Quarter
URL: www.remingtoncollege.edu
Established: Annual Undergrad Tuition & Fees: $14,695
Enrollment: 105 Coed
Affiliation or Control: Independent Non-Profit IRS Status: 501(c)3
Highest Offering: Associate Degree
Program: Occupational
Accreditation: ACICS

01 Campus Director .... Ms. Shirley MCCROY

† Closing January 31, 2014.

Rocky Mountain College of Art & Design (B)

1600 Pierce Street, Lakewood CO 80214-1433
County: Denver FICE Identification: 007649
Unit ID: 127945
Telephone: (303) 753-6046 Carnegie Class: Spec/Arts
FAX Number: (303) 759-4970 Calendar System: Semester
URL: www.rmcad.edu
Established: 1963 Annual Undergrad Tuition & Fees: $21,720
Enrollment: 646 Coed
Affiliation or Control: Proprietary IRS Status: Proprietary
Highest Offering: Master's
Program: Fine Arts Emphasis
Accreditation: NH, ART, CIDA

01 President .... Dr. Maria PUZZIFERRO
88 President of Strategic Development .... Mr. Jim CHRISTIAN
11 VP of Operations .... Mr. Chris MINCHEFF
10 Senior Director of Finance .... Mr. Dave STEWART
07 Director of Admissions .... Mr. Dave HOBLICK
37 Director of Financial Aid .... Ms. Tammy DYBDAHL
05 Dean of Academic Affairs .... Dr. Kiki GILDERHUS
09 Dir Institutional Effectiveness .... Dr. Stephanie FUENTES
15 Director of Human Resources .... Ms. Carrie BRANCHEAU
32 Director of Student Life .... Ms. Emily DMOHOWSKI
35 Director of Student Affairs .... Mr. Yves NAVANT
08 Library Director .... Mr. Hugh THURLOW
06 Registrar .... Mr. Chuck KING
21 Controller .... Ms. Becky SKOUGSTAD

Rocky Vista University (C)

8401 South Chambers Road, Parker CO 80134
County: Douglas Identification: 667002
Telephone: (303) 373-2008 Carnegie Class: Not Classified
FAX Number: N/A Calendar System: Other
URL: www.rvu.edu
Established: 2006 Annual Graduate Tuition & Fees: $46,922
Enrollment: 617 Coed
Affiliation or Control: Proprietary IRS Status: Proprietary
Highest Offering: Doctorate; No Undergraduates
Program: Professional
Accreditation: @NH, OSTEO

01 President .... Dr. Cheryl LOVELL
05 Dean/CAO .... Dr. Bruce DUBIN
20 Vice Dean .... Dr. Thomas MOHR
20 Sr Assoc Dean of Academic Affairs .... Dr. Stephen PUTTHOFF
10 Chief Operating Officer/CFO .... Mr. Peter FREYTAG
06 Registrar .... Ms. Linda CAIRNS

St. John Vianney Theological Seminary (D)

1300 S Steele Street, Denver CO 80210-2526
County: Denver Identification: 666127
Telephone: (303) 282-3427 Carnegie Class: Not Classified
FAX Number: (303) 282-3453 Calendar System: Semester
URL: www.sjvdenver.org
Established: 1999 Annual Graduate Tuition & Fees: $28,567
Enrollment: 130 Male
Affiliation or Control: Roman Catholic IRS Status: 501(c)3
Highest Offering: Master's; No Undergraduates
Program: Professional; Religious Emphasis
Accreditation: THEOL

01 Rector .... Msgr. Michael GLENN
03 Vice Rector .... Rev. Jorge RODRIGUEZ
05 Academic Dean .... Rev. Andreas HOECK
06 Registrar .... Dr. Richard NEYENS

Southwest Acupuncture College (E)

6630 Gunpark Drive Suite 200, Boulder CO 80301-3339
Telephone: (303) 581-9955 Identification: 666618
Accreditation: ACUP

† Main campus is Southwest Acupuncture College in Santa Fe, NM.

Southwest Colorado Community College-East (F)

701 Camino del Rio, Durango CO 81301
Telephone: (970) 247-2929 Identification: 770043
Accreditation: &NH

† Main campus is Pueblo Community College in Pueblo, CO.

Southwest Colorado Community College-West (G)

33057 Highway 160, Mancus CO 81328
Telephone: (970) 564-6200 Identification: 770044
Accreditation: &NH

† Main campus is Pueblo Community College in Pueblo, CO.

Trinidad State Junior College (H)

600 Prospect, Trinidad CO 81082-2396
County: Las Animas FICE Identification: 001368
Unit ID: 128258
Telephone: (719) 846-5621 Carnegie Class: Assoc/Pub-R-M
FAX Number: (719) 846-5667 Calendar System: Semester
URL: www.trinidadstate.edu
Established: 1925 Annual Undergrad Tuition & Fees (In-State): $4,200
Enrollment: 1,714 Coed
Affiliation or Control: State IRS Status: 501(c)3
Highest Offering: Associate Degree
Program: Occupational; 2-Year Principally Bachelor's Creditable
Accreditation: NH, ENGR

01 President .... Dr. Carmen M. SIMONE
05 Vice President of Academic Affairs .... Dr. Paula DAVIS
11 Vice President Administrative Svcs .... Mr. Michael JOLLY
12 Assoc Vice President/Alamosa Campus .... Vacant
32 VP Stdnt Affairs & Sponsored Pgm .... Ms. Kerry GABRIELSON
49 Dean Arts & Sciences .... Ms. Debbie ULIBARRI
20 Associate Dean of Instruction .... Ms. Bonnie ORTEGA
35 Associate Dean Student Services VC .... Mr. Robert MARTINEZ
30 Director of Devel/College Relations .... Ms. Toni DEANGELIS
15 Human Resources Director .... Ms. Lorrie VELASQUEZ
37 Director Financial Aid .... Ms. Wilma ATENCIO
06 Registrar/Institutional Research .... Ms. Annette LUJAN
07 Admission/Recruitment Specialist .... Vacant
18 Director Facilities/Physical Plant .... Mr. Louis MANTELLI
10 Controller .... Ms. Juanita PENA
32 Dir Stdnt Spprt Svcs/Advisory Coord .... Vacant
14 Distance Lrng/Audio Visual Coord .... Mr. Doug BAK
08 Library Resource Manager .... Mr. Wayne RIVERA
35 Coordinator of Student Life .... Vacant

Trinidad State Junior College San Luis Valley Campus (I)

1011 Main Street, Alamusa CO 81101
Telephone: (719) 589-7000 Identification: 770047
Accreditation: &NH

† Main campus is Trinidad State Junior College in Trinidad, CO.

UCH Memorial Hospital School Of Radiologic Technology (J)

1400 East Boulder Street, Colorado Springs CO 80909
County: El Paso Identification: 667097
Telephone: (719) 365-8291 Carnegie Class: Not Classified
FAX Number: N/A Calendar System: Semester
URL: www.uchealth.org
Established: 1969 Annual Undergrad Tuition & Fees: $6,000
Enrollment: 36 Coed
Affiliation or Control: Independent Non-Profit IRS Status: 501(c)3
Highest Offering: Associate Degree
Program: Occupational
Accreditation: RAD

01 Director .... Elaine R. IVAN

*University of Colorado System Office (K)

1800 Grant Street, Suite 800, Denver CO 80203
County: Denver FICE Identification: 007996
Unit ID: 128300
Telephone: (303) 860-5600 Carnegie Class: N/A
FAX Number: (303) 860-5610
URL: www.cu.edu

01 President .... Mr. Bruce D. BENSON
05 Assoc VP & Academic Affairs Officer .... Dr. Kathleen BOLLARD
100 Senior VP & Chief of Staff .... Mr. Leonard DINEGAR
10 VP & Chief Financial Officer .... Mr. Todd SALIMAN
43 VP University Counsel/Secy Board .... Mr. Pat O'ROURKE
16 Sr AVP/Chief Human Resource Ofcr .... Ms. Jill POLLOCK
86 VP Government Relations .... Ms. Tanya KELLY-BOWRY
26 Assoc VP University Relations .... Mr. Ken MCCONNELLOGUE
21 Asst VP & University Controller .... Mr. Robert KUEHLER
13 Asst VP & Chief Information Ofcr .... Mr. Robert WEIR
31 Dir Business & Community Relations .... Ms. Elizabeth COLLINS

*University of Colorado Boulder (L)

Boulder CO 80309-0001
County: Boulder FICE Identification: 001370
Unit ID: 126614
Telephone: (303) 492-1411 Carnegie Class: RU/VH
FAX Number: N/A Calendar System: Semester
URL: www.colorado.edu
Established: 1876 Annual Undergrad Tuition & Fees (In-State): $10,240
Enrollment: 29,278 Coed
Affiliation or Control: State IRS Status: 501(c)3
Highest Offering: Doctorate
Program: Liberal Arts And General; Teacher Preparatory; Professional
Accreditation: NH, AUD, BUS, CEA, CLPSY, CS, ENG, IPSY, JOUR, LAW, MUS, SP, TED

02 Chancellor .... Dr. Phillip P. DISTEFANO
05 Provost & Exec Vice Chancellor .... Dr. Russell MOORE
10 Sr Vice Chanc Budget & Finance .... Ms. Kelly L. FOX
46 Vice Chancellor for Research .... Dr. Stein STURE
11 Vice Chanc Administration .... Ms. Louise VALE
32 Vice Chanc Student Affairs .... Ms. Deborah J. COFFIN
28 Vice Chanc for Diversity/Equity .... Dr. Robert BOSWELL
26 Vice Chanc for Strategic Relations .... Ms. Frances DRAPER
21 Assc VC Budget & Finance/Controller .... Mr. Steven L. MCNALLY
13 Assoc VC & Chief Information Offcr .... Dr. Lawrence M. LEVINE
100 Chief of Staff .... Ms. Catherine SHEA
30 Vice President for Development .... Ms. Carolyn WHITEHEAD
29 Exec Director for Alumni Relations .... Dr. Ron W. STUMP
58 Dean of the Graduate School .... Dr. John A. STEVENSON
61 Dean of Law .... Dr. Philip J. WEISER
49 Dean of Arts & Science .... Dr. Steven R. LEIGH
54 Dean of Engineering .... Dr. Robert H. DAVIS
50 Dean of Business .... Dr. David L. IKENBERRY
53 Dean of Education .... Dr. Lorrie SHEPARD
64 Dean of Music .... Vacant
60 Dir Journalism/Mass Communication ... Dr. Christopher BRAIDER
51 Dean Continuing Ed & Prof Studies .... Ms. Anne K. HEINZ
62 Dean of Libraries .... Mr. James F. WILLIAMS
35 Dean of Students .... Ms. Christina GONZALES
37 Director of Financial Aid .... Ms. Gwen E. POMPER
07 Director of Admissions .... Mr. Kevin L. MACLENNAN
06 Registrar .... Ms. Barbara J. TODD
09 Int Dir of Institutional Research .... Mr. Robert STUBBS
25 Director of Contracts Grants .... Mr. Randall W. DRAPER
15 Asst Vice Chanc of Human Resources .... Ms. Candice BOWEN
41 Interim Athletic Director .... Ms. Ceal R. BARRY
19 Director of Public Safety .... Mr. Joe E. ROY, II
23 Director of Student Health Center .... Dr. Donald MISCH
36 Director of Career Services .... Dr. Lisa E. SEVERY
88 Director of Museum .... Dr. Patrick KOCIOLEK

*University of Colorado Colorado Springs (M)

1420 Austin Bluffs Parkway, Colorado Springs CO 80918
County: El Paso FICE Identification: 004509
Unit ID: 126580
Telephone: (719) 255-8227 Carnegie Class: Master's L
FAX Number: (719) 255-3362 Calendar System: Semester
URL: www.uccs.edu
Established: 1965 Annual Undergrad Tuition & Fees (In-State): $8,658
Enrollment: 8,238 Coed
Affiliation or Control: State IRS Status: 501(c)3
Highest Offering: Doctorate
Program: Liberal Arts And General; Teacher Preparatory; Professional
Accreditation: NH, BUS, CACREP, CLPSY, CS, DIETD, ENG, NURSE, TED

02 Chancellor .... Dr. Pam SHOCKLEY-ZALABAK
05 Provost .... Dr. Mary COUSSONS-READ
10 Exec Chanc Administration & Finance .... Dr. Brian BURNETT
11 Vice Chanc Admin & Finance .... Susan SZPYRKA
32 Vice Chanc Student Success .... Dr. Homer A. WESLEY, III
30 Vice Chanc Univ Advancement .... Martin WOOD
20 Sr Vice Chanc Academic Affairs .... Dr. David MOON
43 Legal Counsel .... Vacant
25 Director of Sponsored Programs .... Gwen GENNARO
08 Dean of Library .... Teri SWITZER
84 Dir of Enrollment Mgmt/Registrar .... Matthew COX
09 Director of Institutional Research .... Dr. Robyn MARSCHKE
15 Human Resources .... Vacant
19 Director of Public Safety .... Brian MCPIKE
29 Director Alumni & Community Rels .... Jennifer HANE
37 Director Finan Aid/Stdnt Employment .... Jevita ROGERS
40 Manager of Bookstore .... Jason VOTRUBA
18 Chief Facilities/Physical Plant .... Gary REYNOLDS
26 Director Media Relations .... Tom HUTTON
38 Director Student Counseling .... Dr. Z. Benek ALTAYLI
41 Director of Athletics .... Stephen W. KIRKHAM
13 Director of Information Technology .... Jerry WILSON

21 Director Resource Management ... Gayanne SCOTT
49 Dean of Letters/Arts/Science ... Dr. Peter BRAZA
50 Dean of Business ... Dr. Venkateshwar REDDY
53 Dean of Education ... Dr. Mary SNYDER
54 Dean of Engineering/Applied Science ... Dr. Ramaswami DANDAPANI
80 Assoc Dean of Public Affairs ... Dr. Terry SCHWARTZ
66 Dean Nursing/Health Sciences ... Dr. Nancy SMITH
58 Dean of Graduate School ... Dr. Kelli KLEBE
28 Assoc Vice Chancellor Diversity ... Dr. Kee WARNER
39 Director Campus Housing ... Ralph GIESE
88 Director of Sustainability ... Linda KOGAN
06 Registrar ... Tracy BARBER

*University of Colorado Denver|Anschutz Medical Campus (A)

1250 14th Street, Denver CO 80204
County: Denver — FICE Identification: 004508
Unit ID: 126562
Telephone: (303) 556-2400 — Carnegie Class: RU/H
FAX Number: N/A — Calendar System: Semester
URL: www.ucdenver.edu
Established: 1912 — Annual Undergrad Tuition & Fees (In-State): $7,494
Enrollment: 18,033 — Coed
Affiliation or Control: State — IRS Status: 501(c)3
Highest Offering: Doctorate
Program: Liberal Arts And General; Teacher Preparatory; Professional
Accreditation: NH, AA, ARCPA, BUS, BUSA, CACREP, CS, DENT, DMS, ENG, HSA, IPSY, LSAR, MED, MIDWF, MUS, NURSE, PH, PHAR, PLNG, PTA, SPAA, TED

02 Chancellor ... Dr. Don ELLIMAN
03 VP Health Affairs/Exec VC AMC ... Ms. Lilly MARKS
10 Vice Chancellor Admin/Finance ... Mr. Jeffrey PARKER
46 Vice Chancellor for Research ... Dr. Richard TRAYSTMAN
17 VC Health Affairs/Dean of Medicine ... Dr. Richard D. KRUGMAN
26 VC of Mkting & Community Engagement ... Ms. Leanna CLARK
05 Provost & VC Academic/Student Affs ... Dr. Roderick NAIRN
52 Dean School of Dental Medicine ... Dr. Denise KASSEBAUM
66 Dean College of Nursing ... Dr. Sarah THOMPSON
67 Dean School of Pharmacy ... Dr. Ralph ALTIERE
69 Dean CO School of Public Health ... Dr. David GOFF
58 Dean Graduate School ... Dr. Barry SHUR
64 Dean College of Arts and Media ... Dr. Laura GOODWIN
80 Dean School of Pubilc Affairs ... Dr. Paul TESKE
49 Dean College of Liberal Arts & Sci ... Dr. Dan J. HOWARD
48 Dean College of Arch/Planning ... Mr. Mark GELERNTER
50 Dean Business School ... Ms. Sueann AMBRON
53 Dean School of Education ... Dr. Rebecca KANTOR
54 Dean College of Engineering ... Dr. Marc INGBER
46 Assoc VC for Research ... Dr. Mary COUSSONS-READ
20 Assoc VC Academic Affairs ... Dr. Laura GOODWIN
32 Assoc VC Student Affairs ... Dr. Raul CARDENAS
21 Assoc VC Budget/Finance ... Ms. Lisa DOUGLAS
18 Assoc VC Facilities Management ... Mr. David C. TURNQUIST
15 Asst VC Human Resources ... Mr. Kevin JACOBS
13 Asst VC Information Technology Svcs ... Mr. Russell POOLE
88 Asst VC Academic Tech/Extd Learning ... Mr. Robert TOLSMA
84 Asst VC Enrollment Management ... Mr. Chris DOWEN
09 Asst VC Institutional Research ... Dr. Christine STROUP-BENHAM
88 Asst VC Student Success ... Ms. Peggy LORE
35 Asst VC Univ Life/Dean of Students ... Dr. Khushnur DADABHOY
06 Registrar ... Ms. Ingrid ESCHHOLZ
28 Director Diversity/Inclusion ... Mr. Dominic MARTINEZ
08 Director Auraria Library ... Dr. Mary SOMERVILLE
08 Director Health Sciences Library ... Mr. Jerry PERRY
26 Director PR/Media Relations ... Ms. Jacque MONTGOMERY
37 Director Financial Aid Svcs ... Mr. James BROSCHEIT
19 Chief of Police ... Mr. Doug ABRAHAM
29 Director Alumni Relations ... Ms. Joy FRENCH
43 Assistant University Counsel ... Mr. Christopher PUCKETT

University of Denver (B)

2199 S. University Blvd., Denver CO 80208-0001
County: Denver — FICE Identification: 001371
Unit ID: 127060
Telephone: (303) 871-2000 — Carnegie Class: RU/H
FAX Number: (303) 871-3301 — Calendar System: Quarter
URL: www.du.edu
Established: 1864 — Annual Undergrad Tuition & Fees: $40,707
Enrollment: 11,656 — Coed
Affiliation or Control: Independent Non-Profit — IRS Status: 501(c)3
Highest Offering: Doctorate
Program: Liberal Arts And General; Teacher Preparatory; Professional
Accreditation: NH, ART, BUS, BUSA, CEA, CLPSY, COPSY, ENG, IPSY, LAW, LIB, MUS, SW

01 Chancellor ... Dr. Robert D. COOMBE
54 Dean Engineering/Comp Science ... Dr. Mike KEABLES
05 Provost ... Dr. Gregg O. KVISTAD
43 University Counsel ... Mr. Paul H. CHAN
10 Vice Chanc Business/Financial Affs ... Mr. Craig WOODY
41 Vice Chanc Athletics and Recreation ... Ms. Peg BRADLEY-DOPPES
30 Vice Chanc University Advancement ... Mr. Scott R. LUMPKIN
26 Vice Chancellor Communications ... Mr. Kevin CARROLL
13 VC Technology/Chief Tech Officer ... Mr. Tim BROOKS
84 Vice Chancellor for Enrollment ... Mr. Thomas WILLOUGHBY
37 Director of Financial Aid ... Mr. Chris GEORGE
04 Assistant to the Chancellor ... Ms. Claire BROWNELL
20 Associate Provost Academic Program ... Dr. Jennifer KARAS
32 Assoc Provost Student Life ... Dr. Patti HELTON
28 Assoc Provost Multicult Excellence ... Dr. Frank TUITT
58 Vice Provost Graduate Studies ... Dr. Barbara WILCOTS
08 Dean Libraries ... Ms. Nancy T. ALLEN
34 Dean Colorado Women's College ... Dr. Lynn GANGONE
45 Associate Provost Planning/Budget ... Ms. Julia MCGAHEY
102 Assc Vice Chanc Annual Giving/Found ... Ms. Kristine CECIL
44 Assoc Vice Chanc Major Gifts ... Mr. Mike MCCALL
06 Registrar ... Mr. Dennis M. BECKER
21 Controller/Assistant Treasurer ... Ms. Margaret HENRY
36 Director Career Center ... Ms. Mary M. HAWKINS
22 EO/ADA Compliance Director ... Ms. Kathryne GROVE
18 Director Facilities Management ... Mr. Jeff BEMELEN
09 Director Institutional Research ... Dr. Gina JOHNSON
15 Director Human Resources ... Ms. Amy KING
19 Director Campus Safety ... Mr. Donald ENLOE
88 Dir Student Financial Services ... Ms. Janet BURKHARDT
88 Asst Vice Chanc Enterprise Services ... Ms. Susan LUTZ
23 Dir of Univ Health Services ... Mr. Chris WERA
79 Interim Dean Arts/Hum/Soc Science ... Dr. Rob ROBERTS
81 Dean Natural Science/Math ... Dr. Andrei KUTATELADZE
50 Interim Dean College of Business ... Dr. Charles H. PATTI
61 Dean College of Law ... Mr. Martin J. KATZ
82 Dean Graduate Sch Intl Studies ... Mr. Christopher R. HILL
70 Dean Graduate Sch Social Work ... Dr. James WILLIAMS
55 Interim Dean University College ... Mr. Michael MCGUIRE
53 Interim Dean College of Education ... Dr. Karen RILEY
64 Director Lamont School of Music ... Ms. Nancy COCHRAN
88 Exec Dir Special Community Programs ... Dr. Cathy GRIEVE
57 Director School of Art/Art History ... Dr. Sarah GJERTSON
07 Director of Enrollment Services ... Ms. Anne GROSS
35 Exec Dir of Campus Life ... Mr. Carl JOHNSON

University of Northern Colorado (C)

501 20th Street, Greeley CO 80639-6900
County: Weld — FICE Identification: 001349
Unit ID: 127741
Telephone: (970) 351-1890 — Carnegie Class: DRU
FAX Number: (970) 351-1880 — Calendar System: Semester
URL: www.unco.edu
Established: 1889 — Annual Undergrad Tuition & Fees (In-State): $6,792
Enrollment: 12,497 — Coed
Affiliation or Control: State — IRS Status: 501(c)3
Highest Offering: Doctorate
Program: Liberal Arts And General; Teacher Preparatory; Professional
Accreditation: NH, ART, AUD, BUS, BUSA, CACREP, CEA, COPSY, CORE, DIETD, DIETI, MUS, NURSE, PH, #SCPSY, SP, TED, THEA

01 President ... Ms. Kay NORTON
05 Provost/Vice Pres Academic Affairs ... Ms. Robbyn WACKER
11 Vice President Administration ... Ms. Michelle QUINN
43 Vice President & University Counsel ... Mr. Dan SATRIANA
26 VP Univ Advancement/Univ Relations ... Mr. Chuck LEONHARDT
30 Vice Pres Development/Alumni Rels ... Ms. Victoria GORRELL
58 Actg Dean Grad School ... Ms. Linda BLACK
20 Ast VP Undergrad Stds/Dean Univ Col ... Dr. Thomas SMITH
10 Asst Vice President Budgets/Analysi ... Ms. Susan SIMMERS
13 Asst VP Information Technology ... Ms. Jeanette VANGALDER
84 Asst Vice Pres for Enrollment Mgmt ... Mr. Tobias GUZMAN
49 Dean Humanities & Social Sciences ... Dr. Michelle BEHR
50 Dean Business Administration ... Dr. Donald GUDMUNDSON
53 Dean Education/Behavorial Sciences ... Dr. Eugene SHEEHAN
76 Actg Dean Natural & Health Sciences ... Dr. Ellen GREGG
57 Dean Performing Visual Arts ... Dr. Leo WELCH
08 Dean University Libraries ... Ms. Helen REED
35 Dean of Students ... Dr. Katrina RODRIGUEZ
102 President University Foundation ... Ms. Cynthia EVANS
06 Registrar ... Mr. Charlie COUCH
07 Director of Admissions ... Dr. Sean M. BROGHAMMER
25 Dir Sponsored Pgms/Academic Res ... Ms. Michele SCHWIETZ
37 Dir Student Financial Resources ... Mr. Marty SOMERO
36 Director of Career Services ... Ms. Renee WELCH
15 Director of Human Resources ... Mr. Marshall PARKS
29 Asst VP Alumni/Donor Relations ... Mr. Matt MANFRA
18 Director Facilities Management ... Mr. Kirk LEICHLITER
41 Director of NCAA Athletics ... Vacant
39 Director of Residence Life ... Ms. Jenna FINLEY
38 Director Student Counseling ... Ms. Kim WILCOX
19 Chief of University Police ... Mr. Dennis PUMPHREY
44 Director of Annual Giving ... Ms. Christina NICHOLS
27 Dir News & Public Relations ... Mr. Nate HAAS
96 Director of Purchasing ... Ms. Cristal SWAIN

University of Phoenix Colorado Main Campus (D)

1000H Park Meadows Drive, Lone Tree CO 80124-5453
Telephone: (303) 755-9090 — Identification: 770195
Accreditation: &NH, ACBSP

† Main campus is University of Phoenix in Tempe, AZ.

University of Phoenix Colorado Springs Main Campus (E)

2 North Cascade Avenue, Suite 100, Colorado Springs CO 80903-1620
Telephone: (719) 527-9000 — Identification: 770194
Accreditation: &NH

† Main campus is University of Phoenix in Tempe, AZ.

University of the Rockies (F)

555 E Pikes Peak Ave, Suite 108, Colorado Springs CO 80903-3612
County: El Paso — FICE Identification: 035453
Unit ID: 441308
Telephone: (719) 442-0505 — Carnegie Class: Spec/Health
FAX Number: (719) 389-0359 — Calendar System: Other
URL: www.rockies.edu
Established: 1998 — Annual Graduate Tuition & Fees: $14,610
Enrollment: 2,015 — Coed
Affiliation or Control: Proprietary — IRS Status: Proprietary
Highest Offering: Doctorate; No Undergraduates
Program: Professional
Accreditation: NH

01 President ... Dr. Charlita SHELTON
03 Vice President/Campus Director ... Dr. Robert EDELBROCK
05 Provost ... Dr. Tina PARSCAL
20 Vice Provost ... Dr. Amy KAHN
88 Director of Academic Services ... Ms. Janet BRUGGER
58 Dean School of Prof Psychology ... Dr. David STEPHENS
106 Dean Sch Organizational Leadership ... Dr. Douglas GILBERT
26 Campus PR/Marketing Specialist ... Vacant
37 Director of Financial Aid ... Ms. Jami FLEMING
15 Director of Human Resources ... Ms. Barbara HENRY-QUINN
06 Registrar ... Ms. Katina JORDAN
28 Director of Diversity ... Ms. Francesca GALARRAGA

U.S. Career Institute (G)

2001 Lowe Street, Fort Collins CO 80525
County: Larimer — Identification: 666776
Telephone: (970) 207-4500 — Carnegie Class: Not Classified
FAX Number: (970) 223-1678 — Calendar System: Other
URL: www.uscareerinstitute.edu
Established: 1981 — Annual Undergrad Tuition & Fees: N/A
Enrollment: N/A — Coed
Affiliation or Control: Proprietary — IRS Status: Proprietary
Highest Offering: Associate Degree
Program: Occupational; Business Emphasis
Accreditation: DETC

01 President ... Ann ROHR
03 Chief Executive Officer ... Cole P. THOMPSON
32 Vice President Student Affairs ... Joyce LINDQUIST
10 Vice President Finance ... Jason STANSBERRY
13 Vice President Information Tech ... Scott LYNCH
05 Director of Education ... Janet PERRY

Western Colorado Community College-Tilman M. Bishop Campus (H)

2508 Blichmann Avenue, Grand Junction CO 81505
Telephone: (970) 255-2600 — Identification: 770030
Accreditation: &NH

† Main campus is Colorado Mesa University in Grand Junction, CO.

Western State Colorado University (I)

600 North Adams, Gunnison CO 81231-0001
County: Gunnison — FICE Identification: 001372
Unit ID: 128391
Telephone: (970) 943-0120 — Carnegie Class: Bac/A&S
FAX Number: (970) 943-7069 — Calendar System: Semester
URL: www.western.edu
Established: 1911 — Annual Undergrad Tuition & Fees (In-State): $7,343
Enrollment: 2,301 — Coed
Affiliation or Control: State — IRS Status: 501(c)3
Highest Offering: Master's
Program: Liberal Arts And General; Teacher Preparatory; Professional
Accreditation: NH, MUS, @TEAC

01 Interim President ... Mr. Brad BACA
05 Interim Vice Pres Academic Affairs ... Dr. Bill NIEMI
10 Interim VP Finance & Administration ... Ms. Julie FEIER
32 Vice President of Student Affairs ... Mr. Gary PIERSON
30 Vice Pres Institutional Advancement ... Mr. Thomas F. BURGGRAF, JR.
20 Assoc Vice Pres Academic Affairs ... Dr. Kevin NELSON
21 Assoc Vice Pres Finance & Admin ... Vacant
07 Director of Admissions ... Mr. Dale GAUBATZ
35 Assoc Vice Pres Student Affairs ... Mr. Chris LUEKENGA
06 Registrar ... Ms. Debra CLARK
37 Director Student Financial Aid ... Mr. Jerry MARTINEZ
104 Dir Intl Student Pgms/Study Abroad ... Ms. Jessica VOGAN
41 Athletic Director ... Dr. R. Greg WAGGONER
15 Director of Human Resources ... Ms. Kim GAILEY
40 Director Retail Operations ... Ms. Teri HAUS
91 Director Administrative Computing ... Mr. Chad ROBINSON
08 Director Library Services ... Ms. Nancy GAUSS
51 Director Extended Studies ... Ms. Erica BOUCHER
39 Director Residence Life ... Mr. Edward KLEIN
36 Director Career Svcs/Internships ... Ms. Svea WHITING
26 Director of Public Relations ... Mr. Brian BARKER
29 Director of Alumni Relations ... Ms. Tonya VANHEE
44 Director Annual & Special Gifts ... Ms. Deb HOSKINS
09 Director Institutional Research ... Mr. Doug DRIVER
18 Chief Facilities/Physical Plant ... Mr. Paul MORGAN
35 Director of Student Affairs ... Vacant

84 Director of Enrollment Management .... Vacant
28 Director of Multicultural Center .... Ms. Sally ROMERO
96 Director of Purchasing .... Ms. Patty LOVE

*Westwood College (A)

7604 Technology Way Suite 400, Denver CO 80237
County: Denver Identification: 667029
Telephone: (303) 846-1700 Carnegie Class: N/A
FAX Number: N/A
URL: www.westwood.edu

01 Chief Executive Officer .... Mr. Dean GOUIN

*Westwood College-Denver North (B)

7350 N Broadway, Denver CO 80221-3653
County: Adams FICE Identification: 007548
Unit ID: 127024
Telephone: (303) 650-5050 Carnegie Class: Bac/Diverse
FAX Number: (303) 426-4647 Calendar System: Other
URL: www.westwood.edu
Established: 1953 Annual Undergrad Tuition & Fees: $14,295
Enrollment: 455 Coed
Affiliation or Control: Proprietary IRS Status: Proprietary
Highest Offering: Baccalaureate
Program: Occupational; Technical Emphasis
Accreditation: **ACICS**

02 Campus President .... Ms. Natalie WILLIAMS

*Westwood College-Denver South (C)

3150 S Sheridan Boulevard, Denver CO 80227-5507
Telephone: (303) 934-1122 Identification: 666512
Accreditation: **ACICS**

† Main campus is Westwood College-Denver North in Denver, CO.

Westwood College-Online (D)

10249 Church Ranch Way, Broomfield CO 80021
Telephone: (720) 887-8888 Identification: 770673
Accreditation: **ACICS**

† Main campus is Westwood College - Los Angeles Campus in Los Angeles, CA.

William Howard Taft University (E)

600 South Cherry Street, Suite 525, Denver CO 80246
County: Denver FICE Identification: 041004
Telephone: (303) 867-1155 Carnegie Class: Not Classified
FAX Number: (303) 867-1156 Calendar System: Other
URL: www.taft.edu
Established: 1976 Annual Undergrad Tuition & Fees: N/A
Enrollment: 60 Coed
Affiliation or Control: Proprietary IRS Status: Proprietary
Highest Offering: Doctorate
Program: Professional
Accreditation: **DETC**

01 President .... Mr. Jerome ALLEY
03 Chief Operating Officer .... Mr. Robert K. STROUSE
11 Director of Administration .... Ms. Christine A. BALDWIN

† Tuition varies by degree program.

Yeshiva Toras Chaim Talmudical Seminary of Denver (F)

1555 Stuart Street, Denver CO 80204
County: Denver Identification: 667113
Unit ID: 128425
Telephone: (303) 629-8200 Carnegie Class: Spec/Faith
FAX Number: (303) 623-5949 Calendar System: Semester
Established: 1967 Annual Undergrad Tuition & Fees: $17,900
Enrollment: 80 Male
Affiliation or Control: Independent Non-Profit IRS Status: 501(c)3
Highest Offering: Second Talmudic Degree
Program: Religious Emphasis
Accreditation: **RABN**

01 President/CEO .... Rabbi Ahron WASSERMAN
00 Board Chair .... H. Michael MILLER
03 Vice President .... Rabbi Aaron KAGAN
30 Dir of Development & Admissions .... Shlomo FISHEROWITZ
33 Dean of Men .... Rabbi Israel KAGAN
40 Events Manager/Bookstore Director .... Sara Gittie NUSSBUAM
10 Business Manager .... Tannis HALEY

CONNECTICUT

Albertus Magnus College (G)

700 Prospect Street, New Haven CT 06511-1189
County: New Haven FICE Identification: 001374
Unit ID: 128498
Telephone: (203) 773-8550 Carnegie Class: Master's L
FAX Number: (203) 773-9539 Calendar System: Semester
URL: www.albertus.edu
Established: 1925 Annual Undergrad Tuition & Fees: $40,485
Enrollment: 1,675 Coed
Affiliation or Control: Independent Non-Profit IRS Status: 501(c)3
Highest Offering: Master's
Program: Liberal Arts And General
Accreditation: **EH**, IACBE

01 President .... Dr. Julia M. MCNAMARA
05 Vice Pres Academic Affairs .... Dr. Sean O'CONNELL
10 Vice President Finance/Treasurer .... Mrs. Jeanne E. MANN
13 VP Information Technology Services .... Mr. Steven GSTALDER
29 VP Development/Alumni Relations .... Ms. Carolyn A. BEHAN KRAUS
32 Dean for Student Services .... Mr. Andrew FOSTER
07 Dean for Admission/Financial Aid .... Mr. Richard J. LOLATTE
35 Asst Dean Campus Activities/Orien .... Ms. Erin MORRELL
06 Registrar .... Mrs. Angela HAGGERTY
08 Director Library/Information Svcs .... Ms. Anne LEENEY-PANAGROSSI
55 Dean for School of New Dimensions .... Dr. Irene RIOS
09 Inst Research & Assessment Analyst .... Dr. Meghan FINLEY
37 Director Financial Aid .... Mrs. Michelle COCHRANE
90 Director Academic Computing .... Mr. Robert HUBBARD
41 Acting Director of Athletics .... Ms. Kristen DECARLI
58 Director MALS Program .... Ms. Julia COASH
89 Director of Freshmen Advising .... Mrs. Corey BRUSHETT
92 Director of Honors Program .... Dr. Christine ATKINS
96 Dir Purchas/Pub Sfty/Spec Projects .... Mr. James A. SCHAFRICK
15 Director Human Resources .... Mrs. Diane L. NUNN
26 Dir Communications/Community Rels .... Ms. Rosanne ZUDEKOFF
36 Director Career Services .... Vacant
42 Director of Campus Ministry .... Sr. Helen KIERAN, OP
18 Supervisor of Facilities Services .... Mr. Edward J. THOMASI, SR.

Beth Benjamin Academy of Connecticut (H)

132 Prospect Street, Stamford CT 06901-1202
County: Fairfield FICE Identification: 029120
Unit ID: 414975
Telephone: (203) 325-4351 Carnegie Class: Not Classified
FAX Number: (203) 323-6073 Calendar System: Trimester
Established: 1976 Annual Undergrad Tuition & Fees: $5,945
Enrollment: 49 Male
Affiliation or Control: Independent Non-Profit IRS Status: 501(c)3
Highest Offering: First Talmudic Degree
Program: Teacher Preparatory; Professional
Accreditation: **RABN**

01 Rosh Hayeshiva .... Rabbi M. HERSHKOWITZ
04 Associate Rosh Hayeshiva .... Rabbi Yeruchom ZEILBERGER
05 Dean .... Rabbi Michael BENDER

Charter Oak State College (I)

55 Paul Manafort Drive, New Britain CT 06053-2142
County: Hartford FICE Identification: 029171
Unit ID: 128780
Telephone: (860) 515-3800 Carnegie Class: Bac/A&S
FAX Number: (860) 606-9615 Calendar System: Other
URL: www.charteroak.edu
Established: 1973 Annual Undergrad Tuition & Fees (In-State): $6,552
Enrollment: 2,240 Coed
Affiliation or Control: State IRS Status: 501(c)3
Highest Offering: Baccalaureate
Program: Liberal Arts And General
Accreditation: **EH**

01 President .... Mr. Edward KLONOSKI
05 Provost .... Dr. Shirley M. ADAMS
20 Dean Undergraduate Programs .... Vacant
10 Chief Financial/Administrative Ofcr .... Mr. Clifford S. WILLIAMS
13 Chief Information Officer .... Mr. George F. CLAFFEY, JR.
09 Dir Institutional Effectiveness .... Mr. Michael BRODERICK
06 Registrar .... Ms. Jennifer WASHINGTON
37 Dir Financial Aid/Veterans Benefits .... Ms. Deborah FLINN
20 Director Academic Services .... Ms. Linda LARKIN
07 Director Admissions .... Ms. Lori GAGNE PENDLETON
45 Coordinator Special Assessments .... Dr. Maryanne LEGROW
106 Director Distance Learning .... Ms. Susan H. ISRAEL
26 Director Marketing/Public Relations .... Ms. Carolyn HEBERT

*Connecticut Board of Regents for Higher Education (J)

39 Woodland Street, Hartford CT 06105-2337
County: Hartford Identification: 666656
Unit ID: 129011
Telephone: (860) 493-0000 Carnegie Class: N/A
FAX Number: (860) 493-0009
URL: www.ct.ed

01 President .... Dr. Gregory W. GRAY
03 Executive Vice President .... Vacant
88 Vice President for CSU .... Dr. Elsa NUNEZ
88 Vice President for CCC .... Dr. David LEVINSON
15 VP for Human Resources .... Mr. Steve WEINBERGER
26 Director PR & Mktg .... Vacant
10 Chief Financial Officer .... Vacant
13 Chief Information Officer .... Vacant
101 Assoc Board Affairs/Secy to BOT .... Ms. Erin FITZGERALD
04 Administrative Assistant .... Ms. Judith S. NOSAL
100 Chief of Staff .... Vacant

*Central Connecticut State University (K)

1615 Stanley Street, New Britain CT 06050-4010
County: Hartford FICE Identification: 001378
Unit ID: 128771
Telephone: (860) 832-3200 Carnegie Class: Master's L
FAX Number: (860) 832-2522 Calendar System: Semester
URL: www.ccsu.edu
Established: 1849 Annual Undergrad Tuition & Fees (In-State): $8,706
Enrollment: 12,091 Coed
Affiliation or Control: State IRS Status: 501(c)3
Highest Offering: Doctorate
Program: Liberal Arts And General; Teacher Preparatory; Professional
Accreditation: **EH**, ANEST, CACREP, CONST, CORE, CS, ENG, ENGT, EXSC, MFCD, MUS, NAIT, NURSE, SW, TED

02 President .... Dr. John W. MILLER
04 Assistant to the President .... Ms. Courtney MCDAVID
05 Provost/Vice Pres Academic Affs .... Dr. Carl R. LOVITT
30 Vice Pres Institutional Advancement .... Mr. Chris GALLIGAN
32 Vice President Student Affairs .... Dr. Laura TORDENTI
35 Asst Vice Pres/Dean of Students .... Vacant
20 Associate VP Academic Affairs .... Dr. Joseph P. PAIGE
44 Assoc VP Institutional Advancement .... Mr. Nicholas PETTINICO, JR.
58 Associate VP Graduate Studies .... Dr. Paulette LEMMA
26 Assoc VP Marketing/Communications .... Dr. Mark W. MCLAUGHLIN
88 Special Assistant to the President .... Ms. Carolyn MAGNAN
11 Chief Administrative Officer .... Dr. Richard R. BACHOO
10 Chief Financial Officer .... Mrs. Charlene CASAMENTO
15 Chief Human Resources Officer .... Mr. Lou PISANO
13 Chief Information Officer .... Mr. James ESTRADA
28 Interim Chief Diversity Officer .... Ms. Rosa RODRIGUEZ
49 Dean School Arts & Sciences .... Dr. Susan PEASE
50 Dean School of Business .... Dr. Siamack SHOJAI
53 Dean School Educ & Prof Studies .... Dr. Michael P. ALFANO
54 Dean School Engineering/Technology .... Dr. Faris MALHUS
82 Dir Center International Education .... Dr. Nancy B. WAGNER
51 Dir Continuing Educ/Cmty Engagement .... Ms. Christa STERLING
07 Director Admissions & Recruitment .... Mr. Lawrence HALL
41 Director Athletics .... Mr. Paul SCHLICKMANN
39 Director Residence Life .... Ms. Jean ALICANDRO
19 Director Public Safety .... Mr. Jason B. POWELL
37 Director Student Financial Aid .... Mr. Richard BISHOP
44 Director Institutional Advancement .... Ms. Cynthia B. CAYER
27 Media Relations Officer .... Ms. Janice PALMER
08 Interim Director Library Services .... Mr. Carl ANTONUCCI
36 Dir Ctr Advising/Career Exploration .... Mr. Kenneth POPPE
23 Director Health Services .... Dr. Christopher R. DIAMOND
24 Director Academic Technology .... Mr. Scott M. ERARDI
06 Registrar .... Mr. Patrick TUCKER
38 Director Counseling & Wellness .... Vacant
18 Asst Chief Admin Ofcr/Dir Facil Mgt .... Mr. Salvatore CINTORINO
21 Director of Business Services .... Ms. Lori JAMES
96 Purchasing Manager .... Mr. Thomas BRODEUR
09 Director of Institutional Research .... Ms. Yvonne KIRBY

*Eastern Connecticut State University (L)

83 Windham Street, Willimantic CT 06226-2295
County: Windham FICE Identification: 001425
Unit ID: 129215
Telephone: (860) 465-5000 Carnegie Class: Master's S
FAX Number: (860) 465-4485 Calendar System: Semester
URL: www.easternct.edu
Established: 1889 Annual Undergrad Tuition & Fees (In-State): $9,376
Enrollment: 5,440 Coed
Affiliation or Control: State IRS Status: 501(c)3
Highest Offering: Master's
Program: 2-Year Principally Bachelor's Creditable; Liberal Arts And General; Teacher Preparatory; Professional
Accreditation: **EH**, SW, TED

02 President .... Dr. Elsa M. NUNEZ
05 Vice President for Academic Affairs .... Dr. Rhona C. FREE
10 VP Finance/Administration .... Mr. James R. HOWARTH
32 Vice Pres Student Affairs .... Mr. Ken BEDINI
30 Vice Pres Institutional Advance .... Mr. Kenneth J. DELISA
28 Int Assoc VP Equity & Diversity .... Mr. Stacey CLOSE
35 Dean of Students .... Mr. Walter DIAZ
09 Asst Dir of Institutional Research .... Dr. Brian R. LASHLEY
41 Director of Athletics .... Mr. Jeff KONIN
08 Director of Library Services .... Ms. Patricia S. BANACH
84 Dir of Enrollment Mgmt/Fin Aid .... Dr. Edwin HARRIS
36 Director of Career Services .... Mr. Clifford MARRETT
29 Director of Alumni Affairs .... Mr. Michael STENKO
06 Interim Registrar .... Ms. Jennifer HUOPPI
19 Director of Public Safety .... Mr. Jeffrey A. GAREWSKI
39 Director Housing/Residence Life .... Mr. Lamar COLEMAN
40 Director of Bookstore .... Mr. Ben BLAKE
42 Director of Campus Ministry .... Rev. Laurence LAPOINTE
18 Dir of Facilities Mgmt/Planning .... Ms. Nancy TINKER
26 Director University Relations .... Mr. Edward H. OSBORN
49 Dean of Arts & Sciences .... Dr. Carmen R. CID
51 Assoc Dean Continuing Education .... Dr. Carol J. WILLIAMS
58 Int Dean Educ/Prof Studies/Grad Pgm .... Dr. Jaime GOMEZ
96 Assoc Dir Fiscal Affs/Acquisition .... Mr. David ROBERTS
38 Director of Counseling & Psych Svcs .... Dr. Mercy ARAIS

*Southern Connecticut State University (A)

501 Crescent Street, New Haven CT 06515-0901

County: New Haven | FICE Identification: 001406
Unit ID: 130493
Telephone: (203) 392-5200 | Carnegie Class: Master's L
FAX Number: (203) 392-7149 | Calendar System: Semester
URL: www.southernct.edu
Established: 1893 | Annual Undergrad Tuition & Fees (In-State): $8,981
Enrollment: 11,117 | Coed
Affiliation or Control: State | IRS Status: 501(c)3
Highest Offering: Doctorate
Program: Liberal Arts And General; Teacher Preparatory; Professional
Accreditation: EH, CACREP, CS, EXSC, #LIB, MFCD, NURSE, PH, SP, SW, TED

02 President .... Dr. Mary A. PAPAZIAN
04 Admin Assistant to the President .... Ms. Beth Ann H. JOHNSON
05 Int Provost/Vice Pres Acad Affairs .... Dr. Marianne KENNEDY
03 Executive Vice President .... Mr. James E. BLAKE
32 Vice Pres Student Affairs .... Dr. Tracy TYREE
30 Vice President Inst Advancement .... Mr. Robert L. STAMP
16 Assoc VP for Human Resources .... Ms. Jaye BAILEY
20 Assoc VP Academic Student Services .... Ms. Kimberly M. CRONE
43 Employment and Labor .... Ms. Diane MAZZA
18 Assoc VP Capitol Budgeting/Fac Ops .... Mr. Robert G. SHEELEY
13 Chief Info Tech Officer .... Dr. Pablo MOLINA
49 Dean School Arts & Sciences .... Mr. Steven BREESE
50 Dean School of Business .... Dr. Ellen DURNIN
53 Interim Dean School Education .... Dr. Deborah NEWTON
58 Int Dean School Graduate Studies .... Dr. Gregory PAVEZA
70 Dean School Health/Human Svcs .... Dr. Gregory PAVEZA
44 Assoc to VP Dir Major/Planned Gifts .... Vacant
41 Director Intercollegiate Athletics .... Ms. Patricia NICOL
26 Director of Public Affairs .... Mr. Patrick DILGER
29 Director Alumni Affairs .... Ms. Michelle JOHNSTON
07 Director Admissions .... Ms. Alexis HAAKONSEN
06 Interim Registrar .... Ms. Kimberly LAING
08 Director of Library Services .... Dr. Christina BAUM
09 Director of Institutional Research .... Vacant
91 Director Computer Svcs/Admin .... Mr. John O. YOUNG
90 Director Computer Svcs/Academic .... Vacant
15 Director of Human Resources .... Vacant
19 Director of Public Safety .... Mr. Joseph M. DOOLEY
25 Director of Sponsored Research .... Ms. Patricia M. ZIBLUK
37 Director of Financial Aid .... Ms. Gloria LEE
36 Director of Career Services .... Vacant
23 Director of Health Services .... Dr. Diane S. MORGENTHALER
35 Director of Student Affairs .... Dr. Peter F. TROIANO
46 Director Ofc of Mgmt/Info/Research .... Dr. Richard RICCARDI
28 Director of Diversity & Equity .... Dr. Pamela LASSITER
38 Director of Counseling Services .... Dr. Julie LIEFELD
96 Purchasing Manager .... Vacant
21 University Controller .... Ms. Lise M. BRULE
92 Director of Honors Program .... Dr. Terese GEMME
94 Director of Women's Studies .... Dr. Yi-Chun Tricia LIN
06 Associate Registrar .... Ms. Monica RAFFONE

*Western Connecticut State University (B)

181 White Street, Danbury CT 06810-6885

County: Fairfield | FICE Identification: 001380
Unit ID: 130776
Telephone: (203) 837-8200 | Carnegie Class: Master's M
FAX Number: (203) 837-8276 | Calendar System: Semester
URL: www.wcsu.edu
Established: 1903 | Annual Undergrad Tuition & Fees (In-State): $8,893
Enrollment: 6,176 | Coed
Affiliation or Control: State | IRS Status: 501(c)3
Highest Offering: Doctorate
Program: Liberal Arts And General; Teacher Preparatory; Professional
Accreditation: EH, CACREP, MUS, NURSE, SW, TED

02 President .... Dr. James W. SCHMOTTER
05 Provost/Vice Pres Academic Affairs .... Dr. Jane MCBRIDE GATES
10 Vice Pres Finance & Administration .... Mr. Paul REIS
30 Assoc VP Inst Advancement .... Mr. Paul M. STEINMETZ
32 Vice Pres Student Affs/Ext Affs .... Dr. Keith BETTS
88 Dean of Visual/Performing Arts .... Dr. Daniel GOBLE
35 Dean of Student Affairs .... Dr. Walter CRAMER
49 Dean of Arts & Sciences .... Dr. Mary STEWART ALEXANDER
50 Int Dean of Ancell Business .... Dr. James DONEGAN
107 Dean of Professional Studies .... Dr. Jess HOUSE
16 Assoc Vice Pres Human Resources .... Mr. Charles P. SPIRIDON
14 Chief Information Officer .... Mr. Thomas DECHIARO
21 Director Fiscal Affairs/Controller .... Mr. Sean LOUGHRAN
44 Director of Development .... Ms. Jane VON TRAPP
22 Ex Asst to Pres/Chief Diversity Ofc .... Ms. Carolyn LANIER
06 Registrar .... Ms. Lourdes CRUZ
08 Director of Library Services .... Dr. Edward O'HARA
09 Director of Inst Research/Assess .... Dr. Jerry WILCOX
25 Director of Grant/Programs .... Ms. Gabrielle E. JAZWIECKI
38 Director of Counseling Svcs .... Dr. Sprague SIMONDS
37 Dir Financial Aid/Veterans Affairs .... Ms. Nancy BARTON
36 Director of Career Devel Center .... Ms. Maureen C. GERNERT
26 Director University Relations .... Mr. Paul STEINMETZ
39 Dir of Housing & Residence Life .... Mr. Ron MASON
35 Director Student Life .... Dr. Paul M. SIMON
41 Director of Athletics .... Mr. Edward FARRINGTON
29 Director of Alumni Affairs .... Ms. Tammy MCINERNEY
07 Director of Admissions .... Mr. Jay MURRAY
15 Director of Employee Relations .... Mr. Frederic CRATTY
45 Dir of Facilities Plng & Engr .... Mr. Peter VISENTIN
11 Director of Administrative Services .... Mr. Mark R. CASE
88 Dir Environmental & Facilities Svcs .... Mr. Luigi MARCONE
88 Dir Facil Utilization & Promotion .... Mr. John MURPHY
21 Director of Fin Planning & Budgets .... Ms. Mary Ann DEASE
88 Police Lieutenant .... Mr. Roger CONNOR

*Asnuntuck Community College (C)

170 Elm Street, Enfield CT 06082-3800

County: Hartford | FICE Identification: 011150
Unit ID: 128577
Telephone: (860) 253-3000 | Carnegie Class: Assoc/Pub-S-SC
FAX Number: (860) 253-3007 | Calendar System: Semester
URL: www.asnuntuck.edu
Established: 1972 | Annual Undergrad Tuition & Fees (In-State): $3,786
Enrollment: 1,677 | Coed
Affiliation or Control: State | IRS Status: 501(c)3
Highest Offering: Associate Degree
Program: Occupational; 2-Year Principally Bachelor's Creditable
Accreditation: EH

02 President .... Dr. Martha MCLEOD
05 Dean of Academic Affairs .... Ms. Barbara MCCARTHY
10 Dean of Administration .... Mr. James LOMBELLA
32 Dean Student Services .... Ms. Kathleen KELLEY
15 Director of Human Resources .... Mr. Joe BLEICHER
07 Director Admissions .... Mr. Tim ST. JAMES
06 Registrar .... Ms. Gail LABBADIA
37 Director Financial Aid .... Ms. Donna JONES-SEARLE
09 Director Institutional Research .... Ms. Qing L. MACK
30 Director Institutional Advancement .... Vacant
51 Assoc Director Continuing Education .... Ms. Eileen PELTIER
18 Bldg Superintendent II/Phys Plant .... Mr. Joseph MULLER

*Capital Community College (D)

950 Main Street, Hartford CT 06103-1207

County: Hartford | FICE Identification: 007635
Unit ID: 129367
Telephone: (860) 906-5000 | Carnegie Class: Assoc/Pub-U-SC
FAX Number: (860) 520-7906 | Calendar System: Semester
URL: www.ccc.commnet.edu
Established: 1967 | Annual Undergrad Tuition & Fees (In-State): $3,811
Enrollment: 4,434 | Coed
Affiliation or Control: State | IRS Status: 501(c)3
Highest Offering: Associate Degree
Program: Occupational; 2-Year Principally Bachelor's Creditable; Business Emphasis
Accreditation: EH, ADNUR, EMT, MAC, #PTAA, RAD

02 President .... Dr. Wilfredo NIEVES
05 Academic Dean .... Dr. Mary Ann AFFLECK
32 Dean of Student Services .... Ms. Doris B. ARRINGTON
11 Dean of Administration .... Mr. Lester PRIMUS
51 Dean Continuing Educ/Community Svcs .... Ms. Linda GUZZO
09 Director of Institutional Research .... Ms. Jenny WANG
10 Director Finance/Administration .... Mr. Ted HALE
06 Registrar .... Ms. Waynette ARNUM
08 Director of Library Services .... Ms. Jessica VANDERHOFF
88 Disabilities Coordinator .... Ms. Glaisma PEREZ-SILVA
07 Director of Admissions .... Ms. Marsha BALL-DAVIS
37 Director of Financial Aid .... Ms. Margaret MALASPINA
14 Director of Computer Services .... Mr. Roger FERRARO
66 Dir Cont Educ Nurse/Allied Health .... Ms. Ruth KREMS
36 Dir of Career Planning/Development .... Ms. Linda DOMENITZ
26 Director of Information/Marketing .... Ms. Jane BRONFMAN
15 Director of Human Resources .... Mr. Henry BURGOS
20 Associate Academic Officer .... Mr. C. Raymond HUGHES
30 Director Institutional Advancement .... Mr. John MCNAMARA

*Gateway Community College (E)

20 Church St., New Haven CT 06510-5970

County: New Haven | FICE Identification: 008037
Unit ID: 130396
Telephone: (203) 285-2000 | Carnegie Class: Assoc/Pub-U-MC
FAX Number: (203) 285-2018 | Calendar System: Semester
URL: www.gwcc.commnet.edu
Established: 1968 | Annual Undergrad Tuition & Fees (In-State): $3,786
Enrollment: 7,976 | Coed
Affiliation or Control: State | IRS Status: 501(c)3
Highest Offering: Associate Degree
Program: Occupational; 2-Year Principally Bachelor's Creditable
Accreditation: EH, ADNUR, DIETT, NMT, RAD, RTT

02 President .... Dr. Dorsey L. KENDRICK
11 Dean of Administrative Services .... Mr. Louis S. D'ANTONIO
46 Dean of Research & Development .... Ms. Mary Ellen CODY
05 Dean of Academics .... Dr. Mark KOSINSKI
31 Dean Community Services .... Ms. Victoria BOZZUTO
15 Director Personnel/Contract Admin .... Ms. Lucille BROWN
04 Executive Assistant to President .... Ms. Carol G. MCHUGH
09 Director Institutional Research .... Dr. Vincent P. TONG
27 Director Public Info & Marketing .... Ms. Evelyn GARD
10 Director Finance & Admin Svcs .... Ms. Jill RAIOLA
30 Director Institutional Advancement .... Vacant
08 Director Library .... Ms. Clara OGBAA
07 Director of Admissions .... Ms. Kim SHEA
36 Director Career Development Center .... Mr. Michael BUCCILLI
06 Registrar .... Vacant
37 Director Financial Aid .... Mr. Raymond ZEEK
38 Director Student Counseling .... Vacant
35 Director of College Life .... Ms. Roberta PRIOR
24 Director Educational Technologies .... Ms. Wendy SAMBERG
25 Grants Facilitator .... Vacant
13 Director Computer Services .... Mr. Lawrence SALAY
24 Director Early Learning Center .... Ms. Marjorie WEINER
88 Coord Center for Education Svcs .... Ms. Clara MENA
50 Chair Business Department .... Mr. Richard REES
79 Chair Humanities Department .... Mr. Chester H. SCHNEPF
83 Chair Social Sciences Department .... Ms. Susan LONGSTON
88 Coord Early Childhood Education .... Ms. Carmelita E. VALENCIA-DAYE
88 Coord Drug/Alcohol Rehab Counseling .... Ms. Cheryl SHANNON
16 Coordinator Human Services Programs .... Mr. Jonah COHEN
67 Coordinator Pharmacy Tech Program .... Ms. Louise A. PETROKA
81 Chair Math/Natural Sci Department .... Mr. Rocky TREMBLAY
50 Director Business & Industry Svcs .... Mr. John VINCZE
88 Director Dietetic Technician Pgm .... Ms. Elaine LICKTIEG
76 Director Allied Health .... Ms. Sheila SOLERNOU
20 Associate Dean of Learning .... Vacant
54 Dir Engineering/Applied Technology .... Mr. Paul SILBERQUIT
18 Chief Facilities/Physical Plant .... Mr. Lucian SIMONE
06 Registrar .... Ms. Maribel LOPEZ

*Housatonic Community College (F)

900 Lafayette Boulevard, Bridgeport CT 06604-4704

County: Fairfield | FICE Identification: 004513
Unit ID: 129543
Telephone: (203) 332-5000 | Carnegie Class: Assoc/Pub-R-M
FAX Number: (203) 332-5123 | Calendar System: Semester
URL: www.hcc.commnet.edu
Established: 1966 | Annual Undergrad Tuition & Fees (In-State): $3,786
Enrollment: 6,097 | Coed
Affiliation or Control: State | IRS Status: 501(c)3
Highest Offering: Associate Degree
Program: Occupational; 2-Year Principally Bachelor's Creditable
Accreditation: EH, OTA, #PTAA

02 President .... Ms. Anita GLINIECKI
05 Academic Dean .... Ms. Elizabeth ROOP
11 Dean of Administration .... Mr. Ralph TYLER
31 Dean of Outreach .... Vacant
32 Dean of Students .... Dr. Avis D. HENDRICKSON
20 Associate Dean Academics .... Mr. Alan BARKLEY
06 Registrar .... Mr. Jim CONNOLLY
07 Director of Admissions .... Ms. Deloris Y. CURTIS
08 Librarian .... Ms. Shelly STROHM
37 Director of Financial Aid .... Ms. Barbara SUROWIEC
26 Public Relations Associate .... Mr. Anson SMITH
19 Director of Security .... Mr. Christopher GOUGH
09 Director of Institutional Research .... Ms. Jan SCHAEFFLER
14 Director of Computer Services .... Mr. Anthony VITOLA
16 Director Personnel/Labor Relations .... Ms. Theresa EISENBACH
30 Director University Advancement .... Mr. Chris CAROLLO
35 Director of Student Life .... Ms. Linda BAYUSIK
10 Director of Finance/Admin Svcs .... Ms. Teresa ORAVETZ
18 Coordinator of Facilities .... Mr. Richard HENNESSEY

*Manchester Community College (G)

PO Box 1046, Great Path, Manchester CT 06045-1046

County: Hartford | FICE Identification: 001392
Unit ID: 129695
Telephone: (860) 512-3000 | Carnegie Class: Assoc/Pub-S-SC
FAX Number: (860) 512-3631 | Calendar System: Semester
URL: www.manchestercc.edu
Established: 1963 | Annual Undergrad Tuition & Fees (In-State): $3,786
Enrollment: 7,692 | Coed
Affiliation or Control: State | IRS Status: 501(c)3
Highest Offering: Associate Degree
Program: Occupational; 2-Year Principally Bachelor's Creditable
Accreditation: EH, ACFEI, COARC, OTA, #PTAA, SURGT

02 President .... Dr. Gena GLICKMAN
05 Interim Dean of Academic Affairs .... Dr. Sandra PALMER
32 Dean of Student Affairs .... Dr. G. Duncan HARRIS
11 Dean of Administrative Affairs .... Mr. James MCDOWELL
30 Dean of Advancement .... Ms. Leia BELL
51 Dean of Continuing Education .... Ms. Melanie HABER
20 Associate Dean of Academic Affairs .... Dr. Pamela MITCHELL-CRUMP
10 Director Finance & Admin Services .... Ms. Regina FERRANTE
07 Director of Admissions .... Mr. Peter HARRIS
06 Registrar .... Ms. Natalie DURANT
08 Dir Library Svcs/Educational Tech .... Ms. Deborah HERMAN
13 Director of Information Technology .... Mr. Barry GRANT
09 Director Plng/Research & Assessment .... Mr. David NIELSEN
15 Interim Director of Human Resources .... Ms. Holly FOETSCH
18 Dir Facilities Management/ Planning .... Ms. Darlene MANCINI-BROWN
26 Dir Marketing and Public Relations .... Ms. Charlene TAPPAN
37 Director of Financial Aid .... Ms. Ivette RIVERA-DREYER
72 Director Business/Engineering/Tech .... Ms. Catherine SEAVER
83 Director Social Science/Hospitality .... Dr. Christopher PAULIN
81 Dir Math/Science/Health Careers .... Ms. Marcia JEHNINGS
79 Director of Liberal Arts .... Mr. Michael STEFANOWICZ
35 Director of Student Life .... Ms. Cynthia WASHBURNE
19 Director of Public Safety .... Ms. Susan GIBBENS

44 Coordinator Annual Giving .... Ms. Sara VINCENT
38 Dir Counseling and Career Svcs .... Mr. Carl OCHNIO
84 Director of Enrollment Management .... Mr. Peter HARRIS
102 Associate Dean of Advancement .... Ms. Endia DECORDOVA
04 Executive Assistant to President .... Ms. Patricia LINDO
103 Director of Business & Industry .... Ms. Janet ALAMPI
90 Director of Academic Support Ctr .... Mr. Brian CLEARY
85 Dir Multicultural/Intl Affairs .... Mr. Joseph MESQUITA

*Middlesex Community College (A)

100 Training Hill Road, Middletown CT 06457-4889
County: Middlesex FICE Identification: 008038
Unit ID: 129756
Telephone: (860) 343-5800 Carnegie Class: Assoc/Pub-S-SC
FAX Number: (860) 344-7488 Calendar System: Semester
URL: www.mxcc.commnet.edu
Established: 1966 Annual Undergrad Tuition & Fees (In-State): $3,862
Enrollment: 2,937 Coed
Affiliation or Control: State IRS Status: 501(c)3
Highest Offering: Associate Degree
Program: Occupational; 2-Year Principally Bachelor's Creditable
Accreditation: EH, OPD, RAD

02 President .... Dr. Anna WASESCHA
05 Dean of Academics .... Dr. Steven MINKLER
10 Dean Finance & Administration .... Mr. David SYKES
32 Dean of Students .... Dr. Adrienne MASLIN
51 Dean Continuing Education .... Vacant
06 Registrar .... Ms. Susan SALOWITZ
08 Director Library Services .... Ms. Lan LIU
37 Director Financial Aid .... Ms. Irene MARTIN
30 Director Institutional Advancement .... Vacant
07 Interim Director of Admissions .... Dr. Darryl REOME
09 Director of Institutional Research .... Dr. Paul CARMICHAEL
13 Director Information Technology .... Ms. Annie SCOTT
18 Chief Facilities/Physical Plant .... Mr. Steven CHESTER
103 Director of Business & Industry .... Vacant
15 Director Personnel Services .... Ms. Mary Lou PHILLIPS
35 Coordinator Student Activities .... Ms. Judy MAZGULSKI
88 Disability Services Coordinator .... Ms. Hilary PHELPS
26 Chief Public Relations Officer .... Ms. Marlene OLSON
50 Chair Business .... Ms. Donna LEONOWICH
83 Chair Social & Behavioral .... Ms. Judith FELTON
81 Chair Mathematics .... Dr. Mary RAYAPPAN
49 Chair Arts & Humanities .... Dr. Donna BONTATIBUS
81 Chair Science & Health .... Dr. Jonathan MORRIS

*Naugatuck Valley Community College (B)

750 Chase Parkway, Waterbury CT 06708-3089
County: New Haven FICE Identification: 006982
Unit ID: 129729
Telephone: (203) 575-8044 Carnegie Class: Assoc/Pub-R-L
FAX Number: (203) 575-8096 Calendar System: Semester
URL: www.nvcc.commnet.edu
Established: 1964 Annual Undergrad Tuition & Fees (In-State): $3,806
Enrollment: 7,427 Coed
Affiliation or Control: State IRS Status: 501(c)3
Highest Offering: Associate Degree
Program: Occupational; 2-Year Principally Bachelor's Creditable
Accreditation: EH, ADNUR, COARC, ENGT, #PTAA, RAD

02 President .... Dr. Daisy Cocco DE FILIPPIS
05 Provost/Senior Dean Administration .... Mr. James TROUP
31 Dean Community/Economic Development .... Vacant
35 Dean of Student Services .... Ms. Lillian ORTIZ
30 Dean of Community Engagement .... Mr. Waldemar KOSTRZEWA
13 Assoc Dean Information Technology .... Mr. Conal LARKIN
20 Interim Dean of Academic Affairs .... Ms. Estela LOPEZ
06 Registrar .... Ms. Joan ARBUSTO
37 Director of Financial Aid .... Ms. Catherine HARDY
07 Director of Admissions .... Ms. Linda STANGO
22 Affirmative Action Officer .... Mr. Ron CLYMER
08 Int Director Learning Resource Ctr .... Ms. Jamie HAMMOND
10 Director of Finance/Admin Services .... Ms. Lisa PALEN
32 Director of Student Activities .... Ms. Karen BLAKE
18 Chief Facilities/Physical Plant .... Mr. Robert DIVJAK
09 Director of Institutional Research .... Ms. Lauren FRIEDMAN
38 Director Student Development Svcs .... Mr. Bernd MATTHEIS
15 Director of Human Resources .... Ms. Kimberly CAROLINA
31 Director of Community Engagement .... Ms. Sydney VOGHEL-OCHS
26 Public Relations Associate .... Ms. Allison O'LEARY

*Northwestern Connecticut Community-Technical College (C)

Park Place E, Winsted CT 06098-1798
County: Litchfield FICE Identification: 001398
Unit ID: 130040
Telephone: (860) 738-6300 Carnegie Class: Assoc/Pub-S-SC
FAX Number: (860) 738-6488 Calendar System: Semester
URL: www.nwctc.commnet.edu
Established: 1965 Annual Undergrad Tuition & Fees (In-State): $3,786
Enrollment: 1,658 Coed
Affiliation or Control: State IRS Status: 501(c)3
Highest Offering: Associate Degree
Program: Occupational; 2-Year Principally Bachelor's Creditable
Accreditation: EH, ADNUR, MAC, #PTAA

02 President .... Dr. Barbara DOUGLASS
11 Dean of Administration .... Dr. Steven R. FRAZIER
05 Dean of Academic & Student Affairs .... Dr. Patricia A. BOUFFARD
07 Director of Admissions .... Ms. Joanne NARDI
08 Director of Library Services .... Mr. James PATTERSON
06 Registrar .... Ms. Debra REYNOLDS
15 Director of Human Resources .... Vacant
37 Financial Aid Officer .... Mr. Louis BRISTOL
14 Director of Computer Services .... Mr. Joseph DANAJOVITS
38 Dir of Student Development .... Ms. Ruth GONZALEZ
09 Director of Institutional Research .... Ms. Caitlin BOGER-HAWKINS
26 Director Marketing/Public Relations .... Mr. Grantley ADAMS
10 Director Financial/Admin Services .... Ms. Kimberly DRAGAN

*Norwalk Community College (D)

188 Richards Avenue, Norwalk CT 06854-1655
County: Fairfield FICE Identification: 001399
Unit ID: 130004
Telephone: (203) 857-7000 Carnegie Class: Assoc/Pub-R-L
FAX Number: (203) 857-7287 Calendar System: Semester
URL: www.ncc.commnet.edu
Established: 1961 Annual Undergrad Tuition & Fees (In-State): $3,786
Enrollment: 6,938 Coed
Affiliation or Control: State IRS Status: 501(c)3
Highest Offering: Associate Degree
Program: Occupational; 2-Year Principally Bachelor's Creditable
Accreditation: EH, ADNUR, COARC, MAC, PTAA

02 President .... Dr. David L. LEVINSON
05 Provost & Dean of Academic Affairs .... Dr. Pamela EDINGTON
11 Dean of Administration .... Dr. Rose R. ELLIS
32 Dean of Students .... Dr. Robert BAER
09 Dean of Institutional Effectiveness .... Dr. Vanessa MOREST
30 Executive Director of Development .... Ms. Jane KIEFER
51 Director of Continuing Education .... Mr. David CHASE
08 Director of Library Services .... Ms. Linda LERMAN
37 Financial Aid Officer .... Ms. Norma L. MCNERNEY
66 Int Director of Nursing Education .... Ms. Coral PRESTI
06 Registrar .... Ms. Danita BROWN
15 Director Human Resources .... Ms. Therese MARROCCO
26 Director of Public Relations .... Ms. Madeline K. BARILLO
36 Director Career Development .... Mr. Patrick O. BOLAND
38 Director Student Counseling .... Ms. Catherine MILLER
35 Acting Director Student Activities .... Vacant
10 Director Finance/Administration .... Ms. Carrie MCGEE-YUROF
18 Chief Facilities/Physical Plant .. Mr. Anthony (Tony) CENTOPANTI

*Quinebaug Valley Community College (E)

742 Upper Maple Street, Danielson CT 06239-1440
County: Windham FICE Identification: 010530
Unit ID: 130217
Telephone: (860) 412-7200 Carnegie Class: Assoc/Pub-R-M
FAX Number: (860) 412-7222 Calendar System: Semester
URL: www.qvcc.commnet.edu
Established: 1971 Annual Undergrad Tuition & Fees (In-State): $3,786
Enrollment: 2,094 Coed
Affiliation or Control: State IRS Status: 501(c)3
Highest Offering: Associate Degree
Program: Occupational; 2-Year Principally Bachelor's Creditable
Accreditation: EH, MAC

02 Interim President .... Dr. Robert MILLER
32 Interim Dean of Student Services .... Mr. Alfred WILLIAMS
11 Dean of Administrative Services .... Mr. Paul MARTLAND
08 Director of Library Services .... Ms. Sharon MOORE
37 Director of Student Financial Aid .... Ms. Kim RICH
51 Director Ctr for Cmty/Profess Lrng .... Ms. Jill O'HAGAN
09 Director of Institutional Research .... Dr. Donna SOHAN
10 Chief Business Officer .... Ms. Michelle WEISS
15 Dir Personnel Svcs/Aff Action Ofcr .... Mr. Dennis SIDOTI
18 Chief Facilities/Physical Plant .... Mr. David STIFEL
26 Chief Public Relations Officer .... Ms. Susan BREAULT
30 Director of College Development .... Ms. Monique WOLANIN
05 Chief Academic Office .... Dr. Amy DESONIA
06 Registrar .... Ms. Amy KACERIK

*Three Rivers Community College (F)

574 New London Turnpike, Norwich CT 06360
County: New London FICE Identification: 009765
Unit ID: 129808
Telephone: (860) 886-0177 Carnegie Class: Assoc/Pub-R-M
FAX Number: (860) 886-0691 Calendar System: Semester
URL: www.trcc.commnet.edu
Established: 1963 Annual Undergrad Tuition & Fees (In-State): $3,786
Enrollment: 4,990 Coed
Affiliation or Control: State IRS Status: 501(c)3
Highest Offering: Associate Degree
Program: Occupational; 2-Year Principally Bachelor's Creditable
Accreditation: EH, ACBSP, ADNUR, ENGT

02 President .... Dr. Grace S. JONES
05 Academic Dean .... Ms. Ann Z. BRANCHINI
11 Dean of Administration .... Mr. Michael LOPEZ
32 Dean of Student Services .... Dr. Karin EDWARDS
06 Registrar .... Ms. Christine LANGUTH
38 Director of Counseling .... Mrs. Jacqueline PHILLIPS
08 Director Learning Resources .... Ms. Mildred HODGE
15 Director Human Resources .... Ms. Louise J. SUMMA
37 Director Student Financial Aid .... Ms. Hong Yu KOVIC
18 Director of Facilities .... Mr. Arnie DE LA ROSSA
30 Int Dir Institutional Advancement .... Ms. Betty BAILLARGEON
09 Director of Institutional Research .... Vacant
26 Public Relations Associate .... Ms. Tracy ROSIENE

*Tunxis Community College (G)

271 Scott Swamp Road, Farmington CT 06032-3187
County: Hartford FICE Identification: 009764
Unit ID: 130606
Telephone: (860) 255-3500 Carnegie Class: Assoc/Pub-S-SC
FAX Number: N/A Calendar System: Semester
URL: www.tunxis.commnet.edu
Established: 1969 Annual Undergrad Tuition & Fees (In-State): $3,786
Enrollment: 4,764 Coed
Affiliation or Control: State IRS Status: 501(c)3
Highest Offering: Associate Degree
Program: Occupational; 2-Year Principally Bachelor's Creditable
Accreditation: EH, ACBSP, DA, DH, #PTAA

02 President .... Dr. Cathryn L. ADDY
05 Dean of Academic Affairs .... Dr. Michael ROOKE
32 Dean of Student Services .... Dr. Kirk PETERS
11 Dean of Administration .... Mr. Charles CLEARY
45 Dean of Institutional Effectiveness .... Dr. David C. ENGLAND
10 Dir Finance/Administrative Services .... Ms. Nancy ESCHENBRENNER
30 Dir of Institutional Advancement .... Vacant
15 Director Human Resources .... Ms. Pamela KOWAR
08 Director Library Services .... Dr. Lisa LAVOIE
13 Director Information Technology .... Mr. Robert WAHL
07 Director of Admissions .... Mr. Peter MCCLUSKEY
35 Director Academic Support Center .... Ms. Kathleen SCHWAGER
09 Director of Institutional Research .... Vacant
37 Director Financial Aid Services .... Mr. David WELSH
26 Dir of Marketing/Public Relations .... Vacant
18 Director of Facilities .... Mr. John LODOVICO
90 Coord Academic Info Technology .... Mr. Steven MEAD
91 Coord Admin Information Technology .... Mrs. Mary Ann DIORIO
06 Registrar .... Ms. Lucretia C. HOLLEY

Connecticut College (H)

270 Mohegan Avenue, New London CT 06320-4125
County: New London FICE Identification: 001379
Unit ID: 128902
Telephone: (860) 447-1911 Carnegie Class: Bac/A&S
FAX Number: (860) 439-2700 Calendar System: Semester
URL: www.conncoll.edu
Established: 1911 Annual Undergrad Tuition & Fees: $46,085
Enrollment: 1,933 Coed
Affiliation or Control: Independent Non-Profit IRS Status: 501(c)3
Highest Offering: Master's
Program: Liberal Arts And General; Teacher Preparatory
Accreditation: EH

01 President .... Mr. Leo I. HIGDON, JR.
05 Dean of the Faculty .... Dr. Roger L. BROOKS
10 Vice President for Finance .... Mr. Paul L. MARONI
30 Vice President College Advancement .... Mr. Gregory T. WALDRON
08 Vice Pres of Info Svcs/Librarian .... Dr. W. Lee HISLE
11 Vice President for Administration .... Mr. Ulyssess B. HAMMOND
26 Vice President College Relations .... Ms. Patricia M. CAREY
07 VP of Admission & Financial Aid .... Ms. Martha C. MERRILL
15 Asst VP HR/Professional Development .... Ms. Cheryl L. MILLER
20 Dean of the College .... Dr. Carolyn C. DENARD
35 Dean of Student Life .... Dr. Victor J. ARCELUS
28 Dean of Multicultural Affairs .... Dr. Elizabeth GARCIA
20 Dean of Studies .... Dr. Theresa P. AMMIRATI
20 Associate Dean of Faculty .... Prof. Abigail A. VAN SLYCK
06 Registrar .... Ms. Elisabeth S. LABRIOLA
09 Director of Institutional Research .... Dr. John D. NUGENT
21 Controller .... Ms. Amanda B. MAYFIELD
36 Director of Placement .... Vacant
37 Director of Financial Aid .... Ms. Elaine F. SOLINGA
41 Director of Athletics .... Mr. Francis SHIELDS
29 Director of Alumni Relations .... Ms. Bridget MCSHANE
38 Director Student Counseling .... Dr. Janet D. SPOLTORE
84 Director Enrollment Management .... Vacant
18 Chief Facilities/Physical Plant .... Mr. James NORTON
96 Director of Purchasing .... Mr. Scott A. SLABODEN
88 Secretary of the College .... Ms. Bonnie WELLS

Fairfield University (I)

1073 N Benson Road, Fairfield CT 06824-5195
County: Fairfield FICE Identification: 001385
Unit ID: 129242
Telephone: (203) 254-4000 Carnegie Class: Master's L
FAX Number: (203) 254-4101 Calendar System: Semester
URL: www.fairfield.edu
Established: 1942 Annual Undergrad Tuition & Fees: $42,320
Enrollment: 4,999 Coed
Affiliation or Control: Roman Catholic IRS Status: 501(c)3
Highest Offering: Doctorate
Program: Liberal Arts And General; Teacher Preparatory; Professional
Accreditation: EH, ANEST, BUS, CACREP, ENG, MFCD, NURSE, TED

01 President .... Rev. Jeffrey P. VON ARX, SJ

42 Univ Chaplain/Special Asst to Pres .....Rev. Charles H. ALLEN, SJ
03 Executive Vice President .....Mr. Kevin P. LAWLOR
05 Sr Vice President Academic Affairs .....Rev. Paul J. FITZGERALD, SJ
11 Sr VP Administration/Chief of Staff .....Dr. Mark C. REED
10 Int Vice Pres Finance/Treasurer .....Mr. Kevin P. LAWLOR
30 Int Vice Pres Univ Advancement .....Dr. Mark C. REED
26 Vice Pres Mktg & Communications .....Ms. Rama SUDHAKAR
32 Vice President of Student Affairs .....Dr. Thomas C. PELLEGRINO
20 Assoc Vice Pres Academic Affairs .....Dr. Mary Frances MALONE
20 Assoc Vice Pres Academic Affairs .....Dr. David SAPP
20 Assoc Vice Pres Academic Affairs .....Dr. Christine SIEGEL
18 Assoc Vice Pres Facilities Mgmt .....Mr. David W. FRASSINELLI
38 Asst Vice Pres/Dir Counseling Svcs .....Dr. Susan N. BIRGE
21 Asst VP of Finance/Controller .....Mr. Kenneth FONTAINE
35 Asst Vice Pres Student Affairs .....Mr. James D. FITZPATRICK
09 Int Dir Institutional Research/Plng .....Ms. Amy BOCZER
84 Dean of Enrollment .....Ms. Karen A. PELLEGRINO
07 Director of Graduate Admission .....Ms. Marianne L. GUMPPER
06 University Registrar .....Mr. Robert C. RUSSO
13 Chief Information Officer .....Ms. Paige FRANCIS
37 Director of Financial Aid .....Vacant
36 Director of Career Planning .....Ms. Cathleen M. BORGMAN
29 Director of Alumni Relations .....Ms. Janet A. CANEPA
42 Int Director of Campus Ministry .....Rev. Paul D. HOLLAND
19 Director of Public Safety .....Mr. Todd A. PELAZZA
41 Director of Athletics .....Mr. Eugene P. DORIS
49 Dean College Arts & Science .....Dr. Robbin D. CRABTREE
50 Dean Charles F Dolan Sch of Bus .....Dr. Donald E. GIBSON
54 Dean School of Engineering .....Dr. Bruce BERDANIER
66 Dean School of Nursing .....Dr. Lynn BABINGTON
53 Int Dean Grad Sch Educ/Allied Prof .....Dr. Faith-Anne DOHM
35 Dean of Students .....Ms. Karen A. DONOGHUE
88 Dir of Conference/Event Management .....Mr. Matthew A. DINNAN
35 Asc Dn Stdnts/Dir Stdnt Miss/Ident .....Dr. Joseph DEFEO
28 Assoc Dn Stdnts/Dir Stdnt Div Pgm .....Mr. William H. JOHNSON
85 Dir of International Programs .....Mr. Christopher JOHNSON
92 Director of Honors Program .....Dr. John E. THIEL
08 Univ Librarian/Dir of Library Svcs .....Ms. Joan T. OVERFIELD
23 Director of Student Health Center .....Ms. Julia A. DUFFY
15 Director Human Resources .....Mr. Mark J. GUGLIELMONI
96 Director of Purchasing .....Mr. Nicholas J. PAPILLO

Goodwin College (A)

One Riverside Drive, East Hartford CT 06118-2777
County: Hartford FICE Identification: 022449
Unit ID: 129154
Telephone: (860) 528-4111 Carnegie Class: Assoc/PrivNFP
FAX Number: (860) 291-9550 Calendar System: Semester
URL: www.goodwin.edu
Established: 1999 Annual Undergrad Tuition & Fees: $18,800
Enrollment: 3,317 Coed
Affiliation or Control: Independent Non-Profit IRS Status: 501(c)3
Highest Offering: Baccalaureate
Program: 2-Year Principally Bachelor's Creditable
Accreditation: EH, ADNUR, COARC, HT, MAAB, MAC, OTA

01 President .....Mr. Mark E. SCHEINBERG
03 Executive Vice President/Provost .....Ms. Ann B. CLARK
10 Vice President for Finance/CFO .....Mr. Jerry D. EMLET
05 Vice President for Academic Affairs .....Ms. Judith D. ZIMMERMAN
45 Vice Pres for Inst Effectiveness .....Ms. Janet L. JEFFORD
30 Vice Pres Col Rels & Advancement .....Mr. Todd J. ANDREWS
18 Vice Pres for Phys Facilities & IT .....Mr. Bryant L. HARRELL
84 Vice President for Enrollment .....Mr. Daniel NOONAN
30 Vice President for Advancement .....Ms. Brooke PENDERS
20 Asst Vice Pres Academic Affairs .....Ms. Danielle S. WILKEN
88 Dean of Magnet Schools .....Mr. Alan KRAMER
35 Dean of Students .....Dr. Sandy WIRTH
07 Director of Admissions .....Mr. Nicholas LENTINO
36 Director of Career Services .....Mr. Lee HAMEROFF
26 Director of Communications .....Mr. Phil MOORE
44 Assoc Dir of Developmnt/Annual Fund .....Ms. Leia BELL
21 Director of Finance & Business Svcs .....Ms. Sharon N. DADDONA
37 Director of Financial Aid .....Mr. William MANGINI
09 Dir Inst Research/Educ Assessment .....Dr. Alan J. STURTZ
08 Director of Library Services .....Ms. Marilyn L. NOWLAN
106 Director of Online Learning .....Dr. Mark FAZIOLI
06 Registrar .....Ms. Allison MISKY
32 Assistant Dean for Student Life .....Ms. Joy CASTELLO-BUTLER
13 Director of Information Technology .....Mr. Dan REGO
29 Alumni Relations Coordinator .....Ms. Vanessa PERGOLIZZI
04 Executive Assistant to President .....Ms. Ann ZAJCHOWSKI
20 Dean of the Faculty .....Dr. Henriette M. PRANGER
66 Dept Chair/Director Nursing .....Ms. Janice COSTELLO
83 Dept Chair Social Sci & Education .....Dr. Clifford THERMER

Hartford Seminary (B)

77 Sherman Street, Hartford CT 06105-2260
County: Hartford FICE Identification: 001387
Unit ID: 129491
Telephone: (860) 509-9500 Carnegie Class: Spec/Faith
FAX Number: (860) 509-9509 Calendar System: Semester
URL: www.hartsem.edu
Established: 1834 Annual Graduate Tuition & Fees: $11,340
Enrollment: 141 Coed
Affiliation or Control: Independent Non-Profit IRS Status: 501(c)3
Highest Offering: Doctorate; No Undergraduates
Program: Professional; Religious Emphasis
Accreditation: EH, THEOL

01 President .....Dr. Heidi HADSELL
05 Academic Dean .....Dr. Uriah KIM
11 Director of Admin and Facilities .....Ms. Roseann LEZAK JANOW
30 Chief Development Officer .....Rev. Jonathan LEE
07 Admissions Manager .....Ms. Tina DEMO
88 Director Religion Research Inst .....Dr. David A. ROOZEN
88 Director Doctor of Ministry Program .....Dr. Scott THUMMA
88 Director of Islamic Center .....Vacant
08 Library Director .....Dr. Steven BLACKBURN
44 Dir of Annual Fund & Database Admin .....Ms. Susan WRIGHT
10 Comptroller .....Ms. Lilyne HOLLINGWORTH
06 Registrar .....Ms. Danielle LAVINE
04 Exec Assistant to the President .....Ms. Mary ZEMAN
27 Director of Communications .....Ms. Susan SCHOENEERGER

Holy Apostles College and Seminary (C)

33 Prospect Hill Road, Cromwell CT 06416-2005
County: Middlesex FICE Identification: 001389
Unit ID: 129534
Telephone: (860) 632-3010 Carnegie Class: Spec/Faith
FAX Number: (860) 632-3030 Calendar System: Semester
URL: www.holyapostles.edu
Established: 1956 Annual Undergrad Tuition & Fees: $10,550
Enrollment: 372 Coed
Affiliation or Control: Roman Catholic IRS Status: 501(c)3
Highest Offering: Beyond Master's But Less Than Doctorate
Program: Liberal Arts And General; Professional
Accreditation: EH

01 President & Rector .....V.Rev. Douglas L. MOSEY
03 Vice Rector .....Rev. Richard FINEO
03 Vice President .....Rev. Gregoire J. FLUET
05 Academic Dean .....Dr. Gerrard NADAL
07 Director of Admissions .....Rev. Bradley W. PIERCE
10 Finance Officer .....Mr. William RUSSELL
08 Director of Library Services .....Ms. Clare ADAMO
06 Registrar .....Dr. Cynthia TOOLIN

Lincoln College of New England (D)

2279 Mount Vernon Road, Southington CT 06489-1057
County: Hartford FICE Identification: 009407
Unit ID: 128683
Telephone: (860) 628-4751 Carnegie Class: Bac/Assoc
FAX Number: (860) 628-6444 Calendar System: Semester
URL: www.lincolncollegene.edu
Established: 1966 Annual Undergrad Tuition & Fees: $19,700
Enrollment: 1,114 Coed
Affiliation or Control: Proprietary IRS Status: Proprietary
Highest Offering: Baccalaureate
Program: Occupational; 2-Year Principally Bachelor's Creditable
Accreditation: EH, CAHIIM, DA, DH, DIETT, FUSER, MAC, NMT, OTA

01 President .....Mrs. Kathryn REGJO
04 Executive Assistant to President .....Mrs. Rita W. SCHOOLNIK
05 Vice Pres Academic Affairs .....Dr. Gil LINNE
11 Vice Pres Operations & Stdnt Affs .....Mr. Spencer MCNIVEN
10 Chief Financial Officer .....Mr. Kevin MILLER
07 Director of Admissions .....Mr. John ALONSO
10 Director of Administrative Services .....Mrs. Denise LEWICKI
32 Associate Dean of Student Life .....Mr. Dwayne CAMERON
35 Assoc Dean of Student Services .....Mrs. Cynthia A. CLARK
20 Associate Dean of Academic Affairs .....Mr. Mark ANDERSON
06 Registrar .....Mr. Christopher DISTISO
08 Director of Library Services .....Mrs. Eileen RHODES
37 Regional Director of Financial Aid .....Mrs. Gina D. SWENTON
09 Dir Institutional Effectiveness .....Mr. Jerome MADSON
19 Director Campus Safety & Security .....Mr. David C. ALLING
36 Director of Career Services .....Mr. Christopher FRYER
36 VP of Career Services .....Mr. Bob MCNAMARA
18 Supt of Buildings & Grounds .....Mr. Leonard ROY
13 IT Administrator-Southington .....Mr. Edward D. CONNELLY
37 Dir of FA & Student Affairs Online .....Ms. Cortni NESBIT

Lincoln College of New England Hartford College Campus (E)

85 Sigourney Street, Hartford CT 06105
Telephone: (860) 895-6100 Identification: 770130
Accreditation: &EH

† Main campus is Lincoln College of New England in Southington, CT.

Lyme Academy College of Fine Arts (F)

84 Lyme Street, Old Lyme CT 06371-2333
County: New London FICE Identification: 030794
Unit ID: 129686
Telephone: (860) 434-5232 Carnegie Class: Spec/Arts
FAX Number: (860) 434-8725 Calendar System: Semester
URL: www.lymeacademy.edu
Established: 1976 Annual Undergrad Tuition & Fees: $42,938
Enrollment: 70 Coed
Affiliation or Control: Independent Non-Profit IRS Status: 501(c)3
Highest Offering: Baccalaureate
Program: Fine Arts Emphasis
Accreditation: EH, ART

01 President .....Mr. Scott COLLEY
30 Vice President Development .....Mr. Fritz JELLINGHAUS
10 Controller .....Ms. Wendy MASSE
05 Actg Dean/Vice Pres Academic Affs .....Ms. Sally SEAMAN
07 Director Admissions/Cont Educ .....Mr. Michael HAYES
06 Registrar & Financial Aid .....Mr. Steve PODESZWA
51 Continuing Education .....Mr. Adam NOWAKOWSKI

Mitchell College (G)

437 Pequot Avenue, New London CT 06320-4498
County: New London FICE Identification: 001393
Unit ID: 129774
Telephone: (860) 701-5000 Carnegie Class: Bac/Diverse
FAX Number: (860) 701-5090 Calendar System: Semester
URL: www.mitchell.edu
Established: 1938 Annual Undergrad Tuition & Fees: $29,458
Enrollment: 760 Coed
Affiliation or Control: Independent Non-Profit IRS Status: 501(c)3
Highest Offering: Baccalaureate
Program: Liberal Arts And General; Teacher Preparatory; Business Emphasis
Accreditation: EH

01 President .....Dr. Mary Ellen JUKOSKI
05 VP Acad Affs/Dean of the College .....Dr. Michael FISHBEIN
10 Vice Pres Administration & Finance .....Ms. Dyann J. BAKER
32 Vice Pres Student Affs/Dean Stdnts .....Mr. Jason EBBELING
84 VP Enrollment Mgmt .....Ms. Susan BIBEAU
41 Director Of Athletics .....Ms. Maureen WHITE
06 Registrar .....Mr. Kevin P. KELLY
88 Director of Thames Academy .....Ms. Tammy BYRON
08 Director of Library Services .....Vacant
15 Director of Human Resources .....Mr. Jonathan HOWELL
09 Dir Institutional Rsrch & Assesment .....Vacant
37 Director of Financial Aid .....Ms. Jacklyn C. STOLTZ
89 Director FYE and Ctr for Teaching .....Ms. Jennifer R. WELSH
35 Director of Student Activities .....Ms. Cheri HENAULT
27 VP Advancement & Communications .....Ms. Crystal NEUHAUSER
51 Ex Dir of Adult & Continuing Stds .....Dr. Catherine ERIK-SOUSSI
36 Director of Career Services .....Ms. Amanda LJUBICIC
31 Title III Activity Director & PM .....Vacant
96 Purchasing Manager .....Ms. Jill RAKOFF
26 Dir Public Relations & Marketing .....Vacant
39 Director of Residence Life .....Ms. Jamia DANZY
18 Director of Facilities .....Mr. Joseph PARDEE
88 Bursar .....Ms. Leah BRENNAN
13 Chief Technology Officer .....Mr. Michael DEPIANO
07 Assoc Director of Admissions .....Mr. Gregg GORNEAULT
21 Comptroller .....Ms. Janet GRANT
04 Executive Assistant to President .....Ms. April HODSON

Paier College of Art (H)

20 Gorham Avenue, Hamden CT 06514-3902
County: New Haven FICE Identification: 007459
Unit ID: 130110
Telephone: (203) 287-3031 Carnegie Class: Spec/Arts
FAX Number: (203) 287-3021 Calendar System: Semester
URL: www.paiercollegeofart.edu
Established: 1946 Annual Undergrad Tuition & Fees: $12,960
Enrollment: 187 Coed
Affiliation or Control: Proprietary IRS Status: Proprietary
Highest Offering: Baccalaureate
Program: Liberal Arts And General
Accreditation: ACCSC

01 President .....Mr. Jonathan E. PAIER
03 Vice President .....Mr. Daniel L. PAIER
05 Dean of the College .....Mr. Francis COOLEY
10 Director Finance .....Mrs. Maureen E. PAIER
57 Director Design/Graphics .....Mr. Peter MISERENDINO
102 Director Foundation/Arts .....Mr. Robert E. ZAPPALORTI
08 Librarian .....Ms. Beth HARRIS
37 Director Student Financial Aid .....Mr. John DE ROSE
32 Director of Student Services .....Mrs. Maureen DEROSE
20 Assistant to the Dean .....Ms. Angela DEROSE
88 Director Interior Design .....Mr. Pierre STRAUCH
88 Director Photography .....Mr. Peter BENSON
07 Admissions Secretary .....Ms. Lynn PASCALE

Post University (I)

800 Country Club Road, Waterbury CT 06723-2540
County: New Haven FICE Identification: 001401
Unit ID: 130183
Telephone: (203) 596-4500 Carnegie Class: Bac/Diverse
FAX Number: (203) 756-5810 Calendar System: Semester
URL: www.post.edu
Established: 1890 Annual Undergrad Tuition & Fees: $27,450
Enrollment: 812 Coed
Affiliation or Control: Proprietary IRS Status: Proprietary
Highest Offering: Master's
Program: Occupational; 2-Year Principally Bachelor's Creditable; Liberal Arts And General; Professional
Accreditation: EH, ACBSP

00 Chief Executive Officer .....Dr. Thomas SAMPH
01 President .....Dr. Donald W. MROZ
84 Sr VP OEI Enrollment .....Ms. Veronica MONTALVO
10 CFO/Vice President Finance & Admin .....Mr. Scott T. ALLEN

16 VP of Human Resources .... Mr. Donald KELLY
06 Registrar .... Mr. Keith GAUVIN
41 Interim Director of Athletics .... Mr. Michael MANNETTI
15 Human Resources Director .... Ms. Madelaine KELSEY
08 Library Director .... Ms. Tracy RALSTON
27 Chief Information Officer .... Mr. Michael STATMORE
26 VP of Marketing Communications .... Ms. Kelly STATMORE
36 Director Career Services .... Dr. Mary RIGALI
35 Dean of Students .... Ms. Erica PERYGA
40 Campus Store Manager .... Mrs. Frances R. KAMINSKY
19 Director of Campus Safety .... Mr. Robert TANSLEY
38 Director Student Counseling .... Ms. Lisa ANTEL
37 Director Financial Aid .... Ms. Regina FAULDS
37 Director Office of Student Finance .... Ms. Michelle GAMBACINI
106 Pres Online Education Institute .... Mr. Frank MULGREW
26 Chief Marketing Officer .... Mr. David HIGLEY
88 Director of Military Programs .... Mr. Edmund LIZOTTE
50 Interim Dean of School of Business .... Ms. Alisa HUNT
53 Dean of School of Education .... Dr. Jill BUBAN
49 Dean of School of Arts & Sciences .... Dr. Elizabeth JOHNSON
80 Dean John P Burke Sch Pub Service .... Dr. Richard STROMPF
88 Executive Asst to the CEO .... Ms. Melissah KOCHERA
04 Executive Asst to the President .... Ms. Patti JENNINGS

Quinnipiac University (A)

275 Mount Carmel Avenue, Hamden CT 06518-1908
County: New Haven | FICE Identification: 001402
Unit ID: 130226
Telephone: (203) 582-8200 | Carnegie Class: Master's L
FAX Number: (203) 582-4703 | Calendar System: Semester
URL: www.quinnipiac.edu
Established: 1929 | Annual Undergrad Tuition & Fees: $39,330
Enrollment: 8,614 | Coed
Affiliation or Control: Independent Non-Profit | IRS Status: 501(c)3
Highest Offering: First Professional Degree
Program: Liberal Arts And General; Professional
Accreditation: EH, ARCPA, BUS, CS, LAW, #MED, NUR, OT, PA, PERF, PTA, RAD, TED

01 President .... Dr. John L. LAHEY
04 Vice President/Exec Assoc to Pres .... Ms. Jean L. HUSTED
03 Executive Vice President/Provost .... Dr. Mark A. THOMPSON
10 Sr Vice Pres Finance .... Dr. Patrick J. HEALY
05 Vice President Academic Affairs .... Dr. Paul TIYAMBE ZELEZA
30 Vice Pres Devel & Alumni Affairs .... Mr. Donald J. WEINBACH
07 Vice Pres Admissions & Fin Aid .... Ms. Joan I. MOHR
32 Vice President & Dean of Students .... Dr. Manuel C. CARREIRO
26 Vice President for Public Affairs .... Ms. Lynn M. BUSHNELL
15 Vice President for Human Resources .... Mr. Ronald E. MASON
21 Assoc VP Budget & Fin Planning .... Mr. Mark VARHOLAK
18 Vice Pres Facilities/Capital Plng .... Mr. Salvatore FILARDI
20 Int Assoc Vice Pres Academic Affs .... Dr. Annalisa ZINN
20 Assoc Vice Pres Academic Affs .... Ms. Sarah STEELE
13 VP/Chief Info & Tech Officer .... Mr. Fred E. TARCA
29 Assoc VP Alumni Affs/Parent Rels .... Ms. Dianna PATEGAS
106 Assoc VP Online Programs .... Ms. Cynthia GALLATIN
28 AVP Acad Affs/Chief Diversity Ofcr .... Dr. Diana M. ARIZA
35 Assoc VP Student Affairs .... Ms. Monique R. DRUCKER
38 Director of Counseling Services .... Ms. Kerry PATTON
19 Chief of Security .... Mr. David BARGER
08 Director of Arnold Bernhard Library .... Vacant
35 Asst Dean & Director Student Center .... Mr. Daniel W. BROWN
41 Director of Athletics & Recreation .... Mr. Jack J. MCDONALD
40 Campus Store Manager .... Ms. Margaret SAMUL
104 Director for Global Education .... Ms. Andrea HOGAN
21 Assoc VP Finance/Controller .... Mr. Daniel R. JOHNSON
96 Director of Shared Services .... Ms. Maria BIMONTE-YERGANIAN
30 Director of Development .... Mr. Nicholas WORMLEY
06 Registrar .... Ms. Dorothy M. LAURIA
37 Assoc VP & Univ Director of Fin Aid .... Mr. Dominic YOIA
09 Director Acad Asses & Research .... Mr. Edward GILLEN
72 Director of Academic Technology .... Ms. Lauren ERARDI
66 Dean School of Nursing .... Dr. Jean LANGE
50 Dean School of Business .... Dr. Matthew L. O'CONNOR
49 Dean College of Arts & Sciences .... Dr. Hans BERGMANN
76 Int Dean School of Health Sciences .... Dr. Kimberly D. HARTMANN
61 Dean School of Law .... Ms. Jennifer BROWN
60 Dean School of Communications .... Mr. Lee KAMLET
53 Dean School of Education .... Dr. Kevin BASMADJIAN
63 Dean School of Med & VP Health Affs .... Dr. Bruce KOEPPEN
94 Director of Women's Studies .... Ms. Michele HOFFNUNG
61 Associate Dean School of Law .... Mr. David S. KING

Rensselaer at Hartford (B)

275 Windsor Street, Hartford CT 06120-2991
Telephone: (860) 548-2400 | FICE Identification: 002804
Accreditation: &M

† Main campus is Rensselaer Polytechnic Institute in Troy, NY.

Sacred Heart University (C)

5151 Park Avenue, Fairfield CT 06825-1000
County: Fairfield | FICE Identification: 001403
Unit ID: 130253
Telephone: (203) 371-7999 | Carnegie Class: Master's L
FAX Number: (203) 365-7652 | Calendar System: Semester
URL: www.sacredheart.edu
Established: 1963 | Annual Undergrad Tuition & Fees: $35,050
Enrollment: 6,434 | Coed
Affiliation or Control: Independent Non-Profit | IRS Status: 501(c)3
Highest Offering: Doctorate
Program: Liberal Arts And General; Teacher Preparatory; Professional; Business Emphasis
Accreditation: EH, BUS, CEA, NURSE, OT, PTA, SW, TED

01 President .... Dr. John J. PETILLO
11 Sr VP for Finance & Administration .... Mr. Michael J. KINNEY
05 Provost/Vice Pres Academic Affairs .... Dr. Laura NIESEN DE ABRUNA
32 Sr VP Student Affairs & Athletics .... Mr. James M. BARQUINERO
15 Vice President for Human Resources .... Mr. Robert M. HARDY
26 VP Marketing & Communication .... Mr. Michael L. IANNAZZI
88 VP for Mission & Catholic Identity .... Dr. Michael J. HIGGINS
10 Vice President for Finance .... Mr. Philip J. MCCABE
13 VP for Information Tech & Security .... Mr. Michael D. TRIMBLE
30 Vice Pres University Advancement .... Ms. Megan ROCK
20 Vice Provost for Special Acad Pgms .... Ms. Mary Lou DEROSA
07 Interim VP Enrollment Management .... Mr. Jim BARQUINERO
43 University General Counsel .... Mr. Michael D. LAROBINA
49 Dean College of Arts & Sciences .... Dr. Seamus CAREY
50 Dean College of Business .... Dr. John CHALYKOFF
76 Dean College of Health Professions .... Dr. Patricia W. WALKER
53 Dean College of Education .... Dr. James C. CARL
35 Dean of Students .... Mr. Larry J. WIELK
21 Controller .... Mr. Peter J. WARD
06 Registrar .... Mrs. Dona J. PERRONE
88 Bursar .... Ms. Alice M. AVERY
08 University Librarian .... Dr. Peter G. FERRIBY
16 Exec Dir for Human Resources .... Mrs. Julia E. NOFRI
37 Exec Dir Univ Financial Asst .... Ms. Julie SAVINO
27 Exec Director of Public Relations .... Mrs. Funda F. ALP
105 Director Web Content Management .... Mrs. Nancy D. BOUDREAU
44 Director of Annual Giving .... Ms. Judite VAMVAKIDES
41 Exec Director of Athletics .... Mr. Bobby VALENTINE
88 Exec Dir Student Affairs Research .... Ms. Deanna FIORENTINO
09 Director of Institutional Research .... Vacant
19 Director of Public Safety .... Mr. Jack FERNANDEZ
25 Director of Foundations and Grants .... Dr. Virginia M. HARRIS
36 Exec Director of Career Developmt .... Mrs. Patricia A. KLAUSER
88 Exec Dir Budgets Student Affairs .... Mrs. JudyAnn RICCIO
38 Director Counseling Center .... Dr. Mary Jo MASON
92 Director Honors Program .... Dr. Jason J. MOLITIERNO
39 Director of Residential Life .... Mr. Joel R. QUINTONG
42 Director Campus Ministry & Chaplain .... Fr. Jerry RYLE
88 Dir GE Foundations Scholar Pgm .... Ms. Virginia L. STEPHENS
88 General Manager WSHU .... Mr. George J. LOMBARDI
96 Purchasing Manager .... Mrs. Donna STERN
29 Director of Alumni Relations .... Ms. Emily GILLETTE

St. Vincent's College (D)

2800 Main Street, Bridgeport CT 06606-4292
County: Fairfield | FICE Identification: 006191
Unit ID: 130448
Telephone: (203) 576-5235 | Carnegie Class: Assoc/PrivNFP
FAX Number: (203) 576-5893 | Calendar System: Semester
URL: www.stvincentscollege.edu
Established: 1991 | Annual Undergrad Tuition & Fees: $19,350
Enrollment: 834 | Coed
Affiliation or Control: Independent Non-Profit | IRS Status: 501(c)3
Highest Offering: Baccalaureate
Program: Occupational; 2-Year Principally Bachelor's Creditable; Nursing Emphasis
Accreditation: EH, ADNUR, MAC, NUR, RAD

01 President .... Dr. Martha K. SHOULDIS
10 Chief Financial Officer .... Mr. Christopher GIVEN
32 VP Enrollment Svcs/Dean of Students .... Dr. L. Christie BORONICO
05 VP Academic Affairs/Dean of Faculty .... Dr. Susan CAPASSO
13 Director Information Technology .... Mrs. Anet SURRRUSCO
09 Institutional Researcher .... Mrs. Sandra SHARP
11 Director of Administrative Services .... Mrs. Janice N. FAYE
29 Director Alumni Relations .... Mrs. Sharon BEASLEY
16 Human Resources Officer .... Ms. Nancy M. MUSANTE
37 Director of Financial Aid .... Mrs. Claire DWYER
06 Registrar .... Mr. Joseph MACIONUS
07 Director of Admissions .... Mr. Joseph MARRONE
51 Director of Continuing Education .... Ms. Tatiana RAMPINO
08 Librarian .... Mrs. Vicky JACOBSON
66 Dean of Nursing .... Dr. Karen L. BARNETTT
66 Chair of Nursing-ADN .... Mrs. Margo M. MCCARTHY
66 Chair of Nursing-BSN .... Dr. Sharon MAKOWSKI
88 Chair of Radiography .... Ms. Terry HINE
97 Chair of General Education .... Dr. Susan CAPASSO
88 Chair of Medical Assisting .... Ms. Holly MULRENAN
21 Director Student Accounts .... Mrs. Alfreda MOZDZER

Sanford-Brown College-Farmington (E)

270 Farminton Avenue, Suite 245,
Farmington CT 06032-1909
County: Hartford | FICE Identification: 012877
Unit ID: 129613
Telephone: (860) 882-1690 | Carnegie Class: Assoc/PrivFP
FAX Number: (860) 882-1691 | Calendar System: Quarter
URL: www.sanfordbrown.edu
Established: | Annual Undergrad Tuition & Fees: $15,714
Enrollment: 272 | Coed
Affiliation or Control: Proprietary | IRS Status: Proprietary
Highest Offering: Associate Degree
Program: Occupational
Accreditation: ACICS

01 President .... Mr. Kurtis M. PETERSON

Trinity College (F)

300 Summit Street, Hartford CT 06106-3100
County: Hartford | FICE Identification: 001414
Unit ID: 130590
Telephone: (860) 297-2000 | Carnegie Class: Bac/A&S
FAX Number: (860) 297-2257 | Calendar System: Semester
URL: www.trincoll.edu
Established: 1823 | Annual Undergrad Tuition & Fees: $47,510
Enrollment: 2,177 | Coed
Affiliation or Control: Independent Non-Profit | IRS Status: 501(c)3
Highest Offering: Master's
Program: Liberal Arts And General
Accreditation: EH, ENG

01 President .... Dr. James F. JONES, JR.
05 Dean of the Faculty .... Dr. Thomas MITZEL
10 Vice Pres Finance & Ops/Treasurer .... Mr. Paul MUTONE
30 Vice Pres College Advancement .... Mr. Jack FRACASSO
32 Dean of Students .... Mr. Frederick ALFORD
101 Secretary of the College .... Mrs. MaryJo KEATING
07 Dean Admissions/Financial Aid .... Mr. Larry DOW
20 Associate Academic Dean .... Dr. Sonia CARDENA
20 Associate Academic Dean .... Dr. Melanie STEIN
27 Director of Media Relations .... Ms. Michele J. JACKLIN
31 Director of Community Relations .... Mr. Jason ROJAS
37 Director of Financial Aid .... Ms. Kelly O'BRIEN
06 Registrar .... Ms. Patricia MCGREGOR
18 Dir of Facilities Mgmt/Plng & Svcs .... Mr. Gary BRICHER
15 Director of Human Resources .... Ms. Beth IACAMPO
21 Director of Business Operations .... Mr. Alan R. SAUER
21 Budget Director .... Ms. Marcia PHELAN JOHNSON
19 Director of Campus Safety .... Mr. Francisco ORTIZ
44 Director of Development .... Mr. Christopher FRENCH
44 Director of Institutional Support .... Ms. Amy F. BROUGH
36 Director of Career Development .... Ms. Violet GANNON
21 Comptroller .... Mr. Guy DRAPEAU
13 Director of Computer/Commun Systems .... Ms. Suzanne ABER
41 Director of Athletics .... Mr. Michael D. RENWICK
09 Director of Institutional Research .... Dr. James J. HUGHES
32 Director of Campus Life .... Ms. Amy DEBAUN
42 College Chaplain .... Rev. Allison READ
28 Dean of Multicultural Affairs .... Ms. Karla SPURLOCK-EVANS
38 Director Student Counseling .... Dr. Randolph LEE
96 Director of Purchasing .... Mr. Michael S. ELLIOTT
88 Dean of Urban and Global Studies .... Dr. Xiangming CHEN
29 Acting Director of Alumni Relations .... Ms. Aliza FINN-WELCH
08 Head Librarian .... Dr. Richard S. ROSS
26 Director of Communications .... Ms. Jenny HOLLAND

University of Bridgeport (G)

126 Park Avenue, Bridgeport CT 06604-5620
County: Fairfield | FICE Identification: 001416
Unit ID: 128744
Telephone: (203) 576-4000 | Carnegie Class: Master's L
FAX Number: (203) 576-4653 | Calendar System: Semester
URL: www.bridgeport.edu
Established: 1927 | Annual Undergrad Tuition & Fees: $29,090
Enrollment: 4,877 | Coed
Affiliation or Control: Independent Non-Profit | IRS Status: 501(c)3
Highest Offering: Doctorate
Program: Occupational; Liberal Arts And General; Teacher Preparatory; Professional
Accreditation: EH, ACBSP, ACUP, #ARCPA, ART, CHIRO, DH, ENG, NATUR

01 President .... Mr. Neil Albert SALONEN
04 Executive Assistant to President .... Ms. Joan E. FLORCZAK
05 Provost & VP for Academic Affairs .... Dr. Hans VAN DER GIESSEN
10 VP Administration & Finance .... Dr. Susan D. WILLIAMS
88 Vice Pres International Programs .... Dr. Thomas J. WARD
30 Vice Pres for University Relations .... Ms. Mary Jane FOSTER
18 VP of Facilities .... Mr. George ESTRADA
09 Exec Asst Pres Plng/Inst Research .... Ms. Barbara A. GABIANELLI
07 Dean of Admissions .... Ms. Karissa L. PECKHAM
32 Dean of Students .... Ms. Edina R. OESTREICHER
08 University Librarian .... Ms. Deborah L. DULEPSKI
15 Dir Human Resources/Affirm Act Ofcr .... Dr. Melitha R. PRZYGODA
21 Controller .... Mr. Thomas A. DEBRIZZI, JR.
27 Systems Architect & Interim CIO .... Mr. Matanya ELCHANANI
37 Director of Financial Aid .... Ms. Christine E. FALZERANO
90 Director of Academic Computing .... Mr. Abdelshakour A. ABUZNEID
19 Exec Director of Campus Security .... Ms. April J. VOURNELIS
38 Director of Counseling Services .... Ms. Jessica M. MILLS
06 University Registrar .... Mr. Christian HANSEN
85 Director of Intl Student Affairs .... Ms. Yumin WANG
39 Dir Residential Life/Stdnt Conduct .... Mr. Robert VASS
96 Director of Purchasing .... Ms. Jacqueline A. REEVES
35 Dir Campus Activit & Cmty Service .... Vacant
12 Director of Waterbury Center .... Ms. Karen K. RINGWOOD
12 Director of Stamford Center .... Ms. Maureen L. MALONEY
29 Director Alumni Relations .... Vacant
26 Dir Public Info & Media Affairs .... Ms. Leslie H. GEARY
43 University Counsel .... Mr. Michael D. BROMLEY
41 Athletic Director .... Mr. James M. MORAN
51 Dean Continuing/Profess Studies .... Mr. Michael J. GIAMPAOLI
23 Director of Health Center .... Ms. Melissa H. LOPEZ
88 Director of Acupuncture Institute .... Dr. Jennifer BRETT
40 Manager of the Bookstore .... Mr. Gary M. REEVES
42 Director of Interfaith Center .... Vacant
36 Director of Career Services .... Ms. Aimee R. MARCELLA

54 VP Grad Stds/Research & Dean Engr ... Dr. Tarek M. SOBH
49 Dean Arts & Sciences ... Dr. Stephen E. HEALEY
53 Dean School of Education ... Dr. Allen P. COOK
88 Dean College of Chiropractic ... Dr. David WICKES
88 Dean College Naturopathic Medicine .. Dr. Elizabeth W. PIMENTEL
50 Dean School of Business ... Dr. Lloyd G. GIBSON
17 Vice Provost Div of Health Science ... Dr. David M. BRADY
97 Director Div of General Studies ... Dr. Edward V. GEIST
89 Director First Year Studies ... Ms. Roxie L. RAY
52 Dean Fones Sch of Dental Hygiene ... Dr. Marcia H. LORENTZEN
56 Director for Distance Learning ... Mr. Kris BICKELL
24 Media Services Coordinator ... Ms. Lynn DORSEY
57 Dir Shintaro Akatsu Sch of Design ... Mr. Richard W. YELLE
88 Dir Physician Assistant Institute ... Dr. Daniel CERVONKA

University of Connecticut (A)

Storrs CT 06269-0001

County: Tolland
FICE Identification: 001417
Unit ID: 129020
Telephone: (860) 486-2000
Carnegie Class: RU/VH
FAX Number: N/A
Calendar System: Semester
URL: www.uconn.edu
Established: 1881
Annual Undergrad Tuition & Fees (In-State): $12,022
Enrollment: 30,256
Coed
Affiliation or Control: State
IRS Status: 501(c)3
Highest Offering: Doctorate
Program: Liberal Arts And General; Teacher Preparatory; Professional
Accreditation: EH, ART, AUD, BUS, BUSA, CACREP, CEA, CGTECH, CLPSY, CS, DIETC, DIETD, DIETI, DMOLS, ENG, JOUR, LAW, LSAR, MFCD, MUS, NURSE, PHAR, PTA, SCPSY, SP, SPAA, SW, TED

01 President ... Susan HERBST
100 Chief of Staff ... Rachel RUBIN
05 Provost/Exec VP Academic Affairs ... Mun CHOI
17 Executive VP for Health Affairs ... Frank TORTI
10 Exec VP for Administration and CFO ... Richard D. GRAY
32 Vice President for Student Affairs ... Michael GILLBERT
46 Vice President for Research ... Jeffrey SEEMANN
88 Vice Pres for Economic Development ... Mary HOLZ-CLAUSE
101 Executive Secretary to the Board ... Rachel RUBIN
26 Vice Pres for Communications ... Tysen KENDIG
41 Director of Athletics ... Warde J. MANUEL
43 Asst Attorney General ... Ralph URBAN
43 General Counsel ... Richard ORR
13 Vice Provost & Chief Info Officer ... Michael MUNDRANE
28 Vice Provost for Diversity ... Jeffrey OGBAR
21 Assoc VP for Budget & Finance ... Lysa TEAL
19 Dir Public Safety/Chief of Police ... Barbara O'CONNOR
28 Assoc VP for Diversity & Equity ... Elizabeth CONKLIN
45 Asst VProv for Inst Rsrch & Effect ... Thulsai KUMAR
102 Pres Univ Connecticut Foundation ... Joshua NEWTON
20 Vice Provost for Acad Admin ... Sally REIS
20 Chief Ops Officer/Academic Admin ... Amy DONAHUE
84 VP Enrollment Planning & Mgmt ... Wayne LOCUST
08 V Provost for University Libraries ... Martha BEDARD
12 Director Stamford Campus ... Sharon WHITE
12 Director Avery Point Campus ... Michael ALFULTIS
12 Director Waterbury Campus ... William J. PIZZUTO
12 Director Hartford Campus ... Michael MENARD
12 Interim Director Torrington Campus ... William J. PIZZUTO
92 AVProv Enrich Pgms/Dir Honors Pgms ... Jennifer LEASE BUTTS
25 Interim Exec Dir Sponsrd Pgms ... Antje HARNISCH
86 Director Government Relations ... Gail GARBER
86 Dir Govt Relations/Health Affairs ... Joann LOMBARDO
06 Registrar ... Lauren DIGRAZIA
27 Director Media Communications ... Vacant
09 Director Institutional Research ... Pamela J. ROELFS
07 Director Undergrad Admissions ... Nathan FUERST
37 Director Student Financial Aid ... Mona LUCAS
29 Int Exec Director Alumni Assoc ... P. Tysen KENDIG
23 Director Student Health Services ... Michael KURLAND
15 Director of Human Resources ... Aliza WILDER
96 Dir Procurement/Logistical Svcs ... Matthew LARSON
47 Dean Col of Agric/Natural Resources ... Gregory WEIDEMANN
50 Dean School of Business ... John ELLIOT
53 Dean Neag School of Education ... Thomas DEFRANCO
54 Interim Dean of Engineering ... Kazem KAZEROUNIAN
51 AVPvst for Exlnce in Teach & Learn ... Peter DIPLOCK
57 Dean of Fine Arts ... Brid GRANT
58 Vice Prov Grad Ed/Dean Grad Sch ... Kent HOLSINGER
82 Exec Director Office Intl Affairs ... Elizabeth MAHAN
61 Dean School of Law ... Timothy FISHER
49 Dean College of Lib Arts/Sciences ... Jeremy TEITELBAUM
66 Dean School of Nursing ... Regina CUSSON
67 Interim Dean School of Pharmacy ... John B. MORRIS
70 Dean School of Social Work ... Salome RAHEIM
52 Dean of Dental Medicine ... R. Lamont MACNEIL
63 Dean School of Medicine ... Frank TORTI
38 Int Dir Stdnt Couns/Mental Hlth Svc ... Elizabeth CRACCO
39 Interim Director Residential Life ... Logan TRIMBLE
88 Deputy Chief of Staff ... Michael KIRK
88 University Master Planner ... Laura CRUICKSHANK
88 Vice Provost for Global Affairs ... Daniel WEINER
36 Asst VProv/Exec Dir Career Services ... James R. LOWE
88 Asst VProvost for Student Success ... Maria D. MARTINEZ
88 Director Marketing Communications ... Patricia FAZIO
88 Ombuds ... James WOHL
20 AVPvst Acad Affairs & Diversity ... Dana WILDER
88 Dir Institute for Materials Science ... Steven L. SUIB

University of Connecticut Health Center (B)

263 Farmington Avenue, Farmington CT 06030-1827
Telephone: (860) 679-2000
FICE Identification: 009867
Accreditation: &EH, DENT, MED, PH

† Main campus is University of Connecticut in Storrs, CT.

University of Connecticut School of Law (C)

55 Elizabeth Street, Hartford CT 06105-2290
Telephone: (860) 570-5000
Identification: 770108
Accreditation: &EH, LAW

† Main campus is University of Connecticut in Storrs, CT.

University of Hartford (D)

200 Bloomfield Avenue, West Hartford CT 06117-1599
County: Hartford
FICE Identification: 001422
Unit ID: 129525
Telephone: (860) 768-4100
Carnegie Class: Master's L
FAX Number: (860) 768-4070
Calendar System: Semester
URL: www.hartford.edu
Established: 1877
Annual Undergrad Tuition & Fees: $33,358
Enrollment: 6,992
Coed
Affiliation or Control: Independent Non-Profit
IRS Status: 501(c)3
Highest Offering: Doctorate
Program: Liberal Arts And General; Teacher Preparatory; Professional
Accreditation: EH, ART, BUS, CLPSY, COARC, DANCE, ENG, ENGT, MT, MUS, NURSE, OPE, PTA, RAD, TED, THEA

01 President ... Dr. Walter HARRISON
05 Provost ... Ms. Sharon VASQUEZ
10 Vice Pres Finance & Administration ... Mr. Arosha JAYAWICKREMA
30 Vice Pres Institutional Advancement ... Ms. Christine M. PINA
32 Vice Pres Student Affs/Dean Stdnts ... Dr. J. Lee PETERS
26 Vice Pres of Univ Relations ... Mr. John J. CARSON
21 Asst Vice Pres Finance/Controller ... Ms. Kimberly KENNISON
35 Asst Vice Pres Student Development ... Ms. DeLois LINDSEY
04 Senior Advisor to the President ... Ms. Susan FITZGERALD
35 Assoc Vice Pres for Student Life ... Mr. Irwin NUSSBAUM
21 Assoc Vice Pres/Treasurer ... Mr. Thomas J. PERRA
43 Vice Pres/Gen Counsel & Secretary ... Mr. Thomas DORER
20 Assoc Provost/Dean UG Studies ... Dr. Guy C. COLARULLI
20 Asst Provost/Dean of Faculty Devel ... Dr. Frederick SWEITZER
07 Dean of Admission ... Mr. Richard A. ZEISER
04 Exec Assistant to the President ... Ms. Ilena ROSENSTEIN
15 Exec Dir Human Resources & Devel ... Ms. Lisa BELANGER
08 Director University Libraries ... Ms. Randi L. ASHTON-PRITTING
37 Director Student Financial Aid ... Ms. Jennifer HORNER
06 Director Registration & Records ... Ms. Doreen LAY
38 Dir Counsel & Personal Development ... Dr. David ALBERT
36 Director Career Center ... Mr. John KNIERING
14 Chief Info Ofcr/Ex Dir Info Tech ... Mr. George BROPHY
19 Director Public Safety ... Mr. John SCHMALTZ
23 Director Health Services ... Ms. Mary NORRIS
24 Director Media Technology Services ... Mr. Sebastian SORRENTINO
25 Dir Inst Prtnrshp/Sponsored Rsrch ... Dr. Peter LISI
29 Director Alumni Relations ... Ms. Heather CORBETT
18 Assoc Vice Pres for Facilities/Mgmt ... Mr. Norman YOUNG
88 Asst Provost for Financial Planning ... Dr. James A. MELLO
41 Director Athletics ... Ms. Patricia MEISER
104 Director International Studies ... Ms. Sarah REUTER
09 Director Institutional Research ... Ms. Sarah NOELL
94 Director of Women's Center ... Ms. Patricia MCKENNA-GRANT
88 Director of Judicial Process ... Ms. Helena SAJKO
96 Director of Purchasing ... Mr. Dennis M. GACIOCH
92 Director of University Honors ... Dr. Donald JONES
88 Dean University Programs ... Mr. R. J. MCGIVNEY
57 Dean Hartford Art School ... Dr. Nancy M. STUART
72 Dean College Engineer/Tech/Arch ... Dr. Louis MANZIONE
58 Interim Dean Graduate Studies ... Dr. Frederick SWEITZER
49 Dean College Arts & Science ... Dr. Joseph VOELKER
50 Dean Barney School of Business ... Dr. James W. FAIRFIELD-SONN
12 Dean Hillyer College ... Dr. David H. GOLDENBERG
53 Dean College of Education ... Dr. Ralph MUELLER
88 Dean Hartt School ... Dr. Aaron FLAGG

University of New Haven (E)

300 Boston Post Road, West Haven CT 06516-1999
County: New Haven
FICE Identification: 001397
Unit ID: 129941
Telephone: (203) 932-7000
Carnegie Class: Master's L
FAX Number: (203) 931-6060
Calendar System: Other
URL: www.newhaven.edu
Established: 1920
Annual Undergrad Tuition & Fees: $33,740
Enrollment: 6,351
Coed
Affiliation or Control: Independent Non-Profit
IRS Status: 501(c)3
Highest Offering: Doctorate
Program: Liberal Arts And General; Professional
Accreditation: EH, CS, DH, DIETD, ENG, FEPAC, TED

01 President ... Dr. Steven H. KAPLAN
05 Provost/Vice Pres Academic Affs ... Dr. Daniel MAY
10 Vice Pres Finance/Treasurer of Univ ... Mr. George S. SYNODI
30 Vice President Univ Advancement ... Mr. Richard J. TUCHMAN
32 Vice President for Student Affairs ... Vacant
84 Vice Pres Enrollment Management ... Dr. James MCCOY
15 Vice President Human Resources ... Ms. Caroline KOZIATEK
100 Chief of Staff & Univ Secretary ... Ms. Gayle S. TAGLIATELA
18 Assoc Vice President for Facilities ... Mr. Louis ANNINO
20 Asc Prov Grad Stds/Rsrch/Fac Devel ... Vacant
21 Assoc Vice Pres for Finance ... Mr. Patrick TORRE
13 Assoc VP Institutional Technology ... Mr. Vincent P. MANGIACAPRA
35 Assc VP Stdnt Affs/Dean of Students .. Ms. Rebecca D. JOHNSON
88 Assoc VP Enrollment Management ... Mr. Kevin J. PHILLIPS
41 Assc Vice Pres Athletics/Recreation ... Ms. Deborah CHIN
37 Assoc Vice Pres Financial Aid ... Ms. Karen FLYNN
88 Asst Provost Undergrad Stds/Assess ... Dr. Gordon SIMERSON
08 University Librarian ... Ms. Hanko H. DOBI
44 Director of Development ... Ms. Roslyn REABACK
06 University Registrar ... Ms. Lynn KOHRN
30 Director Advancement Services ... Mr. Carl PITRUZZELLO
07 Director of Graduate Admissions ... Ms. Eloise GORMLEY
28 Director of Intercultural Relations ... Ms. Wanda TYLER
29 Director of Alumni Events ... Ms. Jennifer PJATAK
38 Director of Counseling ... Dr. Deborah EVERHART
09 Director Institutional Research ... Ms. Susan TURNER
19 Chief of University Police ... Chief Mark DELIETO
85 Director of Intl Student Services ... Ms. Karima JACKSON
35 Director Student Activities ... Mr. Gregory OVEREND
96 Director of Procurement Services ... Mr. Robert STEVENS
85 Director International Admissions ... Mr. Joseph SPELLMAN
88 Dir Student Accounts/Risk Manager ... Mr. Marc MANIATIS
26 Director of Recruiting & Marketing ... Mr. Wayne LEON
49 Dean College Arts & Sciences ... Dr. Lourdes ALVAREZ
50 Dean College Business ... Dr. Elizabeth DAVIS
54 Dean Tagliatela Col Engineering ... Dr. Ronald HARICHANDRAN
88 Dn HCL Col Crimnl Just/Forensic Sci ... Dr. Mario GABOURY
106 AVP & Dean Col Lifelong & eLearning ... Dr. Marsha K. HAM

University of Saint Joseph (F)

1678 Asylum Avenue, West Hartford CT 06117-2791
County: Hartford
FICE Identification: 001409
Unit ID: 130314
Telephone: (860) 232-4571
Carnegie Class: Master's L
FAX Number: (860) 232-6927
Calendar System: Semester
URL: www.usj.edu
Established: 1932
Annual Undergrad Tuition & Fees: $33,417
Enrollment: 2,514
Female
Affiliation or Control: Roman Catholic
IRS Status: 501(c)3
Highest Offering: Doctorate
Program: Liberal Arts And General; Teacher Preparatory; Professional
Accreditation: EH, CACREP, DIETD, DIETI, MFCD, NURSE, @PHAR, SW, TED

01 President ... Dr. Pamela T. REID
05 Provost ... Dr. Michelle KALIS
10 Vice President Finance & Admin ... Mr. Shawn M. HARRINGTON
30 VP Institutional Advancement ... Mr. Douglas NELSON
84 VP Enrollment Management ... Vacant
32 VP Student Affairs/Dean of Students ... Dr. Cheryl A. BARNARD
21 Assoc VP of Finance/Controller ... Mr. William HAWKINS
15 Director of Human Resources ... Ms. Deborah SPENCER
58 Dean Sch of Grad & Prof Studies ... Dr. Daniel NUSSBAUM
67 Dean School of Pharmacy ... Dr. Joseph OFOSU
53 Dean School of Education ... Dr. Kathleen BUTLER
76 Dean School of Health/Nat Sci ... Dr. Sandra AFFENITO
79 Dean School of Humanities/Soc Sci ... Dr. Wayne STEELY
08 Librarian ... Ms. Linda O. GEFFNER
06 Registrar ... Mr. Patrick MARTIN
41 Dir of Athletics/AVP Student Affair ... Mr. William CARDARELLI
26 AVP Marketing & Communications ... Ms. Cynthia WHITCOMB
18 Director of Facilities ... Mr. Kevin COCHRAN
29 Dir of Alumni Rels/Annual Giving ... Mr. Stephen KUMNICK
07 Director of Admissions ... Ms. Eileen HOCKING
37 Director of Financial Aid ... Mr. Daniel SHIELDS
36 Director of Career Services ... Mr. Stephen SEWARD
92 Director of Honors Program ... Dr. Elizabeth VOZZOLA
39 Director Res Life/Assistant Dean ... Ms. Tamara O'DAY-STEVENS
35 Director Student Activities ... Ms. Tracy LAKE
09 Director of Institutional Research ... Ms. Kathleen NEAL

University of Saint Joseph School of Pharmacy (G)

229 Trumbull Street, Hartford CT 06103
Telephone: (860) 231-5858
Identification: 770109
Accreditation: &EH, @PHAR

† Main campus is University of Saint Joseph in West Hartford, CT.

Wesleyan University (H)

Middletown CT 06459-0001
County: Middlesex
FICE Identification: 001424
Unit ID: 130697
Telephone: (860) 685-2000
Carnegie Class: Bac/A&S
FAX Number: (860) 685-2001
Calendar System: Semester
URL: www.wesleyan.edu
Established: 1831
Annual Undergrad Tuition & Fees: $45,928
Enrollment: 3,262
Coed
Affiliation or Control: Independent Non-Profit
IRS Status: 501(c)3
Highest Offering: Doctorate
Program: Liberal Arts And General
Accreditation: EH

01 President ... Dr. Michael S. ROTH

05	Provost/Vice Pres Academic Affairs	Dr. Ruth STRIEGEL WEISSMAN
10	Vice President/Treasurer	Dr. John MEERTS
26	Vice President University Relations	Ms. Barbara-Jan WILSON
28	Int Vice President for Diversity	Dr. Marina MELENDEZ
32	Vice Pres of Student Affairs	Mr. Michael J. WHALEY
29	Assoc VP External Relations	Ms. Gemma F. EBSTEIN
30	Assoc Asst Vice Pres Development	Ms. Ann GOODWIN
20	Senior Associate Provost	Dr. Karen L. ANDERSON
18	Asst Vice President for Facilities	Ms. Joyce TOPSHE
35	Asst Vice Pres/Dean of Students	Mr. Richard CULLITON
07	Dean of Admissions & Financial Aid	Ms. Nancy HARGRAVE MEISLAHN
58	Dir Cont Stds/Graduate Liberal Stds	Ms. Sheryl CULOTTA
06	Registrar	Ms. Anna VAN DER BURG
08	Librarian	Ms. Patricia TULLY
09	Director of Institutional Research	Mr. Michael E. WHITCOMB
37	Director Financial Aid	Mr. John GUDVANGEN
36	Director Career Development	Mr. Michael A. SCIOLA
15	Director Human Resources	Ms. Julia HICKS
19	Director Public Safety	Mr. David A. MEYER
31	Dir Community Svcs/ Volunteerism	Ms. Catherine CRIMMINS LECHOWICZ
41	Director of Athletics	Mr. John S. BIDDISCOMBE
45	Director of Strategic Initiatives	Dr. Charles G. SALAS

Yale University (A)

New Haven CT 06520

County: New Haven | FICE Identification: 001426 | Unit ID: 130794

Telephone: (203) 432-4771 | Carnegie Class: RU/VH

FAX Number: N/A | Calendar System: Semester

URL: www.yale.edu

Established: 1701 | Annual Undergrad Tuition & Fees: $44,000

Enrollment: 11,906 | Coed

Affiliation or Control: Independent Non-Profit | IRS Status: 501(c)3

Highest Offering: Doctorate

Program: Liberal Arts And General; Professional

Accreditation: EH, ARCPA, BUS, CLPSY, ENG, FOR, IPSY, LAW, MED, MIDWF, MUS, NURSE, PH, THEOL

01	President	Peter SALOVEY
05	Provost	Benjamin POLAK
86	Vice Pres & Dir New Haven/State Aff	Bruce D. ALEXANDER
101	Vice President & Secretary	Linda K. LORIMER
10	Vice Pres Finance & Business Ops	Shauna KING
30	Vice President Development	Vacant
43	Vice President & General Counsel	Dorothy K. ROBINSON
16	Vice Pres/Chief HR Officer	Michael A. PEEL
32	Secretary/Vice Pres Student Life	Kimberly M. GOFF-CREWS
20	Deputy Provost Science & Tech	Steven M. GIRVIN
20	Deputy Provost of the Arts	Vacant
20	Deputy Provost Arts and Humanities	Emily P. BAKEMEIR
20	Deputy Prov Health Affairs	Stephanie SPANGLER
20	Deputy Provost Academic Resources	J. Lloyd SUTTLE
11	Assoc VP of Administration	Janet E. LINDNER
18	Assoc VP Facilities	John H. BOLLIER
21	Assoc VP Finance & Univ Controller	Stephen C. MURPHY
27	Chief Comm Ofcr/Dir Ofc Public Affs	Elizabeth STAUDERMAN
96	Assoc VP & Chief Procurement Ofcr	John A. MAYES
102	Assoc VP/Dir Corp & Found Rels	Patricia E. PEDERSEN
08	University Librarian	Susan GIBBONS
09	Acting Dir Institutional Research	Russell K. ADAIR
13	Assoc VP & Univ CIO	Leonard PETERS
19	Chief University Police	Ronnell A. HIGGINS
06	University Registrar	Gabriel G. OLSZEWSKI
07	Dean Undergraduate Admissions	Jeremiah QUINLAN
20	Dean Undergraduate Education	Joseph W. GORDON
35	Dean Student Affairs	Mr. W. Marichal GENTRY
29	Exec Director Assoc of Yale Alumni	Mark R. DOLLHOPF
37	Director University Financial Aid	Caesar T. STORLAZZI
27	Assoc CIO	Charles POWELL
22	Dir Ofc Equal Opportunities	Valarie J. STANLEY
23	Director University Health Services	Dr. Paul GENECIN
90	Sr Dir Academic Technology	Peggy A. MCCREADY
25	Exec Dir Univ Grant & Contract Admn	Michael GLASGOW
36	Director Career Services	Jeanine DAMES
44	Univ Director Planned Giving	Eileen B. DONAHUE
39	Dir Grad & Prof Student Housing	George E. LONGYEAR, JR.
41	Director Athletics	Thomas A. BECKETT
42	University Chaplain	Sharon KUGLER
85	Director Intl Students & Scholars	Ann KUHLMAN
48	Dean of the School of Architecture	Robert A M. STERN
49	Dean of Yale College	Mary MILLER
50	Dean School of Management	Edward A. SNYDER
54	Dean Faculty of Engineering	Ms. T. Kyle VANDERLICK
57	Dean of the School of Art	Robert STORR
58	Dean of Grad Sch Arts & Science	Thomas D. POLLARD
57	Dean of the School of Drama	James A. BUNDY
61	Dean of the Law School	Robert C. POST
64	Dean of the School of Music	Robert L. BLOCKER
65	Dean Sch of Forestry & Environ Stds	Sir Peter CRANE
73	Dean of the Divinity School	Gregory E. STERLING
88	Director Inst of Sacred Music	Martin D. JEAN
63	Dean of School of Medicine	Dr. Robert J. ALPERN
66	Dean of the School of Nursing	Margaret GREY
69	Dean of Public Health	Paul C. CLEARY
28	Chief Diversity Officer	Deborah STANLEY-MCAULAY
104	Dean Intl & Professional Experience	Jane EDWARDS

DELAWARE

Delaware College of Art and Design (B)

600 N Market Street, Wilmington DE 19801-3007

County: New Castle | FICE Identification: 041398 | Unit ID: 432524

Telephone: (302) 622-8000 | Carnegie Class: Assoc/PrivNFP

FAX Number: (302) 622-8870 | Calendar System: Semester

URL: www.dcad.edu

Established: 1997 | Annual Undergrad Tuition & Fees: $21,370

Enrollment: 211 | Coed

Affiliation or Control: Independent Non-Profit | IRS Status: 501(c)3

Highest Offering: Associate Degree

Program: 2-Year Principally Bachelor's Creditable; Fine Arts Emphasis

Accreditation: M, ART

01	President	Mr. Stuart BARON
06	Registrar	Ms. Krista ROTHWELL

Delaware State University (C)

1200 N DuPont Highway, Dover DE 19901-2275

County: Kent | FICE Identification: 001428 | Unit ID: 130934

Telephone: (302) 857-6060 | Carnegie Class: Master's M

FAX Number: (302) 857-6069 | Calendar System: Semester

URL: www.desu.edu

Established: 1891 | Annual Undergrad Tuition & Fees (In-State): $7,336

Enrollment: 4,324 | Coed

Affiliation or Control: State | IRS Status: 501(c)3

Highest Offering: Doctorate

Program: Liberal Arts And General; Teacher Preparatory; Professional

Accreditation: M, BUS, #DIETD, NUR, SW, TED

01	President	Dr. Harry L. WILLIAMS
04	Assistant to the President	Ms. Natasha A. ADAMS
05	Int Provost & V Chair Academic Affs	Dr. Alton THOMPSON
10	Vice Pres Finance & Administration	Mr. Amir MOHAMMADI
30	VP Inst Advancement/Chief of Staff	Mrs. Carolyn CURRY
32	Vice Pres Student Affairs	Mr. Kemal ATKINS
13	Assoc VP Information Technology	Mr. Arthur LEIBLE
09	AVP Inst Research/Planning/Analysis	Dr. Kimberly R. SUDLER
43	General Counsel	Mr. Thomas PRESTON
46	Vice President for Research	Dr. Noureddine MELIKECHI
18	Director of Facilities	Mr. Randy JONES
06	Registrar	Mr. Terrell HOLMES
07	Director of Admissions	Ms. Erin HILL
62	Dean of Library Services	Ms. Rebecca BATSON
37	Director of Financial Aid	Ms. Lynn IOCANO
29	Director of Alumni Relations	Ms. Lorene K. ROBINSON
36	Director Career Services	Ms. Lisa MOODY
38	Director of Student Counseling	Mr. Ralph ROBINSON
27	News Director	Mr. Carlos HOLMES
41	Director of Athletics	Ms. Candy YOUNG SANDERS
15	Director of Human Resources	Ms. Irene HAWKINS

*Delaware Technical Community College, Office of the President (D)

P.O. Box 897, Dover DE 19903-0897

County: Kent | FICE Identification: 008074 | Unit ID: 130882

Telephone: (302) 739-3737 | Carnegie Class: N/A

FAX Number: (302) 739-6225

URL: www.dtcc.edu

01	President	Dr. Orlando J. GEORGE, JR.
05	Vice President for Academic Affairs	Ms. Stephanie S. SMITH
10	Vice President for Finance	Mr. Gerard M. MCNESBY
45	Vice Pres Inst Effect/College Rels	Dr. Judith A. SCIPLE
43	Vice Pres Legal Affs & Human Res	Mr. Brian D. SHIREY
20	Assoc VP for Academic Affairs	Dr. Kimberly L. JOYCE
30	Assoc VP Institutional Advancement	Vacant
21	Asst Vice President for Finance	Ms. Carol C. RHODES
15	Asst Vice Pres Human Resources	Ms. Patricia A. DEPLASCO
26	Asst VP for Marketing & PR	Ms. Tammy K. WATKINS
32	Asst VP for Student Affairs	Dr. Joanne K. DAMMINGER
09	Acting Dir Institutional Research	Mr. Daniel LARSON
106	Asst VP of Technology/E-Learning	Dr. Richard C. KRALEVICH
104	International Education Director	Ms. Taryn E. GASSNER

*Delaware Technical Community College, Owens Campus (E)

Box 610, Georgetown DE 19947-0610

County: Sussex | FICE Identification: 007053 | Unit ID: 130891

Telephone: (302) 856-5400 | Carnegie Class: Assoc/Pub-R-M

FAX Number: (302) 858-5455 | Calendar System: Semester

URL: www.dtcc.edu/owens

Established: 1967 | Annual Undergrad Tuition & Fees (In-State): $3,560

Enrollment: 4,768 | Coed

Affiliation or Control: State | IRS Status: 501(c)3

Highest Offering: Associate Degree

Program: Occupational; 2-Year Principally Bachelor's Creditable

Accreditation: M, ACBSP, ADNUR, COARC, DMS, ENGT, MLTAD, OTA, PTAA, RAD

02	Vice President & Campus Director	Dr. Ileana M. SMITH
05	Dean of Instruction	Bobbi J. BARENDS
32	Dean of Student Services	Dr. Melissa RAKES
20	Assistant Dean of Instruction	Ms. Christy A. MORIARTY
04	Assistant to the Campus Director	Ms. Elizabeth A. RODIER
31	Director Corporate/Community Pgms	Mr. Christopher M. MOODY
15	Human Resources Director	Ms. Maribeth B. DOCKETY
11	Director of Administrative Services	Mr. Linford P. FAUCETT
06	Registrar & Director of Admissions	Mr. Willie G. THOMAS
08	Head Librarian	Ms. Angelynn KING
26	Public Relations Manager	Ms. Christine GILLAN
37	Director of Student Financial Aid	Ms. Veronica E. ONEY
18	Asst Dir of Administrative Services	Mr. George E. BOOTH
10	Business Manager	Mr. Robert W. HEARN, JR.
29	Alumni Coordinator	Ms. Alison BUCKLEY

*Delaware Technical Community College, Stanton-Wilmington Campus (F)

400 Stanton-Christiana Road, Newark DE 19713-2197

County: New Castle | FICE Identification: 021449 | Unit ID: 130916

Telephone: (302) 454-3900 | Carnegie Class: Assoc/Pub-U-MC

FAX Number: (302) 368-6620 | Calendar System: Semester

URL: www.dtcc.edu/stanton

Established: 1968 | Annual Undergrad Tuition & Fees (In-State): $3,560

Enrollment: 7,494 | Coed

Affiliation or Control: State | IRS Status: 501(c)3

Highest Offering: Associate Degree

Program: Occupational; 2-Year Principally Bachelor's Creditable

Accreditation: M, ACBSP, ACFEI, ADNUR, COARC, DH, DMS, ENGT, HT, MAC, NMT, OTA, PTAA, RAD

02	Acting VP & Campus Director	Dr. Kathy A. JANVIER
03	Assistant Campus Director	Dr. Frances H. LEACH
05	Acting Dean of Instruction	Dr. Kathern R. FRIEL
32	Dean Stdnt Svcs Stanton/ Wilmington	Dr. Regan HICKS-GOLDSTEIN
35	Asst Dean Student Svcs Wilmington	Mrs. Cornelia JOHNSON
35	Asst Dean Student Svcs Stanton	Mr. Jeff ROSE
20	Asst Dean of Instruction Stanton	Ms. Mary DOODY
20	Asst Dean of Instruction Wilmington	Dr. Carol BANCROFT-MORELY
04	Assistant to the Campus Director	Dr. Jacquita L. WRIGHT-HENDERSON
04	Assistant to the Campus Director	Ms. Lora A. JOHNSON
31	Dir of Corporate/Community Pgms	Mr. Paul T. MORRIS, JR.
15	Director of Human Resources	Vacant
11	Director Administrative Services	Mr. John A. FOGELGREN
37	Financial Aid Officer	Dr. Debra J. TROXLER
06	Registrar Stanton/Wilmington	Mrs. Collette M. HAYES
08	Head Librarian Stanton	Mrs. Regina A. WELLS
08	Head Librarian Wilmington	Mrs. Donna M. ABED
10	Business Manager	Mr. Daniel R. EHMANN
21	Assistant Business Manager	Dr. Mary M Y. CHEN
88	Asst Director Admin Services	Mr. Eddie CUNNINGHAM
88	Asst Director of Corp/Community	Ms. Rachel L. ANDERSON

*Delaware Technical Community College, Terry Campus (G)

100 Campus Drive, Dover DE 19904-1383

County: Kent | FICE Identification: 011727 | Unit ID: 130907

Telephone: (302) 857-1000 | Carnegie Class: Assoc/Pub-R-M

FAX Number: (302) 857-1296 | Calendar System: Semester

URL: www.dtcc.edu/terry

Established: 1972 | Annual Undergrad Tuition & Fees (In-State): $3,560

Enrollment: 3,206 | Coed

Affiliation or Control: State | IRS Status: 501(c)3

Highest Offering: Associate Degree

Program: Occupational; 2-Year Principally Bachelor's Creditable

Accreditation: M, ACBSP, ACFEI, ADNUR, EMT, PNUR

02	Vice President & Campus Director	Dr. June S. TURANSKY
05	Dean Instruction	Mr. John M. BUCKLEY
32	Dean Student Services	Ms. Jennifer P. PIRES
04	Assistant to the Campus Director	Dr. Martha J. HOFSTETTER
31	Director Corporate & Community Pgms	Ms. Dana L. SAWYER
15	Director of Human Resources	Ms. Charlotte T. LISTER
11	Director of Administrative Services	Mr. William J. AYERS
37	Director Student Financial Aid	Ms. Jennifer J. GRUNDEN
08	Head Librarian	Dr. Margaret R. PROUSE
10	Business Manager	Ms. Christina C. SWEENEY
06	Registrar/Admissions Coordinator	Ms. Nauleen A. PERRY
88	Asst Director of Admin Services	Mr. Ray B. PARSONS
20	Assistant Dean of Instruction	Mr. Bill J. MORROW

Goldey-Beacom College (H)

4701 Limestone Road, Wilmington DE 19808-0551

County: New Castle | FICE Identification: 001429 | Unit ID: 130989

Telephone: (302) 998-8814 | Carnegie Class: Spec/Bus

FAX Number: (302) 998-8631 | Calendar System: Semester

URL: www.gbc.edu

Established: 1886 | Annual Undergrad Tuition & Fees: $22,140

Enrollment: 1,352 | Coed

Affiliation or Control: Independent Non-Profit | IRS Status: 501(c)3

Highest Offering: Master's

Program: Liberal Arts And General; Professional; Business Emphasis

Accreditation: M, ACBSP, IACBE

01 President .... Dr. Mohammad ILYAS
26 Vice President External Affairs .... Dr. Gary L. WIRT
10 Vice Pres Finance/ Administration .... Ms. Kristine M. SANTOMAURO
05 Dean of Academic Affairs .... Ms. Alison Boord WHITE
32 Dean of Students .... Ms. Bernadette H. WIMBERLEY
07 Director of Admissions .... Mr. Larry EBY
84 Dean Enrollment Mgmt/Registrar .... Ms. Jane H. LYSLE
91 Dean of Information Technology/ACC .... Ms. Emily S. JACKSON
21 Controller .... Ms. Susan M. MANNERING
39 Director of Housing/Residence Life .... Mr. Kevin MARTIN
36 Career Service Specialist .... Ms. Elizabeth KIRKER
36 Career Service Specialist .... Ms. Kimberly PLUSCH
18 Director of Facilities .... Mr. Meezie FOSTER
41 Athletic Director .... Mr. Charles A. HAMMOND

Irish American University (A)

404 East Savannah Road, Lewes DE 19958

County: Sussex | Identification: 667120
Telephone: (302) 793-1101 | Carnegie Class: Not Classified
FAX Number: (808) 334-0443 | Calendar System: Semester
URL: www.acd.ie
Established: | Annual Undergrad Tuition & Fees: $7,000
Enrollment: N/A | Coed
Affiliation or Control: Independent Non-Profit | IRS Status: 501(c)3
Highest Offering: Master's
Program: Liberal Arts And General
Accreditation: @M

01 President .... Dr. Donald E. ROSS
05 Academic Dean .... Dr. Rory MCENTERGART

University of Delaware (B)

104 Hullihen Hall, Newark DE 19716

County: New Castle | FICE Identification: 001431
Unit ID: 130943
Telephone: (302) 831-2000 | Carnegie Class: RU/VH
FAX Number: N/A | Calendar System: 4/1/4
URL: www.udel.edu
Established: 1743 | Annual Undergrad Tuition & Fees (In-State): $12,112
Enrollment: 21,856 | Coed
Affiliation or Control: State Related | IRS Status: 501(c)3
Highest Offering: Doctorate
Program: Liberal Arts And General; Teacher Preparatory; Professional
Accreditation: M, BUS, BUSA, CEA, CLPSY, DIETD, DIETI, ENG, ENGT, IPSY, MT, MUS, NURSE, PCSAS, PTA, SPAA, TED

01 President .... Dr. Patrick T. HARKER
05 Provost .... Dr. Domenico GRASSO
03 Exec Vice President/Univ Treasurer .... Mr. Scott R. DOUGLASS
11 Vice President for Finance & Admin .... Vacant
30 VP Development & Alumni Relations .... Ms. Monica M. TAYLOR
26 Vice Pres Communications/Marketing .... Ms. Deborah L. HAYES
13 Vice Pres Information Technologies .... Mr. Carl JACOBSON
43 Vice Pres and General Counsel .... Mr. Lawrence WHITE
100 VP/Chief of Staff .... Ms. Patricia WILSON
18 VP Facilities Real Estate & Aux Svc .... Mr. Alan BRANGMAN
46 Vice Provost for Research .... Dr. Charles RIORDAN
58 Vice Provost Graduate and Prof Educ .... Dr. James G. RICHARDS
20 Deputy Provost .... Dr. Nancy BRICKHOUSE
101 Vice Pres & Univ Secretary .... Mr. Jeffrey W. GARLAND
86 Director of Government Relations .. Mr. Derrick DEADWYLER, JR.
51 Asst Provost Prof Cont Studies .... Dr. James K. BROOMALL
84 Assoc Provost Admin/Enrollment Svcs .... Ms. Margaret B. BOTTORFF
32 Interim Vice Pres for Student Life .... Ms. Dawn M. THOMPSON
88 Interim Assoc Prov Inst Res & Effec .... Dr. John E. SAWYER
09 Director Institutional Research .... Dr. Heather A. KELLY
108 Director Educational Assessment .... Ms. Kathleen L. PUSECKER
28 Dir President Diversity Initiative .... Dr. Margaret ANDERSEN
29 Assistant VP Alumni Relations .... Ms. Cynthia B. CAMPANELLA
08 Vice Provost/Director Libraries .... Ms. Susan BRYNTESON
37 Director Student Financial Services .... Ms. Melissa STONE
36 Director Career Services Center .... Mr. Matthew BRINK
19 Exec Dir Campus & Public Safety .... Mr. Albert J. HOMIAK, JR.
47 Dean Agriculture/Natural Resources .... Dr. Mark RIEGER
49 Dean Arts & Sciences .... Dr. George H. WATSON
50 Dean Business & Economics .... Dr. Bruce W. WEBER
54 Dean College of Engineering .... Dr. Babatunde A. OGUNNAIKE
65 Dean of Earth/Ocean/Environment .... Dr. Nancy M. TARGETT
76 Dean of Health Sciences .... Dr. Kathleen S. MATT
53 Dean Education/Human Development .... Dr. Lynn OKAGAKI
92 Director University Honors Program .... Dr. Michael A. ARNOLD
07 Director Admissions .... Dr. José AVILES
15 Chief Human Resources Officer .... Mr. Thomas LAPENTA
96 Director of Procurement Services .... Ms. Debra C. REESE
06 University Registrar .... Mr. Jeffrey L. PALMER
21 Interim Director Budget .... Mr. Andrew R. KNAB
22 Assoc Director Equity and Inclusion .... Ms. Rebecca R. FOGERTY
35 Dean of Students/AVP Student Life .... Vacant
38 Director Ctr for Couns/Student Dev .... Dr. Charles L. BEALE
39 Director Residence Life & Housing .... Dr. Kathleen G. KERR
104 Assoc Prov Intl Programs .... Dr. Nancy GUERRA
85 Director Intl Students & Scholars .... Mr. Ravi AMMIGAN
41 Director Athletics & Recreation .... Mr. Eric ZIADY

Wesley College (C)

120 N State Street, Dover DE 19901-3876

County: Kent | FICE Identification: 001433
Unit ID: 131098
Telephone: (302) 736-2300 | Carnegie Class: Bac/Diverse
FAX Number: (302) 736-2301 | Calendar System: Semester
URL: www.wesley.edu
Established: 1873 | Annual Undergrad Tuition & Fees: $23,540
Enrollment: 1,723 | Coed
Affiliation or Control: United Methodist | IRS Status: 501(c)3
Highest Offering: Master's
Program: Liberal Arts And General; Teacher Preparatory; Professional
Accreditation: M, NUR, TED

01 President .... Dr. William N. JOHNSTON
05 Vice President for Academic Affairs .... Dr. Patricia DWYER
10 VP Finance/Dir Human Resource .... Mr. Ronald D. RECK
30 Vice Pres Institutional Advancement .... Mr. Chris WOOD
20 Assoc VP for Academic Affairs .... Dr. Colleen DI RADDO
32 Dean of Students .... Ms. Wanda ANDERSON
84 Dean of Enrollment Management .... Dr. Howard BALLENTINE
42 Dir Spiritual Life and Comm Involv .... Rev. Steve LAMOTTE
21 CPA/Controller .... Ms. Adele FOLTZ
43 General Counsel .... Mr. David WILKS
06 Registrar .... Ms. Erin ELSBERRY
12 Part-time Admin Coord DAFB .... Ms. Tracey LUNDBLAD
08 Director of the Parker Library .... Ms. Jessica OLIN
20 Director of Academic Support Svcs .... Ms. Charlene STEPHENS
36 Asst Dir Academic Support Services .Ms. Christine MCDERMOTT
26 Director of Marketing .... Ms. Jessica COOK
09 Director of Institutional Research .... Ms. Jessica WARNER
46 Dir Data Analy & Inst Assessment .... Vacant
07 Director of Undergrad Admissions .... Mr. Chris JESTER
41 Exec Dir of Sports & Recreation .... Mr. Mike DRASS
18 Director of the Physical Plant .... Mr. Rick RICHARDSON
40 Director of the Bookstore .... Mr. Kris MCGLOTHIN
19 Director of Safety/Security .... Mr. Walter BEAUPRE
23 Director Student Health Services .... Ms. Jill MASER
44 Dir of the Annual Wesley Fund .... Ms. Cathy NOSEL
88 Dir of The Wesley Society .... Ms. Cathy ANDERSON
39 Director of Residence Life .... Mr. Kevin HANSBURY
35 Director of Student Activities .... Mr. LaDarius THOMPSON
37 Dir of Student Financial Planning .... Mr. Michael HALL
38 Director of Counseling .... Ms. Ann ROGGE
85 Director of Global Initiatives .... Mr. Kevin CULLEN
29 Director Alumni Affairs .... Ms. Cathy NOSEL
88 Dir Campus Community High School .... Ms. Heidi GREENE
41 Assoc Dir of Sports & Rec .... Vacant
04 Assistant to the President .... Ms. Ellen COLEMAN
88 Supervisor Business Operations .... Ms. Adele FLAMM

Widener University School of Law (D)

PO Box 7474, Wilmington DE 19803-0474

Telephone: (302) 477-2100 | FICE Identification: 012962
Accreditation: &M, LAW

† Main campus is Widener University in Chester, PA.

Wilmington University (E)

320 N Dupont Highway, New Castle DE 19720-6491

County: New Castle | FICE Identification: 007948
Unit ID: 131113
Telephone: (302) 356-4636 | Carnegie Class: DRU
FAX Number: (302) 328-5902 | Calendar System: Trimester
URL: www.wilmu.edu
Established: 1967 | Annual Undergrad Tuition & Fees: $9,985
Enrollment: 13,251 | Coed
Affiliation or Control: Independent Non-Profit | IRS Status: 501(c)3
Highest Offering: Doctorate
Program: Liberal Arts And General; Professional
Accreditation: M, CACREP, IACBE, NURSE, TED

01 President .... Dr. Jack P. VARSALONA
32 University Vice Pres Student Affs .... Dr. LaVerne T. HARMON
11 University Vice Pres Admin Affs .... Ms. Carole D. PITCHER
10 Vice President/CFO Financial Affs .... Ms. Heather A. O'CONNELL
88 Vice Pres Academic Support Services .... Ms. Erin DIMARCO
88 Vice President External Affairs .... Dr. Peter A. BAILEY
05 Vice President Academic Affairs .... Dr. James D. WILSON, JR.
88 Asst Vice Pres/Dean of Locations .... Dr. Richard D. GOCHNAUER
21 Asst Vice President/Controller .... Mr. David R. LEWIS
15 Asst Vice Pres/Chief Human Res Ofcr .... Mr. P. Donald HAGERMANN
26 Asst Vice Pres Public Relations .... Mr. Christopher G. PITCHER
100 Asst Vice Pres/President's Office .... Dr. Angela C. SUCHANIC
88 Asst VP Administrative Affairs .... Ms. Eileen G. DONNELLY
35 Asst VP Student Affairs/Alumni Rel .... Dr. Tina M. BARKSDALE
20 Asst VP Academic Affairs .... Dr. Sheila M. SHARBAUGH
19 Asst VP/University Safety/Athletic .... Dr. Jack L. CUNNINGHAM
08 Director Library .... Mr. James M. MCCLOSKEY
105 Director of Web Communications .... Mr. Kevin G. BARRY
13 Dir Information Technology .... Mr. Bryan E. STEINBERG
41 Director Athletics .... Ms. Linda M. ANDRZJEWSKI
07 Director of Admissions .... Ms. Laura M. MORRIS
18 Sr Director Buildings/Maintenance .... Mr. William P. QUINN
29 Director Alumni Relations .... Ms. Patricia L. JENNINGS
36 Sr Dir Career Svcs/Student Life .... Dr. Regina C. ALLEN-SHARPE
96 Purchasing Specialist .... Mr. Mark S. PARIS
26 Asst Vice President .... Ms. Jacque R. VARSALONA
37 Sr Dir Student Financial Services .... Ms. Trudy E. HITE
88 Asst VP Academic Support Services .... Mrs. Peg P. MITCHELL
27 Director University Information .... Mrs. Meghan R. SCHMEUSSER
78 Director Cooperative Learning .... Mr. David C. CAFFO
16 Senior Director Human Resources .... Mrs. Nicole ROMANO
50 Dean College of Business .... Dr. Donald W. DURANDETTA
53 Dean College of Education .... Dr. John C. GRAY
76 Dean College of Health Professions . Ms. Denise Z. WESTBROOK
83 Dean College Social/Behavioral Sci .... Dr. Christian A. TROWBRIDGE
49 Dean College of Arts and Sciences .... Dr. Doreen B. TURNBO
72 Dean College of Technology .... Dr. Edward L. GUTHRIE
06 Registrar .... Ms. Elizabeth P. JORDAN

DISTRICT OF COLUMBIA

American University (F)

4400 Massachusetts Avenue, NW, Washington DC 20016

FICE Identification: 001434
Unit ID: 131159
Telephone: (202) 885-1000 | Carnegie Class: DRU
FAX Number: N/A | Calendar System: Semester
URL: www.american.edu
Established: 1893 | Annual Undergrad Tuition & Fees: $40,649
Enrollment: 13,165 | Coed
Affiliation or Control: United Methodist | IRS Status: 501(c)3
Highest Offering: Doctorate
Program: Liberal Arts And General; Teacher Preparatory; Professional
Accreditation: M, BUS, CLPSY, IPSY, JOUR, LAW, MUS, SPAA, TED

01 President .... Dr. Cornelius M. KERWIN
05 Provost .... Dr. Scott A. BASS
30 Vice President Development .... Dr. Thomas MINAR
10 Vice President Finance & Treasurer .... Mr. Donald MYERS
32 Vice President Campus Life .... Dr. Gail S. HANSON
43 Vice President General Counsel .... Ms. Mary E. KENNARD
11 Vice Provost for Academic Admin .... Ms. Violeta ETTLE
18 Asst VP Facilities Dev/Real Estate .... Vacant
21 Asst VP Finance & Asst Treasurer .... Mr. Douglas KUDRAVETZ
35 Asst Vice Pres and Dean of Students .... Dr. Robert HRADSKY
35 Asst Vice President Campus Life .... Dr. Fanta AW
29 Asst Vice Pres of Alumni Relations .... Ms. Raina LENNEY
84 Vice Provost Undergrad Enrollment .... Dr. Sharon ALSTON
13 Asst Vice Pres and CIO .... Mr. David L. SWARTZ
100 Chief of Staff President's Office .... Mr. David E. TAYLOR
20 Sr Vice Provost & Dean Acad Affairs .... Dr. Phyllis PERES
58 Vice Provost Grad Studies & Rsrch .... Dr. Jonathan G. TUBMAN
20 Vice Provost Undergrad Studies .....Dr. Virginia (Lyn) STALLINGS
49 Dean College Arts & Sciences .... Dr. Peter STARR
60 Dean Sch of Communication .... Dr. Jeffrey RUTENBECK
50 Dean Kogod School of Business .... Dr. Michael J. GINZBERG
61 Dean Washington College of Law .... Dr. Claudio GROSSMAN
82 Dean School of Intl Service .... Dr. James GOLDGEIER
107 Dean School of Prof & Extended Stds .... Dr. Carola WEIL
80 Dean School of Public Affairs .... Dr. Barbara ROMZEK
15 Exec Director Human Resources .... Ms. Beth MUHA
36 Exec Director Career Center .... Mr. Gihan FERNANDO
09 Dir Institutional Rsrch/ Assessment .... Ms. Karen L. FROSLID JONES
26 Vice Pres University Communications .... Dr. Teresa (Terry) FLANNERY
06 University Registrar .... Dr. Alice POEHLS
08 University Librarian .... Ms. Nancy DAVENPORT
21 Controller .... Mr. John R. SMIELL
88 Dir Student Finance and Collections .... Mr. Mark WELCH
21 Asst Vice Pres Budget & Finance .... Ms. Nana AN
88 Asst VP Risk Mgmt/Safety Svcs .... Ms. Patricia L. KELSHIAN
88 Assoc Director Student Billing .... Ms. Minh N. PHUNG
88 Dir Student Account Operations .... Mr. Darrell COOK
42 University Chaplain .... Dr. Joseph T. ELDRIDGE
30 Asst Vice President Development .... Ms. Abbey FAGIN
19 Exec Dir Univ Safety Programs .... Mr. Daniel NICHOLS
37 Director Financial Aid .... Mr. Brian LEE SANG
38 Director of Counseling Center .... Dr. Wanda COLLINS
25 Director Contracting & Procurement .... Mr. Brian BLAIR
07 Director of Admissions .... Mr. Gregory GRAUMAN
85 Director Intl Student/Scholar Svcs .... Dr. Fanta AW
92 Dir Univ Honors Program .... Dr. Michael L. MANSON
41 Director Athletics & Recreation .... Dr. William "Billy" WALKER
28 Sr Dir Ctr Diversity & Inclusion .... Ms. Tiffany SPEAKS
96 Asst Dir Procurement & Contracts ... Mr. William "Bill" WALTERS
104 Director AU Abroad .... Ms. Sara E. DUMONT

The Catholic University of America (G)

620 Michigan Avenue, NE, Washington DC 20064-0002

FICE Identification: 001437
Unit ID: 131283
Telephone: (202) 319-5000 | Carnegie Class: RU/H
FAX Number: (202) 319-4441 | Calendar System: Semester
URL: www.cua.edu
Established: 1887 | Annual Undergrad Tuition & Fees: $38,000
Enrollment: 6,838 | Coed
Affiliation or Control: Roman Catholic | IRS Status: 501(c)3
Highest Offering: Doctorate
Program: Liberal Arts And General; Teacher Preparatory; Professional
Accreditation: M, CLPSY, ENG, IPSY, LAW, LIB, MUS, NURSE, SW, TED, THEOL

01 President .... Mr. John H. GARVEY
100 VP University Rels/Chief of Staff .... Mr. Frank G. PERSICO
05 Provost .... Dr. James F. BRENNAN
10 Vice Pres Finance & Treasurer .... Ms. Cathy R. WOOD
30 Vice Pres Institutional Advancement .... Mr. John L. HANNAN
32 Vice President Student Life .... Vacant

21 Vice President Business Services ... Vacant
84 Vice Pres Enrollment Management ... Mr. Michael HENDRICKS
35 Assoc VP Student Life/Dean Students ... Mr. Jonathan C. SAWYER
26 Assoc Vice Pres for Public Affairs ... Mr. Victor B. NAKAS
43 University Counsel ... Mr. Lawrence J. MORRIS
15 Assoc VP/Chief Human Resources ... Ms. Christine SPORTES
18 Assoc VP Facilities Operations ... Mr. Jerry CONRAD
41 Assoc VP & Director Athletics ... Dr. Michael S. ALLEN
88 Assoc VP for Campus Services ... Mr. Timothy CARNEY
44 Asst Vice Pres Instnl Advancement ... Mr. David S. MCMULLEN
25 Assoc Prov Sponsored Research ... Mr. Ralph ALBANO
58 Dean Graduate Studies ... Dr. James GREENE
48 Dean of Architecture ... Mr. Randall OTT
49 Dean of Arts & Sciences ... Dr. Lawrence R. POOS
50 Dean Sch of Business & Economics ... Dr. Andrew V. ABELA
54 Dean of Engineering ... Dr. Charles C. NGUYEN
61 Dean of Law ... Mr. Daniel F. ATTRIDGE
64 Dean of Music ... Dr. Grayson WAGSTAFF
70 Dean Natl Catholic Sch Social Svcs ... Dr. William RAINFORD
66 Dean of Nursing ... Dr. Patricia MCMULLEN
73 Dean Theology/Religious Studies ... Rev. Mark MOROZOWICH
55 Dean Metropolitan Sch Profess Stds ... Dr. Sara M. THOMPSON
79 Dean of Philosophy ... Dr. John C. MCCARTHY
88 Dean of Canon Law ... Rev. Robert J. KASLYN, SJ
07 Dean of Admissions ... Ms. Christine MICA
13 Chief Information Officer ... Mr. Ziaeddin MAFAHER
08 Director of Libraries ... Mr. Stephen CONNAGHAN
06 Registrar ... Vacant
36 Director of Career Services ... Mr. Anthony CHIAPPETTA
29 Exec Director Alumni Relations ... Ms. Kyra A. LYONS
19 Director of Public Safety ... Ms. Thomasine JOHNSON
38 Director of Counseling Center ... Dr. T. Monroe RAYBURN
23 Medical Director of Health Center ... Dr. Loretta STAUDT
37 Dir Student Financial Assistance ... Mr. Joe DOBROTA
39 Director of Housing Services ... Ms. Heidi E. ZEICH
44 Director Annual Giving ... Ms. Megan Daly FARMER
42 Dir Univ Campus Ministry ... Rev. Jude DEANGELO, OFM CONV
09 Dir Inst Research/Assessment ... Mr. Brian A. JOHNSTON
92 Director Univ Honors Program ... Dr. Peter SHOEMAKER
96 Sr Director of Procurement Services ... Ms. Debbie JACKSON
22 Equal Opportunity Officer ... Ms. Lisa WOOD
88 Compliance and Ethics Officer ... Mr. Vincent A. LACOVARA
40 Manager Bookstore ... Mr. Jonathan HOWARD

Chicago School of Professional Psychology-Washington DC (A)

901 15th Street NW, Washington DC 20005
Telephone: (202) 706-5052 Identification: 770493
Accreditation: &WC

† Main campus is Chicago School of Professional Psychology Los Angeles Campus in Los Angeles, CA.

Corcoran College of Art and Design (B)

500 17th Street, NW, Washington DC 20006-4804
FICE Identification: 011950
Unit ID: 131308
Telephone: (202) 639-1801 Carnegie Class: Spec/Arts
FAX Number: (202) 639-1802 Calendar System: Semester
URL: www.corcoran.edu
Established: 1890 Annual Undergrad Tuition & Fees: $30,930
Enrollment: 581 Coed
Affiliation or Control: Independent Non-Profit IRS Status: 501(c)3
Highest Offering: Master's
Program: Liberal Arts And General; Fine Arts Emphasis
Accreditation: M, ART

01 Interim Director and President ... Ms. Peggy LOAR
05 Provost & Chief Academic Officer ... Ms. Catherine ARMOUR
10 Interim Vice President of Finance ... Ms. Debbie FEINBERG
26 VP of Marketing and Communications ... Ms. Mimi CARGER
20 Assoc Provost/Dean Undergrad Stds ... Mr. Andy GRUNDBERG
32 Dean of Students ... Mr. John DICKSON
84 Dean of Enrollment ... Ms. Christine LEICHLITER
15 Sr Director of Human Resources ... Ms. Karen WITT
11 Senior Director of Operations ... Mr. Richard CONN
06 Registrar ... Ms. Curren MCLANE
08 Library Director ... Mr. Mario ASCENCIO
37 Director of Financial Aid ... Ms. Diane MORRIS
51 Director of Continuing Education ... Ms. Doris OSTRANDER
09 Dir of Inst Research & Assessment ... Ms. Selila HONIG

Gallaudet University (C)

800 Florida Avenue, NE, Washington DC 20002-3695
FICE Identification: 001443
Unit ID: 131450
Telephone: (202) 651-5000 Carnegie Class: Master's S
FAX Number: (202) 651-5508 Calendar System: Semester
URL: www.gallaudet.edu
Established: 1864 Annual Undergrad Tuition & Fees: $13,898
Enrollment: 1,488 Coed
Affiliation or Control: Independent Non-Profit IRS Status: 501(c)3
Highest Offering: Doctorate
Program: Liberal Arts And General; Teacher Preparatory; Professional
Accreditation: M, ACBSP, AUD, CACREP, CLPSY, SP, SW, TED

01 President ... Dr. T. Alan HURWITZ
05 Provost ... Dr. Stephen F. WEINER
10 Vice Pres Admin & Finance ... Mr. Paul KELLY
30 Vice Pres Dev & Alumni Relations ... Dr. Lynne MURRAY
88 VP Laurent Clerc Nat Deaf Ed Ctr ... Mr. Edward H. BOSSO
100 Chief of Staff ... Mr. Don BEIL
101 Spec Asst to Pres/Board Liaison ... Vacant
84 Interim Chief Enrollmt Mgmt Officer ... Ms. Charity REEDY-HINES
28 Chief Diversity Officer ... Dr. Angela MCCASKILL
27 Chief Information Officer ... Dr. Cynthia KING
53 Int Dean Sch Educ/Bus/Human Svcs ... Dr. Isaac AGBOOLA
58 Asc Prov Rsrch/Dean Graduate School ... Dr. Carol ERTING
32 Dean Student Affs/Academic Support ... Mr. Dwight BENEDICT
49 Dean College Arts & Sciences ... Dr. Genie GERTZ
88 Exec Dir Academic Quality ... Dr. Patricia HULSEBOSCH
21 Executive Director Finance ... Ms. Jean CIBUZAR
45 Director University Budget ... Ms. Debra LIPKEY
96 Exec Dir Business Support Services ... Mr. Gary ALLER
18 Executive Director Facilities ... Dr. Meloyde BATTEN-MICKENS
11 Asst Vice Pres Administration ... Mr. Fred WEINER
102 Dir Corp and Foundations Relations ... Vacant
26 Exec Dir Comm & Public Relations ... Ms. Catherine MURPHY
09 Dir Research & Info Services ... Ms. Sarah DUCRAY
29 Director Alumni Relations ... Mr. Samuel SONNENSTRAHL
15 Director Human Resources Svcs ... Ms. Elaine VANCE
90 Exec Dir Technology Services ... Mr. Earl PARKS
88 Dir Technology Servcies Enterprise ... Mr. Harvey GROSSINGER
14 Info Security Officer/Network Dir ... Vacant
88 Director Library Public Services ... Ms. Sarah HAMRICK
88 University Ombuds ... Ms. Suzanne ROSEN SINGLETON
88 Dir Library Deaf Collection/Archive ... Mr. Ulf HEDBERG
22 Director Equal Opportunity Programs ... Ms. Sharrell MCCASKILL
06 Registrar ... Mr. Randy PREZIOSO

George Washington University (D)

2121 I Street, NW, Washington DC 20052-0002
FICE Identification: 001444
Unit ID: 131469
Telephone: (202) 994-1000 Carnegie Class: RU/VH
FAX Number: (202) 994-0458 Calendar System: Semester
URL: www.gwu.edu
Established: 1821 Annual Undergrad Tuition & Fees: $47,342
Enrollment: 25,653 Coed
Affiliation or Control: Independent Non-Profit IRS Status: 501(c)3
Highest Offering: Doctorate
Program: 2-Year Principally Bachelor's Creditable; Liberal Arts And General; Teacher Preparatory; Professional
Accreditation: M, ARCPA, BUS, BUSA, CACREP, CIDA, CLPSY, CORE, CS, DMS, ENG, FEPAC, HSA, LAW, MED, MT, MUS, NURSE, PH, PTA, SP, SPAA, TED

01 President ... Dr. Steven KNAPP
100 Chief of Staff President's Office ... Ms. Barbara A. PORTER
05 Provost & Exec VP Academic Affairs ... Dr. Steven LERMAN
30 Vice Pres for Dev/Alumni Relations ... Mr. Michael J. MORSBERGER
10 Exec Vice President & Treasurer ... Mr. Louis H. KATZ
43 Senior Vice Pres & General Counsel ... Ms. Beth NOLAN
26 Vice President External Relations ... Ms. Lorraine A. VOLES
20 Sr Vice Provost Academic Affairs ... Dr. Forrest MALTZMAN
28 Vice Provost Diversity & Inclusion ... Dr. Terri Harris REED
20 Vice Provost Teaching and Learning ... Dr. Stephen C. EHRMAN
15 Chief Human Resources Officer ... Ms. Sabrina ELLIS
13 Chief Information Officer ... Mr. David STEINOUR
20 Vice Provost Faculty Affairs ... Dr. Diane C. MARTIN
21 Senior Associate VP for Finance ... Mr. David D. LAWLOR
11 Senior Assoc VP of Operations ... Ms. Alicia M. O'NEIL
35 Senior Assoc VP & Dean of Students ... Dr. Peter A. KONWERSKI
89 Assoc VP & Dean of Freshmen ... Ms. Helen CANNADAY SAULNY
90 Assoc VP for Acad Technologies ... Ms. P. B. GARRETT
88 Assoc VP of Acad Plang & Assessment ... Dr. Cheryl BEIL
46 Vice President for Research ... Dr. Leo M. CHALUPA
21 Chief Budget Officer ... Ms. Vanessa R. ROSE
21 University Comptroller ... Ms. Sharon HEINLE
09 Director Inst Research & Planning ... Mr. Joachim W. KNOP
86 Assistant Vice President DC Affairs ... Mr. Bernard DEMCZUK
87 Associate VP for International Pgms ... Dr. Donna SCARBORO
08 University Librarian ... Mr. Jack A. SIGGINS
26 Asst VP for Communications ... Ms. Sarah GEGENHEIMER BALDASSARO
27 Exec Director of Media Relations ... Ms. Candace E. SMITH
29 Associate VP Alumni Relations ... Ms. Adrienne A. RULNICK
06 Registrar ... Ms. Elizabeth A. AMUNDSON
07 Director of Undergrad Admissions ... Ms. Karen S. FELTON
38 Director Counseling Center ... Dr. John R. DAGES
37 Assoc VP & Director Financial Aid ... Mr. Daniel E. SMALL
36 Exec Director Career Center ... Ms. Marva GUMBS
18 Associate VP Facilities ... Vacant
85 Director International Services ... Mr. Joseph G. LEONARD
19 Sr Assoc VP Safety & Security ... Mr. Darrell L. DARNELL
22 Exec Dir EEO & Affirmative Action ... Mr. Gilberto GARCIA, JR.
23 Director Student Health Services ... Dr. Isabel GOLDENBERG
40 Director GW Bookstore ... Mr. Robert C. BLAKE
107 Dean Col of Professional Studies ... Dr. Ali ESKANDARIAN
49 Dean Columbian Col Arts/Sciences ... Dr. Marguerite BARRATT
63 Interim Dean Medicine & Health Sci ... Dr. Jeffrey S. AKMAN
69 Dean School of Public Health ... Dr. Lynn R. GOLDMAN
61 Interim Dean Law School ... Dr. Gregory E. MAGGS
54 Dean Engineer/Applied Science ... Dr. David DOLLING
53 Dean Education/Human Development ... Dr. Michael J. FEUER
50 Interim Dean School of Business ... Dr. Christopher KAYES
82 Dean Elliott School Intl Affairs ... Dr. Michael E. BROWN
66 Dean School of Nursing ... Dr. Jean JOHNSON
12 Dean GW Virginia Sci/Tech Campus ... Dr. Ali ESKANDARIAN
88 Sen Assoc Dean Military & Veterans ... VAdm. Melvin G. WILLIAMS
41 Director Athletics/Recreation ... Mr. Patrick NERO
84 Asst VP Grad Student Enroll Mgmt ... Dr. Kristin WILLIAMS
92 Director University Honors Program ... Dr. Maria H. FRAWLEY
93 Director Multicultural Student Svc ... Mr. Michael R. TAPSCOTT

Georgetown University (E)

37th & O Streets, NW, Washington DC 20057-1947
FICE Identification: 001445
Unit ID: 131496
Telephone: (202) 687-0100 Carnegie Class: RU/VH
FAX Number: N/A Calendar System: Semester
URL: www.georgetown.edu
Established: 1789 Annual Undergrad Tuition & Fees: $44,280
Enrollment: 17,357 Coed
Affiliation or Control: Roman Catholic IRS Status: 501(c)3
Highest Offering: Doctorate
Program: Liberal Arts And General; Professional
Accreditation: M, ANEST, BUS, CEA, HSA, LAW, MED, MIDWF, NURSE

01 President ... Dr. John (Jack) J. DEGIOIA
46 Sr VP Research/Chief Technology Off ... Dr. Spiros DIMOLITSAS
101 Secretary of the University ... Mr. Edward M. QUINN
100 Chief of Staff ... Mr. Joseph FERRARA
05 Provost ... Dr. Robert M. GROVES
17 Exec Vice Pres Health Sciences ... Dr. Howard J. FEDEROFF
61 Exec Vice Pres/Dean of Law School ... Dr. William M. TREANOR
26 Vice Pres for Advancement ... Mr. R. Bartley MOORE
42 Vice Pres for Mission and Ministry ... Rev. Kevin O'BRIEN, SJ
11 Sr Vice Pres and COO ... Mr. Christopher L. AUGOSTINI
10 Vice Pres Finance & Univ Treasurer ... Mr. David RUBENSTEIN
27 Vice Pres/CIO ... Ms. Lisa DAVIS
15 Acting VP/Chief HR Officer ... Ms. Junie NATHANI
26 VP Public Affairs & Strategic Dev ... Mr. Erik SMULSON
18 VP Planning & Facilities Mgmt ... Mr. Robin MOREY
32 Vice President for Student Affairs ... Dr. Todd OLSON
28 VP for Inst Diversity & Equity ... Ms. Rosemary KILKENNY
19 Chief of Police Dept Public Safety ... Mr. Jay GRUBER
43 VP & General Counsel ... Ms. Lisa M. BROWN
88 VP for Global Engagement ... Dr. Thomas BANCHOFF
29 Associate VP Alumni Relations ... Mr. William G. REYNOLDS
88 Assoc VP for Auxiliary Services ... Mr. Lennie CARTER
90 Asc VP UIS/ED Assessment/Dec Sup ... Dr. Ardoth HASSLER
88 Assc VP Benefits/Chief Benefits Off ... Mr. Charles E. DESANTIS
13 Associate VP & Deputy CIO ... Mr. Judd L. NICHOLSON
20 Vice Provost Education ... Dr. Randall BASS
20 Vice Provost Research ... Dr. Janet MANN
20 Vice Provost Faculty ... Dr. Adriana KUGLER
06 Registrar ... Mr. John Q. PIERCE, IV
07 Dean Undergraduate Admissions ... Mr. Charles A. DEACON
23 Asst VP for Student Health ... Dr. James C. WELSH
08 University Librarian ... Ms. Artemis G. KIRK
09 Interim Director Inst Research ... Dr. Jason P. CASEY
37 Dean Student Financial Svcs ... Ms. Patricia A. MCWADE
25 Associate Dean for Research Admin ... Ms. Mary E. SCHMIEDEL
49 Dean Georgetown College ... Dr. Chester GILLIS
82 Dean School Foreign Service ... Dr. Carol LANCASTER
50 Dean School of Business ... Dr. David A. THOMAS
63 Dean Medical School ... Dr. Stephen R. MITCHELL
66 Dean Sch of Nursing/Health Stds ... Dr. Martin Y. IGUCHI
51 Interim Dean Cont Studies ... Dr. Walter RANKIN
58 Interim Dean of Graduate School ... Dr. G. William REBECK
86 Asst to President Federal Relations ... Mr. Scott S. FLEMING
31 Asst VP Community Engagement/SI ... Ms. Lauralyn B. LEE
85 Exec Dir International Programs ... Ms. Kathryn S. BELLOWS
36 Exec Director Career Center ... Dr. J. Michael SCHAUB
22 Director Affirmative Action Pgm ... Mr. Michael W. SMITH
24 Exec Dir Classroom Educ/Tech Svcs ... Mr. Mark J. COHEN
38 Director Counseling Center ... Dr. Philip W. MEILMAN
41 Director Athletics ... Mr. Lee REED
96 Director Financial Operations ... Ms. Geneva THORNE
39 Director of Residence Life ... Ms. Stephanie J. LYNCH

Graduate School USA (F)

600 Maryland Ave, SW Ste 330, Washington DC 20024
Identification: 667121
Telephone: (202) 314-3300 Carnegie Class: Not Classified
FAX Number: (202) 479-2502 Calendar System: Semester
URL: www.graduateschool.edu
Established: Annual Undergrad Tuition & Fees: $8,100
Enrollment: N/A Coed
Affiliation or Control: Independent Non-Profit IRS Status: 501(c)3
Highest Offering: Associate Degree
Program: Occupational
Accreditation: @M

01 Interim CEO & President ... Dr. Elaine RYAN

Howard University (G)

2400 Sixth Street, NW, Washington DC 20059-0001
FICE Identification: 001448
Unit ID: 131520
Telephone: (202) 806-6100 Carnegie Class: RU/H
FAX Number: (202) 806-5934 Calendar System: Semester
URL: www.howard.edu
Established: 1867 Annual Undergrad Tuition & Fees: $22,883
Enrollment: 10,494 Coed
Affiliation or Control: Independent Non-Profit IRS Status: 501(c)3
Highest Offering: Doctorate

Program: Occupational; Liberal Arts And General; Teacher Preparatory; Professional

Accreditation: M, #ARCPA, ART, BUS, BUSA, CLPSY, #COPSY, CS, DENT, DH, DIETC, ENG, IPSY, JOUR, LAW, MED, MT, MUS, NURSE, OT, PHAR, PTA, #RTT, SP, SW, TED, THEA, THEOL

Code	Title	Name
01	Interim President	Dr. Wayne H. FREDERICK
05	Provost/Chief Academic Officer	Dr. Wayne H. FREDERICK
10	Senior Vice President & CFO	Mr. Robert TAROLA
101	Senior Vice Pres/Secretary of Univ	Ms. Artis G. HAMPSHIRE-COWAN
43	General Counsel	Mr. Kurt L. SCHMOKE
30	Vice President Development	Ms. Nesta BERNARD
100	Chief of Staff	Mr. Andrew RIVERS
17	CEO University Hospital	Mr. Herbert BUCHANAN
20	Associate Provost	Dr. Joseph P. REIDY
46	AVP for Research Health Sciences	Dr. Kristy F. WOODS
32	Vice President Student Affairs	Dr. Barbara GRIFFIN
13	Interim Chief Information Officer	Mr. Tilmon SMITH
21	Deputy Chief Financial Officer	Ms. Bridget SARIKAS
58	Interim Dean Graduate School	Dr. Gary L. HARRIS
49	Interim Dean College Arts/Sciences	Dr. Segun GBADEGESIN
50	Dean School of Business	Dr. Barron H. HARVEY
61	Interim Dean School of Law	Ms. Okianer CHRISTIAN DARK
63	Dean College of Medicine	Dr. Mark S. JOHNSON
52	Dean College of Dentistry	Dr. Leo E. ROUSE
54	Interim Dean Col Engr/Arch/Comp Sc	Dr. Lorraine FLEMING
53	Dean School of Education	Dr. Leslie T. FENWICK
60	Dean School Communications	Dr. Gracie LAWSON-BORDERS
88	Dean Col Nursing/Allied Hlth Sci	Dr. Mary HILL
70	Interim Dean School of Social Work	Dr. Sandra CREWE
73	Dean School of Divinity	Dr. Alton B. POLLARD, III
67	Dean School of Pharmacy	Dr. Anthony WUTOH
48	Director School of Architecture	Prof. Bradford C. GRANT
76	Assoc Dean/Div Allied Health Sci	Dr. Allan JOHNSON
57	Assoc Dean/Division of Fine Arts	Dr. Gwendolyn H. EVERETT
84	Director of Enrollment Management	Vacant
07	Interim Director of Admissions	Ms. Latrice COVINGTON
37	Director Financial Aid	Mr. Derek KINDLE
42	Dean Andrew Rankin Chapel	Dr. Bernard L. RICHARDSON
35	Dean Student Life & Activities	Ms. Tonya L. GUILLORY
39	Dean of Residence Life	Mr. Marc D. LEE
36	Director Career Services Office	Dr. Joan M. BROWNE
23	Director Student Health Center	Dr. Evelyn TREAKLE-MOORE
09	Dir University Research & Plng	Vacant
08	Director University Libraries	Mr. Howard DODSON, JR.
88	Director Health Sciences Library	Ms. Cynthia L. HENDERSON
88	Director Law Library	Ms. Rhea BALLARD-THROWER
24	Dir Teaching Learning & Assmnt Ctr	Dr. Theresa M. REDD
92	Director of Honors Program	Dr. Daniel A. WILLIAMS, III
94	Director of Women's Studies	Vacant
30	Director for Advancement Services	Mr. Jeremy C. RANDALL
29	Director Alumni Relations	Ms. Christie ASKEW
44	Director of Annual Giving	Ms. Christie ASKEW
26	Acting Dir Comm & Marketing	Dr. Kerry-Ann HAMILTON
15	Interim VP for Human Resources	Mr. Michael MCFADDEN
16	Director of Employment	Ms. Kym WILSON
22	Dir Equal Employment Opportunity	Mr. Antwan LOFTON
40	Director University Bookstore	Mr. Antwan D. CLINTON
19	Chief of Campus Police	Mr. Leroy K. JAMES
41	Athletics Director	Mr. Louis PERKINS, JR.
31	Director HU Community Association	Ms. Maybelle T. BENNETT
18	Exec Dir Physical Facilities	Vacant

The Institute of World Politics (A)

1521 16th Street, NW, Washington DC 20036-1464

FICE Identification: 041144
Unit ID: 455804

Telephone: (202) 462-2101 Carnegie Class: Spec/Other
FAX Number: (202) 464-0335 Calendar System: Semester
URL: www.iwp.edu
Established: 1990 Annual Graduate Tuition & Fees: $28,100
Enrollment: 151 Coed
Affiliation or Control: Independent Non-Profit IRS Status: 501(c)3
Highest Offering: Master's; No Undergraduates
Program: Professional
Accreditation: M

Code	Title	Name
01	President	Dr. John LENCZOWSKI
88	VP Professnl Affilations/Ex Dir PP	Ms. Linda STRATING
30	Vice Pres Institutional Advancement	Ms. Tricia LLOYD
05	VP Academic Aff/Chief Academic Ofcr	Dr. J. Michael WALLER
10	Director Financial Operations	Mrs. Elaine PINDER
06	Registrar & Institutional Research	Mrs. Hasanna BENSON-TYUS
84	Director Student Recruitment	Mr. Tim STEBBINS
08	Director Libraries/Info Svcs	Mr. Dmitry KULIK
04	Asst to President/Development Ofcr	Ms. Kathy CARROLL
27	Communications Officer	Mr. Charles VAN SOMEREN
37	Director of Financial Aid	Ms. La Nae HERRARA

Medtech College (B)

529 14th Street, NW, Washington DC 20045
Telephone: (202) 872-4700 Identification: 666591
Accreditation: COE

† Main campus is Medtech College in Falls Church, VA.

Pontifical Faculty of the Immaculate Conception at the Dominican House of Studies (C)

487 Michigan Avenue, NE, Washington DC 20017-1585

FICE Identification: 012803
Unit ID: 131405

Telephone: (202) 495-3820 Carnegie Class: Spec/Faith
FAX Number: (202) 495-3873 Calendar System: Semester
URL: www.dhs.edu
Established: 1902 Annual Graduate Tuition & Fees: $15,370
Enrollment: 97 Coed
Affiliation or Control: Roman Catholic IRS Status: 501(c)3
Highest Offering: Master's; No Undergraduates
Program: Professional; Religious Emphasis
Accreditation: M, THEOL

Code	Title	Name
01	President	Fr. John LANGLOIS, OP
05	Vice President/Academic Dean	Fr. Thomas PETRI, OP
20	Secretary of Studies	Fr. Brian CHRZASTEK, OP
08	Librarian	Fr. John Martin RUIZ, OP
18	Director of Facilities	Br. Gerard THAYER, OP
42	Chaplain to Commuter Students	Fr. John Baptist KU, OP
06	Registrar	Fr. Allen MORAN, OP
10	Treasurer/Director of Financial Aid	Ms. Shauna ROYE
30	Assistant Director of Advancement	Mr. George CERVANTES
14	IT Director	Mr. Carlos MOLINA
88	Writing Tutor	Fr. Raymond VANDEGRIFT, OP
36	Director of Career Placement	Dr. Jem SULLIVAN
04	Executive Assistant	Mrs. Allison LAPARY
88	Administrative Secretary	Ms. Sharon SMITH

Pontifical John Paul II Institute for Studies on Marriage and Family (D)

620 Michigan Ave, NE, McGivney Hall, Washington DC 20064
County: USA FICE Identification: 041427
Unit ID: 455813

Telephone: (202) 526-3799 Carnegie Class: Spec/Other
FAX Number: (202) 269-6090 Calendar System: Other
URL: www.johnpaulii.edu
Established: 1988 Annual Graduate Tuition & Fees: $16,500
Enrollment: 86 Coed
Affiliation or Control: Roman Catholic IRS Status: 501(c)3
Highest Offering: Doctorate; No Undergraduates
Program: Professional; Religious Emphasis
Accreditation: M

Code	Title	Name
01	President	Rev. Livio MELINA
03	Vice President	Carl A. ANDERSON
05	Provost	Fr. Antonio LOPEZ
06	Registrar	Joseph C. ATKINSON
07	Director of Admissions	Sara L. TRUDEAU
20	Dean	Rev. Antonio LOPEZ
20	Associate Dean for Academic Affairs	David S. CRAWFORD
11	Assoc Dean Progams & Administration	Nick J. BAGILEO

† Affiliated with The Catholic University of America, DC.

Radians College (E)

1025 Vermont Avenue, Suite 200, Washington DC 20005
Identification: 667005
Telephone: (202) 291-9020 Carnegie Class: Not Classified
FAX Number: (202) 291-8013 Calendar System: Trimester
URL: www.radianscollege.edu
Established: 2005 Annual Undergrad Tuition & Fees: N/A
Enrollment: N/A Coed
Affiliation or Control: Proprietary IRS Status: Proprietary
Highest Offering: Associate Degree
Program: Occupational; 2-Year Principally Bachelor's Creditable; Nursing Emphasis
Accreditation: ACICS

Code	Title	Name
01	President	Mr. Mark CHESNEY
05	VP Academic Administration	Vacant

Strayer University (F)

1133 15th Street, NW, Washington DC 20005-2710

FICE Identification: 001459
Unit ID: 131803

Telephone: (202) 408-2400 Carnegie Class: Master's L
FAX Number: (202) 419-1423 Calendar System: Quarter
URL: www.strayer.edu
Established: 1892 Annual Undergrad Tuition & Fees: $14,985
Enrollment: 1,517 Coed
Affiliation or Control: Proprietary IRS Status: Proprietary
Highest Offering: Master's
Program: Occupational; Liberal Arts And General; Professional
Accreditation: M, ACBSP, @TEAC

Code	Title	Name
01	President	Dr. Michael PLATER
05	Provost/Chief Academic Ofcr	Dr. Randi REICH COSENTINO
20	Sr Vice Provost of Academic Admin	Vacant
10	Senior VP/Chief Financial Officer	Mr. Mark C. BROWN
32	Senior Vice Provost Student Affairs	Dr. Tracey LACEY
37	Vice Pres Student Financial Svcs	Mr. Richard M. ANTHONY
13	VP/Chief Technology Officer	Mr. Joe P. SCHAEFER
106	Online Academic Dean Global Region	Mr. Matthew MIKO
35	Dean of Students	Ms. Jacqueline PALMER
08	University Librarian	Mr. David A. MOULTON
20	Dir of Acad Program Administration	Ms. Cyndi L. WASTLER
06	University Registrar	Mr. Robert BERWICK
20	Chamblee Campus Dean	Dr. DeNorris HEARD
12	Chamblee Campus Director	Mr. Rick WYLIE
20	Chesterfield Campus Dean	Ms. Carol WILLIAMS
12	Chesterfield Campus Director	Ms. Cheryl VAUGHAN
20	Christiana Campus Dean	Dr. William CREAMER
12	Christiana Campus Director	Ms. Amy CESTONE
20	Charleston Campus Dean	Dr. Andrea BRVENIK
12	Charleston Campus Director	Ms. Colette REID
20	Cobb County Campus Dean	Ms. Andrea BANTO
12	Cobb County Campus Director	Mr. Dion JOHNSON
20	Columbia Campus Dean	Dr. Vincent OSISEK
12	Columbia Campus Director	Ms. Marcia JOHNSON
20	Delaware County Campus Dean	Dr. Wanda ALLEN
12	Delaware County Campus Director	Mr. Paul HINKSMAN
20	Fredericksburg Campus Dean	Vacant
12	Fredericksburg Campus Director	Deon HAMNER
20	Greensboro Campus Dean	Dr. Teresa GREENWOOD
12	Greensboro Campus Director	Ms. Tenika GLENN
20	Interim Henrico Campus Dean	Ms. Carol WILLIAMS
12	Henrico Campus Director	Ms. Amy BREEDEN
20	Lower Bucks Campus Dean	Mr. Gary WHITE
12	Lower Bucks Campus Director	Mr. Lamar FARR
20	Greenville Campus Dean	Mr. Peter MCDANIEL
12	Greenville Campus Director	Ms. Kelly HUMPHRIES
20	King of Prussia Campus Dean	Dr. Eugene GARONE
12	King of Prussia Campus Director	Ms. Monique STERLING
20	Loudoun Campus Dean	Ms. Myra ROBINSON
12	Loudoun Campus Director	Mr. Tyrone TINDELL
20	Manassas Campus Dean	Ms. Melba WILLIAMS
12	Manassas Campus Director	Ms. Shirin SAGHAFI
20	North Raleigh Campus Dean	Dr. Pang-Jen CRAIG KUNG
12	North Raleigh Campus Director	Ms. Kenya DUKES
20	Morrow Campus Dean	Dr. Virgil MENSAH-DARTEY
12	Morrow Campus Director	Ms. Toni STURDIVANT
20	Nashville Campus Dean	Dr. Udoh UDOM
12	Nashville Campus Director	Ms. Denise SILVA
20	Newport News Campus Dean	Dr. Gianpaolo CAPPUZZO
12	Newport News Campus Director	Ms. D'Andre H. WILSON
20	North Charlotte Campus Dean	Dr. Kazem KAN-SHAGHAGHI
12	North Charlotte Campus Director	Ms. Dianna ANDERSON
20	Owings Mills Campus Dean	Mr. Barry THOMAS
12	Owings Mills Campus Director	Dr. Doreen LUCAS
20	Roswell Campus Dean	Dr. Keva YARBROUGH
12	Roswell Campus Director	Ms. Diana BONSIGNORE
20	Shelby Oaks Campus Dean	Dr. Ron DAVIS
12	Shelby Oaks Campus Director	Mr. Torrence EDDIE
20	Penn Center West Campus Dean	Dr. George MARUSCHOCK
12	Penn Center West Campus Director	Ms. Carly BROWN
20	Prince Georges Campus Dean	Mr. Willie STRAIT
12	Prince Georges Campus Director	Ms. Chinneta COLLINS
20	Research Triangle Park Campus Dean	Mr. Donald WEST
12	Research Triangle Park Campus Dir	Ms. Cherry CLARK
20	Rockville Campus Dean	Dr. Jerald L. FEINSTEIN
12	Rockville Campus Director	Mr. Huot HE
20	South Charlotte Campus Dean	Dr. Johnnie D. WOODARD
12	South Charlotte Campus Director	Mr. Mark LOMAS
20	Virginia Beach Campus Dean	Dr. Hermann BAYER
12	Virginia Beach Campus Director	Mr. Tom LOTITO
12	Takoma Park Campus Director	Mr. Melvin MENNS
20	Takoma Park Campus Dean	Mr. Doug EARHART
20	Tampa East Campus Dean	Dr. Yamil GUEVARA
12	Tampa East Campus Director	Mr. Jeffrey KEITH
20	Tampa Westshore Campus Dean	Dr. Mohammad SUMADI
12	Tampa Westshore Campus Director	Ms. Jennifer PORTER
20	Woodbridge Campus Dean	Dr. Michael I. OTAIGBE
12	Woodbridge Campus Director	Ms. Niaomi CARTER
12	Thousand Oakes Campus Director	Ms. Lottie MINOR
20	Thousand Oaks Campus Dean	Dr. Jeannie OLIVER
20	Washington Campus Dean	Dr. Chandra QUAYE
12	Washington Campus Director	Mr. Haroon MOKEL
20	White Marsh Campus Dean	Ms. A. Kobina ARMOO
12	White Marsh Campus Director	Ms. Yanka CAMPBELL
20	Arlington Campus Dean	Ms. E. Maggie SIZER
12	Arlington Campus Director	Ms. Corey ROSSO
20	Alexandria Campus Dean	Dr. Abed H. ALMALA
12	Alexandria Campus Director	Ms. Amy PROPER
20	Center City Campus Dean	Mr. Izzeldin BAKHIT
12	Center City Campus Director	Mr. Isaac WALTERS
20	Anne Arundel Campus Dean	Dr. Twila LINDSAY
12	Anne Arundel Campus Director	Mr. Valtroud HARVEY
20	Birmingham Campus Dean	Dr. Vidal ADADEVOH
12	Birmingham Campus Director	Ms. Stephanie GOWER
20	Chesapeake Campus Dean	Dr. Muleka KIKWEBATI
12	Chesapeake Campus Director	Ms. Jeanne POINDEXTER

Trinity Washington University (G)

125 Michigan Avenue, NE, Washington DC 20017-1090

FICE Identification: 001460
Unit ID: 131876

Telephone: (202) 884-9000 Carnegie Class: Master's L
FAX Number: (202) 884-9229 Calendar System: Semester
URL: www.trinitydc.edu
Established: 1897 Annual Undergrad Tuition & Fees: $20,550
Enrollment: 2,660 Female
Affiliation or Control: Roman Catholic IRS Status: 501(c)3
Highest Offering: Master's
Program: Liberal Arts And General; Teacher Preparatory; Professional

Accreditation: **M**, NURSE, TED

01 President ... Ms. Patricia A. MCGUIRE
04 Assistant to the President ... Ms. Kim MORTON
05 Vice President Academic Affairs ... Dr. Virginia BROADDUS
84 Vice Pres Enrollment Services ... Ms. Cathy GEIER
30 Vice Pres Institutional Advancement ... Ms. Ann PAULEY
07 Vice President of CAS Admissions ... Ms. Kelly GOSNELL
32 Vice President for Student Affairs ... Dr. Karen GERLACH
49 Dean College of Arts & Science ... Vacant
53 Dean School of Education ... Dr. Janet STOCKS
107 Dean School of Professional Studies ... Dr. Telaekah BROOKS
66 Dean Sch Nursing/Health Professions ... Dr. Mary ROMANELLO
32 Dean of Student Services ... Ms. Michelle BOWIE
44 Director of Development ... Ms. Judy TART
15 Director of Human Resources ... Ms. Carole KING
41 Athletic Director ... Ms. Tracy RENKEN
42 Director of Campus Ministry ... Sr. Mary Ellen DOW
18 Exec Director Facilities Services ... Mr. Tim KNIGHT
29 Director Alumnae Affairs ... Ms. Margy REAGAN

University of the District of Columbia (A)

4200 Connecticut Avenue, NW,
Washington DC 20008-1174

FICE Identification: 001441
Unit ID: 131399
Telephone: (202) 274-5000 Carnegie Class: Master's S
FAX Number: (202) 274-5304 Calendar System: Semester
URL: www.udc.edu
Established: 1976 Annual Undergrad Tuition & Fees (In-District): $7,255
Enrollment: 5,110 Coed
Affiliation or Control: Local IRS Status: 501(c)3
Highest Offering: Master's
Program: Occupational; 2-Year Principally Bachelor's Creditable; Liberal Arts And General; Teacher Preparatory; Professional
Accreditation: **M**, ACBSP, ADNUR, CACREP, COARC, CS, DIETD, ENG, #FUSER, LAW, NUR, #SP, SW, TED

01 Interim President ... Dr. James E. LYONS, SR.
05 Provost/Vice Pres Academic Affairs ... Dr. Rachel PETTY
32 Vice President for Student Affairs ... Dr. Valerie EPPS
16 Vice President Human Resources ... Ms. Myrtho BLANCHARD
18 VP Facilities & Real Estate ... Ms. Barbara JUMPER
07 Assoc VP Admission/Recruit ... Ms. Saundra CARTER
12 CEO UDC Community College ... Dr. Calvin WOODLAND
20 Executive Asst to the Provost ... Mr. Herman PRESCOTT
10 Chief Financial Officer ... Mr. Donald RICKFORD
49 Acting Dean Arts & Sciences ... Dr. April MASSEY
50 Dean Sch Business & Public Mgmt ... Dr. Sandra YATES
61 Dean School of Law ... Ms. Katherine S. BRODERICK
54 Dean Engineering/Applied Scis ... Dr. Devdas SHETTY
56 Dean Agriculture Urban Stablity ... Dr. Sabine O'HARA
06 University Registrar ... Ms. LaVerne M. HILL-FLANAGAN
37 Director Student Financial Aid ... Mr. James CONTRERAS
26 Dir Marketing & Communications ... Mr. Michael C. ROGERS
08 Interim Dean Learning Resources ... Ms. Melba BROOME
88 Director Institute Gerontology ... Ms. Jessyna MCDONALD
88 Director Ctr for Res & Urban Policy ... Vacant
25 Director Grants Administration ... Ms. Cassandra PARKER
15 Director Human Resources ... Vacant
41 Athletic Director ... Ms. Patricia A. THOMAS
43 Deputy University Counsel ... Ms. Andrea BAGWELL
88 General Manager UDC Cable TV ... Mr. Edward JONES, JR.
18 Dir of Operations and Maintenance ... Mr. Alvin VENSON
29 Exec Director of Alumni Affairs ... Vacant
30 Exec Director of Development ... Ms. Felicia BRANT
09 Director of Institutional Research ... Vacant
38 Director Student Counseling ... Dr. Sislena LEDBETTER
96 Director of Procurement ... Ms. Mary A. HARRIS
27 Media Liaison and Univ Spokesperson ... Mr. Michael C. ROGERS
88 Dean Student Achievement ... Ms. Hermina P. PETERS
103 Acting Dean Workforce Dept ... Ms. Kim R. FORD
19 Dir Public Safety/Chief of Police ... Mr. Larry E. VOLTZ
92 Director TRIO Program ... Ms. Saundra M. CARTER
36 Director Career Services ... Ms. Katie NAILLER
86 Director State & Local Affairs ... Mr. Thomas E. REDMOND
11 Director Financial Operations ... Mr. David FRANKLIN
88 Director STEM ... Ms. Barbara J. HOLMES
29 Director Alumni Affairs ... Mr. Joseph LIBERTELLI
89 Director of Advising and Retention ... Ms. Kimberly CREWS
102 Director Sponsored Programs ... Ms. Jovita WELLS
13 Dir Information Technology ... Mr. Michael ROGERS
88 Dir Small Business Develop Ctr ... Ms. Candice MILES

University of Phoenix Washington DC Campus (B)

25 Massachusetts Avenue, NW,
Washington DC 20001-1431
Telephone: (202) 423-2520 Identification: 770196
Accreditation: **&NH**, ACBSP

† Main campus is University of Phoenix in Tempe, AZ.

University of the Potomac (C)

1401 H Street NW, Suite 100, Washington DC 20005
FICE Identification: 032183
Unit ID: 384412
Telephone: (202) 686-0876 Carnegie Class: Spec/Bus
FAX Number: (202) 686-0818 Calendar System: Semester
URL: www.potomac.edu
Established: 1991 Annual Undergrad Tuition & Fees: $12,984
Enrollment: 292 Coed
Affiliation or Control: Proprietary IRS Status: Proprietary
Highest Offering: Master's
Program: Technical Emphasis
Accreditation: **M**

01 President/Chief Executive Officer ... Dr. Clinton GARDNER
108 Dir Assessment/Inst Effectiveness ... Walter PERSON
08 Director of Learning Resource Ctr ... Edward ROBINSON

Wesley Theological Seminary (D)

4500 Massachusetts Avenue, NW,
Washington DC 20016-5690
FICE Identification: 001464
Unit ID: 131973
Telephone: (202) 885-8600 Carnegie Class: Spec/Faith
FAX Number: (202) 885-8605 Calendar System: Semester
URL: www.wesleyseminary.edu
Established: 1882 Annual Graduate Tuition & Fees: $17,230
Enrollment: 611 Coed
Affiliation or Control: United Methodist IRS Status: 501(c)3
Highest Offering: Doctorate; No Undergraduates
Program: Professional; Religious Emphasis
Accreditation: **M**, THEOL

01 President ... Dr. David MCALLISTER-WILSON
10 Vice Pres Finance/CFO ... Mr. Jeffrey STRAITS
30 Vice President for Development ... Rev. Terry BRADFIELD
04 Special Assistant to the President ... Ms. Jane S. DELAND
05 Dean ... Dr. Robert MARTIN
32 Assoc Dean Acad Admin/Cmty Life ... Rev. Shelby M. HAGGRAY
07 Director of Admissions ... Rev. William D. ALDRIDGE
06 Registrar ... Ms. Eleanor GEASE
08 Director of Library ... Mr. James ESTES
15 Director Human Resources ... Ms. Yasmin LEWIS-WHITE
18 Chief Facilities/Physical Plant ... Mr. Randall ADAMS
37 Director Student Financial Aid ... Ms. Mary VIBERT
29 Director Alumni Relations ... Ms. Kristin SCHOL
26 Director of Marketing/Communication ... Ms. Amy SHELTON

FLORIDA

Academy for Five Element Acupuncture (E)

305 SE Second Avenue, Gainesville FL 32601-6811
County: Alachua FICE Identification: 035243
Unit ID: 451079
Telephone: (352) 335-2332 Carnegie Class: Spec/Health
FAX Number: (352) 337-2535 Calendar System: Trimester
URL: www.acupuncturist.edu
Established: 1998 Annual Graduate Tuition & Fees: $42,000
Enrollment: 87 Coed
Affiliation or Control: Independent Non-Profit IRS Status: 501(c)3
Highest Offering: Master's; No Undergraduates
Program: Professional
Accreditation: **ACUP**

01 President ... Ms. Misti OXFORD-PICKERAL
11 Vice President Administration ... Ms. Joanne EPSTEIN
05 Academic Dean ... Mr. Chuck GRAHAM
37 Financial Aid Administrator ... Mr. Glenn MORRIS
06 Registrar ... Ms. Angela XISTRIS

Academy for Nursing and Health Occupations (F)

5154 Okeechobee Blvd #201, West Palm Beach FL 33417
County: Palm Beach FICE Identification: 033463
Unit ID: 412173
Telephone: (561) 683-1400 Carnegie Class: Not Classified
FAX Number: (561) 683-6773 Calendar System: Other
URL: www.anho.edu
Established: 1978 Annual Undergrad Tuition & Fees: $18,571
Enrollment: 409 Coed
Affiliation or Control: Independent Non-Profit IRS Status: 501(c)3
Highest Offering: Associate Degree
Program: Occupational; 2-Year Principally Bachelor's Creditable; Nursing Emphasis
Accreditation: **COE**

01 President ... Lois M. GACKENHEIMER

Acupuncture & Massage College (G)

10506 N Kendall Drive, Miami FL 33176-1509
County: Miami-Dade FICE Identification: 034145
Unit ID: 439969
Telephone: (305) 595-9500 Carnegie Class: Spec/Health
FAX Number: (305) 595-2622 Calendar System: Semester
URL: www.amcollege.edu
Established: 1983 Annual Undergrad Tuition & Fees: $45,000
Enrollment: 172 Coed
Affiliation or Control: Proprietary IRS Status: Proprietary
Highest Offering: Master's
Program: Professional; Technical Emphasis
Accreditation: **ACCSC**, ACUP

00 Chief Executive Officer ... Ms. Nancy E. BROWNE
01 President ... Dr. Richard M. BROWNE
05 Academic Dean ... Dr. Gail SHIVEL
17 Clinic Director ... Dr. Wei LU
37 Financial Aid Director ... Mr. Danny CASTELLANOS
07 Admissions Director ... Mr. Joe CALARESO
06 Registrar/Student Services ... Ms. Maria GARCIA

Adventist University of Health Sciences (H)

671 Winyah Drive, Orlando FL 32803-1204
County: Orange FICE Identification: 031155
Unit ID: 133872
Telephone: (407) 303-9798 Carnegie Class: Spec/Health
FAX Number: (407) 303-9408 Calendar System: Trimester
URL: www.adu.edu
Established: 1992 Annual Undergrad Tuition & Fees: $11,830
Enrollment: 2,671 Coed
Affiliation or Control: Seventh-day Adventist IRS Status: 501(c)3
Highest Offering: Master's
Program: Occupational; Professional
Accreditation: **SC**, ADNUR, ANEST, DMS, NMT, NUR, OTA, RAD

01 President ... Dr. David E. GREENLAW
05 Sr VP for Academic Administration ... Dr. Donald E. WILLIAMS
10 Sr VP for Finance/CFO ... Mr. Robert A. CURREN
11 VP for Operations ... Mr. Ruben O. MARTINEZ
32 VP for Student Services ... Mr. Stephen H. ROCHE
26 VP Marketing & Public Relations ... Mr. Lewis HENDERSHOT
106 VP for Educational Tech/Distance Ed ... Dr. Dan LIM
20 Associate VP for Academic Admin ... Dr. Len ARCHER
09 Dir of Accreditation & Inst Effect ... Dr. Roy LUKMAN
37 Director of Financial Aid ... Mrs. Starr S. BENDER
06 Registrar ... Dr. Janet CALDERON
45 Dir of Grant Management ... Ms. Stefanie JOHNSON
88 Director Ctr for Acad Achievement ... Ms. Yvette C. SALIBA
08 Library Director ... Ms. Deanna L. FLORES
42 Campus Chaplain ... Mr. Reynold ACOSTA
07 Director of Enrollment Services ... Mrs. Katie R. SHAW
21 Chief Accountant ... Mr. Grayson GOODMAN
39 Director of Residence Hall ... Mr. David A. BRYANT
30 Development Officer ... Mrs. Carol BRADFIELD
16 Director of Human Resources ... Mr. Fred W. STEPHENS
13 Director of Information Technology ... Mr. Travis WOOLEY
04 Executive Asst to the President ... Mrs. Dawn H. CREFT

Allied Health Institute (I)

51 North State Street, Plantation FL 33317
County: Broward FICE Identification: 041359
Unit ID: 454883
Telephone: (866) 251-3244 Carnegie Class: Not Classified
FAX Number: (877) 493-7416 Calendar System: Other
URL: www.alliedhealthinstitute.edu
Established: Annual Undergrad Tuition & Fees: $13,375
Enrollment: 664 Coed
Affiliation or Control: Proprietary IRS Status: Proprietary
Highest Offering: Associate Degree
Program: Occupational; 2-Year Principally Bachelor's Creditable
Accreditation: **ABHES**

01 President ... Jennifer ANGLIN

American Institute College of Health Professions (J)

1420 Celebration Boulevard, Ste 309,
Celebration FL 34747
Telephone: (407) 738-4488 Identification: 770842
Accreditation: **ACICS**, #COARC, DMS

† Main campus is Salter College in West Boylston, MA.

American InterContinental University (K)

2250 N Commerce Parkway, Weston FL 33326-3233
Telephone: (954) 446-6100 Identification: 666336
Accreditation: **&NH**, ACBSP

† Main campus is American InterContinental University in Schaumburg, IL.

American Medical Academy (L)

12215 SW 112th Street, Miami FL 33186
County: Miami-Dade FICE Identification: 041921
Unit ID: 475714
Telephone: (305) 271-6555 Carnegie Class: Not Classified
FAX Number: (305) 271-6556 Calendar System: Semester
URL: www.ama.edu
Established: 2006 Annual Undergrad Tuition & Fees: $6,500
Enrollment: 220 Coed
Affiliation or Control: Proprietary IRS Status: Proprietary
Highest Offering: Associate Degree
Program: Occupational
Accreditation: **ABHES**

01 Chief Executive Officer ... Mr. Eduardo GUTIERREZ

Ana G. Mendez University System Metro Orlando Campus (A)

5601 S Semoran Boulevard, #55, Orlando FL 32822
Telephone: (407) 207-3363 Identification: 770921
Accreditation: &M

† Main campus is Sistema Universitario Ana G. Mendez in Rio Piedras, PR.

Ana G. Mendez University System South Florida Campus (B)

3520 Enterprise Way, Miramar FL 33025
Telephone: (954) 885-5595 Identification: 770922
Accreditation: &M

† Main campus is Sistema Universitario Ana G. Mendez in Rio Piedras, PR.

Ana G. Mendez University System Tampa Bay Campus (C)

3655 West Waters Avenue, Tampa FL 33614
Telephone: (813) 932-7500 Identification: 770923
Accreditation: &M

† Main campus is Sistema Universitario Ana G. Mendez in Rio Piedras, PR.

Anthem College (D)

3710 Maguire Boulevard, Orlando FL 32803
Telephone: (407) 893-7400 Identification: 770667
Accreditation: ACICS

† Main campus is The Bryman School in Phoenix, AZ.

Argosy University, Sarasota (E)

5250 17th Street, Sarasota FL 34235-8246
Telephone: (941) 379-0404 FICE Identification: 025906
Accreditation: &WC, CACREP

† Main campus is Argosy University, Orange County in Orange, CA.

Argosy University, Tampa (F)

1403 N. Howard Avenue, Tampa FL 33607
Telephone: (813) 393-5290 Identification: 666082
Accreditation: &WC, CLPSY

† Main campus is Argosy University, Orange County in Orange, CA.

The Art Institute of Fort Lauderdale (G)

1799 SE 17th Street, Fort Lauderdale FL 33316-3000
County: Broward FICE Identification: 010195
Unit ID: 132338
Telephone: (954) 463-3000 Carnegie Class: Spec/Arts
FAX Number: (954) 523-7676 Calendar System: Quarter
URL: www.aifl.edu
Established: 1968 Annual Undergrad Tuition & Fees: $17,654
Enrollment: 2,258 Coed
Affiliation or Control: Proprietary IRS Status: Proprietary
Highest Offering: Baccalaureate
Program: Occupational; Liberal Arts And General
Accreditation: ACICS, ACFEI, #CIDA

01 President .... Claude W. TOLAND
32 Dean of Student Affairs .... Kathy F. DEANER
05 Dean of Academic Affairs .... Peter C. WEST
20 Associate Dean of Academic Affairs .... David WALCZAK
10 Director of Finance .... Maria V. BARRON
06 Registrar .... Laura N. TENGERES
07 Senior Director of Admissions .... Judith JOCHEMS
37 Director Student Financial Services .... Joyce CUMMINGS
36 Director of Career Services .... Wendy WAGNER-LIND
15 Human Resources Generalist .... Samantha GORDON

ATA Career Education-Spring Hill (H)

7355 Spring Hill Drive, Spring Hill FL 34609
Telephone: (727) 567-9597 Identification: 770521
Accreditation: ABHES

† Main campus is ATA College in Louisville, KY.

Atlantic Institute of Oriental Medicine (I)

100 E Broward Boulevard, Suite 100,
Fort Lauderdale FL 33301-3510
County: Broward FICE Identification: 034296
Unit ID: 439446
Telephone: (954) 763-9840 Carnegie Class: Spec/Health
FAX Number: (954) 763-9844 Calendar System: Trimester
URL: www.atom.edu
Established: 1994 Annual Graduate Tuition & Fees: $15,000
Enrollment: 145 Coed
Affiliation or Control: Independent Non-Profit IRS Status: 501(c)3
Highest Offering: Master's; No Undergraduates
Program: Professional
Accreditation: ACUP

01 President .... Johanna C. YEN
11 Executive Director .... Dort BIGG
05 Academic Dean .... Yan CHENG

Ave Maria School of Law (J)

1025 Commons Circle, Naples FL 34119
County: Collier FICE Identification: 036914
Unit ID: 442295
Telephone: (239) 687-5300 Carnegie Class: Spec/Law
FAX Number: (239) 353-3173 Calendar System: Semester
URL: www.avemarialaw.edu
Established: 2000 Annual Graduate Tuition & Fees: $37,950
Enrollment: 391 Coed
Affiliation or Control: Roman Catholic IRS Status: 501(c)3
Highest Offering: First Professional Degree; No Undergraduates
Program: Professional
Accreditation: LAW

01 President and Dean .... Mr. Eugene R. MILHIZER
04 Executive Assistant to the Dean .... Ms. Pamela KRAMER
05 Assoc Dean Academic Affairs .... Mr. W. Edward AFIELD
32 Assoc Dean for Student Affairs .... Ms. Kaye A. CASTRO
08 Assoc Dean Library/Information Svcs .... Ms. Roberta STUDWELL
42 Chaplain .... Fr. Michael ORSI
06 Registrar .... Ms. Angela KOJIRO
37 Director of Financial Aid .... Mr. Kevin MCGOWAN
30 Director of Develop & External Affs .... Ms. Donna HEISER
07 Assistant Dean of Admissions .... Ms. Monique MCCARTHY
36 Director of Career Services .... Ms. Laura WESELEY
24 Audio-Visual Coordinator .... Mr. Tony PETRO
11 Director Finance & Administration .... Ms. Virginia TRAVER
40 Bookstore Manager .... Ms. Kathryn LOVE

Ave Maria University (K)

5050 Ave Maria Boulevard, Ave Maria FL 34142-9505
County: Collier FICE Identification: 039413
Unit ID: 446048
Telephone: (239) 280-2500 Carnegie Class: Bac/A&S
FAX Number: (239) 352-2392 Calendar System: Semester
URL: www.avemaria.edu
Established: 2003 Annual Undergrad Tuition & Fees: $23,000
Enrollment: 976 Coed
Affiliation or Control: Independent Non-Profit IRS Status: 501(c)3
Highest Offering: Doctorate
Program: Liberal Arts And General; Religious Emphasis
Accreditation: SC

00 Chancellor .... Mr. Thomas S. MONAGHAN
01 President/CEO .... Mr. James TOWEY
05 VP Academic Affairs .... Dr. Michael DAUPHINAIS
27 Chief Information Officer .... Mr. Eddie DEJTHAI
30 VP Institutional Advancement .... Mr. Kevin JOYCE
32 VP Student Affairs .... Mr. William KIRK
10 Chief Financial Officer .... Ms. Maureen JOYCE
84 VP Enrollment and Marketing .... Dr. Dennis GRACE
07 Director of Admissions .... Mr. Jason FABAZ
06 Registrar .... Ms. Stephanie E. NEGIP
09 Director Institutional Effectivenes .... Dr. Kevin N. SHRINER
37 Managing Financial Aid Director .... Mrs. Anne HART
41 Athletic Director .... Mr. Shawn SUMME
42 Director of Campus Ministry .... Fr. Robert GARRITY
44 Director Planned Giving .... Mr. Jeffrey MCMANUS
35 Director of Student Life .... Ms. Julie COSDEN
88 Director of Mission/Outreach .... Vacant
08 Director of Library Services .... Ms. Jennifer NODES
15 Human Resources & Privacy Ofcr .... Vacant
18 Director Physical Plant & Security .... Mr. Scott SCHNEIDER
21 Controller .... Mr. Anthony BEATA
38 Mental Health Counselor .... Ms. Sharon O'REILLY
39 Director Resident Life .... Ms. Christa MCMAHON
29 Phoneathon Manager .... Mr. Gary HUBER

Aviator College of Aeronautical Science & Technology (L)

3800 St. Lucie Blvd, Fort Pierce FL 34946
County: Saint Lucie FICE Identification: 039863
Unit ID: 447847
Telephone: (772) 466-4822 Carnegie Class: Not Classified
FAX Number: (772) 462-4886 Calendar System: Semester
URL: www.aviator.edu
Established: 1984 Annual Undergrad Tuition & Fees: $67,373
Enrollment: 93 Coed
Affiliation or Control: Proprietary IRS Status: Proprietary
Highest Offering: Associate Degree
Program: Occupational; 2-Year Principally Bachelor's Creditable; Technical Emphasis
Accreditation: ACCSC

01 President .... Mr. Michael E. COHEN
10 Vice Pres & Chief Financial Officer .... Ms. T.J METE
05 Director of Education .... Mr. Pierre LAVIAL
06 Registrar .... Ms. Roxanne PALMER

Azure College (M)

1525 NW 167th Street, Miami Gardens FL 33169
County: Miami-Dade Identification: 667116
Telephone: (305) 751-0001 Carnegie Class: Not Classified
FAX Number: (305) 751-9991 Calendar System: Quarter
URL: www.azure.edu
Established: 2004 Annual Undergrad Tuition & Fees: N/A
Enrollment: N/A Coed
Affiliation or Control: Proprietary IRS Status: Proprietary
Highest Offering: Associate Degree
Program: Occupational
Accreditation: ABHES

01 CEO .... Mr. Jhonson NAPOLEON

The Baptist College of Florida (N)

5400 College Drive, Graceville FL 32440-3306
County: Jackson FICE Identification: 021596
Unit ID: 132408
Telephone: (850) 263-3261 Carnegie Class: Spec/Faith
FAX Number: (850) 263-7506 Calendar System: Semester
URL: www.baptistcollege.edu
Established: 1943 Annual Undergrad Tuition & Fees: $9,700
Enrollment: 558 Coed
Affiliation or Control: Southern Baptist IRS Status: 501(c)3
Highest Offering: Master's
Program: 2-Year Principally Bachelor's Creditable; Teacher Preparatory; Religious Emphasis
Accreditation: SC, MUS

01 President .... Dr. Thomas A. KINCHEN
03 Senior Vice President/CFO .... Dr. R. C. HAMMACK
30 Vice President for Development .... Mr. Charles R. PARKER
05 Dean of Faculty .... Dr. G. Robin JUMPER
06 Registrar .... Ms. Stephanie W. ORR
26 Director of Marketing .... Mrs. Sandra K. RICHARDS
09 Director of Institutional Research .... Dr. R. C. HAMMACK
37 Director of Financial Aid & VA .... Mrs. Stephanie E. POWELL
32 Dean of Students .... Dr. Roger C. RICHARDS
07 Director of Admissions .... Mrs. Sandra K. RICHARDS
18 Maintenance Director .... Mr. Huie G. WILSON
21 Associate Business Officer .... Ms. Polly K. FLOYD
30 Director of Development .... Vacant

Barry University (O)

11300 NE Second Avenue, Miami Shores FL 33161-6695
County: Dade FICE Identification: 001466
Unit ID: 132471
Telephone: (305) 899-3000 Carnegie Class: DRU
FAX Number: (305) 899-3054 Calendar System: Semester
URL: www.barry.edu
Established: 1940 Annual Undergrad Tuition & Fees: $28,160
Enrollment: 9,070 Coed
Affiliation or Control: Roman Catholic IRS Status: 501(c)3
Highest Offering: Doctorate
Program: Liberal Arts And General; Teacher Preparatory; Professional
Accreditation: SC, ANEST, ARCPA, BUS, CACREP, HT, LAW, MACTE, NURSE, OT, PERF, POD, SW, THEOL

01 President .... Sr. Linda BEVILACQUA
00 President Emerita .... Sr. Jeanne O'LAUGHLIN
05 Provost .... Dr. Linda PETERSON
10 Sr Vice Pres Business & Finance .... Mr. Bruce EDWARDS
32 Vice President Student Affairs .... Dr. Scott F. SMITH
30 VP Inst Adv & External Affairs .... Mrs. Sara B. HERALD
88 VP Mission & Inst Effectiveness .... Dr. Christopher STARRATT
43 General Counsel .... Mr. David DUDGEON
49 Dean College of Arts/Sciences .... Dr. Karen A. CALLAGHAN
76 Dean College of Health Sciences .... Dr. John MCFADDEN
51 Dean School of Adult/Cont Ed .... Dr. Andrea ALLEN
50 Dean School of Business .... Dr. Tomislav MANDAKOVIC
53 Dean School of Education .... Dr. Terry PIPER
88 Dean Human Perf/Leisure Sci .... Dr. Darlene KLUKA
61 Dean School of Law .... Dr. Leticia M. DIAZ
63 Dean School of Podiatric Medicine .... Dr. Jeffrey JENSEN
70 Dean School of Social Work .... Dr. Phyllis SCOTT
27 Chief Information Officer .... Ms. Yvette BROWN
84 Assoc Vice Pres Enrollment Mgmt .... Ms. Angela SCOTT
35 Assoc VP Student Affs/Dean Students .... Dr. Maria L. ALVAREZ
35 Assoc Vice Pres Student Affairs .... Dr. Eileen MCDONOUGH
18 Assoc VP Business Svcs & Fac Mgmt .... Ms. Monica SOTO
21 Assoc VP Finance & Chief Acc Office .... Ms. Nicole DIEZ
15 Associate VP Human Resources .... Ms. Jennifer N. BOYD-PUGH
29 Assoc VP Alum Rels & Annual Giving .... Vacant
91 Assoc VP Admin Information Systems .... Ms. Traci SIMPSON
42 Director Campus Ministry .... Dr. Anthony BONTA
105 Assistant VP Web Marketing .... Mr. Michel SILY
19 Executive Director of Public Safety .... Mr. George E. WILHELM
08 Dir Library Svcs/Libr Dir .... Mr. Thomas MESSNER
44 Director for Major Gifts .... Ms. Victoria CHAMPION
44 Director Annual Fund .... Mr. Paul MUITE
06 University Registrar .... Ms. Cynthia A. CHRUSZCZYK
36 Director Career Services .... Mr. John MORIARTY
39 Director Housing and Residence Life .... Mr. Matthew R. CAMERON
92 Director Honors Program .... Dr. Pawena SIRIMANGKALA
96 Director of Purchasing .... Ms. Sandra MADISON
37 Director Financial Aid .... Mr. Howard D. HUMESTON
38 Director Student Counseling Center .... Dr. James SCOTT

40 Manager Bookstore .... Ms. Claudia HADJEZ
07 Director of Undergraduate Admission .... Ms. Sarah RILEY

Bay Medical Center (A)

615 N Bonita Avenue, Panama City FL 32401-3600
County: Bay FICE Identification: 011127
Unit ID: 439464
Telephone: (800) 422-2418 Carnegie Class: Not Classified
FAX Number: (850) 747-6115 Calendar System: Semester
URL: www.baymedical.org/Career-Center.aspx
Established: 1969 Annual Graduate Tuition & Fees: $21,825
Enrollment: 52 Coed
Affiliation or Control: Independent Non-Profit IRS Status: 501(c)3
Highest Offering: Master's; No Undergraduates
Program: Occupational; Professional; Business Emphasis
Accreditation: **ANEST**

01 President/CEO .... Mr. Barry KEEL
10 Chief Financial Officer .... Mr. Chris BROOKS
05 Chief Nursing Officer .... Ms. Kim ADAMS

Beacon College (B)

105 E Main Street, Leesburg FL 34748-5162
County: Lake FICE Identification: 033733
Unit ID: 384254
Telephone: (352) 787-7660 Carnegie Class: Bac/A&S
FAX Number: (352) 787-0721 Calendar System: Semester
URL: www.beaconcollege.edu
Established: 1989 Annual Undergrad Tuition & Fees: $30,396
Enrollment: 186 Coed
Affiliation or Control: Independent Non-Profit IRS Status: 501(c)3
Highest Offering: Baccalaureate
Program: Liberal Arts And General
Accreditation: **SC**

01 President .... Dr. George J. HAGERTY
05 Vice President of Academic Affairs .... Dr. Shelly CHANDLER
32 Vice President of Student Services .... Dr. Robert BRIDGEMAN
30 VP of Institutional Advancement .... Dr. Walter ZIELINSKI
10 VP of Finance & Administration .... Mr. Calvin SANSON
06 Registrar .... Mr. David BROWN
18 Director of Facilities .... Mr. Chris HALL
35 Director of Student Services .... Mr. Rob ROGERS
37 Director of Financial Aid .... Ms. Shawna WELLS-BOOTH
08 Director of Library Resources .... Ms. Tiffany REITZ
13 Director of Information Technology .... Mr. Scott HUGHES
04 Exec Assistant to the President .... Ms. Tamara SYNDER
15 Associate VP of Human Resources .... Ms. Kimberly BEGGETT

Bethune Cookman University (C)

640 Dr. Mary McLeod Bethune Blvd,
Daytona Beach FL 32114-3099
County: Volusia FICE Identification: 001467
Unit ID: 132602
Telephone: (386) 481-2000 Carnegie Class: Bac/Diverse
FAX Number: (386) 481-2010 Calendar System: Semester
URL: www.cookman.edu
Established: 1904 Annual Undergrad Tuition & Fees: $14,410
Enrollment: 3,578 Coed
Affiliation or Control: United Methodist IRS Status: 501(c)3
Highest Offering: Master's
Program: Liberal Arts And General; Teacher Preparatory; Technical Emphasis
Accreditation: **SC**, NUR, TED

01 President .... Dr. Edison O. JACKSON
05 Provost .... Dr. Hiram POWELL
10 Vice President Fiscal Affairs .... Dr. Ronald DOWDY
11 Sr VP Administration & Student Svcs .... Dr. Dwaun J. WARMACK
30 Vice Pres Institutional Advancement .... Dr. Hakim J. LUCAS
32 VP Enrollment Mgmt/Student Dev .... Dr. Dwaun J. WARMACK
09 Vice Pres Inst Research/Plng & Eff .... Dr. Willis WALTER
15 VP HR/Reg/Legal Aff/Counsel to Pres .... Ms. Pamela BROWNE
27 VP Info Tech/Chief Info Officer .... Mr. Franklin PATTERSON
20 Provost for Academic Affairs .... Dr. Makala M. ABDULLAH
21 Assoc Vice Pres Finance/Budget .... Mrs. Melissa PETERS
100 Chief of Staff .... Mr. Fontaine DAVIS
39 Director Resident Life .... Mr. Fulton POSTON
29 Director Alumni Affairs .... Ms. Sharon BOSTICK-ISSAC
44 Planned/Major Gifts Officer .... Vacant
26 Assoc Dir/Communications/Mktg .... Mrs. Meredith RODRIGUEZ
36 Dir Career and Program Services .... Ms. Davita BONNER
08 Director Library/LRC .... Dr. Tasha LUCAS-YOUMANS
06 Registrar .... Mrs. Annie REDD
07 Director Admissions .... Mr. Reynolda BROWN
37 Director Financial Aid .... Mr. Joseph L. COLEMAN
23 Director Health Services .... Ms. Colleen O'BRIEN
41 Athletics Director .... Mr. Lynn THOMPSON
42 Chaplain/Dir of Religious Life .... Rev. Walter MONROE
19 Director of Security .... Capt. Melvin WILLIAMS
18 Chief Facilities/Physical Plant .... Mr. Ervin ROSS, JR.
92 Director of Honors Program .... Dr. Masood POORANDI
66 Dean School of Nursing .... Dr. Willie M. SESSION
50 Dean School of Business .... Dr. Aubrey E. LONG
53 Dean School of Education .... Dr. Carol B. JOHNSON
49 Acting Dean School of Liberal Arts .... Dr. Janice ALLEN-KELSEY
81 Dean Sch Science/Engineering/Math .... Dr. Herbert THOMPSON
107 Dean School of Professional Studies .... Dr. Darryl FRASIER
58 Dean of Graduate Studies .... Dr. Hiram POWELL
89 Dean of Freshman College .... Dr. Michelle THOMPSON
92 Dean of Honors College .... Dr. Alexis WALTER

Broward College (D)

111 E Las Olas Boulevard,
Fort Lauderdale FL 33301-2298
County: Broward FICE Identification: 001500
Unit ID: 132709
Telephone: (954) 201-6500 Carnegie Class: Assoc/Pub-U-MC
FAX Number: (954) 201-7576 Calendar System: Trimester
URL: www.broward.edu
Established: 1959 Annual Undergrad Tuition & Fees (In-State): $3,180
Enrollment: 42,309 Coed
Affiliation or Control: State IRS Status: 501(c)3
Highest Offering: Baccalaureate
Program: Occupational; 2-Year Principally Bachelor's Creditable; Liberal Arts And General; Teacher Preparatory; Professional
Accreditation: **SC**, ADNUR, CAHIIM, COARC, DA, DH, DMS, EMT, MAC, MUS, NUR, OPD, PTAA

01 President .... Mr. J. David ARMSTRONG, JR.
32 Vice Pres Student Affs/Enroll Mgmt .... Mrs. Angelia MILLENDER
05 Sr Vice Pres Acad Affairs/Provost .... Dr. Linda HOWDYSHELL
10 Sr Vice Pres Finance/Administration .... Mr. Thomas OLLIFF
26 VP Public Affairs and Marketing .... Ms. Aileen IZQUIERDO
11 Vice President of Operations .... Mr. John DUNNUCK
102 VP Advanc/Exec Dir BC Foundation .... Ms. Nancy BOTERO
15 Assoc Vice President HR & Equity .... Ms. Denese EDSALL
13 Vice President Info Technology .... Ms. Patti BARNEY
86 VP Govt Policy/Regulatory Affairs .... Mr. Gregory A. HAILE
20 VP of Strategic Intiatives .... Dr. Barbara J. BRYAN
12 President Central Campus .... Dr. Mercedes A. QUIROGA
12 President North Campus .... Dr. Avis PROCTOR
12 President South Campus .... Dr. S. (Sean) MADISON
88 Assoc Vice President Economic Dev .... Mr. Norm SEAVERS
09 Assoc VP Inst Research/Plng/ Effect .... Dr. Rigoberto RINCONES-GÓMEZ
21 Comptroller .... Mr. Jayson IROFF
37 Director of Student Financial Svcs .... Mr. Robert ROBBINS
06 Registrar .... Mr. Willie ALEXANDER
08 Dean of Libraries/Learning Res .... Ms. Jacqueline HENNING
88 Director Enterprise Business Intel .... Ms. Wendy CLINK
29 Director Alumni Relations .... Ms. Danielle SYLVESTER
100 Assistant to the President .... Ms. Adriana FAZZANO
04 Sr Exec Asst to the President .... Mrs. Avis M. MCCOY

Brown Mackie College-Miami (E)

3700 Lakeside Drive, Miramar FL 33027
Telephone: (305) 341-6600 Identification: 666110
Accreditation: **ACICS**

† Main campus is The Art Institute of Phoenix in Phoenix, AZ.

Cambridge Institute of Allied Health & Technology (F)

5150 Linton Boulevard, Suite 340, Delray Beach FL 33484
County: Palm Beach FICE Identification: 040834
Unit ID: 454865
Telephone: (561) 381-4990 Carnegie Class: Assoc/PrivFP
FAX Number: (561) 381-4992 Calendar System: Other
URL: www.cambridgehealth.edu
Established: Annual Undergrad Tuition & Fees: $15,665
Enrollment: 218 Coed
Affiliation or Control: Proprietary IRS Status: Proprietary
Highest Offering: Associate Degree
Program: Occupational
Accreditation: **ABHES**, DMS, #RAD, #RTT

01 President .... Mr. Terry LAPIER

Carlos Albizu University Miami Campus (G)

2173 NW 99th Avenue, Miami FL 33172-2209
Telephone: (305) 593-1223 Identification: 666814
Accreditation: **&M**, CLPSY

† Main campus is Carlos Albizu University in San Juan, PR.

Center of Cinematography, Art & Television (H)

1637 NW 27th Avenue, Miami FL 33125
Telephone: (305) 634-0550 Identification: 770562
Accreditation: **ACCSC**

† Main campus is Colegio de Cinematografia, Artes y Television in Bayamon, PR.

Central Florida Institute (I)

6000 Cinderland Pkwy, Orlando FL 32810
Telephone: (407) 253-5354 Identification: 667022
Accreditation: **ABHES**, DMS

† Main campus is Central Florida Institute in Palm Harbor, FL.

Central Florida Institute (J)

30522 US Highway 19 N, Ste 300,
Palm Harbor FL 34684-4436
County: Pinellas FICE Identification: 034254
Unit ID: 439525
Telephone: (727) 784-0003 Carnegie Class: Assoc/PrivFP
FAX Number: (727) 781-9421 Calendar System: Other
URL: www.cfi.edu
Established: 1998 Annual Undergrad Tuition & Fees: N/A
Enrollment: 250 Coed
Affiliation or Control: Proprietary IRS Status: Proprietary
Highest Offering: Associate Degree
Program: Occupational; Technical Emphasis
Accreditation: **ABHES**, CVT, #DMS, POLYT, SURGT, SURTEC

01 School Director .... Mr. Ray JOLL
05 Director of Education .... Mr. Jimmie SMITH
06 Registrar .... Mr. Steve COLEMAN
07 Director of Admissions .... Mr. Scott FROST
76 Director of Health Education .... Ms. Sondra CRANFORD
37 Director of Financial Aid .... Mr. David ROCK
32 Dir Career/Student Support Svcs .... Ms. Lolita JOHNS
88 Compliance Specialist .... Ms. Caitlin DEVERS-JONES

† Tuition is variable based on program.

Centura College (K)

6359 Edgewater Drive, Orlando FL 32810
County: Orange FICE Identification: 039394
Unit ID: 446446
Telephone: (407) 275-9696 Carnegie Class: Assoc/PrivFP
FAX Number: (407) 275-4499 Calendar System: Semester
URL: www.centura.edu
Established: 2002 Annual Undergrad Tuition & Fees: N/A
Enrollment: 108 Coed
Affiliation or Control: Proprietary IRS Status: Proprietary
Highest Offering: Associate Degree
Program: Occupational
Accreditation: **ACCSC**

01 Director .... Mrs. Danielle BROWN

Chamberlain College of Nursing (L)

2300 SW 145th Avenue, Miramar FL 33027
Telephone: (954) 885-3510 Identification: 770498
Accreditation: **&NH**, NURSE

† Main campus is Chamberlain College of Nursing - Addison in Addison, IL.

Chamberlain College of Nursing-Jacksonville Campus (M)

5200 Belfort Road, Jacksonville FL 32256
Telephone: (904) 251-8100 Identification: 770501
Accreditation: **&NH**, NURSE

† Main campus is Chamberlain College of Nursing - Addison in Addison, IL.

Chipola College (N)

3094 Indian Circle, Marianna FL 32446-3065
County: Jackson FICE Identification: 001472
Unit ID: 133021
Telephone: (850) 526-2761 Carnegie Class: Assoc/Pub4
FAX Number: (850) 718-2388 Calendar System: Semester
URL: www.chipola.edu
Established: 1947 Annual Undergrad Tuition & Fees (In-District): $3,060
Enrollment: 2,414 Coed
Affiliation or Control: State/Local IRS Status: 501(c)3
Highest Offering: Baccalaureate
Program: Occupational; 2-Year Principally Bachelor's Creditable
Accreditation: **SC**

01 President .... Dr. Gene PROUGH
03 Executive Vice President .... Dr. Jason HURST
05 Sr VP Instructional/Student Svcs .... Dr. Sarah CLEMMONS
10 Vice President of Finance .... Mr. Steve YOUNG
32 Vice Pres of Student Affairs .... Dr. Jayne ROBERTS
16 Assoc VP of Human Resources .... Mrs. Karan P. DAVIS
13 Associate VP Information Systems .... Mr. Dennis F. EVERETT
45 Assoc Dean Institutional Dev/Plng .... Mrs. Gail C. HARTZOG
18 Physical Plant Manager .... Mr. Harry FLEENER
26 Director Public Relations .... Mr. Bryan C. CRAVEN
37 Director of Financial Aid .... Ms. Sybil CLOUD
41 Director of Athletics .... Dr. Steven GIVENS
40 Bookstore Manager .... Ms. Barresa ADAMS
06 Registrar .... Ms. Kathy REHBERG

City College (O)

177 Montgomery Road, Altamonte Springs FL 32714
County: Seminole FICE Identification: 030799
Unit ID: 417327
Telephone: (407) 831-9816 Carnegie Class: Assoc/PrivNFP
FAX Number: (407) 831-1147 Calendar System: Quarter
URL: www.citycollegeorlando.edu
Established: 1997 Annual Undergrad Tuition & Fees: $14,000
Enrollment: 320 Coed

Affiliation or Control: Independent Non-Profit IRS Status: 501(c)3
Highest Offering: Associate Degree
Program: Occupational
Accreditation: ACICS, EMT

01 President Mrs. Esther FIKE
05 Executive Director Ms. Donna MCCASKILL
06 Registrar Ms. Cindy BRACERO

City College (A)

2000 W Commercial Boulevard,
Fort Lauderdale FL 33309-1916
County: Broward FICE Identification: 025154
Unit ID: 244233
Telephone: (954) 492-5353 Carnegie Class: Bac/Assoc
FAX Number: (954) 491-1965 Calendar System: Quarter
URL: www.citycollege.edu
Established: 1983 Annual Undergrad Tuition & Fees: $19,200
Enrollment: 1,652 Coed
Affiliation or Control: Independent Non-Profit IRS Status: 501(c)3
Highest Offering: Baccalaureate
Program: Occupational; Business Emphasis
Accreditation: ACICS, EMT, SURTEC

01 President Esther FIKE
03 Executive Director John PADGET
36 Director of Career Development Traci ACKERMAN
05 Director of Education Anie BONILLA
07 Director of Admissions Lesa-Gaye FRANCIS
10 Director of Financial Affairs Ginger RUBACK
13 Director of Technologies Jeffrey A. CLAYTON
08 Director of Library Sharon NEUBAUER
06 Registrar Sanchia WILLIAMS
15 Human Resources Generalist Patricia BURKHART
37 Director Student Financial Aid Kathy JOHNSON

City College (B)

7001 NW Fourth Boulevard, Gainesville FL 32607
Telephone: (352) 335-4000 Identification: 666413
Accreditation: ACICS, EMT

† Main campus is City College in Fort Lauderdale, FL.

City College (C)

6565 Taft Street, Hollywood FL 33024
Telephone: (954) 744-1777 Identification: 770674
Accreditation: ACICS

† Main campus is City College in Fort Lauderdale, FL.

City College (D)

9300 S Dadeland Blvd, Suite PH, Miami FL 33156
Telephone: (305) 666-9242 Identification: 666414
Accreditation: ACICS, EMT, SURTEC

† Main campus is City College in Fort Lauderdale, FL.

Clearwater Christian College (E)

3400 Gulf-to-Bay Boulevard, Clearwater FL 33759-4595
County: Pinellas FICE Identification: 001473
Unit ID: 133085
Telephone: (727) 726-1153 Carnegie Class: Bac/A&S
FAX Number: (727) 723-8566 Calendar System: Semester
URL: www.clearwater.edu
Established: 1966 Annual Undergrad Tuition & Fees: $17,065
Enrollment: 485 Coed
Affiliation or Control: Non-denominational IRS Status: 501(c)3
Highest Offering: Master's
Program: Liberal Arts And General; Teacher Preparatory; Professional
Accreditation: SC

01 President Dr. John F. KLEM
05 Vice President for Academic Affairs Dr. Mary C. DRAPER
30 Senior Vice President Mr. Terry D. WILD
32 Vice President for Student Life Mr. Ryan DUPEE
06 Registrar Mr. Thomas CANNON
26 Dean of Institutional Advancement Mr. Benjamin PUCKETT
35 Dean of Students Mr. Todd BARTON
09 Director Institutional Research Dr. Mary DRAPER
37 Director of Financial Aid Mr. Ryan MCNAMARA
38 Director of Guidance & Career Svcs Mrs. Lisa DOLLENMAYER
41 Athletic Director Mr. Michael TOUMA
29 Alumni Director Mr. Benjamin PUCKETT
08 Director of the Library Mrs. Elizabether WERNER
50 Chair of Business Studies Division Dr. Ian DUNCAN
49 Chair of Arts and Letters Division Dr. Dan HURST
73 Chair of Biblical Studies Division Dr. John F. KLEM
53 Chair of Education Division Dr. Philip LARSEN
81 Chair of Science Division Dr. Jonathan HENRY
07 Director of Admissions Mr. Anthony WILSON
15 Director of Human Resources Mrs. Lynn SMITH
21 Accounting Manager Miss Bethany KAPPLAN
18 Director of Campus Plant Mr. Roy SQUIRES
13 Director of Information Technology Mr. Kevin GAULT
19 Chief of Campus Security Mr. Terry BAUMANN
88 Director of Custodial Services Mrs. Kelly MACLEOD
88 Director of Food Service Mr. Dennis BURGGRAFF
96 Director of Auxiliary Services Mr. Paul SCHMIEL

College of Business and Technology (F)

19151 South Dixie Highway, Cutler Bay FL 33157
Telephone: (305) 273-4499 Identification: 770677
Accreditation: ACICS, CAHIIM

† Main campus is College of Business and Technology in Miami, FL.

College of Business and Technology (G)

935 West 49th Street, Hialeah FL 33012
Telephone: (305) 273-4499 Identification: 770675
Accreditation: ACICS

† Main campus is College of Business and Technology in Miami, FL.

College of Business and Technology (H)

8991 SW 107th Avenue, Suite 200, Miami FL 33176-1412
County: Miami-Dade FICE Identification: 030716
Unit ID: 417318
Telephone: (305) 273-4499 Carnegie Class: Assoc/PrivFP
FAX Number: (305) 270-0779 Calendar System: Semester
URL: www.cbt.edu
Established: 1988 Annual Undergrad Tuition & Fees: $13,600
Enrollment: 922 Coed
Affiliation or Control: Proprietary IRS Status: Proprietary
Highest Offering: Associate Degree
Program: Occupational; 2-Year Principally Bachelor's Creditable; Technical Emphasis
Accreditation: ACICS

01 President Mr. Fernando N. LLERENA
03 Executive Director Mr. Luis E. LLERENA
05 Regional Director of Education Mrs. Gladys P. LLERENA
37 Financial Aid Director Mrs. Yazmin PALMA
36 Career Services Director Ms. Vanessa RODRIGUEZ
06 Registrar Ms. Maria GONZALEZ
84 Director of Enrollment Management Ms. Jane MISKELL
50 Program Director Ms. Carolyn SMITH
10 Finance Director Ms. Maricel SPEZZACATENA
11 Chief Operating Officer Ms. Monica LLERENA
20 Director of Academic Operations Dr. Elizabeth RIOS
12 Campus Director Mr. Kennedy FERNANDEZ
12 Campus Director Mr. Hector DUENAS
12 Campus Director Mr. Russell BATTIATA
12 Campus Director Mr. Anthony RICHIEZ
12 Campus Director Ms. Monica LLERENA

College of Business and Technology (I)

8230 W Flagler Street, Miami FL 33144
Telephone: (305) 273-4499 Identification: 770676
Accreditation: ACICS

† Main campus is College of Business and Technology in Miami, FL.

College of Business and Technology (J)

5190 NW 167 Street, Suite 200, Miami Gardens FL 33014
Telephone: (786) 693-8801 Identification: 770612
Accreditation: ACICS

† Main campus is College of Business and Technology in Miami, FL.

College of Central Florida (K)

3001 S.W. College Road, Ocala FL 34474
County: Marion FICE Identification: 001471
Unit ID: 132851
Telephone: (352) 237-2111 Carnegie Class: Assoc/Pub-R-L
FAX Number: (352) 291-4450 Calendar System: Semester
URL: www.cf.edu
Established: 1957 Annual Undergrad Tuition & Fees (In-District): $3,104
Enrollment: 8,647 Coed
Affiliation or Control: Local IRS Status: 501(c)3
Highest Offering: Baccalaureate
Program: Occupational; 2-Year Principally Bachelor's Creditable; Liberal Arts And General; Teacher Preparatory; Professional
Accreditation: SC, ADNUR, CAHIIM, DA, EMT, PTAA, SURGT

01 President Dr. James D. HENNINGSEN
10 Vice President Adm & Fin Mr. Francis J. MAZUR, III
05 Vice President Academic Affairs Dr. Mark PAUGH
30 Vice Pres Institutional Advancement Mrs. Joan STEARNS
32 Vice President Student Affairs Dr. Timothy WISE
12 Citrus Campus Vice President Dr. Vernon LAWTER, JR.
12 Provost Levy Center Mrs. Marilyn LADNER
86 Exec Dir IE & Govt Relations Dr. Jillian RAMSAMMY
10 Assistant VP for Finance Mr. Steven ASH
75 Assoc VP Careers & Tech Educ Dr. Cheryl FANTE
49 Dean Liberal Arts & Sciences Mr. Allan DANUFF
88 Dean Public Service/Criminal Just Dr. Stacy DICKSON
32 Dean Student Services Dr. Henri BENLOLO
88 Dean Academic Foundations Dr. Rayanne GIDDIS
53 Dean Teacher Education Ms. Debbie BOWE
08 Dean Learning Resources Center Ms. Elizabeth CURRY
84 Dean Enrollment Management Ms. Lyn POWELL
23 Associate Dean Health Sciences Ms. Deanna STENTIFORD
12 Director Hampton Center Ms. LerVerne JACOBS
37 Director Financial Aid Ms. Judy MENADIER
09 Director Inst Effectiveness Dr. Lawrence J. KUSZYNSKI
07 Director Admissions/Records Mrs. Teri LITTLE-BERRY
18 Director Facilities Mr. Tommy MORELOCK
15 Director Human Resources Ms. Tonya KELLY
35 Director Student Life Ms. Marjorie MCGEE
88 Director Student Support Services Ms. Lisa SMITH
41 Director Athletics/Wellness Mr. Bob ZELINSKI
88 Director Access Services Ms. Kimberley SMITH
96 Director Purchasing Mr. Stewart TRAUTMAN
26 Director Marketing/Public Rels Ms. Lois BRAUCKMULLER
88 Director Appleton Museum of Art Ms. Cindi MORRISON
19 Manager Public Safety Mr. Don UGLIANO
25 Manager of Grants Development Mr. Bob HAWKINS
88 Manager Printing & Postal Service Ms. Katharine WADE
88 Manager Conference & Food Service Ms. Cheryl CROSBY
13 Chief Information Officer Ms. Kathy DAVIS
06 Registrar Ms. Devona SEWELL
44 Coordinator Resource Development Ms. Jean IMES
29 Annual Fund/Alumni Devel Coord Ms. Traci MASON
88 Coordinator Sr Svc & Univ Ctr Ms. Edith SHIELDS

Concorde Career Institute (L)

7259 Salisbury Road, Jacksonville FL 32256
County: Duval FICE Identification: 020896
Unit ID: 133845
Telephone: (904) 725-0525 Carnegie Class: Assoc/PrivFP
FAX Number: (904) 721-9944 Calendar System: Semester
URL: www.concorde.edu
Established: 1988 Annual Undergrad Tuition & Fees: $24,400
Enrollment: 548 Coed
Affiliation or Control: Proprietary IRS Status: Proprietary
Highest Offering: Associate Degree
Program: Occupational
Accreditation: ACCSC, COARC, #PTAA, SURGT

01 Campus Director Melissa RYAN

Concorde Career Institute (M)

10933 Marks Way, Miramar FL 33025
County: Broward FICE Identification: 022751
Unit ID: 133854
Telephone: (954) 731-8880 Carnegie Class: Not Classified
FAX Number: (954) 484-2961 Calendar System: Other
URL: www.concorde.edu
Established: Annual Undergrad Tuition & Fees: N/A
Enrollment: 511 Coed
Affiliation or Control: Proprietary IRS Status: Proprietary
Highest Offering: Associate Degree
Program: Occupational; 2-Year Principally Bachelor's Creditable
Accreditation: ACCSC, COARC, OTA, @PTAA, SURGT

01 Campus President Jessie KNIGHT

Concorde Career Institute (N)

3444 McCrory Place, Orlando FL 32803
Telephone: (407) 812-3060 Identification: 770563
Accreditation: ACCSC, #COARC, DA, SURGT

† Main campus is Concorde Career Institute in Jacksonville, FL.

Concorde Career Institute (O)

4202 West Spruce Street, Tampa FL 33607-4127
County: Hillsborough FICE Identification: 021727
Unit ID: 133863
Telephone: (813) 874-0094 Carnegie Class: Not Classified
FAX Number: (813) 872-6884 Calendar System: Other
URL: www.concorde.edu
Established: Annual Undergrad Tuition & Fees: N/A
Enrollment: 614 Coed
Affiliation or Control: Proprietary IRS Status: Proprietary
Highest Offering: Associate Degree
Program: Occupational
Accreditation: ACCSC, COARC, SURGT

01 Campus President Donna HALLAM

Dade Medical College (P)

3721 NW 7th Street, Miami FL 33126
County: Miami-Dade FICE Identification: 038323
Unit ID: 444574
Telephone: (786) 363-4910 Carnegie Class: Assoc/PrivFP
FAX Number: (786) 363-4924 Calendar System: Other
URL: www.dademedical.edu
Established: 1999 Annual Undergrad Tuition & Fees: N/A
Enrollment: 1,800 Coed
Affiliation or Control: Proprietary IRS Status: Proprietary
Highest Offering: Baccalaureate
Program: 2-Year Principally Bachelor's Creditable; Nursing Emphasis
Accreditation: ABHES, DMS, RAD

01 Chief Executive Officer Mr. Ernesto PEREZ
10 Chief Financial Officer Mr. Chris GRESSETT
11 Exec Vice President of Operations Mr. Roger LOPEZ

Dade Medical College-Hollywood (A)
6837 Taft Street, Hollywood FL 33024
Telephone: (954) 843-7930 Identification: 770522
Accreditation: ABHES

† Main campus is Dade Medical College in Miami, FL.

Dade Medical College-Homestead (B)
381 N Krome Avenue, Homestead FL 33030
Telephone: (786) 454-9070 Identification: 770523
Accreditation: ABHES

† Main campus is Dade Medical College in Miami, FL.

Dade Medical College-Jacksonville (C)
9550 Regency Square Blvd, S-1200,
Jacksonville FL 32225
Telephone: (904) 345-5678 Identification: 770524
Accreditation: ABHES

† Main campus is Dade Medical College in Miami, FL.

Dade Medical College-Miami (D)
5875 NW 163rd Street, Suite 101, Miami Lakes FL 33014
Telephone: (786) 363-3340 Identification: 770525
Accreditation: ABHES, RAD

† Main campus is Dade Medical College in Miami, FL.

Dade Medical College-West Palm Beach (E)
2601 South Military Trail, Bay 1-18,
West Palm Beach FL 33415
Telephone: (561) 965-7044 Identification: 770526
Accreditation: ABHES

† Main campus is Dade Medical College in Miami, FL.

Daytona College (F)
425 South Nova Road, Ormond Beach FL 32174-8449
County: Volusia FICE Identification: 039396
Unit ID: 447014
Telephone: (386) 267-0565 Carnegie Class: Assoc/PrivFP
FAX Number: (386) 267-0567 Calendar System: Semester
URL: www.daytonacollege.edu
Established: 1996 Annual Undergrad Tuition & Fees: $27,000
Enrollment: 351 Coed
Affiliation or Control: Proprietary IRS Status: Proprietary
Highest Offering: Associate Degree
Program: Occupational
Accreditation: ACCSC

01 President .... Mr. Roger BRADLEY
05 Director .... Mr. Justin BERKOWITZ

Daytona State College (G)
PO Box 2811, Daytona Beach FL 32120-2811
County: Volusia FICE Identification: 001475
Unit ID: 133386
Telephone: (386) 506-3000 Carnegie Class: Assoc/Pub4
FAX Number: (386) 506-4440 Calendar System: Semester
URL: www.DaytonaState.edu
Established: 1958 Annual Undergrad Tuition & Fees (In-District): $3,134
Enrollment: 15,698 Coed
Affiliation or Control: State/Local IRS Status: 501(c)3
Highest Offering: Baccalaureate
Program: Occupational; 2-Year Principally Bachelor's Creditable
Accreditation: SC, ADNUR, CAHIIM, COARC, DA, DH, EMT, MAC, OTA, PTAA, SURGT

01 President .... Dr. Carol EATON
03 Chief Operating Officer .... Dr. Thomas LOBASSO
03 Executive Vice President .... Mr. Brian T. BABB
05 Chief Academic Officer .... Vacant
10 Chief Business Officer .... Ms. Isalene MONTGOMERY
11 AVP Administrative Services .... Mr. Peter X. MCCARTHY
13 VP Information Technology .... Mr. Roberto LOMBARDO
86 VP Governmental Relations .... Ms. Sharon CROW
32 VP Student Development .... Vacant
50 AVP College of Business Admin .... Dr. Eileen HAMBY
15 AVP Human Resources .... Ms. Robin BARR
103 AVP College of Workforce & CE .... Mrs. Mary BRUNO
84 AVP Enrollment Development .... Mr. Buckley JAMES
46 AVP Institutional Effectiveness .... Dr. Nancy MORGAN
08 Head Librarian .... Ms. Mercedes CLEMENT
108 Director Assessment .... Ms. Janet SLEDGE
17 AVP Col Health Human Pub Svc .... Dr. James GREENE
72 AVP College of Technology .... Dr. Ron EAGLIN
08 AVP/Div Library & Acad Support .... Dr. Michelle MCCRANEY
53 AVP College of Education .... Ms. Kristy PRESSWOOD
106 Exec Director Instructional Resourc .... Dr. Rob SAUM
88 Director Center for Women & Men .... Dr. Katrina BELL
49 AVP College Arts/Music/Science .... Ms. Susan PATE
20 AVP Academic Affairs .... Dr. Rhodella BROWN
35 Dean Student Development .... Mr. Keith KENNEDY
88 Director Facilities Planning .... Mr. Steven ECKMAN
09 Dean Institutional Research .... Ms. Susan ANTILLON
37 Dean Financial Aid .... Mr. Kevin MCCRARY
88 Dean School of Health & Wellness .... Mr. Will DUNNE
19 Director Campus Safety .... Mr. Bill TILLARD
12 Dean DeLand Campus .... Mr. Bill WETHERELL
12 Dean Flagler/Palm Coast Campus .... Mr. Kent RYAN
12 Dean New Smryna Beach Campus .... Mr. Clarence MCCLOUD
12 Dean Deltona Campus .... Ms. Suzette CAMERON
43 College Counsel .... Mr. Brian BABB
51 Director Ctr for Business/Industry .... Mr. Frank MERCER
32 Asst Dean Student Activities .... Mr. Bruce COOK
96 AVP Business Svcs .... Ms. Janet PARISH
38 Director Academic Advising .... Ms. LeeAnn DAVIS
07 Director Admissions/Recruitment .... Ms. Karen SANDERS
22 Director of Equity & Inclusion .... Mr. Lonnie THOMPSON
21 AVP Accounting .... Vacant
06 Director Student Accounts .... Ms. Amy IVERSON
26 Director of Marketing .... Ms. Laurie WHITE

DeVry University - Miramar Campus (H)
2300 SW 145th Avenue, Miramar FL 33027-4150
Telephone: (954) 499-9775 Identification: 666196
Accreditation: &NH, ENGT

† Main campus is DeVry University - Chicago Campus in Chicago, IL.

DeVry University - Orlando Campus (I)
4000 Millenia Boulevard, Orlando FL 32839-2426
Telephone: (407) 345-2800 Identification: 666112
Accreditation: &NH, ENGT

† Main campus is DeVry University - Chicago Campus in Chicago, IL.

Digital Media Arts College (J)
5400 Broken Sound Blvd, Suite 100,
Boca Raton FL 33487
County: Palm Beach FICE Identification: 041274
Unit ID: 451060
Telephone: (561) 391-1148 Carnegie Class: Bac/Diverse
FAX Number: (561) 998-3430 Calendar System: Semester
URL: www.dmac.edu
Established: 2002 Annual Undergrad Tuition & Fees: $24,000
Enrollment: 400 Coed
Affiliation or Control: Proprietary IRS Status: Proprietary
Highest Offering: Master's
Program: Professional; Fine Arts Emphasis
Accreditation: ACICS

01 President .... Mr. Sunny SHARMA
10 Director Accounting & Finance .... Ms. Angela NOVATON

Dragon Rises College of Oriental Medicine (K)
1000 NE 16th Ave., Building F, Gainesville FL 32601-4557
County: Alachua FICE Identification: 038883
Unit ID: 449481
Telephone: (352) 371-2833 Carnegie Class: Spec/Health
FAX Number: (352) 244-0003 Calendar System: Semester
URL: www.dragonrises.edu
Established: 2001 Annual Undergrad Tuition & Fees: $16,000
Enrollment: 52 Coed
Affiliation or Control: Proprietary IRS Status: Proprietary
Highest Offering: Master's
Program: Professional
Accreditation: ACUP

01 Director .... Mr. Bruce PAGEL
05 Academic Dean .... Mr. Kenney EBERSOLE
23 Clinic Director .... Mr. Jamin NICHOLS
32 Dean of Student Services .... Ms. Ruth HAYES-MORRISON
37 Financial Aid Administrator .... Ms. Kate ELLISON

East West College of Natural Medicine (L)
3808 N Tamiami Trail, Sarasota FL 34234-5362
County: Sarasota FICE Identification: 034297
Unit ID: 439394
Telephone: (941) 355-9080 Carnegie Class: Spec/Health
FAX Number: (941) 355-3243 Calendar System: Trimester
URL: www.ewcollege.edu
Established: 1994 Annual Undergrad Tuition & Fees: $48,830
Enrollment: 107 Coed
Affiliation or Control: Proprietary IRS Status: Proprietary
Highest Offering: Master's
Program: Professional
Accreditation: ACUP

01 President/CEO .... Dr. Robyn CRISWELL-BLOOM
05 Academic Dean .... Mr. Jonathan D. WALD
07 Director of Admissions .... Ms. Elyse EAGLE

Eastern Florida State College (M)
1519 Clearlake Road, Cocoa FL 32922-6597
County: Brevard FICE Identification: 001470
Unit ID: 132693
Telephone: (321) 632-1111 Carnegie Class: Assoc/Pub-R-L
FAX Number: (321) 633-4565 Calendar System: Semester
URL: www.easternflorida.edu
Established: 1960 Annual Undergrad Tuition & Fees (In-District): $2,820
Enrollment: 17,139 Coed
Affiliation or Control: Local IRS Status: 501(c)3
Highest Offering: Baccalaureate
Program: Occupational; 2-Year Principally Bachelor's Creditable
Accreditation: SC, DA, DH, EMT, MLTAD, RAD, SURGT

01 President .... Dr. James H. RICHEY
10 VP Financial & Technology Services .... Mr. Richard LAIRD
84 VP Enrollment Mgmt/Student Success .... Dr. John F. DIETRICH
05 VP Academic Affairs/CLO .... Dr. Linda L. MIEDEMA
04 Exec Advisor to the President .... Dr. Joe L. SMITH
18 AVP Facilities .... Dr. Richard PARADISE
10 Chief Financial Officer .... Mr. Mark CHERRY
15 AVP/Exec Dir Human Resources .... Ms. Darla FERGUSON
31 AVP Communications .... Mr. John GLISCH
12 Provost Palm Bay Campus .... Dr. Ethel NEWMAN
12 Provost Melbourne Campus .... Ms. Sandy HANDFIELD
12 Provost Cocoa Campus .... Dr. Beverly J. SLAUGHTER
12 Provost Titusville Campus .... Dr. Philip SIMPSON
12 Provost eBrevard .... Dr. Kathy COBB
103 Exec Dir/Workforce Trng & Devel .... Dr. Linda MIEDEMA
37 Director Student Financial Aid .... Ms. Indira DZADOVSKY
07 Dir Collegewide Admiss/Advsmnt/Test .... Ms. Linda EICHAS
102 Executive Director Foundation .... Ms. Michele MURRELL
04 Executive Asst to the President .... Ms. Gina CLINE
06 Registrar .... Ms. Stephanie BURNETTE

Eckerd College (N)
4200 54th Avenue S, Saint Petersburg FL 33711-4700
County: Pinellas FICE Identification: 001487
Unit ID: 133492
Telephone: (727) 867-1166 Carnegie Class: Bac/A&S
FAX Number: (727) 864-1877 Calendar System: 4/1/4
URL: www.eckerd.edu
Established: 1958 Annual Undergrad Tuition & Fees: $37,362
Enrollment: 2,337 Coed
Affiliation or Control: Presbyterian Church (U.S.A.) IRS Status: 501(c)3
Highest Offering: Baccalaureate
Program: Liberal Arts And General
Accreditation: SC

01 President .... Dr. Donald R. EASTMAN, III
05 Exec Vice Pres/Provost/Dean Faculty .... Dr. Suzan HARRISON
10 CFO .... Mr. Christopher P. BRENNAN
03 Vice President .... Dr. Lisa A. METS
30 Vice President Advancement .... Mr. Matthew S. BISSET
51 Vice Pres/Dean of Special Programs .... Mr. Kelly KIRSCHNER
32 Vice Pres/Dean for Student Life .... Dr. James J. ANNARELLI
07 Dean of Admissions & Financial Aid .... Mr. John SULLIVAN
20 Assistant to the Pres Academic Affs .... Dr. Kathryn J. WATSON
26 Exec Dir Marketing/Communication .... Ms. Valerie GLIEM
21 Associate Chief Financial Officer .... Ms. Luz ARCILA
20 Assoc Dean Institutional Effective .... Dr. David A. EUBANKS
30 Assoc VP Advancement .... Mr. Tom SCHNEIDER
88 Academic Director of PEL .... Dr. Margret SKAFTADOTTIR
105 Dir Web/Marketing/Communication .... Mr. Casey PAQUET
27 Director Media Relations .... Ms. Alizza PUNZALAN HALL
88 Director of ASPEC .... Mr. Ken WOLFE
88 Director of CALA .... Dr. Norman SMITH
88 Director of International Education .... Ms. Diane L. FERRIS
85 Dir International Student Programs .... Mr. Olivier DEBURE
13 Dir of Information Tech .... Dr. John A. DUFF
09 Director Institutional Research .... Ms. Jacqueline MACNEIL
06 Registrar .... Ms. Linda SWINDALL
06 Student Enrollment Manager PEL .... Ms. Lin JORGENSEN
08 Director of Library .... Ms. Jamie W. GILL
38 Director Counseling Center .... Dr. Scott C. STRADER
29 Director Alumni Engagement .... Mr. Chris CONNORS
19 Director Campus Safety .... Mr. Adam COLBY
36 Educ Career Plng/Applied Learning .... Ms. Jessica NEANDER
37 Director Financial Aid .... Dr. Pat E. WATKINS
41 Athletic Director .... Dr. Robert FORTOSIS
07 Director of Admission .... Ms. Maria FURTADO
42 Chaplain .... Rev. Doug MCMAHON
88 Director of Sponsored Research .... Vacant
21 Controller .... Ms. Robin SMALLEY
35 Assistant Dean of Student Affairs .... Ms. Lorisa LORENZO
88 Asst Dean Students for Campus Act .... Mr. Fred SABOTA
28 Assoc Dn Stdnt Affs/Dir Mltcltl-Div .... Ms. Lena L. WILFALK
87 Dir Conferences and Summer School .... Ms. Cheryl GOLD

Edison State College (O)
8099 College Parkway, SW, Fort Myers FL 33919-5566
County: Lee FICE Identification: 001477
Unit ID: 133508
Telephone: (239) 489-9300 Carnegie Class: Assoc/Pub4
FAX Number: (239) 489-9103 Calendar System: Semester
URL: www.edison.edu
Established: 1961 Annual Undergrad Tuition & Fees (In-State): $3,683
Enrollment: 16,052 Coed
Affiliation or Control: State IRS Status: 501(c)3
Highest Offering: Baccalaureate
Program: Occupational; 2-Year Principally Bachelor's Creditable; Liberal Arts And General; Teacher Preparatory; Professional
Accreditation: SC, ADNUR, CAHIIM, COARC, CVT, DH, EMT, NUR, RAD

01 District President .... Dr. Jeffery ALLBRITTEN

05 Provost & VP of Academic Affairs .... Dr. Denis WRIGHT
10 VP Administrative Services .... Ms. Gina DOEBLE
46 VP Research/Tech & Accountability .... Dr. Jeffrey STEWART
32 VP Student Affairs & Enroll Mgmt .... Dr. Christine DAVIS
12 Pres Charlotte County Campus .... Dr. Patricia LAND
12 Pres Collier County Campus .... Dr. Robert JONES
100 Chief of Staff .... Dr. Henry PEEL
43 General Counsel .... Mr. Mark LUPE
102 Executive Director ESC Foundation .... Mr. Kevin MILLER
26 Dir Comm & Public Info Officer .... Ms. Teresa MORGENSTERN
86 Dir Govermental Relations .... Mr. Matthew HOLLIDAY
49 Interim Dean Arts & Sciences .... Dr. Thomas RATH
50 Dean Business & Technology .... Dr. John MEYER
53 Dean Education .... Dr. Erin HARREL
76 Dean Health Professions .... Dr. Marie COLLINS
106 Dean Edison Online .... Ms. Mary MYERS
36 Dean College and Career Readiness .... Dr. Eileen DELUCA
08 Dean Learning Resources .... Dr. Edith PENDLETON
06 Acting Registrar .... Dr. Kevin COUGHLIN
88 Director Academic Services .... Ms. Michelle FANSLAU
12 Director Hendry/Glades Center .... Mr. Jeffery GIBBS
88 Bursar .... Mr. Dwain KEDDO
18 Director Facilities Planning & Dev .... Mr. Steve NICE
15 Director Human Resources .... Mr. Ron DENTE
21 Director Budget & Financial Svcs .... Mr. Tobias DISCENZA
96 Director of Procurement Services .... Ms. Lisa TUDOR
37 Acting Director of Financial Aid .... Ms. Catherine MORGAN
19 Director Public Safety .... Mr. Richard PARFITT
88 Director Auxiliary Services .... Ms. Judith PULTRO
108 Director Effectiveness .... Dr. Susan HIBBARD
09 Director of Institutional Research .... Ms. Abby WILLCOX
13 Director Technology Services .... Mr. Jason DUDLEY
84 Asst VP Enrollment & Student Succes .... Vacant
35 Asst VP Student Affairs .... Vacant
07 Director of Admissions .... Vacant
88 Director of Testing Services .... Ms. Denise SWAFFORD
88 Director of Adaptive Services .... Ms. Angela HARTSELL
88 Director Student Support Services .... Ms. Paula DAILY
29 Coordinator Alumni Relations .... Ms. Rio DE ARMOND
44 Senior Director of Development .... Ms. Arlene KNOX
30 Director of Development .... Mr. Keith CALLAGHAN

Edward Waters College (A)

1658 Kings Road, Jacksonville FL 32209-6199

County: Duval
FICE Identification: 001478
Unit ID: 133526
Telephone: (904) 470-8000
Carnegie Class: Bac/Diverse
FAX Number: (904) 470-8039
Calendar System: Semester
URL: www.ewc.edu
Established: 1866
Annual Undergrad Tuition & Fees: $11,325
Enrollment: 925
Coed
Affiliation or Control: African Methodist Episcopal
IRS Status: 501(c)3
Highest Offering: Baccalaureate
Program: Liberal Arts And General
Accreditation: SC, IACBE

01 President .... Mr. Nathaniel GLOVER
03 Executive Vice President .... Vacant
25 Dir of Title III/Sponsored Programs .... Mrs. Lois M. WASHBURN
88 Executive Business Auditor .... Mr. George DANDELAKE
10 Vice Pres Business & Finance .... Mr. Randolph MITCHELL
32 Vice President Student Affairs .... Dr. Juiliana MOSLEY
84 Asst VP Enrollment Management .... Vacant
05 Interim VP of Academic Affairs .... Dr. Marvin GRANT
101 Secy of the College/Clerk BOT .... Mrs. Linda FOSTER
06 Registrar .... Ms. Loretta LATIMER
08 Director Library Services .... Ms. Carmella MARTIN
15 Director Human Resources .... Mr. Arthur BENDOLPH
37 Director Financial Aid .... Ms. Janice NOWAK
88 Dir of Teacher Education .... Dr. Marie SNOW
20 Assistant VP Academic Affairs .... Dr. Reuben PERECHI
50 Chair Business Administration .... Dr. Francis IKEOKWU
43 General Counsel .... Mr. Michael FREED
09 Dir Inst Planning/Research/Effectiv .... Ms. Bernice PARKER-BELL
88 Director Upward Bound .... Dr. Delacy SANFORD
36 Director Career Planning .... Ms. Kathy FOREMAN
30 Int VP Inst Advancement .... Ms. Wanda J. WILLIS
96 Director of Auxiliary Services .... Vacant
07 Director of Admissions .... Vacant
26 Coord Comm & Marketing .... Mr. Blake HACHT
88 Interim Director of TRIO .... Mr. Selah BISHOP
31 Director Community Resource Center .... Mrs. Marie HEATH
88 Exec Director of CTL .... Dr. Mammie JEFFRIES
89 Director of First-Year Experience .... Vacant
88 Director of FAME .... Mrs. Gladys CLAY
41 Director of Athletics .... Mr. Johnny REMBERT
13 Assistant CIO .... Mr. David SIMFUKWE

Embry-Riddle Aeronautical University (B)

600 S Clyde Morris Boulevard, Daytona Beach FL 32114-3900

County: Volusia
FICE Identification: 001479
Unit ID: 133553
Telephone: (386) 226-6000
Carnegie Class: Master's M
FAX Number: (386) 226-6459
Calendar System: Semester
URL: www.erau.edu
Established: 1926
Annual Undergrad Tuition & Fees: $30,120
Enrollment: 5,120
Coed
Affiliation or Control: Independent Non-Profit
IRS Status: 501(c)3
Highest Offering: Doctorate
Program: Occupational; Liberal Arts And General; Professional
Accreditation: SC, AAB, ACBSP, ENG

01 President .... Dr. John P. JOHNSON
05 Chief Academic Officer .... Dr. Richard HEIST
10 Vice Pres/Chief Financial Officer .... Mr. Eric B. WEEKES
15 Vice President Human Resources .... Vacant
84 VP Enrollment Management .... Mr. William HAMPTON
32 Dean of Students .... Mr. Jason GLENN
88 Assoc VP Enrollment Management .... Mr. Eduardo PRIETO
26 Assistant Director Communications .... Ms. Mary VAN BUREN
37 Director Financial Aid .... Ms. Barbara DRYDEN
09 Director Institutional Research .... Ms. Maria FRANCO
36 Executive Director Career Services .... Mr. Brian M. CARHIDE
07 Director UG Admissions .... Mr. Robert J. ADAMS
13 Chief Information Officer .... Ms. Cindy BIXLER
29 Dir Alum Rels Daytona .... Mr. Edmund ODARTEY-WILLIAMS
06 Registrar Daytona Beach Campus .... Ms. M.J CARO
88 Director Military & Veterans Enroll .... Ms. Faith DESLAURIERS
41 Director of Athletics .... Mr. Steven G. RIDDER
28 Int Director Diversity Initiatives .... Dr. Robin ROBERTS
35 Assoc Director Student Activities .... Ms. Lauren E. MORAN
38 Director Student Academic Support .... Mr. Richard NICOLS

Embry-Riddle Aeronautical University-Worldwide (C)

600 S Clyde Morris Boulevard, Daytona Beach FL 32114-3900

Telephone: (800) 522-6787
Identification: 666089
Accreditation: &SC

† Main campus is Embry-Riddle Aeronautical University in Daytona Beach, FL.

Everest Institute (D)

9020 SW 137th Avenue, Miami FL 33186-1410

County: Miami-Dade
FICE Identification: 030032
Unit ID: 409670
Telephone: (305) 386-9900
Carnegie Class: Assoc/PrivFP
FAX Number: (305) 388-1740
Calendar System: Other
URL: www.everest.edu
Established: 1977
Annual Undergrad Tuition & Fees: $17,000
Enrollment: 525
Coed
Affiliation or Control: Proprietary
IRS Status: Proprietary
Highest Offering: Associate Degree
Program: 2-Year Principally Bachelor's Creditable
Accreditation: ACICS, MAAB, SURGT

01 President .... Darrell RHOTEN
04 Assistant to the President .... Carolina MARTE
05 Academic Dean .... Claudette THOMPSON

Everest Institute (E)

111 NW 183rd Street, Suite 200, Miami FL 33169-4538

County: Miami-Dade
FICE Identification: 021218
Unit ID: 135957
Telephone: (305) 949-9500
Carnegie Class: Assoc/PrivFP
FAX Number: (305) 949-7303
Calendar System: Other
URL: www.everest.edu
Established: 1977
Annual Undergrad Tuition & Fees: $15,950
Enrollment: 592
Coed
Affiliation or Control: Proprietary
IRS Status: Proprietary
Highest Offering: Associate Degree
Program: Occupational; 2-Year Principally Bachelor's Creditable; Technical Emphasis
Accreditation: ACICS

01 Campus President .... Peter BASTIONY
05 Academic Dean .... Mike GIACCHINO
20 Associate Dean .... Rose-Marie MURRAY
07 Director of Admissions .... Kevin WILKINSON
37 Director of Finance .... Angela MACKEY
36 Director of Career Services .... Marissa NICKIE

Everest University-Brandon Campus (F)

3924 Coconut Palm Drive, Tampa FL 33619-1354

Telephone: (813) 621-0041
Identification: 666416
Accreditation: ACICS, ADNUR, MAC, RAD

† Main campus is Everest University-Tampa Campus in Tampa, FL.

Everest University-Jacksonville Campus (G)

8226 Phillips Highway, Jacksonville FL 32256-1240

Telephone: (904) 731-4949
Identification: 666994
Accreditation: ACICS, MAAB

† Main campus is Everest University-Largo in Largo, FL.

Everest University-Lakeland Campus (H)

995 E Memorial Boulevard, Suite 110, Lakeland FL 33801-1919

Telephone: (863) 686-1444
Identification: 666415
Accreditation: ACICS, MAC

† Main campus is Everest University-Largo in Largo, FL.

Everest University-Largo (I)

1199 East Bay Drive, Largo FL 33770-2556

County: Pinellas
FICE Identification: 025998
Unit ID: 137810
Telephone: (727) 725-2688
Carnegie Class: Bac/Assoc
FAX Number: (727) 373-4412
Calendar System: Quarter
URL: www.everest.edu
Established: 1890
Annual Undergrad Tuition & Fees: $22,560
Enrollment: 367
Coed
Affiliation or Control: Proprietary
IRS Status: Proprietary
Highest Offering: Master's
Program: Occupational; 2-Year Principally Bachelor's Creditable; Business Emphasis
Accreditation: ACICS, MAC

01 President .... Mr. Sami FANEK
05 Chief Academic Officer .... Mr. Oluyemi AWOLOLA
07 Director of Admissions .... Ms. Jill MALONE
37 Director of Student Finance .... Mr. Will SCOTT
36 Director of Career Services .... Ms. Lindsey DEMITH
10 Business Manager .... Mr. Will SCOTT
08 Librarian .... Ms. Candice PASCUAL
20 Assoc Dean of Academics .... Ms. Heidi DINDIAL-THOMPSON

Everest University-Melbourne Campus (J)

2401 N Harbor City Boulevard, Melbourne FL 32935-6609

Telephone: (321) 253-2929
Identification: 666417
Accreditation: ACICS, MAC

† Main campus is Everest University-North Orlando Campus in Orlando, FL.

Everest University-North Orlando Campus (K)

5421 Diplomat Circle, Orlando FL 32810-5674

County: Orange
FICE Identification: 001499
Unit ID: 136288
Telephone: (407) 628-5870
Carnegie Class: Bac/Assoc
FAX Number: (407) 628-1344
Calendar System: Quarter
URL: www.everest.edu
Established: 1918
Annual Undergrad Tuition & Fees: $14,616
Enrollment: 978
Coed
Affiliation or Control: Proprietary
IRS Status: Proprietary
Highest Offering: Master's
Program: Business Emphasis
Accreditation: ACICS, MAC

01 President .... Rerrance HARRIS, JR.
12 President of Branch Campus .... Louise A. STEINKEOWAY
12 President of Melbourne Branch .... Mark JUDGE
05 Academic Dean .... Paul VOWINKEL
07 Director of Admissions .... Kenny ANDERSON
08 Librarian .... Tamara DUJARDIAN
37 Financial Aid Supervisor .... Linda KAISRLIK
06 Registrar .... Jasmine RIVIERA
36 Director Student Placement .... Danielle THORNTON
10 Chief Business Officer .... Jessica KINESKEY
35 Director Student Service .... Liane PARDO

Everest University-Orange Park (L)

805 Wells Road, Orange Park FL 32073-2301

Telephone: (904) 264-9122
Identification: 666590
Accreditation: ACICS, MAAB

† Main campus is Everest University-Tampa Campus in Tampa, FL.

Everest University-Pompano Beach Campus (M)

225 N Federal Highway, Pompano Beach FL 33062

County: Broward
FICE Identification: 008146
Unit ID: 134149
Telephone: (954) 783-7339
Carnegie Class: Master's S
FAX Number: (954) 943-2547
Calendar System: Quarter
URL: www.everest.edu
Established: 1940
Annual Undergrad Tuition & Fees: $14,976
Enrollment: 2,452
Coed
Affiliation or Control: Proprietary
IRS Status: Proprietary
Highest Offering: Master's
Program: 2-Year Principally Bachelor's Creditable; Professional; Business Emphasis
Accreditation: ACICS, MAAB

01 President .... Mr. Stephen GUIDRY
05 Academic Dean .... Mr. Esmail ZARIAROW
07 Director Admissions .... Mr. Martin LEVERT
07 Director Admissions .... Ms. Amanda MCLURE
37 Director Student Finance .... Mr. Todd FOX
06 Registrar .... Ms. Dana NGUYEN
20 Associate Academic Dean .... Ms. Indira ST. ONER
36 Director Career Planning/Placement .... Ms. Andrea MITCHELL
08 Librarian .... Ms. Keri ENTERLINE
10 Director Student Accounts .... Mr. Trevor BLOW
04 Admin Assistant to the President .... Ms. Fumiko NYE

Everest University-South Orlando Campus (A)

9200 Southpark Center Loop, Orlando FL 32819-8606
Telephone: (407) 851-2525 Identification: 666418
Accreditation: **ACICS**, MAC

† Main campus is Everest University-North Orlando Campus in Orlando, FL.

Everest University-Tampa Campus (B)

3319 W Hillsborough Avenue, Tampa FL 33614-5801
County: Hillsborough FICE Identification: 001534
Unit ID: 137801
Telephone: (813) 879-6000 Carnegie Class: Bac/Assoc
FAX Number: (813) 871-2483 Calendar System: Quarter
URL: www.everest.edu
Established: 1890 Annual Undergrad Tuition & Fees: $23,396
Enrollment: 687 Coed
Affiliation or Control: Proprietary IRS Status: Proprietary
Highest Offering: Master's
Program: Occupational; 2-Year Principally Bachelor's Creditable; Professional; Business Emphasis
Accreditation: **ACICS**, MAC

01 President .... Mr. Thomas M. **BARLOW**
04 Assistant to the President .... Ms. Catherine **SHERMAN**
05 Academic Dean .... Ms. Theo **EGGLESTON**
07 Director of Admissions .... Mr. Tony **FAULKNER**
37 Director of Financial Aid .... Mr. Brian **JONES**
32 Director of Student Services .... Ms. Yolanda **WILLIAMS**
10 Director of Student Accounts .... Ms. Janet **GENAO**
36 Director of Career Services .... Ms. Regina **HODGSON**
20 Associate Academic Dean .... Ms. Dena **SEIDEN**
06 Lead Registrar .... Ms. Kim **LARKIN**
08 University Librarian .... Ms. Judith **COLE**

Everglades University (C)

5002 T-Rex Avenue, Suite 100,
Boca Raton FL 33431-4493
County: Palm Beach FICE Identification: 031085
Unit ID: 385619
Telephone: (888) 772-6077 Carnegie Class: Bac/Diverse
FAX Number: (561) 912-1191 Calendar System: Semester
URL: www.evergladesuniversity.edu
Established: 1990 Annual Undergrad Tuition & Fees: $26,114
Enrollment: 1,141 Coed
Affiliation or Control: Independent Non-Profit IRS Status: 501(c)3
Highest Offering: Master's
Program: Professional
Accreditation: **SC**

01 President/CEO .... Ms. Kristi L. **MOLLIS**
05 Vice President of Academic Affairs .... Dr. Jayne **MOSCHELLA**
37 Regional Director of Financial Aid .... Mrs. Seeta **SINGH MOONILALL**
84 Regional Dir of Marketing & Enroll .... Mr. Stephen **IACULLO**
88 Director of Fundraising .... Vacant
09 Director Inst Effectiveness .... Dr. Shaun **COWMAN**
08 Director of Library Services .... Mr. Zach **ENGLISH**
12 Vice President Boca Raton Campus ... Mr. David **SHELPMAN, JR.**
12 Vice President Online Division .... Ms. Suzanne **CROWLEY**
12 Vice President Sarasota Campus .... Ms. Caroline **KING**
12 Vice President of Orlando Campus .... Ms. Paulette **THOMAS**
20 Dean of Academics Online .... Dr. Valerie **BURKE**
20 Dean of Academics Sarasota .... Dr. Donette **GORDON**
20 Dean of Academics Orlando .... Dr. Penelope **CARR**
20 Dean of Academics Boca Raton .... Dr. Arlette **PETERSSON**
07 Director of Admissions Boca .... Mrs. Debra **RODRIGUES**
07 Director of Admissions Online Boca .... Ms. Susan **ARONBERG**
07 Director of Admissions Orlando .... Vacant
07 Director of Admission Sarasota .... Ms. Barbara **BEASLEY**
04 Assistant to the President .... Ms. Christina **OAKLEY**
37 Asst Financial Aid Director Online .... Mrs. Anne **RODNE**
37 Asst Financial Aid Director Online .... Ms. Fatima **FLORES**
37 Financial Aid Director Sarasota .... Mrs. Courtney **ROBERTSON**
37 Financial Aid Director Orlando .... Mr. Anthony **CHAMBERS**
37 Financial Aid Director Boca .... Mrs. Alexis **PAULEN**
06 Registrar-Online Division .... Mr. Adrian **KACZOR**
06 Asst. Registrar Online Division .... Ms. Corinna **GILSON**
06 Registrar Boca .... Ms. Sandy **MAZOR**
06 Registrar Orlando .... Mr. Clifton **HURD**
06 Registrar Sarasota .... Ms. Donna **BARANOWSKI**
50 Business Department .... Ms. Celine **MANOOSINGH**
50 Dept Chair of Construction Mgmt .... Vacant
88 Department Chair of Aviation .... Mr. Michael **VAN DUSEN**
76 Department Chair Allied Health .... Mrs. Chelsea **HANSEN**
88 Librarian Boca Raton .... Vacant
88 Librarian Sarasota .... Ms. Anisa **THOMAS**
08 Librarian Orlando .... Vacant
32 Dir of Student Services Online .... Mr. Richard **DELEWSKY**
32 Dir of Student Services Boca Raton .... Mr. Ruben **VALBUENA**
32 Dir of Student Services Sarasota .... Ms. Amy **DISS**
32 Dir of Student Services Orlando .... Ms. Kayli **LEWIS**
88 Bursar Manager Online Division .... Vacant
88 Bursar Online Division .... Ms. Nicolette **DAVIS**
40 Bursar/Bookstore Manager Boca .... Vacant
40 Bookstore Manager Online Division .... Ms. Pamela **PETERSON**
40 Bursar/Bookstore Manager Sarasota .... Ms. Anita **WENDZEL**
40 Bursar/Bookstore Manager Orlando .... Ms. Mabel **RASMUSSEN**
88 Online Trainer .... Mr. Ronnie **ABUKHALAF**

FCC-Anthem College (D)

989 N Semoran Boulevard, Orlando FL 32807
Telephone: (888) 852-7272 Identification: 770613
Accreditation: **ACICS**

† Main campus is Florida Career College in Miami, FL.

Flagler College (E)

74 King Street, Saint Augustine FL 32084-4342
County: Saint Johns FICE Identification: 007893
Unit ID: 133711
Telephone: (904) 829-6481 Carnegie Class: Bac/Diverse
FAX Number: (904) 824-6017 Calendar System: Semester
URL: www.flagler.edu
Established: 1968 Annual Undergrad Tuition & Fees: $16,180
Enrollment: 2,629 Coed
Affiliation or Control: Independent Non-Profit IRS Status: 501(c)3
Highest Offering: Baccalaureate
Program: Liberal Arts And General; Teacher Preparatory; Business Emphasis
Accreditation: **SC**, @TEAC

01 President .... Dr. William T. **ABARE, JR.**
00 Chancellor .... Dr. William L. **PROCTOR**
10 Vice President Business Services .... Mr. Kenneth S. **RUSSOM**
30 Vice President Inst Advancement .... Dr. Beverly C. **CARMICHAEL**
05 Vice President Academic Affairs .... Dr. Alan **WOOLFOLK**
26 Exec Director College Relations .... Ms. Donna **DELORENZO**
21 Executive Director of Finance .... Ms. Pamela F. **LEYDON**
09 Director Inst Research & Planning .... Dr. Will **MILLER**
27 Director of News and Information .... Mr. Brian L. **THOMPSON**
84 Vice President for Enrollment Mgmt .... Mr. Marc G. **WILLIAR**
32 Vice President of Student Services .... Mr. Daniel P. **STEWART**
20 Associate Dean of Academic Affairs .... Mr. Yvan J. **KELLY**
35 Assistant Dean of Student Services .... Dr. Dirk **HIBLER**
38 Associate Dean of Counseling .... Dr. Glenn **GOLDBERG**
06 Registrar .... Mrs. Miriam C. **ROBERSON**
37 Director of Financial Aid .... Mr. Christopher D. **HAFFNER**
36 Director of Career Services .... Ms. Tara **STEVENSON**
08 Director of Library Services .... Mr. Michael A. **GALLEN**
41 Director Intercollegiate Athletics .... Mr. Jud **DAMON**
19 Director of Safety & Security .... Mr. Kerry **DAVIS**
40 Bookstore Manager .... Mr. Bob **SMITH**
24 Director Educational Media Services .... Mr. Steven I. **SKIPP**
13 Director Technology Services .... Mr. Joseph S. **PROVENZA**
39 Director of Residence Life .... Ms. Rachel T. **GREEN**
35 Director of Student Activities .... Ms. Carley **JAMES**
12 Dean Flagler College - Tallahassee .... Dr. Donald K. **PARKS**
88 Dir of Disability Services .... Ms. Eva Lynn **FRANCISCO**
18 Superintendent of Plant & Grounds .... Mr. Victor **CHENEY**
04 Assistant to the President .... Ms. Mary Jane **DILLON**
21 Director of Business Services .... Mr. Larry D. **WEEKS**
29 Director Alumni Relations .... Ms. Margo **BROWN**
44 Director Annual Fund .... Mr. Jeffrey **DAVITT**
15 HR Generalist/Benefits Specialist .... Ms. Tricia **KRISTOFF**
31 Director of College Relations .... Ms. Laura **STEVENSON**
88 Senior Woman Admin Athletic Dept .... Ms. Jennifer **RINNERT**

Florida Career College (F)

1743 N Congress Avenue, Boynton Beach FL 33426
Telephone: (561) 634-7400 Identification: 770678
Accreditation: **ACICS**

† Main campus is Florida Career College in Miami, FL.

Florida Career College (G)

410 Park Place Boulevard, Clearwater FL 33759-3924
Telephone: (727) 724-1037 FICE Identification: 025862
Accreditation: **ACICS**

† Main campus is Florida Career College in Miami, FL.

Florida Career College (H)

3750 West 18th Avenue, Hialeah FL 33012-7028
Telephone: (305) 825-3231 Identification: 666624
Accreditation: **ACICS**

† Main campus is Florida Career College in Miami, FL.

Florida Career College (I)

6600 Youngerman Circle, Jacksonville FL 32244
Telephone: (904) 573-1900 Identification: 770679
Accreditation: **ACICS**

† Main campus is Florida Career College in Miami, FL.

Florida Career College (J)

3383 North State Road 7,
Lauderdale Lakes FL 33319-5617
Telephone: (954) 535-8700 Identification: 666622
Accreditation: **ACICS**

† Main campus is Florida Career College in Miami, FL.

Florida Career College (K)

3271 North State Road 7, Margate FL 33063
Telephone: (954) 862-7260 Identification: 770681
Accreditation: **ACICS**

† Main campus is Florida Career College in Miami, FL.

Florida Career College (L)

1321 SW 107th Avenue, Suite 201B,
Miami FL 33174-2521
County: Miami-Dade FICE Identification: 023058
Unit ID: 133997
Telephone: (305) 553-6065 Carnegie Class: Assoc/PrivFP4
FAX Number: (305) 225-0128 Calendar System: Quarter
URL: www.careercollege.edu
Established: 1982 Annual Undergrad Tuition & Fees: $17,644
Enrollment: 5,793 Coed
Affiliation or Control: Proprietary IRS Status: Proprietary
Highest Offering: Baccalaureate
Program: Occupational; 2-Year Principally Bachelor's Creditable; Technical Emphasis
Accreditation: **ACICS**

01 President/CEO .... Mr. David **KNOBEL**
03 Executive Director .... Ms. Erica **MATTHEW**
05 Director of Education .... Mr. Victor **CALDERON**
88 Associate Executive Director .... Mr. Eduardo **SAMA**
88 Associate Executive Director .... Ms. Muriel **GUTIERREZ**
88 Area Executive Director .... Mr. Gilbert **DELGADO**
88 Area Executive Director .... Mr. Michael **SCHWAM**
37 Financial Aid Director .... Ms. Vanessa **ALFARO**
06 Registrar .... Ms. Nicola **WILLIAMS**
07 Director of Admission .... Mr. Christopher **KAPALKA**

Florida Career College (M)

11731 Mills Drive, Bldg #2, Miami FL 33183
Telephone: (305) 384-7900 Identification: 770680
Accreditation: **ACICS**

† Main campus is Florida Career College in Miami, FL.

Florida Career College (N)

7891 Pines Boulevard, Pembroke Pines FL 33024-6916
Telephone: (954) 965-7272 Identification: 666025
Accreditation: **ACICS**

† Main campus is Florida Career College in Miami, FL.

Florida Career College (O)

2662 S Falkenburg Road, Riverview FL 33569
Telephone: (813) 621-5775 Identification: 770682
Accreditation: **ACICS**, PTAA

† Main campus is Florida Career College in Miami, FL.

Florida Career College (P)

6058 Okeechobee Boulevard, West Palm Beach FL 33417
Telephone: (561) 689-0550 Identification: 770683
Accreditation: **ACICS**

† Main campus is Florida Career College in Miami, FL.

Florida Coastal School of Law (Q)

8787 Baypine, Jacksonville FL 32256-8528
County: Duval FICE Identification: 033743
Unit ID: 434715
Telephone: (904) 680-7700 Carnegie Class: Spec/Law
FAX Number: (904) 680-7777 Calendar System: Semester
URL: www.fcsl.edu
Established: 1995 Annual Graduate Tuition & Fees: $41,351
Enrollment: 1,830 Coed
Affiliation or Control: Proprietary IRS Status: Proprietary
Highest Offering: First Professional Degree; No Undergraduates
Program: Professional
Accreditation: **LAW**

01 Int Dean & Professor of Law .... Mr. Chidi **OGENE**
05 Vice Dean .... Mrs. Cynthia **STROUD**
10 Vice Pres Finance & Administration .... Mr. Bruce **WILSON**
20 Associate Dean Academic Affairs .... Mrs. Cynthia **IRVIN**
32 Associate Dean of Students .... Mr. Thomas **TAGGART**
04 Assistant to the Dean .... Ms. Denise **SACCO**
30 Int Dir Institutional Advancement .... Mrs. Brooks **TERRY**
08 Director of Law Library .... Mrs. Alma (Nickie) **SINGLETON**
36 Int Director of Career Services .... Mrs. Jocelyn **DONAHUE**
06 Registrar .... Ms. Bridgette **WAINES**
37 Director Financial Aid .... Mr. Roger **COLLINS**
14 Director Information Technology .... Mr. Mark **SABATTINI**
26 Asst Dir Marketing/Communications .... Mrs. Brooks **TERRY**
15 Director of Human Resources .... Mrs. Stacie **SMITH**
18 Facilities Manager .... Mr. Jay **LEHMANN**
20 Assistant Dean of Academic Affairs .... Ms. Danielle **NOE**

Florida College (A)

119 N Glen Arven Avenue,
Temple Terrace FL 33617-5578

County: Hillsborough FICE Identification: 001482
Unit ID: 133809
Telephone: (813) 988-5131 Carnegie Class: Bac/Assoc
FAX Number: (813) 899-6772 Calendar System: Semester
URL: www.floridacollege.edu
Established: 1944 Annual Undergrad Tuition & Fees: $14,000
Enrollment: 532 Coed
Affiliation or Control: Independent Non-Profit IRS Status: 501(c)3
Highest Offering: Baccalaureate
Program: Liberal Arts And General; Religious Emphasis
Accreditation: SC, MUS

01 President ... Dr. Harry E. PAYNE, JR.
05 Vice Pres of Acad & Student Affairs ... Dr. Douglas H. NORTHCUTT
20 Dean of Academics ... Dr. Daniel W. PETTY
32 Dean of Student Services ... Dr. Brian CRISPELL
10 Chief Business Officer ... Mr. Ronnie STACKPOLE
37 Director Student Financial Aid ... Mr. Stephen BLAYLOCK
84 Dir of Admissions & Retention Svcs ... Mr. Paul CASEBOLT
09 Director of Institutional Research ... Dr. M. Thaxter DICKEY
06 Registrar ... Ms. Beth A. GRANT
08 Director of Library ... Mrs. Wanda DICKEY
90 Director of Academic Computing ... Mr. M. Ray HINDS
91 Director of Information Technology ... Mr. William J. MCKINNEY
30 Director of Development ... Mr. David CURRY
26 Director of Alumni/Public Relations ... Mr. Ralph R. WALKER, JR.
27 Director of Marketing ... Mr. Jared BARR
40 Manager of Bookstore ... Mr. Jeff NUNLEY

Florida College of Integrative Medicine (B)

7100 Lake Ellenor Drive, Orlando FL 32809-5721

County: Orange FICE Identification: 032383
Unit ID: 434441
Telephone: (407) 888-8689 Carnegie Class: Spec/Health
FAX Number: (407) 888-8211 Calendar System: Semester
URL: www.fcim.edu
Established: 1990 Annual Undergrad Tuition & Fees: $15,125
Enrollment: 135 Coed
Affiliation or Control: Proprietary IRS Status: Proprietary
Highest Offering: Master's; No Lower Division
Program: Professional
Accreditation: ACUP

01 President ... Mr. Larry L. LAN
03 Vice President ... Ms. Jenjen HAN
05 Academic Dean ... Dr. Lin CHAI
11 Chief Administrative Officer ... Mr. Robert P. LYNCH
10 Director of Finance ... Ms. Susan HOEH
07 Director of Admissions ... Ms. Gail L. SPRINGER

Florida College of Natural Health (C)

616 67th Street Circle East, Bradenton FL 34208-6087

Telephone: (941) 744-1244 Identification: 666830
Accreditation: ACCSC, COMTA

† Main campus is Florida College of Natural Health in Pompano Beach, FL.

Florida College of Natural Health (D)

2600 Lake Lucien Drive, Suite 240,
Maitland FL 32751-7253

Telephone: (407) 261-0319 Identification: 666513
Accreditation: ACCSC, COMTA

† Main campus is Florida College of Natural Health in Pompano Beach, FL.

Florida College of Natural Health (E)

7925 NW 12th Street, #201, Miami FL 33126-1821

Telephone: (305) 597-9599 Identification: 666514
Accreditation: ACCSC, COMTA

† Main campus is Florida College of Natural Health in Pompano Beach, FL.

Florida College of Natural Health (F)

2001 W Sample Road, #100,
Pompano Beach FL 33064-1342

County: Broward FICE Identification: 030086
Unit ID: 387925
Telephone: (954) 975-6400 Carnegie Class: Assoc/PrivFP
FAX Number: (954) 975-9633 Calendar System: Other
URL: www.fcnh.com
Established: 1986 Annual Undergrad Tuition & Fees: $12,423
Enrollment: 361 Coed
Affiliation or Control: Proprietary IRS Status: Proprietary
Highest Offering: Associate Degree
Program: Occupational
Accreditation: ACCSC, COMTA

01 President ... Mr. Stephen LAZARUS
10 Controller ... Ms. Barbara KRANE
03 Vice President of Compliance ... Ms. Melissa WADE
05 Vice President of Education ... Ms. Dawnette CABALUNA

Florida Gateway College (G)

149 SE College Place, Lake City FL 32025-2007

County: Columbia FICE Identification: 001501
Unit ID: 135160
Telephone: (386) 752-1822 Carnegie Class: Assoc/Pub-R-M
FAX Number: (386) 755-1521 Calendar System: Semester
URL: www.fgc.edu
Established: 1947 Annual Undergrad Tuition & Fees (In-State): $3,070
Enrollment: 3,073 Coed
Affiliation or Control: State IRS Status: 501(c)3
Highest Offering: Baccalaureate
Program: Occupational; 2-Year Principally Bachelor's Creditable; Liberal Arts And General; Teacher Preparatory; Nursing Emphasis
Accreditation: SC, ADNUR, EMT, PTAA

01 President ... Dr. Charles W. HALL
10 Vice President Business Services ... Ms. Marilyn HAMM
04 Assistant to the President ... Ms. Karyn CONGRESSI
05 Vice President for Academic Pgms ... Dr. Brian DOPSON
75 Vice President Occupational Pgms ... Dr. Tracy HICKMAN
32 Vice President for Student Services ... Dr. Linda CROLEY
14 Exec Dir Info Technology/CIO ... Mr. Mike DAVIS
47 Exec Dir of Industrial & Agricult ... Mr. John PIERSOL
66 Executive Director Nursing & Health ... Ms. Tammy MARTINEAU
53 Exec Dir Ctr for Excell in Teaching ... Ms. Pamela CARSWELL
102 Executive Director Foundation ... Mr. Mike LEE
26 Exec Dir Media & Community Info ... Mr. Mike MCKEE
37 Director Financial Aid ... Mrs. Debberin TUNSIL
84 Director Enrollment Management ... Ms. Sandra JOHNSTON
15 Executive Director Human Resources ... Ms. Sharon BEST
06 Registrar ... Ms. Gayle HUNTER
21 Director Business Services ... Mr. Van SMITHEY
25 Director of Grants ... Dr. Laurel SEMMES
09 Director of Research/Institutional ... Ms. Patty ANDERSON
18 Chief Facilities/Physical Plant ... Mr. George SCOTT
96 Director of Purchasing ... Ms. Tonia LAWSON
36 Director Advising/Student Dev ... Dr. Margaret MCLAUGHLIN
88 Director for Water Resources ... Mr. Tim ATKINSON
88 Director for Criminal Justice ... Mr. John JEWETT
88 Director Title III/Develop Educ ... Ms. Carrie RODESILER
62 Director Library Services ... Ms. Christine BOATRIGHT

Florida Institute of Technology (H)

150 W University Boulevard, Melbourne FL 32901-6975

County: Brevard FICE Identification: 001469
Unit ID: 133881
Telephone: (321) 674-8000 Carnegie Class: DRU
FAX Number: (321) 984-8461 Calendar System: Semester
URL: www.fit.edu
Established: 1958 Annual Undergrad Tuition & Fees: $36,020
Enrollment: 8,816 Coed
Affiliation or Control: Independent Non-Profit IRS Status: 501(c)3
Highest Offering: Doctorate
Program: Liberal Arts And General; Teacher Preparatory; Professional; Technical Emphasis
Accreditation: SC, AAB, CLPSY, CS, ENG

01 President ... Dr. Anthony J. CATANESE
04 Exec Asst to Pres & Ombudsman ... Mrs. Suzee S. LOUCHE
05 Executive Vice Pres & COO ... Dr. T. Dwayne MCCAY
10 Sr Vice Pres Financial Affairs/CFO ... Dr. Robert E. NIEBUHR
88 Sr Vice Pres External Relations ... Capt. Winston SCOTT
30 Sr Vice Pres/Chief Development Ofcr ... Ms. Susan ST. ONGE
20 Deputy COO ... Dr. Donn MILLER-KERMANI
88 Dean College of Aeronautics ... Dr. Kenneth STACKPOOLE
50 Dean College of Business ... Dr. S. Ann BECKER
54 Dean College of Engineering ... Dr. Frederic HAM
83 Dean Col of Psychology/Liberal Arts ... Dr. Mary Beth KENKEL
81 Dean College of Science ... Dr. Hamid RASSOUL
08 Iterim Dean of Libraries ... Ms. Kathy TURNER
30 Vice President Development ... Mr. Michael SEELEY
18 Vice Pres Facilities Ops/Architect ... Mr. Gregory TSARK
13 Vice Pres IT/CIO ... Mr. Eric KLEDZIK
27 Vice Pres Marketing & Communication ... Mr. Wesley SUMNER
88 Vice President Orlando Center ... Ms. Leslie HIELEMA
46 Vice President Research ... Mr. Frank KINNEY
32 Vice President Student Affairs ... Dr. Randall L. ALFORD
11 Vice Pres Support Services ... Dr. Joni OGLESBY
21 Assoc Vice Pres/Fin Plng & Control ... Ms. Claire WURMFELD
84 Assoc Vice Pres Enrollment Mgmt ... Mr. Gary HAMME
108 Assoc Vice Pres Inst Compliance ... Dr. Monica BALOGA
35 Assoc VP Student Affs/Dean of Stdnt ... Mr. Rodney BOWERS
106 Asst Vice Pres/Dir Online Learning ... Mr. Brian EHRLICH
29 Asst VP Alum Rel/Exec Dir Alum Assn ... Mr. Bino CAMPANINI
06 Registrar ... Ms. Charlotte YOUNG
88 Director Academic Support Services ... Mr. Rodd NEWCOMBE
41 Director Athletics ... Mr. William K. JURGENS
19 Director Campus Security ... Mr. Kevin GRAHAM
36 Director Career Services ... Ms. Dona E. GAYNOR
38 Dir Counseling/Psychological Svcs ... Dr. Robyn TAPLEY
88 Director Creative Services ... Ms. Judi E. TINTERA
88 Dir Environ & Regulatory Compliance ... Mr. Greg PEEBLES
18 Director Facilities Operations ... Mr. John M. MILBOURNE
37 Director Financial Aid ... Mr. Jay LALLY
07 Director Grad Adm Online Learning ... Ms. Carolyn P. FARRIOR
58 Director Graduate Programs ... Ms. Rosemary LAYNE
85 Director Intl Students/Scholar Svcs ... Ms. Judith BROOKE
09 Director Institutional Research ... Ms. Leslie L. SAVOIE
07 Director Undergraduate Admission ... Mr. Michael PERRY
88 Director University Museums ... Ms. Carla FUNK
07 Assoc Director Graduate Admissions ... Ms. Cheryl-Ann BROWN

Florida Keys Community College (I)

5901 College Road, Key West FL 33040-4397

County: Monroe FICE Identification: 001485
Unit ID: 133960
Telephone: (305) 296-9081 Carnegie Class: Assoc/Pub-R-S
FAX Number: (305) 292-5155 Calendar System: Trimester
URL: www.fkcc.edu
Established: 1963 Annual Undergrad Tuition & Fees (In-District): $3,776
Enrollment: 1,212 Coed
Affiliation or Control: State/Local IRS Status: 501(c)3
Highest Offering: Associate Degree
Program: Occupational; 2-Year Principally Bachelor's Creditable; Fine Arts Emphasis
Accreditation: SC

01 President ... Dr. Jonathan GUEUERRA
05 Provost ... Mrs. Brittany SYNDER
10 Vice Pres Business & Admin Svcs ... Mrs. Jean MAUK
35 Dean Student Affairs ... Mrs. Erika MACWILLIAMS
32 Director Student Services ... Mrs. Michelle CHERRY
51 Dir Cont Ed/Workforce/Testing ... Mrs. Cathy TORRES
04 Director Pres Office ... Mrs. Debbie LEONARD
26 Director College and Public Rels ... Mrs. Amber ERNST-LEONARD
06 Registrar ... Mrs. Cheryl MALSHEIMER
08 Director Learning Resources ... Mr. Eric DILLALOGUE
37 Dir Student Fin Aid/Enrollment Svcs ... Mrs. Susan URBAN
18 Dir Purchasing and Plant Opers ... Mr. Douglas PRYOR
13 Director of IT ... Mr. Bryan GILCHRIST
15 Director Human Resources ... Ms. LaVonda MEUNIER
25 Director Sponsored Programs ... Ms. Joanne PRESTON
102 Dir Of FKCC Foundation ... Ms. Gavin MCKIERNAN
21 Controller ... Ms. LeeAnne HOLLAND
88 Centers Director ... Mr. Christopher FLETCHER
09 Dir Institutional Effectiveness ... Ms. Linda MACMINN
30 Dir Development/Alumni Rels ... Ms. Gavin MCKIERNAN
76 Director Allied Health & Nursing ... Vacant
88 Dean of Marine Sciences and Tech ... Dr. Jack SEUBERT
49 Dean Arts & Sciences ... Dr. Frank WOOD

Florida Memorial University (J)

15800 NW 42nd Avenue, Miami Gardens FL 33054-6199

County: Miami-Dade FICE Identification: 001486
Unit ID: 133979
Telephone: (305) 626-3600 Carnegie Class: Master's S
FAX Number: (305) 626-3769 Calendar System: Semester
URL: www.fmuniv.edu
Established: 1879 Annual Undergrad Tuition & Fees: $14,445
Enrollment: 1,578 Coed
Affiliation or Control: Independent Non-Profit IRS Status: 501(c)3
Highest Offering: Master's
Program: Liberal Arts And General; Teacher Preparatory
Accreditation: SC, ACBSP, CS, MUS, SW

01 Interim President ... Dr. Roslyn CLARK ARTIS
05 Provost & VP Academic Affairs ... Vacant
05 Associate Provost ... Dr. Denise CALLWOOD-BRATHWAITE
04 Assistant to President ... Ms. Rachel TURNER
49 Interim Dean of Arts and Sciences ... Dr. Keshia N. ABRAHAMN
10 Vice Pres Finance/Administration ... Ms. Cynthia CURRY
32 Vice Pres for Student Affairs ... Ms. Danneal JONES
30 Vice Pres Institutional Advancement ... Dr. John N. BERRY
45 Assc VP Institutional Effectiveness ... Dr. William E. HOPPER
88 Chair Aviation and Safety ... Dr. Arnold J. TOLBERT
50 Dean School of Business ... Dr. Abbass ENTESSARI
53 Dean School of Education ... Dr. Mildred BERRY
81 Chair Health and Natural Sciences ... Dr. Rose Mary STIFFIN
83 Chair Social Sciences ... Vacant
88 Chair Visual and Performing Arts ... Dr. Dawn BATSON-BOREL
77 Chair Comp Science/Math & Tech ... Dr. Ben WONGSAROJ
79 Chair Humanities ... Dr. Keshia N. ABRAHAM
88 Dir Ctrs for Acad Support & Reten ... Dr. Jeffrey SWAIN
08 Interim Director University Library ... Ms. Jauquinda STURDIVANT
84 Director of Enrollment Mgmt ... Mr. Roscoe WARREN
06 Registrar ... Mrs. Lelia A. EFFORD
09 Director of Institutional Research ... Dr. Carlos CANAS
42 Director of Church Relations ... Mrs. Patricia CARTER
15 Director Human Resources Management ... Mrs. Valerie A. WILLIAMS
88 Dir Administrative Support Services ... Mr. Alphonso BURNSIDE
41 Director of Athletics ... Mr. Robert SMITH
36 Director Career Development ... Ms. Athena JACKSON
37 Interim Director Financial Aid ... Mr. Kozman STROMAN
39 Director Residential Life ... Mrs. Jacklan ALEXANDER
07 Director of Admissions ... Mrs. Peggy Murray MARTIN
19 Chief of Security ... Chief Larry COLEMAN
18 Dir Facility Mgmt/Plant Operations ... Mr. David JACCARINO
42 Campus Minister ... Rev. Wendell PARIS, JR.
29 Director Alumni Affairs ... Mrs. Sheila POWELL-COHEN
35 Director Student Development ... Mr. C. Vernon MARTIN, JR.
85 International Student Advisor ... Mr. Trevor LEWIS
13 Actg Chief Information Officer ... Mr. Orlando HUERTAS
88 Director of Assessment ... Dr. Richard YAKLICH

Florida National University Hialeah Campus (A)

4425 W. Jose Regueiro (20th) Ave,
Hialeah FL 33012-4108
County: Dade FICE Identification: 025476
Unit ID: 408844
Telephone: (305) 821-3333 Carnegie Class: Assoc/PrivFP4
FAX Number: (305) 362-0595 Calendar System: Semester
URL: www.fnu.edu
Established: 1982 Annual Undergrad Tuition & Fees: $13,230
Enrollment: 1,497 Coed
Affiliation or Control: Proprietary IRS Status: Proprietary
Highest Offering: Master's
Program: 2-Year Principally Bachelor's Creditable; Business Emphasis
Accreditation: SC, COARC

01 President/CEO .... Mrs. Maria C. REGUEIRO
09 VP of Assessment & Research/FA Dir .... Mr. Omar SANCHEZ
11 Vice President of Operations .... Mr. Frank ANDREU
05 Vice President of Academic Affairs .... Mrs. Caridad HERNANDEZ
10 Controller .... Mrs. Lourdes NIEVES
88 Accreditation Liaison .... Mrs. Barbara J. RODRIGUEZ
07 Director of Admissions .... Mr. Joseph FORTON
06 University Registrar .... Mr. Jose L. VALDES
08 Library Director .... Mr. Patrick BYRNES
32 Director of Student Services .... Mrs. Yesenia DIAZ
105 Campus Dean Online Learning .... Mrs. Sandra LOMENA
12 Campus Dean .... Mr. Jorge ALFONSO
88 Academic Advisor .... Mrs. Jelenny HERNANDEZ
36 Job Placement Officer .... Mr. Candido AVEILLE
50 Business & Economics Division Head .... Dr. James BULLEN
76 Allied Health Division Head .... Dr. Loreto ALMONTE
66 RN Program Nursing Division Dir .... Mrs. Maida BURGOS
79 Humanities and Fine Arts Division .... Mrs. Barbara RODRIGUEZ
88 ESL Division Head .... Mr. Oscar PEREZ
15 Human Resources Director .... Mr. Edward ZALDIVAR
88 Military Recruiter .... Mrs. Vilma ROSARIO
41 Athletic Director .... Mr. Scott J. SCHMIDT
88 Assistant Campus Dean .... Mrs. Olga RODRIGUEZ
88 Assistant Campus Dean .... Mrs. Silvia BORGES
07 Admissions Supervisor Distance .... Mr. Luigi VALDIVIESO
07 Admissions Supervisor .... Mrs. Virginia RABELO
88 Academic Advisor .... Mrs. Carol ROMERO

Florida National University South Campus (B)

11865 SW 26th Street Unit H-3, Miami FL 33175
Telephone: (305) 226-9999 Identification: 666691
Accreditation: &SC

† Main campus is Florida National University Hialeah Campus in Hialeah, FL.

Florida National University Training Center (C)

4206 West 12th Avenue, Hialeah FL 33012
Telephone: (305) 231-3326 Identification: 666690
Accreditation: &SC

† Main campus is Florida National University Hialeah Campus in Hialeah, FL.

Florida Southern College (D)

111 Lake Hollingsworth Drive, Lakeland FL 33801-5698
County: Polk FICE Identification: 001488
Unit ID: 134079
Telephone: (863) 680-4111 Carnegie Class: Bac/Diverse
FAX Number: (863) 680-4112 Calendar System: Semester
URL: www.flsouthern.edu
Established: 1885 Annual Undergrad Tuition & Fees: $28,580
Enrollment: 2,486 Coed
Affiliation or Control: United Methodist IRS Status: 501(c)3
Highest Offering: Master's
Program: Liberal Arts And General
Accreditation: SC, BUS, MUS, NURSE

01 President .... Dr. Anne B. KERR
05 Provost .... Dr. Kyle FEDLER
10 Vice President Finance & Admin .... Mr. Terry DENNIS
26 Vice President External Relations .... Dr. Robert H. TATE
32 Dean of Student Development .... Mr. Bill C. LANGSTON, II
84 Vice Pres/Dean Enrollment Mgmt .... Mr. John GRUNDIG
30 Vice President Advancement .... Vacant
26 Vice President Marketing & Comm .... Vacant
08 Director of the Library .... Mr. Randall M. MACDONALD
07 Director of Admissions .... Ms. Erin ERVIN
06 Registrar .... Ms. Sally L. THISSEN
09 Dir Inst Research/Effectiveness .... Dr. Kenneth M. REAVES
36 Director of Career Development .... Ms. Xuchitl COSO
37 Director of Student Financial Aid .... Mr. William L. HEALY
29 Coordinator of Alumni Services .... Ms. Meredith PROKUSKI
41 Athletic Director .... Mr. Peter E. MEYER
42 Chaplain Director Campus Ministry .... Rev. Timothy S. WRIGHT
19 Director Security/Safety .... Mr. William CAREW
15 Director of Human Resources .... Ms. Katherine PAWLAK
20 Assoc Provost Experiential Educ .... Dr. Mary L. CROWE
31 Director of Community Living .... Ms. Elizabeth CHING-BUSH
38 Director Student Counseling .... Dr. Carol BALLARD
27 Chief Information Officer .... Mr. John L. THOMAS
88 Director of Marketing and Comm .... Ms. Katherine FARLEY

Florida State College at Jacksonville (E)

501 W State Street, Jacksonville FL 32202-4097
County: Duval FICE Identification: 001484
Unit ID: 133702
Telephone: (904) 646-2300 Carnegie Class: Assoc/Pub4
FAX Number: N/A Calendar System: Semester
URL: www.fscj.edu
Established: 1963 Annual Undergrad Tuition & Fees (In-District): $3,086
Enrollment: 30,053 Coed
Affiliation or Control: Local IRS Status: Exempt
Highest Offering: Baccalaureate
Program: Occupational; 2-Year Principally Bachelor's Creditable
Accreditation: SC, ACBSP, ACFEI, ADNUR, CAHIIM, COARC, DA, DH, DIETT, EMT, FUSER, HT, MLTAD, NUR, OTA, PTAA, SURGT

01 Interim College President .... Dr. Willis HOLCOMBE
12 Campus President Kent .... Dr. Christal M. ALBRECHT
12 Campus President Open/Deerwood .... Ms. Jana KOOI
12 Campus President South .... Dr. Margarita A. CABRAL-MALY
12 Campus President North .... Dr. Barbara A. DARBY
12 Campus President Downtown .... Dr. Tracy PIERCE
11 Vice President of Administration .... Dr. Christine C. ARAB
30 Vice Pres Institutional Advancement . Adm. James E. STEVENSON
13 Chief Information Officer .... Dr. Robert J. RENNIE
10 Chief Financial Officer .... Mr. Cleve E. WARREN
20 Assoc VP of Educational Tech .... Mr. Dennis M. REIMAN
18 Assoc VP Facilities & Construction .... Mr. Charles M. STRATMANN
32 Assc VP Student Svcs/Enrollment Mgt .... Mr. Peter J. BIEGEL
96 Assoc VP Purchasing/Auxiliary Svcs .... Mr. Laurence I. SNELL
103 Executive Dean Career/Tech .... Mr. James D. SIMPSON, III
21 Executive Director Financial Svcs .... Ms. Peggy L. BOORD
15 Ex Dir Employee Rels/Col Equity Ofr .... Ms. Lisa J. MOORE
31 Exec Director of Cultural Programs .... Dr. Milton A. RUSSOS
102 Exec Director of the Foundation .... Ms. Maggie W. HIGHTOWER
88 Exec Director Cecil Center .... Mr. Paul D. MCNAMARA
88 Dir Svcs for Stdnts w/Disabilities .... Ms. Denise J. GIARRUSSO
41 Dir Athletics and Physical Educ .... Mr. George E. SANDERS
37 Director Financial Aid .... Vacant
45 Director of Resource Development .... Dr. Phyllis R. RENNIGER
06 Registrar .... Ms. Lori G. COLLINS
07 Director of Admissions .... Ms. Roz DEXTER-HARRIS
09 Director of Institutional Research .... Mr. Greg MICHALSKI
26 Director Communications .... Vacant

Florida Technical College (F)

1199 S Woodland Boulevard, Deland FL 32720-7415
Telephone: (386) 734-3303 Identification: 666419
Accreditation: ACICS, MAAB

† Main campus is Florida Technical College in Orlando, FL.

Florida Technical College (G)

3837 West Vine Street, Kissimmee FL 34741
Telephone: (407) 483-5700 Identification: 770684
Accreditation: ACICS

† Main campus is Florida Technical College in Orlando, FL.

Florida Technical College (H)

4715 South Florida Avenue, Suite 4,
Lakeland FL 33813-2101
Telephone: (866) 967-8822 FICE Identification: 025981
Accreditation: ACICS, MAAB

† Main campus is Florida Technical College in Orlando, FL.

Florida Technical College (I)

12900 Challenger Parkway, Orlando FL 32826
County: Orange FICE Identification: 022187
Unit ID: 134112
Telephone: (407) 447-7300 Carnegie Class: Assoc/PrivFP
FAX Number: (407) 447-7301 Calendar System: Quarter
URL: www.ftccollege.edu
Established: 1982 Annual Undergrad Tuition & Fees: $23,310
Enrollment: 4,000 Coed
Affiliation or Control: Proprietary IRS Status: Proprietary
Highest Offering: Baccalaureate
Program: Occupational; 2-Year Principally Bachelor's Creditable; Liberal Arts And General; Technical Emphasis
Accreditation: ACICS, MAAB

00 President/CEO .... Mr. David RUGGIERI
01 Executive Director .... Mr. John BUCK
05 Director of Education .... Dr. David PENN
07 Director of Admissions .... Mr. Eduardo PEREZ
37 Director of Financial Aid .... Ms. Ivette LUGO

Florida Technical College (J)

12520 Pines Boulevard, Pembroke Pines FL 33027
Telephone: (954) 556-1900 Identification: 770685
Accreditation: ACICS

† Main campus is Florida Technical College in Orlando, FL.

Fortis College (K)

19600 South Dixie Highway, Cutler Bay FL 33157
Telephone: (786) 345-5300 Identification: 770565
Accreditation: ACCSC

† Main campus is Fortis College in Winter Park, FL.

Fortis College (L)

6565 Ulmerton Road, Largo FL 33771
Telephone: (727) 531-5000 Identification: 770564
Accreditation: ACCSC

† Main campus is Fortis College in Winter Park, FL.

Fortis College (M)

7757 West Flagler Street, Ste 230, Miami FL 33144
County: Miami-Dade FICE Identification: 030542
Unit ID: 404921
Telephone: (305) 717-7000 Carnegie Class: Not Classified
FAX Number: (786) 388-5464 Calendar System: Quarter
URL: www.fortis.edu
Established: 1978 Annual Undergrad Tuition & Fees: $13,600
Enrollment: 336 Coed
Affiliation or Control: Proprietary IRS Status: Proprietary
Highest Offering: Associate Degree
Program: Occupational
Accreditation: COE

01 Acting Director .... Ms. Daisy DEBS

Fortis College (N)

560 Wells Road, Orange Park FL 32073-2999
County: Clay FICE Identification: 034343
Unit ID: 439792
Telephone: (904) 269-7086 Carnegie Class: Assoc/PrivFP
FAX Number: (904) 269-6664 Calendar System: Semester
URL: www.fortis.edu
Established: 1985 Annual Undergrad Tuition & Fees: $14,975
Enrollment: 521 Coed
Affiliation or Control: Proprietary IRS Status: Proprietary
Highest Offering: Associate Degree
Program: Occupational; 2-Year Principally Bachelor's Creditable
Accreditation: ACICS, SURGT

01 Campus President .... Mr. Wyman DICKEY

Fortis College (O)

3910 US Highway 301N, Suite 200,
Tampa FL 33619-1283
County: Hillsborough FICE Identification: 023057
Unit ID: 136075
Telephone: (813) 620-1446 Carnegie Class: Assoc/PrivFP
FAX Number: (813) 620-1641 Calendar System: Quarter
URL: www.fortis.edu
Established: 1978 Annual Undergrad Tuition & Fees: $18,606
Enrollment: 309 Coed
Affiliation or Control: Proprietary IRS Status: Proprietary
Highest Offering: Associate Degree
Program: 2-Year Principally Bachelor's Creditable; Nursing Emphasis
Accreditation: ACICS

01 Director .... Mr. Mark GUTMANN
05 Director of Education .... Vacant
66 Director of Nursing .... Dr. Joanna HILL

Fortis College (P)

1573 W Fairbanks Avenue, Suite 100,
Winter Park FL 32789-4679
County: Orange FICE Identification: 022455
Unit ID: 132806
Telephone: (407) 843-3984 Carnegie Class: Assoc/PrivFP
FAX Number: (407) 843-9828 Calendar System: Quarter
URL: www.fortiscollege.edu
Established: 1985 Annual Undergrad Tuition & Fees: $20,949
Enrollment: 265 Coed
Affiliation or Control: Proprietary IRS Status: Proprietary
Highest Offering: Associate Degree
Program: Occupational; Business Emphasis
Accreditation: ACCSC, MAC

01 School Director .... Mr. Ray NUNZIATIA
06 Registrar/Business Manager .... Ms. Giselle RIVIERA
36 Career Services Director .... Ms. Andro MEDA-POLLACK
37 Financial Aid Director .... Ms. Keisha WHITAKER

† Closing in December 2013.

Fortis Institute (Q)

9035 Sunset Drive, Suite 200, Miami FL 33173-3431
Telephone: (305) 596-5553 Identification: 770542
Accreditation: COE, RAD

† Main campus is Fortis Institute in Cookeville, TN.

Fortis Institute (A)

1630 South Congress Avenue, Ste 300,
Palm Springs FL 33461-2171
Telephone: (561) 304-3466 Identification: 770541
Accreditation: COE, MLTAD, RAD, SURGT

† Main campus is Fortis Institute in Cookeville, TN.

Fortis Institute-Pensacola (B)

4081 East Olive Road, Suite B, Pensacola FL 32514
Telephone: (850) 476-7607 Identification: 770513
Accreditation: ABHES

† Main campus is Fortis College in Mobile, AL.

Fortis Institute-Port St. Lucie (C)

9022 South Federal Highway/US-1,
Port St. Lucie FL 34952
Telephone: (772) 221-9799 Identification: 770527
Accreditation: ABHES

† Main campus is Fortis College in Baton Rouge, LA.

Full Sail University (D)

3300 University Boulevard, Winter Park FL 32792
County: Orange FICE Identification: 023621
Unit ID: 134237
Telephone: (407) 679-0100 Carnegie Class: Master's L
FAX Number: (407) 679-9685 Calendar System: Other
URL: www.fullsail.edu
Established: 1979 Annual Undergrad Tuition & Fees: $21,448
Enrollment: 23,497 Coed
Affiliation or Control: Proprietary IRS Status: Proprietary
Highest Offering: Master's
Program: Occupational; 2-Year Principally Bachelor's Creditable
Accreditation: ACCSC

01 President .... Mr. Garry JONES
07 Vice President of Admissions .... Mr. Matt PENGRA

Galen College of Nursing (E)

11101 Roosevelt Blvd N, Suite 100, Petersburg FL 33716
Telephone: (727) 577-1497 Identification: 770539
Accreditation: &SC, COE

† Main campus is Galen College of Nursing in Louisville, KY.

Golf Academy of America (F)

510 South Hunt Club Blvd., Apopka FL 32703
Telephone: (800) 342-7342 Identification: 666186
Accreditation: ACICS

† Main campus is Virginia College in Birmingham, AL.

Gordon-Conwell Theological Seminary-Jacksonville (G)

118 East Monroe Street, Jacksonville FL 32202-3214
Telephone: (904) 354-4800 Identification: 770111
Accreditation: &EH, &THEOL

† Main campus is Gordon-Conwell Theological Seminary in South Hamilton, MA.

Gulf Coast State College (H)

5230 W Highway 98, Panama City FL 32401-1058
County: Bay FICE Identification: 001490
Unit ID: 134343
Telephone: (850) 769-1551 Carnegie Class: Assoc/Pub-R-L
FAX Number: (850) 913-3319 Calendar System: Semester
URL: www.gulfcoast.edu
Established: 1957 Annual Undergrad Tuition & Fees (In-State): $2,370
Enrollment: 6,030 Coed
Affiliation or Control: State Related IRS Status: 501(c)3
Highest Offering: Baccalaureate
Program: Occupational; 2-Year Principally Bachelor's Creditable; Teacher Preparatory
Accreditation: SC, ACFEI, ADNUR, COARC, DA, DH, EMT, PTAA, RAD, SURGA, SURGT

01 President .... Dr. Jim KERLEY
11 Vice Pres Administration & Finance .... Mr. John D. MERCER
05 VP Academic Affairs & Learn Support .... Dr. George BISHOP
75 Chief Economic Dev Officer .... Dr. Jeffry J. STEVENSON
32 VP Student Affairs .... Dr. Melissa LAVENDER
09 VP Institutional Effect/Stratg Plng .... Dr. Cheryl L. FLAX-HYMAN
27 Chief Information Officer .... Ms. Rhonda BARKER
08 Director of Library .... Ms. Lori DRISCOLL
07 Director of Enrollment Services .... Ms. Sharon O. TODD
15 Exec Director of Human Resources .... Ms. Roberta MACKEY
18 Superintendent Grounds & Bldg Svcs .... Mr. Dennis STORCK
28 Assoc Dir Retention/Stdnt Diversity .... Dr. Carrie B. BAKER
26 Exec Director Media & Community Rel .... Mr. Christopher P. THOMES
96 Coordinator of Purchasing .... Mr. Fred BROWN
37 Director of Financial Aid .... Mr. Christopher J. WESTLAKE
88 Coordinator Institutional Research .... Ms. Dee NIELSEN
30 Chief Development Officer .... Vacant

Health Career Institute (I)

1764 N. Congress Avenue, West Palm Beach FL 33409
County: Palm Beach Identification: 667104
Telephone: (561) 586-0121 Carnegie Class: Not Classified
FAX Number: (561) 471-4010 Calendar System: Semester
URL: www.hci.edu
Established: Annual Undergrad Tuition & Fees: N/A
Enrollment: N/A Coed
Affiliation or Control: Independent Non-Profit IRS Status: 501(c)3
Highest Offering: Associate Degree
Program: Occupational
Accreditation: ACCSC

01 President .... Tina PALERMO
03 Vice President .... Marty PALERMO
10 Financial Director .... Cathy WALDRON

Heritage Institute-Fort Myers (J)

6630 Orion Drive, Suite 200, Fort Meyers FL 33912-7130
County: Lee FICE Identification: 025971
Unit ID: 135124
Telephone: (239) 936-5822 Carnegie Class: Assoc/PrivFP
FAX Number: (239) 225-9117 Calendar System: Other
URL: www.heritage-education.com
Established: 2001 Annual Undergrad Tuition & Fees: $24,950
Enrollment: 668 Coed
Affiliation or Control: Proprietary IRS Status: Proprietary
Highest Offering: Associate Degree
Program: Occupational
Accreditation: ABHES

01 Director .... Ms. Eva HUTSON

Heritage Institute-Jacksonville (K)

4130 Salisbury Road, Suite 1100, Jacksonville FL 32216
County: Duval FICE Identification: 030358
Unit ID: 372772
Telephone: (904) 332-0910 Carnegie Class: Assoc/PrivFP
FAX Number: (904) 332-0920 Calendar System: Other
URL: www.heritage-education.com/campus_jacksonville.htm
Established: 2001 Annual Undergrad Tuition & Fees: N/A
Enrollment: 351 Coed
Affiliation or Control: Proprietary IRS Status: Proprietary
Highest Offering: Associate Degree
Program: Occupational
Accreditation: ABHES

01 Director .... Ms. Michelle GRANT

Herzing University (L)

1865 SR 436, Winter Park FL 32792
Telephone: (407) 478-0500 Identification: 666422
Accreditation: &NH, ADNUR, PTAA, SURTEC

† Main campus is Herzing University in Madison, WI.

Hillsborough Community College (M)

PO Box 31127, 39 Columbia Drive, Tampa FL 33631-3127
County: Hillsborough FICE Identification: 007870
Unit ID: 134495
Telephone: (813) 253-7000 Carnegie Class: Assoc/Pub-U-MC
FAX Number: (813) 253-7183 Calendar System: Semester
URL: www.hccfl.edu
Established: 1968 Annual Undergrad Tuition & Fees (In-State): $2,505
Enrollment: 27,754 Coed
Affiliation or Control: State IRS Status: 501(c)3
Highest Offering: Associate Degree
Program: Occupational; 2-Year Principally Bachelor's Creditable
Accreditation: SC, ACFEI, ADNUR, COARC, DA, DH, DIETT, DMS, EMT, MUS, NMT, OPD, RAD, RTT

01 President .... Dr. Ken ATWATER
10 Vice President Administration/CFO .... Dr. Barbara LARSON
03 Senior Vice President .... Mr. Robert WOLF
05 Vice President for Academic Affairs .... Mr. Craig JOHNSON
14 Vice Pres Info Technology .... Mr. Daya PENDHARKAR
32 VP Student Services/Enrollment Mgt .... Dr. Ken RAY
12 Campus President Dale Mabry .... Dr. Robert CHUNN
12 Campus President Ybor City Campus .... Dr. Shawn ROBINSON
12 Campus President Plant City Campus .... Dr. Martyn CLAY
12 Campus President Brandon Campus .... Dr. Carlos SOTO
12 Campus President South Shore Campus .... Dr. Allen WITT
22 Asst to Pres Equity/Special Pgms .... Dr. Joan HOLMES
26 Exec Dir Marketing/Public Relations .... Ms. Ashley CARL
09 Spc Asst to Pres Strat Plng & Analy .... Dr. Paul NAGY
102 Int Exec Director HCC Foundation .... Mr. Farrukh QURAISHI
43 College Attorney .... Ms. Martha Kaye KOEHLER
15 Exec Director Human Resources .... Ms. Donna KEENER
21 Controller .... Ms. Bonnie CARR
75 Director Technical Programs .... Dr. Ginger CLARK
20 Director Assoc in Arts Programs .... Dr. Karen GRIFFIN
90 Director of Academic Technology .... Mr. Richard SENKER
75 Dean Public Services Programs .... Mr. Jack EVANS
88 Dean Environmental Programs .... Vacant
88 Dean of AS Programs - Brandon .... Dr. Sabrina PEACOCK
88 Dean of Arts & Sciences-Dale Mabry .... Dr. Mary BENDICKSON
88 Dean of AS Programs - Dale Mabry .... Dr. Elizabeth JOHNSON
81 Int Dean AA Math/Sci - Dale Mabry .... Dr. James WYSONG
76 Dean Health/Wellness & Sports Tech .... Dr. Amy ANDERSON
37 Financial Aid Director .... Ms. Tierra SMITH
06 Registrar .... Ms. Jennifer WILLIAMS
18 Director Facilities/Physical Plant .... Mr. Ben MARSHALL
96 Director of Purchasing .... Ms. Vonda MELCHIOR
31 Dir of Community & Govt Relations .... Ms. Sarah (Sally) EVERETT

Hobe Sound Bible College (N)

PO Box 1065, Hobe Sound FL 33475-1065
County: Martin FICE Identification: 021889
Unit ID: 134510
Telephone: (772) 546-5534 Carnegie Class: Spec/Faith
FAX Number: (772) 545-1422 Calendar System: Semester
URL: www.hsbc.edu
Established: 1960 Annual Undergrad Tuition & Fees: $5,350
Enrollment: 98 Coed
Affiliation or Control: Independent Non-Profit IRS Status: 501(c)3
Highest Offering: Baccalaureate
Program: Liberal Arts And General; Religious Emphasis
Accreditation: BI

01 President .... Mr. P. Daniel STETLER
05 Academic Dean .... Dr. Clifford W. CHURCHILL
10 Director of Finances .... Mr. Jim OLSEN
11 Director of Administration .... Mr. Wesley HOLDEN
32 Dean of Students .... Mr. John S. JONES
33 Dean of Men .... Mr. Jonathan STRATTON
08 Librarian .... Mr. Phil JONES
26 Public Relations Director .... Mr. Paul STETLER
06 Registrar .... Mrs. Faye PARSONS
07 Director of Admissions .... Mrs. Sarah MILLER
51 Dean of External Studies .... Mr. Dalbert N. WALKER

Hodges University (O)

2655 Northbrooke Drive, Naples FL 34119-7932
County: Collier FICE Identification: 030375
Unit ID: 367884
Telephone: (239) 513-1122 Carnegie Class: Master's S
FAX Number: (239) 598-6253 Calendar System: Trimester
URL: www.hodges.edu
Established: 1990 Annual Undergrad Tuition & Fees: $12,740
Enrollment: 2,750 Coed
Affiliation or Control: Independent Non-Profit IRS Status: 501(c)3
Highest Offering: Master's
Program: Liberal Arts And General; Professional; Business Emphasis
Accreditation: SC, CAHIIM, IACBE, MAC, @PTAA

01 President .... Dr. Jeanette BROCK
05 Exec Vice Pres of Academic Affairs .... Dr. Kim SPIEZIO
11 Exec Vice Pres Administration .... Dr. Joseph PEPE
06 Vice Pres of Student Records Mgt .... Ms. Carol MORRISON
84 Vice President of Enrollment Mgt .... Ms. Rita LAMPUS
32 Dean of Students .... Dr. Marcia TURNER
37 VP of Student Financial Services .... Mr. Joseph GILCHRIST
30 Vice Pres University Advancement .... Mr. Phil MEMOLI
38 Director Student Counseling .... Mr. Micki ERICKSON
26 Chief Public Relations Officer .... Mr. Joe TURNER
09 Dir Institutional Effective/Rsrch .... Dr. Diane BALL
18 Chief Facilities/Physical Plant .... Mr. David RICE
28 Director of Diversity .... Ms. Gail WILLIAMS
29 Director of Alumni Affairs .... Mr. Joe TURNER

Indian River State College (P)

3209 Virginia Avenue, Fort Pierce FL 34981-5596
County: Saint Lucie FICE Identification: 001493
Unit ID: 134608
Telephone: (772) 462-4772 Carnegie Class: Assoc/Pub4
FAX Number: (772) 462-4796 Calendar System: Semester
URL: www.irsc.edu
Established: 1960 Annual Undergrad Tuition & Fees (In-District): $2,810
Enrollment: 17,816 Coed
Affiliation or Control: Local IRS Status: 501(c)3
Highest Offering: Baccalaureate
Program: Occupational; 2-Year Principally Bachelor's Creditable; Liberal Arts And General; Teacher Preparatory
Accreditation: SC, ADNUR, CAHIIM, COARC, DA, DH, DT, EMT, MAC, MLTAD, NUR, PTAA, RAD, SURGT

01 President .... Dr. Edwin R. MASSEY
32 Vice President Student Affairs .... Mr. Frank WATKINS
05 Vice President Academic Affairs .... Dr. Anthony IACONO
10 Actg VP Administration/Finance .... Ms. Sheryl S. VITTITOE
88 Vice Pres Applied Science & Tech .... Dr. Alan L. ROBERTS
45 Associate VP Institutional Effectiv .... Dr. Christina HART
04 Exec Assistant to the President .... Mr. Andrew TREADWELL
12 Vice Pres/Provost-Fort Pierce .... Dr. Mary G. LOCKE
12 Provost Pt St Lucie/St Lucie W .... Dr. Harvey E. ARNOLD
12 Provost Okeechobee .... Mr. Russ BROWN
12 Provost Martin County .... Ms. Elizabeth GASKIN
12 Provost Indian River County .... Dr. David SULLIVAN
12 Dean Northwest Center .... Mr. Andre HAWKINS
18 Dean Auxiliary Services/Facility .... Mr. Allen BOTTORFF

72 Dean Institutional Tech .... Mr. Paul R. O'BRIEN
80 Asst Dean of Public Services Educ .... Mr. Evan BERRY
72 Dean Advanced Technology .... Mr. Jose L. FARINOS
93 Dean Minority Affairs .... Ms. Adriene JEFFERSON
08 Dean Learning Resources .... Ms. Patricia C. PROFETA
49 Dean of Arts & Sciences .... Mr. Casey LUNCEFORD
51 Associate Dean Developmental Ed .... Ms. Libby LIVINGS-EASSA
14 Associate Dean Data Processing .... Ms. Patricia D. PFEIFFER
11 Assoc Dean Administrative Services .... Ms. Jan PAGANO
75 Associate Dean Industrial Education .... Ms. Donna RIVETT
76 Associate Dean of Health Science .... Ms. Jane P. CEBELAK
51 Assoc Dean Baccalaureate Programs .... Mr. Ian NEUHARD
09 Associate Dean Research/Reports .... Mr. Gerald L. MOCK
20 Asst Dean Educational Services .... Mr. Steven W. PAYNE
50 Assistant Dean Business Technology .... Mr. Cedric GIBSON
15 Assistant Dean Human Resources .... Ms. Nancy CUNNINGHAM
21 Assistant Dean Finance .... Mr. Joe MAZUR
66 Administrative Director of Nursing .... Ms. Ann HUBBARD
102 Executive Director Foundation .... Ms. Ann DECKER
30 Director Institutional Advancement .... Ms. Michelle ABALDO
41 Director Athletics .... Mr. Scott KIMMELMAN
36 Director Student Success Services .... Ms. Flossie JACKSON
84 Director Enrollment Management .... Ms. Eileen STORCK
37 Director Student Financial Aid .... Ms. Mary LEWIS
38 Director Student Counseling .... Ms. Dale HAYES
35 Director Student Affairs .... Ms. Sharon LOWE
06 Registrar/Dir Student Affs/Admiss .... Ms. Karen CHAPDELAINE
96 Purchasing Agent .... Mr. Don WINDHAM

Institute of Technical Arts (A)

493 Semoran Blvd, Casselberry FL 32707
County: Seminole FICE Identification: 036183
Unit ID: 441441
Telephone: (407) 869-7387 Carnegie Class: Not Classified
FAX Number: (407) 678-3422 Calendar System: Other
URL: www.myfiaa.com
Established: 1999 Annual Undergrad Tuition & Fees: $13,500
Enrollment: 244 Coed
Affiliation or Control: Proprietary IRS Status: Proprietary
Highest Offering: Associate Degree
Program: Occupational
Accreditation: ACCSC

International Academy of Design and Technology (B)

6039 South Rio Grande Avenue, Orlando FL 32809
Telephone: (407) 857-2300 Identification: 770686
Accreditation: ACICS

† Main campus is International Academy of Design and Technology in Tampa, FL.

International Academy of Design and Technology (C)

5104 Eisenhower Boulevard, Tampa FL 33634-6313
County: Hillsborough FICE Identification: 030314
Unit ID: 134680
Telephone: (813) 881-0007 Carnegie Class: Spec/Arts
FAX Number: (813) 884-9327 Calendar System: Quarter
URL: www.academy.edu
Established: 1984 Annual Undergrad Tuition & Fees: $14,400
Enrollment: 1,387 Coed
Affiliation or Control: Proprietary IRS Status: Proprietary
Highest Offering: Baccalaureate
Program: Fine Arts Emphasis
Accreditation: ACICS, CIDA

01 President .... Dr. Karen O'DONNELL
10 Vice President of Finance .... Vacant
05 Dean/Chief Academic Officer .... Phil BULONE
07 Director of Admissions .... Dawn WOLFF
32 Director of Student Services .... Kim FORTENBERRY
36 Director of Career Services .... Lee SILVERSTEIN
08 Learning Resource Center Coord .... Vashba GREEN

ITT Technical Institute (D)

8039 Cooper Creed Boulevard, Bradenton FL 34201
Telephone: (941) 309-9200 Identification: 770639
Accreditation: ACICS

† Main campus is ITT Technical Institute in Indianapolis, IN.

ITT Technical Institute (E)

700 W Hillsboro Blvd Bdg 1,Ste 100,
Deerfield Beach FL 33441
Telephone: (954) 360-4701 Identification: 770642
Accreditation: ACICS

† Main campus is ITT Technical Institute in Indianapolis, IN.

ITT Technical Institute (F)

3401 S University Drive, Fort Lauderdale FL 33328-2021
Telephone: (954) 476-9300 Identification: 666536
Accreditation: ACICS, CAHIIM

† Main campus is ITT Technical Institute in Indianapolis, IN.

ITT Technical Institute (G)

13500 Powers Court, Suite 100, Fort Myers FL 33912
Telephone: (239) 603-8700 Identification: 666669
Accreditation: ACICS

† Main campus is ITT Technical Institute in Indianapolis, IN.

ITT Technical Institute (H)

7011 A.C. Skinner Parkway, Ste. 140,
Jacksonville FL 32256-6954
Telephone: (904) 573-9100 Identification: 666537
Accreditation: ACICS

† Main campus is ITT Technical Institute in Indianapolis, IN.

ITT Technical Institute (I)

1400 International Parkway South,
Lake Mary FL 32746-1607
Telephone: (407) 660-2900 FICE Identification: 030876
Accreditation: ACICS, CAHIIM

† Main campus is ITT Technical Institute in Indianapolis, IN.

ITT Technical Institute (J)

7955 NW 12th Street, Suite 119, Miami FL 33126-1823
Telephone: (305) 477-3080 Identification: 666026
Accreditation: ACICS, CAHIIM

† Main campus is ITT Technical Institute in Indianapolis, IN.

ITT Technical Institute (K)

8301 South Park Circle, Suite 100, Orlando FL 32819
Telephone: (407) 371-6000 Identification: 770640
Accreditation: ACICS

† Main campus is ITT Technical Institute in Indianapolis, IN.

ITT Technical Institute (L)

6913 North 9th Avenue, Pensacola FL 32504
Telephone: (317) 706-9200 Identification: 770643
Accreditation: ACICS

† Main campus is ITT Technical Institute in Indianapolis, IN.

ITT Technical Institute (M)

877 Executive Ctr. Dr. W, Ste. 100,
St. Petersburg FL 33702
Telephone: (727) 209-4700 Identification: 666163
Accreditation: ACICS

† Main campus is ITT Technical Institute in Indianapolis, IN.

ITT Technical Institute (N)

2639 N Monroe St, Bldg A, Suite 100,
Tallahassee FL 32303
Telephone: (850) 422-6300 Identification: 770638
Accreditation: ACICS

† Main campus is ITT Technical Institute in Indianapolis, IN.

ITT Technical Institute (O)

4809 Memorial Highway, Tampa FL 33634-7350
Telephone: (813) 885-2244 FICE Identification: 022865
Accreditation: ACICS, CAHIIM

† Main campus is ITT Technical Institute in Indianapolis, IN.

ITT Technical Institute (P)

1756 N Congress Avenue, West Palm Beach FL 33409
Telephone: (561) 233-4900 Identification: 770641
Accreditation: ACICS

† Main campus is ITT Technical Institute in Indianapolis, IN.

Jacksonville University (Q)

2800 University Boulevard N, Jacksonville FL 32211-3394
County: Duval FICE Identification: 001495
Unit ID: 134945
Telephone: (904) 256-8000 Carnegie Class: Master's M
FAX Number: N/A Calendar System: Semester
URL: www.ju.edu
Established: 1934 Annual Undergrad Tuition & Fees: $29,900
Enrollment: 3,936 Coed
Affiliation or Control: Independent Non-Profit IRS Status: 501(c)3
Highest Offering: Doctorate
Program: Liberal Arts And General; Teacher Preparatory; Professional; Business Emphasis
Accreditation: SC, AAB, BUS, DANCE, DENT, MUS, NURSE

01 President .... Mr. Timothy P. COST
05 Senior VP for Academic Affairs .... Dr. Lois S. BECKER
10 VP for Finance & Administration .... Mr. George C. SCADUTO
84 Vice Pres Enrollment Management .... Mr. Terry E. WHITTUM
32 Interim VP for Student Life .... Dr. Derek J. HALL
30 Vice Pres University Advancement .... Mr. Michael HOWLAND
26 VP Univ Rel & External Affairs .... Dr. Derek J. HALL
13 VP Info Tech & Chief Info Officer .... Mr. Tom HALL
04 Exec Assistant to the President .... Ms. Dolores STARR
41 Athletic Director .... Mr. Bradford W. EDWARDS
06 Registrar .... Ms. Carolyn BARRETT
09 Director of Institutional Research .... Vacant
08 Director of the Library .... Mr. David JONES
35 Dean of Students .... Dr. Kristie GOVER
36 Director of Career Development .... Ms. Devan COUGHLIN
37 Dir Student Financial Assistance .... Ms. Breanne SIMKIN
29 Asst VP for Institutional Advance .... Vacant
21 Controller .... Ms. Liza MULLINS
11 Exec Dir Budgets/Business Opers .... Ms. Ellen M. PAIGE
96 Director of Purchasing .... Mr. Michael J. BOBBIN
40 Director of the Bookstore .... Ms. Darla LITTLE-VANN
42 Campus Minister .... Mr. Lance BEAUCHAMP
15 Director of Human Resources .... Mr. James V. WILLIAMS
57 Dean College of Fine Arts .... Mr. William E. HILL
49 Dean Col of Arts & Sciences .... Dr. Douglas HAZZARD
50 Dean College of Business .... Dr. Don CAPENER
76 Dean College of Health Sciences .... Dr. Judith ERICKSON
51 Assoc Dean of Continuing Studies .... Vacant
53 Dean School of Education .... Dr. Douglas HAZZARD
64 Chairman Division of Music .... Dr. Thomas HARRISON
66 Dean School of Nursing .... Dr. Judith ERICKSON
79 Chair Div of Humanitites .... Dr. Scott KIMBROUGH
81 Chair Division of Science & Math .... Dr. Lee Ann J. CLEMENTS
38 Director Student Counseling .... Ms. Kristin R. ALBERTS
83 Chair Division of Social Science .... Dr. Sherry JACKSON
88 Chair Division of Naval Science .... Capt. Herbert HADLEY
88 Chair Div of Theatre Arts & Dance .... Mr. Brian PALMER
57 Chair Division Art/Art History .... Ms. Dana L. CHAPMAN
18 Chief Facilities/Physical Plant .... Mr. Joe COLEMAN

Johnson & Wales University (R)

1701 NE 127th Street, North Miami FL 33181-2518
Telephone: (305) 892-7000 Identification: 666423
Accreditation: &EH

† Main campus is Johnson & Wales University in Providence, RI.

Johnson University Florida (S)

1011 Bill Beck Boulevard, Kissimmee FL 34744-5301
Telephone: (407) 847-8966 FICE Identification: 021567
Accreditation: &SC, &BI

† Main campus is Johnson University in Knoxville, TN.

Jones College (T)

5353 Arlington Expressway, Jacksonville FL 32211-5588
County: Duval FICE Identification: 001497
Unit ID: 135063
Telephone: (904) 743-1122 Carnegie Class: Bac/Diverse
FAX Number: (904) 743-4446 Calendar System: Trimester
URL: www.jones.edu
Established: 1918 Annual Undergrad Tuition & Fees: $7,410
Enrollment: 504 Coed
Affiliation or Control: Independent Non-Profit IRS Status: 501(c)3
Highest Offering: Baccalaureate
Program: Business Emphasis
Accreditation: ACICS

00 Corporate President & CEO .... Dorothy D. JONES
01 President of the College .... Dee THORNTON
10 Business Officer .... Kathy DANE
37 Director of Financial Assistance .... Becky DAVIS
07 Director of Admissions .... Vacant
36 Director of Career Development .... Mona WEBB
13 Director IT .... Holly KELLEY
08 Librarian .... Vacant

Jones College (U)

1195 Edgewood Avenue, Jacksonville FL 32205
Telephone: (904) 743-1122 Identification: 770687
Accreditation: ACICS

† Main campus is Jones College in Jacksonville, FL.

Jose Maria Vargas University (V)

8300 S Palm Drive, Pembroke Pines FL 33025
FICE Identification: 041620
Unit ID: 461281
Telephone: (954) 322-4460 Carnegie Class: Not Classified
FAX Number: (954) 322-4131 Calendar System: Semester
URL: www.jmvu.edu
Established: 2003 Annual Undergrad Tuition & Fees: $9,520
Enrollment: 113 Coed
Affiliation or Control: Proprietary IRS Status: Proprietary
Highest Offering: Master's
Program: Occupational; 2-Year Principally Bachelor's Creditable; Teacher Preparatory; Professional
Accreditation: ACICS, @TEAC

01 President .... Dr. Alicia F. PARRA

10 Vice President of Finance ....Lelis Antonio ORTIZ ALVAREZ
08 Library Director ....Maria JIMENEZ
18 Facilities/Purchasing Director ....Fernando ORTIZ PARRA
37 Director of Financial Aid ....Edith PAREDES
06 Registrar ....Lelis ORTIZ PARRA
32 Director of Student Development ....Erika ORTIZ
58 Coord of Research/Grad Studies ....Lori N. KIJANCA
53 Coordinator of Education ....Claudia PARRA
88 Coordinator of Graphic Design ....Henry BALLATE

Kaplan College (A)
7450 Beach Boulevard, Jacksonville FL 32216
Telephone: (904) 855-2400 Identification: 770688
Accreditation: ACICS

† Main campus is Kaplan Career Institute in Harrisburg, PA.

Keiser University (B)
1800 Business Park Blvd, Daytona Beach FL 32114
Telephone: (386) 274-5060 Identification: 770900
Accreditation: &SC, @DIETC, DMS, MAC, OTA, RAD

† Main campus is Keiser University in Fort Lauderdale, FL.

Keiser University (C)
1500 NW 49th Street, Fort Lauderdale FL 33309-3700
County: Broward FICE Identification: 021519
Unit ID: 135081
Telephone: (954) 776-4456 Carnegie Class: Bac/Assoc
FAX Number: (954) 771-4894 Calendar System: Semester
URL: www.keiseruniversity.edu
Established: 1977 Annual Undergrad Tuition & Fees: $16,944
Enrollment: 18,385 Coed
Affiliation or Control: Independent Non-Profit IRS Status: 501(c)3
Highest Offering: Doctorate
Program: Occupational
Accreditation: SC, ADNUR, ARCPA, CAHIIM, COARC, DMS, MAAB, MLTAD, NURSE, OTA, PTAA, RAD

00 Chancellor ....Dr. Arthur KEISER
01 Campus President ....Mr. John SITES
26 Reg Dir Media & Public Relations ....Ms. Kimberly DALE

Keiser University (D)
9100 Forum Corporate Pkwy, Fort Myers FL 33905
Telephone: (239) 277-1336 Identification: 770901
Accreditation: &SC, OTA

† Main campus is Keiser University in Fort Lauderdale, FL.

Keiser University (E)
6430 Southpoint Pkwy, Jacksonville FL 33216
Telephone: (904) 296-3440 Identification: 770902
Accreditation: &SC, ADNUR, OTA, PTAA, RAD

† Main campus is Keiser University in Fort Lauderdale, FL.

Keiser University (F)
2400 Interstate Drive, Lakeland FL 33805
Telephone: (863) 682-6020 Identification: 770903
Accreditation: &SC, ADNUR, @DIETC, MAAB, PTAA, RAD

† Main campus is Keiser University in Fort Lauderdale, FL.

Keiser University (G)
900 South Babcock Street, Melbourne FL 32901
Telephone: (321) 409-4800 Identification: 770904
Accreditation: &SC, ACFEI, ADNUR, DMS, MAAB, OTA, RAD

† Main campus is Keiser University in Fort Lauderdale, FL.

Keiser University (H)
2101 NW 117th Avenue, Miami FL 33172
Telephone: (305) 596-2226 Identification: 770905
Accreditation: &SC, ADNUR, OTA, RAD

† Main campus is Keiser University in Fort Lauderdale, FL.

Keiser University (I)
5600 Lake Underhill Road, Orlando FL 32807
Telephone: (407) 381-1233 Identification: 770906
Accreditation: &SC, ADNUR, HT, OTA

† Main campus is Keiser University in Fort Lauderdale, FL.

Keiser University (J)
1640 SW 145th Avenue, Pembroke Pines FL 33027
Telephone: (954) 431-4300 Identification: 770907
Accreditation: &SC, DIETC, MAAB, OTA

† Main campus is Keiser University in Fort Lauderdale, FL.

Keiser University (K)
10330 S Federal Highway,
Port Saint Lucie FL 34952-5605
Telephone: (772) 398-9990 Identification: 666289
Accreditation: &SC, SURGT

† Main campus is Keiser University in Fort Lauderdale, FL.

Keiser University (L)
6151 Lake Osprey Drive, Sarasota FL 34240
Telephone: (941) 907-3900 Identification: 770908
Accreditation: &SC, ACFEI, ADNUR, MAAB, PTAA, RAD

† Main campus is Keiser University in Fort Lauderdale, FL.

Keiser University (M)
1700 Halstead Blvd, Bldg 2, Tallahassee FL 32309
Telephone: (850) 906-9494 Identification: 770909
Accreditation: &SC, ACFEI, ADNUR, MAAB, OTA

† Main campus is Keiser University in Fort Lauderdale, FL.

Keiser University (N)
5002 West Waters Ave, Tampa FL 33634
Telephone: (813) 885-4900 Identification: 770910
Accreditation: &SC, ADNUR, MAAB, OTA

† Main campus is Keiser University in Fort Lauderdale, FL.

Keiser University (O)
2085 Vista Parkway, West Palm Beach FL 33411-2719
Telephone: (561) 471-6000 Identification: 667032
Accreditation: &SC, ADNUR, OTA

† Main campus is Keiser University in Fort Lauderdale, FL.

Key College (P)
225 E Dania Beach Blvd, Suite 130,
Dania Beach FL 33004-3042
County: Broward FICE Identification: 023251
Unit ID: 134422
Telephone: (954) 923-4440 Carnegie Class: Assoc/PrivFP
FAX Number: (954) 923-9226 Calendar System: Quarter
URL: www.keycollege.edu
Established: 1982 Annual Undergrad Tuition & Fees: $10,785
Enrollment: 85 Coed
Affiliation or Control: Proprietary IRS Status: Proprietary
Highest Offering: Associate Degree
Program: 2-Year Principally Bachelor's Creditable; Business Emphasis
Accreditation: ACICS

01 President ....Mr. Ronald DOOLEY
05 Director of Academic Affairs ....Ms. Marella KING
07 Director of Admissions ....Vacant
37 Director of Financial Aid ....Ms. Terri ANDREWS
06 Registrar ....Mr. Rashad BENNETT

Knox Theological Seminary (Q)
5554 N Federal Highway, Fort Lauderdale FL 33308-3209
County: Broward FICE Identification: 039923
Telephone: (954) 771-0376 Carnegie Class: Not Classified
FAX Number: (954) 351-3343 Calendar System: Semester
URL: www.knoxseminary.edu
Established: 1989 Annual Undergrad Tuition & Fees: $7,850
Enrollment: 450 Coed
Affiliation or Control: Independent Non-Profit IRS Status: 501(c)3
Highest Offering: Doctorate
Program: Religious Emphasis
Accreditation: THEOL

01 President & CEO ....Dr. Luder WHITLOCK
05 Dean of Faculty ....Dr. Michael ALLEN
32 Dir Student Svcs/Dean of Students ......Mr. Jonathan LINEBAUGH

Lake Erie College of Osteopathic Medicine Bradenton (R)
5000 Lakewood Rance Boulevard, Bradenton FL 34211
Telephone: (941) 756-0690 Identification: 770160
Accreditation: &M

† Main campus is Lake Erie College of Osteopathic Medicine in Erie, PA.

Lake-Sumter State College (S)
9501 US Highway 441, Leesburg FL 34788-8751
County: Lake FICE Identification: 001502
Unit ID: 135188
Telephone: (352) 787-3747 Carnegie Class: Assoc/Pub-S-MC
FAX Number: (352) 365-3548 Calendar System: Semester
URL: www.lssc.edu
Established: 1962 Annual Undergrad Tuition & Fees (In-District): $3,232
Enrollment: 4,676 Coed
Affiliation or Control: State/Local IRS Status: 501(c)3
Highest Offering: Baccalaureate
Program: Occupational; 2-Year Principally Bachelor's Creditable
Accreditation: SC, ADNUR, CAHIIM

01 President ....Dr. Charles R. MOJOCK
10 VP Business Affairs ....Mr. Richard M. SCOTT
05 VP Academic-Student Affairs ....Dr. Barbara C. HOWARD
21 Controller ....Mr. John FROMAN
75 Dean Career & Technical Programs ....Dr. Mary Jo RAGER
53 Dean General Ed & Transfer Programs ....Mr. Gary SLIGH
15 Exec Director Human Resources ....Ms. Fran PISTILLI
13 Chief Information Officer ....Mr. Douglas GUILER
09 Exec Dir Planning & IE ....Dr. Kristy LISLE
30 Exec Dir Inst Advance & Foundation ....Ms. Rosanne BRANDEBURG
18 Director College Facilities ....Mr. Donald BALL
08 Director Libraries ....Ms. Denise K. ENGLISH
35 Director Student Development ....Ms. Claire BRADY
21 Director Budget & Accounting ....Ms. Sue FAGAN
66 Director Nursing ....Ms. Cindy GRIFFIN
08 Director Learning Center ....Ms. Marion J. KANE
26 Director College Relations ....Ms. Sasheka TOMLINSON
37 Director Financial Aid ....Ms. Audrey WILLIAMS
84 Director Enrollment Management ....Ms. Debra MARVEL
41 Athletic Director ....Mr. Michael K. MATULIA
88 Director Youth Outreach Programs ....Mr. Reinaldo CORTES
106 Director Distance Learning ....Mr. Mike NATHANSON
06 Registrar ....Ms. Amber OWEN
28 Equity Officer ....Ms. Chris HAMILTON
96 Asst Director of Purchasing ....Mr. Bill PONKO
102 Coord Foundation/Alumni Scholarship ....Ms. Claudia MORRIS

Le Cordon Bleu College of Culinary Arts in Miami (T)
3221 Enterprise Way, Miramar FL 33025-3929
Telephone: (954) 438-8882 Identification: 666369
Accreditation: ACCSC, ACICS, ACFEI

† Main campus is Le Cordon Bleu College of Culinary Arts in Scottsdale in Scottsdale, AZ.

Le Cordon Bleu College of Culinary Arts in Orlando (U)
8511 Commodity Circle, Orlando FL 32819-9002
Telephone: (407) 888-4000 Identification: 666064
Accreditation: ACICS, ACFEI

† Main campus is International Academy of Design and Technology in Tampa, FL.

Lincoln College of Technology (V)
2410 Metrocentre Boulevard,
West Palm Beach FL 33407-3155
County: Palm Beach FICE Identification: 022808
Unit ID: 136066
Telephone: (561) 842-8324 Carnegie Class: Assoc/PrivFP4
FAX Number: (561) 842-9503 Calendar System: Other
URL: www.lincolncollegeoftechnology.com
Established: 1982 Annual Undergrad Tuition & Fees: $15,120
Enrollment: 853 Coed
Affiliation or Control: Proprietary IRS Status: Proprietary
Highest Offering: Baccalaureate
Program: Occupational; Technical Emphasis
Accreditation: ACICS, ACFEI

01 President ....Ms. Helen CARVER

Lincoln Tech Fern Park Orlando Campus (W)
7275 Estapona Circle, Fern Park FL 32730-2351
County: Seminole FICE Identification: 033903
Unit ID: 439437
Telephone: (407) 673-7406 Carnegie Class: Assoc/PrivFP
FAX Number: (407) 339-0295 Calendar System: Quarter
URL: www.lincolntech.com
Established: 1991 Annual Undergrad Tuition & Fees: $26,650
Enrollment: 255 Coed
Affiliation or Control: Proprietary IRS Status: Proprietary
Highest Offering: Associate Degree
Program: Occupational; 2-Year Principally Bachelor's Creditable; Nursing Emphasis
Accreditation: ABHES, DA, SURTEC

01 Executive Director ....Mr. Carl BUTTS
05 Director of Education ....Mr. Jim WILBOUR

Lynn University (X)
3601 N Military Trail, Boca Raton FL 33431-5598
County: Palm Beach FICE Identification: 001505
Unit ID: 132657
Telephone: (561) 237-7000 Carnegie Class: DRU
FAX Number: (561) 237-7100 Calendar System: Semester
URL: www.lynn.edu
Established: 1962 Annual Undergrad Tuition & Fees: $33,600
Enrollment: 2,097 Coed
Affiliation or Control: Independent Non-Profit IRS Status: 501(c)3
Highest Offering: Doctorate
Program: Liberal Arts And General; Business Emphasis

Accreditation: SC, IACBE, MUS

01 President .... Dr. Kevin M. ROSS
100 Chief of Staff .... Dr. Jason L. WALTON
00 President Emeritus .... Dr. Donald E. ROSS
11 Sr Vice Pres Administration .... Mr. Gregory J. MALFITANO
05 Vice President Academic Affairs .... Dr. Gregg COX
84 Vice Pres Enrollment Management .... Dr. Gareth FOWLES
10 Vice President Business & Finance .... Ms. Laurie LEVINE
32 Vice President for Student Life .... Dr. Phil RIORDAN
26 Vice Pres Marketing & Communication .... Vacant
30 Vice Pres Development/Alumni Affs .... Ms. Judith L. NELSON
13 Chief Information Officer .... Mr. Chris G. BONIFORTI
88 Dean of Administration .... Mr. Thomas J. HEFFERNAN
35 Dean of Students .... Mr. Paul S. TURNER
20 Academic Dean .... Dr. Gregg C. COX
43 General Counsel .... Vacant
88 Exec Dir Stdnt Administrative Svcs .... Ms. Evelyn C. NELSON
39 Director Housing & Residence Life .... Vacant
36 Director Career Development .... Vacant
41 Director of Athletics .... Dr. Kristen L. MORAZ
18 Director Auxiliary Services .... Mr. Matthew P. CHALOUX
23 Director Health Center .... Ms. Rita ALBERT
27 Director of Marketing .... Mrs. Carol A. HERZ
31 Director of Public Relations .... Mr. Joshua GLANZER
44 Director of Regional Development .... Mr. Jay J. BRANDT
29 Director Alumni Affairs .... Mr. Matthew R. ROOS
42 Chaplain .... Fr. Martin C. DEVEREAUX
07 Dir Undergraduate Admissions .... Mr. Stefano PAPALEO
37 Dir Student Financial Assistance .... Mrs. Chan J. PARK
38 Director of the Counseling Center .... Ms. Nicole R. OVEDIA
96 Director of Purchasing .... Mr. Alfredo H. BONIFORTI
06 Registrar .... Ms. Angela K. ROGERS
21 Director of Accounting .... Mr. Michael C. BOLDUC
07 Dir Graduate & UG Evening Admiss .... Mr. Steven PRUITT
51 Director Distance Learning .... Vacant
09 Director of Institutional Research .... Mrs. Lara MARTIN
15 Director of Employee Services .... Mrs. Carole E. DODGE
40 Bookstore Manager .... Ms. Rita D. LOUREIRO
50 Dean College Business & Management .... Mr. Thomas KRUCZEK
49 Dean College of Liberal Educ .... Dr. Katrina CARTER-TELLISON
88 Dean School of Aeronautics .... Dr. Jeffrey C. JOHNSON
53 Dean Ross College of Education .... Dr. Craig MERTLER
60 Dean College Intl Communications .... Dr. David L. JAFFE
64 Dean Conservatory of Music .... Dr. Jon H. ROBERTSON
88 Dean Inst Achievement Learning .... Vacant

MedVance Institute of Fort Lauderdale (A)

4850 W Oakland Park Blvd, Suite 224,
Lauderdale Lakes FL 33313-7261
Telophone: (954) 587-7100 Identification: 666269
Accreditation: ABHES, MLTAD, RAD, SURGT, SURTEC

† Main campus is Fortis College in Baton Rouge, LA.

Meridian College (B)

7020 Professional Pkwy E, Sarasota FL 34240
County: Sarasota FICE Identification: 023268
Unit ID: 244279
Telephone: (941) 377-4880 Carnegie Class: Not Classified
FAX Number: (941) 378-2842 Calendar System: Other
URL: www.meridian.edu
Established: 1982 Annual Undergrad Tuition & Fees: $16,900
Enrollment: 148 Coed
Affiliation or Control: Proprietary IRS Status: Proprietary
Highest Offering: Associate Degree
Program: Occupational
Accreditation: ACCSC

01 Campus Director .... Mr. Patrick MCDERMITT

Miami Ad School (C)

955 Alton Road, Miami Beach FL 33139-5203
County: Miami-Dade FICE Identification: 031256
Unit ID: 428000
Telephone: (305) 538-3193 Carnegie Class: Assoc/PrivFP
FAX Number: (305) 538-3724 Calendar System: Quarter
URL: www.miamiadschool.com
Established: 1993 Annual Undergrad Tuition & Fees: $17,400
Enrollment: 171 Coed
Affiliation or Control: Proprietary IRS Status: Proprietary
Highest Offering: Associate Degree
Program: Occupational
Accreditation: COE

01 President .... Ms. Pipa SEICHRIST

Miami Dade College (D)

300 NE Second Avenue, Miami FL 33132-2204
County: Miami-Dade County FICE Identification: 001506
Unit ID: 135717
Telephone: (305) 237-8888 Carnegie Class: Assoc/Pub4
FAX Number: (305) 237-7913 Calendar System: Semester
URL: www.mdc.edu/main/
Established: 1960 Annual Undergrad Tuition & Fees (In-State): $3,426
Enrollment: 62,050 Coed
Affiliation or Control: State IRS Status: 501(c)3
Highest Offering: Baccalaureate
Program: Occupational; 2-Year Principally Bachelor's Creditable; Liberal Arts And General; Teacher Preparatory
Accreditation: SC, ADNUR, ARCPA, ART, CAHIIM, COARC, DANCE, DH, DMS, EMT, FUSER, HT, MLTAD, MUS, NUR, OPD, PTAA, RAD, THEA

01 College President .... Dr. Eduardo J. PADRON
05 College Provost .... Dr. Rolando MONTOYA
10 Sr Vice Provost Business Affairs .... Mr. E. H. LEVERING
13 Interim Vice Provost Info Tech .... Ms. Ruth Ann BALLA
18 Interim Vice Provost Facilities .... Mr. Patrick REBULL
15 Vice Provost Human Resources .... Ms. Iliana CASTILLO-FRICK
09 Vice Provost Inst Effectiveness .... Dr. Michael SELF
12 Campus President Hialeah .... Vacant
12 Campus President Kendall .... Dr. Lourdes OROZA
12 Campus President Medical .... Dr. Armando FERRER
12 Campus President North .... Dr. Jose VICENTE
12 Interim Campus President Wolfson .... Ms. Madeline PUMARIEGA
12 Campus President Homestead .... Dr. Jeanne JACOBS
12 Interim Campus Pres InterAmerican .... Dr. Jorge GUERRA
21 Assoc Vice Prov Business Affs .... Mr. Gregory KNOTT
35 Director Student Services .... Dr. Rene GARCIA
102 Exec Director MDC Foundation .... Ms. Annabelle ROJAS
37 Collegewide Financial Aid Director .... Ms. Mercedes AMAYA
93 Director Employee Relations/EOP/ADA .... Dr. Joy C. RUFF
07 Collegewide Director Admissions .... Ms. Dulce BELTRAN
26 Chief Public Rels Officer/Dir Comm .... Mr. Juan MENDIETA
29 Director Annual Giving/Alumni Rels .... Ms. Nairobi ABRAMS
32 Student Life Manager .... Ms. Yvette SHERAN
36 Dir Testing Admin/Pgm Evaluation .... Mr. Silvio RODRIGUEZ
28 Director of Diversity .... Dr. Joy C. RUFF
38 Director Student Advisement .... Mr. Jose RODRIGUEZ
84 Director Enrollment Management .... Dr. Rene GARCIA
96 Director of Purchasing .... Mr. Roman MARTINEZ
41 Director Athletics & Student Life .... Mr. Anthony FIORENZA
06 Collegewide Registrar .... Ms. Dulce BELTRAN
09 Director of Institutional Research .... Dr. David M. KAISER
43 Legal Counsel .... Ms. Carmen DOMINGUEZ
86 Director Governmental Affairs .... Ms. Victoria HERNANDEZ
100 Chief of Staff .... Mr. George ANDREWS
103 Exec Dir Workforce Educ & Partnrshp .... Dr. Jorge GUERRA
104 Interim Pgm Manager Study Abroad .... Ms. Joanne MICHAUD
105 College Webmaster .... Mr. Andrew SEAGA
08 Head Librarian/Dir Learning Resourc .... Ms. Isabel HERNANDEZ
85 Director Intl Student Services .... Ms. Anoush MCNAMEE

Miami International University of Art & Design (E)

1501 Biscayne Boulevard, Suite 100,
Miami FL 33132-1418
County: Miami-Dade FICE Identification: 008878
Unit ID: 134811
Telephone: (305) 428-5700 Carnegie Class: Spec/Arts
FAX Number: (305) 374-7946 Calendar System: Quarter
URL: www.aimiu.aii.edu
Established: 1965 Annual Undergrad Tuition & Fees: $17,714
Enrollment: 3,517 Coed
Affiliation or Control: Proprietary IRS Status: Proprietary
Highest Offering: Master's
Program: Fine Arts Emphasis
Accreditation: SC, CIDA

01 President .... Ms. Erika FLEMING
05 Chief Academic Officer .... Mr. Paul COX
10 Dir Admin & Financial Services .... Mr. Joseph GIANNATTASIO
32 Dean of Student Affairs .... Mr. John OSBORNE
07 Senior Director of Admissions .... Mr. Kevin RYAN
08 Librarian .... Ms. Lori KELLY

Millennia Atlantic University (F)

3801 NW 97th Avenue, Doral FL 33178
County: Miami-Dade FICE Identification: 041825
Unit ID: 461883
Telephone: (786) 331-1000 Carnegie Class: Not Classified
FAX Number: (305) 503-9680 Calendar System: Semester
URL: www.maufl.edu
Established: Annual Undergrad Tuition & Fees: $9,020
Enrollment: 92 Coed
Affiliation or Control: Proprietary IRS Status: Proprietary
Highest Offering: Master's
Program: Business Emphasis
Accreditation: ACICS

01 President .... Dr. Aristides MAZA-DUERTO
10 CFO .... Mrs. Orianna MAZA-MOSS

National-Louis University Florida Regional Campus (G)

4950 W Kennedy Boulevard, #300, Tampa FL 33609
Telephone: (800) 366-6581 Identification: 770087
Accreditation: &NH

† Main campus is National-Louis University in Chicago, IL.

North Florida Community College (H)

325 NW Turner Davis Drive, Madison FL 32340-1610
County: Madison FICE Identification: 001508
Unit ID: 136145
Telephone: (850) 973-2288 Carnegie Class: Assoc/Pub-R-S
FAX Number: (850) 973-1696 Calendar System: Semester
URL: www.nfcc.edu
Established: 1958 Annual Undergrad Tuition & Fees (In-State): $2,994
Enrollment: 1,430 Coed
Affiliation or Control: State IRS Status: 501(c)3
Highest Offering: Associate Degree
Program: Occupational; 2-Year Principally Bachelor's Creditable
Accreditation: SC

01 President .... Mr. John GROSSKOPF
05 Dean of Academic Affairs/CAO .... Dr. Sharon ERLE
11 Dean Administrative Svcs & CBO .... Ms. Amelia MULKEY
07 Dean of Enrollment/Student Services .... Ms. Mary Anne WHEELER
09 Manager of Networking Systems .... Mr. John SIRMON
15 Director of Personnel Services .... Mr. Bill HUNTER
08 Head Librarian .... Ms. Kay HOGAN
88 SSS and Disability Coordinator .... Dr. Suzie CASHWELL
88 Director of Public Safety Academy .... Mr. Rick DAVIS
06 Registrar .... Ms. Lori PLEASANT
18 Chief Facilities/Physical Plant .... Mr. Dale HACKLE
21 Controller .... Ms. Edna EALY
26 Public Information Officer .... Ms. Kim SCARBORO
29 Dir Foundation Alumni Relations .... Ms. Gina RUTHERFORD
37 Director Student Financial Aid .... Ms. Peggy HARRIS
28 Director of Diversity .... Ms. Denise BELL
32 Director Student Services .... Ms. Kim HALFHILL
96 Director of Purchasing .... Ms. Sarah NEWSOME

Northwest Florida State College (I)

100 College Boulevard, Niceville FL 32578-1295
County: Okaloosa FICE Identification: 001510
Unit ID: 136233
Telephone: (850) 678-5111 Carnegie Class: Assoc/Pub4
FAX Number: (850) 729-5215 Calendar System: Semester
URL: www.nwfsc.edu
Established: 1963 Annual Undergrad Tuition & Fees (In-District): $3,064
Enrollment: 9,412 Coed
Affiliation or Control: Local IRS Status: 501(c)3
Highest Offering: Baccalaureate
Program: Occupational; 2-Year Principally Bachelor's Creditable; Liberal Arts And General; Teacher Preparatory; Professional
Accreditation: SC, DA, NURSE

01 President .... Dr. Ty HANDY
05 Vice Pres for Instruction .... Dr. Sasha JARRELL
11 Vice Pres Administrative Services .... Dr. Gary YANCEY
30 Vice Pres College Advancement .... Mrs. Cristie KEDROSKI
27 Chief Information Officer .... Mr. Greg ELLER
09 Director of Institutional Research .... Dr. Diane W. HODGINS
10 Assoc Vice Pres Business Services .... Vacant
25 Contract Administrator .... Dr. Anne SOUTHARD
15 Director Human Resources/Diversity .... Ms. Nancy MURPHY
07 Director of Admissions .... Ms. Martha LITTLE
29 Assoc Director for Resource/Alumni .... Ms. Carla REINLIE
41 Athletic Director .... Mr. Ramsey ROSS
37 Director Financial Aid/Veteran Affs .... Ms. Patricia BENNETT
18 Facilities Director .... Mr. Sam JONES
36 Director Advising and Testing .... Ms. Marlayna GOOSBY
08 Director Learning Resources Center .... Ms. Janice HENDERSON
26 Director Marketing/Public Relations .... Ms. Stephanie PETTIS
96 Coordinator of Purchasing .... Ms. Dedria LUNDERMAN
32 Dean of Students .... Dr. Sherry AAKER
04 Admin Assistant to President .... Ms. Carolyn LAUX

Northwood University (J)

2600 N Military Trail, West Palm Beach FL 33409
Telephone: (561) 478-5520 Identification: 770279
Accreditation: &NH

† Main campus is Northwood University in Midland, MI.

Nova Southeastern University (K)

3301 College Avenue, Fort Lauderdale FL 33314-7796
County: Broward FICE Identification: 001509
Unit ID: 136215
Telephone: (954) 262-7300 Carnegie Class: RU/H
FAX Number: (954) 262-3800 Calendar System: Other
URL: www.nova.edu
Established: 1964 Annual Undergrad Tuition & Fees: $24,750
Enrollment: 26,808 Coed
Affiliation or Control: Independent Non-Profit IRS Status: 501(c)3
Highest Offering: Doctorate
Program: 2-Year Principally Bachelor's Creditable; Liberal Arts And General; Teacher Preparatory; Professional
Accreditation: SC, AA, ACAE, ARCPA, AUD, CLPSY, DENT, DMS, IACBE, IPSY, LAW, MFCD, NURSE, OPT, OPTR, OSTEO, OT, PH, PHAR, PTA, SP, TED

01 President & CEO .... Dr. George L. HANBURY, II
05 Provost & Exec VP Academic Affairs .... Dr. Frank DE PIANO
11 Exec Vice President/COO .... Ms. Jacqueline A. TRAVISANO
10 VP Finance/CFO .... Ms. Alyson SILVA
23 CEO of Division of Clinical Opers .... Dr. Robert OLLER
00 Chancellor Nova Southeastern Univ .... Mr. Ray FERRERO, JR.
00 University President Emeritus .... Dr. Abraham FISCHLER
17 Chancellor Health Professions Div .... Dr. Fred LIPPMAN
20 Vice Chanc Health Professions Div .... Dr. Irving ROSENBAUM
08 VP Info Svcs/Univ Librarian .... Ms. Lydia M. ACOSTA
43 VP Legal Affairs .... Mr. Joel BERMAN
46 VP Research Tech Transfer .... Dr. Gary S. MARGULES
32 VP Student Affairs .... Dr. Brad WILLIAMS
30 VP Inst Advancement .... Dr. Jennifer O'FLANNERY ANDERSON
18 VP Facilities Mgmt .... Mr. Peter J. WITSCHEN

13 VP Info Tech/Chief Info Ofcr .... Mr. Tom WEST
15 VP Human Resources .... Mr. Robert J. PIETRYKOWSKI
37 VP Enrollment and Stdnt Svcs .... Dr. Stephanie BROWN
21 VP Business Services .... Mr. Marc CROCQUET
26 Exec Director University Relations .... Mr. David DAWSON
19 Director Public Safety .... Mr. James EWING
09 Interim VP Inst Effectiveness .... Dr. Donald J. RUDAWSKY
88 Director Accreditation .... Ms. Jane DUNCAN
24 Exec Dir Ed Tech/Digital Media Prod .... Ms. Diane LIPPE
25 Director Sponsored Programs .... Ms. Cathy HARLAN
86 Exec Dir Licensure/State Relations .... Dr. Greg F. STIBER
84 Exec Director Enrollment Management .... Ms. Maria P. DILLARD
12 Headmaster University School .... Dr. Jerry CHERMAK
27 Director University Publications .... Mr. Ron RYAN
29 Director Alumni Relations .... Ms. Sara DUCUENNOIS
36 Director of Career Development .... Ms. Shari SAPERSTEIN
06 Dir University Registrar's Office .... Ms. G. Elaine N. POFF
41 Director Athletics .... Mr. Michael MOMINEY
39 Dir Residential Life & Housing .... Ms. Aarika CAMP
96 Director Purchasing .... Mr. Mike COROMINAS
88 Director Campus Recreation .... Mr. Tom VITUCCI
26 Director Public Affairs .... Ms. Julie SPECHLER
88 Exec Dir Student Educational Center .... Dr. Ricardo BELMAR
88 Executive Dir Internal Auditing .... Mr. Ron MIDEI
31 Exec Dir Inst & Comm Engagement ... Dr. Barbara PACKER-MUTI
88 Director Compliance .... Ms. Robin SUPPLER
88 Int Exec Dir Museum of Art .... Mr. William STANTON
63 Dean College Osteopathic Medicine .... Dr. Anthony SILVAGNI
67 Dean College Pharmacy .... Dr. Lisa DEZIEL-EVANS
88 Dean College Optometry .... Dr. David LOSHIN
76 Dean College of Hlth Care Services .... Dr. Richard E. DAVIS
77 Dean Grad Sch Computer/Info Sci .... Dr. Eric ACKERMAN
61 Dean Shepard Broad Law Center .... Mr. Athornia STEELE
65 Dean Oceanographic Center .... Dr. Richard DODGE
66 Dean College of Nursing .... Dr. Marcella M. RUTHERFORD
50 Int Dn W Huizenga Grad Sch Bus/Entr .... Dr. J. Preston JONES
49 Dean Farquhar Col Arts & Sciences .... Dr. Donald ROSENBLUM
88 Dean Center Psychological Stds .... Dr. Karen GROSBY
83 Dean Grad Sch Humanities/Social Sci .... Dr. Honggang YANG
53 Dean Abraham S Fischler Sch of Edu ... Dr. H. Wells SINGLETON
88 Dean Mailman Ctr for Human Devel .... Dr. Roni LEIDERMAN
63 Dean College of Medical Sciences .... Dr. Harold LAUBAUCH
52 Dean College of Dental Medicine .... Dr. Robert A. UCHIN
88 Exec Dean Inst Study of Human Svcs .... Dr. Kim DURHAM

Orlando Medical Institute (A)

6220 S. Orange Blossom Tr, Ste 420, Orlando FL 32809
County: Orange — Identification: 667127
Telephone: (407) 251-0007 — Carnegie Class: Not Classified
FAX Number: (407) 251-0352 — Calendar System: Semester
URL: www.orlandomedicalinstitute.com
Established: 2004 — Annual Undergrad Tuition & Fees: $4,000
Enrollment: N/A — Coed
Affiliation or Control: Proprietary — IRS Status: Proprietary
Highest Offering: Associate Degree
Program: Occupational
Accreditation: **ABHES**

01 President .... Felix J. MARQUEZ, JR.

Palm Beach Atlantic University (B)

901 S. Flagler Drive, West Palm Beach FL 33401
County: Palm Beach — FICE Identification: 008849
Unit ID: 136330
Telephone: (561) 803-2000 — Carnegie Class: Master's M
FAX Number: (561) 803-2186 — Calendar System: Semester
URL: www.pba.edu
Established: 1968 — Annual Undergrad Tuition & Fees: $25,500
Enrollment: 3,579 — Coed
Affiliation or Control: Interdenominational — IRS Status: 501(c)3
Highest Offering: Doctorate
Program: Occupational; Liberal Arts And General; Teacher Preparatory; Professional
Accreditation: **SC**, IACBE, MUS, NURSE, PHAR

01 President .... Mr. William B. FLEMING
05 Provost .... Dr. Joseph A. KLOBA
11 Sr VP for Finance Admin & Plng .... Mr. John KAUTZ, III
04 Executive Asst to President .... Mr. Tim WORLEY
30 Vice President Development .... Mrs. Vicki PUGH
32 Vice President Student Development .... Vacant
09 Asst Vice Pres Rsrch/Effectiveness .... Mrs. Carolanne BROWN
27 Assoc VP Campus Information Svcs .... Mr. Phillip MAJOR
26 Assoc VP Univ Relations & Marketing .... Mrs. Rebecca PEELING
51 Dean MacArthur School of Leadership .... Dr. James A. LAUB
49 Dean School of Arts & Sciences .... Dr. J. Barton STARR
50 Interim Dean School of Business .... Dr. Leslie TURNER
53 Dean School of Education .... Dr. Gene SALE
57 Dean School of Music/Fine Arts .... Dr. Lloyd MIMS
66 Dean School of Nursing .... Dr. Joanne MASELLA
67 Dean Gregory School of Pharmacy .... Dr. Mary FERRILL
60 Dean School Communication/Media .... Dr. J. Duane MEEKS
73 Dean School of Ministry .... Dr. Randy RICHARDS
06 Registrar .... Ms. Audrey SCHOFIELD
08 Dean of the Library .... Mr. Steven BAKER
20 Dean of Faculty .... Vacant
15 Assoc VP of Human Resources .... Ms. Mona L. HICKS
18 Director of Physical Plant .... Mr. Matt STEVENS
21 Controller .... Mrs. Renae MURRAY
29 AVP Alumni Relations/Annual Fund .... Ms. Delesa MORRIS
31 Coordinator Community Services .... Mrs. Cindy LAMERSON
38 Director of Student Success Center .... Mrs. Andrea DYBEN
37 Director of Financial Aid .... Mr. Joseph BRYAN
35 Dean of Students .... Mr. Kevin ABEL
40 Director of Campus Store .... Mrs. Abbie ROSEMEYER
41 Director of Athletics .... Mrs. Carolyn STONE
42 Director of Campus Ministries .... Mr. Mark KAPRIVE
19 Director of Safety & Security .... Mr. Terry WHEELER
92 Director of Supper Honors Program .... Dr. Tom ST. ANTOINE
07 Dean of Admissions .... Mr. Joe SHARP

Palm Beach State College (C)

4200 Congress Avenue, Lake Worth FL 33461-4796
County: Palm Beach — FICE Identification: 001512
Unit ID: 136358
Telephone: (561) 967-7222 — Carnegie Class: Assoc/Pub-S-MC
FAX Number: (561) 868-3504 — Calendar System: Semester
URL: www.palmbeachstate.edu
Established: 1933 — Annual Undergrad Tuition & Fees (In-District): $2,947
Enrollment: 29,974 — Coed
Affiliation or Control: Local — IRS Status: 501(c)3
Highest Offering: Baccalaureate
Program: Occupational; 2-Year Principally Bachelor's Creditable
Accreditation: **SC**, ADNUR, CAHIIM, COARC, DA, DH, DMS, EMT, MAC, RAD, SURGT

01 President .... Dr. Dennis P. GALLON
05 Vice President for Academic Affairs .... Dr. Sharon A. SASS
10 Vice President Admin/Business Svcs .... Mr. Richard A. BECKER
32 Vice President for Student Services .... Dr. Peter BARBATIS
102 CEO Foundation .... Ms. Suellen MANN
12 Provost Glades Center .... Dr. Holly L. BENNETT
12 Provost South Campus ..... Dr. Bernadette MENDONEZ RUSSELL
12 Provost Eissey Campus .... Dr. Jean WIHBEY
12 Provost Central Campus .... Dr. Maria M. VALLEJO
35 Dean Student Services/Central .... Ms. Penny J. MCISAAC
35 Dean Student Services/Boca Raton .... Ms. Nicole P. BANKS
35 Dean Student Services/Eissey .... Mr. Scott MACLACHLAN
35 Dean Educational Services/Glades .... Dr. Barry L. MOORE
84 Dean Enrollment Management .... Vacant
103 Dean Workforce .... Ms. Patricia V. RICHIE
37 Director Financial Aid .... Vacant
41 Dir Student Activities/Athletics .... Dr. David HOLSTEIN
09 Dir Institutional Effectiveness .... Dr. Jennifer D. CAMPBELL
86 Director Government Relations .... Ms. Erin S. MCCOLSKEY
18 Director Facilities .... Mr. John T. WASUKANIS
15 Director Human Resources .... Dr. Ellen GRACE
26 Dir College Relations & Marketing .... Dr. Grace H. TRUMAN
21 Controller .... Mr. James E. DUFFIE
06 Registrar/Director Admissions .... Mr. Edward MUELLER
96 Director of Purchasing .... Ms. Jodi HART
27 Chief Information Officer .... Mr. Anthony PARZIALE
13 Director Information Technology .... Mr. Chuck H. ZETTLER
29 Director Alumni Relations .... Ms. Suellen MANN
25 Manager Grant Development .... Ms. Maureen CAPP
88 Project Reports Coordinator .... Ms. Karen M. LIPPE

Palmer College of Chiropractic, Florida Campus (D)

4777 City Center Parkway, Port Orange FL 32129-4153
Telephone: (386) 763-2709 — Identification: 666330
Accreditation: &NH, &CHIRO

† Main campus is Palmer College of Chiropractic in Davenport, IA.

Pasco-Hernando Community College (E)

10230 Ridge Road, New Port Richey FL 34654-5199
County: Pasco — FICE Identification: 010652
Unit ID: 136400
Telephone: (727) 847-2727 — Carnegie Class: Assoc/Pub-S-MC
FAX Number: (727) 816-1815 — Calendar System: Semester
URL: www.phcc.edu
Established: 1972 — Annual Undergrad Tuition & Fees (In-District): $3,035
Enrollment: 10,368 — Coed
Affiliation or Control: State/Local — IRS Status: 501(c)3
Highest Offering: Associate Degree
Program: Occupational; 2-Year Principally Bachelor's Creditable
Accreditation: **SC**, ADNUR, DH, EMT

01 President .... Dr. Katherine M. JOHNSON
05 VP Instruction/Prov West Campus .... Dr. Burt H. HARRES, JR.
32 VP Stdnt Devel/Enrollment Mgmt .... Dr. Timothy L. BEARD
10 Vice Pres Administration & Finance .... Mr. Kenneth R. BURDZINSKI
12 Provost of the East Campus .... Dr. Randall H. STOVALL
12 Associate Provost North Campus .... Ms. Donna R. BURDZINSKI
12 Provost Spring Hill Campus .... Dr. Bonnie M. CLARK
12 Provost Porter Campus at Wiregrass .... Dr. Stanley M. GIANNET
103 Dean of Workforce Development .... Mr. Edwin G. GOOLSBY
24 Dean of Institutional Technology .... Vacant
20 Asst Dean Instructional Services .... Ms. Jeanne F. GASQUE
17 Dean Health Occupations .... Ms. Jayme S. ROTHBERG
49 Dean Arts and Sciences .... Dr. John L. WHITLOCK
21 Dean Admin/Finance/Comptroller .... Mr. Brian S. HORN
84 Dean Student Devel/Enroll Mgmt .... Mr. Robert E. BADE
09 Assoc Dean Institutional Effective .... Dr. Gerardine COCHRAN
13 Director of Management Info Svcs .... Ms. Janice L. SCOTT
30 Dean Inst Advance/Exec Dir Foun .... Ms. Arla S. ALTMAN
66 Associate Dean of Nursing .... Ms. Billie J. GABBARD
07 Dir Admissions & Student Records .... Ms. Estela CARRION
37 Asst Dean Financial Aid/Vet Svcs .... Ms. Rebecca SHANAFELT
43 Gen Counsel/Exec Dir Govt Relations .... Mr. Stephen C. SCHROEDER
08 Director of Libraries .... Mr. Raymond J. CALVERT
41 Athletics Director/Instructor .... Mr. Stephen A. WINTERLING
26 Exec Dir Marketing/Public Relation .... Ms. Lucy T. MILLER
18 Director of Facilities .... Mr. Keith V. BRAUN
15 Exec Director of Human Resources .... Ms. Vivian M. FRIEND
40 Auxiliary Services Manager .... Mr. John D. COLLINS
28 Coord of Disabilities Services .... Mr. Ron THIESSEN
22 Dist Coord Multicul Std Affs/Eq Svc .... Mr. Imani D. ASUKILE
96 Purchasing Agent .... Vacant

Pensacola Christian College (F)

250 Brent Lane, Pensacola FL 32503
County: Escambia — Identification: 667101
Telephone: (850) 478-8496 — Carnegie Class: Not Classified
FAX Number: (850) 479-6577 — Calendar System: Semester
URL: www.pcci.edu
Established: 1974 — Annual Undergrad Tuition & Fees: $5,420
Enrollment: 4,100 — Coed
Affiliation or Control: Independent Non-Profit — IRS Status: 501(c)3
Highest Offering: Doctorate
Program: Religious Emphasis
Accreditation: **@TRACS**

01 President .... Dr. Troy SHOEMAKER
05 Acting Academic Vice President .... Dr. Raylene COCHRAN
06 Registrar .... Ms. Cheryl GREGORY

Pensacola State College (G)

1000 College Boulevard, Pensacola FL 32504-8998
County: Escambia — FICE Identification: 001513
Unit ID: 136473
Telephone: (850) 484-1000 — Carnegie Class: Assoc/Pub-R-L
FAX Number: (850) 484-1826 — Calendar System: Semester
URL: www.pensacolastate.edu
Established: 1948 — Annual Undergrad Tuition & Fees (In-District): $2,902
Enrollment: 11,862 — Coed
Affiliation or Control: Local — IRS Status: 501(c)3
Highest Offering: Baccalaureate
Program: 2-Year Principally Bachelor's Creditable
Accreditation: **SC**, ACFEI, ADNUR, CAHIIM, DH, EMT, MAC, PTAA, RAD, SURGT

01 President .... Dr. Ed MEADOWS
05 Vice Pres for Academic Affairs .... Dr. Erin SPICER
32 Vice President Student Affairs .... Mr. Tom GILLIAM
10 Vice President for Business .... Mrs. Gean Ann EMOND
103 VP Workforce Educ/Academic Support .... Mr. Dan BUSSE
12 Dean Milton Campus .... Ms. Anthea AMOS
12 Dean Warrington Campus .... Ms. Frances DUNCAN
28 Assoc Vice Pres Inst Diversity .... Dr. Gael FRAZER
102 Exec Director College Foundation .... Mr. Aaron WEST
13 Int Director MIS/Telecom Systems .... Mr. Bert MERRITT
86 Exec Director of Govt Relations .... Mr. Larry BRACKEN
26 Director Marketing & College Info .... Ms. Sheila NICHOLS
06 Registrar .... Ms. Martha CAUGHEY
09 Dean Instnl Effectiveness & Grants .... Dr. Debbie DOUMA
18 Director Physical Plant .... Mr. Walt WINTER
14 Director Computer Svcs/Telecommun .... Mr. William MELOY
15 Director Human Resources/EA/EO .... Ms. Tammy HENDERSON
37 Dir Fin Aid/Veteran Affairs/Scholar .... Ms. Karen KESSLER
36 Director Student Job Services .... Mr. Gil BIXEL
19 Public Safety Director .... Mr. Hank SHIRAH
43 General Counsel .... Mr. Thomas J. GILLIAM
08 Int District Dept Head Libraries .... Ms. Winifred BRADLEY
96 Director of Purchasing .... Ms. Cassie BOATWRIGHT
21 Associate Business Officer .... Ms. Jackie PADILLA
29 Exec Director Alumni Affairs .... Ms. Patrice WHITTEN
07 Director of Admissions .... Ms. Martha CAUGHEY
38 Director Student Counseling .... Ms. Kathy DUTREMBLE
41 Director Athletics .... Mr. Bill HAMILTON
84 Director Enrollment Management .... Ms. Kathy DUTREMBLE
12 Director South Santa Rosa Center .... Ms. Michele HORTON
12 Director Century Center .... Ms. Paula JERNIGAN
31 Coordinator Community Education .... Ms. Frances YEO

Polk State College (H)

999 Avenue H, NE, Winter Haven FL 33881-4299
County: Polk — FICE Identification: 001514
Unit ID: 136516
Telephone: (863) 297-1000 — Carnegie Class: Assoc/Pub-R-L
FAX Number: (863) 297-1065 — Calendar System: Trimester
URL: www.polk.edu
Established: 1964 — Annual Undergrad Tuition & Fees (In-District): $3,482
Enrollment: 12,290 — Coed
Affiliation or Control: Local — IRS Status: 501(c)3
Highest Offering: Baccalaureate
Program: Occupational; 2-Year Principally Bachelor's Creditable; Technical Emphasis
Accreditation: **SC**, ADNUR, CAHIIM, COARC, CVT, DMS, EMT, NUR, OTA, PTAA, RAD

01 President .... Dr. Eileen HOLDEN
05 Vice Pres Academic/Student Svcs .... Dr. Ken ROSS
30 Vice Pres Development .... Ms. Tracy PORTER

10 Vice President Administration/CFO ....Mr. Peter A. ELLIOTT
26 Assoc VP Communications/Public Affs ....Mr. David STEELE
32 Dean Student Services-Lakeland ....Mr. Reggie WEBB
32 Dean Student Services-Winter Haven ....Dr. Saul REYES
20 District Dn Academic/Student Svcs ....Dr. Patricia JONES
12 Provost Lakeland Campus ....Mr. Stephen E. HULL
12 Provost Winter Haven Campus ....Dr. Sharon MILLER
66 Director of Nursing ....Dr. Annette HUTCHERSON
06 Registrar ....Ms. Kathy BUCKLEW
21 Comptroller ....Ms. Teresa VOROUS
18 District Director Facilities ....Mr. George URBANO
37 Director Financial Aid ....Ms. Marcia CONLIFFE
22 Director of Equity & Diversity ....Ms. Val BAKER
41 Athletic Diredtor ....Mr. Bing TYUS
09 Dir Inst Research/Effective/Plng ....Mr. Peter USINGER
15 Director Personnel Services ....Ms. Jill HALL
84 Director Enrollment Management ....Mr. Reginald WEBB
96 Director of Purchasing ....Vacant

Polytechnic University of Puerto Rico (A)

8180 NW 36th Street, Suite 401, Miami FL 33166-6674
Telephone: (305) 418-4220 Identification: 666238
Accreditation: &M

† Main campus is Universidad Politecnica De Puerto Rico in San Juan, PR.

Polytechnic University of Puerto Rico-Orlando Campus (B)

550 N Econlockhatchee Trail, Orlando FL 32825
Telephone: (407) 677-7000 Identification: 770172
Accreditation: &M

† Main campus is Universidad Politecnica De Puerto Rico in San Juan, PR.

The Praxis Institute (C)

1850 SW 8th Street, 4th Floor, Miami FL 33135
County: Miami-Dade FICE Identification: 031147
Unit ID: 430582
Telephone: (305) 642-4104 Carnegie Class: Not Classified
FAX Number: N/A Calendar System: Semester
URL: the-praxisinstitute.com
Established: 1988 Annual Undergrad Tuition & Fees: $15,950
Enrollment: 429 Coed
Affiliation or Control: Proprietary IRS Status: Proprietary
Highest Offering: Associate Degree
Program: Occupational
Accreditation: COE, PTAA

01 Executive Director ....Rebeca ALFIE

Professional Golfers Career College (D)

16349 Phil Ritson Way, Winter Garden FL 34787
Telephone: (407) 905-2200 Identification: 666300
Accreditation: ACICS

† Main campus is Professional Golfers Career College in Temecula, CA.

Professional Training Center (E)

13926 SW 47th Street, Miami FL 33175-4404
County: Miami-Dade FICE Identification: 033484
Unit ID: 436702
Telephone: (305) 220-4120 Carnegie Class: Assoc/PrivFP
FAX Number: (305) 220-2889 Calendar System: Other
URL: www.ptcc.edu
Established: 1994 Annual Undergrad Tuition & Fees: $38,595
Enrollment: 574 Coed
Affiliation or Control: Proprietary IRS Status: Proprietary
Highest Offering: Baccalaureate
Program: Occupational; 2-Year Principally Bachelor's Creditable
Accreditation: ACICS, RAD

01 Chief Executive Officer ....Mr. Antonio MATTIA
11 Vice President Operations ....Mr. Marc MATTIA
06 Academic Registrar ....Mr. John KRAMER
07 Director of Admissions ....Ms. Mara GONZALEZ
15 Human Resources Director ....Ms. Jeannie HIDALGO
37 Student Finance Director ....Ms. Angie GUTIERREZ
32 Student Services Director ....Ms. Johanna JIMINEZ
36 Placement Director ....Vacant
08 Librarian ....Ms. Ophelia WIETZ
51 Continuing Education Dept Director ....Ms. Michelle PENA
97 Dir of Assoc & General Education ....Vacant
67 Pharmacy Director ....Mrs. Alicia TUMA
76 Diagnostic Med Sonography Pgm Dir ..Dr. Victor M. FERNANDEZ
88 Imaging Director ....Vacant

Rasmussen College - Fort Myers (F)

9160 Forum Corporate Parkway, Fort Myers FL 33905
Telephone: (239) 477-2100 Identification: 667062
Accreditation: &NH, MAAB

† Main campus is Rasmussen College - St. Cloud in Saint Cloud, MN.

Rasmussen College - Land O'Lakes (G)

18600 Fernview Street, Land O'Lakes FL 34638
Telephone: (813) 435-3601 Identification: 770488
Accreditation: &NH

† Main campus is Rasmussen College Corporate Office in Bloomington, MN.

Rasmussen College - New Port Richey (H)

8661 Citizens Drive, Suite 300, New Port Richey FL 34654
Telephone: (727) 942-0069 Identification: 666425
Accreditation: &NH, MAAB

† Main campus is Rasmussen College - St. Cloud in Saint Cloud, MN.

Rasmussen College - Ocala (I)

4755 SW 46th Court, Ocala FL 34474
Telephone: (352) 629-1941 FICE Identification: 008501
Accreditation: &NH, MAAB

† Main campus is Rasmussen College - St. Cloud in Saint Cloud, MN.

Rasmussen College - Tampa/Brandon (J)

4042 Park Oaks Boulevard, Tampa FL 33610
Telephone: (813) 246-7600 Identification: 667067
Accreditation: &NH, MAAB

† Main campus is Rasmussen College - St. Cloud in Saint Cloud, MN.

Reformed Theological Seminary (K)

1231 Reformation Drive, Oviedo FL 32765-7197
Telephone: (407) 366-9493 Identification: 666628
Accreditation: &SC, &THEOL

† Main campus is Reformed Theological Seminary in Jackson, MS.

Remington College of Nursing (L)

660 Century Point, Lake Mary FL 32746
Telephone: (407) 562-9100 Identification: 770566
Accreditation: ACCSC, NURSE

† Main campus is Remington College-Tampa Campus in Tampa, FL.

Remington College Online (M)

500 International Pkwy, Suite 200,
Heathrow FL 33612-5627
Telephone: (407) 562-5671 Identification: 770567
Accreditation: ACCSC

† Main campus is Remington College-Tampa Campus in Tampa, FL.

Remington College-Tampa Campus (N)

6302 E Martin Luther King Dr, #400, Tampa FL 33619
County: Hillsborough FICE Identification: 007586
Unit ID: 135939
Telephone: (813) 935-5700 Carnegie Class: Bac/Assoc
FAX Number: (813) 935-7415 Calendar System: Quarter
URL: www.remingtoncollege.edu
Established: 1948 Annual Undergrad Tuition & Fees: $15,478
Enrollment: 166 Coed
Affiliation or Control: Independent Non-Profit IRS Status: 501(c)3
Highest Offering: Baccalaureate
Program: Occupational; Technical Emphasis
Accreditation: ACCSC, NURSE

01 President ....Dr. Ken HEINEMANN
06 Registrar ....Ms. Luigidge GUSTIN
36 Director Student Placement ....Ms. Deborah HOFFMAN
37 Director Student Financial Aid ....Ms. Brittany REMLIN

Ringling College of Art and Design (O)

2700 N Tamiami Trail, Sarasota FL 34234-5895
County: Sarasota FICE Identification: 012574
Unit ID: 136774
Telephone: (941) 351-5100 Carnegie Class: Spec/Arts
FAX Number: (941) 359-7517 Calendar System: Semester
URL: www.ringling.edu
Established: 1931 Annual Undergrad Tuition & Fees: $35,490
Enrollment: 1,364 Coed
Affiliation or Control: Independent Non-Profit IRS Status: 501(c)3
Highest Offering: Baccalaureate
Program: Professional; Fine Arts Emphasis
Accreditation: SC, ART, CIDA

01 President ....Dr. Larry R. THOMPSON
04 Spec Asst to Pres Media & Cmty Rels ...Ms. Christine M. LANGE
05 Int Vice President Academic Affairs ....Mr. David H. JACKSON
30 Vice Pres Advancement ....Mr. Michael MOORE
10 Vice President for Finance & Admin ....Ms. Tracy A. WAGNER
15 VP Human/Organizational Development ....Ms. Christine C. DEGEORGE
32 Vice Pres Student Life/Dean Stdnts ....Dr. Tammy S. WALSH
20 Assoc Vice Pres Faculty Affairs ....Mr. David JACKSON
21 Asst VP for Fin & Admn/Controller ....Ms. Monica K. WAID
18 Asst VP/Dir Facilities Operations ....Mr. Jeffrey A. POLESHEK
29 Asst VP Alumni Relations/Advance ....Ms. Terri J. ARNELL
44 Asst Vice Pres of Development ....Ms. Kaye MCHAN
07 Dean of Admissions ....Mr. James H. DEAN
51 Director of Continuing Studies ....Ms. Diane ZORN
06 Dir Advising/Records & Registration ...Ms. Donna M. ANDERSON
90 Director Institutional Technology ....Dr. Mahmoud PEGAH
36 Director Career Services ....Mr. Charles KOVACS
26 Exec Dir Marketing/Communications ....Mr. James H. DEAN
37 Director of Financial Aid ....Mr. Kurt WOLF
19 Director of Public Safety ....Mr. Richard E. TUBBS
08 Director of Library Services ....Ms. Kathleen L. LIST
09 Dir of Student Outcomes Assessment ....Dr. Alison L. WATKINS

The Robert E. Webber Institute for Worship Studies (P)

151 Kingsley Avenue, Orange Park FL 32073-5640
County: Clay Identification: 666616
Telephone: (904) 264-2172 Carnegie Class: Not Classified
FAX Number: (904) 278-2878 Calendar System: Semester
URL: www.iws.edu
Established: 1998 Annual Graduate Tuition & Fees: $5,230
Enrollment: 148 Coed
Affiliation or Control: Independent Non-Profit IRS Status: 501(c)3
Highest Offering: Doctorate; No Undergraduates
Program: Professional; Religious Emphasis
Accreditation: BI

01 Chief Executive Officer ....Dr. James R. HART
05 Chief Academic Officer ....Dr. Eric H. OHLMANN
10 Chief Financial Officer ....Ms. Tracie M. HARLEY
06 Registrar ....Vacant
84 Director of Enrollment Management ....Mr. Mark J. MURRAY
08 Library Director ....Ms. Carol B. SITTEMA
29 Director Alumni Relations ....Dr. Kent L. WALTERS
42 Dean of the Chapel ....Dr. Darrell A. HARRIS
106 Dir of Distance Learning Technology ..Mr. Samuel L. HOROWITZ
88 Administrative Support Coordinator ....Ms. Dianna L. ANDREWS
32 Dir Student Services/Adm Asst Advan ....Ms. Sandy E. DINKINS
45 Dir Strategic Plng/Accreditation ....Dr. Steve E. HUNTLEY
13 Director of Information Technology .Dr. James Kenneth RUSHING

Rollins College (Q)

1000 Holt Avenue, Winter Park FL 32789-4499
County: Orange FICE Identification: 001515
Unit ID: 136950
Telephone: (407) 646-2000 Carnegie Class: Master's L
FAX Number: (407) 646-2600 Calendar System: Semester
URL: www.rollins.edu
Established: 1885 Annual Undergrad Tuition & Fees: $41,460
Enrollment: 3,237 Coed
Affiliation or Control: Independent Non-Profit IRS Status: 501(c)3
Highest Offering: Doctorate
Program: Liberal Arts And General; Teacher Preparatory; Professional
Accreditation: SC, BUS, CACREP, MUS

01 President ....Dr. Lewis DUNCAN
05 Vice President Acad Affairs/Provost ....Dr. Carol BRESNAHAN
32 Vice President Student Affairs ....Dr. Mamta ACCAPADI
10 Vice President Business/Finance ....Mr. Jeffrey EISENBARTH
30 VP for Institutional Advancement ....Dr. Ronald KORVAS
27 Chief Information Officer ....Dr. Pat SCHOKNECHT
49 Dean of College of Arts & Sciences ....Dr. Robert SMITHER
107 Dean Col of Professional Studies ....Dr. Debra WELLMAN
51 Dean of Hamilton Holt School ....Dr. David RICHARD
35 Dean of Student Affairs ....Dr. Karen HATER
84 Dean of Enrollment Management ....Mr. David ERDMANN
50 Dean of Graduate Business School ....Dr. Craig MCALLASTER
42 Dean of the Chapel ....Dr. Patrick POWERS
21 Assoc VP Finance/Asst Treasurer ....Mr. William SHORT
30 Assoc Vice Pres Development ....Ms. Lisa THOMSON
26 Assoc VP Marketing & Communications ....Mr. Thomas HOPE
15 Asst VP Human Res/Risk Management ....Ms. Maria MARTINEZ
20 Assistant Provost ....Dr. Toni STROLLO HOLBROOK
88 Exec Director Student Services ....Ms. Meghan HARTE
08 Director of Olin Library ....Dr. Jonathan MILLER
41 Athletic Director ....Ms. Pennie PARKER
37 Director of Financial Aid ....Mr. Steve BOOKER
09 Director of Institutional Research ....Mr. Udeth LUGO
104 Director of International Programs ....Ms. Giselda BEAUDIN
07 Director of Admission ....Ms. Holly POHLIG
39 Director of Residential Life ....Mr. Leon HAYNER
36 Director of Career Services ....Mr. Ray ROGERS
38 Director of Personal Counseling ....Dr. Joanne VOGEL
35 Dir Student Involvement Leadership ....Mr. Brent TURNER
18 Director of Facilities Management ....Mr. Scott BITIKOFER
96 Director of Business Services ....Ms. Kathy WELCH
19 Campus Director Safety ....Mr. Ken MILLER
29 Senior Director Alumni Relations ....Ms. Leslie CARNEY
44 Director of Planned Giving ....Ms. Amanda HOPKINS
102 Director of Foundation Relations ....Mr. Joseph MONTI
06 Director of Student Records ....Ms. Robin MATEO
28 Director Multicultural Affairs ....Ms. Shelley GENTILE
40 Manager of Bookstore ....Ms. Mary VITELLI
04 Exec Assistant to the President ....Dr. Lorrie KYLE

Saber College (A)

3990 West Flagler St, Ste 103, Miami FL 33134
County: Miami-Dade FICE Identification: 036964
Unit ID: 449506
Telephone: (305) 443-9170 Carnegie Class: Not Classified
FAX Number: (305) 443-8441 Calendar System: Other
URL: www.sabercollege.com
Established: 1972 Annual Undergrad Tuition & Fees: $42,475
Enrollment: 549 Coed
Affiliation or Control: Independent Non-Profit IRS Status: 501(c)3
Highest Offering: Associate Degree
Program: Occupational
Accreditation: **COE**

01 President .... William ALEXANDER

St. John Vianney College Seminary (B)

2900 SW 87th Avenue, Miami FL 33165-3244
County: Miami-Dade FICE Identification: 008075
Unit ID: 137272
Telephone: (305) 223-4561 Carnegie Class: Spec/Faith
FAX Number: (305) 223-0650 Calendar System: Semester
URL: www.sjvcs.edu
Established: 1959 Annual Undergrad Tuition & Fees: $21,000
Enrollment: 92 Male
Affiliation or Control: Roman Catholic IRS Status: 501(c)3
Highest Offering: Baccalaureate
Program: Liberal Arts And General
Accreditation: **SC**

01 Rector & President .... Rev. Roberto GARZA
05 Academic Dean .... Dr. Ramon SANTOS
06 Registrar .... Mrs. Bonnie DE ANGULO
08 Librarian .... Mrs. Maria RODRIGUEZ
32 Dean of Students .... Rev. Scott CIRCE
38 Director of Counseling .... Vacant
09 Institutional Research Director .... Dr. Jose ORTA
42 Spiritual Director .... Rev. Joseph KOTTOYIL

St. Johns River State College (C)

5001 St. Johns Avenue, Palatka FL 32177-3897
County: Putnam FICE Identification: 001523
Unit ID: 137281
Telephone: (386) 312-4200 Carnegie Class: Assoc/Pub-R-L
FAX Number: (386) 312-4229 Calendar System: Semester
URL: www.sjrstate.edu
Established: 1958 Annual Undergrad Tuition & Fees (In-District): $3,240
Enrollment: 7,419 Coed
Affiliation or Control: State/Local IRS Status: 501(c)3
Highest Offering: Baccalaureate
Program: Occupational; 2-Year Principally Bachelor's Creditable; Teacher Preparatory
Accreditation: **SC**, ADNUR, CAHIIM, COARC

01 President .... Mr. Joe PICKENS
03 Exec Vice President/General Counsel .... Dr. Melissa C. MILLER
32 Vice President Student Affairs .... Dr. Gilbert L. EVANS, JR.
05 Vice President Academic Affairs .... Dr. Melanie A. BROWN
10 Vice President Finance & Admin/CFO .... Mr. Albert P. LITTLE
30 Vice Pres Develop/External Affairs .... Mrs. Caroline D. TINGLE
108 VP for Research & Inst Effective .... Dr. Rosalind M. HUMERICK
103 Vice Pres Workforce Development .... Dr. Anna M. LEBESCH
13 Chief Information Officer .... Mr. Paul M. HAWKINS
12 Provost St Augustine Campus .... Dr. Gregory K. MCLEOD
12 Provost Orange Park/Dir Govt Rels .... Mr. James C. ROY
49 Dean of Arts & Sciences .... Dr. Laura L. BOILINI
88 Dean of Crim Justice/Public Safety .... Mr. Gary A. KILLAM
57 Dean of Florida School of the Arts .... Mr. Alain R. HENTSCHEL
08 Dean of Library Services .... Mrs. Carmen M. CUMMINGS
66 Dean Nursing .... Dr. Mary A. LANEY
88 Dean of Adult & Secondary Education .... Dr. Edward K. JORDAN
53 Dean of Teacher Education .... Dr. Myrna L. ALLEN
88 Exec Director TH Center for the Art .... Mr. James A. WALSH
88 Director of Dual Enrollment .... Mrs. Melissa PERRY
103 Director of Workforce Services .... Mrs. Melissa E. O'CONNELL
51 Dir of Cont/Community Education .... Mrs. Meghan DEPUTY
26 Director of Public Relations .... Mrs. Susan B. KESSLER
37 Dir of Financial Aid/Veterans' Aff .... Mr. Wayne BODIFORD
38 Dir of Counsel/Acad Advising .... Ms. Sara J. MYERS
88 Director of Testing & Stdnt Support .... Mrs. Jana S. WILHITE
07 Director of Admissions and Records .... Mrs. Susanne B. LINEBERGER
15 Dir of Benefits/Employee Relations .... Mrs. Ginger C. STOKES
21 Dir of Budget/Employee Compensation .... Ms. Ann KNOTTS

Saint Leo University (D)

33701 State Road 52 W, Saint Leo FL 33574-6665
County: Pasco FICE Identification: 001526
Unit ID: 137032
Telephone: (352) 588-8200 Carnegie Class: Master's L
FAX Number: (352) 588-8654 Calendar System: Semester
URL: www.saintleo.edu
Established: 1889 Annual Undergrad Tuition & Fees: $19,610
Enrollment: 15,932 Coed
Affiliation or Control: Roman Catholic IRS Status: 501(c)3
Highest Offering: Doctorate
Program: Liberal Arts And General; Teacher Preparatory; Professional
Accreditation: **SC**, IACBE, SW

01 President .... Dr. Arthur F. KIRK, JR.
05 VP Academic Affairs .... Dr. Maribeth DURST
51 VP Continuing Ed/Student Services .... Dr. Edward DADEZ
84 VP Enrollment & Online Programs .... Ms. Kathryn MCFARLAND
10 VP Business Affairs .... Ms. Jeanne PLECENIK
30 VP University Advancement .... Vacant
04 Assistant to the President .... Ms. Molly-Dodd ADAMS
20 Associate VP Academic Affairs .... Dr. Jeffrey ANDERSON
108 Director of Assessment .... Dr. Robert LUCIO
51 Associate VP Continuing Education .... Dr. Beth CARTER
43 Associate VP/General Counsel .... Ms. Kelly HILL
84 Associate VP Enrollment .... Ms. Dana DAVIES
90 Associate VP/CIO .... Vacant
42 Asst to the Pres for Univ Ministry .... Fr. Stephan BROWN
32 Associate VP Student Services .... Mr. Kenneth POSNER
38 Director Counseling Services .... Mr. Lawson JOLLY
49 Dean School of Arts & Sciences .... Dr. Mary SPOTO
75 Dean School of Educ/Social Svcs .... Dr. Carol WALKER
50 Dean School of Business .... Dr. Michael NASTANSKI
58 Dir Graduate Studies in Business .... Dr. Lorrie MCGOVERN
58 Dir Grad Studies in Crim Justice .... Dr. Robert DIEMER
58 Dir Grad Studies in Education .... Dr. Sharyn DISABATO
58 Dir Grad Studies in Social Work .... Dr. Cindy LEE
58 Dir Graduate Studies in Theology .... Vacant
06 Registrar .... Mrs. Karen HATFIELD
08 Director Library Services .... Mr. Brent SHORT
07 Assoc VP of Enrollment/Stdnt Svcs .... Mr. Jeff WALSH
88 Asst VP Instructional Technology .... Dr. Susan COLARIC
88 Dir Academic Student Support Svcs .... Dr. Joanne MACEACHRAN
11 Director Academic Administration .... Mr. Joseph TADEO
41 Director Athletics .... Mr. Fran REIDY
26 Director University Communications .... Ms. Maureen MOORE
18 Director Physical Plant .... Mr. Jose CABAN
19 Director Campus Security & Safety .... Mr. Howar MCEVER
23 Director Health Center .... Ms. Teresa DADEZ
88 Asst Director Disability Services .... Ms. Christine GEORGALLIS
35 Asst VP for Student Services .... Ms. Ana DI DONATO
29 Director Alumni Relations .... Mr. Edmond KENNY
44 Exec Director Development .... Ms. Dawn PARISI
85 Assoc Director International Svcs .... Ms. Paige RAMSEY-HAMACHER
15 Human Resources Manager .... Ms. Theresa KLUENDER
36 Director of Career Planning .... Mr. Robert LIDDELL
21 Assoc VP Finance .... Ms. Christine GIBSON
12 Asst VP Continuing Ed Virginia .... Ms. Susan PAULSON
12 Asst VP Continuing Ed Central Reg .... Mr. Jack NUSSEN
12 Asst VP Continuing Ed Florida .... Mr. Stephen HESS
103 Director Professional Development .... Ms. Anne KIBBE
88 Director Dining Services .... Mr. Rich VOGEL

St. Petersburg College (E)

PO Box 13489, Saint Petersburg FL 33733-3489
County: Pinellas FICE Identification: 001528
Unit ID: 137078
Telephone: (727) 341-4772 Carnegie Class: Bac/Assoc
FAX Number: (727) 341-3318 Calendar System: Semester
URL: www.spcollege.edu
Established: 1927 Annual Undergrad Tuition & Fees (In-District): $3,171
Enrollment: 33,128 Coed
Affiliation or Control: Local IRS Status: 501(c)3
Highest Offering: Baccalaureate
Program: Occupational; 2-Year Principally Bachelor's Creditable; Teacher Preparatory; Professional
Accreditation: **SC**, ADNUR, CAHIIM, COARC, DH, EMT, FUSER, NURSE, OPE, PTAA, RAD

01 President .... Dr. William D. LAW
05 Sr VP Instruction/Academic Pgm .... Dr. Anne M. COOPER
32 Sr Vice Pres Student Affairs .... Dr. Tonjua L. WILLIAMS
11 VP Admin/Bus Svcs & Info Technology .... Dr. Douglas S. DUNCAN
46 VP Economic Dev & Innov Projects .... Dennis L. JONES
18 VP Facilities Plng/Inst Svcs .... Mr. James WALCHTER
15 VP Human Resources/Strategic Comm .... Patty JONES
30 VP Inst Advance/Exec Dir Foundation .... Frances NEU
45 Assoc VP Planning/Budget/Compliance .... Jamelle CONNER
84 Assoc VP Enrollment Mgmt .... Dr. Pat RINARD
37 Assoc VP Financial Asst Svcs .... Michael J. BENNETT
20 Assoc VP Academic Affs/Partnership .... Catherine C. KENNEDY
41 Director Athletics .... Mark STRICKLAND
26 Dir Marketing/Public Information .... Michael O'KEEFFE
103 Director Workforce Services .... Dr. Jason KRUPP
43 Acting General Counsel .... Suzanne GARDNER
12 Provost Allstate Center .... J. C. BROCK
12 Provost Clearwater Campus .... Dr. Stanley VITTETOE
12 Provost/Health Education Center .... Dr. Phil NICOTERA
12 Provost St Petersburg Campus .... Dr. Karen K. WHITE
12 Provost Seminole Campus/eCampus .... Dr. James OLLIVER
12 Provost Tarpon Springs Campus .... Dr. Conferlete CARNEY
12 Provost Downtown Center .... Dr. Kevin GORDON
22 Dir Equal Access/Equal Opportunity .... Pam SMITH
96 Dir Procurement & Asset Mgmt .... Paul SPINELLI
38 Dir Student Success .... Joe DVORACSEK
88 Dean College of Public Safety Admin .... Brian FRANK
88 Dean Col of Policy/Legal Studies .... Susan S. DEMERS
83 Dean Social & Behavioral Sciences .... Dr. Joseph SMILEY
88 Principal St Pete Collegiate High .... Starla METZ
88 President Faculty Senate .... Dr. Richard MERCADANTE

St. Thomas University (F)

16401 NW 37th Avenue, Miami Gardens FL 33054-6498
County: Miami-Dade FICE Identification: 001468
Unit ID: 137476
Telephone: (305) 625-6000 Carnegie Class: Master's L
FAX Number: (305) 628-6510 Calendar System: Semester
URL: www.stu.edu
Established: 1961 Annual Undergrad Tuition & Fees: $26,370
Enrollment: 2,439 Coed
Affiliation or Control: Roman Catholic IRS Status: 501(c)3
Highest Offering: Doctorate
Program: Liberal Arts And General; Teacher Preparatory; Professional
Accreditation: **SC**, LAW

01 President .... Msgr. Franklyn M. CASALE
05 Provost & Chief Academic Officer .... Dr. Gregory S. CHAN
10 VP Administration/Chief Exec Ofcr .... Mr. Terrence L. O'CONNER
61 Dean of Law School .... Mr. Douglas RAY
30 Vice Pres University Advancement .... Ms. Beverly BACHRACH
45 Vice Pres for Planning & Enrollment .... Vacant
20 Associate Provost .... Dr. Susan ANGULO
84 Dean Enrollment .... Mr. Andre M. LIGHTBOURN
26 Chief Marketing Officer .... Ms. Marivi PRADO
06 Executive Associate Registrar .... Mrs. Maria ABDEL
37 Assoc Director Financial Aid .... Ms. Yaidany RIVERO
08 University Librarian .... Mr. Lawrence TREADWELL, IV
21 Controller .... Mrs. Maribel SMITH
18 Director Facilities/Physical Plant .... Mr. Juan M. ZAMORA
09 Director Institutional Research .... Dr. Jerry WEINBERG
88 Director Emergency Management .... Mr. Timothy DEPALMA
41 Athletic Director .... Mrs. Laura J. COURTLEY-TODD
07 Director of Admissions .... Mr. Celso J. ALVAREZ
32 Dean of Students .... Vacant
15 Assoc Director Human Resources .... Ms. Lenore M. PRADO
25 Director for Prospect Research .... Ms. Susan M. SMITH
38 Assoc Director Health & Wellness .... Vacant
73 Interim Dean School of Theology .... RevMsg. Terrance E. HOGAN
12 Dean Biscayne College .... Dr. Scott C. ZEMAN
27 Chief Information Officer .... Mr. Rudy IBARRA
29 Director Alumni Affairs .... Ms. Yisel CABRERA
44 Director Annual Giving .... Vacant
11 Director for Administration .... Mrs. Sylvia L. RODRIGUEZ

St. Vincent De Paul Regional Seminary (G)

10701 S Military Trail, Boynton Beach FL 33436-4899
County: Palm Beach FICE Identification: 008223
Unit ID: 136701
Telephone: (561) 732-4424 Carnegie Class: Spec/Faith
FAX Number: (561) 737-2205 Calendar System: Semester
URL: www.svdp.edu
Established: 1963 Annual Graduate Tuition & Fees: $32,000
Enrollment: 86 Coed
Affiliation or Control: Roman Catholic IRS Status: 501(c)3
Highest Offering: Master's; No Undergraduates
Program: Religious Emphasis
Accreditation: **#SC**, THEOL

01 Rector/President .... Rev. David L. TOUPS
03 Vice Rector .... Rev. Jose ALFARO
05 Academic Dean/Registrar .... Deacon Dennis DEMES
10 Treasurer .... Mr. Keith PARKER
08 Director of the Library .... Mr. Arthur QUINN

San Ignacio College (H)

10395 NW 41st St, Ste 125, Doral FL 33178
County: Miami-Dade Identification: 667130
Telephone: (305) 629-2929 Carnegie Class: Not Classified
FAX Number: (305) 629-2910 Calendar System: Semester
URL: www.sanignaciocollege.edu
Established: Annual Undergrad Tuition & Fees: $9,400
Enrollment: N/A Coed
Affiliation or Control: Proprietary IRS Status: Proprietary
Highest Offering: Associate Degree
Program: Occupational; 2-Year Principally Bachelor's Creditable
Accreditation: **ACICS**

01 President .... Alex AZCUY

Sanford-Brown Institute (I)

1201 W Cypress Creek Road, Ste 101,
Fort Lauderdale FL 33309
Telephone: (954) 308-7400 Identification: 667031
Accreditation: **ACICS**, CVT, DH, DMS, SURTEC

† Main campus is Sanford-Brown College in Atlanta, GA.

Sanford-Brown Institute (J)

10255 Fortune Parkway, Suite #501,
Jacksonville FL 32256-0757
County: Duval FICE Identification: 026164
Unit ID: 404505
Telephone: (904) 363-6221 Carnegie Class: Assoc/PrivFP
FAX Number: (904) 363-6824 Calendar System: Other
URL: www.sanfordbrown.edu/Jacksonville
Established: 1977 Annual Undergrad Tuition & Fees: $13,300
Enrollment: 357 Coed

Affiliation or Control: Proprietary IRS Status: Proprietary
Highest Offering: Associate Degree
Program: Occupational
Accreditation: ACICS, CVT, DH

01 President .... Vacant
05 Director of Education .... Ms. Jennifer MULLINGS

Sanford-Brown Institute (A)

5959 Lake Ellenor Drive, Orlando FL 32809
Telephone: (407) 393-1464 Identification: 770689
Accreditation: ACICS

† Main campus is Le Cordon Bleu College of Culinary Arts in Los Angeles in Pasadena, CA.

Sanford-Brown Institute (B)

5701 E Hillsborough Ave, Suite 1417,
Tampa FL 33610-5428
Telephone: (813) 393-4250 Identification: 666027
Accreditation: ACICS

† Main campus is Sanford-Brown Institute in Jacksonville, FL.

Santa Fe College (C)

3000 NW 83rd Street, Gainesville FL 32606-6200
County: Alachua FICE Identification: 001519
Unit ID: 137096
Telephone: (352) 395-5000 Carnegie Class: Assoc/Pub-R-L
FAX Number: (352) 395-5581 Calendar System: Semester
URL: www.sfcollege.edu
Established: 1965 Annual Undergrad Tuition & Fees (In-District): $3,164
Enrollment: 16,867 Coed
Affiliation or Control: Local IRS Status: 501(c)3
Highest Offering: Baccalaureate
Program: Occupational; 2-Year Principally Bachelor's Creditable
Accreditation: SC, ADNUR, CAHIIM, CONST, CVT, DA, DH, DMS, EMT, NMT, PNUR, POLYT, RAD, SURGT

01 President .... Dr. Jackson N. SASSER
05 Provost/Vice Pres Academic Affairs .... Dr. Edward BONAHUE
10 Chief Financial Ofcr/VP Admin Affs .... Ms. Ginger GIBSON
32 Int Vice President Student Affairs .... Dr. Naima BROWN
30 Vice President Development .... Mr. Chuck CLEMONS
108 VP Assessment/Research/Technology .... Dr. Lisa ARMOUR
04 Assistant to the President .... Ms. Cathy KEEN
20 Associate VP Academic Affairs .... Dr. Curtis JEFFERSON
13 Assoc VP Information Tech Services .... Mr. Timothy C. NESLER
18 Assoc VP Facilities Services .... Mr. William REESE
35 Assoc VP Student Affs/Financial Aid .... Dr. Dan RODKIN
88 Assoc Vice Pres Educational Centers .... Ms. Bennye J. ALLIGOOD
25 Asst VP/Development/Grants/Projects .... Ms. Joan M. SUCHORSKI
20 Assoc Vice Pres Academic Affairs .... Dr. Dave YONUTAS
35 Asst Vice Pres Student Affairs .... Dr. Beatrice AWONIYI
43 Legal Counsel .... Ms. Patti P. LOCASCIO
06 College Registrar .... Ms. Lynn SULLIVAN
88 Dir High Sch Dual Enrollment Pgm .... Ms. Linda LANZA-KADUCE
88 Director Advisement Center .... Ms. Kimberly FUGATE-ROBERTS
41 Athletic Director .... Mr. Jim KEITES
08 Director Library Service .... Ms. Myra STERRETT
19 Director Institute of Public Safety .... Capt. Daryl JOHNSTON
35 Director Student Life .... Vacant
96 Director of Purchasing .... Mr. David SHLAFER
28 Director of Diversity .... Ms. Elizabeth O'REGGIO
37 Director Student Financial Aid .... Ms. Maureen MCFARLANE
15 Director Human Resources .... Ms. Lela FRYE

Schiller International University (D)

8560 Ulmerton Road, Largo FL 33771
County: Pinellas FICE Identification: 023141
Unit ID: 404338
Telephone: (727) 736-5082 Carnegie Class: Spec/Bus
FAX Number: (727) 734-0359 Calendar System: Semester
URL: www.schiller.edu
Established: 1964 Annual Undergrad Tuition & Fees: $20,610
Enrollment: 174 Coed
Affiliation or Control: Proprietary IRS Status: Proprietary
Highest Offering: Master's
Program: Occupational; Liberal Arts And General; Business Emphasis
Accreditation: ACICS

01 Chancellor .... Mr. Bill BROOKS
05 Provost .... Dr. Angela CARNEY
07 Director of Admissions .... Mr. Phillip CLARK

Seminole State College of Florida (E)

100 Weldon Boulevard, Sanford FL 32773-6199
County: Seminole FICE Identification: 001520
Unit ID: 137209
Telephone: (407) 708-4722 Carnegie Class: Assoc/Pub-S-SC
FAX Number: (407) 708-2139 Calendar System: Semester
URL: www.seminolestate.edu
Established: 1965 Annual Undergrad Tuition & Fees (In-District): $3,131
Enrollment: 19,572 Coed
Affiliation or Control: Local IRS Status: 501(c)3
Highest Offering: Baccalaureate
Program: Occupational; 2-Year Principally Bachelor's Creditable; Professional
Accreditation: SC, ADNUR, CAHIIM, COARC, EMT, PTAA

01 President .... Dr. E. Ann MCGEE
10 Executive VP/CFO .... Dr. Joseph SARNOVSKY
05 VP Academic Affairs/CAO .... Dr. Laura ROSS
32 VP Student Affairs/CSAO .... Dr. Marcia ROMAN
13 VP Information Resources/CIO .... Mr. Dick T. HAMANN
102 Executive Director Foundation .... Mr. John GYLLIN
21 AVP Finance & Budget .... Ms. Lynn POWERS
26 AVP College Relations .... Mr. Michael GARLICH
30 AVP Student Development .... Dr. Jan LLOYD
12 Provost Altamonte Springs .... Ms. Lynn COLON
12 Provost Oviedo Campus .... Mr. Robert LEDFORD
28 Director Diversity and Inclusion .... Dr. Yolanda WILLIAMS
08 Dean Learning Resources .... Ms. Patricia D. DESALVO
36 AVP Career Programs .... Dr. Angela M. KERSENBROCK
54 Dean Engineering and Design .... Mr. Michael STALEY
51 Dean Academic Foundations .... Dr. Terri DANIELS
86 Director Government Relations .... Mr. Donald PAYTON
91 Director Networks .... Mr. Julio VALENTIN
38 Director Counseling and Advising .... Ms. Deborah LYNCH
20 Director Curriculum .... Ms. Christine BROEKER
15 AVP Human Resources .... Ms. Mae KLINE
07 Dir Enrollment Svcs/Registrar .... Ms. Sonja BOLES
37 Director Student Financial Aid .... Ms. Carmen AFGHANI
09 AVP Institutional Effectiveness .... Dr. Mark MORGAN
41 Director Intercollegiate Athletics .... Mr. John SCARPINO
07 AVP Student Recruitment .... Mrs. Pamela MENNECHEY
36 Director Career Development .... Mrs. Christy KING
14 AVP Information Technology .... Ms. Pilar ACOSTA

South Florida Bible College (F)

1100 South Federal Highway, Deerfield Beach FL 33441
County: Broward FICE Identification: 032643
Unit ID: 366003
Telephone: (954) 545-4500 Carnegie Class: Spec/Faith
FAX Number: (954) 719-3780 Calendar System: Semester
URL: www.sfbc.edu
Established: 1985 Annual Undergrad Tuition & Fees: $5,550
Enrollment: 72 Coed
Affiliation or Control: Interdenominational IRS Status: 501(c)3
Highest Offering: Master's
Program: Professional; Religious Emphasis
Accreditation: BI

01 President .... Dr. Joseph GUADAGNINO
03 Provost .... Mary A. DRABIK
10 Chief Financial Officer .... Beatrice GUADAGNINO
06 Registrar .... Tom DAVIS
08 Librarian .... Paula STEVENSON
05 Dean of Faculty .... Dr. Thomas DRABIK
32 Dean of Students .... Dr. John STEVENSON

South Florida State College (G)

600 W College Drive, Avon Park FL 33825-9399
County: Highlands FICE Identification: 001522
Unit ID: 137315
Telephone: (863) 453-6661 Carnegie Class: Assoc/Pub-R-M
FAX Number: (863) 453-0165 Calendar System: Trimester
URL: www.southflorida.edu
Established: 1965 Annual Undergrad Tuition & Fees (In-District): $3,136
Enrollment: 2,841 Coed
Affiliation or Control: Local IRS Status: 501(c)3
Highest Offering: Baccalaureate
Program: Occupational; 2-Year Principally Bachelor's Creditable
Accreditation: SC, ADNUR, DA, DH, RAD

01 President .... Dr. Thomas C. LEITZEL
05 Vice Pres Educational/Stdnt Svcs .... Dr. Leana REVELL
11 Vice Pres Administrative Services .... Mr. Glenn W. LITTLE
20 Dean Academic Support .... Dr. Michael MCLEOD
75 Dean Applied Science & Tech .... Mr. J. Kevin BROWN
49 Dean Arts & Sciences .... Dr. Kimberly BATTY-HERBERT
88 Dean Cultural Programming .... Mr. Douglas M. ANDREWS
45 Dean Resource Development .... Mr. Donald L. APPELQUIST
32 Dean Student Services .... Mrs. Annie ALEXANDER-HARVEY
12 Director DeSoto Campus .... Mrs. Suzanne DEMERS
12 Director Hardee Campus .... Ms. Teresa CRAWFORD
12 Director Lake Placid Center .... Mr. Randall K. PAEPLOW
21 Controller .... Mrs. Anita A. KOVACS
26 Director Community Relations .... Ms. Deborah LATTER
72 Director Educational Tech Center .... Mrs. Melanie M. JACKSON
15 Director Human Res/EA-EO & ADA Ofcr .... Mrs. Susie HALE
18 Dir Phys Plant/Opers/Maintenance .... Mr. Roberto FLORES
06 Registrar .... Dr. Deborah M. FUSCHETTI
41 Athletic Director .... Mr. Richard J. HITT
36 Director Career Development Center .... Mrs. Colleen RAFATTI
37 Director Financial Aid .... Ms. Susie JOHNSON
13 Dir Information Tech/Inst Research .... Dr. Christopher VAN DER KAAY
38 Director Student Counseling .... Ms. Felecia DOZIER
08 Library Services .... Ms. Lena PHELPS-ELLERKER
40 Manager College Bookstore .... Mr. Gene HALEY
96 Coordinator Purchasing .... Mr. Richard PEAVY
10 Chief Business Officer .... Mrs. Anita A. KOVACS
07 Director of Admissions .... Ms. Lynn HINTZ
09 Director of Institutional Research .... Dr. Christopher VAN DER KAAY

South University (H)

9801 Belevedere Road, Royal Palm Beach FL 33411
Telephone: (561) 273-6500 Identification: 666117
Accreditation: &SC, NURSE, PTAA

† Main campus is South University in Savannah, GA.

South University (I)

4401 North Himes Ave Ste 175, Tampa FL 33614-7095
Telephone: (813) 393-3800 Identification: 770913
Accreditation: &SC, ARCPA, NURSE, PTAA

† Main campus is South University in Savannah, GA.

Southeastern College (J)

6812 Forest Hills Blvd, Suite D-1, Greenacres FL 33413
County: Palm Beach FICE Identification: 031239
Unit ID: 428170
Telephone: (561) 433-2330 Carnegie Class: Not Classified
FAX Number: (561) 433-9025 Calendar System: Other
URL: www.sec.edu
Established: 1988 Annual Undergrad Tuition & Fees: $15,664
Enrollment: 1,341 Coed
Affiliation or Control: Proprietary IRS Status: Proprietary
Highest Offering: Associate Degree
Program: Occupational
Accreditation: ACCSC, MAAB, SURGT

01 Vice President .... Ms. Christine HOOVER

Southeastern College (K)

6700 South Point Pkwy, Ste 400, Jacksonville FL 32216
County: Duval FICE Identification: 035533
Unit ID: 443270
Telephone: (904) 448-9499 Carnegie Class: Assoc/PrivFP
FAX Number: (904) 448-9270 Calendar System: Other
URL: www.sec.edu
Established: 1988 Annual Undergrad Tuition & Fees: $15,664
Enrollment: 194 Coed
Affiliation or Control: Proprietary IRS Status: Proprietary
Highest Offering: Associate Degree
Program: Occupational
Accreditation: ACCSC, SURTEC

01 Campus Vice President .... Mr. Shawn HUMPHREY

Southeastern College (L)

17395 NW 59th Avenue, Miami Lakes FL 33015-5111
Telephone: (305) 820-5003 Identification: 666290
Accreditation: ACCSC, MAAB, SURGT

† Main campus is Southeastern College in Greenacres, FL.

Southeastern College (M)

6014 Hwy 19 North, Suite 250, New Port Richey FL 34652
Telephone: (727) 487-6855 Identification: 770568
Accreditation: ACCSC, DMS

† Main campus is Southeastern College in Greenacres, FL.

Southeastern College (N)

11208 Blue Heron Boulevard, Suite A,
St. Petersburg FL 33716
Telephone: (727) 576-6500 Identification: 666758
Accreditation: ACCSC, MAAB, SURGT

† Main campus is Southeastern College in Greenacres, FL.

Southeastern College (O)

15453 N Dale Mabry Highway, Tampa FL 33618
Telephone: (561) 433-2330 Identification: 770569
Accreditation: ACCSC

† Main campus is Southeastern College in Greenacres, FL.

Southeastern University (P)

1000 Longfellow Boulevard, Lakeland FL 33801-6099
County: Polk FICE Identification: 001521
Unit ID: 137564
Telephone: (863) 667-5000 Carnegie Class: Bac/Diverse
FAX Number: (863) 667-5200 Calendar System: Semester
URL: www.seu.edu
Established: 1935 Annual Undergrad Tuition & Fees: $18,596
Enrollment: 2,703 Coed
Affiliation or Control: Assemblies Of God Church IRS Status: 501(c)3
Highest Offering: Master's
Program: Liberal Arts And General; Teacher Preparatory; Religious Emphasis
Accreditation: SC, IACBE, SW

01 President .... Dr. Kent INGLE
03 Executive Vice President .... Mr. Del CHITTIM
05 Provost .... Dr. William C. HACKET, JR.

10 Vice Pres Finance/Administration ....Dr. Dan MORTENSEN
30 VP for University Advancement ....Mr. Brian C. CARROLL
35 VP for Student Development ....Mr. James (Chris) OWEN
84 VP for Enrollment Management ....Mr. Roy ROWLAND, IV
09 Assoc Provost/Dean Inst Research ....Dr. Andrew H. PERMENTER
08 Dean of Library Services ....Mrs. Grace VEACH
06 Dir Student Records/Registrar ....Mrs. Linda M. KELSO
37 Director Student Financial Services ....Ms. Rebekah BURDICK
07 Director of Admission ....Ms. Betania TORRES
15 Int Director Human Resources ....Ms. Betty KELLEY
29 Director Alumni Relations ....Ms. Jebapriya ARUL
18 Chief Facilities/Physical Plant ....Mr. Norman M. ALDERMAN
88 Director of Academic Success ....Mrs. Pamela CROSBY
36 Director of Career Services ....Mrs. Jacquelyn SMALL
21 Controller ....Mr. Frederick S. GORE
84 Director Enrollment Marketing ....Mr. Edward MANER
38 Director Student Counseling ....Mr. Donald SMITH
88 Dir of Institutional Effectiveness ....Mr. Andrew MILLER

Southern Technical College (A)

2910 South Orlando Drive, Sanford FL 32773
County: Seminole FICE Identification: 039035
Unit ID: 446552
Telephone: (407) 323-4141 Carnegie Class: Assoc/PrivFP
FAX Number: (407) 323-4221 Calendar System: Semester
URL: www.southerntech.edu
Established: 1956 Annual Undergrad Tuition & Fees: $30,975
Enrollment: 1,398 Coed
Affiliation or Control: Proprietary IRS Status: Proprietary
Highest Offering: Associate Degree
Program: Occupational
Accreditation: ACICS

01 Dean ....Mr. Dwayne ORE

Southern Technical College-Auburndale (B)

298 Havendale Boulevard, Auburndale FL 33823
Telephone: (407) 438-6000 Identification: 770705
Accreditation: ACICS

† Main campus is Southern Technical College in Sanford, FL.

Southern Technical College-Brandon (C)

608 E Bloomingdale Avenue, Brandon FL 33511
Telephone: (813) 654-8800 Identification: 770707
Accreditation: ACICS

† Main campus is Southern Technical College in Sanford, FL.

Southern Technical College-Mount Dora (D)

2799 W Old US Highway 441, Mount Dora FL 32757
Telephone: (352) 383-4242 Identification: 770706
Accreditation: ACICS

† Main campus is Southern Technical College in Sanford, FL.

Southern Technical College-Orlando (E)

1485 Florida Mall Avenue, Orlando FL 32809
Telephone: (407) 438-6000 Identification: 770704
Accreditation: ACICS

† Main campus is Southern Technical College in Sanford, FL.

Southwest Florida College (F)

1685 Medical Lane, Fort Myers FL 33907-1158
County: Lee FICE Identification: 022788
Unit ID: 366553
Telephone: (239) 939-4766 Carnegie Class: Bac/Assoc
FAX Number: (239) 790-2118 Calendar System: Quarter
URL: www.swfc.edu
Established: 1974 Annual Undergrad Tuition & Fees: $13,860
Enrollment: 1,284 Coed
Affiliation or Control: Proprietary IRS Status: Proprietary
Highest Offering: Baccalaureate
Program: Occupational; 2-Year Principally Bachelor's Creditable; Teacher Preparatory; Professional; Business Emphasis
Accreditation: ACICS, MAAB, SURTEC

01 President ....Mr. Jim MATHIS
05 VP of Academic Affairs ....Dr. Melanie YERK

Southwest Florida College (G)

950 Tamiami Trail, Unit 109, Port Charlotte FL 33953
Telephone: (239) 274-5860 Identification: 770709
Accreditation: ACICS

† Main campus is Southwest Florida College in Fort Myers, FL.

Southwest Florida College (H)

3910 RIGA Boulevard, Tampa FL 33619-1269
Telephone: (813) 630-4401 Identification: 770708
Accreditation: ACICS

† Main campus is Southwest Florida College in Fort Myers, FL.

State College of Florida, Manatee-Sarasota (I)

PO Box 1849, Bradenton FL 34206-7046
County: Manatee FICE Identification: 001504
Unit ID: 135391
Telephone: (941) 752-5000 Carnegie Class: Assoc/Pub-U-MC
FAX Number: (941) 758-6830 Calendar System: Semester
URL: www.scf.edu
Established: 1957 Annual Undergrad Tuition & Fees (In-District): $3,074
Enrollment: 10,800 Coed
Affiliation or Control: Local IRS Status: 501(c)3
Highest Offering: Baccalaureate
Program: Occupational; 2-Year Principally Bachelor's Creditable
Accreditation: SC, ADNUR, DH, NUR, OTA, PTAA, RAD

01 President ....Dr. Carol F. PROBSTFELD
04 Exec Assistant to President ....Ms. Susan MARROCCO
10 Vice President Business/Admin Svcs ....Ms. Julie JAKWAY
05 VP Academic Affairs ....Mr. Gary T. RUSSELL
32 VP Educational & Student Services ....Dr. Donald R. BOWMAN
12 Provost Bradenton/VP Baccalaureate ....Dr. Michael J. MEARS
12 Provost Venice Campus ....Ms. Darlene WEDLER-JOHNSON
102 Exec Dir SCF Foundation Inc ....Vacant
15 Executive Director Human Resources ....Ms. Margaret Z. BECK
21 Assoc VP Finance ....Ms. Karen A. KESTER
38 Assoc VP Student Development ....Ms. Lynn DREES
06 Assoc VP Student Services ....Ms. MariLynn J. LEWY
31 Assoc VP Corporate & Community Dev ......Ms. Daisy VULOVICH
25 Assoc VP Planning & Inst Effect ....Mr. Bradley W. DAVIS
18 Director Facilities Manager ....Mr. Chris WELLMAN
51 Director Inst of Continuing/Cmty Ed ....Ms. Cynthia HUNTER
19 Director Business Svc/Public Safety ...Mr. Timothy LANGENBACK
22 Equity Officer ....Ms. Gloria TRACY
08 Director Library Services ....Ms. Tracy ELLIOTT
09 Director Institutional Research ....Ms. Su-hua MEN
14 Chief Information Officer ....Mr. Feng HOU
26 Director Public Affairs & Marketing ....Ms. Katherine WALKER
37 Director Financial Aid ....Ms. Sandra SHIMP
40 Manager Bookstore ....Mrs. Betty J. GIBSON
36 Director Career Resource Center ....Ms. Denise D. GATCH
41 Director Athletics ....Mr. Matt ENNIS
88 Director Academic Resource Center ....Ms. Jacquelyn MCNEIL
43 General Counsel ....Mr. Steve PROUTY
88 Head of SCF Collegiate School ....Ms. Kelly MONOD

*State University System of Florida, Board of Governors (J)

325 W Gaines Street, Suite 1614,
Tallahassee FL 32399-0400
County: Leon FICE Identification: 008068
Unit ID: 137449
Telephone: (850) 245-0466 Carnegie Class: N/A
FAX Number: (850) 245-9685
URL: www.flbog.edu

01 Chancellor ....Mr. Frank T. BROGAN
05 Vice Chanc Academic/Student Affairs ....Dr. Jan IGNASH
10 Vice Chanc Budget & Finance ....Mr. Tim JONES
43 General Counsel ....Ms. Vikki SHIRLEY
22 Inspector General & Compliance ....Mr. Derry HARPER
101 Corporate Secretary ....Ms. Monoka VENTERS
100 Chief of Staff ....Mr. Randy A. GOIN, JR.

*Florida Agricultural and Mechanical University (K)

1601 S. Martin Luther King Jr. Blvd, Tallahassee FL 32307
County: Leon FICE Identification: 001480
Unit ID: 133650
Telephone: (850) 599-3000 Carnegie Class: DRU
FAX Number: (850) 599-3952 Calendar System: Semester
URL: www.famu.edu
Established: 1887 Annual Undergrad Tuition & Fees (In-State): $5,785
Enrollment: 12,051 Coed
Affiliation or Control: State IRS Status: 501(c)3
Highest Offering: Doctorate
Program: Occupational; Liberal Arts And General; Teacher Preparatory; Professional
Accreditation: #SC, ACBSP, CAHIIM, COARC, CS, ENG, ENGT, JOUR, LAW, NUR, OT, PH, PHAR, PTA, SW, TED

02 Interim President ....Dr. Larry ROBINSON
05 Provost/Vice Pres Academic Affs ....Dr. Rodner WRIGHT
10 Int Vice Pres Admin & Fin Svcs/CFO ....Mr. Joseph BAKKER
32 Vice Pres Student Affairs ....Dr. William HUDSON, JR.
30 VP University Relations ....Dr. Thomas HAYNES
25 Interim VP for Sponsored Research ....Dr. Kinfe K. REDDA
88 VP Audit and Compliance ....Mr. Richard GIVENS
13 Interim VP/CIO Enterprise Tech ....Mr. Michael JAMES
35 Assoc Vice Pres Student Affairs ....Mr. Henry KIRBY
44 Asst VP for University Development ....Mrs. Shirley RANGE
20 Associate VP for Academic Affairs ....Ms. Linda BARGE-MILES
06 University Registrar ....Dr. Agatha ONWUNLI
43 VP for Legal Affs & General Counsel ....Atty. Avery MCKNIGHT
07 Director of Admissions ....Ms. Barbara COX
08 Director of University Libraries ....Dr. Ruth SWANN
37 Director of Financial Aid ....Ms. Lisa STEWART
36 Director of The Career Center ....Dr. Delores DEAN
09 Director of Institutional Research ....Dr. Kwadwo OWUSU-ADUEMIRI
28 Director of EEO ....Ms. Carrie GAVIN
26 Chief Public Relations Officer ....Mrs. Sharon SAUNDERS
21 University Controller ....Dr. William FEATHERSTONE
15 Assistant VP for Human Resources ....Ms. Sherrye EARST
29 Director of Alumni Affairs ....Mrs. Carmen CUMMINGS
51 Director of Continuing Education ....Mrs. Phyllis WATSON
50 Dean of Business and Industry .....Dr. Shawnta FRIDAY-STROUD
66 Interim Dean of Nursing ....Dr. Ruena NORMAN
67 Dean of Pharmacy ....Dr. Michael THOMPSON
53 Interim Dean of Education ....Dr. Patricia GREEN POWELL
72 Dean College of Science & Tech ....Dr. Maurice EDINGTON
48 Dean of Architecture ....Mr. Rodner B. WRIGHT
60 Dean of Journalism ....Dr. Ann KIMBROUGH
58 Interim Dean of Graduate Studies ....Dr. Verian THOMAS
76 Dean of Allied Health Sciences ......Dr. Cynthia HUGHES HARRIS
54 Dean FAMU/FSU Engineering ....Dr. Yaw D. YEBOAH
61 Dean College of Law ....Mr. Leroy PERNELL
83 Dean Soc Sci/Arts/Humanities ....Dr. Valencia E. MATTHEWS
19 Chief of Police/Dir Public Safety ....Mr. Terence CALLOWAY
23 Director of Student Health Services ....Ms. Tanya TATUM
41 Interim Director of Athletics ....Mr. Michael SMITH
38 Director Counseling Services ....Dr. Yolanda BOGAN
96 Director of Purchasing ....Ms. Stephany FALL
04 Assistant to the President ....Mrs. Ora MUKES
88 Dean of Environmental Sciences ....Dr. Victor IBEANUSI
86 Director of Governmental Relations ....Mr. Tola THOMPSON
47 Dean College of Agri/Food Science ....Dr. Robert TAYLOR

*Florida Atlantic University (L)

PO Box 3091, 777 Glades Road,
Boca Raton FL 33431-0991
County: Palm Beach FICE Identification: 001481
Unit ID: 133669
Telephone: (561) 297-3000 Carnegie Class: RU/H
FAX Number: (561) 297-3942 Calendar System: Semester
URL: www.fau.edu
Established: 1961 Annual Undergrad Tuition & Fees (In-State): $5,388
Enrollment: 30,301 Coed
Affiliation or Control: State IRS Status: 501(c)3
Highest Offering: Doctorate
Program: Liberal Arts And General; Teacher Preparatory; Professional
Accreditation: SC, BUS, CACREP, CORE, CS, ENG, #MED, MUS, NURSE, PLNG, SP, SPAA, SW, TED

02 Interim President ....Mr. Dennis CRUDELE
45 Vice President Strategic Planning ....Dr. Gitanjali KAUL
05 Acting Prov/Chief Academic Officer ....Dr. Diane ALPERIN
10 Int VP Finance/Chief Fiscal Officer ....Ms. Dororthy RUSSELL
32 Vice President Student Affairs ....Dr. Charles L. BROWN
46 Vice President Research ....Dr. Barry ROSSON
102 Int VP Cmty Engag/Exec Dir FAU Fdn ....Ms. Joanne DAVIS
88 Assoc Vice Pres Univ Architect Ofc ....Mr. Tom DONAUDY
46 Associate Vice President Research ....Dr. Jeffrey ANDERSON
20 Assoc Provost Acad Budget/Planning ....Dr. Norman KAUFMAN
13 Assoc Provost Info Resource Mgmt ....Mr. Jason BALL
29 Vice President Alumni Relations ....Mr. Bradford W. CREWS
27 Dir of Marketing and Creative Svcs ....Mr. William PLATE
21 Assoc Bus Ofcr/Assoc VP For Admin ....Ms. Dorothy RUSSELL
35 Assoc Dean Student Affairs ....Mr. Terry MENA
43 General Counsel ....Mr. David KIAN
27 University Ombudsman ....Ms. Julie-Angela GIFFORD
22 Director EEO Programs ....Ms. Paula BEHUL
84 Assoc VP Enrollment Management ....Dr. Robert SELTZER
63 Dean C E Schmidt Col of Medicine ....Dr. David J. BJORKMAN
20 Assoc Provost Personnel & Programs ....Dr. Diane ALPERIN
80 Dean of Design and Social Inquiry ....Dr. Rosalyn Y. CARTER
49 Interim Dean of Arts & Letters ....Dr. Heather COLTMAN
50 Dean of Business ....Dr. Daniel GROPPER
53 Dean of Education ....Dr. Valerie BRISTOR
54 Int Dean of Engineering/Comp Sci ....Dr. Mohammad ILYAS
66 Dean of Nursing ....Dr. Marlaine SMITH
81 Interim Dean of Science ....Dr. Ingrid JOHANSON
92 Dean of Honors College ....Dr. Jeff BULLER
58 Dean Graduate College ....Dr. Barry T. ROSSON
20 Dean Undergraduate Studies ....Dr. Edward E. PRATT
53 Asst Dean/PK-12 Sch/Educational Pgm ....Mr. Joel HERBST
07 Director Undergraduate Admissions ....Ms. Barbara PLETCHER
90 Director Enterprise Computing Svcs . Mr. Mehran BASIRATMAND
91 Dir Univ Administrative Systems ....Ms. Kay RECKTENWALD
25 Dir Sponsored Programs ....Ms. JoAnn MORETTI
09 Director Inst Effective/Analysis ....Mr. Sheng Chien LEE
24 Dir University Learning Resources ....Ms. Molly MUNRO
06 Registrar ....Dr. Wendy KUTCHNER
08 Dean University Library ....Dr. William MILLER
15 Director Human Resources ....Mr. James ACTON
41 Athletics Director ....Mr. Patrick CHUN
39 Int Director Student Housing ....Ms. Artie JAMISON
36 Dir Career Devel Ctr/Student Place ....Ms. Sandra JAKUBOW
21 Director Business Services ....Ms. Stacy VOLNICK
85 Director Intl Students/Scholar Svcs ....Dr. Mihaela METIANU
37 Director Student Financial Aid ....Ms. Tracy BOULUKOS
23 Director Student Health Services ....Ms. Cathie L. WALLACE
19 Dir Safety & Security/Chief Police ....Chief Charles LOWE
86 Director Government Relations ....Ms. Pamela LANDI
45 Director Facilities Planning ....Mr. Robert RICHMAN
18 Director Physical Plant ....Vacant
42 Director Campus Ministries ....Ms. Elise ANGIOLLIO
38 Dir Counseling & Psychological Svcs ....Dr. Kirk M. DOUGHER
96 Director of Purchasing ....Mr. Ed SCHIFF
28 Assoc Dir Multicultural Affairs ....Dr. Ingrid JONES

88 Director Student Union ... Dr. Larry FAERMAN
88 Dir Office Students w/Disabilities ... Ms. Nicole ROKOS
88 Assoc Director Student Orientation ... Ms. Heather BISHARA
88 Assoc Dir Student Dev/Activities ... Ms. Michele PERKINS
21 University Controller ... Mrs. Stacey SEMMEL
57 Director School of the Arts ... Vacant
60 Dir Sch of Comm/Multimedia Studies ... Dr. Noemi MARIN
88 Director School of Accounting ... Dr. Somnath BHATTACHARYA
88 Dir Complex Systems/Brain Sciences ... Dr. Janet BLANKS
70 Director School of Social Work ... Dr. Michele HAWKINS
80 Dir School of Public Administration ... Dr. Khi THAI
48 Director School of Architecture ... Dr. Deirdre HARDY
88 Dir Center for Env/Urban Solutions ... Dr. James MURLEY
104 Director of International Programs ... Dr. Catherine MESCHIEVITZ
88 Assoc Provost Lifelong Learning ... Dr. Herbert SHAPIRO
94 Director Women's Studies ... Dr. Josephine A. BEOKU-BETTS
65 Dir Pine Jog Environ Education Ctr ... Mr. Ray COLEMAN
53 Dir K Slattery Educ Research Ctr ... Ms. Lydia BARTRAM
54 Dir SeaTech Inst for Ocean Engr ... Dr. Manhar DHANAK
54 Dir Intermodal Trans Safety/Sec Ctr ... Dr. Pete SCARLATOS
88 Dir Harbor Brnch Oceanographic Inst ... Dr. Margaret LEINEN

*Florida Gulf Coast University (A)

10501 FGCU Boulevard S, Fort Myers FL 33965-6565
County: Lee FICE Identification: 032553
Unit ID: 433660
Telephone: (239) 590-1000 Carnegie Class: Master's L
FAX Number: (239) 590-1166 Calendar System: Semester
URL: www.fgcu.edu
Established: 1991 Annual Undergrad Tuition & Fees (In-State): $6,172
Enrollment: 13,442 Coed
Affiliation or Control: State IRS Status: 501(c)3
Highest Offering: Doctorate
Program: Liberal Arts And General; Teacher Preparatory; Professional
Accreditation: SC, ANEST, BUS, CACREP, ENG, MT, NURSE, OT, PTA, SPAA, SW, TED

02 President ... Dr. Wilson G. BRADSHAW
05 Provost & VP Academic Affairs ... Dr. Ronald B. TOLL
10 Vice Pres Admin Services/Finance ... Mr. Steve L. MAGIERA
30 VP Univ Advance/Exec Dir Foundation ... Mr. Christopher (Chris) J. SIMONEAU
32 Vice President Student Affairs ... Dr. J. Michael ROLLO
100 Vice President & Chief of Staff ... Ms. Susan EVANS
43 Vice President & General Counsel ... Ms. Vee LEONARD
20 Assoc VP Academic/Curriculum Sppt ... Dr. Cathy DUFF
45 Sr Asc Prov/Asc VP Plng & Inst Perf ... Dr. Paul SNYDER
58 Assoc VP Research/Dean Grad Studies ... Dr. T. C YIH
26 Asst VP Community Rels/Marketing ... Mr. Ken SCHEXNAYDER
04 Asst to Pres/University Ombudsman ... Ms. Helen MAMARCHEV
88 Asst Vice Pres Business Services ... Mr. Joseph MCDONALD
13 Asst VP Business Technology Svcs ... Ms. Mary BANKS
15 Asst Vice Pres/Dir Human Resources ... Ms. Christine LLOYD
21 Controller/Asst VP Admin Services ... Ms. Linda BACHELER
35 Dean Student Affairs ... Dr. Michele YOVANOVICH
49 Int Dean College Arts & Sciences ... Dr. Aswani VOLETY
20 Dean of Undergraduate Studies ... Dr. Jim WOHLPART
50 Dean Lutgert College of Business ... Dr. Hudson ROGERS
53 Dean College of Education ... Dr. Marcia GREENE
76 Dean College Health Professions ... Dr. Mitchell CORDOVA
54 Dean Whitaker Col of Engineering ... Dr. Richard A. BEHR
62 Dean Library Services ... Dr. Kathleen MILLER
45 Assoc Dean Plng/Inst Performance ... Dr. George ALEXANDER
38 Asst Dean Counselng/Stdnt Hlth Svcs ... Dr. Jon L. BRUNNER
43 Asst Dean Judicial Affairs ... Ms. Cindy LYONS
07 Director of Admissions ... Mr. Marc LAVIOLETTE
96 Director of Procurement Services ... Ms. Maryan EGAN
19 Director Campus Police & Safety ... Chief Steven C. MOORE
18 Director Facilities Planning ... Mr. Tom MAYO
37 Director Student Financial Aid ... Mr. Jorge LOPEZ-ROSADO
06 University Registrar ... Ms. Susan BYARS
23 Director Student Health Services ... Ms. Eileen DONDERO
41 Director Intercollegiate Athletics ... Mr. Kenneth KAVANAGH
28 Director Equity & Diversity ... Mr. Jimmy MYERS
85 Director International Services ... Ms. Elaine HOZDIK
106 Dir Web/E-learning/Publication Svcs ... Mr. David JAEGER
72 Director Academic & Event Tech ... Ms. Pat O'CONNOR-BENSON
36 Director Career Development Svcs ... Mr. Reid LENNERTZ
31 Dir Center for Civic Engagement ... Ms. Jessica RHEA
29 Director Alumni Relations ... Ms. Lindsey TOUCHETTE
92 Director Honors Program ... Dr. Sean KELLY
09 Director Inst Research/Analysis ... Dr. Robert VINES
21 Director University Budgets ... Mr. David VAZQUEZ
39 Director University Housing ... Dr. Brian FISHER
86 Director Government Relations ... Ms. Jennifer GOEN
88 Dir Environmental Health/Safety ... Ms. Rhonda HOLTZCLAW
51 Exec Dir Cont Educ/Off-Campus Pgms ... Dr. Paul THORNTON
88 General Manager/WGCU ... Mr. Rick JOHNSON
40 Manager The University Store ... Ms. Laura JENSEN

*Florida International University (B)

University Park, 11200 SW 8 Street, Miami FL 33199-0001
County: Miami-Dade FICE Identification: 009635
Unit ID: 133951
Telephone: (305) 348-2000 Carnegie Class: RU/H
FAX Number: N/A Calendar System: Semester
URL: www.fiu.edu
Established: 1965 Annual Undergrad Tuition & Fees (In-State): $6,541
Enrollment: 46,261 Coed
Affiliation or Control: State IRS Status: 501(c)3
Highest Offering: Doctorate
Program: Liberal Arts And General; Teacher Preparatory; Professional
Accreditation: SC, ANEST, ART, BUS, BUSA, CACREP, CIDA, CONST, CS, DIETC, DIETD, ENG, FEPAC, HSA, IPSY, JOUR, LAW, LSAR, MED, MUS, NURSE, OT, PH, PTA, SP, SPAA, SW, TED, THEA

02 President ... Dr. Mark ROSENBERG
100 Chief of Staff ... Mr. Javier MARQUES
05 Exec VP Academic Affs/Provost ... Dr. Douglas WARTZOK
88 VP for Engagement ... Dr. Irma BECERRA-FERNANDEZ
20 Vice Provost Academic Affairs ... Dr. Elizabeth BEJAR
10 CFO & Sr VP for Administration ... Dr. Kenneth JESSELL
30 Vice President for Advancement ... Mr. Howard LIPMAN
32 VP Student Affairs ... Dr. Larry LUNSFORD
09 Assoc VP Planning & Inst Research ... Mr. Jeffery GONZALEZ
46 VP for Research ... Dr. Andres GIL
13 Vice President/CIO ... Mr. Robert GRILLO
12 Vice Prov Biscayne Bay Campus ... Mr. Stephen MOLL
84 Assoc VP Enrollment Management ... Ms. Luisa HAVENS
35 Assoc VP Student Affairs ... Ms. Cathy AKENS
45 Assoc VP Strategic Development ... Ms. Liane MARTINEZ
15 Assoc Vice Pres Human Resources ... Dr. Jaffus HARDRICK
18 Assoc VP Facilities Operations ... Mr. John CAL
07 Int Dir Undergraduate Admissions ... Ms. Luisa HAVENS
20 Assoc VP Academic Affairs ... Ms. Tonja MOORE
49 Dean College Arts & Sciences ... Dr. Kenneth FURTON
50 Dean College Business Admin ... Dr. David KLOCK
54 Dean Col Engineering/Computing ... Dr. Amir MIRMIRAN
53 Dean College of Education ... Dr. Delia GARCIA
88 Dean Sch Hospitality Management ... Dr. Mike HAMPTON
60 Dean School Journ/Mass Communic ... Dr. Raul REIS
66 Dean Col Nursing/Health Science ... Dr. Ora STRICKLAND
69 Int Dean College of Public Health ... Dr. Michele CICCAZZO
61 Dean College of Law ... Mr. R. Alexander ACOSTA
63 Dean College of Medicine ... Dr. John ROCK
88 Dean Undergraduate Education ... Dr. Douglas ROBERTSON
58 Dean University Graduate School ... Dr. Lakshmi REDDI
92 Dean Honors College ... Dr. Lesley NORTHUP
48 Dean Col Architecture & the Arts ... Mr. Brian SCHRINER
77 Dir Sch Computing/Info Sciences ... Dr. Sundararaj IYENGAR
64 Director School of Music ... Mr. Orlando GARCIA
38 Int AVP Counseling/Psych Svcs ... Dr. Cheryl NOWELL
22 Director Equal Opportunity Program ... Ms. Shirlyon J. MCWHORTER
88 Director School Accounting ... Dr. Ruth MCEWEN
88 Director Multicultural Programs ... Ms. Dorret SAWYERS
62 Dean of Libraries ... Dr. Anne PRESTAMO
25 Assoc VP Sponsored Research ... Dr. Joseph BARABINO
41 Athletics Director ... Mr. Pete GARCIA
86 Asst VP for Government Affairs ... Ms. Michelle PALACIO
06 Int University Registrar ... Ms. Andrea JAY
86 VP for Government Relations ... Mr. Steve SAULS
88 Dir Community Rel/Special Events ... Ms. Lynda RODRIGUEZ
37 Director Student Financial Aid ... Mr. Francisco VALINES
36 Int Director Career Services ... Ms. Ivette DUARTE
23 Director Univ Health Services ... Dr. Oscar LOYNAZ
39 Executive Director Student Housing ... Ms. Lynn HENDRICKS, JR.
85 Director Intl Student/Scholar Svcs ... Ms. Ana M. SIPPIN
88 Director Disability Student Svcs ... Ms. Amanda NIGUIDULA
88 Director Internal Audit ... Mr. Allen VANN
24 Director Media & Technology Support ... Mr. Matthew HAGOOD
21 Associate VP and Univ Controller ... Ms. Cecilia HAMILTON
14 VP/CIO Information Technology ... Mr. Robert GRILLO
88 Dir Environmentl Health/Safety ... Mr. Roger RIDDLEMOSER
19 Chief of Police ... Chief Alexander CASAS
29 Assoc Vice Pres Alumni Affairs ... Mr. Bill DRAUGHON
27 Director Media Relations ... Ms. Maydel SANTANA-BRAVO
43 General Counsel ... Ms. Kristina RAATTAMA

*Florida State University (C)

Tallahassee FL 32306-9936
County: Leon FICE Identification: 001489
Unit ID: 134097
Telephone: (850) 644-2525 Carnegie Class: RU/VH
FAX Number: (850) 644-9936 Calendar System: Semester
URL: www.fsu.edu
Established: 1851 Annual Undergrad Tuition & Fees (In-State): $6,507
Enrollment: 40,695 Coed
Affiliation or Control: State IRS Status: 501(c)3
Highest Offering: Doctorate
Program: Liberal Arts And General; Teacher Preparatory; Professional
Accreditation: SC, AAFCS, ART, BUS, BUSA, CACREP, CIDA, CLPSY, CORE, CS, DANCE, DIETD, DIETI, ENG, IPSY, LAW, LIB, MED, MFCD, MUS, NURSE, PLNG, PSPSY, SP, SPAA, SW, TED, THEA

02 President ... Dr. Eric J. BARRON
05 Prov/Ex Vice Pres Academic Affs ... Dr. Garnett S. STOKES
10 Interim Vice Pres Finance & Admin ... Mr. David K. COBURN
32 Vice President Student Affairs ... Dr. Mary B. COBURN
46 Vice President Research ... Dr. Gary K. OSTRANDER
26 Vice President University Relations ... Ms. Elizabeth MARYANSKI
45 VP Planning and Programs ... Vacant
30 VP University Advancement ... Mr. Thomas W. JENNINGS
102 Exec VP FSU Foundation ... Mr. Andy A. JHANJI
100 Chief of Staff to President ... Mr. David K. COBURN
88 Assoc Vice President for Research ... Dr. Ross ELLINGTON
18 Associate VP for Facilities ... Mr. Dennis A. BAILEY
21 Assoc VP Budget/Planning/Fin Svcs ... Vacant
20 Associate VP for Academic Affairs ... Ms. Anne BLANKENSHIP
16 Asst Vice Pres for Human Resources ... Ms. Joyce A. INGRAM
11 Asst VP for Administrative Services ... Dr. Perry CROWELL
88 Dir Academic Pgm Professional Svcs ... Mr. Bill LINDNER
20 Vice President Faculty Development ... Dr. Sally E. MCRORIE
49 Dean Arts & Sciences ... Dr. Sam HUCKABA
50 Dean Business ... Dr. Caryn BECK-DUDLEY
53 Dean Education ... Dr. Marcy P. DRISCOLL
59 Dean Human Sciences ... Dr. Billie COLLIER
88 Dean Communication & Information ... Dr. Larry DENNIS
66 Interim Dean Nursing ... Dr. Dianne SPEAKE
88 Dean Criminology ... Dr. Thomas BLOMBERG
61 Dean Law ... Mr. Donald WEIDNER
83 Dean Social Sciences ... Dr. David W. RASMUSSEN
70 Dean Social Work ... Dr. Nicholas MAZZA
88 Dean Motion Picture Arts ... Mr. Frank PATTERSON
64 Dean Music ... Dr. Patricia J. FLOWERS
57 Dean Visual Arts/Theatre/Dance ... Mr. Peter WEISHAR
54 Dean Engineering ... Dr. Yaw YEBOAH
63 Dean Medicine ... Dr. John FOGARTY
58 Dean Graduate Studies ... Dr. Nancy MARCUS
88 Dean Undergraduate Studies ... Dr. Karen L. LAUGHLIN
35 Dean of Students ... Dr. Jeanine WARD-ROOF
12 Dean Panama City Branch Campus ... Dr. Ken SHAW
07 Asst VP Admissions and Records ... Mr. John BARNHILL
06 University Registrar ... Ms. Kimberly BARBER
07 Director Admissions ... Ms. Janice FINNEY
92 Director University Honors Program ... Dr. James MATHES
37 Director Student Financial Aid ... Mr. Darryl MARSHALL
08 Director Libraries ... Ms. Julia ZIMMERMAN
27 Chief Information Officer ... Mr. Michael BARRETT
90 Dir University Computing Services ... Mr. Randy MCCAUSLAND
43 General Counsel ... Ms. Carolyn EGAN
88 Asst VP of University Relations ... Dr. Jeanette DEDIEMAR
104 Director International Programs ... Dr. James E. PITTS
88 Chief Budget Officer ... Mr. Michael P. LAKE
09 Director Institutional Research ... Dr. Richard BURNETTE
86 Director Governmental Relations ... Ms. Kathleen M. DALY
41 Athletic Director ... Mr. Stan WILCOX
38 Director Student Counseling ... Dr. Nikki PRITCHETT
19 Director Public Safety ... Mr. David L. PERRY
23 Director Student Health Services ... Dr. Lesley SACHER
36 Director Career Center ... Ms. Myrna HOOVER
29 President Alumni Association ... Mr. Scott ATWELL
88 Chief Audit Officer ... Mr. Sam MCCALL
28 Dir Office of Diversity/Equal Oppty ... Ms. Renisha L. GIBBS
96 Director of Purchasing ... Ms. Martha DOOLITTLE
39 Director Student Housing ... Ms. Adrienne FRAME
88 Director Business Services ... Mr. Harvey BUCHANAN
106 Director Distance Learning ... Ms. Susann RUDASILL
88 Director Sponsored Research ... Mr. Gregory THOMPSON
88 Director Information Technology ... Mr. Kenneth JOHNSON

*New College of Florida (D)

5800 Bay Shore Road, Sarasota FL 34243-2109
County: Sarasota FICE Identification: 001507
Unit ID: 262129
Telephone: (941) 487-4100 Carnegie Class: Bac/A&S
FAX Number: (941) 487-4101 Calendar System: 4/1/4
URL: www.ncf.edu
Established: 1960 Annual Undergrad Tuition & Fees (In-State): $6,938
Enrollment: 833 Coed
Affiliation or Control: State IRS Status: 501(c)3
Highest Offering: Baccalaureate
Program: Liberal Arts And General
Accreditation: SC

02 President ... Dr. Donal E. O'SHEA
05 Provost ... Dr. Stephen MILES
10 Vice Pres Finance & Administration ... Mr. John U. MARTIN
79 Chair of Humanities ... Dr. Alberto PORTUGAL
81 Chair of Natural Sciences ... Dr. Paul SCUDDER
83 Chair of Social Sciences ... Dr. David HARVEY
08 Dean Cook Library ... Dr. Brian DOHERTY
84 Dean of Enrollment & Info Tech ... Ms. Kathleen KILLION
32 Interim Dean of Students ... Mr. Tracy MURRY
07 Associate Dean of Admissions ... Ms. Sonia WU
20 Associate Academic Officer ... Dr. Robert ZAMSKY
21 Associate Business Officer ... Mr. William LAWHON
13 Director of Information Support ... Mr. Jeff SMITH
29 Director Alumnae/i Association ... Ms. Jessica ROGERS
06 Acting Registrar ... Ms. Marta MORENO
26 Director Public Affairs ... Vacant
38 Director Counseling ... Dr. Anne E. FISHER
09 Director of Institutional Research ... Ms. Hui-Men WEN
15 Director Personnel Services ... Ms. Yevette THORNTON
18 Int Chief Facilities/Physical Plant ... Mr. Alan DAWSON
28 Director of Diversity ... Vacant
96 Director of Purchasing ... Mr. Mark LILLQUIST
37 Director Student Financial Aid ... Ms. Tara KARAS
43 Director Legal Svcs/General Counsel ... Mr. Mark ST. LOUIS
25 Contract Administrator ... Ms. Jeanne VIVIANI
72 Director of Technology Support ... Mr. Jeff SMITH
04 Assistant to the President ... Ms. Suzanne L. JANNEY
30 Chief Development ... Ms. Shannon DUVALL
27 Chief Information Officer ... Mr. Ryan NOBLE

*University of Central Florida (E)

PO Box 160000, Orlando FL 32816-0001
County: Orange FICE Identification: 003954
Unit ID: 132903
Telephone: (407) 823-2000 Carnegie Class: RU/VH
FAX Number: N/A Calendar System: Semester
URL: www.ucf.edu
Established: 1963 Annual Undergrad Tuition & Fees (In-State): $6,247
Enrollment: 59,212 Coed
Affiliation or Control: State IRS Status: 501(c)3
Highest Offering: Doctorate

Program: Occupational; Liberal Arts And General; Teacher Preparatory; Professional
Accreditation: SC, BUS, BUSA, CACREP, CAHIIM, CEA, CLPSY, CS, ENG, HSA, IPSY, MED, MT, MUS, NURSE, PTA, SP, SPAA, SW, TED

02 President Dr. John C. HITT
05 Provost/Executive Vice President Dr. Tony G. WALDROP
100 Vice President and Chief of Staff Dr. John SCHELL
10 Vice Pres Admin & Finance/CFO Mr. William F. MERCK, II
26 Vice President University Relations Dr. Daniel HOLSENBECK
43 Vice President/General Counsel Mr. W. Scott COLE
46 VP Research and Commercialization Dr. M. J. SOILEAU
26 VP Strategy/Mktg/Comm/Admissions VAdm. Alfred HARMS, JR.
32 VP Student Dev/Enrollment Svcs Dr. Maribeth EHASZ
30 Vice Pres Development/Alumni Rels Mr. Robert HOLMES, JR.
31 Vice President for Community Rels Ms. Helen DONEGAN
63 VP Medical Affairs/Dean Med College Dr. Deborah GERMAN
49 Dean College of Arts & Humanities Dr. Jose B. FERNANDEZ
50 Dean College of Business Admin Dr. Paul JARLEY
53 Dean College of Education Dr. Sandra L. ROBINSON
54 Dean College of Engr/Comp Sci Dr. Michael GEORGIOPOULOS
76 Dean College of Hlth/Pub Affs Dr. Michael FRUMKIN
88 Dean Rosen College Hospitality Mgt Dr. Abraham PIZAM
66 Dean College of Nursing Dr. Jean LEUNER
88 Dean College of Optics & Photonics Dr. Bahaa SALEH
81 Dean College of Sciences Dr. Michael D. JOHNSON
92 Dean Burnett Honors College Dr. Alvin WANG
20 Vice Provost Academic Affairs Dr. Diane CHASE
13 Vice Provost & CIO Info Tech/Res Dr. Joel L. HARTMAN
88 Vice Provost Space Plng/Anal/Admin Dr. Edward NEIGHBOR
12 Vice Provost Regional Campuses Dr. Jeff JONES
58 Int Vice Provost/Dean Graduate Dr. Charles R. HINKLE
88 Interim Vice Provost/Dean Undergrad Dr. Elliot VITTES
18 Assoc VP Facilities and Safety Ms. Lee KERNEK
29 Assoc Vice Pres Alumni Relations Mr. Tom MESSINA
86 Assoc VP for University Relations Mr. Fred KITTINGER
88 Assoc VP Rsrch & Commercialization Mr. Tom O'NEAL
07 Assoc VP Undergrad Admissions Dr. Gordon CHAVIS
27 Assoc VP Dir Comm & Pub Affairs Mr. Grant HESTON
88 Assoc Vice Provost Fac Relation Dr. Lyman BRODIE
88 Asst VP Inst Knowledge Mgmt Dr. M. Paige BORDEN
37 Exec Dir Student Financial Asst Ms. Mary MCKINNEY
06 University Registrar Mr. Brian BOYD
08 Director Libraries Mr. Barry BAKER
15 Assoc VP Human Res & HR Officer Mr. Mark A. ROBERTS
19 Asst VP Safety & Chief of Police Mr. Richard BEARY
93 Director Multicul Acad Suppt Svcs Mr. Wayne JACKSON
14 Chief Technology Officer Mr. Robert YANCKELLO
38 Director Counseling Center Dr. Stacey PEARSON
41 Vice Pres & Director of Athletics Mr. Todd STANSBURY
22 Director EEO Affirmative Action Ms. Janet BALANOFF
23 Director Health Services Dr. Michael G. DEICHEN
39 Director Housing and Residence Life Mrs. Christi HARTZLER
28 Director of Diversity Initiatives Dr. Valarie G. KING
96 Director of Purchasing Mr. Gregory ROBINSON
36 Exec Director Career Services Ms. Lynn HANSEN

*University of Florida (A)

235 Tigert Hall, Gainesville FL 32611-9500
County: Alachua FICE Identification: 001535
Unit ID: 134130
Telephone: (352) 392-3261 Carnegie Class: RU/VH
FAX Number: N/A Calendar System: Semester
URL: www.ufl.edu
Established: 1853 Annual Undergrad Tuition & Fees (In-State): $6,263
Enrollment: 49,913 Coed
Affiliation or Control: State IRS Status: 501(c)3
Highest Offering: Doctorate
Program: Liberal Arts And General; Teacher Preparatory; Professional
Accreditation: SC, ARCPA, ART, AUD, BUS, BUSA, CACREP, CEA, CIDA, CLPSY, CONST, COPSY, DANCE, DENT, DIETD, DIETI, ENG, ENGR, FOR, HSA, IPSY, JOUR, LAW, LSAR, MED, MIDWF, MUS, NURSE, OT, PH, PHAR, PLNG, PTA, SCPSY, SP, TED, THEA, VET

02 President Dr. James B. MACHEN
05 Provost & Senior Vice President Dr. Joseph GLOVER
47 Sr Vice Pres Agric/Natural Res Dr. Jack M. PAYNE
17 Sr Vice Pres Health Affairs Dr. David S. GUZICK
11 Sr Vice Pres/Chief Operating Ofcr Dr. Winfred M. PHILLIPS
30 Vice President Dev/Alumni Affairs Mr. Thomas J. MITCHELL
10 Vice President Business Affairs Mr. Curtis REYNOLDS
32 Vice President Student Affairs Mr. David KRATZER
26 Vice President Univ Relations Ms. Jane A. ADAMS
15 Vice Pres Human Resources Ms. Paula V. FUSSELL
46 Vice President Research Dr. David P. NORTON
43 Vice President/General Counsel Ms. Jamie L. KEITH
13 Vice President & CIO Mr. Elias G. ELDAYRIE
21 Vice President/Chief Financial Ofcr Mr. Matthew FAJACK
84 Vice Pres Enroll Mgmt/Assoc Provost Dr. Zina EVANS
86 Assoc VP Government Relations Ms. Marion S. HOFFMAN
26 Asst Vice Pres Marketing Mr. Dan WILLIAMS
15 Asst Vice Pres Human Resources Ms. Jodi D. GENTRY
26 Asst VP Media Rels/Public Affairs Ms. Janine SIKES
21 Business Affs/Finance/Admin AVP Mr. Robert MILLER
18 AVP of Facilities/Plng/Construction Ms. Carol WALKER
20 Associate Provost Dr. Angel KWOLEK-FOLLAND
92 Assoc Provost Undergrad Affairs Dr. Bernard A. MAIR
09 Asst Provost/Dir Inst Research/Plng Dr. Marie ZEGLEN
35 Dean Students/Assoc VP Student Affs Dr. Jen D. SHAW
08 Dean University Libraries Ms. Judith RUSSELL
50 Dean of Business Administration Dr. John KRAFT
49 Dean of Liberal Arts & Science Dr. Paul J. D'ANIERI
68 Dean of Health/Human Performance Dr. Michael B. REID
61 Dean of Law Mr. Robert H. JERRY
66 Dean of Nursing Dr. Anna M. MCDANIEL
67 Dean of Pharmacy Dr. William H. RIFFEE
54 Dean of Engineering Dr. Cammy ABERNATHY
47 Dean Agricultural/Life Sciences Dr. Teresa C. BALSER
60 Dean of Journalism/Communications Ms. Diane H. MCFARLIN
76 Dean Pub Health/Health Professions Dr. Michael PERRI
53 Dean of Education Dr. Glenn GOOD
47 Dean IFAS Extension Dr. Nick T. PLACE
74 Dean of Veterinary Medicine Dr. James W. LLOYD
57 Dean of Fine Arts Ms. Lucinda LAVELLI
48 Dean Design Construction Planning Dr. Christopher SILVER
63 Dean of Medicine Dr. Michael L. GOOD
46 Dean of IFAS Research Dr. John HAYES
52 Int Dean of Dentistry Dr. Boyd E. ROBINSON
58 Dean Graduate School Dr. Henry T. FRIERSON
65 Int Dir School Natural Res/Envir Dr. Thomas K. FRAZER
06 University Registrar Mr. Stephen J. PRITZ
23 Int Director of Student Health Dr. Guy NICOLETTE
38 Director of Counseling Center Dr. Sherry BENTON
37 Director Student Financial Aid Mr. Richard D. WILDER
36 Director of Career Resource Center Ms. Heather B. WHITE
14 Director of Computer Center Mr. Timothy J. FITZPATRICK
19 Director of University Police Ms. Linda J. STUMP
27 Senior Director Media Relations Mr. Stephen F. ORLANDO
24 Director of Academic Technology Dr. Fedro S. ZAZUETA
65 Director of Forestry Dr. Timothy L. WHITE
39 Director of Housing Mr. Norbert W. DUNKEL
41 Athletic Director Mr. Jeremy N. FOLEY
29 Exec Director Alumni Affairs Ms. Danita NIAS
28 Director of Diversity Ms. Tamara COHEN
96 Director of Purchasing Ms. Lisa DEAL
07 Director of Admissions Mr. Patrick C. HERRING

*University of North Florida (B)

1 UNF Drive, Jacksonville FL 32224-7699
County: Duval FICE Identification: 009841
Unit ID: 136172
Telephone: (904) 620-1000 Carnegie Class: Master's L
FAX Number: (904) 620-2414 Calendar System: Semester
URL: www.unf.edu
Established: 1965 Annual Undergrad Tuition & Fees (In-State): $6,413
Enrollment: 16,356 Coed
Affiliation or Control: State IRS Status: 501(c)3
Highest Offering: Doctorate
Program: Liberal Arts And General; Teacher Preparatory; Professional
Accreditation: SC, ANEST, BUS, BUSA, CACREP, CONST, CS, DIETD, DIETI, ENG, HSA, MUS, NURSE, PH, PTA, SPAA, @SW, TED

02 President Mr. John A. DELANEY
05 Interim Provost Dr. Earle C. TRAYNHAM
20 Associate Provost Dr. Bobby E. WALDRUP
20 Associate Provost Dr. Newton N. JACKSON
100 VP/Chief of Staff Dr. Thomas S. SERWATKA
86 VP Governmental Affairs Ms. Janet D. OWEN
43 VP/General Counsel Ms. Karen J. STONE
15 VP Human Resources Ms. Rachelle GOTTLIEB
10 VP Administration/Finance Ms. Shari A. SHUMAN
30 Interim VP Inst Advancement Ms. Ann S. MCCULLEN
32 VP Student & International Affairs Dr. Mauricio GONZALEZ
84 Int Asst VP for Enrollment Svcs Mr. John E. YANCEY
88 Assoc VP/Compliance Officer Dr. Joann N. CAMPBELL
21 Assoc VP Admin & Finance Mr. Scott BENNETT
13 Assoc VP Chief Info Officer Mr. Lance TAYLOR
44 Assoc VP Major Gifts Ms. Elizabeth M. HEAD
35 Assoc VP Student Affairs Mr. Everett J. MALCOLM, III
45 Asst VP Research Dr. Imeh D. EBONG
88 Asst VP Development Ms. Ann S. MCCULLEN
26 VP Public Relations Ms. Sharon ASHTON
88 Asst VP Student Affairs Dr. Lucy S. CROFT
89 Dean of Undergraduate Studies Dr. Jeffrey W. COKER
58 Dean of the Graduate School Dr. James L. ROBERSON
08 Dean of the Library Dr. Shirley HALLBLADE
49 Dean College of Arts & Sciences Dr. Barbara HETRICK
50 Dean Coggin College of Business Dr. Ajay SAMANT
53 Dean College of Education Dr. Larry DANIEL
76 Dean Brooks College of Health Dr. Pam CHALLY
77 Dean Computing Engineering & Constr Dr. Mark A. TUMEO
51 Dean Continuing Education Mr. Robert WOOD
04 Executive Director Pres Office Mr. Donald A. SHEA
16 Dir Human Resources Ms. Teresa L. SANDROCK
88 Dir Internal Auditing Mr. Robert L. BERRY
22 Dir Equal Oppty Programs Ms. Cheryl N. GONZALEZ
88 Dir Professional Dev Training Ms. Kelly G. HARRISON
21 Chief Budget Officer Mr. Ricky B. ARJUNE
21 Controller Ms. Valerie O. STEVENSON
88 Dir Environment Health/Safety Mr. Daniel D. ENDICOTT
88 Dir ADA Compliance Ms. Rocelia T. GONZALEZ
88 Treasurer Mr. Michael S. NEGLIA
18 Dir Univ Facilities Planning Mr. Zak OVADIA
88 Dir University Center Mr. George ANDROUIN
29 Dir Alumni Services Ms. Faith M. HALL
19 Dir Safety Security Mr. John E. DEAN
36 Dir Career Development Services Mr. Rick ROBERTS
85 Dir Intercultural Ctr for Peace Dr. Oupa SEANE
88 Dir Child Development Research Ctr Ms. Pam BELL
23 Chief Medical Officer Dr. Lisa DYNAN-DOBBERTIEN
38 Dir Univ Counseling Center Dr. Rene MONTESINOS
88 Dir Women's Center Ms. Sheila D. SPIVEY
85 Dir The International Center Dr. Timothy ROBINSON
39 Dir Housing Residence Life Mr. Robert J. BOYLE
41 Athletic Director Mr. Lee L. MOON
88 Dir Office of Faculty Dr. Francis D. RICHARD
88 Exec Dir of Assessment Dr. Judith E. MILLER
92 Dir Honors Program Dr. Leslie G. KAPLAN
37 Dir Student Financial Aid Mrs. Anissa AGNE
06 Registrar Mrs. Megan R. KUEHNER
44 Director Annual Giving Ms. Heather A. VARIAN
88 Associate Vice Pres for Major Gifts Ms. Elizabeth HEAD
07 Interim Dir Admissions Mr. Chad N. LEARCH
25 Dir Contracts and Grants Acct Ms. Cheresa Y. HAMILTON
09 Dir Institutional Research Dr. Richard S. POWELL
88 Exec Dir FL Inst of Education Dr. Cheryl A. FOUNTAIN
104 Dir Study Abroad Ms. Anne S. FUGARD
88 Dir Small Business Dev Ctr Ms. Janice W. DONALDSON
88 Dir Disability Resource Center Dr. Kristine W. WEBB
96 Dir Purchasing Ms. Kathy RITTER
103 Dir Continuing Education Mr. Timothy W. GILES

*University of South Florida (C)

4202 E Fowler Avenue, Tampa FL 33620-6100
County: Hillsborough FICE Identification: 001537
Unit ID: 137351
Telephone: (813) 974-2011 Carnegie Class: RU/VH
FAX Number: (813) 974-5530 Calendar System: Semester
URL: www.usf.edu
Established: 1956 Annual Undergrad Tuition & Fees (In-State): $6,410
Enrollment: 41,212 Coed
Affiliation or Control: State IRS Status: 501(c)3
Highest Offering: Doctorate
Program: Liberal Arts And General; Teacher Preparatory; Professional; Nursing Emphasis
Accreditation: SC, ANEST, ART, AUD, BUS, BUSA, CACREP, CEA, CLPSY, CORE, CS, ENG, ENGR, HSA, IPSY, LIB, MED, MUS, NURSE, PCSAS, PH, @PHAR, PTA, SCPSY, SP, SPAA, SW, TED, THEA

02 President Dr. Judy L. GENSHAFT
100 Chief of Staff/President's Office Dr. Cynthia S. VISOT
05 Prov/Exec Vice Pres Academic Affs Dr. Ralph WILCOX
20 AVP USF World/Vice Prov Acad Affs Dr. Roger BRINDLEY
46 Sr Vice Pres Research & Innovation Dr. Paul SANBERG
17 Sr Vice Pres USF Health Dr. Stephen K. KLASKO
20 Sr Vice Prov Faculty & Development Dr. Dwayne SMITH
10 Vice Pres Business & Finance Mr. Nick TRIVUNOVICH
11 Vice Pres Administrative Services Ms. Sandy LOVINS
30 Sr Vice Pres University Advancement Mr. Joel MOMBERG
32 Int Vice President Student Affairs Dr. Thomas E. MILLER
13 Vice Pres Information Technology Mr. Michael PEARCE
26 VP Univ Communication/Marketing Vacant
29 Assoc Vice Pres Alumni Affairs Mr. Bill MCCAUSLAND
44 Assoc Vice Pres Development Vacant
14 Assoc Vice Pres Info Technologies Mr. George W. ELLIS
22 Assoc VP for Diversity/Equal Oppty Dr. Jose HERNANDEZ
84 Assoc VP Enrollment Planning & Mgmt Dr. Paul J. DOSAL
15 Assoc Vice Pres Personnel Services Ms. Theresea DRYE
86 Asst Vice Pres Government Rels Mr. Mark WALSH
35 Asst Vice Pres Student Affairs Dr. Michael A. FREEMAN
35 Asst Vice Pres Student Affairs Mr. Guy CONWAY
40 Asst VP Auxiliary Services Mr. Jeffrey A. MACK
43 General Counsel Mr. Steven D. PREVAUX
39 Dean Housing/Residential Educ Ms. Ana HERNANDEZ
83 Dean Behavioral/Community Sci Dr. Julianne SEROVICH
50 Dean Business Administration Dr. Moez LIMAYEM
53 Dean Education Dr. Vasti TORRES
54 Dean Engineering Dr. John M. WIENCEK
57 Dean College of the Arts Dr. James S. MOY
49 Dean Arts & Sciences Dr. Eric EISENBERG
66 Dean Nursing Dr. Dianne MORRISON-BEEDY
69 Dean Public Health Dr. Donna PETERSEN
58 Dean Graduate School Dr. Karen D. LILLER
89 Dean of Undergraduate Studies Dr. W. Robert SULLINS
51 Interim Dean University College Dr. Judy ASHCROFT
48 Dir Sch of Architecture/Cmty Design Mr. Robert MACLEOD
12 Regional Chanc Sarasota-Manatee Dr. Arthur M. GUILFORD
12 Regional Chanc USF St Petersburg Dr. Sophia WISNIEWSKA
21 Controller Ms. Jennifer CONDON
27 Director of News Ms. Lara WADE
06 University Registrar Ms. Angela W. DEBOSE
07 Director Admissions Mr. David HENRY
18 Interim Director Physical Plant Mr. Siva PRAKASH
21 University Budget Officer Ms. Bertha P. ALEXANDER
37 Director Financial Aid Ms. Billy Jo HAMILTON
38 Director Counseling Center Dr. Ann JARONSKI
36 Director of the Career Center Dr. Drema K. HOWARD
19 Director University Police Mr. Thomas F. LONGO
08 USF Libraries Dean Dr. William GARRISON
41 Director of Athletics Mr. Doug WOOLARD
28 Director of Diversity & Inclusion Ms. Patsy FELICIANO
96 Director Purchasing & Property Svcs Mr. Michael ABERNETHY
09 Director of Institutional Planning Ms. Valeria GARCIA

*University of South Florida St. Petersburg (D)

140 7th Avenue S, Saint Petersburg FL 33701-5016
County: Pinellas FICE Identification: 009016
Unit ID: 448840
Telephone: (727) 873-4873 Carnegie Class: Master's M
FAX Number: (727) 873-4131 Calendar System: Semester
URL: www.usfsp.edu
Established: 1956 Annual Undergrad Tuition & Fees (In-District): $5,720
Enrollment: 4,690 Coed
Affiliation or Control: State/Local IRS Status: 501(c)3
Highest Offering: Master's

Program: Liberal Arts And General; Teacher Preparatory; Professional
Accreditation: SC, BUS, BUSA, JOUR, TED

02 Regional Chancellor .... Dr. Sophia T. WISNIEWSKA
04 Special Asst to Regional Chancellor .... Vacant
05 Reg Vice Chanc Academic Affairs .... Dr. Vivian FUEYO
11 Reg Vice Chanc Admin/Financial Svcs .... Vacant
26 Reg Vice Chanc External Affairs .... Dr. Helen LEVINE
32 Reg Assoc Vice Chanc Std Affs .... Dr. Julie WONG
49 Dean College of Arts & Sciences .... Dr. Frank BIAFORA
50 Dean College of Business .... Dr. Maling EBRAHIMPOUR
53 Dean College of Education .... Dr. William HELLER
08 Dean of the Library .... Ms. Carol HIXSON
09 Reg Asst Vice Chanc Inst Research .... Dr. J. E. GONZALEZ
19 Chief of Police .... Vacant
13 Director of Campus Computing .... Mr. Jeff REISBERG
16 Director Human Resources .... Ms. Sandra CONWAY
37 Director of Financial Aid .... Ms. Erin DUNN
06 Director Records and Registration .... Ms. Linda CROSSMAN
07 Director Admissions & Marketing .... Ms. Holly KICKLITER
18 Dir Facil Plng/Construction Svcs .... Mr. John DICKSON
96 Purchasing Manager .... Mr. Bill BENJAMIN
10 Budget Director .... Mr. David EVERINGHAM
31 Communications Director .... Mr. Tom SCHERBERGER
30 Asst Dir Development .... Ms. Jennifer GONZALEZ-BOHNERT
30 Asst Dir Development .... Ms. Alexis SEARFOSS
105 Director Web Services .... Mr. Michel FOUGERES

*University of South Florida Sarasota-Manatee (A)

8350 Tamiami Trail, Sarasota FL 34243-2049
County: Manatee Identification: 667058
Unit ID: 451671
Telephone: (941) 359-4200 Carnegie Class: Master's M
FAX Number: N/A Calendar System: Semester
URL: www.usfsm.edu
Established: 1956 Annual Undergrad Tuition & Fees (In-State): $5,587
Enrollment: 1,952 Coed
Affiliation or Control: State IRS Status: 501(c)3
Highest Offering: Master's; No Lower Division
Program: Liberal Arts And General; Teacher Preparatory; Professional
Accreditation: SC

02 Regional Chancellor .... Dr. Arthur M. GUILFORD
10 Vice Chancellor Business & Finance .... Mr. Ben ELLINOR
05 Vice Chancellor Academic Affairs .... Dr. Bonnie JONES
32 Dean of Students .... Ms. Mary Beth WALLACE
30 Vice Chancellor Advancement .... Mr. Dennis L. STOVER
49 Dean College of Arts & Sciences .... Dr. Jane ROSE
50 Dean College of Business .... Dr. Robert ANDERSON
53 Dean College of Education .... Dr. Terry OSBORN
88 Dean Sch Hotel & Restaurant Mgmt .... Dr. Cihan COBANOGLU

*University of West Florida (B)

11000 University Parkway, Pensacola FL 32514-5750
County: Escambia FICE Identification: 003955
Unit ID: 138354
Telephone: (850) 474-2000 Carnegie Class: DRU
FAX Number: (850) 474-3131 Calendar System: Semester
URL: uwf.edu
Established: 1963 Annual Undergrad Tuition & Fees (In-State): $6,238
Enrollment: 12,652 Coed
Affiliation or Control: State IRS Status: 501(c)3
Highest Offering: Doctorate
Program: Occupational; Liberal Arts And General; Teacher Preparatory; Professional; Business Emphasis
Accreditation: SC, BUS, ENG, MT, MUS, NURSE, PH, SW, TED

02 President .... Dr. Judy A. BENSE
05 Provost .... Dr. Martha SAUNDERS
32 Vice President Student Affairs .... Dr. Kevin BAILEY
30 Vice Pres University Advancement .... Dr. Brendan KELLY
20 Vice Provost .... Dr. George B. ELLENBERG
27 Sr Assoc VP University Affairs/CIO .... Mr. Mike F. DIECKMANN
84 Asst Vice Pres Enrollment Mgt .... Mrs. Joffery GAYMON
18 Assoc VP Facilities Dev/Operations .... Dr. James R. BARNETT
35 Associate Vice Pres Student Affairs .... Dr. James R. HURD
58 AVP Res & Dean of Grad Students .... Dr. Richard S. PODEMSKI
21 Asc VP Internal Audit/Mgmt Consultg .... Ms. J. Betsy BOWERS
15 Associate Vice Pres Human Resources .... Mrs. Cindy FARIA
88 Assoc VP Business & Property Dev .... Mr. David J. O'BRIEN
28 Assoc VP Diversity/Intl Educ/Pgms .... Dr. Angela E. MCCORVEY
88 Executive Director .... Mr. J. Patrick CRAWFORD
43 Associate General Counsel .... Ms. Patricia D. LOTT
35 Assistant VP/Dean of Students .... Dr. Brandon FRYE
50 Dean of Business .... Dr. F. Edward RANELLI
49 Dean of Arts & Sciences .... Dr. Jane S. HALONEN
107 Dean of Professional Studies .... Dr. Pamela NORTHRUP
100 Chief of Staff & Vice President .... Dr. Kimberly S. BROWN
08 Dean University Libraries .... Mr. Robert DUGAN
35 Associate Dean of Students .... Dr. LuSharon WILEY
10 Vice President and CFO .... Dr. Susan E. STEPHENSON
21 Asst VP Financial Services .... Ms. Colleen M. ASMUS
84 AVP of Enrollment Management .... Dr. David MARKER
13 Deputy Chief CIO & CTO .... Mrs. Melanie J. HAVEARD
07 Interim Director of Admissions .... Ms. Katherine CONDON
92 Director of Honors Program .... Dr. Gregory W. LANIER
37 Director of Financial Aid .... Ms. Jan BASS
19 Director of University Police .... Mr. John S. WARREN
39 Director of Housing/Residence Life .... Dr. Ruth L. DAVISON
38 Assistant VP Health & Counseling .... Dr. Rebecca E. KENNEDY
88 Director Facilities Planning .... Mr. Kenneth C. KLINDT
29 Director of Alumni Relations .... Ms. Katherine C. EHEREDGE
41 Athletic Director .... Mr. David L. SCOTT
26 Director Mktg & Creative Services .... Ms. Sabrina MCLAUGHLIN
09 Director Institutional Research .... Vacant
44 Director of Development .... Ms. Martha Lee BLODGETT
21 Director University Budgets .... Ms. Valerie Z. MONEYHAM
21 Director Business/Auxiliary Svcs .... Ms. Ellen P. TILL
57 Dir Sch Fine/Performing/Comm Arts .... Dr. Brendan B. KELLY

Stetson University (C)

421 N Woodland Boulevard, DeLand FL 32723-0001
County: Volusia FICE Identification: 001531
Unit ID: 137546
Telephone: (386) 822-7000 Carnegie Class: Master's L
FAX Number: (386) 822-8832 Calendar System: 4/1/4
URL: www.stetson.edu
Established: 1883 Annual Undergrad Tuition & Fees: $38,330
Enrollment: 3,961 Coed
Affiliation or Control: Independent Non-Profit IRS Status: 501(c)3
Highest Offering: Doctorate
Program: Liberal Arts And General; Teacher Preparatory; Professional
Accreditation: SC, BUS, BUSA, CACREP, LAW, MUS, TED

01 President .... Dr. Wendy B. LIBBY
05 Provost & Vice Pres Acad Affairs .... Dr. Beth PAUL
10 VP for Business & CFO .... Mr. F. Robert HUTH
88 Spec Advsr to Pres for Philanthropy .... Ms. Linda P. DAVIS
30 Vice Pres for University Relations .... Ms. Carol JULIAN
84 VP Enrollment Management .... Mr. Joel BAUMAN
26 VP for University Marketing .... Mr. Gregory CARROLL
32 Vice President for Student Affairs .... Mr. Christopher KANDUS-FISHER
61 Dean College of Law .... Mr. Christopher PIETRUSZKIEWICZ
49 Dean of College of Arts & Sciences .... Dr. Karen RYAN
50 Dean of School of Business Admin .... Dr. Thomas SCHWARZ
64 Dean of School of Music .... Dr. Thomas G. MASSE
20 Assoc Provost for Faculty Devlpmnt .... Vacant
20 Assoc VP for Boundless Learning .... Dr. Emily RICHARDSON
20 Asst Provost for Student Success .... Dr. Lua HANCOCK
06 Registrar .... Ms. Kristina BRANTLEY
08 Dean of duPont-Ball Library .... Ms. Susan RYAN
27 Assoc VP Technology & CIO .... Mr. R. William PENNEY
15 Assoc VP for Human Resources .... Ms. Shelia DANIELS
18 Assoc Vice Pres Facilities Mgmt .... Mr. Al ALLEN
21 Assoc Vice Pres for Finance .... Mr. Jeffrey MARGHEIM
09 Assoc Vice Pres of Analytics .... Dr. Raymond BARCLAY
88 Asst Vice Pres for Univ Relations .... Ms. Rina TOVAR
32 Asst Dean of Students .... Ms. Rosalie CARPENTER
07 Exec Dir of Admission .... Mr. Rodney SAN JOSE
36 Exec Dir Career Dev & Advising .... Mr. Joseph PROTOPAPA
39 Exec Dir of Housing & Res Life .... Mr. Ben FALTER
38 Exec Dir of Holistic Wellness .... Ms. Lynn SCHOENBERG
42 University Chaplain .... Rev. Michael R. FRONK
44 Director of Annual Giving .... Mr. Mark ERNEST
44 Director of Planned Giving .... Ms. Katheryn P. PEARCE
29 Director Alumni Engagement .... Ms. Colleen M. COOPER
51 Director Continuing Education .... Mr. William R. O'CONNOR
104 Director of International Learning .... Mr. Eric CANNY
41 Director of Athletics .... Mr. Jeffrey P. ALTIER
15 Director Human Resources .... Ms. Betty WHITEMAN
96 Director of Purchasing .... Ms. Valinda WIMER
19 Chief Pubic Safety .... Mr. Robert MATUSICK

Tallahassee Community College (D)

444 Appleyard Drive, Tallahassee FL 32304-2895
County: Leon FICE Identification: 001533
Unit ID: 137759
Telephone: (850) 201-6200 Carnegie Class: Assoc/Pub-R-L
FAX Number: (850) 201-8682 Calendar System: Semester
URL: www.tcc.fl.edu
Established: 1966 Annual Undergrad Tuition & Fees (In-District): $2,569
Enrollment: 14,511 Coed
Affiliation or Control: Local IRS Status: 501(c)3
Highest Offering: Associate Degree
Program: Occupational; 2-Year Principally Bachelor's Creditable; Nursing Emphasis
Accreditation: SC, ADNUR, COARC, DA, DH, EMT

01 President .... Dr. Jim MURDAUGH
10 Vice Pres Administrative Svcs/CFO .... Dr. Teresa SMITH
13 VP Information Technology .... Mr. Bret INGERMAN
05 Provost and VP for Academic Affairs .... Dr. Barbara SLOAN
32 Vice President for Student Affs .... Dr. Sally SEARCH
103 Vice Pres Workforce Development .... Ms. Kimberly MOORE
88 Assoc VP Inst Effectiveness .... Dr. Lei WANG
100 Chief of Staff .... Mr. Scott BALOG
57 Dean Communications & Humanities .... Dr. Marge BANOCY-PAYNE
83 Dean History & Social Sciences .... Dr. Monte FINKELSTEIN
81 Associate Dean Mathematics .... Dr. Eddy STRINGER
72 Dean Technology & Professional Pgms .... Ms. Kate STEWART
88 Assoc Dean Dev Comm & Col Success .... Ms. Sharisse TURNER
88 Associate Dean Developmental Math .... Mr. David DELROSSI
88 Associate Dean Natural Sciences .... Mr. Anthony JONES
08 Director of Library Services .... Ms. Deborah P. ROBINSON
76 Dean Health Care Professions .... Dr. Alice NIED
37 Director of Financial Aid .... Mr. William SPIERS
84 Dir of Student Success & Retention .... Dr. Shanna AUTRY
15 Director of Human Resources .... Ms. Renae TOLSON
102 Director of TCC Foundation .... Mr. Robin JOHNSTON
41 Director of Athletics .... Mr. Rob CHANEY
35 Dir of Campus & Civic Engagement .... Mr. Mike COLEMAN
27 Director of Communications .... Ms. Alice MAXWELL
88 Exec Dir Florida Public Safety Inst .... Mr. E. E. EUNICE
18 Dir Facilities/Construction/Plng .... Mr. David WILDES
21 Controller .... Ms. Patricia MANNING
45 Director of Educational Research .... Dr. Barbara J. GILL
09 Director of Institutional Research .... Ms. Margaret WINGATE
106 Dir Center for Distance Learning .... Dr. Marilyn DICKEY
88 Dir Ctr for Teach/Learn/Ldrshp .... Dr. Karinda BARRETT
13 Director of User Services .... Mr. Chip SINGLETARY
18 Construction Coordinator .... Mr. Bill HUNTER
85 International Students Coordinator .... Ms. Betty JENSEN
14 Director of Enterprise Systems .... Mr. Mike ROBECK
25 Contracts and Grants Manager .... Ms. Vanessa LAWRENCE
88 Director Grants & Special Projects .... Mr. Charles WOOD
96 Purchasing Manager .... Mr. Bobby HINSON
19 Chief of Police .... Mr. David HENDRY
06 Registrar .... Ms. Renee R. GREEN
20 Dean of Curriculum and Instruction .... Mrs. Calandra STRINGER
07 Director of Admissions & Enrollment .... Ms. Lourena MAXWELL
36 Director of Career Services .... Ms. Catie GOODMAN

Talmudic College of Florida (E)

4000 Alton Road, Miami Beach FL 33140
County: Dade FICE Identification: 025089
Unit ID: 137777
Telephone: (305) 534-7050 Carnegie Class: Spec/Faith
FAX Number: (305) 534-8444 Calendar System: Semester
URL: www.talmudicu.edu
Established: 1974 Annual Undergrad Tuition & Fees: $12,250
Enrollment: 55 Male
Affiliation or Control: Independent Non-Profit IRS Status: 501(c)3
Highest Offering: Doctorate
Program: Teacher Preparatory; Professional; Religious Emphasis
Accreditation: RABN

01 President .... Rabbi Yitzchak ZWEIG
05 Dean/Vice President .... Rabbi Yochanan ZWEIG
06 Registrar .... Rabbi Ira HILL
37 Director Student Financial Aid .... Ms. Stacy BROWN
20 Director Educational Programs .... Rabbi Yeshaya GREENBERG
07 Director of Admissions .... Rabbi Yaakov BURSTYN

Thomas M. Cooley Law School Tampa Bay Campus (F)

9445 Camden Field Parkway, Riverview FL 33578
Telephone: (813) 419-5100 Identification: 770290
Accreditation: &NH

† Main campus is Thomas M. Cooley Law School in Lansing, MI.

Touro College South (G)

1703 Washington Avenue, Miami Beach FL 33139
Telephone: (305) 535-1066 Identification: 770147
Accreditation: &M

† Main campus is Touro College in New York, NY.

Trinity Baptist College (H)

800 Hammond Boulevard, Jacksonville FL 32221-1398
County: Duval FICE Identification: 031019
Unit ID: 137953
Telephone: (904) 596-2400 Carnegie Class: Spec/Faith
FAX Number: (904) 596-2532 Calendar System: Semester
URL: www.tbc.edu
Established: 1974 Annual Undergrad Tuition & Fees: $15,360
Enrollment: 283 Coed
Affiliation or Control: Baptist IRS Status: 501(c)3
Highest Offering: Master's
Program: 2-Year Principally Bachelor's Creditable; Teacher Preparatory; Religious Emphasis
Accreditation: TRACS

00 Chancellor .... Dr. Thomas C. MESSER
01 President/CEO .... Mr. Mac HEAVENER
03 Senior Vice President .... Dr. Matthew BEEMER
32 Dean of Students .... Mr. Jeremiah STANLEY
84 Director of Enrollment Management .... Mr. Brandon WILLIS
37 Director of Financial Aid .... Mr. Mark ELKINS

Trinity College of Florida (I)

2430 Welbilt Boulevard, Trinity FL 34655-4401
County: Pasco FICE Identification: 030282
Unit ID: 137962
Telephone: (727) 376-6911 Carnegie Class: Spec/Faith
FAX Number: (727) 376-0781 Calendar System: Semester
URL: www.trinitycollege.edu
Established: 1932 Annual Undergrad Tuition & Fees: $13,320
Enrollment: 219 Coed
Affiliation or Control: Independent Non-Profit IRS Status: 501(c)3
Highest Offering: Baccalaureate
Program: Religious Emphasis
Accreditation: BI

01 President ....Dr. Mark T. O'FARRELL
32 Vice President Student Affairs ....Rev. Al DEPOUTOT
05 Vice President Academic Affairs ....Dr. David BENEDICT
30 Vice President for Advancement ....Dr. Charlie MARTIN
10 Vice Pres for Business & Finance ....Mr. Paul S. WILLARD
07 Vice Pres for Enrollment/Adult Ed ....Vacant
06 Registrar ....Mr. Zachary T. RANES
26 Asst VP Marketing/Communications ....Mr. Kevin D. O'FARRELL

Trinity International University, Florida Regional Center (A)

8190 W State Road 84, Davie FL 33324-4611
Telephone: (954) 382-6400 FICE Identification: 012314
Accreditation: &NH

† Main campus is Trinity International University in Deerfield, IL.

Ultimate Medical Academy-Clearwater (B)

1255 Cleveland Street, Clearwater FL 33756
County: Pinellas FICE Identification: 035493
Unit ID: 441371
Telephone: (727) 298-8685 Carnegie Class: Not Classified
FAX Number: (727) 446-2489 Calendar System: Semester
URL: www.ultimatemedical.edu
Established: 1998 Annual Undergrad Tuition & Fees: $13,500
Enrollment: 414 Coed
Affiliation or Control: Proprietary IRS Status: Proprietary
Highest Offering: Associate Degree
Program: Occupational
Accreditation: ABHES

01 Campus Director ....Ms. Lori LEGROW

Ultimate Medical Academy Online-Tampa (C)

3101 W Martin Luther King Boulevard, Tampa FL 33607
Telephone: (813) 386-6350 Identification: 770528
Accreditation: ABHES

† Main campus is Ultimate Medical Academy-Clearwater in Clearwater, FL.

Unilatina International College (D)

3130 Commerce Pkwy, Miramar FL 33025
County: Broward Identification: 667155
Telephone: (954) 607-4344 Carnegie Class: Not Classified
FAX Number: (954) 357-1766 Calendar System: Quarter
URL: www.unilatina.edu
Established: 2001 Annual Undergrad Tuition & Fees: $14,800
Enrollment: N/A Coed
Affiliation or Control: Proprietary IRS Status: Proprietary
Highest Offering: Associate Degree
Program: Occupational
Accreditation: ACICS

01 President ....Lydia B. BAUTISTA MOLLER
05 Academic Director ....Angelica MOYANO

University of Fort Lauderdale (E)

4069 NW 16th Street, Lauderhill FL 33313-5809
County: Broward FICE Identification: 041563
Unit ID: 457402
Telephone: (954) 486-7728 Carnegie Class: Not Classified
FAX Number: (954) 486-7667 Calendar System: Other
URL: www.uftl.edu
Established: Annual Undergrad Tuition & Fees: N/A
Enrollment: 59 Coed
Affiliation or Control: Non-denominational IRS Status: 501(c)3
Highest Offering: Doctorate
Program: Professional; Religious Emphasis
Accreditation: TRACS

01 Chancellor and CEO ....Dr. Henry B. FERNANDEZ
05 Dean of College ....Dr. Owen FACEY
10 Chief Financial Officer ....Mr. Brian HANKERSON
32 VP for Academic & Student Services ..Ms. Chloris UNDERWOOD
06 Registrar ....Ms. Lenice BARNETT
07 Director of Admissions ....Ms. Lynda NATION

University of Miami (F)

1252 Memorial Drive, Coral Gables FL 33124
County: Miami-Dade FICE Identification: 001536
Unit ID: 135726
Telephone: (305) 284-2211 Carnegie Class: RU/VH
FAX Number: N/A Calendar System: Semester
URL: www.miami.edu
Established: 1925 Annual Undergrad Tuition & Fees: $42,852
Enrollment: 16,172 Coed
Affiliation or Control: Independent Non-Profit IRS Status: 501(c)3
Highest Offering: Doctorate
Program: Liberal Arts And General; Teacher Preparatory; Professional
Accreditation: SC, ANEST, BUS, BUSA, CEA, CLPSY, COPSY, DENT, ENG, HSA, IPSY, LAW, MED, MIDWF, MUS, NURSE, PH, PTA, @TEAC

01 President ....Dr. Donna E. SHALALA
05 Exec Vice President & Provost ....Dr. Thomas J. LEBLANC
10 Sr Vice Pres for Business & Finance ....Mr. Joseph T. NATOLI
63 Sr VP & Dean School of Medicine ....Dr. Pascal J. GOLDSCHMIDT
30 Sr VP Univ Advancement/Ext Affairs ....Mr. Sergio M. GONZALEZ
21 Vice President Finance & Treasurer ....Mr. John R. SHIPLEY
43 Vice Pres Gen Counsel/Sec of Univ ....Ms. Aileen M. UGALDE
32 Vice President Student Affairs ....Dr. Patricia A. WHITELY
17 Vice Pres Medical Administration ....Mr. Joseph T. NATOLI
15 Vice President Human Resources ....Ms. Nerissa E. MORRIS
13 Vice Pres Information Tech/CIO ....Mr. Steve CAWLEY
21 Vice President Budget & Planning ....Mr. Mark DIAZ
18 Vice Pres Real Estate & Facilities ....Mr. Larry D. MARBERT
27 Vice Pres University Communications ....Ms. Jacqueline R. MENENDEZ
86 Vice Pres Government Affairs ....Mr. Rodolfo J. FERNANDEZ
100 President's Chief of Staff ....Dr. Rudolph J. FERNANDEZ
20 Sr Vice Prov/Dean Undergrad Educ ....Dr. William S. GREEN
46 Vice Provost for Research ....Dr. John L. BIXBY
20 Vice Provost Faculty Affairs ....Dr. David J. BIRNBACH
20 Vice Prov Acad Affs/Dean Grad Sch ....Mr. M. Brian BLAKE
41 Director of Athletics ....Mr. Blake JAMES
29 Associate VP Alumni Relations ....Ms. Donna A. ARBIDE
21 Assoc Vice President/Controller ....Ms. Theresa L. ASHMAN
06 Assoc Vice President & Registrar ....Dr. Scott INGOLD
31 Asst Vice Pres Community Relations ....Ms. Sarah N. ARTECONA
84 Asst VP of Enrollment Management ....Mr. James M. BAUER
26 Exec Director Media Relations ....Mrs. Elizabeth AMORE
86 Director of Government Affairs ....Ms. Shira KASTAN
09 Asst VP Planning & Inst Research ....Dr. Mary M. SAPP
19 Chief of Police ....Major David A. RIVERO
49 Dean College of Arts & Sciences ....Dr. Leonidas G. BACHAS
48 Dean School of Architecture ..Ms. Elizabeth M. PLATER-ZYBERK
50 Dean Business Administration ....Dr. Eugene ANDERSON
60 Dean School Communication ....Dr. Gregory J. SHEPHERD
53 Dean of Education/Human Development ....Dr. Isaac PRILLELTENSKY
54 Dean College of Engineering ....Dr. James M. TIEN
61 Dean of Law ....Ms. Patricia WHITE
64 Dean Frost School of Music ....Dr. Shelton G. BERG
65 Dean Marine & Atmospheric Science ....Dr. Roni AVISSAR
66 Dean of Nursing & Health Studies ....Dr. Nilda P. PERAGALLO
58 Dean of the Graduate School ....Dr. Teresa A. SCANDURA
08 Interim Dean of Libraries ....Ms. Yolanda COOPER
35 Dean of Students ....Dr. Ricardo D. HALL
12 Director Center Hemisphere Policy ....Dr. Susan K. PURCELL
38 Director Student Counseling ....Dr. Ernesto R. ESCOTO
36 Executive Director Career Services ....Mr. Christian GARCIA
85 Director Intl Student & Scholar Svc ....Ms. Teresa S. DE LA GUARDIA
39 Director Student Housing ....Mr. James G. SMART
96 Chief Purchasing Officer ....Ms. Susan R. MONTES
28 Exec Dir Equality Administration ....Ms. Wilhemena BLACK

University of Phoenix North Florida Campus (G)

4500 Salisbury Road, Jacksonville FL 32216-0959
Telephone: (904) 636-6645 Identification: 770197
Accreditation: &NH, ACBSP

† Main campus is University of Phoenix in Tempe, AZ.

University of Phoenix South Florida Main Campus (H)

2400 SW 145th Avenue, Miramar FL 33207-4145
Telephone: (954) 382-5303 Identification: 770237
Accreditation: &NH, ACBSP

† Main campus is University of Phoenix in Tempe, AZ.

University of St. Augustine for Health Sciences (I)

1 University Boulevard, Saint Augustine FL 32086-5799
County: Saint Johns FICE Identification: 031713
Unit ID: 367954
Telephone: (904) 826-0084 Carnegie Class: Spec/Health
FAX Number: (904) 826-0085 Calendar System: Trimester
URL: www.usa.edu
Established: 1979 Annual Undergrad Tuition & Fees: $41,448
Enrollment: 1,541 Coed
Affiliation or Control: Proprietary IRS Status: Proprietary
Highest Offering: Doctorate
Program: Professional
Accreditation: DETC, OT, PTA

01 President ....Dr. Wanda NITSCH
03 Vice President ....Dr. Cindy MATHENA
10 Chief Financial Officer ....Ms. Rachelle AGATHA
88 Dir Inst of Occupational Therapy ....Dr. Karen HOWELL
88 Program Dir Occupational Therapy-CA ....Dr. Judith OLSON
88 Program Dir Physical Therapy-CA ....Dr. Ellen LOWE
88 Program Dir Physical Therapy-FL ....Dr. Jeffrey ROT
88 Program Dir Physical Therapy-TX ....Dr. Patricia KING
88 Dir Trans Doctor Physical Therapy ....Dr. Jodi LIPHART
88 Director Trans Doctor Occup Therapy ....Dr. Anne HULL
88 Director of DHSc/EdD Programs ....Dr. Dan LOFALD
06 Registrar ....Ms. Diane RONDINELLI
07 Director of Admissions ....Mr. Steve JONES
51 Director of Continuing Education ....Ms. Lori HANKINS

University of Southernmost Florida (J)

9550 Regency Square Blvd.Suite 1100, Jacksonville FL 32225
County: Duval FICE Identification: 025982
Unit ID: 134121
Telephone: (904) 345-2840 Carnegie Class: Assoc/PrivFP
FAX Number: (904) 520-7295 Calendar System: Quarter
URL: www.usmf.edu
Established: 1960 Annual Undergrad Tuition & Fees: $23,000
Enrollment: 185 Coed
Affiliation or Control: Proprietary IRS Status: Proprietary
Highest Offering: Associate Degree
Program: Occupational; 2-Year Principally Bachelor's Creditable; Nursing Emphasis
Accreditation: ACICS

01 Campus Director ....Mr. Orlando CASARIEGO
05 Director of Education ....Ms. Katrina BROOKS

University of Southernmost Florida-Coral Gables Campus (K)

178 Giralda Avenue, Coral Gables FL 33134
Telephone: (305) 644-1171 Identification: 770614
Accreditation: ACICS

† Main campus is University of Southernmost Florida in Jacksonville, FL.

University of Tampa (L)

401 W Kennedy Boulevard, Tampa FL 33606-1490
County: Hillsborough FICE Identification: 001538
Unit ID: 137847
Telephone: (813) 253-3333 Carnegie Class: Master's L
FAX Number: (813) 258-7207 Calendar System: Other
URL: www.ut.edu
Established: 1931 Annual Undergrad Tuition & Fees: $25,772
Enrollment: 7,200 Coed
Affiliation or Control: Independent Non-Profit IRS Status: 501(c)3
Highest Offering: Master's
Program: Liberal Arts And General; Teacher Preparatory; Professional
Accreditation: SC, BUS, MUS, NUR

01 President ....Dr. Ronald L. VAUGHN
05 Provost/Vice Pres Academic Affairs ....Dr. David STERN
10 Vice Pres Administration/Finance ....Mr. Richard W. OGOREK
84 Vice President Enrollment ....Mr. Dennis L. NOSTRAND
30 Vice Pres Development/Univ Rels ....Mr. Daniel T. GURA
45 Vice Pres Operations & Planning ....Dr. Linda W. DEVINE
13 Vice President Info Technology ....Ms. Donna R. ALEXANDER
21 Assistant Vice Pres Admin/Finance ....Mr. T. Kevin LAFFERTY
32 Dean of Students ....Ms. Stephanie R. KREBS
20 Assoc Provost & Dean of Acad Svcs ....Dr. Katharine H. COLE
06 Registrar ....Ms. Michelle PELAEZ
08 Director of the Library ....Ms. Marlyn PETHE-COOK
29 Director of Alumni Relations ....Mr. James HARDWICK
44 Director of Annual Giving ....Mrs. Taylor A. PINKE
37 Director of Financial Aid ....Ms. Jacqueline LATORELLA
27 Director of Public Information ....Mr. Eric D. CARDENAS
36 Director of Career Services ....Mr. Mark W. COLVENBACH
18 Director of Facilities Management ....Mr. David RAMSEY
91 Director Information Systems ....Mr. Jon ALBRECHT
15 Exec Director of Human Resources ....Ms. Donna B. POPOVICH
07 Sr Associate Director of Admissions ....Mr. Brent W. BENNER
41 Athletic Director ....Mr. Larry J. MARFISE
40 Manager Campus Store ....Vacant
39 Director of Residence Life ....Ms. Krystal R. SCHOFIELD
22 Affirmative Action Officer ....Ms. Donna B. POPOVICH
19 Director Safety & Security ....Mr. Kevin A. HOWELL
23 Dir Health Center/Stdnt Counseling ....Ms. Sharon P. SCHAEFER
44 Director of Planned Giving ....Vacant
38 Director Student Counseling ....Ms. Sharon P. SCHAEFER
96 Director of Procurement ....Ms. Cyn D. EZELL
09 Dir Institutional Effectiveness ....Dr. Jeanne M. ROBERTS
92 Director of Honors Program ....Dr. Gary S. LUTER
50 Dean College of Business ....Dr. F. Frank GHANNADIAN
83 Dean Social Science/Math Education ....Dr. Jack M. GELLER
81 Dean College Natural/Health Sci ....Dr. James A. GORE
57 Dean College of Arts/Letters ....Dr. Haig MARDIROSIAN
51 Assoc Dean Graduate/Continuing Stds ....Dr. Donald D. MORRILL

Valencia College (M)

PO Box 3028, Orlando FL 32802-3028
County: Orange FICE Identification: 006750
Unit ID: 138187
Telephone: (407) 299-5000 Carnegie Class: Assoc/Pub-U-MC
FAX Number: (407) 426-8970 Calendar System: Semester
URL: www.valenciacollege.edu
Established: 1967 Annual Undergrad Tuition & Fees (In-State): $2,972
Enrollment: 42,802 Coed
Affiliation or Control: State IRS Status: 501(c)3
Highest Offering: Baccalaureate
Program: Occupational; 2-Year Principally Bachelor's Creditable
Accreditation: SC, ADNUR, CEA, COARC, COARCP, CVT, DH, DMS, EMT, RAD

01 President ....Dr. Sanford C. SHUGART
05 VP Academic Affairs & Planning ....Dr. Susan E. LEDLOW
32 Vice President Student Affairs ....Dr. Joyce C. ROMANO
10 Vice President Operations & Finance ....Mr. Keith W. HOUCK

30 Vice Pres Institutional Advancement .... Vacant
43 Vice Pres Policy & General Counsel .... Dr. William J. MULLOWNEY
16 Interim VP Human Resources/Div .... Dr. Amy N. BOSLEY
26 Vice Pres Marketing/Strategic Comm .... Ms. Lucy BOUDET
12 Campus President East Campus .... Dr. Stacey R. JOHNSON
12 Campus President Osceola Campus .... Dr. Kathleen A. PLINSKE
12 Campus President West Campus .... Dr. Falecia D. WILLIAMS
27 Chief Information Officer .... Mr. William A. WHITE
102 Foundation President and CEO . Ms. Geraldine M P. GALLAGHER
15 Asst VP Human Resources .... Mr. Joe A. LIVINGSTON
18 Asst VP Facilities & Sustain .... Ms. Helene LOISELLE
103 Asst VP Career & Workforce Ed .... Dr. Nasser HEDAYAT
21 Asst VP Financial Svcs .... Ms. Jacqueline D. LASCH
35 Asst VP Student Affairs .... Dr. Sonya F. JOSEPH
88 Asst VP College Transition .... Ms. Amy KLEEMAN
07 Asst VP Admissions & Records .... Dr. Renee K. SIMPSON
31 Asst VP College/Community Rels .... Vacant
28 Asst VP Diversity & Inclusion .... Dr. Martha W. WILLIAMS
20 Asst VP Academic Affairs .... Vacant
19 Asst VP Safety/Security Risk Mgmt .... Mr. Thomas LOPEZ
108 Asst VP Assessment & IE .... Mr. Kurt E. EWEN
88 Asst VP Curriculum Dev & Art .... Dr. Karen M. BORGLUM
88 Asst VP Budget/Aux Services .... Ms. Sherri L. DIXON
88 Foundation VP & COO .... Ms. Michelle D. MATIS
25 Asst VP Resource Development .... Ms. Kristeen R. CHRISTIAN
35 Dean of Students East .... Mr. Joseph M. SARRUBBO
35 Dean of Students West .... Ms. Linda K. HERLOCKER
35 Dean of Students Osceola .... Ms. Jillian M. SZENTMIKLOSI
35 Dean of Students Winter Park .... Dr. Cheryl ROBINSON
40 Director College Bookstore .... Mr. Todd A. HUNT
92 Director Honors Program .... Dr. Valerie C. BURKS
96 Director Procurement/Aux Svcs .... Mr. W. Edward AMES
105 Director Web and Portal Services .... Vacant
09 Managing Director Research .... Vacant
04 Senior Executive Assistant .... Ms. Barbara HALSTEAD

Virginia College (A)

5940 Beach Boulevard, Jacksonville FL 32207
Telephone: (904) 520-7400 Identification: 770839
Accreditation: ACICS, MAAB, SURGT

† Main campus is Virginia College in Birmingham, AL.

Virginia College (B)

19 W Garden Street, Pensacola FL 32502-5678
Telephone: (850) 436-8838 FICE Identification: 031005
Accreditation: ACICS, MAAB, SURGT

† Main campus is Virginia College in Birmingham, AL.

Warner University (C)

13895 Highway 27, Lake Wales FL 33859-2549
County: Polk FICE Identification: 008848
Unit ID: 138275
Telephone: (863) 638-1426 Carnegie Class: Master's S
FAX Number: (863) 638-1472 Calendar System: Semester
URL: www.warner.edu
Established: 1968 Annual Undergrad Tuition & Fees: $24,828
Enrollment: 1,108 Coed
Affiliation or Control: Church Of God IRS Status: 501(c)3
Highest Offering: Master's
Program: Liberal Arts And General; Teacher Preparatory
Accreditation: SC, SW

01 President .... Dr. Gregory V. HALL
05 Exec Vice Pres/Chief Academic Ofcr .... Dr. James G. MOYER
10 Vice Pres for Finance & Business .... Mr. Greg A. RODDEN
30 Vice President for Advancement .... Mrs. Doris B. GUKICH
84 VP for Enrollment Mgmt & Marketing .... Mrs. Dawn M. RAFOOL
50 Dean of School of Business .... Vacant
49 Dean of Ministry/Arts & Sciences .... Dr. Steven DARR
53 Dean of School of Education .... Dr. Bill RIGEL
32 Dean of Student Life .... Rev. Dawn MEADOWS
43 General Counsel .... Dr. Norman WHITE
06 Registrar .... Mrs. Sara F. KANE
07 Director of Admissions .... Mr. Bob MOBLEY
37 Director Student Financial Aid .... Mrs. Lorrie STEEDLEY
21 Controller .... Mr. Dean MEADOWS
08 Librarian .... Mrs. Sherill HARRIGER
29 Director Alumni Relations .... Miss Kareen PICKETT
106 Dean of School of Online Education .... Dr. Jeff HAYES
42 Campus Pastor .... Vacant
83 Chair Social & Natural Science .... Mrs. Erica SIRRINE
68 Chair Physical Educ/Rec/Health .... Mr. Trevor HALL
09 Director of Institutional Research .... Mrs. Lisa B. MURPHY
18 Chief Facilities/Physical Plant .... Mr. Bill BROWN
97 Director of General Studies .... Mrs. Kelly MILLS
79 Chair Ministry & Humanities .... Dr. Michael SANDERS
88 Chair of Traditional BA .... Dr. Melodi GUILBAULT
40 Director Bookstore .... Ms. Monica HAMILTON
13 Director of Institutional Tech .... Mr. Mark THOMAS
19 Director Campus Security .... Mr. Brian ROWLES

Webber International University (D)

1201 Scenic Highway N/P.O. Box 96,
Babson Park FL 33827-0096
County: Polk FICE Identification: 001540
Unit ID: 138293
Telephone: (863) 638-1431 Carnegie Class: Bac/Diverse
FAX Number: (863) 638-2823 Calendar System: Semester
URL: www.webber.edu
Established: 1927 Annual Undergrad Tuition & Fees: $22,115
Enrollment: 729 Coed
Affiliation or Control: Independent Non-Profit IRS Status: 501(c)3
Highest Offering: Master's
Program: Business Emphasis
Accreditation: SC, IACBE

01 President .... Dr. H. Keith WADE
05 Academic Dean .... Dr. Charles SHIEH
10 Vice President Finance .... Ms. Christina JORDON
30 VP Institutional Advancement .... Dr. Steve WARNER
32 Dean of Student Life .... Ms. Johanna DEVERTEUIL
06 Registrar/Dir of Financial Aid .... Mrs. Kathy A. WILSON
36 Director Career Services .... Vacant
08 Head Librarian .... Ms. Sue DUNNING
26 Dir Public Relations/Athletic Dir .... Mr. Bill HEATH
13 Director Information Technology .... Mr. Bob M. WEIS
55 Director for Adult Education .... Vacant
18 Director of Campus Svcs/Maintenance .... Mr. Matt YENTES
40 Director of Bookstore .... Mr. Jay CULVER
07 Director of Admissions .... Vacant
09 Director of Institutional Effectiv .... Dr. Bill LOFTUS
50 Chair of Business Education .... Dr. Jeanette EBERLE
53 Chair of General Education Division .... Dr. Charles WUNKER

Wolford College (E)

1336 Creekside Boulevard, Suite 2,
Naples FL 34108-1931
County: Collier FICE Identification: 039393
Unit ID: 451130
Telephone: (239) 513-1135 Carnegie Class: Spec/Health
FAX Number: (239) 513-1368 Calendar System: Semester
URL: www.wolford.edu
Established: 2004 Annual Graduate Tuition & Fees: N/A
Enrollment: 211 Coed
Affiliation or Control: Independent Non-Profit IRS Status: 501(c)3
Highest Offering: Master's; No Undergraduates
Program: Professional
Accreditation: ANEST

01 President .... Dr. Norman R. WOLFORD
00 Chancellor .... Dr. Thomas COOK
37 Director of Financial Aid Services .... Mr. Gilbert CHANG
84 Dir Enrollment & Student Services .... Ms. Lori ELLISON
04 Administrative Assistant .... Ms. Eve N. OLVERA

WyoTech (F)

470 Destination Daytona Lane, Ormond Beach FL 32174
County: Volusia FICE Identification: 023462
Unit ID: 132268
Telephone: (386) 255-0295 Carnegie Class: Not Classified
FAX Number: (386) 252-3523 Calendar System: Quarter
URL: www.wyotech.edu
Established: Annual Undergrad Tuition & Fees: $26,500
Enrollment: 1,010 Coed
Affiliation or Control: Proprietary IRS Status: Proprietary
Highest Offering: Associate Degree
Program: Occupational
Accreditation: ACCSC

Yeshiva Gedolah Rabbinical College (G)

1140 Alton Road, Miami Beach FL 33139-4708
County: Dade FICE Identification: 032563
Unit ID: 363712
Telephone: (305) 653-8770 Carnegie Class: Spec/Faith
FAX Number: (305) 653-6790 Calendar System: Semester
Established: 1973 Annual Undergrad Tuition & Fees: $8,400
Enrollment: 47 Male
Affiliation or Control: Independent Non-Profit IRS Status: 501(c)3
Highest Offering: Master's
Program: Teacher Preparatory; Professional
Accreditation: @RABN

01 Executive Vice President .... Rabbi Benzion KORF
05 Dean .... Rabbi Abraham KORF
06 Registrar .... Ayelet BORTUNK

GEORGIA

Abraham Baldwin Agricultural College (H)

ABAC 1 - 2802 Moore Highway, Tifton GA 31793-2601
County: Tift FICE Identification: 001541
Unit ID: 138558
Telephone: (229) 391-5050 Carnegie Class: Assoc/Pub4
FAX Number: (229) 391-5051 Calendar System: Semester
URL: www.abac.edu
Established: 1908 Annual Undergrad Tuition & Fees (In-State): $3,920
Enrollment: 3,226 Coed
Affiliation or Control: State IRS Status: 501(c)3
Highest Offering: Baccalaureate
Program: Occupational; 2-Year Principally Bachelor's Creditable; Liberal Arts And General; Professional; Business Emphasis
Accreditation: SC, ADNUR

01 President .... Dr. David BRIDGES
05 VP for Academic Affairs .... Dr. Niles REDDICK
10 VP for Planning & Operations .... Mr. John CLEMENS
30 VP External Affairs/Chief of Staff .... Mr. Paul WILLIS
08 Director of Library Services .... Ms. Marie DAVIS
32 Dean of Students .... Ms. Bernice HUGHES
41 Athletic Director .... Mr. Alan KRAMER
13 Chief Data Officer & Registrar .... Ms. Amy WILLIS
38 Director of Student Development .... Dr. Maggie MARTIN
37 Director of Student Financial Svcs .... Ms. Traci BRYAN
44 Director of Capital Planning .... Mr. Melvin MERRILL
15 Director of Human Resources .... Mr. Richard SPANCAKE
26 Director of Public Relations .... Ms. Ashley MOCK
108 Director of Assessment .... Ms. Amy HOWELL
84 Director Enrollment Management .... Ms. Donna WEBB
96 Director of Procurement .... Ms. Teri MATHIS
19 Chief of Police .... Mr. Bryan A. GOLDEN

† Part of the University System of Georgia.

Agnes Scott College (I)

141 E College Avenue, Decatur GA 30030-3797
County: DeKalb FICE Identification: 001542
Unit ID: 138600
Telephone: (404) 471-6000 Carnegie Class: Bac/A&S
FAX Number: (404) 471-6067 Calendar System: Semester
URL: www.agnesscott.edu
Established: 1889 Annual Undergrad Tuition & Fees: $34,788
Enrollment: 885 Female
Affiliation or Control: Presbyterian Church (U.S.A.) IRS Status: 501(c)3
Highest Offering: Baccalaureate
Program: Liberal Arts And General
Accreditation: SC

01 President .... Dr. Elizabeth KISS
05 VP Acad Affs/Dean of the College .... Dr. Carolyn J. STEFANCO
32 VP Student Life/Dean of Students .... Ms. Donna A. LEE
10 Vice President Business/Finance .... Mr. John P. HEGMAN
30 Vice Pres College Advancement .... Mr. Robert PARKER
84 Vice Pres Enrollment & Admission .... Ms. Laura MARTIN
13 Assoc VP Technology .... Ms. LaNeta COUNTS
20 Associate Dean of the College .... Dr. James K. DIEDRICK
35 Associate Dean of Students .... Ms. Suzanne ONORATO
42 Chaplain .... Rev. Kate COLUSSY-ESTES
04 Director Office of the President .... Ms. Lea Ann HUDSON
27 Senior Director of Communications .... Mr. J. D. FITE
44 Senior Director of Development .... Ms. Elizabeth K. WILSON
06 Registrar .... Ms. Gail N. MEIS
35 Associate Dean of Students .... Dr. Kijua SANDERS-MCMURTRY
08 Director of Library Services .... Ms. Elizabeth BAGLEY
29 Director of Alumnae Relations .... Ms. Kimberly VICKERS
36 Director Career Planning .... Ms. Catherine NEINER
18 Director of Facilities .... Mr. Tim BLANKENSHIP
15 Director of Human Resources .... Ms. Karen GILBERT
41 Director of Athletics .... Ms. Joeleen AKIN
28 Director of Multicultural Affairs .... Mr. Hiram RAMIREZ
37 Director of Student Financial Aid .... Mr. Patrick BONONES
38 Director Personal Counseling .... Dr. Holly BYRD
09 Director of Institutional Research .... Ms. Katherine MCGUIRE
07 Director of Admissions .... Ms. Alexa GAETA
23 Director of Student Health .... Ms. Marcia J. PETERS
26 Director of Public Relations .... Ms. Megan TERRASO

Albany State University (J)

504 College Drive, Albany GA 31705-2796
County: Dougherty FICE Identification: 001544
Unit ID: 138716
Telephone: (229) 430-4600 Carnegie Class: Master's M
FAX Number: (229) 430-4830 Calendar System: Semester
URL: www.asurams.edu
Established: 1903 Annual Undergrad Tuition & Fees (In-State): $6,024
Enrollment: 4,275 Coed
Affiliation or Control: State IRS Status: 501(c)3
Highest Offering: Beyond Master's But Less Than Doctorate
Program: Liberal Arts And General; Teacher Preparatory; Professional
Accreditation: SC, ACBSP, FEPAC, NUR, SPAA, SW, TED

01 President .... Dr. Everette J. FREEMAN
43 Chief of Staff & University Counsel . Ms. Sharon "Nyota" TUCKER
05 Provost/VP Academic Affairs .... Dr. Richard GREEN
32 Interim Vice Pres Student Affairs .... Dr. Rhonda BRYANT
10 Vice President Fiscal Affairs .... Mr. Larry WAKEFIELD
30 Vice Pres Institutional Advance .... Mr. Clifford PORTER
13 Vice Pres Information Tech/CIO .... Mr. Erwin CARROW
20 Asst Vice Pres Academic Affairs .... Dr. Linda GRIMSLEY
46 Assoc Prov Research Sponsored Pgms .... Dr. Chanta HAYWOOD
83 Dean Arts & Humanities .... Dr. Leroy BYNUM
76 Dean Sciences Health Professions .... Dr. Joyce JOHNSON
50 Interim Dean College of Business .... Dr. Michael ROGERS
53 Interim Dean College of Education .... Dr. Kimberly FIELDS
06 Registrar/Chief Data Officer .... Mrs. Tarrah MIRUS
84 Assoc Provost Enrollment Svcs .... Dr. Mike MILLER
08 Director Library Services .... Dr. LaVerne MCLAUGHLIN
88 Director Title III .... Mrs. Connie LEGGETT
27 Director University Communications .... Ms. Vickie OLDHAM
88 Interim Director Sports Information .... Mr. Stanley MCCORMICK
38 Director Counseling/Disability Svcs .... Dr. Stephanie HARRIS-JOLLY
88 Director Budgets and Contracts .... Mrs. Marion RYANT

37 Director Financial Aid ... Mr. Thomas HARRIS, JR.
23 Director Student Health Services ... Dr. Vickie PHILLIPS
15 Director Human Resources Mgmt ... Mr. Steve GRANT
19 Chief of Police ... Mr. John FIELDS
41 Director of Athletics ... Dr. Richard WILLIAMS
18 Director Facilities Management ... Mr. James OLIVER
35 Director Student Life/Judicial Affs ... Ms. Gwinetta L. TRICE
38 Director Career Services ... Ms. Glorya E. WILLIAMS
29 Interim Director Alumni Affairs ... Ms. Sue POLITE-SOLOMON
96 Director Business Services ... Ms. Lori W. BURNETT
21 Controller ... Ms. Dorothy MARTIN
25 Director Grants and Contracts ... Mr. Andrew FLOYD
39 Director Housing Residence Life ... Mrs. Bonisha PORTER
88 Exec Asst Ctr African American Male ... Mr. Antonio LEROY
88 Dir Academic Advising Retention ... Dr. Kimberly BURGESS

† Part of the University System of Georgia.

Albany Technical College (A)

1704 S Slappey Boulevard, Albany GA 31701-3587
County: Dougherty FICE Identification: 005601
Unit ID: 138682
Telephone: (229) 430-3500 Carnegie Class: Assoc/Pub-R-M
FAX Number: (229) 430-3594 Calendar System: Semester
URL: www.albanytech.edu
Established: 1961 Annual Undergrad Tuition & Fees (In-State): $3,044
Enrollment: 3,935 Coed
Affiliation or Control: State IRS Status: 501(c)3
Highest Offering: Associate Degree
Program: Occupational; 2-Year Principally Bachelor's Creditable; Technical Emphasis
Accreditation: SC, DA, MAC, RAD, SURGT

01 President ... Dr. Anthony O. PARKER
05 Exec Vice Pres Academic Affairs ... Ms. Shirley ARMSTRONG
32 VP Student Affairs/Enrollment Mgmt ... Ms. Lisa DEJESUS
46 Vice President Economic Development ... Mr. Matt TRICE
11 Vice Pres Administrative Services ... Mrs. Kathy SKATES
45 Vice Pres of Inst Effectiveness ... Dr. Kimberly LEE
88 Associate Vice Pres of Adult Educ ... Mrs. Linda COSTON
04 Special Assistant to the President ... Mr. Joe NAJJAR
06 Registrar ... Ms. Suzann CULPEPPER
37 Director of Financial Aid ... Ms. Helen CATT
36 Dir of Job Placement/Career Svcs ... Ms. Judy JIMMERSON
21 Director of Accounting Services ... Mrs. Karen THOMAS
20 Dean of Academic Affairs ... Dr. Debra JONES
20 Dean of Academic Affairs ... Ms. Joy KNIGHTON
20 Dean of Academic Affairs ... Mr. Emmett GRISWOLD
55 Dean of Evening Administration ... Dr. Ed COOPER
88 Director of Business & Industry Svc ... Mr. Gary FRAGE
51 Dir Manufacturing Tech Ctr/Contg Ed ... Ms. Valerie WILLIAMS
09 Director of Institutional Research ... Mr. Joe NAJJAR
26 Director of Public Relations ... Ms. Wendy HOWELL
14 Director of Computer/Info Systems ... Mr. Bobby WIDNER
88 Director of Special Programs ... Vacant
18 Campus Operations Manager ... Mr. Lavon ACKLEY
56 Dir Spec Proj/Tech in Curriculum ... Ms. Elizabeth DEMING
35 Director Student Activities ... Dr. Mary RICHARDSON

Altamaha Technical College (B)

1777 W Cherry Street, Jesup GA 31545-0612
County: Wayne FICE Identification: 030321
Unit ID: 366447
Telephone: (912) 427-5800 Carnegie Class: Assoc/Pub-R-S
FAX Number: (912) 427-5823 Calendar System: Semester
URL: www.altamahatech.edu
Established: 1989 Annual Undergrad Tuition & Fees (In-State): $3,046
Enrollment: 1,405 Coed
Affiliation or Control: State IRS Status: 501(c)3
Highest Offering: Associate Degree
Program: Occupational; 2-Year Principally Bachelor's Creditable
Accreditation: SC

01 Acting President ... Mr. Lonnie V. ROBERTS
05 Vice President for Academic Affairs ... Dr. Al CUNNINGHAM
11 Vice Pres Administrative Services ... Ms. Monica S. O'QUINN
32 Vice President for Student Affairs ... Ms. Karla C. EUBANKS
09 VP of Institutional Effectiveness ... Mr. Lonnie V. ROBERTS
06 Registrar ... Mr. Chris MISSEL
07 Director of Admissions ... Mr. Chris JEANCAKE
15 Director Personnel Services ... Ms. Katrina HOWARD
20 Dean of Academic Affairs ... Ms. Bridget ATKINS
20 Dean of Academic Affairs ... Mr. Walt PINDER
20 Dean of Academic Affairs ... Ms. Patsy WILKERSON
21 Director of Accounting ... Mrs. Melissa LAMB
30 Dir of Institutional Advancement ... Mrs. Melinda LAAGER
36 Career Placement & Dev Coord ... Ms. Markisha BUTLER
37 Financial Aid Coordinator ... Mrs. Tina MANNING
28 Special Services Coordinator ... Ms. Tracy JORDAN
96 Purchasing Technician ... Ms. Kathy KOVACH
08 Acting Director of Library Services ... Mr. Ben BRYSON
14 Director of Information Tech ... Mr. Richard COTHERN
40 Bookstore Manager ... Ms. Bertie SHIPES
18 Director of Facilities ... Mr. Randy SMITH
38 Counseling & Special Svcs Director ... Ms. Cathy MONTGOMERY
29 Director Alumni Relations ... Vacant
20 Dean of Academic Support ... Ms. Sandra WILLIAMS
106 Distance Education Coordinator ... Mr. Chad SWANSON
51 Executive Director of Economic Dev ... Ms. Jan MELCHER
103 Director of Contract Training ... Dr. Henry HOBBS
97 Chair of General Education ... Mr. David BAILEY

American InterContinental University (C)

6600 Pchtree-Dunwdy Rd, 500 Embassy,
Atlanta GA 30328
Telephone: (404) 965-6500 Identification: 666723
Accreditation: &NH, ACBSP, CIDA

† Main campus is American InterContinental University in Schaumburg, IL.

Andrew College (D)

501 College Street, Cuthbert GA 39840-5550
County: Randolph FICE Identification: 001545
Unit ID: 138761
Telephone: (229) 732-2171 Carnegie Class: Assoc/PrivNFP
FAX Number: (229) 732-2176 Calendar System: Semester
URL: www.andrewcollege.edu
Established: 1854 Annual Undergrad Tuition & Fees: $21,785
Enrollment: 292 Coed
Affiliation or Control: United Methodist IRS Status: 501(c)3
Highest Offering: Associate Degree
Program: 2-Year Principally Bachelor's Creditable; Fine Arts Emphasis
Accreditation: SC

01 President ... Dr. David C. SEYLE
04 Executive Asst to the President ... Mrs. Pennie R. SCROGGINS
10 Chief Financial Officer ... Vacant
07 Director Admissions & Financial Aid ... Mr. Blake COTY
21 Controller ... Mrs. Julie CADLE
30 Director of Development ... Mr. Andy BRUBAKER
32 Director of Student Life ... Dr. Sherri TAYLOR
41 Athletic Director ... Dr. Edith SMITH
42 Chaplain ... Vacant
08 Librarian ... Mrs. Karan PITTMAN
37 Coordinator Student Financial Aid ... Mrs. Amy THOMPSON
40 Director of Bookstore ... Mrs. Karan PITTMAN
88 Student Support Services Director ... Ms. Santee ARCHER
05 Dean of Academic Affairs ... Dr. Jason GOODNER
06 Registrar ... Ms. Rachel BUSH
13 Director Computer Services ... Mr. Paul MOORE
18 Director of Maintenance ... Mr. David HARPER
19 Chief of Police ... Mr. Al ROBINSON
39 Director of Resident Housing ... Ms. Desi FRAZIER
105 Web Services ... Mr. Brice HERRIN
88 Director of AndrewServes ... Mrs. Rebecca WHITE
88 FOCUS Director ... Mrs. Bennie MATTOX
88 Director of Student Success Center ... Mr. Stephen ADAMS

Anthem College (E)

2450 Piedmont Road, Atlanta GA 30324
Telephone: (678) 279-7000 Identification: 770670
Accreditation: ACICS

† Main campus is Anthem College in Phoenix, AZ.

Argosy University, Atlanta (F)

980 Hammond Drive, Suite 100, Atlanta GA 30328-6162
Telephone: (770) 671-1200 Identification: 666735
Accreditation: &WC, CACREP, CLPSY

† Main campus is Argosy University, Orange County in Orange, CA.

Armstrong Atlantic State University (G)

11935 Abercorn Street, Savannah GA 31419-1997
County: Chatham FICE Identification: 001546
Unit ID: 138789
Telephone: (912) 344-2503 Carnegie Class: Master's L
FAX Number: N/A Calendar System: Semester
URL: www.armstrong.edu
Established: 1935 Annual Undergrad Tuition & Fees (In-State): $5,085
Enrollment: 7,439 Coed
Affiliation or Control: State IRS Status: 501(c)3
Highest Offering: Doctorate
Program: Occupational; Liberal Arts And General; Teacher Preparatory; Professional
Accreditation: SC, COARC, CS, HSA, MT, MUS, NMT, NURSE, PH, PTA, RAD, RTT, SP, TED

01 President ... Dr. Linda M. BLEICKEN
05 Provost & VP for Academic Affairs ... Dr. Carey ADAMS
10 Vice President Business & Finance ... Mr. David CARSON
32 Vice President Student Affairs ... Dr. Keith BETTS
30 Vice President for Advancement ... Mr. William KELSO
100 Chief of Staff ... Dr. Amy HEASTON
43 University Counsel ... Mr. Lee DAVIS
27 Chief Information Officer ... Mr. Robert P. HOWARD
84 Assoc VP Enrollment Mgmt ... Dr. Patrice B. MITCHELL
21 Associate VP Business & Finance ... Mr. Marc MASCOLO
20 Int Assistant VP Academic Affairs ... Dr. John KRAFT
53 Dean College of Education ... Dr. Patricia WACHHOLZ
76 Dean Health Professions ... Dr. David WARD
49 Dean College of Liberal Arts ... Dr. Laura BARRETT
72 Dean Science and Technology ... Dr. Robert GREGERSON
08 University Librarian ... Mr. Doug FRAZIER
06 Registrar ... Ms. Judy GINTER
19 Chief Campus Police ... Mr. Wayne WILLCOX
41 Athletic Director ... Ms. Lisa SWEANY
07 Director of Admissions ... Ms. Stephanie WHALEY
88 Director Faculty Development ... Dr. Teresa WINTERHALTER
37 Director Financial Aid ... Ms. Lee Ann KIRKLAND
89 Director First Year Experience ... Vacant
92 Director Honors Program ... Dr. Jonathan ROBERTS
36 Director of Career Services ... Ms. Elizabeth WILSON
09 Int Director Institutional Research ... Ms. Laura J. MILLS
104 Director of International Education ... Dr. James ANDERSON
12 Director Liberty Center ... Mr. Peter HOFFMAN
106 Director Online & Blended Learning ... Vacant
15 Director of Human Resources ... Ms. Rebecca CARROLL
18 Director Plant Operations ... Mr. David FAIRCLOTH
38 Director Counseling Services ... Mr. John MITCHELL
39 Director Housing & Residence Life ... Vacant
28 Director Multicultural Affairs ... Ms. Nashia WHITTENBURG
35 Director Student Activities ... Vacant
29 Director Alumni Development ... Ms. Cheryl ANDERSON
44 Director Major & Planned Giving ... Ms. Julie GERBSCH
26 Director Marketing & Communications ... Ms. Brenda FORBIS

† Part of the University System of Georgia.

The Art Institute of Atlanta (H)

6600 Peachtree Dunwoody Road, Atlanta GA 30328-1635
County: Fulton FICE Identification: 009270
Unit ID: 138813
Telephone: (770) 394-8300 Carnegie Class: Spec/Arts
FAX Number: (770) 394-0008 Calendar System: Quarter
URL: www.artinstitutes.edu/atlanta/
Established: 1949 Annual Undergrad Tuition & Fees: $24,200
Enrollment: 3,367 Coed
Affiliation or Control: Proprietary IRS Status: Proprietary
Highest Offering: Baccalaureate
Program: Fine Arts Emphasis
Accreditation: SC, ACFEI, CIDA

01 President ... Mr. Newton MYVETT
10 Dir of Admin and Financial Svcs ... Mr. Shane PATILLA
15 Director of Human Resources ... Ms. Ashley UNO
07 Senior Director of Admissions ... Mr. Doug LOCHBAUM
05 Dean of Academic Affairs ... Dr. Ameeta JADAV
32 Dean of Student Affairs ... Ms. April SHAVKIN
37 Director of Student Financial Svcs ... Mr. Bela AKBASHEVA
09 Dir of Inst Effectiveness/Research ... Dr. Suzanne Valle KILLEEN
08 Director of Library ... Ms. Lametric PATTERSON
13 Director of Technology ... Mr. Patrick SLUDER
06 Registrar ... Ms. Diana HILL
36 Director of Career Services ... Mr. Jerry HEILPERN
26 Director of Communications ... Vacant
18 Director of Facilities ... Mr. Tom MORGAN
39 Director of Residence Life/Housing ... Mr. Richard SMITH
04 Exec Assistant to the President ... Ms. Rebecca CROWFOOT

Ashworth College (I)

6625 The Corners Parkway, Norcross GA 30092-3406
County: Gwinnett Identification: 666106
Telephone: (770) 729-8400 Carnegie Class: Not Classified
FAX Number: (770) 729-9296 Calendar System: Semester
URL: www.ashworthcollege.edu
Established: 2000 Annual Undergrad Tuition & Fees: $4,153
Enrollment: 12,000 Coed
Affiliation or Control: Proprietary IRS Status: Proprietary
Highest Offering: Master's
Program: Occupational; 2-Year Principally Bachelor's Creditable; Professional
Accreditation: DETC

01 President ... Mr. Robert KLAPPER
05 Chief Academic Officer ... Dr. Leslie GARGIULO

Athens Technical College (J)

800 US Highway 29 N, Athens GA 30601-1500
County: Clarke FICE Identification: 005600
Unit ID: 246813
Telephone: (706) 355-5000 Carnegie Class: Assoc/Pub-R-M
FAX Number: (706) 369-5753 Calendar System: Semester
URL: www.athenstech.edu
Established: 1958 Annual Undergrad Tuition & Fees (In-State): $2,230
Enrollment: 4,788 Coed
Affiliation or Control: State IRS Status: 501(c)3
Highest Offering: Associate Degree
Program: Occupational; 2-Year Principally Bachelor's Creditable; Technical Emphasis
Accreditation: SC, ACBSP, ADNUR, CAHIIM, DA, DH, DMS, PTAA, RAD, SURGT

01 President ... Dr. Flora W. TYDINGS
05 Vice President Academic Affairs ... Dr. Joyce SANSING
32 Vice President Student Affairs ... Ms. Andrea DANIEL
11 Vice Pres Administrative Services ... Ms. Kathryn S. THOMAS
45 Vice Pres Economic Devel Services ... Mr. Jerry BARROW
12 Vice President of Off Campus Sites ... Dr. Larry D. SIEFFERMAN
09 Executive Vice President ... Dr. Daniel J. SMITH
13 Vice Pres Information Technology ... Mr. Dennis ASHWORTH
72 Dean Technical Education ... Ms. Susan LARSON
76 Dean Life Sciences ... Dr. Scott MARTIN
06 Exec Dir of Registration & Records ... Ms. Caroline ANGELO
07 Director Admissions ... Mr. Lenzy REID
08 Director Library Services ... Ms. Carol STANLEY
08 Librarian Elbert County Campus ... Ms. Marci MANGLITZ

36 Director Student Support/Career Dev .... Ms. Keli FEWOX
37 Director Financial Aid .... Ms. Wanda HICKS
88 Director Adult Education Programs .... Ms. Gwenn EVANS
12 Director Walton County Campus .... Ms. Lesley BOWICK
12 Director Greene County Campus .... Mr. Sibley BRYAN
50 Dean Business/Personal Services Div .... Ms. Diane CAMPBELL
35 Student Activities Director .... Dr. Yancey GULLEY
15 Executive Director Human Resources .... Dr. Leslie CRICKENBERGER
18 Facilities Director .... Mr. Jim WALTER
30 Director Institutional Advancement .... Ms. Liz DALTON
21 Director of Accounting .... Mr. Ryan STANLEY
97 Dean of General Education .... Dr. Carol MYERS
88 Exec Director Inst Effectiveness .... Ms. Stephanie G. BENSON

Atlanta Metropolitan State College (A)

1630 Metropolitan Parkway, SW, Atlanta GA 30310-4498
County: Fulton FICE Identification: 012165
Unit ID: 138901
Telephone: (404) 756-4000 Carnegie Class: Assoc/Pub-U-SC
FAX Number: (404) 756-4460 Calendar System: Semester
URL: www.atlm.edu
Established: 1974 Annual Undergrad Tuition & Fees (In-State): $3,526
Enrollment: 2,871 Coed
Affiliation or Control: State IRS Status: 501(c)3
Highest Offering: Baccalaureate
Program: Occupational; 2-Year Principally Bachelor's Creditable
Accreditation: SC, ACBSP

01 President .... Dr. Gary A. MCGAHA, SR.
05 Interim Vice Pres Academic Affairs .... Dr. Bonita FLOURNOY
10 Vice President Fiscal Affairs .... Mr. Freddie JOHNSON
32 Vice President Student Affairs .... Mrs. Cynthia EVERS
30 Vice Pres Institutional Advancement .... Mr. Larion WILLIAMS
21 Assoc VP Fiscal Affairs .... Mrs. Michelle ALSTON-BROWN
50 Dean Div Business/Computer Sci .... Dr. Eze NWAOGU
79 Dean Div Humanities/Fine Arts .... Dr. Frank JOHNSON
81 Dean Div of Sci/Math/Health Profess .... Mr. Bryan MITCHELL
83 Dean Div of Social Science .... Dr. Grady CULPEPPER
06 Dir Enrollment Services/Registrar .... Ms. Candace PERRY
15 Director of Human Resources .... Ms. Regina Ray SIMMONS
08 Director of the Library .... Mr. Robert QUARLES
35 Director of Student Activities .... Ms. Iris SHANKLIN
37 Interim Director of Financial Aid .... Ms. Michelle CHAPMAN
38 Director Counseling/Disability Svcs .... Ms. Dorothy WILLIAMS
14 Data Processing Manager .... Vacant
13 Chief Information Officer .... Mr. Antonio TRAVIS
09 Director Inst Effectiveness .... Dr. Mark CUNNINGHAM
19 Director of Campus Safety .... Mr. Antonio LONG
35 Dir of Student Outreach & Access .... Mr. Stephen WOODALL
18 Dir Plant Operations/Facilities .... Mr. E. Keith WILLIAMS
40 Bookstore Manager .... Ms. Barbara SMITH

† Part of the University System of Georgia.

Atlanta Technical College (B)

1560 Metropolitan Parkway, SW, Atlanta GA 30310-4446
County: Fulton FICE Identification: 008543
Unit ID: 138840
Telephone: (404) 225-4400 Carnegie Class: Assoc/Pub-U-SC
FAX Number: (404) 225-4445 Calendar System: Semester
URL: www.atlantatech.edu
Established: 1967 Annual Undergrad Tuition & Fees (In-State): $2,401
Enrollment: 4,874 Coed
Affiliation or Control: State IRS Status: 501(c)3
Highest Offering: Associate Degree
Program: Occupational; 2-Year Principally Bachelor's Creditable; Technical Emphasis
Accreditation: SC, ACFEI, CAHIIM, DA, DH, DT, EMT, MAC, @PTAA

01 President .... Dr. Alvetta P. THOMAS
05 Vice President Academic Affairs .... Dr. Murray WILLIAMS
11 Vice Pres Administrative Services .... Mrs. Teresa BROWN
32 Vice President Student Affairs .... Dr. Rushton JOHNSON
30 Vice President Economic Development .... Mr. Harold CRAIG
04 Assistant to the President .... Mrs. Joni WILLIAMS
45 Executive Vice President .... Vacant
26 Director Communications & Marketing ..... Mrs. Terreta RODGERS
37 Director of Financial Aid .... Mrs. Deborah CLARK
07 Director of Admissions .... Mr. Vory BILLUPS
88 Dean Industrial and Transportation .... Dr. Constance RUSSELL
51 Director of Continuing Education .. Dr. Deborah JOHNSON-BLAKE
36 Director Career Placement .... Mr. Michael BURNSIDE
50 Dean Business and Public Services .... Mrs. Phoebe COQUEREL
88 Dean Health and Public Safety .... Dr. Queenston THORPE
06 Registrar .... Mrs. Niya EADY
15 Director Human Resources .... Ms. Marilyn SMITH-ROBINSON
18 Director of Facilities .... Mr. Isaac VINING
09 Director of Curriculum and Planning .... Vacant

Atlanta's John Marshall Law School (C)

1422 West Peachtree Street NW, Atlanta GA 30309
County: Fulton FICE Identification: 031733
Unit ID: 138929
Telephone: (404) 872-3593 Carnegie Class: Spec/Law
FAX Number: (404) 873-3802 Calendar System: Semester
URL: www.johnmarshall.edu
Established: 1933 Annual Graduate Tuition & Fees: $37,335
Enrollment: 669 Coed
Affiliation or Control: Proprietary IRS Status: Proprietary
Highest Offering: First Professional Degree; No Undergraduates
Program: Professional
Accreditation: LAW

01 Dean .... Mr. Richardson R. LYNN
05 Assoc Dean Academics .... Mr. Kevin CIEPLY
32 Assoc Dean of Students .... Ms. Sheryl E. HARRISON
10 Chief Financial Officer .... Mr. Allen BREZEL
11 Asst Dean for Administration .... Ms. Michelle HARRIS

Augusta Technical College (D)

3200 Augusta Tech Drive, Augusta GA 30906-3399
County: Richmond FICE Identification: 005599
Unit ID: 138956
Telephone: (706) 771-4000 Carnegie Class: Assoc/Pub-R-M
FAX Number: (706) 771-4016 Calendar System: Semester
URL: www.augustatech.edu
Established: 1961 Annual Undergrad Tuition & Fees (In-District): $4,512
Enrollment: 4,339 Coed
Affiliation or Control: State/Local IRS Status: 501(c)3
Highest Offering: Associate Degree
Program: Occupational; Technical Emphasis
Accreditation: SC, COARC, CVT, DA, ENGT, MAC, OTA, PNUR, SURGT

01 President .... Mr. Terry D. ELAM
05 Sr Vice President Academic Affairs .... Dr. C. Rick HALL
11 Vice Pres Administrative Services .... Ms. Sheila HILL
32 Vice Pres Student Affairs .... Mr. Eddie J. HOWARD
88 Vice President Economic Development .... Dr. Lisa PALMER
12 Dean/Director Waynesboro Campus .... Ms. Johnica MITCHELL
35 Dean Student Services .... Vacant
37 Director Financial Aid .... Ms. Beverly SMYRE HINES
07 Director Admissions .... Ms. Christine BALL
30 Director Institutional Advancement .... Ms. Beverly PELTIER
06 Registrar .... Mr. Mike VIOLETTE
45 Sr Vice Pres Inst Effectiveness .... Dr. Melissa F. ALSTON
21 Director Accounting .... Ms. Sherrick L. JOHNSON
26 Dir Marketing/Public Relations .... Ms. Bonita JENKINS
15 Payroll/Benefits Manager .... Ms. Lori USRY
12 Dean Director Thomson Campus .... Ms. Julie LANGHAM
36 Director Career Services .... Ms. Donna WENDT
88 High School Coordinator .... Mrs. Evett DAVIS
76 Dean Allied Health Science .... Dr. Gwen TAYLOR
72 Dean Industrial Technology .... Mr. James PRICE
50 Dean Business/Personal Svcs .... Ms. Elizabeth A. JULIAN
97 Dean Gen Ed & Learning Support .... Mr. John RICHARDSON
54 Dean Information & Engineering Tech .... Mr. John ARENA

Bainbridge College (E)

2500 E Shotwell Street, PO Box 990,
Bainbridge GA 39818-0990
County: Decatur FICE Identification: 011074
Unit ID: 139010
Telephone: (229) 248-2500 Carnegie Class: Assoc/Pub-R-M
FAX Number: (229) 248-2547 Calendar System: Semester
URL: www.bainbridge.edu
Established: 1970 Annual Undergrad Tuition & Fees (In-State): $2,914
Enrollment: 2,887 Coed
Affiliation or Control: State IRS Status: 501(c)3
Highest Offering: Associate Degree
Program: Occupational; 2-Year Principally Bachelor's Creditable
Accreditation: SC, ADNUR

01 President .... Dr. Richard CARVAJAL
05 Vice Pres Academic Affairs .... Dr. Tonya STRICKLAND
10 Vice Pres of Business & Operations .... Mr. Shawn MCGEE
32 Vice President of Student Affairs .... Dr. Rodney CARR
49 Chair School of Arts & Sciences .... Dr. Michael STEWART
75 Chr Sch Health Sci/Profess Studies .... Ms. Kathleen KETTERER
88 Director of Learning Support .... Mr. Wesley WHITEHEAD
08 Director Library .... Ms. Susan RALPH
51 Director of Continuing Education .... Mr. Martin DAVIS
26 Chief Public Relations Officer .... Vacant
37 Director of Financial Aid .... Ms. Helen CATT
21 Controller .... Ms. Kay LIVINGSTON
18 Director of Plant Operations .... Vacant
91 Director of Technology Services .... Mr. Scott DUNN
35 Director Student Affairs .... Mr. Sam MAYHEW
30 Director of Development .... Ms. Dale FULLER
07 Director of Admissions .... Mr. Spencer STEWART
09 Research Analyst .... Vacant
38 Dir of Disability Services/Testing .... Ms. Arlene COOK
15 Director of Human Resources .... Dr. Lisa BURROUGHS
19 Director of Public Safety .... Mr. James SPOONER
06 Assistant Registrar .... Mr. Ridge HARPER

† Part of the University System of Georgia.

Bauder College (F)

384 Northyards Blvd, Ste 190 & 400,
Atlanta GA 30313-2439
County: Fulton FICE Identification: 011574
Unit ID: 139074
Telephone: (404) 237-7573 Carnegie Class: Bac/Assoc
FAX Number: (404) 237-1642 Calendar System: Quarter
URL: atlanta.bauder.edu
Established: 1964 Annual Undergrad Tuition & Fees: $44,251
Enrollment: 1,198 Coed
Affiliation or Control: Proprietary IRS Status: Proprietary
Highest Offering: Baccalaureate
Program: Occupational; 2-Year Principally Bachelor's Creditable
Accreditation: SC

01 Interim President .... Dr. Carolyn NORDSTROM
11 Interim Director of Operations .... Susan SHERWOOD
05 Academic Dean .... Vacant
07 Director of Admissions .... Terri HOLTE
37 Director of Financial Aid .... Catherine BARTON
36 Director of Career Services .... Wendolyn LARKINS
66 Director of Nursing .... Maxinee BLACK-ARIAS
06 Head Registrar .... Hannah LEONARD-HINDS
09 Institutional Research .... Vacant
08 Head Librarian .... Randall JAMES
04 Executive Assistant .... Shannon GILMER
21 Business Office Manager .... LaTanya HARTSFIELD
32 Director Student Services .... Carolyn JENKINS

Berry College (G)

2277 Martha Berry Highway, NW,
Mount Berry GA 30149-0001
County: Floyd FICE Identification: 001554
Unit ID: 139144
Telephone: (706) 232-5374 Carnegie Class: Bac/A&S
FAX Number: (706) 236-2238 Calendar System: Semester
URL: www.berry.edu
Established: 1902 Annual Undergrad Tuition & Fees: $29,090
Enrollment: 2,166 Coed
Affiliation or Control: Independent Non-Profit IRS Status: 501(c)3
Highest Offering: Beyond Master's But Less Than Doctorate
Program: Liberal Arts And General; Teacher Preparatory; Professional
Accreditation: SC, BUS, MUS, TED

01 President .... Dr. Stephen R. BRIGGS
05 Vice President & Provost .... Dr. Kathy Brittain RICHARDSON
10 Vice President Finance .... Mr. Brian I. ERB
32 VP Student Affairs and Enrollment .... Ms. Debbie HEIDA
30 Vice Pres Institutional Advancement .... Ms. Bettyann O'NEILL
84 VP of Enrollment Management .... Dr. Gary WATERS
100 Chief of Staff .... Mr. Whit WHITAKER
42 Chaplain .... Rev. Jonathan HUGGINS
35 Assoc Vice Pres Student Affairs .... Ms. Julie A. BUMPUS
26 Asst VP Public Rels and Marketing .... Ms. Jeanne MATHEWS
20 Associate Provost .... Dr. Andrew BRESSETTE
50 Dean Campbell School of Business .... Dr. John GROUT
53 Dean Charter School of Education .... Dr. Jackie MCDOWELL
79 Dean School Humanities/Arts/Soc Sci .... Dr. Thomas D. KENNEDY
66 Dean of Nursing .... Dr. Vanice ROBERTS
81 Interim Dean School of Math/Nat Sci .... Dr. Gary BRETON
78 Dean Stdnt Work/Experiential Lrng .... Mr. Rufus MASSEY
07 Director of Admissions .... Mr. Brett E. KENNEDY
08 Director of the Library .... Ms. Sherre Lee HARRINGTON
29 Director of Alumni Affairs .... Ms. Christina WATTERS
27 Chief Information Officer .... Ms. Penny EVANS-PLANTS
38 Director of Counseling Center .... Dr. J. Marshall JENKINS
37 Director of Financial Aid .... Ms. Marcia MCCONNELL
36 Director of Career Center .... Mrs. Sue TARPLEY
09 Dir Institutional Rsrch & Registrar .... Dr. Bryce DURBIN
88 Dir Faculty Rsrch & Sponsored Pgm .... Mrs. Donna DAVIN
18 Director Physical Plant .... Mr. Mark HOPKINS
89 Director First Year Experience .... Mrs. Katherine POWELL
92 Director Honors Program .... Dr. Brian CARROLL
94 Director Women's Studies .... Dr. Susan CONRADSEN
96 Director Purchasing .... Mr. Brad BARRRIS
85 Director International Programs .... Ms. Sarah EGERER
15 Director Human Resources .... Mr. Harold NALLY
43 Director of Legal Services .... Mr. Danny PRICE
28 Director of Multicultural Affairs .... Dr. Tasha TOY
78 Dir Stdnt Work/Experiential Lrng .... Mr. Michael BURNES
88 Director of Employee Development .... Mr. Mark KOZERA

Beulah Heights University (H)

892 Berne Street, SE, PO Box 18145,
Atlanta GA 30316-1873
County: Fulton FICE Identification: 030763
Unit ID: 139153
Telephone: (404) 627-2681 Carnegie Class: Spec/Faith
FAX Number: (404) 627-0702 Calendar System: Semester
URL: www.beulah.org
Established: 1918 Annual Undergrad Tuition & Fees: $5,760
Enrollment: 750 Coed
Affiliation or Control: Other Protestant IRS Status: 501(c)3
Highest Offering: Doctorate
Program: Religious Emphasis
Accreditation: BI, TRACS

01 President .... Dr. Benson M. KARANJA
05 Vice Pres/Dean Academic Affairs .... Dr. James B. KEILLER
32 VP Student Life/Enrollment Mgmt .... Pastor Shawn ADAMS
11 Assoc Vice Pres Operations .... Mr. Peter KARANJA
42 Dean of Chapel .... Bishop Johnathan E. ALVARADO
20 Associate Academic Officer .... Dr. Mark HARDGROVE
37 Director of Financial Aid .... Ms. Robin HARRELL
08 Director of Library Services .... Mr. Pradeep K. DAS
06 Registrar .... Mr. John DREHER
07 Director of Admissions .... Ms. Charlotte DUDLEY
106 Director of Online Studies .... Dr. Angelita HOWARD
18 Facilities Director .... Mr. Harvey BRUMELOW
15 Human Resources Coordinator .... Ms. Bernadette ASHER
58 Chair Div of Graduate Studies .... Dr. Mark HARDGROVE

73 Chair Dept of Religious Studies ... Mr. Walter TURNER
88 Chair Dept of Leadership Studies ... Ms. Betty G. PALMER

Brenau University (A)

500 Washington Street, SE, Gainesville GA 30501-3668
County: Hall | FICE Identification: 001556
Unit ID: 139199
Telephone: (770) 534-6299 | Carnegie Class: Master's L
FAX Number: (770) 534-6114 | Calendar System: Semester
URL: www.brenau.edu
Established: 1878 | Annual Undergrad Tuition & Fees: $23,330
Enrollment: 2,777 | Coed
Affiliation or Control: Independent Non-Profit | IRS Status: 501(c)3
Highest Offering: Doctorate
Program: Liberal Arts And General; Teacher Preparatory; Professional
Accreditation: SC, ACBSP, CIDA, DANCE, NURSE, OT, TED

01 President ... Dr. Ed L. SCHRADER
03 Sr VP/Chief Financial Ofcr ... Dr. David L. BARNETT
05 Provost & VP For Academic Affairs ... Dr. Nancy F. KRIPPEL
100 Chief of Staff ... Ms. Jody Y. WALL
10 Vice President Financial Services ... Mr. Toby R. HINTON
32 Sr VP Enrollment Mgt/Student Svcs ... Mr. Scott A. BRIELL
30 Vice Pres External Relations ... Mr. J. Matthew THOMAS
13 Vice Pres Information Technology ... Mr. Chip L. ANDREWS
09 Director of Research & Planning ... Dr. Robert E. CUTTINO
37 Assoc VP of EM & Dir Financial Aid ... Ms. Pam J. BARRETT
21 Controller ... Ms. Holly REYNOLDS
15 Director of Human Resources ... Ms. Kelley L. MADDOX
18 Director Facilities & Logistics ... Mr. Mike HOLLIMON
26 VP Communications/Publications ... Mr. David MORRISON
35 Dean of Student Success & Retention ... Ms. Valerie SIMMONS-WALSTON
36 Director of Career Services ... Mr. George BAGEL
24 Director of Learning Center ... Dr. Vince J. YAMILKOSKI
41 Athletic Director ... Mr. Mike LOCHSTAMPFOR
23 Chaplain ... Dr. Don HARRISON
53 Dean College of Education ... Dr. Sandra LESLIE
76 Dean College of Health & Sciences ... Dr. Gale H. STARICH
50 Dean College Business/Mass Commun ... Dr. Bill LIGHTFOOT
79 Dean College of Fine Arts & Human ... Dr. Andrea C. BIRCH
08 Dean of Library Svcs & SACS Liaison ... Ms. Marlene GIGUERE
88 Executive Director for Recruitment ... Mr. Nathan R. GOSS
06 Registrar & Dir of Student Records ... Ms. Barbara WILSON
29 Director Alumni Relations ... Ms. Jennifer DELL
19 Director Campus Safety & Security ... Ms. Paula DAMPIER

Brewton-Parker College (B)

201 David-Eliza Fountain Circle,
Mount Vernon GA 30445-0197
County: Montgomery | FICE Identification: 001557
Unit ID: 139205
Telephone: (912) 583-2241 | Carnegie Class: Bac/Diverse
FAX Number: (912) 583-4498 | Calendar System: Semester
URL: www.bpc.edu
Established: 1904 | Annual Undergrad Tuition & Fees: $12,410
Enrollment: 655 | Coed
Affiliation or Control: Baptist | IRS Status: 501(c)3
Highest Offering: Baccalaureate
Program: 2-Year Principally Bachelor's Creditable; Liberal Arts And General; Teacher Preparatory; Business Emphasis
Accreditation: #SC, TED

01 President ... Dr. Mike SIMONEAUX
43 General Counsel ... Mr. John MANNING
03 Exec VP Finance & Operations ... Mr. Randy F. MINTON
05 Vice President Academic Services ... Dr. Tim SEARCY
84 Vice Pres of Enrollment Services ... Mr. Jim BEALL
30 Interim VP Col Advancement ... Mr. Dave WALLACE
09 Dir of Assessment & Inst Research ... Vacant
15 Director Human Resources ... Ms. Nikki JONES
37 Director of Financial Aid ... Mr. Rick WOOLVERTON
18 Director of Plant Operations ... Mr. DeWayne BYNUM
06 Registrar ... Mrs. Sara CROWE
38 Dir Counseling & Career Services ... Mrs. Tonia SPAULDING
41 Athletic Director ... Ms. Sheila SIMMONS
08 Librarian ... Mrs. Ann HUGHES
26 Marketing Associate ... Ms. Amanda CORBIN
32 Director of Student Activities ... Ms. Jennifer L. WOOTEN
39 Director of Housing ... Ms. Kim KERN
40 Bookstore Manager ... Mrs. Lynn ADDISON
50 Interim Chair Business Division ... Dr. Don WALLACE
53 Chair Education Division ... Dr. Susan E. WHITE
49 Chair Arts & Sciences Division ... Dr. Ron MELTON
73 Chair Christian Studies ... Dr. Jerry RAY
42 Director of Campus Ministry ... Ms. Lauren PARNELL

Brown College of Court Reporting (C)

1900 Emery St. NW, Atlanta GA 30318
County: Fulton | FICE Identification: 020609
Unit ID: 139214
Telephone: (404) 876-1227 | Carnegie Class: Assoc/PrivFP
FAX Number: (404) 876-4415 | Calendar System: Quarter
URL: www.bccr.edu
Established: 1972 | Annual Undergrad Tuition & Fees: $16,600
Enrollment: 235 | Coed
Affiliation or Control: Proprietary | IRS Status: Proprietary
Highest Offering: Associate Degree
Program: Occupational; 2-Year Principally Bachelor's Creditable
Accreditation: COE

01 Director ... Marita CAREY
07 Director of Admissions ... Vacant
05 Director of Education ... Tami EDWARDS

Brown Mackie College-Atlanta (D)

4370 Peachtree Road NE, Atlanta GA 30319
Telephone: (404) 799-4500 | FICE Identification: 026214
Accreditation: ACICS, OTA, SURTEC

† Main campus is The Art Institute of Phoenix in Phoenix, AZ.

Carver College (E)

3870 Cascade Road SW, Atlanta GA 30331-2184
County: Fulton | FICE Identification: 036353
Unit ID: 139287
Telephone: (404) 527-4520 | Carnegie Class: Not Classified
FAX Number: (404) 527-4526 | Calendar System: Semester
URL: www.carver.edu
Established: 1943 | Annual Undergrad Tuition & Fees: $7,920
Enrollment: 120 | Coed
Affiliation or Control: Independent Non-Profit | IRS Status: 501(c)3
Highest Offering: Baccalaureate
Program: Religious Emphasis
Accreditation: BI

01 President and CEO ... Mr. Robert W. CRUMMIE
05 Vice Pres Academic Affs/Acad Dean ... Dr. Sujaya JAMES
10 Vice President of Business Affairs ... Mr. Terry ALEXANDER
30 Vice President of Advancement ... Mrs. Carla M. CRUMMIE
32 Dean of Students ... Mr. Damon D. BYRD
07 Director of Admissions ... Mr. Richard A. FEILDS
06 Registrar ... Mrs. Olive JACKS
09 Dir Institutional Effectiveness ... Ms. Traonah PATTERSON
29 Director Alumni Affairs ... Mr. Troy MAMON
42 Stdnt Director of Chapel Services ... Mr. Danny HUDSON
73 Director of Bible/Theology Division ... Dr. Sujaya JAMES
97 Director of General Studies ... Dr. Benjamin JACKS
107 Director of Professional Studies ... Dr. John JENKINS
08 Director of Library Services ... Mrs. Tosha BUSSEY
18 Chief of Facilities/Physical Plant ... Mr. Andre HARVEY
41 Athletic Dir/Mens Basketball Coach ... Mr. Martin CARTER
40 Director of Bookstore ... Mrs. Lyn VAUGHN
04 Assistant to the President ... Ms. Iverna SHELTON

Central Georgia Technical College (F)

3300 Macon Tech Drive, Macon GA 31206-3699
County: Bibb | FICE Identification: 005763
Unit ID: 140304
Telephone: (478) 757-3400 | Carnegie Class: Assoc/Pub-R-L
FAX Number: (478) 757-3454 | Calendar System: Quarter
URL: www.centralgatech.edu
Established: 1966 | Annual Undergrad Tuition & Fees (In-State): $3,550
Enrollment: 4,631 | Coed
Affiliation or Control: State | IRS Status: 501(c)3
Highest Offering: Associate Degree
Program: Occupational; Technical Emphasis
Accreditation: SC, DH, MLTAD, RAD, SURGT

01 President ... Dr. Ivan ALLEN
05 Vice President Academic Affairs ... Dr. Amy HOLLOWAY
10 Vice President Admin/Fin Svcs ... Ms. Michelle SINIARD
32 Vice President Student Affairs ... Mr. Craig JACKSON
31 Vice President Econ Dev ... Ms. Rebecca LEE
11 Vice Pres Facilities/Ancillary Svcs ... Ms. Dana DAVIS
13 Vice Pres Technology ... Mr. Gardner LONG, II
20 Assoc Vice Pres Academic Affairs ... Dr. Joan THOMPSON
35 Dean of Student Affairs ... Vacant
88 Asst VP for Academic Affairs ... Dr. Hazel STRUBY
06 Registrar ... Ms. Sonja JENKINS
07 Exec Director of Admissions ... Mr. Dann WEBB
21 Exec Dir of Student Fin Svcs ... Mr. Chris JOHNSON
30 Asst VP for Advancement ... Mrs. Tonya MCCLURE
36 Director Career Services ... Mr. Pat IVEY
08 Director Library & Media Services ... Mr. Neil MCARTHUR
37 Director of Financial Aid ... Ms. Jackie WHITE
15 Executive Director Human Resources ... Ms. Carol JONES
105 Web Developer/Data Analyst ... Ms. Margo S. KENIREY
18 Facilities Director ... Mr. Robert DOMINY
13 Director of Information Technology ... Mr. Michael CLOUGH
51 Director of Continuing Education ... Mr. Clay TEAGUE

Central Georgia Technical College (G)

80 Cohen Walker Drive, Warner Robins GA 31088-2729
County: Houston | FICE Identification: 025086
Unit ID: 140085
Telephone: (478) 988-6800 | Carnegie Class: Assoc/Pub-R-M
FAX Number: (478) 988-6813 | Calendar System: Quarter
URL: www.centralgatech.edu
Established: 1973 | Annual Undergrad Tuition & Fees (In-State): $2,700
Enrollment: 3,771 | Coed
Affiliation or Control: State | IRS Status: 501(c)3
Highest Offering: Associate Degree
Program: Occupational; 2-Year Principally Bachelor's Creditable; Technical Emphasis
Accreditation: SC, COARC, DH, RAD, SURGT

01 President ... Dr. Ivan H. ALLEN
05 Vice President for Academic Affairs ... Dr. Amy L. HOLLOWAY
32 Vice President for Student Affairs ... Mr. Craig JACKSON
09 VP Economic Develop/Inst Support ... Mr. Jeffrey SCRUGGS
11 VP for Administrative Services ... Mrs. Michelle SINIARD
88 Vice President for Adult Education ... Ms. Brenda L. BROWN
07 Director of Admissions ... Mr. Dann WEBB
37 Director of Financial Aid ... Ms. Shirley GLOVER
06 Registrar ... Ms. Sonja JENKINS
08 Director of Library Services ... Dr. Dumont C. BUNN
15 Director of Human Resources ... Ms. Carol F. JONES
30 Director of Advancement ... Ms. Janet H. KELLY
26 Marketing & PR Director ... Mrs. Janet H. KELLY
18 Maintenance Superintendent ... Mr. Joe PETERSDORFF

Chamberlain College of Nursing-Atlanta (H)

5775 Peachtree Dunwoody Rd NE,A100,
Atlanta GA 30342
Telephone: (404) 250-8500 | Identification: 770504
Accreditation: &NH, NURSE

† Main campus is Chamberlain College of Nursing - Addison in Addison, IL.

Chattahoochee Technical College (I)

980 South Cobb Drive, Marietta GA 30060
County: Barton | FICE Identification: 030290
Unit ID: 366456
Telephone: (770) 528-4545 | Carnegie Class: Not Classified
FAX Number: (770) 975-4126 | Calendar System: Quarter
URL: www.chattahoocheetech.edu
Established: 1981 | Annual Undergrad Tuition & Fees (In-State): $2,289
Enrollment: 11,679 | Coed
Affiliation or Control: State | IRS Status: 501(c)3
Highest Offering: Associate Degree
Program: Occupational
Accreditation: SC, ACFEI, MAC, OTA, PTAA, RAD

01 President ... Dr. Ron NEWCOMB
04 Administrative Asst to President ... Ms. Tammy COLLUM
03 Executive Vice President ... Dr. Trina BOTELER
05 Actg Vice President for Academics ... Dr. Brenda WHITE
11 Vice Pres for Administrative Svcs ... Ms. Catrice HUFSTETLER
32 VP Student Affairs/Technology ... Dr. Scott RULE
31 Vice Pres External Affairs ... Ms. Jennifer NELSON
18 Vice President for Facilities ... Mr. David SIMMONS
15 Vice President Human Resources ... Dr. Randall REECE
30 Vice Pres Economic Development ... Mr. Rex BISHOP
26 Exec Dir External Affs/Brd Liaison ... Ms. Jennifer NELSON
06 Registrar ... Ms. Shannon POLLOCK

Clark Atlanta University (J)

223 James P. Brawley Drive, SW, Atlanta GA 30314-4391
County: Fulton | FICE Identification: 001559
Unit ID: 138947
Telephone: (404) 880-8000 | Carnegie Class: DRU
FAX Number: N/A | Calendar System: Semester
URL: www.cau.edu
Established: 1988 | Annual Undergrad Tuition & Fees: $21,100
Enrollment: 3,419 | Coed
Affiliation or Control: United Methodist | IRS Status: 501(c)3
Highest Offering: Doctorate
Program: Liberal Arts And General; Teacher Preparatory; Professional
Accreditation: SC, BUS, CACREP, SPAA, SW, TED

01 President ... Dr. Carlton E. BROWN
05 Int Provost/VP for Academic Affairs ... Dr. James A. HEFNER
30 VP for Inst Advancement/Univ Rels ... Mr. Henry W. TAYLOR
10 VP for Finance/Business Svcs ... Ms. Lucille MAUGE
84 VP for Enroll Svcs/Student Affairs ... Dr. Carl JONES
88 VP for Research & Sponsored Pgms ... Dr. Marcus W. SHUTE
20 Assoc VP for Academic Affairs ... Dr. Jeffrey J. PHILLIPS
13 Assoc VP/Chief Info Ofcr ... Mr. Reginald BRINSON
21 Interim Assoc VP/Controller ... Mr. Leighton O'SULLIVAN
35 Interim Director of Student Affairs ... Ms. Ernita HEMMITT
09 Asst VP Planning Assess/Inst Rsrch ... Mr. Narendra H. PATEL
43 General Counsel ... Mr. Lance DUNNINGS
06 Interim University Registrar ... Ms. Susan GIBSON
26 Director Strategic Communications ... Ms. Donna BROCK
29 Director Alumni Relations ... Ms. Gay-linn JASHO
15 Director Human Resources ... Ms. Valerie VINSON
07 Dir Recruitment & Admissions ... Mr. Dwight B. SANCHEZ
38 Director University Counseling Ctr ... Dr. Marilyn LINEBERGER
36 Career Planning/Placement ... Mr. Andre MCKINNEY
37 Director Student Financial Aid ... Mr. Nigel EDWARDS
96 Director of Purchasing ... Ms. Donna BYRD
41 Director of Athletics ... Dr. Tamica JONES
42 University Chaplain ... Dr. Valerie GREEN
49 Dean Arts & Sciences ... Dr. Shirley WILLIAMS-KIRKSEY
50 Acting Dean Business Admin ... Dr. Charles MOSES
53 Dean Education ... Dr. Sean WARNER
70 Dean Social Work ... Dr. Vimala PILLARI
58 Dean Graduate Studies ... Dr. Bettye CLARK
19 Chief of Public Safety ... Chief Thomas TRAWICK
23 Director Health Services ... Ms. Janet SINGLETON
25 Dir Accts Payable Grants/Contracts ... Ms. Rotesha HARRIS
39 Director of Residence Life ... Mr. Ernest MOORE
88 Director Instructional Media ... Mr. Frank EDWARDS
101 Coordinator for Board Relations ... Ms. Natalie BAKER

104 Dir International Educ/Study Abroad ....Dr. Paul M. BROWN
22 University Compliance Officer ....Mr. Robert CLARK
100 Chief of Staff/Spec Asst to Pres ....Ms. Cynthia BUSKEY
44 Exec Dir for Fund Dev & Annual Giv ....Ms. Nicole BLOUNT
18 Director of Facilities ....Mr. Victor PANCHUK

Clayton State University (A)

2000 Clayton State Boulevard, Morrow GA 30260-0285
County: Clayton FICE Identification: 008976
Unit ID: 139311
Telephone: (678) 466-4000 Carnegie Class: Bac/Diverse
FAX Number: (770) 961-3700 Calendar System: Semester
URL: www.clayton.edu
Established: 1969 Annual Undergrad Tuition & Fees (In-State): $5,153
Enrollment: 7,140 Coed
Affiliation or Control: State IRS Status: 501(c)3
Highest Offering: Master's
Program: Occupational; Liberal Arts And General; Teacher Preparatory
Accreditation: SC, BUS, DH, MUS, NURSE, TED

01 President ....Dr. Thomas HYNES
05 Provost/Vice Pres Academic Affairs ....Dr. Michael CRAFTON
10 VP for Operations/Planning/Budget ....Ms. Corlis CUMMINGS
32 Vice President for Student Affairs ....Dr. Brian HAYNES
26 Vice President External Affairs ....Ms. Kate TROELSTRA
13 Vice Pres Information Tech & Svcs ....Dr. John S. BRYAN
20 Assoc Vice President Academic Affs ....Dr. Robert A. VAUGHAN, JR.
35 Assoc Vice Pres Student Affairs ....Dr. Elaine MANGLITZ
84 Assoc VP Enroll Mgmt/Acad Success ....Dr. Mark DADDONA
41 Executive Director of Athletics ....Mr. Carl MCALOOSE
88 Executive Director of Spivey Hall ....Mr. Samuel DIXON
15 Exec Dir Human Resources & Services ....Vacant
49 Dean of Arts & Sciences ....Dr. Nasser MOMAYEZI
36 Dean of Retention & Stdnt Placement ....Vacant
50 Dean of Business ....Dr. Michael DEIS
76 Dean of Health Sciences ....Dr. Lisa EICHELBERGER
81 Dean Information/Mathematical Sci ....Dr. Lila ROBERTS
08 Dean of Library Services ....Dr. Gordon BAKER
46 Dean Assessmnt/Instructnl Developmt ....Dr. Jill LANE
51 Director of Continuing Education ....Ms. Janet WINKLER
06 University Registrar ....Ms. Rebecca GMEINER
07 Director of Admissions ....Ms. Betty MOMAYEZI
31 Director of Auxiliary Services ....Ms. Carolina AMERO
26 Director of University Relations ....Mr. John SHIFFERT
18 Director of Plant Operations ....Mr. Harun BISWAS
19 Director of Public Safety ....Mr. Bobby HAMIL
30 Dir of Development/Alumni Relations ....Ms. Reda ROWELL
09 Director of Institutional Research ....Dr. Narem REDDY
24 Director Media Services ....Mr. Paul BAILEY
38 Director of Counseling Services ....Dr. Christine SMITH
37 Director Student Financial Aid ....Ms. Pat BARTON
96 Director of Purchasing ....Ms. Marcia JONES
29 Director Alumni Relations ....Mr. Gid ROWELL

† Part of the University System of Georgia.

College of Coastal Georgia (B)

One College Drive, Brunswick GA 31520-3632
County: Glynn FICE Identification: 001558
Unit ID: 139250
Telephone: (912) 279-5700 Carnegie Class: Assoc/Pub-R-M
FAX Number: (912) 262-3072 Calendar System: Semester
URL: www.ccga.edu
Established: 1961 Annual Undergrad Tuition & Fees (In-State): $4,238
Enrollment: 3,156 Coed
Affiliation or Control: State IRS Status: 501(c)3
Highest Offering: Baccalaureate
Program: Occupational; 2-Year Principally Bachelor's Creditable; Liberal Arts And General; Teacher Preparatory; Professional
Accreditation: SC, ACFEI, ADNUR, MLTAD, NUR, RAD

01 President ....Dr. Gregory F. ALOIA
05 Vice President Academic Affairs ....Dr. Phil MASON
10 Vice President Business Affairs ....Mr. Jeffrey H. PRESTON
32 Vice President Student Affairs ....Dr. Heidi LEMING
20 Associate VP Academic Affairs ....Ms. Kay HAMPTON
84 Asst VP Enrollment Management ....Mr. Clayton DANIELS
30 Chief Advancement Officer ....Ms. Elizabeth WEATHERLY
21 Asst VP Business Affairs ....Mr. C. Tom SAUNDERS
88 Asst VP Construction and Design ....Mr. Greg CARVER
37 Director Student Financial Aid ....Ms. Terral HARRIS
06 Registrar ....Ms. Lisa LESSEIG
08 Dean of Library Services ....Ms. Debra HOLMES
09 Director Institutional Effectivenes ....Dr. James LYNCH
12 Director Camden Center ....Ms. Holly CHRISTENSEN
15 Director of Human Resources ....Ms. Phyllis BROADWELL
18 Director of Facilities and Plant Op ....Mr. Gary STRICKLAND
50 Dean Sch of Business & Public Affs ....Dr. William MOUNTS
49 Dean School of Arts and Sciences ....Dr. Keith E. BELCHER
53 Dean School of Education & Teacher .... Dr. Michael HAZELKORN
66 Dean School of Nursing & Health Sci ....Dr. Patricia KRAFT
19 Chief of Police ....Mr. Brian SIPE
35 Dean of Students ....Dr. Michael BUTCHER
41 Director of Athletics ....Dr. William CARLTON
27 Chief Information Officer ....Mr. Tim MOODY
13 Director of Technology Services ....Vacant
106 Director of E-Learning ....Dr. Kevin MOBBS
26 Director of Marketing & Public Rels ....Mr. John CORNELL
88 Coordinator Faculty & Admin Svcs ....Ms. Sandra J. BUNN
96 Purchasing Officer ....Ms. Karen O. MARTIN

04 Executive Assistant President's Off ....Ms. Judy JOHNSTON

† Part of the University System of Georgia. The Annual Tuition and Fees reported for 2012-2013 included a 30-meal pack fee. This fee is not included in the Annual Tuition and Fees reported for 2013-2014.

Columbia Theological Seminary (C)

P.O. Box 520, 701 Columbia Drive, Decatur GA 30031-0520
County: DeKalb FICE Identification: 001560
Unit ID: 139348
Telephone: (404) 378-8821 Carnegie Class: Spec/Faith
FAX Number: (404) 377-9696 Calendar System: 4/1/4
URL: www.ctsnet.edu
Established: 1828 Annual Graduate Tuition & Fees: N/A
Enrollment: 363 Coed
Affiliation or Control: Presbyterian Church (U.S.A.) IRS Status: 501(c)3
Highest Offering: Doctorate; No Undergraduates
Program: Professional; Religious Emphasis
Accreditation: SC, THEOL

01 President ....Dr. Stephen A. HAYNER
05 Exec VP Acad Affs/Dean of Faculty ....Dr. Deborah F. MULLEN
10 Vice Pres Business and Finance ....Mr. Martin SADLER
32 Vice President Student Services ....Rev. John WHITE
30 Vice Pres Institutional Advancement ....Mr. Doug TAYLOR
20 Assoc Dean Academic Administration ....Dr. Ann Clay ADAMS
08 Director of Library ....Dr. Kelly D. CAMPBELL
107 Assoc Dean Advanced Prof Studies ....Dr. Kevin PARK
06 Registrar ....Mr. Mike MEDFORD
07 Director of Admissions & Recruiting ....Rev. Monica WEDLOCK
26 Director of Communications ....Mr. Michael THOMPSON

Columbus State University (D)

4225 University Avenue, Columbus GA 31907-5645
County: Muscogee FICE Identification: 001561
Unit ID: 139366
Telephone: (706) 507-8800 Carnegie Class: Master's L
FAX Number: (706) 568-2123 Calendar System: Semester
URL: www.columbusstate.edu
Established: 1958 Annual Undergrad Tuition & Fees (In-State): $6,774
Enrollment: 8,239 Coed
Affiliation or Control: State IRS Status: 501(c)3
Highest Offering: Doctorate
Program: 2-Year Principally Bachelor's Creditable; Liberal Arts And General; Teacher Preparatory; Professional
Accreditation: SC, ART, BUS, CACREP, MUS, NURSE, TED, THEA

01 President ....Dr. Timothy S. MESCON
05 Provost/VP Academic Affairs ....Dr. Tom HACKETT
10 Vice President Business & Finance ....Mr. Tom HELTON
32 VP Student Affairs & Enrollment Mgt ....Dr. Gina SHEEKS
30 VP University Advancement ....Dr. Alan MEDDERS
14 Chief Information Officer ....Mr. Abraham GEORGE
20 Assoc Provost Undergraduate Educ ....Dr. Tina BUTCHER
20 Interim Asst VP Academic Affairs ....Dr. Ellen ROBERTS
30 Assoc VP for Development ....Mr. Spence SEALY
21 Asst Vice Pres Business & Finance ....Mrs. Lougene BROWN
84 Asst VP for Enrollment Mgmt ....Mr. John MCELVEEN
26 Asst VP for University Relations ....Mr. John LESTER
50 Dean College of Business & Comp Sci ....Dr. Linda HADLEY
81 Interim Dean COLS ....Dr. Pat MCHENRY
53 Dean College of Education ....Dr. Barbara BUCKNER
57 Dean College of the Arts ....Dr. Richard L. BAXTER
08 Dean of Libraries ....Mr. Mark FLYNN
35 Dean of Students ....Mr. Aaron J. REESE
35 Sr Dir Student Life & Development ....Dr. Kimberly MULLEN
44 Dir Annual Giving ....Mr. Brett EVANS
29 Director Alumni Relations ....Mrs. Jennifer JOYNER
15 Human Resources Director ....Ms. Laurie S. JONES
09 Director Institutional Research ....Dr. Sri SITHARAMAN
41 Athletic Director ....Mr. Jay SPARKS
19 Chief Campus Police ....Mr. Rus DREW
51 Director Continuing Education ....Ms. Susan WIRT
39 Director Residence Life ....Mr. Jonathan LUCIA
37 Assoc Director Financial Aid ....Ms. Patricia GARRETT
38 Director Counseling Center ....Dr. Dan ROSE
85 Director Center International Educ ....Dr. Neal R. MCCRILLIS
07 Director of Admissions ....Ms. Susan LOVELL
92 Director Honors Program ....Dr. Cindy HENNING
23 Director Student Health Services ....Ms. Rebecca TEW

† Part of the University System of Georgia.

Columbus Technical College (E)

928 Manchester Expressway, Columbus GA 31904-6572
County: Muscogee FICE Identification: 005624
Unit ID: 139357
Telephone: (706) 649-1800 Carnegie Class: Assoc/Pub-R-M
FAX Number: (706) 649-1885 Calendar System: Semester
URL: www.columbustech.edu
Established: 1961 Annual Undergrad Tuition & Fees (In-State): $3,822
Enrollment: 4,267 Coed
Affiliation or Control: State IRS Status: 501(c)3
Highest Offering: Associate Degree
Program: Occupational; 2-Year Principally Bachelor's Creditable; Technical Emphasis
Accreditation: SC, ADNUR, CAHIIM, COARC, DA, DH, DMS, MAC, PNUR, RAD, SURGT

01 President ....Ms. Lorette M. HOOVER
11 Vice President Administrative Svcs ....Ms. Betty JACKSON
05 Vice President Academic Affairs ....Dr. Linn STOREY
32 Vice President Student Affairs ....Ms. Tara ASKEW
18 Vice President Operations ....Mr. Tommy WILSON
46 VP Institutional Effectiveness ....Dr. Michael LAMB
88 Vice President Economic Development ....Mr. James LOYD
51 Assoc VP of Adult Education ....Dr. Sarah BEECHAM
15 Director of Human Resources ....Ms. Patricia HOOD
26 Director of Communications ....Ms. Cheryl MYERS
37 Associate VP of Financial Aid ....Ms. Debbie HENSHAW
38 Director Student Counseling ....Ms. Olive VIDAL-KENDALL
30 Director Institutional Advancement ....Ms. Gloria DODDS

Covenant College (F)

14049 Scenic Highway, Lookout Mountain TN 30750-4164
County: Dade FICE Identification: 003484
Unit ID: 139393
Telephone: (706) 820-1560 Carnegie Class: Bac/Diverse
FAX Number: (706) 820-2165 Calendar System: Semester
URL: www.covenant.edu
Established: 1955 Annual Undergrad Tuition & Fees: $29,100
Enrollment: 1,135 Coed
Affiliation or Control: Presbyterian Church In America IRS Status: 501(c)3
Highest Offering: Master's
Program: Liberal Arts And General; Teacher Preparatory
Accreditation: SC

01 President ....Dr. J. Derek HALVORSON
05 Vice Pres Academic Affairs ....Dr. Jeffrey B. HALL
30 Vice President Advancement ....Mr. Troy DUBLE
32 Vice Pres Student Development ....Mr. Brad VOYLES
10 Vice Pres for Business & Finance ....Mr. Dan WYKOFF
08 Librarian ....Mr. Tad MINDEMAN
06 Dean of Records ....Mr. Rodney E. MILLER
42 Chaplain ....Mr. Lowe GRANT
58 Director of Master of Education Pgm ....Dr. Jim DREXLER
21 Controller ....Mr. Robert E. HARBERT
18 Director of Physical Plant ....Mr. David NORTHCUTT
37 Director of Student Financial Plng ....Ms. Beth BAILEY
15 Director of Human Resources ....Mr. Pat SEMTNER
41 Athletic Director ....Mr. Kyle TAYLOR
13 Chief Information Officer ....Ms. Marjorie CROCKER
29 Director of Alumni Relations ....Mr. Marshall K. ROWE
24 Director of AV Services ....Mr. Matt WRIGHT
23 Director of Health Services ....Mrs. Barbara M. MICHAL
07 Dir Admissions & Church Relations ....Mr. Matthew BRYANT
09 Director of Institutional Research ....Dr. Karen NELSON
26 Chief Communications Officer ....Ms. Jen ALLEN
20 Director of Academic Support ....Mrs. Janet HULSEY
36 Dir of Center for Calling & Career ....Mr. Anthony TUCKER

Dalton State College (G)

650 College Drive, Dalton GA 30720-3797
County: Whitfield FICE Identification: 003956
Unit ID: 139463
Telephone: (706) 272-4436 Carnegie Class: Bac/Assoc
FAX Number: (706) 272-4588 Calendar System: Semester
URL: www.daltonstate.edu
Established: 1963 Annual Undergrad Tuition & Fees (In-State): $3,750
Enrollment: 5,200 Coed
Affiliation or Control: State IRS Status: 501(c)3
Highest Offering: Baccalaureate
Program: Occupational; 2-Year Principally Bachelor's Creditable; Liberal Arts And General; Teacher Preparatory; Professional
Accreditation: SC, ADNUR, BUS, COARC, MAC, MLTAD, PHLEB, RAD, SW, TED

01 President ....Dr. John O. SCHWENN
05 Vice President for Academic Affairs ....Dr. Sandra STONE
10 Vice President Fiscal Affairs ....Mr. Scott BAILEY
84 Vice Pres Enrollment & Student Svcs ....Dr. Jodi S. JOHNSON
20 Asst Vice President Academic Affs ....Dr. Andy MEYER
37 Director of Financial Aid/Vet Svcs ....Ms. Carol JONES
08 Librarian ....Ms. Lydia KNIGHT
09 Director Inst Research & Planning ....Dr. Henry M. CODJOE
21 Asst Director of Business Office ....Mr. Nick HENRY
07 Asst VP for Enrollment Services ....Dr. Angela HARRIS
18 Chief Facilities/Physical Plant ....Mr. Jack REYNOLDS
26 Director Marketing & Communication ....Ms. Pam PARTAIN
102 Director Foundation ....Mr. David ELROD
32 Director Student Life ....Ms. Jami HALL
38 Director Student Counseling ....Ms. Linda WHEELER
15 Director Human Resources ....Ms. Faith MILLER
96 Interim Director of Purchasing ....Ms. Penny CORDELL
13 Director Computing & Info Services ....Mr. Terry BAILEY
19 Interim Director Public Safety ....Mr. Michael MASTERS
29 Director Alumni Relations ....Mr. Josh WILSON
39 Director Student Housing ....Mr. Jonathan JOHNSON
50 Interim Dean School of Business ....Dr. Larry JOHNSON
53 Interim Dean School of Education ....Dr. Sharon HIXON
49 Dean School of Liberal Arts ....Ms. Mary NIELSEN
81 Dean School of Science/Tech/Math ....Mr. Randall GRIFFUS
66 Interim Dean Health Professions ..... Dr. Gina KERTULIS-TARTAR
06 Registrar ....Mr. Rob WINGFIELD
41 Director Intercollegiate Athletics ....Mr. Derek WAUGH

† Part of the University System of Georgia.

Darton State College (A)

2400 Gillionville Road, Albany GA 31707-3098

County: Dougherty — FICE Identification: 001543
Unit ID: 138691
Telephone: (229) 317-6000 — Carnegie Class: Assoc/Pub-R-M
FAX Number: (229) 317-6604 — Calendar System: Semester
URL: www.darton.edu
Established: 1963 — Annual Undergrad Tuition & Fees (In-State): $3,241
Enrollment: 6,405 — Coed
Affiliation or Control: State — IRS Status: 501(c)3
Highest Offering: Baccalaureate
Program: Occupational; 2-Year Principally Bachelor's Creditable
Accreditation: SC, ADNUR, CAHIIM, COARC, CVT, DH, EMT, HT, MLTAD, OTA, PTAA

Code	Title	Name
01	President	Dr. Peter J. SIRENO
10	Vice Pres Business/Financial Svcs	Mr. Ronnie A. HENRY
05	VP Academic Affairs	Dr. F. Gary BARNETTE
32	VP Student Affs/Dean of Students	Dr. F. Gary BARNETTE
21	Asst VP Business/Financial Svcs	Mr. Stan BROWN
51	Interim Dir Cont Ed/Economic Dev	Mr. Blake COOK
08	Director Learning Resources Ctr	Mrs. Mary WASHINGTON
07	Director Admissions	Ms. Susan BOWEN
13	Director Office of Information Tech	Mr. Tracy COSPER
18	Director Physical Plant	Mr. D. Steve HARRIS
26	Director College Relations	Mr. Tracy GOODE
41	Athletic Director	Mr. Michael KIEFER
06	Registrar	Mrs. Frances CARR
37	Director Student Financial Aid	Ms. Haley HOOKS
15	Director Personnel Services	Mr. Ronnie HENRY
85	International Student Coordinator	Ms. Karly BOYD
29	Director Alumni Relations	Mrs. Lisa MALINOWSKI
36	Director Student Placement	Mr. Jason SWORDS
38	Director Student Counseling	Vacant
96	Director of Purchasing	Mrs. Joy CAUSEY
89	Director Freshmen Studies	Ms. Gloria RIDGEWAY
92	Director Honors Program	Ms. Shani CLARK
93	Director Minority Students	Ms. Wendy WILSON
09	Director of Institutional Research	Dr. Richard BALSLEY

† Part of the University System of Georgia.

DeVry University - Decatur Campus (B)

One West Court Square, Ste. 100,
Decatur GA 30030-2556

Telephone: (404) 270-2700 — FICE Identification: 009224
Accreditation: &NH, ENGT

† Main campus is DeVry University - Chicago Campus in Chicago, IL.

East Georgia State College (C)

131 College Circle, Swainsboro GA 30401-3643

County: Emanuel — FICE Identification: 010997
Unit ID: 139621
Telephone: (478) 289-2000 — Carnegie Class: Assoc/Pub-R-S
FAX Number: (478) 289-2038 — Calendar System: Semester
URL: www.ega.edu
Established: 1973 — Annual Undergrad Tuition & Fees (In-State): $3,432
Enrollment: 2,944 — Coed
Affiliation or Control: State — IRS Status: 501(c)3
Highest Offering: Baccalaureate
Program: Occupational; 2-Year Principally Bachelor's Creditable
Accreditation: SC

Code	Title	Name
01	President	Dr. Robert G. BOEHMER
05	Vice President for Academic Affairs	Dr. Timothy D. GOODMAN
10	Vice President for Business Affairs	Mr. Cliff GAY
32	Vice Pres for Student Affairs	Mr. Donald AVERY
13	Vice Pres Information Technology	Mr. Mike ROUNTREE
100	Chief of Staff/Legal Counsel	Mrs. Mary C. SMITH
04	Executive Assistant to President	Mrs. Susan GRAY
08	Librarian	Mrs. Amanda MCKENZIE
06	Registrar	Mrs. Janet STRACHER
12	Director of EGSC-Augusta	Dr. Jeff EDGENS
27	Director of Public Information	Mr. Gerald D. HOOKS
09	Director of Institutional Research	Mr. David GRIBBIN
37	Director of Financial Aid	Mrs. Karen S. JONES
15	Director of Human Resources	Mrs. Tracy WOODS
30	Director of External Affairs	Ms. Elizabeth GILMER
18	Director of Facilities	Mrs. Michelle GOFF
26	Director of Marketing	Ms. Norma KENNEDY
12	Director of EGSC-Statesboro	Ms. Caroline MCMILLAN
19	Director of Security	Mr. Drew DURDEN
35	Director of Student Life	Ms. Vicki SHERROD
07	Director of Admissions	Ms. Georgia EDMOND
21	Comptroller	Vacant
38	Dir Counseling/Disability Services	Ms. Anna Marie REICH
39	Director of Housing	Ms. Missie CRAWFORD
41	Director of Athletics	Mr. Neil BAILEY
12	Dir Sudie A Fulford Cmty Lrng Ctr	Mrs. Jean D. SCHWABE
18	Director of Plant Operations	Mr. David STEPTOE
88	Director of Accounting Services	Ms. Becky FOSKEY
106	Director of Distance Education	Dr. Dee MCKINNEY
88	Director of Academic Advisement	Ms. Deborah KITTRELL-MIKELL
88	Interim Director Learning Support	Ms. Jordyn NAIL
88	Auditor	Ms. Rebecca VINCENT
88	Director of Auxiliary Services	Ms. Ruth UNDERWOOD
88	Director of Student Conduct	Ms. Sherrie HELMS
81	Chair of Mathematics & Sciences	Dr. Robert BROWN
79	Chair of Humanities	Dr. Carmine PALUMBO
83	Chair of Social Sciences	Dr. Lee CHEEK
81	Chair of Biology Department	Dr. Jimmy WEDINCAMP

† Part of the University System of Georgia.

Emmanuel College (D)

181 Springs Street, Franklin Springs GA 30639

County: Franklin — FICE Identification: 001563
Unit ID: 139630
Telephone: (706) 245-7226 — Carnegie Class: Bac/Diverse
FAX Number: (706) 245-4424 — Calendar System: Semester
URL: www.ec.edu
Established: 1919 — Annual Undergrad Tuition & Fees: $16,800
Enrollment: 806 — Coed
Affiliation or Control: Pentecostal Holiness Church — IRS Status: 501(c)3
Highest Offering: Baccalaureate
Program: Liberal Arts And General; Teacher Preparatory; Professional; Business Emphasis
Accreditation: SC

Code	Title	Name
01	President	Dr. Michael S. STEWART
32	Vice President for Student Life	Mr. Jason CROY
05	Vice President for Academic Affairs	Dr. John R. HENZEL, JR.
10	Vice President for Finance	Dr. Kevin CRAWFORD
30	Vice President for Development	Mr. W. Brian JAMES
84	Vice Pres Enrollment Mgmt/Marketing	Ms. Wendy VINSON
08	Director of Library Services	Ms. Austina JORDAN
06	Registrar	Mrs. Debra F. GRIZZLE
37	Director of Financial Aid	Mr. Vince WELCH
13	Director of Information Technology	Mr. Glenn TONEY
11	Director of Campus Operations	Mr. Ron MCCULLAR
41	Athletics Director	Mr. Jose LARIOS
42	Dir Spiritual Life/Campus Pastor	Mr. Chris MAXWELL
15	Director of Human Resources	Mrs. Joann HARPER
26	Chief Public Relations Officer	Mrs. Paula DIXON
38	Director of Student Counseling	Mr. Sean WILLIAMSON
96	Director of Accounting Services	Mrs. Anita RAY
18	Physical Plant Director	Mr. Wayne CRIDER
09	Director of Institutional Research	Dr. Brian PEEK
29	Director Alumni Relations	Mr. Harrell W. QUEEN
36	Director Career Services	Mr. Sean WILLIAMSON

Emory University (E)

201 Dowman Drive, Atlanta GA 30322-0001

County: DeKalb — FICE Identification: 001564
Unit ID: 139658
Telephone: (404) 727-6123 — Carnegie Class: RU/VH
FAX Number: (404) 727-5997 — Calendar System: Semester
URL: www.emory.edu
Established: 1836 — Annual Undergrad Tuition & Fees: $44,008
Enrollment: 14,236 — Coed
Affiliation or Control: United Methodist — IRS Status: 501(c)3
Highest Offering: Doctorate
Program: Occupational; 2-Year Principally Bachelor's Creditable; Liberal Arts And General; Teacher Preparatory; Professional
Accreditation: SC, AA, ARCPA, BUS, CLPSY, DENT, IPSY, LAW, MED, MIDWF, NURSE, PH, PTA, RAD, TED, THEOL

Code	Title	Name
01	President	Dr. James W. WAGNER
05	Provost/Exec VP Acad Affs	Dr. Claire E. STERK
03	Exec Vice Pres for Finance/Admin	Mr. Michael J. MANDL
17	Exec Vice Pres Health Affairs	Dr. S. Wright CAUGHMAN
101	VP/Secretary of the University	Dr. Rosemary MAGEE
04	VP/Deputy to the President	Dr. Gary S. HAUK
43	Sr Vice Pres & General Counsel	Mr. Stephen D. SENCER
30	Sr Vice Pres Devel/Alumni Rels	Ms. Susan CRUSE
32	Sr Vice President/Dean Campus Life	Dr. Ajay NAIR
46	Vice President for Research Admin	Dr. David L. WYNES
29	Vice President Alumni Relations	Ms. Allison DYKES
10	Vice President for Finance	Ms. Edith C. MURPHREE
58	Vice Provost/Dean Graduate Sch	Dr. Lisa A. TEDESCO
15	Vice President Human Resources	Mr. Peter BARNES
26	Interim Vice Pres Comm/Marketing	Ms. Nancy SEIDEMAN
86	Acting Vice President Govt Affairs	Ms. Jane JORDAN
18	Vice President Campus Services	Mr. Matthew EARLY
25	Assoc Vice Pres for Research Admin	Ms. Kathleen BIENKOWSKI
10	Assoc Vice President & Controller	Ms. Belva WHITE
35	Special Asst to Sr VP Campus Life	Dr. Carolyn LIVINGSTON
28	Sr Vice Provost Community/Diversity	Mr. Ozzie HARRIS
20	Assoc Vice Prov for Academic Affs	Ms. Dorothy BROWN
20	Sr Vice Prov Undergrad & Cont Ed	Dr. Lynn ZIMMERMAN
88	Assoc Vice Prov Oper Student Svcs	Ms. Heather MUGG
08	Sr Vice Provost for Lib Svcs/CIO	Dr. Richard A. MENDOLA
07	AVP Undergrad Enroll/Dean of Admiss	Dr. John LATTING
49	Dean of Emory College	Dr. Robin FORMAN
12	Dean & CEO Oxford College	Dr. Stephen H. BOWEN
63	Dean of Medicine	Dr. Christian P. LARSEN
66	Dean of Nursing	Dr. Linda MCCAULEY
73	Dean of Theology	Dr. Jan LOVE
61	Dean of Law	Mr. Robert SCHAPIRO
50	Dean of the Business School	Dr. Lawrence M. BENVENISTE
69	Dean of Public Health	Dr. James W. CURRAN
85	Dir Intl Student Scholar Program	Ms. Lelia CRAWFORD
80	Pres & CEO of the Carter Center	Dr. John HARDMAN
42	Dean of the Chapel & Religious Life	Rev. Susan HENRY-CROWE
06	University Registrar	Ms. JoAnn MCKENZIE
27	Executive Director Marketing	Ms. Jan GLEASON
37	Director Financial Aid	Mr. Dean BENTLEY
36	Director Placement Service	Mr. Paul FOWLER
19	Chief of Police	Mr. Craig T. WATSON
23	Pres & CEO Emory Healthcare	Mr. John T. FOX
41	Director Athletics/Recreation	Mr. Timothy DOWNES
88	Director Yerkes Research Ctrs	Dr. Stuart M. ZOLA
49	Director Institute Liberal Arts	Dr. Kevin CORRIGAN
88	Director M C Carlos Museum	Ms. Bonnie SPEED
40	University Bookstore Liaison	Mr. Bruce COVEY
39	Exec Dir Res Life & Housing	Dr. Andrea TRINKLEIN
38	Director Univ Counseling Center	Dr. Mark MCLEOD
09	Director Institutional Research	Dr. Melissa BOLYARD
96	Director Contract Admin/Compliance	Mr. Rex HARDAWAY
44	Executive Director of Annual Giving	Ms. Kimberly JULIAN

Everest College (F)

2841 Greenbriar Parkway SW, Atlanta GA 30331

Telephone: (678) 600-3400 — Identification: 770570
Accreditation: ACCSC, MAAB

† Main campus is Everest College-Reseda in Reseda, CA.

Everest Institute (G)

1750 Beaver Ruin Road, Suite 500, Norcross GA 30093

Telephone: (770) 921-1085 — Identification: 770571
Accreditation: ACCSC

† Main campus is Everest College-Gardena in Gardena, CA.

Fort Valley State University (H)

1005 State University Drive, Fort Valley GA 31030-4313

County: Peach — FICE Identification: 001566
Unit ID: 139719
Telephone: (478) 825-6211 — Carnegie Class: Bac/Diverse
FAX Number: (478) 825-6394 — Calendar System: Semester
URL: www.fvsu.edu
Established: 1895 — Annual Undergrad Tuition & Fees (In-State): $5,278
Enrollment: 3,755 — Coed
Affiliation or Control: State — IRS Status: 501(c)3
Highest Offering: Beyond Master's But Less Than Doctorate
Program: Occupational; Liberal Arts And General; Teacher Preparatory
Accreditation: SC, AAFCS, CACREP, CORE, ENGT, TED

Code	Title	Name
01	President	Dr. Ivelaw L. GRIFFITH
03	Inerim Exeutive Vice President	Dr. Canter BROWN, JR.
32	Vice Pres Student Affairs	Mr. Willie WILLIAMS
10	Int Vice Pres Business & Finance	Mr. Henry SPINKS
31	Vice President External Affairs	Dr. Melody CARTER
05	Int Vice Pres for Academic Affairs	Dr. Julius SCIPIO
09	VP Inst Research/Plng & Effec	Dr. B. Donta TRUSS
88	Assoc VP for Land Grant Affair	Dr. Mark LATTIMORE
04	Spec Asst to the Pres/Legal Counsel	Dr. Canter BROWN
49	Dean Arts & Sciences	Dr. Victor BROWN
21	Comptroller	Mr. Kevin HOWARD
06	Registrar	Mrs. Sharee LAWRENCE
13	Director for Information Technology	Mr. Gary MILLER
08	Dir University Libraries	Dr. Annie PAYTON
07	Director Admissions	Mr. Johnny C. NIMES
37	Int Director Financial Aid	Ms. Lakisia SANDERS
88	Director Title III	Dr. Melody CARTER
29	Director Alumni Affairs	Ms. Clara BRASWELL
15	Director of Human Resources	Ms. Erika GRAVETT
19	Director Campus Safety	Mr. Ken MORGAN
47	Int Dean Agriculture	Dr. Gavindarajan KANNON
23	Director Health Services	Vacant
18	Director Plant & Maintenance	Dr. Dwayne CREW
36	Director Counsel/Career Development	Ms. Simmons ROMELDA
26	Director Marketing/Communications	Vacant
41	Director of Athletics	Vacant
88	Int Exec Dir Academic Success Ctr	Dr. Jerry HAYWOOD
58	Dean Grad Studies/Extended Educ	Dr. Anna HOLLOWAY
53	Dean College of Education	Dr. Edward HILL

† Part of the University System of Georgia.

Georgia Christian University (I)

6789 Peachtree Industrial Boulevard, Atlanta GA 30360

County: DeKalb — FICE Identification: 041565
Unit ID: 461236
Telephone: (770) 279-0507 — Carnegie Class: Not Classified
FAX Number: (770) 279-0308 — Calendar System: Other
URL: www.gcuniv.edu
Established: 1986 — Annual Undergrad Tuition & Fees: $21,500
Enrollment: 280 — Coed
Affiliation or Control: Independent Non-Profit — IRS Status: 501(c)3
Highest Offering: Doctorate
Program: Professional; Religious Emphasis
Accreditation: TRACS

Code	Title	Name
01	President	Dr. Paul C. KIM
07	Director of Admissions	Ms. Younghee HAN
05	Chief Academic Officer	Dr. Seung-ju BAICK
45	Director Of Planning	Dr. HeeSook SONG
10	Chief Financial Officer	Ms. Eunice KIM
12	Director of Branch Campus	Ms. Sun Hee CHOI
18	Chief Facilities/Physical Plant	Rev. Min Soo KIM
19	Director Security/Safety	Mr. Samuel KIM
21	Director of Business Affairs	Mr. Daniel D. KIM
29	Director Alumni Relations	Rev. Min Soo KIM
26	Chief Public Relations Officer	Dr. Hyun Sung CHO

06 Registrar ... Ms. Sara KIM
37 Director Student Financial Aid ... Dr. Younghee HAN
50 Dean School of Business ... Dr. Kyung-il GHYMN
53 Dean School of Education ... Dr. HeeSook SONG
88 Dean Divinity School ... Dr. Ho Woo LEE
64 Dean School of Music ... Dr. Mi Sun CHUN
88 Dn Mission Stds/World Christianity ... Dr. Youngwoo LEE
73 Dean School of Theology ... Dr. Jong Sik CHANG
88 International Student Advisor ... Ms. Younghee HAN
30 Dir of Institutional Advancement ... Dr. Yong Soo JO
42 Chaplain ... Rev. Chang Sun PYO

Georgia College & State University (A)

231 West Hancock Street, Milledgeville GA 31061-0490
County: Baldwin FICE Identification: 001602
Unit ID: 139861
Telephone: (478) 445-5004 Carnegie Class: Master's L
FAX Number: (478) 445-1191 Calendar System: Semester
URL: www.gcsu.edu
Established: 1889 Annual Undergrad Tuition & Fees (In-State): $8,790
Enrollment: 6,444 Coed
Affiliation or Control: State IRS Status: 501(c)3
Highest Offering: Doctorate
Program: Liberal Arts And General; Teacher Preparatory; Professional; Nursing Emphasis
Accreditation: SC, BUS, MUS, NUR, SPAA, TED

01 President ... Dr. Steve M. DORMAN
04 Exec Assistant to the President ... Ms. Monica STARLEY
05 Provost/VP for Academic Affairs ... Dr. Kelli BROWN
11 Sr VP for Finance & Administration ... Dr. Paul A. JONES
32 Vice President for Student Affairs ... Dr. Bruce HARSHBARGER
30 Interim VP University Advancement ... Mr. Bill DOERR
88 Dir of Comm Engagement/Economic Dev ... Mr. Johnny GRANT
20 Assoc Provost for Academic Affs ... Dr. Tom ORMOND
51 Assoc VP for Extended University ... Dr. Mark PELTON
35 Dean of Students ... Dr. Andy LEWTER
26 Assoc VP Strategic Communications ... Mr. John HACHTEL
84 Asst VP for Enrollment Management ... Ms. Suzanne PITTMAN
31 Asst VP for Auxiliary Services ... Mr. Kyle CULLARS
21 Asst VP Institutional Budget/Plng ... Ms. Susan ALLEN
49 Dean College of Arts & Sciences ... Mr. Ken PROCTER
50 Interim Dean College of Business ... Dr. Dale YOUNG
53 Dean College of Education ... Dr. Jane HINSON
76 Dean College of Health Sciences ... Dr. Sandra GANGSTEAD
39 Exec Director of University Housing ... Mr. Larry CHRISTENSON
88 Univ Architect/Dir Facilities Plng ... Mr. Michael RICKENBAKER
18 Director of Plant Operations ... Mr. Mark DUCLOS
19 Director of Public Safety ... Mr. Scott BECKNER
09 Director of Institutional Research ... Dr. Ed HALE
12 Director Macon Graduate Center ... Dr. Kendra RUSSELL
13 Chief Information Officer ... Mr. Robert ORR
08 Director of University Libraries ... Dr. Joe MOCNIK
36 Director Career Center ... Ms. Mary ROBERTS
40 Director of University Bookstore ... Ms. Lynda GRABLE
16 Director of Human Resources ... Mr. Rod KELLY
22 Director of Instl Equity/Diversity ... Dr. Veronica WOMACK
91 Director Enterprise Applications ... Mr. James CARLISLE
07 Director of Admissions ... Mr. Stephen LAZOWSKI
06 Registrar ... Ms. Kay ANDERSON
41 Director of Athetics ... Mr. Wendell STATON
29 Director Alumni & Parent Relations ... Mr. Matt MIZE
43 General Counsel ... Mr. Marc CARDINALLI
38 Director of Counseling Services ... Vacant
37 Director of Financial Aid ... Ms. Cathy CRAWLEY
88 Dir Materials Mgmt/Central Services ... Mr. Mark MEEKS
88 Dir for Internal Audit/Advisory Ser ... Ms. Julia HANN
35 Director of Campus Life ... Mr. Tom MILES

Georgia Gwinnett College (B)

1000 University Center Lane, Lawrenceville GA 30043
County: Gwinnett FICE Identification: 041429
Unit ID: 447689
Telephone: (678) 407-5000 Carnegie Class: Bac/Diverse
FAX Number: N/A Calendar System: Semester
URL: www.ggc.edu
Established: 2005 Annual Undergrad Tuition & Fees (In-District): $5,290
Enrollment: 9,397 Coed
Affiliation or Control: State/Local IRS Status: 501(c)3
Highest Offering: Baccalaureate
Program: Liberal Arts And General
Accreditation: SC

01 Interim President ... Dr. Stanley PRECZEWSKI
05 Vice Pres Academic/Student Affairs ... Dr. Stanley PRECZEWSKI
18 Vice Pres Facilities/Operations ... Mr. Eddie BEAUCHAMP
88 Vice Pres Educational Technology ... Dr. Mark IKEN
44 Vice President for Resources ... Ms. Laura MAXWELL
30 Vice President Advancement ... Ms. Renee BYRD-LEWIS
41 Athletic Director ... Dr. Darin WILSON
07 Dir Student Recruitment/Admission ... Mr. Tee MITCHELL

Georgia Highlands College (C)

3175 Cedartown Highway SE, Rome GA 30161-3897
County: Floyd FICE Identification: 009507
Unit ID: 139700
Telephone: (706) 802-5000 Carnegie Class: Assoc/Pub-R-M
FAX Number: (706) 295-6610 Calendar System: Semester
URL: www.highlands.edu
Established: 1970 Annual Undergrad Tuition & Fees (In-State): $2,596
Enrollment: 5,532 Coed
Affiliation or Control: State IRS Status: 501(c)3
Highest Offering: Baccalaureate
Program: Occupational; 2-Year Principally Bachelor's Creditable
Accreditation: SC, ADNUR, DH

01 Interim President ... Dr. Renva WATTERSON
03 Interim Vice President ... Dr. Laura MUSSELWHITE
10 Vice Pres Finance/Administration ... Mr. Jeff DAVIS
15 Director Human Resources ... Ms. Ginni SILER
38 Student Support Services Coord ... Ms. Angie WHEELUS
37 Director Financial Aid ... Ms. Megan SIMPSON
06 Registrar ... Ms. Sandie DAVIS
09 Director of Institutional Research ... Dr. Laura MUSSELWHITE
21 Director of Accounting ... Mr. Jamie PETTY
29 Director Alumni Relations ... Ms. Alison LAMPKIN
32 Student Life Coordinator ... Mr. John SPRANZA
08 Librarian ... Mr. Elijah SCOTT
19 Director Security ... Mr. John UPTON
30 Development Officer ... Mr. Raymond CARNLEY
18 Chief Facilities/Physical Plant ... Mr. Phillip KIMSEY
96 Director of Purchasing ... Ms. Cynthia PARKER
12 Campus Dean Marietta Campus ... Mr. Ken REAVES
12 Campus Dean Paulding Campus ... Dr. Cathy LEDBETTER
12 Cmapus Dean Douglasville Campus ... Dr. Cathy LEDBETTER
12 Campus Dean Floyd Campus ... Mr. Todd JONES
12 Campus Dean Cartersville Campus ... Ms. Carolyn HAMRICK
83 Dean Social Sciences ... Dr. Robert PAGE
76 Dean Health Sciences ... Dr. Janet ALEXANDER
88 Dean Acadamic Success ... Dr. Diane LANGSTON
68 Dean Science/PE ... Ms. Donna DAUGHERTY
81 Dean Mathematics ... Mr. Brent GRIFFIN
79 Dean Humanities ... Dr. Jonathan HERSHEY
14 Dir Info Tech/Inst Computer Ctr ... Mr. Jeff PATTY
41 Director of Athletics ... Mr. Phillip GAFFNEY

† Part of the University System of Georgia.

Georgia Institute of Technology (D)

225 North Avenue, NW, Atlanta GA 30332-0002
County: Fulton FICE Identification: 001569
Unit ID: 139755
Telephone: (404) 894-2000 Carnegie Class: RU/VH
FAX Number: (404) 894-1277 Calendar System: Semester
URL: www.gatech.edu
Established: 1885 Annual Undergrad Tuition & Fees (In-State): $10,650
Enrollment: 21,557 Coed
Affiliation or Control: State IRS Status: 501(c)3
Highest Offering: Doctorate
Program: Professional
Accreditation: SC, ART, BUS, CONST, CS, ENG, IPSY, OPE, PLNG

01 President ... Dr. G. P. (Bud) PETERSON
05 Provost/Exec VP Academic Affairs ... Dr. Rafael BRAS
10 Executive Vice Pres Admin/Finance ... Mr. Steven SWANT
46 Executive Vice President Research ... Dr. Stephen CROSS
100 Assistant Vice Pres/Chief of Staff ... Ms. Lynn DURHAM
30 Vice President Development ... Mr. Barrett H. CARSON
26 Vice Pres Communications/Marketing ... Mr. Michael L. WARDEN
32 Vice President Student Affairs ... Dr. William SCHAFER
88 VP/Director GA Tech Res Inst ... Dr. Robert MCGRATH
46 Vice President Research ... Ms. Jilda GARTON
86 Exec Dir Government/Cmty Relations ... Mr. Dene SHEHEANE
88 Vice Prov Entrprse Innovation Inst ... Mr. Stephen FLEMING
29 President Georgia Tech Alumni Assoc ... Mr. Joseph IRWIN
20 Vice Prov Grad Ed & Faculty Affairs ... Dr. Susan COZZENS
84 Vice Prov Enrollment Services ... Dr. Paul KOHN
88 Vice Prov Undergraduate Education ... Dr. Colin POTTS
43 Vice Pres Legal Affairs/Risk Mgt ... Mr. Patrick MCKENNA
28 Vice President Institute Diversity ... Dr. Archie ERVIN
16 Assoc VP Human Resources ... Mr. M. Scott MORRIS
18 Vice President Facilities ... Mr. Charles G. RHODE
31 Vice President Campus Services ... Mr. Paul STROUTS
13 Vice President Information Tech/CIO ... Mr. James O'CONNOR
41 Director of Athletics ... Mr. Michael BOBINSKI
22 Senior Director Diversity Mgmt ... Ms. Pearl ALEXANDER
12 Dean Ivan Allen College ... Dr. Jacqueline J. ROYSTER
35 Dean of Students/Asst Vice Pres ... Mr. John STEIN
48 Dean College of Architecture ... Dr. Steve FRENCH
77 Dean College of Computing ... Dr. Zvi GALIL
54 Dean College of Engineering ... Dr. Gary S. MAY
08 Vice Prov Lrng Excel/Dean Libraries ... Ms. Catherine MURRAY-RUST
82 Dean Scheller College of Business ... Dr. Steven C. SALBU
81 Dean College of Sciences ... Dr. Paul GOLDBART
06 Registrar ... Ms. Reta PIKOWSKY
40 Director Bookstore ... Mr. Gerald J. MALONEY
19 Director of Security & Police ... Ms. Teresa CROCKER
107 Dean Professional Education ... Dr. Nelson BAKER
78 Exec Dir Prof Practice Div ... Dr. Patrick ANTHONY
37 Director Student Financial Aid ... Ms. Marie MONS
23 Sr Director Student Health Svcs ... Dr. Gregory MOORE
39 Executive Director Housing ... Mr. Michael BLACK
09 Exec Dir Inst Research & Planning ... Ms. Sandra J. BRAMBLETT
85 Vice Provost Intl Initiatives ... Dr. Yves BERTHELOT
104 Exec Dir International Education ... Ms. Amy HENRY
93 Dir Minority Education Development ... Mr. Gordon MOORE
36 Director Career Services ... Mr. Ralph MOBLEY
38 Director Counseling Center ... Dr. Ruperto PEREZ
53 AVP Learning Excel/Director CETL ... Dr. Donna C. LLEWELLYN
88 Senior Director Auxiliary Svcs ... Mr. Richard STEELE
07 Director Undergraduate Admission ... Mr. Richard CLARK
96 Director of Procurement Services ... Mr. Frans BARENDS
88 Exec Dir Inst Budget Plng & Admin ... Mr. James KIRK
88 Director Capital Planning/Spce Mgt ... Mr. Howard WERTHEIMER
88 Exec Director Organizational Devel ... Vacant
88 Bursar ... Ms. Carol PAYNE
88 Associate Vice President Fin Svcs ... Mr. James FORTNER

† Part of the University System of Georgia.

Georgia Military College (E)

201 E Greene Street, Milledgeville GA 31061-3398
County: Baldwin FICE Identification: 001571
Unit ID: 139904
Telephone: (478) 387-4900 Carnegie Class: Assoc/Pub-Spec
FAX Number: N/A Calendar System: Quarter
URL: www.gmc.cc.ga.us
Established: 1879 Annual Undergrad Tuition & Fees: $4,633
Enrollment: 7,015 Coed
Affiliation or Control: Independent Non-Profit IRS Status: 501(c)3
Highest Offering: Associate Degree
Program: 2-Year Principally Bachelor's Creditable; Business Emphasis
Accreditation: SC

01 President ... LTG. William B. CALDWELL, IV
03 Executive Vice President ... COL. Fredrick VAN HORN
05 Vice Pres Academic Affs/Dn Faculty ... Dr. Phillip M. HOLMES
10 Vice President Business Affairs ... Mr. Charles E. MADDEN
84 Vice Pres for Enrollment Management ... Ms. Donna FINDLEY
32 Vice Pres Student Svcs/Commandant ... COL. Patrick BEER
30 Vice Pres Institutional Advancement ... Mrs. Elizabeth SHEPPARD
13 Vice Pres Information Technology ... Ms. Jody YEARWOOD
21 Assoc Vice Pres Business Affairs ... Ms. Susan MEEKS
09 Director Institutional Research ... Ms. Wendy KALLINA
41 Athletic Director ... Mr. Bert WILLIAMS
18 Director Facilities/Engineer ... Mr. Jeff GRAY
06 Registrar ... Mrs. Robin KNIGHT
08 Librarian ... Mr. Glen PHILLIPS
19 Chief of Security/Safety ... Mr. James HODNETT

Georgia Northwestern Technical College (F)

One Maurice Culberson Drive, Rome GA 30161
County: Floyd FICE Identification: 005257
Unit ID: 141273
Telephone: (706) 295-6963 Carnegie Class: Not Classified
FAX Number: (706) 295-6944 Calendar System: Semester
URL: www.gntc.edu
Established: 1966 Annual Undergrad Tuition & Fees (In-State): $2,048
Enrollment: 6,187 Coed
Affiliation or Control: State IRS Status: 501(c)3
Highest Offering: Associate Degree
Program: Occupational; 2-Year Principally Bachelor's Creditable
Accreditation: SC, ADNUR, CAHIIM, COARC, DA, DMS, EMT, MAC, OTA, RAD, RTT, SURGT

01 President ... Dr. Pete MCDONALD
05 Provost ... Mr. Jeff KING
11 Vice Pres Administrative Services ... Ms. Kelly BARNES
30 Vice Pres Econ Development ... Mr. Pete MCDONALD
20 Vice President Academic Affairs ... Dr. Mindy MCCANNON
09 Vice Pres Inst Effectiveness ... Ms. Heidi POPHAM
51 Vice President Adult Education ... Ms. Connie SMITH
32 Assoc Vice Pres Student Services ... Dr. Steve BRADSHAW
06 Registrar ... Ms. Selena MAGNUSSON
08 Director of Library Services ... Mr. John LASSITER
35 Director of Student Affairs ... Mr. David MCBURNETT
37 Exec Director of Financial Aid ... Mr. Stephen ANDERSEN
18 Director Facilities Management ... Mr. Johnny TROTTER
26 Dir Marketing/Public Relations ... Ms. Amber JORDAN
15 Director of Human Resources ... Ms. Peggy CORDELL

Georgia Perimeter College (G)

3251 Panthersville Road, Decatur GA 30034-3897
County: DeKalb FICE Identification: 001562
Unit ID: 244437
Telephone: (678) 891-2300 Carnegie Class: Assoc/Pub-S-MC
FAX Number: N/A Calendar System: Semester
URL: www.gpc.edu
Established: 1963 Annual Undergrad Tuition & Fees (In-State): $3,094
Enrollment: 23,681 Coed
Affiliation or Control: State IRS Status: 501(c)3
Highest Offering: Baccalaureate
Program: Occupational; 2-Year Principally Bachelor's Creditable
Accreditation: SC, ADNUR, DH

01 Interim President ... Mr. Robert E. WATTS
05 Int Vice President Academic Affairs ... Mr. Philip A. SMITH
10 Exec Vice Pres Financial/Admin Affs ... Mr. Ronald B. STARK
30 Vice Pres Institutional Advancement ... Mr. Jeffrey TARNOWSKI
32 Vice Pres Student Affairs ... Dr. Vincent JUNE
21 Assoc Vice Pres Financial Affairs ... Ms. Diane HICKEY
13 Assoc VP/Chief Information Officer ... Dr. Mark HOETING
35 Asst Vice Pres for Student Affairs ... Ms. Coletta CARTER
21 Asst VP Budgets/Strategic Planning ... Ms. Jamie FERNANDES
88 Dir Center for Teaching & Learning ... Dr. Pamela MOOLENAR-WIRSY
12 Academic Dean Alpharetta Campus ... Dr. Susan CODY
106 Academic Dean Online Campus ... Dr. Ingrid THOMPSON-SELLERS
12 Academic Dean Decatur Campus ... Dr. Stuart NOEL

12	Academic Dean Dunwoody Campus	Dr. Margaret EHRLICH
12	Academic Dean Newton Campus	Dr. Paulos YOHANNES
12	Academic Dean Clarkston Campus	Ms. Marla CALICO
15	Exec Director Human Resources	Mr. James RASMUS
15	Dir HR Employment/Acad Svcs	Ms. Eyvon MITCHELL
26	Director Public Relations	Ms. Barbara OBRENTZ
88	Dir Human Res Conflict Management	Ms. Karen TRUESDALE
45	Int Dir Institutional Research/Plng	Ms. Patti GREGG
41	Director Athletics	Mr. Alfred BARNEY
29	Director Alumni Relations	Mr. Collins FOSTER
37	Dir Student Financial Services	Ms. Robin WINSTON
25	Director Grants/Sponsored Programs	Ms. Ethel BROWN
28	Director of Disability Services	Ms. Bonnie MARTIN
88	Dir Hum Res Cmp/Aff Act/Opn Rec Ofr	Ms. Amanda REDDICK
88	Director of College Services	Mr. Brian Keith CHAPMAN
07	Director Admissions & Records	Mr. Richard BEAUBIEN
06	Director of Records/Registrar	Mr. Douglas RUCH
18	Dir Facil/Physical Plant Operations	Mr. Scott E. HARDY
88	Director Facilities/Planning	Mr. Lewis GODWIN
19	Chief of Police	Mr. Nicholas MARINELLI

† Part of the University System of Georgia.

Georgia Piedmont Technical College (A)

495 N Indian Creek Drive, Clarkston GA 30021-2397

County: DeKalb — FICE Identification: 005622 — Unit ID: 244446
Telephone: (404) 297-9522 — Carnegie Class: Assoc/Pub-S-MC
FAX Number: (404) 297-4234 — Calendar System: Semester
URL: www.gptc.edu
Established: 1961 — Annual Undergrad Tuition & Fees (In-State): $2,458
Enrollment: 4,283 — Coed
Affiliation or Control: State — IRS Status: 501(c)3
Highest Offering: Associate Degree
Program: Occupational; 2-Year Principally Bachelor's Creditable; Technical Emphasis
Accreditation: SC, EMT, ENGT, MAC, MLTAD

01	President	Dr. Jabari SIMAMA
04	Exec Dir & Spec Asst to President	Mr. Keith SAGERS
11	Vice Pres of Business & Financial	Ms. Heather PENCE
03	Executive Vice President	Vacant
05	Vice President Academic Affairs	Dr. Mariam DITTMANN
46	Vice Pres of Economic Development	Mr. Richard SMITH
30	Vice President Inst Advancement	Ms. Judy TAYLOR
31	VP Cmty Outreach & Engagement	Ms. Cynthia EDWARDS
20	Dean Academic Operations	Vacant
20	Dean of Academic Programs	Mr. Marcus HICKS
20	Dean of Academic Success	Dr. Daisy DAVIS
20	Dean of Academic Programs	Dr. Debra GORDON
32	Vice President Student Affairs	Dr. Irvin CLARK
15	Director of Human Resources	Ms. Lolita MORRISON
26	Director of Public Relations & Info	Ms. Zaundra BROWN
06	Registrar	Ms. Patricia LEWIS
07	Director of Admissions	Vacant
108	Dir Inst Assess/Eval/Effectiveness	Dr. Sue CHANDLER
50	Director Business & Comm Services	Ms. Loretta HICKS
37	Director of Financial Aid	Vacant
18	Director of Facilities & Auxil Svcs	Vacant
88	Dean of Adult Literacy	Dr. Jacqueline ECHOLS
29	Director Alumni Relations	Vacant
36	Director Assessment & Career Svcs	Vacant
35	Dean of Students	Ms. Amanda TAYLOR-RODRIGUEZ
108	Dean of Quality Initiatives	Dr. Catrenia MCLENDON
13	Director of Information Technology	Mr. Keith PERRY

Georgia Regents University (B)

1120 Fifteenth Street, Augusta GA 30912-0004

County: Richmond — FICE Identification: 001579 — Unit ID: 140401
Telephone: (706) 721-0211 — Carnegie Class: Spec/Med
FAX Number: N/A — Calendar System: Semester
URL: www.gru.edu
Established: 1828 — Annual Undergrad Tuition & Fees (In-State): $5,118
Enrollment: 9,557 — Coed
Affiliation or Control: State — IRS Status: 501(c)3
Highest Offering: Doctorate
Program: Occupational; 2-Year Principally Bachelor's Creditable; Liberal Arts And General; Teacher Preparatory; Professional
Accreditation: SC, ANEST, ARCPA, ART, BUS, CACREP, CAHIIM, COARC, DENT, DH, IPSY, MED, MIL, MT, MUS, NMT, NUR, NURSE, OT, PH, PTA, RTT, SPAA, SW, TED

01	President	Dr. Ricardo AZZIZ
05	Exec VP for Acad Affairs/Provost	Dr. Gretchen CAUGHMAN
17	Exec Vice Pres Clinical Affairs	Mr. David S. HEFNER
10	Chief Business Officer	Mr. Anthony E. WAGNER
46	Senior Vice President for Research	Dr. Mark W. HAMRICK
100	Interim Chief of Staff	Mr. Michael SHAFFER
43	Interim General Counsel	Ms. Lee LITTLE
21	Chief Audit Officer	Mr. Clay SPROUSE
88	Chief Integrity Officer	Mr. James RUSH, JR.
41	Director of Athletics	Mr. Clint BRYANT
27	Enterprise CIO	Mr. Charles ENICKS
88	Director Cancer Center	Dr. Samir KHLEIF
76	Dean College of Allied Health	Dr. E. Andrew BALAS
49	Dean College of Arts/Hum/Soc Sci	Dr. Charles CLARK
50	Dean College of Business	Dr. Marc MILLER
52	Interim Dean College of Dental Med	Dr. Carol LEFEBVRE
53	Dean College of Education	Dr. Cindi CHANCE
66	Dean College of Nursing	Dr. Lucy N. MARION
81	Interim Dean College of Sci & Math	Dr. Sam ROBINSON
63	Dean of Medical College	Dr. Peter F. BUCKLEY
58	Dean College of Graduate Studies	Dr. Mitchell WATSKY
20	Vice Provost	Dr. Roman M. CIBIRKA
32	VP for Student Affairs	Dr. Kevin B. FRAZIER
28	VP for Diversity & Inclusion	Dr. Kent GUION
88	VP Institutional Effectiveness	Mrs. Beth P. BRIGDON
88	VP Academic & Faculty Affairs	Dr. Carol RYCHLY
88	VP for Military Affairs	Mr. Jeff FOLEY
15	Enterprise VP Human Resources	Ms. Susan A. NORTON
18	VP Facilities Service	Mr. Philip HOWARD
19	Director of Public Safety	Mr. Bill MCBRIDE, JR.
35	Director of Auxiliary Services	Mr. Karl MUNSCHY
88	Director of Supply Chain	Mr. Clay TROVER
21	Assoc VP for Finance/Controller	Mr. Jim JONES
88	AVP Budget Planning & Analysis	Mr. Russ WILLIAMS
86	VP Gov Rel/Chief Advocacy Officer	Mr. Michael SHAFFER
30	Sr VP Advance/Cmty Relations/CDO	Ms. Susan L. BARCUS
26	Enterprise SVP Comm & Marketing	Mr. David BROND
37	Director of Financial Aid	Ms. Cynthia PARKS
06	Registrar	Ms. Heather METRESS
08	Director of Libraries	Dr. Brenda SEAGO
07	Director of Admissions	Ms. Katherine SWEENEY
88	Bursar	Ms. Beth WELSH

† Part of the University System of Georgia.

Georgia Southern University (C)

PO Box 8033, Statesboro GA 30460-8033

County: Bulloch — FICE Identification: 001572 — Unit ID: 139931
Telephone: (912) 478-4636 — Carnegie Class: DRU
FAX Number: N/A — Calendar System: Semester
URL: www.georgiasouthern.edu
Established: 1906 — Annual Undergrad Tuition & Fees (In-State): $7,066
Enrollment: 20,574 — Coed
Affiliation or Control: State — IRS Status: 501(c)3
Highest Offering: Doctorate
Program: Liberal Arts And General; Teacher Preparatory; Professional
Accreditation: SC, ART, BUS, BUSA, CACREP, CIDA, CONST, CS, DIETD, @DIETI, ENGT, MUS, NRPA, NURSE, PH, SPAA, TED, THEA

01	President	Dr. Brooks A. KEEL
05	Provost/Vice Pres Academic Affairs	Dr. Jean BARTELS
10	Vice Pres Business & Finance	Mr. Rob WHITAKER
32	VP Student Affairs & Enroll Mgmt	Dr. Teresa THOMPSON
30	VP Univ Advance/GSU Foundation Pres	Ms. Salinda ARTHUR
27	VP Information Technology/CIO	Mr. Steve BURRELL
86	VP Governmtl Rels/Cmty Engagement	Mr. Russell KEEN
46	Vice Pres for Research	Dr. Charles PATTERSON
09	Assoc VP Strategic Rsrch & Analysis	Dr. Jayne PERKINS BROWN
20	Associate Provost	Dr. Diana CONE
35	Assoc VP & Dean of Students	Ms. Patrice BUCKNER JACKSON
43	Assoc Vice Pres for Legal Affairs	Ms. Maura COPELAND
04	Exec Associate to the President	Ms. Leigh PRICE
07	Interim Dir of Admissions	Ms. Amy SMITH
58	Dean College of Graduate Studies	Dr. Charles PATTERSON
50	Dean College Business Admin	Dr. Bill WELLS
53	Dean College Education	Dr. Thomas KOBALLA
76	Dean College Health/Human Sci	Dr. Barry JOYNER
49	Dean Col Liberal Arts/Social Sci	Dr. Curtis RICKER
81	Dean College Science & Mathematics	Dr. Martha ABELL
54	Dean AEP Col Engr/Info Tech	Dr. Mohammad DAVOUD
51	Interim Assoc VP Continuing Ed	Dr. Barbara PRICE
69	Dean College of Public Health	Dr. R. Gregory EVANS
62	Dean University Library	Dr. Bede MITCHELL
88	Dir NCAA Compliance/Stdnt-Athl Svcs	Mr. Keith ROUGHTON
88	Director Audit & Advisory Services	Ms. Jana BRILEY
43	Associate University Attorney	Mr. Geoffrey CARSON
26	Interim Assoc VP Mktg & Comm	Ms. Angela HARN
88	Director Academic Success Center	Ms. Kathleen L. O'BRIEN
37	Director Financial Aid	Ms. Connie MURPHEY
06	Registrar	Dr. Velma BURDEN
88	Assoc VP Auxiliary Services	Mr. Edward D. MILLS
21	Senior Assoc VP/Controller	Ms. Kim THOMPSON BROWN
15	Assoc VP Human Resources	Mr. Paul MICHAUD
41	Athletic Director	Mr. Tom KLEINLEIN
18	Assoc VP Facilities	Mr. Marvin MILLS
19	Director Public Safety	Mr. Michael RUSSELL
36	Director Career Services	Mr. Philip BRUCE
38	Director Counseling Services	Dr. Jodi K. CALDWELL
88	Director Educ Opportunity Programs	Dr. Joyya SMITH
23	Director Health Services	Mr. Paul FERGUSON
39	Director University Housing	Mr. Christopher MACDONALD
28	Dir Multicultural Student Center	Ms. Dorsey BALDWIN
88	Director Leadership/Outreach Pgms	Dr. Todd DEAL
88	Director Advancement IT	Ms. Janice WEST
29	Sr Dir Alumni Rels/Annual Giving	Mr. Wendell TOMPKINS, JR.
88	Director Garden of Coastal Plain	Ms. Carolyn ALTMAN
13	Director Technical Services	Mr. Joey REEVES
90	Director Info Tech for Acad Affairs	Ms. Pamela DEAL
31	Director Museum	Mr. Brent THARP
40	Director Stores & Shops	Mr. Richie AKINS
88	Director Wildlife Educ/Raptor Ctr	Mr. Steven M. HEIN
96	Director of Materials Management	Mr. George HORN
28	Director of Diversity Services	Mr. Gary P. GAWEL

† Part of the University System of Georgia.

Georgia Southwestern State University (D)

800 GA Southwestern State Univ Dr, Americus GA 31709-4693

County: Sumter — FICE Identification: 001573 — Unit ID: 139764
Telephone: (800) 338-0082 — Carnegie Class: Master's S
FAX Number: N/A — Calendar System: Semester
URL: www.gsw.edu
Established: 1906 — Annual Undergrad Tuition & Fees (In-State): $13,558
Enrollment: 2,973 — Coed
Affiliation or Control: State — IRS Status: 501(c)3
Highest Offering: Beyond Master's But Less Than Doctorate
Program: Occupational; Liberal Arts And General; Teacher Preparatory; Professional
Accreditation: SC, BUS, NUR, TED

01	President	Dr. Kendall A. BLANCHARD
05	Vice President Academic Affairs	Dr. Brian U. ADLER
10	Vice Pres Business & Finance	Mr. W. Cody KING
32	Vice President for Student Affairs	Dr. Samuel T. MILLER
26	Vice Pres for University Relations	Vacant
84	Vice Pres Enroll Mgmt/Dir Admiss	Dr. Gaye HAYES
20	Assoc Vice Pres Academic Affairs	Dr. Helen TATE
09	Director Institutional Research	Dr. Lisa A. COOPER
08	Dean Library Services	Ms. Ru STORY-HUFFMAN
91	Dir Information/Instructional Tech	Mr. Royce HACKETT
30	Director of Development	Mr. Stephen E. SNYDER
06	Registrar	Ms. Krista SMITH
36	Director Career Services Center	Ms. Sandra FOWLER
37	Director Student Financial Aid	Ms. Angela V. BRYANT
85	Director Foreign Students	Mr. John FOX
27	Director Public Relations	Mr. Stephen E. SNYDER
32	Dean of Students	Dr. Gaye HAYES
53	Dean of Education	Dr. Lettie WATFORD
50	Dean of Business	Dr. Elizabeth WILSON
66	Dean of Nursing	Dr. Sandra D. DANIEL
49	Dean of Arts & Sciences	Dr. J. Kelly MCCOY
77	Dean Computing & Mathematics	Dr. Boris PELTSVERGER
15	Director of Human Resources	Ms. Janet SIDERS
41	Athletic Director	Ms. Jaclyn DONOVAN
51	Director of Continuing Education	Ms. Karen HOLLOWAY
18	Interim Director of Physical Plant	Mr. Hugh SLATON
38	Director Student Counseling	Ms. Alma G. KEITA
96	Director of Purchasing	Ms. Michelle UNDERWOOD
29	Coord Alumni Relations/Annual Fund	Ms. Kimberly COMER

† Part of the University System of Georgia.

Georgia State University (E)

PO Box 3999, Atlanta GA 30302-3999

County: Fulton — FICE Identification: 001574 — Unit ID: 139940
Telephone: (404) 413-2000 — Carnegie Class: RU/VH
FAX Number: (404) 413-1380 — Calendar System: Semester
URL: www.gsu.edu
Established: 1913 — Annual Undergrad Tuition & Fees (In-State): $9,928
Enrollment: 32,092 — Coed
Affiliation or Control: State — IRS Status: 501(c)3
Highest Offering: Doctorate
Program: Liberal Arts And General; Teacher Preparatory; Professional
Accreditation: SC, ART, BUS, BUSA, CACREP, CEA, CLPSY, COARC, COPSY, CORE, DIETC, DIETD, EXSC, HSA, IPSY, LAW, MUS, NURSE, PH, PTA, SCPSY, SP, SPAA, SW, TED

01	President	Dr. Mark P. BECKER
05	Sr VP Academic Affairs & Provost	Dr. Risa I. PALM
10	Sr VP Finance & Administration	Dr. Jerry J. RACKLIFFE
46	Vice President Research & Econ Dev	Dr. James A. WEYHENMEYER
32	Vice President Student Affairs	Dr. Douglass F. COVEY
30	Vice President Development	Mr. Walter T. MASSEY
26	VP PR & Mktg Communications	Mr. Don HALE
20	Vice Provost & Chief Enroll Ofc	Dr. Timothy M. RENICK
43	University Attorney	Dr. Kerry L. HEYWARD
49	Dean Arts & Sciences	Dr. William J. LONG
50	Dean Business	Dr. H. Fenwick HUSS
53	Interim Dean Education	Dr. Paul A. ALBERTO
76	Dean Nursing/Health Professions	Dr. Margaret C. WILMOTH
69	Dean Public Health	Dr. Michael P. ERIKSEN
61	Dean Law	Dr. Steven J. KAMINSHINE
80	Dean Policy Studies	Dr. Mary Beth WALKER
92	Dean Honors College	Dr. Larry S. BERMAN
08	Dean University Library	Dr. Nancy H. SEAMANS
88	Assoc Provost Strategic Initiatives	Dr. Robert D. MORRIS
09	Assoc Provost Inst Effectiveness	Dr. Peter LYONS
82	Assc Prov International Initiatives	Dr. Jun LIU
20	Assoc Provost Faculty Affairs	Dr. Lynda BROWN WRIGHT
45	Assoc VP Research Integrity	Dr. Brenda J. CHAPMAN
45	Assoc Vice President Research	Dr. Monica H. SWAHN
13	Assoc VP Info Sys & Technology	Mr. J. L. ALBERT
18	Assoc VP Facilities	Mr. Ramesh VAKAMUDI
21	Assoc Vice President Finance	Ms. Elizabeth R. JONES
21	Assoc VP Finance & Comptroller	Mr. Bruce R. SPRATT
30	Assoc VP Central Development	Mr. John D. CLARK
30	Assoc VP Advancement Resources	Ms. Charlotte P. PARKS
30	Assoc VP Constituent Programs Dev	Mr. David J. FRABONI
102	Assoc VP GSU Foundation	Mr. Dale J. PALMER
35	Assoc VP Stdnt Affs/Dean Students	Dr. Rebecca Y. STOUT
07	Asst VP Undergraduate Admissions	Mr. Scott M. BURKE

84 Asst VP Student Retention .... Dr. Allison CALHOUN-BROWN
88 Asst VP Multicultural Affairs .... Dr. Darryl B. HOLLOMAN
88 Asst VP Student Affairs Admin .... Mr. Jeff W. WALKER
29 Asst VP Alumni Relations .... Ms. Christina C. MILLION
40 Asst VP Auxiliary Enterprises .... Mr. Wayne E. REED
15 Asst VP Human Resources .... Ms. Linda J. NELSON
22 Asst VP Opp Dev/Diversity Educ .... Ms. Linda J. NELSON
19 Asst VP/Chief University Police .... Ms. Connie B. SAMPSON
25 Asst VP Research/Awards Admin .... Vacant
06 Registrar .... Ms. Shari P. SCHWARTZ
85 Dir Intl Students/Scholars Svcs .... Ms. Heather L. HOUSLEY
39 Director University Housing .... Ms. Marilyn A. DE LAROCHE
38 Director Psychological & Health Svc .... Dr. Jill LEE-BARBER
28 Director Diversity Programs .... Mr. John R. DAY
14 Director Business Support Services .... Mr. William F. PARASKA
13 Director Tech Support & Prof Svcs .... Mr. Julian O. ALLEN
88 Director Application Engineering .... Mr. John M. BANDY, JR.
13 Director Technology Engineering .... Mr. Keith E. CAMPBELL
88 Director Production Services .... Mr. William GRUSZKA
36 Director University Career Svcs .... Mr. Kevin E. GAW
37 Director Financial Aid .... Mr. Louis B. SCOTT
96 Director of Business Services .... Mr. Larry J. MCCALOP
88 Dir Univ Auditing & Advisory Svcs .... Mr. Sterling ROTH
88 Director Design/Construction Svcs .... Ms. Kimberly P. BAUER
88 Director Emergency Management .... Mr. Keith P. SUMAS
26 Director Govt & Community Affairs .... Ms. Julia M. KERLIN
41 Athletic Director .... Ms. Cheryl L. LEVICK
88 Special Advisor to President .... Mr. Thomas C. LEWIS
04 Assistant to the President .... Ms. Ethel M. BROWN
88 Assistant to the Provost .... Dr. Edgar C. TORBERT

† Part of the University System of Georgia.

Gordon State College (A)

419 College Dr., Barnesville GA 30204-1746
County: Lamar FICE Identification: 001575
Unit ID: 139968
Telephone: (678) 359-5021 Carnegie Class: Assoc/Pub4
FAX Number: (678) 359-5080 Calendar System: Semester
URL: www.gordonstate.edu
Established: 1972 Annual Undergrad Tuition & Fees (In-State): $3,992
Enrollment: 4,171 Coed
Affiliation or Control: State IRS Status: 501(c)3
Highest Offering: Baccalaureate
Program: Occupational; 2-Year Principally Bachelor's Creditable; Teacher Preparatory
Accreditation: SC, ADNUR, NUR

01 President .... Dr. Max BURNS
05 Provost & VP Academic Affairs .... Dr. Margaret VENABLE
20 Associate VP Academic Affairs .... Dr. Richard BASKIN
10 VP Business Affairs .... Mr. Lee FRUITTICHER
32 VP Student Affairs .... Dr. Dennis R. CHAMBERLAIN
30 VP Institutional Advancement .... Mrs. Rhonda TOON
08 Head Librarian .... Vacant
37 Director of Financial Aid .... Mr. Larry G. MITCHAM
06 Registrar .... Ms. Janet BARRAS
15 Director of Human Resources .... Ms. Tonya L. JOHNSON
18 Director of Facilities .... Mr. Richard VEREEN
38 Director of Counseling Services .... Mrs. Laura BOWEN
07 Director of Admissions .... Mr. Bennett FERGUSON
27 Chief Public Information Officer .... Mrs. Tamara BOATWRIGHT
09 Director of Institutional Research .... Dr. Kimbrely S. CLARK
19 Director of Public Safety .... Chief Jeff MASON
40 Bookstore Manager .... Mrs. Connie H. WADE
41 Athletic Director .... Mr. Todd DAVIS
39 Director of Resident Life .... Ms. Tonya R. COLEMAN
35 Director of Student Activities .... Mrs. Sharon LLOYD
13 Director of Computer Services .... Mr. Jeff HAYES
20 Director of Student Success Center .... Mr. Peter J. HIGGINS
21 Director of Business Services .... Ms. Sharon ELLIS
88 Controller .... Mr. Clint CHASTAIN
29 Director of Alumni Relations .... Mrs. Natalie RISCHBIETER

† Part of the University System of Georgia.

Gupton Jones College of Funeral Service (B)

5141 Snapfinger Woods Drive, Decatur GA 30035-4022
County: DeKalb FICE Identification: 010771
Unit ID: 139995
Telephone: (770) 593-2257 Carnegie Class: Assoc/PrivNFP
FAX Number: (770) 593-1891 Calendar System: Quarter
URL: www.gupton-jones.edu
Established: 1920 Annual Undergrad Tuition & Fees: $10,500
Enrollment: 115 Coed
Affiliation or Control: Independent Non-Profit IRS Status: 501(c)3
Highest Offering: Associate Degree
Program: Occupational; 2-Year Principally Bachelor's Creditable; Technical Emphasis
Accreditation: FUSER

01 President .... Ms. Patty S. HUTCHESON
05 Dean .... Mr. James HINZ
06 Registrar .... Ms. Felicia SMITH

Gwinnett College (C)

4230 Highway 29, Suite 11, Lilburn GA 30047-3447
County: Gwinnett FICE Identification: 025830
Unit ID: 140003
Telephone: (770) 381-7200 Carnegie Class: Assoc/PrivFP
FAX Number: (770) 381-0454 Calendar System: Other
URL: www.gwinnettcollege.com
Established: 1976 Annual Undergrad Tuition & Fees: $9,925
Enrollment: 347 Coed
Affiliation or Control: Proprietary IRS Status: Proprietary
Highest Offering: Associate Degree
Program: Occupational; 2-Year Principally Bachelor's Creditable
Accreditation: ACICS

01 President .... Mr. Michael DAVIS

Gwinnett Technical College (D)

5150 Sugarloaf Parkway, Lawrenceville GA 30043-5702
County: Gwinnett FICE Identification: 022884
Unit ID: 140012
Telephone: (770) 962-7580 Carnegie Class: Assoc/Pub-S-SC
FAX Number: (770) 962-7985 Calendar System: Semester
URL: www.gwinnetttech.edu
Established: 1984 Annual Undergrad Tuition & Fees (In-State): $2,700
Enrollment: 6,682 Coed
Affiliation or Control: State IRS Status: 501(c)3
Highest Offering: Associate Degree
Program: Occupational; 2-Year Principally Bachelor's Creditable; Technical Emphasis
Accreditation: SC, ACFEI, ADNUR, COARC, DA, EMT, MAC, RAD, SURGT

01 President .... Mrs. Sharon J. BARTELS
11 Executive VP of Administration .... Mr. David WELDEN
05 VP of Academic Affairs .... Dr. Victoria SEALS
26 VP of Economic Development .... Mr. Dave MCCULLOCH
32 VP of Student Affairs .... Dr. Julie POST
30 VP of Institutional Advancement .... Vacant
88 Dir of Economic Development .... Ms. Ann SECHRIST
16 Director of Human Resources .... Ms. Becky BURTON
09 Dir of Institutional Effectiveness .... Vacant
21 Director of Accounting .... Mrs. Valerie STRICKLAND
06 Registrar .... Ms. Arlene CLARKE
36 Director of Career Services .... Ms. Ave MILLER
37 Director of Financial Aid .... Ms. Ginny YANCY
53 Dean of Adult Education .... Ms. Stephanie ROOKS
07 Dir of Admissions and Assessment .... Ms. Brenda PYLE
18 Supervisor of Facilities .... Ms. Janice BOLTON
19 Chief of Campus Police & Security .... Mr. Joseph MARKHAM
08 Manager of Library Services .... Ms. Elissa CHECOV
04 Assistant to the President .... Mrs. Stephanie SMITH

Herzing University (E)

3393 Peachtree Road NE, Suite 1003, Atlanta GA 30326-1332
Telephone: (404) 816-4533 FICE Identification: 020897
Accreditation: &NH

† Main campus is Herzing University in Madison, WI.

Interactive College of Technology (F)

5303 New Peachtree Road, Chamblee GA 30341-2818
County: DeKalb FICE Identification: 022843
Unit ID: 138655
Telephone: (770) 216-2960 Carnegie Class: Assoc/PrivFP
FAX Number: (770) 216-2988 Calendar System: Semester
URL: www.ict.edu
Established: 1986 Annual Undergrad Tuition & Fees: $8,400
Enrollment: 464 Coed
Affiliation or Control: Proprietary IRS Status: Proprietary
Highest Offering: Associate Degree
Program: Occupational
Accreditation: #COE

01 President .... Mr. Elmer R. SMITH
05 Dean of the College .... Mr. Thomas BLAIR
12 Campus Director Pasadena Texas .... Mr. Gregory WEAVER
12 Campus Dir SW Houston Texas .... Ms. Cynthia BRYSON
12 Campus Dir North Houston Texas .... Ms. Jennifer DUROUCHIC
12 Campus Director - Newport KY .... Ms. Sophia BATISTE
12 Campus Director - Morrow GA .... Mr. Jonathon BONDS
12 Campus Director - Gainesville GA .... Ms. Sophia BATISTE

Interactive College of Technology (G)

2323-C Browns Bridge Road, Gainesville GA 30504
Telephone: (678) 456-0550 Identification: 770533
Accreditation: COE

† Main campus is Interactive College of Technology in Chamblee, GA.

Interactive College of Technology (H)

1580 Southdale Parkway, Suite C, Morrow GA 30260
Telephone: (770) 960-1298 Identification: 770534
Accreditation: COE

† Main campus is Interactive College of Technology in Chamblee, GA.

Interdenominational Theological Center (I)

700 Martin L. King, Jr. Drive, SW, Atlanta GA 30314-4143
County: Fulton FICE Identification: 001568
Unit ID: 140146
Telephone: (404) 527-7700 Carnegie Class: Spec/Faith
FAX Number: (404) 527-0901 Calendar System: Semester
URL: www.itc.edu
Established: 1958 Annual Graduate Tuition & Fees: $11,780
Enrollment: 425 Coed
Affiliation or Control: Interdenominational IRS Status: 501(c)3
Highest Offering: Doctorate; No Undergraduates
Program: Professional; Religious Emphasis
Accreditation: SC, THEOL

01 Interim President .... Dr. Edward P. WIMBERLY
05 Interim VP for Acad Svcs/Provost .... Dr. Temba L. MAFICO
10 Vice Pres of Admin Services .... Dr. Charles E. THOMAS, JR.
30 VP for Institutional Advancement .... Ms. Christal M. CHERRY
06 Registrar .... Ms. Bobbie HALL
37 Financial Aid Director .... Ms. Tina GARNIGAN
15 Human Resource Director .... Ms. Kathryn J. WEBB
42 Chaplain .... Dr. Keith SLAUGHTER
32 Int Dean of Student Services .... Dr. Wille GOODMAN

ITT Technical Institute (J)

485 Oak Place, Suite 800, Atlanta GA 30349
Telephone: (404) 765-4600 Identification: 666595
Accreditation: ACICS

† Main campus is ITT Technical Institute in Indianapolis, IN.

ITT Technical Institute (K)

5905 Stewart Parkway, Douglasville GA 30135
Telephone: (678) 715-2100 Identification: 770655
Accreditation: ACICS

† Main campus is ITT Technical Institute in Indianapolis, IN.

ITT Technical Institute (L)

10700 Abbotts Bridge Road, Duluth GA 30097-8460
Telephone: (678) 957-8510 Identification: 666325
Accreditation: ACICS

† Main campus is ITT Technical Institute in Indianapolis, IN.

ITT Technical Institute (M)

2065 ITT Tech Way N.W., Kennesaw GA 30144
Telephone: (770) 426-2300 Identification: 666378
Accreditation: ACICS

† Main campus is ITT Technical Institute in Indianapolis, IN.

Kennesaw State University (N)

1000 Chastain Road #0101, Kennesaw GA 30144-5591
County: Cobb FICE Identification: 001577
Unit ID: 140164
Telephone: (770) 423-6000 Carnegie Class: Master's L
FAX Number: (770) 423-6543 Calendar System: Semester
URL: www.kennesaw.edu
Established: 1963 Annual Undergrad Tuition & Fees (In-State): $6,807
Enrollment: 24,604 Coed
Affiliation or Control: State IRS Status: 501(c)3
Highest Offering: Doctorate
Program: Liberal Arts And General; Teacher Preparatory; Professional
Accreditation: SC, ART, BUS, BUSA, CGTECH, CS, MACTE, MUS, NURSE, SPAA, SW, TED, THEA

01 President .... Dr. Daniel S. PAPP
10 Chief Business Officer .... Dr. Randy C. HINDS
05 Provost/Vice Pres Academic Affs .... Dr. W. Ken HARMON
30 VP University Advancement & Devel .... Mr. Michael HARDERS
32 Vice Pres Student Success .... Dr. Jerome RATCHFORD
11 Vice President for Operations .... Dr. Randy C. HINDS
58 VP Research/Dean Graduate College .... Dr. Charles J. AMLANER
26 Vice President External Affairs .... Ms. Arlethia PERRY-JOHNSON
20 Senior Vice Provost Academic Affs .... Dr. Teresa M. JOYCE
43 Univ Attorney/Sp Asst Pres Leg Affs .... Dr. Flora B. DEVINE
04 Faculty Exec Assistant to President .... Dr. Maureen MCCARTHY
20 Assoc Vice Pres for Curriculum .... Dr. Valerie D. WHITTLESEY
21 Assoc Vice Pres for Operations .... Ms. Maria BRITT
20 Assoc VP Acad Affairs/Dean Univ Col .... Dr. Ralph J. RASCATI
15 Asst Vice Pres Human Resources Svcs .... Mr. Rodney BOSSERT
84 Asst Vice Pres Enrollment Services .... Mr. Kim WEST
08 Asst Vice Pres for Library Services .... Mr. J. David EVANS
18 Asst Vice Pres Facilities Services .... Mr. John A. ANDERSON
26 Asst VP Communications//Marketing .... Mr. David ARNOLD
46 Asst VP Enterprise Info Mgmt .... Mr. Erik R. BOWE
04 Exec Admin/Chief of Protocol .... Ms. Lynda K. JOHNSON
79 Dean Humanities/Social Science .... Dr. Robert DORFF
81 Dean Science & Mathematics .... Dr. Mark R. ANDERSON
53 Dean Bagwell College of Education .... Dr. Arlinda EATON
50 Dean Coles College of Business .... Dr. Kathy S. SCHWAIG
76 Dean WellStar Col Health/Human Svcs .... Dr. Richard L. SOWELL
49 Dean College of the Arts .... Dr. Patricia S. POULTER
35 Dean of Student Success .... Dr. Michael L. SANSEVIRO
51 Dean Continuing/Professional Educ .... Ms. Barbara S. CALHOUN
07 Asc Dn Enrol Svs/Ex Dir Univ Admiss .... Ms. Susan N. BLAKE
38 Asst Dean/Dir Student Success Svs .... Dr. Robert J. MATTOX
28 Chief Diversity Officer .... Dr. Erik MALEWSKI
06 Registrar .... Ms. Ana EDWARDS
13 Chief Technology Officer .... Dr. John L. ISENHOUR
91 Dir Enterprise Systems & Services .... Mr. T. Wayne DENNISON
37 Director Student Financial Aid .... Mr. Rondall H. DAY

07 Dir Student Recruitment/Admissions Dr. Angela J. EVANS
25 Director Procurement & Contracting Ms. Laura MCMILLAN
36 Director of Career Services Center Ms. Karen B. ANDREWS
41 Director of Athletics Mr. Vaughn A. WILLIAMS
29 Interim Director Alumni Affairs Ms. Caryn YOUNG
44 Director Annual Giving Vacant
19 Director Public Safety Mr. Theodore J. COCHRAN
35 Director Student Life Ms. Katherine E. ALDAY
88 Dir Enterprise Academic Reporting Ms. Donna R. HUTCHESON
96 Director of Purchasing Vacant

† Part of the University System of Georgia.

LaGrange College (A)

601 Broad Street, La Grange GA 30240-2999
County: Troup FICE Identification: 001578
Unit ID: 140234
Telephone: (706) 880-8000 Carnegie Class: Bac/Diverse
FAX Number: (706) 880-8358 Calendar System: 4/1/4
URL: www.lagrange.edu
Established: 1831 Annual Undergrad Tuition & Fees: $25,400
Enrollment: 902 Coed
Affiliation or Control: United Methodist IRS Status: 501(c)3
Highest Offering: Master's
Program: Liberal Arts And General; Teacher Preparatory; Professional
Accreditation: SC, ACBSP, NUR

01 President Dr. Dan MCALEXANDER
04 Executive Assistant to President Mrs. Carla RHODES
31 Events Coordinator Ms. Tammy ROGERS
41 Athletic Director Mrs. Jennifer D. CLAYBROOK
05 Provost and Chief Academic Officer Dr. David GARRISON
32 Dean of Student Engagement Dr. Mark SHOOK
06 Registrar Mr. Jimmy G. HERRING
08 Director Library Mr. Loren L. PINKERMAN
55 Director Evening College Vacant
09 Director Inst Effectiveness Dr. Carol YIN
88 Director of SOURCE Center Mr. Todd PRATER
36 Director Student Placement Mrs. Diana GOLDWIRE
38 Director Student Counseling Mrs. Pamela TREMBLAY
104 Associate Provost and Professor Mrs. Sarah Beth MALLORY
39 Director Res Educ & Housing Mr. Vernon JAMES
30 Vice President Advancement Mr. William JONES
26 Director Communications/Marketing Mr. Dean A. HARTMAN
37 Director Student Financial Aid Ms. Sylvia A. SMITH
44 Director Major Gifts Ms. Rebecca ROTH
29 Director Alumni & Cmty Relations Mrs. Martha PIRKLE
84 Dean of Enrollment Management Mr. Joseph C. MILLER
44 Director of Planned Giving Mr. Wendell CLARK
07 Director of Admissions Mr. Michael THOMAS
105 Asst Director Communications Mr. David BEARD
10 Vice Pres Finance & Operations Mr. Martin E. PIRRMAN
21 Director of Finance Mrs. Patti D. HOXSIE
15 Director Human Resources Mrs. Dawn COKER
13 Chief Information Officer Mr. Paul COPELAND
18 Manager Facilities/Physical Plant Mr. Michael CONIGLIO
19 Director of Security Mr. Michael A. THOMAS
14 Director Infomation Technology Mr. James BLACKWOOD
42 VP Spiritual Life & Church Relation Dr. Quincy D. BROWN

Lanier Technical College (B)

2990 Landrum Education Drive, Oakwood GA 30566-3405
County: Hall FICE Identification: 005254
Unit ID: 140243
Telephone: (770) 531-6300 Carnegie Class: Assoc/Pub-R-M
FAX Number: (770) 531-6328 Calendar System: Semester
URL: www.laniertech.edu
Established: 1964 Annual Undergrad Tuition & Fees (In-State): $3,789
Enrollment: 3,389 Coed
Affiliation or Control: State IRS Status: 501(c)3
Highest Offering: Associate Degree
Program: Occupational; 2-Year Principally Bachelor's Creditable; Technical Emphasis
Accreditation: SC, COE, DA, DH, EMT, MAC, RAD, SURGT

01 President Mr. Ray PERREN
103 Vice President Economic Development Mr. Tim MCDONALD
05 Vice President Academic Affairs Dr. Linda M. BARROW
12 Vice President Operations Forsyth Dr. Joanne P. TOLLESON
32 Vice President Student Affairs Ms. Lisa WILSON
10 Vice Pres Administrative Services Ms. Laura ELDER
13 Vice President Technology Mr. Robbie VICKERS
04 Executive Assistant to President Ms. Karen MINOR
20 Dean Academic Affairs Ms. Dana NICHOLS
20 Dean Academic Affairs Ms. Donna BRINSON
09 Dir of Institutional Effectiveness Mr. Brad GADBERRY
30 Director of Development Ms. Chris PERKINS
26 Director Public Relations Officer Mr. Dave PARRISH
12 Director Satellite Campus Ms. Lisa MALOOF
12 Director Satellite Campus Mr. Troy LINSEY
12 Director Satellite Campus Dr. Howard LEDFORD
07 Director of Admissions Ms. Sue CRONC
06 Registrar Ms. Sandi J. BAKER
37 Director Student Financial Aid Ms. Patsy GRIFFIN
84 Director Enrollment Management Ms. Deanna ORZA
21 Director Administrative Services Ms. Janet BOHANON
15 Director of Human Resources Ms. Jill CANTRELL
18 Director of Facilities Mr. Guy ABBS
36 Student Placement Specialist Ms. Melissa LAWRENCE
28 Coord Special Svcs/Minority Affairs Ms. Mallory SAFLEY

Le Cordon Bleu College of Culinary Arts in Atlanta (C)

1927 Lakeside Parkway, Tucker GA 30084-5865
Telephone: (770) 938-4711 Identification: 666298
Accreditation: ACICS, ACFEI

† Main campus is Le Cordon Bleu College of Culinary Arts in Portland in Portland, OR.

Life University (D)

1269 Barclay Circle, Marietta GA 30060-2996
County: Cobb FICE Identification: 020748
Unit ID: 140252
Telephone: (770) 426-2600 Carnegie Class: Bac/A&S
FAX Number: (770) 429-4819 Calendar System: Quarter
URL: www.life.edu
Established: 1974 Annual Undergrad Tuition & Fees: $9,747
Enrollment: 2,647 Coed
Affiliation or Control: Independent Non-Profit IRS Status: 501(c)3
Highest Offering: Doctorate
Program: 2-Year Principally Bachelor's Creditable; Liberal Arts And General; Professional
Accreditation: SC, CHIRO, DIETD, DIETI

01 President Dr. Guy F. RIEKEMAN
10 Exec Vice President for Finance Mr. William JARR
05 VP of Academic Affairs Dr. Rob SCOTT
30 Vice Pres of University Advancement Mr. Greg HARRIS
32 Vice President for Student Services Dr. Marc SCHNEIDER
11 Vice President for Admin Services Dr. Tim GROSS
84 Executive Dir of Enrollment & Mktg Dr. Cynthia BOYD
41 Director of Athletics Mr. John BARRETT
15 Director of Human Resources Ms. Stella PETERSON
27 Chief Information Officer Mr. John ALTIKULAC
13 Director Information Technology Mr. Thorton MUIR
104 Director of Global Initiatives Dr. John DOWNES
76 Dean College of Chiropractic Dr. Ralph DAVIS
49 Dean College Undergraduate Studies Dr. Michael SMITH
23 Dean of Clinics Vacant
06 Registrar Ms. Tiffany SMITH
07 Director of Admissions Operations Mr. Brian GIPSON
08 Director of Learning Resources Ms. Karen PRESTON
46 Director of Research Dr. Stephanie SULLIVAN
29 Alumni Relations Manager Ms. Mary Ellen LEFFARD
108 Director of Inst Effectiveness Dr. Vince ERARIO
09 Director of Institutional Research Mr. Tiannan ZHOU
18 Director Facilities/Physical Plant Mr. Michael STERLING
38 Director Student Success Dr. Lisa RUBIN
37 Director Student Financial Aid Ms. Melissa WATERS
35 Exec Dir of Student Services Ms. Jennifer VALTOS
36 Director of Career Planning Ms. Susan DUDT
88 Dir of Student Administrative Svcs Ms. Kay FREELAND
26 Director of Communications Mr. Craig DEKSHENIEKS
28 Director of Diversity Dr. Jerry HARDEE
21 Budget Director Ms. Amy MCILVANE
44 Director of Development Ms. Erin DANCER

Luther Rice University (E)

3038 Evans Mill Road, Lithonia GA 30038-2454
County: DeKalb FICE Identification: 031009
Unit ID: 135364
Telephone: (770) 484-1204 Carnegie Class: Spec/Faith
FAX Number: (770) 484-1155 Calendar System: Semester
URL: www.lru.edu
Established: 1962 Annual Undergrad Tuition & Fees: $7,290
Enrollment: 1,315 Coed
Affiliation or Control: Independent Non-Profit IRS Status: 501(c)3
Highest Offering: Doctorate
Program: Liberal Arts And General; Professional
Accreditation: TRACS

01 President Dr. James L. FLANAGAN
10 Vice President Financial Affairs Mr. Louis B. HARDCASTLE
32 Vice Pres for Student Development Dr. Dennis D. DIERINGER
05 Vice President for Academic Affairs Dr. Brad K. ARNETT
30 Vice Pres Institutional Advancement Mr. Russ L. SORROW
09 VP for Institutional Effectiveness Dr. Ralph J. MCCANN
08 Director of Library Services Mr. Daryl FLETCHER
37 Director Student Financial Aid Mr. Gary W. COOK
88 Asst to the Pres for Asian Affairs Dr. Kyung C. LIM
85 Asst to the Pres Global Strategy Dr. Ronald B. LONG

Medtech College (F)

4501 Circle 75, Pkwy SE, Ste D-4100, Atlanta GA 30339
County: Cobb FICE Identification: 038044
Unit ID: 444714
Telephone: (770) 859-9779 Carnegie Class: Not Classified
FAX Number: (770) 859-9778 Calendar System: Quarter
URL: www.medtech.edu
Established: Annual Undergrad Tuition & Fees: $14,200
Enrollment: 574 Coed
Affiliation or Control: Proprietary IRS Status: Proprietary
Highest Offering: Associate Degree
Program: Occupational
Accreditation: COE

01 Executive Director Chris ARMSTRONG

Medtech College (G)

2800 Century Pkwy NE, Suite 100, Atlanta GA 30345
Telephone: (678) 218-0600 Identification: 770536
Accreditation: COE

† Main campus is Medtech College in Atlanta, GA.

Mercer University (H)

1400 Coleman Avenue, Macon GA 31207-0003
County: Bibb FICE Identification: 001580
Unit ID: 140447
Telephone: (478) 301-2700 Carnegie Class: Master's L
FAX Number: (478) 301-2108 Calendar System: Semester
URL: www.mercer.edu
Established: 1833 Annual Undergrad Tuition & Fees: $33,120
Enrollment: 8,341 Coed
Affiliation or Control: Independent Non-Profit IRS Status: 501(c)3
Highest Offering: Doctorate
Program: Liberal Arts And General; Teacher Preparatory; Professional
Accreditation: SC, ARCPA, BUS, CACREP, CS, ENG, LAW, MED, MFCD, MUS, NURSE, PH, PHAR, PTA, TED, THEOL

01 President and CEO Mr. William D. UNDERWOOD
00 Chancellor Dr. R. Kirby GODSEY
100 Senior VP and Chief of Staff Mr. Larry D. BRUMLEY
05 Provost Dr. D. Scott DAVIS
10 Executive VP for Admin & Finance Dr. James S. NETHERTON
12 Sr VP Atlanta Campus Dr. Richard V. SWINDLE
30 Sr VP for University Advancement Mr. John A. PATTERSON
84 Sr Vice Pres Enrollment Mgmt Dr. Penny L. ELKINS
43 Vice President and General Counsel Mr. William G. SOLOMON
13 Chief Technology Officer Mr. Michael R. BELOTE
17 Sr VP Health Sciences/Dean Phar/HS Dr. Hewitt MATTHEWS
32 Vice President & Dean of Students Dr. Doug R. PEARSON
46 Sr V Prov Research/Dean Grad Stds Dr. Wayne C. GLASGOW
21 Treasurer & Assoc VP Finance Ms. Julia T. DAVIS
18 Assoc Vice President for Facilities Mr. Russell VULLO
15 Associate Vice Pres Personnel Admin Ms. Rhonda W. LIDSTONE
26 Sr Asst VP for Marketing Commun Mr. Richard L. CAMERON
37 Assoc VP Student Financial Planning Ms. Maria A. HAMMETT
49 Dean College of Liberal Arts Dr. Lake LAMBERT
61 Dean School of Law Mr. Gary J. SIMSON
63 Dean School of Medicine Dr. William F. BINA, III
54 Dean School of Engineering Dr. Wade H. SHAW
50 Dean Sch Business/Econ Dr. Susan P. GILBERT
73 Dean School of Theology Dr. R. Alan CULPEPPER
53 Interim Dean College of Education Dr. Paige L. TOMPKINS
66 Dean College of Nursing Dr. Linda A. STREIT
51 Dean College Cont/Prof Stds Dr. Priscilla R. DANHEISER
64 Dean School of Music Dr. C. David KEITH
76 Int Dn Col of Health Professions Dr. Lisa M. LUNDQUIST
08 Dean of University Libraries Ms. Elizabeth D. HAMMOND
06 Registrar Ms. Lucy P. WILSON
41 Athletic Director Mr. Jim COLE
19 Chief Police Department Mr. Gary COLLINS
09 Director of Institutional Research Ms. Sarah E. MAY
96 Director of Purchasing Mr. Charles MIZE
07 Asst VP & Director of Admissions Mr. C. Ray TATUM

Middle Georgia State College (I)

100 College Station Drive, Macon GA 31206-5145
County: Bibb FICE Identification: 007728
Unit ID: 140322
Telephone: (478) 471-2700 Carnegie Class: Bac/Diverse
FAX Number: (478) 471-2846 Calendar System: Semester
URL: www.mga.edu
Established: 1884 Annual Undergrad Tuition & Fees (In-State): $3,910
Enrollment: 8,800 Coed
Affiliation or Control: State IRS Status: 501(c)3
Highest Offering: Baccalaureate
Program: Liberal Arts And General
Accreditation: SC, ADNUR, CAHIIM, CS, NUR, OTA, TED

01 Interim President Dr. John BLACK
05 Vice President Academic Affairs Dr. Martha L. VENN
10 Vice President Fiscal Affairs Ms. Nancy STROUD
31 Vice President External Affairs Mr. Albert J. ABRAMS
32 Vice Pres Student Affs/Enroll Mgmt Vacant
20 Asst VP for Student Success Dr. Pamela BEDWELL
84 VP Enrollment Management Dr. Sherri ROWLAND
21 Asst Vice Pres Fiscal Affairs Vacant
30 Assoc Vice Pres Development/Alumni Ms. Sue CHIPMAN
09 Assoc VP Institutional Research Vacant
07 Director of Admissions Ms. Margo WOODHAM
51 Director Continuing Education Mr. Albert J. ABRAMS
12 Dean of Warner Robins Campuses Mr. David CARPENTER
13 Chief Information Officer Mr. Roger DIXON
06 Interim Registrar Ms. Brenda HOGAN
08 Director Library Services Ms. Pat BORCK
37 Director Financial Aid Ms. Pat SIMMONS
15 Dir Human Resources Ms. Lisa CHASTAIN
18 Assistant VP Facilities Mr. David SIMS
44 Director Development Ms. Beth BYERS
36 Director Counseling Mr. Allen CHASTAIN
35 Asst VP Student Affairs Mr. Michael STEWART
88 Director Student Support Services Ms. Yolanda PETTY
27 Director Communications Mr. William H. WEAVER
21 Controller Mr. Brian STANLEY
96 Purchasing Manager Vacant

50 Dean of Business .... Dr. Varkey K. TITUS
66 Dean School of Nursing/Health .... Dr. Rebecca J. CORVEY
49 Dean Arts & Sciences .... Dr. Ron WILLIAMS
50 Dean Education .... Dr. Ann LEVETT
72 Dean Information Technology .... Dr. Alex KOOHANG
36 Director Career Services .... Ms. Barbara WARREN
90 Director Academic Resource Center .... Mr. Paul JOHNSON
91 Director Administrative Systems .... Ms. Beverly BERGMAN
41 Director Athletics .... Mr. Charles MULLIS
39 Director of Residence Life .... Dr. Chris SUMMERLIN
19 Director of Public Safety .... Mr. Shawn DOUGLAS
40 Director Auxillary Services .... Mr. Kevin REID

† Part of the University System of Georgia.

Miller-Motte Technical College (A)

621 NW Frontage Road, Augusta GA 30907

Telephone: (706) 396-8000 Identification: 770710
Accreditation: ACICS

† Main campus is Miller-Motte Technical College in Clarksville, TN.

Miller-Motte Technical College (B)

1800 Box Road, Columbus GA 31907

Telephone: (706) 225-5000 Identification: 770711
Accreditation: ACICS

† Main campus is Miller-Motte Technical College in Clarksville, TN.

Miller-Motte Technical College (C)

175 Tom Hill Sr Boulevard, Macon GA 31210

Telephone: (478) 803-4800 Identification: 770844
Accreditation: ACICS

† Main campus is McCann School of Business & Technology in Pottsville, PA.

Morehouse College (D)

830 Westview Drive SW, Atlanta GA 30314-3773

County: Fulton FICE Identification: 001582
Unit ID: 140553
Telephone: (404) 681-2800 Carnegie Class: Bac/A&S
FAX Number: (404) 681-2650 Calendar System: Semester
URL: www.morehouse.edu
Established: 1867 Annual Undergrad Tuition & Fees: $25,460
Enrollment: 2,375 Male
Affiliation or Control: Independent Non-Profit IRS Status: 501(c)3
Highest Offering: Baccalaureate
Program: Liberal Arts And General; Teacher Preparatory
Accreditation: SC, BUS, MUS

01 President .... Dr. John S. WILSON, JR.
05 Provost/SVP Academic Affairs .... Dr. Garikai CAMPBELL
11 Vice President Campus Operations .... Mr. Andre E. BERTRAND
30 Vice Pres Institutional Advancement .... Mr. Phillip D. HOWARD
100 Chief of Staff .... Ms. Karen MILLER
32 Acting Vice Pres Student Services .... Dr. Renardo HALL
10 Vice Pres Business Affairs/CFO .... Dr. Alan ROBERTSON
20 Assoc Vice Pres Academic Affairs .... Vacant
15 Interim AVP Human Resource .... Ms. Shirley CARPENTER
44 Exec Asst to Pres-Capital Campaign .... Ms. Kathleen JOHNSON
42 Dean Martin Luther King Jr Chapel .... Dr. Lawrence E. CARTER
06 Int Assoc Dean Records/Registration .... Ms. Kasi ROBINSON
07 Dean Admissions & Recruitment .... Mr. Darryl ISOM
37 Interim Director of Financial Aid .... Ms. Sheryl SPIVEY
29 Dir Alumni Rels/Annual Giving Pgm .... Mr. Henry GOODGAME
26 Director of Communications .... Ms. Toni O'NEAL MOSLEY
36 Director of Placement .... Mr. Doug COOPER
41 Athletic Director .... Mr. Andre PATTILLO
39 Director Student Housing .... Mr. Maurice WASHINGTON
19 Interim Chief of Campus Police .... Chief Jared SMITH
18 Int Superintendent Physical Plant .... Mr. Curtis DAVIS
85 Interim Dir Andrew Young Ctr .... Mr. Julius COLES
86 Director Government Relations .. Ms. Denise MOORE BERTRAND
09 Director of Institutional Research .... Dr. Michael FLEMING
35 Director Student Services .... Mr. Kevin BOOKER
38 Director of Student Counseling .... Dr. Gary WRIGHT
96 Purchasing Manager .... Mr. Kevin BRANCH
27 Publications Manager .... Ms. Vickie HAMPTON
50 Interim Dean Business & Economics .... Dr. Cheryl ALLEN
81 Dean Div of Science & Mathematics .... Dr. John K. HAYNES
79 Dean Div of Humanities & Soc Sci .... Dr. Clarissa MYRICK HARRIS
84 Interim Director of Enrollment .... Mr. Terrance DIXON

Morehouse School of Medicine (E)

720 Westview Drive, SW, Atlanta GA 30310-1495

County: Fulton FICE Identification: 024821
Unit ID: 140562
Telephone: (404) 752-1500 Carnegie Class: Spec/Med
FAX Number: (404) 752-1027 Calendar System: Semester
URL: www.msm.edu
Established: 1975 Annual Graduate Tuition & Fees: $49,652
Enrollment: 341 Coed
Affiliation or Control: Independent Non-Profit IRS Status: 501(c)3
Highest Offering: Doctorate; No Undergraduates
Program: Professional
Accreditation: SC, MED, PH

01 President .... Dr. John E. MAUPIN, JR.
05 Dean and Executive Vice President .... Dr. Valerie MONTGOMERY RICE
86 Exec Director of Government Affairs .... Mr. Daniel DAWES
43 Interim General Counsel .... Ms. Santhia CURTIS
30 VP Institutional Advancement .... Vacant
46 VP & Sr Assoc Dean OSRA .... Dr. Sandra HARRIS-HOOKER
20 Sr Assoc Dean for Educ/Faculty UME .... Dr. Martha ELKS
11 Director Faculty Affairs .... Ms. Sandra E. WATSON
37 Director 1- Student Fiscal Affairs .... Ms. Cynthia H. HANDY
08 Library Manager .... Mr. Joe SWANSON, JR.
09 Director II .... Ms. Andrea D. FOX
26 VP of Marketing & Communications .... Ms. Necole MERITT
25 Director of Grants & Contracts .... Ms. Sherry BALLENGER
29 Alumni Affairs Coordinator .... Ms. Carrie M. DUMAS
84 Director I Admissions .... Mr. Brandon HUNTER
96 Director I Purchasing .... Mr. Linwood HILTON
15 Associate VP of Human Resources .... Ms. Denise BRITT
102 Assoc VP for Inst Adv Found/Corp .... Ms. Wendi NANCE
44 Major Gifts Officer .... Ms. Kelly BROWN MORRIS
22 Chief Compliance Officer .... Mr. Jonathan WILLIAMS
100 Chief of Staff/Int General Counsel .... Santhia CURTIS
06 Registrar .... Vacant
88 Sr Assoc Dean for Clinical Affairs .... Dr. Derrick BEECH, JR.
27 Director II .... Ms. Annmarie EADES
19 Director I Chief of Police .... Mr. Joseph CHEVALIER, JR.
105 Communications Specialist II .... Ms. Chrystal NEELY
44 Assoc VP Alumni Affairs/Annual Fund .... Ms. Trina STEELE OLIDGE

Moultrie Technical College (F)

800 Veterans Parkway North, Moultrie GA 31788-1919

County: Colquitt FICE Identification: 005255
Unit ID: 140599
Telephone: (912) 891-7000 Carnegie Class: Assoc/Pub-R-M
FAX Number: (912) 891-7010 Calendar System: Semester
URL: www.moultrietech.edu
Established: 1964 Annual Undergrad Tuition & Fees (In-State): $4,491
Enrollment: 2,000 Coed
Affiliation or Control: State IRS Status: 501(c)3
Highest Offering: Associate Degree
Program: Occupational; 2-Year Principally Bachelor's Creditable; Technical Emphasis
Accreditation: ®SC, COE, MAC, RAD, SURGT

01 President .... Dr. Tina K. ANDERSON
05 Vice President for Academic Affairs .... Jim GLASS
11 VP of Administrative Services .... Ken STRICKLAND
32 Vice President of Student Services .... Leigh WALLACE
21 Vice President Operations .... David EVANS
09 VP Institutional Effectiveness .... Tavarez HOLSTON
51 Asst Vice President of Adult Educ .... Jerry SMITH
12 Dean of Instruction Moultrie Campus .... Tina STRICKLAND
12 Dean of Instruction Tifton Campus .... Becky RICHARDSON
06 Registrar .... Wendi TOSTENSON
32 Director Student Affairs .... Lisa GRIFFIN
15 Director Human Resources .... Michael HEARD
18 Chief Facilities/Physical Plant .... Steve PEACOCK
26 Director of Marketing .... Jana WIGGINS
37 Director Student Financial Aid .... Judi LOVVORN
36 Career Services Specialist .... Bridgett ADAMS

North Georgia Technical College (G)

PO Box 65, Clarkesville GA 30523-0065

County: Habersham FICE Identification: 005619
Unit ID: 140678
Telephone: (706) 754-7700 Carnegie Class: Assoc/Pub-R-M
FAX Number: (706) 754-7777 Calendar System: Semester
URL: www.northgatech.edu
Established: 1943 Annual Undergrad Tuition & Fees (In-State): $4,667
Enrollment: 2,605 Coed
Affiliation or Control: State IRS Status: 501(c)3
Highest Offering: Associate Degree
Program: Occupational; 2-Year Principally Bachelor's Creditable; Technical Emphasis
Accreditation: SC, ACFEI, MAC, MLTAD

01 President .... Dr. Gail THAXTON
05 Vice President of Academic Affairs .... Kathie IVESTER
35 Vice President for Student Affairs .... Dr. Michael KING
10 Vice President of Administration .... Carol CARSON
30 Vice Pres of Economic Development .... Dr. Mark IVESTER
06 Registrar .... Caroline FRICK
07 Director of Admissions .... Amanda MITCHELL
15 Director Personnel Services .... Marcia PEYTON
18 Chief Facilities/Physical Plant .... Michael BOYD
26 Chief Public Relations Officer .... Sandra MAUGHON
29 Director Alumni Relations .... Cynthia BROWN
32 Chief Student Life Officer .... Sherry SEAL
36 Director Job Placement .... Daniel GREGG
37 Director Student Financial Aid .... Kim KELLEY
38 Director Student Counseling .... Vacant
84 Director Enrollment Management .... Amanda MITCHELL
96 Procurement Officer .... Jeannie BARRETT
09 Director of Institutional Research .... Vacant
46 Dir Institutional Effectiveness .... Janet HENDERSON
20 Dean of Academics .... Dan PRESSLEY
20 Dean of Academics .... Mindy GLANDER

Oconee Fall Line Technical College-North Campus (H)

1189 Deepstep Road, Sandersville GA 31082-9337

County: Washington FICE Identification: 031555
Unit ID: 420431
Telephone: (478) 553-2050 Carnegie Class: Assoc/Pub-R-S
FAX Number: (478) 553-2118 Calendar System: Semester
URL: www.oftc.edu
Established: 1996 Annual Undergrad Tuition & Fees (In-State): $1,726
Enrollment: 1,886 Coed
Affiliation or Control: State IRS Status: 501(c)3
Highest Offering: Associate Degree
Program: Occupational
Accreditation: COE

01 President .... Dr. Lloyd HORADAN
05 Vice Pres Academic/Student Affs .... Ms. Erica HARDEN
11 Vice Pres Administrative Services .... Ms. Rosemary SELBY
30 Vice Pres Economic Development .... Ms. Leigh EVANS
49 Dean Arts & Sciences/Business Svcs .. Ms. Michele STRICKLAND
32 Dean Student Affairs .... Ms. Johnnie EDGE
06 Registrar .... Ms. Geri CLEMENTS
07 Director of Admissions .... Ms. Raydor CONEWAY
15 Director Human Resources .... Ms. Sharon VEAL
21 Director of Administrative Services .... Ms. Penny KITCHENS
18 Director Facilities/Physical Plant .... Mr. Jim HARRISON
26 Exec Director Marketing .... Ms. Jennifer AHRENS
37 Financial Aid Director .... Ms. Betty YOUNG
28 Dir of Spec Populations/Stdnt Life .... Ms. Dessie HALL

Oconee Fall Line Technical College-South Campus (I)

560 Pinehill Road, Dublin GA 31021-1599

County: Laurens FICE Identification: 022795
Unit ID: 140076
Telephone: (478) 275-6589 Carnegie Class: Assoc/Pub-R-M
FAX Number: (478) 275-6642 Calendar System: Semester
URL: www.oftc.edu
Established: 1984 Annual Undergrad Tuition & Fees (In-State): $1,514
Enrollment: 1,885 Coed
Affiliation or Control: State IRS Status: 501(c)3
Highest Offering: Associate Degree
Program: Occupational; Technical Emphasis
Accreditation: COE, COARC, MAC, RAD

01 President .... Dr. Lloyd HORADAN
05 Provost South Campus .... Mrs. Beth CRUMPTON
09 Vice Pres Inst Effectiveness .... Dr. Katie DAVIS
32 Dean Student Affairs .... Mr. Jay MULLIS
06 Assistant Registrar .... Ms. Kimberly NOLES
18 Director Facilities .... Mr. Ragan GREEN
30 Exec Dir Institutional Advancement .... Mrs. Jenny SHUMAN
19 Director Safety & Security .... Mr. Rick SWANSON
36 Director of Career Development .... Ms. Cecile MILLER
76 Dean Allied Health/Prof Svcs .... Ms. Tammy BAYTO
37 Asst Director Financial Aid .... Ms. Teresa CRAFTON
08 Director Library Services .... Ms. Wendi MORRIS

Ogeechee Technical College (J)

One Joseph E. Kennedy Boulevard, Statesboro GA 30458-8049

County: Bulloch FICE Identification: 030300
Unit ID: 366465
Telephone: (912) 681-5500 Carnegie Class: Assoc/Pub-R-M
FAX Number: (912) 486-7704 Calendar System: Semester
URL: www.ogeecheetech.edu
Established: 1987 Annual Undergrad Tuition & Fees (In-State): $3,156
Enrollment: 2,236 Coed
Affiliation or Control: State IRS Status: 501(c)3
Highest Offering: Associate Degree
Program: Occupational; 2-Year Principally Bachelor's Creditable
Accreditation: COE, CAHIIM, DA, DMS, FUSER, MAC, OPD, RAD, SURGT

01 President .... Dr. Dawn H. CARTEE
04 Exec Assistant to the President .... Ms. Karen MOBLEY
05 Executive VP for Academic Affairs .... Dr. Charlene LAMAR
31 Vice President Economic Development .... Ms. Lori DURDEN
108 VP Institutional Effectiveness .... Ms. Brandy TAYLOR
32 Vice President Student Affairs .... Mr. Ryan FOLEY
10 Vice President for Administration .... Ms. Evyonne HART
13 VP Technology & Institutional Supp .... Mr. Jeff DAVIS
30 VP for College Advancement .... Mr. Barry TURNER
09 Director Inst Research & Planning .... Ms. YLonne HODGES
20 Dean for Academic Affairs .... Mr. John GROOVER
20 Dean for Academic Affairs .... Mr. Bill BARTON
08 Dean for Library Services .... Dr. Lynn FUTCH
51 Dir Continuing Ed & Ind Training .... Ms. Kathleen KOSMOSKI
84 Director for Admissions .... Ms. Laura SAUNDERS
06 Registrar .... Ms. Michelle STUBBS
37 Director for Financial Aid .... Ms. Letrell THOMAS
21 Director for Accounting .... Ms. Patsy POWELL
15 Director for Human Resources .... Mr. Steve MILLER
40 Director for Auxiliary Services .... Mr. J.J ALTMAN
18 Director for Plant Operations .... Mr. Buddy SAPP
19 Director Campus Safety & Security .... Mr. Stan YORK
88 Director for Adult Education .... Mr. Paul MIZELL
20 Assistant VP for Academic Affairs .... Dr. Linda ROBERTS

Oglethorpe University (A)

4484 Peachtree Road, NE, Atlanta GA 30319-2797
County: DeKalb FICE Identification: 001586
Unit ID: 140696
Telephone: (404) 261-1441 Carnegie Class: Bac/A&S
FAX Number: (404) 364-8500 Calendar System: Semester
URL: www.oglethorpe.edu
Established: 1835 Annual Undergrad Tuition & Fees: $31,000
Enrollment: 1,079 Coed
Affiliation or Control: Independent Non-Profit IRS Status: 501(c)3
Highest Offering: Master's
Program: Liberal Arts And General; Teacher Preparatory; Business Emphasis
Accreditation: SC

01 President ... Dr. Lawrence M. SCHALL
05 Provost ... Vacant
10 Vice Pres for Business & Finance ... Mr. Michael D. HORAN
30 Vice Pres Devel & Alumni Relations ... Mr. Kevin A. SMYRL
84 Vice Pres for Enrollment Management ... Ms. Lucy LEUSCH
32 VP Stdnt Affairs/Dean of Students ... Ms. Michelle HALL
20 Assoc Provost ... Dr. Keith AUFDERHEIDE
20 Interim Assoc Provost ... Dr. John NARDO
04 Exec Assistant to the President ... Ms. Colleen D'ALESSANDRO
20 Asst Provost ... Mr. Eric TACK
08 Librarian ... Ms. Anne SALTER
06 Registrar ... Vacant
09 Director of Institutional Research ... Dr. Amy PALDER
26 Exec Dir Marketing/Public Relations ... Mr. Todd BENNETT
41 Athletic Director ... Ms. Becky HALL
37 Director of Financial Aid ... Mr. Chris SUMMERS
39 Director of Residence Life ... Mr. Danny GLASSMAN
21 Director of Finance/Controller ... Ms. Amy RENTENBACH
91 Director Administrative Computing ... Vacant
27 Chief Information Officer ... Vacant
29 Director of Alumni Relations ... Ms. Barbara HENRY
36 Director of Career Counseling ... Ms. Caroline WEIMAR
44 Director of Development Operations ... Mr. John CARR
15 Director Human Resources ... Vacant
31 Dir Center for Civic Engagement ... Ms. Tamara NASH
18 Director Facilities/Physical Plant ... Mr. Walter HALL
40 Bookstore Manager ... Ms. Ashley GANDY

Okefenokee Technical College (B)

1701 Carswell Avenue, Waycross GA 31503-4016
County: Ware FICE Identification: 005511
Unit ID: 248776
Telephone: (912) 287-6584 Carnegie Class: Assoc/Pub-R-M
FAX Number: (912) 287-4865 Calendar System: Semester
URL: www.okefenokeetech.edu
Established: 1965 Annual Undergrad Tuition & Fees (In-State): $4,395
Enrollment: 1,348 Coed
Affiliation or Control: State IRS Status: 501(c)3
Highest Offering: Associate Degree
Program: Occupational; Technical Emphasis
Accreditation: SC, COARC, MAC, MLTAD, RAD, SURGT

01 President ... Dr. Glenn DEIBERT
05 Vice Pres for Academic Affairs ... Dr. Melanie THORNTON
11 VP of Administrative Services ... Ms. Pamela FARR
46 Vice Pres for Economic Development ... Mr. Andy BRANNEN
32 Vice President for Student Affairs ... Ms. Danita CANNON
06 Registrar ... Ms. Tara EICHFIELD
26 Public Relations/Information Dir ... Ms. Cindy TANNER
18 Facilities Director ... Mr. Chad BOYETT
36 Career Services Director ... Mr. Charlie GIBSON
37 Director Student Financial Aid ... Mr. Josh DASHER
09 Institutional Effectiveness Dir ... Ms. Teresa ALLEN
07 Director of Admissions ... Mr. Neal MURPHY
15 Human Resources Coordinator ... Ms. Cynthia LINDER
30 Coord of Resource Development ... Ms. Cindy TANNER

Paine College (C)

1235 15th Street, Augusta GA 30901-3182
County: Richmond FICE Identification: 001587
Unit ID: 140720
Telephone: (706) 821-8200 Carnegie Class: Bac/Diverse
FAX Number: (706) 821-8373 Calendar System: Semester
URL: www.paine.edu
Established: 1882 Annual Undergrad Tuition & Fees: $13,332
Enrollment: 837 Coed
Affiliation or Control: Multiple Protestant Denominations
IRS Status: 501(c)3
Highest Offering: Baccalaureate
Program: Liberal Arts And General; Teacher Preparatory; Professional
Accreditation: SC, ACBSP, TED

01 President ... Dr. George C. BRADLEY
05 Interim Provost/VP Acad Affs ... Dr. Samuel SULLIVAN
10 VP of Administrative & Fiscal Affs ... Mr. Roger MCLEAN
30 VP of Institutional Advancement ... Mr. Brandon BROWN
32 VP and Dean of Student Affairs ... Dr. Elias ETINGE
45 Dir Plng/Eval & Title III Coord ... Dr. Cheryl EVANS JONES
88 Special Asst to the President ... Dr. Walter C. HOWARD
42 Campus Pastor ... Dr. Luther FELDER
41 Athletics Director ... Mr. Timothy DUNCAN
20 Assoc VP of Acad Affairs ... Dr. Tina MARSHALL-BRADLEY
20 Asst VP for Academic Affairs ... Dr. Edem TETTEH
44 Asst VP of Inst Advancement ... Ms. Helene CARTER
49 Interim Provost/VP Acad Affs ... Dr. Samuel SULLIVAN
107 Dean School of Professional Studies ... Dr. David CHAMBLEE
19 Chief of Campus Safety ... Mr. Joseph D. NELSON
23 College Nurse ... Ms. Harriett S. JONES
21 Controller ... Mrs. Burshunda HARDEN
07 Director Admissions ... Mr. Marshall RAINEY
88 Director Athletics Compliance ... Ms. Taura HATNEY
36 Director Career Services ... Mrs. April EWING
38 Director Counseling Center ... Ms. Brooke ROBERTSON
18 Dir Facilities Mgmt/Environ Svcs ... Mr. Michael SUMMERS
37 Director Financial Aid ... Ms. Gerri BOGAN
13 Dir Information Technology Svcs ... Mr. Michael HICKS
08 Head Librarian ... Mrs. Alana LEWIS
09 Director Inst Research ... Mrs. Alice M. SIMPKINS
39 Director Residence Life ... Ms. Lauren DEVILLE
25 Director Sponsored Programs ... Mr. Geno CLARK
35 Director Student Activities ... Ms. Sasha MCCRAW
88 Dir Transportation/Maintenance ... Mr. Charlie WOODLEY
16 Dir of Human Resources ... Mrs. Jannette HENRY-DAVENPORT
40 Manager of The Lion's Shop ... Vacant
06 Registrar ... Mrs. Castine RHOADES WILLIAMS
29 Director Alumni Relations ... Mrs. Mildred KENDRICK
26 Asst Dir Communications & Marketing ... Ms. Leah SUGGS
96 Junior Buyer ... Ms. Linda BEASLEY
104 Student Services Specialist ... Mr. Yaw BANGOLAME

Philadelphia College of Osteopathic Medicine Georgia Campus (D)

625 Old Peachtree Road NW, Suwanee GA 30024
Telephone: (678) 225-7500 Identification: 770165
Accreditation: &M

† Main campus is Philadelphia College of Osteopathic Medicine in Philadelphia, PA.

Piedmont College (E)

PO Box 10, Demorest GA 30535-0010
County: Habersham FICE Identification: 001588
Unit ID: 140818
Telephone: (706) 778-3000 Carnegie Class: Master's L
FAX Number: (706) 776-0701 Calendar System: Semester
URL: www.piedmont.edu
Established: 1897 Annual Undergrad Tuition & Fees: $20,730
Enrollment: 2,473 Coed
Affiliation or Control: Christian Churches And Churches of Christ
IRS Status: 501(c)3
Highest Offering: Doctorate
Program: Liberal Arts And General; Teacher Preparatory
Accreditation: SC, ACBSP, NUR

01 President ... Dr. James F. MELLICHAMP
05 Vice Pres Academic Affairs ... Dr. Perry RETTIG
03 Exec VP for Institutional Resources ... Dr. John MISNER
11 Asst VP for Administrative Services ... Mr. Parks MILLER
10 Asst VP Finance/Human Resources ... Ms. Margie MEANS
12 Vice President Athens Campus ... Dr. Mel PALMER
30 Vice President for Advancement ... Ms. Amy AMASON
35 Asst VP Student Svcs/Dn Admissions . Ms. Cynthia L. PETERSON
88 Special Assistant to the President ... Ms. Jane KIDD
44 Director of Development ... Mr. Justin SCALI
09 Director of Institutional Research ... Ms. Kim LOVELL
29 Dir Special Projects/Community Rels ... Mr. Bill LOYD
04 Assistant to the President ... Ms. Kristen GRAY
04 Assistant to the President ... Ms. Ann SUTTON
32 Dean Student Affairs ... Mr. Andrew B. DAVIS
42 Chaplain/Church Relations ... Rev Dr. Ashley CLEERE
07 Director Graduate Admissions ... Ms. Penny LOGGINS
06 Registrar ... Ms. Carla EDENFIELD
08 College Librarian ... Mr. Robert GLASS, JR.
37 Director of Financial Aid ... Mr. David MCMILLION
07 Director Undergraduate Admissions ... Ms. Brenda BOONSTRA
13 Director Information Technology ... Dr. Shahryar HEYDARI
15 Human Resources Specialist ... Ms. Debbie ZIMMERMAN
26 Director of Public Relations ... Mr. David E. PRICE
41 Dir of Intercollegiate Athletics ... Mr. John L. DZIK
21 Compliance & Treasurery Officer ... Ms. Leesa P. ANDERSON
36 Director Counseling/Career Services ... Ms. Emily PETIT
19 Director Security/Campus Police ... Mr. Richard D. MARTIN
66 Dean School of Nursing/Health Sci ... Dr. Linda SCOTT
50 Dean School of Business Admin ... Dr. John MISNER
49 Dean School of Arts & Sciences ... Dr. Steven NIMMO
53 Dean School of Education ... Dr. Donald GNECCO

Point University (F)

507 W 10th St, West Point GA 31833
County: Troup FICE Identification: 001547
Unit ID: 138868
Telephone: (706) 385-1000 Carnegie Class: Bac/Diverse
FAX Number: N/A Calendar System: Semester
URL: www.point.edu
Established: 1937 Annual Undergrad Tuition & Fees: $17,400
Enrollment: 1,483 Coed
Affiliation or Control: Christian Churches And Churches of Christ
IRS Status: 501(c)3
Highest Offering: Baccalaureate
Program: 2-Year Principally Bachelor's Creditable; Liberal Arts And General; Teacher Preparatory; Religious Emphasis
Accreditation: SC, TED

01 President ... Mr. Dean C. COLLINS
05 Chief Academic Officer ... Dr. W. Darryl HARRISON
20 Vice Pres for Academic Affairs ... Dr. Kimberly C. MACENCZAK
108 Vice Pres for Inst Effectiveness ... Dr. Dennis E. GLENN
88 Vice Pres for Educ Initiatives ... Ms. Emma W. MORRIS
55 Dean of Acad & Stdnt Svcs - Access ... Mr. Richard BUMPERS
08 Library Director ... Mr. Michael L. BAIN
84 Vice Pres for Enrollment Management ... Ms. Stacy BARTLETT
06 Registrar ... Ms. Betsy CLIFTON
07 Director of Admission ... Ms. Tiffany WOOD
37 Director of Financial Aid ... Ms. Karen BAILEY
32 Director of Student Life ... Mr. Chris BEIRNE
88 Asst VP of Enroll Mgmt - Access ... Ms. Tonya CANNON
07 Director of Enrollment - Access ... Mr. Doug JOHNSON
11 Chief Operations Officer ... Mr. Lance FRANCIS
16 Director of Human Resources ... Ms. Chasta RAUCCIO
10 Vice Pres for Finance and CFO ... Mr. Joseph BOTANA
21 Controller ... Ms. Merinda THROWER
42 Vice Pres for Spiritual Formation ... Mr. Wye HUXFORD
30 Vice President for Advancement ... Vacant
44 Major Gifts Officer ... Mr. Mike MCCAFFERTY
88 Chancellor ... Dr. R. Edwin GROOVER
29 Director of Alumni Relations ... Ms. Pam ROSS
27 Communications Manager ... Ms. Weslynn BIGGERS
13 Vice Pres for Info Technology ... Mr. Jose' DIEUDONNE'
41 Athletic Director ... Vacant
18 Dir of Facilities and Maintenance ... Mr. Jim ALDRIDGE
19 Director of Security ... Mr. Fred BERKELEY

† Formerly Atlanta Christian College

Reinhardt University (G)

7300 Reinhardt Circle, Waleska GA 30183-2981
County: Cherokee FICE Identification: 001589
Unit ID: 140872
Telephone: (770) 720-5600 Carnegie Class: Bac/Diverse
FAX Number: (770) 720-5602 Calendar System: Semester
URL: www.reinhardt.edu
Established: 1883 Annual Undergrad Tuition & Fees: $18,670
Enrollment: 1,223 Coed
Affiliation or Control: United Methodist IRS Status: 501(c)3
Highest Offering: Master's
Program: Liberal Arts And General
Accreditation: SC, MUS

01 President ... Dr. J. Thomas ISHERWOOD
04 Executive Assistant to President ... Mrs. Bonnie H. DEBORD
05 VP & Dean for Academic Affairs ... Dr. Mark A. ROBERTS
10 Vice Pres Finance & Administration ... Mr. Robert G. MCKINNON
30 VP for Advancement ... Mrs. JoEllen B. WILSON
32 VP Student Affairs/Dean of Students ... Dr. Roger R. LEE
58 Assoc Vice Pres Graduate Studies ... Dr. Margaret M. MORLIER
101 Asst Secretary Board of Trustees ... Mrs. Bonnie H. DEBORD
18 Exec Director of Physical Plant ... Mr. John W. YOUNG
26 Exec Dir Marketing/Communications ... Mrs. Marsha S. WHITE
13 Exec Dir & CIO for Information Tech ... Mrs. Virginia R. TOMLINSON
88 Exec Director of Funk Heritage Ctr ... Dr. Joseph H. KITCHENS
07 Director of Admissions ... Mrs. Julie C. FLEMING
06 Registrar ... Ms. Janet M. RODNING
09 Dir Instnl Research/Effectiveness ... Mr. Rob W. DUNNAM
08 Director of Library Services ... Mr. Joel C. LANGFORD
19 Director of Public Safety ... Ms. Sherry N. CORNETT
29 Dir Alumni Rel & Alumni Giving ... Mrs. Kathy A. BOUYETT
42 University Chaplain ... Rev. Jordan S. THRASHER
21 Controller ... Mr. Peter J. BROMSTAD
37 Director Student Financial Aid ... Mrs. Angie D. HARLOW
41 Director of Athletics ... Mr. William C. POPP
16 Director Human Resources ... Ms. Nikki WEHUNT
39 Director Residence Life ... Ms. Shalyn J. HERNANDEZ
23 University Nurse ... Mrs. Alicia C. MILES
35 Asst Dean of Students/Dir Stdnt Act ... Dr. Walter P. MAY
38 Director of Counseling Svcs ... Mr. Derek L. STRUCHTEMEYER
88 Dir Center for Student Success ... Dr. Catherine B. EMANUEL
36 Director of Career Services ... Mrs. Peggy C. FEEHERY
40 Bookstore Manager ... Ms. Janet TASKER
105 Web Communication Manager ... Mr. John C. PETTIBONE
106 Coordinator Online Education ... Dr. Katherine E. HYATT
49 Dean School of Arts & Humanities ... Dr. Arthur W. GLOWKA
81 Dean School of Maths & Sciences ... Dr. Bill J. DEANGELIS
50 Int Dean McCamish School Business ... Dr. Donald D. WILSON, JR.
53 Dean Price School of Education ... Dr. James L. CURRY, JR.
64 Int Dean School of Music ... Dr. Dennis K. MCINTIRE
107 Int Dean Sch Professional Studies ... Mr. Lester W. DRAWDY

SAE Institute Atlanta (H)

215 Peachtree St NE #300, Atlanta GA 30303-1739
County: Fulton FICE Identification: 042066
Unit ID: 476948
Telephone: (404) 247-3529 Carnegie Class: Not Classified
FAX Number: (404) 526-9366 Calendar System: Semester
URL: atlanta.sae.edu
Established: 1976 Annual Undergrad Tuition & Fees: $18,040
Enrollment: 113 Coed
Affiliation or Control: Proprietary IRS Status: Proprietary
Highest Offering: Associate Degree
Program: Occupational
Accreditation: ACICS

Sanford-Brown College (A)

1140 Hammond Drive NE, Suite A 1150,
Atlanta GA 30328

County: Fulton FICE Identification: 021160
Unit ID: 420495
Telephone: (770) 576-4498 Carnegie Class: Assoc/PrivFP
FAX Number: (773) 601-3881 Calendar System: Other
URL: www.sanfordbrown.edu/Atlanta
Established: Annual Undergrad Tuition & Fees: $15,776
Enrollment: 488 Coed
Affiliation or Control: Proprietary IRS Status: Proprietary
Highest Offering: Associate Degree
Program: Occupational; Technical Emphasis
Accreditation: ACICS, CVT, DMS

01 Campus President .... Mr. Steven IROFF

Savannah College of Art and Design (B)

342 Bull Street, PO Box 3146, Savannah GA 31402-6263

County: Chatham FICE Identification: 021415
Unit ID: 140951
Telephone: (912) 525-5000 Carnegie Class: Spec/Arts
FAX Number: (912) 525-6263 Calendar System: Quarter
URL: www.scad.edu
Established: 1978 Annual Undergrad Tuition & Fees: $32,950
Enrollment: 11,415 Coed
Affiliation or Control: Independent Non-Profit IRS Status: 501(c)3
Highest Offering: Master's
Program: Fine Arts Emphasis
Accreditation: SC, CIDA

01 President .... Mrs. Paula WALLACE
03 COO .... Vacant
11 VP for Business Operations .... Mr. J.J WALLER
88 VP for Student Financial Services .... Mr. Scott LINZEY
46 Sr Vice Pres University Resources ... Mr. Glenn E. WALLACE, JR.
05 Chief Academic Officer .... Dr. Gokhan OZAYSIN
10 Chief Financial Officer .... Mr. John WHALEY
20 Assoc VP for Academic Support .... Mrs. Hannah CROCKETT
12 Vice President for SCAD Atlanta .... Ms. Teresa GRIFFIS
12 Assoc VP for SCAD Hong Kong .... Mr. Grant PREISSER
88 VP for Creative Direction .... Ms. Kari HERRIN
13 VP for Educational Technology .... Mr. Andrew FULP
32 Vice President for Student Success .... Dr. Philip ALLETTO
15 Vice President for Human Resources .... Ms. Lesley HANAK
13 Vice President for IM&T .... Mr. Brad GRANT
106 VP for Strategy & Innovation .... Mr. John Paul ROWAN
07 Assoc VP for Admissions .... Mr. David PUGH
88 Assoc VP for University Resources .... Mr. Charles SMITH
26 Director of Public Relations .... Ms. Sunny NELSON
35 Assoc Dean of Students .... Mr. David BLAKE
08 Dean of Library/Academic Services .... Vacant
18 Exec Dir for Physical Resources .... Ms. Helen MORGAN
37 Director of Financial Aid .... Ms. Kim BEVERIDGE
06 Registrar .... Vacant
07 Exec Dir Admissions/Recruit & Eve .... Ms. Jenny JAQUILLARD
30 Sr VP for Marketing & Public Rel .... Mr. Jose MALLABO
19 Director of Security .... Mr. John BUCKOVICH
41 Athletics Director (Savannah) .... Mr. Doug WOLLENBURG
41 Athletics Director (Atlanta) .... Ms. Stephany RAINES
38 Dir Counseling/Student Support Svc .. Dr. Tamara KNAPP-GROSZ
58 Director of Graduate Studies .... Ms. Sarah MCCARN
88 Dean of School of Building Arts .... Mr. Christian SOTTILE
88 Dean of School Communication Arts .... Mr. Anthony FISHER
88 Dean of School of Design .... Mr. Victor ERMOLI
88 Dean of School of Digital Media .... Ms. Tina O'HAILEY
57 Dean of School of Fine Arts .... Mr. Steve BLISS
49 Dean of School of Liberal Arts .... Ms. Beth CONCEPCION
88 Dean School of Fashion .... Mr. Michael FINK
88 Dean School of Foundation Studies .... Ms. Maureen GARVIN
88 Dean of Entertainment Arts .... Vacant
36 Exec Dir of Career & Alumni Success .... Ms. Kristine FAXON
44 Director of Development .... Ms. Allison MARTIN

Savannah State University (C)

3219 College Street, Savannah GA 31404-5308

County: Chatham FICE Identification: 001590
Unit ID: 140960
Telephone: (912) 358-4778 Carnegie Class: Bac/A&S
FAX Number: (912) 356-2256 Calendar System: Semester
URL: www.savannahstate.edu
Established: 1890 Annual Undergrad Tuition & Fees (In-State): $6,340
Enrollment: 4,582 Coed
Affiliation or Control: State IRS Status: 501(c)3
Highest Offering: Master's
Program: Liberal Arts And General
Accreditation: SC, BUS, ENGT, JOUR, SPAA, SW

01 University President .... Dr. Cheryl DOZIER
05 Provost/VP Academic Affairs .... Dr. Reynold VERRET
10 Vice Pres Business & Finance .... Mr. Edward B. JOLLEY, JR.
32 Int Vice President Student Affairs .... Dr. David SMITH
30 VP Advancement/Ex Dir SSU Foundatn .... Mr. Phillip D. ADAMS
20 Asst Vice Pres Academic Affairs .... Dr. Larry STOKES
84 Dir Enrollment Services/Registrar .... Mr. Timothy CRANFORD
07 Asst Director of Admissions .... Ms. Carol DOLAN
15 Director Human Resources .... Dr. Sandra M. BEST
08 Librarian .... Mrs. MaryJo FAYOYIN
26 Director Marketing/Communications .... Ms. Loretta HEYWARD
27 Chief Information Officer .... Dr. Mable MOORE
18 Director Facilities/Physical Plant .... Mr. Ervin OGDEN
09 Dir Inst Resrch/Planning/Assessment .... Dr. Michael G. CROW
29 Director Alumni Relations .... Ms. Barbara S. MYERS
37 Director Financial Aid .... Mrs. Adrienne BROWN
41 Director Athletics .... Mr. Sterling STEWARD, JR.
19 Chief of Police .... Mr. Creighton ROBERTS
35 Director of Student Development .... Ms. Jacqueline AWE
50 Asst Dean College Business Admin .... Dr. Reginald LESEANE
83 Interim Dean Col Lib Arts/Soc Sci .... Dr. Michael SCHROEDER
72 Int Dean Col Science & Technology .... Dr. Jonathan LAMBRIGHT

† Part of the University System of Georgia.

Savannah Technical College (D)

5717 White Bluff Road, Savannah GA 31405-5521

County: Chatham FICE Identification: 005618
Unit ID: 140942
Telephone: (912) 443-5700 Carnegie Class: Assoc/Pub-R-M
FAX Number: (912) 443-5705 Calendar System: Quarter
URL: www.savannahtech.edu
Established: 1967 Annual Undergrad Tuition & Fees (In-State): $2,922
Enrollment: 4,748 Coed
Affiliation or Control: State IRS Status: 501(c)3
Highest Offering: Associate Degree
Program: Occupational; 2-Year Principally Bachelor's Creditable; Technical Emphasis
Accreditation: SC, ACFEI, DA, DH, ENGT, MAC, PNUR, SURGT

01 President .... Dr. Kathy S. LOVE
05 Vice Pres Academic Affairs .... Dr. Ken BOYD
11 Vice Pres Administrative Services .... Ms. Sue Z. TURNER
32 Vice President Student Affairs .... Mr. Jim NORDONE
45 Vice Pres Economic Development .... Mr. Kevin WERNTZ
84 Exec Director Enroll Mgmt/Marketing .... Ms. Gail EUBANKS
07 Director Admissions .... Ms. Gwendolyn MOORE
37 Director Financial Aid .... Ms. Faith ANDERSON
06 Registrar .... Ms. Regina THOMAS-WILLIAMS
18 Director Facilities/Operations .... Dr. Vic BURKE
37 Exec Dir Student Financial Services .... Ms. Teresa POTTS
38 Director Student Support Services .... Ms. Laurie HERRINGTON
15 Director Human Resources .... Ms. Melissa BANKS
12 Campus Dean Liberty Campus .... Ms. Terrie O. SELLERS
12 Campus Dean Effingham Campus .... Mr. Robert SOLOMON
96 Purchasing Manager .... Mr. Kevin CHIEVES
88 Dean Public Services .... Dr. Gayle TREMBLE
76 Dean Health Science .... Mr. Larry ROBERSON
50 Dean Business and Technology .... Vacant
97 Dean General Studies .... Ms. Christina CAVAGE
88 Dean Industrial Technology .... Vacant
20 Dean Curriculum/Special Projects .... Dr. Kathleen MERRIGAN
88 Dean Aviation .... Mr. Tal LOOS
56 Dean Adult Education .... Mr. Brent STUBBS
88 Director Learning Enrichment Center .... Dr. Ethel BERKSTEINER

Shorter University (E)

315 Shorter Avenue, Rome GA 30165-4298

County: Floyd FICE Identification: 001591
Unit ID: 140988
Telephone: (706) 291-2121 Carnegie Class: Bac/A&S
FAX Number: (706) 236-1515 Calendar System: Semester
URL: www.shorter.edu
Established: 1873 Annual Undergrad Tuition & Fees: $19,670
Enrollment: 2,971 Coed
Affiliation or Control: Baptist IRS Status: 501(c)3
Highest Offering: Master's
Program: Liberal Arts And General; Teacher Preparatory; Professional
Accreditation: SC, MUS, NURSE

01 President .... Dr. Donald V. DOWLESS
05 Executive Vice President & Provost .... Dr. Donald L. MARTIN
11 VP for Administrative Affairs .... Vacant
10 Interim VP for Finance & CFO .... Ms. Susan ZEIRD
84 Vice Pres Enrollment Management .... Ms. Emily MESSER
30 Vice President for Advancement .... Mr. Bert EPTING
32 VP Student Affairs/Dean of Students .... Mr. Corey HUMPHRIES
26 Assoc VP University Communications .... Dr. Dawn C. TOLBERT
104 Asst Vice Pres International Pgms .... Mrs. Linda PALUMBO-OLSZANSKI
06 Registrar .... Mrs. Brandi BERGER
29 Director of Alumni Relations .... Mrs. Sheri RANSOME
35 Director of Student Activities .... Vacant
08 Director of Libraries .... Mr. DeWayne WILLIAMS
09 Director of Inst Planning/Research .... Ms. Julie HENSEL
37 Director of Financial Aid .... Ms. Colleen LASSITER
15 Director Human Resources .... Mr. Tommy CURTIS
90 Director of Academic Computing .... Mr. Anthony J. NICHOLS
56 Director Special Programs .... Vacant
13 Director of Information Technology .... Mr. Torey BRADLEY
18 Director of Facilities Management .... Mr. Dickerson E. TAYLOR
38 Director of Student Support Svcs .... Ms. Sara BAKER
23 Director of Health Services .... Mrs. Mary SHOTWELL SMITH
41 Athletic Director .... Mr. Bill PETERSON
44 Director of Annual Giving .... Mr. Neely RAPER
07 Director of Admissions .... Mr. Patrick MCELHANEY
39 Dir Residence Life/Student Conduct .... Mr. Joshua ARNOLD
40 Bookstore Manager .... Ms. Dre FILLMORE
57 Dean School of the Arts .... Dr. Alan B. WINGARD
50 Dean College of Business .... Dr. Robert H. DARVILLE
49 Dean School of Liberal Arts .... Dr. Sabrena PARTON
53 Dean School of Education .... Dr. Norma HARPER
56 Dean Coll Adult/Professional Pgms .... Dr. Jacqueline AVANT
66 Dean School of Nursing .... Dr. Angela HAYNES
106 Dean of Online Programs .... Mr. Sean BUTCHER
81 Assoc Dean Sciences & Mathematics .... Ms. Lisa M. KEITH
79 Assoc Dean Humanities/Social Sci .... Dr. Benjamin MCFRY
73 Chair Dept of Christian Studies .... Dr. Earle KELLETT
53 Chair Department of Education .... Dr. Gary ROSS
77 Chair Dept of Math/Computer Science .... Dr. Diana SWANAGAN
60 Chair Dept of Communication Arts .... Dr. Cassandra JOHNSON
83 Chr Dpt Hist/Poli Sci/Psych/Soclgy .... Dr. Barsha PICKELL
42 Campus Minister .... Rev. David E. ROLAND

South Georgia State College (F)

100 W College Park Drive, Douglas GA 31533-5098

County: Coffee FICE Identification: 001592
Unit ID: 140997
Telephone: (912) 260-4394 Carnegie Class: Assoc/Pub-R-S
FAX Number: (912) 260-4454 Calendar System: Semester
URL: www.sgsc.edu
Established: 1906 Annual Undergrad Tuition & Fees (In-State): $3,626
Enrollment: 2,226 Coed
Affiliation or Control: State IRS Status: 501(c)3
Highest Offering: Baccalaureate
Program: 2-Year Principally Bachelor's Creditable; Liberal Arts And General
Accreditation: SC, ADNUR

01 President .... Dr. Virginia M. CARSON
05 Vice Pres Academic Affairs .... Vacant
32 Vice President for Student Success .... Mr. Wes S. BROWN
10 Vice President for Fiscal Affairs .... Mr. Mark LATHAM
30 Vice President for External Affairs .... Ms. Walda KIGHT
18 Vice President for Operations .... Mr. Keith NEWELL
20 Asst Vice Pres for Academic Affairs .... Dr. Rick REIMAN
08 Director of Libraries .... Ms. Jacqueline VICKERS
06 Registrar .... Ms. Ame WILKERSON
37 Director Financial Aid .... Ms. Becky RUMKER
15 Director Human Resources .... Mr. Jamie TANNER
07 Director of Admissions .... Ms. Angie EVANS
12 Dir of Entry Programs and Planning .... Ms. Valerie WEBSTER
72 Director of Technology .... Vacant
40 Director of Bookstore .... Ms. Daphne FRENCH
21 Director of Business Services .... Vacant
41 Athletic Director .... Dr. Greg TANNER
09 Dir of Institutional Effectiveness .... Ms. Danielle BUEHRER
39 Director of Residence Life .... Mr. Andy JOHNSON
35 Director of Student Life .... Ms. Sharon KOMANECKY
19 Director of Security .... Ms. Sonja MCCULLOCH

† Part of the University System of Georgia.

South Georgia Technical College (G)

900 South Georgia Tech Parkway,
Americus GA 31709-8167

County: Sumter FICE Identification: 005617
Unit ID: 141006
Telephone: (229) 931-2394 Carnegie Class: Assoc/Pub-R-M
FAX Number: (229) 931-2924 Calendar System: Semester
URL: www.southgatech.edu
Established: 1948 Annual Undergrad Tuition & Fees (In-State): $4,707
Enrollment: 1,901 Coed
Affiliation or Control: State IRS Status: 501(c)3
Highest Offering: Associate Degree
Program: Occupational; Technical Emphasis
Accreditation: SC, COE

01 President .... Sparky REEVES
11 Vice Pres Administrative Services .... Janice DAVIS
10 Vice Pres Business & Industry Svcs .... Wally SUMMERS
05 Vice President for Academic Affairs .... John WATFORD
09 Vice Pres of Institutional Support .... Karen J. WERLING
04 Special Assistant to the President .... Don SMITH
20 Assistant Vice Pres Academic Affair .... David KUIPERS
20 Dean of Academic Affairs .... Raymond HOLT
26 Vice Pres Resource Dev & Marketing .... Su Ann BIRD
13 Technology Director .... Wray SKIPPER
37 Director of Financial Aid .... Michael WRIGHT
15 Director Personnel Services .... Sandy LARSON
36 Director of Career Services .... Cynthia CARTER
32 Director of Campus Life .... Cynthia CARTER
21 Director of Accounting .... Lea COE
88 Director of Administrative Services .... Mark BROOKS
55 Evening Coordinator .... John WILDER
06 Registrar .... Julie PARTAIN
08 Librarian .... Jerry STOVALL
07 Director of Admissions .... Whitney CRISP
29 Director Alumni Relations .... SuAnn BIRD
38 Director Student Counseling .... LaKenya JOHNSON
84 Director Enrollment Management .... Whitney CRISP
18 Chief Facilities/Physical Plant .... Don SMITH
96 Purchasing Agent .... Gail CLARY

South University (H)

709 Mall Boulevard, Savannah GA 31406-4881

County: Chatham FICE Identification: 013039
Unit ID: 139579
Telephone: (912) 201-8000 Carnegie Class: Master's L
FAX Number: (912) 201-8070 Calendar System: Quarter
URL: www.southuniversity.edu
Established: 1899 Annual Undergrad Tuition & Fees: $21,580

Enrollment: 21,932 Coed
Affiliation or Control: Proprietary IRS Status: Proprietary
Highest Offering: Doctorate
Program: 2-Year Principally Bachelor's Creditable; Liberal Arts And General; Professional; Business Emphasis
Accreditation: SC, AA, ARCPA, MAC, NURSE, PHAR, PTAA

01 Chancellor .... Mr. John T. SOUTH, III
88 Vice Chanc Art Institute Campuses .... Dr. Thomas NEWSOM
12 President Ai Charlotte Campus .... Mr. Maurice LEE
12 President Ai Raleigh-Durham Campus .... Mr. Christopher MESECAR
12 President Ai Dallas Campus .... Dr. Thomas NEWSOM
12 President Ai Fort Worth Campus .... Ms. Lourdes GIPSON
11 Interim Vice Chanc South Campuses .... Mr. Chad THOMPSON
12 President Montgomery Campus ...... Mr. Victor K. BIEBIGHAUSER
12 President West Palm Beach Campus .... Mr. David MCGUIRE
12 President Columbia Campus .... Mr. Greg SHIELDS
12 President Novi Campus .... Dr. Theodore BLASHAK
12 President Richmond Campus .... Mr. Troy RALSTON
12 President Tampa Campus .... Dr. Dan COBLE
12 President Virginia Beach Campus .... Mr. Richard KRIOFSKY
12 President Austin Campus .... Ms. Shelby FRUTCHEY
12 President Cleveland Campus .... Mr. Scott BEHMER
12 President High Point Campus .... Mr. Michael TREMBLEY
12 President Savannah Campus .... Mr. Todd CELLINI
12 Director Accelerated Grad Programs .... Mr. Edward HOOD, IV
13 Assoc Chanc Information Technology ... Mr. James FREYBURGER
13 Regional Campus Technology Manager .... Mr. Dustin BARRETT
106 Vice Chanc Online & Strat Operation .... Mr. Andrew HURST
05 Vice Chancellor Academic Affairs .... Dr. Steven K. YOHO
20 Assoc Vice Chanc Academic Operation .... Dr. Joseph HARM
20 Assoc Vice Chan Academic Affairs .... Dr. Jay STUBBLEFIELD
08 Asst Vice Chanc University Librarie .... Ms. Kate SAWYER
06 University Registrar .... Ms. Anita MACIAS
20 Asst Vice Chanc Academic Services .... Dr. Lucas B. KAVLIE
09 Sr Dir Inst Research & Effectivenes .... Dr. Fran OB
20 Dir QEP & Academic Project Manager ..... Dr. Reinhold GERBSCH
20 Asst Vice Chanc Online Acad Ops .... Dr. Destini COPP
20 Asst Vice Chanc Campus Acad Ops .... Vacant
49 Dean College of Arts and Sciences .... Dr. Michael BROOKS
50 Acting Dean College of Business .... Dr. Susan DAVIS
107 Dean College of Health Professions .... Dr. Devin BYRD
66 Acting Dean College of Nursing & P .... Dr. Charles HOSSLER
67 Dean School of Pharmacy .... Dr. Curtis JONES
57 Dean College Creative Art & Design .... Dr. Leslie BAUGHMAN
73 Dean College of Theology .... Vacant
07 Vice Chancellor for Admissions .... Mr. Matthew MILLS
84 Regional Director of Admissions .... Ms. Kathy DEVINE
84 Regional Director of Admissions .... Mr. Charlie PARKER
26 Asst Chancellor for Communications .... Vacant
26 Director of Communications .... Ms. Ally HUGHES
16 Assoc Chancellor of Human Resources .... Ms. Lynne HAINES
88 Senior Human Resources Generalist .... Ms. Christy SHAPARD
88 Human Resources Generalist .... Ms. Jamie FRAZIER-HELD
88 Senior Human Resources Coordinator .... Ms. Allison MCCRAY
37 Asst Chancellor for Student Service .... Ms. Alisa KROUSE
29 University Director Career Services .... Ms. Paula ABSHIRE
10 Vice Chancellor for Finance .... Mr. Chad THOMPSON
21 Associate Chancellor for Finance .... Ms. Katrina WIGREN
37 Director of Student Financial Aid .... Ms. Tressa BRUSH
27 Associate Chancellor for Marketing .... Mr. Bruce CHONG
88 Senior Marketing Manager .... Ms. Kalani ROBINSON
88 Senior Marketing Manager .... Ms. Hope DAVID
88 Senior Marketing Manager .... Ms. Teresa FOOTE

Southeastern Technical College (A)

3001 E First Street, Vidalia GA 30474-8817
County: Toombs FICE Identification: 030665
Unit ID: 368911
Telephone: (912) 538-3100 Carnegie Class: Assoc/Pub-R-S
FAX Number: (912) 538-3156 Calendar System: Semester
URL: www.southeasterntech.edu
Established: 1989 Annual Undergrad Tuition & Fees (In-State): $3,648
Enrollment: 1,747 Coed
Affiliation or Control: State IRS Status: 501(c)3
Highest Offering: Associate Degree
Program: Occupational; Technical Emphasis
Accreditation: SC, DH, EMT, MAC, MLTAD, RAD, SURGT

01 President .... Dr. Cathryn MITCHELL
03 Provost .... Mr. Larry CALHOUN
05 Vice Pres Academic Affairs .... Ms. Teresa COLEMAN
11 Vice Pres Administrative Services .... Ms. Denise POWELL
10 Vice President Fiscal Affairs .... Vacant
32 Vice President Student Affairs .... Dr. Barry DOTSON
84 Director Enrollment Services .... Mr. Brad HART
06 Registrar .... Ms. Karen VEREEN
37 Director Financial Aid .... Mr. Mitchell FAGLER
36 Director Job Placement .... Mr. Lance HELMS
103 Special Populations Coordinator .... Ms. Helen THOMAS
88 Fatherhood Initiative Coordinator .... Vacant
40 Bookstore Manager .... Ms. Ashley MCINTYRE

Southern Crescent Technical College (B)

501 Varsity Road, Griffin GA 30223-2042
County: Spalding FICE Identification: 005621
Unit ID: 139986
Telephone: (770) 228-7348 Carnegie Class: Assoc/Pub-S-MC
FAX Number: (770) 229-3227 Calendar System: Semester
URL: www.sctech.edu
Established: 1963 Annual Undergrad Tuition & Fees (In-State): $3,213
Enrollment: 5,543 Coed
Affiliation or Control: State IRS Status: 501(c)3
Highest Offering: Associate Degree
Program: Occupational; 2-Year Principally Bachelor's Creditable; Technical Emphasis
Accreditation: SC, CAHIIM, COARC, COARCP, DA, MAC, SURGT

01 President .... Dr. Randall PETERS
03 Provost .... Mr. Steve DANIEL
05 Vice Pres for Academic Affairs .... Dr. Dawn HODGES
32 Vice Pres for Student Affairs .... Ms. Xenia JOHNS
103 Vice Pres for Economic Development .... Mr. Mark ANDREWS
10 Vice Pres Administrative Services .... Ms. Miriam CASLIN
18 Vice Pres Facilities/Operations .... Mr. Jim BROWN
30 Vice President Advancement .... Ms. Barbara Jo COOK
46 Vice Pres for Tech/Inst Research .... Mr. Brent MAYES
88 Int Vice Pres for Adult Education .... Ms. Melissa GORDON
08 Director of Library Services .... Ms. Kate WILLIAMS
06 Registrar .... Ms. Kathlyn BURDEN
26 Dir Marketing & Public Relations .... Ms. Anna TAYLOR
37 Director of Financial Aid .... Ms. Kimberly MORRIS
49 Dean Business Tech Arts & Sciences/ ..... Ms. Rebecca JOHNSON
76 Dean Allied Health .... Dr. John POPE
75 Dean Personal Svcs/Public Safety .... Mr. Lemuel MERCADO
75 Dean Industrial Technical Studies .... Mr. Steve CROMER
106 Dean Computer Info Services .... Ms. Tempie KITCHENS
07 Director of Admissions .... Dr. Jasper FOUST
15 Director of Human Resources .... Ms. Sharon IRBY
35 Director of Student Affairs .... Ms. Cherryl GILBERT
21 Director of Administrative Services .... Ms. Gina BYRD
36 Director of Career Services .... Ms. Susan MURRAY
88 Director of Satellite Operations .... Mr. Scott ROSS
19 Campus Police Chief .... Mr. Kenneth TROISI
27 Chief Information Officer .... Mr. Michael SHIVER

Southern Polytechnic State University (C)

1100 South Marietta Parkway, Marietta GA 30060-2896
County: Cobb FICE Identification: 001570
Unit ID: 141097
Telephone: (678) 915-7778 Carnegie Class: Master's M
FAX Number: (678) 915-7483 Calendar System: Semester
URL: www.spsu.edu/
Established: 1948 Annual Undergrad Tuition & Fees (In-State): $6,810
Enrollment: 6,202 Coed
Affiliation or Control: State IRS Status: 501(c)3
Highest Offering: Master's
Program: 2-Year Principally Bachelor's Creditable; Liberal Arts And General; Teacher Preparatory; Professional; Technical Emphasis
Accreditation: SC, ACBSP, CONST, CS, ENG, ENGR, ENGT

01 President .... Dr. Lisa A. ROSSBACHER
05 Vice President for Academic Affairs .... Dr. Zvi SZAFRAN
32 Vice Pres Student/Enrollment Svcs .... Dr. Ron R. KOGER
30 VP for University Advancement .... Dr. Ron D. DEMPSEY
10 Vice President for Business/Finance .... Dr. Bill PRIGGE
13 Vice President for UITS/CIO .... Dr. Sam CONN
88 Exec Dir Strategic Mktg/Sustainblty .... Mr. James W. COOPER
22 Affirmative Action Officer .... Ms. Mary E. MCGEE
20 Assoc VP for Academic Affairs .... Mr. Dave CAUDILL
54 Dean of Engineering .... Dr. Thomas CURRIN
48 Dean of Architecture & Const Mgmt .... Dr. Wilson C. BARNES
49 Dean of Arts & Sciences .... Dr. Thomas NELSON
77 Dean of Computing/Software Eng .... Dr. Han REICHGELT
72 Dean of Engr Technology/Mgmt .... Dr. Jeffrey RAY
56 Dean of Extended University .... Dr. Ruston HUNT
93 Dir of Adv/Tutoring/Tst/Intl Center .... Dr. Jeff ORR
58 Director of Graduate Studies .... Ms. Nikki PALAMIOTIS
104 Director of International Programs .... Dr. Richard BENNETT
08 Interim Director of Library .... Yongli C. MA
78 Dir Center for Teaching Excellence .... Ms. Dawn RAMSEY
92 Director of Honors Program/Admin .... Ms. Alda WOOD
36 Director of Career/Counseling Svcs ... Ms. Phyllis N. WEATHERLY
88 Director of Recreational Sports .... Mr. Karl D. STABER
07 Dir Admissions/Student Recruitment .... Mr. Gary W. BUSH
37 Dir of Scholarships/Financial Aid .... Mr. Gary MANN
06 Registrar .... Mr. Stephen A. HAMRICK
44 Director of Development .... Ms. Kit TRENSCH
26 Director of Public Relations .... Ms. Sylvia CARSON
21 Controller .... Mr. Arthur VAUGHN
21 Director of Budget and Grants .... Ms. Robin WADE
15 Director of Human Resources .... Dr. I. Charles AZEBEOKHAI
19 Chief of University Police .... Chief John BAUER
18 Dir of Facilities Management .... Mr. Steve KITCHEN
96 Director Material Management .... Mr. Robert P. FORBES
31 Director of Campus Services .... Ms. Kasey HELTON
90 Director of Technical Support .... Mr. Dave PARHAM
13 Dir of IT Enterprise Applications .... Mr. Ken HILL
91 Director of Information Systems .... Mr. Ronald J. SKOPITZ
14 Director of Information Technology .... Mr. Jim HERBERT
41 Director of Athletics .... Mr. Matthew GRIFFIN
88 Internal Auditor .... Mr. William KETCHUM
43 University Counsel .... Ms. Alana KYRIAKAKIS
09 Assoc VP for Inst Effectiveness .... Ms. Becky RUTHERFOORD
35 Associate Director of Student Life .... Mr. Ron LUNK
88 Financial Operations Manager .... Ms. Lawanda COLEMAN-WHITE
29 Assoc Director of Alumni Relations .... Ms. Pierrette MAILLET

† Part of the University System of Georgia. Most of the tutition increase is due to a change in the definition of "full-time student" from 24 credit hour annually to 30.

Southwest Georgia Technical College (D)

15689 US Highway 19 N, Thomasville GA 31792-2622
County: Thomas FICE Identification: 005615
Unit ID: 141158
Telephone: (229) 225-4096 Carnegie Class: Assoc/Pub-R-S
FAX Number: (229) 225-4330 Calendar System: Semester
URL: www.southwestgatech.edu
Established: 1947 Annual Undergrad Tuition & Fees (In-State): $4,497
Enrollment: 1,649 Coed
Affiliation or Control: State IRS Status: 501(c)3
Highest Offering: Associate Degree
Program: Occupational
Accreditation: SC, ADNUR, COARC, MAC, MLTAD, SURGT

01 President .... Dr. Craig R. WENTWORTH
11 Vice Pres Administrative Services .... Mr. Paul ROBERTS
05 Vice Pres Academic Affairs .... Dr. Annie MCELROY
32 Vice President Student Affairs .... Ms. Joyce HALSTEAD
30 Vice President Economic Development .... Mr. Gary PITTS
09 VP Institutional Effectiveness .... Dr. Debbie GOODMAN
76 Dean Allied Health/Gen Education .... Ms. Carla BARROW
50 Dean Bus/Computer/Prof Svcs/T&I .... Mr. Dennis LEE
37 Director Financial Aid .... Ms. Amy SCOGGINS
26 Dir Marketing/Inst Devel/Pub Rels .... Ms. Amy MAISON
88 Executive Director Adult Education .... Mr. Dale ALDRIDGE
07 Director Admissions .... Ms. Wanda HANCOCK
06 Registrar .... Ms. Deborah GRAY
08 Director Library & Media Services .... Ms. Gail ROBERTS
36 Dir Career Placement & Development .... Dr. Jeanine LONG
15 Director Personnel Services .... Ms. Jennifer SIMPSON
18 Chief Facilities/Physical Plant .... Mr. Gary ALDRIDGE

Spelman College (E)

350 Spelman Lane, SW, Atlanta GA 30314-4399
County: Fulton FICE Identification: 001594
Unit ID: 141060
Telephone: (404) 681-3643 Carnegie Class: Bac/A&S
FAX Number: N/A Calendar System: Semester
URL: www.spelman.edu
Established: 1881 Annual Undergrad Tuition & Fees: $24,634
Enrollment: 2,145 Female
Affiliation or Control: Independent Non-Profit IRS Status: 501(c)3
Highest Offering: Baccalaureate
Program: Liberal Arts And General; Teacher Preparatory
Accreditation: SC, MUS

01 President .... Dr. Beverly Daniel TATUM
05 Provost & VP of Academic Affairs .... Dr. Johnnella E. BUTLER
20 Vice Provost .... Dr. Myra BURNETT
10 VP Business/Financial Affairs/ Treas .... Mr. Robert D. FLANIGAN, JR.
32 Vice President for Student Affairs .... Dr. Darnita KILLIAN
30 Vice Pres for College Relations .... Ms. Eloise ALEXIS
84 Vice Pres Enrollment Management .... Ms. Lenora JACKSON
30 Vice President for Development .... Ms. Kassandra JOLLEY
21 Assoc VP Business/Financial Affairs ...... Mr. John CUNNINGHAM
88 Dir Investments & Financial Plng .... Ms. Rhonda HONEGAN
21 Controller .... Ms. April AUSTIN
100 Secretary of College .... Ms. Tamaria DAVIS
26 Exec Dir of Communications .... Ms. Tomika DEPRIEST
04 Assistant to President .... Ms. Yvonne SKILLINGS
13 VP & CIO Media & Information Tech .... Ms. Delores BARTON
105 Dir Bonner Comm Svcs/Student Dev .... Vacant
20 Dean of Undergraduate Studies .... Dr. Desiree PEDESCLEAUX
42 Director Sisters Center for WISDOM .... Rev. Lisa D. RHODES
06 Registrar .... Dr. Frederick FRESH
07 Director of Admissions .... Ms. Erica JOHNSON
27 Director Publications .... Ms. Jo Moore STEWART
29 Director of Alumnae Affairs .... Ms. Sharon OWENS
37 Director of Student Financial Svcs .... Ms. Thresa GAY
36 Director Career Planning/Devel .... Mr. Harold BELL
78 Director of Cooperative Education .... Mr. Keith WEBB
15 Director Human Resources .... Ms. Bernadette COHEN
38 Director Counseling Services .... Dr. Ave MARSHALL
09 Dir Inst Rsrch/Assessment/Planning .... Ms. Jill TRIPLETT
88 Director Women's Resource Center ... Dr. Beverly GUY-SHEFTALL
18 Director Facilities/Mgmt & Svcs .... Mr. Arthur E. FRAZIER, III
19 Director of Public Safety .... Mr. Steve BOWSER
24 Dir Educational Technology Svcs .... Vacant
46 Associate Provost of Research .... Dr. Carmen SIDBURY
44 Director of Annual Giving .... Ms. DeShanna BROWN
102 Dir of Corp & Foundation Relations .... Ms. Shelese LANE
88 Director of Special Events .... Ms. Heather HAWES
39 Director Housing & Residential Life .... Ms. Alison CUMMINGS
86 Director Title III/Government Rels .... Ms. Helga GREENFIELD
88 Coordinator Commuter Students .... Ms. Letitia DENARD
85 Coordinator International Students .... Ms. Asha ROBINSON
08 Library Director/CEO .... Ms. Loretta PARHAM
23 Director Health Services .... Ms. Brenda DALTON
25 Director Sponsored Programs .... Dr. Carmen SIDBURY
102 Assoc VP for College Relations .... Ms. Helga GREENFIELD
35 Dean Students .... Ms. Kimberly FERGUSON
40 Director Bookstore .... Ms. Tiffani HODGE
41 Dir Phys Ed & Athletics/Sr Instr .... Ms. Germaine MCAULEY
96 Dir Adminstrative Support Svcs .... Ms. Jacqueline JAMES

Thomas University (F)

1501 Millpond Road, Thomasville GA 31792-7499
County: Thomas FICE Identification: 001555
Unit ID: 141167

Telephone: (229) 226-1621 Carnegie Class: Bac/Diverse
FAX Number: (229) 226-1653 Calendar System: Semester
URL: www.thomasu.edu
Established: 1950 Annual Undergrad Tuition & Fees: $14,890
Enrollment: 1,124 Coed
Affiliation or Control: Independent Non-Profit IRS Status: 501(c)3
Highest Offering: Master's
Program: Liberal Arts And General; Professional
Accreditation: SC, CORE, IACBE, MT, NUR, SW

01 President .... Dr. Gary BONVILLIAN
05 Provost & Exec Vice President .... Dr. Ann LANDIS
30 Vice Pres for Instnl Advancement .... Mr. Richard MUNROE
08 Univ Librarian/Dir Info Services .... Ms. Amber BROCK
06 Registrar .... Mrs. Lacey HARRISON
09 Director of Institutional Research .... Ms. Danae JOHNSON
07 Director of Admissions .... Ms. Kerri KNIGHT
38 Director of Student Support Svcs .... Ms. Faye R. JOHNSON
37 Director of Financial Aid .... Mr. Michael RAYBURN
41 Director of Athletics .... Mr. Michael D. LEE
10 Controller .... Ms. Sue STONE
18 Director of Physical Plant .... Mr. Randy WILCOX
32 Director of Student Life .... Mr. Deryl OUZTS
44 Director of Annual Fund .... Ms. Melinda FRIDDELL
26 Director of Communications .... Mrs. Cindy MONTGOMERY
04 Assistant to the President .... Ms. Linda M. HERNDON

Toccoa Falls College (A)

107 Kincaid Drive, Toccoa Falls GA 30598-0068
County: Stephens FICE Identification: 001596
Unit ID: 141185
Telephone: (706) 886-6831 Carnegie Class: Bac/Diverse
FAX Number: (706) 282-6005 Calendar System: Semester
URL: www.tfc.edu
Established: 1907 Annual Undergrad Tuition & Fees: $18,900
Enrollment: 723 Coed
Affiliation or Control: Independent Non-Profit IRS Status: 501(c)3
Highest Offering: Baccalaureate
Program: Liberal Arts And General; Teacher Preparatory
Accreditation: SC, BI, MUS

01 President .... Dr. Robert M. MYERS
04 Sr Exec Administrative Assistant .... Mrs. Paula S. ELKINS
32 VP Student Development .... Mr. Lee P. YOWELL
30 VP for Advancement .... Mr. James HANSEN
10 Vice President for Finance .... Mr. R. Gregg SCHULTE
05 VP for Academic Affairs .... Dr. W. Brian SHELTON
84 Dean of Enrollment & Marketing .... Mr. Daniel GRIFFIN
42 Director Spiritual Formation .... Dr. Stephen WOODWORTH
09 Director Institutional Research .... Vacant
08 Director Info Svcs/IT Dept/Library .... Miss Heather SAMSA
39 Director Residence/Community Life .... Dr. Debbie MOORE
29 Director Alumni Assoc/Col Relations .... Vacant
38 Dir Stdnt Health/Career Servs .... Mr. Johnathan C. KERR
37 Director Student Financial Aid .... Mr. Truitt FRANKLIN
07 Director of Admissions .... Mrs. Cathy DOAN
06 Registrar .... Mr. Kelly G. VICKERS
41 Athletic Director .... Mr. Jason MEHL
18 Chief Facilities/Physical Plant .... Mr. Gerald WILLIAMSON
26 Chief Public Relations Officer .... Vacant
15 Director Human Resources .... Ms. Mary K. RITCHEY

Truett McConnell College (B)

100 Alumni Drive, Cleveland GA 30528-1264
County: White FICE Identification: 001597
Unit ID: 141237
Telephone: (706) 865-2134 Carnegie Class: Bac/Assoc
FAX Number: (706) 243-4968 Calendar System: Semester
URL: www.truett.edu
Established: 1946 Annual Undergrad Tuition & Fees: $16,410
Enrollment: 1,339 Coed
Affiliation or Control: Baptist IRS Status: 501(c)3
Highest Offering: Baccalaureate
Program: Liberal Arts And General; Religious Emphasis
Accreditation: SC, MUS

01 President .... Dr. Emir CANER
05 Vice Pres Academic Services .... Dr. Brad REYNOLDS
11 Vice Pres Administrative Svcs .... Mr. David ARMSTRONG
32 Vice President of Student Services .... Mr. Chris EPPLING
04 Executive Assistant to President .... Mrs. Jeanavon BURROW
41 Athletic Director .... Dr. Stacy HALL
06 Registrar/Dir Inst Research .... Mrs. Melissa FORTNER
37 Director of Financial Aid .... Mrs. Becky MOORE
08 Librarian .... Mrs. Teresa HAYMORE
29 Director of Alumni Relations .... Dr. John YARBROUGH
07 Director of Admissions .... Mr. Scott SMITH
42 Director of Collegiate Ministries .... Mr. Keith WADE
40 Bookstore Manager .... Mr. Eddie O'BRIEN

University of Georgia (C)

Athens GA 30602-0001
County: Clarke FICE Identification: 001598
Unit ID: 139959
Telephone: (706) 542-3000 Carnegie Class: RU/VH
FAX Number: N/A Calendar System: Semester
URL: www.uga.edu
Established: 1785 Annual Undergrad Tuition & Fees (In-State): $10,262
Enrollment: 34,519 Coed
Affiliation or Control: State IRS Status: 501(c)3
Highest Offering: Doctorate
Program: Liberal Arts And General; Teacher Preparatory; Professional
Accreditation: SC, AAFCS, ART, BUS, BUSA, CACREP, CIDA, CLPSY, COPSY, DANCE, DIETD, DIETI, ENG, FOR, JOUR, LAW, LSAR, MFCD, MUS, NRPA, PH, PHAR, SCPSY, SP, SPAA, SW, TED, THEA, VET

01 President .... Dr. Jere W. MOREHEAD
100 Chief of Staff .... Dr. Kathy R. PHARR
04 Assistant to the President .... Mr. Charles G. TONEY
04 Assistant to the President .... Mr. Matthew M. WINSTON, JR.
05 Interim Sr VP Acad Affs/Provost .... Dr. Libby V. MORRIS
20 Vice Provost Academic Affairs .... Dr. Hugh RUPPERSBURG
10 Int Vice Pres for Finance & Admin .... Mr. Ryan A. NESBIT
26 Vice Pres for Dev & Alumni Relation ... Mr. Thomas S. LANDRUM
20 Vice President for Instruction .... Dr. Laura D. JOLLY
46 Vice President for Research .... Dr. David C. LEE
88 Vice Pres Public Svc/Outreach .... Dr. Jennifer L. FRUM
32 Vice President Student Affairs .... Dr. Victor K. WILSON
86 Vice President for Govt Relations .... Mr. J. Griffin DOYLE
26 Vice President Public Affairs .... Dr. Thomas H. JACKSON, JR.
92 Assoc Prov/Dir of Honors Program .... Dr. David S. WILLIAMS
104 Assoc Prov for International Educ .... Dr. Kavita K. PANDIT
28 Assoc Prov/Chief Diversity Officer .... Dr. Michelle G. COOK
45 Assoc Provost Academic Planning .... Dr. Jerome S. LEGGE
20 Assoc Provost Academic Programs .... Dr. Margaret AMSTUTZ
88 Assoc VP Economic Development .... Dr. Margaret W. DAHL
13 Associate Provost & CIO .... Dr. Timothy M. CHESTER
08 Assoc Provost/University Librarian .... Dr. William G. POTTER
07 Assoc VP Admissions/Enroll Mgmt .... Ms. Nancy G. MCDUFF
21 Interim Sr Assoc VP Finance/Admin . Ms. Holley W. SCHRAMSKI
18 Assoc VP Facilities Management .... Mr. Ralph F. JOHNSON
15 Int Associate VP Human Resources .... Mr. Duane J. RITTER
43 Int Executive Director Legal Aff .... Ms. S. Elizabeth BAILEY
49 Dean of Arts & Sciences .... Dr. Alan T. DORSEY
47 Dean of Agricultural & Environ Sci .... Dr. J. Scott ANGLE
61 Dean of Law .... Ms. Rebecca H. WHITE
67 Dean of Pharmacy .... Dr. Svein OIE
65 Dean Forestry & Natural Resources .... Dr. Michael L. CLUTTER
53 Dean of Education .... Dr. Craig H. KENNEDY
58 Dean of the Graduate School .... Dr. Maureen GRASSO
50 Interim Dean of Business .... Dr. Charles B. KNAPP
60 Dean Journalism & Mass Comm .... Dr. Charles N. DAVIS
59 Dean of Family & Consumer Sci .... Dr. Linda K. FOX
74 Dean of Veterinary Medicine .... Dr. Sheila W. ALLEN
70 Dean of Social Work .... Dr. Maurice C. DANIELS
48 Dean of Environment & Design .... Mr. Daniel J. NADENICEK
80 Dean of Public/International Affs .... Dr. Stefanie A. LINDQUIST
69 Dean of Public Health .... Dr. Phillip L. WILLIAMS
88 Dean School of Ecology .... Dr. John L. GITTLEMAN
88 Dean GHSU/UGA Medical .... Dr. Barbara L. SCHUSTER
41 Athletic Director .... Mr. William G. MCGARITY
22 Director of Equal Opportunity .... Ms. E. Janyce DAWKINS
06 Registrar .... Dr. Jan M. HATHCOTE
19 Chief of Police .... Chief James E. WILLIAMSON
37 Director of Student Financial Aid .... Ms. Bonnie C. JOERSCHKE
36 Director of Career Services Center .... Mr. Scott T. WILLIAMS
39 Executive Director of Housing .... Dr. Gerard J. KOWALSKI
23 Exec Director of Health Services .... Dr. Jean E. CHIN
35 Dean of Students .... Dr. William M. MCDONALD
38 Dir Counseling/Psychological Svcs .... Dr. Gayle M. ROBBINS
51 Dir of Georgia Ctr Continuing Educ .... Dr. William R. CROWE
29 Exec Director of Alumni Relations .... Ms. Deborah H. DIETZLER
30 Assoc Vice Pres Development .... Mr. Mac CORRY
09 Director of Institutional Research .... Dr. Meihua ZHAI
88 Director of Academic Enhancement .... Dr. Earl GINTER
94 Director Inst of Women's Studies . Dr. Juanita JOHNSON-BAILEY
96 Director of Purchasing .... Ms. Annette EVANS

† Part of the University System of Georgia.

University of North Georgia (D)

82 College Circle, Dahlonega GA 30597-1001
County: Lumpkin FICE Identification: 001585
Unit ID: 140669
Telephone: (706) 864-1400 Carnegie Class: Master's L
FAX Number: (706) 864-1478 Calendar System: Semester
URL: www.ung.edu
Established: 1873 Annual Undergrad Tuition & Fees (In-State): $6,692
Enrollment: 15,072 Coed
Affiliation or Control: State IRS Status: 501(c)3
Highest Offering: Doctorate
Program: 2-Year Principally Bachelor's Creditable; Liberal Arts And General; Teacher Preparatory; Professional
Accreditation: SC, ACBSP, ADNUR, BUS, CACREP, NUR, PTA, TED

01 President .... Dr. Bonita JACOBS
11 Vice Pres of Exec Affairs .... Mr. Billy WELLS
05 Sr Vice President & Provost .... Dr. Patricia DONAT
10 Sr VP Business & Finance .... Mr. Frank J. MCCONNELL
03 Sr VP University Affairs .... Dr. Al PANU
30 Vice Pres of University Advancement .... Dr. Andrew LEAVITT
32 Vice Pres Student Affairs .... Dr. Tom WALTER
20 Assoc Provost Acad Administration .... Dr. Richard OATES
20 Assoc Provost for Acad Affairs .... Dr. Maryellen COSGROVE
84 Assoc VP Enrollment Management .... Ms. Jennifer CHADWICK
88 Assoc VP & Dean Univ College .... Dr. Kristen RONEY
29 Assoc VP Alumni Relations & Annual .... Mr. Phil COLLINS
21 Associate VP for Financial Services .... Dr. Brenda FINDLEY
18 Assoc VP Facilities & Auxiliary Ent .... Vacant
88 Assoc VP Univ Affairs & Academic .... Dr. Chaudron GILLE
88 Assoc VP for Executive Affairs .... Ms. Mary TRANSUE
44 Asst VP Development .... Mr. Perry ROBERTS
20 Asst VP for Budgets & Personnel .... Dr. Kathy SISK
88 Asst VP Advancement Svcs .... Ms. Amanda BRIDGES
35 Asst VP Stdnt Affs & Dean of Stdnts .... Dr. Michelle BROWN
35 Asst VP Stdnt Affs & Dean of Stdnts .... Ms. Alyson PAUL
88 Asst VP Institutional Effectiveness .... Dr. Denise YOUNG
106 Dir Distance Ed & Tech Integration .... Dr. Irene KOKKALA
07 Exec Director Undergrad Admissions .... Mr. Keith ANTONIA
07 Director of Cadet Admissions .... Vacant
92 Director Honors Pgm/Grad Studies .... Dr. Eric SKIPPER
41 Director of Athletics .... Ms. Lindsay REEVES
27 Chief Information Officer .... Mr. Brandon HAAG
06 University Registrar .... Ms. Janice HARTSOE
25 Director of Grants & Contracts .... Dr. Kelley ROBERTS
37 Director of Financial Aid .... Ms. Jill RAYNER
58 Exec Director Regional Engagement .... Dr. Donna GESSELL
09 Director Institutional Research .... Ms. Linda ROWLAND
88 Assoc Dean Academic Administration .... Dr. Kelly MANLEY
35 Assoc Dean Student Life .... Dr. Cara RAY
08 Dean of Libraries .... Dr. Deborah PROSSER
88 Dir of Public Services .... Ms. Jane O'GORMAN
49 Dean College of Arts & Letters .... Dr. Christopher JESPERSEN
50 Dean M C College of Business .... Dr. Donna MAYO
53 Dean of College of Education .... Dr. Bob MICHAEL
81 Dean College of Sci & Mathematics .... Dr. Michael BODRI
76 Int Dean College of Health Sc .... Dr. Robert MICHAEL
104 Exec Director Global Engagement .... Dr. John WILSON
15 Director Human Resources .... Ms. Beth ARBUTHNOT
18 Director of Facilities - North .... Mr. Todd BERMANN
18 Director of Facilities - South .... Mr. Bill MOODY
19 Director of Public Safety .... Mr. Michael F. STAPLETON
13 Assoc CIO IT Services-Dah .... Mr. Steve MCLOAD
26 Director of University Relations .... Ms. Kate MAINE
20 Commandant Corp of Cadets .... Col. James PALMER
36 Director of Career Services .... Ms. Dora DITCHFIELD
38 Director Counseling Services .... Dr. Simon CORDERY
39 Director of Residence Life .... Ms. Treva SMITH
23 Director of Student Health Services .... Ms. Karen TOMLINSON
12 Actg Exec Dir Cumming Campus .... Mr. Jason PRUITT
12 Actg CEO Oconee Campus .... Dr. Eric SKIPPER
108 Dir Accreditation & Assessment .... Ms. Betty CANTRELL
102 Dir Corporate & Foundation Relation .... Mr. Jeff BOGGAN
51 Dir Continuing Education .... Ms. Wendy THELLMAN
31 Dir Community Engagement .... Ms. Sloan JONES
96 Director Purchasing .... Mr. Alan SILBERT
88 Dir Student Disability Services .... Dr. Nicole DOVEY
22 Dir Diversity Initiatives .... Mr. Robert ROBINSON
44 Director Planned Giving .... Mr. Bruce HOWERTON
88 Executive Director NISTS .... Dr. Janet MARLING

† Part of the University System of Georgia.

University of Phoenix Atlanta Campus (E)

8200 Roberts Drive, Sandy Springs GA 30350-4147
Telephone: (678) 731-0555 Identification: 770200
Accreditation: &NH, ACBSP

† Main campus is University of Phoenix in Tempe, AZ.

University of Phoenix Augusta Campus (F)

3150 Perimeter Parkway, Augusta GA 30909-4583
Telephone: (706) 868-2000 Identification: 770198
Accreditation: &NH, ACBSP

† Main campus is University of Phoenix in Tempe, AZ.

University of Phoenix Columbus GA Campus (G)

7200 North Lake Drive, Columbus GA 31909
Telephone: (706) 320-1266 Identification: 770199
Accreditation: &NH, ACBSP

† Main campus is University of Phoenix in Tempe, AZ.

University of Phoenix Savannah Campus (H)

8001 Chatham Center Drive, Savannah GA 31405-7400
Telephone: (912) 232-0531 Identification: 770201
Accreditation: &NH, ACBSP

† Main campus is University of Phoenix in Tempe, AZ.

University of West Georgia (I)

1601 Maple Street, Carrollton GA 30118-0001
County: Carroll FICE Identification: 001601
Unit ID: 141334
Telephone: (678) 839-5000 Carnegie Class: Master's L
FAX Number: N/A Calendar System: Semester
URL: www.westga.edu
Established: 1906 Annual Undergrad Tuition & Fees (In-State): $6,832
Enrollment: 11,769 Coed
Affiliation or Control: State IRS Status: 501(c)3
Highest Offering: Doctorate
Program: Occupational; Liberal Arts And General; Teacher Preparatory; Professional
Accreditation: SC, ART, BUS, BUSA, CACREP, CS, MUS, NURSE, SP, SPAA, TED, THEA

01 President .... Dr. Kyle MARRERO
05 Provost & VP for Academic Affairs .... Dr. Michael HORVATH

10 Vice President Business & Finance ....Mr. Jim SUTHERLAND
32 Vice President for Student Affairs ....Dr. Scott LINGRELL
26 Vice President of Univ Advancement ....Mr. Bill ESTES
30 Director of Development ....Ms. Diane HOMESLEY
20 Deputy Provost ....Dr. Jon ANDERSON
84 Assoc VP for Enrollment Mgt ....Dr. John HEAD
20 Associate VP for Academic Affairs ....Dr. Myrna GANTNER
35 Assoc VP for Student Life ....Dr. Alicia CAUDILL
21 University Controller ....Mr. Richard SEARS
83 Dean of Social Sciences ....Dr. N. Jane MCCANDLESS
50 Dean of Business ....Dr. Faye S. MCINTYRE
53 Dean of Education ....Dr. Dianne HOFF
79 Dean College of Arts and Humanities ....Dr. Randy HENDRICKS
81 Dean Science and Mathematics ....Dr. Farooq A. KHAN
92 Dean & Director of Honors College ....Dr. Michael D. HESTER
06 Registrar ....Ms. Donna HALEY
07 Director of Admissions ....Mr. Justin BARLOW
08 Director of Libraries ....Ms. Lorene FLANDERS
37 Director of Financial Aid ....Dr. Philip HAWKINS
36 Director of Career Services ....Vacant
27 Chief Information Officer ....Mrs. Kathy KRAL
51 Director of Continuing Education ....Ms. Rachael L. ROBINSON
15 Dir of Human Res/Affirm Action Ofcr ....Ms. Juanita HICKS
18 Asst VP Campus Planning/Facilities ....Mr. Brendan BOWEN
19 Director of University Police ....Mr. Thomas J. MACKEL
23 Director of Health Services ....Dr. Leslie COTTRELL
35 Director of the Campus Center ....Mr. Matthew MILLER
39 Director of Residence Life ....Mr. Stephen WHITLOCK
41 Director of Athletics ....Mr. Daryl DICKEY
38 Dir of Counseling & Career Dev ....Dr. Lisa ADAMS
88 Dir Business Svcs/Auxiliary Enterpr ....Mr. Mark REEVES
09 Director Inst Research/Planning ....Vacant
29 Director of Alumni Relations ....Mr. H. Franklin PRITCHETT
89 Director of EXEL Center ....Mrs. Cheryl A. RICE
26 Asst Vice President of UA ....Ms. Jami BOWER
40 Bookstore Manager ....Mr. Mark RHODES
25 Assoc VP Research & Spons Projects ....Dr. Charles MARIS
55 Dean of USG eCore ....Dr. Melanie N. CLAY
12 Director-Newnan Campus ....Ms. Cathy WRIGHT
44 Assoc Director of Legacy Giving ....Mr. Baylor BASSETT
28 Director of Diversity ....Vacant
24 Assistant Dir for Classroom Support ....Mr. Brian MCCRARY
43 University Legal Counsel ....Ms. Jane SIMPSON
104 Dir of International Svcs & Pgms ....Vacant
102 Assoc Exec Dir of WG Foundation ....Mr. Bart GILLESPIE
66 Dean School of Nursing ....Dr. Kathyrn GRAMS

† Part of the University System of Georgia.

*University System of Georgia Office (A)

270 Washington Street, SW, Atlanta GA 30334-9007
County: Fulton FICE Identification: 008290
Telephone: (404) 656-2202 Carnegie Class: N/A
FAX Number: (404) 962-3013
URL: www.usg.edu

01 Chancellor ....Mr. Henry M. HUCKABY
04 Executive Assistant to Chancellor ....Ms. Sabrina THOMPSON
11 Exec Vice Chanc Administration ....Mr. Steve WRIGLEY
05 Exec Vice Chanc/Chief Academic Ofcr ....Dr. Houston DAVIS
45 Assoc Vice Chanc Planning & Impleme .....Ms. Shelley C. NICKEL
10 Vice Chancellor Fiscal Affairs ....Mr. John BROWN
21 Chief Audit Officer ....Mr. John M. FUCHKO, III
26 Sr Vice Chanc External Affairs ....Mr. Thomas E. DANIEL
18 Vice Chancellor Facilities ....Mr. Jim JAMES
13 Vice Chanc/Chief Info Officer ....Dr. Curt CARVER
27 Assoc Vice Chanc Media/Publications ....Mr. John MILLSAPS

Valdosta State University (B)

1500 N Patterson Street, Valdosta GA 31698-0010
County: Lowndes FICE Identification: 001599
Unit ID: 141264
Telephone: (229) 333-5800 Carnegie Class: Master's L
FAX Number: (229) 333-7400 Calendar System: Semester
URL: www.valdosta.edu
Established: 1906 Annual Undergrad Tuition & Fees (In-State): $5,889
Enrollment: 12,515 Coed
Affiliation or Control: State IRS Status: 501(c)3
Highest Offering: Doctorate
Program: 2-Year Principally Bachelor's Creditable; Liberal Arts And General; Teacher Preparatory
Accreditation: SC, ART, BUS, CACREP, #LIB, MFCD, MUS, NURSE, SP, SPAA, SW, TED, THEA

01 President ....Dr. William MCKINNEY
05 Acting VP Academic Affairs ....Dr. Sharron GRAVETT
10 Vice President for Finance & Admin ......Ms. Sue E. FUCIARELLI
30 Vice President for Advancement ....Mr. John D. CRAWFORD
32 VP for Student Affairs ....Mr. Russell F. MAST
84 Int VP for Enroll/Marketing & Comm ....Mr. Andy T. CLARK
21 Assoc VP Finance & Administration ....Ms. Traycee F. MARTIN
58 Interim Asst VP Rsrch & Grad Dean ....Dr. James T. LAPLANT
20 Asst VP Academic Affairs ....Dr. Sharon L. GRAVETT
86 Asst to Pres Gov & Corp Relations ....Mr. Philip D. ALLEN
49 Dean College of Arts & Sciences ....Dr. Connie L. RICHARDS
50 Dean College of Business Admin ....Dr. Wayne L. PLUMLY
57 Dean College of the Arts ....Mr. Arthur B. PEARCE
53 Acting Dean College of Education ....Dr. Brian GERBER
66 Dean College of Nursing ....Dr. Anita G. HUFFT
92 Interim Dean of Honors College ....Mr. Michael P. SAVOIE

08 University Librarian ....Dr. Alan BERNSTEIN
06 Registrar ....Mr. Stanley JONES
13 Director Information Tech Services ....Mr. Joseph A. NEWTON
13 Dir Enterprise Apps and Analytics .... Mr. Brian A. HAUGABROOK
39 Director Housing & Residence Life ....Dr. Thomas W. HARDY
07 Director Admissions/Enrollment Mgmt .... Mr. Walter H. PEACOCK
41 Director of Athletics ....Mr. Herb REINHARD
37 Director of Financial Aid ....Mr. Douglas R. TANNER
31 Director of Public Services ....Mr. Bill MUNTZ
88 Dir of Publication & Design Service ....Mr. Jeff GRANT
36 Dir Career Services/Cooperative Ed ....Vacant
15 Director of Human Resources ....Dr. Denise BOGART
88 Director Division Aerospace Studies .... LtCol. Marsha ALEEM
22 Director of Social Equity ....Dr. Maggie J. VIVERETTE
43 University Attorney ....Ms. Laverne L. GASKINS
18 Dir Phys Plant & Facilities Plng ....Mr. Ray SABLE
26 Dir Marketing & Cmty Relations ....Ms. Mary B. GOODING
38 Director of Counseling Center ....Dr. John GROTGEN
40 Director of Bookstore ....Ms. Bethanie B. BROGDON
23 Director of Student Health Services ....Dr. Edwin L. HIATT
19 Director of University Police ....Mr. Scott DONER
108 Director of Inst Effectiveness ....Dr. Michael M. BLACK
44 Director of Annual Giving ....Ms. Karen A. JOHNSON
96 Director of Purchasing ....Ms. Terri M. GERHARDT

† Part of the University System of Georgia.

Virginia College (C)

2807 Wylds Road Extension, Suite B, Augusta GA 30909
Telephone: (706) 288-2500 Identification: 770833
Accreditation: ACICS, MAAB, SURGT

† Main campus is Virginia College in Birmingham, AL.

Virginia College (D)

5601 Veterans Parkway, Columbus GA 31904
Telephone: (762) 207-1600 Identification: 770835
Accreditation: ACICS, MAAB

† Main campus is Virginia College in Birmingham, AL.

Virginia College (E)

1901 Paul Walsh Drive, Macon GA 31206
Telephone: (478) 803-4600 Identification: 770834
Accreditation: ACICS, MAAB

† Main campus is Virginia College in Birmingham, AL.

Virginia College (F)

14045 Abercorn Street, Suite 1503, Savannah GA 31419
Telephone: (912) 721-5600 Identification: 770836
Accreditation: ACICS

† Main campus is Virginia College in Birmingham, AL.

Wesleyan College (G)

4760 Forsyth Road, Macon GA 31210-4462
County: Bibb FICE Identification: 001600
Unit ID: 141325
Telephone: (478) 477-1110 Carnegie Class: Bac/A&S
FAX Number: (478) 757-4030 Calendar System: Semester
URL: www.wesleyancollege.edu
Established: 1836 Annual Undergrad Tuition & Fees: $19,500
Enrollment: 710 Female
Affiliation or Control: United Methodist IRS Status: 501(c)3
Highest Offering: Master's
Program: Liberal Arts And General; Teacher Preparatory
Accreditation: SC, MUS

01 President ....Ms. Ruth A. KNOX
05 Provost/VP for Academic Affairs ....Dr. Vivia L. FOWLER
30 VP Institutional Advancement .... Mr. Douglas B. MACMILLAN
10 Vice Pres Finance/Treasurer ....Mr. Richard P. MAIER
32 Vice Pres for Student Affairs ....Ms. Patricia M. GIBBS
84 Vice Pres for Enrollment Services ....Mr. C. Stephen FARR
06 Assistant Dean/Registrar ....Ms. Patricia R. HARDEMAN
04 Assistant to the President ....Mrs. Denise W. HOLLOWAY
04 Assistant to the President ....Mrs. Sally A. HEMINGWAY
08 Library Director ....Ms. Sybil MCNEIL
13 Director of Information Services ....Mr. Kevin L. ULSHAFER
29 Director of Alumnae Affairs ....Ms. Cathy C. SNOW
26 Director of Communications ....Ms. Mary Ann HOWARD
44 Director of Annual Fund ....Ms. Andrea G. WILLIFORD
37 Director of Financial Aid ....Ms. Danielle LODGE
39 Director of Residence Life ....Ms. Stefanie SWANGER
18 Director of Physical Plant ....Ms. Kelly BLEDSOE
41 Athletic Director ....Ms. Patty GIBBS
42 Chaplain ....Rev. Bill HURDLE
19 Director Security/Safety ....Mr. Clinton BRANTLEY
15 Director Human Resources ....Ms. Meagon DAVIS
07 Director of Admissions ....Ms. Danielle LODGE
09 Director of Institutional Research ....Ms. Angie WRIGHT
32 Chief Student Life Officer ....Ms. Stefanie SWANGER
36 Director Career Development ....Ms. Monica MOODY
38 Director Student Counseling ....Ms. Jamie THAMES
96 Director of Purchasing ....Ms. Lindsay TIMMS
20 Associate Academic Officer ....Ms. Patricia R. HARDEMAN
21 Associate Business Officer ....Ms. Dawn P. NASH
40 Bookstore Manager ....Ms. Lindsay TIMMS

West Georgia Technical College (H)

176 Murphy Campus Boulevard, Waco GA 30182-2407
County: Haralson FICE Identification: 010487
Unit ID: 139278
Telephone: (770) 537-6000 Carnegie Class: Assoc/Pub-S-SC
FAX Number: (770) 537-7976 Calendar System: Semester
URL: www.westgatech.edu
Established: 1968 Annual Undergrad Tuition & Fees (In-State): $3,942
Enrollment: 6,639 Coed
Affiliation or Control: State IRS Status: 501(c)3
Highest Offering: Associate Degree
Program: Occupational; 2-Year Principally Bachelor's Creditable; Technical Emphasis
Accreditation: SC, ACBSP, ADNUR, DH, MAC, MLTAD, RAD, SURGT

01 President ....Dr. Skip SULLIVAN
05 Vice President Academic Affairs ....Mr. Patrick K. HANNON
32 Vice President Student Affairs ....Mrs. Tonya WHITLOCK
30 Vice Pres Institutional Advancement ....Mrs. Dawn COOK
09 VP Institutional Effectiveness ....Dr. Kristen DOUGLAS
20 Asst Vice Pres For Curriculum ....Dr. Sindi MCGOWAN
08 Director Library Services ....Mr. Emanuel MITCHELL
06 Registrar ....Mrs. Laura JAKUBIAK
13 Exec Dir Information Technology ....Mr. Sam JENKINS
07 Director of Admissions ....Mrs. Mary ADERHOLD
18 Director Facilities ....Mr. Michael JILES

Westwood College-Atlanta Midtown (I)

1100 Spring Street, Suite 102, Atlanta GA 30309-2824
Telephone: (404) 745-9862 Identification: 666421
Accreditation: ACICS

† Main campus is Westwood College-DuPage in Woodridge, IL.

Westwood College-Atlanta Northlake (J)

2309 Parklake Drive NE, Atlanta GA 30345-2906
Telephone: (866) 821-6145 Identification: 666597
Accreditation: ACICS

† Main campus is Westwood College-O'Hare Airport in Chicago, IL.

Wiregrass Georgia Technical College (K)

4089 Val Tech Road, Valdosta GA 31602
County: Lowndes FICE Identification: 005256
Unit ID: 141255
Telephone: (229) 333-2100 Carnegie Class: Assoc/Pub-R-M
FAX Number: (229) 333-2129 Calendar System: Semester
URL: www.wiregrass.edu
Established: 1963 Annual Undergrad Tuition & Fees (In-State): $2,492
Enrollment: 4,143 Coed
Affiliation or Control: State IRS Status: 501(c)3
Highest Offering: Associate Degree
Program: Occupational; 2-Year Principally Bachelor's Creditable; Technical Emphasis
Accreditation: SC, CAHIIM, DA, DH, MLTAD, SURGT

01 President ....Dr. Tina K. ANDERSON
31 Exec VP Cmty/College Relations ....Dr. Shawn UTLEY
10 Vice President Operations ....Ms. Lisa TOMBERLIN
05 VP for Academic Affairs ....Dr. Ron O'MEARA
11 VP for Administrative Services ....Ms. Keren WYNN
32 VP for Student Affairs ....Ms. Connie SUMNER
09 VP for Institutional Effectiveness ....Dr. Helen PENNY
51 VP for Adult Education Services ....Mr. Alvin PAYTON
46 Exec VP for Business Development ....Mr. John FISHER
26 Executive Dir for Public Relations ....Ms. Angela HOBBY
07 Director Recruitment ....Ms. Brooke JARAMILLO

Young Harris College (L)

1 College Street, Young Harris GA 30582-0098
County: Towns FICE Identification: 001604
Unit ID: 141361
Telephone: (706) 379-3111 Carnegie Class: Assoc/PrivNFP
FAX Number: (706) 379-4319 Calendar System: Semester
URL: www.yhc.edu
Established: 1886 Annual Undergrad Tuition & Fees: $24,500
Enrollment: 1,034 Coed
Affiliation or Control: United Methodist IRS Status: 501(c)3
Highest Offering: Baccalaureate
Program: Liberal Arts And General
Accreditation: SC, MUS

01 President ....Ms. Cathy COX
05 Vice Pres for Academic Affairs ....Dr. Gary MYERS
11 Senior VP for Finance & Admin ....Mr. David LEOPARD
10 Vice Pres for Business/Controller ....Mr. Wade M. BENSON
32 Vice President for Student Affairs ....Ms. Angi SMITH
84 Vice Pres for Enrollment Management ....Mr. Clinton G. HOBBS
30 Vice President of Advancement ....Mr. Jay STROMAN
45 VP for Planning and Assessment ......Ms. Rosemary R. ROYSTON
14 Vice President of Campus Technology ....Mr. Ken FANEUFF
29 Director of Alumni Relations ....Ms. Dana ENSLEY
20 Associate Academic Officer ....Dr. Keith DEFOOR
08 Librarian ....Ms. Dawn LAMADE
38 Counselor ....Ms. Lynne GRADY

06 Registrar .... Ms. Tammy GIBSON
37 Director Student Financial Aid .... Ms. Linda ADAMS
07 Director of Admissions .... Vacant
15 Director Personnel Services .... Mr. Vince ROBELOTTO
26 Chief Public Relations Officer .... Ms. Krystin DEAN
18 Chief Facilities/Physical Plant .... Mr. Jim RAWSKI
19 Director of Safety & Compliance .... Vacant
41 Athletic Director .... Mr. Randy DUNN
42 Campus Minister .... Rev. Tim MOORE

HAWAII

Argosy University, Hawaii (A)

400 ABS Tower, 1001 Bishop Street, Honolulu HI 96813
Telephone: (808) 536-5555 Identification: 666787
Accreditation: &WC, CLPSY

† Main campus is Argosy University, Orange County in Orange, CA.

Babel University Professional School of Translation (B)

1833 Kalakaua Avenue, #208, Honolulu HI 96815
County: Honolulu Identification: 666350
Telephone: (808) 946-3773 Carnegie Class: Not Classified
FAX Number: (808) 946-3993 Calendar System: Other
URL: www.babel.edu
Established: 2000 Annual Graduate Tuition & Fees: $19,450
Enrollment: 69 Coed
Affiliation or Control: Proprietary IRS Status: Proprietary
Highest Offering: Master's; No Undergraduates
Program: Professional
Accreditation: DETC

01 Chancellor .... Dr. Miyoko YUASA
05 Head of Deans .... Mr. Yoshiharu ISHIDA

Brigham Young University Hawaii (C)

55-220 Kulanui Street, Laie Oahu HI 96762-1294
County: Honolulu FICE Identification: 001606
Unit ID: 230047
Telephone: (808) 675-3211 Carnegie Class: Bac/Diverse
FAX Number: (808) 675-3329 Calendar System: Semester
URL: www.byuh.edu
Established: 1955 Annual Undergrad Tuition & Fees: $4,770
Enrollment: 3,166 Coed
Affiliation or Control: Latter-day Saints IRS Status: 501(c)3
Highest Offering: Baccalaureate
Program: Liberal Arts And General; Teacher Preparatory; Professional
Accreditation: WC, SW

01 President .... Dr. Steven C. WHEELWRIGHT
05 Vice President for Academics .... Dr. Max L. CHECKETTS
11 VP for Administrative Services .... Mr. Michael B. BLISS
32 VP for Student Development & Svcs .... Dr. Debbie HIPPOLITE WRIGHT
18 VP Construction Facilities & Maint .... Mr. David A. LEWIS
04 Administrative Asst to the Pres .... Ms. Lisa FEHOKO
108 Assoc Academic VP for Assessment .... Dr. Rosalind RAM
20 Assoc Academic VP for Instruction .... Dr. D. Chad COMPTON
20 Assoc Academic VP for Curriculum .... Dr. Jennifer LANE
81 Dean College of Math and Sciences .... Dr. W. Jeffrey BURROUGHS
88 Dean College of Bus/Computing/Govt .... Dr. Glade TEW
88 Dean College of Human Development .... Dr. John BAILEY
88 Dean College of Lang/Culture & Arts .... Dr. Phillip MCARTHUR
13 University Technology Officer .... Mr. Kevin SCHLAG
07 Director Enrollment Services .... Mr. Arapata MEHA
41 Director of Athletics .... Mr. Ken WAGNER
08 Director University Library .... Mr. Michael ALDRICH
88 Director Budget Services .... Mr. Michael CHRISTENSEN
96 Director of Purchasing & Travel .... Mr. Robert OWAN
19 Director Safety/Security & Risk Mgt .... Mr. Roy YAMAMOTO
15 Director of Human Resources .... Mrs. Tessie FAUSTINO
18 Director Facilities Management .... Mr. Randy SHARP
10 Director Financial Services .... Mr. Eric MARLER
23 Director Health Center .... Dr. P. Douglas NIELSON
88 Dir Compliance & Internal Audit .... Mr. Adam R. JACOBSMEYER
36 Director Career Services .... Mrs. Jodi CHOWEN
38 Director of Counseling Services .... Vacant
35 Director Student Leadership & Honor .... Ms. Alison WHITING
88 Director Food Services .... Mr. David KEALA
26 Director Communications .... Mr. Michael JOHANSON
88 Director Testing and Assessment .... Dr. Paul H. FREEBAIRN
06 Registrar .... Mr. Daryl WHITFORD
51 Manager of Educational Outreach .... Mrs. Edna OWAN
40 Manager Bookstore .... Mr. Corbin THOMANDER
39 Manager Housing & Residential Life .... Ms. Lorraine MATAGI

† Affiliated with Brigham Young University, Provo, UT.

Chaminade University of Honolulu (D)

3140 Waialae Avenue, Honolulu HI 96816-1578
County: Honolulu FICE Identification: 001605
Unit ID: 141486
Telephone: (808) 735-4711 Carnegie Class: Master's L
FAX Number: (808) 735-4870 Calendar System: Semester
URL: www.chaminade.edu
Established: 1955 Annual Undergrad Tuition & Fees: $20,090
Enrollment: 2,766 Coed
Affiliation or Control: Independent Non-Profit IRS Status: 501(c)3
Highest Offering: Master's
Program: Liberal Arts And General; Teacher Preparatory; Professional
Accreditation: WC, CIDA, IACBE, MACTE, NURSE

01 President .... Bro. Bernard PLOEGER, SM
88 Exec Director of Compliance & Pers .... Ms. Maile LU'UWAI
05 Provost .... Dr. Helen WHIPPY
30 VP for Institutional Advancement .... Ms. Diane PETERS-NGUYEN
10 Vice President Finance/Facilities .... Ms. Aulani KAANOI
13 Dean of Info Technologies & Service .... Mr. Kyle JOHNSON
84 Dean of Enrollment Management .... Ms. Joy BOUEY
32 Dean of Students .... Ms. Grissel BENITZ-HODGE
35 Associate Dean of Students .... Ms. Allison JEROME
88 Dir Academic Advising/Retention .... Mr. Curtis WASHBURN
90 Director Network/Desktop Services .... Mr. Eddie PANG
55 Dir Adult & Graduate Services .... Vacant
91 Director of Management Info Svcs .... Mr. Jorge HERNANDEZ
29 Director of Alumni Relations .... Ms. Be-Jay KODAMA
41 Director of Athletics .... Mr. William VILLA
42 Director of Campus Ministry .... Mr. Danny O'REGAN
36 Dir Career Develop/Job Placement .... Vacant
18 Director of Facilities Operations .... Mr. Michael HAISEN
11 Director of Administrative Services .... Ms. Elaine OISHI
21 Director of Finance .... Mr. Jeoffrey VERANO
07 Director of Admissions .... Ms. Joy BOUEY
08 Director of Library .... Ms. Sharon LEPAGE
15 Director Personnel Services .... Mrs. Lucy STREETER
19 Director of Security .... Mr. Melvin DECOSTA
38 Director of Student Counseling .... Dr. June YASUHARA
06 Registrar .... Mr. John MORRIS
37 Director of Financial Aid .... Ms. Amy TAKIGUCHI
09 Dir of Institutional Research .... Mr. Hieu NGUYEN
26 Director of Communications .... Ms. Kapono RYAN

Hawaii College of Oriental Medicine (E)

93 Banyan Drive, Suite 504, Hilo HI 96720
County: Hawaii FICE Identification: 039994
Unit ID: 449579
Telephone: (808) 981-2790 Carnegie Class: Spec/Health
FAX Number: (808) 933-1369 Calendar System: Trimester
URL: www.hicom.edu
Established: 1986 Annual Graduate Tuition & Fees: $14,628
Enrollment: 20 Coed
Affiliation or Control: Independent Non-Profit IRS Status: 501(c)3
Highest Offering: Master's; No Undergraduates
Program: Professional
Accreditation: ACUP

01 President & CEO .... Mr. Grif FROST
05 Dean of Oriental Medicine .... Mr. William PETTIS
10 COO/CFO/Financial Aid Officer .... Mr. Greg BAKER

Hawaii Pacific University (F)

1164 Bishop Street, Suite 800, Honolulu HI 96813-2882
County: Honolulu FICE Identification: 007279
Unit ID: 141644
Telephone: (808) 544-0200 Carnegie Class: Master's L
FAX Number: (808) 544-1136 Calendar System: Semester
URL: www.hpu.edu
Established: 1965 Annual Undergrad Tuition & Fees: $19,980
Enrollment: 7,463 Coed
Affiliation or Control: Independent Non-Profit IRS Status: 501(c)3
Highest Offering: Master's
Program: Liberal Arts And General; Teacher Preparatory; Professional
Accreditation: WC, NURSE, SW, @TEAC

01 President .... Dr. Geoff BANNISTER
00 President Emeritus .... Mr. Chatt G. WRIGHT
05 Vice President of Academic Affairs .... Dr. Andrew BRITTAIN
20 Assistant VP Academic Affairs .... Mr. Joe SCHMIEDL
56 Assoc VP Off-Campus/Military Pgm .... Mr. Robert CYBORON
88 Director Instructional Innovation .... Vacant
35 Exec Dir Student Academic Services .... Ms. Deborah NAKASHIMA
84 Vice Pres Enrollment Management .... Vacant
10 VP/Chief Financial Officer .... Mr. William KLINE
09 Vice Pres Institutional Research .... Dr. Leslie H. CORREA
15 Vice President Human Resources .... Ms. Christine GODFREY
30 Vice Pres Alumni & Univ Relations .... Ms. Mary Ellen MCGILLAN
21 Associate VP/Controller .... Ms. Kathleen CLARK
50 Dean Business Administration .... Dr. Deborah CROWNE
66 Acting Dean Nursing/Health Sciences .... Dr. Dale ALLISON
81 Dean Natural/Computational Sciences .... Dr. Andrew BRITTAIN
60 Dean Humanities & Social Sciences .... Dr. Steven COMBS
89 Dean of Students .... Ms. Marites MCKEY
13 Chief Application Officer .... Mr. Robert SLIKE
106 Assistant Dean Distance Ed Policy .... Dr. Asoke DATTA
85 Dir Intl Admis/Recruit/Student Srvs .... Ms. Lilian HALLSTROM
97 Assistant Dean General Education .... Dr. Malia SMITH
07 Director of Admissions .... Ms. Sara SATO
09 Academic Information Analyst .... Mr. John IGE
104 Director Intl Exchange/Study Abroad .... Dr. Jon DAVIDANN
36 Director Career Svcs Ctr/Co-op Educ .... Mr. Joseph BARRIENTOS
06 Registrar .... Ms. Jean LANG
37 Director Financial Aid .... Mr. Adam HATCH
41 Athletic Director .... Mr. Darren VORDERBRUEGGE
51 Assoc Dir Adult Learning Program .... Ms. Jill MERL
105 Director Web Services .... Mr. Abe TOMA
08 University Librarian .... Ms. Kathleen CHEE
42 University Chaplain .... Rev. Dale BURKE
14 Director Computing Services .... Ms. Lisa CARPENTER
88 Dir Admin Support Operations .... Ms. Jamie KEMP
19 Assoc Director Security and Safety .... Mr. Wayne FERNANDEZ
18 Manager Facilities/Physical Plant .... Mr. Steve HENDRICKS
40 Bookstore Manager .... Ms. Shellee HEEN
29 Alumni/Parent Relations Coordinator .... Ms. Kris SMITH
38 Director Counseling/Behavioral Hlth .... Dr. Kevin BOWMAN
96 Procurement Director .... Mr. Kevin WETTER
06 Associate Registrar .... Ms. Carole KOMATSUBARA
27 Chief Information Ofcr/Vice Pres .... Dr. Sharon BLANTON

Hawaii Tokai International College (G)

2241 Kapiolani Boulevard, Honolulu HI 96826-4310
County: Honolulu FICE Identification: 037603
Telephone: (808) 983-4100 Carnegie Class: Not Classified
FAX Number: (808) 983-4107 Calendar System: Quarter
URL: www.hawaiitokai.edu
Established: 1992 Annual Undergrad Tuition & Fees: $15,240
Enrollment: 129 Coed
Affiliation or Control: Independent Non-Profit IRS Status: 501(c)3
Highest Offering: Associate Degree
Program: 2-Year Principally Bachelor's Creditable; Liberal Arts And General
Accreditation: WJ

01 Chancellor .... Dr. Naoto YOSHIKAWA
05 Vice Chancellor .... Dr. Douglas FUQUA
11 Exec Director of Administration .... Mr. Yuzo OIDA
20 Dean of Instruction .... Dr. Deanna MADDEN
46 Director Program Development .... Ms. Wanda SAKO
08 Librarian .... Ms. Suzanne HARTER
32 Director Student Services .... Ms. Jaelee HEUPEL
15 Human Resources Officer .... Ms. Janice DAWSON
21 Finance Department .... Mr. Mark GREENE
29 Alum Rel Coord/Std Sup Specialist .... Mr. Andrew FUJIMOTO

Heald College, Honolulu (H)

1500 Kapiolani Boulevard, Honolulu HI 96814-3797
Telephone: (808) 955-1500 FICE Identification: 004546
Accreditation: &WC, CAHIIM, DA, MAC

† Main campus is Heald College, San Francisco in San Francisco, CA.

Institute of Clinical Acupuncture and Oriental Medicine (I)

100 N Beretania Street, Suite 203 B,
Honolulu HI 96817-4709
County: Honolulu FICE Identification: 037353
Unit ID: 444699
Telephone: (808) 521-2288 Carnegie Class: Spec/Health
FAX Number: (808) 521-2271 Calendar System: Semester
URL: www.orientalmedicine.edu
Established: 1996 Annual Graduate Tuition & Fees: $12,810
Enrollment: 50 Coed
Affiliation or Control: Proprietary IRS Status: Proprietary
Highest Offering: Master's; No Undergraduates
Program: Professional; Business Emphasis
Accreditation: ACUP

01 President .... Dr. Wai Hoa LOW
05 Chancellor Academic Affairs .... Dr. Edmund BERNAUER
63 Clinic Director .... Dr. Catherine Yu-Ling LOW

New Hope Christian College-Hawaii (J)

290 Sand Island Access Road, Honolulu HI 96819
Telephone: (808) 853-1040 Identification: 667010
Accreditation: &BI

† Main campus is New Hope Christian College in Eugene, OR.

Remington College-Honolulu Campus (K)

1111 Bishop Street, Suite 400, Honolulu HI 96813-2811
Telephone: (808) 942-1000 Identification: 666028
Accreditation: ACCSC

† Main campus is Remington College, Mobile Campus in Mobile, AL.

*University of Hawaii System Office (L)

2444 Dole Street, Honolulu HI 96822
County: Honolulu FICE Identification: 007885
Unit ID: 141963
Telephone: (808) 956-8207 Carnegie Class: N/A
FAX Number: (808) 956-5286
URL: www.hawaii.edu

01 President .... Dr. M. R. C GREENWOOD
05 Exec VP for Academic Affs/Provost .... Dr. Linda K. JOHNSRUD
46 Vice President for Research .... Dr. James R. GAINES
43 VP Legal Affs/Univ Gen Counsel .... Ms. Darolyn LENDIO
10 VP Budget and Finance/CFO .... Mr. Howard TODO
88 Vice President Community Colleges .... Dr. John MORTON
32 VP Student Affs and Univ/Comm Rels .... Vacant
27 Vice President Info Tech/CIO .... Dr. David K. LASSNER
35 Interim Assoc VP Student Affairs .... Dr. Jan M. JAVINAR
26 Assoc VP External Affs & Univ Rels .... Ms. Lynne T. WATERS
18 Assoc VP Capital Improvements .... Mr. Brian MINAAI

102 President UH Foundation .... Ms. Donna VUCHINICH
21 Director of Budget .... Ms. Laurel A. JOHNSTON
16 System Director Human Resources .... Ms. Debra ISHII
13 Director Management Info Systems .... Ms. Susan K. INOUYE
45 Director Off Research Services .... Ms. Yaa-Yin FONG
21 Interim Dir Financial Management .... Ms. Barbara K. KAWAMOTO
09 Dir Admin Operations/EVAAP .... Ms. Sandra FURUTO
22 Director EEO/AA .... Ms. Mie WATANABE
88 Director Media Production .... Mr. Dan MEISENZAHL
88 Director Communications .... Ms. Jodi LEONG

*University of Hawaii at Hilo (A)

200 W Kawili Street, Hilo HI 96720-4091
County: Hawaii FICE Identification: 001611
Unit ID: 141565
Telephone: (808) 974-7444 Carnegie Class: Bac/A&S
FAX Number: (808) 974-7622 Calendar System: Semester
URL: www.uhh.hawaii.edu
Established: 1947 Annual Undergrad Tuition & Fees (In-State): $6,184
Enrollment: 4,157 Coed
Affiliation or Control: State IRS Status: 501(c)3
Highest Offering: Doctorate
Program: Liberal Arts And General; Teacher Preparatory; Professional
Accreditation: WC, BUS, CEA, NUR, PHAR, @TEAC

02 Chancellor .... Dr. Donald O. STRANEY
05 Vice Chancellor Academic Affair .... Dr. Matthew PLATZ
10 Vice Chanc Administrative Affs .... Dr. Marcia SAKAI
46 Int Vice Chancellor for Research .... Vacant
32 Vice Chancellor Student Affairs .... Dr. Luoluo HONG
20 Asst VC for Academic Affairs .... Vacant
21 Budget Director .... Ms. Lois M. FUJIYOSHI
88 Director University Disability Svcs .... Ms. Susan SHIRACHI
15 Director Human Resources .... Ms. Claire SHIGEOKA
18 Director Facilities Planner .... Mr. Lo-Li CHIH
26 Director University Relations .... Mr. Jerry CHANG
08 University Librarian .... Ms. Helen ROGERS
24 Director Media Relations ...... Ms. Alyson Y. KAKUGAWA-LEONG
07 Director Admissions .... Mr. Curtis NISHIOKA
38 Acting Director Counseling .... Ms. Leslie ARMENOIX
39 Director Housing .... Mr. Miles K. NAGATA
35 Director Campus Center .... Ms. Ellen I. KUSANO
37 Director Financial Aid .... Mr. Jeff SCOFIELD
06 University Registrar .... Ms. Cathy TRAVIS
49 Dean College of Arts & Sciences .... Dr. Randy HIROKAWA
50 Actg Dean College of Business/Econ .... Dr. Kelly BURKE
67 Dean College of Pharmacy .... Dr. John PEZZUTO
47 Int Dean Col Agri/For/Nat Res Mgmt .... Dr. Bruce MATHEWS
51 Int Dean Cont Educ/Community Svcs ...... Dr. Farrahmarie GOMES
41 Director of Athletics .... Mr. Dexter IRVIN
40 Bookstore Manager .... Mr. Jason K. TANAKA
85 Dir International Student Services .... Mr. James P. MELLON
36 Director Career Services .... Dr. Norman S. STAHL
22 Director EEO/AA .... Mr. Jubilee KUEWA
09 Institutional Research Analyst .... Mr. Mason KUO
29 Director Marketing & Alumni .... Ms. Yu Yok PEARRING
30 Interim Sr Director of Development .... Ms. Andrea FURULI
94 Coordinator Women's Center .... Ms. Hannah WU
23 Asst Director Medical Services .... Ms. Heather HIRATA
92 Honors Director .... Vacant
88 Dir College of Hawaiian Language .... Keiki KAWAI`AE`A

*University of Hawaii at Manoa (B)

2500 Campus Road, Honolulu HI 96822-2217
County: Honolulu FICE Identification: 001610
Unit ID: 141574
Telephone: (808) 956-8111 Carnegie Class: RU/VH
FAX Number: N/A Calendar System: Semester
URL: www.manoa.hawaii.edu
Established: 1907 Annual Undergrad Tuition & Fees (In-State): $9,904
Enrollment: 20,246 Coed
Affiliation or Control: State IRS Status: 501(c)3
Highest Offering: Doctorate
Program: Liberal Arts And General; Teacher Preparatory; Professional
Accreditation: WC, BUS, CEA, CLPSY, CORE, DH, DIETD, ENG, IPSY, LAW, LIB, MED, MT, MUS, NURSE, PH, PLNG, #SP, SW, TED

02 Chancellor .... Dr. Thomas M. APPLE
11 Vice Chanc Admin/Finance/ Operations .... Ms. Kathleen D. CUTSHAW
05 Vice Chanc Academic Affs .... Dr. Reed W. DASENBROCK
45 Int Vice Chancellor for Research .... Dr. Brian TAYLOR
32 Vice Chancellor for Students .... Dr. Francisco J. HERNANDEZ
06 University Registrar .... Mr. Stuart LAU
08 University Librarian .... Dr. Irene HEROLD
37 Director Financial Aid Services .... Ms. Jodie M. KUBA
38 Director Counsel/Student Devel Ctr .... Dr. Allyson M. TANOUYE
23 Director University Health Center .... Dr. Andrew W. NICHOLS
39 Director Student Housing .... Mr. Michael W. KAPTIK
40 Director Campus Svcs (Bookstore) .... Ms. Deborah T. HEUBLER
41 Athletic Director .... Mr. Ben JAY
56 Dean Outreach College .... Dr. William G. CHISMAR
50 Dean Shidler College of Business .... Dr. V. Vance ROLEY
58 Dean Graduate Division .... Dr. Patricia A. COOPER
88 Int Dean Sch of Travel Industry Mgt .... Dr. Juanita C. LIU
53 Dean College of Education .... Dr. Donald B. YOUNG
54 Dean College of Engineering .... Dr. Peter E. CROUCH
47 Dean Col Trop Agric & Human Res .... Dr. Maria GALLO
63 Dean John A Burns Sch of Med .... Dr. Jerris R. HEDGES
66 Dean Sch Nursing & Dental Hygiene .... Dr. Mary G. BOLAND
70 Dean M P Thompson Sch of Soc Work ... Dr. Noreen K. MOKUAU
61 Dean Wm S Richardson Sch of Law .... Mr. Aviam SOIFER
48 Int Dean School of Architecture .... Mr. Thomas E. BINGHAM
49 Dean College Arts & Humanities .... Mr. Peter ARNADE
65 Dean College Natural Sciences .... Dr. William L. DITTO
83 Dean College Social Sciences .... Dr. Denise E. KONAN
79 Dean College Lang Ling & Lit .... Dr. Robert BLEY-VROMAN
88 Dean Sch Ocean & Earth Sci & Tech .... Dr. Brian TAYLOR
88 Int Dean Pac and Asian Stds .... Dr. R. Anderson SUTTON
88 Dn Hawaiinuiakea Sch Hawn Knowledge .... Dr. Maenette BENHAM
86 Director of Cmty/Govt Affairs .... Mr. Elmer KAAI
28 Dir Stdnt Equity/Exclnce/Diversity .... Dr. Amefil AGBAYANI
36 Dir Manoa Career Center .... Ms. Myrtle CHING-RAPPA
15 Director Human Resources .... Ms. Tammy KUNIYOSHI
88 Director Cancer Center .... Dr. Michele CARBONE
88 Director Institute for Astronomy .... Dr. Guenther HASINGER
88 Director Waikiki Aquarium .... Dr. Andrew ROSSITER
88 Int Assc Dr Pac Biosci Research Ctr .... Dr. Marilyn DUNLAP

*University of Hawaii - West Oahu (C)

91-1001 Farrington Highway, Kapolei HI 96707
County: Honolulu FICE Identification: 021078
Unit ID: 141981
Telephone: (808) 689-2770 Carnegie Class: Bac/Diverse
FAX Number: (808) 689-2771 Calendar System: Semester
URL: www.uhwo.hawaii.edu
Established: 1976 Annual Undergrad Tuition & Fees (In-State): $5,602
Enrollment: 1,997 Coed
Affiliation or Control: State IRS Status: 501(c)3
Highest Offering: Baccalaureate
Program: Liberal Arts And General; Teacher Preparatory
Accreditation: WC, TED

02 Chancellor .... Dr. Rockne C. FREITAS
05 Vice Chanc Academic Affairs .... Dr. Linda RANDALL
32 Int Vice Chanc for Student Affairs .... Dr. Jan JAVINAR
11 Vice Chanc Administrative Services .... Ms. Donna KIYOSAKI
84 Director for Enrollment Management .... Mr. James CROMWELL
09 Director of Institutional Research .... Dr. Elaine LEE
26 Dir Public Relations & Marketing .... Vacant
08 Head Librarian .... Ms. Sarah S. GILMAN
06 Registrar .... Ms. Robyn OSHIRO
37 Financial Aid Officer .... Mr. Lester ISHIMOTO
15 Director of Human Resources .... Ms. Nancy K. NAKASONE
18 Facilities/Auxiliary Services Mgr .. Mr. James (Kimo) YAMAGUCHI
10 Director of Business Affairs .... Ms. Linda SAIKI
13 Director of Information Technology .... Mr. Earl BETHKE

*University of Hawaii Community Colleges (D)

2444 Dole Street, Honolulu HI 96822-2411
County: Honolulu FICE Identification: 006751
Unit ID: 420592
Telephone: (808) 956-7038 Carnegie Class: N/A
FAX Number: (808) 956-9219
URL: www.hawaii.edu

01 Vice Pres for Community Colleges .... Dr. John F. MORTON
05 Assoc Vice Pres Academic Affairs .... Dr. Peter QUIGLEY
11 Assoc Vice Pres Admin/Cmty Col Oper .... Mr. Michael T. UNEBASAMI
04 Executive Assistant to the VP .... Ms. Deborah NAKAGAWA

*Kapiolani Community College (E)

4303 Diamond Head Road, Honolulu HI 96816-4496
County: Honolulu FICE Identification: 001613
Unit ID: 141796
Telephone: (808) 734-9000 Carnegie Class: Assoc/Pub2in4
FAX Number: (808) 734-9162 Calendar System: Semester
URL: www.kcc.hawaii.edu
Established: 1957 Annual Undergrad Tuition & Fees (In-State): $2,604
Enrollment: 8,892 Coed
Affiliation or Control: State IRS Status: 501(c)3
Highest Offering: Associate Degree
Program: Occupational; 2-Year Principally Bachelor's Creditable
Accreditation: WJ, ACFEI, ADNUR, COARC, MAC, MLTAD, OTA, PHLEB, PTAA, RAD

02 Chancellor .... Dr. Leon RICHARDS
05 Vice Chancellor for Acad Affs .... Dr. Louise PAGOTTO
10 Vice Chancellor for Admin Services .... Mr. Milton HIGA
32 Vice Chanellor for Student Services .... Ms. Mona LEE
49 Dean Arts and Sciences .... Dr. Charles SASAKI
50 Dean Hospitality/Business/Legal .... Dr. Frank HAAS
66 Dean Health Programs .... Dr. Patricia O'HAGAN
51 Dean Community & Continuing Educ .... Ms. Carol HOSHIKO
04 Special Asst to the Chancellor .... Dr. Salvatore LANZILOTTI
88 Dir Culinary Inst of the Pacific .... Mr. Conrad NONAKA
09 Dir Institutional Effectiveness .... Dr. Robert FRANCO
08 Librarian .... Ms. Susan MURATA
06 Registrar .... Ms. Jerilyn LORENZO
37 Financial Aid Officer .... Ms. Jennifer BRADLEY
18 Auxiliary Services Officer .... Mr. Gordon MAN
29 Alumni Relations Coordinator .... Ms. Louise YAMAMOTO
30 Development Officer .... Ms. Linh HOANG
15 Director Personnel Office .... Vacant
21 Fiscal Officer .... Ms. Carol MASUTANI
35 Student Activities Coordinator .... Mr. Keith KASHIWADA

*University of Hawaii Hawaii Community College (F)

200 W Kawili Street, Hilo HI 96720-4091
County: Hawaii FICE Identification: 005258
Unit ID: 383190
Telephone: (808) 934-2500 Carnegie Class: Assoc/Pub2in4
FAX Number: (808) 934-2501 Calendar System: Semester
URL: www.hawaii.hawaii.edu
Established: 1941 Annual Undergrad Tuition & Fees (In-State): $2,678
Enrollment: 3,686 Coed
Affiliation or Control: State IRS Status: 501(c)3
Highest Offering: Associate Degree
Program: Occupational; 2-Year Principally Bachelor's Creditable
Accreditation: WJ, ACFEI, ADNUR, CEA

02 Chancellor .... Ms. Noreen YAMANE
05 Vice Chanc Academic Affairs .... Ms. Joni ONISHI
11 Vice Chanc Administrative Affairs .... Mr. James YOSHIDA
32 Vice Chanc Student Affairs .... Mr. Jason CIFRA
51 Int Dir Continuing Educ/Training .... Ms. Deborah SHIGEHARA
37 Student Financial Aid Officer .... Ms. Vivian LAMOTHE
12 Int Dir UH Center at West Hawaii .... Ms. Beth SANDERS
06 Registrar .... Mr. David LOEDING
15 Personnel Services Officer .... Ms. Mari CHANG
07 Admissions Specialist .... Ms. Dorinna MANUEL-CORTEZ
21 Budget Specialist .... Ms. Jodi MINE

*University of Hawaii Honolulu Community College (G)

874 Dillingham Boulevard, Honolulu HI 96817-4598
County: Honolulu FICE Identification: 001612
Unit ID: 141680
Telephone: (808) 845-9211 Carnegie Class: Assoc/Pub2in4
FAX Number: (808) 845-9173 Calendar System: Semester
URL: www2.honolulu.hawaii.edu
Established: 1920 Annual Undergrad Tuition & Fees (In-State): $2,574
Enrollment: 4,582 Coed
Affiliation or Control: State IRS Status: 501(c)3
Highest Offering: Associate Degree
Program: Occupational; 2-Year Principally Bachelor's Creditable; Technical Emphasis
Accreditation: WJ

02 Chancellor .... Ms. Erika LACRO
05 Int Vice Chancellor of Acad Affairs .... Mr. Russell UYENO
11 Int Vice Chancellor of Admin Svcs .... Mr. Brian FURUTO
32 Dean of Student Services .... Ms. Katy HO
88 Int Dir PCATT .... Ms. Rosemary SUMAJIT
88 Interim Dean Transport & Trades .... Mr. Michael BARROS
27 Dean Communications & Services .... Mr. Russell UYENO
24 Director Educational Media .... Dr. Jon BLUMHARDT
21 Fiscal Officer .... Ms. Myrna PATTERSON
08 Librarian in Charge .... Ms. Irene MESINA
37 Financial Aid Officer .... Ms. Jannine OYAMA
15 Director Personnel Services .... Ms. Sharene MORIWAKI
18 Chief Facilities/Physical Plant .... Mr. Brian FURUTO
35 Director Student Affairs .... Ms. Emily Ann KUKULIES
04 Executive Asst to the Chancellor .... Ms. Billie LUEDER
06 Registrar .... Ms. Nova SUNIGA
09 Director Management Info & Research .... Mr. Steven SHIGEMOTO
36 Dir Student Placement/Counselor .... Ms. Silvan CHUNG
20 Dean University College .... Ms. Marcia ROBERTS-DEUTSCH
07 Director of Admissions .... Ms. Janis DELA CRUZ
10 Chief Business Officer .... Mr. Derek INAFUKU
26 Chief Public Relations Officer .... Ms. Billie LUEDER
28 Director of Diversity .... Ms. Sharene MORIWAKI
29 Director Alumni Relations .... Ms. Billie LUEDER
30 Chief Development .... Ms. Billie LUEDER
38 Director Student Counseling .... Ms. Lara SUGIMOTO
84 Dean of Academic Support .... Mr. Wayne SUNAHARA
96 Director of Purchasing .... Mr. Derek INAFUKU

*University of Hawaii Kauai Community College (H)

3-1901 Kaumualii Highway, Lihue HI 96766-9500
County: Kauai FICE Identification: 001614
Unit ID: 141802
Telephone: (808) 245-8311 Carnegie Class: Assoc/Pub2in4
FAX Number: (808) 245-8220 Calendar System: Semester
URL: kauai.hawaii.edu/
Established: 1964 Annual Undergrad Tuition & Fees (In-State): $3,288
Enrollment: 1,433 Coed
Affiliation or Control: State IRS Status: 501(c)3
Highest Offering: Associate Degree
Program: Occupational; 2-Year Principally Bachelor's Creditable
Accreditation: WJ, ACFEI, ADNUR

02 Chancellor .... Dr. Helen COX
05 Vice Chanc Academic Affairs .... Dr. James DIRE
32 Vice Chanc Student Affairs .... Mr. Earl K. NISHIGUCHI
11 Vice Chanc Administrative Services ..... Mr. Brandon SHIMOKAWA
20 Director Acad Supp/Univ Ctr Dir .... Ms. Ramona KINCAID
51 Director Continuing Educ/Training .... Mr. Bruce GETZEN
08 Librarian .... Mr. Robert KAJIWARA
06 Registrar .... Mr. Leighton ORIDE
18 Chief Facilities/Physical Plant .... Mr. Calvin SHIRAI
21 Associate Business Officer .... Ms. Phyllis VIDINHA

37 Financial Aid Officer .... Ms. Rebecca THOMPSON
22 AA/EEO Coordinator .... Ms. Jo Rae BAPTISTE
35 Counselor .... Mr. John CONSTANTINO
09 Institutional Researcher .... Mr. Jonathan KALK

*University of Hawaii Leeward Community College (A)

96-045 Ala Ike, Pearl City HI 96782-3393
County: Honolulu FICE Identification: 004549
Unit ID: 141811
Telephone: (808) 455-0011 Carnegie Class: Assoc/Pub2in4
FAX Number: (808) 455-0471 Calendar System: Semester
URL: www.leeward.hawaii.edu
Established: 1968 Annual Undergrad Tuition & Fees (In-State): $3,207
Enrollment: 7,960 Coed
Affiliation or Control: State IRS Status: 501(c)3
Highest Offering: Associate Degree
Program: Occupational; 2-Year Principally Bachelor's Creditable
Accreditation: WJ, ACFEI

02 Chancellor .... Mr. Manuel J. CABRAL
05 Vice Chancellor/CAO .... Mr. Michael PECSOK
11 Vice Chancellor Admin Services .... Mr. Mark LANE
32 Dean Student Services .... Mr. Christopher MANASERI
72 Asst Dean Career & Tech Education .... Mr. Ron UMEHIRA
49 Asst Dean Arts & Sciences .... Mr. James GOODMAN
08 Librarian .... Mr. Christopher MATZ
06 Registrar .... Mr. Grant HELGESON
37 Financial Aid Officer .... Ms. Aileen LUM-AKANA
18 Chief Facilities/Physical Plant .... Ms. Sandy MAEDA
09 Dir Policy/Planning & Assessment .... Ms. Della ANDERSON
10 Chief Business Officer .... Ms. Cecilia LUCAS
26 Chief Public Relations Officer .... Ms. Kathleen CABRAL
15 Human Resources/EEO/AA Officer .... Mr. Michael WONG
14 Computer Center Manager .... Ms. Penny UYEHARA
19 Security Supervisor .... Mr. Talbort HOOK
12 Coord Waianae Education Center .... Ms. Laurie LAWRENCE
24 Media Coordinator .... Ms. Leanne CHUN
35 Student Activities Coordinator .... Ms. Lexer CHOU
36 Placement Officer .... Vacant

*University of Hawaii Maui College (B)

310 Kaahumanu Avenue, Kahului HI 96732-1644
County: Maui FICE Identification: 001615
Unit ID: 141839
Telephone: (808) 984-3500 Carnegie Class: Assoc/Pub4
FAX Number: (808) 984-3546 Calendar System: Semester
URL: maui.hawaii.edu
Established: 1931 Annual Undergrad Tuition & Fees (In-State): $1,335
Enrollment: 4,382 Coed
Affiliation or Control: State IRS Status: 501(c)3
Highest Offering: Baccalaureate
Program: Occupational; 2-Year Principally Bachelor's Creditable; Nursing Emphasis
Accreditation: WC, ACFEI, ADNUR, DA, DH

02 Chancellor .... Dr. Clyde SAKAMOTO
05 Vice Chanc Academic Affairs .... Dr. Jonathon MCKEE
32 Interim Vice Chanc of Student Affs .... Ms. Cathy BIO
11 Vice Chanc of Administrative Affs .... Mr. David TAMANAHA
13 Interim Vice Chanc Information Tech .... Dr. Debasis BHATTACHARYA
20 Int Assistant Dean of Instruction .... Mr. David GROOMS
51 Director Continuing Educ/Training .... Ms. Lori TERAGAWACHI
08 Librarian .... Ms. Lisa SEPA
06 Registrar .... Mr. Stephen KAMEDA
12 Director University Center Maui .... Ms. Tamone Karen HANADA
07 Director of Admissions .... Mr. Stephen KAMEDA
09 Director of Institutional Research .... Dr. Jean PEZZOLI
15 Director Personnel Services .... Ms. Debbi BROWN
18 Chief Facilities/Physical Plant .... Mr. Robert BURTON
21 Associate Fiscal Officer .... Ms. Cindy YAMAMOTO
30 Chief Development .... Mr. Ray TSUCHIYAMA
36 Director Student Placement .... Mr. Stephen KAMEDA
37 Acting Dir Student Financial Aid .... Mr. Kilohana MILLER
38 Director Student Counseling .... Mr. Shane PAYBA

*University of Hawaii Windward Community College (C)

45-720 Keaahala Road, Kaneohe HI 96744-3598
County: Honolulu FICE Identification: 011220
Unit ID: 141990
Telephone: (808) 235-7400 Carnegie Class: Assoc/Pub2in4
FAX Number: (808) 247-5362 Calendar System: Semester
URL: www.wcc.hawaii.edu
Established: 1972 Annual Undergrad Tuition & Fees (In-State): $2,464
Enrollment: 2,741 Coed
Affiliation or Control: State IRS Status: 501(c)3
Highest Offering: Associate Degree
Program: Occupational; 2-Year Principally Bachelor's Creditable
Accreditation: WJ

02 Chancellor .... Mr. Doug DYKSTRA
05 Int Vice Chancellor Academic Affs .... Dr. Ellen ISHIDA-BABINEAU
32 Vice Chancellor Student Services .... Ms. Ardis ESHENBERG
11 Vice Chanc Administrative Services .... Mr. Kevin ISHIDA
75 Dir Vocational/Cmty Education .... Mr. Mike MOSER
08 Head Librarian .... Ms. Nancy HEU
06 Registrar .... Ms. Geri IMAI
09 Director of Institutional Research .... Mr. Jeffrey HUNT
37 Director Student Financial Aid .... Mr. Steven CHIGAWA
15 Personnel Officer .... Ms. Karen CHO
26 Marketing/Public Relations Dir .... Ms. Bonnie BEATSON

University of Phoenix Hawaii Campus (D)

745 Fort Street, Suite 2000, Honolulu HI 96813-3800
Telephone: (808) 536-2686 Identification: 770202
Accreditation: &NH, ACBSP

† Main campus is University of Phoenix in Tempe, AZ.

World Medicine Institute (E)

931 University Avenue, Suite 104, Honolulu HI 96826-3266
County: Honolulu FICE Identification: 030725
Unit ID: 141936
Telephone: (808) 947-4788 Carnegie Class: Spec/Health
FAX Number: (808) 373-4341 Calendar System: Semester
URL: www.wmi.edu
Established: 1970 Annual Graduate Tuition & Fees: $10,640
Enrollment: 57 Coed
Affiliation or Control: Independent Non-Profit IRS Status: 501(c)3
Highest Offering: Master's; No Undergraduates
Program: Professional
Accreditation: ACUP

01 President .... Dr. Lillian CHANG
05 Academic Dean .... Dr. Gayle TODOKI

IDAHO

Boise Bible College (F)

8695 W Marigold Street, Boise ID 83714-1220
County: Ada FICE Identification: 022345
Unit ID: 142090
Telephone: (208) 376-7731 Carnegie Class: Spec/Faith
FAX Number: (208) 376-7743 Calendar System: Semester
URL: www.boisebible.edu
Established: 1945 Annual Undergrad Tuition & Fees: $10,540
Enrollment: 197 Coed
Affiliation or Control: Christian Churches And Churches of Christ
IRS Status: 501(c)3
Highest Offering: Baccalaureate
Program: Religious Emphasis
Accreditation: BI

01 President .... Mr. Terry E. STINE
05 Academic Dean .... Mr. Charles FABER
32 Dean of Students .... Mr. Travis JACOB
10 Business Officer .... Ms. Val WELCH
30 Director of Development .... Mr. David DAVOLT
84 Director of Enrollment Services .... Mr. Ross KNUDSEN
07 Director of Admissions .... Mr. Russell GROVE
08 Librarian .... Ms. Amber GROVE
37 Financial Aid Director .... Mrs. Joyce ANDERSON
18 Supt of Building & Grounds .... Mr. Scott OR
04 Assistant to the President .... Mrs. Ricki CARR
40 Director of Bookstore .... Mrs. Debby GRAF
29 Alumni Relations Coordinator .... Dr. James BYERLY

Boise State University (G)

1910 University Drive, Boise ID 83725-1000
County: Ada FICE Identification: 001616
Unit ID: 142115
Telephone: (208) 426-1000 Carnegie Class: Master's L
FAX Number: (208) 426-3765 Calendar System: Semester
URL: www.boisestate.edu
Established: 1932 Annual Undergrad Tuition & Fees (In-State): $6,292
Enrollment: 22,678 Coed
Affiliation or Control: State IRS Status: 501(c)3
Highest Offering: Doctorate
Program: Liberal Arts And General; Teacher Preparatory; Professional; Business Emphasis
Accreditation: NW, ACFEI, ART, BUS, BUSA, CACREP, CAHIIM, COARC, CONST, CS, DMS, ENG, MUS, NUR, RAD, SPAA, SW, TED, THEA

01 President .... Dr. Robert W. KUSTRA
05 Provost/Vice Pres Academic Affairs .... Dr. Martin SCHIMPF
10 Vice President Finan/Administration .... Ms. Stacy PEARSON
32 Vice President Student Affairs .... Dr. Lisa HARRIS
30 Vice Pres University Advancement .... Ms. Laura SIMIC
43 Vice Pres Gen Counsel & Campus Op .... Mr. Kevin SATTERLEE
20 Associate VP for Academic Planning .... Dr. James MUNGER
20 Assoc VP for Undergraduate Studies .... Dr. Sharon MCGUIRE
21 Associate Vice Pres for Finance .... Ms. Jo Ellen DI NUCCI
46 VP Research & Economic Development .... Dr. Mark RUDIN
13 Assoc VP Information Technologies .... Mr. Max DAVIS-JOHNSON
08 Dean of Library Services .... Ms. Tracy BICKNELL-HOLMES
84 Assoc Vice Pres Enrollment Managmt .... Mr. James ANDERSON
29 Executive Director Alumni Affairs .... Vacant
17 Medical Services Director .... Dr. Vincent SERIO
06 Registrar .... Ms. Kristine COLLINS
18 Exec Director Campus Security .... Mr. Jon UDA
40 Director Bookstore .... Mr. Mike REED
24 Director Academic Technologies .... Mr. Dale PIKE
09 Director Institutional Research .... Ms. Shari ELLERTSON
07 Director of Admissions .... Vacant
35 Director Student Affairs .... Ms. Lynn HUMPHREY
26 Assoc VP Communications & Marketing .... Mr. Greg HAHN
41 Director Athletics .... Mr. Mark COYLE
22 Director Affirmative Action/EEO .... Vacant
15 Assoc VP Human Resource Services .... Mr. Pablo COBLENTZ
38 Director Counseling Services .... Ms. Karla WEST
37 Dir Financial Aid & Scholarships .... Ms. Diana FAIRCHILD
96 Director of Purchasing .... Ms. Terri SPINAZZA
51 Dean Extended Studies .... Mr. Mark WHEELER
49 Dean of Arts & Sciences .... Dr. Tony ROARK
83 Dean of Social Science/Public Affs .... Dr. Melissa LAVITT
50 Dean of Business & Economics .... Dr. Pat SHANNON
53 Dean of Education .... Dr. Diane BOOTHE
58 Dean of the Graduate College .... Dr. Jack PELTON
76 Dean of Health Sciences .... Dr. Tim DUNNAGAN
54 Dean College of Engineering .... Dr. Amy MOLL

Brigham Young University-Idaho (H)

Rexburg ID 83460-1650
County: Madison FICE Identification: 001625
Unit ID: 142522
Telephone: (208) 496-1411 Carnegie Class: Bac/Diverse
FAX Number: (208) 496-1103 Calendar System: Semester
URL: www.byui.edu
Established: 1888 Annual Undergrad Tuition & Fees: $3,650
Enrollment: 16,263 Coed
Affiliation or Control: Latter-day Saints IRS Status: 501(c)3
Highest Offering: Baccalaureate
Program: Occupational; Liberal Arts And General
Accreditation: NW, ADNUR, CIDA, EMT, ENG, MAC, MUS, NUR, SW

01 President .... Dr. Kim B. CLARK
05 Academic Vice President .... Dr. Fenton L. BROADHEAD
46 University Resources Vice President ... Mr. Charles N. ANDERSEN
35 Student Svcs & Activities Vice Pres .... Mr. Kevin T. MIYASAKI
30 Advancement Vice President .... Dr. Henry J. EYRING
20 Assoc Academic VP Instruction .... Mr. Kelly T. BURGENER
20 Assoc Academic Vice Pres Curriculum .... Dr. Edwin A. SEXTON
20 Assoc Acad VP Support Services .... Dr. Richard K. PAGE
20 Assoc Acad VP Student Connections .... Dr. Ralph M. KERN
32 Dean of Students .... Mr. Kip B. HARRIS
32 Student Well Being Mng Director .... Mr. Wynn N. HILL
51 Continuing Education Director .... Mr. Chad P. PRICE
13 Interim Chief Technology Officer .... Dr. Barbara A. WHITE
09 Inst Research & Assessment Director ....Dr. Scott J. BERGSTROM
06 Student Records & Registration .... Mr. Kyle R. MARTIN
37 Student Fin Aid/Scholarship Dir .... Mr. Aaron D. SANNS
08 University Librarian .... Vacant
21 Univ Operations Managing Director .... Mr. Wayne N. CLARK
15 Human Resources Director .... Mr. Kevin L. PRICE
23 Student Health Services Director .... Mr. Shaun ORR
38 Student Counseling Center Director .... Mr. Reed J. STODDARD
19 University Security & Safety .... Mr. Garth M. GUNDERSON
07 Admissions Director .... Mr. Tyler R. WILLIAMS
29 Alumni Director .... Mr. Steven J. DAVIS
35 Student Activities Mng Director .... Mr. Derek R. FAY
26 University Relations Mng Director .... Mr. Merv R. BROWN
30 Philanthropies Director .... Mr. Christopher W. MOORE
44 Annual Giving Director .... Mr. D. Alton HANSEN
39 Housing & Student Living Director .... Dr. Troy J. DOUGHERTY
43 Legal Counsel .... Mr. Michael R. ORME
21 Financial Services Mng Director .... Mr. Russel K. BENEDICT
88 Academic Discovery Center Director .... Mrs. Amy R. LABAUGH
96 Purchasing & Travel Director .... Mr. Darin N. LEE
84 Enrollment Svcs Managing Director .... Mr. Rob J. GARRETT
40 University Store Manager .... Mr. Doug R. MASON
104 International Services Manager .... Mr. Mike R. OSWALD
04 Asst to Pres Strategy & Planning .... Mrs. Betty A. OLDHAM

Broadview University (I)

2750 East Gala Court, Meridian ID 83642
Telephone: (208) 577-2900 Identification: 770712
Accreditation: ACICS

† Main campus is Broadview University in West Jordan, UT.

Brown Mackie College-Boise (J)

9050 West Overland Road, Ste. 101, Boise ID 83709
Telephone: (208) 321-8800 Identification: 666780
Accreditation: ACICS, OTA, SURGT, SURTEC

† Main campus is The Art Institute of Phoenix in Phoenix, AZ.

Carrington College - Boise (K)

1122 N Liberty Street, Boise ID 83704-8742
County: Ada FICE Identification: 022180
Unit ID: 142054
Telephone: (208) 377-8080 Carnegie Class: Assoc/PrivFP
FAX Number: (208) 322-7658 Calendar System: Semester
URL: www.carrington.edu
Established: 1980 Annual Undergrad Tuition & Fees: $53,975
Enrollment: 508 Coed
Affiliation or Control: Proprietary IRS Status: Proprietary
Highest Offering: Associate Degree
Program: Occupational; 2-Year Principally Bachelor's Creditable

Accreditation: ACICS, DA, DH, MAAB, PNUR, PTAA

01 Executive Director .... Ms. Danielle HORRAS
05 Dean of Academic Affairs .... Ms. Julia BENNETT
36 Director Career Services .... Ms. Valerie DICKERSON

The College of Idaho (A)

2112 Cleveland Boulevard, Caldwell ID 83605-9990
County: Canyon FICE Identification: 001617
Unit ID: 142294
Telephone: (208) 459-5011 Carnegie Class: Bac/A&S
FAX Number: (208) 454-2077 Calendar System: Other
URL: www.collegeofidaho.edu
Established: 1891 Annual Undergrad Tuition & Fees: $24,055
Enrollment: 1,059 Coed
Affiliation or Control: Independent Non-Profit IRS Status: 501(c)3
Highest Offering: Master's
Program: Liberal Arts And General; Teacher Preparatory
Accreditation: NW

01 President .... Dr. Marvin HENBERG
05 Vice President Academic Affairs .... Dr. John OTTENHOFF
10 Vice Pres Finance/Administration .... Ms. Petra CARVER
32 Vice President Student Affairs .... Mr. Paul BENNION
30 Vice President for Advancement .... Mr. Michael VANDERVELDEN
84 Dean of Enrollment .... Mr. Brian BAVA
20 Associate Dean .... Dr. Kathy SEIBOLD
06 Registrar .... Ms. Susan HINES
41 Director of Athletics .... Mr. Marty HOLLY
26 Dir of Marketing & Communications .... Mr. Dustin WUNDERLICH
29 Director of Alumni .... Ms. Sally SKINNER
44 Director of Boone Fund .... Ms. Tara WENSEL
08 Director of Library .... Ms. Christine SCHUTZ
18 Director of Facilities .... Mr. Kyle ABRAHAMSON
21 Controller .... Ms. Deanna ROSS
37 Director of Financial Services .... Mrs. Juanitta PEARSON
15 Human Resources Director .... Ms. Bev ROBINSON
36 Director Student Placement .... Ms. Dora GALLEGOS
85 Director of International Education .... Dr. Ellen BATT
92 Director of Honors Program .... Dr. Sue SCHAPER
89 Director of Freshman Studies .... Dr. Lynn WEBSTER
39 Director of Residential Life .... Ms. Jen NELSON
93 Director of Multicultural Affairs .... Mr. Arnold HERNANDEZ
42 Campus Minister/Asc Dean Students .... Dr. Phil ROGERS
19 Director of Campus Safety .... Mr. Allan LAIRD
96 Director of Purchasing .... Ms. Peta CARVER
90 Director of Network Services .... Mr. Zane HOWE
09 Director Institutional Research .... Dr. Kristina MAZURAK
30 Director Development .... Mr. Jack CAFFERTY
40 Bookstore Manager .... Ms. Susan HUNSBERGER
38 Counselor .... Ms. Marilyn SIMMONDS

College of Southern Idaho (B)

PO Box 1238, 315 Falls Avenue,
Twin Falls ID 83303-1238
County: Twin Falls FICE Identification: 001619
Unit ID: 142559
Telephone: (208) 733-9554 Carnegie Class: Assoc/Pub-R-L
FAX Number: (208) 736-3015 Calendar System: Semester
URL: www.csi.edu
Established: 1964 Annual Undergrad Tuition & Fees (In-District): $2,640
Enrollment: 9,086 Coed
Affiliation or Control: Local IRS Status: 501(c)3
Highest Offering: Associate Degree
Program: Occupational; 2-Year Principally Bachelor's Creditable
Accreditation: NW, ADNUR, DH, EMT, MAC, RAD, SURGA, SURGT

01 Interim President .... Mr. Curtis H. EATON
05 Exec VP/Chief Academic Officer .... Dr. D. Jeff FOX
11 Vice President of Administration .... Mr. J. Mike MASON
32 VP of Student Svc/Plng & Grant Dev .... Dr. Edit SZANTO
102 Executive Director Foundation .... Ms. Debra J. WILSON
20 Instructional Dean .... Dr. John S. MILLER
20 Instructional Dean .... Dr. Cindy R. BOND
20 Instructional Dean .... Mr. Terry L. PATTERSON
76 Dean Health Sci/Human Svcs/Biology .... Dr. Mark A. SUGDEN
21 Dean of Finance .... Mr. Jeff M. HARMON
09 Dean of Information Tech Svcs .... Dr. Ken B. CAMPBELL
35 Dean of Students .... Mr. J. Scott A. SCHOLES
06 Director of Admissions & Records .... Ms. Gail SCHULL
38 Director of Advising .... Mr. Cesar PEREZ GARCIA
37 Director of Student Financial Aid .... Ms. Jennifer J. ZIMMERS
15 Director Human Resources .... Mr. Monty J. ARROSSA
18 Director Physical Plant .... Mr. Randy G. DILL
08 Director Library .... Ms. Teri L. FATTIG
26 Public Information Director .... Mr. Doug L. MAUGHAN
14 Director Data Services .... Mr. Jay N. SNEDDON
19 Director Security & Safety .... Mr. Jim ELLINGTON
41 Athletic Director .... Mr. Joel C. BATE
27 Sports Information Director .... Ms. Karen D. BAUMERT
85 Director of Foreign Students .... Ms. Samra CULUM
92 Coordinator Honors Program .... Ms. Kimberly PRESTWICH
04 Admin Assistant to the President .... Ms. Kathy S. DEAHL

College of Western Idaho (C)

P.O. Box 3010, Nampa ID 83653
County: Canyon FICE Identification: 042118
Unit ID: 455114
Telephone: (208) 562-3000 Carnegie Class: Assoc/Pub-R-M
FAX Number: (888) 562-3216 Calendar System: Semester
URL: cwidaho.cc
Established: 2007 Annual Undergrad Tuition & Fees (In-District): $3,264
Enrollment: 9,107 Coed
Affiliation or Control: Local IRS Status: 501(c)3
Highest Offering: Associate Degree
Program: Occupational; 2-Year Principally Bachelor's Creditable
Accreditation: @NW, ADNUR, DA, SURGT

01 President .... Dr. Bert GLANDON
10 VP Finance & Administration .... Ms. Cheryl WRIGHT
05 VP of Instruction/Student Services .... Mr. David SHELLBERG
06 Registrar .... Ms. Connie BLACK

Eastern Idaho Technical College (D)

1600 S 25th E, Idaho Falls ID 83404-5788
County: Bonneville FICE Identification: 011133
Unit ID: 142179
Telephone: (208) 524-3000 Carnegie Class: Assoc/Pub-R-S
FAX Number: (208) 524-3007 Calendar System: Semester
URL: www.eitc.edu/
Established: 1969 Annual Undergrad Tuition & Fees (In-State): $2,773
Enrollment: 709 Coed
Affiliation or Control: State IRS Status: 501(c)3
Highest Offering: Associate Degree
Program: Occupational; 2-Year Principally Bachelor's Creditable; Technical Emphasis
Accreditation: NW, MAC, SURGT

01 President .... Mr. Steve K. ALBISTON
10 Vice President of Finance and Admin .... Mr. James STRATTON
05 VP of Instruction & Student Affairs .... Dr. Sharee ANDERSON
06 Registrar .... Mrs. Suzanne FELT
10 Controller .... Mr. Don E. BOURNE
103 Mgr Workforce Trng/Cmty Education . Mr. Kenneth W. ERICKSON
08 Librarian .... Mrs. Suzy RICKS
37 Financial Aid Director .... Mrs. Shayna SHARP
04 President Administrative Assistant .... Mrs. Jacque LARSEN
26 Director of College Relations .... Mr. Todd WIGHTMAN
102 Foundation Director .... Mrs. Michelle P. ZIEL
07 Director of Admissions/Placement ..... Mrs. Rae Lynn PATTERSON
40 Bookstore Operator .... Mr. Devon H. GLOVER
50 Business/Office/Technology Div Mgr .... Mr. Christian J. GODFREY
97 General Education Division Manager .... Mrs. Peggy L. NELSON
76 Health Care Technology Div Manager .... Dr. Lynn DURTSCHI
88 Trades/Industry Division Manager .... Mr. Kent E. BERGGREN
88 Adult Basic Education Div Manager .... Mrs. Melody CLEGG
09 Director of Institutional Research .... Mrs. Marina MEIER
15 Director Human Resources .... Mrs. Isela GUTIERREZ
18 Chief Facilities/Physical Plant .... Mr. William C. BRYANT
29 Director Alumni Relations .... Mrs. Michelle ZIEL

Idaho State University (E)

921 S 8th, Pocatello ID 83209-0009
County: Bannock FICE Identification: 001620
Unit ID: 142276
Telephone: (208) 282-0211 Carnegie Class: RU/H
FAX Number: (208) 282-4000 Calendar System: Semester
URL: www.isu.edu
Established: 1901 Annual Undergrad Tuition & Fees (In-State): $6,344
Enrollment: 13,852 Coed
Affiliation or Control: State IRS Status: 501(c)3
Highest Offering: Doctorate
Program: Occupational; Liberal Arts And General; Teacher Preparatory; Professional
Accreditation: NW, ACFEI, ADNUR, ARCPA, AUD, BUS, BUSA, CACREP, CAHIIM, CLPSY, COARC, CS, DENT, DH, DIETD, DIETI, EMT, ENG, ENGR, ENGT, MAC, MT, MUS, NAIT, NURSE, OT, PH, PHAR, PTA, PTAA, RAD, SP, SW, TED, THEA

01 President .... Dr. Arthur C. VAILAS
05 ProvostVP for Acad Affairs .... Dr. Laura WOODWORTH-NEY
10 Vice President for Finance & Admin .... Mr. James A. FLETCHER
30 Vice Pres University Advancement .... Dr. Kent M. TINGEY
32 Vice Pres of Student Affairs .... Dr. Patricia TERRELL
46 VP for Research & Econ Dev .... Dr. Howard GRIMES
43 University Legal Counsel .... Mr. David ALEXANDER
41 Athletic Director .... Mr. Jeff TINGEY
20 AVP/Exec Dean Div Health Sciences .... Dr. Linda HATZENBUEHLER
20 AVP for Academic Affairs .... Vacant
20 AVP for Academic Affairs .... Vacant
30 Interim AVP for Development .... Mr. Scott TURNER
18 AVP for Facilities Services .... Mr. Phillip MOESSNER
58 Dean of Graduate School .... Dr. Cornelis VAN DER SCHYF
54 Interim Dean College Science & Eng .... Dr. Richard BREY
67 Dean College of Pharmacy .... Dr. Paul S. CADY
50 Dean College of Business .... Dr. Thomas OTTAWAY
49 Dean College of Arts & Letters .... Dr. Kandi TURLEY-AMES
53 Dean College of Education .... Dr. Deborah L. HEDEEN
75 Dean College of Technology .... Dr. Scott RASMUSSEN
12 Dean of Academic Pgm ISU-Meridian .... Dr. Bessie KATSILOMETES
12 Dean of Academic Pgm ISU-Id Falls .... Dr. Lyle W. CASTLE
08 University Librarian & Dean .... Ms. Sandra SHOPSHIRE
06 Registrar & Dir of Undergrad Admiss .... Ms. Laura MCKENZIE
14 Chief Information Officer .... Mr. Randy GAINES
29 Director Alumni Relations .... Ms. K.C FELT
09 Director Institutional Research .... Mr. Vince MILLER
37 Director Student Financial Aid .... Mr. Kent D. LARSON
15 Director Human Resources .... Mr. Brian SAGENDORF
23 Director Student Health Center .... Dr. Ronald SOLBRIG
22 Dir EEO/Affirm Action & Diversity .... Ms. Stacey GIBSON
19 Director Public Safety .... Mr. Stephen A. CHATTERTON
26 Director Marketing & Communication .... Mr. Mark LEVINE
86 Director Government Relations .... Mr. Kent KUNZ
88 Director Events Management .... Mr. George CASPER
35 Director of Student Life .... Dr. Jane COE-SMITH
38 Director of Counseling & Testing .... Dr. Don PAULSON
85 Director of International Programs .... Ms. Maria FLETCHER

ITT Technical Institute (F)

12302 W Explorer Drive, Boise ID 83713-1529
Telephone: (208) 322-8844 FICE Identification: 004553
Accreditation: ACICS

† Main campus is ITT Technical Institute in Indianapolis, IN.

Lewis-Clark State College (G)

500 8th Avenue, Lewiston ID 83501-2698
County: Nez Perce FICE Identification: 001621
Unit ID: 142328
Telephone: (208) 792-5272 Carnegie Class: Bac/Diverse
FAX Number: (208) 792-2831 Calendar System: Semester
URL: www.lcsc.edu
Established: 1893 Annual Undergrad Tuition & Fees (In-State): $5,784
Enrollment: 4,525 Coed
Affiliation or Control: State IRS Status: 501(c)3
Highest Offering: Baccalaureate
Program: Occupational; 2-Year Principally Bachelor's Creditable; Liberal Arts And General; Teacher Preparatory; Professional; Nursing Emphasis
Accreditation: NW, IACBE, MAC, NURSE, RAD, SW, TED

01 President .... Dr. J. Anthony FERNANDEZ
05 Interim Provost/VP Academic Affairs .... Dr. Lori STINSON
10 VP Finance and Administration .... Mr. Chet HERBST
75 Dean Professional/Technical Pgms .... Dr. Robert LOHRMEYER
51 Dean Community Programs .... Ms. Kathy MARTIN
20 Dean Academic Programs .... Ms. Mary FLORES
32 Vice President Student Affairs .... Dr. Andrew HANSON
08 Director of Library Services .... Ms. Susan NIEWENHOUS
103 Director of Workforce Training .... Dr. Linda STRICKLIN
07 Director of Admissions/Registrar .... Ms. Nikol LUTHER
09 Dir Planning/Research/Assessment .... Mr. Howard ERDMAN
13 Chief Technology Officer .... Mr. Allen SCHMOOCK
41 Athletic Director .... Mr. Gary PICONE
15 Director of Human Resources .... Ms. Vikki SWIFT
27 Director of College Communications .... Mr. Greg MEYER
29 Director of Alumni Relations .... Ms. Renee OLSEN
37 Director of Student Financial Aid .... Ms. Laura HUGHES
30 Director of College Advancement .... Ms. Mary HASENOEHRL
18 Director of Physical Plant .... Mr. Matt GRAVES
36 Director Career & Advising Services .... Ms. Debra LYBYER
96 Director of Purchasing .... Ms. Sheila KOM

New Saint Andrews College (H)

PO Box 9025, Moscow ID 83843-1525
County: Latah Identification: 666166
Unit ID: 440396
Telephone: (208) 882-1566 Carnegie Class: Bac/A&S
FAX Number: (208) 882-4293 Calendar System: Other
URL: www.nsa.edu
Established: 1994 Annual Undergrad Tuition & Fees: $11,200
Enrollment: 165 Coed
Affiliation or Control: Independent Non-Profit IRS Status: 501(c)3
Highest Offering: Master's
Program: Liberal Arts And General; Religious Emphasis
Accreditation: TRACS

01 President .... Dr. Roy A. ATWOOD
03 Executive Vice President .... Mr. Bob HIERONYMUS
58 Dean of Graduate Studies .... Dr. Jonathan MCINTOSH
10 Dir Financial & Facility Services .... Mr. Eric BURNETT
08 Head Librarian .... Mr. Ed IVERSON
06 Registrar .... Mrs. Beverlee ATWOOD
20 Dean of Undergraduate Studies .... Mr. Ben MERKLE
07 Director Admissions .... Mrs. Brenda SCHLECT
40 Bookstore Manager .... Mr. Eric BURNETT
09 Dir Institutional Effectiveness .... Mr. Ed IVERSON
84 Director Student Recruitment .... Mr. John SAWYER

North Idaho College (I)

1000 W Garden Avenue, Coeur d'Alene ID 83814-2199
County: Kootenai FICE Identification: 001623
Unit ID: 142443
Telephone: (208) 769-3300 Carnegie Class: Assoc/Pub-R-M
FAX Number: (208) 765-2761 Calendar System: Semester
URL: www.nic.edu
Established: 1933 Annual Undergrad Tuition & Fees (In-District): $2,974
Enrollment: 6,542 Coed
Affiliation or Control: Local IRS Status: 501(c)3
Highest Offering: Associate Degree
Program: Occupational; 2-Year Principally Bachelor's Creditable
Accreditation: NW, ADNUR, MAC, RAD

01 President .... Dr. Joe H. DUNLAP
05 Vice President for Instruction .... Dr. Lita BURNS
10 Vice President for Resource Mgmt .... Mr. Ronald DORN
32 Vice President for Student Services .... Mr. Graydon STANLEY

26 VP for Community Relations & Mktg .... Mr. Mark BROWNING
103 Dean of Prof/Tech/Workforce Educ .... Mr. Mike MIRES
97 Dean of General Studies .... Vacant
66 Dean of Nursing & Health Prof .... Ms. Christy DOYLE
06 Registrar .... Ms. Tami HAFT
09 Director of Inst Effectiveness .... Ms. Ann LEWIS
08 Librarian .... Vacant
13 Director of Information Technology .... Mr. Stephen A. RUPPEL
37 Director of Financial Aid .... Mr. Joseph BEKKEN
07 Director of Admissions .... Ms. Tami HAFT
15 Executive Dir of Human Resources .... Ms. Laura HILL
18 Director of Facilities .... Mr. Mike HALPERN
26 Director of Comm & Marketing .... Ms. Stacy HUDSON
30 Development Director .... Ms. Rayelle ANDERSON
35 Director Student Development .... Mr. Alex HARRIS
36 Dir of Academic & Support Services .... Ms. Sally HINDERS
21 Controller .... Ms. Sarah GARCIA
72 Technology Coordinator .... Mr. Andy FINNEY
29 Alumni Relations Coordinator .... Ms. Katie ELWELL

Northwest Nazarene University (A)

623 S. University Blvd., Nampa ID 83686-5897
County: Canyon — FICE Identification: 001624
Unit ID: 142461
Telephone: (208) 467-8011 — Carnegie Class: Master's L
FAX Number: (208) 467-8099 — Calendar System: Semester
URL: www.nnu.edu
Established: 1913 — Annual Undergrad Tuition & Fees: $30,150
Enrollment: 2,052 — Coed
Affiliation or Control: Church Of The Nazarene — IRS Status: 501(c)3
Highest Offering: Doctorate
Program: Liberal Arts And General; Teacher Preparatory; Professional
Accreditation: NW, ACBSP, CACREP, MUS, NURSE, SW, TED

01 President .... Dr. David C. ALEXANDER
05 Vice Pres Academic Affairs/Dean .... Dr. Burton J. WEBB
30 Vice Pres University Advancement .... Dr. Joel K. PEARSALL
10 Vice Pres Financial Affairs .... Mr. David S. TARRANT
84 Vice Pres Enrollment & Marketing .... Mrs. Stacey L. BERGGREN
32 Vice President Student Development .... Dr. Carey W. COOK
88 Vice Pres Spiritual & Ldrshp Dev .... Dr. Fred C. FULLERTON
06 Registrar .... Mrs. Nancy A. AYERS
08 Director of the Library .... Dr. Sharon I. BULL
29 Director of Alumni Relations .... Mr. Darl L. BRUNER
51 Dir Center for Professional Devel .... Mr. Dave R. COVINGTON
42 Dean of the Chapel .... Rev. M. Gene SCHANDORFF
42 Director of Campus Ministry .... Ms. Julene M. TEGERSTRAND
40 Bookstore Manager .... Ms. Gail D. WALKER
39 Director of Residential Life .... Mrs. Karen L. PEARSON
38 Director of Wellness Center .... Mrs. Terri BLACKBURN
07 Director of Admissions .... Mr. Mike B. MARSTON
21 Controller .... Mrs. Shirley J. HAIDLE
26 Director of Marketing & Media .... Mrs. Hollie M. LINDNER
35 Director of Campus Life .... Mr. Tim R. MILBURN
36 Director of Career Center .... Ms. Amanda F. MARBLE
13 Exec Director of Info Technology .... Mr. Sal SIMILI
24 Director of Tech & Media Resources .... Mr. Frank E. ESTELL
37 Director of Financial Aid .... Mr. David KLAFFKE
93 Director of Multicultural Affairs .... Rev. Jamie COLEMAN
16 Director of Human Resources .... Ms. Sherry L. HARTMAN
41 Athletic Director .... Mr. Bill RAPP
88 Network Systems Administrator .... Vacant
91 Dir of Administrative Computing .... Mr. Brian C. STILLMAN
18 Chief Facilities/Physical Plant .... Mr. C. Richard VAN SCHYNDEL

Stevens-Henager College (B)

901 Pier View Drive, Suite 105, Idaho Falls ID 83404
Telephone: (205) 522-0887 — Identification: 770573
Accreditation: ACCSC

† Main campus is Stevens-Henager College in Ogden, UT.

Stevens-Henager College-Boise (C)

1444 S. Entertainment Avenue, Boise ID 83709
Telephone: (208) 383-4540 — Identification: 666329
Accreditation: ACCSC, COARC

† Main campus is Stevens-Henager College in Ogden, UT.

University of Idaho (D)

Campus Drive, PO Box 443151, Moscow ID 83844-3151
County: Latah — FICE Identification: 001626
Unit ID: 142285
Telephone: (208) 885-6111 — Carnegie Class: RU/H
FAX Number: (208) 885-5540 — Calendar System: Semester
URL: www.uidaho.edu
Established: 1889 — Annual Undergrad Tuition & Fees (In-State): $6,524
Enrollment: 12,420 — Coed
Affiliation or Control: State — IRS Status: 501(c)3
Highest Offering: Doctorate
Program: Liberal Arts And General; Teacher Preparatory; Professional
Accreditation: NW, ART, BUS, BUSA, CEA, CIDA, CORE, CS, DIETC, ENG, FOR, IPSY, LAW, LSAR, MUS, NRPA, TED

01 Interim President .... Dr. Donald L. BURNETT
05 Interim Provost & Executive VP .... Dr. Katherine AIKEN
10 Vice Pres Finance & Administration .... Mr. Ron SMITH
30 Vice Pres University Advancement .... Mr. Christopher D. MURRAY
46 Vice President Research .... Dr. John MCIVER
12 Assoc Vice Pres for Northern Idaho .... Dr. Charles BUCK
12 Assoc VP and CEO Boise Center .... Dr. Trudy J. ANDERSON
12 Assoc Vice Pres Idaho Falls Center .... Dr. Robert W. SMITH
27 Assoc Vice Pres Mktg/Strat Comm .... Vacant
18 Assistant Vice President Facilities .... Mr. Brian D. JOHNSON
21 Asst VP Aux Svcs/Ad Ops/Cap Plng .... Mr. Tyrone W. BROOKS
84 Asst Vice Pres Enrollmnt Managemnt .... Mr. Steve NEIHEISEL
28 Asst to Pres Diversity/Equity/Cmty .... Vacant
19 Manager Parking & Trans Services .... Mr. Carl ROOT
20 Vice Provost Academic Affairs .... Dr. Jeanne M. CHRISTIANSEN
35 Vice Provost Student Affairs .... Dr. Bruce M. PITMAN
08 Dean Library Services .... Ms. Lynn N. BAIRD
15 Associate VP Human Resources .... Mr. Greg WALTERS
32 Dean of Students .... Dr. Bruce M. PITMAN
22 Dir Human Rights/Access/Inclusion .... Ms. Carmen A. SUAREZ
06 Registrar .... Ms. Nancy A. KROGH
07 Director of Admissions .... Mr. Cezar MESQUITA
09 Director Inst Research & Assessment .... Dr. Archie A. GEORGE
24 Director Information Tech Services .... Mr. Daniel EWART
29 Director Alumni Relations .... Mr. Steven C. JOHNSON
36 Dir Career & Professional Planning .... Ms. Suzanne K L. BILLINGTON
37 Director Student Financial Aid .... Dr. Daniel D. DAVENPORT
38 Director Counseling & Testing Ctr .... Dr. Joan PULAKOS
39 Director University Residences .... Mr. Ray GASSER
41 Athletic Director .... Dr. Robert SPEAR
42 Director Campus Christian Center .... Ms. Sharon A. KEHOE
43 General University Counsel .... Mr. Kent E. NELSON
44 Director Annual Giving .... Ms. Mandy HANOUSEK
87 Director Summer & Dual Enrol Prog .... Ms. Nancy KROGH
92 Director Honors Program .... Dr. Alton CAMPBELL
93 Int Director Multicultural Affairs .... Mr. Eddy A. RUIZ
94 Director Women's Center .... Ms. Lysa SALSBURY
40 Director Bookstore .... Mr. John Anthony BALES
96 Manager Purchasing .... Ms. Julia MCILROY
47 Dean College of Agri/Life Sciences .... Dr. John FOLTZ
48 Dean College of Art & Architecture .... Mr. Mark E. HOVERSTEN
49 Dean Col of Letters/Arts Soc Sci .... Dr. Katherine G. AIKEN
50 Dean College of Business & Econ .... Dr. Mario S. REYES
53 Dean College of Education .... Dr. Corinne MANTLE-BROMLEY
54 Dean College of Engineering .... Dr. Larry STAUFFER
58 Dean Graduate Studies .... Dr. Jie CHEN
61 Interim Dean College of Law .... Mr. Michael SATZ
65 Dean College of Natural Resources .... Dr. Kurt PREGITZER
81 Interim Dean College of Science .... Dr. Paul JOYCE

University of Phoenix Idaho Campus (E)

1420 South Tech Lane, Meridian ID 83642-5114
Telephone: (208) 898-2000 — Identification: 770204
Accreditation: &NH, ACBSP

† Main campus is University of Phoenix in Tempe, AZ.

ILLINOIS

Adler School of Professional Psychology (F)

17 North Dearborn, Chicago IL 60602
County: Cook — FICE Identification: 020681
Unit ID: 142832
Telephone: (312) 662-4000 — Carnegie Class: Spec/Health
FAX Number: (312) 662-4099 — Calendar System: Semester
URL: www.adler.edu
Established: 1952 — Annual Graduate Tuition & Fees: $36,000
Enrollment: 1,168 — Coed
Affiliation or Control: Independent Non-Profit — IRS Status: 501(c)3
Highest Offering: Doctorate; No Undergraduates
Program: Professional
Accreditation: NH, CLPSY, IPSY

01 President .... Dr. Raymond E. CROSSMAN
101 Board Secy/Dir Ofc of the Pres .... Ms. Mitzi NORTON
11 Vice President Administration .... Mrs. Jo Beth CUP
05 Vice President Academic Affairs .... Dr. Wendy PASZKIEWICZ
30 VP for Institutional Advancement .... Mr. Anthony CHIMERA
28 VP Leadership in Social Justice .... Dr. Lynn TODMAN
07 Associate Vice President Admissions .... Mr. Craig HINES
07 Director of Admissions .... Ms. Michelle BRICE
26 Assoce Vice President Marketing .... Mr. Mark BRANSON
06 Registrar .... Ms. Sheba JONES
32 Assoc Vice President Student Affair .... Mr. Greg MACVARISH
35 Asst Director Student Affairs .... Ms. Jennifer POPE
37 Director Student Financial Aid .... Ms. Terri ESCH
20 AVP Academic Affairs/Cmty Engagemt .... Dr. Kevin OSTEN
88 Director MA Counseling Training .... Dr. Paul FITZGERALD
88 Director of Doctoral Training .... Dr. Eunice KIM
24 Director Learning & Educ Technology .... Mr. Zoaib MIRZA
10 Vice President Finance & IT .... Mr. Jeffrey GREEN
18 Director of Facilities .... Ms. Hope POPA
21 Controller .... Ms. Eve HERDEA
13 Associate VP Technology .... Mr. Paul COLLINS
16 Assoc VP Human Resources .... Ms. Elinor HITE
23 Director Adler Community Health Svc .... Dr. Dan BARNES
08 Director Library .... Ms. Kerry COCHRANE
09 Director of Institutional Research .... Mr. Don HUFFMAN
12 Dean Vancouver Campus .... Dr. Larry AXELROD
102 Director Corp & Foundation Rels .... Vacant
36 Director Career Services .... Vacant
28 Director IPSSJ .... Dr. Elena QUINTANA
29 Director Alumni Relations .... Vacant
31 Director of Community Engagement .... Dr. Kevin L. JAMES

Ambria College of Nursing (G)

5210 Trillium Blvd, Hoffman Estates IL 60192
County: Cook — FICE Identification: 041247
Unit ID: 457527
Telephone: (847) 397-0300 — Carnegie Class: Not Classified
FAX Number: (847) 397-0313 — Calendar System: Other
URL: www.ambria.edu
Established: 2006 — Annual Undergrad Tuition & Fees: $25,400
Enrollment: 397 — Coed
Affiliation or Control: Proprietary — IRS Status: Proprietary
Highest Offering: Associate Degree
Program: Occupational; Nursing Emphasis
Accreditation: ACICS

01 President .... Jon OLIVEROS

American Academy of Art (H)

332 S Michigan Avenue, Chicago IL 60604-4302
County: Cook — FICE Identification: 001628
Unit ID: 142887
Telephone: (312) 461-0600 — Carnegie Class: Spec/Arts
FAX Number: (312) 294-9570 — Calendar System: Semester
URL: www.aaart.edu
Established: 1923 — Annual Undergrad Tuition & Fees: $28,600
Enrollment: 432 — Coed
Affiliation or Control: Proprietary — IRS Status: Proprietary
Highest Offering: Baccalaureate
Program: Professional; Fine Arts Emphasis
Accreditation: NH, ACCSC

01 Director .... Mr. Richard H. OTTO
05 Academic Dean .... Mr. Duncan WEBB
06 Registrar .... Ms. Marcia R. THOMAS
36 Career Services Coordinator .... Ms. Lindsay SANDBOTHE
37 Financial Aid Director .... Ms. Ione FITZGERALD
08 Faculty Librarian .... Ms. Lindsay HARMON
88 Cultural Coordinator .... Ms. Lou Ann BURKHARDT
07 Director of Admissions .... Mr. Stuart ROSENBLOOM

American InterContinental University (I)

231 North Martingale Rd, 6th Fl, Schaumburg IL 60173
County: Cook — FICE Identification: 021136
Unit ID: 445027
Telephone: (877) 701-3800 — Carnegie Class: Master's L
FAX Number: N/A — Calendar System: Quarter
URL: www.aiuonline.edu
Established: 1970 — Annual Undergrad Tuition & Fees: N/A
Enrollment: 16,538 — Coed
Affiliation or Control: Proprietary — IRS Status: Proprietary
Highest Offering: Master's
Program: 2-Year Principally Bachelor's Creditable; Professional
Accreditation: NH, ACBSP, @TEAC

01 President & Chancellor .... Dr. George P. MILLER
05 Provost/Chief Academic Officer .... Dr. Gregory WASHINGTON
32 Vice President Student Affairs .... Ms. Betsy BALACHANDRAN

Argosy University, Chicago (J)

225 North Michigan Ave., Suite 1300, Chicago IL 60601
Telephone: (312) 777-7600 — Identification: 666736
Accreditation: &WC, CACREP, CLPSY

† Main campus is Argosy University, Orange County in Orange, CA.

Argosy University, Schaumburg (K)

999 N. Plaza Drive, Suite 111, Schaumburg IL 60173-5403
Telephone: (847) 969-4900 — Identification: 666789
Accreditation: &WC, CACREP, CLPSY

† Main campus is Argosy University, Orange County in Orange, CA.

Augustana College (L)

639-38th Street, Rock Island IL 61201-2296
County: Rock Island — FICE Identification: 001633
Unit ID: 143084
Telephone: (309) 794-7000 — Carnegie Class: Bac/A&S
FAX Number: (309) 794-7422 — Calendar System: Trimester
URL: www.augustana.edu
Established: 1860 — Annual Undergrad Tuition & Fees: $35,835
Enrollment: 2,551 — Coed
Affiliation or Control: Evangelical Lutheran Church In America
IRS Status: 501(c)3
Highest Offering: Baccalaureate
Program: Liberal Arts And General; Teacher Preparatory
Accreditation: NH, MUS, TED

01 President .... Mr. Steven C. BAHLS
05 Dean of College .... Dr. Pareena G. LAWRENCE
10 Vice Pres Business & Finance .... Mr. David ENGLISH
30 Vice President Advancement .... Ms. Lynn E. JACKSON

32 Vice Pres/Dean of Student Services ...... Dr. Evelyn S. CAMPBELL
84 VP Enrollment/Communication/Plng ....Mr. W. Kent BARNDS
20 Associate Dean of the College ....Dr. Margaret E. FARRAR
25 Director Assessments/Grants Officer ....Vacant
42 Chaplain ....Rev. Richard W. PRIGGIE
06 College Registrar ....Ms. Liesl A. FOWLER
14 Director of ITS ....Mr. Chris VAUGHAN
08 Director of the Library ....Ms. Carla B. TRACY
26 Director of Public Relations ....Ms. Keri RURSCH
36 Director of Career Development ....Ms. Johnna ADAM
29 Director Alumni/Parent Relations ....Ms. Kelly NOACK
37 Director of Student Financial Aid ....Ms. Susan STANDLEY
38 Director Student Counseling ....Mr. Michael W. TENDALL
09 Director of Institutional Research ....Mr. Mark SALISBURY
41 Director of Athletics ....Mr. Mike ZAPOLSKI
15 Director Human Resources ....Mrs. Laura C. FORD
18 Director Facilities Services ....Mr. Dennis M. HITTLE
07 Director of Admissions/Recruitment ....Ms. Meghan M. COOLEY
28 Director of Diversity ....Mr. Greg AGUILAR
96 Director of Purchasing ....Mr. Tom SCHAUBROECK

Aurora University (A)

347 S Gladstone Avenue, Aurora IL 60506-4892
County: Kane FICE Identification: 001634
Unit ID: 143118
Telephone: (630) 892-6431 Carnegie Class: Master's L
FAX Number: (630) 844-5463 Calendar System: Semester
URL: www.aurora.edu
Established: 1893 Annual Undergrad Tuition & Fees: $20,500
Enrollment: 4,702 Coed
Affiliation or Control: Independent Non-Profit IRS Status: 501(c)3
Highest Offering: Doctorate
Program: Liberal Arts And General; Teacher Preparatory; Professional
Accreditation: NH, NURSE, SW, TED

01 President ....Dr. Rebecca L. SHERRICK
05 Provost ....Dr. Andrew P. MANION
30 Exec Vice Pres Univ Advancement ....Mr. Theodore C. PARGE
20 VP for Academic Affairs ....Dr. Dale H. SIMMONS
10 Vice President for Finance .... Dr. Beth W. REISSENWEBER
11 Vice President for Administration ....Mr. Thomas HAMMOND
84 VP Enrollment/Exec Dean Adult/Grad ....Dr. Donna DE SPAIN
32 Vice President for Student Life ....Dr. Lora DE LACEY
26 Vice Pres University Communications ....Mr. Steven MCFARLAND
31 Vice President Community Relations ....Ms. Sarah R. RUSSE
30 VP for Development/Alumni Relations ....Ms. Teri TOMASZKIEWICZ
35 Asst Vice Pres for Student Life ....Dr. Amy GRAY
21 Assistant VP/Controller ....Ms. Sharon MAXWELL
37 Dean of Student Financial Services ....Mrs. Heather L. MCKANE
13 Assoc VP/Chief Information Officer ......Ms. Celeste E. BRANDING
20 Assistant Provost ....Ms. Ellen J. GOLDBERG
06 Registrar ....Ms. Lisa WISNIOWICZ
08 Director of the Library ....Mr. John W. LAW
15 Director of Human Resources ....Vacant
19 Director of Campus Safety ....Mr. Gary BOLT
88 Dir Rsrch on Retention/Tchng Effect .... Ms. Brynn LANDWEHR
44 Director Special Gifts ....Mr. Roger K. PAROLINI
41 Athletic Director ....Mr. James HAMAD
28 Director of Diversity Affairs ....Vacant
38 Director of Counseling Center ....Vacant
66 Director of School of Nursing ....Dr. Barbara LOCKWOOD
70 Director of School of Social Work ....Dr. Fred R. MCKENZIE
49 Dean College of Arts/Sciences ....Dr. Saib OTHMAN
88 Dean of Faculty ....Dr. Alicia C. COSKY
53 Dean College of Education ....Dr. Donald C. WOLD
106 Dean Undergrad/Dean Aurora Online .... Dr. Carmella MORAN
68 Dir of School of Health/Phys Educ ....Dr. Jennifer BUCKLEY

Benedictine University (B)

5700 College Road, Lisle IL 60532-0900
County: DuPage FICE Identification: 001767
Unit ID: 145619
Telephone: (630) 829-6000 Carnegie Class: DRU
FAX Number: (630) 960-1126 Calendar System: Semester
URL: www.ben.edu
Established: 1887 Annual Undergrad Tuition & Fees: $26,940
Enrollment: 6,516 Coed
Affiliation or Control: Roman Catholic IRS Status: 501(c)3
Highest Offering: Doctorate
Program: Liberal Arts And General; Teacher Preparatory; Professional
Accreditation: NH, DIETD, DIETI, NURSE

01 President ....Dr. William J. CARROLL
03 Executive Vice President ....Mr. Charles GREGORY
05 Provost/Vice Pres Academic Affs ....Dr. Donald TAYLOR
10 VP Business & Finance ....Mr. Allan GOZUM
88 Exec Dir of Stewardship Development ....Ms. Pat ARIANO
32 Vice Pres Student Life ....Mr. Marco MASINI
09 Assoc Prov/Dir Inst Effectiveness ......Dr. David SONNENBERGER
42 Director University Ministry ....Mr. Mark KUROWSKI
84 VP for Enrollment Services ....Ms. Kari GIBBONS
06 Registrar ....Ms. Betty MORRISON
08 Director Library Services ....Mr. Jack FRITTS
37 Sr Associate Dean Financial Aid ....Ms. Diane BATTISTELLA
09 Director Institutional Research ....Mr. Robert STANLEY
36 Director Career Development ....Ms. Julie COSIMO
23 Director Health Services ....Vacant
26 Exec Dir Marketing/Communications ....Ms. Mercy ROBB
50 Dean College of Business ....Dr. Sandra GILL
81 Dean College of Science ....Dr. Bart NG
49 Dean College of Liberal Arts ....Dr. Maria DE LA CAMARA
51 Dean Col of Adult Profess Studies ....Dr. Steve NUNES
53 Dean Col Education/Health Services ....Dr. Alan GORR
19 Chief of Police ....Mr. Michael SALATINO
18 Director Campus Services ....Mr. Jay L. STUART
31 Director Community Development ....Ms. Denise WEST
15 Director of Personnel Resources ....Ms. Betsy RHINESMITH
35 Student Activ & Commuter Svcs Coord ....Ms. Katie BUELL
27 Chief Information Officer ....Mr. Charles WILLIAMS

Benedictine University at Springfield (C)

1500 N 5th Street, Springfield IL 62702
Telephone: (217) 525-1420 Identification: 770067
Accreditation: &NH

† Main campus is Benedictine University in Lisle, IL.

Bexley Seabury (D)

8765 W. Higgins Road, Chicago IL 60631
County: Cook FICE Identification: 001754
Unit ID: 148724
Telephone: (773) 380-6780 Carnegie Class: Spec/Faith
FAX Number: (847) 328-9624 Calendar System: Semester
URL: www.seabury.edu
Established: 1858 Annual Graduate Tuition & Fees: N/A
Enrollment: 38 Coed
Affiliation or Control: Protestant Episcopal IRS Status: 501(c)3
Highest Offering: Doctorate; No Undergraduates
Program: Professional; Religious Emphasis
Accreditation: THEOL

01 President ....Rev. Roger A. FERLO
05 Academic Dean ....Rev. Ellen WONDRA
10 Director of Finance ....Mr. Robert DOAK
04 Exec Assistant to the Dean ....Br. Ronald A. FOX, BSG
51 Director of Continuing Education ....Vacant
08 Director United Library ....Ms. Lucy CHUNG
06 Registrar & Admissions ....Ms. Peggy PEARSON
30 Director of Development ....Vacant
42 Dir of Congregational Development ....Ms. Susan HARLOW
15 Mgr Acctng/Human Res/Spec Events .... Ms. Lynn BOWERS
44 Annual Campaign Coordinator ....Ms. Susan QUIGLEY

Black Hawk College (E)

6600 34th Avenue, Moline IL 61265-5899
County: Rock Island FICE Identification: 001638
Unit ID: 143279
Telephone: (309) 796-5000 Carnegie Class: Assoc/Pub-R-L
FAX Number: (309) 792-5976 Calendar System: Semester
URL: www.bhc.edu
Established: 1946 Annual Undergrad Tuition & Fees (In-District): $3,450
Enrollment: 6,403 Coed
Affiliation or Control: Local IRS Status: 501(c)3
Highest Offering: Associate Degree
Program: Occupational; 2-Year Principally Bachelor's Creditable
Accreditation: NH, ADNUR, EMT, PTAA

01 President ....Dr. Thomas B. BAYNUM
05 VP of Instructional Services ....Dr. Bettie TRUITT
10 Vice President for Finance ....Ms. Leslie ANDERSON
11 VP Administration ....Mr. Mike PHILLIPS
32 VP Student Svcs/Dean of Students ....Dr. Richard VALLANDINGHAM
12 Vice President for East Campus ....Ms. Chanda DOWELL
15 Director of Human Resources ....Ms. Karen BOYD
13 Chief Information Officer ....Mr. Sam SCOMA
09 Director Plng & Inst Effectiveness ....Ms. Kathy MALCOLM
20 Dean Instruction/Academic Support ....Vacant
20 Dean of Business and Technology ....Dr. Michael RIVERA
51 Dean Adult/Continuing Educ ....Ms. Glenda NICKE
35 Asst Dean of Student Support Svcs ....Dr. Kim ARMSTRONG
88 Asst Dean of Student Support Svc/EC ....Mr. B. J MCCULLUM
44 Exec Dir BHC Foundation QC Campus ....Ms. Shelly CAIN
88 Director Small Business Devel Ctr ....Mr. Joel YOUNGS
26 Director Marketing/Public Relations ....Mr. John MEINEKE
37 Director of Financial Aid ....Ms. Joanna DYE
36 Director Career Services Center ....Dr. Bruce STOREY
41 Division Director Athletics/Coach ....Mr. Gary HUBER
08 Librarian ....Ms. Charlet KEY
19 Chief of Police ....Mr. Shawn CISNA
22 EEO/Affirmative Action Officer ....Ms. Jo JOHNSON
24 Dir Teaching Lrng Ctr/Online Lrng ....Vacant
31 Professional and Continuing Educ ....Ms. Brenda BROWN
51 Director Adult Education ....Ms. Diane FALL
06 Registrar ....Ms. Sandi GIESON
40 Bookstore Manager Quad Cities ....Ms. Nyla WOOLARD
96 Purchasing Manager ....Mr. Mike MELEG
51 Department Chair Adult Education ....Ms. Constance KAPPAS
72 Dept Chair Bus & Office Tech ....Ms. Diana MCCABE
57 Dept Chair Comm & Fine Arts ....Ms. Michelle JOHNSON
79 Dept Chair Human/Languages/Journal ....Mr. Bill DESMOND
81 Dept Chair Math/Comp Science ....Mr. Peter NODZENSKI
54 Dept Chair Natural Science/Engrng ....Mr. Brian GLASER
83 Dept Chair Social/Behav/Educ Stds ....Dr. Bruce LEBLANC
47 Department Chair Applied Science ....Mr. William GOOD
49 Dept Chair Liberal Arts/Sciences ....Mr. Kirk WATSON
66 Dept Chair Assoc Degree/Prac Nurs ....Ms. Karen BABER
76 Dept Chair Allied Health/HPE ....Ms. Betsey MORTHLAND
88 Dept Chair Counseling ....Ms. Wendy BOCK
62 Dept Chair Lrg Resource Center ....Ms. Charlet KEY

Black Hawk College East Campus (F)

26230 Black Hawk Road, Galva IL 61434
Telephone: (309) 854-1700 Identification: 770069
Accreditation: &NH

† Main campus is Black Hawk College in Moline, IL.

Blackburn College (G)

700 College Avenue, Carlinville IL 62626-1498
County: Macoupin FICE Identification: 001639
Unit ID: 143288
Telephone: (217) 854-3231 Carnegie Class: Bac/Diverse
FAX Number: (217) 854-5700 Calendar System: Semester
URL: www.blackburn.edu
Established: 1837 Annual Undergrad Tuition & Fees: $18,506
Enrollment: 550 Coed
Affiliation or Control: Presbyterian Church (U.S.A.) IRS Status: 501(c)3
Highest Offering: Baccalaureate
Program: Liberal Arts And General; Teacher Preparatory
Accreditation: NH

01 President ....Dr. John COMERFORD
05 Provost ....Dr. Jeffery P. APER
10 Vice Pres Administration & Finance ....Ms. Heather BIGARD
30 VP for Institutional Advancement ....Mr. Glen KRUPICA
32 Vice Pres of Student Affairs ....Ms. Heidi HEINZ
101 Exec Asst to Pres/Sec Bd Trustees ....Ms. Ann M. ALLEN
07 Director of Admissions ....Ms. Alisha KAPP
88 Director of Transfer Admissions ....Mr. John MALIN
29 Sr Develop Ofcr/Alumni/Staff Rels ....Mr. Nate RUSH
37 Director of Financial Aid ....Ms. Jane KELSEY
08 Head Librarian ....Mr. Spencer BRAYTON
38 College Counselor ....Mr. Robert M. WEIS
06 College Registrar ....Ms. Dianna RUYLE
15 Director Personnel Services ....Ms. Ann ALLEN
36 Director Student Placement ....Ms. Suzanne KRUPICA
18 Director Physical Plant ....Mr. Samuel HARDING
41 Dir of Athletics/Recreational Pgms ....Ms. Angela MORENZ
42 Chaplain ....Rev. Erica BROWN
26 Director of Public Relations ....Mr. Peter OSWALD
09 Director of Institutional Research ....Dr. Kristi NELMS
21 Controller ....Ms. Dawn KIPER
44 Director of Annual Giving ....Ms. Jodi ROWE

Blessing-Rieman College of Nursing (H)

Broadway at 11th, PO Box 7005, Quincy IL 62305-7005
County: Adams FICE Identification: 006214
Unit ID: 143297
Telephone: (217) 228-5520 Carnegie Class: Spec/Health
FAX Number: (217) 223-4661 Calendar System: Semester
URL: www.brcn.edu
Established: 1891 Annual Undergrad Tuition & Fees: $19,782
Enrollment: 282 Coed
Affiliation or Control: Independent Non-Profit IRS Status: 501(c)3
Highest Offering: Master's
Program: Professional; Nursing Emphasis
Accreditation: NH, NURSE

01 President College of Nursing ....Dr. Pamela S. BROWN
06 Registrar ....Ms. Rachel CRAMSEY

Bradley University (I)

1501 W Bradley Avenue, Peoria IL 61625-0001
County: Peoria FICE Identification: 001641
Unit ID: 143358
Telephone: (309) 676-7611 Carnegie Class: Master's L
FAX Number: N/A Calendar System: Semester
URL: www.bradley.edu
Established: 1897 Annual Undergrad Tuition & Fees: $29,664
Enrollment: 5,451 Coed
Affiliation or Control: Independent Non-Profit IRS Status: 501(c)3
Highest Offering: Doctorate
Program: Liberal Arts And General; Teacher Preparatory; Professional
Accreditation: NH, ART, BUS, BUSA, CACREP, CONST, DIETD, @DIETI, ENG, ENGT, MUS, NUR, PTA, SW, TED, THEA

01 President ....Ms. Joanne K. GLASSER
05 Provost/Vice Pres Academic Affairs ....Dr. David GLASSMAN
20 Assistant Provost Academic Affairs ....Mrs. Linda J. PIZZUTI
10 Vice President Business Affairs ....Mr. Gary M. ANNA
30 Vice President Advancement ....Mr. Pat VICKERMAN
32 Interim Vice Pres Student Affairs ....Mr. Nathan THOMAS
84 VP Enrollment Management ....Mr. Paul SCHROEDER
26 Assoc VP University Marketing ....Ms. Susan ANDREWS
88 Assoc VP Enrollment Management ....Mr. Justin BALL
58 Assoc Provost Dean Graduate School .... Dr. Jeffrey BAKKEN
50 Dean Foster Col Business ....Dr. Darrell J. RADSON
57 Dean Slane Col Communic/Fine Arts ...Dr. Jeffrey H. HUBERMAN
53 Dean Education & Health Sciences ....Dr. Joan L. SATTLER
54 Dean Engineering & Technology ....Dr. Lex A. AKERS
49 Int Dean Liberal Arts & Sciences .... Dr. Stacey ROBERTSON
84 Ex Dir Enrollment Mgmt Office Oper ..Ms. Angela M. ROBERSON
13 Assoc Provost Info Resources & Tech ....Mr. J. Chuck RUCH

08 Exec Director of the Library .... Ms. Barbara GALIK
38 Ex Dir Ctr For Stdnt Dev/Hlth Svcs .... Vacant
39 Ex Dir Ctr Residential Lvgn/Ldrshp .... Vacant
88 Exec Dir Student Involvement .... Mr. Mike KEUP
36 Exec Director Smith Career Center .... Ms. Jane C. LINNENBURGER
14 Exec Dir Computing Services .... Ms. Sandra BURY
24 Ex Dir Instruct Tech/Media Svcs .... Mr. Nial L. JOHNSON
29 Exec Director of Alumni Relations .... Ms. Lori FAN
51 Executive Director Continuing Educ .... Ms. Janet LANGE
06 Registrar .... Mrs. Katherine M. BEATY
37 Exec Dir Enroll Mgmt/Dir Fin Asst .... Mr. David L. PARDIECK
19 Chief of Campus Police .... Mr. Brian JOSCHKO
15 Director of Human Resources .... Ms. Nena PEPLOW
18 Director Facilities Management .... Vacant
23 Medical Director Health Services .... Dr. Jessica HIGGS
27 Senior Director Public Relations .... Ms. M. Kathleen CONVER
41 Director Athletics .... Dr. Michael CROSS
78 Associate Director Springer Center .... Mrs. Dawn KOELTZOW
87 Assoc Dir Summer/Interim Sessions .... Mr. Jon NEIDY
25 Int Dir Off/Teaching Excel/Fac Dev .... Mrs. Kim WILLIS
22 Director Affirmative Action/EEO .... Ms. Nena PEPLOW
28 Dir Multicultural Student Services .... Ms. Frances JONES
92 Director of Honors Program .... Dr. Kyle DZAPOP
94 Int Director of Women's Studies .... Dr. Amy SCOTT
09 Dir of Institutional Improvement .... Ms. Jennifer GRUENING
40 Manager Bookstore .... Mr. Paul KROENKE
88 Dir of PreProfessional Health Adv .... Dr. Valesie BENNETT
88 Dir Pre Law Center .... Mrs. Nicole MEYER
07 Asst Dir Admissions .... Mr. Joshua JONES

Carl Sandburg College (A)

2400 Tom L. Wilson Boulevard, Galesburg IL 61401-9576
County: Knox FICE Identification: 007265
Unit ID: 143613
Telephone: (309) 344-2518 Carnegie Class: Assoc/Pub-R-M
FAX Number: (309) 344-1395 Calendar System: Semester
URL: www.sandburg.edu
Established: 1966 Annual Undergrad Tuition & Fees: $4,200
Enrollment: 2,460 Coed
Affiliation or Control: Independent Non-Profit IRS Status: 501(c)3
Highest Offering: Associate Degree
Program: Occupational; 2-Year Principally Bachelor's Creditable
Accreditation: NH, ADNUR, DH, FUSER, PNUR

01 President .... Dr. Lori L. SUNDBERG
32 VP of Student Services/AD .... Mr. Steve NORTON
05 VP of Academic Services .... Ms. Julie GIBB
11 VP Administrative Services & CIO .... Dr. Samuel SUDHAKAR
08 Dean of Library .... Mr. Michael WALTERS
76 Dean of Career Technical and Health .... Ms. Lauri WHITE
12 Dean of Extension Services .... Ms. Debra MILLER
56 Director of Extension Services .... Ms. Linda THOMAS
96 Director of Business Services .... Mr. Larry BYRNE
37 Director Financial Aid .... Ms. Lisa HANSON
26 Director Marketing/Public Relations .... Ms. Robin DEMOTT
10 Chief Financial Officer/Treasurer .... Ms. Lisa BLAKE
102 Dir Foundation & Bus & Comm Ed .... Ms. Gena ALCORN
88 Director TRIO Upward Bound .... Mr. Tony BENTLEY
88 Dean of Student Success .... Ms. Misty LYON
07 Director of Recuitment .... Ms. Dylana CARLSON
66 Associate Dean of Nursing .... Ms. Rosemary O'DANIEL
06 Director of Admissions & Records .... Mr. Rick EDDY
46 Dean HR/Organizational Development .... Dr. Constance THURMAN

Carl Sandburg College The Branch Campus (B)

305 Sandburg Drive, Carthage IL 62321
Telephone: (217) 357-3129 Identification: 770071
Accreditation: &NH

† Main campus is Carl Sandburg College in Galesburg, IL.

Carl Sandburg College The Extension Center (C)

380 E Main Street, Bushnell IL 61422
Telephone: (309) 772-2177 Identification: 770070
Accreditation: &NH

† Main campus is Carl Sandburg College in Galesburg, IL.

Catholic Theological Union (D)

5401 S Cornell Avenue, Chicago IL 60615-5698
County: Cook FICE Identification: 009232
Unit ID: 143659
Telephone: (773) 371-5400 Carnegie Class: Spec/Faith
FAX Number: (773) 324-8490 Calendar System: Semester
URL: www.ctu.edu
Established: 1967 Annual Graduate Tuition & Fees: $20,115
Enrollment: 480 Coed
Affiliation or Control: Roman Catholic IRS Status: 501(c)3
Highest Offering: Doctorate; No Undergraduates
Program: Professional; Religious Emphasis
Accreditation: THEOL

01 President .... Rev. Mark R. FRANCIS, CSV
05 Vice President/Academic Dean .... Sr. Barbara REID, OP
10 Vice Pres Administration & Finance .... Mr. Michael W. CONNORS
30 Director of Development .... Ms. Anne M. TIRPAK
26 Dir of Marketing & Communications .... Ms. Nancy NICKEL
08 Director of the Library .... Ms. Melody L. MCMAHON
06 Registrar .... Mrs. Maria De Jesus LEMUS
07 Director of Admissions .... Mrs. Angela PAVIGLIANITI
21 Comptroller .... Mrs. Dionne DAY
88 Director of Educational Technology .... Mr. Darnell PAYNE
04 Assistant to the President .... Sr. Pam PAULOSKI, SP
32 Events & Student Services Manager .... Ms. Christine HENDERSON
37 Director Student Financial Aid .... Ms. Kathy VAN DUSER

Chamberlain College of Nursing (E)

3300 North Campbell Avenue, Chicago IL 60618
Telephone: (773) 961-3000 Identification: 770495
Accreditation: &NH, NURSE

† Main campus is Chamberlain College of Nursing - Addison in Addison, IL.

*Chamberlain College of Nursing (F)

3005 Highland Parkway, Downers Grove IL 60515
County: DuPage Identification: 667149
Telephone: (877) 751-5783 Carnegie Class: N/A
FAX Number: (630) 512-8888
URL: www.chamberlain.org

01 President .... Dr. Susan GROENWALD
03 Vice President Campus Operations .... Ms. Marie HALLINAN
05 Vice President Academic Affairs .... Dr. William Richard COWLING
10 Vice President Finance .... Ms. Sonya EVANOSKY
26 Vice President Marketing .... Mr. Thomas WILLIAMS
07 National Senior Dir of Admissions .... Mr. Larry VEENEMAN
32 National Senior Dir of Student Svcs .... Ms. June MARLOWE

† Part of DeVry University, IL.

Chamberlain College of Nursing - Addison (G)

1221 N. Swift Road, Addison IL 60101
County: DuPage FICE Identification: 006385
Unit ID: 466921
Telephone: (630) 953-3680 Carnegie Class: Spec/Health
FAX Number: (630) 628-1154 Calendar System: Semester
URL: www.chamberlain.edu
Established: 1889 Annual Undergrad Tuition & Fees: $17,360
Enrollment: 540 Coed
Affiliation or Control: Proprietary IRS Status: Proprietary
Highest Offering: Doctorate
Program: Nursing Emphasis
Accreditation: NH, NURSE

01 President .... Ms. Susan L. GROENWALD
12 Campus President .... Dr. Janice DEMASTERS
05 Vice President of Academic Affairs .... Dr. William Richard COWLING
106 Dean Online Programs .... Ms. Margi WHEELER
88 Director Accreditation .... Ms. Kathleen R. MODENE
32 Senior Director Student Services .... Ms. June MARLOWE
26 Director of Marketing .... Ms. Stephanie L. GALLO

† Master's and Doctorate programs are only offered online.

Chamberlain College of Nursing Tinley Park (H)

18624 Wests Creek Drive, Tinley Park IL 60471
Telephone: (708) 560-2000 Identification: 770496
Accreditation: &NH, NURSE

† Main campus is Chamberlain College of Nursing - Addison in Addison, IL.

Chicago School of Professional Psychology-Chicago (I)

325 N Wells Street, Chicago IL 60654-8158
Telephone: (312) 329-6600 Identification: 770349
Accreditation: &WC, CLPSY

† Main campus is Chicago School of Professional Psychology Los Angeles Campus in Los Angeles, CA.

Chicago State University (J)

9501 S King Drive, Chicago IL 60628-1598
County: Cook FICE Identification: 001694
Unit ID: 144005
Telephone: (773) 995-2000 Carnegie Class: Master's L
FAX Number: (773) 995-2563 Calendar System: Semester
URL: www.csu.edu
Established: 1867 Annual Undergrad Tuition & Fees (In-State): $10,964
Enrollment: 6,107 Coed
Affiliation or Control: State IRS Status: 501(c)3
Highest Offering: Doctorate
Program: Liberal Arts And General; Teacher Preparatory; Professional
Accreditation: NH, ACBSP, CACREP, CAHIIM, MUS, NRPA, NUR, OT, PHAR, SW, TED

01 President .... Dr. Wayne D. WATSON
100 Chief of Staff .... Dr. Napoleon W. MOSES
05 Provost/Sr VP for Academic Affairs .... Dr. Angela HENDERSON
43 VP Gen Counsel for Labor/Legal Affs .... Mr. Patrick CAGE
21 VP of Administration and Finance .... Mr. Lawrence PINKELTON
10 Acting Director Budget & Risk Mgmt .... Mrs. Arrileen PATAWARAN
13 Chief Information Officer .... Mr. Prashant SHINDE
84 Vice Pres of Enrollment Management .... Mrs. LaShondra PEEBLES
09 Director Inst Research/Evaluations .... Dr. Resche HINES
49 Interim Dean Arts & Sciences .... Dr. David R. KANIS
53 Dean Education .... Dr. Sylvia GIST
67 Dean College of Pharmacy .... Dr. Miriam MOBLEY-SMITH
76 Dean College of Health Sciences .... Dr. Leslie A. ROUNDTREE
50 Dean College of Business .... Mr. Derrick K. COLLINS
08 Acting Dean of Library/Instruct Svc .... Dr. Richard DARGA
51 Interim Dean Cont Educ Nontrad Pgms .... Ms. Nelly MAYNARD
06 Registrar .... Mrs. Victoria SMITH-MURPHY
21 Bursar .... Ms. Miesha V. DALEY
84 Assoc Vice President Enroll Mgmt .... Ms. Cheri SIDNEY
37 Director of Financial Aid .... Mrs. Cathy DAVIS
07 Director of Admissions .... Mr. Matthew HARRISON
29 Director Alumni Affairs .... Vacant
26 Director of Marketing & Communicati .... Mrs. Sabrina LAND
15 Director Human Resources .... Dr. Renee D. MITCHELL
36 Director of Career Development .... Dr. Renee D. MITCHELL
88 Dir Latino Resource Center .... Mr. Fernando DIAZ
96 Director of Purchasing .... Ms. Janielle GRAHAM
18 Int Dir Facilities/Physical Plant .... Mr. Alan O'NEAL
20 Associate VP Academic Officer .... Dr. Debrah JEFFERSON
35 Dir of Student Act & Leadership Dev .... Vacant
38 Director Counseling Center .... Dr. Michael C. EDWARDS
27 Dir of Public Relations & Communica .... Ms. Deborah DOUGLAS

Chicago Theological Seminary (K)

1407 East 60th Street, Chicago IL 60637-1284
County: Cook FICE Identification: 001661
Unit ID: 144014
Telephone: (773) 896-2400 Carnegie Class: Spec/Faith
FAX Number: (773) 643-1284 Calendar System: Semester
URL: www.ctschicago.edu
Established: 1855 Annual Graduate Tuition & Fees: $14,568
Enrollment: 242 Coed
Affiliation or Control: United Church Of Christ IRS Status: 501(c)3
Highest Offering: Doctorate; No Undergraduates
Program: Professional; Religious Emphasis
Accreditation: NH, THEOL

01 President .... Dr. Alice HUNT
05 Academic Dean .... Dr. Ken STONE
10 Vice President for Finance & Admin .... Mr. Stephen MANNING
30 Vice President for Advancement .... Ms. Megan DAVIS OCHI
06 Registrar .... Ms. Elena JIMENEZ
08 Head Librarian .... Rev. Neil W. GERDES
07 Director Recruitment/Admission .... Ms. Lisa SEIWERT

Christian Life College (L)

400 E Gregory Street, Mount Prospect IL 60056-2522
County: Cook FICE Identification: 031993
Unit ID: 260947
Telephone: (847) 259-1840 Carnegie Class: Spec/Faith
FAX Number: (847) 259-3888 Calendar System: Semester
URL: www.christianlifecollege.edu
Established: 1950 Annual Undergrad Tuition & Fees: $11,110
Enrollment: 49 Coed
Affiliation or Control: Pentecostal/Charismatic Non-Denominational
IRS Status: 501(c)3
Highest Offering: Baccalaureate
Program: Religious Emphasis
Accreditation: TRACS

01 President .... Mr. Harry R. SCHMIDT
05 Academic Dean .... Mr. Wayne R. WACHSMUTH
08 Director of Library Services .... Mr. Christopher C. ULLMAN
10 Director of Finance .... Mr. Roger K. STEVENS
32 Dean of Students .... Mr. Michael BELL
06 Registrar .... Mrs. Christina BELL

*City Colleges of Chicago (M)

226 W Jackson Boulevard, Chicago IL 60606-6998
County: Cook FICE Identification: 001647
Unit ID: 144500
Telephone: (312) 553-2500 Carnegie Class: N/A
FAX Number: (312) 553-2699
URL: www.ccc.edu

01 Chancellor .... Ms. Cheryl HYMAN
05 Interim Provost .... Ms. Vernese EDGHILL-WALDEN
10 Interim Vice Chancellor Finance .... Ms. Melanie SHAKER
13 Vice Chanc/Chief Information Ofcr .... Ms. Arshele STEVENS
09 Vice Chanc Strategy & Instnl Intel .... Mr. Rasmus LYNNERUP
11 Vice Chanc Administrative Services .... Ms. Diane MINOR
04 Executive Board Administrator .... Ms. Candace MONTGOMERY
43 General Counsel .... Mr. Eugene MUNIN
27 Vice Chanc Institutional Advan .... Mr. Laurent PERNOT

*City Colleges of Chicago Harold Washington College (N)

30 E Lake Street, Chicago IL 60601-2449
County: Cook FICE Identification: 001652
Unit ID: 144209
Telephone: (312) 553-5600 Carnegie Class: Assoc/Pub-U-MC
FAX Number: (312) 553-5964 Calendar System: Semester

URL: www.ccc.edu
Established: 1962 Annual Undergrad Tuition & Fees (In-District): $3,010
Enrollment: 8,840 Coed
Affiliation or Control: State/Local IRS Status: 501(c)3
Highest Offering: Associate Degree
Program: Occupational; 2-Year Principally Bachelor's Creditable; Business Emphasis
Accreditation: NH, ACBSP

02 President .... Mr. Donald J. LAACKMAN
05 Vice Pres Academic Affairs .... Dr. Margaret MARTYN
11 Vice President Operations .... Mr. Kent LUSK
37 Director of Financial Aid .... Mr. Pedro LADINO
18 Chief Facilities/Physical Plant .... Mr. Richard WREN
21 Director Bus Admin & Aux Services .... Vacant
08 Librarian .... Mr. John KIERALDO
15 Human Resources Admin .... Mr. Brandon PENDLETON
20 Dean of Instruction .... Mr. Armen SARRAFIAN
32 Dean of Student Services .... Mr. Wendell BLAIR
04 Assistant to the President .... Ms. Angela GUERNICA
88 Int Dean Public Agency/Special Pgms .... Mr. John HADER
20 Associate Dean of Instruction .... Mr. George BICKFORD
13 Director Information Technology .... Ms. Ewa BEJNAROWICZ
35 Assoc Dean of Student Services .... Mr. Robert BROWN
46 Asst Director Research/Planning .... Dr. George W. CALISTO
06 Registrar .... Ms. Crystal NAPIER

*City Colleges of Chicago Harry S Truman College (A)

1145 W Wilson Avenue, Chicago IL 60640-5691
County: Cook FICE Identification: 001648
Unit ID: 144184
Telephone: (773) 907-4700 Carnegie Class: Assoc/Pub-U-MC
FAX Number: (773) 907-4464 Calendar System: Semester
URL: www.trumancollege.edu
Established: 1956 Annual Undergrad Tuition & Fees (In-District): $3,070
Enrollment: 6,212 Coed
Affiliation or Control: State/Local IRS Status: 501(c)3
Highest Offering: Associate Degree
Program: Occupational; 2-Year Principally Bachelor's Creditable
Accreditation: NH, ADNUR

02 President .... Dr. Reagan F. ROMALI
05 Vice Pres Student/Academic Affs .... Dr. Pervez RAHMAN
06 Registrar .... Ms. My Linh TRAN
32 Dean of Student Services .... Ms. Marilyn DEMENT
35 Associate Dean of Student Services .... Ms. Indra PELAEZ
35 Associate Dean of Student Services .... Mr. Jason WIEDENHOEFT
56 Dean of Adult Education .... Mr. Armando MATA
51 Director of Continuing Education .... Ms. Kyla WILSON
20 Dean of Instruction .... Ms. Loretta BAILES
20 Associate Dean of Instruction .... Ms. DeShaunta STEWART
20 Associate Dean of Instruction .... Ms. Maggie RICE AYALA
10 Exec Dir Business/Operational Svcs .... Mr. Thomas DUNHAM
19 Director of Security .... Mr. Andres DURBAK
37 Director of Financial Aid .... Mr. Robert EVANS
15 Human Resource Administrator .... Mr. Michael ROBERTS
27 Director of Public Relations .... Ms. Lisa HERNANDEZ
18 Chief Engineer .... Mr. Brian MCCUE
72 Asst Dean Information Technology .... Vacant
24 Director Lakeview Learning Center .... Vacant
09 Asst Dir of Research & Planning .... Ms. Ericka KILBURN
88 Business Manager .... Ms. Nina CAO
20 Director of Developmental Education .... Ms. Elizabeth ROSENTHAL

*City Colleges of Chicago Kennedy-King College (B)

6301 South Halsted Street, Chicago IL 60621-3798
County: Cook FICE Identification: 001654
Unit ID: 144157
Telephone: (773) 602-5000 Carnegie Class: Assoc/Pub-U-MC
FAX Number: N/A Calendar System: Semester
URL: www.kennedyking.ccc.edu
Established: 1934 Annual Undergrad Tuition & Fees (In-District): $3,070
Enrollment: 6,234 Coed
Affiliation or Control: State/Local IRS Status: 501(c)3
Highest Offering: Associate Degree
Program: Occupational; 2-Year Principally Bachelor's Creditable
Accreditation: NH, DH

02 President .... Dr. Joyce C. ESTER
05 Vice President for Academic Affairs .... Dr. Erica HOLMES
32 Dean Student Services .... Dr. De Reese REID-HART
12 Interim Dean-Dawson Tech Institute .... Mr. Selmon ASSIGNON
36 Dean Career Programs .... Ms. Kimberly CHAVIS
51 Dean Adult/Continuing Education .... Mr. John MCCLURE
35 Assistant Dean Student Services .... Ms. Cynthia TORRES
37 Director Financial Aid .... Ms. Tabitha O'NEIL
20 Director Academic Support Services .... Mr. Brandon NICHOLS
10 Director Business/Operation Svcs .... Vacant
06 Assistant Registrar .... Mr. Iman RIDDICK
09 Director of Institutional Research .... Vacant
18 Chief Facilities/Physical Plant .... Mr. Jerome DABNEY
26 Marketing Director .... Ms. Angela O'CONNOR
15 Director Human Resources .... Mrs. Araceli CABRALES-MEDINA
04 Assistant to the President .... Mrs. Keli LEVESQUE

*City Colleges of Chicago Malcolm X College (C)

1900 W Van Buren Street, Chicago IL 60612-3197
County: Cook FICE Identification: 001650
Unit ID: 144166
Telephone: (312) 850-7000 Carnegie Class: Assoc/Pub-U-MC
FAX Number: (312) 850-7039 Calendar System: Semester
URL: www.ccc.edu/malcolmx
Established: 1911 Annual Undergrad Tuition & Fees (In-District): $4,236
Enrollment: 4,846 Coed
Affiliation or Control: State/Local IRS Status: 501(c)3
Highest Offering: Associate Degree
Program: Occupational; 2-Year Principally Bachelor's Creditable
Accreditation: NH, #ARCPA, COARC, EMT, FUSER, RAD, SURGT

02 President .... Dr. Anthony E. MUNROE
05 Vice Pres Academic Affairs .... Dr. Darrylinn TODD
32 Interim Dean Student Services .... Dr. Tasha WILLIAMS
10 Exec Director Business Operations .... Ms. Kimberly TYLER
04 Executive Assistant to President . Mrs. Alanna S. WITHERSPOON
15 Human Resources Administrator .... Mr. Stanley BEAMON
20 Interim Dean Instruction .... Ms. Kimberly HOLLINGSWORTH
09 Assoc Dir Inst Research & Planning .... Mr. Byron A. JAVIER
13 Asst Dean Information Technology .... Ms. Debra CRONIN
06 Registrar .... Mr. Alex UNDERWOOD
35 Assoc Dean Student Services .... Mr. Mario DIAZ
37 Assistant Director Financial Aid .... Ms. Tamika DAVENPORT
88 Director Child Care Center .... Ms. Aisha RUTHER
19 Director Security/Public Safety .... Mr. Walter GREEN
18 Chief Facilites/Physical Plant .... Mr. John MORLEY
08 Librarian .... Ms. CM WINTERS-PALACIO
21 Business Manager .... Ms. Latasha JOHNSON
40 Director Bookstore .... Ms. Kristen ROMAN
76 Dean Health Sciences Programs .... Dr. Micah YOUNG
56 Interim Dean Adult Education Pgms .... Dr. Lemario JACKSON
51 Dean Continuing Education .... Dr. Sharon BRYANT
88 Assoc Dean Student Development .... Ms. Lisa WILLIS
88 Executive Director H2P .... Dr. Ebbin DOTSON

*City Colleges of Chicago Olive-Harvey College (D)

10001 S Woodlawn Avenue, Chicago IL 60628-1645
County: Cook FICE Identification: 009767
Unit ID: 144175
Telephone: (773) 291-6100 Carnegie Class: Assoc/Pub-U-MC
FAX Number: (773) 291-6304 Calendar System: Semester
URL: www.ccc.edu/colleges/olive-harvey/pages/default.aspx
Established: 1970 Annual Undergrad Tuition & Fees (In-District): $3,130
Enrollment: 5,120 Coed
Affiliation or Control: State/Local IRS Status: 501(c)3
Highest Offering: Associate Degree
Program: Occupational; 2-Year Principally Bachelor's Creditable
Accreditation: NH

02 President .... Dr. Craig FOLLINS
04 Assistant to President .... Ms. Joann WASHINGTON
05 VP Academic & Student Affairs .... Dr. David MARSHALL
32 Interim Dean Student Services .... Ms. Michelle ADAMS
51 Dean Adult & Continuing Education .... Mr. Robert REIMER
09 Asst Dean of Research/Planning .... Vacant
13 Director Information Technology .... Mr. Savio PINTO
20 Dean of Instruction .... Dr. Addie DAVIS
36 Dir Career Planning/ Placement .... Ms. Kassandra MCGHEE JOHNSON
35 Assoc Dean of Student Services .... Dr. Ria PINKSTON-MCKEE
35 Interim Dean of Student Services .... Ms. Michelle ADAMS
36 Assoc Dean of College to Career .... Ms. Joanne IVORY
36 Assoc Dean of College to Career .... Mr. George BROWN
10 Exec Dir Business/Admin/Aux Svc .... Ms. Angela ARRINGTON-JONES
12 Director of South Chicago Lrng Ctr .... Mr. John ROSALES
37 Director Financial Aid .... Mr. Stacey ROBBINS
38 Manager Wellness Center .... Ms. Mary DYER
06 Registrar .... Ms. Dorian THOMAS
19 Director Security .... Mr. Phillip JONES
88 Director Child Development Center .... Ms. Tiffany CARTER
41 Director of Athletics .... Mr. James COOPER
15 Human Resource Administrator .... Ms. Sharon PRAYOR
26 Director Public Relations .... Vacant
18 Chief Engineer .... Mr. Tom SIEFERT

*City Colleges of Chicago Richard J. Daley College (E)

7500 S Pulaski Road, Chicago IL 60652-1299
County: Cook FICE Identification: 001649
Unit ID: 144193
Telephone: (773) 838-7500 Carnegie Class: Assoc/Pub-U-MC
FAX Number: (773) 838-7524 Calendar System: Semester
URL: daley.ccc.edu
Established: 1960 Annual Undergrad Tuition & Fees (In-District): $3,070
Enrollment: 4,872 Coed
Affiliation or Control: State/Local IRS Status: 501(c)3
Highest Offering: Associate Degree
Program: Occupational; 2-Year Principally Bachelor's Creditable
Accreditation: NH, ADNUR

02 President .... Dr. Jose M. AYBAR
03 Vice President .... Dr. Keith MCCOY
05 Dean of Instruction .... Vacant
36 Dean Career & Economic Programs .... Vacant
88 Dean Adult Education .... Mr. Victor CASTILLO
32 Dean of Student Services .... Vacant
51 Dean Continuing Education .... Mrs. Jean JOHNSON
10 Exec Director Business Operations .... Vacant
37 Director Financial Aid .... Vacant
18 Chief Engineer/Physical Plant .... Mr. Tim SMITH
19 Director Security .... Mr. Frank LIMON
21 Asst Director Business/Oper Svcs .... Ms. Crystal WASHINGTON
35 Assoc Dean Student Services .... Ms. Eileen LYNCH
06 Registrar .... Mr. Milton WRIGHT
09 Director of Institutional Research .... Ms. Mary MCLEAN
15 Administrator Human Resources .... Ms. Elinore MOORE

*City Colleges of Chicago Wilbur Wright College (F)

4300 N Narragansett Avenue, Chicago IL 60634-1591
County: Cook FICE Identification: 001655
Unit ID: 144218
Telephone: (773) 777-7900 Carnegie Class: Assoc/Pub-U-MC
FAX Number: (773) 481-8185 Calendar System: Semester
URL: www.ccc.edu/wright
Established: 1934 Annual Undergrad Tuition & Fees (In-District): $3,070
Enrollment: 12,725 Coed
Affiliation or Control: State/Local IRS Status: 501(c)3
Highest Offering: Associate Degree
Program: Occupational; 2-Year Principally Bachelor's Creditable
Accreditation: NH, ACBSP, OTA, RAD

02 President .... Dr. David POTASH
05 Vice President Academic Affairs .... Mr. Michael DAVIS
32 Dean Student Services .... Ms. Romell MURDEN-WALDU
20 Dean of Instruction .... Mr. Kevin LI
35 Assoc Dean Student Svcs .... Ms. Maria LLOPIZ
35 Assoc Dean Student Svcs .... Ms. Linda HUERTAS
20 Associate Dean of Instruction .... Ms. Nancy KOLL
20 Associate Dean of Instruction .... Mr. Jeffrey JANULIS
88 Director Developmental Education .... Dr. Sara SCHUPACK
10 Director Business .... Ms. Phoebe WOOD
37 Director Financial Aid .... Vacant
09 Dir Institutional Research/Plng .... Mr. Brian TRZEBIATOWSKI
14 Director Information Technology .... Mr. Brad SEXTON
18 Director of Facilities .... Ms. Jackie LONQUIST
08 Librarian .... Ms. Linda NEIL
15 Director Personnel Services .... Ms. Kimberly WILLIAMSON
38 Director Student Counseling .... Ms. Anne WYSOGLAD
19 Director of Security .... Mr. Jack MURPHY
06 Registrar .... Ms. Mai ALY
41 Athletic Director .... Mr. John MCDONNELL
76 Dean Allied Health .... Vacant
53 Dean Adult Education .... Ms. Magxina WAGEMAN
51 Dean of Continuing Education .... Dr. Alba PEZZAROSSI
12 Dean Humboldt Park Center .... Ms. Madeline ROMAN-VARGAS
12 Assoc Dean Humboldt Park Center .... Mr. Kenneth SANTIAGO

College of DuPage (G)

425 Fawell Boulevard, Glen Ellyn IL 60137-6599
County: DuPage FICE Identification: 006656
Unit ID: 144865
Telephone: (630) 942-2800 Carnegie Class: Assoc/Pub-S-SC
FAX Number: (630) 858-9399 Calendar System: Semester
URL: www.cod.edu
Established: 1965 Annual Undergrad Tuition & Fees (In-District): $4,224
Enrollment: 26,155 Coed
Affiliation or Control: State/Local IRS Status: 501(c)3
Highest Offering: Associate Degree
Program: Occupational; 2-Year Principally Bachelor's Creditable
Accreditation: NH, ACFEI, ADNUR, ART, CAHIIM, COARC, CONST, DH, DMS, MAC, NMT, PNUR, PTAA, RAD, SURGT

01 President .... Dr. Robert L. BREUDER
03 Executive Vice President .... Dr. Joseph COLLINS
05 Vice President Academic Affairs .... Dr. Jean V. KARTJE
11 Senior Vice Pres Administration .... Mr. Thomas J. GLASER
13 Vice Pres Information Technology .... Mr. Chuck CURRIER
45 VP Planning & Inst Effectiveness .... Mr. James BENTE
15 Vice President Human Resources ... Ms. Linda SANDS-VANKERK
30 VP Develop/Exec Dir COD Foundation .... Ms. Catherine BROD
24 Asst VP Info Sys/Multimedia Svcs .... Ms. Donna BERLINER
20 Assoc VP Academic Affairs .... Vacant
27 Vice Pres Marketing & Communication .... Mr. Joseph MOORE
32 Assoc VP Student Affairs .... Mr. Earl DOWLING
49 Dean Liberal Arts .... Dr. Daniel LLOYD
50 Dean Business & Technology .... Dr. Donna H. STEWART
75 Dean Health & Sciences .... Mr. Thomas CAMERON
51 Dean Cont Ed/Extended Learning .... Dr. Joseph CASSIDY
08 Dean Learning Resources .... Dr. Lisa A. STOCK
35 Dean Student Affairs .... Ms. Susan M. MARTIN
21 Asst VP Financial Affs/Controller .... Ms. Lynn SAPYTA
18 Dir Facilities Planning and Dev .... Mr. Bruce SCHMIEDL
06 Dean Admiss/Registration/Records .... Ms. Jane L. SMITH
09 Director Research & Analytics .... Eugene YE
30 Asst VP Resource Development .... Vacant
88 Internal Auditor .... Mr. James E. MARTNER
57 Director Performing Arts .... Mr. Stephen CUMMINS
41 Director Athletics .... Mr. Paul ZAKOWSKI
25 Director of Grants .... Ms. Barbara ABROMITIS
86 Director Legislative Relations .... Ms. Mary Ann MILLUSH

19 Director & Chief COD Police Dept ... Mr. Joseph MULLIN
18 Director Facilities Operations ... Mr. Jim MA
79 Associate Dean Humanities ... Ms. Laura ORTIZ
60 Associate Dean English & Acad ESL ... Ms. Beverly REED
26 Dir Marketing & Creative Svcs ... Ms. Laurie JORGENSEN
88 Dir Academic Partnerships ... Vacant
57 Assoc Dean Fine & Applied Arts ... Ms. Cathryn WILKINSON
66 Director Nursing Programs ... Ms. Vickie GUKENBERGER
16 Director Labor & Emp Relations ... Ms. Mia IGYARTO
72 Assoc Dean Technology ... Mr. John KRONENBURGER
83 Assoc Dean Social & Behav Sciences . Ms. Marianne HUNNICUTT
81 Assoc Dean Math & Physical Sciences ... Mr. Thomas SCHRADER
88 Assoc Dean Health & Bio Sciences ... Ms. Karen SOLT
88 Associate Dean Learning Resources ... Ms. Ellen SUTTON

College of Lake County (A)

19351 W Washington Street, Grayslake IL 60030-1198
County: Lake | FICE Identification: 007694
Unit ID: 146472
Telephone: (847) 543-2000 | Carnegie Class: Assoc/Pub-S-MC
FAX Number: (847) 223-1017 | Calendar System: Semester
URL: www.clcillinois.edu
Established: 1967 | Annual Undergrad Tuition & Fees (In-District): $3,348
Enrollment: 17,575 | Coed
Affiliation or Control: Local | IRS Status: 501(c)3
Highest Offering: Associate Degree
Program: Occupational; 2-Year Principally Bachelor's Creditable
Accreditation: NH, ADNUR, CAHIIM, DH, MAC, PHLEB, RAD, SURGT

01 President ... Dr. Girard W. WEBER
05 Vice President Educ Affairs ... Dr. Richard J. HANEY
11 Vice Pres Administrative Affs ... Mr. David AGAZZI
32 Vice Pres Student Development ... Vacant
35 Assoc Vice Pres of Student Devel ... Ms. Karen HLAVIN
35 Asst Dir Student Develop Operation ... Ms. Jennifer MALLER
26 Exec Dir Public Relations & Mktg ... Ms. Evelyn R. SCHIELE
12 Dean Southlake Campus ... Ms. Vicky CVITKOVIC
12 Dean Lakeshore Campus ... Dr. Alphonso BALDWIN
08 Dean Libraries/Instruction Svcs ... Mr. Brian BEECHER
88 Dir Workplace Lrng/Perform/Prof Dev ... Ms. Sonia CROSIER
10 Dir Business & Auxilliary Svcs ... Vacant
21 Controller/Controller's Office ... Mr. Wright WILLIAMS
50 Dean of Business/Workforce Bus Div ... Ms. Lourdene HUHRA
76 Dean Biological/Health Sciences ... Mr. Steven HOLMAN
83 Dean Social Sciences ... Dr. Jeffrey A. STOMPER
79 Dean Comm Arts/Humanities/Fine Arts ... Mr. Roland G. MILLER
54 Int Dean Engr/Math/Physical Science ... Mr. Rob TWARDOCK
51 Dean Adult Basic Education/GED/ESL ... Dr. Raiana MEARNS
38 Dean Counsel/Advising/Transfer Ctr ... Vacant
31 Assoc Dean Community Education ... Ms. Michele VAUGHN
103 Exec Dir Workforce/Prof Dev Inst ... Ms. Roneida MARTIN
41 Dir Athletics/Physical Activities ... Dr. Darryl POPE
86 Dir Resource Dev/Legislative Affrs ... Mr. Nick C. KALLIERIS
13 Chief Info Ofcr/Info Tech Svcs ... Mr. Kamlesh SANGHVI
14 Director User Services/User Spport ... Mr. Edward BOCKMAN
88 Dir Application Svcs/Applic Develop ... Mr. Jay MEYER
35 Int Exec Dir Student Life ... Ms. Teresa AGUINALDO
102 Executive Director CLC Foundation ... Vacant
16 Exec Director Human Resources ... Ms. Susan YASECKO
88 Director Student Services Lakeshore ... Mr. David WEATHERSPOON
18 Director Facilities ... Vacant
88 Dir Children's Learning Center ... Ms. Sandra GROENINGER
88 Dir Ofc Students with Disabilities ... Mr. Thomas CROWE
19 Chief of Police/CLC Police Dept ... Mr. Thomas GUENTHER
36 Exec Dir Career/Placement Services ... Ms. Sylvia M. JOHNSON JONES
20 Asst Vice Pres Educational Affairs ... Ms. Alyssa O'BRIEN
88 Asst Dir Educational Affairs Oper .. Ms. Arlene SANTOS-GEORGE
66 Director Nursing Education ... Dr. Deborah JEZUIT
88 Exec Dir James Lumber Ctr Perf Arts ... Ms. Gwethalyn BRONNER
88 Director Procurement Tech Asst Ctr ... Mr. Marc N. VIOLANTE
88 Director Judicial Services ... Ms. Margaret C. MILLER
29 Dir Alumni Relations/Special Events ... Ms. Julie SHROKA
23 Director Health Services ... Ms. Michelle M. GRACE
37 Director Financial Aid ... Ms. Erin FOWLES
88 Dir Active Lrng Technologies ... Mr. Scott RIAL
88 Director Continuing Prof Devel ... Ms. Carol EWING
88 Director of Business Services ... Ms. Melanie SCHERER
84 Asst Director Enrollment Services ... Ms. Debra MICHELINI
15 Assistant Director Human Resources ... Ms. Kathleen SCATLIFFE-WALLACE
88 Director Green Jobs Initiative ... Mr. Stephen BELL
35 Director Student Support Services ... Ms. Zandra GENOUS
88 Director Technical Services ... Mr. James SENFT
38 Director of Advising ... Ms. Trisha ANDREWS
88 Project Dir IGEN Career Pathways ... Dr. Theresa BERRYMAN
09 Exec Dir/Inst Effect/Plan/Research ... Dr. Sean HOGAN
100 Chief of Staff ... Mr. Derrick HARDEN
88 Dir Construction Management ... Mr. Ted JOHNSON
88 Assistant Controller ... Mr. David HITTENMILLER

College of Lake County Lakeshore Campus (B)

33 North Genesee Street, Waukegan IL 60085
Telephone: (847) 543-2191 | Identification: 770073
Accreditation: &NH

† Main campus is College of Lake County in Grayslake, IL.

College of Lake County Southlake Campus (C)

1120 South Milwaukee Avenue, Vernon Hills IL 60061
Telephone: (847) 543-6501 | Identification: 770072
Accreditation: &NH

† Main campus is College of Lake County in Grayslake, IL.

Columbia College Chicago (D)

600 S Michigan Avenue, Chicago IL 60605-1996
County: Cook | FICE Identification: 001665
Unit ID: 144281
Telephone: (312) 369-1000 | Carnegie Class: Master's M
FAX Number: (312) 369-8069 | Calendar System: Semester
URL: www.colum.edu
Established: 1890 | Annual Undergrad Tuition & Fees: $22,752
Enrollment: 10,783 | Coed
Affiliation or Control: Independent Non-Profit | IRS Status: 501(c)3
Highest Offering: Master's
Program: Liberal Arts And General
Accreditation: NH, CIDA

01 President ... Dr. Kwang-Wu KIM
03 Senior Vice President ... Dr. Warren CHAPMAN
10 VP Bus Affairs/Chief Financial Ofcr ... Mr. Ken GOTSCH
43 Senior Counsel ... Ms. Patricia BERGESON
30 Vice Pres Institutional Advancement ... Dr. Eric WINSTON
88 Vice President Campus Environment ... Ms. Alicia M. BERG
45 Assoc VP/Planning and Compliance ... Ms. Anne FOLEY
20 VP Academic Affairs/Interim Provost ... Dr. Louise LOVE
35 Vice President Student Affairs ... Mr. Mark KELLY
49 Dean School Liberal Arts/Sciences ... Dr. Deborah HOLDSTEIN
57 Dean School of Fine/Performing Arts ... Mr. John GREEN
88 Dean School of Media Arts ... Dr. Robin BARGAR
21 Associate VP of Business Affairs ... Mr. Timothy BAUHS
84 Assoc Vice Pres for Enrollment Mgmt ... Ms. Debra MCGRATH
18 Assoc VP Facilities/Operations ... Mr. John KAVOURIS
32 Assoc Vice Pres/Dean of Students ... Ms. Sharon WILSON-TAYLOR
26 Assoc VP PR/Marketing/Advertising ... Ms. Diane DOYNE
13 Assoc VP & CIO Info Technology .. Ms. Bernadette B. MCMAHON
21 Assoc Vice President & Controller ... Mr. Kevin DOHERTY
19 Assoc Vice Pres Safety & Security ... Mr. Robert KOVERMAN
07 Executive Director of Admissions ... Mr. Murphy MONROE
44 Assoc VP Institutional Advancement ... Mr. Michael ANDERSON
37 Exec Dir of Student Financial Svcs ... Ms. Jennifer WATERS
35 Asst Dean of Student Development ... Mr. William FRIEDMAN
88 Director of Degree Evaluation ... Ms. Susan SINDLINGER
26 Senior Director of Public Relations ... Mr. Steve KAUFFMAN
15 Int Assoc Vice Pres of Human Res ... Ms. Patricia RIOS
29 National Director Alumni Relations ... Mr. Charles BONILLA
96 Director of Purchasing ... Mr. Thomas RUSSELL
28 Exec Director Multicultural Affs ... Ms. Sheila CARTER
85 Dir International Student Affairs ... Ms. Gigi POSEJPAL
06 Director of Records/Registrar ... Mr. Marvin COHEN
36 Director of Portfolio Center ... Mr. Tim LONG
39 Director of Residence Life ... Ms. Mary OAKES
09 AVP Planning/Dir Inst Research ... Mr. Royal DAWSON

Concordia University Chicago (E)

7400 Augusta Street, River Forest IL 60305-1499
County: Cook | FICE Identification: 001666
Unit ID: 144351
Telephone: (708) 771-8300 | Carnegie Class: Master's L
FAX Number: (708) 209-3176 | Calendar System: Semester
URL: www.cuchicago.edu
Established: 1864 | Annual Undergrad Tuition & Fees: $27,324
Enrollment: 5,453 | Coed
Affiliation or Control: Lutheran Church - Missouri Synod
IRS Status: 501(c)3
Highest Offering: Doctorate
Program: Liberal Arts And General; Teacher Preparatory; Professional
Accreditation: NH, CACREP, MUS, TED

01 President ... Dr. John F. JOHNSON
05 Sr Vice President for Academics ... Dr. Marilyn REINECK
30 Sr Vice Pres Development/Alumni ... Ms. Cindy SIMPSON
45 Sr VP for Planning & Research ... Mr. Alan E. MEYER
10 Vice President for Finance ... Mr. Tom HALLETT
11 Vice President for Administration ... Dr. Dennis E. WITTE
84 Vice Pres Enrollment/Student Svcs ... Ms. Evelyn P. BURDICK
32 Vice President Student Services ... Mr. Jeff HYNES
44 Asst Vice President of Major Gifts ... Mr. Tom J. FOOTE
84 Asst Vice President for Enrollment ... Ms. Gwen E. KANELOS
26 Asst Vice Pres Marketing ... Mr. Eric MATANYI
49 Dean College Arts & Sciences ... Dr. Pamela KALBFLEISCH
53 Dean College Education ... Dr. Kevin BRANDON
50 Dean College of Business ... Vacant
58 Dean Col Graduate Innovative Pgms ... Dr. Thomas JANDRIS
88 Associate Director of CURES ... Ms. Elizabeth M. BECKER
37 Director Student Financial Planning .... Ms. Aida ASENCIO-PINTO
06 Registrar ... Ms. Connie PETTINGER
08 Director of Library Services ... Ms. Yana V. SERDYUK
88 Director of Degree Completion ... Dr. Carol J. REISECK
36 Director Career Plng/Placement Svcs ... Mr. Gerald PINOTTI
15 Director of Human Resources ... Ms. Elizabeth WOTEN
18 Director of Physical Plant ... Ms. Linda HOLOWICKI
11 Dean of Administration ... Mr. Glen D. STEINER
29 Director of Alumni Relations ... Ms. Paige CRAIG
38 Director Schmieding Counseling Ctr ... Dr. Carol A. JABS
31 Director of Auxiliary Services ... Mr. Pete D. BECKER
41 Director of Athletics ... Mr. Peter D. GNAN
21 Director of Business Services ... Ms. Anne FARMER
88 Director of Budget Services ... Ms. Tina NEPOMUCENO
39 Director Campus Housing ... Mr. Scott HENDRICKS
42 Campus Pastor ... Rev. Jeffrey LEININGER
24 Dir of Media Production Services ... Mr. James A. KOSINSKY
19 Director of Public Safety ... Ms. Amberleigh BIRKHOLZ
88 Director of Academic Advising ...... Ms. Rosemarie GARCIA-HILLS
96 Director of Purchasing ... Ms. Kathryn KLEMENT
91 Manager of Admin Information System ... Ms. Linda C. BERRY
85 International Student Coordinator ... Mr. Robert HAYES

Coyne College (F)

330 North Green Street, Chicago IL 60607-1300
County: Cook | FICE Identification: 007549
Unit ID: 144485
Telephone: (773) 577-8100 | Carnegie Class: Assoc/PrivFP
FAX Number: (312) 226-3818 | Calendar System: Semester
URL: www.coynecollege.edu
Established: 1899 | Annual Undergrad Tuition & Fees: $15,500
Enrollment: 885 | Coed
Affiliation or Control: Proprietary | IRS Status: Proprietary
Highest Offering: Associate Degree
Program: Occupational; 2-Year Principally Bachelor's Creditable; Technical Emphasis
Accreditation: ACCSC, MAAB

01 President ... Mr. Russell T. FREEMAN
03 Director ... Mr. John L. MUELLER

Danville Area Community College (G)

2000 E Main Street, Danville IL 61832-5199
County: Vermilion | FICE Identification: 001669
Unit ID: 144564
Telephone: (217) 443-3222 | Carnegie Class: Assoc/Pub-R-L
FAX Number: (217) 443-8560 | Calendar System: Semester
URL: www.dacc.edu
Established: 1949 | Annual Undergrad Tuition & Fees (In-District): $3,600
Enrollment: 5,563 | Coed
Affiliation or Control: State/Local | IRS Status: 501(c)3
Highest Offering: Associate Degree
Program: Occupational; 2-Year Principally Bachelor's Creditable
Accreditation: NH, CAHIIM, RAD

01 President ... Dr. Alice M. JACOBS
04 Admin Asst to the Pres/Board Sec ... Ms. Kerri L. THURMAN
05 VP Instruction & Student Svcs ... Mr. David L. KIETZMANN
15 Director Human Resources/AA Ofcr ... Ms. Jill A. CRANMORE
10 Chief Financial Officer ... Ms. Tammy L. CLARK-BETANCOURT
11 Director Administrative Services ... Mr. R. Michael CUNNINGHAM
84 Dean Student Services ... Ms. Stacy L. EHMEN
25 Director Grants and Planning ... Mr. Patrick BAYARD
102 Foundation Executive Director ... Ms. Tracy D. WAHLFELDT
26 Director Marketing/Col Relations ... Ms. Lara L. CONKLIN
09 Dir Institutional Effectiveness ... Ms. Nancy A. BOESDORFER
103 Executive Director of JTP ... Mr. Brian C. HENSGEN
21 Controller ... Ms. Debra L. KNIGHT
37 Director of Financial Aid ... Ms. Janet M. INGARGIOLA
31 Dir Corporate/Community Education ... Mr. Andy PERRY
91 Director of Admin Data Systems ... Mr. Kim H. COLWELL
90 Director Computer & Network Svcs ... Mr. Jefferson D. WILLIAMS
88 Director of Adult Education ... Ms. Laura M. WILLIAMS
50 Dean Business & Technology ... Mr. Bruce M. RAPE
49 Dean Liberal Arts and Library Servi .... Dr. Penny J. MCCONNELL
81 Dean Math & Sciences ... Ms. Kathy R. STURGEON
41 Athletic Director ... Mr. Tim M. BUNTON
88 Director Small Business Development ... Ms. Carol NICHOLS
07 Director Admissions & Registrar ... Ms. Cindy J. PECK
38 Director Student Support Services ... Ms. Vicky L. WELGE
36 Coordinator Career Services ... Ms. Carla M. BOYD
24 Director Instructional Media ... Mr. Jonathon L. SPORS
40 Coordinator Bookstore ... Ms. Cindy A. PARR-BARRETT
88 Coordinator Recruitment ... Ms. Dawn S. NASSER

DePaul University (H)

1E Jackson Boulevard, Chicago IL 60604-2287
County: Cook | FICE Identification: 001671
Unit ID: 144740
Telephone: (312) 362-8000 | Carnegie Class: DRU
FAX Number: (312) 362-5322 | Calendar System: Quarter
URL: www.depaul.edu
Established: 1898 | Annual Undergrad Tuition & Fees: $33,990
Enrollment: 32,295 | Coed
Affiliation or Control: Roman Catholic | IRS Status: 501(c)3
Highest Offering: Doctorate
Program: Liberal Arts And General; Teacher Preparatory; Professional
Accreditation: NH, ANEST, BUS, BUSA, CLPSY, LAW, MUS, NURSE, PH, SPAA, SW

01 President ... Rev. Dennis H. HOLTSCHNEIDER
00 Chancellor ... Rev. John T. RICHARDSON, CM
05 Provost ... Dr. Donald B. POPE-DAVIS
03 Executive Vice President ... Mr. Robert KOZOMAN
11 Vice President Admin/Sec of Univ ... Rev. Edward R. UDOVIC
32 Interim VP Student Affairs ... Ms. Cindy SUMMERS
84 Sr Vice Pres Enrollment Management ..... Dr. David H. KALSBEEK
10 Vice President for Finance ... Ms. Bonnie FRANKEL

15 Vice President Human Resources ....Ms. Stephanie SMITH
18 Vice President Facilities Operation ....Mr. Robert J. JANIS
43 Vice President & General Counsel ....Dr. Jose D. PADILLA
88 VP Teaching/Learning Resources ....Rev. Edward R. UDOVIC
29 Asst VP Alumni Engagement/Outreac ....Tracy KRAHL
28 VP Inst Diversity & Equity ....Ms. Elizabeth F. ORTIZ
27 VP Public Relations & Communication ....Ms. Cynthia LAWSON
30 Sr Vice President for Advancement ....Ms. Mary FINGER
20 Assoc VP Academic Affairs ....Ms. Caryn CHADEN
20 Assoc VP Academic Affairs Online .... Mr. GianMario BESANA
45 VP Planning & Presidential Admin ....Dr. Jay BRAATZ
21 Sr Assoc VP Fiscal Admin .... Ms. Alyssa KUPKA
35 AVP Student Advocacy & Comm Affairs .... Ms. Cindy SUMMERS
88 Assoc VP Faculty Development ....Dr. Rafaela WEFFER
35 Assoc Vice Pres Student Development ....Dr. Peggy BURKE
22 Assoc VP Diversity Education ....Mr. Rico TYLER
20 Assoc Vice Pres Academic Affairs ....Ms. Kelly JOHNSON
09 Asst VP Inst Rsrch & Mkt Analytic ....Dr. Liz SANDERS
36 Assoc Vice President Career Svcs ....Ms. Carol MONTGOMERY
42 Assoc VP University Ministry ....Mr. Mark LABOE
21 Assoc VP Operations ....Mr. Mark TITZER
26 Assoc VP Univ Marketing Comm ....Ms. Gwyn FRIEND
46 Assoc VP Research ....Ms. Joanne ROMAGNI
88 Senior Executive University
Mission ....Rev. Edward R. UDOVIC, CM
88 Treasurer ....Mr. Jeffrey BETHKE
21 Controller ....Mr. Mark HAWKINS
90 Director Instruc Technology Devel ....Dr. Sharon GUAN
91 VP Information Services ....Mr. Robert MCCORMICK
37 Assoc VP Financial Aid ....Ms. Paula LUFF
25 Director Sponsored Programs Rsrch .... Dr. Douglas PETCHER
26 Director News & Information Bureau ....Ms. Carol HUGHES
07 Director of Transfer Admission ....Ms. Pamela LEE KADIRIFU
19 Director Public Safety ....Mr. Robert WACHOWSKI
38 Director Student Counseling ....Dr. Jeffery LANFEAR
41 Athletic Director ....Ms. Jean PONSETTO
06 Director of Registration ....Ms. Patricia HUERTA
07 Director of Freshman Admission ....Ms. Sacha THIEME
88 Asst VP Grad & Adult Recruit & Adm ......Ms. Suzanne DEPEDER
07 Dean of Undergraduate Admission ....Ms. Carlene KLAAS
77 Dean Computing & Digital Media ....Dr. David MILLER
49 Dean Liberal Arts & Sciences ....Dr. Charles S. SUCHAR
50 Dean Driehaus Business College ....Dr. Ray WHITTINGTON
60 Interim Dean Col of Communication ....Dr. Jean-Claude TEBOUL
64 Dean School of Music ....Dr. Donald E. CASEY
61 Dean College of Law ....Mr. Gregory A. MARK
57 Dean Theatre School ....Mr. John CULBERT
53 Dean School of Education ....Dr. Paul ZIONTS
51 Dean School for New Learning ....Ms. Marisa ALICEA
76 Interim Dean Col of Sci & Health ....Dr. Jerry CLELAND

*DeVry University - Home Office (A)

3005 Highland Parkway, Downers Grove IL 60515-5799
County: DuPage FICE Identification: 001672
Unit ID: 144777
Telephone: (800) 733-3879 Carnegie Class: N/A
FAX Number: (630) 571-0317
URL: www.devry.edu

00 President & Chief Executive Officer .... Mr. Daniel HAMBURGER
01 President of DeVry University ....Mr. David J. PAULDINE
86 SVP External Rel & Global Comp/
CCO ....Ms. Sharon THOMAS-PARROTT
26 Chief Marketing Officer ....Mr. John BIRMINGHAM
32 VP of Student & Career Services ....Ms. Madeleine SLUTSKY
10 SVP/CFO/Treasurer ....Mr. Timothy WIGGINS
106 President DeVry Online Services ....Mr. Eric DIRST
43 SVP/General Counsel/Corp Secretary ....Mr. Gregory DAVIS
84 VP Enrollment Management ....Ms. Erika ORRIS
88 VP Enrollment Management - Online ....Mr. Mark BUCK
05 Provost/VP Academic Affairs ....Ms. Donna LORAINE
16 SVP Human Resources ....Ms. Donna JENNINGS
88 VP Regulatory Affairs ....Mr. Thomas BABEL
88 Pres K-12/Prof & Intl Education/DMI ....Mr. Steven RIEHS
12 Chief Operating Officer ....Ms. Jill ALBRINCK
07 Group VP Admissions - California ....Vacant
07 Group VP Admissions - Mountain ....Mr. Russell GILL
07 VP of Admissions - Northeast ....Ms. Jamie JAYNES
07 Group VP Admissions - Southeast .... Mr. Matt DEARSMAN
07 Group VP Admissions - North Central ...... Ms. Virginia MECHNIG
07 Group VP Admissions - South Central ....Mr. David WOOD
12 Group VP - North Central ....Ms. Terri JOHNSON
12 Group VP - South Central ....Mr. Mark CAMERON
12 Group VP - California ....Ms. Shelly DUBOIS
12 Group VP - Mountain ....Mr. Jim DUGAN
12 Group VP - Northeast ....Mr. Darryl FIELD
12 Group VP - Southeast ....Mr. Julio TORRES

*DeVry University - Chicago Campus (B)

3300 N Campbell Avenue, Chicago IL 60618-5994
County: Cook FICE Identification: 010727
Unit ID: 144759
Telephone: (773) 929-8500 Carnegie Class: Master's L
FAX Number: (773) 348-1780 Calendar System: Semester
URL: www.devry.edu
Established: 1931 Annual Undergrad Tuition & Fees: $16,156
Enrollment: 1,776 Coed
Affiliation or Control: Proprietary IRS Status: Proprietary
Highest Offering: Master's
Program: Occupational; Professional; Business Emphasis
Accreditation: NH, CAHIIM, ENGT

02 Campus President ....Ms. Candace GOODWIN
06 Registrar ....Ms. Becky MCALISTER
07 Director of Admissions ....Mr. Kelvin EASTER
05 Dean Academic Affairs ....Ms. Deborah ZELECHOWSKI
36 Director of Career Services ....Ms. Keely DENENBERG
37 Manager Student Finance ....Ms. Inesha KELLY
08 Director Library Services ....Mr. Jason ROSSI
26 Director of Community Outreach ....Ms. Karen KUSHINO
32 Dean Student Central ....Ms. Allison VALENTIN

† Regional accreditation is carried under the parent institution in Downers Grove, IL.

Dominican University (C)

7900 W Division Street, River Forest IL 60305-1099
County: Cook FICE Identification: 001750
Unit ID: 148496
Telephone: (708) 366-2490 Carnegie Class: Master's L
FAX Number: (708) 524-5990 Calendar System: Semester
URL: www.dom.edu
Established: 1901 Annual Undergrad Tuition & Fees: $28,690
Enrollment: 3,589 Coed
Affiliation or Control: Roman Catholic IRS Status: 501(c)3
Highest Offering: Doctorate
Program: Liberal Arts And General; Teacher Preparatory; Professional
Accreditation: NH, ACBSP, DIETC, DIETD, LIB, SW, TED

01 President ....Dr. Donna M. CARROLL
05 Provost ....Dr. Cheryl JOHNSON-ODIM
20 Associate Provost ....Dr. David H. KRAUSE
10 Sr VP for Finance & Administration .... Ms. Amy MCCORMACK
42 Vice Pres for Mission & Ministry ....Mrs. Claire NOONAN
30 Vice Pres University Advancement ...... Mrs. Grace J. CICHOMSKA
84 Interim VP Enrollment Management ....Ms. Ann HURLEY
07 AVP Enroll Mgt/Dir Undergrad Admiss ....Mr. Glenn HAMILTON
32 Dean of Students ....Ms. Trudi GOGGIN
50 Dean Brennan School of Business ....Ms. Molly BURKE
62 Dean Grad School Library Science ....Ms. Kate MAREK
53 Dean School of Education ....Dr. Colleen REARDON
70 Dean Graduate School Social Work ....Mr. Charles STOPPS
49 Dean College of Arts & Science ....Dr. Jeffrey CARLSON
88 Assistant Provost ....Mr. Matthew J. HLINAK
08 University Librarian ....Ms. Felice E. MACIEJEWSKI
26 Chief Marketing/Communications Ofcr ....Vacant
27 Chief Information Officer ....Mrs. Jill ALBIN-HILL
06 Registrar ....Mr. Michael Patrick MILLER
36 Director Career Development ....Ms. Keli WOJCIECHOWSKI
29 Dir Alumnae/i Relations ....Ms. Alysha COMSTOCK
88 Promoter of Mission
Integration ....Sr. Mary Ann MEUNINGHOFF, OP
09 Dir Institutional Rsch & Assessment ....Ms. Elizabeth SILK
15 Director Human Resources ....Ms. Roberta MCMAHON
18 Director/Physical Plant ....Mr. Daniel BULOW
07 Director Transfer/Adult Admission ...... Mr. Michael MORSOVILLO
37 Director Financial Aid ....Ms. Marie VON EBERS
23 Director Wellness Center ....Ms. Elizabeth RITZMAN
41 Director Athletics ....Mr. Erick BAUMANN
104 Director International Studies ....Dr. Sue PONREMY

East-West University (D)

816 S Michigan Avenue, Chicago IL 60605-2185
County: Cook FICE Identification: 021686
Unit ID: 144883
Telephone: (312) 939-0111 Carnegie Class: Bac/A&S
FAX Number: (312) 939-0083 Calendar System: Quarter
URL: www.eastwest.edu
Established: 1980 Annual Undergrad Tuition & Fees: $12,795
Enrollment: 899 Coed
Affiliation or Control: Independent Non-Profit IRS Status: 501(c)3
Highest Offering: Baccalaureate
Program: Liberal Arts And General
Accreditation: NH

01 Chancellor ....Dr. M. Wasiullah KHAN
05 Provost ....Dr. Madhu JAIN
20 Associate Provost ....Dr. Ekkehard T. WILKE
88 Assistant Provost for Acad Quality ....Dr. Lawrence J. GORMAN
84 Director of Enrollment Management .... Mr. Bryan S. LAMBERT
30 Assoc Dean Development/Univ Rels ....Mr. Zafar A. MALIK
32 Director Counseling/Student Affairs .... Mr. Bryan S. LAMBERT
37 Director of Financial Aid ....Mr. Cesar CAMPOS
06 Registrar ....Mr. Matt S. MCCAW
04 Assistant to the Chancellor ....Ms. Carolyn J. FOWLKES
19 Director of Security ....Mr. Tasleem RAJA
26 Chief Public Relations Officer ....Mr. John THOMAS
18 Chief Facilities/Physical Plant ....Mr. Tasleem RAJA
10 Chief Business Officer ....Dr. Madhu JAIN
44 Chief Development Officer ....Ms. Barbara ABRAJANO
38 Academic Counselor ....Ms. Sonja M. SIMS
85 International Student Advisor ....Mr. Rashed JAHANGIR

Eastern Illinois University (E)

600 Lincoln Avenue, Charleston IL 61920-3099
County: Coles FICE Identification: 001674
Unit ID: 144892
Telephone: (217) 581-5000 Carnegie Class: Master's L
FAX Number: (217) 581-2722 Calendar System: Semester
URL: www.eiu.edu
Established: 1895 Annual Undergrad Tuition & Fees (In-State): $11,144
Enrollment: 10,417 Coed
Affiliation or Control: State IRS Status: 501(c)3
Highest Offering: Beyond Master's But Less Than Doctorate
Program: Liberal Arts And General; Teacher Preparatory; Professional
Accreditation: NH, AAFCS, ART, BUS, BUSA, CACREP, DIETD, DIETI, JOUR, MUS, NAIT, NRPA, NURSE, SP, TED, THEA

01 President ....Dr. William L. PERRY
05 Provost/Vice Pres Academic Affairs ....Dr. Blair M. LORD
10 Vice President Business Affairs ....Dr. William V. WEBER
32 Vice President Student Affairs ....Dr. Daniel P. NADLER
30 Vice Pres University Advancement ....Mr. Robert K. MARTIN
20 Associate VP Academic Affairs ....Mr. Jeffrey F. CROSS
35 Special Asst to VP Student Affairs ....Ms. Jennifer L. SIPES
13 Asst VP for Information Tech Svcs ....Ms. Kathy S. REED
26 Asst VP Integ Marketing/Communic .... Mr. Patrick M. EARLY
08 Dean of Library Services ....Dr. Allen K. LANHAM
84 Asst VPAA/Enrollment
Management ....Ms. Mary C. HERRINGTON-PERRY
92 Dean Honors College ....Dr. Richard ENGLAND
15 Director Human Resources ....Dr. Richard K. ENYARD
43 General Counsel ....Mr. Robert L. MILLER
22 Director Civil Rights ....Ms. Cynthia D. NICHOLS
45 Dir Planning/Budgeting/Research .... Mr. Michael S. MAURER
07 Director of Admissions ....Ms. Brenda L. MAJOR
37 Director of Financial Aid ....Mr. Jerry A. DONNA
06 Registrar ....Vacant
29 Director Alumni Svc/Community Rels ....Mr. Steven W. RICH
09 Director of Institutional Research .... Mr. Michael S. MAURER
18 Int Dir Facilities/Planning Mgmt .... Mr. Dave CROCKETT
96 Int Dir Procur/Disburs/Contract Svc ....Ms. Kay E. MCELWEE
38 Director of Counseling Center ....Ms. Sandra K. COX
25 Director of Research & Grants ....Dr. Robert W. CHESNUT
41 Director of Athletics ....Ms. Barbara A. BURKE
93 Director of Minority Affairs ....Ms. Mona DAVENPORT
39 Director of Housing/Dining Service ....Mr. Mark A. HUDSON
21 Director Business Svcs/Treasurer ....Mr. Paul A. MCCANN
28 Director of Civil Rights ....Ms. Cynthia D. NICHOLS
36 Director of Career Services ....Ms. Linda L. MOORE
51 Dean Continuing Education ....Dr. Regis M. GILMAN
58 Dean Graduate School ....Dr. Robert M. AUGUSTINE
81 Dean College Sciences ....Dr. W. Harold ORNES
50 Dean Lumpkin Col Bus/Appl Sci ....Dr. Mahyar IZADI
79 Dean College Arts/Humanities ....Dr. Bonnie IRWIN
53 Dean College Education ....Dr. Diane H. JACKMAN

Elgin Community College (F)

1700 Spartan Drive, Elgin IL 60123-7193
County: Kane FICE Identification: 001675
Unit ID: 144944
Telephone: (847) 697-1000 Carnegie Class: Assoc/Pub-S-MC
FAX Number: (847) 214-7995 Calendar System: Semester
URL: www.elgin.edu
Established: 1949 Annual Undergrad Tuition & Fees (In-District): $2,616
Enrollment: 11,554 Coed
Affiliation or Control: Local IRS Status: 501(c)3
Highest Offering: Associate Degree
Program: Occupational; 2-Year Principally Bachelor's Creditable
Accreditation: NH, ADNUR, COMTA, DA, HT, MLTAD, PTAA, RAD, SURGT

01 President ....Dr. David SAM
10 Vice Pres Business/Finance ....Ms. Sharon KONNY
05 VP Teaching/Learning/Stdnt Dev ....Ms. Rose DIGERLANDO
20 Asst VP Teach/Lrng/Stdnt Dev ....Ms. Marcy THOMPSON
20 Dean Academic Dev/Learning Resource ....Dr. Mi HU
88 Dean Sustain/Safety & Career Tech ....Dr. Jeff BOYD
83 Dean Comm/Behavioral Sciences ....Dr. Ruixuan MAO
57 Dean Liberal/Visual/Performing Arts ....Ms. Mary HATCH
81 Dean Math/Science & Engineer ....Dr. James MCGEE
32 Dean of Student Services ....Dr. Gregory ROBINSON
88 Dean Adult Basic Education ....Ms. Peggy HEINRICH
76 Dean Health Professions ....Ms. Wendy MILLER
38 Assoc Dean Counsel/Career Svcs ....Mr. John COFFIN
84 Assoc Dean Enrollment Management ....Dr. Mary PERKINS
106 Assoc Dean Inst Improve/Dist Lrng ....Mr. Timothy MOORE
88 Asc Dean TRIO/Reten/Stdnt Outreach .... Dr. L. Bruce AUSTIN
18 Managing Director Facilities ....Mr. Cal BYRD
16 Chief Human Resources Officer ....Ms. Janelle CROWLEY
13 Chief Information Officer ....Mr. Ned COONEN
26 Exec Dir Communications ....Mr. Jeff JULIAN
30 Exec Dir Inst Advance/ECC Found .... Ms. Katherine SAWYER
20 Managing Dir Inst Comp/Curr ....Ms. Sharon WILSON
45 Executive Dir Planning/Inst Effect ....Dr. Philip GARBER
09 Director Institutional Research ....Mr. David RUDDEN
37 Director Financial Aid/Scholarships ....Ms. Amy PERRIN
19 Chief of Police ....Mr. Emad EASSA
21 Controller ....Ms. Heather SCHOLL
84 Managing Dir Enrollment Svcs ....Dr. Jennifer MCCLURE
90 Director Academic Computing ....Ms. Karin STACY
22 Paralegal/EEO/AA Title IX/FOIA Ofcr ....Ms. Marilyn PRENTICE
07 Director of Admissions/Recruitment ....Mr. Trevell EDDINS
41 Director Athletics & Wellness ....Mr. Kent PAYNE
40 Exec Dir Aux Enterprises & Cont Ed .... Mr. Frank HERNANDEZ
96 Director Business Services ....Ms. Melissa TAIT
36 Director Career Services ....Ms. Peggy GUNDRUM
26 Senior Director of Marketing ....Mr. Jeffrey ARENA
35 Director Orientation/Student Life ....Ms. Amybeth MAURER
88 Dir Small Business Devel Center ....Ms. Sybil EGE
14 Sr Director Technology Services ....Mr. Phil HOWARD
86 Dir Cmty Engagemnt/Legislative Affs ....Ms. Paula AMENTA
101 Secretary to Board of Trustees ....Mr. John DUFFY
04 Sr Exec Asst to the President ....Ms. Kathleen J. STOVER

Elmhurst College (A)

190 Prospect, Elmhurst IL 60126-3296
County: DuPage FICE Identification: 001676
Unit ID: 144962
Telephone: (630) 279-4100 Carnegie Class: Master's M
FAX Number: (630) 617-3282 Calendar System: 4/1/4
URL: www.elmhurst.edu
Established: 1871 Annual Undergrad Tuition & Fees: $32,720
Enrollment: 3,298 Coed
Affiliation or Control: United Church Of Christ IRS Status: 501(c)3
Highest Offering: Master's
Program: Liberal Arts And General; Teacher Preparatory; Professional
Accreditation: NH, NURSE, @SP

01 President .... Dr. S. Alan RAY
10 VP of Finance & Administration .... Mr. James CUNNINGHAM
05 Sr VP Acad Affs/Dean of Faculty .... Dr. Alzada TIPTON
27 VP and Chief Information Officer .... Dr. James KULICH
26 VP for Communications & Public Affs .... Mr. James W. WINTERS
29 VP for Development/Alumni Relations .... Mr. Joseph R. EMMICK
32 Dean of Students .... Dr. Eileen G. SULLIVAN
07 Dean of Admission .... Mr. Gary F. ROLD
107 Dean School for Professional Stds .... Dr. Timothy RICORDATI
20 Associate Dean of Faculty .... Dr. Heather HALL
20 Associate Dean of Faculty .... Dr. Theodore LERUD
88 Exec Dir Center for Pro Excellence .... Dr. Lawrence B. CARROLL
18 Exec Director Facilities Management .... Mr. Bruce J. MATHER
42 Chaplain .... Rev. H. Scott MATHENEY
06 Registrar .... Mr. S. Dean ELLENS
08 Director of the Library .... Ms. Susan S. STEFFEN
36 Director of Career Education .... Ms. Peggy KILLIAN
21 Controller .... Mr. Richard A. SCHEPLER
38 Director of Counseling Services .... Dr. Amy SWARR
28 Director of Intercultural Education .... Dr. Kathleen RUST
14 Director of Computer Services .... Mr. James M. FRANCIS
88 Director Development Services .... Ms. LaTonya FOSTER
29 Director of Alumni Relations .... Mr. Thomas NEWTON
88 Managing Dir of Public Affairs .... Ms. Desiree CHEN
15 Director of Human Resources .... Ms. Lynita GEBHARDT
19 Exec Director of Campus Security .... Mr. Jeff KEDROWSKI
37 Director of Financial Aid .... Ms. Ruth PUSICH
07 Director of Admission .... Ms. Stephanie LEVENSON
07 Managing Dir Adult/Grad Admission .... Mr. Tim PANFIL
39 Director of Residence Life .... Ms. Christine J. SMITH
41 Director Intercollegiate Athletics .... Mr. Paul KROHN

Erikson Institute (B)

451 N. Lasalle Street, Chicago IL 60654
County: Cook FICE Identification: 035103
Unit ID: 409254
Telephone: (312) 755-2250 Carnegie Class: Spec/Other
FAX Number: (312) 755-0928 Calendar System: Semester
URL: www.erikson.edu
Established: 1966 Annual Graduate Tuition & Fees: $16,380
Enrollment: 256 Coed
Affiliation or Control: Independent Non-Profit IRS Status: 501(c)3
Highest Offering: Master's; No Undergraduates
Program: Professional
Accreditation: NH

01 Int President of External Affairs .... Barbara BOWMAN
01 Int President of Internal Affairs .... Frances SCOTT
05 Sr VP Academic Affs/Dean of Faculty .... Aisha RAY
10 Vice President Finance/Operations .... Susan WALLACE
45 Vice President Planning/Enrollment .... Jeanne LOCKRIDGE
30 Vice Pres Institutional Advancement .... Randy L. HOLGATE
84 Dean of Enrollment Management .... Michel FRENDIAN
13 Chief Information Officer .... Jonathan FRANK
27 Director of Communications .... Anne DIVITA KOPACZ
88 Dir of Professional Development .... Deborah MANTIA
44 Asst Dir Data Systems/Donor Svcs .... Christine VILLAS

Eureka College (C)

300 E College Avenue, Eureka IL 61530-1500
County: Woodford FICE Identification: 001678
Unit ID: 144971
Telephone: (309) 467-3721 Carnegie Class: Bac/Diverse
FAX Number: (309) 467-6386 Calendar System: Semester
URL: www.eureka.edu
Established: 1855 Annual Undergrad Tuition & Fees: $20,060
Enrollment: 754 Coed
Affiliation or Control: Christian Church (Disciples Of Christ)
IRS Status: 501(c)3
Highest Offering: Baccalaureate
Program: Liberal Arts And General; Teacher Preparatory
Accreditation: NH

01 President .... Dr. J. David ARNOLD
04 Administrative Asst to President .... Mrs. Jyl ZUBIATE
05 Provost & Dean of the College .... Dr. Philip Acree CAVALIER
10 VP Fin/Fac/Chief Financial Officer .... Mr. Marc PASTERIS
32 Dean of Student Services .... Mrs. Brooke CAMPBELL
30 Vice Pres Dev & Alumni Relations .... Mr. Michael MURTAGH
26 Director of Marketing and Comm .... Ms. Corrie HECK
06 Registrar .... Mr. Scott WIGNALL
08 Library Director .... Mr. Tony GLASS
18 Director of Physical Plant .... Mr. Rob MCCHESNEY
42 Chaplain .... Rev. Bruce M. FOWLKES
14 Director of Computer Services .... Dr. Kanaka VIJITHA-KUMARA
37 Director of Financial Aid .... Mrs. Ellen M. RIGSBY
41 Athletic Director .... Mr. Paul BRYANT
29 Director Alumni Relations .... Mrs. Shellie SCHWANKE

Fox College (D)

6640 South Cicero Avenue, Bedford Park IL 60638
County: Cook FICE Identification: 025228
Unit ID: 145239
Telephone: (708) 444-4500 Carnegie Class: Assoc/PrivFP
FAX Number: (708) 802-6585 Calendar System: Semester
URL: www.foxcollege.edu
Established: 1932 Annual Undergrad Tuition & Fees: $15,080
Enrollment: 500 Coed
Affiliation or Control: Proprietary IRS Status: Proprietary
Highest Offering: Associate Degree
Program: Occupational; 2-Year Principally Bachelor's Creditable; Business Emphasis
Accreditation: NH, MAAB, PTAA

01 President .... Mr. Carey CRANSTON
11 Operations Administrator .... Ms. Nicole BROWN

Garrett-Evangelical Theological Seminary (E)

2121 Sheridan Road, Evanston IL 60201-3298
County: Cook FICE Identification: 001682
Unit ID: 145275
Telephone: (847) 866-3900 Carnegie Class: Spec/Faith
FAX Number: (847) 866-3957 Calendar System: Semester
URL: www.garrett.edu
Established: 1853 Annual Graduate Tuition & Fees: $18,415
Enrollment: 390 Coed
Affiliation or Control: United Methodist IRS Status: 501(c)3
Highest Offering: Doctorate; No Undergraduates
Program: Professional; Religious Emphasis
Accreditation: NH, THEOL

01 President .... Dr. Philip A. AMERSON
11 VP for Admin/External Programming .... Dr. James A. NOSEWORTHY
05 Acad Dean/Vice Pres Acad Affairs .... Dr. Lallene J. RECTOR
30 Vice President for Development .... Dr. David L. HEETLAND
10 Vice President Business Affairs/CFO .... Mr. Arnold HENNING
32 Dean of Students .... Rev. Cynthia A. WILSON
84 Associate VP for Enrollment Mgmt .... Rev. Becky J. EBERHART
04 Executive Asst to the President .... Ms. Erin B. MOORE
21 Controller .... Vacant
06 Registrar/Dir of Academic Studies .... Rev. Vince MCGLOTHIN-ELLER
08 Director of United Library .... Dr. Jaeyeon L. CHUNG
13 Director of Information Technology .... Mr. James D. CASH
18 Director of Buildings & Grounds .... Mr. John CARTER
39 Director of Housing & Food Service .... Ms. Barbara B. ADAMS
29 Dir Annual Gvg/Alum Rel/Hospitality .... Ms. Kay A. BURLINGHAM
88 Director of Stewardship .... Ms. Elizabeth P. CAMPBELL
37 Director of Financial Aid .... Mr. Jason GILL
26 Manager of Communications & Events .... Mr. Shane NICHOLS

Governors State University (F)

1 University Parkway, University Park IL 60484-0975
County: Will FICE Identification: 009145
Unit ID: 145336
Telephone: (708) 534-5000 Carnegie Class: Master's L
FAX Number: (708) 534-4107 Calendar System: Semester
URL: www.govst.edu
Established: 1969 Annual Undergrad Tuition & Fees (In-State): $9,386
Enrollment: 5,609 Coed
Affiliation or Control: State IRS Status: 501(c)3
Highest Offering: Doctorate
Program: Liberal Arts And General; Teacher Preparatory; Professional
Accreditation: NH, ACBSP, CACREP, HSA, NUR, OT, PTA, SP, SPAA, SW, TED

01 President .... Dr. Elaine P. MAIMON
03 Executive VP & Chief of Staff/Treas .... Dr. Gebeyehu EJIGU
05 Provost/VP Academic Affairs .... Dr. Deborah BORDELON
10 Vice Pres Admininstration & Finance .... Ms. Karen KISSEL
11 Interim Vice Pres Admin & Planning .... Dr. Gebeyehu EJIGU
30 VP Advancement/CEO Foundation .... Mr. William DAVIS
26 VP Enrollment Mgmt & Marketing .... Ms. Courtney KOHN SANDERS
43 Legal Counsel .... Ms. Alexis KENNEDY
22 Affirmative Action/EO .... Mr. Tony A. TYMKOW
45 Director Budget Planning/Inst Rsrch .... Dr. Jeffrey SLOVAK
09 Assoc Dir of Institutional Research .... Ms. Kirstan MEUKAM
29 Interim Director of Alumni Assoc .... Ms. Cheri GAREY
26 Asst VP of Marketing/Communication .... Ms. Rhonda BROWN
50 Dean Col Business/Public Admin .... Dr. Ellen FOSTER CURTIS
49 Dean College Arts Sciences .... Dr. Reinhold HILL
76 Dean Col Health Professions .... Dr. Elizabeth CADA
53 Interim Dean College Education .... Dr. Karen D'ARCY
32 Dean Student Affairs & Services .... Dr. Aurelio VALENTE
84 Exec Director Enrollment Services .... Vacant
08 Dean Library Svc/Academic Computing .... Vacant
56 Dean Extend Lrng/Community Svcs .... Vacant
06 Registrar .... Mr. Christopher HUANG
37 Director Financial Aid .... Mr. John PERRY
35 Acting Executive Dir Student Life .... Ms. Vanessa NEWBY

20 Associate Provost/AVP Academic Affs .... Dr. Angela LATHAM
21 Director Business Operations .... Ms. Karen KISSEL
13 Exec Director Information Tech Svcs .... Mr. Peter J. MIZERA
15 Director Human Resources .... Ms. Gail BRADSHAW
18 Director Physical Plant .... Mr. Sajid MAIN
19 Int Director Dept Public Safety .... Mr. James MCGEE
38 Dir Stdnt Develop/Counseling Center .... Ms. Kelly MCCARTHY
36 Director of Career Services .... Ms. Darcie R. CAMPOS
96 Dir of Procurement/Auxillary Svcs .... Ms. Tracy SULLIVAN

Greenville College (G)

315 E College, Greenville IL 62246
County: Bond FICE Identification: 001684
Unit ID: 145372
Telephone: (618) 664-2800 Carnegie Class: Bac/Diverse
FAX Number: (618) 664-6841 Calendar System: 4/1/4
URL: www.greenville.edu
Established: 1892 Annual Undergrad Tuition & Fees: $23,612
Enrollment: 1,463 Coed
Affiliation or Control: Free Methodist IRS Status: 501(c)3
Highest Offering: Master's
Program: Liberal Arts And General; Teacher Preparatory; Professional
Accreditation: NH, @TEAC

01 President .... Dr. Ivan FILBY
04 Assistant to the President .... Ms. Tamie HEICHELBECK
05 Interim VPAA .... Dr. Brad SHAW
30 Vice Pres for Advancement .... Vacant
10 Vice President for Finance .... Mrs. Dana FUNDERBURK
32 Vice Pres for Student Development .... Dr. Norman D. HALL
84 Vice Pres for Enrollment .... Mr. Michael RITTER
45 Assoc VP Planning/Dn Prof Stds .... Dr. Dave HOLDEN
08 Director of Library .... Ms. Jane L. HOPKINS
06 Registrar .... Mrs. Michelle SUSSENBACH
29 Director Alumni Relations .... Ms. Pam TAYLOR
37 Director of Financial Aid .... Mrs. Marilae LATHAM
30 Director of Advancement .... Vacant
42 Dean Chapel & Dir Spiritual Form .... Mrs. Lori GAFFNER
18 Director of Facilities .... Mr. Mark OWENS
26 Director of Marketing .... Mr. Nathan BREWER
09 Dean of College Planning/Assessment .... Vacant
49 Dean School Arts & Sciences .... Dr. Brian HARTLEY
53 Dean School of Education .... Dr. Mark LAMB
41 Athletic Director .... Dr. Doug FAULKNER
13 Assoc VP Innovation & Technology .... Dr. Vickie COOK
07 Dir of Undergraduate Admissions .... Mr. John MASSENA
28 Dean of Diversity .... Dr. Eugene DUNKLEY

Harper College (H)

1200 W Algonquin Road, Palatine IL 60067-7398
County: Cook FICE Identification: 003961
Unit ID: 149842
Telephone: (847) 925-6000 Carnegie Class: Assoc/Pub-S-SC
FAX Number: (847) 925-6034 Calendar System: Semester
URL: www.harpercollege.edu
Established: 1965 Annual Undergrad Tuition & Fees (In-District): $3,102
Enrollment: 16,470 Coed
Affiliation or Control: State/Local IRS Status: 501(c)3
Highest Offering: Associate Degree
Program: Occupational; 2-Year Principally Bachelor's Creditable
Accreditation: NH, ACBSP, ADNUR, CAHIIM, CEA, DH, DIETT, DMS, MAC, MUS, RAD

01 President .... Dr. Kenneth L. ENDER
100 Chief of Staff/VP Plng/Inst Effect .... Ms. Sheila QUIRK-BAILEY
103 Sr Exec to the Pres/VP Wkfrce Strat .... Dr. Maria COONS
10 Exec VP Finance & Admin Services .... Dr. Ron ALLY
05 Provost .... Dr. Judith MARWICK
30 Chief Advancement Officer .... Dr. Mary KNIGHT
26 Chief Communications Officer .... Mr. Phil BURDICK
20 Assoc Provost/Interdis Student Succ .... Dr. Joan KINDLE
16 Chief Human Resources Officer .... Mr. Roger SPAYER
27 Chief Information Officer .... Mr. Patrick BAUER
21 Controller .... Mr. Bret BONNSTETTER
18 Exec Director of Facilities Mgmt .... Mr. Thomas CRYLEN
75 Dean Career & Technical Programs .... Dr. Mary Beth OTTINGER
76 Dean Health Careers .... Ms. Kimberly CHAVIS
88 Dean Acad Enrichment/Engagement .... Dr. Kenya AYERS
08 Dean Resources for Learning .... Ms. Njambi KAMOCHE
32 Dean Stdnt Affs/Welln & Campus Act .... Dr. Ashley KNIGHT
84 Asst Provost/Dean Enrollment Svcs .... Ms. Maria MOTEN
51 Dean Cont Education & Bus Outreach .... Dr. Mark MROZINSKI
35 Asst Provost Student Development .... Ms. Sheryl OTTO
50 Dean Business & Social Science .... Ms. Michele' ROBINSON
81 Interim Dean Mathematics & Sciences .... Ms. Julie ELLEFSON-KUEHN
88 Asst Dean Acad Enrch/Engmt/Dir AED .... Ms. Darice TROUT
72 Asst Dean Ctr for Adjunct Fac Engag .... Mr. Jack HENDERSON
49 Dean Liberal Arts .... Mr. Brian KNETL
88 Assoc Dean Ctr Adjunct Fac Engag .... Vacant
93 Assoc Dean Multicultural Lrng .... Ms. Laura LABAUVE-MAHER
23 Director Health Services .... Dr. Bridget CAHILL
88 Dir New Student Programs/Retention .... Ms. Vicki ATKINSON
13 Director IT Enterprise Systems .... Dr. Mike BABB
26 Director Marketing Services .... Mr. Mike BARZACCHINI
36 Director Career Svs & Women's Pgm .... Ms. Kathleen CANFIELD
88 Director IT Client Services .... Ms. Sue CONTARINO
09 Director Institutional Research .... Mr. Doug EASTERLING
106 Director Ctr for Innov Instruction .... Mr. Matthew ENSENBERGER
88 Dir Disability Svcs/ADA Compliance .... Mr. Scott FRIEDMAN

Code	Title	Name
88	Director Physical Plant	Mr. Darryl KNIGHT
37	Dir Student Financial Assistance	Ms. Laura MCGEE
66	Director Nursing	Ms. Julie D'AGOSTINO
14	Director IT Technical Services	Mr. James BATSON
35	Director Student Involvement	Mr. Ernie KIMLIN
07	Dir Student Recruitment & Outreach	Mr. Robert PARZY
88	Campus Architect	Mr. Stephen PETERSEN
38	Dir Academic Advising & Counseling	Dr. Eric ROSENTHAL
44	Asc Exec Dir Found/Dir Major Gifts	Vacant
108	Dir Inst Effect/Outcomes Assess	Ms. Darlene SCHLENBECKER
41	Director of Athletics & Fitness	Mr. Doug SPIWAK

Harrington College of Design (A)

200 W Madison, 2nd Floor, Chicago IL 60606-3433
County: Cook — FICE Identification: 020552
Unit ID: 145460
Telephone: (312) 939-4975 — Carnegie Class: Spec/Arts
FAX Number: (312) 939-8005 — Calendar System: Semester
URL: www.harrington.edu
Established: 1931 — Annual Undergrad Tuition & Fees: $19,300
Enrollment: 615 — Coed
Affiliation or Control: Proprietary — IRS Status: Proprietary
Highest Offering: Master's
Program: Professional; Fine Arts Emphasis
Accreditation: NH, CIDA

Code	Title	Name
01	President	Mr. Max S. SHANGLE
05	Director of Academic Affairs	Ms. Gretchen FRICKX
07	Director of Admissions	Ms. Jessie MCEWEN
10	Regional Controller	Ms. Gladys CHINCHILLA
13	Manager of IT & Facilities	Mr. Bryan STYER
36	Director Career Services	Ms. Camille HARRIS
08	Head Librarian	Ms. Leigh GATES
21	Campus Business Operations Manager	Mr. Ryan FROEHLE
06	Registrar	Mr. Sam DELAROSA
35	Director Student Services	Mr. Sam DELAROSA
09	Director of Institutional Research	Ms. Renee DAROSKY

Heartland Community College (B)

1500 W Raab Road, Normal IL 61761-9446
County: McLean — FICE Identification: 030838
Unit ID: 384342
Telephone: (309) 268-8000 — Carnegie Class: Assoc/Pub-R-L
FAX Number: (309) 268-7999 — Calendar System: Semester
URL: www.heartland.edu
Established: 1990 — Annual Undergrad Tuition & Fees (In-District): $3,336
Enrollment: 5,456 — Coed
Affiliation or Control: State/Local — IRS Status: 501(c)3
Highest Offering: Associate Degree
Program: Occupational; 2-Year Principally Bachelor's Creditable
Accreditation: NH, ADNUR, RAD

Code	Title	Name
01	President	Dr. Robet D. WIDMER
05	Vice Pres Learning/Student Success	Dr. Rick PEARCE
10	Vice President Business Services	Mr. Robert D. WIDMER
30	Vice President of Advancement	Ms. Mary Beth TRAKINAT
88	Dean Student Success	Dr. Amy MUNSON
84	Dean Enrollment Services	Mr. Padriac SHINVILLE
18	Executive Director of Facilities	Mr. James HUBBARD
11	Director of Administrative Services	Ms. Valerie CRAWFORD
13	Chief Information Officer	Mr. Doug MINTER
21	Controller	Ms. Sue GILPIN
37	Director of Financial Aid	Mr. Todd BURNS
15	Exec Director Human Resources	Mrs. Barb LEATHERS
86	Exec Dir Governmental Relations	Ms. Janet HILL GETZ
09	Exec Director Inst Effectiveness	Mr. David COOK
41	Director of Athletics	Mr. Nate METZGER
29	Director Alumni Relations/Outreach	Ms. Colleen REYNOLDS
36	Director Testing Services	Ms. Kimberly KELLEY
06	Assoc Director of Records	Ms. Jeannie HILL
26	Director of Marketing	Ms. Amy HUMPHREYS

Hebrew Theological College (C)

7135 N Carpenter Road, Skokie IL 60077-3263
County: Cook — FICE Identification: 001685
Unit ID: 145497
Telephone: (847) 982-2500 — Carnegie Class: Spec/Faith
FAX Number: (847) 674-6381 — Calendar System: Semester
URL: www.htc.edu
Established: 1922 — Annual Undergrad Tuition & Fees: $18,305
Enrollment: 464 — Coordinate
Affiliation or Control: Independent Non-Profit — IRS Status: 501(c)3
Highest Offering: Master's
Program: Liberal Arts And General; Teacher Preparatory; Professional; Religious Emphasis
Accreditation: NH

Code	Title	Name
01	Chancellor	Rabbi Jerold ISENBERG
05	Rosh Hayeshiva-Chief Academic	Rabbi Avraham FRIEDMAN
11	Vice President for Administration	Rabbi Sender KUTNER
20	Dean Blitstein Institute	Dr. Esther SHKOP
20	Dean AHS & LAS Men's Division	Rabbi Michael MYERS
33	Mashgiach Ruchani-Dean	Rabbi Zvi ZIMMERMAN
34	Menahel Ruchani-Dean	Rabbi Binyamin OLSTEIN
34	Assistant Dean Blitstein Institute	Ms. Rita LIPSHITZ
06	Registrar	Rabbi Shmuel SCHUMAN
07	Director of Admissions	Rabbi Joshua ZISOOK
30	Director of Development	Rabbi Gershon SEIF
44	Development Coordinator	Rabbi Yaakov FRIEDMAN
08	Librarian	Ms. Eti BERLAND
88	Israel Program Liaison - Blitstein	Mrs. Chaya FISH
88	Israel Program Liaison - Beis Midra	Rabbi Joshua KANTER

† Separate campuses for male and female students.

Highland Community College (D)

2998 W Pearl City Road, Freeport IL 61032-9341
County: Stephenson — FICE Identification: 001681
Unit ID: 145521
Telephone: (815) 235-6121 — Carnegie Class: Assoc/Pub-R-M
FAX Number: (815) 235-6130 — Calendar System: Semester
URL: www.highland.edu
Established: 1962 — Annual Undergrad Tuition & Fees (In-District): $3,930
Enrollment: 1,733 — Coed
Affiliation or Control: State/Local — IRS Status: 501(c)3
Highest Offering: Associate Degree
Program: Occupational; 2-Year Principally Bachelor's Creditable
Accreditation: NH, MAC

Code	Title	Name
01	President	Dr. Joe M. KANOSKY
05	Vice Pres Academic Services	Mr. Tim HOOD
11	Vice Pres Administrative Services	Ms. Jill M. JANSSEN
15	Associate VP Human Resources	Mrs. Rose A. FERGUSON
32	Assoc VP Student Services	Mrs. Elizabeth L. GERBER
50	Dean Business & Technology	Mr. Scott R. ANDERSON
79	Dean Humanities/Soc Science	Dr. Thompson A. BRANDT
66	Assoc Dean Nursing & Allied Health	Ms. Donna KAUKE
81	Assoc Dean Natural Science & Math	Vacant
51	Director Adult Education	Mr. Mark JANSEN
41	Director Athletics	Mr. Peter E. NORMAN
84	Director Enrollment/Records	Mr. Jeremy BRADT
37	Director Financial Aid	Ms. Kathy BANGASSER
90	Director ITS	Mr. Nathan HENSAL
09	Director Institutional Research	Dr. Michelle THRUMAN
88	Director Learning & Transitional Ed	Ms. Carolyn PETSCHE
08	Director Library Services	Mrs. Judy MOORE
31	Director Marketing & Cmty Relations	Mr. Pete WILLGING
18	Director Physical Plant/Maint	Mr. Kurt SIMPSON
88	Director Retired & Senior Vol Pgm	Mr. Michael J. SHORE
88	Director Title IV Student Support	Mr. Anthony SAGO
21	Manager Accounting	Ms. Mary J. LLOYD
40	Manager Bookstore	Ms. Madonna KEENEY
101	Exec Asst to President/Board Sec	Ms. Terri A. GRIMES
96	Purchasing & Insurance Specialist	Ms. Teresa WILLIAMS
102	Executive Director Foundation	Mr. James M. BERBERET

Illinois Central College (E)

1 College Drive, East Peoria IL 61635-0001
County: Tazewell — FICE Identification: 006753
Unit ID: 145682
Telephone: (309) 694-5422 — Carnegie Class: Assoc/Pub-R-L
FAX Number: (309) 694-5450 — Calendar System: Semester
URL: www.icc.edu
Established: 1966 — Annual Undergrad Tuition & Fees (In-District): $3,450
Enrollment: 11,125 — Coed
Affiliation or Control: State/Local — IRS Status: 501(c)3
Highest Offering: Associate Degree
Program: Occupational; 2-Year Principally Bachelor's Creditable
Accreditation: NH, ADNUR, COARC, DH, EMT, MAC, MLTAD, MUS, OTA, PTAA, RAD, SURGT

Code	Title	Name
01	President	Dr. John S. ERWIN
05	Provost	Dr. William TAMMONE
10	Exec VP Administration/Finance	Mr. Bruce BUDDE
26	Vice President of Marketing & Comm	Dr. Cheryl FLIEGE
20	Vice Pres of Academic Affairs	Dr. Margaret A. SWANSON
30	Vice President/Chief Devel Officer	Ms. Robin BALLARD
32	Vice President of Student Affairs	Mr. Guy GOODMAN
15	Vice President of Human Resources	Ms. Marti BLOODSAW
28	Vice President of Diversity	Dr. Rita ALI
14	Director Technology Services	Dr. Susan WHEELER
38	Director Advisement/Assess/Counsel	Ms. Pam WILFINGER
37	Director Student Financial Services	Ms. Beth MCCLAIN
07	Director Enrollment Services	Ms. Angela DREESSEN
18	Dir of Facilities Planning & Design	Mr. Troy HATTERMANN
51	Dean Corporate/Community Education	Ms. Ellen GEORGE
88	Assoc Dean Inst Innov & Learning	Ms. Janice KINSINGER
83	Dean English/Soc Sciences & Lang	Dr. Jill WRIGHT
81	Dean Math/Science/Engineering	Mr. Tom PILAT
50	Dean Business/Info Services	Vacant
57	Dean Arts & Communications	Mr. Christopher GRAY
47	Dean Agriculture/Industrial Tech	Mr. Michael SLOAN
31	Dean Cmty Outreach/ICC S Coord	Ms. Kay SUTTON
52	Dean Health Careers	Ms. Wendee GUTH
60	Associate Dean English	Dr. Michael BOYD
106	Associate Dean Online Learning	Dr. Patrice HESS
21	Director Business Services	Ms. Kim MALCOLM
06	Registrar	Ms. Nikisha WRIGHTANDERSON
29	Coordinator Alumni Relations	Ms. Elaine GOSLIN

Illinois College (F)

1101 W College Avenue, Jacksonville IL 62650-2299
County: Morgan — FICE Identification: 001688
Unit ID: 145691
Telephone: (217) 245-3000 — Carnegie Class: Bac/A&S
FAX Number: (217) 245-3034 — Calendar System: Semester
URL: www.ic.edu
Established: 1829 — Annual Undergrad Tuition & Fees: $27,800
Enrollment: 965 — Coed
Affiliation or Control: Independent Non-Profit — IRS Status: 501(c)3
Highest Offering: Master's
Program: Liberal Arts And General; Teacher Preparatory
Accreditation: NH

Code	Title	Name
01	President	Dr. Barbara A. FARLEY
05	Vice President Academic Affairs	Dr. Elizabeth H. TOBIN
10	Vice President Business Affairs	Mr. Frank G. WILLIAMS
30	Vice President Advancement	Vacant
84	Vice President for Enrollment	Ms. Stephanie CHIPMAN
32	VP Student Affairs/Dean of Students	Dr. Malinda L. CARLSON
18	Director of Campus Facilities	Mr. Al DILLOW
20	Associate Dean of the College	Dr. Adam PORTER
07	Associate Director Admissions	Mr. Richard L. BYSTRY
29	Director Alumni Relations	Ms. Kristin E. JAMISON
26	Director of Marketing & Communicati	Ms. Mary Ellen ROY
08	Librarian	Mr. Jan FIGA
37	Director Student Financial Aid	Ms. Katherine A. TAYLOR
36	Director of Career Center	Ms. Susan K. DRAKE
06	Registrar	Ms. Helen KUHN
21	Controller	Ms. Melissa J. DYSSON
35	Director Student Activities	Ms. Karen K. HOMOLKA
42	Chaplain	Rev. Katrina E. JENKINS
88	Assoc Dir of Admissions/Recruitment	Ms. Kristen REED
09	Advisor to Pres for Inst Research	Dr. Robert A. SWEATMAN
15	Director Personnel Services	Ms. Teresa C. SMITH
38	Director Student Counseling	Mr. William TENNILL
28	Director of Diversity	Mr. Justin MALLETT

Illinois College of Optometry (G)

3241 S Michigan Avenue, Chicago IL 60616-3878
County: Cook — FICE Identification: 001689
Unit ID: 145628
Telephone: (312) 225-1700 — Carnegie Class: Spec/Health
FAX Number: (312) 225-1724 — Calendar System: Quarter
URL: www.ico.edu
Established: 1872 — Annual Graduate Tuition & Fees: $35,086
Enrollment: 639 — Coed
Affiliation or Control: Independent Non-Profit — IRS Status: 501(c)3
Highest Offering: First Professional Degree; No Undergraduates
Program: Professional
Accreditation: NH, OPT, OPTR

Code	Title	Name
01	President	Dr. Arol R. AUGSBURGER
05	Vice Pres for Academic Affairs/Dean	Dr. Stephanie MESSNER
11	Vice President Administration	Mrs. Laura L. ROUNCE
17	Vice Pres for Patient Care Services	Dr. Leonard V. MESSNER
10	VP for Finance & Business/CFO	Mr. John BUDZYNSKI
30	VP Student/Alumni/College Devel	Dr. Mark COLIP
22	VP Compliance/Cmty Based Services	Dr. Valarie CONRAD
20	Associate Dean Academic Affairs	Dr. Barclay BAKKUM
06	Asst Dean Academic Admin/Registrar	Mrs. Lavern YOUNG
07	Director of Admissions	Ms. Teisha JOHNSON
35	Sr Director Student Development	Ms. Beth KARMIS
37	Director Student Financial Aid	Ms. Melissa BARTOLD
29	Director Alumni Relations	Ms. Connie M. SCAVUZZO
18	Chief Facilities/Physical Plant	Mr. Opie NIMON
36	Director Student Placement	Vacant

*Illinois Eastern Community Colleges System Office (H)

233 E Chestnut Street, Olney IL 62450-2298
County: Richland — FICE Identification: 009135
Unit ID: 443368
Telephone: (618) 393-2982 — Carnegie Class: N/A
FAX Number: (618) 392-4816
URL: www.iecc.edu

Code	Title	Name
01	Chief Executive Officer	Mr. Terry BRUCE
05	Dean Acad/Student Support Svc/CAO	Mrs. Chris CANTWELL
10	Chief Finance Officer/Treasurer	Mr. Roger BROWNING
103	Dean Workforce Education	Mr. Michael THOMAS
30	Assoc Dean Grants/Inst Development	Mrs. LeAnn HARTLEROAD
20	Pgm Director College Support Svcs	Ms. Rita S. ADAMS
88	Program Director SBDC	Mr. Byron BRUMFIEL
85	Pgm Dir Intl Std/Dir Dist Std Rctmt	Ms. Pamela SWANSON-MADDEN
15	Director of Human Resources	Mrs. Tara BUERSTER
88	TRiO Upward Bound Director DO/OCC	Ms. Tiffany COWGER
88	TRiO Upward Bound Director DO/LTC	Mr. Brandon WEGER
88	Director Student Advantage Network	Vacant
88	TRiO Talent Search Director DO	Ms. Gina HUTTON

*Illinois Eastern Community Colleges Frontier Community College (I)

Frontier Drive, Fairfield IL 62837-9801
County: Wayne — FICE Identification: 020744
Unit ID: 403469
Telephone: (618) 842-3711 — Carnegie Class: Assoc/Pub-R-L
FAX Number: (618) 842-4425 — Calendar System: Semester
URL: www.iecc.edu/fcc
Established: 1976 — Annual Undergrad Tuition & Fees (In-District): $2,954
Enrollment: 2,597 — Coed
Affiliation or Control: State/Local — IRS Status: 501(c)3
Highest Offering: Associate Degree
Program: Occupational; 2-Year Principally Bachelor's Creditable
Accreditation: &NH, ADNUR

02 President ....Dr. Tim TAYLOR
05 Dean of Instruction ....Mr. Bob BOYLES
32 Asst Dean of Student Services ....Mrs. Jan WILES
51 Assoc Dean Adult & Cont Education ....Mrs. Jervaise MCDANIEL
10 Director of Business ....Mrs. Mary JOHNSTON
08 Director of Learning Resource Ctr ....Ms. Merna YOUNGBLOOD
88 Pgm Dir Emerg Prep/Indu Qual Mgmt ....Vacant
18 Supervisor of Building & Grounds ....Mr. Galen DUNN
37 Coordinator of Financial Aid ....Mr. Adam BOWLES
26 Coord of Public Info & Marketing ....Mrs. Karen BRYANT
88 Coord Literary Development Program ....Ms. Linda SARGENT
06 Coordinator of Registration/Records ....Ms. Amy LOSS

† Regional accreditation is carried under the parent institution Illinois Eastern Community Colleges System Office in Olney, IL.

*Illinois Eastern Community Colleges Lincoln Trail College (A)

11220 State Highway 1, Robinson IL 62454-5707
County: Crawford FICE Identification: 009786
Unit ID: 403478
Telephone: (618) 544-8657 Carnegie Class: Assoc/Pub-R-M
FAX Number: (618) 544-7423 Calendar System: Semester
URL: www.iecc.edu/ltc
Established: 1969 Annual Undergrad Tuition & Fees (In-District): $2,954
Enrollment: 1,055 Coed
Affiliation or Control: State/Local IRS Status: 501(c)3
Highest Offering: Associate Degree
Program: Occupational; 2-Year Principally Bachelor's Creditable
Accreditation: &NH, ADNUR

02 President ....Mr. Mitch HANNAHS
05 Dean of the College ....Ms. Kathy HARRIS
37 Director of Financial Aid ....Ms. Jennifer BARTHELEMY
07 Director of Admissions ....Ms. Becky L. MIKEWORTH
08 Director of Learning Resource Ctr ....Ms. Vicky BONELLI
10 Director of Business ....Ms. Jamie HENRY
36 Career Advisor ....Ms. Gayle ZARING
41 Interim Sports Center Manager/Coach ....Mr. Kevin BOWERS
18 Groundskeeper ....Mr. Dan LEGGITT
26 Coord Public Information/Marketing ....Ms. Danelle HEVRON

† Regional accreditation is carried under the parent institution Illinois Eastern Community Colleges System Office in Olney, IL.

*Illinois Eastern Community Colleges Olney Central College (B)

305 North West Street, Olney IL 62450-1099
County: Richland FICE Identification: 001742
Unit ID: 145707
Telephone: (618) 395-7777 Carnegie Class: Assoc/Pub-R-M
FAX Number: (618) 392-3293 Calendar System: Semester
URL: www.iecc.edu/occ
Established: 1962 Annual Undergrad Tuition & Fees (In-District): $2,954
Enrollment: 1,477 Coed
Affiliation or Control: State/Local IRS Status: 501(c)3
Highest Offering: Associate Degree
Program: Occupational; 2-Year Principally Bachelor's Creditable
Accreditation: &NH, ADNUR, RAD

02 President ....Mr. Rodney RANES
05 Dean of Instruction ....Mr. Jeff CUTCHIN
32 Assistant Dean Student Services ....Mrs. Chris WEBBER
76 Assoc Dean Nursing Allied Health ....Ms. Tamara FRALICKER
08 Director Learning Resource Center ....Ms. Brittany BASS
88 Director Cosmetology ....Ms. Linda MILLER
10 Director Business ....Mr. Doug SHIPMAN
41 Athletic Director/Coach ....Mr. Dennis CONLEY
37 Financial Aid Coordinator ....Mrs. Vicki STUCKEY

† Regional accreditation is carried under the parent institution Illinois Eastern Community Colleges System Office in Olney, IL.

*Illinois Eastern Community Colleges Wabash Valley College (C)

2200 College Drive, Mount Carmel IL 62863-2657
County: Wabash FICE Identification: 001779
Unit ID: 403487
Telephone: (618) 262-8641 Carnegie Class: Assoc/Pub-R-L
FAX Number: (618) 262-5347 Calendar System: Semester
URL: www.iecc.edu/wvc
Established: 1960 Annual Undergrad Tuition & Fees (In-District): $2,954
Enrollment: 4,706 Coed
Affiliation or Control: State/Local IRS Status: 501(c)3
Highest Offering: Associate Degree
Program: Occupational; 2-Year Principally Bachelor's Creditable
Accreditation: &NH, ADNUR

02 President ....Mr. Matt FOWLER
05 Dean of Instruction ....Mr. Steve PATBERG
32 Assistant Dean Student Services ....Mrs. Diana SPEAR
20 Director of Academic Advising ....Mr. Tim ZIMMER
08 Director of LRC ....Ms. Sandy CRAIG
60 Director of Broadcasting ....Mr. Kyle PEACH
41 Athletic Director ....Mr. Mike CARPENTER
26 Director of Public Info & Marketing ....Vacant
10 Director of Business ....Ms. Reilly BAUMGART
37 Financial Aid Coordinator ....Ms. Mary JOHNSON
18 Groundskeeper ....Mr. Ron MARTIN

† Regional accreditation is carried under the parent institution Illinois Eastern Community Colleges System Office in Olney, IL.

The Illinois Institute of Art (D)

350 N Orleans, Suite 136, Chicago IL 60654-1514
County: Cook FICE Identification: 012584
Unit ID: 148177
Telephone: (312) 280-3500 Carnegie Class: Spec/Arts
FAX Number: (312) 777-8780 Calendar System: Quarter
URL: www.artinstitutes.edu/chicago
Established: 1916 Annual Undergrad Tuition & Fees: $21,996
Enrollment: 2,263 Coed
Affiliation or Control: Proprietary IRS Status: Proprietary
Highest Offering: Baccalaureate
Program: Professional; Technical Emphasis
Accreditation: NH, ACFEI, CIDA

01 President/Chicago ....David W. RAY
04 Exec Assistant to the President ....Allison SANTOS
05 Interim Dean of Academic Affairs ....Karen JANKO
07 VP/Senior Director of Admissions ....Janis K. ANTON
06 Registrar ....Donohue MICHAEL
108 Director of Assessment ....Dr. James BORLAND
08 Librarian ....Sean MCCARTHY
79 Program Coordinator Humanities ....Karine BRAVAIS-SLYMAN
88 Media Arts Dept Director ....Scott PERRY
81 Program Coordinator Math/Science ....Deann GROSSI
88 Culinary Arts/Hospitality Dept Dir ....Richard VALENTE
88 Fashion Department Director ....Dan ROBISON
88 Program Coordinator Interior Design ....Lisa GODSEY
88 Program Coordinator Visual Arts ....Suchi PAHWA
88 Design Department Directors ....Jodie LAWRENCE
10 Director of Finance ....Daniel LEAVITT
21 Director of Accounting ....Diosa COLLADO
37 Director Student Financial Aid ....Terry LEPPELLERE
32 Dean of Student Affairs ....Catherine BROKENSHIRE
35 Asst Dean of Student Affairs ....Valarie RAND
38 Student Support Coordinator ....Sara SPIEGEL
40 Supply Store Manager ....Ricardo OLAVE
36 Director of Career Services ....Vanessa JACKSON
15 Human Resources Generalist ....Rae DEROSE
13 Director of Technology ....Terence HAHN

The Illinois Institute of Art-Schaumburg (E)

1000 Plaza Drive, Suite 100, Schaumburg IL 60173-4913
Telephone: (847) 619-3450 Identification: 770074
Accreditation: &NH

† Main campus is The Illinois Institute of Art in Chicago, IL.

Illinois Institute of Technology (F)

3300 S Federal Street, Chicago IL 60616-3793
County: Cook FICE Identification: 001691
Unit ID: 145725
Telephone: (312) 567-3000 Carnegie Class: RU/H
FAX Number: (312) 567-3004 Calendar System: Semester
URL: www.iit.edu
Established: 1890 Annual Undergrad Tuition & Fees: $38,512
Enrollment: 7,684 Coed
Affiliation or Control: Independent Non-Profit IRS Status: 501(c)3
Highest Offering: Doctorate
Program: Liberal Arts And General; Teacher Preparatory; Professional; Technical Emphasis
Accreditation: NH, BUS, CLPSY, CORE, CS, ENG, LAW, LSAR

01 President ....Dr. John L. ANDERSON
05 Provost ....Dr. Alan W. CRAMB
10 VP Finance & Administration ....Dr. Patricia LAUGHLIN
21 AVP & Controller ....Mr. Brian LAFFEY
21 AVP Finance ....Mr. David ULASZEK
18 VP Facilities & Public Safety ....Mr. Bruce WATTS
30 Vice Pres Institutional Advancement ....Ms. Elizabeth HUGHES
88 Vice Pres International Affairs ....Dr. Darsh T. WASAN
86 Vice President External Affairs ....Mr. David E. BAKER
43 Vice President General Counsel ....Mr. Anthony D'AMATO
31 VP Community Affairs & Outreach ....Mr. Leroy E. KENNEDY
27 Vice Pres Marketing/Communications ....Ms. Jeanne HARTIG
88 Sr VP & Dir IIT Research Inst ....Dr. David MCCORMICK
88 VP & Dir Inst Food Safety & Health ....Dr. Robert BRACKETT
13 Chief Information Officer ....Mr. Ophir TRIGALO
04 Director President's Office ....Ms. Sandra LAPORTE
18 AVP Facilities/Real Estate & Const ....Mr. Terence FRIGO
28 Vice Provost Student Diversity ....Mr. Gerald DOYLE
16 Associate VP Human Resources ....Ms. Antoinette MURRIL
07 Vice Provost Admission & Fin Aid ....Dr. Michael GOSZ
20 Vice Provost Academic Affairs ....Dr. Christopher WHITE
88 Vice Provost for Research ....Mr. Dennis ROBERSON
84 Assoc Vice Provost Enrollment Mgmt ....Ms. Caryn SCHNIERLE
88 Assoc Vice Provost Acad Affairs ....Ms. Carol ORZE
26 Senior Dir Communications ....Mr. Evan VENIE
32 Dean of Students ....Ms. Katherine MURPHY-STETZ
61 Dean Chicago-Kent College of Law ....Mr. Harold J. KRENT
49 Dean College of Science & Letters ....Dr. Russell BETTS
54 Dean Armour Col of Engineering ....Dr. Natacha DEPAOLA
50 Dean Stuart School of Business ....Dr. Harvey KAHALAS
48 Dean College of Architecture ....Mr. Wiel ARETS
83 Dean College of Psychology ....Dr. M. Ellen MITCHELL
88 Dean Institute of Design ....Mr. Patrick F. WHITNEY
58 Dean Graduate Col & VP Research ....Dr. Ali CINAR
72 Dean School of Applied Technology ....Dr. C. Robert CARLSON
06 Registrar ....Mr. Peter ZACHOCKI
25 Director Sponsored Research ....Ms. Domenica G. PAPPAS
108 Director of Assessment ....Dr. Carol-Ann EMMONS
44 Director Annual Giving ....Mr. Jason SMITH
29 Director Alumni & Donor Relations ....Mr. James ACTON
37 Director Financial Aid ....Ms. Abigail MCGRATH
41 Athletic Director ....Mr. Enzley MITCHELL, IV
19 Director Public Safety ....Mr. Carl DOBRICH
08 Dean of Libraries ....Ms. Sharon BOSTICK
22 Dir Equal Opp/Affirmative Action ....Ms. Candida MIRANDA
96 Director of Purchasing ....Mr. Frank FIORITO
28 Director Student Ctr for Diversity ....Ms. Lisa MONTGOMERY
35 Director Student Life ....Ms. Erin GRAY
88 Dir Environmental Health & Safety ....Ms. Cynthia CHAFFEE

Illinois Institute of Technology Downtown Campus (G)

565 W Adams Street, Chicago IL 60661
Telephone: (312) 906-5000 Identification: 770075
Accreditation: &NH

† Main campus is Illinois Institute of Technology in Chicago, IL.

Illinois Institute of Technology Institute of Design (H)

350 N LaSalle Street, Chicago IL 60610
Telephone: (312) 595-4900 Identification: 770076
Accreditation: &NH

† Main campus is Illinois Institute of Technology in Chicago, IL.

Illinois Institute of Technology Rice Campus (I)

201 East Loop Road, Wheaton IL 60189
Telephone: (630) 682-6000 Identification: 770077
Accreditation: &NH

† Main campus is Illinois Institute of Technology in Chicago, IL.

Illinois State University (J)

School and North Streets, Normal IL 61790-0001
County: McLean FICE Identification: 001692
Unit ID: 145813
Telephone: (309) 438 2111 Carnegie Class: DRU
FAX Number: (309) 438-2768 Calendar System: Semester
URL: www.ilstu.edu
Established: 1857 Annual Undergrad Tuition & Fees (In-State): $13,009
Enrollment: 20,706 Coed
Affiliation or Control: State IRS Status: 501(c)3
Highest Offering: Doctorate
Program: Liberal Arts And General; Teacher Preparatory; Professional
Accreditation: NH, AAFCS, ART, AUD, BUS, BUSA, CAHIIM, CIDA, CONST, CS, DIETD, DIETI, IPSY, MT, MUS, NAIT, NRPA, NURSE, SCPSY, SP, SW, TED, THEA

01 President ....Dr. Timothy FLANAGAN
05 Vice Pres Academic Affs & Provost ....Dr. Sheri N. EVERTS
10 Vice President Finance & Planning ....Dr. Daniel LAYZELL
32 Vice President Student Affairs ....Dr. Larry DIETZ
26 Vice President Univ Advancement ....Ms. Erin MINNE
20 Associate Provost ....Dr. Jim JAWAHAR
35 Sr Assoc VP Student Affairs ....Dr. Brent PATERSON
21 Sr Assoc VP Finance & Planning ....Ms. Debra K. SMITLEY
91 Assoc Vice President Technology ....Dr. Mark WALBERT
58 Assoc VP Grad Std/Res/Intern Educ ....Dr. John BAUR
84 Assoc VP Enrollment Management ....Dr. Troy JOHNSON
15 Asst VP Human Resources ....Ms. Tammy CARLSON
86 Asst to Pres/Government Relations ....Mr. Jay HOFFMAN
08 Interim Dean University Libraries ....Mr. Dane WARD
06 University Registrar ....Mr. Jess D. RAY
07 Acting Director Admissions ....Ms. Stacy RAMSEY
20 Director University College ....Ms. Amelia NOEL-ELKINS
30 Exec Director of Development ....Ms. Joy D. HUTCHCRAFT
21 Asst VP Financial Admin/Comptroller ....Mr. Greg L. ALT
37 Director Financial Aid ....Ms. Jana ALBRECHT
29 Exec Director Alumni Engagement ....Ms. Doris GROVES
18 Exec Director Facilities Management ....Mr. Charles SCOTT
19 Chief University Police ....Mr. Aaron WOODRUFF
28 Dir Off of Eq Oppty/Ethics & Access ....Mr. Shane MCCREERY
23 Director Student Health Services ....Ms. Laura KNOBLAUCH
39 Director University Housing ....Ms. Maureen BLAIR
41 Director Intercollegiate Athletics ....Mr. Larry LYONS
85 Director International Studies ....Dr. Momar NDIAYE
92 Director Honors Program ....Dr. Tim FREDSTROM
94 Director Women's Studies ....Dr. Alison BAILEY
96 Director of Purchasing ....Ms. Judy JOHNSON
49 Dean College Arts & Sciences ....Dr. Gregory SIMPSON
50 Interim Dean College Business ....Dr. Gerry MCKEAN
53 Dean College Education ....Dr. Perry SCHOON
72 Dean College Applied Science/Tech ....Dr. Jeffrey A. WOOD
57 Dean College Fine Arts ....Dr. James MAJOR
66 Dean Mennonite College of Nursing ....Dr. Janet KREJCI
100 Chief of Staff ....Mr. Jay GROVES
35 Dean of Students ....Dr. Janet PATERSON
88 Asst VP Acad Admin ....Dr. Sam CATANZARO
88 Associate VP Acad Fiscal Mgmt ....Dr. Mardell WILSON
88 Assoc VP Admin Tech/Chief Tech ....Ms. Andrea BALLINGER
21 Assoc VP Budget Plng & Analysis ....Ms. Barb BLAKE

35 Asst VP Student Affairs .... Mr. Dwayne SACKMAN
44 Exec Dir Annual Giving .... Ms. Lora WEY
88 Exec Dir University Marketing/Comm .... Mr. Brian BEAM
45 Dir Planning/Rsch/Policy Analysis .... Ms. Kristen HENDRICKSON

Illinois Valley Community College (A)

815 N Orlando Smith Road, Oglesby IL 61348-9692
County: La Salle FICE Identification: 001705
Unit ID: 145831
Telephone: (815) 224-2720 Carnegie Class: Assoc/Pub-R-L
FAX Number: (815) 224-3033 Calendar System: Semester
URL: www.ivcc.edu
Established: 1966 Annual Undergrad Tuition & Fees (In-District): $3,040
Enrollment: 3,944 Coed
Affiliation or Control: Local IRS Status: 501(c)3
Highest Offering: Associate Degree
Program: Occupational; 2-Year Principally Bachelor's Creditable
Accreditation: NH, ADNUR, DA

01 President .... Dr. Jerry M. CORCORAN
05 VP Learning/Student Development .... Dr. Lori E. SCROGGS
10 Vice Pres Business Svcs/Finance .... Ms. Cheryl E. ROELFSEMA
20 AVP Academic Affs/Dean Wrkfce Devel .... Ms. Sue L. ISERMANN
32 Assoc Vice Pres Student Services .... Ms. Tracy L. MORRIS
24 Director of Learning Technologies .... Ms. Emily B. VESCOGNI
31 Director Cmty Relations & Marketing .... Mr. Francis R. BROLLEY
13 Dir of Information Technology Svcs .... Mr. Harold B. BARNES
51 Dir Cont Educ/Business Services .... Ms. Jamie L. GAHM
15 Director Human Resources .... Ms. Glenna S. JONES
37 Director of Financial Aid .... Ms. Patricia A. WILLIAMSON
07 Director of Admissions/Records .... Mr. Mark J. GRZYBOWSKI
08 Head Librarian .... Ms. Frances A. WHALEY
30 Director of Development .... Mr. Francis R. BROLLEY
96 Director of Purchasing .... Ms. Michelle L. CARBONI
18 Director of Facilities .... Mr. Gary K. JOHNSON
09 Director of Institutional Research .... Ms. Amy J. SMITH
81 Dean Natural Science/Business .... Mr. Ron W. GROLEAU
66 Dean Health Professions/ Nursing .... Ms. Bonnie L. BENNETT-CAMPBELL
79 Int Dn Humanities/Fine Arts/Soc Sci .... Mr. Stephen R. ALVIN
88 Dean English/Mathematics/Education .... Ms. Marianne DZIK

Illinois Wesleyan University (B)

PO Box 2900, 1312 Park Street,
Bloomington IL 61702-2900
County: McLean FICE Identification: 001696
Unit ID: 145646
Telephone: (309) 556-1000 Carnegie Class: Bac/A&S
FAX Number: (309) 556-3411 Calendar System: Other
URL: www.iwu.edu
Established: 1850 Annual Undergrad Tuition & Fees: $39,136
Enrollment: 2,013 Coed
Affiliation or Control: Independent Non-Profit IRS Status: 501(c)3
Highest Offering: Baccalaureate
Program: Liberal Arts And General; Teacher Preparatory; Professional
Accreditation: NH, MUS, NURSE

01 President .... Dr. Richard F. WILSON
05 Provost & Dean of Faculty .... Dr. Jonathan D. GREEN
10 Vice President Business & Finance .... Mr. Daniel P. KLOTZBACH
30 Vice President for Advancement .... Mr. Martin W. SMITH
26 Vice President for Communications .... Mr. Matt KURZ
32 VP Student Affairs/Dean Students .... Dr. Karla CARNEY-HALL
07 Dean of Admissions .... Mr. Tony BANKSTON
84 Dean of Enrollment Management .... Mr. Robert MURRAY
09 AVP Instl Research/Plng/Evaluation .... Dr. Michael THOMPSON
86 Dir Government/Community Relations .... Mr. Carl F. TEICHMAN
04 Exec Assistant to the President .... Ms. Susan E. BASSI
20 Assoc Provost Acad Plng/Standards .... Dr. Frank A. BOYD
20 Assoc Dean Curriculum/Faculty Devel .... Prof. Lynda DUKE
16 Assoc VP for Human Resources .... Ms. Catherine SPITZ
13 Asst Provost/Chief Technology Ofcr .... Mr. Trey SHORT
44 Associate Vice Pres for Advancement .... Vacant
88 Associate Vice Pres for Advancement .... Mr. Steve D. SEIBRING
35 Asc Dean Stdnts/Co-Curricular/Pgmng .... Ms. Darcy L. GREDER
38 Asst Dean/Dir Student Counseling .... Dr. Annorrah MOORMAN
35 Asst Dean of Students .... Mr. Matthew DAMSCHRODER
08 University Librarian .... Dr. Karen SCHMIDT
06 Registrar .... Dr. Leslie BETZ
42 University Chaplain .... Rev. Elyse NELSON WINGER
21 Controller .... Mr. John BRYANT
37 Director of Financial Aid .... Mr. Scott SEIBRING
64 Director of School of Music .... Dr. Mario J. PELUSI
57 Director of School of Art .... Prof. Kevin STRANDBERG
57 Director of School of Theatre Arts .... Dr. Curtis C. TROUT
66 Director of School of Nursing .... Dr. Victoria FOLSE
41 Director of Athletics .... Prof. Dennis BRIDGES
29 Director of Alumni Relations .... Ms. Ann HARDING
102 Dir Grants/Foundation Relations .... Mr. Carlo ROBUSTELLI
44 Dir of Wesleyan Annual Fund .... Mr. Jeffrey MAVROS
36 Director of Career Center .... Mr. Warren KISTNER
18 Director of Physical Plant .... Mr. James J. BLUMBERG
88 Director of Sports Information .... Mr. Stewart I. SALOWITZ
93 Director Multicultural Student Affs .... Mr. George E. JACKSON, III
35 Dir Student Act/Leadership Programs .... Mr. Colin STEWART
94 Director of Women's Studies Program .... Dr. Carole MYSCOFSKI
104 Director of International Office .... Ms. Stacey SHIMIZU
40 Bookstore Manager .... Mr. Thaddeus SUTTER

Institute for Clinical Social Work (C)

401 South State Street, Suite 822, Chicago IL 60605
County: Cook FICE Identification: 025737
Unit ID: 145886
Telephone: (312) 935-4232 Carnegie Class: Spec/Health
FAX Number: (312) 935-4255 Calendar System: Semester
URL: www.icsw.edu
Established: 1981 Annual Graduate Tuition & Fees: $18,215
Enrollment: 118 Coed
Affiliation or Control: Independent Non-Profit IRS Status: 501(c)3
Highest Offering: Doctorate; No Undergraduates
Program: Professional
Accreditation: NH

01 President .... Dr. Marty LAUB
05 Dean .... Dr. Alan LEVY
88 Director of Degree Programs .... Dr. Jennifer TOLLESON
20 Associate Dean .... Dr. Scott HARMS ROSE
11 Director of Operations .... Maureen A. HEWITT
37 Admin Fin Aid/Instl Operations .... Pierre SMITH
08 Librarian .... Casey GIBBS
32 Coordinator Student/Faculty Svcs .... Elizabeth OLER
07 Director of Marketing/Enrollment .... Mina GERALL

International Academy of Design and Technology (D)

1 N State Street, Suite 500, Chicago IL 60602-9736
County: Cook FICE Identification: 021603
Unit ID: 146010
Telephone: (312) 980-9200 Carnegie Class: Spec/Arts
FAX Number: (312) 541-3929 Calendar System: Quarter
URL: www.iadtchicago.edu
Established: 1977 Annual Undergrad Tuition & Fees: $14,400
Enrollment: 538 Coed
Affiliation or Control: Proprietary IRS Status: Proprietary
Highest Offering: Baccalaureate
Program: Occupational
Accreditation: ACICS

01 President .... Mr. Anthony WILLIAMS
05 Campus Director of Education .... Ms. Kathleen EMBRY
88 Regulatory Operations Consultant .... Ms. Audrey HENRY
07 Campus Director of Admissions .... Mr. A.J JABER
06 Associate Registrar .... Vacant
08 Regional Director Library Services .... Ms. Amanda HENDERSON
36 Director of Career Services .... Ms. Cheryl PERILLO
37 Student Finance Manager .... Mr. Willis JORDAN

International Academy of Design and Technology-Schaumburg (E)

935-E National Parkway, Schaumburg IL 60173-5160
Telephone: (847) 969-2800 Identification: 666141
Accreditation: ACICS

† Main campus is International Academy of Design and Technology in Chicago, IL.

ITT Technical Institute (F)

1401 Feehanville Drive, Mount Prospect IL 60056-6005
Telephone: (847) 375-8800 Identification: 666538
Accreditation: ACICS

† Main campus is ITT Technical Institute in Indianapolis, IN.

ITT Technical Institute (G)

800 Jorie Blvd., Suite 100, Oak Brook IL 60523
Telephone: (630) 472-7000 Identification: 666118
Accreditation: ACICS

† Main campus is ITT Technical Institute in Indianapolis, IN.

ITT Technical Institute (H)

11551 184th Place, Orland Park IL 60467-4900
Telephone: (708) 326-3200 Identification: 666539
Accreditation: ACICS

† Main campus is ITT Technical Institute in Indianapolis, IN.

ITT Technical Institute (I)

2501 Wabash Avenue, Springfield IL 62704
Telephone: (217) 793-5700 Identification: 770649
Accreditation: ACICS

† Main campus is ITT Technical Institute in Indianapolis, IN.

John A. Logan College (J)

700 Logan College Road, Carterville IL 62918-2500
County: Williamson FICE Identification: 008076
Unit ID: 146205
Telephone: (618) 985-3741 Carnegie Class: Assoc/Pub-R-L
FAX Number: (618) 985-2248 Calendar System: Semester
URL: www.jalc.edu
Established: 1967 Annual Undergrad Tuition & Fees (In-District): $2,910
Enrollment: 6,400 Coed
Affiliation or Control: State/Local IRS Status: 501(c)3
Highest Offering: Associate Degree
Program: Occupational; 2-Year Principally Bachelor's Creditable
Accreditation: NH, CAHIIM, CONST, DA, DH, DMS, MLTAD, OTA, SURGT

01 President .... Dr. Michael DREITH
05 Vice President Instruction Services .... Dr. Deborah PAYNE
10 VP Business Svcs/College Facilities .... Mr. Brad MCCORMICK
11 Vice President Administration .... Dr. Tim DAUGHERTY
06 Dean Student Services .... Mr. Terry CRAIN
21 Dean Financial Operations .... Ms. Stacy BUCKINGHAM
20 Dean Instruction .... Vacant
103 Dean Workforce Dev/Comm Educ .... Mr. Phil MINNIS
88 Assoc Dean Baccalaureate Transfer .... Mr. Mark HENSON
76 Assoc Dean Health/Public Svcs .... Dr. Valerie BARKO
51 Assoc Dean Continuing Education .... Mr. Barry HANCOCK
88 Assoc Dean Adult Basic/Secondary Ed .... Ms. Kay FLEMING
13 Assoc Dean Information Technology .... Mr. Mark KINKADE
07 Associate Dean Admissions .... Vacant
37 Director of Student Financial Asst .... Ms. Sherry SUMMARY
08 Assoc Dean for Library Services .... Ms. Judy VINEYARD
30 Director of Development .... Vacant
26 Dir Community Relations/Marketing .... Mr. Steve O'KEEFE
35 Director of Student Activities .... Ms. Adrienne BARKLEY-GIFFIN
36 Director of Placement .... Ms. Lisa HUDGENS
102 Executive Director of Foundation .... Ms. Staci BYNUM
66 Director of Nursing .... Ms. Marilyn FALASTER
88 Director of Career Dev/Acad Support .... Ms. Christy MCBRIDE
15 Director of Human Resources/AAO .... Mr. Clay BREWER
18 Dir Building/Grounds/Campus Safety .... Mr. Dwight HOFFARD
09 Director Institutional Research .... Mr. Eric PULLEY
29 Dir of Scholarships/Alumni Svcs .... Ms. Stacy HOLLOWAY

John Hancock University (K)

1 Mid America Plaza, Suite 130,
Oakbrook Terrace IL 60181-4701
County: DuPage FICE Identification: 041433
Unit ID: 452133
Telephone: (877) 355-4762 Carnegie Class: Bac/A&S
FAX Number: (630) 560-6299 Calendar System: Semester
URL: www.hancocku.edu
Established: 2008 Annual Undergrad Tuition & Fees: $4,500
Enrollment: 81 Coed
Affiliation or Control: Proprietary IRS Status: Proprietary
Highest Offering: Master's
Program: Professional; Business Emphasis
Accreditation: DETC

01 President .... Dr. Virginia A. CARLIN
10 Chief Financial Officer .... Randy WILLY
11 VP of Operations .... Raymond RODRIGUEZ
20 Chief Academic Officer .... Dr. Andrew CARPENTER
06 Registrar .... Yahana TEGEGNE
07 Director of Academic Advising .... LePra GEORGE

John Marshall Law School (L)

315 S Plymouth Court, Chicago IL 60604-3968
County: Cook FICE Identification: 001698
Unit ID: 146241
Telephone: (312) 427-2737 Carnegie Class: Spec/Law
FAX Number: (312) 427-8307 Calendar System: Semester
URL: www.jmls.edu
Established: 1899 Annual Graduate Tuition & Fees: $41,144
Enrollment: 1,617 Coed
Affiliation or Control: Independent Non-Profit IRS Status: 501(c)3
Highest Offering: First Professional Degree; No Undergraduates
Program: Professional
Accreditation: NH, LAW

01 Dean .... Mr. John E. CORKERY
05 Assoc Dean Academic Affairs .... Dean Ralph RUEBNER
07 Assoc Dean Admissions/Stdnt Affairs .... Mr. William B. POWERS
10 Chief Financial Officer .... Ms. Cynthia SAH
13 Chief Technology Officer .... Ms. June LIEBERT
20 Asst Dean for Academic Services .... Ms. Jodie NEEDHAM
15 Asst Dean Human Resources .... Mr. Martin D'AMBROSE
36 Director Career Services .... Ms. Chante SPANN
06 Registrar .... Mr. Ray GRANT
29 Director Alumni Relations/Aux Svcs .... Ms. Sherri BERENDT
37 Director Student Financial Aid .... Ms. Yara SANTANA
09 Director of Institutional Affairs .... Ms. Anna KRUG

John Wood Community College (M)

1301 S 48th Street, Quincy IL 62305-8736
County: Adams FICE Identification: 012813
Unit ID: 146278
Telephone: (217) 224-6500 Carnegie Class: Assoc/Pub-R-M
FAX Number: (217) 224-4208 Calendar System: Semester
URL: www.jwcc.edu
Established: 1974 Annual Undergrad Tuition & Fees (In-District): $3,990
Enrollment: 2,172 Coed
Affiliation or Control: State/Local IRS Status: 501(c)3
Highest Offering: Associate Degree
Program: Occupational; 2-Year Principally Bachelor's Creditable
Accreditation: NH, SURGT

01 President .... Dr. John LETTS
05 Vice President for Instruction .... Dr. Ron DAVIS
10 Vice Pres for Finance/Business Svcs .... Ms. Mary ARP

32 Vice President for Student Services ... Mr. Michael ELBE
09 Dir Institutional Effectiveness ... Mr. Josh WELKER
49 Dean Arts and Sciences ... Dr. David SHINN
75 Dean Careers and Technology ... Ms. Pam FOUST
84 Dean Enrollment Svcs/Dir Finan Aid ... Ms. Melanie LECHTENBERG
88 Associate Dean Arts and Sciences ... Mr. Kent HAWLEY
103 Assoc Dn Careers and Technology ... Mr. Terry JENKINS
07 Director Admissions ... Ms. Rachel BUHR
06 Registrar/Dir Career/Advising Svcs ... Mr. Cody BAGGETT
21 Director Fiscal Services ... Ms. Jennifer KELTY
35 Director Support Services ... Vacant
13 Director Information Technology ... Mr. Joshua BRUECK
76 Assoc Dean Health Sciences ... Vacant
08 Director Learning Resource Center ... Ms. Barbara LIEBER
26 Director Public Relations/Marketing ... Ms. Tracy ORNE
30 Director Advancement ... Ms. Barbara HOLTHAUS
15 Director Human Resources ... Ms. Stacey O'BRIEN
18 Director Physical Plant ... Mr. Lou BARTA
37 Director Financial Aid ... Ms. Melanie LECHTENBERG
19 Chief of Campus Police ... Mr. Bill LATOUR
41 Manager Athletics & Intramurals ... Mr. Brad HOYT
40 Manager Campus Services ... Ms. Lynn BLICKHAN
96 Purchasing Coordinator ... Ms. Darla SNYDER
47 Dept Chair Ag Sciences ... Mr. Gary SHUPE
77 Dept Chair Ofc Technology/Comp Sci ... Mr. Nick KRIZMANIC
50 Dept Chair Business ... Ms. Cathy STEPHENS
57 Dept Chair Fine Arts ... Mr. Gary DECLUE
81 Department Chair Mathematics ... Mr. David RIGSBEE
65 Dept Chair Natural Sciences ... Dr. Ivan PAUL
79 Dept Chair Language/Literature/Hum ... Ms. Valerie VLAHAKIS
88 Dept Chair Developmental Education ... Ms. Joyce MILLER-BOREN
83 Dept Chair Social/Behavior Science ... Mr. Randall EGDORF

Joliet Junior College (A)

1215 Houbolt Road, Joliet IL 60431-8938

County: Will FICE Identification: 001699
Unit ID: 146296

Telephone: (815) 729-9020 Carnegie Class: Assoc/Pub-S-SC
FAX Number: (815) 729-4256 Calendar System: Semester
URL: www.jjc.edu
Established: 1901 Annual Undergrad Tuition & Fees (In-District): $3,210
Enrollment: 15,589 Coed
Affiliation or Control: State/Local IRS Status: 501(c)3
Highest Offering: Associate Degree
Program: Occupational; 2-Year Principally Bachelor's Creditable
Accreditation: NH, ACBSP, ACFEI, ADNUR, CAHIIM, MUS

01 President ... Dr. Debra S. DANIELS
05 Vice President Academic Affairs ... Vacant
11 VP Administrative Services ... Dr. Judy MITCHELL
13 Int Exec Dir Information Technology ... Mr. Jim SERR
32 VP Student Development ... Dr. Yolanda ISAACS
31 Dean Community/Economic Development ... Vacant
07 Director Admissions & Recruitment ... Ms. Jennifer KLOBERDANZ
88 Dir Adult & Family Services ... Ms. Emilie MCCALLISTER
37 Director Financial Aid ... Mr. David SEWARD
15 Executive Director Human Resources ... Ms. Joyce COLEMAN
06 Registrar ... Mr. Keith TILLMAN
18 Director Facility Services ... Mr. Patrick VAN DUYNE
21 Director Business/Auxiliary Svcs ... Ms. Janice REEDUS
26 Dir Commun/External Relations ... Ms. Kelly ROHDER
36 Director Career Services ... Ms. Bridgett LARKIN-BEENE
41 Director Athletics ... Mr. Wayne KING
21 Director Financial Svcs/Controller ... Mr. Jeffrey HEAP
19 Dir Campus Safety & Police Chief ... Mr. Peter COMANDA
30 Ex Dir Inst Adv Exec Dir JJC Found ... Ms. Kristin MULVEY
08 Director Library ... Mr. Thomas URBANSKI
09 Director of Institutional Research ... Mr. Joseph OFFERMANN
29 Director Alumni Relations ... Ms. Amanda QUINN
40 Manager Bookstore ... Mr. Michael M. MAIER
88 Coord GSD ... Dr. Angie KAYSEN-LUZBETAK
74 Dept Chair Veterinary Medicine Tech ... Dr. Scott KELLER
38 Counselor/Dept Chair ... Ms. Jennifer KIMBAROVSKY

Judson University (B)

1151 N State Street, Elgin IL 60123-1498

County: Kane FICE Identification: 001700
Unit ID: 146339

Telephone: (847) 628-2500 Carnegie Class: Bac/Diverse
FAX Number: (847) 628-1027 Calendar System: Semester
URL: www.judsonu.edu
Established: 1913 Annual Undergrad Tuition & Fees: $27,530
Enrollment: 1,127 Coed
Affiliation or Control: American Baptist IRS Status: 501(c)3
Highest Offering: Doctorate
Program: Liberal Arts And General; Teacher Preparatory; Professional
Accreditation: NH

01 President ... Dr. Gene CRUME
04 Exec Assistant to the President ... Mrs. Tena ROBOTHAM
05 Provost/Chief Academic Officer ... Dr. Wilbert FRIESEN
10 Interim VP Business Affairs ... Mr. John POTTER
30 Vice President Advancement ... Vacant
06 University Registrar ... Ms. Virginia GUTH
84 Exec Dir of Enrollment Services ... Ms. Nancy BINGER
49 Dean Liberal Arts and Sciences ... Dr. Lanette POTEETE-YOUNG
48 Dean Art/Design and Architecture ... Dr. Curtis SARTOR
53 Dean Education ... Dr. Kathy MILLER
50 Dean Leadership and Business ... Dr. Thomas BERLINER
32 Dean of Students ... Mrs. Lisa JAROT
08 Library Director ... Mr. Larry WILD
13 Director of Information Technology ... Mr. Brent RICHARDSON
44 Senior Director of Development ... Dr. Angelo BRAVOS
88 Dir of Advancement Operations ... Ms. Jean BEDNAR
29 Director of Alumni Relations ... Mrs. Bonnie BIENERT
37 Director of Financial Aid ... Dr. Roberto SANTIZO
07 Assoc Director of Admissions ... Mr. Nate MCNEELY
27 Director of Comm & Marketing ... Ms. Mary DULABAUM
36 Director of Career Development ... Mrs. Doris HAUGEN
38 Director of Counseling Center ... Dr. Donald FERRELL
19 Director of Campus Safety ... Mr. Nick SALZMANN
41 Athletic Director ... Mr. Joel COTTON
88 Director of Retention & Orientation ... Miss Jaimee BARTHA
39 Coord Student Services/Dir Housing ... Mr. Rafael HECK
85 Director of Intercultural Relations ... Mrs. Lisa JAROT
35 Associate Dean of Students ... Ms. Casey SUNDSEDT
23 Campus Nurse ... Ms. Susan WEBER
88 Dir of Acad & Accessibility Service ... Dr. Rolanda BURRIS
92 Honors Director ... Dr. Craig KAPLOWITZ
15 Director of Human Resources ... Mr. Jeremiah THOMPSON
101 Asst Sec to Board of Trustees ... Mrs. Tena ROBOTHAM
105 Webmaster ... Mr. Eric SECKER

Kankakee Community College (C)

100 College Drive, Kankakee IL 60901-6505

County: Kankakee FICE Identification: 007690
Unit ID: 146348

Telephone: (815) 802-8100 Carnegie Class: Assoc/Pub-R-L
FAX Number: (815) 802-8101 Calendar System: Semester
URL: www.kcc.edu
Established: 1966 Annual Undergrad Tuition & Fees (In-District): $3,510
Enrollment: 3,572 Coed
Affiliation or Control: State/Local IRS Status: 501(c)3
Highest Offering: Associate Degree
Program: Occupational; 2-Year Principally Bachelor's Creditable
Accreditation: NH, COARC, MLTAD, PHLEB, PTAA

01 President ... Dr. John AVENDANO
04 Executive Secretary to President ... Ms. Rose MITCHELL
05 VP of Instructional & Stdnt Success ... Mr. Dennis SORENSEN
06 Registrar ... Mr. David HERMANN
32 Dean of Student Development ... Ms. Julia WASKOSKY
09 Director Institutional Research ... Dr. Vicki MAGEE
31 Asst Dean Adult & Community Educ ... Ms. Margaret COOPER
103 Director of Workforce Development ... Ms. Dana WASHINGTON
37 Director Financial Aid ... Ms. Deanna THOMPSON
35 Coordinator Student Life ... Mrs. Lindsey ZERBIAN
88 Director Fitness Center ... Mr. Dennis CLARK
41 Director Athletics ... Mr. Ted PETERSEN
15 Director Human Resources ... Mr. David CAGLE
21 Director Financial Affairs ... Ms. Beth NUNLEY
50 Assoc Dean Business & Technology ... Mr. Paul CARLSON
51 Asst Dean Cont Educ & Career Svcs ... Ms. Mary POSING
18 Dir Campus Facilities & Security ... Mr. Rich SODERQUIST
88 Coordinator Small Business Devel ... Mr. Ken CRITE
81 Assoc Dean Math/Science Division ... Mr. Fred COOPER
76 Assoc Dean Health Careers Div ... Ms. Sheri CAGLE
88 Director Student Advisement ... Ms. Meredith PURCELL
76 Director Respiratory Therapist Pgm ... Ms. Nancy OZEE
76 Director Medical Lab Technology ... Ms. Glenda FORNERIS
83 Assoc Dean Humanities/Social Sci ... Mr. Mark LANTING
76 Director Radiology Technology Pgm ... Ms. Darla JEPSON
13 Director Information Tech Svcs ... Mr. Michael O'CONNOR
102 Exec Director of KCC Foundation ... Ms. Kelly MYERS
07 Coord Admissions & Recruitment ... Mrs. Oshunda CARPENTER-WILLIAMS
88 Director Institutional Tech/Fac Dev ... Mr. Craig KEIGHER
62 Director Learning Resource Center ... Ms. Karen BECKER
26 Director Marketing ... Ms. Kari SARGEANT
88 Dean of Sustainability ... Dr. Bert JACOBSON

Kaskaskia College (D)

27210 College Road, Centralia IL 62801-7878

County: Clinton FICE Identification: 001701
Unit ID: 146366

Telephone: (618) 545-3000 Carnegie Class: Assoc/Pub-R-L
FAX Number: (618) 532-1990 Calendar System: Semester
URL: www.kaskaskia.edu
Established: 1940 Annual Undergrad Tuition & Fees (In-District): $3,330
Enrollment: 5,104 Coed
Affiliation or Control: State/Local IRS Status: 501(c)3
Highest Offering: Associate Degree
Program: Occupational; 2-Year Principally Bachelor's Creditable
Accreditation: NH, ADNUR, CAHIIM, COARC, DA, MLTAD, OTA, PTAA, RAD, SURGT

01 President ... Dr. James C. UNDERWOOD
11 Vice Pres Administrative Services ... Mrs. Nancy KINSEY
05 Vice Pres Instructional Services ... Dr. Gregory LABYAK
32 Vice President of Student Services ... Mrs. Susan BATCHELOR
75 Dean Career & Technical Education ... Mr. George EVANS
49 Dean of Arts & Sciences ... Ms. Kellie HENEGAR
66 Dean of Nursing ... Mrs. Janet GARRETSON
09 Int Dir Inst Effectiveness ... Mr. Jeffrey EBEL
08 Director of LRC ... Vacant
15 Dir Human Resources/Legal Counsel ... Ms. Rhonda BOEHNE
18 Director Facilities/Physical Plant ... Mr. Phillip ELLRICH
96 Director Purchasing/Auxiliary Svcs ... Mr. Craig ROPER
06 Manager of Records & Registration ... Ms. Jan RIPPERDA
37 Director of Financial Aid ... Ms. Lisa COLLIER
88 Director of Radiologic Technology ... Mrs. Mimi POLCZYNSKI
88 Dir Physical Therapist Asst Pgm ... Ms. Jane HERRMANN
91 Director of Information Technology ... Ms. Gina SCHUETZ
27 Director of Public Information ... Ms. Cathy KARRICK
26 Director of Marketing ... Mr. Travis HENSON
40 Bookstore Manager ... Ms. Cheryl JOHNSON
88 Director Adult Education ... Ms. Lisa ATKINS
88 Project Director Business Svc Ctr ... Mr. Steve GRONER
50 Business Services Field Rep ... Mr. Art BORUM
41 Athletic Director ... Mr. Shane LARSON
10 Controller ... Ms. Mary DANT
88 Coordinator of Student Recruitment ... Ms. Amy TROUTT
38 Director of Reten & Stdnt Develop ... Ms. Christin DALAVARIS
84 Dean of Enrollment Management ... Ms. Denise DERRICK
07 Dir Admissions/Records & Dual Cred ... Mrs. Cheryl BOEHNE
88 Director of Title III Program ... Mrs. Jill KLOSTERMANN
88 Dir Centralia Correctional Ctr Pgm ... Ms. Tina WOLFE
30 Coord Inst Advancement Programs ... Mrs. Suzanne CHRIST
108 Dir Assess & Strategic Initiatives ... Mr. Scott CROTHERS

Kendall College (E)

900 N North Branch Street, Chicago IL 60642

County: Cook FICE Identification: 001703
Unit ID: 146393

Telephone: (312) 752-2000 Carnegie Class: Bac/Diverse
FAX Number: (312) 752-2021 Calendar System: Quarter
URL: www.kendall.edu
Established: 1934 Annual Undergrad Tuition & Fees: $24,246
Enrollment: 1,812 Coed
Affiliation or Control: Proprietary IRS Status: Proprietary
Highest Offering: Baccalaureate
Program: Occupational; 2-Year Principally Bachelor's Creditable; Liberal Arts And General; Teacher Preparatory; Professional; Business Emphasis
Accreditation: NH, ACFEI

01 President ... Ms. Emily WILLIAMS KNIGHT
05 Provost ... Dr. Gwen HILLESHEIM
32 Dean of Student Affairs ... Ms. Kimberly SKARR
26 Director of Marketing ... Ms. Genevieve BURKE
04 Assistant to the President ... Mrs. Helena VASILOPOULOS
10 Director of Finance ... Mr. Scott LESHT
06 Registrar ... Ms. Amanda MOLLER
15 Manager of Human Resources ... Ms. Barbara SLOAN
29 Alumni Affairs ... Ms. Marguerite ALLGRETTI
38 Director of Advising ... Mr. Frank ARCE
08 Director Library Services ... Mrs. Iva M. FREEMAN
84 Director of Enrollment Management ... Mr. Ross ROSENBURG
13 Director of Information Technology ... Ms. Laura WELMERS
37 Director of Financial Aid ... Mr. Frank ARCE
39 Director of Residence Life ... Ms. Jena HENSON
106 Academic Director ... Ms. Cheryl BONCUORE
97 Director of General Education ... Mr. Ryan BARTELMAY
18 Chief Facilities/Physical Plant ... Mr. Philip LITTLE
35 Director Student Life ... Ms. Chaya SANDLER
09 Director of Institutional Research ... Mrs. Stacy VLAHAKIS
96 Procurement Manager ... Ms. Lara ENGERT

Kishwaukee College (F)

21193 Malta Road, Malta IL 60150-9600

County: De Kalb FICE Identification: 007684
Unit ID: 146418

Telephone: (815) 825-2086 Carnegie Class: Assoc/Pub-S-SC
FAX Number: (815) 825-2072 Calendar System: Semester
URL: www.kishwaukeecollege.edu
Established: 1967 Annual Undergrad Tuition & Fees (In-District): $3,100
Enrollment: 4,921 Coed
Affiliation or Control: State/Local IRS Status: 501(c)3
Highest Offering: Associate Degree
Program: Occupational; 2-Year Principally Bachelor's Creditable
Accreditation: NH, COMTA, RAD

01 President ... Dr. Thomas L. CHOICE
05 Vice President Instruction ... Vacant
10 Vice Pres of Finance/Administration ... Mr. Robert GALICK
32 Vice President Student Services ... Mr. Sedgwick HARRIS
09 Assoc VP Institutional Effectivenes ... Mr. Kevin J. FUSS
83 Dean Arts/Communic/Social Science ... Ms. Jaime LONG
72 Dean Career Technologies ... Mrs. Sara POHL
76 Dean Health & Education ... Ms. Bette CHILTON
35 Dean of Student Services ... Ms. Nancy PARTCH
81 Dean Math/Science/Business ... Mr. Steven SQUIER
51 Dean Adult Educ/Transition Pgms ... Ms. Joanne KANTNER
21 Dean of Business Affairs ... Ms. Beth YOUNG
88 Exec Dir Bus Dev & Cont Ed ... Ms. Karen SCHMITT
102 Exec Dir Kish Col Foundation Devel ... Mr. Marshall HAYES
07 Dir Admissions/Registration/Records ... Ms. Jill BIER
27 Dir of Marketing & Public Relations ... Ms. Kayte HAMEL
37 Director Student Financial Aid ... Mrs. Pam WAGENER
14 Director Information Technology ... Mr. Scott ARMSTRONG
40 Director Bookstore ... Mrs. Lynne DURIN
08 Director Library Services ... Ms. Anne-Marie EGGLESTON
15 Director Human Resources ... Vacant
41 Athletic Director ... Ms. Karen WILEY
18 Chief Facilities/Physical Plant ... Mr. Jim PURDIE

Knowledge Systems Institute (G)

3420 Main Street, Skokie IL 60076-2453

County: Cook FICE Identification: 026227
Unit ID: 260956

Telephone: (847) 679-3135 Carnegie Class: Spec/Tech

FAX Number: (847) 679-3166 Calendar System: Semester
URL: www.ksi.edu
Established: 1978 Annual Graduate Tuition & Fees: $7,900
Enrollment: 125 Coed
Affiliation or Control: Independent Non-Profit IRS Status: 501(c)3
Highest Offering: Master's; No Undergraduates
Program: Professional; Technical Emphasis
Accreditation: NH

01 Chancellor ....Dr. Shi-Kuo CHANG
03 Executive Director ....Ms. Judy PAN
05 Academic Dean ....Dr. Cheng-Yuan HSIEH
07 Chr Computer Sci/Admiss Committee ....Dr. Cheng-Yuan HSIEH
11 Administrative Manager ....Mr. Noorjhan ALI

Knox College (A)

2 E South Street, Galesburg IL 61401-4999
County: Knox FICE Identification: 001704
Unit ID: 146427
Telephone: (309) 341-7000 Carnegie Class: Bac/A&S
FAX Number: (309) 341-7090 Calendar System: Trimester
URL: www.knox.edu
Established: 1837 Annual Undergrad Tuition & Fees: $38,652
Enrollment: 1,405 Coed
Affiliation or Control: Independent Non-Profit IRS Status: 501(c)3
Highest Offering: Baccalaureate
Program: Liberal Arts And General; Teacher Preparatory
Accreditation: NH, @TEAC

01 President ....Dr. Teresa L. AMOTT
05 VP Acad Affairs/Dean of College ....Dr. Laura L. BEHLING
10 Vice Pres for Finance & Admin Svcs ....Mr. Thomas B. AXTELL
30 Vice President for Advancement ....Ms. Beverly HOLMES
07 Vice Pres Enrollment/Dean of Admn ....Mr. Paul R. STEENIS
27 Assoc VP/Communications ....Ms. Megan SCOTT
06 Registrar ....Dr. Chuck SCHULZ
32 Dean of Students ....Ms. Debbie SOUTHERN
20 Associate Dean of College ....Dr. Lori HASLEM
37 Director Financial Aid ....Ms. Ann BRILL
08 Librarian ....Mr. Jeffrey A. DOUGLAS
36 Director Ctr Career Pre-Prof Dev ....Ms. Terrie SALINE
14 VP/CIO Information Technology Svcs ....Mr. Steven HALL
15 Director Human Resources ....Ms. Gina ZINDT
18 Director Facilities Services ....Mr. Scott MAUST
21 Controller ....Ms. Bobby Jo MAURER
86 Dir Government & Community Relation ....Ms. Karrie HEARTLEIN
29 Dir Alumni & Constituent Programs ....Ms. Carol J. BROWN
38 Director of Counseling Services ....Dr. Daniel L. LARSON
41 Director of Athletics ....Mr. Chad EISELE
19 Director Campus Safety ....Mr. John SCHLAF
09 Dir Institutional Research/Assess ....Mr. Charles L. CLARK
102 Dir Corporate/Foundation Relations ....Ms. Anne-Marie BERK

Lake Forest College (B)

555 N Sheridan Road, Lake Forest IL 60045-2338
County: Lake FICE Identification: 001706
Unit ID: 146481
Telephone: (847) 234-3100 Carnegie Class: Bac/A&S
FAX Number: (847) 735-6291 Calendar System: Semester
URL: www.lakeforest.edu
Established: 1857 Annual Undergrad Tuition & Fees: $39,842
Enrollment: 1,525 Coed
Affiliation or Control: Independent Non-Profit IRS Status: 501(c)3
Highest Offering: Master's
Program: Liberal Arts And General
Accreditation: NH

01 President ....Mr. Stephen D. SCHUTT
05 Provost/Dean of Faculty ....Dr. Michael ORR
10 Vice Pres of Business/Treasurer ....Mrs. Leslie T. CHAPMAN
30 VP of Development & Alumni Pgms ....Mr. Philip HOOD
07 Vice Pres Admissions/Career Svcs ..Mr. William G. MOTZER, JR.
45 VP Budget/Planning/Controller ....Ms. Lori H. SUNDBERG
04 Executive Assistant to President ....Ms. Elizabeth A. PALM
32 Dean of Students ....Mr. Rob FLOT
35 Director of Residence Life ....Ms. Carolyn GOLZ
28 Director Intercult Relelations ....Ms. Erin HOFFMAN
20 Asc Dean Facul/Dir Ctr Chicago Pgms ....Dr. Davis SCHNEIDERMAN
20 Assoc Dean Facul/Dir Lrng/Tchng Ctr ....Dr. Richard MALLETTE
31 Director of Community Education ....Mr. Dan LEMAHIEU
37 Director of Financial Aid ....Mr. Gerard J. CEBRZYNSKI
41 Athletic Director ....Ms. Jacqueline SLAATS
08 Librarian & Director Info Svcs/Tech ....Mr. James R. CUBIT
06 Registrar ....Ms. Ruthane I. BOPP
38 Director of Counseling Services ....Dr. Jennifer JEZIORSKI
29 Assoc Vice Pres for Alumni Relation ....Mr. Timothy STATE
09 Director of Institutional Research ....Ms. Lori H. SUNDBERG
15 Director of Human Resources ....Ms. Silvana PRESTA
36 Director of Career Services ....Ms. Lisa HINKLEY
18 Director of Facilities Management ....Mr. David J. SIEBERT
26 Assoc VP for Comm//Mktg ....Ms. Elizabeth LIBBY
19 Director of Public Safety ....Mr. Richard L. COHEN

Lake Forest Graduate School of Management (C)

1905 W Field Court, Lake Forest IL 60045-4824
County: Lake FICE Identification: 023192
Unit ID: 146490
Telephone: (847) 234-5005 Carnegie Class: Spec/Bus
FAX Number: (847) 295-3656 Calendar System: Quarter
URL: www.lakeforestmba.edu
Established: 1946 Annual Graduate Tuition & Fees: $3,156
Enrollment: 650 Coed
Affiliation or Control: Independent Non-Profit IRS Status: 501(c)3
Highest Offering: Master's; No Undergraduates
Program: Professional; Business Emphasis
Accreditation: NH

01 President ....Mr. John N. POPOLI
05 Exec VP Educ Pgms & Solutions ....Mr. Christopher MULTHAUF
10 VP Finance & CFO ....Mr. Malcolm C. DOUGLAS
26 Vice President Marketing ....Mr. Peter DRUMMOND
20 VP Corporate Learning Solutions ....Ms. Kathleen M. LECK
16 VP Human Resources & Fundraising ....Ms. Stasia ZWISLER
27 VP Information Technology & CIO ....Mr. Gregory KOZAK
20 Dean Degree Programs & Faculty Rel ....Ms. Ellen MCMAHON
20 Dean Corporate Learning Solutions ....Mr. Neil HOLMAN
06 Registrar ....Ms. Christine L. PERLSTROM
29 Manager Alumni Relations & Events ....Ms. Jessica GARDNER
37 Associate Director of Financial Aid ....Ms. Rebecca KIM
07 Director of Admissions ....Ms. Carolyn BRUNE
36 Director Career Services ....Ms. Laura PALEY
35 Manager Student Services ....Ms. Roxanne GREENBURGER

Lake Land College (D)

5001 Lake Land Boulevard, Mattoon IL 61938-9366
County: Coles FICE Identification: 007644
Unit ID: 146506
Telephone: (217) 234-5253 Carnegie Class: Assoc/Pub-R-L
FAX Number: (217) 234-5400 Calendar System: Semester
URL: www.lakeland.cc.il.us
Established: 1966 Annual Undergrad Tuition & Fees (In-District): $3,024
Enrollment: 6,818 Coed
Affiliation or Control: State/Local IRS Status: 501(c)3
Highest Offering: Associate Degree
Program: Occupational; 2-Year Principally Bachelor's Creditable
Accreditation: NH, ADNUR, DH, PNUR, PTAA

01 President ....Dr. Josh BULLOCK
04 Admin Assistant to President ....Ms. Lana FULLER
10 Vice President Business Services ....Mr. Ray RIECK
05 VP Academic Services ....Dr. Jim HULL
32 Vice President Student Services ....Dr. Tina STOVALL
30 Vice President Development ....Vacant
88 Dean Correctional Pgms-South ....Mr. Brandon YOUNG
103 Assoc Vice Pres Workforce Devel ....Ms. Linda VON BEHREN
20 Assoc Vice Pres Educational Svcs ....Dr. Deb HUTTI
88 Exec Dean Correctional Pgms ....Mr. Tom KERKHOFF
07 Dean of Admissions Services ....Mr. Jon VAN DYKE
88 Assoc Dean Corrections-Taylorville ....Mr. John ALLEN
88 Assoc Dean Corrections-Graham ....Mr. Dennis MIHLBACHLER
88 Assoc Dean Corrections-Dwight ....Mr. Alan MORTENSEN
88 Assoc Dean Corrections-Western ....Mr. Tom THEISS
88 Assoc Dean Correction-IL River ....Mr. Tom ZABORAC
88 Assoc Dean Corrections-Jacksonville ....Mr. Steve BAHNEY
88 Assoc Dean Corrections-Lawrence ....Mr. Tim WATSON
88 Assoc Dean Corrections-Robinson ....Mr. Glen DONALDSON
88 Assc Dean Corrections-SW & Vandalia ....Mr. Steve DRAKE
88 Site Director Corrections-Hill ....Ms. Christine LEHR
88 Site Director Corr-Vienna & Shawnee ....Mr. Blake MCCONNELL
21 Comptroller ....Ms. Madge SHOOT
50 Dir Center for Business & Industry ....Mr. Charles BOVARD
08 Library Director ....Mr. Scott DRONE-SILVERS
26 Dir Communications/Creative Svcs ....Mrs. Kelly ALLEE
14 Director of Information Systems/Svc ....Mr. Lee SPANIOL
37 Director Financial Aid/Veteran Svcs ....Ms. Paula CARPENTER
18 Director Facilities Planning ....Mr. Michael KASDORF
15 Director of Human Resources ....Ms. Dawn SCHLECHTE
88 Director Learning Technologies ....Mr. Steve GARREN
25 Director Grants Development ....Ms. Emily RAMAGE
40 Director Auxiliary Services ....Ms. Chris KRAMER
29 Director Foundation & Alumni ....Mr. Dave COX
36 Director of Career Services ....Ms. Tina MOORE
38 Director of Student Counseling ....Ms. Emily HARTKE
18 Dir of Physical Plant Operations ....Mr. Matthew JANSEN
41 Director of Athletics ....Mr. Dennis THRONEBURG
09 Director of Institutional Research ....Dr. Mary BREER

Lakeview College of Nursing (E)

903 N Logan Avenue, Danville IL 61832-3788
County: Vermilion FICE Identification: 010501
Unit ID: 146533
Telephone: (217) 709-0920 Carnegie Class: Spec/Health
FAX Number: (217) 709-0954 Calendar System: Semester
URL: www.lakeviewcol.edu
Established: 1987 Annual Undergrad Tuition & Fees: $13,500
Enrollment: 339 Coed
Affiliation or Control: Independent Non-Profit IRS Status: 501(c)3
Highest Offering: Baccalaureate
Program: Professional; Nursing Emphasis
Accreditation: NH, NURSE

01 Interim Dean of Nursing ....Ms. Irene STEWARD
11 Associate CEO ....Ms. Sheila MINGEE
06 Registrar/Dir Enrollment ....Ms. Connie YOUNG
08 Library Dir/IT Coordinator ....Ms. Miranda SHAKE

Le Cordon Bleu College of Culinary Arts In Chicago (F)

361 W Chestnut Street, Chicago IL 60610
County: Cook FICE Identification: 023522
Unit ID: 144467
Telephone: (312) 944-0882 Carnegie Class: Assoc/PrivFP
FAX Number: (312) 944-8557 Calendar System: Semester
URL: www.chefs.edu/chicago
Established: 1983 Annual Undergrad Tuition & Fees: $19,530
Enrollment: 1,349 Coed
Affiliation or Control: Proprietary IRS Status: Proprietary
Highest Offering: Associate Degree
Program: Occupational; 2-Year Principally Bachelor's Creditable
Accreditation: NH, ACFEI

01 President ....Mr. Kirk T. BACHMANN
05 VP Academic Affs/Dean Student Svcs ....Mr. Marshall J. SHAFKOWITZ

Lewis and Clark Community College (G)

5800 Godfrey Road, Godfrey IL 62035-2466
County: Madison FICE Identification: 010020
Unit ID: 146603
Telephone: (618) 466-7000 Carnegie Class: Assoc/Pub-S-SC
FAX Number: (618) 466-2798 Calendar System: Semester
URL: www.lc.edu
Established: 1970 Annual Undergrad Tuition & Fees (In-District): $3,540
Enrollment: 8,483 Coed
Affiliation or Control: State/Local IRS Status: 501(c)3
Highest Offering: Associate Degree
Program: Occupational; 2-Year Principally Bachelor's Creditable
Accreditation: NH, ADNUR, DA, DH, OTA

01 President ....Dr. Dale T. CHAPMAN
05 Vice President Academic Affairs ....Dr. Linda CHAPMAN
84 Vice President Enrollment Services ....Mr. Kent SCHEFFEL
102 Vice Pres Media & Foundation Rels ....Mrs. Lori ARTIS
32 Vice President Student Services ....Dr. Sean HILL
11 Vice President Administration ....Mr. Gary AYRES
10 Assoc Vice Pres Finance ....Mrs. Mary SCHULTE
10 Assoc Vice President Accounting ....Mrs. Nancy KAISER
76 Dean Science/Math/Technology ....Dr. Sue CZERWINSKI-ALJETS
72 Dean Business & Liberal Arts ....Mrs. Jill LANE
88 Director Corp & Comm Learning ....Mrs. Kathy WILLIS
27 Assoc Vice Pres Telecommunications ....Mrs. Julie MCPIKE
18 Assoc Vice Pres Cap Proj/Campus ..Mr. Christopher BACHMANN
20 Dir Academic Operations & Planning ....Mr. Jeff COLES
09 Dir Institutional Res/Library Svcs ....Mr. Dennis KRIEB
51 Director Adult Education Program ....Mrs. Valorie HARRIS
88 Director Enrollment Center/Advising ....Mrs. Delfina DORNES
37 Dir Financial Aid/Stdnt Employment ....Mrs. Angela WEAVER
38 Dir Student Dev & Counseling ....Mrs. Kathy HABERER
35 Int Dir Student Support Services ....Mr. Kehven WILLIAMS
15 Director Human Resources ....Mr. Bob BECHERER
06 Registrar ....Ms. Heidi SCOTT
41 Director Athletics ....Mr. Deon THOMAS

Lewis University (H)

One University Parkway, Romeoville IL 60446-2200
County: Will FICE Identification: 001707
Unit ID: 146612
Telephone: (815) 838-0500 Carnegie Class: Master's L
FAX Number: (815) 838-9456 Calendar System: Semester
URL: www.lewisu.edu
Established: 1932 Annual Undergrad Tuition & Fees: $25,770
Enrollment: 6,539 Coed
Affiliation or Control: Roman Catholic IRS Status: 501(c)3
Highest Offering: Doctorate
Program: Occupational; Liberal Arts And General; Teacher Preparatory; Professional
Accreditation: NH, ACBSP, NURSE, SW, TED

01 President ....Bro. James GAFFNEY, FSC
03 Executive Vice President ....Mr. Wayne J. DRAUDT
05 Provost ....Dr. Stephany S. SCHLACHTER
32 Sr Vice President Student Services ....Mr. Joseph T. FALESE
10 Senior Vice Pres/CFO ....Mr. Robert C. DE ROSE
84 Sr VP Enrollment Mgmt/Marketing ....Mr. Raymond KENNELLY
30 Vice Pres University Advancement ....Mr. Leonard BERTOLINI
07 Director of Admission ....Mr. Ryan COCKERILL
35 Dean of Student Services ....Ms. Kathryn SLATTERY
28 VP Mission & Academic Services ....Dr. Kurt SCHACKMUTH
49 Dean College Arts & Sciences ....Dr. Bonnie BONDAVALLI
50 Dean College Business ....Dr. Rami KHASAWNEH
66 Dean Col Nursing/Health Professions ....Dr. Peggy RICE
15 Assoc Vice Pres Human Resources ....Ms. Graciela DUFOUR
09 Assoc VP Inst Research/Planning ....Dr. Jion YEN
08 Director of Library ....Vacant
06 Registrar ....Mr. Robert KEMPIAK
37 Director of Financial Aid ....Ms. Janeen DECHARINTE
26 Director Marketing/Communications ....Ms. Ramona LAMONTAGNE
41 Director of Athletics ....Mr. John PLANEK
23 Dir of Health & Counseling Services ....Ms. Michele MANASSAH
19 Chief of Police ....Mr. James MONTANARI
42 Director of University Ministry ....Mr. Steve ZLATIC
31 Dir of Meetings/Events/Conferences ....Mr. Robert ARNOLD

13 Chief Info Technology Officer .... Vacant
85 Director International Student Svcs .... Mr. Michael FEKETE
14 Director Instl Data Administration .... Ms. Tammy KUSE
29 Exec Dir Alumni/Development Svcs .... Ms. Julie PENNER
96 Director of Purchasing .... Mr. Jim KOENIG
36 Director of Career Services .... Ms. Kristi KELLY

Lexington College (A)

310 S Peoria, Suite 512, Chicago IL 60607-3534
County: Cook FICE Identification: 025276
Unit ID: 146621
Telephone: (312) 226-6294 Carnegie Class: Spec/Bus
FAX Number: (312) 226-6405 Calendar System: Semester
URL: www.lexingtoncollege.edu
Established: 1977 Annual Undergrad Tuition & Fees: $24,075
Enrollment: 45 Female
Affiliation or Control: Independent Non-Profit IRS Status: 501(c)3
Highest Offering: Baccalaureate
Program: Professional
Accreditation: NH

01 President .... Ms. Mary HUNT
05 Academic Dean .... Mrs. Jolene BIRMINGHAM
10 Manager of Business Office .... Ms. Estela GODINA
26 Mgr Communications & Marketing .... Ms. Veronica NORTH
37 Director of Financial Aid .... Ms. Maria LEBRON
06 Registrar .... Ms. Christy ACOSTA
21 Associate Business Officer .... Ms. Diane MCDERMOTT
30 Director of Development .... Ms. Katherine CASKEY
35 Director Student Affairs .... Ms. Meg RAY

Lincoln Christian University (B)

100 Campus View Drive, Lincoln IL 62656-2167
County: Logan FICE Identification: 001708
Unit ID: 146667
Telephone: (217) 732-3168 Carnegie Class: Spec/Faith
FAX Number: (217) 732-5718 Calendar System: Semester
URL: www.lincolnchristian.edu
Established: 1944 Annual Undergrad Tuition & Fees: $15,810
Enrollment: 1,066 Coed
Affiliation or Control: Christian Churches And Churches of Christ
IRS Status: 501(c)3
Highest Offering: Doctorate
Program: Liberal Arts And General; Religious Emphasis
Accreditation: NH, BI, THEOL

01 President .... Dr. Keith H. RAY
05 Provost .... Dr. Clay HAM
10 Vice President of Finance .... Vacant
32 Vice Pres of Student Development .... Mr. Brian MILLS
30 VP of University Advancement .... Mr. Gordon D. VENTURELLA
84 VP of Enrollment Management .... Mrs. Krista BROOKS
29 Assoc VP of Alumni Services .... Mr. Lynn LAUGHLIN
06 Registrar .... Mr. Shawn SMITH
08 Librarian .... Ms. Nancy OLSON
37 Director of Financial Aid .... Ms. Nancy SIDDENS
101 Admin Asst to Pres/Secy Bd of Gov .... Mrs. Linda SEGGELKE
13 Director of Campus Technology .... Mr. Larry WOOLARD

Lincoln College (C)

300 Keokuk Street, Lincoln IL 62656-1699
County: Logan FICE Identification: 001709
Unit ID: 146676
Telephone: (217) 732-3155 Carnegie Class: Bac/Assoc
FAX Number: (217) 732-8859 Calendar System: Semester
URL: www.lincolncollege.edu
Established: 1865 Annual Undergrad Tuition & Fees: $17,500
Enrollment: 1,275 Coed
Affiliation or Control: Independent Non-Profit IRS Status: 501(c)3
Highest Offering: Baccalaureate
Program: 2-Year Principally Bachelor's Creditable
Accreditation: NH, IACBE

01 President .... Mr. John D. BLACKBURN
05 Vice Pres Academic Affairs .... Dr. A. Gigi FANSLER
30 Vice President for Advancement .... Ms. Debbie ACKERMAN
10 Vice Pres Finance & Administration .... Mr. Greg A. EIMER
84 VP for Enroll Mgmt & Student Svcs .... Mr. Rick SAMUELS
37 Director of Financial Aid .... Mr. Chris STECKMANN
06 Registrar .... Mrs. Debra J. HARMON
29 Coordinator Alumni Relations .... Ms. Kerri TAYLOR
38 Director of Counseling .... Ms. Michelle BAUER
08 Head Librarian .... Mr. Mike STARASTA
18 Director of Building & Grounds .... Ms. Ronda PIATT
23 Director of Health Services .... Ms. Diane STEPHENSON
21 Controller .... Mrs. Katherine PAPESCH
15 Director of Human Resources .... Mrs. Kathy STEFFENS
40 Bookstore Manager .... Mrs. Donna HUTCHISON
32 Dean of Students .... Mrs. Bridgett THOMAS
13 Director of Information Technology .... Mr. Tim FOSTER
27 Director of Communications .... Vacant
35 Director of Student Development .... Vacant
07 Director of Admissions .... Mrs. Gretchen BREE
09 Director of Institutional Research .... Mr. David SMALLEY

Lincoln College- Normal (D)

715 W Raab Road, Normal IL 61761
Telephone: (309) 452-0500 Identification: 770078
Accreditation: &NH

† Main campus is Lincoln College in Lincoln, IL.

Lincoln College of Technology (E)

8317 West North Avenue, Melrose Park IL 60160-1605
FICE Identification: 010316
Unit ID: 146700
Telephone: (708) 344-4700 Carnegie Class: Assoc/PrivFP
FAX Number: (708) 345-4065 Calendar System: Semester
URL: www.lincolnedu.com
Established: 1950 Annual Undergrad Tuition & Fees: $31,502
Enrollment: 700 Coed
Affiliation or Control: Proprietary IRS Status: Proprietary
Highest Offering: Associate Degree
Program: Occupational
Accreditation: ACCSC

01 President .... Ms. Jody WASMER

Lincoln Land Community College (F)

5250 Shepherd Road, PO Box 19256,
Springfield IL 62794-9256
County: Sangamon FICE Identification: 007170
Unit ID: 146685
Telephone: (217) 786-2200 Carnegie Class: Assoc/Pub-R-L
FAX Number: (217) 786-2468 Calendar System: Semester
URL: www.llcc.edu
Established: 1967 Annual Undergrad Tuition & Fees (In-District): $3,300
Enrollment: 7,193 Coed
Affiliation or Control: Local IRS Status: 501(c)3
Highest Offering: Associate Degree
Program: Occupational; 2-Year Principally Bachelor's Creditable; Nursing Emphasis
Accreditation: NH, ADNUR, COARC, NDT, OTA, RAD, SURGT

01 President .... Dr. Charlotte J. WARREN
11 Vice President Administrative Svcs .... Mr. Richard W. VERTREES
05 Vice President Academic Svcs .... Dr. Eileen G. TEPATTI
32 Vice President Student Services .... Ms. Lesley J. FREDERICK
103 Vice President Workforce Systems .... Dr. Judy JOZAITIS
13 Chief Information Officer .... Mr. Esteban CRUZ
04 Asst to Pres Planning & Inst Impr .... Vacant
15 Assoc Vice Pres Human Resources .... Ms. Junell A. RANSDELL
84 Assoc VP Enrollment Svcs/Registrar .... Ms. Tyra TAYLOR
10 Associate Vice President Finance .... Ms. Karie L. LONGHTA
45 Asc VP Budget/Finan Plng/Analysis .... Ms. Mary A. MCGEE
37 Asst Vice President Financial Aid .... Ms. Lisa COLLIER
86 Asst VP Corp/Gov Trng & Econ Devel .... Ms. Paula J. LUEBBERT
18 Asst VP Construction .... Mr. Hugh GARVEY
12 Exec Director Educ Service Area .... Mr. Scott R. STALLMAN
12 Exec Director Educ Service Area .... Ms. Jan M. TERRY
102 Exec Director LLCC Foundation .... Ms. Karen A. SANDERS
26 Exec Dir Public Relations/Marketing .... Ms. Lynn WHALEN
24 Exec Director Learning Lab .... Mrs. Julie CLEVENGER
88 Director Small Business Devel Ctr .... Mr. Kevin LUST
07 Director Admissions & Records .... Mr. Ronald J. GREGOIRE
22 Dir Employ Bnft Svc/Eq Opty Cmpl Of .... Ms. Nicole M. RALPH
09 Director Institutional Research .... Ms. Susan SIMPSON
30 Director Development .... Ms. Janet SEMANIK
36 Director Placement/Testing .... Ms. Tricia A. KUJAWA
32 Director Student Life .... Ms. Marci ROCKEY
19 Police Chief .... Mr. Bradley D. GENTRY
50 Dean Business & Technologies .... Mr. David A. GREEN
83 Dean Social Sciences .... Dr. Victor K. BRODERICK
72 Dean District Learning Resources .... Ms. Wendy L. HOWERTER
57 Dean Arts & Humanities .... Mr. David E. LAUBERSHEIMER
81 Dean Mathematics and Sciences .... Mr. William D. BADE
76 Dean Health Professions .... Dr. Cynthia L. MASKEY
08 Assoc Dean Library .... Mrs. Tamara SCHNELL
56 Asc Dean Instruct Tech/Distance Ed .... Mrs. Becky PARTON

Lindenwood University Belleville Campus (G)

2600 West Main Street, Belleville IL 62226
Telephone: (618) 239-6000 Identification: 770322
Accreditation: &NH, ACBSP

† Main campus is Lindenwood University in Saint Charles, MO.

Loyola University Chicago (H)

1032 W. Sheridan Road, Chicago IL 60660
County: Cook FICE Identification: 001710
Unit ID: 146719
Telephone: (773) 274-3000 Carnegie Class: RU/H
FAX Number: (312) 915-7003 Calendar System: Semester
URL: www.luc.edu
Established: 1870 Annual Undergrad Tuition & Fees: $36,660
Enrollment: 15,720 Coed
Affiliation or Control: Roman Catholic IRS Status: 501(c)3
Highest Offering: Doctorate
Program: Liberal Arts And General; Teacher Preparatory; Professional; Business Emphasis
Accreditation: NH, BUS, BUSA, CLPSY, COPSY, DENT, DIETI, EMT, FEPAC, LAW, MED, NURSE, SCPSY, SW, TED, THEA

01 President/CEO .... Rev. Michael J. GARANZINI, SJ
17 Sr VP & Provost Health Sciences .... Dr. Richard GAMELLI
05 Provost .... Dr. John P. PELISSERO
11 COO Health Sciences .... Rev. Dennis YESALONIA, SJ
10 Sr Vice President Finance & CFO .... Mr. William G. LAIRD
30 Sr Vice President Advancement .... Mr. Jonathan R. HEINTZELMAN
45 Sr VP Cap Planning & Campus Mgmt .... Mr. Wayne MAGDZIARZ
15 Sr VP Admin Svcs & Chief HR Officer .... Mr. Thomas M. KELLY
43 Vice President & General Counsel .... Ms. Pam COSTAS
32 Vice President Student Development .... Dr. Robert KELLY
12 Vice President & Director Rome Ctr .... Mr. Emilio IODICE
16 Vice President Government Affairs .... Mr. Philip P. HALE
27 Vice President Information Services .... Ms. Susan M. MALISCH
04 Special Assistant to the President .... Rev. John COSTELLO, SJ
26 VP Marketing & Communications .... Ms. Kelly SHANNON
88 VP Planning & Strategy Health Sci .... Mr. Steve BERGFELD
30 Assoc VP Development .... Ms. Jamie ORSINI
88 Assoc VP Administration/Finance/SSM .... Ms. Cindy D. GONYA
88 Assoc VP Informatics/System Devel .... Mr. Ronald N. PRICE
21 Assoc VP Finance & Controller .... Ms. Andrea SABITSANA
21 Actg Assoc VP Finance Sponsored Pgm .... Ms. Donna QUIRK
21 Associate VP Campus Services .... Mr. Timothy MCGURIMAN
26 Assoc VP Campus/Community Planning .... Ms. Jennifer R. CLARK
21 Assoc VP for Budget & Finance .... Dr. Thomas F. HICKEY
18 Associate VP of Facilities .... Ms. Kana WIBBENMEYER
35 Assoc VP & Dean of Students .... Ms. Jane F. NEUFELD
35 Assistant VP Student Development .... Mr. Jack MCLEAN
44 Asst VP Dev & University Engagement .... Ms. Shena KEITH
88 Asst VP/Asst to Pres/Chairman .... Ms. Donna B. CURIN
30 Asst VP Advancement Health Sci .... Mr. Shawn VOGEN
88 Asst VP Student Development .... Dr. Kenechukwu MMEJE
88 Vice Provost Health Sciences .... Dr. Richard KENNEDY
85 Vice Provost Acad Ctrs/Global Inits .... Dr. Patrick M. BOYLE
11 Vice Provost Acad & Faculty Res .... Dr. David P. PRASSE
84 Associate Provost Enrollment Management .... Mr. Paul G. ROBERTS
46 Assoc Provost Research .... Dr. Samuel A. ATTOH
11 Associate Provost Administration .... Dr. Marian A. CLAFFEY
20 Associate Provost Academic Services .... Rev. Justin DAFFRON, SJ
88 Assoc Provost for Mission & Identit .... Dr. John HARDT
62 Assoc Provost & Dir HSD Library .... Ms. Gail HENDLER
88 Assoc Provost Curriculum Dev .... Dr. Jo Beth D'AGOSTINO
88 Asst Provost & Dir Faculty Admin .... Dr. Beverly KASPER
100 Special Assistant to the President .... Ms. Lorraine G. SNYDER
08 Dean University Libraries .... Mr. Robert A. SEAL
49 Dean of Arts & Sciences .... Dr. Reinhard ANDRESS
50 Dean School of Business Admin .... Dr. Kathleen A. GETZ
51 Acting Dean Continuing & Prof Educ .... Dr. Janet DEATHERAGE
58 Dean of Graduate School .... Dr. Samuel A. ATTOH
60 Dean School of Communication .... Dr. Donald B. HEIDER
61 Dean School of Law .... Dr. David N. YELLEN
63 Dean School of Medicine .... Dr. Linda BRUBAKER
66 Dean School of Nursing .... Dr. Vicki A. KEOUGH
70 Dean School of Social Work .... Dr. Darrell P. WHEELER
15 Dean Faculty Rome Center .... Dr. Susana CAVALLO
51 Dean School of Cont & Prof Stds .... Mr. Walter S. PEARSON
53 Dean School of Education .... Dr. Michael DANTLEY
18 Superintendent Lakeside Facilities .... Mr. Wliam SHERRY
88 Exec Director Conference Services .... Mr. Dana ADAMS
26 Exec Dir Development Major Gifts .... Ms. Nicole MEEHAN
96 Manager of Purchasing .... Mr. Sam J. PERRY
90 Director Academic Tech Services .... Mr. Bruce A. MONTES
21 Director Academic Business Ops .... Ms. Joanna PAPPAS
88 Dir Budgeting & Financial Planning .... Mr. Joseph M. FILIPIAK
46 Dir Enrollment Systems & Analysis .... Mr. Timothy HEUER
28 Dir Student Diversity & Multicultur .... Ms. Sadika SULAIMAN-HARA
88 Director Special Events .... Mr. Richard WILLIAMS
29 Director Alumni Relations HSD .... Ms. Mary WEINGARTNER
37 Acting Dir Student Fin Assistance .... Mr. Edward MOORE
15 Director of Human Resources .... Ms. Joan C. STASIAK
90 Dir of System Implementation & Cons .... Mr. Kevin J. SMITH
88 Director of Communications .... Ms. Maeve M. KILEY
102 Dir of Corporate & Foundation Rels .... Ms. Angela LIEGEL
88 Dir Advancement Info Services .... Ms. Stacy HUGHES
21 Treasurer .... Mr. Eric JONES
23 Director Wellness Center .... Ms. Diane C. ASARO
09 Director Institutional Research .... Dr. Richard S. HURST
06 Director of Registration & Records .... Ms. Clare M. KORINEK
07 Director Undergraduate Admissions .... Ms. Lori A. GREENE
36 Director Career Development Center .... Dr. Stephanie STEWART
39 Director Residence Life .... Mr. Cass M. COUGHLIN
41 Director of Athletics .... Dr. M.Grace CALHOUN
18 Director Infrastructure Services .... Mr. Dan VONDER HEIDE
88 Dir Enterprise Architecture & Promo .... Mr. Jim SIBENALLER
28 Dir Cultural Affairs & LUMA .... Ms. Pam AMBROSE
42 Director Campus Ministry .... Dr. Lisa REITER
85 Director Chicago Center .... Mr. Jason OBIN
88 Director Compensation & Benefits .... Ms. Debra MEISTER
88 Director Strategic Financing/Risk .... Ms. Susan BODIN
88 Director Environmental Services .... Mr. William CURTIN
88 Director Business Operations .... Mr. David BEALL
29 Special Asst Alumni Relations .... Rev. Patrick DORSEY
88 Dir Institute Pastoral Studies .... Dr. Brian SCHMISEK
84 Dir Graduate/Professional Admiss .... Ms. Ann TALBOT
88 Director Adult & Transfer Center .... Ms. Jill SCHUR
88 Director Enrollment Marketing .... Ms. Nicole BARRON
19 Director Campus Safety .... Vacant
29 Director Alumni Relations .... Vacant

Loyola University Health Sciences Campus (I)

2160 S First Avenue, Maywood IL 60153
Telephone: (708) 216-9000 Identification: 770080
Accreditation: &NH

† Main campus is Loyola University Chicago in Chicago, IL.

Loyola University Water Town Campus (A)

820 N Michigan Avenue, Chicago IL 60611
Telephone: (312) 915-6000 Identification: 770079
Accreditation: &NH

† Main campus is Loyola University Chicago in Chicago, IL.

Lutheran School of Theology at Chicago (B)

1100 E 55th Street, Chicago IL 60615-9985
County: Cook FICE Identification: 001712
Unit ID: 146728
Telephone: (773) 256-0700 Carnegie Class: Spec/Faith
FAX Number: (773) 256-0782 Calendar System: Semester
URL: www.lstc.edu
Established: 1860 Annual Graduate Tuition & Fees: $14,656
Enrollment: 257 Coed
Affiliation or Control: Evangelical Lutheran Church In America
IRS Status: 501(c)3
Highest Offering: Doctorate; No Undergraduates
Program: Professional; Religious Emphasis
Accreditation: NH, THEOL

01 President ....Dr. James NIEMAN
04 Assistant to the President ....Ms. Patti DEBIAS
108 Exec for Administration/Assess/Plng ....Ms. Laura WILHELM
05 Dean/Vice Pres for Academic Affairs ....Dr. Michael SHELLEY
88 Director of the MDiv Programs ....Dr. Kathleen BILLMAN
88 Director of the MA Programs ....Dr. Kurt HENDEL
58 Director of Advanced Studies ....Dr. Esther MENN
88 Pastor to the Community ....Rev. Joan BECK
11 Vice President for Operations ....Mr. Bob BERRIDGE
30 Vice President for Advancement ....Mr. Mark H. VAN SCHARREL
10 Chief Financial Officer ....Mr. David WEISZ
07 Director of Admissions ....Dr. Scott CHALMERS
06 Registrar ....Ms. Patricia A. BARTLEY
26 Director of Communications/Mktg ....Ms. Janet BODEN
08 Director of Library ....Dr. Christine WENDEROTH
13 Dir of Information Technology Svcs ....Mr. Kenesa DEBELA
37 Assoc Dir Admissions/Financial Aid ....Ms. Rachel BROCKER

MacCormac College (C)

29 E Madison Street 2nd Floor, Chicago IL 60602-4405
County: Cook FICE Identification: 001716
Unit ID: 146816
Telephone: (312) 922-1884 Carnegie Class: Assoc/PrivNFP
FAX Number: (312) 922-4286 Calendar System: Semester
URL: www.maccormac.edu
Established: 1904 Annual Undergrad Tuition & Fees: $12,930
Enrollment: 194 Coed
Affiliation or Control: Independent Non-Profit IRS Status: 501(c)3
Highest Offering: Associate Degree
Program: 2-Year Principally Bachelor's Creditable
Accreditation: NH

01 President ....Dr. Marnelle ALEXIS
05 Academic Dean ....Dr. Mary Ann ROWAN
10 Director of Finance/Human Resources ....Mr. Matt GAWENDA
06 Registrar ....Ms. Mariza SILVA
37 Director of Financial Aid ....Mr. Robert GOMEZ
32 Assoc Dir Admission/Student Svcs ....Mr. Marcus TROUTMAN
07 Assoc Dir Admissions/Financial Aid ....Mr. Roberto TORRES

MacMurray College (D)

447 E College Avenue, Jacksonville IL 62650-2590
County: Morgan FICE Identification: 001717
Unit ID: 146825
Telephone: (217) 479-7041 Carnegie Class: Bac/Diverse
FAX Number: (217) 245-0405 Calendar System: 4/1/4
URL: www.mac.edu
Established: 1846 Annual Undergrad Tuition & Fees: $21,900
Enrollment: 585 Coed
Affiliation or Control: United Methodist IRS Status: 501(c)3
Highest Offering: Baccalaureate
Program: Liberal Arts And General; Teacher Preparatory; Professional
Accreditation: NH, NURSE, SW

01 President ....Dr. Colleen HESTER
03 CFO & Vice President of Finance ....Ms. Jackie LOOSER
05 VP Academic Affairs & Student Life ....Dr. James MAXWELL
32 Dean of Student Affairs ....Mr. Martin SABOLO
30 Exec Dir Institutional Advancement ....Ms. Bridget PHILLIPS
84 Chief Admissions Officer ....Ms. Alicia ZEONE
10 Controller ....Mr. Andrew SIDOCK
13 Director of IT/System Administrator ....Mr. Bob LOOSER
06 Registrar ....Dr. Glen CLATTERBUCK
08 Librarian ....Ms. Susan EILERING
37 Director of Financial Aid ....Ms. Laci ENGELBRECHT
36 Coordinator Career Services ....Ms. Cori WAGNER
29 Director Alumni Relations ....Ms. Christina WELLS
09 Director of Institutional Research ....Vacant
18 Director of Facilities ....Mr. Larry TROWBRIDGE
26 Director of Public Relations ....Mr. Ted ROTH

McCormick Theological Seminary (E)

5460 S University Avenue, Chicago IL 60615-5108
County: Cook FICE Identification: 001721
Unit ID: 146977
Telephone: (773) 947-6300 Carnegie Class: Spec/Faith
FAX Number: (773) 288-2612 Calendar System: Semester
URL: www.mccormick.edu
Established: 1829 Annual Graduate Tuition & Fees: $19,665
Enrollment: 207 Coed
Affiliation or Control: Presbyterian Church (U.S.A.) IRS Status: 501(c)3
Highest Offering: Doctorate; No Undergraduates
Program: Professional; Nursing Emphasis
Accreditation: NH, THEOL

01 President ....Rev. Frank M. YAMADA
10 Exec Vice Pres/Chief Business Ofcr ....Mr. David CRAWFORD
05 Vice Pres Acad Affs/Dean Faculty ....Dr. Luis R. RIVERA
32 Vice President for Student Affairs ....Rev Dr. Christine VOGEL
30 Vice Pres Seminary Rels/Development ....Ms. Lisa M. DAGHER
06 Registrar ....Mr. Jim COURTNEY
29 Dir of Alumni/ae & Church Rels ....Ms. Veronica JOHNSON
08 Director of JKM Library ....Dr. Christine WENDEROTH
15 Director Human Resources ....Ms. Ashley WOODFAULK
37 Dir Student Financial Aid/Planning ....Ms. Tabitha CLARK

McHenry County College (F)

8900 US Highway 14, Crystal Lake IL 60012-2796
County: McHenry FICE Identification: 007691
Unit ID: 147004
Telephone: (815) 455-3700 Carnegie Class: Assoc/Pub-S-SC
FAX Number: (815) 455-3999 Calendar System: Semester
URL: www.mchenry.edu
Established: 1967 Annual Undergrad Tuition & Fees (In-District): $3,531
Enrollment: 6,976 Coed
Affiliation or Control: State/Local IRS Status: 501(c)3
Highest Offering: Associate Degree
Program: Occupational; 2-Year Principally Bachelor's Creditable
Accreditation: NH, OTA

01 President ....Dr. Vicky SMITH
101 Asst to the President/Board Liaison ....Mrs. Pat KRIEGERMEIER
05 VP Academic & Student Affairs ....Dr. Tony MIKSA
30 Vice Pres Institutional Advancement ....Ms. Laura J. BROWN
13 Chief Information Officer ....Dr. Allen P. BUTLER
10 CFO/Treasurer ....Mr. Bob TENUTA
19 Exec Director Campus Public Safety ....Mr. Michael CLESCERI
75 Exec Dean Career & Technical Educ ....Mr. James FALCO
51 Exec Dean Cont & Professional Ed ....Ms. Kay MOORMANN
79 Exec Dean Humanities & Soc Sciences ....Vacant
81 Exec Dean Math/Sciences Health Pro ....Dr. Amy MAXEINER
26 Chief Communications Officer ....Mrs. Christina HAGGERTY
32 AVP Academic & Student Affairs ....Ms. Julietta PATRICK
18 AVP Physical Facilities ....Mr. Gregory EVANS
16 AVP of Human Resources ....Ms. Angelina CASTILLO
103 Exec Dir Workforce Community Pgm ....Ms. Catherine JONES
102 Executive Director MCC Foundation ....Vacant
88 Dir Fieldwork Occ Therapy Asst Pgm ....Ms. Marlene VOGT
66 Director Nursing ....Vacant
106 Director of Online Learning ....Dr. Raymond LAWSON
88 Directory of Sustainability ....Ms. Kim HANKINS
20 Dean of Academic Development ....Ms. Adriane HUTCHINSON
84 Dean Enrollment Services ....Ms. Marianne DEVENNY
08 Dean of Library ....Ms. Kathy HARGER
88 Dean of Student Development ....Dr. Flecia THOMAS
21 Controller ....Vacant
88 Assoc Dean College/Career Readiness ....Mr. Tony CAPALBO
72 Assoc Dean Educ Career & Tech Ed ....Mr. Peter LINDEN
79 Assoc Dean Humanities/Social Sci ....Ms. Loreen KELLER
81 Assoc Dean Math Science Health ....Ms. Sharon BUTTON
14 Director Application Solutions ....Ms. Marilyn SCHICK
96 Director of Business Services ....Ms. Jennifer JONES
09 Director Institutional Effectivenes ....Ms. Patricia STEJSKAL
88 Director of Network Services ....Mr. Rob RASMUSSEN
25 Director of Resource Development ....Dr. Marcella RECA ZIPP
06 Director of Registration & Records ....Ms. Amy HALLER
41 Director Athletics-Intramural & Rec ....Mr. Wally REYNOLDS
51 Dir of Continuing Education ....Ms. Dori SULLINS
15 Director Employment Svcs/Diversity ....Ms. Sandra HESS MOLL
88 Director End User Services ....Mr. Geary SMITH
37 Director of Financial Aid ....Vacant
88 Director of Learning Support ....Ms. Emma HENDRIETH
40 Director Bookstore ....Ms. Karen SMITH
88 Director Food Services ....Ms. Sandra JOHNSTON
23 Director of Health and Wellness ....Ms. Lena KALEMBA
15 Manager of Human Resources ....Ms. Anita ROEWER
88 Mgr IL Small Business Development ....Ms. Kristi PATTERSON
07 Manager New Student Transitions ....Ms. Kellie CARPER
88 Manager of Special Needs ....Ms. Bev ALBRIGHT
19 Supervisor Campus Public Safety ....Mr. Scott SOSNOWSKI
35 Mgr of Student Conduct/Campus Life ....Ms. Talia KORONKIEWICZ

McKendree University (G)

701 College Road, Lebanon IL 62254-9990
County: Saint Clair FICE Identification: 001722
Unit ID: 147013
Telephone: (618) 537-4481 Carnegie Class: Master's L
FAX Number: (618) 537-6259 Calendar System: Semester
URL: www.mckendree.edu
Established: 1828 Annual Undergrad Tuition & Fees: $25,050
Enrollment: 3,032 Coed
Affiliation or Control: United Methodist IRS Status: 501(c)3
Highest Offering: Doctorate
Program: Liberal Arts And General; Teacher Preparatory; Professional
Accreditation: NH, IACBE, NURSE

01 President ....Dr. James M. DENNIS
03 Senior Vice President ....Ms. Victoria A. DOWLING
04 Assistant to the President ....Ms. Patti J. DANIELS
05 Provost/Dean of the University ....Dr. Christine M. BAHR
10 Vice Pres Finance/Administration ....Mrs. Sally A. MAYHEW
07 Vice Pres Admission & Financial Aid ....Mr. Chris HALL
32 Vice President Student Affairs ....Dr. Joni BASTIAN
09 Vice Pres Research Plng & Tech ....Dr. Mary E. BORNHEIMER
30 Asst VP Dev/Alumni/Parent Relations ....Ms. Kimberly A. MAYDEN
20 Associate Dean of the University ....Dr. Tami EGGLESTON
12 Assoc Dean McKendree-at-Scott ....Mr. Thomas A. PAWLOW
56 External Programs ....Dr. Joseph J. CIPFL
13 Director Technology Information ....Mr. George KRISS
06 Registrar/Asst Dean ....Ms. Debra LARSON
08 Librarian ....Ms. Rebecca SCHREINER
21 Comptroller/Budget Manager ....Mr. Paul ZINK
26 Exec Dir Marketing/Communications ....Mrs. Krysti H. CONNELLY
29 Director Alumni Relations ....Mrs. Whitney FRAIER
44 Director of Annual Giving ....Mr. Vincent PIAZZA
37 Director Financial Aid ....Mrs. Elizabeth JUEHNE
36 Director Career Services ....Ms. Jennifer K. PICKERELL
18 Director of Operations ....Mr. Tom P. JENSEN
15 Director Human Resources ....Ms. Shirley A. RENTZ
27 Director Media Relations ....Ms. Lisa K. BRANDON
39 Director of Residence Life ....Mr. Mitch NASSER
35 Director of Campus Activities ....Mr. Craig L. ROBERTSON
41 Athletic Director ....Mr. Chuck BRUEGGEMANN
42 Chaplain/Director Church Relations ....Rev Dr. B. Timothy HARRISON
40 Bookstore Director ....Ms. Rebecca B. MATHEWS
30 Director of Advancement Services ....Mr. Scott L. BILLHARTZ
19 Director Safety & Security ....Mr. Ranodore M. FOGGS
44 Director of Major Gifts ....Ms. Tricia POETTKER
88 Director of Student Accounts ....Mrs. Marsha GILES
28 Director of Diversity ....Mr. Brent W. REEVES

Meadville Lombard Theological School (H)

610 South Michigan Avenue, Chicago IL 60605
County: Cook FICE Identification: 001723
Unit ID: 147031
Telephone: (773) 256-3000 Carnegie Class: Spec/Faith
FAX Number: (312) 327-7002 Calendar System: Semester
URL: www.meadville.edu
Established: 1844 Annual Graduate Tuition & Fees: $17,460
Enrollment: 128 Coed
Affiliation or Control: Unitarian Universalist IRS Status: 501(c)3
Highest Offering: Doctorate; No Undergraduates
Program: Professional; Religious Emphasis
Accreditation: THEOL

01 President ....Dr. Lee BARKER
05 Provost ....Dr. Sharon WELCH
10 Vice Pres Finance & Administration ....Ms. Deborah BIEBER
08 Dean of Library ....Rev. Neil W. GERDES
30 Dir of Development & Communications ....Ms. Madeleine ROBINS
32 Senior Director Student Services ....Ms. Tina PORTER

Methodist College (I)

415 St. Mark Court, Peoria IL 61603
County: Peoria FICE Identification: 006228
Unit ID: 147129
Telephone: (309) 672-5530 Carnegie Class: Spec/Health
FAX Number: (309) 671-8303 Calendar System: Semester
URL: www.methodistcol.edu
Established: 2000 Annual Undergrad Tuition & Fees: $17,610
Enrollment: 528 Coed
Affiliation or Control: Independent Non-Profit IRS Status: 501(c)3
Highest Offering: Baccalaureate
Program: Nursing Emphasis
Accreditation: NH, NUR, NURSE

01 President ....Dr. Kimberly JOHNSTON
05 Vice Pres Academic Affairs ....Dr. Linda PENDERGAST
84 Dean Enrollment Management ....Mr. Keith BRANHAM
10 Director of Finance ....Mr. Steve ROLLINS
20 Director of Educational Tech ....Mr. Matthew HERTZOG
30 Director Marketing/Alumni Affairs ....Ms. Kirstin MARSHALL
15 Director Human Resources ....Ms. Linda MOORE
09 Dir Institutional Research/Analysis ....Ms. Staci PAUER
13 Director Information Management ....Vacant
06 Registrar ....Ms. Ann GAREY

Midstate College (J)

411 W Northmoor Road, Peoria IL 61614-3558
County: Peoria FICE Identification: 004568
Unit ID: 147165
Telephone: (309) 692-4092 Carnegie Class: Bac/Assoc
FAX Number: (309) 692-3893 Calendar System: Quarter
URL: www.midstate.edu
Established: 1888 Annual Undergrad Tuition & Fees: $21,640
Enrollment: 592 Coed
Affiliation or Control: Proprietary IRS Status: Proprietary
Highest Offering: Baccalaureate
Program: Occupational; 2-Year Principally Bachelor's Creditable; Business Emphasis
Accreditation: NH, CAHIIM, MAC

01 President .... Meredith N. BUNCH
05 Dean of Academics .... Ruth E. SHAFFER
32 Dean of Students .... Vicki DRAKSLER
10 Controller .... Angie HATTEN
37 Director of Financial Assistance .... Irene BIMROSE
26 Director of Marketing & Enrollment .... Ashley SPAIN
32 Director of Student Affairs .... Rhonda P. URBAN
36 Director of Career Services .... Jennie GREENAN
08 Director of Library Resources .... Zachary M. BROWN

Midwest College of Oriental Medicine (A)

4334 N Hazel, Suite 102, Chicago IL 60613-1429
Telephone: (773) 975-1295 Identification: 666090
Accreditation: ACUP

† Main campus is Midwest College of Oriental Medicine in Racine, WI.

Midwestern University (B)

555 31st Street, Downers Grove IL 60515-1200
County: DuPage FICE Identification: 001657
Unit ID: 143853
Telephone: (630) 969-4400 Carnegie Class: Spec/Med
FAX Number: N/A Calendar System: Quarter
URL: www.midwestern.edu
Established: 1900 Annual Undergrad Tuition & Fees: N/A
Enrollment: 2,547 Coed
Affiliation or Control: Independent Non-Profit IRS Status: 501(c)3
Highest Offering: Doctorate
Program: Professional
Accreditation: NH, ARCPA, DENT, OSTEO, OT, PHAR, PTA, @SP

01 President/CEO .... Dr. Kathleen H. GOEPPINGER
03 Exec VP/Chief Operating Officer .... Dr. Arthur G. DOBBELAERE
10 Sr VP/Chief Financial Officer .... Mr. Gregory J. GAUS
21 Vice President Business Services .... Mr. Dean P. MALONE
26 Vice President University Relations .... Dr. Karen D. JOHNSON
05 VP/CAO Dental & Medical Education .... Dr. Dennis J. PAULSON
05 VP/CAO Pharmacy & Health Sci Educ .... Dr. Mary W L. LEE
11 VP Human Resources & Administration .... Ms. Angela L. MARTY
63 Dean Chicago Col of Osteo Medicine .... Dr. Karen J. NICHOLS
67 Dean Chicago College of Pharmacy .... Dr. Nancy F. FJORTOFT
76 Dean Col Health Sciences .... Dr. Fred D. ROMANO
52 Dean College of Dental Medicine IL .... Dr. M. A. J. Lex MACNEIL
32 Dean for Student Services .... Dr. Teresa A. DOMBROWSKI
88 Director Finance .... Dr. Kimberly A. BROWN
08 University Librarian .... Ms. Natalie K. REED
06 Registrar .... Ms. Sue C. HARDWIDGE
46 Director Research & Sponsored Pgms .... Dr. James M. WOODS
07 Director of Admissions .... Mr. Michael J. LAKEN
30 Dir Development/Alumni Relations .... Ms. Karen L. WYSOCKI
09 Director of Institutional Research .... Dr. Kevin P. HYNES
14 Director Information Technology Svc .... Mr. Erik P. CARROLL
15 Director Human Resources .... Ms. Amy B. GIBSON
24 Director Media Resources .... Ms. Kathleen A M. DOOLEY
18 Director Campus Facilities .... Mr. Kevin M. MCCORMICK
37 Director Student Financial Services .... Mr. Nathan ERNST

† Tuition rates vary by program

Millikin University (C)

1184 W Main Street, Decatur IL 62522-2084
County: Macon FICE Identification: 001724
Unit ID: 147244
Telephone: (217) 424-6211 Carnegie Class: Bac/Diverse
FAX Number: (217) 424-3993 Calendar System: Semester
URL: www.millikin.edu
Established: 1901 Annual Undergrad Tuition & Fees: $27,852
Enrollment: 2,347 Coed
Affiliation or Control: Presbyterian Church (U.S.A.) IRS Status: 501(c)3
Highest Offering: Doctorate
Program: Liberal Arts And General; Teacher Preparatory; Professional; Nursing Emphasis
Accreditation: NH, ACBSP, ANEST, MUS, NURSE, TED

01 Interim President .... Dr. Patrick E. WHITE
05 Vice President Academic Affairs .... Vacant
10 Int Vice Pres Finance/Business Affs .... Mrs. Ruby F. BRASE
30 Vice Pres University Development .... Mr. Dave E. BRANDON
84 Interim Vice President Enrollment .... Ms. Sarah SHUPENUS
32 Dean of Student Development .... Mrs. Raphaella PRANGE
100 Chief of Staff/Board Secretary .... Ms. Marilyn S. DAVIS
49 Dean of Arts & Sciences .... Dr. Randy M. BROOKS
57 Dean of Fine Arts .... Ms. Laura LEDFORD
107 Dean Col of Professional Studies .... Dr. Deborah L. SLAYTON
50 Acting Dean Tabor School Business .... Dr. Susan KRUML
06 Registrar .... Mr. Walter G. WESSEL
29 Sr Director Alumni/Donor Engagement .... Vacant
44 Director of Major Gifts/Grant Devel .... Ms. Dawn SANDONE
36 Director of Career Center .... Ms. Pamela M. FOLGER
13 Director of Technology .... Mrs. Patricia A. PETTIT
08 Director of the Library .... Ms. Cindy FULLER
44 Sr Director of Development .... Mrs. Stacey HUBBARD
41 Director of Athletics .... Dr. Craig WHITE
53 Director of School of Education .... Dr. Nancy I. GAYLEN
88 Director Kirkland Fine Arts Center .... Mrs. Janiece L. SADDORIS-TRAUGHBER
28 Asst Dean Inclusion/Stdt Engagement .... Mr. Quantrell WILLIS
104 Director Center for Intl Education .... Mrs. Carmen ARAVENA
15 Director Human Resources .... Ms. Diane L. LANE
21 Director of Fiscal Operations .... Mrs. Ruby F. BRASE
21 Controller .... Mrs. Vicki A. WRIGLEY
38 Director of Counseling Services .... Mr. Kevin C. GRAHAM
92 Director of Honors Program .... Dr. Cheryl L. CHAMBLIN
35 Director Student Development .... Mrs. Elizabeth J. DOORES
37 Director of Financial Aid .... Ms. Cheryl L. HOWERTON
51 Director of PACE Program .... Mrs. Gail CROOKSHANK
58 Director of MBA Program .... Dr. Anthony F. LIBERATORE
64 Director School of Music .... Dr. Stephen B. WIDENHOFER
87 Director of Summer School .... Dr. Randy M. BROOKS
19 Director of Dept of Public Safety .... Mr. Chris BALLARD
66 Director School of Nursing .... Dr. Kathy J. BOOKER
07 Director of Admission .... Mr. Joe HAVIS
39 Director of Residence Life .... Mr. Paul LIDY
18 Director of Facilities Services .... Mr. Ken JORDAN
26 Director of Marketing .... Ms. Sarah SHUPENUS
09 Coord of Institutional Research .... Mrs. Laura A. BIRCH
105 Web Developer .... Mr. Derek ISHMAEL

Monmouth College (D)

700 E Broadway, Monmouth IL 61462-1963
County: Warren FICE Identification: 001725
Unit ID: 147341
Telephone: (309) 457-2311 Carnegie Class: Bac/A&S
FAX Number: (309) 457-2141 Calendar System: Semester
URL: www.monmouthcollege.edu
Established: 1853 Annual Undergrad Tuition & Fees: $39,100
Enrollment: 1,247 Coed
Affiliation or Control: Presbyterian Church (U.S.A.) IRS Status: 501(c)3
Highest Offering: Baccalaureate
Program: Liberal Arts And General; Teacher Preparatory
Accreditation: NH

01 President .... Dr. Mauri A. DITZLER
05 Dean of Faculty .... Dr. David M. TIMMERMAN
10 Vice President Finance & Business .... Mr. Donald L. GLADFELTER
30 Vice Pres Devel/College Relations .... Ms. Molly A. BALL
32 Vice Pres Student Life/Dn Students .... Ms. Jacquelyn S. CONDON
84 Vice President for Enrollment Mgmt .... Mr. Timothy KEEFAUVER
06 Registrar .... Ms. Christine D. JOHNSTON
08 Director Hewes Library .... Mr. Richard SAYRE
37 Director of Financial Aid .... Ms. Jayne A. SCHRECK
29 Director of Alumni Programs .... Ms. Hannah MAHER
26 Director College Communications .... Mr. Jeffrey D. RANKIN
44 Director of Annual Giving .... Ms. Hannah MAHER
15 Director of Personnel Services .... Mr. Mike MCNALL
18 Director Facilities Management .... Mr. Earl WILFONG
20 Associate Dean of the Faculty .... Dr. Frank GERSICH
21 Controller .... Mrs. Debbie CLARK

Moody Bible Institute (E)

820 N Lasalle Boulevard, Chicago IL 60610-3263
County: Cook FICE Identification: 001727
Unit ID: 147369
Telephone: (312) 329-4000 Carnegie Class: Spec/Faith
FAX Number: (312) 329-4109 Calendar System: Semester
URL: www.moody.edu
Established: 1886 Annual Undergrad Tuition & Fees: $10,098
Enrollment: 3,600 Coed
Affiliation or Control: Independent Non-Profit IRS Status: 501(c)3
Highest Offering: First Professional Degree
Program: Liberal Arts And General; Professional; Religious Emphasis
Accreditation: NH, BI, MUS, THEOL

01 President .... Dr. J. Paul NYQUIST
05 Provost & Dean of Education .... Dr. Junias V. VENUGOPAL
11 Exec VP & Chief Operating Officer .... Mr. Steven A. MOGCK
43 Vice President & General Counsel .... Mrs. Elizabeth A. BROWN
20 VP/Dean of Undergraduate School .... Dr. Larry J. DAVIDHIZAR
58 VP/Dean of Graduate School .... Dr. John A. JELINEK
16 Vice President Human Resources .... Mr. Lloyd R. DODSON
88 Vice President Broadcasting .... Mr. Collin LAMBERT
30 Vice President Stewardship .... Mr. James ELLIOTT
13 Vice President Information Systems .... Mr. Frank W. LEBER
26 Vice Pres Corporate Communications .... Mrs. Christine GORZ
45 Vice Pres/Dean of MDL .... Vacant
84 Vice President of Student Services .... Dr. Tom A. SHAW
18 Division Manager Facilities .... Mr. Konrad FINCK
56 Dir Customer Rels/Distance Lrng Ctr .... Vacant
32 Dean of Students .... Dr. Timothy E. ARENS
07 Dean of Admissions .... Mr. Charles E. DRESSER
38 Associate Dean Counseling Services .... Mr. Steve BRASEL
35 Associate Dean for Student Programs .... Mr. Joseph M. GONZALES, JR.
36 Assoc Dean of Career Development .... Mr. Patrick FRIEDLINE
39 Associate Dean Residence Life .... Mr. Bruce R. NORQUIST
37 Director of Financial Aid .... Vacant
06 Registrar/Director of Acad Records .... Mr. George MOSHER
08 Department Manager Library .... Mr. James PRESTON
29 Exec Director Alumni Association .... Mrs. Nancy HASTINGS
41 Athletic Director .... Mr. Daniel DUNN
10 Chief Fin Ofcr/Treasurer/Asst Secy .... Mr. Ken HEULITT
21 Controller .... Miss Linda WAHR
23 Admin of Health Service .... Miss Ann MEYER
96 Manager of Procurement Services .... Mr. Paul BRACKLEY
09 Institutional Researcher .... Mr. Gregory GAERTNER

† Tuition is paid through donor contributions. Fees are $1,950.00 per year.

Moraine Valley Community College (F)

9000 W College Parkway, Palos Hills IL 60465-0937
County: Cook FICE Identification: 007692
Unit ID: 147378
Telephone: (708) 974-4300 Carnegie Class: Assoc/Pub-S-SC
FAX Number: (708) 974-1184 Calendar System: Semester
URL: www.morainevalley.edu
Established: 1967 Annual Undergrad Tuition & Fees (In-District): $3,786
Enrollment: 16,650 Coed
Affiliation or Control: State/Local IRS Status: 501(c)3
Highest Offering: Associate Degree
Program: Occupational; 2-Year Principally Bachelor's Creditable
Accreditation: NH, CAHIIM, COARC, COMTA, MAC, PHLEB, POLYT, RAD

01 President .... Dr. Sylvia JENKINS
05 Vice President Academic Affairs .... Dr. Pamela HANEY
32 Vice President Student Devel .... Dr. Normah SALLEH-BARONE
11 Exec Vice Pres Administrative Svcs .... Mr. Andrew M. DUREN
10 Chief Financial Officer .... Mr. Robert STERKOWITZ
13 Chief Information Officer .... Vacant
50 Dean Science/Business/Comp Tech .... Dr. Ryen NAGLE
49 Dean Liberal Arts .... Mr. Walter FRONCZEK
38 Dean Counseling & Advising .... Ms. Joann WRIGHT
84 Dean Enrollment Services .... Mr. Severo BALASON
51 Dean Corporate/Cmty & Cont Educ .... Mr. Albert LEWIS
36 Dean Career Programs .... Dr. Margaret MACHON
35 Dean Student Services .... Mr. Chester SHAW
88 Dean Learn Enrich & Col Readiness .... Mr. Michael MORSCHES
56 Asst Dean/Dir Academic Outreach .... Vacant
32 Asst Dean Code of Conduct & St Life .... Mr. Kent MARSHALL
37 Director Financial Aid .... Ms. Laurie ANEMA
09 Dir Institutional Research/Planning .... Ms. Elizabeth REIS
19 Chief of Police .... Mr. Patrick O'CONNOR
15 Director Human Resources .... Ms. Lynn HARRINGTON
07 Director of Admissions/Recruitment .... Ms. Claudia ROSELLI
26 Director College & Cmty Relations .... Mr. Mark HORSTMEYER
18 Director Campus Operations .... Mr. Rick BRENNAN
40 Director Auxiliary Svcs .... Mr. Kashif SHAH
88 Director Health Education Well Ctr .... Mr. William FINN
85 Asst Dean Intl Student Admissions .... Ms. Diane VIVERITO
27 Director Mktg & Creative Services .... Ms. Delores J. BROOKS
44 Dir Res Devel/Extended Programs .... Dr. Sharon KATTERMAN
21 Controller .... Ms. Theresa O'CARROLL
42 Campus Minister .... Mr. Bill DROEL
88 Director Center Disability Services .... Ms. Debbie SIEVERS
96 Director of Purchasing .... Ms. Jane BENTLEY

Morrison Institute of Technology (G)

701 Portland Avenue, Morrison IL 61270-2959
County: Whiteside FICE Identification: 008880
Unit ID: 147396
Telephone: (815) 772-7218 Carnegie Class: Assoc/PrivNFP
FAX Number: (815) 772-7584 Calendar System: Semester
URL: www.morrisontech.edu
Established: 1973 Annual Undergrad Tuition & Fees: $15,590
Enrollment: 82 Coed
Affiliation or Control: Independent Non-Profit IRS Status: 501(c)3
Highest Offering: Associate Degree
Program: 2-Year Principally Bachelor's Creditable; Technical Emphasis
Accreditation: COE, ENGT

01 Chief Executive Officer .... Mr. Christopher D. SCOTT
05 Vice President of Academic Affairs .... Mr. Greg J. TULLY
06 Registrar .... Ms. Judy TURNEY

Morton College (H)

3801 S Central Avenue, Cicero IL 60804-4398
County: Cook FICE Identification: 001728
Unit ID: 147411
Telephone: (708) 656-8000 Carnegie Class: Assoc/Pub-S-SC
FAX Number: (708) 656-3297 Calendar System: Semester
URL: www.morton.edu
Established: 1924 Annual Undergrad Tuition & Fees (In-District): $3,188
Enrollment: 4,785 Coed
Affiliation or Control: State/Local IRS Status: 501(c)3
Highest Offering: Associate Degree
Program: Occupational; 2-Year Principally Bachelor's Creditable
Accreditation: NH, ADNUR, PTAA

01 President .... Dr. Dana GROVE
05 VP Academic/Student Development .... Mr. Muhammad SIDDIQI
32 Director of Student Development .... Vacant
51 Dean Adult Educ/Cmty Prgms/Outreach .... Mr. James YOUNG
08 Director of Library .... Ms. Jennifer BUTLER
15 Director of Human Resources .... Mr. Kenneth STOCK
31 Director Community & Business Svcs .... Ms. Susan FELICE
09 Director Institutional Research .... Ms. Magda BANDA
18 Director of Facilities & Operations .... Mr. John S. POTEMPA
37 Director of Financial Aid .... Ms. Yolanda FREEMON

National-Louis University (I)

122 S Michigan Avenue, Chicago IL 60603
County: Cook FICE Identification: 001733
Unit ID: 147536
Telephone: (888) 658-8632 Carnegie Class: DRU
FAX Number: N/A Calendar System: Quarter
URL: www.nl.edu
Established: 1886 Annual Undergrad Tuition & Fees: $18,540
Enrollment: 8,376 Coed
Affiliation or Control: Independent Non-Profit IRS Status: 501(c)3
Highest Offering: Doctorate
Program: Teacher Preparatory; Professional
Accreditation: NH, CACREP, IACBE, TED

01 President .... Dr. Nivine MEGAHED
05 Provost .... Dr. Christine J. QUINN
30 Vice Pres Institutional Advancement .... Mr. John BERGHOLZ
15 Vice President Human Resources .... Mr. Tom BERGMANN
10 Vice Pres Finance & Administration .... Mr. Marty MICKEY
84 Vice Pres Enrollment Mgmt .... Ms. Bobbi BIRINGER
26 Vice Pres Marketing/Communications .... Dr. Tom EHRHARDT
09 Vice Provost Institutional Effect .... Dr. Marsha WATSON
20 Vice Prov Acad Pgm & Fac Dev ... Dr. Generosa LOPEZ-MOLINA
88 Asst Vice Prov Advising/Retention .... Mr. Stephen NEER
50 Dean College of Mgmt/Business .... Dr. Christopher CASSIRER
53 Dean Natl College of Education .... Dr. Alison HILSABECK
49 Dean College of Arts & Science .... Dr. Christopher CASSIRER
08 Dean University Library .... Ms. Kathleen WALSH
32 Exec Dir Stdnt Affs/Ombudsperson .... Mr. Steve DIBENEDETTO
12 Exec Director Milwaukee/Beloit .... Mr. Robert VANCE
12 Exec Director Florida Regional .... Dr. George VALCOURT
43 Exec Director of Legal Services .... Mrs. McCeil J. JOHNSON
28 Director of Employment/Diversity .... Ms. Erin HAULOTTE
37 Director of Student Finance .... Mr. Steve DIBENEDETTO
07 Director of Admissions/Registrar .... Mr. Ken KASPRZAK
36 Director of Career Services .... Ms. Julie BECHTOLD
51 Director Outreach Academic Pgm .... Ms. Karen HAWORTH
35 Director of Student Life .... Ms. Maria MEINTANIS

National-Louis University Elgin Campus (A)

620 Tollgate Road, Elgin IL 60123
Telephone: (800) 443-5522 Identification: 770083
Accreditation: &NH

† Main campus is National-Louis University in Chicago, IL.

National-Louis University Lisle Campus (B)

850 Warrenville Road, Lisle IL 60532
Telephone: (800) 443-5522 Identification: 770084
Accreditation: &NH

† Main campus is National-Louis University in Chicago, IL.

National-Louis University North Shore Campus (C)

5202 Old Orchard Road, Skokie IL 60077
Telephone: (800) 443-5522 Identification: 770085
Accreditation: &NH

† Main campus is National-Louis University in Chicago, IL.

National-Louis University Wheeling Campus (D)

1000 Capitol Drive, Wheeling IL 60090
Telephone: (800) 443-5522 Identification: 770086
Accreditation: &NH

† Main campus is National-Louis University in Chicago, IL.

National University of Health Sciences (E)

200 E Roosevelt Road, Lombard IL 60148-4583
County: DuPage FICE Identification: 001732
Unit ID: 147590
Telephone: (630) 629-2000 Carnegie Class: Spec/Health
FAX Number: (630) 889-6600 Calendar System: Trimester
URL: www.nuhs.edu
Established: 1906 Annual Undergrad Tuition & Fees: $9,224
Enrollment: 848 Coed
Affiliation or Control: Independent Non-Profit IRS Status: 501(c)3
Highest Offering: First Professional Degree
Program: Liberal Arts And General; Professional; Technical Emphasis
Accreditation: NH, ACUP, CHIRO, COMTA, NATUR

01 President .... Dr. Joseph P D. STIEFEL
05 Vice President Academic Services .... Dr. Nicholas A. TRONGALE
10 Vice President Business Services .... Mr. Ron MENSCHING
11 Vice Pres Administrative Services .... Ms. Tracy MCHUGH
76 Dean College Allied Health Sciences .... Dr. Randy L. SWENSON
51 Dean Col Postprofessional Educ .... Dr. Jenna GLENN
23 Dean of Clinics .... Dr. Theodore JOHNSON
107 Dean Col Professional Studies FL .... Dr. Daniel STRAUSS
107 Dean Col Professional Studies IL .... Dr. Nicholas TRONGALE
46 Dean of Research .... Dr. Gregory D. CRAMER
32 Dean of Students .... Dr. Daniel R. DRISCOLL
108 Dean Academic Assessment .... Vacant
88 Dean Accreditation .... Vacant
08 Chair Learning Resource Center .... Ms. Joyce E. WHITEHEAD
06 University Registrar .... Ms. Izabela DUBAK
07 Dir Communication/Enrollment Svcs .... Ms. Victoria SWEENEY
21 Director of Financial Services .... Ms. Sue UNGER
37 Director of Financial Aid .... Mr. Robert DAME
18 Director Maintenance & Facilities .... Mr. Tom ROHNER
15 Director of Human Resources .... Mr. Andrew WOZNIAK
26 Chief Public Relations Officer .... Ms. Christine LUCENTA
30 Director Alumni & Development .... Ms. Shawna MCDONOUGH
13 Dir Management Information Services .... Mr. Kurt FALER
29 Director Alumni Relations .... Ms. Shawna MCDONOUGH
40 Bookstore Manager .... Ms. Mary BASSETT
39 Coordinator of Housing .... Ms. Pam THOMAS

North Central College (F)

30 N Brainard Street, Naperville IL 60540-4607
County: DuPage FICE Identification: 001734
Unit ID: 147660
Telephone: (630) 637-5100 Carnegie Class: Master's M
FAX Number: (630) 637-5121 Calendar System: Trimester
URL: www.northcentralcollege.edu
Established: 1861 Annual Undergrad Tuition & Fees: $32,613
Enrollment: 3,042 Coed
Affiliation or Control: United Methodist IRS Status: 501(c)3
Highest Offering: Master's
Program: Liberal Arts And General
Accreditation: NH

01 President .... Dr. Troy D. HAMMOND
04 Exec Secy/Assistant to President .... Ms. Margaret A. WHITE
05 Vice President Academic Affairs .... Dr. R. Devadoss PANDIAN
10 Vice President Business Affairs .... Mr. Paul H. LOSCHEIDER
30 Vice Pres Institutional Advancement .... Mr. Rick E. SPENCER
84 VP Enrollment Management/Stdnt Svcs .... Ms. Laurie M. HAMEN
16 Asst Vice Pres Human Resources .... Ms. Michelle M. SKINDER
26 Asst Vice President Mktg/Communic .... Mr. James GODO
21 Asst VP for Business Operations .... Mr. Michael J. HUDSON
20 Associate Academic Dean .... Dr. Marti S. BOGART
07 Dean of Admissions .... Mr. Marty R. SAUER
32 Dean of Students .... Ms. Kimberly SLUIS
58 Dean of Graduate Pgms/Continuing Ed .... Vacant
06 Registrar .... Mr. Jonathan M. PICKERING
08 Director of the Library .... Mr. John J. SMALL
36 Director of Career Development .... Mr. Jeffrey D. DENARD
37 Director of Financial Aid .... Mr. Marty ROSSMAN
23 Director of the Wellness Center .... Vacant
31 Director of Cmty Educ/Conf/Camps .... Mr. Michael E. SQUIRE
41 Athletic Director .... Mr. James MILLER
21 AVP Finance/Controller .... Mr. David S. MISSURELLI
39 Director of Residence Life .... Mr. Kevin E. MCCARTHY
42 Campus Chaplain .... Rev. Lynn L. PRIES
90 Director of Technology Services .... Mr. Matthew BURDEN
44 Director of Planned Giving .... Mr. Bruce NORTELL
09 Director of Institutional Research .... Mr. Jonathan M. PICKERING
29 Director Alumni Relations .... Mr. Adrian M. ALDRICH
28 Director of Multicultural Affairs .... Ms. Dorothy J. PLEAS

North Park University (G)

3225 W Foster Avenue, Chicago IL 60625-4895
County: Cook FICE Identification: 001735
Unit ID: 147679
Telephone: (773) 244-6200 Carnegie Class: Master's L
FAX Number: (773) 244-4953 Calendar System: Semester
URL: www.northpark.edu
Established: 1891 Annual Undergrad Tuition & Fees: $23,290
Enrollment: 3,142 Coed
Affiliation or Control: Evangelical Covenant Church Of America
IRS Status: 501(c)3
Highest Offering: Doctorate
Program: Liberal Arts And General; Teacher Preparatory; Professional
Accreditation: NH, IACBE, MUS, NURSE, THEOL

01 President .... Dr. David L. PARKYN
10 Executive Vice President/CFO .... Mr. Carl E. BALSAM
05 Provost .... Dr. Joseph JONES
84 Vice Pres for Enrollment/Marketing .... Mr. Nathan MOUTTET
30 Vice President for Development .... Ms. Mary M. SURRIDGE
73 Seminary Dean .... Dr. Davide W. KERSTEN
49 Dean of Arts & Sciences .... Dr. Charles I. PETERSON
51 Dean School of Adult Learning .... Dr. Bryan WATKINS
50 Dean School of Business & NFP Mgmt .... Dr. Wesley LINDAHL
53 Dean School of Education .... Dr. Rebecca NELSON
64 Dean School of Music .... Dr. Craig JOHNSON
66 Dean School of Nursing .... Dr. Linda DUNCAN
09 Director of Institutional Research .... Vacant
28 Dean of Diversity & Intercult Pgm .... Dr. Terry LINDSAY
32 VP for Student Engagement .... Dr. Jodi KOSLOW MARTIN
08 Director of Library .... Vacant
07 Director of Undergrad Recruitment .... Ms. Jennifer DIXON
38 Director Counseling/Health Services .... Ms. Juanita BARRETT
37 Director Financial Aid Services .... Dr. Lucy G. SHAKER
14 Director of Computer Center .... Mr. Steven P. CLARK
15 Director of Human Resources .... Ms. Ingrid K. TENGLIN
18 Director of Environmental Services .... Mr. Carl H. WISTROM
19 Director of Security .... Mr. Daniel GOORIS
21 Director of Finance .... Mr. Lester H. CARLSTROM
26 University Marketing & Communic .... Mr. Nathan MOUTTET
41 Athletic Director .... Mr. Jack F. SURRIDGE
42 Director University Ministries .... Mr. Anthony ZAMBLE
36 Director of Career Planning .... Vacant
06 Registrar .... Mr. Aaron D. SCHOOF
29 Alumni Relations Manager .... Ms. Melissa VELEZ LUCE

Northeastern Illinois University (H)

5500 N Saint Louis Avenue, Chicago IL 60625-4699
County: Cook FICE Identification: 001693
Unit ID: 147776
Telephone: (773) 583-4050 Carnegie Class: Master's L
FAX Number: (773) 442-4900 Calendar System: Semester
URL: www.neiu.edu
Established: 1867 Annual Undergrad Tuition & Fees (In-State): $8,460
Enrollment: 11,149 Coed
Affiliation or Control: State IRS Status: 501(c)3
Highest Offering: Master's
Program: Liberal Arts And General; Teacher Preparatory; Professional; Fine Arts Emphasis
Accreditation: NH, ART, CACREP, CORE, MUS, SW, TED

01 President .... Dr. Sharon K. HAHS
05 Provost & VP Academic Affairs .... Dr. Richard HELLDOBLER
10 Vice Pres Finance & Administration .... Mr. Mark WILCOCKSON
32 Vice President for Student Affairs .... Dr. Frank E. ROSS
30 Vice President Inst Advancement .... Ms. Melba RODRIGUEZ
28 Asst VP Divrsty/Intercultural Affs .... Dr. Juan R. GUARDIA
35 Associate VP for Student Affairs .... Dr. Daniel LOPEZ, JR.
36 Asst VP for Student Affairs .... Dr. Jermaine F. WILLIAMS
07 Associate VP Enrollment Services .... Dr. Janice HARRING-HENDON
21 Director of Univ Budgets .... Ms. Ann M. MCNABB
08 Int Dean Libraries & Learning Res .... Mr. Carlos MELIAN
09 Director Institutional Research .... Mr. Blase E. MASINI
15 Human Resources Director .... Ms. Marta E. MASO
25 Coordinator Sponsored Programs . Mr. John L. BUTLER-LUDWIG
26 Asst VP for Communications .... Ms. Erika M. KREHBIEL
37 Director Financial Aid .... Ms. Maureen T. AMOS
50 Dean College Business/Management .... Vacant
58 Interim Dean of Graduate College .... Dr. Marcelo O. SZTAINBERG
53 Dean College of Education .... Dr. Maureen D. GILLETTE
49 Dean College of Arts & Sciences .... Dr. Wamucii E. NJOGU
13 Chief Information Officer .... Mr. Kim TRACY
18 Asst Vice Pres Facilities Mgmt .... Ms. Nancy MEDINA
19 Director University Police Dept .... Mr. James C. LYON, JR.
21 Director Financial Affs/Controller .... Ms. Peggy HO
22 Dir Univ Outreach/Equal Employment .... Vacant
86 Executive Dir Government Relations .... Dr. Suleyma PEREZ
06 University Registrar .... Mr. Daniel R. WEBER
29 Director of Alumni Relations .... Ms. Damaris TAPIA
38 Dir of Student Health & Counseling .... Dr. Christine ASIDAO
96 Asst VP of Purchasing/Auxil Svcs .... Mr. Robert B. FILIPP

Northern Illinois University (I)

De Kalb IL 60115-2825
County: De Kalb FICE Identification: 001737
Unit ID: 147703
Telephone: (815) 753-1000 Carnegie Class: RU/H
FAX Number: (815) 753-0198 Calendar System: Semester
URL: www.niu.edu
Established: 1895 Annual Undergrad Tuition & Fees (In-State): $11,916
Enrollment: 21,869 Coed
Affiliation or Control: State IRS Status: 501(c)3
Highest Offering: Doctorate
Program: Liberal Arts And General; Teacher Preparatory; Professional
Accreditation: NH, ART, AUD, BUS, BUSA, CACREP, CLPSY, CORE, DIETD, DIETI, ENG, ENGT, IPSY, LAW, MFCD, MT, MUS, NAIT, NURSE, PH, PTA, SCPSY, SP, SPAA, TED, THEA

01 President .... Douglas D. BAKER
05 Executive Vice Pres & Provost .... Raymond W. ALDEN, III
20 Vice Provost Academic Planning/Dev .... Carolinda DOUGLASS
10 Acting Exec VP/Chief of Operations .... Steven CUNNINGHAM
30 Vice Pres Univ Advance/Development .... Michael P. MALONE
45 Vice Prov Resource Planning .... Susan MINI
11 VP Admin/University Outreach .... Anne C. KAPLAN
32 Vice Pres Student Affs/Enroll Mgmt .... Eric WELDY
46 Vice Pres for Research/Grad Studies .... Lisa C. FREEMAN
26 Vice Pres University Relations .... Kathryn A. BUETTNER
43 VP/General Counsel/Legal Svcs .... Jerry D. BLAKEMORE
102 Vice Pres University Advancement .... Michael MALONE
13 Assoc Vice Pres Info Tech Services .... Walter L. CZERNIAK
18 Assoc VP Facilities Planning & Op .... Jeffrey DAURER
15 Assoc VP Admin/Human Resources .... Steven D. CUNNINGHAM
35 Assoc VP for Student Affairs .... Kelley WESENER-MICHAEL
51 Assoc Vice President NIU Outreach .... Vacant
23 Director Health Services .... Christine GRADY
84 Actg Assoc VP Stdnt Affs/Enrol Mgmt .... Kimberley BUSTER-WILLIAMS
28 Asst Vice Pres Diversity/Equity .... Katrina CALDWELL
20 Vice Provost .... Anne BIRBERICK
50 Dean of Business .... Denise SCHOENBACHLER
53 Dean of Education .... La Vonne NEAL
54 Dean of Engineering/Engr Tech .... Promod VOHRA
61 Dean of Law .... Jennifer ROSATO
49 Dean Liberal Arts & Sciences .... Christopher MCCORD
76 Dean Health & Human Sciences .... Derryl BLOCK
57 Dean Visual & Performing Arts .... Richard HOLLY
58 Dean Grad Sch/AVP Grad Studies .... Bradley BOND
85 Assoc Prov International Programs .... Deborah L. PIERCE
84 Asst Vice Prov Enrollment Services .... Vacant
31 Exec Dir Community Relations .... Rena COTSONES
12 Director Lorado Taft Field Campus .... Diana DENNIS
12 Director Outreach Centers .... Brian VOLLMERT
12 Director NIU Naperville .... Brian BECKER
06 Director Registration & Records .... Jerry MONTAG
09 Director of Institutional Research .... J. Daniel HOUSE
24 Director of Media Services .... Jay ORBIK
25 Director of Sponsored Projects .... David STONE
36 Exec Director of Career Services .... Cindy HENDERSON
37 Director of Student Financial Aid .... Rebecca BABEL
38 Director of Counseling/Student Dev .... Brooke RUXTON
40 Director of University Bookstore .... Mitch KIELB
19 Police Chief/Public Safety .... Darren MITCHELL
41 Athletic Director .... Sean FRAZIER
91 Director Enterprise Info Systems .... Kimberly S. HENSLEY
39 Executive Director Housing & Dining .... Michael STANG
88 Director Access-Ability Resources .... Randall WARD
29 Director Alumni Relations .... Joseph MATTY
96 Director of Purchasing .... Al MUELLER

Northern Seminary (A)

660 E Butterfield Road, Lombard IL 60148-5698
County: DuPage FICE Identification: 001736
Unit ID: 147697
Telephone: (630) 620-2180 Carnegie Class: Spec/Faith
FAX Number: (630) 620-2190 Calendar System: Quarter
URL: www.seminary.edu
Established: 1913 Annual Graduate Tuition & Fees: $13,320
Enrollment: 202 Coed
Affiliation or Control: American Baptist IRS Status: 501(c)3
Highest Offering: Doctorate; No Undergraduates
Program: Professional; Religious Emphasis
Accreditation: NH, THEOL

01 President/Chief Academic Officer ... Dr. Alistair BROWN
05 Vice President of Academic Programs ... Dr. Karen WALKER-FREEBURG
20 Vice Pre of Academic Administration ... Mr. Blake WALTER
30 Vice President of Advancement ... Mr. Greg HENSON
06 Registrar ... Ms. Marilyn R. MAST HEWITT
88 Director Doctoral Studies ... Dr. Karen WALKER-FREEBURG
32 Director Student Services ... Ms. Marilyn MAST HEWITT
15 Director Human Resources ... Vacant
13 Director of Information Technology ... Mr. Rich ROBOTHAM

Northwestern College (B)

9501 Technology Blvd; Suite 425, Rosemont IL 60018
County: Cook FICE Identification: 012362
Unit ID: 147749
Telephone: (847) 233-7700 Carnegie Class: Assoc/PrivFP
FAX Number: (847) 233-7705 Calendar System: Quarter
URL: www.northwesterncollege.edu
Established: 1902 Annual Undergrad Tuition & Fees: $16,600
Enrollment: 1,427 Coed
Affiliation or Control: Proprietary IRS Status: Proprietary
Highest Offering: Associate Degree
Program: Occupational; 2-Year Principally Bachelor's Creditable
Accreditation: NH, ACBSP, CAHIIM, MAC, RAD

01 President ... Mr. Lawrence SCHUMACHER
03 Executive VP of Operations ... Mrs. Gail SCHUMACHER
11 Vice President of Campus Operations ... Mrs. Cynthia REYNOLDS
84 VP of Enrollment & Marketing ... Mr. Dimitrios KRIARAS
10 Controller ... Ms. Leslie RODRIGUEZ
05 VP of Academic Affairs ... Mrs. Diane MAREK
13 VP of Technology ... Mr. David HOMAN
32 VP of Student Affairs ... Mrs. Barbara ANDERSON-SAPATA
86 Government & Public Relations Mgr ... Ms. Laura POLLASTRINI
08 Director of Library Services ... Ms. Sarah DULAY
12 Director of Bridgeview Campus ... Mr. Tony SAPATA
12 Director of NC Online ... Ms. Mary REYNOLDS
12 Director of Chicago Campus ... Mrs. Laura SORIA
16 Chief Human Resources Officer ... Ms. Cheri CANFIELD
37 Director of Financial Assistance ... Mrs. Ethel ARROYO
38 Director of Counseling ... Ms. Alexandra DELLUTRI
106 Distance Education Director ... Ms. Jenifer VIENCEK
07 Director of Admissions ... Mr. Shahed KASEM
07 Director of Admissions ... Mr. Scott KAWALL
11 Dir of Administration Bridgeview ... Mrs. Margie BENNECKE
11 Director of Administration Chicago ... Mrs. Nubia CASTILLO
66 Director of Nursing ... Vacant
06 Registrar ... Ms. Sharon FORBES
36 Career Development Coordinator ... Ms. Amy BUOSCIO
97 Program Director - GE ... Mr. David COOPER
61 Program Director - LS ... Mr. Joseph PECKO

Northwestern College-SW Campus (C)

7725 S Harlem Avenue, Bridgeview IL 60455
Telephone: (888) 205-2283 Identification: 770089
Accreditation: &NH

† Main campus is Northwestern College in Rosemont, IL.

Northwestern University (D)

633 Clark Street, Evanston IL 60208-3854
County: Cook FICE Identification: 001739
Unit ID: 147767
Telephone: (847) 491-3741 Carnegie Class: RU/VH
FAX Number: (847) 491-7364 Calendar System: Quarter
URL: www.northwestern.edu
Established: 1851 Annual Undergrad Tuition & Fees: $48,339
Enrollment: 20,778 Coed
Affiliation or Control: Independent Non-Profit IRS Status: 501(c)3
Highest Offering: Doctorate
Program: Liberal Arts And General; Teacher Preparatory; Professional
Accreditation: NH, ARCPA, AUD, BUS, CLPSY, ENG, IPSY, JOUR, LAW, MED, MFCD, MUS, OPE, PCSAS, PH, PTA, SP

01 President ... Dr. Morton O. SCHAPIRO
05 Provost ... Dr. Daniel I. LINZER
10 Sr Vice Pres Business/Finance ... Mr. Eugene S. SUNSHINE
32 Vice President Student Affairs ... Dr. Patricia TELLES-IRVIN
26 Vice President University Relations ... Mr. Alan K. CUBBAGE
45 Vice Pres Administration & Planning ... Ms. Marilyn MCCOY
13 Vice Pres Information Technology ... Mr. Sean B. REYNOLDS
30 Vice Pres for Alumni Rel & Devel ... Mr. Robert MCQUINN
46 Vice President Research ... Mr. Joseph T. WALSH
88 Vice Pres/Chief Investment Officer ... Mr. William H. MCLEAN
43 Vice President/General Counsel ... Mr. Thomas G. CLINE
84 Associate Provost Univ Enrollment ... Mr. Michael E. MILLS
53 Associate Provost Undergrad Educ ... Dr. Ronald R. BRAEUTIGAM
20 Associate Provost Faculty Affairs ... Dr. James B. YOUNG
20 Assoc VP & Assoc Provost Academic ... Mr. Jake JULIA
21 Assoc Prov Budget/Facil/Analysis ... Ms. Jean E. SHEDD
86 Spec Asst to Pres for Govt Rels ... Mr. Bruce LAYTON
04 Assistant to the President ... Mr. Eugene Y. LOWE, JR.
100 Director Office of the President ... Ms. Judith V. REMINGTON
41 Vice Pres Athletics and Recreation ... Mr. James J. PHILLIPS
72 Dean Sch Engr/Applied Science ... Dr. Julio M. OTTINO
50 Dean Graduate School of Management ... Dr. Sally E. BLOUNT
60 Dean School of Journalism ... Dr. Bradley J. HAMM
64 Dean School of Music ... Dr. Toni-Marie MONTGOMERY
63 Lewis Landsberg Deanship/Deans Ofc ... Dr. Eric G. NEILSON
51 Dean/Assoc Prov Conting Educ ... Dr. Thomas F. GIBBONS
58 Dean Graduate School ... Mr. Dwight A. MCBRIDE
60 Dean School of Communication ... Dr. Barbara J. O'KEEFE
53 Dean School of Ed & Social Policy ... Dr. Penelope L. PETERSON
49 Dean College Arts & Science ... Dr. Sarah C. MANGELSDORF
61 Dean School of Law ... Dr. Daniel B. RODRIGUEZ
08 University Librarian ... Ms. Sarah M. PRITCHARD
36 Director of Univ Career Services ... Dr. Lonnie J. DUNLAP
35 Assistant VP of Student Engagement ... Mr. Burgwell HOWARD
29 Assoc VP Alumni Relations & Develop ... Ms. Catherine L. STEMBRIDGE
88 Assoc Vice President for Research ... Mr. Lewis SMITH
88 Assoc Vice President for Research ... Mr. Jian CAO
88 Assoc VP for Rsrch Innov & New Vent ... Ms. Alicia LOFFLER
88 Assoc Vice President for Research ... Ms. Ann ADAMS
88 Assoc Vice Pres for Research ... Mr. Rex CHISHOLM
21 Assoc Vice Pres Budget Planning ... Mr. James M. HURLEY
18 Assoc Vice Pres Facilities Mgmt ... Mr. Ronald NAYLER
16 Assoc Vice Pres for Human Resources ... Ms. Pamela BEEMER
21 Assoc Vice Pres Finance/Controller ... Ms. Ingrid S. STAFFORD
07 Dean of Undergraduate Admissions ... Mr. Christopher WATSON
88 Exec Dir Intl Research Partnerships ... Ms. Indrani MUKHARJI
23 Medical Director of Health Services ... Dr. John ALEXANDER
39 Director of Residential Life ... Ms. Mary GOLDENBERG
38 Director of Counseling/Psych Svcs ... Dr. John H. DUNKLE
42 University Chaplain ... Dr. Timothy S. STEVENS
09 Director Analytical Studies ... Vacant
88 Director University Housing ... Ms. Theresa M. DELIN
88 Dir Program Review/Spec Project ... Mr. Jeremy HUNSUCKER
71 Planning/Special Projects Director ... Ms. Evelyn CALIENDO
88 Ex Dir Univ Center/Student Aux Svcs ... Ms. Kelly A. SCHAEFER
88 Director University Services ... Mr. Brian S. PETERS
06 University Registrar ... Ms. Jacqualyn CASAZZA
37 Director Financial Aid ... Ms. Carolyn V. LINDLEY
15 Dir HR Consulting Svcs/Staffing ... Mr. Paul CORONA
19 Chief of University Police ... Mr. Bruce LEWIS
21 Director Auditing ... Ms. Betty L. MCPHILIMY
22 Dir Equal Emply Oppprty/Affirm Act ... Ms. Tasha SHELTON
96 Director University Svcs Purchasing ... Mr. Jim KONRAD
28 Asst Provost Diversity & Inclusion ... Ms. Dona CORDERO

Northwestern University Chicago Downtown Campus (E)

676 N St. Clair Street, Chicago IL 60611
Telephone: (312) 503-8649 Identification: 770090
Accreditation: &NH

† Main campus is Northwestern University in Evanston, IL.

Oakton Community College (F)

1600 E Golf Road, Des Plaines IL 60016-1256
County: Cook FICE Identification: 009896
Unit ID: 147800
Telephone: (847) 635-1600 Carnegie Class: Assoc/Pub-S-MC
FAX Number: (847) 635-1992 Calendar System: Semester
URL: www.oakton.edu
Established: 1969 Annual Undergrad Tuition & Fees (In-District): $2,840
Enrollment: 5,743 Coed
Affiliation or Control: Local IRS Status: 501(c)3
Highest Offering: Associate Degree
Program: Occupational; 2-Year Principally Bachelor's Creditable; Business Emphasis
Accreditation: NH, ADNUR, CAHIIM, MLTAD, PTAA

01 President ... Dr. Margaret B. LEE
05 Vice President Academic Affairs ... Dr. Thomas HAMEL
20 Assistant VP Academic Affairs ... Dr. Nancy PRENDERGAST
32 Vice President Student Affairs ... Dr. Joianne SMITH
28 AVP for Access/Equity & Diversity ... Dr. Michael ANTHONY
10 Vice President Business & Finance ... Mr. Robert NOWAK
51 AVP Cont Ed & Trng/Wrkforce Dev ... Dr. Merrill IRVING
13 Vice Pres Information Technology ... Ms. Bonnie LUCAS
76 Dean Science & Health Careers ... Dr. Adam HAYASHI
81 Dean Math & Technology ... Dr. Robert SOMPOLSKI
60 Dean Language/Humanities & the Arts ... Ms. Linda KORBEL
83 Dean Social Science/Business ... Mr. Bradley WOOTEN
26 Exec Director College Advancement ... Dr. Carlee DRUMMER
09 Director Research ... Dr. Trudy H. BERS
08 Director Library & Media Svcs ... Mr. Gary NEWHOUSE
84 Dir of Student Recruitment/Outreach ... Ms. Michele BROWN
06 Director of Registrar Services ... Mr. Bruce OATES
35 Director of Student Life ... Ms. Ann Marie BARRY
88 Director of Student Success ... Mr. Sebastian CONTRERAS, JR.
88 Asst Director of Student Success ... Ms. Leana CUELLAR
41 Director of Athletics ... Mr. Bruce OATES
13 Director Systems & Network Svcs ... Mr. John WADE
50 Dir Business Institute/Prof Educ ... Ms. Lynn SEINFELD
21 Director of Accounting Services ... Mr. Raul GARCIA
21 Director of Business Services ... Ms. Doreen SCHWARTZ
15 Associate VP Human Resources ... Mr. D. Arnie OUDENHOVEN
18 Director of Facilities ... Ms. Leah SWANQUIST
14 Dir of Educ Computing/End User Svcs ... Ms. Renee KOZIMOR
07 Director of Enrollment Services ... Ms. Cheryl WARMANN
25 Dir of Grants & Alternative Funding ... Ms. Roxann MARSHBURN
31 Dir of Community & Adult Education ... Ms. Robyn BAILEY
28 Ethics Officer ... Mr. D. Arnie OUDENHOVEN
75 Dir of Wrkforce Dev & Corp Trng ... Dr. Colette HANDS
38 Director of Counseling ... Dr. Mark KIEL

Oakton Community College Ray Hartstein Campus (G)

7701 N Lincoln Avenue, Skokie IL 60077
Telephone: (847) 635-1600 Identification: 770091
Accreditation: &NH

† Main campus is Oakton Community College in Des Plaines, IL.

Olivet Nazarene University (H)

One University Avenue, Bourbonnais IL 60914-2345
County: Kankakee FICE Identification: 001741
Unit ID: 147828
Telephone: (815) 939-5011 Carnegie Class: Master's L
FAX Number: (815) 935-4998 Calendar System: Semester
URL: www.olivet.edu
Established: 1907 Annual Undergrad Tuition & Fees: $29,050
Enrollment: 4,544 Coed
Affiliation or Control: Church Of The Nazarene IRS Status: 501(c)3
Highest Offering: Doctorate
Program: Liberal Arts And General; Teacher Preparatory; Professional
Accreditation: NH, DIETD, ENG, MUS, NURSE, SW, TED

01 President ... Dr. John C. BOWLING
05 Vice President Academic Affairs ... Dr. Dennis CROCKER
10 Vice President for Finance ... Dr. Douglas E. PERRY
32 Vice President Student Development ... Dr. Walter W. WEBB
26 Vice Pres Institutional Advancement ... Dr. Brian ALLEN
88 Vice Pres of Strategic Expansion ... Mr. Ryan SPITTAL
49 Dean College of Arts & Sciences ... Dr. Janna MCLEAN
73 Dn Sch Theology/Christian Ministry ... Dr. Carl LETH
53 Dean School of Education ... Dr. Jim UPCHURCH
107 Dean School of Professional Studies ... Vacant
29 Dir Alumni & University Relations ... Mr. Gary GRIFFIN
07 Director of Admissions ... Mrs. Susan WOLFF
06 Registrar ... Dr. Jim D. KNIGHT
08 Director of the Library ... Mrs. Kathy R. BOYENS
37 Director of Financial Aid ... Mr. Greg BRUNER
14 Director of Computer Center ... Mr. Dennis SEYMOUR
41 Athletic Director ... Mr. Gary NEWSOME
42 Chaplain ... Rev. Mark HOLCOMB
30 Exec Director of Development ... Mr. Dan J. FERRIS
35 Director Student Activities ... Mrs. Kathy STEINACKER
38 Director Student Counseling ... Mrs. Lisa VANDER VEER
15 Director of Human Resources ... Mr. David PICKERING
18 Chief Facilities/Physical Plant ... Mr. Matt WHITIS
40 Bookstore Manager ... Mrs. Rachel PIAZZA
36 Career Specialist ... Mrs. Mary ANDERSON
85 International Student Advisor ... Mr. Tony GRIMM
27 Coord of Strategic Comm & Web ... Mrs. Heather DAY

Pacific College of Oriental Medicine (I)

65 East Wacker Place 21st Floor, Chicago IL 60601
Telephone: (888) 729-4811 Identification: 666615
Accreditation: ACCSC, ACUP

† Main campus is Pacific College of Oriental Medicine in San Diego, CA.

Parkland College (J)

2400 W Bradley Avenue, Champaign IL 61821-1899
County: Champaign FICE Identification: 007118
Unit ID: 147916
Telephone: (217) 351-2200 Carnegie Class: Assoc/Pub-R-L
FAX Number: (217) 351-2581 Calendar System: Semester
URL: www.parkland.edu
Established: 1966 Annual Undergrad Tuition & Fees (In-District): $3,360
Enrollment: 8,679 Coed
Affiliation or Control: State/Local IRS Status: 501(c)3
Highest Offering: Associate Degree
Program: Occupational; 2-Year Principally Bachelor's Creditable
Accreditation: NH, ADNUR, COARC, DH, OTA, RAD, SURGT

01 President ... Dr. Thomas R. RAMAGE
04 Asst to President/Board of Trustees ... Ms. Nancy R. WILLAMON
05 Vice President Academic Services ... Dr. Kristine M. YOUNG
32 Vice President Student Services ... Dr. Linda H. MOORE
10 Vice Pres Administrative Svcs/CFO ... Mr. Christopher M. RANDLES
30 Vice Pres Institutional Advancement ... Dr. Seamus REILLY
35 Dean of Students ... Ms. Marietta TURNER
75 Dean of Career & Transfer Prgms ... Mr. Randy FLETCHER
50 Dept Chair Bus & Agri Industries ... Mr. Bruce HENRIKSON
77 Department Chair Comp Science & IT ... Ms. Maria MOBASSERI
54 Dept Chair Engineering Science/Tech ... Ms. Catherine STALTER
79 Dept Chair Humanities ... Mr. Tom BARNARD

57 Dept Chair Fine & Applied Arts .... Ms. Nancy SUTTON
76 Dept Chair Health Professions .... Ms. Roberta SCHOLZE
81 Department Chair Mathematics .... Mr. Geoffrey GRIFFITHS
65 Dept Chair Natural Sciences .... Ms. Kathy BRUCE
83 Dept Chair Social Sci & Human Svcs ..... Mr. Paul SARANTAKOS
88 Dir Center for Academic Success ....Ms. Becky OSBORNE
09 Director Accountability & Research .... Mr. Kevin KNOTT
88 Director of Adult Basic Education .... Ms. Tawanna NICKENS
26 Dir Marketing & Public Relations ....Ms. Patty LEHN
103 Exec Director Workforce Development .... Mr. Minor JACKSON
102 Exec Dir Foundation/Alumni Affairs ....Ms. Linda MYETTE
08 Director Library .... Ms. Anna Maria S. WATKIN
31 Director Community Education .... Ms. Jan SIMON
25 Director Grants and Contracts ....Mr. Ray SPENCER
07 Director Admissions/Enrollment Mgmt ....Mr. Reo WILHOUR
35 Director Student Life ....Dr. Thomas M. CAULFIELD
41 Director Athletics ....Mr. Rod M. LOVETT
36 Director Career Center ....Ms. Sandra L. SPENCER
38 Dir Counseling & Advising Center .... Mr. John SHEAHAN
37 Director Financial Aid .... Mr. Tim WENDT
19 Director Public Safety .... Mr. Von YOUNG
18 Director Physical Plant ....Mr. James BUSTARD
15 Director Human Resources ....Ms. Kathleen CHARLESTON
21 Controller .... Mr. Dave DONSBACH
40 Manager of Bookstore ....Ms. Diane M. KIEST
44 Dir Planned and Major Gifts .... Mr. Michael HAGAN
88 Director Assessment Center ....Dr. Michael TRAME

Prairie State College (A)

202 S Halsted Street, Chicago Heights IL 60411-8226
County: Cook FICE Identification: 001640
Unit ID: 148007
Telephone: (708) 709-3500 Carnegie Class: Assoc/Pub-S-SC
FAX Number: (708) 755-2587 Calendar System: Semester
URL: www.prairiestate.edu
Established: 1957 Annual Undergrad Tuition & Fees (In-District): $3,480
Enrollment: 5,416 Coed
Affiliation or Control: State/Local IRS Status: 501(c)3
Highest Offering: Associate Degree
Program: Occupational; 2-Year Principally Bachelor's Creditable
Accreditation: NH, ADNUR, DH, SURGT

01 President ....Dr. Terri L. WINFREE
10 Vice Pres Finance & Administration ....Dr. Alan D. ROBERTSON
05 Vice Pres Acad Affs/Dean Faculty ....Vacant
31 Vice President Community/Econ Devel ....Vacant
32 VP Student Affairs/Dean of Students .....Mr. Gregory A. THOMAS
49 Dean Liberal Arts ....Dr. Susan R. SOLBERG
50 Dean Business/Mathematics & Science ....Dr. Debra L. PRENDERGAST
17 Dean Health & Industrial Technology ....Dr. Marie C. HANSEL
15 Exec Dir Human Resources ....Mr. David CRONAN
14 Exec Dir Info Technology Resources .... Ms. Diane CONATSER
56 Dean Adult Education ....Ms. Kim M. KUNCE
21 Controller/Dir of Business Svcs ....Mr. James M. EATON
08 Assoc Dean/Library & Instruct Svcs ....Vacant
51 Dean Corporate/Cont Professional Ed .... Mr. Edward JODELKA
35 Dean Student Dev & Campus Life ....Dr. Shawn L. GOVAN
20 Associate Dean Faculty Affairs ....Ms. Patricia ZUCCARELLO
18 Director Facilities and Operations ...Mr. Timothy J. KOZIEK
26 Exec Dir Communications & Marketing .. Ms. Jennifer E. STONER
102 Executive Director Foundation ....Ms. Deborah S. HAVIGHORST
91 Assoc Dir Admin Computer Services ....Mr. Roy E. MAURER
07 Exec Dir Enrollment/Fin Aid Svcs .... Ms. Jaime M. MILLER
19 Dir Police/Campus Safe/Chief Police ....Mr. John MURPHY
88 Director Children's Learning Center ....Ms. Kellie E. CLARK
88 Director Advising/Disability Svcs .... Ms. Diane J. JANOWIAK
37 Director Financial Aid/Vet Affairs .... Ms. Grace MCGINNIS
09 Director Inst Research/Planning ....Dr. Adane G. KASSA
88 Director Institutional Support Svcs ....Ms. Paulette A. MAURER
41 Director of Athletics ....Vacant
88 Director Test Svcs/Intent Advising .... Ms. Lee A. HELBERT
04 Exec Assistant to the President .... Ms. Patricia G. TROST

Principia College (B)

1 Maybeck Place, Elsah IL 62028-9799
County: Jersey FICE Identification: 001744
Unit ID: 148016
Telephone: (618) 374-2131 Carnegie Class: Bac/A&S
FAX Number: (618) 374-5500 Calendar System: Semester
URL: www.principiacollege.edu
Established: 1898 Annual Undergrad Tuition & Fees: $25,980
Enrollment: 496 Coed
Affiliation or Control: Independent Non-Profit IRS Status: 501(c)3
Highest Offering: Baccalaureate
Program: Liberal Arts And General; Teacher Preparatory
Accreditation: NH

01 President and Chief Executive ....Dr. Jonathan PALMER
05 Dean of Academics ....Dr. Scott SCHNEBERGER
88 Chief Investment Officer ....Mr. Howard E. BERNER, JR.
10 Chief Financial Officer .... Mr. Doug GIBBS
20 Associate Dean of Academics ....Dr. Joe RITTER
06 Registrar ....Ms. Alice DERVIN
07 Dean of Enrollment Mgt/Admissions ....Mr. Brian MCCAULEY
08 Director of Libraries ....Mrs. Lisa ROBERTS
13 Chief Technology Officer ....Mr. Richard BOOTH
104 Director of Principia Abroads .... Ms. Linda A. BOHAKER
41 Director of Athletics .... Mr. Lee ELLIS
15 Human Resources Manager ....Ms. SharonAnn SMITH
18 Director of Facilities .... Mr. Ed GOEWERT
11 Director of Administration ....Mrs. Karen D. GRIMMER
21 Controller .... Mrs. Sara THORNDIKE
29 Director of Alumni Relations .... Mrs. Donna GIBBS
32 Dean of Students .... Ms. Dorsie GLEN
37 Director of College Financial Aid .... Mrs. Tami GAVALETZ
96 Purchasing Manager ....Vacant
38 Director Academic Career Advising ....Mrs. Midge BROWNING
09 Director of IEP ....Vacant

Quincy University (C)

1800 College Avenue, Quincy IL 62301-2699
County: Adams FICE Identification: 001745
Unit ID: 148131
Telephone: (217) 222-8020 Carnegie Class: Master's S
FAX Number: (217) 228-5257 Calendar System: Semester
URL: www.quincy.edu
Established: 1860 Annual Undergrad Tuition & Fees: $25,834
Enrollment: 1,632 Coed
Affiliation or Control: Roman Catholic IRS Status: 501(c)3
Highest Offering: Master's
Program: Liberal Arts And General; Teacher Preparatory
Accreditation: NH

01 President ....Dr. Robert GERVASI
05 Vice Pres for Academic Affairs ....Dr. Teresa REED
42 Vice Pres for Mission & Ministry ....Fr. John DOCTOR, OFM
10 Vice President for Business/Finance .... Mr. Tim WEIS
84 Vice Pres for Enrollment Management ....Mrs. Syndi PECK
32 Vice Pres for Student Affairs .... Dr. Tiffany NOLAN
30 Vice President for Advancement ....Mrs. Julie BELL
04 Exec Assistant to the President ....Mrs. Julie BUDINE
101 Corporate Secretary ....Dr. Teresa REED
21 Assoc VP for Finance/Controller ....Mrs. Jean M. GREEN
50 Associate Dean School of Business ....Dr. Cynthia HALIEMUN
50 Associate Dean School of Business ....Dr. John PALMER
53 Dean School of Education ....Dr. Ann BEHRENS
79 Chair Division of Humanities .... Dr. Robert MANNING
81 Chair Division Science & Technology ....Dr. Lee ENGER
83 Chair Div Behavioral/Social Sci ....Dr. Wendy BELLER
57 Chr Div Communication & Fine Arts .... Dr. Barbara SCHLEPPENBACH
20 Dean Academic Support Services ....Vacant
08 Dean of Library/Info Resources .... Ms. Patricia TOMCZAK
92 Director of Honors Program ....Dr. Daniel STRUDWICK
06 Registrar ....Mrs. Barbara WELLMAN
09 Institution Research Specialist .... Mrs. Roberta PAUL
42 Director of Campus Ministry ....Fr. Ferd CHERI, OFM
106 Director of Online & Non-traditiona .... Dr. George HOEMANN
29 Director Development/Alumni Svc ....Mr. Matthew BERGMAN
37 Director of Financial Aid .... Ms. Lisa FLACK
13 Director Information Technology Svc ....Mr. Tony HAYES
27 Director of Communications ....Mrs. Heidi MEYER
36 Director Career Planning/Placement .... Ms. Kristen LIESEN
41 Director of Athletics ....Mr. Marty BELL
18 Director of Facilities Management .... Mr. Rob GOEBEL
39 Director of Residence Life .... Ms. Laryssa LAVENDER
28 Dir Multicultural/Leadership Pgms ....Ms. Natasha RAMSEY
19 Director of Safety & Security .... Mr. Sam LATHROP
15 Director of Human Resources .... Ms. Dana KEPPNER
38 Director of the Counseling Center .....Mrs. Molly DUNN-STEINKE
96 Director of Purchasing .... Mrs. Jennifer TRUITT
25 Grant Writer .... Ms. Julie BOLL
40 Manager of the Bookstore ....Mr. Ben MEANS

Rasmussen College - Aurora (D)

2363 Sequoia Drive, Suite 131, Aurora IL 60506
Telephone: (630) 888-3500 Identification: 667060
Accreditation: &NH, CAHIIM, MAAB

† Main campus is Rasmussen College - St. Cloud in Saint Cloud, MN.

Rasmussen College - Mokena/Tinley Park (E)

8650 W. Spring Lake Drive, Mokena IL 60448
Telephone: (815) 534-3300 Identification: 667064
Accreditation: &NH, MAAB

† Main campus is Rasmussen College - St. Cloud in Saint Cloud, MN.

Rasmussen College - Rockford (F)

6000 E. State Street, 4th Floor, Rockford IL 61108
Telephone: (815) 316-4800 Identification: 667065
Accreditation: &NH, CAHIIM, MAAB

† Main campus is Rasmussen College - St. Cloud in Saint Cloud, MN.

Rasmussen College - Romeoville/Joliet (G)

1400 West Normantown Road, Romeoville IL 60446
Telephone: (815) 306-2600 Identification: 667066
Accreditation: &NH, MAAB

† Main campus is Rasmussen College - St. Cloud in Saint Cloud, MN.

Rend Lake College (H)

468 N Ken Gray Parkway, Ina IL 62846-9801
County: Jefferson FICE Identification: 007119
Unit ID: 148256
Telephone: (618) 437-5321 Carnegie Class: Assoc/Pub-R-L
FAX Number: (618) 437-5677 Calendar System: Semester
URL: www.rlc.edu
Established: 1967 Annual Undergrad Tuition & Fees (In-District): $3,136
Enrollment: 3,815 Coed
Affiliation or Control: State/Local IRS Status: 501(c)3
Highest Offering: Associate Degree
Program: Occupational; 2-Year Principally Bachelor's Creditable
Accreditation: NH, CAHIIM, MLTAD, OTA, RAD, SURGT

01 President .... Mr. Terry WILKERSON
05 VP of Academic Instruction ....Ms. Chris KUBERSKI
10 VP of Finance & Administration ....Mrs. Angie KISTNER
20 VP of Career Technical Instruction ....Ms. Lisa PAYNE
09 VP of Institutional Effectiveness .... Ms. Andrea WITTHOFT
38 Vice Pres of Student Services ....Ms. Lisa PRICE
26 Director Marketing & Information ....Mr. Chad COPPLE
37 Director Student Financial Aid .... Ms. Cheri RUSHING
41 Athletic Director .... Mr. Tim WILLS
18 Director Physical Plant ....Mr. C. Randall SHIVELY
102 CEO of RLC Foundation ....Ms. Shawna MANION
06 Director of Student Records ....Ms. Kelly DOWNES
09 Director of Institutional Research ....Ms. Vickie SCHULTE

Resurrection University (I)

1431 N. Claremont Street 6th Floor, Chicago IL 60622
County: Cook FICE Identification: 006250
Unit ID: 149763
Telephone: (773) 252-6464 Carnegie Class: Spec/Health
FAX Number: (773) 227-3838 Calendar System: Semester
URL: www.resu.edu
Established: 1982 Annual Undergrad Tuition & Fees: $23,542
Enrollment: 462 Coed
Affiliation or Control: Independent Non-Profit IRS Status: 501(c)3
Highest Offering: Master's
Program: Liberal Arts And General; Nursing Emphasis
Accreditation: NH, CAHIIM, NURSE

01 President ....Dr. Beth A. BROOKS
66 Dean of Nursing ....Dr. Sandie SOLDWISCH
26 Dir of Marketing & Communications ....Ms. Jeri BINGHAM
10 Chief Financial Officer ....Dr. Therese A. SCANLAN
32 Director of Student Services ....Ms. Heather PIERCE
29 Asst Dir Alumni Rels/Career Svcs ....Ms. Esther WALLEN
04 Administrative Asst to President ....Ms. Barbara BAILEY
90 Program Analyst ....Mr. Zbigniew KUSNIERZ
37 Student Financial Aid ....Ms. Shirley HOWELL
06 Registrar .... Mr. Michael SHERMAN

Richland Community College (J)

One College Park, Decatur IL 62521-8513
County: Macon FICE Identification: 010879
Unit ID: 148292
Telephone: (217) 875-7200 Carnegie Class: Assoc/Pub-R-M
FAX Number: (217) 875-6961 Calendar System: Semester
URL: www.richland.edu
Established: 1971 Annual Undergrad Tuition & Fees (In-District): $3,042
Enrollment: 3,272 Coed
Affiliation or Control: State/Local IRS Status: 501(c)3
Highest Offering: Associate Degree
Program: Occupational; 2-Year Principally Bachelor's Creditable
Accreditation: NH, ADNUR, SURGT

01 President .... Dr. Gayle M. SAUNDERS
10 Vice President of Finance & Admin ....Mr. Greg E. FLORIAN
05 Vice Pres Academic Services ....Dr. Denise CREWS
32 Vice Pres of Student Success ....Mr. Marcus BROWN
103 VP Econ Dev/Innov Wkfce Solutions .... Dr. Douglas BRAUER
106 Director Online Learning ....Mrs. Kona JONES
30 Exec Director Foundation & Develop .... Mr. Richard MCGOWAN
29 Dir Scholarships/Alumni Development ... Mrs. Tricia CORDULACK
51 Dean Continuing & Prof Educ Div ......Mrs. Darbe BRINKOETTER
27 Exec Dir Public Info/Chief of Staff ....Ms. Lisa GREGORY
07 Dean Enrollment Services ....Mr. Marcus BROWN
06 Director Advising & Registration ......Ms. Stephanie ZIMMERMAN
32 Director Student Engagement .... Mrs. Heather KIND-KEPPEL
38 Director Counseling and Advising ....Mrs. Deborah MCGEE
53 Dean Teaching/Learning Support Svcs ....Mrs. Sheryl BLAHNIK
81 Dean of Math & Sciences ....Dr. John CORDULACK
72 Dean of Business & Technology .... Dr. Jack ADWELL
37 Dir Financial Aid/Veteran Affairs ....Ms. Carmin E. ROSS
36 Director Career Services ....Mr. Michael DIGGS
16 Director Human Resources ....Mr. Richard GSCHWEND
57 Dean of Communications/Fine Arts ....Dr. Lily SIU
76 Dean of Health Professions .... Ms. Ellen COLBECK
18 Dir Tech Services & Operations ....Mr. David HOLTFRETER
19 Dir Campus Safety ....Mr. Greg FIRKUS

Robert Morris University (K)

401 South State Street, Chicago IL 60605-1225
County: Cook FICE Identification: 001746
Unit ID: 148335
Telephone: (312) 935-6800 Carnegie Class: Master's M
FAX Number: (312) 935-6660 Calendar System: Other
URL: www.robertmorris.edu
Established: 1913 Annual Undergrad Tuition & Fees: $22,800
Enrollment: 3,758 Coed
Affiliation or Control: Independent Non-Profit IRS Status: 501(c)3
Highest Offering: Master's
Program: Occupational; 2-Year Principally Bachelor's Creditable; Liberal Arts And General; Professional; Business Emphasis

Accreditation: NH, ADNUR, IACBE, MAC, SURGT

01 President ... Michael P. VIOLLT
05 Provost ... Mablene KRUEGER
45 Sr VP for Resource Administration ... Deborah BRODZINSKI
84 Sr VP for Enrollment Management ... Nicole FARINELLA
84 Sr VP for Adult & Grad Enrollment ... Catherine LOCKWOOD
20 VP of Academic Administration ... Kathleen SUHAJDA
88 VP of Brand and Image ... Christine FISHER
10 VP of Business Affairs ... Ronald M. ARNOLD
41 VP of Extracurricular Activities ... Megan SMITH-EGGERT
09 VP of External Affairs ... Marie A. GIACOMELLI
37 VP of Financial Services ... Leigh BRINSON
15 VP of Human Resources ... Nicole SKALUBA
14 VP of Information Systems ... Lisa CONTRERAS
26 VP of Marketing/Communications ... Connie ESPARZA
32 VP of Student Affairs ... Angela JORDAN
97 Dean of College of Liberal Arts ... Paula DIAZ
66 Dean College of Nurs & Health Stds ... Lora TIMMONS
49 Dean of Institute of Art & Design ... Janice KAUSHAL
72 Dean of Inst of Technology & Media ... Basim KHARTABIL
58 Dean of Morris Grad School of Mgmt ... Kayed AKKAWI
50 Dean of Business Administration ... Larry NIEMAN
88 Exec Dir/Dean Inst of Culinary Arts ... Nancy ROTUNNO
36 Dean of Career Management ... Stefanie COLEMAN
106 Dean of Distance Learning ... Jill MCGINTY
07 Dean of Day Div Enrollment ... Michelle CASINI
07 Dean of Eve Div Enrollment ... Ana MENDEZ
07 Dean of Graduate Enrollment ... Fernando VILLEDA
07 Dean of Admissions Athletic Enroll ... Justin MERRIS
07 Dean of Admissions Athletic Enroll ... Betsy MALM
88 Director of Recruitment & Out of St ... Danielle NAFFZIGER
88 Sr Dir of Academic Administration ... Kathleen VIOLLT
88 Dir of Admissions Info Systems ... Damaris RIVERA
88 Dir of High School Relations ... Veronica SAUCEDO
96 Dir of Culinary Purchasing & Facil ... Amy KECK
88 Director of Data Administration ... Deana MIRANDA
88 Director of Food Service Operations ... Nick JARMUZ
88 Dir of Human Capital Management ... Gregory TALL
88 Director of Internal Relations ... Joe TAKASH
13 Director of Networking Services ... Gloria PLAZA
26 Director of Public Relations ... Nancy DONOHOE
88 Director of Student Center ... Daniel MARTIN
06 Director of Student Information ... Stella MACH
39 Dir of Student Life and Housing ... Janely RIVERA
88 Dir of Student Support Services ... Pinkey STEWART
88 Dir of System Integration/Integrity ... Arlene REGNERUS
88 Director of Title VII Grant ... Lauren MILLER
88 Dir of Upward Bound and ETS ... Carolyn BASLEY
88 Associate Registrar ... Nancy SMITH-IRONS
21 Controller ... Melanie CARLIN
08 Institutional Library Director ... Sue DUTLER
18 Institutional Dir of Operations ... Nino RANDAZZO

Rock Valley College (A)

3301 N Mulford Road, Rockford IL 61114-5699
County: Winnebago | FICE Identification: 001747
Unit ID: 148380
Telephone: (815) 921-7821 | Carnegie Class: Assoc/Pub-R-L
FAX Number: N/A | Calendar System: Semester
URL: www.rockvalleycollege.edu
Established: 1964 | Annual Undergrad Tuition & Fees (In-District): $2,924
Enrollment: 8,312 | Coed
Affiliation or Control: Local | IRS Status: 501(c)3
Highest Offering: Associate Degree
Program: Occupational; 2-Year Principally Bachelor's Creditable
Accreditation: NH, COARC, DH, SURGT

01 President ... Dr. Jack J. BECHERER
05 Interim VP Academic Affairs/CAO ... Dr. Brian SAGER
102 Executive Director Foundation ... Ms. Pamela OWENS
10 Vice Pres Administrative Services ... Mr. Sam OVERTON, JR.
32 VP Student Development ... Dr. Amy DIAZ
51 VP Career & Technical Education ... Mr. Michael MASTROIANNI
20 Assoc VP Academic Affairs ... Vacant
13 Managing Dir Information Technology ... Ms. Diann JABUSCH
15 Executive Dir Human Resources ... Ms. Jessica JONES
96 Director Business Services ... Mr. Michael PHILLIPS
35 Dean of Students ... Ms. Lynn PERKINS
18 Director Facilities Planning & POM ... Vacant
26 Director Public Relations ... Ms. Nancy CHAMBERLAIN
88 Director Theatre & Arts Park ... Mr. Michael WEBB
19 Director Public Safety ... Mr. Joe DROUGHT
37 Director Financial Aid ... Ms. Cyndi STONESIFER
09 Executive Director Inst Research ... Dr. Lisa MEHLIG
06 Registrar/Director Records/Rgstn ... Ms. Michelle ROTHMEYER
36 Coordinator Career Svcs/Placement ... Ms. Kelly COOPER
07 Director of Admissions ... Ms. Jennifer THOMPSON
84 Dean Enrollment Management ... Dr. Patrick PEYER
04 Assistant to the President ... Ms. Ann KERWITZ

Rockford Career College (B)

1130 S. Alpine Road, Rockford IL 61108
County: Winnebago | FICE Identification: 008545
Unit ID: 148399
Telephone: (815) 965-8616 | Carnegie Class: Assoc/PrivFP
FAX Number: (815) 965-0360 | Calendar System: Quarter
URL: www.rockfordcareercollege.edu
Established: 1862 | Annual Undergrad Tuition & Fees: $9,632
Enrollment: 537 | Coed
Affiliation or Control: Proprietary | IRS Status: Proprietary
Highest Offering: Associate Degree
Program: Occupational; 2-Year Principally Bachelor's Creditable
Accreditation: ACCSC, MAC

01 President/CEO ... Mr. Kevin PULS
10 Vice President/Dir of Finance ... Mr. Guary BERNADELLE
05 Dean of Academics ... Ms. Amy SEMENCHUCK
32 Dean of Students ... Ms. Karen GILBERT
22 Dir of Institutional Compliance ... Mr. Jack MARTIN
84 Director of Enrollment ... Mr. David JULIUS
15 Director of Human Resources ... Mr. Jim LAIBLE
36 Director Student Placement ... Ms. Monica WILLIAMS
37 Director of Financial Aid ... Ms. Lisa RUCH
26 Director of College Relations ... Mr. Jeff SWANBERG

Rockford University (C)

5050 E State Street, Rockford IL 61108-2393
County: Winnebago | FICE Identification: 001748
Unit ID: 148405
Telephone: (815) 226-4000 | Carnegie Class: Master's L
FAX Number: (815) 226-4119 | Calendar System: Semester
URL: www.rockford.edu
Established: 1847 | Annual Undergrad Tuition & Fees: $26,610
Enrollment: 1,030 | Coed
Affiliation or Control: Independent Non-Profit | IRS Status: 501(c)3
Highest Offering: Master's
Program: Liberal Arts And General; Teacher Preparatory; Professional
Accreditation: NH, IACBE, NUR

01 President ... Dr. Robert L. HEAD
05 VP of Academic Affairs & Provost ... Dr. Steven SICONOLFI
30 VP for Institutional Advancement ... Mr. Bernard SUNDSTEDT
88 Senior Development Officer ... Mr. John MCNAMARA
10 VP for Business/Operations/CFO ... Ms. Christina ANDERSON
21 Business Office Accounting Manager ... Mr. Justin KRUEGER
84 VP Enrollment Management ... Dr. Eric FULCOMER
07 Assoc VP Undergraduate Admission ... Ms. Jennifer NORDSTROM
37 Assistant VP for SAS ... Mr. Todd FISCHER-FREE
11 Associate Vice President Operations ... Mr. Matthew PHILLIPS
13 Director of Information Technology ... Mr. Philip (PJ) WAY
32 Dean of Students ... Mr. Bradley KNOTTS
58 Director of MBA ... Mr. Jeffrey FAHRENWALD
58 Director of MAT ... Vacant
06 Registrar ... Ms. Anna J. JATTKOWSKI-HUDSON
04 Exec Assistant to the President ... Ms. Brenda PERRONE
04 Assistant to the President ... Ms. Teddy PHILLIPS
41 Athletic Director ... Mrs. Kristyn KING
15 Director of Human Resources ... Ms. Kim ADAMS
36 Director Career Services ... Vacant
26 Director of Communications ... Ms. Rita ELLIOTT
09 Coordinator of IR ... Dr. Chih-Ming (Ryan) CHUNG
88 Director of Intl Student Success ... Mr. Todd FLEMING
38 Director Counseling ... Mrs. Sallyann ROBERTS
23 Director Health Services ... Mrs. Cecelia M. BRISTOL
18 Director Physical Plant ... Mr. Jerry BERG
19 Security Officer ... Mr. Roy RONCAL
08 Head Librarian ... Ms. Kelly JAMES

Roosevelt University (D)

430 S Michigan Avenue, Chicago IL 60605-1394
County: Cook | FICE Identification: 001749
Unit ID: 148487
Telephone: (312) 341-3500 | Carnegie Class: Master's L
FAX Number: (312) 341-3655 | Calendar System: Semester
URL: www.roosevelt.edu
Established: 1945 | Annual Undergrad Tuition & Fees: $26,625
Enrollment: 6,343 | Coed
Affiliation or Control: Independent Non-Profit | IRS Status: 501(c)3
Highest Offering: Doctorate
Program: Liberal Arts And General; Teacher Preparatory; Professional
Accreditation: NH, ACBSP, CACREP, CLPSY, MUS, @PHAR, TED

01 President ... Dr. Charles R. MIDDLETON
05 Exec Vice President/Univ Provost ... Dr. Doug KNERR
88 Vice Provost Acad Supt/Retention ... Mr. Michael FORD
20 Vice Provost Faculty/Acad Admin ... Dr. Samuel ROSENBERG
10 Sr VP of Finance/Admin and CFO ... Ms. Miroslava MEJIA KRUG
86 VP Govt Relations/Univ Outreach ... Ms. Lesley SLAVITT
84 VP Enrollment Mgmt & Student Svcs ... Vacant
15 Vice President Human Resources ... Ms. Gretchen VAN NATTA
100 Chief of Staff & Asst Secy to BOT ... Mr. Brigham J. TIMPSON
30 VP Inst Advancement and CAO ... Mr. Patrick WOODS
29 Asst VP Alumni Relations/Campaigns ... Ms. Janice PARKIN
44 Asst Vice President Planned Giving ... Ms. Denise A. BRANSFORD
39 Asst VP of Residence Life ... Ms. Bridget COLLIER
26 Asst VP Public Relations ... Mr. Thomas R. KAROW
07 Int Dir Undergraduate Admissions ... Mr. Eric TAMMES
35 Assoc VP Communication & Retention ... Mr. Eric TAMMES
09 Assoc Provost Inst Research ... Mr. Joseph P. REGAN
21 Associate VP Finance ... Ms. Tangella MADDOX
32 Senior Assoc VP Student Services ... Ms. Tanya L. WOLTMANN
18 Assoc VP Campus Planning & Op ... Mr. Steven A. HOSELTON
96 Assoc Vice President for Admin Svcs ... Ms. Laurie CASHMAN
85 Asst Dir of International Programs ... Ms. Dawn HOUGLAND
13 Chief Information Officer ... Mr. Neeraj KUMAR
58 Assoc Provost Research & Grad Stds ... Dr. Kimberly N. RUFFIN
49 Int Dean College Arts & Sciences ... Dr. Bonnie GUNZENHAUSER
50 Dean College Business Admin ... Dr. Terri L. FRIEL
64 Dean College of Performing Arts ... Mr. Henry FOGEL
107 Dean College of Professional Stds ... Dr. D. Bradford HUNT
53 Dean College of Education ... Dr. Holly STADLER
67 Dean College of Pharmacy ... Dr. George MACKINNON
88 Exec Dir of Auditorium Theatre/RU ... Mr. Brett BATTERSON
08 University Librarian ... Mr. Richard UTTICH
06 University Registrar ... Ms. Sheila COFFIN
37 Sr Assoc VP Admission & Fin Aid ... Vacant
38 Director Counseling Center ... Dr. Susan STOCK
36 Director of Career Development ... Ms. Tina GADDY

Roosevelt University Albert A. Robin Campus (E)

1400 N Roosevelt Boulevard, Schaumburg IL 60173
Telephone: (847) 619-7300 | Identification: 770092
Accreditation: &NH

† Main campus is Roosevelt University in Chicago, IL.

Rosalind Franklin University of Medicine & Science (F)

3333 Green Bay Road, North Chicago IL 60064-3095
County: Lake | FICE Identification: 001659
Unit ID: 145558
Telephone: (847) 578-3000 | Carnegie Class: Spec/Med
FAX Number: (847) 578-3401 | Calendar System: Quarter
URL: www.rosalindfranklin.edu
Established: 1912 | Annual Undergrad Tuition & Fees: N/A
Enrollment: 2,084 | Coed
Affiliation or Control: Independent Non-Profit | IRS Status: 501(c)3
Highest Offering: Doctorate; No Lower Division
Program: Professional; Technical Emphasis
Accreditation: NH, ANEST, ARCPA, CLPSY, MED, PA, @PHAR, POD, PTA

01 President/Chief Executive Officer ... Dr. Michael WELCH
03 Exec Vice Pres/Chief Operating Ofcr ... Ms. Margot SURRIDGE
17 VP Medical Affs/Dean Medical School ... Dr. Russell ROBERTSON
05 VP Acad Affs/Dean Col Hlth Prof ... Dr. Wendy RHEAULT
46 VP Research ... Dr. Ronald S. KAPLAN
67 Dean Col of Pharmacy ... Dr. Gloria MEREDITH
58 Dean Sch Grad PostDoc Stds ... Dr. Joseph X. DIMARIO
63 Dean Scholl Col Podiatric Med ... Dr. Nancy L. PARSLEY
10 Chief Financial Officer ... Ms. Roberta LANE
88 VP Faculty Affairs ... Dr. Timothy R. HANSEN
30 VP Institutional Advancement ... Ms. Tina M. ERICKSON
45 Assoc VP Financial Plng/Analysis ... Mr. Eugene DAUN
88 Assoc VP Technology/Learning Res ... Mr. Rick LOESCH
09 Assoc VP Institutional Research ... Ms. Maryann DECAIRE
11 Assoc VP Operations ... Mr. Daniel ESTA
84 Assoc VP Stdnt Aff/Enrollment Mgmt ... Ms. Rebecca DURKIN
106 Assoc VP Online/Distance Education ... Dr. Melanie SHURAN
27 Chief Information Officer ... Mr. Richard LOESCH
29 Exec Dir Alumni/Community Affairs ... Ms. Martha KELLY BATES
15 Exec Dir of Human Resources ... Ms. Sherry BAGNO
26 Exec Dir Marketing/Communications ... Ms. Lee CONCHA
100 Director Office of the President ... Ms. Donna AGNEW
88 Chief Compliance Officer ... Mr. Bret MOBERG
19 Director Campus Security ... Mr. Gordon BLANCHARD
18 Dir Facilities Management ... Mr. Robert D. JACKSON
25 Dir Sponsored Research ... Ms. Dora ESPINOZA
06 Registrar ... Mr. Timothy CARROLL
37 Dir Student Financial Services ... Ms. Maryann DECAIRE
88 Dir Academic/Retention Svcs ... Mr. Steven WEIAND
07 Dir Admissions/Recruitment ... Vacant
32 Director Student Life ... Ms. Shelly BLOHOWIAK

Rush University (G)

600 S Paulina, Chicago IL 60612-3832
County: Cook | FICE Identification: 009800
Unit ID: 148511
Telephone: (312) 942-7100 | Carnegie Class: Spec/Med
FAX Number: (312) 942-2219 | Calendar System: Quarter
URL: www.rushu.rush.edu
Established: 1971 | Annual Undergrad Tuition & Fees: $31,209
Enrollment: 2,206 | Coed
Affiliation or Control: Independent Non-Profit | IRS Status: 501(c)3
Highest Offering: Doctorate
Program: Professional
Accreditation: NH, ANEST, #ARCPA, AUD, BBT, COARC, DIETI, DMS, HSA, IPSY, MED, MT, NURSE, OT, PERF, SP

01 President ... Dr. Larry J. GOODMAN
03 Executive Vice President/COO ... Mr. Peter W. BUTLER
05 Sr Vice Pres Medical Affs/Provost ... Dr. Thomas A. DEUTSCH
26 Sr Vice Pres Corp/External Affairs ... Mr. Terry PETERSON
10 Senior Vice President Finance ... Mr. John MORDACH
30 Senior Vice President Philanthropy ... Ms. Diane M. MCKEEVER
13 Sr Vice Pres/Chief Information Ofcr ... Mr. Lac VAN TRAN
43 Sr Vice President Legal Affairs ... Ms. Anne MURPHY
15 Sr Vice President Human Resource ... Ms. Mary E. SCHOPP
46 Vice President Research ... Dr. James L. MULSHINE
25 Vice Pres Chief Compliance Office ... Dr. Cynthia E. BOYD
22 Assoc VP Equal Oppty Academic Affs ... Ms. Beverly B. HUCKMAN
20 Vice Provost ... Dr. Lois A. HALSTEAD
32 Assoc Prov Student Svcs/Registrar ... Dr. Gayle WARD
108 Assoc Prov Inst Res/Assess/Accred ... Dr. Rosemarie SUHAYDA
76 Dean College of Health Sciences ... Dr. David SHELLEDY
58 Acting Dean Graduate College ... Dr. James L. MULSHINE
66 Dean College of Nursing ... Dr. Melanie DREHER
63 Dean Rush Medical College ... Dr. Thomas A. DEUTSCH
20 Assoc Dean Med/Student Pgm ... Dr. Keith BOYD
27 Asst Vice President Marketing ... Ms. Lori ALLEN
08 Director Library ... Ms. Christine D. FRANK

35 Director Student Affairs .... Ms. Jill GABBERT
37 Director Student Financial Aid .... Mr. Michael FRECHETTE
09 Director of Institutional Research .... Dr. James L. MULSHINE
38 Director Student Counsel Center .... Dr. Hilarie TEREBESSY
29 Director Alumni Relations .... Mr. James LOWENBERG
85 Director International Services .... Ms. Helen LAVELLE
96 Director of Purchasing .... Mr. Michael MULROE
90 Asst Dir Library Educ Tech Ctr .... Mr. Max ANDERSON
21 Manager of Financial Affairs .... Ms. Diane HEALY

Saint Anthony College of Nursing (A)

5658 E State Street, Rockford IL 61108-2468

County: Winnebago | FICE Identification: 009987 | Unit ID: 149028
Telephone: (815) 395-5091 | Carnegie Class: Spec/Health
FAX Number: (815) 395-2275 | Calendar System: Semester
URL: www.sacn.edu
Established: 1915 | Annual Undergrad Tuition & Fees: $21,352
Enrollment: 286 | Coed
Affiliation or Control: Roman Catholic | IRS Status: 501(c)3
Highest Offering: Master's
Program: Professional; Nursing Emphasis
Accreditation: NH, NURSE

01 President .... Dr. Terese A. BURCH
05 Dean Undergraduate Affairs .... Dr. Elizabeth M. CARSON
58 Dean Graduate Affairs & Research .... Dr. Shannon K. LIZER
32 Associate Dean Support Services .... Ms. Nancy A. SANDERS
08 College LRC/Med Library Director .... Ms. Heather A. KLEPITSCH

St. Augustine College (B)

1333-45 W Argyle Street, Chicago IL 60640-3501

County: Cook | FICE Identification: 021854 | Unit ID: 148876
Telephone: (773) 878-8756 | Carnegie Class: Assoc/PrivNFP4
FAX Number: (773) 878-0937 | Calendar System: Semester
URL: www.staugustine.edu
Established: 1980 | Annual Undergrad Tuition & Fees: $9,120
Enrollment: 1,612 | Coed
Affiliation or Control: Independent Non-Profit | IRS Status: 501(c)3
Highest Offering: Baccalaureate
Program: 2-Year Principally Bachelor's Creditable; Liberal Arts And General
Accreditation: NH, COARC, SW

01 President .... Mr. Andrew C. SUND
05 Dean of Academic & Student Affairs .... Dr. Bruno BONDAVALLI
20 Dean of Instruction .... Mr. Lee MALTBY
10 VP for Finance .... Ms. Saundra FLEMING
30 VP for Institutional Advancement .... Vacant
103 VP for Workforce Development .... Mr. Norman RUANO
09 VP Technology/Research & Systems .... Mr. Paul HECK
37 Director of Financial Aid .... Ms. Maria ZAMBONINO
15 Director Human Resources .... Mr. Teofilo CALERO
18 Director of Physical Facilities .... Mr. Francisco MICHEL
07 Director of Admission .... Mr. Honorio MORALES
12 Director West Satellite .... Ms. Carmen RIVERA
12 Director South Satellite .... Ms. Gloria QUIROZ
24 Dir of Learning Resources Center .... Ms. Elizabeth GRUBY

Saint Francis Medical Center College of Nursing (C)

511 NE Greenleaf Street, Peoria IL 61603-3783

County: Peoria | FICE Identification: 006240 | Unit ID: 148575
Telephone: (309) 655-2201 | Carnegie Class: Spec/Health
FAX Number: (309) 624-8973 | Calendar System: Semester
URL: www.sfmccon.edu
Established: 1985 | Annual Undergrad Tuition & Fees: $16,694
Enrollment: 638 | Coed
Affiliation or Control: Roman Catholic | IRS Status: 501(c)3
Highest Offering: Doctorate
Program: Professional; Nursing Emphasis
Accreditation: NH, NUR

01 President of the College .... Dr. Patricia A. STOCKERT
05 Dean Undergraduate Program .... Dr. Sue C. BROWN
58 Dean Graduate Program .... Dr. Janice F. BOUNDY
32 Asst Dean of Support Services .... Mr. Kevin N. STEPHENS
07 Director of Admissions/Registrar .... Ms. Janice E. FARQUHARSON
08 Librarian .... Ms. Leslie E. MENZ
38 College Counselor .... Mrs. Jennifer CARLOCK
37 Coord Student Fin/Financial Assist .... Mrs. Nancy S. PERRYMAN
21 Coord Student Finance/Accts Rec .... Ms. Laura L. SIMMONS
04 Administrative Assistant .... Ms. Luann MORELOCK

St. John's College (D)

729 E. Carpenter Street, Springfield IL 62702-5317

County: Sangamon | FICE Identification: 030980 | Unit ID: 148593
Telephone: (217) 525 5628 | Carnegie Class: Spec/Health
FAX Number: (217) 757-6870 | Calendar System: Semester
URL: www.stjohnscollegespringfield.edu
Established: 1991 | Annual Undergrad Tuition & Fees: $17,642
Enrollment: 122 | Coed
Affiliation or Control: Independent Non-Profit | IRS Status: 501(c)3
Highest Offering: Baccalaureate
Program: Professional; Nursing Emphasis
Accreditation: NH, NUR

01 Chancellor .... Dr. Brenda R. JEFFERS
05 Academic Dean .... Dr. Jane DIERS
07 Admissions Officer/Registrar .... Ms. Anne K. KLINGBORG
30 Development Officer .... Ms. Kristine MYSZKA
51 Director of Continuing Education .... Dr. Judy SHACKELFORD
37 Financial Aid Officer .... Ms. Mary BROWN

Saint Xavier University (E)

3700 W 103rd Street, Chicago IL 60655-3105

County: Cook | FICE Identification: 001768 | Unit ID: 148627
Telephone: (773) 298-3000 | Carnegie Class: Master's L
FAX Number: (773) 779-9061 | Calendar System: Semester
URL: www.sxu.edu
Established: 1846 | Annual Undergrad Tuition & Fees: $28,110
Enrollment: 4,384 | Coed
Affiliation or Control: Roman Catholic | IRS Status: 501(c)3
Highest Offering: Master's
Program: Liberal Arts And General; Professional
Accreditation: NH, ACBSP, MUS, NURSE, SP, TED

01 President .... Ms. Christine M. WISEMAN
05 Provost .... Dr. Paul L. DEVITO
10 Vice President Business & Finance .... Mr. Raymond P. CATANIA
30 Executive Director Development .... Dr. Steven J. MURPHY
26 Vice President University Relations .... Mr. Robert C. TENCZAR, JR.
32 Vice President Student Affairs .... Mr. John P. PELRINE, JR.
45 Vice Pres Administration/Planning .... Sr. Susan M. SANDERS, RSM
84 VP Enrollment Mgmt/Inst Research .... Dr. Kathleen CARLSON
35 Asst Vice Pres Student Affairs .... Ms. Carrie SCHADE
18 Asst Vice Pres Facilities Mgmt .... Mr. Peter SKACH
20 Associate Provost .... Dr. Richard VENNERI
20 Asst Provost/Director Retention .... Ms. Maureen WOGAN
35 Dean of Students .... Ms. Eileen DOHERTY
18 Director Auxilliary Services .... Ms. Linda MORENO
37 Director Financial Aid .... Ms. Susan SWISHER
21 Controller .... Ms. Tina FRODYMA
07 Director of Admission .... Mr. Brian HOTZFIELD
26 Executive Director Media Relation .... Ms. Karla THOMAS
24 Director Media Services .... Mr. Lee VAN SICKLE
08 Director Library .... Mr. Mark A. VARGAS
06 Director Records/Registration Svcs .... Ms. Barbara SUTTON
19 Dir Public Safety/Chief of Police .... Mr. Jack TOUHY
29 Director Alumni/Parent Relations .... Ms. Jamie MANAHAN
41 Director Athletics .... Mr. Robert HALLBERG
42 Exec Dir Office of Mission/Ministry .... Mr. Graziano MARCHESCHI
85 Director Center for Intl Education .... Ms. Colleen O'HARA
40 Director Bookstore Operations .... Ms. Donna GASIOR
36 Director of Career Services .... Ms. Jean RIORDAN
96 Purchasing Coordinator .... Ms. Donna PAVLIK
51 Dean School Cont Prof Studies .... Dr. Leslie PETTY
49 Dean College Arts/Sciences .... Dr. Kathleen ALAIMO
53 Dean School of Education .... Dr. S. Beverly GULLEY
50 Dean Graham School of Management .... Dr. John EBER
66 Dean School of Nursing .... Dr. Gloria JACOBSON

Saint Xavier University Orland Park Campus (F)

18230 Orland Parkway, Orland Park IL 60467

Telephone: (708) 802-6200 | Identification: 770093
Accreditation: &NH

† Main campus is Saint Xavier University in Chicago, IL.

Sanford-Brown College (G)

1101 Eastport Plaza Drive, Collinsville IL 62234

Telephone: (618) 344-5600 | Identification: 666753
Accreditation: ACICS, MLTAD

† Main campus is Le Cordon Bleu College of Culinary Arts in Austin in Austin, TX.

Sanford-Brown College (H)

4600 Roosevelt Road, Hillside IL 60162

Telephone: (708) 836-3200 | Identification: 770691
Accreditation: ACICS

† Main campus is Le Cordon Bleu College of Culinary Arts in Los Angeles in Pasadena, CA.

Sanford-Brown College (I)

4930 Oakton Street, Skokie IL 60077

Telephone: (847) 983-1200 | Identification: 770690
Accreditation: ACICS

† Main campus is Le Cordon Bleu College of Culinary Arts in Los Angeles in Pasadena, CA.

Sanford-Brown College (J)

8525 West 183rd Street, Suite K, Tinley Park IL 60487

Telephone: (708) 781-2035 | Identification: 770692
Accreditation: ACICS

† Main campus is Le Cordon Bleu College of Culinary Arts in Los Angeles in Pasadena, CA.

Sauk Valley Community College (K)

173 Illinois Route 2, Dixon IL 61021-9188

County: Lee | FICE Identification: 001752 | Unit ID: 148672
Telephone: (815) 288-5511 | Carnegie Class: Assoc/Pub-R-M
FAX Number: (815) 288-1880 | Calendar System: Semester
URL: www.svcc.edu
Established: 1965 | Annual Undergrad Tuition & Fees (In-State): $3,243
Enrollment: 2,829 | Coed
Affiliation or Control: State | IRS Status: 501(c)3
Highest Offering: Associate Degree
Program: Occupational; 2-Year Principally Bachelor's Creditable
Accreditation: NH, RAD

01 President .... Dr. George J. MIHEL
05 Academic Vice President .... Mr. Alan D. PFEIFER
32 Dean of Student Services .... Mr. Luis S. MORENO
20 Dean of Instructional Services .... Mr. Jon MANDRELL
09 Dean Institutional Research/Plng .... Mr. Steve NUNEZ
76 Dean Health & Sciences .... Ms. Janet D. LYNCH
10 Director of Business Services .... Ms. Melissa DYE
18 Director Buildings & Grounds .... Mr. Frank MURPHY
15 Director of Human Resources .... Ms. Kathryn SNOW
06 Registrar .... Ms. Pam MEDEMA
102 Director of Foundation and Grants .... Vacant
13 Dean of Information Services .... Ms. Chris SHELLEY
41 Director of Athletics .... Mr. Russ DAMHOFF
26 Coordinator College Relations .... Ms. Rachel MARCO
37 Coord Student Financial Assistance .... Ms. Debra STIEFEL
91 Director Instructional Technology .... Dr. Molly BAKER

School of the Art Institute of Chicago (L)

37 S Wabash, Chicago IL 60603-3103

County: Cook | FICE Identification: 001753 | Unit ID: 143048
Telephone: (312) 899-5100 | Carnegie Class: Spec/Arts
FAX Number: (312) 263-0141 | Calendar System: Semester
URL: www.saic.edu
Established: 1866 | Annual Undergrad Tuition & Fees: $39,020
Enrollment: 3,310 | Coed
Affiliation or Control: Independent Non-Profit | IRS Status: 501(c)3
Highest Offering: Master's
Program: Teacher Preparatory; Fine Arts Emphasis
Accreditation: NH, ART

01 President .... Mr. Walter E. MASSEY
00 Chancellor .... Mr. Tony JONES
05 Provost .... Ms. Elissa TENNY
11 Senior VP Planning & COO .... Mr. Edward J. MCNULTY
84 Vice Pres Enrollment Management .... Ms. Rose MILKOWSKI
30 VP for Institutional Advancement .... Ms. Cheryl JESSOGNE
10 Vice President of Finance .... Mr. Brian ESKER
15 Vice President for Human Resources .... Mr. Michael NICOLAI
32 Vice Pres/Dean of Student Affairs .... Dr. Felice DUBLON
20 Vice Provost .... Mr. Paul COFFEY
18 Assoc VP Facilities/Operations .... Mr. Thomas BUECHELE
20 Dean of Faculty .... Ms. Lisa WAINWRIGHT
35 Dean of Student Life .... Ms. Deborah MARTIN
21 Exec Dir Academic Accounting .... Ms. Sherry MISGEN
26 Exec Dir Enroll Mktg & Operations .... Ms. Maryann SCHAEFER
27 Exec Director Mktg & Graphics .... Ms. Ann WIENS
29 Assoc Director Alumni Relations .... Ms. Emily CHAPMAN
38 Exec Director Student Counseling .... Dr. Joseph BEHEN
84 Exec Director Enrollment Services .... Ms. Jane BRUMITT
06 Director Registration & Records .... Mr. Brad ERZ
08 Director of School Library .... Ms. Claire EIKE
36 Asst Dean/Dir Career Development .... Ms. Katharine SCHUTTA
07 Director of Undergrad Admissions .... Mr. Scott RAMON
07 Director of Graduate Admissions .... Mr. Andre VAN DE PUTTE
105 Exec Director Web E-Communication .... Ms. Rae ULRICH
37 Director of Student Financial Svcs .... Mr. Patrick JAMES
28 Director of Multicultural Affairs .... Mr. James BRITT
23 Director of Health Services .... Vacant
09 Enrollment Analyst .... Mr. Bruce FELKNOR
49 Int Dean Undergraduate Studies .... Ms. Tiffany HOLMES
58 Chair of Graduate Division .... Mr. Werner HERTERICH

Shawnee Community College (M)

8364 Shawnee College Road, Ullin IL 62992-2206

County: Pulaski | FICE Identification: 007693 | Unit ID: 148821
Telephone: (618) 634-3200 | Carnegie Class: Assoc/Pub-R-L
FAX Number: (618) 634-3300 | Calendar System: Semester
URL: www.shawneecc.edu
Established: 1967 | Annual Undergrad Tuition & Fees (In-District): $2,850
Enrollment: 3,986 | Coed
Affiliation or Control: Local | IRS Status: 501(c)3
Highest Offering: Associate Degree
Program: Occupational; 2-Year Principally Bachelor's Creditable
Accreditation: NH, CAHIIM, MLTAD, OTA, SURGT

01 President .... Dr. Tim BELLAMEY
05 Vice Pres Instructional Services .... Dr. Vicky ARTMAN
32 Int Vice President Student Svcs .... Ms. Carolyn KINDLE
04 Asst to President/Human Res Ofcr .... Ms. Beth DARDEN
20 Dean Instructional Services .... Ms. Jean Ellen BOYD
51 Dean Adult Educ/Alternative Instruc .... Mr. James DARDEN

10 Chief Financial Officer Ms. Tiffiney RYAN
38 Student Support Services Director Mr. Jeff MCGOY
35 Dean of Student Services Ms. Dee BLAKELY
37 Dir Fin Aid/Coord Vet & Mil Personl Dr. Tammy CAPPS
41 Athletic Director Mr. Mike FITZGERALD
13 Director MIS Mr. Chris CLARK
12 Director Metro Center Dr. Sally WEST
66 Director of Nursing Ms. Denise GRIFFITH
08 Head Librarian Ms. Tracey JOHNSON
06 Registrar Ms. Danielle BOYD
102 Dir Resource Development/Foundation Vacant
21 Director of Business Services Ms. Brandy WOODS
18 Facilities Director Mr. Don KOCH
09 Director of Institutional Research Mrs. Pamela BARNES
40 Bookstore Manager Ms. Erica POAT
88 Special Needs Counselor Ms. Annie HUBBARD
88 Coord Ctr for Cmty/Economic Devel Ms. Candy EASTWOOD
26 Public Relations Coordinator Ms. Sharon FELKER
36 Career Services Coordinator Ms. Leslie WELDON
50 Div Chair Business/Occup/Tech Dp Mr. Jerry AINSWORTH
81 Division Chair Math/Science Ms. Rhonda DILLOW
79 Div Chr Social Stds/Humanities/Comm Ms. Sharon WALKER
76 Div Chair Allied Health Ms. Tracy LOHSTROH

Shimer College (A)

3424 S State Street, Second Floor,
Chicago IL 60616-3893

County: Cook FICE Identification: 001756
Unit ID: 148849
Telephone: (312) 235-3500 Carnegie Class: Bac/A&S
FAX Number: (312) 235-3502 Calendar System: Semester
URL: www.shimer.edu
Established: 1853 Annual Undergrad Tuition & Fees: $30,780
Enrollment: 112 Coed
Affiliation or Control: Independent Non-Profit IRS Status: 501(c)3
Highest Offering: Baccalaureate
Program: Liberal Arts And General
Accreditation: NH

01 President Dr. Susan HENKING
10 Chief Financial Officer Ms. Sandra COLLINS
11 Chief Operating Officer Mr. Joseph FITZPATRICK
05 Dean of the College Dr. Barbara STONE
32 Dean of Students Mr. Joseph FITZPATRICK
30 Director of Development Ms. Mary Pat BARBARI
37 Director of Financial Aid Ms. Janet HENTHORN
07 Director of Admissions Ms. James BOWERS
08 Library Director Ms. Colleen MCCARROLL
06 Registrar Mr. James ULRICH

SOLEX College (B)

350 E. Dundee Road, Suite 200, Wheeling IL 60090

County: Cook FICE Identification: 045816
Unit ID: 459356
Telephone: (847) 229-9595 Carnegie Class: Not Classified
FAX Number: (847) 229-1919 Calendar System: Other
URL: www.solex.edu/locations/wheeling/
Established: 2004 Annual Undergrad Tuition & Fees: $17,200
Enrollment: 80 Coed
Affiliation or Control: Proprietary IRS Status: Proprietary
Highest Offering: Associate Degree
Program: Occupational; 2-Year Principally Bachelor's Creditable; Technical Emphasis
Accreditation: ACICS, COMTA, @PTAA

01 Executive Director Mr. Leon E. LINTON

South Suburban College of Cook County (C)

15800 S State Street, South Holland IL 60473-1270

County: Cook FICE Identification: 001769
Unit ID: 149365
Telephone: (708) 596-2000 Carnegie Class: Assoc/Pub-S-SC
FAX Number: (708) 210-5710 Calendar System: Semester
URL: www.ssc.edu
Established: 1927 Annual Undergrad Tuition & Fees (In-District): $3,866
Enrollment: 6,211 Coed
Affiliation or Control: State/Local IRS Status: 501(c)3
Highest Offering: Associate Degree
Program: Occupational; 2-Year Principally Bachelor's Creditable
Accreditation: NH, ADNUR, MAC, OTA, PHLEB

01 President Mr. Don MANNING
05 Vice President Academic Services Dr. Linda STOKES-WILSON
11 Vice Pres Administration Mr. Martin LAREAU
32 Vice President Student Development Ms. Songie ADEBIYI
84 VP Enrollment/Community Education Mrs. Jane Ellen STOCKER
35 Dean Student Development Mr. Greg LAWRENCE
83 Dean Legal Studies/Soc & Behav Sci Mr. Ronald KAWANNA, JR.
50 Dean Business & Technology Mr. James COATES
76 Dean Health Professions & Sciences Mr. Jeff WADDY
57 Dean Fine Arts/Soc & Behav Sci/Bus Mr. Tom GOVAN, JR.
66 Dean Nursing/Fine Arts/English/Hum Ms. Miriam ANTHONY
51 Director Continuing Education Ms. Shirley DREWENSKI
10 Treasurer/Controller Mr. Tim POLLERT
26 Director Public Rels/Pub & Found Mr. Patrick RUSH
14 Exec Dir Information Technology Mr. John MCCORMACK
35 Dean Student Services Mrs. Patrice BURTON
88 Dir New Student Ctr & Retenion Svcs Mrs. Jazaer FARRAR
84 Director Enrollment Services Mrs. Robin RIHACEK
37 Director of Financial Aid Mr. John SEMPLE
18 Director Physical Plant Services Mr. Justin PAPP
24 Dir Communication Svcs/Media Design Mrs. Lisa MILLER
41 Athletic Director Mr. Steve RUZICH
09 Director of Institutional Research Mr. Kevin RIORDAN
15 Director Human Resources Ms. Kimberly PIGATTI

South Suburban College of Cook County University and College Center (D)

16333 Kilbourne Avenue, Oak Forest IL 60452
Telephone: (708) 225-6029 Identification: 770094
Accreditation: &NH

† Main campus is South Suburban College of Cook County in South Holland, IL.

Southeastern Illinois College (E)

3575 College Road, Harrisburg IL 62946-4925

County: Saline FICE Identification: 001757
Unit ID: 148937
Telephone: (618) 252-5400 Carnegie Class: Assoc/Pub-R-L
FAX Number: (618) 252-3156 Calendar System: Semester
URL: www.sic.edu
Established: 1960 Annual Undergrad Tuition & Fees (In-District): $5,700
Enrollment: 2,223 Coed
Affiliation or Control: State/Local IRS Status: 501(c)3
Highest Offering: Associate Degree
Program: Occupational; 2-Year Principally Bachelor's Creditable
Accreditation: NH, MLTAD, OTA, SURGT

01 President Dr. Jonah RICE
05 Vice President Instruction Dr. Dana KEATING
10 VP Administration/Business Affairs Mr. Tim WALKER
32 Dean of Enrollment Mgt & Stdnt Dev Mr. Chad FLANNERY
20 Dean of Career & Technical Educ Mrs. Karen WEISS
103 Assoc Dean of Workforce & Cmty Ed Mrs. Lori COX
08 Head Librarian Mr. Gary JONES
84 Director Enrollment Services Ms. Sarah ADAMS
26 Marketing Coordinator Ms. Angela WILSON
37 Financial Aid Director Ms. Emily HENSON
13 Chief Information Officer Mr. Greg MCCULLOCH
76 Director Allied Health & Nursing Ms. Gina SIRACH
15 Human Resources Administrator Mrs. Barbara POTTER
06 Registrar Ms. Sarah ADAMS
18 Director of Environmental Services Mr. Ed FITZGERALD

*Southern Illinois University (F)

Stone Center - 1400 Douglas Drive, Carbondale IL 62901

County: Jackson FICE Identification: 008237
Unit ID: 149240
Telephone: (618) 536-3331 Carnegie Class: N/A
FAX Number: (618) 536-3404
URL: www.southernillinois.edu

01 President Dr. Glenn POSHARD
05 Vice President Academic Affairs Dr. Paul SARVELA
10 Sr VP Financial/Admin Affs/Bd Treas Dr. Duane STUCKY
88 Director Risk Management Ms. Chris GLIDEWELL
86 Exec Dir of Governmental Public Aff Mr. John CHARLES
21 Exec Dir of Internal Audits Ms. Kim LABONTE
43 Interim General Counsel Mr. Lucas CRATER
04 Assistant to the President Ms. Paula S. KEITH

*Southern Illinois University Carbondale (G)

425 Clocktower Drive, Carbondale IL 62901-4701

County: Jackson FICE Identification: 001758
Unit ID: 149222
Telephone: (618) 453-2121 Carnegie Class: RU/H
FAX Number: (618) 453-3250 Calendar System: Semester
URL: siu.edu
Established: 1869 Annual Undergrad Tuition & Fees (In-State): $12,092
Enrollment: 18,847 Coed
Affiliation or Control: State IRS Status: 501(c)3
Highest Offering: Doctorate
Program: Occupational; 2-Year Principally Bachelor's Creditable; Liberal Arts And General; Teacher Preparatory; Professional
Accreditation: NH, AAB, ARCPA, ART, BUS, BUSA, CACREP, CEA, CIDA, CLPSY, COPSY, CORE, CS, DH, DIETD, DIETI, DMS, ENG, ENGT, FOR, FUSER, IFSAC, IPSY, JOUR, LAW, MLTAD, MUS, NAIT, PH, PTAA, RADDOS, RTT, SP, SPAA, SW, TED, THEA

02 Chancellor Dr. Rita CHENG
05 Provost & Vice Chancellor Dr. John NICKLOW
32 Interim Dean of Students Dr. Katherine SERMERSHEIM
30 VC for Development & Alumni Rels Mr. Jim SALMO
10 VC for Administration and Finance Mr. Kevin BAME
46 Interim VC for Research Dr. James GARVEY
28 Assoc Chancellor Diversity Dr. Linda MCCABE-SMITH
102 Asst Director SIU Foundation Ms. Elizabeth BANYCKY
13 Asst Provost & Chief Info Officer Mr. Ronald D. CRAIN
84 Asst Provost Enrollment Mgmt Vacant
20 Assoc Provost for Academic Admin Dr. David DILALLA
20 Assoc Provost for Academic Programs Dr. James S. ALLEN
04 Assistant to the Chancellor Mr. Matthew BAUGHMAN
49 Dean Liberal Arts Dr. Kimberly LEONARD
50 Dean College of Business Dr. James D. CRADIT
53 Dean Educ & Human Services Dr. Keith WILSON
54 Dean Engineering Dr. John J. WARWICK
58 Dean Graduate School Dr. Susan M. FORD
61 Dean School of Law Dr. Cynthia FOUNTAINE
81 Interim Dean College of Science Dr. Laurie ACHENBACH
63 Dean School of Medicine Dr. John K. DORSEY
47 Dean Agricultural Sciences Dr. Mickey A. LATOUR
72 Dean Col Applied Sciences & Arts Dr. JuAn WANG
57 Interim Dean Mass Comm/Media Arts Dr. Dafna P. LEMISH
08 Dean Library Affairs Dr. Anne C. MOORE
07 Director Undergrad Admissions Ms. Katharine J. SUSKI
37 Director Student Financial Aid Ms. Terry HARFST
29 Associate VC Alumni Services Ms. Michelle SUAREZ
21 Interim Budget Director Ms. Judith MARSHALL
09 Int Director Institutional Research Dr. George VINEYARD
13 Exec Dir Finance Ms. Judith MARSHALL
27 Chief Marketing & Comm Officer Rae GOLDSMITH
15 Director Human Resources Ms. Jennifer WATSON
39 Interim Director University Housing Ms. Lisa M. MARKS
36 Director Univ Career Services Ms. Keri YOUNG
85 Director International Education Ms. Carla E. COPPI
18 Director Plant/Service Operations Mr. Philip S. GATTON
19 Director of Public Safety Mr. Todd D. SIGLER
23 Director Student Health Services Dr. Ted W. GRACE
41 Director Intercollegiate Athletics Mr. Mario L. MOCCIA
106 Director Distance Education Ms. Gayla STONER
06 Director Registrar's Office Ms. Tiffany SPENCER
38 Director Student Counseling Center Dr. Rosemary E. SIMMONS
96 Int Director Procurement Services Ms. Debbie ABELL
35 Acting Assoc Dean of Students Mr. Andy L. MORGAN

*Southern Illinois University Edwardsville (H)

Edwardsville IL 62026-0001

County: Madison FICE Identification: 001759
Unit ID: 149231
Telephone: (618) 650-2000 Carnegie Class: Master's L
FAX Number: (618) 650-2270 Calendar System: Semester
URL: www.siue.edu
Established: 1957 Annual Undergrad Tuition & Fees (In-State): $9,666
Enrollment: 14,055 Coed
Affiliation or Control: State IRS Status: 501(c)3
Highest Offering: Doctorate
Program: Liberal Arts And General; Teacher Preparatory; Professional
Accreditation: NH, ANEST, BUS, BUSA, CONST, CS, DENT, ENG, JOUR, MLTAD, MUS, NURSE, PHAR, SP, SPAA, SW, TED, THEA

02 Chancellor Dr. Julie FURST-BOWE
05 Interim Prov & VC for Academic Affs Dr. Ann M. BOYLE
11 Vice Chancellor for Administration Mr. Kenneth R. NEHER
26 VC Univ Rel & CEO SIUE Foundation Mr. Patrick HUNDLEY
32 Vice Chanc for Student Affairs Dr. Narbeth R. EMMANUEL
100 Executive Asst to the Chancellor Ms. Kimberly H. DURR
22 Asst Chanc for Institutional Compli Mr. Paul PITTS
20 Assoc Prov for Acad Plng & Pgm Dev Dr. Susan L. THOMAS
20 Assoc Prov Rsch/Dean Grad Sch Dr. Jerry B. WEINBERG
35 Assoc VC Stdnt Affs/Dean of Stdnts Dr. James W. KLENKE
35 Assoc VC for Student Affairs Ms. Lora MILES
13 Assoc VC for IT & CIO Ms. Jennifer VANDEVER
28 Assoc Prov Inst Diversity/Inclusion Dr. Venessa BROWN
88 Asst Prov for Acad Innov & Eff Dr. P. Denise COBB
41 Asst VC Athletic Dev/Dir Athletics Dr. Bradley L. HEWITT
84 Asst VC for Enrollment Mgmt Mr. Scott BELOBRAJDIC
45 Asst VC for Planning & Budgeting Mr. Richard WALKER
49 Dean College of Arts & Sciences Dr. Aldemaro ROMERO
50 Interim Dean School of Business Dr. John NAVIN
52 Dean Sch of Dental Medicine Dr. Bruce E. ROTTER
53 Dean School of Education Dr. Bette BERGERON
54 Dean School of Engineering Dr. Hasan SEVIM
66 Interim Dean School of Nursing Dr. Anne PERRY
67 Dean School of Pharmacy Dr. Gireesh V. GUPCHUP
62 Dean Library & Information Services Dr. Regina MCBRIDE
21 Budget Director Mr. William F. WINTER, JR.
27 Asst VC Univ Rel/Exec Dir Univ M&C Ms. Elizabeth M. KESERAUSKIS
51 Director Educational Outreach Mr. Tim ENGELMAN
12 Dir Grant Funded Pgm East StL Ctr Dr. Andrew THEISING
88 Director Academic Advising Ms. Cheryle L. TUCKER-LOEWE
07 Director Admissions Mr. Todd C. BURRELL
29 Director Alumni Affairs Mr. Stephen E. JANKOWSKI
36 Director Career Dev Center Ms. Susan SEIBERT
38 Director Counseling Services Dr. Andrew B. KING
18 Director Facilities Management Mr. Paul FULIGNI
23 Director Health Services Ms. Riane B. GREENWALT
15 Director Human Resources Ms. Sherrie SENKFOR
09 Dir Institutional Rsrch & Studies Mr. Phillip M. BROWN
85 Director Ctr for International Pgms Dr. Ronald P. SCHAEFER
96 Director of Purchasing Ms. Nancy J. UFERT FAIRLESS
37 Acting Dir Student Financial Aid Ms. Sally MULLEN
102 Dir Univ Advancement/Foundation Ops Mr. Kevin MARTIN
39 Director University Housing Mr. Michael J. SCHULTZ
19 Director University Police Ms. Regina M. HAYS
06 Registrar Ms. Laura A. STROM

*Southern Illinois University Carbondale School of Medicine (I)

PO Box 19620, Springfield IL 62794-9620
Telephone: (217) 545-8000 Identification: 770181

Accreditation: &NH, MED

† Main campus is Southern Illinois University Carbondale in Carbondale, IL.

Southwestern Illinois College (A)

2500 Carlyle Avenue, Belleville IL 62221-5899
County: Saint Clair FICE Identification: 001636
Unit ID: 143215
Telephone: (618) 235-2700 Carnegie Class: Assoc/Pub-S-MC
FAX Number: (618) 277-0631 Calendar System: Semester
URL: www.swic.edu
Established: 1946 Annual Undergrad Tuition & Fees (In-District): $3,240
Enrollment: 7,437 Coed
Affiliation or Control: State/Local IRS Status: 501(c)3
Highest Offering: Associate Degree
Program: Occupational; 2-Year Principally Bachelor's Creditable
Accreditation: NH, ACFEI, ADNUR, CAHIIM, COARC, MAC, MLTAD, PTAA, RAD

01 President - District ... Dr. Georgia COSTELLO
10 Controller ... Ms. Deborah MASSENA
11 VP Administrative Svcs/Treasurer ... Mr. Bernie J. YSURSA, JR.
05 Vice Pres Instruction ... Mr. Clay L. BAITMAN
31 Vice Pres Community Svcs ... Dr. Mark P. EICHENLAUB
26 Vice Pres Mktg/Institutional Adv ... Mr. Mike R. FLEMING
15 Director Human Resources ... Ms. Sherry FAVRE
32 Vice Pres Student Development ... Ms. Staci G. CLAYBORNE
20 Assoc Dean Instructional Services ... Ms. Patricia POU
12 Executive Director SWGCC ... Vacant
12 Executive Director Red Bud Campus ... Mr. Mike REED
30 Interim Exec Director Foundation ... Mr. Gary E. GRAY
08 Dean Learning Resources ... Mrs. Laurie A. BINGEL
37 Director of Financial Aid/Placement ... Mr. Robert TEBBE
13 Chief Information Officer ... Dr. James RIHA
18 Director of Physical Plant ... Mr. Ron R. HENDERSON
19 Director of Public Safety ... Mr. Mark A. GREEN
96 Director of Purchasing ... Mr. Mike R. THOMAS
76 Dean Hlth Sci and Homeland Security ... Ms. Julie A. MUERTZ
50 Dean of Business Division ... Ms. Janet S. FONTENOT
72 Dean of Technical Education ... Mr. Brad SPARKS
81 Dean of Math & Science ... Ms. Amanda M. STARKEY
49 Dean of Liberal Arts ... Mr. Richard SPENCER
51 Director Adult Education/Cont Educ ... Dr. Lea MAUE
07 Dean of Enrollment Services ... Ms. Michelle L. BIRK
28 Director of Diversity ... Ms. Donna MOODY
88 Dean of Success Programs ... Ms. Deborah ALFORD
88 Treasurer IL Green Economy Network ... Mr. Robert J. HILGENBRINK

Southwestern Illinois College Granite City Campus (B)

4950 Maryville Road, Granite City IL 62040
Telephone: (618) 931-0600 Identification: 770095
Accreditation: &NH

† Main campus is Southwestern Illinois College in Belleville, IL.

Southwestern Illinois College Red Bud Campus (C)

500 W South 4th Street, Red Bud IL 62278
Telephone: (618) 282-6682 Identification: 770096
Accreditation: &NH

† Main campus is Southwestern Illinois College in Belleville, IL.

Spertus Institute for Jewish Learning and Leadership (D)

610 S Michigan Avenue, Chicago IL 60605-1994
County: Cook FICE Identification: 001663
Unit ID: 148982
Telephone: (312) 322-1700 Carnegie Class: Spec/Other
FAX Number: (312) 922-6406 Calendar System: Quarter
URL: www.spertus.edu
Established: 1924 Annual Graduate Tuition & Fees: $20,000
Enrollment: 250 Coed
Affiliation or Control: Independent Non-Profit IRS Status: 501(c)3
Highest Offering: Doctorate; No Undergraduates
Program: Liberal Arts And General; Teacher Preparatory; Professional
Accreditation: NH

01 President ... Dr. Hal M. LEWIS
05 Dean ... Dr. Dean BELL
51 Director for Public Programing ... Ms. Beth SCHENKER
10 Director Finance & Administration ... Mr. Robert TENUTA
88 Director Nonprofit Admin Program ... Dr. Karen BAIRD
37 Student Records/Financial Aid Mgr ... Ms. Pamela FELTON

Spoon River College (E)

23235 N County Road 22, Canton IL 61520-9801
County: Fulton FICE Identification: 001643
Unit ID: 148991
Telephone: (309) 647-4645 Carnegie Class: Assoc/Pub-R-M
FAX Number: (309) 649-6235 Calendar System: Semester
URL: www.src.edu
Established: 1959 Annual Undergrad Tuition & Fees (In-District): $3,750
Enrollment: 2,382 Coed
Affiliation or Control: Local IRS Status: 501(c)3
Highest Offering: Associate Degree
Program: Occupational; 2-Year Principally Bachelor's Creditable
Accreditation: NH

01 President ... Mr. Curt OLDFIELD
05 Vice President Inst/Student Svcs ... Dr. Randall GREENWELL
11 Vice President Admin Services ... Mr. Brett STOLLER
31 Vice President Community Outreach ... Ms. Carol DAVIS
04 Executive Asst to the President ... Ms. Julie HAMPTON
36 Dean Career & Technical Education ... Mr. Michael DENUM
32 Dean Student Services ... Ms. Missy WILKINSON
66 Director Nursing ... Ms. Tamatha SCHLEICH
88 Dean Transfer Education ... Ms. Holly NORTON
18 Director Facilities ... Mr. Bob A. HAILE
55 Dir Adult and Outreach Education ... Mr. Chad MURPHY
08 Director Library Services ... Ms. Kathleen A. MENANTEAUX
13 Chief Information Officer ... Mr. Raj SIDDARAJU
41 Director Athletics/Student Life ... Mr. Ron CLARK
21 Director Business Services ... Ms. Sarah GRAY
37 Director Financial Aid ... Ms. Salinda Jo BRANSON
40 Dir Purchasing & Auxiliary Services ... Mr. Brad T. O'BRIEN
15 Director Human Resources ... Ms. Michelle L. BUGOS
14 Director Technology Services ... Mr. Dean CLARY
84 Director Enrollment Services ... Ms. Janet MUNSON
13 Director Information Services ... Ms. Patty SCHMIDT
09 Coord Institutional Reporting ... Mr. Aaron ROE
26 Director Marketing ... Ms. Sherri RADER
27 Coordinator Public Information ... Ms. Sally SHIELDS

Spoon River College-Macomb Campus (F)

208 S Johnston Street, Macomb IL 61455
Telephone: (309) 837-5727 Identification: 770097
Accreditation: &NH

† Main campus is Spoon River College in Canton, IL.

Taylor Business Institute (G)

318 W Adams Street, Suite 500, Chicago IL 60606
County: Cook FICE Identification: 011810
Unit ID: 149310
Telephone: (312) 658-5100 Carnegie Class: Assoc/PrivFP
FAX Number: (312) 658-0867 Calendar System: Quarter
URL: www.tbiil.edu
Established: 1962 Annual Undergrad Tuition & Fees: $13,500
Enrollment: 245 Coed
Affiliation or Control: Proprietary IRS Status: Proprietary
Highest Offering: Associate Degree
Program: Occupational
Accreditation: @NH, ACICS

01 President ... Mrs. Janice C. PARKER

Telshe Yeshiva-Chicago (H)

3535 W Foster Avenue, Chicago IL 60625-5598
County: Cook FICE Identification: 020732
Unit ID: 149329
Telephone: (773) 463-7738 Carnegie Class: Spec/Faith
FAX Number: (773) 463-2849 Calendar System: Semester
Established: 1960 Annual Undergrad Tuition & Fees: $12,000
Enrollment: 81 Male
Affiliation or Control: Independent Non-Profit IRS Status: 501(c)3
Highest Offering: Second Talmudic Degree
Program: Professional; Business Emphasis
Accreditation: RABN

01 President ... Rabbi Avrohom C. LEVIN
03 Executive Vice President ... Rabbi Yitzchok LEVIN
05 Vice President ... Rabbi Chaim D. KELLER
05 Vice President ... Rabbi Moshe SCHMELCZER
11 Administrative Director/Secretary ... Rabbi Shmuel ADLER

Toyota Technological Institute at Chicago (I)

6045 South Kenwood Avenue, Chicago IL 60637
County: Cook Identification: 666367
Unit ID: 445054
Telephone: (773) 834-2500 Carnegie Class: Assoc/PrivNFP4
FAX Number: (773) 834-9881 Calendar System: Quarter
URL: www.ttic.edu
Established: 2003 Annual Graduate Tuition & Fees: $30,000
Enrollment: 22 Coed
Affiliation or Control: Independent Non-Profit IRS Status: 501(c)3
Highest Offering: Doctorate; No Undergraduates
Program: Professional; Technical Emphasis
Accreditation: NH

01 President ... Dr. Sadaoki FURUI
05 Chief Academic Officer ... Dr. David MCALLESTER
10 Treasurer/Secretary of the Board ... Mr. Masashi HISAMOTO
11 Chief Administrator ... Mr. Gary HAMBURG
58 Admin Director of Graduate Studies ... Ms. Christina NOVAK
21 Controller ... Ms. Anna RUFFULO
15 Human Resources Coordinator ... Ms. Liv LEADER

Tribeca Flashpoint Media Arts Academy (J)

28 North Clark Street, Suite 500, Chicago IL 60602
County: Cook Identification: 667083
Unit ID: 460747
Telephone: (312) 332-0707 Carnegie Class: Not Classified
FAX Number: (312) 506-0708 Calendar System: Semester
URL: www.tfa.edu
Established: 2007 Annual Undergrad Tuition & Fees: $26,000
Enrollment: 555 Coed
Affiliation or Control: Proprietary IRS Status: Proprietary
Highest Offering: Associate Degree
Program: Occupational; 2-Year Principally Bachelor's Creditable
Accreditation: ACICS

01 President ... Todd STEELE
05 Exec VP/Dean Academic Affairs ... Paula M. FROEHLE
10 Exec VP/Chief Financial Officer ... Mario CHRISTOPHER
11 Sr VP/Associate Academic Dean ... John MURRAY
15 Sr VP/Human Resources/Career Svcs ... Jill GEIMER
07 Sr VP/Director Admissions ... Joy MCCLURE
11 Sr VP Operations ... Ernesto PARAS
26 VP Marketing/Business Development ... Edward GLASSMAN
32 VP/Assoc Dean of Students ... Benjamin J. SPANNER
06 Registrar ... Jason CALIZ
21 Controller ... Laura PETRY

Trinity Christian College (K)

6601 W College Drive, Palos Heights IL 60463-0929
County: Cook FICE Identification: 001771
Unit ID: 149505
Telephone: (708) 597-3000 Carnegie Class: Bac/Diverse
FAX Number: (708) 385-5665 Calendar System: 4/1/4
URL: www.trnty.edu
Established: 1959 Annual Undergrad Tuition & Fees: $23,980
Enrollment: 1,369 Coed
Affiliation or Control: Independent Non-Profit IRS Status: 501(c)3
Highest Offering: Master's
Program: Liberal Arts And General; Teacher Preparatory; Professional
Accreditation: NH, ACBSP, NURSE, SW

01 President ... Dr. Steven TIMMERMANS
05 Provost ... Dr. Elizabeth RUDENGA
10 Vice Pres for Business & Finance ... Mr. James E. BELSTRA
07 Dean of Admissions ... Mr. Pete HAMSTRA
32 VP Student Development & Retention ... Mrs. Rebekah L. STARKENBURG
30 Vice Pres for Development ... Mr. Larryl HUMME
08 Director of Library Services ... Ms. Marcille FREDERICK
06 Registrar ... Ms. Jaynn TOBIAS-JOHNSON
07 Director of Admissions ... Mr. Jeremy KLYN
36 Director Career Planning/Placement ... Vacant
55 Director of Adult Studies Programs ... Dr. Lori SCREMENTI
29 Director of Alumni Relations ... Mr. Travis BANDSTRA
27 Dir of Marketing and Communications ... Ms. Kim FABIAN
88 Asst Dir Marketing/Graphic Designer ... Mr. Peter CLEVERING
44 Campaign Gifts Manager ... Vacant
14 Director of Computer Services ... Mr. Joe VELDERMAN
41 Director of Athletics ... Mr. Bill SCHEPEL
31 Director of Community Partnerships ... Vacant
42 Chaplain ... Dr. Willis VAN GRONINGEN
85 Director of Off-Campus Programs ... Dr. Burton J. ROZEMA
37 Director Financial Aid ... Mr. Ryan ZANTINGH
18 Director of Building/Grounds ... Mr. Tim TIMMONS
44 Director of Planned Giving ... Mr. Ken BOSS
21 Controller ... Mr. Mike TROCHUCK
28 Dir of Diversity/Acad Dean/Ed Prof ... Mr. Don WOO
92 Director of Honors Program ... Dr. Craig MATTSON
35 Director Student Affairs/Counseling ... Mrs. Ginny CARPENTER
04 Director Enrollment Management ... Mr. Pete HAMSTRA
09 Asst Registar for Inst Research ... Ms. Kimberly WILLIAMS
15 Human Resources Manager ... Mr. Larry BOER
20 Acad Dean/Mathematics Prof ... Dr. Sharon ROBBERT
20 Acad Dean/Social Work Prof ... Dr. Mackenzi HUYSER

Trinity College of Nursing & Health Sciences (L)

2122 25th Avenue, Rock Island IL 61201-5317
County: Rock Island FICE Identification: 006225
Unit ID: 146755
Telephone: (309) 779-7700 Carnegie Class: Spec/Health
FAX Number: (309) 779-7748 Calendar System: Semester
URL: www.trinitycollegeqc.edu
Established: 1994 Annual Undergrad Tuition & Fees: $23,590
Enrollment: 232 Coed
Affiliation or Control: Independent Non-Profit IRS Status: 501(c)3
Highest Offering: Master's
Program: Professional; Nursing Emphasis
Accreditation: NH, ADNUR, COARC, NURSE, RAD

01 Chancellor ... Dr. Susan C. WAJERT
05 Dean of Nursing & Health Sciences ... Ms. Tracy L. POELVOORDE
06 Registrar ... Ms. Cara BANKS

Trinity International University (M)

2065 Half Day Road, Deerfield IL 60015-1284
County: Lake FICE Identification: 001772
Unit ID: 149514
Telephone: (847) 945-8800 Carnegie Class: DRU
FAX Number: (847) 317-8090 Calendar System: Semester
URL: www.tiu.edu
Established: 1897 Annual Undergrad Tuition & Fees: $25,840
Enrollment: 2,284 Coed
Affiliation or Control: Evangelical Free Church Of America
IRS Status: 501(c)3

Highest Offering: Doctorate
Program: Liberal Arts And General; Teacher Preparatory; Professional
Accreditation: NH, THEOL

01 Interim President .... Mr. Neil NYBERG
04 Director of the President's Office .... Ms. Mindy WILKERSON
03 Exec Vice President & Provost .... Vacant
05 Co-Provost/Sr VP Educ/Dean TEDS .... Dr. Tite TIENOU
05 Co-Provost/Sr VP Academic Affairs .... Dr. Jeanette HSIEH
84 Sr VP for Enrollment Management .... Mr. Roger L. KIEFFER
32 Sr VP Stdnt Affs/Dn Stdnts/Athl Dir .... Dr. William O. WASHINGTON
13 Sr VP Information Technology/Plng .... Mr. Steven GEGGIE
30 Sr Vice Pres University Advancement .... Dr. David HOAG
10 Sr VP of Business & Finance/CFO .... Mr. Mike PICHA
44 Vice President of Development .... Mr. Carl JOHNSON
26 Director Marketing .... Ms. Rachel YANTIS
21 University Controller .... Mr. Paul EISENMENGER
73 Assoc Academic Dean Divinity School .... Dr. James R. MOORE
88 Interim Dean of Nontraditional Educ .... Mr. Jay SIMALA
35 Assoc Dean of Undergraduate Stdnts .... Ms. Karen WROBBEL
90 Director of Acad/Desktop Computing .... Mr. Chris MILLER
91 Director Administrative Computing .... Ms. Katie KEMP
23 Director of Health Services .... Ms. Barbara VIETMEIER
58 Assoc Dean of Graduate School .... Dr. Joyce A. SHELTON
61 Dean of Law School .... Mr. Myron R. STEEVES
35 Dean of Students TEDS & TGS .... Mr. Felix THEONUGRAHA
42 Chaplain .... Rev. Scott SAMUELSON
07 Director Undergraduate Admissions .... Mr. Aaron MAHL
07 Director TEDS & TGS Admissions .... Mr. Jared CHRISTIENSEN
19 Director of Security Services .... Mr. Bob TOPOREK
96 Director of Facilities .... Mr. Ryan HUST
15 Director of Human Resources .... Mr. Kevin MOON
06 Assoc University Registrar .... Mr. David SKINNER
37 Director of Financial Aid .... Ms. Patricia COLES
36 Director of Career Services .... Ms. Jan VICTOR
36 Director of Placement .... Dr. Eugene SWANSTROM
08 University Librarian .... Dr. Robert H. KRAPOHL
29 Director of Alumni .... Mr. Ryan L. FINNELLY
27 Director of Publications .... Mr. Chris DONOTO
38 Director of Counseling Center .... Ms. Cathy CONWAY
28 Director of Ethnic Diversity .... Mr. Orlando FELICIANO
92 Director of Honors Program .... Vacant
35 Director of Student Activities .... Ms. Heather CORDERO
85 International Student Coordinator .... Ms. Kate REED
39 Housing Coordinator .... Mrs. Amy HORTON

Triton College (A)

2000 Fifth Avenue, River Grove IL 60171-1995
County: Cook   FICE Identification: 001773
Unit ID: 149532
Telephone: (708) 456-0300   Carnegie Class: Assoc/Pub-S-SC
FAX Number: (708) 583-3112   Calendar System: Semester
URL: www.triton.edu
Established: 1964   Annual Undergrad Tuition & Fees (In-District): $3,090
Enrollment: 15,024   Coed
Affiliation or Control: Local   IRS Status: 501(c)3
Highest Offering: Associate Degree
Program: Occupational; 2-Year Principally Bachelor's Creditable; Business Emphasis
Accreditation: NH, ADNUR, DMS, NMT, RAD, SURGT

01 President .... Dr. Patricia GRANADOS
10 Vice President Business Services .... Mr. Sean SULLIVAN
05 VP Student and Academic Affairs .... Dr. Douglas OLSON
101 Secretary for Brd of Trustees .... Ms. Susan PAGE
100 Chief of Staff .... Ms. Lindsey WESTLEY
13 Assoc Vice Pres Information Systems .... Mr. Michael GARRITY
21 Assoc VP Business Operations .... Mr. Kevin KENNEDY
18 Assoc VP Facilities .... Mr. John LAMBRECHT
20 Assoc Vice Pres Academic Affairs .... Ms. Cheryl ANTONICH
35 Dean of Student Services .... Mr. Corey WILLIAMS
84 Dean of Enrollment Services .... Dr. Amanda TURNER
37 Assoc Dean of Financial Aid .... Ms. Patricia ZINGA
21 Director Finance .... Mr. James REYNOLDS
45 Director Planning & Accreditation .... Ms. Pamela PERRY
25 Director of Grants Development .... Dr. Sherry BURLINGAME
88 Director Teaching & Learning .... Dr. Mary Ann TOBIN
26 Executive Director Marketing .... Mr. Sam TOLIA
07 Director Admissions Services .... Ms. Izabela ZURAWSKA
19 Chief of Police .... Mr. Jeffrey SARGENT
102 Director Triton Foundation .... Vacant
09 Dir Institutional Effectiveness .... Ms. Mary MCLEAN-SCANLON
14 Sr Data and System Admin .... Mr. Robert HAUSKNECHT
91 Director Programming Services .... Vacant
102 Director Corporate Outreach .... Ms. Susan SMEDINGHOFF
90 Manager Online Technology .... Vacant
88 Public Relations Associate .... Ms. Brenda JONES WATKINS
72 Instructional Technologist .... Ms. Marie-Ange ZICHER
49 Dean Arts & Sciences .... Mr. Ricardo SEGOVIA
51 Dean of Continuing Education .... Mr. Paul JENSEN
76 Dean Health Careers & Pub Svc Pro .... Dr. Sue COLLINS
55 Dean of Adult Education .... Dr. Virginia CABASA-HESS
09 Dean of Academic Success .... Dr. Deborah BANESS KING
49 Asst Dean of Arts & Sciences .... Mr. Gabriel GUZMAN
51 Asst Dean Continuing Education ..Ms. Colleen MAZZUCA-PESCE
29 Director Alumni Relations .... Ms. Lisa SCALESSI
50 Dean Business & Technology .... Vacant
100 Coord for Brd of Trustees/Exec Asst .... Vacant
32 AVP of Student Affairs .... Dr. Quincy MARTIN
45 AVP of Strategic Planning .... Ms. Mary Rita MOORE
13 VP of Technology & Innovation .... Mr. Humberto ESPINO

University of Chicago (B)

5801 S Ellis Avenue, Chicago IL 60637-1496
County: Cook   FICE Identification: 001774
Unit ID: 144050
Telephone: (773) 702-1234   Carnegie Class: RU/VH
FAX Number: N/A   Calendar System: Quarter
URL: www.uchicago.edu
Established: 1891   Annual Undergrad Tuition & Fees: $46,386
Enrollment: 15,539   Coed
Affiliation or Control: Independent Non-Profit   IRS Status: 501(c)3
Highest Offering: Doctorate
Program: Liberal Arts And General; Teacher Preparatory; Professional
Accreditation: NH, BUS, IPSY, LAW, MED, SW, THEOL

01 President .... Mr. Robert J. ZIMMER
05 Provost .... Mr. Thomas F. ROSENBAUM
03 Executive Vice President .... Mr. David A. GREENE
10 VP of Administration/CFO .... Mr. Nim CHINNIAH
86 Vice President for Civic Engagement .... Mr. Derek DOUGLAS
101 VP/Sec of the University .... Mr. David FITHIAN
46 VP for Research/Argonne Natl Lab .... Mr. Donald LEVY
17 EVP for Medical Affairs/Dean of BSD .... Dr. Kenneth POLONSKY
30 VP for Alumni Rel & Development .... Mr. Ken MANOTTI
43 Vice President & General Counsel .... Ms. Beth A. HARRIS
88 Vice Pres/Chief Investment Officer .... Mr. Mark A. SCHMID
88 VP for Global Engagement .... Mr. Ian H. SOLOMON
84 VP/Dean Col Enroll/Financial Aid .... Mr. James NONDORF
42 Dean Rockefeller Memorial Chapel .... Ms. Elizabeth DAVENPORT
32 VP/Campus Life Student Services .... Ms. Karen W. COLEMAN
26 Vice Pres for Communications .... Ms. Julie PETERSON
88 Assoc VP University Architect .... Mr. Steve WIESENTHAL
16 VP and Chief HR Officer .... Mr. Richard F. IORIO
09 Assoc VP Rsrch/Dir Rsrch Admin .... Ms. Carol ZUICHES
21 Exec Director of Risk Management .... Mr. Luke FIGORA
31 Vice President for Civic Engagement .... Mr. Derek DOUGLAS
35 Ast VP Stdnt Life/Assoc Dean Col .... Ms. Eleanor DAUGHERTY
49 Dean of the College .... Mr. John W. BOYER
83 Dean of Social Sciences Division .... Mr. Mario SMALL
79 Dean of Humanities Division .... Ms. Martha T. ROTH
61 Dean of the Law School .... Mr. Michael H. SCHILL
88 Dean Harris Sch Public Policy .. Mr. Colm O'MUIRCHEARTAIGH
81 Dean Physical Sciences Division .... Mr. Edward W. KOLB
88 Dean of Molecular Engineering .... Mr. Matthew TIRRELL
88 Dean of the Divinity School .... Ms. Margaret MITCHELL
50 Dean of Booth School of Business .... Mr. Sunil KUMAR
51 Dean of Graham School .... Mr. Daniel SHANNON
70 Dean Social Svcs Admin .... Mr. Neil GUTERMAN
04 Assoc Provost and Budget Director .... Mr. David L. MURPHY
04 Associate Provost .... Ms. Ingrid GOULD
04 Associate Provost .... Ms. Diana JERGOVIC
88 Deputy Provost for Research .... Dr. Roy E. WEISS
20 Deputy Provost for Grad Education .... Ms. Deborah L. NELSON
88 Exec Dir/Center for Performing Arts .... Mr. William MICHEL
28 Deputy Provost for Minority Affairs .... Mr. William MCDADE
20 Deputy Provost for the Arts .... Mr. Lawrence ZBIKOWSKI
22 Assoc Provost/Affirm Action Ofcr .... Ms. Aneesah ALI
45 Assoc Provost for Planning .... Ms. Blair ARCHAMBEAU
04 Director of Admin and Operations .... Ms. Susan BOONE
20 Associate Provost .... Mr. Stephen H. GABEL
20 Associate Provost .... Ms. Mary J. HARVEY
21 AVP for Finance .... Mr. John R. KROLL
06 Registrar .... Mr. Scott CAMPBELL
37 Executive Director University Aid .... Ms. Amanda FIJAL
36 Director Career Adv & Planning Svcs .... Ms. Meredith DAW
08 Director University Library .... Ms. Judith NADLER
38 Interim Dir Stdnt Counseling Svc .... Dr. Linda M. TARTOF
38 Interim Medical Dir Stdnt Coun Svc .... Dr. David BERRIER
96 Exec Dir Payroll/Procurement .... Mr. Mark FEHLBERG

*University of Illinois University Administration (C)

506 S Wright Street, Urbana IL 61801-3689
County: Champaign   FICE Identification: 008001
Unit ID: 149587
Telephone: (217) 333-6400   Carnegie Class: N/A
FAX Number: (217) 333-5733
URL: www.uillinois.edu

01 President .... Dr. Robert A. EASTER
12 Chancellor/Vice President (Chicago) .... Dr. Paula ALLEN-MEARES
12 Chancellor/Vice President (Sprfld) .... Dr. Susan KOCH
12 Chancellor/Vice President (Urbana) .... Dr. Phyllis WISE
10 CFO/VP and Comptroller .... Mr. Walter KNORR
05 Vice Pres for Academic Affairs .... Dr. Christophe PIERRE
17 Vice Pres for Health Affairs .... Dr. Joe GARCIA
09 Vice Pres for Research .... Dr. Lawrence SCHOOK
43 University Counsel .... Mr. Thomas R. BEARROWS
86 Exec Director for Govt Relations .... Ms. Katherine LAING
26 Exec Dir for University Relations .... Mr. Thomas P. HARDY
13 Executive CIO .... Dr. Michael HITES
16 Executive Director HR .... Ms. Maureen PARKS
101 Secretary Board of Trustees/Univ .... Dr. Susan M. KIES
102 President/CEO Univ Foundation .... Dr. Thomas J. FARRELL
29 Pres/CEO Univ Alumni Association .... Mr. Loren R. TAYLOR

*University of Illinois at Chicago (D)

601 S Morgan, M/C 102, Chicago IL 60607-7128
County: Cook   FICE Identification: 001776
Unit ID: 145600
Telephone: (312) 996-7000   Carnegie Class: RU/VH
FAX Number: (312) 413-3393   Calendar System: Semester
URL: www.uic.edu
Established: 1896   Annual Undergrad Tuition & Fees (In-State): $13,410
Enrollment: 27,875   Coed
Affiliation or Control: State   IRS Status: 501(c)3
Highest Offering: Doctorate
Program: Liberal Arts And General; Teacher Preparatory; Professional
Accreditation: NH, ART, BUS, BUSA, CAHIIM, CEA, CLPSY, CS, DENT, DIETC, DIETD, ENG, ENGR, FEPAC, HSA, IPSY, MED, MIDWF, MIL, NURSE, OT, PH, PHAR, PLNG, PTA, SPAA, SW

02 Chancellor .... Dr. Paula ALLEN-MEARES
05 Vice Chancellor Acad Affs/Provost .... Dr. Lon KAUFMAN
32 Vice Chancellor Student Affairs .... Dr. Barbara HENLEY
11 Vice Chanc for Administrative Svcs .... Mr. Mark DONOVAN
46 Vice Chancellor for Research .... Dr. Mitra DUTTA
26 Exec Assoc Chanc External Affairs .... Mr. Michael REDDING
17 Assoc VP Hospital Operations .... Dr. Bryan BECKER
29 Vice President Alumni Association .... Ms. Arlene NORSYM
30 Interim Vice Chancellor Development .... Mr. Edward EWALD
84 Vice Prov Acad/Enrollment Svcs .... Mr. Kevin BROWNE
35 Assoc Vice Chanc/Dean Student Affs .... Dr. Linda DEANNA
27 Assoc Chancellor Public Affairs .... Mr. William BURTON
23 Interim Vic Pres for Health Affairs .... Dr. Jerry BAUMAN
10 Exec Asst VP Business/Finance .... Dr. Heather J. HABERAECKER
48 Dean College Arch/Arts .... Mr. Steve EVERETT
50 Dean College Business Admin .... Dr. Michael B. MIKHAIL
52 Dean College Dentistry .... Dr. Bruce GRAHAM
53 Interim Dean College of Education .... Dr. Alfred TATUM
54 Dean College Engineering .... Dr. Peter C. NELSON
76 Dean Col Applied Health Sciences .... Dr. Bo FERNHALL
58 Dean Graduate College .... Dr. Karen COLLEY
92 Dean of the Honors College .... Dr. Bette L. BOTTOMS
49 Dean Liberal Arts & Sciences .... Dr. Astrida ORLE TANTILLO
63 Dean College Medicine .... Dr. Dimitri AZAR
66 Dean College Nursing .... Dr. Terri E. WEAVER
67 Dean College Pharmacy .... Dr. Jerry BAUMAN
70 Dean College Social Work .... Dr. Creasie HAIRSTON
69 Dean School of Public Health .... Dr. Paul BRANDT-RAUF
26 Dean Urban Planning/Public Affs .... Dr. Michael A. PAGANO
43 University Counsel .... Mr. Thomas R. BEARROWS
08 University Librarian .... Ms. Mary CASE
88 Asst Univ Librarian Health Sciences . Ms. Kathryn H. CARPENTER
07 Managing Director Admissions .... Ms. Malinda LORKOVICH
41 Director Athletics .... Mr. James W. SCHMIDT
38 Director Student Counseling .... Dr. Joseph HERMES
37 Director Student Financial Aid .... Mr. Timothy OPGENORTH
09 Director of Institutional Research .... Ms. Mary LELIK
15 Director Faculty Affairs HR .... Ms. Angela L. YUDT
22 Director Access & Equity .... Ms. Caryn A. BILLS-WINDT
36 Director Career Services .... Mr. Thy NGUYEN
14 Exec Dir Acad Computer/Communica .... Ms. Cynthia E. HERRERA LINDSTROM
51 Exec Dir School Cont Studies .... Ms. Cordelia MALONEY
06 Registrar .... Mr. Robert DIXON
96 Interim Director of Purchasing .... Mr. Kevin FAIR
18 Director Operations & Maintenance .... Mr. Clarence E. BRIDGES

*University of Illinois at Springfield (E)

One University Plaza, Springfield IL 62703-5407
County: Sangamon   FICE Identification: 009333
Unit ID: 148654
Telephone: (217) 206-6600   Carnegie Class: Master's L
FAX Number: (217) 206-6511   Calendar System: Semester
URL: www.uis.edu
Established: 1969   Annual Undergrad Tuition & Fees (In-State): $9,282
Enrollment: 5,048   Coed
Affiliation or Control: State   IRS Status: 501(c)3
Highest Offering: Doctorate
Program: Liberal Arts And General; Teacher Preparatory; Professional
Accreditation: NH, BUS, CACREP, MT, SPAA, SW

02 Chancellor .... Dr. Susan KOCH
27 Assoc Chancellor/Constituent Rels .... Mr. Edward WOJCICKI
05 Vice Chancellor Acad Affs .... Ms. Lynn PARDIE
32 Vice Chanc Student Affairs .... Dr. Timothy L. BARNETT
20 Vice Chanc Undergrad Education .... Ms. Karen MORANSKI
29 Vice President Alumni Relations .... Mr. Charles SCHRAGE
30 Vice Chanc Dev/Sr VP UL Found .... Dr. Jeffrey D. LORBER
18 Asc Chanc Admin/Exec Dir Facil Svcs .... Mr. David BARROWS
22 Asc Chanc Access/Equal Opportunity .... Ms. Deanie BROWN
49 Dean College Liberal Arts/Science .... Dr. James ERMATINGER
50 Dean College Business/Management .... Dr. Ronald D. MCNEIL
80 Dean College Public Affs/Admin .... Dr. Mark WRIGHTON
53 Dean College Educ/Human Svcs .... Dr. Hanfu MI
15 Director of Human Resources .... Ms. Laura ALEXANDER
84 Director of Enrollment Management .... Vacant
43 Legal Counsel .... Dr. Mark HENSS
08 University Librarian .... Ms. Jane B. TREADWELL
26 Director Public Information .... Mr. Derek SCHNAPP
20 Associate Provost .... Mr. Aaron G. SHURES
19 Chief Campus Police Department .... Mr. Donald MITCHELL
06 Registrar .... Mr. Brian CLEVENGER
35 Director of Student Life .... Ms. Cynthia THOMPSON
41 Director of Athletics .... Ms. Kim PATE
90 Director Campus Technology Service .... Vacant
09 Director Institutional Research .... Ms. Laura DORMAN
96 Director of Purchasing .... Mr. Michael BLOECHLE
37 Director Financial Assistance .... Dr. Gerard JOSEPH
38 Director Counseling Center .... Dr. Judith SHIPP
85 Director International Programs .... Dr. Jonathan GOLDBERGBELLE
24 Assoc Prov Educational Technology .... Mr. Farokh ESLAHI
39 Director Campus Housing .... Mr. John RINGLE

*University of Illinois at Urbana-Champaign (A)

601 E John Street, Champaign IL 61820-5711
County: Champaign FICE Identification: 001775
Unit ID: 145637
Telephone: (217) 333-1000 Carnegie Class: RU/VH
FAX Number: (217) 333-9758 Calendar System: Semester
URL: www.illinois.edu
Established: 1867 Annual Undergrad Tuition & Fees (In-State): $15,258
Enrollment: 31,901 Coed
Affiliation or Control: State IRS Status: 501(c)3
Highest Offering: Doctorate
Program: Occupational; Liberal Arts And General; Teacher Preparatory; Professional
Accreditation: NH, ART, AUD, BUS, BUSA, CLPSY, COPSY, CS, DANCE, DIETD, DIETI, ENG, FOR, IPSY, JOUR, LAW, LIB, LSAR, MUS, NRPA, PCSAS, PH, PLNG, SP, SW, THEA, VET

02 Vice President & Chancellor .... Dr. Phyllis M. WISE
05 Vice Chancellor Acad Affs & Provost .... Dr. Ilesanmi ADESIDA
46 Vice Chancellor Research .... Dr. Peter E. SCHIFFER
32 Vice Chancellor Student Affairs .... Dr. C. Renee ROMANO
30 Vice Chanc for Inst Advancement .... Mr. Daniel C. PETERSON
31 Associate Chanc Public Engagement .... Dr. Pradeep KHANNA
20 Vice Provost Academic Affairs .... Dr. Barbara WILSON
88 Associate Chancellor .... Mr. Michael DELORENZO
88 Associate Chancellor .... Dr. Menah PRATT-CLARKE
26 Associate Chanc Public Affairs .... Ms. Robin KALER
04 Associate Chancellor .... Dr. Reginald ALSTON
29 Int Assoc Chanc Alumni Relations .... Vacant
15 Associate Provost Human Resources .... Ms. Elyne COLE
07 Asst Prov Enrollment Management .... Ms. Stacey KOSTELL
82 Int Assoc Provost Intl Pgms/Studies .... Dr. Wolfgang SCHLOER
21 Vice Provost Budgetary Planning .... Mr. Mike ANDRECHAK
09 Asst Provost Management Info .... Dr. Amy EDWARDS
49 Int Dean Liberal Arts & Sciences .... Dr. Brian ROSS
61 Dean Law .... Dr. Bruce SMITH
74 Dean Veterinary Medicine .... Dr. Herbert E. WHITELEY
54 Dean Engineering .... Dr. Andreas C. CANGELLARIS
47 Dean Agric/Consumer/Environ Sci .... Dr. Robert HAUSER
50 Dean Business .... Dr. Larry DEBROCK
57 Dean Fine & Applied Arts .... Dr. Edward FESER
70 Dean School of Social Work .... Dr. Wynne S. KORR
68 Dean Col Applied Health Sciences .... Dr. Tanya M. GALLAGHER
60 Dean College of Media .... Dr. Janet SLATER
58 Dean Graduate College .... Dr. Debasish DUTTA
62 Int Dean Grad Sch Library/Info Sci .... Dr. Allen H. RENEAR
53 Dean Education .... Dr. Mary KALANTZIS
63 Int Reg Dean Col Med/Urbana-Champ .... Dr. Uretz S. OLIPHANT
88 Int Dean Labor & Employment Rels .... Dr. Fritz DRASGOW
08 University Librarian & Dean .... Mr. John P. WILKIN
88 Dir Acad Aff Institute of Aviation .... Mr. Tom EMANUEL
13 Chief Information Officer .... Mr. Paul HIXSON
35 Dean of Students .... Dr. Kenneth BALLOM
56 Int Assoc Dean Extension & Outreach .... Dr. Robert HOEFT
41 Director Athletics .... Mr. Michael J. THOMAS
10 Asst Vice Pres Bus/Fin Affairs .... Ms. Ginger VELAZQUEZ
43 Campus Legal Counsel .... Mr. Scott RICE
88 Deputy CIO Information Technology .... Mr. Joseph G. GULICK
22 Dir Equal Opportunity & Access .... Dr. Menah PRATT-CLARKE
19 Director Public Safety .... Mr. Jeffrey T. CHRISTENSEN
18 Exec Director Facilities .... Mr. Allan M. STRATMAN
23 Director McKinley Health Center .... Dr. Robert D. PALINKAS
36 Director Career Services Center .... Dr. Gail ROONEY
37 Director Student Financial Aid .... Mr. Daniel R. MANN
38 Director Counseling Center .... Dr. Carla MCCOWAN
39 Director Housing Division .... Ms. Alma SEALINE
51 Int Dir Cont Educ/Public Service .... Dr. Faye LESHT
06 Int Registrar .... Mr. Rodney E. HOEWING

*University of Illinois at Chicago College of Medicine at Peoria (B)

Box 1649, Peoria IL 61656-1649
Telephone: (309) 671-3000 Identification: 770182
Accreditation: &NH

† Main campus is University of Illinois at Chicago in Chicago, IL.

*University of Illinois at Chicago College of Medicine at Rockford (C)

1601 Parkview Avenue, Rockford IL 61107
Telephone: (815) 395-0600 Identification: 770183
Accreditation: &NH

† Main campus is University of Illinois at Chicago in Chicago, IL.

*University of Illinois at Chicago College of Medicine at Urbana (D)

506 South Matthews Avenue, Urbana IL 61801
Telephone: (217) 333-5465 Identification: 770184
Accreditation: &NH

† Main campus is University of Illinois at Chicago in Chicago, IL.

University of Phoenix Chicago Campus (E)

1500 McConnor Parkway, Suite 700,
Schaumburg IL 60173-4395
Telephone: (847) 413-1922 Identification: 770205
Accreditation: &NH, ACBSP

† Main campus is University of Phoenix in Tempe, AZ.

University of St. Francis (F)

500 N Wilcox Street, Joliet IL 60435-6188
County: Will FICE Identification: 001664
Unit ID: 148584
Telephone: (815) 740-3400 Carnegie Class: Master's L
FAX Number: (815) 740-4285 Calendar System: Semester
URL: www.stfrancis.edu
Established: 1920 Annual Undergrad Tuition & Fees: $27,970
Enrollment: 3,452 Coed
Affiliation or Control: Roman Catholic IRS Status: 501(c)3
Highest Offering: Doctorate
Program: Liberal Arts And General; Teacher Preparatory; Professional
Accreditation: NH, ACBSP, NRPA, NURSE, RTT, SW, TED

01 President .... Dr. Arvid C. JOHNSON
05 Provost/VP Academic Affairs .... Dr. Frank H. PASCOE
10 VP Finance & Administration .... Ms. Elizabeth A. LAKEN
84 VP Admissions/Enrollment Svcs .... Mr. Charles M. BEUTEL
88 VP Mission Int & Ministry .... Sr. Mary Elizabeth IMLER
27 CIO .... Dr. Gerard H. KICKUL
30 Chief Advancement Officer .... Ms. Regina M. BLOCK
04 Executive Assistant to President .... Ms. Barbara S. INGOLD
26 Exec Dir Univ Rels/Pres Liaison .... Ms. Nancy A. POHLMAN
18 Exec Dir Operations & Facil Mgmt .... Mr. Mike DECMAN
21 Controller .... Ms. Michelle L. MAHONEY
49 Dean Col Arts & Sciences .... Dr. Robert KASE
50 Dean Col Business/Health Admin .... Dr. Christopher CLOTT
53 Dean Col Education .... Dr. John S. GAMBRO
66 Dean Col Nursing .... Dr. Carol J. WILSON
32 Dean of Students .... Mr. Damon N. SLOAN
29 Dir Alumni Relations .... Ms. Aubrey L. DURISH
41 Dir Athletics .... Mr. Dave LAKETA
38 Dir Counseling Services .... Mr. Carlos AQUINO
28 Dir Diversity .... Dr. Billie P. TERRELL
37 Dir Financial Aid .... Ms. Mary V. SHAW
07 Dir Undergrad Admissions .... Ms. Cynthia A. CRUZ
07 Dir Grad/Degree Completion Admiss .... Ms. Sandra L. SLOKA
07 Asst Dir Undergraduate Admissions .... Mr. Eric A. RUIZ
15 Dir Human Resources .... Mr. John D. BYRNES
09 Dir Institutional Effectiveness .... Ms. Janine M. HICKS
08 Dean Acad Tech & Library Services .... Mr. Terrance L. COTTRELL
14 Dir Network Support Services .... Mr. Mark T. SNODGRASS
39 Int Dir Residence Life .... Ms. Mollie ROCKAFELLOW
19 Dir Security .... Mr. Thomas S. URASKI
35 Dir Student Development .... Ms. Dominique A. ANNIS
42 Dir University Ministry .... Mr. Joseph T. WYSOCKI
06 Registrar .... Ms. Laura A. KOGA
23 Coordinator of Health Services .... Ms. Phyllis M. PETERSON
36 Dir Career Services .... Ms. Kelly LAPETINO
24 Head of Tech Svcs .... Ms. Gail GAWLIK
105 Web Communications Manager .... Mr. Michael PLANETA

University of Saint Mary of the Lake-Mundelein Seminary (G)

1000 E Maple Avenue, Mundelein IL 60060-1174
County: Lake FICE Identification: 001765
Unit ID: 148885
Telephone: (847) 566-6401 Carnegie Class: Spec/Faith
FAX Number: (847) 566-7330 Calendar System: Quarter
URL: www.usml.edu
Established: 1844 Annual Graduate Tuition & Fees: $22,885
Enrollment: 174 Male
Affiliation or Control: Roman Catholic IRS Status: 501(c)3
Highest Offering: Doctorate; No Undergraduates
Program: Professional; Religious Emphasis
Accreditation: THEOL

00 Chancellor .... Card. Francis GEORGE
01 Rector/President .... Rev. Robert E. BARRON
03 Vice Rector for Seminary Admin .... Rev. James PRESTA
05 Vice Rector for Academic Affairs .... Rev. Thomas A. BAIMA
73 Pres/Pontifical Faculty of Theology .... Dr. Elizabeth NAGEL
32 Vice President/Dean of Formation .... Rev. Ronald HICKS
20 Vice President & Provost .... Rev. Thomas FRANZMAN
10 Vice President for Finance .... Mr. John F. LEHOCKY
30 Vice President Inst Advancement .... Mr. Mark TERESI
18 Director of Facilities .... Mr. Clayton KALWEIT
20 Assistant Academic Dean .... Mr. Christopher MCATEE
73 Director Pre-Theology Program .... Rev. August J. BELAUSKAS
08 Library Director .... Mrs. Lorraine OLLEY
06 Registrar .... Mrs. Mary Ann ULZ
88 Director of Pastoral Internships .... Rev. Martin BARNUM
88 Director of Liturgy .... Rev. Ronald T. KUNKEL
88 Director of Spiritual Life .... Rev. Brian WELTER
39 Director of Seminary Residence Hall .... Rev. Christopher HOUSE
14 Director Computer Services .... Mr. Eric ALBERT
85 Director of International Students .... Rev. Martin BARNUM

VanderCook College of Music (H)

3140 S Federal Street, Chicago IL 60616-3731
County: Cook FICE Identification: 001778
Unit ID: 149639
Telephone: (312) 225-6288 Carnegie Class: Spec/Arts
FAX Number: (312) 225-5211 Calendar System: Semester
URL: www.vandercook.edu
Established: 1909 Annual Undergrad Tuition & Fees: $24,890
Enrollment: 227 Coed
Affiliation or Control: Independent Non-Profit IRS Status: 501(c)3
Highest Offering: Master's
Program: Teacher Preparatory; Professional; Music Emphasis
Accreditation: NH, MUS

01 President .... Dr. Charles T. MENGHINI
06 Registrar .... Mrs. Carolyn BERGHOFF
08 Head Librarian .... Mr. Robert DELAND
05 Dean of Undergraduate Studies .... Ms. Stacey L. DOLAN
58 Dean of Graduate Studies .... Ms. Ruth RHODES
07 Director of Admissions & Retention .... Ms. Amy L. LENTING
10 Controller .... Ms. Diane KELLY
37 Director of Financial Aid .... Ms. Sirena COVINGTON
13 Director Information Technologies .... Mr. Rick MALIK
04 President's Assistant .... Ms. Cindy TOVAR
51 Director of Continuing Education .... Mr. Rick PALESE

Vatterott College-Quincy (I)

3609 North Marx Drive, Quincy IL 62305
County: Adams FICE Identification: 020693
Unit ID: 148140
Telephone: (217) 224-0600 Carnegie Class: Assoc/PrivFP
FAX Number: (217) 223-6771 Calendar System: Other
URL: www.vatterott-college.edu
Established: 1995 Annual Undergrad Tuition & Fees: $11,965
Enrollment: 206 Coed
Affiliation or Control: Proprietary IRS Status: Proprietary
Highest Offering: Associate Degree
Program: Occupational; 2-Year Principally Bachelor's Creditable
Accreditation: ACCSC

01 CEO & President .... Ms. Pam BELL
10 Chief Financial Officer .... Mr. Dennis BEAVERS
05 Vice President Academic Affairs .... Mr. Brandon SHEDRON
30 VP Regulatory Affs/Strategic Devel .... Mr. Aaron LACEY
43 General Counsel/Chief Administrator .... Mr. Scott CASANOVER
12 Campus Director .... Mr. Tom LOCKETT

Waubonsee Community College (J)

Route 47 at Waubonsee Drive,
Sugar Grove IL 60554-9799
County: Kane FICE Identification: 006931
Unit ID: 149727
Telephone: (630) 466-7900 Carnegie Class: Assoc/Pub-S-SC
FAX Number: (630) 466-7550 Calendar System: Semester
URL: www.waubonsee.edu
Established: 1966 Annual Undergrad Tuition & Fees (In-District): $2,448
Enrollment: 11,146 Coed
Affiliation or Control: Local IRS Status: 501(c)3
Highest Offering: Associate Degree
Program: Occupational; 2-Year Principally Bachelor's Creditable
Accreditation: NH, MAC, SURGT

01 President .... Dr. Christine J. SOBEK
05 Exec VP Educ Affs/Chief Lrng Ofcr .... Dr. Deborah F. LOVINGOOD
10 Exec VP Finance & Operations .... Mr. David QUILLEN
09 VP Quality/Strategic Development .... Dr. Karen STEWART
32 Vice Pres of Student Development .... Dr. Melinda L. JAMES
21 Asst Vice President of Finance .... Ms. Darla S. CARDINE
106 Asst VP Onlne Lrng/Instruction Sup .... Ms. Renee TONIONI
88 Asst VP Workforce Sol/Comm Learning .... Mr. Gary KECSKÉS
13 Chief Information Officer .... Mr. Terence FELTON
16 Exec Director Human Resources .... Ms. Michele NEEDHAM
26 Exec Dir Marketing/Communications .... Mr. Jeff NOBLITT
76 Dean Health Professions/Public Svc .... Dr. Jess TOUSSAINT
83 Dean Social Sciences/Edu/World Lang .... Dr. William MARZANO
79 Dean Communic/Humanities/Fine Arts .... Ms. Cynthia SPARR
88 Dean Development Ed/Coll Read .... dr. Medea RAMBISH
81 Dean Mathematics/Sciences .... Ms. Mary Edith BUTLER
35 Dean Counseling/Student Support .... Ms. Kelli SINCLAIR
56 Dean Adult Education .... Ms. Jeri L. DIXON
30 Director Fund Development .... Ms. Katharine RICHARDS
50 Dean Business/Career Technologies .... Ms. Suzette MURRAY
103 Dean Workforce Development .... Ms. Lesa NORRIS
84 Dean Enrollment Mgmt .... Ms. Faith LASHURE
31 Dean Community Education .... Mr. Douglas L. GRIER
04 Senior Executive to President .... Ms. Kimberly CAPONI
37 Director Student Fin Aid Services .... Dr. Charles BOUDREAU
09 Dir Institutional Effectiveness .... Dr. Stacey RANDALL
28 Dir Governmental/Multicultural Affa .... Ms. Lourdes BLACKSMITH
19 Dir Emergency/Preparednes/Safety .... Mr. John WU
88 Dir Accounting/Business Services .... Mr. Bruce HARTMANN
18 Director Campus Operations .... Mr. Dale WILLERTH
06 Registrar .... Mr. Marc DALE

Western Illinois University (K)

1 University Circle, Macomb IL 61455-1390
County: McDonough FICE Identification: 001780
Unit ID: 149772
Telephone: (309) 298-1414 Carnegie Class: Master's L
FAX Number: (309) 298-2400 Calendar System: Semester
URL: www.wiu.edu
Established: 1899 Annual Undergrad Tuition & Fees (In-State): $10,940
Enrollment: 12,205 Coed
Affiliation or Control: State IRS Status: 501(c)3
Highest Offering: Doctorate
Program: Liberal Arts And General; Teacher Preparatory

Accreditation: NH, ART, BUS, BUSA, CACREP, CEA, DIETD, ENG, MUS, NAIT, NRPA, NURSE, SP, SW, TED, THEA

01 President .... Dr. Jack THOMAS
05 Provost/Vice Pres Academic Affairs .... Dr. Kenneth HAWKINSON
20 Assoc Provost/Assoc VP Acad Affs .... Dr. Kathleen NEUMANN
20 Asst VP for Academic Affairs .... Dr. Ronald WILLIAMS
20 Int Assoc Provost/Undergrad & Grad .... Dr. Nancy P. PARSONS
11 VP Administrative Services .... Ms. Julie DEWEES
32 Vice President Student Services .... Dr. Gary M. BILLER
26 Vice Pres Advancement/Public Svcs .... Mr. Bradley BAINTER
29 Director Alumni Programs .... Ms. Amy SPELMAN
35 Assoc VP Student Support Svcs .... Mr. W. Earl BRACEY
39 Assoc Vice Pres Student Services .... Mr. John BIERNBAUM
45 VP for QC & Planning .... Dr. Joseph RIVES
86 Asst to Pres Government Relations .... Ms. Jeanette MALAFA
49 Dean College Arts/ Sciences .... Dr. Susan MARTINELLI-FERNANDEZ
50 Dean College Business/Technology .... Dr. Thomas L. EREKSON
53 Dean College Ed & Human Svcs .... Dr. Sterling SADDLER
57 Dean Fine Arts & Comm .... Mr. William T. CLOW
08 Dean University Libraries .... Dr. Michael LORENZEN
92 Dir Illinois Centennial Honors Col .... Dr. Richard J. HARDY
64 Director School of Music .... Dr. Bart SHANKLIN
06 Registrar .... Dr. Angela LYNN
21 Director Business Services .... Ms. Dana BIERNBAUM
13 Dir Admin Information Mgmt Systems .... Ms. Brenda PARKS
90 Director of University Technology .... Mr. Daniel A. ROMANO
27 Director University Relations .... Ms. Darcie R. SHINBERGER
09 Director Inst Research & Planning .... Ms. Rhonda K. KLINE
22 Director Equal Opportunity & Access .... Ms. Andrea HENDERSON
37 Director Financial Aid .... Mr. Robert ANDERSEN
36 Director Placement .... Mr. Martin J. KRAL
15 Director Human Resources .... Ms. Pamela L. BOWMAN
18 Director Physical Plant .... Mr. Scott A. COKER
19 Director Public Safety .... Mr. Scott HARRIS
23 Director Health Center .... Ms. Mary M. HARRIS
31 Dir Distance Learning and Outreach .... Dr. Richard CARTER
40 Director University Bookstore .... Mr. Jude KIAH
41 Interim Director Athletics .... Ms. Lisa MELZ-JENNINGS
102 Director WIU Foundation .... Mr. Bradley BAINTER
30 Director of Development .... Vacant
07 Director Admissions .... Dr. Andrew BORST
38 Director Student Counseling .... Mr. James E. DITULIO
96 Director of Purchasing .... Ms. Dana BIERNBAUM
85 Dir Center International Studies .... Dr. Richard CARTER

Western Illinois University Quad Cities (A)

3300 River Drive, Moline IL 61265
Telephone: (309) 762-9481 Identification: 770100
Accreditation: &NH

† Main campus is Western Illinois University in Macomb, IL.

Westwood College-Chicago Loop (B)

1 North State Street, Suite 1000, Chicago IL 60602
Telephone: (312) 739-0850 Identification: 666424
Accreditation: ACICS

† Main campus is Westwood College - Los Angeles Campus in Los Angeles, CA.

Westwood College-DuPage (C)

7155 Janes Avenue, Woodridge IL 60517-2321
County: DuPage FICE Identification: 030792
Unit ID: 406194
Telephone: (866) 721-7646 Carnegie Class: Bac/Diverse
FAX Number: (630) 963-1420 Calendar System: Quarter
URL: www.westwood.edu
Established: Annual Undergrad Tuition & Fees: $25,852
Enrollment: 273 Coed
Affiliation or Control: Proprietary IRS Status: Proprietary
Highest Offering: Baccalaureate
Program: Occupational; Liberal Arts And General
Accreditation: ACICS

01 Campus President .... Jeff HILL
05 Campus Academic Dean .... Jennifer SHARP
11 Director of Campus Operations .... Diana GARCIA
07 Director of Admissions .... Vacant
36 Assistant Director of Career Svcs .... Lizzie HARRINGTON
37 Director of Student Finance .... Pertrina BRIGGS

Westwood College-O'Hare Airport (D)

8501 W Higgins Road, Suite 100, Chicago IL 60631-2814
County: Cook FICE Identification: 023139
Unit ID: 178226
Telephone: (773) 380-6800 Carnegie Class: Bac/Diverse
FAX Number: (773) 380-6820 Calendar System: Other
URL: www.westwood.edu
Established: 2000 Annual Undergrad Tuition & Fees: $13,950
Enrollment: 333 Coed
Affiliation or Control: Proprietary IRS Status: Proprietary
Highest Offering: Baccalaureate
Program: Occupational; 2-Year Principally Bachelor's Creditable; Professional; Technical Emphasis
Accreditation: ACICS

01 President .... Ms. Deann FITZGERALD
05 Academic Dean .... Dr. Ellen CROWE
32 Assistant Director of Student Svcs .... Vacant
10 Director of Campus Operations .... Ms. Zena WILLIAMS
07 Director of Admissions .... Mr. Lou BELLSOM
36 Director of Career Services .... Ms. Hope GREEN
37 Director of Student Finance .... Ms. Tracy WALKER

Westwood College-River Oaks (E)

96 River Oaks Center Drive, Dept 45, Calumet City IL 60409-5555
Telephone: (708) 832-1988 Identification: 666440
Accreditation: ACICS

† Main campus is Westwood College - Los Angeles Campus in Los Angeles, CA.

Wheaton College (F)

501 College Avenue, Wheaton IL 60187-5593
County: DuPage FICE Identification: 001781
Unit ID: 149781
Telephone: (630) 752-5000 Carnegie Class: Bac/A&S
FAX Number: (630) 752-5555 Calendar System: Semester
URL: www.wheaton.edu
Established: 1860 Annual Undergrad Tuition & Fees: $30,880
Enrollment: 3,034 Coed
Affiliation or Control: Independent Non-Profit IRS Status: 501(c)3
Highest Offering: Doctorate
Program: Liberal Arts And General; Teacher Preparatory; Professional
Accreditation: NH, CLPSY, MUS, TED

01 President .... Dr. Philip G. RYKEN
05 Provost .... Dr. Stanton L. JONES
03 Vice President for Finance .... Mr. Dale A. KEMP
32 Vice President Student Development .... Mr. Paul O. CHELSEN
30 Vice Pres Advancement/Alumni Rels .... Dr. R. Mark DILLON
04 Exec Asst to the President .... Miss Marilee A. MELVIN
58 Acting Dean of the Graduate School .... Dr. Nicholas PERRIN
79 Dean Humanities/Theol Studies .... Dr. Jill P. BAUMGAERTNER
49 Dean Conservatory/Arts & Comm .... Dr. Michael WILDER
83 Dean Natural & Social Sciences .... Dr. Dorothy F. CHAPPELL
104 Dean Global & Exper Learning .... Dr. Laura M. MONTGOMERY
09 Dean Information and Technology .... Dr. Gary N. LARSON
35 Dean of Student Engagement .... Dr. Steve IVESTER
06 Registrar .... Mrs. Peggy KING
08 College Librarian .... Mrs. Lisa T. RICHMOND
20 Director Billy Graham Center .... Dr. Lon J. ALLISON
21 Auxilary Services Director .... Mr. Tony DAWSON
21 Senior Dir of Financial Operations .... Mr. Patrick T. BROOKE
29 Director of Alumni Relations .... Ms. Cindra STACKHOUSE TAETZCH
24 Director Academic Media & Tech .... Mr. J. R. SMITH
36 Director of Career Services .... Mrs. Ita FISCHER
16 Director of Human Resources .... Mrs. Karen TUCKER
13 Director of Computing Services .... Mr. Lowell W. BALLARD
07 Director Undergraduate Admissions .... Ms. Shawn B. LEFTWICH
07 Director Graduate Admissions .... Mr. Dusty DI SANTO
37 Director of Student Financial Aid .... Ms. Karen BELLING
41 Director of Athletics .... Ms. Julie DAVIS
39 Associate Dean of Residence Life .... Mr. Justin HETH
38 Director of Counseling .... Dr. Doug B. DEMERCHANT
42 Chaplain .... Dr. Stephen B. KELLOUGH
23 Director of Student Health Services .... Ms. Britt BLACK
26 Director of Media Relations .... Ms. LaTonya TAYLOR
40 Manager of Bookstore .... Ms. Jennifer HAMPTON
18 Director of Physical Plant .... Mr. James M. JOHNSON
19 Chief of Public Safety .... Mr. Robert F. NORRIS
26 Director Marketing Communications .... Ms. Kimberly MEDAGLIA
88 Editor & Director of Special Proj .... Mrs. Georgia DOUGLASS
93 Director Multicultural Development .... Mr. Rodney K. SISCO
96 Director of Purchasing .... Mr. Gregory S. DOTY
88 Director Risk Management .... Mr. Daniel CLARK

Worsham College of Mortuary Science (G)

495 Northgate Parkway, Wheeling IL 60090-2646
County: Cook FICE Identification: 001783
Unit ID: 369455
Telephone: (847) 808-8444 Carnegie Class: Assoc/PrivFP
FAX Number: (847) 808-8493 Calendar System: Quarter
URL: www.worshamcollege.com
Established: 1911 Annual Undergrad Tuition & Fees: $20,700
Enrollment: 100 Coed
Affiliation or Control: Proprietary IRS Status: Proprietary
Highest Offering: Associate Degree
Program: Occupational
Accreditation: FUSER

01 Director .... Ms. Stephanie J. KANN

Zarem/Golde ORT Technical Institute (H)

5440 W. Fargo Avenue, Skokie IL 60077
County: Cook FICE Identification: 041184
Unit ID: 393180
Telephone: (847) 324-5588 Carnegie Class: Assoc/PrivNFP
FAX Number: (847) 324-5580 Calendar System: Other
URL: www.chicagotrainingschool.com
Established: 1991 Annual Undergrad Tuition & Fees: $5,550
Enrollment: 500 Coed
Affiliation or Control: Independent Non-Profit IRS Status: 501(c)3
Highest Offering: Associate Degree
Program: Occupational; 2-Year Principally Bachelor's Creditable; Nursing Emphasis
Accreditation: CNCE

01 Director .... Marina CHUDNOVSKY

INDIANA

American College of Education (I)

101 West Ohio St., Suite 1200, Indianapolis IN 46204
County: Marion Identification: 666242
Unit ID: 449889
Telephone: (800) 280-0307 Carnegie Class: Spec/Other
FAX Number: (317) 829-9401 Calendar System: Semester
URL: www.ace.edu
Established: 2005 Annual Graduate Tuition & Fees: $6,950
Enrollment: 3,410 Coed
Affiliation or Control: Proprietary IRS Status: Proprietary
Highest Offering: Doctorate; No Undergraduates
Program: Teacher Preparatory
Accreditation: NH, TEAC

01 Interim President .... Dr. Shawntel D. LANDRY
05 Associate Provost .... Dr. Shawntel D. LANDRY
10 Vice President Regulatory Affairs .... Ms. Amber YING
26 Sr VP Marketing and Enrollment .... Mr. Dan HOLESTINE

Anabaptist Mennonite Biblical Seminary (J)

3003 Benham Avenue, Elkhart IN 46517-1999
County: Elkhart FICE Identification: 001823
Unit ID: 151865
Telephone: (574) 295-3726 Carnegie Class: Spec/Faith
FAX Number: (574) 295-0092 Calendar System: 4/1/4
URL: www.ambs.edu
Established: 1946 Annual Graduate Tuition & Fees: $14,190
Enrollment: 104 Coed
Affiliation or Control: Mennonite Church IRS Status: 501(c)3
Highest Offering: Master's; No Undergraduates
Program: Professional
Accreditation: NH, THEOL

01 President .... Dr. Sara W. SHENK
05 Academic Dean .... Dr. Rebecca SLOUGH
11 Administrative Vice President .... Mr. Ron RINGENBERG
30 Director of Development .... Ms. Missy K. SCHROCK
10 Chief Financial Officer .... Mr. Jeff MILLER
06 Registrar .... Mr. Scott JANZEN
08 Librarian .... Ms. Eileen SANER
84 Director of Enrollment Services .... Mr. Bob ROSA
73 Director of Inst Mennonite Studies .... Dr. Mary H. SCHERTZ

Ancilla College (K)

PO Box 1, Donaldson IN 46513-0001
County: Marshall FICE Identification: 001784
Unit ID: 150048
Telephone: (574) 936-8898 Carnegie Class: Assoc/PrivNFP
FAX Number: (574) 935-1773 Calendar System: Semester
URL: www.ancilla.edu
Established: 1937 Annual Undergrad Tuition & Fees: $13,000
Enrollment: 420 Coed
Affiliation or Control: Roman Catholic IRS Status: 501(c)3
Highest Offering: Associate Degree
Program: 2-Year Principally Bachelor's Creditable
Accreditation: NH

01 President .... Dr. Ron MAY
04 Assistant to the President .... Ms. Diana CALDWELL
05 Dean of Academic & Student Services .... Dr. Joanna BLOUNT
10 Exec Director Finance & Admin .... Mr. Mike BROWN
30 Exec Dir of Institutional Advance .... Mr. Todd ZELTWANGER
07 Interim Exec Dir of Admissions .... Mr. Eric WIGNALL
42 Coord Mission Integration .... Sr. Carleen WRASMAN, PHJC
21 Director of Business Affairs .... Mr. Raymond GIRRES
37 Director of Financial Aid .... Mrs. Katherine MILLS
41 Athletic Director .... Mr. Robert REESE
30 Assoc Dir Inst Advancement/Alumni .... Mr. Thomas SIBAL
13 Director of Information Technology .... Mr. John LINBACK
09 Dir Inst Research/Assessment .... Vacant
18 Chief Facilities/Physical Plant .... Mr. Tom NOWAK
32 Director Student Development .... Mr. Jim CAWTHON
06 Interim Registrar .... Vacant
40 Bookstore Manager .... Ms. Nena HASKINS
08 Librarian .... Ms. Cassaundra BASH
17 Director Nursing & Health Science .... Ms. Ann FITZGERALD

Anderson University (L)

1100 E Fifth Street, Anderson IN 46012-3495
County: Madison FICE Identification: 001785
Unit ID: 150066
Telephone: (765) 649-9071 Carnegie Class: Master's L
FAX Number: (765) 641-3851 Calendar System: Semester
URL: www.anderson.edu
Established: 1917 Annual Undergrad Tuition & Fees: $35,230
Enrollment: 2,516 Coed

Affiliation or Control: Church Of God IRS Status: 501(c)3
Highest Offering: Doctorate
Program: Liberal Arts And General; Teacher Preparatory; Professional
Accreditation: NH, ACBSP, MUS, NURSE, SW, TED, THEOL

01 President Dr. James L. EDWARDS
05 Provost Dr. Marie S. MORRIS
10 Vice President Finance/Treasurer Mrs. Dana S. STUART
30 Vice President for Advancement Mr. Robert L. COFFMAN
32 VP Student Affairs Dr. Brent A. BAKER
73 Dean School of Theology Dr. David L. SEBASTIAN
79 Dean College of the Arts Dr. Jeffrey E. WRIGHT
81 Dean College of Science/Humanities Dr. D. Blake JANUTOLO
50 Dean Falls School of Business Dr. Terry C. TRUITT
42 Campus Pastor Rev. J. Todd FAULKNER
06 University Registrar Mr. Arthur J. LEAK
26 Exec Director for Advancement Mr. Tom S. BRUCE
08 Director of Libraries Dr. Janet L. BREWER
07 Director of Admissions Mr. Joe M. DAVIS
21 Assistant Treasurer/Controller Mrs. Vanessa J. TIJERINA
36 Dir Career Development Mrs. Laurie L. JUDGE
14 Director of Info Technology Svcs Mr. Michael A. TUCKER
37 Student Financial Services Mr. Kenneth F. NIEMAN
27 Dir Univ Communications/Cmty Rels Mr. Chris J. WILLIAMS
18 Exec Dir Facilities & Property Mgmt Mr. Joseph M. ROYER
16 Director of Human Resources Mrs. Denise A T. KRIEBEL
19 Director Police & Security Services Mr. Walter L. SMITH
24 Director of Ctr for Educ Technology Mr. Shelby D. CANTLEY
85 Dean Intercultural Engagement Dr. Aleza D. BEVERLY
40 Bookstore Manager Mr. Dustin MARTIN
41 Athletic Director Ms. Marcie J. TAYLOR
38 Director Counseling Services Ms. Christal R. HELVERING
29 Director of Alumni Relations Mr. Benjamin A. DAVIS
51 Director Department Adult Studies Mrs. Ellen E. DANIELS

The Art Institute of Indianapolis (A)

3500 Depauw Boulevard Suite 1010,
Indianapolis IN 46268
Telephone: (317) 613-4800 Identification: 666247
Accreditation: ACICS

† Main campus is The Art Institute of Phoenix in Phoenix, AZ.

Ball State University (B)

2000 W University Avenue, Muncie IN 47306-1099
County: Delaware FICE Identification: 001786
Unit ID: 150136
Telephone: (765) 289-1241 Carnegie Class: RU/H
FAX Number: (765) 285-1461 Calendar System: Semester
URL: www.bsu.edu
Established: 1918 Annual Undergrad Tuition & Fees (In-State): $9,160
Enrollment: 21,053 Coed
Affiliation or Control: State IRS Status: 501(c)3
Highest Offering: Doctorate
Program: Occupational; Liberal Arts And General; Teacher Preparatory; Professional
Accreditation: NH, AAFCS, ART, AUD, BUS, BUSA, CACREP, CEA, CIDA, CONST, COPSY, CORE, DANCE, DIETD, DIETI, ENGT, IPSY, JOUR, LSAR, MUS, NURSE, PLNG, RAD, SCPSY, SP, SW, TED, THEA

01 President Dr. Jo Ann M. GORA
05 Provost/Vice Pres Academic Affs Dr. Terry KING
84 VP Marketing/Comm/Enroll Mgmt Mr. Tom TAYLOR
10 VP Business Affairs & Treasurer Dr. Randy B. HOWARD
30 Vice Pres University Advancement Mr. Hudson AKIN
13 VP for Information Technology Mr. Philip C. REPP
32 VP Student Affairs/Dean of Students Dr. Kay BALES
41 Dir Intercollegiate Athletics Mr. Bill SCHOLL
43 VP & General Counsel Ms. Sali K. FALLING
21 Assoc VP Business/Aux Svcs Ms. Leisa JULIAN
86 Assoc VP Governmental Relations Ms. Gretchen GUTMAN
21 Assoc VP Finance/Asst Treasurer Mr. Bernard HANNON
85 Exec Director International Pgms Mr. Imara V. DAWSON
20 Assoc Provost/Dean Univ College Dr. Marilyn M. BUCK
18 Assoc VP Facilities Planning/Mgmt Mr. Kevin S. KENYON
07 Director Admissions & Orientation Mr. Christopher T. MUNCHEL
32 Asc VP Student Affairs/Dir Housing Dr. Alan L. HARGRAVE
29 Exec Director Alumni Programs Ms. Julie STROH
26 Assoc VP Marketing & Communications Mr. Tony PROUDFOOT
38 Director Counseling/Health Services Dr. June P. PAYNE
14 Asst VP IT for Strategic/Fiscal Mgt Mr. Donald (Jr.) KING
88 Dir Unified Techonology Support Mr. Dan LUTZ
36 Director Career Center Mr. Jim MCATEE
37 Director Scholarships/Financial Aid Dr. John MCPHERSON
06 Reg/Dir Registration/Acad Pgms Mrs. Nancy L. CRONK
09 Int Dir Inst Effectiveness Mrs. Andrea INGLE
30 Exec Director Univ Development Vacant
96 Director of Purchasing Services Mr. Roger HASSENZAHL
24 Director of Teleplex Mr. William B. CAHOE
88 Asst to VP/Coord Title IX Mrs. Katie SLABAUGH
25 Director Contracts & Grants Ms. Kathy A. LUCAS
19 Director Public Safety Mr. Gene BURTON
15 Director of Human Resources Svcs Ms. Judith A. BURKE
28 Asst Provost Diversity Dr. Charlene ALEXANDER
08 Dean University Libraries Dr. Arthur W. HAFNER
57 Dean College of Fine Arts Dr. Robert A. KVAM
50 Dean Miller College of Business Dr. Rajib N. SANYAL
48 Dean College Architecture/Planning Dr. Guillermo P. VASQUEZ DE VELASCO
53 Dean of Teachers College Dr. John E. JACOBSON
58 Asc Provost/Research/Dean Grad Sch Dr. Robert J. MORRIS
49 Dean Col of Science/Humanities Dr. Michael A. MAGGIOTTO
60 Dean Col of Comm/Info/Media Mr. Roger LAVERY
72 Dean Col Applied Science/Technology Dr. Mitchell H. WHALEY
92 Dean of Honors College Dr. James S. RUEBEL
103 Assoc VP Econ Dev/Community Engage Dr. John A. FALLON, III
88 Assoc Provost Learning Initiatives Dr. Jennifer BOTT

Bethany Theological Seminary (C)

615 National Road W, Richmond IN 47374-4019
County: Wayne FICE Identification: 001637
Unit ID: 143233
Telephone: (800) 287-8822 Carnegie Class: Spec/Faith
FAX Number: (765) 983-1840 Calendar System: Semester
URL: www.bethanyseminary.edu
Established: 1905 Annual Graduate Tuition & Fees: $12,150
Enrollment: 67 Coed
Affiliation or Control: Church Of The Brethren IRS Status: 501(c)3
Highest Offering: Master's; No Undergraduates
Program: Professional
Accreditation: NH, THEOL

01 President RevDr. Jeffrey W. CARTER
05 Academic Dean Dr. Steven J. SCHWEITZER
10 Exec Dir of Student/Business Svcs Ms. Brenda J. REISH
30 Exec Dir Institutional Advancement Mr. Lowell FLORY
20 Director of Academic Services Ms. April VANLONDEN
26 Director of Communications Ms. Jennifer L. WILLIAMS
32 Director of Student Development Ms. Amy S. GALL RITCHIE
12 Exec Director Brethren Academy Ms. Julie M. HOSTETTER
88 Director Inst Ministry with Youth Mr. Russell HAITCH
07 Director of Admissions Ms. Tracy PRIMOZICH
88 Dir Peace/Cross Cultural Studies Mr. Scott HOLLAND
88 Director of the MA Program Ms. Malinda BERRY
88 Dir of Electronic Communications Mr. Enten ELLER

Bethel College (D)

1001 Bethel Circle, Mishawaka IN 46545-5509
County: Saint Joseph FICE Identification: 001787
Unit ID: 150145
Telephone: (574) 259-8511 Carnegie Class: Bac/Diverse
FAX Number: (574) 257-3326 Calendar System: Semester
URL: www.bethelcollege.edu
Established: 1947 Annual Undergrad Tuition & Fees: $24,620
Enrollment: 1,850 Coed
Affiliation or Control: Missionary Church IRS Status: 501(c)3
Highest Offering: Master's
Program: 2-Year Principally Bachelor's Creditable; Liberal Arts And General; Teacher Preparatory; Professional; Nursing Emphasis
Accreditation: NH, ADNUR, IACBE, MUS, NUR, TED

01 President Dr. Gregg A. CHENOWETH
05 VP for Academic Services Dr. Barbara K. BELLEFEUILLLE
30 VP for Development Dr. Terry A. ZEITLOW
10 VP & Chief Financial Officer Mr. Clair W. KNAPP
32 VP for Student Development Dr. Shawn M. HOLTGREN
36 Director of Student Success Dr. Joel BOEHNER
84 Asst VP for Enrollment/Marketng Mr. Randy BEACHY
13 Senior Director of IT Ms. Patti FISHER
66 Dean Division of Nursing Dr. Deborah GILLUM
81 Dean Division of Sciences Vacant
88 Director of Nontraditional Studies Mr. Dale GADD
79 Dean Humanities & Education Dr. Thomas L. VISKER
83 Dean Natural & Social Sciences Dr. Bradley D. SMITH
35 Director of Student Life Mrs. Julie BEAM
06 Registrar Mrs. Jeanne FOX
36 Director Student Enrichment Vacant
37 Director Financial Aid Mr. Guy FISHER
26 Assistant Director Marketing Mrs. Erin KINZEL
41 Director Athletics Mr. Jody MARTINEZ
08 Director Library Services Dr. Clyde ROOT
88 Director Teacher Certification Mrs. Joyce LAURENT
18 Director Physical Plant Mr. Steve YAW
09 Director Institutional Research Dr. Ray WHITEMAN
19 Director Campus Safety Mr. Paul NEEL
85 Director International Students Mrs. Emily SHERWOOD
91 Director Administrative Computing Mr. Harold RODGERS
23 Director Wellness Center Mrs. Carol BEMIS
29 Director Alumni Services Mrs. Justine LIGHTFOOT
28 Director Intercultural Development Vacant
07 Director Admissions Ms. Andrea HELMUTH
15 Director Human Resources Mr. Mike NICHOLAS

Brown Mackie College-Fort Wayne (E)

3000 E Coliseum Boulevard, Sute 100,
Fort Wayne IN 46805-1565
Telephone: (260) 484-4400 Identification: 666435
Accreditation: ACICS, MAC, OTA, PTAA, SURGT, SURTEC

† Main campus is The Art Institute of Phoenix in Phoenix, AZ.

Brown Mackie College-Indianapolis (F)

1200 N. Meridian Street, Suite 100, Indianapolis IN 46204
Telephone: (317) 554-8300 Identification: 666394
Accreditation: ACICS, OTA

† Main campus is The Art Institute of Phoenix in Phoenix, AZ.

Brown Mackie College-Merrillville (G)

1000 E 80th Place, Suite 205M, Merrillville IN 46410-5602
Telephone: (219) 769-3321 FICE Identification: 021032
Accreditation: ACICS, MAAB, OTA, SURGT

† Main campus is The Art Institute of Phoenix in Phoenix, AZ.

Brown Mackie College-Michigan City (H)

1001 E. US Highway 20, Michigan City IN 46360-7362
Telephone: (219) 877-3100 Identification: 666426
Accreditation: ACICS, MAAB, SURGT

† Main campus is The Art Institute of Phoenix in Phoenix, AZ.

Brown Mackie College-South Bend (I)

3454 Douglas Road, South Bend IN 46635
Telephone: (574) 237-0774 FICE Identification: 004583
Accreditation: ACICS, MAC, OTA, #PTAA

† Main campus is The Art Institute of Phoenix in Phoenix, AZ.

Butler University (J)

4600 Sunset Avenue, Indianapolis IN 46208-3443
County: Marion FICE Identification: 001788
Unit ID: 150163
Telephone: (317) 940-8000 Carnegie Class: Master's M
FAX Number: (317) 940-9930 Calendar System: Semester
URL: www.butler.edu
Established: 1855 Annual Undergrad Tuition & Fees: $34,368
Enrollment: 4,712 Coed
Affiliation or Control: Independent Non-Profit IRS Status: 501(c)3
Highest Offering: Doctorate
Program: Liberal Arts And General; Teacher Preparatory; Professional
Accreditation: NH, ARCPA, BUS, CACREP, DANCE, IPSY, MUS, PHAR, TED, THEA

01 President Mr. James M. DANKO
05 Provost/VP Acad Affs Dr. Kathryn MORRIS
10 Vice President for Finance Mr. Bruce E. ARICK
30 VP University Advancement Mr. D. Mark HELMUS
84 Vice Pres Enrollment Management Mr. Thomas D. WEEDE
32 Vice President of Student Affairs Dr. Levester JOHNSON
20 Assoc Provost Student Acad Affs Dr. Mary M. RAMSBOTTOM
20 Assoc Prov Faculty Affs Dr. Laura L. BEHLING
57 Dean Jordan College Fine Arts Dr. Ronald CALTABIANO
50 Dean Business Administration Dr. Chuck R. WILLIAMS
49 Dean Liberal Arts & Science Dr. Jay R. HOWARD
53 Dean Education Dr. Ena M. SHELLEY
67 Dean Pharmacy & Health Sciences Dr. Mary H. ANDRITZ
60 Dean College of Communication Dr. Gary EDGERTON
35 Dean Student Services Dr. Sally E. CLICK
35 Dean Student Life Dr. Irene E. STEVENS
38 Asst Dean & Director Counseling Ctr Dr. Keith B. MAGNUS
08 Dean of Libraries Mr. Lewis R. MILLER
29 Exec Dir Alumni/Development Pgms Ms. M. Rachel STEPHEN BURT
15 Exec Dir HR/Chief Diversity Officer Mr. Jonathan A. SMALL
88 Exec Director Clowes Memorial Hall Ms. Elise J. KUSHIGIAN
37 Director Financial Aid Ms. Melissa J. SMURDON
21 Executive Budget Director Mr. Robert J. MARCUS
26 Exec Director University Relations Ms. Marcia A. DOWELL
07 Dean of Admission Mr. Scott D. HAM
31 Director Conference/Special Events Ms. Beth A. ALEXANDER
39 Director Residence Life Ms. Karla K. CUNNINGHAM
09 Director Institutional Research Dr. Nandini RAMASWAMY
85 Director International Programs Dr. C. Montgomery BROADED
06 Registrar Ms. Sondrea S. OZOLINS
36 Director Career Services Mr. Gary R. BEAULIEU
41 Director of Athletics Mr. Barry S. COLLIER
27 Chief Information Officer Mr. Scott A. KINCAID
19 Chief of Staff/Exec Dir Pub Safety Mr. Ben D. HUNTER
21 Controller Ms. Susan M. WESTERMEYER
26 Dir Print Marketing/Communications Ms. Sally M. CUTLER
28 Director of Diversity Programs Ms. Valerie J. DAVIDSON
40 Manager Bookstore Ms. Janine L. FRAINIER
96 Manager of Purchasing Ms. Shelly S. RABIDEAU
101 Executive Assistant to the Board Dr. Carol WROBLEWSKI

Calumet College of Saint Joseph (K)

2400 New York Avenue, Whiting IN 46394-2195
County: Lake FICE Identification: 001834
Unit ID: 150172
Telephone: (219) 473-7770 Carnegie Class: Master's S
FAX Number: (219) 473-4259 Calendar System: Semester
URL: www.ccsj.edu
Established: 1951 Annual Undergrad Tuition & Fees: $15,620
Enrollment: 1,030 Coed
Affiliation or Control: Roman Catholic IRS Status: 501(c)3
Highest Offering: Master's
Program: Liberal Arts And General; Teacher Preparatory; Professional; Business Emphasis
Accreditation: NH, TED

01 President Dr. Daniel LOWERY
05 Vice President Academic Affairs Dr. Joi PATTERSON
30 Vice President for Development Vacant
15 Vice President of Human Resources Ms. Melisha HENDERSON

10 VP Business & Finance .... Ms. Lynn MISKUS
32 Assoc VP of Student Life & Retent .... Ms. Dionne JONES-MALONE
06 Registrar .... Ms. Diana FRANCIS
08 Librarian .... Ms. Marcia KEITH
09 Institutional Researcher .... Mr. Darren HENDERSON
26 Director of Marketing & Pub Rel .... Ms. Linda GAJEWSKI
41 Athletic Director .... Mr. Peter HARING
42 Director of Campus Ministry .... Br. Jerry SCHWIETERMAN
18 VP of Facilities & Technology .... Mr. Gene KESSLER
07 Director of Admissions .... Mr. Carl CUTTONE
37 Dir of Business Office & Fin Aid Op .... Ms. Gina PIRTLE
13 Director of Computer Services .... Mr. Kevin KRIEPS
105 Assoc Dir of Marketing/Webmaster .... Mr. Darren JASIENIECKI
29 Alumni Relations .... Ms. Angela HUGHES
40 Bookstore Manager .... Ms. Erren TAPIA
88 Asst to President for Development .... Mr. Michael SPICCIA

Chamberlain College of Nursing Indianapolis Campus (A)

9100 Keystone Crossing, Indianapolis IN 46240
Telephone: (317) 816-7335 Identification: 770503
Accreditation: &NH, NURSE

† Main campus is Chamberlain College of Nursing - Addison in Addison, IL.

Christian Theological Seminary (B)

1000 W. 42nd Street, Indianapolis IN 46208-3301
County: Marion FICE Identification: 001789
Unit ID: 150215
Telephone: (317) 924-1331 Carnegie Class: Spec/Faith
FAX Number: (317) 923-1961 Calendar System: Semester
URL: www.cts.edu
Established: 1925 Annual Graduate Tuition & Fees: $14,148
Enrollment: 223 Coed
Affiliation or Control: Christian Church (Disciples Of Christ)
IRS Status: 501(c)3
Highest Offering: Doctorate; No Undergraduates
Program: Professional; Religious Emphasis
Accreditation: NH, MFCD, THEOL

01 President .... Dr. Matthew M. BOULTON
05 Int Vice Pres & Co-Academic Dean .... Dr. Edwin D. APONTE
30 Vice President Development .... Ms. Melissa HICKMAN
32 Dean of Students .... Rev. Mary HARRIS
10 Chief Operating Officer .... Ms. Julie SHEWMAKER
16 Executive Admin/HR Director .... Ms. Kathleen BELL
44 Director Annual Fund .... Ms. Karen HORSMAN
21 Director of Business Affairs .... Mr. Al MIZEN
42 Chaplain .... Dr. Tercio B. JUNKER
08 Director of Library .... Vacant
06 Registrar .... Mr. Matt SCHLIMGEN
75 Director of Field Education .... Dr. William KINCAID
18 Director of Physical Plant .... Mr. Richard DAVIS
37 Director of Student Financial Aid .... Mr. Ed DETAMORE
40 Director of Bookstore .... Mrs. Sarah EVANS
27 Communications Associate .... Mr. Chris VARNAU

College of Court Reporting, Inc. (C)

111 W 10th, Suite 111, Hobart IN 46342-5969
County: Lake FICE Identification: 026158
Unit ID: 150251
Telephone: (866) 294-3974 Carnegie Class: Assoc/PrivFP
FAX Number: (219) 942-1631 Calendar System: Semester
URL: www.ccr.edu
Established: 1984 Annual Undergrad Tuition & Fees: $13,250
Enrollment: 256 Coed
Affiliation or Control: Proprietary IRS Status: Proprietary
Highest Offering: Associate Degree
Program: Occupational
Accreditation: ACICS

01 President .... Mr. Jeff T. MOODY
03 Executive Director .... Mr. Jay VETTICKAL
05 Director of Education .... Ms. Kay MOODY
07 Director of Admissions .... Ms. Nicky M. RODRIQUEZ
37 Director of Financial Aid .... Ms. Lisa MORTON
32 Director of Student Services .... Ms. Kathleen LAZART

Concordia Theological Seminary (D)

6600 N Clinton Street, Fort Wayne IN 46825-4996
County: Allen FICE Identification: 020876
Unit ID: 150288
Telephone: (260) 452-2100 Carnegie Class: Spec/Faith
FAX Number: (260) 452-2121 Calendar System: Quarter
URL: www.ctsfw.edu
Established: 1846 Annual Graduate Tuition & Fees: $26,166
Enrollment: 294 Male
Affiliation or Control: Lutheran Church - Missouri Synod
IRS Status: 501(c)3
Highest Offering: Doctorate; No Undergraduates
Program: Professional
Accreditation: NH, THEOL

01 President .... Dr. Lawrence R. RAST
05 Academic Dean .... Dr. Charles A. GIESCHEN
36 Dean Pastoral Education/ Placement .... Dr. Carl C. FICKENSCHER, II
32 Dean of Students .... Rev. Thomas P. ZIMMERMAN
10 Vice President Business Affairs .... Rev. Albert B. WINGFIELD
06 Registrar .... Mrs. Barbara A. WEGMAN
07 Director of Admissions .... Rev. John M. DREYER
08 Head Librarian .... Prof. Robert V. ROETHEMEYER

Crossroads Bible College (E)

601 N Shortridge Road, Indianapolis IN 46219-4912
County: Marion FICE Identification: 034567
Unit ID: 439613
Telephone: (317) 789-8255 Carnegie Class: Spec/Faith
FAX Number: (317) 789-8253 Calendar System: Semester
URL: www.crossroads.edu
Established: 1980 Annual Undergrad Tuition & Fees: $9,980
Enrollment: 219 Coed
Affiliation or Control: Independent Non-Profit IRS Status: 501(c)3
Highest Offering: Baccalaureate
Program: Religious Emphasis
Accreditation: BI

01 President .... Dr. A. Charles WARE
03 Executive Vice President .... Dr. John A. CRABTREE, JR.
05 Vice President Academic Affairs .... Dr. Mark ECKEL
11 Dean of Administration .... Mr. Marcus SCHRADER
84 Dean of Enrollment Management .... Mr. John CROWDER
06 Acting Registrar .... Ms. Cheryl PLOTROWSKI

DePauw University (F)

313 S Locust Street, Greencastle IN 46135-1772
County: Putnam FICE Identification: 001792
Unit ID: 150400
Telephone: (765) 658-4800 Carnegie Class: Bac/A&S
FAX Number: (765) 658-4177 Calendar System: 4/1/4
URL: www.depauw.edu
Established: 1837 Annual Undergrad Tuition & Fees: $40,640
Enrollment: 2,336 Coed
Affiliation or Control: United Methodist IRS Status: 501(c)3
Highest Offering: Baccalaureate
Program: Liberal Arts And General
Accreditation: NH, MUS

01 President .... Dr. Brian W. CASEY
04 Executive Assistant to President .... Ms. Elizabeth DEMMINGS
100 Dir of Strategic Comm .... Mr. Jonathan COFFIN
05 VP for Academic Affairs .... Dr. Larry STIMPERT
32 VP Student Life .... Dr. Cynthia BABINGTON
45 VP for Comm & Strat Initiatives .... Mr. Christopher J. WELLS
10 VP for Finance/Administration .... Mr. Bradley A. KELSHEIMER
84 VP for Admissions/Financial Aid .... Mr. Daniel L. MEYER
64 Dean of the School of Music .... Dr. Mark MCCOY
30 VP for Development .... Ms. Melanie NORTON
88 Dean of Experiential Learning .... Dr. Raj BELLANI
27 Chief Information Officer .... Ms. Carol L. SMITH
35 Dean of Campus Life .... Mr. Dorian SHAGER
06 Registrar .... Dr. Kenneth J. KIRKPATRICK
35 Director of Student Life .... Ms. Julia SUTHERLIN
20 Dean of Academic Life .... Dr. Pedar W. FOSS
16 Director of Human Resources .... Ms. Amy HAUG
37 Director of Financial Aid .... Mr. Craig A. SLAUGHTER
41 Director of Athletics .... Ms. Stevie BAKER-WATSON
29 Associate VP for Alumni Engagement .... Mr. Steven J. SETCHELL
21 Assoc VP for Finance .... Mr. Kevin S. KESSINGER
08 Director of Libraries .... Mr. Rick E. PROVINE
44 Director of Gift Planning .... Ms. Lisa MAXWELL-FRIEDEN
44 Director of Annual Giving .... Ms. Lindsay STEGMAN
19 Director of Public Safety .... Ms. Angela D. NALLY
07 Director of Admission .... Ms. Dani WEATHERFORD
96 Director of Purchasing .... Mr. Richard SHUCK
18 Director of Facilities .... Mr. Richard N. VANCE
21 Exec Director of Finance/Controller .... Mr. Keith ARCHER
35 Assoc Dean of Students .... Ms. Cara SETCHELL
20 Dean of the Faculty .... Dr. Terri BONEBRIGHT
26 Exec Director of Media Relations .... Mr. Ken OWEN
09 Director of Institutional Research .... Dr. William M. TOBIN
23 Director of Health Services .... Dr. Scott A. RIPPLE
38 Director of Student Counseling .... Dr. Bud EDWARDS
39 Director of Housing .... Mr. Greg DILLON

Earlham College and Earlham School of Religion (G)

801 National Road W, Richmond IN 47374-4095
County: Wayne FICE Identification: 001793
Unit ID: 150455
Telephone: (765) 983-1200 Carnegie Class: Bac/A&S
FAX Number: (765) 983-1304 Calendar System: Semester
URL: www.earlham.edu
Established: 1847 Annual Undergrad Tuition & Fees: $49,710
Enrollment: 1,001 Coed
Affiliation or Control: Friends IRS Status: 501(c)3
Highest Offering: Master's
Program: Liberal Arts And General; Teacher Preparatory; Professional; Religious Emphasis
Accreditation: NH, THEOL

01 President .... John David DAWSON
03 Provost .... Nelson BINGHAM
05 Vice President Academic Affairs .... Greg MAHLER
10 Vice President Business Affairs .... Sena LANDEY
30 Vice President Advancement .... Jim MCKEY
88 Vice President School of Religion .... Jay MARSHALL
31 Vice President for Community Rels .... Avis STEWART
07 VP of Enrollment & Communications .... Jonathan STROUD
32 VP Stdnt Develop/Dean of Stdnts .... Laura HUTCHINSON
44 Assoc VP for Institutional Advance .... Kim TANNER
06 Registrar .... Bonita WASHINGTON-LACEY
41 Athletic Director .... Mike BERGUM
21 Assistant VP for Business .... Dana NORTH
21 Controller .... Cathy HABSCHMIDT
88 Director Academic Support Services .... Donna KEESLING
29 Director of Alumni Relations .... Gail CLARK
42 Director of Religious Life .... Kelly BURK
36 Interim Director of Career Services .... Michelle THOMAS
14 Director of Computing Services .... Thomas STEFFES
37 Director of Financial Aid .... Robert ARNOLD
23 Director of Health Services .... Mary Ann STIENBARGER
16 Asst Director of Human Resources .... Emily STEWART
09 Director of Institutional Research .... Nelson BINGHAM
85 Director of International Programs .... Patty O'MALEY-LAMSON
18 Director of Physical Plant .... Ian SMITH
26 AVP for Marketing & Communications .... Tamara CISSNA
27 Director of Public Information .... Vacant
19 Director of Public Safety .... Tom KEARNS
08 Director of Library .... Neal BAKER
40 Bookstore Manager .... Dee Dee CUMMINGS
73 Admissions School of Religion .... Matt HISRICH
06 Registrar School of Religion .... April VANLONDEN
35 Director Student Affairs .... Rich DORNBERGER
20 Associate Academic Dean .... Amy MILLER
28 Director of Multicultural Affairs .... Trayce PETERSON
84 Director Enrollment Management .... Nancy SINEX
96 Director of Purchasing .... Alice LAFUZE

Fortis College (H)

9001 N Wesleyan Road, Indianapolis IN 46268
Telephone: (317) 808-4800 Identification: 770574
Accreditation: ACCSC, MAAB

† Main campus is Fortis College in Winter Park, FL.

Franklin College of Indiana (I)

101 Branigin Boulevard, Franklin IN 46131-2623
County: Johnson FICE Identification: 001798
Unit ID: 150604
Telephone: (317) 738-8000 Carnegie Class: Bac/Diverse
FAX Number: (317) 736-6030 Calendar System: 4/1/4
URL: www.franklincollege.edu
Established: 1834 Annual Undergrad Tuition & Fees: $27,510
Enrollment: 1,053 Coed
Affiliation or Control: American Baptist IRS Status: 501(c)3
Highest Offering: Baccalaureate
Program: Liberal Arts And General; Teacher Preparatory; Fine Arts Emphasis
Accreditation: NH, TED

01 President .... Dr. James G. MOSELEY
04 Assistant to the President .... Ms. Janet D. SCHANTZ
10 Vice President Finance .... Mr. Daniel SCHLUGE
45 Vice Pres Planning/Plant/Technology .... Mrs. Lisa FEARS
05 Vice Pres Academic Affs/Dean of Col .... Dr. David G. BRAILOW
84 Vice Pres Enrollment and Marketing .... Mr. Alan P. HILL
20 Assoc VP Acad Affs/Instl Effective .... Dr. Timothy L. GARNER
32 Dean of Students .... Mr. Ellis F. HALL
29 Dean Alumni/Student Engagement .... Mrs. Brooke A. WORLAND
06 Registrar .... Ms. Jennifer Anne DUZINSKI
18 Dir Facilities/Energy Management .... Mr. Thomas PATZ
39 Director of Residence Life .... Mr. Jacob E. KNIGHT
38 Director of Counseling .... Dr. John R. SHAFER
30 VP of Development/Alumni Engagement .... Mrs. Gail LOWRY
35 Dir Stdnt Activities/Organizations .... Ms. Keri ELLINGTON
46 Dir of Devel Research & Records .... Ms. Betsy SCHMIDT
44 Dir Advancement/Leadership Giving .... Mr. Thomas W. ARMOR
37 Director of Financial Aid .... Mrs. Elizabeth SAPPENFIELD
42 Campus Minister .... Rev. David WEATHERSPOON
41 Athletic Director .... Mr. Kerry N. PRATHER
13 Dir of Information Tech Services .... Ms. Lisa E. MAHAN
36 Dir Career Svcs/Asst Dean Students .... Mr. Kirk J. BIXLER
88 Director of Leadership Development .... Mrs. Bonnie L. PRIBUSH
104 Dir Intercultural/Off-Campus Stds .... Ms. Jennifer CATALDI
88 Director of Dining Services-Sodexo .... Mr. Les PETROFF
44 Annual Fund Director .... Mrs. Madeleine SMITH
07 Director of Admissions .... Ms. Jennifer BOSTROM
27 Director of Communications .... Ms. Deidra BAUMGARDNER
26 Director of Marketing .... Ms. Theresa LEHMAN
08 Director of the Library .... Mr. Ronald L. SCHUETZ
19 Director of Campus Security .... Mr. Steve LEONARD
105 Interim Webmaster .... Mrs. Renee KNIGHT
15 Manager of Employee Resources .... Mrs. Maureen PINNICK
22 Proj Mgr Organization Devel/Safety .... Mr. Thomas PATZ
40 Bookstore Manager (Follett) .... Ms. Yvette THOMAS
21 Business Office Manager .... Mr. Brad JONES
23 Coordinator Student Health Center .... Ms. Catherine DECLEENE
28 Coord Multicultural/Diversity Svcs .... Ms. Terri L. ROBERTS
50 Head Business/Computing/Math Div .... Mr. James C. WILLIAMS
53 Head Education Division .... Mrs. Katherine M. REMSBURG
79 Head Humanities Division .... Dr. Sara COLBURN-ALSOP
60 Head Journalism Division .... Mr. Joel CRAMER
65 Head Natural Sciences Division .... Dr. Steven K. BROWDER

83 Head Social Sciences Division ....Dr. Denise M. BAIRD
57 Head Fine Arts Division ....Mr. Robin ROBERTS

Goshen College (A)

1700 S Main Street, Goshen IN 46526-4794

County: Elkhart FICE Identification: 001799
Unit ID: 150668
Telephone: (574) 535-7000 Carnegie Class: Bac/A&S
FAX Number: (574) 535-7060 Calendar System: Semester
URL: www.goshen.edu
Established: 1894 Annual Undergrad Tuition & Fees: $28,500
Enrollment: 832 Coed
Affiliation or Control: Mennonite Church IRS Status: 501(c)3
Highest Offering: Master's
Program: Liberal Arts And General; Teacher Preparatory; Professional
Accreditation: NH, NURSE, SW, TED

01 President ....Dr. James E. BRENNEMAN
05 VP Academic Affairs/Academic Dean ....Dr. Anita K. STALTER
10 Vice President for Finance ....Mr. James L. HISTAND
30 Vice Pres Institutional Advancement ....Mr. James K. CASKEY
84 VP for Enroll Management/Marketing ...Mr. James R. TOWNSEND
28 Assc Dean for Intercultural Dev ....Dr. Rebecca HERNANDEZ
32 VP Student Life/Dean of Students ....Mr. Bill BORN
20 Associate Academic Dean ....Dr. Ross PETERSON-VEATCH
66 Director of Undergraduate Nursing ....Ms. Vicki S. KIRKTON
58 Director of Graduate Nursing ....Dr. Brenda S. SROF
70 Director of Social Work ....Dr. Jeanne M. LIECHTY
53 Director of Elementary Teacher Educ ....Dr. Kathryn MEYER REIMER
08 Librarian ....Ms. Lisa G. GUEDEA CARRENO
82 Director of International Education ....Dr. Tom J. MEYERS
88 Director of Secondary Education ....Dr. Kevin GARY
14 Director of Information Tech Svcs ....Mr. Michael SHERER
09 Director of Institutional Research ....Dr. Scott BARGE
06 Registrar ....Mr. Stan W. MILLER
37 Director Student Financial Aid ....Mr. Joel D. SHORT
26 Director of Public Relations ....Mr. Richard AGUIRRE
29 Director of Alumni/Parent Relations ....Ms. Kelli B. KING
42 Campus Minister ....Mr. Robert E. YODER
36 Director of Career Services ....Ms. Anita R. YODER
18 Director of Facilities ....Mr. Clay E. SHETLER
15 Director of Human Resources ....Mr. Norm BAKHIT
106 Director of Adult/Online Pgms ....Dr. Ross PETERSON-VEATCH
39 Director of Residence Life ....Mr. Chad COLEMAN
38 Director Student Counseling ....Mrs. Jenny BEER
04 Admin Assistant to the President ....Ms. Betty SCHRAG
07 Director of Admissions ....Dr. Dan KOOP LIECHTY

Grace College and Seminary (B)

200 Seminary Drive, Winona Lake IN 46590-1294

County: Kosciusko FICE Identification: 001800
Unit ID: 150677
Telephone: (574) 372-5100 Carnegie Class: Bac/Diverse
FAX Number: (574) 372-5139 Calendar System: Semester
URL: www.grace.edu
Established: 1948 Annual Undergrad Tuition & Fees: $23,970
Enrollment: 1,821 Coed
Affiliation or Control: Fellowship Of Grace Brethren Churches
IRS Status: 501(c)3
Highest Offering: Doctorate
Program: 2-Year Principally Bachelor's Creditable; Liberal Arts And General; Teacher Preparatory; Religious Emphasis
Accreditation: NH, CACREP, IACBE, TED, THEOL

01 President ....Dr. William J. KATIP
04 Exec Assistant to the President ....Mrs. Nancy L. WEIMER
05 VP Academic Affairs ....Vacant
73 VP & Dean Seminary & School of Min ....Dr. Jeffery A. GILL
30 VP Advancement ....Vacant
11 VP Administration & Compliance ....Dr. Carrie A. YOCUM
84 VP Enrollment Management ....Mrs. Cindy N. SISSON
10 VP Financial Affairs/CFO ....Vacant
45 VP Strategic Initiatives & Planning ....Mr. Thomas A. DUNN
32 VP Student Affairs & Academic Svcs ......Dr. James E. SWANSON
51 Dean of Adult & Community Educ ....Dr. Stephen A. GRILL
49 Dean of School of Arts & Sciences ....Dr. Mark M. NORRIS
83 Dean of Schl of Behavioral Science ...Dr. Thomas J. EDGINGTON
50 Dean of School of Business ....Dr. Jeffrey K. FAWCETT
53 Dean of School of Education ....Mrs. Laurinda A. OWEN
106 Dean of Online Education ....Mr. Timothy J. ZIEBARTH
42 Dean of Chapel & Global Ministries ....Mr. J. Carlos TELLEZ
06 Registrar ....Mr. Steven T. CARLSON
08 Librarian ....Mrs. Tonya L. FAWCETT
13 Dir Information Technology ....Mr. Donald W. FLUKE
23 Dir Student Health & Counseling ....Dr. Debra S. MUSSER
37 Dir Student Financial Aid ....Mrs. Charlette R. SAUDERS
15 Dir of Human Resource ....Mrs. Audrey L. RUSSELL
27 Dir of Marketing & Communication ....Mr. David GROUT
18 Director Physical Plant ....Mr. Randy KLEINHANS
29 Director Alumni Relations ....Mrs. Tammy DENLINGER
41 Athletic Director ....Mr. Chad BRISCOE
36 Dir Career Services ....Mrs. Denise TERRY
09 Dir Institutional Effectiveness ....Dr. Mark H. RAIKES

Hanover College (C)

PO Box 108, Hanover IN 47243-0108

County: Jefferson FICE Identification: 001801
Unit ID: 150756
Telephone: (812) 866-7000 Carnegie Class: Bac/A&S
FAX Number: (812) 866-2164 Calendar System: Other
URL: www.hanover.edu
Established: 1827 Annual Undergrad Tuition & Fees: $31,760
Enrollment: 1,118 Coed
Affiliation or Control: Presbyterian Church (U.S.A.) IRS Status: 501(c)3
Highest Offering: Baccalaureate
Program: Liberal Arts And General; Teacher Preparatory
Accreditation: NH, TED

01 President ....Dr. Sue DEWINE
04 Executive Asst to the President ....Treva SHELTON
10 Vice President Business Affairs ....J. Michael BRUCE
41 Director of Athletics ....Lynn HALL
30 Vice President College Advancement ....Dennis HUNT
05 Vice President Academic Affairs ....Dr. Steve JOBE
84 Vice Pres Enrollment Management ....Jon RIESTER
32 Vice President Student Life ....Dr. David YEAGER
88 Exec Director-Rivers Institute ....Dr. Larry DEBUHR
88 Exec Dir Business Scholars Program ....Jerry JOHNSON
07 Dean of Admission ....Chris GAGE
06 Registrar ....Dr. Ken PRINCE
13 Chief Technology Officer ....John COLLINS
35 Associate Dean of Students ....Katy LOWE-SCHNEIDER
42 Chaplain ....Laura ARICO
29 Director of Alumni Relations ....Ann INMAN
19 Director of Campus Safety ....Jim HICKERSON
36 Director of Career Center ....Margaret KRANTZ
26 Dir of Communications & Marketing ....Rhonda BURCH
08 Director of Duggan Library ....Ken GIBSON
37 Director of Financial Aid ....Richard NASH
23 Director of Health Services ....Sandi ALEXANDER-LEWIS
15 Director of Human Resources ....Shelley PREOCANIN
28 Director of Multi-Cultural Affairs ....Taran MCZEE
18 Director of Physical Plant ....Scott KLEIN
104 Director of Study Abroad ....Uschi APPELT
38 Director of Student Counseling ....Catherine LE SAUX
39 Director of Student Housing ....Casey HECKLER
35 Asst Dir Fraternities/Sororities ....Matthew DEEG

Harrison College - Anderson Campus (D)

140 E 53rd Street, Anderson IN 46013-1717

Telephone: (765) 644-7514 Identification: 666030
Accreditation: &@NH, ACICS, MAC

† Main campus is Harrison College - Indianapolis Downtown Campus in Indianapolis, IN.

Harrison College - Columbus Indiana Campus (E)

2222 Poshard Drive, Columbus IN 47203-1843

Telephone: (812) 379-9000 Identification: 666428
Accreditation: &@NH, ACICS, MAC

† Main campus is Harrison College - Indianapolis Downtown Campus in Indianapolis, IN.

Harrison College - Elkhart Campus (F)

56075 Parkway Avenue, Elkhart IN 46516-9325

Telephone: (574) 522-0397 Identification: 666143
Accreditation: &@NH, ACICS, MAC

† Main campus is Harrison College - Indianapolis Downtown Campus in Indianapolis, IN.

Harrison College - Evansville Campus (G)

4601 Theater Drive, Evansville IN 47715-3901

Telephone: (812) 476-6000 Identification: 666429
Accreditation: &@NH, ACICS, MAC

† Main campus is Harrison College - Indianapolis Downtown Campus in Indianapolis, IN.

Harrison College - Fort Wayne Campus (H)

6413 N Clinton Street, Fort Wayne IN 46825-4911

Telephone: (260) 471-7667 Identification: 666029
Accreditation: &@NH, ACICS, MAC, SURGT

† Main campus is Harrison College - Indianapolis Downtown Campus in Indianapolis, IN.

Harrison College - Indianapolis Downtown Campus (I)

550 E Washington Street, Indianapolis IN 46204-2611

County: Marion FICE Identification: 021584
Unit ID: 151166
Telephone: (317) 447-6200 Carnegie Class: Bac/Assoc
FAX Number: (317) 686-9190 Calendar System: Quarter
URL: www.harrison.edu
Established: 1902 Annual Undergrad Tuition & Fees: N/A
Enrollment: 2,071 Coed
Affiliation or Control: Proprietary IRS Status: Proprietary
Highest Offering: Baccalaureate
Program: Occupational; 2-Year Principally Bachelor's Creditable; Business Emphasis
Accreditation: @NH, ACICS, ACFEI, MAC

01 President ....Mr. Jason T. KONESCO
12 Campus President ....Mr. Steve D. HARDIN

† Includes online and The Chef's Academy.

Harrison College - Indianapolis East Campus (J)

8150 Brookville Road, Indianapolis IN 46239-8903

Telephone: (317) 375-8000 Identification: 666430
Accreditation: &@NH, ACICS, ADNUR, MAC, #MLTAD, SURGT

† Main campus is Harrison College - Indianapolis Downtown Campus in Indianapolis, IN.

Harrison College - Indianapolis Northwest Campus (K)

6300 Technology Center Drive, Indianapolis IN 46278-6022

Telephone: (317) 873-6500 Identification: 666388
Accreditation: &@NH, ACICS

† Main campus is Harrison College - Indianapolis Downtown Campus in Indianapolis, IN.

Harrison College - Lafayette Campus (L)

4705 Meijer Court, Lafayette IN 47905-4859

Telephone: (765) 447-9550 Identification: 666431
Accreditation: &@NH, ACICS, MAC

† Main campus is Harrison College - Indianapolis Downtown Campus in Indianapolis, IN.

Harrison College - Terre Haute Campus (M)

1378 S State Road 46, Terre Haute IN 47803-9787

Telephone: (812) 877-2100 Identification: 666433
Accreditation: &@NH, ACICS, MAC

† Main campus is Harrison College - Indianapolis Downtown Campus in Indianapolis, IN.

Holy Cross College (N)

PO Box 308, Notre Dame IN 46556-0308

County: Saint Joseph FICE Identification: 007263
Unit ID: 150774
Telephone: (574) 239-8400 Carnegie Class: Bac/A&S
FAX Number: (574) 239-8323 Calendar System: Semester
URL: www.hcc-nd.edu
Established: 1966 Annual Undergrad Tuition & Fees: $24,500
Enrollment: 431 Coed
Affiliation or Control: Roman Catholic IRS Status: 501(c)3
Highest Offering: Baccalaureate
Program: Liberal Arts And General
Accreditation: NH

01 President ....Bro. John R. PAIGE, CSC
03 Senior Vice President ....Dr. Tina S. HOLLAND
11 VP for Operations ....Mr. Dan HAVERTY
30 VP for Mission Advancement ....Mr. Robert L. KLOSKA
04 Executive Assistant ....Ms. Jodie L. SWEET
20 Dean of Faculty ....Mr. Justin WATSON
32 Dean of Students ....Mr. Daniel J. COCHRAN
06 Registrar ....Mr. Richard J. SULLIVAN
84 Director of Enrollment Management ....Mr. Brian STUDEBAKER
37 Director of Financial Aid ....Mrs. Shelly BARNES
38 Director of Student Counseling Svcs .Bro. Chris J. DREYER, CSC
13 Director of Campus Technology ...Bro. Charles D. DREVON, CSC
18 Director of Building & Grounds ....Mr. Randy MCKINLEY
39 Director of Residence Life ....Dr. Christopher TORRIJAS
08 Director of Library Services ....Mrs. Mary Ellen HEGEDUS
36 Director of Discernment & Prep ....Mr. Charles BALL
42 Director of Campus Ministry ....Mr. Andrew POLANIECKI
41 Athletic Director ....Mr. Robert SCHERMERHORN
26 Dir of Marketing/Comm/Public Rels ....Mr. Jeff PENNEY

Huntington University (O)

2303 College Avenue, Huntington IN 46750-9986

County: Huntington FICE Identification: 001803
Unit ID: 150941
Telephone: (260) 356-6000 Carnegie Class: Bac/Diverse
FAX Number: (260) 359-4086 Calendar System: 4/1/4
URL: www.huntington.edu
Established: 1897 Annual Undergrad Tuition & Fees: $24,140
Enrollment: 1,211 Coed
Affiliation or Control: United Brethren Church IRS Status: 501(c)3
Highest Offering: Master's
Program: Liberal Arts And General; Teacher Preparatory; Professional
Accreditation: NH, NURSE, SW, TED

01 President ....Dr. Sherilyn R. EMBERTON
05 Int Sr Vice Pres Academic Affairs ....Dr. Delbert D. DOUGHTY
10 Interim VP for Business/Finance ....Mrs. Julie A. HENDRYX
84 Sr VP Enrollment Mgmt & Marketing ..Mr. Jeffrey C. BERGGREN
45 Sr VP Strategy & Grad/Adult Program ..Dr. Ann C. MCPHERREN
30 Vice President for Advancement ....Mr. Vincent D. HAUPERT
32 Vice President for Student Life ....Dr. Ron L. COFFEY
45 VP for Strategy & Innovation ....Mr. Troy D. IRICK
04 Admin Assistant to President ....Mrs. Barbara A. THOMPSON
42 Campus Pastor ....Rev. Arthur L. WILSON
58 Dean of Graduate & Adult Programs .....Dr. Stephen D. HOLTROP

36 Assoc Dean Student Life/Career Dev ... Ms. Martha J. SMITH
35 Assoc Dean of Student Development ... Mr. Jesse M. BROWN
44 Senior Director of Gift Planning ... Mr. Richard W. MCCONNELL
21 Controller & Budget Director ... Mr. Scott A. BERRY
26 Director of Communications ... Mrs. Heather R. BARKLEY
37 Director of Financial Aid ... Mr. Robert E. SOMMERS
06 Registrar ... Mrs. Sarah J. HARVEY
08 Director of Library Services ... Ms. Anita GRAY
13 Director of Technology Services ... Mr. Adam L. SKILES
38 Director of Learning Assistance ... Mrs. Kristal L. CHAFIN
41 Athletic Director ... Ms. Lori L. CULLER
18 Director of Physical Plant ... Mr. Jerry A. GRESSLEY
15 Dir Human Resources/Auxiliary Svcs ... Mrs. Rachel L. WUST
29 Director of Alumni ... Mrs. Margaret A. ROUSH
19 Director of Campus Police ... Mr. Barry A. COCHRAN
88 Dir of Horizon Leadership Program ... Mr. Jesse M. BROWN
26 Assoc Director of Media Relations ... Ms. Ashley SMITH
40 Bookstore Manager ... Mrs. Lisa M. SNYDER

Indiana State University (A)

200 N 7th Street, Terre Haute IN 47809-1902
County: Vigo FICE Identification: 001807
Unit ID: 151324
Telephone: (812) 237-6311 Carnegie Class: DRU
FAX Number: (812) 237-2291 Calendar System: Semester
URL: web.indstate.edu
Established: 1865 Annual Undergrad Tuition & Fees (In-State): $8,056
Enrollment: 12,114 Coed
Affiliation or Control: State IRS Status: 501(c)3
Highest Offering: Doctorate
Program: Liberal Arts And General; Teacher Preparatory; Professional
Accreditation: NH, AAFCS, #ARCPA, ART, BUS, CACREP, CIDA, CLPSY, CONST, COPSY, DIETC, ENGT, MUS, NAIT, NUR, SCPSY, SP, SW, TED

01 President ... Dr. Daniel J. BRADLEY
100 Chief of Staff ... Ms. Teresa D. EXLINE
86 Exec Dir of Government Relations ... Mr. Greg J. GOODE
88 Chief Strategic Officer ... Dr. Karl BURGHER
05 Provost/Vice Pres Academic Affs ... Dr. Richard "Biff" WILLIAMS
10 VP Business Affs & Fin/Treas ... Ms. Diann E. MCKEE
84 VP Enrollment Mgmt/Mktg/Comm ... Mr. John BEACON
32 VP Student Affairs/Dean of Students ... Ms. Carmen TILLERY
43 General Council/Univ Secretary ... Ms. Melony A. SACOPULOS
20 Assoc VP Academic Affairs ... Dr. Joshua POWERS
13 Assoc VP Chief Info Officer ... Dr. Lisa SPENCE
18 Assoc VP Univ Facilities Management ... Mr. Kevin L. RUNION
26 Interim Asst VP Comm/Marketing ... Mr. Santhana NAIDU
07 Assoc VP Enroll/Mgmt/Adm/HS Rel ... Mr. Richard J. TOOMEY
29 Director of Alumni Affairs ... Mr. Rex KENDALL
15 Assoc VP Human Resources ... Mr. Wil DOWNS
14 Exec Dir Information Technology ... Mr. Yancy PHILLIPS
21 Business Officer ... Ms. Diann E. MCKEE
06 Registrar ... Ms. April HAY
22 Compliance Dir of Affirm Action ... Mrs. Bonita MCGEE
28 University Diversity Officer ... Ms. Elonda ERVIN
41 Director of Athletics ... Mr. Ronald PRETTYMAN
36 Interim Executive Dir Career Svcs ... Dr. Darby C. SCISM
88 Assoc Vice Pres Comm Engagement ... Dr. Nancy B. ROGERS
25 Director Sponsored Programs ... Ms. Dawn UNDERWOOD
09 Director of Institutional Research ... Ms. Patty MCCLINTOCK
19 Director of Public Safety ... Mr. William C. MERCIER
96 Dir Purchasing/Central Receiving ... Mr. Kevin BARR
39 Executive Dir of Residential Life ... Mr. Amanda KNERR
38 Director of Student Counseling ... Dr. Kenneth CHEW
37 Director Student Financial Aid ... Ms. Crystal BAKER
49 Dean of Arts & Sciences ... Dr. John MURRAY
50 Dean of Business ... Dr. Brien N. SMITH
53 Dean of Education ... Dr. Kandi HILL-CLARKE
68 Dean Nursing/Health & Human Svcs ... Vacant
72 Dean of Technology ... Dr. Bradford (Brad) SIMS
58 Dean of Grad/Professional Studies ... Dr. Jay GATRELL
08 Dean of Library Services ... Ms. Alberta COMER
56 Dean of Extended Learning ... Dr. Ken BRAUCHLE

Indiana Tech (B)

1600 E Washington Boulevard, Fort Wayne IN 46803-1297
County: Allen FICE Identification: 001805
Unit ID: 151290
Telephone: (260) 422-5561 Carnegie Class: Spec/Bus
FAX Number: (260) 420-1453 Calendar System: Semester
URL: www.indianatech.edu
Established: 1930 Annual Undergrad Tuition & Fees: $24,450
Enrollment: 5,256 Coed
Affiliation or Control: Independent Non-Profit IRS Status: 501(c)3
Highest Offering: Doctorate
Program: Professional; Business Emphasis
Accreditation: NH, ENG

01 President ... Dr. Arthur E. SNYDER
05 Vice President for Academic Affairs ... Dr. Douglas P. CLARK
03 Exec VP Finance & Administration ... Ms. Judy K. ROY
84 VP for Enrollment Management ... Mr. Steve A. HERENDEEN
30 Vice President of Inst Advancement ... Mr. Mark H. RICHTER
07 Assoc VP Enrollment Management ... Ms. Monica L. CHAMBERLAIN
50 Dean of Business ... Dr. Jeffrey A. ZIMMERMAN
97 Dean of General Studies ... Dr. Doty A. LATUSZEK
54 Dean of Engineering/Computer Sci ... Mr. David A. ASCHLIMAN
61 Dean Law School ... Mr. Peter C. ALEXANDER
77 Assoc Dean of Computer Sciences ... Mr. Gary A. MESSICK
20 Assoc Dean of CPS ... Dr. Andrew I. NWANNE
06 Registrar ... Mr. Travis A. BLUME
37 Director of Financial Aid ... Mr. Scott W. THUM
18 Director of Facilities Management ... Mr. R. Mike TOWNSLEY
13 Director of Information Technology ... Mr. Jeff S. LEICHTY
15 Human Resources Director ... Mr. Christopher B. BLACK
21 Controller ... Ms. Shelly R. MUSOLF
58 Director Global Leadership Program ... Dr. Kenneth E. RAUCH
53 Director of Teacher Education ... Dr. Brad L. YODER
26 Marketing Director ... Ms. Janet L. SCHUTTE
36 Dir of Career Planning & Devel Ctr ... Ms. Cynthia P. VERDUCE
11 Director of Operations-CPS ... Ms. Sharon LOKUTA
12 Operations Manager-Indianapolis ... Ms. Phyllis E. HOGAN
08 Director McMillen Library ... Ms. Constance E. SCOTT
88 Director of Criminal Sciences ... Dr. Dominic P. LOMBARDO
106 Director of Online Learning ... Dr. Y. Ben LEE
89 Director of Freshman College & SSS ... Ms. Mary C. SCUDDER
39 Assoc VP Student Services ... Mr. Chris M. DICKSON
29 Dir Annual Fund & Alumni Relations ... Mr. Michael E. PETERSON
04 Executive Asst to the President ... Ms. Jennifer A. ROSS
04 Executive Secretary to President ... Ms. Donna L. SARK
42 Faith Services Coordinator ... Mr. Gregory P. BYMAN
41 Athletic Director ... Mr. Martin C. NEUHOFF
32 Director Student Life ... Ms. Andrea G. CHECK
88 Title III Director ... Ms. Danielle L. WITZIGREUTER
84 Enrollment Manager-Fort Wayne ... Mr. Yiani DEMITSAS
84 Enrollment Manager-Indy ... Mr. Shayne D. ABRAHAMS
88 Associate VP Advancement ... Ms. Mary V. SLAFKOSKY
88 CPS Development Manager ... Ms. A. Nicole SCOTT
35 Student Life Coordinator ... Vacant

Indiana Tech-Elkhart (C)

333 Middleburg Street, Elkhart IN 46516
Telephone: (574) 296-7075 Identification: 770102
Accreditation: &NH

† Main campus is Indiana Tech in Fort Wayne, IN.

Indiana Tech-Indianapolis (D)

3500 DePaul W Boulevard, Indianapolis IN 46268
Telephone: (317) 466-2121 Identification: 770103
Accreditation: &NH

† Main campus is Indiana Tech in Fort Wayne, IN.

*Indiana University (E)

Bryan Hall, Bloomington IN 47405-7000
County: Monroe FICE Identification: 008002
Telephone: (812) 855-4613 Carnegie Class: N/A
FAX Number: N/A
URL: www.indiana.edu

01 President ... Dr. Michael A. MCROBBIE
05 Exec Vice President/Provost IUB ... Lauren ROBEL
45 Exec Vice Pres/Chancellor IUPUI ... Dr. Charles BANTZ
45 Exec VP Univ Regional Affs/Plng/Pol ... Mr. John APPLEGATE
46 Vice Pres for Research ... Dr. Jorge JOSE
28 VP Diversity/Equity/Multicultural ... Dr. Edwin MARSHALL
18 Vice Pres Facilities ... Dr. Thomas MORRISON
10 Vice President/CFO ... Ms. MaryFrances MCCOURT
26 VP Public Affairs & Govt Relations ... Mr. Michael SAMPLE
100 Chief of Staff ... Dr. Karen H. ADAMS
13 Vice President Info Tech/CIO ... Dr. Brad C. WHEELER
43 Vice Pres and University Counsel ... Ms. Jacqueline A. SIMMONS
104 Vice Pres for International Affairs ... Dr. David ZARET
88 Vice President for Engagement ... Mr. William B. STEPHAN
41 VP & Dir of Intercoll Athletics ... Mr. Fred GLASS
63 VP Univ Clinical Affs/Dean Sch Med ... Dr. Jay HESS
21 University Treasurer ... Ms. Mary Frances MCCOURT
22 Director of Affirmative Action ... Ms. Julie KNOST
29 Exec Dir IU Alumni Association ... Mr. J. Thomas FORBES
15 Director of Human Resources ... Mr. Dan RIVES
27 Director of Media Relations ... Mr. Mark LAND
102 President IU Foundation ... Dr. Gene TEMPEL

*Indiana University Bloomington (F)

107 S. Indiana Ave., Bloomington IN 47405-7000
County: Monroe FICE Identification: 001809
Unit ID: 151351
Telephone: (812) 855-4848 Carnegie Class: RU/VH
FAX Number: (812) 855-5678 Calendar System: Semester
URL: www.iub.edu/
Established: 1820 Annual Undergrad Tuition & Fees (In-State): $10,209
Enrollment: 42,133 Coed
Affiliation or Control: State IRS Status: 501(c)3
Highest Offering: Doctorate
Program: Liberal Arts And General; Teacher Preparatory; Professional
Accreditation: NH, ART, AUD, BUS, CACREP, CEA, CIDA, CLPSY, COPSY, DIETD, IPSY, JOUR, LAW, LIB, MUS, NRPA, OPD, OPT, OPTR, OPTT, PH, SCPSY, SP, SPAA, TED, THEA

02 President ... Dr. Michael MCROBBIE
05 Exec Vice Pres & Provost ... Ms. Lauren ROBEL
03 Exec Vice Pres & Chanc IUPUI ... Dr. Charles BANTZ
09 Exec VP Univ Reg Affs/Plng/Policy ... Mr. John S. APPLEGATE
88 Senior Advisor to Provost & Exec VP ... Dr. Maynard THOMPSON
10 Vice President/CFO & Treasurer ... Ms. MaryFrances MCCOURT
63 VP Univ Clin Affrs/Dean Sch of Med ... Dr. D. Craig BRATER
18 Vice Pres Capital Plng/Facilities ... Dr. Tom MORRISON
28 VP Diversity/Equity & Multicul Affs ... Dr. Edwin MARSHALL
46 Vice President for Research ... Dr. Jorge JOSE
26 VP for Public Affs & Govt Relations ... Mr. Mike SAMPLE
88 Vice President for Engagement ... Mr. William B. STEPHAN
20 Vice Provost for Undergraduate Educ ... Dr. Sonya STEPHENS
20 Vice Prov Faculty & Academic Affs ... Dr. Thomas GIERYN
88 Assoc VP Rsrch/Vice Provost Rsrch ... Dr. P. Sarita SONI
84 Vice Provost Enrollment Mgmt ... Dr. David JOHNSON
30 Sr Vice Pres Development/IU Fdn ... Ms. Marti HEIL
15 Associate Vice Pres Human Resources ... Mr. Dan RIVES
09 Assoc VP Univ Inst Rsrch/Reporting ... Dr. Vic BORDEN
91 Assoc VP Enterprise Infrastructure ... Mr. Dennis CROMWELL
21 Asst V Prov Budget & Admin/IUB ... Mr. James DONGES
13 Vice Pres Info Technology & CIO ... Dr. Brad WHEELER
58 Dean University Graduate School ... Dr. James WIMBUSH
102 Pres & CEO IU Foundation ... Dr. Daniel C. SMITH
20 Assoc Vice Prov Faculty & Acad Affs ... Dr. Sara PRYOR
20 Assoc Vice Prov Faculty & Acad Affs ... Dr. Anne MASSEY
85 Assoc VP for International Svcs ... Mr. Christopher VIERS
49 Dean College Arts & Sciences ... Dr. Larry SINGELL
08 Ruth Lilly Dean Univ Libraries ... Dr. Brenda JOHNSON
32 Dean of Students ... Dr. Pete GOLDSMITH
50 Dean Kelley School of Business ... Dr. Idalene KENSER
53 Dean School of Education ... Dr. Gerardo GONZALEZ
68 Dean School of Public Health ... Dr. Mohammed TORABI
88 Dean School of Optometry ... Dr. Joseph BONANNO
61 Interim Dean School of Law ... Ms. Hannah BUXBAUM
64 Dean Jacobs School of Music ... Mr. Gwyn RICHARDS
60 Int Dean School of Journalism ... Dr. Michael EVANS
88 Dean School of Informatics ... Dr. Bobby SCHNABEL
80 Dean SPEA ... Dr. John D. GRAHAM
62 Dean Sch of Library/Info Science ... Dr. Debora SHAW
82 Vice Pres International Affairs ... Dr. David ZARET
92 Dean Hutton Honors College ... Dr. Matthew AUER
35 Assoc Dean for Student Affairs ... Ms. Carol MCCORD
29 Exec Dir IU Alumni Association ... Mr. J.T FORBES
39 Exec Dir Residential Pgm & Svcs ... Mr. Pat CONNOR
36 Director Career Dev Center ... Mr. Patrick DONAHUE
16 Bloomington Dir Employee Rels Svcs ... Ms. Suzanne RYAN
06 Assoc Vice Provost/Registrar ... Mr. Mark MCCONAHAY
23 Exec Dir IU Health Center ... Dr. Pete GROGG
43 VP & General Counsel ... Ms. Jacqueline SIMMONS
88 Director IU Press ... Dr. Janet RABINOWITCH
22 Director Affirmative Action ... Ms. Julie KNOST
40 Manager of IU Bookstore ... Mr. Joe BENDER
19 Acting Chief of Police ... Mr. Laury FLINT
88 Exec Dir Indiana Memorial Union ... Mr. Bruce JACOBS
88 Director Radio/TV Services ... Mr. Perry METZ
88 Operations Mgr Campus Bus Service ... Mr. Perry MAULL
88 Director IU Auditorium ... Mr. Doug BOOHER
18 Asst VP Facilities Operations ... Mr. Hank HEWETSON
38 Director Counseling & Psych Svs ... Dr. Nancy STOCKTON
41 VP & Dir Intercollegiate Athletics ... Mr. Fred GLASS
96 Asst VP for Procurement ... Ms. Jill SCHUNK
25 Exec Dir Grant & Contract Services ... Mr. Jim BECKER
90 Asocc Dean Rsrch Tech/ED PTI/Prof ... Dr. Craig STEWART
07 Director of Admissions ... Ms. Mary Ellen ANDERSON

*Indiana University East (G)

2325 Chester Boulevard, Richmond IN 47374-1289
County: Wayne FICE Identification: 001811
Unit ID: 151388
Telephone: (765) 973-8200 Carnegie Class: Bac/Diverse
FAX Number: (765) 973-8364 Calendar System: Semester
URL: www.iue.edu
Established: 1946 Annual Undergrad Tuition & Fees (In-State): $8,269
Enrollment: 4,186 Coed
Affiliation or Control: State IRS Status: 501(c)3
Highest Offering: Master's
Program: Liberal Arts And General; Teacher Preparatory
Accreditation: NH, ACBSP, NUR, TED

02 Chancellor ... Dr. Kathyrn CRUZ-URIBE
05 Exec Vice Chanc Academic Affairs ... Dr. Laurence D. RICHARDS
26 Vice Chanc External Affs/Marketing ... Mr. Rob ZINKAN
10 Vice Chancellor Admin & Finance ... Mr. Dan DOOLEY
32 Dean of Students ... Ms. Mary BLAKEFIELD
13 Director Information Technology ... Mr. Todd DUKE
30 Director of Gift Development ... Ms. Stephanie HAYS-MUSSOINI
06 Registrar ... Mr. Dennis HICKS
08 Director Library/Media Services ... Dr. Frances YATES
15 Director Human Resources ... Ms. Dianne S. CHANDLER
36 Director Career Services ... Ms. Liz FERRIS
07 Director of Admissions ... Ms. Molly VANDERPOOL
37 Dir Fin Aid & Scholarships ... Ms. Sarah SOPER
20 Director University College ... Ms. Carrie REISNER
40 Manager of Barnes & Noble Bookstore ... Ms. Kristy FRASHER
35 Director of Campus Life ... Ms. Rebeckah HESTER
21 Bursar ... Ms. Shelley DODSON
22 Director Affirmative Action ... Ms. Patricia CRAWFORD
70 Director Social Work/Human Services ... Mr. Ed FITZGERALD
27 Director Communications & Marketing ... Mr. John DALTON
97 Assoc VC & Director General Studies ... Dr. Ross ALEXANDER
29 Director Alumni Relations ... Ms. Terry WIESEHAN
28 Director of Multicultural Affairs ... Vacant
50 Dean Business/Technology ... Dr. David FRANTZ
79 Dean Humanities & Social Sciences ... Dr. Katherine FRANK
81 Dean Natural Math & Science ... Dr. Neil SABINE
66 Dean of Nursing ... Ms. Karen CLARK
53 Dean Education ... Dr. Marilyn WATKINS

*Indiana University Kokomo (A)

2300 S Washington, Box 9003, Kokomo IN 46904-9003
County: Howard FICE Identification: 001814
Unit ID: 151333
Telephone: (765) 453-2000 Carnegie Class: Bac/Diverse
FAX Number: (765) 455-9444 Calendar System: Semester
URL: www.iuk.edu
Established: 1945 Annual Undergrad Tuition & Fees (In-State): $6,674
Enrollment: 3,719 Coed
Affiliation or Control: State IRS Status: 501(c)3
Highest Offering: Master's
Program: Occupational; Liberal Arts And General; Teacher Preparatory; Professional
Accreditation: NH, BUS, NURSE, RAD, TED

Code	Title	Name
02	Interim Chancellor	Dr. Susan SCIAME-GIESECKE
05	Int Vice Chanc Academic Affairs	Dr. Kathy PARKISON
32	Vice Chanc Student Affs/Enroll Mgmt	Dr. Todd GAMBILL
30	Vice Chancellor for Advancement	Vacant
72	Director Division Purdue Tech	Mr. Jeff GRIFFIN
08	Dean of the Library	Vacant
37	Associate Director Financial Aid	Ms. Karen SHAW
10	Director of Budget Administration	Dr. Philemon YEBEI
15	Director Human Resources	Ms. Cathy VALCKE
06	Registrar	Ms. Stacey THOMAS
88	Exec Dir Office of the Chancellor	Ms. Gerry G. STROMAN
36	Manager Career Services	Ms. Tracy SPRINGER
29	Director Alumni Relations	Mr. Ryan BOWMAN
27	Director Communications & Marketing	Ms. Marie RADEL
07	Director of Admissions	Ms. Angie SIDERS
28	Director of Diversity	Ms. Maria AHMAD
35	Dean of Students	Ms. Sarah SARBER
18	Director Facilities/Physical Plant	Mr. John SARBER
50	Interim Dean School of Business	Dr. Erv BOSCHMANN
49	Dean Sch Humanities/Social Sciences	Dr. Scott JONES
66	Dean School of Nursing	Dr. Linda WALLACE
53	Dean Division of Education	Dr. Paul PAESE
81	Dean Sch Sciences/Math/Information	Dr. Christian CHAURET
79	Chair Humanities	Vacant

*Indiana University Northwest (B)

3400 Broadway, Gary IN 46408-1197
County: Lake FICE Identification: 001815
Unit ID: 151360
Telephone: (219) 980-6500 Carnegie Class: Master's M
FAX Number: (219) 980-6670 Calendar System: Semester
URL: www.iun.edu
Established: 1921 Annual Undergrad Tuition & Fees (In-State): $6,739
Enrollment: 6,184 Coed
Affiliation or Control: State IRS Status: 501(c)3
Highest Offering: Master's
Program: Occupational; Liberal Arts And General; Teacher Preparatory; Professional
Accreditation: NH, BUS, CAHIIM, DA, DH, NUR, RAD, RTT, SPAA, TED

Code	Title	Name
02	Chancellor	Dr. William J. LOWE
04	Exec Asst to the Chancellor	Mrs. Kathy MALONE
05	Exec Vice Chanc Academic Affairs	Dr. David J. MALIK
11	Vice Chancellor Administration	Dr. Joseph PELLICCIOTTI
32	Vice Chancellor Student Services	Dr. Georj LEWIS
10	Campus Chief Financial Officer	Mrs. Marianne MILICH
26	Vice Chancellor External Affairs	Ms. Jeri Pat GABBERT
27	Chief Information Officer	Ms. Beth VAN GORDON
20	Assoc Vice Chanc Academic Affs	Dr. Cynthia O'DELL
09	Asst VC Inst Effectiveness & Rsrch	Mr. John NOVAK
49	Dean College of Arts & Sciences	Dr. Mark HOYERT
88	Dean Col of Health & Human Svcs	Dr. Patrick BANKSTON
50	Dean School of Business & Economics	Dr. Anna ROMINGER
53	Dean School of Education	Dr. Lora BAILEY
80	Director Public & Environ Affs	Dr. Barbara PEAT
70	Director Social Work	Dr. Darlene LYNCH
06	Registrar	Mr. Craig DEMYER
88	Director Pre-Professional Pgm	Dr. Michael LAPOINTE
07	Director Admissions	Ms. Linda B. TEMPLETON
37	Director Financial Aid	Mr. Harold BURTLEY
36	Director Career & Placement	Ms. Sharese DUDLEY
35	Director Student Life	Mr. Scott FULK
19	Director Security	Ms. Patricia NOWAK
29	Director Alumni Relations	Ms. Paulette LAFATA-JOHNSON
66	Director Division of Nursing	Dr. Linda DELUNAS
24	Director Instructional Media Svcs	Mr. Paul SHARPE
08	Director Library	Mr. Timothy SUTHERLAND
18	Director Physical Plant	Mr. Otto JEFIMENKO
21	Manager Student Accounts	Ms. Sandra MENDOZA
25	Director Research/Sponsored Pgms	Ms. T.J STOOPS
15	Director Human Resources	Ms. Carolyn HARTLEY
28	Int Dir of Diversity Programming	Mr. James WALLACE, JR.
38	Director of Counseling Services	Ms. Barbara A. BULLOCK
22	Director Affirmative Action	Ms. Ida GILLIS
88	Dir Schlrshp in Teaching & Learning	Dr. Christopher YOUNG
88	Dir Urban & Regional Excellence	Dr. Ellen SZARLETA

*Indiana University-Purdue University Fort Wayne (C)

2101 E Coliseum Boulevard, Fort Wayne IN 46805-1499
County: Allen FICE Identification: 001828
Unit ID: 151102
Telephone: (260) 481-6100 Carnegie Class: Master's L
FAX Number: (260) 481-6880 Calendar System: Semester
URL: www.ipfw.edu
Established: 1964 Annual Undergrad Tuition & Fees (In-State): $7,013
Enrollment: 13,771 Coed
Affiliation or Control: State IRS Status: 501(c)3
Highest Offering: Master's
Program: Liberal Arts And General; Teacher Preparatory; Professional
Accreditation: NH, BUS, CS, DA, DH, DT, ENG, ENGT, MUS, NUR, RAD, SPAA, TED, THEA

Code	Title	Name
02	Chancellor	Dr. Vicky L. CARWEIN
05	Vice Chanc Academic Affairs	Dr. Jeffrey R. ANDERSON
10	Vice Chancellor Financial Affairs	Mr. Walter J. BRANSON
32	Vice Chancellor Student Affairs	Dr. George S. MCCLELLAN
45	Assoc Vice Chancellor Inst Research	Dr. Robert WILKINSON
30	Executive Director Development	Ms. Linda L. RUFFOLO
26	Exec Dir Univ Relations/Commun	Ms. Irene A. WALTERS
14	Director Information Tech Services	Mr. Robert M. KOSTRUBANIC
18	Director Physical Plant	Mr. Jay H. HARRIS
29	Interim Director Alumni Relations	Ms. Jessica BUTLER
08	Library Dean	Ms. Cheryl B. TRUESDELL
15	Director Human Resources	Ms. Rose M. COSTELLO
41	Director of Athletics	Mr. Tommy BELL
21	Comptroller	Mr. Daniel L. GEBHART
06	Registrar	Mr. Patrick A. MCLAUGHLIN
96	Director Purchasing	Ms. Cynthia M. ELICK
19	Chief University Police	Mr. Jeffrey W. DAVIS
22	Director Institutional Equity	Ms. Christine M. MARCUCCILLI
85	Director International Program	Mr. Brian MYLREA
37	Director Financial Aid	Mr. David PETERSON
07	Director of Admissions	Ms. Carol B. ISAACS
38	Assoc Vice Chanc Student Success	Dr. Bruce BUSBY
84	Director Enrollment Management	Mr. Mark A. FRANKE
49	Dean Arts & Sciences	Dr. Carl N. DRUMMOND
76	Dean Health Sciences	Dr. Ann OBERGFELL
51	Exec Director Continuing Stds	Ms. Deborah M. CONKLIN
72	Dean Engr Tech/Computer Science	Mr. S.C. Max YEN
53	Interim Dean Educ & Public Policy	Dr. James BURG
50	Dean Business	Dr. Otto H. CHANG
57	Dean Visual/Performing Arts	Dr. John O'CONNELL
46	Assoc Vice Chanc Rsrch Ext Support	Dr. J. ALBAYYARI
20	Associate Academic Officer	Dr. Steve T. SARRATORE
35	Dean of Students	Dr. Eric M. NORMAN
28	Assoc Vice Chancellor Diversity	Mr. Kenneth C. CHRISTMON
100	Chief of Staff	Ms. Kimberly WAGNER

*Indiana University-Purdue University Indianapolis (D)

355 N Lansing Street, Indianapolis IN 46202-2896
County: Marion FICE Identification: 001813
Unit ID: 151111
Telephone: (317) 274-5555 Carnegie Class: RU/H
FAX Number: N/A Calendar System: Semester
URL: www.iupui.edu
Established: 1969 Annual Undergrad Tuition & Fees (In-State): $7,081
Enrollment: 30,451 Coed
Affiliation or Control: State IRS Status: 501(c)3
Highest Offering: Doctorate
Program: Occupational; Liberal Arts And General; Teacher Preparatory; Professional
Accreditation: NH, #ARCPA, ART, CAHIIM, CIDA, CLPSY, CS, CYTO, DA, DENT, DH, DIETI, EMT, ENG, ENGT, FEPAC, HSA, HT, IPSY, LAW, MED, MT, MUS, NDT, NMT, NUR, NURSE, OT, PA, PH, PTA, RAD, RADDOS, RTT, SPAA, SW

Code	Title	Name
02	Chancellor	Dr. Charles R. BANTZ
100	Chief of Staff	Dr. Jeffrey A. DEAN
28	Vice Chanc Diversity/Equity/Incl	Vacant
04	Assistant to Chancellor for Comm	Ms. Sylvia M. PAYNE
05	Exec Vice Chanc/Chief Academic Ofcr	Dr. Nasser H. PAYDAR
10	Vice Chanc Administration & Finance	Ms. Dawn M. RHODES
26	Vice Chancellor External Affairs	Ms. Amy C. WARNER
32	Vice Chancellor Student Life	Dr. Zebulun R. DAVENPORT
46	Vice Chancellor Research	Dr. Kody VARAHRAMYAN
13	Dean Information Technologies	Dr. Anastasia MORRONE
08	Dean University Library	Mr. David W. LEWIS
84	Director Enrollment Services	Dr. Rebecca E. PORTER
06	Registrar	Ms. Mary Beth MYERS
21	Bursar	Mr. Dan YOUNGBLOOD
22	Director Equal Opportunity	Ms. Kim D. KIRKLAND
38	Director Student Counseling	Dr. Julie LASH
39	Director Campus Housing	Mr. Aaron HART
40	Bookstore Manager	Ms. Michele GRETCH-CARTER
36	Career Services Council	Mr. Joshua D. KILLEY
41	Athletic Director	Mr. Michael R. MOORE
29	Director Alumni Relations	Mr. Stefan S. DAVIS
27	Director News & Media	Ms. Margie SMITH-SIMMONS
09	Director Institutional Research	Dr. Gary PIKE
07	Dir of Undergraduate Admissions	Mr. Chris J. FOLEY
37	Director Student Financial Aid	Ms. Kathy PURVIS
15	Assoc Vice Chanc Human Resources	Ms. Carlene M. THOMPSON
23	Medical Director Student Health Svc	Dr. Stephen F. WINTERMEYER
18	Director Campus Facility Services	Ms. Emily C. WREN
19	Chief Campus Police	Mr. Paul E. NORRIS
92	Dean Honors College	Dr. E. Jane LUZAR
96	Director Purchasing	Mr. Robert HALTER
45	Senior Advisor/Academic Planning	Dr. Trudy W. BANTA
12	Dean Columbus Campus	Dr. Marwan A. WAFA
76	Dean School Health/Rehab Sci	Dr. Austin O. AGHO
57	Dean Herron School of Art	Ms. Valerie EICKMEIER
52	Dean School of Dentistry	Dr. John N. WILLIAMS
54	Dean School of Engr/Technology	Dr. David J. RUSSOMANNO
88	Exec Assoc Dean of Informatics	Dr. Mathew J. PALAKAL
61	Dean McKinney Sch of Law	Mr. Andrew R. KLEIN
49	Dean School of Liberal Arts	Dr. William A. BLOMQUIST
63	Dean School of Medicine	Dr. Jay L. HESS
66	Dean School of Nursing	Dr. Marion E. BROOME
68	Dean School of Physical Education	Dr. James M. GLADDEN
81	Dean School of Science	Dr. Simon RHODES
70	Dean School of Social Work	Dr. Michael PATCHNER
69	Dean Fairbanks Sch of Public Health	Dr. Paul K. HALVERSON
88	Dean Lilly Fam Sch of Philanthropy	Dr. Eugene R. TEMPEL
53	Exec Assoc Dean School of Education	Dr. Patricia M. ROGAN
60	Int Ex Assoc Dean Sch of Journalism	Dr. Dan DREW
62	Int Ex Assoc Dean Library/Info Sci	Dr. Rachel APPLEGATE
80	Exec Assoc Dean Public/Environ Affs	Dr. Lilliard RICHARDSON
85	Assoc Vice Chanc International Affs	Dr. Gil LATZ
50	Assoc Dean School of Business	Dr. Philip L. COCHRAN
58	Associate Dean Graduate School	Dr. Sherry F. QUEENER
89	Dean University College	Dr. Kathy JOHNSON

*Indiana University South Bend (E)

1700 Mishawaka Avenue, South Bend IN 46634-7111
County: Saint Joseph FICE Identification: 001816
Unit ID: 151342
Telephone: (574) 520-4872 Carnegie Class: Master's M
FAX Number: (574) 520-4834 Calendar System: Semester
URL: www.iusb.edu
Established: 1940 Annual Undergrad Tuition & Fees (In-State): $6,815
Enrollment: 8,490 Coed
Affiliation or Control: State IRS Status: 501(c)3
Highest Offering: Master's
Program: Occupational; Liberal Arts And General; Teacher Preparatory; Professional
Accreditation: NH, BUS, CACREP, DH, MACTE, NURSE, RAD, SPAA, TED

Code	Title	Name
02	Chancellor	Dr. Terry L. ALLISON
05	Int Exec Vice Chanc Acad Affairs	Dr. John MCINTOSH
10	Vice Chancellor Finance & Admin	Mr. Bill J. O'DONNELL
26	Vice Chanc Public Affs/Univ Advance	Dr. Ilene SHEFFER
32	Vice Chanc Student Affs/Enroll Mgmt	Vacant
13	Regional Chief Information Officer	Ms. Elizabeth VAN GORDON
20	Int Assoc Vice Chanc Academic Affs	Dr. Linda CHEN
88	Assoc VC Student Acad Support Svcs	Ms. Karen L. WHITE
84	Asst Vice Chanc for Enrollment Svcs	Ms. Cathy M. BUCKMAN
06	Registrar	Mr. Jeff JOHNSTON
36	Director Career Services Office	Vacant
35	Dir Student Activit Ctr/Athletics	Mr. Gary DEMSKI
18	Director Facilities Management	Mr. Michael PRATER
19	Director of Safety & Security	Mr. Martin L. GERSEY
15	Director of Human Resources	Ms. Sara ERMETI
24	Dir of Instructional Media Svcs	Mr. Jim YOCOM
29	Dir Alumni Affs/Campus Ceremonies	Ms. Jeanie METZGER
27	Director Communications/Marketing	Mr. Kenneth W. BAIERL
52	Director of Dental Auxiliary Educ	Ms. Kristyn QUIMBY
51	Director of Extended Learning	Mr. Tim RYAN
97	Director of General Studies	Dr. David A. VOLLRATH
85	Director of International Programs	Dr. Scott SERNAU
38	Director Student Counseling Ctr	Mr. James HURST
07	Director of Admissions	Vacant
09	Director of Institutional Research	Mr. Biniam TESFAMARIAM
28	Director of Diversity	Vacant
30	Director of Development	Ms. Dina HARRIS
39	Director of Student Housing	Vacant
21	Director of Accounting	Ms. Kathleen PIZANA
37	Associate Director of Financial Aid	Ms. Cyndi LANG
49	Dean of Liberal Arts & Science	Dr. Elizabeth E. DUNN
50	Dean of Business & Economics	Dr. Robert DUCOFFE
53	Dean of Education	Dr. Marvin LYNN
57	Dean of the Arts	Dr. Marvin CURTIS
66	Dean of Nursing/Health Profess	Dr. Mario ORTIZ
08	Dean of Library Services	Ms. Vicki BLOOM

*Indiana University Southeast (F)

4201 Grant Line Road, New Albany IN 47150-6405
County: Floyd FICE Identification: 001817
Unit ID: 151379
Telephone: (812) 941-2000 Carnegie Class: Master's L
FAX Number: (812) 941-2475 Calendar System: Semester
URL: www.ius.edu
Established: 1941 Annual Undergrad Tuition & Fees (In-State): $6,700
Enrollment: 6,904 Coed
Affiliation or Control: State IRS Status: 501(c)3
Highest Offering: Master's
Program: Occupational; Liberal Arts And General; Teacher Preparatory; Professional
Accreditation: NH, BUS, NURSE, TED

Code	Title	Name
02	Interim Chancellor	Dr. Barbara A. BICHELMEYER
05	Exec Vice Chanc Academic Affairs	Dr. Uric DUFRENE
10	Vice Chanc Administration/Finance	Mr. Dana C. WAVLE
32	Vice Chancellor Student Affairs	Mr. Jason L. MERIWETHER
29	Int Vice Chanc Alumni/Cmty Rels	Mr. Jerry A. WAYNE
20	Assoc Vice Chanc Academic Affairs	Dr. Annette M. WYANDOTTE
13	Chief Information Officer	Mr. Thomas SAWYER
07	Director Admissions	Ms. Anne M. SKUCE
04	Admin Assistant to the Chancellor	Ms. Charla K. STONECIPHER
35	Dean for Student Life	Mr. Seuth CHALEUNPHONH
06	Registrar	Mr. Patrick FAWCETT
37	Director Student Financial Aid	Ms. Brittany HUBBARD
08	Director Library Services	Mr. C. Martin ROSEN
36	Director Career Development Center	Mr. James E. LEWIS, III

18 Director Physical Plant .... Mr. James WOLFE, JR.
14 Dir IT Communications & Support .... Mr. Nicholas T. RAY
21 Director Accounting Services .... Mr. Michael J. KERSTIENS
41 Director Athletics .... Mr. Joseph M. GLOVER
72 Purdue Pgms Site Administrator .... Dr. Andy SCHAFFER
15 Director Human Resources .... Ms. Ann B. LEE
09 Director Institutional Research .... Dr. Tanlee T. WASSON
19 Chief Safety & Security .... Mr. Charles EDELEN
38 Dir Advis Center-Exploratory Stdnts .... Ms. Rebecca B. TURNER
22 Staff Equity & Diversity .... Ms. Darlene P. YOUNG
26 Dir of University Communication .... Ms. Jennifer J. WOLF
39 Director Residence Life & Housing .... Ms. Amanda G. STONECIPHER
51 Manager Continuing Studies .... Ms. Saundra E. GORDON
79 Dean School Arts & Letters .... Dr. Samantha EARLEY
81 Dean School Natural Sciences .... Dr. Elaine HAUB
83 Dean School Social Sciences .... Dr. Joseph L. WERT
50 Dean School Business .... Dr. A. Jay WHITE
53 Dean School Education .... Dr. Gloria J. MURRAY
66 Int Dean School Nursing .... Dr. Jacquelyn C. REID
46 Dean for Research .... Dr. Diane E. WILLE

* *Indiana University-Purdue University Columbus* (A)

4601 Central Avenue, Columbus IN 47203
Telephone: (812) 348-7271 Identification: 770185
Accreditation: &NH

† Main campus is Indiana University-Purdue University Indianapolis in Indianapolis, IN.

Indiana Wesleyan University (B)

4201 S Washington Street, Marion IN 46953-4999
County: Grant FICE Identification: 001822
Unit ID: 151801
Telephone: (765) 674-6901 Carnegie Class: Master's L
FAX Number: (765) 677-2499 Calendar System: 4/1/4
URL: www.indwes.edu
Established: 1920 Annual Undergrad Tuition & Fees: $23,628
Enrollment: 15,580 Coed
Affiliation or Control: Wesleyan Church IRS Status: 501(c)3
Highest Offering: Doctorate
Program: Liberal Arts And General; Teacher Preparatory; Professional; Business Emphasis
Accreditation: NH, CACREP, EXSC, MUS, NURSE, SW, TED, @THEOL

01 President .... Dr. David WRIGHT
03 Executive Vice President .... Dr. Keith NEWMAN
05 Interim Provost .... Dr. Larry LINDSAY
10 Vice President Finance/CFO .... Dr. Duane KILTY
49 VP & Dean College of Arts & Science .... Dr. Darlene BRESSLER
51 Int VP & Dean Adult & Prof Studies .... Dr. Audrey HAHN
88 Vice President Wesley Seminary .... Dr. Wayne SCHMIDT
58 Dean Graduate School .... Dr. Jim FULLER
76 Dean School of Health Sciences .... Dr. Scott MCPHEE
88 Dean of the Seminary .... Dr. Ken SCHENCK
66 Exec Director School of Nursing .... Dr. Barbara IHRKE
32 Vice Pres Student Development .... Dr. Michael MOFFITT
84 Vice Pres Enrollment Management .... Mrs. Janelle VERNON
13 VP Info Tech/CIO/Facil Svcs/Cmp Pln .... Mr. John JONES
09 Asst Provost Inst Research & Accred .... Dr. Don SPROWL
88 Assistant Provost for Scholarship .... Dr. Jerry PATTENGALE
20 Assistant Provost for Acad Svcs .... Mrs. Karen ROORBACH
37 Associate VP Financial Aid .... Mr. Thomas RATLIFF
08 Director Library Resources .... Mrs. Shelia CARLBLOM
08 Director Off-campus Library Svcs .... Mrs. Jule KIND
29 Director of Alumni .... Mr. Rick CARDER
07 Director Admissions .... Mr. Daniel SOLMS
15 Director Personnel Services .... Mrs. Diane MCDANIEL
06 University Registrar .... Mrs. Kim NICHOLSON
21 Controller .... Mrs. Tiffany LEWIS
36 Director Center for Life Calling .... Dr. Bill MILLARD
41 Athletic Director .... Mr. Mark DEMICHAEL
42 Dean of the Chapel .... Dr. Jim LO
44 Director Planned Giving .... Mr. Brian LEWIS
92 Exec Director of Honors College .... Mr. David RIGGS

International Business College (C)

5699 Coventry Lane, Fort Wayne IN 46804-9990
County: Allen FICE Identification: 004579
Unit ID: 151458
Telephone: (260) 459-4500 Carnegie Class: Bac/Assoc
FAX Number: (260) 436-1896 Calendar System: Semester
URL: www.ibcfortwayne.edu
Established: 1889 Annual Undergrad Tuition & Fees: $13,560
Enrollment: 438 Coed
Affiliation or Control: Proprietary IRS Status: Proprietary
Highest Offering: Baccalaureate
Program: Occupational; 2-Year Principally Bachelor's Creditable
Accreditation: ACICS, MAC

01 President .... Mr. Steve KINZER
05 Director of Education .... Ms. Amee AUGENSTEIN
07 Director of Admissions .... Ms. Gena HOPKINS
32 Student Services Director .... Ms. Roxanna SHULL
51 Director Continuing Education .... Mr. Amee AUGENSPEIN
36 Director of Placement .... Vacant
06 Registrar .... Ms. Cara CLAPPER

International Business College (D)

7205 Shadeland Station, Indianapolis IN 46256-3997
Telephone: (317) 813-2300 Identification: 666929
Accreditation: ACICS, DA, MAC

† Main campus is International Business College in Fort Wayne, IN.

ITT Technical Institute (E)

2810 Dupont Commerce Court,
Fort Wayne IN 46825-2393
Telephone: (260) 497-6200 FICE Identification: 008329
Accreditation: ACICS

† Main campus is ITT Technical Institute in Indianapolis, IN.

ITT Technical Institute (F)

9511 Angola Court, Indianapolis IN 46268-1119
County: Marion FICE Identification: 007329
Unit ID: 151519
Telephone: (317) 875-8640 Carnegie Class: Master's S
FAX Number: (317) 875-8641 Calendar System: Quarter
URL: www.itt-tech.edu
Established: 1956 Annual Undergrad Tuition & Fees: N/A
Enrollment: 5,597 Coed
Affiliation or Control: Proprietary IRS Status: Proprietary
Highest Offering: Master's
Program: Technical Emphasis
Accreditation: ACICS, CAHIIM

ITT Technical Institute (G)

2525 N Shadeland Avenue, Suite 103,
Indianapolis IN 46219
Telephone: (317) 351-3800 Identification: 770651
Accreditation: ACICS

† Main campus is ITT Technical Institute in Indianapolis, IN.

ITT Technical Institute (H)

8488 Georgia Street, Merrillville IN 46410
Telephone: (219) 738-6100 Identification: 770650
Accreditation: ACICS

† Main campus is ITT Technical Institute in Indianapolis, IN.

ITT Technical Institute (I)

10999 Stahl Road, Newburgh IN 47630-7429
Telephone: (812) 858-1600 FICE Identification: 007327
Accreditation: ACICS

† Main campus is ITT Technical Institute in Indianapolis, IN.

ITT Technical Institute (J)

17390 Dugdale Drive, Suite 100, South Bend IN 46635
Telephone: (574) 247-8300 Identification: 666700
Accreditation: ACICS

† Main campus is ITT Technical Institute in Indianapolis, IN.

* Ivy Tech Community College of Indiana-Central Office (K)

50 W Fall Creek Parkway N Drive,
Indianapolis IN 46208-5752
County: Marion FICE Identification: 008546
Unit ID: 363563
Telephone: (317) 921-4882 Carnegie Class: N/A
FAX Number: (317) 921-4753
URL: www.ivytech.edu

01 President .... Mr. Thomas J. SNYDER
05 Sr VP Academic Affairs/Provost .... Dr. Mary E. OSTRYE
30 Sr Vice Pres Ivy Tech Foundation .... Mr. John MURPHY
88 Sr VP Pgm Analysis/Instl Efficiency .... Mr. Jeff TERP
10 VP Finance/Treasurer/Gen Counsel .... Mr. Chris RUHL
32 Vice Pres Stdnt Affairs/Enrol Mgmt .... Dr. Benjamin YOUNG
103 Vice Pres Workforce & Econ Dev .... Dr. Rebecca NICKOLI
27 Vice Pres Marketing/Communications .... Mr. Jeff FANTER
12 President Corporate College .... Vacant
20 Assoc Vice Pres Academic Affairs .... Dr. Russell D. BAKER
18 AVP Facilities Inst Planning .... Mrs. Lori DUNLAP
53 Exec Dir Academic Policy/Assessment .... Vacant
88 Chief Finan Student Resources Offcr .... Mr. Ben BURTON
15 Executive Director Human Resources .... Mrs. Julie LORTON-ROWLAND
09 Exec Dir Institutional Research .... Mrs. Jill KRAMER
21 Assistant Treasurer .... Mr. Mark A. HUSK
13 Chief Technology Officer .... Mrs. Anne BRINSON

* Ivy Tech Community College-Central Indiana (L)

50 W Fall Creek Parkway North Drive,
Indianapolis IN 46208-5752
County: Marion FICE Identification: 009917
Unit ID: 150987
Telephone: (317) 921-4882 Carnegie Class: Assoc/Pub-U-SC
FAX Number: (317) 921-4753 Calendar System: Semester
URL: www.ivytech.edu/indianapolis/
Established: 1966 Annual Undergrad Tuition & Fees (In-State): $3,455
Enrollment: 22,150 Coed
Affiliation or Control: State IRS Status: 501(c)3
Highest Offering: Associate Degree
Program: Occupational; 2-Year Principally Bachelor's Creditable
Accreditation: NH, ACBSP, ACFEI, ADNUR, CAHIIM, COARC, COARCP, FUSER, MAC, NAIT, PNUR, RAD, SURGT

02 Chancellor .... Dr. Kathleen F. LEE
05 VC of Academic Affairs .... Dr. Frank MOMAN
32 Vice Chancellor of Student Affairs .... Dr. Darrell CAIN
10 Executive Director of Finance .... Mr. Michael DAVIDSON
15 Exec Director of Human Resources .... Ms. Angie SCANLON
11 Exec Dir of Administrative Services .... Mr. James N. BARNEY
103 Exec Dir Workforce & Economic Devel .... Ms. Stephanie TAYLOR
30 Exec Dir Institutional Advancement .... Mr. Randy ROGERS
35 Asst Vice Chanc Student Affairs .... Mr. Jerry H. HARRELL
37 Director of Financial Aid .... Vacant
06 Registrar .... Ms. Amanda OWEN
07 Director of Admissions .... Dr. Tracy FUNK
09 Director of Institutional Research .... Mr. Jeff CORNETT
36 Director of Career Services .... Dr. Rebecca PATTEN-LEMONS
96 Director of Purchasing .... Mr. Jerry L. KOENIG
20 Asst Vice Chanc Academic Affairs .... Mr. Gary PELLICO
26 Director Marketing/Communications .... Ms. Kelli FORD
46 Director of Resource Development .... Mr. Paul ST. ANGELO

* *Ivy Tech Community College of Indiana-Anderson* (M)

104 West 53rd Street, Anderson IN 46013-1502
Telephone: (800) 644-4882 Identification: 770239
Accreditation: &NH

† Main campus is Ivy Tech Community College of Indiana-Central Office in Indianapolis, IN.

* *Ivy Tech Community College of Indiana-Bloomington* (N)

200 N Daniels Way, Bloomington IN 47404-9772
Telephone: (812) 332-1559 FICE Identification: 035213
Accreditation: &NH, ACBSP, ACFEI, ADNUR, CAHIIM, COARC, EMT, NAIT, PNUR, RTT

† Main campus is Ivy Tech Community College of Indiana-Central Office In Indianapolis, IN.

* *Ivy Tech Community College of Indiana-Columbus* (O)

4475 Central Avenue, Columbus IN 47203-1868
Telephone: (812) 372-9925 FICE Identification: 010038
Accreditation: &NH, ART, ACBSP, ADNUR, DA, EMT, MAC, NAIT, PNUR, SURGT

† Main campus is Ivy Tech Community College of Indiana-Central Office in Indianapolis, IN.

* *Ivy Tech Community College of Indiana-East Central* (P)

4301 Cowan Road, Muncie IN 47302-9448
Telephone: (765) 289-2291 FICE Identification: 009924
Accreditation: &NH, ACBSP, ACFEI, ADNUR, COARC, DA, DH, MAC, NAIT, PNUR, PTAA, RAD, SURGT

† Main campus is Ivy Tech Community College of Indiana-Central Office in Indianapolis, IN.

* *Ivy Tech Community College of Indiana-East Chicago* (Q)

410 East Columbus Drive, East Chicago IN 46312
Telephone: (219) 392-3600 Identification: 770240
Accreditation: &NH

† Main campus is Ivy Tech Community College of Indiana-Central Office in Indianapolis, IN.

* *Ivy Tech Community College of Indiana-Elkhart* (R)

22531 County Road 18, Goshen IN 46528
Telephone: (574) 830-0375 Identification: 770241
Accreditation: &NH

† Main campus is Ivy Tech Community College of Indiana-Central Office in Indianapolis, IN.

* *Ivy Tech Community College of Indiana-Kokomo* (S)

1815 E Morgan Street, Box 1373, Kokomo IN 46903-1373
Telephone: (765) 459-0561 FICE Identification: 010041
Accreditation: &NH, ACBSP, ADNUR, DA, EMT, MAC, NAIT, PNUR, SURGT

† Main campus is Ivy Tech Community College of Indiana-Central Office in Indianapolis, IN.

*Ivy Tech Community College of Indiana-Lafayette (A)

3101 S Creasy Lane, Box 6299, Lafayette IN 47903-6299
Telephone: (765) 269-5000 FICE Identification: 010039
Accreditation: &NH, ACBSP, ADNUR, COARC, DA, MAC, NAIT, PNUR, SURGT

† Main campus is Ivy Tech Community College of Indiana-Central Office in Indianapolis, IN.

*Ivy Tech Community College of Indiana-Lawrenceburg-Riverfront (B)

50 Walnut Street, Lawrenceburg IN 47025
Telephone: (812) 573-4010 Identification: 770242
Accreditation: &NH, MAC

† Main campus is Ivy Tech Community College of Indiana-Central Office in Indianapolis, IN.

*Ivy Tech Community College of Indiana-Logansport (C)

1 Ivy Tech Way, Logansport IN 46947
Telephone: (866) 753-5102 Identification: 770243
Accreditation: &NH

† Main campus is Ivy Tech Community College of Indiana-Central Office in Indianapolis, IN.

*Ivy Tech Community College of Indiana-Marion (D)

261 S Commerce Drive, Marion IN 46953
Telephone: (800) 644-4882 Identification: 770244
Accreditation: &NH, MAC

† Main campus is Ivy Tech Community College of Indiana-Central Office in Indianapolis, IN.

*Ivy Tech Community College of Indiana-Michigan City (E)

3714 Franklin Drive, Michigan City IN 46360
Telephone: (219) 879-9137 Identification: 770245
Accreditation: &NH, MAC

† Main campus is Ivy Tech Community College of Indiana-Central Office in Indianapolis, IN.

*Ivy Tech Community College of Indiana-North Central (F)

220 Dean Johnson Boulevard, South Bend IN 46601-3415
Telephone: (574) 289-7001 FICE Identification: 008423
Accreditation: &NH, ART, ACBSP, ACFEI, ADNUR, COARC, DA, DH, EMT, MAC, MLTAD, NAIT, PHLEB, PNUR

† Main campus is Ivy Tech Community College of Indiana-Central Office in Indianapolis, IN.

*Ivy Tech Community College of Indiana-Northeast (G)

3800 N Anthony Boulevard, Fort Wayne IN 46805-1489
Telephone: (260) 482-9171 FICE Identification: 009926
Accreditation: &NH, ACBSP, ACFEI, ADNUR, COARC, EMT, MAC, NAIT, PNUR

† Main campus is Ivy Tech Community College of Indiana-Central Office in Indianapolis, IN.

*Ivy Tech Community College of Indiana-Northwest (H)

1440 E 35th Avenue, Gary IN 46409-1499
Telephone: (219) 981-1111 FICE Identification: 010040
Accreditation: &NH, ACBSP, ACFEI, ADNUR, COARC, #FUSER, MAC, NAIT, PNUR, PTAA, SURGT

† Main campus is Ivy Tech Community College of Indiana-Central Office in Indianapolis, IN.

*Ivy Tech Community College of Indiana-Richmond (I)

2357 Chester Boulevard, Richmond IN 47374-1298
Telephone: (765) 966-2656 FICE Identification: 010037
Accreditation: &NH, ACBSP, ADNUR, MAC, NAIT, PNUR

† Main campus is Ivy Tech Community College of Indiana-Central Office in Indianapolis, IN.

*Ivy Tech Community College of Indiana-Southeast (J)

590 Ivy Tech Drive, Madison IN 47250-1883
Telephone: (812) 265-2580 FICE Identification: 009923
Accreditation: &NH, ACBSP, ADNUR, MAC, PNUR

† Main campus is Ivy Tech Community College of Indiana-Central Office in Indianapolis, IN.

*Ivy Tech Community College of Indiana-Southern Indiana (K)

8204 Highway 311, Sellersburg IN 47172-1897
Telephone: (812) 246-3301 FICE Identification: 010109
Accreditation: &NH, ACBSP, ADNUR, COARC, MAC, MLTAD, NAIT, PNUR, #PTAA

† Main campus is Ivy Tech Community College of Indiana-Central Office in Indianapolis, IN.

*Ivy Tech Community College of Indiana-Southwest (L)

3501 First Avenue, Evansville IN 47710-1881
Telephone: (812) 426-2865 FICE Identification: 009925
Accreditation: &NH, ACBSP, ADNUR, ART, EMT, MAC, NAIT, PNUR, SURGT

† Main campus is Ivy Tech Community College of Indiana-Central Office in Indianapolis, IN.

*Ivy Tech Community College of Indiana-Valparaiso (M)

3100 Ivy Tech Drive, Valparaiso IN 46383
Telephone: (219) 464-8514 Identification: 770246
Accreditation: &NH

† Main campus is Ivy Tech Community College of Indiana-Central Office in Indianapolis, IN.

*Ivy Tech Community College of Indiana-Wabash (N)

277 N Thorne Street, Wabash IN 46992
Telephone: (260) 563-8828 Identification: 770247
Accreditation: &NH

† Main campus is Ivy Tech Community College of Indiana-Central Office in Indianapolis, IN.

*Ivy Tech Community College of Indiana-Wabash Valley (O)

8000 S. Education Drive, Terre Haute IN 47802-4833
Telephone: (812) 299-1121 FICE Identification: 008547
Accreditation: &NH, ACBSP, ADNUR, COARC, EMT, MAC, MLTAD, NAIT, PNUR, RAD, SURGT

† Main campus is Ivy Tech Community College of Indiana-Central Office in Indianapolis, IN.

*Ivy Tech Community College of Indiana-Warsaw (P)

2545 Silreus Crossing, Warsaw IN 46582
Telephone: (574) 267-5428 Identification: 770248
Accreditation: &NH

† Main campus is Ivy Tech Community College of Indiana-Central Office in Indianapolis, IN.

Kaplan College (Q)

7833 Indianapolis Boulevard, Hammond IN 46324-3347
County: Lake FICE Identification: 022018
Unit ID: 152415
Telephone: (219) 844-0100 Carnegie Class: Assoc/PrivFP
FAX Number: (219) 844-0105 Calendar System: Quarter
URL: www.getinfo.kaplancollege.com
Established: 1969 Annual Undergrad Tuition & Fees: $14,895
Enrollment: 397 Coed
Affiliation or Control: Proprietary IRS Status: Proprietary
Highest Offering: Associate Degree
Program: Occupational
Accreditation: ACICS

01 Campus President .... Mr. Johnny CRAIG

Kaplan College (R)

7302 Woodland Drive, Indianapolis IN 46278-1736
County: Marion FICE Identification: 009777
Unit ID: 152220
Telephone: (317) 299-6001 Carnegie Class: Assoc/PrivFP
FAX Number: (317) 298-6342 Calendar System: Semester
URL: www.getinfo.kaplancollege.com
Established: 1967 Annual Undergrad Tuition & Fees: $15,735
Enrollment: 322 Coed
Affiliation or Control: Proprietary IRS Status: Proprietary
Highest Offering: Associate Degree
Program: Occupational
Accreditation: ACCSC, DA

05 Director of Education .... Ms. Kimberly WILSON

† School is in teach-out mode. Will close December 2013.

Kaplan College (S)

4200 South East Street, Indianapolis IN 46227
Telephone: (317) 782-0315 Identification: 770575
Accreditation: ACCSC, ACICS

† Main campus is Kaplan College in Indianapolis, IN.

Lincoln College of Technology (T)

7225 Winton Drive, Building 128, Indianapolis IN 46268-4198
County: Marion FICE Identification: 007938
Unit ID: 151661
Telephone: (317) 632-5553 Carnegie Class: Assoc/PrivFP
FAX Number: (317) 687-0475 Calendar System: Semester
URL: www.lincolntech.com
Established: 1962 Annual Undergrad Tuition & Fees: $30,000
Enrollment: 979 Coed
Affiliation or Control: Proprietary IRS Status: Proprietary
Highest Offering: Associate Degree
Program: Occupational
Accreditation: ACCSC

01 President .... Todd CLARK
05 Vice President of Education .... Dale SHEPPERSON
11 Director Administrative Services .... LaTrina JOHNSON
36 Director Student Placement .... Jennifer FINESILVER

Manchester University (U)

604 E College Avenue, North Manchester IN 46962-1225
County: Wabash FICE Identification: 001820
Unit ID: 151777
Telephone: (260) 982-5000 Carnegie Class: Bac/Diverse
FAX Number: (260) 982-5043 Calendar System: 4/1/4
URL: www.manchester.edu
Established: 1889 Annual Undergrad Tuition & Fees: $27,920
Enrollment: 1,345 Coed
Affiliation or Control: Church Of The Brethren IRS Status: 501(c)3
Highest Offering: Doctorate
Program: Liberal Arts And General; Teacher Preparatory; Professional
Accreditation: NH, @PHAR, SW, TED

01 President .... Dr. Jo YOUNG SWITZER
03 Executive Vice President .... Dr. David F. MCFADDEN
05 Vice President Academic Affairs .... Dr. Glenn R. SHARFMAN
10 Vice Pres Financial Affairs/Treas .... Mr. Jack A. GOCHENAUR
32 Vice President Student Development .... Dr. Beth E. SWEITZER-RILEY
30 Vice President College Advancement .... Mr. Michael EASTMAN
84 VP Enrollment & Marketing .... Mr. Scott OCHANDER
07 Director of Admissions .... Mr. Adam HOHMAN
20 Associate Academic Dean .... Dr. Mark W. HUNTINGTON
29 Exec Director of Alumni Relations .... Ms. Jennifer SHEPHERD
30 Director of Development .... Mr. Drew FLAMM
15 Director Human Resources .... Mr. Dale E. CARPENTER
08 Director of the Library .... Ms. Jill LICHTSINN
06 Registrar .... Ms. Lila D. HAMMER
24 Director of Audio-Visual Services .... Mr. Stanley G. PITTMAN
38 Director of Counseling .... Ms. Danette NORMAN TILL
36 Director of Career Services .... Ms. Elizabeth J. BUSHNELL
39 Director of Residence Life .... Mr. Allen J. MACHIELSON
42 Campus Pastor .... Mr. Walt WILTSCHEK
41 Director of Athletics .... Mr. Rick ESPESET
13 Director of Mgmt Info Services .... Mr. Michael CASE
19 Director of Security .... Mr. Leslie L. GAHL
44 Director of the Manchester Fund .... Ms. Janeen W. KOOI
37 Director of Student Financial Aid .... Ms. Sherri L. SHOCKEY
88 Director of Multicultural Affairs .... Mr. Michael G. DIXON
26 Director of Public Relations .... Ms. Jeri S. KORNEGAY
18 Director of Physical Plant .... Mr. Christopher W. GARBER
23 Director of Health Services .... Ms. Heather R. BANKS
21 Senior Accountant .... Mr. Michael J. LECKRONE
35 Director Student Affairs .... Ms. Shanon L. FAWBUSH
96 Director of Purchasing .... Mr. Quentin J. MOUDY
40 Bookstore Manager .... Ms. Heather K. GOCHENAUR

Marian University (V)

3200 Cold Spring Road, Indianapolis IN 46222-1997
County: Marion FICE Identification: 001821
Unit ID: 151786
Telephone: (317) 955-6000 Carnegie Class: Bac/Diverse
FAX Number: (317) 955-6448 Calendar System: Semester
URL: www.marian.edu
Established: 1851 Annual Undergrad Tuition & Fees: $28,400
Enrollment: 2,582 Coed
Affiliation or Control: Roman Catholic IRS Status: 501(c)3
Highest Offering: Doctorate
Program: Liberal Arts And General; Teacher Preparatory; Professional
Accreditation: NH, IACBE, NURSE, @OSTEO, TED

01 President .... Mr. Daniel J. ELSENER
05 Executive VP and Provost .... Dr. Thomas ENNEKING
45 Sr VP Planning/Marketing/Advanceme .... Mr. Dan CONWAY
10 VP for Finance & Business Opers .... Mr. Greg GINDER
26 VP for Marketing Communications .... Mr. Mark APPLE
30 VP for Institutional Advancement .... Mr. John FINKE
32 VP Student Affairs/Dean of Students .... Ms. Ruth RODGERS
63 VP and Dean College of Osteopathic .... Dr. Paul EVANS
84 AVP Enrollment Management .... Vacant
37 Dean Financial Aid/Enroll Mgmt .... Mr. Chad BIR
20 Dean for Academic Affairs .... Mr. William HARTING
18 Director of Projects & Procurement .... Ms. Audra BLASDEL
41 Director of Athletics .... Mr. Steve DOWNING

29 Director of Alumni Relations ..... Ms. Nicholle ELLIS
06 Registrar ..... Ms. Jennifer SCHWARTZ
08 Director of Graduate Library Svcs ..... Ms. Nancy KIRKPATRICK
35 Director of Student Act/Orientation ..... Mr. Ben BRAKSICK
19 Director of Safety & Police Svcs ..... Mr. Scott RALPH
13 Chief Information Office ..... Mr. Peter E. WILLIAMS
27 Manager of Event Marketing and Spon ..... Ms. Maggie KUCIK
36 Dir of Internships & Career Svcs ..... Dr. Leanne MALLOY
42 Director of Campus Ministry ..... Mr. Adam SETMEYER
38 Director Academic Support Services ..... Mrs. Marjorie BATIC
07 AVP for Enrollment Management ..... Vacant
55 Exec Director Adult Programs ..... Ms. Amy BENNETT
38 Director of Counseling Services ..... Ms. Leanne MALLOY
88 Director of Advancement Information ..... Vacant
23 Director of Health & Wellness Svcs ..... Ms. Jan CARNAGHI
09 Director of Institutional Research ..... Mr. William HARTING
15 Director of Human Resources ..... Ms. Anita HERBERTZ
21 Director of Business Services ..... Ms. Alice SHELTON
40 Bookstore Manager ..... Ms. Allison BONEZ

Martin University (A)

2171 Avondale Place, PO 18567,
Indianapolis IN 46218-3878
County: Marion FICE Identification: 021408
Unit ID: 151810
Telephone: (317) 543-3235 Carnegie Class: Bac/A&S
FAX Number: (317) 543-3257 Calendar System: Semester
URL: www.martin.edu
Established: 1977 Annual Undergrad Tuition & Fees: $14,180
Enrollment: 718 Coed
Affiliation or Control: Independent Non-Profit IRS Status: 501(c)3
Highest Offering: Master's
Program: Liberal Arts And General
Accreditation: NH

01 President ..... Vacant
03 Executive Vice President ..... Ms. Ruby BOWMAN
05 Int Vice President Academic Affairs ..... Dr. Martin GREENAN
09 Vice Pres of Institutional Research ..... Dr. Laura-Lee DAVIDSON
32 Vice President Student Services ..... Dr. Stanley SINGLETON
10 Vice Pres Fiscal Affairs ..... Mr. Michael MOOS
30 VP of Sponsored Programs ..... Dr. David VANDERSTEL
37 Director Financial Aid ..... Ms. Corrine FURTICK
18 Manager of Facilities ..... Mr. William WOODSON
31 Director of Community Relations ..... Mr. Ricky ELMORE
06 Registrar ..... Vacant
21 Bursar ..... Mrs. Virginia GOODWIN
40 Manager Bookstore ..... Ms. Tanya DOUGLAS
96 Purchasing Manager ..... Ms. Pam HOOD

MedTech College (B)

7230 Engle Road, Suite 200, Fort Wayne IN 46804
Telephone: (260) 436-3272 Identification: 666677
Accreditation: ACICS, MAC, MLTAD

† Main campus is MedTech College in Indianapolis, IN.

MedTech College (C)

1500 American Way, Greenwood IN 46143
Telephone: (317) 534-0322 Identification: 666678
Accreditation: ACICS, MAC, MLTAD

† Main campus is MedTech College in Indianapolis, IN.

MedTech College (D)

6612 East 75th Street Suite 300, Indianapolis IN 46250
County: Marion FICE Identification: 007362
Unit ID: 448415
Telephone: (317) 845-0100 Carnegie Class: Assoc/PrivFP
FAX Number: (317) 845-1800 Calendar System: Quarter
URL: www.medtechcollege.edu
Established: 2004 Annual Undergrad Tuition & Fees: $15,648
Enrollment: 1,147 Coed
Affiliation or Control: Proprietary IRS Status: Proprietary
Highest Offering: Associate Degree
Program: Occupational
Accreditation: ACICS, #MAC, MLTAD, PNUR

01 Executive Director ..... Ms. Amye MELTON

Mid-America College of Funeral Service (E)

3111 Hamburg Pike, Jeffersonville IN 47130-9630
County: Clark FICE Identification: 010618
Unit ID: 151962
Telephone: (812) 288-8878 Carnegie Class: Spec/Other
FAX Number: (812) 288-5942 Calendar System: Quarter
URL: www.mid-america.edu
Established: 1905 Annual Undergrad Tuition & Fees: $14,000
Enrollment: 90 Coed
Affiliation or Control: Independent Non-Profit IRS Status: 501(c)3
Highest Offering: Associate Degree
Program: Occupational
Accreditation: FUSER

01 President ..... Vacant
32 Dean of Students ..... Mr. Richard D. NELSON
06 Registrar/Director of Admissions ..... Ms. Angela PERRSINGER
29 Director Alumni Relations ..... Vacant
37 Director Student Financial Aid ..... Mr. Richard D. NELSON

Mid-America Reformed Seminary (F)

229 Seminary Drive, Dyer IN 46311-1069
County: Lake FICE Identification: 039893
Unit ID: 373030
Telephone: (219) 864-2400 Carnegie Class: Not Classified
FAX Number: (219) 864-2410 Calendar System: Semester
URL: www.midamerica.edu
Established: 1981 Annual Undergrad Tuition & Fees: $8,250
Enrollment: 40 Coed
Affiliation or Control: Independent Non-Profit IRS Status: 501(c)3
Highest Offering: Master's
Program: Religious Emphasis
Accreditation: THEOL, TRACS

01 President ..... Dr. Cornelius VENEMA
32 Dean of Students ..... Rev. Alan STRANGE
06 Registrar ..... Rev. Alan STRANGE
30 Director of Development ..... Mr. Keith LEMAHIEU
96 Office Manager/Director Purchasing ..... Ms. Florence KOOIMAN
36 Director of Apprenticeship Program ..... Rev. Mark VANDERHART

National American University-Indianapolis (G)

3600 Woodview Terrace, Suite 200, Indianapolis IN 46268
Telephone: (800) 609-1430 Identification: 770393
Accreditation: &NH

† Main campus is National American University in Rapid City, SD.

National College (H)

6131 N Clinton Street, Fort Wayne IN 46825
Telephone: (260) 483-1605 Identification: 770696
Accreditation: ACICS

† Main campus is American National University in Salem, VA.

National College (I)

6060 Castleway West Drive, Indianapolis IN 46250
County: Marion FICE Identification: 010489
Telephone: (317) 578-7353 Carnegie Class: Not Classified
FAX Number: (317) 578-7721 Calendar System: Quarter
URL: www.ncbt.edu
Established: 1886 Annual Undergrad Tuition & Fees: N/A
Enrollment: N/A Coed
Affiliation or Control: Proprietary IRS Status: Proprietary
Highest Offering: Baccalaureate
Program: Occupational
Accreditation: ACICS, CAHIIM, MAC, SURGT

01 Campus Director ..... Mr. Jim ABRAHAM
04 Admin Asst to Campus Director ..... Ms. May MOORE

National College (J)

1030 E Jefferson Boulevard, South Bend IN 46617
Telephone: (574) 307-7100 Identification: 770695
Accreditation: ACICS

† Main campus is American National University in Salem, VA.

Oakland City University (K)

138 N Lucretia Street, Oakland City IN 47660-1099
County: Gibson FICE Identification: 001824
Unit ID: 152099
Telephone: (812) 749-4781 Carnegie Class: Master's M
FAX Number: (812) 749-1233 Calendar System: Semester
URL: www.oak.edu
Established: 1885 Annual Undergrad Tuition & Fees: $18,600
Enrollment: 2,575 Coed
Affiliation or Control: Baptist IRS Status: 501(c)3
Highest Offering: Doctorate
Program: Occupational; 2-Year Principally Bachelor's Creditable; Liberal Arts And General; Teacher Preparatory; Professional; Business Emphasis
Accreditation: NH, IACBE, TED, THEOL

01 President ..... Dr. Ray G. BARBER
11 Vice Pres Administration & Finance ..... Dr. Robert E. YEAGER
05 Provost ..... Dr. Jeffrey MCNABB
44 Vice Pres Planning & Research ..... Dr. Bernard MARLEY
30 Director of Development ..... Mr. Brian BAKER
32 Director Student Affairs/Housing ..... Dr. James PRATT
12 Director Bedford College Center ..... Dr. L. Kay COLLINS
42 Campus Chaplain ..... Rev. Mark GRIMES
06 Registrar ..... Ms. Betty BURNS
07 Director of Admissions ..... Mr. Dave MCFARLAND
37 Director Student Financial Aid ..... Mrs. Cassie SCRAPER
09 Director of Institutional Research ..... Dr. Morris PELZEL
15 Director Personnel Services ..... Mrs. Kris PRATT
91 Director Information Technology ..... Mr. Clint WOOLSEY
88 Director Institutional Assessment ..... Mrs. Amy SATTERLY
08 Learning Resources Center ..... Mrs. Denise PINNICK
29 Dir Alumni Rels/Chief Pub Rels Ofcr ..... Ms. Susan SULLIVAN
36 Director Placement ..... Dr. James PRATT
36 Dir Career & College Directions ..... Mrs. Charity JULIAN
35 Director Student Support Services ..... Mrs. Cinda K. PHILLIPS
88 Director Upward Bound Program ..... Ms. Mary HEALY
10 Business Mgr/Chief Financial Ofcr ..... Mrs. Elizabeth BARBER
88 Dean Sch Adult Degree/Prof Stds ..... Dr. John SUTTON
73 Dean Graduate School of Theology ..... Dr. Douglas LOW
18 Chief Facilities/Physical Plant ..... Mr. Wayne ROWLAND
53 Dean School of Education ..... Dr. Mary Jo BEAUCHAMP
50 Dean School of Business ..... Mr. Norman REYNOLDS
21 Assistant Chief Financial Officer ..... Mrs. Elizabeth CARLISLE
49 Dean School of Arts & Sciences ..... Dr. Claudine CUTCHIN
22 Compliance Officer ..... Ms. Patricia ENDICOTT

Ottawa University Jeffersonville (L)

287 Quarter Master Court, Jeffersonville IN 47130-3669
Telephone: (785) 242-5200 Identification: 666088
Accreditation: &NH

† Main campus is Ottawa University in Ottawa, KS.

Purdue University Main Campus (M)

610 Purdue Mall, West Lafayette IN 47907-2040
County: Tippecanoe FICE Identification: 001825
Unit ID: 243780
Telephone: (765) 494-4600 Carnegie Class: RU/VH
FAX Number: N/A Calendar System: Semester
URL: www.purdue.edu
Established: 1869 Annual Undergrad Tuition & Fees (In-State): $9,992
Enrollment: 39,256 Coed
Affiliation or Control: State IRS Status: 501(c)3
Highest Offering: Doctorate
Program: Liberal Arts And General; Teacher Preparatory; Professional
Accreditation: NH, AAB, ART, AUD, BUS, CACREP, CIDA, CLPSY, CONST, COPSY, CS, DIETC, DIETD, ENG, ENGR, ENGT, FOR, IPSY, LSAR, MFCD, NAIT, NURSE, PHAR, SP, TED, THEA, VET

01 President ..... Mr. Mitchell E. DANIELS, JR.
10 Exec Vice President & Treasurer ..... Mr. Alphonso V. DIAZ
05 Exec VP Acad Affairs/Provost ..... Dr. Timothy D. SANDS
30 Interim Vice Pres for Development ..... Ms. Amy NOAH
16 Vice President Ethics & Compliance ..... Prof. Alysa C. ROLLOCK
10 Sr VP Business Svcs/Asst Treas ..... Mr. James S. ALMOND
13 Vice Pres Information Technology ..... Dr. William G. MCCARTNEY
15 Vice President Human Resources ..... Mr. Luis E. LEWIN
18 Vice President Physical Facilities ..... Mr. Michael B. CLINE
26 Vice President for Public Affairs ..... Ms. Julie K. GRIFFITH
39 Assoc Vice Pres Housing/Food Serv ..... Ms. Beth M. MCCUSKEY
32 Vice President of Student Affairs ..... Dr. Melissa E. EXUM
20 Vice Provost Undergrad Acad Affairs ..... Dr. A. Dale WHITAKER
46 Vice President for Research ..... Dr. Richard O. BUCKIUS
88 Assoc VP for Engagement ..... Dr. Suresh GARIMELLA
86 Assoc VP Governmental Relations ..... Mr. Timothy J. SANDERS
20 Interim VP Faculty Affairs ..... Dr. S. L. WELDON
20 Assistant Provost ..... Dr. Candiss VIBBERT
20 Assistant Provost/Financial Affairs ..... Ms. Connie L. LAPINSKAS
47 Dean College of Agriculture ..... Dr. Jay T. AKRIDGE
59 Dean College Health & Human Science ..... Dr. Christine M. LADISCH
53 Dean College of Education ..... Dr. Maryann SANTOS DE BARONA
54 Dean College of Engineering ..... Dr. Leah H. JAMIESON
49 Dean College of Liberal Arts ..... Dr. Irwin H. WEISER
50 Dean School of Management ..... Dr. P. Christopher EARLEY
67 Dean College of Pharmacy ..... Dr. Craig K. SVENSSON
81 Dean College of Science ..... Dr. Jeffrey T. ROBERTS
72 Dean College of Technology ..... Dr. Gary R. BERTOLINE
74 Dean College of Veterinary Medicine ..... Dr. Willie M. REED
58 Dean of Graduate School ..... Dr. Mark J. SMITH
104 Dean International Programs ..... Dr. Michael A. BRZEZINSKI
08 Dean of Libraries ..... Dr. James L. MULLINS
29 Exec Dir & CEO Alumni Association ..... Mr. Kirk R. CERNY
41 Director Intercollegiate Athletics ..... Mr. Morgan J. BURKE
09 Director of Institutional Research ..... Dr. Jacque L. FROST
36 Director Center Career Opportunity ..... Mr. Timothy B. LUZADER
31 Assistant VP External Relations ..... Vacant
85 Dir Intl Students & Scholars ..... Dr. Joe D. POTTS
25 Director Sponsored Program Svcs ..... Mr. Michael R. LUDWIG
94 Director Women's Studies ..... Dr. Tracey J. BOISSEAU
07 Dean Admiss/Asst VP Enroll Mgmt ..... Dr. Pamela T. HORNE
35 Dean of Students ..... Vacant
04 Executive Assistant to President ..... Ms. Sharon K. WHITLOCK
37 Director Financial Aid ..... Mr. Ted E. MALONE
06 Registrar ..... Vacant
28 Vice Provost Diversity & Inclusion ..... Dr. G. Christine TAYLOR
38 Associate Dean Student Counseling ..... Mr. Robert L. MATE
96 Director of Procurement Services ..... Mr. Phillip D. O'KEEFFE
21 Comptroller ..... Ms. Mary Catherine GAISBAUER
84 Asst VP/Dir Enroll Mgmt/Analys/Rep ..... Mr. Brent M. DRAKE

Purdue University Calumet (N)

2200 169th Street, Hammond IN 46323-2094
County: Lake FICE Identification: 001827
Unit ID: 152248
Telephone: (219) 989-2204 Carnegie Class: Master's L
FAX Number: (219) 989-2581 Calendar System: Semester
URL: www.purduecal.edu
Established: 1946 Annual Undergrad Tuition & Fees (In-State): $7,132
Enrollment: 10,054 Coed
Affiliation or Control: State IRS Status: 501(c)3
Highest Offering: Master's
Program: Liberal Arts And General; Teacher Preparatory; Professional

Accreditation: NH, CACREP, CS, ENG, ENGT, IACBE, MFCD, NAIT, NUR, TED

01 Chancellor .... Thomas L. KEON
05 Vice Chanc Acadmic Affs & Provost .... Ralph V. ROGERS
10 Vice Chanc Administrative Services .... James K. JOHNSTON
30 Vice Chanc for Advancement .... Regina D. BIDDINGS-MURO
13 Interim Vice Chanc Info Services .... Sarah HOWARD
32 Vice Chanc Enroll Mgmt & Stdnt Affs .... Carmen PANLILIO
46 Interim Assoc VC Rsrch & Grad Stds .... Chenn ZHOU
26 Interim Assoc Vice Chanc Marketing .... Kris FALZONE
09 Asst VC Academic Quality & Outreach .... M. Beth PELLICCIOTTI
11 Asst Vice Chancellor for Admin Svcs .... Michael KULL
27 Asst Vice Chanc Advance/Univ Rels .... Wes K. LUKOSHUS
35 Assoc Vice Chanc Stdnt Affs/EOP .... Roy HAMILTON
21 Asst VC Business Svcs/Comptroller .... Randal FREEBOURN
15 Asst Vice Chanc Human Resources .... Mary Beth RINCON
49 Dean Sch Liberal Arts/Social Sc .... Ronald CORTHELL
54 Dean School Engr/Math/Sci .... William R. LAW
72 Dean School of Technology .... Niaz LATIF
50 Dean School of Management .... Jane MUTCHLER
66 Dean School of Nursing .... Gerard S. PEGGY
53 Dean School of Educ/Teacher Educ .... Alice ANDERSON
06 Registrar .... Anne Agosto SEVERA
21 Asst Comptroller/Budget/Fiscal Plng .... Donna ADELSPERGER
37 Director Student Financial Services .... Beatriz CONTRERAS
41 Director of Athletics .... Richard J. COSTELLO
38 Director Counseling Center .... Kenneth JACKSON
08 Dir Research/Learning & Res Svcs .... Tammy GUERRERO
29 Dir Alumni Relations/Annual Giving .... Vacant
22 Director Office of Equity Diversity .... Linda KNOX
19 Chief University Police .... Anthony MARTIN, SR.
85 Exec Dir of International Programs .... Vacant
96 Dir of Procurement/General Services .... Phillip BROWN
39 Director of Housng Residental Educ .... Scott IVERSON
92 Director of the Honors Program .... Rowan JOHN
84 Assoc Dean Enroll Mgmt & Grad Pgms .... Lori FELDMAN
86 Dir Government/Corp & Found Rels .... Vacant

Purdue University North Central Campus (A)

1401 S US 421, Westville IN 46391-9542

County: La Porte | FICE Identification: 001826 | Unit ID: 152266
Telephone: (219) 785-5200 | Carnegie Class: Bac/Diverse
FAX Number: (219) 785-5355 | Calendar System: Semester
URL: www.pnc.edu
Established: 1943 | Annual Undergrad Tuition & Fees (In-State): $7,185
Enrollment: 6,048 | Coed
Affiliation or Control: State | IRS Status: 501(c)3
Highest Offering: Master's
Program: Liberal Arts And General; Teacher Preparatory; Professional
Accreditation: NH, ACBSP, ENGT, NUR, TED

01 Chancellor .... Dr. James B. DWORKIN
04 Executive Asst to the Chancellor .... Mrs. Debra A. NIELSEN
30 Director of Development .... Mrs. Melissa C. WESTPHAL-BENEFIEL
05 Vice Chanc Academic Affairs .... Dr. Karen L. SCHMID
20 Assoc Vice Chanc Acad Affairs .... Dr. Kumara JAYASURIYA
10 Vice Chanc for Admin .... Mr. Stephen R. TURNER
84 VC for Enroll Mgmt & Student Svcs .... Mr. Paul M. MCGUINNESS
32 Asst VC & Dean of Students .... Mr. John WEBER
10 Assoc VC Business Svcs/Budget .... Mr. Phillip E. JANKOWSKI
15 Assoc Vice Chanc Human Resources .... Mrs. Susan T. MILLER
50 Dean College of Business .... Dr. Cynthia ROBERTS
72 Dean College of Engr & Tech .... Dr. Thomas F. BRADY
49 Dean College of Liberal Arts .... Dr. S. Rex MORROW
88 Dean College of Science .... Dr. K. Chris HOLFORD
66 Interim Chair Nursing Department .... Dr. Diane SPOLJORIC
83 Chair Social Sciences Department .... Dr. Michael LYNN
81 Int Chair Biology/Chem Department .... Dr. Jason CURTIS
81 Chair Math/Physics/Statistics Dept .... Dr. Purna DAS
53 Acting Chair Education Department .... Dr. David FEIKES
88 Int Chair English/Foreign Lang Dept .... Dr. Jerry HOLT
60 Chair Communication Dept .... Dr. V. Scott SMITHSON
54 Chair Engr Tech Dept .... Vacant
88 Interim Chr Business & Leadershp .... Dr. Carolyn ROPER
22 Asst Dir EEO & Training .... Ms. Laura ODOM
21 Bursar .... Mrs. Beverly J. PULLER
21 Accounting Manager .... Mr. Brock MARTIN
96 Dir Auxiliary Svcs & Resource Plng .... Mrs. Elizabeth DEPEW
08 Librarian .... Mr. Kent R. JOHNSON
07 Director Enroll & Outreach .... Mrs. Janice WHISLER
06 Assistant Registrar .... Mrs. Jennifer WOLSZCZAK
36 Director of Career Development .... Ms. Natalie CONNORS
37 Dir of Financial Aid & Compliance .... Mr. Brad REMMENGA
38 Director Student Counseling .... Ms. Diana MAROVICH
19 Director of Public Safety .... Mr. Robert GAEKLE
27 Director Media & Comm Services .... Mrs. Carol CONNELLY
41 Director Student Athletics .... Vacant
35 Director Student Activities .... Mrs. Keri MARRS DE BARRON
18 Director Facilities Management .... Mr. L. James SALLEE
09 Institutional Research Specialist .... Mr. Joseph P. WARD
09 Data Specialist .... Mrs. Madonna TRITLE
26 Asst VC of Mktg & Campus Relations .... Mrs. Judy N. JACOBI
88 Coord Special Events & Marketing .... Ms. Liz BERNEL
29 Coord Alumni & Annual Giving .... Mr. Thomas ALBANO
58 Coord Graduate & Extended Learning .... Mrs. Cassandra BOEHLKE
88 Director of Food Service .... Mr. Keith PEFFERS
40 Bookstore Manager .... Ms. Susan PEARSON
88 Coord Service Learning .... Ms. Laura WEAVER
88 Dir School Partnerships .... Mrs. Susan WILSON
88 Dir Student Success Center .... Dr. Jane BROOKS

06 Asst Vice Chanc Enroll Mgmt .... Ms. Sandra CZEKAJ
88 Asst Dean of Enroll Access .... Ms. Mary A. BISHEL
27 Chief Information Officer .... Mrs. Robin BROWN
88 Development Officer .... Mrs. Marie C. FOSTER
88 Wellness Coordinator .... Ms. Kendra GARDIN
88 Dir of Academic Advising .... Ms. Kathleen JOHNSON

Radiological Technologies University-VT (B)

100 E. Wayne St., Ste 140, South Bend IN 46601

County: St. Joseph | Identification: 667156
Telephone: (574) 232-2468 | Carnegie Class: Not Classified
FAX Number: (574) 232-2200 | Calendar System: Semester
URL: www.rtuvt.com
Established: 2009 | Annual Graduate Tuition & Fees: $25,000
Enrollment: N/A | Coed
Affiliation or Control: Proprietary | IRS Status: Proprietary
Highest Offering: Master's; No Undergraduates
Program: Professional
Accreditation: ACICS

01 President .... Brent D. MURPHY

Rose-Hulman Institute of Technology (C)

5500 Wabash Avenue, Terre Haute IN 47803-3920

County: Vigo | FICE Identification: 001830 | Unit ID: 152318
Telephone: (812) 877-1511 | Carnegie Class: Spec/Engg
FAX Number: (812) 877-9925 | Calendar System: Quarter
URL: www.rose-hulman.edu
Established: 1874 | Annual Undergrad Tuition & Fees: $39,462
Enrollment: 2,214 | Coed
Affiliation or Control: Independent Non-Profit | IRS Status: 501(c)3
Highest Offering: Master's
Program: Professional; Technical Emphasis
Accreditation: NH, CS, ENG

01 President .... Dr. James C. CONWELL
03 Senior VP/Chief Admin Officer .... Mr. Robert A. COONS
05 Vice Pres Academic Affairs .... Dr. Phillip J. CORNWELL
30 Vice President Inst Advancement .... Mr. Rickey N. MCCURRY
32 Vice President Student Affairs .... Mr. Peter A. GUSTAFSON
26 VP Communications/Marketing .... Ms. Mary G. BARR
21 Assoc VP for Finance/Controller .... Mr. Matthew D. DAVIS
84 Vice President Enrollment Mgmt .... Mr. James A. GOECKER
03 Vice Pres for Rose-Hulman Ventures .... Dr. Elizabeth M. HAGERMAN
20 Dean of Innovation/Engagement .... Dr. William KLINE
20 Interim Dean of Faculty .... Dr. Richard E. STAMPER
20 Associate Dean of Faculty .... Dr. Azad SIAHMAKOUN
20 Assoc Dean Learning/Technology .... Dr. Kay C. DEE
104 Associate Dean Global Programs .... Dr. Luchen LI
13 Vice Pres Instruct/Admin/Info Tech .... Dr. Louis H. TURCOTTE
18 Sr Director Facilities Operations .... Mr. Michael A. TAYLOR
36 Dir Career Services/Employer Rels .... Mr. Kevin L. HEWERDINE
07 Director of Admissions .... Ms. Lisa M. NORTON
29 Executive Director Alumni Affairs .... Mr. Jim BERTOLI
45 Exec Dir Inst Rsrch/Plng/Assessment .... Dr. Julia M. WILLIAMS
15 Director of Human Resources .... Ms. Kimberly D. MILLER
37 Director of Financial Aid .... Ms. Melinda L. MIDDLETON
41 Director of Athletics .... Mr. Jeffrey L. JENKINS
28 Director Center for Diversity .... Dr. Luanne TILSTRA
44 Director of Planned Giving .... Mr. Chris AIMONE
44 Annual Fund Coordinator .... Ms. Jennifer KENZOR
06 Registrar .... Ms. Jan LIND
08 Library Director .... Ms. Bernadette EWEN
19 Director of Public Safety .... Mr. John S. WOLFE
40 Bookstore Manager .... Ms. Sheryl E. FULK
85 Dir Intl Stdnt Svcs/Disability Svcs .... Ms. Karen A. DEGRANGE
04 Exec Assistant to the President .... Ms. Kerry SCHAFFER
25 Dir Fin Svcs/Sponsored Programs .... Ms. Linda L. PRICE
96 Director Administrative Services .... Mr. Dan WELLS
09 Director of Institutional Research .... Dr. Timothy CHOW
102 Director Corporate & Foundation Rel .... Mr. Richard D. BOYCE
39 Associate Dean of Student Affairs .... Mr. Erik Z. HAYES
35 Dean of Student Affairs .... Mr. Thomas D. MILLER
35 Dean of Student Services .... Ms. Donna J. GUSTAFSON
101 Dir Donor Relations/Exec Asst Board .... Ms. Tammy SHAFFER
105 Web Content Director .... Ms. Marianne MESSINA
108 Director of Assessment .... Ms. Shannon M. SIPES
24 Instructional Technology Manager .... Ms. Janie SZABO
24 Emerging Digital Technologies Mgr .... Mr. Alan WARD
38 Director of Counseling Services .... Dr. Michael LATTA

St. Anthony School of Echocardiography (D)

1201 S. Main Street, Crown Point IN 46307

County: Lake | Identification: 667119
Telephone: (219) 757-6132 | Carnegie Class: Not Classified
FAX Number: (219) 681-6725 | Calendar System: Semester
URL: www.franciscanalliance.org/hospitals/crownpoint
Established: 2004 | Annual Undergrad Tuition & Fees: $11
Enrollment: 13 | Coed
Affiliation or Control: Independent Non-Profit | IRS Status: 501(c)3
Highest Offering: Associate Degree
Program: Occupational; Technical Emphasis
Accreditation: DMS

01 Co-Program Director .... Tracy BULT
01 Co-Program Director .... Karin KOLISZ

Saint Joseph's College (E)

PO Box 870, US Highway 231, Rensselaer IN 47978-0870

County: Jasper | FICE Identification: 001833 | Unit ID: 152363
Telephone: (219) 866-6000 | Carnegie Class: Bac/Diverse
FAX Number: (219) 866-6100 | Calendar System: Semester
URL: www.saintjoe.edu
Established: 1889 | Annual Undergrad Tuition & Fees: $27,350
Enrollment: 1,011 | Coed
Affiliation or Control: Roman Catholic | IRS Status: 501(c)3
Highest Offering: Master's
Program: Liberal Arts And General; Teacher Preparatory; Professional
Accreditation: NH, IACBE, NURSE, TED

01 President .... Dr. F. Dennis RIEGELNEGG
04 Admin Asst to the President .... Mrs. Sheila K. HANEWICH
05 Vice President for Academic Affairs .... Dr. Daniel J. BLANKENSHIP
10 Vice President Business Affairs .... Mr. Hoa NGUYEN
30 Vice Pres Inst Advancement/Mrktng .... Dr. Maureen V. EGAN
44 Asst VP Institutional Advancement .... Mrs. Elizabeth GRAF
32 Dean of Students .... Dr. Leslie FRERE
06 Registrar .... Mrs. Maureen HEALEY
07 Director of Admissions .... Mr. Michael RAMIAN
08 Librarian .... Mrs. Catherine A. SALYERS
14 Director of Computer Center .... Mr. Paul PHAM
38 Director of Counseling Services .... Ms. Laura WAGNER
18 Chief Facilities/Physical Plant .... Mr. Randal FLINN
15 Director Human Resources .... Ms. Nancy STUDER
26 Director of Integrated Marketing .... Ms. Christine BABICK-SAQUI
29 Director Alumni Relations .... Mrs. Kendra ILLINGWORTH
37 Director Student Financial Services .... Mrs. Debra SIZEMORE
28 Director of Diversity .... Mr. Ernest WATSON
36 Director Career Development .... Vacant
41 Athletic Director .... Mr. William MASSOELS
40 Director Bookstore .... Mrs. Rhonda ELIJAH
42 Chaplain/Director Campus Ministry .... Vacant

Saint Mary-of-the-Woods College (F)

St Mary of the Woods IN 47876-0067

County: Vigo | FICE Identification: 001835 | Unit ID: 152381
Telephone: (812) 535-5151 | Carnegie Class: Bac/Diverse
FAX Number: (812) 535-5231 | Calendar System: Semester
URL: www.smwc.edu
Established: 1840 | Annual Undergrad Tuition & Fees: $27,672
Enrollment: 1,031 | Coed
Affiliation or Control: Roman Catholic | IRS Status: 501(c)3
Highest Offering: Master's
Program: Liberal Arts And General
Accreditation: NH, MUS, TED

01 President .... Dr. Dottie KING
30 Vice President for Advancement .... Ms. Karen DYER
10 Vice Pres Finance & Administration .... Mr. Gordon AFDAHL
05 Vice President for Academic Affairs .... Dr. Janet CLARK
32 Vice President for Student Life .... Ms. Vicki KOSOWSKY
84 Vice Pres Enrollment Management .... Ms. Beth TERRELL
06 Registrar .... Mr. Jeff GARDNER
08 Director of the Library .... Ms. Judy TRIBBLE
29 Director Alumnae Affairs .... Ms. Chanel REEDER
26 Executive Dir of College Relations .... Ms. Dee REED
106 Director Woods Online Program .... Ms. Gwen HAGEMEYER
13 Exec Dir Information Technology .... Vacant
21 Controller .... Ms. Susie THOMPSON
36 Director of Career Development .... Ms. Susan GRESHAM
15 Director Human Resources .... Ms. Diana WARREN
18 Chief Facilities/Physical Plant .... Mr. John MORREALE
35 Director Campus Life .... Mr. Jeffrey MALLOY
37 Director Financial Aid .... Ms. Darla HOPPER
44 Dir Major and Planned Gifts .... Ms. April SIMMA
64 Dir Grad Pgm Music Therapy .... Ms. Tracy RICHARDSON
88 Dir Grad Pgm Art Therapy .... Ms. Kathy GOTSHALL
88 Dir Grad Pgm Leadership Development .... Ms. Susan DECKER

Saint Mary's College (G)

Notre Dame IN 46556

County: Saint Joseph | FICE Identification: 001836 | Unit ID: 152390
Telephone: (574) 284-4000 | Carnegie Class: Bac/A&S
FAX Number: (574) 284-4716 | Calendar System: Semester
URL: www.saintmarys.edu
Established: 1844 | Annual Undergrad Tuition & Fees: $34,600
Enrollment: 1,469 | Female
Affiliation or Control: Roman Catholic | IRS Status: 501(c)3
Highest Offering: Baccalaureate
Program: Liberal Arts And General; Teacher Preparatory; Professional
Accreditation: NH, ART, MUS, NURSE, SW, TED

01 President .... Dr. Carol Ann MOONEY
04 Executive Asst to the President .... Ms. Susan C. DAMPEER
05 Provost/Sr VP Academic Affairs .... Dr. Patricia A. FLEMING
26 Vice President College Relations .... Ms. Shari M. RODRIGUEZ
32 Vice President for Student Affairs .... Ms. Karen A. JOHNSON
10 Vice Pres Finance & Administration .... Ms. Susan BOLT
84 Vice Pres for Enrollment Management .... Ms. Mona BOWE

88 Vice President for Mission ... Sr. Veronique WIEDOWER, CSC
89 Associate Dean for Advising ... Ms. Susan VANEK
06 Registrar ... Mr. Todd NORRIS
07 Director of Admission ... Ms. Kristin MCANDREW
08 Director of Library ... Ms. Janet S. FORE
09 Director of Institutional Research ... Ms. Jessica ICKES
29 Director of Alumnae Relations ... Ms. Kara O'LEARY
37 Director of Financial Aid ... Ms. Kathleen M. BROWN
27 Director of Publicity & Cmty Rels ... Ms. Gwen O'BRIEN
38 Director of Women's Health ... Ms. Elizabeth FOURMAN
13 Chief Information Officer ... Mr. Michael BOEHM
15 Director of Human Resources ... Mr. Richard NUGENT
19 Director of Safety & Security ... Mr. David GARIEPY
40 Manager Bookstore ... Vacant
41 Director of Athletics ... Ms. Julie SCHROEDER-BIEK
42 Director of Campus Ministry ... Ms. Judith FEAN
18 Director of Facilities ... Vacant
35 Dir Stdt Involvement/Multicult Pgm ... Ms. Stephanie STEWARD-BRIDGES
96 Director of Purchasing ... Mr. Daniel P. DEETER

Saint Meinrad School of Theology (A)

200 Hill Drive, St. Meinrad IN 47577-1030
County: Spencer FICE Identification: 007276
Unit ID: 152451
Telephone: (812) 357-6611 Carnegie Class: Spec/Faith
FAX Number: (812) 357-6964 Calendar System: Semester
URL: www.saintmeinrad.edu
Established: 1861 Annual Graduate Tuition & Fees: $21,973
Enrollment: 252 Coed
Affiliation or Control: Roman Catholic IRS Status: 501(c)3
Highest Offering: Master's; No Undergraduates
Program: Professional; Religious Emphasis
Accreditation: NH, THEOL

01 President & Rector ... Rev. Denis ROBINSON, OSB
03 Vice Rector ... Rev. Tobias COLGAN, OSB
05 Academic Dean ... Dr. Robert ALVIS
84 Director of Enrollment ... Rev. Brendan MOSS, OSB
42 Director of Spiritual Formation ... Rev. Peter MARSHALL
20 Director of Lay Degree Programs ... Mr. Kyle KRAMER
30 Vice President of Development ... Mr. Michael ZIEMIANSKI
10 Business Manager & Treasurer ... Mrs. Lisa CASTLEBURY
08 Library Director ... Dr. Daniel KOLB
06 Registrar ... Mrs. Donna M. BALBACH
88 Dir Inst for Priests & Presbyterate ... Rev. Ronald KNOTT
21 Director of Budget ... Mrs. Pam DOWLAND
37 Director of Student Financial Aid ... Mrs. Ruth KRESS
26 Director of Communications ... Mrs. Mary Jeanne SCHUMACHER
29 Director of Alumni Relations ... Mr. Tim HERRMANN
38 Director of Student Counseling Ctr ... Sr. Diane PHARO, SCN
09 Director of Institutional Research ... Rev. Bede CISCO, OSB
23 Director of Health Services ... Mrs. Ann ROHLEDER
108 Director of Assessment ... Sr. Jeana VISEL, OSB

Sanford-Brown College (B)

4030 Vincennes Road, Indianapolis IN 46268
Telephone: (317) 532-8300 Identification: 770848
Accreditation: ACICS

† Main campus is Le Cordon Bleu College of Culinary Arts in Los Angeles in Pasadena, CA.

Taylor University (C)

West 236 Reade Avenue, Upland IN 46989-1001
County: Grant FICE Identification: 001838
Unit ID: 152530
Telephone: (765) 998-2751 Carnegie Class: Bac/Diverse
FAX Number: (765) 998-4910 Calendar System: 4/1/4
URL: www.taylor.edu
Established: 1846 Annual Undergrad Tuition & Fees: $28,753
Enrollment: 2,364 Coed
Affiliation or Control: Independent Non-Profit IRS Status: 501(c)3
Highest Offering: Master's
Program: Liberal Arts And General; Teacher Preparatory; Fine Arts Emphasis
Accreditation: NH, CEA, ENG, MUS, SW, TED

01 President ... Dr. Eugene B. HABECKER
05 Provost ... Dr. Jeff MOSHIER
11 VP Business Administration ... Mr. Ronald SUTHERLAND
30 VP University Advancement ... Dr. Ben SELLS
32 VP Student Dev/Dean of Students ... Dr. Skip TRUDEAU
84 VP Enroll Mgmt & Marketing ... Mr. Stephen MORTLAND
10 VP Finance & CFO ... Mr. Stephen OLSON
20 Vice Provost ... Dr. Jeff GROELING
49 Dean Sch Hum/Arts & Bible Studies ... Dr. Thomas JONES
83 Dean Sch of Soc Sciences/Educ & Bus ... Dr. Connie LIGHTFOOT
81 Dean Sch Natural & Applied Sciences ... Dr. William TOLL
104 Dean International Programs ... Dr. Chris BENNETT
13 Chief Information Officer ... Mr. Rob LINEHAN
41 Director of Athletics ... Dr. Angie FINCANNON
20 Dean Faculty Development/Dir CTLE ... Dr. Faye CHECHOWICH
26 Assoc VP for University Relations ... Ms. Joyce WOOD
44 Assoc VP for Campaigns ... Mr. David RITCHIE
44 Assoc VP for Major & Planned Gifts ... Mr. Mike FALDER
29 Assoc VP Alumni & Parent Relations ... Vacant
36 Assoc Dean Students/Dir Career Dev ... Mr. Drew MOSER
37 Assoc Dean Enroll Mgmt/Dir Fin Aid ... Mr. Timothy NACE
08 University Librarian ... Mr. Daniel BOWELL
39 Residence Life Pgm/Asc Dn Stdnt ... Mr. Steve MORLEY
06 Registrar ... Ms. Janet ROGERS
106 Director of Online Learning ... Ms. Carrie MEYER
42 Campus Pastor/Assoc Dean Students ... Rev. Randall GRUENDYKE
15 Asst Director of Human Resources ... Ms. April EVANS
07 Director Admissions ... Ms. Amy BARNETT
18 Director of Physical Plant ... Mr. Greg ELEY
38 Director of Counseling Center ... Mr. Robert NEIDECK
19 Chief of Police/Taylor Police ... Mr. Jeff WALLACE
09 Director IR/Assoc Registrar ... Dr. Edwin WELCH
21 Controller ... Mr. David LLOYD
108 Director Assessment/Quality Improv ... Dr. Kim CASE
88 Payroll Manager ... Ms. Toni NEWLIN
88 University Bursar ... Ms. Cathy MOORMAN
24 Director of Academic Technology ... Mr. Gary FRIESEN

TCM International Institute (D)

6337 Hollister Drive, Indianapolis IN 46224
Identification: 666333
Telephone: (317) 299-0333 Carnegie Class: Not Classified
FAX Number: (317) 290-8607 Calendar System: Semester
URL: www.tcmi.org
Established: 1991 Annual Graduate Tuition & Fees: N/A
Enrollment: N/A Coed
Affiliation or Control: Independent Non-Profit IRS Status: 501(c)3
Highest Offering: Master's; No Undergraduates
Program: Religious Emphasis
Accreditation: NH

01 President ... Dr. Tony TWIST

Trine University (E)

1 University Avenue, Angola IN 46703-1764
County: Steuben FICE Identification: 001839
Unit ID: 152567
Telephone: (260) 665-4100 Carnegie Class: Bac/Diverse
FAX Number: (260) 665-4292 Calendar System: Semester
URL: www.trine.edu
Established: 1884 Annual Undergrad Tuition & Fees: $28,700
Enrollment: 2,465 Coed
Affiliation or Control: Independent Non-Profit IRS Status: 501(c)3
Highest Offering: Master's
Program: Teacher Preparatory; Professional; Business Emphasis
Accreditation: NH, ACBSP, ENG, TED

01 President ... Dr. Earl D. BROOKS, II
03 Senior Vice President ... Mr. Mike BOCK
05 Vice President for Academic Affairs ... Dr. John SHANNON
10 Vice President Finance ... Ms. Jody GREER
30 Vice Pres for Alumni & Development ... Mr. Kent D. STUCKY
84 Vice Pres Enrollment Management ... Dr. Stuart JONES
32 Vice President for Student Services ... Mr. Randy WHITE
51 Asst Vice Pres for Adult Learning ... Dr. Jean DELLER
49 Dean Jannen School of Arts & Sci ... Mr. Craig LAKER
107 Dean of Professional Studies ... Ms. Mersiha ALIC
15 Human Resources ... Mr. Robert MORELAND
41 Athletic Director ... Mr. Matt LAND
06 Registrar ... Ms. Debra F. HELMSING
27 Dir Integrated & Brand Marketing ... Vacant
04 Assistant to the President ... Ms. Gretchen MILLER
37 Director Student Financial Planning ... Ms. Kim BENNETT
13 Chief Information Officer-IT ... Ms. Michelle DUNN
08 Director of the Library ... Ms. Kristina BREWER
36 Int Director of Placement/Coop Educ ... Ms. Linda BATEMAN
09 Director Inst Planning/Analysis ... Ms. Christina ZUMBRUN

Trine University-Fort Wayne Regional Campus (F)

9910 Dupont Circle Dr East, Ste 130, Fort Wayne IN 46825
Telephone: (260) 483-4949 Identification: 770105
Accreditation: &NH

† Main campus is Trine University in Angola, IN.

Trine University-South Bend Regional Campus (G)

4101 Edison Lakes Parkway, Ste 250, Mishawaka IN 46545
Telephone: (574) 243-0500 Identification: 770106
Accreditation: &NH

† Main campus is Trine University in Angola, IN.

University of Evansville (H)

1800 Lincoln Avenue, Evansville IN 47722-1586
County: Vanderburgh FICE Identification: 001795
Unit ID: 150534
Telephone: (812) 488-2000 Carnegie Class: Master's S
FAX Number: (812) 488-2320 Calendar System: Semester
URL: www.evansville.edu
Established: 1854 Annual Undergrad Tuition & Fees: $30,596
Enrollment: 2,498 Coed
Affiliation or Control: United Methodist IRS Status: 501(c)3
Highest Offering: Doctorate
Program: Liberal Arts And General; Teacher Preparatory; Professional
Accreditation: NH, BUS, CS, ENG, MUS, NUR, PTA, PTAA, TED

01 President ... Dr. Thomas A. KAZEE
05 Sr Vice President Academic Affairs ... Dr. John MOSBO
30 VP Development ... Mr. John C. BARNER
10 Vice President Fiscal Affairs/Admin ... Mr. Jeffery M. WOLF
32 VP Student Affairs/Dean of Students ... Ms. Dana CLAYTON
84 Vice President Enrollment Services ... Dr. Shane DAVIDSON
26 VP Marketing and Communication ... Mr. Donald JONES
25 Assoc VP Academic Affs/Grants Dir ... Dr. Jennifer L. GRABAN
35 Asst VP Student Affs/Dir Res Life ... Mr. Michael A. TESSIER
21 Asst VP for Fiscal Affairs ... Ms. Donna O. TEAGUE
13 Asst VP & Chief Technology Office ... Mr. Donald HUDSON
49 Dean of Arts & Sciences ... Dr. Ray LUTGRING
50 Dean of Business Administration ... Dr. Stephen STANDIFIRD
53 Dean of Education/Health Science ... Dr. Lynn R. PENLAND
54 Dean Engineering/Computer Science ... Dr. Phillip M. GERHART
88 Director of Adult Education ... Vacant
85 Exec Dir International Programs ... Dr. Wesley MILNER
41 Director of Athletics ... Mr. John STANLEY
26 Director of University Relations ... Ms. Lucy HIMSTEDT
09 Asst VP Institutional Effectiveness ... Ms. Amy BRANDEBURY
06 University Registrar ... Vacant
08 University Librarian ... Mr. William F. LOUDEN
42 University Chaplain ... Rev. Tammy GIESELMAN
11 Director of Administrative Services ... Mr. Mark J. LOGEL
29 Director of Alumni/Parent Relations ... Ms. Sylvia Y. DEVAULT
44 Dir Gift Planning/Capital Support ... Ms. Abigail MILEY
36 Director of Career Svcs/Placement ... Mr. C. Gene WELLS
38 Director of Counseling/Health Educ ... Ms. Sylvia T. BUCK
37 Director of Financial Aid ... Ms. JoAnn E. LAUGEL
15 Director of Human Resources ... Mr. Keith GEHLHAUSEN
18 Director of Physical Plant ... Mr. Larry S. HORN
19 Director of Safety & Security ... Mr. Harold P. MATTHEWS
104 Director of Study Abroad/Harlaxton ... Mr. Earl D. KIRK
40 Director of Bookstore ... Mr. Douglas GUSTWILLER
28 Director of Diversity ... Vacant
44 Asst Director of Gift Giving ... Ms. Cathy RENNER
27 Coordinator of News Services ... Ms. Kristen LUND
07 Dean of Admissions ... Vacant

University of Indianapolis (I)

1400 E Hanna Avenue, Indianapolis IN 46227-3697
County: Marion FICE Identification: 001804
Unit ID: 151263
Telephone: (317) 788-3368 Carnegie Class: Master's L
FAX Number: (317) 788-3300 Calendar System: Other
URL: www.uindy.edu
Established: 1902 Annual Undergrad Tuition & Fees: $24,420
Enrollment: 5,432 Coed
Affiliation or Control: United Methodist IRS Status: 501(c)3
Highest Offering: Doctorate
Program: Occupational; Liberal Arts And General; Teacher Preparatory; Professional
Accreditation: NH, ACBSP, ADNUR, ART, CLPSY, EXSC, MIDWF, MUS, NURSE, OT, PTA, PTAA, SW, TED

01 President ... Dr. Robert L. MANUEL
05 Exec VP Academic Affairs/Provost ... Dr. Deborah Ware BALOGH
84 Exec VP for Campus Affs/Enroll Svcs ... Mr. Mark T. WEIGAND
46 VP Research/Plng/Strategic Ptnrship ... Dr. Mary C. MOORE
10 VP of Business & Finance/ Treasurer ... Mr. Michael L. BRAUGHTON
26 VP Communications & Marketing ... Ms. Mary WADE ATTEBERRY
30 Vice President for Univ Advancement ... Mr. Christopher H. MOLLOY
31 Assoc VP of Community Relations ... Dr. David W. WANTZ
41 VP for Intercollegiate Athletics ... Dr. Sue C. WILLEY
42 Dean Ecumenical and Interfaith Pgm ... Dr. Michael G. CARTWRIGHT
43 Vice President/General Counsel ... Ms. Samantha KARN
32 VP for Stdnt/Campus Affs/Dn of Std ... Ms. Kory M. VITANGELI
100 Special Asst to the President ... Ms. Lara G. MANN
09 Asst VP of Inst Planning & Rsrch ... Dr. Patrick ALLES
06 Registrar ... Ms. Kristine L. DOZIER
13 Associate VP Information Systems ... Mr. Steven R. HERRIFORD
58 Assoc Provost & Dean Grad School ... Dr. John MCILVRIED
49 Dean College of Arts & Sciences ... Dr. Jennifer A. DRAKE
50 Dean School of Business ... Dr. Karl KNAPP
53 Dean School of Education ... Dr. Kathryn A. MORAN
66 Dean School of Nursing ... Dr. Anne C. THOMAS
76 Dean College of Health Sciences ... Dr. Stephanie KELLY
88 Dean School of Adult Learning ... Dr. Judy APPLE VANALSTINE
90 Assoc Provost for Academic Systems ... Dr. Mary Beth BAGG
07 Director of Admissions ... Mr. Ronald W. WILKS
08 Librarian ... Ms. Christine GUYONNEAU
15 Director Human Resources ... Mr. Stant CLARK
26 Director Marketing ... Mr. Joe P. SOLARI
36 Dir Career Svcs/Employer Relations ... Vacant
37 Director Student Financial Aid ... Mrs. Linda B. HANDY
58 Director Graduate Business Pgms ... Mr. Stephen A. TOKAR
18 Director Physical Plant ... Mr. Kenneth M. PIEPENBRINK
19 Director Safety & Police Services ... Mr. David K. SELBY
29 Director Alumni Relations ... Vacant
31 Director Univ Cmty Bridge Program ... Dr. Mary E. BUSCH
42 Co-Chaplain ... Dr. L. Lang BROWNLEE
42 Co-Chaplain/Dir Lantz Center ... Rev. Jeremiah GIBBS
44 Executive Director of Development ... Mr. Andy M. KOCHER
85 Director International Division ... Ms. Marilyn O. CHASE
24 Asst VP of Information Systems ... Mr. Robert A. JONES
38 Director Counseling Center ... Dr. Kelly M. MILLER
40 Bookstore Manager ... Mr. Bradley A. ZURCHER
96 Procurement & Ancillary Services ... Ms. Stacie L. NEUHAUS

University of Notre Dame (A)

400 Main Building, Notre Dame IN 46556
County: Saint Joseph FICE Identification: 001840
Unit ID: 152080
Telephone: (574) 631-5000 Carnegie Class: RU/VH
FAX Number: (574) 631-6700 Calendar System: Semester
URL: www.nd.edu
Established: 1842 Annual Undergrad Tuition & Fees: $44,605
Enrollment: 12,126 Coed
Affiliation or Control: Roman Catholic IRS Status: 501(c)3
Highest Offering: Doctorate
Program: Liberal Arts And General; Professional; Business Emphasis
Accreditation: NH, ART, BUS, BUSA, CS, ENG, IPSY, LAW, THEOL

01 President ... Rev. John I. JENKINS, CSC
05 Provost ... Dr. Thomas G. BURISH
03 Executive Vice President ... Dr. John F. AFFLECK-GRAVES
20 Vice Pres/Sr Associate Provost ... Dr. Christine M. MAZIAR
20 Vice Pres/Associate Provost ... Dr. Daniel J. MYERS
20 Vice Pres/Associate Provost ... Dr. Donald B. POPE-DAVIS
82 VP/Provost Internationalization ... Dr. Nicholas ENTRIKIN
32 Vice President for Student Affairs ... Ms. Erin HOFFMANN HARDING
10 Vice President for Finance ... Mr. John A. SEJDINAJ
46 Vice President for Research ... Dr. Robert J. BERNHARD
43 Vice President & General Counsel ... Ms. Marianne CORR
88 Vice Pres/Chief Investment Ofcr ... Mr. Scott C. MALPASS
41 Vice Pres & Director of Athletics ... Mr. John "Jack" B. SWARBRICK
15 Vice Pres Human Resources ... Mr. Robert K. MCQUADE
26 Vice President University Relations ... Mr. Louis M. NANNI
13 VP & Chief Information Officer ... Mr. Ronald D. KRAEMER
88 VP Mission Engagmnt/Church Affairs . Rev. William M. LIES, CSC
100 Chief of Staff ... Ms. Ann M. FIRTH
28 Chief Diversity Officer ... Vacant
84 Assoc VP Undergraduate Enrollment ... Mr. Donald BISHOP
18 Assoc VP Facilities & Design ... Mr. Douglas K. MARSH
06 Registrar ... Mr. Charles T. HURLEY
96 Director Procurement ... Mr. Vaibhav AGARWAL
50 Dean of College of Business ... Dr. Roger D. HUANG
61 Dean of Law School ... Prof. Nell J. NEWTON
54 Dean College of Engineering ... Dr. Peter K. KILPATRICK
58 Acting Dean Graduate School ... Dr. Christine M. MAZIAR
49 Dean of Arts & Letters ... Dr. John T. MCGREEVY
81 Dean of Science ... Dr. Gregory P. CRAWFORD
48 Dean of Architecture ... Dr. Michael N. LYKOUDIS
88 Dean First Year of Studies ... Dr. Hugh R. PAGE
29 Exec Director Alumni Assoc ... Ms. Dolly DUFFY
08 Dir of University Libraries ... Ms. Diane PARR WALKER
27 Chief Communications Executive ... Mr. Matthew V. STORIN
42 Director of Campus Ministry ... Rev. James B. KING, CSC
37 Dir of Student Financial Aid ... Ms. Mary B. NUCCIARONE
36 Director of Career Center ... Mr. Lee J. SVETE
38 Director of Counseling Center ... Dr. Susan STEIBE-PASALICH
45 Assoc VP Strategic Planning ... Mr. David C. BAILEY
19 Director of Security/Police ... Mr. Phillip A. JOHNSON

University of Phoenix Indianapolis Campus (B)

7999 Knue Road, Indianapolis IN 46250-1932
Telephone: (317) 585-8610 Identification: 770206
Accreditation: &NH, ACBSP

† Main campus is University of Phoenix in Tempe, AZ.

University of Saint Francis (C)

2701 Spring Street, Fort Wayne IN 46808-3994
County: Allen FICE Identification: 001832
Unit ID: 152336
Telephone: (260) 399-7700 Carnegie Class: Master's S
FAX Number: N/A Calendar System: Semester
URL: www.sf.edu
Established: 1890 Annual Undergrad Tuition & Fees: $25,180
Enrollment: 2,292 Coed
Affiliation or Control: Roman Catholic IRS Status: 501(c)3
Highest Offering: Master's
Program: Occupational; 2-Year Principally Bachelor's Creditable; Liberal Arts And General; Teacher Preparatory; Professional
Accreditation: NH, ACBSP, ADNUR, ARCPA, ART, NURSE, PTAA, RAD, SURGT, SW, TED

01 President ... Sr. M. Elise KRISS, OSF
05 Vice President Academic Affairs ... Dr. J. Andrew PRALL
03 Executive Vice President ... Dr. Stacy J. ADKINSON
20 Vice President Adult Learning ... Dr. Toni M. PAULS
30 Vice President Advancement ... Dr. Matthew J. SMITH
10 Vice President Finance & Operations ... Mr. Richard A. BIENZ
11 Associate Vice President ... Mrs. Teresa A. SORDELET
84 Assoc VP Enrollment Management ... Mr. Jean Paul SPAGNOLO
26 Assoc Vice President Marketing ... Mrs. Trois K. HART
42 Associate VP Mission Integration ... Sr. M. Anita HOLZMER, OSF
12 Dean Crown Point Site ... Vacant
49 Interim Dean School Arts & Sciences ... Dr. Earl T. KUMFER
50 Interim Dean School of Business ... Mr. Robert W. LEE
57 Dean School of Creative Arts ... Mr. Rick E. CARTWRIGHT
17 Dean School of Health Sciences ... Dr. Mindy J. YODER
107 Dean School of Professional Studies ... Dr. Jane M. SWISS
32 Dean of Students ... Ms. Sharon K. MEJEUR
35 Associate Dean of Students ... Mrs. Elizabeth A. GROMAN
35 Assoc Dean Student Services ... Ms. Jennifer M. FAWBUSH
06 Registrar ... Mr. Francis P. CONNOR
07 Executive Dir Enrollment Services ... Mrs. Jamie M. MCGRATH
08 Exec Dir Information/Instruc Svcs ... Mrs. Karla K. ALEXANDER
13 Exec Dir Univ Technology Services ... Mr. Robert H. SOULLIERE
29 Director Alumni Relations ... Mrs. Jessica L. SWINFORD
41 Director Athletics ... Mr. Michael H. MCCAFFREY
88 Director Campaigns & Major Gifts ... Mr. William J. SLAYTON
42 Director Campus Ministry ... Mr. Joshua C. STAGNI
19 Director Campus Safety & Security ... Mr. Richard E. ROBBINS
36 Director Career Services ... Vacant
88 Dir Center for Service Engagement ... Ms. Katrina P. BOEDEKER
88 Dir College Adult Learn Enroll Svcs ... Mrs. Michelle L. KUHLHORST
102 Dir Corp/Found Relations and Grants ... Mrs. Lynnette MCKENNA-FRAZIER
21 Dir Financial Planning/Accounting ... Mrs. Cathy L. CRAWFORD
88 Director Financial Reporting ... Mr. Craig M. TEETSEL
58 Director Graduate School ... Dr. Douglas A. BARCALOW
88 Dir Health Science Sim Lab ... Dr. Dawn M. MABRY
88 Dir Hlth Sci Strategic Initiatives ... Dr. Lorene R. ARNOLD
92 Director Honors Program ... Dr. Lance B. RICHEY
39 Director Housing & Residence Life ... Mr. Andrew MCKEE
15 Director Human Resources ... Mrs. Norma J. BOENKER
108 Dir Inst Effectiveness/Accredit ... Dr. Marcia K. SAUTER
09 Director Institutional Research ... Dr. Stephanie J. OETTING
91 Dir Network & Information Mgmt ... Mr. Mark ROBBINS
88 Director Operations ... Mr. Thomas BUUCK
44 Director Planned Giving ... Sr. M. Marilyn OLIVER, OSF
28 Director Retention & Diversity ... Mr. Garien L. HUDSON
88 Director Sports Information ... Mr. William J. SCOTT
88 Dir Student Academic Services ... Mrs. Tricia J. BUGAJSKI
88 Dir Tech Security & Compliance ... Mr. Randy D. TROY
14 Dir Tech User Support Services ... Mr. A. Drew REPP
88 Director TRiO ... Mr. Tellis S. YOUNG
88 Mgr & Exec Chef AVI Food Service ... Mr. Brian D. SMITH
40 Mgr Barnes & Noble Campus Shoppe ... Mrs. Robin HUFFMAN

University of Southern Indiana (D)

8600 University Boulevard, Evansville IN 47712-3596
County: Vanderburgh FICE Identification: 001808
Unit ID: 151306
Telephone: (812) 464-8600 Carnegie Class: Master's L
FAX Number: (812) 464-1960 Calendar System: Semester
URL: www.usi.edu
Established: 1965 Annual Undergrad Tuition & Fees (In-State): $6,358
Enrollment: 10,467 Coed
Affiliation or Control: State IRS Status: 501(c)3
Highest Offering: Doctorate
Program: Liberal Arts And General; Teacher Preparatory; Professional
Accreditation: NH, ART, BUS, BUSA, COARC, DA, DH, @DIETD, DMS, ENG, JOUR, NURSE, OT, OTA, RAD, SW, TED

01 President ... Dr. Linda L M. BENNETT
100 Assistant to the President ... Ms. Janel S. ALLEN
05 Provost ... Dr. Ronald S. ROCHON
10 Vice President Business Affairs ... Mr. Mark ROZEWSKI
86 Vice Pres Govt and Univ Relations ... Ms. Cynthia S. BRINKER
26 Asst VP Marketing/Communications ... Mrs. Kindra STRUPP
56 Assoc Provost Outreach Engagement ... Dr. Mark C. BERNHARD
20 Asst Provost for Academic Affairs ... Dr. Shelly B. BLUNT
32 Assoc Provost for Student Affairs ... Dr. Marcia K. KIESSLING
21 Asst Vice Pres Business Affairs ... Ms. Mary A. HUPFER
09 Exec Director Plng/Research/Assess . Dr. Katherine A. DRAUGHON
58 Director of Graduate Studies ... Dr. Wes T. DURHAM
06 Registrar ... Ms. Sandy K. FRANK
07 Director of Admission ... Mr. Eric H. OTTO
08 Director of Library Svcs ... Ms. Marna M. HOSTETLER
30 Director of Development/USI Fndtn ... Mr. David A. BOWER
92 Director Honors Program ... Dr. Antonia D. BAMBINA
38 Director of Counseling ... Dr. B. Thomas LONGWELL
29 Director of Alumni Affairs ... Mrs. Janet L. JOHNSON
37 Director of Student Financial Asst ... Ms. Mary J. HARPER
15 Director of Human Resources ... Ms. Donna J. EVINGER
36 Director Career Svcs & Internships ... Mr. Philip L. PARKER
35 Dean of Students ... Dr. Angela E. BATISTA
85 Director of Intl Student Services ... Mrs. Heidi GREGORI-GAHAN
28 Director Multicultural Center ... Ms. Pamela F. HOPSON
14 Exec Dir of Information Technology ... Mr. Richard TOENISKOETTER
90 Academic Services Coordinator ... Mr. Juzar AHMED
18 Director of Facilities Operations ... Mr. Stephen P. HELFRICH
96 Director Procurement Services ... Mr. Daniel R. MARTENS
27 Director of News & Information Svcs ... Mr. John A. FARLESS
19 Director of Security ... Mr. Stephen WOODALL
39 Director of Residence Life ... Ms. Laurie M. BERRY
40 Bookstore Manager ... Mr. Michael J. GOELZHAUSER
41 Athletic Director ... Mr. Jon Mark HALL
50 Dean College of Business ... Dr. Mohammed KHAYUM
49 Dean College of Liberal Arts ... Mr. Michael K. AAKHUS
66 Dean College Nursing/Health Profess ... Dr. Ann H. WHITE
81 Dean College of Science/Engineering ... Dr. Scott A. GORDON
21 Asst Vice Pres Finance Admin Treas ... Mr. Steven J. BRIDGES
51 Director Continuing Education ... Ms. Linda L. CLEEK
106 Asst Provost for Distance Learning ... Ms. Megan W. LINOS

Valparaiso University (E)

Valparaiso IN 46383-9978
County: Porter FICE Identification: 001842
Unit ID: 152600
Telephone: (219) 464-5000 Carnegie Class: Master's L
FAX Number: (219) 464-5381 Calendar System: Semester
URL: valpo.edu
Established: 1859 Annual Undergrad Tuition & Fees: $32,400
Enrollment: 4,081 Coed
Affiliation or Control: Lutheran IRS Status: 501(c)3
Highest Offering: Doctorate
Program: Liberal Arts And General; Teacher Preparatory; Professional
Accreditation: NH, BUS, CACREP, ENG, LAW, MUS, NURSE, SW, TED

01 President ... Mr. Mark A. HECKLER
05 Provost/Exec VP for Acad Affs ... Dr. Mark R. SCHWEHN
20 Senior Associate Provost ... Dr. Renu JUNEJA
32 VP for Student Affairs ... Dr. Bonnie L. HUNTER
10 VP for Finance & Administration ... Mr. Matt DELNICK
84 VP for Enrollment Mgt & Mktg ... Mr. Michael JOSEPH
58 Asc Provost/Dean Grad Sch/Cont Ed ... Dr. David L. ROWLAND
30 VP for Advancement ... Ms. Lisa HOLLANDER
43 VP University Counsel ... Mr. Darron C. FARHA
11 VP for Administration & Finance ... Ms. Susan SCROGGINS
92 Dean of Christ College ... Dr. Peter KANELOS
49 Dean College Arts & Sciences ... Dr. Jon T. KILPINEN
61 Interim Dean School of Law ... Mr. Ivan BODENSTEINER
54 Dean College of Engineering ... Dr. Eric JOHNSON
50 Dean College of Business Admin ... Dr. James BRODZINSKI
66 Dean College of Nursing ... Dr. Janet M. BROWN
08 Dean Library Services ... Dr. Bradford L. EDEN
35 Dean of Students ... Dr. Timothy S. JENKINS
84 AVP Enrollment Management ... Mr. David FEVIG
42 Exec Dir of Campus Ministries ... Rev. Brian T. JOHNSON
06 Registrar ... Ms. Shelly KOOI
19 Chief University Police ... Ms. Rebecca A. WALKOWIAK
39 Asst Dean Students/Residential Life ... Mr. Ryan BLEVINS
104 Director of Study Abroad Programs ... Ms. Julie A. MADDOX
85 Dir International Students/Scholars ... Mr. Holly SINGH
29 Director Alumni Relations ... Ms. Linda ROETTGER
15 Dir Human Resource Services ... Ms. Nora WIERGACZ
88 Exec Dir for Capital Planning ... Mr. Fred W. PLANT
36 Director Career Center ... Mr. Tom CATH
38 Director of Counseling Services ... Dr. Stewart E. COOPER
41 Director Athletics ... Mr. Mark LABARBERA
20 Assistant Provost ... Dr. Rick GILLMAN
21 Controller ... Ms. Diana BLANEY
28 Director of Multicultural Programs ... Ms. Jane M. BELLO-BRUNSON
96 Director of Procurement ... Ms. Nancy K. MURRAY
09 Exec Dir Instnl Effectiveness ... Mr. Greg STINSON
42 University Pastor ... Rev. Charlene COX
42 University Pastor ... Rev. James WETZSTEIN
37 Director of Financial Aid ... Ms. Karen KLIMCZYK
100 Chief of Staff ... Mr. Rick AMRHEIN

Vincennes University (F)

1002 N First Street, Vincennes IN 47591-1504
County: Knox FICE Identification: 001843
Unit ID: 152637
Telephone: (812) 888-8888 Carnegie Class: Assoc/Pub4
FAX Number: (812) 888-5868 Calendar System: Semester
URL: www.vinu.edu
Established: 1801 Annual Undergrad Tuition & Fees (In-State): $5,022
Enrollment: 9,952 Coed
Affiliation or Control: State IRS Status: 501(c)3
Highest Offering: Baccalaureate
Program: Occupational; 2-Year Principally Bachelor's Creditable; Liberal Arts And General
Accreditation: NH, ACBSP, ADNUR, ART, CAHIIM, EMT, FUSER, NUR, PNUR, PTAA, SURGT, TED, THEA

01 President ... Dr. Richard E. HELTON
05 Provost/Vice Pres Institutional Svc ... Mr. Charles R. JOHNSON, JR.
10 Vice Pres Financial Svcs/Govt Rels ... Mr. Phillip S. RATH
103 VP Workforce Dev/Comm Services ... Mr. David C. TUCKER
12 Assistant VP/Dean Jasper Campus ... Dr. Alan D. JOHNSON
21 Associate Vice President/Controller ... Ms. Linda L. WALDROUP
32 Asst Provost Student Affairs ... Ms. Lynn WHITE
20 Int Asst Provost Curriculum & Inst ... Dr. Laurel A. SMITH
35 Dean of Students ... Mr. John T. LIVERS
26 Sr Director External Relations ... Ms. Kristi R. DEETZ
07 Director of Admissions ... Mrs. Heidi M. WHITEHEAD
08 Director of Learning Resources/Tech ... Mr. David M. PETER
09 Int Dir of Inst Research/Planning ... Ms. Kimela A. MEEKS
13 Director of Mgmt Information Center ... Mr. Carmin A. SCHNARR
27 Director Public Information ... Mr. Duane H. CHATTIN
88 Director of University Events ... Ms. Brenda L. THOMPSON
36 Dir Ctr for Career & Empl Relations ... Mr. Richard A. COLEMAN
37 Director of Student Financial Aid ... Mr. Stanley J. WERNE
88 Director Disability Services ... Ms. Leslie M. SMITH
38 Director of Student Counseling ... Dr. Lisa J. BISHOP
39 Director of Housing Facilities ... Ms. Patricia A. JOST
40 Manager of Bookstore ... Mr. Ronald L. KOTTER
102 President of VU Foundation ... Mr. Bumper R. HOSTETLER
41 Athletic Director ... Mr. Harry L. MEEKS
88 Director of Project Excel/Proj Link ... Ms. Heather MOFFAT
29 Director of Alumni Programs ... Ms. Jennifer D. GILMORE
85 Dir Multicultural/Intl Student Affs ... Ms. Schvalla RIVERA
18 Director of Physical Plant ... Mr. James W. MINDERMAN
19 Director of Campus Police ... Mr. James M. JONES
88 Bursar ... Ms. Lori J. HOSTETLER
23 Coordinator Student Health Office ... Ms. Margaret J. MILLIGAN
24 Director of Media Services ... Mr. Jay D. WOLF
06 Registrar ... Ms. Rebecca K. LITTLE
39 Director Residential Life ... Ms. Dawn M. BREWER
88 Director Marketing Services ... Ms. Andrea G. TSCHERTER
96 Director of Procurement ... Mr. Michael L. MORRISON
38 Director Academic Advising ... Mr. Thomas E. KONKLE

88 Director Architectural Services ....Mr. Andrew YOUNG
16 Director Human Res/AAO ....Ms. Regina L. MCCORD-FITHIAN
76 Dean College Health Sci/Human Perf ....Dr. Jana L. VIECK
50 Int Dean Business/Convergent Tech ....Ms. Mary L. HOLLARS
72 Dean College of Technology ....Mr. Arthur H. HAASE
81 Dean College of Science/Math ....Dr. Paul J. WILDER
83 Dean Social Sci/Performing Arts ....Mr. Eric W. MARGERUM
51 Dean Extended Studies ....Mr. Donald E. KAUFMAN
79 Dean College of Humanities ....Dr. Charles W. REINHART
88 Dir Avia Tech Ctr Indianapolis ....Mr. Michael D. GEHRICH
88 Dir Marketing Communications ....Ms. Krystal F. SPENCER
88 Dir Institutional Effectiveness ....Mr. Michael E. GRESS
20 Interim Dir Early College ....Dr. Carolyn K. JONES
88 Director Military Education Pgm ....Mr. Matthew J. SCHWARTZ
88 Director Veterans Affairs ....Mr. Alex SIEVERS
88 Dir Gibson Ctr Adv Mfg/Logistics ....Mr. Dennis G. LIECHTY
88 Dir Plainfield Logistics Ctr ....Mr. James E. DOLAN

Vincennes University-Jasper Center (A)

850 College Avenue, Jasper IN 47546
Telephone: (812) 482-3030 Identification: 770107
Accreditation: &NH

† Main campus is Vincennes University in Vincennes, IN.

Wabash College (B)

301 W Wabash, PO Box 352,
Crawfordsville IN 47933-0352
County: Montgomery FICE Identification: 001844
Unit ID: 152673
Telephone: (765) 361-6100 Carnegie Class: Bac/A&S
FAX Number: (765) 361-6461 Calendar System: Semester
URL: www.wabash.edu
Established: 1832 Annual Undergrad Tuition & Fees: $35,000
Enrollment: 906 Male
Affiliation or Control: Independent Non-Profit IRS Status: 501(c)3
Highest Offering: Baccalaureate
Program: Liberal Arts And General
Accreditation: NH

01 President ....Dr. Gregory D. HESS
05 Dean of the College ....Dr. Gary A. PHILLIPS
10 Chief Financial Officer & Treasurer ....Mr. Larry GRIFFITH
32 Dean of Students ....Mr. Michael P. RATERS
30 Dean for Advancement ....Mr. Jonathan S. STERN
35 Associate Dean of Students ....Mr. George W. OPRISKO
06 Registrar and Assoc Dean ....Dr. Jonathon D. JUMP
07 Dean of Admissions & Financial Aid ....Mr. Steven J. KLEIN
37 Director of Financial Aid ....Ms. Heidi A. CARL
08 Head Librarian & Dir Lilly Library ....Mr. John E. LAMBORN
13 Director of IT Services ....Mr. Bradley K. WEAVER
36 Director of Career Development ....Mr. R. Scott CRAWFORD
29 Dir of Alumni & Parent Relations ....Mr. Thomas G. RUNGE
26 Senior Director of Communications a ....Mr. James L. AMIDON
40 Director of Business Auxilaries ....Mr. Thomas E. KEEDY
41 Dir of Athletics & Campus Wellness ....Mr. Joseph R. HAKLIN
44 Director of Development ....Mr. James J. BREHM
15 Director of Human Resources ....Ms. Catherine A. METZ
18 Director of Campus Services ....Mr. David MORGAN
21 Controller ....Ms. Cathy VANARSDALL
38 Director of Counseling Services ....Mr. Kevin C. SWAIM
28 Int Director of Malcolm X Institute ....Mr. Willyerd R. COLLIER
88 Director of Inquiries CILA ....Dr. Charles F. BLAICH
88 Dir Wabash Ctr Teaching/Learning ....Dr. Nadine S. PENCE
19 Director of Safety and Security ....Mr. Richard G. WOODS
09 Director of Institutional Research ....Dr. Preston R. BOST

IOWA

AIB College of Business (C)

2500 Fleur Drive, Des Moines IA 50321-1799
County: Polk FICE Identification: 003963
Unit ID: 152822
Telephone: (515) 244-4221 Carnegie Class: Spec/Bus
FAX Number: (515) 244-6773 Calendar System: Quarter
URL: www.aib.edu
Established: 1921 Annual Undergrad Tuition & Fees: $14,850
Enrollment: 921 Coed
Affiliation or Control: Independent Non-Profit IRS Status: 501(c)3
Highest Offering: Baccalaureate
Program: Business Emphasis
Accreditation: NH

01 President ....Ms. Nancy WILLIAMS
05 Vice President for Academic Affairs ....Dr. M. Susan CIGELMAN
10 VP & Chief Financial Officer ....Mr. Paul WINGET
88 Vice President for Enrollment ....Mr. Terry PETERS
32 Dean of Students ....Vacant
36 Director of Career Services ....Ms. Jane DEHAVEN
37 Director of Financial Aid Services ....Mr. Tristan LYNN
38 Director of Student Counseling ....Ms. Sheila KEENE
88 Director of Academic Advising ....Ms. Jessica HANSEN
31 Director of Community Engagement ....Ms. Julie SPICER
88 Director of Activities Center ....Mr. Mike MCCOY
88 Director of Facilities Management ....Mr. Mike LARSON
29 Alumni Director ....Ms. Reonna SNYDER
06 Registrar ....Mr. Randy TERRONEZ
08 Library Director ....Ms. Leslie BINTNER
15 Director of Human Resources ....Mr. Kirk TROW
18 Chief Facilities Officer ....Mr. Chris SCHMIDT
20 Chief Academic Officer ....Ms. Christy ROLAND
21 Director of Financial Services ....Ms. Laurie SANDERS
04 Executive Assistant to President ....Ms. Ronette SMITH
50 Department Chair Accounting ....Ms. Kelly SWINTON
50 Dept Chair Business Administration ....Ms. Ann WRIGHT
49 Dept Chair Comm & General Studies ....Ms. Dianne LEONARD
13 Senior Director of Information Tech ....Ms. Denise CODY
41 Athletics Director ....Vacant
90 Assistant Dean/Academic Resources ....Ms. Danielle EDWARDS
26 Director of Public Relations ....Ms. Jane MEISNER
07 Director of Admissions ....Ms. Megan PITZ
30 Senior Dir of Advancement ....Ms. Dawn ROBERTS
09 Dir of Inst Acct/Compliance ....Vacant
39 Director of Student Life ....Ms. Danielle SCHMIDT
88 Director of Marketing ....Ms. Deborah LANDON
40 Bookstore Manager ....Ms. Cassandra HUFF

Allen College (D)

1825 Logan Avenue, Waterloo IA 50703-1999
County: Black Hawk FICE Identification: 030691
Unit ID: 152798
Telephone: (319) 226-2000 Carnegie Class: Spec/Health
FAX Number: (319) 226-2010 Calendar System: Semester
URL: www.allencollege.edu
Established: 1989 Annual Undergrad Tuition & Fees: $20,029
Enrollment: 551 Coed
Affiliation or Control: Independent Non-Profit IRS Status: 501(c)3
Highest Offering: Doctorate
Program: Professional; Nursing Emphasis
Accreditation: NH, MT, NMT, NURSE, RAD

01 Chancellor ....Dr. Jerry DURHAM
05 Vice Chancellor of Academic Affairs ....Dr. Nancy KRAMER
10 Dir Business/Administrative Svcs ....Ms. Denise HANSON
66 Dean School of Nursing ....Dr. Kendra WILLIAMS-PEREZ
76 Dean School of Health Sciences ....Dr. Peggy FORTSCH
32 Dir of Student Services/
Internation ....Ms. Joanna RAMSDEN-MEIER
37 Financial Aid Coordinator ....Ms. Kathie ASWEGAN
24 Media Specialist ....Ms. Robin NICHOLSON
06 Registrar ....Ms. Michelle KOEHN
08 Coordinator Library/Media Services ....Dr. Ruth YAN
07 Admissions Counselor ....Ms. Molly QUINN
37 Financial Aid Coordinator ....Ms. Molly CORDES

Antioch School of Church Planting and Leadership Development (E)

2400 Oakwood Road, Ames IA 50014
County: Story Identification: 667026
Telephone: (515) 292-9694 Carnegie Class: Not Classified
FAX Number: (515) 292-1933 Calendar System: Other
URL: www.antiochschool.edu
Established: 2006 Annual Undergrad Tuition & Fees: $1,800
Enrollment: N/A Coed
Affiliation or Control: Independent Non-Profit IRS Status: 501(c)3
Highest Offering: Doctorate
Program: Religious Emphasis
Accreditation: DETC

01 President ....Jeff REED
05 Academic Dean ....Stephen KEMP

Ashford University (F)

400 N Bluff Boulevard, Clinton IA 52732-3997
County: Clinton FICE Identification: 001881
Unit ID: 154022
Telephone: (563) 242-4023 Carnegie Class: Master's L
FAX Number: (563) 242-2003 Calendar System: Semester
URL: www.ashford.edu
Established: 1918 Annual Undergrad Tuition & Fees: $13,928
Enrollment: 77,734 Coed
Affiliation or Control: Proprietary IRS Status: Proprietary
Highest Offering: Master's
Program: Liberal Arts And General; Teacher Preparatory
Accreditation: NH, WC, IACBE

01 University President ....Dr. Richard PATTENAUDE
05 Provost ....Dr. Rebecca WARDLOW
10 VP of Finance ....Mr. Tom MEAD
84 Sr VP of Enrollment Management ....Mr. Sean GOUSHA
11 Sr VP of Administrative Operations ....Ms. Sheri JONES
45 VP of Planning and Effectiveness ....Dr. Christina LEIMER
100 Executive VP and Chief of Staff ....Dr. Joseph HOEY
88 VP and Campus Director ....Mr. John BALLHEIM
09 AVP of Institutional Research ....Dr. Kristina CRAGG
49 Dean College Liberal Arts ....Dr. Suzanne POWER
50 Dean Col Business/Professional Stds ....Dr. Michael REILLY
53 Dean College Education ....Dr. Andrew SHEAN
76 Dean College Health ....Dr. Mihaela TANASESCU
06 University Registrar ....Mr. Kirk MORRISON
41 Director of Athletics ....Ms. Meg SCHEBLER
37 VP of Financial Aid ....Mr. Matthew VALLEJO
32 VP of Student and Alumni Affairs ....Ms. Amber ECKERT

*Board of Regents, State of Iowa (G)

11260 Aurora Avenue, Urbandale IA 50322-7405
County: Polk FICE Identification: 033443
Telephone: (515) 281-3934 Carnegie Class: N/A
FAX Number: (515) 281-6420
URL: www.regents.iowa.gov

01 Executive Director ....Mr. Bob DONLEY
05 Chief Academic Officer ....Dr. Diana GONZALEZ
10 Chief Business Officer ....Mrs. Patrice M. SAYRE
43 General Counsel ....Mr. Thomas A. EVANS

*Iowa State University (H)

Ames IA 50011-0002
County: Story FICE Identification: 001869
Unit ID: 153603
Telephone: (515) 294-4111 Carnegie Class: RU/VH
FAX Number: (515) 294-2592 Calendar System: Semester
URL: www.iastate.edu
Established: 1858 Annual Undergrad Tuition & Fees (In-State): $7,726
Enrollment: 31,040 Coed
Affiliation or Control: State IRS Status: 501(c)3
Highest Offering: Doctorate
Program: Liberal Arts And General; Teacher Preparatory; Professional
Accreditation: NH, ART, BUS, BUSA, CIDA, COPSY, CS, DIETD, DIETI, ENG, FOR, IPSY, JOUR, LSAR, MUS, NAIT, PLNG, VET

02 President ....Dr. Steven LEATH
100 Assoc VP/Chief of Staff ....Mr. Miles LACKEY
05 Sr Vice President and Provost ....Dr. Jonathan A. WICKERT
10 Sr Vice Pres for Business & Finance ....Mr. Warren R. MADDEN
32 Sr Vice Pres for Student Affairs ....Dr. Thomas L. HILL
46 Int Vice Pres Research/Econ Dev ....Dr. David J. OLIVER
56 Vice Pres Extension/Outreach ....Dr. Cathann A. KRESS
24 Vice Provost Info Technology & CIO ....Dr. James A. DAVIS
20 Associate Provost Academic Programs ....Dr. David K. HOLGER
20 Assoc Prov Faculty ....Dr. Dawn BRATSCH-PRINCE
21 Associate Vice President/Univ Sec ....Ms. Pam ELLIOTT CAIN
18 Assoc Vice Pres Facilities ....Mr. David J. MILLER
15 Assoc Vice Pres Human Resources ....Vacant
84 Assoc Vice Pres Student Affairs ....Mr. Martino HARMON
38 Asst VP for Counseling Service ....Dr. Terry W. MASON
04 Sr Policy Adv to the President ....Dr. Tahira K. HIRA
102 President of ISU Foundation ....Mr. Roger NEUHAUS
29 President of Alumni Association ....Mr. Jeffrey W. JOHNSON
37 Director of Financial Aid ....Ms. Roberta L. JOHNSON
06 Registrar ....Ms. Laura DOERING
07 Int Director of Admissions ....Mr. Darin B. WOHLGEMUTH
22 Director of Equal Opportunity ....Ms. Robinette KELLEY
08 Dean of Library Services ....Ms. Olivia M. MADISON
09 Director of Institutional Research ....Dr. Gebre H. TESFAGIORGIS
19 Director of Public Safety ....Mr. Jerry D. STEWART
26 Director of University Relations ....Mr. John F. MCCARROLL
35 Dean of Students ....Dr. Pamela ANTHONY
23 Director of Student Health ....Ms. Michelle HENDRICKS
39 Director of Residence ....Dr. Peter D. ENGLIN
91 Associate CIO/Admin Info Systems ....Mr. Maury M. HOPE
25 Director of Sponsored Program Admin ....Ms. Rochelle ATHEY
41 Director of Athletics ....Mr. Jamie B. POLLARD
88 Int Director Ames Laboratory ....Dr. Thomas LOGRASSO
43 University Counsel ....Mr. Paul N. TANAKA
96 Director of Purchasing ....Ms. Nancy S. BROOKS
40 Director University Bookstore ....Ms. Rita M. PHILLIPS
58 Dean Graduate College ....Dr. David K. HOLGER
47 Dean College of Agriculture ....Dr. Wendy WINTERSTEEN
50 Dean College of Business ....Mr. David SPALDING
48 Dean College of Design ....Mr. Luis C. RICO-GUTIERREZ
53 Dean College of Human Sciences ....Dr. Pamela WHITE
54 Dean College of Engineering ....Dr. Sarah RAJALA
49 Dean Col of Lib Arts & Sciences ....Dr. Beate SCHMITTMANN
74 Dean College of Veterinary Medicine ....Dr. Lisa NOLAN

*University of Iowa (I)

Iowa City IA 52242-0001
County: Johnson FICE Identification: 001892
Unit ID: 153658
Telephone: (319) 335-3500 Carnegie Class: RU/VH
FAX Number: (319) 335-0807 Calendar System: Semester
URL: www.uiowa.edu
Established: 1847 Annual Undergrad Tuition & Fees (In-State): $8,061
Enrollment: 31,498 Coed
Affiliation or Control: State IRS Status: 501(c)3
Highest Offering: Doctorate
Program: Liberal Arts And General; Teacher Preparatory; Professional
Accreditation: NH, ANEST, ARCPA, AUD, BUS, BUSA, CACREP, CEA, CLPSY, COPSY, CORE, DANCE, DENT, DIETI, DMS, EMT, ENG, ENGR, HSA, IPSY, JOUR, LAW, LIB, MED, MUS, NMT, NURSE, PCSAS, PERF, PH, PHAR, PLNG, PTA, RAD, RTT, SCPSY, SP, SW, THEA

02 President ....Dr. Sally MASON
05 Exec Vice President & Provost ....Dr. Patrick B. BUTLER
46 Vice President Research ....Dr. Daniel REED
10 VP Finance/Operations/Univ Treas ....Mr. Douglas K. TRUE
32 VP Student Life ....Dr. Thomas R. ROCKLIN
17 Vice President for Medical Affairs ....Dr. Jean E. ROBILLARD
102 Vice Pres University Foundation ....Mr. David R. DIERKS
26 Interim VP Strategic Communication ....Mr. Mark BRAUN
20 Associate Provost Faculty ....Dr. Tom W. RICE
51 Assoc Provost Continuing Education ....Dr. Chet S. RZONCA

28 Chief Diversity Officer/AP ..... Dr. Georgina DODGE
88 Assoc Provost/Dean Univ College ..... Dr. Beth INGRAM
45 Assoc Vice President Research ..... Dr. Richard D. HICHWA
11 Assoc VP/Dir of Admin and Planning .. Mr. Donald J. SZESZYCKI
16 Assoc VP Finan/Univ Svcs/Dir HR ..... Ms. Susan C. BUCKLEY
18 Assoc VP/Dir Facilities Management ..... Mr. Donald J. GUCKERT
13 Assoc Vice President & CIO ..... Mr. Steven R. FLEAGLE
23 Assoc VP/CEO Univ Hosp & Clinics ..... Mr. Kenneth KATES
25 Executive Dir Sponsored Pgms ..... Ms. Jennifer LASSNER
19 Asst VP/Director Public Safety ..... Mr. Charles D. GREEN
85 Dean International Programs ..... Dr. Downing THOMAS
43 VP Legal Affairs & Gen Coun ..... Ms. Carroll REASONER
08 University Librarian ..... Mr. John P. CULSHAW
29 Exec Director Alumni Association ..... Mr. Vincent C. NELSON
30 President University Foundation ..... Ms. Lynette L. MARSHALL
07 Director Admissions ..... Mr. Michael BARRON
37 Director Student Financial Aid ..... Mr. Mark S. WARNER
06 Registrar ..... Mr. Lawrence J. LOCKWOOD
36 Director Career Center ..... Mr. David A. BAUMGARTNER
38 Director Univ Counseling Services ..... Dr. Sam V. COCHRAN, III
39 Director Residence Services ..... Mr. Von STANGE
41 Director Athletics Administration ..... Mr. Gary BARTA
49 Dean Col of Liberal Arts & Sciences ..... Dr. Chaden DJALALI
50 Dean College of Business Admin ..... Dr. Sarah GARDIAL
52 Dean College of Dentistry ..... Dr. David C. JOHNSEN
53 Dean College of Education ..... Vacant
54 Dean College of Engineering ..... Dr. Alec SCRANTON
58 Dean Graduate College ..... Dr. John C. KELLER
61 Dean College of Law ..... Dr. Gail B. AGRAWAL
66 Dean College of Nursing ..... Dr. Rita A. FRANTZ
67 Dean College of Pharmacy ..... Dr. Donald E. LETENDRE
69 Dean College of Public Health ..... Dr. Susan CURRY
04 Special Assistant to President ..... Dr. Thomas K. DEAN
22 Dir Equal Opportunity/Diversity ..... Ms. Jennifer A. MODESTOU
86 Director State Relations ..... Mr. Keith SAUNDERS
40 Director University Bookstore ..... Mr. George E. HERBERT
96 Director Purchasing ..... Ms. Deborah J. ZUMBACH
92 Director Honors Program ..... Dr. Art L. SPISAK
87 Director Summer Session ..... Dr. Chet RZONCA
24 Manager Audiovisual Center ..... Mr. Daniel G. LIND
35 Dean of Students ..... Dr. David L. GRADY

*University of Northern Iowa (A)

1227 W 27th Street, Cedar Falls IA 50614-0001

County: Black Hawk FICE Identification: 001890
Unit ID: 154095
Telephone: (319) 273-2311 Carnegie Class: Master's L
FAX Number: (319) 273-2885 Calendar System: Semester
URL: www.uni.edu
Established: 1876 Annual Undergrad Tuition & Fees (In-State): $7,685
Enrollment: 12,273 Coed
Affiliation or Control: State IRS Status: 501(c)3
Highest Offering: Doctorate
Program: Liberal Arts And General; Teacher Preparatory
Accreditation: NH, BUS, CACREP, CEA, ENGT, MUS, NAIT, NRPA, SP, SW

02 President ..... Dr. William N. RUUD
05 Executive Vice President & Provost ..... Dr. Gloria J. GIBSON
32 Vice Pres for Student Affairs ..... Dr. Terrence HOGAN
10 VP Administration/Financial Svcs ..... Mr. Michael A. HAGER
18 Assoc VP for Facilities Management ... Mr. Morris E. MIKKELSEN
04 Spec Asst to Pres for Board/Gov Rel ..... Dr. Patricia L. GEADELMANN
26 Interim Dir University Relations ..... Ms. Kimberly BRISLAWN
39 Executive Director of Residence ..... Mr. Glenn GRAY
20 Assoc Provost for Academic Affairs ..... Dr. Michael J. LICARI
20 Assoc Provost for Faculty Affairs ..... Dr. Nancy LIPPENS
13 Chief Information Officer ..... Dr. Shashidhar KAPARTHI
62 Dean of Library Services ..... Mr. Christopher COX
06 Registrar ..... Mr. Philip L. PATTON
37 Director of Financial Aid ..... Ms. Joyce MORROW
15 Dir Human Resource Services ..... Ms. Michelle C. BYERS
36 Director of Career Services ..... Mr. Robert J. FREDERICK
83 Int Dean Col Social/Behav Science ..... Dr. Brenda BASS
53 Dean College of Education ..... Dr. Dwight C. WATSON
49 Dean Col Humanities/Arts & Science ..... Dr. Joel HAACK
51 Dean Cont Educ/Special Programs ..... Dr. Kent M. JOHNSON
50 Dean College Business Admin ..... Dr. Farzad MOUSSAVI
35 Dean of Students ..... Dr. Leslie K. WILLIAMS
07 Director of Admissions ..... Ms. Christie KANGAS
10 Controller/Secretary/Treasurer ..... Mr. Gary B. SHONTZ
38 Counseling Center Director ..... Dr. David C. TOWLE
22 Asst to Pres Compliance/Equity Mgmt .. Ms. Leah K. GUTKNECHT
41 Athletic Director ..... Mr. Troy A. DANNEN
21 Director of Business Operations ..... Ms. Kelly A. FLEGE

Briar Cliff University (B)

3303 Rebecca Street, Sioux City IA 51104-2100

County: Woodbury FICE Identification: 001846
Unit ID: 152992
Telephone: (712) 279-5321 Carnegie Class: Bac/Diverse
FAX Number: (712) 279-5410 Calendar System: 4/1/4
URL: www.briarcliff.edu
Established: 1929 Annual Undergrad Tuition & Fees: $26,650
Enrollment: 1,150 Coed
Affiliation or Control: Roman Catholic IRS Status: 501(c)3
Highest Offering: Doctorate
Program: Liberal Arts And General; Teacher Preparatory; Professional
Accreditation: NH, NURSE, SW

01 President ..... Mrs. Beverly A. WHARTON
05 Vice President Academic Affairs ..... Dr. William MANGAN
10 Vice President Finance & Treasurer ..... Mrs. Beth GRIGSBY
30 Vice Pres University Relations ..... Mr. Craig MCGARRY
84 Vice Pres Enrollment Management ..... Mrs. Sharisue WILCOXON
32 Vice President Student Development ..... Vacant
06 Registrar ..... Mrs. Deidre ENGEL
08 Librarian/Dir Information Services ..... Ms. Debora ROBERTSON
14 Director Computer Center ..... Ms. Leah WARD
29 Activities/Events & E-Coordinator ..... Ms. Lorna DAUGHERTY
36 Director Career Development ..... Ms. Nancy MCGUIRE
37 Director Financial Aid ..... Mr. Brian EBEN
40 Director Bookstore ..... Ms. Nancy WATSON
41 Athletic Director ..... Mr. Steve GAST
42 Director Campus Ministry ..... Sr. Janet MAY
18 Director Physical Plant ..... Mr. Eric HOLMQUIST
26 Director Marketing & Communications ..... Ms. Paula DAMON
07 Director of Admissions ..... Mr. Jeff LAFAVOR
15 Director Human Resources ..... Mrs. JoAnn PETERSON
39 Director Residence Life ..... Mr. Dave ARENS
38 Director Student Counseling ..... Ms. Laurel MEINE
09 Director of Institutional Research ..... Ms. Deidre ENGEL
44 Director of Development ..... Mrs. Tina STROUD

Brown Mackie College-Quad Cities (C)

2119 East Kimberly Road, Bettendorf IA 52722

Telephone: (563) 344-1500 Identification: 666792
Accreditation: ACICS, OTA

† Main campus is The Art Institute of Phoenix in Phoenix, AZ.

Buena Vista University (D)

610 W Fourth Street, Storm Lake IA 50588-1798

County: Buena Vista FICE Identification: 001847
Unit ID: 153001
Telephone: (712) 749-2351 Carnegie Class: Bac/Diverse
FAX Number: (712) 749-2037 Calendar System: 4/1/4
URL: www.bvu.edu
Established: 1891 Annual Undergrad Tuition & Fees: $29,448
Enrollment: 971 Coed
Affiliation or Control: Presbyterian Church (U.S.A.) IRS Status: 501(c)3
Highest Offering: Master's
Program: Liberal Arts And General; Teacher Preparatory
Accreditation: NH, SW, @TEAC

01 President ..... Dr. Frederick V. MOORE
04 Assistant to the President ..... Ms. Emily A. LAMPE
05 VP Academic Affairs/Dean of Faculty ..... Dr. David R. EVANS
10 Vice President Business Services ..... Ms. Elizabeth MERTEN
84 Vice Pres for Enrollment Management ..... Mr. Michael FRANTZ
32 VP Student Affairs/Dean Students ..... Dr. Meg MCKEON
30 Vice Pres for Inst Advancement ..... Mr. Kenneth L. CONVERSE
81 Dean School of Science ..... Mr. Ben DONATH
50 Dean HWS School of Business ..... Dr. Ashok SUBRAMANIAN
53 Dean School of Education ..... Dr. Paul THEOBALD
60 Dean School Communication & Arts . Dr. Michael D. WHITLATCH
83 Dean School Social Sci/Phil/Relig ..... Dr. Dixee BARTHOLOMEW-FEIS
20 Associate Dean of Faculty ..... Dr. Peter K. STEINFELD
20 AVP Acad Affs/Dn Graduate/Prof Stds ..... Dr. Susan KALSOW
06 Registrar ..... Ms. Nila HOUSKA
07 Director of Admissions ..... Ms. Bridget KURKOWSKI
15 Human Resources Manager ..... Ms. Beth MCNALLY
08 Actg Dir of Library/Ref Librarian ..... Ms. Jodie MORIN
27 Dir University Marketing & Comm ..... Ms. Jennifer FELTON
29 Director of Alumni Rels/Annual Fund ..... Ms. Amy J. JONES
13 Managing Director Univ Info Svcs ..... Vacant
18 Director of Physical Plant ..... Mr. Keith E. SCHMIDT
36 Director of Career Services ..... Ms. Carol J. LYTLE
37 Director of Financial Assistance ..... Ms. Leanne VALENTINE
28 Director of Intercultural Programs ..... Mr. Yorgun MARCEL
41 Athletic Director ..... Ms. Christyn ABARAY
42 Chaplain ..... Rev. Ken MEISSNER
19 Director of Campus Security ..... Mr. Mark KIRKHOLM
38 Director of Counseling Services ..... Ms. Mandy BOOTHBY
09 Institutional Researcher ..... Mr. James E. HEWETT
96 Purchasing Administrator ..... Ms. Tanya LANDGRAF

Central College (E)

812 University, Pella IA 50219-1999

County: Marion FICE Identification: 001850
Unit ID: 153108
Telephone: (641) 628-9000 Carnegie Class: Bac/A&S
FAX Number: (641) 628-5316 Calendar System: Semester
URL: www.central.edu
Established: 1853 Annual Undergrad Tuition & Fees: $30,700
Enrollment: 1,486 Coed
Affiliation or Control: Reformed Church In America IRS Status: 501(c)3
Highest Offering: Baccalaureate
Program: Liberal Arts And General; Teacher Preparatory; Professional
Accreditation: NH, MUS

01 President ..... Dr. Mark L. PUTNAM
05 VP Academic Affairs/Dean of Faculty ..... Dr. Mary M. STREY
30 Vice President Advancement ..... Mr. Bill NORTHUP
84 Vice Pres Enrollment Management ..... Mrs. Carol WILLIAMSON
32 Vice Pres Student Development ..... Dr. Peggy FITCH
10 Vice Pres for Finance & Admin ..... Ms. Margaret TUNGSETH
20 Director of Academic Resources ..... Mr. Eric JONES
35 Dean of Students ..... Mr. Charles STREY
07 Director of Admission ..... Mr. Chevy FREIBURGER
38 Director of Counseling ..... Ms. Michelle KELLAR
39 Director of Residence Life ..... Ms. Melissa SHARKEY
08 Director of Library ..... Mrs. Natalie N. HUTCHINSON
88 Associate Dean for Global Education ..... Ms. Lyn R. ISAACSON
36 Director of Career Center ..... Mrs. Patricia JOACHIM KITZMAN
29 Director of Alumni Relations ..... Ms. Kathy THOMPSON
37 Director Financial Aid ..... Mr. Wayne DILLE
104 Manager On-Campus Rels/Study Abroad ..... Mr. Brian ZYLSTRA
13 Chief Information Officer ..... Ms. Terri JENSEN
90 Director of Academic Computing ..... Ms. Debra BRUXVOORT
42 Chaplain ..... Rev. Joe BRUMMEL
44 Director Planned Giving ..... Mr. Don MORRISON
15 Director of Human Resources ..... Ms. Gena GARBER
41 Athletics Director ..... Mr. Eric VAN KLEY
18 Dir Facilities Planning/Management ..... Mr. Mike LUBBERDEN
28 Director of Intercultural Life ..... Mr. Brandyn WOODARD
06 Registrar ..... Ms. Stephanie HENNING

Clarke University (F)

1550 Clarke Drive, Dubuque IA 52001-3198

County: Dubuque FICE Identification: 001852
Unit ID: 153126
Telephone: (563) 588-6300 Carnegie Class: Bac/Diverse
FAX Number: (563) 588-6789 Calendar System: Semester
URL: www.clarke.edu
Established: 1843 Annual Undergrad Tuition & Fees: $28,000
Enrollment: 1,191 Coed
Affiliation or Control: Roman Catholic IRS Status: 501(c)3
Highest Offering: Doctorate
Program: Liberal Arts And General; Teacher Preparatory; Professional
Accreditation: NH, MUS, NURSE, PTA, SW

01 President ..... Dr. Joanne M. BURROWS, SC
04 Exec Admin Assistant to President ..... Ms. Kathy TEIG
05 Provost/Vice Pres Academic Affs ..... Dr. Joan LINGEN, BVM
30 Vice Pres Institutional Advancement ..... Mr. Bill BIEBUYCK
32 Vice President Student Life ..... Ms. Kate ZANGER
10 Vice President Business & Finance ..... Ms. Daisy HALVORSON
84 Vice President Enrollment Mgmt ..... Dr. Beth TRIPLETT
51 Director Adult & Continuing Educ ..... Mr. Scott SCHNEIDER
06 Registrar ..... Ms. Kristi BAGSTAD
08 Director of Library ..... Ms. Susanne LEIBOLD
20 Academic Dean of Undergraduate Stds ..... Dr. Graciela CANEIRO-LIVINGSTON
20 Academic Dean of Graduate Studies ..... Vacant
37 Director of Financial Aid ..... Ms. Amy NORTON
26 Exec Director of Marketing & Comm ..... Mr. Ken BROWN
14 Director of Computer Center ..... Ms. Karen GERHARD
18 Director of Facilities ..... Mr. Brian SCHULTES
38 Dir of Counseling/Career Services ..... Ms. Lorie MURPHY-FREEBOLIN
15 Director of Human Resources ..... Ms. Megan LUCAS
41 Director of Athletics ..... Mr. Curt LONG
42 Director of Campus Ministry ..... Ms. Anastasia NICKLAUS SCHMELZER
40 Director of the Bookstore ..... Ms. Sarah MERZ
23 Director of Health Services ..... Ms. Julie BURGMEIER
90 Director of Academic Support Center ..... Mr. Brian GOMOLL
07 Director of Admissions ..... Ms. Emily KRUSE
44 Director of Development ..... Ms. Kari NICKOL
09 Director of Institutional Research ..... Mr. Glen LANTZ
29 Director of Alumni Relations ..... Ms. Nicole BREITBACH
85 International Students Advisor ..... Ms. Evelyn NADEAU

Coe College (G)

1220 1st Avenue, NE, Cedar Rapids IA 52402-5092

County: Linn FICE Identification: 001854
Unit ID: 153144
Telephone: (319) 399-8000 Carnegie Class: Bac/A&S
FAX Number: (319) 399-8830 Calendar System: Semester
URL: www.coe.edu
Established: 1851 Annual Undergrad Tuition & Fees: $35,730
Enrollment: 1,367 Coed
Affiliation or Control: Independent Non-Profit IRS Status: 501(c)3
Highest Offering: Master's
Program: Liberal Arts And General; Teacher Preparatory; Professional
Accreditation: NH, MUS, NURSE

01 President ..... Dr. David W. MCINALLY
05 Vice Pres Acad Affs/Dean of Faculty ..... Dr. Marie BAEHR
11 Vice President Admin/Enrollment ..... Mr. Michael L. WHITE
32 Interim Vice Pres Student Affairs ..... Mr. Erik ALBINSON
30 Vice President Advancement ..... Mr. Richard E. MEISTERLING
21 Controller ..... Mr. Richard E. RHEINSCHMIDT
07 Dean of Admission ..... Ms. Julie STAKER
06 Registrar ..... Dr. Evelyn J. MOORE
08 Director Library Services ..... Ms. Jill JACK
29 Director Alumni Programs ..... Ms. Jean A. JOHNSON
09 Director of Institutional Research ..... Dr. Wendy L. DUNN
26 Dir of Marketing/Public Relations ..... Mr. Rod PRITCHARD
37 Director of Financial Aid ..... Ms. Barbara HOFFMAN
20 Associate Dean ..... Dr. Terry MCNABB
35 Dean of Students ..... Mr. Erik ALBINSON
85 International Student Advisor ..... Ms. Deanna L. JOBE
42 Chaplain ..... Rev. Kristin E. HUTSON
23 Director of Health Services ..... Ms. Melinda S. BROKAW
41 Director of Athletics ..... Mr. John M. CHANDLER
18 Director of Physical Plant ..... Ms. Lisa CIHA

36 Career Services Coordinator .... Ms. Michelle MCILLECE
36 Dir of Internships/Career Services .... Ms. Diana R. PATTEN

Cornell College (A)

600 First Street SW, Mount Vernon IA 52314-1098
County: Linn FICE Identification: 001856
Unit ID: 153162
Telephone: (319) 895-4000 Carnegie Class: Bac/A&S
FAX Number: (319) 895-4492 Calendar System: Other
URL: www.cornellcollege.edu
Established: 1853 Annual Undergrad Tuition & Fees: $44,930
Enrollment: 1,174 Coed
Affiliation or Control: United Methodist IRS Status: 501(c)3
Highest Offering: Baccalaureate
Program: Liberal Arts And General; Teacher Preparatory
Accreditation: NH

01 President ....Mr. Jonathan BRAND
05 VP Acad Affairs/Dean of College ....Dr. R. Joseph DIEKER
10 Vice President Business Affairs .... Ms. Karen MERCER
84 Vice President for Enrollment ....Ms. Colleen MURPHY
32 Vice President Student Affairs .... Mr. John W. HARP
44 VP for Alumni & College Advancement ....Ms. Pam GERARD
04 Special Asst to the President ....Dr. James W. BROWN
35 Dean of Students .... Dr. Heidi LEVINE
20 Associate Dean of the College .... Dr. Benjamin GREENSTEIN
09 Director of Institutional Research ....Dr. Becki S. ELKINS
37 Director of Student Financial Asst ....Vacant
06 Interim Registrar .... Ms. Robbin REKEMEYER
08 College Librarian .... Mr. Paul WAELCHLI
29 Director of Alumni & Annual Giving .... Mr. Dustin ROSS
30 Director of Development ....Ms. Kristi COLUMBUS
27 Director of College Communications .... Ms. Dee A. REXROAT
96 Director of Purchasing/Admin Svcs ....Ms. Lisa M. LARSON
42 Chaplain .... Ms. Catherine M. QUEHL-ENGEL
22 Affirmative Action Officer ....Ms. Vickie L. FARMER
41 Athletics Director ....Mr. John T. COCHRANE
18 Director of Facilities .... Mr. Joel C. MILLER
36 Director Career Engagement Center .... Mr. R.J HOLMES
38 Director Student Counseling ....Dr. Brenda C. LOVSTUEN
15 Director of Human Resources ....Ms. Vickie L. FARMER
07 Senior Director of Admissions ....Ms. Sharon GRICE
28 Director of Intercultural Life .... Mr. Kenneth W. MORRIS
13 Director of Information Technology ....Mr. Mike J. CERVENY
40 Manager Bookstore .... Mr. Tyler WEDIG

Des Moines Area Community College (B)

2006 S Ankeny Boulevard, Ankeny IA 50023-3993
County: Polk FICE Identification: 007120
Unit ID: 153214
Telephone: (515) 964-6200 Carnegie Class: Assoc/Pub-R-L
FAX Number: N/A Calendar System: Semester
URL: www.dmacc.edu
Established: 1966 Annual Undergrad Tuition & Fees (In-District): $4,080
Enrollment: 23,685 Coed
Affiliation or Control: State/Local IRS Status: 501(c)3
Highest Offering: Associate Degree
Program: Occupational; 2-Year Principally Bachelor's Creditable
Accreditation: NH, ACBSP, ACFEI, ADNUR, COARC, DA, DH, FUSER, MAC, MLTAD, SURGT

01 President/CEO ....Dr. Rob DENSON
05 Exec Vice Pres Academic Affairs .... Dr. Kim LINDUSKA
10 Vice President Business Svcs .... Mr. Greg MARTIN
103 Vice Pres Cmty/Workforce Partnershp ....Vacant
13 Vice Pres Information Solutions ....Vacant
12 Provost Urban Campus ....Dr. Laura DOUGLAS
12 Provost Boone Campus .... Mr. Tom LEE
12 Provost Carroll Campus .... Mr. Steve SCHULZ
12 Provost Newton Campus .... Ms. Mary ENTZ
12 Provost West Campus ....Dr. Tony PAUSTIAN
32 Exec Dean Student Services .... Dr. Laurie WOLF
15 Executive Director Human Resources ....Dr. Sandy TRYON
102 Executive Director Foundation .... Ms. Tara CONNOLLY
09 Exec Director Inst Effectiveness ....Dr. Joe DEHART
51 Exec Dir Continuing Education .... Mr. Michael HOFFMAN
50 Exec Dir Business Resources .... Ms. Kim DIDIER
84 Exec Dir Enrollment Management ....Vacant
37 Director Financial Aid .... Ms. DeLores HAWKINS
26 Director of Marketing ....Mr. Todd JONES
25 Director Grants/Contracts ....Ms. Deb KOUA
06 Registrar ....Ms. Rachel ERKKILA
18 Chief Facilities/Physical Plant .... Mr. Mark BAETHKE
38 Director Student Development ....Ms. Wendy ROBINSON
96 Director of Purchasing ....Mr. Tim HAGER
27 Media Liaison .... Mr. Dan IVIS
70 Dean Sciences & Humanities .... Mr. Jim STICK
72 Dean Industrial & Technology .... Mr. Scott OCKEN
76 Dean Health Service & Science .... Ms. Sally SCHROEDER
50 Dean Business/Mgmt/Information Tech .... Mr. MJ ISLEY
55 Dean Evening & Weekend College ....Ms. Shanna FOUNTAIN

Des Moines Area Community College Boone Campus (C)

1125 Hancock Drive, Boone IA 50036
Telephone: (515) 432-7203 Identification: 770048
Accreditation: &NH

† Main campus is Des Moines Area Community College in Ankeny, IA.

Des Moines Area Community College Carroll Campus (D)

906 North Grant Road, Carroll IA 51401-2525
Telephone: (712) 792-1755 Identification: 770049
Accreditation: &NH

† Main campus is Des Moines Area Community College in Ankeny, IA.

Des Moines Area Community College Newton Campus (E)

600 N 2nd Avenue West, Newton IA 50208
Telephone: (641) 791-3622 Identification: 770051
Accreditation: &NH

† Main campus is Des Moines Area Community College in Ankeny, IA.

Des Moines Area Community College Urban Campus (F)

1100 7th Street, Des Moines IA 50314
Telephone: (515) 244-4226 Identification: 770050
Accreditation: &NH

† Main campus is Des Moines Area Community College in Ankeny, IA.

Des Moines Area Community College West Des Moines Campus (G)

5959 West Grand Avenue, West Des Moines IA 50266
Telephone: (515) 633-2407 Identification: 770052
Accreditation: &NH

† Main campus is Des Moines Area Community College in Ankeny, IA.

Des Moines University (H)

3200 Grand Avenue, Des Moines IA 50312-4198
County: Polk FICE Identification: 001855
Unit ID: 154156
Telephone: (515) 271-1400 Carnegie Class: Spec/Med
FAX Number: (515) 271-1532 Calendar System: Other
URL: www.dmu.edu
Established: 1898 Annual Graduate Tuition & Fees: N/A
Enrollment: 1,801 Coed
Affiliation or Control: Independent Non-Profit IRS Status: 501(c)3
Highest Offering: First Professional Degree; No Undergraduates
Program: Professional
Accreditation: NH, ARCPA, OSTEO, PH, POD, PTA

01 President/CEO ....Dr. Angela L. WALKER FRANKLIN
05 Provost ....Dr. Karen P. MCLEAN
32 Vice President Student Services ....Ms. Mary Ann ZUG
30 Vice Pres for Advancement ....Ms. Susan HUPPERT
46 Vice President for Research ....Dr. Jeffrey GRAY
06 Registrar ....Ms. Kathy L. SCAGLIONE
08 Director of Library .... Mr. Larry MARQUARDT
15 Director of Human Resources ....Ms. Becky LADE
27 Chief Information Officer .... Ms. Carolyn WEAVER
37 Director of Financial Aid ....Ms. Mary PAYNE
18 Director of Facilities Management ....Mr. David MCNERNEY
19 Director University Services ....Mr. John BRUECKEN
88 Chief Compliance Officer ....Ms. Erika LINDEN
21 Chief Financial Officer ....Mr. Mark J. PEIFFER
69 Director Public Health Program ....Dr. Mary Mincer HANSEN
76 Director Healthcare Administration ....Dr. Carla STEBBINS
26 Director Marketing & Communication ....Ms. Kendall DILLON
38 Director Educational Support Svcs ....Ms. Lynn MARTIN
84 AVP for Enrollment Management ....Dr. Karen LEWIS
76 Dean College Health Sciences ....Dr. Jodi CAHALAN
63 Dean Col Podiatric Medicine/Surg ....Dr. Robert YOHO
63 Dean Col Osteopathic Medicine/Surg ....Dr. JD POLK

† Tuition varies by program.

Divine Word College (I)

102 Jacoby Drive, SW, PO Box 380,
Epworth IA 52045-0380
County: Dubuque FICE Identification: 001858
Unit ID: 153241
Telephone: (563) 876-3353 Carnegie Class: Spec/Faith
FAX Number: (563) 876-3407 Calendar System: Semester
URL: www.dwci.edu
Established: 1918 Annual Undergrad Tuition & Fees: $12,310
Enrollment: 123 Male
Affiliation or Control: Roman Catholic IRS Status: 501(c)3
Highest Offering: Baccalaureate
Program: Religious Emphasis
Accreditation: NH

01 President .... Fr. Timothy A. LENCHAK
05 Academic Dean/Vice President ...... Dr. Mathew KANJIRATHINKAL
10 Vice Pres for Finances/Fin Aid Dir ....Mr. Mark PASKER
32 Dean of Students ....Rev. Khien LUU
07 Director Admissions/VP Recruitment ....Mr. Len UHAL
30 Development Director ....Mr. Terrance SYKORA
26 Public Relations Director ....Ms. Sandy WILGENBUSCH
08 Librarian ....Mr. Daniel BOICE
06 Registrar ....Mrs. Deborah HIRSCH
38 Counselor .... Mrs. Nan PECK

Dordt College (J)

498 4th Avenue, NE, Sioux Center IA 51250-1697
County: Sioux FICE Identification: 001859
Unit ID: 153250
Telephone: (712) 722-6000 Carnegie Class: Bac/Diverse
FAX Number: (712) 722-6035 Calendar System: Semester
URL: www.dordt.edu
Established: 1955 Annual Undergrad Tuition & Fees: $26,540
Enrollment: 1,391 Coed
Affiliation or Control: Christian Reformed Church IRS Status: 501(c)3
Highest Offering: Master's
Program: 2-Year Principally Bachelor's Creditable; Liberal Arts And General; Teacher Preparatory
Accreditation: NH, ENG, NURSE, SW

01 President .... Dr. Erik HOEKSTRA
05 Provost ....Dr. Eric A. FORSETH
30 Vice President College Advancement .... Mr. John BAAS
10 Vice President Business ....Mr. Arlan NEDERHOFF
11 Vice President for Administration ....Dr. Bethany SCHUTTINGA
84 Vice President for Enrollment ....Mr. Howard WILSON
88 Dean of Off Campus Programs ....Dr. Curtis J. TAYLOR
07 Executive Director Admissions .... Mr. Quentin VAN ESSEN
37 Director Financial Aid .... Mr. Michael EPEMA
06 Registrar .... Mr. James BOS
88 Dean for Research and Scholarship .... Dr. John H. KOK
20 Dean for Curriculum & Instruction ....Dr. Leah ZUIDEMA
58 Director Graduate Education ....Dr. Timothy VAN SOELEN
36 Director of Career Services ....Vacant
26 Marketing and Public Relations .. Ms. Sonya JONGSMA KNAUSS
18 Director Physical Plant .... Mr. Stan OORDT
32 Interim Dean of Campus Life ....Mr. Robert TAYLOR
42 Campus Pastor ....Rev. Aaron BAART
41 Director of Athletics ....Mr. Glenn BOUMA
40 Director Bookstore/Purchasing .... Ms. Lora DEVRIES
44 Director of Planned Giving ....Mr. Dave VANDER WERF
29 Director Alumni/Church Relations ....Vacant
15 Director Human Resources ....Mrs. Sue DROOG
96 Director of Purchasing ....Mr. Fred HAAN
91 Director of Computer Services ....Mr. Brian VAN DONSELAAR
44 Development Programs Coordinator ......Ms. Barbara J. MELLEMA
08 Director of Library Services ....Ms. Sheryl S. TAYLOR
23 Director of Health Sciences ....Ms. Pamela L. HULSTEIN
88 Director Academic Skills Center ....Ms. Pamala S. DE JONG

Drake University (K)

2507 University Avenue, Des Moines IA 50311-4505
County: Polk FICE Identification: 001860
Unit ID: 153269
Telephone: (515) 271-2011 Carnegie Class: Master's L
FAX Number: (515) 271-3016 Calendar System: Semester
URL: www.drake.edu
Established: 1881 Annual Undergrad Tuition & Fees: $30,734
Enrollment: 5,270 Coed
Affiliation or Control: Independent Non-Profit IRS Status: 501(c)3
Highest Offering: Doctorate
Program: Liberal Arts And General; Teacher Preparatory; Professional
Accreditation: NH, ART, BUS, BUSA, CORE, JOUR, LAW, MUS, PHAR

01 President .... Dr. David E. MAXWELL
05 Provost .... Dr. Deneese JONES
10 Vice President Business & Finance ....Ms. Deborah NEWSOM
30 Vice Pres Alumni and Development ....Mr. John SMITH
07 Vice Pres Admissions/Financial Aid ....Mr. Tom DELAHUNT
20 Associate Provost of Curriculum .... Mr. Art SANDERS
09 Associate Provost ....Dr. Raylene ROSPOND
32 Interim Vice Prov Student Affairs ......Ms. Melissa STURM-SMITH
35 Dean of Students .... Dr. Sentwali BAKARI
15 Human Resources Director .... Ms. Venessa MACRO
27 Chief Tech Information Officer ....Vacant
04 Executive Asst to Pres/Secy of Univ ....Ms. Linda S. RYAN
18 Director Facility Services ....Ms. Jolene SCHMIDT
06 Director of Student Records .... Mr. Kevin P. MOENKHAUS
08 Dean Cowles Library ....Mr. Rodney N. HENSHAW
85 Vice Provost of Intl Programs .... Dr. Christa OLSON
91 Director Campus Information Svcs .... Ms. Angela EMBREE
19 Chief Campus Security Services ....Vacant
26 Exec Dir Marketing & Communications ..... Ms. Debra LUKEHART
29 Alumni/Parent Programs .... Mr. Blake CAMPBELL
49 Dean Arts & Sciences ....Dr. Joseph LENZ
53 Dean School Education .... Dr. Janet M. MCMAHILL
61 Dean Law School ....Mr. Allan VESTAL
50 Dean Business/Public Administration .... Mr. Charles EDWARDS, JR.
67 Dean Pharmacy/Health Science ....Dr. Wendy DUNCAN
60 Dean Journ/Mass Communications .. Mr. Charles EDWARDS, JR.
44 Director of Planned Giving ....Vacant
41 Director Intercollegiate Athletics ....Ms. Sandy Hatfield CLUBB
37 Director Financial Aid ....Ms. Susan K. LADD
38 Director University Counseling Ctr .... Dr. Mark KLOBERDANZ
92 Assistant Director Honors Program .... Ms. Charlene SKIDMORE
94 Director Women's Studies ....Dr. Nancy REINCKE
31 Dir Community Outreach/Development ....Vacant
39 Director Office of Residence Life ....Ms. Lorissa LIEURANCE

*Eastern Iowa Community College District (L)

306 W River Drive, Davenport IA 52801-1221
County: Scott FICE Identification: 004075
Unit ID: 153311
Telephone: (563) 336-3300 Carnegie Class: N/A

FAX Number: (563) 336-3350
URL: www.eicc.edu

01	Chancellor	Dr. Donald S. DOUCETTE
30	Exec Dir Resource Development	Dr. Ellen KABAT LENSCH
103	Vice Chanc Workforce Dev/Cont Educ	Dr. Nancy KOTHENBEUTEL
31	Exec Dir Community & Econ Devel	Mr. Mark KAPFER
26	Associate Director for Marketing	Ms. Karen FARLEY
11	Exec Dir Administrative Services	Ms. Lana J. DETTBARN
09	Dir Institutional Effectiveness	Ms. Laurie R. HANSON
27	Associate Director Communications	Mr. Alan CAMPBELL

*Clinton Community College (A)

1000 Lincoln Boulevard, Clinton IA 52732-6299
County: Clinton — FICE Identification: 001853 — Unit ID: 153135
Telephone: (563) 244-7001 — Carnegie Class: Not Classified
FAX Number: (563) 244-7107 — Calendar System: Semester
URL: www.eicc.edu
Established: 1966 — Annual Undergrad Tuition & Fees (In-District): $134
Enrollment: 1,769 — Coed
Affiliation or Control: State/Local — IRS Status: 501(c)3
Highest Offering: Associate Degree
Program: Occupational; 2-Year Principally Bachelor's Creditable
Accreditation: &NH, EMT

02	President	Dr. Karen VICKERS
05	Dean of the College	Mr. Ron SERPLISS
32	Dean of Student Development	Ms. Lisa MILLER
102	Asst to Pres/Exec Dir Sharar Found	Ms. Ann EISENMAN
04	Assistant to President/Admin	Ms. Deborah RICHTER

*Muscatine Community College (B)

152 Colorado Street, Muscatine IA 52761-5396
County: Muscatine — FICE Identification: 001882 — Unit ID: 154040
Telephone: (563) 288-6001 — Carnegie Class: Not Classified
FAX Number: (563) 288-6074 — Calendar System: Semester
URL: www.eicc.edu
Established: 1929 — Annual Undergrad Tuition & Fees (In-District): $134
Enrollment: 1,840 — Coed
Affiliation or Control: State/Local — IRS Status: 501(c)3
Highest Offering: Associate Degree
Program: Occupational; 2-Year Principally Bachelor's Creditable
Accreditation: &NH, EMT

02	President	Mr. Bob ALLBEE
04	Assistant to the President	Ms. Lisa WIEGEL
05	Dean of the College	Dr. Gail SPIES
32	Dean of Student Development	Ms. Shelly CRAM-RAHLF
31	Director Business/Industry Center	Mr. Marvin SMITH
06	Registrar	Ms. Robin MITCHELL
08	Library Specialist	Ms. Nancy LUIKART

*Scott Community College (C)

500 Belmont Road, Bettendorf IA 52722-6804
County: Scott — FICE Identification: 001885 — Unit ID: 154314
Telephone: (563) 441-4001 — Carnegie Class: Not Classified
FAX Number: (563) 441-4154 — Calendar System: Semester
URL: www.eicc.edu
Established: 1966 — Annual Undergrad Tuition & Fees (In-District): $134
Enrollment: 4,865 — Coed
Affiliation or Control: State/Local — IRS Status: 501(c)3
Highest Offering: Associate Degree
Program: Occupational; 2-Year Principally Bachelor's Creditable
Accreditation: &NH, CAHIIM, DA, EMT, NDT, RAD, SURGT

02	President	Dr. Teresa A. PAPER
32	Dean of Student Development/Affs	Ms. Lisa BROWN
36	Dean Career Assistance Center	Ms. Peg GARRISON
05	Dean of the College	Ms. Janet COOGAN
08	Librarian	Ms. Michelle BAILEY
11	Asst to President Administration	Mr. Matt SCHMIT
06	Registrar	Mr. Arnold THODE
18	Chief Facilities/Physical Plant	Mr. Ken MIROCHA
37	Director Student Financial Aid	Ms. Jeannine INGELSON
36	Job Placement Specialist	Mr. Wayne COLE

Emmaus Bible College (D)

2570 Asbury Road, Dubuque IA 52001-3096
County: Dubuque — FICE Identification: 023289 — Unit ID: 153302
Telephone: (563) 588-8000 — Carnegie Class: Spec/Faith
FAX Number: (563) 588-1216 — Calendar System: Semester
URL: www.emmaus.edu
Established: 1941 — Annual Undergrad Tuition & Fees: $15,390
Enrollment: 209 — Coed
Affiliation or Control: Independent Non-Profit — IRS Status: 501(c)3
Highest Offering: Baccalaureate
Program: 2-Year Principally Bachelor's Creditable; Teacher Preparatory; Professional
Accreditation: NH, BI

01	President	Mr. Philip BOOM
10	VP for Administration and Finance	Mr. Mark A. PRESSON
05	Vice President for Academic Affairs	Mrs. Lisa L. BEATTY
30	Vice President for Advancement	Mr. Jon W. GLOCK
32	Dean for Student Development	Vacant
88	Dean for Biblical Studies	Dr. David J. MACLEOD
08	Librarian	Mr. John H. RUSH
37	Financial Aid Officer	Mr. Steve C. SEEMAN
21	Controller	Mr. Steve M. JENSEN
06	Registrar	Mrs. Kathryn L. VAN DINE
07	Enrollment Services Manager	Mr. Israel CHAVEZ

Faith Baptist Bible College and Seminary (E)

1900 NW 4th Street, Ankeny IA 50023-2152
County: Polk — FICE Identification: 007121 — Unit ID: 153320
Telephone: (515) 964-0601 — Carnegie Class: Spec/Faith
FAX Number: (515) 964-1638 — Calendar System: Semester
URL: www.faith.edu
Established: 1921 — Annual Undergrad Tuition & Fees: $15,546
Enrollment: 300 — Coed
Affiliation or Control: Independent Non-Profit — IRS Status: 501(c)3
Highest Offering: First Professional Degree
Program: Liberal Arts And General; Teacher Preparatory; Religious Emphasis
Accreditation: NH, BI

01	President	Dr. James D. MAXWELL, III
05	VP for Academic Services	Dr. Paul HARTOG
73	Dean of Seminary	Dr. Doug E. BROWN
10	VP for Business/CFO	Mr. Daniel H. BJOKNE
30	VP for Advancement/Church Rels	Mr. Eugene M. MATLOCK
34	Dean of Women	Mrs. Carrie A. AUGSBURGER
32	Dean of Students	Mr. Lance A. AUGSBURGER
27	Director of Communications	Mr. Don K. ANDERSON
06	Registrar	Mr. David L. STOUT
37	Director Student Financial Aid	Mr. Breck H. APPELL
08	Head Librarian	Dr. John HARTOG, II

Graceland University (F)

1 University Place, Lamoni IA 50140-1699
County: Decatur — FICE Identification: 001866 — Unit ID: 153366
Telephone: (641) 784-5000 — Carnegie Class: Master's L
FAX Number: (641) 784-5480 — Calendar System: 4/1/4
URL: www.graceland.edu
Established: 1895 — Annual Undergrad Tuition & Fees: $23,530
Enrollment: 2,222 — Coed
Affiliation or Control: Other — IRS Status: 501(c)3
Highest Offering: Doctorate
Program: Liberal Arts And General; Teacher Preparatory
Accreditation: NH, TED

01	President	Dr. John SELLARS
05	Vice Pres Acad Affs/Dean of Faculty	Dr. Parris R. WATTS
09	VP Institutional Effectiveness	Dr. Kathleen M. CLAUSON
10	Vice Pres Business & Admin Svcs	Ms. Janice TIFFANY
32	Dean of Students	Mrs. Marian KILLPACK
84	Vice Pres Enrollment/Dean Admission	Mr. Kirk BJORLAND
30	Vice Pres Institutional Advancement	Mr. Kelly EVERETT
51	Director for Graduate/Continuing Ed	Mr. Paul BINNICKER
39	Director of Residence Life	Ms. Deb SKINNER
06	Registrar	Mrs. M. Joyce LIGHTHILL
29	Director of Alumni Relations	Mr. Paul DAVIS
36	Director Career/Acad/CAP Couns Ctr	Mrs. Michele MAGUIRE-BECK
23	Director Health Service	Mrs. Benna EASTER
18	Director Facility Services	Mr. Kurt REMMENGA
15	Director Human Resources	Mrs. Ondrea DORY
26	Chief Public Relations Officer	Mr. Randy MELINE
04	Executive Asst to President	Ms. Jodi L. SEYMOUR
41	Athletic Director	Mr. Jeff FALKNER
44	Director of Annual Fund/Stewardship	Mrs. Peggy STURDEVANT
85	Director International Programs	Ms. Diana JONES
86	Director Government Relations	Dr. Tom MORAIN
50	Dean School of Business	Dr. Steven ANDERS
53	Dean School of Education	Dr. Tammy EVERETT
66	Dean School of Nursing	Dr. Claudia HORTON
07	Director of Admissions	Mr. Kevin BROWN

Grand View University (G)

1200 Grandview Avenue, Des Moines IA 50316-1599
County: Polk — FICE Identification: 001867 — Unit ID: 153375
Telephone: (515) 263-2800 — Carnegie Class: Bac/Diverse
FAX Number: (515) 263-6095 — Calendar System: Semester
URL: www.grandview.edu
Established: 1896 — Annual Undergrad Tuition & Fees: $22,628
Enrollment: 2,232 — Coed
Affiliation or Control: Evangelical Lutheran Church In America — IRS Status: 501(c)3
Highest Offering: Master's
Program: Liberal Arts And General; Professional
Accreditation: NH, NURSE

01	President	Mr. Kent L. HENNING
04	Executive Asst to the President	Mr. Lucas J. CASEY
05	Provost/Vice Pres Academic Affairs	Dr. Mary Elizabeth STIVERS
79	Dean College of Humanities & Educ	Dr. Ross WASTVEDT
83	Dean College of Social/Nat Science	Dr. Katherine VAN BLAIR
10	Vice Pres Administration & Finance	Mr. Adam J. VOIGTS
30	Vice President Advancement	Mr. William H. BURMA
84	Vice Pres Enrollment Management	Ms. Debbie M. BARGER
26	Vice Pres Marketing/Communications	Ms. Carol M. BAMFORD
32	Vice President Student Affairs	Dr. Jay B. PRESCOTT
37	Director Financial Aid	Ms. Michele A. DUNNE
20	Special Assistant to the Provost	Ms. Pamela M. CHRISTOFFERS
51	Dean Graduate/Adult Programs	Dr. Patricia A. WILLIAMS
35	Associate VP for Student Affairs	Mr. Jason K. BAUER
06	Registrar	Ms. Debbie K. GANNON
42	Senior Campus Pastor	Rev. Russell L. LACKEY
09	Director Inst Planning/Research	Ms. Debbie M. BARGER
36	Director Career Center	Ms. Susan M. STEARNS
91	Vice President Information Svcs/CIO	Mr. Tim T. WHEELDON
08	Director of the Library	Ms. Pamela D. REES
40	Director Bookstore & Campus Svcs	Mr. Michael D. SHUPP
07	Director of Admissions	Ms. Diane S. JOHNSON
18	Director Buildings & Grounds	Ms. Kim I. BUTLER
38	Director Leadership & Counseling	Mr. Kent A. SCHORNACK
28	Dir Multicultural & Cmty Outreach	Mr. Alex H. PIEDRAS
41	Athletic Director	Mr. Troy A. PLUMMER
15	Human Resources Manager	Ms. Erica L. KLUVER

Grinnell College (H)

1121 Park Street, Grinnell IA 50112-1690
County: Poweshiek — FICE Identification: 001868 — Unit ID: 153384
Telephone: (641) 269-4000 — Carnegie Class: Bac/A&S
FAX Number: (641) 269-3408 — Calendar System: Semester
URL: www.grinnell.edu
Established: 1846 — Annual Undergrad Tuition & Fees: $43,656
Enrollment: 1,635 — Coed
Affiliation or Control: Independent Non-Profit — IRS Status: 501(c)3
Highest Offering: Baccalaureate
Program: Liberal Arts And General; Teacher Preparatory
Accreditation: NH

01	President	Raynard S. KINGTON
100	Spec Asst to Pres/VP Strat Planning	Angela VOOS
05	Int Vice Pres Acad Affs/Dean Col	David LOPATTO
30	Vice President Dev/Alumni Rel	Beth HALLORAN
88	Chief Investment Officer	David S. CLAY
32	Vice Pres Student Affairs	W. Houston DOUGHARTY
88	Vice President of College Services	John KALKBRENNER
10	Vice President for Finance/Treas	Karen VOSS
20	Associate Dean of College	Mark SCHNEIDER
20	Associate Dean of College	Heather LOBBAN-VIRAVONG
07	VP Enroll/Dean Adm & Fin Aid	Joseph P. BAGNOLI
30	Director of Development Operations	Jacquelyn AANES
37	Director of Student Financial Aid	Arnold A. WOODS, JR.
15	Director of Human Resources	Kristin LOVIG
26	Director of Communication	Jim REISCHE
06	Registrar	Cheryl CHASE
08	Librarian	Richard FYFFE
29	Director of Alumni Relations	Jayn CHANEY
14	Dir of Information Technology Svcs	Vacant
09	Assoc VP Analytics/Inst Rsch	Randall STILES
85	Director Intl Student Services	Karen K. EDWARDS
40	Manager/Bookstore	Cassandra J. WHERRY
41	Athletic Director	Greg WALLACE
23	Director of Health Service	Deb SHILL
38	Assoc Dean/Dir Academic Advising	Joyce STERN
18	Interim Director Facilities Mgmt	Richard WHITNEY
19	Director of Safety & Security	Stephen A. BRISCOE
42	Chaplain/Dean of Rel Life	Deanna SHORB
102	Director Corp/Founda/Govt Rels	Karen WIESE
39	Asst Dean/Director Residence Life	Andrea CONNER
35	Dean of Students	Travis GREENE
31	Dir Community Enhancement/Engagemnt	Monica CHAVEZ-SILVA
36	Assoc Dean and Director/Career Dev	Mark PELTZ

Hamilton Technical College (I)

1011 E 53rd Street, Davenport IA 52807-2616
County: Scott — FICE Identification: 012064 — Unit ID: 153427
Telephone: (563) 386-3570 — Carnegie Class: Spec/Tech
FAX Number: (563) 386-6756 — Calendar System: Semester
URL: www.hamiltontechcollege.com
Established: 1969 — Annual Undergrad Tuition & Fees: $11,025
Enrollment: 218 — Coed
Affiliation or Control: Proprietary — IRS Status: Proprietary
Highest Offering: Baccalaureate
Program: Occupational; Technical Emphasis
Accreditation: ACCSC

01	President	Mrs. Maryanne HAMILTON

Hawkeye Community College (J)

Box 8015, Waterloo IA 50704-8015
County: Black Hawk — FICE Identification: 004595 — Unit ID: 153445
Telephone: (319) 296-2320 — Carnegie Class: Assoc/Pub-R-L
FAX Number: (319) 296-2874 — Calendar System: Semester
URL: www.hawkeyecollege.edu
Established: 1966 — Annual Undergrad Tuition & Fees (In-District): $4,410
Enrollment: 5,942 — Coed
Affiliation or Control: State/Local — IRS Status: 501(c)3
Highest Offering: Associate Degree
Program: Occupational; 2-Year Principally Bachelor's Creditable

Accreditation: NH, COARC, DA, DH, MLTAD, OTA, PTAA

01 President .... Dr. Linda A. ALLEN
05 Vice Pres Academic Affairs .... Dr. Jane BRADLEY
10 Vice Pres Administration & Finance .... Mr. Dan GILLEN
30 Vice Pres Institutional Advancement .... Ms. Kathy A. FLYNN
102 Executive Director Foundation .... Vacant
15 Exec Dir Human Resource Services .... Mr. John D. CLOPTON
81 Dean Math/Natural & Social Sciences .... Dr. Cynthia BOTTRELL
79 Dean Comm/Humanities/Educ/Fine Arts .... Dr. Laurel KLINKENBERG
75 Dean Applied Science/Eng Technology .... Mr. A. Ray BEETS
76 Dean Health Sciences .... Dr. Candace CROFT
50 Dean Business & Public Services .... Mr. Bryan RENFRO
32 Dean of Students .... Ms. Nancy HENDERSON
07 Director Admissions & Recruitment .... Mr. Dave BALL
21 Director Business Services .... Vacant
13 Director Communication/Info Systems .... Vacant
62 Director Library Services .... Ms. Candace HAVELY
51 Exec Director Business & Cmty Ed .... Mr. Aaron SAUERBREI
18 Director Plant & Facilities .... Ms. Lindsey NISSEN
06 Dir Student Records & Registration .... Ms. Patricia A. EAST
24 Director Teaching/Learning Services .... Vacant
09 Director Institutional Research .... Ms. Connie BUHR
26 Director Public Relations/Mktg .... Ms. Mary Pat MOORE
28 Assoc Dir of Multicultural Affairs .... Mr. Quentin HART
35 Student Life Coordinator .... Ms. Stephanie CHERRY
44 Development Officer .... Ms. Karen GEBEL
101 Board Secretary .... Ms. Denise A. DUNN

Indian Hills Community College (A)

525 Grandview, Ottumwa IA 52501-1398
County: Wapello FICE Identification: 008403
Unit ID: 153472
Telephone: (641) 683-5111 Carnegie Class: Assoc/Pub-R-M
FAX Number: (641) 683-5184 Calendar System: Quarter
URL: www.indianhills.edu
Established: 1966 Annual Undergrad Tuition & Fees (In-District): $4,470
Enrollment: 4,885 Coed
Affiliation or Control: State/Local IRS Status: 501(c)3
Highest Offering: Associate Degree
Program: Occupational; 2-Year Principally Bachelor's Creditable
Accreditation: NH, ACFEI, CAHIIM, DA, EMT, MLTAD, OTA, PTAA, RAD

01 President .... Dr. Marlene SPROUSE
10 Chief Financial Officer .... Mr. Bill MECK
05 Vice President Academic Affairs .... Dr. Matt THOMPSON
86 Assoc Dean Govt Affs & Cmty Rels .... Ms. Martha WICK
49 Executive Dean Arts & Sciences .... Ms. Darlas SHOCKLEY
103 Exec Dean Reg Economic Advancement .... Mr. Tom RUBEL
32 Dean Student Services .... Mr. Chris BOWSER
76 Dean Health Occupations .... Dr. Jill BUDDE
12 Dean Centerville Campus .... Mr. Joe STARCEVICH
15 Director Human Resources .... Ms. Bonnie CAMPBELL
18 Director Maintenance .... Mr. Rick FOSDYCK
06 Registrar .... Vacant
41 Athletic Director .... Mr. Mike HAGEN
26 Director for Media/Public Rels .... Mr. Kevin PINK
88 Chair Aviation Programs .... Vacant
07 Director of Admissions .... Mr. Mark THOMPSON
09 Director of Institutional Research .... Dr. Stephanie HOLLIMAN
29 Director of Alumni Relations .... Dr. Bianca MYERS
35 Chief Development .... Ms. Rhonda CONRAD

Indian Hills Community College Centerville (B)

721 N First Street, Centerville IA 52544
Telephone: (641) 856-2143 Identification: 770054
Accreditation: &NH

† Main campus is Indian Hills Community College in Ottumwa, IA.

Inste Bible College (C)

2302 SW 3rd Street, Ankeny IA 50023-2453
County: Polk Identification: 666461
Telephone: (515) 289-9200 Carnegie Class: Not Classified
FAX Number: (515) 289-9201 Calendar System: Semester
URL: www.inste.edu
Established: 1982 Annual Undergrad Tuition & Fees: $2,024
Enrollment: 28 Coed
Affiliation or Control: Interdenominational IRS Status: 501(c)3
Highest Offering: Baccalaureate
Program: Liberal Arts And General; Religious Emphasis
Accreditation: DETC

01 President .... Dr. Nicholas VENDITTI
05 Vice President & Academic Dean .... Dr. Leona VENDITTI
20 Assistant Dean .... Rev. Victor COLÓN

Iowa Central Community College (D)

One Triton Circle, Fort Dodge IA 50501-5798
County: Webster FICE Identification: 001865
Unit ID: 153524
Telephone: (515) 576-7201 Carnegie Class: Assoc/Pub-R-M
FAX Number: (515) 576-7207 Calendar System: Semester
URL: www.iowacentral.edu
Established: 1966 Annual Undergrad Tuition & Fees (In-District): $4,530
Enrollment: 6,216 Coed
Affiliation or Control: Local IRS Status: 501(c)3
Highest Offering: Associate Degree
Program: Occupational; 2-Year Principally Bachelor's Creditable
Accreditation: NH, DH, MAC, MLTAD, RAD

01 President .... Dr. Daniel P. KINNEY
04 Assistant to the President .... Mrs. Karen L. LOMBARD
05 Vice President of Instruction .... Mr. David E. GROSLAND
32 Vice Pres Enroll Mgmt/Student Devel .... Mr. Thomas J. BENEKE
86 VP External Affairs/Govt Rels .... Mr. James B. KERSTEN
30 VP Development/Alumni Rels .... Mrs. Laurie M. HENDRICKS
10 Vice President of Business Affairs .... Mrs. Angela A. MARTIN
72 Dean Business & Ind Technology .... Mr. Neale J. ADAMS
66 Dean Health Sciences .... Ms. Trina J. STATON
49 Dean Liberal Arts & Sciences .... Mrs. Jennifer M. CONDON
106 Dean Distance Learning .... Mr. Timothy J. MARTIN
21 Director Business Office .... Mr. Luke J. GROVE
16 Director Human Resources .... Ms. Kimberly N. WHITMORE
15 Coordinator Human Resources .... Ms. Sandi J. PIEPER
06 Registrar .... Ms. Courtney A. KOPP
84 Director Enrollment Management .... Ms. Sara A. CONDON
37 Director Financial Aid .... Mrs. Darci M. BANGERT
41 Director Intercollegiate Athletics .... Mr. Rick A. SANDQUIST
39 Director Housing .... Mr. Jeremy D. CONLEY
35 Dir Student Life & Activities .... Mr. David L. PEARSON
88 Director Academic Resource Services .... Ms. Lori WOLTEN
18 Director Physical Facilities .... Mr. Troy A. BRANDT
12 Director Storm Lake Center .... Mr. Dan J. ANDERSON
12 Director Webster City Center .... Mrs. Kelly J. WIRTZ
27 Director Public Information .... Mr. Paul A. DECOURSEY
13 Director Institutional Technology .... Mr. Jeff A. NELSEN
13 Director Institutional Technology .... Mr. Troy D. CRAMPTON
14 Computer System Analyst .... Mr. Warren K. BAUER
40 Bookstore Manager .... Mrs. Samantha E. MCCLAIN

Iowa Lakes Community College (E)

19 S Seventh Street, Estherville IA 51334-2234
County: Emmet FICE Identification: 001864
Unit ID: 153533
Telephone: (712) 362-2604 Carnegie Class: Assoc/Pub-R-M
FAX Number: (712) 362-8363 Calendar System: Semester
URL: www.iowalakes.edu
Established: 1967 Annual Undergrad Tuition & Fees (In-District): $5,324
Enrollment: 2,954 Coed
Affiliation or Control: State/Local IRS Status: 501(c)3
Highest Offering: Associate Degree
Program: Occupational; 2-Year Principally Bachelor's Creditable
Accreditation: NH, MAC, SURGT

01 President .... Ms. Valerie K. NEWHOUSE
03 Executive Vice President .... Mr. Robert W. L'HEUREUX
12 Exec Dean Emmetsburg Campus .... Mr. Thomas S. BROTHERTON
27 Exec Director of Marketing .... Ms. Jane S. CAMPBELL
05 Exec Dean Instruction/Development .... Mr. Mark A. GRUWELL
18 Exec Dir of Facilities Management .... Ms. Delaine S. HINEY
51 Exec Dir Cmty & Business Relations .... Ms. Jolene R. ROGERS
12 Exec Dean Estherville Campus .... Mr. Scott M. STOKES
32 Executive Dean of Students .... Ms. Julie R. WILLIAMS

Iowa Lakes Community College Emmetsburg Campus (F)

3200 College Drive, Emmetsburg IA 50536
Telephone: (712) 852-3554 Identification: 770055
Accreditation: &NH

† Main campus is Iowa Lakes Community College in Estherville, IA.

Iowa Lakes Community College Spencer Campus (G)

Gateway N 1900 Grand Ave, Ste B-1, Spencer IA 51301
Telephone: (712) 262-7141 Identification: 770056
Accreditation: &NH

† Main campus is Iowa Lakes Community College in Estherville, IA.

*Iowa Valley Community College District (H)

3702 S Center Street, Marshalltown IA 50158-4760
County: Marshall FICE Identification: 033436
Telephone: (641) 752-4643 Carnegie Class: N/A
FAX Number: (641) 754-1336
URL: www.ivccd.com

01 Chancellor .... Mr. Christopher DUREE
51 Vice Chanc Continuing Educ/Training .... Ms. Jacque GOODMAN
11 Vice Chanc Administrative Services .... Ms. Colleen SPRINGER
10 Chief Financial Officer .... Ms. Kathleen PINK
12 Provost of ECC .... Dr. Nancy MUECKE
12 Provost of MCC .... Dr. Robin SHAFFER LILIENTHAL
12 Dean of Iowa Valley Grinnell .... Ms. Mary Anne NICKLE
26 Director of Marketing .... Ms. Robin ANCTIL
09 Institutional Researcher .... Dr. Lisa BREJA
04 Admin Assistant to the Chancellor .... Ms. Barbara JENNINGS
13 Dir Computing and Info Management .... Mr. Jim WILSON

*Ellsworth Community College (I)

1100 College Avenue, Iowa Falls IA 50126-1199
County: Hardin FICE Identification: 001862
Unit ID: 153296
Telephone: (641) 648-4611 Carnegie Class: Assoc/Pub-R-S
FAX Number: (641) 648-3128 Calendar System: Semester
URL: www.iavalley.edu/ecc/
Established: 1890 Annual Undergrad Tuition & Fees (In-District): $4,080
Enrollment: 1,100 Coed
Affiliation or Control: State/Local IRS Status: 501(c)3
Highest Offering: Associate Degree
Program: Occupational; 2-Year Principally Bachelor's Creditable
Accreditation: &NH, MAC

02 Provost .... Dr. Nancy MUECKE
05 Dean of Students & Academic Affairs .... Dr. Kelly FAGA
08 Director of Libraries .... Ms. Sandra GREUFE
32 Dean of Student Serv/Athletic Dir .... Mr. Nate FORSYTH
39 Director Student Housing .... Mr. O. J. PAYNE
37 Director Financial Aid .... Ms. Tara MILLER
44 Dir Annual Plan Giving/Dir Alum Rel .... Ms. Kaitlyn BARTLING
32 Associate Dean Student Services .... Ms. Annie KALOUS
84 Director Enrollment Mgmt/Registrar .... Ms. Barb KLEIN

† Regional accreditation is carried under the parent institution Iowa Valley Community College District in Marshalltown, IA.

*Marshalltown Community College (J)

3700 S Center Street, Marshalltown IA 50158-4760
County: Marshall FICE Identification: 001875
Unit ID: 153922
Telephone: (641) 752-7106 Carnegie Class: Assoc/Pub-R-S
FAX Number: (641) 752-8149 Calendar System: Semester
URL: www.iavalley.edu
Established: 1927 Annual Undergrad Tuition & Fees (In-District): $4,080
Enrollment: 2,005 Coed
Affiliation or Control: State/Local IRS Status: 501(c)3
Highest Offering: Associate Degree
Program: Occupational; 2-Year Principally Bachelor's Creditable
Accreditation: &NH, DA

02 Chancellor .... Dr. Christopher A. DUREE
11 Vice Chanc Administrative Services .... Ms. Colleen SPRINGER
10 Chief Financial Officer .... Ms. Kathy PINK
51 Vice Chancellor of Cont Educ/Trng .... Ms. Jacque GOODMAN
03 Povost .... Dr. Robin SHAFFER LILIENTHAL
05 Dean of Students & Academic Affairs .... Dr. Chris A. RUSSELL
20 Dir of Retention & Learning Svcs .... Mr. Nate CHUA
06 Registrar .... Ms. Zoe THORNTON
76 Assoc Dean of Health Occupations .... Ms. Linda HANSON
102 Executive Director of Foundation .... Ms. Carol GEIL
84 Assoc Dean of Enrollment Services .... Ms. Angie REDMOND
37 Director Student Financial Aid .... Mr. Matt DANIELS
26 Director of Marketing .... Ms. Robin ANCTIL
41 Athletic Director .... Mr. Daniel HUNTLEY
35 Coordinator of Student Engagement .... Mr. Chris BREES
38 Senior Student Success Specialist .... Mr. Dan KEY
39 Dir Residence Life & Housing .... Mr. Phil HERNANDEZ
08 Library Supervisor .... Mr. Eric GRACZKOWSKI
40 Bookstore Supervisor .... Ms. Meghan TOMLINSON

† Regional accreditation is carried under the parent institution Iowa Valley Community College District in Marshalltown, IA.

Iowa Wesleyan College (K)

601 N Main, Mount Pleasant IA 52641-1398
County: Henry FICE Identification: 001871
Unit ID: 153621
Telephone: (319) 385-8021 Carnegie Class: Bac/Diverse
FAX Number: (319) 385-6296 Calendar System: Semester
URL: www.iwc.edu
Established: 1842 Annual Undergrad Tuition & Fees: $25,530
Enrollment: 651 Coed
Affiliation or Control: United Methodist IRS Status: 501(c)3
Highest Offering: Baccalaureate
Program: Liberal Arts And General; Teacher Preparatory; Professional
Accreditation: NH

01 President .... Dr. Steven E. TITUS
100 Special Assistant to the President .... Vacant
10 Senior VP/Chief Financial Officer .... Ms. Phyllis WHITNEY
05 VP Academic Affairs and Dean .... Vacant
30 Vice Pres Institutional Relations .... Vacant
32 Vice Pres and Dean for Student Life .... Dr. Linda R. BUCHANAN
51 Associate VP for Extended Learning .... Mr. David C. FILE
27 Assoc VP/Chief Information Officer .... Dr. Kit NIP
07 Assoc VP & Dean for Admissions .... Vacant
06 Registrar .... Ms. Patty BROKKEN
37 Director of Financial Aid .... Ms. Renae ARMENTROUT
08 Library Director .... Ms. Paula KINNEY
15 Director of Human Resources .... Ms. Kathy MOOTHART
30 Development Officer .... Ms. Dawn DUNNEGAN
44 Director of Annual Fund .... Mr. James A. PEDRICK
26 Director of Marketing/Communication .... Ms. Martha POTTS-BELL
26 Publications Manager .... Ms. Sheri MICHAELS
29 Director of Alumni/Parent Relations .... Ms. Anita HAMPTON
42 Director of Church Relations .... Vacant
41 Athletic Director .... Mr. Mike HAMPTON
18 Director of Physical Plant .... Mr. Bob VITALE
35 Director of Student Activities .... Ms. Kat NIEMANN
36 Director of Career Development .... Ms. Ashlee WHIPPLE
40 Bookstore Director .... Ms. Amy MABEUS
04 Senior Exec Asst to the President .... Ms. Rebecca ROWE

Iowa Western Community College (L)

2700 College Road, Council Bluffs IA 51503-0567
County: Pottawattamie FICE Identification: 004598
Unit ID: 153630
Telephone: (712) 325-3200 Carnegie Class: Assoc/Pub-S-MC

FAX Number: (712) 325-3424 Calendar System: Semester
URL: www.iwcc.edu
Established: 1966 Annual Undergrad Tuition & Fees (In-District): $4,380
Enrollment: 7,367 Coed
Affiliation or Control: State/Local IRS Status: 501(c)3
Highest Offering: Associate Degree
Program: Occupational; 2-Year Principally Bachelor's Creditable
Accreditation: NH, ACFEI, DA, DH, MAC, SURGT

01 President Dr. Dan KINNEY
04 Assistant to the President Ms. Erin STOPAK
10 Vice Pres of Finance & Operations Mr. Thomas JOHNSON
05 Vice President for Academic Affairs Dr. Dorothy DURAN
32 Vice President for Student Services Ms. Tori CHRISTIE
26 Vice Pres of Marketing/Public Rels Mr. Donald KOHLER
30 Vice Pres Institutional Advancement Ms. Rene COUGHLIN
09 Dean of Institutional Research Ms. Karna LOEWENSTEIN
84 Dean Enrollment Services Ms. Chris LAFERLA
35 Dean Student Services Ms. Kimberly HENRY
12 Director of Clarinda Campus Mr. Chad WELLHAUSEN
06 Registrar Ms. Jill CLARK
15 Director of Human Resources Ms. Nancy SCHRAGE
29 Director of Alumni Relations Ms. Stacy SHOCKEY
37 Director of Student Financial Aid Vacant
21 Director Accounting Mr. Eddie HOLTZ
14 Director Computer Center Mr. James A. MAHLBERG
88 Exec Dir Economic Development Mr. Mark STANLEY
41 Athletic Director Ms. Brenda HAMPTON
39 Director of Residence Life Ms. Desirae BACHMAN
18 Chief Facilities/Physical Plant Mr. Greg CLAUSEN
07 Director of Admissions/Advising Ms. Keri ZIMMER
96 Director of Purchasing Mrs. Diane OSBAHR
40 Director Food Svcs/Bookstore Mgr Ms. Eddie HOLTZ
76 Area Nursing Coordinator Ms. Rita BERTHELSEN

Iowa Western Community College Clarinda Center (A)

923 East Washington Street, Clarinda IA 51632
Telephone: (712) 542-5117 Identification: 770057
Accreditation: &NH

† Main campus is Iowa Western Community College in Council Bluffs, IA.

ITT Technical Institute (B)

3735 Queen Court SW, Cedar Rapids IA 52404
Telephone: (319) 654-8200 Identification: 770648
Accreditation: ACICS

† Main campus is ITT Technical Institute in Indianapolis, IN.

ITT Technical Institute (C)

1860 NW 118th Street, Suite 110, Clive IA 50325-8278
Telephone: (515) 327-5500 Identification: 666596
Accreditation: ACICS

† Main campus is ITT Technical Institute in Indianapolis, IN.

Kaplan University (D)

3165 Edgewood Parkway SW,
Cedar Rapids IA 52404-2998
Telephone: (319) 363-0481 FICE Identification: 004220
Accreditation: &NH, ACBSP, MAC

† Main campus is Kaplan University in Davenport, IA.

Kaplan University (E)

1801 East Kimberly Road, Suite 1,
Davenport IA 52807-2095
County: Scott FICE Identification: 004586
Unit ID: 260901
Telephone: (563) 355-3500 Carnegie Class: Master's L
FAX Number: (563) 355-1320 Calendar System: Quarter
URL: www.kucampus.edu
Established: 1937 Annual Undergrad Tuition & Fees: $13,665
Enrollment: 48,865 Coed
Affiliation or Control: Proprietary IRS Status: Proprietary
Highest Offering: Doctorate
Program: Occupational
Accreditation: NH, ACBSP, CAHIIM, MAC, NURSE

01 Campus President Ms. Liza ZERBONIA
04 Assistant to the Campus President Ms. Sara SKELTON
32 Director of Student Services Ms. Connie BONNE
37 Director of Financial Aid Ms. Sharon BARBER
07 Director of Admissions Mr. Jason WILEVSKI
36 Employment Search Coordinator Ms. Sandra WAKEFIELD
08 Librarian Ms. Jillian FLAHAVEN
06 Registrar Ms. Janet GEHRLS

Kaplan University (F)

Plaza West 2570 4th Street, SW,
Mason City IA 50401-3102
Telephone: (641) 423-2530 Identification: 666438
Accreditation: &NH, ACBSP, MAC

† Main campus is Kaplan University in Davenport, IA.

Kaplan University (G)

4655 121st Street, Urbandale IA 50323-2311
Telephone: (515) 727-2100 Identification: 666437
Accreditation: &NH, ACBSP, MAC

† Main campus is Kaplan University in Davenport, IA.

Kaplan University-Cedar Falls (H)

7009 Nordic Drive, Cedar Falls IA 50613
Telephone: (319) 277-0220 Identification: 770058
Accreditation: &NH, ACBSP, MAC

† Main campus is Kaplan University in Davenport, IA.

Kaplan University-Council Bluffs (I)

1751 Madison Avenue, Suite 750, Council Bluffs IA 51503
Telephone: (712) 328-4212 Identification: 770059
Accreditation: &NH

† Main campus is Kaplan University in Davenport, IA.

Kirkwood Community College (J)

PO Box 2068, Cedar Rapids IA 52406-2068
County: Linn FICE Identification: 004076
Unit ID: 153737
Telephone: (319) 398-5411 Carnegie Class: Assoc/Pub-R-L
FAX Number: (319) 398-1037 Calendar System: Semester
URL: www.kirkwood.edu
Established: 1966 Annual Undergrad Tuition & Fees (In-District): $4,200
Enrollment: 16,661 Coed
Affiliation or Control: Local IRS Status: 501(c)3
Highest Offering: Associate Degree
Program: Occupational; 2-Year Principally Bachelor's Creditable
Accreditation: NH, ACBSP, ACFEI, CAHIIM, COARC, DA, DH, DT, EMT, MAC, NDT, OTA, PTAA, SURGT

01 President Dr. Mick STARCEVICH
51 VP Cont Education/Training Svcs Dr. Kim JOHNSON
10 Vice President/Chief Fin/Oper Ofcr Mr. Jim CHOATE
30 Vice President Resource Development Ms. Kathy HALL
05 Vice President Academic Affairs Dr. Bill LAMB
32 Vice President Student Services Dr. Kristie FISHER
20 Assoc Vice President Acad Affairs Mr. John HENIK
12 Dean Iowa City Campus Dr. Dale SIMON
35 Dean of Students Mr. Jon BUSE
15 Director Human Resources Mr. Mike ROBERTS
13 Associate VP IT Mr. Jon NEFF
09 Associate VP Institutional Research Mr. Al ROWE
86 Associate VP Governmental Rels Mr. Steven J. OVEL
106 Dean Distance Lrng & Secondary Pgm Mr. Todd PRUSHA
84 Director Enrollment Management Ms. Peg JULIUS
08 Director Library Mr. Arron WINGS
07 Director Admissions Mr. Douglas F. BANNON
18 Associate VP Facilities Mr. Tom KALDENBERG
25 Director Grants & Fed Programs Ms. Heather CONLEY
41 Athletic Director Mr. Doug WAGEMESTER
06 Registrar Ms. Dena RAUCH
29 Scholarship & Alumni Director Ms. Jody DONALDSON
37 Director Student Financial Aid Ms. Peg JULIUS
47 Dean Agriculture Mr. Scott ERMER
72 Dean Industrial Technology Mr. Jeff MITCHELL
88 Dean English Ms. Allison YORK
79 Dean Arts & Humanities Dr. Jennifer BRADLEY
76 Dean Health Sciences Ms. Nancy GLAB
83 Dean Social Sciences/Career Option Dr. Milford MUSKETT
81 Dean Math/Science Dr. Lori WOESTE
66 Dean Nursing Dr. Jimmy REYES
76 Dean Health Occupations Dr. Mike MCLAUGHLIN
50 Dean Business & Information Tech Ms. Lisa DUTCHIK
88 Dean Learning Services Vacant

Kirkwood Community College-Iowa City (K)

1816 Lower Muscatine Road, Iowa City IA 52240
Telephone: (819) 887-3658 Identification: 770062
Accreditation: &NH

† Main campus is Kirkwood Community College in Cedar Rapids, IA.

Loras College (L)

1450 Alta Vista, Dubuque IA 52004-0178
County: Dubuque FICE Identification: 001873
Unit ID: 153825
Telephone: (563) 588-7100 Carnegie Class: Bac/Diverse
FAX Number: (563) 588-7964 Calendar System: Semester
URL: www.loras.edu
Established: 1839 Annual Undergrad Tuition & Fees: $28,822
Enrollment: 1,558 Coed
Affiliation or Control: Roman Catholic IRS Status: 501(c)3
Highest Offering: Master's
Program: Liberal Arts And General; Teacher Preparatory
Accreditation: NH, SW

01 President Mr. James E. COLLINS
05 Provost & Academic Dean Dr. Cheryl R. JACOBSEN
10 Vice President Finance/Admin Svcs Dr. David W. EISINGER
84 Vice Pres Enrollment Management Mr. Omar CORREA
30 Vice Pres Institutional Advancement Mr. Michael J. DOYLE
32 Vice President Student Development Mr. Arthur W. SUNLEAF
04 Executive Assistant to President Ms. Barbara J. SIMON
20 Assoc Vice Pres Academic Affairs Dr. Mary E. CARROLL
42 Dean of Campus Spiritual Life Rev. William JOENSEN
91 Sr Dir Technology Support Services Mr. Jim ANDERSON
29 Exec Dir Alumni & Communications Ms. Bobbi L. EARLES
15 Dir Human/Organization Development Vacant
09 Director of Institutional Research Vacant
38 Director Center for Counseling Dr. Michael J. BOYD
07 Director of Admissions Ms. Sharon K. LYONS
08 Director of Academic Resource Ctr Ms. Joyce A. MELDREM
19 Director of Safety/Security Vacant
44 Director of Major & Planned Giving Mr. Eric J. SOLBERG
41 Director of Athletics Mr. Robert E. QUINN
18 Director of Physical Plant Mr. John R. MCDERMOTT
40 Director of Bookstore Ms. Renee A. MENNE
23 Director of Health Center Mrs. Tammy S. MARTI
42 Director of Campus Ministry Ms. Colleen M. KUHL
06 Registrar Mr. JT BROWN
39 Dir of Residence Life/Campus Safety Ms. Molly A. BURROWS-SCHUMACHER
35 Director of Student Life Ms. Kimberly A. WALSH
37 Director of Financial Planning Ms. Julie A. DUNN
25 Grant Writing Director Ms. Valorie A. WOERDEHOFF
26 Dir Communication/Media Relations Ms. Susan P. HAFKEMEYER
96 Controller for Business Office Ms. Sandy M. RECKER
36 Academic Internship Coordinator Ms. Faye A. FINNEGAN

Luther College (M)

700 College Drive, Decorah IA 52101-1045
County: Winneshiek FICE Identification: 001874
Unit ID: 153834
Telephone: (563) 387-2000 Carnegie Class: Bac/A&S
FAX Number: (563) 387-2158 Calendar System: 4/1/4
URL: www.luther.edu
Established: 1861 Annual Undergrad Tuition & Fees: $37,530
Enrollment: 2,473 Coed
Affiliation or Control: Evangelical Lutheran Church In America
IRS Status: 501(c)3
Highest Offering: Baccalaureate
Program: Liberal Arts And General; Teacher Preparatory; Professional
Accreditation: NH, MUS, NURSE, SW, TED

01 Interim President Dr. David L. TIEDE
05 Vice Pres Acad Affs/Dean of College Dr. Kevin KRAUS
20 Assistant Dean Ms. Arleen ORVIS
30 Vice President for Development Mr. Keith J. CHRISTENSEN
10 Vice President for Finance & Admin Ms. Diane L. TACKE
32 Vice Pres/Dean for Student Life Mr. Corey LANDSTROM
84 Vice Pres Enrollment Management Mr. Scot SCHAEFFER
26 Vice Pres Communications/Marketing Dr. Rob K. LARSON
13 Exec Dir Library & Info Tech Svcs Mr. Paul R. MATTSON
21 Controller Ms. Peggy LENSING
18 Exec Director Campus Services Mr. Jay L. UTHOFF
91 Director Information Systems Ms. Marcia A. GULLICKSON
44 Senior Development Officer Mr. Doug NELSON
06 Registrar Mr. Douglas KOSCHMEDER
20 Associate Dean Dr. Jeffrey WILKERSON
15 Director Human Resources Ms. Lora STEIL
41 Director Intercollegiate Athletics Dr. Joe H. THOMPSON
29 Director of Alumni Relations Ms. Sherry B. ALCOCK
26 Coordinator of Campus News Ms. Julie SHOCKEY
04 Assistant to the President Ms. Karen B. MARTIN-SCHRAMM
35 Associate Dean Student Life Ms. Jane HILDEBRAND
36 Director Career Center Vacant
38 Director Counseling Service Dr. Pamela C. TORRESDAL
37 Director Student Financial Planning Ms. Janice K. CORDELL
42 Dir Campus Ministry & Cong Rels Rev. Michael R. BLAIR
40 Director Book Shop/Union Services Ms. Deanna CASTERTON
27 Director of Publications Ms. Ellen E. MODERSOHN
39 Assistant Dean & Dir Res Life Ms. Kristine FRANZEN
85 Exec Dir Ctr Glo Learning & Int Adm Mr. Jon LUND
23 Director Health Services Vacant
19 Director Security/Safety Mr. Robert HARRI
88 Director Campus Programing Ms. Tanya M. GERTZ
28 Exec Director of Diversity Dr. Sheila RADFORD-HILL
09 Director Assessment/Inst Research Dr. Jon A. CHRISTY
07 Director of Recruiting Services Mr. Kirk NEUBAUER
35 Coordinator Student Activities Ms. Trish NEUBAUER
88 Asst Dean & Health Res Adv Ms. Janet HUNTER

Maharishi University of Management (N)

1000 N 4th Street, Fairfield IA 52557-0001
County: Jefferson FICE Identification: 011113
Unit ID: 153861
Telephone: (641) 472-7000 Carnegie Class: Master's L
FAX Number: (641) 472-1179 Calendar System: Other
URL: www.mum.edu
Established: 1971 Annual Undergrad Tuition & Fees: $24,850
Enrollment: 1,267 Coed
Affiliation or Control: Independent Non-Profit IRS Status: 501(c)3
Highest Offering: Doctorate
Program: Liberal Arts And General; Teacher Preparatory
Accreditation: NH, IACBE

01 President Dr. Bevan H. MORRIS
03 Executive Vice President Dr. Craig PEARSON
45 Vice President of Expansion Dr. David TODT

05 Dean of Faculty ... Dr. Cathy GORINI
10 Treasurer ... Mr. Michael SPIVAK
88 International Vice President ... Dr. Michael DILLBECK
88 International Vice President ... Dr. Susan DILLBECK
11 Chief Administrative Officer ... Dr. David STREID
43 Legal Counsel/Dean Global Develop ... Mr. Bill GOLDSTEIN
07 Dean of Admissions ... Mr. Bradford MYLETT
32 Co-Dean of Student Life ... Mr. Rod EASON
32 Co-Dean of Student Life ... Ms. Ellen AKST JONES
33 Associate Dean of Men ... Mr. Graham TORPEY
34 Associate Dean of Women ... Ms. Elaine POMFREY
06 Registrar ... Mr. Tom ROWE
26 Media Director ... Mr. Ken CHAWKIN
51 Dir Distance Educ/Intl Programs ... Mr. Dennis HEATON
27 Director of Press ... Mr. Harry BRIGHT
39 Director of Housing ... Mr. Britt ZEIGER
37 Director of Student Financial Aid ... Mr. Bill CHRISTENSEN
14 Director of Information Services ... Mr. Tom HIRSCH
09 Director of Assessment ... Mr. Raoul CALDERON
15 Director of Personnel ... Mr. John KENNEDY
29 Director Alumni Relations ... Ms. Jennine FELLMER
30 Co-Director of Development ... Mr. Nick ROSANIA
30 Co-Director of Development ... Ms. Sandra ROSANIA
36 Director Student Placement ... Dr. Rachel GOODMAN
18 Chief Facilities/Physical Plant ... Mr. De Armond BRIGGS
49 Dean College of Arts & Sciences ... Dr. Scott HERRIOTT
77 Dn College of Computer Sci & Math ... Mr. Gregory GUTHRIE
58 Dean of Graduate School ... Dr. Frederick TRAVIS

Mercy College of Health Sciences (A)

928 Sixth Avenue, Des Moines IA 50309-1239
County: Polk FICE Identification: 006273
Unit ID: 153977
Telephone: (515) 643-3180 Carnegie Class: Spec/Health
FAX Number: (515) 643-6698 Calendar System: Semester
URL: www.mchs.edu
Established: 1995 Annual Undergrad Tuition & Fees: $15,040
Enrollment: 846 Coed
Affiliation or Control: Roman Catholic IRS Status: 501(c)3
Highest Offering: Baccalaureate
Program: Liberal Arts And General; Professional; Nursing Emphasis
Accreditation: NH, ADNUR, DMS, EMT, MAC, MT, NMT, NURSE, POLYT, PTAA, RAD, SURGT

01 President ... Dr. Barbara Q. DECKER
05 VP of Academic Affairs and Provost ... Dr. Steven D. LANGDON
26 VP of External Affairs ... Mr. Brian P. TINGLEFF
10 VP of Business & Regulatory Affairs ... Dr. Thomas LEAHY
66 Dean of Nursing ... Dr. Shirley BEAVER
49 Dean of Liberal Arts & Sciences ... Dr. Jeannine MATZ
76 Dean of Allied Health ... Dr. Theresa SMITH
09 Dean Inst Rsrch/Assess/Dist Educ ... Dr. Joan M. MCCLEISH
08 Dir of Library and Media Services ... Mr. Roy MEADOR
06 Registrar ... Ms. Carolyn BUCKLIN
15 Human Resources Business Partner ... Ms. Anne DENNIS
37 Director of Financial Aid ... Ms. Lisa CROAT
38 Manager of Student Success ... Dr. Kristine OWENS
13 Director of Information Technology ... Mr. Jeff BOUZEK
18 Facilities Manager ... Mr. David STEENHOEK
07 Director of Admissions ... Ms. Kara DONOVAN
26 Marketing Coordinator ... Mr. Jim TAGYE
32 Dean of Student Affairs ... Dr. Karen ANDERSON

Morningside College (B)

1501 Morningside Avenue, Sioux City IA 51106-1751
County: Woodbury FICE Identification: 001879
Unit ID: 154004
Telephone: (712) 274-5000 Carnegie Class: Bac/Diverse
FAX Number: (712) 274-5101 Calendar System: Semester
URL: www.morningside.edu
Established: 1894 Annual Undergrad Tuition & Fees: $25,950
Enrollment: 2,224 Coed
Affiliation or Control: United Methodist IRS Status: 501(c)3
Highest Offering: Master's
Program: Liberal Arts And General; Teacher Preparatory; Professional
Accreditation: NH, MUS, NURSE

01 President ... Mr. John C. REYNDERS
05 Vice President/Dean of College ... Dr. William C. DEEDS
10 Vice President Business & Finance ... Mr. Ronald A. JORGENSEN
32 Vice Pres Student Life & Enrollment ... Mrs. Terri A. CURRY
30 Vice Pres Institutional Advancement ... Mr. Ahmad BOURA
35 Dean for Advising/Assoc Dean Stdnts ... Dr. Mary LEIDA
20 Associate Dean for Acad Affairs ... Dr. Susan BURNS
09 Asc Dean Assessment/Inst Research ... Dr. John PINTO
06 Registrar ... Ms. Mary PESHEK
37 Director Student Financial Planning ... Ms. Karen GAGNON
14 Dir Info Tech/Dean Learning Center ... Mr. Andrew HEISER
26 Vice Pres Communications & Mktg ... Mr. Rick WOLLMAN
29 Director of Alumni Relations ... Mr. Gene AMBROSON
58 Director of Graduate Studies ... Dr. Glenna J. TEVIS
18 Director of Physical Plant ... Mr. Kirk JOHNSON
19 Director of Security ... Mr. Jim CORNELIA
23 Director of Student Health ... Ms. Carol GARVEY
36 Director of Career Services ... Ms. Stacie HAYS
40 Director of Bookstore ... Mr. Duane BENSON
41 Athletic Director ... Mr. Tim JAGER
42 Campus Ministry ... Rev. Kathy MARTIN
44 Director of Gift Planning ... Mr. Fred S. ERBES
15 Director Human Resources ... Ms. Cindy WELP
38 Director Student Counseling ... Ms. Bobbi MEISTER
21 Controller ... Mr. Paul TREFT

Mount Mercy University (C)

1330 Elmhurst Drive, NE, Cedar Rapids IA 52402-4797
County: Linn FICE Identification: 001880
Unit ID: 154013
Telephone: (319) 363-8213 Carnegie Class: Bac/Diverse
FAX Number: (319) 363-5270 Calendar System: 4/1/4
URL: www.mtmercy.edu
Established: 1928 Annual Undergrad Tuition & Fees: $26,160
Enrollment: 1,810 Coed
Affiliation or Control: Roman Catholic IRS Status: 501(c)3
Highest Offering: Master's
Program: Liberal Arts And General; Teacher Preparatory; Professional
Accreditation: NH, NURSE, SW

01 Interim President ... Dr. Norm R. NIELSEN
05 Interim Provost ... Dr. Jan HANDLER
10 Vice President Finance ... Vacant
84 Vice Pres Enrollment Management ... Mr. Robert CALLAHAN
30 Vice Pres Develop & Alumni Rels ... Mr. Duff RIDGEWAY
11 Vice President for Administration ... Ms. Vicky SMITH
20 Vice Provost Academic Affairs ... Dr. Janet R. HANDLER
07 Dean of Admissions ... Mr. Scott BAUMLER
06 Registrar ... Mr. Jason CLAPP
08 Director of Library Services ... Mrs. Marilyn J. MURPHY
36 Director of Career Services ... Ms. Cheryl TABARELLA-REED
29 Asst VP Develop & Alumni Relations ... Ms. Lonna DREWELOW
37 Director of Financial Aid ... Ms. Bethany RINDERKNECHT
26 Asst VP Communications/Marketing ... Ms. Lisa LAFLER
41 Director of Athletics ... Mr. Scot H. REISINGER
42 Director Campus Ministry ... Mr. William MULCAHEY
32 Dean of Students ... Ms. Checka LEINWALL
44 Director of Major & Planned Gifts ... Vacant
88 Director of Faculty Development ... Dr. Edy PARSONS
38 Director of Counseling Services ... Vacant
13 Director of Technology Operations ... Ms. Connie SNITKER
19 Director of Public Safety ... Mr. Blake MIKESELL
24 Academic Technology Librarian ... Ms. Vicky MALOY
35 Director of Student Activities ... Ms. Sarah L. BOTKIN
15 Director Human Resources ... Vacant
18 Director Facilities/Physical Plant ... Mr. Dave D. DENNIS
92 Director Honors Program ... Dr. Joy E. OCHS
40 Bookstore Manager ... Ms. Janie A. MILLS
04 Exec Assistant to President ... Mrs. Dianne M. AUSTAD
09 Exec Dir of Institutional Research ... Ms. Lori HEYING

North Iowa Area Community College (D)

500 College Drive, Mason City IA 50401-7299
County: Cerro Gordo FICE Identification: 001877
Unit ID: 154059
Telephone: (641) 423-1264 Carnegie Class: Assoc/Pub-R-M
FAX Number: (641) 423-1711 Calendar System: Semester
URL: www.niacc.edu
Established: 1917 Annual Undergrad Tuition & Fees (In-District): $4,596
Enrollment: 3,279 Coed
Affiliation or Control: State/Local IRS Status: 501(c)3
Highest Offering: Associate Degree
Program: Occupational; 2-Year Principally Bachelor's Creditable
Accreditation: NH, ADNUR, MAC, PTAA

01 Interim President ... Dr. David BUETTNER
05 Vice Pres Academic/Student Affairs ... Dr. Lyn A. BRODERSEN
10 Vice Pres Administrative Services ... Mrs. Kathy M. GROVE
32 Dean of Student Development ... Dr. Terri L. EWERS
30 VP of Inst Advancement & JPEC ... Mr. Jamie T. ZANIOS
09 VP Inst Effectiveness & Organiz Dev ... Dr. Shelly M. SCHMIT
06 Registrar ... Mrs. Michelle L. PETZNICK
07 Director of Admissions ... Mrs. Rachel L. MCGUIRE
49 Chair Arts & Science Division ... Dr. William W. BACKLIN
47 Chair Ag & Industrial Division ... Mr. Kevin D. MUHLENBRUCH
50 Chair Business Division ... Mrs. Laura L. MERFELD
66 Chair Health Division ... Mrs. Donna J. ORTON
51 Dean of Cont Ed & Economic Dev ... Mr. Terry W. SCHUMAKER
37 Director of Financial Aid ... Mrs. Mary E. BLOOMINGDALE
20 Director Learning Support Division ... Mrs. Jessica J. PUTNAM
14 Director of Technology Services ... Mr. Mark D. GREENWOOD
103 Regional Dir of Iowa Works ... Ms. Angela A. KONIG
40 Bookstore Manager ... Mrs. Rhonda K. NESHEIM-KAUFFMAN
41 Director of Athletics ... Mr. Dan J. MASON
18 Director of Facilities Management ... Mr. Tony A. PAPPAS
21 Accountant/Business Office Manager ... Ms. Mindy R. EASTMAN
24 Instructional Technology Coord ... Mr. Bruce G. MCKEE
39 Director Student Housing ... Mr. Travis J. HERGERT
08 Librarian ... Vacant
88 Director of Food Service ... Mr. Ken P. WEBBER
26 Dir Marketing/Public Affs/Govt Affs ... Mrs. Michele R. APPELGATE
88 Dir Incubation & Acceleration Svcs ... Mr. Daniel J. WINEGARDEN
88 Director of School Partnerships ... Mrs. Jean M. OSTRANDER
88 Director of Operations ... Mrs. Constance J. GLANDON
88 Director of Programming & Sales ... Mrs. Jody L. EAST

Northeast Iowa Community College (E)

Box 400, Calmar IA 52132-0400
County: Winneshiek FICE Identification: 004587
Unit ID: 154110
Telephone: (563) 562-3263 Carnegie Class: Assoc/Pub-R-M
FAX Number: (563) 562-3719 Calendar System: Semester
URL: www.nicc.edu
Established: 1966 Annual Undergrad Tuition & Fees (In-District): $5,216
Enrollment: 5,018 Coed
Affiliation or Control: Local IRS Status: 501(c)3
Highest Offering: Associate Degree
Program: Occupational; 2-Year Principally Bachelor's Creditable; Technical Emphasis
Accreditation: NH, CAHIIM, COARC, DA, RAD

01 President ... Dr. Liang C. WEE
10 Vice Pres Finance & Administration ... Mr. John D. NOEL
05 Chief Acad Ofcr/VP Academic Affairs ... Dr. Kathy J. NACOS-BURDS
46 Vice Pres Bus & Community Solutions ... Dr. Wendy A. MIHM-HEROLD
12 Peosta Provost ... Dr. Amy H. ESTERHUIZEN
12 Calmar Provost ... Ms. Rhonda K. SEIBERT
32 Vice Pres Student Services ... Dr. Linda M. PETERSON
51 Exec Dir Town Clock/Dubuque Centers ... Ms. Wendy S. KNIGHT
102 Exec Director of NICC Foundation ... Ms. Julie A. WURTZEL
21 Executive Director of Finance ... Mr. Thomas M. RIDOUT
45 Exec Dir of Inst Effectiveness ... Ms. Kristin A. DIETZEL
15 Exec Director of Human Resources ... Dr. Julie G. HUISKAMP
106 Director Distance Learning ... Dr. Christopher M. OSTWINKLE
13 Director Computer Information Sys ... Mr. Leonard B. FIELDS
09 Director of Institutional Research ... Ms. Dolores M. MILLER
88 Director Economic Devel/Peosta ... Mr. Gregory A. WILLGING
37 Director of Financial Aid ... Ms. Kim M. BAUMLER
06 District Registrar ... Ms. Karla R. WINTER
06 Dir of Advising/Registr/Persistence ... Ms. Sheila R. BECKER
36 Career Services Manager ... Mr. Chris E. ENTRINGER
07 Director of Admissions ... Ms. Kristi L. STRIEF

Northeast Iowa Community College Peosta Campus (F)

8342 Nicc Drive, Peosta IA 52068
Telephone: (800) 728-7367 Identification: 770063
Accreditation: &NH

† Main campus is Northeast Iowa Community College in Calmar, IA.

Northwest Iowa Community College (G)

603 W Park Street, Sheldon IA 51201-1046
County: Sioux FICE Identification: 004600
Unit ID: 154129
Telephone: (712) 324-5061 Carnegie Class: Assoc/Pub-R-S
FAX Number: (712) 324-4136 Calendar System: Semester
URL: www.nwicc.edu
Established: 1966 Annual Undergrad Tuition & Fees (In-District): $4,128
Enrollment: 1,621 Coed
Affiliation or Control: State/Local IRS Status: 501(c)3
Highest Offering: Associate Degree
Program: Occupational; 2-Year Principally Bachelor's Creditable; Technical Emphasis
Accreditation: NH, CAHIIM

01 President ... Dr. Alethea F. STUBBE
05 VP Student & Academic Services ... Dr. John HARTOG
30 VP Inst Adv & External Affairs ... Dr. Jan E. SNYDER
10 VP Operations & Finance ... Mr. Mark BROWN
49 Dean Arts & Sci/Business/Health ... Dr. Rhonda R. PENNINGS
72 Dean Applied Technology ... Mr. Steve WALDSTEIN
53 Dean Center for Teaching & Learning ... Ms. Gretchen G. BARTELSON
21 Director of Business Services ... Ms. Jessica WILLIAMS
37 Director Financial Aid ... Ms. Karna HOFMEYER
84 Director Enrollment Management ... Ms. Lisa L. STORY
08 Director of Library Services ... Ms. Molly D. GALM
13 Director of Technology & Info Svcs ... Mr. Mike OLDENKAMP
88 Director of TRIO ... Ms. Laurie L. EDWARDS
51 Dean Workforce and Continuing Educ ... Mr. Frank DE MILIA
06 Registrar/Assoc Dean of Students ... Ms. Beth SIBENALLER-WOODALL
15 Director of Human Resources ... Ms. Sandy BRUNS
88 Director of Alt HS/Learning Center ... Ms. Susan SCHMIDT
26 Director Community Relations ... Ms. Kristin E. KOLLBAUM
18 Director Physical Facilities ... Mr. Doug RODGER

Northwestern College (H)

101 Seventh Street, SW, Orange City IA 51041-1996
County: Sioux FICE Identification: 001883
Unit ID: 154101
Telephone: (712) 707-7000 Carnegie Class: Bac/Diverse
FAX Number: (712) 707-7247 Calendar System: Semester
URL: www.nwciowa.edu
Established: 1882 Annual Undergrad Tuition & Fees: $26,764
Enrollment: 1,241 Coed
Affiliation or Control: Reformed Church In America IRS Status: 501(c)3
Highest Offering: Baccalaureate
Program: Liberal Arts And General; Teacher Preparatory; Professional
Accreditation: NH, IACBE, NURSE, SW, TED

01 President ... Mr. Gregory E. CHRISTY
05 Provost ... Dr. Jasper LESAGE
20 Dean of Faculty ... Dr. Adrienne M. FORGETTE
32 Dean of Student Life ... Dr. Julie VERMEER ELLIOTT

10 Vice President Financial Affairs .... Mr. Doug D. BEUKELMAN
30 Vice President Advancement .... Mr. Jay WIELENGA
84 Dean of Enrollment Management .... Mr. Kenton PAULS
88 Assoc Dean of Spiritual Formation .... Ms. Barb DEWALD
104 Associate Dean for Global Education .... Dr. Douglas W. CARLSON
42 Chaplain .... Rev. Harlan VAN OORT
41 Director of Athletics .... Mr. Barry M. BRANDT
08 Director of the Library .... Mr. Tim SCHLAK
06 Registrar .... Ms. Sandy VAN KLEY
37 Director of Financial Aid .... Mr. Eric ANDERSON
14 Director of Computing Services .... Mr. Harlan R. JORGENSEN
26 Director of Public Relations .... Mr. Duane L. BEESON
36 Director of Career Development .... Mr. William C. MINNICK
38 Dir Student Counseling Services .... Dr. Sally EDMAN
18 Director of Maintenance/Operations .... Mr. Scott K. SIMMELINK
29 Director Alumni Relations .... Mr. Mark R. BLOEMENDAAL
15 Director of Human Resources .... Mrs. Deb SANDBULTE
09 Director of Institutional Research .... Vacant

Palmer College of Chiropractic (A)

1000 Brady Street, Davenport IA 52803-5287
County: Scott FICE Identification: 012300
Unit ID: 154174
Telephone: (563) 884-5000 Carnegie Class: Spec/Health
FAX Number: (563) 884-5409 Calendar System: Trimester
URL: www.palmer.edu
Established: 1897 Annual Undergrad Tuition & Fees: $31,845
Enrollment: 2,168 Coed
Affiliation or Control: Independent Non-Profit IRS Status: 501(c)3
Highest Offering: First Professional Degree
Program: Professional
Accreditation: NH, CHIRO

00 Chancellor .... Dr. Dennis M. MARCHIORI
01 Campus Provost .... Dr. Daniel J. WEINERT
05 Vice Chancellor for Academics .... Dr. Robert E. PERCUOCO
32 Vice Chancellor Student Success .... Dr. Kevin A. CUNNINGHAM
11 Vice Chancellor Support Services .... Mr. Robert E. LEE
84 Vice Chancellor for Enrollment .... Mr. J. Michael NOVAK
10 Vice Chancellor for Administration .... Mr. Thomas L. TIEMEIER
17 Vice Chancellor for Clinic Affairs .... Dr. Kurt W. WOOD
46 Vice Chancellor for Research .... Dr. Christine GOERTZ
26 Exec Dir for Marketing & PR .... Mr. James O'CONNOR
29 Executive Director for Alumni .... Dr. Mickey G. BURT
20 Dean of Academic Programs .... Dr. Kevin PAUSTIAN
88 Director of Undergrad Studies .... Ms. Cathy EBERHART
06 Senior Director/Registrar .... Ms. Mindy S. LEAHY
09 Sr Dir Institutional Plng/Research .... Dr. Dustin C. DERBY
21 Senior Dir for Financial Affairs .... Ms. Alexis A. VANDER HORN
13 Senior Director of IT .... Mr. Mike A. BENEDICT
15 Senior Director of Human Resources .... Ms. Michelle K. WALKER
18 Senior Director of Facilities .... Mr. Stanley E. CARLSON
07 Senior Director of Admissions .... Ms. Julie BEHN
37 Senior Dir of Financial Planning .... Ms. Jennifer L. RANDAZZO
108 Senior Director for Assessment .... Dr. Andrea HAAN
24 Sr Dir/Center for Teaching/Lrng .... Dr. Dana J. LAWRENCE
51 Senior Dir of Continuing Education .... Vacant
38 Senior Dir of Counseling Services .... Dr. Lori L. NEWMAN
08 Senior Director of Library .... Ms. Chabha TEPE
40 Senior Director of Bookstores .... Ms. Carol A. HOYT
88 Sr Dir Quality Assurance/Sys Organ .... Ms. Earlye A. JULIEN
96 Purchasing Manager .... Ms. Cheryl L. KOFRON

St. Ambrose University (B)

518 W Locust Street, Davenport IA 52803-2898
County: Scott FICE Identification: 001889
Unit ID: 154235
Telephone: (563) 333-6000 Carnegie Class: Master's L
FAX Number: (563) 333-6243 Calendar System: Semester
URL: www.sau.edu
Established: 1882 Annual Undergrad Tuition & Fees: $26,740
Enrollment: 3,357 Coed
Affiliation or Control: Roman Catholic IRS Status: 501(c)3
Highest Offering: Doctorate
Program: Liberal Arts And General; Fine Arts Emphasis
Accreditation: NH, ACBSP, ENG, NURSE, OT, PTA, @SP, SW, TEAC

01 President .... Sr. Joan LESCINSKI, CSJ
05 VP for Academic & Student Affairs .... Dr. Paul KOCH
10 Vice President Finance .... Mr. Michael C. POSTER
42 Chaplain .... Rev. Charles A. ADAM
30 Vice President Advancement .... Mr. James R. STANGLE
84 Vice Pres Enrollment Management .... Mr. John D. COOPER
88 Assoc Vice Pres for Advancement .... Mr. Edward J. FINN
46 Assoc Vice Pres Assess/
Research .... Dr. Tracy SCHUSTER-MATLOCK
21 Assistant Vice President Finance .... Ms. Carol A. GLINES
26 Asst Vice Pres Communications/Mktg .... Ms. Linda R. HIRSCH
32 Asst VP Student Svcs/Dean of Stdnts .... Mr. Timothy PHILLIPS
15 Director Human Resources .... Ms. Audrey D. HEIN
07 Director Admissions .... Ms. Meg F. HALLIGAN
14 Exec Dir of Information Resources .... Ms. Mary B. HEINZMAN
29 Director Alumni Rels & Spec Project .... Ms. Anne A. GANNAWAY
37 Director Financial Aid .... Ms. Julie A. HAACK
38 Director Counseling .... Mr. Stephen TENDALL
18 Director Physical Plant .... Mr. Jim M. HANNON
06 Registrar .... Mr. Dan L. ZEIMET
23 Director of Health Services .... Ms. Nancy A. HINES
19 Director of Security .... Mr. Robert CHRISTOPHER
39 Director of Resident Life .... Mr. Matt B. HANSEN
08 Director Library .... Ms. Mary B. HEINZMAN
36 Director Career Development .... Ms. Angela P. ELLIOTT
41 Athletic Director .... Mr. Raymond J. SHOVLAIN
94 Director of Women's Studies .... Dr. Beatrice F. JACOBSON
40 Manager of Bookstore .... Ms. Linda K. MACUMBER
85 Asst VP International Education .... Dr. Ryan D. DYE
88 Chair Masters Pastoral Studies .... Rev. Bud GRANT
88 Chair Masters Criminal Justice .... Mr. Waylyn C. MCCULLOH
49 Dean College Arts & Sciences .... Dr. Aron R. AJI
50 Dean College Business .... Dr. David J. O'CONNELL
71 Dean Education and Health Sciences .... Dr. Sandra L. CASSADY
88 Dean for Academic Adult
Programming .... Dr. Regina M. MATHESON
54 Dir Ambrose Industrial Engineering .... Dr. Michael E. OPAR
57 Director Fine Arts .... Mr. Lance A. SADLEK
88 Director Occupational Therapy .... Dr. Lynn J. KILBURG
88 Director Masters of Accounting .... Mr. Lew D. MARX
58 Director Academic Svcs MBA Pgm .... Ms. Allison S. AMBROSE
58 Director Graduate Student Recruit .... Ms. Elizabeth B. LOVELESS
28 Director of Diversity .... Dr. Paul C. KOCH

St. Luke's College (C)

2720 Stone Park Boulevard, Sioux City IA 51104-0010
County: Woodbury FICE Identification: 007291
Unit ID: 154262
Telephone: (712) 279-3149 Carnegie Class: Assoc/PrivNFP
FAX Number: (712) 233-8017 Calendar System: Semester
URL: www.stlukescollege.edu
Established: 1995 Annual Undergrad Tuition & Fees: $18,090
Enrollment: 213 Coed
Affiliation or Control: Independent Non-Profit IRS Status: 501(c)3
Highest Offering: Baccalaureate
Program: Occupational; 2-Year Principally Bachelor's Creditable; Nursing Emphasis
Accreditation: NH, ADNUR, COARC, MT, RAD

01 Chancellor .... Mr. Michael D. STILES
05 Exec Dean/Chief Academic Officer .... Dr. Richard S. AYI
32 Dept Chair Student Services .... Ms. Danelle D. JOHANNSEN

Shiloh University (D)

100 Shiloh Drive, Kalona IA 52247
County: Washington Identification: 667095
Unit ID: 480499
Telephone: (319) 656-2447 Carnegie Class: Not Classified
FAX Number: (319) 656-2448 Calendar System: Trimester
URL: www.shilohuniversity.edu
Established: 2006 Annual Undergrad Tuition & Fees: $4,510
Enrollment: 39 Coed
Affiliation or Control: Independent Non-Profit IRS Status: 501(c)3
Highest Offering: Master's
Program: 2-Year Principally Bachelor's Creditable; Liberal Arts And General; Professional; Religious Emphasis
Accreditation: DETC

00 Chancellor/Chairman of the Board .... Mr. Gary HARGRAVE
01 President .... Mr. Christopher REEVES
05 Vice President of Academics .... Dr. Daniel SALVADOR
11 Vice President of Administration .... Mr. Frank POTTORFF
13 Vice President of Technology .... Mr. James WIRTHLIN
58 Dean of Biblical Studies .... Dr. John BUCKINGHAM
97 Dean of General Education .... Dr. Marsha SMITH
06 Registrar .... Mrs. Judy BREWER
07 Admissions Coordinator .... Mr. Andy THOMPSON
09 Manager of Academic Effectiveness .... Mrs. Gayle WIRTHLIN

Simpson College (E)

701 North C Street, Indianola IA 50125-1297
County: Warren FICE Identification: 001887
Unit ID: 154350
Telephone: (515) 961-6251 Carnegie Class: Bac/A&S
FAX Number: (515) 961-1498 Calendar System: Other
URL: www.simpson.edu
Established: 1860 Annual Undergrad Tuition & Fees: $30,423
Enrollment: 1,844 Coed
Affiliation or Control: United Methodist IRS Status: 501(c)3
Highest Offering: Master's
Program: Liberal Arts And General; Teacher Preparatory; Business Emphasis
Accreditation: NH, MUS

01 President .... Dr. Jay K. SIMMONS
05 Vice Pres/Dean Academic Affairs .... Dr. Steven J. GRIFFITH
10 Vice President Business/Finance .... Mr. Kenneth I. BIRKENHOLTZ
30 Vice President College Advancement .... Mr. Robert J. LANE
32 Vice President Student Development .... Mr. James D. THORIUS
84 Vice President Enrollment .... Ms. Deborah J. TIERNEY
91 VP Info Svcs/Chief Info Officer .... Ms. Kelley L. BRADDER
37 Asst VP Enrollment/Financial Aid .... Ms. Tracie PAVON
06 Registrar & Associate Dean .... Ms. Jody RAGAN
26 Executive Director Marketing and PR .... Ms. Jill JOHNSON
08 Director of Library .... Ms. Cynthia M. DYER
27 Director of Information Services .... Mr. Allan APPENZELLER
44 Director of Annual Giving .... Ms. Sherry FULLER
15 Director of Human Resources .... Ms. Mary E. BARTLEY
36 Director of Career Services .... Ms. Jennifer DEL PINO
07 Director of Admissions .... Ms. Alison SWANSON
41 Athletic Director .... Mr. John F. SIRIANNI
96 Director of Procurement .... Ms. Marilyn J. LEEK
35 Assistant Dean of Students .... Mr. Richard O. RAMOS
42 Chaplain .... Mr. Fritz WEHRENBERG
39 Director of Residence Life .... Mr. Luke BEHAUNEK
18 Director Campus Services .... Mr. John HARRIS
21 Controller .... Ms. Heather TRAVIS
19 Coordinator of Campus Security .... Mr. Chris FRERICHS
51 Associate Dean Adult Learning .... Dr. Rosemary J. LINK
28 International Educ Coordinator .... Mr. Jay WILKINSON

Simpson College West Des Moines (F)

1415 28th Street, #250, West Des Moines IA 50266
Telephone: (515) 309-3099 Identification: 770064
Accreditation: &NH

† Main campus is Simpson College in Indianola, IA.

Southeastern Community College (G)

1500 W Agency Road, PO Box 180,
West Burlington IA 52655-0180
County: Des Moines FICE Identification: 001848
Unit ID: 154378
Telephone: (319) 752-2731 Carnegie Class: Assoc/Pub-R-M
FAX Number: (319) 752-4957 Calendar System: Semester
URL: www.scciowa.edu
Established: 1966 Annual Undergrad Tuition & Fees (In-District): $4,260
Enrollment: 3,112 Coed
Affiliation or Control: State/Local IRS Status: 501(c)3
Highest Offering: Associate Degree
Program: Occupational; 2-Year Principally Bachelor's Creditable
Accreditation: NH, COARC, EMT, MAC

01 President .... Dr. Michael ASH
05 Int Vice Pres of Academic Affairs .... Mr. David SCHACHTSIEK
32 Vice President of Student Services .... Ms. Joan WILLIAMS
11 Vice Pres Administrative Services .... Mr. Bill MECK
30 Exec Director for Inst Advancement .... Ms. Rebecca RUMP
37 Financial Aid Officer .... Mr. Ean FREELS
84 Enrollment Coordinator .... Ms. Dana CHRISMAN
06 Registrar .... Mr. Tim GRAY
15 Director Human Resources .... Ms. Michelle FOSTER
49 Dean Arts and Sciences .... Dr. Tim AHERN
12 Dean Keokuk Campus/Trans Studies .... Dr. Teresa GARCIA
75 Dean Career/Technical/Health Educ .... Vacant

Southeastern Community College Keokuk Campus (H)

335 Messenger Road, PO Box 6007, Keokuk IA 52632
Telephone: (319) 524-3221 Identification: 770065
Accreditation: &NH

† Main campus is Southeastern Community College in West Burlington, IA.

Southwestern Community College (I)

1501 W Townline Street, Creston IA 50801-1098
County: Union FICE Identification: 001857
Unit ID: 154396
Telephone: (641) 782-7081 Carnegie Class: Assoc/Pub-R-S
FAX Number: (641) 782-3312 Calendar System: Semester
URL: www.swcciowa.edu
Established: 1966 Annual Undergrad Tuition & Fees (In-State): $4,440
Enrollment: 1,666 Coed
Affiliation or Control: State IRS Status: 501(c)3
Highest Offering: Associate Degree
Program: Occupational; 2-Year Principally Bachelor's Creditable
Accreditation: NH

01 Superintendent/President .... Dr. Barbara J. CRITTENDEN
03 Vice President Economic Development .... Mr. Thomas L. LESAN
10 Chief Financial Officer .... Mrs. Teresa KREJCI
05 Vice President Instruction .... Mr. Bill TAYLOR
32 Dean of Student Services .... Dr. Matt THOMPSON
30 Director Institutional Advancement .... Dr. Matt THOMPSON
20 Asst Vice Pres of Instruction .... Vacant
106 Director of Distance Education .... Mr. Doug GREENE
15 Director of Human Resources .... Mrs. Jolene GRIFFITH
26 Director Marketing .... Mrs. Terri HIGGINS
08 Head Librarian .... Mrs. Ann COULTER
13 Director of Information Technology .... Mr. Scott HELM
37 Director Financial Aid .... Mrs. Tracy DAVIS
06 Registrar .... Ms. Sandy WEBB

University of Dubuque (J)

2000 University Avenue, Dubuque IA 52001-5099
County: Dubuque FICE Identification: 001891
Unit ID: 153278
Telephone: (563) 589-3000 Carnegie Class: Master's S
FAX Number: (563) 589-3682 Calendar System: 4/1/4
URL: www.dbq.edu
Established: 1852 Annual Undergrad Tuition & Fees: $25,520
Enrollment: 2,015 Coed
Affiliation or Control: Presbyterian Church (U.S.A.) IRS Status: 501(c)3
Highest Offering: Doctorate
Program: Liberal Arts And General; Teacher Preparatory; Professional
Accreditation: NH, AAB, NURSE, THEOL

01 President ... Dr. Jeffrey F. BULLOCK
04 Exec Assistant to the President ... Mrs. Deborah L. BUOL
05 Vice President/Dean of the College ... Dr. Mark WARD
10 Vice President Finance & Treasurer ... Mr. James D. STEINER
84 Vice Pres Enrollment/Univ Rels ... Mr. Peter L. SMITH
20 Vice Pres/Dean of Seminary ... Dr. Bradley J. LONGFIELD
30 Vice President for Philanthropy ... Mr. David DENDY
32 Vice President/Dean of Student Life ... Dr. Michael H. MIYAMOTO
13 Network Administrator ... Ms. Sherry CUSICK
07 Dean of Admission ... Mr. Jesse L. JAMES
06 Registrar ... Ms. Elizabeth OLESON
08 Director of Libraries ... Ms. Mary Anne KNEFEL
16 Director of Human Resources ... Ms. Julie MACTAGGART
37 Dean of Student Financial Planning ... Mr. Timothy KREMER
09 Dir Institutional Research ... Ms. Keri SAMSON
36 Director of Career Services ... Dr. Amy BAUS
29 Director Alumni Relations ... Vacant
40 Director Bookstore ... Ms. Margo KETELS
41 Athletic Director ... Mr. Dan RUNKLE
18 Director of Facilities ... Mr. Craig KLOFT
04 Special Assistant to the President ... Dr. John R. STEWART
88 Exec Dir Heritage Center ... Mr. Thomas J. ROBBINS

University of Phoenix Des Moines Campus (A)

317 6th Avenue, Suite 102, Des Moines IA 50309-4109
Telephone: (866) 229-5743 Identification: 770203
Accreditation: &NH, ACBSP

† Main campus is University of Phoenix in Tempe, AZ.

Upper Iowa University (B)

605 Washington, Box 1857, Fayette IA 52142-1857
County: Fayette FICE Identification: 001893
Unit ID: 154493
Telephone: (563) 425-5200 Carnegie Class: Master's M
FAX Number: (563) 425-5271 Calendar System: Semester
URL: www.uiu.edu
Established: 1857 Annual Undergrad Tuition & Fees: $24,400
Enrollment: 6,182 Coed
Affiliation or Control: Independent Non-Profit IRS Status: 501(c)3
Highest Offering: Master's
Program: Liberal Arts And General; Teacher Preparatory; Business Emphasis
Accreditation: NH, NURSE

01 President ... Dr. William R. DUFFY, II
05 Interim Provost ... Dr. Oliver EVANS
10 Interim CFO ... Mr. Randy FEHE
20 VP for Academic Extension ... Mr. Fritz OPPENLANDER
82 VP International Programs ... Mr. Ismael J. BETANCOURT VELEZ
15 VP for Human Resources ... Ms. Melissa MACTAGGART
84 SVP Strategic Pos/Chief Enroll Ofcr ... Vacant
07 Exec Dir of Admissions ... Mr. Storm SCHMITT
30 VP of External Affairs ... Mr. Andrew WENTHE
09 Assoc VP Inst Effect & Assessment ... Ms. Janet SHEPHERD
32 Dean of Student Development ... Ms. Louise SCOTT
36 Assoc Dean Stdnts/Dir Res Life ... Ms. Jean MERKLE
12 Director South Central Region ... Ms. Shawn WILSON
12 Director Mid-West Region ... Mr. Walter BEMBRY
12 Director North Central Region ... Mr. Marshall WHITLOCK
12 Director Mid-Central Region ... Ms. Kathy FRANKEN
06 Registrar ... Mrs. Holly STREETER
08 Director Library Services ... Mrs. Becky WADIAN
41 Athletic Director ... Mr. David MILLER
04 Exec Assistant to the President ... Ms. Holly D. WOLFF
56 Dir Ctr for Distance Educ ... Ms. Barb SCHULTZ
105 Director Internet Development ... Mr. Joel KUNZE
21 Associate Business Ofcr/Controller ... Ms. Laura MATT
36 Director of Career Development ... Mr. Darren NOBLE
35 Dir Student Leadership & Activities ... Mr. Daryl GROVE
26 Assoc VP for Comm and Marketing ... Ms. Monica HEATON
86 Director External Affairs ... Mr. Andrew WENTHE
13 Director Information Technology ... Mr. Terry SMID
15 Director Payroll & Benefits ... Ms. Tammy CAROLAN
88 Director Sports Info Services ... Mr. Howard THOMPSON
18 Chief Facilities/Physical Plant ... Mr. Ron CROOKER
40 Bookstore Manager ... Ms. Becky WISSMILLER

Vatterott College-Des Moines (C)

7000 Fleur Drive, Des Moines IA 50321-2414
County: Polk FICE Identification: 026092
Unit ID: 373058
Telephone: (515) 309-9000 Carnegie Class: Assoc/PrivFP
FAX Number: (515) 309-0366 Calendar System: Other
URL: www.vatterott-college.edu
Established: 1997 Annual Undergrad Tuition & Fees: $11,907
Enrollment: 284 Coed
Affiliation or Control: Proprietary IRS Status: Proprietary
Highest Offering: Associate Degree
Program: Occupational
Accreditation: ACCSC, DA, MAAB

01 CEO & President ... Ms. Pam BELL
12 Campus Director ... Ms. Sarah BOUMA

Waldorf College (D)

106 S 6th Street, Forest City IA 50436-1713
County: Winnebago FICE Identification: 001895
Unit ID: 154518
Telephone: (641) 585-2450 Carnegie Class: Bac/Diverse
FAX Number: (641) 585-8194 Calendar System: Semester
URL: www.waldorf.edu
Established: 1903 Annual Undergrad Tuition & Fees: $20,316
Enrollment: 594 Coed
Affiliation or Control: Proprietary IRS Status: Proprietary
Highest Offering: Baccalaureate
Program: Liberal Arts And General
Accreditation: NH

01 President ... Dr. Robert ALSOP
05 Dean of Col/Vice Pres Acad Affs ... Dr. Scott SEARCY
10 Vice President Business Affairs ... Mr. Mason HARMS
04 Assistant to the President ... Ms. Cindy CARTER
32 Dean of Students ... Mr. Jason RAMAKER
92 Dean of Honors Program ... Dr. Suzanne FALCK-YI
07 Director Admissions ... Mr. Scott PITCHER
08 Library Director ... Ms. Elizabeth KISCADEN
29 Director of Alumni Affairs ... Ms. Rita GILBERTSON
06 Registrar ... Mr. Darrell BARBOUR
37 Director of Financial Aid ... Mr. Duane POLSDOFER
18 Director of Facilities Services ... Mr. Allan EGGEBRAATEN
26 Communications Director ... Ms. Barbara BARROWS
44 Director of Annual Fund ... Ms. Nancy OLSON
38 Counselor ... Mr. James AMELSBERG
41 Athletic Director ... Mr. Michael SCARANO
36 Director Student Placement ... Ms. Mary REISETTER
40 Bookstore Manager ... Ms. Karla SCHAEFER
15 Director Human Resources ... Ms. Dawn RAMAKER

Wartburg College (E)

PO Box 1003, 100 Wartburg Boulevard, Waverly IA 50677-0903
County: Bremer FICE Identification: 001896
Unit ID: 154527
Telephone: (319) 352-8200 Carnegie Class: Bac/A&S
FAX Number: (319) 352-8514 Calendar System: Other
URL: www.wartburg.edu
Established: 1852 Annual Undergrad Tuition & Fees: $34,250
Enrollment: 1,747 Coed
Affiliation or Control: Evangelical Lutheran Church In America
IRS Status: 501(c)3
Highest Offering: Baccalaureate
Program: Liberal Arts And General; Teacher Preparatory
Accreditation: NH, MUS, SW, TED

01 President ... Dr. Darrel D. COLSON
05 VP Acad Affs/Dean Faculty ... Dr. Mark L. BIERMANN
32 VP Student Life/Dean Students ... Dr. Deborah L. LOERS
10 VP for Finance and Administration ... Mr. Richard SEGGERMAN
30 Vice Pres Institutional Advancement ... Mr. Scott C. LEISINGER
84 Vice Pres Enrollment Management ... Dr. Edith J. WALDSTEIN
07 Asst VP Admiss/Alumni/Parent Pgms ... Mr. Jay T. COLEMAN
06 Registrar ... Ms. Sheree S. COVERT
26 VP for Mktg and Comm ... Mr. Graham GARNER
91 Dir of Info Technology Svcs/CIO ... Mr. Gary L. WIPPERMAN
08 College Librarian ... Ms. Curtis BRUNDY
29 Dir of Alumni/Parent Rel & Ann Giv ... Ms. Renee VOVES
37 Director of Financial Aid ... Ms. Jen L. SASSMAN
41 Director of Athletics ... Mr. Eric R. WILLIS
42 Dean of the Chapel ... Rev. Ramona S. BOUZARD
18 Director of Physical Plant ... Mr. John A. WUERTZ
39 Asst Dean/Dir of Residential Life ... Mr. Wesley H. BROOKS
36 Assoc Dir of Pathways/Career Svcs ... Mr. Derek N. SOLHEIM
38 Director of Counseling Svcs ... Mrs. Stephanie R. NEWSOM
40 Bookstore Manager ... Ms. Janet HUEBNER
85 Director of International Programs ... Ms. Jenna RINEHART
35 Director of Campus Programming ... Ms. Ashley LANG
88 Campus Pastor ... Rev. Brian A. BECKSTROM
23 Dir of Health & Wellness Promotion ... Ms. Dawn R. WIEGMANN
21 Chief Business Officer & Treasurer ... Mr. Richard W. SEGGERMAN
15 Director of Human Resources ... Ms. Jane J. JUCHEMS
30 Director of Development ... Mr. Donald J. MEYER
09 Dir of Inst Research/Prof of Psych ... Dr. Fred D. RIBICH
92 Director Honors Program ... Dr. Mariah H. BIRGEN
04 Assistant to the President ... Ms. Janeen K. STEWART
20 Asst Dean for Academic Affairs ... Ms. Stephanie S. TEKIPPE

Wartburg Theological Seminary (F)

333 Wartburg Place, PO Box 5004, Dubuque IA 52004-5004
County: Dubuque FICE Identification: 001897
Unit ID: 154536
Telephone: (563) 589-0200 Carnegie Class: Spec/Faith
FAX Number: (563) 589-0333 Calendar System: 4/1/4
URL: www.wartburgseminary.edu
Established: 1854 Annual Graduate Tuition & Fees: $14,900
Enrollment: 166 Coed
Affiliation or Control: Evangelical Lutheran Church In America
IRS Status: 501(c)3
Highest Offering: Master's; No Undergraduates
Program: Professional
Accreditation: NH, THEOL

01 President ... Dr. Stanley N. OLSON
05 Academic Dean of the Seminary ... Dr. Craig L. NESSAN
10 Vice Pres for Finance & Operations ... Mr. Andy B. WILLENBORG
30 Vice President for Mission Support ... Rev. Len HOFFMANN
15 Assistant to President & Dir of HR ... Ms. Eileen LEMAY
88 Dean for Vocation ... Rev. Amy L. CURRENT
08 Library Director ... Ms. Susan J S. EBERTZ
06 Registrar/Admin Assistant to Dean ... Dr. Kevin L. ANDERSON
13 Director of Information Technology ... Mr. Richard ROBLEDO

Western Iowa Tech Community College (G)

PO Box 5199, 4647 Stone Avenue, Sioux City IA 51102-5199
County: Woodbury FICE Identification: 007316
Unit ID: 154572
Telephone: (712) 274-6400 Carnegie Class: Assoc/Pub-R-L
FAX Number: (712) 274-6412 Calendar System: Semester
URL: www.witcc.edu
Established: 1966 Annual Undergrad Tuition & Fees (In-District): $4,410
Enrollment: 7,570 Coed
Affiliation or Control: State/Local IRS Status: 501(c)3
Highest Offering: Associate Degree
Program: Occupational; 2-Year Principally Bachelor's Creditable
Accreditation: NH, DA, EMT, MAC, PNUR, PTAA, SURGT

01 President ... Dr. Terry MURRELL
05 VP Instruction/Stdnt Svc Admin ... Ms. Juline ALBERT
10 VP Finance/Administrative Svcs ... Mr. Troy JASMAN
31 Dean of Corporate College ... Mr. Martin REIMER
15 Exec Director of Human Resources ... Ms. Brenda BRADLEY
13 Dean of Information Technologies ... Mr. Mike LOGAN
30 Exec Director College Development ... Ms. Carolyn ELLWANGER
32 Dean of Students ... Dr. Tricia SUTHERLAND
88 Dean of Outreach ... Ms. Janet GILL
20 Dean of Instruction ... Mr. Darin MOELLER
88 Director of Economic Development ... Ms. Angela LAWSON
08 Library Manager ... Ms. Sharon DYKSHOORN
88 KWIT/KOJI-FM General Manager ... Ms. Gretchen GONDEK
88 Director Small Business Devel Ctr ... Mr. Todd RAUSCH
18 Director Physical Plant ... Mr. Kyle HUESER
09 Dir Instl Rsrch/Resource Dev Coord ... Mr. Larry OBERMEYER
06 Registrar ... Ms. Lora VANDER ZWAAG
26 Director Marketing/Publications ... Ms. Emma HEWITT
37 Director of Financial Aid ... Mr. Don DUZIK

William Penn University (H)

201 Trueblood Avenue, Oskaloosa IA 52577-1799
County: Mahaska FICE Identification: 001900
Unit ID: 154590
Telephone: (641) 673-1001 Carnegie Class: Bac/Diverse
FAX Number: (641) 673-1396 Calendar System: Semester
URL: www.wmpenn.edu
Established: 1873 Annual Undergrad Tuition & Fees: $23,210
Enrollment: 1,865 Coed
Affiliation or Control: Friends IRS Status: 501(c)3
Highest Offering: Master's
Program: Liberal Arts And General; Teacher Preparatory
Accreditation: NH

01 President ... Dr. Ann FIELDS
05 Vice Pres Academic Affs/Acad Dean ... Dr. Noel STAHLE
30 Vice President for Advancement ... Ms. Sherri TAYLOR
32 Exec Vice President Student Svcs ... Mr. John OTTOSSON
10 VP Financial Operations ... Ms. Bonnie JOHNSON
41 VP Athletics ... Mr. Greg HAFNER
56 VP of College for Working Adults ... Ms. Marjorie WELCH
30 Assoc VP for Advancement ... Ms. Marsha RIORDAN
108 Assoc VP Assessment/Devel/Planning ... Dr. Mary Pat WOHLFORD
29 Assoc Vice Pres Alumni Relations ... Ms. Jill DURSKY
07 Director of Admissions ... Ms. Kira STRONG
06 Registrar ... Dr. Michael EDWARDS
37 Director of Financial Aid ... Ms. Cyndi PEIFFER
36 Career Services Coordinator ... Ms. Debbie STEVENS
08 Head Librarian ... Ms. Julie HANSEN
26 Dir Public Relations/Marketing ... Ms. Amber LAKE
31 Director of Community Relations ... Ms. Jill DURSKY
15 Human Resource Director ... Ms. Louise BLAINE
35 Director of Student Activities ... Mr. Levi TARBELL
38 Student Counselor ... Mr. Frank SIMS
09 Director of Institutional Research ... Vacant
42 Campus Minister ... Mr. Spencer THURY
40 Bookstore Manager ... Ms. Heidi PARKER
18 Director of Buildings & Grounds ... Mr. Milt CAMPBELL
83 Chair Div of Social/Behavioral Sci ... Dr. Michael COLLINS
72 Chair Div of Applied Technology ... Dr. Jim DROST
53 Chair Division of Education ... Dr. Pamela MARTIN
50 Chair Div of Business Admin ... Dr. Lonny L. WILSON
79 Chair Division of Humanities ... Dr. Jared PEARCE
76 Chair Div of Health & Life Sciences ... Dr. James A. NORTH

KANSAS

Allen County Community College (I)

1801 N Cottonwood, Iola KS 66749-1698
County: Allen FICE Identification: 001901
Unit ID: 154642
Telephone: (620) 365-5116 Carnegie Class: Assoc/Pub-R-M
FAX Number: (620) 365-7406 Calendar System: Semester
URL: www.allencc.edu
Established: 1923 Annual Undergrad Tuition & Fees (In-District): $2,304
Enrollment: 2,952 Coed
Affiliation or Control: State/Local IRS Status: 501(c)3
Highest Offering: Associate Degree

Program: Occupational; 2-Year Principally Bachelor's Creditable
Accreditation: NH

01 President Mr. John A. MASTERSON
05 Vice Pres for Academic Affairs Mr. Jon MARSHALL
10 Vice Pres for Finance & Operations Mr. Steve TROXEL
32 Vice Pres Student Affairs Ms. Cynthia JACOBSON
12 Dean for the Iola Campus Mrs. Tosca HARRIS
12 Dean for the Burlingame Campus Mr. Bob REAVIS
106 Dean for Online Learning Mrs. Regena BAILEY-AYE
08 Director of Library Mr. Steven ANDERSON
13 Director of MIS Mr. Doug DUNLAP
38 Director of Guidance Services Dr. Valis MCLEAN
37 Director of Financial Aid Mrs. Vicki CURRY
30 Director of Development Mrs. Cynthia ADAMS
18 Director of Physical Plant Opers Mr. Don BAUER
07 Director of Admissions Ms. Rebecca BILDERBACK
41 Director of Athletics Ms. Jessica PETERS
40 Director of Bookstore Mrs. Donna CASON
17 Allied Health Director Vacant
85 Foreign Student Advisor Mr. John STEEL
90 Director Academic Computing Vacant
09 Director Inst Research/Assessment Vacant
35 Director Student Life Mr. Ryan BILDERBACK
06 Registrar Mrs. Bobbie HAVILAND
26 Public Relations Coordinator Mrs. Nancy FORD

Allen County Community College Burlingame Campus (A)

100 Bloomquist, Burlingame KS 666413
Telephone: (785) 654-2416 Identification: 770249
Accreditation: &NH

† Main campus is Allen County Community College in Iola, KS.

The Art Institutes International - Kansas City (B)

8208 Melrose Drive, Lenexa KS 66214
Telephone: (913) 217-4600 Identification: 666765
Accreditation: ACICS

† Main campus is The Art Institute of Phoenix in Phoenix, AZ.

Baker University (C)

618 Eighth Street, Baldwin City KS 66006-0065
County: Douglas FICE Identification: 001903
Unit ID: 154688
Telephone: (785) 594-6451 Carnegie Class: Master's L
FAX Number: (785) 594-2522 Calendar System: 4/1/4
URL: www.bakeru.edu
Established: 1858 Annual Undergrad Tuition & Fees: $25,200
Enrollment: 3,208 Coed
Affiliation or Control: United Methodist IRS Status: 501(c)3
Highest Offering: Doctorate
Program: 2-Year Principally Bachelor's Creditable; Liberal Arts And General; Teacher Preparatory; Professional
Accreditation: NH, ACBSP, MUS, NURSE, TED

01 President Dr. Patricia N. LONG
11 COO & Exec VP for Admin Services Dr. Susan LINDAHL
05 Exec VP Acad Affs/Dn Col Arts/Scis Dr. Brian POSLER
58 VP/Dean School of Education Dr. Peggy HARRIS
12 VP/Dean SPGS Dr. Brian MESSER
88 Chief External Relations Officer Mrs. Mary LARSON-DIAZ
13 Chief Information Officer Mr. Andy JETT
66 VP/Dean of School of Nursing Dr. Kathleen HARR
44 VP for Endowment/Planned Giving Mr. Jerry WEAKLEY
26 Director of Marketing & Comm Mr. Neil KULBISKI
06 University Registrar Ms. Ruth MILLER
42 Minister to the University Dr. Ira L. DESPAIN
32 Dean of Students Dr. Cassy BAILEY
30 Sr Dir of University Advancement Mr. Patrick MIKESIC
09 Dir of Inst Research/Math Prof Dr. Jean JOHNSON
88 Asst Dean Stdnt Engage & Success Dr. Judith SMRHA
20 CAS Asst Dean for Academic Affairs Mrs. Martha HARRIS
35 Assoc Dean of Students & Dir MCA Dr. Teresa CLOUNCH
08 Director of Library Services Ms. Kay BRADT
84 Director of Enrollment Management Mr. Kevin KROPF
37 Director of Financial Aid Mrs. Jeanne MOTT
36 Director of Career Services Ms. Susan WADE
41 Director Of Athletics Ms. Theresa YETMAR
23 Dir of Student Health Services Ms. Ruth SARNA
18 Director of Physical Plant Mr. Jeremy PORTLOCK
21 University Controller Ms. Melissa VAN LEIDEN
29 Dir of Alumni & Corporate Relations Mr. Doug BARTH
38 Director Counseling Center Dr. Tim HODGES
26 Public Relations Director Mr. Steve ROTTINGHAUS
15 Dir of Human Resources & Staff Dev Ms. Connie DEEL

Baker University School of Professional and Graduate Studies (D)

8001 College Boulevard, Suite 100,
Overland Park KS 66210
Telephone: (913) 491-4432 Identification: 770250
Accreditation: &NH

† Main campus is Baker University in Baldwin City, KS.

Barclay College (E)

607 N Kingman, Haviland KS 67059-0288
County: Kiowa FICE Identification: 001917
Unit ID: 155070
Telephone: (620) 862-5252 Carnegie Class: Spec/Faith
FAX Number: (620) 862-5242 Calendar System: Semester
URL: www.barclaycollege.edu
Established: 1917 Annual Undergrad Tuition & Fees: $13,990
Enrollment: 255 Coed
Affiliation or Control: Independent Non-Profit IRS Status: 501(c)3
Highest Offering: Baccalaureate
Program: Liberal Arts And General; Religious Emphasis
Accreditation: BI

01 President Dr. Royce FRAZIER
05 VP Academics Dr. Jim LS SHANA
10 VP Business Services Mr. Lee ANDERS
32 VP Student Services Mr. Kevin LEE
30 VP Institutional Advancement Dr. Herb FRAZIER
06 VP Registration and Records Dr. Glenn W. LEPPERT
37 Director Student Financial Aid Mr. Ryan HAASE
07 Admissions Counselor Mr. Justin KENDALL
08 Librarian Mr. Pat HALL
29 Alumni Relations Dr. Herb FRAZIER

Barton County Community College (F)

245 NE 30th Road, Great Bend KS 67530-9107
County: Barton FICE Identification: 004608
Unit ID: 154697
Telephone: (620) 792-2701 Carnegie Class: Assoc/Pub-R-L
FAX Number: (620) 792-5624 Calendar System: Semester
URL: www.bartonccc.edu
Established: 1965 Annual Undergrad Tuition & Fees (In-District): $2,912
Enrollment: 5,027 Coed
Affiliation or Control: State/Local IRS Status: 501(c)3
Highest Offering: Associate Degree
Program: Occupational; 2-Year Principally Bachelor's Creditable
Accreditation: NH, ADNUR, EMT, MLTAD

01 President Dr. Carl R. HEILMAN
05 VP of Instruction & Student Svcs Dr. Penny QUINN
11 Dean of Administration Mr. Mark E. DEAN
27 Dean of Information Services Mr. Charles PERKINS
32 Dean of Student Services Mrs. Angela M. MADDY
20 Dean of Academics Dr. Richard L. ABEL
88 Dean Ft Riley Lrng Svcs/Mil Ops Mr. Gene KINGSLIEN
103 Dean Workforce Training & Cmty Educ Mrs. Elaine R. SIMMONS
37 Asst Dean Stndt Svcs/Dir Fin Aid Mrs. Myrna L. PERKINS
30 Exec Dir Institutional Advancement Mrs. Darnell HOLOPIREK
66 Exec Dir of Nursing & Healthcare Ed Dr. Kathy KOTTAS
50 Exec Dir of Business/Tech/Cmty Educ Ms. Jane HOWARD
103 Exec Dir of Workforce Trn & Cmty Ed Ms. Mary FOLEY
26 Dir of Public Relations & Marketing Mr. Brandon STEINERT
04 Assistant to President Mrs. Amye SCHNEIDER
41 Director of Athletics Mr. Trevor ROLFS
08 Director of Learning Resources Mrs. ReGina REYNOLDS-CASPER
15 Director of Human Resources Mrs. Julie A. KNOBLICH
07 Director of Admissions Ms. Tana COOPER
19 Coordinator of Facility Management Mr. Jim D. IRELAND
25 Director of Grants Ms. Cathie R. OSHIRO
06 Registrar Mrs. Lori D. CROWTHER
40 Bookstore Manager Mrs. Connie M. KERNS
09 Coord of Instruct & Instnl Research Mrs. Caicey L. CRUTCHER
39 Coordinator of Student Housing Vacant

Barton County Community College Fort Riley Campus (G)

PO Box 2463, Bldg 217, Rm 105, Fort Riley KS 66442
Telephone: (877) 620-6606 Identification: 770251
Accreditation: &NH

† Main campus is Barton County Community College in Great Bend, KS.

Benedictine College (H)

1020 N 2nd Street, Atchison KS 66002-1499
County: Atchison FICE Identification: 010256
Unit ID: 154712
Telephone: (913) 367-5340 Carnegie Class: Bac/Diverse
FAX Number: (913) 367-6566 Calendar System: Semester
URL: www.benedictine.edu
Established: 1858 Annual Undergrad Tuition & Fees: $23,650
Enrollment: 2,149 Coed
Affiliation or Control: Roman Catholic IRS Status: 501(c)3
Highest Offering: Master's
Program: Liberal Arts And General; Teacher Preparatory; Business Emphasis
Accreditation: NH, MUS, NURSE, TED

01 President Mr. Stephen D. MINNIS
05 Dean of the College Dr. Kimberly C. SHANKMAN
10 Chief Financial Officer Mr. Ronald J. OLINGER
30 Vice President Advancement Ms. Kelly J. VOWELS
84 Dean of Enrollment Management Mr. Pete HELGESEN
32 Vice President of Student Life Dr. Linda HENRY
35 Dean of Students Dr. Joseph WURTZ
42 Director for Mission and Ministry David TROTTER
41 Athletic Director Mr. Charles GARTENMAYER
26 Vice President for College Rels Mr. Tom HOOPES
20 Assoc Dean & Registrar Sr. Linda HERNDON, OSB
09 Director of Institutional Research Jennifer HELLER
58 Exec Dir of Grad Business Programs Mr. Dave GEENENS
58 Director of MASL/Asst Prof Educ Dr. Cheryl REDING
37 Director of Student Financial Aid Mr. Tony TANKING
27 Dir of Marketing & Communications Mr. Steve JOHNSON
38 Director of Counseling Center Mr. Kerry A. MARVIN
23 Director of Student Health Services Ms. Janet ADRIAN
18 Director of Operations Mr. Matt FASSERO
14 Dir of Tech & Information Sys Mr. Randy ROWLAND
88 Director of International Program Mr. Daniele MUSSO
08 Librarian Mr. Steven GROMATZKY
39 Director of Residence Life Mr. Sean MULCAHY
21 Bursar Ms. Becky MILLER
36 Director of Career Development Katie MCDOWELL
29 Director of Planned Giving & Alumni Mr. Tim ANDREWS

Bethany College (I)

335 E Swensson Street, Lindsborg KS 67456-1895
County: McPherson FICE Identification: 001904
Unit ID: 154721
Telephone: (785) 227-3311 Carnegie Class: Bac/Diverse
FAX Number: (785) 227-2004 Calendar System: 4/1/4
URL: www.bethanylb.edu
Established: 1881 Annual Undergrad Tuition & Fees: $23,305
Enrollment: 549 Coed
Affiliation or Control: Evangelical Lutheran Church In America
IRS Status: 501(c)3
Highest Offering: Baccalaureate
Program: Liberal Arts And General; Teacher Preparatory; Professional
Accreditation: NH, MUS, TED

01 President Dr. Edward F. LEONARD, III
05 Provost and Dean of the College Dr. Kenneth M. MACUR
30 VP for Advancement Mr. Galen BUNNING
10 VP for Finance and Operations Mr. Dennis STUGELMEYER
21 Accountant Mr. John COYKENDALL
32 Dean for Student Development Dr. Daniel DENTINO
35 Assoc Dean for Student Development Dr. Robin LEE
84 VP for Recruitment & Marketing Ms. Tricia HARTSHORN
88 Assoc Vice Pres for Development Mr. Warren OLSON
06 Registrar Ms. Jill MEGREDY
08 Dir of Wallerstedt Learning Center Mrs. Denise K. CARSON
41 Dean of Athletics Mr. Dane PAVLOVICH
37 Director of Financial Aid Ms. Nichole WESTENDORF
18 Director of Campus Facilities Mr. Randy JIRAK
13 Director of Technology Services Mr. Matthew CARVER
88 Director of Information Services Ms. Christi PAULSEN
26 Director of Communications Ms. Stephanie MCDOWELL
29 Director Alumni Relations Ms. Molly B. JOHNSON
36 Director Career Services Vacant
39 Residential Education Director Vacant
42 Campus Pastor Rev. Naomi M. STRAND
35 Director Campus Activities Ms. Roxie L. SJOGREN
88 Program Dir Athletic Training Dr. David SLACK
53 Program Director Teacher Education Mr. Gail KONZEM
64 Music Department Chair Dr. Melody STEED
15 Director of Human Resources Ms. Lisa EASTER
09 Director of Assessment and Research Ms. Joanne GUNSOLLEY
40 Bookstore Manager Mrs. Brenda C. SMITH
92 Honors Program Coordinator Dr. Kristin VAN TASSEL
38 Student Counselor Ms. Valoree BARRETT
85 Coord Student Dev & Intl Program Ms. Charlotte ANDERSON

Bethel College (J)

300 E 27th Street, North Newton KS 67117-0531
County: Harvey FICE Identification: 001905
Unit ID: 154749
Telephone: (316) 283-2500 Carnegie Class: Bac/Diverse
FAX Number: (316) 284-5286 Calendar System: 4/1/4
URL: www.bethelks.edu
Established: 1887 Annual Undergrad Tuition & Fees: $23,500
Enrollment: 472 Coed
Affiliation or Control: Mennonite Church IRS Status: 501(c)3
Highest Offering: Baccalaureate
Program: Liberal Arts And General; Teacher Preparatory; Professional
Accreditation: NH, NURSE, SW, TED

01 President Dr. Perry D. WHITE
04 Assistant to the President Ms. Rosa BARRERA
05 Vice President Academic Affairs Dr. Brad BORN
32 Vice President Student Life Mr. Aaron L. AUSTIN
41 Athletic Director Mr. Kent ALLSHOUSE
30 Vice President Advancement Ms. Sondra KOONTZ
10 Vice President for Business Affairs Mr. Allen WEDEL
26 VP for Marketing and Communications Ms. Lori LIVENGOOD
06 Registrar Ms. Marcia K. MILLER
44 Director of Development Mr. Fred GOERING
07 Vice President for Admissions Mr. Todd H. MOORE
37 Director of Financial Aid Mr. Tony GRABER
29 Director of Alumni Relations Mr. David LINSCHEID
08 Head Librarian Ms. Gail STUCKY
42 Director of Church Relations Mr. Dale SCHRAG
18 Chief Facilities/Physical Plant Mr. Les GOERZEN

Brown Mackie College-Kansas City (A)

9705 Lenexa Drive, Lenexa KS 66215-1345
Telephone: (913) 768-1900 Identification: 666091
Accreditation: &NH, OTA

† Main campus is Brown Mackie College-Salina in Salina, KS.

Brown Mackie College-Salina (B)

2106 S 9th Street, Salina KS 67401-7307
County: Saline FICE Identification: 006755
Unit ID: 154776
Telephone: (785) 825-5422 Carnegie Class: Assoc/PrivFP
FAX Number: (785) 827-7623 Calendar System: Other
URL: www.brownmackie.edu
Established: 1892 Annual Undergrad Tuition & Fees: $12,024
Enrollment: 557 Coed
Affiliation or Control: Proprietary IRS Status: Proprietary
Highest Offering: Baccalaureate
Program: Occupational; 2-Year Principally Bachelor's Creditable; Business Emphasis
Accreditation: NH, OTA

01 President .... Ms. Judy HOLMES
05 Dean of Academic Affairs .... Ms. Vanessa DAVIS-WARNER
07 Senior Director of Admissions .... Ms. Diann HEATH
06 Registrar .... Ms. Amanda JEARDOE
36 Director of Career Services .... Ms. Robin NASH

Bryan University (C)

1527 SW Fairlawn Road, Topeka KS 66604
County: Shawnee FICE Identification: 030662
Unit ID: 154794
Telephone: (785) 272-0889 Carnegie Class: Assoc/PrivFP
FAX Number: (785) 272-4538 Calendar System: Other
URL: www.bryanu.edu
Established: 1982 Annual Undergrad Tuition & Fees: $136
Enrollment: 14,415 Coed
Affiliation or Control: Proprietary IRS Status: Proprietary
Highest Offering: Associate Degree
Program: Occupational; 2-Year Principally Bachelor's Creditable
Accreditation: ACICS

01 Executive Director .... Mr. Wayne MAJOR

Butler Community College (D)

901 S. Haverhill Road, El Dorado KS 67042-3225
County: Butler FICE Identification: 001906
Unit ID: 154800
Telephone: (316) 321-2222 Carnegie Class: Assoc/Pub-S-MC
FAX Number: (316) 322-3109 Calendar System: Semester
URL: www.butlercc.edu
Established: 1927 Annual Undergrad Tuition & Fees (In-District): $2,280
Enrollment: 9,951 Coed
Affiliation or Control: Local IRS Status: 501(c)3
Highest Offering: Associate Degree
Program: Occupational; 2-Year Principally Bachelor's Creditable; Liberal Arts And General
Accreditation: NH, ACBSP, ADNUR, ENGT

01 President .... Dr. Kimberly KRULL
05 Vice President of Academics .... Dr. Karla FISHER
10 Vice President of Finance .... Mr. Kent WILLIAMS
32 Vice President of Student Services .... Mr. Bill RINKENBAUGH
08 Reference Librarian .... Ms. Judy BASTIN
06 Registrar .... Ms. Rhonda MORRISON
09 Director of Institutional Research .... Dr. Gene GEORGE
15 Director Personnel Services .... Ms. Vicki LONG
21 Associate Business Officer .... Ms. Edith WAUGH
26 Director Public Information/Rels .... Vacant
29 Director Alumni Relations .... Vacant
30 Chief Development .... Ms. Stacy COFER
35 Director Student Affairs/Counseling .... Ms. Karen GELVIN
36 Director Student Placement .... Ms. Loretta PATTERSON
37 Director Student Financial Aid .... Ms. Susie EDWARDS
84 Director Enrollment Management .... Ms. Jessica OHMAN
18 Director Facilities .... Mr. Roger NEIFERT
96 Director of Purchasing .... Ms. Regina KIEFFER
07 Director of Admissions .... Ms. Kirsten ALLEN
38 Director Student Counseling .... Ms. Jessica OHMAN

Butler of Andover (E)

1810 N Andover Road, Andover KS 67002
Telephone: (316) 733-0071 Identification: 770253
Accreditation: &NH

† Main campus is Butler Community College in El Dorado, KS.

Butler of Council Grove (F)

131 West Main, Council Grove KS 66846
Telephone: (620) 767-5158 Identification: 770254
Accreditation: &NH

† Main campus is Butler Community College in El Dorado, KS.

Butler of Marion (G)

412 N Second Street, Marion KS 66861
Telephone: (620) 382-2183 Identification: 770255
Accreditation: &NH

† Main campus is Butler Community College in El Dorado, KS.

Butler of McConnell (H)

Ed Ctr, Bldg 412, 53474 Lawrence Ct, McConnell AFB KS 67221
Telephone: (316) 681-3522 Identification: 770257
Accreditation: &NH

† Main campus is Butler Community College in El Dorado, KS.

Butler of Rose Hill (I)

712 Rosehill Road, Rose Hill KS 67133
Telephone: (316) 776-9429 Identification: 770256
Accreditation: &NH

† Main campus is Butler Community College in El Dorado, KS.

Central Baptist Theological Seminary (J)

6601 Monticello Road, Shawnee KS 66226-3513
County: Johnson FICE Identification: 001907
Unit ID: 154837
Telephone: (913) 667-5700 Carnegie Class: Spec/Faith
FAX Number: (913) 371-8110 Calendar System: Semester
URL: www.cbts.edu
Established: 1901 Annual Graduate Tuition & Fees: $6,780
Enrollment: 189 Coed
Affiliation or Control: Baptist IRS Status: 501(c)3
Highest Offering: Doctorate; No Undergraduates
Program: Professional; Religious Emphasis
Accreditation: NH, THEOL

01 President .... Dr. Molly T. MARSHALL
05 Dean of the Seminary .... Dr. Robert E. JOHNSON
03 Executive Vice President .... Mr. George TOWNSEND
30 VP for Institutional Advancement .... Dr. John GRAVLEY
06 Assistant to the Dean/Registrar .... Mr. Stephen GUINN
26 Director of Seminary Relations .... Ms. Robin SANDBOTHE
07 Dir Recruitment/Foundation Coord .... Mrs. Debra SERMONS

Central Christian College of Kansas (K)

1200 S Main, PO Box 1403, McPherson KS 67460-5799
County: McPherson FICE Identification: 001908
Unit ID: 154855
Telephone: (620) 241-0723 Carnegie Class: Bac/Diverse
FAX Number: (620) 241-6032 Calendar System: 4/1/4
URL: www.centralchristian.edu
Established: 1884 Annual Undergrad Tuition & Fees: $19,500
Enrollment: 650 Coed
Affiliation or Control: Free Methodist IRS Status: 501(c)3
Highest Offering: Baccalaureate
Program: Liberal Arts And General
Accreditation: NH

01 President .... Mr. Hal HOXIE
05 Vice President of Academics .... Dr. Leonard FAVARA, JR.
30 Vice President of Development .... Mr. Dave JEFFREY
53 Dean of Professional Education .... Dr. Dean KROEKER
32 Chief Student Affairs Officer .... Rev. Chris SMITH
06 Registrar .... Ms. Ruth PARRY
41 Athletic Director .... Mr. Chad KERR
07 Director of Admissions .... Mr. Patrick MASAR
09 Director of Institutional Research .... Mr. AJ ELLIS
37 Director of Financial Aid .... Mr. Andy OLSEN
10 Business Office Manager .... Mr. Phil NELSON

Cleveland University - Kansas City (L)

10850 Lowell Avenue, Overland Park KS 66210
County: Johnson FICE Identification: 020907
Unit ID: 177038
Telephone: (913) 234-0600 Carnegie Class: Spec/Health
FAX Number: (913) 234-0904 Calendar System: Trimester
URL: www.cleveland.edu
Established: 1922 Annual Undergrad Tuition & Fees: $8,899
Enrollment: 522 Coed
Affiliation or Control: Independent Non-Profit IRS Status: 501(c)3
Highest Offering: First Professional Degree
Program: Professional
Accreditation: NH, CHIRO

01 President .... Dr. Carl S. CLEVELAND, III
10 Chief Operating Officer .... Mr. Jeff KARP
05 Provost .... Dr. Ashley CLEVELAND
26 VP of Campus and Alumni Relations .... Dr. Clark BECKLEY
20 Dean of Pre-Clinical Education .... Dr. Paul BARLETT
21 Controller .... Ms. Marla COPE
06 Director of Academic Records .... Mr. David FOOSE
37 Director of Financial Aid .... Ms. Caprice CALAMAIO
16 Director of Human Resources .... Mr. Dale MARRANT
09 Director of Institutional Reporting .... Dr. Christena NICHOLSON
09 Director of Research .... Dr. Mark T. PFEFER
35 Director of Student Services .... Ms. Jalonna BOWIE
07 Director of Admissions .... Ms. Melissa DENTON
20 Dean of Clinical Education .... Dr. Julia BARTLETT
08 Library Director .... Ms. Marcia M. THOMAS
13 Systems Administrator .... Mr. Calvin DANIELS
04 Assistant to the President .... Ms. Marjorie BRADSHAW
18 Director of Facilities Mgmt .... Mr. Frank HANEY

Cloud County Community College (M)

2221 Campus Drive, Concordia KS 66901-1002
County: Cloud FICE Identification: 001909
Unit ID: 154907
Telephone: (785) 243-1435 Carnegie Class: Assoc/Pub-R-M
FAX Number: (785) 243-1459 Calendar System: Semester
URL: www.cloud.edu
Established: 1965 Annual Undergrad Tuition & Fees (In-District): $3,000
Enrollment: 2,917 Coed
Affiliation or Control: State/Local IRS Status: 501(c)3
Highest Offering: Associate Degree
Program: Occupational; 2-Year Principally Bachelor's Creditable
Accreditation: NH, ADNUR

01 President .... Dr. Danette TOONE
05 Vice President for Academic Affairs .... Dr. Kimberly KRULL
84 VP Enrollment Mgmt/Student Services .... Mr. Joel FIGGS
11 Vice Pres for Administrative Svcs .... Mr. Robert MAXSON
30 Director Institutional Advancement .... Vacant
07 Director of Admissions .... Vacant
08 Director of Library Services .... Ms. Jennifer SCHROEDER
41 Athletic Director .... Mr. Matthew BECHARD
06 Registrar .... Mrs. Linda PETERSEN
18 Chief Facilities/Physical Plant .... Mr. Rex E. SICARD
26 Chief Public Relations Officer .... Ms. Jenny ACREE
102 Ex Dir Cloud County Cmty Col Found .. Ms. Kimberly REYNOLDS
37 Director Student Financial Aid .... Ms. Suzi KNOETTGEN
38 Director Advising & Retention .... Ms. Ashley DOUGLAS
15 Coordinator of Human Resources .... Ms. Christine WILSON

Cloud County Community College Geary County Campus (N)

631 Caroline Avenue, Junction City KS 66441
Telephone: (785) 238-8010 Identification: 770258
Accreditation: &NH

† Main campus is Cloud County Community College in Concordia, KS.

Coffeyville Community College (O)

400 W 11th Street, Coffeyville KS 67337-5064
County: Montgomery FICE Identification: 001910
Unit ID: 154925
Telephone: (620) 251-7700 Carnegie Class: Assoc/Pub-R-S
FAX Number: (620) 252-7098 Calendar System: Semester
URL: www.coffeyville.edu
Established: 1923 Annual Undergrad Tuition & Fees (In-District): $2,080
Enrollment: 1,792 Coed
Affiliation or Control: State/Local IRS Status: 501(c)3
Highest Offering: Associate Degree
Program: Occupational; 2-Year Principally Bachelor's Creditable
Accreditation: NH, EMT, MAC

01 President .... Ms. Linda MOLEY
05 Vice President for Academic Service .... Mrs. Alysia JOHNSTON
10 Vice Pres for Operations & Finance .... Mr. Jeff MORRIS
88 VP for Innovation/Bus Initiatives .... Mr. Marlon THORNBURG
102 Exec Director-CCC Foundation .... Mr. Dickie ROLLS
32 Dean of Student Life .... Mr. Ryan MCCUNE
09 Dean Institutional Research/Records .... Mrs. Deborah OESTMANN
26 Director of Marketing .... Mrs. Lisa KUEHN
20 Director Academic Advising/SSC .... Mrs. Kim LAY
45 Director Institutional Effectivenes .... Mr. Marty EVENSVOLD
37 Director of Financial Aid .... Mrs. Pam FEERER
15 Director of Human Resources .... Mrs. Kelli BAUER
41 Athletics Director .... Mr. Jeff LEIKER
18 Director of Maintenance .... Ms. Vivian FROST
106 Director of Distance Learning .... Mr. Brad WEBER
40 Bookstore Manager .... Mrs. Karen STRIMPLE
12 Director Columbus Technical Campus .... Mrs. Cindy HARROLD

Colby Community College (P)

1255 S Range, Colby KS 67701-4099
County: Thomas FICE Identification: 001911
Unit ID: 154934
Telephone: (785) 462-3984 Carnegie Class: Assoc/Pub-R-M
FAX Number: (785) 460-4699 Calendar System: Semester
URL: www.colbycc.edu
Established: 1964 Annual Undergrad Tuition & Fees (In-District): $3,136
Enrollment: 1,400 Coed
Affiliation or Control: State/Local IRS Status: 501(c)3
Highest Offering: Associate Degree
Program: Occupational; 2-Year Principally Bachelor's Creditable
Accreditation: NH, ADNUR, PTAA

01 President .... Dr. Stephen M. VACIK
05 Dean of Academic Affairs .... Mr. Gregory NICHOLS
32 VP of Student Affairs .... Vacant

10 Vice President of Business Affairs .... Mr. Alan WAITES
06 Registrar .... Mrs. Brette HANKIN
08 Librarian .... Mrs. Tara SCHROER
26 Director of Public Information .... Mrs. Deborah SCHWANKE
09 Director Institutional Effectivenes .... Dr. Xuemei YANG
07 Director of Admissions .... Vacant
18 Dean of External Affairs .... Mr. Barry KAAZ
37 Director of Student Financial Aid .... Vacant
29 Director Alumni Relations .... Mr. Nick WELLS
41 Athletic Director .... Mr. Ryan STURDY
14 Director of IT .... Mr. Brooks WEDERSKI

Cowley County Community College (A)

125 S Second, PO Box 1147,
Arkansas City KS 67005-1147
County: Cowley FICE Identification: 001902
Unit ID: 154952
Telephone: (620) 442-0430 Carnegie Class: Assoc/Pub-R-M
FAX Number: (620) 441-5350 Calendar System: Semester
URL: www.cowley.edu
Established: 1922 Annual Undergrad Tuition & Fees (In-District): $2,356
Enrollment: 3,966 Coed
Affiliation or Control: Local IRS Status: 501(c)3
Highest Offering: Associate Degree
Program: Occupational; 2-Year Principally Bachelor's Creditable
Accreditation: NH, EMT

01 President .... Mr. Clark WILLIAMS
10 Exec Vice Pres of Business Services .... Mr. Tony CROUCH
32 Int VP of Student Affairs .... Mr. Ben SCHEARS
05 Vice President of Academic Affairs .... Mr. Slade GRIFFITHS
30 Vice Pres Institutional Development .... Mr. Ben SCHEARS
13 Vice Pres of Research & Technology .... Mr. Charles MCKOWN
41 Int Athletic Director .... Mr. Dave BURROUGHS
06 Registrar .... Mr. Mark BRITTON
15 Dir of Human Resources .... Ms. Linda KREUTZER
26 Dir Inst Comm/Public Relations .... Mr. Rama PEROO

Dodge City Community College (B)

2501 N 14th Avenue, Dodge City KS 67801-2399
County: Ford FICE Identification: 001913
Unit ID: 154998
Telephone: (620) 225-1321 Carnegie Class: Assoc/Pub-R-M
FAX Number: (620) 227-9366 Calendar System: Semester
URL: www.dc3.edu
Established: 1935 Annual Undergrad Tuition & Fees (In-District): $2,100
Enrollment: 1,865 Coed
Affiliation or Control: State/Local IRS Status: 501(c)3
Highest Offering: Associate Degree
Program: Occupational; 2-Year Principally Bachelor's Creditable
Accreditation: NH, ADNUR, PNUR

01 President .... Dr. Don A. WOODBURN
05 Exec VP College Affairs/Learning .... Mr. Michael AHERN
10 Vice Pres of Operations & Finance .... Ms. Vada HERMON
103 VP Innovation/Workforce Development .... Mr. Danny GILLUM
31 VP Community & Industry Relations .... Mr. Anthony LYONS
32 Dean of Student Services .... Mrs. Beverly TEMAAT
72 Dean Technology/Distance Education .... Mr. Thad RUSSELL
84 Dean of Enrollment Management .... Mrs. Kelly RUSSELL
102 Exec Director of DCCC Foundation .... Mr. Roger PROFFITT
51 Dir Bus/Technology/Continuing Educ .... Vacant
24 Director Adult Learning Center .... Mr. Ryan AUSMUS
26 Dir of Marketing/Human Resources .... Mr. David WETMORE
07 Dir Admissions Placement & Testing .... Vacant
08 Director Learning Resource Center .... Mrs. Shelly HUELSMAN
66 Director Nursing Allied Health .... Mrs. Mary BENJAMIN
41 Athletic Director .... Mr. Casey MALEK
06 Registrar .... Ms. Stephanie LANNING
37 Director of Financial Aid .... Mr. Russ MCBEE
21 Director of Business Services .... Ms. Debbie BISCH
40 Director Bookstore .... Mrs. Debby MALEK
13 Director Information Technology .... Mrs. Judith MAXFIELD
39 Director of Residence Life .... Mr. Lewis MIZE
18 Director of Facilities & Operations .... Mr. Greg PATEE
15 Asst Director of Human Resources .... Ms. Sheila BERGKAMP
04 Exec Assistant to the President .... Mrs. Carla PATEE

Donnelly College (C)

608 N 18th Street, Kansas City KS 66102-4298
County: Wyandotte FICE Identification: 001914
Unit ID: 155007
Telephone: (913) 621-8700 Carnegie Class: Bac/Assoc
FAX Number: (913) 621-8719 Calendar System: Semester
URL: www.donnelly.edu
Established: 1949 Annual Undergrad Tuition & Fees: $7,074
Enrollment: 650 Coed
Affiliation or Control: Roman Catholic IRS Status: 501(c)3
Highest Offering: Baccalaureate
Program: Occupational; 2-Year Principally Bachelor's Creditable; Liberal Arts And General
Accreditation: NH

01 President .... Dr. Steven M. LANASA
03 Vice President .... Mrs. Frances SANDERS
32 Vice President of Student Affairs .... Ms. Donette ALONZO
85 Dean of International Students .... Mr. Mark BLEVINS
88 Director Student Success .... Dr. Mary PFLANZ
06 Registrar .... Ms. Jennifer BALES
26 Marketing Coordinator .... Vacant
30 Director of Development .... Mrs. Emily BUCKLEY
36 Career Center Coord/Library Dir .... Mrs. Jane BALLAGH DE TOVAR
37 Director of Financial Aid .... Mrs. Belinda OGAN
10 Dir Business Affairs/Personnel Svcs .... Ms. Laurie LOETHEN
18 Director of Facilities .... Ms. Donette ALONZO
09 Dir Institutional Rsrch/Plng/Assess .... Mrs. Frances SANDERS
14 Director of Computer Services .... Vacant
07 Director of Admissions .... Mr. Edward MARQUEZ
29 Alumini Relations .... Mr. Roger BERG

Emporia State University (D)

1200 Commercial Street, Emporia KS 66801-5087
County: Lyon FICE Identification: 001927
Unit ID: 155025
Telephone: (620) 341-1200 Carnegie Class: Master's L
FAX Number: (620) 341-5553 Calendar System: Semester
URL: www.emporia.edu
Established: 1863 Annual Undergrad Tuition & Fees (In-State): $5,614
Enrollment: 5,867 Coed
Affiliation or Control: State IRS Status: 501(c)3
Highest Offering: Doctorate
Program: Liberal Arts And General; Teacher Preparatory
Accreditation: NH, ART, BUS, CACREP, CORE, LIB, MUS, NUR, TED

01 President .... Dr. Michael SHONROCK
05 Provost/VP for Academic Affairs .... Dr. David CORDLE
11 Vice President Admin & Fiscal Affs .... Mr. Raymond A. HAUKE
32 Vice President Student Affairs .... Dr. James E. WILLIAMS
14 Assoc Vice Pres Tech/Computing Svcs .... Mr. Michael ERICKSON
09 Asst Provost Inst Research/Assess .... Dr. JoLanna KORD
85 Dean of International Education .... Mr. Gonzalo BRUCE
35 Dean of Students .... Ms. Lynn M. HOBSON
10 Assoc Vice Pres Fiscal Affairs .... Ms. Diana E. KUHLMANN
102 President ESU Foundation .... Ms. DenaSue POTESTIO
29 Director of Alumni/Govt Rels .... Mr. K. Tyler CURTIS
88 Director Natl Teachers Hall of Fame .... Ms. Carol STRICKLAND
22 Affirmative Action Officer .... Ms. Judy ANDERSON
53 Dean/The Teachers College .... Dr. Kenneth WEAVER
49 Dean College of Liberal Arts/Sci .... Dr. Marie MILLER
50 Dean School of Business .... Dr. Kristie OGILVIE
62 Dean School of Library/Info Mgmt .... Dr. Gwendolyn ALEXANDER
58 Dean Graduate Studies .... Dr. Kathy ERMLER
88 Exec Dir Jones Inst Educ Excel .... Dr. Roger CASWELL
06 Registrar .... Ms. M. Elaine HENRIE
08 Dean University Libraries/Archives .... Mr. John SHERIDAN
106 Director Distance Education .... Dr. Kathy ERMLER
37 Director Student Financial Aid .... Ms. M. Elaine HENRIE
07 Director Admissions .... Ms. Laura M. EDDY
36 Director Career Services .... Ms. June COLEMAN
38 Director Student Life & Counseling .... Dr. Jaqueline L. SCHMIDT
26 Director Marketing & Media Relation .... Mr. Umair ABBASI
41 Director Athletics .... Mr. Kent L. WEISER
18 Director Facilities/Physical Plant .... Mr. Mark S. RUNGE
15 Director Human Resources .... Ms. Judy ANDERSON
23 Director Health Services .... Dr. Jaqueline L. SCHMIDT
39 Dir Residential Life/Orientation .... Mr. Wade REDEKER
40 Manager Bookstore .... Mr. Michael MCRELL
19 Director Police & Safety .... Capt. Chris HOOVER
43 General Counsel .... Mr. Kevin JOHNSON
21 Controller .... Ms. Mary MINGENBACK
92 Director Honors Program .... Dr. William H. CLAMURRO
28 Director Multicultural Affairs .... Mr. Jason BROOKS

Flint Hills Technical College (E)

3301 W 18th Avenue, Emporia KS 66801-5957
County: Lyon FICE Identification: 005264
Unit ID: 155052
Telephone: (620) 343-4600 Carnegie Class: Assoc/Pub-R-S
FAX Number: (620) 343-4610 Calendar System: Semester
URL: www.fhtc.edu
Established: 1965 Annual Undergrad Tuition & Fees (In-District): $4,480
Enrollment: 702 Coed
Affiliation or Control: State/Local IRS Status: 501(c)3
Highest Offering: Associate Degree
Program: Occupational; Technical Emphasis
Accreditation: NH, DA, DH

01 President .... Dr. Dean HOLLENBECK
05 Vice Pres Instructional Services .... Mr. Steve LOEWEN
32 Vice Pres Student Services .... Ms. Lisa KIRMER
10 Vice Pres Business Services .... Mrs. Nancy THOMPSON
06 Registrar .... Ms. Brenda CARMICHAEL
15 Director Personnel Services .... Mrs. Sheri KNIGHT
37 Director Student Financial Aid .... Ms. Sandra SCHROEDER
84 Director Enrollment Management .... Ms. Brenda CARMICHAEL

Fort Hays State University (F)

600 Park Street, Hays KS 67601-4099
County: Ellis FICE Identification: 001915
Unit ID: 155061
Telephone: (785) 628-4000 Carnegie Class: Master's L
FAX Number: (785) 628-4096 Calendar System: Semester
URL: www.fhsu.edu
Established: 1902 Annual Undergrad Tuition & Fees (In-State): $4,358
Enrollment: 14,972 Coed
Affiliation or Control: State IRS Status: 501(c)3
Highest Offering: Beyond Master's But Less Than Doctorate
Program: Liberal Arts And General; Teacher Preparatory; Professional
Accreditation: NH, MUS, NURSE, RAD, SP, SW, TED

01 President .... Dr. Edward H. HAMMOND
05 Provost .... Dr. Lawrence V. GOULD
10 Vice Pres Administration & Finance .... Mr. Mike BARNETT
32 Vice President Student Affairs .... Dr. Tisa MASON
35 Asst Vice Pres Student Affairs .... Ms. Keegan NICHOLS
09 Asst Provost Quality Improvement .... Dr. Chris CRAWFORD
58 Dean Graduate Studies and Research .... Dr. Tim CROWLEY
04 Exec Assistant to the President .... Mr. Todd POWELL
04 Assistant to President .... Ms. Lisa M. KARLIN
06 Registrar .... Dr. Joseph G. LINN
07 Admissions Director .... Ms. Tricia CLINE
29 Exec Director Alumni & Govt Rels .... Ms. Debra K. PRIDEAUX
45 Director Budget & Planning .... Mr. Larry R. GETTY
36 Director Career Services .... Mr. Daniel B. RICE
37 Director Student Financial Aid .... Mr. Craig E. KARLIN
26 Director University Relations .... Mr. Kent L. STEWARD
14 Director Computing/Telecom Center .... Dr. David E. SCHMIDT
08 Director Library .... Mr. John A. ROSS
15 Director Personnel Services .... Ms. Shannon LINDSEY
51 Dean Virtual College .... Mr. Dennis KING
53 Dean College Education .... Dr. Robert F. SCOTT
49 Dean College Liberal Arts/Sciences .... Dr. Paul W. FABER
50 Dean College Business .... Dr. Mark BANNISTER
76 Dean Coll Health/Life Science .... Dr. Jeff BRIGGS
18 Co-Dir Chief Facil/Physical Plant .... Mr. Jim SCHREIBER
18 Co-Dir Chief Facil/Physical Plant .... Mr. Ken JACOBS
38 Dir Acad Advis/Career Exploration .... Dr. Patricia L. GRIFFIN
28 Diversity Coordinator .... Vacant

Fort Scott Community College (G)

2108 S Horton, Fort Scott KS 66701-3140
County: Bourbon FICE Identification: 001916
Unit ID: 155098
Telephone: (620) 223-2700 Carnegie Class: Assoc/Pub-R-M
FAX Number: (620) 223-4927 Calendar System: Semester
URL: www.fortscott.edu
Established: 1919 Annual Undergrad Tuition & Fees (In-District): $2,610
Enrollment: 1,903 Coed
Affiliation or Control: State/Local IRS Status: 501(c)3
Highest Offering: Associate Degree
Program: Occupational; 2-Year Principally Bachelor's Creditable
Accreditation: NH, ADNUR

01 President .... Dr. Clayton TATRO
05 Interim Dean of Instruction .... Dr. Regena LANCE
32 Dean of Student Services .... Robert GOETRA
10 Dean of Finance and Operations .... Karla FARMER
07 Director Admissions .... Tom GORMAN
08 Library Director .... Wendy WILMOTH
06 Registrar .... Courtney CRAYS
26 Director Public Relations .... Juliana HUGHES
66 Director Nursing .... Bill RHOADS
41 Athletic Director .... JD ETTORE
13 Information Technology Director .... Morgan BECK
12 Associate Dean Crawford Campuses .... Santos MANRIQUE
12 Associate Dean Paola .... Buddy Jo TANCK
38 Director of Advising .... Steve KRAMER
15 Human Resource Director .... Juley MCDANIEL
18 Director Facilities & Operations .... Joel RAMSEY
30 Director of Development/Alumni .... Gary PALMER
37 Director Student Financial Aid .... Lillie GRUBB
28 Director of Diversity .... Jill WARFORD
35 Director of Student Life .... Marci MYERS
21 Director Business Operations .... Mindy RUSSELL

Friends University (H)

2100 W University Avenue, Wichita KS 67213-3397
County: Sedgwick FICE Identification: 001918
Unit ID: 155089
Telephone: (316) 295-5000 Carnegie Class: Master's L
FAX Number: (316) 295-5060 Calendar System: Semester
URL: www.friends.edu
Established: 1898 Annual Undergrad Tuition & Fees: $23,250
Enrollment: 2,502 Coed
Affiliation or Control: Independent Non-Profit IRS Status: 501(c)3
Highest Offering: Master's
Program: Liberal Arts And General; Teacher Preparatory; Professional
Accreditation: NH, MFCD, MUS, TED

01 President .... Dr. TJ ARANT
04 Executive Secretary .... Ms. Nancy GRAF
10 Vice Pres Administration & Finance .... Mr. Randall C. DOERKSEN
32 Vice President of Student Life .... Dr. Carole OBERMEYER
30 Vice President Inst Advancement .... Ms. Tracy MUIRHEAD
84 Vice President of Enrollment Mgmt .... Mr. Steven KLEIN
20 Assoc VP of Academic Affairs .... Dr. Darcy ZABEL
15 Assoc VP Admn Finance/Dir of HR .... Ms. Kelley WILLIAMS
06 Assoc VP Registrar/Enrollment Svcs .... Ms. Heidi HOSKINSON
49 Dean College of Bus/Art/Sci & Educ .... Dr. Steve PETERS
107 Dean Adult and Professional Studies .... Dr. Jo LOBERTINI
58 Dean Graduate School .... Dr. David HOFMEISTER
50 Chair Business & IT .... Dr. Arlen HONTS
57 Chair Fine Arts .... Dr. Stephen EAVES
81 Chair Natural Science/Math .... Dr. Nora STRASSER
73 Chair Religion/Humanities .... Dr. Stan HARSTINE
53 Chair Teacher Education .... Dr. Jan WILSON
83 Chair Social/Behavioral Science .... Mr. Bill ALLAN

46 Dir Inst Research & Assessment ...... Dr. Stephanie J. HARGRAVE
08 Director Library ...... Mr. Max BURSON
18 Chief Facilities/Physical Plant ...... Mr. Paul WINCHESTER
96 Director of Purchasing/Aux Services ...... Mr. Ryan ARCHER
07 Dir Traditional Undergrad Admiss ...... Mr. Jim ALLEN
41 Director Athletics ...... Mr. Joe ZIMMERMAN
37 Director Financial Aid ...... Mr. Brandon PIERCE
42 Chaplain ...... Mr. Patrick SEHL, JR.
35 Director of Campus Life ...... Mr. Gary RAPP
39 Director Residence Life ...... Ms. Kelley MARTIN
26 Director Communications ...... Ms. Gisele MCMINIMY
29 Exec Dir Alumni/Annual Fund ...... Ms. Lisa TILMA
88 Director of Northeast Region ...... Ms. Hilary PEGUERO

Garden City Community College (A)

801 Campus Drive, Garden City KS 67846-6398
County: Finney FICE Identification: 001919
Unit ID: 155104
Telephone: (620) 276-7611 Carnegie Class: Assoc/Pub-R-M
FAX Number: (620) 276-9573 Calendar System: Semester
URL: www.gcccks.edu
Established: 1919 Annual Undergrad Tuition & Fees (In-District): $2,560
Enrollment: 2,059 Coed
Affiliation or Control: Local IRS Status: 501(c)3
Highest Offering: Associate Degree
Program: Occupational; 2-Year Principally Bachelor's Creditable
Accreditation: NH, ADNUR, EMT

01 President ...... Dr. Herbert SWENDER
03 Executive Vice President ...... Ms. Dee WIGNER
05 Vice Pres of Instructional Services ...... Dr. Bruce EXSTROM
32 Vice Pres of Student Services/AD ...... Mr. Ryan RUDA
08 Library Director ...... Mr. Trent SMITH
06 Registrar ...... Ms. Nancy UNRUH
07 Director of Admissions ...... Ms. Jayre LEE
15 Director of Human Resources ...... Ms. Cricket TURLEY
18 Interim Physical Plant Director ...... Mr. Derek RAMOS
26 Exec Director Marketing & PR ...... Ms. Cathy MCKINLEY
37 Director Student Financial Aid ...... Ms. Kathy BLAU
39 Director Residential Life ...... Ms. Kate COVINGTON
38 Director Student Counseling ...... Mr. Colin LAMB
75 Dean Technical Education ...... Ms. Lenora COOK

Haskell Indian Nations University (B)

155 Indian Avenue, #5030, Lawrence KS 66046-4800
County: Douglas FICE Identification: 010438
Unit ID: 155140
Telephone: (785) 749-8404 Carnegie Class: Tribal
FAX Number: (785) 749-8406 Calendar System: Semester
URL: www.haskell.edu
Established: 1884 Annual Undergrad Tuition & Fees: $80
Enrollment: 846 Coed
Affiliation or Control: Federal IRS Status: Exempt
Highest Offering: Baccalaureate
Program: 2-Year Principally Bachelor's Creditable; Liberal Arts And General; Teacher Preparatory
Accreditation: NH, TED

01 Acting President ...... Mr. Michael LEWIS
05 Vice President for Academics ...... Dr. Venida CHENAULT
11 Vice President University Services ...... Mr. Clyde PEACOCK
10 Chief Finance Officer ...... Mr. Michael LEWIS
27 Chief Information Officer ...... Mr. Joshua ARCE
08 Librarian/Dir Academic Support Ctr ...... Dr. Marilyn RUSSELL
39 Dir Resident Housing/Mgr Stdnt Life ...... Mr. Jim TUCKER
37 Financial Aid Officer ...... Ms. Reta BREWER
06 Registrar ...... Mr. Manny KING
07 Director of Admissions ...... Ms. Dorothy D. STITES
09 Dir Instl Research/Sponsored Pgms ...... Ms. Freda GIPP
36 Actg Career Development Specialist ...... Mr. Burgess TAPEDO
38 Director Student Counseling ...... Ms. Brenda SCHILDT
15 Human Resources Liason ...... Ms. Mona GONZALES
96 Acquisitions ...... Ms. Janice BEGAY
26 Executive Asst/Public Relations ...... Mr. Stephen PRUE
18 Director Facilities Management ...... Mr. Lee PAHCODDY, JR.

Heritage College-Wichita (C)

2800 South Rock Road, Wichita KS 67210
Telephone: (316) 681-1615 Identification: 770529
Accreditation: ABHES

† Main campus is Heritage College in Denver, CO.

Hesston College (D)

Box 3000, Hesston KS 67062-2093
County: Harvey FICE Identification: 001920
Unit ID: 155177
Telephone: (620) 327-4221 Carnegie Class: Assoc/PrivNFP
FAX Number: (620) 327-8300 Calendar System: Semester
URL: www.hesston.edu
Established: 1909 Annual Undergrad Tuition & Fees: $23,174
Enrollment: 447 Coed
Affiliation or Control: Mennonite Church IRS Status: 501(c)3
Highest Offering: Associate Degree
Program: Occupational; 2-Year Principally Bachelor's Creditable
Accreditation: NH, ADNUR

01 President ...... Dr. Howard KEIM
05 Vice President of Academics ...... Dr. Sandra ZERGER
30 Vice President of Advancement ...... Mrs. Yvonne SIEBER
07 Vice President of Admissions ...... Mrs. Rachel S. MILLER
10 Vice Pres of Finance & Auxil Svcs ...... Mr. Mark LANDES
32 Vice President of Student Life ...... Mr. Lamar ROTH
29 Director of Alumni & Church Rels ...... Mr. Dallas STUTZMAN
06 Registrar ...... Mr. Brent YODER
21 Business Manager ...... Mr. Karl BRUBAKER

Highland Community College (E)

606 W Main, Highland KS 66035-0068
County: Doniphan FICE Identification: 001921
Unit ID: 155186
Telephone: (785) 442-6000 Carnegie Class: Assoc/Pub-R-M
FAX Number: (785) 442-6100 Calendar System: Semester
URL: www.highlandcc.edu
Established: 1858 Annual Undergrad Tuition & Fees (In-District): $2,940
Enrollment: 3,093 Coed
Affiliation or Control: Local IRS Status: 501(c)3
Highest Offering: Associate Degree
Program: Occupational; 2-Year Principally Bachelor's Creditable
Accreditation: NH

01 President ...... Mr. David REIST
05 Vice President for Academic Affairs ...... Ms. Peggy FORSBERG
32 Vice President for Student Services ...... Dr. Cheryl RASMUSSEN
10 Vice Pres for Finance/Operations ...... Ms. Cynthia HAGGARD
88 Director of Technical Education ...... Ms. Terri BALL
30 Vice Pres Institutional Advancemntn ...... Dr. Craig E. MOSHER
06 Registrar ...... Ms. Alice HAMILTON
37 Financial Aid Director ...... Ms. Amy LACKEY
13 Director of Information Systems ...... Vacant
09 Director of Institutional Research ...... Dr. Harold ARNETT
38 Director Student Counseling ...... Ms. Kristin WOODRUFF
41 Athletic Director ...... Mr. Greg DELZEIT
08 Library Director ...... Ms. Penny DONALDSON
18 Supervisor of Buildings & Grounds ...... Mr. Rick CROSSLAND
26 Chief Public Relations Officer ...... Dr. Craig MOSHER
29 Director Alumni Relations ...... Dr. Craig MOSHER
35 Director of Student Life ...... Mr. Bradley DIXON
15 Human Resource Manager ...... Ms. Eileen C. GRONNIGER
40 Bookstore Coordinator ...... Vacant

Hutchinson Community College and Area Vocational School (F)

1300 N Plum Street, Hutchinson KS 67501-5894
County: Reno FICE Identification: 001923
Unit ID: 155195
Telephone: (620) 665-3500 Carnegie Class: Assoc/Pub-R-L
FAX Number: (620) 665-3310 Calendar System: Semester
URL: www.hutchcc.edu
Established: 1928 Annual Undergrad Tuition & Fees (In-District): $2,520
Enrollment: 6,112 Coed
Affiliation or Control: State/Local IRS Status: 501(c)3
Highest Offering: Associate Degree
Program: Occupational; 2-Year Principally Bachelor's Creditable
Accreditation: NH, ACBSP, ADNUR, CAHIIM, #COARC, EMT, PNUR, PTAA, RAD, SURGT

01 President ...... Dr. Edward E. BERGER
05 Vice President of Academic Affairs ...... Dr. Cindy HOSS
10 Vice President Finance/Operations ...... Mr. Carter FILE
103 VP Workforce Development/Outreach ...... Mr. Steve PORTER
32 Vice President of Students ...... Mr. Randy E. MYERS
26 Director of Marketing & Info ...... Ms. M. L. HINKLE
13 Director of Data Processing ...... Mr. Loren L. MORRIS
06 Registrar ...... Mrs. Christina LONG
41 Athletic Director ...... Mr. Randy STANGE
15 Director of Personnel ...... Mr. Brooks E. MANTOOTH
37 Financial Aid Officer ...... Mr. Nathan BUCHE
07 Director of Admissions ...... Mr. Corbin STROBEL
18 Director of Plant Facilities ...... Mr. Don ROSE
39 Director of Residence Life ...... Ms. Dana HINSHAW
29 Director Alumni Relations ...... Mrs. Cindy KEAST
08 Coordinator of Library Services ...... Mr. Robert KELLY
09 Coord of Institutional Research ...... Mr. Rex CHEEVER

Independence Community College (G)

Brookside Drive and College Avenue, Independence KS 67301-0708
County: Montgomery FICE Identification: 001924
Unit ID: 155201
Telephone: (620) 331-4100 Carnegie Class: Assoc/Pub-R-S
FAX Number: (620) 331-5344 Calendar System: Semester
URL: www.indycc.edu
Established: 1925 Annual Undergrad Tuition & Fees (In-District): $2,130
Enrollment: 764 Coed
Affiliation or Control: State/Local IRS Status: 501(c)3
Highest Offering: Associate Degree
Program: Occupational; 2-Year Principally Bachelor's Creditable
Accreditation: NH

01 President ...... Dr. Daniel W. BARWICK
10 VP Financial and Employee Services ...... Mr. Jan FISCHER
05 VP Academic Affairs ...... Dr. Sara HARRIS
32 VP Student Affairs/Athletics ...... Ms. Tammie GELDENHUYS
11 VP Information/Operations ...... Mr. Greg EYTCHESON
26 VP Marketing/Resource Dev ...... Ms. Misty GITHENS
102 Foundation Director ...... Ms. Lori SHAW
06 Registrar ...... Ms. Sonja CONLEY
08 Director Library/Lrng Resource Ctr ...... Ms. Lily MORGAN
18 Director Maintenance/Custodial ...... Mr. Mario LOPEZ
12 Director William Inge Center ...... Mr. Peter ELLENSTEIN
07 Recruiting/Admissions Specialist ...... Ms. Brittany THORNTON
37 Financial Aid Coordinator ...... Ms. Wendy ISLE
13 MIS Coordinator ...... Mr. Darrin MCFARLAND
09 Dir of Institutional Research ...... Ms. Debbie PHELPS
04 Executive Asst to President ...... Ms. Beverly HARRIS
40 Bookstore Manager ...... Ms. Teresa VESTAL
25 Grants/New Program Development ...... Vacant
88 Upward Bound Program Director ...... Ms. Nicole PERCIVAL
72 Associate VP Career/Technical Ed ...... Mr. Travis GITHENS
15 Human Resources Coordinator ...... Ms. Keli TUSCHMAN

ITT Technical Institute (H)

7600 West 119th Street, Suite 100, Overland Park KS 66213
Telephone: (913) 253-1300 Identification: 770652
Accreditation: ACICS

† Main campus is ITT Technical Institute in Indianapolis, IN.

ITT Technical Institute (I)

8111 E. 32nd St. N, Suite 103, Wichita KS 67226
Telephone: (316) 609-4100 Identification: 666168
Accreditation: ACICS

† Main campus is ITT Technical Institute in Indianapolis, IN.

Johnson County Community College (J)

12345 College Boulevard, Overland Park KS 66210-1299
County: Johnson FICE Identification: 008244
Unit ID: 155210
Telephone: (913) 469-8500 Carnegie Class: Assoc/Pub-S-SC
FAX Number: (913) 469-2559 Calendar System: Semester
URL: www.jccc.edu
Established: 1969 Annual Undergrad Tuition & Fees (In-District): $1,275
Enrollment: 20,443 Coed
Affiliation or Control: State/Local IRS Status: 501(c)3
Highest Offering: Associate Degree
Program: Occupational; 2-Year Principally Bachelor's Creditable
Accreditation: NH, ACBSP, ACFEI, ADNUR, COARC, DH, EMT, IFSAC, POLYT

01 President ...... Dr. Joe SOPCICH
10 Exec Vice Pres Administrative Svcs ...... Vacant
05 Exec Vice Pres Academic Affairs ...... Dr. Marilyn RHINEHART
15 Executive Vice Pres Instruction/COO ...... Dr. Judy KORB
32 Vice Pres Student Success/Engagemnt ...... Dr. Dennis DAY
27 Vice President Information Services ...... Ms. Denise MOORE
04 Exec Asst to the President & Board ...... Ms. Terri SCHLICHT
26 AVP Marketing Communications ...... Ms. Julie HAAS
21 AVP Financial Services ...... Mr. Don PERKINS
18 AVP Campus Services ...... Mr. Rex HAYS
72 Dean Technology ...... Mr. Bill BROWN
13 Director Admin Computing Services ...... Ms. Sandra WARNER
96 AVP Business Services ...... Mr. Mitch BORCHERS
35 Dean Student Success ...... Mr. Paul KYLE
76 AVP Instruction ...... Dr. Clarissa CRAIG
37 Director Student Financial Aid ...... Vacant
36 Director Testing and Assessment ...... Ms. Mary Ann DICKERSON
06 Registrar ...... Ms. Leslie QUINN
08 Director Library Services ...... Mr. Mark DAGANAAR
68 Dir Physical Education/Athletics ...... Mr. Carl HEINRICH
07 Director of Admissions ...... Mr. Peter BELK
84 Asst Dean Enrollment Management ...... Ms. MargE SHELLEY
92 Program Facilitator Honors ...... Dr. Pat DECKER
35 Asst Dean Student Activ/Ldrshp Dev ...... Ms. Pam VASSAR

Kansas City College and Bible School (K)

7401 Metcalf, Overland Park KS 66204-1995
County: Johnson Identification: 667134
Telephone: (913) 722-0272 Carnegie Class: Not Classified
FAX Number: (913) 403-0595 Calendar System: Semester
URL: www.kccbs.edu
Established: 1938 Annual Undergrad Tuition & Fees: $4,800
Enrollment: N/A Coed
Affiliation or Control: Independent Non-Profit IRS Status: 501(c)3
Highest Offering: Baccalaureate
Program: Religious Emphasis
Accreditation: @BI

01 President ...... Delbert SCOTT

Kansas City Kansas Community College (L)

7250 State Avenue, Kansas City KS 66112-3003
County: Wyandotte FICE Identification: 001925
Unit ID: 155292
Telephone: (913) 334-1100 Carnegie Class: Assoc/Pub-U-SC
FAX Number: (913) 288-7609 Calendar System: Semester
URL: www.kckcc.edu
Established: 1923 Annual Undergrad Tuition & Fees (In-District): $2,490

Enrollment: 7,479 Coed
Affiliation or Control: State/Local IRS Status: 501(c)3
Highest Offering: Associate Degree
Program: Occupational; 2-Year Principally Bachelor's Creditable
Accreditation: NH, ACBSP, ADNUR, COARC, EMT, FUSER, PTAA

01 President Dr. Doris F. GIVENS
11 VP Student & Administrative Svcs Mr. Brian BODE
05 VP of Accademic Affairs Dr. Tamara AGHA-JAFFAR
50 Dean Business & Continuing Educ Dr. Marvin HUNT
81 Dean Engineering/Math/Science Dr. Edward KREMER
84 Dean Enrollment Mgmt/Registrar Dr. Denise MCDOWELL
16 Dean Human Resources/Affirm Action Ms. Leota MARKS
79 Dean Humanities & Fine Arts Dr. Cherilee WALKER
13 Dean Information Services Mr. Baz ABOUELENEIN
45 Dean Institutional Services Dr. Sangki MIN
66 Dean Nursing Educ/Allied Health Dr. Shirley A. WENDEL
83 Dean Social & Behavioral Sciences Dr. Charles WILSON
32 Dean of Student Services Vacant
75 Dean Technical Education Center Mr. Cliff SMITH
88 Exec Director Leavenworth Center Ms. Karalin ALSDURF
88 Director of Academic Resource Ctr Ms. Jaclyn ANDERSON
41 Director of Athletics Mr. Anthony "Tony" TOMPKINS
40 Director of Bookstore Operations Mr. John BURRIGHT
18 Director of Buildings/Grounds Mr. Jeff SIXTA
19 Director of Campus Police Mr. Greg SCHNEIDER
36 Director of Career Planning/Plcmnt Ms. Linda L. WYATT
30 Director of Endowment Mr. Patrick S. MCCARTNEY
14 Director of Computing Mr. James BENNETT
31 Director of Cont Educ & Cmty Svcs Ms. Rosemary L. LISCHKA
38 Director of Counseling Mr. Shawn DERRITT
09 Director Ctr for Rsrch & Cmty Devel Ms. Kaaren FIFE
37 Director of Financial Aid Ms. Mary I. DORR
21 Director of Financial Records Ms. Marie BRANSTETTER
92 Director of Honors/Phi Theta Kappa Ms. Stacy TUCKER
28 Director of Intercultural Center Ms. Barbara CLARK-EVANS
08 Director of Library Ms. Cheryl POSTLEWAIT
24 Director Media Services Technology Mr. Michael J. KIMBROUGH
106 Director of Online Services Ms. Susan STUART
96 Director of Purchasing & Risk Mgr Mr. David ROOT
35 Director of Student Activities Ms. Linda SUTTON
07 Director of Admissions Ms. Sherri A. NEFF
06 Assistant Registrar Ms. Theresa HOLLIDAY
88 Director Community Outreach Counsel Ms. Andrea J. CHASTAIN
15 Director Human Resources Ms. Cheryl C. COLEMAN
88 Director Forensic Laboratory Vacant
88 Director Wellness Center Mr. Rob M. CRANE
103 Director of Cultural Outreach Mr. Brian PATRICK
66 Director Nursing Ms. Anita M. KRONDAK
66 Director Practical Nursing Ms. Susan K. WHITE
88 Assistant Director Student Develop Ms. Tamara D. MILLER
88 Director Technical Programs Mr. Richard PIPER
88 Director Technical Programs Perkins Ms. Donna S. SHAWN
88 Assistant Director Academic Resourc Ms. Amanda WILLIAMS
88 Director Performing Arts Center Mr. Bill YEAZEL

Kansas State University (A)

Manhattan KS 66506
County: Riley FICE Identification: 001928
Unit ID: 155399
Telephone: (785) 532-6250 Carnegie Class: RU/H
FAX Number: (785) 532-2120 Calendar System: Semester
URL: www.k-state.edu
Established: 1863 Annual Undergrad Tuition & Fees (In-State): $8,585
Enrollment: 24,378 Coed
Affiliation or Control: State IRS Status: 501(c)3
Highest Offering: Doctorate
Program: Liberal Arts And General; Teacher Preparatory; Professional
Accreditation: NH, ART, BUS, BUSA, CACREP, CEA, CIDA, CONST, CS, DIETC, DIETD, ENG, IPSY, JOUR, LSAR, MFCD, MUS, NRPA, PLNG, SP, SPAA, SW, TED, THEA, VET

01 President Dr. Kirk H. SCHULZ
05 Provost and Senior Vice President Dr. April C. MASON
10 Interim VP Admin & Finance Ms. Cindy A. BONTRAGER
46 Vice President Research Dr. Ronald W. TREWYN
32 VP Student Life/Dean of Students Dr. Pat J. BOSCO
26 VP for Communications & Marketing Mr. Jeffery B. MORRIS
100 Chief of Staff/Dir Community Rels Dr. Jackie L. HARTMAN
20 Senior Vice Provost Dr. Ruth DYER
86 Dir for Governmental Relations Dr. Susan K. PETERSON
04 Admin Asst to the President Ms. Dana M. HASTINGS
13 Vice Provost Info Tech Svcs Mr. Kenneth STAFFORD
108 Assoc Prov Institutional Effectiv Dr. Brian A. NIEHOFF
88 Director Military Affairs Mr. Arthur S. DE GROAT
08 Dean of Libraries Dr. Lori A. GOETSCH
47 Dean of Agriculture Dr. John FLOROS
48 Dean Architecture/Planning/Design Mr. Timothy DE NOBLE
49 Dean of Arts & Sciences Dr. Peter K. DORHOUT
50 Dean of Business Administration Dr. Ali R. MALEKZADEH
51 Dean of Continuing Education Dr. Sue C. MAES
53 Dean of Education Dr. Debbie K. MERCER
54 Interim Dean of Engineering Dr. Gary A. CLARK
58 Dean of Graduate School Dr. Carol SHANKLIN
59 Dean of Human Ecology Dr. John B. BUCKWALTER
72 Dean of Technology & Aviation Dr. Verna M. FITZSIMMONS
74 Dean of Veterinary Medicine Dr. Ralph C. RICHARDSON
30 President/CEO of Foundation Dr. Fred A. CHOLICK
29 Alumni Association President Ms. Amy Button RENZ
41 Athletic Director Mr. John CURRIE
56 Dir Research and Extension Dr. John FLOROS
21 Director of Budget Ms. Cindy A. BONTRAGER
37 Asst VP Student Financial Assist Mr. Lawrence E. MOEDER
36 Director Career & Employment Svcs Ms. Kerri D. KELLER
06 Registrar Dr. Monty E. NIELSEN
07 Asst VP/Director of Admissions Mr. Lawrence E. MOEDER
15 Asst VP for Human Resources Mr. Gary E. LEITNAKER
28 Assoc Prov for Diversity Dr. Myra E. GORDON

Kansas State University-Salina, College of Technology and Aviation (B)

2310 Centennial Road, Salina KS 67401-8196
Telephone: (785) 826-2601 FICE Identification: 004611
Accreditation: &NH, AAB, ENGT

† Main campus is Kansas State University in Manhattan, KS.

Kansas Wesleyan University (C)

100 E Claflin Avenue, Salina KS 67401-6196
County: Saline FICE Identification: 001929
Unit ID: 155414
Telephone: (785) 827-5541 Carnegie Class: Bac/Diverse
FAX Number: (785) 827-0927 Calendar System: Semester
URL: www.kwu.edu
Established: 1886 Annual Undergrad Tuition & Fees: $23,800
Enrollment: 745 Coed
Affiliation or Control: United Methodist IRS Status: 501(c)3
Highest Offering: Master's
Program: Liberal Arts And General; Teacher Preparatory; Professional
Accreditation: NH, NUR, TED

01 President and CEO Dr. Matthew R. THOMPSON
04 Executive Assistant to President Ms. Jan M. SHIRK
10 Vice Pres Finance/Administration Mr. Wayne R. SCHNEIDER
21 Controller/Business Officer Ms. Cheri L. BOYD
84 Vice Pres Enrollment Management Dr. Mark A. BANDRE
37 Director Student Financial Planning Ms. Lois MADSEN
06 Registrar Mrs. Krista L. LOUGH
07 Director of Admissions Mr. Esteban PAREDES
05 Exec Vice President/Provost Dr. Wayne LOWEN
30 Exec Dir Institutional Advancement Mr. Jeffrey D. CHAPMAN
29 Director of Alumni Relations Ms. Jennifer L. REIN
26 Dir PR/Marketing/Communications Ms. Mary J. GORDON
44 Institutional Development Ms. Sophie A. LAMB
32 Exec Director Student Development Ms. Bridget R. WEISER
36 Director of Career Services Vacant
108 Director of Assessment Prof. Raymond A. TUCKER
08 Director of Library Svcs Mr. James E. CORBLY
13 Director of Information Systems Mr. Jay C. KROB
18 Director of Plant Operations Mr. Darrell D. VICTORY
40 Manager Yotee's Bookstore Mr. Steve G. CARRIER
42 Chaplain Univ United Meth Church Rev. Mike ROSE
41 Athletic Director Vacant
58 Director of MBA Program Prof. Daniel J. BOTZ
66 Division Nursing Education Chair Vacant
53 Director of Teacher Education Dr. Martha S. ROBERTSON
79 Division Chair Humanities Dr. Michael RUSSELL
49 Div Chair Applied Art & Sciences Prof. Bryan K. MINNICH
83 Division Chair Social Sciences Prof. John K. BURCHILL
57 Division Chair Fine Arts Prof. Barbara J. NICKELL
81 Division of Natural Sciences Chair Dr. Stephanie WELTER

Labette Community College (D)

200 S 14th, Parsons KS 67357-4299
County: Labette FICE Identification: 001930
Unit ID: 155450
Telephone: (620) 421-6700 Carnegie Class: Assoc/Pub-R-M
FAX Number: (620) 421-0921 Calendar System: Semester
URL: www.labette.edu
Established: 1923 Annual Undergrad Tuition & Fees (In-District): $2,580
Enrollment: 2,056 Coed
Affiliation or Control: Local IRS Status: 501(c)3
Highest Offering: Associate Degree
Program: Occupational; 2-Year Principally Bachelor's Creditable
Accreditation: NH, ADNUR, COARC, DA, DMS, PTAA, RAD

01 President Dr. George C. KNOX
04 Executive Assistant to President Ms. Megan A. FUGATE
05 Vice President Academic Affairs Mr. Joe BURKE
10 Vice President Finance & Operations Ms. Leanna J. NEWBERRY
32 Vice President Student Affairs Ms. Tammy FUENTEZ
20 Dean of Instruction Mr. Mark WATKINS
13 Director of Information Technology Mrs. Jody BURZINSKI
30 Dir Resource Devel/Alumni Rels Mrs. Lindi D. FORBES
08 Director of Library Services Mr. Scott M. ZOLLARS
18 Director of Physical Plant Mr. Kevin DOHERTY
66 Director of Nursing Mrs. Delyna BOHNENBLUST
41 Athletic Director Mr. Aaron J. KEAL
31 Director of Community Services Vacant
26 Director of Public Relations Mrs. Bethany KENDRICK
06 Registrar/Dir Student Financial Aid Ms. Kathy JOHNSTON
07 Director of Admissions Ms. Kathy JOHNSTON
15 Director of Human Relations Ms. Janice S. GEORGE
37 Director Student Financial Aid Ms. Kathy JOHNSTON
35 Student Life Coordinator Mrs. Melissa NANCE
40 Bookstore Specialist Mrs. Lois D. HEMBREE

Manhattan Area Technical College (E)

3136 Dickens Avenue, Manhattan KS 66503-2499
County: Riley FICE Identification: 005500
Unit ID: 155487
Telephone: (785) 587-2800 Carnegie Class: Assoc/Pub-R-S
FAX Number: (785) 587-2804 Calendar System: Semester
URL: www.matc.net
Established: 1965 Annual Undergrad Tuition & Fees (In-District): $4,895
Enrollment: 755 Coed
Affiliation or Control: State/Local IRS Status: 501(c)3
Highest Offering: Associate Degree
Program: Occupational; 2-Year Principally Bachelor's Creditable; Technical Emphasis
Accreditation: NH, ADNUR, DH

01 President/CEO Dr. Robert J. EDLESTON
05 Vice Pres of Instructional Services Ms. Marilyn MAHAN
10 Vice President of Business Services Ms. Jane BLOODGOOD
32 Vice President of Student Services Mr. Joel LUNDSTROM
30 Assoc VP Institutional Advancement Dr. Richard FOGG
15 Director Human Resources Ms. Trysta WILLIAMS
07 Director of Admissions Ms. Nicole BOLLIG
37 Director Financial Aid Ms. Sarah SAUERESSIG

Manhattan Christian College (F)

1415 Anderson, Manhattan KS 66502-4081
County: Riley FICE Identification: 001931
Unit ID: 155496
Telephone: (785) 539-3571 Carnegie Class: Spec/Faith
FAX Number: (785) 539-0832 Calendar System: Semester
URL: www.mccks.edu
Established: 1927 Annual Undergrad Tuition & Fees: $13,152
Enrollment: 356 Coed
Affiliation or Control: Christian Churches And Churches of Christ
IRS Status: 501(c)3
Highest Offering: Baccalaureate
Program: Liberal Arts And General; Professional; Religious Emphasis
Accreditation: NH, BI

01 President Mr. J. Kevin INGRAM
05 Vice President Academic Affairs Mr. Randall L. INGMIRE
10 Vice President Business Affairs Ms. Lori J. STANFIELD
32 Vice President Student Life Dr. Rick L. WRIGHT
06 Registrar Mr. Jeff DAVIS
26 Asst to Institutional Advancement Mrs. Jolene K. RUPE
37 Director of Financial Aid Ms. Lori J. STANFIELD
08 Library Director Ms. Mary Ann BUHLER
41 Athletic Director Mr. Shawn M. CONDRA
29 Alumni Relations Director Mrs. Genae DENVER
04 Admin Asst to President Ms. Juanita (Nita) M. PRICKETT

McPherson College (G)

1600 E Euclid, PO Box 1402, McPherson KS 67460-1402
County: McPherson FICE Identification: 001933
Unit ID: 155511
Telephone: (620) 242-0400 Carnegie Class: Bac/Diverse
FAX Number: (620) 241-8443 Calendar System: 4/1/4
URL: www.mcpherson.edu
Established: 1887 Annual Undergrad Tuition & Fees: $21,801
Enrollment: 585 Coed
Affiliation or Control: Church Of The Brethren IRS Status: 501(c)3
Highest Offering: Master's
Program: Liberal Arts And General; Teacher Preparatory
Accreditation: NH, TED

01 President Mr. Michael P. SCHNEIDER
05 Provost Dr. Kent EATON
30 Vice President for Advancement Ms. Amanda GUTIERREZ
10 Vice President for Finance Mr. Rick TUXHORN
26 Vice President for Marketing Ms. Christi HOPKINS
07 Vice President for Admissions Mr. David BARRETT
32 Dean of Students Dr. Sharonda MACLIN
41 Athletic Director Mr. Doug QUINT
06 Assoc Dean of Academic Records Mrs. Karlene M. TYLER
88 Special Projects Coordinator Ms. Abbey ARCHER-RIERSON
37 Director of Financial Aid Ms. Brenda KREHBIEL
08 Director of Library Services Ms. Mary HESTER
36 Director of Career Services Mrs. Chris WIENS
26 Director Marketing & Communications Ms. Nancy YOUNG
40 Director of Bookstore Mrs. Linda BARRETT
42 Director of Campus Ministry Dr. Steve CRAIN
13 Director of Computer Services Mr. David GITCHELL

MidAmerica Nazarene University (H)

2030 E College Way, Olathe KS 66062-1899
County: Johnson FICE Identification: 007032
Unit ID: 155520
Telephone: (913) 782-3750 Carnegie Class: Master's M
FAX Number: (913) 971-3290 Calendar System: Semester
URL: www.mnu.edu
Established: 1966 Annual Undergrad Tuition & Fees: $21,200
Enrollment: 2,006 Coed
Affiliation or Control: Church Of The Nazarene IRS Status: 501(c)3
Highest Offering: Master's
Program: 2-Year Principally Bachelor's Creditable; Liberal Arts And General; Teacher Preparatory; Professional
Accreditation: NH, CACREP, MUS, NURSE, TED

01 President Dr. David J. SPITTAL
05 Provost and Chief Academic Officer Dr. Mary JONES
10 Vice President Finance Mr. Kevin P. GILMORE
30 Vice Pres University Advancement Mr. Jon D. NORTH

32 Vice President Community Formation ... Dr. Randy BECKUM
42 University Chaplain ... Dr. Randy BECKUM
20 Associate Academic Vice President ... Dr. Mark C. FORD
27 Chief Technology Officer ... Dr. Martin CROSSLAND
53 Dean School of Education ... Dr. Nancy DAMRON
66 Dean Sch Nursing/Health Sci ... Dr. Susan LARSON
50 Dean School of Business ... Mrs. Jamie MYRTLE
83 Dean Sch Behav Sci/Counseling ... Dr. Earl BLAND
49 Dean College Arts & Sciences ... Dr. Cindy PETERSON
06 Registrar ... Mr. James R. GARRISON
08 Director of the Library ... Mr. Bruce FLANDERS
26 Assoc VP University Advancement ... Mr. Tim KEETON
07 Interim Director of Admissions ... Ms. Lisa DOWNS
39 Director of Residential Life ... Mrs. Kristi KEETON
29 Director of Alumni ... Mr. Kevin S. GARBER
37 Director of Student Financial Svcs ... Mr. Perry DIEHM
41 Athletic Director ... Mr. Kevin L. STEELE
15 Director of Human Resources ... Ms. Nancy S. MERIMEE
27 Marketing Strategist ... Mrs. Kimberly CAMPBELL
18 Director of Facility Services ... Mr. Denis JOHNSON
40 Bookstore Manager ... Mr. Nikos KELLEPOURIS
19 Director of Campus Safety ... Mr. Emil F. SCHELLACK

National American University-Overland Park (A)

10310 Mastin Street, Overland Park KS 66212
Telephone: (913) 981-8700 　Identification: 770394
Accreditation: &NH, &MAC

† Main campus is National American University in Rapid City, SD.

National American University-Wichita (B)

7309 E 21st Street, Suite G40, Wichita KS 67206
Telephone: (316) 448-5400 　Identification: 770395
Accreditation: &NH, &MAC

† Main campus is National American University in Rapid City, SD.

National American University-Wichita West (C)

8428 W 13th Street N, Suite 120, Wichita KS 67212
Telephone: (316) 448-3150 　Identification: 770396
Accreditation: &NH

† Main campus is National American University in Rapid City, SD.

Neosho County Community College (D)

800 W 14th Street, Chanute KS 66720-2699
County: Neosho 　FICE Identification: 001936
Unit ID: 155566
Telephone: (620) 431-2820 　Carnegie Class: Assoc/Pub-R-M
FAX Number: (620) 431-0082 　Calendar System: Semester
URL: www.neosho.edu
Established: 1935 　Annual Undergrad Tuition & Fees (In-District): $2,430
Enrollment: 2,656 　Coed
Affiliation or Control: Local 　IRS Status: 501(c)3
Highest Offering: Associate Degree
Program: Occupational; 2-Year Principally Bachelor's Creditable
Accreditation: NH, ACBSP, ADNUR, CAHIIM, OTA, SURGT

01 President ... Dr. Brian L. INBODY
05 Vice President Student Learning ... Mr. James GENANDT
11 Vice President for Operations ... Mr. Benjamin J. SMITH
10 Chief Financial Officer ... Ms. Sondra K. SOLANDER
32 Dean of Students ... Mr. Jason KEGLER
51 Dean of Outreach and Workforce Dev ... Ms. Brenda L. KRUMM
12 Dean Ottawa Campus ... Mr. Dale E. ERNST
84 Dean of Enrollment Management ... Ms. Kerrie COOMES
15 Director of HR ... Ms. Terri DALE
106 Dean for Online Campus ... Ms. Marie GARDNER
13 Dean for Operations/CIO ... Mr. Kerry D. RANABARGAR
30 Director of Development/Alumni Rels ... Ms. Claudia CHRISTIANSEN
08 Director Library Services ... Ms. Susan D. WEISENBERGER
37 Director Student Financial Aid ... Ms. Kara B. HALE
66 Director of Nursing ... Ms. Pamela COVAULT
13 Director of Technology Services ... Mr. Jon SEIBERT
46 Director of Assessment/Research ... Ms. Sarah ROBB
41 Athletic Director ... Ms. Amber BURDGE
07 Director of Admissions ... Vacant
85 Dir International Student Services ... Ms. Sarah CADWALLADER
06 Registrar ... Ms. Susan HADDAN
09 Coordinator/Institutional Research ... Ms. LuAnn HAUSER
40 Chanute Bookstore Coordinator ... Ms. Mary Jo SECHLER
40 Ottawa Bookstore Coordinator ... Ms. Diane HOWELL
26 Advertising/Media Coordinator ... Ms. Nancy ISAAC
38 Director Student Counseling ... Vacant
39 Residence/Student Life Coordinator ... Ms. Allison OUELLETTE
04 Admin Asst to the President ... Ms. Denise GILMORE
88 Dir of Recruitment/College Relation ... Ms. Leslie BEDDO

Newman University (E)

3100 McCormick, Wichita KS 67213-2097
County: Sedgwick 　FICE Identification: 001939
Unit ID: 155335
Telephone: (316) 942-4291 　Carnegie Class: Master's L
FAX Number: (316) 942-4483 　Calendar System: Semester
URL: www.newmanu.edu
Established: 1933 　Annual Undergrad Tuition & Fees: $23,880
Enrollment: 3,108 　Coed
Affiliation or Control: Roman Catholic 　IRS Status: 501(c)3
Highest Offering: Master's
Program: Occupational; 2-Year Principally Bachelor's Creditable; Liberal Arts And General; Teacher Preparatory; Professional
Accreditation: NH, ANEST, COARC, NURSE, OTA, RAD, SW, TED

01 President ... Dr. Noreen CARROCCI
04 Exec Assistant to the President ... Ms. Tracy MCGAREY
05 Provost & Vice Pres Acad Affairs ... Dr. Michael AUSTIN
30 Vice Pres University Advancement ... Mr. Troy HORINE
10 Vice Pres Finance/Administration ... Ms. Jennifer GANTZ
15 Vice President Human Resources ... Ms. Rhonda CANTRELL
20 Assoc VP Acad Svcs/Student Dev ... Ms. Rosemary NIEDENS
42 Director of Campus Ministry ... Fr. Michael LINNEBUR
29 Director of Alumni Relations ... Ms. Sarah CUNDIFF
26 Director of Communications ... Ms. Kelly SNEDDEN
09 Director of Institutional Research ... Sr. JoAnn MARK, ASC
08 Library Director ... Mr. Joseph FORTE
06 Registrar ... Ms. Shirley RUEB
37 Director of Financial Aid ... Ms. Charly SMITH
41 Director of Athletics ... Mr. Victor TRILLI
40 Director of Bookstore ... Mr. Larry WILLIAMS
13 Chief Information Officer ... Mr. Icer VAUGHAN
19 Director of Safety & Security ... Mr. Richard OLIVERSON
21 Controller ... Mr. Don WIESNER
07 Dean of Admissions ... Mr. John CLAYTON
32 Dean of Students ... Ms. Laura HUPACH
58 Dean College of Grad/Cont Studies ... Dr. Audrey CURTIS HANE
49 Dean College of Undergrad Studies ... Dr. David SHUBERT

North Central Kansas Technical College (F)

PO Box 507, Beloit KS 67420-0507
County: Mitchell 　FICE Identification: 005265
Unit ID: 155593
Telephone: (785) 738-2276 　Carnegie Class: Assoc/Pub-R-S
FAX Number: (785) 738-2903 　Calendar System: Semester
URL: www.ncktc.edu
Established: 1964 　Annual Undergrad Tuition & Fees (In-District): $4,485
Enrollment: 819 　Coed
Affiliation or Control: State/Local 　IRS Status: 501(c)3
Highest Offering: Associate Degree
Program: Occupational; 2-Year Principally Bachelor's Creditable; Technical Emphasis
Accreditation: NH, ADNUR

01 President ... Mr. Eric BURKS
05 Dean of Instruction ... Mr. Corey ISBELL
11 Dean of Administrative Services ... Mrs. Brandi ZIMMER
66 Director of Nursing ... Mrs. Sandy GOTTSCHALK
06 Registrar ... Ms. Judy HEIDRICK
07 Director of Admissions ... Mr. David HUGHES
09 Coordinator Institutional Research ... Mrs. Jennifer BROWN
32 Dean of Student Services ... Mr. David HUGHES
37 Director Student Financial Aid ... Mr. Gary ODLE

North Central Kansas Technical College (G)

2205 Wheatland Avenue, Hays KS 67601
Telephone: (785) 625-2437 　Identification: 770259
Accreditation: &NH

† Main campus is North Central Kansas Technical College in Beloit, KS.

Northwest Kansas Technical College (H)

1209 Harrison Street, PO Box 668, Goodland KS 67735-3441
County: Sherman 　FICE Identification: 005267
Unit ID: 155618
Telephone: (785) 890-3641 　Carnegie Class: Assoc/Pub-R-S
FAX Number: (785) 899-5711 　Calendar System: Semester
URL: www.nwktc.edu
Established: 1964 　Annual Undergrad Tuition & Fees (In-District): $10,647
Enrollment: 562 　Coed
Affiliation or Control: State/Local 　IRS Status: 501(c)3
Highest Offering: Associate Degree
Program: Occupational; Technical Emphasis
Accreditation: NH, COARC, MAC

01 President ... Dr. Ed MILLS
05 Vice Pres Instruct & Student Svcs ... Ms. Brenda L. CHATFIELD
35 Asst Vice Pres of Student Affairs ... Ms. Reina BRANUM

Ottawa University (I)

1001 S Cedar Street, Ottawa KS 66067-3399
County: Franklin 　FICE Identification: 001937
Unit ID: 155627
Telephone: (785) 242-5200 　Carnegie Class: Bac/Diverse
FAX Number: (785) 229-1020 　Calendar System: Semester
URL: www.ottawa.edu
Established: 1865 　Annual Undergrad Tuition & Fees: $23,364
Enrollment: 944 　Coed
Affiliation or Control: American Baptist 　IRS Status: 501(c)3
Highest Offering: Master's
Program: Liberal Arts And General; Teacher Preparatory
Accreditation: NH, TED

01 President ... Mr. Kevin EICHNER
05 Univ Provost/Chief Academic Officer ... Dr. Terry HAINES
20 Vice Pres & Provost of the College ... Dr. Dennis TYNER
10 Vice Pres Administration/CFO ... Mr. J. Clark RIBORDY
26 VP & Chief Marketing Officer ... Ms. Nancy WINGER
30 Vice Pres University Advancement ... Mr. Paul BEAN
86 VP Regulatory/Governmental Affairs ... Dr. Donna LEVENE
09 Assoc VP Governmental/Reg Affairs ... Ms. Jan STONE
32 Dean Student Affairs ... Mr. Tom TALDO
84 Mgr New Student Enrollment Service ... Ms. Jessica HOMOLKA
06 University Registrar ... Ms. Karen ADAMS
21 Director Finance/Controller ... Ms. Noelle TESTA
21 Director Business Operations ... Mr. Thomas CORLEY
15 Director Human Resources ... Ms. Joanna WALTERS
37 Director Financial Aid ... Mr. Howard FISCHER
13 Director Information Technology ... Dr. Jack MAXWELL
29 Director Alumni Programs ... Ms. Nori HALE
08 Director Library Services ... Ms. Gloria CREED-DIKEOGU
41 Director Athletics ... Ms. Arabie CONNER
18 Chief Facilities/Physical Plant ... Mr. Herb ORR
04 Executive Assistant to President ... Ms. Gaynia MENNINGER
11 Chief Operations Officer ... Mr. Keith JOHNSON
20 Dean of Instruction ... Dr. Karen OHNESORGE
53 Dean School of Education ... Dr. Amy HOGAN
88 VP and COO APOS ... Mr. Shane SMEED
84 Enrollment Director Online ... Ms. Sarah TIPPING
50 Dean Angell Snyder Sch of Business ... Dr. Kirk WESSEL

† The Online division is included in this institution's Enrollment count.

Ottawa University Kansas City (J)

4370 W. 109th Street, Suite 200, Overland Park KS 66211-1302
Telephone: (913) 266-8600 　Identification: 666083
Accreditation: &NH

† Main campus is Ottawa University in Ottawa, KS.

Pinnacle Career Institute (K)

1601 W. 23rd Street, Ste 200, Lawrence KS 66046
County: Douglas 　FICE Identification: 026130
Unit ID: 367097
Telephone: (785) 841-9640 　Carnegie Class: Assoc/PrivFP
FAX Number: (785) 841-4854 　Calendar System: Quarter
URL: www.pcitraining.edu
Established: 1953 　Annual Undergrad Tuition & Fees: $13,470
Enrollment: 118 　Coed
Affiliation or Control: Proprietary 　IRS Status: Proprietary
Highest Offering: Associate Degree
Program: Occupational
Accreditation: ACICS

01 Executive Director ... Mr. Brian LAHARGOUE

Pittsburg State University (L)

1701 S Broadway, Pittsburg KS 66762-7500
County: Crawford 　FICE Identification: 001926
Unit ID: 155681
Telephone: (620) 231-7000 　Carnegie Class: Master's L
FAX Number: (620) 235-4080 　Calendar System: Semester
URL: www.pittstate.edu
Established: 1903 　Annual Undergrad Tuition & Fees (In-State): $5,906
Enrollment: 7,289 　Coed
Affiliation or Control: State 　IRS Status: 501(c)3
Highest Offering: Beyond Master's But Less Than Doctorate
Program: Liberal Arts And General; Teacher Preparatory; Professional
Accreditation: NH, BUS, CACREP, ENGT, MUS, NRPA, NURSE, SW, TED

01 President ... Dr. Steven A. SCOTT
05 Provost & VP for Academic Affairs ... Dr. Lynette OLSON
11 VP Administration & Campus Life ... Mr. John D. PATTERSON
30 Vice Pres University Advancement ... Dr. J. Bradford HODSON
06 Registrar ... Ms. Debbie GREVE
32 Assoc VP Campus Life/Auxil Svcs ... Dr. Steve ERWIN
88 Assoc VP for Communication & Mktg ... Mr. Chris KELLY
84 Assoc Vice Pres Enrollment Mgmt ... Dr. William IVY
51 Dean Graduate & Continuing Studies ... Dr. Pawan KAHOL
49 Dean of Arts & Sciences ... Dr. Karl KUNKEL
50 Dean of Business ... Dr. Paul GRIMES
53 Dean of Education ... Dr. Howard W. SMITH
72 Dean of Technology ... Dr. Bruce D. DALLMAN
08 Interim Dean of Library Services ... Mr. Randy ROBERTS
108 Director Assessment ... Dr. Patricia LINDLEY
26 Director of Media Relations ... Mr. Ron WOMBLE
29 Dir Alumni Rels/Constituent Svcs ... Ms. Johnna M. SCHREMMER
27 Chief Information Officer ... Ms. Angela NERIA
15 Director Human Resource Svcs/Budget ... Dr. Michele D. SEXTON
85 Director of International Affairs ... Dr. Cathy L. ARCUINO
04 Dir of Community & Govt Relations ... Mr. Shawn NACCARATO
18 Director of Trades & Landscape Svcs ... Mr. Tom AMERSHEK
18 Director Gen & Custodial Services ... Ms. Wanda ENDICOTT
19 Director of University Police ... Mr. Mike MCCRACKEN
22 Dir Equal Opportunity/Affirm Action ... Ms. Cindy JOHNSON
37 Director of Financial Aid ... Ms. Tammy HIGGINS
41 Dir of Intercollegiate Athletics ... Mr. James JOHNSON
07 Director of Admissions ... Ms. Melinda A. ROELFS
36 Director Career Services ... Ms. Mindy E. CLONINGER
09 Director of Institutional Research ... Dr. Dai LI
38 Dir University Counseling Services ... Dr. Steven MAYHEW
30 Director of University Development ... Ms. Kathleen FLANNERY

96 Director of Purchasing .... Mr. Jim HUGHES
28 Director of Diversity .... Ms. Deatrea ROSE
10 Controller .... Ms. Barbara J. WINTER

Pratt Community College (A)

348 NE SR 61, Pratt KS 67124-8432
County: Pratt FICE Identification: 001938
Unit ID: 155715
Telephone: (620) 672-5641 Carnegie Class: Assoc/Pub-R-S
FAX Number: (620) 672-5288 Calendar System: Semester
URL: www.prattcc.edu
Established: 1938 Annual Undergrad Tuition & Fees (In-District): $3,040
Enrollment: 965 Coed
Affiliation or Control: State/Local IRS Status: 501(c)3
Highest Offering: Associate Degree
Program: Occupational; 2-Year Principally Bachelor's Creditable
Accreditation: NH, ACBSP, ADNUR

01 President .... Dr. William A. WOJCIECHOWSKI
05 Vice President Instruction .... Dr. Joe VARRIENTOS
10 Vice President Finance/Operations .... Mr. Kent ADAMS
84 Vice Pres Student Enroll Management .... Ms. Lisa MILLER
66 Dean of Nursing .... Ms. Gail WITHERS
41 Director of Athletics .... Mr. Kurt MCAFEE
20 Dean of Academic Instruction .... Vacant
75 Dean of Technical Instruction .... Vacant
07 Director of Admissions .... Mr. Frank STAHL
06 Registrar .... Mr. Brian ELKINS
13 Director of Information Technology .... Mr. Jerry SANKO
37 Director of Financial Aid .... Ms. Nikki POWELL
30 Director Development .... Vacant
08 Dir Linda Hunt Memorial Library .... Ms. Sandra WAGNER
16 Director of Personnel .... Ms. Rita PINKALL
38 Director Student Success Center .... Ms. Amy JACKSON
21 Controller .... Ms. Christy ALLEY
18 Director of Buildings & Grounds .... Mr. Dan PETZ
39 Director of Residence Life .... Vacant
26 Chief Public Relations Officer .... Vacant

Rasmussen College Topeka (B)

620 SW Governor View, Topeka KS 66606
Telephone: (785) 228-7320 Identification: 770490
Accreditation: &NH

† Main campus is Rasmussen College Corporate Office in Bloomington, MN.

Rasmussen College-Kansas City/Overland Park (C)

11600 College Boulevard, Overland Park KS 66210
Telephone: (913) 491-7870 Identification: 770489
Accreditation: &NH

† Main campus is Rasmussen College Corporate Office in Bloomington, MN.

Saint Paul School of Theology (D)

4370 West 109th Street, Suite 300,
Overland Park KS 66211
County: Johnson FICE Identification: 002509
Unit ID: 179317
Telephone: (816) 483-9600 Carnegie Class: Spec/Faith
FAX Number: (816) 483-9605 Calendar System: Other
URL: www.spst.edu
Established: 1958 Annual Graduate Tuition & Fees: $18,150
Enrollment: 196 Coed
Affiliation or Control: United Methodist IRS Status: 501(c)3
Highest Offering: Doctorate; No Undergraduates
Program: Professional; Religious Emphasis
Accreditation: NH, THEOL

01 President .... Dr. Myron F. MCCOY
05 VP Academic Affairs/Dean .... Dr. Harold WASHINGTON
30 Vice President for Advancement .... Mr. David SISNEY
10 Chief Financial Officer .... Ms. Laura SNOW
12 Academic Dean for OCU Extens Site .... Dr. Elaine ROBINSON
08 Librarian .... Dr. Logan S. WRIGHT
07 Director of Admissions .... Mr. Philip GEBAUER
04 Executive Assistant to President .... Ms. Leigh PRECISE
26 Director of Communications .... Ms. Heather CHAMBERLIN

Salina Area Technical College (E)

2562 Centennial Road, Salina KS 67401
County: Saline FICE Identification: 005499
Unit ID: 155830
Telephone: (785) 309-3100 Carnegie Class: Not Classified
FAX Number: (785) 309-3101 Calendar System: Semester
URL: www.salinatech.edu
Established: 1965 Annual Undergrad Tuition & Fees (In-District): $4,019
Enrollment: 432 Coed
Affiliation or Control: State/Local IRS Status: 501(c)3
Highest Offering: Associate Degree
Program: Occupational
Accreditation: @NH, DA

01 President .... Mr. Gregg R. GOODE
06 Registrar .... Ms. Denise HOEFFNER

Seward County Community College/Area Technical School (F)

1801 N Kansas Avenue, Liberal KS 67901-2054
County: Seward FICE Identification: 008228
Unit ID: 155858
Telephone: (620) 624-1951 Carnegie Class: Assoc/Pub-R-S
FAX Number: (620) 417-1169 Calendar System: Semester
URL: www.sccc.edu
Established: 1967 Annual Undergrad Tuition & Fees (In-District): $2,220
Enrollment: 1,968 Coed
Affiliation or Control: State/Local IRS Status: 501(c)3
Highest Offering: Associate Degree
Program: Occupational; 2-Year Principally Bachelor's Creditable
Accreditation: NH, ACBSP, ADNUR, COARC, MLTAD, SURGT

01 President .... Dr. Duane M. DUNN
05 Dean of Academic Affairs .... Ms. Cynthia K. RAPP
10 Dean of Finance & Operations .... Mr. Dennis M. SANDER
32 Dean of Student Services .... Ms. Celeste DONOVAN
88 Dean of Career and Technical Ed .... Dr. Janese V. THATCHER
06 Registrar .... Ms. Alaina M. RICE
13 Director of Information Technology .... Mr. Mark W. MERRIHEW
37 Financial Aid Director .... Mrs. Donna M. FISHER
26 Dir of Public and Alumni Relations .... Mrs. Andrea G. YOXALL
50 Director of Business & Industry .... Mrs. Norma Jean DODGE
24 Director of Multi-media .... Mr. Doug BROWNE
08 Director of Library .... Mr. Matthew PANNKUK
41 Athletic Director .... Mr. Galen W. MCSPADDEN
18 Dir of Buildings Grounds & Security .... Mr. Roger SCHEIB
40 Director of Bookstore .... Ms. Jerri L. LYDDON
30 Director of Development/Alumni Rels .... Ms. Tammy DOLL
39 Student Housing Manager .... Ms. Kate A. MULLIGAN
09 Institutional Research/Data Analyst .... Ms. Teresa WEHMEIER
21 Fiscal Officer/Admin Assistant .... Mr. Mike BAILEY
19 Safety and Security Supervisor .... Mr. Dennis K. MULANAX
15 Director of Human Resources .... Ms. Deborah WEILERT
07 Admissions Coordinator/Events .... Ms. Nereida LUJAN
07 Admissions Coordinator/Recruiting .... Ms. Alyson CALL
36 Career Services and Admissions Coor .... Ms. Veronica THOR
38 Counselor/Retention Specialist .... Ms. Rhonda L. KINSER
35 Director Student Activities .... Mr. Wade LYON
04 Adm Asst to Pres & Brd of Trustees .... Mrs. Pamela M. PERKINS
66 Dir of Nursing and Allied Health .... Mrs. Veda KING
75 Div Chair of Industrial Technology .... Mr. Larry A. MCLEMORE

Southwestern College (G)

100 College Street, Winfield KS 67156-2499
County: Cowley FICE Identification: 001940
Unit ID: 155900
Telephone: (620) 229-6000 Carnegie Class: Master's M
FAX Number: (620) 229-6224 Calendar System: Semester
URL: www.sckans.edu
Established: 1885 Annual Undergrad Tuition & Fees: $23,736
Enrollment: 1,637 Coed
Affiliation or Control: United Methodist IRS Status: 501(c)3
Highest Offering: Doctorate
Program: Liberal Arts And General; Teacher Preparatory; Professional
Accreditation: NH, MUS, NURSE, TED

01 President .... Dr. William R. MERRIMAN, JR.
05 Vice President Academic Affairs .... Dr. James A. SHEPPARD
10 Vice President Finance .... Ms. Sheila R. KRUG
32 Vice President Student Life .... Dr. Dawn E. PLEAS-BAILEY
107 Vice President Professional Studies .... Ms. Pamela MONACO
45 VP Planning/New Programs .... Dr. Stephen K. WILKE
30 Vice Pres Institutional Advancement .... Vacant
26 Vice President Communications .... Ms. Sara S. WEINERT
13 Vice Pres Information Technology .... Mr. Ben LIM
35 Dean of Student Life .... Mr. Dan FALK
29 Director Alumni Programs .... Ms. Susan G. LOWE
44 Director Development .... Vacant
44 Director Major Gifts .... Vacant
20 Director Academic Affairs .... Ms. Lolita REPP
08 Library Director .... Ms. Dalene MCDONALD
84 Vice President for Enrollment Mgmt .... Ms. Marla SEXSON
37 Director Financial Aid .... Ms. Brenda D. HICKS
06 Registrar .... Ms. Donna BOESE
35 Director Campus Life .... Ms. Lai-L CLEMONS
09 Director of Institutional Research .... Ms. Margaret A. ROBINSON
41 Director Athletics .... Mr. David DENLY
42 Campus Minister .... Ms. Ashlee E. ALLEY
87 Director Human Resources .... Ms. Lonnie BOYD
96 Director of Purchasing .... Mr. David H. DOLSEN
36 Director Advising/Student Success .... Ms. Tami P. PULLINS
04 Administrative Asst to President .... Ms. Skye BROWNING

Southwestern College Wichita East (H)

2040 S Rock Road, Wichita KS 67207
Telephone: (316) 684-5335 Identification: 770260
Accreditation: &NH

† Main campus is Southwestern College in Winfield, KS.

Sterling College (I)

125 W Cooper Street, Sterling KS 67579-1533
County: Rice FICE Identification: 001945
Unit ID: 155937
Telephone: (620) 278-2173 Carnegie Class: Bac/Diverse
FAX Number: (620) 278-4411 Calendar System: 4/1/4
URL: www.sterling.edu
Established: 1887 Annual Undergrad Tuition & Fees: $21,200
Enrollment: 653 Coed
Affiliation or Control: Presbyterian Church (U.S.A.) IRS Status: 501(c)3
Highest Offering: Baccalaureate
Program: Liberal Arts And General; Teacher Preparatory
Accreditation: NH, TED

01 President .... Mr. Scott RICH
05 Vice President Academic Affairs .... Dr. Greg KERR
30 Vice President for Inst Advancement .... Dr. Marvin DEWEY
10 Vice President Financial Services .... Mr. Scott RICH
32 Vice President Student Life .... Mrs. Tina WOHLER
27 Dir Marketing/Pres Communications .... Ms. Karin SWIHART
06 Registrar .... Ms. Janet CAYWOOD
08 Head Librarian .... Ms. Brooke SUTTON
37 Director of Financial Aid .... Ms. Mitzi SUHLER
29 Director of Alumni/Parent Services .... Ms. Amy THOMPSON
41 Athletic Director .... Mr. Gary KEMPF
20 Director Academic Support .... Mrs. Carol LUDWICK
44 Director of Annual Giving .... Ms. Sheila BIRD
18 Chief Facilities/Physical Plant .... Mr. Clay THOMAS
36 Director Student Placement .... Ms. Lisa PARSON
38 Director Student Counseling .... Ms. Teri ANDERSON
21 Associate Business Officer .... Ms. Michelle HALL
26 Public Relations Coordinator .... Ms. Ashley BARNES

Tabor College (J)

400 S Jefferson Street, Hillsboro KS 67063-1753
County: Marion FICE Identification: 001946
Unit ID: 155973
Telephone: (620) 947-3121 Carnegie Class: Bac/Diverse
FAX Number: (620) 947-2607 Calendar System: 4/1/4
URL: www.tabor.edu
Established: 1908 Annual Undergrad Tuition & Fees: $22,730
Enrollment: 768 Coed
Affiliation or Control: Mennonite Brethren Church IRS Status: 501(c)3
Highest Offering: Master's
Program: Liberal Arts And General; Teacher Preparatory
Accreditation: NH, MUS, NURSE, TED

01 President .... Dr. Jules GLANZER
05 Vice President Academic Affairs .... Dr. Frank JOHNSON
10 Sr Vice President Business/Finance .... Mr. Kirby FADENRECHT
30 Vice President Advancement .... Mr. Ronald BRAUN
41 Vice President of Athletics .... Mr. Rusty ALLEN
32 Vice President of Student Life .... Dr. Jim PAULUS
06 Registrar .... Ms. Deanne DUERKSEN
08 Director of Library Services .... Vacant
84 Director Enrollment Management .... Mr. Rusty ALLEN
37 Dir of Student Financial Services .... Mr. Scott FRANZ
29 Director Alumni & Parent Relations .... Ms. Marlene FAST
27 Director of Communications .... Mrs. Beth RIFFEL
18 Director Facilities/Physical Plant .... Mr. Doug GRABER
35 Director Student Success .... Vacant
09 Institutional Research .... Mrs. Deborah PENN
13 Director of Information Services .... Mr. Chris GLANZER
27 Chief Information Officer .... Mrs. Joy MARK
15 Human Resources Coordinator .... Mrs. Ruth FUNK

University of Kansas Edwards Campus (K)

12600 Quivira Road, Overland Park KS 66213
Telephone: (913) 897-8400 Identification: 770261
Accreditation: &NH

† Main campus is University of Kansas Main Campus in Lawrence, KS.

University of Kansas Main Campus (L)

1450 Jayhawk Boulevard, Room 230,
Lawrence KS 66045-7418
County: Douglas FICE Identification: 001948
Unit ID: 155317
Telephone: (785) 864-3131 Carnegie Class: RU/VH
FAX Number: (785) 864-4120 Calendar System: Semester
URL: www.ku.edu
Established: 1866 Annual Undergrad Tuition & Fees (In-State): $9,279
Enrollment: 27,939 Coed
Affiliation or Control: State IRS Status: 501(c)3
Highest Offering: Doctorate
Program: Liberal Arts And General; Teacher Preparatory; Professional
Accreditation: NH, ART, AUD, BUS, BUSA, CEA, CLPSY, COPSY, CS, ENG, HSA, IPSY, JOUR, LAW, MUS, PH, PHAR, PLNG, SCPSY, SP, SPAA, SW, TED

01 Chancellor .... Dr. Bernadette GRAY-LITTLE
05 Exec Vice Chancellor/Provost .... Dr. Jeffrey S. VITTER
12 Vice Chancellor/Dean Edwards Campus .... Dr. David COOK
26 Vice Chancellor for Public Affairs .... Dr. Timothy CABONI
04 Executive Assistant to Chancellor .... Ms. Mary G. BURG
43 General Counsel .... Mr. James P. POTTORFF, JR.
20 Sr Vice Provost Academic Affairs .... Dr. Sara ROSEN
20 Vice Provost .... Dr. Mary Lee HUMMERT
20 Vice Provost .... Ms. Diane H. GODDARD
32 Vice Provost for Student Affairs .... Dr. Tammara DURHAM
46 Vice Provost Research/Grad Studies .... Dr. Steven F. WARREN
28 Vice Provost Diversity & Equity .... Vacant
13 Chief Information Officer .... Mr. Bob LIM
45 Asst Vice Provost Research .... Ms. Kristi M. BILLINGER
58 Assoc VP/Dean Research & Grad Stds .... Dr. Thomas W. HEILKE

104 Assoc VP International Programs .... Ms. Susan GRONBECK-TEDESCO
96 Assoc Vice Provost of Purchasing .... Mr. Barry K. SWANSON
84 AVP Recruitment/Enrollment .... Dr. Matt MELVIN
30 President Endowment Association .... Mr. Dale SEUFERLING
29 President Alumni Association .... Mr. Kevin J. CORBETT
07 Director Admissions .... Ms. Lisa P. KRESS
10 Chief Business/Financial Plng Ofcr .... Ms. Theresa K. GORDZICA
21 Comptroller .... Ms. Katrina M. YOAKUM
21 Director Budget Office .... Mr. Richard L. MCKINNEY
06 University Registrar .... Ms. Cindy DERRITT
09 Univ Director Inst Research Plng .... Ms. Deborah J. TEETER
15 Director Human Resources .... Ms. Ola FAUCHER
85 Director International Student Svcs .... Dr. Chuck OLCESE
38 Director Counseling/Psych Services .... Dr. Michael LYNCH MAESTAS
18 Director Design & Construction Mgmt .... Mr. James E. MODIG
37 Director Student Financial Aid .... Ms. Brenda MAIGAARD
36 Director Career/Employment Svcs .... Mr. David GASTON
41 Director Intercollegiate Athletics .... Dr. Sheahon ZENGER
18 Director Facilities Service .... Mr. Jay PHILLIPS
22 Director Inst Oppty & Access .... Ms. Jane MCQUEENY
88 Director Multicultural Affairs .... Mr. Blane HARDING
23 Director Student Health Services .... Ms. Carol SEAGER
24 Director Media Services .... Dr. Susan M. ZVACEK
39 Director Housing .... Dr. Diana ROBERTSON
86 Director State Relations .... Ms. Kathy DAMRON
92 Director Honors Program .... Dr. Kathleen A. MCCLUSKEY-FAWCETT
86 Director Federal Relations .... Mr. Jack CLINE
40 Director Bookstores .... Ms. Estella MCCOLLUM
51 Exec Dir Continuing Education .... Mr. Frederick W. PAWLICKI
25 Manager Contract Negotiations .... Ms. Lucille MARINO
91 Project Coord Information Systems .... Mr. David M. GARDNER
49 Dean Liberal Arts/Science .... Dr. Danny J. ANDERSON
61 Dean of Law .... Mr. Stephen W. MAZZA
54 Dean of Engineering .... Dr. Michael BRANICKY
48 Dean Architecture/Design/Planning .... Mr. John C. GAUNT
50 Dean of Business .... Dr. Neeli BENDAPUDI
67 Dean of Pharmacy .... Dr. Kenneth L. AUDUS
60 Dean of Journalism .... Dr. Ann M. BRILL
53 Dean of Education .... Dr. Rick GINSBERG
64 Dean of Music .... Dr. Robert L. WALZEL, JR.
70 Dean of Social Welfare .... Dr. Mary Ellen KONDRAT
08 Dean of Library .... Ms. Lorraine J. HARICOMBE
57 Assoc Dean School of the Arts .... Ms. Elizabeth KOWALCHUK

† Medical Center and Main campus enrollments should be combined for the total institution enrollment.

University of Kansas Medical Center (A)

3901 Rainbow Boulevard, Kansas City KS 66160-0001
Telephone: (913) 588-5000 FICE Identification: 024579
Accreditation: &NH, ANEST, CAHIIM, COARC, CYTO, DIETI, DMOLS, DMS, MED, MIDWF, MT, NMT, NURSE, OT, PTA

† Main campus is University of Kansas Main Campus in Lawrence, KS.

University of Saint Mary (B)

4100 S 4th Street Trafficway, Leavenworth KS 66048-5082
County: Leavenworth FICE Identification: 001943
Unit ID: 155812
Telephone: (913) 682-5151 Carnegie Class: Master's M
FAX Number: (913) 758-6140 Calendar System: Semester
URL: www.stmary.edu
Established: 1923 Annual Undergrad Tuition & Fees: $22,600
Enrollment: 1,187 Coed
Affiliation or Control: Roman Catholic IRS Status: 501(c)3
Highest Offering: Doctorate
Program: Liberal Arts And General; Teacher Preparatory; Professional
Accreditation: NH, IACBE, NURSE, @PTA, TED

01 President .... Dr. Diane STEELE
05 Academic Vice President .... Dr. Bryan LEBEAU
10 Vice President for Finance .... Mr. Dale CULVER
30 Director of Development .... Ms. Karolyn DREILING
26 Director Marketing & Communication .... Mr. John SHULTZ
32 Vice President for Student Life .... Dr. Wendi SANTEE
84 Director of Enrollment Management .... Mr. Ken WUERZEBERGER
06 Interim Registrar .... Ms. Wanda OWENS
08 Director of the Library .... Ms. Penny LONERGAN
09 Data Analyst .... Ms. Veronica DONOVAN
29 Alumni and Events Coordinator .... Ms. Sharon CLAY
37 Director of Financial Aid .... Ms. Annissa EPPERSON
42 Director of Campus Ministry .... Sr. Julie MARSH
44 Development Officer Planned Giving .... Ms. Jane LIEBERT
41 Athletic Director .... Mr. Rob MILLER
15 Director Human Resources .... Ms. Teresa LEE
39 Director of Residence Life .... Mr. Josh CASE
21 Controller .... Ms. Sherry WELLS
38 Counselor .... Ms. Deborah SHADDY
18 Plant Manager .... Mr. Mark GIESEMAN
40 Bookstore Manager .... Ms. Cynthia FORRESTER
12 Site Coordinator Johnson County .... Ms. Patricia HOWARD
14 Coordinator of Computer Operations .... Mr. Kevin GANTT
04 Executive Administrative Assistant .... Ms. Kathryn MUSTAIN
35 Director of Student Activities .... Ms. Lisa POTOKA

Vatterott College - Wichita (C)

8853 East 37th Street North, Wichita KS 67226-2018
Telephone: (316) 634-0066 Identification: 666583
Accreditation: ACCSC

† Main campus is Vatterott College-NorthPark in Berkeley, MO.

Washburn University (D)

1700 SW College Avenue, Topeka KS 66621-0001
County: Shawnee FICE Identification: 001949
Unit ID: 156082
Telephone: (785) 670-1010 Carnegie Class: Master's M
FAX Number: (785) 670-1089 Calendar System: Semester
URL: www.washburn.edu
Established: 1865 Annual Undergrad Tuition & Fees (In-District): $5,774
Enrollment: 7,204 Coed
Affiliation or Control: Local IRS Status: 501(c)3
Highest Offering: Doctorate
Program: Liberal Arts And General; Teacher Preparatory; Professional
Accreditation: NH, ART, BUS, CAHIIM, COARC, DMS, LAW, MUS, NURSE, OTA, PTAA, RAD, SW, TED

01 President .... Dr. Jerry B. FARLEY
05 Vice President Acad Affairs .... Dr. Randall G. PEMBROOK
10 Vice Pres Admin & Treasurer .... Mr. Rick L. ANDERSON
32 Vice President for Student Life .... Dr. Denise OTTINGER
04 Special Assistant to the President .... Dr. Cynthia A. HORNBERGER
84 Director Enrollment Management .... Mr. Richard W. LIEDTKE
43 University Legal Counsel .... Ms. Lisa R. JONES
20 Assoc Vice Pres Acad Affairs .... Dr. Nancy A. TATE
30 President WU Foundation .... Dr. Juliann MAZACHEK
06 Registrar .... Dr. Carla RASCH
08 Dean of Libraries .... Dr. Alan BEARMAN
35 Dean of Students .... Mr. Meredith KIDD
37 Director Student Financial Aid .... Ms. Gail PALMER
07 Director of Admissions .... Ms. Kris KLIMA
15 Director of Human Resources .... Ms. Deborah D. MOORE
90 Director Info Systems & Services .... Mr. Floyd DAVENPORT
09 Director Institutional Research .... Ms. Melodie E. CHRISTAL
49 Interim Dean College Arts/Sciences .... Dr. Laura STEPHENSON
88 Interim Dean School Applied Studies .... Dr. Pat MUNZER
61 Dean School of Law .... Mr. Thomas J. ROMIG
50 Dean School of Business .... Dr. David SOLLARS
66 Dean School of Nursing .... Dr. Monica S. SCHEIBMEIR
41 Athletic Director .... Mr. Loren FERRE
35 Director Student Services .... Ms. Jeanne D. KESSLER
22 Interim Director Equal Opportunity .... Mr. Ken HACKLER
18 Int Director Facilities Services .... Mr. Ed SCHMIDT
23 Director Health Services .... Dr. Shirley DINKEL
29 Alumni Director .... Ms. Susie HOFFMANN
96 Director of Purchasing .... Mr. Mel RAGAR
92 Dean Honors Program .... Dr. Michael J. MCGUIRE
88 Assistant Dean of Student Success .... Dr. John DAHLSTRAND
39 Director Student Housing .... Ms. Mindy P. RENDON
40 Director Bookstore .... Ms. Kay FARLEY
35 Director Student Activities .... Ms. Jessica BARRACLOUGH
38 Director Student Counseling .... Ms. Marilynn KOELLIKER
26 Chief Public Relations Officer .... Ms. Dena ANSON
36 Director Student Placement .... Mr. Kent MCANALLY

Wichita Area Technical College (E)

4004 N Webb Road, Wichita KS 67226-8101
County: Sedgwick FICE Identification: 005498
Unit ID: 156107
Telephone: (316) 677-9400 Carnegie Class: Assoc/Pub-U-MC
FAX Number: (316) 677-9510 Calendar System: Semester
URL: www.watc.edu
Established: 1965 Annual Undergrad Tuition & Fees (In-District): $6,634
Enrollment: 2,677 Coed
Affiliation or Control: State/Local IRS Status: 501(c)3
Highest Offering: Associate Degree
Program: 2-Year Principally Bachelor's Creditable; Technical Emphasis
Accreditation: NH, DA, MAC, PNUR, SURGT

01 President .... Dr. Anthony G. KINKEL
05 Vice Pres Academic Affairs .... Ms. Sheree UTASH
10 Vice Pres Finance/Administration .... Mr. Chris MARTIN
26 Vice Pres Marketing/Student Svcs .... Mr. Joe ONTJES
30 Exec Dir Advancements/Workforce Dev .... Mr. Jim FLY
13 Exec Dir Tech/Instl Effectiveness .... Mr. Randy ROEBUCK
15 Exec Director Human Resources .... Ms. Judy MOUNT
06 Registrar .... Ms. Willow DEAN

Wichita State University (F)

1845 N Fairmount, Wichita KS 67260-0001
County: Sedgwick FICE Identification: 001950
Unit ID: 156125
Telephone: (316) 978-3456 Carnegie Class: RU/H
FAX Number: (316) 978-3770 Calendar System: Semester
URL: www.wichita.edu
Established: 1895 Annual Undergrad Tuition & Fees (In-State): $6,929
Enrollment: 14,972 Coed
Affiliation or Control: State IRS Status: 501(c)3
Highest Offering: Doctorate
Program: Liberal Arts And General; Teacher Preparatory; Professional
Accreditation: NH, ARCPA, ART, AUD, BUS, BUSA, CLPSY, DANCE, DENT, DH, ENG, IPSY, MT, MUS, NURSE, #PTA, SP, SPAA, SW, TED

01 President .... Dr. John W. BARDO
05 VP Academic Affairs .... Dr. Anthony VIZZINI
11 VP Administration & Finance .... Ms. Mary L. HERRIN
32 VP Campus Life/Univ Relations .... Dr. Wade A. ROBINSON
43 VP and General Counsel .... Mr. Ted D. AYRES
26 Assoc VP University Relations .... Mr. Barth A. HAGUE
20 Assoc VP Academic Affairs .... Dr. David WRIGHT
20 Senior Assoc VP Academic Affairs .... Dr. Richard D. MUMA
27 VP Information Technologies .... Dr. Ravi PENDSE
20 Associate VP Academic Affairs .... Dr. Linnea GLENMAYE
46 VP Research & Technology Transfer .... Dr. John S. TOMBLIN
49 Dean Liberal Arts & Sciences .... Dr. Ronald R. MATSON
50 Dean Barton School of Business .... Dr. Cindy CLAYCOMB
53 Dean Education .... Dr. Shirley LEFEVER-DAVIS
54 Dean Engineering .... Dr. Vish PRASAD
57 Dean Fine Arts .... Dr. Rodney E. MILLER
76 Dean Health Professions .... Dr. Keith PICKUS
58 Dean Graduate School .... Dr. Abu MASUD
08 Dean Libraries .... Dr. Don GILSTRAP
84 Dean Enrollment Services .... Ms. Christine SCHNEIKART-LUEBBE
86 Exec Director Government Relations .... Mr. Andrew SCHLAPP
24 Dir Media Resources Center .... Ms. Tonya WITHERSPOON
29 CEO & President Alumni Association .... Ms. Deborah KENNEDY
41 Athletic Director .... Dr. Eric L. SEXTON
88 Director Creative Services .... Mr. Craig LINDEMAN
15 Director Human Resources .... Ms. Frankie M. BROWN
21 Director Budgets .... Mr. Paul F. WERNER
06 Registrar .... Ms. Gina D. CRABTREE
07 Director Admissions .... Mr. Bobby GANDU
37 Director Financial Aid .... Ms. Deborah BYERS
36 Director Placement/Career Services .... Ms. Jill M. PLETCHER
38 Director Counseling & Testing .... Dr. Maureen DASEY-MORALES
18 Director Physical Plant .... Mr. Woodrow DEPONTIER
45 Director Facilities Planning .... Mr. James FREED
19 Campus Police Chief .... Ms. Sara B. MORRIS
23 Director Student Health Services .... Ms. Camille CHILDERS
39 Director Stdnt Housing & Resid Life .... Mr. Steve M. LARSON
28 Int Director Multicultural Affairs .... Dr. Wade ROBINSON
40 Manager Bookstore .... Mr. Kevin J. KONDA
21 Controller .... Mr. Steven D. LAFEVER
42 Campus Minister .... Rev. Christopher ESHELMAN
96 Director of Purchasing .... Mr. Steven WHITE
102 Foundation CEO & President .... Dr. Elizabeth KING
22 Director of EEO .... Vacant

Wichita Technical Institute (G)

2051 South Meridian, Wichita KS 67213-1927
County: Sedgwick FICE Identification: 010503
Unit ID: 156134
Telephone: (316) 943-2241 Carnegie Class: Not Classified
FAX Number: (316) 943-5438 Calendar System: Quarter
URL: www.wti.edu
Established: Annual Undergrad Tuition & Fees: $19,540
Enrollment: 1,166 Coed
Affiliation or Control: Proprietary IRS Status: Proprietary
Highest Offering: Associate Degree
Program: Occupational
Accreditation: ACCSC

Wright Career College (H)

10700 Metcalf Avenue, Overland Park KS 66210
FICE Identification: 025909
Unit ID: 406200
Telephone: (913) 385-7700 Carnegie Class: Assoc/PrivNFP
FAX Number: (913) 647-8073 Calendar System: Other
URL: www.wrightcc.edu
Established: 1997 Annual Undergrad Tuition & Fees: N/A
Enrollment: 1,837 Coed
Affiliation or Control: Independent Non-Profit IRS Status: 501(c)3
Highest Offering: Baccalaureate
Program: Occupational
Accreditation: ACICS

01 Campus Director .... Ms. Rachelle BUTTS

Wright Career College (I)

7700 East Kellogg, Wichita KS 67207
Telephone: (913) 381-2577 Identification: 770721
Accreditation: ACICS

† Main campus is Wright Career College in Overland Park, KS.

KENTUCKY

Alice Lloyd College (J)

Purpose Road, Pippa Passes KY 41844-9703
County: Knott FICE Identification: 001951
Unit ID: 156189
Telephone: (606) 368-2101 Carnegie Class: Bac/Diverse
FAX Number: (606) 368-6212 Calendar System: Semester
URL: www.alc.edu
Established: 1923 Annual Undergrad Tuition & Fees: $10,620
Enrollment: 608 Coed
Affiliation or Control: Independent Non-Profit IRS Status: 501(c)3
Highest Offering: Baccalaureate
Program: Liberal Arts And General; Teacher Preparatory
Accreditation: SC

01 President .... Dr. Joe A. STEPP
03 Executive Vice President .... Dr. Jim STEPP

05 Vice President Academic Affairs ... Dr. Claude CRUM
10 Vice President of Business Affairs ... Mr. David JOHNSON
32 Dean of Students & Community Life ... Mr. Scott CORNETT
07 Director of Admissions ... Ms. Angela PHIPPS
06 Registrar ... Mrs. Thelmarie THORNSBERRY
08 Director of Library ... Mr. Andrew BUSROE
37 Director of Financial Aid ... Mrs. Jacqueline STEWART
88 Director of Student Work Program ... Mr. Kerry RATLIFF
53 Director of Teacher Education ... Dr. Sherry LONG
18 Director of Physical Plant ... Mr. Ryan GIBSON
39 Director of Student Housing ... Mr. John MILLS
29 Director of Alumni Relations ... Mrs. Teresa GRENDER
35 Director of Student Activities ... Ms. Christine STUMBO
26 Dir of Marketing & Communications ... Mrs. Tiffany COMBS
09 Director of Institutional Research ... Dr. Sherry LONG
30 Director of Development ... Mrs. Margo SPARKMAN

† Cost of tuition is guaranteed for students from 108 county territories.

Asbury Theological Seminary (A)

204 N Lexington Avenue, Wilmore KY 40390-1199
County: Jessamine FICE Identification: 001953
Unit ID: 156222
Telephone: (859) 858-3581 Carnegie Class: Spec/Faith
FAX Number: N/A Calendar System: 4/1/4
URL: www.asburyseminary.edu
Established: 1923 Annual Graduate Tuition & Fees: $542
Enrollment: 1,512 Coed
Affiliation or Control: Independent Non-Profit IRS Status: 501(c)3
Highest Offering: Doctorate; No Undergraduates
Program: Professional
Accreditation: SC, THEOL

01 President ... Dr. Timothy C. TENNENT
03 Vice President/COO ... Mr. Robert S. LANDREBE
05 Provost/VP Academic for Affairs ... Dr. Douglas K. MATTHEWS
10 Vice President for Finance ... Mr. Bryan P. BLANKENSHIP
30 Vice President for Advancement ... Mr. Jay MANSUR
31 Vice Pres Community Formation ... Dr. Marilyn ELLIOTT
84 Vice Pres Enrollment Management ... Mr. Kevin BISH
13 Chief Technology Officer ... Mr. Patrick GARDELLA
06 Registrar ... Vacant
07 Director of Admissions ... Mrs. Carolyn CLAYTON
37 Director of Student Financial Aid ... Mrs. Jenny BURKHART
18 Director of Physical Plant ... Mr. Lanny SPEARS
09 Dir of Institutional Effectiveness ... Dr. Alexandra HENCHY
15 Director of Human Resources ... Mrs. Barbara ANTROBUS
29 Director Alumni Relations ... Ms. Tammy CESSNA
73 Dean School of Theology & Formation ... Dr. James THOBABEN
88 Dean Beeson Center ... Dr. Tom TUMBLIN
88 Dean ESJ School World of Missions ... Dr. Gregg OKESSON
88 Dean School Biblical Interpretation ... Dr. David BAUER
88 Dean School of Practical Theology ... Dr. Anne GATOBU
88 Dean Advanced Research Programs ... Dr. Lalsangkima PACHUAU

Asbury University (B)

1 Macklem Drive, Wilmore KY 40390-1198
County: Jessamine FICE Identification: 001952
Unit ID: 156213
Telephone: (859) 858-3511 Carnegie Class: Bac/Diverse
FAX Number: (859) 858-3921 Calendar System: Semester
URL: www.asbury.edu
Established: 1890 Annual Undergrad Tuition & Fees: $32,038
Enrollment: 1,750 Coed
Affiliation or Control: Independent Non-Profit IRS Status: 501(c)3
Highest Offering: Master's
Program: Liberal Arts And General; Teacher Preparatory
Accreditation: SC, MUS, SW, TED

01 President ... Dr. Sandra C. GRAY
05 Provost ... Dr. Jon S. KULAGA
10 Vice Pres Business Affairs & Treas ... Dr. Charlie D. FISKEAUX
84 Vice Pres of Enrollment Management ... Dr. Mark J. TROYER
32 Vice Pres Student Dev/Dean Students ... Dr. Douglas A. WILCOXSON
30 Vice President for Inst Advancement ... Mr. Charles SHEPARD
11 Asst Vice President Operations ... Mr. Glenn R. HAMILTON
20 Academic Dean ... Dr. Bonnie BANKER
49 Dir of College of Arts & Sciences ... Dr. Stephen K. CLEMENTS
53 Director of School of Education ... Dr. Sherry POWERS
60 Dir of School of Communication Arts ... Dr. James R. OWENS
58 Dir of School of Grad & Prof Stud ... Dr. William HALL, JR.
51 Dir of Adult Professional Studies ... Mr. T. Joshua FEE
106 Director of Online Education ... Mrs. Sara PORTER
44 Senior Advancement Director ... Rev. Stuart A. SMITH
37 Director of Financial Aid ... Mr. Ronald M. ANDERSON
42 Assoc Dean for Campus Ministries ... Rev. Gregory K. HASELOFF
39 Assoc Dean for Residence Life ... Mr. Joe W. BRUNER
06 Registrar ... Mrs. Sheryl VOIGTS
29 Dir of Alumni Relations/Parents Pgm ... Miss Carolyn L. RIDLEY
08 Director of Library Services ... Mr. Morgan A. TRACY
13 Director of Information Services ... Mr. Paul J. DUPREE
07 Director of Admissions ... Mrs. Lisa D. HARPER
26 Dir of Marketing & Communications ... Mr. Brad JOHNSON
18 Director of Physical Plant ... Mr. Eric C. MCMILLION
23 Supervisor of Clinic ... Miss Carol J. AMEY
36 Dir Center for Career & Calling ... Mr. Jason CLAYTON
38 Director of Counseling Center ... Mrs. Melissa COZART
19 Dir of Security & Environ Safety ... Mr. Jerry MARCHAL
40 Manager of Bookstore ... Mr. C. David TRAMMELL
21 Associate Business Officer ... Mr. Gary E. HOWARD

04 Admin Asst to the President ... Mrs. Dana MOUTZ
85 Coordinator of Intercultural Pgms ... Mrs. Esther JADHAV
41 Athletics Director ... Mr. Mark PERDUE

ATA College (C)

10180 Linn Station Road, Ste A-200, Louisville KY 40223
County: Jefferson FICE Identification: 040383
Unit ID: 447935
Telephone: (502) 371-8330 Carnegie Class: Assoc/PrivFP
FAX Number: (502) 371-8598 Calendar System: Quarter
URL: www.ata.edu
Established: 1994 Annual Undergrad Tuition & Fees: N/A
Enrollment: 489 Coed
Affiliation or Control: Proprietary IRS Status: Proprietary
Highest Offering: Associate Degree
Program: Occupational
Accreditation: ABHES

01 President ... Mr. Donald A. JONES

Beckfield College (D)

16 Spiral Drive, Florence KY 41042-4866
County: Boone FICE Identification: 024911
Unit ID: 247065
Telephone: (859) 371-9393 Carnegie Class: Assoc/PrivFP4
FAX Number: (859) 371-5096 Calendar System: Quarter
URL: www.beckfield.edu
Established: 1984 Annual Undergrad Tuition & Fees: $15,120
Enrollment: 758 Coed
Affiliation or Control: Proprietary IRS Status: Proprietary
Highest Offering: Baccalaureate
Program: Professional; Business Emphasis
Accreditation: ACICS

00 Chief Executive Officer ... Ms. Diane G. WOLFER
01 President Florence Campus ... Mr. Richard F. COSTA, JR.
05 Dean of Academic Affairs ... Mr. Steven LAKES
12 Campus Director of Florence ... Mr. Keith GRANT
32 Director of Student Services ... Ms. Alisha WOODESHICK
37 Director of Financial Aid ... Mrs. Patricia A. NETTLETON
13 Director of Information Technology ... Mr. James BRUN
07 Director Admissions ... Mr. John AVILES
36 Director Career Services ... Ms. Christin JACKSON
22 Director of Compliance ... Mr. Peter NETTLETON
06 Registrar ... Ms. Jocelyn ROY
08 Librarian ... Ms. Emily STEELE
12 Interim Campus Dean-Florence ... Dr. Jerry LINGER, JR.
50 Dean of Business/Technology ... Mr. Charles RICHARDSON
66 Dean Division of Nursing ... Mrs. Deborah SMITH-CLAY
76 Dean of Allied Health ... Ms. Ruth GABBARD
97 Dean of General Education ... Ms. Brittaney HARP
88 Dean of Criminal Justice ... Dr. Rachel MCARTHUR
04 Assistant to the President ... Ms. Cheryl A. KUNKEL

Bellarmine University (E)

2001 Newburg Road, Louisville KY 40205-0671
County: Jefferson FICE Identification: 001954
Unit ID: 156286
Telephone: (502) 272-8000 Carnegie Class: Master's L
FAX Number: (502) 272-8033 Calendar System: Semester
URL: www.bellarmine.edu
Established: 1950 Annual Undergrad Tuition & Fees: $34,890
Enrollment: 3,602 Coed
Affiliation or Control: Independent Non-Profit IRS Status: 501(c)3
Highest Offering: Doctorate
Program: Liberal Arts And General; Teacher Preparatory; Professional
Accreditation: SC, BUS, COARC, MT, NURSE, PTA, TED

01 President ... Dr. Joseph J. MCGOWAN
03 Executive Vice President & Provost ... Dr. Doris A. TEGART
10 Vice President Admin & Finance ... Mr. Robert L. ZIMLICH
32 Vice President Acad & Student Life ... Dr. Fred W. RHODES
30 Vice President Development & Alumni ... Mr. Glenn F. KOSSE
26 Vice President Comm/Public Affairs ... Mr. Hunt C. HELM
84 Vice President Enrollment Mgmt ... Dr. Sean J. RYAN
100 Exec Assistant to the President ... Ms. Marisa ZOELLER
20 Vice President Academic Affairs ... Dr. Carole PFEFFER
20 Asst VP Academic Affairs ... Dr. Graham ELLIS
20 Asst VP for Acadeic Affairs ... Dr. Cindy G. GNADINGER
66 Dn Lansing Sch of Nursing/Hlth Sci ... Dr. Mark WIEGAND
50 Dean Rubel School of Business ... Dr. Daniel L. BAUER
107 Dean of Professional Studies ... Dr. Sean J. RYAN
53 Dean Annsley Frazier Thornton Ed ... Dr. Robert B. COOTER
47 Dean Regional Environmental Studies ... Dr. Robert KINGSOLVER
49 Dean Bellarmine College ... Dr. William E. FENTON
15 Chief Human Resources Officer ... Ms. Lynn M. BYNUM
21 Asst VP for Admin and Finance ... Ms. Denise BROWN-CORNELIUS
28 Asst VP & Dir Multicultural Pgms ... Dr. Hannah CLAYBORNE
85 Director of International Programs ... Ms. Gabriele BOSLEY
35 Dean of Students ... Dr. Helen G. RYAN
89 Dean Academic Advising ... Vacant
92 Director Honors Program ... Dr. Hank J. ROTHGERBER
41 Athletic Director ... Mr. Scott P. WIEGANDT
18 Chief Facilities/Physical Plant ... Mr. Jeffrey DEAN
07 Dean of Admission ... Mr. Timothy A. STURGEON
08 Director of the Library ... Mr. John K. STEMMER
19 Director Safety & Security ... Mr. Joseph FRYE

07 Dean of Graduate School Admission ... Dr. Sara YOUNT-PETTINGILL
06 Registrar ... Ms. Ann E. OLSEN
96 Purchasing Manager ... Mr. Patrick COONS
42 Director Campus Ministry ... Dr. Melanie P. SULLIVAN
39 Director Residence Life ... Ms. Leslie M. MAXIE-ASHFORD
13 Director Information Technology ... Mr. Eric SATTERLY
37 Director Student Financial Aid ... Ms. Heather BOUTELL
09 Director of Institutional Research ... Vacant
36 Asst Dean Career Services ... Vacant
29 Executive Director Alumni Relations ... Mr. Peter W. KREMER
26 Director of News/Media/Social Netwk ... Mr. Jason A. CISSELL
38 Director Student Counseling ... Dr. Gary PETIPRIN
92 Director of Brown Scholars Program ... Dr. Matisa WILBON

Berea College (F)

101 Chestnut Street, Berea KY 40404-0003
County: Madison FICE Identification: 001955
Unit ID: 156295
Telephone: (859) 985-3000 Carnegie Class: Bac/A&S
FAX Number: (859) 985-3917 Calendar System: Semester
URL: www.berea.edu
Established: 1855 Annual Undergrad Tuition & Fees: $1,070
Enrollment: 1,658 Coed
Affiliation or Control: Independent Non-Profit IRS Status: 501(c)3
Highest Offering: Baccalaureate
Program: Liberal Arts And General; Teacher Preparatory; Professional
Accreditation: SC, NURSE, TED

01 President ... Dr. Lyle D. ROELOFS
10 Vice President Finance ... Mr. Jeff S. AMBURGEY
30 Vice President Alumni College Rels ... Ms. Michelle JANSSEN
32 Vice President Labor & Student Life ... Ms. Gail WOLFORD
11 Interim VP Operations & Sustain ... Mr. Derrick SINGLETON
04 Assistant to President ... Ms. Teri THOMPSON
35 Asst Vice Pres for Student Life ... Mr. Gus GERASSIMIDES
05 Academic VP/Dean of the Faculty ... Dr. Chad BERRY
37 Dir of Student Financial Aid Svcs ... Ms. Nancy MELTON
38 Dir Counseling/Psychological Svcs ... Ms. Sue REIMONDO
44 Director of Gift Planning ... Ms. Amy SHEHEE
20 Assoc VP for Academic Affairs ... Dr. Linda LEEK
20 Director of Academic Assessment ... Dr. Robet SMITH
20 Dean of Curriculum/Student Learning ... Dr. Scott STEELE
13 Chief Information Officer ... Dr. John LYMPANY
07 Director of Admissions Operations ... Mr. Luke HODSON
29 Acting Director of Alumni Relations ... Ms. Diane KERBY
15 Director of People Services ... Ms. Erin FARRELL
18 Director of Facilities Management ... Mr. Jon METCALF
88 Director of Appalachian Center ... Mr. Chris GREEN
09 Director of Inst Rsrch/Assessment ... Ms. Judith WECKMAN
23 Director of College Health Service ... Dr. Miriam DAVID
26 Assoc VP for Integrated Marketing ... Mr. James C. MAGUIRE
08 Director of Library Services ... Ms. Anne CHASE
41 Dir Athletics/Seabury Ctr Complex ... Mr. Mark CARTMILL
42 Director Campus Christian Center ... Rev. Gail BOWMAN
43 General Counsel ... Mr. Judge WILSON
19 Director of Public Safety ... Mr. V. Lavoyed HUDGINS
28 Director Black Cultural Center ... Ms. Monica JONES
88 Dean of Labor ... Mr. David K. TIPTON
85 Director International Center ... Dr. Richard CAHILL
40 College Bookstore Director ... Ms. Marty WAYLAND
96 Purchasing Manager ... Ms. Aurelia BRANDENBURG
24 Media Services Coordinator ... Mr. Rob LEWIS
06 Director of Academic Services ... Mr. Curtis SANDBERG
88 Center for Transformative Learning ... Ms. Leslie ORTQUIST-AHRENS
88 Woodson Center for Interracial Educ ... Dr. Alicestyne TURLEY
88 Director of CELTS ... Ms. Ashley COCHRANE

Brescia University (G)

717 Frederica Street, Owensboro KY 42301-3023
County: Daviess FICE Identification: 001958
Unit ID: 156356
Telephone: (270) 685-3131 Carnegie Class: Bac/Diverse
FAX Number: (270) 686-6422 Calendar System: Semester
URL: www.brescia.edu
Established: 1950 Annual Undergrad Tuition & Fees: $19,000
Enrollment: 877 Coed
Affiliation or Control: Roman Catholic IRS Status: 501(c)3
Highest Offering: Master's
Program: Liberal Arts And General; Teacher Preparatory
Accreditation: SC, SW

01 President ... Rev. Larry HOSTETTER
05 Vice President & Academic Dean ... Dr. Cheryl CLEMONS
10 Vice President Business & Finance ... Mr. Dale CECIL
84 Vice President of Enrollment ... Mr. Christopher HOUK
30 Vice Pres Institutional Advancement ... Mr. Todd BROCK
32 Vice Pres/Dean Student Development ... Vacant
39 Asst Dean Students Residence Life ... Mr. Jeffrey A. RUDNIK
35 Asst Dean Stdnts Act/Leadership Dev ... Vacant
06 Registrar ... Sr. Helena FISCHER, OSU
71 Director of Weekend College ... Ms. Shanda LARUE
38 Director of Counseling Center ... Ms. Eva G. ATKINSON
08 Director of Library Services ... Sr. Judith N. RINEY, OSU
88 Director Student Support Services ... Dr. Dolores KIESLER
15 Director of Human Resources ... Ms. Tammy S. KELLER
13 Director of Information Technology ... Mr. Chris FORD
18 Director of Physical Plant ... Mr. Mike WARD
37 Director of Financial Aid ... Ms. Kristi EIDSON

41 Director of Athletics ... Mr. Brian SKORTZ
26 Director of Public Relations ... Ms. Tina KASEY
29 Director of Alumni ... Mr. Jason COX
44 Director of Annual Giving ... Ms. Sydney WARREN
09 Director of Institutional Research ... Ms. Tracy NAYLOR
58 Director of Graduate Program-MBA ... Dr. Sandra O. OBILADE
58 Director of Graduate Program-MSCI ... Dr. Patricia A. AKOJIE
42 Director of Campus Ministry ... Sr. Pam MUELLER, OSU
07 Director of Admissions ... Ms. Christy ROHNER
21 Asst Director Business & Finance ... Ms. Nancy W. REYNOLDS
36 Coordinator of Career Services ... Ms. Helen BENNETT
20 Associate Academic Officer ... Mr. Keith HUDSON
40 Bookstore Manager ... Ms. Beverly MCCANDLESS

Brown Mackie College-Hopkinsville (A)

4001 Fort Campbell Boulevard,
Hopkinsville KY 42240-4948
Telephone: (270) 886-1302 Identification: 666516
Accreditation: ACICS, OTA

† Main campus is The Art Institute of Phoenix in Phoenix, AZ.

Brown Mackie College-Louisville (B)

3605 Fern Valley Road, Louisville KY 40219-1916
Telephone: (502) 810-6000 FICE Identification: 021082
Accreditation: ACICS, OTA, SURGT, SURTEC

† Main campus is The Art Institute of Phoenix in Phoenix, AZ.

Brown Mackie College-Northern Kentucky (C)

309 Buttermilk Pike, Fort Mitchell KY 41017-2191
Telephone: (859) 341-5627 Identification: 666446
Accreditation: ACICS, OTA, SURGT

† Main campus is The Art Institute of Phoenix in Phoenix, AZ.

Campbellsville University (D)

1 Universty Drive, Campbellsville KY 42718-2799
County: Taylor FICE Identification: 001959
Unit ID: 156365
Telephone: (270) 789-5000 Carnegie Class: Master's M
FAX Number: (270) 789-5050 Calendar System: Semester
URL: www.campbellsville.edu
Established: 1906 Annual Undergrad Tuition & Fees: $21,696
Enrollment: 3,664 Coed
Affiliation or Control: Baptist IRS Status: 501(c)3
Highest Offering: Master's
Program: Liberal Arts And General; Teacher Preparatory; Professional
Accreditation: SC, IACBE, MUS, SW, TED

01 President ... Dr. Michael CARTER
10 Vice Pres Finance & Administration ... Mr. Otto TENNANT
05 Vice President Academic Affairs ... Dr. Frank CHEATHAM
30 Vice President for Development ... Mr. Benji KELLY
26 VP for Church & External Rels ... Mr. John E. CHOWNING
07 VP for Admissions/Student Svcs ... Mr. Dave WALTERS
32 Dean of Student Services ... Mrs. Jodi ALLEN
20 Associate Academic Officer ... Vacant
21 Comptroller ... Mr. Tim JUDD
09 Director of Institutional Research ... Mr. Paul DAMERON
38 Director of Student Counseling ... Vacant
28 Director of Diversity ... Mr. John E. CHOWNING
92 Director of Honors Program ... Dr. Craig L. ROGERS
41 Director of Athletics ... Mr. Rusty HOLLINGSWORTH
40 Director of Bookstore ... Mrs. Donna WRIGHT
42 Director of Campus Ministries ... Mr. Edwin C. PAVY
13 Director of Computing/Communication ... Mr. Hermano QUEIROZ
37 Director of Financial Aid ... Ms. Chris TOLSON
29 Director of Alumni Relations ... Mrs. Paula SMITH
08 Director of Library Services ... Mr. John BURCH
15 Director of Personnel Services ... Mr. Terry VANMETER
18 Director of Maintenance ... Mr. Steve MORRIS
27 Director of News Information ... Mrs. Joan C. MCKINNEY
06 Director of Student Records ... Mrs. Rita A. CREASON
04 Secretary to the President ... Mrs. Kellie VAUGHN
96 Dir of Purchasing/Special Projects ... Mr. Marion HALL
88 Director of Custodial Services ... Mr. Bob STOTTS

Centre College (E)

600 W Walnut Street, Danville KY 40422-1394
County: Boyle FICE Identification: 001961
Unit ID: 156408
Telephone: (859) 238-5200 Carnegie Class: Bac/A&S
FAX Number: (859) 238-6977 Calendar System: Other
URL: www.centre.edu
Established: 1819 Annual Undergrad Tuition & Fees: $45,100
Enrollment: 1,343 Coed
Affiliation or Control: Independent Non-Profit IRS Status: 501(c)3
Highest Offering: Baccalaureate
Program: Liberal Arts And General; Teacher Preparatory
Accreditation: SC

01 President ... Dr. John A. ROUSH
05 Vice President & Dean of College ... Dr. Stephanie L. FABRITIUS
10 Vice Pres for Finance & Treasurer ... Mr. Robert L. KEASLER
26 Vice President College Relations ... Dr. Richard W. TROLLINGER
32 Vice Pres/Dean of Student Life ... Mr. Wm. Randy HAYS
30 Assoc VP Development/Alumni Affairs ... Mr. Shawn LYONS
43 Assoc VP for Legal Affs/Gift Plng ... Mr. James P. LEAHEY
88 Professor of Education ... Dr. Donna M. PLUMMER
28 Asst Vice Pres Diversity ... Mr. James H. ATKINS
07 Dean Admiss/Student Financial Plng ... Mr. Robert M. NESMITH
20 Associate Dean of the College ... Dr. Beth GLAZIER-MCDONALD
38 Assoc Dean & Dir Residence Life ... Ms. Sarah S. HALL
45 Asst to the President for Planning ... Dr. Clarence R. WYATT
85 Director of International Programs ... Dr. Milton M. REIGELMAN
08 Director of Library Services ... Mr. Stanley R. CAMPBELL
04 Exec Assistant to the President ... Ms. Yvonne Y. MORLEY
37 Director of Student Financial Plng ... Vacant
06 Registrar ... Mr. Timothy P. CULHAN
15 Director Human Resources/Admin Svcs ... Mrs. Kay L. DRAKE
27 Director of Communications ... Dr. Michael P. STRYSICK
36 Director of Career Services ... Ms. Deborah A. JONES
35 Director Student Life & Housing ... Ms. Ann S. YOUNG
41 Director of Athletics & Recreation ... Mr. W. Bradley FIELDS
19 Co-Director of Public Safety ... Mr. Kevin S. MILBY
19 Co-Director of Public Safety ... Mr. Gary D. BUGG
09 Director of Institutional Research ... Mr. J. Patrick NOLTEMEYER
13 Director of Info Technology Service ... Mr. J. Keith FOWLKES
24 Director Ctr for Teaching/Learning ... Dr. Sarah E. LASHLEY
18 Director of Facilities Management ... Mr. D. Wayne KING
21 Controller ... Mr. Steven A. JAMISON
42 College Chaplain ... Dr. Richard D. AXTELL
96 Dir Purchasing/Campus Interiors ... Ms. Ann T. SMITH
29 Director of Alumni Affairs ... Ms. Megan H. MILBY
57 Mgr Director Norton Center for Arts ... Mr. Steven A. HOFFMAN

Clear Creek Baptist Bible College (F)

300 Clear Creek Road, Pineville KY 40977-9754
County: Bell FICE Identification: 025356
Unit ID: 156417
Telephone: (606) 337-3196 Carnegie Class: Spec/Faith
FAX Number: (606) 337-2372 Calendar System: Semester
URL: www.ccbbc.edu
Established: 1926 Annual Undergrad Tuition & Fees: $6,436
Enrollment: 171 Coed
Affiliation or Control: Southern Baptist IRS Status: 501(c)3
Highest Offering: Baccalaureate
Program: Religious Emphasis
Accreditation: SC, BI

01 President ... Dr. Donnie S. FOX
05 Academic Dean ... Dr. Malcolm HESTER
32 Dean of Students ... Rev. David WADE
11 Dean of Administrative Affairs ... Mr. Jeromy ANDERSON
30 Dean of Institutional Advancement ... Dr. Jay SULFRIDGE
08 Librarian ... Mrs. Marge CUMMINGS
42 Christian Service Director ... Rev. Gerald SIMMONS
18 Dir of Maintenance and Facilities ... Mr. Ronnie WASHAM
37 Director Financial Aid ... Mr. Sam RISNER
06 Registrar ... Mr. Jacob YATES
07 Admissions ... Rev. Billy HOWELL
26 Director of College Relations ... Rev. Richard L. WITHERITE
14 Director of Computer Operations ... Mr. Shane KAHKOLA
56 Director of Distance Education ... Dr. Jay BARNETT

Daymar College Online (G)

3309 Collins Lane, Louisville KY 40245
Telephone: (270) 926-1188 Identification: 770615
Accreditation: ACICS

† Main campus is Daymar College-Owensboro in Owensboro, KY.

Daymar College-Bellevue (H)

119 Fairfield Avenue, Bellevue KY 41073
Telephone: (859) 291-0800 Identification: 666390
Accreditation: ACICS

† Main campus is Daymar College-Owensboro in Owensboro, KY.

Daymar College-Bowling Green (I)

2421 Fitzgerald Industrial Drive,
Bowling Green KY 42101-4071
Telephone: (270) 843-6750 Identification: 666439
Accreditation: ACICS

† Main campus is Daymar Institute in Nashville, TN.

Daymar College-Louisville (J)

4112 Fern Valley Road, Louisville KY 40219-1973
Telephone: (502) 495-1040 Identification: 666391
Accreditation: ACICS

† Main campus is Daymar College-Owensboro in Owensboro, KY.

Daymar College-Louisville East (K)

3309 Collins Lane, Louisville KY 40245
Telephone: (502) 400-4075 Identification: 667081
Accreditation: ACICS

† Main campus is Daymar College-Owensboro in Owensboro, KY.

Daymar College-Madisonville (L)

1105 National Mine Drive, Madisonville KY 42431
Telephone: (270) 643-0312 Identification: 667079
Accreditation: ACICS

† Main campus is Daymar College-Owensboro in Owensboro, KY.

Daymar College-Owensboro (M)

3361 Buckland Square, PO Box 22150,
Owensboro KY 42304-2150
County: Daviess FICE Identification: 009313
Unit ID: 157465
Telephone: (270) 926-4040 Carnegie Class: Assoc/PrivFP
FAX Number: (270) 685-4090 Calendar System: Quarter
URL: www.daymarcollege.edu
Established: 1963 Annual Undergrad Tuition & Fees: $16,610
Enrollment: 150 Coed
Affiliation or Control: Proprietary IRS Status: Proprietary
Highest Offering: Baccalaureate
Program: Technical Emphasis
Accreditation: ACICS

01 President/CEO ... Dan INMAN
12 Campus President ... Michael TRAAS
05 Director of Education ... Tim FERGUSON
07 Director of Admissions ... Latasha SHEMWELL

Daymar College-Paducah (N)

509 S 30th Street, Paducah KY 42002-4181
County: McCracken FICE Identification: 008425
Unit ID: 156903
Telephone: (270) 444-9676 Carnegie Class: Assoc/PrivFP
FAX Number: (270) 441-7202 Calendar System: Quarter
URL: www.daymarcollege.edu
Established: 1964 Annual Undergrad Tuition & Fees: $18,000
Enrollment: 150 Coed
Affiliation or Control: Proprietary IRS Status: Proprietary
Highest Offering: Baccalaureate
Program: Technical Emphasis
Accreditation: ACICS

01 President ... Mr. Mark A. GABIS
12 Campus President ... Mr. Greg WEBB
07 Director of Admissions ... Ms. Connie HOLLEY
37 Director of Financial Services ... Ms. Jo Ann PRICE
32 Director of Student Services ... Ms. Peggy TIPPIN
05 Director of Education ... Mr. Steve DAVIDSON
36 Dir of Career Svc & Cmty Relations ... Mr. Ken AVERILL

Daymar College-Scottsville (O)

1138 Old Gallatin Road, Scottsville KY 42164
Telephone: (270) 237-3577 Identification: 667080
Accreditation: ACICS

† Main campus is Daymar College-Owensboro in Owensboro, KY.

Eastern Kentucky University (P)

521 Lancaster Avenue, Richmond KY 40475-3102
County: Madison FICE Identification: 001963
Unit ID: 156620
Telephone: (859) 622-1000 Carnegie Class: Master's L
FAX Number: (859) 622-1020 Calendar System: Semester
URL: www.eku.edu
Established: 1906 Annual Undergrad Tuition & Fees (In-State): $7,536
Enrollment: 15,968 Coed
Affiliation or Control: State IRS Status: 501(c)3
Highest Offering: Doctorate
Program: Occupational; Liberal Arts And General; Teacher Preparatory; Professional
Accreditation: SC, AAFCS, ADNUR, BUS, CACREP, CAHIIM, CONST, CS, DIETD, DIETI, EMT, FEPAC, IFSAC, MLTAD, MT, MUS, NAIT, NRPA, NURSE, OT, PH, SP, SPAA, SW, TED

01 President ... Dr. Michael BENSON
05 Provost/Vice Pres Academic Affairs ... Dr. Janna VICE
32 Int Assoc Provost/VP Student Affs ... Dr. Claire GOOD
10 VP Financial Affs/Treasurer/Admin ... Mr. Barry POYNTER
30 Vice Pres University Advancement ... Mr. Michael EASTMAN
84 Act VP Enrol Mgt/Mrktng/Univ Rels ... Ms. Elizabeth WACHTEL
45 Assoc VP University Programs ... Dr. Sara ZEIGLER
26 Assoc VP Public Relations/Marketing ... Mr. Marc WHITT
35 Assoc Vice Pres Student Affairs ... Dr. Mike REAGLE
76 Dean Health Sciences ... Dr. Deborah WHITEHOUSE
49 Dean Arts & Sciences ... Dr. John WADE
50 Dean Business & Technology ... Dr. Robert ROGOW
53 Dean Education ... Dr. Verna LOWE
88 Dean Justice & Safety ... Dr. Allen AULT
86 Exec Dir Government Relations ... Mr. David MCFADDIN
43 University Counsel ... Mrs. Judy SPAIN
19 Chief of Police ... Mr. Brian MULLINS
08 Director Libraries ... Ms. Betina GARDNER
06 Registrar ... Ms. Tina DAVIS
88 Director Advising ... Mr. Benton SHIREY
07 Director Admissions ... Mr. Brett MORRIS
36 Director Career Services ... Mrs. Gladys JOHNSON
25 Director Sponsored Programs ... Mr. Gus BENSON

92 Interim Director Honors Program ....Dr. David COLEMAN
09 Director Institutional Research ....Vacant
85 Director International Education ....Dr. William HOLMES
38 Director Counseling Center ....Dr. Jen C. WALKER
39 Director Housing ....Mrs. Kenna MIDDLETON
88 Director Judicial Affairs/Disabled ....Mrs. Betsy BOHANNON
37 Director Student Financial Assist ....Mrs. Shelley S. PARK
23 Director Student Health Services ....Dr. Pradeep BOSE
40 Director Bookstore ....Ms. Lisa CROWE
15 Director Human Resources ....Mr. Gary BARKSDALE
90 Director Info Tech/Delivery Svcs ....Ms. Mona ISAACS
29 Director Alumni Relations ....Ms. Jackie COLLIER
88 Dir Student Involvement/Leadership ....Ms. April BARNES
24 Director Media Resources ....Ms. Jo BROSIUS
18 Int Director Facilities Services ....Mr. David WILLIAMS
28 Director of Diversity ....Ms. Sandra MOORE
96 Director of Purchasing ....Ms. Lora SNIDER
42 Chaplain ....Dr. Patrick C. NNOROMELE
04 Admin Asst to the President ....Ms. Lisa KELLEY
04 Admin Asst to the President ....Mrs. Dreidre DE LEON

Frontier Nursing University (A)

PO Box 528, Hyden KY 41749-0528
County: Leslie FICE Identification: 030070
Unit ID: 156727
Telephone: (606) 672-2312 Carnegie Class: Spec/Health
FAX Number: (606) 672-3776 Calendar System: Quarter
URL: www.frontier.edu
Established: 1939 Annual Graduate Tuition & Fees: $15,660
Enrollment: 1,398 Coed
Affiliation or Control: Independent Non-Profit IRS Status: 501(c)3
Highest Offering: Doctorate; No Undergraduates
Program: Professional; Nursing Emphasis
Accreditation: **SC**, MIDWF, NUR

01 President & Dean ....Dr. Susan STONE
11 Chief Operations Officer ....Ms. Shelley ALDRIDGE
10 Vice President of Finance ....Mr. Michael STEINMETZ
05 Associate Dean of Academic Affairs ....Dr. Joyce KNESTRICK
88 Assoc Dean Midwifery/Women's Health ....Vacant
66 Assoc Dean of Family Nursing ....Dr. Julie MARFELL
88 Associate Dean of Research ....Dr. Janet ENGSTROM
88 PM-DNP Program Director ....Dr. Barbara ANDERSON
88 Bridge Option Director ....Dr. Trish VOSS
29 Director of Development and Alumni ....Ms. Denise BARRETT
07 Director of Recruitment & Retention ....Ms. Stephanie BOYD
06 Registrar ....Ms. Sherri DAVIS
37 Director of Financial Aid ....Ms. Rainie BOGGS
08 Director of Library Services ....Ms. Billie Anne GEBB
13 Information Technology Manager ....Mr. Chad MILLER

Galen College of Nursing (B)

1031 Zorn Avenue, Suite 400, Louisville KY 40207-1064
County: Jefferson FICE Identification: 030837
Unit ID: 156471
Telephone: (502) 410-6200 Carnegie Class: Assoc/PrivFP
FAX Number: (502) 581-0425 Calendar System: Quarter
URL: www.galencollege.edu
Established: 1989 Annual Undergrad Tuition & Fees: $16,875
Enrollment: 2,261 Coed
Affiliation or Control: Proprietary IRS Status: Proprietary
Highest Offering: Associate Degree
Program: 2-Year Principally Bachelor's Creditable; Nursing Emphasis
Accreditation: **SC**, COE

01 President ....Mr. Mark A. VOGT
10 Executive VP and CFO ....Mr. Joseph R. PETERS
05 VP of Academic Affairs ....Dr. Tracy A. ORTELLI
84 VP of Enrollment Management ....Mr. Thomas DWYER
09 VP of Institutional Research ....Mr. David RAY
32 VP and Chief People Officer ....Ms. Audria DENKER
11 VP of Operations ....Ms. Kathleen GOOKIN
106 VP of Online ....Dr. Steve HYNDMAN
37 Financial Aid Director ....Ms. Joni M. PENLAND
07 Asst VP of Enrollment Management ....Mr. Carter SMITH
20 Special Asst to VP Academic Affairs ....Ms. Kathy BURLINGAME
66 Dean of the Cincinnati Campus ....Ms. Carol BUSCHUR
66 Dean of the Main Campus-Louisville ....Dr. Joan L. FREY
66 Dean of the Tampa Bay Campus ....Vacant
66 Dean of the San Antonio Campus ....Dr. Vivian C. LILLY
26 Dir of Communications & Marketing ....Ms. Stephanie FRENCH
13 Director of Information Technology ....Mr. Duane HELLUMS
15 Director of Human Resources ....Ms. Robin LUCKETT

Georgetown College (C)

400 E College Street, Georgetown KY 40324-1696
County: Scott FICE Identification: 001964
Unit ID: 156745
Telephone: (502) 863-8000 Carnegie Class: Bac/A&S
FAX Number: (502) 868-8891 Calendar System: Semester
URL: www.georgetowncollege.edu
Established: 1787 Annual Undergrad Tuition & Fees: $32,310
Enrollment: 1,543 Coed
Affiliation or Control: Baptist IRS Status: 501(c)3
Highest Offering: Master's
Program: Liberal Arts And General
Accreditation: **SC**, TED

01 Acting President ....Mrs. Granotta BINGHAM BLEVINS
05 Provost/Dean of the College ....Dr. Rosemary ALLEN
10 Vice President/CFO/Treasurer ....Mr. James A. MOAK, JR.
43 General Counsel & Spec Asst to Pres ....Mr. James H. NEWBERRY, JR.
30 Assoc VP/Chief Development Officer ....Vacant
32 VP Student Life/Dean of Students ....Vacant
84 Vice President for Enrollment ....Ms. Michelle LYNCH
13 Assoc VP for Info Tech Services ....Mr. Donald L. BLAKEMAN
26 Assoc VP Inst Adv/Dir Comm & Mktg ....Mr. Jim ALLISON
21 Controller ....Mr. David WILHITE
88 Bursar ....Ms. Marianne RIDDLE
06 Registrar ....Ms. Winnie BRATCHER
15 Director of Human Resources ....Ms. Tracie SHAPIRO
28 VP of Diversity and Inclusion ....Mr. Brian EVANS
53 Dean of Education ....Dr. Yolanda CARTER
07 Director of Admissions ....Vacant
37 Dir of Student Financial Planning ....Ms. Tiffany HORNBERGER
09 Institutional Research Associate ....Ms. Jane BENARD
08 Director of Library Services ....Ms. Susan MARTIN
29 Director of Alumni Relations ....Ms. Laura OWSLEY
41 Athletic Director ....Mr. Brian EVANS
42 Director of Religious Life ....Mr. H.K KINGKADE
36 Dir Graves Ctr for Calling & Career ....Mr. Ray CLERE
19 Director Campus Safety ....Mr. Dan BROWN
38 Director of Counseling/Health Svcs ....Dr. Lloyd CLARK
18 Dir Facilities and Grounds ....Mr. Bart HORNE

Indiana Tech-Louisville (D)

11855 Commonwealth Drive, Louisville KY 40299
Telephone: (502) 708-2363 Identification: 770104
Accreditation: **&NH**

† Main campus is Indiana Tech in Fort Wayne, IN.

Interactive College of Technology (E)

76 Caruthers Road, Newport KY 41071
Telephone: (859) 282-8989 Identification: 770535
Accreditation: **COE**

† Main campus is Interactive College of Technology in Chamblee, GA.

ITT Technical Institute (F)

2473 Fortune Drive, Suite 180, Lexington KY 40509-4253
Telephone: (859) 246-3300 Identification: 666158
Accreditation: **ACICS**

† Main campus is ITT Technical Institute in Indianapolis, IN.

ITT Technical Institute (G)

9500 Ormsby Station Road, Suite 100, Louisville KY 40223
Telephone: (502) 327-7424 Identification: 666540
Accreditation: **ACICS**

† Main campus is ITT Technical Institute in Indianapolis, IN.

Kentucky Christian University (H)

100 Academic Parkway, Grayson KY 41143-2205
County: Carter FICE Identification: 001965
Unit ID: 157100
Telephone: (606) 474-3000 Carnegie Class: Bac/Diverse
FAX Number: (606) 474-3155 Calendar System: Semester
URL: www.kcu.edu
Established: 1919 Annual Undergrad Tuition & Fees: $17,088
Enrollment: 615 Coed
Affiliation or Control: Christian Churches And Churches of Christ
IRS Status: 501(c)3
Highest Offering: Master's
Program: Liberal Arts And General; Fine Arts Emphasis
Accreditation: **SC**, NURSE, SW

01 President/CEO ....Dr. Jeff K. METCALF
05 VP of Academic Affairs ....Dr. Marvin L. ELLIOTT
10 VP of Business & Finance ....Mr. William S. BONDURANT
84 VP of Enrollment Services ....Vacant
30 VP of University Advancement ....Mr. James W. PATTON
88 Director of Church Relations ....Mr. Jeff W. GREENE
06 Registrar ....Mrs. Andrea L. STAMPER
13 Director of Campus Technology ....Mr. Greg C. RICHARDSON
08 Librarian ....Mrs. Naulayne R. ENDERS
108 Director Institutional Assessment ....Mr. Kenneth L. BECK
32 Dean of Student Services ....Mr. Ron W. ARNETT
42 Campus Minister ....Mr. Larry W. MARSHALL
37 Director Financial Aid ....Mrs. Jennie M. BENDER
15 Human Resources Officer ....Mr. Terry L. YANKEY
38 Student Counseling Coordinator ....Ms. Lori A. SMITH-WARD
41 Athletic Director ....Mr. Bruce W. DIXON
39 Director of Residence Services ....Mr. Kris A. LANGSTAFF
18 Director of Maintenance ....Mr. Troy E. ROUSH
29 Alumni Relations Officer ....Mr. Jeff W. GREENE
58 Dean of the Graduate School ....Dr. David A. FIENSY
07 Director of Enrollment Services ....Miss Heather J. STACEY
26 Public Relations Officer ....Mr. James W. PATTON
40 Bookstore Director ....Mrs. Sandra L. BROOKS

*Kentucky Community and Technical College System (I)

300 N Main Street, Versailles KY 40383-1245
County: Woodford FICE Identification: 006724
Unit ID: 157854
Telephone: (859) 256-3100 Carnegie Class: N/A
FAX Number: (859) 256-3119
URL: www.kctcs.edu

01 President ....Dr. Michael B. MCCALL
00 Chancellor ....Dr. Jay BOX
10 Vice President Finance ....Mr. Ken WALKER
13 Vice Pres Technology Solutions ....Mr. Paul CZARAPATA
30 Vice Pres Devel & Public Relations ....Mr. Timothy R. BURCHAM, CFRE
04 Sr Exec Assistant to the President ....Ms. Beth HILLIARD

*Ashland Community and Technical College (J)

1400 College Drive, Ashland KY 41101-3617
County: Boyd FICE Identification: 001990
Unit ID: 156231
Telephone: (606) 326-2000 Carnegie Class: Assoc/Pub-R-M
FAX Number: (606) 326-2187 Calendar System: Semester
URL: www.ashland.kctcs.edu
Established: 1938 Annual Undergrad Tuition & Fees (In-State): $3,360
Enrollment: 3,948 Coed
Affiliation or Control: State IRS Status: 501(c)3
Highest Offering: Associate Degree
Program: Occupational; 2-Year Principally Bachelor's Creditable
Accreditation: **SC**, ADNUR, IFSAC, SURGT

02 President & CEO ....Dr. Kay ADKINS
05 Dean of Academic Affairs ....Dr. Janie KITCHEN
32 Dean of Student Affairs ....Ms. Willie MCCULLOUGH
10 Dean of Business Affairs ....Ms. Karen BLEVINS
103 Dean Cmty Workforce/Economic Devel ....Dr. Larry FERGUSON
09 Dean of Institutional Effectiveness ....Mr. Steve FLOUHOUSE
26 Dean Mktg/Community Relations ....Mr. John MCGLONE
08 Director of Library Services ....Mr. Matthew ONION
07 Assoc Dean Admissions/Registrar ....Mr. Kevin COOTS
13 Assoc Dean Information Technology ....Mr. Farnoosh RAFIEE
28 Director of Cultural Diversity ....Mr. Alvin BAKER
15 Director of Human Resources ....Ms. Kellie ALLEN
25 Director of Grants & Contracts ....Ms. Sarah DIAMOND BURROWAY
37 Director of Financial Aid ....Ms. Robin LEWIS
36 Coordinator of Career Services ....Ms. Nancy MENSHOUSE
79 Division Chair Humanities ....Dr. Carol GREENE
76 Division Chair Health Sciences ....Ms. Michelle NAPIER
81 Div Chair Math & Natural Sciences ....Dr. Keith BRAMMELL

*Big Sandy Community and Technical College (K)

1 Bert T. Combs Drive, Prestonburg KY 41653-9502
County: Floyd FICE Identification: 001996
Unit ID: 157553
Telephone: (606) 886-3863 Carnegie Class: Assoc/Pub-R-M
FAX Number: (606) 886-2677 Calendar System: Semester
URL: www.bigsandy.kctcs.edu
Established: 1964 Annual Undergrad Tuition & Fees (In-State): $3,456
Enrollment: 5,217 Coed
Affiliation or Control: State IRS Status: 501(c)3
Highest Offering: Associate Degree
Program: Occupational; 2-Year Principally Bachelor's Creditable
Accreditation: **SC**, COARC, DH

02 President/CEO ....Dr. George EDWARDS
03 Vice Pres Institutional Services ....Mr. Bobby MCCOOL
05 Provost ....Dr. Nancy JOHNSON
35 Assoc Dean of Student Affairs ....Mr. Jimmy WRIGHT
10 Int Chief Business Affairs Officer ....Ms. Michelle MEEK
08 Director of Library Services ....Ms. Melissa FORSYTH
15 Int Director of Human Resources ....Ms. Bryen GOBLE
06 Registrar ....Ms. Della PACK
37 Director of Financial Aid ....Ms. Denise TRUSTY
09 Dir Institutional Effectiveness ....Ms. Denese ATKINSON
13 Director of Information Technology ....Mr. John DOVE
18 Dir Facilities/Safety/Auxil Svcs ....Mr. John HERALD
40 Bookstore Manager ....Ms. Stephanie WEST
26 Public Relations ....Mr. Randall ROBERTS
30 Director of Advancement ....Ms. Kelli HALL
07 Director of Admissions ....Vacant
28 Director of Cultural Diversity ....Ms. Tina TERRY
103 Int Director Workforce Solutions ....Mr. Harold BURTON
32 Mgr Transformation Communications ....Ms. Melinda JUSTICE

*Bluegrass Community and Technical College (L)

470 Cooper Drive, Lexington KY 40506-0001
County: Fayette FICE Identification: 009707
Unit ID: 156392
Telephone: (859) 246-6200 Carnegie Class: Assoc/Pub-R-L
FAX Number: (859) 246-4664 Calendar System: Semester
URL: www.bluegrass.kctcs.edu
Established: 1965 Annual Undergrad Tuition & Fees (In-State): $3,456
Enrollment: 6,513 Coed

Affiliation or Control: State IRS Status: 501(c)3
Highest Offering: Associate Degree
Program: Occupational; 2-Year Principally Bachelor's Creditable
Accreditation: SC, ADNUR, COARC, DA, DH, DT, IFSAC, MAC, NMT, POLYT, RAD, SURGT

02 President & CEO .... Dr. Augusta A. JULIAN
103 VP Workforce/Institutional Devel .... Mr. Mark MANUEL
13 Vice Pres of Information Technology .... Mr. Ren BATES
05 VP of Academics .... Dr. David M. HELLMICH
32 VP Student Dev/Enrollment Svcs .. Dr. Palisa WILLIAMS RUSHIN
10 VP Finance & Administration .... Ms. Lisa G. BELL
28 VP Multiculturalism & Inclusion .... Ms. Charlene WALKER
56 VP Regional Campuses/ Outreach .... Mr. Francis (Tri) A. ROBERTS, III
20 Dean of Academic Affairs .... Dr. Sandra CAREY
20 Dean of Academic Affairs .... Ms. Bonnie NICHOLSON
06 Registrar .... Ms. Becky HARP-STEPHENS
37 Financial Aid Director .... Ms. Runan PENDERGRAST
07 Admissions Director .... Ms. Shelbie HUGLE
15 Associate VP Institutional Develop .... Ms. Deborrah L. CATLETT
26 Chief Communications Officer .... Ms. Vernal L. KENNEDY
38 Director of Advising & Assessment .... Ms. Pamela BATES
30 Chief Resource Development Officer .... Ms. Linda EPLING
79 Assistant Dean Humanities .... Ms. Angella DAVIS
88 Assistant Dean Natural Sciences .... Ms. Tammy LILES
66 Assistant Dean Nursing .... Ms. Susan HAYES
76 Assistant Dean Allied Health .... Mr. Marty A. BAXTER
81 Asst Dean Mathematics .... Ms. Ruth SIMMS
77 Asst Dean Computer Sci/Info Systems .... Ms. Debbie HOLT
72 Asst Dean Trades/Technologies/Equn .... Mr. William FRANKLIN
88 Asst Dean Mfg Industrial Technology .... Mr. Paul TURNER
50 Asst Dean Business/Education .... Ms. Jenny JONES
83 Asst Dean Comm/Hist/Lang/Social Sci .... Ms. Vicki WILSON
08 Asst Dean Learning Resources Center .... Mr. Charles JAMES
88 Asst Dean Adult Educ/Opportunity .... Dr. Rebecca SIMMS
106 Assistant Dean Distance Learning .... Mr. Ben WORTH
18 Director of Maintenance/Operations .... Mr. Michael BALL
96 Director of Purchasing .... Ms. Tammy HORN

*Elizabethtown Community and Technical College (A)

600 College Street Road, Elizabethtown KY 42701
County: Hardin FICE Identification: 001991
Unit ID: 156648
Telephone: (270) 769-2371 Carnegie Class: Assoc/Pub-R-M
FAX Number: (270) 769-0736 Calendar System: Semester
URL: www.elizabethtown.kctcs.edu
Established: 1963 Annual Undergrad Tuition & Fees (In-State): $144
Enrollment: 7,586 Coed
Affiliation or Control: State IRS Status: 501(c)3
Highest Offering: Associate Degree
Program: Occupational; 2-Year Principally Bachelor's Creditable
Accreditation: SC, ADNUR, COARC, IFSAC, RAD

02 President .... Dr. Thelma WHITE
05 Provost (Interim) .... Dr. Diane OWSLEY
32 Chief Student Affairs Officer .... Dr. Dale BUCKLES
11 Chief Operations .... Mr. Keith JOHNSON
12 Campus Education Center Director .... Mr. Darrin POWELL
103 Dean of Workforce Development .... Dr. Thomas DAVENPORT
10 Dean of Business Affairs .... Mr. Jonathan THOMPSON
08 Library Director .... Ms. Ann THOMPSON
15 Director of Human Resources .... Ms. Kris WOOD
06 Registrar .... Mr. Bryan SMITH
13 Director of Information Technology .... Mr. Chris LEE
37 Director of Financial Aid .... Mr. Michael BARLOW
30 Chief Development .... Mr. Ronald HARRELL
26 Director of Public Relations .... Ms. Mary Jo KING
24 Learning Center Coordinator .... Ms. Pam HARPER
36 Counselor .... Ms. Sharon SPRATT
38 Counselor .... Mr. Charles SPATARO
40 Bookstore Manager .... Ms. Pamela BENTLEY
46 Assoc Dean of Inst Effectiveness .... Dr. Jack DILBECK
18 Maintenance/Operations Supervisor .... Mr. Charles COBB
57 Chair Div of Arts/Humanities .... Ms. Jacqueline HAWKINS
81 Chair Div of Biological Science .... Dr. Penelope LOGSDON
81 Chair Div of Physical Science .... Mr. Paul STURGEON
75 Chair Div Occupational Technology .... Mr. Mike HAZZARD
83 Chair Div Social & Behavioral Sci .... Ms. Theresia STEWART
28 Director of Diversity .... Ms. Felicia TOLIVER

*Gateway Community and Technical College (B)

500 Technology Way, Florence KY 41042
County: Boone FICE Identification: 005273
Unit ID: 157438
Telephone: (859) 441-4500 Carnegie Class: Assoc/Pub-S-MC
FAX Number: (859) 292-6415 Calendar System: Semester
URL: www.gateway.kctcs.edu
Established: 1961 Annual Undergrad Tuition & Fees (In-State): $4,320
Enrollment: 4,648 Coed
Affiliation or Control: State IRS Status: 501(c)3
Highest Offering: Associate Degree
Program: Occupational; 2-Year Principally Bachelor's Creditable
Accreditation: SC, IFSAC

02 President/CEO .... Dr. Ed HUGHES
04 Executive Assistant to President .... Ms. Sharon POORE
05 Provost/Vice Pres Academic Affairs .... Dr. Laura URBAN
30 VP Resource Devel/External Affairs .... Ms. Laura KROEGER
32 Vice Pres Student Development .... Ms. Ingrid WASHINGTON
10 VP Administration & Business Affs .... Mr. Mike BAKER
09 VP Knowledge Mgmt/Strategic Initiat .... Dr. Patricia GOODMAN
103 VP Business Solutions & Innovations .... Dr. Angie TAYLOR
20 Assoc Provost Academic Affairs .... Dr. Teri VONHANDORF
20 Assoc Provost Academic Affairs .... Ms. Marinell BROWN
20 Assoc Provost Academic Affairs .... Dr. Ross SANTELL
84 Dean of Enrollment Services .... Mr. Andre WASHINGTON
06 Registrar .... Ms. Robin WRIGHT
15 Director of Human Resources .... Ms. Phyllis YEAGER
18 Director Maintenance & Operations .... Mr. George HALL
26 Dir Marketing & Public Relations .... Ms. Margaret THOMSON
37 Director of Financial Aid .... Mr. Justin CRISTELLO
88 Director Early College Initiatives .... Ms. Shelby KRENTZ
08 Director Library/Information Svcs .... Vacant
25 Director of Grants .... Dr. Amber DECKER
28 Dir Inclusion/Cultural Initiatives .... Mr. Michael LEE
21 Director Budget & Accounting .... Mr. Jamie YOUNGER

*Hazard Community and Technical College (C)

One Community College Drive, Hazard KY 41701-2402
County: Perry FICE Identification: 006962
Unit ID: 156790
Telephone: (606) 436-5721 Carnegie Class: Assoc/Pub-R-M
FAX Number: (606) 439-2988 Calendar System: Semester
URL: www.hazard.kctcs.edu
Established: 1968 Annual Undergrad Tuition & Fees (In-State): $3,456
Enrollment: 3,804 Coed
Affiliation or Control: State IRS Status: 501(c)3
Highest Offering: Associate Degree
Program: Occupational; 2-Year Principally Bachelor's Creditable
Accreditation: SC, DMS, IFSAC, PTAA, RAD, SURGT

02 President/CEO .... Dr. Stephen GREINER
05 Provost/Vice Pres of Academic Svcs .... Dr. Kathy SMOOT
32 Vice President of Student Services .... Mr. Doug FRALEY
10 Chief Financial Officer .... Ms. Connie WATTS
04 Exec Admin Asst to President .... Ms. Delcie COMBS
13 Chief Information Officer .... Ms. Donna ROARK
15 Senior Director of Human Resources .... Ms. Vickie COMBS
21 Dean of Business Services .... Ms. Jackie HALL
08 Director Library Services .... Mrs. Cathy BRANSON
20 Academic Dean Lees College Campus .... Ms. Leila SMITH
103 Occup Tech & Workforce Sol Dean .... Ms. Jeniffer LINDON
20 Academic Dean Hazard Campus .... Ms. Anna NAPIER
09 Coordinator of Inst Research .... Mrs. Anna L. PUFFER
26 Director of Public Relations .... Mrs. Evelyn WOOD
37 Director of Financial Aid .... Mr. Charles ANDERSON, JR.
06 Registrar .... Ms. Libby PETERS
07 Director of Admissions .... Mr. Scott GROSS
45 Dean of Inst Effectiv/Plng & Rsrch .... Ms. Germaine SHAFFER
28 Diversity Liaison .... Ms. Alexis MALEPEAI
18 Dir of Maintenance and Operations .... Mr. Ronald HOLMES

*Henderson Community College (D)

2660 S Green Street, Henderson KY 42420-4699
County: Henderson FICE Identification: 001993
Unit ID: 156851
Telephone: (270) 827-1867 Carnegie Class: Assoc/Pub-R-M
FAX Number: (270) 831-9600 Calendar System: Semester
URL: www.henderson.kctcs.edu
Established: 1960 Annual Undergrad Tuition & Fees (In-State): $3,360
Enrollment: 1,964 Coed
Affiliation or Control: State IRS Status: 501(c)3
Highest Offering: Associate Degree
Program: Occupational; 2-Year Principally Bachelor's Creditable
Accreditation: SC, ADNUR, DH, MAC, MLTAD

02 President/CEO .... Dr. Kris WILLIAMS
05 Provost .... Dr. David F. BRAUER
32 Dean Student Affairs .... Vacant
10 Chief Business Affairs Officer .... Mr. Jerry H. GENTRY
08 Library Director .... Mr. Mike W. KNECHT
13 Chief Information Technology Ofcr .... Ms. Kimberley S. CONLEY
15 Director of Human Resources .... Ms. Doris J. LAKE
57 Director of Fine Arts Center .... Ms. Rachael BAAR
06 Registrar .... Ms. Brenda L. KNIGHT
88 Dean Success Grants .... Ms. Pamala P. WILSON
28 Director of Cultural Diversity .... Mr. William DIXON
30 Chief Institutional Advance Ofcr .... Ms. Susanne WILSON
09 Asst Dean/Dir Plng & Rsrch .... Mr. Mike THURMAN
18 Maintenance/Oper Supervisor .... Mr. David CAMPBELL
35 Student Activities Coordinator .... Mr. Larry TUTT
36 Career Services Coordinator .... Ms. Angela WATSON
37 Director Financial Aid .... Mr. Andrew ZELLERS
103 Interim Dir Workforce Solutions .... Ms. Victoria REED
88 Dir Advising and Assessment .... Mr. Cary CONLEY
88 Professional Development Coord .... Ms. Cathy HUNT
57 Division Chair Arts/Humanities .... Mr. Mike A. KNECHT
81 Div Chair Physical Sciences .... Ms. Rebecca WELLS
83 Div Chair Social/Behavior Sciences .... Mr. Eugene PATSALIDES
76 Div Chair Biological Sciences .... Ms. Kim DEAN

*Hopkinsville Community College (E)

720 North Drive, PO Box 2100,
Hopkinsville KY 42241-2100
County: Christian FICE Identification: 001994
Unit ID: 156860
Telephone: (270) 707-3700 Carnegie Class: Assoc/Pub-R-M
FAX Number: (270) 886-0237 Calendar System: Semester
URL: www.hopkinsville.kctcs.edu
Established: 1965 Annual Undergrad Tuition & Fees (In-State): $3,456
Enrollment: 3,827 Coed
Affiliation or Control: State IRS Status: 501(c)3
Highest Offering: Associate Degree
Program: Occupational; 2-Year Principally Bachelor's Creditable
Accreditation: SC, ADNUR

02 Interim President/CEO .... Dr. Patrick R. LAKE
04 Exec Admin Asst to President .... Ms. Cheryle DYMEK
05 Chief Academic Affairs Officer .... Dr. Kristin WILSON
06 Registrar .... Ms. Melissa STEVENSON
08 Library Services Director .... Ms. Cynthia A. ATKINS
09 Institutional Effectiveness Dean .... Dr. Lance R. ANGELL
10 Chief Business Affairs Officer .... Ms. Beverly A. ATWOOD
12 Campus/Educ Center Director FTC .... Ms. Allisha LCC
13 Technology Solutions Director .... Mr. Terry DUNCAN
16 Human Resources Director .... Ms. Yvonne GLASMAN
18 Maintence/Operations Director .... Mr. Dan HAMBY
19 Safety and Security Director .... Mr. John BRAUN
20 Dean of Academic Affairs .... Dr. Alissa YOUNG
21 Business Affairs Associate Dean .... Ms. Ann T. HOLLAND
26 Marketing & Communication Director .... Ms. Rena YOUNG
28 Cultural Diversity Director .... Ms. Tracey Y. FOLDEN
30 Chief Institutional Advancement Ofc .... Ms. Yvette EASTHAM
32 Chief Student Affairs Officer .... Dr. Jason D. WARREN
36 Career & Transfer Director .... Ms. Kanya ALLEN
37 Financial Aid Director .... Ms. Janet GUNTHER
38 Advising Center Director .... Ms. Deloria SCOTT
40 Bookstore Director .... Ms. Diane CUNNINGHAM
51 Continuing Education Associate Dean .... Ms. Carol KIRVES
57 Arts and Sciences Division Chair .... Dr. Ken CASEY
72 Professional & Technical Studies .... Mr. Gregory BRIDGEMAN
76 Allied Health Div Chair .... Ms. Peggy I. BOZARTH
81 Mathmatics & Sciences Div Chair .... Mr. Ted H. WILSON
103 Interim Workforce Transitions Ofcr .... Ms. Carol KIRVES

*Jefferson Community and Technical College (F)

109 E Broadway, Louisville KY 40202-2000
County: Jefferson FICE Identification: 006961
Unit ID: 156921
Telephone: (502) 213-5333 Carnegie Class: Assoc/Pub-U-MC
FAX Number: N/A Calendar System: Semester
URL: www.jefferson.kctcs.edu
Established: 1967 Annual Undergrad Tuition & Fees (In-State): $4,090
Enrollment: 14,346 Coed
Affiliation or Control: State IRS Status: 501(c)3
Highest Offering: Associate Degree
Program: Occupational; 2-Year Principally Bachelor's Creditable
Accreditation: SC, ACFEI, ADNUR, CAHIIM, COARC, DMS, IFSAC, MAC, OTA, PTAA, RAD, SURGT

02 President .... Dr. Anthony NEWBERRY
05 Provost/Chief Academic Affairs Ofcr .... Dr. Diane CALHOUN-FRENCH
10 Chief Business Officer .... Ms. Norma NORTHERN
20 Dean Academic Affs Tech Prorgrams .... Mr. Robert SILLIMAN
20 Dean Academic Affs Downtown .... Dr. Randy DAVIS
20 Dean Academic Affairs Southwest .... Dr. Katy VARNER
32 Dean of Student Affairs Southwest .... Dr. Denise GRAY-LACKEY
32 Dean Student Affairs Downtown .... Dr. Laura SMITH
21 Associate Dean of Business Affairs .... Vacant
08 Library Services Director .... Ms. Sheree WILLIAMS
08 Library Svcs Director Southwest .... Vacant
13 Director Information Technology .... Mr. Thomas ROGERS
09 Director of Institutional Research .... Dr. Mary C. JONES
06 Registrar .... Ms. Amanda TINDALL
28 Director of Cultural Diversity .... Vacant
26 Dir of Marketing/Public Relations .... Ms. Lisa BROSKY
15 Director of Human Resources .... Mr. Kent ROBINSON
18 Facilities Director .... Mr. Craig TURPIN
37 Director of Financial Aid .... Vacant
30 Dir Inst Advance/Development Coord .... Ms. Jo Carole DICKSON
88 Director CE/CS/Business/ Industry .... Ms. Mary Ann HYLAND-MURR
07 Director of Admissions .... Ms. Melanie VAUGHAN-COOKE
38 Director of Student Counseling .... Dr. Telly SELLARS
96 Director of Purchasing .... Ms. Pamela DUMM
12 Director of Carrolton Campus .... Ms. Susan CARLISLE
12 Director of Shelby Campus .... Dr. John WIELAND
12 Int Dir Bullitt County Campus .... Ms. Donna MILLER
44 Manager of Advancement .... Ms. Karla HALL
31 Coord Cont Education/Cmty Services .... Ms. Donna HILL
24 Learning Center Coord Downtown .... Ms. Reneau WAGGONER
79 Chairperson Humanities Southwest .... Dr. Donna ELKINS
50 Chairperson Business Downtown .... Dr. Pamela BESSER
65 Div Chair Natural Sci Downtown .... Ms. Caroline MARTINSON
66 Dean Nursing/Allied Health .... Dr. Carolyn O'DANIEL
76 Chair Allied Health Jefferson Tech .... Ms. Eva OLTMAN
83 Div Chair Behav/Soc Sci Downtown .... Mr. Ron WALFORD
83 Chair Behav/Soc Sci Southwest .... Ms. Cathy WRIGHT
50 Chairperson Business Southwest .... Mr. Pete RODSKI

79 Chairperson Humanities Downtown ... Ms. Marlisa AUSTIN
81 Chrpsn Natural Science Southwest ... Mr. Gerry JOHNSON
72 Chair Technology/Related Sci-SW ... Mr. Bruce JOST
72 Chair Technology & Industry ... Mr. Andrew KORNOWSKI

*Madisonville Community College (A)

2000 College Drive, Madisonville KY 42431-9199
County: Hopkins FICE Identification: 009010
Unit ID: 157304
Telephone: (270) 824-8573 Carnegie Class: Assoc/Pub-R-M
FAX Number: (270) 824-1864 Calendar System: Semester
URL: www.madisonville.kctcs.edu
Established: 1968 Annual Undergrad Tuition & Fees (In-State): $3,500
Enrollment: 4,555 Coed
Affiliation or Control: State IRS Status: 501(c)3
Highest Offering: Associate Degree
Program: Occupational; 2-Year Principally Bachelor's Creditable
Accreditation: SC, ADNUR, COARC, IFSAC, MLTAD, OTA, PTAA, RAD, SURGA, SURGT

02 President ... Dr. Judith L. RHOADS
05 Chief Academic Affairs Officer ... Dr. Deborah M. COX
10 Chief Business Affairs Officer ... Mr. Ray GILLASPIE
32 Dean of Student Affairs ... Mr. Jonathan V. PARRENT
72 Division Chair Applied Technology ... Ms. Darlena GALLEGOS
66 Div Chr Nursing/Related Tech ... Ms. Patricia SIMMONS
79 Div Chr Humanities/Related Tech ... Dr. Scott VANDER PLOEG
83 Div Chr Social Science/Related Tech ... Mr. Chester M. CUNNINGHAM
81 Div Chr Mathematics and Sciences ... Dr. John LOWBRIDGE
76 Div Chr Allied Health/Related Tech ... Ms. Karol A. CONRAD
08 Director of Library Services ... Ms. Cherry L. BERGES
06 Registrar ... Ms. Tiffanie WITT
15 Director of Human Resources ... Ms. May F. WRIGHT
36 Counselor ... Ms. Sherry D. HEWELL
30 Director of Advancement ... Mr. John E. PETERS
37 Director of Financial Aid ... Ms. Martha PHELPS
26 Public Relations Officer ... Ms. Joyce RIGGS
56 Extended Campus Director ... Dr. George G. HUMPHREYS
25 Dir Grants/Planning & Effectiveness ... Mr. David A. SCHUERMER
28 Director of Cultural Diversity ... Mr. James H. BOWLES
103 Director Workforce Solutions ... Mr. Mike DAVENPORT
20 Associate Academic Officer ... Ms. Lisa A. HOWERTON
21 Manager Business Operations ... Mr. Michael L. JOHNSON
40 Bookstore Manager ... Ms. Sonya L. BURNS
84 Coord of Enrollment Management ... Ms. Aimee J. WILKERSON

*Maysville Community and Technical College (B)

1755 US 68, Maysville KY 41056-8910
County: Mason FICE Identification: 006960
Unit ID: 157331
Telephone: (606) 759-7141 Carnegie Class: Assoc/Pub-R-M
FAX Number: (606) 759-7174 Calendar System: Semester
URL: www.maysville.kctcs.edu
Established: 1966 Annual Undergrad Tuition & Fees (In-State): $4,050
Enrollment: 4,634 Coed
Affiliation or Control: State IRS Status: 501(c)3
Highest Offering: Associate Degree
Program: Occupational; 2-Year Principally Bachelor's Creditable; Music Emphasis
Accreditation: SC, IFSAC, MAC

02 President ... Dr. Ed STORY
05 Chief Academic Officer ... Dr. Juston PATE
10 Chief Finance & Facilities Officer ... Mr. George A. JONES
32 Dean Student Development ... Ms. Patricia MASSIE
20 Assoc Dean Academic Support Svc ... Dr. Dana CALLAND
09 Assoc Dean Institutional Rsch/Plng ... Ms. Pam STAFFORD
21 Associate Dean of Finance ... Mr. Steve WINFREY
08 Director Library Services ... Ms. Sonja EADS
13 Director Information Technology ... Mr. Henry JEFFERSON
30 Dir Resource Development/Foundation ... Ms. Cara CLARKE
103 Chief Officer Workforce Solutions ... Ms. Barbara CAMPBELL
37 Director Student Financial Aid ... Ms. Leslie STORIE
06 Registrar ... Ms. Lori GAUNCE
26 Public Relations Director ... Ms. Tina CURTIS
28 Director of Diversity ... Mr. Noel WILLIAMS
15 Director of Human Resources ... Ms. Sandi L. ESTILL
40 Bookstore Manager ... Ms. Kaye HIGH
24 Coordinator of Assessment/Testing ... Ms. Frances PETERSON
20 Coordinator of Academic Programs ... Mr. Stanley CLICK
50 Div Chr Bus/Inform Technologies ... Ms. Darla HUNT
49 Div Chair Liberal Arts/Education ... Mr. John KLEE
81 Div Chair Math/Science/Agriculture ... Dr. Angela FULTZ
66 Division Chair of Health Sciences ... Ms. Deborah NOLDER
72 Division Chair Industrial Tech ... Mr. Stanley W. CLICK

*Owensboro Community and Technical College (C)

4800 New Hartford Road, Owensboro KY 42303-1899
County: Daviess FICE Identification: 030345
Unit ID: 247940
Telephone: (270) 686-4400 Carnegie Class: Assoc/Pub-R-M
FAX Number: (270) 686-4496 Calendar System: Semester
URL: www.octc.kctcs.edu
Established: 1986 Annual Undergrad Tuition & Fees (In-State): $3,456
Enrollment: 4,762 Coed
Affiliation or Control: State IRS Status: 501(c)3
Highest Offering: Associate Degree
Program: Occupational; 2-Year Principally Bachelor's Creditable
Accreditation: SC, IFSAC, RAD, SURGT

02 President ... Dr. James S. KLAUBER
04 Assistant to the President ... Ms. Kittridge MIDKIFF
05 VP of Academic Affairs ... Dr. Scott WILLIAMS
32 VP of Student Affairs ... Mr. Kevin BEARDMORE
30 VP Institutional Advancement ... Mr. Larry S. MILLER
10 VP of Business Affairs ... Ms. Sarah PRICE
13 VP Information Technology ... Mr. James HARTZ
103 VP Workforce Solutions ... Ms. Cynthia FIORELLA
35 Assoc Dean of Student Affairs ... Ms. Sandy CARDEN
08 Library Services Director ... Ms. Donna ABELL
06 Registrar ... Ms. Sandy CARDEN
15 Director of Human Resources ... Ms. Victoria HOHIEMER
09 Director of Institutional Research ... Mr. Kevin BEARDMORE
29 Dir Advancement/Alumni Relations ... Ms. Linda TAYLOR
37 Financial Aid Director ... Ms. Bernice AYER
26 Director of Public Relations ... Ms. Bernadette TOYE-HALE
28 Director of Diversity ... Mr. Lewatis MCNEAL
38 Director Student Counseling ... Ms. Barbara TIPMORE
84 Director Enrollment Management ... Mr. Kevin BEARDMORE
96 Director of Purchasing ... Ms. Sarah PRICE
24 Dir of Teaching & Learning Center ... Ms. Judy COOMES
40 Bookstore Manager ... Ms. Sonya SOUTHARD
88 TV Production Manager ... Mr. John BRYENTON
07 Senior Admissions Advisor ... Ms. Linda CALHOUN
36 Career Resource/Placemnt Ctr Coord ... Ms. Katie BALLARD
79 Associate Dean Humanities ... Dr. Julia LEDFORD
83 Assoc Dean Soc Sci/Bus/Public Svc ... Dr. Marc MALTBY
81 Assoc Dean Math/Sci/Allied Health ... Dr. Veena SALLAN
75 Assoc Dean Advanced Technologies ... Mr. Dean AUTRY
66 Associate Dean Nursing ... Ms. Melissa ALSTOTT
88 Assc Dean Personal Svc/Skill Trades ... Mr. Mike RODGERS
20 Assoc Dean Academic Affairs ... Dr. Stacy EDDS-ELLIS
09 Coord Institutional Effectiveness ... Ms. Joy BOWLDS

*Somerset Community College (D)

808 Monticello Street, Somerset KY 42501-2973
County: Pulaski FICE Identification: 001997
Unit ID: 157711
Telephone: (877) 629-9722 Carnegie Class: Assoc/Pub-R-L
FAX Number: N/A Calendar System: Semester
URL: somerset.kctcs.edu
Established: 1965 Annual Undergrad Tuition & Fees (In-State): $3,456
Enrollment: 8,000 Coed
Affiliation or Control: State IRS Status: 501(c)3
Highest Offering: Associate Degree
Program: Occupational; 2-Year Principally Bachelor's Creditable
Accreditation: SC, ADNUR, COARC, IFSAC, MLTAD, PTAA, RAD, SURGT

02 President/CEO ... Dr. Jo MARSHALL
05 Provost ... Dr. Tony L. HONEYCUTT
49 Dean of Arts and Sciences ... Ms. Sharon F. WHITEHEAD
09 Dir of Institutional Effectiveness ... Ms. Amy L. BEAUDOIN
32 Dean of Student Affairs ... Ms. Tracy L. CASADA
106 Assoc Dean for Distance Education ... Ms. Linda D. BOURNE
10 Chief Business Affairs Officer ... Mr. Timothy ZIMMERMAN
11 Chief Operations Officer ... Mr. Larry ABBOTT
30 Dir of Institutional Advancement ... Ms. Cindy D. CLOUSE
103 Chief Cmty Wkfc & Economic Dev Ofc ... Mr. David A. WILES
76 Dean for Health Sciences ... Ms. Nancy L. POWELL
79 Assoc Dean Humanities/Fine Arts/SS ... Mr. Jon BURLEW
83 Assoc Dean Math/Natural Science ... Mr. Clint R. HAYES
88 Assoc Dean Const/Manuf/Trans ... Mr. Daniel C. BURNETT
50 Assoc Dean Bus/IT/Crim Just/Ed/Cons ... Ms. Lois A. MCWHORTER
88 Dean Academic Support Services ... Mr. Bruce GOVER
46 Dir of Prof and Org Development ... Ms. Karen M. WRIGHT
20 Assoc Dean for Learning ... Ms. Margo HAMM
37 Director of Financial Aid ... Mr. Tony MEEKS
06 Registrar ... Ms. Paula J. GUFFEY
15 Director of Human Resources ... Ms. Jill N. MEECE
26 Director of Public Relations ... Ms. Cindy D. CLOUSE
28 Director of Cultural Diversity ... Ms. Elaine WILSON
12 Director of McCreary Center ... Mr. Steve HAMMONS
88 Dean of Applied Technology ... Mr. Roger L. ANGEVINE
12 Director of Clinton Center ... Ms. Judy TALLENT
12 Director of Casey Center ... Ms. Judy SAPP
12 Director of Russell Center ... Ms. Winfrey BATES

*Southcentral Kentucky Community and Technical College (E)

1845 Loop Drive, Bowling Green KY 42101-9202
County: Warren FICE Identification: 005271
Unit ID: 156338
Telephone: (270) 901-1000 Carnegie Class: Assoc/Pub-R-M
FAX Number: (270) 901-1145 Calendar System: Semester
URL: www.bowlinggreen.kctcs.edu
Established: 1939 Annual Undergrad Tuition & Fees (In-State): $3,456
Enrollment: 5,301 Coed
Affiliation or Control: State IRS Status: 501(c)3
Highest Offering: Associate Degree
Program: Occupational; 2-Year Principally Bachelor's Creditable; Technical Emphasis
Accreditation: SC, ACFEI, COARC, DMS, IFSAC, POLYT, RAD, SURGT

02 President & CEO ... Dr. Phillip W. NEAL
05 Vice President Academic Affairs ... Dr. Maggie SHELTON
32 Vice President Student Affairs ... Dr. Gerald NAPOLES
06 Registrar ... Ms. Brooke JUSTICE
10 Vice President Business Affairs ... Mr. Chris CUMENS
15 Director of Human Resources ... Ms. Sherri L. FORESTER
26 Director of Public Relations ... Mr. Mark D. BROOKS
30 Director of Advancement ... Ms. Donna P. MARTIN
37 Director of Financial Aid ... Mr. Rickie W. WILSON
09 Director Institutuion Effectiveness ... Mr. Mark GARRETT
103 Dean of Workforce Solutions ... Mr. Lewis BURKE, JR.

*Southeast Kentucky Community and Technical College (F)

700 College Road, Cumberland KY 40823-1099
County: Harlan FICE Identification: 001998
Unit ID: 157739
Telephone: (606) 589-2145 Carnegie Class: Assoc/Pub-R-M
FAX Number: (606) 589-4941 Calendar System: Semester
URL: www.southeast.kctcs.edu
Established: 1960 Annual Undergrad Tuition & Fees (In-State): $3,456
Enrollment: 5,123 Coed
Affiliation or Control: State IRS Status: 501(c)3
Highest Offering: Associate Degree
Program: Occupational; 2-Year Principally Bachelor's Creditable
Accreditation: SC, ADNUR, COARC, MLTAD, PNUR, PTAA, RAD, SURGT

02 President ... Dr. Lynn MOORE
05 Chief Academic Officer ... Dr. Wheeler CONOVER
10 Chief Business Affairs Officer ... Vacant
12 Branch Campus Director ... Ms. Deborah YOUNG
12 Campus/Education Center Director ... Mr. Stephen STURGILL
06 Dean Student Affairs/Registrar ... Vacant
21 Dean Administration Services ... Mr. Tom POPE
11 Chief Operations Officer ... Mr. Larry WARF
103 Chief Community Workforce ... Mr. Vic ADAMS
20 Chief Learning Officer ... Mr. Rick MASON
26 Director of Public Relations ... Mr. Chris JONES
16 Human Resources Director ... Ms. Billie FRANKS
08 Head Librarian ... Mr. Warren GRAY
13 Director of Information Technology ... Mr. Merrill GALLOWAY
09 Director of Institutional Research ... Vacant
28 Director of Diversity ... Ms. Carolyn SUNDY
30 Chief Institutional Advancement Ofc ... Ms. Susan CALDWELL
32 Chief Student Affairs Officer ... Ms. Rebecca PARROTT
96 Dean of Finance ... Ms. Angela SIMPSON
07 Director of Admissions ... Ms. Veria BALDWIN
40 Bookstore Manager ... Ms. Tammy DEAL
37 Coordinator Financial Aid ... Ms. Charlotte LOCKABY
76 Div Chr Allied Hlth/Coord Clin Lab ... Ms. Kathy GUYN
83 Div Chair Soc Sci/Business/Rel Tech ... Mr. Kevin LAMBERT
79 Div Chair Humanities/Comm/Fine Arts ... Ms. Terry MACUILA
88 Div Chair Industrial Technology ... Mr. Ronnie DANIELS
65 Div Chair Natural Sciences ... Ms. Pat SCOPA

*West Kentucky Community and Technical College (G)

4810 Alben Barkley Drive, Paducah KY 42002-7380
County: McCracken FICE Identification: 001979
Unit ID: 157483
Telephone: (270) 554-9200 Carnegie Class: Assoc/Pub-R-L
FAX Number: (270) 554-6217 Calendar System: Semester
URL: www.westkentucky.kctcs.edu
Established: 1909 Annual Undergrad Tuition & Fees (In-State): $4,320
Enrollment: 7,245 Coed
Affiliation or Control: State IRS Status: 501(c)3
Highest Offering: Associate Degree
Program: Occupational; 2-Year Principally Bachelor's Creditable
Accreditation: SC, ACBSP, ACFEI, ADNUR, COARC, DA, DMS, IFSAC, MLTAD, POLYT, PTAA, RAD, SURGT

02 President ... Dr. Barbara VEAZEY
103 VP of Workforce Solutions ... Mr. Jim PAPE
05 VP of Academic Affairs ... Dr. Tena PAYNE
32 VP of Student Affairs ... Dr. Belinda DALTON-RUSSELL
10 VP of Administrative Services ... Mr. John CARRICO
88 VP Learning Initiatives ... Ms. Sherry ANDERSON
45 VP Institutional Development ... Dr. Steve FREEMAN
10 VP Business Affairs ... Ms. Susan GRAVES
08 Library Services Director ... Mr. Ken BRADSHAW
37 Financial Aid Director ... Mr. Nathanial SLATON
26 Public Relations Director ... Ms. Janett BLYTHE
13 Director Information Technology ... Ms. Ruby RODGERS
15 Director Human Resources ... Ms. Bridget CANTER
30 Dir Institutional Advancement ... Ms. Kay TRAVIS
40 Bookstore Manager ... Mr. Todd MITCHELL
06 Int Registrar/Dir of Admissions ... Ms. Jess PUFFENBARGER
35 Student Activities Coordinator ... Ms. Amy ELMORE
79 Dean Humanities/Fine Arts/Soc Sci ... Ms. Sharla KRUPANSKY
66 Dean Nursing Division ... Ms. Shari GHOLSON
50 Dean Business/Comp Related Tech Div ... Ms. Tammy POTTER
76 Dean Allied Health Division ... Ms. Peggy BLOCK
75 Dean Applied Tech Division ... Ms. Stephanie MILLIKEN
81 Dean Science & Math Division ... Dr. Karen HLINKA
97 Dean Transition Education Div ... Ms. Maria FLYNN
09 Associate VP of IE ... Dr. Renea AKIN
28 Director of Diversity ... Ms. Jipaum ASKEW-ROBINSON

Kentucky Mountain Bible College (H)

855 Highway 541, Jackson KY 41339
County: Breathitt FICE Identification: 030021
Unit ID: 157030

Telephone: (606) 693-5000 Carnegie Class: Spec/Faith
FAX Number: (606) 693-4884 Calendar System: Semester
URL: www.kmbc.edu
Established: 1931 Annual Undergrad Tuition & Fees: $6,690
Enrollment: 84 Coed
Affiliation or Control: Independent Non-Profit IRS Status: 501(c)3
Highest Offering: Baccalaureate
Program: 2-Year Principally Bachelor's Creditable; Liberal Arts And General; Religious Emphasis
Accreditation: BI

01 President .... Dr. Philip E. SPEAS
05 Exec Vice Pres/VP Academic Affs .... Rev. Thomas H. LORIMER
10 Chief Business Manager .... Ms. Joy PAUL
32 Dean of Student Affairs .... Mr. Jim NELSON
13 Director IT .... Mr. Stephen A. LORIMER
08 Head Librarian .... Ms. Patricia A. BOWEN
06 Registrar .... Mr. Richard ENGLEHARDT
07 Chief Admissions Counselor .... Mr. David W. LORIMER
37 Director Student Financial Aid .... Ms. Rosita MARSHALL
26 Dir PR/Foreign Stdnts/Dean of Men .... Mr. James H. NELSON
34 Dean of Women .... Ms. Wanda SPEAS

Kentucky State University (A)

400 E Main Street, Frankfort KY 40601-2355
County: Franklin FICE Identification: 001968
Unit ID: 157058
Telephone: (502) 597-6000 Carnegie Class: Bac/A&S
FAX Number: (502) 597-6490 Calendar System: Semester
URL: www.kysu.edu
Established: 1886 Annual Undergrad Tuition & Fees (In-State): $8,235
Enrollment: 2,524 Coed
Affiliation or Control: State IRS Status: 501(c)3
Highest Offering: Master's
Program: Liberal Arts And General; Teacher Preparatory; Business Emphasis
Accreditation: SC, ACBSP, ADNUR, MUS, NUR, SPAA, SW, TED

01 President .... Dr. Mary E. SIAS
05 Provost/Vice Pres Academic Affs .... Dr. Joel THIERSTEIN
10 Chief Financial Officer .... Ms. Anita LOCKRIDGE
32 VP Student Success/Enrollment Mgmt .... Dr. Lorenzo ESTERS
30 Exec VP External Relation & Dev .... Mr. Hinfred MCDUFFIE
07 Director of Admissions .... Mr. Juan ALEXANDER
23 Director Student Health Services .... Ms. Floarine WILSON
31 Int Director Educational Outreach .... Ms. Irma JOHNSON
06 Director Records/Registrar .... Vacant
08 Director Libraries .... Ms. Shella STUCKEY
100 Chief of Staff/Exec Asst to Pres .... Mr. Stephen MASON
36 Dir Couns/Career Plng/Placement .... Mr. Ronald BANKS
14 Director Information Technology .... Mr. Eric BERGQUIST
15 Director Human Resources .... Mr. Gary MEISELES
29 Director Alumni Affairs .... Mr. Garland HIGGINS
39 Director Residence Life .... Ms. Renee' WATSON
37 Director Student Financial Aid .... Ms. Victoria OWENS
25 Dean Col of Ag (CAFSSS)/Land Grant .... Dr. Teferi TSEGAYE
26 Director Public Relations .... Ms. Felicia LEWIS
43 General Counsel .... Ms. Lori A. DAVIS
21 Internal Auditor .... Vacant
18 Director Physical Plant .... Mr. Jack MCNEAR
41 Director Athletics .... Dr. Denisha HENDRICKS
19 Chief University Police .... Vacant
45 Budget Director .... Vacant
84 Director Enrollment Management .... Dr. Antonio BOYLE
96 Director of Purchasing .... Ms. Tonya MONTGOMERY
49 Dean College of Arts & Science .... Dr. Sam OLEKA
107 Dean College of Prof Studies .... Dr. Gashaw LAKE
09 Coord Instl Research/Effectivenes .... Dr. Robin GEIGER

Kentucky Wesleyan College (B)

3000 Frederica Street, Owensboro KY 42301
County: Daviess FICE Identification: 001969
Unit ID: 157076
Telephone: (270) 926-3111 Carnegie Class: Bac/Diverse
FAX Number: (270) 926-3112 Calendar System: Semester
URL: www.kwc.edu
Established: 1858 Annual Undergrad Tuition & Fees: $21,200
Enrollment: 678 Coed
Affiliation or Control: United Methodist IRS Status: 501(c)3
Highest Offering: Baccalaureate
Program: Liberal Arts And General; Teacher Preparatory
Accreditation: SC, IACBE

01 President .... Dr. Craig TURNER
05 VP Acad Affairs/Dean of the College .... Dr. Paula DEHN
03 Executive Vice President .... Vacant
10 Vice Pres for Finance/Treasurer .... Ms. Cindra K. STIFF
30 VP for Development/Alumni Relations .... Vacant
32 VP of Student Affairs .... Mr. Scott E. KRAMER
07 Director of Admissions .... Mr. Rashad SMITH
06 Registrar .... Ms. Jennifer VAUGHN
09 Director of Institutional Research .... Mr. Mark C. HEDGES
15 Director of Personnel Services .... Mrs. Linda B. KELLER
37 Director of Student Financial Aid .... Ms. Samantha HAYES
89 Director of the PLUS Center .... Ms. Marisue S. COY
08 Director of Library Learning Center . Mrs. Patricia G. MCFARLING
41 Athletic Director .... Vacant
21 Controller .... Ms. Courtney LEMASTER
26 Director of Public Relations .... Ms. Kathy RUTHERMAN
42 Campus Minister .... Mr. Kent LEWIS

Lexington Theological Seminary (C)

631 S Limestone, Lexington KY 40508-3288
County: Fayette FICE Identification: 001971
Unit ID: 157207
Telephone: (859) 252-0361 Carnegie Class: Spec/Faith
FAX Number: (859) 281-6042 Calendar System: Semester
URL: www.lextheo.edu
Established: 1865 Annual Graduate Tuition & Fees: $10,840
Enrollment: 75 Coed
Affiliation or Control: Christian Church (Disciples Of Christ)
IRS Status: 501(c)3
Highest Offering: Doctorate; No Undergraduates
Program: Professional; Religious Emphasis
Accreditation: THEOL

01 President .... Dr. Charisse L. GILLETT
05 Dean .... Dr. Richard WEIS
30 Vice President for Advancement .... Mr. Mark BLANKENSHIP
10 Chief Financial Officer .... Mrs. Laura DAVIS
06 Registrar .... Ms. Windy KIDD
08 Librarian .... Ms. Dolores YILIBUW
36 Director Student Placement .... Rev. Jan EHRMANTRAUT
13 Director Information Services .... Mr. Ben WYATT
07 Director Admission .... Rev. Erin CASH

Lindsey Wilson College (D)

210 Lindsey Wilson Street, Columbia KY 42728-1298
County: Adair FICE Identification: 001972
Unit ID: 157216
Telephone: (270) 384-2126 Carnegie Class: Master's M
FAX Number: (270) 384-8200 Calendar System: Semester
URL: www.lindsey.edu
Established: 1903 Annual Undergrad Tuition & Fees: $29,230
Enrollment: 2,700 Coed
Affiliation or Control: United Methodist IRS Status: 501(c)3
Highest Offering: Master's
Program: 2-Year Principally Bachelor's Creditable; Liberal Arts And General; Teacher Preparatory
Accreditation: SC, CACREP, IACBE

01 President .... Dr. William T. LUCKEY, JR.
03 Chancellor .... Dr. John B. BEGLEY
05 Vice President Academic Affairs .... Dr. Bettie C. STARR
10 Vice President Administration .... Dr. Mark COLEMAN
30 Vice President Advancement .... Mr. Kevin A. THOMPSON
04 Executive Assistant .... Mrs. Nancy SINCLAIR
32 Vice President Student Services .... Dr. Dean ADAMS
37 VP Educ Outreach/Stdnt Finan Svcs .... Mrs. Denise G. FUDGE
35 Dean of Students .... Mr. Christopher SCHMIDT
20 Associate Academic Dean .... Ms. Leslie KORB
88 Dean of Chapel .... Dr. Terry W. SWAN
07 Dean of Admissions .... Mrs. Traci M. POOLER
07 Director of Admissions .... Mrs. Charity F. FERGUSON
55 Director of Evening College .... Ms. Regina HAUGEN
41 Athletic Director .... Mr. Willis POOLER, III
06 Registrar .... Mrs. Sue B. COOMER
15 Director of Human Resources .... Mrs. Karen F. WRIGHT
31 Dir of Civic Engagement & Std Ldrsp .... Mrs. Amy C. THOMPSON-WELLS
36 Director Career Services .... Mrs. Ashley MILLER
08 Librarian .... Mr. C. Phil HANNA
18 Director of Physical Plant .... Mr. Michael L. NEWTON
21 Director of Auxiliary Services .... Mr. Jeff WILLIS
40 Bookstore Manager .... Mrs. Amy M. COOPER
35 Director of Student Activities .... Mrs. Jayne S. HOPKINS
85 Dir of International Stdnt Programs .... Mrs. Suzy MCALPINE
14 Director Information Services .... Mrs. Harriet B. GOLD
13 Director of Information Systems .... Mr. Anthony MOORE
26 Public Relations Officer .... Mr. Duane BONIFER
29 Assistant to Pres Alumni Affairs .... Mr. Randy BURNS
19 Director Safety/Security .... Mr. Michael STATEN
42 Chaplain .... Rev. Troy A. ELMORE
09 Dir Plng/Instl Effective/Research .... Vacant
37 Director Student Financial Services .... Ms. Marilyn RADFORD
38 Director Student Counseling .... Dr. Jeff CRANE
66 Director of Nursing .... Mrs. Marian SMITH

Louisville Bible College (E)

8013 Damascus Road, Louisville KY 40228
County: Jefferson FICE Identification: 041418
Unit ID: 157234
Telephone: (502) 231-5221 Carnegie Class: Spec/Faith
FAX Number: (502) 231-5222 Calendar System: Semester
URL: www.myLBC.us
Established: 1948 Annual Undergrad Tuition & Fees: $4,800
Enrollment: 118 Coed
Affiliation or Control: Independent Non-Profit IRS Status: 501(c)3
Highest Offering: Master's
Program: Religious Emphasis
Accreditation: BI

01 President .... Dr. Tracy W. MARX
30 VP for Operations & Advancement .... Danny L. DYE
05 Academic Dean .... Dr. Peter RASOR

Louisville Presbyterian Theological Seminary (F)

1044 Alta Vista Road, Louisville KY 40205-1798
County: Jefferson FICE Identification: 001974
Unit ID: 157298
Telephone: (502) 895-3411 Carnegie Class: Spec/Faith
FAX Number: (502) 895-1096 Calendar System: 4/1/4
URL: www.lpts.edu
Established: 1853 Annual Graduate Tuition & Fees: $10,546
Enrollment: 219 Coed
Affiliation or Control: Presbyterian Church (U.S.A.) IRS Status: 501(c)3
Highest Offering: Doctorate; No Undergraduates
Program: Professional; Religious Emphasis
Accreditation: SC, MFCD, THEOL

01 President .... Dr. Michael JINKINS
30 Vice Pres for Inst Advancement .... Ms. Linda S. MEDLEY
10 Vice President & CFO .... Mr. Patrick A. CECIL
05 Dean of the Seminary .... Dr. Susan R. GARRETT
32 Dean of Students .... Rev. Kilen GRAY
06 Registrar .... Dr. Steve COOK
102 Sr Director of Development .... Ms. Sally PENDLETON
29 Director of Seminary Relations .... Mr. Greg CLARK
44 Director of Seminary Fund .... Ms. Judy JOHNSTON
14 Director of Data Management .... Ms. Heather GRIFFIN
27 Director of Communications .... Ms. Ashley SCHAFFNER
08 Director of Library Services .... Dr. Matthew COLLINS
21 Controller .... Ms. Marti F. MARSH
51 Director of DMin & Continuing Ed .... Dr. David HESTER
07 Director of Recruitment & Admiss .... Rev. Cheri HARPER
13 Director of IT Services .... Mr. Jack SHARER
18 Director of Facilities .... Mr. Tim WILLIAMS

MedTech College-Lexington (G)

1648 McGrathiana Pkwy, Suite 200, Lexington KY 40511
Telephone: (859) 410-2110 Identification: 770722
Accreditation: ACICS, MAC

† Main campus is MedTech College in Indianapolis, IN.

Mid-Continent University (H)

99 Powell Road E, Mayfield KY 42066-9007
County: Graves FICE Identification: 025762
Unit ID: 157359
Telephone: (270) 247-8521 Carnegie Class: Bac/Diverse
FAX Number: (270) 247-3115 Calendar System: Semester
URL: www.midcontinent.edu
Established: 1949 Annual Undergrad Tuition & Fees: $13,350
Enrollment: 2,264 Coed
Affiliation or Control: Southern Baptist IRS Status: 501(c)3
Highest Offering: Master's
Program: Liberal Arts And General; Business Emphasis
Accreditation: SC

01 President .... Dr. Robert J. IMHOFF
04 Assistant to the President .... Mrs. Mitzi TURNER
03 Executive Vice President .... Dr. Charles W. FORD
05 Acting VP Academic Affairs .... Dr. Debra HUDSON
10 VP Finance & Administration .... Col. Andrew B. STRATTON
84 Dean of Enrollment Management .... Mr. Karl HATTON
55 VP Adult Pgms/Dir Advantage Pgm .... Dr. Jacquelyn IMHOFF
09 VP Inst Effectiveness/Planning .... Dr. Cynthia TWEEDELL
08 Dean of the Markham Library .... Mr. Ben GRAVES
30 Director of External Relations .... Mr. David SMITH
06 Advantage Registrar .... Mr. Keenan FORD
06 Traditional Registrar .... Mrs. Tracey THORNTON
21 Director of Budget & Planning .... Col. Andrew B. STRATTON
07 Director Admissions/Advantage Pgm .... Mr. Chris AUSTIN
07 Director of Graduate Admissions .... Mrs. Wendy PUCKETT
07 Traditional Admissions Director .... Ms. Teresa PROCTOR
37 Executive Director of Financial Aid .... Ms. Paula CLENDENEN
41 Athletic Director .... Mr. Kevin IMHOFF
18 Director of Facilities .... Mr. Tim BLALOCK
14 Director of Information Services .... Mr. David ROSS
15 Director of Human Resources .... Mrs. Angela LOCKARD
19 Director of Campus Security .... Mr. Wayne CHAPMAN
21 Business Office Manager .... Mrs. Deborah NALL
49 Dean Baptist Col of Arts & Science .... Dr. Jamie SUMMERVILLE
73 Dean Baptist College of Bible .... Dr. Stephen WILLIAMS
58 Dean of Graduate Studies .... Dr. David WILLIAMS

Midway College (I)

512 E Stephens Street, Midway KY 40347-1120
County: Woodford FICE Identification: 001975
Unit ID: 157377
Telephone: (859) 846-4421 Carnegie Class: Bac/Diverse
FAX Number: (859) 846-5349 Calendar System: Semester
URL: www.midway.edu
Established: 1847 Annual Undergrad Tuition & Fees: $22,000
Enrollment: 1,662 Female
Affiliation or Control: Christian Church (Disciples Of Christ)
IRS Status: 501(c)3
Highest Offering: Master's
Program: 2-Year Principally Bachelor's Creditable; Liberal Arts And General; Teacher Preparatory; Professional
Accreditation: SC, ADNUR, NUR

01	President	Dr. John P. MARSDEN
05	Provost and VP of Academic Affairs	Dr. Laura ARMESTO
04	Admin Assist to the President	Ms. Sheila K. HOLSCLAW
10	Vice Pres of Business Affairs	Vacant
30	Vice President of Advancement	Vacant
84	Dean of Admissions	Dr. Johnie E. DEAN
26	Vice Pres of Marketing & Comm	Mrs. Ellen D. GREGORY
36	Dean of School for Career Dev	Dr. William (Bill) BROWN
32	Dean of Student Life	Mrs. Karen PETKO
07	Associate Dean of Admissions	Mrs. Rachel LINARES
58	Director of Graduate Admissions	Mrs. Rebecca SERRANO
06	Registrar	Mrs. Linda P. ELDRIDGE
08	Director of Library Services	Ms. Catherine L. REILENDER
41	Athletic Director	Dr. Wendy HOFFMAN
07	Director of Admissions Women's Col	Mrs. Stacy M. SHARP
13	Director of Information Systems	Mrs. C. Joan MCDANIEL
15	Director of Human Resources	Mrs. Anne COCKLEY
21	Director of Student Accounts	Mr. Robert L. NORTON
29	Director of Development/Alumni Affs	Ms. Christy c. SMITH
37	Director of Financial Aid	Ms. Katie A. CONRAD
18	Director of Physical Plant	Mr. Stephen D. GOODWIN
39	Dir Residence Life/Stdnt Activities	Ms. Leigh OAKLEY
27	Chief Information Officer	Dr. Salah SHAKIR

Morehead State University (A)

150 University Boulevard, Morehead KY 40351-1689

County: Rowan — FICE Identification: 001976 — Unit ID: 157386

Telephone: (606) 783-2221 — Carnegie Class: Master's L

FAX Number: N/A — Calendar System: Semester

URL: www.moreheadstate.edu

Established: 1887 — Annual Undergrad Tuition & Fees (In-State): $7,498

Enrollment: 11,172 — Coed

Affiliation or Control: State — IRS Status: 501(c)3

Highest Offering: Doctorate

Program: Occupational; Liberal Arts And General; Teacher Preparatory; Professional

Accreditation: SC, ADNUR, BUS, DMS, MUS, NAIT, NURSE, RAD, RADMAG, SPAA, SW, TED, THEA

01	President	Dr. Wayne D. ANDREWS
05	Acting Provost & VP Acad Affairs	Dr. Gerald L. DEMOSS
10	Chief Financial Officer/VP AFS	Ms. Beth G. PATRICK
32	Vice President Student Life	Ms. Madonna WEATHERS
30	Vice Pres for Univ Advancement	Mr. James A. SHAW
45	Executive Assistant to President	Dr. John P. ERNST
20	Assoc VP Academic Affairs/Programs	Dr. Clarenda M. PHILLIPS
04	Assistant to the President	Ms. Carol JOHNSON
06	Registrar	Ms. Roslyn PERRY
46	Director Undergrad Research Pgm	Dr. Bruce A. MATTINGLY
51	Asst VP Adult Ed & College Access	Dr. Dan J. CONNELL
84	Asst Vice Pres Enrollment Services	Mr. Jeffrey R. LILES
26	Asst VP Communication & Marketing	Ms. Jami M. HORNBUCKLE
18	Asst VP Facilities Management	Mr. Richard T. LINIO
40	Asst Vice Pres Auxiliary Services	Mr. William REDWINE
08	Dean of Library Services	Dr. David L. GREGORY
07	Dir of Undergraduate Admissions	Ms. Holly L. POLLOCK
09	Dir Inst Research & Analysis	Ms. Erin D. WRIGHT
15	Director of Human Resources	Mr. Phillip E. GNIOT
19	Chief of Police	Mr. Matt SPARKS
21	Director Accounting/Financial Svcs	Mrs. Kelli D. OWEN
21	Exec Dir Budgets & Financial Plng	Ms. Teresa C. LINDGREN
88	Dir Stdnt Act Inclusion/Ldrshp Dev	Mr. Ricardo NAZARIO-COLON
29	Director Alumni Relations	Ms. Tami B. JONES
36	AVP Student Life/Dean of Students	Mr. Kevin S. KOETT
37	Director Financial Aid	Ms. Donna J. KING
36	Director Career Services	Ms. Julia L. HAWKINS
39	Director of Housing/Residence Educ	Dr. Christopher A. SUMMERLIN
41	Director of Athletics	Mr. Brian A. HUTCHINSON
43	General Counsel	Dr. Jane FITZPATRICK
44	Director of Development	Ms. Melinda C. HIGHLEY
27	Media Relations Director	Mr. Jason BLANTON
85	Director International Education	Dr. Philip KRUMMRICH
96	Director Support Services	Ms. Ladonna M. PURCELL
38	Director of Counseling & Health Svc	Dr. Brenda K. WILBURN
50	Dean Col of Business & Public Affs	Dr. Robert ALBERT
53	Interim Dean College of Education	Dr. Kathryn N. POLMANTEER
72	Dean College Science & Technology	Dr. Roger R. MCNEIL
79	Dean Col of Arts/Human/Soc Studies	Dr. Scott MCBRIDE
27	Asst VP Technology	Mr. Steve RICHMOND
20	Asst VP Academic Affairs/IRSA	Ms. Jill C. RATLIFF

Murray State University (B)

218 Wells Hall, Murray KY 42071-3318

County: Calloway — FICE Identification: 001977 — Unit ID: 157401

Telephone: (270) 809-3011 — Carnegie Class: Master's L

FAX Number: (270) 809-3413 — Calendar System: Semester

URL: www.murraystate.edu

Established: 1922 — Annual Undergrad Tuition & Fees (In-State): $7,044

Enrollment: 10,832 — Coed

Affiliation or Control: State — IRS Status: 501(c)3

Highest Offering: Doctorate

Program: 2-Year Principally Bachelor's Creditable; Liberal Arts And General; Teacher Preparatory; Professional

Accreditation: SC, ANEST, ART, BUS, DIETD, DIETI, ENG, ENGR, ENGT, EXSC, JOUR, MUS, NURSE, SP, SW, TED, THEA

01	Interim President	Dr. Thomas I. MILLER
100	Chief of Staff	Dr. Joshua E. JACOBS
101	Sr Exec Coord for Pres/Coord Bd Rel	Ms. Jill HUNT
05	Provost/VP Academic Affairs	Dr. Jay MORGAN
10	Interim VP Finance & Admin Svcs	Ms. Jacklyn K. DUDLEY
32	VP Student Affairs	Dr. Don E. ROBERTSON
30	VP Institutional Advancement	Mr. James F. CARTER
58	Int Assoc Provost Grad Educ & Rsrch	Dr. Robert PERVINE
20	Assoc Prov/Undergrad Education	Dr. Renae D. DUNCAN
35	Assoc VP Student Affairs	Mr. Michael E. YOUNG
26	Asst VP Communications	Ms. Catherine M. SIVILLS
43	General Counsel	Mr. John P. RALL
50	Dean Bauernfeind Col of Business	Dr. Timothy S. TODD
53	Dean College of Education	Dr. David WHALEY
76	Dean Col of Health Sci & Human Svcs	Dr. Susan M. MULLER
79	Dean Col of Humanities & Fine Arts	Dr. O. Ted BROWN
81	Dean Col Science/Engineering/Tech	Dr. Stephen H. COBB
47	Dean Hutson School of Agriculture	Dr. Tony L. BRANNON
66	Dean School of Nursing	Dr. Marcia B. HOBBS
08	Dean University Libraries	Mr. Adam L. MURRAY
51	Dn Cont Educ/Academic Outreach	Dr. Brian W. VAN HORN
24	Asst Dn/Dir Dist Learn/Noncrdt Pgm	Mr. Daniel A. LAVIT
97	Coordinator University Studies	Dr. Peter F. MURPHY
92	Director Honors Program	Dr. Warren EDMINSTER
85	Director Institute for Intl Studies	Dr. Luis CANALES
104	Assoc Director Education Abroad	Ms. Melanie C. MCCALLON
84	Exec Director Enrollment Mgmt	Mr. Fred K. DIETZ
07	Dir Undgrad Admissions Svcs	Ms. Lesa C. HARRIS
06	Registrar	Ms. Tracy ROBERTS
37	Dir Student Fin Aid/Scholarships	Ms. Lori A. MITCHUM
39	Director Housing	Dr. J. David WILSON
38	Dir University Counseling Services	Dr. Angie TRZEPACZ
28	Dir African-American Student Svcs	Mr. Sidney G. CARTHELL
36	Director Career Services	Dr. Ross B. MELOAN
23	Interim Director Health Services	Ms. Kimberly S. PASCHALL
16	Director Human Resources	Mr. Thomas E. HOFFACKER
21	Sr Director Accounting & Fin Svcs	Ms. Jacklyn K. DUDLEY
21	Dir Fiscal Plng/Analysis/Budget Ofc	Mr. Carl F. PRESTFELDT
102	Executive Director MSU Foundation	Dr. Robert L. JACKSON
96	Director Procurement Services	Ms. Deanne TOBY
22	Exec Dir Inst Divrsty/Equity/Access	Ms. Cami DUFFY
88	Exec Director Regional Outreach	Ms. Gina S. WINCHESTER
13	Chief Information Officer	Ms. Linda G. MILLER
91	Manager Administrative Computing	Mr. Brantly D. TRAVIS
90	Dir Ctr for Teaching/Learn/Tech	Mr. Howard T. RICE
09	Coordinator Institutional Research	Vacant
41	Athletic Director	Mr. C. Allen WARD
18	Interim VP Finance & Admin Svcs	Ms. Jacklyn K. DUDLEY
19	Dir Public Safety/Emergency Mgmt	Mr. David V. DEVOSS
40	Director University Store	Ms. R. Karol HARDISON
25	Director Sponsored Programs	Mr. John A. ROARK
29	Assoc Director Alumni Affairs	Vacant
105	Web Manager	Mr. R. Tony A. POWELL
108	Director Institutional Assessment	Dr. Kelley C. WEZNER

National College (C)

115 E Lexington Avenue, Danville KY 40422-1517

Telephone: (859) 236-6991 — Identification: 666441

Accreditation: ACICS, MAC

† Main campus is National College in Indianapolis, IN.

National College (D)

7627 Ewing Boulevard, Florence KY 41042-1812

Telephone: (859) 525-6510 — Identification: 666442

Accreditation: ACICS, MAC, SURGT

† Main campus is National College in Indianapolis, IN.

National College (E)

2376 Sir Barton Way, Lexington KY 40509-2256

County: Fayette — Identification: 667202 — Unit ID: 157021

Telephone: (859) 253-0621 — Carnegie Class: Assoc/PrivFP4

FAX Number: (859) 254-7664 — Calendar System: Quarter

URL: www.ncbt.edu

Established: 1941 — Annual Undergrad Tuition & Fees: $11,544

Enrollment: 1,351 — Coed

Affiliation or Control: Proprietary — IRS Status: Proprietary

Highest Offering: Baccalaureate

Program: Occupational; 2-Year Principally Bachelor's Creditable

Accreditation: ACICS, MAC, SURGT

01	President	Mr. Frank LONGAKER
05	Campus Director	Ms. Kim THOMASSON
03	Vice President	Ms. Charlotte BRINNEMAN
32	Director of Student Services	Mr. Raymond BROOK
07	Regional Director of Admissions	Ms. Donna STOUTENBOROUGH

National College (F)

4205 Dixie Highway, Louisville KY 40216-4147

Telephone: (502) 447-7634 — Identification: 666443

Accreditation: ACICS, CAHIIM, MAC, SURGT

† Main campus is National College in Indianapolis, IN.

National College (G)

50 National College Boulevard, Pikeville KY 41501-3176

Telephone: (606) 478-7200 — Identification: 666444

Accreditation: ACICS, MAC

† Main campus is National College in Indianapolis, IN.

National College (H)

125 S Killarney Lane, Richmond KY 40475-2309

Telephone: (859) 623-8956 — Identification: 666445

Accreditation: ACICS, MAC

† Main campus is National College in Indianapolis, IN.

Northern Kentucky University (I)

Nunn Drive, Highland Heights KY 41099-0000

County: Campbell — FICE Identification: 009275 — Unit ID: 157447

Telephone: (859) 572-5100 — Carnegie Class: Master's L

FAX Number: (859) 572-5566 — Calendar System: Semester

URL: www.nku.edu

Established: 1968 — Annual Undergrad Tuition & Fees (In-State): $8,088

Enrollment: 15,660 — Coed

Affiliation or Control: State — IRS Status: 501(c)3

Highest Offering: Doctorate

Program: 2-Year Principally Bachelor's Creditable; Liberal Arts And General; Teacher Preparatory; Professional

Accreditation: SC, BUS, CACREP, COARC, CONST, ENGT, LAW, MUS, NUR, RAD, SPAA, SW, TED

01	President	Mr. Geoffrey S. MEARNS
04	Exec Asst to President	Ms. Kathryn J. HERSCHEDE
05	Vice Pres Academic Affairs/Provost	Dr. Gail W. WELLS
10	Vice Pres Admin & Finance	Mr. Kenneth H. RAMEY
32	Vice Pres Student Affairs	Dr. Peter GITAU
30	Vice Pres University Advancement	Mr. Gerard A. ST. AMAND
45	Vice Pres Planning/Policy/Budget	Dr. Sue HODGES MOORE
43	VP Legal Affairs & General Counsel	Ms. Sara L. SIDEBOTTOM
86	Vice Pres Govt/Community Relations	Mr. Joseph E. WIND
20	Vice Provost University Programs	Mr. J. Patrick MOYNAHAN
44	Asst VP University Development	Mr. Donald A. GORBANDT
26	Asst VP Marketing & Communications	Mr. Rick MEYERS
84	Assoc VP Enrollment Management	Mr. Paul ORSCHELN
88	Assoc Provost for Reg Stewardship	Dr. Jan HILLARD
20	Assoc Provost Academic Affs/Admin	Ms. Beth SWEENEY
13	Assoc Provost & CIO	Mr. Timothy FERGUSON
08	Assoc Provost Library Services	Mr. Arne J. ALMQUIST
35	Dean of Students	Dr. Jeffrey WAPLE
49	Dean College of Arts & Sciences	Dr. Samuel ZACHARY
50	Dean College of Business	Dr. Rick KOLBE
88	Dean College of Informatics	Dr. Kevin KIRBY
53	Int Dean College of Ed/Human Svcs	Dr. Carol RYAN
61	Dean Chase College of Law	Mr. Jeffrey STANDEN
66	Dean College of Health Professions	Dr. Denise ROBINSON
11	Director of Administration	Ms. Linda REYNOLDS
18	Asst VP Facilities Management	Mr. Larry BLAKE
18	Director Operations & Maintenance	Mr. Ray MIRIZZI
21	Dir Fin & Operational Auditing	Mr. Larry MEYER
21	Dir Business/Auxiliary Services	Mr. Andy MEEKS
88	Dir Univ Architect/Design/Const/Mgt	Mr. Steve NIENABER
45	Director Campus Space and Planning	Ms. Mary Paula SCHUH
15	Senior Director Human Resources	Ms. Lori SOUTHWOOD
21	Comptroller	Mr. Russell A. KERDOLFF
19	Director University Police	Mr. Jason WILLIS
13	Director IT Policy & Compliance	Ms. Kimberly HEIMBROCK
96	Director Procurement Services	Mr. Jeffrey STRUNK
92	Interim Director Honors Program	Ms. Belle ZEMBRODT
07	Director Undergraduate Admissions	Ms. Melissa GORBANDT
104	Exec Dir Intl Education Center	Dr. Francois LEROY
27	Assoc Provost/Chief Info Officer	Mr. Timothy FERGUSON
06	Registrar	Ms. Marla HERRON
37	Dir Student Financial Assistance	Ms. Leah STEWART
78	Exec Dir Ctr for Civic Engagement	Mr. Mark NEIKIRK
51	Director Community Connections	Ms. Melinda SPONG
25	Director Research/Grants/Contracts	Mr. William THOMPSON
89	Assoc Director First Year Programs	Ms. Jeanne PFTTIT
88	Sr Director Office of the Budget	Mr. Kenneth KLINE
45	Exec Director Planning/Performance	Ms. Vickie NATALE
09	Exec Dir Institutional Research	Ms. Katherine A. BONTRAGER
88	Director Campus Recreation	Mr. Matthew HACKETT
38	Dir Health/Counseling/Prevention	Ms. Barbara SWEEN
35	Director Student Life	Ms. Betty MULKEY
38	Director Testing & Disability Svcs	Mr. Ben ANDERSON
39	Director University Housing	Mr. Arnie SLAUGHTER
36	Director Career Services	Mr. Bill FROUDE
85	Dir International Students/Scholars	Ms. Elizabeth CHAULK
41	Athletic Director	Mr. Ken BOTHOF
102	Executive Director Foundation	Ms. Karen ZERHUSEN KRUER
29	Director Alumni Programs	Ms. Deidra FAJACK

St. Catharine College (J)

2735 Bardstown Road, Saint Catharine KY 40061-9499

County: Washington — FICE Identification: 001983 — Unit ID: 157632

Telephone: (859) 336-5082 — Carnegie Class: Bac/Assoc

FAX Number: (859) 336-5031 — Calendar System: Semester

URL: www.sccky.edu

Established: 1931 — Annual Undergrad Tuition & Fees: $17,976

Enrollment: 925 — Coed

Affiliation or Control: Roman Catholic — IRS Status: 501(c)3

Highest Offering: Master's
Program: Occupational; 2-Year Principally Bachelor's Creditable
Accreditation: **SC**, ADNUR, DMS, RAD, RTT, SURGT

01 President ... Mr. William D. HUSTON
03 Executive Vice President ... Mr. Roger L. MARCUM
05 Vice President for Academic Affairs ... Dr. Don GILES
10 Vice President Finance ... Mr. Gary ROBINSON
30 Vice President for Advancement ... Ms. Molly Keene SMITH
84 Vice Pres Enrollment Management ... Ms. Melinda LYNCH
32 Dean of Students ... Mr. Ticha CHIKUNI
06 Registrar ... Ms. Anita FOSTER
07 Director of Admissions ... Vacant
08 Head Librarian ... Ms. Ilona BURDETTE
37 Financial Aid Officer ... Ms. Melinda LYNCH
27 Director of Communications ... Mr. Jesse OSBOURNE
38 Director of Counseling ... Vacant
15 Director of Personnel Services ... Mrs. Carlotta BRUSSELL
18 Chief Facilities/Physical Plant ... Mr. Dwight COTTON
21 Associate Business Officer ... Mr. Jim SNYDER
26 Chief Public Relations Officer ... Mr. Jesse OSBOURNE
09 Director of Institutional Research ... Vacant
29 Director of Alumni Relations ... Ms. Angela HOFFMAN

Simmons College of Kentucky (A)

1018 South 7th Street, Louisville KY 40203-3322
County: Jefferson FICE Identification: 041780
Unit ID: 461759
Telephone: (502) 776-1443 Carnegie Class: Not Classified
FAX Number: (502) 776-2227 Calendar System: Semester
URL: www.simmonscollegeky.edu
Established: 1879 Annual Undergrad Tuition & Fees: $4,620
Enrollment: N/A Coed
Affiliation or Control: Baptist IRS Status: 501(c)3
Highest Offering: Baccalaureate
Program: Religious Emphasis
Accreditation: @BI

01 President ... Mr. Kevin W. COSBY
05 Vice Pres Academic Affairs ... Dr. Brian J. WELLS
32 Vice Pres Student Affs/Dir Admiss ... Ms. Kathleen BROWN
06 Registrar ... Ms. Deborah THOMAS

The Southern Baptist Theological Seminary (B)

2825 Lexington Road, Louisville KY 40280-2899
County: Jefferson FICE Identification: 001982
Unit ID: 157748
Telephone: (502) 897-4011 Carnegie Class: Spec/Faith
FAX Number: (502) 899-1770 Calendar System: Other
URL: www.sbts.edu
Established: 1859 Annual Undergrad Tuition & Fees: $14,774
Enrollment: 3,088 Coed
Affiliation or Control: Southern Baptist IRS Status: 501(c)3
Highest Offering: Doctorate
Program: Professional; Religious Emphasis
Accreditation: **SC**, MUS, THEOL

01 President ... Dr. R. Albert MOHLER, JR.
100 Exec Asst to the President ... Mr. J. T ENGLISH
04 Admin Assistant to the President ... Miss Rachel HULTZ
05 Sr VP Academic Administration ... Dr. Randy STINSON
11 Sr VP Institutional Administration ... Mr. Dan DUMAS
10 Vice Pres of Business Operations ... Vacant
11 Vice President of Operations ... Mr. Andrew VINCENT
26 Vice President Communications ... Mr. Steve WATTERS
13 Assoc VP Information Technology ... Mr. Jason HEATH
30 VP Institutional Advancement ... Dr. Craig PARKER
32 Vice President Academic Services ... Dr. Matthew HALL
106 Assoc VP Online Education ... Dr. Timothy Paul JONES
84 Assoc VP Enrollment Management ... Dr. Matthew HALL
108 Director Institutional Assessment ... Mr. Joseph C. HARROD
15 Director Human Resources ... Mr. Jim STITZINGER
18 Chief Facilities/Physical Plant ... Mr. Bob SNIP
41 Director of Health & Recreation ... Mr. Matt EMADI
07 Director of Admissions ... Mr. John POWELL
08 Librarian ... Mr. Bruce L. KEISLING
29 Director Strategic Initiatives ... Mr. Benjamin DOCKERY
37 Manager of Financial Aid ... Mrs. Erin JOINER
73 Dean of School of Theology ... Dr. Greg WILLS
88 Dean Missions Evang Ch Growth ... Mr. Adam GREENWAY
88 Dean Boyce College ... Dr. Dan DEWITT

Spalding University (C)

845 S Third Street, Louisville KY 40203-2213
County: Jefferson FICE Identification: 001960
Unit ID: 157757
Telephone: (502) 585-9911 Carnegie Class: DRU
FAX Number: (502) 585-7158 Calendar System: Other
URL: www.spalding.edu
Established: 1814 Annual Undergrad Tuition & Fees: $21,450
Enrollment: 2,515 Coed
Affiliation or Control: Independent Non-Profit IRS Status: 501(c)3
Highest Offering: Doctorate
Program: Liberal Arts And General; Teacher Preparatory; Professional
Accreditation: **SC**, CLPSY, IACBE, NURSE, OT, SW, TED

01 President ... Ms. Tori MURDEN MCCLURE
05 Provost ... Dr. Randy STRICKLAND
30 Dir of Advancement & Philanthropy ... Ms. Bobbie RAFFERTY
32 Dean of Students ... Dr. Richard HUDSON
10 Chief Financial Officer ... Mr. Mark HOHMANN
43 General Counsel ... Ms. Emily NORRIS
84 Dean of Enrollment Management ... Mr. Chris HART
53 Dean of College of Education ... Dr. Beverly C. KEEPERS
83 Dean College Social Science/Hum ... Dr. John JAMES
88 Chair Adult Accelerated Programs ... Dr. Linda BEATTIE
76 Dean College Health & Nat Science ... Ms. Joanne BERRYMAN
26 Chief Marketing Officer ... Mr. Rick BARNEY
20 Sr Dir Academic Resource Center ... Ms. Judith LUTHER
06 Registrar ... Ms. Jennifer GOHMANN
27 Chief Information Officer ... Mr. Ezra KRUMHANSL
08 Director Library ... Ms. Jackie YOUNG
37 Director Student Financial Aid ... Ms. Gina KUZUOKA
15 Human Resources Manager ... Ms. Jennifer BROCKHOFF
09 Dir of Institutional Effectiveness ... Ms. Kay VETTER
26 Director of Executive Communication ... Ms. Beth NEWBERRY
88 Dir Student Achievement/Retention ... Ms. Judith LUTHER
41 Director of Athletics ... Mr. Roger BURKMAN
88 Admin Dir/Mstr Fin Arts in Writing ... Ms. Karen MANN
21 Business Manager ... Ms. Jamie JOHNSON
18 JLL Facilities Manager ... Mr. Kevin WEBER
40 Bookstore Manager ... Vacant
88 Director Applied Behavior Analysis ... Dr. Erick DUBUQUE
88 Director Masters of Business Commu ... Dr. Denise CUMBERLAND

Spencerian College (D)

1575 Winchester Road, Lexington KY 40505-4520
Telephone: (859) 223-9608 Identification: 666448
Accreditation: **ACICS**, MAC, MLTAB, RAD

† Main campus is Spencerian College in Louisville, KY.

Spencerian College (E)

4627 Dixie Highway, Louisville KY 40216-2605
County: Jefferson FICE Identification: 004618
Unit ID: 157766
Telephone: (502) 447-1000 Carnegie Class: Assoc/PrivFP
FAX Number: (502) 447-4574 Calendar System: Quarter
URL: www.spencerian.edu
Established: 1892 Annual Undergrad Tuition & Fees: $16,320
Enrollment: 695 Coed
Affiliation or Control: Proprietary IRS Status: Proprietary
Highest Offering: Associate Degree
Program: Occupational
Accreditation: **ACICS**, #COARC, CVT, MAC, MLTAB, RAD, SURGT

01 Executive Director ... Ms. Jan M. GORDON
05 Academic Dean ... Ms. Linda BLAIR
37 Director of Financial Planning ... Ms. Jill SCHULER
07 Director of Admissions ... Ms. Charmaine POWELL
36 Director of Career Services ... Ms. Heather FUQUA
32 Director of Student Services ... Ms. Amanda HICKERSON

Sullivan College of Technology and Design (F)

3901 Atkinson Square Drive, Louisville KY 40218-4549
County: Jefferson FICE Identification: 012088
Unit ID: 157270
Telephone: (502) 456-6509 Carnegie Class: Spec/Arts
FAX Number: (502) 456-2341 Calendar System: Quarter
URL: www.sctd.edu
Established: 1961 Annual Undergrad Tuition & Fees: $17,340
Enrollment: 467 Coed
Affiliation or Control: Proprietary IRS Status: Proprietary
Highest Offering: Baccalaureate
Program: Occupational
Accreditation: **ACICS**

00 Chancellor ... Dr. A. R. SULLIVAN
01 President ... Mr. Glenn D. SULLIVAN
11 Senior Vice President ... Mr. Thomas F. DAVISSON
05 Dean of Academic Affairs ... Dr. Sheree KOPPEL
10 Vice President Finance ... Mr. Shelton BRIDGES
84 Vice Pres Enrollment Management ... Mr. James CRICK
12 Executive Director ... Mr. Chris ERNST
06 Registrar ... Ms. Cathy DRUIN
07 Director of Admissions ... Mr. Aamer CHAUHDRI
37 Dir of Student Financial Planning ... Ms. Karen WILLIAM
08 Head Librarian ... Ms. Jill SHERMAN
36 Placement Director ... Mr. Gerald BEAVERS
55 Evening Division Dean ... Mr. Robert MITCHELL
96 Director of Purchasing ... Ms. Ann VEST
13 Chief Technology Officer ... Mr. Mike GROSSE
29 Director Alumni Relations ... Ms. Hazel MATTHEWS

Sullivan University (G)

3101 Bardstown Road, Louisville KY 40205-3000
County: Jefferson FICE Identification: 004619
Unit ID: 157793
Telephone: (502) 456-6504 Carnegie Class: Master's M
FAX Number: (502) 456-0040 Calendar System: Quarter
URL: www.sullivan.edu
Established: 1962 Annual Undergrad Tuition & Fees: $17,520
Enrollment: 5,445 Coed
Affiliation or Control: Proprietary IRS Status: Proprietary
Highest Offering: Doctorate
Program: Occupational; Professional
Accreditation: **SC**, ACFEI, IACBE, MAC, PHAR

00 Chancellor ... Dr. A. R. SULLIVAN
01 President ... Mr. Glenn D. SULLIVAN
03 Chief Executive Officer ... Dr. Jay MARR
05 Provost ... Dr. Ken MILLER
88 Senior Vice President ... Mr. Thomas F. DAVISSON
10 Vice President Finance ... Mr. Shelton BRIDGES
84 Vice Pres Enrollment Management ... Mr. James CRICK
07 Vice President of Admissions ... Ms. Nina MARTINEZ
58 Assoc Provost/Dean Graduate School ... Dr. Tim SWENSON
32 Dean of Students ... Mr. Gabe GHAMMACHI
88 Dean Natl Ctr Hospitality Studies ... Mr. Keith LERME
20 Associate Dean of Students ... Ms. Aubree ALVAREZ
06 Registrar ... Ms. Kim MITCHELL
08 Librarian ... Mr. Charles BROWN
13 Chief Technology Officer ... Mr. Mike GROSSE
36 Director of Career Services ... Mr. Sam MANNINO
37 Director Student Financial Planning ... Vacant
55 Director Evening Division ... Mr. James TAYLOR
40 Director Bookstore ... Ms. Brenda HOOKS
12 Director Lexington Branch ... Mr. David KEENE
96 Director of Purchasing ... Ms. Ann VEST
56 Director of Extension Campus ... Ms. Barbara DEAN
88 University Ombudsman ... Mr. Jim KLEIN
29 Director Alumni Relations ... Ms. Hazel MATTHEWS
09 Director Institutional Research ... Dr. Forrest HOULETTE
18 Manager Campus Facilities ... Mr. Mike FOWLER
35 Student Life Coordinator ... Ms. Kim ATWOOD
67 Dean College of Pharmacy ... Dr. Walter SOJA
50 Dean College of Business Admin ... Mr. Ken MORAN
72 Dean Col Information/Computer Tech ... Dr. Emmanuel UDOH

Thomas More College (H)

333 Thomas More Parkway,
Crestview Hills KY 41017-3495
County: Kenton FICE Identification: 002001
Unit ID: 157809
Telephone: (859) 341-5800 Carnegie Class: Master's S
FAX Number: (859) 344-3345 Calendar System: Semester
URL: www.thomasmore.edu
Established: 1921 Annual Undergrad Tuition & Fees: $27,200
Enrollment: 1,486 Coed
Affiliation or Control: Roman Catholic IRS Status: 501(c)3
Highest Offering: Master's
Program: Liberal Arts And General; Teacher Preparatory; Professional
Accreditation: **SC**, NUR, TED

01 President ... Mr. David A. ARMSTRONG
04 Assistant to the President ... Ms. Charlene BARLOW
10 Vice President of Finance ... Mr. Peter W. AAMODT
05 Vice President for Academic Affairs ... Dr. Bradley A. BIELSKI
30 Vice Pres for Inst Advancement ... Ms. Cathy SILVERS
32 Vice Pres of Student Services ... Mr. Matthew H. WEBSTER
35 Dean of Students ... Ms. Ebony GRIGGS-GRIFFIN
09 Dir of Inst Planning/Effectiveness ... Ms. Genie M. WAMBAUGH
06 Registrar ... Ms. Kelly FRENCH
08 Director of Library ... Mr. James M. MCKELLOGG
37 Director of Financial Aid ... Ms. Mary GIVHAN
13 Director of IT ... Mr. William K. SWISHER
26 Dir Communications/Media Relations ... Vacant
38 Director of Counseling ... Ms. Veronica A. LUBBE
42 Chaplain ... Rev. Gerald E. TWADDELL
84 Director of Enrollment for TAP ... Dr. Bradley A. BIELSKI
41 Athletic Director ... Mr. Terry D. CONNOR
19 Director of Campus Safety ... Mr. Robert MARSHALL
15 Director of Human Resources ... Ms. Laura CUSTER
18 Director of Facilities ... Mr. Jeffrey KORDENBROCK
29 Director of Alumni ... Ms. Monica GINNEY
36 Dir of Career Planning/Coop Educ ... Ms. Julie MUELLER
73 Director of Campus Ministry ... Mr. Robert SHEARN
21 Controller ... Ms. Judy STRICKLING
51 Director of Lifelong Learning ... Mr. Nathan HARTMAN
92 Director of Honors Program ... Dr. Catherine SHERRON
44 Dir Annual Giving/Special Events ... Ms. Beth MALEY
07 Associate Director of Admissions ... Mr. Billy SARGE
35 Coordinator of Student Activities ... Ms. Monica RUSCHER
39 Coordinator of Residence Life ... Vacant
28 Director of Diversity ... Ms. Elizabeth DANSBERRY

Transylvania University (I)

300 N Broadway, Lexington KY 40508-1797
County: Fayette FICE Identification: 001987
Unit ID: 157818
Telephone: (859) 233-8300 Carnegie Class: Bac/A&S
FAX Number: (859) 233-8797 Calendar System: Other
URL: www.transy.edu
Established: 1780 Annual Undergrad Tuition & Fees: $31,560
Enrollment: 1,074 Coed
Affiliation or Control: Christian Church (Disciples Of Christ)
IRS Status: 501(c)3
Highest Offering: Baccalaureate
Program: Liberal Arts And General; Teacher Preparatory
Accreditation: **SC**, TED

01 President ... Dr. R. Owen WILLIAMS
20 Interim Dean of the College ... Dr. Kathleen JAGGER
10 Vice President Finance & Business ... Mr. Marc MATHEWS
30 Vice Pres Advancement ... Mr. Kirk PURDOM

32 Dean of Students Dr. Barbara LOMONACO
06 Registrar Ms. Michelle RAWLINGS
09 Director of Institutional Research Mr. Rhyan M. CONYERS
07 Vice President for Enrollment Mr. Bradley L. GOAN
08 Librarian Ms. Susan M. BROWN
37 Director of Financial Aid Mr. David J. CECIL
26 Director of Public Relations Ms. Sarah EMMONS
36 Director of Placement Services Ms. Susan S. RAYER
13 Director of Information Technology Mr. Jason WHITAKER
104 Dir Study Abroad & Special Programs Ms. Kathryn C. SIMON
15 Director Personnel Services Mr. Jeff MUDRAK
18 Chief Facilities/Physical Plant Mr. Darrell L. BANKS
96 Director of Purchasing Ms. Shawn T. SINGLETON
29 Director Alumni Relations Ms. Natasa PAJIC
28 Director of Campus Diversity Mr. Eduardo NINO-MORENO

Union College (A)

310 College Street, Barbourville KY 40906-1499
County: Knox FICE Identification: 001988
Unit ID: 157863
Telephone: (606) 546-4151 Carnegie Class: Master's L
FAX Number: (606) 546-1217 Calendar System: Other
URL: www.unionky.edu
Established: 1879 Annual Undergrad Tuition & Fees: $22,000
Enrollment: 1,200 Coed
Affiliation or Control: United Methodist IRS Status: 501(c)3
Highest Offering: Master's
Program: Liberal Arts And General; Teacher Preparatory
Accreditation: SC, NURSE, SW

01 President Dr. Marcia HAWKINS
01 VP for Academic Affairs Dr. David JOHNS
30 Vice President for Advancement Ms. Jessica BERGMAN
84 Director Undergraduate Enrollment Ms. Summer JACKSON
32 Interim Dean of Students Ms. Stephanie SMITH
53 Head of Educational Studies Dept Dr. Jason REEVES
35 Associate Dean Student Life Ms. Barbara TEAGUE
96 Dir Purchasing/Act Pyable/Staff Act Ms. Jennifer JONES
06 Registrar Ms. Kathy WEBB
18 Director of Physical Plant (NMRC) Mr. James JAMERSON
41 Athletic Director Mr. Tim CURRY
29 Director of Alumni Relations Vacant
09 Director of Institutional Research Ms. Anisa JAMES
10 Chief Business Officer Mr. Steve HOSKINS
26 Director of Public Relations Ms. Melissa REID
88 Director of Sports Information Mr. Jay STANCIL
88 Director of Special Programs Ms. Stephanie SMITH
08 Head Librarian Ms. Tara L. COOPER
42 College Minister Rev. David MILLER
31 Director of Common Partners Mr. Austin SEBALD
37 Assistant Director of Financial Aid Ms. Andra BUTLER
38 Director of Counseling Mrs. Jodi CARROLL
15 Benefits Coordinator Ms. Lynn SMITH
19 Safety Team Leader Vacant
50 Chair Department of Business Dr. Carolyn PAYNE
88 Chair Dept Wellness/Human Perf/Rec Dr. Larry INKSTER
79 Chair Dept Engr/Comm/Language Dr. James GARRETT
57 Chr Dpt Hist/Relig Std/Fn/Perf Arts Dr. Russell SISSON
81 Chair Dept of Natural Sciences Dr. Dan COVINGTON
83 Chair Dept Social/Behav Science Dr. Robert ARMOUR
04 Coordinator President's Office Ms. Monica SHANNON-CLOUSE
88 Events Coordinator Ms. Bobbie DOOLIN

University of the Cumberlands (B)

6191 College Station Drive, Williamsburg KY 40769-1372
County: Whitley FICE Identification: 001962
Unit ID: 156541
Telephone: (606) 549-2200 Carnegie Class: Master's M
FAX Number: (606) 539-4280 Calendar System: Semester
URL: www.ucumberlands.edu
Established: 1888 Annual Undergrad Tuition & Fees: $20,000
Enrollment: 4,297 Coed
Affiliation or Control: Baptist IRS Status: 501(c)3
Highest Offering: Doctorate
Program: Liberal Arts And General; Teacher Preparatory
Accreditation: SC, ARCPA

01 President Dr. James H. TAYLOR
30 Vice Pres Institutional Advancement Mrs. Sue WAKE
05 Vice President Academic Affairs Dr. Larry L. COCKRUM
32 Vice President Student Services Dr. Michael COLEGROVE
10 Vice President Business Services Mr. Steve MORRIS
21 Vice President Finance Ms. Jana K. BAILEY
11 Vice President Operations Mr. Kyle GILBERT
37 Vice Pres Student Financial Plng Mr. Steve ALLEN
41 Vice Pres Athletics/Athletic Dir Mr. Randy VERNON
27 Vice President Information Services Mr. Donnie GRIMES
07 Director of Admissions Mrs. Erica HARRIS
06 Registrar Mr. Charles DUPIER
20 Associate Dean Dr. Thomas E. FISH
09 Institutional Research Mr. Charles DUPIER
26 Dir Multimedia/Athletic Services Ms. Jennifer FLOYD
35 Dean Student Life Ms. Linda CARTER
15 Director of Human Resources Ms. Pearl BAKER
90 Director of Information Technology Mr. Donnie GRIMES
42 Dir International Pgm/Church Rels Dr. Rick FLEENOR
36 Director of Career Services Ms. Debbie HARP
08 Director of Library Ms. Jan WREN
58 Director Graduate Program Dr. Fred SAGESTER
18 Director of Physical Plant Mr. David ROOT
21 Bursar Ms. Jo DUPIER
29 Director Alumni Relations Mr. Dave BERGMAN

University of Kentucky (C)

Lexington KY 40506-0003
County: Fayette FICE Identification: 001989
Unit ID: 157085
Telephone: (859) 257-9000 Carnegie Class: RU/VH
FAX Number: (859) 257-4000 Calendar System: Semester
URL: www.uky.edu
Established: 1865 Annual Undergrad Tuition & Fees (In-State): $9,676
Enrollment: 28,034 Coed
Affiliation or Control: State IRS Status: 501(c)3
Highest Offering: Doctorate
Program: Liberal Arts And General; Teacher Preparatory; Professional
Accreditation: SC, AAFCS, ARCPA, ART, BUS, BUSA, CIDA, CLPSY, COPSY, CORE, CS, DENT, DIETC, DIETD, DIETI, ENG, FOR, HSA, JOUR, LAW, LIB, LSAR, MED, MFCD, MT, MUS, NURSE, PCSAS, PH, PHAR, PTA, #SCPSY, SP, SPAA, SW, TED, THEA

01 President Dr. Eli CAPILOUTO
46 Vice President Research Dr. James W. TRACY
05 Provost Dr. Christine RIORDAN
100 Chief of Staff Mr. Bill SWINFORD
10 Exec VP Finance/Administration Mr. Eric N. MONDAY
17 Executive VP for Health Affairs Dr. Michael KARPF
13 Senior Vice Provost Info Technology Mr. Vincent J. KELLEN
32 Vice Pres Student Affairs Dr. Robert C. MOCK, JR.
28 Vice Pres Institutional Diversity Dr. Judy J. JACKSON
30 Vice President for Development Dr. D. Michael RICHEY
10 VP Health Affs/Chief Financial Ofcr Mr. Murray B. CLARK
45 VP Financial Operations/Treasurer Ms. Angela S. MARTIN
18 Vice President Facilities Mgmt Mr. Bob WISEMAN
22 Assoc VP Institutional Equity Mr. Terry D. ALLEN
26 VP University Relations Mr. Thomas W. HARRIS
35 Assoc VP Stdnt Affs/Dean of Stdnts Dr. Victor A. HAZARD
15 Assoc VP Human Resources Admin Ms. Kimberly P. WILSON
88 Asst Vice Pres Public Safety Mr. Anthany BEATTY
31 Assoc Vice Pres Auxiliary Services Mr. Ben CRUTCHER
25 Assoc VP Res Admin & Fiscal Affs Mr. Jack SUPPLEE, JR.
88 Exec Director Sponsored Projects Ms. Debbie DAVIS
20 Assoc Provost International Center Dr. Susan CARVALHO
17 Assoc VP Clinical Network Devel Mr. Joe CLAYPOOL
58 Dean Graduate School Dr. Jeannine BLACKWELL
20 Assoc Provost Undergrad Education Dr. Ben WITHERS
20 Assoc Provost Faculty Advancement Dr. Gene T. LINEBERRY
84 Assoc Provost Enroll Mgmt/Registrar Mr. Don WITT
08 Dean of Libraries Dr. Terry L. BIRDWHISTELL
27 Director University Press Dr. Stephen WRINN
43 General Counsel Mr. William E. THRO
41 Director Athletics Mr. Mitch BARNHART
37 Director Student Financial Aid Dr. Nimmi WIGGINS
09 Director of Institutional Research Dr. Roger P. SUGARMAN
36 Director Career Center Ms. Francene GILMER
38 Director Counseling & Testing Dr. Mary BOLIN-REECE
29 Director Alumni Affairs Mr. Stan KEY
26 Exec Director Public Relations Mr. Jay BLANTON
21 Controller Ms. Ronda BECK
47 Dean of Agriculture Dr. M. Scott SMITH
19 Chief of Police Mr. Joseph W. MONROE
48 Interim Dean College of Design Dr. Ann DICKSON
88 Director Student Center Mr. John H. HERBST
49 Dean of Arts & Sciences Dr. Mark KORNBLUH
50 Dean of Business & Economics Dr. David BLACKWELL
53 Dean of Education Dr. Mary J. O'HAIR
54 Dean of Engineering Dr. John WALZ
57 Dean of Fine Arts Dr. Michael TICK
60 Dean of Communication/Information Dr. Dan O'HAIR
61 Dean of Law Mr. David BRENNEN
70 Dean of Social Work Dr. James P. ADAMS, JR.
76 Interim Dean of Health Sciences Dr. Sharon STEWART
52 Dean of Dentistry Dr. Sharon P. TURNER
63 Dean of Medicine/VP Clinical Affs Dr. Fredrick C. DE BEER
66 Interim Dean of Nursing Dr. Patricia HOWARD
67 Dean of Pharmacy Dr. Tim TRACY
69 Dean Public Health Dr. Steve WYATT
96 Purchasing Director Mr. William L. HARRIS
23 Director Univ Student Health Svcs Dr. Gregory R. MOORE

University of Louisville (D)

2301 S Third Street, Louisville KY 40292-0001
County: Jefferson FICE Identification: 001999
Unit ID: 157289
Telephone: (502) 852-5555 Carnegie Class: RU/VH
FAX Number: (502) 852-7013 Calendar System: Semester
URL: www.louisville.edu
Established: 1798 Annual Undergrad Tuition & Fees (In-State): $9,750
Enrollment: 22,293 Coed
Affiliation or Control: State IRS Status: 501(c)3
Highest Offering: Doctorate
Program: Liberal Arts And General; Teacher Preparatory; Professional
Accreditation: SC, AUD, BUS, BUSA, CACREP, CIDA, CLPSY, COPSY, CS, DENT, DH, ENG, EXSC, IPSY, LAW, MED, MFCD, MUS, NURSE, PH, PLNG, SP, SPAA, SW, TED, THEA

01 President Dr. James R. RAMSEY
05 Exec Vice Pres/University Prov Dr. Shirley C. WILLIHNGANZ
17 Exec Vice Pres for Health Affairs Dr. David DUNN
46 Executive VP for Research Dr. Bill PIERCE
32 Vice President Student Affairs Dr. Tom JACKSON, JR.
11 Vice President for Business Affairs Mr. Larry L. OWSLEY
30 Vice Pres Univ Advancement Mr. Keith INMAN
13 Vice Pres Information Tech Dr. Priscilla HANCOCK
86 VP for Community Engagement Mr. Daniel HALL
10 Vice President for Finance Mr. Michael J. CURTIN
16 Vice Pres Human Resources Mr. Sam CONNALLY
41 Vice President for Athletics Mr. Tom JURICH
44 Sr Assoc VP Advancement Ms. Rebecca SIMPSON
18 Assoc VP Facilities/Physical Plant Mr. Larry DETHERAGE
29 Asst Vice Pres for Alumni Relations Mr. Jimmy FORD
100 Chief of Staff for the President Ms. Kathleen M. SMITH
43 University Counsel Ms. Angela D. KOSHEWA
20 Vice Prov Undergraduate Affairs Dr. Dale B. BILLINGSLEY
58 Dean Graduate School Dr. Beth A. BOEHM
28 Vice Prov for Diversity/Intl Affs Dr. Mordean TAYLOR-ARCHER
88 Assoc Prov Acad Acct/IR & Effect Mr. Robert S. GOLDSTEIN
106 Assoc Univ Provost Distance Ed/Delp Dr. Gale RHODES
88 Asst Prov for Accreditation Ms. Connie C. SHUMAKE
21 Controller Mr. Larry W. ZINK
07 Executive Director Admissions Ms. Jenny L. SAWYER
06 University Registrar Mr. Scott A. BURKS
37 Exec Director Financial Aid Ms. Patricia O. ARAUZ
26 Director of Comm/Marketing Ms. Cindy HESS
25 Director Contract Admin/Risk Mgmt Mr. David MARTIN
15 Dir of Staff Dev/Employee Rel Ms. Mary E. MILES
19 Director Public Safety Mr. Wayne HALL
09 Director Inst Research and Planning Ms. Becky PATTERSON
45 Director Inst Effectiveness Ms. Cheryl B. GILCHRIST
39 Director Student Housing Ms. Shannon D. STATEN
105 Director of Digital Media Mr. Jeffery A. RUSHTON
27 Director Media Relations Mr. Mark HEBERT
88 Assoc Vice Pres for Audit Services Mr. David F. BARKER
14 Director IT Enterprise Security Ms. Brenda B. GOMBOSKY
92 Director of Honors Program Dr. John F. RICHARDSON
96 Director Purchasing Mr. David MARTIN
88 Dir Planning/Design & Construction Mr. Kenneth DIETZ
36 Director Career Services Ms. Leslye A. ERICKSON
38 Director Counseling Services Dr. Kathy J. PENDLETON
08 Dean of University Libraries Mr. Robert FOX
49 Acting Dean College Arts & Sciences Dr. John P. FERRE'
50 Dean College of Business Dr. R. Charles MOYER
52 Dean School of Dentistry Dr. John J. SAUK
53 Int Dean Col of Educ/Human Develop Dr. Blake HASELTON
70 Dean Kent School Social Work Dr. Terry L. SINGER
64 Dean School of Music Dr. Christopher DOANE
61 Interim Dean Brandeis School of Law Ms. Susan DUNCAN
66 Dean School of Nursing Dr. Marcia J. HERN
54 Dean Speed School of Engineering Dr. Neville PINTO
63 Dean School of Medicine Dr. Toni GANZEL
69 Dean Public Health/Information Sci Dr. Craig H. BLAKELY
35 Dean of Students/Assoc VP Stdnt Aff Dr. Michael MARDIS

University of Phoenix Louisville Campus (E)

10400 Linn Station Road, Louisville KY 40223-3839
Telephone: (502) 423-0149 Identification: 770207
Accreditation: &NH, ACBSP

† Main campus is University of Phoenix in Tempe, AZ.

University of Pikeville (F)

147 Sycamore Street, Pikeville KY 41501-1194
County: Pike FICE Identification: 001980
Unit ID: 157535
Telephone: (606) 218-5250 Carnegie Class: Bac/A&S
FAX Number: (606) 218-5269 Calendar System: Semester
URL: www.upike.edu
Established: 1889 Annual Undergrad Tuition & Fees: $17,750
Enrollment: 2,032 Coed
Affiliation or Control: Presbyterian Church (U.S.A.) IRS Status: 501(c)3
Highest Offering: Doctorate
Program: Liberal Arts And General; Teacher Preparatory
Accreditation: SC, NUR, OSTEO, SW

00 Chancellor Mr. Paul E. PATTON
01 President Dr. James L. HURLEY
05 VPAA/Dean College Arts/Sciences Dr. Thomas R. HESS
50 Dean College of Business Dr. Howard V. ROBERTS
10 Vice Pres Finance/Business Affairs Mr. Douglas J. LANGE
30 Vice President for Advancement Dr. Eric BECHER
26 Asst Vice President Public Affairs Mrs. Lucy HOLMAN
63 VP Health Affairs/Dean KYCOM Dr. Boyd R. BUSER
32 VP Student Svcs/Dean of Students Mr. Ron DAMRON
07 Director Admissions/ Mrs. Amber COLLINS
08 Director of Library Services Ms. Karen S. CHAFIN-EVANS
06 Asst VP Academic Affairs/Registrar Mrs. Gia POTTER
09 Director of Institutional Research Dr. Meg SIDLE
14 Senior Info Services Administrator Mr. Randy SCARBERRY
18 Director of Operations Mr. John HOLMAN
37 Director of Student Financial Svcs Mrs. Judy BRADLEY
15 Director of Human Resources Vacant

Western Kentucky University (G)

1906 College Heights Blvd, Bowling Green KY 42101-3576
County: Warren FICE Identification: 002002
Unit ID: 157951
Telephone: (270) 745-0111 Carnegie Class: Master's L
FAX Number: (270) 745-5387 Calendar System: Semester
URL: www.wku.edu
Established: 1906 Annual Undergrad Tuition & Fees (In-State): $8,722
Enrollment: 21,110 Coed
Affiliation or Control: State IRS Status: 501(c)3

Highest Offering: Doctorate
Program: 2-Year Principally Bachelor's Creditable; Liberal Arts And General; Teacher Preparatory; Professional
Accreditation: **SC**, ADNUR, ART, BUS, BUSA, CACREP, CAHIIM, CONST, DANCE, DH, DIETD, @DIETI, ENG, JOUR, MUS, NAIT, NRPA, NURSE, PH, @PTA, SP, SPAA, SW, TED, THEA

01 President .... Dr. Gary A. RANSDELL
05 Provost/VP Academic Affairs .... Dr. A. Gordon EMSLIE
46 VP for Research .... Dr. Gordon BAYLIS
26 VP for Public Affairs .... Ms. Robbin M. TAYLOR
30 VP Development & Alumni Rels .... Ms. Kathryn COSTELLO
13 VP Information Technology .... Dr. Bob OWEN
32 Vice President Student Affairs .... Mr. Howard E. BAILEY
10 Vice President Finance & Admin .... Ms. K. Ann MEAD
100 Chief of Staff/General Counsel .... Ms. Deborah T. WILKINS
20 Vice Provost Academic Affairs .... Dr. Richard C. MILLER
11 Vice Pres Campus Svcs & Facilities .... Mr. John N. OSBORNE
84 Assoc Vice Pres for Enrollment Mgmt .... Dr. Brian MEREDITH
106 Assoc VP Ext Learning & Outreach .... Dr. Beth LAVES
79 Dean Arts & Letters .... Dr. David D. LEE
50 Dean Business .... Dr. Jeffrey KATZ
53 Dean Education/Behavioral Sci .... Dr. Sam EVANS
76 Dean Health & Human Services .... Dr. John A. BONAGURO
81 Dean Science/Engineering .... Dr. Cheryl L. STEVENS
58 Dean Grad Studies & Research .... Dr. Carl A. FOX
97 Dean University College .... Dr. Dennis K. GEORGE
62 Dean Libraries .... Ms. Connie FOSTER
88 Assoc VP Enrichment & Effectiveness .... Dr. Doug MCELROY
88 Assoc VP Planning & Program Develop .... Dr. Sylvia GAIKO
21 Chief Financial Officer .... Mr. Jim CUMMINGS
21 Budget Director .... Ms. Kimberly REED
07 Director Admissions .... Mr. Scott S. GORDON
88 Assoc VP Academic Budgets & Admin .... Mrs. Ladonna L. HUNTON
30 Assoc VP Research and Development .... Mr. Douglas ROHRER
06 Registrar .... Ms. Freida K. EGGLETON
91 Director Admin Systems/Applications .... Mr. Gordon L. JOHNSON
15 Director Human Resources .... Mr. Tony L. GLISSON
18 Director Facilities Management .... Mr. Charles E. JONES
12 Regional Chancellor .... Dr. Sally RAY
12 Regional Chancellor .... Dr. Gene E. TICE
90 Director Academic Technology .... Mr. John BOWERS
88 Dir Acad Advising & Retention Ctr .... Dr. Russell L. CURLEY
28 Director Diversity Programs .... Ms. Andrea GARR-BARNES
39 Director Housing & Residence Life .... Mr. Brian KUSTER
19 Chief of Police .... Mr. Robert DEANE
102 President College Heights Found .... Mr. Donald SMITH
29 Asst VP/Exec Dir Alumni Relations .... Mr. Richard A. DUBOSE
88 Asst VP Retention & Student Svcs .... Dr. Joelle CARTER
44 Associate VP Major Gifts .... Mr. John P. BLAIR
36 Director Career Services Center .... Dr. Lynne HOLLAND
37 Dir Student Financial Assistance .... Ms. Cindy BURNETTE
88 Director Student Support Svcs .... Mr. Terrance C. GEORGE
38 Int Director Counseling & Testing .... Dr. Peggy A. CROWE
40 Director Bookstore .... Ms. Shawna C. TURNER
09 Director Institutional Research .... Dr. Tuesdi HELBIG
22 Equal Oppty/ADA/Compliance Director .... Ms. Huda N. MELKY
24 Director Educ Television Svcs .... Mr. James MORGESE
41 Athletics Director .... Mr. Todd M. STEWART
85 Director Intl Student & Sch Service .... Mr. Tarek EL SHAYEB
92 Executive Director Honors College .... Dr. Craig COBANE
96 Director Purchasing/Accts Payable .... Mr. Ken BAUSHKE
101 Senior Administrative Assistant .... Ms. Julia J. MCDONALD
101 Executive Administrative Assistant .... Ms. Torie COCKRIEL
104 Director Study Abroad/Global Lrng .... Vacant
23 Executive Director Health Services .... Ms. Vicky ROSA
27 Director of Media Relations .... Mr. Bob SKIPPER
86 Dir Govt/Community Relations .... Ms. Jennifer B. SMITH
04 Executive Admininstrative Assistant .... Ms. Shelia E. HOUCHINS

LOUISIANA

Baton Rouge School of Computers (A)

9352 Interline Avenue, Baton Rouge LA 70809-1909
County: East Baton Rouge — FICE Identification: 021975
Unit ID: 158343
Telephone: (225) 923-2524 — Carnegie Class: Assoc/PrivFP
FAX Number: (225) 923-2979 — Calendar System: Other
URL: www.brsc.edu
Established: 1979 — Annual Undergrad Tuition & Fees: $16,504
Enrollment: 72 — Coed
Affiliation or Control: Proprietary — IRS Status: Proprietary
Highest Offering: Associate Degree
Program: Occupational
Accreditation: **ACCSC**

01 President/Director .... Mrs. Betty D. TRUXILLO
05 Chief Academic Officer .... Ms. Pauline ROBERTS
37 Financial Aid Assistant .... Vacant
06 Registrar .... Vacant

Blue Cliff College (B)

120 James Comeaux Road, Lafayette LA 70508
County: Lafayette — FICE Identification: 034226
Unit ID: 439491
Telephone: (337) 269-0620 — Carnegie Class: Assoc/PrivFP
FAX Number: (337) 269-0688 — Calendar System: Quarter
URL: www.bluecliffcollege.com
Established: 1987 — Annual Undergrad Tuition & Fees: $14,394
Enrollment: 14,624 — Coed
Affiliation or Control: Proprietary — IRS Status: Proprietary
Highest Offering: Associate Degree
Program: Occupational; Technical Emphasis
Accreditation: **ACCSC**

01 Director .... Ms. Teresa RICE
07 Director of Admissions .... Mr. Dalton DURAL
37 Director of Financial Aid .... Mrs. Verna TAYLOR

Blue Cliff College (C)

3200 Cleary Avenue, Metairie LA 70002-5714
County: Jefferson — FICE Identification: 032943
Unit ID: 434821
Telephone: (504) 456-3141 — Carnegie Class: Assoc/PrivFP
FAX Number: (504) 456-7849 — Calendar System: Quarter
URL: www.bluecliffcollege.com
Established: 1987 — Annual Undergrad Tuition & Fees: N/A
Enrollment: 549 — Coed
Affiliation or Control: Proprietary — IRS Status: Proprietary
Highest Offering: Associate Degree
Program: Occupational
Accreditation: **ACCSC**

01 President/CEO .... Mr. Reggie MOORE
05 Campus Director .... Mr. Doug ROBERTSON

Blue Cliff College (D)

8731 Park Plaza Drive, Shreveport LA 71105-5682
County: Caddo — FICE Identification: 034225
Unit ID: 439482
Telephone: (318) 798-6868 — Carnegie Class: Assoc/PrivFP
FAX Number: (318) 798-6880 — Calendar System: Quarter
URL: www.bluecliffcollege.com
Established: 1995 — Annual Undergrad Tuition & Fees: N/A
Enrollment: 423 — Coed
Affiliation or Control: Proprietary — IRS Status: Proprietary
Highest Offering: Associate Degree
Program: Occupational
Accreditation: **ACCSC**

01 Campus Director .... Mr. James POWELL
05 Director of Education .... Ms. Stacie BOLEY

Cameron College (E)

2740 Canal Street, New Orleans LA 70119-5500
County: Orleans — FICE Identification: 022340
Unit ID: 158440
Telephone: (504) 821-5881 — Carnegie Class: Assoc/PrivFP
FAX Number: (504) 822-3467 — Calendar System: Other
URL: www.cameroncollege.com
Established: 1981 — Annual Undergrad Tuition & Fees: $10,950
Enrollment: 175 — Coed
Affiliation or Control: Proprietary — IRS Status: Proprietary
Highest Offering: Associate Degree
Program: Occupational
Accreditation: **COE**

01 President .... Ms. Eleanor W. CAMERON

Career Technical College (F)

2319 Louisville Avenue, Monroe LA 71201-6126
County: Ouachita — FICE Identification: 026068
Unit ID: 367112
Telephone: (318) 323-2889 — Carnegie Class: Assoc/PrivFP
FAX Number: (318) 324-9883 — Calendar System: Quarter
URL: www.careertc.edu
Established: 1988 — Annual Undergrad Tuition & Fees: $14,160
Enrollment: 600 — Coed
Affiliation or Control: Proprietary — IRS Status: Proprietary
Highest Offering: Associate Degree
Program: Occupational; 2-Year Principally Bachelor's Creditable; Technical Emphasis
Accreditation: **ACICS**, COE, MAC, RAD, SURGT

01 College Director .... Ms. Cheryl P. LOKEY

Career Technical College (G)

1227 Shreveport-Barksdale Highway, Shreveport LA 71105
Telephone: (318) 629-2889 — Identification: 770723
Accreditation: **ACICS**, COE, MAC, SURGT

† Main campus is Career Technical College in Monroe, LA.

Centenary College of Louisiana (H)

PO Box 41188, Shreveport LA 71134-1188
County: Caddo — FICE Identification: 002003
Unit ID: 158477
Telephone: (318) 869-5011 — Carnegie Class: Bac/A&S
FAX Number: (318) 869-5010 — Calendar System: Semester
URL: www.centenary.edu
Established: 1825 — Annual Undergrad Tuition & Fees: $30,740
Enrollment: 776 — Coed
Affiliation or Control: United Methodist — IRS Status: 501(c)3
Highest Offering: Master's
Program: Liberal Arts And General; Teacher Preparatory; Professional
Accreditation: **SC**, MUS, @TEAC

01 President .... Dr. B. David ROWE
04 Exec Assistant to the President .... Mrs. Connie WHITTINGTON
05 Dean of the College & Provost .... Dr. Michael R. HEMPHILL
50 Dean of the School of Business .... Dr. Christopher L. MARTIN
64 Dean of the School of Music .... Dr. Gale ODOM
03 Executive Vice President .... Mr. Scott RAWLES
84 Vice President of Enrollment Svcs .... Mr. Monty L. CURTIS
10 Vice President for Finance/Admin .... Mrs. Stephanie OWENS
32 VP Student Development .... Vacant
30 Associate VP for Advancement .... Mr. Fred LANDRY
13 Director of Information Technology .... Mr. Scott MERRITT
21 Controller .... Mrs. Loretta SALVATORE
41 Director of Athletics & Wellness .... Mrs. Ronda SEAGRAVES
32 Dean of Students .... Dr. Mark MILLER
38 Director of Counseling .... Ms. Tina FELDT
37 Director of Financial Aid .... Mrs. Lynette VISKOZKI
06 Registrar/Director of Re-Enrollment .... Ms. Nicole DEESE
08 Librarian .... Ms. Christy WRENN
26 Director Marketing & Communications .... Mrs. Dena PRUETT
29 Director of Alumni Relations .... Ms. Saige WILHITE
38 Director of Career Services .... Mr. Dennis TAYLOR
18 Director of Facilities .... Mr. Chris SAMPITE
46 Director Sponsored Research .... Ms. Patty J. ROBERTS
88 Director of Church Relations .... Vacant
44 Sr Director of Philanthropy .... Ms. Margo SHIDELER
07 Director of Admissions .... Mr. Thomas NEWTON
15 Human Resources Director .... Ms. Tracy MARANTO-PHILLIPS
19 Director of Public Safety .... Mr. Eddie WALKER

Delta College of Arts & Technology (I)

7380 Exchange Place, Baton Rouge LA 70806-3851
County: East Baton Rouge — FICE Identification: 025383
Unit ID: 366270
Telephone: (225) 928-7770 — Carnegie Class: Assoc/PrivFP
FAX Number: (225) 927-9096 — Calendar System: Other
URL: www.deltacollege.com
Established: 1983 — Annual Undergrad Tuition & Fees: $22,600
Enrollment: 687 — Coed
Affiliation or Control: Proprietary — IRS Status: Proprietary
Highest Offering: Associate Degree
Program: Occupational; 2-Year Principally Bachelor's Creditable; Nursing Emphasis
Accreditation: **ACCSC**

01 President .... Mr. Billy L. CLARK

Delta School of Business & Technology, DBA Delta Tech (J)

517 Broad Street, Lake Charles LA 70601-4334
County: Calcasieu — FICE Identification: 020555
Unit ID: 158723
Telephone: (337) 439-5765 — Carnegie Class: Assoc/PrivFP
FAX Number: (337) 436-5151 — Calendar System: Quarter
URL: www.deltatech.edu
Established: 1970 — Annual Undergrad Tuition & Fees: $9,590
Enrollment: 300 — Coed
Affiliation or Control: Proprietary — IRS Status: Proprietary
Highest Offering: Associate Degree
Program: Occupational
Accreditation: **ACICS**

01 Chief Executive Officer .... Mr. Jeff EDWARDS
10 Chief Fiscal Officer/Corp Secretary .... Mrs. Nina LEBLANC

Dillard University (K)

2601 Gentilly Boulevard, New Orleans LA 70122-3097
County: Orleans — FICE Identification: 002004
Unit ID: 158802
Telephone: (504) 283-8822 — Carnegie Class: Bac/A&S
FAX Number: N/A — Calendar System: Semester
URL: www.dillard.edu
Established: 1869 — Annual Undergrad Tuition & Fees: $15,860
Enrollment: 1,307 — Coed
Affiliation or Control: United Methodist — IRS Status: 501(c)3
Highest Offering: Baccalaureate
Program: Liberal Arts And General; Teacher Preparatory; Professional; Fine Arts Emphasis
Accreditation: **SC**, NUR

01 President .... Dr. Walter M. KIMBROUGH
03 Executive Vice President .... Mr. Marc BARNES
05 Provost/Sr VP for Academic Affairs .... Dr. Yolanda PAGE
32 Vice President for Student Success .... Dr. Toya BARNES-TEAMER
43 VP for Legal Affairs .... Dr. Denise WALLACE
10 VP for Finance & CFO .... Mr. Gerald COLEMAN
20 Associate Provost .... Vacant
07 Asst VP of Admissions .... Dr. Alecia CYPRIAN
18 Assoc Vice Pres Facilities Mgmt .... Mr. Keith MCKENDALL
36 Director of Career/Prof Services .... Dr. Dawn WILLIAMS
06 Director of Records & Registration .... Mr. Robert MITCHELL
37 Int Dir Financial Aid/Scholarships .... Ms. Shannon NEAL
102 Assoc VP Research & Spons Programs .... Mr. Theodore CALLIER
30 Int Assistant VP for Development .... Vacant
100 Assistant to the President .... Mrs. Kathy T. ANCAAR

09 Director of Institutional Research .... Dr. Willie KIRKLAND
27 Asst Vice Pres Community Devel .... Mr. Nick L. HARRIS
19 Chief of Police .... Vacant
16 Director of Human Resources .... Ms. Lori KNIGHT
26 Sr Dir of Marketing Communications .. Ms. Mona DUFFEL-JONES
97 Dean of College of General Studies .... Dr. Dorothy SMITH
08 Interim Dean of Library/Learning .... Ms. Cynthia CHARLES
49 Dean of College of Arts & Sciences .... Dr. Robert COLLINS
96 Purchasing Officer .... Ms. Anlatear KIRKLIN

Fortis College (A)

9255 Interline Avenue, Baton Rouge LA 70809
County: East Baton Rouge FICE Identification: 034803
Unit ID: 439738
Telephone: (225) 248-1015 Carnegie Class: Assoc/PrivFP
FAX Number: (225) 248-9517 Calendar System: Other
URL: www.fortis.edu
Established: 1991 Annual Undergrad Tuition & Fees: $14,480
Enrollment: 411 Coed
Affiliation or Control: Proprietary IRS Status: Proprietary
Highest Offering: Associate Degree
Program: Occupational
Accreditation: ABHES, MLTAD, RAD, SURGT, SURTEC

01 Campus Director .... Mr. Vaughn HARTUNIAS

Herzing University (B)

2500 Williams Boulevard, Kenner LA 70062
Telephone: (504) 733-0074 Identification: 666450
Accreditation: &NH, MAAB, SURTEC

† Main campus is Herzing University in Madison, WI.

ITI Technical College (C)

13944 Airline Highway, Baton Rouge LA 70817-5998
County: East Baton Rouge FICE Identification: 021662
Unit ID: 159197
Telephone: (225) 752-4230 Carnegie Class: Assoc/PrivFP
FAX Number: (225) 756-0903 Calendar System: Quarter
URL: www.iticollege.edu
Established: 1973 Annual Undergrad Tuition & Fees: $27,950
Enrollment: 585 Coed
Affiliation or Control: Proprietary IRS Status: Proprietary
Highest Offering: Associate Degree
Program: Occupational; Technical Emphasis
Accreditation: ACCSC

01 President .... Mr. Earl Joe MARTIN, III
03 Vice President .... Mr. Mark WORTHY
05 Dean of Education .... Mr. Louis BABIN

ITT Technical Institute (D)

14111 Airline Hwy, Suite 101,
Baton Rouge LA 70817-6241
Telephone: (225) 754-5800 Identification: 666164
Accreditation: ACICS

† Main campus is ITT Technical Institute in Indianapolis, IN.

ITT Technical Institute (E)

140 James Drive East, Saint Rose LA 70087-4005
Telephone: (504) 463-0338 Identification: 666031
Accreditation: ACICS

† Main campus is ITT Technical Institute in Indianapolis, IN.

Louisiana College (F)

1140 College Drive, Pineville LA 71359-0001
County: Rapides FICE Identification: 002007
Unit ID: 159568
Telephone: (318) 487-7011 Carnegie Class: Bac/Diverse
FAX Number: (318) 487-7191 Calendar System: Semester
URL: www.lacollege.edu
Established: 1906 Annual Undergrad Tuition & Fees: $14,120
Enrollment: 1,511 Coed
Affiliation or Control: Southern Baptist IRS Status: 501(c)3
Highest Offering: Master's
Program: Liberal Arts And General; Teacher Preparatory
Accreditation: SC, ACBSP, MUS, NURSE, PTAA, SW, @TEAC, TED

01 President .... Dr. Joe AGUILLARD
03 Exec VP/VP Integration Faith/Lrng .... Dr. Argile SMITH
05 Vice Pres Academic Affairs .... Dr. Travis WRIGHT
10 Vice President for Business Affairs .... Mr. Randall HARGIS
30 VP Inst Advancement/New Projects .... Dr. Rod MASTELLER
09 Vice Pres Campus-Wide Inst Advance .... Dr. Fred GUILBERT
32 Dean of Students .... Mr. Eric JOHNSON
20 Assistant Dean of the College .... Dr. Wade WARREN
06 Registrar .... Ms. Carolyn DENNIS
84 Director Enrollment Mgmt/Admissions .... Mr. Byron MCGEE
37 Director of Financial Aid .... Mr. Jeff MASSEY
08 Director of the Library .... Mr. Terry MARTIN
26 Director of Marketing .... Mr. John WILLIE
14 Director Computer Services .... Mr. Shane DAVIS
18 Director of Physical Plant .... Mr. Randall HARGIS
21 Director of Business Office .... Ms. Beverly INGRAM
39 Director of Housing .... Mr. Clay MATCHETT
41 Athletic Director .... Mr. Darrell PAYNE
42 Baptist Student Union Director .... Mr. Shannon LANE
44 Director Constituent Relations .... Vacant
35 Director Student Activities .... Ms. K. B THOMAS
36 Director Career Development .... Mrs. Leneil MERCER
09 Director of Institutional Research .... Mr. Bruce DEATON
38 Director Student Counseling .... Ms. Leneil MERCER
07 Director of Admissions .... Mr. Byron MCGEE
15 Director Personnel Services .... Ms. Shannon TASSIN
40 Bookstore Manager .... Mrs. Linda BILLINGSLEY
29 Coord Alumni Affairs/Fdn Rels .... Ms. Luana CUNNINGHAM
19 Coordinator of Safety & Security .... Mr. Dwayne ROGERS
23 Coordinator of Health Services .... Ms. Carla MARTIN
04 Assistant to the President .... Ms. Susan NIXON

*Louisiana Community & Technical College System (G)

265 S Foster Drive, Baton Rouge LA 70806-4104
County: East Baton Rouge Identification: 666188
Telephone: (225) 922-2800 Carnegie Class: N/A
FAX Number: (225) 922-2392
URL: www.lctcs.edu

01 President .... Dr. Joe MAY
03 Executive Vice President .... Dr. Neil MATKIN
10 Sr Vice Pres Finance & Admin .... Ms. Jan JACKSON
05 Vice Pres Academic Affs/Instl Res .... Dr. Derrick MANNS
103 Sr Vice Pres Workforce Solutions .... Dr. Jimmy SAWTELLE
30 Sr Vice Pres System Advancement .... Ms. Leah GOSS
09 Asst VP Institutional Research/Plng .... Dr. Sandra KINNEY
26 Exec Director Media Relations .... Mr. Quinton TAYLOR
04 Exec Assistant to the President .... Ms. Jean Ann KOZLOWSKI
106 Director of Client Services .... Ms. Tiffany SNELL

*Baton Rouge Community College (H)

201 Community College Drive,
Baton Rouge LA 70806-4156
County: East Baton Rouge FICE Identification: 037303
Unit ID: 437103
Telephone: (225) 216-8000 Carnegie Class: Assoc/Pub-U-SC
FAX Number: (225) 216-8100 Calendar System: Semester
URL: www.mybrcc.edu
Established: 1998 Annual Undergrad Tuition & Fees (In-District): $3,366
Enrollment: 8,893 Coed
Affiliation or Control: State/Local IRS Status: 501(c)3
Highest Offering: Associate Degree
Program: Occupational; 2-Year Principally Bachelor's Creditable
Accreditation: SC, ACBSP, ADNUR, NAIT

02 Chancellor .... Dr. Andrea L. MILLER
04 Exec Asst to the Chancellor .... Mr. Howard O. GIBSON
32 Vice Chancellor Student Affairs .... Vacant
30 Vice Chanc Economic Development .... Ms. Phyllis MOUTON
05 Vice Chancellor Acad Affairs .... Ms. Monique CROSS
10 Int Vice Chanc Finance .... Ms. Helen HARRIS
25 Dir Grants Resource Center .... Ms. Ann ZANDERS
84 Int Exec Director Enrollment Svcs .... Dr. Teresa JONES
09 Vice Chanc Rsrch/Assess & Account .... Vacant
15 Director of HR/Payroll .... Mr. William DALTON
18 Acting Dir of Fac/Phys Plant .... Mr. Anthony BROWN
26 Spec Asst to the Chan for Med Rel .... Mr. Steve MITCHELL
29 Director of External Resources .... Ms. Georgia SCOBEE
35 Dir Student Support Services .... Ms. Stacia HARDY
36 Director Career and Job Placement .... Ms. Lisa HIBNER
37 Director Student Financial Aid .... Ms. Rosie TONEY
38 Exec Dir for Advising & Counseling .... Ms. Vinetta FRIE
41 Athletic Director .... Mr. Neil HAYHURST
88 Director of Disability Services .... Ms. Wendy DEVALL
88 Dir of Academic Learning Center .... Ms. Jeanne STACY
25 Project Director Title III .... Ms. Tanasha BROWN
88 Upward Bound Program Director .... Ms. Darica SIMON
96 Director of Purchasing .... Mr. Michael CONSTANTIN
88 Int Dir of Recruit .... Mr. Johnny MELANA
06 Registrar .... Ms. Erin BLAKE
07 Director of Admissions .... Ms. Shontell BLAKE
31 Exec Dir of Comm Rels .... Ms. Gerri HOBDY
19 Chief of Police .... Ms. Genoria TILLEY

*Bossier Parish Community College (I)

6220 E Texas Street, Bossier City LA 71111-6922
County: Bossier FICE Identification: 020554
Unit ID: 158431
Telephone: (318) 678-6000 Carnegie Class: Assoc/Pub-R-M
FAX Number: (318) 678-6389 Calendar System: Semester
URL: www.bpcc.edu
Established: 1966 Annual Undergrad Tuition & Fees (In-District): $2,911
Enrollment: 7,917 Coed
Affiliation or Control: State/Local IRS Status: 501(c)3
Highest Offering: Associate Degree
Program: Occupational; 2-Year Principally Bachelor's Creditable
Accreditation: SC, ACFEI, ADNUR, COARC, EMT, MAC, NAIT, OTA, PHLEB, PTAA, SURGT

02 Chancellor .... Mr. James B. HENDERSON
05 VC for Academic Affairs .... Dr. Stan WILKINS
11 VC Business Affs/Economic Devel .... Mr. Tom WILLIAMS
32 VC of Student Affairs .... Ms. Karen RECCHIA
10 Chief Financial Officer .... Ms. Michelle BREWER
20 Assoc VC Planning/Instruction .... Ms. Lesa TAYLOR-DUPREE
60 Dean of Comm & Performing Arts .... Mr. Ray Scott CRAWFORD
103 Dean of Workforce Develop/Cont Educ .... Ms. Lisa WARGO
08 Dean of Learning Resources .... Ms. Brenda BRANTLEY
88 Dean for Innovative Learning .... Ms. Donna WOMACK
21 Comptroller .... Ms. Carol BATES
38 Student Counselor .... Mr. Morris ROBINSON
37 Director Student Financial Aid .... Ms. Vickie TEMPLE
06 Registrar .... Ms. Patty H. STEWART
26 Director of Public Relations .... Ms. Tracy MCGILL
16 Director of Human Resources .... Mrs. Teri BASHARA
35 Director of Student Life .... Ms. Marjoree HARPER
13 Chief Information Officer .... Mr. Gary HOLLATZ
22 Diversity/Multicultural Affairs .... Ms. Cindy DARBY
72 Director of Educational Technology .... Ms. Kathleen GAY
18 Dir Physical Plant & Maintenance .... Mr. Joe ST. ANDRE
29 Director Alumni Relations .... Ms. Stephanie ROGERS
09 Dir Inst Research/Assessment/Grants .... Ms. Lisa WHEELER
96 Director of Purchasing .... Ms. Gayle DOUCET

*Central Louisiana Technical College Avoyelles Campus (J)

508 Choupique Street, Cottonport LA 71327-3743
County: Avoyelles FICE Identification: 008317
Unit ID: 158237
Telephone: (318) 876-2401 Carnegie Class: Not Classified
FAX Number: (318) 876-2634 Calendar System: Semester
URL: www.ltc.edu
Established: 1938 Annual Undergrad Tuition & Fees (In-District): $1,631
Enrollment: 378 Coed
Affiliation or Control: State/Local IRS Status: 501(c)3
Highest Offering: Associate Degree
Program: Occupational; Technical Emphasis
Accreditation: COE

02 Campus Dean .... Mr. Jude PITRE

*Central Louisiana Technical College Huey P. Long Campus (K)

5960 Highway 167 N, Winnfield LA 71483-5075
County: Winn FICE Identification: 005480
Unit ID: 159090
Telephone: (318) 628-4342 Carnegie Class: Not Classified
FAX Number: (318) 628-7768 Calendar System: Semester
URL: www.ltc.edu
Established: 1938 Annual Undergrad Tuition & Fees (In-District): $1,631
Enrollment: 310 Coed
Affiliation or Control: State/Local IRS Status: 501(c)3
Highest Offering: Associate Degree
Program: Occupational; Technical Emphasis
Accreditation: COE

02 Campus Dean .... Mr. Danny KEYES

*Central Louisiana Technical College Oakdale Campus (L)

117 Highway 1152, Oakdale LA 71463-3536
County: Allen FICE Identification: 030026
Unit ID: 160047
Telephone: (318) 335-3944 Carnegie Class: Assoc/Pub-R-S
FAX Number: (318) 335-3347 Calendar System: Quarter
URL: www.ltc.edu
Established: Annual Undergrad Tuition & Fees (In-District): $1,631
Enrollment: 456 Coed
Affiliation or Control: State/Local IRS Status: 501(c)3
Highest Offering: Associate Degree
Program: Occupational; Technical Emphasis
Accreditation: COE

02 Campus Coordinator .... Ms. Donnis POE

*Central Louisiana Technical Community College (M)

4311 S. Macarthur Drive, Alexandria LA 71301
County: Rapides FICE Identification: 005489
Unit ID: 158088
Telephone: (318) 487-5439 Carnegie Class: Assoc/Pub-R-S
FAX Number: (318) 487-5970 Calendar System: Trimester
URL: www.region6.ltc.edu
Established: 1965 Annual Undergrad Tuition & Fees (In-State): $1,431
Enrollment: 1,691 Coed
Affiliation or Control: State IRS Status: 501(c)3
Highest Offering: Associate Degree
Program: Occupational; Technical Emphasis
Accreditation: COE

02 Chancellor .... Dr. Rodney ELLIS
05 Chief Academic/Student Svcs Officer .... Ms. Carol HEBERT
10 Controller .... Ms. Elizabeth BYNOG

*Delgado Community College (A)

615 City Park Avenue, New Orleans LA 70119-4399
County: Orleans FICE Identification: 004625
Unit ID: 158662
Telephone: (504) 671-5000 Carnegie Class: Assoc/Pub-U-MC
FAX Number: (504) 361-6699 Calendar System: Semester
URL: www.dcc.edu
Established: 1921 Annual Undergrad Tuition & Fees (In-District): $3,750
Enrollment: 18,093 Coed
Affiliation or Control: State/Local IRS Status: 501(c)3
Highest Offering: Associate Degree
Program: Occupational; 2-Year Principally Bachelor's Creditable
Accreditation: SC, ACBSP, ACFEI, ADNUR, CAHIIM, COARC, DIETT, DMS, EMT, ENGT, FUSER, MLTAD, NAIT, NMT, OTA, PHLEB, PTAA, RAD, RTT, SURGT

02 Chancellor ... Dr. Monty SULLIVAN
10 Vice Chanc Business/Admin Affairs ... Mr. Aristide C. EAGAN, III
05 Vice Chanc Acad Affs/Col Provost ... Ms. Deborah R. LEA
103 Asst Vice Chanc Workforce Dev/Educ ... Dr. Leroy KENDRICK
66 Exec Dean School of Nursing Campus ... Dr. Cheryl MYERS
76 Dean of Allied Health ... Mr. Harold GASPARD
50 Dean Business & Technology ... Mr. Warren PUNEKY
60 Dean of Communication Division ... Mr. Lester ADELSBERG
81 Dean Science & Math ... Mr. Thomas GRUBER
79 Dean of Arts and Humanities ... Ms. Patrice MOORE
106 Dean of Dist Learn and Instr Tech ... Ms. Melissa LACOUR
12 Dean Northshore ... Ms. Ashley CHITWOOD
12 Exec Dean West Bank Campus ... Dr. Kristine STRICKLAND
32 Asst VC of Student Affairs ... Ms. Arnel COSEY
15 Asst Vice Chanc for Human Resources ... Vacant
14 Asst VC of Information Technology ... Mr. Thomas LOVINCE
21 Asst VC of Budget & Finance ... Mr. Steve CAZAUBON
18 Asst VC of Dir Facilities/Planning ... Mr. Adolfo GIRAU
21 Asst VC/Comptroller ... Mr. Ronald RODRIGUEZ
88 Senior Compliance Officer ... Vacant
04 Executive Asst to the Chancellor ... Ms. Traci SMOTHERS
72 Asst Dean Business & Technology ... Mr. Rene CINTRON
55 Asst Dean Evening and Weekend Div ... Vacant
09 Exec Dir Planning & Research ... Ms. Jennifer DALY
88 Exec Dir of Curriculum & Pgm Devel ... Mr. Timothy STAMM
08 Librarian ... Ms. Denise REPMAN
37 Director Financial Aid ... Ms. Rhonda KING
41 Athletic Director ... Mr. Tommy SMITH
06 College Registrar ... Ms. Maria CISNEROS
07 Director Admissions/Enrollment Svcs ... Ms. Gwen BOUTTE
25 Director of Grants Development ... Vacant
35 Director of Student Life ... Mrs. Michelle GRECO
88 Director Ofc of Advising & Testing ... Ms. Tania CARRADINE
96 Director of Purchasing ... Ms. Susan VARBLE
19 Director of Campus Police ... Mr. Ronald DOUCETTE
26 Asst Director of Public Relations ... Mr. Tony COOK

*L.E. Fletcher Technical Community College (B)

1407 Highway 311, Schriever LA 70395
County: Terrebonne FICE Identification: 005761
Unit ID: 160481
Telephone: (985) 448-7900 Carnegie Class: Assoc/Pub-U-MC
FAX Number: (985) 446-3308 Calendar System: Semester
URL: www.fletcher.edu
Established: 1948 Annual Undergrad Tuition & Fees (In-State): $2,831
Enrollment: 2,502 Coed
Affiliation or Control: State IRS Status: Exempt
Highest Offering: Associate Degree
Program: Occupational; 2-Year Principally Bachelor's Creditable
Accreditation: SC, COARC, COE, NAIT, PHLEB, PNUR

02 Chancellor ... Mr. F. Travis LAVIGNE, JR.
05 Vice Chancellor Instruction ... Mr. William H. TULAK
06 Registrar ... Ms. Lisa HIDALGO
09 Dean/Planning & Inst Effectiveness ... Mr. Stanton MCNEELY
10 Vice Chancellor Finance & Admin ... Mr. Bryan E. GLATTER
30 Director Philanthrophy & Stewrdship ... Ms. Jessica THORNTON
32 Dean of Student Services ... Mr. Mickey DIEZ
75 Dean of Technical Education ... Ms. Fathia WILLIAMS
66 Dean of Nursing and Allied Health ... Ms. Sonia CLARKE
07 Director of Admissions ... Vacant
15 HR Manager ... Ms. Gina MARCEL
37 Director of Financial Aid ... Mrs. Shawn TRAVIS
04 Assistant to the Chancellor ... Ms. Brenda FAUCHEUX
08 Head Librarian ... Mrs. Suzanne MARTIN
26 Exec Dir Inst Adv & External Rels ... Vacant
49 Dean Art and Sciences ... Mrs. Donna ESTRADA
103 Director of Workforce Education ... Mrs. Catherine BARBER
75 Director of LAMPI ... Mr. Breck CHAISSON

*Louisiana Delta Community College (C)

7500 Millhaven Road, Monroe LA 71203
County: Ouachita Parish FICE Identification: 041301
Unit ID: 440624
Telephone: (318) 345-9000 Carnegie Class: Assoc/Pub-R-S
FAX Number: N/A Calendar System: Semester
URL: www.ladelta.edu
Established: 2001 Annual Undergrad Tuition & Fees (In-District): $2,931
Enrollment: 2,518 Coed
Affiliation or Control: State/Local IRS Status: 501(c)3
Highest Offering: Associate Degree
Program: Occupational; 2-Year Principally Bachelor's Creditable; Business Emphasis
Accreditation: SC, ADNUR

02 Interim Chancellor ... Dr. Jerry RYAN
05 Interim V Chancellor of Academic ... Mrs. Margie MIXON
10 Interim V C of Finance & Administra ... Mrs. Melissa DUCOTE
20 Registrar ... Mr. Joe MANSOUR
32 Interim V C of Student Affairs ... Ms. Alvina THOMAS
30 Dir of Institutional Advancement ... Mr. Keith ADAMS
13 Chief Information Officer ... Mr. Bradley MASTERS

*Northshore Technical Community College (D)

1710 Sullivan Drive, Bogalusa LA 70427-5866
County: Washington FICE Identification: 006756
Unit ID: 160667
Telephone: (985) 732-6640 Carnegie Class: Assoc/Pub-U-MC
FAX Number: (985) 732-6603 Calendar System: Semester
URL: www.northshorecollege.edu
Established: 1930 Annual Undergrad Tuition & Fees (In-District): $3,266
Enrollment: 3,111 Coed
Affiliation or Control: State/Local IRS Status: 501(c)3
Highest Offering: Associate Degree
Program: Occupational; 2-Year Principally Bachelor's Creditable; Technical Emphasis
Accreditation: COE

02 Chancellor ... Dr. William S. WAINWRIGHT
05 Associate Dean ... Mr. William POTTER
32 Dean of Student Services ... Mr. Mack JACKSON, III
72 Dean of Technical Studies ... Ms. Gayle LADNER
76 Dean of Health Sciences ... Ms. Katherine M. LYONS
35 Student Services Officer ... Ms. Debra SHERMAN
09 Dir of Institutional Research & Eff ... Ms. Shelia SINGLETARY
10 Vice Chancellor Finance & Admin ... Mr. Marc CHAUVIN
15 Human Resources Director ... Ms. Joanna DILLMAN
18 Chief Facilities/Physical Plant ... Mr. Gerald BLAPPERT
103 Chief Workforce Development ... Ms. Stephanie BADEAUX
37 Director of Financial Aid ... Ms. Angela MARSHALL
96 Director of Purchasing ... Ms. Ann LUMPKIN

*Northwest Louisiana Technical College Northwest Campus (E)

PO Box 835, Minden LA 71058-0835
County: Webster FICE Identification: 009975
Unit ID: 160010
Telephone: (318) 371-3035 Carnegie Class: Assoc/Pub-R-S
FAX Number: (318) 371-3055 Calendar System: Trimester
URL: www.ltc.edu
Established: 1952 Annual Undergrad Tuition & Fees (In-District): $1,631
Enrollment: 2,633 Coed
Affiliation or Control: State/Local IRS Status: 501(c)3
Highest Offering: Associate Degree
Program: Occupational; 2-Year Principally Bachelor's Creditable; Technical Emphasis
Accreditation: COE

02 Campus Dean ... Mr. Charles T. STRONG
05 Assistant Dean ... Mr. David RHODES
09 Director Institutional Research ... Mr. David RHODES
15 Director Personnel Services ... Ms. Lisa SNIDER
20 Assistant Dean ... Ms. Diane CLARK
37 Director Student Financial Aid ... Ms. Annette CHANLER

*Nunez Community College (F)

3710 Paris Road, Chalmette LA 70043-1297
County: Saint Bernard FICE Identification: 021661
Unit ID: 158884
Telephone: (504) 278-6200 Carnegie Class: Assoc/Pub-S-SC
FAX Number: (504) 278-6480 Calendar System: Semester
URL: www.nunez.edu
Established: 1992 Annual Undergrad Tuition & Fees (In-District): $3,256
Enrollment: 2,294 Coed
Affiliation or Control: State/Local IRS Status: 501(c)3
Highest Offering: Associate Degree
Program: Occupational; 2-Year Principally Bachelor's Creditable
Accreditation: SC, NAIT

02 Chancellor ... Dr. Thomas R. WARNER
05 Vice Chanc for Acad & Student Affs ... Mrs. Annette ACCOMANDO
30 Ex Dir Inst Advanc/Ex Asst to Chanc ... Ms. Teresa L. SMITH
10 Chief Financial Officer ... Mr. Louis LEHR
32 Dean for Student Affairs ... Ms. Becky MAILLET
72 Dean of Business/Technology ... Vacant
45 Dir Planning/Inst Effectiveness ... Mr. Leonard UNBEHAGEN
08 Director of Library Services ... Mr. Richard DEFOE
15 Dir Human Res/Exec Asst to Chanc ... Dr. Carol MCLEOD
38 Student Counselor ... Vacant
06 Registrar ... Ms. Meg GREENFIELD
07 Director of Admissions ... Ms. Angie JONES
26 Chief Public Relations Officer ... Ms. Arifah LIGHTBURN
37 Director Financial Aid ... Mr. John WHISNANT
103 Director Workforce Development ... Mr. Ernest T. FRAZIER, JR.
25 Director of Sponsored Programs ... Ms. Kimberly RUTHERFORD
29 Director Alumni Relations ... Vacant
18 Coordinator of Facilities ... Ms. Dawn HART-THORE
41 Coord Student Activities/Athletics ... Vacant
13 Computer Services Coordinator ... Mr. Jason HOSCH

*River Parishes Community College (G)

PO Box 310, Sorrento LA 70778-0310
County: Ascension FICE Identification: 037894
Unit ID: 436304
Telephone: (225) 675-8270 Carnegie Class: Assoc/Pub-S-SC
FAX Number: (225) 675-5478 Calendar System: Semester
URL: www.rpcc.edu
Established: 1999 Annual Undergrad Tuition & Fees (In-District): $2,803
Enrollment: 3,566 Coed
Affiliation or Control: State/Local IRS Status: 501(c)3
Highest Offering: Associate Degree
Program: 2-Year Principally Bachelor's Creditable
Accreditation: SC, NAIT

02 Chancellor ... Dr. Joe Ben WELCH
03 Executive Vice Chancellor ... Dr. William MARTIN
10 VC Business/Finance/Administration ... Rodney JOHNSON, JR.
84 Dean of Students/Enrollment Mgmt ... Allison D. VICKNAIR
05 Dean of Academic Studies ... Dr. Crystal LEE
21 Director of Accounting & Payroll ... Lisa JACKSON
06 Registrar ... Cara LANDRY
37 Director Financial Aid ... Terry MARTIN
38 Director Student Counseling ... Jennifer KLEINPETER
08 Director of Library Services ... Wendy JOHNSON
15 Human Resource Manager ... Donna WHITTINGTON
07 Admissions Counselor ... Dianna GILBERT
09 Director of Institutional Research ... Vacant

*South Central Louisiana Technical College Young Memorial Campus (H)

900 Youngs Road, Morgan City LA 70380-2931
County: Saint Mary FICE Identification: 005526
Unit ID: 160913
Telephone: (985) 380-2957 Carnegie Class: Assoc/Pub-S-MC
FAX Number: (985) 380-2440 Calendar System: Semester
URL: www.scl.edu
Established: 1965 Annual Undergrad Tuition & Fees (In-District): $1,902
Enrollment: 2,918 Coed
Affiliation or Control: State/Local IRS Status: 501(c)3
Highest Offering: Associate Degree
Program: Occupational; Technical Emphasis
Accreditation: COE

02 Campus Administrator ... Mr. Karl J. YOUNG, JR.
05 Chief Academic Officer ... Ms. Melanie HENRY
07 Dir of Admissions/Student Affairs ... Ms. Tammie L. MOORE
09 Director of Institutional Research ... Ms. Katherine FALGOUT
10 Chief Business Officer ... Mr. Darryl DAIGLE
15 Director Human Resources ... Ms. Pam MILLER

*South Louisiana Community College (I)

320 Devalcourt Street, Lafayette LA 70506-4124
County: Lafayette FICE Identification: 039563
Unit ID: 434061
Telephone: (337) 521-8896 Carnegie Class: Assoc/Pub-R-M
FAX Number: (337) 262-2100 Calendar System: Semester
URL: www.solacc.edu
Established: 1998 Annual Undergrad Tuition & Fees (In-District): $3,262
Enrollment: 4,015 Coed
Affiliation or Control: State/Local IRS Status: 501(c)3
Highest Offering: Associate Degree
Program: Occupational; 2-Year Principally Bachelor's Creditable
Accreditation: SC, EMT, NAIT

02 Chancellor ... Dr. Natalie HARDER
04 Assistant to the Chancellor ... Ms. Ziuta BLAES
05 Vice Chanc Academic Affairs ... Dr. Michael GLISSON
10 Vice Chanc Finance & Administration ... Mr. Rudy GONZALES
11 Vice Chanc Business & Industry ... Mr. Willie SMITH
32 Vice Chanc of Student Services ... Ms. Rochelle MOORE
20 Assoc Dean Instruction ... Ms. Karol HOWERTON
32 Dean of Students ... Ms. Meltida WILSON
09 Asc Vice Chanc Institutional Effect ... Dr. Charles MILLER
06 Director of Admissions/Advising ... Ms. Rachel ALEXANDER
37 Director of Financial Aid ... Ms. Kelly KNIGHT
08 Director of Library Services ... Ms. Katherine ROLFES
21 Business Manager ... Ms. Janet LAGRANGE
96 Financial Manager ... Ms. Gloria SMITH
18 Facilities Coordinator ... Mr. Ed LOPEZ
15 Human Resources Director ... Ms. Alicia HULIN

*South Louisiana Community College Ardoin Campus (J)

1101 Bertrand Drive, Lafayette LA 70506-4115
County: Lafayette FICE Identification: 022148
Unit ID: 159443
Telephone: (337) 262-5962 Carnegie Class: Assoc/Pub-R-S
FAX Number: (337) 262-5122 Calendar System: Semester
URL: www.solacc.edu
Established: 1978 Annual Undergrad Tuition & Fees (In-State): $1,631
Enrollment: 1,398 Coed
Affiliation or Control: State IRS Status: 501(c)3
Highest Offering: Associate Degree
Program: Occupational; Technical Emphasis

Accreditation: COE, ACFEI, MLTAD, NAIT, SURGT

02 Campus Dean .... Ms. Darcee BEX
06 Registrar .... Ms. Connie CHOPIN
37 Director of Financial Aid .... Ms. Kelly KNIGHT

*South Louisiana Community College Charles B Coreil Campus (A)

1124 Vocational Dr Ward 1, Ville Platte LA 70586-0296
County: Evangeline FICE Identification: 022402
Unit ID: 160816
Telephone: (337) 363-2197 Carnegie Class: Not Classified
FAX Number: (337) 363-7984 Calendar System: Semester
URL: www.ltc.edu
Established: 1976 Annual Undergrad Tuition & Fees (In-District): $1,474
Enrollment: 230 Coed
Affiliation or Control: State/Local IRS Status: 501(c)3
Highest Offering: Associate Degree
Program: Occupational; Technical Emphasis
Accreditation: COE

02 Campus Dean .... Ms. Laurie FONTENOT

*South Louisiana Community College Gulf Area Campus (B)

1301 Clover Street, Abbeville LA 70510-3811
County: Vermilion FICE Identification: 005482
Unit ID: 159018
Telephone: (337) 893-4984 Carnegie Class: Assoc/Pub-R-S
FAX Number: (337) 893-4991 Calendar System: Other
URL: www.solacc.edu
Established: 1952 Annual Undergrad Tuition & Fees (In-District): $1,631
Enrollment: 422 Coed
Affiliation or Control: State/Local IRS Status: 501(c)3
Highest Offering: Associate Degree
Program: Occupational; Technical Emphasis
Accreditation: COE

02 Campus-Dean .... Ms. Nicole LEARSON
32 Director Student Services .... Ms. Tobi EDWARDS
37 Financial Aid Officer .... Ms. Kelly KNIGHT

*South Louisiana Community College T.H. Harris Campus (C)

332 East South Street, Opelousas LA 70570-6114
County: Saint Landry FICE Identification: 005466
Unit ID: 160676
Telephone: (337) 948-0239 Carnegie Class: Assoc/Pub-R-S
FAX Number: (337) 948-0243 Calendar System: Semester
URL: www.solacc.edu
Established: 1938 Annual Undergrad Tuition & Fees (In-District): $1,631
Enrollment: 666 Coed
Affiliation or Control: State/Local IRS Status: 501(c)3
Highest Offering: Associate Degree
Program: Occupational; 2-Year Principally Bachelor's Creditable; Technical Emphasis
Accreditation: COE

02 Campus Dean .... Mrs. Laurie FONTENOT
37 Financial Aid Officer .... Mrs. Kelly KNIGHT
32 Student Affairs Officer .... Mrs. Erika MILTON

*South Louisiana Community College Teche Area Campus (D)

PO Box 11057, 609 Ember Drive,
New Iberia LA 70562-1057
County: Iberia FICE Identification: 005528
Unit ID: 160694
Telephone: (337) 373-0011 Carnegie Class: Assoc/Pub-R-S
FAX Number: (337) 373-0039 Calendar System: Semester
URL: www.solacc.edu
Established: 1951 Annual Undergrad Tuition & Fees (In-District): $1,631
Enrollment: 750 Coed
Affiliation or Control: State/Local IRS Status: 501(c)3
Highest Offering: Associate Degree
Program: Occupational; Technical Emphasis
Accreditation: COE

02 Campus Dean .... Ms. Douglas Anne TAYLOR
06 Registrar .... Ms. Connie CHOPIN

*Sowela Technical Community College (E)

PO Box 16950, Lake Charles LA 70616-6950
County: Calcasieu FICE Identification: 005467
Unit ID: 160579
Telephone: (337) 421-6565 Carnegie Class: Assoc/Pub-R-S
FAX Number: (337) 491-2135 Calendar System: Semester
URL: www.sowela.edu
Established: 1938 Annual Undergrad Tuition & Fees (In-District): $4,070
Enrollment: 2,741 Coed
Affiliation or Control: State/Local IRS Status: 501(c)3
Highest Offering: Associate Degree
Program: 2-Year Principally Bachelor's Creditable; Technical Emphasis

Accreditation: @SC, COE, NAIT

02 Chancellor .... Dr. Neil ASPINWALL
04 Assistant to the Chancellor .... Ms. Amy THIBODEAUX
05 Vice Chanc Acad Affs/Stdnt Success .... Dr. Rick BATEMAN, JR.
10 Vice Chancellor Finance .... Ms. Jeanine NEWMAN
46 Vice Chancellor Economic Devel .... Vacant
27 Chief Info Resources & Tech Officer .... Dr. Charles NWANKWO
84 Exec Dean Enrollment Mgmt/Registrar .... Ms. Erin BLAKE
21 Controller .... Mr. Francis PORCHE, JR.
37 Director of Financial Aid .... Ms. Anna DAIGLE
08 Director of Library Services .... Ms. Mary Frances SHERWOOD
15 Director of Human Resources .... Dr. FitzPatrick ANYANWU
103 Director of Workforce Development .... Dr. Joseph FLEISHMAN
35 Director of Student Support Service .... Ms. Christine COLLINS
18 Director Facilities Planning & Mgmt .... Mr. Davidson DARBONE
09 Exec Director Planning & Analysis ... Dr. Fitzpatrick U. ANYANWU
30 Exec Dir Institutional Advancement .... Mr. Randy JOLLY

*Baton Rouge Community College, Acadian Branch (F)

3250 N Acadian Thruway East,
Baton Rouge LA 70805-6699
Telephone: (225) 359-9201 FICE Identification: 005488
Accreditation: COE, ACFEI, NAIT

† Main campus is Baton Rouge Community College in Baton Rouge, LA.

*Baton Rouge Community College, Jackson Branch (G)

3337 Highway 10 E, Jackson LA 70748-6240
Telephone: (225) 634-2636 FICE Identification: 025099
Accreditation: COE

† Main campus is Baton Rouge Community College in Baton Rouge, LA.

*Baton Rouge Community College, New Roads Branch (H)

PO Box 725, New Roads LA 70760-0725
Telephone: (225) 638-8613 FICE Identification: 005478
Accreditation: COE

† Main campus is Baton Rouge Community College in Baton Rouge, LA.

*Northwest Louisiana Technical College Natchitoches Campus (I)

6587 Highway 1 Bypass (3110),
Natchitoches LA 71458-0657
Telephone: (318) 357-3162 FICE Identification: 021602
Accreditation: COE

† Main campus is Northwest Louisiana Technical College Northwest Campus in Minden, LA.

*Northwest Louisiana Technical College Shreveport Campus (J)

Box 78527, 2010 N Market Street,
Shreveport LA 71137-8527
Telephone: (318) 676-7811 FICE Identification: 005469
Accreditation: COE

† Main campus is Northwest Louisiana Technical College Northwest Campus in Minden, LA.

*South Central Louisiana Technical College Lafourche Campus (K)

1425 Tiger Drive, Thibodaux LA 70301-4336
Telephone: (985) 447-0924 FICE Identification: 030091
Accreditation: COE, SURGT

† Main campus is South Central Louisiana Technical College Young Memorial Campus in Morgan City, LA.

*South Central Louisiana Technical College River Parishes Campus (L)

PO Drawer AQ, 181 Regala Park Road,
Reserve LA 70084-0542
Telephone: (985) 536-4418 FICE Identification: 023334
Accreditation: COE, NAIT

† Main campus is South Central Louisiana Technical College Young Memorial Campus in Morgan City, LA.

Louisiana Culinary Institute (M)

10550 Airline Highway, Baton Rouge LA 70816-4109
County: East Baton Rouge FICE Identification: 041123
Unit ID: 449612
Telephone: (225) 769-8820 Carnegie Class: Assoc/PrivFP
FAX Number: (225) 769-8792 Calendar System: Semester
URL: www.louisianaculinary.com
Established: 2002 Annual Undergrad Tuition & Fees: $28,300
Enrollment: 183 Coed
Affiliation or Control: Proprietary IRS Status: Proprietary
Highest Offering: Associate Degree
Program: Occupational

Accreditation: COE, ACFEI

01 Chief Executive Officer .... Keith RUSH

*Louisiana State University System Office (N)

3810 W Lakeshore Drive, Baton Rouge LA 70808-4600
County: East Baton Rouge FICE Identification: 002009
Unit ID: 159638
Telephone: (225) 578-2111 Carnegie Class: N/A
FAX Number: (225) 578-5524
URL: www.lsusystem.edu

01 President .... Dr. F. King ALEXANDER
05 VP Academic Affairs .... Dr. Carolyn H. HARGRAVE
17 Exec VP HC/Med Educ Redesign .... Dr. Frank OPELKA
88 Asst Vice Pres for System Relations . Dr. Robert H. RASMUSSEN
10 CFO/Asst Vice Pres & Comptroller .... Mrs. Wendy SIMONEAUX
18 System Director Facility Planning .... Mr. Danny MAHAFFEY
43 LSU Lead Counsel .... Mr. W. Shelby MCKENZIE
15 System Dir Human Resource/Risk Mgt ... Ms. Sharyon LIPSCOMB
21 System Director Internal Audit .... Mr. Chad BRACKIN

*Louisiana State University and Agricultural and Mechanical College (O)

Baton Rouge LA 70803-0100
County: East Baton Rouge FICE Identification: 002010
Unit ID: 159391
Telephone: (225) 578-3202 Carnegie Class: RU/VH
FAX Number: (225) 578-6400 Calendar System: Semester
URL: www.lsu.edu
Established: 1860 Annual Undergrad Tuition & Fees (In-State): $7,873
Enrollment: 30,225 Coed
Affiliation or Control: State IRS Status: 501(c)3
Highest Offering: Doctorate
Program: Liberal Arts And General; Teacher Preparatory; Professional
Accreditation: SC, AAFCS, ART, BUS, CACREP, CIDA, CLPSY, CONST, CS, DIETD, EMT, ENG, FOR, IPSY, JOUR, LIB, LSAR, MUS, SCPSY, SP, SPAA, SW, TED, THEA, VET

02 President & Chancellor .... Dr. King ALEXANDER
05 Exec Vice Chanc/Provost Acad Affs .... Dr. Stuart R. BELL
26 Assoc Vice Chanc Comm & Univ Rel .... Mr. Herb VINCENT
10 Int Vice Chanc Fin & Adm/Controller .... Mr. Robert KUHN
46 Vice Chanc Research & Econ Dev .... Dr. Kalliat T. VALSARAJ
45 Vice Chanc Strategic Initiatives .... Dr. Isiah M. WARNER
32 Vice Chanc Student Life/Enroll Svcs .... Dr. Kurt J. KEPPLER
102 President/CEO LSU Foundation .... MajGen. Lee G. GRIFFIN
28 Vice Prov Campus Equity/Diversity .... Mr. Kenneth O. MILES
20 Vice Prov Academic Affairs .... Dr. Jane CASSIDY
20 Vice Provost Academics & Planning .... Dr. Gilmore REEVE
15 Assoc VC Human Resources Mgmt .... Mr. A. G. MONACO
84 Assoc VC Enrollment Management .... Dr. David KURPIUS
30 Exec Director Inst Advancement .... Ms. Bunnie CANNON
86 External & Legislative Affairs Dir .... Dr. Jason DRODDY
85 Assoc VC International Programs .... Dr. Hector ZAPATA
37 Assoc Dir Student Aid/Scholarships .... Ms. Amy MARIX
08 Dean LSU Libraries .... Dr. Jennifer S. CARGILL
79 Dean College of Humanities .... Dr. Gaines FOSTER
58 Dean of Graduate School .... Dr. Gary R. BYERLY
54 Dean College of Engineering .... Dr. Richard KOUBEK
47 Dean College of Agriculture .... Dr. Kenneth L. KOONCE
50 Dean Ourso College of Business .... Dr. Richard D. WHITE
64 Dean College Music & Dramatic Arts .... Dr. Laurence KAPTAIN
81 Int Dean College of Science .... Dr. Guillermo FERREYRA
62 Dean Sch of Library & Info Science .... Dr. Beth M. PASKOFF
53 Int Dean Col of Human Sci & Educ .... Dr. Damon P. ANDREW
49 Int Dean College of Art & Design .... Mr. Kenneth CARPENTER
74 Dean Veterinary Medicine .... Dr. Peter F. HAYNES
60 Dean Manship Sch of Mass Comm .... Dr. Jerry CEPPOS
92 Dean Honors College .... Dr. Nancy L. CLARK
65 Dean Sch of Coast & Environ .... Dr. Christopher D'ELIA
88 Assoc Dean University College .... Mr. Paul IVEY
38 Assc Dean Advising & Counseling Ctr .... Mr. R. Paul IVEY
35 Assistant Dean Student Services .... Ms. Angela GUILLORY
88 Sr Ex Dir SN Ctr Security Rsch Trng .... Mr. Jim FERNANDEZ
88 Exec Director Center Energy Stds .... Dr. Allan G. PULSIPHER
51 Exec Director Continuing Education .... Mr. Doug WEIMER
29 President Alumni Association .... Dr. Charlie W. ROBERTS
59 Director School Human Ecology .... Dr. Roy J. MARTIN
88 Exec Director Museum of Art .... Dr. Jordana POMEROY
18 Exec Director Facility Services .... Mr. Tony LOMBARDO
13 Int Chief Info Ofcr/Info Tech Svcs .... Mr. Brian NICHOLS
75 Dir Sch Human Res Ed/Workforce Dev .. Dr. Michael F. BURNETT
80 Director Public Admin Institute .... Dr. James A. RICHARDSON
88 Director LSU Press .... Ms. MaryKatherine CALLAWAY
41 Athletic Director .... Mr. Joe ALLEVA
06 Registrar .... Mr. Robert K. DOOLOS
36 Director Career Services .... Dr. Mary D. FEDUCCIA
09 Director of Institutional Research .... Mr. Thomas M. SMITH
93 Director Multicultural Affairs .... Ms. Chaunda ALLEN
94 Director Women's/Gender Studies .... Ms. Kate BRATTON
65 Director Museum of Natural Science ... Dr. Frederick H. SHELDON
88 Director Rural Life Museum .... Mr. David J W. FLOYD
96 Exec Dir of Purch & Property Mgmt .... Ms. Marie FRANK
07 Assoc Director of Admissions .... Ms. Lupe LAMADRID

*Louisiana State University at Alexandria (A)

8100 Highway 71 S, Alexandria LA 71302-9121
County: Rapides FICE Identification: 002011
Unit ID: 159382
Telephone: (318) 445-3672 Carnegie Class: Bac/A&S
FAX Number: (318) 473-6418 Calendar System: Semester
URL: www.lsua.edu
Established: 1959 Annual Undergrad Tuition & Fees (In-State): $5,337
Enrollment: 2,430 Coed
Affiliation or Control: State IRS Status: 501(c)3
Highest Offering: Baccalaureate
Program: Liberal Arts And General; Teacher Preparatory
Accreditation: SC, ADNUR, MLTAD, NUR, RAD, TED

02 Interim Chancellor ... Dr. Paul D. CORIEL
05 Vice Chanc Academic & Student Affs ... Dr. Barbara S. HATFIELD
10 Vice Chanc Finance/Admin Services ... Mr. David WESSE
30 Director Institutional Advancement ... Ms. Melinda F. ANDERSON
20 Asst VC Academic/Student Affairs ... Dr. Eamon HALPIN
21 Asst VC Finance/Admin Services ... Ms. Belinda AARON
50 Dept Chair Business Administration ... Dr. Robert BUSH
49 Dept Chair Arts/English/Humanities ... Dr. Arthur RANKIN
83 Dept Chair Behavioral & Social Sci ... Dr. Jerry SANSON
81 Dept Chair Math & Physical Sciences ... Dr. Nathan PONDER
53 Deparment Chair Education ... Dr. Judy RUNDELL
76 Department Chair Allied Health ... Dr. Haywood JOINER
66 Department Chair Nursing ... Dr. Elizabeth BATTALORA
49 Dept Chair Biological Sciences ... Dr. Carol CORBAT
18 Exec Director of Facility Services ... Mr. Robert KARAM
84 Exec Director Enrollment Management ... Ms. Teresa SEYMOUR
08 Director Library ... Dr. Bonnie HINES
37 Director of Financial Aid ... Mr. Paul MONTELEONE
15 Director Human Resource Management ... Ms. Lynette BURLEW
14 Dir Information/Educ Technology ... Mr. Deron THAXTON
51 Director Continuing Education ... Mr. Robert S. SAVAGE
32 Director Student Services ... Dr. Eamon HALPIN
09 Dir Inst Research/Effectiveness ... Mr. Reed BLALOCK
96 Dir Procurement Svcs/Property Mgmt ... Mr. Larry WILLIAMS
27 Chief Information Officer ... Mr. Deron THAXTON
41 Director Athletics ... Mr. Charles ZEILMAN, JR.
07 Director of Admissions & Recruiting ... Ms. Shelly KIEFFER
06 Registrar ... Ms. Teresa SEYMOUR
26 Director of University Relations ... Ms. Sarah BLACK

*Louisiana State University at Eunice (B)

2048 Johnson Highway, Eunice LA 70535-6726
County: Acadia FICE Identification: 002012
Unit ID: 159407
Telephone: (337) 457-7311 Carnegie Class: Assoc/Pub2in4
FAX Number: (337) 546-6620 Calendar System: Semester
URL: www.lsue.edu
Established: 1964 Annual Undergrad Tuition & Fees (In-State): $3,102
Enrollment: 3,074 Coed
Affiliation or Control: State IRS Status: 501(c)3
Highest Offering: Associate Degree
Program: Occupational; 2-Year Principally Bachelor's Creditable
Accreditation: SC, ADNUR, #COARC, DMS, RAD

02 Chancellor ... Dr. William J. NUNEZ, III
05 Vice Chancellor Academic Affairs ... Dr. Renee ROBICHAUX
32 Vice Chancellor Student Affairs ... Ms. Judy DANIELS
10 Vice Chancellor Business Affairs ... Ms. Arlene C. TUCKER
26 Director of Public Relations ... Mr. Van REED
08 Director of the Library ... Mr. Gerald PATOUT
06 Registrar/Director Admissions ... Mr. Jason SAMPLER
37 Director of Financial Aid ... Ms. Jacqueline LA CHAPELLE
30 Director Institutional Development ... Ms. Madelaine LANDRY
51 Director of Continuing Education ... Mr. David PULLING
18 Director Physical Plant ... Mr. Michael BROUSSARD
25 Director Grants ... Ms. Jane SPRADLING
15 Director Personnel Services ... Vacant
81 Interim Head Division of Sciences ... Dr. John HAMLIN
50 Head Div Bus/Nursing/Allied Health ... Ms. Dotty MCDONALD
49 Interim Head Div of Liberal Arts ... Dr. Michael ALLEMAN

*Louisiana State University Health Sciences Center-New Orleans (C)

433 Bolivar Street, New Orleans LA 70112-2223
County: Orleans FICE Identification: 002014
Unit ID: 159373
Telephone: (504) 568-4808 Carnegie Class: Spec/Med
FAX Number: N/A Calendar System: Semester
URL: www.lsuhsc.edu
Established: 1931 Annual Undergrad Tuition & Fees (In-State): $6,288
Enrollment: 2,788 Coed
Affiliation or Control: State IRS Status: 501(c)3
Highest Offering: Doctorate
Program: Occupational; 2-Year Principally Bachelor's Creditable; Liberal Arts And General; Professional
Accreditation: SC, ANEST, #ARCPA, AUD, COARC, CORE, CVT, DENT, DH, DT, IPSY, MED, MT, NURSE, OT, PTA, SP

00 Chancellor Emeritus ... Dr. John ROCK
02 Chancellor ... Dr. Larry H. HOLLIER
05 Vice Chanc Acad Aff/Dean Grad Stds ... Dr. Joseph M. MOERSCHBAECHER
10 Vice Chancellor Admin & Finance ... Vacant
17 Vice Chanc Clinic/Cmty/Security Aff ... Mr. Ronald E. GARDNER
63 Dean Medicine NO ... Dr. Steve NELSON
52 Dean School of Dentistry ... Dr. Henry GREMILLION
66 Dean of Nursing ... Dr. Demetrius PORCHE
69 Dean of Public Health ... Dr. Elizabeth FONTHAM
76 Dean Allied Health Professions ... Dr. Jim R. CAIRO
04 Assistant to the Chancellor ... Mrs. Patricia MAGEE
86 Director of International Services ... Ms. Remy E. ALLEN
14 Director Computer Services ... Ms. Bettina OWENS
13 Director Information Services ... Ms. Leslie L. CAPO
08 Int Director Library Administration ... Ms. Debra H. SIBLEY
15 Director Human Resource Mgmt ... Mr. Duane LEBBE
06 Registrar ... Mr. William Bryant FAUST
37 Assoc Dir Student Financial Aid ... Ms. Kimberly BRUNO
09 Director of Institutional Research ... Dr. Ken KRATZ
31 Director of Community Relations ... Ms. Diane E. BAJOIE
18 Chief Facilities/Physical Plant ... Mr. John BALL
96 Director of Purchasing ... Mr. Brent HEROLD
26 Director of External Relations ... Mr. Christopher VIDRINE

*Louisiana State University Health Sciences Center at Shreveport (D)

1501 Kings Highway, Shreveport LA 71103
County: Caddo FICE Identification: 008067
Unit ID: 435000
Telephone: (318) 675-5000 Carnegie Class: Spec/Med
FAX Number: N/A Calendar System: Semester
URL: www.lsuhscshreveport.edu
Established: Annual Undergrad Tuition & Fees (In-District): $7,723
Enrollment: 888 Coed
Affiliation or Control: State/Local IRS Status: 501(c)3
Highest Offering: Doctorate
Program: Professional
Accreditation: SC, COARC, DENT, MED, MT, OT, PTA, SP

02 Chancellor ... Dr. Robert A. BARISH
11 Vice Chancellor Administration ... Mr. John T. DAILEY
06 Registrar ... Ms. Kim CARMEN
10 Chief Financial Officer ... Ms. Sheila FAOUR
63 Dean School of Medicine ... Dr. Andrew L. CHESSON, JR.
76 Dean Sch Allied Health Professions ... Dr. Joseph MCCULLOCH
58 Dean School of Graduate Studies ... Dr. Sandra C. ROERIG

† Tuition varies by degree program.

*Louisiana State University Paul M. Hebert Law Center (E)

1 East Campus Drive, Baton Rouge LA 70803
County: East Baton Rouge Identification: 667028
Telephone: (225) 578-8491 Carnegie Class: Not Classified
FAX Number: (225) 578-8202 Calendar System: Semester
URL: www.law.lsu.edu
Established: 1906 Annual Graduate Tuition & Fees: $19860.75
Enrollment: 681 Coed
Affiliation or Control: State IRS Status: 501(c)3
Highest Offering: Doctorate; No Undergraduates
Program: Professional
Accreditation: SC, LAW

02 Chancellor ... Jack M. WEISS
10 Vice Chanc Business/Financial Affs ... Gregory SMITH
05 Vice Chancellor for Academic Affair ... Cheney C. JOSEPH, JR.
20 Vice Chancellor Faculty Develop ... Raymond T. DIAMOND
06 Registrar ... Michele FORBES

*Louisiana State University in Shreveport (F)

One University Place, Shreveport LA 71115-2399
County: Caddo FICE Identification: 002013
Unit ID: 159416
Telephone: (318) 797-5000 Carnegie Class: Master's M
FAX Number: (318) 797-5180 Calendar System: Semester
URL: www.lsus.edu
Established: 1967 Annual Undergrad Tuition & Fees (In-State): $5,485
Enrollment: 4,535 Coed
Affiliation or Control: State IRS Status: 501(c)3
Highest Offering: Beyond Master's But Less Than Doctorate
Program: Liberal Arts And General; Teacher Preparatory; Professional
Accreditation: SC, ARCPA, BUS, CS, TED

02 Interim Chancellor ... Dr. Paul D. SISSON
05 Interim Provost/VC Academic Affairs ... Dr. John S. VASSAR
10 Vice Chancellor Business Affairs ... Mr. Michael T. FERRELL
32 Vice Chancellor for Student Affairs ... Dr. Randy R. BUTTERBAUGH
29 Director Alumni Affairs ... Ms. Dianne B. HOWELL
09 Director Planning/Inst Research ... Vacant
15 Director of Human Resource Mgmt ... Mr. Bill WOLFE
08 Dean Noel Memorial Library ... Dr. Alan D. GABEHART
37 Director of Student Financial Aid ... Mrs. Betty M. MCCRARY
07 Registrar ... Ms. Darlenna M. ATKINS
36 Dir Student Devel & Counseling ... Mrs. Paula B. ATKINS
14 Director of Computing Services ... Mr. Shelby C. KEITH
18 Director of Facility Services ... Mr. Donald R. BLOXOM
40 Director of Bookstore ... Ms. Brenda P. BARTLEBAUGH
96 Interim Director of Purchasing ... Mr. Bill WOLFE
26 Director of Media/Public Relations ... Mrs. Brooke H. RINAUDO
04 Assistant to the Chancellor ... Mrs. Viki P. FENTRESS
19 Director of University Police ... Ms. Rebecca CHILES
41 Athletic Director ... Mr. Chad MCDOWELL
49 Dean of Arts and Sciences ... Dr. Larry ANDERSON
58 Dean of Graduate Studies ... Dr. Paul D. SISSON
51 Director of Continuing Education ... Mrs. Tisha L. SAMHAN
53 Interim Dean Business/Ed/Human Dev ... Dr. Doug S. BIBLE

*University of New Orleans (G)

2000 Lakeshore Drive, New Orleans LA 70148-2000
County: Orleans FICE Identification: 002015
Unit ID: 159939
Telephone: (504) 280-6000 Carnegie Class: RU/H
FAX Number: (504) 280-5522 Calendar System: Semester
URL: www.uno.edu/
Established: 1958 Annual Undergrad Tuition & Fees (In-State): $5,850
Enrollment: 10,071 Coed
Affiliation or Control: State IRS Status: 501(c)3
Highest Offering: Doctorate
Program: Liberal Arts And General; Teacher Preparatory
Accreditation: SC, ART, BUS, BUSA, CACREP, CS, ENG, MUS, PLNG, SPAA, TED, THEA

02 President ... Dr. Peter J. FOS
05 Provost ... Dr. James PAYNE
46 VP Research ... Dr. Kenneth SEWELL
10 VP Business Affairs ... Mr. Gregg LASSEN
27 VP for External Affairs ... Ms. Rachel A. KINCAID
13 Chief Information Officer ... Mr. Jim E. BURGARD
50 Dean of Business Administration ... Dr. John WILLIAMS
53 Dean of Education & Human Dev ... Dr. Darrell KRUGER
54 Interim Dean of Engineering ... Dr. Norman WHITLEY
49 Interim Dean of Liberal Arts ... Dr. Kevin GRAVES
08 Dean of Library ... Dr. Sharon B. MADER
81 Dean of Sciences ... Dr. Steve JOHNSON
06 University Registrar ... Mr. Matt MOORE
29 Director Alumni Affairs ... Ms. Pamela MEYER
26 Director of Public Relations ... Mr. Adam NORRIS
07 Director of Admissions ... Mr. Dave MEREDITH
19 Asst Vice Chanc for Public Safety ... Mr. Thomas HARRINGTON
19 Chief of UNO Police Operations ... Mr. H. David ALLY
85 Director International Students ... Ms. Christiana J. THOMAS
96 Director of Purchasing ... Ms. Deborah K. BRIDGES
41 Director Intercollegiate Athletics ... Mr. Derek MOREL
32 Interim Dean of Student Affairs ... Dr. Pamela V. RAULT
39 Director Student Housing ... Mr. Mike BRAUNINGER

Loyola University New Orleans (H)

6363 Saint Charles Avenue, New Orleans LA 70118-6195
County: Orleans FICE Identification: 002016
Unit ID: 159656
Telephone: (504) 865-2011 Carnegie Class: Master's L
FAX Number: (504) 865-3851 Calendar System: Semester
URL: www.loyno.edu
Established: 1912 Annual Undergrad Tuition & Fees: $34,952
Enrollment: 5,008 Coed
Affiliation or Control: Roman Catholic IRS Status: 501(c)3
Highest Offering: Doctorate
Program: Liberal Arts And General; Teacher Preparatory; Professional
Accreditation: SC, BUS, CACREP, LAW, MUS, NUR, NURSE

01 President ... Rev. Kevin W. WILDES, SJ
101 Exec Asst to Pres for Board Rels ... Ms. Kristine D. LELONG
05 Provost/Vice Pres Academic Affs ... Dr. Marc MANGANARO
10 Vice Pres Finance/Administration ... Mr. John J. CALAMIA
30 Vice Pres Institutional Advance ... Mr. William BISHOP
32 VP Student Affairs/Assoc Provost ... Dr. Marcia L. PETTY
88 Vice Pres for Mission & Ministry ... Rev. Ted DZIAK, SJ
84 Int VP for Enrollment Management ... Ms. Roberta KASKEL
13 Vice Prov Information Tech/CIO ... Mr. Bret JACOBS
21 Assoc Vice Pres Financial Affairs ... Mr. Leon MATHES
44 Assoc Vice Pres Development ... Mr. Chris WISEMAN
27 Asst VP Marketing/Communications ... Ms. Terrell F. FISHER
11 Asst Vice Pres Administration ... Mr. Paul C. FLEMING
35 Asst Vice Pres of Student Affairs ... Mr. Robert A. REED
20 Sr Vice Provost of Academic Affairs ... Dr. Thom SPENCE
42 Director of University Ministry ... Mr. Kurt BINDEWALD
09 Co-Director Institutional Research ... Ms. Donna BOURGEOIS
09 Co-Director Institutional Research ... Ms. Cynthia D. CAIRE
26 Dir Public Affairs/External Rels ... Ms. Meredith HARTLEY
43 General Counsel ... Ms. Gita BOLT
29 Director Alumni Relations ... Ms. Monique G. GARDNER
06 Dir Stdnt Records/Registration Svcs ... Ms. Kathy R. GROS
07 Dean Admissions ... Mr. Keith E. GRAMLING
15 Director of Human Resources ... Mr. Ross D. MATTHEWS
40 Bookstore Manager ... Ms. Maleta WILSON
41 Director Athletics & Wellness ... Dr. Michael GIORLANDO
36 Director Career Development Center ... Ms. Roberta KASKEL
23 Director Student Health Services ... Dr. Alicia BOURQUE
19 Director University Police ... Mr. Patrick X. BAILEY
37 Director Scholarships/Financial Aid ... Ms. Carrie GLASS
08 Director of the Law Library ... Mr. P. Michael WHIPPLE
85 Director Ctr for International Ed ... Ms. Debra DANNA
86 Dir Government Relations ... Mr. Tommy SCREEN
38 Director Student Counseling ... Dr. Alicia BOURQUE
96 Director of Purchasing ... Mr. Bret PENNISON
28 Dir Intercultural Understanding ... Ms. Lisa MARTIN
06 Dir Admin Services-Student Records ... Mr. Michael RACHAL

39 Director of Residential Life .... Mr. Craig BEEBE
08 Dean of Libraries .... Dr. Michael OLSON
49 Dean Humanities/Natural Science .... Dr. Maria CALZADA
61 Dean of Law .... Ms. Maria LOPEZ
64 Dean of Music and Fine Arts .... Dr. Donald BOOMGAARDEN
50 Dean of Business .... Dr. William LOCANDER
83 Dean of Social Sciences .... Dr. Roger WHITE

New Orleans Baptist Theological Seminary (A)

3939 Gentilly Boulevard, New Orleans LA 70126-4858
County: Orleans FICE Identification: 002019
Unit ID: 159948
Telephone: (504) 282-4455 Carnegie Class: Spec/Faith
FAX Number: (504) 283-3631 Calendar System: Semester
URL: www.nobts.edu
Established: 1917 Annual Undergrad Tuition & Fees: $5,745
Enrollment: 2,277 Coed
Affiliation or Control: Southern Baptist IRS Status: 501(c)3
Highest Offering: Doctorate
Program: Professional; Religious Emphasis
Accreditation: SC, MUS, THEOL

01 President .... Dr. Charles S. KELLEY, JR.
05 Provost .... Dr. Steve W. LEMKE
09 Dir Institutional Effectiveness .... Dr. C. Scott DRUMM
10 Vice President for Business Affairs .... Mr. Clay L. CORVIN
30 Vice President for Development .... Mr. Randy DRIGGERS
58 Dean Graduate Studies .... Dr. Jerry N. BARLOW
12 Dean Leavell College .... Dr. L. Thomas STRONG, III
32 Dean of Students .... Mr. J. Craig GARRETT
07 Dean of Admissions & Registrar .... Dr. Paul E. GREGOIRE, JR.
08 Dean of Libraries .... Dr. Jeff D. GRIFFIN
18 Associate VP of Facilities .... Dr. Jim O. PARKER
13 Assoc VP Information Technology .... Dr. Laurie S. WATTS
73 Assoc Dean Prof Doctoral Pgms .... Dr. Reggie R. OGEA
106 Associate Dean of Online Learning .... Dr. W. Craig PRICE
20 Associate Dean of Graduate Studies .... Dr. Michael H. EDENS
58 Assoc Dean Research Doctoral Pgms .... Dr. Charles A. RAY, JR.
35 Assoc Dean of Students .... Dr. Judi JACKSON
88 Director of Leavell Center .... Dr. Preston L. NIX
15 Director of Human Resources .... Ms. Pattie SHOENER
26 Chief Public Relations Officer .... Mr. Gary D. MYERS
29 Director of Alumni Relations .... Dr. Dennis L. PHELPS
36 Director of Student Enlistment .... Mr. J. Craig GARRETT
37 Director of Student Financial Aid .... Mr. Owen NEASE
38 Director of Testing & Counseling .... Dr. Jeffery W. NAVE

Notre Dame Seminary, Graduate School of Theology (B)

2901 S Carrollton Avenue, New Orleans LA 70118-4391
County: Orleans FICE Identification: 002022
Unit ID: 160029
Telephone: (504) 866-7426 Carnegie Class: Spec/Faith
FAX Number: (504) 866-3119 Calendar System: Semester
URL: www.nds.edu
Established: 1923 Annual Graduate Tuition & Fees: $20,265
Enrollment: 154 Coed
Affiliation or Control: Roman Catholic IRS Status: 501(c)3
Highest Offering: Master's; No Undergraduates
Program: Professional; Religious Emphasis
Accreditation: SC, THEOL

01 President/Rector .... V.Rev. James A. WEHNER, STD
05 Academic Dean .... Dr. Thomas NEAL
10 Business Manager .... Ms. Michelle W. KLEIN
08 Director of Library .... Mr. Thomas R. BENDER
06 Registrar .... Dr. Debora PANEPINTO
09 Director IE/Planning/Faculty Devel .... Dr. Rebecca S. MALONEY

Our Lady of Holy Cross College (C)

4123 Woodland Drive, New Orleans LA 70131-7399
County: Orleans FICE Identification: 002023
Unit ID: 160065
Telephone: (504) 394-7744 Carnegie Class: Master's S
FAX Number: (504) 391-2421 Calendar System: Semester
URL: www.olhcc.edu
Established: 1916 Annual Undergrad Tuition & Fees: $9,950
Enrollment: 1,072 Coed
Affiliation or Control: Roman Catholic IRS Status: 501(c)3
Highest Offering: Doctorate
Program: Liberal Arts And General; Teacher Preparatory; Professional; Nursing Emphasis
Accreditation: SC, CACREP, IACBE, NUR, RAD, TED

01 President .... Dr. Ronald J. AMBROSETTI
05 Provost/Vice Pres Academic Affairs .... Dr. Patricia PRECHTER
10 Vice Pres for Finance & Operations .... Mrs. Arlean WEHLE
30 Vice Pres for Philanthropy .... Mr. David CATHERMAN
84 VP for Enrollment Management .... Ms. Meredith REED
20 Director of CTL .... Dr. Victoria DAHMES
08 Director of Library Services .... Ms. Diana SCHAUBHUT
49 Dean Liberal Arts and Science .... Dr. Michael LABRANCHE
06 Registrar .... Ms. Shannon CHIASSON
09 Director Inst Research & Planning .... Vacant
42 Director of Campus Ministry .... Fr. John LYDON
15 Human Resources Manager .... Ms. Cathy WAGUESPACK
44 Director of Annual Fund .... Mr. David CATHERMAN
13 Director of Technology Services .... Mr. Jeff MCCOY
37 Coordinator of Financial Aid .... Mrs. Anna VAUGHAN

Our Lady of the Lake College (D)

5414 Brittany Drive, Baton Rouge LA 70808
County: East Baton Rouge FICE Identification: 031062
Unit ID: 160074
Telephone: (225) 768-1700 Carnegie Class: Spec/Health
FAX Number: (225) 768-0811 Calendar System: Semester
URL: www.ololcollege.edu
Established: 1923 Annual Undergrad Tuition & Fees: $12,200
Enrollment: 1,757 Coed
Affiliation or Control: Roman Catholic IRS Status: 501(c)3
Highest Offering: Master's
Program: Occupational; 2-Year Principally Bachelor's Creditable; Liberal Arts And General; Professional
Accreditation: SC, ADNUR, ANEST, #ARCPA, COARC, MT, NUR, PTAA, RAD, SURGT

01 President .... Vacant
05 Exec VP for Academics and Students .... Dr. David ENGLAND
30 VP for Institutional Advancement .... Mr. H. Ken DEDOMINICIS
10 Director of Finance .... Ms. Beverly S. PLAISANCE
66 Dean School of Nursing .... Dr. Jennifer BECK
49 Dean School of A&S and Health Prof .... Dr. Katherine KRIEG
32 Dean Student Services .... Dr. Phyllis SIMPSON
26 Director of Public Relations .... Ms. Denise DOKEY
37 Director Financial Aid .... Ms. Tiffany MAGEE
06 Registrar .... Mr. Brad DUFFY
84 Director Enrollment Management .... Ms. Rebecca CANNON
88 Director Physician Asst Studies .... Mr. John ALLGOOD
58 Director Nurse Anesthetist Program .... Ms. Phyllis PEDERSEN
76 Director Radiologic Technology .... Ms. Liza MAYEUX
76 Director Clinical Lab Sciences .... Dr. Debbie FOX
76 Director Physical Therapist Asst .... Ms. Leah GEHEBER
88 Dir Health Service Administration .... Ms. Elizabeth BERZAS
76 Director Respiratory Therapy .... Ms. Sue DAVIS
88 Director Writing Center .... Mr. Angus WOODWARD
90 Director Acad & Admin Technology .... Mr. Eric SENECA
91 Manager Student Info System .... Mr. Janssen BURRIS

Remington College-Baton Rouge Campus (E)

10551 Coursey Boulevard, Baton Rouge LA 70816-4040
Telephone: (225) 236-3200 Identification: 666449
Accreditation: ACCSC

† Main campus is Remington College Cleveland Campus in Cleveland, OH.

Remington College-Lafayette Campus (F)

303 Rue Louis XIV, Lafayette LA 70508-5700
Telephone: (337) 981-4010 FICE Identification: 005203
Accreditation: ACCSC

† Main campus is Remington College Cleveland Campus in Cleveland, OH.

Remington College-Shreveport (G)

2106 Bert Kouns Industrial Loop, Shreveport LA 71118
Telephone: (318) 671-4001 Identification: 666302
Accreditation: ACCSC

† Main campus is Remington College Cleveland Campus in Cleveland, OH.

Saint Joseph Seminary College (H)

75376 River Road, Saint Benedict LA 70457-9999
County: Saint Tammany FICE Identification: 002027
Unit ID: 160409
Telephone: (985) 867-2225 Carnegie Class: Spec/Faith
FAX Number: (985) 867-2270 Calendar System: Semester
URL: www.sjasc.edu
Established: 1891 Annual Undergrad Tuition & Fees: $29,260
Enrollment: 106 Male
Affiliation or Control: Roman Catholic IRS Status: 501(c)3
Highest Offering: Baccalaureate
Program: Liberal Arts And General; Religious Emphasis
Accreditation: SC

01 President - Rector .... V.Rev. Gregory M. BOQUET, OSB
05 Academic Dean .... Rev. Charles BENOIT, OSB
03 Vice-Rector .... Rev. Matthew CLARK, OSB
08 Librarian .... Ms. Bonnie WOOD
56 Director Extension Programs .... Vacant
10 Business Officer .... Mrs. Judith GAUBERT
37 Director Financial Aid .... Mr. George BINDER
29 Director of Alumni Affairs .... Rev. Matthew CLARK, OSB
30 Director of Development .... Mrs. Vanessa CROUERE
27 Director of Communications .... Bro. Simon STUBBS, OSB
32 Dean of Students .... Rev. Jude ISRAEL, OSB

*Southern University and Agricultural & Mechanical College System Office (I)

JS Clark Admin Building, 4th Floor,
Baton Rouge LA 70813-0001
County: East Baton Rouge FICE Identification: 009637
Unit ID: 160533
Telephone: (225) 771-4680 Carnegie Class: N/A
FAX Number: (225) 771-5522
URL: www.sus.edu

01 President .... Dr. Ronald F. MASON, JR.
100 Chief of Staff .... Ms. Evola C. BATES
43 General Counsel to the System/Board .... Ms. Tracie J. WOODS
10 Vice Pres Finance/Business Affairs .... Mr. Kevin APPLETON
13 Vice Pres Information Technology .... Mr. Tony MOORE
05 System Officer for Academic Affairs .... Mr. Walter T. TILLMAN, JR.
30 VP Sys Advance/Exec Dir Foundation .... Dr. Ernie T. HUGHES
43 Exec Counsel/Legislative Liaison .... Mr. Byron C. WILLIAMS
29 Director of Alumni Affairs .... Ms. Robyn MERRICK
26 Director of Publications .... Mr. Henry TILLMAN
18 Director of Facilities Planning .... Mr. Endas VINCENT
21 System Director of Internal Audit .... Ms. Linda H. CATALON

*Southern University and A&M College (J)

Baton Rouge LA 70813-0001
County: East Baton Rouge FICE Identification: 002025
Unit ID: 160621
Telephone: (225) 771-4500 Carnegie Class: Master's L
FAX Number: (225) 771-2018 Calendar System: Semester
URL: www.subr.edu
Established: 1880 Annual Undergrad Tuition & Fees (In-State): $6,534
Enrollment: 6,700 Coed
Affiliation or Control: State IRS Status: 501(c)3
Highest Offering: Doctorate
Program: Liberal Arts And General; Teacher Preparatory
Accreditation: SC, AAFCS, ART, BUS, CACREP, CORE, CS, DIETD, DIETI, ENG, ENGT, #JOUR, LAW, MUS, NURSE, SP, SPAA, SW, TED

02 Chancellor .... Dr. James LLORENS
05 Int Exec Vice Chancellor & Provost .... Dr. Verjanis PEOPLES
32 Vice Chanc Student Affairs .... Dr. Brandon DUMAS
10 Vice Chanc of Finance & Admin .... Mr. Flandus MCCLINTON, JR.
46 VC Research/Strategic Initiative .... Dr. Michael STUBBLEFIELD
20 Int Assoc Vice Chan Academic Affs .... Dr. Ella KELLEY
26 Asst to Chanc for Media Relations .... Mr. Edward PRATT
45 Dir Planning Assess/Instnl Research .... Mr. Urban WIGGINS
29 Director of Alumni Affairs .... Ms. Robyn MERRICK
15 Director Human Resources .... Mr. Lester POURCIAU
21 Chief Budget Officer .... Ms. Pamela JONES
06 Registrar .... Mr. Arthur GILLIS
07 Director Admissions/Recruitment .... Vacant
35 Dean of Students .... Mr. Marcus COLEMAN
39 Int Director Residential Housing .... Ms. Tracie ABRAHAM
37 Director of Financial Aid .... Ms. Ursula SHORTY
13 Chief Information Officer .... Mr. Carlos THOMAS
51 Dir Intl Educ/Dir Svc Learning/CE .... Dr. Barbara CARPENTER
41 Athletic Director .... Mr. William BROUSSARD
18 Director Facilities Planning .... Mr. Endas VINCENT
88 Director School of Accountancy .... Ms. Mary A. DARBY
96 Director of Purchasing .... Mrs. Linda B. ANTOINE
38 Director Student Counseling .... Dr. ValaRay IRVIN
62 Dean of Libraries .... Mrs. Emma BRADFORD-PERRY
88 Dean University College .... Dr. Dana CARPENTER
92 Dean of Honors College .... Dr. Ella KELLEY
58 Interim Dean of the Graduate School .... Dr. Doze BUTLER
54 Dean College of Engineering .... Dr. Habib P. MOHAMADIAN
50 Dean College of Business .... Dr. Donald R. ANDREWS
53 Interim Dean College of Education .... Dr. Luria YOUNG
47 Int Dean Col Agri/Family/Consum Sci .... Dr. Grace NAMWAMBA
49 Dean College Arts/Humanities .... Dr. Joyce O'ROURKE
80 Dean School of Public Policy .... Dr. William ARP
48 Dean School Architecture .... Mr. Lonnie WILKINSON
66 Dean of School of Nursing .... Dr. Janet RAMI
81 Dean of College of Science .... Dr. Robert H. MILLER

*Southern University at New Orleans (K)

6400 Press Drive, New Orleans LA 70126-1009
County: Orleans FICE Identification: 002026
Unit ID: 160630
Telephone: (504) 286-5000 Carnegie Class: Master's M
FAX Number: (504) 286-5131 Calendar System: Semester
URL: www.suno.edu
Established: 1956 Annual Undergrad Tuition & Fees (In-State): $4,850
Enrollment: 3,239 Coed
Affiliation or Control: State IRS Status: 501(c)3
Highest Offering: Master's
Program: Liberal Arts And General; Teacher Preparatory; Business Emphasis
Accreditation: SC, BUS, CAHIIM, SW, TED

02 Chancellor .... Dr. Victor UKPOLO
04 Exec Assoc to the Chancellor .... Mr. Harold E. CLARK
05 VC for Academic Affairs & SACS .... Dr. David S. ADEGBOYE
10 VC for Admin & Finance .... Mr. Jullin RENTHROPE

09 Dir IR & Strategic Initiatives ....Vacant
09 Director Quality Enhancement Plan ....Dr. Donalyn L. LOTT
108 Learning Outcomes/Assessment Coord ....Ms. Tamika SAUL
84 VC Student Affs & Enroll Services ....Dr. Donna GRANT
29 Vice Chan Cmty Outreach/Univ Advanc ....Mrs. Gloria B. MOULTRIE
21 Director of Facilities Management ....Mr. Shaun M. LEWIS
25 Dir Grants & Sponsored Programs ....Dr. William R. BELISLE
06 Registrar ....Ms. Gilda DAVIS
21 Comptroller ....Ms. Shawn M. GULLEY
08 Director of Library ....Mrs. Shatiqua A. MOSBY-WILSON
36 Dir Career Counseling & Vet Liaison ....Mr. Joseph MARION
14 Director of Information Technology ..Mr. Edmond M. CUMMINGS
15 Director of Human Resources ....Ms. Monique MALDONADO
19 Police Captain Campus Police ....Mr. Ira THOMAS, SR.
20 Assoc VC Academic Affairs Faculty ....Mr. Wesley T. BISHOP
41 Director of Athletics ....Mr. Elston H. KING
07 Asst VC for Enrollment Management ...Ms. Leatrice D. LATIMORE
26 Director of Public Relations ....Mr. David GRUBB
96 Director of Purchasing ....Ms. Marilyn G. MANUEL
106 Director of E-Learning ....Ms. Shelia WOOD
70 Dean School of Social Work ....Dr. Beverly C. FAVRE
50 Dean College of Business/Pub Admin ....Dr. Igwe E. UDEH
88 Director of Museum Studies ....Dr. Sara HOLLIS
58 Dean of Graduate Studies ....Vacant
49 Dean College of Arts & Sciences ....Dr. Henry E. MOKOSSO
53 Int Dean College Educ & Human Dev ....Dr. Louise KALTENBAUGH
88 Dir Services for Students w/Disab ....Ms. Yolanda L. MIMS
35 Int Dir of Student Activities & Org ....Ms. Shawanda M. HOWARD
38 Dir of Student Development Center ....Mrs. Josephine OKORONKWO
39 Director of Residential Life ....Dr. Adrell L. PINKNEY
88 Director of Title III Programs ....Dr. Brenda W. JACKSON
88 Dir Student Support Services Pgm ....Ms. Linda D. FREDERICK
88 Dir Ctr for African & American Stds ....Dr. Romanus EJIAGA

*Southern University at Shreveport-Louisiana (A)

3050 Martin Luther King Drive, Shreveport LA 71107-4795
County: Caddo FICE Identification: 007686
Unit ID: 160649
Telephone: (318) 670-6000 Carnegie Class: Assoc/Pub2in4
FAX Number: (318) 670-6374 Calendar System: Semester
URL: www.susla.edu
Established: 1964 Annual Undergrad Tuition & Fees (In-State): $3,195
Enrollment: 2,831 Coed
Affiliation or Control: State IRS Status: 501(c)3
Highest Offering: Associate Degree
Program: Occupational; 2-Year Principally Bachelor's Creditable
Accreditation: SC, ADNUR, CAHIIM, COARC, DH, MLTAD, PHLEB, RAD, SURGT

02 Chancellor ....Dr. Ray L. BELTON
26 Spec Asst to Chanc IR/Div Univ Rels ....Ms. Theron JACKSON
04 Admin Assistant to the Chancellor ....Mrs. Carolyn S. WEBB
05 Vice Chanc Academic Affairs ....Dr. Orelia BRAZILE
10 Vice Chanc Finance/Administration ....Mr. Benjamin W. PUGH
103 VC Cmty Outreach/Workforce Develop ....Mrs. Janice SNEED
32 Vice Chanc Student Affairs ....Dr. Sharon F. GREEN
21 Comptroller ....Mrs. Brandy JACOBSEN
21 Bursar ....Ms. LaSonia MORRIS
84 Assoc Vice Chanc Enrollment Mgmt ....Vacant
06 Registrar ....Ms. Mahailier L. BROOM
08 Librarian ....Mrs. Jane O'RILEY
35 Asst Vice Chanc for Student Affairs ....Vacant
20 Asst Vice Chanc for Academic Affs ....Dr. Regina ROBINSON
51 Director of Continuing Education ....Mrs. Beverly PARKER
07 Director of Admission & Recruitment ....Mrs. Rhalanda JACKSON
37 Director of Financial Aid ....Ms. Katraya WILLIAMS
27 Director University Communications ....Mr. William STROTHER
83 Div Chair Behavioral Sciences/Educ ....Mrs. Roslyn J. HOLT
50 Division Chair Business Studies ....Ms. Cynthia L. HESTER
79 Division Chair for Humanities ....Mrs. June PHILLIPS
72 Div Chair Science & Technology ....Dr. Barry C. HESTER
76 Div Chair for Respiratory Therapy ....Mrs. JoAnn BROWN
46 Dir Inst Rsrch/Grants & Spnsrd Pgms ....Vacant
13 Dir Information Technology Center ....Dr. Gabriel FAGBEYIRO
88 Director Student Support Services ....Ms. Karen COCO
75 Director Aerospace Technology ....Mr. David FOGLEMAN
38 Director Counseling Center ....Ms. Rubie J. SCERE
15 Director Human Resources ....Mr. Wayne H. BRYANT
96 Director of Purchasing ....Ms. Sophia JACKSON-LEE
18 Dir Physical Plant Facilities ....Mr. Joseph LACOUR
88 Director of Testing Center ....Ms. Kaye WASHINGTON
21 University Budget Officer ....Ms. Regina WINN
72 Director Radiologic Technology ....Ms. Sheila SWIFT
88 Ex Dir TRIO Cmty Outrch/Talent Srch ....Mrs. Carrie ROBINSON
88 Director Dental Hygiene ....Mrs. Kheysia H. WASHINGTON
09 Director Inst Plng/Assessment/Rsrch ....Mr. Martin FORTNER
66 Dean of School of Nursing ....Dr. Sandra TUCKER
88 Director Biomedical Research Devel ....Dr. Joseph ORBAN
83 Dean Behav Sci/Educ/Bus Standards ....Vacant

Southwest University (B)

2200 Veterans Memorial Boulevard,
Kenner LA 70062-4005
County: Jefferson Identification: 666310
Telephone: (504) 468-2900 Carnegie Class: Not Classified
FAX Number: (504) 468-3213 Calendar System: Semester
URL: www.southwest.edu
Established: 1982 Annual Undergrad Tuition & Fees: $9,000
Enrollment: 415 Coed
Affiliation or Control: Proprietary IRS Status: Proprietary
Highest Offering: Master's
Program: 2-Year Principally Bachelor's Creditable; Liberal Arts And General; Professional; Business Emphasis
Accreditation: DETC

01 President ....Dr. Grayce LEE
11 Chief Administrative Officer ....Mr. Neil FESER
07 Admissions ....Mrs. Lydia OCMAND

Tulane University (C)

6823 St. Charles Avenue, New Orleans LA 70118-5698
County: Orleans FICE Identification: 002029
Unit ID: 160755
Telephone: (504) 865-5000 Carnegie Class: RU/VH
FAX Number: (504) 865-5202 Calendar System: Semester
URL: www.tulane.edu
Established: 1834 Annual Undergrad Tuition & Fees: $46,930
Enrollment: 13,486 Coed
Affiliation or Control: Independent Non-Profit IRS Status: 501(c)3
Highest Offering: Doctorate
Program: Liberal Arts And General; Teacher Preparatory; Professional
Accreditation: SC, BUS, DIETI, ENG, ENGR, HSA, IPSY, LAW, MED, PH, SCPSY, SW, TEAC

01 President ....Dr. Scott S. COWEN
05 Sr Vice Pres Acad Affairs/Provost ....Prof. Michael BERNSTEIN
26 COO/Sr VP External Affairs ....Ms. Yvette M. JONES
10 Sr Vice Pres for Operations & CFO ....Mr. Anthony P. LORINO
63 Sr Vice Pres/Dn School of Medicine ....Dr. L. L. HAMM
17 VP/Vice Dean Health Sciences ....Ms. Mary BROWN
43 General Counsel ....Ms. Victoria D. JOHNSON
13 VP Information Technology/CTO ....Mr. Charles P. MCMAHON
20 Senior Associate Provost ....Ms. Ana LOPEZ
32 VP Student Affairs ....Dr. John NONNAMAKER
20 Associate Provost ....Dr. Brian S. MITCHELL
58 Assoc Prov Graduate Studies ....Dr. Brian S. MITCHELL
100 Chief of Staff & Vice President ....Ms. Anne BANOS
22 VP Inst Equity/Asst to Pres Dvrsity ....Ms. Deborah E. LOVE
84 Vice Pres Enrollment Mgmt/Registrar ....Mr. Earl RETIF
18 VP Operations & Facilities Services ....Mr. James ALTY
26 Vice Pres University Communications ....Ms. Deborah L. GRANT
46 Assoc Sr Vice President Research ....Ms. Laura LEVY
30 Vice Pres Constituency Programs ....Ms. Luann D. DOZIER
86 Assoc VP Government Relations ....Ms. Sharon P. COURTNEY
35 Assoc VP Auxiliary Svcs/Student Ctr ....Mr. Robert C. HAILEY
18 Assoc Vice President Facilities ....Mr. Sylvester C. JOHNSON
44 Assoc Vice President Development ....Mr. Jeffrey A. BUSH
37 Assoc Vice President Financial Aid ....Mr. Michael GOODMAN
21 Director Budget ....Mr. Gene MEYERS
22 Exec Dir Empl Rels/Inst Equity ....Ms. Stephanie ALLWEISS
29 VP for Alumni Affairs ....Mr. James STOFAN
21 Controller ....Mr. Frank (Doug) HARRELL
19 Director of Public Safety ....Mr. John BARNWELL
08 Dean Library & Academic Information ....Dr. Lance QUERY
38 Exec Dir Educ Resources/Couns ....Ms. Kim CROWLEY
36 Exec Director Career Svcs Ctr ....Dr. Amjad AYOUBI
12 Dir Tulane Natl Primate Res Ctr ....Mr. Andrew LACKNER
24 Executive Director Publications ....Ms. Carol J. SCHLUETER
39 Assoc VP Housing Services/Residence ....Mr. W. Ross BRYAN
96 Director Central Procurement Svcs ....Mr. William VAN CLEAVE
91 Asst VP Academic & Admin Computing ....Ms. Mary T. WALSH
41 Director Athletics ....Mr. Richard P. DICKSON
51 Dean Sch Cont Stds/Summer Sch ....Dr. Rick MARKSBURY
49 Dean School of Liberal Arts ....Dr. Carole HABER
49 Dean Newcomb-Tulane College ....Dr. James MACLAREN
61 Dean School of Law ....Mr. David D. MEYER
69 Dean Sch Public Health/Trop Med ....Dr. Pierre BUEKENS
54 Dean School Science & Engineering ....Dr. Nicholas J. ALTIERO
48 Dean School of Architecture ....Mr. Kenneth SCHWARTZ
50 Dean AB Freeman School of Business ....Dr. Ira SOLOMON
70 Dean School of Social Work ....Dr. Ronald MARKS
09 Director of Institutional Research ....Mr. Shawn POTTER
88 Exec Dir of CELT ....Dr. Michael CUNNINGHAM

*University of Louisiana System Office (D)

1201 N Third Street, Suite 7-300,
Baton Rouge LA 70802-5243
County: East Baton Rouge FICE Identification: 033444
Unit ID: 247083
Telephone: (225) 342-6950 Carnegie Class: N/A
FAX Number: (225) 342-6473
URL: www.ulsystem.net

01 President ....Dr. Sandra K. WOODLEY
05 Int Provost & VP Acad/Student Affs ....Dr. Richard HANSEN
10 VP Business & Finance ....Mr. Robbie ROBINSON
09 VP Research & Performance Assess ....Dr. Beatrice BALDWIN
11 VP Administration and General Couns ....Ms. Dianne IRVINE
21 Asst VP for Budget & Finance ....Dr. Edwin LITOLFF

*Grambling State University (E)

Grambling LA 71245-3091
County: Lincoln FICE Identification: 002006
Unit ID: 159009
Telephone: (318) 247-3811 Carnegie Class: Master's M
FAX Number: (318) 274-6172 Calendar System: Semester
URL: www.gram.edu
Established: 1901 Annual Undergrad Tuition & Fees (In-State): $5983.75
Enrollment: 5,277 Coed
Affiliation or Control: State IRS Status: 501(c)3
Highest Offering: Doctorate
Program: 2-Year Principally Bachelor's Creditable; Liberal Arts And General; Teacher Preparatory; Professional
Accreditation: SC, BUS, CS, ENGT, JOUR, MUS, NRPA, NUR, SPAA, SW, TED, THEA

02 President ....Dr. Frank G. POGUE
05 Provost/Vice Pres Academic Affairs ....Dr. Connie WALTON
10 Vice President for Finance and Admn ....Mr. Leon SANDERS
32 Vice President Student Affairs ....Dr. Stacey DUHON
30 Vice President Inst Advancement ....Vacant
86 Exec Assoc VP of CIAP ....Mr. Mahmoud LAMADANIE
18 Director of Facilties Management ....Mr. Lavoyd R. DUDLEY
14 Assoc VP of Information Technology ....Mr. Winfred JONES
45 Assoc VP of Planning & Research ....Ms. Nettie DANIELS
19 University Police Chief ....Vacant
15 AVP of Human Resources ....Mrs. Monica BRADLEY
53 Dean College of Education ....Dr. Larnell FLANNAGAN
50 Dean College of Business ....Vacant
58 Dean Division Grad Studies/Research ....Dr. Janet A. GUYDEN
88 Interim Dean Col of Prof Studies ....Dr. Rama TUNUGUNTLA
49 Dean College of Arts & Sci ....Vacant
92 Assistant Dean Honors College ....Dr. Ellen SMILEY
41 Director of Athletics ....Mr. Aaron JAMES
22 EEO Officer & Wage & Salary Officer ....Mrs. Monica BRADLEY
07 Director of Admissions ....Mrs. Annie MOSS
06 University Registrar ....Mrs. Patricia J. HUTCHERSON
37 Dir Student Financial Aid ....Vacant
91 Dir of Administrative Computing ....Mrs. Peggy HANLEY
04 Executive Asst to the President ....Dr. Ellen SMILEY
29 Director Alumni Relations ....Ms. Debra JOHNSON
23 Director of Health Services ....Mrs. Patrice OUTLEY
38 Director Counseling Center ....Dr. Coleen SPEED
39 Dir of Residential Life and Housing ....Mr. James PAYNE
42 Director of Campus Ministry ....Vacant
96 Director of Purchasing ....Ms. Connie HAMPTON
40 Manager University Bookstore ....Ms. Rosalyn LEWIS
106 Director of Distance Learning ....Mr. Eldrie HAMILTON
20 Special Assistant to Provost and VP ....Ms. Joann BROWN
36 Director of Career Services ....Mr. Johnny PATTERSON
44 Dir Annual Fund Coord ....Ms. Kimlin A. HALL

*Louisiana Tech University (F)

PO Box 3168, Ruston LA 71272-0001
County: Lincoln FICE Identification: 002008
Unit ID: 159647
Telephone: (318) 257-0211 Carnegie Class: RU/H
FAX Number: (318) 257-2928 Calendar System: Quarter
URL: www.latech.edu
Established: 1894 Annual Undergrad Tuition & Fees (In-State): $7,416
Enrollment: 11,360 Coed
Affiliation or Control: State IRS Status: 501(c)3
Highest Offering: Doctorate
Program: Liberal Arts And General; Teacher Preparatory; Professional
Accreditation: SC, AAB, AAFCS, ADNUR, ART, AUD, BUS, BUSA, CACREP, CAHIIM, CIDA, COPSY, CS, DIETD, DIETI, ENG, ENGT, FOR, MUS, SP, TED

02 President ....Dr. Leslie K. GUICE
05 Vice Pres Academic Affairs ....Dr. Terry M. MCCONATHY
32 Vice President for Student Affairs ....Dr. Jim M. KING
11 Vice Pres Finance/Administration ....Mr. Joe R. THOMAS
30 Vice President for Univ Advancement ....Ms. Corre A. STEGALL
10 Comptroller ....Mrs. Lisa COLE
50 Dean of Business ....Dr. James LUMPKIN
49 Dean of Liberal Arts ....Dr. Don KACZVINSKY
53 Dean of Education ....Dr. Lawrence LEONARD
54 Int Dean of Engineering & Science ....Dr. Hisham HEGAB
65 Dean of Applied & Natural Sciences ....Dr. James D. LIBERATOS
84 Dean of Enrollment Management ....Mrs. Pamela R. FORD
26 Exec Dir University Communications ....Mr. David GUERIN
07 Interim Director of Admissions ....Mrs. Joan B. EDINGER
21 Business Officer ....Mr. Jerry S. DREWETT
14 Director of Computer Center ....Mr. Roy S. WATERS
37 Director Student Financial Aid ....Ms. Aimee F. BAXTER
09 Director Institutional Research ....Mrs. Lori C. THEIS
06 Registrar ....Mr. Robert D. VENTO
08 Interim Director of Libraries ....Ms. Rita FRANKS
15 Director of Personnel ....Mrs. Sheila TRAMMEL
29 Director of Alumni Relations ....Mr. Ryan RICHARD
36 Dir Career Ctr/Student Counseling ....Mr. Ron CATHEY
89 Director of Freshmen Studies ....Vacant
92 Director of Honors Program ....Dr. Rick SIMMONS
93 Director of Multicultural Affairs ....Vacant
96 Director of Purchasing ....Ms. Karen MURPHY
18 Int Chief Facilities/Physical Plant ....Mr. Doug WILLIS
35 Director Student Affairs ....Dr. Jim KING
41 Athletics Director ....Mr. Thomas H. MCCLELLAND, II

*McNeese State University (G)

4205 Ryan Street, Lake Charles LA 70609-4510
County: Calcasieu FICE Identification: 002017
Unit ID: 159717
Telephone: (337) 475-5000 Carnegie Class: Master's L
FAX Number: (337) 475-5012 Calendar System: Semester
URL: www.mcneese.edu
Established: 1939 Annual Undergrad Tuition & Fees (In-State): $5,575
Enrollment: 8,588 Coed
Affiliation or Control: State IRS Status: 501(c)3
Highest Offering: Beyond Master's But Less Than Doctorate
Program: Liberal Arts And General; Teacher Preparatory; Professional

Accreditation: SC, AAFCS, ADNUR, ART, BUS, CS, DIETD, DIETI, ENG, ENGT, MT, MUS, NURSE, RAD, TED

02 President ... Dr. Philip C. WILLIAMS
05 Provost/VP Academic & Student Affs ... Dr. Jeanne M. DABOVAL
10 VP Business Affairs/University Svcs ... Mr. Eddie P. MECHE
30 Vice Pres University Advancement ... Mr. Richard H. REID
84 Assoc VP Enrollment Management ... Ms. Stephanie B. TARVER
32 AVP University Services ... Mr. Toby W. OSBURN
81 Dean College of Science ... Dr. George F. MEAD, JR.
50 Dean College Business ... Dr. Musa M. ESSAYYAD
53 Dean of College of Education ... Dr. Wayne R. FETTER
49 Dean College Liberal Arts ... Dr. Ray MILES
54 Dean Col of Engr & Engr Technology ... Dr. Nikos KIRITSIS
66 Dean of College of Nursing ... Dr. Peggy L. WOLFE
58 Exec Dir Dore Sch Graduate Studies ... Dr. Dustin HEBERT
18 Director Facilities & Plant Opers ... Mr. Richard R. RHODEN
13 Director of Univ Computing Services ... Mr. Stanley HIPPLER
31 Dir Community Service and Outreach ... Mrs. Betty H. ANDERSON
15 Dir Human Res/Student Employment ... Ms. Charlene R. ABBOTT
09 Director Institutional Research ... Ms. Kathleen S. DOUGAY
37 Director Student Financial Aid ... Ms. Taina J. SAVOIT
08 Director of Library ... Ms. Debbie L. JOHNSON-HOUSTON
19 University Police Chief ... Mr. Robert SPINKS
29 Director Alumni Affairs ... Ms. Joyce D. PATTERSON
38 Dir Career Services/Scholarships ... Ms. Ralynn F. CASTETE
07 Dir of Admissions and Recruiting ... Ms. Kara SMITH
41 Athletic Director ... Vacant
45 Dir Inst Effectiveness/Acad Support ... Dr. Tom DVORSKE
96 Director Purchasing/Property Cntrl ... Ms. Roxane FONTENOT
92 Director of Honors College ... Dr. Scott E. GOINS
14 Chief Information Technology ... Mr. Chad THIBODEAUX
46 Dir Ofc of Research/Sponsored Pgm ... Ms. Janet R. WOOLMAN
85 International Student Advisor ... Mr. Aaron WEBSTER
26 Director Public Relations ... Ms. Candace V. TOWNSEND
23 RN Supervisor-Student Health ... Vacant
40 Bookstore Manager ... Ms. Sharamie T. MOORE
06 Coordinator Alternative Learning ... Vacant
90 Coord of Col of Science Computing ... Vacant
106 Director of Electronic Learning ... Ms. Helen B. WARE
28 Chief Diversity Officer ... Dr. Michael T. SNOWDEN

*Nicholls State University (A)

University Station, Thibodaux LA 70310-0001
County: Lafourche FICE Identification: 002005
Unit ID: 159966
Telephone: (985) 446-8111 Carnegie Class: Master's M
FAX Number: (985) 448-4920 Calendar System: Semester
URL: www.nicholls.edu
Established: 1948 Annual Undergrad Tuition & Fees (In-State): $6,312
Enrollment: 6,606 Coed
Affiliation or Control: State IRS Status: 501(c)3
Highest Offering: Beyond Master's But Less Than Doctorate
Program: 2-Year Principally Bachelor's Creditable; Liberal Arts And General; Teacher Preparatory
Accreditation: SC, AAFCS, ART, BUS, BUSA, DIETD, ENGR, JOUR, MUS, NAIT, NURSE, TED

02 President ... Vacant
05 VP for Academic Affairs ... Dr. Allayne BARRILLEAUX
03 Executive Vice President ... Mr. Lawrence W. HOWELL
32 Vice Pres Student Affs/Enroll Svcs ... Dr. Eugene A. DIAL
30 Vice President for Inst Advancement ... Dr. David E. BOUDREAUX
21 Asst Vice Pres for Facilities ... Mr. Michael G. DAVIS
21 Assoc Vice Pres for Finance/CFO ... Mr. Michael P. NAQUIN
45 Exec Dir of Planning/Effectiveness ... Mrs. Renee G. HICKS
49 Dean of Arts & Sciences ... Dr. John DOUCET
66 Dean of Nursing and Allied Health ... Dr. Velma S. WESTBROOK
50 Dean Business Administration ... Dr. Shawn MAULDIN
53 Dean of Education ... Dr. Leslie JONES
88 Dean of University College ... Dr. Albert DAVIS
32 Dean of Student Life ... Vacant
09 Dir Assess/Institutional Research ... Mrs. Leslie B. DISHMAN
08 Director of Library ... Dr. Robert BREMET
19 Director of University Police ... Mr. Craig M. JACCUZZO
36 Director of Student Placement ... Ms. Kristie R. TAUZIN
37 Director of Student Financial Aid ... Ms. Casie TRICHE
14 Director of Computing Center ... Mr. Charles R. ORDOYNE
15 Director of Human Resources ... Vacant
18 Dir Facility Plng/Special Projects ... Mr. Michael G. DAVIS
26 Director of University Relations ... Mrs. Renee PIPER
51 Assoc Dir of Continuing Education ... Ms. Simone HARRIS
41 Athletic Director ... Mr. Robert BERNARDI
29 Director of Alumni Affairs ... Miss Monique CROCHET
06 Director Records & Registration ... Mr. Kelly J. RODRIGUE
07 Director of Admissions ... Mrs. Becky L. DUROCHER
23 Director University Health Services ... Dr. Diane GARVEY
38 Director of Student Services ... Dr. Michele E. CARUSO
39 Director Residence Life ... Mr. Hayward GUENARD
90 Director Academic Computing ... Vacant
84 Director of Enrollment Services ... Mrs. Courtney CASSARD
96 Director of Purchasing ... Mr. Terry G. DUPRE
88 Director Research & Sponsored Pgms ... Mrs. Debra BENOIT
58 Director of Graduate Programs ... Mrs. Deshey PLAISANCE
88 Director of Printing & Design ... Mr. Bruno RUGGIERO
88 Director of Auxiliary Services ... Mrs. Brenda HASKINS
88 Coordinator of Veterans Services ... Mr. Gilberto BURBANTE

*Northwestern State University (B)

140 Central Avenue, Natchitoches LA 71497-0002
County: Natchitoches FICE Identification: 002021
Unit ID: 160038
Telephone: (318) 357-6361 Carnegie Class: Master's L
FAX Number: (318) 357-4223 Calendar System: Semester
URL: www.nsula.edu
Established: 1884 Annual Undergrad Tuition & Fees (In-State): $9219.65
Enrollment: 9,447 Coed
Affiliation or Control: State IRS Status: 501(c)3
Highest Offering: Doctorate
Program: Liberal Arts And General; Teacher Preparatory; Professional
Accreditation: SC, AAFCS, ADNUR, ART, BUS, ENGT, MUS, NURSE, RAD, SW, TED, THEA

02 President ... Dr. Randall J. WEBB
04 Exec Assistant to the President ... Vacant
05 Provost/VP Academic & Student Affs ... Dr. Lisa ABNEY
11 Vice Pres for University Affairs ... Dr. Marcus JONES
26 Vice President for External Affairs ... Mr. Jerry D. PIERCE
46 Vice Pres for Tech/Research/Eco Dev ... Dr. Darlene WILLIAMS
10 Vice President Business Affairs ... Mr. Carl JONES
20 Vice Provost ... Dr. Steve HORTON
32 Dean of Students ... Mrs. Frances CONINE
53 Dean Col of Education & Human Dev ... Dr. Vickie GENTRY
49 Dean Col of Arts/Letters/Grad Stds ... Dr. Steve HORTON
66 Dean Col of Nursing & Allied Health ... Dr. Norann PLANCHOCK
72 Dean Col of Science/Tech/Business ... Dr. Austin TEMPLE
88 Director Scholars College ... Dr. Davina MCCLAIN
12 Exec Dir CENLA & Ft Polk Campuses ... Mr. Jason PARKS
09 Director Institutional Research ... Mr. Curtis PENROD
06 Registrar ... Mrs. Lillie F. BELL
08 Director of Libraries ... Ms. Abbie LANDRY
29 Director Alumni Affairs & Devel ... Dr. Chris MAGGIO
37 Director Student Financial Aid ... Ms. Lauren JACKSON
27 Director News Bureau ... Mr. David WEST
36 Director Counseling & Career Svcs ... Mrs. Rebecca BOONE
41 Athletic Director ... Mr. Greg BURKE
23 Director of Health Services ... Mrs. Stephanie CAMPBELL
07 Director of University Recruiting ... Mrs. Jana LUCKY
15 Director Human Resources ... Mr. Cecil KNOTTS
18 Physical Plant Director ... Mr. Chuck BOURG
96 Director of Purchasing ... Mr. Dale MARTIN
21 Associate Business Officer ... Ms. Rita GRAVES

*Southeastern Louisiana University (C)

548 Western Avenue, Hammond LA 70402-0001
County: Tangipahoa FICE Identification: 002024
Unit ID: 160612
Telephone: (985) 549-2000 Carnegie Class: Master's L
FAX Number: (985) 549-2061 Calendar System: Semester
URL: www.selu.edu
Established: 1925 Annual Undergrad Tuition & Fees (In-State): $5,242
Enrollment: 15,602 Coed
Affiliation or Control: State IRS Status: 501(c)3
Highest Offering: Doctorate
Program: Liberal Arts And General; Teacher Preparatory; Professional
Accreditation: SC, AAFCS, ART, BUS, BUSA, CACREP, CS, ENGR, MUS, NAIT, NURSE, SP, SW, TED

02 President ... Dr. John L. CRAIN
05 Provost/VP Academic Affairs ... Dr. Tammy BOURG
10 Interim VP Administration/Finance ... Mr. Sam DOMIANO
30 Vice Pres University Advancement ... Ms. Wendy LAUDERDALE
32 Vice President Student Affairs ... Dr. Marvin L. YATES
20 Asst VP Academic Affairs ... Dr. Josie WALKER
13 Chief Information Officer ... Dr. Mike M. ASOODEH
04 Exec Assistant to the President ... Ms. Erin K. COWSER
21 Controller ... Ms. Nettie L. BURCHFIELD
06 Director Records & Registration ... Ms. Paulette M. POCHE
08 Director of Library ... Mr. Eric W. JOHNSON
36 Director Career Development Svcs ... Mr. Ken W. RIDGEDELL
31 Interim Director Auxiliary Services ... Ms. Connie DAVIS
29 Director of Alumni Services ... Ms. Kathy L. PITTMAN
39 Dir Student Housing & Resident Svcs ... Dr. Kay MAURIN
15 Director Human Resources ... Mr. Kevin BRADY
19 Interim Director University Police ... Mr. Carmen BRAY
46 Dir Sponsored Research/Programs ... Ms. Cheryl HALL
41 Athletic Director ... Mr. Bart BELLAIRS
18 Director Facility Planning ... Mr. Ken D. HOWE
92 Director Honors Program ... Dr. Kent NEUERBURG
23 Director Health Services ... Ms. Michelle REED
38 Director Counseling Center ... Dr. Barbara B. HEBERT
07 Director Admissions ... Mr. Richard BEAUGH
37 Director Financial Aid ... Ms. Mary LACOUR
09 Director Inst Research/Assessment ... Dr. Michelle HALL
26 Director Public Information ... Mr. Rene G. ABADIE
96 Dir Purchasing/Property Control ... Mr. Ed E. GAUTIER
85 Dir Multicultural/Intl Stdnt Affs ... Mr. Eric J. SUMMERS
22 Coordinator EEO/ADA ... Mr. Gene E. PREGEANT
49 Int Dn Col Arts/Human/Soc Sciences ... Dr. Karen FONTENOT
50 Dean of College of Business ... Dr. Randy P. SETTOON
53 Interim Dean College Education ... Dr. Shirley JACOB
66 Dean Col of Nursing & Health Sci ... Dr. Ann CARRUTH
72 Dean Col of Science & Technology ... Dr. Daniel MCCARTHY
56 Asst VP Extended Studies ... Ms. Joan GUNTER

*University of Louisiana at Lafayette (D)

104 University Circle, Lafayette LA 70503-0001
County: Lafayette FICE Identification: 002031
Unit ID: 160658
Telephone: (337) 482-1000 Carnegie Class: RU/H
FAX Number: (337) 482-6195 Calendar System: Semester
URL: www.louisiana.edu
Established: 1898 Annual Undergrad Tuition & Fees (In-State): $5,343
Enrollment: 16,687 Coed
Affiliation or Control: State IRS Status: 501(c)3
Highest Offering: Doctorate
Program: Liberal Arts And General; Teacher Preparatory; Professional
Accreditation: SC, ART, BUS, BUSA, CAHIIM, CIDA, CS, DIETD, DIETI, ENG, JOUR, MUS, NAIT, NURSE, SP, TED

02 President ... Dr. E. Joseph SAVOIE
05 Interim VP for Academic Affairs ... Dr. Bradd CLARK
10 VP Administration & Finance ... Mr. Jerry L. LEBLANC
32 Interim VP for Student Affairs ... Ms. Patricia COTTONHAM
30 Vice Pres University Advancement ... Mr. Ken ARDOIN
46 Vice Pres for Research/Grad Studies ... Dr. Ramesh KOLLURU
84 VP for Enrollment Mgmt ... Dr. DeWayne BOWIE
13 Chief Information Officer ... Dr. Gene FIELDS
11 Director of Administrative Services ... Ms. Lisa C. LANDRY
21 Asst Vice Pres Financial Services ... Ms. Debra CALAIS
21 Comptroller ... Vacant
45 Asst VP Institutional Planning ... Dr. Paula P. CARSON
108 Asst VP Institutional Plng & Effect ... Dr. Paula CARSON
20 Asst VP Academic Affairs ... Ms. Ellen D. COOK
35 Associate Dean of Students ... Ms. Heidie LINDSEY
35 Assoc Dean Students/Dir Stdnt Life ... Mr. Greg ZERANGUE
25 Director Research/Sponsored Pgms ... Ms. Ruth LANDRY
91 Director of Information Systems ... Mr. Sam F. BULLARD
14 Director Computing Support Services ... Mr. Patrick LANDRY
08 Dean of University Libraries ... Dr. Charles W. TRICHE, III
07 Dir of UN Admissions & Recruitment ... Mr. Andy BENOIT
88 Director Information Networks ... Mr. Stephen J. MAHLER
09 Director of Institutional Research ... Ms. Lisa LORD
55 Director University College ... Ms. Amanda DOYLE
37 Director of Financial Aid ... Ms. Cindy SHOWS-PEREZ
96 Director Purchasing ... Mr. Joseph FLOYD
27 Assoc Director Publications ... Ms. Kathleen A. THAMES
36 Director Career Services ... Ms. Kim A. BILLEAUDEAU
19 Chief of Police ... Chief Joey STURM
23 Director Student Health Svcs ... Dr. Marelle YONGUE
49 Dean Liberal Arts ... Dr. Jordan KELLMAN
54 Dean of Engineering ... Dr. Mark E. ZAPPI
53 Dean of Education ... Dr. Gerald P. CARLSON
66 Dean of Nursing ... Dr. Gail P. POIRRIER
58 Dean of Graduate School ... Dr. Mary FARMER-KAISER
50 Dean of Business Administration ... Dr. Joby JOHN
81 Dean of Sciences ... Dr. Bradd CLARK
97 Dean of General Studies ... Vacant
57 Dean College of the Arts ... Mr. H. Gordon BROOKS, II
77 Director Ctr Adv Computer Studies ... Dr. Magdy A. BAYOUMI
18 Director Physical Plant ... Mr. William J. CRIST
22 Director Operational Review/EEO Off ... Ms. Christine BRASHER
39 Director Housing ... Ms. Lisa L. LANDRY
40 Manager Bookstore ... Mr. Robert RICHARD
24 Director Univ Media/Printing Svcs ... Mr. Steve MAHLER
41 Athletic Director ... Mr. Scott FARMER
85 Director Office of Intl Affairs ... Dr. Rose HONEGGER
51 Director of Continuing Education ... Ms. Elaine D. LIVERS
31 Dean of Community Service ... Mr. David YARBROUGH
86 Coordinator Governmental Relations ... Vacant
26 Dir of Communication and Marketing ... Mr. Aaron MARTIN
29 Director Alumni Affairs ... Mr. David EDMINSTON
44 Planned Giving Officer ... Mr. David P. COMEAUX
38 Director Counseling and Testing ... Mr. Brian FREDERICK
16 Director of Human Resources ... Mr. John BROOKS
06 Registrar ... Mr. Chip JACKSON
106 Director of Distance Learning ... Dr. Luke DOWDEN
92 Director of Honors Program ... Dr. Julia FREDERICK
89 Director of First-Year Experience ... Dr. Theresa WOZENCRAFT

*University of Louisiana at Monroe (E)

700 University Avenue, Monroe LA 71209-0001
County: Ouachita FICE Identification: 002020
Unit ID: 159993
Telephone: (318) 342-1000 Carnegie Class: Master's L
FAX Number: (318) 342-5161 Calendar System: Semester
URL: www.ulm.edu
Established: 1931 Annual Undergrad Tuition & Fees (In-State): $5,443
Enrollment: 8,545 Coed
Affiliation or Control: State IRS Status: 501(c)3
Highest Offering: Doctorate
Program: 2-Year Principally Bachelor's Creditable; Liberal Arts And General; Teacher Preparatory; Professional; Business Emphasis
Accreditation: SC, AAB, BUS, BUSA, CACREP, CONST, CS, DH, EXSC, MFCD, MT, MUS, NURSE, OTA, PHAR, RAD, SP, SW, TED

02 President ... Dr. Nick J. BRUNO
03 Executive VP ... Dr. Stephen P. RICHTERS
10 Chief Business Officer ... Mr. William T. GRAVES
32 Vice President for Student Affairs ... Dr. Wendell W. BRUMFIELD
05 Academic Affairs VP ... Dr. Eric A. PANI
84 Asst VP for Enrollment Mgmt ... Mrs. Lisa R. MILLER
07 Director of Admissions ... Ms. Jennifer MALONE
29 Exec Director Alumni ... Mr. Keith A. BROWN
41 Director of Athletics ... Vacant
27 Director Media Relations ... Mrs. Laura J. WOODARD
88 Director Internal Audit ... Mr. Kirby D. CAMPBELL
49 Dean College of Arts & Sciences ... Dr. Michael CAMILLE
50 Dean Col Business Administration ... Dr. Ronald BERRY
88 Dir Ctr Business/Economic Research ... Dr. Robert C. EISENSTADT
53 Dean Col of Education/Human Devel ... Dr. Sandra M. LEMOINE
76 Dean College of Health Sciences ... Dr. Denny G. RYMAN
67 Dean College of Pharmacy ... Dr. Benny BLAYLOCK
58 Interim Dean of Graduate Programs ... Dr. William MCCOWN
108 Director Assessment and Evaluation ... Mrs. Allison L. THOMPSON

09 Exec Dir Univ Planning/Analysis ... Mr. Ruslan HEMED
08 Dean of the Library ... Mr. Donald R. SMITH
51 Director Continuing Education ... Ms. Paula THORNHILL
06 Registrar ... Mr. Anthony MALTA
37 Director of Financial Aid ... Ms. Cori SMIT
88 Director Testing ... Ms. Denise M. DUPLECHIN
85 Dir Intl Student Program and Svcs ... Vacant
88 Director of University Retention ... Mrs. Barbara MICHAELIDES
39 Director Residential Life ... Ms. Tresea L. BUCKHAULTS
45 Budget Officer ... Ms. Gail C. PARKER
21 Controller ... Ms. Sandra WALKER
15 Director Human Resources ... Mr. Fred BARAGONA
96 Director Purchasing ... Mr. Larry M. ESTESS
14 Director Computer Center ... Mr. Chance W. EPPINETTE
88 Exec Dir Auxiliary Enterprises ... Mr. Michael R. TREVATHAN
40 Manager University Bookstore ... Ms. Rebecca BOOTHBY
18 Director Physical Plant Admin ... Mr. Lawrence B. THORN
88 Director Facilities Mgmt & Ehs ... Mr. Jason S. ROUBIQUE
35 Director of Student Services ... Ms. Pamela JACKSON
38 Director Counseling Center ... Ms. Karen FOSTER
23 Director Student Health Services ... Ms. Yolanda CAMPER
19 Interim Director University Police ... Mr. Steven MAHON
36 Director Career Connections/Exp ... Ms. Roslynn POGUE
88 Dir Recreational Svcs/Facilities ... Ms. Treina LANDRUM
88 Director of Development ... Ms. Anne A. LOCKHART
105 Director of Web Services ... Mr. Lindsey S. WILKERSON
102 Chief Finan Ofcr Univ Foundations ... Mr. Mark S. LABUDE
29 Associate Director Alumni Relations ... Mr. Tommy A. WALPOLE

University of Phoenix Baton Rouge Campus (A)

2431 S Acadian Thruway, Baton Rouge LA 70808-2300
Telephone: (225) 927-4443 Identification: 770208
Accreditation: &NH, ACBSP

† Main campus is University of Phoenix in Tempe, AZ.

Virginia College (B)

9501 Cortana Place, Baton Rouge LA 70815-8604
Telephone: (225) 236-3900 Identification: 770826
Accreditation: ACICS, MAAB

† Main campus is Virginia College in Birmingham, AL.

Virginia College (C)

2950 East Texas Street, Suite C, Bossier City LA 71111
Telephone: (888) 342-0014 Identification: 770827
Accreditation: ACICS

† Main campus is Virginia College in Birmingham, AL.

Xavier University of Louisiana (D)

One Drexel Drive, New Orleans LA 70125-1098
County: Orleans FICE Identification: 002032
Unit ID: 160904
Telephone: (504) 486-7411 Carnegie Class: Bac/A&S
FAX Number: (504) 520-7904 Calendar System: Semester
URL: www.xula.edu
Established: 1925 Annual Undergrad Tuition & Fees: $18,500
Enrollment: 3,178 Coed
Affiliation or Control: Roman Catholic IRS Status: 501(c)3
Highest Offering: Doctorate
Program: Liberal Arts And General; Teacher Preparatory; Professional
Accreditation: SC, ACBSP, MUS, PHAR, TED

01 President ... Dr. Norman C. FRANCIS
11 Sr Vice Pres for Administration ... Mr. Ralph JOHNSON
05 Sr Vice Pres for Academic Affairs ... Dr. Loren BLANCHARD
30 Sr VP for Resource Development ... Dr. Gene D'AMOUR
32 Vice President for Student Services ... Mr. Joseph K. BYRD
30 Vice President for Inst Advancement ... Dr. Kenneth ST.CHARLES
10 Vice President for Finance ... Mr. Edward PHILLIPS
13 Interim VP for Office of Technology ... Mrs. Melva WILLIAMS
45 VP Planning Inst Res & Assessment ... Dr. Ronald R. DURNFORD
18 Vice President Facilities Planning ... Mr. Marion BRACY
26 Assoc VP Public Affairs/Comm ... Vacant
20 Assoc VP for Academic Affairs ... Dr. Marguerite GIGUETTE
31 Assoc Vice Pres Auxiliary Services ... Mr. William JEFFRION
07 Dean of Admissions ... Mr. Winston D. BROWN
06 Registrar ... Ms. Avis STUARD
42 Director of Campus Ministry ... Vacant
21 Director of Accounting ... Ms. Joyce SANDIFER
21 Director of Operations ... Ms. Lori GIE
21 Dir Fin Reporting & External Audit ... Mrs. Ingenue S. SCHEXNIDER-FIELDS
15 Director of Human Resources ... Mr. Larry CALVIN
49 Dean of Arts & Sciences ... Dr. Anil KUKREJA
67 Dean of College of Pharmacy ... Dr. Kathleen KENNEDY
79 Director of Freshmen Studies ... Sr. Monica LOUGHLIN
108 Dir of Inst Effectiv & Assessment ... Dr. Danielle DUFFOURC
09 Dir Inst Compliance & Plng Init ... Dr. Treva A. LEE
08 Director of the Library ... Dr. Lynette RALPH
36 Director of Career Services ... Mrs. Carolyn D. THOMAS
37 Director of Financial Aid ... Ms. Emily LONDON-JONES
19 Director of Campus Police ... Mr. Duane CARKUM
23 Director Student Health Services ... Ms. Brenda MEDLEY
38 Director of Counseling Services ... Ms. Eloise DOXIE-DIXON
29 Director of Alumni Relations ... Ms. Kimberly REESE
40 Manager Bookstore ... Ms. Rose NAQUIN
41 Athletic Director ... Mr. Dennis COUSIN

MAINE

Bangor Theological Seminary (E)

Two College Circle, Bangor ME 04402
County: Penobscot FICE Identification: 002035
Unit ID: 160968
Telephone: (207) 942-6781 Carnegie Class: Spec/Faith
FAX Number: (207) 990-1267 Calendar System: Semester
URL: www.bts.edu
Established: 1814 Annual Graduate Tuition & Fees: $11,760
Enrollment: 58 Coed
Affiliation or Control: United Church Of Christ IRS Status: 501(c)3
Highest Offering: Doctorate; No Undergraduates
Program: Professional; Religious Emphasis
Accreditation: EH

01 President ... Rev Dr. Robert GROVE-MARKWOOD
05 Academic Dean ... Rev Dr. Steven LEWIS
06 Registrar ... Ms. Danielle R. LAVINE
08 Library & Information Services ... Ms. Laurie MCQUARRIE
10 Controller ... Mrs. Caroline HAMMOND
04 Assistant to the President ... Mrs. Patricia O. ANNIS

Bates College (F)

2 Andrews Road, Lewiston ME 04240-6047
County: Androscoggin FICE Identification: 002036
Unit ID: 160977
Telephone: (207) 786-6255 Carnegie Class: Bac/A&S
FAX Number: (207) 786-6123 Calendar System: Other
URL: www.bates.edu
Established: 1855 Annual Undergrad Tuition & Fees: $58,950
Enrollment: 1,753 Coed
Affiliation or Control: Independent Non-Profit IRS Status: 501(c)3
Highest Offering: Baccalaureate
Program: Liberal Arts And General
Accreditation: EH

01 President ... Dr. A. Clayton SPENCER
05 VP Academic Affairs/Dean of Faculty ... Dr. Matthew R. AUER
10 VP Finance & Admin/Treasurer ... Ms. Terry J. BECKMANN
08 VP Info & Libr Services/Librarian ... Dr. Eugene L. WIEMERS
30 VP Advancement ... Ms. Sarah R. PEARSON
32 Dean of Students ... Mr. Tedd GOUNDIE
21 Asst Vice Pres Financial Planning ... Mr. Douglas W. GINEVAN
20 Associate Dean of Faculty ... Dr. Kathryn G. LOW
20 Assoc Dean of Faculty ... Mr. Kirk D. READ
31 Director of Community Partnerships ... Ms. Darby K. RAY
06 Registrar ... Ms. Mary MESERVE
09 Dir Inst Rsch/Analysis and Planning ... Ms. Anne Marie T. RUSSELL
15 Asst VP Human Resources ... Ms. Mary MAIN
18 Dir Physical Plant Operations ... Mr. Daniel F. NEIN
88 Dir Capital Planning/Construction ... Ms. Pamela J. WICHROSKI
07 Dean of Admissions & Financial Aid ... Ms. Leigh WEISENBURGER
29 Dir Alumni & Parent Engagement ... Ms. Marianne COWAN
19 Dir Security & Campus Safety ... Mr. Thomas P. CAREY
23 Dir Health Services ... Ms. Christy TISDALE
26 Asst VP Communications/Media Rels ... Ms. Margaret KIMMEL
37 Dir Student Financial Services ... Ms. Wendy G. GLASS
40 Dir Bookstore/Contract Officer ... Ms. Sarah POTTER
36 Dir of Career Services ... Mr. David MCDONOUGH
91 Dir Sys Development & Integration ... Ms. Eileen P. ZIMMERMAN
24 Dir of Academic Technology Services ... Mr. Andrew W. WHITE
41 Athletic Director ... Mr. Kevin MCHUGH
42 College Chaplain ... Mr. William BLAINE-WALLACE
39 Asst Dean of Students/Housing ... Ms. Erin FOSTER ZSIGA
102 Dir of the Office for External Grnt ... Mr. Philip WALSH
104 Assoc Dean of Students/Study Abroad ... Mr. Stephen SAWYER

† Tuition figure is a comprehensive fees figure.

Beal College (G)

99 Farm Road, Bangor ME 04401-6831
County: Penobscot FICE Identification: 005204
Unit ID: 160995
Telephone: (207) 947-4591 Carnegie Class: Assoc/PrivFP
FAX Number: (207) 947-0208 Calendar System: Other
URL: www.bealcollege.edu
Established: 1891 Annual Undergrad Tuition & Fees: $7,260
Enrollment: 457 Coed
Affiliation or Control: Proprietary IRS Status: Proprietary
Highest Offering: Associate Degree
Program: 2-Year Principally Bachelor's Creditable
Accreditation: ACICS, CAHIIM, MAC

01 President ... Mr. Allen T. STEHLE
05 Director of Education ... Ms. Deborah CROCKETT
08 Chief Librarian ... Mrs. Ann W. REA
37 Director Student Financial Aid ... Ms. Maggie MAGEE
18 Superintendent Physical Plant ... Mr. Kevin HARDY
10 Associate Business Officer ... Ms. Pollyanne HEWES
88 Dir Early Child Ed/Hospitality Svcs ... Ms. Susan XIRINACHS
76 Director Allied Health ... Ms. Barbara MARCHELLETTA
88 Director Criminal Justice ... Mr. Allen STEHLE
40 Director Bookstore ... Ms. Lisa PORTER
36 Director Student Placement ... Ms. Donna GILLETTE
06 Registrar ... Ms. Ellen EDWARDS

07 Director of Admissions ... Ms. Erin LEIGHTON
32 Director of Student Affairs ... Ms. Debbie LEBLANC
50 Director Business Studies ... Ms. Katrin TEEL
83 Director Social & Human Svcs Asst ... Ms. Russ DUBOIS
75 Director Welding Technology ... Mr. Jesse CROSBY

Bowdoin College (H)

5700 College Station, Brunswick ME 04011-8448
County: Cumberland FICE Identification: 002038
Unit ID: 161004
Telephone: (207) 725-3000 Carnegie Class: Bac/A&S
FAX Number: (207) 725-3123 Calendar System: Semester
URL: www.bowdoin.edu
Established: 1794 Annual Undergrad Tuition & Fees: $44,118
Enrollment: 1,839 Coed
Affiliation or Control: Independent Non-Profit IRS Status: 501(c)3
Highest Offering: Master's
Program: Liberal Arts And General
Accreditation: EH

01 President ... Dr. Barry MILLS
10 Sr VP Finance/Admin & Treasurer ... Ms. S. Catherine LONGLEY
46 Sr VP Devel & Alumni Relations ... Mr. Kelly K. KERNER
32 Dean of Student Affairs ... Mr. Timothy W. FOSTER
05 Dean for Academic Affairs ... Dr. Cristle Collins JUDD
07 Dean of Admissions ... Mr. Scott A. MEIKLEJOHN
26 VP/Dir Comm/Public Affairs ... Mr. Scott W. HOOD
09 VP Institutional Planning & Assess ... Mrs. Becky BRODIGAN
30 Sr VP for Devel & Alumni Relations ... Mr. Kelly KERNER
13 Chief Information Officer ... Mr. Mitchel W. DAVIS
29 Director Alumni Relations ... Ms. Rodie F. LLOYD
08 Librarian ... Marjorie HASSEN
37 Director of Student Aid ... Mr. Michael D. BARTINI
21 Controller ... Mr. Matthew ORLANDO
06 Registrar ... MS. Jan BRACKETT
15 Director of Human Resources ... Ms. Tamara D. SPOERRI
19 Director of Security ... Mr. Randall NICHOLS
36 Director of Career Planning ... Mr. Timothy DIEHL
38 Director of Counseling Service ... Dr. Bernie HERSHBERGER
41 Director of Athletics ... Mr. Timothy M. RYAN
23 Director of Health Services ... Ms. Sandra J. HAYES
18 Director Facilities Ops/Maintenance ... Mr. Theodore R. STAM
24 Instructional Media Librarian ... Ms. Carmen M. GREENLEE
21 Director of Finance & Campus Svcs ... Mr. Delwin C. WILSON
39 Director of Residential Life ... Ms. Mary Pat MCMAHON
40 Dir Dining & Bookstore Services ... Ms. Mary M. KENNEDY
35 Director of Student Activities ... Dr. Allen W. DELONG
35 Sr Associate Dean Student Affairs ... Vacant
88 Co-Dir of the Museum of Art ... Ms. Anne GOODYEAR
88 Co-Dir of the Musuem of Art ... Mr. Frank GOODYEAR
18 Director of Capital Projects ... Mr. Donald V. BORKOWSKI
20 Assoc Dean for Academic Affairs ... Dr. Barry LOGAN
88 Associate Dean for Faculty ... Dr. Jennifer SCANLON

Central Maine Medical Center College of Nursing and Health Professions (I)

70 Middle Street, Lewiston ME 04240-7027
County: Androscoggin FICE Identification: 006305
Unit ID: 161022
Telephone: (207) 795-2840 Carnegie Class: Assoc/PrivNFP
FAX Number: (207) 795-2849 Calendar System: Semester
URL: www.cmmccollege.edu
Established: 1891 Annual Undergrad Tuition & Fees: $9,550
Enrollment: 217 Coed
Affiliation or Control: Independent Non-Profit IRS Status: 501(c)3
Highest Offering: Associate Degree
Program: Occupational; 2-Year Principally Bachelor's Creditable; Nursing Emphasis
Accreditation: EH, ADNUR, NMT, RAD

01 President ... Mrs. Susan C. BALTRUS
05 Director ... Ms. Nancy J. ROSS
05 Director ... Mrs. Judith RIPLEY
07 Chair Admissions ... Mrs. Jacqueline F. COLLINS
06 Registrar ... Mrs. Kathleen C. JACQUES
37 Student Financial Aid Specialist ... Mrs. Jenna ROCQUE
24 Educational Media Coordinator ... Vacant

Colby College (J)

4000 Mayflower Hill, Waterville ME 04901-8840
County: Kennebec FICE Identification: 002039
Unit ID: 161086
Telephone: (207) 859-4000 Carnegie Class: Bac/A&S
FAX Number: (207) 859-4603 Calendar System: 4/1/4
URL: www.colby.edu
Established: 1813 Annual Undergrad Tuition & Fees: $57,510
Enrollment: 1,863 Coed
Affiliation or Control: Independent Non-Profit IRS Status: 501(c)3
Highest Offering: Baccalaureate
Program: Liberal Arts And General
Accreditation: EH

01 President ... Dr. William D. ADAMS
05 Vice Pres Acad Affs/Dean of Faculty ... Dr. Lori G. KLETZER
10 Vice President Admin & Treasurer ... Mr. Douglas C. TERP
30 Vice Pres Development & Alumni Rels ... Vacant

03 Vice President/Secy of the Corp ....Ms. Sally A. BAKER
32 VP Student Affairs/Dean of Students ....Mr. James S. TERHUNE
27 Vice President Communications ....Mr. Michael D. KISER
07 Vice Pres/Dean Admiss & Fin Aid ....Dr. Terry E. COWDREY
20 Assoc VP Acad Affs/Assoc Dn Faculty .Dr. Paul G. GREENWOOD
32 Asst Vice Pres/Sr Associate Dean ....Ms. Barbara E. MOORE
35 Senior Associate Dean of Students ....Mr. Paul E. JOHNSTON
06 Registrar ....Ms. Elizabeth N. SCHILLER
08 Director of Libraries ....Mr. Clement P. GUTHRO
36 Director of Career Center ....Ms. Alisa M. JOHNSON
88 Director of Special Programs ....Mr. Jacques MOORE
37 Director of Financial Aid ....Vacant
29 Director of Alumni Relations ....Ms. Margaret M. BOYD
35 Assoc Dean Stdnts/Dir Campus Life ....Mr. Jed W. WARTMAN
16 Director Human Resources ....Mr. Mark CROSBY
19 Director of Security ....Mr. Peter S. CHENEVERT
13 Director of Info-Tech Services ....Dr. Raymond B. PHILLIPS
18 Director of Physical Plant ....Ms. Patricia C. WHITNEY
23 Medical Director ....Dr. Paul D. BERKNER
38 Director of Counseling Services ....Ms. Patricia N. NEWMEN
41 Director of Athletics ....Ms. Marcella K. ZALOT
09 Dir Instnl Research & Assessment ....Dr. William P. WILSON
21 Controller ....Mr. Ruben L. RIVERA
40 Director of the Bookstore ....Ms. Barbara C. SHUTT
104 Director of Off-Campus Study ....Dr. Nancy DOWNEY
102 Dir Corp/Found/Govt Relations ....Ms. Marcella J. BERNARD

College of the Atlantic (A)

105 Eden Street, Bar Harbor ME 04609-1198
County: Hancock FICE Identification: 011385
Unit ID: 160959
Telephone: (207) 288-5015 Carnegie Class: Bac/A&S
FAX Number: (207) 288-3780 Calendar System: Trimester
URL: www.coa.edu
Established: 1969 Annual Undergrad Tuition & Fees: $37,701
Enrollment: 340 Coed
Affiliation or Control: Independent Non-Profit IRS Status: 501(c)3
Highest Offering: Master's
Program: Liberal Arts And General; Teacher Preparatory
Accreditation: EH

01 President ....Dr. Darron COLLINS
05 Academic Dean ....Dr. Ken HILL
10 Administrative Dean ....Mr. Andy GRIFFITHS
32 Dean for Student Life ....Ms. Sarah LUKE
30 Dean Institutional Advancement ....Ms. Lynn BOULGER
07 Dean of Admission ....Ms. Heather ALBERT-KNOPP
06 Registrar ....Ms. Judy ALLEN
08 Director of Thorndike Library ....Ms. Jane HULTBERG
21 Comptroller ....Mrs. Melissa COOK
37 Director of Financial Aid ....Mr. Bruce HAZAM
36 Director of Internship/Career Svcs ....Ms. Jill BARLOW-KELLEY
26 Public Relations Manager ....Ms. Heather ANDERSON

Husson University (B)

1 College Circle, Bangor ME 04401-2929
County: Penobscot FICE Identification: 002043
Unit ID: 161165
Telephone: (207) 941-7000 Carnegie Class: Master's M
FAX Number: (207) 941-7139 Calendar System: Semester
URL: www.husson.edu
Established: 1898 Annual Undergrad Tuition & Fees: $15,130
Enrollment: 3,077 Coed
Affiliation or Control: Independent Non-Profit IRS Status: 501(c)3
Highest Offering: Doctorate
Program: Liberal Arts And General; Professional
Accreditation: EH, IACBE, NURSE, OT, @PHAR, PTA

01 President ....Dr. Robert A. CLARK
05 Provost ....Dr. Lynne COY-OGAN
10 Vice Pres for Finance & Treasurer ....Craig HADLEY
30 Vice President for Advancement ....Thomas MARTZ
11 VP of Administration ....John RUBINO
32 Dean of Students ....Sharon WILSON-BARKER
50 Dean School of Business ....Marie HANSEN
67 Dean School of Pharmacy ....Rodney LARSON
53 Dean College of Health & Education ....Paula TINGLEY
58 Dean of Graduate Studies ....Vacant
53 Director School of Education ....Barbara MOODY
07 Director of Admissions ....Carlena BEAN
37 Director of Financial Aid ....Linda HILL
08 Librarian ....Amy AVERRE
06 Registrar ....Nancy FENDERS
49 Dean Science/Humanities ....Francis HUBBARD
29 Director of Alumni Affairs ....Buffie MCQUE
36 Director Career Services ....James WESTHOFF
41 Director of Athletics ....Vacant
26 Dir of Public Affs/Govt Relations ....Julia GREEN
39 Director of Student Life ....Pamela KROPP-ANDERSON
16 Human Resources Director ....Mary DEMERS
14 Director of Institutional Research ....Gail TUDOR
18 Director of Maintenance ....Vacant
13 Exec Dir of Information Resources ....Kevin CASEY
44 Director of Advancement Services ....Christina CARON

Institute for Doctoral Studies in the Visual Arts (C)

130 Neal Street, Portland ME 04102
County: Cumberland FICE Identification: 041888
Unit ID; 462044
Telephone: (207) 879-8757 Carnegie Class: Not Classified
FAX Number: N/A Calendar System: Semester
URL: www.idsva.org
Established: 2007 Annual Graduate Tuition & Fees: $27,500
Enrollment: 42 Coed
Affiliation or Control: Independent Non-Profit IRS Status: 501(c)3
Highest Offering: Doctorate; No Undergraduates
Program: Professional
Accreditation: @EH

01 President ....George SMITH
03 Executive Vice President ....Amy CURTIS

Kaplan University-Augusta (D)

14 Marketplace Drive, Augusta ME 04330
Telephone: (207) 213-2500 Identification: 770060
Accreditation: &NH

† Main campus is Kaplan University in Davenport, IA.

Kaplan University-Lewiston (E)

475 Lisbon Street, Lewiston ME 04240
Telephone: (207) 333-3300 Identification: 770061
Accreditation: &NH

† Main campus is Kaplan University in Davenport, IA.

Kaplan University-Maine (F)

265 Western Avenue, South Portland ME 04106
Telephone: (207) 774-6126 FICE Identification: 009292
Accreditation: &NH, ACBSP

† Main campus is Kaplan University in Davenport, IA.

The Landing School (G)

286 River Road, Arundel ME 04046
County: York FICE Identification: 023613
Unit ID: 161208
Telephone: (207) 985-7976 Carnegie Class: Not Classified
FAX Number: (207) 985-7942 Calendar System: Other
URL: www.landingschool.edu
Established: 1978 Annual Undergrad Tuition & Fees: $19,220
Enrollment: 68 Coed
Affiliation or Control: Independent Non-Profit IRS Status: 501(c)3
Highest Offering: Associate Degree
Program: Occupational
Accreditation: ACCSC

01 President ....Mr. Robert J. DECOLFMACKER
05 Director of Education ....Mr. Ken RUSINEK
10 Controller ....Ms. Kristy WIGGINS

Maine College of Art (H)

522 Congress St, Portland ME 04101
County: Cumberland FICE Identification: 011673
Unit ID: 161509
Telephone: (207) 775-3052 Carnegie Class: Spec/Arts
FAX Number: (207) 775-5087 Calendar System: Semester
URL: www.meca.edu
Established: 1882 Annual Undergrad Tuition & Fees: $30,990
Enrollment: 402 Coed
Affiliation or Control: Independent Non-Profit IRS Status: 501(c)3
Highest Offering: Master's
Program: Liberal Arts And General; Professional; Fine Arts Emphasis
Accreditation: EH, ART

01 President ....Mr. Donald TUSKI
03 Executive Vice President ....Ms. Beth ELICKER
05 Dean/Vice Pres Academic Affairs ....Mr. Ian ANDERSON
30 VP for Institutional Advancement ....Ms. Rebecca CONRAD
06 Registrar ....Ms. Anne DENNISON
32 Director of Student Involvement ....Ms. Anna SCHWARTZ
07 Director of Admissions ....Mr. Liam SULLIVAN
14 Director Technology ....Mr. David BRANSON
26 Dir Public Relations & Publications ..Ms. Jessica J. TOMLINSON
10 Director of Business Services ....Mr. Phil STEVENS
37 Director of Financial Aid ....Ms. Carri FROCHETTE
51 Director Continuing Studies ....Ms. Sara GIBSON
18 Chief Facilities/Physical Plant ....Mr. Douglas DOERING
08 Librarian ....Ms. Moira STEVENS

*Maine Community College System (I)

323 State Street, Augusta ME 04330-7131
County: Kennebec Identification: 666092
Unit ID: 409713
Telephone: (207) 629-4000 Carnegie Class: N/A
FAX Number: (207) 629-4048
URL: www.mccs.me.edu

01 President ....Dr. John FITZSIMMONS

*Central Maine Community College (J)

1250 Turner Street, Auburn ME 04210-6498
County: Androscoggin FICE Identification: 005276
Unit ID: 161077
Telephone: (207) 755-5100 Carnegie Class: Assoc/Pub-R-M
FAX Number: (207) 755-5491 Calendar System: Semester
URL: www.cmcc.edu
Established: 1964 Annual Undergrad Tuition & Fees (In-State): $3,384
Enrollment: 3,004 Coed
Affiliation or Control: State IRS Status: 501(c)3
Highest Offering: Associate Degree
Program: Occupational; 2-Year Principally Bachelor's Creditable; Technical Emphasis
Accreditation: EH, ADNUR, ENGT

02 President ....Dr. Scott E. KNAPP
05 Dean Academic Affairs ....Dr. Judy WILDER
06 Registrar ....Ms. Sonya SAMPSON
10 Dean of Finance and General Service ....Ms. Pamela REMIERES-MORIN
37 Director of Financial Aid ....Mr. John BOWIE
31 Dean Corporate/Community Services ....Ms. Diane DOSTIE
32 Dean of Student Services/Admissions ....Ms. Betsy LIBBY
26 Dean Planning/Development/PR ....Mr. Roger PHILIPPON
72 Director of Technology/Prep ....Mr. Andrew MORONG
08 Head Librarian ....Ms. Judith FROST
18 Chief Physical Plant ....Mr. Raymond MASSE
22 Affirmative Action Officer ....Ms. Barbara OWEN
39 Director of Housing/Athletic Dir ....Mr. David GONYEA
40 Director of Bookstore ....Ms. Christine MORIN
15 Director of Human Resources ....Ms. Barbara OWEN
30 Director of Development ....Mr. Marc GOSSELIN

*Eastern Maine Community College (K)

354 Hogan Road, Bangor ME 04401-4280
County: Penobscot FICE Identification: 005277
Unit ID: 161138
Telephone: (207) 974-4600 Carnegie Class: Assoc/Pub-R-M
FAX Number: (207) 974-4608 Calendar System: Semester
URL: www.emcc.edu
Established: 1966 Annual Undergrad Tuition & Fees (In-State): $3,920
Enrollment: 2,472 Coed
Affiliation or Control: State IRS Status: 501(c)3
Highest Offering: Associate Degree
Program: Occupational; 2-Year Principally Bachelor's Creditable; Technical Emphasis
Accreditation: EH, ADNUR, MAC, RAD, SURGT

02 President ....Dr. Lawrence M. BARRETT
05 Academic Dean ....Dr. Pamela PROULX-CURRY
10 Dir Finance & Auxiliary Services ....Mr. Eric MACDONALD
09 Dean Inst Research/Enrollment Mgmt ....Mr. Daniel CROCKER
88 Dean Professional/Industry Services ....Vacant
07 Director of Admissions ....Vacant
15 Director of Human Resources ....Ms. Jody BOYD
08 Librarian ....Ms. Janet BLOOD
37 Director of Financial Aid ....Ms. Candace WARD
13 Dean of Communication/Info Tech ....Mr. Timothy CONROY
18 Dir Facilities Mgmt/Student Life ....Mr. Daniel BELYEA
20 Assistant Academic Dean ....Ms. Merlene SANBORN
30 Dir of Institutional Advancement ....Ms. CarolAnne DUBE

*Kennebec Valley Community College (L)

92 Western Avenue, Fairfield ME 04937-1367
County: Somerset FICE Identification: 009826
Unit ID: 161192
Telephone: (207) 453-5000 Carnegie Class: Assoc/Pub-R-M
FAX Number: (207) 453-5010 Calendar System: Semester
URL: www.kvcc.me.edu
Established: 1970 Annual Undergrad Tuition & Fees (In-State): $3,258
Enrollment: 2,470 Coed
Affiliation or Control: State IRS Status: 501(c)3
Highest Offering: Associate Degree
Program: Occupational; 2-Year Principally Bachelor's Creditable
Accreditation: EH, ACBSP, ADNUR, CAHIIM, COARC, DMS, MAC, OTA, PTAA, RAD

02 President ....Dr. Richard HOPPER
05 Academic Dean/Vice President ....Mrs. Karen WHITE
13 Dean of Information Technology ....Mr. Ryan CONNON
32 Dean of Student Affairs ....Ms. Karen NORMANDIN
10 Dean of Finance & Administration ....Mr. John DELILE
06 Registrar ....Mrs. Lisa YORK-LEMELIN
30 Director of Development ....Ms. Michelle WEBB
07 Director of Admissions ....Mr. Jim BOURGOIN
37 Director Student Financial Aid ....Ms. Anne CONNORS
09 Director of Institutional Research ....Ms. Karen GLEW

*Northern Maine Community College (M)

33 Edgemont Drive, Presque Isle ME 04769-2099
County: Aroostook FICE Identification: 005760
Unit ID: 161484
Telephone: (207) 768-2700 Carnegie Class: Assoc/Pub-R-S
FAX Number: (207) 768-2831 Calendar System: Semester
URL: www.nmcc.edu
Established: 1961 Annual Undergrad Tuition & Fees (In-State): $3,408
Enrollment: 1,040 Coed
Affiliation or Control: State IRS Status: 501(c)3
Highest Offering: Associate Degree
Program: Occupational; 2-Year Principally Bachelor's Creditable
Accreditation: EH, ACBSP, ADNUR, EMT, MAC

02 President .... Mr. Timothy D. CROWLEY
05 Academic Dean .... Dr. Dorothy MARTIN
32 Dean of Students .... Dr. William G. EGELER
10 Director of Finance .... Mr. Larry LAPLANTE
51 Dean of Continuing Education .... Vacant
30 Director Development & College Rels .... Ms. Sue BERNARD
07 Director of Admissions .... Mr. Eugene MCCLUSKEY
06 Registrar .... Ms. Betsy A. HARRIS
37 Asst Director for Financial Aid .... Ms. Norma M. SMITH
39 Director of Housing & Resident Life ...... Mr. Thomas J. RICHARD
38 Director of Counseling .... Ms. Tammy NELSON
18 Director of Facilities .... Mr. Barry INGRAHAM
21 Business Manager .... Mr. Philip R. BROWN
15 Human Resource Manager .... Mr. Thomas J. RICHARD
40 Bookstore Manager .... Ms. Rebecca A. MAYNARD
88 Tech Prep Coordinator .... Ms. Elizabeth M. MORGAN

*Southern Maine Community College (A)

Fort Road, South Portland ME 04106-1698
County: Cumberland　FICE Identification: 005525
Unit ID: 161545
Telephone: (207) 741-5500　Carnegie Class: Assoc/Pub-R-M
FAX Number: (207) 741-5751　Calendar System: Semester
URL: www.smccme.edu
Established: 1946　Annual Undergrad Tuition & Fees (In-State): $4,281
Enrollment: 7,574　Coed
Affiliation or Control: State　IRS Status: 501(c)3
Highest Offering: Associate Degree
Program: Occupational; 2-Year Principally Bachelor's Creditable
Accreditation: EH, ACFEI, ADNUR, COARC, DIETT, EMT, RAD, RTT

02 President/CEO .... Ronald G. CANTOR
05 Vice President/Academic Dean .... Janet M. SORTOR
32 Dean of Student Life/Affiirm Action .... Tiffanie L. BENTLEY
26 Dean of Effectiveness & Engagement .... Kaylene WAINDLE
04 Asst to the Pres/Strategic Initiat .... Darla JEWETT
04 Exec Assistant to the President .... Laura J. ZANDSTRA
12 Dean of the Midcoast Campus .... James WHITTEN
10 Dean of Finance .... Robert COOMBS
11 Dean of Administration .... Scott BEATTY
13 Dean of Information Technology/CIO .... Mitch DAVIDSON
30 Dean of Advancement .... Vacant
88 Int Dean Bus & Cmty Partnerships .... Julie CHASE
35 Associate Dean of Student Services .... Mark A. KROGMAN
20 Associate Dean of Academic Affairs .... Paul CHARPENTIER
06 Assistant Dean of Records/Reten .... Jeremy DILL
21 Director of Budget & Financial Rpt .... Shaun GRAY
37 Director of Financial Aid .... Vacant
07 Director of Admissions .... Amy LEE
88 Director of Student Success .... Kathleen DOAN
39 Dir of Residence Life & Stdnt Dev .... Shane LONG
88 Director of the Learning Commons .... Lisa MCDANIELS
19 Director Campus Security .... Joseph MANHARDT
41 Director of Athletics .... Matthew RICHARDS
18 Plant Maintenance Engineer III .... James RENY
40 Manager Campus Store .... Cherie BRYANT
21 Business Mgr Student Billing/Bursar .... Irene FINCH
15 HR & Benefits Manager .... Denise RENY

*Washington County Community College (B)

One College Drive, Calais ME 04619-9704
County: Washington　FICE Identification: 009231
Unit ID: 161581
Telephone: (207) 454-1000　Carnegie Class: Assoc/Pub-R-S
FAX Number: (207) 454-1092　Calendar System: Semester
URL: www.wccc.me.edu
Established: 1969　Annual Undergrad Tuition & Fees (In-State): $3,500
Enrollment: 477　Coed
Affiliation or Control: State　IRS Status: 501(c)3
Highest Offering: Associate Degree
Program: Occupational; 2-Year Principally Bachelor's Creditable
Accreditation: EH, MAC

02 President .... Mr. Joseph CASSIDY
05 Academic Dean .... Dr. David SOUSA
10 Dean of Finance & Admin Services .... Ms. Desiree THOMPSON
15 Director of HR and Public Relations .... Ms. Tina ERSKINE
84 Assoc Dean Enroll/Retention Svcs .... Ms. Susan MINGO
31 Dean of Community Education .... Mr. Scott HARRIMAN
07 Director of Admissions .... Ms. Susan MINGO

*York County Community College (C)

112 College Drive, Wells ME 04090-0529
County: York　FICE Identification: 031229
Unit ID: 420440
Telephone: (207) 646-9282　Carnegie Class: Assoc/Pub-R-S
FAX Number: (207) 646-9675　Calendar System: Semester
URL: www.yccc.edu
Established: 1994　Annual Undergrad Tuition & Fees (In-State): $3,420
Enrollment: 1,524　Coed
Affiliation or Control: State　IRS Status: 501(c)3
Highest Offering: Associate Degree
Program: Occupational; 2-Year Principally Bachelor's Creditable
Accreditation: EH

02 Interim President .... Dr. Christopher HALL
05 Vice President/Academic Dean .... Ms. Paula GAGNON
32 Dean of Students .... Dr. Corinne KOWPAK
10 Dean of Finance & Administration .... Ms. Nancy DROUIN
26 Director Marketing & PR .... Ms. Stacy CHILICKI
51 Director of Continuing Education .... Ms. Paulette MILLETTE
04 Admin Assistant to the President .... Ms. Erin HAYE
20 Associate Academic Dean .... Ms. Doreen ROGAN
08 Director Library/Learning Resources .... Ms. Amber TATNALL
88 Faculty Development Coordinator .... Ms. Stefanie FORSTER
07 Director of Admissions .... Mr. Fred QUISTGARD
84 Director of Enrollment Services .... Ms. Jessica MASI
37 Director Financial Aid .... Mr. David DAIGLE
13 Director of Technology .... Mr. Tim DUNNE
21 Business Manager .... Mr. Samuel ELLIS
15 Human Resources & Benefits Manager .... Ms. Ellen HARFORD
18 Manager of Facilities .... Mr. Dana PETERSEN
09 Director of Institutional Research .... Mr. Nicholas GILL

Maine Maritime Academy (D)

Castine ME 04420-0001
County: Hancock　FICE Identification: 002044
Unit ID: 161299
Telephone: (207) 326-4311　Carnegie Class: Bac/Diverse
FAX Number: (207) 326-2218　Calendar System: Semester
URL: www.mma.edu
Established: 1941　Annual Undergrad Tuition & Fees (In-State): $16,850
Enrollment: 931　Coed
Affiliation or Control: State　IRS Status: 501(c)3
Highest Offering: Master's
Program: Professional
Accreditation: EH, ENG, ENGT

01 President .... Dr. William J. BRENNAN
05 Academic Dean .... Dr. John BARLOW
11 Vice Pres of Operations .... Mr. Jeffery LOUSTAUNAU
84 VP Stdnt Svcs/Enrollment Mgmt .... Dr. Elizabeth TRUE
30 Vice President for Advancement .... Ms. Ellie WILLMANN
15 Human Resource Officer .... Ms. Virginia ALTEMUS
32 Chief Student Life Officer .... Ms. Kristen WENTWORTH
35 Dean of Student Services .... Ms. Deidra DAVIS
36 Placement Director .... Mr. Timothy LEACH
07 Director of Admissions .... Mr. Jeffrey WRIGHT
06 Registrar .... Ms. Christina STEPHENS
29 Director Alumni Relations .... Mr. Paul MERCER
37 Director Student Financial Aid .... Ms. Kathy HEATH
38 Director Student Counseling .... Mr. Paul FERREIRA
08 Head Librarian .... Ms. Wendy GIRVEN
10 Chief Business Officer .... Ms. Diana SNAPP
18 Chief Facilities/Physical Plant .... Mr. Adam POTTER
20 Associate Academic Dean .... Dr. Joceline BOUCHER
26 Chief Public Relations Officer .... Mrs. Jennifer DEJOY
09 Director of Institutional Research .... Dr. Darrell DONOHUE
96 Director of Purchasing .... Mrs. Alice HERRICK

New England Bible College (E)

879 Sawyer St, Box 2886, South Portland ME 04116
County: Cumberland　Identification: 667135
Telephone: (207) 799-5979　Carnegie Class: Not Classified
FAX Number: (207) 799-6586　Calendar System: Semester
URL: www.nebc.edu
Established: 1980　Annual Undergrad Tuition & Fees: $7,600
Enrollment: N/A　Coed
Affiliation or Control: Independent Non-Profit　IRS Status: 501(c)3
Highest Offering: Baccalaureate
Program: Religious Emphasis
Accreditation: @BI

01 Interim President .... Dr. David CHRISTENSEN

New England School of Communications (F)

1 College Circle, Bangor ME 04401-2999
County: Penobscot　FICE Identification: 023471
Unit ID: 373827
Telephone: (207) 941-7176　Carnegie Class: Spec/Other
FAX Number: (207) 941-7139　Calendar System: Semester
URL: www.nescom.edu
Established: 1981　Annual Undergrad Tuition & Fees: $14,004
Enrollment: 499　Coed
Affiliation or Control: Independent Non-Profit　IRS Status: 501(c)3
Highest Offering: Baccalaureate
Program: Occupational
Accreditation: ACCSC

01 President .... Mr. Thomas C. JOHNSTON
03 Exec Vice President/Academic Dean .... Mr. Benjamin E. HASKELL
07 Director of Admissions .... Mrs. Louise G. GRANT
84 Dir of Enrollment Mgmt/Registrar .... Ms. Anne E. REED
37 Director of Student Financial Aid .... Ms. Nicole VACHON
29 Director Alumni Relations .... Mr. Mark NASON

Saint Joseph's College of Maine (G)

278 Whites Bridge Road, Standish ME 04084-5236
County: Cumberland　FICE Identification: 002051
Unit ID: 161518
Telephone: (207) 892-6766　Carnegie Class: Master's M
FAX Number: (207) 893-7861　Calendar System: Semester
URL: www.sjcme.edu
Established: 1912　Annual Undergrad Tuition & Fees: $30,990
Enrollment: 3,371　Coed
Affiliation or Control: Roman Catholic　IRS Status: 501(c)3
Highest Offering: Master's
Program: Liberal Arts And General; Teacher Preparatory; Professional
Accreditation: EH, NURSE

01 President .... Dr. James S. DLUGOS
05 VP & Chief Officer of Learning .... Dr. Michael PARDALES
30 VP & Chief Advancement Officer .... Vacant
84 Vice Pres Enrollment .... Ms. Kathleen DAVIS
88 Vice Pres for Sponsorship & Mission .... Sr. Kathleen SULLIVAN
58 Dean Graduate/Prof Studies .... Vacant
10 VP & Chief Financial Officer .... Ms. Evan BERRY
37 Director of Financial Aid .... Vacant
32 Dean of Student Life .... Mr. Reis HAGERMAN
06 Director of Academic Records .... Mr. Kevin PAQUETTE
08 Director of the Library .... Ms. Shelly DAVIS
29 Dir Alumni & Parent Communications .... Ms. Kristina GREEN
44 Director of Annual Giving .... Ms. Heather PLATI
18 Chief Facilities/Physical Plant .... Mr. Charles DAWES
41 Athletic Director .... Mr. Brian CURTIN
26 Director Public Relations .... Mr. Robert HAND
38 Director Student Counseling .... Dr. Elizabeth WIESEN
13 Director Information Systems .... Ms. Gayle LANGIS
23 Director Health Services .... Dr. Sue-Anne HAMMOND
36 Director Career Services .... Mr. Thomas NOVAK
96 Director of Purchasing .... Ms. Carlene P. LEMIEUX
39 Director Student Housing .... Mr. Jon BLANCHARD
11 Director Human Resources .... Ms. Kristine AVERY
20 Associate Dean .... Mrs. Elaine TRUMBLE
09 Director of Institutional Research .... Dr. Paul J. WOODWARD

Thomas College (H)

180 W River Road, Waterville ME 04901-5097
County: Kennebec　FICE Identification: 002052
Unit ID: 161563
Telephone: (207) 859-1111　Carnegie Class: Bac/Diverse
FAX Number: (207) 859-1114　Calendar System: Semester
URL: www.thomas.edu
Established: 1894　Annual Undergrad Tuition & Fees: $22,160
Enrollment: 1,201　Coed
Affiliation or Control: Independent Non-Profit　IRS Status: 501(c)3
Highest Offering: Master's
Program: Liberal Arts And General; Teacher Preparatory; Professional; Business Emphasis
Accreditation: EH

01 President .... Ms. Laurie G. LACHANCE
05 Provost .... Dr. Thomas EDWARDS
20 Dean of Academic Affairs .... Dr. James LIBBY
20 Assistant Academic Dean .... Ms. Jamie BALLINGER
10 Senior Vice President/CFO/Treasurer .... Ms. Beth B. GIBBS
30 Vice Pres Advancement .... Mr. Robert M. MOORE
88 Dean of Advancement .... Ms. Erin BALTES
88 Asst Dean Alumni & Career Svcs .... Ms. Lucy C. PELSMA
84 Vice Pres Enrollment Management .... Mr. Jonathan KENT
07 Dean of Admissions .... Ms. Wendy MARTIN
32 Vice President Student Affairs .. Ms. Lisa DESAUTELS-POLIQUIN
35 Assistant Dean of Students .... Ms. Hannah GLADSTONE
13 Vice President Information Services .... Mr. Christopher RHODA
08 Director Library Services .... Ms. Lisa AURIEMMA
37 Director Student Financial Services .... Ms. Jeannine BOSSE
36 Director Career Services .... Vacant
18 Director Physical Plant .... Mr. James PARSONS
15 Director Human Resources .... Ms. Michelle JOLER-LABBE
26 Director Public Relations .... Ms. Jennifer BUKER
06 Registrar .... Ms. Lindsey NELSON
29 Director Alumni Relations .... Ms. Cathy DUMONT
40 Manager of Bookstore .... Ms. Katie THOMAS

Unity College (I)

90 Quaker Hill Road, Unity ME 04988-9502
County: Waldo　FICE Identification: 006858
Unit ID: 161572
Telephone: (207) 948-9100　Carnegie Class: Bac/Diverse
FAX Number: (207) 948-9771　Calendar System: Semester
URL: www.unity.edu
Established: 1965　Annual Undergrad Tuition & Fees: $25,000
Enrollment: 540　Coed
Affiliation or Control: Independent Non-Profit　IRS Status: 501(c)3
Highest Offering: Baccalaureate
Program: Occupational; 2-Year Principally Bachelor's Creditable; Liberal Arts And General; Teacher Preparatory
Accreditation: EH

01 President .... Dr. Stephen MULKEY
101 Secretary to Board .... Ms. Chris MELANSON
05 Provost & VP for Academic Affairs .... Dr. Michael EVANS
10 Vice Pres Finance & Administration .... Ms. Deborah CRONIN
31 Sr Vice President External Affairs .... Dr. Melik Peter KHOURY
32 Vice Pres for Student Affairs .... Mr. Gary ZANE
06 Registrar .... Ms. Holly A. HEIN
07 Sr Associate Director Admissions .. Mr. Joseph SALTALAMACHIA
88 Director Outdoor Adventure Center .... Ms. Jessica STEELE
41 Director of Athletics .... Mr. Chris KEIN
88 Director Dining Services .... Ms. Sandy DONAHUE
18 Director Facilities & Public Safety .... Mr. Daniel LAFORGE
37 Director Financial Aid .... Mr. Rand E. NEWELL
23 Director Health & Wellness Center .... Ms. Anna MCGALLIARD

16	Director Human Resources	Ms. Sarah CONROY
13	Director Information Technology	Mr. Bert AUDETTE
24	Director Learning Resource Center	Vacant
08	Director Quimby Library	Mrs. Melora NORMAN
53	Co-Director of Teacher Education	Mr. Gerry SAUNDERS
26	Director of Marketing	Mr. Robert FITZPATRICK
30	Director of College Development	Ms. Martha NORDSTROM
39	Director Residence Life	Mr. Stephen S. NASON
35	Director Student Accounts	Ms. Jeri ROBERTS
88	Director Writing Center	Ms. Judy WILLIAMS
88	Sustainability Director	Mr. Jesse PYLES
88	Assoc Dir College Communications	Mr. Mark TARDIF
29	Alumni/Parent Relations Coordinator	Ms. Debora NOONE
40	Manager Bookstore	Ms. Leigh JUSKEVICE
88	Community-Based Learning Coord	Ms. Jen OLIN
36	Career Consultant/Internship Coord	Ms. Nicole COLLINS
19	Chief Public Safety Officer	Mr. Dean BESSEY
04	Executive Assistant	Ms. Kimberly SHEFF

† The 2011-2012 tuition should have been lited as $23,540.

*University of Maine System Office (A)

16 Central Street, Bangor ME 04401-5106
County: Penobscot FICE Identification: 008012
Unit ID: 161280
Telephone: (207) 973-3200 Carnegie Class: N/A
FAX Number: (207) 973-3296
URL: www.maine.edu

01	Chancellor	Dr. James H. PAGE
10	CFO & Treasurer	Dr. Rebecca WYKE
43	University Counsel/Clerk of Board	Mr. J. Kelley WILTBANK
86	Asst to Chanc Governmental Rels	Mr. Ryan LOW
15	Exec Director of Human Resources	Ms. Tracy BIGNEY
32	Chief Student Affairs Officer	Ms. Rosa REDONNETT
27	Chief Information Officer	Mr. Dick THOMPSON
18	Director of Facilities	Mr. M. F. Chip GAVIN

*University of Maine (B)

Orono ME 04469-0001
County: Penobscot FICE Identification: 002053
Unit ID: 161253
Telephone: (207) 581-1110 Carnegie Class: RU/H
FAX Number: (207) 581-1604 Calendar System: Semester
URL: www.umaine.edu
Established: 1865 Annual Undergrad Tuition & Fees (In-State): $10,600
Enrollment: 8,778 Coed
Affiliation or Control: State IRS Status: 501(c)3
Highest Offering: Doctorate
Program: Liberal Arts And General; Teacher Preparatory; Professional
Accreditation: EH, ART, BUS, CLPSY, CS, DIETD, DIETI, ENG, ENGT, FOR, IPSY, MUS, NURSE, SP, SW, TED

02	President	Dr. Paul W. FERGUSON
05	Exec VP Academic Affairs/Provost	Dr. Susan J. HUNTER
10	Sr Vice Pres Administration/Finance	Ms. Janet E. WALDRON
30	VP Development/Alumni Relations	Mr. Eric F. ROLFSON
32	VP Student Affs/Dean of Students	Dr. Robert Q. DANA
46	Vice President for Research	Dr. Michael J. ECKARDT
84	Vice Pres Enrollment Management	Dr. Jimmy JUNG
88	VP Innovation/Economic Development	Mr. James WARD, IV
15	Assoc VP Human Res/Administration	Ms. Judith S. RYAN
21	Asst VP of Financial/Budget Svcs	Mrs. Claire I. STRICKLAND
20	Assoc Provost/Dean Undergrad Educ	Dr. Stuart L. MARRS
04	Senior Advisor to the President	Ms. Julie D. HOPWOOD
08	Dean of Libraries	Ms. Joyce V. RUMERY
13	Exec Dir of Information Technology	Dr. John H. GREGORY
18	Exec Dir Facilities/Capital Mgt Svc	Mr. Stewart A. HARVEY
26	Sr Dir Univ Relations/Operations	Ms. Margaret A. NAGLE
39	Exec Director of Auxiliary Services	Mr. Daniel H. STURRUP
25	Director Research & Sponsor Program	Mr. Michael M. HASTINGS
06	Director Student Records	Ms. Kimberly D. PAGE
07	Director of Admissions	Ms. Sharon M. OLIVER
37	Director of Financial Aid	Ms. Gianna F. MARRS
36	Director of Career Center	Ms. Patricia B. COUNIHAN
09	Director Institutional Studies	Mr. Ted T. COLADARCI
85	Director International Programs	Dr. CK KWAI
41	Athletic Director	Mr. Steven W. ABBOTT
28	Director Equal Employment Diversity	Ms. Karen D. KEMBLE
19	Dir of Public Safety/Transportation	Chief Roland J. LACROIX
29	Director Alumni Relations	Mr. Todd SAUCIER
40	Interim Director of Bookstore	Mr. Richard YOUNG
96	Dir Purchasing/AP Shared Services	Mr. Michael NOBLET
38	Director Student Counseling	Mr. Douglas P. JOHNSON
49	Dean Liberal Arts & Sciences	Dr. Jeffrey E. HECKER
50	Dean Bus/Public Policy/Health	Dr. Ivan M. MANEV
53	Dean Education/Human Development	Dr. William D. NICHOLS
54	Dean Engineering	Dr. Dana N. HUMPHREY
65	Dean Natural Science/Forestry/Agric	Dr. Edward N. ASHWORTH
51	Dean Lifelong Learning	Dr. Lucille A. ZEPH
58	Dean Graduate School	Dr. Daniel H. SANDWEISS

*University of Maine at Augusta (C)

46 University Drive, Augusta ME 04330-9410
County: Kennebec FICE Identification: 006760
Unit ID: 161217
Telephone: (207) 621-3000 Carnegie Class: Bac/Assoc
FAX Number: (207) 621-3116 Calendar System: Semester
URL: www.uma.edu
Established: 1965 Annual Undergrad Tuition & Fees (In-State): $7,380
Enrollment: 4,990 Coed
Affiliation or Control: State IRS Status: 501(c)3
Highest Offering: Baccalaureate
Program: 2-Year Principally Bachelor's Creditable; Liberal Arts And General; Professional
Accreditation: EH, ADNUR, DA, DH, MLTAD

02	President	Dr. Allyson HUGHES HANDLEY
05	Executive Vice President/Provost	Dr. Joe S. SZAKAS
10	Vice President of Finance and Admin	Vacant
84	Dean of Enrollment Services	Ms. Sheri FRASER
11	Exec Director of Admin Services	Ms. Sheri R. STEVENS
100	Chief of Staff	Ms. Joyce BLANCHARD
08	Dean of Libraries & Distance Ed	Dr. Thomas E. ABBOTT
12	Dean Bangor Campus	Ms. Gillian JORDAN
32	Dean of Students	Ms. Kathleen A. DEXTER
107	Dean College of Prof Studies	Ms. Brenda MCALEER
37	Director of Financial Aid	Ms. Sherry MCCOLLETT
06	Registrar	Ms. Ann CORBETT
15	Director Personnel Services	Mr. David LANE
18	Chief Facilities/Physical Plant	Mr. Peter ST. MICHEL
38	Dir of Cornerstone & Counseling	Ms. Dorrea FELLMAN
88	Director of Advising	Ms. Tricia DYER
35	Director of Student Life	Mr. Warren NEWTON
40	Director Bookstore	Mr. Jerry GARTHOFF
26	Exec Director of External Relations	Mr. Bob STEIN
09	Exec Director of IR & Planning	Mr. Gregory LAPOINTE
49	Dean College of Arts & Sciences	Mr. Greg FAHY

*University of Maine at Farmington (D)

224 Main Street, Farmington ME 04938-1911
County: Franklin FICE Identification: 002040
Unit ID: 161226
Telephone: (207) 778-7000 Carnegie Class: Bac/Diverse
FAX Number: (207) 778-7247 Calendar System: Semester
URL: www.umf.maine.edu
Established: 1864 Annual Undergrad Tuition & Fees (In-State): $9,167
Enrollment: 2,028 Coed
Affiliation or Control: State IRS Status: 501(c)3
Highest Offering: Master's
Program: Liberal Arts And General; Teacher Preparatory
Accreditation: EH, TED

02	President	Dr. Kathryn A. FOSTER
05	Interim VP Academic Affairs/Provost	Dr. Daniel P. GUNN
10	Exec Dir Finance & Administration	Ms. Laurie A. GARDNER
32	Vice Pres Student & Community Svcs	Ms. Celeste BRANHAM
07	Director of Admissions	Mr. Jamie E. MARCUS
84	Vice Pres Enrollment Mgmt & Mktg	Vacant
88	Sustainability Coordinator	Dr. Lucas C. KELLETT
53	Assoc Provost & Dean of Education	Dr. Katherine W. YARDLEY
20	Assoc Provost & Dean of Acad Svcs	Dr. Robert L. LIVELY
89	Asst to Dean First Year Experience	Vacant
92	Director of Honors Program	Dr. Scott D. ERB
88	Dir of Learning Assistance Center	Ms. Claire N. NELSON
08	Director of Library	Mr. Franklin D. ROBERTS
37	Financial Aid Director	Mr. Ronald P. MILLIKEN
15	Dir Human Resources & Finance	Ms. Kathleen P. FALCO
06	Director Adm Sys/Student Records	Ms. Sharon L. NADEAU
88	Dir Center for Student Development	Mr. Robert A. PEDERSON
44	Dir Gift Planning & Stewardship	Ms. Patricia A. CARPENTER
27	Director of Media Relations	Ms. April C. MULHERIN
14	Ex Dir Information Technolog Svcs	Mr. Frederick L. BRITTAIN
41	Dir Athletics/Fitness & Recreation	Ms. Julie A. DAVIS
88	Dir Fitness & Recreation Center	Mr. James D. TONER
88	Coordinator of Outdoor Recreation	Vacant
39	Director Residential Life	Mr. Brian K. UFFORD
35	Dir Center for Stdnt Involvement	Ms. Kirsten SWAN
23	Dir Clinical Svcs Stdnt Health Ctr	Dr. Susan E. COCHRAN
18	Director of Facilities Management	Mr. Bernard PRATT
19	Director of Public Safety	Vacant
29	Director of Alumni Relations	Ms. Jennifer A. ERIKSEN
88	Director of Dining Services	Mr. Andrew HUTCHINS
09	Director of Institutional Research	Dr. Sarah HARDY

*University of Maine at Fort Kent (E)

23 University Drive, Fort Kent ME 04743-1292
County: Aroostook FICE Identification: 002041
Unit ID: 161235
Telephone: (207) 834-7500 Carnegie Class: Bac/Diverse
FAX Number: (207) 834-7503 Calendar System: Semester
URL: www.umfk.maine.edu
Established: 1878 Annual Undergrad Tuition & Fees (In-State): $9,572
Enrollment: 1,169 Coed
Affiliation or Control: State IRS Status: 501(c)3
Highest Offering: Baccalaureate
Program: Occupational; 2-Year Principally Bachelor's Creditable; Liberal Arts And General; Teacher Preparatory; Professional; Nursing Emphasis
Accreditation: EH, IACBE, NURSE

02	President	Mr. Wilson G. HESS
05	Vice President Academic Affairs	Dr. Rachel E. ALBERT
11	Vice President for Administration	Mr. John D. MURPHY
31	Dean of Community Education	Mr. Scott A. VOISINE
84	Dean of Enrollment Management	Ms. Ellia SABLAN-ZEBEDY
36	Assistant Dean of Student Success	Ms. Eleanor B. HESS
06	Registrar	Mr. Humberto PORTELLEZ
15	Acting Director of Human Resources	Mr. John D. MURPHY
66	Nursing Division Director	Ms. Erin SOUCY
08	Dir of Information Svcs/Library	Ms. Leslie E. KELLY
07	Director of Admissions	Ms. Jill CAIRNS
37	Director of Financial Aid	Ms. Elizabeth VIOLETTE
26	Dir University Relations/Alum Affs	Mr. Terence KELLY
18	Director of Facilities Management	Mr. Andrew C. JACOBS
21	Director of Business Systems	Ms. Leslie R. GUERRETTE
29	Director Alumni Relations	Mr. Terence KELLY
28	Assoc Dir Res Life & Diversity Pgms	Mr. Raymond R. PHINNEY
09	Assoc Dir of Institutional Research	Mr. Joseph R. BJERKLIE
30	Development Officer	Ms. Linda DEPREY

*University of Maine at Machias (F)

116 O'Brien Avenue, Machias ME 04654-1397
County: Washington FICE Identification: 002055
Unit ID: 161244
Telephone: (207) 255-1200 Carnegie Class: Bac/A&S
FAX Number: (207) 255-4864 Calendar System: Semester
URL: www.umm.maine.edu
Established: 1909 Annual Undergrad Tuition & Fees (In-State): $7,480
Enrollment: 925 Coed
Affiliation or Control: State IRS Status: 501(c)3
Highest Offering: Baccalaureate
Program: Liberal Arts And General; Teacher Preparatory
Accreditation: EH, NRPA

02	President	Dr. Cynthia E. HUGGINS
05	Vice Pres Academic Affairs/Provost	Dr. Stuart G. SWAIN
10	Vice Pres Finance/Administration	Mr. Thomas L. POTTER
32	Director Student Life	Mr. Melvin ADAMS
06	Registrar	Ms. Mary STOVER
08	Director Library	Vacant
07	Dean of Admissions	Mr. Michael MATTISON
15	Director Human Resources	Ms. Kim PAGE
37	Director Student Financial Aid	Mrs. Katie KURZ
18	Director Physical Facilities	Mr. Robert FARRIS
26	Director Public Relations	Mr. Erik SMITH
13	Director Information Technology	Mr. Michael MATIS
41	Director Athletics	Vacant

*University of Maine at Presque Isle (G)

181 Main Street, Presque Isle ME 04769-2888
County: Aroostook FICE Identification: 002033
Unit ID: 161341
Telephone: (207) 768-9400 Carnegie Class: Bac/Diverse
FAX Number: (207) 768-9608 Calendar System: Semester
URL: www.umpi.edu
Established: 1903 Annual Undergrad Tuition & Fees (In-State): $7,300
Enrollment: 1,463 Coed
Affiliation or Control: State IRS Status: 501(c)3
Highest Offering: Baccalaureate
Program: Liberal Arts And General; Teacher Preparatory; Professional
Accreditation: EH, MLTAD, @PTAA, SW

02	President	Dr. Linda K. SCHOTT
05	Vice President Academic Affairs	Dr. Michael E. SONNTAG
11	Vice Pres Administration & Finance	Mr. Charles G. BONIN
35	Dean of Students	Vacant
07	Director of Admissions	Ms. Erin V. BENSON
15	Asst Director of Human Resources	Ms. Jennie R. SAVAGE
27	Director of Information Services	Ms. JoAnne L. WALLINGFORD
06	Director of Student Records	Ms. Kathy K. DAVIS
37	Director of Financial Aid	Mr. Christopher A R. BELL
36	Director Student Placement	Ms. Barbara J. DEVANEY
39	Director Residence Life	Mr. James D. STEPP
41	Director of Athletics	Vacant
26	Director of Media Relations	Ms. Rachel RICE
29	Director of Alumni Relations	Mr. Keith L. MADORE
40	Bookstore Manager	Mr. Greg DOAK
18	Director of Facilities Management	Mr. Robert AUGHINBAUGH

*University of Southern Maine (H)

96 Falmouth Street, PO Box 9300,
Portland ME 04101-9300
County: Cumberland FICE Identification: 002054
Unit ID: 161554
Telephone: (207) 780-4141 Carnegie Class: Master's L
FAX Number: (207) 780-4933 Calendar System: Semester
URL: www.usm.maine.edu
Established: 1878 Annual Undergrad Tuition & Fees (In-State): $7,590
Enrollment: 9,385 Coed
Affiliation or Control: State IRS Status: 501(c)3
Highest Offering: Doctorate
Program: Liberal Arts And General; Teacher Preparatory; Professional
Accreditation: EH, ART, BUS, CACREP, CORE, CS, ENG, EXSC, HSA, LAW, MUS, NAIT, NURSE, OT, SW, TEAC

02	President	Dr. Theodora J. KALIKOW
05	Provost/VPAA	Dr. Michael STEVENSON
10	Chief Financial Officer/VP Admin	Mr. Richard CAMPBELL
32	Chief Student Success Officer	Dr. Susan CAMPBELL
30	Vice President for Advancement	Ms. Cecile AITCHISON
09	Assoc Dir Institutional Research	Ms. Patricia DAVIS
18	Exec Director Facilities Management	Mr. Bob BERTRAM
96	Director of Purchasing and Paybles	Mr. Gregg N. ALLEN
08	University Librarian	Mr. David NUTTY
108	Director Academic Assessment Ctr	Ms. Susan L. KING
38	Director of Health & Counseling	Dr. Kristine BERTINI
15	Chief Human Resources Office	Ms. Martha FREEMAN
26	Executive Director Public Affairs	Mr. Robert S. CASWELL

37 Director of Financial Aid ... Mr. Keith DUBOIS
35 Executive Director Student Success ... Ms. Elizabeth HIGGINS
07 Interim Director Admissions ... Ms. Rachel MORALES
06 Registrar ... Mr. Steven RAND
22 Director of Equal Opportunity ... Mr. Daryl MCLLWAIN
72 Interim Director CTEL ... Ms. Barbara STEBBINS
25 Dir of Office of Sponsored Programs ... Mr. Lawrence WAXLER
31 Director of Community Standards ... Ms. Joy PUFHAL
41 Director of Athletics & Rec Sports ... Mr. Al BEAN
51 Director of Prof & Continuing Educ ... Dr. Monique LAROCQUE
39 Director of Residential Life ... Ms. Joy PUFHAL
40 Director of USM Bookstore ... Ms. Nicole PIAGET
61 Dean School of Law ... Mr. Peter PITEGOFF
50 Dean College of Mgmt & Human Svcs ... Dr. Joseph MCDONNELL
72 Dean College of Sci/Tech & Health ... Dr. Andrew ANDERSON
49 Dean of Arts/Humanities & Soc Sci ... Dr. Lynn KUZMA
12 Dean Lewiston-Auburn College ... Dr. Joyce GIBSON
35 Executive Director Student Success ... Mr. Joseph M. AUSTIN
24 Manager Audiovisual/Media Services ... Ms. Angela COOK
94 Director of Women's Studies ... Dr. Wendy CHAPKIS
20 Assoc Provost Undergraduate Educ ... Dr. Dahlia LYNN
88 Coordinator Multicultural Affairs ... Mr. Reza JALALI
29 Director of Alumni Relations ... Ms. Melissa DUDLEY
88 Director of Marketing ... Ms. Traci ST. PIERRE
102 President & CEO USM Foundation ... Ms. Cecile AITCHISON
46 Assoc VP Research/Dean Grad Stds ... Dr. Samantha LANGLEY-TURNBAUGH
36 Director of Student Placement ... Mr. Joseph M. AUSTIN

University of New England (A)

11 Hills Beach Road, Biddeford ME 04005-9988
County: York FICE Identification: 002050
Unit ID: 161457
Telephone: (207) 283-0171 Carnegie Class: Master's L
FAX Number: (207) 282-6379 Calendar System: Semester
URL: www.une.edu
Established: 1831 Annual Undergrad Tuition & Fees: $31,980
Enrollment: 5,666 Coed
Affiliation or Control: Independent Non-Profit IRS Status: 501(c)3
Highest Offering: Doctorate
Program: Occupational; 2-Year Principally Bachelor's Creditable; Liberal Arts And General; Teacher Preparatory; Professional
Accreditation: EH, ACBSP, ADNUR, ANEST, ARCPA, DENT, DH, NUR, OSTEO, OT, PH, PHAR, PTA, SW

01 President ... Dr. Danielle RIPICH
04 Executive Asst to the President ... Ms. Holly HAMMOND NASS
05 Vice Pres Academic Affairs/Provost ... Dr. James KOELBL
23 Sr Vice Pres for Health Affairs ... Mr. Douglas WOOD
18 Vice Pres of Operations ... Mr. William BOLA
88 Vice President Clinical Affairs ... Dr. Dora MILLS
10 Vice Pres Fiscal Services ... Ms. Nicole TRUFANT
30 Vice Pres Institutional Advancement ... Mr. John NORTON
32 Vice Pres Student Affairs ... Dr. Cynthia FORREST
26 Vice Pres of Communications ... Vacant
102 Asst VP Institutional Advancement ... Mr. Scott MARCHILDON
15 Exec Dir Human Resources ... Ms. Sharen BEAULIEU
30 Assoc VP Institutional Advancement ... Mr. William CHANCE
82 Vice Pres Global Affairs ... Dr. Anouar MAJID
46 VP for Research & Scholarship ... Dr. Edward BILSKY
106 Assoc Provost of On Line Education ... Dr. Martha WILSON
49 Dean College Arts & Sciences ... Dr. Jeanne HEY
17 Dean College Health Professions ... Dr. Tim FORD
63 Dean College Osteopathic Medicine ... Dr. Douglas WOOD
67 Dean College of Pharmacy ... Dr. Gayle BRAZEAU
52 Dean College of Dental Medicine ... Dr. James KOELBL
58 Interim Dean Graduate Studies ... Ms. Ellen BEAULIEU
63 Director School of Nurse Anesthesia ... Ms. Maribeth MASSIE
62 Dean Library Services ... Mr. Andrew GOLUB
35 Dean of Students ... Mr. Mark NAHORNEY
88 Asst Dean Student Support Svcs ... Mr. John LANGEVIN
17 Assoc Dean College Health Prof ... Mrs. Karen PARDUE
66 Assoc Director of Nursing ... Ms. Patricia MORGAN
49 Assoc Dean College Arts & Sciences ... Ms. Paulette ST. OURS
76 Assoc Dean Health Professions ... Dr. Clay GRAYBEAL
29 Director Alumni Relations ... Ms. Amy HAIL
39 Asst Dean of Students Res Life ... Ms. Jennifer DEBURRO
41 Interim Director of Athletics ... Mr. Curt SMYTH
09 Director for Institutional Research ... Mr. Kuldeep PUPPALA
88 Director Campus Planning ... Mr. Alan THIBEAULT
19 Director Campus Safety & Security ... Mr. Donald CLARK
52 Director of Dental Hygiene ... Ms. Bernice MILLS
88 Director Exercise & Sport Perf ... Mr. Wayne LAMARRE
66 Director of Nursing HSM ... Ms. Bonnie DAVIS
63 Director Occupational Therapy ... Mr. Regi ROBNETT
63 Director of Physical Therapy ... Mr. Michael SHELDON
96 Director Purch/Risk Mgmt/Contract ... Mr. William BOLA
62 Director Reference Services ... Ms. Barbara SWARTZLANDER
28 Director Multi-Cultural Affairs ... Ms. Donna GASPAR JARVIS
70 Interim Director Social Work ... Dr. Clay GRAYBEAL
88 Director Sponsored Programs ... Mr. Nicholas GERE
38 Director Student Counseling ... Dr. John LANGEVIN
37 Exec Director Student Fiscal Svcs ... Mr. Paul HENDERSON
07 Exec Director for U Admissions ... Mrs. Stacy GATO
06 Registrar ... Ms. Joan MOYNAHAN

MARYLAND

Allegany College of Maryland (B)

12401 Willowbrook Road, SE,
Cumberland MD 21502-2596
County: Allegany FICE Identification: 002057
Unit ID: 161688
Telephone: (301) 784-5000 Carnegie Class: Assoc/Pub-R-M
FAX Number: (301) 784-5050 Calendar System: Semester
URL: www.allegany.edu
Established: 1961 Annual Undergrad Tuition & Fees (In-District): $3,388
Enrollment: 3,672 Coed
Affiliation or Control: Local IRS Status: 501(c)3
Highest Offering: Associate Degree
Program: Occupational; 2-Year Principally Bachelor's Creditable
Accreditation: M, ADNUR, COARC, COMTA, DH, MAC, MLTAD, OTA, PTAA, RAD

01 President ... Dr. Cynthia S. BAMBARA
05 Int Vice Pres Instructional Affairs ... Dr. David HINDS
10 Vice President Finance ... Mr. David DEWITT
30 VP Col Advancement/Enroll Mgmt ... Mrs. Linda A. PRICE
11 VP Administrative Services ... Mrs. Mona CLITES
32 VP Student Services ... Dr. B. Renee CONNER
51 VP of Continuing Education ... Mr. Jeff KIRK
14 Assoc Dean Computer Services ... Mr. Tim PELESKY
21 Associate Dean of Finance ... Vacant
30 Director of Grants & Development ... Mr. David R. JONES
37 Director Student Financial Aid ... Mrs. Vicki SMITH
07 Director Admissions/Registration ... Mrs. Cathy M. NOLAN
18 Director of Physical Plant ... Mr. Adam PHIPPS
08 Interim Director Learning Resources ... Mrs. Teresa WILMES
26 Dir Public Relations/Recruitment ... Ms. Shauna N. MCQUADE
41 Interim Athletic Director ... Mr. Steve BAZARNIC
29 Secretary Alumni Association ... Vacant
50 Director of Business/Indus Training ... Vacant
51 Director Professional Cont Educ ... Mrs. Becky L. RUPPERT
09 Director of Institutional Research ... Mr. Scott HARRAH
69 Director Health Prof Cont Education ... Ms. Linda ATKINSON
38 Director Student Counseling ... Vacant
15 Director Personnel ... Mrs. Rhonda WILES

Ana G. Mendez University System Capital Area Campus (C)

11006 Veirs Mill Road, Wheaton MD 20902
Telephone: (301) 949-2224 Identification: 770924
Accreditation: &M

† Main campus is Sistema Universitario Ana G. Mendez in Rio Piedras, PR.

Anne Arundel Community College (D)

101 College Parkway, Arnold MD 21012-1895
County: Anne Arundel FICE Identification: 002058
Unit ID: 161767
Telephone: (410) 777-2222 Carnegie Class: Assoc/Pub-S-SC
FAX Number: (410) 777-2489 Calendar System: Semester
URL: www.aacc.edu
Established: 1961 Annual Undergrad Tuition & Fees (In-District): $3,750
Enrollment: 17,650 Coed
Affiliation or Control: State/Local IRS Status: 501(c)3
Highest Offering: Associate Degree
Program: Occupational; 2-Year Principally Bachelor's Creditable
Accreditation: M, ACFEI, ADNUR, ARCPA, CAHIIM, EMT, MAC, MLTAD, PTAA, RAD, SURGT

01 President ... Dr. Dawn LINDSAY
05 VP for Learning ... Dr. Karen L. HAYS
10 VP Learning Resources Management ... Ms. Melissa A. BEARDMORE
03 VP for Learner Support Services ... Ms. Felicia L. PATTERSON
106 Dean of Virtual Campus ... Ms. Jean M. RUNYON
20 Associate VP for Learning ... Ms. Trish A. CASEY-WHITEMAN
30 Director of Development ... Vacant
32 Dean of Student Services ... Dr. Ivan L. HARRELL
76 Dean School Health/Wellness/Phys Ed ... Dr. Claire L. SMITH
66 Director of Nursing ... Ms. Beth Anne BATTURS
49 Dean School Arts & Sciences ... Dr. Daniel F. SYMANCYK
72 Dean Sch Bus/Computing/Tech Stds ... Ms. Kelly A. KOERMER
51 Dean Sch of Continuing/Prof Studies ... Dr. Faith A. HARLAND-WHITE
103 Dean of Workforce Development ... Dr. Laura E. WEIDNER
22 Controller ... Ms. Martha D. ROTHSCHILD
21 Executive Director of Finance ... Mr. Andrew P. LITTLE
14 Chief Technology Officer/Info Svcs ... Ms. Shirin M. GOODARZI
08 Director of Library ... Ms. Cynthia K. STEINHOFF
06 Registrar ... Ms. Nancy A. BEIER
09 Dean Plng/Rsrch/Inst Assess ... Dr. Ricka K. FINE
15 Exec Director of Human Resources ... Ms. Suzanne L. BOYER
26 Exec Director PR & Marketing ... Mr. Daniel B. BAUM
37 Director of Financial Aid ... Mr. Richard C. HEATH
07 Dir Admissions/Enroll Development ... Mr. Thomas J. MCGINN, III
11 Exec Dir of Administrative Services ... Mr. Maury L. CHAPUT, JR.
35 Asst Dean Student Devel & Success ... Ms. Terry M. CLAY
84 Asst Dean Enrollment Services ... Dr. John F. GRABOWSKI
36 Dir Counseling/Advising/Reten Svcs ... Ms. Bonnie J. GARRETT
35 Director of Student Life ... Ms. Christine M. STORCK
22 Federal Compliance Officer ... Ms. Kelly A. KOERMER

40 College Bookstore Manager ... Mr. Steven M. PEGG
19 Director Public Safety ... Mr. J. Gary LYLE
96 Director Purchasing/Contracting ... Vacant
29 Coordinator Alumni Relations ... Ms. Leslie H. SALVAIL
23 Coordinator Health Services ... Ms. Beth A. MAYS
41 Intercollegiate Athletics Coordntor ... Mr. D. Bruce SPRINGER
28 Coordinator of Minority Recruitment ... Mr. James T. JACKSON, JR.
94 Coordinator of Women's Studies ... Dr. Suzanne J. SPOOR
88 Director of Environmental Center ... Dr. M. Stephen AILSTOCK
88 Director Center Study Local Issues ... Dr. Daniel D. NATAF
88 Dir Homeland Sec/Crim Justice Inst ... Dr. Tyrone POWERS
53 Director TEACH Institute ... Ms. Colleen K. EISENBEISER
88 Director Hosp/Cul Arts/Tourism Inst ... Ms. Mary Ellen MASON
38 Coordinator Inst for the Future ... Mr. Steven T. HENICK
88 Dir Sarbanes Center/Pub & Cmty Svc ... Ms. Cathleen H. DOYLE

Bais HaMedrash & Mesivta of Baltimore (E)

6823 Old Pimlico Road, Baltimore MD 21209
County: Baltimore FICE Identification: 041884
Unit ID: 476601
Telephone: (410) 486-0006 Carnegie Class: Not Classified
FAX Number: (410) 602-9738 Calendar System: Semester
Established: 1997 Annual Undergrad Tuition & Fees: $16,300
Enrollment: 42 Male
Affiliation or Control: Independent Non-Profit IRS Status: 501(c)3
Highest Offering: First Talmudic Degree
Program: Professional; Religious Emphasis
Accreditation: RABN

01 Rosh Yeshiva ... Rabbi Zvi Dov SLANGER

Baltimore City Community College (F)

2901 Liberty Heights Avenue, Baltimore MD 21215-7893
County: Baltimore City FICE Identification: 002061
Unit ID: 161864
Telephone: (410) 462-8300 Carnegie Class: Assoc/Pub-U-MC
FAX Number: (410) 462-7795 Calendar System: Semester
URL: www.bccc.edu
Established: 1947 Annual Undergrad Tuition & Fees (In-District): $3,062
Enrollment: 5,474 Coed
Affiliation or Control: State/Local IRS Status: 501(c)3
Highest Offering: Associate Degree
Program: Occupational; 2-Year Principally Bachelor's Creditable
Accreditation: M, ACBSP, ADNUR, CAHIIM, COARC, DH, PTAA, SURGT

01 Interim President ... Dr. Carolyn HULL ANDERSON
10 Vice President Business & Finance ... Ms. Susan NIEHOFF
32 Vice President for Student Affairs ... Vacant
05 Vice Pres Academic Affairs ... Dr. Peggy BRADFORD
51 Interim Vice Pres Bus & Cont Educ ... Mr. Gregory MASON
84 Dean of Enrollment Management ... Ms. Julia PITTMAN
30 Int VP of Institutional Advancement ... Mr. Patrick ONLEY
18 Int Dir Facilities/Plng/Operations ... Mr. Gregorio GOMEZ
21 Controller/Chief of Accounting ... Ms. Sabina SILKWORTH
37 Director Student Financial Aid ... Ms. Vera BROOKS
13 Chief Information Tech Officer ... Mr. Antonio HERRERA
08 Director Library/Media Services ... Ms. Stephanie REIDY
06 Exec Director Records/Registrar ... Ms. Kathleen STYLES
15 Interim Exec Director of HR ... Ms. Sheryl NELSON
09 Director Institutional Research ... Mr. Gerard REICHENBERG
102 Director of Foundation ... Ms. Leslie REED
100 Interim Chief of Staff ... Dr. Sheila WHITE-DANIELS
96 Chief Procurement Officer ... Mr. Dan COLMAN

Capitol College (G)

11301 Springfield Road, Laurel MD 20708-9759
County: Prince Georges FICE Identification: 001436
Unit ID: 162061
Telephone: (301) 369-2800 Carnegie Class: Spec/Engg
FAX Number: (301) 953-1442 Calendar System: Semester
URL: www.capitol-college.edu
Established: 1927 Annual Undergrad Tuition & Fees: $21,648
Enrollment: 904 Coed
Affiliation or Control: Independent Non-Profit IRS Status: 501(c)3
Highest Offering: Doctorate
Program: Technical Emphasis
Accreditation: M, ENG, ENGT, IACBE

01 President ... Dr. Michael T. WOOD
05 Vice President for Academic Affairs ... Dr. W. Vic MACONACHY
10 Vice Pres Finance/Administration ... Derick A. VEENSTRA
46 Vice Pres for Planning/Assessment ... Dianne M. VEENSTRA
30 Vice President Advancement ... Dr. Donna THOMAS
88 Dean Mgmt and Info Sciences ... Dr. Helen G. BARKER
32 Dean Student Life & Retention ... Melinda A. BUNNELL-RHYNE
54 Dean Engineering/Computer Sci/Tech ... Dr. Robert WEILER
06 Director of Registration & Records ... Sallie MCKEVITT
08 Dir Library/Information Literacy ... Rick A. SAMPLE
11 Dir Administration/Human Resources ... Jacquelyn K. ENRIGHT
07 Senior Director Admissions ... George H. WALLS
26 Director Marketing Communications ... Megan CAMPBELL
29 Assistant Dir Development ... Rachel BURNS
07 Dir Admissions Operations ... Meghan YOUNG
37 Director of Financial Aid ... Suzanne THOMPSON
21 Director of Finance ... Kathleen WERNER
51 Director of Continuing Education ... Vacant

91 Director Administrative Computing .... Allen EXNER
18 Director of Maintenance .... Harry TRAPP

Carroll Community College (A)

1601 Washington Road, Westminster MD 21157-6913
County: Carroll FICE Identification: 031007
Unit ID: 405872
Telephone: (410) 386-8000 Carnegie Class: Assoc/Pub-S-SC
FAX Number: (410) 386-8181 Calendar System: Semester
URL: www.carrollcc.edu
Established: 1993 Annual Undergrad Tuition & Fees (In-District): $3,302
Enrollment: 5,473 Coed
Affiliation or Control: Local IRS Status: 501(c)3
Highest Offering: Associate Degree
Program: Occupational; 2-Year Principally Bachelor's Creditable
Accreditation: M, PTAA

01 President .... Dr. Faye PAPPALARDO
11 Exec Vice Pres Administration .... Mr. Alan M. SCHUMAN
05 VP of Academic & Student Affairs .... Dr. James D. BALL
45 VP Planning Marketing & Assessment .... Dr. Craig A. CLAGETT
51 VP Continuing Education/Training .... Ms. Karen L. MERKLE
04 Executive Assistant to President .... Ms. Sylvia BLAIR
30 Exec Dir Inst Devel/College Found .... Mr. Steven WANTZ
88 Integrity & Judicial Affairs Advoca .... Mr. Joel M. HOSKOWITZ
88 Director Transfer .... Ms. Toyette SULLIVAN
35 Dean of Student Affairs .... Dr. Michael KIPHART
76 Dean of STEM & Allied Health .... Mr. Robert BROWN
49 Dean of Arts/Letters & Soc Sci .... Mr. Steve GEPPI
88 Director of Learning Outcomes .... Dr. Janet OHLEMACHER
38 Director of Advising/Counseling .... Ms. Janenne CORCORAN
07 Director of Admissions .... Ms. Candace EDWARDS
89 Dir Student Life/1st Yr Pgm/Honor .... Ms. Kristie CRUMLEY
06 Registrar .... Ms. Lauren SHIELDS
37 Director of Financial Aid .... Mr. John GAY
66 Director of Nursing .... Ms. Nancy PERRY
08 Sr Dir Library/Media/Dist Lrn .... Mr. Alan BOGAGE
106 Director Distance Lrng Programs .... Dr. Susan BIRO
26 Director Publications/Comm Design .... Ms. Eleni SWENGLER
09 Director Institutional Research .... Ms. Janet NICKELS
103 Sr Dir Cont Ed/Workforce/Bus Devel . Ms. Kathleen T. MENASCHE
31 Sr Dir Lifelong Lrng/Pgm Support .... Ms. Sally LONG
105 Director of Network & Tech Services .... Ms. Patti DAVIS
21 Director Fiscal Affairs .... Mr. Timothy LEAGUE
15 Director Human Resources .... Ms. Bridget S. LEIMBACH
18 Director Facilities Management .... Ms. Terry BOWEN

Cecil College (B)

One Seahawk Drive, North East MD 21901-1999
County: Cecil FICE Identification: 008308
Unit ID: 162104
Telephone: (410) 287-6060 Carnegie Class: Assoc/Pub-S-SC
FAX Number: (410) 287-1026 Calendar System: Semester
URL: www.cecil.edu
Established: 1968 Annual Undergrad Tuition & Fees (In-District): $3,240
Enrollment: 2,708 Coed
Affiliation or Control: State/Local IRS Status: 501(c)3
Highest Offering: Associate Degree
Program: Occupational; 2-Year Principally Bachelor's Creditable
Accreditation: M, ADNUR, EMT, MAC

01 President .... Dr. W. Stephen PANNILL
05 Vice President Academic Programs .... Dr. Mary WAY BOLT
11 Vice Pres Administrative Services .... Dr. Christine A. VALUCKAS
32 VP Students/Instit Effectiveness .... Dr. Diane C. LANE
13 VP/Chief Information Officer .... Mr. Steve DIFILIPO
30 Vice Pres Institutional Advancement .... Ms. Chris Ann SZEP
15 Director Human Resources .... Dr. Jim WILBURN
20 Dean of Academic Programs .... Dr. David LINTHICUM
31 Dean of Career/Community Education .... Ms. Debbie KLENK
66 Dean Nursing Ed/Alld Hlth/Hlth Sci .... Dr. Christy DRYER
18 Director of Facilities .... Mr. James PETTUS
37 Director of Financial Aid Services .... Mr. Stephen AMPERSAND
26 Director of Marketing .... Ms. Charlene CONOLLY
84 Director of Enrollment Management .... Ms. Cindy MISHOE
93 Director Minority Student Services .... Ms. Laney HOXTER
09 Director of Institutional Research .... Mr. Dan STOICESCU
06 Registrar/Dir Admiss & Registration .... Ms. S. Tomeka SWAN
08 Director of Library Services .... Ms. Lorraine MARTORANA
41 Director Athletics .... Mr. Ed DURHAM
29 Coordinator Alumni Relations .... Ms. Mary MOORE
04 Assistant to the President .... Ms. Dawn KISNER

Chesapeake College (C)

PO Box 8, 1000 College Circle, Wye Mills MD 21679-0008
County: Queen Annes FICE Identification: 004650
Unit ID: 162168
Telephone: (410) 822-5400 Carnegie Class: Assoc/Pub-R-M
FAX Number: (410) 827-5875 Calendar System: Semester
URL: www.chesapeake.edu
Established: 1965 Annual Undergrad Tuition & Fees (In-District): $4,110
Enrollment: 2,660 Coed
Affiliation or Control: State/Local IRS Status: 501(c)3
Highest Offering: Associate Degree
Program: Occupational; 2-Year Principally Bachelor's Creditable
Accreditation: M, ADNUR, PTAA, RAD, SURGT

01 President .... Dr. Barbara A. VINIAR
05 VP Academic Affairs & Econ Develop .... Dr. Kathryn A. BARBOUR
11 Vice Pres for Administrative Svcs .... Mr. Tim JONES
32 VP Student Success/Enrollment Svcs .... Dr. Richard D. MIDCAP
18 Director of Facilities .... Mr. Anthony PATTERSON
51 Continuing Education Dean .... Mr. Michael DUGAN
49 Dean for Liberal Arts & Sciences .... Dr. Eleanor WELSH
107 Dean for Career & Professional Stds .... Ms. Maureen A. GILMARTIN
72 VP Technology & Academic Support .... Mr. Douglass P. GRAY
08 Dean Lrng Res/Acad Sppt Svcs .... Ms. Chandra M. GIGLIOTTI-GURIDI
15 Director of Human Resources .... Ms. Susan A. CIANCHETTA
37 Director of Financial Aid .... Ms. Mindy M. SCHAFFER
30 Director Resource Development .... Ms. Lauren C. HALTERMAN
09 Dir Inst Planning/Research & Assmnt ..... Ms. Kimberly A. MILLER
07 Dean for Recruitment Services ..... Ms. Kathleen J. PETRICHENKO
26 Director of Public Information .... Ms. Marcie A. MOLLOY
06 Registrar .... Mr. James A. DAVIDSON
20 Dean for Retention Services .... Ms. Joan M. SEITZER

College of Southern Maryland (D)

PO Box 910, La Plata MD 20646-0910
County: Charles FICE Identification: 002064
Unit ID: 162122
Telephone: (301) 934-2251 Carnegie Class: Assoc/Pub-S-MC
FAX Number: (301) 934-7698 Calendar System: Semester
URL: www.csmd.edu
Established: 1958 Annual Undergrad Tuition & Fees (In-District): $4,170
Enrollment: 9,217 Coed
Affiliation or Control: Local IRS Status: 501(c)3
Highest Offering: Associate Degree
Program: Occupational; 2-Year Principally Bachelor's Creditable
Accreditation: M, ACBSP, ADNUR, PNUR, PTAA

01 President .... Dr. Bradley GOTTFRIED
05 Vice Pres Academic Affairs .... Dr. Sue SUBOCZ
12 Vice President Leonardtown Campus .... Dr. Tracy HARRIS
12 VP Prince Frederick Campus .... Dr. Richard FLEMING
102 VP Corporate/Cmty Training Inst .... Dr. Daniel MOSSER
10 VP Financial & Admin Services .... Mr. Tony JERNIGAN
32 VP Student/Instruc Support Svcs .... Dr. William COMEY
30 Vice President for Advancement .... Ms. Michelle GOODWIN
43 Vice President/General Counsel .... Mr. Craig PATENAUDE
20 Inter Assoc VP Academic Affairs .... Dr. Patrick ALLEN
09 Assoc VP Plng/Inst Effective/Rsrch .... Dr. Kelly MCMURRAY
84 Assoc VP Enrollment Mgmt Team .... Ms. Joan MIDDLETON
18 Director of Facilities .... Mr. Dave DALO
15 Exec Director Human Resources .... Dr. Denise BAILEY CLARK
26 Exec Director Community Relations .... Ms. Karen SMITH-HUPP
37 Director Financial Assistance .... Mr. Christian ZIMMERMANN
06 Registrar .... Ms. Carol HARRISON
08 Director of Library .... Mr. Thomas REPENNING
66 Chair Nursing Dept .... Dr. Laura POLK
35 Director of Athletics/Student Life .... Ms. Michelle RUBLE
40 General Mgr College Store .... Ms. Marcy GANNON
07 Int Director Admissions Department .... Ms. Joan MIDDLETON
38 Director Advisement/Career Services .... Ms. Susan STRAUS
96 Director of Procurement .... Mr. Tom KELLEY
28 Ex Dir Diversity/Equal Opportunity .... Ms. Makeba CLAY

The Community College of Baltimore County (E)

7201 Rossville Blvd., Baltimore MD 21237-3899
County: Baltimore FICE Identification: 002063
Unit ID: 434672
Telephone: (443) 840-2222 Carnegie Class: Assoc/Pub-S-MC
FAX Number: (443) 840-1100 Calendar System: Semester
URL: www.ccbcmd.edu
Established: Annual Undergrad Tuition & Fees (In-District): $4,077
Enrollment: 25,188 Coed
Affiliation or Control: Local IRS Status: 501(c)3
Highest Offering: Associate Degree
Program: Occupational; 2-Year Principally Bachelor's Creditable
Accreditation: M, ACBSP, ADNUR, CAHIIM, COARC, COMTA, DH, EMT, FUSER, MLTAD, MUS, OTA, POLYT, RAD, RTT, SURGT, THEA

01 President .... Dr. Sandra L. KURTINITIS
30 Vice Pres Institutional Advancement .... Mr. Kenneth WESTARY
10 Vice Pres Finance/Administration .... Ms. Melissa HOPP
05 Vice Pres Instruction .... Dr. Mark MCCOLLOCH
84 VP Enrollment & Student Services .... Dr. Richard LILLEY
26 Sr Director for Public Relations .... Ms. Mary DELUCA
16 Senior Director Human Resources .... Ms. Penny MILSOM

Faith Theological Seminary (F)

529 Walker Avenue, Baltimore MD 21212
County: Baltimore City Identification: 667016
Telephone: (410) 323-6211 Carnegie Class: Not Classified
FAX Number: (410) 323-6331 Calendar System: Semester
URL: www.faiththeological.org
Established: 1937 Annual Undergrad Tuition & Fees: $5,800
Enrollment: 134 Coed
Affiliation or Control: Non-denominational IRS Status: 501(c)3
Highest Offering: Doctorate; No Lower Division
Program: Religious Emphasis
Accreditation: @TRACS

01 President .... Dr. Norman J. MANOHAR
05 Academic Dean .... Dr. Stephen T. HAGUE
06 Registrar .... Ms. Aruna S. MANOHAR
07 Admissions Director .... Mr. Michael DEWALT

Fortis College (G)

4351 Garden City Drive, Landover MD 20785
Telephone: (301) 459-3650 Identification: 770731
Accreditation: ACICS, DH

† Main campus is Fortis Institute in Erie, PA.

Frederick Community College (H)

7932 Opossumtown Pike, Frederick MD 21702-2097
County: Frederick FICE Identification: 002071
Unit ID: 162557
Telephone: (301) 846-2400 Carnegie Class: Assoc/Pub-S-SC
FAX Number: (301) 846-2498 Calendar System: Semester
URL: www.frederick.edu
Established: 1957 Annual Undergrad Tuition & Fees (In-District): $4,022
Enrollment: 7,629 Coed
Affiliation or Control: State/Local IRS Status: 501(c)3
Highest Offering: Associate Degree
Program: Occupational; 2-Year Principally Bachelor's Creditable
Accreditation: M, ADNUR, COARC, NMT, SURGT

01 President .... Mr. Douglas D. BROWNING
05 Interim Vice Pres for Learning .... Mr. David CROGHAN
11 Int Vice Pres for Administration .... Ms. Dana MCDONALD
32 Int Vice Pres for Learning Support .... Dr. Rich HANEY
30 Chief Development Officer .... Mr. Christopher A. MASSI
13 Chief Technology Officer .... Mr. Wayne KELLER
84 Assoc VP Enrollment Management .... Ms. Laura MEARS
15 Assoc VP Human Resources .... Mr. Donald FRANCIS
10 Int Assoc VP for Fiscal & Aux Svcs .... Ms. Angela LUDEMAN
06 Assoc Registrar .... Ms. Deidre WEILMINSTER
51 Int Assoc VP Learning/Dean CE & WD .... Ms. Karen REILLY
88 Assoc VP Teaching & Learning .... Dr. Christine HELFRICH
35 Int Assoc VP/Dean of Students .... Ms. Jeanni WINSTON-MUIR
20 Assoc VP Lrng/Dean Academic & Prof .... Dr. Gerald L. BOYD
18 Exec Dir Facilities Management .... Vacant
08 Exec Dir Library .... Mr. Mick O'LEARY
09 Exec Dir Outcome Assess/Plng/Res .... Dr. Gohar FARAHANI
19 Exec Dir Risk Mgmt/Public Services .... Mr. Walter SMITH
26 Exec Dir Marketing/Public Relations . Mr. Michael H. PRITCHARD
38 Exec Dir Advising & Counseling .... Ms. Debra SANFORD
37 Exec Dir Financial Aid .... Ms. Brenda DAYHOFF
88 Exec Dir Academic Ops & Ext Lng .... Ms. Michelle HALL
04 Exec Asst to the President & Board .... Ms. Diane MORTON
88 Director Monroe Center .... Ms. Patricia TORRES
14 Exec Dir of Software Development .... Mr. Adam RENO
41 Director of Athletics .... Dr. Tom JANDOVITZ
88 Director Children's Center .... Ms. Teri BICKEL
88 Director Learning Technologies .... Mr. Alberto RAMIREZ
106 Director Distance Learning .... Mr. Jurgen HILKE
88 Dir Student Engagement/Student Life .... Ms. Jeanni WINSTON-MUIR
88 Dir Multicultural Student Services .... Mr. Chad ADERO
88 Director Office of Adult Services .... Ms. Janice BROWN
88 Dir Svcs for Students w/ Disbilities .... Ms. Kate KRAMER-JEFFERSON
07 Director of Admissions .... Ms. Lisa FREEL
88 Dir Career & Transfer Services .... Ms. Lorraine DODSON
28 Director of Diversity .... Vacant
14 Dir Network Info Security & Telecom .... Mr. Joe MARSHALL
105 Director Web Services .... Ms. Cindy OSBON
88 Coordinator Veterans Services .... Ms. Rachel NACHLAS
45 Ex Dir Strategic Plng/Inst Effect .... Dr. Bonnie L. THOMAS
31 Exec Director Auxillary Services .... Mr. Frederick HOCKENBERRY
88 Dir Business Systems & Compliance .... Ms. Karen REILLY
88 Director Administrative Projects .... Ms. Linda SEEK
30 Asst Dir Institutional Advancement .... Ms. Amanda GLENN
88 Manager Food Services .... Ms. Donna S. SOWERS

Garrett College (I)

687 Mosser Road, McHenry MD 21541-1265
County: Garrett FICE Identification: 010014
Unit ID: 162609
Telephone: (301) 387-3000 Carnegie Class: Assoc/Pub-R-S
FAX Number: (301) 387-3038 Calendar System: Semester
URL: www.garrettcollege.edu
Established: 1966 Annual Undergrad Tuition & Fees (In-District): $3,368
Enrollment: 874 Coed
Affiliation or Control: State/Local IRS Status: 501(c)3
Highest Offering: Associate Degree
Program: Occupational; 2-Year Principally Bachelor's Creditable
Accreditation: M, EMT

01 President .... Dr. Richard MACLENNAN
04 Executive Assistant to President .... Ms. Marcia KNEPP
10 Dean of Administration & Finance .... Ms. Josephine GILMAN
05 Interim Dean of Instruction .... Mr. James ALLEN, JR.
51 Dean of Cont Educ/Workforce Devel .... Ms. Julie YODER
13 Interim Director of IT .... Ms. Jami REYNOLDS
26 Dean of Marketing & Enrollment Mgmt .... Ms. Ann WELLHAM
32 Dean of Student Life .... Dr. George BRELSFORD
30 Dir Develop/Exec Dir Foundation .... Ms. Cherie KRUG
06 Director of Records & Registration .... Ms. Kim DEGIOVANNI
37 Director of Financial Aid .... Ms. Cissy VANSICKLE
08 Interim Library Director .... Ms. Ellen SHEAFFER

21 Director of Business Office .... Ms. Katherine BROWNING
18 Plant Manager ....Mr. Hugh SCHRIER
15 Director of Human Resources ....Ms. Linda K. FIKE
65 Dir of Natural Res/Wildlife Tech ....Mr. Kevin DODGE
41 Interim Director of Athletics ....Mr. Dennis GIBSON
50 Director of Business/Info Tech ....Dr. Qing YUAN
36 Dir Acad Career & Trans Advising ....Ms. Judy CARBONE
96 Purchasing/Accounts Payable ....Ms. Bonnie BROADWATER
09 Asst Dir Institutional Research ....Ms. Kalie ASHBY
40 Bookstore Manager .... Ms. Margi L. PERFETTI
07 Director of Admissions ....Ms. Rachelle DAVIS
38 Coordinator of Counseling Services ....Ms. Madonna POOL
17 Coordinator of Health Services .... Ms. Jamie RESH-KAMP
39 Coordinator of Residential Services .... Ms. Tracy BARCUS
45 Director of Institutional Planning ....Mr. James ALLEN, JR.
105 Webmaster ....Ms. Linda STEVANUS
79 Dir of Humanities & Social Sciences .... Mr. Ron SKIDMORE
88 Director of Adventure Sports ....Mr. Michael LOGSDON
81 Dir of Math/Science & Teacher Educ ....Mr. Alexander TUEL

Goucher College (A)

1021 Dulaney Valley Road, Towson MD 21204-2780
County: Baltimore FICE Identification: 002073
Unit ID: 162654
Telephone: (410) 337-6000 Carnegie Class: Bac/A&S
FAX Number: (410) 337-6123 Calendar System: Semester
URL: www.goucher.edu
Established: 1885 Annual Undergrad Tuition & Fees: $39,084
Enrollment: 2,254 Coed
Affiliation or Control: Independent Non-Profit IRS Status: 501(c)3
Highest Offering: Master's
Program: Liberal Arts And General; Teacher Preparatory
Accreditation: M

01 President ....Mr. Sanford J. UNGAR
05 Provost & Chief Academic Officer ....Dr. Marc ROY
32 Vice Pres/Dean of Students ....Dr. Bryan F. COKER
30 Vice Pres Devel/Alumni Affs ....Vacant
84 Vice President Enrollment Mgmt .... Mr. Michael O'LEARY
26 Vice President for Communications ....Vacant
13 VP for Technology and Planning ....Mr. Bill LEIMBACH
43 VP & General Counsel ....Ms. Laura BURTON-GRAHAM
20 Associate Dean Academic Affairs ....Ms. Janine BOWEN
82 Assoc Dean International Studies ....Mr. Daniel NORTON
35 Assoc Dean for Student Engagement ....Ms. Emily PERL
15 Vice President for Human Resources ....Ms. Deborah LUPTON
21 Controller ....Mr. Alex ANTKOWIAK
07 Director of Admissions ....Mr. Carlton E. SURBECK, III
08 Librarian ....Ms. Nancy MAGNUSON
29 Exec Dir for Alumnae/i Engagement ....Ms. Holly SELBY
36 Director of Career Development ....Ms. Traci MARTIN
58 Director Grad Program in Education .... Ms. Phyllis SUNSHINE
06 Registrar ....Mr. Andrew WESTFALL
09 Director of Institutional Research ....Ms. Pallabi ROY
10 Dir Business/Auxiliary Services ....Mr. Calvin GLADDEN
18 Dir Facilities Management Services ....Mr. Harold TINSLEY
37 Director Financial Aid ....Ms. Stephanie BENDER
93 Asst Dean for Multicultural Stds ....Ms. Mary TANDIA

Hagerstown Community College (B)

11400 Robinwood Drive, Hagerstown MD 21742-6590
County: Washington FICE Identification: 002074
Unit ID: 162690
Telephone: (240) 500-2000 Carnegie Class: Assoc/Pub-R-M
FAX Number: (301) 393-3682 Calendar System: Semester
URL: www.hagerstowncc.edu
Established: 1946 Annual Undergrad Tuition & Fees (In-District): $2,986
Enrollment: 5,106 Coed
Affiliation or Control: State/Local IRS Status: 501(c)3
Highest Offering: Associate Degree
Program: Occupational; 2-Year Principally Bachelor's Creditable
Accreditation: M, ADNUR, DA, EMT, PNUR, RAD

01 President ....Dr. Guy ALTIERI
05 Vice President of Academic Affairs ....Dr. David WARNER
11 Vice Pres Administration/Finance ....Ms. Anna M. BARKER
32 Dean of Students ....Dr. Jessica A. CHAMBERS
09 Dean of Plng/Inst Effectiveness ....Ms. Barbara E. MACHT
51 Dean Continuing Educ/Bus Svcs ....Ms. Theresa M. SHANK
18 Dir Facilities Management & Plng ....Vacant
07 Dir Admissions/Records/ Registration ....Ms. Robin A. BECKER-CORNBLATT
30 Exec Director College Advancement .... Ms. Stacey L. LOWMAN
26 Director Marketing/Public Info ......Ms. Elizabeth L. KIRKPATRICK
37 Director of Financial Aid ....Ms. Carolyn S. COX
106 Assoc Dean Inst Tech/Online Educ ....Dr. Julian K. HORTON
14 Dir Technology/Computer Studies ....Ms. Margaret C. SPIVEY
21 Director of Business Services ....Ms. Lita J. ORNER
66 Director of Nursing ....Ms. Karen S. HAMMOND
15 Director of Human Resources ....Ms. Donna M. MARRIOTT
41 Dir Athletics/Phys Ed/Leisure Stds ....Mr. Bernard A. JOHNSON
20 Director of Instruction ....Mr. Gerald C. HAINES
13 Director of Information Technology ....Mr. Craig M. FENTRESS
21 Director of Finance ....Mr. David C. BITTORF
88 Dir Organization Devel/Special Proj ....Vacant
76 Director of Health Sciences ....Ms. Angela D. STOOPS

Harford Community College (C)

401 Thomas Run Road, Bel Air MD 21015-1698
County: Harford FICE Identification: 002075
Unit ID: 162706
Telephone: (443) 412-2000 Carnegie Class: Assoc/Pub-S-SC
FAX Number: (443) 412-2120 Calendar System: Semester
URL: www.harford.edu
Established: 1957 Annual Undergrad Tuition & Fees (In-District): $2,593
Enrollment: 6,139 Coed
Affiliation or Control: Local IRS Status: 501(c)3
Highest Offering: Associate Degree
Program: Occupational; 2-Year Principally Bachelor's Creditable
Accreditation: M, ADNUR, HT, MAC

01 President ....Dr. Dennis GOLLADAY
05 Vice President Academic Affairs ....Dr. M. Annette HAGGRAY
10 Vice President Finance & Operations ... Mr. Fredrick P. JOHNSON
32 VP Student Affairs/Inst Effective ....Dr. Deborah J. CRUISE
31 VP Mkting/Dev/Community Relations .Ms. Brenda M. MORRISON
13 Chief Information Officer ....Dr. Christopher DELA ROSA
96 Asst Vice Pres Procurement ....Mr. Victor H. DODSON
84 Assoc VP Enrollment Services ....Dr. Karen L. SEMIEN
32 Assoc VP Student Development ....Dr. Diane L. RESIDES
21 Assoc VP Finance & Budget ....Mr. Stephen S. PHILLIPS
51 Assoc VP Continuing Educ & Training ....Dr. Zoann J. PARKER
18 Assoc VP Campus Operations ....Dr. Gregory A. DEAL
37 Director Financial Aid ....Ms. D. Lynn LEE
06 Registrar ....Vacant
26 Dir Marketing & Public Relations ....Ms. Nancy J. DYSARD
15 Dir Human Resources/Employee Dev ....Ms. Cheryl E. HICKSON
29 Director College/Alumni Development .... Ms. Denise M. DREGIER
08 Director Library & Info Resources .... Ms. Carol M. ALLEN
106 Dir eLearning & Instr Resources ....Mr. LeRoy A. TRUSTY
09 Dir Inst Research/Plng/Effective ....Vacant
38 Dir Advising/Career/Transfer Svcs .... Ms. J. Bonnie SULZBACH
40 Coordinator College Store ....Ms. Linda L. FIFE
07 Coordinator for Admissions ....Mr. Brian J. HAMMOND
29 Alumni Coordinator ....Ms. Lanell PATRICK
81 Dean Science/Tech/Engr/Math ....Ms. Deborah R. WROBEL
83 Dean Behavioral & Social Sciences ....Mr. Avery W. WARD
79 Dean Humanities ....Dr. Karry L. HATHAWAY
57 Dean Visual/Performing/Applied Arts ....Mr. Paul E. LABE
50 Dean Bus/Computing/Applied Tech ....Mr. John F. MAYHORNE
88 Dean Educ & Transitional Studies ....Mr. Carl E. HENDERSON
66 Dean Nursing & Allied Health Profs ....Ms. Laura C. PRESTON

Hood College (D)

401 Rosemont Avenue, Frederick MD 21701-8575
County: Frederick FICE Identification: 002076
Unit ID: 162760
Telephone: (301) 663-3131 Carnegie Class: Master's M
FAX Number: (301) 694-7653 Calendar System: Semester
URL: www.hood.edu
Established: 1893 Annual Undergrad Tuition & Fees: $33,280
Enrollment: 2,422 Coed
Affiliation or Control: Independent Non-Profit IRS Status: 501(c)3
Highest Offering: Master's
Program: Liberal Arts And General; Teacher Preparatory; Fine Arts Emphasis
Accreditation: M, ACBSP, SW, TED

01 President ....Dr. Ronald J. VOLPE
05 Provost/Dean of Faculty ....Dr. Katherine CONWAY-TURNER
10 Vice Pres Finance ....Mr. Charles G. MANN
30 VP for Institutional Advancement ....Ms. Nancy E. GILLECE
32 VP Student Life/Dean of Students ....Dr. Olivia G. WHITE
84 VP Undergrad/Grad Enrollment ....Dr. Kathleen BANDS
07 Director of Admissions ....Vacant
58 Dean of Graduate School ....Dr. Maria GREEN COWLES
20 Director CAAR ....Vacant
26 Exec Dir Marketing/Communications ....Mr. Dave DIEHL
29 Director of Alumnae/i Programs ....Ms. Linda ROTH
06 Registrar ....Mrs. Nanette MARKEY
08 Librarian ....Mrs. Jan SAMET
37 Director of Financial Aid ....Ms. Carol SCHROYER
15 Director of Human Resources ....Ms. Carol M. WUENSCHEL
18 Director of Facilities ....Mr. John WICHSER
13 Chief Technology Officer ....Mr. Cornelius R. FAY, III
09 Director of Institutional Research ....Ms. Cynthia EMORY

Howard Community College (E)

10901 Little Patuxent Parkway, Columbia MD 21044-3197
County: Howard FICE Identification: 008175
Unit ID: 162779
Telephone: (443) 518-1000 Carnegie Class: Assoc/Pub-S-SC
FAX Number: N/A Calendar System: Semester
URL: www.howardcc.edu
Established: 1966 Annual Undergrad Tuition & Fees (In-District): $4,318
Enrollment: 10,152 Coed
Affiliation or Control: State/Local IRS Status: 501(c)3
Highest Offering: Associate Degree
Program: Occupational; 2-Year Principally Bachelor's Creditable
Accreditation: M, ADNUR, CVT, EMT, MUS, PNUR, @PTAA, RAD

01 President ....Dr. Kathleen B. HETHERINGTON
32 Vice President of Student Services ....Dr. Cynthia J. PETERKA
05 Vice President of Academic Affairs ....Dr. Sharon PIERCE
10 Vice Pres of Administration/Finance .... Ms. Lynn C. COLEMAN
13 Vice President for Information Tech .... Mr. Thomas J. GLASER
51 Assoc Vice Pres Cont Education ....Ms. JoAnn HAWKINS
84 Assoc Vice Pres for Enroll Svcs ....Ms. Alison BUCKLEY
35 Assoc Vice Pres for Student Devel ....Ms. Janice L. MARKS
15 Associate Vice Pres Human Resources ....Mr. Dave JORDAN
21 Associate Vice Pres of Finance ....Ms. Janet L. CULLISON

09 Exec Dir Plng/Research & Org Dev ....Ms. Zoe A. IRVIN
18 Exec Dir Capital Proj/Facilities .... Mr. Charles NIGHTINGALE
101 Executive Associate to President ....Ms. Linda EMMERICH
27 Director of Strategic Marketing ....Ms. Jane SHARP
88 Director of Finance ....Ms. Amanda HUFFMAN
30 Exec Director of Development ....Ms. Melissa MATTEY
40 Director Auxiliary Services ....Ms. Arla J. WEBB
19 Director of Public Safety ....Mr. Ken MCGLYNN
35 Director Student Life ....Ms. Llatetra D. BROWN
04 Exec Assistant to the President ....Ms. Farida GUZDAR
96 Director of Purchasing ....Ms. Elizabeth H. MOSS
06 Registrar ....Ms. Catherine MUND

ITT Technical Institute (F)

7030 Dorsey Road, Suite 100, Hanover MD 21076
Telephone: (410) 694-4700 Identification: 770644
Accreditation: ACICS

† Main campus is ITT Technical Institute in Indianapolis, IN.

ITT Technical Institute (G)

11301 Red Run Boulevard, Owings Mills MD 21117-3246
Telephone: (443) 394-7115 Identification: 666377
Accreditation: ACICS

† Main campus is ITT Technical Institute in Indianapolis, IN.

Johns Hopkins University (H)

Charles and 34th Streets, Baltimore MD 21218-2680
County: Independent City FICE Identification: 002077
Unit ID: 162928
Telephone: (410) 516-8000 Carnegie Class: RU/VH
FAX Number: N/A Calendar System: Semester
URL: www.jhu.edu
Established: 1876 Annual Undergrad Tuition & Fees: $45,470
Enrollment: 20,871 Coed
Affiliation or Control: Independent Non-Profit IRS Status: 501(c)3
Highest Offering: Doctorate
Program: Liberal Arts And General; Teacher Preparatory; Professional
Accreditation: M, BBT, CACREP, CS, DIETC, DMS, ENG, ENGR, HSA, IPSY, MED, MIL, MUS, NMT, NURSE, PDPSY, PH, TED

01 President ....Mr. Ronald J. DANIELS
100 Sr Vice President/Chief of Staff ....Vacant
05 Provost & Sr VP Acad Affs ....Dr. Robert LIEBERMAN
17 CEO Johns Hopkins Medicine ....Dr. Paul B. ROTHMAN
10 Sr VP Finance & Administration ....Mr. Daniel G. ENNIS
29 VP for Development & Alum Relations ......Mr. Fritz SCHROEDER
45 Vice Pres Strategic Initiatives ....Mr. Phillip SPECTOR
26 Vice Pres Comm/Public Affairs ....Mr. Glenn M. BIELER
43 Vice Pres/General Counsel ....Mr. Mark B. ROTENBERG
43 Deputy General Counsel ....Mr. Frederick SAVAGE
86 Vice Pres Govt/Community Affairs ....Mr. Thomas LEWIS
18 Vice Pres Real Estate/Campus Svcs ....Mr. Alan FISH
16 Vice Pres Human Resources ....Ms. Charlene M. HAYES
21 Vice Pres Finance & CFO ....Ms. Helene GRADY
21 Vice Pres Chief Investment Officer ...... Dr. Kathryn J. CRECELIUS
21 Chief Risk Officer ....Dr. Jonathan LINKS
20 Vice Provost for Student Affairs .... Dr. Kevin SHOLLENBERGER
20 Vice Provost Faculty Affairs ....Dr. Barbara LANDAU
20 Asst Vice Provost Accred/Acad Svcs ....Mr. Philip TANG
84 Vice Provost for Admiss & Fin Aid ....Mr. David PHILLIPS
58 Vice Provost Grad/Post-Doc Programs .. Dr. Jonathan A. BAGGER
88 Vice Provost International Programs ....Dr. Pam CRANSTON
27 Vice Provost Info Technology/CIO ....Ms. Stephanie REEL
22 Vice Provost Institutional Equity ....Ms. Caroline LAGUERRE-BROWN
46 Vice Provost Research ....Dr. Scott L. ZEGER
09 Vice Provost Institutional Research ....Mr. Sean FAHEY
09 Asst Provost Institutional Research ....Dr. Cathy J. LEBO
88 Asst Prov Intl Student Scholar Svc ....Mr. James BRAILER
82 Dean Nitze School Adv Intl Studies .... Dr. Vali NASR
49 Dean Krieger School Arts & Sciences ....Dr. Kathleen NEWMAN
50 Dean Carey Business School ....Dr. Bernard FERRARI
53 Dean School of Education ....Dr. David W. ANDREWS
54 Int Dean Whiting Sch Engineering ....Dr. Andrew DOUGLAS
63 Dean School of Medicine ....Dr. Paul ROTHMAN
66 Dean School of Nursing ....Dr. Patricia DAVIDSON
69 Dean Bloomberg School Public Health ....Dr. Michael J. KLAG
08 Dean Sheridan Libraries and Museums .... Mr. Winston G. TABB
64 Director Peabody Institute ....Vacant
81 Director Applied Physics Lab ....Mr. Ralph SEMMEL
96 Director Purchasing ....Mr. Paul N. BEYER
21 Controller ....Mr. Gregory S. OLER
19 Exec Director Safety & Security ....Mr. Edmund SKRODZKI
21 Exec Director Internal Audits ....Mr. Francis X. BOSSLE
27 Exec Director Comm & Public Affairs .... Mr. Dennis O'SHEA
88 Exec Director JH Real Estate ....Mr. Brian B. DEMBECK

Kaplan University (I)

18618 Crestwood Drive, Hagerstown MD 21742-2797
Telephone: (301) 766-3600 FICE Identification: 007946
Accreditation: &NH, ACBSP, CAHIIM, MAC, PHLEB

† Main campus is Kaplan University in Davenport, IA.

Lincoln College of Technology (J)

9325 Snowden River Parkway, Columbia MD 21046
County: Howard FICE Identification: 007936
Unit ID: 163028

Telephone: (410) 290-7100 Carnegie Class: Assoc/PrivFP
FAX Number: (410) 290-7880 Calendar System: Quarter
URL: www.lincolntech.com
Established: 1978 Annual Undergrad Tuition & Fees: $29,211
Enrollment: 800 Coed
Affiliation or Control: Proprietary IRS Status: Proprietary
Highest Offering: Associate Degree
Program: Occupational
Accreditation: ACCSC

01 Campus Director ....Mr. David DOCKMAN

Loyola University Maryland (A)

4501 N Charles Street, Baltimore MD 21210-2694
County: Independent City FICE Identification: 002078
Unit ID: 163046
Telephone: (410) 617-2000 Carnegie Class: Master's L
FAX Number: (410) 322-2768 Calendar System: Semester
URL: www.loyola.edu
Established: 1852 Annual Undergrad Tuition & Fees: $56,960
Enrollment: 5,978 Coed
Affiliation or Control: Roman Catholic IRS Status: 501(c)3
Highest Offering: Doctorate
Program: Liberal Arts And General; Teacher Preparatory
Accreditation: M, BUS, BUSA, CACREP, CLPSY, CS, ENG, SP, TED

01 President ....Rev. Brian F. LINNANE, SJ
03 Executive Vice President ....Dr. Susan DONOVAN
04 Assistant to the President ....Ms. Vicki WELLER
05 Vice President for Academic Affairs ....Dr. Timothy L. SNYDER
10 Vice Pres for Finance & Treasurer ....Mr. Randall GENTZLER
11 Vice President for Administration ....Dr. Terrence M. SAWYER
30 Vice President Advancement ....Ms. Megan GILLICK
32 VP Student Devel/Dean of Students .Dr. Sheilah SHAW HORTON
84 Vice Pres Enrollment Management ....Mr. Marc CAMILLE
20 Assoc Vice Pres Academic Affairs ....Ms. Jenny LOWRY
28 Asst VP Academic Affrs/Diversity ....Dr. Martha L. WHARTON
37 Asst Vice Pres of Financial Aid ....Mr. Mark L. LINDENMEYER
09 Asst VP of Institutional Research ....Ms. Terra SCHEHR
18 Assoc VP Facilities/Campus Services ....Ms. Helen SCHNEIDER
13 Asst VP of Technology Services/CIO ....Ms. Louise FINN
26 Dir Institutional Communications ....Vacant
35 Asst Vice Pres Student Development ....Mr. Xavier COLE
15 Asst Vice Pres for Human Resources ....Ms. Kathleen PARNELL
21 Asst Vice Pres for Administration ....Ms. Joan FLYNN
26 Asst VP Marketing/Communications ....Ms. Sharon HIGGINS
41 Asst VP/Director of Athletics ....Mr. James PAQUETTE
38 Dir Counsel Ctr/Ast VP Student Dev ....Dr. Donelda COOK
102 Dir Corporation & Foundation Rels ....Mr. Thomas BRUSH
07 Director Undergraduate Admissions ....Ms. Elena HICKS
07 Director of Graduate Admissions ....Ms. Maureen FAUX
06 Director of Records ....Ms. Rita L. STEINER
85 Director of International Programs ....Dr. Andre COLOMBAT
08 Director of Library ....Ms. Barbara PREECE
42 Interim Director of Campus Ministry .... Rev. Timothy BROWN, SJ
88 Dir Center Community Svc/ Justice ....Sr. Catherine GUGERTY, SSND
36 Director of The Career Center ....Dr. CreSaundra SILLS
88 Dir Alcohol/Drug Ed/Support Svcs ....Mr. Jan WILLIAMS
88 Director Recreational Sports ....Ms. Pamela WETHERBEE-METCALF
35 Director Student Activities ....Mr. Mark C. BRODERICK
88 Director ALANA Services ....Mr. Rodney PARKER
21 Temporary Controller ....Ms. Kelly NELSON
45 Director of Resource Management ....Mr. David DAUGHADAY
31 Director Event Svcs/Auxiliary Mgmt ....Mr. Joseph BRADLEY
88 Director of Project Management ....Mr. Laszlo PELY
88 Director Environment Health/Safety ....Mr. Thomas HETTLEMAN
19 Dir of Public Safety/Campus Police ....Mr. Timothy FOX
29 Director Alumni Relations ....Mr. Daniel BARNETT
44 Director of Annual Giving ....Ms. Jane Curley HOGGE
27 Director of Creative Services ....Mr. Brian HATCHER
88 Director Advancement Services ....Mr. Ian WEBSTER
89 Dean of Freshman & Academic Svcs ....Dr. Ilona MCGUINESS
49 Dean College of Arts & Sciences ....Rev. James F. MIRACKY, SJ
50 Dean Sellinger Sch Business & Mgmt ....Ms. Karyl LEGGIO
49 Assistant Dean Arts & Sciences ....Dr. Suzanne KEILSON
50 Assistant Dean for Business Program ....Ms. Ann ATTANASIO
88 Associate Dean of Students ....Ms. Michelle CHEATEM
58 AVP for Graduate Studies ....Ms. Amanda THOMAS
18 Dir Facilities Management ....Mr. Robert WALLETT

Maple Springs Baptist Bible College & Seminary (B)

4130 Belt Road, Capitol Heights MD 20743-5712
County: Prince Georges FICE Identification: 038224
Unit ID: 446394
Telephone: (301) 736-3631 Carnegie Class: Spec/Faith
FAX Number: (301) 735-6507 Calendar System: Semester
URL: www.msbbcs.edu
Established: 1986 Annual Undergrad Tuition & Fees: $4,590
Enrollment: 99 Coed
Affiliation or Control: Baptist IRS Status: 501(c)3
Highest Offering: Doctorate
Program: Religious Emphasis
Accreditation: TRACS

01 President ....Dr. Larry W. JORDAN
04 Executive Assistant to President ....Dr. Jerome S. TARVER
03 Executive Vice President ....Dr. Vivian E. BESS
05 Vice President Academic Affairs ....Mr. Lewis ANTHONY
11 Vice Pres Administration & Finance ....Dr. Jerrye B. FELICIANA
73 Chair Dept Church Vocations ....Dr. Carl KEELS
88 Academic Dean Seminary Div ....Dr. Daryl WATSON
06 Director Records/Admissions ....Ms. Esther BIRCH
09 Dir Institutional Plng/Assessment ....Ms. Veronica GRAVES
10 Director Business Affairs ....Mrs. Fannie G. THOMPSON
32 Director Student Affairs ....Dr. James THOMPSON
08 Dir Library/Instrnl Resource Center ....Mr. Darren JONES
37 Financial Aid Coordinator ....Ms. Patricia JONES

Maryland Institute College of Art (C)

1300 Mount Royal Avenue, Baltimore MD 21217-4191
County: Independent City FICE Identification: 002080
Unit ID: 163295
Telephone: (410) 669-9200 Carnegie Class: Spec/Arts
FAX Number: (410) 669-9206 Calendar System: Semester
URL: www.mica.edu
Established: 1826 Annual Undergrad Tuition & Fees: $2,282
Enrollment: 39,340 Coed
Affiliation or Control: Independent Non-Profit IRS Status: 501(c)3
Highest Offering: Master's
Program: Fine Arts Emphasis
Accreditation: M, ART

01 President ....Mr. Fred LAZARUS, IV
05 Vice Pres Academic Affairs/Provost ....Mr. Ray ALLEN
10 Vice Pres Fiscal Affairs ....Mr. Douglas MANN
30 Vice Pres Advancement ....Mr. Michael R. FRANCO
32 Vice Pres/Dean Student Affairs ..Mr. J. Davidson (Dusty) PORTER
84 Vice Pres/Dean Admiss/Finan Aid ....Ms. Theresa BEDOYA
13 Vice Pres Technology Systems & Svcs ....Mr. Tom HYATT
11 Vice Pres Operations ....Mr. Mike MOLLA
20 Vice Prov Ugrad Studies & Faculty ....Ms. Jan STINCHCOMB
46 Vice Provost Research ....Ms. Gwynne KEATHLEY
04 Executive Assistant to President ....Ms. Marian SMITH
37 Assoc VP Financial Aid ....Ms. Diane PRENGAMAN
44 Assoc VP Dev Constituent Rels ....Ms. Alison DAVITT
27 Assoc VP Institutnal Communication ....Mr. Cedric MOBLEY
44 Assoc VP Advancement/Plan/Sp Projct .Ms. Mary Ann LAMBROS
14 Assoc VP Technology ....Ms. Susan MILTENBERGER
18 Assoc VP Facilities Management ....Mr. Timothy MILLNER
16 Assoc VP Human Resources ....Ms. Estevanny TURNS
20 Dean Academic Services ....Ms. Cynthia BARTH
53 Dean Art Education ....Ms. Karen CARROLL
51 Dean Continuing & Professnl Studies ....Mr. David GRACYALNY
35 Assoc Dean Stdnt Life/Judicial Affs ....Mr. Michael PATTERSON
88 Assoc Dean Student Health Wellness ....Mr. James DAVIS
07 Assoc Dean Undergraduate Admissions ....Ms. Christine SEESE
88 Assoc Dean Graduate Admissions ....Mr. Scott KELLY
88 Assoc Dean Continuing Studies ....Mr. Peter DUBEAU
06 Assoc Dean Enrollment Svs/Registrar ....Ms. Christine PETERSON
28 Asst Dean Diversity Intercultur Dev ....Mr. Clyde JOHNSON, JR.
21 Director Accounting ....Ms. Jessica RURKA
88 Director Budget ....Ms. Brigitte SULLIVAN
39 Director Residence Life ....Mr. Scott STONE
36 Director Career Development ....Ms. Megan MILLER
31 Director Community Engagement ....Ms. Karen STULTS
31 Director Community Art Partnerships ....Vacant
38 Director Counseling Center ....Ms. Pat FARRELL
88 Director Student Activities ....Ms. Karol MARTINEZ
88 Director Admissions Operations ....Ms. Cheryl ISSOD
08 Director & Head Librarian ....Mr. Anthony WHITE
88 Director Annual Fund ....Ms. Carolyn STRATFORD-YOUNCE
88 Director Advancement Services ....Ms. Dana COSTELLO
88 Director Stewardships ....Ms. Erin CHREST
26 Director Public Relations ....Ms. Jessica WEGLEIN
88 Director Exhibitions ....Mr. Gerald ROSS
85 Director International Affairs ....Ms. Mary ALLEN
88 Director Writing St/Learn Res Cnt ....Mr. Daniel GUTSTEIN
88 Dir Data Mgmt/Registration Cont Std ....Ms. Sarah MARAVETZ
88 Director Marketing & Enrollment Svs ....Vacant
09 Director Student Records & Research ....Mr. Hadley GARBART
19 Director of Campus Safety ....Mr. Stephen DAVIS
88 Director Events ....Ms. Anne SOUTH
88 Director Operation Services ....Mr. Chris BOHASKA
29 Dir Alumni & Parent Rels ....Vacant
102 Director Corp/Found/Govt Relations ....Ms. Sara WARREN
105 Director of Web Communications ....Vacant
24 Director Technical Support Services ....Mr. John RHODES
91 Director Administrative Systems ....Vacant
88 Director Network Services ....Mr. David APAW
90 Dir Instructional Advance & Tech ....Ms. Pamela STEFANUCA
40 Manager College Store ....Ms. Kerri LITZ

Maryland University of Integrative Health (D)

7750 Montpelier Road, Laurel MD 20723-6010
County: Howard FICE Identification: 025784
Unit ID: 164085
Telephone: (410) 888-9048 Carnegie Class: Master's S
FAX Number: (410) 888-9004 Calendar System: Trimester
URL: www.muih.edu
Established: 1981 Annual Graduate Tuition & Fees: $26,500
Enrollment: 758 Coed
Affiliation or Control: Independent Non-Profit IRS Status: 501(c)3
Highest Offering: Master's; No Undergraduates
Program: Professional
Accreditation: M, ACUP

01 President & CEO ....Mr. Frank VITALE
05 Provost/Vice Pres Academic Affairs ....Dr. Judith BROIDA
11 VP Administration/General Counsel ....Ms. Louise GUSSIN
30 VP Inst Adv & Chief Values Officer ....Ms. Cheryl WALKER
26 VP Marketing/Enrollment Mgmt ....Ms. Gail DOERR
10 VP/CFO & Treasurer ....Mr. Marc LEVIN
06 Assoc VP Student Svcs/Registrar ....Mr. Reginald GARCON
37 Director Student Financial Aid ....Ms. Christa DEAN
08 Director of Library Services ....Ms. Jenifer KIRIN
29 Director Cont Ed & Alumni Affairs ....Ms. Patricia DELORENZO
32 Academic & Student Affairs Advisor ....Mr. Reginald GARCON

McDaniel College (E)

2 College Hill, Westminster MD 21157-4390
County: Carroll FICE Identification: 002109
Unit ID: 164270
Telephone: (410) 848-7000 Carnegie Class: Bac/A&S
FAX Number: (410) 857-2279 Calendar System: Semester
URL: www.mcdaniel.edu
Established: 1867 Annual Undergrad Tuition & Fees: $36,690
Enrollment: 3,284 Coed
Affiliation or Control: Independent Non-Profit IRS Status: 501(c)3
Highest Offering: Master's
Program: Liberal Arts And General; Teacher Preparatory
Accreditation: M, SW, TED

01 President ....Dr. Roger N. CASEY
05 Provost/Dean of Faculty ....Dr. Jeanine STEWART
10 Vice Pres Administration & Finance ....Dr. Ethan A. SEIDEL
44 Vice Pres Institutional Advancement ....Ms. Lori LEWIS
32 Vice Pres/Dean of Student Affairs ....Ms. Beth R. GERL
84 VP Enroll Mgt/Dean of Admissions ....Ms. Florence W. HINES
30 Assoc Vice Pres/Director Devel ....Mr. Lawrence JUNKIN
29 Assoc Vice Pres of Alumni Relations ....Ms. Robin A. BRENTON
27 Assoc Vice Pres Comm/Marketing ....Ms. Joyce D. MULLER
04 Int Exec Assistant to the President .. Ms. Patricia LIVELSBERGER
58 Dean Graduate/Professional Stds ....Dr. Tom ZIRPOLI
20 Associate Dean of Academic Affairs ....Dr. Debora JOHNSON-ROSS
88 Assoc Dean Student Acad Life ....Ms. Lisa BRESLIN
102 Dir Corp & Foundation Relations ....Ms. Kathleen M. CURTIN
08 Director of Library ....Ms. Jessame E. FERGUSON
37 Interim Director Financial Aid ....Ms. Ellie GEIMAN
06 Registrar ....Ms. Jan A. KIPHART
41 Director Athletics ....Mr. Paul MOYER
36 Director Career Advising ....Vacant
38 Director Counseling ....Ms. Susan J. GLORE
35 Director Student Engagement ....Ms. Christine WORKMAN
21 Director Financial Services/Treas ....Mr. Arthur S. WISNER
15 Director Human Resources ....Mr. Thomas G. STEBACK
45 Dir Facility Plng/Capital Projects ....Mr. Edgar S. SELL, JR.
18 Director Physical Plant ....Mr. Stafford TORGESEN
19 Director of Campus Safety ....Mr. Michael N. WEBSTER
40 Manager Bookstore ....Mr. Kyle MELOCHE
18 Director Conferences/Auxil Svcs ....Ms. Mary J. COLBERT
13 Chief Information Officer ....Dr. Esther IGLICH
28 Director of Multicultural Services ....Ms. Jennifer MARANA
92 Director of Honors Program ....Dr. Stephanie D. MADSEN
96 Director of Purchasing/Receiving ....Ms. Margaret G. BELL
88 Coord of Deaf Education Program ....Dr. Mark M. RUST
09 Director Institutional Research ....Dr. Brian AULT
101 Int Secretary of Board of Trustees ... Ms. Patricia LIVELSBERGER
86 Director of Government Relations ....Dr. Herbert C. SMITH

Montgomery College (F)

900 Hungerford Drive, Rockville MD 20850-1733
County: Montgomery FICE Identification: 006911
Unit ID: 163426
Telephone: (240) 567-5000 Carnegie Class: Assoc/Pub-S-MC
FAX Number: (240) 567-6397 Calendar System: Semester
URL: www.montgomerycollege.edu
Established: 1946 Annual Undergrad Tuition & Fees (In-District): $4,452
Enrollment: 27,453 Coed
Affiliation or Control: Local IRS Status: 501(c)3
Highest Offering: Associate Degree
Program: Occupational; 2-Year Principally Bachelor's Creditable
Accreditation: M, ADNUR, CAHIIM, DMS, MUS, POLYT, PTAA, RAD, SURGT

01 President ....Dr. DeRionne P. POLLARD
05 Sr VP for Academic Affairs ....Dr. Donald PEARL
32 Sr VP for Student Services ....Dr. Beverly WALKER-GRIFFEA
11 Interim SVP for Adm & Fiscal Svcs ....Dr. Janet WORMACK
12 Vice Pres/Provost Rockville Campus ....Dr. Judy ACKERMAN
12 Vice Pres/Provost Germantown Campus ....Dr. Sanjay RAI
12 Vice Pres/Prov Takoma Park Campus ....Dr. Brad J. STEWART
103 VP for Workforce Dev & Contuing Ed ....Mr. George M. PAYNE
100 Chief of Staff/Chief Strategy Ofcr ....Dr. Stephen D. CAIN
30 Sr VP Advancement & Comm Engagement ....Mr. David SEARS
45 VP for Planning and Inst Effective ....Ms. Kathleen WESSMAN
13 Acting VP of Instructional & IT/CIO ....Ms. Donna SCHENA
09 Dir Institutional Rsrch & Analysis ....Dr. Robert LYNCH
86 Chief Government Relations Officer ....Ms. Susan MADDEN
43 General Counsel ....Mr. Clyde H. SORRELL
15 VP of Human Res/Dev & Engagement ....Ms. Sarah ESPINOSA
18 VP of Facilities & Security ....Dr. Dewey YEATTS
28 Chief Diversity Officer ....Dr. Michelle T. SCOTT
37 Chief Enrollment Svcs/Fin Aid Ofc ....Ms. Melissa GREGORY
07 Asst Dir of Enrollment Services ....Mr. Ernest CARTLEDGE
31 Director of Auxiliary Services ....Dr. Kathi CAREY-FLETCHER
26 Director of Communications ....Ms. Elizabeth HOMAN

29 Alumni Coordinator .... Mr. John LIBBY
96 Director of Procurement .... Mr. Patrick JOHNSON
10 VP of Finance/CFO .... Ms. Ruby SHERMAN
88 VP of Audit & Business Process Mgmt .... Mr. Robert PRESTON
88 Deputy Chief of Staff and Strategy .... Dr. Brian K. BAKER

Morgan State University (A)

1700 East Cold Spring Lane, Baltimore MD 21251-0001
County: Independent City FICE Identification: 002083
Unit ID: 163453
Telephone: (443) 885-3333 Carnegie Class: DRU
FAX Number: (443) 885-3698 Calendar System: Semester
URL: www.morgan.edu
Established: 1867 Annual Undergrad Tuition & Fees (In-State): $7,218
Enrollment: 7,952 Coed
Affiliation or Control: State IRS Status: 501(c)3
Highest Offering: Doctorate
Program: Liberal Arts And General; Teacher Preparatory; Professional
Accreditation: M, BUS, BUSA, DIETD, ENG, LSAR, MT, MUS, PH, PLNG, SW, TED

01 President .... Dr. David WILSON
05 Int Provost/Vice Pres Academic Affs .... Dr. Keith JACKSON
88 VP Academic Outreach and Engagement .... Dr. Maurice TAYLOR
10 Vice President Finance & Management .... Mr. Raymond VOLLMER
45 Vice President Planning .... Dr. Joseph POPOVICH
32 Vice Pres Student Affairs .... Dr. Kevin BANKS
30 Vice Pres Institutional Advancement .... Ms. Cheryl Y. HITCHCOCK
20 Assoc VP for Academic Affairs .... Dr. Kara TURNER
21 Asst Vice President for Finance .... Mr. Bickram JANAK
35 Associate VP Student Affairs .... Ms. Tanya RUSH
100 Chief of Staff .... Dr. Willie LARKIN
49 Acting Dean College of Liberal Arts .... Dr. Pamela SCOTT-JOHNSON
50 Dean School Business & Management .... Dr. Fikru BOGHOSSIAN
53 Dean School of Education .... Dr. Patricia WELCH
54 Dean School of Engineering .... Dr. Eugene DELOATCH
58 Dean of the Graduate School .... Dr. Mark GARRISON
48 Dean School of Architecture .... Dr. Mary Anne AKERS
70 Dean School of Social Work .... Dr. Anna MCPHATTER
69 Act Dean School of Community Health .... Dr. Kim SYDNOR
37 Director of Financial Aid .... Ms. Tanya WILKERSON
38 Director of Counseling Services .... Ms. Nina DOBSON-HOPKINS
08 Director of Library .... Dr. Richard BRADBERRY
06 Director of Records/Registration .... Mr. Paul THOMPSON
07 Director of Admissions .... Ms. Shonda GRAY
36 Director of Placement .... Mr. William CARSON
15 Director Human Resources .... Mrs. Armada GRANT
29 Director Alumni Association .... Mrs. Joyce BROWN
14 Director Computer Center .... Mr. Gilbert MORGAN
86 Director State Relations .... Mr. Claude E. HITCHCOCK
09 Director of Institutional Research .... Ms. Cheryl ROLLINS
18 Director Physical Plant .... Mr. Kenneth ELLIS
26 Director Public Relations .... Mr. Clinton R. COLEMAN
84 Director Enrollment Management .... Mr. Joseph C. BOZEMAN
96 Director of Purchasing .... Mr. Churchill B. WORTHERLY
28 Director of Diversity .... Vacant

Mount St. Mary's University (B)

16300 Old Emmitsburg Road,
Emmitsburg MD 21727-7799
County: Frederick FICE Identification: 002086
Unit ID: 163462
Telephone: (301) 447-6122 Carnegie Class: Master's M
FAX Number: (301) 447-5634 Calendar System: Semester
URL: www.msmary.edu
Established: 1808 Annual Undergrad Tuition & Fees: $34,644
Enrollment: 2,350 Coed
Affiliation or Control: Roman Catholic IRS Status: 501(c)3
Highest Offering: Master's
Program: Liberal Arts And General; Teacher Preparatory; Professional; Religious Emphasis
Accreditation: M, IACBE, TED, THEOL

01 President .... Dr. Thomas H. POWELL
03 Vice President/Rector .... Msgr. Steven ROHLFS
03 Executive Vice President .... Mr. Dan SOLLER
88 Vice President University Affairs .... Ms. Pauline ENGLESTATTER
05 Provost .... Dr. David B. REHM
10 Vice Pres for Business & Finance .... Mr. William E. DAVIES
30 Vice President for Advancement .... Mr. Robert J. BRENNAN
84 Vice Pres Enrollment Management .... Mr. Michael POST
20 Assoc Provost .... Dr. Leona SEVICK
50 Dean Richard J Bolte Sr Sch of Bus .... Dr. Karl W. EINOLF
53 Dean Sch Education & Human Services .... Dr. Barbara MARTIN PALMER
81 Dean School Natural Science & Math .... Vacant
79 Dean College of Liberal Arts .... Dr. Joshua HOCHSCHILD
41 Director of Athletics .... Ms. Lynne P. ROBINSON
42 Chaplain .... Fr. Brian NOLAN
32 Dean of Students .... Mr. Michael TABERSKI
51 Director Professional/Cont Studies .... Mr. Joe LEBHERZ
08 Dean of the Library .... Mr. Charles KUHN
09 Director Institutional Research .... Ms. Linda K. JUNKER
06 Registrar .... Vacant
50 Director of Grad/Adult Business Pgm .... Ms. Deborah POWELL
88 Director Conferences/Special Pgms .... Ms. Marianne DEMPSEY
23 Director of Health Services .... Dr. Bonnie PORTIER
24 Director of the Media Center .... Mr. John B. BREWER, JR.
37 Director of Financial Aid .... Mr. David C. REEDER

36 Director Career Center .... Ms. Claire TAURIELLO
13 Chief Information Officer .... Mr. Bobby L. FLACK
26 Director of Communications .... Mr. Duffy ROSS
44 Director of Annual Giving .... Ms. Marie CACACE
16 Director of Human Resources .... Ms. Barbara R. MILLER
19 Director of Public Safety .... Mr. R. Barry TITLER
29 Director of Alumni Relations .... Ms. Maureen C. PLANT
18 Director of Physical Plant .... Mr. Bruce NORMAN
88 Director Office of Social Justice .... Mr. Jeff ABEL
28 Director Ctr for Student Diversity .... Ms. Chianti BLACKMON
35 Dir Campus Activ/Student Ldrshp .... Mr. Kenneth MCVEARRY
92 Director of the Honors Program .... Dr. Caroline EICK
40 Manager of College Store .... Ms. Amanda CASALE
96 Purchasing Agent .... Ms. Maria L. TOPPER

National Labor College (C)

10000 New Hampshire Avenue,
Silver Spring MD 20903-1706
County: Montgomery FICE Identification: 034555
Unit ID: 434034
Telephone: (301) 431-6400 Carnegie Class: Spec/Bus
FAX Number: (301) 434-5411 Calendar System: Semester
URL: www.nlc.edu
Established: 1997 Annual Undergrad Tuition & Fees: $6,048
Enrollment: 741 Coed
Affiliation or Control: Independent Non-Profit IRS Status: 501(c)3
Highest Offering: Baccalaureate
Program: Liberal Arts And General
Accreditation: M

01 President & CEO .... Dr. Paula PEINOVICH
04 Executive Asst to the President .... Laura BARRANTES
05 Provost .... Dr. Daniel KATZ
10 VP for Finance & CFO .... Bruce PANKEY
86 VP Govt Rels/Legal Cous/HR Dir .... James GENTILE
30 Advancement Officer .... Beth SHANNON
26 VP for Marketing & Communications .... Lara MANZIONE
09 Institutional Research Director .... Dr. Ann STEHNEY
06 Registrar .... Jeff BRIA
07 Director of Enrollment Management .... Lucas SIFUENTES
37 Financial Aid Director .... D. DENNY
21 Finance Director .... Jacinta KELLY

Ner Israel Rabbinical College (D)

400 Mount Wilson Lane, Baltimore MD 21208-1198
County: Baltimore FICE Identification: 002087
Unit ID: 163532
Telephone: (410) 484-7200 Carnegie Class: Spec/Faith
FAX Number: (410) 484-3060 Calendar System: Semester
Established: 1933 Annual Undergrad Tuition & Fees: $1,000
Enrollment: 580 Male
Affiliation or Control: Independent Non-Profit IRS Status: 501(c)3
Highest Offering: Doctorate
Program: Teacher Preparatory; Professional; Religious Emphasis
Accreditation: RABN

01 President .... Rabbi Sheftel M. NEUBERGER
05 Chief Academic Officer .... Rabbi Aharon FELDMAN
03 Executive Director .... Mr. Jerome H. KADDEN
04 Assistant to the President .... Rabbi Boruch NEUBERGER
07 Director of Admissions .... Rabbi Beryl WEISBORD
13 Director of Administrative Services .... Mr. Larry RIBAKOW
06 Registrar .... Rabbi Chaim D. LAPIDUS
37 Director Student Financial Aid .... Rabbi Shmuel SCHACHTER
85 Foreign Student Advisor .... Rabbi Eliyahu HAKKAKIAN
30 Director of Development .... Rabbi Louis HOFFMAN
45 Director of Planning .... Rabbi Leonard OBERSTEIN
26 Director Community Relations .... Rabbi Jonathan SEIDEMANN
18 Chief Physical Plant .... Mr. David FRIEDMAN
08 Head Librarian .... Rabbi Avrohom SHNIDMAN
39 Director of Student Housing .... Rabbi Emanuel GOLDFEIZ
29 Associate Director Alumni Relations .... Rabbi Eli GREENGART

Notre Dame of Maryland University (E)

4701 N Charles Street, Baltimore MD 21210-2404
County: Independent City FICE Identification: 002065
Unit ID: 163578
Telephone: (410) 435-0100 Carnegie Class: Master's L
FAX Number: (410) 532-5791 Calendar System: Semester
URL: www.ndm.edu
Established: 1873 Annual Undergrad Tuition & Fees: $30,981
Enrollment: 2,863 Female
Affiliation or Control: Roman Catholic IRS Status: 501(c)3
Highest Offering: Doctorate
Program: Liberal Arts And General; Teacher Preparatory; Professional
Accreditation: M, NUR, PHAR, TED

01 Interim President .... Ms. Joan DEVELIN COLEY
05 Vice President Academic Affairs .... Sr. Christine DE VINNE
32 Vice President Student Life .... Dr. Rebecca SAWYER
30 Vice Pres Institutional Advancement .... Ms. Patricia A. BOSSE
84 Vice Pres Enrollment Management .... Ms. Heidi L. FLETCHER
10 Vice Pres Finance & Administration .... Ms. Deanna MCCORMICK
20 Associate VP Academic Affairs .... Dr. Kathryn DOHERTY
35 Dean of Students .... Vacant
04 Special Assistant to the President .... Dr. Candace CARACO
06 Assoc VP Enrollment/Registrar .... Ms. Sharon BOGDAN
37 Director of Financial Aid .... Ms. Zhanna GOLTSER

36 Dir Academic & Career Enrichment .... Ms. Diane MCCANN
13 Director Information Technology .... Mr. Warren SZELISTOWSKI
29 Director of Alumnae Relations .... Ms. Emilia POITER
08 Librarian .... Ms. Barbara PREECE
85 Director International Program .... Vacant
07 Director of Admissions .... Ms. Angela BAUMLER
09 Sr Dir Inst Research/Effectiveness .... Ms. Shuang LIU
15 Director of Human Resources .... Ms. Geri LARSEN
18 Director of Facility Management .... Mr. Mario CANDIELLO
21 Controller .... Ms. Barbara MORRIS
38 Director Counseling Center .... Ms. Amy PROVAN
19 Director of Public Safety .... Mr. Jeff MUNCHEL
40 Bookstore Manager .... Ms. Allegra WOODALL
41 Athletic Director .... Ms. Erin FOLEY
42 Director Campus Ministry .... Ms. Melissa LEES
67 Dean School of Pharmacy .... Dr. Anne LIN
07 Director Pharmacy Admissions .... Mr. Larry SHATTUCK

Prince George's Community College (F)

301 Largo Road, Largo MD 20774-2199
County: Prince Georges FICE Identification: 002089
Unit ID: 163657
Telephone: (301) 336-6000 Carnegie Class: Assoc/Pub-S-SC
FAX Number: (301) 808-0960 Calendar System: Semester
URL: www.pgcc.edu
Established: 1958 Annual Undergrad Tuition & Fees (In-District): $3,360
Enrollment: 13,824 Coed
Affiliation or Control: Local IRS Status: 501(c)3
Highest Offering: Associate Degree
Program: Occupational; 2-Year Principally Bachelor's Creditable
Accreditation: M, ADNUR, CAHIIM, COARC, EMT, NMT, RAD

01 President .... Dr. Charlene M. DUKES
05 Vice Pres Academic Affairs .... Dr. Sandra F. DUNNINGTON
32 Vice Pres Student Services .... Dr. Tyjaun A. LEE
10 Vice Pres Administrative Services .... Mr. Tom E. KNAPP
103 Interim VP Workforce Devel/Cont Ed .... Mr. Joseph L. MARTINELLI
72 Vice Pres Technology Services .... Dr. Joseph G. ROSSMEIER
20 Sr Acad Admin to VP for Acad Affs .... Ms. Catherine LAPALOMBARA
38 Dean Student Development Svcs .... Dr. Scheherazade W. FORMAN
84 Interim Dean of Enrollment Services .... Ms. Cindy D. CHILDS
09 Dean Planning/Institutional Rsrch .... Dr. Andrea A. LEX
51 Dean Wrkfrce Dev/Cont Educ Pgms .... Mr. Joseph I. MARTINELLI
15 Dean Human Resources .... Ms. Lark T. DOBSON
88 Dean of Learning Foundations .... Dr. Beverly S. REED
21 Dean Financial Affairs .... Ms. Nancy E. BURGESS
100 Chief of Staff .... Ms. Alonia C. SHARPS
08 Dir Library/Learning Resources .... Ms. Priscilla C. THOMPSON
06 Director Admissions & Records .... Ms. Vera L. BAGLEY
07 Director Recruitment .... Vacant
18 Dean Facilities Management .... Dr. David C. MOSBY
88 Director Physical Facilities .... Vacant
86 Dir Community & Government Affairs .... Dr. Jacqueline L. BROWN
30 Exec Dir Institutional Advancement .... Ms. Brenda S. MITCHELL
26 Director Marketing & Creative Svcs .... Dr. Deidra W. HILL
13 Chief Technology Officer .... Mr. William L. ANDERSON
96 Director of Procurement .... Mr. Andrew G. ROBINSON
37 Director Financial Aid .... Ms. Sharon E. HASSAN
36 Manager Career & Job Services .... Ms. Stephanie S. PAIR-CUNNINGHAM
79 Dean of Liberal Arts .... Dr. Carolyn F. HOFFMAN
35 Dean College Life Services .... Mr. Malverse A. NICHOLSON, JR.
76 Dean of Health Science .... Ms. Angela D. ANDERSON
81 Dean Science/Tech/Engr/Math .... Dr. Christine E. BARROW
83 Int Dean Soc Sci/Bus Studies Div .... Dr. Lorraine P. BASSETTE

St. John's College (G)

PO Box 2800, Annapolis MD 21404-2800
County: Anne Arundel FICE Identification: 002092
Unit ID: 163976
Telephone: (410) 263-2371 Carnegie Class: Bac/A&S
FAX Number: (410) 626-2886 Calendar System: Semester
URL: www.sjca.edu
Established: 1784 Annual Undergrad Tuition & Fees: $45,846
Enrollment: 509 Coed
Affiliation or Control: Independent Non-Profit IRS Status: 501(c)3
Highest Offering: Master's
Program: Liberal Arts And General
Accreditation: M

01 President .... Mr. Christopher B. NELSON
30 Vice Pres Advancement Annapolis .... Ms. Barbara GOYETTE
05 Dean .... Ms. Pamela KRAUS
10 Treasurer .... Ms. Bronte JONES
06 Registrar .... Ms. Jacqueline THOMS
07 Director of Admissions .... Ms. Sarah MORSE
102 Director Corporate/Foundation Rels .... Ms. Susan BORDEN
37 Director of Financial Aid .... Ms. Dana KENNEDY
08 Library Director .... Ms. Cathy DIXON
15 Director of Human Resources .... Ms. Deborah ANAWALT
18 Supt of Buildings & Grounds .... Mr. Sid PHIPPS
19 Chief of Security .... Mr. Timon LINN
23 Director of Student Health .... Ms. Nancy CALABRESE
27 Director of Communications .... Ms. Patricia DEMPSEY
32 Director of Student Services .... Ms. Taylor WATERS
20 Assistant Dean .... Ms. Katherine HEINES
36 Director of Career Services .... Ms. Jaime DUNN
40 Bookstore Manager .... Mr. Robin DUNN

41 Director of Athletics ..... Mr. Michael MCQUARRIE
58 Director of Graduate Institute ..... Mr. Jeff BLACK
21 Controller ..... Ms. Diane SAWYER
29 Director of Alumni Relations ..... Mr. Leo PICKENS

† See Affiliate: St. John's College at Santa Fe, NM.

St. Mary's College of Maryland (A)

18952 E Fisher Road, Saint Mary's City MD 20686-3001
County: Saint Mary's FICE Identification: 002095
Unit ID: 163912
Telephone: (240) 895-2000 Carnegie Class: Bac/A&S
FAX Number: (240) 895-4462 Calendar System: Semester
URL: www.smcm.edu
Established: 1840 Annual Undergrad Tuition & Fees (In-State): $14,773
Enrollment: 1,933 Coed
Affiliation or Control: State IRS Status: 501(c)3
Highest Offering: Master's
Program: Liberal Arts And General
Accreditation: M

01 Interim President ..... Dr. Ian NEWBOULD
05 Dean of Faculty/VP for Acad Affairs ..... Dr. Beth RUSHING
10 VP Business & Finance ..... Mr. Charles C. JACKSON
30 Vice President for Advancement ..... Dr. Maureen C. SILVA
84 Vice Pres Enrollment Management ..... Mr. Gary SHERMAN
44 Asst Vice Pres for Development ..... Vacant
26 Assoc VP for Marketing/Public Rels ..... Vacant
29 Director Alumni Relations ..... Mr. David M. SUSHINSKY
09 Assoc Dir Institutional Research ..... Ms. Elizabeth A. CLUNE-KNEUER
06 Registrar ..... Ms. Susan A. BENNETT
20 Assoc Dean of Faculty ..... Dr. Rich PLATT
20 Dean of the Core Curric/1st-yr Exp ..... Dr. Elizabeth N. WILLIAMS
07 VP Dean Admissions/Financial Aid ..... Vacant
37 Director of Financial Aid ..... Vacant
88 Asst VP for Academic Administration ..... Mr. Mark W. HEIDRICH
35 Interim Dean of Students ..... Dr. Roberto IFILL
38 Director of Counseling Services ..... Dr. Kyle K. BISHOP
41 Director of Athletics/Recreation ..... Mr. Scott W. DEVINE
83 Chair Anthropology ..... Dr. William C. ROBERTS
57 Chair of Arts & Art History ..... Ms. Carrie C. PATTERSON
88 Chair of Biology ..... Dr. Holly GORTON
88 Chair of Chemistry ..... Dr. Randolph K. LARSEN, III
83 Chair of Economics ..... Dr. Michael H. YE
83 Chair Educational Studies ..... Dr. Katy ARNETT
79 Chair of English ..... Dr. Ben A. CLICK
83 Chair of History ..... Dr. Charles J. HOLDEN
79 Chair of Intl Languages/Cultures ..... Dr. Katie L. GANTZ
81 Chair of Math/Computer Science ..... Dr. Susan GOLDSTINE
64 Chair of Music ..... Dr. Deborah A. LAWRENCE
79 Chair Philosophy/Religious Studies ..... Dr. Michael S. TABER
77 Chair of Physics ..... Dr. Charles M. ADLER
82 Chair of Political Science ..... Dr. Sahar SHAFQAT
83 Chair of Psychology ..... Dr. Aileen M. BAILEY
83 Acting Chair of Sociology ..... Dr. Curt RANEY
57 Chair of Threatre/Film/Media Stds ..... Dr. Joanne R. KLEIN
51 Asst Vice Pres Lifelong Learning ..... Vacant
20 Asst Vice Pres Academic Services ..... Vacant
18 Assoc Vice President of Facilities ..... Vacant
19 Director of Public Safety ..... Mr. Sean M. TALLARICO
40 Director of the Campus Store ..... Mr. Richard T. WAGNER
15 Director of HR ..... Vacant
23 Director of Health Services ..... Ms. Linda WALLACE
35 Associate Dean of Students ..... Ms. Joanne A. GOLDWATER
13 Asst VP of Information Technology ..... Dr. C. Michael GASS
44 Senior Development Officer ..... Ms. Karen C. RALEY
08 Director of the Library/Media Svcs ..... Dr. Celia E. RABINOWITZ
102 Director of Development & Campaigns ..... Ms. Liisa E. FRANZEN
21 Comptroller/Director of Accounting ..... Mr. Gabriel A. MBOMEH
43 Assistant Attorney General ..... Ms. Sara SLAFF
22 Affirm Act/Equal Opportunity Office ..... Mr. Melvin A. MCCLINTOCK
25 Director of Sponsored Research ..... Mrs. Sabine DILLINGHAM
28 Fair Practices Officer ..... Vacant
96 Procurement Officer/Director of Aux ..... Mr. Patrick G. HUNT

Saint Mary's Seminary and University (B)

5400 Roland Avenue, Baltimore MD 21210-1994
County: Independent City FICE Identification: 002096
Unit ID: 163842
Telephone: (410) 864-4000 Carnegie Class: Spec/Faith
FAX Number: (410) 864-4278 Calendar System: Semester
URL: www.stmarys.edu
Established: 1791 Annual Undergrad Tuition & Fees: $29,450
Enrollment: 208 Coed
Affiliation or Control: Roman Catholic IRS Status: 501(c)3
Highest Offering: First Professional Degree
Program: Liberal Arts And General; Professional; Religious Emphasis
Accreditation: M, THEOL

01 President/Rector ..... Rev. Thomas R. HURST
10 Vice President for Finance ..... Mr. Richard G. CHILDS
30 Vice Pres Advancement/Human Res ..... Mrs. Elizabeth L. VISCONAGE
05 Dean School Theology ..... Rev. Timothy A. KULBICKI, OFM CONV
73 Dean Ecumenical Institute Theology ..... Dr. D. Brent LAYTHAM
73 Dean Ecclesiastical Faculty ..... Rev. Timothy A. KULBICKI, OFM CONV
06 University Registrar ..... Ms. Paula M. THIGPEN
37 Director Financial Aid ..... Mrs. Victoria F. GAUNT
08 Director of Knott Library ..... Mr. Thomas RASZEWSKI

The SANS Technology Institute (C)

8120 Woodmont Avenue, Suite 205, Bethesda MD 20814
County: Montgomery Identification: 667006
Telephone: (301) 654-7267 Carnegie Class: Not Classified
FAX Number: (301) 951-0140 Calendar System: Semester
URL: www.sans.edu
Established: Annual Graduate Tuition & Fees: $17,800
Enrollment: 81 Coed
Affiliation or Control: Independent Non-Profit IRS Status: 501(c)3
Highest Offering: Master's; No Undergraduates
Program: Professional
Accreditation: @M

01 President ..... Mr. Alan PALLER
05 Provost ..... Dr. Toby GOUKER
84 Director Enrollment Management ..... Ms. Mary Kay PORTER

Sojourner-Douglass College (D)

200 North Central Avenue, Baltimore MD 21202
County: Baltimore FICE Identification: 021279
Unit ID: 163921
Telephone: (410) 276-0306 Carnegie Class: Bac/Diverse
FAX Number: (410) 675-1810 Calendar System: Trimester
URL: www.sdc.edu
Established: 1980 Annual Undergrad Tuition & Fees: $14,055
Enrollment: 1,408 Coed
Affiliation or Control: Independent Non-Profit IRS Status: 501(c)3
Highest Offering: Master's
Program: Liberal Arts And General
Accreditation: M, @SW

01 President ..... Dr. Charles W. SIMMONS
03 Executive Vice President ..... Dr. Howard L. SIMMONS
05 Provost/Vice Pres Academic Affairs ..... Dr. Marian STANTON
10 Vice Pres for Admin & Fiscal Affs ..... Mr. Donald L. HUTCHINS
04 Special Assistant to the President ..... Ms. Carolyn J. ECHOLS
15 Department Chair Human Services ..... Dr. Monica POINDEXTER-KERR
36 Dept Chair Human Growth/Development ..... Dr. Deborah KING
20 Dean of Academic Affairs ..... Ms. Shirley EVANS
12 Dean of Lanham Campus ..... Dr. Bernard M. GROSS
12 Dean of Annapolis Campus ..... Dr. Charlestine FAIRLEY
12 Dean of Salisbury Campus ..... Ms. Constance STEWART
12 Dean of Cambridge Campus ..... Mr. Jeff DIGGS
12 Dean of Nassau Bahamas Campus ..... Hon. Theresa MOXEY-INGRAHAM
12 Dean of Owings Mills Campus ..... Ms. Doris W. CARROLL
06 Registrar ..... Ms. Andrea MANNING
51 Director of Continuing Education ..... Dr. Ann BOSTIC
37 Director of Financial Aid ..... Ms. Rebecca CHALK
31 Director Community Outreach ..... Mr. Jamal MUBDI-BEY
18 Director Facilities/Physical Plant ..... Mr. Gilbert RAWLINGS
08 Director of Library ..... Ms. Marlene JONES
19 Director Security/Safety ..... Col. Mahdi EL-HAQQ
21 Bursar ..... Mr. Bert LEE
29 Director Alumni Relations ..... Vacant
58 Director of Graduate Studies ..... Dr. Linda FASSETT
09 Dir of Institutional Research/Plng ..... Mr. Kareem AZIZ
35 Chief Admin Stdt Dev/Stdt Sppt Svcs ..... Mr. Lewis ANDREWS
38 Director Student Counseling ..... Ms. Kimberly ECHOLS
07 Director of Admissions ..... Ms. Diana SAMUELS
13 Director Information Technology ..... Mr. Tacuma SIMMONS
96 Director of Purchasing ..... Mr. Gilbert RAWLINGS

Stevenson University (E)

1525 Greenspring Valley Road,
Stevenson MD 21153-0641
County: Baltimore FICE Identification: 002107
Unit ID: 164173
Telephone: (410) 486-7000 Carnegie Class: Master's S
FAX Number: (410) 486-3552 Calendar System: Semester
URL: www.stevenson.edu
Established: 1947 Annual Undergrad Tuition & Fees: $27,082
Enrollment: 4,418 Coed
Affiliation or Control: Independent Non-Profit IRS Status: 501(c)3
Highest Offering: Master's
Program: Liberal Arts And General; Teacher Preparatory
Accreditation: M, MT, NURSE, TED

01 President ..... Dr. Kevin J. MANNING
04 Assistant to President ..... Ms. Ruth HUBBARD
03 Exec Vice President/Academic Dean ..... Dr. Paul D. LACK
10 Exec Vice Pres/Chief Financial Ofcr ..... Mr. Timothy M. CAMPBELL
05 Chief Academic Officer ..... Dr. Paul D. LACK
30 Vice Pres University Advancement ..... Mr. Steve CLOSE
84 Vice Pres Enrollment Management ..... Mr. Mark J. HERGAN
32 Vice Pres Student Affairs ..... Ms. Claire E. MOORE
27 VP Marketing & Digital Comms ..... Ms. Glenda G. LE GENDRE
15 Vice Pres for Human Resources ..... Ms. Brenda BALZER
100 VP & Chief of Staff ..... Ms. Sue KENNEY
20 Asst Vice Pres for Academic Affairs ..... Dr. Jo-Ellen ASBURY
36 VP for Career Services ..... Ms. Anne SCHOLL-FIEDLER
58 Dean Graduate/Professional Studies ..... Ms. Joyce K. BECKER
50 Dean School of Business ..... Dr. Norman A. ENDLICH
81 Dean School of Science ..... Dr. Susan GORMAN
83 Dean Sch of Humanities/Social Sci ..... Dr. James SALVUCCI
88 Dean School of Design ..... Mr. Keith KUTCH
53 Dean School of Education ..... Dr. Deborah KRAFT
18 Asst VP Fac & Campus Svcs ..... Mr. Leland BEITEL
21 Asst VP Finan Affs/Controller ..... Ms. Melanie M. EDMONDSON
07 Asst VP Enrollment Management ..... Vacant
37 Director of Financial Aid ..... Ms. Barbara MILLER
35 Assoc VP/Dean of Students ..... Dr. Jeffrey M. KELLY
14 Chief Information Officer/Asst VP ..... Mr. Tom ALLEN
88 Assistant VP for Acad Supp Svcs ..... Ms. Nicole MARANO
09 Assoc Dean Inst Rsrch & Assess ..... Vacant
23 Assoc Dean/Dir of Wellness Center ..... Ms. Linda REYMANN
66 Associate Dean GPS Nursing ..... Dr. Judith FEUSTLE
66 Associate Dean for Nursing Educ ..... Dr. Denise SEIGART
106 Associate Dean Distance Education ..... Dr. Barbara ZIRKIN
08 Director of Library Services ..... Ms. Maureen A. BECK
06 Registrar ..... Ms. Tracy L. BOLT
19 Director of Safety & Security ..... Mr. Timothy OSTENDARP
41 Athletic Director ..... Mr. Brett C. ADAMS
40 Director Auxiliary Services ..... Mr. Robert REED
28 Director of Multicultural Affairs ..... Ms. Cheryl HINTON
29 Director Alumni Rels ..... Mr. James MYERS
88 Director Acad Link and PASS ..... Ms. Christine FLAX
88 Director of Developmental Studies ..... Dr. Terri WRIGHT

Stratford University Baltimore Campus (F)

219 S. Central Avenue, Baltimore MD 21202
Telephone: (410) 752-4710 Identification: 770616
Accreditation: ACICS

† Main campus is Stratford University in Falls Church, VA.

TESST College of Technology (G)

1520 S Caton Avenue, Baltimore MD 21227-1063
County: Baltimore City FICE Identification: 007491
Unit ID: 163736
Telephone: (410) 644-6400 Carnegie Class: Assoc/PrivFP
FAX Number: (410) 644-6481 Calendar System: Quarter
URL: www.tesst.com
Established: 1956 Annual Undergrad Tuition & Fees: N/A
Enrollment: 698 Coed
Affiliation or Control: Proprietary IRS Status: Proprietary
Highest Offering: Associate Degree
Program: Occupational
Accreditation: ACCSC

01 President ..... Ms. Amy BEAUREGARD
11 Director of Operations ..... Vacant

TESST College of Technology (H)

4600 Powder Mill Road, Suite 500,
Beltsville MD 20705-2649
County: Prince Georges FICE Identification: 020836
Unit ID: 164058
Telephone: (301) 937-8448 Carnegie Class: Assoc/PrivFP
FAX Number: (301) 937-5327 Calendar System: Quarter
URL: www.tesst.com
Established: 1956 Annual Undergrad Tuition & Fees: N/A
Enrollment: 413 Coed
Affiliation or Control: Proprietary IRS Status: Proprietary
Highest Offering: Associate Degree
Program: Occupational
Accreditation: ACCSC, ACICS

01 President ..... Mr. Kevin BEAVER
06 Registrar ..... Mrs. LaDonna DAVIS
07 Director of Admissions ..... Ms. Cathy MCKINNEY
36 Director of Career Services ..... Ms. Marsha D. HUNT
37 Director of Financial Aid ..... Mr. Michael YAGER

TESST College of Technology (I)

803 Glen Eagles Court, Towson MD 21286-2201
County: Baltimore FICE Identification: 010410
Unit ID: 161776
Telephone: (410) 296-5350 Carnegie Class: Assoc/PrivFP
FAX Number: (410) 296-5356 Calendar System: Quarter
URL: www.tesst.com
Established: 1956 Annual Undergrad Tuition & Fees: $15,137
Enrollment: 322 Coed
Affiliation or Control: Proprietary IRS Status: Proprietary
Highest Offering: Associate Degree
Program: Occupational
Accreditation: ACCSC, ACICS

01 Executive Director ..... Ms. Sue SHERWOOD
07 Director of Admissions ..... Mr. Nicholas BUIZZARD

University of Phoenix Maryland Campus (J)

8830 Stanford Boulevard, Suite 100,
Colulmbia MD 21045-5423
Telephone: (410) 872-9001 Identification: 770210
Accreditation: &NH, ACBSP

† Main campus is University of Phoenix in Tempe, AZ.

*The University System of Maryland Office (A)

3300 Metzerott Road, Adelphi MD 20783-1690
County: Prince Georges
FICE Identification: 007959
Unit ID: 164146
Telephone: (301) 445-1901
Carnegie Class: N/A
FAX Number: (301) 445-1931
URL: www.usmd.edu

01 Chancellor Dr. William KIRWAN
12 Pres Univ of Md Ctr Environment Sci Dr. Donald F. BOESCH
05 Sr VC Academic Affairs Dr. Joann BOUGHMAN
11 COO/Vice Chanc Admin & Finance Mr. Joseph F. VIVONA
30 Vice Chancellor Advancement Mr. Leonard R. RALEY
86 VC Governmental Relations Mr. Patrick J. HOGAN
26 VC for Communications Ms. Anne MOULTRIE
100 USM Chief of Staff Ms. Janice B. DOYLE
10 Assoc VC Financial Affairs Vacant
20 Assoc Vice Chanc Academic Affairs Ms. Teri HOLLANDER
13 Assoc VC Information Technology Mr. Donald Z. SPICER
21 Assoc VC Administration & Finance Ms. JoAnn GOEDERT
21 Director Internal Audit Mr. David MOSCA
21 Director Budget Analysis Ms. Monica WEST

*University of Maryland College Park (B)

College Park MD 20742-0001
County: Prince Georges
FICE Identification: 002103
Unit ID: 163286
Telephone: (301) 405-1000
Carnegie Class: RU/VH
FAX Number: (301) 314-9560
Calendar System: Semester
URL: www.umd.edu
Established: 1856
Annual Undergrad Tuition & Fees (In-State): $9,162
Enrollment: 37,200
Coed
Affiliation or Control: State
IRS Status: 501(c)3
Highest Offering: Doctorate
Program: Liberal Arts And General; Teacher Preparatory; Professional
Accreditation: M, AUD, BUS, CACREP, CEA, CLPSY, COPSY, DIETD, DIETI, ENG, IACBE, IPSY, JOUR, LIB, LSAR, MFCD, MUS, PH, PLNG, SCPSY, SP, SPAA, TED

02 President Dr. Wallace D. LOH
05 Sr Vice President & Provost Dr. Mary Ann RANKIN
11 Vice President Administrative Affs Mr. Carlo COLELLA
43 General Counsel Mr. J. Terrance ROACH
26 Vice President University Relations Mr. Peter B. WEILER
32 Vice President Student Affairs Dr. Linda M. CLEMENT
13 Vice President & CIO Mr. Brian D. VOSS
46 Vice President Research Dr. Patrick G. O'SHEA
47 Dean Col Agric/Natural Resources Dr. Cheng-I WEI
48 Dean Sch Architecture/Plng/Preserv Mr. David CRONRATH
79 Dean College Arts & Humanities Dr. Bonnie T. DILL
83 Dean Col Behavioral/Social Sciences Dr. John R. TOWNSHEND
50 Dean Smith School of Business Dr. G. Anand ANANDALINGAM
81 Dean Computer/Math/Natural Science Dr. Jayanth R. BANAVAR
53 Dean of College of Education Dr. Donna WISEMAN
54 Dean Clark School of Engineering Dr. Darryll J. PINES
69 Dean School of Public Health Dr. Jane E. CLARK
60 Dean Merrill College of Journalism Ms. Lucy DALGLISH
62 Dean College Info Studies Dr. Jennifer J. PREECE
80 Dean School Public Policy Dr. Donald F. KETTL
20 Dean Undergraduate Studies Dr. Donna B. HAMILTON
58 Dean Graduate School Dr. Charles A. CARAMELLO
08 Dean of Libraries Dr. Patricia A. STEELE
88 Assoc Provost International Affairs Dr. Ross LEWIN
09 Assoc VP/Inst Research & Planning Dr. Mona LEVINE
18 Int Assoc VP Facilities/Management Mr. John FARLEY
28 Assoc VP & Chief Diversity Officer Dr. Kumea SHORTER-GOODEN
39 Asst VP/Director Resident Life Dr. Deborah F. GRANDNER
25 Assoc VP/Dir Research Adv & Admin Ms. Denise CLARK
35 Asst Vice Pres Student Affairs Mr. John ZACKER
07 Asst Vice Pres Admissions Ms. Barbara A. GILL
06 Asst VP Records/Registration Mr. Chuck A. WILSON
37 Asst VP Student Financial Aid Ms. Sarah J. BAUDER
27 Asst VP Marketing & Communications Mr. Brian ULLMANN
20 Professor/Assoc Prov Faculty Affs Dr. Juan URIAGEREKA
29 Exec Director Alumni Association Mr. Ralph AMOS
36 Executive Director Career Center Mr. Kelley BISHOP
64 Director School of Music Dr. Robert L. GIBSON
85 Int Dir International Services Ms. Barbara VARSA
41 Director Athletics Mr. Kevin ANDERSON
40 Director University Book Center Mr. Mike GORE
23 Director Health Center Dr. Sacared A. BODISON
38 Director Counseling Center Dr. Sharon E. KIRKLAND-GORDON
19 Chief Campus Police Mr. David B. MITCHELL
15 Director University Human Resources Mr. Dale O. ANDERSON
92 Director University Honors Program Dr. William DORLAND
96 Director Procurement & Supply Mr. James S. STIRLING
31 Asst Director Community Service Mr. Craig SLACK

*University of Maryland Baltimore (C)

620 W. Lexington Street, Baltimore MD 21201-1508
County: Independent City
FICE Identification: 002104
Unit ID: 163259
Telephone: (410) 706-7004
Carnegie Class: Spec/Med
FAX Number: (410) 706-0500
Calendar System: 4/1/4
URL: www.umaryland.edu
Established: 1807
Annual Undergrad Tuition & Fees (In-State): $9,448
Enrollment: 6,368
Coed
Affiliation or Control: State
IRS Status: 501(c)3
Highest Offering: Doctorate
Program: Professional
Accreditation: M, ANEST, DENT, DH, DIETI, IPSY, LAW, MED, MT, NURSE, PA, PH, PHAR, PTA, RADDOS, SW

02 President Dr. Jay A. PERMAN
05 Sr VP/Chief Acad & Research Officer Dr. Bruce E. JARRELL
11 Sr VP/Chief Operating Officer Mr. Peter N. GILBERT
17 Vice President Medical Affairs/Dean Dr. E. Albert REECE
10 Chief Admin & Finance Officer/VP Ms. Kathleen M. BYINGTON
13 Vice President and CIO Dr. Peter J. MURRAY
46 Chief Enterprise & Econ Dev Ofcr/VP Mr. James L. HUGHES
26 Int Chief Communications Ofcr/VP Ms. Jennifer B. LITCHMAN
30 Chief Development Officer/VP Mr. Michael B. DOWDY
43 Chief University Counsel Ms. Susan GILLETTE
20 Assoc VP AA/Ch Accountability Ofc Dr. Roger J. WARD
18 Assoc VP Facilities & Operations Mr. Robert M. ROWAN
16 Assoc VP Human Resource Services Ms. Marjorie L. POWELL
86 Assoc VP Govt & Community Affairs Ms. Barbara A. KLEIN
21 Assoc Vice Pres Budget & Finance Mr. Scott BITNER
25 AVP Research & Global Health Init Ms. Marjorie FORSTER
14 Asst VP Information Technology Mr. Christopher G. PHILLIPS
24 Asst VP Technology Svcs & Support Mr. Paul S. PETROSKI
22 Asst Vice President for Compliance Vacant
09 Asst VP Institutional Research Mr. Gregory C. SPENGLER
37 Asst VP Student Financial Assist Ms. Patricia A. SCOTT
27 Asst VP Communications & Ext Aff Ms. Laura A. KOZAK
32 AVP Student Affairs & Wellness Mr. Flavius R. LILLY
88 AVP Sponsored Projects Accounting Ms. Lynn M. MCGINLEY
19 Chief of Police/AVP Public Safety Mr. Antonio WILLIAMS
08 Exec Dir Health Sci/Human Svc Libr Ms. Mary J. TOOEY
06 Director Records & Registration Mr. Thomas C. DAY
41 Dir Univ Recreation & Fitness Mr. William P. CROCKETT
88 Director Auxiliary Services Ms. Marion A. LIPINSKI
88 Director Benefits & Compensation Ms. Patricia ILOWITE
88 Coordinator Community Affairs Mr. Brian C. STURDIVANT
15 Exec Dir Human Resource Services Mr. Joseph T. SMITH
38 Director Counseling Ms. Emilia K. PETRILLO
35 Director Student Services Ms. Cynthia E. RICE
88 Director of Financial Services Ms. Susan E. MCKECHNIE
96 Director of Procurement Services Mr. Joseph EVANS
52 Interim Dean School of Dentistry Dr. Mark A. REYNOLDS
58 Dean Graduate School Dr. Bruce E. JARRELL
61 Dean School of Law Ms. Phoebe A. HADDON
63 Dean School of Medicine Dr. E. Albert REECE
66 Dean School of Nursing Dr. Jane M. KIRSCHLING
67 Dean School of Pharmacy Dr. Natalie D. EDDINGTON
70 Dean School of Social Work Dr. Richard P. BARTH
84 Asst Dean Grad Admin/Enrollment Mgt Mr. Keith BROOKS
45 Dir of Capital Budget and Planning Ms. Angela FOWLER-YOUNG

*University of Maryland Baltimore County (D)

1000 Hilltop Circle, Baltimore MD 21250-0001
County: Baltimore
FICE Identification: 002105
Unit ID: 163268
Telephone: (410) 455-1000
Carnegie Class: RU/H
FAX Number: (410) 455-1210
Calendar System: 4/1/4
URL: www.umbc.edu
Established: 1966
Annual Undergrad Tuition & Fees (In-State): $9,764
Enrollment: 13,637
Coed
Affiliation or Control: State
IRS Status: 501(c)3
Highest Offering: Doctorate
Program: Liberal Arts And General; Teacher Preparatory
Accreditation: M, CLPSY, CS, DANCE, DMS, EMT, ENG, SPAA, SW, TED

02 President Dr. Freeman A. HRABOWSKI
05 Provost/Sr Vice Pres Acad Affs Dr. Philip ROUS
10 Vice Pres Finance/Administration Ms. Lynne SCHAEFER
32 Vice President Student Affairs Dr. Nancy YOUNG
30 Vice Pres Institutional Advancement Mr. Gregory SIMMONS
27 Vice Pres Information Technology Mr. Jack J. SUESS
46 Vice President of Research Dr. Karl V. STEINER
49 Dean Col of Arts/Humanities/Soc Sci Dr. Scott CASPER
81 Int Dean Col Natural/Math Sciences Dr. William LACOURSE
54 Dean College of Engr/Info Tech Dr. Warren R. DEVRIES
84 Asst Dean Graduate Enrollment Mgmt Ms. K. Jill BARR
20 Vice Provost/Dean Undergrad Educ Dr. Diane M. LEE
51 VP Cont/Prf Std/Ex Dir Shriver Ctr Dr. John S. MARTELLO
20 Vice Provost Academic Affairs Dr. Antonio R. MOREIRA
58 Dean/Vice Provost for Graduate Educ Dr. Janet RUTLEDGE
15 Vice Provost Faculty Affairs Dr. Patrice MCDERMOTT
84 Associate Provost Enrollment Mgmt Dr. Yvette MOZIE-ROSS
21 Assoc VP Financial Services Mr. Benjamin LOWENTHAL
26 Assistant to Pres/Assoc VP Mktg/PR Ms. Lisa G. AKCHIN
11 Assoc VP Administrative Services Ms. Terry COOK
15 Associate VP for Human Resources Ms. Valerie A. THOMAS
29 Director Alumni Relations Ms. Stanyell BRUCE
88 Asst VP New Media/Instruction Tech Mr. John FRITZ
18 Asst VP Facilities Management Mr. Rusty POSTLEWATE
04 Senior Advisor to the President Dr. Peter HENDERSON
96 Director of Procurement Ms. Sharon QUINN
92 Acting Director Honors College Dr. Simon STACEY
41 Director Physical Educ & Recreation Dr. Tim HALL
19 Director University Police Mr. Mark SPARKS
36 Asst VP Career & Corp Partnership Ms. Caroline BAKER
23 Director Health Services Ms. Jennifer LEPUS
37 Director Financial Aid Ms. Stephanie JOHNSON
27 Senior Manager Communications Ms. Chelsea HADDAWAY-WILLIAMS
25 Director Sponsored Programs Ms. Christina STANGER
40 Director of UMBC Bookstore Mr. Robert J. SOMERS
85 Director International Educ Svcs Dr. Arlene V. ODENWALD
08 Director Library Dr. Larry M. WILT
06 Registrar Mr. Steven SMITH
35 Director Student Life Ms. Lee CALIZO
43 General Counsel Mr. David GLEASON
07 Dir Undergrd Admissions Mr. Dale BITTINGER
39 Director Residential Life Ms. Katherine B. BOONE
09 Director of Institutional Research Dr. Michael DILLON
38 Director Student Counseling Dr. Bruce HERMAN
100 Chief of Staff President's Office Ms. Elyse ASHBURN

*University of Maryland Eastern Shore (E)

Princess Anne MD 21853-1299
County: Somerset
FICE Identification: 002106
Unit ID: 163338
Telephone: (410) 651-2200
Carnegie Class: Master's S
FAX Number: (410) 651-6105
Calendar System: Semester
URL: www.umes.edu
Established: 1886
Annual Undergrad Tuition & Fees (In-State): $6,998
Enrollment: 4,454
Coed
Affiliation or Control: State
IRS Status: 501(c)3
Highest Offering: Doctorate
Program: Liberal Arts And General; Teacher Preparatory; Professional
Accreditation: M, ARCPA, BUS, CONST, CORE, DIETD, DIETI, PHAR, PTA, TED

02 President Dr. Juliette B. BELL
04 Executive Assistant to President Vacant
05 Provost/VP Academic Affairs Dr. Ronald A. NYKIEL
10 Vice Pres Administrative Affairs Dr. Ronnie E. HOLDEN
30 Vice President Inst Advancement Ms. Kimberly C. DUMPSON
32 Vice President Student Affairs Dr. Anthony L. JENKINS
88 VP Research/Economic Development Dr. Garlen D. WESSON
20 Asst Vice Pres Academic Affairs Vacant
20 Assoc Vice Pres Academic Affairs Dr. Bernita M. SIMS-TUCKER
11 Asst Vice President Admin Affairs Mr. Alverne W. CHESTERFIELD
88 Asst to VP Administrative Affairs Dr. Maurice C. NGWABA
21 Asst VP Admin Affs/Budget Director Ms. Nelva G. COLLIER-WHITE
15 Asst VP Human Resources Ms. Marie H. BILLIE
84 Assoc VP Student Life/Enroll Mgt Dr. James M. WHITE
04 Special Assistant to the President Ms. Rolanda C. BURNEY
91 Director Administrative Computing Mr. Kenneth GASTON
56 Assoc Dir Cooperative Extension Dr. Henry M. BROOKS
29 Director Alumni Affairs Vacant
08 Dean Library Services Dr. Ellis B. BETECK
37 Director Financial Aid Mr. James W. KELLAM
23 Director Student Health Services Ms. Sharone V. GRANT
96 Director Procurement Ms. Jacqueline M. COLLINS
88 Director Univ Dining Services Mr. David SCOTT
07 Director Admissions Mr. Tyrone YOUNG
06 Registrar Ms. Cheryl HOLDEN-DUFFY
12 Director Richard A Henson Center Dr. Corey J. BOWEN
36 Director Career Services Dr. Theresa QUEENAN
09 Director Inst Research/Plng/Assess Dr. Stanley M. NYIRENDA
19 Director Public Safety Mr. Ernest LEATHERBURY, JR.
18 Director Physical Plant Mr. Leon J. BIVENS
39 Director Residence Life Mr. Marvin L. JONES
41 Athletic Director Mr. Keith S. DAVIDSON
21 Comptroller Ms. Bonita E. BYRD
46 Director Sponsored Research Ms. Catherine BOLEK
88 Director Student Retention & Svcs Ms. Stephanie L. KRAH
88 Director Rural Development Vacant
88 Director Upward Bound Dr. Nicole L. GALE
35 Director Student Activities Mr. James G. LUNNERMON, JR.
88 Director Title III Program Dr. Frances H. MCKINNEY
26 Director Public Relations Mr. William ROBINSON
44 Director Development Dr. Veronique L. DIRIKER
88 Director Advancement Services Mrs. Chenita R. KOLLOCK
51 Coordinator Continuing Education Ms. Gretchen M. BOGGS
38 Coordinator Counseling Services Dr. Patricia E. TILGHMAN
58 Dean Graduate Studies Dr. Jennifer M. KEANE-DAWES
47 Dean School Agric/Natural Sciences Dr. Moses T. KAIRO
49 Dean School of Arts & Professions Dr. Ray J. DAVIS
50 Dean School Business & Technology Dr. Ayodele J. ALADE
67 Dean Sch Pharmacy/Health Profession Dr. Nicholas R. BLANCHARD

*University of Maryland University College (F)

3501 University Boulevard East, Adelphi MD 20783-7998
County: Prince Georges
FICE Identification: 011644
Unit ID: 163204
Telephone: (301) 985-7000
Carnegie Class: Master's L
FAX Number: (301) 985-7678
Calendar System: Semester
URL: www.umuc.edu
Established: 1947
Annual Undergrad Tuition & Fees (In-State): $6,384
Enrollment: 42,268
Coed
Affiliation or Control: State
IRS Status: 501(c)3
Highest Offering: Doctorate
Program: Liberal Arts And General; Professional
Accreditation: M, CAHIIM

02 President Mr. Javier MIYARES
11 Chief Operating Officer Mr. George SHOENBERGER
10 Vice Pres Chief Financial Officer Mr. Eugene D. LOCKETT, JR.

05 Provost/Sr Vice Pres Academic Affs ......Dr. Marie CINI
26 Sr Vice President Communications ......Mr. Michael FREEDMAN
45 Sr VP Institutional Effectiveness ......Vacant
86 Sr VP Partnerships Mktg Enroll Mgmt ......Mr. James H. SELBE
13 Sr Vice Pres Analytics/Plng/Tech ......Mr. Peter C. YOUNG
43 Sr Vice President & General Counsel ...Ms. Nancy WILLIAMSON
15 Act VP/Chief Human Resources Ofcr ......Mr. John PETROV
84 Vice Pres Enrollment Management ......Mr. Sean CHUNG
86 Vice Pres Fed Government ......Ms. Sarah DUFENDACH
28 Ombudsman/VP Diversity Initiatives ......Dr. Blair HAYES
18 Associate Vice President Facilities ......Mr. George TRUJILLO
88 Associate VP State Government ......Ms. Susan O'BRIEN
37 AVP Student Financial Aid ......Ms. Cheryl STORIE
58 Vice Prov/Dean The Graduate School ......Mr. Aric KRAUSE
08 Assoc Provost of Library Services ......Mr. Stephen MILLER
06 Assoc Vice Provost/Registrar ......Ms. Joellen SHENDY
49 Acting Dean The Undergrad School ......Ms. Cynthia DAVIS
09 Sr Director Institutional Research ......Wei ZHOU
07 Director of Admissions ......Ms. Insiya JIWANJI

*Bowie State University (A)

14000 Jericho Park Road, Bowie MD 20715-3318

County: Prince Georges FICE Identification: 002062
Unit ID: 162007
Telephone: (301) 860-4000 Carnegie Class: DRU
FAX Number: (301) 860-3510 Calendar System: Semester
URL: www.bowiestate.edu
Established: 1865 Annual Undergrad Tuition & Fees (In-State): $6,971
Enrollment: 5,421 Coed
Affiliation or Control: State IRS Status: 501(c)3
Highest Offering: Doctorate
Program: Liberal Arts And General; Teacher Preparatory
Accreditation: M, ACBSP, NUR, SPAA, SW, TED

02 President ......Dr. Mickey L. BURNIM
05 Provost/Vice Pres Academic Affs ......Dr. Weldon JACKSON
10 Vice Pres Finance & Administration ......Dr. Karl B. BROCKENBROUGH
30 Vice Pres Institutional Advancement ......Dr. Richard LUCAS, JR.
32 VP Student Affairs/Campus Life ......Dr. Artie L. TRAVIS
43 Vice Pres & General Counsel ....Ms. Karen JOHNSON-SHAHEED
35 Student Code of Conduct ......Mrs. Thomaice BOARDLEY
13 VP Office of Information Technology ......Dr. E. Wayne ROSE
84 Asst VP Enrollment Management ......Mr. Clayton STEEN
88 Asst to Prov Institutional Effec ......Ms. Gayle M. FINK
06 University Registrar ......Ms. Patricia MITCHELL
08 Assoc Library Dir/Interim Dean ......Ms. Marian RUCKER-SHAMU
36 Director Career Services ......Ms. April JOHNOSON
15 Sr Director of Human Resources ......Ms. Sheila HOBSON
19 Chief of Campus Police ......Mr. Ernest WAITERS
58 Int Dean Sch of Grad Stds/Research ....Dr. Cosmos NWOKEAFOR
49 Dean School of Arts & Sciences ......Dr. George ACQUAAH
50 Dean School of Business ......Dr. Anthony NELSON
53 Dean Sch of Education ......Dr. Traki TAYLOR-WEBB
107 Dean School of Professional Studies ......Dr. Jerome H. SCHIELE
92 Director UCE Honors Program ......Dr. Monika GROSS
23 Director University Wellness Center ......Dr. Rita WUTHO
41 Director Athletics ......Mr. Anton GOFF
26 Dir University Relations/ Marketing ......Ms. Cassandra M. ROBINSON
88 Director University Wiseman Centre ......Mr. Frank WALLER
37 Director Financial Aid ......Ms. Deborah STANLEY
18 Director Facilities ......Mr. Darryl WILLIFORD
07 Director Undergraduate Admissions ......Mr. Lonnie MORRIS
29 Director of Alumni Relations ......Ms. Anette WEDDERBURN
96 Director of Purchasing ......Mr. Steve A. JOST
09 Director of Institutional Research ......Dr. Doug NUTTER
100 Chief of Staff ......Mrs. Tammi L. THOMAS

*Coppin State University (B)

2500 W North Avenue, Baltimore MD 21216-3698

County: Baltimore City FICE Identification: 002068
Unit ID: 162283
Telephone: (410) 951-3000 Carnegie Class: Master's S
FAX Number: (410) 333-5369 Calendar System: Semester
URL: www.coppin.edu
Established: 1900 Annual Undergrad Tuition & Fees (In-State): $6,065
Enrollment: 2,729 Coed
Affiliation or Control: State IRS Status: 501(c)3
Highest Offering: Doctorate
Program: Liberal Arts And General; Teacher Preparatory; Professional
Accreditation: M, CAHIIM, CORE, NUR, NURSE, SW, TED

02 President ......Dr. Mortimer H. NEUFVILLE
05 Provost/VP Academic Affairs ......Dr. Sadie R. GREGORY
30 VP Institutional Advancement ......Mr. Douglas DALZELL
10 VP Administration & Finance ......Mr. John SPINARD
32 Vice Pres Student Affairs ......Dr. Franklin D. CHAMBERS
13 VP Information Systems/CIO ......Dr. Ahmed EL-HAGGAN
84 Acting VP Enrollment Management ......Dr. Monica RANDALL
45 Assoc VP Planning/Assessment ......Dr. Scott J. DANTLEY
20 Actg Assoc Vice Pres Academic Affs ......Dr. Habtu BRAHA
21 Assoc Vice Pres Admin/Finance ......Vacant
32 Associate VP Student Affairs ....Dr. Joann CHRISTOPHER-HICKS
18 Assoc VP Capital Plng/Constr & Cont ......Mr. Maqbool PATEL
86 Assoc VP of Pub Policy & Govt Rel ......Dr. Monica E. RANDALL
07 Director of Admissions ......Ms. Michelle R. GROSS
06 Interim Registrar ......Ms. Karen BARLAND
21 Controller ......Mrs. Crystal MOSLEY
08 Director of the Library ......Dr. Mary WANZA
37 Director of Financial Aid ......Mr. Mose CARTIER
36 Director of Career Services Center ......Mrs. Linda BOWIE
15 Director of Human Resorces ......Mrs. Lisa EARLY
19 Chief of Public Safety ......Chief Leonard HAMM
39 Director of Housing/Residence Life ......Mrs. Vallyn MERRICK
41 Director of Athletics ......Mr. Derrick RAMSEY
35 Director Student Support Services ......Ms. Leila WASHINGTON
88 Director Academic Resource Center ......Vacant
88 Director of Academic Advisement ......Vacant
29 Director Alumni Relations ......Ms. Tara TURNER
96 Director of Purchasing ......Mr. Thomas E. DAWSON, JR.
26 Director of University Relations ......Vacant
88 Director Client Computing Services ......Mr. Emmanuel OWUSU-SEKYERE
88 Director Coppin Academy ......Mr. Frank WHORLEY
35 Director of Student Activities ......Mrs. Jocelyn BRYANT
27 Director Telecommunications ......Mr. Claude K. RADER
105 Director Web & Multimedia ......Mr. Andrew C. BAIN
31 Exec Dir of Community Partnerships ......Mr. Albert ROBINSON
92 Dean Honors College & McNair Pgms ......Mr. Ronnie L. COLLINS, SR.
58 Dean Graduate School ......Dr. Mary E. OWENS-SOUTHHALL
66 Dean of Nursing ......Dr. Marcella COPES
04 Executive Assistant to President ......Mrs. Sherie JOHNSON
88 Chair Interdisciplinary Studies ......Ms. Tondelaya BLACKSTONE
97 Chair General & Adult Education ......Dr. Jacqueline H. WILLIAMS
88 Int Chr Applied Psych/Rehab Counsel ......Mr. James STEWART
61 Chair Crim Justice/Law Enforcement ......Dr. Dilip DAS
53 Chair Curriculum & Instruction ......Dr. Glynis BARBER
57 Chair Fine Arts ......Dr. Garey HYATT
82 Chair History Geography/Global Stds ......Dr. Katherine BANKOLE-MEDINA
79 Interim Chair Humanities ......Dr. Seth FORREST
50 Chr Mgmt Sci & Economics (Business) ......Dr. Habtu BRAHA
77 Int Chair Math & Computer Science ......Dr. Sean BROOKS
65 Chair Natural Sciences ......Dr. Gilbert OGONJI
83 Chair Social Sciences ......Dr. John L. HUDGINS
70 Chair Social Work ......Dr. Errol BOLDEN
68 Chair Health/Physical Education ......Dr. Edna SIMMONS
88 Chair Special Education ......Dr. Daniel P. JOSEPH

*Frostburg State University (C)

101 Braddock Road, Frostburg MD 21532-2303

County: Allegany FICE Identification: 002072
Unit ID: 162584
Telephone: (301) 687-4000 Carnegie Class: Master's L
FAX Number: (301) 687-4737 Calendar System: Semester
URL: www.frostburg.edu
Established: 1898 Annual Undergrad Tuition & Fees (In-State): $7,728
Enrollment: 5,421 Coed
Affiliation or Control: State IRS Status: 501(c)3
Highest Offering: Doctorate
Program: Liberal Arts And General; Teacher Preparatory
Accreditation: M, BUS, NRPA, NURSE, SW, TED

02 President ......Dr. Jonathan GIBRALTER
05 Interim Provost & VP Acad Affairs ......Dr. William P. CHILDS
32 Vice Pres Student/Education Svcs ......Dr. Thomas L. BOWLING
10 Vice President for Admin & Finance ......Mr. David C. ROSE
30 Vice Pres Univ Advancement ......Dr. Rosemary M. THOMAS
84 Assoc VP for Enrollment Management ......Mr. Wray BLAIR
86 Chief of Staff/VP for Govt Relation ......Mr. Steven SPAHR
15 Vice President Human Resources ......Ms. Katherine SNYDER
43 University Counsel ......Ms. Karen A. TREBER
20 Interim Associate Provost ......Dr. Randall RHODES
21 Assoc VP Finance & Controller ......Mr. Richard A. REPAC
35 Asst VP Student Svcs/Dean of Stdnts ......Dr. Jesse KETTERMAN
88 Associate VP Univ Advancement ......Ms. Colleen STUMP
35 Asst Vice Pres Student Services ......Mr. Bernard WYNDER
45 Assoc Director Budget & Planning ......Ms. Denise MURPHY
20 Vice Provost ......Dr. John BOWMAN
49 Dean Col Liberal Arts & Science ......Dr. Joseph M. HOFFMAN
50 Dean College of Business ......Dr. Ahmad TOOTOONCHI
53 Dean College of Education ......Dr. Clarence GOLDEN
08 Director of the Library ......Dr. David M. GILLESPIE
37 Director of Financial Aid ......Mrs. Angela L. HOVATTER
108 Asst Vice Pres Planning and Assess ......Mr. Robert E. SMITH
09 Director of Institutional Research ......Vacant
58 Director of Graduate Services ......Ms. Vickie MAZER
18 Director Facilities/Physical Plant ......Mr. Robert BOYCE
27 Director News & Media Services ......Ms. Elizabeth MEDCALF
36 Director Career Services ......Dr. Robbie L. CORDLE
38 Director Counseling & Psyc Svcs ......Dr. Spencer F. DEAKIN
40 Director Bookstore & ID Services ......Ms. Melissa HILLER
41 Athletic Director ......Mr. Troy DELL
19 Chief University Police ......Col. Cynthia SMITH
90 Director of Academic Computing ......Ms. Beth KENNEY
91 Director of Admin Computing ......Mr. Bruce LEHMAN
44 Director Annual Giving ......Ms. Shannon L. GRIBBLE
22 Director of AA/EEO ......Mrs. Beth HOFFMAN
25 Dir Research/Sponsored Programs ......Mr. Aaron HOEL
07 Director of Admissions ......Ms. Trisha GREGORY
28 Director of Diversity ......Ms. Robin WYNDER
29 Director Alumni Programs ......Ms. Laura C. MCCULLOUGH
13 Dir Networking/Telecommunications ......Vacant
96 Coord Procurement/Material Handling ......Mr. Alan R. SNYDER
23 Director Health Services ......Ms. Mary A. TOLA
39 Director Residence Life ......Mr. Dana A. SEVERANCE
06 Registrar ......Mr. Jay HEGEMAN

*Salisbury University (D)

1101 Camden Avenue, Salisbury MD 21801-6860

County: Wicomico FICE Identification: 002091
Unit ID: 163851
Telephone: (410) 543-6000 Carnegie Class: Master's L
FAX Number: (410) 548-2587 Calendar System: Semester
URL: www.salisbury.edu
Established: 1925 Annual Undergrad Tuition & Fees (In-State): $8,128
Enrollment: 8,657 Coed
Affiliation or Control: State IRS Status: 501(c)3
Highest Offering: Doctorate
Program: Liberal Arts And General; Teacher Preparatory; Professional
Accreditation: M, BUS, COARC, EXSC, MT, MUS, NURSE, SW, TED

02 President ......Dr. Janet E. DUDLEY-ESHBACH
05 Provost & Sr VP of Acad Affairs ......Dr. Diane D. ALLEN
100 Chief of Staff ......Ms. Amy S. HASSON
10 Vice Pres Administration/Finance ......Mrs. Betty P. CROCKETT
32 Vice Pres of Student Affairs ......Dr. Dane R. FOUST
30 Vice Pres Advancement/External Affs ......Mr. T. Greg PRINCE
84 Asst VP of Enrollment Management ......Mr. Aaron M. BASKO
28 Chief Diversity Officer ......Vacant
35 Associate VP of Student Affairs ......Ms. Mentha HYNES-WILSON
20 Associate Provost ......Dr. Melanie L. PERREAULT
20 Asst Vice Pres Academic Affairs ......Ms. Melissa M. BOOG
18 Assoc VP Facilities & Cap Mgmt ......Mr. Eric J. BERKHEIMER
35 Dean of Students ......Vacant
27 Chief Information Officer ......Mr. Simeon ANANOU
26 Director of Public Relations ......Mr. Richard W. CULVER
88 Director of University Dining Svcs ......Vacant
41 Director of Athletics ......Dr. Michael P. VIENNA
92 Director Honors Program ......Dr. James BUSS
06 Registrar ......Ms. Jacqueline M. MAISEL
07 Director of Admissions ......Ms. Elizabeth A. SKOGLUND
09 Special Asst to Pres/UARA ......Dr. Kara O. SIEGERT
08 Dean of Libraries & Instr Resources ......Dr. Beatriz B. HARDY
38 Director of Counseling Center ......Dr. Kathleen J. SCOTT
36 Director of Career Services ......Dr. Rebecca A. EMERY
37 Director of Financial Aid ......Ms. Barri ZIMMERMAN
15 Assoc VP of Admin & Finance for HR ......Mr. Marvin L. PYLES
29 Dir Alumni Relations & Gift Develop ......Mr. Jayme E. BLOCK
23 Director of Student Health Services ......Vacant
35 Int Director of Student Activities ......Ms. Sara LOWERY
86 Dir of Govt & Community Relations ......Mr. Robert J. SHEEHAN
43 Interim General Counsel ......Mr. Todd ENSMINGER
39 Director Housing/Residence Life ......Mr. David P. GUTOSKEY
19 Director of Public Safety ......Mr. Edwin L. LASHLEY
40 Director of Bookstore ......Ms. Lisa G. GRAY
18 Director of Physical Plant ......Mr. Kevin J. MANN
96 Director of Purchasing ......Ms. Tonia NIXON
75 Dean Henson Sch Science/Tech ......Dr. Karen L. OLMSTEAD
50 Dean Perdue School of Business ......Dr. Bob G. WOOD
49 Dean Fulton School of Liberal Arts ......Dr. Maarten L. PEREBOOM
53 Dean Seidel Sch Ed/Prof Studies ......Dr. Cheryl PARKS
58 Dean Graduate Studies/Research ......Dr. Clifton P. GRIFFIN
88 Dir Ctr for Student Achievement ......Dr. Heather W. HOLMES

*Towson University (E)

8000 York Road, Baltimore MD 21252-0001

County: Baltimore FICE Identification: 002099
Unit ID: 164076
Telephone: (410) 704-2000 Carnegie Class: Master's L
FAX Number: N/A Calendar System: 4/1/4
URL: www.towson.edu
Established: 1866 Annual Undergrad Tuition & Fees (In-State): $8,132
Enrollment: 21,960 Coed
Affiliation or Control: State IRS Status: 501(c)3
Highest Offering: Doctorate
Program: Liberal Arts And General; Teacher Preparatory; Professional
Accreditation: M, ARCPA, AUD, BUS, BUSA, CS, DANCE, FEPAC, IPSY, MUS, NURSE, OT, SP, TED, THEA

02 President ......Dr. Maravene S. LOESCHKE
05 Provost/Vice Pres Academic Affairs ......Dr. Timothy CHANDLER
10 Vice Pres Admin & Finance ......Mr. Joseph J. OSTER
30 Vice Pres University Advancement ......Dr. Gary N. RUBIN
32 Vice President Student Affairs ......Dr. Debra MORIARTY
46 VP Div of Innovation/Applied Rsrch ...Ms. Dyan L. BRASINGTON
100 Chief of Staff ......Ms. Jennifer GAJEWSKI
88 Deputy Chief of Staff ......Ms. Marina COOPER
04 Spec Asst to the Pres Div & Equ Opp ......Dr. Debra SEEBERGER
20 Vice Provost ......Dr. James DILISIO
84 Interim Sr Assoc VP Enrollment Mgmt ......Mr. Robert GIORDANI
44 Assoc Vice President Development ......Mr. Michael CATHER
26 Int Sr Dir Marketing/ Communications ......Ms. Josianne E. PENNINGTON
29 Assoc Vice Pres Alumni Relations ......Ms. Lori B. ARMSTRONG
13 Assoc Vice President OTS/CIO ......Mr. Jeffrey SCHMIDT
31 Actg Assoc Vice Pres Auxiliary Svcs ......Mr. Robert CAMPBELL
18 Assoc Vice Pres Facilities Mgmt ......Mr. Roger HAYDEN
21 Assoc VP Fiscal Planning & Svcs ......Vacant
15 Associate Vice Pres Human Resources ......Mr. Phillip ROSS, III
35 Assoc Vice Pres Student Affairs ......Dr. Jana VARWIG
45 Assoc Prov Academic Res & Plng ......Dr. Gary LEVY
88 Assoc Vice President Campus Life ......Dr. Teresa HALL
28 Asst VP Ctr for Student Diversity ......Mr. L. Victor COLLINS
39 Asst VP/Dir Housing/Residence Life ....Mr. Jerome T. DIERINGER
37 Acting Director for Financial Aid ......Mr. David HORNE
25 Asst VP University Research Svcs ......Ms. Amy TAYLOR
07 Acting Director of Admissions ......Mr. David FEDORCHAK

19 Asst VP Public Sfty/Chief of Police .... Chief Bernard GERST
53 Dean College of Education .... Dr. Raymond LORION
50 Dean College of Business/Economics .... Dr. Shohreh KAYNAMA
49 Dean College of Liberal Arts .... Dr. Terry COONEY
81 Dean J&M Fisher Col of Science/Math .... Dr. David VANKO
57 Dean Col Fine Arts/Communications .... Ms. Susan PICINICH
76 Dean College of Health Professions .... Dr. Charlotte E. EXNER
92 Dean Honors College .... Dr. Joseph MCGINN
43 University Counsel .... Mr. Michael A. AMSELMI
08 Dean of University Libraries .... Ms. Deborah NOLAN
104 Director Study Abroad .... Dr. Rebecca L. PISANO
94 Chair Women's Studies .... Dr. Karen DUGGER
09 Director Institutional Research .... Vacant
27 Dir Communications/Media Relations .... Mr. Raymond C. FELDMANN
41 Interim Director of Athletics .... Ms. Tricia BRANDENBURG
23 Director of Health Services .... Dr. Jane L. HALPERN
40 Director of University Bookstore .... Ms. Stacey ELOFIR
96 Director of Procurement .... Ms. Lucy SLAICH
88 Exec Dir Technology Support Svcs .... Vacant
38 Director Counseling Center .... Dr. Gregory REISING
36 Director of Career Services .... Ms. Lorie LOGAN-BENNETT
06 Associate Registrar .... Ms. Susan HYMAN

*University of Baltimore (A)

1420 N Charles Street, Baltimore MD 21201-5779
County: Independent City — FICE Identification: 002102
Unit ID: 161873
Telephone: (410) 837-4200 — Carnegie Class: Master's L
FAX Number: N/A — Calendar System: Semester
URL: www.ubalt.edu
Established: 1925 — Annual Undergrad Tuition & Fees (In-State): $8,838
Enrollment: 6,558 — Coed
Affiliation or Control: State — IRS Status: 501(c)3
Highest Offering: Doctorate
Program: Liberal Arts And General; Professional
Accreditation: M, BUS, LAW, SPAA

02 President .... Mr. Robert L. BOGOMOLNY
05 Provost & Sr VP Academic Affairs .... Dr. Joseph S. WOOD
10 Sr VP Admin & Finance .... Mr. Harry SCHUCKEL
100 Exec Dir Pres Operations & Projects .... Ms. Susan SCHUBERT
84 Sr Vice Pres Enrollment Management .... Ms. Miriam E. KING
30 Vice Pres Institutional Advancement .... Ms. Theresa SILANSKIS
45 Vice Pres Planning/External Affairs .... Mr. Peter TORAN
86 VP Government & Community Relations .... Ms. Anita THOMAS
18 VP Facil Mgmt/Capital Planning .... Mr. Steve CASSARD
13 Vice Pres Technology/CIO .... Mr. David BOBART
15 Asst Vice Pres Human Resources .... Ms. Mary MAHER
20 Associate Provost .... Dr. Beverly SCHNELLER
09 AVP for Institutional Research .... Mr. Paul MONIODIS
35 Assoc Vice Pres Student Affairs .... Ms. Shelia BURKHALTER
32 Dean of Students .... Ms. Kathleen ANDERSON
35 Director Center Student Involvement .... Ms. Kari OSBORNE
28 Dir Diversity and Culture Center .... Ms. Karla M. SHEPHERD
07 Actg Executive Director Admissions .... Ms. Janet WHELAN
08 Director of Library .... Ms. Lucy HOLMAN
19 Chief of Police .... Mr. Samuel D. TRESS
07 AVP for Enrollment Services .... Ms. Anne HAMILL
96 Director of Procurement & Supply .... Mr. Blair BLANKINSHIP
44 Dir Annual Giving/Alumni Relations .... Ms. Kate CRIMMINS
38 Director Counseling Services .... Dr. Myra WATERS
36 Director Career & Professional Dev .... Mr. Ray MCCREE
06 Registrar .... Mr. Michael DRISCOLL
09 Director Institutional Research .... Mr. Merrill R. PRITCHETT
27 Manager Public Information .... Mr. Chris HART
80 Dean College of Public Affairs .... Dr. Steve PERCY
49 Dean College of Arts & Sci .... Dr. Laura BRYAN
61 Dean of the School of Law .... Dr. Ronald WEICH
50 Dean School of Business .... Dr. Darlene SMITH
88 Dir Center for Education Access .... Ms. Karyn SCHULZ
21 AVP Admin & University Budget Dir .... Ms. Barbara AUGHENBAUGH
07 AVP Admissions .... Mr. David WAGGONER

Washington Adventist University (B)

7600 Flower Avenue, Takoma Park MD 20912-7794
County: Montgomery — FICE Identification: 002067
Unit ID: 162210
Telephone: (301) 891-4000 — Carnegie Class: Bac/Diverse
FAX Number: (301) 270-1618 — Calendar System: Semester
URL: www.wau.edu
Established: 1904 — Annual Undergrad Tuition & Fees: $20,180
Enrollment: 1,403 — Coed
Affiliation or Control: Seventh-day Adventist — IRS Status: 501(c)3
Highest Offering: Master's
Program: Liberal Arts And General; Teacher Preparatory; Professional
Accreditation: M, COARC, NUR

01 President .... Dr. Weymouth SPENCE
10 Exec VP Financial Administration .... Mr. Patrick FARLEY
32 Vice Pres Student Life .... Ms. Jean WARDEN
13 Assoc VP for Info Tech Systems .... Mr. Gregory INGRAM
58 Dean Sch Grad/Professional Studies .... Vacant
33 Dean of Men .... Mr. Tim NELSON
34 Dean of Women .... Ms. Adrienne MATTHEWS
08 Librarian .... Ms. Lee Marie WISEL
30 Director of Development .... Vacant
06 Director of Records/Admissions .... Vacant
19 Director Safety & Security .... Vacant
42 Chaplain .... Baraka MUGANDA
41 Athletic Director .... Vacant
84 Director of Student Recruiting .... Vacant
29 Director of Alumni .... Vacant
15 Director of Human Resources .... Ms. Erytheia JONES
27 Director Marketing & Communications .... Mr. William JACKSON
78 Dir Coop Educ/Acad Support & Test .... Mr. Fitzroy THOMAS
18 Chief Facilities/Physical Plant .... Mr. Steve LAPHAM
37 Director Student Financial Aid .... Ms. Sharon CONWAY
38 Director Student Counseling .... Vacant
09 Director of Institutional Research .... Ms. Janette NEUFVILLE
40 Manager the College Bookstore .... Mr. Lloyd YUTUC

Washington College (C)

300 Washington Avenue, Chestertown MD 21620-1197
County: Kent — FICE Identification: 002108
Unit ID: 164216
Telephone: (410) 778-2800 — Carnegie Class: Bac/A&S
FAX Number: (410) 778-7850 — Calendar System: Semester
URL: www.washcoll.edu
Established: 1782 — Annual Undergrad Tuition & Fees: $41,120
Enrollment: 1,512 — Coed
Affiliation or Control: Independent Non-Profit — IRS Status: 501(c)3
Highest Offering: Master's
Program: Liberal Arts And General; Teacher Preparatory; Fine Arts Emphasis
Accreditation: M

01 President .... Dr. Mitchell B. REISS
05 Provost/Dean of College .... Dr. Emily CHAMLEE-WRIGHT
100 Chief of Staff .... Mr. Joseph L. HOLT
10 Senior Vice Pres Finance & Mgmt .... Mr. James V. MANARO
30 Sr Vice Pres College Advancement .... Mrs. Barbara H. HECK
44 Vice President College Advancement .... Mr. Gary B. GRANT
84 Vice Pres Enrollment Mgmt .... Mr. Satyajit DATTAGUPTA
26 Asst VP College Relations/Marketing .... Vacant
32 Vice President & Dean of Students .... Vacant
29 Dir Alumni Rels/Ldrship Annual Gvng .... Ms. Rebekah L. HARDY
09 Asst Provost Inst Research & Assmt .... Mr. Dale W. TRUSHEIM
20 Asst Dean Academic Initiatives .... Dr. Andrea G. LANGE
31 Director of Campus Special Events .... Mrs. Laura J. WILSON
41 Director of Athletics .... Dr. Bryan L. MATTHEWS
06 Registrar .... Mr. James A. THIEMANN
08 Director of Miller Library .... Dr. Ruth C. SHOGE
27 Chief Information Officer .... Mrs. Billie S. DODGE
91 Director of Admin Computing .... Mr. Kenneth W. SUTTON
58 Director of Graduate Program .... Dr. Andrea LANGE
21 Controller .... Ms. Penelope L. FARLEY
18 Director of Physical Plant .... Mr. Reid C. RAUDENBUSH
15 Director of Human Resources .... Dr. Alan P. CHESNEY
19 Director of Public Safety .... Mr. Gerald K. RODERICK
37 Director of Financial Aid .... Ms. Jeani M. NARCUM
35 Dir of Student Development Programs .... Dr. Sarah R. FEYERHERM
39 Dir Resid Life/Assoc Dean of Stdnts .... Mr. Carl CROWE
85 Director International Programs .... Ms. Kathryn S. MCCLEARY
23 Clinical Director Health Services .... Mrs. Lisa MARX
38 Director of Counseling Center .... Dr. Bonnie MICHAELSON FISHER
36 Director of Career Development .... Mr. James M. ALLISON, JR.
28 Director of Multi-Cultural Affairs .... Mr. Darnell PARKER
27 Director of Media Relations .... Mrs. Kay H. MACINTOSH
40 Bookstore Manager .... Ms. Shannon WYBLE

Wor-Wic Community College (D)

32000 Campus Drive, Salisbury MD 21804-1486
County: Wicomico — FICE Identification: 020739
Unit ID: 164313
Telephone: (410) 334-2800 — Carnegie Class: Assoc/Pub-R-M
FAX Number: (410) 334-2951 — Calendar System: Semester
URL: www.worwic.edu
Established: 1975 — Annual Undergrad Tuition & Fees (In-District): $3,240
Enrollment: 3,739 — Coed
Affiliation or Control: Local — IRS Status: 501(c)3
Highest Offering: Associate Degree
Program: Occupational; 2-Year Principally Bachelor's Creditable
Accreditation: M, ACFEI, RAD

01 President .... Dr. Murray K. HOY
05 Vice Pres Academic & Student Affs .... Dr. Stephen L. CAPELLI
11 Vice Pres Administrative Services .... Ms. Jennifer A. SANDT
26 Vice Pres Institutional Affairs .... Dr. Reenie MCCORMICK
32 Dean Student Development .... Dr. Lynn M. WILJANEN
51 Dean Continuing Education .... Mrs. Ruth E. BAKER
97 Dean General Education .... Dr. Colleen C. DALLAM
75 Dean Occupational Education .... Dr. Trevor H. JONES
07 Director Admissions .... Mr. Richard C. WEBSTER
14 Director Information Technology .... Ms. Ruth GILL
36 Director Career Services .... Ms. Lori SMOOT
37 Director Financial Aid .... Ms. Deborah D. JENKINS
21 Director Accounting .... Mr. Thomas N. TYSON
15 Director Human Resources .... Ms. Karen BERKHEIMER
38 Director Counseling .... Ms. Suzanne T. ALEXANDER
27 Director Marketing .... Ms. Janet S. KENNINGTON
09 Director Institutional Research .... Ms. Carol A. MENZEL
30 Director Development .... Ms. Janice MURPHY
06 Registrar .... Ms. Kelly HEWETT
88 Dir Retention & Student Success .... Ms. Deirdra G. JOHNSON
35 Director Student Activities .... Ms. Katherine JONES
08 Director of Library Services .... Ms. Cheryl MICHAEL
18 Director Plant Management .... Mr. Paul MACE
96 Director Purchasing & Auxiliary Svc .... Ms. Allison M. CANADA
105 Webmaster .... Mr. Joshua W. TOWNSEND

Yeshiva College of the Nation's Capital (E)

1216 Arcola Avenue, Silver Spring MD 20902-3408
County: Montgomery — FICE Identification: 039373
Unit ID: 434937
Telephone: (301) 593-2534 — Carnegie Class: Spec/Faith
FAX Number: (301) 593-2534 — Calendar System: Semester
Established: 1995 — Annual Undergrad Tuition & Fees: $9,400
Enrollment: 45 — Male
Affiliation or Control: Independent Non-Profit — IRS Status: 501(c)3
Highest Offering: Second Talmudic Degree
Program: Teacher Preparatory; Professional; Religious Emphasis
Accreditation: RABN

01 President .... Rabbi Yitzchok MERKIN
05 Rosh Yeshiva .... Rabbi Aaron LOPIANSKY
37 Financial Aid Director .... Ms. Irene LAWSON
11 Administrator .... Mr. Matthew MANES

MASSACHUSETTS

American International College (F)

1000 State Street, Springfield MA 01109-3155
County: Hampden — FICE Identification: 002114
Unit ID: 164447
Telephone: (413) 737-7000 — Carnegie Class: Master's L
FAX Number: (413) 205-3943 — Calendar System: Semester
URL: www.aic.edu
Established: 1885 — Annual Undergrad Tuition & Fees: $30,040
Enrollment: 3,607 — Coed
Affiliation or Control: Independent Non-Profit — IRS Status: 501(c)3
Highest Offering: Doctorate
Program: Liberal Arts And General; Teacher Preparatory; Professional; Nursing Emphasis
Accreditation: EH, IACBE, NURSE, OT, PTA

01 President .... Dr. Vincent M. MANIACI
05 Provost .... Dr. Todd G. FRITCH
11 Exec VP Administration .... Mr. Mark R. BERMAN
41 Executive VP for Athletics .... Mr. Richard F. BEDARD
27 Chief Information Officer .... Ms. Mimi ROYSTON
16 Vice President for Human Resources .... Ms. Nicolle M. CESTERO
09 VP for Institutional Effectiveness .... Dr. Gregory T. SCHMUTTE
10 Vice President for Finance .... Mr. Thomas DYBICK
51 VP for Graduate and Adult Education .... Ms. Ellen R. NOONAN
30 Assoc VP for Institutional Advance .... Ms. Heather CAHILL
18 Assoc VP for Facilities .... Vacant
88 Dean of Academic Success .... Dr. Carol SITTERLY
76 Dean Health Sciences .... Dr. Cesarina THOMPSON
49 Dean Business/Arts & Sciences .... Vacant
32 Dean of Students .... Mr. Brian J. O'SHAUGHNESSY
07 Dean for Admissions .... Ms. Janelle HOLMBOE
06 Registrar .... Ms. Diane H. FURTEK
08 Director of Library .... Ms. Estelle H. SPENCER
60 Dir for Marketing & Communications .... Mr. Timothy GRADER
38 Director Counseling Center .... Dr. Rose L. ANDREJCZYK
36 Dir of Career Services .... Vacant
76 Director Occupational Therapy Pgm .... Dr. Cathy A. DOW-ROYER
76 Director Physical Therapy Program .... Dr. Gail STERN
66 Director of Division of Nursing .... Ms. Karen S. ROUSSEAU
37 Director for Financial Aid .... Ms. Sage CRARY-STACHOWIAK
21 Comptroller .... Mr. Christopher GARRITY
96 Director Auxiliary Svcs/Purchasing .... Ms. Katherine M. TOOHEY

Amherst College (G)

PO Box 5000, Amherst MA 01002-5000
County: Hampshire — FICE Identification: 002115
Unit ID: 164465
Telephone: (413) 542-2000 — Carnegie Class: Bac/A&S
FAX Number: (413) 542-2621 — Calendar System: Semester
URL: www.amherst.edu
Established: 1821 — Annual Undergrad Tuition & Fees: $46,574
Enrollment: 1,817 — Coed
Affiliation or Control: Independent Non-Profit — IRS Status: 501(c)3
Highest Offering: Baccalaureate
Program: Liberal Arts And General
Accreditation: EH

01 President .... Dr. Carolyn (Biddy) A. MARTIN
100 Chief of Staff .... Ms. Susan PIKOR
05 Dean of the Faculty .... Dr. Gregory S. CALL
32 Dean of Students .... Mr. James A. LARIMORE
07 Dean Admission/Financial Aid .... Mr. Thomas H. PARKER
37 Dean of Financial Aid .... Ms. Gail W. HOLT
20 Associate Dean of the Faculty .... Dr. John CHENEY
20 Associate Dean of the Faculty .... Dr. Austin D. SARAT
10 Chief Financial Officer .... Mr. Kevin C. WEINMAN
30 Chief Advancement Officer .... Ms. Megan MOREY
43 Chief Policy Ofcr/General Counsel .... Ms. Lisa H. RUTHERFORD
29 Exec Director Alumni/Parent Pgms .... Ms. Elizabeth CANNON SMITH
06 Registrar .... Ms. Kathleen GOFF
15 Director of Human Resources .... Ms. Maria-Judith RODRIGUEZ
21 Comptroller .... Mr. Stephen M. NIGRO

09 Director of Institutional Research .... Ms. Marian F. MATHESON
26 Director of Public Affairs .... Mr. Peter J. ROONEY
08 College Librarian .... Mr. Bryn GEFFERT
13 Chief Information Officer .... Ms. Gayle R. BARTON
23 Director of Student Health Services .... Dr. Warren H. MORGAN
38 Director of Counseling Center .... Dr. Jacqueline S. BEARCE
36 Director of the Career Center .... Ms. Ursula J. OLENDER
39 Director of Resident Life .... Mr. Torin Y. MOORE
41 Director of Athletics .... Dr. Suzanne R. COFFEY
18 Dir Facilities/Assc Treas Camp Svcs .... Mr. James D. BRASSORD
19 Chief of Campus Police .... Mr. John B. CARTER
88 Director of Dining Services .... Mr. Charles G. THOMPSON

Andover Newton Theological School (A)

210 Herrick Road, Newton Centre MA 02459-2243

County: Middlesex FICE Identification: 002116
Unit ID: 164474
Telephone: (617) 964-1100 Carnegie Class: Spec/Faith
FAX Number: (617) 965-9756 Calendar System: Semester
URL: www.ants.edu
Established: 1807 Annual Graduate Tuition & Fees: $15,960
Enrollment: 268 Coed
Affiliation or Control: Independent Non-Profit IRS Status: 501(c)3
Highest Offering: Doctorate; No Undergraduates
Program: Professional; Religious Emphasis
Accreditation: EH, THEOL

01 President .... Dr. Nick CARTER
05 Dean of the Faculty .... Dr. Sarah B. DRUMMOND
10 Vice President for Finance .... Mr. Peter CHINETTI
30 Vice Pres Institutional Advance .... Ms. Jennifer CRAIG
29 Director of the Annual Fund .... Rev. Ruth EDENS
06 Registrar .... Ms. Nayda G. AGUILA
84 Director of Recruitment .... Ms. Alison MCCARTY
08 Co-Director of the Library .... Ms. Diana YOUNT
08 Co-Director of the Library .... Mr. Jeffrey BRIGHAM
32 Dean of Students .... Dr. Nancy E. NIENHUIS
04 Assistant to the President .... Ms. Marjorie BELL
18 Director Physical Plant .... Mr. Frank CAVACO
27 Chief Information Office .... Mr. Mugur ROZ
37 Coordinator Financial Aid .... Ms. Rosemary TURANO
39 Director Housing & Events Planning .... Mr. Frank NOVO

Anna Maria College (B)

50 Sunset Lane, Paxton MA 01612-1198

County: Worcester FICE Identification: 002117
Unit ID: 164492
Telephone: (508) 849-3300 Carnegie Class: Master's M
FAX Number: (508) 849-3334 Calendar System: 4/1/4
URL: www.annamaria.edu
Established: 1946 Annual Undergrad Tuition & Fees: $32,164
Enrollment: 1,432 Coed
Affiliation or Control: Roman Catholic IRS Status: 501(c)3
Highest Offering: Beyond Master's But Less Than Doctorate
Program: Liberal Arts And General; Teacher Preparatory; Professional
Accreditation: EH, MUS, NUR, SW

01 President .... Dr. Jack P. CALARESO
03 Executive Vice President .... Ms. Mary Louise RETELLE
10 VP for Finance and Admin/CFO .... Mr. David M. ROSATI
21 Controller .... Ms. Yvonnie MALCOLM
05 Vice President for Academic Affairs .... Dr. Billye W. AUCLAIR
32 VP for Student Success & Retention .... Mr. Andrew O. KLEIN
84 VP for Marketing/College Relations .... Ms. Paula L. GREEN
09 Director of Institutional Research .... Ms. Irene IRUDAYAM
06 Registrar .... Ms. Barbara ZAWALICH
30 Director Institutional Advancement .... Ms. Susan A. WOJTAS
38 Director Counseling Services .... Mr. Dennis VANASSE
23 Director of Health Services .... Ms. Linda ARONSON
08 Director of Library .... Ms. Janice WILBUR
29 Director Alumni Relations .... Mr. Wesley DUNHAM
36 Director Career Counsel/Placement ... Ms. Judith M. SPARANGES
37 Director Financial Aid .... Ms. Sandra PEREIRA
13 Director of Information Technology .... Mr. Michael MIERS
04 Administrative Assistant .... Ms. Renee J. MARKIEWICZ
04 Senior Asst to the President .... Mrs. Kay PRENTISS
18 Director Physical Plant .... Mr. Mark COLLETTE
66 Director of Nursing Program .... Dr. Carol GABRIELE
35 Dean of Students .... Ms. Elizabeth BONNEAU
41 Athletic Director .... Mr. Stanley VIEIRA
42 Director Campus Ministry .... Fr. Manuel CLAVIJO
15 Director of Human Resources .... Ms. Lisa DRISCOLL
44 Director of Annual Fund .... Ms. Jodi WALSH
88 Dean of Mission Effectiveness .... Sr. Rollande QUINTAL
07 Dean of Admissions & Financial Aid .... Mr. Peter MILLER
20 Director of Academic Advising .... Mr. Adam DUGGAN
28 Chief Diversity Officer .... Mr. Oscar MAYORGA

Assumption College (C)

500 Salisbury Street, Worcester MA 01609-1296

County: Worcester FICE Identification: 002118
Unit ID: 164562
Telephone: (508) 767-7000 Carnegie Class: Master's M
FAX Number: (508) 756-1780 Calendar System: Semester
URL: www.assumption.edu
Established: 1904 Annual Undergrad Tuition & Fees: $34,975
Enrollment: 2,792 Coed
Affiliation or Control: Roman Catholic IRS Status: 501(c)3
Highest Offering: Beyond Master's But Less Than Doctorate
Program: Liberal Arts And General; Teacher Preparatory; Professional
Accreditation: EH, CORE

01 President .... Dr. Francesco C. CESAREO
03 Executive Vice President .... Mr. Christian MCCARTHY
05 Provost/Academic Vice Pres .... Dr. Francis M. LAZARUS
32 Vice President for Student Affairs .... Dr. Catherine M. WOODBROOKS
30 Vice Pres Institutional Advancement ...... Mr. Timothy R. STANTON
42 Vice President Mission .... Rev. Dennis M. GALLAGHER, AA
84 Vice Pres for Enrollment Management .... Mr. Evan E. LIPP
43 General Counsel .... Dr. Michael H. RUBINO
20 Associate Provost .... Dr. Louise CARROLL KEELEY
51 Dir of Career and Continuing Ed .... Mr. Dennis BRAUN
07 Dean of Admissions .... Ms. Kathleen M. MURPHY
20 Dean of Undergraduate Studies .... Dr. Eloise KNOWLTON
58 Dean of Graduate Studies .... Vacant
89 Associate Dean for the First Year .... Dr. Jennifer K. MORRISON
42 Director of Campus Ministry .... Mr. James RIZZA
35 Dean of Student Development .... Dr. Neil R. CASTRONOVO
08 Director of Library Services .... Ms. Doris Ann SWEET
10 Director of Finance .... Mr. Peter WELLS
21 Dir of Facilities Planning & Projs .... Vacant
09 Director Inst Research and Ac Asst .... Mr. Stuart J. MUNRO
58 Director Grad Enrollment Mgmt/Svcs .... Ms. Barbara Z. BENOIT
06 Registrar .... Mr. David W. AALTO
13 Exec Dir Info Tech & Media Svcs .... Dr. Dawn M. THISTLE
15 Director of Human Resources/AAO .... Ms. Grace BLUNT
26 Director of Public Affairs .... Vacant
29 Director of Alumni Relations .... Ms. Diane LASKA-NIXON
44 Director of Annual Giving .... Mr. Timothy R. MARTIN
88 Director of Academic Support Center .... Dr. Allen A. BRUEHL
35 Dean of Campus Life .... Mr. Conway CAMPBELL
39 Assoc Dean Campus Life/Dir Res Life .... Mr. Joseph ZITO
41 Director of Athletics .... Mr. Nichloas A. SMITH
19 Director of Public Safety .... Mr. Robert MURPHY
23 Director of Health Services .... Ms. Elizabeth DREXLER-HINES
24 Director of Media Services .... Mr. Ted HALEY
37 Director of Financial Aid .... Mr. William C. SMITH
88 Director of Auxiliary Services .... Mr. John LANGLOIS
25 Director of Grant Development .... Dr. Landy C. JOHNSON
35 Dean of Students .... Mr. Robert G. RAVENELLE
28 Director of the Cross Cultural Ctr .... Ms. Beatriz PATINO-MANCUELLO
96 Director of Purchasing .... Ms. Gail M. RACINE
86 Exec Asst for Govt/Cmty Relations .... Mr. Daniel F. DITULLIO
36 Director of Career Services .... Ms. Nicole DIORIO

Babson College (D)

231 Forest Street, Babson Park MA 02457-0310

County: Norfolk FICE Identification: 002121
Unit ID: 164580
Telephone: (781) 235-1200 Carnegie Class: Spec/Bus
FAX Number: (781) 239-5231 Calendar System: Semester
URL: www.babson.edu
Established: 1919 Annual Undergrad Tuition & Fees: $43,520
Enrollment: 3,250 Coed
Affiliation or Control: Independent Non-Profit IRS Status: 501(c)3
Highest Offering: Master's
Program: Professional; Business Emphasis
Accreditation: EH, BUS

01 President .... Dr. Kerry MURPHY HEALEY
12 CEO Babson Global .... Dr. Shahid ANSARI
05 Vice President & Provost .... Dr. Dennis HANNO
10 VP for Finance and CFO .... Mr. Philip SHAPIRO
18 VP Facilities Mgt & Construct/CIO .... Mr. Samuel DUNN
30 Vice President of Development .... Ms. Diana P. ZAIS
29 VP Alumni and Friends Network .... Ms. Carol J. HACKER
15 Vice Pres Human Resources .... Ms. Donna BONAPARTE
43 VP and General Counsel .... Mr. Jonathan MOLL
07 VP Enrollment & Dean of Admissions .... Mr. Grant M. GOSSELIN
32 VP Student Affairs/Program Strategy .... Ms. Elizabeth NEWMAN
18 Assoc VP Facilities/Services .... Mr. Shelley KAPLAN
21 Assoc VP Fin Services/Controller .... Mr. Richard BOWMAN
11 Chief Operating Officer .... Mr. Ranch KIMBALL
13 Chief Information Officer .... Mr. Samuel DUNN
26 Chief Marketing Officer .... Ms. Sarah SYKORA
35 Dean of Student Affairs .... Dr. Shannon FINNING
20 Dean of Faculty .... Ms. Carolyn HOTCHKISS
100 Chief of Staff .... Ms. Tracee PETRILLO
50 Dean/Undergraduate School .... Dr. Scott MOORE
51 Dean of Babson Exec Education .... Ms. Elaine EISENMAN
37 Assoc Dean UG Sch/Dir Std Fin Svcs .... Ms. Melissa J. SHAAK
06 Registrar .... Ms. Linda KEAN
88 Exec Dir Ctr for Women's Leadership .... Dr. Susan DUFFY
07 Director Graduate Admissions .... Ms. Barbara J. SELMO
36 Dir Graduate Career Svcs .... Ms. Cheri PAULSON
36 Dir Undergraduate Career Services .... Ms. Megan HOULKER
09 Director of Institutional Research .... Ms. Anne Marie DELANEY
26 Sr Dir Institutional Communications .... Ms. Kelly LYNCH
72 Digital Marketing Director .... Mr. Gene BEGIN
26 Director Public Relations .... Mr. Michael CHMURA
96 Director of Business Services .... Ms. Teresa PITARO
28 Chief Diversity & Inclusion Officer .... Dr. Sadie BURTON-GOSS

Bard College at Simon's Rock (E)

84 Alford Road, Great Barrington MA 01230-9702

County: Berkshire FICE Identification: 009645
Unit ID: 167792
Telephone: (413) 644-4400 Carnegie Class: Bac/Assoc
FAX Number: (413) 528-7365 Calendar System: Semester
URL: www.simons-rock.edu
Established: 1964 Annual Undergrad Tuition & Fees: $45,818
Enrollment: 343 Coed
Affiliation or Control: Independent Non-Profit IRS Status: 501(c)3
Highest Offering: Baccalaureate
Program: Liberal Arts And General
Accreditation: EH

01 President .... Dr. Leon BOTSTEIN
03 Executive Vice President .... Mr. Dimitri PAPADIMITRIOU
05 Vice President/Provost .... Dr. Peter LAIPSON
04 Asst to Vice President & Provost .... Ms. Lisa CLAYTON
84 VP Early College Policies/Programs .... Mr. U. Ba WIN
32 Dean of the College .... Ms. Leslie DAVIDSON
20 Dean of Academic Affairs .... Dr. Anne O'DWYER
35 Dean of Students .... Mr. Robert GRAVES
27 Director of Communications .... Ms. Paige ORLOFF
06 Registrar .... Ms. Heidi ROTHBERG
08 Library Director .... Mr. Brian MIKESELL
37 Director of Financial Aid .... Ms. Ellen MAMMEN
18 Director Physical Plant .... Mr. Steven CARIGNAN
10 Dir of Finance/Administration/HR .... Ms. Pat MARCELLA
38 Dir Counseling Services .... Dr. Judith WIN
23 Director of Student Health Services .... Ms. Jodi TULLER, RN
90 Director of ITS .... Ms. Janice GILDAWIE
19 Director of Security .... Mr. Kenneth GEREMIA
44 Director of Annual Fund .... Mr. Richard MONTONE
41 Athletic Center Manager .... Mr. David COLLOPY
57 Division Head Arts .... Ms. Karen BEAUMONT
81 Division Head Science/Math/Computer .... Dr. Eric KRAMER
83 Division Head Social Studies .... Dr. Asma ABBAS
79 Division Head Language & Literature .... Dr. Colette VAN KERCKVOORDE

Bay Path College (F)

588 Longmeadow Street, Longmeadow MA 01106-2292

County: Hampden FICE Identification: 002122
Unit ID: 164632
Telephone: (413) 565-1000 Carnegie Class: Bac/A&S
FAX Number: (413) 565-1105 Calendar System: Semester
URL: www.baypath.edu
Established: 1897 Annual Undergrad Tuition & Fees: $29,959
Enrollment: 2,370 Female
Affiliation or Control: Independent Non-Profit IRS Status: 501(c)3
Highest Offering: Master's
Program: Liberal Arts And General; Teacher Preparatory; Professional
Accreditation: EH, #ARCPA, OT

01 President .... Dr. Carol A. LEARY
05 Vice Pres Academic Affairs/Provost .... Dr. Melissa MORRISS-OLSON
10 VP Finance/Administrative Services ...... Mr. Michael GIAMPIETRO
30 VP for Institutional Advancement .... Ms. Kathleen BOURQUE
45 Chief Strategy Officer Springfield .... Ms. Caron T. HOBIN
88 Chief Operating Officer Spfld .... Dr. David DEMERS
04 Assistant to the President .... Ms. Barbara KOCHON
21 Associate Vice President Finance .... Ms. Donna GUERTIN
20 Founding Dean of Research .... Ms. Ann DOBMEYER
12 Director of the Burlington Campus .... Vacant
12 Director CMC Campus .... Ms. Kathy JARRETT
26 Director of Communications .... Ms. Kathleen WROBLEWSKI
37 Director of Student Financial Svcs .... Ms. Stephanie KING
36 Exec Dir Career & Life Planning .... Ms. Laureen CIRILLO
07 Exec Director Graduate Admissions .... Ms. Lisa ADAMS
08 Director of the Library .... Mr. Michael MORAN
06 Registrar .... Ms. Laura LANDER
36 Director Career Services .... Ms. Sally J. SCHIRMER-SMITH
29 Dir of Alumni Relations .... Ms. Kathleen COTNOIR
23 Director of Health Services .... Ms. Margaret ANDERSON
19 Captain Campus Public Safety .... Mr. Vincent ROSSI
15 Asst VP & Dir of Human Resources .... Ms. Kathleen HALPIN-ROBBINS
14 Mgr of Info Systems and Telecommun ... Mrs. Linda A. SIMONDS
18 Director Facilities/Campus Svcs .... Mr. Paul E. STANTON
41 Director of Athletics .... Mr. Steven J. SMITH
88 Dir Masters of Sci Commun/Info Mgmt .... Vacant
32 Director of Student Life .... Ms. Natalie STOTHART
88 Sr Dir Bus Pgm Online/Ongrnd Spfld ... Ms. Shakeena WILLIAMS
88 Dir MBA Entrepr Thnkg/Innov Practic .... Mr. Mo SATTAR
88 Dir Grad Pgms Nonprofit Mgmt/Philan .... Mr. Jeffrey GREIM
09 Dir Institutional Research & Data .... Ms. Kathleen MARTIN
88 Director of Health & Wellness .... Ms. Katie JONES
88 Dir Center for Teaching & Learning .... Dr. Charlotte BRIGGS
17 Director of Clinical Education .... Mr. Stephen LEE
96 Exec Dir of Purchasing/Office Svcs ...... Mr. Ted LETH-STEENSEN
102 Dir Foundation/Corporate Relations .... Ms. Janine MCVAY
49 Dean College of Arts & Sciences .... Dr. Michael KONIG
53 Dean School of Education & Psych .... Dr. Elizabeth FLEMING
88 Dean School of Mgmt/Social Justice .... Dr. Thomas LOPER
107 Chief Learning Officer Springfield .... Dr. Vana NESPOR
88 Dean of Planning & Student Develop .... Mr. Dave YELLE
83 Fndg Dean Sch Health Sci/Hum Behav .... Vacant
88 Dir Occupational Therapy Program .... Dr. Lori VAUGHN
51 Dean Cont Educ & Grad Recruitment .... Ms. Diane RANALDI
108 Exec Dir Academic Ops/Assessment .... Dr. Jacqueline SNYDER
88 Director of Analytics .... Ms. Amanda GOULD
57 Director MFA Program .... Ms. Leanna JAMES BLACKWELL
53 Director ABA Program .... Dr. Susan AINSLEIGH
88 Director PA Program .... Dr. Jennifer HIXON

Bay State College (G)

122 Commonwealth Avenue, Boston MA 02116-2975

County: Suffolk FICE Identification: 003965
Unit ID: 164641

Telephone: (617) 217-9000 Carnegie Class: Assoc/PrivFP4
FAX Number: (617) 249-0400 Calendar System: Semester
URL: www.baystate.edu
Established: 1946 Annual Undergrad Tuition & Fees: $24,060
Enrollment: 1,721 Coed
Affiliation or Control: Proprietary IRS Status: Proprietary
Highest Offering: Baccalaureate
Program: Occupational; 2-Year Principally Bachelor's Creditable
Accreditation: EH, ADNUR, MAAB, PTAA

01 President ....Craig PFANNENSTIEHL
05 Vice President of Academic Affairs ....Dr. William CARROLL
32 Vice President of Student Services ....Sylvia REIFLER
10 Vice Pres Administration & Finance ....Meg TRANT
84 Vice Pres of Enrollment & Marketing ....Chip BERGSTROM
37 Director of Financial Aid ....Christine WRIGHT
06 Registrar ....Ray BARNES
08 Librarian ....Jessica NEAVE
32 Chief Student Life Officer ....Kristin STAINE
35 Director Student Affairs ....Kate ACKERMAN
07 Director of Admissions ....Kim OLDS
18 Chief Facilities/Physical Plant ....Kate AKERMAN
21 Bursar ....Jeff MCMASTER
36 Director Career Services ....Tom CORRIGAN
38 Director Student Counseling ....Cheryl RAICHE

Becker College-Worcester (A)

61 Sever Street, Worcester MA 01609-2165
County: Worcester FICE Identification: 002123
Unit ID: 164720
Telephone: (508) 791-9241 Carnegie Class: Bac/Diverse
FAX Number: (508) 831-7505 Calendar System: Semester
URL: www.becker.edu
Established: 1887 Annual Undergrad Tuition & Fees: $31,200
Enrollment: 1,826 Coed
Affiliation or Control: Independent Non-Profit IRS Status: 501(c)3
Highest Offering: Baccalaureate
Program: 2-Year Principally Bachelor's Creditable; Liberal Arts And General; Nursing Emphasis
Accreditation: EH, ADNUR, NUR

01 President ....Dr. Robert E. JOHNSON
10 Senior Vice President & CFO ....Mr. David A. ELLIS
05 Vice President of Academic Affairs ....Ms. Elizabeth FULLER
30 Vice President Advancement ....Mr. Dean J. HICKEY
32 Vice President of Student Affairs ....Dr. Nancy P. CRIMMIN
84 Vice Pres of Enrollment Management ....Mr. Kevin MAYNE
15 Assoc Vice Pres of Human Resources .Mrs. Kathleen M. GARVEY
41 Asst Vice Pres/Athletics Director ....Mr. Frank E. MILLERICK
66 Dean of Nursing/Health Stds ....Ms. Linda ESPER
08 Director of the Libraries ....Mr. Garrett EASTMAN
27 Chief Information officer ....Ms. Patty PATRIA
06 Registrar ....Ms. Nikki ANDREWS
29 Assistant Director Alumni Affairs ....Ms. Caitlin VISSCHER
35 Dir of Student Services - Leicester ....Ms. Michelle FATCHERIC
38 Director of Counseling ....Ms. Wendy MILES
20 Dir Center for Academic Success ....Ms. Dolores RADLO
88 Director for BA in Design ....Mr. Paul COTNOIR
74 Director Animal Science Programs ....Dr. James KNIGHT
27 Communications Director ....Ms. Sandy LASHIN-CUREWITZ
96 Director of Business Services ....Mr. Mike MONGEON
26 Director Marketing/Strategic Comm ....Ms. Amy DEAN
21 Controller ....Mr. Richard NAYLOR
19 Campus Police Chief ....Mr. David BOUSQUET
36 Director of Career Services ....Mr. Eric SACZAWA

Benjamin Franklin Institute of Technology (B)

41 Berkeley Street, Boston MA 02116-6296
County: Suffolk FICE Identification: 002151
Unit ID: 165884
Telephone: (617) 423-4630 Carnegie Class: Spec/Tech
FAX Number: (617) 482-3706 Calendar System: Semester
URL: www.bfit.edu
Established: 1908 Annual Undergrad Tuition & Fees: $16,950
Enrollment: 484 Coed
Affiliation or Control: Independent Non-Profit IRS Status: 501(c)3
Highest Offering: Baccalaureate
Program: Occupational; 2-Year Principally Bachelor's Creditable; Technical Emphasis
Accreditation: EH, OPD

01 Acting President ....Anthony BENOIT
05 Dean of Academic Affairs ....Anthony BENOIT
32 Dean of Students ....Brian BICKNELL
10 Chief Financial Officer ....Keith DROPKIN
11 Director of Operations ....Stephen LOZEN
06 Registrar ....James KLASEN
08 Librarian ....Sharon B. BONK
84 Dean of Enrollment Management ....Mike BOSCO
07 Director of Admissions ....Marvin LOISEAU
30 Chief Advancement Officer ....Vacant
20 Director of Advising ....Rachel ARNO
09 Director of Institutional Research ....James KLASEN
15 Director Human Resources ....Shelley DROPKIN
19 Director of Facilities ....Myftar MYRTAJ
36 Director of Career Services ....Phyllis MOLTA
37 Director Student Financial Aid ....Tatjana HASKAJ

Bentley University (C)

175 Forest Street, Waltham MA 02452-4705
County: Middlesex FICE Identification: 002124
Unit ID: 164739
Telephone: (781) 891-2000 Carnegie Class: Master's L
FAX Number: (781) 891-2569 Calendar System: Semester
URL: www.bentley.edu
Established: 1917 Annual Undergrad Tuition & Fees: $39,628
Enrollment: 5,647 Coed
Affiliation or Control: Independent Non-Profit IRS Status: 501(c)3
Highest Offering: Doctorate
Program: Liberal Arts And General; Professional; Business Emphasis
Accreditation: EH, BUS, BUSA

01 President ....Ms. Gloria C. LARSON
43 General Counsel ....Ms. Judith A. MALONE
102 Director Foundation Relations ....Mr. Paul K. CARBERRY
05 VP Academic Affairs/Provost ....Dr. Michael J. PAGE
10 VP Business/Finance/Treas ....Vacant
30 VP University Advancement ....Mr. John PINI
32 VP Student Affairs ....Dr. Andrew J. SHEPARDSON
13 COO & VP for Information Technology ....Ms. Traci A. LOGAN
84 VP Enrollment Management ....Ms. Joann C. MCKENNA
49 Dean of Arts and Sciences ....Dr. Daniel L. EVERETT
50 Dean of Business/McCallum Grad Sch ....Dr. Michael J. PAGE
09 Reporting Specialist/Inst Research ....Ms. Lindsey C. LEWIS
49 Assoc Dean of Arts and Sciences ....Dr. Juliet GAINSBOROUGH
44 Senior Director of Special Gifts ....Mr. John A. PINI
29 Mng Dir Alumni/Parents & Friends ....Ms. Leigh GASPAR
27 Exec Director Mktg/Communication ....Ms. Katherine H. BLAKE
16 Exec Director of Human Resources ....Ms. Ann DEXTER
11 Assoc Dean of Administration ....Ms. Judy KAMM
21 Exec Dir Financial Operations ....Ms. Marianne F. CWALINA
06 Registrar ....Ms. Patricia A. ROGERS
22 Pres Assistant Equal Opportunity ....Dr. Earl L. AVERY
38 Assoc Dean/Dir Couns & Student Dev ....Dr. Roger A. DANCHISE
41 Director of Athletics ....Mr. Robert A. DEFELICE
37 Exec Dir Enroll Mgmt & Fin Assist ....Ms. Donna M. KENDALL
39 Dir Housing & Student Systems ....Mr. Ronald M. ARDIZZONE
90 Dir Academic Tech/Library/Rsch Svcs ....Dr. Phillip G. KNUTEL
31 Director Service-Learning Center ....Mr. Franklyn P. SALIMBENE
19 Executive Director of Public Safety ....Mr. Ernest H. LEFFLER
26 Director Public & Media Relations ....Ms. Michele M. WALSH
88 Mng Dir Corp Fin & Sponsored Pgms ..Mr. Leonard MORRISON
23 Asst Dean/Dir Health & Wellness ....Ms. Geraldine S. TAYLOR
25 Director of Sponsored Programs ....Ms. Mary Louise PAULI
88 Director of Conference Services ....Mr. Robert L. WEBB
07 Asst Dean/Dir of Grad Admission ....Ms. Sharon F. HILL
58 Director of MBA Programs ....Vacant
88 Senior Associate Dir Reunion Pgms ....Mr. Gary E. KELLY
18 Director Facilities Management ....Mr. Thomas W. KANE
96 Director Purchasing/Contract Svcs ....Ms. Julianne BRITT
28 Director of Diversity ....Vacant
35 Dean of Student Affairs ....Dr. J. Andrew SHEPARDSON

Berklee College of Music (D)

1140 Boylston Street, Boston MA 02215-3693
County: Suffolk FICE Identification: 002126
Unit ID: 164748
Telephone: (617) 266-1400 Carnegie Class: Spec/Arts
FAX Number: (617) 247-6878 Calendar System: Semester
URL: www.berklee.edu
Established: 1945 Annual Undergrad Tuition & Fees: $37,586
Enrollment: 4,447 Coed
Affiliation or Control: Independent Non-Profit IRS Status: 501(c)3
Highest Offering: Master's
Program: Music Emphasis
Accreditation: EH

01 President ....Roger H. BROWN
05 Sr Vice Pres Academic Affs/Provost ....Lawrence J. SIMPSON
32 Vice Pres Student Affs/Dean Stdnts ....Lawrence E. BETHUNE
102 Sr VP Institutional Advancement ....Cindy ALBERT LINK
10 Chief Financial Officer ....Richard M. HISEY
11 Vice President Administration ....John ELDERT
21 Vice President Finance ....Amelia KOCH
30 Vice Pres Institutional Advancement ....David MCKAY
13 Vice Pres Technology/Educ Outreach ....David MASH
28 Vice Pres for Cultural Diversity ....Myra HINDUS
88 Assoc VP for Administration ....Nancy EAGEN
84 Vice President Enrollment ....Mark CAMPBELL
14 Assoc VP Information Technology ....Scott V. STREET
15 Vice Pres Human Res/Diversity/Incl ....Christine M. CONNORS
88 Assoc Ed Outreach/Ex Dir BC Music ....J. Curtis WARNER, JR.
82 Asst Vice Pres Intl Programs ....Greg BADOLATO
35 Asst VP Student Affs/Student Devel ....Steven LIPMAN
20 Assoc VP Academic Affs/Assoc Prov ....Jay S. KENNEDY
27 Asst VP for Public Information ....Rob HAYES
88 Asst VP Academic Technology ....Matt MARVUGLIO
88 Dean Prof Writing Div/Music Tech ....Kari JUUSELA
53 Dean of Prof Education Division ....Darla S. HANLEY
08 Dean of Learning Resources ....Gary HAGGERTY
09 Director Inst Reseach & Assessment ....Susan Coia GAILEY
91 Director Telecom/Networking Svcs ....Norman E. SILVER
06 Registrar ....Michael HAGERTY
39 Director of Housing ....William M. MACKAY
37 Director of Financial Aid ....Frank MULLEN
38 Director of Counseling ....Sara REGAN
07 Director of Admissions ....Damien S. BRACKEN
29 Director Alumni Relations ....Karen BELL

36 Director Career Development Center ....Peter SPELLMAN
18 Assoc Director of Physical Plant ....George O'MEARA

Blessed John XXIII National Seminary (E)

558 South Avenue, Weston MA 02493-2699
County: Middlesex FICE Identification: 002202
Unit ID: 167464
Telephone: (781) 899-5500 Carnegie Class: Spec/Faith
FAX Number: (781) 899-9057 Calendar System: Semester
URL: www.blessedjohnxxiii.edu
Established: 1964 Annual Graduate Tuition & Fees: $27,000
Enrollment: 67 Male
Affiliation or Control: Roman Catholic IRS Status: 501(c)3
Highest Offering: Master's; No Undergraduates
Program: Professional
Accreditation: THEOL

01 Rector and President ....Rev. William B. PALARDY
05 Academic Dean/Registrar ....Dr. Anthony KEATY
08 Librarian ....Sr. Jacqueline MILLER
10 Business Manager ....Mrs. Kyle RYAN
06 Registrar ....Dr. Anthony KEATY

Boston Architectural College (F)

320 Newbury Street, Boston MA 02115-2795
County: Suffolk FICE Identification: 003966
Unit ID: 164872
Telephone: (617) 262-5000 Carnegie Class: Spec/Arts
FAX Number: (617) 585-0111 Calendar System: Semester
URL: www.the-bac.edu
Established: 1889 Annual Undergrad Tuition & Fees: $18,622
Enrollment: 907 Coed
Affiliation or Control: Independent Non-Profit IRS Status: 501(c)3
Highest Offering: Master's
Program: Professional; Technical Emphasis
Accreditation: EH, CIDA, LSAR

01 President/CEO ....Dr. Theodore C. LANDSMARK
04 Assistant to the President ....Ms. Kristin KOCHANCZYK
101 Assistant to the Exec VP & Board ....Ms. Amyjo HOFNER
05 Provost ....Ms. Julia HALEVY
10 Vice President for Finance/Admin ....Ms. Kathleen C. ROOD
30 VP Institutional Advancement ....Mr. Evan GALLIVAN
107 VP of Prof & Cont Education ....Ms. Karen MUNCASTER
18 Associate VP of Facilities ....Mr. Arthur BYERS
88 Head School of Interior Design ....Mr. Crandon GUSTAFSON
88 Head School of Landscape Architect ....Ms. Maria BELLALTA
88 Head School of Design Studies ....Mr. Donald HUNSICKER
48 Head School of Architecture ....Ms. Karen L. NELSON
51 Head Continuing Ed Pgms/Curriculum ....Ms. Jane TOLAND
88 Head of Practice ....Mr. Len CHARNEY
32 Assoc Provost/Dean of Students ....Mr. Richard M. GRISWOLD
14 Director of IT Operations ....Mr. Timothy OGAWA
88 Dir of Master's Thesis Arch ....Mr. Ian TABERNER
88 Director of Design Computing ....Mr. Diego L. MATHO
88 Director of Media Arts ....Mr. Luis MONTALVO
88 Director of Distance M Arch ....Mr. Tom PARKS
08 Library Director ....Ms. Susan A. LEWIS
06 Registrar ....Ms. Ann ROYALL
07 Dean Enrollment & Student Fin Svcs ....Mr. James RYAN
86 Director of External/Gov Relations ....Ms. Janet OBERTO
35 Director of Student Development ....Ms. Kara PEET
11 Dir of Administrative Operations ....Ms. Patti VAUGHN
20 Director of Academic Services ....Ms. Rebecca CHABOT-WIEFERICH
88 Director of Foundation Studies ....Mr. Lee PETERS
106 Director of Distance M. Arch ....Mr. Michael WOLFSON
88 Director of Practice Instruction ....Mr. David ECCLESTON
88 Director of Sustainable Design Inst ....Mr. Lance FLETCHER
88 Director of the Landscape Institute ....Ms. Heather HEIMARCK
88 Director of Global Initiatives ....Ms. Sharon MATTHEWS
88 Dir of Historic Preservation Stds ....Mr. Robert OGLE
58 Dean Grad Studies & Dir of Liberal ....Ms. Diana RAMIREZ-JASSO
88 Dir of Sustainable Design Studies ....Mr. Shaun O'ROURKE

Boston Baptist College (G)

950 Metropolitan Avenue, Boston MA 02136-4000
County: Suffolk FICE Identification: 032483
Unit ID: 164614
Telephone: (617) 364-3510 Carnegie Class: Spec/Faith
FAX Number: (775) 245-1498 Calendar System: Semester
URL: www.boston.edu
Established: 1976 Annual Undergrad Tuition & Fees: $15,026
Enrollment: 88 Coed
Affiliation or Control: Baptist IRS Status: 501(c)3
Highest Offering: Baccalaureate
Program: Religious Emphasis
Accreditation: TRACS

01 President ....Rev. David V. MELTON
05 Vice President for Academics ....Rev. Kenneth D. GILLMING
32 Vice President for Student Affairs ....Vacant
11 Vice President for Operations ....Mr. Randall WARD
84 Director of Enrollment Services ....Mrs. Wendi WEBBER
07 Director of Admissions ....Ms. Brianna VILLANUEVA
08 Head Librarian ....Mr. Fred TATRO
31 Community Relations Officer ....Vacant

Boston College (A)

140 Commonwealth Avenue, Chestnut Hill MA 02467-3934
County: Middlesex FICE Identification: 002128
Unit ID: 164924
Telephone: (617) 552-8000 Carnegie Class: RU/H
FAX Number: (617) 552-8828 Calendar System: Semester
URL: www.bc.edu
Established: 1863 Annual Undergrad Tuition & Fees: $45,622
Enrollment: 14,640 Coed
Affiliation or Control: Roman Catholic IRS Status: 501(c)3
Highest Offering: Doctorate
Program: Liberal Arts And General; Teacher Preparatory; Professional
Accreditation: EH, ANEST, BUS, COPSY, LAW, NURSE, SW, TEAC, THEOL

01 President ... Rev. William P. LEAHY, SJ
00 Chancellor ... Rev. J. Donald MONAN, SJ
05 Int Provost/Dean of Faculties ... Dr. Joseph F. QUINN
03 Executive Vice President ... Dr. Patrick J. KEATING
26 Senior Vice President ... Dr. James P. MCINTYRE
30 Sr Vice Pres University Advancement ... Mr. James J. HUSSON
04 Executive Assistant to President ... Mr. Kevin J. SHEA
100 Chief of Staff Provost's Office ... Dr. Anita TIEN
10 Financial Vice President/Treasurer ... Mr. Peter C. MCKENZIE
101 Vice President/University Secretary .. Mr. Terrence P. DEVINO, SJ
32 Vice Pres Student Affairs ... Dr. Barbara JONES
15 Vice President for Human Resources ... Mr. Leo V. SULLIVAN
44 Vice Pres for Development ... Mr. Thomas P. LOCKERBY
13 Vice Pres Information Technology ... Mr. Michael J. BOURQUE
88 Vice Pres Univ Mission & Ministry ... Rev. John T. BUTLER, SJ
86 Vice Pres Govt/Community Affairs ... Mr. Thomas J. KEADY
18 Vice Pres Facilities Management ... Mr. Daniel F. BOURQUE
04 Vice Pres/Special Asst to President .. Rev. William B. NEENAN, SJ
45 Vice Pres Planning & Assessment ... Dr. Kelli J. ARMSTRONG
20 Vice Provost for Undergrad Affairs ... Dr. Donald L. HAFNER
46 Vice Provost for Research ... Dr. Larry MCLAUGHLIN
20 Vice Provost for Faculties ... Dr. Patricia DE LEEUW
14 Assoc VP Information Technology ... Mrs. Mary C. CORCORAN
44 Assoc VP Capital Giving/Development ... Ms. Beth MCDERMOTT
20 Assoc Vice Provost Undergrad Acad ... Dr. J. Joseph BURNS
18 Assoc VP Capital Projects ... Ms. Mary S. NARDONE
29 Associate VP for Alumni Relations ... Mr. John A. FEUDO
49 Dean College Arts & Sciences ... Dr. David QUIGLEY
87 Int Dn Col Adv Stds/Summer Session ... Rev. James R. BURNS
53 Interim Dean School of Education ... Ms. Maureen E. KENNY
61 Dean Law School ... Mr. Vincent D. ROUGEAU
50 Dean School of Management ... Dr. Andrew C. BOYNTON
66 Dean of School of Nursing ... Dr. Susan GENNARO
70 Dean Grad School of Social Work ... Dr. Alberto A. GODENZI
84 Dean of Enrollment Management ... Mr. Robert S. LAY
35 Dean of Students Office ... Mr. Paul J. CHEBATOR
08 University Librarian Emeritus ... Dr. Thomas WALL
90 Exec Director Academic Technology ... Mrs. Rita OWENS
28 Exec Dir Institutional Diversity ... Mr. Richard P. JEFFERSON
06 Exec Director Student Services ... Dr. Louise M. LONABOCKER
07 Director of Admission ... Mr. John L. MAHONEY, JR.
26 Exec Dir/Special Asst to Pres/Mktg ... Mr. Ben BIRNBAUM
27 Dir Office of News & Public Affairs ... Mr. John B. DUNN
102 Director Corp & Foundation Rels ... Mrs. Ginger K. SAARIAHO
41 Director Athletic Department ... Mr. Brad BATES
36 Director of Career Center ... Vacant
42 Director Campus Ministry ... Rev. Anthony PENNA
31 Director of Community Affairs ... Mr. William R. MILLS
38 Director Univ Counseling Services . Dr. Thomas P. MCGUINNESS
37 Director Financial Aid ... Mrs. Mary S. MCGRANAHAN
23 Director Health Services ... Dr. Thomas I. NARY
39 Director of Residential Life ... Mr. George A. AREY
25 Dir Pre-Award Admin Sponsored Pgms ... Mrs. Sharon COMVALIUS-GODDARD
25 Dir Post-Award Admin Sponsored Pgms ... Ms. Susan ZIPKIN
19 Dir Public Safety/Chief of Police ... Mr. John M. KING
40 Director Bookstore ... Mr. Robert STEWART
43 General Counsel ... Mr. Joseph M. HERLIHY
24 Director Media Technology Services ... Mr. David CORKUM
85 Director International Programs ... Dr. Nick GOZIK
92 Director Honors Program A & S ... Dr. Mark F. O'CONNOR
93 Director AHANA Student Programs ... Dr. Ines MATURANA SENDOYA
86 Director Governmental Relations ... Ms. Jeanne LEVESQUE
94 Director of Women's Studies ... Dr. Sharlene HESSE-BIBER
96 Director Procurement Services ... Mr. Paul MCGOWAN
09 Director Institutional Research ... Dr. Jessica A. GREENE

The Boston Conservatory (B)

8 The Fenway, Boston MA 02215-4006
County: Suffolk FICE Identification: 002129
Unit ID: 164933
Telephone: (617) 536-6340 Carnegie Class: Spec/Arts
FAX Number: (617) 912-9101 Calendar System: Semester
URL: www.bostonconservatory.edu
Established: 1867 Annual Undergrad Tuition & Fees: $40,900
Enrollment: 748 Coed
Affiliation or Control: Independent Non-Profit IRS Status: 501(c)3
Highest Offering: Master's
Program: Teacher Preparatory; Professional; Music Emphasis
Accreditation: EH, MUS

01 President ... Mr. Richard ORTNER
05 VP Academic Affairs/Dean/CAO ... Dr. Patricia HOY
11 VP for Finance and Planning ... Mr. Eric NORMAN
30 VP for Institutional Advancement ... Ms. Leslie J. KAYE
10 Director of Finance ... Ms. Leigh Ann LUETZEN
32 Vice Pres Stdnt Affs/Dean Students ... Dr. Carmen S. GRIGGS
20 Assoc Dean Academic Operations ... Mr. James O'DELL
07 Director of Admissions ... Ms. Meghan CADWALLADER
64 Director Music Division ... Dr. Abra BUSH
88 Director Dance Division ... Ms. Cathy YOUNG
57 Director Theater Division ... Mr. Neil DONOHOE
06 Registrar ... Ms. Florence BERGERON
37 Director Student Financial Aid ... Ms. Nicole BRENNAN
08 Director of the Library ... Ms. Jennifer HUNT
13 Director of Information Technology ... Mr. Bob XAVIER
18 Director Facilities & Plant ... Mr. Christopher HAYDEN
35 Asst Dean for Student Affairs ... Mr. Christopher READE
26 Director Marketing & Communications ... Mr. Jake MESSIER
85 Director International Student Svcs ... Mr. Gordon HOMANN
15 Manager HR Employment ... Ms. Carrie BOURQUE
15 Manager HR Benefits ... Ms. Alyssa OZIMEK-MAIER
29 Dir of Alumni and Parent Relations ... Ms. Tracy SMITH
26 Director of External Relations ... Ms. Kim HAACK

Boston Graduate School of Psychoanalysis (C)

1581 Beacon Street, Brookline MA 02446-4602
County: Norfolk FICE Identification: 031943
Unit ID: 164915
Telephone: (617) 277-3915 Carnegie Class: Spec/Health
FAX Number: (617) 277-0312 Calendar System: Semester
URL: www.bgsp.edu
Established: 1973 Annual Graduate Tuition & Fees: $21,375
Enrollment: 165 Coed
Affiliation or Control: Independent Non-Profit IRS Status: 501(c)3
Highest Offering: Doctorate; No Undergraduates
Program: Professional
Accreditation: EH

01 President ... Dr. Jane SYNDER
10 Vice President Finance ... Dr. Carol PANETTA
58 Dean of Graduate Studies ... Dr. Lynn PERLMAN
07 Director of Admissions ... Ms. Jill SOLOMON
26 Director of Marketing ... Ms. Paula BERMAN
06 Registrar ... Ms. Allison WILLIAMS
37 Director of Financial Aid ... Ms. Stephanie WOOLBERT
21 Controller ... Ms. Gayle DOLAN

Boston University (D)

One Silber Way, Boston MA 02215-1700
County: Suffolk FICE Identification: 002130
Unit ID: 164988
Telephone: (617) 353-2000 Carnegie Class: RU/VH
FAX Number: (617) 353-2053 Calendar System: Semester
URL: www.bu.edu
Established: 1839 Annual Undergrad Tuition & Fees: $44,910
Enrollment: 33,226 Coed
Affiliation or Control: Independent Non-Profit IRS Status: 501(c)3
Highest Offering: Doctorate
Program: Liberal Arts And General; Teacher Preparatory; Professional
Accreditation: EH, BUS, CEA, CLPSY, DIETD, DIETI, ENG, FEPAC, HSA, IPSY, LAW, MUS, OT, PTA, SP, SW, THEOL

01 President ... Robert A. BROWN
05 University Provost ... Jean MORRISON
17 Provost Medical Campus ... Karen H. ANTMAN
100 VP & Chief of Staff to President ... Douglas SEARS
49 Dean Col/Grad Sch Arts & Sciences ... Virginia SAPIRO
60 Dean College of Communication ... Thomas FIEDLER
53 Dean School of Education ... Hardin L. COLEMAN
54 Dean College of Engineering ... Kenneth R. LUTCHEN
57 Dean College of Fine Arts ... Benjamin JUAREZ
97 Dean College General Studies ... Vacant
61 Dean of School of Law ... Maureen A. O'ROURKE
50 Dean School Management ... Kenneth W. FREEMAN
55 Interim Dean Met Col/Ext Educ ... Tanya ZLATEVA
76 Interim Dean Health & Rehab Sci ... Kathleen MORGAN
88 Dean School of Hospitality Admin ... Arun UPNEJA
70 Dean School of Social Work ... Gail STEKETEE
73 Dean School of Theology ... Mary E. MOORE
63 Dean School of Medicine ... Karen H. ANTMAN
52 Dean Sch of Dental Medicine ... Jeffery W. HUTTER
69 Dean School of Public Health ... Robert F. MEENAN
32 Dean of Students ... Kenneth ELMORE
42 Dean of Marsh Chapel ... Robert A. HILL
88 VP/Assoc Provost Global Programs ... Willis G. WANG
84 VP Enrollment & Student Affairs ... Laurie POHL
46 VP & Assoc Provost Research ... Gloria WATERS
20 Assoc Provost Graduate Affairs ... Timothy BARBARI
20 Assoc Provost Strategic Initiatives ... Nicole HAWKES
20 Assoc Provost Undergraduate Affairs ... Elizabeth LOIZEAUX
20 Assoc Provost for Faculty Affairs ... Julie SANDELL
18 Senior Vice President Operations ... Gary W. NICKSA
10 Senior Vice Pres/CFO & Treasurer ... Martin J. HOWARD
26 Senior VP Marketing & Comm ... Stephen P. BURGAY
43 Sr VP/General Counsel & Board Secy ... Todd L C. KLIPP
30 Senior VP Devel/Alumni Relations ... Scott G. NICHOLS
90 VP Information Systems & Technology ... Tracy SCHROEDER
45 VP Budget and Planning ... Derek HOWE
21 Vice President Auxiliary Services ... Peter SMOKOWSKI
86 Vice Pres Government & Cmty Affairs ... Robert DONAHUE
102 VP Federal Relations ... Jennifer GRODSKY
11 Vice Pres Administrative Services ... Peter FIEDLER
41 Asst VP/Exec Dir of Athletics ... Mike LYNCH
06 Assistant VP & Registrar ... Jeffrey VON MUNKWITZ-SMITH
07 Assoc VP/Exec Dir Undergraduate Adm ... Kelly WALTER
08 University Librarian ... Robert HUDSON
09 Asst VP Institutional Research ... Melanie MADAIO-O'BRIEN
09 Director Institutional Research ... Linette DECARIE
15 Chief Human Resouce Officer ... Diane P. TUCKER
19 Chief of Police ... Thomas G. ROBBINS
20 Assoc Provost Budget & Planning ... Christopher GOSS
23 Director Student Health Services ... David R. MCBRIDE
27 Asst VP Strategic Communication ... Amy HOOK
28 Director Thurman Center ... Katherine KENNEDY
29 VP Development & Alumni Rels ... Steven A. HALL
35 Assoc VP Enroll & Student Affairs ... Denise MOONEY
35 Assoc Director Student Activities ... Raul FERNANDEZ
36 Director Career Planning Services ... Kimberley DELGIZZO
37 Assoc VP/Dir Financial Assistance ... Christine MCGUIRE
39 Exec Director of Housing/Dining ... Marc ROBILLARD
44 Assistant VP Annual Giving ... Daniel ALLENBY
44 Assoc VP Sch-based Dev & Alum Rels ... Adam K. WISE
46 VP Research Finance & Operations ... Andrew HORNER
68 Exec Director Physical Education ... Timothy MOORE
85 Director Intl Student/Scholars Ofc ... Jeanne KELLEY
87 Assistant Dean Summer Term ... Donna SHEA
96 Director Sourcing and Procurement ... Richard STACK

Boston University Medical Campus (E)

72 East Concord Street, Boston MA 02118
Telephone: (617) 638-5300 Identification: 770110
Accreditation: &EH, DENT, MED, PH

† Main campus is Boston University in Boston, MA.

Brandeis University (F)

415 South Street, Waltham MA 02454-9110
County: Middlesex FICE Identification: 002133
Unit ID: 165015
Telephone: (781) 736-2000 Carnegie Class: RU/VH
FAX Number: (781) 736-8699 Calendar System: Semester
URL: www.brandeis.edu
Established: 1948 Annual Undergrad Tuition & Fees: $46,106
Enrollment: 5,808 Coed
Affiliation or Control: Independent Non-Profit IRS Status: 501(c)3
Highest Offering: Doctorate
Program: Liberal Arts And General; Professional
Accreditation: EH, BUS

00 Chairman of the Board ... Mr. Perry TRAQUINA
01 President ... Mr. Frederick M. LAWRENCE
04 Executive Asst to the President ... Ms. Celia D. HARRIS
03 Senior Vice President and COO ... Mr. Steve MANOS
05 Provost/Sr Vice Pres for Acad Affs ... Dr. Steve GOLDSTEIN
20 Asst Provost for Academic Affairs ... Ms. Kim GODSOE
30 Sr Vice Pres Inst Advancement ... Ms. Nancy K. WINSHIP
29 Vice President of Development ... Mr. Myles E. WEISENBERG
84 Sr Vice Pres for Students/Enroll ... Mr. Andrew FLAGEL
26 Sr VP Communication & External Affs ... Ms. Ellen DE GRAFFENREID
43 Sr VP and General Counsel ... Ms. Judith R. SIZER
100 Chief of Staff ... Mr. David A. BUNIS
88 Chief Investment Officer ... Mr. Nicholas WARREN
10 Sr VP for Finance and CFO ... Ms. Marianne CWALINA
90 VP for IT/Vice Provost for Library ... Mr. John UNSWORTH
11 Senior VP for Administration ... Mr. Mark COLLINS
18 Associate VP for Facilities ... Mr. Peter C. SHIELDS
19 Director of Public Safety ... Mr. Edward CALLAHAN
15 Vice Pres Human Resources ... Mr. Scot R. BEMIS
18 VP for Planning & Inst Research ... Mr. Dan FELDMAN
58 Exec Director Div Grad Prof Studies ... Ms. Anne MARANDO
49 Dean of Arts & Sciences ... Dr. Susan J. BIRREN
58 Dean Grad School/Arts & Sciences ... Dr. Malcolm W. WATSON
70 Dean Heller School Social Pol & Mgt ... Dr. Lisa LYNCH
50 Dean International Business School ... Dr. Bruce R. MAGID
32 Assoc VP & Dean of Student Life ... Mr. Rick SAWYER
35 Associate Dean of Student Life ... Mr. Jamele ADAMS
35 Associate Dean of Student Life ... Ms. Maggie BALCH
41 Director of Athletics ... Ms. Sheryl A. SOUSA
07 Director of Admissions ... Vacant
37 Dean of Student Financial Svcs ... Mr. Peter M. GIUMETTE
08 Chief University Librarian ... Dr. John UNSWORTH
06 University Registrar ... Dr. Mark S. HEWITT
88 Asst Provost for Research Admin ... Mr. Paul O'KEEFE
36 Director Hiatt Career Center ... Mr. Joseph DUPONT
38 Director Psych Counseling Center ... Mr. Robert Y. BERLIN
96 Director of Strategic Procurement ... Mr. John STORTI
42 Coordinator Interfaith Chaplaincy ... Fr. Walter CUENIN
104 Asst Dean/Director of Study Abroad . Mr. J. Scott VAN DER MEID
88 Director of the Rose Art Museum ... Mr. Chris BEDFORD

Cambridge College (G)

1000 Massachusetts Avenue, Cambridge MA 02138-5304
County: Middlesex FICE Identification: 021829
Unit ID: 165167
Telephone: (617) 868-1000 Carnegie Class: Master's L
FAX Number: (617) 349-3545 Calendar System: Trimester
URL: www.cambridgecollege.edu
Established: 1971 Annual Undergrad Tuition & Fees: $13,140
Enrollment: 3,757 Coed
Affiliation or Control: Independent Non-Profit IRS Status: 501(c)3
Highest Offering: Doctorate
Program: Liberal Arts And General; Professional

Accreditation: EH, @TEAC

01 President .... Deborah JACKSON
05 Provost .... Dr. Elwood ROBINSON
10 CFO/VP of Finance .... Helen OULETTE
43 General Counsel .... R. Yvette CLARK
30 Vice Pres Institutional Advancement .... Ariadne VALSAMIS
16 Director of Human Resources .... Lauretta SIGGERS
37 Director of Financial Aid .... Frank LAUDER
21 Controller .... Lynn WOOD
06 Registrar .... Mark SLAWSON
84 Vice Pres of Enrollment Management .... Robin PEEVEY
90 Director of Information Technology .... Richard PAPAZIAN
18 Director of Business Operations .... Joe GIBREE
12 Director Chesapeake VA Reg Ctr .... Dr. Ella BENSON
12 Director of Merrimack Valley Center .... Joseph MIGLIO
12 Director Springfield Center .... Teresa (Terrie) FORTE
12 Interim Dir of Inland Empire Center .... Dr. Rita CLEMONS
12 Director Puerto Rico Center .... Dr. Jose R. IRIZARRY
12 Director Memphis Regional Center .... Karen STREETER
12 Director Augusta Regional Center .... Sharlotte EVANS
56 Exec Dir Regional Centers/NITE .... Dr. Kristin POPPO
26 Director of PR & Communications .... Jacqueline CONRAD
86 Dir of Govt/Bus & Comm Partnership .... Phillip PAGE

Clark University (A)

950 Main Street, Worcester MA 01610-1477
County: Worcester FICE Identification: 002139
Unit ID: 165334
Telephone: (508) 793-7711 Carnegie Class: RU/H
FAX Number: (508) 793-7780 Calendar System: Semester
URL: www.clarku.edu
Established: 1887 Annual Undergrad Tuition & Fees: $39,200
Enrollment: 3,503 Coed
Affiliation or Control: Independent Non-Profit IRS Status: 501(c)3
Highest Offering: Doctorate
Program: Liberal Arts And General; Teacher Preparatory; Professional
Accreditation: EH, BUS, CLPSY

01 President .... Dr. David P. ANGEL
03 Executive Vice President .... Ms. Julie L. DOLAN
10 Chief Investment Officer .... Mr. James E. COLLINS
05 Provost & Vice Pres Academic Affs .... Dr. Davis BAIRD
20 Vice Provost .... Ms. Andrea P. MICHAELS
30 Vice Pres University Advancement .... Mr. C. Andrew MCGADNEY
26 Vice Pres Marketing & Communication .... Ms. Paula DAVID
13 Vice Pres for Information Tech/CIO .... Ms. Pennie TURGEON
86 VP Government/Cmty Affs/Campus Svcs .... Mr. John FOLEY
32 VP Student Affairs/Dean of Students .... Ms. Denise M. DARRIGRAND
46 Assoc Provost/Dean of Research .... Dr. Nancy BUDWIG
58 Assoc Provost/Dean Graduate Studies .... Dr. William FISHER
49 Assoc Provost/Dean of College .... Dr. Mary-Ellen BOYLE
35 Associate Dean of Students .... Mr. Jason ZELESKY
38 Associate Dean Academic Advising .... Dr. Kevin M. MCKENNA
50 Dean Graduate School Mgmt .... Dr. Catherine USOFF
51 Dean Col Profess & Cont Education .... Dr. Thomas P. MASSEY
07 Dean of Admissions & Financial Aid .... Mr. Donald HONEMAN
37 Director of Financial Aid .... Ms. Mary Ellen SEVERANCE
08 University Librarian .... Dr. Gwendolynne ARTHUR
21 Controller .... Ms. Katherine CANNON
36 Interim Director Career Services .... Ms. Vickie COX-LANYON
29 Dir of Stewardship/Donor Relations .... Ms. Aixa L. KIDD
06 Registrar .... Ms. Rebecca HUNTER
15 Dir of Human Resources/Affirm Act .... Ms. Jacqueline CAPOMACCHIO
18 Director of Physical Plant .... Mr. Michael DAWLEY
41 Director of Athletics .... Mr. Sean SULLIVAN
19 Chief of Campus Police .... Mr. Stephen P. GOULET
23 Director of Health Services .... Ms. Robin MCNALLY
28 Chief Officer Diversity/Inclusion .... Dr. Betsy HUANG
04 Assistant to the President .... Ms. Joanne MILLER
21 Business Manager .... Mr. Paul WYKES
09 Manager of Institutional Research .... Mr. Jeffrey HIMMELBERGER

College of the Holy Cross (B)

1 College Street, Worcester MA 01610-2322
County: Worcester FICE Identification: 002141
Unit ID: 166124
Telephone: (508) 793-2011 Carnegie Class: Bac/A&S
FAX Number: (508) 793-3030 Calendar System: Semester
URL: www.holycross.edu
Established: 1843 Annual Undergrad Tuition & Fees: $44,272
Enrollment: 2,891 Coed
Affiliation or Control: Roman Catholic IRS Status: 501(c)3
Highest Offering: Baccalaureate
Program: Liberal Arts And General
Accreditation: EH, THEA

01 President .... Rev. Philip L. BOROUGHS, SJ
03 Senior Vice President .... Dr. Frank VELLACCIO
05 Int VP Academic Affairs/Dean of Col .... Ms. Margaret FREIJE
10 Treasurer/VP Admin & Finance .... Mr. Michael LOCHHEAD
10 Chief Investment Officer .... Mr. Timothy JARRY
32 VP Student Affairs/Dean of Students .... Ms. Jacqueline D. PETERSON
30 VP for Development/Alumni Relations .... Ms. Tracy BARLOK
88 Vice President for Mission .... Rev. Paul F. HARMAN, SJ
20 Associate Dean of the College .... Mr. Ronald JARRET
20 Associate Dean of the College .... Dr. Amy WOLFSON
21 Director of Finance/Asst Treasurer .... Ms. Dottie HAUVER
06 Registrar .... Ms. Patricia RING
07 Director of Admissions .... Ms. Ann B. MCDERMOTT
08 Director of Library Services .... Ms. Kathleen CARNEY
37 Director of Financial Aid .... Ms. Lynne M. MYERS
25 Director Grants/Found & Corp Giving .... Dr. Charles S. WEISS
42 Director Ofc of College Chaplains .... Ms. Marybeth KEARNS-BARRETT
71 Director Ctr Interdisc/Spec Studies .... Dr. Richard E. MATLAK
36 Director of Career Planning .... Ms. Amy MURPHY
13 Director Information Tech Services .... Ms. Ellen J. KEOHANE
26 Director of Public Affairs .... Ms. Ellen RYDER
29 Director of Alumni Relations .... Ms. Kristyn M. DYER
19 Director of Public Safety .... Mr. Robert HART
35 Director of Campus Center .... Mr. Jeremiah O'CONNOR
15 Human Resources Director .... Ms. Donna C. WRENN
18 Director of Physical Plant .... Mr. Scott M. MERRILL
41 Director of Athletics .... Mr. Richard M. REGAN
21 Controller .... Mr. Charles F. ESTAPHAN
45 Director of Planning .... Ms. Judy A. HANNUM
38 Director Counseling Center .... Dr. Paul GALVINHILL
23 Director Student Health Services .... Ms. Martha SULLIVAN
11 Director Administrative Services .... Mr. William J. CONLEY
96 Manager of Purchasing .... Ms. Joan E. ANDERSON
09 Ofc of Assessment/Research .... Ms. Denise BELL
86 Dir of Government/Cmty Relations .... Mr. Edward AUGUSTUS

College of Our Lady of the Elms (C)

291 Springfield Street, Chicopee MA 01013-2839
County: Hampden FICE Identification: 002140
Unit ID: 167394
Telephone: (413) 594-2761 Carnegie Class: Bac/Diverse
FAX Number: (413) 592-4871 Calendar System: Semester
URL: www.elms.edu
Established: 1928 Annual Undergrad Tuition & Fees: $29,676
Enrollment: 1,576 Coed
Affiliation or Control: Roman Catholic IRS Status: 501(c)3
Highest Offering: Master's
Program: Liberal Arts And General; Teacher Preparatory; Professional
Accreditation: EH, IACBE, NURSE, SW

01 President .... Dr. Mary REAP
05 Vice President of Academic Affairs .... Dr. Walter C. BREAU
10 Vice Pres Finance/Administration .... Mr. Brian E. DOHERTY
32 Vice Pres of Student Affairs .... Mr. John KELLER
30 Vice Pres of Instl Advancement .... Mr. Kevin M. EDWARDS
35 Associate Dean of Students .... Ms. Teresa WINTERS-DUNN
20 Assoc Acad Dean Grad Studies/CE .... Dr. Elizabeth HUKOWICZ
44 Director of Development .... Ms. Bernadette NOWAKOWSKI
07 Director of Admissions .... Mr. Joseph WAGNER
42 Director of Campus Ministry .... Sr. Carol ALLAN
06 Registrar .... Ms. Frances BLISS
08 Director of Library .... Mr. Anthony FONSECA
18 Director of Campus Operations .... Mr. Michael SULLIVAN
19 Director of Public Safety .... Mr. Michael SULLIVAN
26 Director of Institutional Marketing .... Ms. Nancy FARRELL
37 Director of Financial Aid .... Ms. Kristin HMIELESKI
36 Director of Career Services .... Ms. Nancy DAVIS
14 Director Information Technology .... Ms. Mary KASELOUSKAS
38 Director Student Counseling Svcs .... Mr. John COAN
41 Director of Athletics .... Mr. Peter KRASNY
15 Director Human Resources/Personnel .... Ms. Marie PHILLIPS
35 Director of Student Activities .... Ms. Megan KIELTY
85 Dir of ESL/International Program .... Dr. Joyce HAMPTON
09 Dir of Institutional Research .... Dr. Chul LEE
29 Dir of Constituent Relations .... Ms. Valerie BONATAKIS

Conway School of Landscape Design (D)

332 S Deerfield Road, PO Box 179,
Conway MA 01341-0179
County: Franklin FICE Identification: 022743
Unit ID: 165495
Telephone: (413) 369-4044 Carnegie Class: Spec/Arts
FAX Number: (413) 369-4032 Calendar System: Trimester
URL: www.csld.edu
Established: 1972 Annual Graduate Tuition & Fees: $31,450
Enrollment: 18 Coed
Affiliation or Control: Independent Non-Profit IRS Status: 501(c)3
Highest Offering: Master's; No Undergraduates
Program: Professional
Accreditation: EH

01 President/Director .... Mr. Paul C. HELLMUND
32 Assoc Dir Student Svcs/Fin/Fac .... Mr. David NORDSTROM
07 Assoc Dir Admissions/Comm .... Ms. Mollie BABIZE
30 Director of Development .... Ms. Priscilla NOVITT

Curry College (E)

1071 Blue Hill Avenue, Milton MA 02186-2395
County: Norfolk FICE Identification: 002143
Unit ID: 165529
Telephone: (617) 333-0500 Carnegie Class: Master's M
FAX Number: (617) 979-3540 Calendar System: Semester
URL: www.curry.edu
Established: 1879 Annual Undergrad Tuition & Fees: $34,415
Enrollment: 3,097 Coed
Affiliation or Control: Independent Non-Profit IRS Status: 501(c)3
Highest Offering: Master's
Program: Liberal Arts And General; Professional
Accreditation: EH, NURSE

01 President .... Mr. Kenneth K. QUIGLEY, JR.
05 Chief Academic Officer .... Vacant
30 Vice Pres Institutional Advancement .... Mr. Christopher LAWSON
10 Chief Financial Officer .... Mr. Richard F. SULLIVAN, JR.
07 Dean of Admission .... Ms. Jane P. FIDLER
32 Dean of Student Affairs .... Ms. Maryellen M. KILEY
45 Dean for Institutional Planning .... Dr. Susan W. PENNINI
04 Assistant to the President .... Ms. Amy M. BIANCHI
08 Librarian .... Mr. Edward TALLENT
14 Chief Information Officer .... Mr. Dennis THIBEAULT
15 Director of Human Resources .... Ms. Mary E. DUNN
20 Associate Dean Academic Affairs .... Vacant
84 Asst Dean Enrollment Mgt/Registrar .... Ms. Sally A. BUCKLEY
18 Chief Facilities/Physical Plant .... Mr. Robert G. O'CONNELL
26 Chief Public Relations Officer .... Ms. Frances L. JACKSON
29 Director of Alumni Relations .... Vacant
36 Director of Student Placement .... Ms. Maureen A. ASHBURN
37 Dir of Student Financial Services .... Ms. Stephanny J. ELIAS
38 Director of Student Counseling .... Dr. Alison W. MARKSON
51 Dean of Continuing Ed/Graduate Stds .... Dr. Ruth D. SHERMAN

Dean College (F)

99 Main Street, Franklin MA 02038-1994
County: Norfolk FICE Identification: 002144
Unit ID: 165574
Telephone: (508) 541-1508 Carnegie Class: Assoc/PrivNFP4
FAX Number: (508) 541-8726 Calendar System: Semester
URL: www.dean.edu
Established: 1865 Annual Undergrad Tuition & Fees: $33,230
Enrollment: 1,322 Coed
Affiliation or Control: Independent Non-Profit IRS Status: 501(c)3
Highest Offering: Baccalaureate
Program: 2-Year Principally Bachelor's Creditable; Liberal Arts And General
Accreditation: EH

01 President .... Dr. Paula M. ROONEY
04 Exec Assistant to President .... Ms. Sandra CAIN
05 Vice President Academic Affairs .... Dr. Linda RAGOSTA
84 VP Enrollment Services/Marketing .... Mr. John MARCUS
10 Vice Pres Financial Svcs/Treasurer .... Mr. Dan MODELANE
32 VP Student Development & Retention .... Ms. Cindy T. KOZIL
30 Vice Pres Institutional Advancement .... Ms. Coleen RESNICK
27 VP/Chief Information Officer .... Mr. Darrell KULESZA
44 Assoc Vice Pres Leadership Gifts .... Mr. Peter MOLLO
21 Assoc VP/Controller/Asst Treasurer .... Ms. Kathleen MCGUIRE
07 Asst VP Enrollment/Dean Admission .... Mr. James FOWLER
20 Asst VP Student Success/Career Plng .... Ms. Wendy ADLER
20 Asst Vice Pres Academic Affairs .... Ms. Melissa P. READ
45 Asst VP Capital Planning/Facilities .... Mr. Brian KELLY
26 AVP Marketing/Communications .... Mr. Gregg CHALK
35 Dean of Students .... Mr. David DRUCKER
51 Dean School of Continuing Studies .... Ms. Veatrice CARABINE
15 Chief Human Resources Officer .... Dr. Gary CONVERTINO
06 Registrar .... Mr. Daniel O'DRISCOLL
19 Dir Public Safety/Risk Management .... Mr. Kenneth F. CORKRAN
08 Director of the Library .... Mr. Ted BURKE
41 Athletic Director .... Mr. John A. JACKSON
39 Director Residence Life .... Ms. Shannon OVERCASH
35 Dir Student Activities/Orientation .... Ms. Jennifer BOTHWELL
40 Director of Bookstore .... Ms. Kathleen EKBOLM
37 Director of Financial Aid .... Ms. Jenny AGUIAR
84 Director Enrollment Operations .... Ms. Kathleen RYAN
36 Dir Career Planning/Internships .... Mr. Richard DAVINO
38 Coordinator of Counseling Services .... Ms. Mary Ann SILVESTRI

Eastern Nazarene College (G)

23 E Elm Avenue, Quincy MA 02170-2999
County: Norfolk FICE Identification: 002145
Unit ID: 165644
Telephone: (617) 745-3000 Carnegie Class: Bac/A&S
FAX Number: (617) 745-3907 Calendar System: 4/1/4
URL: www.enc.edu
Established: 1918 Annual Undergrad Tuition & Fees: $26,884
Enrollment: 1,459 Coed
Affiliation or Control: Church Of The Nazarene IRS Status: 501(c)3
Highest Offering: Master's
Program: Liberal Arts And General; Teacher Preparatory
Accreditation: EH, SW

01 President .... Dr. Corlis A. MCGEE
05 Provost & Dean of the College .... Dr. Timothy T. WOOSTER
10 Vice President Financial Affairs .... Mr. Jan G. WEISEN
32 Vice Pres Student Devel & Retention .... Mr. Jeff KIRKSEY
07 VP of Admissions/Financial Aid .... Dr. Timothy T. WOOSTER
30 Vice President Inst Advancement .... Dr. Scott TURCOTT
32 Assoc Dean Students/Residence Life .... Vacant
06 Registrar .... Mrs. Margaret BALLARD
37 Director Financial Aid .... Mr. Lerick FANFANX
08 Director of Library Services .... Ms. Susan J. WATKINS
19 Director Safety/Security/Risk Mgmt .... Mr. Jan G. WEISEN
38 Dir Counseling & Career Services .... Mr. Bradford E. THORNE
58 Dean of Div of Graduate/Prof Stds .... Vacant
41 Athletic Director .... Dr. Nancy DETWILER
18 Director of Facilities .... Mr. Jim HARDING
45 Director of Instructional Resources .... Ms. Patricia VASQUEZ
21 Controller .... Mrs. Myrna GIBERTSON
42 Chaplain/VP Spiritual Development .... Dr. Corey MACPHERSON
22 Director Human Resources .... Mrs. Francine WRIGHT
40 Director Bookstore .... Vacant

13 Director of Information Technology .... Mr. Charles BURT
58 Director Adult/Graduate Studies .... Dr. Jossie OWENS
04 Admin Assistant to the President .... Mrs. Sheryl WEISEN
39 Dir Resident Life/Multicultural Aff .... Mr. Robert BENJAMIN

Emerson College (A)

120 Boylston Street, Boston MA 02116-4624
County: Suffolk FICE Identification: 002146
Unit ID: 165662
Telephone: (617) 824-8500 Carnegie Class: Master's L
FAX Number: (617) 824-8511 Calendar System: Semester
URL: www.emerson.edu
Established: 1880 Annual Undergrad Tuition & Fees: $35,072
Enrollment: 4,492 Coed
Affiliation or Control: Independent Non-Profit IRS Status: 501(c)3
Highest Offering: Doctorate
Program: Liberal Arts And General; Professional
Accreditation: EH, SP

01 President .... Mr. M. Lee PELTON
43 Vice President & General Counsel .... Ms. Christine HUGHES
11 Vice President for Admin & Finance .... Ms. Maureen MURPHY
05 Vice President for Academic Affairs .... Ms. Michaele WHELAN
13 VP for Information Technology .... Dr. William GILLIGAN
26 Vice Pres Communications/Marketing .... Mr. Andrew TIEDEMANN
28 VP Diversity & Inclusion .... Ms. Sylvia SPEARS
10 Assoc Vice Pres for Finance .... Vacant
15 Assoc Vice Pres for Human Resources .... Ms. Alexa JACKSON
29 AVP Inst Advance/Dir Alumni Affrs .... Ms. Barbara RUTBERG
86 Assoc Vice Pres Govt/Community Rels ..... Ms. Margaret Ann INGS
58 Dean Grad Studies/AVP Acad Affairs .... Dr. Richard ZAUFT
32 Dean of Students .... Dr. Ronald LUDMAN
107 Exec Director Professional Studies .... Mr. Henry W. ZAPPALA
08 Exec Director of Library Services .... Mr. Robert FLEMING
07 Director of Graduate Admission .... Ms. Kristin BURKE
36 Director of Career Services .... Ms. Carol SPECTOR
38 Director Counseling Center .... Dr. Cheryl ROSENTHAL
19 Director of Public Safety .... Mr. Robert SMITH
41 Int Director Athletics/Head Coach .... Mr. Stan NANCE
85 Director International Student Affs .... Ms. Virga MOHSINI
96 Director Purchasing/Risk Management .... Ms. Margaret ROGAN
39 Assoc Dean Housing/Residence Life .... Mr. David W. HADEN
21 Controller .... Ms. Nancy TREVETHICK
06 Registrar .... Mr. William DEWOLF
42 Chair Center for Spiritual Life .... Mr. Albert S. AXELRAD
101 Exec Asst to the Board of Trustees ..... Ms. Anne SHAUGHNESSY
18 Int Assoc Director of Facilities .... Mr. Joseph KNOLL
37 Director Financial Aid .... Ms. Kerri JACOBS
07 Sr Assoc Director of Admissions .... Ms. Sara CUMMINGS
09 Director of Institutional Research .... Mr. Eric SYKES

Emmanuel College (B)

400 The Fenway, Boston MA 02115-5798
County: Suffolk FICE Identification: 002147
Unit ID: 165671
Telephone: (617) 277-9340 Carnegie Class: Master's S
FAX Number: (617) 735-9877 Calendar System: Semester
URL: www.emmanuel.edu
Established: 1919 Annual Undergrad Tuition & Fees: $34,670
Enrollment: 2,867 Coed
Affiliation or Control: Roman Catholic IRS Status: 501(c)3
Highest Offering: Master's
Program: Liberal Arts And General; Teacher Preparatory; Professional
Accreditation: EH, NURSE

01 President .... Sr. Janet EISNER, SND
03 Exec Asst to the President .... Ms. Michelle H. ERICKSON
04 Senior Assistant to President .... Ms. Lori SULLIVAN
05 Vice President of Academic Affairs .... Dr. Joyce DE LEO
10 Exec Vice Pres & Chief Oper Ofcr .... Vacant
26 Vice President Govt/Cmty Relations .... Ms. Sarah WELSH
32 Vice President of Student Affairs .... Dr. Patricia RISSMEYER
84 VP of Enrollment Mgmt & Marketing .... Ms. Lynn FAWTHROP
37 Assoc VP Student Financial Services ...... Ms. Jennifer C. PORTER
26 Assoc Vice President of Mktg/Comm .... Ms. Molly HONAN
07 Dean of Enrollment .... Ms. Sandra ROBBINS
35 Dean of Students .... Dr. Joseph ONOFRIETTI
49 Dean of Arts & Sciences .... Dr. William LEONARD
06 Associate Dean & Registrar .... Ms. Elizabeth ROSS
38 Director of Academic Advising .... Sr. Susan THORNELL
08 Director of Library .... Ms. Susan VON DAUM THOLL
15 Director Human Resources .... Ms. Erin FARMER NOONAN
41 Director of Athletics & Recreation .... Ms. Pamela ROECKER
42 Assoc VP of Mission & Ministry .... Fr. John SPENCER
20 Assoc Dean of Academic Pgm Support .... Ms. Cindy O'CALLAGHAN
38 Director Counseling Services .... Dr. Linda JURGELA
90 Director Academic Resource Ctr .... Ms. Wendy LABRON
88 Asst Dean Cmty Stdrds & Family Pgms . Ms. Mary Beth THOMAS

Endicott College (C)

376 Hale Street, Beverly MA 01915-2098
County: Essex FICE Identification: 002148
Unit ID: 165699
Telephone: (978) 927-0585 Carnegie Class: Master's M
FAX Number: (978) 927-0084 Calendar System: 4/1/4
URL: www.endicott.edu
Established: 1939 Annual Undergrad Tuition & Fees: $28,426
Enrollment: 4,408 Coed
Affiliation or Control: Independent Non-Profit IRS Status: 501(c)3
Highest Offering: Doctorate
Program: Liberal Arts And General; Professional
Accreditation: EH, ART, CIDA, NUR

01 President .... Dr. Richard E. WYLIE
05 Vice President & Academic Dean .... Dr. Laura ROSSI-LE
03 Executive VP/Vice President Finance .... Ms. Lynne B. O'TOOLE
84 Vice Pres Admissions/Financial Aid .... Mr. Thomas J. REDMAN
58 VP/Dean Graduate & Prof Stds .... Dr. Mary HUEGEL
32 Dean of Students .... Mr. Brandon DAWSON
30 Vice Pres Institutional Advancement .... Mr. David VIGNERON
11 Vice Pres Special Proj/Omudsperson .... Ms. Denise BILODEAU
04 Assistant to the President .... Ms. Joanne L. WALDNER
90 Assoc Dean of Academic Technology .... Mr. Kent BARCLAY
07 Associate Dean of Admission .... Mr. George M. SHERMAN
45 Executive Director of Research .... Mr. Peter L. HART
15 Director Human Resources .... Ms. Sally ARNOLD
21 Treasurer .... Ms. Donna L. COUTURE
06 Registrar .... Ms. Rosa CADENA
08 Library Director .... Mr. Brian COURTEMANCHE
29 Director Alumni Relations .... Ms. Sarah EARNEST
37 Director Financial Aid .... Ms. Marcia D. TOOMEY
41 Athletic Director .... Mr. Brian WYLIE
91 Chief Information Systems Officer .... Mr. Gary F. KELLEY
38 Senior Counselor .... Mr. Scott RUSSELL
39 Director of Residence Life .... Ms. Erica HEDRICK
18 Director of Physical Plant .... Mr. Dennis MONACO
26 Director Communications .... Ms. Carol RAICHE
36 Director of Career Services .... Ms. Dale MCLENNAN
09 Assoc Dir of Institutional Research .... Mr. Donald FEMINO
96 Purchasing Agent .... Mr. Terry SCHWENK
85 Dean of Undergrad International Ed .... Dr. Warren JAFERIAN
20 Dean of Academic Resources .... Dr. Kathleen BARNES
49 Dean of Arts & Sciences .... Dr. Gene WONG
53 Dean of Education .... Dr. Sara QUAY
57 Dean of Art & Design .... Mr. Mark TOWNER
59 Dean of Hospitality Management .... Dr. William H. SAMENFINK
68 Dean of Sports Science .... Dr. Deborah SWANTON
66 Dean of Nursing .... Dr. Kelly FISHER
50 Dean of Business & Technology .... Dr. Michael PAIGE
60 Dean of Communication .... Dr. Laurel HELLERSTEIN

Episcopal Divinity School (D)

99 Brattle Street, Cambridge MA 02138-3494
County: Middlesex FICE Identification: 002149
Unit ID: 165705
Telephone: (617) 868-3450 Carnegie Class: Spec/Faith
FAX Number: (617) 864-5385 Calendar System: Semester
URL: www.eds.edu
Established: 1857 Annual Graduate Tuition & Fees: $13,781
Enrollment: 80 Coed
Affiliation or Control: Protestant Episcopal IRS Status: 501(c)3
Highest Offering: Doctorate; No Undergraduates
Program: Professional; Religious Emphasis
Accreditation: THEOL

01 President and Dean .... Rev. Katherine H. RAGSDALE
05 Academic Dean .... Dr. Angela BAUER-LEVESQUE
100 Dean of Student & Community Life .... Rev. Miriam GELFER
30 VP Institutional Advancement .... Mr. Christopher HARTLEY
08 Director of the Library .... Ms. Pat PAYNE
27 Dir of Communications & Marketing .... Vacant
10 Chief Financial and Planning Office .... Mr. William JUDGE
21 Comptroller .... Ms. Joanne MANNING
07 Director of Recruitment .... Vacant
06 Registrar/Manager Academic Affairs .... Ms. Cecelia CULL
88 Director Congregational Studies .... Vacant
88 Director Field Education .... Dr. William KONDRATH
18 Superintendent Buildings & Grounds ..... Mr. Gustavo VILLATORO
04 Exec Assistant to President & Dean .... Ms. Jane WAGNER
37 Director Student Financial Aid .... Ms. Valerie PATERSON
15 Director of Human Resources .... Ms. Samaria WILSON-STALLINGS

FINE Mortuary College (E)

150 Kerry Place, Norwood MA 02062
County: Norfolk FICE Identification: 033164
Unit ID: 436599
Telephone: (781) 762-1211 Carnegie Class: Assoc/PrivFP
FAX Number: (781) 762-7177 Calendar System: Quarter
URL: www.fine-ne.com
Established: 1996 Annual Undergrad Tuition & Fees: $22,890
Enrollment: 80 Coed
Affiliation or Control: Proprietary IRS Status: Proprietary
Highest Offering: Associate Degree
Program: Occupational; Business Emphasis
Accreditation: FUSER

01 President .... Dr. Louis MISANTONE
03 Executive Vice President .... Dr. Lyn PRENDERGAST
11 Chief Financial & Operating Officer .... Ms. Susan BURKE
37 Director Financial Aid .... Ms. Brenda SWANSON

Fisher College (F)

118 Beacon Street, Boston MA 02116-1500
County: Suffolk FICE Identification: 002150
Unit ID: 165802
Telephone: (617) 236-8800 Carnegie Class: Bac/Assoc
FAX Number: (617) 236-8858 Calendar System: Semester
URL: www.fisher.edu
Established: 1903 Annual Undergrad Tuition & Fees: $27,595
Enrollment: 2,037 Coed
Affiliation or Control: Independent Non-Profit IRS Status: 501(c)3
Highest Offering: Baccalaureate
Program: Occupational; 2-Year Principally Bachelor's Creditable; Liberal Arts And General; Business Emphasis
Accreditation: EH, CAHIIM

01 President .... Dr. Thomas MCGOVERN
05 Vice President Academic Affairs .... Ms. Janet KUSER
10 VP for Finance .... Mr. Steven RICH
84 Dean of Enrollment Management .... Mr. Robert MELARAGNI
32 Dean of Students .... Ms. Shiela LALLY
88 Dean Intl Acad Oper/Curriculum Dev .... Ms. Nancy PITHIS
49 Chairman Div of Arts & Sciences .... Dr. Dean WALTON
06 College Registrar .... Mr. Gregory KARAS
41 Director of Athletics .... Mr. Scott DULIN
21 Director of Accounting .... Mr. Jeffrey CONRAD
13 Director of Information Services .... Mr. Jonathan BARTSCH
18 Director of Facilities .... Mr. Paul MCBRINE
37 Director of Financial Aid .... Ms. Colleen WOODS
66 Director of Nursing Services .... Ms. Bonnie CHUK
100 Chief of Staff .... Ms. Melinda COOK
88 Dir of Acad Center for Enrichment ..... Mrs. Jennifer MANDOLESE
35 Director of Student Activities .... Ms. Margarita ASCENCIO
42 Director of Spiritual Life .... Dr. Ann CLARKE
19 Chief Dept of Public Safety .... Mr. William CHASE
26 Dir Communications/Special Projects .... Ms. Jennie MOORE
36 Director of Career Services .... Ms. Heather CARPENTER
88 Director of Accessibility Service . Ms. Wanda CAMACHO-MARON
15 Sr Director of Human Resources .... Dr. Jack ROCHE
21 College Bursar .... Ms. Joy NELSON
08 College Librarian .... Mr. Joshua MCKAIN
29 Director Alumni Relations .... Ms. Kristen SHERMAN
09 Director of Institutional Research .... Mr. Alex WAGNER
51 Dean Div Cont Ed/Sch Hlth Professn .... Dr. Neil TROTTA

Franklin W. Olin College of Engineering (G)

Olin Way, Needham MA 02492-1200
County: Norfolk FICE Identification: 039463
Unit ID: 441982
Telephone: (781) 292-2300 Carnegie Class: Spec/Engg
FAX Number: (781) 292-2210 Calendar System: Semester
URL: www.olin.edu
Established: 2002 Annual Undergrad Tuition & Fees: $42,000
Enrollment: 355 Coed
Affiliation or Control: Independent Non-Profit IRS Status: 501(c)3
Highest Offering: Baccalaureate
Program: Professional
Accreditation: EH, ENG

01 President .... Dr. Richard K. MILLER
04 Asst to President .... Ms. Nancy SULLIVAN
10 Executive Vice President/Treasurer .. Mr. Stephen P. HANNABURY
07 VP External Rels/Dean of Admission .... Dr. Charles S. NOLAN
05 Provost/Dean of Faculty .... Dr. Vincent P. MANNO
11 VP Operations/Chief Info Officer .... Ms. Joanne KOSSUTH
32 Dean of Student Life .... Ms. Rae-Anne BUTERA
26 Chief Marketing Officer .... Ms. Michelle DAVIS
30 VP Development/Family & Alumni Rel .. Mr. J. Thomas KRIMMEL
29 Director Family & Alumni Relations .... Ms. Kristina RAPOSA
09 Dir Inst Research & Eval .... Mr. Jeremy GOODMAN
06 Registrar .... Ms. Linda T. CANAVAN

† All admitted students who enroll at Olin College receive an Olin Scholarship covering half tuition during the eight semesters of the baccalaureate program.

Gordon College (H)

255 Grapevine Road, Wenham MA 01984-1899
County: Essex FICE Identification: 002153
Unit ID: 165936
Telephone: (978) 927-2300 Carnegie Class: Bac/A&S
FAX Number: (978) 867-4659 Calendar System: Semester
URL: www.gordon.edu
Established: 1889 Annual Undergrad Tuition & Fees: $33,230
Enrollment: 1,580 Coed
Affiliation or Control: Independent Non-Profit IRS Status: 501(c)3
Highest Offering: Master's
Program: Liberal Arts And General
Accreditation: EH, MUS, SW

01 President .... Dr. D. Michael LINDSAY
03 Exec VP and Chief of Staff .... Mr. Daniel TYMANN
05 Provost .... Dr. Janel CURRY
10 Vice President for Finance/CFO .... Mr. Michael J. AHEARN
07 Executive Director of Admissions .... Ms. June BODONI
32 Vice President/Dean of Students .... Mr. Barry J. LOY
26 VP of Marketing and Communications .... Mr. Rick SWEENEY
26 Sr VP External Affairs .... Dr. Paul MAURER
20 Academic Dean .... Dr. Daniel RUSS
45 Legal Counsel .... Dr. Stephen C. MACLEOD
42 Dean of Christian Life .... Dr. Gregory W. CARMER
08 Director Library .... Mr. Myron SCHIRER-SUTER
06 Registrar .... Mrs. Alice A. FALCONE
13 Dir Technology and Administration .... Mr. Christopher JONES
37 Dir of Student Financial Services .... Mr. Daniel O'CONNELL
15 Director Human Resources .... Ms. Nancy ANDERSON
18 Chief Facilities/Physical Plant .... Mr. Paul HELGESEN
21 Controller .... Ms. Kim MATHER

29 Director Alumni & Parent Relations .... Ms. Adrienne COOK
36 Director Student Placement .... Ms. Pam LAZARAKIS
96 Purchasing Manager .... Mr. Michael NAWOICHIK
09 Sr Dir Institutional Research .... Mr. Robert VAN CLEEF

Gordon-Conwell Theological Seminary (A)

130 Essex Street, South Hamilton MA 01982-2317
County: Essex FICE Identification: 009747
Unit ID: 165945
Telephone: (978) 468-7111 Carnegie Class: Spec/Faith
FAX Number: (978) 468-6691 Calendar System: Semester
URL: www.gordonconwell.edu
Established: 1884 Annual Graduate Tuition & Fees: $17,100
Enrollment: 2,033 Coed
Affiliation or Control: Independent Non-Profit IRS Status: 501(c)3
Highest Offering: Doctorate; No Undergraduates
Program: Professional; Religious Emphasis
Accreditation: EH, THEOL

01 President .... Dr. Dennis HOLLINGER
10 Vice President Finance/CFO .... Mr. Jay S. TREWERN
05 Vice Pres for Academic Affairs .... Dr. Richard LINTS
30 Vice President of Advancement .... Mr. Kurt W. DRESCHER
12 Dean of Boston Campus .... Dr. Mark HARDEN
12 Academic Dean - Charlotte .... Dr. Timothy S. LANIAK
32 Dean of Students/Dir Stdnt Life Svc .... Mrs. Lita SCHLUETER
16 Director of Human Resources .... Ms. Susan ARSLANIAN
13 Chief Information Officer .... Mrs. Amy E. DONOVAN
84 Dean Enrollment Mgmt/Registrar .... Mr. Scott B. POBLENZ
18 Director of Physical Plant .... Mr. Timothy INGRAHAM
08 Director of Goddard Library .... Mr. Meredith KLINE
88 Director of the Ockenga Institute .... Dr. David G. HORN
37 Director of Financial Aid .... Mr. Stacey T. GLIDDEN
40 Director of Support Services .... Mr. David SHOREY
19 Director of Campus Safety .... Mr. Cabot W. DODGE
26 Dir of Communications & Marketing .... Mr. Michael L. COLARERI
07 Director of Admissions & Marketing .... Ms. Jill M. BARLOW
21 Controller & Dir Financial Svcs .... Mr. Gregg HANSEN
30 Chief Advancement Ofcr Charlotte .... Dr. Neely GASTON
42 Dir Doctor of Ministry Programs .... Mr. Dave CURRIE

Hampshire College (B)

893 West Street, Amherst MA 01002-3372
County: Hampshire FICE Identification: 004661
Unit ID: 166018
Telephone: (413) 549-4600 Carnegie Class: Bac/A&S
FAX Number: (413) 559-5584 Calendar System: 4/1/4
URL: www.hampshire.edu
Established: 1965 Annual Undergrad Tuition & Fees: $46,100
Enrollment: 1,545 Coed
Affiliation or Control: Independent Non-Profit IRS Status: 501(c)3
Highest Offering: Baccalaureate
Program: Liberal Arts And General
Accreditation: EH

01 President .... Dr. Jonathan LASH
101 Secretary of the College .... Ms. Beth I. WARD
05 Vice President & Dean of Faculty .... Dr. Eva RUESCHMANN
32 Dean of Students .... Mr. Byron MCCRAE
10 Vice Pres for Finance & Admin .... Mr. Mark SPIRO
15 Assoc Vice Pres Human Resources ..... Ms. Ann Michele RUOCCO
30 Chief Advancement Officer .... Mr. Clay BALLANTINE
07 Dean of Admissions & Financial Aid ...... Ms. Julie RICHARDSON
08 Director of Library/Info Services .... Ms. Jennifer KING
06 Director of Central Records .... Ms. Roberta P. STUART
37 Director of Financial Aid .... Ms. Jennifer G. LAWTON
09 Director of Institutional Research .... Ms. Meredith TWOMBLY
18 Director of Facilities and Grounds .... Mr. Larry ARCHEY
20 Sr Assc Dean Faculty Acad Fin/Admin ... Ms. Yaniris FERNANDEZ
26 Chief Public Relations Officer .... Ms. B. Elaine THOMAS
29 Director Alumni Relations .... Ms. Killara BURN
36 Director Student Placement .... Ms. Carin RANK
38 Director Student Counseling .... Dr. Eliza MCARDLE
100 Chief of Staff .... Ms. Joanna OLIN
28 Director of Diversity .... Ms. Diana FERNANDEZ

Harvard University (C)

1350 Massachusetts Ave, Cambridge MA 02138-3800
County: Middlesex FICE Identification: 002155
Unit ID: 166027
Telephone: (617) 495-1000 Carnegie Class: RU/VH
FAX Number: (617) 495-0500 Calendar System: Semester
URL: www.harvard.edu
Established: 1636 Annual Undergrad Tuition & Fees: $42,292
Enrollment: 28,147 Coed
Affiliation or Control: Independent Non-Profit IRS Status: 501(c)3
Highest Offering: Doctorate
Program: Liberal Arts And General; Teacher Preparatory; Professional
Accreditation: EH, BUS, CLPSY, DENT, ENG, IPSY, LAW, LSAR, MED, PCSAS, PH, PLNG, THEOL

01 President .... Drew G. FAUST
05 Provost .... Alan M. GARBER
03 Executive Vice President .... Katherine N. LAPP
88 Treasurer .... James ROTHENBERG
49 Dean Faculty Arts & Sciences .... Michael D. SMITH
20 Dean of Harvard College .... Vacant
58 Dean Grad School of Arts & Science .... Xiao-Li MENG
54 Dean of Engineering/Applied Science .... Cherry A. MURRAY
50 Dean of Harvard Business School .... Nitin NOHRIA
52 Dean of Dental Medicine .... R. Bruce DONOFF
48 Dean Graduate School of Design .... Mohsen MOSTAFAVI
73 Dean of the Divinity School .... David N. HEMPTON
51 Dean of Continuing Education .... Huntington D. LAMBERT
53 Acting Dean Graduate School of Educ .... Richard J. MURNANE
61 Dean of the Law School .... Martha MINOW
63 Dean of the Medical School .... Dr. Jeffrey S. FLIER
80 Dean of Government .... David ELLWOOD
69 Dean of Public Health .... Julio FRENK
88 Int Dean Radcliffe Inst Advance Std .... Lizabeth COHEN
88 Vice Pres for Strategy & Programs .... Leah ROSOVSKY
10 Vice President for Finance and CFO .... Daniel SHORE
11 Vice President for Campus Services .... Lisa HOGARTY
43 Vice President & General Counsel .... Robert W. IULIANO
26 Vice Pres Public Aff/Communications .... Christine HEENAN
29 Vice Pres Alumni Affs & Development .... Tamara E. ROGERS
15 Vice President for Human Resources ...... Marilyn HAUSAMMANN
18 Vice President for Campus Services .... Lisa HOGARTY
13 VP Harvard Information Technology .... Anne MARGULIES
28 Sr Vice Prov Fac Devel & Diversity .... Judith SINGER
09 Assc Provost Institutional Research .... Erin DRIVER-LINN
25 Sr Director Sponsored Programs .... Catherine BREEN
28 Chief Diversity Ofc/Sp Asst to Pres .... Lisa M. COLEMAN
07 Dean of Admissions/Financial Aid .... William R. FITZSIMMONS
06 Registrar/Faculty Arts & Sciences .... Michael P. BURKE
08 Exec Director for Harvard Library .... Helen SHENTON
23 Director Health Services .... Paul J. BARREIRA
19 Dir Police/Security/Chief of Police .... Francis D. RILEY
37 Director Student Financial Aid .... Sally C. DONAHUE

Hebrew College (D)

160 Herrick Road, Newton Centre MA 02459-2237
County: Middlesex FICE Identification: 002157
Unit ID: 166045
Telephone: (617) 559-8600 Carnegie Class: Spec/Faith
FAX Number: (617) 559-8601 Calendar System: Semester
URL: www.hebrewcollege.edu
Established: 1921 Annual Undergrad Tuition & Fees: $19,200
Enrollment: 228 Coed
Affiliation or Control: Independent Non-Profit IRS Status: 501(c)3
Highest Offering: Beyond Master's But Less Than Doctorate
Program: Professional; Religious Emphasis
Accreditation: EH

01 President .... Rabbi Daniel LEHMANN
10 Vice Pres Finance & Administration .... Mr. Leon ZAIMES
05 Provost .... Dr. Barry MESCH
84 Director of Enrollment Management .... Ms. Sara SHALVA
06 Registrar/Financial Aid Services .... Ms. Marilyn JAYE
30 Director of Development .... Mr. Paul ROSENSTEIN
15 Director Personnel Services .... Ms. Steffi BOBBIN
04 Assistant to the President .... Ms. Annette ASHIN

Hellenic College-Holy Cross Greek Orthodox School of Theology (E)

50 Goddard Avenue, Brookline MA 02445-7496
County: Norfolk FICE Identification: 002154
Unit ID: 166054
Telephone: (617) 731-3500 Carnegie Class: Spec/Faith
FAX Number: (617) 850-1460 Calendar System: Semester
URL: www.hchc.edu
Established: 1937 Annual Undergrad Tuition & Fees: $21,268
Enrollment: 206 Coed
Affiliation or Control: Greek Orthodox IRS Status: 501(c)3
Highest Offering: Master's
Program: Teacher Preparatory; Professional
Accreditation: EH, THEOL

01 President .... Rev. Nicholas C. TRIANTAFILOU
73 Dean School of Theology .... Rev Dr. Thomas FITZGERALD
05 Dean Hellenic College .... Dr. Demetrios KATOS
32 Dean of Students .... Dean Nicholas BELCHER
11 Chief Operating Officer .... Mr. James D. KARLOUTSOS
10 Interim Chief Financial Officer .... Mr. Kevin DERRIVAN
07 Director of Admissions & Records .... Mr. Gregory FLOOR
08 Director Library .... Rev. Joachim COTSONIS
37 Financial Aid Officer .... Mrs. Christine BURKE
06 Registrar .... Ms. Alba PAGAN
13 Director Computing/Information Mgmt .... Mr. Mugur ROZ
42 Chaplain .... Rev. Peter CHAMBERAS
38 Director Student Counseling .... Ms. Athina-Eleni MAVROUDHIS
30 Director Institutional Advancement .... Rev. James KATINAS
29 Director of Alumni Office .... Mr. Gregory FLOOR
21 Interim Controller .... Mr. Alan B. BOYER
40 Bookstore Manager .... Ms. Tanya CONTOS
26 Director of Public Relations .... Mr. Joshua COLE
39 Director of Housing/Security .... Mr. George GEORGENES
04 Administrator of President's Office .... Mrs. Joanna BAKAS

Hult International Business School (F)

One Education Street, Cambridge MA 02141-1805
County: Middlesex FICE Identification: 041432
Unit ID: 164368
Telephone: (617) 746-1990 Carnegie Class: Not Classified
FAX Number: (617) 746-1991 Calendar System: Other
URL: www.hult.edu
Established: 1964 Annual Undergrad Tuition & Fees: $65,800
Enrollment: 2,036 Coed
Affiliation or Control: Proprietary IRS Status: Proprietary
Highest Offering: Master's
Program: Professional; Business Emphasis
Accreditation: EH

01 President .... Dr. Stephen HODGES
05 Chief Academic Officer .... Dr. Mukul KUMAR
20 Vice President for Academic Affairs .... Dr. Richard JOSEPH
12 Dean Boston Campus .... Mr. Henrik TOTTERMAN
12 Dean San Francisco Campus .... Mr. Larry LOUIE
84 Dir of Recruiting .... Mr. Steve WYNN
36 Dir of Career Services Boston .... Mr. James MORRISON
35 Dir Student Services Boston .... Mr. David HIETT
06 Registrar Boston Campus .... Mr. Alec FISHER
06 Asst Registrar San Francisco Campus .... Ms. Caroline CONNOR

ITT Technical Institute (G)

333 Providence Highway, Norwood MA 02062
Telephone: (781) 278-7200 Identification: 666541
Accreditation: ACICS

† Main campus is ITT Technical Institute in Indianapolis, IN.

ITT Technical Institute (H)

200 Ballardvale Street, Suite 200, Wilmington MA 01887
Telephone: (978) 658-2636 Identification: 666119
Accreditation: ACICS

† Main campus is ITT Technical Institute in Indianapolis, IN.

Laboure College (I)

2120 Dorchester Avenue, Boston MA 02124-5698
County: Suffolk FICE Identification: 006324
Unit ID: 165264
Telephone: (617) 296-8300 Carnegie Class: Assoc/PrivNFP
FAX Number: (617) 296-7947 Calendar System: Semester
URL: www.laboure.edu
Established: 1892 Annual Undergrad Tuition & Fees: $32,412
Enrollment: 743 Coed
Affiliation or Control: Roman Catholic IRS Status: 501(c)3
Highest Offering: Baccalaureate
Program: Occupational; 2-Year Principally Bachelor's Creditable; Nursing Emphasis
Accreditation: EH, ADNUR, CAHIIM, DIETT, NDT, NURSE, RTT

01 President .... Ms. Maureen A. SMITH
10 Chief Financial Officer .... Mr. Mark VIRELLO
05 Dean Academic Affairs .... Ms. Paula VOSBURGH
32 Vice Pres/Dean Student Affairs .... Mrs. Karen MASTERS
08 Director Learning Resources Center .... Mr. Andrew CALO
06 Registrar .... Mr. John SACCO
84 Director of Enrollment Services .... Vacant
30 VP Institutional Advancement .... Ms. Catherine PHILBIN
26 Director Public Relations/Marketing .... Ms. Katelyn DWYER
37 Director Student Financial Aid .... Ms. Erin HANLON
66 Chair of Nursing Division .... Ms. Anne JACOBY
78 Chair of Dietetic Division .... Mrs. Anne MANION
76 Div Chair Health Info Tech .... Ms. Elise BELANGER
88 Div Chair Radiation Technology .... Mrs. Pauline CLANCY
88 Div Chair Electroneuro Technology .... Mrs. Jean FARLEY

Langley School of Music of Bard College (J)

27 Garden Street, Cambridge MA 02138
Telephone: (617) 876-0956 Identification: 770137
Accreditation: &M

† Main campus is Bard College in Annandale-On-Hudson, NY.

Lasell College (K)

1844 Commonwealth Avenue, Newton MA 02466-2716
County: Middlesex FICE Identification: 002158
Unit ID: 166391
Telephone: (617) 243-2000 Carnegie Class: Bac/Diverse
FAX Number: (617) 243-2389 Calendar System: Semester
URL: www.lasell.edu
Established: 1851 Annual Undergrad Tuition & Fees: $30,000
Enrollment: 1,980 Coed
Affiliation or Control: Independent Non-Profit IRS Status: 501(c)3
Highest Offering: Master's
Program: Liberal Arts And General
Accreditation: EH, EXSC

01 President .... Michael B. ALEXANDER
04 Exec Assistant to the President .... Pamela FARIA
05 VP Academic Affairs .... James OSTROW
10 VP Business & Finance .... Michael HOYLE
84 VP Enrollment Management .... Kathleen O'CONNOR
88 VP Lasell Village .... Paula PANCHUCK
32 VP Student Affairs .... Diane AUSTIN
26 VP Comm/Community & Govt Rels .... Ruth SHUMAN
30 VP Development & Alumni Relations .... Dean HICKEY
07 Dean Undergraduate Admission .... James TWEED
20 Assoc VP/Dean Undergraduate Educ .... Steven BLOOM
58 Dean Grad & Prof Studies .... Joan DOLAMORE
89 Dean Advis & First Year Programs .... Helena SANTOS
35 Dean Student Affairs .... David HENNESSEY

21 Asst VP Finance Diane PARKER
37 Dir Student Financial Planning Michele KOSBOTH
09 Dir Institutional Research Melanie LARSON
06 Registrar Dianne POLIZZI
44 Dir Annual Giving/Const Rel Haegan FORREST
18 Dir Plant Operations/Sustainability Marc FOURNIER
27 Dir Communications Michelle GASSEAU
30 Dir Development Mark LAFRANCE
30 Senior Advancement Officer Katharine URNER-JONES
29 Assoc Dir Alumni Relations Lauren MCCAUSLIN
35 Dir Student Act & Orientation Jennifer GRANGER
23 Dir Health Services Ann SHERMAN
08 Dir Library Marilyn NEGIP
41 Dir Athletics Kristy WALTER
15 Dir Human Resources Kathryn BRYNE
38 Dir Counseling Center Janice FLETCHER
07 Dir Graduate Admission Adrienne FRANCIOSI
42 Dir Center for Spirtual Life Thomas SULLIVAN
13 Chief Information Officer Deborah GELCH
39 Dir Residential Life Peter WIERNICKI

Le Cordon Bleu College of Culinary Arts in Cambridge (A)

215 First Street, Cambridge MA 02142
Telephone: (617) 218-8000 Identification: 770576
Accreditation: ACCSC

† Main campus is Le Cordon Bleu College of Culinary Arts in Scottsdale in Scottsdale, AZ.

Lesley University (B)

29 Everett Street, Cambridge MA 02138-2790
County: Middlesex FICE Identification: 002160
Unit ID: 166452
Telephone: (617) 868-9600 Carnegie Class: Master's L
FAX Number: (617) 349-8717 Calendar System: Semester
URL: www.lesley.edu
Established: 1909 Annual Undergrad Tuition & Fees: $32,000
Enrollment: 5,896 Coed
Affiliation or Control: Independent Non-Profit IRS Status: 501(c)3
Highest Offering: Doctorate
Program: Liberal Arts And General; Teacher Preparatory; Professional
Accreditation: EH, ART, TEAC

01 President Dr. Joseph B. MOORE
05 Provost Dr. Selase W. WILLIAMS
11 Vice President for Administration Ms. Marylou BATT
10 Vice President/CFO Ms. Bernice BRADIN
30 Vice President of Advancement Mr. Randy STABILE
84 VP of Enrollment Management Mr. Timothy ROBISON
21 VP for Budgeting & Fin Planning Ms. M. L. DYMSKI
43 General Counsel Ms. Shirin PHILIPP
100 Chief of Staff Dr. MaryPat LOHSE
20 Associate Provost Ms. Lisa IJIRI
22 Dir Equal Opportunity & Inclusion Dr. Barbara ADDISON REID
58 Dean Grad Sch Arts & Social Sci Dr. Catherine KOVEROLA
53 Dean School of Education Dr. Jack GILLETTE
32 Dean of Student Life & Academic Dev Dr. Nathaniel MAYS
88 Dean Art Institute of Boston Mr. Stan TRECKER
49 Dean College of Liberal Arts & Sci Dr. Mary COLEMAN
18 Dir Operations & Campus Planning Mr. George SMITH
13 Chief Information Officer Mr. Daryl FORD
07 Director of Graduate Admissions Ms. Martha SHEEHAN
91 Director Admin Applications UT Mr. Scott BOULET
90 Assoc VP Academic Programming Ms. Lisa IJIRI
15 Director of Human Resources Ms. Jane JOYCE
37 Director of Financial Aid Mr. Scott JEWELL
19 Captain of Security Ms. Nicole O'LEARY
88 Budget Director Ms. Anne GROGAN
88 Director Student Accounts Ms. Heather CLANG
21 Controller Ms. Karen BAYTCH
40 Manager of Bookstore/Campus Shop Ms. Lee-Ann LANZILLO
44 Dir of Annual Giving & Alumni Rels Ms. Pattyanne LYONS
08 Director of Libraries Ms. Patricia PAYNE
06 Registrar Ms. Melissa JANOT
36 Assoc Dean Career/Community Service Ms. Alice DIAMOND
41 Director of Athletics Mrs. Jennifer BENWAY
07 Dir Undergrad Admissions Lesley Col Ms. Deb KOCAR
39 Director Residence Life Ms. Nancy GALVIN
38 Director Counseling Center Ms. Magi MCKINNIES
85 Dir International Student Services Ms. Janie BESS
09 Dir of Assessment/Inst Research Dr. Linda PURSLEY
26 Assistant VP of Marketing Mr. Jeremy THOMPSON
27 Dir of Advancement Communications Ms. Carol KREMS
96 Director of Purchasing Mr. William HOYT

Marian Court College (C)

35 Littles Point Road, Swampscott MA 01907-2896
County: Essex FICE Identification: 006873
Unit ID: 166601
Telephone: (781) 595-6768 Carnegie Class: Assoc/PrivNFP
FAX Number: (781) 595-3560 Calendar System: Semester
URL: www.mariancourt.edu
Established: 1964 Annual Undergrad Tuition & Fees: $16,200
Enrollment: 160 Coed
Affiliation or Control: Roman Catholic IRS Status: 501(c)3
Highest Offering: Baccalaureate
Program: Occupational; 2-Year Principally Bachelor's Creditable
Accreditation: EH

01 Interim President Dr. Denise HAMMON
10 Chief Financial Officer Ms. Maribeth FORBES
30 VP Development and Marketing Ms. Sarah JOHNSON
05 Dean of Academic & Student Affairs Dr. Denise HAMMON
06 Registrar Ms. Linda LUNDSTROM
07 Sr Assoc Director of Admissions Mr. Peter SCHILLING
08 Librarian & Career Info Specialist Ms. Mia MORGAN
38 Dir of Academic & Career Services Ms. Megan PENYACK
37 Director of Financial Aid Ms. Stacy BONSANG
13 Director of Information Technology Mr. Jorge CORREIA
50 Chair Business Dept Ms. Joan THOMPSON
79 Chair Liberal Studies Dr. Tom HALLORAN
88 Chair Criminal Justice Mr. Fran BRENNAN

*Massachusetts Board of Higher Education (D)

One Ashburton Place, Room 1401,
Boston MA 02108-1696
County: Suffolk FICE Identification: 029283
Unit ID: 166531
Telephone: (617) 994-6950 Carnegie Class: N/A
FAX Number: (617) 727-6397
URL: www.mass.edu

01 Commissioner Dr. Richard M. FREELAND
103 Assoc Comm of Workforce Development Mr. David C. CEDRONE
05 Deputy Comm Academic Policy Ms. Aundrea KELLEY
43 General Counsel Ms. Constantia PAPANIKOLAOU
10 Dep Comm Administration and Finance Mr. Sean NELSON
09 Assoc Comm Institutional Research Dr. Jonathan KELLER
37 Sr Dep Comm Student Financial Aid Dr. Clantha MCCURDY

*University of Massachusetts Central Office (E)

225 Franklin Street, 33rd Floor, Boston MA 02110
County: Suffolk FICE Identification: 008017
Unit ID: 166665
Telephone: (617) 287-7050 Carnegie Class: N/A
FAX Number: (617) 287-7167
URL: www.massachusetts.edu

01 President Dr. Robert L. CARET
03 Exec VP/Chief Operating Officer Mr. James JULIAN
05 Sr VP Acad Affs/Stdnt & Intl Affs Dr. Marcellette WILLIAMS
11 Sr VP Administration and Finance Ms. Christine WILDA
30 Vice President for Advancement Mr. Charles PAGNAM
46 Vice President Economic Development Mr. Thomas CHMURA
26 VP Strategic Comm/Univ Spokesperson Mr. Robert CONNOLLY
104 Deputy Chief Operating Officer Ms. Susan KELLY
86 Special Asst to Pres Govt Relation Mr. David MCDERMOTT
43 General Counsel Ms. Deirdre HEATWOLE
27 Assoc VP and Chief Info Officer Mr. Robert SOLIS
101 Secretary to Board of Trustees Ms. Zunilka BARRETT
21 Director for University Auditing Mr. Kyle DAVID
15 Dir of Human Resources & Labor Rels Mr. Mark PREBLE
106 Interim CEO UMass Online Dr. John CUNNINGHAM

*University of Massachusetts (F)

Amherst MA 01003-0001
County: Hampshire FICE Identification: 002221
Unit ID: 166629
Telephone: (413) 545-0111 Carnegie Class: RU/VH
FAX Number: N/A Calendar System: Semester
URL: www.umass.edu
Established: 1863 Annual Undergrad Tuition & Fees (In-State): $13,258
Enrollment: 28,236 Coed
Affiliation or Control: State IRS Status: 501(c)3
Highest Offering: Doctorate
Program: Liberal Arts And General; Teacher Preparatory; Professional
Accreditation: EH, AUD, BUS, BUSA, CLPSY, DIETD, DIETI, ENG, FOR, IPSY, LSAR, MUS, NURSE, PH, #PLNG, SCPSY, SP, TED

02 Chancellor Dr. Kumble R. SUBBASWAMY
05 Provost/Sr Vice Chancellor Dr. James V. STAROS
10 Vice Chancellor Admin/Finance Mr. James P. SHEEHAN
30 Vice Chancellor Univ Advancement Mr. Michael A. LETO
46 Vice Chancellor Research Dr. Michael F. MALONE
32 VC Student Affairs & Campus Life Ms. Enku GELAYE
31 Vice Chanc University Relations Mr. John KENNEDY
41 Director of Athletics Mr. John F. MCCUTCHEON
43 Senior Counsel Mr. Brian W. BURKE
13 Special Asst to Chancellor & CIO Dr. John F. DUBACH
13 VC Information Services & CIO Ms. Julie L. BUEHLER
22 Assoc Chanc Equal Oppty/Diversity Ms. Debora D. FERREIRA
28 Faculty Adv Diversity & Excellence Dr. Amilcar SHABAZZ
04 Asst to the Chancellor Ms. Becky DEAN
20 Vice Provost Undegrad & Cont Educ Dr. Carol A. BARR
58 Vice Provost/Dean of Grad School Dr. John J. MCCARTHY
88 Vice Provost/Dean of Faculty Dr. Joel W. MARTIN
88 Assoc Provost Faculty Development Mr. John BRYAN
88 Assoc Provost Center for Teaching Dr. Mary Deane SORCINELLI
85 Assoc Provost Intl Programs Dr. Jack AHERN
84 Assoc Provost Enrollment Management Dr. James ROCHE
45 Assoc Provost Academic Plng/Assess Dr. Bryan C. HARVEY
20 Asst Provost Advising/Acad Support Dr. Pamela R. MARSH-WILLIAMS
09 Asst Provost Institutional Research Dr. Marilyn H. BLAUSTEIN
108 Asst Provost Assessment/Educ Effect Dr. Martha L. STASSEN
87 Assistant Provost Summer Programs Dr. Edmund J. FERSZT
51 Exec Director Continuing Education Mr. William S. MCCLURE
07 Director Undergraduate Admissions Mr. Kevin KELLY
37 Director Financial Aid Services Ms. Suzanne PETERS
06 University Registrar Mr. John LENZI
92 Dean Commonwealth Honors College Dr. Daniel L. GORDON
79 Dean Col Humanities & Fine Arts Dr. Julie C. HAYES
81 Dean Col Natural Science Dr. Steve GOODWIN
83 Dean Col Social & Behavioral Sci Dr. Robert S. FELDMAN
53 Dean School of Education Dr. Christine B. MCCORMICK
54 Dean College of Engineering Dr. Timothy J. ANDERSON
50 Dean School of Management Dr. Mark A. FULLER
66 Dean School of Nursing Dr. Stephen CAVANAGH
69 Dean Sch Public Health/Health Sci Dr. C. Marjorie AELION
08 Director of Libraries Mr. Jay SCHAFER
56 Director of Extension Ms. Nancy GARRABRANTS
47 Dir Stockbridge School Agriculture Dr. Wesley AUTIO
88 Director Fine Arts Center Dr. Willie L. HILL
15 Asst Vice Chanc Human Resources Mr. Juan A. JARRETT
21 Assoc VC/Budget Director/Controller Mr. Andrew P. MANGELS
18 Assoc VC Facilities Planning Ms. Juanita M. HOLLER
19 Director Public Safety/Chief Police Mr. John K. HORVATH
96 Director of Purchasing Mr. John O. MARTIN
40 Manager Univ Store/Retail Services Mr. Ken KAHLER
35 Dean Student Affairs Ms. Enku GELAYE
39 Exec Director Housing & Res Life Mr. Edward C. HULL
23 Director University Health Services Dr. George A. COREY
38 Director Mental Health/Health Svcs Dr. Harry S. ROCKLAND-MILLER
36 Director Career Services Ms. Candice J. SERAFINO
29 Exec Director Alumni Relations Dr. JC SCHNABL
44 Director Annual Giving Ms. Sarah SLIGO
27 Exec Director News & Media Mr. Edward F. BLAGUSZEWSKI
26 Assoc VC University Relations Ms. Amy C. GLYNN
86 Dir Public/Constituent Relations Mr. Christopher DUNN
102 Director Corporate/Foundation Rels Ms. Jennifer VEILLEUX
31 Dir Cmty Relations/Special Events Dr. Nancy BUFFONE
25 Director Grant & Contract Admin Ms. Carol SPRAGUE
91 Associate CIO/Dir Admin Applics Ms. Heidi DOLLARD
90 Director OIT Academic Computing Ms. Heidi DOLLARD
24 Director Educational Media Mr. Stephen PIELOCK
105 Web Manager Ms. Nina SOSSEN

*University of Massachusetts Boston (G)

100 Morrissey Boulevard, Boston MA 02125-3393
County: Suffolk FICE Identification: 002222
Unit ID: 166638
Telephone: (617) 287-5000 Carnegie Class: RU/H
FAX Number: (617) 265-7173 Calendar System: Semester
URL: www.umb.edu
Established: 1964 Annual Undergrad Tuition & Fees (In-State): $13,075
Enrollment: 15,874 Coed
Affiliation or Control: State IRS Status: 501(c)3
Highest Offering: Doctorate
Program: Liberal Arts And General; Teacher Preparatory; Professional; Business Emphasis
Accreditation: EH, BUS, CLPSY, CORE, CS, MFCD, NURSE, @TEAC

02 Chancellor Dr. J. Keith MOTLEY
88 Assistant Chancellor Dr. Theresa MORTIMER
100 Chief of Staff Mr. Christopher HOGAN
05 Provost Dr. Winston LANGLEY
10 Vice Chanc for Admin & Finance Ms. Ellen O'CONNOR
30 VC Chanc for Univ Advancement Ms. Gina CAPPELLO
84 Vice Chanc Enrollment Management Ms. Kathleen TEEHAN
32 Int Vice Chancellor for Student Aff Ms. Lisa BUENAVENTURA
32 Int Vice Chancellor for Student Aff Mr. James OVERTON
41 VC for Athletics & Special Projects Mr. Charlie TITUS
86 VC for Govt Rel/Public Aff Mr. Edward LAMBERT
14 Int Vice Provost Inf Tech/CIO Mr. Apurva MEHTA
84 Assoc Vice Chanc Enrollment Mgmt Dr. Lisa JOHNSON
15 Asst Vice Chanc for Human Resources Ms. Becky HSU
29 Asst VC Alumni Relations Ms. Elizabeth FREEDMAN DOHERTY
31 Asst Vice Chanc Community Relations Ms. Gail HOBIN
23 Int Asst VC Std Aff/Ex Dir Hlth Svc Dr. Kathleen YORKIS
20 Associate Provost Ms. Kristine ALSTER
20 Assoc Provost Assess and Planning Dr. Peter LANGER
53 Int Dean Col of Educ & Human Dev Ms. Felicia WILCZENSKI
51 Dean of University College Dr. Philip DISALVIO
81 Dean of Math & Science Dr. Andrew GROSOVSKY
79 Int Dean of Liberal Arts Dr. Emily MCDERMOTT
50 Dean College of Management Dr. Philip L. QUAGLIERI
66 Dean College of Nursing & Health Sc Dr. Anahid KULWICKI
80 Int Dean of CPCS Dr. Anna MADISON
35 Dean of Students Vacant
43 Interim General Counsel Ms. Deirdre HEATWOLE
26 Director of Communications Mr. DeWayne LEHMAN
38 Director Univ Advising Center Ms. Gail STUBBS
09 Director Institutional Research Dr. Jennifer A. BROWN
06 Director of Registration & Records Mr. David R. CESARIO
07 Director of Undergrad Admissions Mr. John DREW
37 Director Financial Aid Services Ms. Judy KEYES
08 Director of Libraries Dr. Daniel ORTIZ
22 Int Chief Diversity Officer ODI Ms. Georgianna MELENDEZ
18 Director of Facilities Devel & Mgmt Ms. Dorothy RENAGHAN
19 Int Director of Public Safety Mr. Donald BAYNARD
40 Director of Campus Services Ms. Diane D'ARRIGO
41 Senior Assoc Director of Athletics Ms. Terry CONDON
36 Director of Career Services Mr. Mark KENYON
24 Media Services Manager Mr. John POTTER
96 Director of Procurement Mr. Darryl MAYERS

92 Director of Honors Programs ... Ms. Rajini SRIKANTH
20 Asst Vice Provost Undergrad Studies ... Ms. Maura MAST

*University of Massachusetts Dartmouth (A)

285 Old Westport Road, North Dartmouth MA 02747-2300
County: Bristol FICE Identification: 002210
Unit ID: 167987
Telephone: (508) 999-8000 Carnegie Class: Master's L
FAX Number: (508) 999-8901 Calendar System: Semester
URL: www.umassd.edu
Established: 1895 Annual Undergrad Tuition & Fees (In-State): $11,681
Enrollment: 9,210 Coed
Affiliation or Control: State IRS Status: 501(c)3
Highest Offering: Doctorate
Program: Liberal Arts And General; Teacher Preparatory; Professional
Accreditation: EH, ART, BUS, CS, ENG, #LAW, MT, NUR

02 Chancellor ... Dr. Divina GROSSMAN
05 Provost/VC Acad & Student Affairs ... Dr. Mohammad KARIM
10 Vice Chanc Admin/Fiscal Services ... Ms. Deborah MCLAUGHLIN
30 Interim Vice Chancellor Advancement ... Ms. Wendy SKINNER
04 Special Assistant to the Chancellor ... Mr. Richard TONETTI
51 Special Asst to Provost/PCE Pgm ... Ms. Karen RHODA
20 Vice Provost for Academic Affairs ... Dr. Magali CARRERA
20 Int Assc Provost Grad Stds/Research ... Dr. Tesfay MERESSI
84 Assc VC Enrollment Management ... Ms. Teresa MAUK
21 Int Assoc Vice Chancellor Finance ... Ms. Marilyn SCUDELLARI-PRESTO
18 Associate VC Facilities Management ... Mr. Peter DUFFY
58 Dir Graduate Studies/Admissions ... Mr. Scott WEBSTER
22 Int Asst Chanc Diversity/Equity/Inc ... Ms. Deborah MAJEWSKI
31 Asst Chanc Economic Development ... Mr. Paul VIGEANT
88 Assistant VC Student Success ... Ms. Carol SPENCER
35 Assoc Vice Chanc Student Affairs ... Dr. David M. MILSTONE
13 CIO & Assoc VC IT ... Ms. Donna R. MASSANO
91 Asst VC IT System & Planning ... Vacant
88 Asst VC for Pgm Planning/Fiscal Mgt ... Ms. Joanne ZANELLA-LITKE
49 Interim Dean College Arts & Science ... Dr. Jeannette RILEY
50 Dean Charlton Col of Business ... Dr. Angappa GUNASEKARAN
54 Dean College of Engineering ... Dr. Robert PECK
66 Dean College of Nursing ... Dr. James FAIN
57 Dean College Visual Perform Arts ... Mr. Adrian TIO
88 Dean School Marine Science/Tech ... Dr. Steven LOHRENZ
96 Asst VC for Administrative Services ... Mr. Michael LAGRASSA
21 Assistant Financial Controller ... Ms. Suzanne AUDET
92 Director Honors Program ... Mr. Avery PLAW
94 Dir Center Women/Gender/Sexuality ... Ms. Juli PARKER
88 Assoc Dir Academic Advising Center ... Ms. Suzanne MELLONI
06 Interim University Registrar ... Ms. Christine KAYLOR
07 Director of Admissions ... Mr. Michael LYNCH
09 Director of Institutional Research ... Ms. Tammy A. SILVA
08 Dean Library Services ... Mr. Terrance BURTON
19 Dir Public Safety/Chief of Police ... Col. Emil FIORAVANTI
36 Director Career Development Center ... Ms. Gail L. BERMAN-MARTIN
37 Associate Director Financial Aid ... Ms. Audra CALLAHAN
38 Dir Counseling/Stdnt Develop Ctr ... Dr. Christine FRIZZELL
90 Exec Dir IT Service Assurance ... Ms. Margaret S. DIAS
29 AVC Alumni Relations ... Vacant
29 Director of Alumni Relations ... Mr. C. Chad ARGOSINGER
15 Asst VC Human Resources ... Ms. Carol SANTOS
18 Director Facilities/Physical Plant ... Mr. Jeffrey LOURO
41 Director of Athletics ... Mr. Ian DAY
23 Director of Health Services ... Ms. Sheila DORGAN
39 Director of Housing/Residence Life ... Ms. Lucinda POUDRIER-AARONSON
40 Interim Manager Campus Store ... Ms. Jann STAHL
44 Director Annual Giving/Development ... Ms. Jen RAXTER
26 Asst Chancellor Public Affairs ... Mr. John T. HOEY
88 Bursar ... Ms. Kathleen L. EUBANKS
35 Asst VC Student Affairs ... Ms. Cynthia CUMMINGS
35 Associate Dean of Students ... Ms. Shelly METIVIER SCOTT
104 Dir Intl Exch/Study Abroad Programs ... Ms. Kristen KALBRENER
85 Dir International Student Center ... Ms. Christina M. BRUEN
93 Assoc Dir Fred Douglas Unity House ... Ms. Nicole WILLIAMS
88 Director Academic Resource Center ... Mr. Thomas DAIGLE
105 Webmaster ... Mr. Don KING
108 Dir of Learning Assessment ... Dr. Edward MORGAN

*University of Massachusetts Lowell (B)

1 University Avenue, Lowell MA 01854-2881
County: Middlesex FICE Identification: 002161
Unit ID: 166513
Telephone: (978) 934-4000 Carnegie Class: RU/H
FAX Number: (978) 934-3000 Calendar System: Semester
URL: www.uml.edu
Established: 1894 Annual Undergrad Tuition & Fees (In-State): $12,097
Enrollment: 16,294 Coed
Affiliation or Control: State IRS Status: 501(c)3
Highest Offering: Doctorate
Program: 2-Year Principally Bachelor's Creditable; Liberal Arts And General; Teacher Preparatory; Professional
Accreditation: EH, ART, BUS, ENG, ENGR, ENGT, MT, MUS, NURSE, PTA, TED

02 Chancellor ... Mr. Martin T. MEEHAN
03 Executive Vice Chancellor ... Dr. Jacqueline MOLONEY
05 Provost ... Dr. Ahmed ABDELAL
20 Vice Provost Undergrad Education ... Dr. Charlotte MANDELL
58 Vice Provost Graduate Education ... Dr. Donald PIERSON
84 Vice Provost for Enrollment ... Dr. John TING
10 Vice Chancellor Finance & Operation ... Ms. Joanne YESTRAMSKI
30 Vice Chancellor for Advancement ... Mr. Edward CHIU
46 Vice Provost for Research ... Dr. Julie CHEN
18 Assoc VC Facilities Mgmt ... Mr. Thomas DREYER
88 Assoc VC Entrepreneurship Econ Dev ... Mr. Steven TELLO
31 Asst VC Community Outreach ... Mr. Paul MARION
49 Dean Col Fine Arts/Hum/Soc Sci ... Dr. Luis FALCON
81 Dean College of Sciences ... Dr. Mark HINES
53 Dean of Education ... Dr. Anita GREENWOOD
51 Exec Dir Academic Svcs/Cont Educ ... Ms. Pauline CARROLL
54 Dean College of Engineering ... Dr. Joseph HARTMAN
76 Dean School of Health & Environment ... Dr. Shortie MCKINNEY
50 Dean Manning School of Business ... Dr. Kathryn CARTER
13 Exec Dir Information Technology ... Mr. Richard ZERA
09 Director of Institutional Research ... Dr. Julie ALIG
08 Director of Libraries ... Mr. George HART
06 Registrar ... Ms. Kerry DONOHOE
37 Director of Financial Aid ... Ms. Joyce MCLAUGHLIN
35 Dean of Students ... Mr. Larry SIEGEL
38 Director of Counseling Svcs ... Dr. John PAKSTIS
36 Assoc Dir of Career Services ... Ms. Priscilla MARCH
41 Director of Athletics ... Mr. Dana SKINNER
29 Dir of Alumni Relations ... Ms. Heather MAKREZ
15 Assoc VC Human Resources and EOO ... Ms. Lauren TURNER
19 Chief Univ Police Dir Public Safe ... Mr. Randolph BRASHEARS
23 Exec Director Health Services ... Ms. Nancy QUATTROCCHI
88 Dir Graduate Admissions ... Ms. Linda SOUTHWORTH
96 Dir Purchasing & Campus Services ... Mr. Thomas HOOLE
88 Dir Outreach & Recruitment ... Mr. Michael BELCHER
07 Assoc Dean Enroll & Dir UG Admiss ... Ms. Kerri JOHNSTON
88 Assoc Director UCAPS ... Mr. Jon VICTORINE
28 Dir Equal Opportunity & Outreach ... Ms. Clara ORLANDO
88 Dean Enrollment & Student Success ... Mr. Thomas TAYLOR
26 VC University Relations ... Ms. Patricia MCCAFFERTY
21 Assoc Vice Chancellor for Finance ... Mr. Steven O'RIORDAN
88 Director Student Disability Svcs ... Ms. Jody GOLDSTEIN
39 Dir of Student Residence Life ... Mr. James KOHL
88 Director Graduate Administration ... Ms. Deborah WHITE
88 Director Cooperative Education ... Ms. Diane HEWITT

*University of Massachusetts Medical School (C)

55 Lake Avenue N, Worcester MA 01655-0001
County: Worcester FICE Identification: 009756
Unit ID: 166708
Telephone: (508) 856-8989 Carnegie Class: Spec/Med
FAX Number: (508) 856-8181 Calendar System: Semester
URL: www.umassmed.edu
Established: 1962 Annual Graduate Tuition & Fees: $20,662
Enrollment: 1,160 Coed
Affiliation or Control: State IRS Status: 501(c)3
Highest Offering: Doctorate; No Undergraduates
Program: Professional
Accreditation: EH, IPSY, MED, NMT, NURSE, PDPSY, RTT

02 Chancellor & SVP Health Sciences ... Dr. Michael F. COLLINS
05 Dean Provost & Exec Dep Chancellor ... Dr. Terence R. FLOTTE
10 VC Administration & Finance ... Mr. Robert E. JENAL
30 Vice Chancellor for Development ... Mr. Charles J. PAGNAM
88 Exec Vice Chancellor MassBiologics ... Dr. Mark D. KLEMPNER
11 Exec VC Commonwealth Medicine ... Ms. Joyce A. MURPHY
16 Vice Chancellor HR & Diversity ... Dr. Deborah L. PLUMMER
86 VC Government/Community Relations ... Mr. James LEARY
26 Vice Chancellor of Communications ... Mr. Edward J. KEOHANE
18 Assoc Vice Chanc Facilities Mgmt ... Mr. John T. BAKER
88 Vice Provost Faculty Affairs ... Dr. Luanne THORNDYKE
88 Vice Provost School Services ... Dr. Deborah-Harmon HINES
43 General Counsel/AVP Management ... Mr. James HEALY
46 Vice Provost for Research ... Dr. John L. SULLIVAN
53 Sr Assoc Dean Educational Affairs ... Dr. Michele P. PUGNAIRE
63 Sr Assc Dean Clin Aff/Assc Dean GME ... Dr. Deborah DEMARCO
66 Dean Graduate School of Nursing ... Dr. Paulette SEYMOUR-ROUTE
32 Associate Dean Student Affairs ... Dr. Mai-Lan A. ROGOFF
58 Dean Grad School Biomedical Science ... Dr. Anthony CARRUTHERS
06 Registrar ... Mr. Michael F. BAKER
13 Chief Information Officer ... Mr. Greg WOLF
07 Assoc Dean for Admissions ... Dr. John A. PARASKOS
37 Director Financial Aid ... Shawn MORRISSEY
08 Director of Library ... Ms. Elaine R. MARTIN
100 Chief of Staff ... Mr. Brendan H. CHISHOLM
04 Exec Assistant to the Chancellor ... Mrs. Stephanie H. RENK
17 Sr Assoc Dean UMass Medical Group ... Vacant
88 Assoc Provost for Global Health ... Dr. Katherine LUZURIAGA
88 Asst Dean for Admin/Chief of Staff ... Ms. Lisa B. BEITTEL
09 Institutional Research Officer ... Dr. Mary L. ZANETTI

*Bridgewater State University (D)

131 Summer Street, Bridgewater MA 02325-0001
County: Plymouth FICE Identification: 002183
Unit ID: 165024
Telephone: (508) 531-1000 Carnegie Class: Master's L
FAX Number: N/A Calendar System: Semester
URL: www.bridgew.edu
Established: 1840 Annual Undergrad Tuition & Fees (In-State): $8,228
Enrollment: 11,417 Coed
Affiliation or Control: State IRS Status: 501(c)3
Highest Offering: Master's
Program: Liberal Arts And General; Teacher Preparatory; Professional
Accreditation: EH, ART, CACREP, MUS, SPAA, SW, TED

02 President ... Dr. Dana MOHLER-FARIA
03 Exec VP/VP for External Affairs ... Mr. Fred CLARK
05 Provost & VP Academic Affairs ... Dr. Howard LONDON
11 Vice Pres Administration/Finance ... Mr. Miguel GOMES, JR.
32 Vice President Student Affairs ... Dr. Jason PINA
30 VP Univ Advance/Strategic Planning ... Mr. Bryan BALDWIN
10 Assoc Vice Pres Finance ... Mr. Douglas SHROPSHIRE
15 Assoc Vice Pres Human Resources ... Ms. Keri POWERS
22 Asst to Pres Affirmative Action ... Dr. Alan V. COMEDY
32 Asst Vice Pres Student Affairs ... Mr. Brian SALVAGGIO
35 Assoc Vice Pres Student Affairs ... Dr. Catherine HOLBROOK
84 Assoc Vice Pres for Enrollment Svcs ... Dr. Heather C. SMITH
20 Assoc Provost Faculty Affs ... Dr. Pamela M. WITCHER
45 Assoc Provost Academic Plng/Admin ... Dr. Michael YOUNG
79 Dean Col of Humanities/Social Sci ... Dr. Paula M. KREBS
53 Dean Col Education/Allied Stds ... Dr. Lisa BATTAGLINO
50 Dean Ricciardi College of Business ... Dr. Marian EXTEJT
100 Chief of Staff ... Dr. Brenda MOLIFE
07 Dean of University Admissions ... Mr. Gregg A. MEYER
13 Vice Pres for Information Tech ... Mr. Patrick CRONIN
06 Registrar ... Ms. Irene C. CHECKOVICH
88 Director Academic Achievement Ctr ... Ms. Alicia D'OYLEY
29 Director Alumni Relations ... Ms. Shana MURRELL
30 Director of Development ... Mr. Todd AUDYATIS
41 Director Athletics/Recreation ... Dr. Marybeth LAMB
21 Director University Services ... Ms. Margarida VIEIRA
19 Chief of Police ... Mr. David TILLINGHAST
36 Director Career Services ... Mr. John PAGANELLI
88 Director Children's Center ... Ms. Judith RITACCO
37 Director of Financial Aid ... Ms. Janet GUMBRIS
23 Sr Dir Counseling/Health Services ... Dr. Mary Lou FRIAS
08 Director Library Administration ... Mr. Michael SOMERS
51 Dir Continuing/Distance Education ... Dr. Mary FULLER
22 Director Multicultural Affairs ... Vacant
27 Director of Publications ... Ms. Marie MURPHY
25 Director Grants/Sponsored Projects ... Ms. Mia ZOINO
96 Director of Purchasing ... Ms. Jennifer PACHECO
28 Director of Institutional Diversity ... Dr. Sabrina GENTLEWARRIOR
18 Assoc VP Facilities Management/Plng ... Ms. Karen JASON
81 Dean Bartlett Col Science & Math ... Dr. Arthur GOLDSTEIN
88 Exec Dir University Initiatives ... Dr. Anna BRADFIELD
58 Dean College of Graduate Studies ... Dr. William S. SMITH
09 Director of Institutional Research ... Ms. Melanie SULLIVAN
88 Director Teaching and Learning ... Dr. Roben TOROSYAN
46 Director Undergraduate Research ... Dr. Jenny SHANAHAN
85 Dir International Students/Scholar ... Dr. Roopa RAWJEE
88 Dir Regional Partnerships ... Dr. Diana E. JENNINGS
104 Director Study Abroad ... Ms. Lisa MCADAM DONEGAN
88 Asst VP Applications & Development ... Mr. Raymond LEFEBVRE
91 Dir Administrative Systems ... Ms. Dona ALEXANDER
88 Act Asst VP Infrastructure Netwk Sy ... Mr. Steven ZUROMSKI
105 Director of Web Development ... Ms. Eileen O'SULLIVAN
26 Dir Intergrated Marketing and Comm ... Ms. Eva GAFFNEY
27 Director of University News ... Mr. John WINTERS
38 Director Counseling Center ... Mr. Philip ROBERTS
39 Dir Residence Life and Housing ... Ms. Beth MORIARTY

*Fitchburg State University (E)

160 Pearl Street, Fitchburg MA 01420-2697
County: Worcester FICE Identification: 002184
Unit ID: 165820
Telephone: (978) 345-2151 Carnegie Class: Master's L
FAX Number: (978) 665-3693 Calendar System: Semester
URL: www.fitchburgstate.edu
Established: 1894 Annual Undergrad Tuition & Fees (In-State): $8,985
Enrollment: 6,888 Coed
Affiliation or Control: State IRS Status: 501(c)3
Highest Offering: Master's
Program: Liberal Arts And General; Teacher Preparatory; Professional
Accreditation: EH, CS, IACBE, NURSE, TED

02 President ... Dr. Robert V. ANTONUCCI
05 Vice President Academic Affairs ... Dr. Robin E. BOWEN
10 Vice Pres Finance & Administration ... Mr. Jay BRY
20 Associate VP Academic Affairs ... Dr. Paul WEIZER
26 Exec Asst to Pres for External Affs ... Mr. Michael V. SHANLEY
32 Dean of Student & Academic Life ... Dr. Stanley BUCHOLC
84 Dean Enrollment Mgmt ... Ms. Pamela MCCAFFERTY
51 Dean of Graduate Cont Educ ... Ms. Catherine E. CANNEY
53 Dean of Education ... Dr. Pamela HILL
30 Vice President of Inst Advancement ... Mr. Christopher HENDRY
35 Assistant Dean for Student Devel ... Dr. Henry C. PARKINSON, III
06 Registrar ... Ms. Linda DUPELL
09 Director of Institutional Research ... Mr. Anthony WILCOX
08 Director Library ... Mr. Robert A. FOLEY
41 Director Athletics ... Ms. Sue M. LAUDER
07 Director of Admissions ... Ms. Kay REYNOLDS
36 Director of Career Services ... Ms. Erin C. KELLEHER
38 Director Counseling ... Dr. Robert HYNES
23 Director Student Health Services ... Ms. Martha FAVRE
29 Asst Director of Alumni Relations ... Ms. Emily AUSTIN-BRUNS
19 Director of Campus Police ... Chief James HAMEL
44 Director of Annual Giving ... Mr. Michael KUSHMEREK
96 Director of Procurement ... Ms. Doreen ARES
15 Asst VP of Human Resources/Payroll ... Ms. Jessica MURDOCH
18 Dir of Operations & Maint ... Mr. Joseph LOBUONO
18 Dir Capital Planning & Construction ... Mr. Doug THOMAS
102 Director Grants & Sponsored Pgm ... Ms. Karen FRANK MAYS
37 Director Financial Aid ... Mr. Matthew SANCHEZ

*Framingham State University (A)

100 State Street, PO Box 9101,
Framingham MA 01701-9101
County: Middlesex FICE Identification: 002185
Unit ID: 165866
Telephone: (508) 620-1220 Carnegie Class: Master's L
FAX Number: (508) 626-4592 Calendar System: Semester
URL: www.framingham.edu
Established: 1839 Annual Undergrad Tuition & Fees (In-State): $8,080
Enrollment: 6,506 Coed
Affiliation or Control: State IRS Status: 501(c)3
Highest Offering: Master's
Program: Liberal Arts And General; Teacher Preparatory
Accreditation: EH, DIETC, DIETD, NURSE

02 Interim President .... Dr. Robert MARTIN
03 Executive Vice President .... Dr. Dale M. HAMEL
05 Vice President Academic Affairs .... Dr. Linda VADEN-GOAD
88 Vice President Enrollment & Student .... Dr. Susanne H. CONLEY
43 Vice President General Counsel .... Ms. Rita COLUCCI
20 Associate Vice President .... Dr. Ellen ZIMMERMAN
20 Associate Vice President .... Dr. Scott B. GREENBERG
13 Associate Vice President .... Mr. Patrick LAUGHRAN
18 Assistant Vice President .... Mr. Warren FAIRBANKS
84 Dean of Enrollment Management .... Mr. Jeremy SPENCER
32 Dean of Student Affairs .... Dr. Melinda K. STOOPS
39 Associate Dean Student Affairs .... Mr. Glenn COCHRAN
07 Associate Dean Undergrad Admissions .... Ms. Shayna EDDY
35 Assistant Dean Student Affairs .... Mr. David N. BALDWIN
35 Assistant Dean Student Affairs .... Dr. Christopher GREGORY
06 Executive Director/Registrar .... Mr. Mark R. POWERS
15 Director Human Resources .... Ms. Erin NECHIPURENKO
19 Chief Public Safety .... Mr. Brad MEDEIROS
88 Director Academic Support .... Ms. LaDonna BRIDGES
108 Director Assessment .... Vacant
41 Director Athletics .... Mr. Thomas KELLEY
36 Director Career Services .... Mr. Jacob LIVENGOOD
37 Director Financial Aid .... Ms. Susan LANZILLO
10 Director Financial Services .... Ms. Rachel TRANT
89 Director First Year Programs .... Mr. Benjamin J. TRAPANICK
23 Director Health Services .... Ms. Ilene HOFRENNING
104 Director International Education .... Ms. Jane DECATUR
08 Director Library Services .... Mrs. Bonnie MITCHELL
38 Director Counseling Center .... Dr. Paul WELCH
35 Director Student Involvement .... Ms. Rachel LUCKING
88 Director Student Accounts .... Ms. Deborah DALTON
30 Director Development .... Mr. Eric GUSTAFSON
25 Director Grants Sponsored Programs .... Mr. Jonathan LEE
09 Director Institutional Research .... Ms. Ann CASO
04 Administrative Assistant .... Ms. Katie RESTUCCIA

*Massachusetts College of Art and Design (B)

621 Huntington Avenue, Boston MA 02115-5882
County: Suffolk FICE Identification: 002180
Unit ID: 166674
Telephone: (617) 879-7000 Carnegie Class: Spec/Arts
FAX Number: (617) 566-4034 Calendar System: Semester
URL: www.massart.edu
Established: 1873 Annual Undergrad Tuition & Fees (In-State): $10,400
Enrollment: 1,970 Coed
Affiliation or Control: State IRS Status: 501(c)3
Highest Offering: Master's
Program: Teacher Preparatory; Professional; Fine Arts Emphasis
Accreditation: EH, ART

02 President .... Ms. Dawn BARRETT
03 Executive Vice President .... Mr. Kurt STEINBERG
05 Provost/Vice Pres Academic Affairs .... Mr. Ken STRICKLAND
32 Vice President Student Development .... Dr. Maureen KEEFE
30 Vice Pres Institutional Advancement .... Mr. Hunter O'HANIAN
09 Assoc VP of Planning/Research .... Ms. Kathleen KEENAN
20 Associate VP Academic Affairs .... Ms. Michele FURST
21 Asst Vice Pres of Fiscal Affairs .... Mr. Donald ARPINO
100 Chief of Staff President's Office .... Ms. Susana SEGAT
86 Executive Dir Government/Cmty Rels .... Mr. Robert CHAMBERS
07 Dean of Admissions .... Ms. Karen TOWNSEND
35 Dean Students/Multi-Cultural Affrs .... Dr. Jamie COSTELLO
06 Registrar .... Mr. Jonathan RAND
37 Director of Financial Aid .... Mr. Aurelio RAMIREZ
88 Dir Curatorial Pgms/Prof Galleries .... Ms. Lisa TUNG
08 Director Library .... Mr. Paul DOBBS
15 Director Human Resources .... Ms. Elaine O'SULLIVAN
22 Dir Civil Rights Compliance/Dvrsty .... Ms. Mercedes EVANS
18 Director Facilities/Physical Plant .... Mr. Howie LAROSEE
11 Director of Administrative Services .... Mr. James MCDAID
29 Director of Alumni Relations .... Ms. Emily FOSTER-DAY

*Massachusetts College of Liberal Arts (C)

375 Church Street, North Adams MA 01247-4100
County: Berkshire FICE Identification: 002187
Unit ID: 167288
Telephone: (413) 662-5000 Carnegie Class: Bac/A&S
FAX Number: (413) 662-5010 Calendar System: Semester
URL: www.mcla.edu
Established: 1894 Annual Undergrad Tuition & Fees (In-State): $8,525
Enrollment: 1,799 Coed
Affiliation or Control: State IRS Status: 501(c)3
Highest Offering: Master's
Program: Liberal Arts And General; Teacher Preparatory; Professional
Accreditation: EH

02 President .... Dr. Mary K. GRANT
05 VP Academic Affairs .... Dr. Cynthia F. BROWN
10 VP Administration & Finance .... Dr. James M. STAKENAS
84 VP Enrollment & External Relations .... Ms. Denise RICHARDELLO
30 Chief Advancement Officer .... Ms. Marianne DRAKE
32 VP Student Affairs .... Ms. Charlotte DEGEN
20 Dean Academic Affairs .... Dr. Monica JOSLIN
04 Executive Assistant to President .... Mr. Thomas BERNARD
26 Dir of Marketing & Communications .... Ms. Bernadette LUPO
27 Chief Information Officer .... Mr. Curt KING
21 Treasurer .... Mr. Gerald DESMARAIS
07 Dean Admissions and Enrollment .... Ms. Annette S. JEFFES
58 Dean Gradaute & Continuing Educ .... Dr. Howard EBERWEIN
108 Assoc Dean Assessment & Planning .... Dr. Kristina BENDIKAS
08 Assoc Dean Library Services .... Ms. Maureen HORAK
90 Assoc Dean Information Technology .... Mr. Peter ALLMAKER
35 Asst Dean of Students .... Ms. Theresa M. O'BRYANT
06 Asst Dean Enrollment Services .... Mr. Steven KING
37 Director Financial Aid .... Ms. Elizabeth PETRI
39 Director Residential Programs .... Ms. Dianne M. MANNING
41 Director Athletics .... Mr. Scott NICHOLS
18 Director Facilities Management .... Mr. Charles L. KIMBERLING
44 Dir Annual Fund & Alumni Relations .... Ms. Jocelyn MERRICK
21 Director Student Accounts/ Bursar .... Ms. Jennifer MACKSEY-ETHIER
23 Director Health Services .... Ms. JoAnn TIERNEY
15 Director Human Resources .... Vacant
19 Director Public Safety .... Mr. Joseph CHARON
38 Director Counseling Services .... Ms. Heidi A. RIELLO
102 Dir Corporate & Foundation Relation .... Ms. Theresa MILLER
09 Staff Assoc Institutional Research .... Mr. Jason G. CANALES

*Massachusetts Maritime Academy (D)

101 Academy Drive, Buzzards Bay MA 02532-3400
County: Barnstable FICE Identification: 002181
Unit ID: 166692
Telephone: (508) 830-5000 Carnegie Class: Bac/Diverse
FAX Number: (508) 830-5004 Calendar System: Semester
URL: www.maritime.edu
Established: 1891 Annual Undergrad Tuition & Fees (In-State): $7,519
Enrollment: 1,415 Coed
Affiliation or Control: State IRS Status: 501(c)3
Highest Offering: Master's
Program: Professional
Accreditation: EH

02 President .... RADM. R. G. GURNON
05 Vice President/Dean .... CAPT. Brad LIMA
10 Vice Pres Finance .... Ms. Rose CASS
30 Vice Pres Advancement .... Ms. Holly KNIGHT
32 Dean of Students .... CAPT. Edward ROZAK
36 Assoc Dir Career/Professional Svcs .... CDR. Maryanne RICHARDS
84 Vice Pres Enrollment Management .... CAPT. Elizabeth STEVENSON
06 Director Student Records/Registrar .... Mr. Michael CUFF
08 Director Library .... Ms. Susan BERTEAUX
15 Director Personnel Services .... Mrs. Elizabeth BENWAY
18 Chief Facilities/Physical Plant .... Mr. Paul O'KEEFE
26 Chief Public Relations Officer .... Mr. Christopher RYAN
29 Director Alumni Relations .... Mr. Ian MACLEOD
37 Director Student Financial Aid .... Mrs. Cathy KEDSKI
96 Director of Purchasing .... Mr. Paul AIROZO

*Salem State University (E)

352 Lafayette Street, Salem MA 01970-5353
County: Essex FICE Identification: 002188
Unit ID: 167729
Telephone: (978) 542-6000 Carnegie Class: Master's L
FAX Number: (978) 542-6970 Calendar System: Semester
URL: www.salemstate.edu
Established: 1854 Annual Undergrad Tuition & Fees (In-State): $8,530
Enrollment: 9,456 Coed
Affiliation or Control: State IRS Status: 501(c)3
Highest Offering: Master's
Program: Liberal Arts And General; Teacher Preparatory; Professional
Accreditation: EH, ART, CS, MUS, NMT, NURSE, OT, SW, TED, THEA

02 President .... Dr. Patricia M. MESERVEY
05 Provost & Academic VP .... Dr. Kristin G. ESTERBERG
84 VP Enrollment Mgmt & Student Life .... Dr. Scott JAMES
03 Executive Vice President .... Dr. Stanley P. CAHILL
10 VP Finance & Facilities .... Mr. Andrew SOLL
30 VP Institutional Advancement .... Ms. Cynthia MCGURREN
100 Chief of Staff .... Ms. Beth A. BOWER
26 VP Marketing & Communications .... Mr. Tom TORELLO
45 Asst Provost Planning & Evaluation .... Dr. Neal FOGG
13 CIO-CISO/Interim Exec Dir Finance .... Ms. Patricia AINSWORTH
15 Assistant VP for HR & EEO .... Ms. Beth A. MARSHALL
20 Assoc Provost and Dean Human Svcs .... Dr. Neal DECHILLO
20 Asst Provost .... Dr. Amie M. GOODWIN
86 Director of External Affairs .... Ms. Adria LEACH
08 Dean Library & Instr/Learning Supp .... Dr. Susan E. CIRILLO
50 Dean School of Business .... Dr. K. Brewer DORAN
58 Dean Graduate School .... Dr. Carol A. GLOD
51 Int Dean Sch Cont & Prof Studies .... Dr. Mary CHURCHILL
49 Dean School of Arts & Sciences .... Dr. Jude NIXON
21 Assoc VP Financial Svcs .... Mr. Joseph DONOVAN
32 Assoc VP & Dean of Student Life .... Dr. James G. STOLL
44 Asst VP Alumni Affairs/Annual Giv .... Ms. Eileen M. O'BRIEN
101 Exec Asst to President/Secy to BOT .... Ms. Jean FLEISCHMAN
19 Dir Public Safety/Int Ex Dir Facil .... Mr. Gene R. LABONTE
41 Director Athletics .... Mr. Timothy P. SHEA
06 Registrar .... Ms. Megan MILLER
07 Assoc Dean for Admissions .... Ms. Bonnie GALINSKI
18 Director of Facilities .... Mr. Daniel BURKE
28 Dir Diversity & Multicult Affairs .... Ms. Rebecca COMAGE
29 Director Alumni Affairs .... Ms. Mandy RAY
37 Director of Financial Aid .... Ms. Judy CRAMER
38 Dir Counseling and Health Service .... Ms. Elisa CASTILLO
96 Director Purchasing & Vendor Rel .... Ms. Evelyn WILSON
25 Dir Sponsored Programs & Res Adm .... Ms. Mary MADER

*Westfield State University (F)

577 Western Avenue, Westfield MA 01086-1630
County: Hampden FICE Identification: 002189
Unit ID: 168263
Telephone: (413) 572-5300 Carnegie Class: Master's M
FAX Number: (413) 572-8147 Calendar System: Semester
URL: www.westfield.ma.edu
Established: 1838 Annual Undergrad Tuition & Fees (In-State): $8,694
Enrollment: 6,079 Coed
Affiliation or Control: State IRS Status: 501(c)3
Highest Offering: Beyond Master's But Less Than Doctorate
Program: Liberal Arts And General; Teacher Preparatory
Accreditation: EH, MUS, CS, EXSC, SW, TED

02 President .... Dr. Evan S. DOBELLE
05 Vice Pres Academic Affairs .... Dr. Elizabeth PRESTON
32 Vice Pres Student Affairs .... Dr. Carlton PICKRON
84 Vice Pres Enrollment Management .... Dr. Carol PERSSON
10 Vice Pres Administration & Finance .... Mr. Milton SANTIAGO
30 Vice Pres Advancement/Univ Rels .... Ms. Nanci SALVIDIO
20 Dean of Faculty .... Dr. Stephen ADAMS
49 Dean of Undergraduate Programs .... Dr. Marsha MAROTTA
51 Dean Graduate/Continuing Educ .... Dr. Kimberly TOBIN
53 Dean of Education .... Dr. Cheryl STANLEY
35 Dean Student Affairs .... Ms. Susan LAMONTAGNE
06 Registrar .... Mr. John OHOTNICKY
09 Assoc Dean Institutional Reseach .... Dr. Lisa PLANTEFABER
22 Director Multicult Affairs/AA/EO .... Ms. Waleska LUGO-DEJESUS
08 Director Library .... Mr. Thomas RAFFENSPERGER
11 Asst Vice Pres Administration .... Dr. Curt D. ROBIE
39 Exec Director Residential Life .... Dr. Jon CONLOGUE
19 Director Public Safety .... Mr. Michael NOCKUNAS
27 Asst to President Communications .... Mr. Robert PLASSE
36 Director Career Services .... Mr. Junior DELGADO
13 Exec Dir Information Technology .... Mr. Christopher HIRTLE
91 Director Admin Systems .... Mr. Rudolph HEBERT
44 Assoc VP Advancement .... Vacant
18 Asst Dir Facilities/Physical Plant .... Mr. Terry FENSTAD
41 Director Athletics .... Mr. Richard LENFEST
24 Director Media Services .... Vacant
38 Director Counseling Center .... Ms. Tammy BRINGAZE
23 Director Health Services .... Ms. Patricia BERUBE
37 Director of Financial Aid .... Ms. Catherine RYAN
07 Director of Admissions .... Dr. Kelly HART
21 Assoc VP Administration/Finance .... Ms. Lisa FREEMAN
29 Assoc VP Alumni Relations .... Ms. Nanci SALVIDIO
96 Director of Purchasing .... Mr. Chris RAYMOND
16 Director of Human Resources .... Mr. Rafael BONES
86 VP of Government Relations .... Mr. Ken LEMANSKI
25 Director Grants Sponsored Programs .... Ms. Louann D'ANGELO

*Worcester State University (G)

486 Chandler Street, Worcester MA 01602-2597
County: Worcester FICE Identification: 002190
Unit ID: 168430
Telephone: (508) 929-8000 Carnegie Class: Master's M
FAX Number: (508) 929-8191 Calendar System: Semester
URL: www.worcester.edu
Established: 1874 Annual Undergrad Tuition & Fees (In-State): $8,630
Enrollment: 6,221 Coed
Affiliation or Control: State IRS Status: 501(c)3
Highest Offering: Master's
Program: Occupational; Liberal Arts And General; Teacher Preparatory; Professional
Accreditation: EH, NMT, NURSE, OT, SP, @TEAC

02 President .... Mr. Barry M. MALONEY
05 Provost/Vice President Academic Aff .... Dr. Charles CULLUM
10 Vice Pres Administration & Finance .... Ms. Kathleen EICHELROTH
32 Vice President Student Affairs .... Dr. Sibyl BROWNLEE
30 Vice Pres University Advancement .... Mr. Thomas MCNAMARA
84 Interim VP for Enrollment Mgmt .... Dr. Donald VESCIO
20 Assoc VP for Academic Affairs .... Dr. Patricia A. MARSHALL
21 Assoc VP Administration & Finance .... Ms. Robin QUILL
35 Associate VP/Dean of Students .... Ms. Julie KAZARIAN
13 Assoc VP/CIO Univ Technology Svcs .... Dr. Anthony ADADE
58 Acting Assoc VP CE & Dean Grad Stds .... Dr. Roberta KYLE
108 Asst VP for Assessment & Planning .... Dr. Carol LERCH
22 Dir Diversity/Inclusion & Equal Op .... Dr. Calvin HILL
88 Dean Sch of Educ Health & Nat Sci .... Dr. Frank HALL
88 Dean Sch of Humanities & Soc Sci .... Dr. Charles FOX
55 Assoc Dean of Graduate/Cont Educ .... Vacant
35 Assoc Dean & Dir Stdnt Ctr/Activ .... Mr. Timothy J. SULLIVAN
93 Asst Dean/Dir Multicultural Affairs .... Ms. Marcela URIBE-JENNINGS
19 Chief of Campus Police .... Ms. Rosemary NAUGHTON

26 Asst to Pres for Intl/Cmty & Govt .... Mr. Carl HERRIN
08 Executive Director of the Library ...... Mr. Sainath CHINNASWAMY
29 Exec Dir Univ Advancement & Alumni .... Ms. Karen SHARPE
15 Director Human Resources .... Mr. Russell E. VICKSTROM
18 Director of Facilities .... Ms. Sandra OLSON
37 Director of Financial Aid .... Ms. Jayne MCGINN
07 Director of Admissions .... Mr. Joseph DICARLO
06 Registrar .... Ms. Julie CHAFEE
39 Director Residence Life & Housing .... Mr. Adrian GAGE
88 Manager of Student Accounts .... Ms. Julie CARMEL
96 Director of Procurement/Bus Mgr .... Ms. Brenda BUSSEY
09 Director of Institutional Research .... Mr. Kenneth SMITH
38 Director Student Counseling .... Ms. Laura MURPHY
85 Int Dir of International Students .... Ms. Katey PALUMBO
36 Director of Career Services .... Ms. Jillian ANDERSON
41 Interim Sr Assoc Athletic Director .... Mr. John MEANY
84 Assoc VP Enrollment Services .... Ms. Kathleen TORPEY GARGANTA
27 VP College Communications .... Ms. Sally C. CAMERON
29 Dir Alumni Relations/Special Events .... Vacant
88 Dean Disability Svcs & Student Engm .... Ms. Susan BOISSONEAULT
78 Director Coop Education .... Ms. Margaret (Peg) CURRO
103 Dean Ctr for Workforce/Community Ed ...... Ms. Carmen AGUILAR
23 Health Services Coordinator .... Ms. Carol CONSTANTINE
56 Asst Dean Instructional Lrng Tech .... Ms. April BELLAFIORE
09 VP Inst Research/Plng & Assesssment .. Ms. Rhonda GABOVITCH
92 Director Honors Program .... Mr. J. Thomas GRADY
96 Director of Purchasing .... Ms. Philicia PACHECO
36 Career Services - Sr Acad Counselor .... Ms. Patricia CONDON
41 Athletic Director .... Mr. Derek VIVEIROS
04 Executive Assistant to President .... Ms. Kathleen A. WORDELL
88 Dean Developmental Educ .... Ms. Sarah MORRELL

*Berkshire Community College (A)

1350 West Street, Pittsfield MA 01201-5786

County: Berkshire FICE Identification: 002167
Unit ID: 164775
Telephone: (413) 499-4660 Carnegie Class: Assoc/Pub-R-M
FAX Number: (413) 447-7840 Calendar System: Semester
URL: www.berkshirecc.edu
Established: 1960 Annual Undergrad Tuition & Fees (In-State): $5,810
Enrollment: 2,503 Coed
Affiliation or Control: State IRS Status: 501(c)3
Highest Offering: Associate Degree
Program: Occupational; 2-Year Principally Bachelor's Creditable
Accreditation: EH, ADNUR, COARC, PTAA

02 President .... Dr. Ellen KENNEDY
05 Vice President for Academic Affairs .... Dr. Frances FEINERMAN
10 Vice President for Admin/Finance .... Mr. John LAW
32 Vice Pres Student Affs/Enroll Svcs .... Mr. Michael BULLOCK
30 Vice Pres Institutional Advancement .... Mr. Jeffrey DOSCHER
103 VP Community Ed/Workforce Dev ..... Mr. William MULHOLLAND
15 VP Human Res/Affirm Action Officer .... Ms. Deborah COTE
54 Dean Engineering/Sciences .... Dr. Charles KAMINSKI
79 Dean Humanities .... Mr. Thomas CURLEY
66 Dean Nursing/Allied Hlth .... Ms. Anna FOSS
06 Registrar .... Mr. Donald PFEIFER
31 Dir Development/Alumni Relations .... Ms. Jennifer KERWOOD
18 Director of Facilities .... Mr. Scott RICHARDS
13 Director Information Technology .... Mr. Richard WIXSOM
09 Acting Dir IR/Plng/Grants .... Ms. Gina STEC
08 Director of Library .... Ms. Nancy WALKER
07 Dir of Marketing/Stdnt Recruitment .... Ms. Christina BARRETT
12 Director of Off-Campus Centers .... Ms. Julie HANNUM
96 Director of Procurement .... Mr. William MANNIX
32 Director of Student Engagement .... Ms. Beth WALLACE
37 Director Student Financial Aid .... Ms. Anne MOORE
20 Comptroller .... Mr. Mitchell SAVISKI
88 Coord of Transfer Affairs/Artic .... Mr. Geoff TABOR
40 Manager Bookstore .... Ms. Kristen SCALA
26 Public Relations Manager .... Ms. Heidi WEBER
38 Senior Academic Counselor .... Ms. Lisa MATTILA

*Bristol Community College (B)

777 Elsbree Street, Fall River MA 02720-7395

County: Bristol FICE Identification: 002176
Unit ID: 165033
Telephone: (508) 678-2811 Carnegie Class: Assoc/Pub-U-MC
FAX Number: (508) 730-3270 Calendar System: Semester
URL: www.bristolcc.edu
Established: 1965 Annual Undergrad Tuition & Fees (In-State): $4,178
Enrollment: 9,022 Coed
Affiliation or Control: State IRS Status: 501(c)3
Highest Offering: Associate Degree
Program: Occupational; 2-Year Principally Bachelor's Creditable
Accreditation: EH, ADNUR, CAHIIM, COMTA, DH, MAC, MLTAD, OTA

02 President .... Dr. John J. SBREGA
03 Executive Vice President .... Mr. David F. FEENEY
05 Acting VP of Academic Affairs .... Mr. Greg SETHARES
50 Dean of Business & Info Tech .... Mr. William BERARDI
79 Dean of Humanities & Education .... Ms. Joanne PRESTON
83 Dean of Behavioral & Soc Sciences .... Dr. Calvin MCFADDEN
76 Dean of Health Sciences .... Ms. Patricia DENT
81 Dean of Math/Science & Engineering .... Dr. Sarmad SAMAN
10 VP of Administration & Finance .... Mr. Steven KENYON
30 VP of Resource Development .... Ms. Elizabeth K. MCCARTHY
84 VP of Students and Enrollment Mgt .... Mr. Steve OZUG
91 VP of Information Technology .... Ms. Jo-Ann M. PELLETIER
32 Director Student Engagement .... Ms. Kathleen BURNS
07 Dean of Admissions .... Ms. Shilo HENRIQUES
12 Dean of New Bedford Campus .... Mr. P. Wesley LUNDBURG
12 Dean of Attleboro Center .... Mr. Rodney CLARK
06 Acting Registrar .... Mr. Benjamin BAUMANN
08 Assistant Dean of the Library .... Vacant
25 Dean of Grant Development .... Ms. Marianne TAYLOR
37 Director Student Financial Aid .... Mr. David ALLEN
38 Director Counseling Services .... Mr. Michael BENSINK
15 VP of Human Resources/Affirm Action .... Mr. Tafa AWOLAJU
18 Director of Facilities Management .... Mr. Leo RACINE
19 Director of Public Safety .... Mr. Wayne WOOD
21 Comptroller .... Mr. Keith TONI
11 Associate VP of Administration .... Ms. Linda DANZELL
20 Assoc VP Academic Affairs .... Dr. Michael VIEIRA
20 Acting Assoc VP of Academic Affairs .... Mr. Anthony UCCI

*Bunker Hill Community College (C)

250 New Rutherford Avenue, Boston MA 02129-2925

County: Suffolk FICE Identification: 011210
Unit ID: 165112
Telephone: (617) 228-2000 Carnegie Class: Assoc/Pub-U-MC
FAX Number: (617) 228-2082 Calendar System: Semester
URL: www.bhcc.mass.edu
Established: 1973 Annual Undergrad Tuition & Fees (In-State): $3,384
Enrollment: 13,600 Coed
Affiliation or Control: State IRS Status: 501(c)3
Highest Offering: Associate Degree
Program: Occupational; 2-Year Principally Bachelor's Creditable
Accreditation: EH, ADNUR, #COARC, DMS, MLTAD, RAD, SURGT

02 President .... Dr. Pam Y. EDDINGER
03 Executive Vice President & CFO .... Mr. Jesse M. THOMPSON
05 VP Academic Affairs/Student Service .... Dr. James F. CANNIFF
28 Director Diversity & Inclusion .... Mr. Thomas L. SALTONSTALL
09 Exec Dean Inst Effectiveness .... Dr. Emily DIBBLE
20 Associate Academic Dean .... Ms. Judith GRAHAM-ROBEY
35 Dean of Students .... Ms. Janice M. BONANNO
26 Exec Director of Communications .... Ms. Karen NORTON
18 Director Facilities Management .... Mr. Paul A. RIGHI
81 Dean of Mathematics/Behav Sciences .... Dr. Valerie T. SMITH
79 Dean of Humanities .... Ms. Lori A. CATALLOZZI
54 Dean Science/Engineering .... Dr. Laurie K. MCCORRY
107 Dean of Professional Studies ...... Dr. Bogusia WOJCIECHOWSKA
66 Interim Dean Nurse Education .... Dr. Patti-Ann COLLINS
12 Dean Chelsea Campus .... Dr. Vanessa SHANNON
21 Comptroller .... Mr. Wesui A. TAFAWA
25 Director of Grants Development .... Mr. Steven A. ROLLER
06 Registrar .... Ms. Debra A. BOYER
08 Director Library/Info Center .... Dr. Vivica D. PIERRE
27 Chief Information Officer .... Mr. Bret MOELLER
15 Dir Human Resources/Labor Relations .... Ms. Molly B. AMBROSE
19 Director of Public Safety .... Mr. Robert BARROWS
37 Director of Financial Aid .... Ms. Melissa HOLSTER
96 Director of Purchasing .... Mr. Richard J. PISHKIN
38 Dir Advising/Counseling/Assessment .... Ms. Anne BROWN
30 Executive Director of Development .... Ms. Anne HYDE
07 Director of Admissions .... Ms. Vanessa WHALEY

*Cape Cod Community College (D)

2240 Iyannough Road, West Barnstable MA 02668-1599

County: Barnstable FICE Identification: 002168
Unit ID: 165194
Telephone: (508) 362-2131 Carnegie Class: Assoc/Pub-R-M
FAX Number: (508) 362-3988 Calendar System: Semester
URL: www.capecod.edu
Established: 1960 Annual Undergrad Tuition & Fees (In-State): $5,090
Enrollment: 4,201 Coed
Affiliation or Control: State IRS Status: 501(c)3
Highest Offering: Associate Degree
Program: Occupational; 2-Year Principally Bachelor's Creditable
Accreditation: EH, ADNUR, DH, MAC

02 President .... Dr. John L. COX
05 Vice Pres Academic/Student Affairs .... Dr. Susan MILLER
10 Vice President Finance & Operations .... Mr. Walter T. BROOKS
21 Asst VP Administration & Finance .... Ms. Cynthia CROSSMAN
18 Asst VP Sustainability/Facil Mgmt .... Mr. John LEBICA
13 Asst VP Information Technology .... Mr. Gregory BANWARTH
49 Dean Arts & Humanities .... Dr. Lore DEBOWER
81 Dean Science/Tech/Math/Business .... Dr. Robert CODY
08 Dean Learning Res & Student Success .... Mr. David ZIEMBA
84 Dean Enroll Mgmt/Advising Services .... Ms. Roseanna PENA-WARFIELD
83 Dean Health/Social Sci/Human Svcs .... Ms. Susan MADDIGAN
15 Asst VP Human Resources .... Mr. Victor SANTOS
08 Assoc Dean Learning Resources .... Ms. Jeanmarie FRASER
07 Director Admissions .... Mr. Matthew CORMIER
37 Director of Financial Aid .... Ms. Sherry ANDERSEN
27 Director College Communications .... Mr. Michael GROSS
06 Registrar .... Ms. Sandra BRITO
19 Director Public Safety .... Mr. Philip RYAN
04 Staff Assoc to President .... Ms. Linda HOULE
36 Coord Career Plng & Placement .... Ms. Kristina IERARDI
09 Dir Institutional Research & Effec .... Ms. Maureen O'SHEA

*Greenfield Community College (E)

1 College Drive, Greenfield MA 01301-9739

County: Franklin FICE Identification: 002169
Unit ID: 165981
Telephone: (413) 775-1000 Carnegie Class: Assoc/Pub-S-SC
FAX Number: (413) 774-4676 Calendar System: Semester
URL: www.gcc.mass.edu
Established: 1962 Annual Undergrad Tuition & Fees (In-State): $5,357
Enrollment: 2,437 Coed
Affiliation or Control: State IRS Status: 501(c)3
Highest Offering: Associate Degree
Program: Occupational; 2-Year Principally Bachelor's Creditable
Accreditation: EH, ADNUR

02 President .... Dr. Robert L. PURA
05 Chief Academic/Student Affairs Ofcr .... Dr. Sheryl HRUSKA
10 Chief Financial Officer .... Mr. Barry BRAIM
31 Dean of Community Education .... Mr. Robert BARBA
84 Dean Enrollment Services .... Mr. Shane HAMMOND
79 Dean Humanities .... Mr. Leo HWANG
81 Dean Engr/Math/Nat & Soc Sciences .... Dr. Peter ROSNIK
50 Dean Business/Info Tech/HO/Prof Std .... Mr. Terence LYNN
15 Interim Exec Dir of Human Resources .... Mr. Peter SENNETT
30 Exec Director Resource Development .... Ms. Regina CURTIS
13 Chief Information Officer .... Mr. Michael ASSAF
28 Chief Diversity Officer .... Mr. Peter SENNETT
18 Director Physical Plant .... Mr. Jeffrey MARQUES
07 Admissions Director .... Ms. Colleen KUCINSKI
37 Director Financial Aid .... Ms. Linda DESJARDINS
19 Director Public Safety .... Mr. William MAYROSE
96 Director of Purchasing .... Mr. Ryan AIKEN
08 Director Library .... Ms. Deborah CHOWN
21 Comptroller .... Ms. Karen PHILLIPS
06 Registrar .... Ms. Holly FITZPATRICK
38 Co-Coord Learning Asst Programs .... Ms. Mary Ellen KELLY
38 Co-Coord Learning Asst Programs .... Mr. Norman BEEBE
36 Coordinator of Student Assessment .... Ms. Jean BOUCIAS
08 Coordinator Library .... Mr. Eric POULIN
35 Coordinator of Student Life .... Ms. Melissa EICH

*Holyoke Community College (F)

303 Homestead Avenue, Holyoke MA 01040-1099

County: Hampden FICE Identification: 002170
Unit ID: 166133
Telephone: (413) 538-7000 Carnegie Class: Assoc/Pub-S-SC
FAX Number: (413) 552-2045 Calendar System: Semester
URL: www.hcc.edu
Established: 1946 Annual Undergrad Tuition & Fees (In-State): $518
Enrollment: 7,000 Coed
Affiliation or Control: State IRS Status: 501(c)3
Highest Offering: Associate Degree
Program: Occupational; 2-Year Principally Bachelor's Creditable
Accreditation: EH, ACFEI, ADNUR, MUS, RAD

02 President .... Dr. William F. MESSNER
11 Vice Pres Administration & Finance .... Mr. William FOGARTY
05 Vice President Academic Affairs .... Dr. Matthew REED
32 Vice President Student Affairs .... Ms. Yanina VARGAS
30 Vice Pres Institutional Development .... Ms. Erica BROMAN
28 Assistant Vice Pres of Diversity .... Ms. Idelia SMITH
08 Dean Library .... Mr. Carl TODD
15 Dean Human Resources .... Ms. Clara ELLIOTT
36 Dean Coop Education & Career Svcs ... Ms. Christine HOLBROOK
06 Registrar .... Mr. Anthony SBALBI
07 Director of Admissions .... Ms. Marcia ROSBURY-HENNE
37 Director of Financial Aid .... Ms. Karen DEROUIN
91 Director Administrative Computing .... Vacant
18 Director of Facilities .... Mr. Dan CAMPBELL
10 Comptroller .... Mr. John O'ROURKE
13 Chief Information Officer .... Ms. Linda SZALANKIEWICZ
21 Dir Business Services/Purchasing .... Ms. Tara WOLMAN
09 Director Institutional Research .... Ms. Michelle RIBERDY
26 Dir of Marketing/Public Relations .... Ms. JoAnne ROME
29 Director of Alumni Relations .... Ms. Joanna BROWN
35 Dean of Student Services .... Vacant
20 Director of Academic Administration .... Ms. Idelia SMITH
38 Dir Retention & Adult Support Svcs .... Vacant

*Massachusetts Bay Community College (G)

50 Oakland Street, Wellesley Hills MA 02481-5357

County: Norfolk FICE Identification: 002171
Unit ID: 166647
Telephone: (781) 239-3000 Carnegie Class: Assoc/Pub-S-MC
FAX Number: (781) 237-1061 Calendar System: Semester
URL: www.massbay.edu
Established: 1961 Annual Undergrad Tuition & Fees (In-State): $4,600
Enrollment: 5,427 Coed
Affiliation or Control: State IRS Status: 501(c)3
Highest Offering: Associate Degree
Program: Occupational; 2-Year Principally Bachelor's Creditable
Accreditation: EH, ADNUR, RAD, SURGT

02 President .... Dr. John O'DONNELL
05 Provost/Chief Academic Officer .... Dr. Francesca PURCELL
10 VP Admin & Finance/CFO .... Mr. Richard HASKELL
26 Associate VP for Marketing .... Mr. Jeremy SOLOMON
84 Asst VP Enrol Mgmt/Student Affairs .... Ms. Marva PERRY
15 Assistant VP of Human Resources ... Ms. Robin NELSON-BAILEY
30 Asst VP of Inst Adv & Alumni Rel .... Ms. Mary SHIA
106 Dean of eLearning .... Dr. Lynn HUNTER
09 Dean Inst Planning Res & Assessment .... Dr. Yves SALOMON-FERNÁNDEZ

32 Project Director Title III ... Dr. Craig MACK
76 Dean Health Sciences Division ... Dr. Lynne DAVIS
107 Dean Social Sci & Profess Studies ... Dr. Jane O'BRIEN FRIEDERICHS
81 Dean STEM Division ... Dr. Chitra JAVDEKAR
88 Dean Transportation & Energy ... Mr. Howard FERRIS
55 Dean Evening & Weekend Programming ... Ms. Carol STAFFIER
51 Dean Corporate/Community Education ... Vacant
32 Dean of Students (Wellesley Hills) ... Dr. Elizabeth BLUMBERG
20 Dean Academic Advancement ... Dr. David COLEMAN
07 Director of Admissions ... Ms. Donna RAPOSA
37 Director of Financial Aid ... Ms. Elizabeth ENOS
06 Registrar ... Mr. Ali GUVENDIREN
88 Director Acad Achievement Ctr ... Ms. Jennifer JEFFERSON
20 Director of Academic Advising ... Ms. Sarah READING
38 Director of Counseling ... Mr. Jon EDWARDS
36 Director of Career Services ... Ms. Julie KOMACK
90 Dir Ctr for Teaching & Learning ... Dr. Linda GRISHAM
85 Director of International Education ... Ms. Marie Lourdes ELGIRUS
41 Dir Athletics Recreation & Wellness ... Mr. Bill RAYNOR
35 Coordinator of Student Activities ... Ms. Julie SCHLEICHER
21 Controller ... Ms. Linda FAZIO
96 Budget Analyst/Purchasing Manager ... Mr. Kevin FLYNN
96 Purchasing Supervisor ... Ms. Lauren CURLEY
88 Director of Grants Development ... Dr. Cheryl WEST
13 Chief Information Officer ... Mr. Michael LYONS
91 Director Administrative Computing ... Mr. Terry KRAMER
08 Director of Learning Services ... Mr. Timothy RIVARD
18 Director of Facilities ... Mr. Marco BRANCATO
19 Manager of Public Safety ... Mr. John MCCUNE
04 Exec Assistant to the President ... Ms. Vivian ORTIZ

*Massasoit Community College (A)

1 Massasoit Boulevard, Brockton MA 02302-3996
County: Plymouth FICE Identification: 002177
Unit ID: 166823
Telephone: (508) 588-9100 Carnegie Class: Assoc/Pub-R-L
FAX Number: (508) 427-1202 Calendar System: Semester
URL: www.massasoit.mass.edu
Established: 1966 Annual Undergrad Tuition & Fees (In-State): $5,070
Enrollment: 8,209 Coed
Affiliation or Control: State IRS Status: 501(c)3
Highest Offering: Associate Degree
Program: Occupational; 2-Year Principally Bachelor's Creditable
Accreditation: EH, ADNUR, COARC, DA, MAC, RAD

02 President ... Dr. Charles WALL
05 Sr Vice Pres/VP Faculty & Instruct ... Dr. Barbara E. FINKELSTEIN
10 Chief Financial Officer ... Mr. William MITCHELL
32 Vice Pres Student Svcs/Enroll Mgmt ... Mr. David TRACY
12 Vice Pres/Dean of Canton Campus ... Mr. Nicholas PALANTZAS
15 VP & Director of Human Resources ... Ms. Lisa LOWERY
09 Assoc Dean Institutional Research ... Ms. Mary GOODHUE LYNCH
25 Associate Dean of Grants ... Ms. Hollyce STATES
04 Exec Dir Extrnl Affs/Asst to Pres ... Mr. Phillip SHEPPARD
26 Public Relations Director ... Ms. Laurie MAKER
84 Dean of Enrollment Management ... Ms. Nancy SULLIVAN
35 Dean Student Affairs ... Vacant
07 Director of Admissions ... Ms. Michelle HUGHES
37 Director Student Financial Aid ... Ms. Mary Beth COURTRIGHT
06 Registrar ... Ms. Jannie GILSON
38 Director Student Counseling ... Ms. Christine DYMENT
28 Director of Diversity ... Vacant
13 CIO ... Mr. Alfred WILLIAMS
21 Comptroller ... Ms. Sophie LEE
36 Director of Career Placement ... Ms. Kathyrn PRYLES
18 Director Facilities/Physical Plant ... Mr. Richard HADLEY
96 Director of Purchasing ... Ms. Diane PIQUETTE
41 Director of Athletics ... Ms. Julie MULVEY
29 Director Alumni Relations ... Ms. Sheryl SAVAGE
50 Acting Dean Business & Technology ... Ms. Lynda THOMPSON
79 Dean Humanities/Social Science ... Ms. Deanna YAMEEN
76 Dean Allied Health ... Dr. Anne SCALZO-MCNEIL
83 Dean Public Svc/Social Science ... Ms. Karyn BOUTIN
81 Dean Science & Math ... Mr. Douglas BROWN
72 Dean of Emergent Technologies ... Vacant
88 Dean of Academic Advising ... Mr. Peter JOHNSTON

*Middlesex Community College (B)

591 Springs Road, Bedford MA 01730-1197
County: Middlesex FICE Identification: 009936
Unit ID: 166887
Telephone: (781) 280-3200 Carnegie Class: Assoc/Pub-S-MC
FAX Number: (781) 275-0741 Calendar System: Semester
URL: www.middlesex.mass.edu
Established: 1969 Annual Undergrad Tuition & Fees (In-State): $4,274
Enrollment: 9,664 Coed
Affiliation or Control: State IRS Status: 501(c)3
Highest Offering: Associate Degree
Program: Occupational; 2-Year Principally Bachelor's Creditable
Accreditation: EH, ADNUR, DA, DH, DMS, DT, MAC, RAD

02 President ... Dr. Carole A. COWAN
05 Provost/VP of Academic Affairs ... Mr. Philip J. SISSON
32 Int Provost/VP Student Affairs ... Ms. Ann MONTMINY
03 Executive Vice President ... Mr. James F. LINNEHAN, JR.
84 VP Enrollment Svcs/Rsrch & Plng ... Dr. Paula R. PITCHER
04 Assistant to the President ... Ms. Lura SMITH
20 Associate Provost ... Ms. Clea ANDREADIS
32 Dean of Students ... Ms. Pamela B. FLAHERTY
88 Dean of International Arts ... Mr. Kent H. MITCHELL
79 Dean Humanities and Social Sciences ... Mr. Matthew OLSON
72 Dean of Business/Education & Publi ... Ms. Judith HOGAN
17 Dean of Health and STEM ... Ms. Kathleen J. SWEENEY
88 Dean Professional/Instructional Dev ... Ms. Mary Anne DEAN
22 Asst Dir HR/Affirm Action Officer ... Ms. Darcy ORELLANA
12 Dean of Lowell Campus ... Dr. Maureen H. SHEEHY
12 Dean Fac Mgmt/Bedford Campus Mgr ... Mr. Matt SEPE
84 Dean of Enrollment Services ... Ms. Audrey NAHABEDIAN
26 Dean External Affs/Col Advancement ... Mr. Dennis MALVERS
07 Dean of Admissions ... Ms. Marilynn GALLAGAN
26 Director Marketing Communication ... Ms. Jennifer M. ARADHYA
35 Associate Dean of Students ... Ms. Susan WOODS
09 Assoc Dean Institutional Planning ... Vacant
27 Director Public Affairs ... Mr. Daniel J. MARTIN
10 Director of Budget & Financial Svcs ... Ms. Gina SPAZIANI
16 Director Human Resources ... Mr. Gary R. MCPHEE
37 Director of Financial Aid ... Mr. Robert BAUMAL
21 Comptroller ... Ms. Kathy RICH
21 Bursar ... Mr. Christopher FIORI
08 Director Library Services ... Ms. Maryann NILES
23 Director of Health Services ... Vacant
06 Registrar ... Mr. Kevin GATELY
96 Coordinator of Purchasing ... Ms. Maureen HUDSON

*Mount Wachusett Community College (C)

444 Green Street, Gardner MA 01440-1000
County: Worcester FICE Identification: 002172
Unit ID: 166957
Telephone: (978) 632-6600 Carnegie Class: Assoc/Pub-R-M
FAX Number: (978) 632-6155 Calendar System: Semester
URL: www.mwcc.mass.edu
Established: 1963 Annual Undergrad Tuition & Fees (In-State): $4,900
Enrollment: 4,731 Coed
Affiliation or Control: State IRS Status: 501(c)3
Highest Offering: Associate Degree
Program: Occupational; 2-Year Principally Bachelor's Creditable; Business Emphasis
Accreditation: EH, ADNUR, DA, DH, MAC, MLTAD, PNUR, PTAA

02 President ... Dr. Daniel M. ASQUINO
03 Exec VP & VP of Enrollment Services ... Ms. Ann M. MCDONALD
05 Vice Pres of Academic Affairs ... Dr. Melissa FAMA
51 VP Lifelong Learning/Workforce Dev ... Ms. Jacqueline BELROSE
11 VP Finance & Administration ... Mr. Robert LABONTE
15 VP HR/Affirmative Action Officer ... Ms. Diane RUKSNAITIS
30 Assoc VP Institutional Advancement ... Mr. Joseph STISO
84 Assoc VP Enroll Mgt/Stdnt Fin Aid ... Mr. Ryan FORSYTH
12 Dean Leominster Campus ... Mr. John WALSH
72 Dean Academic & Inst Technology ... Mr. Vincent IALENTI
76 Dean School of Health Sciences ... Ms. Eileen COSTELLO
08 Dean Library and Academic Support ... Ms. Heidi MCCANN
09 Asst Dean of Records/Instl Research ... Ms. Rebecca FOREST
36 Dir North Central Career Services ... Ms. Cynthia KRUSEN
18 Director Maintenance/Mechanical Sys ... Mr. William SWIFT
68 Director Fitness & Wellness Center ... Mr. Stephen WASHKEVICH
19 Chief Public Safety & Security ... Ms. Karen KOLIMAGA
35 Assistant Dean of Student Services ... Mr. Gregory CLEMENT
38 Director of Counseling ... Vacant
84 Assoc Dean Enrollment Services ... Mr. Glenn ROBERTS
29 Dir Alumni Affairs/Annual Giving ... Ms. Carol JACOBSON
06 Registrar ... Ms. Rebecca FOREST

*North Shore Community College (D)

1 Ferncroft Road, PO Box 3340, Danvers MA 01923-0840
County: Essex FICE Identification: 002173
Unit ID: 167312
Telephone: (978) 762-4000 Carnegie Class: Assoc/Pub-S-MC
FAX Number: (978) 762-4020 Calendar System: Semester
URL: www.northshore.edu
Established: 1965 Annual Undergrad Tuition & Fees (In-State): $5,070
Enrollment: 7,912 Coed
Affiliation or Control: State IRS Status: 501(c)3
Highest Offering: Associate Degree
Program: 2-Year Principally Bachelor's Creditable
Accreditation: EH, AAB, ADNUR, COARC, MAC, OTA, PTAA, RAD, SURGT

02 Interim President ... Ms. Janice M. FORSSTROM
05 Interim VP Academic Affairs ... Dr. Maureen O'NEILL
84 Vice Pres Enrollment Mgmt/Students ... Dr. Donna L. RICHEMOND
30 Vice Pres Institutional Advancement ... Dr. Sandra B. EDWARDS
11 Interim Chief Financial Officer ... Ms. Mariflor UVA
15 Vice President Human Res/Affirm Act ... Ms. Madeline WALLIS
31 Dean of Community Svcs/Corp Ed ... Ms. Dianne PALTER-GILL
90 Dean Academic Technology ... Mr. Michael BADOLATO
84 Dean of Enrollment ... Dr. Joanne LIGHT
32 Dean of Students ... Dr. Lloyd A. HOLMES
20 Assistant Dean Academic Affairs ... Dr. Laura VENTIMIGLIA
08 Director of Learning Resources ... Ms. Karen PANGALLO
14 Dir of Networking/Info Services ... Mr. Gary HAM
37 Dean of Financial Aid ... Mr. Stephen CREAMER
09 Director Inst Research/Planning ... Ms. Laurie LACHAPELLE
18 Director of Facilities Mgmt ... Mr. Richard RENEY
19 Campus Police Chief ... Mr. Douglas P. PUSKA
21 Comptroller ... Ms. Patricia CALLAHAN
26 Director Public Relations/Marketing ... Ms. Linda BRANTLEY
29 Director Alumni Relations ... Ms. Sandra ROCHON
35 Chief Student Life Officer ... Ms. Lisa MILSO
36 Director Student Placement ... Ms. Lynn MARCUS
07 Director of Recruitment ... Ms. Jennifer KIRK
38 Director Student Support Center ... Mr. Daniel O'NEILL
40 Bookstore Manager ... Mr. Shawn CRONIN
06 Associate Registrar ... Ms. Mel POTOCZAK

*Northern Essex Community College (E)

100 Elliott Street, Haverhill MA 01830-2399
County: Essex FICE Identification: 002174
Unit ID: 167376
Telephone: (978) 556-3000 Carnegie Class: Assoc/Pub-S-MC
FAX Number: (978) 556-3723 Calendar System: Semester
URL: www.necc.mass.edu
Established: 1960 Annual Undergrad Tuition & Fees (In-State): $4,860
Enrollment: 7,312 Coed
Affiliation or Control: State IRS Status: 501(c)3
Highest Offering: Associate Degree
Program: Occupational; 2-Year Principally Bachelor's Creditable; Fine Arts Emphasis
Accreditation: EH, ADNUR, COARC, DA, MAC, PNUR, POLYT, RAD

02 President ... Dr. Lane A. GLENN
05 Vice President of Academic Affairs ... Dr. William HEINEMAN
30 Vice Pres Institutional Advancement ... Ms. Jean C. POTH
84 Exec VP Enroll Mgmt/Student Svcs ... Ms. Mary Ellen ASHLEY
11 Vice President of Administration ... Mr. David GINGERELLA
15 Vice President of Human Resources ... Mr. Stephen W. FABBRUCCI
07 Assoc VP Enroll Svcs/Admissions ... Ms. Nora SHERIDAN
12 Dean of Lawrence Campus ... Ms. Mary Ellen ASHLEY
09 Dean of Institutional Research ... Mr. Thomas FALLON
44 Assistant Dean of Development ... Ms. Wendy SHAFFER
38 Asst Dean/Dir Counseling Center ... Vacant
103 Exec Dir Workforce Devel/Cont Ed ... Mr. George MORIARTY
27 Chief Information Officer ... Mr. Jeffrey BICKFORD
06 Registrar ... Ms. Sue SHAIN
37 Director of Financial Aid ... Ms. Alexis FISHBONE
26 Director of Public Relations ... Ms. Ernestine GREENSLADE
29 Director Alumni Relations ... Ms. Lindsey MAYO
32 Chief Student Life Officer ... Ms. Nita LAMBORGHINI
35 Director Student Affairs ... Ms. Dina BROWN
18 Chief Facilities/Physical Plant ... Mr. Richard GOULET
96 Director of Purchasing ... Vacant

*Quinsigamond Community College (F)

670 W Boylston Street, Worcester MA 01606-2092
County: Worcester FICE Identification: 002175
Unit ID: 167534
Telephone: (508) 853-2300 Carnegie Class: Assoc/Pub-U-SC
FAX Number: (508) 852-6943 Calendar System: Semester
URL: www.qcc.edu
Established: 1963 Annual Undergrad Tuition & Fees (In-State): $5,430
Enrollment: 8,991 Coed
Affiliation or Control: State IRS Status: 501(c)3
Highest Offering: Associate Degree
Program: Occupational; 2-Year Principally Bachelor's Creditable; Business Emphasis
Accreditation: EH, ADNUR, COARC, DA, DH, MAC, OTA, PNUR, RAD, SURGT

02 President ... Dr. Gail E. CARBERRY
05 Vice President of Academic Affairs ... Ms. Patricia A. TONEY
11 VP of Administration ... Mr. Stephen T. MARINI
32 Int VP Enrollment & Student Svcs ... Mr. Steven BUDD
26 Vice Pres of Community Engagement ... Mr. Dale ALLEN
88 Asst VP for Policy & Governance ... Ms. Susan LAPRADE
20 Assistant VP Academic Affairs ... Ms. Jane SHEA
04 Executive Assistant to President ... Ms. Patricia A. SOLITRO
21 Asst VP for Finance/Comptroller ... Ms. Debra A. LAFLASH
88 Dean Public Service & Social Sci ... Mr. James BROWN
79 Dean Humanities & Education ... Dr. Clarence ATES
76 Dean Health Care ... Dr. Jane JUNE
50 Dean Business/Engineer/Technology ... Ms. Kathleen RENTSCH
81 Dean Science & Mathematics ... Dr. Leslie HORTON
84 Asst VP of Enrollment Management ... Ms. Iris GODES
15 Assoc VP of Human Resources ... Mr. William DARING
06 Assoc Dean Enrollment/Registrar ... Ms. Tara F. JENKINS
62 Dean of Library Services ... Ms. Andrea MACRITCHIE
09 Dir Institutional Research/Planning ... Dr. Ingrid SKADBERG
07 Assoc Dean Enrollment Management ... Ms. Michelle TUFAU-AFRIYIE
13 Chief Technology Officer ... Mr. Ken DWYER
26 Dir Community Affairs& Site Facilit ... Mr. Victor SOMMA
35 Director Student Life ... Mr. Jonathan MILLER
18 Director of Facilities ... Mr. Donny HALL
37 Director Student Financial Aid ... Ms. Karen GRANT
96 Director of Purchasing ... Ms. Paula CAREY
19 Chief of Campus Police ... Mr. Kevin RITACCO
88 Dir Institutional Communications ... Mr. Joshua MARTIN
22 Employment & Equity Officer ... Ms. Anita BOWDEN
38 Coordinator Student Counseling ... Ms. Karen COX
88 Director Disability Services ... Ms. Kristen PROCTOR

*Roxbury Community College (G)

1234 Columbus Avenue,
Roxbury Crossing MA 02120-3423
County: Suffolk FICE Identification: 011930
Unit ID: 167631
Telephone: (617) 427-0060 Carnegie Class: Assoc/Pub-S-MC
FAX Number: (617) 541-5351 Calendar System: Semester
URL: rcc.mass.edu
Established: 1973 Annual Undergrad Tuition & Fees (In-State): $3,962

Enrollment: 2,725 Coed
Affiliation or Control: State IRS Status: 501(c)3
Highest Offering: Associate Degree
Program: Occupational; 2-Year Principally Bachelor's Creditable
Accreditation: EH, ADNUR, RAD

02 President .... Dr. Valerie R. ROBERSON
04 Executive Asst to the President .... Ms. Shirley Y. LESLIE
05 Vice President of Academic Affairs ..... Dr. Brenda W. MERCOMES
10 Vice President of Admin & Finance .... Mr. Chuks OKOLI
84 VP Enrollment Mgmt/Student Affairs .... Vacant
13 Chief Information Tech Officer .... Mr. Patrick JEAN-LOUIS
81 Dean of Science/Tech/Eng/Math .... Vacant
66 Dean of Health Sciences .... Dr. Gloria H. CATER
49 Dean of Liberal Arts .... Dr. Nancy A. TEEL
09 Dean of Inst Research & Planning .... Mr. Mike WALKER
90 Dean of Academic Technology .... Ms. Jenene COOK
07 Dean of Enroll Mgmt/Stdnt Jud Affs .... Mr. Charles DIGGS
88 Dean of Student Success .... Vacant
51 Asst Dean Continuing Education .... Mr. Morisset ST. PREUX
20 Assoc Dean of Academic Affairs .... Dr. Jose ALICEA
41 Director of RLTAC & Athletics .... Mr. A. Keith MCDERMOTT
29 Director of Alumni Affairs .... Ms. Carol BLISS-FURR
21 Comptroller .... Ms. Florence CRAIG
21 Budget Director .... Mr. Gib PORNKITTICHOTCHAROEN
88 Bursar .... Vacant
37 Director Financial Aid .... Mr. Raymond O'ROURKE
08 Director of Library .... Mr. Mark LAWRENCE
23 Director of Health Services .... Ms. Ruth HINES
06 Registrar .... Mr. Martin GRACE
88 Assistant Registrar .... Ms. Carrie L. MONESTIME
35 Director of Student Life .... Ms. Elizabeth CLARK
18 Director of Facilities .... Mr. Nicholas PIRELLI
15 Director of Human Resources/AA .... Mr. P. Paul ALEXANDER
26 Director Marketing/Communications .... Mr. Milton SAMUELS
36 Director Testing & Assessment .... Ms. Colleen SPENCE
25 Director of Grants Development .... Ms. Theresa BREWER
103 Dir of Corp & Community Education .... Vacant
57 Dir of Visual/Performing/Media Arts .... Mr. Marshall HUGHES
88 Director of the Writing Center Lab .... Ms. Judith KAHALAS
88 Director of Academic Advising .... Ms. Lisa CARTER

*Springfield Technical Community College (A)

Armory Square, Springfield MA 01105-1296
County: Hampden FICE Identification: 008078
Unit ID: 167905
Telephone: (413) 781-7822 Carnegie Class: Assoc/Pub-U-SC
FAX Number: (413) 755-6309 Calendar System: Semester
URL: www.stcc.edu
Established: 1967 Annual Undergrad Tuition & Fees (In-State): $5,106
Enrollment: 7,011 Coed
Affiliation or Control: State IRS Status: 501(c)3
Highest Offering: Associate Degree
Program: Occupational; 2-Year Principally Bachelor's Creditable; Technical Emphasis
Accreditation: EH, ADNUR, CA, COARC, DA, DH, DMS, ENGT, MAC, MLTAD, #NMT, OTA, PTAA, RAD, SURGT

02 President .... Dr. Ira H. RUBENZAHL
05 Exec Vice Pres Academic Affairs .... Mr. Stephen H. KELLER
10 VP of Finance/CFO .... Mr. Joseph DASILVA
20 Dean of Curriculum .... Mr. Matthew GRAVEL
32 VP Student/Multicultural Affairs .... Mrs. Myra D. SMITH
04 Assistant to the President .... Mr. Michael J. SUZOR
50 Dean School of Business/Info Tech .... Dr. Leona R. ITTLEMAN
66 Dean of Nursing .... Ms. Mary TARBELL
72 Dean Engineering Technologies .... Ms. Adrienne SMITH
76 Dean School of Health .... Mr. Michael C. FOSS
79 Dean Arts/Humanities/Social Sci .... Dr. Arlene RODRIGUEZ
81 Dean Math/Science/Engineering .... Dr. Robert DICKERMAN
51 Dean School Continuing Education .... Dr. Debbie BELLUCCI
35 Dean of Student Affairs .... Mr. Ray BLAIR
07 Dean of Admissions .... Ms. Louisa M. DAVIS FREEMAN
09 Dean of Institutional Effectiveness .... Dr. Barb CHALFONTE
06 Registrar .... Mrs. Theresa REMILLARD
41 Director of Athletics .... Mr. J. Vincent GRASSETTI
102 VP Foundation/Workforce Options .... Mr. Bob LEPAGE
19 Director of Public Safety .... Ms. Wendy MASIUK
18 Sr Director of Facilities .... Mrs. Maureen SOCHA
38 Director of Academic Advising .... Mr. Kamari COLLINS
23 Coordinator of Health Services .... Mr. Jonathan L. MILLER
26 Director of Marketing .... Mrs. Joan THOMAS
36 Director of Coop/Career Placement .... Ms. Pamela WHITE
15 Director of Human Resources .... Ms. Michelle CAPDEVILLE
37 Director Student Financial Aid .... Mr. Jeremy GREENHOUSE
88 Fiscal/Financial Project Manager .... Mr. Jason COHEN
96 Asst Dir Purchasing/Business Svcs .... Ms. Francene CLINTON
35 Coord Student Activities/Devel .... Ms. Andrea TARPEY
27 Coordinator of Media Relations .... Ms. Carla POTTS
88 Senior Director Finance/Budgets .... Mrs. Cathy OLSON
14 SR Director of IT Applications .... Mr. Clifton PORTER
13 Sr Director of IT Infrastructure .... Mr. Robert TRUSCH
16 Sr Director of Human Resouces .... Ms. Debra DOWER
62 Dean Library Services .... Ms. Barbara WURTZEL
88 Controller .... Mr. Jonathan TUDRYN
09 Director of Institutional Research .... Ms. Suzanne SMITH
108 Director of Assessment .... Ms. Laura HENDERSON
88 Director of Grants .... Ms. Deborah KOCH
96 Director of Purchasing .... Mr. Roger BESSETTE
88 Director of Student Support Service .... Mr. Roosevelt CHARLES
88 Director of Gateway to College .... Ms. Rachel JONES
44 Director of Annual Giving .... Ms. Christina TUOHEY

Massachusetts Institute of Technology (B)

77 Massachusetts Avenue, Cambridge MA 02139-4307
County: Middlesex FICE Identification: 002178
Unit ID: 166683
Telephone: (617) 253-1000 Carnegie Class: RU/VH
FAX Number: N/A Calendar System: 4/1/4
URL: web.mit.edu
Established: 1861 Annual Undergrad Tuition & Fees: $43,498
Enrollment: 11,189 Coed
Affiliation or Control: Independent Non-Profit IRS Status: 501(c)3
Highest Offering: Doctorate
Program: Technical Emphasis
Accreditation: EH, BUS, CS, ENG, PLNG

01 President .... Dr. L. Rafael REIF
00 Chairman of the Corporation .... Mr. John REED
05 Provost .... Dr. Chris A. KAISER
88 Chancellor .... Prof. W. Eric L. GRIMSON
03 Exec Vice President & Treasurer .... Mr. Israel RUIZ
101 VP and Secretary of the Corporation .... Dr. Kirk D. KOLENBRANDER
30 Vice Pres for Resource Development .... Mr. Jeffrey L. NEWTON
43 Vice President & General Counsel .... Mr. R. Gregory MORGAN
10 Vice President for Finance .... Mr. Michael W. HOWARD
15 Vice President for Human Resources .... Dr. Alison ALDEN
46 Vice President for Research .... Prof. Maria T. ZUBER
88 Vice President .... Prof. Claude R. CANIZARES
29 Exec VP & CEO Alumni Association .... Ms. Judith M. COLE
88 President MIT Investment Mgmt Co .... Mr. Seth ALEXANDER
20 Associate Provost .... Prof. Martin A. SCHMIDT
20 Associate Provost .... Prof. Philip S. KHOURY
20 Institute Community & Equity Ofcr .... Prof. Edmund BERTSCHINGER
48 Dean Sch of Architecture & Planning .. Prof. Adele Naude SANTOS
54 Dean School of Engineering .... Prof. Ian A. WAITZ
79 Dean Sch Hum/Arts/Soc Sciences . Prof. Deborah K. FITZGERALD
50 Dean Sloan School of Management .... Prof. David C. SCHMITTLEIN
81 Dean School of Science .... Prof. Marc A. KASTNER
58 Dean Graduate for Education .... Dr. Christine ORTIZ
88 Dean for Undergraduate Education .... Prof. Dennis FREEMAN
32 Dean for Student Life .... Mr. Chris COLOMBO
106 Director of Digital Learning .... Prof. Sanjay SARMA
08 Director of Libraries .... Ms. Ann J. WOLPERT
88 Director Lincoln Laboratory .... Dr. Eric D. EVANS
86 Director MIT Washington Office .... Mr. William B. BONVILLIAN
27 Associate VP for Communications .... Mr. Nate NICKERSON
07 Dean of Admissions .... Mr. Stuart SCHMILL
37 Exec Dir Student Financial Services .... Ms. Elizabeth M. HICKS
23 Medical Dir & Head MIT Medical .... Dr. William M. KETTYLE
13 Head of Info Services & Technology .... Vacant
18 Dir Facilities Operations/Security .... Chief John DI FAVA
45 Director Campus Planning & Design ... Ms. Pamela DELPHENICH
102 Exec Dir Resource Development .... Ms. Lindley HUEY
25 Dir Office of Sponsored Programs .... Ms. Michelle D. CHRISTY
96 Asst Dir of Strategic Sourcing .... Ms. Sara MALCONIAN
41 Director of Athletics .... Ms. Julie SORIERO
09 Director of Institutional Research .... Mrs. Lydia S. SNOVER
85 Dir International Students Office .... Ms. Danielle GUICHARD-ASHBROOK
36 Exec Dir Global Educ/Career Dev Ctr .... Ms. Melanie L. PARKER
93 Associate Dean and Director OME .... Ms. DiOnetta JONES
06 Registrar .... Ms. Mary CALLAHAN
40 Director MIT Press .... Ms. Ellen W. FARAN
39 Director of Housing Operations .... Mr. Daniel RODERICK
42 Chaplain to the Institute .... Dr. Robert M. RANDOLPH
38 Assoc Dean Student Support Services .... Mr. David RANDALL
94 Women's and Gender Studies Director .... Prof. Sally HASLANGER
104 Associate Dean Global Education ..... Ms. Malgorzata HEDDERICK
105 Web Manager .... Mr. Patrick GILLOOLY
24 Manager Audio Visual .... Mr. Louis W. GRAHAM, JR.

Massachusetts School of Law at Andover (C)

500 Federal Street, Andover MA 01810-1094
County: Essex FICE Identification: 032353
Unit ID: 369002
Telephone: (978) 681-0800 Carnegie Class: Spec/Law
FAX Number: (978) 681-6330 Calendar System: Semester
URL: www.mslaw.edu
Established: 1988 Annual Graduate Tuition & Fees: $19,500
Enrollment: 625 Coed
Affiliation or Control: Independent Non-Profit IRS Status: 501(c)3
Highest Offering: Doctorate; No Undergraduates
Program: Professional
Accreditation: EH

01 Dean .... Mr. Lawrence R. VELVEL
05 Chief Acad Ofcr/Dir Personnel Svc .... Prof. Michael COYNE
10 Chief Business Officer .... Prof. Paula KALDIS
37 Director Student Financial Aid .... Ms. Lynn BOWAB
06 Registrar .... Ms. Louise ROSE
07 Director of Admissions .... Ms. Paula COLBY CLEMENTS
26 Chief Public Relations Officer .... Vacant
29 Director Alumni Relations .... Vacant

Massachusetts School of Professional Psychology (D)

1 Wells Avenue, Newton MA 02459-3211
County: Norfolk FICE Identification: 021636
Unit ID: 166717
Telephone: (617) 327-6777 Carnegie Class: Spec/Health
FAX Number: (617) 327-4447 Calendar System: Semester
URL: www.mspp.edu
Established: 1974 Annual Graduate Tuition & Fees: $36,880
Enrollment: 650 Coed
Affiliation or Control: Independent Non-Profit IRS Status: 501(c)3
Highest Offering: Doctorate; No Undergraduates
Program: Professional
Accreditation: EH, CLPSY, IPSY

01 President .... Dr. Nicholas COVINO
04 Executive Asst to the President .... Ms. Lilly MANOLIS
10 VP Finance and Operations .... Mr. Patrick CAPOBIANCO
05 Assoc Vice Pres Academic Affairs .... Dr. Stacey LAMBERT
21 Assoc VP Finance .... Mr. Daniel BRENT
46 Assoc VP for Research .... Dr. Edward DEVOS
37 Director Financial Aid .... Mrs. Elaine TOOMEY
06 Director of Student Services .... Ms. Eileen O'DONNELL
32 Dean of Students .... Dr. Frances MERVYN
88 Director of Multicultural Affairs .... Mrs. Gretchen NASH
07 Director of Admissions .... Mr. Mario MURGA
51 Director Continuing Prof Education .... Mr. Dean ABBY
36 Director Career Services .... Mrs. Tricia KRZYWICKI
27 Director of Marketing .... Mrs. Katie O'HARE
13 Dir Information Technology .... Mr. Jeff CHOO
78 Assoc Dir Community Education .... Mrs. Beth BASNIGHT
08 Head Librarian .... Mr. Matt KRAMER
15 Human Resource Manager .... Mrs. Ellen COLLINS
18 Facilities Manager .... Mr. Kevin COSTELLO
26 Chief Public Relations Officer .... Ms. Patti JACOBS
96 Director of Purchasing .... Ms. Marice NICHOLS
29 Director Alumni Relations .... Dr. Alan BECK

MCPHS University (E)

179 Longwood Avenue, Boston MA 02115-5896
County: Suffolk FICE Identification: 002165
Unit ID: 166656
Telephone: (617) 732-2800 Carnegie Class: Spec/Health
FAX Number: (617) 732-2801 Calendar System: Semester
URL: www.mcphs.edu
Established: 1823 Annual Undergrad Tuition & Fees: $28,470
Enrollment: 6,010 Coed
Affiliation or Control: Independent Non-Profit IRS Status: 501(c)3
Highest Offering: Doctorate
Program: Professional
Accreditation: EH, ARCPA, DH, NMT, NURSE, @OPT, PHAR, @PTA, RAD, RTT

01 President .... Mr. Charles F. MONAHAN, JR.
05 VP Academic Affairs/Provost .... Dr. George E. HUMPHREY
10 Exec Vice Pres Finance & Admin/COO .. Mr. Richard J. LESSARD
30 VP for Development & Chief of Staff ... Ms. Marguerite JOHNSON
12 Vice President Wor/Manch Campuses .... Vacant
20 Assoc Provost for Academic Affairs .... Dr. Lily HSU
20 Assoc Provost for Undergraduate Ed .... Dr. David TANNER
106 Assoc Provost Online Education/CEO .... Dr. Barbara MACAULAY
43 Legal Counsel .... Ms. Deborah A. O'MALLEY
32 Dean of Students-Boston .... Dr. Jean JOYCE-BRADY
32 Dean of Students-W/M .... Dr. Shuli XU
67 Dean Pharmacy Boston .... Dr. Douglas J. PISANO
67 Dean Pharmacy Worcester .... Dr. Michael J. MALLOY
08 Dean Library & Learning Resources .... Mr. Richard KAPLAN
49 Dean School of Arts and Sciences .... Dr. Delia C. ANDERSON
66 Dean School of Nursing .... Dr. Carol ELIADI
52 Dean Forsyth School for Dental Hyg .... Dr. Linda D. BOYD
88 Dean School of Physical Therapy .... Dr. Linda J. TSOUMAS
88 Dean Sch Medical Imaging & Therap .... Dr. Douglas J. PISANO
37 Exec Dir Student Enrollment Svcs .... Ms. Carrie GLASS
15 Director of Human Resources .... Ms. Mary LILLY
06 Registrar .... Ms. Stacey TAYLOR
13 Director of Information Services .... Mr. Tom SCANLON
21 Chief Business Officer .... Mr. Keith BELLUCCI
12 Exec Director Manchester Campus .... Mr. Seth P. WALL
29 Exec Director Alumni Relations .... Ms. Dawn BALLOU
07 Executive Director of Admissions .... Ms. Kathleen RYAN
96 Director of Purchasing .... Ms. Margaret EATON-CRAWFORD
38 Director Counseling Services .... Ms. Molly PAYNE
27 Director of Communications .... Mr. Michael RATTY
39 Director of Residence Life .... Ms. Jennifer KOSSES
35 Asst Dean Campus Life & Leadership .... Ms. Jennifer MICHAEL
18 Director of Facilities .... Mr. Michael O'NEIL
19 Chief of Public Safety .... Mr. Jack KELLY
105 Director of Web Services .... Ms. Linda DANGELO
21 Dean of Optometry .... Dr. Shilpa REGISTER
09 Dir Institutional Res & Assessment .... Mr. Rajiv MALHOTRA

MCPHS-Worcester Campus (F)

19 Foster Street, Worcester MA 01608-1715
Telephone: (508) 890-8855 Identification: 770112
Accreditation: &EH

† Main campus is MCPHS University in Boston, MA.

Merrimack College (A)

315 Turnpike Street, North Andover MA 01845-5800
County: Essex FICE Identification: 002120
Unit ID: 166850
Telephone: (978) 837-5000 Carnegie Class: Bac/Diverse
FAX Number: (978) 837-5222 Calendar System: Semester
URL: www.merrimack.edu
Established: 1947 Annual Undergrad Tuition & Fees: $35,085
Enrollment: 2,694 Coed
Affiliation or Control: Roman Catholic IRS Status: 501(c)3
Highest Offering: Master's
Program: Liberal Arts And General; Teacher Preparatory; Professional
Accreditation: EH, ENG

01 President .... Dr. Christopher E. HOPEY
100 Chief of Staff .... Mr. Jeffrey DOGGETT
43 Vice President Admin & Gen Counsel .... Ms. Alexa ABOWITZ
04 Director Office of the President .... Ms. Lisa JEBALI
05 Provost .... Dr. Josephine MODICA-NAPOLITANO
20 Vice Provost .... Dr. Patricia SENDALL
20 Vice Provost .... Dr. Russell MAYER
20 Vice Provost .... Dr. Cynthia MCGOWAN
84 VP for Enrollment & Retention .... Mr. David HAUTANEN
88 Vice Pres Mission/Student Affairs .. Rev. Raymond DLUGOS, OSA
10 Vice Pres Finance & Budget/CFO .... Mr. William KLINE
30 VP Development and Alumni Affairs .... Ms. Sara BRAZDA
26 VP Communications and Marketing .... Vacant
88 Assoc VP/Chief of Staff to Provost .... Mr. Mark GOULD
86 AVP for External Affairs .... Mr. Felipe SCHWARZ
09 Asst VP Inst Research & Planning .... Ms. Kim BRIDGEO
15 Asst VP of Admin & Personnel .... Ms. Linda MURPHY
88 Asst VP for Marketing .... Ms. Zoe COHEN
07 Dean of Admissions .... Mr. Mark BARRETT
37 Director of Student Financial Aid .... Ms. Adrienne MONTGOMERY
21 Dir of Fiscal Affairs & Controller .... Ms. Caitlin BLUNDELL
50 Dean Girard Sch Business/Intl Comm .... Dr. Mark CORDANO
54 Interim Dean Science & Engineering .... Ms. Mary NOONAN
49 Dean of Liberal Arts .... Dr. Kathleen TIEMANN
53 Dean School of Education .... Dr. Dan BUTIN
06 Registrar .... Ms. Elaine GRELLE
32 Dean of Campus Life .... Dr. Donna L. SWARTWOUT
13 Chief Information Officer .... Mr. Chip STILES
36 Director Career Services/Co-op Educ .... Dr. Heather MAIETTA
46 Special Asst to Pres for Res Dev .... Mr. Michael ACCARDI
08 Director of the Library .... Ms. Kathryn GEOFFRION-SCANNELL
41 Director of Athletics .... Mr. Jeremy GIBSON
29 Exec Director of Alumni Relations .... Joanne MERMELSTEIN
42 Director of Campus Ministry .... Rev. Keith HOLLIS
23 Director Counseling & Health Svcs .... Dr. Suzanne SLATTERY
35 Assistant Dean of Campus Life .... Ms. Allison GILL
104 Director of International Programs .... Ms. Lauren BENT
39 Director of Residence Life .... Ms. Sara HICKS
19 Director of Police Services .... Mr. Michael DELGRECO
28 Director Diversity Education .... Mr. J. Scott GAGE
18 Director of Physical Plant .... Vacant
31 Dir of Stevens Service Learning Ctr .... Ms. Mary MCHUGH
24 Dir of Media Instructional Services .... Mr. Kevin SALEMME

MGH Institute of Health Professions (B)

36 1st Avenue, Boston MA 02129-4557
County: Suffolk FICE Identification: 022316
Unit ID: 166869
Telephone: (617) 726-2947 Carnegie Class: Spec/Health
FAX Number: (617) 726-3716 Calendar System: Semester
URL: www.mghihp.edu
Established: 1977 Annual Undergrad Tuition & Fees: $1,092
Enrollment: 1,230 Coed
Affiliation or Control: Independent Non-Profit IRS Status: 501(c)3
Highest Offering: Doctorate
Program: Professional
Accreditation: EH, NURSE, PTA, SP

01 President .... Dr. Janis P. BELLACK
05 Provost/VP of Academic Affairs .... Dr. Alex F. JOHNSON
10 VP for Finance & Administration .... Mr. Atlas D. EVANS
26 Chief Information Officer .... Mr. Denis G. STRATFORD
30 Chief Development Officer .... Ms. Harriet S. KORNFELD
32 Dean of Student Affairs .... Ms. Carolyn LOCKE
66 Dean of Nursing .... Dr. Laurie LAUZON CLABO
76 Int Dean School of Hlth & Rehab Sci .... Dr. Leslie PORTNEY
88 Chair Comm Sciences & Disorders .... Dr. Gregory LOF
20 Assoc Provost for Acad Affairs .... Dr. Peter CAHN
06 Asst Dean of Students/Registrar .... Mr. James V. VITAGLIANO
04 Executive Assistant to President .... Ms. Elizabeth M. PIPES
37 Director Student Financial Aid .... Mrs. Kathy ANDERSON
09 Director of Inst Effectiveness .... Ms. Cynthia P. KING
84 Assistant Director of Admissions .... Mr. Anthony MICELI
21 Student Accounts Manager .... Ms. Joyce DESANCTIS
07 Director of Admissions .... Ms. Maureen JUDD
27 Director of Communications .... Mr. Paul W. MURPHY
15 Director Personnel Services .... Ms. Sarah WELCH
18 Chief Facilities/Physical Plant .... Mr. Denis G. STRATFORD
29 Director Alumni Relations .... Ms. Kami CRARY

Montserrat College of Art (C)

23 Essex Street, Box 26, Beverly MA 01915-4508
County: Essex FICE Identification: 020630
Unit ID: 166911
Telephone: (978) 922-8222 Carnegie Class: Spec/Arts
FAX Number: (978) 922-4268 Calendar System: Semester
URL: www.montserrat.edu
Established: 1970 Annual Undergrad Tuition & Fees: $27,770
Enrollment: 385 Coed
Affiliation or Control: Independent Non-Profit IRS Status: 501(c)3
Highest Offering: Baccalaureate
Program: Liberal Arts And General
Accreditation: EH, ART

01 President .... Dr. Stephen D. IMMERMAN
05 Dean Faculty/Academic Affairs .... Ms. Laura TONELLI
84 Dean Admissions/Enrollment Mgmt .... Mr. Rick LONGO
32 Dean of Students .... Ms. Maureen WARK
30 Dean of Development .... Mr. Howard AMIDON
26 Dean College Rels/Spec Asst to Pres .... Ms. Jo BRODERICK
10 Chief Financial Officer .... Mr. James MACDONALD
13 Director of Information Technology .... Mr. Jake SYNDER
08 Library Director .... Ms. Cheri COE
06 Registrar .... Mrs. Theresa SKELLY
37 Director of Financial Aid .... Ms. Anne MCDERMOTT
15 Human Resources Director .... Ms. Jennifer THOMAS TROUPE

Mount Holyoke College (D)

50 College Street, South Hadley MA 01075-1424
County: Hampshire FICE Identification: 002192
Unit ID: 166939
Telephone: (413) 538-2000 Carnegie Class: Bac/A&S
FAX Number: (413) 538-2391 Calendar System: Semester
URL: www.mtholyoke.edu
Established: 1837 Annual Undergrad Tuition & Fees: $41,270
Enrollment: 2,344 Female
Affiliation or Control: Independent Non-Profit IRS Status: 501(c)3
Highest Offering: Master's
Program: Liberal Arts And General; Teacher Preparatory
Accreditation: EH

01 President .... Lynn PASQUERELLA
05 Dean of Faculty/Vice Pres Acad Affs .... Sonya STEPHENS
10 Vice Pres Finance/Administration .... Shannon GUREK
84 Vice Pres Enrollment .... Diane ANCI
30 Vice President for Advancement .... MaryAnne YOUNG
32 Dean of the College/VP Student Affs .... Cerri BANKS

Mount Ida College (E)

777 Dedham Street, Newton MA 02459
County: Middlesex FICE Identification: 002193
Unit ID: 166948
Telephone: (617) 928-4500 Carnegie Class: Bac/Diverse
FAX Number: (617) 928-4746 Calendar System: Semester
URL: www.mountida.edu
Established: 1899 Annual Undergrad Tuition & Fees: $28,162
Enrollment: 1,389 Coed
Affiliation or Control: Independent Non-Profit IRS Status: 501(c)3
Highest Offering: Master's
Program: Liberal Arts And General; Professional
Accreditation: EH, ART, CIDA, DH, FUSER

01 President .... Mr. Barry BROWN
05 Vice Pres Acad Aff/Enroll Mgmt/Mktg .... Mr. Ronald E. AKIE
30 Vice President for Development .... Dr. Deborah HIRSCH
10 Vice Pres Finance/ Administration .... Ms. Cheryl ST. PIERRE-SLEBODA
32 Vice President of Student Affairs .... Ms. Laura DEVEAU
21 Assoc Vice Pres for Finance .... Mr. Edward MOLLER
35 Associate Dean of Students .... Mr. William CRIBBY
06 Registrar .... Ms. Kathy POSEY
08 Director of Learning Resources .... Vacant
29 Dir Alumni Relations/Annual Giving .... Ms. Candace CRABTREE
37 Director Financial Aid .... Ms. Dyan TEEHAN
36 Director of Career Services .... Mr. Robert BROOKS
15 Director of Human Resources .... Ms. Omaira ROY
26 Director of Mkting & Communications .. Ms. Annmarie FARRETTA
85 Director of Intl Student Affairs .... Vacant
41 Athletic Director .... Mr. Matthew BURKE
19 Director Campus Security .... Mr. Ben KATZ
18 Director of Facilities .... Ms. Donna LEMIERE
09 Director of Institutional Research .... Mr. Jerome DEAN
88 Dean of College Academic Services .... Ms. Alyce CURTIS
24 Director of Educational Media .... Mr. Manouche MADANIPOUR
96 Director of Business Services .... Ms. Leah WEBBER
28 Director of Multicultural Affairs .... Ms. Roxanne LONGORIA
42 College Chaplain .... Vacant
14 Director Network Services .... Mr. David VALENTINE
23 Director Health Services .... Ms. Marsha WELBURN
35 Director Student Activities .... Ms. Adebimpe DARE
58 Dean Graduate Studies/Cont Educ .... Ms. Lois NUNEZ

The National Graduate School of Quality Systems Management (F)

186 Jones Road, Falmouth MA 02540-2908
County: Barnstable FICE Identification: 035043
Unit ID: 441478
Telephone: (508) 457-1313 Carnegie Class: Spec/Bus
FAX Number: (508) 457-5347 Calendar System: Other
URL: www.ngs.edu
Established: 1993 Annual Undergrad Tuition & Fees: $20,500
Enrollment: 294 Coed
Affiliation or Control: Independent Non-Profit IRS Status: 501(c)3
Highest Offering: Doctorate
Program: Business Emphasis
Accreditation: EH

01 Interim President/CEO .... Dr. R. Clinton MINER
84 Director Enrollment Management .... Ms. Marcie TREFNEY
88 Director Regulatory Affairs .... Ms. Maureen REARDON
06 Registrar .... Ms. Catherine KING
10 Comptroller .... Ms. Mary ORLANDO

New England College of Business and Finance (G)

10 High Street, Suite 204, Boston MA 02110
County: Suffolk FICE Identification: 039653
Unit ID: 164438
Telephone: (617) 951-2350 Carnegie Class: Assoc/PrivFP4
FAX Number: (617) 951-2533 Calendar System: Other
URL: www.necb.edu
Established: 1909 Annual Undergrad Tuition & Fees: $11,575
Enrollment: 1,211 Coed
Affiliation or Control: Proprietary IRS Status: Proprietary
Highest Offering: Master's
Program: Business Emphasis
Accreditation: EH

01 President .... Mr. Howard E. HORTON
11 Chief Operating Officer .... Mr. Jeff HERLE
05 Provost .... Dr. Sharon FROSS
20 Associate Provost .... Ms. Debra LEAHY
32 Sr Vice Pres of Student Services .... Ms. Paula BRAMANTE
10 Controller .... Mr. William MCDONALD
97 Dean of Undergraduate Studies .... Mr. Roger PAO
88 Program Chair MBE .... Ms. Deborah SEMENTA
88 Program Chair MBA .... Dr. Carla PATALANO
04 Asst to the President/Office Mgr .... Ms. Kathy CANTALUPA
06 Registrar .... Mr. Robert WAGSTAFF
88 Dean of Student Advising .... Ms. Caitrin BRISSON
07 Director of Enrollment .... Ms. Kirsten THOMPSON
37 Director of Financial Aid .... Vacant

The New England College of Optometry (H)

424 Beacon Street, Boston MA 02115-1129
County: Suffolk FICE Identification: 002164
Unit ID: 167093
Telephone: (617) 266-2030 Carnegie Class: Spec/Health
FAX Number: (617) 424-9202 Calendar System: Semester
URL: www.neco.edu
Established: 1894 Annual Undergrad Tuition & Fees: $38,358
Enrollment: 472 Coed
Affiliation or Control: Independent Non-Profit IRS Status: 501(c)3
Highest Offering: Doctorate
Program: Professional
Accreditation: EH, OPT, OPTR

01 President .... Dr. Clifford SCOTT
05 VP & Dean of Academic Affairs .... Dr. Barry FISCH
10 VP Business Development .... Mr. Robert GORDON
17 VP Clinical Affairs & CEO of NEEI .... Ms. Jody FLEIT
30 VP of Philanthropy .... Ms. Nancy BROUDE
32 Assoc Dean Students/Dir Stdnt Svcs .... Ms. Barbara MCGINLEY
07 Assoc Dean of Admissions .... Dr. Taline FARRA
37 Director Student Financial Aid .... Ms. Carol RUBEL
15 Director of Human Resources .... Ms. Patricia DAHILL
06 Registrar .... Ms. Glenda UNDERWOOD
08 Director of Library Services .... Ms. Kristin MOTTE
04 Executive Asst to the President .... Ms. Marie HILL

New England Conservatory of Music (I)

290 Huntington Avenue, Boston MA 02115-5018
County: Suffolk FICE Identification: 002194
Unit ID: 167057
Telephone: (617) 585-1100 Carnegie Class: Spec/Arts
FAX Number: (617) 262-0500 Calendar System: Semester
URL: www.necmusic.edu
Established: 1867 Annual Undergrad Tuition & Fees: $39,500
Enrollment: 750 Coed
Affiliation or Control: Independent Non-Profit IRS Status: 501(c)3
Highest Offering: Doctorate
Program: Liberal Arts And General; Teacher Preparatory; Professional
Accreditation: EH, MUS

01 President .... Mr. Tony WOODCOCK
05 Provost/Dean of the College .... Mr. Thomas NOVAK
10 Sr Vice Pres Finance/Operations .... Mr. Edward R. LESSER
30 Exec Vice Pres Institutional Advanc .... Mr. Don JONES
26 Vice Pres Marketing/Communications .... Ms. Carol PHELAN
100 Chief of Staff .... Ms. Suzanne WILSON
56 Dean of Extension Division .... Mr. Mark CHURCHILL
32 Dean of Students .... Mr. Tom HANDEL
07 Asst Dean for Admissions .... Ms. Christina DALY
11 Head of Operations/Inst Planning .... Ms. Hilary FIELD
21 Controller .... Ms. Amanda GATES
18 Exec Dir Facilities/Engrng/Constr .... Mr. Michael RYAN
06 Registrar .... Mr. Robert WINKLEY
08 Director of Libraries .... Ms. Jean MORROW
37 Director Financial Aid .... Ms. Lauren URBANEK
35 Director Student Activities .... Ms. Colleen PALMER

36 Director of Career Services .... Dr. Angela Myles BEECHING
29 Director of Alumni Relations .... Ms. Cheryl WEBER
15 Director of Human Resources .... Ms. Elise COMEAU
13 Director ITS .... Mr. Charles MEMBRINO
09 Director of Institutional Research .... Ms. Sarah DOW
20 Asst Dean of Academic Studies .... Vacant
38 Director Student Counseling .... Ms. Jan LERBINGER
51 Director of Continuing Education .... Mr. Sean P. HAGON
88 Dir of Entrepreneurial Musicianship .... Ms. Rachel ROBERTS

The New England Institute of Art (A)

10 Brookline Place W, Brookline MA 02445-7295
County: Norfolk — FICE Identification: 007486
Unit ID: 167321
Telephone: (617) 739-1700 — Carnegie Class: Spec/Arts
FAX Number: (617) 582-4500 — Calendar System: Semester
URL: www.artinstitutes.edu/boston
Established: 1952 — Annual Undergrad Tuition & Fees: $27,000
Enrollment: 1,052 — Coed
Affiliation or Control: Proprietary — IRS Status: Proprietary
Highest Offering: Baccalaureate
Program: Occupational; Fine Arts Emphasis
Accreditation: EH

01 President .... Dr. Christine MURPHY
05 Dean of Academic Affairs .... Dr. Rick KETTNER-POLLEY
32 Dean of Student Affairs .... Ms. Michele TRACIA
06 Registrar .... Ms. Dawn NORRIS
07 Senior Director of Admissions .... Ms. Mary BURNE
10 Director of Admin & Financial Svcs .... Mr. Ross SORACI
13 Campus Technology Manager .... Ms. Connie BURKE
15 Human Resources Generalist .... Ms. Ashley JENKINS
36 Director of Career Services .... Mr. John LAY
37 Director Student Financial Services .... Mr. Michael CARDENAS
40 Bookstore Manager .... Ms. Stephanie VINCENT

New England Law | Boston (B)

154 Stuart Street, Boston MA 02116-5687
County: Suffolk — FICE Identification: 008916
Unit ID: 167215
Telephone: (617) 451-0010 — Carnegie Class: Spec/Law
FAX Number: (617) 422-7333 — Calendar System: Semester
URL: www.nesl.edu
Established: 1908 — Annual Undergrad Tuition & Fees: $42,490
Enrollment: 1,166 — Coed
Affiliation or Control: Independent Non-Profit — IRS Status: 501(c)3
Highest Offering: First Professional Degree
Program: Professional
Accreditation: LAW

01 Dean .... Mr. John F. O'BRIEN
05 Associate Dean .... Mr. Victor HANSEN
11 Associate Dean of Administration .... Ms. Susan S. CALAMARE
20 Asst Dean .... Ms. Sandra GOLDSMITH
07 Director of Admission .... Ms. Michelle L'ETOILE
10 Chief Financial Officer .... Mr. Fred COVELLE
08 Librarian .... Ms. Anne ACTON
36 Director Career Services .... Ms. Mandie A. LEBEAU
37 Director of Financial Aid .... Mr. Eric A. KRUPSKI
06 Registrar .... Mr. David M. BERTI
18 Director of Facilities/Security .... Mr. Anthony GIORDANO
35 Director of Student Services .... Ms. Jacqueline PILGRIM

New England School of Acupuncture (C)

150 California Street, Newton MA 02458-1005
County: Middlesex — FICE Identification: 025798
Unit ID: 167181
Telephone: (617) 558-1788 — Carnegie Class: Spec/Health
FAX Number: (617) 558-1789 — Calendar System: Trimester
URL: www.nesa.edu
Established: 1975 — Annual Undergrad Tuition & Fees: $20,000
Enrollment: 180 — Coed
Affiliation or Control: Independent Non-Profit — IRS Status: 501(c)3
Highest Offering: Master's; No Lower Division
Program: Professional
Accreditation: ACUP

01 President/Executive Dean .... Susan L. GORMAN
05 Academic Dean .... Meredith ST. JOHN
07 Admissions Director .... Jason POWERS
06 Registrar .... Julia MABUCHI

Newbury College (D)

129 Fisher Avenue, Brookline MA 02445-5796
County: Norfolk — FICE Identification: 007484
Unit ID: 167251
Telephone: (617) 730-7000 — Carnegie Class: Bac/Diverse
FAX Number: (617) 731-9618 — Calendar System: Semester
URL: www.newbury.edu
Established: 1962 — Annual Undergrad Tuition & Fees: $28,950
Enrollment: 1,003 — Coed
Affiliation or Control: Independent Non-Profit — IRS Status: 501(c)3
Highest Offering: Baccalaureate
Program: Liberal Arts And General
Accreditation: EH

01 President .... Ms. Hannah M. MCCARTHY
05 VP Academic Affairs/Dean of the Col .... Dr. Hannah LEVERTOV
10 Vice President Finance/CFO .... Ms. Joyce HANLON
03 Executive Vice President .... Mr. Joseph CHILLO
32 Vice President of Student Affairs .... Mr. Paul MARTIN
30 VP for Development .... Ms. Clare MCCULLY
35 Dean of Student Affairs .... Vacant
20 Assoc Dean for Academic Services .... Ms. Sara D'ANJOU
08 Director of Library Services .... Mr. Peter G. OBUCHAN
37 Exec Dir Student Financial Services .... Mr. Elreo CAMPBELL
06 Registrar .... Ms. Rachelle E. MAZZA
27 Chief Information Officer .... Mr. Gary HAMMON
15 Director Human Resources .... Ms. Amy DOWNING
36 Director of Career Services .... Ms. Sara SHECKELLS
38 Director Counseling/Health Educ .... Ms. Susan CHAMANDY
18 Director of Facilities .... Mr. Ron MINERVINI
88 Asst VP for Adult Enrollment .... Ms. Eileen SHERIDAN
41 Director of Athletics .... Ms. Jessica GOULD
07 Interim Director of Admissions .... Ms. Jillian ANELAUSKAS
39 Director of Residence Life .... Ms. Jennifer FORRY

Nichols College (E)

Center Road, PO Box 5000, Dudley MA 01571-5000
County: Worcester — FICE Identification: 002197
Unit ID: 167260
Telephone: (508) 213-1560 — Carnegie Class: Bac/Diverse
FAX Number: N/A — Calendar System: Semester
URL: www.nichols.edu
Established: 1815 — Annual Undergrad Tuition & Fees: $32,370
Enrollment: 1,368 — Coed
Affiliation or Control: Independent Non-Profit — IRS Status: 501(c)3
Highest Offering: Master's
Program: Liberal Arts And General; Teacher Preparatory; Professional; Business Emphasis
Accreditation: EH, IACBE

01 President .... Susan WEST ENGELKEMEYER
05 Provost and Senior Vice President .... Alan J. REINHARDT
10 Vice President Administration .... Michael J. STANTON
30 Vice President for Advancement .... William C. PIECZYNSKI
88 VP Marketing & Intl Partnerships .... Thomas R. CAFARO
32 Dean of Students .... Pamela J. BOGGIO
13 Vice Pres for Information Services .... Kevin F. BRASSARD
58 Exec Dir Graduate & Prof Studies .... Kerry CALNAN
21 Assoc Vice Pres for Finance .... Patricia A. HERTZFELD
04 Exec Assistant to the President .... Cynthia L. BROWN
06 Assoc Dean Academic Admin/Records .... Peter M. ENGH
41 Assoc Dn Stdt Svcs/Dir Athletics .... Charlyn A. ROBERT
07 Director Admissions .... Paul O. BROWER
06 Registrar .... Betin ROBICHAUD
08 Director of Library .... Jim DOUGLAS
15 Director of Human Resources .... Rick WOODS
29 Director of Alumni Relations .... Brianne S. CALLAHAN
21 Controller .... Jamie SKOWYRA
35 Dir Student Activities/Orientation .... Brian QUINLAN
36 Director of Career Services .... Elizabeth HORGAN
37 Director of Financial Aid .... Denise BRINDLE
38 Director Mental Health Services . Monica GOODRICH PELLETIER
26 Director of Communications .... Ronald SCHACHTER
18 Assoc VP for Facilities Management .... Robert W. LAVIGNE
07 Associate Director of Admissions .... Paul A. MAY
96 Director Procurement & Contract Svc .... Kay F. YOUNG
19 Director Public Safety .... Jack CAULFIELD
23 Director Health Services .... Katherine NICOLETTI
39 Interim Director Residence Life .... Frank KUSTER

Northeastern University (F)

360 Huntington Avenue, Boston MA 02115-0195
County: Suffolk — FICE Identification: 002199
Unit ID: 167358
Telephone: (617) 373-2000 — Carnegie Class: RU/H
FAX Number: N/A — Calendar System: Semester
URL: www.northeastern.edu
Established: 1898 — Annual Undergrad Tuition & Fees: $40,780
Enrollment: 31,891 — Coed
Affiliation or Control: Independent Non-Profit — IRS Status: 501(c)3
Highest Offering: Doctorate
Program: Liberal Arts And General; Teacher Preparatory; Professional
Accreditation: EH, ANEST, ARCPA, AUD, BUS, CS, ENG, ENGT, LAW, NURSE, PH, PHAR, PSPSY, PTA, SP, SPAA

01 President .... Dr. Joseph E. AOUN
04 Executive Asst to the President .... Ms. Susie C. GUSZCZA
05 Sr VP Academic Affairs and Provost .... Dr. Stephen W. DIRECTOR
100 Chief of Staff .... Mr. J.D LAROCK
88 Sr Advisor to President .... Mr. John H. MCCARTHY
88 Sr VP Enroll Mgmt & Student Affairs .... Dr. Philomena V. MANTELLA
30 Sr VP University Advancement .... Ms. Diane N. MACGILLIVRAY
43 Sr VP and General Counsel .... Mr. Ralph C. MARTIN II
26 Sr VP External Affairs .... Mr. Michael A. ARMINI
11 Sr VP & Chief Operating Officer .... Mr. Steven KADISH
88 VP & Senior Counsel .... Mr. Vincent J. LEMBO
10 VP & Chief Financial Officer .... Mr. Thomas NEDELL
32 VP Student Affairs .... Dr. Laura A. WANKEL
84 VP Enrollment Management .... Ms. Jane B. BROWN
18 VP Facilities .... Ms. Nancy S. MAY
16 VP Human Resources Management .... Ms. Katherine N. PENDERGAST
29 VP Alumni Rel & Northeastern Fund .... Mr. Jack MOYNIHAN
88 VP Public Affairs .... Mr. Robert P. GITTENS
86 VP Government Relations .... Mr. Tim E. LESHAN
13 VP Information Services .... Mr. Rehan KHAN
31 VP City & Community Affairs .... Mr. John M. TOBIN
88 VP Advancement & Campaign Director .... Mr. Joseph DONNELLY, JR.
88 VP Enterprise Risk Management .... Ms. Deloris PETTIS
45 VP Campus Planning & Development .... Ms. Kathy SPIEGELMAN
88 VP Development .... Ms. Luanne KIRWIN
46 Sr Vice Provost Research & Grad Ed .... Dr. Melvin BERNSTEIN
20 Vice Provost for Undergrad Ed .... Dr. Bruce E. RONKIN
20 Vice Provost Academic Affairs .... Dr. Mary LOEFFELHOLZ
88 Vice Provost Budget/Planning/Admin .... Dr. Anthony RINI
89 Vice Provost Honors & FY Programs .... Dr. Susan G. POWERS-LEE
88 Vice Prov Hlth Rsch/Dean Acad Affs .... Dr. Stephen ZOLOTH
28 Vice Prov Inst Diversity & Inclsn .... Dr. John ARMENDARIZ
108 Vice Provost Teaching & Learning .... Dr. Susan AMBROSE
88 VP Business Affs Graduate Campuses . Mr. M. Seamus HARREYS
36 Assoc VP Career Services & Co-Op .... Ms. Maria K. STEIN
07 AVP Enrollment .... Ms. Ronne PATRICK-TURNER
35 AVP Student Affairs .... Ms. Madeleine A. ESTABROOK
09 AVP Institutional Rsch & Data Admin .... Dr. Nancy M. LUDWIG
25 AVP Research Administration ...... Ms. Deborah GRUPP-PATRUTZ
88 AVP Graduate Affairs .... Dr. Phil HE
76 Dean Bouve College Health Science .... Dr. Terry FULMER
77 Dean Col Computer & Info Science ..... Dr. Larry A. FINKELSTEIN
54 Dean College of Engineering .... Dr. Nadine AUBRY
81 Dean College of Science .... Dr. J. Murray GIBSON
50 Dean D'Amore-McKim School of Bus .... Dr. Hugh COURTNEY
61 Dean School of Law .... Dr. Jeremy PAUL
57 Dean College of Arts/Media & Design .... Dr. Xavier COSTA
83 Dean Col of Soc Sci & Humanities .... Dr. Uta POIGER
107 Dean Col Prof Studies/VP Prof Educ .... Dr. John G. LABRIE
08 Dean University Libraries .... Mr. William M. WAKELING
06 University Registrar .... Ms. Linda D. ALLEN
42 Exec Dir Sprituality & Dialogue .... Mr. Alexander KERN
92 Director of Honors Program .... Dr. Maureen E. KELLEHER
21 Director of Finance & Treasurer .... Dr. Samuel B. SOLOMON
19 Director of Public Safety .... Mr. D. Joseph GRIFFIN
27 Director of Communications .... Ms. Renata NYUL
41 Director of Athletics .... Mr. Peter P. ROBY

Northpoint Bible College (G)

320 South Main Street, Haverhill MA 01835
County: Essex — FICE Identification: 035705
Unit ID: 217606
Telephone: (978) 478-3400 — Carnegie Class: Spec/Faith
FAX Number: (978) 478-3406 — Calendar System: Semester
URL: www.northpoint.edu
Established: 1924 — Annual Undergrad Tuition & Fees: $10,543
Enrollment: 402 — Coed
Affiliation or Control: Assemblies Of God Church — IRS Status: 501(c)3
Highest Offering: Master's
Program: Religious Emphasis
Accreditation: BI

01 President .... Rev Dr. David J. ARNETT
03 Executive Vice President .... Rev Dr. Patrick G. GALLAGHER
32 Vice President of Student Affairs ...... Rev. David HANSHUMAKER
10 Director of Finance .... Mr. Ed LAUGHLIN
07 Director of Admissions .... Rev. David HODGE
08 Head Librarian .... Miss Ginger MCDONALD
37 Director of Financial Aid .... Miss Patricia STAUFFER

Pine Manor College (H)

400 Heath Street, Chestnut Hill MA 02467-2332
County: Norfolk — FICE Identification: 002201
Unit ID: 167455
Telephone: (617) 731-7000 — Carnegie Class: Bac/A&S
FAX Number: (617) 731-7199 — Calendar System: Semester
URL: www.pmc.edu
Established: 1911 — Annual Undergrad Tuition & Fees: $24,300
Enrollment: 317 — Coed
Affiliation or Control: Independent Non-Profit — IRS Status: 501(c)3
Highest Offering: Master's
Program: Liberal Arts And General
Accreditation: #EH

01 Interim President .... Dr. Joseph LEE
05 Dean of College .... Dr. William VOGELE
11 Vice President for Finance .... Mr. Neil BUCKLEY
30 Vice President for Development .... Mr. Ken SPRITZ
32 Dean Student Affs/Cmty Engagement .... Ms. Jamica LOVE
84 Director of Enrollment .... Vacant
10 Director of Finance .... Mr. Timothy JOHNSON
15 Director of Human Resources .... Mr. William OPAVA
06 Registrar .... Mr. Jeffrey MEI
26 Dir Publications/Media Relations .... Ms. Efrat ZINNAR-SHAVIT
08 Interim Library Director .... Ms. Sarah WOOLF

Quincy College (I)

1250 Hancock Street, Quincy MA 02169-4324
County: Norfolk — FICE Identification: 002205
Unit ID: 167525
Telephone: (617) 984-1700 — Carnegie Class: Assoc/Pub-S-MC
FAX Number: (617) 984-1779 — Calendar System: Semester
URL: www.quincycollege.edu
Established: 1956 — Annual Undergrad Tuition & Fees (In-District): $5,675
Enrollment: 4,495 — Coed
Affiliation or Control: Local — IRS Status: 501(c)3

Highest Offering: Associate Degree
Program: Occupational; 2-Year Principally Bachelor's Creditable
Accreditation: **EH**, ADNUR, MLTAD, PNUR, SURGT

01 President .... Mr. Peter H. TSAFFARAS
05 Vice Pres Academic Affairs .... Vacant
11 Vice Pres Administration/Finance .... Vacant
100 Assistant to the President .... Dr. Robert BAKER
10 Chief Financial Officer .... Vacant
04 Admin Asst to President .... Ms. Donna M. BRUGMAN
06 Dir of Student Records & Registrar .... Ms. Catherine MALONEY
66 Dean of Nursing .... Ms. Roxanne MIHAL
49 Dean of Liberal Arts .... Dr. Robert BAKER
50 Dean of Business & Public Service .... Dr. Sandra SMALES
81 Dean of Natural & Health Sciences .... Vacant
21 Director of Finance .... Mr. Martin AHERN
13 Assoc VP/Comm & Info Technology .... Mr. Tom C. PHAM
12 Dean of Plymouth Campus .... Ms. Mary BURKE
37 Assoc VP for Financial Aid .... Ms. Rose M. DEVITO
18 Dir of Admin Services & Facilities .... Mr. William C. HALL
32 Assoc VP for Student Development .... Ms. Susan G. BOSSA
15 Vice Pres for Human Resources .... Ms. Mary SCOTT
26 Dir Strategic Mktg/Brand Mgmt .... Mr. Taggart BOYLE
07 Interim Director of Admissions .... Ms. Catherine MALONEY
07 Associate Director of Admission .... Ms. Fotini AROCHO
85 Director of Int'l Student Services .... Ms. Lisa STACK
103 Dir of Workforce Development .... Mr. Gary G. WALLRAPP
09 Assoc VP for Inst Research & Assess .... Dr. Kimberly PUHALA
35 Director of Student Development .... Ms. Kathi SCHAEFFER
08 Director of Library Services .... Ms. Susan WHITEHEAD

Regis College (A)

235 Wellesley Street, Weston MA 02493-1571
County: Middlesex — FICE Identification: 002206
Unit ID: 167598
Telephone: (781) 768-7000 — Carnegie Class: Spec/Health
FAX Number: (781) 768-8339 — Calendar System: Semester
URL: www.regiscollege.edu
Established: 1927 — Annual Undergrad Tuition & Fees: $34,380
Enrollment: 1,991 — Coed
Affiliation or Control: Independent Non-Profit — IRS Status: 501(c)3
Highest Offering: Doctorate
Program: Liberal Arts And General; Teacher Preparatory; Professional
Accreditation: **EH**, ADNUR, NMT, NUR, RAD, SW

01 President .... Dr. Antoinette M. HAYS
10 Vice President Finance/Business .... Mr. Thomas G. PISTORINO
84 Vice Pres Enrollment & Marketing .... Mr. Paul VACCARO
20 Assoc Vice Pres Academic Affairs .... Vacant
07 Director of Admission .... Ms. Wanda SURIEL
37 Director of Financial Aid .... Ms. Bonnie QUINN
06 Registrar .... Ms. Esther A. GHAZARIAN
09 Dean of Institutional Research .... Dr. Susan TAMMARO
15 Director of Human Resources .... Ms. Joan D. SULLIVAN
18 Director of Physical Plant .... Mr. Joseph SHAUGHNESSY
21 Director Finance & Business .... Mr. Steven SAVAS
29 Director of Alumni Relations .... Mrs. Christina DUGGAN
32 Dean of Students .... Ms. Kara KOLOMITZ
23 Director of Health Services .... Ms. Dianna JONES
04 Special Assistant to President .... Ms. Mary Jane DOHERTY
08 Director of Library .... Ms. Lynn TRIPLETT
13 Director ITS .... Ms. Marla BOTELHO
41 Director Athletics & Physical Ed .... Mr. Robert RILEY
42 Director Campus Ministry .... Sr. Elizabeth CONWAY
96 Director of Purchasing .... Ms. Diep SHEEHAN
31 Director of Community Living .... Mr. Shawn EDIE
44 Director Annual Fund .... Ms. Tara BRADY
35 Director of Student Programs .... Ms. Jessica HOMER
30 Chief Development Officer .... Ms. Miriam FINN-SHERMAN

Saint John's Seminary (B)

127 Lake Street, Brighton MA 02135-3898
County: Suffolk — FICE Identification: 002214
Unit ID: 167677
Telephone: (617) 254-2610 — Carnegie Class: Spec/Faith
FAX Number: (617) 787-2336 — Calendar System: Semester
URL: www.sjs.edu
Established: 1884 — Annual Undergrad Tuition & Fees: $26,000
Enrollment: 197 — Male
Affiliation or Control: Roman Catholic — IRS Status: 501(c)3
Highest Offering: Master's
Program: Professional; Religious Emphasis
Accreditation: **EH**, THEOL

01 Rector .... Msgr. James MORONEY
03 Vice Rector .... Rev. Christopher K. O'CONNOR
05 Dean of Faculty .... Rev. Paul METILLY
32 Dean of Students .... Rev. Edward RILEY
07 Director of Admissions & Records .... Mrs. Maureen DEBERNARDI
08 Librarian .... Rev. Raymond VAN DE MOORTELL
10 Director Finance and Operations .... Mr. Richard A. FLAHERTY
73 Director Pre-Theology Program .... Rev. Joseph SCORZELLO
21 Asst Finance Director .... Mr. Armand DILANDO

Salter College (C)

645 Shawinigan Drive, Chicopee MA 01020-3744
Telephone: (508) 853-1074 — Identification: 770724
Accreditation: **ACICS**

† Main campus is Salter College in West Boylston, MA.

Salter College (D)

184 West Boylston Street, West Boylston MA 01583
County: Worcester — FICE Identification: 004666
Unit ID: 167738
Telephone: (508) 853-1074 — Carnegie Class: Assoc/PrivFP
FAX Number: (508) 853-1674 — Calendar System: Semester
URL: www.saltercollege-us.com
Established: 1937 — Annual Undergrad Tuition & Fees: N/A
Enrollment: 465 — Coed
Affiliation or Control: Proprietary — IRS Status: Proprietary
Highest Offering: Associate Degree
Program: Occupational; 2-Year Principally Bachelor's Creditable
Accreditation: **ACICS**, ACFEI, DA, MAC

01 Campus Director .... Dr. David GOODWIN

Sanford-Brown College of Boston, Inc. (E)

126 Newbury Street, Boston MA 02116-2904
County: Suffolk — FICE Identification: 007481
Unit ID: 166276
Telephone: (617) 578-7100 — Carnegie Class: Assoc/PrivFP
FAX Number: (617) 262-6210 — Calendar System: Other
URL: www.sanfordbrown.edu/boston
Established: 1917 — Annual Undergrad Tuition & Fees: $15,220
Enrollment: 246 — Coed
Affiliation or Control: Proprietary — IRS Status: Proprietary
Highest Offering: Associate Degree
Program: Occupational; 2-Year Principally Bachelor's Creditable; Technical Emphasis
Accreditation: **ACICS**, CVT

01 President .... Dr. Richard FARMER
05 Academic Dean .... Ms. Debra HESSELL
08 Librarian .... Mr. William GREALISH
07 Director of Admissions .... Ms. Jaimee TYLER
37 Director of Financial Aid .... Mr. Jay BEIRNE
06 Registrar .... Ms. Elisa ADAMS
36 Director Career Services .... Ms. Laura MEYER

School of the Museum of Fine Arts-Boston (F)

230 The Fenway, Boston MA 02115-5518
County: Suffolk — FICE Identification: 004667
Unit ID: 166984
Telephone: (617) 267-6100 — Carnegie Class: Spec/Arts
FAX Number: (617) 424-6271 — Calendar System: Semester
URL: www.smfa.edu
Established: 1876 — Annual Undergrad Tuition & Fees: $39,170
Enrollment: 644 — Coed
Affiliation or Control: Independent Non-Profit — IRS Status: 501(c)3
Highest Offering: Master's
Program: Liberal Arts And General; Teacher Preparatory; Fine Arts Emphasis
Accreditation: **ART**

01 President .... Chris BRATTON
04 Executive Assistant .... Christine WILLIS
05 Senior VP for Academic Affairs/Dean .... Sarah MCKINNON
06 Registrar .... Taylor HORNER
30 VP for Inst Advance/Ext Relations .... Anne COWIE
84 VP and Dean of Enrollment .... Eric THOMPSON
10 Chief Financial Officer .... Mark KERWIN
21 Director of Financial Operations .... Barbara DONNELLAN
09 Assoc VP Operations and Research .... Mary ROETZEL
32 Dean of Students .... Vacant
45 Budget and Planning Officer .... Christopher FOX
51 Director Artist's Res Ctr/Cont Educ .... Debra SAMDPERIL
20 Assoc VP Academic Administration .... Greg D'ANGELO
58 Assoc Dean Graduate Studies .... David BROWN
37 Director of Financial Aid .... Beth GOREHAM
20 Assoc Dean Undergraduate Studies .... Susan LUSH
88 Bursar .... Rosalyn NAZZARO
07 Director of Admissions .... Lorie KOMLYN
27 Dir of Marketing & Communications .... Amanda KARR
44 Senior Development Officer .... Alexandra HUFF
26 Press Coordinator .... Brooke DANIELS
29 Dir Alum Relations/Special Projects .... Stephanie BOYE'
08 Librarian .... Darin MURPHY
90 Mgr of Instructional Technology .... Matthew GIRARD
40 School Store Manager .... Terri NORDONE
88 Assoc Dir Artist Resource Center .... Catherine TUTTER
35 Asst Director of Student Life .... Ryan O'CONNELL
39 Asst Dir of Residential Housing .... Holly GOULD
18 Director SMFA Campus Facilities .... Arthur TRENOWITH
15 Director Human Resources .... Jane O'REILLY
96 Director of Purchasing .... Brendan MULLIGAN
19 Director of Protective Services .... Craig MCQUATE
88 Curator .... Joanna SOLTAN

Simmons College (G)

300 The Fenway, Boston MA 02115-5898
County: Suffolk — FICE Identification: 002208
Unit ID: 167783
Telephone: (617) 521-2000 — Carnegie Class: Master's L
FAX Number: (617) 521-3065 — Calendar System: Semester
URL: www.simmons.edu
Established: 1899 — Annual Undergrad Tuition & Fees: $35,370
Enrollment: 4,830 — Coordinate
Affiliation or Control: Independent Non-Profit — IRS Status: 501(c)3
Highest Offering: Doctorate
Program: Liberal Arts And General; Teacher Preparatory; Professional
Accreditation: **EH**, BUS, DIETD, DIETI, HSA, LIB, NURSE, PTA, SW

01 President .... Helen G. DRINAN
04 Assistant to the President .... Marianne FIGUEIREDO
05 Provost .... Sheila "Katie" CONBOY
20 Associate Provost .... Andrew EFFRAT
62 Dean Grad Sch Library/Info Science .... Eileen G. ABELS
76 Dean Sch Nursing & Health Sciences .... Judy BEAL
70 Dean School of Social Work .... Stefan KRUG
50 Dean School of Management .... Cathy MINEHAN
49 Dean College of Arts & Sciences .... Renee WHITE
104 Program Manager Study Abroad .... Laura BEY
06 Asst VP Acad Operations & Registrar .... Donna M. DOLAN
108 Director Assessment .... Vacant
08 Director Library .... Daphne HARRINGTON
25 Director Sponsored Programs .... Jon KIMBALL
09 Director Institutional Research .... Heather S. ROSCOE
36 Director Career Education Center .... Andrea WOLF
10 Sr VP Finance/Admin/Treasurer .... Stefano FALCONI
21 Asst VP Finance .... Patricia C. FALLON
37 Director Student Financial Services .... Daniel FORSTER
13 Executive Director Technology CIO .... Debra ORR
14 Sr Dir Enterprise Applications & Sv .... Michael PENNACHIO
11 Asst VP Administration .... Janet FISHSTEIN
19 Director Public Safety .... Sean COLLINS
96 Director Purchasing & Procurement .... Kathy PERONI-CALLAHAN
26 VP Marketing & Admissions .... Cheryl HOWARD
07 Asst VP Undergrad Admission & Mktg .... Catherine CAPOLUPO
07 Assistant VP Graduate Admissions .... Kristen HAACK
26 Director Marketing Communications .... Allyson IRISH
30 VP Advancement .... Marianne E. LORD
30 Assoc VP Capital Giving .... Laura BRINK
102 Director Corp/Foundation Relations .... Amy FISHER
44 Asst VP Annual Fund and Alumnae/i .... Janice TAYLOR
32 Dean Student Life .... Sarah NEILL
42 Spiritual Life Program Manager .... Bonnie-Jeanne CASEY
38 Clinical Director Counseling Svcs .... Sherri ETTINGER
39 Director Residence Life .... Jessica FAULK
41 Director Athletics .... Ali KANTOR
35 Assoc Dean Office for Student Life .... Lisa SMITH-MCQUEENIE
43 VP & General Counsel .... Kathleen R. ROGERS
15 VP Talent & Human Capital Strategy .... Regina SHERWOOD

Smith College (H)

Northampton MA 01063-0001
County: Hampshire — FICE Identification: 002209
Unit ID: 167835
Telephone: (413) 584-2700 — Carnegie Class: Bac/A&S
FAX Number: (413) 585-2123 — Calendar System: Semester
URL: www.smith.edu
Established: 1871 — Annual Undergrad Tuition & Fees: $42,840
Enrollment: 3,209 — Female
Affiliation or Control: Independent Non-Profit — IRS Status: 501(c)3
Highest Offering: Doctorate
Program: Liberal Arts And General; Teacher Preparatory; Professional
Accreditation: **EH**, ENG, SW

01 President .... Kathleen MCCARTNEY
04 Secretary to the President .... Beth BERG
10 Vice Pres Finance & Administration .... Ruth H. CONSTANTINE
05 Provost & Dean of the Faculty .... Marilyn R. SCHUSTER
20 Dean for Academic Development .... Joseph O'ROURKE
32 Dean of the College .... Maureen A. MAHONEY
35 Dean of Students .... Julianne OHOTNICKY
70 Dean School for Social Work .... Carolyn JACOBS
39 Director of Residence Life .... Becky SHAW
85 Assoc Dean International Students .... Hrayr TAMZARIAN
30 Associate VP for Development .... Sandra DOUCETT
38 Assoc Dir Health Svcs/Stdnt Counsel .... Pamela MCCARTHY
26 VP for Public Affairs .... Laurie FENLASON
29 Exec Director Alumnae Association .... Jennifer S. CHRISLER
13 Exec Director Info Technology Svcs .... David D. GREGORY
09 Dir Inst Research and Edu Assess .... Cate ROWEN
08 Director of Libraries .... Christopher LORING
15 Assoc VP for Human Resources .... Lawrence HUNT
07 Dean of Admission .... Debra D. SHAVER
58 Director of Graduate Study .... Danielle D. RAMDATH
37 Dir Student Financial Services .... David J. BELANGER
06 Registrar .... Patricia A. O'NEIL
36 Director Career Development Office .... Stacie HAGENBAUGH
28 Dir for Inst Diversity and Equity .... Pamela NOLAN YOUNG
88 Associate Dean of the Faculty .... Danielle D. RAMDATH
18 Assoc VP for Facilities Management .... John SHENETTE
23 Director of Health Services .... Leslie R. JAFFE
41 Director of Athletics .... Lynn OBERBILLIG
42 Dean of Religious Life .... Jennifer L. WALTERS
43 Office of General Counsel .... Vacant
84 Assoc VP for Enrollment .... Audrey Y. SMITH
96 Procurement Director .... Linda HIESIGER

Springfield College (I)

263 Alden Street, Springfield MA 01109-3788
County: Hampden — FICE Identification: 002211
Unit ID: 167899
Telephone: (413) 748-3000 — Carnegie Class: Master's L
FAX Number: (413) 748-3746 — Calendar System: Semester
URL: www.spfldcol.edu
Established: 1885 — Annual Undergrad Tuition & Fees: $31,690

Enrollment: 3,284 Coed
Affiliation or Control: Independent Non-Profit IRS Status: 501(c)3
Highest Offering: Doctorate
Program: Liberal Arts And General; Professional
Accreditation: EH, ARCPA, CORE, EXSC, IACBE, NRPA, OT, PTA, SW

01 President ... Dr. Mary-Beth COOPER
45 Executive Vice President ... Dr. Jill F. RUSSELL
04 Special Assistant to President ... Ms. Mary Lou DYJAK
05 Vice President Academic Affairs ... Dr. Jean A. WYLD
29 Vice President Devel & Alumni Rels ... Mr. John A. WHITE
10 VP for Administration/Finance ... Mr. John MAILHOT
32 VP Student Affairs/Dean of Students ... Dr. David BRAVERMAN
20 Assistant VP Academic Affairs ... Dr. Mary Ann COUGHLIN
15 Asst Vice President Admin/Finance ... Ms. Rosanne CAPTAIN
21 Treasurer ... Mr. Michael DOBISE
30 Associate VP Development ... Mr. Scott M. BERG
84 Dir Enrollment Management ... Ms. Mary DEANGELO
06 Registrar ... Mr. Keith INGALLS
07 Dir Undergrad Admission ... Mr. Richard VERES
08 Director Library ... Ms. Andrea S. TAUPIER
29 Director Alumni Programs ... Ms. Tamie KIDESS LUCEY
37 Director of Financial Aid ... Mr. Edward CIOSEK
36 Director Career Services ... Ms. Barbara K. KAUTZ
13 Chief Information Officer ... Mr. Danny DAVIS
90 Director Academic Computer Center ... Mr. Thomas F. LARKIN
26 Director of Marketing/Communication ... Mr. Stephen ROULIER
38 Director of Counseling Center ... Mr. Brian KRYLOWICZ
19 Director Campus Police Department ... Ms. L. Judy JACKSON
88 Director YMCA Programs ... Mr. Harry ROCK
85 Director of International Center ... Dr. Deborah ALM
42 Director Campus Ministry ... Mr. David MCMAHON
18 Director of Facilities & Campus Svc ... Mr. Stephen LEFEVER
39 Director of Residence Life ... Mr. Tarome ALFORD
41 Director of Athletics ... Dr. Cathie SCHWEITZER
96 Director of Purchasing ... Ms. Lita ADAMS
28 Director Multicultural Affairs ... Mr. John WILSON

Stonehill College (A)

320 Washington Street, Easton MA 02357-6110
County: Bristol FICE Identification: 002217
Unit ID: 167996
Telephone: (508) 565-1000 Carnegie Class: Bac/A&S
FAX Number: (508) 565-1500 Calendar System: Semester
URL: www.stonehill.edu
Established: 1948 Annual Undergrad Tuition & Fees: $49,970
Enrollment: 2,602 Coed
Affiliation or Control: Roman Catholic IRS Status: 501(c)3
Highest Offering: Master's
Program: Liberal Arts And General; Teacher Preparatory; Professional
Accreditation: EH, BUS

01 President ... Rev. John F. DENNING, CSC
05 Provost/VP for Acad Affairs ... Dr. Joseph FAVAZZA
10 Vice Pres for Finance & Treasurer ... Ms. Jeanne FINLAYSON
30 Vice President for Advancement ... Mr. Francis X. DILLON
32 Interim VP of Student Affairs ... Ms. Pauline DOBROWSKI
88 Vice President for Mission ... Rev. James LIES, CSC
84 VP for Enrollment Mgmt & Marketing ... Mr. Christopher LYDON
21 AVP for Finance & Operations ... Mr. Craig BINNEY
35 Assoc VP for Students Affairs ... Ms. Pauline DOBROWSKI
20 Assoc VP for Academic Affairs ... Dr. Joseph FAVAZZA
18 Assoc VP for Operations ... Vacant
37 Asst VP/Dir of Student Aid/Finance ... Mrs. Eileen K. O'LEARY
04 Sr Executive Asst to the President ... Mrs. Jessica L. GRACIA
20 Dean of the Faculty ... Dr. Maria CURTIN
43 General Counsel ... Mr. Thomas V. FLYNN
21 Controller ... Ms. Jennifer MATHEWS
07 Dean of Admissions ... Mr. Daniel MONAHAN
06 Registrar ... Mr. John PESTANA
09 Director Planning/Inst Research ... Ms. Laura J. UERLING
08 Director of College Library ... Ms. Cheryl MCGRATH
26 Dir of Media Rels & Communications ... Mr. Martin P. MCGOVERN
29 Director of Alumni Affairs ... Ms. Anne M. SANT
15 Director of Human Resources ... Ms. Maryann B. PERRY
38 Dir of Counseling & Testing Center ... Ms. Maria A. KAVANAUGH
27 Chief Information Officer ... Ms. Tamara ANDERSON
19 Chief of Police ... Mr. Peter CARNES
42 Director Campus Ministry ... Rev. Hugh CLEARY, CSC
90 Manager of Instructional Technology ... Ms. Janice HARRISON
45 Director of Academic Development ... Ms. Bonnie L. TROUPE
88 Dir of Enterprise Infrastructure ... Mr. Thomas MCGRATH
23 Director of Health Services ... Mrs. Maria SULLIVAN
36 Director of Career Services ... Ms. Heather HEERMAN
41 Dir of Intercollegiate Athletics ... Mr. Brendan SULLIVAN
92 Director of Honors Program ... Prof. John LANCI
44 Director of Development ... Mr. Douglas J. SMITH
20 Asst Dean for Academic Services ... Mr. Kevin PISKADLO
96 Director of Purchasing ... Mr. Gregory WOLFE
45 Asst VP for Planning & Budgeting ... Mr. Stephen BEAUREGARD
39 Director of Residence Life ... Ms. Ali HICKS
24 Dir of Media/Videography Services ... Mr. Michael PIETROWSKI
40 Manager of College Bookstore ... Mrs. Mary DUNCKLEE
88 Dean of Academic Achievement ... Dr. Craig ALMEIDA
97 Dir Gen Educ/First Year Experience ... Dr. Todd S. GERNES
18 Dir of Facilities Management ... Mr. Bruce BOYER
88 Dir of Ctr for Teaching & Learning ... Ms. Stacy GROOTERS
104 Director International Programs ... Ms. Alice CRONIN
31 Campus Minister for Community Svc ... Ms. Mary Anne CAPPELLERI
88 Dir Ctr for Academic Achievement ... Dr. Martha UCCI
28 Director of Intercultural Affairs ... Ms. Liza TALUSAN

Suffolk University (B)

8 Ashburton Place, Boston MA 02108-2770
County: Suffolk FICE Identification: 002218
Unit ID: 168005
Telephone: (617) 573-8000 Carnegie Class: Master's L
FAX Number: (617) 573-8353 Calendar System: Semester
URL: www.suffolk.edu
Established: 1906 Annual Undergrad Tuition & Fees: $30,792
Enrollment: 9,192 Coed
Affiliation or Control: Independent Non-Profit IRS Status: 501(c)3
Highest Offering: Doctorate
Program: Liberal Arts And General; Teacher Preparatory; Professional
Accreditation: EH, ART, BUS, BUSA, CIDA, CLPSY, ENG, IPSY, LAW, RADDOS, RTT, SPAA

01 President ... Dr. James MCCARTHY
05 Sr VP Academic Affs/Provost ... Dr. Bernard KEENAN
10 Sr VP Finance/Admin/Treasurer ... Ms. Danielle MANNING
30 Sr Vice Pres for Advancement ... Mr. Stephen MORIN
84 Vice Pres Enrollment Mgmt ... Mr. Walter CAFFEY, III
26 VP Marketing/Communications ... Mr. Greg GATLIN
86 VP Government/Community Affairs ... Mr. John A. NUCCI
20 Vice Prov Faculty Devel/Curriculum ... Mr. Jeffrey POKORAK
37 AVP/Dir of Financial Aid ... Ms. Christine M. PERRY
100 Chief of Staff ... Ms. Jen MURRAY
32 Dean of Student Affairs ... Dr. Nancy C. STOLL
50 Dean Sawyer Business School ... Mr. William J. O'NEILL, JR.
61 Dean of the Law School ... Ms. Camile NELSON
49 Dean College Arts & Science ... Dr. Kenneth S. GREENBERG
22 Chief Diversity/Inclusion Officer ... Ms. Nicole G. PRICE
07 Director Undergraduate Admission ... Mr. John HAMEL
07 Director Graduate Admission ... Ms. Judith L. REYNOLDS
08 Director of Sawyer Library ... Mr. Robert E. DUGAN
06 College Registrar ... Miss Mary LALLY
36 Director Career Plng & Placement ... Mr. Paul TANKLEFSKY
15 Director of Human Resources ... Ms. Judy MINARDI
29 Director of Alumni Affairs/Law Sch ... Ms. Diane SCHOENFELD
13 Chief Information Officer ... Mr. Fouad YATIM
19 Captain University Police ... Mr. John PAGLIARULO
35 Director of Student Activities ... Mr. John SILVERIA
41 Int Director of Athletics ... Mr. Cary MCCONNELL
18 Sr Dir Facilites Plng & Mgmt ... Mr. Gordon B. KING
07 Director of Law School Admission ... Ms. Gail ELLIS
06 Law School Registrar ... Ms. Lorraine D. COVE
36 Director of Law School Placement ... Mr. David JAMES
08 Law Librarian ... Ms. Elizabeth MCKENZIE
09 Director of Institutional Research ... Mr. Michael B. DUGGAN
38 Director of Student Counseling ... Dr. Kenneth F. GARNI
21 Associate Business Officer ... Mr. Gregory HARRIS

Tufts University (C)

Medford MA 02155-5555
County: Middlesex FICE Identification: 002219
Unit ID: 168148
Telephone: (617) 628-5000 Carnegie Class: RU/VH
FAX Number: N/A Calendar System: Semester
URL: www.tufts.edu
Established: 1852 Annual Undergrad Tuition & Fees: $46,598
Enrollment: 10,838 Coed
Affiliation or Control: Independent Non-Profit IRS Status: 501(c)3
Highest Offering: Doctorate
Program: Liberal Arts And General; Teacher Preparatory; Professional
Accreditation: EH, #ARCPA, CS, DENT, DIETI, ENG, IPSY, MED, OT, PH, PLNG, VET

01 President ... Dr. Anthony P. MONACO
100 Chief of Staff ... Mr. Michael BAENEN
03 Executive Vice President ... Ms. Patricia CAMPBELL
05 Sr Vice President/Provost ... Mr. David R. HARRIS
26 Sr Vice Pres University Relations ... Ms. Mary R. JEKA
30 Vice Pres University Advancement ... Mr. Eric C. JOHNSON
11 Vice President for Operations ... Ms. Linda SNYDER
10 Vice President Finance/Treasurer ... Mr. Thomas S. MCGURTY
16 Vice President for Human Resources ... Ms. Linda CATALDO
13 VP & Chief Information Officer ... Mr. David J. KAHLE
46 Vice Provost for Research ... Ms. Diane SOUVAINE
09 Assoc Provost Inst Res & Eval ... Dr. Dawn G. TERKLA
20 Associate Provost ... Dr. Mary Y. LEE
20 Assistant Provost ... Vacant
21 Assistant Provost for Admin/Finance ... Ms. Celia K. CAMPBELL
29 Exec Director Alumni Relations ... Mr. Tim BROOKS
45 Exec Dir Planning & Administration ... Ms. Martha POKRAS
22 Exec Director Inst Diversity ... Vacant
15 Sr Director Human Res & Talent Mgmt ... Ms. Alison A. BLACKBURN
23 Sr Director Health/Wellness Svcs ... Ms. Michelle D. BOWDLER
43 Senior Legal Counsel ... Mr. Martin OPPENHEIMER
37 Director of Financial Aid ... Ms. Patricia REILLY
26 Director Public Relations ... Ms. Kimberly M. THURLER
36 Director Career Services ... Ms. Jean M. PAPALIA
08 Director Tisch Library ... Ms. Laura WOOD
18 Director of Facilities Services ... Mr. Bob BURNS
28 Director Equal Opportunity ... Ms. Jill A. ZELLMER
38 Director Mental Health Services ... Dr. Julie S. ROSS
19 Director Public & Env Safety ... Mr. Kevin C. MAGUIRE
49 Dean Arts & Sciences ... Dr. Joanne E. BERGER-SWEENEY
54 Dean of Engineering ... Dr. Linda ABRIOLA
58 Dean Grad School of Arts & Science ... Vacant
82 Dean Fletcher Sch Law & Diplomacy ... Adm. James STAVRIDIS
52 Dean of Dental Medicine ... Dr. Huw F. THOMAS
74 Dean Cummings Sch of Veterinary Med ... Dr. Deborah KOCHEVAR
63 Dean Medical School ... Dr. Harris BERMAN
88 Dean Sackler School ... Dr. Naomi ROSENBERG
88 Interim Dean Friedman School Nutri ... Dr. Robin KANAREK
88 Dean Tisch College ... Mr. Alan SOLOMONT
53 Dean Undergrad & Grad Educ ... Mr. John BARKER
88 Dean Academic Adv & Undergrad Study ... Dr. Carmen LOWE
88 Dean of Student Services/Art & Sci ... Mr. Paul STANTON
32 Dean of Campus Life & Stdnt Ldrshp ... Mr. Bruce REITMAN
07 Dean Undergrad Admiss/Enroll Mgt ... Mr. Lee A. COFFIN
06 Registrar ASE & Stdnt Svcs Desk Mgr ... Ms. Jo Ann JACK
96 Purchasing Director ... Ms. Diane M. DEVLIN
41 Director Athletics ... Mr. William GEHLING
42 Interim Chaplain ... Rev. Patricia BUDD KEPLER

University of Phoenix Boston Campus (D)

19 Granite Street, Suite 300, Braintree MA 02184-1744
Telephone: (866) 867-3678 Identification: 770209
Accreditation: &NH, ACBSP

† Main campus is University of Phoenix in Tempe, AZ.

Urban College of Boston (E)

178 Tremont Street, Boston MA 02111-1093
County: Suffolk FICE Identification: 031305
Unit ID: 429128
Telephone: (617) 348-6359 Carnegie Class: Assoc/PrivNFP
FAX Number: (617) 423-4758 Calendar System: Semester
URL: www.urbancollege.edu
Established: 1993 Annual Undergrad Tuition & Fees: $8,880
Enrollment: 510 Coed
Affiliation or Control: Independent Non-Profit IRS Status: 501(c)3
Highest Offering: Associate Degree
Program: 2-Year Principally Bachelor's Creditable
Accreditation: #EH

01 President ... Mr. Michael TAYLOR
05 Academic Dean ... Ms. Nancy C. DANIEL
84 Dean Enrollment Svcs & Registrar ... Vacant
32 Dean of Students/Dir Student Affs ... Ms. Carmen PINEDA
37 Director of Financial Aid ... Ms. Mia TAYLOR
88 Director of Special Projects ... Ms. Amanda NORRIS
07 Director of Admissions ... Ms. Jane DOLLOFF
20 Curriculum Coordinator ... Ms. Tong FENG
10 Business Manager ... Ms. Denise HARGAN

Wellesley College (F)

106 Central Street, Wellesley MA 02481-8203
County: Norfolk FICE Identification: 002224
Unit ID: 168218
Telephone: (781) 283-1000 Carnegie Class: Bac/A&S
FAX Number: (781) 283-3639 Calendar System: Semester
URL: www.wellesley.edu
Established: 1875 Annual Undergrad Tuition & Fees: $57,042
Enrollment: 2,481 Female
Affiliation or Control: Independent Non-Profit IRS Status: 501(c)3
Highest Offering: Baccalaureate
Program: Liberal Arts And General
Accreditation: EH

01 President ... Kim BOTTOMLY
05 Provost & Dean of the College ... Andrew SHENNAN
30 VP for Resources & Public Affairs ... Cameran MASON
10 Vice Pres Finance Administration ... Ben HAMMOND
18 Asst VP Facilities Management/Plng ... Peter ZURAW
27 Chief Information Officer ... Ganesan RAVISHANKER
07 Dean of Admission/Financial Aid ... Jennifer DESJARLAIS
32 Dean of Students ... Debra DEMEIS
42 Dn Intercult Educ/Relig/Spirit Life ... Victor H. KAZANJIAN
20 Dean of Academic Affairs ... Richard G. FRENCH
20 Dean of Faculty Affairs ... Kathryn LYNCH
09 Asc Prov Institutional Plng/Assess ... Elena BERNAL
28 Asc Prov/Acad Dir Diversity/Inclsn ... Robbin CHAPMAN
06 Registrar ... Carol SHANMUGARATNAM
29 Executive Director Alumnae Assn ... Susan CHALLENGER
37 Director of Student Financial Svcs ... Scott JUEDES
15 Acting Dir Human Res/Auxiliary Svcs ... Carolyn SLABODEN
36 Director Center for Work & Service ... Joanne S. MURRAY
26 Chief Public Relations Officer ... Elizabeth T. GILDERSLEEVE
35 Assoc Director Student Involvement ... Megan K. JORDAN
38 Administrative Counseling Svcs ... Robin COOK-NOBLES
101 Clerk Board of Trustees ... Marianne B. COOLEY
96 Purchasing Manager ... Tina M. DOLAN

Wentworth Institute of Technology (G)

550 Huntington Avenue, Boston MA 02115-5998
County: Suffolk FICE Identification: 002225
Unit ID: 168227
Telephone: (617) 989-4590 Carnegie Class: Bac/Diverse
FAX Number: (617) 989-4591 Calendar System: Semester
URL: www.wit.edu
Established: 1904 Annual Undergrad Tuition & Fees: $27,950
Enrollment: 4,124 Coed
Affiliation or Control: Independent Non-Profit IRS Status: 501(c)3
Highest Offering: Master's
Program: Professional; Technical Emphasis
Accreditation: EH, ART, CIDA, CONST, CS, ENG, ENGT, IACBE

01 President ... Dr. Zorica PANTIC
100 Chief of Staff ... Ms. Amy INTILLE
05 Sr VP Academic Affairs/Provost ... Dr. Russell PINIZZOTTO
10 Vice Pres Finance ... Mr. Robert TOTINO
21 Vice President Business ... Mr. David A. WAHLSTROM
30 Vice Pres Institutional Advancement ... Vacant
32 VP Enrollment Mgmt/Student Affairs ... Ms. Keiko BROOMHEAD
15 Vice Pres Human Resources ... Ms. Anne M. GILL
13 VP of Information Technology ... Mr. Mark STAPLES
04 Exec Assistant to the President ... Ms. Nancy BANDOIAN
20 Assoc Provost ... Mr. Charles HOTCHKISS
35 Assoc Vice Pres of Student Affairs ... Ms. Annamaria WENNER
21 Assoc Vice President Finance ... Mr. Peter MADDOCKS
84 Assoc VP of Enrollment Management ... Ms. Dianne PLUMMER
31 Assoc VP Community Affairs ... Ms. Sandra E. PASCAL
91 Assoc VP Information Technology ... Mr. Leslie VAUGHAN
90 Assoc VP Learning & Development ... Ms. Monique FUCHS
20 Assoc Provost for Acad Operations ... Ms. Susan PARIS
51 Dean of College of Prof & Cont Educ ... Mr. Larry CARR
07 Executive Director of Admissions ... Ms. Maureen DISCHINO
06 Registrar ... Ms. Nichole MANCONE
08 Director of Library ... Mr. Walter PUNCH
35 Dir Student Financial Services ... Ms. Wen-Hsin CHEN
18 Associate VP Physical Facilities ... Mr. Michael PANKIEVICH
29 Director of Alumni Programs ... Ms. Monica KEY
27 Director of Publications ... Mr. Caleb COCHRAN
35 Associate Dean of Students ... Mr. Peter FOWLER
102 Director of Corporate Relations ... Mr. Jonathan CARROLL
37 Director Financial Aid ... Ms. Anne-Marie CARUSO
38 Director of Counseling ... Ms. Maura MULLIGAN
26 Associate Vice Pres Public Affairs ... Mr. Jamie KELLY
19 Director of Public Safety ... Mr. William POWERS
41 Associate Athletic Director ... Mr. William P. GORMAN
36 Director of Career Services ... Mr. Gregory DENON
39 Director Housing & Residential Life ... Mr. Philip BERNARD
41 Director of Athletics ... Ms. Angel AYRES
09 Director of Institutional Research ... Mr. Bradford WILD
96 Director of Purchasing ... Mr. Gerald INMAN
09 Institutional Researcher ... Mr. Alan T. WHITEMORE
49 Dean for Arts & Sciences ... Mr. Patrick HAFFORD
48 Dean for Arch/Design & Const Mgmt ... Dr. Glenn WIGGINS
54 Dean for Engineering & Technology ... Mr. Frederick DRISCOLL
88 Director of Marketing & Comm ... Mr. Robert YEE
18 Director of Physical Plant ... Mr. Robert FERRO
88 Dir of Stdnt Lead Pgm & Camp Ctr ... Ms. Carissa DURFEE

Western New England University (A)

1215 Wilbraham Road, Springfield MA 01119-2684
County: Hampden FICE Identification: 002226
Unit ID: 168254
Telephone: (413) 782-3111 Carnegie Class: Master's M
FAX Number: (413) 782-1746 Calendar System: Semester
URL: www.wne.edu
Established: 1919 Annual Undergrad Tuition & Fees: $33,020
Enrollment: 3,800 Coed
Affiliation or Control: Independent Non-Profit IRS Status: 501(c)3
Highest Offering: Doctorate
Program: Liberal Arts And General; Professional; Fine Arts Emphasis
Accreditation: EH, BUS, ENG, LAW, @PHAR, SW

01 President ... Dr. Anthony S. CAPRIO
05 Provost/Vice Pres Academic Affairs ... Dr. Jerry A. HIRSCH
26 Vice Pres Marketing & External Affs ... Mrs. Barbara A. CAMPANELLA
10 Vice Pres Finance & Administration ... Mr. William J. KELLEHER
84 Vice President for Enrollment Mgmt ... Dr. Charles R. POLLOCK
32 VP Student Affairs/Dean of Students ... Dr. Jeanne S. STEFFES
30 Vice President Advancement ... Ms. Beverly J. DWIGHT
14 Asst Vice Pres Information Tech ... Mr. Scott J. COOPEE
88 Vice Pres for Strategic Initiatives ... Dr. Richard S. KEATING
61 Dean of Law ... Prof. Arthur R. GAUDIO
54 Dean of Engineering ... Dr. S. Hossein CHERAGHI
50 Dean School of Business ... Dr. Julie SICILIANO
49 Dean of Arts & Sciences ... Dr. Saeed GHAHRAMANI
89 Dean Freshmen/Transfer Students ... Ms. Kerri P. JARZABSKI
08 Assoc Dean Library/Info Resources ... Ms. Pat NEWCOMBE
39 Assistant Dean for Residence Life ... Mr. Thomas P. WOZNIAK
15 Exec Dir Human Res/Career Ctr ... Ms. Joanne OLLSON
09 Director Inst Research & Planning ... Dr. Richard A. WAGNER
29 Dir Alumni Relations/Annual Giving ... Ms. Kathrine PAPPAS
20 Academic Schdl Contr/Info Analyst ... Ms. Linda M. CHOJNICKI
08 Director of D'Amour Library ... Mrs. Priscilla L. PERKINS
37 Director of Student Admin Services ... Mr. Rodney W. PEASE
38 Director of Counseling Services ... Dr. Wayne D. CARPENTER
18 Director of Facilities Management ... Mr. Michael C. DUNCAN
41 Director of Athletics ... Dr. Michael THEULEN
31 Cultural Liaison Coordinator ... Rabbi Jerome S. GURLAND
23 Director of Health Services ... Mrs. Kathleen A. REID
19 Director of Public Safety ... Mr. Adam WOODROW
28 Director of Diversity Programs ... Mrs. Yvonne BOGLE
11 Director Administrative Services ... Ms. Arlene M. ROCK

Wheaton College (B)

26 E Main Street, Norton MA 02766-2322
County: Bristol FICE Identification: 002227
Unit ID: 168281
Telephone: (508) 285-7722 Carnegie Class: Bac/A&S
FAX Number: (508) 286-8270 Calendar System: Semester
URL: www.wheatonma.edu
Established: 1834 Annual Undergrad Tuition & Fees: $43,774
Enrollment: 1,616 Coed
Affiliation or Control: Independent Non-Profit IRS Status: 501(c)3
Highest Offering: Baccalaureate
Program: Liberal Arts And General
Accreditation: EH

01 President ... Dr. Ronald A. CRUTCHER
05 Provost ... Dr. Linda EISENMANN
10 Vice Pres Finance/Administration ... Mr. Brian DOUGLAS
30 Vice President College Advancement ... Ms. Mary M. CASEY
84 Vice President Enrollment/Marketing ... Ms. Gail BERSON
32 VP Student Affairs/Dean of Students ... Ms. Lee B. WILLIAMS
37 Asst VP Enroll/Stdnt Finan Svcs ... Ms. Robin RANDALL
26 Asst Vice Pres for Communications ... Mr. Michael GRACA
06 Registrar/Dean Academic Systems ... Ms. Patricia SANTILLI
29 Dir Alumni Rels/Annual Giving ... Ms. Jill LAWLOR
105 Director College Web Strategy ... Mr. David CALDWELL
15 Asst VP/Director Human Resources ... Ms. Barbara LEMA
38 Director College Counseling ... Ms. Martha LAMB
07 Director of Admissions ... Ms. Lynne STACK
18 Asst VP Business Svcs/Phys Plant ... Mr. John M. SULLIVAN
96 Director of Purchasing ... Vacant
26 Director Public Affairs ... Vacant
09 Director of Institutional Research ... Ms. Audrey ADAM
39 Assoc Dean Stdnt Affs/Dir Res Life ... Ms. Kathryn E. MCCAFFREY
19 Director Public Safety ... Mr. Charles A. FURGAL

Wheelock College (C)

200 The Riverway, Boston MA 02215-4176
County: Suffolk FICE Identification: 002228
Unit ID: 168290
Telephone: (617) 879-2000 Carnegie Class: Master's M
FAX Number: (617) 566-7369 Calendar System: Semester
URL: www.wheelock.edu
Established: 1888 Annual Undergrad Tuition & Fees: $31,880
Enrollment: 904 Coed
Affiliation or Control: Independent Non-Profit IRS Status: 501(c)3
Highest Offering: Beyond Master's But Less Than Doctorate
Program: Liberal Arts And General; Teacher Preparatory
Accreditation: EH, SW, TED

01 President ... Ms. Jackie JENKINS-SCOTT
04 Executive Assistant to President ... Ms. Valerie THORNHILL-HUDSON
32 VP Campus Life/Information Svcs ... Mr. Roy SCHIFILLITI
05 Vice Pres for Academic Affairs ... Dr. Joan GALLOS
30 Vice Pres for Inst Advancement ... Ms. Linda Allaire WELTER
10 Vice Pres/Chief Financial Officer ... Ms. Anne Marie MARTORANA
84 VP Enrollment Mgt/Student Success ... Dr. Adrian K. HAUGABROOK
35 Dean of Students ... Ms. Barbara MORGAN
49 Dean of Arts & Sciences ... Dr. Shirley MALONE-FENNER
104 Dean International Pgms/Prtrnshp ... Dr. Linda DAVIS
53 Assoc Dean of Education/Social Work ... Dr. Donna MCKIBBENS
07 Director of Undergrad Admissions ... Ms. Lisa SLAVIN
07 Director of Graduate Admissions ... Mr. Brian MINCHELLO
06 Interim Registrar ... Ms. Michelle ORMEROD
08 Director of Academic Resc & Library ... Ms. Brenda ECSEDY
15 Director of Human Resources ... Ms. Michele CREWS
13 Director of Information Technology ... Mr. Jonathan LAPIERRE
37 Director Financial Aid ... Ms. Roxanne DUMAS
36 Dir Center for Career Development ... Vacant
85 Int Director Center for Intl Educ ... Dr. Linda DAVIS
18 Chief Facilities/Physical Plant ... Mr. Ed JACQUES
38 Director Counseling Center ... Ms. Eileen THOMPSON
86 Dir of Government and Ext Affairs ... Ms. Marta ROSA
29 Dir of Development/Alumni Relations ... Ms. Lauren MARQUIS
41 Athletic Director ... Ms. Diana CUTAIA
26 Communications Manager ... Ms. Beth KAPLAN

Williams College (D)

Williamstown MA 01267
County: Berkshire FICE Identification: 002229
Unit ID: 168342
Telephone: (413) 597-3131 Carnegie Class: Bac/A&S
FAX Number: N/A Calendar System: 4/1/4
URL: www.williams.edu
Established: 1793 Annual Undergrad Tuition & Fees: $46,330
Enrollment: 2,106 Coed
Affiliation or Control: Independent Non-Profit IRS Status: 501(c)3
Highest Offering: Master's
Program: Liberal Arts And General
Accreditation: EH

01 President ... Adam F. FALK
05 Dean of Faculty ... Peter T. MURPHY
45 Provost ... William C. DUDLEY
10 VP for Fin & Admin and Treasurer ... Frederick W. PUDDESTER
32 Vice President for Campus Life ... Stephen P. KLASS
30 Vice Pres for College Relations ... John M. MALCOLM
28 VP Strategic Plng/Inst Diversity ... Michael E. REED
26 Vice President for Public Affairs ... James G. KOLESAR
04 Asst to Pres/Secretary of the Col ... Keli A. KAEGI
20 Dean of the College ... Sarah R. BOLTON
18 Exec Director Facilities Management ... Robert F. WRIGHT
06 Registrar ... Barbara A. CASEY
07 Director of Admission ... Richard L. NESBITT
37 Director of Financial Aid ... Paul J. BOYER
08 Librarian ... David M. PILACHOWSKI
21 Controller ... Susan S. HOGAN
29 Director Alumni Relations ... Brooks L. FOEHL
15 Director of Human Resources ... Martha R. TETRAULT
36 Director of Career Center ... John H. NOBLE
88 Director of Dining Services ... Robert P. VOLPI
14 Chief Technology Officer ... Dinny S. TAYLOR
09 Director of Institutional Research ... Courtney WADE
23 Director of Health Services ... Ruth G. HARRISON
35 Director Office of Student Life ... Douglas J. SCHIAZZA
41 Director of Athletics/PE ... Lisa M. MELENDY
42 Chaplain ... Richard E. SPALDING

Woods Hole Oceanographic Institution (E)

266 Woods Hole Road, Woods Hole MA 02543-1535
County: Barnstable FICE Identification: 002230
Unit ID: 166610
Telephone: (508) 289-2252 Carnegie Class: Not Classified
FAX Number: N/A Calendar System: 4/1/4
URL: www.whoi.edu
Established: 1930 Annual Graduate Tuition & Fees: $57,605
Enrollment: 126 Coed
Affiliation or Control: Independent Non-Profit IRS Status: 501(c)3
Highest Offering: Doctorate; No Undergraduates
Program: Professional
Accreditation: EH

01 President and Director ... Dr. Susan AVERY
09 Director of Research ... Dr. Laurence P. MADIN
05 VP of Academic Programs and Dean ... Dr. James A. YODER
10 Vice Pres of Finance & Admin/CFO ... Mr. Jeffrey FERNANDEZ
20 Associate Dean ... Dr. Margaret K. TIVEY
06 Registrar ... Ms. Julia WESTWATER
08 Research Librarian ... Ms. Holly N. MILLER

Worcester Polytechnic Institute (F)

100 Institute Road, Worcester MA 01609-2280
County: Worcester FICE Identification: 002233
Unit ID: 168421
Telephone: (508) 831-5000 Carnegie Class: DRU
FAX Number: (508) 831-5753 Calendar System: Semester
URL: www.wpi.edu
Established: 1865 Annual Undergrad Tuition & Fees: $42,178
Enrollment: 5,575 Coed
Affiliation or Control: Independent Non-Profit IRS Status: 501(c)3
Highest Offering: Doctorate
Program: Liberal Arts And General; Professional; Technical Emphasis
Accreditation: EH, BUS, CS, ENG

01 Interim President ... Mr. Philip B. RYAN
05 Sr Vice President and Provost ... Dr. Eric OVERSTROM
10 Executive Vice President & CFO ... Mr. Jeffrey S. SOLOMON
30 VP for University Advancement ... Mr. William MCAVOY
26 Chief Marketing Officer ... Ms. Amy M. MORTON
13 CIO ... Ms. Deborah C. SCOTT
84 Sr VP Enrollment & Instnl Strategy ... Ms. Kristin R. TICHENOR
18 Asst Vice President for Facilities ... Mr. Alfred DIMAURO, JR.
15 Vice President of Human Resources ... Ms. A. Tracy HASSETT
20 VP Acad & Corp Devel ... Mr. Stephen P. FLAVIN
35 Dean of Students/Chief SA Ofcr ... Mr. Philip N. CLAY
22 University Compliance Officer ... Mr. Michael J. CURLEY
36 Director of Career Devel Center ... Mr. Steve KOPPI
08 Dean of Library Services ... Dr. Tracey LEGER-HORNBY
100 Asst VP/Sec of the Corp ... Ms. Stephanie PASHA
07 Dean of Admissions ... Mr. Edward J. CONNOR
06 University Registrar ... Ms. Heather JACKSON
27 Director of Research/Communications ... Mr. Michael W. DORSEY
96 Manager of Procurement Services ... Ms. Laurie COLELLA
21 University Controller ... Ms. Charlene M. BELLOWS
09 Assistant VP of Budget Planning ... Ms. Judith L. TRAINOR
38 Asst Dean of Stdnt Dev/Dir SDCC ... Mr. Charles C. MORSE
88 Director Life Sciences Center ... Mr. Donald D. EASSON
37 Director Student Financial Aid ... Ms. Monica M. BLONDIN
19 Mgr Env Occupational Safety ... Mr. David H. MESSIER
28 Director of Multicultural Affair ... Ms. Bonnie HALL
29 Exec Director of Alumni Relations ... Mr. Peter A. THOMAS

MICHIGAN

Adrian College (G)

110 S Madison Street, Adrian MI 49221-2575
County: Lenawee FICE Identification: 002234
Unit ID: 168528
Telephone: (517) 265-5161 Carnegie Class: Bac/Diverse
FAX Number: (517) 264-3331 Calendar System: Semester
URL: www.adrian.edu
Established: 1859 Annual Undergrad Tuition & Fees: $29,156
Enrollment: 1,767 Coed
Affiliation or Control: United Methodist IRS Status: 501(c)3
Highest Offering: Master's
Program: Liberal Arts And General; Teacher Preparatory
Accreditation: NH, SW, TEAC

01 President ... Dr. Jeffrey R. DOCKING
05 Vice Pres/Dean for Academic Affairs ... Dr. Agnes CALDWELL
30 Vice Pres Institutional Advancement ... Mr. James MAHONY
84 Vice President of Enrollment ... Mr. Frank J. HRIBAR
10 Vice Pres Business Affairs/CFO ... Mr. Jerry WRIGHT
32 Dean of Student Affairs ... Mr. Troy SCHMIDLI
20 Asst Dean of Academic Affairs ... Ms. Bridgette WINSLOW
21 Asst Vice Pres of Business Affairs ... Mr. David DREWS

44 Asst Vice President for Development ....Mr. Ryan EFF
07 Associate Director of Admissions ....Ms. Erin VANDERWORP
42 Chaplain/Director Church Relations ..Dr. Christopher P. MOMANY
26 Director of Public Relations ....Ms. Jennifer COMPTON
06 Registrar ....Vacant
35 Associate Dean for Student Life ....Ms. Mallory FRAILING
21 Controller ....Ms. Nicole MEGALE
86 Dir of Govt & Foundation Relations ....Ms. Amy CAMPBELL
15 Director of Human Resources ....Mrs. Ann FORRISTER
40 Bookstore Manager ....Ms. Rachelle M. DUFFY
93 Dir Multicultural Cultural Programs ....Ms. Idali FELICIANO
29 Director Alumni Relations ....Mrs. Marsha FIELDER
41 Director of Athletics ....Mr. Michael DUFFY
19 Director of Campus Safety ....Mr. Wade BIETELCHIES
36 Director of Career Planning ....Mrs. Janna D'AMICO
88 Director of Conferences ....Ms. Denise HEIN
38 Director of Counseling ....Ms. Monique J. SAVAGE
08 Head Librarian ....Mr. David CRUSE
23 Director of Health Center ....Ms. Dawn MARSH
96 Director of Purchasing ....Ms. Robin RUMLER
37 Director of Financial Aid ....Vacant
18 Director of Facilities ....Mr. John E. JOHNSTON
09 Director of Institutional Research ....Dr. Jason M. HARTZ
88 Director of Academic Services ....Ms. Linda JACOBS
88 Assoc Director of Academic Services ....Ms. Carolyn QUINLAN
27 Asst Dir of Information Services ....Mr. Bradley MAGGARD

Albion College (A)

611 E Porter Street, Albion MI 49224-1831

County: Calhoun FICE Identification: 002235
Unit ID: 168546
Telephone: (517) 629-1000 Carnegie Class: Bac/A&S
FAX Number: (517) 629-0509 Calendar System: Semester
URL: www.albion.edu
Established: 1835 Annual Undergrad Tuition & Fees: $34,194
Enrollment: 1,382 Coed
Affiliation or Control: United Methodist IRS Status: 501(c)3
Highest Offering: Baccalaureate
Program: Liberal Arts And General; Teacher Preparatory
Accreditation: NH, MUS, TEAC

01 Interim President ....Dr. Michael L. FRANDSEN
10 Int Vice Pres Business & Finance ....Mr. James GALBALLY
05 Provost ....Dr. Susan CONNER
30 Vice Pres Institutional Advancement ....Mr. Joshua MERCHANT
84 Vice Pres Enrollment Management ....Mr. Joshua D. MERCHANT
32 Vice Pres & Dean Student Affairs ....Dr. Sally J. WALKER
13 Assoc Vice Pres Info Svcs/CIO ....Mr. Richard ZERA
07 Director of Admissions ....Ms. Mandy DUBIEL
39 Director Residential Life ....Mr. Michael WADSWORTH
08 Director of Libraries ....Dr. Michael VAN HOUTEN
26 Director of Communications ....Ms. Sarah F. BRIGGS
29 Director of Alumni Engagement ....Ms. Elinor MARSH
38 Director of Counseling ....Dr. Frank KELEMEN
37 Director of Financial Aid ....Ms. Ann WHITMER
06 Registrar ....Dr. Andrew DUNHAM
88 Director Dining & Hospitality Svcs ....Mrs. Pat MILLER
18 Director of Facilities Operations ....Mr. Donald MASTERNAK
19 Director of Campus Safety ....Mr. Kenneth SNYDER
41 Athletic Director ....Mr. Matthew AREND
42 College Chaplain ....Rev. Daniel MCQUOWN
15 Director of Human Resources ....Mrs. Lisa LOCKE
09 Director of Institutional Research ....Dr. Andrew DUNHAM
96 Director of Purchasing ....Mrs. Susan CLARK
20 Associate Academic Officer ....Dr. John WOELL
28 Assoc Director Multicultural Affs ....Vacant
40 Manager of Bookstore ....Mr. Nick ANGLE

Alma College (B)

614 W Superior, Alma MI 48801-1599

County: Gratiot FICE Identification: 002236
Unit ID: 168591
Telephone: (989) 463-7111 Carnegie Class: Bac/A&S
FAX Number: (989) 463-7277 Calendar System: Other
URL: www.alma.edu
Established: 1886 Annual Undergrad Tuition & Fees: $33,135
Enrollment: 1,438 Coed
Affiliation or Control: Independent Non-Profit IRS Status: 501(c)3
Highest Offering: Baccalaureate
Program: Liberal Arts And General; Teacher Preparatory
Accreditation: NH, MUS, TEAC

01 President ....Dr. Jeff ABERNATHY
05 Provost & Vice Pres for Acad Affs ....Dr. Michael L. SELMON
10 Vice Pres for Business Affairs ....Mr. David V. BUHL
30 Vice President for Advancement ....Ms. Carol F. HYBLE
84 Vice President for Enrollment ....Mr. Bob GARCIA
32 Vice President for Student Life ....Dr. Nicholas A. PICCOLO
26 Vice Pres Communication/Marketing ....Ms. Ann HALL
04 Executive Asst to the President ....Ms. Sandee A. GADDE
20 Assistant Provost ....Ms. Julie WILLIAMS
06 Registrar ....Ms. Susan M. DEEL
42 Chaplain ....Vacant
37 Director of Financial Aid ....Ms. Michelle MCNIER
08 Director of Library ....Ms. Carol ZEILE
26 Director of College Communications ....Mr. Mike SILVERTHORN
14 Chief Technology Officer ....Dr. Keith R. NELSON
18 Director Facilities & Service Mgmt ....Mr. Douglas DICE
15 Director Human Resources ....Mr. Kenneth L. BORGMAN
21 Controller ....Mr. Dan HENRIS

29 Director Alumni Relations ....Ms. Lou ECKEN
35 Director Campus Life ....Mr. David K. BLANDFORD
38 Director Counseling & Wellness ....Ms. Anne K. LAMBRECHT
07 Director Admissions ....Ms. Amanda SLENSKI
09 Director of Institutional Research ....Mr. Robert ROE

Alpena Community College (C)

665 Johnson Street, Alpena MI 49707-1495

County: Alpena FICE Identification: 002237
Unit ID: 168607
Telephone: (989) 356-9021 Carnegie Class: Assoc/Pub-R-M
FAX Number: (989) 358-7553 Calendar System: Semester
URL: www.alpenacc.edu
Established: 1952 Annual Undergrad Tuition & Fees (In-District): $3,810
Enrollment: 1,953 Coed
Affiliation or Control: Local IRS Status: 501(c)3
Highest Offering: Associate Degree
Program: Occupational; 2-Year Principally Bachelor's Creditable
Accreditation: NH, MAC

01 President ....Dr. Olin JOYNTON
05 Vice Pres Academic/Student Affairs ....Ms. Kathleen MARSH
10 Vice President Admin & Finance ....Mr. Richard SUTHERLAND
32 Assoc VP Academic/Student Affairs ....Ms. Nancy SEGUINN
21 Controller ....Ms. Lyn KOWALEWSKY
20 Dean Learning Resource Center ....Ms. Wendy BROOKS
103 Dean Workplace Partnership Program ..Mr. Donald MACMASTER
13 Co-Director Computing/Info Mgmt ....Ms. Vicky KROPP
13 Co-Director Computing/Info Mgmt ....Mr. Mark GRUNDER
26 Director Public Information ....Mr. Jay WALTERREIT
40 Director Bookstore ....Mr. William MATZKE
102 Foundation Director ....Ms. Penny BOLDREY
18 Director of Facilities Management ....Mr. Thomas LUDWIG
88 Director Volunteer Center ....Ms. Kathleen BRUSKI
06 Registrar ....Ms. Lori DZIESINSKI
15 Director Personnel Services ....Ms. Carolyn DAOUST
07 Director of Admissions ....Mr. Mike KOLLIEN
37 Director Student Financial Aid ....Mr. Robert ROOSE

Andrews University (D)

8975 U.S. 31, Berrien Springs MI 49104-0001

County: Berrien FICE Identification: 002238
Unit ID: 168740
Telephone: (269) 471-7771 Carnegie Class: DRU
FAX Number: (269) 471-6900 Calendar System: Semester
URL: www.andrews.edu
Established: 1074 Annual Undergrad Tuition & Fees: $25,470
Enrollment: 3,551 Coed
Affiliation or Control: Seventh-day Adventist IRS Status: 501(c)3
Highest Offering: Doctorate
Program: Liberal Arts And General; Teacher Preparatory; Professional
Accreditation: NH, CACREP, DIETD, DIETI, ENG, IACBE, MT, MUS, NUR, PTA, SW, TED, THEOL

01 President ....Dr. Niels-Erik A. ANDREASEN
05 Provost ....Dr. Andrea T. LUXTON
20 Associate Provost ....Dr. Emilio GARCIA-MARENKO
20 Associate Provost for Faculty Dev ....Dr. Christon ARTHUR
20 Assistant Provost Inst Assessment ....Dr. Lynn MERKLIN
10 Vice President for Financial Admin ....Mr. Lawrence E. SCHALK
32 Vice President for Student Life ....Dr. Frances M. FAEHNER
26 Vice Pres Marketing & Communication ....Mr. Stephen D. PAYNE
84 Vice Pres for Enrollment Management ....Mr. Randy K. GRAVES
30 Vice President for Advancement ....Dr. David A. FAEHNER
43 General Counsel ....Mr. Brent G T. GERATY
06 Registrar ....Dr. Emilio GARCIA-MARENKO
49 Dean College Arts & Sciences ....Dr. Keith E. MATTINGLY
76 Dean School of Health Professions ....Dr. Emmanuel RUDATSIKIRA
50 Dean School of Business Admin ....Dr. Allen F. STEMBRIDGE
53 Dean School of Education ....Dr. James R. JEFFERY
48 Dean Sch Architecture/Art & Design ....Mr. Carey CARSCALLEN
73 Dean of Theological Seminary ....Dr. Denis FORTIN
58 Dean School of Grad Studies ....Dr. Christon ARTHUR
106 Dean School of Distance Education ....Dr. Alayne THORPE
08 Dean of Libraries ....Mr. Lawrence W. ONSAGER
21 Associate Business Officer ....Mr. Glenn A. MEEKMA
90 Chief Information Officer ....Ms. Lorena L. BIDWELL
39 Dir of University Apartment Life ....Mr. Alfredo RUIZ
34 Dir of the Women's Residence Halls ....Ms. Jennifer R. BURRILL
33 Dir of the Men's Residence Halls ....Mr. Spencer D. CARTER
85 Dir of International Student Svcs ....Mr. Robert BENJAMIN
92 Director of Honors Program ....Dr. L. Monique PITTMAN
15 Director of Human Resources ....Mr. Daniel E. AGNETTA
37 Director Student Financial Aid ....Ms. Elynda A. BEDNEY
07 Director of Undergrad Admissions ....Ms. Shanna LEAK
07 Director of Graduate Admissions ....Ms. Monica WRINGER
88 Media Relations Specialist ....Ms. Becky ST. CLAIR
29 Director of Alumni Services ....Ms. Tami CONDON
38 Dir of Counseling/Testing Center ....Dr. Judith FISHER
40 Manager of Bookstore ....Ms. Cheryl KEAN
19 Director of Campus Safety ....Mr. Dale B. HODGES
23 Director of Medical Services ....Dr. Dan REICHERT
42 University Chaplain ....Mr. Japhet DE OLIVEIRA
09 Director Institutional Research ....Mr. James R. MASSENA
18 Director of Facilities Management ....Mr. Richard L. SCOTT

Aquinas College (E)

1607 Robinson Road, SE, Grand Rapids MI 49506-1799

County: Kent FICE Identification: 002239
Unit ID: 168786
Telephone: (616) 632-8900 Carnegie Class: Master's M
FAX Number: (616) 732-4469 Calendar System: Semester
URL: www.aquinas.edu
Established: 1886 Annual Undergrad Tuition & Fees: $26,280
Enrollment: 2,093 Coed
Affiliation or Control: Roman Catholic IRS Status: 501(c)3
Highest Offering: Master's
Program: Liberal Arts And General; Teacher Preparatory; Professional
Accreditation: NH, TEAC

01 President ....Dr. Juan OLIVAREZ
05 Provost/Dean of Faculty ....Dr. Charles GUNNOE, JR.
30 Vice Pres Institutional Advancement ....Mr. Greg MEYER
10 Vice President Finance ....Dr. Leonard KOGUT
84 Vice Pres Enrollment Management ....Ms. Paula T. MEEHAN
04 Assistant to President ....Ms. Monica EDISON
26 Assoc VP Marketing & Communication ....Ms. Meg DERRER
06 Registrar ....Mrs. Cecelia MESLER
07 Assoc VP for Admissions ....Mr. Thomas MIKOWSKI
32 Assoc VP for Student Services ....Mr. Brian MATZKE
35 Associate Dean of Student Affairs ....Dr. Jennifer DAWSON
38 Director of Career/Counseling Svcs ....Ms. Sharon E. SMITH
104 Dir International Education Pgms ....Ms. Joelle BALDWIN
94 Director of Women's Studies ....Ms. Amy DUNHAM STRAND
92 Director of Honors Program ....Dr. Michelle DEROSE
58 Director of Graduate Management ....Mr. Brian DIVITA
08 Co-Director Woodhouse Library ....Ms. Shellie JEFFRIES
08 Co-Director Woodhouse Library ....Ms. Francine PAOLINI
21 Controller ....Ms. Cathy LUCK
18 Director of Maintenance ....Mr. Dale HAISMA
39 Director Residence Life ....Ms. Julie BLASZAK
07 Director of Admissions ....Ms. Angela SCHLOSSER-BACON
37 Director of Financial Aid ....Mr. David J. STEFFEE
41 Director Athletics ....Mr. Terry M. BOCIAN
42 Director Campus Ministry ....Ms. Mary CLARK-KAISER
13 Dir Information Technology & Svcs ....Ms. Joyce LAFLEUR
29 Director of Alumni Relations ....Ms. Brigid AVERY
09 Director of Institutional Research ....Dr. Susan ENGLISH
35 Director of Campus Life ....Ms. Heather HALL
44 Director of Major Gifts ....Ms. Cecelia CUNNINGHAM
44 Director of Corporate Giving ....Dr. Ali ERHAN
20 Director of Academic Advising ....Ms. Cecelia MESLER
28 Director of Diversity & Inclusion ....Ms. Latoya BOOKER
40 Director Bookstore ....Ms. Marian TODISH
23 Manager of Health and Wellness ....Ms. Veronica BEITNER
24 Media Coordinator ....Ms. Francine PAOLINI
42 Campus Chaplain ....Rev. Stanley DRONGOWSKI, OP

The Art Institute of Michigan (F)

28125 Cabot Drive, Novi MI 48377

Telephone: (248) 675-3800 Identification: 666692
Accreditation: &NH, ACFEI

† Main campus is The Illinois Institute of Art in Chicago, IL.

*Baker College System (G)

1050 W Bristol Road, Flint MI 48507-5508

County: Genesee Identification: 666923
Unit ID: 419572
Telephone: (810) 766-4280 Carnegie Class: N/A
FAX Number: (810) 766-4279
URL: www.baker.edu

00 Chairman of the Board ....Mr. Edward J. KURTZ
01 CEO/President of System ....Mr. F. James CUMMINS
05 Vice President for Academics ....Dr. Denise A. BANNAN
13 Vice President for Computer Systems ....Ms. Jacqueline SPICER
32 Vice President for Student Services ....Mr. Ellis P. SALIM
15 Vice President of Human Resources ....Ms. Rosemary ZAWACKI
26 Vice Pres Marketing/Admissions/PR ....Mr. Richard DELONG
10 Vice President for Finance ....Ms. Tiffany DAVIS
12 Campus Director-Cass City ....Ms. Karen EASTERLING
07 System Director for Admissions ....Mr. Bruce LUNDEEN
35 Director of Student Life ....Vacant
45 Director of Assessment ....Ms. Debra BILLINGS
20 Director Curriculum ....Ms. Kim L. LUTZ
36 Director of Career Services ....Ms. Beth NUCCIO
13 Director Computer Programming ....Vacant
14 Director Computer Operations ....Mrs. Sheryl L. DEAN
08 Director of Library Services ....Mr. Eric PALMER
58 President Graduate Studies ....Dr. Michael HEBERLING

*Baker College of Flint (H)

1050 W Bristol Road, Flint MI 48507-5508

County: Genesee FICE Identification: 004673
Unit ID: 168847
Telephone: (810) 766-4000 Carnegie Class: Bac/Assoc
FAX Number: (810) 766-4293 Calendar System: Quarter
URL: www.baker.edu
Established: 1911 Annual Undergrad Tuition & Fees: $8,100
Enrollment: 5,510 Coed
Affiliation or Control: Independent Non-Profit IRS Status: 501(c)3
Highest Offering: Doctorate
Program: Occupational; 2-Year Principally Bachelor's Creditable; Liberal Arts And General; Business Emphasis
Accreditation: NH, CAHIIM, ENG, ENGT, IACBE, MAC, NURSE, OT, POLYT, PTAA, SURGT, @TEAC

02 President ....Dr. Julianne T. PRINCINSKY

05 Vice President of Academics .... Dr. Candace JOHNSON
07 Vice President of Admissions .... Ms. Jodi CUNEAZ
15 Vice President of Human Resources .... Ms. Rosemary ZAWACKI
32 Vice President of Student Services .... Mr. Gerald MCCARTY, II
88 Dean of Developmental Education .... Mrs. Connie WARNER
50 Dean of Business Administration .... Dr. John C. COTE
97 Dean of General Education .... Dr. Mary Ann THAYER
76 Dean of Health/Human Services .... Vacant
72 Dean of Technical Division .... Mrs. Anca SALA
08 Director of Library Services .... Mr. Eric PALMER
06 Registrar .... Mr. Robert MARTIN
13 Director of Computer Operations .... Mr. Michael MEYERS
18 Director of Facilities .... Mr. Marvin DEAN
38 Director of Counseling/Assessment .... Mr. Paul ZANG
19 Director of Safety/Security .... Mr. Thomas POKORA
40 Director of Bookstore .... Mr. James ROTTA
54 Dir Engineering/Computer Science .... Mrs. Anca SALA
26 Actg Director Community Relations .. Dr. Julianne T. PRINCINSKY
10 Business Officer .... Mrs. Rebecca AYRE-BOGGS
36 Director of Career Services .... Mrs. Janie STEWART
37 Director Student Financial Aid .... Ms. Veta NORRIS
31 Director Corporate/Community Svcs .... Ms. Karen EASTERLING
23 Director of Health and Fitness .... Ms. Maureen PARMANN
39 Housing Coordinator .... Mr. Leon CARTER

* *Baker College of Allen Park* (A)

4500 Enterprise Drive, Allen Park MI 48101-3033
Telephone: (313) 425-3700 Identification: 666996
Accreditation: &NH, CAHIIM, IACBE, MAC, MLTAD, OTA, PTAA, SURGT

† Main campus is Baker College of Flint in Flint, MI.

* *Baker College of Auburn Hills* (B)

1500 University Drive, Auburn Hills MI 48326-2642
Telephone: (248) 340-0600 Identification: 666940
Accreditation: &NH, COARC, DA, DH, DMS, IACBE, MAC, PHLEB, @PTAA

† Main campus is Baker College of Flint in Flint, MI.

* *Baker College of Cadillac* (C)

9600 E 13th Street, Cadillac MI 49601-9600
Telephone: (231) 876-3100 Identification: 666941
Accreditation: &NH, IACBE, MAC, SURGT

† Main campus is Baker College of Flint in Flint, MI.

* *Baker College of Clinton Township* (D)

34950 Little Mack Avenue,
Clinton Township MI 48035-4701
Telephone: (586) 791-6610 Identification: 666942
Accreditation: &NH, CAHIIM, IACBE, MAC, RAD, SURGT

† Main campus is Baker College of Flint in Flint, MI.

* *Baker College of Jackson* (E)

2800 Springport Road, Jackson MI 49202-1290
Telephone: (517) 788-7800 FICE Identification: 004680
Accreditation: &NH, CAHIIM, IACBE, MAC, MLTAD, OPD, RTT, SURGT

† Main campus is Baker College of Flint in Flint, MI.

* *Baker College of Muskegon* (F)

1903 Marquette Avenue, Muskegon MI 49442-1490
Telephone: (231) 777-5200 FICE Identification: 002296
Accreditation: &NH, ACFEI, IACBE, MAC, OTA, PTAA, RAD, SURGT

† Main campus is Baker College of Flint in Flint, MI.

* *Baker College of Owosso* (G)

1020 S Washington Street, Owosso MI 48867-4400
Telephone: (989) 729-3370 Identification: 666937
Accreditation: &NH, ADNUR, DMS, IACBE, MAC, MLTAD, PHLEB, RAD

† Main campus is Baker College of Flint in Flint, MI.

* *Baker College of Port Huron* (H)

3403 Lapeer Road, Port Huron MI 48060-2597
Telephone: (810) 985-7000 Identification: 666943
Accreditation: &NH, DA, DH, IACBE, MAC, MLTAD, SURGT

† Main campus is Baker College of Flint in Flint, MI.

Bay College West Campus (I)

2801 North US 2, Iron Mountain MI 49801
Telephone: (906) 774-8547 Identification: 770262
Accreditation: &NH

† Main campus is Bay Noc Community College in Escanaba, MI.

Bay Mills Community College (J)

12214 W Lakeshore Drive, Brimley MI 49715-9750
County: Chippewa FICE Identification: 030666
Unit ID: 380359
Telephone: (906) 248-3354 Carnegie Class: Tribal
FAX Number: (906) 248-3351 Calendar System: Semester
URL: www.bmcc.edu
Established: 1984 Annual Undergrad Tuition & Fees: $3,200
Enrollment: 536 Coed
Affiliation or Control: Tribal Control IRS Status: 501(c)3
Highest Offering: Associate Degree
Program: Occupational; 2-Year Principally Bachelor's Creditable; Business Emphasis
Accreditation: NH

01 President .... Michael C. PARISH
05 Vice President of Academic Affairs .... Samantha CAMERON
10 VP of Business & Finance .... Laura POSTMA
32 Dean of Student Services .... Debra J. WILSON
13 Technology Director .... Chet KASPER
06 Registrar .... Sherri SCHOFIELD
37 Director Student Financial Aid .... Tina MILLER
07 Director of Admissions .... Elaine LEHRE

Bay Noc Community College (K)

2001 N Lincoln Road, Escanaba MI 49829-2510
County: Delta FICE Identification: 002240
Unit ID: 168883
Telephone: (906) 786-5802 Carnegie Class: Assoc/Pub-R-M
FAX Number: (906) 789-6952 Calendar System: Semester
URL: www.baycollege.edu
Established: 1962 Annual Undergrad Tuition & Fees (In-District): $3,888
Enrollment: 2,445 Coed
Affiliation or Control: Local IRS Status: 501(c)3
Highest Offering: Associate Degree
Program: Occupational; 2-Year Principally Bachelor's Creditable
Accreditation: NH, ADNUR

01 President .... Dr. Laura L. COLEMAN
05 VP Instruction & Student Learning .... Dr. Catherine GATEWOOD
10 VP of Administrative Services .... Mrs. Tanya L. HOAR
12 VP of West Campus .... Dr. Patrick KENNEDY
32 VP of Student Services .... Mr. Matthew R. SOUCY
49 Dean of Arts and Sciences .... Dr. Deborah ANDERSON
72 Dean of Business and Tech .... Mr. Mark KINNEY
30 VP of Institutional Advancement .... Ms. Kim CARNE
13 Chief Info & Sustainability Officer .... Ms. Christine WILLIAMS
37 Director of Financial Aid .... Ms. Laurie SPANGENBERG
07 Director of Admissions .... Ms. Cynthia A. CARTER
15 Director of Human Resources .... Mr. Thomas J. GRIGGS
18 Superintendent Buildings/Grounds .... Mr. Ralph W. CURRY
76 Dean of Allied Health/Wellness .... Ms. Patti HENNING
51 Manager Continuing Educ & Prof Dev .... Ms. Lori L. SHEA
36 Career/Academic Advisor .... Ms. Annette M. JOHNSON
35 Director of Student Life .... Mr. Douglas S. KENDRICK
103 Director of Workforce Development .... Mr. Mark KINNEY

Calvin College (L)

3201 Burton Street, SE, Grand Rapids MI 49546-4388
County: Kent FICE Identification: 002241
Unit ID: 169080
Telephone: (616) 526-6000 Carnegie Class: Bac/A&S
FAX Number: (616) 526-8551 Calendar System: 4/1/4
URL: www.calvin.edu
Established: 1876 Annual Undergrad Tuition & Fees: $28,025
Enrollment: 4,008 Coed
Affiliation or Control: Christian Reformed Church IRS Status: 501(c)3
Highest Offering: Master's
Program: Liberal Arts And General; Teacher Preparatory; Professional
Accreditation: NH, CS, ENG, MUS, NURSE, @SP, SW, TEAC

01 President .... Dr. Michael K. LE ROY
04 Senior Executive Associate .... Mr. Robert A. BERKHOF
88 Exec Assoc to the Pres for Comm .... Dr. Douglas KOOPMAN
05 Provost .... Dr. Claudia BEVERSLUIS
10 Vice Pres Admin/Finance .... Ms. Sally VANDER PLOEG
30 Vice President for Advancement .... Mr. Kenneth ERFFMEYER
84 Vice Pres Enrollment Management .... Mr. Russell J. BLOEM
32 Vice President Student Life .... Dr. Shirley VOGELZANG HOOGSTRA
21 Director of Finance .... Vacant
08 Director of the Library .... Mr. Glenn A. REMELTS
29 Director Alumni/Parent Relations ..... Mr. Michael J. VAN DENEND
06 Director Academic Svcs/Registrar .... Mr. Thomas L. STEENWYK
39 Dean of Residence Life .... Mr. John WITTE
35 Dean of Student Development .... Mr. C. Robert CROW
88 Dean of Students for Judicial Affs ...... Ms. Jane E. HENDRIKSMA
46 Dean of Research & Scholarship .... Dr. Matthew WALHOUT
108 Dean Institutional Effectiveness .... Dr. Michael STOB
83 Academic Dean Soc Sci/Context Disc .... Dr. Cheryl BRANDSEN
79 Acad Dean Arts/Language/Education .... Dr. Mark WILLIAMS
81 Academic Dean Natural Science/Math .... Dr. Stanley L. HAAN
28 Dean of Multicultural Academic Affs .... Dr. Michelle LOYD-PAIGE
15 Assoc Vice Pres Human Resources .... Mr. Todd K. HUBERS
36 Director of Career Development .... Mr. Glenn E. TRIEZENBERG
09 Dir Institutional/Enroll Research .... Mr. Thomas A. VAN ECK
31 Director Conferences/Campus Events .... Mr. Jeffrey A. STOB
26 Director of Communic & Marketing .... Mr. Timothy L. ELLENS
88 Director Social Research Center .... Dr. Neil CARLSON
19 Director of Campus Safety .... Mr. William T. CORNER
18 Director Physical Plant .... Mr. Philip D. BEEZHOLD
24 Director Instruc Resources Center .... Mr. Randal G. NIEUWSMA
38 Director Broene Counseling Center .... Dr. Cynthia KOK
23 Director Health Services .... Dr. Laura CHAMPION
92 Director Honors Program .... Dr. Bruce BERGLUND
42 College Chaplain .... Dr. Mary HULST
40 Manager of the College Store .. Mr. Thomas J. VAN WINGERDEN
41 Athletic Director Men .... Dr. James TIMMER, JR.
41 Athletic Director Women .... Dr. Nancy L. MEYER

Calvin Theological Seminary (M)

3233 Burton Street, SE, Grand Rapids MI 49546-4387
County: Kent FICE Identification: 002242
Unit ID: 169099
Telephone: (616) 957-6036 Carnegie Class: Spec/Faith
FAX Number: (616) 957-8621 Calendar System: Semester
URL: www.calvinseminary.edu
Established: 1876 Annual Graduate Tuition & Fees: $14,190
Enrollment: 294 Coed
Affiliation or Control: Christian Reformed Church IRS Status: 501(c)3
Highest Offering: Doctorate; No Undergraduates
Program: Professional; Religious Emphasis
Accreditation: THEOL

01 President .... Rev. Julius T. MEDENBLIK
05 Dean of Academic Programs .... Dr. Ronald J. FEENSTRA
20 Dean of the Faculty .... Vacant
06 Registrar .... Ms. Joan BEELEN
32 Dean of Students .... Rev. Jeff SAJDAK
08 Theological Librarian .... Rev. Lugene L. SCHEMPER
10 Chief Financial & Operations Ofcr .... Ms. Jinny DE JONG
30 Director of Development .... Mr. Robert KNOOR
36 Director of Mentored Ministries .... Rev. Alvern GELDER
07 Director of Admissions .... Mr. Matthew COOKE
37 Director of Financial Aid .... Mrs. Jennifer SETTERGREN

Central Michigan University (N)

Mount Pleasant MI 48859-0001
County: Isabella FICE Identification: 002243
Unit ID: 169248
Telephone: (989) 774-4000 Carnegie Class: DRU
FAX Number: (989) 774-3537 Calendar System: Semester
URL: www.cmich.edu
Established: 1892 Annual Undergrad Tuition & Fees (In-State): $11,220
Enrollment: 27,626 Coed
Affiliation or Control: State IRS Status: 501(c)3
Highest Offering: Doctorate
Program: Liberal Arts And General; Teacher Preparatory; Professional
Accreditation: NH, ART, ACAE, ARCPA, AUD, BUS, BUSA, CIDA, CLPSY, DIETD, DIETI, ENG, JOUR, #MED, MUS, NAIT, NRPA, PTA, SCPSY, SP, SPAA, SW, TEAC

01 President .... Dr. George E. ROSS
05 Executive VP/Provost .... Dr. Michael A. GEALT
10 Vice Pres Finance/Admin Svcs .... Mr. David A. BURDETTE
30 Vice Pres Development/Ext Relations .... Ms. Kathleen M. WILBUR
84 Vice Pres Enrollment & Student Svcs ..... Mr. Steven L. JOHNSON
88 Vice Pres Global Campus .... Vacant
14 Vice President Technology/CIO .... Dr. Roger E. REHM
21 AVP Fin Svcs & Reporting/Controller .... Mr. Barrie J. WILKES
26 AVP University Communications .... Ms. Sherry S. KNIGHT
18 Assoc Vice Pres Facilities Mgmt .... Mr. Stephen P. LAWRENCE
39 Assoc VP Residence/Auxiliary Svcs .... Mr. John S. FISHER
28 Interim Assoc VP Diversity .... Dr. Traci L. GUINN
15 Assoc VP Human Resources .... Ms. Lori L. HELLA
20 Interim Vice Provost Acad Affairs .... Dr. Claudia B. DOUGLASS
88 Vice Provost Academic Admin .... Dr. Ray L. CHRISTIE
46 Vice President Research .... Dr. John J. MCGRATH
44 Asst Vice President Development .... Mr. Edward A. TOLCHER
08 Dean of Libraries .... Mr. Thomas J. MOORE
32 Asst Vice President Student Affairs .... Mr. Anthony A. VOISIN
35 Executive Director Campus Life .... Mr. Shaun HOLTGREIVE
88 Exec Dir Acad Advis/Assistance .... Ms. Michelle L. HOWARD
29 Exec Dir of Alumni Relations .... Ms. Marcie M. OTTEMAN
09 Exec Dir Institutional Research .... Dr. Robert ROE
22 Director Civil Rights/Inst Equity .... Ms. Katherine M. LASHER
07 Director Undergraduate Admissions .. Mr. Thomas W. SPEAKMAN
43 General Counsel .... Dr. Manuel R. RUPE
06 Registrar .... Ms. Karen E. HUTSLAR
37 Director Scholarships/Financial Aid .... Mr. Kirk M. YATS
36 Director Career Services .... Ms. Julia B. SHERLOCK
41 Assoc VP/Director of Athletics .... Mr. David W. HEEKE, JR.
38 Director Counseling Center .... Mr. Ross J. RAPAPORT
45 Director Financial Plan & Budgets .... Ms. Carol A. HAAS
27 Director Public Relations .... Mr. Steven F. SMITH
19 Chief of Police .... Mr. William YEAGLEY, JR.
40 Director CMU Bookstore .... Mr. Barry D. WATERS
81 Dean College of Sci & Tech .... Dr. Ian R. DAVISON
76 Dean Col of Health Professions .... Dr. Chris INGERSOLL
63 Founding Dean College of Medicine .... Dr. Ernest L. YODER
83 Dean Col Hum/Soc/Behav Sci .... Dr. Pamela S. GATES
57 Dean College Comm/Fine Arts .... Dr. Salma I. GHANEM
50 Dean College of Business Admin .... Dr. Charles T. CRESPY
53 Dean College Education/Human Svcs .... Dr. Dale-Elizabeth PEHRSSON
58 Interim Dean Graduate Studies .... Dr. Roger L. COLES
04 Executive Assistant to President .... Ms. Mary Jane FLANAGAN
85 Exec Dir International Affairs .... Vacant
96 Dir Contract & Purchasing Svcs .... Mr. Thomas P. TRIONFI
92 Director Honors Program .... Dr. Phame M. CAMARENA
93 Int Dir Multicultural Acad/Stdnt Sv .... Ms. Jamie L. BROWN
86 Director Government Relations .... Mr. Toby ROTH, JR.
102 Dir Corp & Foundation Relations .... Ms. Kimberly R. HOUSTON-PHILPOT
104 Director Study Abroad .... Ms. Dianne S. DESALVO

Cleary University (A)

3601 Plymouth Road, Ann Arbor MI 48105-2659
County: Washtenaw FICE Identification: 002246
Unit ID: 169327
Telephone: (800) 686-1886 Carnegie Class: Spec/Bus
FAX Number: (734) 332-4646 Calendar System: Quarter
URL: www.cleary.edu
Established: 1883 Annual Undergrad Tuition & Fees: $390
Enrollment: 704 Coed
Affiliation or Control: Independent Non-Profit IRS Status: 501(c)3
Highest Offering: Master's
Program: Occupational; Professional; Business Emphasis
Accreditation: NH

01 President & CEO .... Mr. Thomas P. SULLIVAN
05 Provost & VP Academic Affairs .... Dr. Vincent P. LINDER
10 VP Finance & Administration .... Ms. Judy WALKER
06 Asst VP Academic Svcs/Registrar .... Ms. Dawn M. FISER
04 Exec Asst to Pres/Board of Trustees .... Ms. Linda T. RENTZ
72 Dn Col Bus Innovation/Applied Tech .... Ms. Dawn MARKELL
20 Academic Dean .... Ms. Sadhana ALANGAR
13 Exec Director/Chief Info Officer .... Mr. David G. BOWERS
09 Dir Institutional Research/Analysis .... Mr. Tim VEENSTRA
18 Director Facilities .... Mr. Gary BACHMAN
30 Exec Dir Development/Alumni Rel .... Ms. Janet FILIP
37 Director Financial Aid .... Ms. Vesta SMITH-CAMPBELL
36 Dir Career Services & Placement .... Ms. Corrie WILLIAMS
40 Director Bookstore Services .... Ms. Sheila THOMPSON
07 Director of Admissions .... Ms. Carrie BONOFIGLIO

Cleary University-Livingston Campus (B)

3750 Cleary Drive, Howell MI 48843
Telephone: (800) 686-1883 Identification: 770263
Accreditation: &NH

† Main campus is Cleary University in Ann Arbor, MI.

College for Creative Studies (C)

201 E Kirby, Detroit MI 48202-4034
County: Wayne FICE Identification: 006771
Unit ID: 169442
Telephone: (313) 664-7400 Carnegie Class: Spec/Arts
FAX Number: (313) 872-8377 Calendar System: Semester
URL: www.collegeforcreativestudies.edu
Established: 1906 Annual Undergrad Tuition & Fees: $35,710
Enrollment: 1,404 Coed
Affiliation or Control: Independent Non-Profit IRS Status: 501(c)3
Highest Offering: Master's
Program: Teacher Preparatory; Professional; Fine Arts Emphasis
Accreditation: NH, ART, CIDA

01 President .... Mr. Richard L. ROGERS
100 Executive Assistant/Chief of Staff .... Ms. Sandra BRADEN
04 Admin Assistant to the President .... Ms. Brigette NEAL
05 Provost .... Vacant
10 Vice Pres Administration & Finance .... Ms. Anne D. BECK
84 Vice Pres Enrollmnt & Student Svcs .... Ms. Julie HINGELBERG
30 Vice Pres Institutional Advancement .... Ms. Nina HOLDEN
20 Assoc Provost .... Ms. Sharon PROCTER
58 Dean Graduate Studies .... Ms. Joanne HEALY
57 Dean Undergraduate Studies .... Mr. Vince CARDUCCI
32 Dean of Students .... Mr. Daniel LONG
06 Registrar & Acad Advising Director .... Ms. Nadine ASHTON
102 Sr Dir Corp/Foundation Relations .... Ms. Anne MASTERSON
07 Director of Admissions .... Ms. Lori WATSON
37 Director Financial Aid .... Ms. Kristin MOSKOVITZ
35 Director Student Life .... Mr. Michael COLEMAN
85 Director Intl Student Services .... Ms. Jennifer DICKEY
28 Director of Multicultural Affairs .... Mr. Cliff HARRIS
51 Dir Continuing & Precollege Studies .... Ms. Carla GONZALEZ
31 Dir of Community Arts Partnerships .... Mr. Mikel BRESEE
08 Director Library .... Ms. Beth WALKER
19 Director of Safety & Security .... Mr. Garrett OCHALEK
18 Director Facilities & Admin Svcs .... Mr. Geoffrey SLEEMAN
13 Director Information Technology .... Mr. Greg FRASER
90 Director of Academic Technologies .... Ms. Laurie EVANS
21 Director Business Services .... Ms. Kerri MCKAY
16 Director Human Resources .... Mr. Gregory KNOFF
26 Director Marketing & Communications .... Mr. Marcus POPIOLEK
44 Dir Annual Giving/Donor Services .... Ms. Elizabeth KLOS
36 Director Career Services .... Ms. Terese NEHRA
29 Alumni Coordinator .... Ms. Lauren MORRIS
38 Personal Counselor .... Mr. James BAUER
40 Manager Bookstore .... Ms. Lauren HART

Compass College of Cinematic Arts (D)

41 Sheldon Blvd, SE, Grand Rapids MI 49503
County: Kent FICE Identification: 041633
Unit ID: 459417
Telephone: (616) 988-1000 Carnegie Class: Not Classified
FAX Number: (616) 458-4676 Calendar System: Other
URL: www.compass.edu
Established: 2003 Annual Undergrad Tuition & Fees: $20,405
Enrollment: 80 Coed
Affiliation or Control: Independent Non-Profit IRS Status: 501(c)3
Highest Offering: Associate Degree
Program: Occupational
Accreditation: ACCSC

01 President .... Keri LOWE
11 Vice President Administration .... Jill POSTMA
32 Student Svcs Coord/Acad Advising .... Rachel VANDER STELT
07 Admissions/Marketing Coordinator .... Stephanie BERGMAN

Concordia University (E)

4090 Geddes Road, Ann Arbor MI 48105-2797
County: Washtenaw FICE Identification: 002247
Unit ID: 169363
Telephone: (734) 995-7300 Carnegie Class: Bac/Diverse
FAX Number: (734) 995-4610 Calendar System: Semester
URL: www.cuaa.edu
Established: 1962 Annual Undergrad Tuition & Fees: $23,363
Enrollment: 668 Coed
Affiliation or Control: Lutheran Church - Missouri Synod
IRS Status: 501(c)3
Highest Offering: Master's
Program: Liberal Arts And General; Teacher Preparatory; Religious Emphasis
Accreditation: NH, TED

01 President .... Rev. Patrick FERRY
11 VP of Admin/Campus Chief Exec .... Dr. Curt GIELOW
03 Exec VP & COO .... Mr. Allen PROCHNOW
05 Interim VP Academic Affairs .... Dr. Ross STUEBER
07 Director of Admissions .... Mr. Jonathon BAHR
06 Registrar .... Mr. Steven MONTREAL
32 Director Student Services .... Mr. Eric CHAMBERS
37 Director Financial Aid .... Mr. Steven TAYLOR
41 Director of Athletics .... Mr. Lonnie PRIES
13 Director IT Services .... Mr. Woodrow HOLBERT
30 Director of Development .... Mr. Martin MORO
09 Director of Institutional Research .... Dr. Mae KELLER
18 Chief Facilities/Physical Plant .... Mr. Jerry NOVAK
38 Director Student Counseling .... Mrs. Gina VERSEMAN
42 Director of Spiritual Life .... Mr. Robert MCKINNEY
15 Director Personnel Services .... Mrs. Barb WALTHER
19 Director Security/Safety .... Mr. Steven DEGNAN
39 Director Residence Life .... Mr. Dauthan KEENER
08 Coordinator of Library Services .... Mr. Michael O'LEARY
36 Director Student Placement .... Mrs. Susan GRESE
96 Director of Purchasing .... Mr. Dean ROE

Cornerstone University (F)

1001 E Beltline Avenue, NE, Grand Rapids MI 49525-5897
County: Kent FICE Identification: 002266
Unit ID: 170037
Telephone: (616) 949-5300 Carnegie Class: Master's L
FAX Number: (616) 222-1540 Calendar System: Semester
URL: www.cornerstone.edu
Established: 1941 Annual Undergrad Tuition & Fees: $23,598
Enrollment: 2,858 Coed
Affiliation or Control: Independent Non-Profit IRS Status: 501(c)3
Highest Offering: Master's
Program: Liberal Arts And General; Teacher Preparatory; Professional
Accreditation: NH, MUS, SW, @TEAC, THEOL

01 President .... Dr. Joseph M. STOWELL
03 Executive Vice President .... Mr. Marc FOWLER
05 Provost .... Dr. Richard OSTRANDER
30 Exec Vice President Advancement .... Mr. William KNOTT
88 Vice President of Broadcasting .... Mr. Chris LEMKE
42 Vice Pres Spiritual Formation .... Mr. Gerald LONGJOHN
58 Assoc Prov/Professional & Grad Stds .... Dr. Robert SIMPSON
97 Dean of Undergraduate Education .... Dr. Martin HUGHES
73 Dean Grand Rpds Theol Seminary .... Mr. John VER BERKMOES
32 Dean of Student Engagement .... Mr. Chip HUBER
09 Dean Institutional Effectiveness .... Dr. Tim DETWILER
35 Director of Student Services .... Mr. Keith DEBOER
08 Director of Miller Library .... Mr. Fred SWEET
37 Director Financial Services .... Mrs. Carol CARPENTER
21 Controller .... Mr. Scott STEWART
88 Director of Retention .... Mrs. Kay LANDRUM
41 Athletic Director .... Mr. Dave GRUBE
15 Director of Human Resources .... Mrs. Emilie AZKOUL
18 Director of Campus Services .... Mr. Bob PRIOLO
19 Director of Campus Safety .... Mr. Brandan BISHOP
36 Director of Career Services .... Mr. John WARREN
29 Director of Alumni .... Mr. Nate CLASON
06 Registrar .... Mrs. Gail DUHON
24 Director of Technical Support .... Mr. Dan MILLS
38 Director of the Counseling Center .... Mr. Scott COUREY
92 Director of Honors Program .... Mr. Michael STEVENS
07 Director of Admissions .... Mrs. Lisa LINK
10 Chief Financial Officer .... Mrs. Nancy SCHOONMAKER
26 Chief Public Relations Officer .... Mr. Bob SACK

Cranbrook Academy of Art (G)

39221 Woodward Avenue, PO Box 801, Bloomfield Hills MI 48303-0801
County: Oakland FICE Identification: 002248
Unit ID: 169424
Telephone: (248) 645-3300 Carnegie Class: Spec/Arts
FAX Number: (248) 645-3591 Calendar System: Semester
URL: www.cranbrook.edu
Established: 1932 Annual Graduate Tuition & Fees: $31,793
Enrollment: 155 Coed
Affiliation or Control: Independent Non-Profit IRS Status: 501(c)3
Highest Offering: Master's; No Undergraduates
Program: Professional; Fine Arts Emphasis
Accreditation: NH, ART

01 Director .... Mr. Reed KROLOFF
06 Registrar/Fin Aid & Admiss Mgr .... Ms. Leslie TOBAKOS

Davenport University (H)

6191 Kraft Avenue, S.E., Grand Rapids MI 49512
County: Kent FICE Identification: 002249
Unit ID: 169479
Telephone: (616) 698-7111 Carnegie Class: Master's M
FAX Number: N/A Calendar System: Semester
URL: www.davenport.edu
Established: 1866 Annual Undergrad Tuition & Fees: $16,920
Enrollment: 10,477 Coed
Affiliation or Control: Independent Non-Profit IRS Status: 501(c)3
Highest Offering: Master's
Program: Professional; Business Emphasis
Accreditation: NH, CAHIIM, IACBE, MAC, NUR, PNUR

01 President .... Dr. Richard J. PAPPAS
30 Exec VP Advancement .... Ms. Peg LUY
26 Exec VP Univ Relations & Communic .... Ms. Kimberly A. BRUYN
46 Exec VP of Quality & Effectiveness .... Dr. Scott EPSTEIN
15 Exec VP Human/Organizational Devel .... Mr. Dave VENEKLASE
07 Exec VP Admission & Student Svcs .... Mr. Walter O'NEILL
10 Exec Vice President for Finance/CFO .... Mr. Michael S. VOLK
05 Exec VP Academics/Provost .... Dr. Linda RINKER
13 Vice Pres Information Technology .... Mr. Brian MILLER
09 VP for Institutional Research .... Dr. Kathy ABOUFADEL
18 Vice President for Plant & Security .... Mr. Shallan SPIELMAKER
50 Dean College of Business .... Dr. Michael BOWERS
72 Dean College of Technology .... Vacant
76 Dean College of Health Professions .... Dr. Karen DALEY
49 Dean College of Arts and Sciences .... Dr. Thomas LONERGAN
106 Dean Online .... Dr. Christine WALLACE
37 Exec Director Financial Aid .... Mr. David DE BOER
26 Executive Dir of Communications .... Mr. Robyn LUYMES
29 Director of Alumni Relations .... Ms. Cathie ROGG
21 Controller .... Mr. Michael SLEVA
06 University Registrar .... Ms. Donna MILHAM
96 Director of Purchasing .... Vacant
41 Director of Athletics .... Mr. Paul LOWDEN

Davenport University Battle Creek (I)

200 West Van Buren Street, Battle Creek MI 49017
Telephone: (269) 968-6105 Identification: 770264
Accreditation: &NH, MAC

† Main campus is Davenport University in Grand Rapids, MI.

Davenport University Flint (J)

4318 Miller Road, Flint MI 48507
Telephone: (810) 732-9977 Identification: 770265
Accreditation: &NH

† Main campus is Davenport University in Grand Rapids, MI.

Davenport University Holland (K)

643 S Waverly Road, Holland MI 49423
Telephone: (616) 395-4600 Identification: 770266
Accreditation: &NH

† Main campus is Davenport University in Grand Rapids, MI.

Davenport University Kalamazoo (L)

4123 West Main Street, Kalamazoo MI 49006
Telephone: (269) 382-2835 Identification: 770267
Accreditation: &NH

† Main campus is Davenport University in Grand Rapids, MI.

Davenport University Lansing (M)

220 E Kalamazoo, Lansing MI 48933
Telephone: (517) 484-2600 Identification: 770268
Accreditation: &NH, MAC

† Main campus is Davenport University in Grand Rapids, MI.

Davenport University Livonia (N)

19499 Victor Parkway, Livonia MI 48152
Telephone: (734) 943-2800 Identification: 770269
Accreditation: &NH

† Main campus is Davenport University in Grand Rapids, MI.

Davenport University Midland (O)

3555 E Patrick Road, Midland MI 48642
Telephone: (989) 835-5588 Identification: 770270
Accreditation: &NH

† Main campus is Davenport University in Grand Rapids, MI.

Davenport University Saginaw (A)

5300 Bay Road, Saginaw MI 48604
Telephone: (989) 799-7800 Identification: 770271
Accreditation: &NH

† Main campus is Davenport University in Grand Rapids, MI.

Davenport University Warren (B)

27650 Dequindre Road, Warren MI 48092
Telephone: (586) 558-8700 Identification: 770272
Accreditation: &NH

† Main campus is Davenport University in Grand Rapids, MI.

Delta College (C)

1961 Delta Rd., University Center MI 48710-0001
County: Bay FICE Identification: 002251
Unit ID: 169521
Telephone: (989) 686-9000 Carnegie Class: Assoc/Pub-R-L
FAX Number: (989) 667-0620 Calendar System: Semester
URL: www.delta.edu
Established: 1961 Annual Undergrad Tuition & Fees (In-District): $3,604
Enrollment: 10,791 Coed
Affiliation or Control: Local IRS Status: 501(c)3
Highest Offering: Associate Degree
Program: Occupational; 2-Year Principally Bachelor's Creditable
Accreditation: NH, ADNUR, COARC, DA, DH, DMS, PTAA, RAD, SURGT

01 President .... Dr. Jean GOODNOW
10 Vice President Finance/Treasurer .... Ms. Debra K. LUTZ
32 Vice President Student & Educ Svcs ... Ms. Margarita MOSQUEDA
05 Vice Pres Instruction/Learning Svcs .... Vacant
20 Dean of Teaching & Learning .... Vacant
20 Dean of Student and Acad Services .... Ms. Judy MILLER
36 Dean Career Educ/Learning Part .... Ms. Ginny PRZYGOCKI
26 Marketing & Public Info Director .... Ms. Leanne GOVITZ
24 Dir Broadcasting/General Mgr .... Mr. Barry BAKER
30 Ex Dir Delta Col Found/Inst Advance .... Ms. Pam CLARK
11 Asst to Pres/Dir Strat Plng/Bd Secy .... Ms. Andrea L. URSUY
25 Interim Dir of Corporate Services .... Mr. Greg LUCZAK
13 Chief Information Officer .... Mr. Jason STAHL
37 Director of Student Financial Aid .... Mr. David URBANIAK
15 Director of Human Resources .... Ms. Mary L. GMEINER
18 Director of Facilities Management .... Mr. Larry E. RAMSEYER
35 Dean of Student & Educational Svcs .... Vacant
40 Bookstore Manager .... Ms. Barbara POWERS
07 Director of Admissions .... Mr. Gary BRASSEUR
06 Registrar .... Mr. Keith MALKOWSKI
19 Interim Director Law Enforce .... Mr. Steve WITZKE
08 Library Learning Info Center Dir .... Mr. Jack WOOD
38 Dir Counseling Advising/Career Svcs .... Ms. Diana GUTIERREZ
21 Business Services Director .... Ms. Barbara WEBB
09 Director of Institutional Research .... Mr. Wm. Michael WOOD
44 Coordinator of Development .... Ms. Mary HARDING
31 Dean of Community Development .... Ms. Teresa STITT

Eastern Michigan University (D)

Ypsilanti MI 48197-2207
County: Washtenaw FICE Identification: 002259
Unit ID: 169798
Telephone: (734) 487-1849 Carnegie Class: Master's L
FAX Number: (734) 481-1095 Calendar System: Semester
URL: www.emich.edu
Established: 1849 Annual Undergrad Tuition & Fees (In-State): $9,364
Enrollment: 23,547 Coed
Affiliation or Control: State IRS Status: 501(c)3
Highest Offering: Doctorate
Program: Liberal Arts And General; Teacher Preparatory; Professional
Accreditation: NH, BUS, CACREP, CIDA, CLPSY, CONST, DIETC, ENGT, MT, MUS, NURSE, OPE, OT, PLNG, SP, SPAA, SW, TED

01 President .... Dr. Susan W. MARTIN
05 Provost and Vice President .... Dr. Kim SCHATZEL
10 Chief Financial Officer .... Mr. John LUMM
26 Vice President Communications .... Mr. Walter KRAFT
30 VP Advancement & Exec Director .... Mr. Thomas STEVICK
101 VP & Sec to the Board of Regents .... Ms. Vicki REAUME
41 VP and Dir Intercol Athletics .... Ms. Heather LYKE
20 Assoc Provost & VP for Research Adm .... Dr. James J. CARROLL, III
58 Assc Provost & Assc VP Grad Studies .... Dr. Jeffrey KENTOR
26 Assoc VP Marketing & Communication .... Mr. Theodore G. COUTILISH
15 Chief Human Resources Officer .... Dr. James GALLAHER
84 Assoc Vice Pres Enrollment Mgmt .... Mr. Kevin KUCERA
21 Associate Vice President Finance .... Ms. Andrea JAECKEL
86 VP Government & Community Relations .... Mr. Leigh GREDEN
18 VP for Operations and Facilities .... Mr. John P. DONEGAN
69 Dean Col Health & Human Svcs .... Dr. Murali NAIR
106 Int Dir EMU Online/Exten/Reg Sites .... Ms. Julie KNUTSON
49 Dean of Art & Sciences .... Dr. Thomas VENNER
50 Dean of Business .... Dr. Michael TIDWELL
53 Dean of Education .... Dr. Jann JOSEPH
72 Interim Dean of Technology .... Dr. Wade TORNQUIST
43 General Counsel/University Attorney .... Ms. Gloria HAGE
13 Asst VP/CIO Information Technolog .... Dr. Carl POWELL
23 Asst VP of Student Well-Being .... Ms. Ellen GOLD
09 Asst VP & Exec Dir Inst Rsrch/Info .... Dr. Bin NING
32 Asst VP of Student Life .... Vacant
20 Asst VP for Academic Affairs .... Dr. David WOIKE
21 Asst VP Bus Oper/Student Svcs .... Mr. Brian KULPA
88 Asst VP for Academic Success Partn .... Dr. Lynette FINDLEY
102 Exec Dir Foundation Operations/CFO .... Ms. Laura WILBANKS
88 Interim Ombudsman .... Dr. Perry FRANCIS
29 Exec Dir Alumni Relations .... Ms. Ann THOMPSON
19 Exec Dir Public Safety .... Mr. Robert HEIGHES
08 Dean Halle Library .... Dr. Tara L. FULTON
88 Dir Charter Schools Program .... Dr. Malverne WINBORNE
92 Director Honors College .... Dr. Rebecca SIPE
39 Director of Housing & Residence .... Ms. Marney BUSS
27 Executive Director Media Relations .... Mr. Geoffrey LARCOM
21 Exec Dir Financial Plng & Budget .... Mr. Michael F. FOX
88 Dir University Convocation Center .... Mr. Mark MONAHAN
44 Sr Development Officer/Central Svcs .... Ms. Susan RINK
88 Chief Development Officer .... Ms. Jill HUNSBERGER
88 Exec Dir Integrated Content .... Ms. Darcy GIFFORD
88 Dir Special Events & Public Engagem .... Vacant
88 Gen Mgr WEMU-FM Public Rad .... Ms. Molly MOTHERWELL

Ecumenical Theological Seminary (E)

2930 Woodward Avenue, Detroit MI 48201-3035
County: Wayne FICE Identification: 040024
Unit ID: 247162
Telephone: (313) 831-5200 Carnegie Class: Spec/Faith
FAX Number: (313) 831-1353 Calendar System: Quarter
URL: www.etseminary.edu
Established: 1980 Annual Undergrad Tuition & Fees: $12,300
Enrollment: 159 Coed
Affiliation or Control: Independent Non-Profit IRS Status: 501(c)3
Highest Offering: Doctorate
Program: Professional; Technical Emphasis
Accreditation: THEOL

01 President .... Dr. Marsha FOSTER BOYD
05 Vice Pres Academic Affs/Acad Dean .... Dr. Anneliese SINNOTT
11 Vice President of Administration .... Rev. Margaret PRIEST
30 Director of Advancement .... Ms. Cathy MAHER
06 Registrar .... Ms. Jean D. MURPHY
08 Head Librarian .... Rev. Dianne VAN MARTER

Ferris State University (F)

1201 S. State Street, Big Rapids MI 49307-2295
County: Mecosta FICE Identification: 002260
Unit ID: 169910
Telephone: (231) 591-2000 Carnegie Class: Master's L
FAX Number: (231) 591-2990 Calendar System: Semester
URL: www.ferris.edu
Established: 1884 Annual Undergrad Tuition & Fees (In-State): $10,220
Enrollment: 14,533 Coed
Affiliation or Control: State IRS Status: 501(c)3
Highest Offering: First Professional Degree
Program: Occupational; 2-Year Principally Bachelor's Creditable; Liberal Arts And General; Teacher Preparatory; Professional
Accreditation: NH, ACBSP, ART, CAHIIM, CIDA, COARC, CONST, DH, DMS, ENG, ENGT, MLTAD, MT, NMT, NRPA, NUR, OPT, OPTR, PHAR, RAD, SW, @TEAC

01 President .... Dr. David L. EISLER
05 Provost & VP for Academic Affairs .... Dr. Fritz J. ERICKSON
43 Vice President & General Counsel .... Mr. Miles J. POSTEMA
10 VP of Administration & Finance .... Mr. Jerry L. SCOBY
30 Interim VP of Advancement & Mktg .... Ms. Shelly ARMSTRONG
32 Vice President Student Affairs .... Dr. Don FLICKINGER
12 President/Vice Chancellor KCAD .... Dr. David ROSEN
88 Vice Chancellor Admin & Fin KCAD .... Ms. Sandra DAVISON-WILSON
12 VP for Extended and Intl Operations .... Dr. Donald GREEN
28 VP for Diversity and Inclusion .... Dr. David PILGRIM
20 Associate Provost .... Dr. Roberta TEAHEN
20 Associate Provost .... Dr. Paul BLAKE
20 Associate Provost .... Dr. William POTTER
21 Assoc Vice President Finance .... Mr. Patrick BRIGGS
35 Assoc Vice Pres Student Affairs .... Vacant
16 Assoc Vice Pres Human Resources .... Ms. Tamie GRUNOW
30 Assoc Vice Pres for Advancement .... Ms. Carla MILLER
18 Assoc Vice Pres Plant Management .... Mr. Mike HUGHES
84 Associate Dean Enrollment Services .... Ms. Kathy LAKE
06 Dean Enroll Svc/Dir Admiss & Rec .... Dr. Kristen SALOMONSON
88 Associate VP Auxiliary Enterprises .... Mr. James HESSLER
45 Director Budget Planning/Analysis .... Ms. Sally DEPEW
14 Chief Technology Officer .... Mr. John URBANICK
22 Director of Equal Opportunity .... Mr. Matthew OLOVSON
19 Director of Public Safety .... Mr. Bruce BORKOVICH
36 Mgr Stdnt Employment & Career Svcs .... Mr. John RANDLE
88 Director Rankin Student Center .... Mr. Mark SCHUELKE
38 Interim Director Counseling Center .... Ms. Renee DOUGLAS
23 Interim Director Health Center .... Ms. Renee DOUGLAS
35 Dean of Student Life .... Mr. Leroy WRIGHT
88 Dir Multicultural Student Svcs .... Dr. Matthew CHANEY
88 Dir Student Leadership/Activities .... Vacant
88 Director University Recreation .... Ms. Cindy HORN
29 Dir Alumni Relations/Annual Giving .... Mr. Jeremy MISHLER
09 Director of Institutional Research .... Dr. Kristen SALOMANSON
39 Director Residential Life .... Vacant
40 Director Bookstore .... Ms. Karen BOHREN
41 Director of Athletics .... Mr. Perk WEISENBURGER
44 Director Planned Giving .... Mr. Todd JACOBS
96 Director Purchasing .... Mr. Michael PETHICK
49 Dean of Arts & Sciences .... Dr. Rick KURTZ
50 Dean of Business .... Dr. David NICOL
51 Dean of Professional & Tech Studies .... Dr. Donald GREEN
53 Dean of Education & Human Services .... Dr. Michelle JOHNSTON
67 Dean of Pharmacy .... Dr. Steve DURST
76 Dean of Health Professions .... Dr. Matthew ADEYANJU
63 Dean Michigan College Optometry .... Dr. David DAMARI
72 Dean of Engineering Technology .... Dr. JK YATES
92 Dean Retention & Student Success .... Dr. William POTTER
08 Dean of FLITE .... Dr. Scott GARRISON

Finlandia University (G)

601 Quincy Street, Hancock MI 49930-1882
County: Houghton FICE Identification: 002322
Unit ID: 172440
Telephone: (906) 482-5300 Carnegie Class: Bac/Diverse
FAX Number: (906) 487-7366 Calendar System: Semester
URL: www.finlandia.edu
Established: 1896 Annual Undergrad Tuition & Fees: $20,480
Enrollment: 571 Coed
Affiliation or Control: Evangelical Lutheran Church In America
IRS Status: 501(c)3
Highest Offering: Baccalaureate
Program: Liberal Arts And General; Professional
Accreditation: NH, MAC, NURSE, PTAA

01 President .... Dr. Philip JOHNSON
10 Exec Vice Pres Business/Finance .... Mr. Nick STEVENS
05 Executive Vice Pres/Provost .... Ms. TyAnn LINDELL
26 Exec VP External Relations/CAO .... Mr. Duane AHO
04 Executive Administrative Assistant .... Ms. Doreen KORPELA
27 Executive Director Communications .... Ms. Karen JOHNSON
20 Assistant Provost .... Ms. Carol BATES
102 Director Foundation Relations .... Ms. Robin BONINI
08 Librarian .... Ms. Elizabeth MARTIN
32 Director of Living and Learning .... Mr. Michael BAILY
42 University Chaplain .... Mr. Soren SCHMIDT
06 Registrar .... Ms. Evelyn GOKE
29 Director Alumni Relations .... Ms. Cheryl RIES
38 Director Student Support Services .... Vacant
13 Director Information Technology .... Mr. Scott BLAKE
41 Athletic Director .... Mr. Chris SALANI
44 Advancement Officer .... Vacant
18 Director of Plant and Facilities .... Mr. Curt HAHKA
21 Controller .... Ms. Lori BAAKKO
37 Director Student Financial Aid .... Ms. Sandra TURNQUIST
36 Career Services Manager .... Mr. Mark CAVIS
09 Institutional Research Analyst .... Mr. Hannu LEPPANEN
40 Bookstore Manager .... Ms. Alana EVANS
96 Purchaser .... Ms. Janine NOTTKE
15 Director of Human Resources .... Ms. Karin VAN DYKE
07 Director of Admissions .... Ms. Julie JENNERJOHN
19 Director of Campus Safety/Security .... Mr. Jim HARDEN
39 Residence Life Coordinator .... Vacant
49 Dean College of Arts & Sciences .... Dr. Christine O'NEIL
57 Dean Intl School of Art & Design .... Ms. Denise VANDEVILLE
76 Dean College of Health Science .... Dr. Fredi DE YAMPERT
104 Dean Intl School of Business .... Dr. Terry MONSON

Glen Oaks Community College (H)

62249 Shimmel Road, Centreville MI 49032-9719
County: Saint Joseph FICE Identification: 002263
Unit ID: 169974
Telephone: (269) 467-9945 Carnegie Class: Assoc/Pub-R-S
FAX Number: (269) 467-4114 Calendar System: Semester
URL: www.glenoaks.edu
Established: 1965 Annual Undergrad Tuition & Fees (In-District): $3,914
Enrollment: 1,333 Coed
Affiliation or Control: Local IRS Status: 501(c)3
Highest Offering: Associate Degree
Program: Occupational; 2-Year Principally Bachelor's Creditable
Accreditation: NH, MAC

01 President .... Dr. Gary WHEELER
05 Dean of Teaching & Learning .... Dr. Ana GAILLAT
10 Dean of Finance/Administrative Svcs .... Ms. Marilyn WIESCHOWSKI
32 Dean of Students .... Dr. Margaret HALE-SMITH
66 Asst Dean of Nursing .... Mr. Allan PUPLIS
84 Asst Dean Enrollment Svcs/Registrar .... Ms. Beverly ANDREWS
20 Assoc Dean Extend Lrng/Wrkfce Devel .... Dr. Patricia MORGENSTERN
08 Director Learning Resources Center .... Ms. Betsy S. MORGAN
21 Accountant .... Ms. Jennifer DODSON
18 Director of Buildings/Grounds .... Mr. Nick MILLIMAN
07 Director of Admissions .... Ms. Tonya HOWDEN
37 Dir of Financial Aid/Scholarships .... Ms. Jean ZIMMERMAN
41 Director of Athletics .... Mr. Steve PROEFROCK
09 Institutional Effect/Rsrch Analyst .... Ms. Tammy RUSSELL
15 Personnel Coordinator .... Ms. Candy BOHACZ
26 Public Relations/Marketing .... Ms. Valorie JUERGENS

Gogebic Community College (I)

E4946 Jackson Road, Ironwood MI 49938-1366
County: Gogebic FICE Identification: 002264
Unit ID: 169992
Telephone: (906) 932-4231 Carnegie Class: Assoc/Pub-R-S
FAX Number: (906) 932-5541 Calendar System: Semester
URL: www.gogebic.edu
Established: 1931 Annual Undergrad Tuition & Fees (In-District): $4,114
Enrollment: 1,050 Coed

Affiliation or Control: Local IRS Status: 501(c)3
Highest Offering: Associate Degree
Program: Occupational; 2-Year Principally Bachelor's Creditable
Accreditation: NH

01 President Mr. James A. LORENSON
05 Dean of Instruction/Dir Exten Pgm Mr. Ken J. TRZASKA
10 Dean of Business Services Mr. Erik M. GUENARD
32 Dean of Student Services Ms. Jeanne GRAHAM
37 Dir Financial Aid/Veterans Svcs Ms. Suzetta R. FORBES
76 Director of Allied Health Program Ms. Dawn MCPHERSON
18 Director of Buildings & Grounds Vacant
88 Director of Ski Area Management Mr. James VANDERSPOEL
08 Dir Learning Resource/Instruct Tech Mr. Walter LESSUN
14 Director of Computer Services Ms. Kathie A. MUNN
07 Dir of Admission/Public Information Ms. Kim ZECKOVICH
30 Dir of Institutional Development Ms. Kelly MARZCAK
15 Director of Human Resources Ms. Ashley PAQUETTE
88 Transfer Coordinator Ms. Therese PAWLAK
06 Asst Registrar/Institutional Rschr Ms. Miranda LAWVER

Grace Bible College (A)

1011 Aldon Street, SW, Grand Rapids MI 49509-1998
County: Kent FICE Identification: 002265
Unit ID: 170000
Telephone: (616) 538-2330 Carnegie Class: Bac/Diverse
FAX Number: (616) 538-0599 Calendar System: Semester
URL: www.gbcol.edu
Established: 1939 Annual Undergrad Tuition & Fees: $16,000
Enrollment: 272 Coed
Affiliation or Control: Independent Non-Profit IRS Status: 501(c)3
Highest Offering: Baccalaureate
Program: Liberal Arts And General; Teacher Preparatory; Religious Emphasis
Accreditation: NH, BI

01 President Dr. Kenneth B. KEMPER
05 Vice President for Academics Mrs. Kim PILIECI
10 Vice Pres Finance/Bus Operations Mr. Douglas VRIESMAN
30 Vice Pres Institutional Advancement Mr. Gregory HEATH
11 Vice Pres Cmty Life/Operations Mr. Brian P. SHERSTAD
106 Vice Pres Adult & Online Education Mr. Mike STOWELL
35 Dean of Students Mr. Kyle BOHL
04 Executive Assistant to President Mrs. Joyce A. STORMS
06 Registrar Ms. Linda K. SILER
46 Fund Development Director Mr. Steve HILBRANDS
08 Director Library Services Mrs. Kathy L. MOLENKAMP
37 Director of Financial Aid Mr. Kurt POSTMA
84 Director of Enrollment Mr. Kevin E. GILLIAM
13 Information Technology Director Mr. James PETERS
18 Director of Maintenance Mr. Nathan JOHNSON
41 Sports Information Director Mr. Gary BAILEY
42 Director of Campus Ministries Vacant
88 Dir Recruitment Online & Adult Stds Mr. Zak SORENSEN
108 Director Institutional Assessment Dr. Mat LOVERIN

Grand Rapids Community College (B)

143 Bostwick Avenue, NE, Grand Rapids MI 49503-3295
County: Kent FICE Identification: 002267
Unit ID: 170055
Telephone: (616) 234-4000 Carnegie Class: Assoc/Pub-U-SC
FAX Number: (616) 234-4005 Calendar System: Semester
URL: www.grcc.edu
Established: 1914 Annual Undergrad Tuition & Fees (In-District): $4,008
Enrollment: 17,448 Coed
Affiliation or Control: Local IRS Status: 501(c)3
Highest Offering: Associate Degree
Program: Occupational; 2-Year Principally Bachelor's Creditable
Accreditation: NH, ACFEI, ADNUR, ART, DA, DH, MAC, MUS, OTA, PNUR, RAD

01 President Dr. Steven C. ENDER
05 Exec Vice Pres Academic Affairs Dr. Gilda G. GELY
10 Exec VP Business/Financial Services Ms. Lisa FREIBURGER
13 VP & CIO Lrng Res/Tech Solutions Mr. Kevin O'HALLA
30 Assoc VP Advancement/Exec Dir Found Mr. Donald MACKENZIE
88 Dean of Adult & Developmental Educ Mr. John COWLES
103 Director Workforce Training Ms. Julie PARKS
75 Dean Sch Workforce Development Ms. Fiona HERT
32 Dean Student Affairs Ms. Tina OEN-HOXIE
09 Dean Inst Research & Planning Ms. Donna KRAGT
49 Dean School of Arts & Science Dr. Laurie CHESLEY
72 Dean Instruct Design/Info Tech Ms. Patti TREPKOWSKI
07 Assoc Dean Admiss/Enrollment Mgmt Ms. Diane D. PATRICK
26 Director of Communications Ms. Leah NIXON
37 Exec Dir Student Financial Services Ms. Jill M. NUTT
16 Executive Director Human Resources Ms. Cathy WILSON
06 Registrar Ms. Diane PATRICK
35 Director Student Activities Mr. Eric MULLEN
36 Assoc Director Student Employment Ms. Luann WEDGE
08 Director of Library Services Ms. Pat INGERSOLL
18 Executive Director of Facilities Mr. Thomas J. SMITH
88 Director MTEC/Employment Training Mr. George WAITE
19 Chief of Campus Police Ms. Rebecca R. WHITMAN
43 General Counsel Ms. Kathy KEATING
96 Director Purchasing Mr. Mansfield MATTHEWSON
12 Dean of Lakeshore Campus & Outreach Mr. Daniel CLARK
22 Exec Dir Equity/Community/Legis Mr. Eric WILLIAMS
28 Dir Diversity Learning Center Ms. Christina ARNOLD

Grand Valley State University (C)

1 Campus Drive, Allendale MI 49401-9403
County: Ottawa FICE Identification: 002268
Unit ID: 170082
Telephone: (616) 331-5000 Carnegie Class: Master's L
FAX Number: (616) 331-3503 Calendar System: Semester
URL: www.gvsu.edu
Established: 1960 Annual Undergrad Tuition & Fees (In-State): $10,454
Enrollment: 24,654 Coed
Affiliation or Control: State IRS Status: 501(c)3
Highest Offering: Doctorate
Program: Liberal Arts And General; Teacher Preparatory; Professional
Accreditation: NH, ARCPA, ART, BUS, BUSA, CS, CVT, DMS, ENG, IPSY, MT, MUS, NURSE, OT, PTA, RTT, @SP, SPAA, SW, TED

01 President Dr. Thomas J. HAAS
05 Provost/VP Academic & Stdnt Affairs Dr. Gayle R. DAVIS
10 Vice President Finance/Admin Mr. James BACHMEIER
26 Vice President University Relations Mr. Matthew E. MCLOGAN
30 Vice President of Development Ms. Karen M. LOTH
22 Vice President Inclusion and Equity Dr. Jeanne J. ARNOLD
43 University Counsel Mr. Thomas A. BUTCHER
04 Special Assistant to President Ms. Teri L. LOSEY
32 Vice Provost/Dean Student Services Dr. H. Bart MERKLE
20 Vice Provost/Dean Academic Svcs Ms. Lynn BLUE
20 Vice Provost for Student Success Dr. Nancy GIARDINA
88 Vice Provost for Research Admin Dr. Robert SMART
20 V Pvst Instruct Develop & Innov Dr. Christine RENER
88 Vice Provost for Health Dr. Jean NAGELKERK
20 Assoc Vice Pres Academic Affairs Mr. Jon A. JELLEMA
20 Assoc Vice Pres Academic Affairs Dr. Joseph H. GODWIN
20 Asst Vice Pres Academic Affairs Dr. Julia GUEVARA
20 Asst Vice Pres Academic Affairs Dr. Maria CIMITILE
21 Associate VP Business/Finance Mr. Brian COPELAND
21 Asst VP for University Budgets Mr. Jeff MUSSER
15 Assoc Vice Pres Human Resources Mr. D. Scott RICHARDSON
26 Assoc VP Institutional Marketing Ms. Rhonda LUBBERTS
27 Assoc VP News & Information Svcs Ms. Mary Eilleen LYON
18 Assoc Vice Pres Facilities Services Mr. Timothy THIMMESCH
88 Assoc VP for Facilities Planning Mr. James MOYER
12 Asst VP for Pew Campus Operations Ms. Lisa HAYNES
22 Asst VP for Affirmative Action Mr. Dwight HAMILTON
88 Asst VP for Inclusion Initiatives Dr. Adriel HILTON
49 Dean Col of Liberal Arts & Sciences Dr. Frederick ANTCZAK
50 Int Dean Seidman Col of Business Dr. John REIFEL
70 Dean College of Cmty/Public Service Dr. George GRANT
53 Dean College of Education Dr. Elaine COLLINS
54 Dean Padnos Col Engr & Computing Dr. Paul PLOTKOWSKI
76 Dean College of Health Professions Dr. Roy OLSSON
88 Dean College Interdisciplin Studies Dr. Anne HISKES
66 Dean Kirkhof College of Nursing Dr. Cynthia MCCURREN
58 Dean Graduate Studies Dr. Jeffrey POTTEIGER
08 Dean University Libraries Dr. Lee VAN ORSDEL
07 Director of Admissions Ms. Jodi CHYCINSKI
37 Director of Financial Aid Ms. Michelle RHODES
06 Interim Registrar Dr. Sherril SOMAN
36 Director Career Center Mr. Troy FARLEY
14 Director of Information Technology Ms. Sue KORZINEK
29 Director of Alumni Relations Mr. Chris W. BARBEE
09 Director of Institutional Analysis Dr. Philip BATTY
39 Dir of Housing and Residence Life Dr. Andrew J. BEACHNAU
85 Chief International Officer Dr. Mark SCHAUB
28 Director of Multicultural Affairs Ms. Connie DANG
88 Dir Intercult Trng/Learning & Devel Mr. Sean HUDDLESTON
88 Dir of Disability Support Resources Ms. Kathleen VANDERVEEN
19 Director of Public Safety Services Vacant
88 Exec Dir Van Andel Global Trade Ctr Ms. Sonja JOHNSON
88 Dir Sm Business/Technology Dev Ctr Ms. Carol LOPUCKI
96 Director of Procurement Services Mr. Kim PATRICK
41 Athletic Director Mr. Tim SELGO
88 Director Annis Water Resources Inst Dr. Alan STEINMAN
88 Dir Michigan Alt/Renwble Energy Ctr Mr. Arn BOEZAART
38 Director Univ Counseling Center Dr. Amber ROBERTS
88 Director of Hauenstein Center Mr. Gleaves WHITNEY
88 Spec Asst for Charter Schools Mr. Tim WOOD
88 General Manager WGVU TV & Radio Mr. Michael WALENTA
40 Bookstore Manager Mr. Jerrod NICKELS

Grand Valley State University Meijer Campus (D)

515 South Waverly Road, Holland MI 49423
Telephone: (616) 331-3910 Identification: 770275
Accreditation: &NH

† Main campus is Grand Valley State University in Allendale, MI.

Grand Valley State University Pew Campus (E)

401 Fulton Street, Grand Rapids MI 49504
Telephone: (616) 331-7220 Identification: 770274
Accreditation: &NH

† Main campus is Grand Valley State University in Allendale, MI.

Great Lakes Christian College (F)

6211 Willow Highway, Lansing MI 48917-1299
County: Eaton FICE Identification: 002269
Unit ID: 170091
Telephone: (517) 321-0242 Carnegie Class: Spec/Faith
FAX Number: (517) 321-5902 Calendar System: Semester
URL: www.glcc.edu
Established: 1949 Annual Undergrad Tuition & Fees: $15,600
Enrollment: 200 Coed
Affiliation or Control: Christian Churches And Churches of Christ
IRS Status: 501(c)3
Highest Offering: Baccalaureate
Program: Professional; Religious Emphasis
Accreditation: NH, BI

01 President Mr. Lawrence L. CARTER
10 Vice President Finance/Operations Mr. William D. BROSSMANN
05 Vice President of Academic Affairs Mr. David J. RICHARDS
30 Vice Pres Institutional Advancement Mr. Philip E. BEAVERS
84 Vice Pres of Enrollment Management Mr. Lloyd S. SCHARER
06 Registrar Mr. Brian SLENSKI
08 Director of Library Services Mr. James ORME
37 Financial Aid Director Mr. Tedd C. KEES
32 Director of Student Life Mr. Ryan BUSHNELL
41 Athletic Director Mr. John PIERCEFIELD
88 Director of Outreach Ministries Mrs. Judy BEAVERS
18 Maintenance Supervisor Mr. Brian SMITH
27 Publications Coordinator Mrs. Robyn ORME

Griggs University (G)

8903 N US Highway 31, Suite 2,
Berrien Springs MI 49104-1900
County: Berrien FICE Identification: 009454
Telephone: (800) 782-4769 Carnegie Class: Not Classified
FAX Number: (269) 471-2804 Calendar System: Semester
URL: www.griggs.edu
Established: 1990 Annual Undergrad Tuition & Fees: $11,190
Enrollment: 2,756 Coed
Affiliation or Control: Seventh-day Adventist IRS Status: 501(c)3
Highest Offering: Master's
Program: Religious Emphasis
Accreditation: DETC

01 President/Dean Dr. Alayne D. THORPE
03 Vice President/Assoc Dean Dr. Janine LIM
05 Chief Academic Officer Dr. Janine LIM
32 Director of Student Services Dr. Glynis BRADFIELD
07 Director of Admissions/Registrar Dr. Emilio GARCIA-MARENKO
10 Chief Financial Officer Mr. Nantoo BANERJEE
07 Graduate Admissions Ms. M. Angelica MUNOZ
21 Administrative Services Manager Vacant
15 Human Resources Manager Mr. Daniel AGNETTA
09 Director of Institutional Research Ms. Charlotte CONWAY
26 Chief Public Relations Officer Mr. Stephen D. PAYNE

Henry Ford Community College (H)

5101 Evergreen Road, Dearborn MI 48128-1495
County: Wayne FICE Identification: 002270
Unit ID: 170240
Telephone: (313) 845-9615 Carnegie Class: Assoc/Pub-S-MC
FAX Number: (313) 845-9658 Calendar System: Semester
URL: www.hfcc.edu
Established: 1938 Annual Undergrad Tuition & Fees (In-District): $3,112
Enrollment: 17,338 Coed
Affiliation or Control: Local IRS Status: 501(c)3
Highest Offering: Associate Degree
Program: Occupational; 2-Year Principally Bachelor's Creditable
Accreditation: NH, ACFEI, ADNUR, COARC, MAC, PTAA, RAD, SURGT

01 President Dr. Stan C. JENSEN
10 Vice President/Controller Dr. John SATKOWSKI
32 Vice Pres/Dean Student Services Dr. Lisa COPPRUE
05 Vice Pres/Chief Academic Officer Dr. Tracy PIERNER
30 Executive Director of Development Mr. A. Reginald BEST, JR.
06 Director of Registration and Record Ms. Holly DIAMOND
38 Division Director Counseling Mr. Imad NOURI
51 Director Corporate Training Ms. Tricia LEWELLYN
66 Director of Nursing Ms. Susan SHUNKWILER
08 Director Library Mr. Terrence POTVIN
13 Director Data & Voice Mr. Sandro SILVESTRI
21 Director Financial Services Dr. David CUNNINGHAM
26 Communications Director Mr. Gary ERWIN
37 Director Student Financial Aid Mr. Kevin J. CULLER
15 Executive Director Human Resources Dr. Cynthia ESCHENBURG
92 Director Honors Program Dr. Nabeel ABRAHAM
94 Director Women's Studies Vacant
96 Director Purchasing Mr. Fred STEINER
09 Executive Director Research/Plng Ms. Becky J. CHADWICK
40 Manager of College Store Ms. Pamela HALL
24 Instructional Technologist Dr. Vivian BEATY
19 Coordinator of Security Mr. Mark LABERGE

Hillsdale College (I)

33 East College Street, Hillsdale MI 49242-1298
County: Hillsdale FICE Identification: 002272
Unit ID: 170286
Telephone: (517) 437-7341 Carnegie Class: Bac/A&S
FAX Number: (517) 437-3923 Calendar System: Semester
URL: www.hillsdale.edu
Established: 1844 Annual Undergrad Tuition & Fees: $22,890
Enrollment: 1,399 Coed
Affiliation or Control: Independent Non-Profit IRS Status: 501(c)3
Highest Offering: Baccalaureate
Program: Liberal Arts And General; Teacher Preparatory
Accreditation: NH

01 President ...Dr. Larry P. ARNN, III
05 Provost ...Dr. David WHALEN
30 Vice Pres Institutional Advancement ...Mr. John CERVINI
10 Chf Admin Ofcr/VP Fin Affs & Treas ...Mr. Patrick FLANNERY
11 VP Admin & Sec of Board of Trustees ...Mr. Richard P. PEWE
26 VP of External Affairs ...Mr. Douglas JEFFREY
32 VP Student Affairs/Dean of Women ...Mrs. Diane PHILIPP
88 Vice Pres for Dow Leadership Center ...Mr. Jack OXENRIDER
100 Chief of Staff/Asst to President ...Mr. Mike HARNER
20 Associate Provost ...Dr. Mark MAIER
33 Dean of Men ...Mr. Aaron PETERSEN
07 Director of Admissions ...Mr. Jeffrey S. LANTIS
27 Exec Director of Media Relations ...Mr. Douglas JEFFREY
37 Director of Financial Aid ...Mr. Richard MOEGGENBERG
41 Athletic Director ...Mr. Don BRUBACHER
06 Registrar ...Mr. Douglas MCARTHUR
29 Director of Alumni Affairs ...Mr. Grigor HASTED
36 Director Career Planning ...Mr. Michael MURRAY
08 Librarian ...Mr. Daniel L. KNOCH
40 Bookstore Manager ...Mrs. Vicki NASH
42 Chaplain ...R.Rev. Peter BECKWITCH
18 Physical Plant Director ...Mr. Todd CLOW
90 Director of Academic Computing ...Mr. David M. ZENZ
15 Director Personnel Services ...Ms. Janet MARSH

Hope College (A)

141 E 12th Street, Holland MI 49423-3607
County: Ottawa FICE Identification: 002273
Unit ID: 170301
Telephone: (616) 395-7000 Carnegie Class: Bac/A&S
FAX Number: (616) 395-7922 Calendar System: Semester
URL: www.hope.edu
Established: 1866 Annual Undergrad Tuition & Fees: $28,720
Enrollment: 3,343 Coed
Affiliation or Control: Reformed Church In America IRS Status: 501(c)3
Highest Offering: Baccalaureate
Program: Liberal Arts And General; Teacher Preparatory; Professional
Accreditation: NH, ART, DANCE, ENG, MUS, NURSE, SW, TEAC, THEA

01 President ...Dr. John C. KNAPP
05 Provost ...Dr. R. Richard RAY, JR.
10 Vice Pres and Chief Fiscal Officer ...Mr. Thomas W. BYLSMA
07 Vice President for Admissions ...Mr. William VANDERBILT
30 Interim VP for College Advancement ...Mr. David VANDERWEL
32 VP Student Devel/Dean of Students ...Dr. Richard A. FROST
20 Associate Provost ...Mr. Alfredo M. GONZALES
26 Assoc VP Public & Community Rels ...Mr. Tom L. RENNER
08 Librarian ...Ms. Kelly G. JACOBSMA
39 Dir of Residential Life & Housing ...Dr. John E. JOBSON
22 Director of Multicultural Life ...Ms. Vanessa GREENE
94 Director of Women's Studies ...Ms. Priscilla D. ATKINS
81 Dean for Natural Sciences ...Dr. James GENTILE
79 Dean for Arts & Humanities ...Dr. Patrice RANKINE
83 Dean for Social Sciences ...Dr. Scott D. VANDER STOEP
88 Dean of the Chapel ...Rev. Trygve D. JOHNSON
06 Registrar ...Ms. Carol DEJONG
37 Director of Financial Aid ...Ms. Jill NUTT
36 Director Career Services ...Mr. Dale F. AUSTIN
21 Director of Finance & Business Svcs ...Mr. Douglas VAN DYKEN
13 Director of Operations & Technology ...Mr. Greg MAYBURY
14 Director of Computing & Info Tech ...Mr. Carl E. HEIDEMAN
15 Director Human Resources ...Mrs. Lori MULDER
18 Director Physical Plant ...Mr. Greg MAYBURY
40 Manager of Bookstore ...Mr. Mark COOK
29 Dir of Parent & Alumni Relations ...Mr. Scott TRAVIS
41 Co-Director of Athletics ...Mr. Tim SCHOONVELD
41 Co-Director of Athletics ...Mrs. Eva Dean FOLKERT
42 Senior Chaplain ...Rev. Paul H. BOERSMA
38 Asst Dean/Director Counseling Ctr ...Dr. Kristen GRAY

International Academy of Design and Technology (B)

1850 Research Drive, Troy MI 48083
Telephone: (248) 457-2700 Identification: 666632
Accreditation: ACICS, CIDA

† Main campus is International Academy of Design and Technology in Chicago, IL.

ITT Technical Institute (C)

1905 S Haggerty Road, Canton MI 48188-2025
Telephone: (734) 397-7800 Identification: 666323
Accreditation: ACICS

† Main campus is ITT Technical Institute in Indianapolis, IN.

ITT Technical Institute (D)

19855 West Outer Drive, L10W, Dearborn MI 48124
Telephone: (313) 278-5208 Identification: 770645
Accreditation: ACICS

† Main campus is ITT Technical Institute in Indianapolis, IN.

ITT Technical Institute (E)

3518 Plainfield Avenue NE, Grand Rapids MI 49525
Telephone: (616) 365-4800 Identification: 770646
Accreditation: ACICS

† Main campus is ITT Technical Institute in Indianapolis, IN.

ITT Technical Institute (F)

26700 Lahser Road, Suite 100, Southfield MI 48033
Telephone: (248) 603-6100 Identification: 770647
Accreditation: ACICS

† Main campus is ITT Technical Institute in Indianapolis, IN.

ITT Technical Institute (G)

6359 Miller Road, Swartz Creek MI 48473-1520
Telephone: (810) 628-2500 Identification: 666146
Accreditation: ACICS

† Main campus is ITT Technical Institute in Indianapolis, IN.

ITT Technical Institute (H)

1522 E Big Beaver Road, Troy MI 48083-1905
Telephone: (248) 524-1800 Identification: 666542
Accreditation: ACICS

† Main campus is ITT Technical Institute in Indianapolis, IN.

ITT Technical Institute (I)

1980 Metro Court S.W., Wyoming MI 49519
Telephone: (616) 406-1200 FICE Identification: 010627
Accreditation: ACICS

† Main campus is ITT Technical Institute in Indianapolis, IN.

Jackson College (J)

2111 Emmons Road, Jackson MI 49201-8399
County: Jackson FICE Identification: 002274
Unit ID: 170444
Telephone: (517) 787-0800 Carnegie Class: Assoc/Pub-R-L
FAX Number: (517) 789-1623 Calendar System: Semester
URL: www.jccmi.edu
Established: 1928 Annual Undergrad Tuition & Fees (In-District): $3,504
Enrollment: 6,247 Coed
Affiliation or Control: Local IRS Status: 501(c)3
Highest Offering: Associate Degree
Program: Occupational; 2-Year Principally Bachelor's Creditable
Accreditation: NH, ACBSP, COARC, DMS, MAC, RAD

01 President/CEO ...Dr. Daniel J. PHELAN
10 Vice Pres Finance & College Opers ...Vacant
32 Executive Dean of Students ...Mrs. Nancy MILLER
05 Provost ...Dr. Rebekah WOODS
11 Vice Pres of Administration ...Ms. Cindy ALLEN
102 President of JCC Foundation ...Mr. Jason VALENTE
15 Exec Director of HR & Org Develop ...Mr. William HENDRY

Kalamazoo College (K)

1200 Academy Street, Kalamazoo MI 49006-3295
County: Kalamazoo FICE Identification: 002275
Unit ID: 170532
Telephone: (269) 337-7000 Carnegie Class: Bac/A&S
FAX Number: (269) 337-7251 Calendar System: Quarter
URL: www.kzoo.edu
Established: 1833 Annual Undergrad Tuition & Fees: $47,825
Enrollment: 1,366 Coed
Affiliation or Control: Independent Non-Profit IRS Status: 501(c)3
Highest Offering: Baccalaureate
Program: Liberal Arts And General
Accreditation: NH

01 President ...Dr. Eileen B. WILSON-OYELARAN
05 Provost ...Dr. Michael A. MCDONALD
10 Vice President Business & Finance ...Mr. James E. PRINCE
30 Vice President College Advancement ...Mr. Albert J. DESIMONE
32 VP Student Devel & Dean of Students ...Dr. Sarah B. WESTFALL
20 Associate Provost ...Dr. Paul R. SOTHERLAND
85 Associate Provost for Intl Pgms ...Dr. Joseph L. BROCKINGTON
13 Associate Provost for Info Services ...Mr. Gregory S. DIMENT
09 Asst Provost Inst Support/Research ...Ms. Anne T. DUEWEKE
89 Dean of First Year & Advising ...Dr. Zaide E. PIXLEY
06 Registrar ...Mr. Ted WITRYK
15 Human Resources Manager ...Ms. Laura A. ANDERSEN
07 Dean of Admission and Financial Aid ...Mr. Eric P. STAAB
37 Director of Financial Aid ...Ms. Marian STOWERS
27 Director of College Communication ...Mr. James A. VANSWEDEN
18 Director of Facilities Management ...Mr. Paul W. MANSTROM
40 Director Bookstore ...Ms. Deborah L. THOMPSON
29 Director of Alumni Relations ...Ms. Kimberly J. ALDRICH
38 Director of Student Counseling ...Dr. Patricia A. PONTO
36 Dir Ctr Career/Professional Devel ...Ms. Joan HAWXHURST
20 Associate Provost ...Dr. Amy L. SMITH

Kalamazoo Valley Community College (L)

6767 West O Avenue, PO Box 4070,
Kalamazoo MI 49003-4070
County: Kalamazoo FICE Identification: 006949
Unit ID: 170541
Telephone: (269) 488-4400 Carnegie Class: Assoc/Pub-R-L
FAX Number: (269) 488-4555 Calendar System: Semester
URL: www.kvcc.edu
Established: 1966 Annual Undergrad Tuition & Fees (In-District): $2,630
Enrollment: 13,200 Coed
Affiliation or Control: Local IRS Status: 501(c)3
Highest Offering: Associate Degree
Program: Occupational; 2-Year Principally Bachelor's Creditable
Accreditation: NH, COARC, DH, EMT, MAC

01 President ...Dr. Marilyn J. SCHLACK
05 Vice President Academic Services ...Dr. Dennis BERTCH
10 Vice President Financial Services ...Ms. Louise ANDERSON
32 Exec VP Instructional/Student Svcs ...Mr. Michael COLLINS
15 Vice President of Human Resources ...Ms. Sandra BOHNET
13 Vice Pres for Admin Svc/Info Tech ...Mr. Terrel F. HUTCHINS
50 VP Econ & Business Development ...Vacant
86 Exec Dir Govt Rels/Special Projects ...Ms. Kathy JOHNSON
19 Director of Public Safety ...Mr. Richard IVES
08 Director of Libraries ...Ms. Janet ALM
07 Dir Admissions/Records/Registrar ...Mr. Michael MCCALL
09 Dir Planning/Research/Assessment ...Mr. Stephen CANNELL
30 Director Development ...Mr. Steve DOHERTY
37 Director Financial Aid ...Mr. Roger MILLER
18 Facilities/Construction Management ...Mr. Daniel MALEY
96 Director of Purchasing ...Ms. Kathy CAMPBELL
21 Business Manager ...Ms. Muriel HICE
35 Director of Student Success ...Ms. Laura COSBY
66 Director of Nursing ...Ms. Susan MOTT

Kalamazoo Valley Community College Arcadia Commons Campus (M)

202 North Rose Street, Kalamazoo MI 49007
Telephone: (269) 373-7800 Identification: 770276
Accreditation: &NH

† Main campus is Kalamazoo Valley Community College in Kalamazoo, MI.

Kaplan Career Institute (N)

18440 Ford Road, Detroit MI 48228
Telephone: (313) 425-4300 Identification: 770732
Accreditation: ACICS

† Main campus is Kaplan Career Institute in Harrisburg, PA.

Kellogg Community College (O)

450 North Avenue, Battle Creek MI 49017-3397
County: Calhoun FICE Identification: 002276
Unit ID: 170550
Telephone: (269) 965-3931 Carnegie Class: Assoc/Pub-R-L
FAX Number: (269) 962-4260 Calendar System: Semester
URL: www.kellogg.edu
Established: 1956 Annual Undergrad Tuition & Fees (In-District): $2,868
Enrollment: 6,002 Coed
Affiliation or Control: Local IRS Status: 501(c)3
Highest Offering: Associate Degree
Program: Occupational; 2-Year Principally Bachelor's Creditable
Accreditation: NH, DH, MLTAD, PTAA, RAD

01 President ...Dr. Dennis BONA
05 Vice President Instruction ...Ms. Catherine HENDLER
11 Vice Pres Administration/Finance ...Mr. Mark O'CONNELL
32 Vice President Student Services ...Dr. Kay KECK
10 Chief Financial Officer ...Mr. Richard SCOTT
13 Chief Information Officer ...Mr. Robert REYNOLDS
57 Chair Arts & Communication Dept ...Ms. Barbara SUDEIKIS
81 Int Chair Math & Science Dept ...Ms. Carole DAVIS
49 Dean Arts/Sciences/Regional Educ ...Dr. Kevin RABINEAU
102 Executive Director KCC Foundation ...Ms. Ginger CUTSINGER
96 Director Purchasing ...Ms. Angela CLEVELAND
06 Registrar ...Dr. Colleen WRIGHT
08 Director Library Services ...Ms. Martha STILWELL
41 Director Athletics & PE ...Mr. Tom SHAW
12 Director of Grahl Center ...Ms. Roberta GAGNON
12 Director Fehsenfeld Center ...Mr. Timothy SLEEVI
12 Director Eastern Academic Center ...Mr. Colin MCCALEB
15 Director Human Resources ...Ms. Ali ROBERTSON
18 Dir Inst Facilities/Public Safety ...Mr. John DIPIERRO
51 Director Lifelong Learning ...Ms. Mary GREEN
09 Director Institutional Research ...Ms. Doris LEWIS
21 Director of Finance ...Ms. Tracy BEATTY
12 Dir Reg Manufacturing Tech Center ...Vacant
38 Dir Academic Advising/Student Life ...Ms. Terah ZAREMBA
26 Dir Public Information & Marketing ...Mr. Eric GREENE
07 Director of Admissions ...Ms. Meredith STRAVERS
40 Bookstore Manager ...Ms. Catherine JAMES

Kendall College of Art & Design (P)

17 Fountain Street, NW, Grand Rapids MI 49503
Telephone: (800) 676-2787 Identification: 770273
Accreditation: &NH

† Main campus is Ferris State University in Big Rapids, MI.

Kettering University (Q)

1700 University Avenue, Flint MI 48504-6214
County: Genesee FICE Identification: 002262
Unit ID: 169983
Telephone: (810) 762-9500 Carnegie Class: Master's M
FAX Number: (810) 762-9837 Calendar System: Semester
URL: www.kettering.edu
Established: 1919 Annual Undergrad Tuition & Fees: $35,600

Enrollment: 2,048 Coed
Affiliation or Control: Independent Non-Profit IRS Status: 501(c)3
Highest Offering: Master's
Program: Professional
Accreditation: NH, ACBSP, CS, ENG

01	President	Dr. Robert K. MCMAHAN
04	Executive Assistant to President	Ms. Evelyn YAEGER
04	Assistant to President	Ms. Tabitha BOURASSA
05	Provost & VP Academic Affairs	Dr. Robert L. SIMPSON
10	VP Administration & Finance	Mr. Tom AYERS
84	VP Enrollment Services	Mr. Kip DARCY
32	VP Student Life & Dean of Students	Ms. Betsy E. HOMSHER
30	VP Univ Advancement/Ext Relations	Ms. Susan DAVIES
13	VP Instruct/Admin & Info Technology	Ms. Viola SPRAGUE
20	Vice Provost/Assoc VP Acad Services	Dr. Jacqueline A. EL-SAYED
15	Director Human Resources	Ms. Beth EWALD
102	Dir of Philanthropy Corp/Found	Ms. Eve VITALE
29	Dir of Alumni Engagement	Mr. Robert NICHOLS
88	Dir of Philanthropy Indiv Giving	Mr. Jack P. STOCK
19	Chief Campus Safety	Mr. James R. BENFORD
37	Director Student Financial Aid	Ms. Diane K. BICE
21	Controller	Ms. Beth A. COVERS
09	Director Institution Effectiveness	Dr. Edwin IMASUEN
58	Director Graduate Programs	Mr. Todd J. STEELE
18	Director Physical Plant	Mr. Joseph ASPERGER
08	Director Library Services	Dr. Charles D. HANSON
07	Director Intl & Undergrad Admiss	Ms. Karen A. FULL
41	Director Athletics/Rec Service	Mr. Michael L. SCHAAL
93	Director Minority Student Affairs	Mr. Dwight L. TAVADA
104	Director International Office	Dr. Basem ALZAHABI
88	Director Auxilliary Services	Ms. Nadine L. THOR
27	Director of Marketing	Ms. Julie A. ULSETH
06	Registrar	Ms. Sheila R. RUPP
23	Director Wellness Center	Ms. Cristina REED
39	Director Residence Life	Ms. Katherine BOSIO
78	Director Coop Educ & Career Svcs	Dr. Jacqueline A. EL-SAYED
88	MI SBTDC Regional Director	Ms. Marsha J. LYTTLE
96	Purchasing Manager	Ms. Kathleen A. REMENDER
44	Director of Annual Giving	Ms. Michelle D. LOPER
14	Director of IT Operations	Mr. Daniel GARCIA
25	Contract/Grant Specialist	Ms. Jodi L. DORR
105	Webmaster	Ms. Donna WICKS
88	Dir Center Excellence Teach & Learn	Dr. Terri LYNCH-CARIS
88	Dir Enrollment Events/Visitor Rels	Ms. Sheila ADAMS COWES
88	Director Special Events	Ms. Diane ALDERSON
88	Director Academic Service Center	Ms. Natalie CANDELA

Keweenaw Bay Ojibwa Community College (A)

111 Beartown Rd, PO Box 519, Baraga MI 49908
County: Baraga FICE Identification: 041647
Unit ID: 461315
Telephone: (906) 353-4600 Carnegie Class: Not Classified
FAX Number: N/A Calendar System: Semester
URL: www.kbocc.org
Established: 1975 Annual Undergrad Tuition & Fees (In-District): $2,660
Enrollment: 86 Coed
Affiliation or Control: Local IRS Status: 501(c)3
Highest Offering: Associate Degree
Program: Occupational; 2-Year Principally Bachelor's Creditable
Accreditation: NH

01	President	Ms. Debra J. PARRISH
05	Dean of Instruction	Ms. Lynn AHO
07	Interim Admissions Officer	Mr. Patrick RACETTE
10	Business Officer	Ms. Megan SHANAHAN
32	Dean of Student Services	Ms. Danise CADEAU
37	Director Financial Aid/Enroll Coord	Ms. Elizabeth JULIO
88	Cultural Advisor	Ms. Liz JULIO

Kirtland Community College (B)

10775 N Saint Helen Road, Roscommon MI 48653-9721
County: Roscommon FICE Identification: 007171
Unit ID: 170587
Telephone: (989) 275-5000 Carnegie Class: Assoc/Pub-R-M
FAX Number: (989) 275-8210 Calendar System: Semester
URL: www.kirtland.edu
Established: 1966 Annual Undergrad Tuition & Fees (In-District): $3,235
Enrollment: 1,807 Coed
Affiliation or Control: Local IRS Status: 501(c)3
Highest Offering: Associate Degree
Program: Occupational; 2-Year Principally Bachelor's Creditable
Accreditation: NH

01	President	Dr. Thomas QUINN
05	Dean of Instruction	Ms. Julie LAVENDER
32	Dean of Student Services	Ms. Michelle VYSKOCIL
76	Associate Dean Health Sciences	Ms. Julie LAVENDER
20	Associate Dean Instruction	Mr. Nick HOLTON
20	Associate Dean of Instruction	Ms. Laura PERCIVAL
08	Director of Library	Ms. Deb SHUMAKER
37	Director of Financial Aid	Ms. Christin HORNDT
10	Chief Financial Officer	Mr. Jason BROGE
26	Director of Institutional Services	Mr. Tim SCHERER
18	Director of Physical Plant	Ms. Evelyn SCHENK
06	Registrar	Ms. Michelle VYSKOCIL
15	Director of Human Resources	Mr. Dale SHANTZ
09	Director of Institutional Research	Mr. Nick BAKER

102	Foundation Director	Ms. Lynne RUDEN
07	Admissions Coordinator	Ms. Michelle DEVINE

Kuyper College (C)

3333 East Beltline Avenue, NE,
Grand Rapids MI 49525-9749
County: Kent FICE Identification: 002311
Unit ID: 171881
Telephone: (616) 222-3000 Carnegie Class: Bac/Diverse
FAX Number: (616) 988-3608 Calendar System: Semester
URL: www.kuyper.edu
Established: 1939 Annual Undergrad Tuition & Fees: $18,454
Enrollment: 323 Coed
Affiliation or Control: Independent Non-Profit IRS Status: 501(c)3
Highest Offering: Baccalaureate
Program: Professional; Religious Emphasis
Accreditation: NH, BI, SW

01	President	Dr. Nicholas V. KROEZE
05	Provost	Dr. Patricia R. HARRIS
06	Registrar	Ms. Joy MILANO
30	Vice Pres College Advancement	Mr. Ken CAPISCIOLTO
44	Director Annual/Planned Giving	Ms. Teresa JANZEN
10	Vice Pres Business Administration	Mr. Duane BRAS
84	Vice Pres Enrollment Management	Mr. Dale KUIPER
07	Director of Admissions	Ms. Sung-Ae REED
37	Financial Aid Director	Ms. Agnes M. RUSSELL
04	Assistant to the President	Ms. Dawn A. LYNEMA
08	Librarian	Ms. Dianne V. ZANDBERGEN
32	Director of Student Life	Mr. Curt ESSENBURG
19	Director of Facilities/Safety	Mr. Eric ROOSMA
18	Director of Physical Plant	Mr. Tim CHUPP
29	Director of Alumni/Public Relations	Ms. Hannah SCHIERBEEK
15	Director Personnel Services	Ms. Mary CARLSON
13	Director Computing/Info Management	Mr. Keith TORNO
41	Athletic Director	Ms. Christine MORAN
49	Arts and Sciences	Ms. Teresa RENKEMA
64	Music	Dr. Kai Ton CHAU
70	Social Work	Mr. Greg SCOTT
73	Theology	Dr. Branson PARLER
85	International Student Services	Ms. Mary VANDERMEER

Lake Michigan College (D)

2755 E Napier, Benton Harbor MI 49022-1899
County: Berrien FICE Identification: 002277
Unit ID: 170620
Telephone: (269) 927-8861 Carnegie Class: Assoc/Pub-R-M
FAX Number: N/A Calendar System: Semester
URL: www.lakemichigancollege.edu
Established: 1946 Annual Undergrad Tuition & Fees (In-District): $1,464
Enrollment: 4,654 Coed
Affiliation or Control: Local IRS Status: 501(c)3
Highest Offering: Associate Degree
Program: Occupational; 2-Year Principally Bachelor's Creditable
Accreditation: NH, ADNUR, DA, RAD

01	President	Dr. Robert HARRISON
05	Vice President of Instruction	Dr. Sarah DEMPSEY
11	VP Administrative Services	Ms. Anne C. ERDMAN
30	VP Institutional Advance/Planning	Mr. Greg A. KOROCH
10	Vice President Financial Services	Ms. Kelli HAHN
04	Exec Assistant to the President	Ms. Rebecca STEFFEN
49	Exec Dean Arts & Sciences	Vacant
50	Dean Tech/Health Sciences/Business	Dr. Leslie KELLOGG
12	Exec Dean South Haven Campus	Ms. Janice VARNEY
12	Exec Dean Bertrand Crossing	Mrs. Barbara CRAIG
32	Vice President Student Services	Dr. Clinton GABBARD
88	Manager Mainstage Services	Vacant
18	Director Facilities Management	Mr. Lee H. VAN GINHOVEN
13	Exec Dir Informational Technology	Mr. Randall MELTON
26	Director Marketing	Ms. Laura KRAKLAU
37	Director of Financial Aid	Ms. Anne TEWS
06	Associate Registrar	Mr. Tezuko HIROKO
51	Dir Cmty Outreach/Continuing Educ	Vacant
102	Director Foundations & Grants	Vacant
96	Purchasing Manager	Mr. Nathan MAIN
88	Dir Conference and Event Services	Vacant
91	Network Systems/Database Admin	Ms. Alecia LIN
90	Activity Dir/Instruction Technology	Mr. Mark KELLY
09	Director Institutional Research	Ms. Alissa SHEFTIC

Lake Michigan College Bertrand Crossing (E)

1905 Foundation Drive, Niles MI 49120
Telephone: (269) 695-1391 Identification: 770277
Accreditation: &NH

† Main campus is Lake Michigan College in Benton Harbor, MI.

Lake Michigan College South Haven (F)

125 Veterans Boulevard, South Haven MI 49090
Telephone: (269) 639-8442 Identification: 770278
Accreditation: &NH

† Main campus is Lake Michigan College in Benton Harbor, MI.

Lake Superior State University (G)

650 W Easterday Avenue,
Sault Sainte Marie MI 49783-1699
County: Chippewa FICE Identification: 002293
Unit ID: 170639
Telephone: (906) 632-6841 Carnegie Class: Bac/Diverse
FAX Number: (906) 635-2111 Calendar System: Semester
URL: www.lssu.edu
Established: 1946 Annual Undergrad Tuition & Fees (In-State): $10,025
Enrollment: 2,590 Coed
Affiliation or Control: State IRS Status: 501(c)3
Highest Offering: Master's
Program: Liberal Arts And General; Teacher Preparatory; Professional
Accreditation: NH, ENG, ENGT, IFSAC, NUR, @TEAC

01	President	Dr. Tony L. MCLAIN
05	Vice President/Provost	Mr. Maurice WALWORTH
32	Vice President Student Affairs	Dr. Kenneth PERESS
10	Vice President Finance	Ms. Sherry L. BROOKS
84	Vice President Enrollment Services	Mr. William EILOLA
108	Assoc Provost Assess/Grad/Educ	Dr. David MYTON
49	Interim Dean ALSS & Emerg Svcs	Dr. Paige GORDIER
81	Dean Natural & Math Sciences	Dr. Barbara KELLER
66	Dean Nursing/Rec Studies/ExSc	Vacant
50	Dean Business & Engineering	Dr. David FINLEY
53	Asst Dean Education	Dr. Donna FIEBELKORN
13	Interim Dir IT/Network Admin	Mr. Scott OLSON
18	Director Physical Plant	Ms. Sherry BROOKS
06	Registrar	Ms. Nancy NEVE
07	Director of Admissions	Mr. Allan CASE
16	Director Human Resources	Ms. Marta WARREN
36	Director of Career Services	Ms. Theresa WEAVER
37	Director of Financial Aid	Ms. Deborah FAUST
38	Director of Counseling	Ms. Kristin LARSON
39	Director Housing/Residential Life	Mr. Scott M. KORB
26	Director of Public Affairs	Mr. Thomas A. PINK
29	Director Alumni Relations	Ms. Susan FITZPATRICK
102	Director of Foundation	Mr. Tom COATES
96	Director of Purchasing	Ms. Colleen RYE
23	Director Health Services	Ms. Karen STOREY
28	Dir Native American Ctr/Diversity	Ms. Stephanie SABATINE
41	Athletic Director	Ms. Kristin DUNBAR
35	Director Student Life	Mr. Scott KORB
40	Bookstore Manager	Ms. Amber MCLEAN
09	Institutional Research Analyst	Ms. Cynthia F. MERKEL

Lansing Community College (H)

419 N Capitol Avenue, Lansing MI 48901-7211
County: Ingham FICE Identification: 002278
Unit ID: 170657
Telephone: (517) 483-1957 Carnegie Class: Assoc/Pub-R-L
FAX Number: (517) 483-1845 Calendar System: Semester
URL: www.lcc.edu
Established: 1957 Annual Undergrad Tuition & Fees (In-District): $2,720
Enrollment: 19,367 Coed
Affiliation or Control: Local IRS Status: 501(c)3
Highest Offering: Associate Degree
Program: Occupational; 2-Year Principally Bachelor's Creditable
Accreditation: NH, ADNUR, COMTA, DH, DMS, EMT, HT, IFSAC, RAD, SURGT

01	President	Dr. Brent KNIGHT
05	Provost	Dr. Richard PRYSTOWSKY
10	Sr VP Finance/Admin & Advancement	Ms. Lisa WEBB SHARPE
21	Acting Chief Financial Officer	Mr. Don WILSKE
13	Chief Information Officer	Mr. Kevin BUBB
11	Int Exec Dir Administrative Svcs	Mr. Tim MARTZ
20	Associate VP Academic Affairs	Vacant
30	Assoc VP External Affs/Development	Ms. Elva REVILLA
56	Dean Ext Learning & Prof Studies	Dr. Jean MORCIGLIO
88	Dean Health & Human Services	Ms. Margie CLARK
49	Dean Arts & Sciences	Dr. Michael NEALON
32	Dean Student Affairs	Dr. Evan MONTAGUE
72	Dean Technical Careers	Mr. George BERGHORN
15	Exec Director Human Resources	Ms. Ann KRONEMAN
26	Director Public Affairs	Ms. Ellen JONES

Lawrence Technological University (I)

21000 W Ten Mile Road, Southfield MI 48075-1058
County: Oakland FICE Identification: 002279
Unit ID: 170675
Telephone: (248) 204-4000 Carnegie Class: Master's L
FAX Number: (248) 204-3727 Calendar System: Semester
URL: www.ltu.edu
Established: 1932 Annual Undergrad Tuition & Fees: $29,000
Enrollment: 4,154 Coed
Affiliation or Control: Independent Non-Profit IRS Status: 501(c)3
Highest Offering: Doctorate
Program: Liberal Arts And General; Professional
Accreditation: NH, ACBSP, ART, CIDA, ENG, IACBE

01	President	Dr. Virinder K. MOUDGIL
04	Exec Assistant to the President	Ms. Louise M. GARRETT
05	Provost	Dr. Maria J. VAZ
10	Vice Pres Finance/Admin	Ms. Linda L. HEIGHT
30	VP of University Advancement	Mr. Stephen E. BROWN
88	Assoc VP Advance/Chief Dev Officer	Mr. Dennis J. HOWIE
58	Assoc Provost/Dean Grad Program	Dr. S. Alan MCCORD
84	Asst Provost Enrollment Management	Ms. Lisa R. KUJAWA

48 Dean of Architecture & Design ....Mr. Glen S. LEROY
49 Dean of Arts & Sciences ....Dr. Hsiao-Ping H. MOORE
54 Dean of Engineering ....Dr. Nabil F. GRACE
50 Dean of Management ....Dr. Bahman MIRSHAB
32 Dean of Students ....Mr. Kevin FINN
26 Exec Dir Marketing & Public Affs ....Mr. Bruce J. ANNETT, JR.
10 Director Business Services ....Vacant
07 Director Admissions ....Ms. Jane T. ROHRBACK
06 Interim Registrar ....Ms. Noreen FERGUSON
08 Director Library ....Mr. Gary R. COCOZZOLI
18 Director Campus Facilities ....Mr. Carey G. VALENTINE
14 Ex Dir IT Svc Delivery Organization ....Mr. Tim CHAVIS
37 Int Dir Financial Aid & Vet Affs ....Ms. Dee KING
35 Dir Stdnt Rec/Athletics & Wellness ....Mr. Scott TRUDEAU
36 Director of Career Services ....Ms. Peg PIERCE
44 Asst Vice Pres/Campaign Director ....Vacant
85 Exec Dir of Student Affairs ....Ms. Cyndi MCMICHAEL
24 Director Audio Visual Media Svcs ....Mr. Walter G. BIZON
39 Director Residence Life ....Ms. Kimberly OSANTOWSKI
86 Exec Dir Econ Dev & Govt Relations ....Mr. Mark J. BRUCKI
102 Dir of Corp & Foundation Relations ....Mr. Howard DAVIS
44 Philanthropy Director ....Ms. Julie VULAJ
44 Philanthropy Director ....Ms. Angeline ZELENAK
13 Director Help Desk/Services ....Ms. Charlene RAMOS
28 Director of Diversity ....Mr. Kevin FINN
89 Director of Freshman Studies ....Vacant
15 Human Resources Director ....Ms. Deshawn JOHNSON
40 Manager Campus Bookstore ....Mr. Carl CAMPANELLA
88 Manager Dining Services ....Ms. Nancy THOMAS
27 Managing Editor News Bureau ....Mr. Eric POPE
19 Director of Campus Safety ....Mr. Harry P. BUTLER
29 Manager Alumni Rels/Alumni Giving ....Ms. Mary RANDAZZO
31 Dir of University Special Events ....Ms. Robin LECLERC
26 Dir Univ Comm & Academic Editor ....Ms. Anne M G. ADAMUS
44 Mgr Advancement Svcs/Annual Giving ....Vacant
88 University Architect ....Mr. Joseph C. VERYSER
88 Director of Student Engagement ....Vacant
88 Dir of Academic Achievement Center ....Dr. Gladys M. AVILES
09 Dir of Inst Research/Academic Plng ....Vacant
96 Purchasing Agent ....Ms. Michelle BUTKOVICH

Macomb Community College (A)

14500 Twelve Mile Road, Warren MI 48088-9838
County: Macomb FICE Identification: 008906
Unit ID: 170790
Telephone: (586) 445-7999 Carnegie Class: Assoc/Pub-S-MC
FAX Number: (586) 445-7886 Calendar System: Semester
URL: www.macomb.edu
Established: 1954 Annual Undergrad Tuition & Fees (In-District): $2,770
Enrollment: 24,160 Coed
Affiliation or Control: Local IRS Status: 501(c)3
Highest Offering: Associate Degree
Program: Occupational; 2-Year Principally Bachelor's Creditable
Accreditation: NH, ACFEI, ADNUR, CAHIIM, COARC, MAC, MLTAD, OTA, PTAA, SURGT

01 President ....Dr. James JACOBS
05 Vice Pres/Provost Learning Unit ....Dr. James SAWYER
10 Vice President for Business ....Ms. Elizabeth ARGIRI
16 Vice President for Human Resources ....Ms. Denise WILLIAMS
26 VP College Adv/Community Relations ....Ms. Casandra ULBRICH
88 Dean University Relations ....Ms. Donna PETRAS
32 Vice President for Student Services ....Ms. Jill M. LITTLE
49 Dean Arts & Sciences ....Ms. Katherine GRENDA
76 Dean Health/Public Services ....Ms. Charlene MCPEAK
54 Dean Engineering & Adv Tech ....Mr. Joseph PETROSKY
50 Dean Business & Info Technology ....Mr. David CORBA
35 Dean of Student Success ....Ms. Susan BOYD
31 Dean Student & Community Services ....Mr. Geary MAIURI
45 Exec Director Planning & Research ....Ms. Gerri Lynn PAVONE
21 Director Finance & Investments ....Ms. Roberta REMIAS
19 Captain College Police ....Mr. Thomas WILK
88 Director Public Service Institute ....Mr. Carl SEITZ
26 Director Marketing & Recruitment ....Ms. Audrey TAKACS
09 Director Institutional Research ....Ms. Deirdre SYMS
88 Director Special Research Projects ....Mr. Randall HICKMAN
06 Registrar/Dir Enrollment Services ....Ms. Carrie JEFFERS
102 Director Macomb College Foundation ....Ms. Dawn MAGRETTA
38 Dir Counseling & Academic Advising ....Mr. Gerald KNESEK
96 Purchasing Administrator ....Mr. Dennis COSTELLO
41 Manager Athletics/Sports Clubs ....Mr. Brent BIEBUYCK
18 Director Facilities Management ....Mr. Stevan ALTON
37 Director of Financial Aid ....Mr. Douglas LEVY
36 Director Career Employment Services ....Mr. Robert PENKALA
51 Dir Workforce Continuing Education ....Ms. Elise JOHNSON
27 CIO/Exec Dir Communications & IT ....Mr. Michael ZIMMERMAN
08 Dean Libraries/Learning Resources ....Mr. Michael BALSAMO
43 General Counsel ....Mr. Hunter WENDT

Madonna University (B)

36600 Schoolcraft Road, Livonia MI 48150-1176
County: Wayne FICE Identification: 002282
Unit ID: 170806
Telephone: (734) 432-5300 Carnegie Class: Master's M
FAX Number: (734) 432-5333 Calendar System: Semester
URL: www.madonna.edu
Established: 1947 Annual Undergrad Tuition & Fees: $16,340
Enrollment: 4,428 Coed
Affiliation or Control: Roman Catholic IRS Status: 501(c)3
Highest Offering: Doctorate
Program: Liberal Arts And General; Teacher Preparatory; Professional
Accreditation: NH, DIETD, DMS, NURSE, SW, TED

01 President ....Sr. Rose Marie KUJAWA
30 Vice President for Advancement ....Ms. Andrea NODGE
05 Provost and VP for Academic Admin ....Dr. Ernest NOLAN
10 Vice Pres for Finance/Operations ....Mr. Leonard WILHELM
32 Vice President for Student Affairs ... Dr. Connie TINGSON-GATUZ
84 Vice Pres Planning/Enrollment Mgmt ....Mr. Michael KENNEY
12 Dean Outreach and Distance Learning ....Dr. James NOVAK
42 Director of Campus Ministry ....Mr. Patrick WATERS
06 Registrar ....Ms. Dina DUBUIS
07 Director of Admissions ....Mr. Mike QUATTRO
28 Director Diversity/Multicultural ....Mr. Bryant GEORGE
08 Director of Library Services ....Ms. Joanne LUMETTA
37 Director of Financial Aid ....Mr. Chris ZIEGLER
13 Director Information Systems ....Sr. Serafina Marie DIXON
15 Director of Human Resources ....Ms. Tracey DURDEN
36 Director of Career Services ....Ms. Christine BRANT
30 Director Corp Devel/Special Events ....Ms. Ashley FREDRICK
19 Director Public Safety ....Mr. David HAMMERSCHMIDT
41 Director Athletics ....Mr. Bryan RIZZO
40 Bookstore Manager ....Ms. Debbie MITCHELL
39 Director Residence Hall ....Ms. Tanisha MCINTOSH
24 Director Media Services ....Ms. Patricia DERRY
23 Director Instruction Center ....Dr. Patricia VINT
09 Director of Institutional Research ....Dr. Edith RALEIGH
18 Chief Facilities/Physical Plant ....Mr. Craig FLICKINGER
29 Director Alumni Relations ....Ms. Carole BOOMS
26 Director of Marketing ....Ms. Karen SANBORN
79 Dean Arts & Humanities ....Dr. Kathleen O'DOWD
50 Dean Business ....Dr. Stuart ARENDS
58 Dean Graduate Studies ....Dr. Edith RALEIGH
66 Dean Nursing & Health ....Dr. Teresa THOMPSON
72 Dean Science & Mathematics ....Dr. Theodore BIERMANN
83 Dean Social Sciences ....Dr. Karen ROSS
53 Dean Education ....Dr. Karen OBSNIUK

Manthano Christian College (C)

6420 Newburgh Road, Westland MI 48185
County: Wayne Identification: 667140
Telephone: (734) 895-3280 Carnegie Class: Not Classified
FAX Number: N/A Calendar System: Other
URL: manthanochristian.org
Established: Annual Undergrad Tuition & Fees: N/A
Enrollment: 5,280 Coed
Affiliation or Control: Non-denominational IRS Status: 501(c)3
Highest Offering: Baccalaureate
Program: Religious Emphasis
Accreditation: @TRACS

Marygrove College (D)

8425 W McNichols Road, Detroit MI 48221-2599
County: Wayne FICE Identification: 002284
Unit ID: 170842
Telephone: (313) 927-1200 Carnegie Class: Master's L
FAX Number: (313) 927-1345 Calendar System: Semester
URL: www.marygrove.edu
Established: 1905 Annual Undergrad Tuition & Fees: $19,850
Enrollment: 1,963 Coed
Affiliation or Control: Roman Catholic IRS Status: 501(c)3
Highest Offering: Master's
Program: 2-Year Principally Bachelor's Creditable; Liberal Arts And General; Teacher Preparatory; Professional
Accreditation: NH, SW, TEAC

01 President ....Dr. David J. FIKE
04 Exec Assistant to the President ....Ms. Maryann S. KUMMER
05 VP Academic Affairs ....Vacant
30 Vice Pres Institutional Advancement ....Mr. Kenneth MALECKE
10 VP Finance/Admin & CFO ....Vacant
20 Dean of Academic Programs ....Dr. Judith A. HEINEN
88 Dean of the Faculty ....Dr. Donald E. LEVIN
88 Asst to the Pres New Pgm Develpmnt ....Dr. Sally WELCH
51 Exec Dir of Continuing Education ....Ms. Jo Ann M. CUSMANO
06 Registrar ....Ms. Gladys SMITH
07 Chief Recruitment & Enrollment Ofcr ....Ms. Anna NASH
09 Director of Institutional Research ....Mr. John SENKO
29 Director of Alumni Relations ....Ms. Diane PUHL
37 Dir Fin Aid and Student Svc Ctr ....Ms. Patricia M. CHAPLIN
41 Athletic Director ....Mr. David SICHTERMAN
88 Director of Mission Integration ....Ms. Janice M. MACHUSAK
42 Director of Campus Ministry ....Mr. Jesse COX
88 Dir of Urban Leadership Initiatives ....Ms. Brenda G. PRICE
15 Director of Human Resources ....Vacant
32 Assistant Dean for Student Develop ....Dr. Carolyn ROBERTS
39 Director Residential Life ....Ms. Helena GARDNER
104 Director of International Programs ....Ms. Michelle A. CADE
19 Dir of Campus Security & Services ....Mr. Horace DANDRIDGE
26 Communications & Marketing Officer ....Ms. Karen E. CAMERON
36 Director of Career Services ....Vacant
88 Dir of Retention and Student Succ ....Ms. Veronica KILLEBREW

MIAT College of Technology (E)

2955 South Haggerty Rd, Canton MI 48188
County: Wayne FICE Identification: 020603
Unit ID: 169655
Telephone: (734) 423-2139 Carnegie Class: Not Classified
FAX Number: (734) 858-5000 Calendar System: Other
URL: www.miat.edu
Established: Annual Undergrad Tuition & Fees: $12,950
Enrollment: 764 Coed
Affiliation or Control: Proprietary IRS Status: Proprietary
Highest Offering: Associate Degree
Program: Occupational
Accreditation: ACCSC

Michigan Jewish Institute (F)

6890 West Maple Road, West Bloomfield MI 48322
County: Oakland FICE Identification: 032843
Unit ID: 434414
Telephone: (248) 414-6900 Carnegie Class: Bac/A&S
FAX Number: (248) 414-6907 Calendar System: Semester
URL: www.mji.edu
Established: 1994 Annual Undergrad Tuition & Fees: $11,200
Enrollment: 1,529 Coed
Affiliation or Control: Independent Non-Profit IRS Status: 501(c)3
Highest Offering: Baccalaureate
Program: Business Emphasis
Accreditation: ACICS

01 President/CFO/VP Financial Affs ....Rabbi Kasriel SHEMTOV
05 VP Inst Adv & Dean Academic Admin ....Dr. T. Hershel GARDIN
06 Registrar ....Ms. Alicia JAMES
20 Director of Academics ....Mr. Dov STEIN
37 Financial Aid Administrator ....Ms. Fran HERMAN
105 Web & Lan Services ....Mr. Philip KLUMP

Michigan School of Professional Psychology (G)

26811 Orchard Lake Road,
Farmington Hills MI 48334-4512
County: Oakland FICE Identification: 021989
Unit ID: 169220
Telephone: (248) 476-1122 Carnegie Class: Spec/Health
FAX Number: (248) 476-1125 Calendar System: Semester
URL: www.mispp.edu
Established: 1981 Annual Graduate Tuition & Fees: $27,639
Enrollment: 165 Coed
Affiliation or Control: Independent Non-Profit IRS Status: 501(c)3
Highest Offering: Doctorate; No Undergraduates
Program: Professional
Accreditation: NH

01 President/Chief Executive Officer ....Dr. Diane BLAU
03 Vice President/Chief Operating Ofcr ....Ms. Diane ZALAPI
05 Program Director/Chief Academic Ofc ....Dr. Lee BACH
88 Director of Clinical Training ....Dr. Fran BROWN
13 Director of Info Tech & Bldg Svcs ....Mr. Jeffrey CROSS
37 Financial Aid Coordinator ....Ms. Sandra BUTTERWORTH
08 Head Academic Librarian ....Ms. Michelle WHEELER
06 Registrar ....Ms. Heather RIGBY
07 Admissions/Recruitment Coordinator ....Ms. Amanda MING
11 Dir of Administrative Operations ....Ms. Laura LANE

Michigan State University (H)

426 Auditorium Road, East Lansing MI 48824-1046
County: Ingham FICE Identification: 002290
Unit ID: 171100
Telephone: (517) 355-1855 Carnegie Class: RU/VH
FAX Number: N/A Calendar System: Semester
URL: www.msu.edu
Established: 1855 Annual Undergrad Tuition & Fees (In-State): $13,579
Enrollment: 48,906 Coed
Affiliation or Control: State IRS Status: 501(c)3
Highest Offering: Doctorate
Program: Liberal Arts And General; Teacher Preparatory; Professional
Accreditation: NH, ANEST, BUS, BUSA, CEA, CIDA, CLPSY, CONST, CORE, CS, DIETD, DIETI, DMOLS, ENG, FEPAC, FOR, IPSY, JOUR, LAW, LSAR, MED, MFCD, MT, MUS, NURSE, OSTEO, #PLNG, SCPSY, SP, SW, TEAC, VET

01 President ....Dr. Lou Anna K. SIMON
05 Actg Provost/Exec VP Academic Affs ....Dr. June P. YOUATT
03 Exec Vice Pres for Admin Services ....Dr. Satish S. UDPA
101 Vice President/Secretary to Board ....Mr. William R. BEEKMAN
46 Vice President Research & Grad Stds ....Dr. Stephen HSU
32 Interim VP Student Affairs & Svcs ....Dr. Denise B. MAYBANK
86 Vice President Governmental Affairs ....Mr. Mark A. BURNHAM
10 Vice Pres Finance Opers/Treasurer ....Mr. Mark HAAS
30 Vice Pres Univ Advancement ....Mr. Robert GROVES
43 Vice Pres Legal Affairs & Gen Coun ....Mr. Robert A. NOTO
18 VP Infrastructure Planning & Facil ....Mr. Ronald T. FLINN
88 Vice President Auxillary Services ....Mr. Vennie GORE
26 VP Communication & Brand Strategy ....Ms. Heather C. SWAIN
22 Dir Incl/Intrcult Init/Sr Adv P Dvr ....Ms. Paulette GRANBERRY-RUSSELL
88 Assoc VP Research/Graduate Studies ....Dr. Paul M. HUNT
58 Assoc Prov and Dean Grad School ....Dr. Karen L. KLOMPARENS
20 Assoc Prov & Dean Ungrad Studies ....Dr. Douglas ESTRY
88 Assoc Prov Univ Outreach/ Engagement ....Dr. Hiram E. FITZGERALD
88 Assoc Provost Academic Svcs ....Dr. Linda O. STANFORD
15 Assoc Prov/VP Academic Human Res ....Mr. Theodore H. CURRY, II
45 Asst VP & Director of Plng/Budgets ....Mr. David S. BYELICH
16 Asst Vice Pres for Human Resources ....Ms. Sharon BUTLER
13 CIO and Dir IT Svcs Techology ....Mr. Thomas DAVIS
88 Asst VP Ofc of Sponsored Programs ....Dr. Twila REIGHLEY
21 Controller ....Mr. Greg DEPPONG

07 Director of Admissions ....Mr. James W. COTTER
29 Assoc VP University Advancement ....Mr. W. Scott WESTERMAN, III
25 Director Contract & Grant Admin ....Mr. Daniel T. EVON
36 Assoc Dir Career Services/Placement ....Dr. Linda GROSS
38 Assoc Director Counseling Center ....Dr. Scott BECKER
88 Dir MI AgBioResearch ....Dr. Doug BUHLER
56 Director MSU Extension ....Dr. Thomas G. COON
37 Director of Financial Aid ....Mr. Richard SHIPMAN
06 Registrar ....Dr. Nicole ROVIG
85 Director Intl Students/Scholars ....Mr. Peter F. BRIGGS
23 Director MSU Student Health Ctr ....Dr. Glynda M. MOORER
92 Dean Honors College ....Dr. Cynthia JACKSON-ELMOORE
41 Director Intercollegiate Athletics ....Mr. Mark J. HOLLIS
08 Director of Libraries ....Mr. Clifford H. HAKA
88 Dir Natl Supercond Cyclotron Lab ....Dr. Konrad GELBKE
19 Police Chf/Dir Police & Pub Safety ....Mr. James H. DUNLAP
88 Director Undergraduate Univ Div ....Dr. Bonita P. CURRY
47 Dean Col Ag & Nat Resources ....Dr. Fred POSTON
79 Dean College Arts & Letters ....Dr. Karin A. WURST
79 Dean Res Col Arts/Humanities ....Dr. Stephen L. ESQUITH
50 Dean Eli Broad Col of Business ....Dr. Stefanie A. LENWAY
60 Dean Col Communication Arts & Sci ....Dr. Pamela WHITTEN
53 Dean College of Education ....Dr. Donald E. HELLER
54 Acting Dean College of Engineering ....Dr. Leo KEMPEL
63 Dean College Human Medicine ....Dr. Marsha D. RAPPLEY
82 Dean James Madison College ....Dr. Sherman W. GARNETT
61 Dean College of Law ....Ms. Joan W. HOWARTH
81 Dean Lyman Briggs College ....Dr. Elizabeth H. SIMMONS
64 Dean College of Music ....Mr. James FORGER
81 Dean College Natural Science ....Dr. R. James KIRKPATRICK
66 Dean College of Nursing ....Dr. Mary H. MUNDT
63 Dean College Osteopathic Medicine ....Dr. William D. STRAMPEL
83 Dean College of Social Science ....Dr. Marietta BABA
74 Dean College Veterinary Medicine ....Dr. Christopher M. BROWN
82 Int Dean Intl Studies & Programs ....Dr. Steven D. HANSON

Michigan Technological University (A)

1400 Townsend Drive, Houghton MI 49931-1295

County: Houghton FICE Identification: 002292
Unit ID: 171128
Telephone: (906) 487-1885 Carnegie Class: RU/H
FAX Number: (906) 487-2935 Calendar System: Semester
URL: www.mtu.edu
Established: 1885 Annual Undergrad Tuition & Fees (In-State): $13,188
Enrollment: 6,945 Coed
Affiliation or Control: State IRS Status: 501(c)3
Highest Offering: Doctorate
Program: Liberal Arts And General; Teacher Preparatory; Professional
Accreditation: NH, BUS, CONST, ENG, ENGT, FOR, TEAC

01 President ....Dr. Glenn D. MROZ
05 Provost/Vice Pres Academic Affairs ....Dr. Max SEEL
86 Vice Pres Governmental Relations ....Dr. Dale R. TAHTINEN
11 Vice President for Administration ....Ms. Ellen S. HORSCH
46 Vice President for Research ....Dr. David D. REED
32 VP for Student Affairs/Advancement ....Dr. Les P. COOK
84 Asst VP for Enrollment Services ....Mr. John B. LEHMAN
35 Dean of Students ....Ms. Bonnie GORMAN
10 Chief Financial Officer ....Mr. Daniel D. GREENLEE
26 Director Marketing/Communications ....Ms. Linda BAKER
08 Director of the Library ....Ms. Ellen MARKS
09 Institutional Analysis ....Mr. Richard ELENICH
29 Director Alumni Association ....Ms. Brenda RUDIGER
06 Registrar ....Ms. Theresa K. JACQUES
07 Director Undergraduate Recruitment ....Ms. Allison A. CARTER
15 Director Human Resources ....Ms. Theresa COLEMAN-KAISER
37 Director of Financial Aid ....Mr. William R. ROBERTS
36 Director University Career Center ....Mr. James TURNQUIST
18 Int Dir Facilities/Physical Plant ....Mr. George BUTVILAS
21 Director Planning & Budgeting ....Ms. Deborah L. LASSILA
38 Director Counseling Services ....Mr. Donald S. WILLIAMS
19 Director Public Safety ....Mr. Daniel P. BENNETT
22 Director Affirmative Programs ....Dr. Jill HODGES
96 Director of Purchasing ....Mr. Raymond E. LASANEN
58 Dean Graduate School ....Dr. Jacqueline E. HUNTOON
50 Dean Business & Economics ....Dr. Gene KLIPEL
54 Interim Dean of Engineering ....Dr. Wayne PENNINGTON
65 Dean of Forestry ....Dr. Terry SHARIK
49 Dean Sciences/Arts ....Dr. Bruce E. SEELY
72 Dean of Technology ....Dr. James FRENDEWEY, JR.

Mid Michigan Community College (B)

1375 S Clare Avenue, Harrison MI 48625-9447

County: Clare FICE Identification: 006768
Unit ID: 171155
Telephone: (989) 386-6622 Carnegie Class: Assoc/Pub-R-M
FAX Number: (989) 386-2411 Calendar System: Semester
URL: www.midmich.edu
Established: 1965 Annual Undergrad Tuition & Fees (In-District): $3,412
Enrollment: 4,694 Coed
Affiliation or Control: State/Local IRS Status: 501(c)3
Highest Offering: Associate Degree
Program: Occupational; 2-Year Principally Bachelor's Creditable
Accreditation: NH, CAHIIM, MAC, PHLEB, PTAA, RAD

01 President ....Ms. Carol A. CHURCHILL
05 Vice President of Academic Services . Dr. Michael W. JANKOVIAK
32 VP Community/Student Relations ....Dr. Matt MILLER
10 Vice President for Admin & Finance ....Ms. Lillian K. FRICK
04 Executive Assistant to President ....Ms. Tonya M. CLAYTON
15 Exec Director of Human Resources ....Ms. Gail NUNAMAKER
27 College Info/Org Dev Officer ....Mr. Anthony FREDS
20 Dean of Instruction ....Mr. Chris GOFFNETT
84 Exec Dean of Student Services ....Ms. Kimberly BARNES
81 Assoc Dean of Math & Science ....Mr. Peter VELGUTH
69 Associate Dean of Health Sciences ....Ms. Maggie MAGOON
14 IT Systems Manager ....Mr. Chris KLIEWONEIT
13 Director IT ....Mr. Kirk A. LEHR
09 Dir of Inst Research/Grants Mgr ....Ms. Carol DARLINGTON
26 Assoc Dean of Student Services ....Mr. Scott MERTES
21 Director of Accounting ....Mr. Gene SCHMIDT
96 Purchasing Manager ....Mr. Jeffery PUNCHES
88 Recruiter/Advisor ....Mr. Chris PELLERITO
88 SBTDC Director ....Mr. Anthony FOX
07 Director of Marketing & Admissions ....Ms. Jessica GORDON
08 Dir Library/Learning Services ....Mr. Corey GOETHE
37 Director of Financial Aid ....Mr. Gale M. CRANDELL
40 Director Auxiliary Services ....Ms. Kelly KOCH
18 Director of Facilities ....Mr. William D. WHITMAN
88 Recruiter ....Ms. Julie FORTINO SHURTIFF
76 Director Radiology ....Ms. LouAnn GOODWIN
25 Title III Coordinator ....Ms. Lori CORTEZ
88 Radiology Tech Clinical Coordinator ....Mr. Galen P. MILLER
50 Associate Dean Liberal Arts ....Mr. Shawn TROY
103 Exec Dir Econ/Workforce Dev ....Mr. Scott GOVITZ
25 NSF Plastics Grant Coordinator ....Mr. Steven FOSGARD
88 Dir Of Educational Talent Search ....Mr. Brent MISHLER

Monroe County Community College (C)

1555 S Raisinville Road, Monroe MI 48161-9746

County: Monroe FICE Identification: 002294
Unit ID: 171225
Telephone: (734) 242-7300 Carnegie Class: Assoc/Pub-S-SC
FAX Number: (734) 242-9711 Calendar System: Semester
URL: www.monroeccc.edu
Established: 1964 Annual Undergrad Tuition & Fees (In-District): $3,190
Enrollment: 4,071 Coed
Affiliation or Control: Local IRS Status: 170(c)1
Highest Offering: Associate Degree
Program: Occupational; 2-Year Principally Bachelor's Creditable
Accreditation: NH, ADNUR, COARC

01 President ....Dr. Kojo QUARTEY
05 Vice President of Instruction ....Dr. Grace B. YACKEE
10 Vice Pres of Admin & Exec Dir Fdn ....Ms. Suzanne M. WETZEL
32 Vice Pres Student & Information Svc ....Mr. Randell W. DANIELS
50 Dean of Business ....Mr. Paul L. KNOLLMAN
76 Dean of Health Sciences ....Ms. Kimberly LINDQUIST
79 Dean of Humanities/Social Science ....Dr. Paul HEDEEN
72 Dean of Industrial Technology ....Mr. Parmeshwar COOMAR
81 Dean of Science/Mathematics ....Mr. Vincent MALTESE
31 Dean of Corporate/Cmty Svcs ....Mr. John A. JOY
08 Director Learning Resources ....Ms. Barbara MCNAMEE
06 Registrar ....Ms. Tracy VOGT
07 Director of Admissions/Guidance ....Mr. Mark HALL
88 Director of Upward Bound ....Mr. Anthony QUINN
88 Director of Respiratory Therapy ....Ms. Bonnie B. BOGGS
21 Director of Financial Services ....Ms. Deborah BEAGLE
18 Director Physical Plant ....Vacant
96 Dir Auxiliary Services/Purchasing ....Ms. Jean FORD
14 Director Data Processing Services ....Mr. James A. ROSS
37 Director of Financial Aid ....Ms. Valerie CULLER
36 Dir Business Devel/Employment Svcs ....Mr. Barry C. KINSEY
56 Director of Extension Centers ....Vacant
88 Director of Lifelong Learning ....Ms. Tina PILLARELLI
13 Manager Information Services ....Mr. Brian K. LAY
27 Director of Marketing ....Mr. Joseph VERKENNES
15 Director of Human Resources ....Ms. Molly M. MCCUTCHAN

Montcalm Community College (D)

2800 College Drive, Sidney MI 48885-9723

County: Montcalm FICE Identification: 002295
Unit ID: 171234
Telephone: (989) 328-2111 Carnegie Class: Assoc/Pub-R-M
FAX Number: (989) 328-2950 Calendar System: Semester
URL: www.montcalm.edu
Established: 1965 Annual Undergrad Tuition & Fees (In-District): $3,150
Enrollment: 2,011 Coed
Affiliation or Control: Local IRS Status: 501(c)3
Highest Offering: Associate Degree
Program: Occupational; 2-Year Principally Bachelor's Creditable; Liberal Arts And General
Accreditation: NH, MAC

01 President ....Mr. Robert C. FERRENTINO
11 Vice Pres Administrative Services ....Mr. James D. LANTZ
05 Vice Pres for Student/Acad Affairs ....Mr. Robert SPOHR
30 Vice Pres Institutional Advancement ....Ms. Therese A. SMITH
10 Chief Business Officer ....Mr. James D. LANTZ
32 Dean Student & Enrollment Svcs ....Ms. Debra ALEXANDER
31 Dean of Community/Workforce Dev ....Ms. Susan HATTO
76 Dean of Health Occupations ....Ms. Amy EADY
37 Director of Financial Aid ....Ms. Traci NICHOLS
21 Director of Accounting ....Ms. Kire WIERDA
18 Director of Facilities ....Mr. George F. GERMAIN
13 Director Information Tech Svcs ....Mr. Rodney C. MIDDLETON
66 Director of Nursing ....Ms. Beth MOWATT
09 Director Institutional Effectivenes ....Ms. Lisa LUND

26 Communications Director ....Ms. Shelly STRAUTZ-SPRINGBORN
20 Dean of Instruction & Student Dev ....Mr. Gary HAUCK
15 Director of Human Resources ....Ms. Connie STEWART

Moody Theological Seminary-Michigan (E)

41550 E Ann Arbor Trail, Plymouth MI 48170-4308

Telephone: (734) 207-9581 FICE Identification: 031353
Accreditation: &NH, THEOL

† Main campus is Moody Bible Institute in Chicago, IL.

Mott Community College (F)

1401 E Court Street, Flint MI 48503-2089

County: Genesee FICE Identification: 002261
Unit ID: 169275
Telephone: (810) 762-0200 Carnegie Class: Assoc/Pub-R-L
FAX Number: (810) 762-0257 Calendar System: Semester
URL: www.mcc.edu
Established: 1923 Annual Undergrad Tuition & Fees (In-District): $3,675
Enrollment: 10,500 Coed
Affiliation or Control: Local IRS Status: 501(c)3
Highest Offering: Associate Degree
Program: Occupational; 2-Year Principally Bachelor's Creditable; Business Emphasis
Accreditation: NH, ACBSP, ADNUR, COARC, DA, DH, OTA, PTAA

01 President ....Dr. Dick SHAINK
30 Exec Dir Inst Developmnt/Foundation ....Ms. Lennetta CONEY
05 Vice Pres Academic Affairs ....Dr. Amy FUGATE
11 VP Student & Administrative Svcs ....Mr. Scott JENKINS
10 Chief Financial Officer ....Mr. Larry GAWTHROP
16 Chief Human Resources Officer ....Mr. Mark KENNEDY
88 Exec Dean Regional Tech Ctr Project ....Mr. Tom CRAMPTON
51 Exec Dir Corporate Svcs & Cont Educ ....Mr. Chuck THIEL
32 Interim Exec Dean Student Services ....Mr. Troy BOQUETTE
37 Exec Dir Student Fin Svcs ....Ms. Jennifer DOW-MCDONALD
81 Dean of Math & Science ....Dr. Johanna BROWN
76 Interim Dean of Health Sciences ....Dr. Steve ROBINSON
38 Dean Counseling & Student Devlop ....Vacant
83 Dean Social Sciences & Fine Arts ....Ms. Mary CUSACK
50 Interim Dean of Business ....Ms. Dolores SHARPE
72 Dean of Technology ....Mr. Clark HARRIS
26 Exec Director Marketing & PR ....Mr. Michael KELLY
27 Chief Technology Officer ....Ms. Cheryl BASSETT
06 Registrar ....Mr. Chris ENGLE
36 Exec Dir Career Ctr/Job Placement ....Mrs. Cindy MCDANIEL
62 Executive Director Library ....Mrs. Kathy IRWIN
18 Exec Dir Physical Plant/Architect ....Mr. Larry KOEHLER
41 Director Athletics/Campus Rec ....Mr. Tom HEALEY
09 Exec Dir Institutional Research ....Mrs. Lori HANCOCK
35 Director Student Life ....Ms. Dawn VANNIMAN
96 Director of Purchasing ....Ms. Jody MICHAEL

Muskegon Community College (G)

221 S Quarterline Road, Muskegon MI 49442-1493

County: Muskegon FICE Identification: 002297
Unit ID: 171304
Telephone: (231) 773-9131 Carnegie Class: Assoc/Pub-U-SC
FAX Number: (231) 777-0255 Calendar System: Semester
URL: www.muskegoncc.edu
Established: 1926 Annual Undergrad Tuition & Fees (In-District): $3,085
Enrollment: 5,067 Coed
Affiliation or Control: Local IRS Status: Exempt
Highest Offering: Associate Degree
Program: Occupational; 2-Year Principally Bachelor's Creditable
Accreditation: NH, ADNUR, COARC

01 President ....Dr. Dale K. NESBARY
05 VP of Academic Affairs and Finance ....Ms. Teresa STURRUS
32 VP Student Svcs and Administration ....Dr. John SELMON
06 Dean of Academic Svcs/Registrar ....Ms. Jean ROBERTS
20 Dean of Instruction & Assessment ....Mr. Ed BREITENBACH
31 Dean of Community Outreach ....Ms. Trynette Lottie HARPS
84 Dean of Enrollment Services ....Ms. Cindy REUSS
10 Director of Finance ....Ms. Beth DICK
13 Chief Information Officer ....Mr. Mike ALSTROM
37 Director Financial Aid ....Mr. Bruce WIERDA
09 Director of Institutional Research ....Mr. Eduardo BEDOYA
102 Dir Foundation/Strategic Initiative ....Ms. Tina DEE
15 Adm Dir of Human Resources ....Mr. Aaron HILLIARD
41 Athletic Director ....Mr. Marty MCDERMOTT

North Central Michigan College (H)

1515 Howard Street, Petoskey MI 49770-8717

County: Emmet FICE Identification: 002299
Unit ID: 171395
Telephone: (231) 348-6600 Carnegie Class: Assoc/Pub-R-M
FAX Number: (231) 348-6628 Calendar System: Semester
URL: www.ncmich.edu
Established: 1958 Annual Undergrad Tuition & Fees (In-District): $1,233
Enrollment: 2,757 Coed
Affiliation or Control: Local IRS Status: 501(c)3
Highest Offering: Associate Degree
Program: Occupational; 2-Year Principally Bachelor's Creditable
Accreditation: NH

01 President ....Dr. Cameron BRUNET-KOCH

05 Dean of Instruction Dr. Christine HAMMOND
10 Dean Finance & Facilities Mr. Todd MCDONALD
32 Dean of Students Dr. Naomi DEWINTER
102 Executive Director Foundation Mr. Sean POLLION
08 Librarian Mrs. Eunice TEEL
37 Director of Financial Aid Mrs. Virginia PANOFF
18 Director of Physical Plant Mr. Jeff GARDNER
84 Dir Enrollment Services/Registrar Ms. Renee DEYOUNG
21 Controller Mr. Troy SLATER
29 Director Alumni Relations Mr. Sean POLLION
35 Dir Student Activities/Camp Housing Mr. Josh DEAL
15 Human Resources Ms. Diana SOUZA
40 Bookstore Manager Ms. Julie WEAVER
09 Director of Institutional Research Dr. Robert MARSH

Northern Michigan University (A)

1401 Presque Isle Avenue, Marquette MI 49855-5301
County: Marquette FICE Identification: 002301
Unit ID: 171456
Telephone: (906) 227-1000 Carnegie Class: Master's M
FAX Number: (906) 227-2204 Calendar System: Semester
URL: www.nmu.edu
Established: 1899 Annual Undergrad Tuition & Fees (In-State): $9,037
Enrollment: 9,159 Coed
Affiliation or Control: State IRS Status: 501(c)3
Highest Offering: Beyond Master's But Less Than Doctorate
Program: Occupational; 2-Year Principally Bachelor's Creditable; Liberal Arts And General; Teacher Preparatory; Professional
Accreditation: NH, BUS, CA, CGTECH, COARC, DMOLS, ENGT, MLTAD, MT, MUS, NURSE, RAD, SURGT, SW, TEAC

01 President Dr. David S. HAYNES
10 VP for Finance & Administration Mr. R. Gavin LEACH
30 Vice Pres Advancement Ms. Martha B. HAYNES
84 Vice Pres Enrollment & Stdnt Svcs Vacant
09 Assoc VP for Inst Research Dr. Linda WANG
21 Assoc VP Business & Auxiliary Svcs Mr. Arthur J. GISCHIA
05 Provost/VP Academic Affairs Dr. Paul L. LANG
20 Asc Provost Acad Affs/Undergrad Pgm Dr. Dale P. KAPLA
58 Asst Provost Graduate Educ/Research Dr. Brian CHERRY
90 Dean Academic Information Services Ms. Leslie A. WARREN
35 Dean of Students Ms. Christine G. GREER
49 Dean of Arts & Sciences Dr. Michael J. BROADWAY
50 Int Dean Walker L. Cisler Col Bus Dr. David RAYOME
107 Interim Dean College Prof Studies Dr. Harvey A. WALLACE
06 Registrar Ms. Kim M. ROTUNDO
44 Director Major/Planned Giving Ms. Amy M. HUBINGER
27 Director Communications & Marketing Ms. Cindy L. PAAVOLA
36 Dir of Acad & Career Advisement Mr. James G. GADZINSKI
37 Director of Financial Aid Mr. Michael R. ROTUNDO
38 Head Counseling Center Vacant
88 Dir US Olympic Education Center Mr. Forrest KARR
88 Director Glenn T. Seaborg Center Ms. Debra L. HOMEIER
41 Athletic Director Mr. Forrest KARR
19 Dir Public Safety/Police Services Mr. Michael J. BATH
39 Director Housing/Residence Life Mr. Carl D. HOLM
07 Director of Admissions Ms. Gerri L. DANIELS
23 Chief of Staff/Physician Dr. David M. LOUMA
15 Director of Human Resources Ms. Ann M. SHERMAN
26 Marketing Director Ms. Anne M. STARK
28 Dir Multicult Educ/Resource Center Vacant
85 Exec Dir International Programs Vacant
92 Director of Honors Program Dr. David H. WOOD
88 Director of Support/Consulting Svcs Ms. Felecia J. FLACK
24 Director Broadcast & AV Services Mr. Eric L. SMITH
29 Exec Dir Alumni Ops/Annual Giving Ms. Robyn L. STILLE
40 Bookstore Manager Mr. Michael J. KUZAK
18 Associate VP Eng & Plan/Facilities Ms. Kathy A. RICHARDS
13 Chief Technology Officer Mr. David W. MAKI

Northwestern Michigan College (B)

1701 E Front Street, Traverse City MI 49686-3061
County: Grand Traverse FICE Identification: 002302
Unit ID: 171483
Telephone: (231) 995-1000 Carnegie Class: Assoc/Pub-R-M
FAX Number: (231) 995-1339 Calendar System: Semester
URL: www.nmc.edu
Established: 1951 Annual Undergrad Tuition & Fees (In-District): $2,621
Enrollment: 4,847 Coed
Affiliation or Control: Local IRS Status: 501(c)3
Highest Offering: Associate Degree
Program: 2-Year Principally Bachelor's Creditable
Accreditation: NH, ACFEI, DA

01 President Mr. Timothy J. NELSON
05 Vice Pres for Educational Services Dr. Stephen N. SICILIANO
107 VP Lifelong/Professional Learning Ms. Marguerite C. COTTO
10 VP of Finance & Administration Ms. Vicki COOK
04 Exec Assistant to President & Board Ms. Holly J. GORTON
08 Exec Director Lrng Res/Technologies Mr. Craig A. MULDER
15 Director of Human Resources Mr. Aaron T. BEACH
88 Exec Dir of Dennos Museum Center Mr. Eugene A. JENNEMAN
32 VP for Enrollment & Student Svcs Dr. Chris WEBER
24 Director Educational Media Tech Ms. Janet W. OLIVER
12 Supt Great Lakes Maritime Academy RAdm. Gerard ACHENBACH, USMS
20 Dir Academic Affairs/Business Div Ms. Susan DECAMILLIS
31 Director Extended Educ Services Ms. Carol A. EVANS
06 Registrar Ms. Carol J. TABERSKI
23 Director of Health Services Ms. Renee R. JACOBSON
09 Dir Research Planning Effectiveness Dr. Darby L. HILLER-FREUND
18 Director of Campus Services Mr. Paul PERRY
26 Exec Dir of PR & Marketing Mr. Andrew B. DOLAN
44 Exec Dir of Resource Dev & Found Ms. Rebecca M. TEAHEN
62 Director of Library Services Ms. Tina J. ULRICH
88 Director Great Lakes Culinary Inst Mr. Frederick L. LAUGHLIN
88 Director Upward Bound Ms. Patty ROTH
88 Director Training & Research Mr. Richard R. WOLIN
21 Controller Ms. Cheryl SULLIVAN
96 Purchasing Manager Mr. Stephen A. WESTPHAL
19 Asst Dir Campus Safety & Security Mr. Jim WHITE
07 Director of Admissions Mr. James S. BENSLEY
37 Director of Financial Aid Ms. Pam PALERMO
36 Director of Learning Services Ms. Kari L. KAHLER
68 Coordinator Physical Education Mr. Peter W. LACOURSE
60 Communications Chair Ms. Deirdre M. MAHONEY
75 Director of Technical Division Mr. Ed BAILEY
88 Director of Aviation Mr. Aaron COOK
79 Humanities Chair Mr. Jim PRESS
81 Science & Math Chair Mr. Keith OVERBAUGH
76 Health Occupations Chair Ms. Jean M. ROKOS

Northwood University (C)

4000 Whiting Drive, Midland MI 48640-2398
County: Midland FICE Identification: 004072
Unit ID: 171492
Telephone: (989) 837-4200 Carnegie Class: Spec/Bus
FAX Number: (989) 837-4111 Calendar System: Semester
URL: www.northwood.edu
Established: 1959 Annual Undergrad Tuition & Fees: $22,130
Enrollment: 4,719 Coed
Affiliation or Control: Independent Non-Profit IRS Status: 501(c)3
Highest Offering: Master's
Program: Liberal Arts And General; Business Emphasis
Accreditation: NH

01 President & Chief Executive Officer Dr. Keith A. PRETTY
03 EVP/CAO/COO Dr. Kristin STEHOUWER
10 Vice President Finance & Treasurer Mr. W. Karl STEPHAN
30 Vice President Alumni & Advancement Mr. Arnold D'AMBROSIO
88 VP Strategic/Corporate Alliances Dr. Timothy G. NASH
84 VP Enrollment Management Dr. Brian SANDUSKY
12 President Northwood Texas Dr. Kevin G. FEGAN
12 President Michigan Campus Dr. William K. BATEMAN
12 President Northwood Florida Dr. Tom L. DUNCAN
26 Associate VP Mktg/Comm/PR Mr. William GAGLIARDI
51 Associate Dean Adult Degree Program Ms. Rhonda C. ANDERSON
07 Director of Admissions Mr. Gregory S. STIFFLER
32 Dean of Students Mr. Larry J. LINDSEY
85 Dean International Programs Ms. Mamiko REEVES
96 Director of Asset Management Mr. David L. BENDER
88 Director of Communications Mr. Michael D. CURRY
06 Registrar Ms. Marisa L. TOSCHKOFF
09 Dir of Institutional Effectiveness Mr. Michael THOMAS
37 System Financial Aid Director Mr. Mark A. MARTIN
15 Director of Human Resources Ms. Pamela L. CHRISTIE
21 Business Office Mgr/System Director Ms. Susan M. RIDGWAY
29 Executive Director Alumni Relations Ms. Julie L. FELSKE

Oakland Community College (D)

2480 Opdyke Road, Bloomfield Hills MI 48304-2266
County: Oakland FICE Identification: 002303
Unit ID: 171535
Telephone: (248) 341-2000 Carnegie Class: Assoc/Pub-S-MC
FAX Number: (248) 341-2118 Calendar System: Semester
URL: www.oaklandcc.edu
Established: 1964 Annual Undergrad Tuition & Fees (In-District): $2,473
Enrollment: 27,503 Coed
Affiliation or Control: State/Local IRS Status: 501(c)3
Highest Offering: Associate Degree
Program: Occupational; 2-Year Principally Bachelor's Creditable
Accreditation: NH, ACFEI, ADNUR, COARC, DH, DMS, MAC, RAD, SURGT

01 Chancellor Dr. Timothy R. MEYER
05 Vice Chanc Academic Affairs Dr. Richard E. HOLCOMB
45 Vice Chanc for Planning & Devel Vacant
11 Vice Chanc Administrative Services Mr. Clarence E. BRANTLEY
26 Vice Chancellor External Affairs Ms. Sharon MILLER
16 Vice Chancellor Human Resources Mr. William J. MACQUEEN
32 Assoc Vice Chanc Acad/Student Affs Dr. Mary MAZE
04 Exec Assistant to Chancellor Ms. Cherie A. FOSTER
12 Int President Highland Lakes Campus Dr. Cynthia ROMAN
12 President Royal Oak/Southfield Camp Dr. Steven J. REIF
12 President Auburn Hills Campus Dr. Gordon F. MAY
12 President Orchard Ridge Campus Dr. Jacqueline SHADKO
20 Dean Academic Services Vacant
14 Exec Director Tech Applications Mr. David M. DUNSHEE
09 Exec Dir Institutional Research Ms. Nancy C. SHOWERS
88 Executive Director of Curriculum Mr. Martin A. ORLOWSKI
27 Director College Communication Vacant
13 Chief Information Officer Mr. Robert MONTGOMERY
84 Exec Director Enrollment Mgmt Mrs. Carla R. MATHEWS
76 Int Dean Nursing/Health Professions Ms. Lori A. PRZYMUSINSKI
26 Executive Director Marketing Ms. Janet ROBERTS
72 Int Exec Dir Inform Technologies Mr. Chuck S. FLAGG
88 Director of Training Ms. Pamela L. DORRIS
06 Registrar Mr. Stephen M. LINDEN
18 Director Physical Facilities Mr. Daniel P. CHEREWICK
19 Director Public Safety Mr. Terry L. MCCAULEY
30 Chief Strategic Devel Officer Vacant
21 Controller Mrs. Gail S. PITTS
22 Director Employee Relations Mr. Gary S. CASEY
102 Director of OCC Foundation Vacant
36 Director Placement/Coop Education Mr. Willie L. LLOYD
41 Athletic Director Ms. Laurie G. HUBER
96 Director Purchasing/Auxiliary Svcs Ms. Gheretta R. HARRIS
21 Director Financial Services Ms. Sharon K. CONVERSE
37 Director Financial Res/Scholarships Ms. Wilma B. PORTER
15 Director of Personnel Services Mrs. Margaret R. CARROLL
35 Exec Director Student Services Vacant
29 Coordinator Alumni Association Ms. Cynthia A. TANNER

Oakland Community College Auburn Hills (E)

2900Featherstone Road, Auburn Hills MI 48326-2845
Telephone: (248) 232-4100 Identification: 770281
Accreditation: &NH

† Main campus is Oakland Community College in Bloomfield Hills, MI.

Oakland Community College High Lakes (F)

7350 Cooley Lake Road, Waterford MI 48327-4187
Telephone: (248) 942-3100 Identification: 770285
Accreditation: &NH

† Main campus is Oakland Community College in Bloomfield Hills, MI.

Oakland Community College Orchard Ridge (G)

27055 Orchard Lake Road,
Farmington Hills MI 48334-4579
Telephone: (248) 522-3400 Identification: 770282
Accreditation: &NH

† Main campus is Oakland Community College in Bloomfield Hills, MI.

Oakland Community College Royal Oak (H)

739 South Washington, Royal Oak MI 48067-3898
Telephone: (248) 246-2400 Identification: 770283
Accreditation: &NH

† Main campus is Oakland Community College in Bloomfield Hills, MI.

Oakland Community College Southfield (I)

22322 Rutland Drive, Southfield MI 48075-4793
Telephone: (248) 233-2700 Identification: 770284
Accreditation: &NH

† Main campus is Oakland Community College in Bloomfield Hills, MI.

Oakland University (J)

2200 N. Squirrel Road, Rochester MI 48309-4401
County: Oakland FICE Identification: 002307
Unit ID: 171571
Telephone: (248) 370-2100 Carnegie Class: DRU
FAX Number: N/A Calendar System: Semester
URL: www.oakland.edu
Established: 1957 Annual Undergrad Tuition & Fees (In-State): $10,612
Enrollment: 19,740 Coed
Affiliation or Control: State IRS Status: 501(c)3
Highest Offering: Doctorate
Program: Liberal Arts And General; Teacher Preparatory; Professional
Accreditation: NH, ANEST, BUS, BUSA, CACREP, CS, DANCE, ENG, ENGR, #MED, MUS, NURSE, PTA, SPAA, SW, TEAC, THEA

01 Interim President Dr. Betty J. YOUNGBLOOD
04 Executive Asst to the President Vacant
05 Sr VP Academic Affairs/Provost Dr. James P. LENITNI
32 Int VP Student Affs/Enrollment Mgmt Mr. Glenn MCINTOSH
30 VP Dev/Alumni Community Engagement Mr. Eric D. BARRITT
10 VP Finance & Administration Mr. John W. BEAGHAN
43 VP Legal Affairs & General Counsel Mr. Victor A. ZAMBARDI
86 VP Government & Comm Relations Ms. Rochelle A. BLACK
12 Interim Exec Dir OU Macomb Julie TRUBE
66 Dean of Nursing Dr. Kerri D. SCHUILING
54 Dean Engineer & Computer Science Dr. Louay M. CHAMRA
76 Dean School Health Sciences Dr. Kenneth R. HIGHTOWER
53 Interim Dean Educ & Human Services Ms. Mary T. STEIN
49 Dean College Arts & Sciences Dr. Kevin J. CORCORAN
50 Dean School of Business Admin Dr. Mohan R. TANNIRU
63 Dean School of Medicine Dr. Robert FOLBERG
62 Dean of the Library Ms. Adriene I. LIM
20 Senior Associate Provost Dr. Susan M. AWBREY
46 Vice Provost Research Dr. Dorothy A. NELSON
27 Chief Information Officer Ms. Theresa M. ROWE
09 Dir Inst Research & Assessment Ms. Laura A. SCHARTMAN
24 Asst VP Classrm Spprt/Instruct Tech Mr. George T. PREISINGER
90 Int Dir E-Learning/Instr Support Mr. John COUGHLIN
20 Asst VP Academic Affairs Ms. Peggy S. COOKE
88 Dir Ctr Excellence Tchg Lrng Dr. Judith ABLESER
88 Dir Eye Research Institute Dr. Frank GIBLIN
88 Director FAJRI Dr. Sayed NASSAR
21 Asst VP Finance & Administration Mr. Thomas P. LEMARBE
18 Assoc VP Facilities Mgmt Mr. Terry STOLLSTEIMER
15 Asst VP University Human Resources Mr. Ronald P. WATSON

102 Campaign Director ....Ms. Brenda WEHRLI
07 Asst VP Student Affs Admissions ....Ms. Eleanor L. REYNOLDS
35 Asst VP SA/Int Dean Students ....Ms. Nancy A. SCHMITZ
19 Chief of Police ....Mr. Samuel C. LUCIDO
06 Registrar ....Mr. Steven J. SHABLIN
44 Exec Dir Planned/Annual Giving ....Ms. Angie SCHMUCKER
37 Director of Financial Aid ....Ms. Cindy L. HERMSEN
29 Dir Alumni Cmty Engagement ....Ms. Sue HELDEROP
27 Assoc VP Univ Comm & Mktg ....Mr. John O. YOUNG
41 Director of Athletics ....Mr. Tracy A. HUTH
28 Dir Inclus Intercu Initiatives/Atty ....Ms. Joi M. CUNNINGHAM
39 Director of University Housing ....Mr. James R. ZENTMEYER
36 Director Career Services ....Mr. Wayne J. THIBODEAU
38 Director Counseling Center ....Dr. David J. SCHWARTZ
85 Director International Students ....Mr. David J. ARCHBOLD
88 Director Disability Support Svcs ....Ms. Linda G. SISSON
96 Purchasing Manager ....Ms. Maria E. EBNER-SMITH

Olivet College (A)

320 S Main Street, Olivet MI 49076-9406
County: Eaton FICE Identification: 002308
Unit ID: 171599
Telephone: (269) 749-7000 Carnegie Class: Bac/Diverse
FAX Number: (269) 749-7600 Calendar System: Semester
URL: www.olivetcollege.edu
Established: 1844 Annual Undergrad Tuition & Fees: $22,995
Enrollment: 1,152 Coed
Affiliation or Control: Independent Non-Profit IRS Status: 501(c)3
Highest Offering: Master's
Program: Liberal Arts And General; Teacher Preparatory
Accreditation: NH, TEAC

01 President ....Dr. Steven M. COREY
05 Provost and Dean of the College ....Dr. Maria DAVIS
10 Sr Vice Pres/Chief Financial Ofcr ....Mr. William KURTZ
11 Vice President Admin/Physical Plant ....Mr. Larry COLVIN
84 Vice Pres Enrollment Management ....Vacant
32 Vice President/Dean Student Life ....Dr. Linda LOGAN
30 Vice Pres Development/Inst Advance ....Mr. William HULL
06 Registrar ....Ms. Leslie SULLIVAN
41 Athletic Director ....Vacant
42 Director of Church Relations ....Mr. Michael F. FALES
36 Int Dir Career Services Network ....Ms. Joanne WILLIAMS
37 Director of Student Financial Aid ....Ms. Libby JEAN
07 Asst Vice President of Admissions ....Ms. Melissa CASAREZ
94 Director of Women's Resource Center ....Ms. Dianne THOMAS
39 Student Housing ....Ms. Tamyra WALTERS
13 Asst Vice President of ITS ....Mr. Suresh ACHARYA
15 Director of Human Resources ....Mrs. Terri GLASGOW
29 Director of Alumni Relations ....Ms. Martha MASON JENNINGS

Puritan Reformed Theological Seminary (B)

2965 Leonard St NE, Grand Rapids MI 49525
County: Kent Identification: 667099
Telephone: (616) 977-0599 Carnegie Class: Not Classified
FAX Number: (616) 285-3246 Calendar System: Semester
URL: puritanseminary.org
Established: 1995 Annual Graduate Tuition & Fees: $5,400
Enrollment: 57 Coed
Affiliation or Control: Independent Non-Profit IRS Status: 501(c)3
Highest Offering: Master's; No Undergraduates
Program: Religious Emphasis
Accreditation: @THEOL

01 President ....Dr. Joel R. BEEKE
05 Academic Dean/VP Academic Affairs ....Dr. Michael BARRETT

Robert B. Miller College (C)

450 North Avenue, Battle Creek MI 49017-3397
County: Calhoun FICE Identification: 040943
Unit ID: 448804
Telephone: (269) 660-8021 Carnegie Class: Bac/Diverse
FAX Number: (269) 565-2180 Calendar System: Semester
URL: www.millercollege.edu
Established: 2002 Annual Undergrad Tuition & Fees: $10,590
Enrollment: 367 Coed
Affiliation or Control: Independent Non-Profit IRS Status: 501(c)3
Highest Offering: Baccalaureate
Program: Liberal Arts And General; Teacher Preparatory; Business Emphasis
Accreditation: NH, NURSE, @TEAC

01 President ....Dr. Paul OHM
05 Vice President/Provost ....Ms. Gloria ROBERTSON
37 Dean Student Svcs & Financial Aid ..Ms. Kimberly F. CVITKOVIC
10 Executive Director of Finance ....Ms. Janet MCGHEE
11 Director of Administrative Services ....Ms. Lorene E. FRISBIE
84 Director of Enrollment Management ....Mr. Chad DANIELSON

Rochester College (D)

800 W Avon Road, Rochester Hills MI 48307-2764
County: Oakland FICE Identification: 002288
Unit ID: 170967
Telephone: (248) 218-2000 Carnegie Class: Bac/Diverse
FAX Number: (248) 218-2025 Calendar System: Semester
URL: www.rc.edu
Established: 1959 Annual Undergrad Tuition & Fees: $20,010
Enrollment: 1,183 Coed
Affiliation or Control: Independent Non-Profit IRS Status: 501(c)3
Highest Offering: Master's
Program: Liberal Arts And General
Accreditation: NH, NURSE, @TEAC

00 Chancellor ....Dr. Thomas R. SHELLY
01 President ....Dr. John TYSON
05 Provost ....Dr. John D. BARTON
84 Vice President Enrollment ....Mr. Klint PLEASANT
10 Chief Financial Officer ....Mr. Mark VANRHEENEN
07 Assoc Vice Pres Admissions ....Mr. Scott SAMUELS
21 Controller ....Ms. Amy MAUST
18 Director Operational Support ....Mr. Mark JOHNSON
50 Int Dir School of Bus/Prof Studies ....Mr. Danny CAGNET
79 Dean School of Humanities ....Dr. David KELLER
15 Director of Human Resources ....Ms. Lindsey M. DUNFEE
26 Dir of Communication Services ....Ms. Lora HUTSON
32 Dean of Students ....Ms. Candace CAIN
37 Director of Student Financial Svcs ....Ms. Jessica BRISTOW
08 Director of Library Services ....Ms. Alison KELLER
06 Registrar ....Ms. Rebekah PINCHBACK
108 Director of Assessment ....Mr. J. Mark MANRY
29 Director of Alumni/Bookstore Mgr ....Mr. Larry STEWART
35 Assoc Dean of Students/Campus Life ....Mr. Cole YOAKUM
41 Director of Athletics ....Mr. Klint PLEASANT
42 Campus Minister ....Mr. Chris SHIELDS
19 Director of Safety & Security ....Mr. Shawn WESTAWAY
04 Assistant to the President ....Ms. Karen HART

Sacred Heart Major Seminary (E)

2701 Chicago Boulevard, Detroit MI 48206-1799
County: Wayne FICE Identification: 002313
Unit ID: 172033
Telephone: (313) 883-8500 Carnegie Class: Spec/Faith
FAX Number: (313) 868-6440 Calendar System: Semester
URL: www.shms.edu
Established: 1919 Annual Undergrad Tuition & Fees: $16,700
Enrollment: 429 Coed
Affiliation or Control: Roman Catholic IRS Status: 501(c)3
Highest Offering: Master's
Program: Liberal Arts And General; Professional
Accreditation: NH, THEOL

01 Rector & President ....Msgr. Todd LAJINESS
32 Vice Rector/Dean of Seminarians ....Rev. Gerard BATTERSBY
05 Dean of Studies ....Rev. Timothy LABOE
73 Dean of the Institute for Ministry ....Mrs. Janet DIAZ
10 Director Finance/Treasurer ....Ms. Ann Marie CONNOLLY
06 Registrar ....Mr. John MELDRUM
35 Director Undergraduate Seminarians ....Rev. Stephen BURR
38 Graduate Spiritual Director ....Rev. Daniel TRAPP
08 Library Director ....Mr. Christopher SPILKER
38 Undergraduate Spiritual Director ....Rev. Robert SPEZIA
58 Dir Graduate Pastoral Formation ....Rev. John VANDENAKKER
13 Dir of Educational Technology ....Mr. Chad HUGHES

Saginaw Chippewa Tribal College (F)

2274 Enterprise Drive, Mount Pleasant MI 48858-2335
County: Isabella FICE Identification: 037723
Unit ID: 441070
Telephone: (989) 775-4123 Carnegie Class: Tribal
FAX Number: (989) 775-4528 Calendar System: Semester
URL: www.sagchip.edu
Established: 1998 Annual Undergrad Tuition & Fees: $2,040
Enrollment: 129 Coed
Affiliation or Control: Tribal Control IRS Status: 501(c)3
Highest Offering: Associate Degree
Program: 2-Year Principally Bachelor's Creditable
Accreditation: NH

01 President ....Ms. Carla SINEWAY
05 Dean of Instruction ....Ms. Karmen FOX
32 Dean of Student Services ....Ms. Kathryn DENHEETEN
07 Admissions Officer/Registrar ....Ms. Patricia ALONZO
37 Financial Aid Officer ....Ms. Tracy REED

Saginaw Valley State University (G)

7400 Bay Road, University Center MI 48710-0001
County: Saginaw FICE Identification: 002314
Unit ID: 172051
Telephone: (989) 964-4000 Carnegie Class: Master's L
FAX Number: (989) 964-0180 Calendar System: Semester
URL: www.svsu.edu
Established: 1963 Annual Undergrad Tuition & Fees (In-State): $8,423
Enrollment: 10,552 Coed
Affiliation or Control: State IRS Status: 501(c)3
Highest Offering: Beyond Master's But Less Than Doctorate
Program: Liberal Arts And General; Teacher Preparatory; Professional; Business Emphasis
Accreditation: NH, BUS, ENG, MT, MUS, NURSE, OT, SW, TED

01 President ....Dr. Eric R. GILBERTSON
05 Provost/VP Academic Affairs ....Dr. Donald J. BACHAND
10 Exec VP Admin & Business Affairs ....Mr. James G. MULADORE
84 Vice Pres Enrollment Management ....Mr. James P. DWYER
32 VP Student Affairs/Dean of Students ....Ms. Merry Jo BRANDIMORE
86 Spec Asst to Pres/Government Rels ....Dr. Eugene J. HAMILTON
28 Spec Asst to Pres/Diversity Pgms ....Dr. Mamie T. THORNS
84 Exec Asst Pres/Dir Public Affairs ....Dr. Carlos RAMET
45 Assoc Provost ....Dr. Marc PERETZ
21 Assoc VP Admin & Business Affairs ....Mr. Ronald E. PORTWINE
18 Asst Vice Pres Campus Facilities ....Mr. Stephen L. HOCQUARD
21 Assistant VP & Controller ....Ms. Susan L. CRANE
13 Exec Dir Information Tech Svcs ....Mr. James MAHER
85 Director International Programs ....Ms. Stephanie SIEGGREEN
07 Director Admissions ....Ms. Jennifer PAHL
06 Registrar/Dir Institutional Rsrch ....Dr. Clifford DORNE
26 Dir of Branding & Marketing Support ....Ms. Jan R. POPPE
36 Director Career Services ....Mr. Michael MAJOR
21 Director Business Services ....Ms. Connie J. SCHWEITZER
88 University Ombudsman ....Mr. Richard P. THOMPSON
29 Director Alumni ....Mr. Kevin J. SCHULTZ
14 Director Information Tech Svcs ....Mr. Patrick C. SAMOLEWSKI
31 Dir Media & Community Relations ....Mr. J. J BOEHM
08 Director Library/Learning Resources ....Ms. Linda J. FARYNK
25 Dir Sponsored Pgms/IRB Rsrch Compl ....Ms. Janet D. RENTSCH
15 Director Human Resources ....Dr. Jack VANHOORELBEKE
19 Chief University Police ....Mr. Ronald E. TREPKOWSKI
37 Director Scholarships/Financial Aid ....Mr. Robert L. LEMUEL
51 Assoc Dir Ctr Business/Economic Dev ....Ms. Monica B. REYES
38 Dir Student Counseling Center ....Ms. Jennifer N. ORDWAY
41 Director of Athletics ....Mr. Michael E. WATSON
44 Director Annual & Planned Giving ....Mr. Joseph A. VOGL
88 Dir Sch & University Partnerships ....Mr. Joseph ROUSSEAU
88 Dir Enviornmental Health & Safety ....Mr. Robert J. TUTSOCK
88 Exec Dir Ctr for Business/Econ Dev ....Mr. Harold L. LEAVER
93 Director Multicultural Services ....Mr. Shawn WILSON
20 Associate Provost ....Dr. Marc H. PERETZ
26 Dir Media & Community Relations ....Mr. J. J. BOEHM
102 Executive Director SVSU Foundation ....Mr. Andrew J. BETHUNE
40 Bookstore Manager ....Mr. Chris J. PAWLOSKI
96 Purchasing Manager ....Mr. Joshua M. WEBB
35 Asst Dean Student Life ....Vacant
49 Dean Arts & Behavioral Science ....Dr. Joni BOYE-BEAMAN
50 Dean Business & Management ....Dr. Rama YELKUR
53 Dean College of Education ....Dr. Mary R. HARMON
76 Dean of Health & Human Services ....Dr. Judith RULAND
54 Dean Science Engr & Technology ....Dr. Deborah HUNTLEY

St. Clair County Community College (H)

323 Erie Street, PO Box 5015, Port Huron MI 48061-5015
County: St. Clair FICE Identification: 002310
Unit ID: 172291
Telephone: (810) 984-3881 Carnegie Class: Assoc/Pub-S-SC
FAX Number: (810) 984-4730 Calendar System: Semester
URL: www.sc4.edu
Established: 1923 Annual Undergrad Tuition & Fees (In-District): $3,330
Enrollment: 4,661 Coed
Affiliation or Control: Local IRS Status: 501(c)3
Highest Offering: Associate Degree
Program: Occupational; 2-Year Principally Bachelor's Creditable
Accreditation: NH, ADNUR, RAD

01 President ....Dr. Kevin A. POLLOCK
04 Executive Assistant to President ....Ms. Mary L. HAWTIN
10 Vice Pres Administrative Services ....Mr. Kirk A. KRAMER
05 Vice President Academic Services ....Mrs. Denise M. MCNEIL
32 Vice President Student Services ....Mr. Pete LACEY
15 Senior Labor Relations Executive ....Mr. Kenneth M. LORD
35 Dean of Students & Grants ....Dr. Patricia Y. LEONARD
23 Director of Health/Human Services ....Ms. Cindy NICHOLSON
37 Dir of Financial Assistance/Svcs ....Ms. Josephine R. CASSAR
06 Registrar ....Ms. Carrie BEARSS
18 Director of Physical Plant ....Mr. Thomas R. DONOVAN
21 Controller ....Ms. Mary K. BRUNNER
41 Dir Campus Activities/Athletics ....Mr. Dale R. VOS
88 Dean of Instructional Support ....Ms. Linda DAVIS
30 Dir Advancement/Alumni Relations ....Mr. David GOETZE
08 Director of Library Services ....Mr. Christopher RENNIE
20 Associate Dean ....Mr. James NEESE

Sanford-Brown College (I)

5900 Mercury Drive, Dearborn MI 48126
Telephone: (313) 203-3541 Identification: 770693
Accreditation: ACICS, CVT, DMS

† Main campus is Le Cordon Bleu College of Culinary Arts in Los Angeles in Pasadena, CA.

Sanford-Brown College (J)

4020 Sparks Drive SE, Grand Rapids MI 49546
Telephone: (616) 977-8400 Identification: 770694
Accreditation: ACICS

† Main campus is Le Cordon Bleu College of Culinary Arts in Los Angeles in Pasadena, CA.

South University (K)

41555 Twelve Mile Road, Novi MI 48377
Telephone: (248) 675-0200 Identification: 770914
Accreditation: &SC, NURSE, @PTAA

† Main campus is South University in Savannah, GA.

Schoolcraft College (A)

18600 Haggerty Road, Livonia MI 48152-2696
County: Wayne FICE Identification: 002315
Unit ID: 172200
Telephone: (734) 462-4400 Carnegie Class: Assoc/Pub-S-SC
FAX Number: (734) 462-4507 Calendar System: Semester
URL: www.schoolcraft.edu
Established: 1961 Annual Undergrad Tuition & Fees (In-District): $3,242
Enrollment: 12,522 Coed
Affiliation or Control: Local IRS Status: 501(c)3
Highest Offering: Associate Degree
Program: Occupational; 2-Year Principally Bachelor's Creditable
Accreditation: NH, ACFEI, ADNUR, CAHIIM, MAC

01 President .... Dr. Conway A. JEFFRESS
10 Vice Pres/Chief Financial Officer .... Mr. Glenn CERNY
05 Vice Pres of Instruction .... Mr. Richard WEINKAUF
32 Vice Pres of Student Services .... Ms. Cheryl M. HAGEN
49 Dean Liberal Arts & Sciences .... Ms. Cheryl HAWKINS
75 Dean Occupational Prog/Econ Dev .... Mr. Robert LEADLEY
45 Assoc Dean Learning Support Svcs .... Dr. Deborah DAIEK
88 Assoc Dean College Centers .... Dr. Bonnie HECKARD
56 Assoc Dean Distance Learning .... Ms. Cheri HOLMAN
51 Assoc Dean Cont Educ/Prof Develop .... Dr. Leslie PETTY
35 Assoc Dean Counseling/Student Sppt .... Ms. Michelle KOSS
84 Assoc Dean Enrollment Management .... Mr. Martin HEATOR
72 Asst Dean Occupational Programs .... Ms. Amy JONES
30 Exec Director Devel/Govt Relations .... Dr. James RYAN
15 Exec Director of Human Resources .... Ms. Cindy J. KOENIGSKNECHT
21 Exec Dir Business Services/Risk Mgt . Mr. James R. POLKOWSKI
09 Director of Business Intelligence .... Mr. Rob STIRTON
06 Registrar .... Ms. Nicole WILSON-FENNELL
37 Exec Dir Student Financial Services .... Ms. Regina MOSLEY
19 Campus Security Police Chief .... Mr. Steven KAUFMAN
21 Director of Finance .... Mr. Jeffrey LILLEY
96 Director of Purchasing .... Mr. Matthew WILSON

Siena Heights University (B)

1247 Siena Heights Drive, Adrian MI 49221-1796
County: Lenawee FICE Identification: 002316
Unit ID: 172264
Telephone: (517) 263-0731 Carnegie Class: Master's M
FAX Number: (517) 264-7704 Calendar System: Semester
URL: www.sienaheights.edu
Established: 1919 Annual Undergrad Tuition & Fees: $21,890
Enrollment: 2,631 Coed
Affiliation or Control: Roman Catholic IRS Status: 501(c)3
Highest Offering: Beyond Master's But Less Than Doctorate
Program: Occupational; Liberal Arts And General; Teacher Preparatory; Professional
Accreditation: NH, ART, NURSE, SW, TEAC

01 President .... Dr. Peg ALBERT, OP
10 Sr Vice Pres for Business/Finance .... Dr. J. Lee JOHNSON
30 Vice President for Advancement .... Mr. Mitchell P. BLONDE
05 Vice President for Academic Affairs .... Dr. Sharon R. WEBER, OP
84 Vice Pres of Enrollment Mgmt Svcs .... Mr. George WOLF
26 Assoc Vice Pres Advancement .... Mrs. Jennifer H. CHURCH
58 Dean of Graduate Studies .... Dr. Linda PETTIT
107 Dean College Professional Studies .... Mrs. Deborah CARTER
49 Dean College of Arts and Science .... Dr. Mark SCHERSTEN
32 Dean for Students .... Mr. Michael ORLANDO
06 Registrar .... Mrs. Brenda K. DOREMUS
08 Library Director .... Dr. Robert W. GORDON
13 Director Computer Systems/Services .... Mr. Robert C. METZ
41 Director of Athletics .... Mr. Frederick M. SMITH
15 Human Resource Director .... Mr. Michael L. KARABETSOS
42 Director of Campus Ministry .... Mr. Thomas PUSZCZEWICZ
38 Director of Counseling Services .... Mrs. Sandy MORLEY
20 Director of Academic Advising .... Ms. Wiona PORATH
18 Supt of Buildings & Grounds .... Mr. Brian BERTRAM
39 Director of Residence Life .... Mr. Justin LANDIS
19 Director of Campus Security .... Mrs. Cindy A. BIRDWELL
23 Director of Health Services .... Mrs. Marlene WALDVOGEL
29 Director of Alumni Relations .... Mrs. Jennifer H. CHURCH
36 Director of Career Services .... Mrs. Melissa A. GROWDEN
44 Director of Donor Relations .... Mrs. Jenn BROOKET
28 Director of Diversity .... Mr. Paul SPRADLEY
88 Dir of Integrated Univ Marketing .... Mr. Doug GOODNOUGH
37 Director Student Financial Aid .... Mrs. Lori KOSARUE
21 Controller .... Ms. Mary KRUSE
07 Director of Admissions .... Vacant
44 Coordinator of Annual Fund .... Mrs. Kate HAMILTON

Southwestern Michigan College (C)

58900 Cherry Grove Road, Dowagiac MI 49047-9793
County: Cass FICE Identification: 002317
Unit ID: 172307
Telephone: (269) 782-1000 Carnegie Class: Assoc/Pub-R-M
FAX Number: (269) 782-8414 Calendar System: Semester
URL: www.swmich.edu
Established: 1964 Annual Undergrad Tuition & Fees (In-District): $5,292
Enrollment: 2,639 Coed
Affiliation or Control: State/Local IRS Status: 501(c)3
Highest Offering: Associate Degree
Program: Occupational; 2-Year Principally Bachelor's Creditable
Accreditation: NH, CAHIIM

01 President .... Dr. David MATHEWS
100 Chief of Staff .... Mr. Thomas ATKINSON
10 Vice President/Chief Business Ofcr .... Ms. Susan COULSTON
27 Vice President/Chf Information Ofcr .... Mr. Ronald YOUNG
05 Vice President of Instruction .... Dr. David FLEMING
32 Vice President of Student Services .... Ms. Eileen CROUSE
07 Executive Dir Admissions/Advising .... Ms. Angela PALSAK
88 Dean of Academic Studies .... Dr. Scott TOPPING
50 Dean NAC/School of Business .... Dr. Stacy HORNER
66 Dean School Nursing/Human Services .... Ms. Rebecca JELLISON
88 Dir of Acad Assess & Testing Svcs .... Ms. Charlotte MCGOWAN
18 Director of Buildings & Grounds .... Mr. George DIERICKX
44 Director of Development .... Ms. Eileen TONEY
88 Director of Developmental Studies .... Dr. Naomi LUDMAN
88 Dir of Educational Talent Srch Prgm .... Ms. Amy ANDERSON
07 Director of Admissions .... Mr. Brent BREWER
35 Director of EXCEL .... Ms. Laura SKILLINGS
37 Director of Financial Aid .... Ms. Christine PASSER
15 Director of Human Resources .... Ms. Kate DORNER
09 Director of Institutional Research .... Dr. Angela CARRICO
08 Director of Library Services .... Ms. Colleen WELSCH
26 Director of Marketing .... Vacant
06 Director of Records/Registrar .... Ms. Carol LEE
39 Director of Student Housing .... Mr. Jason WILT
88 Senior Budget Analyst .... Ms. Breighan BROWN
88 Controller .... Ms. Michelle KITE
88 Manager of Accounting .... Ms. Christy MANGUS
88 Manager of Student Activity Center .... Mr. Shawn RAWSON

Southwestern Michigan College Niles Area Campus (D)

33890 U.S. Highway 12, Niles MI 49120
Telephone: (800) 456-8675 Identification: 770286
Accreditation: &NH

† Main campus is Southwestern Michigan College in Dowagiac, MI.

Spring Arbor University (E)

106 E Main Street, Spring Arbor MI 49283-9799
County: Jackson FICE Identification: 002318
Unit ID: 172334
Telephone: (517) 750-1200 Carnegie Class: Master's L
FAX Number: (517) 750-6620 Calendar System: Semester
URL: www.arbor.edu
Established: 1873 Annual Undergrad Tuition & Fees: $23,400
Enrollment: 4,125 Coed
Affiliation or Control: Free Methodist IRS Status: 501(c)3
Highest Offering: Master's
Program: Liberal Arts And General
Accreditation: NH, MUS, NURSE, SW, TEAC

01 President .... Dr. Brent ELLIS
05 Provost/Chief Academic Officer .... Dr. Kimberly RUPERT
10 Vice Pres Finance & Administration .... Mr. Jerry L. WHITE
30 Vice Pres University Advancement .... Vacant
32 VP Student Development/Learning . Mrs. Kimberly K. HAYWORTH
84 VP for Enrollment Services .... Vacant
13 VP Technology Services/CIO .... Mr. Jeff E. EDWARDS
20 Associate Provost .... Mr. Rod S. STEWART
100 Chief of Staff .... Mr. Damon M. SEACOTT
58 Interim Dean Sch Grad/Prof Studies .... Mrs. Natalie GIANETTI
58 Associate Dean Graduate Programs .... Dr. Carl E. PAVEY
107 Associate Dean Professional Studies . Mrs. Tamara L. DINDOFFER
49 Dean School Arts & Sciences .... Vacant
50 Dean Gainey School of Business .... Dr. Caleb K. CHAN
53 Dean School of Education .... Dr. Linda G. SHERRILL
106 Dean SAU Online .... Mr. Todd MARSHALL
06 Registrar .... Mr. Tim WIEGERT
21 Controller .... Mrs. Dawn I. SCHNITKEY
41 Athletic Director .... Mr. Ryan T. COTTINGHAM
91 Asst VP Technology Services .... Mr. Michael K. DEVER
26 Asst VP for Marketing & Comm .... Mr. Malachi D. CRANE
105 Web Architect .... Mr. Peter J. SHACKELFORD
88 Director of Support Services .... Mrs. Christina E. RANDALL
106 Director Content and eLearning .... Vacant
44 Executive Director of Development .... Mrs. Linda SCHAUB
07 Executive Director of Admissions .... Mr. Randy C. COMFORT
15 Assistant VP for Human Resources .... Mr. Randy S. ROSSMAN
08 Director Library .... Mr. Robert D. BOLTON
37 Director Student Financial Aid .... Mr. Geoff A. MARSH
29 Director Alumni Relations .... Mrs. Irene L. PRICE
09 Director Institutional Research .... Mr. Thomas P. KORMAN
18 Director of Physical Plant .... Mr. Larry OUSLEY
35 Asst VP Student Development .... Mr. Dan VANDERHILL
39 Asst Dean Students/Dir of Housing .... Mr. Robert C. PRATT
31 Asst Dean Students/Dir of Outreach .... Mr. Steven D. NEWTON
89 Director Retention & Fresh Programs .... Mrs. Robin R. SMITH
36 Director Career Svcs/Acad Advising .... Mr. John BECK
42 Chaplain .... Mr. Ronald L. KOPICKO
19 Director Campus Safety .... Mr. Tom D. FIERO
104 Director Cross Cultural Studies .... Mrs. Diane L. KURTZ
23 Director Student Health Services .... Mrs. Mary A. RICK

SS. Cyril and Methodius Seminary (F)

3535 Indian Trail, Orchard Lake MI 48324-1623
County: Oakland FICE Identification: 037384
Unit ID: 260211
Telephone: (248) 683-0310 Carnegie Class: Not Classified
FAX Number: (248) 738-6735 Calendar System: Semester
URL: www.sscms.edu
Established: 1885 Annual Graduate Tuition & Fees: $16,016
Enrollment: 56 Coed
Affiliation or Control: Roman Catholic IRS Status: 501(c)3
Highest Offering: Master's; No Undergraduates
Program: Professional
Accreditation: THEOL

01 Rector/President .... RevMsg. Thomas MACHALSKI
05 Interim Academic Dean .... Rev. Leonard OBLOY

Thomas M. Cooley Law School (G)

300 S Capitol Avenue, Lansing MI 48933
County: Ingham FICE Identification: 012627
Unit ID: 172477
Telephone: (517) 371-5140 Carnegie Class: Spec/Law
FAX Number: (517) 334-5718 Calendar System: Semester
URL: www.cooley.edu
Established: 1972 Annual Graduate Tuition & Fees: $40,640
Enrollment: 3,220 Coed
Affiliation or Control: Independent Non-Profit IRS Status: 501(c)3
Highest Offering: First Professional Degree; No Undergraduates
Program: Professional
Accreditation: NH, LAW

01 President .... Don LEDUC
04 Executive Asst to the President .... Cherie BECK
05 Dean .... Don LEDUC
10 Chief Financial Officer .... Kathleen CONKLIN
11 Chief Operating Officer .... Layne MALONEY
07 Dean Admissions .... Paul ZELENSKI
08 Associate Dean Library/Info Svcs .... Duane STROJNY
20 Associate Dean for Faculty .... Charles CERCONE
45 Associate Dean Planning/Programs .... Laura LEDUC
36 Assoc Dean Career Prof Development .... Charles TOY
32 Assoc Dean Students/Professionalism .... Amy TIMMER
30 Associate Dean for Development .... James ROBB
13 Associate Dean for Information Tech .... Charles MICKENS
84 Assoc Dean for Enrollment Services .... Paul ZELENSKI
26 Assoc Dean for Community Relations .... Helen MICKENS
12 Associate Dean Auburn Hills .... John NUSSBAUMER
12 Associate Dean Grand Rapids .... Nelson MILLER
12 Asst Dean Tampa Bay .... Jeffre MARTLEW
23 Assoc Dean Ann Arbor .... Joan VESTRAND
104 Assoc Dean International Programs .... Charles CERCONE
88 Assistant Dean Auburn Hills .... Lisa HALUSHKA
88 Assistant Dean Ann Arbor .... Martha MOORE
88 Assistant Dean Grand Rapids .... Tracey BRAME
06 Registrar & Assistant Dean .... Sherida WYSOCKI
37 Director Financial Aid .... Richard BORUSZEWSKI
40 Director Bookstore .... Joelle TOPP
21 Controller .... Ronda BECK
29 Director Alumni Donor Relations .... Pamela HEOS
27 Director Communications .... Terry CARELLA
15 Director Human Resources .... Scott HARRISON
35 Director Student Services .... Christopher LEWIS
96 Purchasing Manager .... Theresa ISKRA

Thomas M. Cooley Law School Ann Arbor Campus (H)

3475 Plymouth Road, Ann Arbor MI 48105
Telephone: (734) 372-4900 Identification: 770287
Accreditation: &NH

† Main campus is Thomas M. Cooley Law School in Lansing, MI.

Thomas M. Cooley Law School Auburn Hills Campus (I)

2630 Featherstone, Auburn Hills MI 48326
Telephone: (248) 751-7800 Identification: 770288
Accreditation: &NH

† Main campus is Thomas M. Cooley Law School in Lansing, MI.

Thomas M. Cooley Law School Grand Rapids Campus (J)

111 Commerce Avenue, SW, Grand Rapids MI 49503
Telephone: (606) 301-6800 Identification: 770289
Accreditation: &NH

† Main campus is Thomas M. Cooley Law School in Lansing, MI.

University of Detroit Mercy (K)

4001 W McNichols Road, Detroit MI 48221-3038
County: Wayne FICE Identification: 002323
Unit ID: 169716
Telephone: (313) 993-1000 Carnegie Class: Master's L
FAX Number: (313) 993-1229 Calendar System: Semester
URL: www.udmercy.edu
Established: 1877 Annual Undergrad Tuition & Fees: $35,920
Enrollment: 5,231 Coed
Affiliation or Control: Roman Catholic IRS Status: 501(c)3
Highest Offering: Doctorate
Program: Liberal Arts And General; Teacher Preparatory; Professional
Accreditation: NH, ANEST, ARCPA, BUS, CACREP, CLPSY, DENT, DH, ENG, LAW, NURSE, SW, TEAC

01 President .... Dr. Antoine M. GARIBALDI
05 Provost and VP for Academic Affairs .... Ms. Pamela ZARKOWSKI

10 VP for Business & Finance and CFO . Mr. Vincent ABATEMARCO
30 VP for University Advancement Ms. Barbara MILBAUER
84 Interim VP Enrollment & Stdnt Affs Ms. Deborah STIEFFEL
101 University Secretary & Senior Atty Ms. Monica BARBOUR
18 Assoc Vice Pres Facil Management Ms. Tamara BATCHELLER
15 Associate Vice Pres Human Resources Mr. Steven J. NELSON
26 Assoc VP Marketing & Public Affairs Ms. Liz PATTERSON
14 Associate Vice President ITS Mr. Edward TRACY, II
06 Associate VP/Registrar Ms. Diane M. PRAET
44 Exec Director of Annual Giving Ms. Ann FISHER
32 Dean of Students Ms. Monica WILLIAMS
08 Dean of Libraries Ms. Margaret AUER
09 Director Institutional Research Mr. E. Rob STIRTON
37 Director Scholarships & Aid Ms. Jenny MCALONAN
35 Associate Director of Student Life Ms. Dorothy STEWART
41 Director of Athletics Mr. Robert VOWELS
42 Director University Ministry Mr. David NANTAIS
49 Dean College of Liberal Arts/Ed Dr. Mark DENHAM
61 Interim Dean School of Law Dr. Troy HARRIS
54 Dean College Engineering & Science Dr. Gary KULECK
48 Dean School of Architecture Mr. William WITTIG
50 Dean Col Business Admin Dr. Joseph EISENHAUER
52 Dean School of Dentistry Dr. Mert AKSU
76 Dean CHP/Nursing Dr. Christine PACINI
88 Dean Coop Education/Career Ctr Ms. Sheryl MCGRIFF
39 Director Residence Life Ms. Lanae GILL
04 Exec Asst to the President Ms. Lisa MACDONNELL
85 Director International Services Ms. Amanda DENTLER
38 Director of Wellness Center Ms. Annmarie SILVERI
92 Director of Honors Program Mr. Jason ROCHE
96 Director of Purchasing Ms. Tina A. MAITLAND
88 Coordinator of Advancement Systems Ms. Stephanie LANDERS
07 Director of Admissions Ms. Tyra ROUNDS

University of Detroit Mercy Corktown Campus (A)

2700 Martin Luther King Jr. Blvd, Detroit MI 482082576
Telephone: (313) 494-6700 Identification: 770291
Accreditation: &NH

† Main campus is University of Detroit Mercy in Detroit, MI.

University of Detroit Mercy Riverfront Campus (B)

651 E Jefferson Avenue, Detroit MI 482264349
Telephone: (313) 596-0200 Identification: 770292
Accreditation: &NH

† Main campus is University of Detroit Mercy in Detroit, MI.

University of Michigan-Ann Arbor (C)

Ann Arbor MI 48109-1318
County: Washtenaw FICE Identification: 002325
Unit ID: 170976
Telephone: (734) 764-1817 Carnegie Class: RU/VH
FAX Number: N/A Calendar System: Trimester
URL: www.umich.edu
Established: 1817 Annual Undergrad Tuition & Fees (In-State): $13,142
Enrollment: 43,426 Coed
Affiliation or Control: State IRS Status: 501(c)3
Highest Offering: Doctorate
Program: Liberal Arts And General; Teacher Preparatory; Professional
Accreditation: NH, DANCE, ART, BUS, CLPSY, CS, DENT, DH, DIETD, DIETI, ENG, ENGR, HSA, IPSY, LAW, LIB, LSAR, MED, MIDWF, MUS, NURSE, PDPSY, PH, PHAR, PLNG, SW, TEAC

01 President Dr. Mary Sue COLEMAN
05 Provost/Exec VP Academic Affs Dr. Martha E. POLLACK
10 Exec VP/Chief Financial Officer Mr. Timothy P. SLOTTOW
17 Exec VP for Medical Affairs Dr. Ora H. PESCOVITZ
30 Vice President Development Mr. Jerry A. MAY
32 Vice President Student Affairs Dr. E. Royster HARPER
46 Vice President for Research Dr. Stephen R. FORREST
86 Vice Pres Governmental Relations Ms. Cynthia H. WILBANKS
26 Vice Pres Global Communications Ms. Lisa M. RUDGERS
43 Int Vice Pres/General Counsel Mr. Timothy G. LYNCH
101 Vice Pres/Sec of the University Ms. Sally J. CHURCHILL
20 Sr Vice Provost Academic Affairs Dr. Lester P. MONTS
04 Exec Asst to the President Ms. Erika J. HRABEC
100 Chief of Staff to the Provost Ms. Stephanie L. RIEGLE
20 Vice Provost Acad/Budget Affairs Dr. Alfred FRANZBLAU
20 Vice Provost Acad & Faculty Affairs Dr. Lori J. PIERCE
20 Vice Provost Acad & Faculty Affairs Dr. Christina WHITMAN
58 Vice Provost Acad Affs Grad Stds Dr. Janet A. WEISS
104 Vice Provost Global & Engaged Educ .. Dr. James P. HOLLOWAY
09 Assoc Vice Provost & Exec Dir OBP Ms. Glenna L. SCHWEITZER
07 Assoc VP/Exec Dir UG Admissions Mr. Theodore L. SPENCER
88 Assoc Vice Provost/Exec Dir OAMI Dr. John H. MATLOCK
88 Assoc Vice Provost/Exec Dir CRLT Dr. Constance E. COOK
15 Assoc Vice Provost & Sr Dr Acad HR Mr. Jeffery R. FRUMKIN
22 Assoc Vice Prov/Sr Dir Inst Equity Mr. Anthony J. WALESBY
18 Assoc VP Facilities/Operations Mr. Henry D. BAIER
21 Assoc VP Finance Dr. Rowan A. MIRANDA
88 Chief Investment Officer Mr. Erik LUNDBERG
30 Assoc VP for Development Mr. Dondi L. CUPP
17 Assoc VP for Medical Affairs Dr. John E. BILLI
46 Assoc VP for Research Dr. Volker SICK
46 Assoc VP for Research Dr. J. Brian FOWLKES
46 Assoc VP for Research Dr. Toni C. ANTONUCCI
46 Assoc VP for Research Mr. Marvin G. PARNES
35 Assoc VP Student Affs/Dean Stdnts Ms. Laura B. JONES
35 Assoc VP Student Affairs Ms. Anjali N. ANTURKAR
35 Assoc VP Student Affairs Dr. Simone HIMBEAULT-TAYLOR
35 Assoc VP Student Affairs Mr. Loren J. RULLMAN
16 Assoc VP for Human Resources Ms. Laurita E. THOMAS
13 Assoc VP Info Tech/Chief Info Ofcr Ms. Laura M. PATTERSON
06 University Registrar Mr. Paul A. ROBINSON
96 Director Procurement Services Ms. Nancy A. HOBBS
38 Director Counseling & Psych Service Dr. Todd D. SEVIG
39 Director University Housing Ms. Linda L. NEWMAN
23 Director University Health Service Dr. Robert A. WINFIELD
19 Interim Exec Dir Pub Safety/Secur Mr. Joseph G. PIERSANTE
37 Exec Director Financial Aid Ms. Pamela W. FOWLER
18 Executive Director Plant Operations Mr. Richard W. ROBBEN
41 Athletic Director Mr. David A. BRANDON
48 Dean Col Architecture & Urban Plng Ms. Monica PONCE DE LEON
49 Dean Col Literature/Science/Arts Vacant
54 Dean College of Engineering Dr. David C. MUNSON
61 Dean Law School Mr. Mark D. WEST
63 Dean Medical School Dr. James O. WOOLLISCROFT
67 Dean College of Pharmacy Dr. Frank J. ASCIONE
65 Dean Sch Natural Resrc/Environ Dr. Marie L. MIRANDA
64 Dean School Music Theatre & Dance Mr. Christopher W. KENDALL
57 Dean School of Art & Design Dr. Gunalan L. NADARAJAN
50 Dean School of Business Dr. Alison DAVIS-BLAKE
52 Dean School of Dentistry Dr. Laurie K. MCCAULEY
53 Dean School of Education Dr. Deborah L. BALL
62 Dean School of Information Dr. Jeffrey K. MACKIE-MASON
68 Dean School of Kinesiology Dr. Ronald F. ZERNICKE
66 Dean School of Nursing Dr. Kathleen M. POTEMPA
80 Dean School of Public Policy Dr. Susan M. COLLINS
70 Dean School of Social Work Dr. Laura LEIN
69 Dean School of Public Health Dr. Martin A. PHILBERT
29 President Alumni Association Mr. Steve C. GRAFTON

University of Michigan-Dearborn (D)

4901 Evergreen Road, Dearborn MI 48128-1491
County: Wayne FICE Identification: 002326
Unit ID: 171137
Telephone: (313) 593-5000 Carnegie Class: Master's L
FAX Number: (313) 593-5452 Calendar System: Trimester
URL: www.umd.umich.edu
Established: 1959 Annual Undergrad Tuition & Fees (In-State): $10,854
Enrollment: 9,083 Coed
Affiliation or Control: State IRS Status: 501(c)3
Highest Offering: Doctorate
Program: Liberal Arts And General; Teacher Preparatory; Professional
Accreditation: NH, BUS, CS, ENG, TEAC

01 Chancellor Dr. Daniel LITTLE
05 Prov/Vice Chanc Academic Affs Dr. Catherine A. DAVY
10 Vice Chancellor Business Affairs Mr. Jeffrey L. EVANS
84 Vice Chanc Enrollment Management .Mr. Stanley E. HENDERSON
30 Vice Chanc Inst Advancement Ms. Mallory M. SIMPSON
31 Vice Chanc for External Relations Mr. Kenneth KETTENBEIL
21 Director of Financial Services Mr. Noel HORNBACHER
06 Registrar Ms. Janice LEWIS-BOYD
100 Chief of Staff Mr. Ray METZ
26 Director Communications/Marketing Ms. Beth MARMARELLI
86 Government Relations Manager Mr. Mike LATVIS
15 Director of Human Resources Ms. Ginny ZARRAS
29 Alumni Engagement Ms. Peggy PATTISON
20 Associate Provost Mr. Ismael AHMED
13 Director IT Strategy/Operations Mr. Robert GOFFENEY
08 Director of Library Ms. Elaine LOGAN
09 Director of Institutional Research Ms. Roma E. HEANEY
84 Asst VC for Enrollment Management Vacant
07 Director of Admissions Ms. Deb PEFFER
37 Director of Financial Aid Ms. Katherine ALLEN
38 Director of Counseling Dr. David SCHROAT
36 Director of Career Services Ms. Regina M. STORRS
85 Director of International Affairs Dr. Monica PORTER
35 Director of Student Engagement ... Ms. Reetha PERANANAMGAM
18 Exec Dir of Facilities Operations Ms. Carol GLICK
19 Director of Campus Safety Mr. Richard GORDON
22 Institutional Equity Officer Ms. Anita GREEN
28 Asst to Chancellor for Inclusion ... Dr. Ann LAMPKIN-WILLIAMS
49 Dean Col Arts/Science/Letters Dr. Martin HERSHOCK
54 Interim Dean Col of Engr/Comp Sci Dr. A. W. ENGLAND
50 Dean College of Business Dr. Raju BALAKRISHNAN
53 Dean School of Education Dr. Edward SILVER

University of Michigan-Flint (E)

303 E Kearsley Street, Flint MI 48502-1950
County: Genesee FICE Identification: 002327
Unit ID: 171146
Telephone: (810) 762-3000 Carnegie Class: Master's L
FAX Number: (810) 762-5725 Calendar System: Semester
URL: www.umflint.edu
Established: 1956 Annual Undergrad Tuition & Fees (In-State): $9,028
Enrollment: 8,289 Coed
Affiliation or Control: State IRS Status: 501(c)3
Highest Offering: Doctorate
Program: Liberal Arts And General; Teacher Preparatory; Professional
Accreditation: NH, ANEST, BUS, CEA, MUS, NURSE, PTA, RTT, SW

01 Chancellor Dr. Ruth J. PERSON
05 Provost/VC Academic Affairs Dr. Gerard VOLAND
32 Vice Chancellor for Student Affairs Dr. Mary Jo S. SEKELSKY
11 Vice Chanc for Business and Finance ... Mr. David BARTHELMES
35 Asst VC for Student Affairs Vacant
21 Asst Vice Chanc Business & Finance ..Mr. William C. WEBB, JR.
58 Assoc Provost/Dean Grad Pgms Dr. Vahid LOTFI
20 Asst Prov/Dean Undergrad Studies Ms. Christine WATERS
26 Exec Director University Relations Ms. Jennifer HOGAN
86 Director Government Relations Mr. David E. LOSSING
28 Exec Director Educational Oppty Mr. Tendaji W. GANGES
08 Director of Library Mr. Robert L. HOUBECK, JR.
06 Registrar Ms. Karen A. ARNOULD
07 Interim Admissions Director Mr. Jon DAVIDSON
37 Director Financial Aid Ms. Lori VEDDER
15 Director Human Res/Affirm Action Ms. Diana T. CURRAN
49 Dean College Arts & Sciences Dr. D. J. TRELA
50 Interim Dean School of Management Dr. Vahid LOTFI
66 Director Nursing Program Dr. Margaret ANDREWS
76 Dean Sch Health Prof & Studies Dr. David GORDON
53 Int Dean Sch Education & Human Svcs Dr. Robert BARNETT
51 Director of Extended Learning Ms. Deborah WHITE
19 Director of Public Safety Mr. Raymond D. HALL
18 Director Facilities Mgmt/Auxil Svcs Mr. George HAKIM
14 Director Info Technology Services Mr. Scott ARNST
36 Director Acad Advis & Career Center Ms. Aimi MOSS
46 Director of Research Dr. Terry VAN ALLEN
21 Director of Financial Svcs & Budget Mr. Gerald GLASCO
88 Int Director University Outreach Mr. Jonathan JAROSZ
29 Exec Dir of Dev and Alumni Relation Vacant
96 Director of Purchasing Mr. Gregory J. SNYDER
09 Director of Institutional Analysis Ms. Fawn SKARSTEN

University of Phoenix Detroit Main Campus (F)

26261 Evergreen Road, Southfield MI 48076-4400
Telephone: (248) 675-3700 Identification: 770211
Accreditation: &NH

† Main campus is University of Phoenix in Tempe, AZ.

Van Andel Institute Graduate School (G)

333 Bostwick Avenue NE, Grand Rapids MI 49503
County: Kent Identification: 667085
Telephone: (616) 234-5708 Carnegie Class: Not Classified
FAX Number: (616) 234-5709 Calendar System: Other
URL: www.vai.org/education/graduateschool.aspx
Established: 1996 Annual Graduate Tuition & Fees: $25,000
Enrollment: N/A Coed
Affiliation or Control: Independent Non-Profit IRS Status: 501(c)3
Highest Offering: Doctorate; No Undergraduates
Program: Professional
Accreditation: @NH

01 President/Dean of the Graduate Sch . Dr. Steven J. TREIZENBERG

Walsh College Novi Campus (H)

41500 Gardenbrook Road, Novi MI 48375-1313
Telephone: (248) 349-5454 Identification: 770293
Accreditation: &NH

† Main campus is Walsh College of Accountancy and Business Administration in Troy, MI.

Walsh College of Accountancy and Business Administration (I)

3838 Livernois Road, Box 7006, Troy MI 48007-7006
County: Oakland FICE Identification: 004071
Unit ID: 172608
Telephone: (248) 689-8282 Carnegie Class: Spec/Bus
FAX Number: (248) 689-9066 Calendar System: Semester
URL: www.walshcollege.edu
Established: 1922 Annual Undergrad Tuition & Fees: $12,015
Enrollment: 2,982 Coed
Affiliation or Control: Independent Non-Profit IRS Status: 501(c)3
Highest Offering: Doctorate
Program: Professional; Business Emphasis
Accreditation: NH, ACBSP, IACBE

01 President & CEO Ms. Stephanie W. BERGERON
05 Exec VP/Chief Academic Officer Dr. David SHIELDS
10 Vice President/CFO/Treasurer . Ms. Helen C. KIEBA-TOLKSDORF
84 VP/Chief Mktg & Enrollment Mgt Ofcr Vacant
16 VP/Chief Human Resources/Admin Ofcr Ms. Elizabeth A. BARNES
30 Vice President/Chief Devel Officer Ms. Audrey OLMSTEAD
04 Exec Assistant to the President Ms. Rosemarie E. ZOOK
08 Assoc VP Acad Admin/Librarian Vacant
32 Asst VP Student Services/Marketing Ms. Victoria R. SCAVONE
20 Asst VP Academic Administration Ms. Terri WASHBURN
106 Dean Office of Online Learning Vacant
20 Director Academic Administration Ms. Monique CARDENAS
37 Director Financial Aid Ms. Catherine BERRAHOU
18 Director Facilities/Auxiliary Svcs Ms. Chris STOUT
21 Director Accounting/Business Ofcr Mr. Brant WRIGHT
07 Director Admissions/Acad Advising Mr. Jeremy GUC
06 Director of Records/Registrar Ms. Karen HILLEBRAND
13 Exec Dir Ofc of Info Technology Mr. Joseph ESDALE
12 Director Novi Campus Mr. Ed BATAYEH

36 Director Career Services .... Ms. Laurie SIEBERT
88 Director of MBA/MSM Program .... Dr. Sheila R. RONIS
88 Director Doctoral Program .... Dr. Linda HAGAN
88 Director Undergrad Business Program .... Dr. Michael LEVENS
88 Director Corporate Rel/BLI .... Ms. Janet HUBBARD
88 Director Information Assurance .... Ms. Nanette POULIOS
88 Dir Center for Entrepreneurship .... Ms. Tara MICELI
26 Director of Marketing .... Ms. Brenda MELLER
29 Manager of Alumni Relations .... Ms. Duc ABRAHAMSON
26 Public Relations Coordinator .... Vacant
72 Int Chair Business Info Tech/IA .... Ms. Terri WASHBURN
88 Chair Accounting/Taxation/Bus Law .... Mr. Dan HOOPS
88 Chair Economics & Finance .... Dr. Linda WIECHOWSKI

Washtenaw Community College (A)

4800 E Huron River Dr, Ann Arbor MI 48105-4800
County: Washtenaw FICE Identification: 002328
Unit ID: 172617
Telephone: (734) 973-3300 Carnegie Class: Assoc/Pub-U-SC
FAX Number: (734) 677-5413 Calendar System: Semester
URL: www.wccnet.edu
Established: 1965 Annual Undergrad Tuition & Fees (In-District): $3,500
Enrollment: 12,476 Coed
Affiliation or Control: Local IRS Status: 501(c)3
Highest Offering: Associate Degree
Program: Occupational; 2-Year Principally Bachelor's Creditable
Accreditation: NH, ACFEI, ADNUR, DA, PTAA, RAD

01 President .... Dr. Rose BELLANCA
11 Vice President Admin & Finance .... Vacant
05 Int Vice President for Instruction .... Dr. William ABERNETHY
16 Assoc VP Human Resources Mgmt .... Mr. Douglas KRUZEL
32 VP Student & Academic Services .... Ms. Linda S. BLAKEY
18 Assoc VP Facilities Devel & Opers .... Mr. Damon FLOWERS
30 Vice Pres of College Advancement .... Ms. Wendy LAWSON
88 Assoc VP Econ Devel/Cmty/Corp .... Ms. Michelle MUELLER
45 Exec Associate to the President .... Ms. Julie MORRISON
79 Int Dean Humanities & Social Sci .... Ms. Dena BLAIR
20 Dean Supp Svcs & Student Advocacy .... Dr. Patricia TAYLOR
62 Dean Learning Resources .... Mr. Victor LIU
50 Dean Business & Computer Tech .... Ms. Rosemary WILSON
81 Dean Math/Natural & Behavioral Sci .... Ms. Martha SHOWALTER
88 Dean Adv Manuf Trades/Publ Svcs .... Ms. Marilyn DONHAM
106 Dean Distance Learning .... Mr. James EGAN
07 Dean Admissions & Student Life .... Mr. Arnett CHISHOLM
13 Chief Information Officer .... Mr. Amin LADHA
10 Controller .... Ms. Lynn MARTIN
21 Dir Budget Purchasing Aux Svcs .... Ms. Barbara FILLINGER
15 Director Human Resource Svcs .... Ms. Christine MIHALY
37 Director Financial Aid .... Ms. Lori TRAPP
09 Director Institutional Research .... Dr. Roger MOURAD
20 Director Educational Services .... Vacant
19 Director Safety & Security .... Mr. Jacque DESROSIERS
35 Dir Student Development/Activities .... Mr. Pete LESHKEVICH
84 Dean of Enrollment Mgmt/Ombudsman .... Mr. Larry AEILTS
88 Student Svcs Info Officer .... Ms. Kathryn STAFFORD
26 Exec Dir Public Rels & Marketing .... Ms. Annessa CARLISLE
86 Dir of Governement Relations .... Mr. Jason MORGAN
88 Exec Dir Econ & Cmty Develop .... Mr. Brandon TUCKER
43 General Counel .... Vacant

Wayne County Community College District (B)

801 W Fort Street, Detroit MI 48226-3010
County: Wayne FICE Identification: 009230
Unit ID: 172635
Telephone: (313) 496-2600 Carnegie Class: Assoc/Pub-U-MC
FAX Number: (313) 961-9439 Calendar System: Semester
URL: www.wcccd.edu
Established: 1967 Annual Undergrad Tuition & Fees (In-District): $2,716
Enrollment: 28,677 Coed
Affiliation or Control: State/Local IRS Status: 501(c)3
Highest Offering: Associate Degree
Program: Occupational; 2-Year Principally Bachelor's Creditable
Accreditation: NH, DA, DH, SURGA, SURGT

01 Chancellor .... Dr. Curtis L. IVERY
03 Executive Vice Chancellor Dist Ofc .... Mr. John BOLDEN
05 Vice Chanc Educational Affairs .... Dr. Stephanie BULGER
26 Vice Chanc External Affairs .... Dr. George W. SWAN, III
32 Vice Chanc Student Services .... Mr. Brian SINGLETON
51 Vice Chanc Sch Cont Ed/Wrkforce Dev .... Ms. Shawna FORBES
10 Vice Chanc Admin/Finance .... Ms. Kim DICARO
15 Vice Chanc HR/Accountability .... Mr. Mirza F. AHMED
09 District VC IE/Info Management .... Ms. Johnesa HODGE
35 Dist Assoc Vice Chanc Student Svcs .... Mr. Adrian PHILLIPS
12 Campus President Downriver .... Mr. Anthony ARMINIAK
12 Campus President Downtown .... Ms. Denise SHANNON
12 Campus President Western .... Mr. Michael P. DOTSON
12 Campus President Northwest .... Dr. Letitia UDUMA
12 Campus President Eastern/Corp Col .... Ms. Mawine DIGGS
88 Asst to Chanc Instruct/Stdnt Succes .... Dr. Patrick MCNALLY

Wayne County Community College District Downriver Campus (C)

21000 Northline Road, Taylor MI 48180
Telephone: (734) 946-3500 Identification: 770297
Accreditation: &NH

† Main campus is Wayne County Community College District in Detroit, MI.

Wayne County Community College District Eastern Campus (D)

5901 Conner, Detroit MI 48213
Telephone: (313) 922-3311 Identification: 770295
Accreditation: &NH

† Main campus is Wayne County Community College District in Detroit, MI.

Wayne County Community College District Northwest Campus (E)

8200 West Outer Drive, Detroit MI 48219
Telephone: (313) 943-4000 Identification: 770296
Accreditation: &NH

† Main campus is Wayne County Community College District in Detroit, MI.

Wayne County Community College District Western Campus (F)

9555 Haggerty Road, Belleville MI 481111404
Telephone: (734) 699-7008 Identification: 770294
Accreditation: &NH, SURGT

† Main campus is Wayne County Community College District in Detroit, MI.

Wayne State University (G)

656 W. Kirby, Room # 4070, Detroit MI 48202-4095
County: Wayne FICE Identification: 002329
Unit ID: 172644
Telephone: (313) 577-2424 Carnegie Class: RU/VH
FAX Number: (313) 577-8154 Calendar System: Semester
URL: www.wayne.edu
Established: 1868 Annual Undergrad Tuition & Fees (In-State): $11,093
Enrollment: 28,938 Coed
Affiliation or Control: State IRS Status: 501(c)3
Highest Offering: Doctorate
Program: Occupational; Liberal Arts And General; Teacher Preparatory; Professional
Accreditation: NH, ANEST, ARCPA, AUD, BUS, CACREP, CLPSY, CORE, DANCE, DIETC, ENG, ENGR, ENGT, FUSER, LAW, LIB, MED, MIDWF, MT, MUS, NURSE, OT, PA, PH, PHAR, PLNG, PTA, RAD, RTT, SP, SPAA, SW, TEAC, THEA

01 President .... Dr. M. Roy WILSON
100 Chief of Staff/VP Marketing & Comm .... Mr. Michael G. WRIGHT
05 Interim Provost/Sr VP Acad Affairs .... Dr. Margaret E. WINTERS
10 VP Finance & Business/Treasurer/CFO .... Mr. Richard NORK
43 Vice President and General Counsel .... Mr. Louis A. LESSEM
46 Vice President for Research .... Dr. Hilary H. RATNER
30 VP Development and Alumni Affairs .... Mr. David W. RIPPLE
86 VP Government and Community Affairs .... Mr. Patrick O. LINDSEY
20 Associate VP Undergraduate Affairs .... Mr. Joseph RANKIN
84 Associate VP for Enrollment .... Ms. Corinne M. WEBB
101 Sec to the BOG/Exec Asst to Pres .... Ms. Julie H. MILLER
04 Assistant to the President .... Ms. Allison GUILLIOM
29 Senior Director Alumni Relations .... Mr. Ty S. STEVENSON
15 Associate VP of Human Resources .... Mr. James FARRELL
18 Assoc VP Facilities/Planning/Mgmt .... Mr. James R. SEARS
21 Assoc VP Budget/Planning/Analysis .... Mr. Robert KOHRMAN
32 Dean of Students .... Dr. David J. STRAUSS
07 Senior Director of UG Admissions .... Ms. Judy B. TATUM
26 Director of Communications .... Mr. Matthew T. LOCKWOOD
25 Asst VP Sponsored Program Admin .... Ms. Gail L. RYAN
37 Int Sr Director Student Fin Aid .... Ms. Gabriela GARFIELD
38 Director of Career Services .... Mr. Ronald H. KENT
62 Dean College of Lib & Info Science .... Dr. Sandra G. YEE
06 University Registrar .... Ms. Linda K. FALKIEWICZ
09 Associate VP for Research .... Dr. Gloria HEPPNER
49 Dean College of Liberal Arts/Sci .... Dr. Wayne RASKIND
61 Interim Dean Law School .... Ms. Jocelyn BENSON
63 Dean School of Medicine .... Dr. Valerie M. PARISI
66 Dean College of Nursing .... Dr. Barbara K. REDMAN
54 Dean College of Engineering .... Dr. Farshad FOTOUHI
50 Int Dean School of Business Admin .... Dr. Margaret WILLIAMS
70 Dean School of Social Work .... Dr. Cheryl E. WAITES
67 Dean College of Pharm/Health Svcs .... Dr. Lloyd Y. YOUNG
53 Dean College of Education .... Dr. Carolyn M. SHIELDS
57 Dean College Fine/Perf & Comm Arts .... Dr. Matthew SEEGER
92 Dean Honors College .... Dr. Jerry HERRON
58 Interim Dean Grad School .... Dr. Ambika MATHUR
96 Assistant VP of Purchasing .... Mr. Kenneth DOHERTY
104 Associate VP Outreach & Intl Pgms .... Dr. Ahmad EZZEDDINE
21 Associate VP Business & Aux Ops .... Mr. Timothy MICHAEL
46 Assoc VP Tech Commerc & Research .... Dr. Joan DUNBAR
27 Associate VP CIO .... Mr. Joseph SAWASKY
41 Director of Athletics .... Mr. Robert FOURNIER

West Shore Community College (H)

3000 N. Stiles Rd., Scottville MI 49454-0277
County: Mason FICE Identification: 007950
Unit ID: 172671
Telephone: (231) 845-6211 Carnegie Class: Assoc/Pub-R-S
FAX Number: (231) 845-0207 Calendar System: Semester
URL: www.westshore.edu
Established: 1967 Annual Undergrad Tuition & Fees (In-District): $2,250
Enrollment: 1,470 Coed
Affiliation or Control: Local IRS Status: 501(c)3
Highest Offering: Associate Degree
Program: Occupational; 2-Year Principally Bachelor's Creditable
Accreditation: NH

01 President .... Dr. Charles T. DILLON
11 VP of Administrative Services .... Mr. Scott WARD
05 VP of Academic and Student Services .... Ms. Lisa STICH
32 Dean of Student Services .... Mr. Chad E. INABINET
40 Director of Bookstore & Food Svcs .... Ms. Cheryl HOGAN
04 Executive Assistant to President .... Ms. Lisa STANKOWSKI
37 Director Financial Aid .... Ms. Juliann MURPHY
91 Manager of Adm Computing Systems .... Mr. Stephen VON PFAHL
88 Director of Criminal Justice .... Mr. Dan DELLAR
88 Director of Recreational Services .... Mr. Michael A. MOORE
15 Director of Human Resources .... Ms. Debbie CAMPBELL
88 Director of Women's Resource Center .... Ms. Carla E. SHAY
26 Director of College Relations .... Mr. Thomas A. HAWLEY
23 Director of Wellness Center .... Ms. Julie PAGE-SMITH
10 Director of Accounting .... Ms. Kristen BIGGS
106 Director Distance Learning & Info .... Mr. John GERTS

Western Michigan University (I)

1903 W Michigan Avenue, Kalamazoo MI 49008-5202
County: Kalamazoo FICE Identification: 002330
Unit ID: 172699
Telephone: (269) 387-1000 Carnegie Class: RU/H
FAX Number: (269) 387-0958 Calendar System: Semester
URL: www.wmich.edu
Established: 1903 Annual Undergrad Tuition & Fees (In-State): $10,355
Enrollment: 24,598 Coed
Affiliation or Control: State IRS Status: 501(c)3
Highest Offering: Doctorate
Program: Liberal Arts And General; Teacher Preparatory; Professional
Accreditation: NH, AAB, ARCPA, ART, AUD, BUS, BUSA, CACREP, CEA, CIDA, CLPSY, COPSY, CORE, CS, DANCE, DIETD, DIETI, ENG, ENGT, IPSY, #MED, MUS, NURSE, OT, SP, SPAA, SW, TED, THEA

01 President .... Dr. John M. DUNN
05 Provost/Vice Pres Academic Affairs .... Dr. Timothy J. GREENE
10 Vice Pres Business & Finance/CFO .... Ms. Jan VAN DER KLEY
32 VP Student Affairs/Dean of Students .... Dr. Diane K. ANDERSON
46 Vice President for Research .... Dr. Daniel M. LITYNSKI
30 VP Development & Alumni Relations .... Mr. James THOMAS
43 VP Legal Affairs/General Counsel .... Ms. Carol L J. HUSTOLES
86 VP Governmental Affs/University Rel .... Mr. Greg J. ROSINE
28 Vice Pres Diversity/Inclusion .... Dr. Martha B. WARFIELD
27 Vice Provost Budget Personnel/CIO .... Dr. James A. GILCHRIST
84 Vice Provost for Enrollment Mgmt .... Mr. Christopher W. TREMBLAY
09 Assoc Provost Inst Effectiveness .... Dr. Jody BRYLINSKY
108 Assoc VP Assessment/Undergrad Stdnt .... Dr. David REINHOLD
51 Assoc Prov Extended Univ Pgms .... Dr. Dawn GAYMER
82 Assoc VP Haenicke Inst Global Ed .... Vacant
21 Assoc Vice President of Finance .... Ms. Patti VANWALBECK
15 Assoc Vice Pres Human Resource .... Mr. Warren HILLS
18 Assoc Vice Pres Facilities Mgmt .... Mr. Peter J. STRAZDAS
35 Assoc Vice Pres Student Affairs .... Ms. Suzie NAGEL
35 Assoc VP for Student Affairs .... Mr. Vernon PAYNE
45 Assoc VP Budget and Planning .... Mr. Dean HONSBERGER
88 Exec Director Institutional Equity .... Ms. Evelyn WINFIELD-THOMAS
31 Assoc VP Community Outreach .... Mr. Robert MILLER
101 Secretary Board of Trustees .... Ms. Betty A. KOCHER
58 Dean Graduate College .... Dr. Susan STAPLETON
49 Dean of Arts & Sciences .... Dr. Alexander ENYEDI
88 Dean of Aviation .... Capt. Dave POWELL
50 Dean of Business .... Dr. Kay PALAN
53 Int Dean of Educ & Human Dev .... Dr. Walter BURT
54 Int Dean of Engr & Applied Sciences .... Dr. Edmund TSANG
57 Dean of Fine Arts .... Dr. Daniel GUYETTE
76 Dean Health & Human Services .... Dr. Earlie WASHINGTON
63 Dean School of Medicine .... Dr. Hal B. JENSON
92 Dean of Honors College .... Dr. Carla M. KORETSKY
08 Dean of Libraries .... Dr. Joseph G. REISH
26 Exec Dir of University Relations .... Ms. Cheryl ROLAND
29 Executive Director Alumni Relations .... Mr. James THOMAS
36 Exec Dir Career & Employment Svcs .... Ms. Lynn KELLY ALBERTSON
06 Registrar .... Ms. Carrie CUMMING
07 Director Admissions/Orientation .... Ms. Penny BUNDY
37 Director Student Financial Aid .... Mr. Mark J. DELOREY
38 Dir Counseling Services Sindecuse .... Dr. Geniene M. GERSH
41 Dir Intercollegiate Athletics .... Ms. Kathy BEAUREGARD
96 Dir Logistical Svcs (Purchasing) .... Mr. Donald PENSKAR

Western Theological Seminary (J)

101 E 13th Street, Holland MI 49423-3622
County: Ottawa FICE Identification: 002331
Unit ID: 172705
Telephone: (616) 392-8555 Carnegie Class: Spec/Faith
FAX Number: (616) 392-7717 Calendar System: Semester
URL: www.westernsem.edu
Established: 1866 Annual Graduate Tuition & Fees: $12,480
Enrollment: 255 Coed
Affiliation or Control: Reformed Church In America IRS Status: 501(c)3
Highest Offering: Doctorate; No Undergraduates
Program: Professional; Religious Emphasis
Accreditation: THEOL

01 President .... Dr. Timothy BROWN
05 Dean/Vice Pres Academic Affairs .... Dr. Leanne VAN DYK

30 Vice President Advancement/Comm ....Rev. Jeffrey MUNROE
10 Vice President of Finance ....Mr. Norman DONKERSLOOT
08 Director of the Library ....Rev. Paul M. SMITH

Yeshiva Beth Yehuda - Yeshiva Gedolah of Greater Detroit (A)

24600 Greenfield, Oak Park MI 48237-1544
County: Oakland FICE Identification: 023638
Unit ID: 247773
Telephone: (248) 968-3360 Carnegie Class: Spec/Faith
FAX Number: (248) 968-8613 Calendar System: Semester
Established: 1985 Annual Undergrad Tuition & Fees: $6,200
Enrollment: 79 Male
Affiliation or Control: Independent Non-Profit IRS Status: 501(c)3
Highest Offering: Doctorate
Program: Professional
Accreditation: **RABN**

01 Dean ....Rabbi Y. BAKST
05 Assistant Dean ....Rabbi M. S. BAKST
11 Executive Administrator ....Rabbi P. RUSHNAWITZ
37 Director of Financial Aid ....Rabbi Y. BLITZ

MINNESOTA

Academy College (B)

1101 E 78th Street, Suite 100,
Minneapolis MN 55420-1402
County: Hennepin FICE Identification: 020503
Unit ID: 172866
Telephone: (952) 851-0066 Carnegie Class: Bac/Assoc
FAX Number: (952) 851-0094 Calendar System: Quarter
URL: www.academycollege.edu
Established: 1936 Annual Undergrad Tuition & Fees: $18,111
Enrollment: 152 Coed
Affiliation or Control: Proprietary IRS Status: Proprietary
Highest Offering: Baccalaureate
Program: 2-Year Principally Bachelor's Creditable
Accreditation: **ACICS**, MAC

01 Director ....Ms. Mary ERICKSON

Adler Graduate School (C)

1550 E 78th Street, Richfield MN 55423
County: Hennepin FICE Identification: 030519
Unit ID: 374024
Telephone: (612) 861-7554 Carnegie Class: Spec/Health
FAX Number: (612) 861-7559 Calendar System: Quarter
URL: www.alfredadler.edu
Established: 1969 Annual Graduate Tuition & Fees: $11,880
Enrollment: 359 Coed
Affiliation or Control: Independent Non-Profit IRS Status: 501(c)3
Highest Offering: Master's; No Undergraduates
Program: Professional
Accreditation: **NH**

01 President ....Dr. Daniel HAUGEN
05 Academic Vice President ....Dr. Chris HELGESTAD
10 Vice President for Finance ....Ms. Leslie ROHDE
07 Director of Admissions/Student Svcs ....Ms. Evelyn HAAS
37 Director of Student Financial Aid ....Ms. Jeanette MAYNARD NELSON

American Academy of Acupuncture and Oriental Medicine (D)

1925 W County Road B2, Roseville MN 55113-2703
County: Ramsey FICE Identification: 038333
Unit ID: 446002
Telephone: (651) 631-0204 Carnegie Class: Spec/Health
FAX Number: (651) 631-0361 Calendar System: Trimester
URL: www.aaaom.org
Established: 1997 Annual Graduate Tuition & Fees: $11,212
Enrollment: 88 Coed
Affiliation or Control: Proprietary IRS Status: Proprietary
Highest Offering: Master's; No Undergraduates
Program: Professional
Accreditation: **ACUP**

01 President ....Dr. Changzhen GONG
05 Academic Dean ....Dr. Yubin LU
11 Administrative Director ....Leila NIELSEN
37 Financial Aid Officer ....Lillian CHEUNG

Anthem College (E)

5100 Gamble Drive, Suite 200, St. Louis Park MN 55416
Telephone: (952) 417-2200 Identification: 770671
Accreditation: **ACICS**, SURTEC

† Main campus is Anthem College in Phoenix, AZ.

Argosy University, Twin Cities (F)

1515 Central Parkway, Eagan MN 55121-1756
Telephone: (888) 844-2004 FICE Identification: 007619
Accreditation: **&WC**, CLPSY, DH, DMS, HT, MAC, MFCD, MLTAD, MT, RTT

† Main campus is Argosy University, Orange County in Orange, CA.

The Art Institutes International Minnesota (G)

15 S 9th Street, Minneapolis MN 55402-2808
County: Hennepin FICE Identification: 010248
Unit ID: 173887
Telephone: (612) 332-3361 Carnegie Class: Spec/Arts
FAX Number: (612) 904-1541 Calendar System: Quarter
URL: www.artinstitutes.edu/minneapolis
Established: 1964 Annual Undergrad Tuition & Fees: $17,616
Enrollment: 1,437 Coed
Affiliation or Control: Proprietary IRS Status: Proprietary
Highest Offering: Baccalaureate
Program: Occupational
Accreditation: **ACICS**, ACFEI

01 President ....Dr. Jennifer SORENSON
05 Dean of Academic Affairs ....Dr. Susan TARNOWSKI
32 Dean of Student Affairs ....Pam BOERSIG
36 Director of Career Services ....Becky BATES
07 Director of Admissions ....Amanda KARLSTAD

Augsburg College (H)

2211 Riverside Avenue, Minneapolis MN 55454-1398
County: Hennepin FICE Identification: 002334
Unit ID: 173045
Telephone: (612) 330-1000 Carnegie Class: Master's L
FAX Number: (612) 330-1649 Calendar System: Semester
URL: www.augsburg.edu
Established: 1869 Annual Undergrad Tuition & Fees: $33,208
Enrollment: 3,700 Coed
Affiliation or Control: Evangelical Lutheran Church In America
IRS Status: 501(c)3
Highest Offering: Doctorate
Program: Liberal Arts And General; Teacher Preparatory; Professional
Accreditation: **NH**, ARCPA, MUS, NURSE, SW, TED

01 President ....Dr. Paul C. PRIBBENOW
05 Provost and Chief Academic Officer ....Dr. Karen KAIVOLA
10 CFO/Vice Pres Finance/Admin ....Ms. Tammy MCGEE
30 VP Institutional Advancement ....Ms. Heather RIDDLE
84 Vice Pres Enrollment Management ....Dr. William MULLEN
32 Vice President Student Affairs ....Ms. Ann L. GARVEY
44 Director of Development Initiatives ....Ms. Donna D. MCLEAN
58 Asst VP/Dean of Grad & Prof Stds ....Dr. Lori PETERSON
12 Director Rochester Program ....Dr. Karl WOLFE
26 Vice President of Marketing/Comm ....Ms. Rebecca JOHN
42 Campus Pastor ....Vacant
37 Director Student Financial Services ....Mr. Paul L. TERRIO
06 Registrar ....Ms. Crystal COMER
07 Director Undergraduate Admissions ....Vacant
07 Director Graduate Admissions ....Mr. Nathan GORR
13 Director of Information Technology ....Mr. Scott KRAJEWSKI
18 Director of Facilities ....Mr. Dennis STUCKEY
29 AVP Advancement/Sr Dir Alumni Rels ....Ms. Kim STONE
27 VP & Chief Information Officer ....Mr. Leif B. ANDERSON
38 Director Counseling & Health Promo ....Ms. Nancy G. GUILBEAULT
15 Interim AVP Human Resources ....Ms. Dionne DOERING
35 Dean of Students ....Dr. Sarah GRIESSE
35 Dir Campus Activities/Orientation ....Ms. Joanne REECK-IRBY
08 Director Library Services ....Ms. Jane A. NELSON
19 Director Public Safety ....Mr. Jesse CASHMAN
102 Dir Corp/Foundation/Govt Relations ....Ms. Laura ROLLER
31 Director Community Relations ....Mr. Steve PEACOCK
88 Director Parent/Family Relations .....Ms. Sally DANIELS HERRON
88 Director StepUp Program ....Ms. Patrice SALMERI
88 Director Advancement Services ....Mr. Kevin HEALY
40 Bookstore Manager ....Ms. Laura FORGEY
85 Dir Intl Student & Scholar Service ....Mr. James TRELSTAD-PORTER
49 Asst Vice Pres/Dean of Arts & Sci ....Dr. Amy GORT
41 Athletic Director ....Mr. Jeffrey F. SWENSON
21 Controller ....Ms. Staney ROSTAD
88 Director Event & Conf Planning ....Ms. Jodi COLLEN
20 Senior Analyst Academic Affairs ....Mr. Nathan HALLANGER
88 Director News and Media Services ....Ms. Stephanie WEISS

Bethany College of Missions (I)

6820 Auto Club Rd, Ste B, Bloomington MN 55438
County: Hennepin Identification: 667136
Telephone: (952) 944-2121 Carnegie Class: Not Classified
FAX Number: (952) 829-2753 Calendar System: Semester
URL: www.bcom.org
Established: 1948 Annual Undergrad Tuition & Fees: $9,970
Enrollment: 95 Coed
Affiliation or Control: Interdenominational IRS Status: 501(c)3
Highest Offering: Master's
Program: Religious Emphasis
Accreditation: **@BI**

01 President ....Dan BROKKE

Bethany Lutheran College (J)

700 Luther Drive, Mankato MN 56001-6163
County: Blue Earth FICE Identification: 002337
Unit ID: 173142
Telephone: (507) 344-7000 Carnegie Class: Bac/A&S
FAX Number: (507) 344-7376 Calendar System: Semester
URL: www.blc.edu
Established: 1911 Annual Undergrad Tuition & Fees: $24,010
Enrollment: 621 Coed
Affiliation or Control: Evangelical Lutheran Synod IRS Status: 501(c)3
Highest Offering: Baccalaureate
Program: Liberal Arts And General
Accreditation: **NH**

01 President ....Dr. Dan R. BRUSS
42 Dir Campus Spiritual Life/Chaplain ....Rev. Donald L. MOLDSTAD
05 Dean of Academic Affairs ....Dr. Eric K. WOLLER
32 Vice President for Student Affairs ....Mr. Steven C. JAEGER
10 Chief Financial/Administrative Ofcr ....Mr. Daniel L. MUNDAHL
30 Chief Advancement Officer ....Mr. Arthur P. WESTPHAL
35 Dean of Student Services ....Dr. Theodore E. MANTHE
37 Director of Financial Aid ....Mr. Jeffrey W. YOUNGE
06 Registrar ....Ms. Mary Jo H. STARKSON
07 Dean of Admissions ....Mr. Donald M. WESTPHAL
16 Manager of Human Resources .....Ms. Paulette L. TONN BOOKER
08 Director of Library Services ....Mr. Orrin J. AUSEN
13 Director of Information Technology ....Mr. John M. SEHLOFF
26 Dir of Institutional Communication ....Mr. Lance W. SCHWARTZ
57 Director of Fine Arts ....Vacant
41 Director of Athletics ....Mr. Karl E. FAGER
29 Manager of Alumni Relations ....Mr. Jacob C. KRIER
88 Mgr Acad & Institutional Research ....Ms. Lisa A. SHUBERT
90 Manager of Academic Computing ....Mr. Mark S. MEYER
40 Bookstore Manager ....Mr. Paul G. WOLD
21 Controller ....Mr. Gregory W. COSTELLO
28 Coord Ctr for Intercultural Develop ....Mr. Thomas G. FLUNKER
36 Coord Career Svcs & Internships ....Ms. Brittany D. NASH
38 Coord of Student Counseling ....Mrs. Patricia J. REAGLES
18 Director of Facilities ....Mr. Juel O. MERSETH
108 Director of Assessment ....Dr. Theodore E. MANTHE

Bethel University (K)

3900 Bethel Drive, Saint Paul MN 55112-6999
County: Ramsey FICE Identification: 009058
Unit ID: 173160
Telephone: (651) 638-6400 Carnegie Class: Master's L
FAX Number: (651) 638-6001 Calendar System: Semester
URL: www.bethel.edu
Established: 1871 Annual Undergrad Tuition & Fees: $31,760
Enrollment: 5,355 Coed
Affiliation or Control: Baptist IRS Status: 501(c)3
Highest Offering: Doctorate
Program: Liberal Arts And General; Teacher Preparatory; Professional
Accreditation: **NH**, #ARCPA, MFCD, NURSE, SW, TEAC, THEOL

01 President ....Dr. James H. BARNES, III
100 Executive Assistant to President ....Vacant
05 Executive Vice Pres and Provost ....Dr. Debra HARLESS
10 Sr Vice Pres Business Affs ....Ms. Kathleen J. NELSON
46 Sr VP Strategic Plng & Opers Effect ....Mr. Joseph LALUZERNE
26 Sr VP Communications/Marketing ....Ms. Sherie J. LINDVALL
30 Sr VP University Relations ....Mr. Patrick MAZOROL
44 Vice President Development ....Mr. Bruce W. ANDERSON
07 VP for Admiss/Fin Aid & Retention ....Mr. Daniel NELSON
90 Vice President Information Tech ....Mr. Mark POSNER
29 Vice Pres Constituent Relations ....Mr. Ralph GUSTAFSON
32 Vice President Student Life ....Dr. Edee SCHULZE
49 Acting Dean of Arts & Sciences ....Dr. Barrett FISHER
49 Acting Dean of CAS ....Dr. Deborah SULLIVAN-TRAINOR
58 Vice Pres Dean Cont Stds/Grad Pgm ....Mr. Richard CROMBIE
51 Dean Acad of Cont Studies/Grad Pgm ....Vacant
73 VP and Dean BSSP ....Dr. David CLARK
79 Associate Dean Arts & Humanities ....Dr. Barrett FISHER
20 Assoc Dean Gen Educ & Fac Develop ....Dr. Deborah SULLIVAN-TRAINOR
46 Actg Assoc Dean Inst Assess Accred .....Dr. Joel FREDERICKSON
81 Acting Assoc Dean Nat Behav Sci ....Dr. Deborah SULLIVAN-TRAINOR
107 Assoc Dean of Prof Programs ....Dr. Pamela ERWIN
104 Assoc Dean Off-Campus Programs ....Mr. Vincent PETERS
12 Dean/Exec Ofcr Bethel Sem San Diego ....Dr. John R. LILLIS
12 Dean/Exec Ofcr Bethel Sem East ....Dr. Douglas W. FOMBELLE
35 Dean of Students ....Dr. Marie WISNER
08 Director of Libraries ....Mr. David R. STEWART
15 Director of Human Resources ....Ms. Cara WALD
41 Athletic Director ....Mr. Robert B. BJORKLUND
37 Financial Aid Officer ....Mr. Jeffery D. OLSON
42 Dean Campus Ministries/Campus Pastor ....Ms. Laurel BUNKER
07 Director of CAS Admissions ....Mr. Jay T. FEDJE
07 Dir Seminary/CAPS/GS Admissions ....Mr. Joseph V. DWORAK
06 University Registrar ....Ms. Katrina CHAPMAN
36 Director Career Counsel/Placement ....Mr. Dave BROZA
19 Chief of Security and Safety ....Mr. Andrew LUCHSINGER
40 Director Campus Stores ....Ms. Jill SONSTEBY
23 Director of Health Services ....Mrs. Elizabeth K. MILLER
96 Director of Purchasing ....Vacant
21 Associate Business Officer ....Vacant
38 Director Student Counseling ....Dr. James KOCH
18 Director of Facilities Mgmt ....Mr. Tom TRAINOR

28 Chief Diversity Officer .... Dr. Leon RODRIGUES

† The marriage and family therapy master's program at Bethel Seminary San Diego is accredited by the Commission on Accreditation for Marriage and Family Therapy Education (COAMFTE) of the American Association for Marriage and Family Therapy (AAMFT)

Brown College (A)

5951 Earle Brown Drive, Brooklyn Center MN 55430
Telephone: (763) 279-2400 Identification: 770733
Accreditation: ACICS

† Main campus is Brown College in Mendota Heights, MN.

Brown College (B)

1340 Mendota Heights Road, Mendota Heights MN 55120
County: Dakota FICE Identification: 007351
Unit ID: 174394
Telephone: (651) 905-3400 Carnegie Class: Bac/Assoc
FAX Number: (651) 905-3550 Calendar System: Other
URL: www.browncollege.edu
Established: 1946 Annual Undergrad Tuition & Fees: $19,850
Enrollment: 700 Coed
Affiliation or Control: Proprietary IRS Status: Proprietary
Highest Offering: Baccalaureate
Program: Occupational; 2-Year Principally Bachelor's Creditable; Professional; Business Emphasis
Accreditation: ACICS

01 President/Dir Brooklyn Ctr Campus .... Dr. Michelle ERNST
05 Dean of Education .... Ms. Lisa THOMAS
07 Director of Admissions .... Ms. Jennifer HUSTON
36 Director of Career Services .... Mr. Paul KRAIMER
13 Director of Information Technology .... Mr. John HANS
06 Registrar .... Ms. Debra NEWGARD
08 Librarian .... Mr. Philip DUDAS
10 Business Office Manager .... Ms. Jennifer BOLISH

Capella University (C)

225 S 6th Street, 9th Floor, Minneapolis MN 55402-4319
County: Hennepin FICE Identification: 032673
Unit ID: 413413
Telephone: (888) 227-3552 Carnegie Class: DRU
FAX Number: (612) 977-5066 Calendar System: Other
URL: www.capella.edu
Established: 1993 Annual Undergrad Tuition & Fees: $11,952
Enrollment: 36,375 Coed
Affiliation or Control: Proprietary IRS Status: Proprietary
Highest Offering: Doctorate
Program: Professional
Accreditation: NH, CACREP, CS, MFCD, NURSE, TED

01 President .... Mr. Scott KINNEY
05 Chief Academic Officer .... Dr. Amy DONOVAN
04 Executive Asst to the President .... Ms. Lauri GIBSON
27 Vice President/Chief Info Officer .... Mr. Scott HENKEL
26 Sr Vice Pres/Chief Marketing Ofcr .... Ms. Mary MILLER
84 Vice President Enrollment Services .... Ms. Leslie BRONK
15 Vice President Human Resources .... Ms. Sally CHIAL
43 VP Govt Affs/Gen Counsel/Secretary .... Mr. Greg THOM
88 Vice Pres Academic Innovation .... Dr. Deborah BUSHWAY
72 Dean School of Business/Tech .... Dr. Barbara BUTTS WILLIAMS
53 Dean School of Education .... Dr. Fernanda WILLIAMSON
88 Dean School of Psychology .... Dr. Curtis BRANT
09 Assessment & Inst Rsch Director .... Ms. Kim PEARCE
06 Registrar .... Ms. Nancy PENNA
10 Chief Financial Officer .... Ms. Lois MARTIN
21 Corporate Controller .... Ms. Amy DRIFKA
21 Director of Finance .... Mr. Andy WATT
88 Director Next Generation Learning .... Mr. Keith KOCH
31 Director Events & Outreach .... Mr. Tom CLEMENS
26 Director of Public Relations .... Ms. Irene SILBER
46 Director Academic Research .... Dr. Tsuey-Hwa CHEN
18 Director of Facilities .... Ms. Carla BUSTROM
08 Manager Library Services .... Ms. Kathe PELLETIER
88 Licensing Specialist .... Mr. Dick BUTALA
07 Asst Reg/Mgr Operational Strategies .... Ms. Debra NEWGARD
43 Corp Attorney/Govt Affs/Compliance .... Ms. Priscilla MCNULTY

Carleton College (D)

1 N College Street, Northfield MN 55057-4001
County: Rice FICE Identification: 002340
Unit ID: 173258
Telephone: (507) 222-4000 Carnegie Class: Bac/A&S
FAX Number: (507) 222-4204 Calendar System: Trimester
URL: www.carleton.edu
Established: 1866 Annual Undergrad Tuition & Fees: $46,167
Enrollment: 2,035 Coed
Affiliation or Control: Independent Non-Profit IRS Status: 501(c)3
Highest Offering: Baccalaureate
Program: Liberal Arts And General; Teacher Preparatory
Accreditation: NH

01 President .... Mr. Steven G. POSKANZER, JR.
05 Dean of the College .... Ms. Beverly NAGEL
10 VP Business & Finance/Treasurer .... Mr. Fred A. ROGERS
30 Vice President External Relations .... Mr. Donald HASSELTINE
32 VP for Student Dev/Dean of Students .... Ms. Hudlin WAGNER
07 VP and Dean of Admissions/Fin Aid .... Mr. Paul THIBOUTOT
100 Assoc Vice President/Chief of Staff .... Ms. Elise ESLINGER
26 Assoc VP Ext Relations/Dir Develop .... Ms. Gayle MCJUNKIN
26 Assoc VP Ext Relations/Dir Col Rels .... Mr. Joe HARGIS
20 Associate Dean of the College .... Mr. Fernan JARAMILLO
20 Associate Dean of the College .... Mr. George SHUFFELTON
20 Assoc Dean and Director of Advising .... Mr. Louis NEWMAN
35 Associate Dean of Students .... Ms. Julie THORNTON
35 Associate Dean of Students .... Mr. Joseph BAGGOT
35 Associate Dean of Students .... Ms. Cathy CARLSON
37 Assoc Dean Admiss/Dir Stdnt Fin Svc .... Mr. Rod M. OTO
42 Chaplain .... Rev. Carolyn FURE-SLOCUM
06 Registrar .... Mr. Roger LASLEY
08 College Librarian .... Mr. Bradley SCHAFFNER
09 Dir of Inst Research and Assessment .... Mr. James FERGERSON
44 Asst VP Alum/Par Rel/Dir Annual Fnd .... Ms. Becky ZRIMSEK
29 Director of Alumni Relations .... Ms. Sarah FORSTER
13 Chief Technology Officer .... Ms. Janet SCANNELL
105 Dir Web Communications/Development .... Ms. Jaye LAWRENCE
27 Director of Media/Public Relations .... Mr. Eric SIEGER
15 Director of Human Resources .... Ms. Kerstin CARDENAS
39 Director of Residential Life .... Ms. Andrea ROBINSON
88 Dir Intercult/International Life .... Ms. Joy KLUTTZ
85 Assoc Dir Intercult/Internatnl Life .... Mr. Luyen PHAN
104 Director of Off-Campus Studies .... Ms. Helena KAUFMAN
36 Director of the Career Center .... Ms. Kimberly BETZ
23 Dir Student Health and Counseling .... Ms. Marit LYSNE
18 Dir of Facilities/Capital Planning .... Mr. Steven SPEHN
21 Comptroller .... Ms. Linda THORNTON
102 Dir Corporate/Foundation Relations .... Mr. Mark GLEASON
88 Dir of Curricular/Research Support .... Ms. Andrea NIXON
88 Dir Center for Learning/Teaching .... Mr. Fred HAGSTROM
88 Director of Auxiliary Services .... Mr. Daniel BERGESON
40 Director of Carleton Bookstore .... Mr. David SCHLOSSER
41 Athletic Director .... Mr. Gerald YOUNG
19 Director of Security Services .... Mr. Wayne EISENHUTH

Central Baptist Theological Seminary of Minneapolis (E)

900 Forestview Lane N, Plymouth MN 55441-5934
County: Hennepin Identification: 666050
Telephone: (763) 417-8250 Carnegie Class: Not Classified
FAX Number: (763) 417-8258 Calendar System: Semester
URL: www.centralseminary.edu
Established: 1956 Annual Undergrad Tuition & Fees: $6,800
Enrollment: 90 Coed
Affiliation or Control: Baptist IRS Status: 501(c)3
Highest Offering: Doctorate
Program: Religious Emphasis
Accreditation: TRACS

01 President .... Dr. Samuel E. HORN
05 VP of Academic Affairs .... Dr. Jonathan R. PRATT
06 Registrar .... Mr. Jeff STRAUB

*College of Medicine, Mayo Clinic (F)

200 First Street, Rochester MN 55905-3712
County: Olmsted Identification: 666719
Telephone: (507) 284-2511 Carnegie Class: N/A
FAX Number: (507) 284-0999
URL: www.mayo.edu

01 Chief Executive Officer .... Dr. John H. NOSEWORTHY
05 Exec Dean for Education Mayo Clinic .... Dr. Mark WARNER
46 Exec Dean for Research Mayo Clinic .... Dr. Greg GORES
22 Affirmative Action Administrator .... Mr. Kenneth J. SCHNEIDER
26 Chief Marketing Officer .... Mr. John H. WESTON
43 Immigration Attorney .... Mr. Bruce R. LARSON
37 Financial Aid Officer .... Mr. David L. DAHLEN
08 Director of Libraries .... Mr. J. Michael HOMAN
29 Director Mayo Clinic Alumni Center .... Ms. Judith ANDERSON
30 Director of Development .... Dr. Michael CAMILLERI
86 Director Government Relations .... Dr. Patricia SIMMONS

*Mayo Medical School (G)

200 1st Street, SW, Rochester MN 55905-0001
County: Olmsted FICE Identification: 011732
Unit ID: 173957
Telephone: (507) 538-4897 Carnegie Class: Spec/Med
FAX Number: (507) 284-2634 Calendar System: Other
URL: www.mayo.edu/mms
Established: 1971 Annual Undergrad Tuition & Fees: $29,355
Enrollment: 343 Coed
Affiliation or Control: Independent Non-Profit IRS Status: 501(c)3
Highest Offering: First Professional Degree
Program: Professional
Accreditation: NH, MED

02 Dean .... Dr. Sherine GABRIEL
05 Assoc Dean Academic Affairs .... Dr. Darcy REED
32 Assoc Dean Student Affairs .... Dr. Alexandra A. WOLANSKYJ
20 Assoc Dean Faculty Affairs .... Dr. Thomas R. VIGGIANO
11 Administrator for Mayo Med School .... Mr. Jonathan TORRENS-BURTON
22 Chief Human Resources .... Ms. Jill RAGSDALE
26 Chief Mrktng Ofcr/Chair Public Affs .... Mr. John W. LAFORGIA
88 Internatl Personnel Practice Group .... Ms. Ann H. LANCE
37 Financial Aid Officer .... Mr. David L. DAHLEN
08 Head Librarian .... Mr. J. Michael HOMAN

*Mayo Clinic College of Medicine-Mayo Graduate School (H)

200 First Street, SW, Rochester MN 55905-0001
Telephone: (507) 538-1160 FICE Identification: 011516
Accreditation: &NH

† Main campus is Mayo Medical School in Rochester, MN.

*Mayo School of Health Sciences (I)

200 First St. SW, Siebens Bldg 11, Rochester MN 55905-0001
Telephone: (507) 284-3678 FICE Identification: 008182
Accreditation: &NH, ANEST, COARC, CYTO, DENT, DIETI, DMS, HT, MT, NDT, NMT, PDPSY, PHLEB, PTA, RAD, RTT

† Main campus is Mayo Medical School in Rochester, MN.

College of Saint Benedict (J)

37 S College Avenue, Saint Joseph MN 56374-2099
County: Stearns FICE Identification: 002341
Unit ID: 174747
Telephone: (320) 363-5011 Carnegie Class: Bac/A&S
FAX Number: (320) 363-6099 Calendar System: Semester
URL: www.csbsju.edu
Established: 1913 Annual Undergrad Tuition & Fees: $37,926
Enrollment: 2,070 Coordinate
Affiliation or Control: Roman Catholic IRS Status: 501(c)3
Highest Offering: Baccalaureate
Program: Liberal Arts And General; Teacher Preparatory
Accreditation: NH, DIETD, MUS, NURSE, TED

01 President .... Dr. MaryAnn BAENNINGER
05 Provost Academic Affairs .... Dr. Rita KNUESEL
32 Vice President Student Development .... Ms. Mary A. GELLER
30 Vice Pres Institutional Advancement .... Ms. Kimberly FERLAAK MOTES
84 VP Planning and Public Affairs .... Mr. Jon D. MCGEE
10 Vice Pres Finance/Administration .... Ms. Susan M. PALMER
07 VP Admission & Financial Aid .... Dr. Calvin MOSLEY
18 Exec Director Facilities .... Mr. Brad SINN
20 Vice Provost .... Dr. Joseph DESJARDINS
20 Academic Dean .... Dr. Richard ICE
27 Director of Media Relations .... Ms. Diane HAGEMAN
34 Dean of Students .... Ms. Jody L. TERHAAR
06 Registrar .... Ms. Julie E. GRUSKA
08 Director Library .... Ms. Kathleen PARKER
37 Exec Director Financial Aid .... Mr. Stuart PERRY
15 Director Human Resources .... Ms. Carol ABELL
38 Director of Counseling .... Dr. Mike J. EWING
42 Director of Campus Ministry .... Sr. Sharon NOHNER, OSB
41 Athletic Director .... Ms. Carol L. HOWE-VEENSTRA
13 Director of Info Technology Svc .... Mr. Jim J. KOENIG
19 Director of Security .... Mr. Darren SWANSON
21 Controller .... Ms. Anne OBERMAN
44 Director of Planned Giving .... Mr. Bill HICKEY
36 Director of Career Services .... Dr. Heidi HARLANDER
09 Assoc Dir of Institutional Research .... Ms. Karen KNUTSON
40 Director of Bookstores .... Mr. Don L. FORBES
100 Chief of Staff/Exec Asst to Pres .... Ms. Kathryn ENKE
44 Senior Director Advancement .... Ms. Heather PIEPER-OLSON
28 Dir of Intercultural/International .... Mr. Brandyn WOODARD
29 Asst Director Alumnae Relations .... Ms. Kristin LYMAN
96 Purchasing Coordinator .... Ms. Briana WENTLAND

The College of Saint Scholastica (K)

1200 Kenwood Avenue, Duluth MN 55811-4199
County: Saint Louis FICE Identification: 002343
Unit ID: 174899
Telephone: (218) 723-6000 Carnegie Class: Master's M
FAX Number: (218) 723-6290 Calendar System: Semester
URL: www.css.edu
Established: 1912 Annual Undergrad Tuition & Fees: $31,416
Enrollment: 4,144 Coed
Affiliation or Control: Roman Catholic IRS Status: 501(c)3
Highest Offering: Doctorate
Program: Liberal Arts And General; Teacher Preparatory; Professional
Accreditation: NH, CAHIIM, NURSE, OT, PTA, SW, TEAC

01 President .... Dr. Larry GOODWIN
10 Vice President Finance .... Mr. Patrick FLATTERY
05 Vice Pres Academic Affairs .... Dr. Elizabeth DOMHOLDT
30 Vice Pres College Advancement .... Ms. Margot ZELENZ
32 Vice President for Student Affairs .... Mr. Steve LYONS
84 Vice Pres for Enrollment Management .... Mr. Eric BERG
15 VP for HR & Chief Diversity Officer .... Ms. Patricia PRATT-COOK
88 Assoc Vice Pres College Advancement .... Ms. Janet S. ROSEN
06 Registrar .... Mr. George A. BEATTIE
26 Exec Dir Public & Media Relations .... Mr. Robert J. ASHENMACHER
13 Chief Information Officer .... Dr. Lynne HAMRE
08 Director of Library .... Mr. Kevin MCGREW
09 Director of Institutional Research .... Dr. Iwalani ELSE
18 Director of Facilities Services .... Mr. Tom BREKKE
88 Director OneStop Student Service .... Ms. Linda ROGENTINE
29 Director Alumni Relations .... Ms. Lisa ROSETH
07 Director of Freshman Admissions .... Mr. Joe WICKLUND
07 Director of Transfer Admissions .... Mr. Clarence SHARPE
41 Athletic Director .... Mr. Don OLSON

42 Director of Campus Ministry .... Mr. Nathan LANGER
37 Director Student Financial Aid .... Mr. Jon ERICKSON
38 Dir Stdnt Ctr Health/Well-Being .... Mr. Tad SEARS
96 Purchasing Manager .... Ms. Lisa ANDERSON
79 Dean School of Arts & Letters .... Dr. Tammy OSTRANDER
50 Dean Sch of Business & Technology .... Mr. Kurt LINBERG
53 Dean School of Education .... Dr. Jo OLSEN
76 Dean School of Health Sciences .... Dr. Rondell BERKELAND
66 Dean School of Nursing .... Dr. Marty WITRAK
81 Dean School of Sciences .... Dr. Aileen BEARD
85 International Student Advisor .... Ms. Alison CHAMPEAUX
104 Director of International Eduction .... Mr. Thomas HOMAN
45 Vice Pres for Strategic Initiatives .... Mr. Donald WORTHAM
04 Exec Admin Asst to President .... Ms. Joan HOLTER
19 Safety and Security Manager .... Mr. Michael TURNER
39 Asst Dean of Students-Campus Life .... Ms. Elizabeth KNEEPKENS
92 Director Honors Program .... Dr. Debra SCHROEDER
44 Exec Dir of Dev/Planned Giving .... Mr. Gary GARLIE
40 Bookstore Manager .... Ms. Ksenia OLSON
97 Director of General Education .... Dr. Darryl DIETRICH
88 Assoc Vice Pres of Mission Integrat .... Sr. Mary ROCHEFORT
88 Exec Dir Ctr for Healthcare Innovat .... Ms. Tami LICHTENBERG
88 Virtual Campus Director .... Mr. Craig BRIDGES
35 Dean of Students .... Ms. Megan PERRY-SPEARS
88 Asst Dean Advising & Retention .... Mr. David BAUMAN
28 Director of Institutional Diversity .... Ms. Emily SEGAR-JOHNSON

Concordia College (A)

901 8th Street S, Moorhead MN 56562-0001
County: Clay FICE Identification: 002346
Unit ID: 173300
Telephone: (218) 299-4000 Carnegie Class: Bac/A&S
FAX Number: (218) 299-3947 Calendar System: Semester
URL: www.cord.edu
Established: 1891 Annual Undergrad Tuition & Fees: $32,814
Enrollment: 2,631 Coed
Affiliation or Control: Evangelical Lutheran Church In America
IRS Status: 501(c)3
Highest Offering: Master's
Program: Liberal Arts And General; Teacher Preparatory
Accreditation: NH, DIETD, DIETI, MUS, NURSE, SW, @TEAC

01 President .... Dr. William J. CRAFT
05 Dean of College/VP Academic Affairs .... Dr. Eric ELIASON
10 Vice Pres Finance/Treasurer .... Ms. Linda J. BROWN
84 Vice President for Enrollment .... Mr. Steven M. SCHUETZ
88 VP Concordia Language Villages .... Dr. Christine L. SCHULZE
30 Vice Pres Advancement .... Ms. Teresa L. HARLAND
32 VP Student Affairs/Dean of Students .... Dr. J. Sue OATEY
04 Senior Associate to the President .... Ms. Tracey A. MOORHEAD
13 Chief Info Ofcr/Assoc Vice Pres .... Mr. Bruce W. VIEWEG
07 Director of Admissions .... Mr. Scott D. ELLINGSON
06 Registrar .... Ms. Ericka K. PETERSON
37 Director Financial Aid .... Mr. Eric J. ADDINGTON
08 Librarian .... Mrs. Laura K. PROBST
36 Director of Career Center .... Mr. Jay H. THORESON
15 Director Human Resources .... Ms. Peggy L. TORRANCE
29 Director Alumni Relations .... Mr. Eric P. JOHNSON
27 Sr Dir of Communications/Marketing .... Mr. Roger E. DEGERMAN
09 Director of Institutional Research .... Dr. Polly A. FASSINGER
18 Director of Facilities Management .... Mr. Wayne R. FLACK
38 Director of Student Counseling .... Ms. Monica R. KERSTING
41 Athletic Director .... Mr. Rich GLAS
42 Campus Pastor .... Rev. Timothy M. MEGORDEN
85 Director Intercultural Affairs .... Dr. Per ANDERSON

Concordia University, St. Paul (B)

275 Syndicate Street N, Saint Paul MN 55104-5494
County: Ramsey FICE Identification: 002347
Unit ID: 173328
Telephone: (651) 641-8278 Carnegie Class: Master's L
FAX Number: (651) 659-0207 Calendar System: Semester
URL: www.csp.edu
Established: 1893 Annual Undergrad Tuition & Fees: $19,700
Enrollment: 2,941 Coed
Affiliation or Control: Lutheran Church - Missouri Synod
IRS Status: 501(c)3
Highest Offering: Beyond Master's But Less Than Doctorate
Program: Liberal Arts And General; Teacher Preparatory
Accreditation: NH, ACBSP, TED

01 President .... Rev. Thomas Karl RIES
03 Executive Vice President .... Dr. Cheryl T. CHATMAN
05 Vice President Academic Affairs .... Mr. Lonn D. MALY
10 Vice President for Finance .... Rev. Michael H. DORNER
30 Vice President for Advancement .... Mr. Paul SELTZ
11 Sr Vice Pres for Administration .... Dr. Eric E. LAMOTT
20 Assc VP Academic Affs/Stdnt Svcs .... Dr. Miriam E. LUEBKE
32 Assc VP Stdnt Life/Conf & Event Svc .... Mr. Jason M. RAHN
53 Dean College of Education & Science .... Dr. Donald W. HELMSTETTER
49 Dean College of Arts & Letters .... Dr. David A. LUMPP
58 Dean of Graduate School .... Dr. Michael WALCHESKI
73 Dean College of Vocation/Ministry .... Dr. David A. LUMPP
50 Dean College of Bus/Org Leadership .... Vacant
28 Dean of Diversity .... Dr. Cheryl T. CHATMAN
39 Associate Dean of Residence Life .... Ms. Sharon R. SCHEWE
06 Registrar .... Mrs. Toni SQUIRES
23 Director Health Services .... Mrs. Cher A. RAFFTERY
08 Director of Library Services .... Dr. Charlotte M. KNOCHE
07 Director Undergraduate Admission .... Mrs. Kristin M. SCHOON
27 Dir Univ Communications/Mrktng .... Mr. Jason DEBOER-MORAN
102 Dir Foundation/Corporate Relations .... Dr. Alan D. WINEGARDEN
15 Director of Human Resources .... Mrs. Mary M. ARNOLD
37 Director of Financial Aid .... Ms. Jeanie PECK
04 Executive Assistant to President .... Mrs. Jill K. SIMON
42 Interim Campus Chaplain .... Rev. Richard CARTER
88 Director of Traditional Advising .... Ms. Renee L. RERKO
09 Director of Institutional Research .... Ms. Beth C. PETER
29 Director of Alumni Relations .... Mrs. Rhonda K. BEHM
41 Director of Athletics .... Mr. Thomas J. RUBBELKE
18 Director of Operations .... Mr. James P. ORCHARD
36 Director of Placement/Prof .... Ms. Mary LEWIS
40 Bookstore Manager .... Mr. Anthony J. ROSS
90 Director of Computer Services .... Mr. Jonathan S. BREITBARTH
91 Director Administrative Computing .... Ms. Beth C. PETER
38 Director of Counseling Services .... Mr. Daniel HESS
19 Risk Manager .... Mrs. Sara K. MULSO
24 Help Desk Coordinator .... Ms. Brianna TRAQUAIR

Crossroads College (C)

920 Mayowood Road, SW, Rochester MN 55902-2382
County: Olmsted FICE Identification: 002366
Unit ID: 174206
Telephone: (507) 288-4563 Carnegie Class: Spec/Faith
FAX Number: (507) 288-9046 Calendar System: Semester
URL: www.crossroadscollege.edu
Established: 1913 Annual Undergrad Tuition & Fees: $15,280
Enrollment: 152 Coed
Affiliation or Control: Christian Churches And Churches of Christ
IRS Status: 501(c)3
Highest Offering: Baccalaureate
Program: 2-Year Principally Bachelor's Creditable; Religious Emphasis
Accreditation: BI

01 President .... Michael KILGALLIN
05 Vice President of Academics .... Claudio DIVINO
11 Vice Pres Administration & Finance .... Roger LANGSETH
30 VP of Institutional Advancement .... Vacant
32 Director Student Development .... Brad JORDE
06 Registrar .... Emily HOLTER
08 Director of the Library .... Jim GODSEY
07 Director of Admissions .... Christopher WILLIAMS
37 Director of Financial Aid .... Polly KELLOGG-BRADLEY
10 Business Manager .... Roger W. LANGSETH

Crown College (D)

8700 College View Drive, Saint Bonifacius MN 55375-9001
County: Carver FICE Identification: 002383
Unit ID: 174862
Telephone: (952) 446-4100 Carnegie Class: Bac/Diverse
FAX Number: (952) 446-4149 Calendar System: Semester
URL: www.crown.edu
Established: 1916 Annual Undergrad Tuition & Fees: $29,910
Enrollment: 1,245 Coed
Affiliation or Control: The Christian And Missionary Alliance
IRS Status: 501(c)3
Highest Offering: Master's
Program: Liberal Arts And General; Teacher Preparatory
Accreditation: NH, NURSE

01 President .... Dr. David J. WIGGINS
04 Exec Assistant to the President .... Mrs. Shirley M. GRANLUND
10 VP Finance .... Mrs. Susan WILSON
05 VP Academic Affairs .... Dr. Scott MOATS
32 VP Student Development .... Dr. Paul BLEZIEN
84 VP Enrollment & Marketing Services .... Mr. Mike PRICE
30 VP Advancement .... Dr. James HUNTER
20 Dean for Undergraduate Pgms .... Dr. Scott MOATS
66 Director of Nursing .... Mrs. Teresa NEWBY
21 Controller .... Mr. Ronald STRAKA
41 Athletic Director .... Mr. Joshua DUNWOODY
08 Director of Media Services .... Dr. Dennis INGOLFSLAND
06 Registrar .... Mrs. Cheryl FISK
37 Director of Financial Aid .... Mrs. Shannon SCHAAF
35 Dir Leadership Dev/Student Activit .... Vacant
84 Director of Enrollment Services .... Ms. Maggie UNGER
18 Director of Facilities Services .... Mr. Rick LARSON
40 Director of Bookstore Services .... Vacant
58 Director/Adult & Graduate Studies .... Dr. Fawn MCCRACKEN
44 Director of Development .... Vacant
42 Chaplain .... Mr. Bill KUHN
07 Director Undergraduate Admissions .... Mr. Bret HYDER
15 Director of Human Resources .... Mrs. Amy LUESSE
36 Dir Career Svcs/Academic Advising .... Vacant
13 Director of Technology Services .... Mr. Jeff AUNE
26 Director of Marketing .... Mr. Brian WRIGHT
29 Director Alumni Relations .... Mr. Michael WOOD

Duluth Business University, Inc. (E)

4724 Mike Colalillo Drive, Duluth MN 55807-2723
County: Saint Louis FICE Identification: 009892
Unit ID: 173489
Telephone: (218) 722-4000 Carnegie Class: Assoc/PrivFP
FAX Number: (218) 628-2127 Calendar System: Quarter
URL: www.dbumn.edu
Established: 1891 Annual Undergrad Tuition & Fees: $15,785
Enrollment: 247 Coed
Affiliation or Control: Proprietary IRS Status: Proprietary
Highest Offering: Baccalaureate
Program: Occupational; 2-Year Principally Bachelor's Creditable; Technical Emphasis
Accreditation: ACICS, MAC

01 President .... Mr. James R. GESSNER
12 Campus Director .... Mrs. Bonnie L. KUPCZYNSKI
05 Associate Director .... Mr. David LUTZKA
91 Dir Info Technology/Dist Educ Oper .... Mr. David R. LUTZKA
06 Registrar .... Ms. Lisa E. NAGURSKI
08 Librarian .... Ms. Joyce C. PETERSON
36 Career Services Manager .... Mr. David E. COOK
37 Financial Aid Advisor .... Mrs. Gloria G. COOLE

Dunwoody College of Technology (F)

818 Dunwoody Boulevard, Minneapolis MN 55403-1192
County: Hennepin FICE Identification: 004641
Unit ID: 175227
Telephone: (612) 374-5800 Carnegie Class: Assoc/PrivNFP4
FAX Number: (612) 381-9620 Calendar System: Semester
URL: www.dunwoody.edu
Established: 1914 Annual Undergrad Tuition & Fees: $18,514
Enrollment: 1,131 Coed
Affiliation or Control: Independent Non-Profit IRS Status: 501(c)3
Highest Offering: Baccalaureate
Program: 2-Year Principally Bachelor's Creditable; Technical Emphasis
Accreditation: NH, CIDA, RAD

01 President .... Mr. Rich WAGNER
05 Provost .... Mr. Jeff YLINEN
20 Associate Provost .... Ms. Ann IVERSON
10 Chief Financial Officer .... Vacant
84 Vice President Enrollment Mgmt .... Ms. Collette GARRITY
15 Director of Human Resources .... Ms. Patricia EDMAN

Globe University (G)

80 South Eighth Street, Suite 51, Minneapolis MN 55402
Telephone: (651) 332-8042 Identification: 770734
Accreditation: ACICS

† Main campus is Globe University in Woodbury, MN.

Globe University (H)

8089 Globe Drive, Woodbury MN 55125-3388
County: Washington FICE Identification: 004642
Unit ID: 173629
Telephone: (651) 730-5100 Carnegie Class: Bac/Assoc
FAX Number: (651) 730-5151 Calendar System: Quarter
URL: www.globeuniversity.edu
Established: 1885 Annual Undergrad Tuition & Fees: $15,300
Enrollment: 1,284 Coed
Affiliation or Control: Proprietary IRS Status: Proprietary
Highest Offering: Master's
Program: Occupational
Accreditation: ACICS, MAAB

01 Campus Director .... Ms. Lisa PALERMO
05 Dean of Faculty .... Ms. Denise RADCLIFFE
32 Dean of Students .... Mr. Brian RAICHE
37 Director of Financial Aid .... Mr. Ben FLIKEID
07 Director of Admissions .... Ms. Sonia SULTAN
36 Director of Career Services .... Ms. Teresa DYE

Gustavus Adolphus College (I)

800 W College Avenue, Saint Peter MN 56082-1498
County: Nicollet FICE Identification: 002353
Unit ID: 173647
Telephone: (507) 933-8000 Carnegie Class: Bac/A&S
FAX Number: (507) 933-7041 Calendar System: Semester
URL: www.gustavus.edu
Established: 1862 Annual Undergrad Tuition & Fees: $38,660
Enrollment: 2,524 Coed
Affiliation or Control: Evangelical Lutheran Church In America
IRS Status: 501(c)3
Highest Offering: Baccalaureate
Program: Liberal Arts And General
Accreditation: NH, MUS, NURSE, TED

01 President .... Mr. Jack R. OHLE
05 Provost and Dean of the College .... Dr. Mark J. BRAUN
10 VP for Finance and Treasurer .... Mr. Kenneth C. WESTPHAL
07 VP for Enrollment Management .... Dr. Thomas M. CRADY
30 VP for Institutional Advancement .... Mr. Thomas W. YOUNG
32 VP for Student Life .... Dr. JoNes R. VANHECKE
26 VP Marketing & Communication .... Mr. Timothy R. KENNEDY
28 Dir of Diversity/Asst Dean Stdnts .... Mr. Virgil E. JONES
09 Director Institutional Research .... Dr. David A. MENK
08 Head Librarian .... Mr. Daniel MOLLNER
88 Director Church Relations .... Rev. Grady I. ST. DENNIS
29 Dir Alumni and Parent Engagement .... Vacant
36 Director Career Development .... Ms. Cynthia L. FAVRE
06 Registrar .... Ms. Kristianne R. WESTPHAL
13 Dir Gustavus Technology Services .... Mr. Bruce N. AARSVOLD
18 Director Physical Plant .... Mr. Warren P. WUNDERLICH
37 AVP and Dean of Financial Aid .... Mr. Doug O. MINTER
39 Director Residential Life .... Mr. Lawrence C. POTTS
42 Chaplain .... Rev. Siri C. ERICKSON
42 Chaplain .... Rev. Brian E. KONKOL
35 Associate Dean of Students .... Dr. Stephen R. BENNETT

41 Athletics Director .... Mr. Thomas W. BROWN
15 Director Human Resources .... Dr. Kirk D. BEYER
19 Director Campus Security .... Mr. Raymond H. THROWER
40 Manager Book Mark .... Ms. Molly L. YONKERS
27 Director Media Relations .... Mr. Matthew D. THOMAS
04 Asst to the Pres & Sec of the Board .... Ms. Jolene D. CHRISTENSEN

Hamline University (A)

1536 Hewitt Avenue, Saint Paul MN 55104-1284
County: Ramsey FICE Identification: 002354
Unit ID: 173665
Telephone: (651) 523-2800 Carnegie Class: Master's L
FAX Number: (651) 523-2899 Calendar System: 4/1/4
URL: www.hamline.edu
Established: 1854 Annual Undergrad Tuition & Fees: $34,570
Enrollment: 3,623 Coed
Affiliation or Control: United Methodist IRS Status: 501(c)3
Highest Offering: Doctorate
Program: Liberal Arts And General; Teacher Preparatory; Professional
Accreditation: NH, LAW, MUS, TED

01 President .... Dr. Linda N. HANSON
05 Provost .... Dr. Eric JENSEN
10 Vice President Finance .... Mr. Douglas P. ANDERSON
26 Vice Pres Marketing/Enrollment Mgmt .... Ms. Ann NESS
30 VP Development & Alumni Relations .. Mr. Tony GRUNDHAUSER
32 Dean of Students .... Dr. Alan A. SICKBERT
43 VP HR/General Counsel .... Ms. Catherine WASSBERG
13 Assoc VP/Dir IT .... Mr. Mark KONDRAK
26 Assoc VP Marketing Communications .... Vacant
28 Dir Multicult and Div Initiatives .... Dr. Veena DEO
18 Assoc VP Facilities/Physical Plant .... Mr. Lowell BROMANDER
61 Dean School of Law .... Mr. Donald M. LEWIS
50 Dean School of Business .... Ms. Anne MCCARTHY
53 Dean School of Education .... Dr. Nancy SORENSON
49 Dean College Liberal Arts .... Dr. John MATACHEK
28 Ast Dn/Dir Multicult/Intl Stdt Affs .... Mr. Carlos SNEED
06 Registrar Undergrad/Grad Schools .... Mr. Tim TRAFFIE
29 Exec Director Assoc of Hamline Alum .... Ms. Elizabeth L. RADTKE
37 Director Financial Aid .... Ms. Lynette WAHL
06 Registrar Law School .... Ms. Colleen CLISH
07 Director Law School Admissions .... Ms. Robin C. INGLI
07 Dean of Undergraduate Admission .... Mr. Milyon TRULOVE
15 Director Human Resources .... Ms. Dorcas M. MICHAELSON
36 Interim Dir Career Development .... Mr. Terry MIDDENDORF
41 Athletic Director .... Mr. Jason VERDUGO
19 Director of Safety & Security .... Mr. James SCHUMANN
23 Director Counseling & Health Center .... Ms. Heidi FAUL
35 Dir Student Leadership & Activities .... Ms. Wendy BURNS
42 Chaplain & Director .... Ms. Nancy M. VICTORIN-VANGERUD
96 Director of Purchasing .... Ms. Susan BORNUS
04 Exec Assistant to the President .... Ms. Jane A. TELLEEN
09 Director of Institutional Research .... Ms. Tracy WILLIAMS
38 Director of Student Counseling .... Mr. Hussein RAJPUT

Hazelden Graduate School of Addiction Studies (B)

PO Box 11 (CO9), Center City MN 55012-0011
County: Chisago FICE Identification: 040443
Unit ID: 173683
Telephone: (651) 213-4175 Carnegie Class: Spec/Health
FAX Number: (651) 213-4710 Calendar System: Semester
URL: www.hazelden.edu
Established: 1999 Annual Graduate Tuition & Fees: $29,360
Enrollment: 111 Coed
Affiliation or Control: Independent Non-Profit IRS Status: 501(c)3
Highest Offering: Master's; No Undergraduates
Program: Professional
Accreditation: NH

01 President and CEO .... Mr. Mark MISHEK
05 Chief Academic Officer & Provost .... Dr. Valerie SLAYMAKER
88 Asst to the Chief Academic Officer .... Ms. Heidi SOLOMONSON
20 Dean .... Dr. Roy KAMMER
07 Admissions Specialist .... Ms. Jennifer URCIAGA
06 Registrar .... Ms. Debra MATTISON
09 Dir of Institutional Effectiveness .... Dr. Timothy SHEEHAN
06 Registrar of Administrative Service .... Ms. Twyla RAMSDELL

* *Hennepin Technical College* (C)

131000 College View, Eden Prairie MN 55347
Telephone: (952) 995-1300 Identification: 770299
Accreditation: &NH

† Main campus is Hennepin Technical College in Brooklyn Park, MN.

Herzing University (D)

5700 West Broadway, Minneapolis MN 55428
Telephone: (763) 535-3000 FICE Identification: 011017
Accreditation: &NH, DA, DH, MAC, NURSE, OTA

† Main campus is Herzing University in Madison, WI.

Institute of Production and Recording (E)

300 N. 1st Avenue, Suite 500, Minneapolis MN 55401
County: Hennepin FICE Identification: 041302
Unit ID: 454616
Telephone: (612) 375-1900 Carnegie Class: Assoc/PrivFP
FAX Number: (612) 375-1919 Calendar System: Other
URL: www.ipr.edu
Established: 2002 Annual Undergrad Tuition & Fees: $16,560
Enrollment: 300 Coed
Affiliation or Control: Proprietary IRS Status: Proprietary
Highest Offering: Associate Degree
Program: Occupational
Accreditation: ACCSC

01 President .... Brian JACOBY
12 Campus Director .... Norbert KRUEZER
03 Vice President .... Vacant
05 Dean of Faculty .... Madeline HENGEL
07 Director of Admissions .... Suzanne FERKINGSTAD
32 Director of Student Services .... Karah BARR
08 Librarian .... Tina HALFMANN

ITT Technical Institute (F)

6120 Earle Brown Drive, Suite 100, Brooklyn Center MN 55430
Telephone: (763) 549-5900 Identification: 770653
Accreditation: ACICS

† Main campus is ITT Technical Institute in Indianapolis, IN.

ITT Technical Institute (G)

8911 Columbine Road, Eden Prairie MN 55347-4143
Telephone: (952) 914-5300 Identification: 666319
Accreditation: ACICS

† Main campus is ITT Technical Institute in Indianapolis, IN.

Le Cordon Bleu College of Culinary Arts in Minneapolis/St Paul (H)

1315 Mendota Heights Road, Mendota Heights MN 55120-1129
Telephone: (651) 675-4700 Identification: 666370
Accreditation: ACICS, ACFEI

† Main campus is Le Cordon Bleu College of Culinary Arts in Portland in Portland, OR.

Leech Lake Tribal College (I)

P.O. Box 180, Cass Lake MN 56633-0180
County: Cass FICE Identification: 030964
Unit ID: 413626
Telephone: (218) 335-4200 Carnegie Class: Tribal
FAX Number: (218) 335-4282 Calendar System: Semester
URL: www.lltc.edu
Established: 1990 Annual Undergrad Tuition & Fees: $4,430
Enrollment: 338 Coed
Affiliation or Control: Tribal Control IRS Status: 501(c)3
Highest Offering: Associate Degree
Program: Occupational; 2-Year Principally Bachelor's Creditable
Accreditation: NH

01 President .... Dr. Donald DAY
32 Vice Pres Student Devel/Enrollment .... Dr. Beverly RODGERS
05 Dean of Academics .... Dr. Sharon MARCOTTE
10 Chief Financial Officer .... Shelly PEMBERTON
30 Director Institutional Advancement .... Kyle ERICKSON

Luther Seminary (J)

2481 Como Avenue, Saint Paul MN 55108-1496
County: Ramsey FICE Identification: 002357
Unit ID: 173896
Telephone: (651) 641-3456 Carnegie Class: Spec/Faith
FAX Number: (651) 641-3425 Calendar System: Semester
URL: www.luthersem.edu
Established: 1869 Annual Graduate Tuition & Fees: $15,000
Enrollment: 764 Coed
Affiliation or Control: Evangelical Lutheran Church In America
IRS Status: 501(c)3
Highest Offering: Doctorate; No Undergraduates
Program: Professional; Religious Emphasis
Accreditation: NH, THEOL

01 President .... Rev. Rick FOSS
05 Dean of Academic Affairs .... Dr. Craig KOESTER
11 VP Administration & Finance .... Dr. William V. FRAME
26 VP Seminary Relations .... Mr. Thomas JOLIVETTE
32 VP Student Affairs & Enrollment .... Ms. Carrie CARROLL
15 VP Human Resources .... Ms. Sandra MIDDENDORF
42 Seminary Pastor .... Dr. Laura THELANDER
07 Director of Admissions .... Ms. Jennifer OLSEN KRENGEL
06 Registrar .... Ms. Diane DONCITS

Lutheran Brethren Seminary (K)

815 West Vernon Avenue, Fergus Falls MN 56537-2676
County: Otter Tail Identification: 666644
Telephone: (218) 739-3375 Carnegie Class: Not Classified
FAX Number: (218) 739-1259 Calendar System: Semester
URL: www.lbs.edu
Established: 1903 Annual Undergrad Tuition & Fees: $10,206
Enrollment: 25 Coed
Affiliation or Control: Other IRS Status: 501(c)3
Highest Offering: Master's
Program: Liberal Arts And General; Religious Emphasis
Accreditation: TRACS

01 President .... Dr. David VEUM
05 Dean .... Dr. Eugene BOE
06 Registrar .... Dr. Gaylan MATHIESEN

Macalester College (L)

1600 Grand Avenue, Saint Paul MN 55105-1801
County: Ramsey FICE Identification: 002358
Unit ID: 173902
Telephone: (651) 696-6000 Carnegie Class: Bac/A&S
FAX Number: (651) 696-6689 Calendar System: Semester
URL: www.macalester.edu
Established: 1874 Annual Undergrad Tuition & Fees: $45,388
Enrollment: 2,070 Coed
Affiliation or Control: Presbyterian Church (U.S.A.) IRS Status: 501(c)3
Highest Offering: Baccalaureate
Program: Liberal Arts And General
Accreditation: NH

01 President .... Dr. Brian C. ROSENBERG
05 Dean of the Faculty & Provost .... Dr. Kathleen M. MURRAY
88 Chief Investment Officer .... Mr. Mansco PERRY
30 Vice President College Advancement .... Mr. Thomas P. BONNER
32 Vice President Student Affairs .... Ms. Laurie B. HAMRE
11 Vice President for Admin/Finance .... Mr. David M. WHEATON
08 Associate Vice President ITS .... Mr. Jerry R. SANDERS
07 Dean of Admissions/Financial Aid .... Mr. Lorne T. ROBINSON
85 Inst for Global Citizenship .... Ms. Christy L. HANSON
20 Director of Academic Programs .... Ms. Ann M. MINNICK
28 Dean of Multicultural Life .... Mr. Chris A. MACDONALD-DENNIS
09 Assoc Provost/Inst Research .... Mr. Daniel J. BALIK
35 Dean of Students .... Mr. Jim HOPPE
37 Director Student Financial Aid .... Mr. Brian LINDEMAN
06 Registrar .... Ms. Jayne L. NIEMI
36 Assoc Dean for Student Services .... Ms. Denise WARD
15 Director Human Resources .... Mr. Bob GRAF
18 Director Facilities Management .... Mr. Mark D. DICKINSON
41 Athletic Director .... Ms. Kim CHANDLER
04 Assistant to the President .... Ms. Cynthia L. HENDRICKS
21 Assistant Vice President Finance .... Ms. Kate WALKER
26 Director Communications and PR .... Mr. David P. WARCH
29 Director Alumni Relations .... Ms. Gabrielle S. LAWRENCE
38 Director Health and Wellness Center .... Ms. Denise WARD
96 Dir Purchasing/Accounts Payable .... Ms. Kathleen L. JOHNSON

Martin Luther College (M)

1995 Luther Court, New Ulm MN 56073-3300
County: Brown FICE Identification: 002361
Unit ID: 173452
Telephone: (507) 354-8221 Carnegie Class: Bac/Diverse
FAX Number: (507) 354-8225 Calendar System: Semester
URL: www.mlc-wels.edu
Established: 1995 Annual Undergrad Tuition & Fees: $12,300
Enrollment: 777 Coed
Affiliation or Control: Wisconsin Evangelical Lutheran Synod
IRS Status: 501(c)3
Highest Offering: Master's
Program: Liberal Arts And General; Teacher Preparatory
Accreditation: NH

01 President .... Rev. Mark G. ZARLING
05 Vice President for Academics .... Dr. David O. WENDLER
11 Vice President for Administration .... Prof. Steven R. THIESFELDT
84 Vice President for Enrollment Mgmt .... Vacant
32 Vice President Student Life .... Prof. Jeffrey L. SCHONE
53 Academic Dean Educational Ministry .. Prof. Jeffery P. WIECHMAN
73 Academic Dean Pastoral Ministry .... Prof. Daniel N. BALGE
10 Director of Finance .... Mrs. Carla J. HULKE
08 Librarian .... Prof. David M. GOSDECK
37 Director of Financial Aid .... Mr. Gene A. SLETTEDAHL
07 Director of Admissions .... Prof. Mark A. STEIN
58 Director Graduates Studies/Cont Edu .... Prof. John E. MEYER
88 Director of Clinical Experiences .... Prof. Paul A. TESS
41 Director of Athletics .... Prof. James M. UNKE
42 Campus Pastor .... Rev. John C. BOEDER
14 Director of Technology .... Mr. James A. RATHJE
26 Director of Public Relations .... Prof. William A. PEKRUL
40 Bookstore Manager .... Mrs. Linette M. SCHARLEMANN
90 Director of Academic Computing .... Dr. James R. GRUNWALD
29 Director Alumni Relations .... Mr. Stephen J. BALZA

McNally Smith College of Music (N)

19 Exchange Street, Saint Paul MN 55101-2220
County: Ramsey FICE Identification: 030012
Unit ID: 367194
Telephone: (651) 291-0177 Carnegie Class: Spec/Arts
FAX Number: (651) 291-0366 Calendar System: Semester

URL: www.mcnallysmith.edu
Established: 1985　Annual Undergrad Tuition & Fees: $24,690
Enrollment: 644　Coed
Affiliation or Control: Proprietary　IRS Status: Proprietary
Highest Offering: Baccalaureate
Program: Occupational; Liberal Arts And General; Professional; Music Emphasis
Accreditation: @NH, MUS

01 President ... Harry CHALMIERS
10 Chief Financial Officer ... Jakki EDWARDS
37 Financial Aid Director ... Jeffrey R. AALBERS
07 Admissions Director ... Matthew EDLUND

Minneapolis Business College (A)

1711 W County Road B, Roseville MN 55113-4056
County: Ramsey　FICE Identification: 004645
Unit ID: 174118
Telephone: (651) 636-7406　Carnegie Class: Assoc/PrivFP
FAX Number: (651) 636-8185　Calendar System: Semester
URL: www.minneapolisbusinesscollege.edu
Established: 1874　Annual Undergrad Tuition & Fees: $14,500
Enrollment: 250　Coed
Affiliation or Control: Proprietary　IRS Status: Proprietary
Highest Offering: Associate Degree
Program: Occupational; 2-Year Principally Bachelor's Creditable; Business Emphasis
Accreditation: ACICS, MAC

01 President ... Mr. David WHITMAN
05 Director of Education ... Mr. Jon BLUMENTHAL
32 Director of Student Services ... Mrs. Marie MARTIN
36 Placement Coordinator ... Mrs. Suzanne ERICKSON

Minneapolis College of Art Design (B)

2501 Stevens Avenue, Minneapolis MN 55404-4343
County: Hennepin　FICE Identification: 002365
Unit ID: 174127
Telephone: (612) 874-3700　Carnegie Class: Spec/Arts
FAX Number: (612) 874-3704　Calendar System: Semester
URL: www.mcad.edu
Established: 1886　Annual Undergrad Tuition & Fees: $32,550
Enrollment: 725　Coed
Affiliation or Control: Independent Non-Profit　IRS Status: 501(c)3
Highest Offering: Master's
Program: Liberal Arts And General; Professional; Fine Arts Emphasis
Accreditation: NH, ART

01 President ... Mr. Jay COOGAN
04 Executive Assistant to President ... Ms. Kate MOHN
05 Vice President Academic Affairs ... Ms. Karen WIRTH
30 Vice Pres Institutional Advancement ... Ms. Joan G. OLSON
11 Vice President Administration ... Ms. Pam NEWSOME
20 Assoc VP Academic Affairs ... Dr. Thomas O. HAAKENSON
84 Assoc VP Enrollment Management ... Ms. Melissa HUYBRECHT
18 Assoc VP Facilities/Public Safety ... Mr. Brock RASMUSSEN
13 Assoc Vice President Technology ... Mr. R. Hal WELLS
32 Dean of Student Affairs ... Ms. Jen ZUCCOLA
06 Registrar ... Ms. Jacki L. CHESTNUT
51 Director of Continuing Education ... Ms. Lara ROY
08 Director of Library ... Ms. Amy NAUGHTON
24 Director of Media Center ... Mr. Scott BOWMAN
36 Director of Career Services ... Ms. Meghana SHROFF
29 Director Major and Alumni Giving ... Mr. Brian GIOIELLI
39 Director Student Housing ... Mr. Nate K. LUTZ
26 Director Communications ... Mr. Ann BENRUD
37 Director Student Financial Aid ... Ms. Laura LINK
40 Manager of Bookstore ... Ms. Allyson R. HARPER

Minneapolis Media Institute (C)

4100 West 76th Street, Edina MN 55435
Telephone: (952) 897-1111　Identification: 770578
Accreditation: ACCSC

† Main campus is Madison Media Institute-College of Media Arts in Madison, WI.

Minnesota School of Business (D)

3680 Pheasant Ridge Drive NE, Blaine MN 55449
Telephone: (763) 225-8000　Identification: 770718
Accreditation: ACICS

† Main campus is Minnesota School of Business in Richfield, MN.

Minnesota School of Business (E)

5910 Shingle Creek Parkway, #200,
Brooklyn Center MN 55430-2319
Telephone: (763) 566-7777　Identification: 666453
Accreditation: ACICS, MAAB

† Main campus is Minnesota School of Business in Richfield, MN.

Minnesota School of Business (F)

11500 193rd Avenue NW, Elk River MN 55330
Telephone: (763) 367-7000　Identification: 770719
Accreditation: ACICS

† Main campus is Minnesota School of Business in Richfield, MN.

Minnesota School of Business (G)

17685 Juniper Path, Lakeville MN 55044
Telephone: (952) 892-9000　Identification: 770720
Accreditation: ACICS

† Main campus is Minnesota School of Business in Richfield, MN.

Minnesota School of Business (H)

2777 34th Street South, Moorhead MN 56560
Telephone: (218) 422-1000　Identification: 770717
Accreditation: ACICS

† Main campus is Minnesota School of Business in Richfield, MN.

Minnesota School of Business (I)

1455 County Road 101 North, Plymouth MN 55447
Telephone: (763) 476-2000　Identification: 770713
Accreditation: ACICS

† Main campus is Minnesota School of Business in Richfield, MN.

Minnesota School of Business (J)

1401 W 76th Street, Suite 500, Richfield MN 55423-3846
County: Hennepin　FICE Identification: 004646
Unit ID: 174279
Telephone: (612) 861-2000　Carnegie Class: Master's S
FAX Number: (612) 861-5548　Calendar System: Quarter
URL: www.msbcollege.edu
Established: 1877　Annual Undergrad Tuition & Fees: $15,300
Enrollment: 1,252　Coed
Affiliation or Control: Proprietary　IRS Status: Proprietary
Highest Offering: Master's
Program: Occupational
Accreditation: ACICS, MAAB, NURSE

01 Campus Director ... Mrs. Stacy SEVERSON
05 Dean of Faculty ... Ms. Alisa KILMER
32 Dean of Students ... Ms. Shelby NAFUS
07 Director of Admissions ... Ms. Sonia SULTAN
36 Director of Career Services ... Ms. Sara SHORE
37 Director of Financial Aid ... Ms. Nicole PAULSON

Minnesota School of Business (K)

2521 Pennington Drive NW, Rochester MN 55901
Telephone: (507) 536-9500　Identification: 770716
Accreditation: ACICS

† Main campus is Minnesota School of Business in Richfield, MN.

Minnesota School of Business (L)

1200 Shakopee Town Square, Shakopee MN 55379
Telephone: (952) 345-1200　Identification: 770714
Accreditation: ACICS

† Main campus is Minnesota School of Business in Richfield, MN.

Minnesota School of Business (M)

1201 2nd Street South, Waite Park MN 56387
Telephone: (320) 257-2000　Identification: 770715
Accreditation: ACICS

† Main campus is Minnesota School of Business in Richfield, MN.

*Minnesota State Colleges and Universities System Office (N)

30 7th Street East, Suite 350, Saint Paul MN 55101-4901
County: Ramsey　FICE Identification: 009346
Unit ID: 428453
Telephone: (651) 201-1800　Carnegie Class: N/A
FAX Number: (651) 297-5550
URL: www.mnscu.edu

01 Chancellor ... Steven J. ROSENSTONE
03 Vice Chancellor ... Mark CARLSON
05 Vice Chanc Academic/Student Affairs ... Douglas D. KNOWLTON
10 Vice Chanc Finance/Administration ... Laura M. KING
16 Int Vice Chancellor Human Resources ... Sheila REGER
13 Vice Chanc Information Technology ... Chris MCCOY
30 Vice Chanc Advancement ... Michael I. DOUGHERTY
18 Assoc Vice Chancellor Facilities ... Brian D. YOLITZ
46 Assoc Vice Chanc Research/Planning ... Leslie K. MERCER
35 Assoc Vice Chanc Student Affairs ... Mike LOPEZ
22 Exec Dir Diversity/Multiculturalism ... Whitney Stewart HARRIS
102 Exec Dir System/Foundation Rels ... Maria R. MCLEMORE
43 General Counsel ... Gail M. OLSON
09 System Director for Research ... Craig V. SCHOENECKER
21 Exec Director of Internal Auditing ... Beth H. BUSE

*Alexandria Technical & Community College (O)

1601 Jefferson Street, Alexandria MN 56308-2796
County: Douglas　FICE Identification: 005544
Unit ID: 172918
Telephone: (320) 762-0221　Carnegie Class: Assoc/Pub-R-M
FAX Number: (320) 762-4501　Calendar System: Semester
URL: www.alextech.edu
Established: 1961　Annual Undergrad Tuition & Fees (In-State): $5,385
Enrollment: 2,877　Coed
Affiliation or Control: State　IRS Status: 501(c)3
Highest Offering: Associate Degree
Program: Occupational; 2-Year Principally Bachelor's Creditable; Technical Emphasis
Accreditation: NH, MLTAD

02 President ... Dr. Kevin KOPISCHKE
05 Exec VP Academic/Student Affairs ... Dr. Jan DOEBBERT
41 Vice Pres/Athletic Director ... Vacant
51 Vice Pres Custom Services ... Dr. Chad COAUETTE
10 Chief Financial Officer ... Mr. David BJELLAND
05 Dean of Academic Affairs ... Mr. Gregg RAISANEN
32 Dean of Student Affairs ... Vacant
72 Dean of Technology ... Mr. Steve RICHARDS
20 Associate Dean of Academic Affairs ... Ms. Kellie TATGE
19 Associate Dean of Law Enforcement ... Mr. Scott BERGER
37 Financial Aid Director ... Mr. Steve RICHARDS
22 Human Rights Officer ... Ms. Tamzin BUKOWSKI
36 Director Student Placement ... Mr. Patrick RUNNING
30 Exec Dir Advancement/Foundation ... Ms. Kathy NOHRE
06 Registrar ... Ms. Debra LE DOUX
18 Director of Facilities ... Mr. Tim TOUGAS
15 Chief Human Resources Officer ... Ms. Shari MALONEY
09 Director Institutional Research ... Ms. Rebekah SUMMER
07 Director of Admissions/Diversity ... Vacant
35 Director of Student Activities ... Ms. Michelle AHLQUIST
38 Dir Testing Center/PSEO Specialist ... Ms. Mary LENZ
04 Asst to Pres/Dir of Office Services ... Ms. Annette PAVEK
21 Accounting Supervisor ... Ms. Joan STICH
40 Bookstore Manager ... Ms. Karen SLACK
29 Alumni Coordinator ... Ms. Linda DOLAN
88 Support Services Coordinator ... Ms. Mary ACKERMAN

*Anoka-Ramsey Community College (P)

11200 Mississippi Boulevard NW,
Coon Rapids MN 55433-3499
County: Anoka　FICE Identification: 002332
Unit ID: 172963
Telephone: (763) 433-1100　Carnegie Class: Assoc/Pub-S-MC
FAX Number: (763) 433-1121　Calendar System: Semester
URL: www.anokaramsey.edu
Established: 1965　Annual Undergrad Tuition & Fees (In-State): $4,987
Enrollment: 9,497　Coed
Affiliation or Control: State　IRS Status: 501(c)3
Highest Offering: Associate Degree
Program: Occupational; 2-Year Principally Bachelor's Creditable
Accreditation: NH, ADNUR, MUS, PTAA

02 President ... Dr. Kent HANSON
10 VP Finance & Administration ... Mr. Don LEWIS
05 VP Academic/Student Affairs ... Ms. Deidra PEASLEE
32 Dean/Chief Student Affairs Officer ... Vacant
18 Physical Plant Manager ... Mr. Roger FREEMAN
16 Chief HR Director ... Mr. Darren HOFF
57 Dean of Arts & Letters ... Mr. Greg RATHERT
88 Dean CE/CT/Bus/Tech/Wellness ... Ms. Luanne KANE
35 Interim Dean Student Life ... Ms. Lisa HARRIS
76 Dean of Allied Health ... Ms. Natasha BAER
21 Director Fiscal & Auxillary Svcs ... Ms. Marilyn SMITH
81 Dean of STEM ... Ms. Kim LYNCH
09 Dean of Research & Assessment ... Ms. Nora MORRIS
28 Director of Multicultural Affairs ... Ms. Merlita LOCKMAN
102 Director of Foundations ... Mr. Marc JOHNSON
26 Director of Mktg/Public Relations ... Ms. Mary JACOBSON
19 Director of Safety & Security ... Mr. Orrin NYHUS
35 Director of Student Life ... Ms. Joyce TRACZYK
13 Interim Director of Technology ... Mr. Tim ZONDLO
21 Business Manager ... Ms. Kim BIENFANG

*Anoka Technical College (Q)

1355 W Highway 10, Anoka MN 55303-1590
County: Anoka　FICE Identification: 007350
Unit ID: 172954
Telephone: (763) 576-4700　Carnegie Class: Assoc/Pub-S-MC
FAX Number: (763) 576-4715　Calendar System: Semester
URL: www.anokatech.edu
Established: 1967　Annual Undergrad Tuition & Fees (In-District): $5,590
Enrollment: 2,184　Coed
Affiliation or Control: State/Local　IRS Status: 501(c)3
Highest Offering: Associate Degree
Program: Occupational; 2-Year Principally Bachelor's Creditable; Technical Emphasis
Accreditation: NH, CAHIIM, MAC, OTA, SURGT

02 President ... Dr. Kent HANSON
05 Int Vice Pres of Acad/Student Affs ... Heidi HAAGENSON
13 Chief Information Officer ... William BEAR
10 Vice Pres Finanance & Admin ... Donald LEWIS
20 Academic Dean ... Sherry WICKSTROM
20 Academic Dean ... James CLARK
04 Assistant to the President ... Pamela ZINKEN
15 Chief Human Res Ofcr/Dir Diversity ... Jay NELSON
26 Director of Marketing ... Mary JACOBSON
06 Registrar ... Kimberly ROAN
32 Intermin Dean of Student Affairs ... LeAnn BROWN
37 Financial Aid Director ... Lucy ROSS

*Bemidji State University (A)

1500 Birchmont Drive NE, Bemidji MN 56601-2699
County: Beltrami FICE Identification: 002336
Unit ID: 173124
Telephone: (218) 755-2001 Carnegie Class: Master's S
FAX Number: N/A Calendar System: Semester
URL: www.bemidjistate.edu
Established: 1919 Annual Undergrad Tuition & Fees (In-State): $8,124
Enrollment: 5,017 Coed
Affiliation or Control: State IRS Status: 501(c)3
Highest Offering: Master's
Program: Liberal Arts And General; Teacher Preparatory
Accreditation: NH, IACBE, MUS, NAIT, NURSE, SW

02 President .... Dr. Richard A. HANSON
05 Provost & VP Academic Affairs .... Dr. Martin TADLOCK
84 VP Student Development & Enrollment .... Dr. James PARKER
10 VP Finance & Administration .... Mr. William D. MAKI
20 Int VP Innovation & Ext Learning .... Mr. Robert J. GRIGGS
20 Assoc VP Academic Affairs .... Dr. Patrick G. GUILFOILE
66 Dean Nursing .... Dr. Jeanine GANGENESS
49 Int Dean Arts & Sciences .... Dr. Colleen GREER
50 Dean Business/Tech & Communication .... Dr. Shawn STRONG
76 Int Dean Health Sci/Human Ecology .... Dr. James BARTA
94 Director Women's Studies .... Vacant
92 Director Honors Program .... Dr. Marsha DRISCOLL
06 Registrar .... Ms. Michelle FRENZEL
09 Director Inst Rsrch/Effectiveness .... Mr. Douglas P. OLNEY
106 Int Director Distance Learning .... Ms. Lynn JOHNSON
07 Assoc VP Admissions/Enrollment .... Mr. Michael HEITKAMP
36 Director Career Services .... Ms. Margie T. GIAUQUE
85 Director International Program Ctr .... Ms. Cherish HAGEN-SWANSON
39 Director Residential Life .... Vacant
88 Director American Indian Ctr .... Dr. Anton TREUER
37 Director Financial Aid .... Mr. Paul G. LINDSETH
15 Director Human Resources .... Ms. Marybeth CHRISTENSON-JONES
21 Business Manager .... Ms. Diane ILLIES
96 Director Procurement & Logistics .... Ms. Belinda S. LINDELL
19 Director Public Safety .... Mr. Casey J. MCCARTHY
18 Director Physical Plant .... Mr. Jeff A. SANDE
22 Int Asst to Pres Affirmative Action .... Dr. Mary WARD
30 Exec Dir for University Advancement .... Mr. Robert D. BOLLINGER
29 Director Alumni Relations .... Ms. Caroline NORELIUS
27 Chief Information Officer .... Mr. Jim PULLIAM
26 Director Communications & Marketing .... Mr. Scott FAUST
41 Athletic Director .... Mr. Tracy DILL

*Central Lakes College (B)

501 W College Drive, Brainerd MN 56401-3900
County: Crow Wing FICE Identification: 002339
Unit ID: 173203
Telephone: (218) 855-8000 Carnegie Class: Assoc/Pub-R-M
FAX Number: (218) 855-8057 Calendar System: Semester
URL: www.clcmn.edu
Established: 1938 Annual Undergrad Tuition & Fees (In-State): $5,745
Enrollment: 1,901 Coed
Affiliation or Control: State IRS Status: 501(c)3
Highest Offering: Associate Degree
Program: Occupational; 2-Year Principally Bachelor's Creditable
Accreditation: NH, DA, MAC

02 President .... Dr. Larry A. LUNDBLAD
05 Vice Pres Academic Affairs .... Dr. Douglas BINSFELD
11 VP Administrative Svcs/Facilities .... Ms. Kari CHRISTIANSEN
12 Dean Technical Pgms/Staples Campus .... Mr. Christopher HADFIELD
32 Dean of Students .... Ms. Beth ADAMS
13 Dean of Academic/Technology Svcs .... Mr. Michael AMICK
49 Dean of Liberal Arts .... Mr. Kelly MCCALLA
30 Dir Resource Development/CLC Fndtn .... Ms. Pamela THOMSEN
15 Director of Human Resources .... Ms. Nancy PAULSON
07 Director of Admissions & Advising .... Mr. Nick HEISSERER
06 Registrar .... Ms. Michelle KANGAS
08 Librarian .... Mr. David BISSONETTE
37 Director Financial Aid .... Mr. Mike BARNABY
27 Public Information Officer .... Mr. Kenn DOLS
21 Director of Business Services .... Ms. Christina VOPATEK
18 Physical Plant Director .... Mr. James MCARDELL
28 Director of Diversity .... Ms. Mary SAM

*Century College (C)

3300 Century Avenue N, White Bear Lake MN 55110-1894
County: Ramsey FICE Identification: 010546
Unit ID: 175315
Telephone: (651) 779-3200 Carnegie Class: Assoc/Pub-S-SC
FAX Number: (651) 779-3417 Calendar System: Semester
URL: www.century.edu
Established: 1967 Annual Undergrad Tuition & Fees (In-State): $5,361
Enrollment: 10,476 Coed
Affiliation or Control: State IRS Status: 501(c)3
Highest Offering: Associate Degree
Program: Occupational; 2-Year Principally Bachelor's Creditable
Accreditation: NH, ADNUR, DA, DH, EMT, MAC, OPE, RAD

02 President .... Dr. Ron ANDERSON
05 VP Academic Affairs/CAO .... Dr. Suresh TIWARI
32 VP Student Services .... Dr. Michael BRUNER
51 VP Continuing Educ/Customized Train .... Ms. Jeralyn JARGO
10 VP Finance & Administration .... Dr. Patrick OPATZ
13 Assoc VP Information Tech/Admn Svcs .... Mr. John ROHLEDER
96 Purchasing & Auxiliary Svcs Suprvr .... Mr. Todd OSEBY
21 Director of Finance .... Ms. Bonnie MEYERS
102 Executive Director Foundation .... Ms. Jill GREENHALGH
06 Registrar .... Ms. Susan DICKENS
15 Director of Human Resources .... Ms. Mary NIENABER
07 Director of Admissions .... Ms. Christine PAULOS
45 Director of Resource Development .... Mr. Donald LONG
37 Director of Financial Aid .... Ms. Pam ENGEBRETSON
18 Mgr of Physical Plant/Super of Bld .... Mr. Michael HOUFER
28 Director of Diversity .... Mr. Herbert KING
26 Dir Cmty Rels/College Advanc/Alumni .... Ms. Nancy LIVINGSTON
19 Director of Public Safety .... Mr. Mark HOLPER
66 Dean Nursing/Allied Health .... Ms. Kathleen BELL
75 Dean Trades/Public Safety/Svcs .... Ms. Jane NICHOLSON
72 Dean Science/Technology .... Ms. Brenda LYSENG
81 Dean English/ESOL/Reading/Math .... Dr. Susan EHLERS
83 Dean Social & Behav Sci/Lang/Com .... Ms. Pakou VANG
35 Dean of Student Services .... Mr. Jason CARDINAL
35 Dean of Student Services .... Ms. Andrea RYSTROM
35 Dean of Student Services .... Ms. Kristin HAGEMAN
09 Dean of Institutional Effectiveness .... Ms. Lisa SCHLOTTERHAUSEN

*Dakota County Technical College (D)

145th Street E, Rosemount MN 55068-2999
County: Dakota FICE Identification: 010402
Unit ID: 173416
Telephone: (651) 423-8000 Carnegie Class: Assoc/Pub-S-SC
FAX Number: (651) 423-8775 Calendar System: Semester
URL: www.dctc.edu
Established: 1970 Annual Undergrad Tuition & Fees (In-District): $5,850
Enrollment: 3,710 Coed
Affiliation or Control: State/Local IRS Status: 501(c)3
Highest Offering: Associate Degree
Program: Occupational; 2-Year Principally Bachelor's Creditable; Technical Emphasis
Accreditation: NH, DA, MAC

02 Interim President .... Mr. Tim WYNES
05 VP Academic & Student Affairs .... Dr. Kelly MURTAUGH
88 Dean Transportation Indust Careers .... Dr. Mike OPP
50 Dean of Business/Technology and GE .... Ms. Gayle LARSON
32 Dean of Student Affairs .... Mr. Greg MCCALLEY
06 Registrar .... Ms. Jodie SWEARINGEN
15 Human Resources Director .... Ms. Susan RADDATZ
18 Chief Facilities/Physical Plant .... Mr. Paul DEMUTH
32 Chief Student Life Officer .... Ms. Nicole MEULEMANS
103 Dean of Customized Training .... Mr. Pat MCQUILLAN
07 Admissions Coordinator .... Mr. Patrick LAIR
30 Director Institutional Advancement .... Ms. Erin LARSEN
37 Financial Aid Coordinator .... Mr. Scott ROELKE
09 Director of Institutional Research .... Ms. Carrie SCHNEIDER

*Fond du Lac Tribal and Community College (E)

2101 14th Street, Cloquet MN 55720-2984
County: Carlton FICE Identification: 031291
Unit ID: 380368
Telephone: (218) 879-0800 Carnegie Class: Tribal
FAX Number: (218) 879-0814 Calendar System: Semester
URL: www.fdltcc.edu
Established: 1987 Annual Undergrad Tuition & Fees (In-State): $5,256
Enrollment: 2,842 Coed
Affiliation or Control: State IRS Status: 501(c)3
Highest Offering: Associate Degree
Program: Occupational; 2-Year Principally Bachelor's Creditable; Liberal Arts And General
Accreditation: NH

02 President .... Mr. Larry ANDERSON
05 Vice President of Instruction .... Dr. Anna FELLEGY
10 Chief Financial Officer .... Ms. Stephanie HAMMITT
32 Interim Dean of Student Affairs .... Mr. Keith TURNER
27 Director of Public Information .... Mr. Tom URBANSKI
06 Registrar .... Ms. Leah TOLLEFSON
88 Disability Services/Student Service .... Ms. Shelia SUMNER
13 Information Technology Specialist .... Mr. Loran WAPPES
37 Director of Financial Aid .... Mr. David SUTHERLAND
07 Director of Admissions .... Ms. Susan BUMANN
09 Director of Institutional Research .... Vacant
35 Dir of Student Support Services .... Ms. Roberta TORGERSON
62 Library Services .... Ms. Nancy BROUGHTON
30 Director of Development .... Mr. Larry ANDERSON
39 Director of Housing .... Mr. Jesse STIREWALT
15 Director of Human Resources .... Ms. Louise LIND
18 Chief Facilities/Physical Plant .... Mr. Mark BERNHARDSON
40 Bookstore Coordinator .... Ms. Bonnie BERNHARDSON
04 Executive Assistant to President .... Ms. Mary SOYRING

*Hennepin Technical College (F)

9000 Brooklyn Boulevard, Brooklyn Park MN 55445-2399
County: Hennepin FICE Identification: 010491
Unit ID: 173708
Telephone: (952) 995-1300 Carnegie Class: Assoc/Pub-S-MC
FAX Number: (763) 488-2956 Calendar System: Semester
URL: www.hennepintech.edu
Established: 1972 Annual Undergrad Tuition & Fees (In-District): $5,122
Enrollment: 6,587 Coed
Affiliation or Control: State/Local IRS Status: 501(c)3
Highest Offering: Associate Degree
Program: Occupational; 2-Year Principally Bachelor's Creditable; Technical Emphasis
Accreditation: NH, ACBSP, ACFEI, DA, IFSAC, MAC

02 President .... Dr. Cecillia Y M. CERVANTES
05 Int Vice President Academic Affairs .... Dr. Marilyn KRASOWSKI
11 Vice Pres Administrative Services .... Mr. Craig ERICKSON
32 Int Vice President Student Affairs .... Dr. Marilyn KRASOWSKI
06 Registrar .... Ms. Julie HIGDEM
15 Chief Human Resources Officer .... Ms. Sharon MOHR
30 Dir Development/Alumni Relations .... Ms. Jeanne MORPHEW
28 Director of Diversity .... Ms. Jean MAIERHOFER
07 Director of Admissions .... Ms. Monir JOHNSON
09 Director of Institutional Research .... Ms. Donna S. STATZELL
26 Exec Dir Inst Adv & Marketing .... Ms. Annette ROTH
37 Director of Financial Aid .... Mr. Tim JACOBSON
84 Dean of Enrollment .... Mr. Nathan STRATTON
88 Dean of Student Success .... Ms. Dara HAGAN

*Hibbing Community College, A Technical and Community College (G)

1515 E 25th Street, Hibbing MN 55746-3300
County: Saint Louis FICE Identification: 002355
Unit ID: 173735
Telephone: (218) 262-7200 Carnegie Class: Assoc/Pub-R-S
FAX Number: (218) 262-6717 Calendar System: Semester
URL: www.hibbing.edu
Established: 1916 Annual Undergrad Tuition & Fees (In-State): $5,438
Enrollment: 1,332 Coed
Affiliation or Control: State IRS Status: 501(c)3
Highest Offering: Associate Degree
Program: Occupational; 2-Year Principally Bachelor's Creditable
Accreditation: NH, ADNUR, DA, MLTAD

02 President .... Dr. M. Sue COLLINS
03 Provost .... Dr. Ken SIMBERG
05 Dean of Acad Affairs & Student Svcs .... Dr. Mike RAICH
32 Associate Dean of Student Services .... Vacant
10 Chief Fiscal Officer .... Mr. Bill MANNEY
09 Institutional Research .... Ms. Tracey ROY
37 Director Student Financial Aid .... Mr. Paul HATCH
18 Plant Maintenance Engineer .... Mr. Jimmer HODGE
26 Director of Public Information .... Ms. Susan DEGNAN

*Inver Hills Community College (H)

2500 80th Street E, Inver Grove Heights MN 55076-3224
County: Dakota FICE Identification: 009740
Unit ID: 173799
Telephone: (651) 450-3000 Carnegie Class: Assoc/Pub-S-SC
FAX Number: (651) 450-3679 Calendar System: Semester
URL: www.inverhills.edu
Established: 1970 Annual Undergrad Tuition & Fees (In-State): $6,326
Enrollment: 6,099 Coed
Affiliation or Control: State IRS Status: 501(c)3
Highest Offering: Associate Degree
Program: Occupational; 2-Year Principally Bachelor's Creditable
Accreditation: NH, ACBSP, ADNUR, EMT

02 President .... Mr. Timothy WYNES
05 Prov/VP Academic Affs & Student Dev .... Dr. Christina ROYAL
10 Vice Pres Administrative Services .... Ms. Dee BERNARD
32 Vice Pres for Student Affairs .... Mr. Jason HOSENEY
35 Dean of Student/Enroll Svcs .... Mr. Tom WILLIAMSON
50 Dean of Business & Social Sciences .... Ms. Anne JOHNSON
76 Dean of Allied Health Sciences .... Dr. Doris HILL
79 Int Dean of Fine Arts/Humanities .... Dr. Jason KAUFMAN
81 Dean of STEM .... Dr. Kevin GYOLAI
30 Exec Dir of Foundation & Advancemnt .... Mrs. Gail MORRISON
15 Director of Human Resources .... Ms. Elizabeth NEWBERRY
51 Dean of Continuing Education .... Mr. Pat MCQUILLAN
08 Librarian .... Ms. Julie BENOLKEN
84 Director of Enrollment Services .... Mr. Matt TRAXLER
88 Dir Paralegal Pgm/Ofc Sys-Legal .... Ms. Sally DAHLQUIST
90 Director Acad Tech/Computing Svcs .... Mr. Mark PETERSON
18 Director Facilities Plng/Management .... Mr. Pat BUHL
88 Director of Emergency Health Svcs .... Ms. Tia RADANT
28 Director of Access & Opportunity .... Mr. Tadael EMIRU
37 Director of Financial Aid .... Mr. Steve YANG
09 Director of Institutional Research .... Ms. Wendy MARSON
26 Interim Director of Marketing .... Ms. Marie MARCOGLIESE
28 Director of Equity and Inclusion .... Ms. Sarah NAPOLI-RANGEL
45 Interim Assoc Dean of Acad Affair .... Mr. Matt SIMONEAU

*Itasca Community College (I)

1851 E Highway 169, Grand Rapids MN 55744-3397
County: Itasca FICE Identification: 002356
Unit ID: 173805
Telephone: (800) 996-6422 Carnegie Class: Assoc/Pub-R-S
FAX Number: (218) 322-2332 Calendar System: Semester
URL: www.itascacc.edu
Established: 1922 Annual Undergrad Tuition & Fees (In-State): $5,306
Enrollment: 1,269 Coed
Affiliation or Control: State IRS Status: 501(c)3
Highest Offering: Associate Degree
Program: 2-Year Principally Bachelor's Creditable

Accreditation: NH

02 Provost .... Dr. Barbara MCDONALD
05 Academic Dean .... Mr. Bart JOHNSON
10 Director of Finance & Facilities .... Ms. Patricia LEISTIKOW
84 Dir of Enrollment Mgmt/Admissions .... Ms. Candace PERRY
06 Registrar .... Ms. Gwen LITCHKE
29 Director of Alumni Relations .... Ms. Beth ANDERSON
30 Director of College Development .... Ms. Janet NEURAUTER
37 Director of Student Financial Aid .... Mr. Nathan WRIGHT
08 Head Librarian .... Mr. Steve BEAN
18 Chief Facilities/Physical Plant .... Mr. Chad HAATVEDT
40 Director of Bookstore .... Vacant
28 Director of Diversity .... Mr. Harold ANNETTE
09 Director of Institutional Research .... Ms. Tracey ROY

*Lake Superior College (A)

2101 Trinity Road, Duluth MN 55811-3399

County: Saint Louis FICE Identification: 005757
Unit ID: 173461
Telephone: (218) 733-7600 Carnegie Class: Assoc/Pub-R-L
FAX Number: (218) 733-4921 Calendar System: Semester
URL: www.lsc.edu
Established: 1995 Annual Undergrad Tuition & Fees (In-State): $5,083
Enrollment: 5,422 Coed
Affiliation or Control: State IRS Status: 501(c)3
Highest Offering: Associate Degree
Program: Occupational; 2-Year Principally Bachelor's Creditable
Accreditation: NH, ADNUR, COARC, DH, MAC, MLTAD, PTAA, RAD, SURGT

02 President .... Dr. Patrick JOHNS
05 Vice Pres Academic/Student Affairs .... Mr. Mark MAGNUSON
10 Vice President of Administration .... Mr. Al FINLAYSON
49 Dean of Liberal Arts & Sciences .... Ms. Hanna ERPESTAD
75 Dean of Business/Industry Division .... Ms. Jenni SWENSON
76 Dean of Allied Health & Nursing .... Ms. Pamela ELSTAD
103 Exec Dir Workforce/Cmty Develop .... Mr. Steve WAGNER
09 Dir IR/Accred Assessment/Research .... Mr. Kent RICHARDS
15 Director of Human Resources .... Ms. Colleen CONLEY
26 Dir of Public Affairs/Advancement .... Mr. Gary KRUCHOWSKI
06 Registrar .... Ms. Jean STOJEVICH
07 Director of Admissions .... Ms. Melissa LENO
18 Director Physical Plant .... Mr. Gary ADAMS
28 Dir Diversity & Stdnt Support Svcs .... Mr. Wade GORDON
36 Director Student Placement .... Ms. Betsy JACOBSON
37 Director Student Financial Aid .... Ms. LaNita ROBINSON
29 Director Alumni Relations .... Ms. LuAnne ANDERSON
35 Dir Student Life/Student Senate .... Mr. Roger JOHNSON
21 Director Business Services .... Ms. Kathy DUGDALE
102 Foundation Director .... Ms. Kim PARMETER
13 Director Information Technology .... Ms. Kim PARMETER
96 Purchasing Agent .... Ms. Joyce CLOCK

*Mesabi Range Community & Technical College (B)

1001 Chestnut Street West, Virginia MN 55792-3401

County: Saint Louis FICE Identification: 005739
Unit ID: 173993
Telephone: (218) 741-3095 Carnegie Class: Assoc/Pub-R-S
FAX Number: (218) 748-2419 Calendar System: Semester
URL: www.mesabirange.edu
Established: 1963 Annual Undergrad Tuition & Fees (In-State): $2,556
Enrollment: 2,345 Coed
Affiliation or Control: State IRS Status: Exempt
Highest Offering: Associate Degree
Program: Occupational; 2-Year Principally Bachelor's Creditable; Fine Arts Emphasis
Accreditation: NH, EMT

02 President .... Dr. Sue COLLINS
05 Provost .... Ms. Carol HELLAND
32 Dean of Students .... Mr. David DAILEY
10 Chief Finance and Facilities Office .... Mr. Roy TROUSDELL
15 Director Human Resources .... Ms. Carmen BRADACH
37 Director Student Financial Aid .... Ms. Jodi PONTINEN
06 Registrar .... Vacant
07 Director of Admissions .... Ms. Brenda KOCHEVAR
09 Director of Institutional Research .... Ms. Tracey ROY
26 Chief Public Relations Officer .... Ms. Brenda KOCHEVAR
38 Director Student Counseling .... Ms. Kelly BAKK
36 Director Student Placement .... Mr. Toby ANDERSON
84 Director Enrollment Management .... Ms. Brenda KOCHEVAR

*Metropolitan State University (C)

700 E 7th Street, Saint Paul MN 55106-5000

County: Ramsey FICE Identification: 010374
Unit ID: 174020
Telephone: (651) 793-1300 Carnegie Class: Master's M
FAX Number: (651) 793-1235 Calendar System: Semester
URL: www.metrostate.edu
Established: 1971 Annual Undergrad Tuition & Fees (In-State): $6,340
Enrollment: 8,527 Coed
Affiliation or Control: State IRS Status: 501(c)3
Highest Offering: Doctorate
Program: Liberal Arts And General; Teacher Preparatory; Professional
Accreditation: NH, NURSE, SW

02 President .... Dr. Sue K. HAMMERSMITH
05 Provost/Vice Pres Academic Affs .... Ms. Virginia ARTHUR
11 Vice Pres Administrative Affairs .... Mr. Murtuza SIDDIQUI
32 Vice President Student Affairs .... Mr. Andrew MELENDRES
30 Vice Pres University Advancement .... Mr. Jesse BETHKE-GOMEZ
35 Interim Dean of Students .... Mr. Tadael EMIRU
18 Assoc Vice Pres Admin Affairs .... Mr. Daniel HAMBROCK
13 Assoc VP Info/Telecom/Tech/CIO .... Vacant
10 Assoc VP Financial Management .... Mr. Ronald BECKSTROM
15 Director Human Resources .... Dr. Edna COMEDY
06 Registrar .... Mr. Daryl JOHNSON
37 Director Financial Aid .... Ms. Lois LARSON
26 Int Dir Communications/ Marketing .... Ms. Diane DEROSIER DOUGLASS
27 Publication/News Services Director .... Ms. Susan M. AMOS PALMER
29 Director Alumni Relations .... Ms. Vicki LOFQUIST
22 Director Affirmative Action .... Ms. Truly WEBB
09 Director Institutional Research .... Ms. Cynthia DEVORE
07 Director of Admissions .... Mr. Daryl JOHNSON
49 Dean College of Arts & Sciences .... Dr. Becky OMDAHL
58 Int Dean of College of Management .... Dr. Roger PRESTWICH
107 Dean Col Health/Cmty/Profess Stds .... Dr. Ann LEJA
88 Int Dean Col Individualized Stds .... Dr. Leah HARVEY
88 Dean School of Urban Education .... Dr. Rose CHU
66 Int Exec Dir School of Nursing .... Dr. Judith GRAZIANO
88 Int Dean Sch Law Enforce/Crim Just .... Dr. Everett DOOLITTLE

*Minneapolis Community and Technical College (D)

1501 Hennepin Avenue, Minneapolis MN 55403-9810

County: Hennepin FICE Identification: 002362
Unit ID: 174136
Telephone: (612) 659-6000 Carnegie Class: Assoc/Pub-U-SC
FAX Number: (612) 659-6210 Calendar System: Semester
URL: www.minneapolis.edu
Established: 1996 Annual Undergrad Tuition & Fees (In-State): $5,349
Enrollment: 10,090 Coed
Affiliation or Control: State IRS Status: 501(c)3
Highest Offering: Associate Degree
Program: Occupational; 2-Year Principally Bachelor's Creditable
Accreditation: NH, ADNUR, DA, NDT, PHLEB, PNUR, POLYT

02 President .... Mr. Phillip L. DAVIS
05 Vice Pres Academic/Student Affairs .... Dr. Lois BOLLMAN
10 Vice President Finance/Operations .... Mr. Scott ERICKSON
32 Int Vice President Student Affairs .... Ms. Laura FEDOCK
09 Int Assoc VP Strat/Plng/Account .... Ms. Jessica SHRYACK
103 Assoc VP Workforce Development .... Mr. Mike CHRISTENSON
84 Dean of Enrollment Management .... Ms. Laura FEDOCK
49 Dean of Liberal Arts .... Dr. Linnea STENSON
81 Dean of Science & Math .... Mr. Chuck PAULSON
51 Dean of Continuing Education .... Mr. Reede WEBSTER
66 Dean of Nursing & Allied Health .... Mr. Robert MUSTER
72 Dean of Technical Programs .... Mr. Mick COLEMAN
35 Interim Dean of Students .... Ms. Becky NORDIN
20 Dean Academic Development .... Vacant
43 Director Legal Affairs .... Ms. Dianna CUSICK
15 Director of Human Resources .... Mr. Keith BALASKI
13 Chief Information Officer .... Mr. Jim DILLEMUTH
07 Director of Admissions .... Ms. Kerri CARLSON
06 Interim Registrar .... Ms. Jeanne MAANUM
08 Librarian .... Mr. Tom ELAND
37 Financial Aid Director .... Ms. Angela CHRISTENSEN
09 Director of Institutional Research .... Vacant
18 Director Facilities .... Mr. Roger BROZ
19 Director of Public Safety .... Mr. Curt SCHMIDT
26 Chief Public Relations Officer .... Ms. Dawn SKELLY
32 Chief Student Life Officer .... Ms. Tara MARTINEZ

*Minnesota State College - Southeast Technical (E)

1250 Homer Road, PO Box 409, Winona MN 55987-4897

County: Winona FICE Identification: 002393
Unit ID: 175263
Telephone: (507) 453-2700 Carnegie Class: Assoc/Pub-R-M
FAX Number: (507) 453-2795 Calendar System: Semester
URL: www.southeastmn.edu
Established: 1949 Annual Undergrad Tuition & Fees (In-District): $5,164
Enrollment: 2,301 Coed
Affiliation or Control: State/Local IRS Status: 501(c)3
Highest Offering: Associate Degree
Program: Occupational; 2-Year Principally Bachelor's Creditable
Accreditation: NH, RAD

02 President .... Mr. James J. JOHNSON
04 Assistant to President .... Ms. Casie JOHNSON
05 Vice President Academic Affairs .... Mr. Ron SELLNAU
32 Vice Pres Student Affairs .... Mr. Nate EMERSON
10 Vice Pres Finance/Administration .... Mr. Mike KROENING
20 Dean of Academic Affairs .... Dr. Jolene PONCELET
49 Dean of Liberal Arts & Sciences .... Ms. Jolene PONCELET
15 Chief Human Resource Officer .... Ms. Deanna VOTH
26 Director of Public Relations .... Ms. Erin LATTEN
13 Chief Information Officer .... Mr. Rick NAHRGANG
06 Registrar .... Ms. Mary JOHNSON
37 Director Financial Aid .... Ms. Anne DAHLEN
09 Director of Institutional Research .... Mr. Josh BUBLITZ
84 Dir of Enrollment Svcs/Stdnt Plcmt .... Vacant
30 Exec Dir Institutional Advancement .... Ms. Cheryl HANCOCK
84 Director Student Enrollment .... Ms. Jackie BRIGGS
07 Admissions Counselor .... Ms. Melissa CARRINGTON-IRWIN
07 Admissions Counselor .... Mr. Gale LANNING
18 Chief Facilities/Physical Plant .... Mr. Thomas HOFFMAN
51 Dir Continuing/Workforce Education .... Ms. Cheryl HANCOCK

*Minnesota State Community and Technical College (F)

1414 College Way, Fergus Falls MN 56537-1000

County: Otter Tail FICE Identification: 005541
Unit ID: 173559
Telephone: (218) 736-1500 Carnegie Class: Assoc/Pub-R-L
FAX Number: (218) 736-1510 Calendar System: Semester
URL: www.minnesota.edu
Established: 1960 Annual Undergrad Tuition & Fees (In-State): $5,824
Enrollment: 6,778 Coed
Affiliation or Control: State IRS Status: 501(c)3
Highest Offering: Associate Degree
Program: Occupational; 2-Year Principally Bachelor's Creditable; Liberal Arts And General
Accreditation: NH, CAHIIM, DA, MLTAD, RAD

02 President .... Dr. Peggy KENNEDY
05 Chief Academic Officer .... Ms. Kathy BROCK
16 Director of Human Resources .... Mrs. Dacia JOHNSON
13 Interim Chief Information Officer .... Mr. Dan KNUDSON
10 Chief Financial Officer .... Mr. Pat NORDICK
84 Dean of Student Access .... Mr. Anthony SCHAFFHAUSER
26 Dir of Communications & Marketing .... Ms. Mary DEVINE
32 Assoc VP of Acad & Student Affairs .... Mrs. Carrie BRIMHALL
18 Supt of Buildings & Grounds .... Mr. Matt SHEPPARD
88 Senior Dean for Student Success .... Mr. Shawn ANDERSON
12 Vice President - Wadena and CSSO .... Dr. Peter WIELINSKI
106 Senior Dean eCampus .... Dr. Jill ABBOTT
20 Sr Dean Academic - Detroit Lakes .... Mr. Tom WHELIHAN
20 Sr Dean Academic - Fergus Falls .... Dr. Gary HENRICKSON
20 Sr Dean Academic - Wadena .... Mr. Monty JOHNSON
88 Dean of CTS/BES .... Mr. G.L TUCKER
66 Dean of Nursing .... Mrs. Jennifer JACOBSON

*Minnesota State University, Mankato (G)

309 Wigley Administration Center,
Mankato MN 56001-6062

County: Blue Earth FICE Identification: 002360
Unit ID: 173920
Telephone: (507) 389-1111 Carnegie Class: Master's L
FAX Number: (507) 389-6200 Calendar System: Semester
URL: www.mnsu.edu
Established: 1868 Annual Undergrad Tuition & Fees (In-State): $10,709
Enrollment: 15,441 Coed
Affiliation or Control: State IRS Status: Exempt
Highest Offering: Doctorate
Program: Liberal Arts And General; Teacher Preparatory; Professional
Accreditation: NH, ART, BUS, CACREP, CONST, CORE, DH, DIETD, ENG, ENGT, MUS, NRPA, NURSE, SP, SW, TED

02 President .... Dr. Richard DAVENPORT
05 VP Academic & Student Affairs .... Vacant
10 Vice Pres Finance & Administration .... Mr. Richard STRAKA
30 VP Univ Advance/Chief Dev Ofcr .... Mr. Jeff ISEMINGER
13 VP Technology/CIO .... Mr. Ed CLARK
88 VP Strategic/Busnss/Ed/Reg Prtrshps .... Dr. Robert HOFFMAN
28 Interm Dean Institutional Diversity .... Mr. Henry MORRIS
32 Assoc VP for Student Affairs .... Dr. David JONES
20 Asso Vice Pres for Academic Affairs .... Dr. Warren SANDMANN
04 Assistant to the President .... Ms. DeeAnn SNAZA
20 Asst VP for Undergrad Stds Intl Ed .... Dr. Becky COPPER-GLENZ
27 Asst VP Integrated Marketing/Comm .... Mr. Jeff ISEMINGER
18 Int Asst Vice Pres Facilities Mgmt .... Mr. David COWAN
06 University Registrar .... Mr. Marcius BROCK
07 Director of Admissions .... Mr. Brian JONES
08 Dean Library Services .... Dr. Joan ROCA
15 Director of Human Resources .... Ms. Sheri SARGENT
36 Director Career Development .... Ms. Pamela WELLER-DENGEL
26 Director Media Relations .... Mr. Daniel BENSON
41 Dir of Intercollegiate Athletics .... Mr. Kevin BUISMAN
29 Director of Alumni Relations .... Ms. Jennifer MYERS
22 Director Affirmative Action .... Ms. Linda HANSON
37 Director Student Financial Services .... Ms. Jan MARBLE
58 Dean Graduate Studies/Research .... Dr. Barry RIES
79 Dean of Arts & Humanities .... Dr. Walter ZAKAHI
53 Dean of Education .... Dr. Jean HAAR
50 Dean of Business .... Dr. Brenda FLANNERY
76 Interim Dean Allied Health/Nursing .... Dr. Harry KRAMPF
81 Dean Science/Engineering/Technology .... Dr. Vijendra AGARWAL
83 Dean Social/Behavioral Science .... Dr. Kimberly GREER
38 Director Student Counseling .... Ms. Kari MUCH

*Minnesota State University Moorhead (H)

1104 7th Avenue S, Moorhead MN 56563-2996

County: Clay FICE Identification: 002367
Unit ID: 174358
Telephone: (218) 477-4000 Carnegie Class: Master's M
FAX Number: (218) 477-2168 Calendar System: Semester
URL: www.mnstate.edu
Established: 1887 Annual Undergrad Tuition & Fees (In-State): $7,816
Enrollment: 6,904 Coed

Affiliation or Control: State IRS Status: 501(c)3
Highest Offering: Doctorate
Program: Liberal Arts And General; Teacher Preparatory; Professional
Accreditation: NH, ART, BUS, CACREP, CONST, DH, MUS, NAIT, NURSE, SP, SW, TED

02 President Dr. Edna M. SZYMANSKI
05 Provost & Sr VP Academic Affairs Dr. Anne E. BLACKHURST
10 VP Finance & Administration Ms. Janet L. MAHONEY
84 VP Enrollment Mgmt/Student Affairs Dr. Yvette UNDERDUE MURPH
29 VP Alumni Foundation Ms. Laura L. HUTH
45 AVP F&A/Univ Plng & Budget Ofcr Ms. Jean R. HOLLAAR
04 Assistant to the President Ms. Kathleen J. MCNABB
20 AVP Acad Affairs Ms. Ginny V. BAIR
28 AVP Div/Inclusion/Affirm Action Dr. Donna L. BROWN
88 AVP for Academic Planning Ms. Denise M. GORSLINE
41 Director of Athletics Mr. Doug D. PETERS
14 Chief Information Officer Mr. Daniel A. HECKAMAN
21 Comptroller Ms. Karen K. LESTER
50 Dean Business & Innovation Dr. Marsha L. WEBER
49 Dean Arts/Media/Communication Dr. Timothy A. BORCHERS
53 Int Dean Educ/Human Svcs/Grad Stds Dr. Boyd L. BRADBURY
83 Dean Sciences/Health/Environment Dr. Michelle L. MALOTT
08 Dean Instructional Resources Ms. Brittney G. GOODMAN
79 Int Dean of Col Humanities/Soc Sci Dr. Randy L. CAGLE
15 Director Human Resources Mr. Mark A. YURAN
06 Interim Registrar Ms. Heather M. SOLEIM
26 Director Marketing/Communications Mr. David C. WAHLBERG
19 Director of Security Mr. Gregory J. LEMKE
37 Dir Financial Aid & Scholarships Ms. Carolyn F. ZEHREN
23 Dir Health/Wellness/Counseling Ctrs Ms. Carol M. GRIMM
88 Director Disabilities Mr. Greg A. TOUTGES
36 Director of Career Development Ms. Sarah A. MILLER
07 Director of Admissions Mr. Rance LARSEN
35 Exec Dir Student Union Ms. Karen B. MEHNERT-MELAND
39 Dir Housing & Residential Life Ms. Heather PHILLIPS
85 Director International Student Affs Ms. Janet M. HOHENSTEIN
18 Manager Physical Plant Mr. Jeffrey D. GOEBEL
40 Bookstore Supervisor Ms. Kim M. SAMSON

*Minnesota West Community and Technical College (A)

1450 Collegeway, Worthington MN 56187
County: Nobles FICE Identification: 005263
Unit ID: 173638
Telephone: (507) 372-3400 Carnegie Class: Assoc/Pub-R-M
FAX Number: (507) 372-5801 Calendar System: Semester
URL: www.mnwest.edu
Established: 1985 Annual Undergrad Tuition & Fees (In-State): $5,660
Enrollment: 3,467 Coed
Affiliation or Control: State IRS Status: 501(c)3
Highest Offering: Associate Degree
Program: Occupational; 2-Year Principally Bachelor's Creditable
Accreditation: NH, ADNUR, DA, MAC, MLTAD, RAD, SURGT

02 President Dr. Richard SHRUBB
05 College Provost Dr. Jeff WILLIAMSON
11 Vice President of Administration Ms. Lori VOSS
106 Dean Technology/Distance Learning Ms. Kayla WESTRA
84 Director of Enrollment Management Vacant
37 Director of Student Financial Aid Ms. Jodi LANDGAARD
18 Chief Facilities/Physical Plant Mr. Jeff HARMS
06 Registrar Ms. Crystal STROUTH
15 Director Human Resources Ms. Karen MILLER
102 Foundation Director Ms. Lori VOSS

*Normandale Community College (B)

9700 France Avenue S, Bloomington MN 55431-4399
County: Hennepin FICE Identification: 007954
Unit ID: 174428
Telephone: (952) 358-8200 Carnegie Class: Assoc/Pub-S-SC
FAX Number: (952) 358-8101 Calendar System: Semester
URL: www.normandale.edu
Established: 1968 Annual Undergrad Tuition & Fees (In-State): $5,694
Enrollment: 9,901 Coed
Affiliation or Control: State IRS Status: 501(c)3
Highest Offering: Associate Degree
Program: Occupational; 2-Year Principally Bachelor's Creditable
Accreditation: NH, ACBSP, ADNUR, ART, DH, DIETT, MUS, THEA

02 President Dr. Joe OPATZ
10 Vice Pres Finance & Operations Mr. Ed WINES
05 Vice President Academic Affairs Ms. Julie GUELICH
32 Vice President Student Affairs Dr. Lisa WHEELER
09 Assoc VP Planning & Inst Research Mr. Michael BERNDT
35 Dean of Students Dr. Orinthia MONTAGUE
50 Dean Bus/Tech/Library/Social Sci Mr. Michael KIRCH
79 Dean of Humanities/Col Readiness Mr. Jeff JUDGE
81 Dean Natural Science/Mathematics Mr. Cary KOMOTO
76 Dean of Health Sciences Dr. Colleen BRICKLE
35 Associate Dean of Students Ms. Wanda L. KANWISCHER
10 Director Fiscal Services Vacant
15 Director Human Resources Ms. Michelle THOM
13 Director of Information Tech Svcs Mr. Stephen WINCKELMAN
18 Director of Building Services Mr. Michael KOREEN
102 Exec Dir Foundation/Resource Devel Ms. Colleen SIMPSON
84 Dean of Enroll/Marketing/Multicul Mr. Matt CRAWFORD
26 Chief Public Relations Officer Mr. Steve GELLER
06 Registrar Ms. Tonya HANSON HUBER

07 Director of Admissions Ms. Nancy PATES
38 Director Student Counseling Mr. Torrion AMIE

*North Hennepin Community College (C)

7411 85th Avenue N, Brooklyn Park MN 55445-2299
County: Hennepin FICE Identification: 002370
Unit ID: 174376
Telephone: (763) 424-0702 Carnegie Class: Assoc/Pub-S-SC
FAX Number: (763) 424-0929 Calendar System: Semester
URL: www.nhcc.edu
Established: 1966 Annual Undergrad Tuition & Fees (In-State): $5,582
Enrollment: 7,736 Coed
Affiliation or Control: State IRS Status: 501(c)3
Highest Offering: Associate Degree
Program: Occupational; 2-Year Principally Bachelor's Creditable
Accreditation: NH, ACBSP, ADNUR, HT, MLTAD

02 Acting President Dr. Lisa LARSON
05 Vice Pres Academic Affairs Ms. Jane REINKE
32 Vice Pres of Student Affairs Dr. Landon PIRIUS
10 Vice Pres of Finance & Facilities Mr. Daniel HALL
72 Int Dean Academics/Technology Svcs Ms. Kristine BOIKE
35 Assoc Dean Student Affairs Mr. Jim BORER
37 Assoc Dean Financial Aid Ms. Jackie OLSSON
08 Librarian Mr. Craig LARSON
06 Director Records & Registration Ms. Lori KIRKEBY
07 Director Admissions & Outreach Ms. Melissa LEIMBEK
15 Chief Human Resources Officer Mr. Michael FREER
45 Director Planning & Research Vacant
18 Director of Plant Services Mr. Larry MEYERS
30 Director of Development Ms. Jennifer LAMBRECHT
28 Director Diversity/Multiculturalism Mr. Michael BIRCHARD
26 Interim Director of Communications Ms. Janet MCCLELLAND
09 Director of Institutional Research Ms. Sheryl OLSON
19 Director of Security/Safety Mr. Erik PAKIESER
21 Business Manager Ms. Dawn BELKO
49 Dean Liberal Arts Ms. Suellen RUNDQUIST
50 Dean Business & Career Programs Ms. Renae FRY
76 Dean Health Careers/Science Dr. Elaina BLEIFIELD
51 Dean of Cont Educ/Custom Trng Vacant

*Northland Community and Technical College (D)

1101 Highway 1 E, Thief River Falls MN 56701-2598
County: Pennington FICE Identification: 002385
Unit ID: 174473
Telephone: (218) 683-8800 Carnegie Class: Assoc/Pub-R-M
FAX Number: (218) 683-8980 Calendar System: Semester
URL: www.northlandcollege.edu
Established: 1965 Annual Undergrad Tuition & Fees (In-State): $5,517
Enrollment: 5,358 Coed
Affiliation or Control: State IRS Status: 501(c)3
Highest Offering: Associate Degree
Program: Occupational; 2-Year Principally Bachelor's Creditable; Technical Emphasis
Accreditation: NH, ADNUR, COARC, CVT, EMT, OTA, PTAA, RAD, SURGT

02 President Dr. Anne T. TEMTE
05 VP Academic Affairs/Student Svcs Vacant
04 Assistant to the President Ms. Cindy CEDERGREN
20 Dean of Academic Affairs Dr. Brian HUSCHLE
32 Dean of Student Development Mr. Steve CRITTENDEN
32 Dean of Students East Grand Forks Ms. Mary FONTES
103 Dean Workforce & Econ Development Mr. James RETKA
08 Learning Center Director Mr. Dean DALEN
10 Chief Finance Officer Ms. Shannon JESME
38 Counselor Ms. Kelsy BLOWERS
38 Counselor Ms. Kate SCHMALENBERG
66 Dean of Nursing Ms. Jodi STASSEN
84 Director of Enrollment Management Mr. Jason TRAINER
37 Director Student Financial Aid Mr. Gerald SCHULTE
09 Director of Institutional Research Mr. Rocky AMMERMAN
15 Director Personnel Services Ms. Becky LINDSETH
18 Chief Facilities/Physical Plant Mr. Clinton CASTLE
26 Director Marketing/Communication Mr. Jason TRAINER
44 Dir Annual Giving/Alumni Relations Mr. Lars DYRUD
06 Registrar Mr. Rocky AMMERMAN
07 Director of Admissions Mr. Gene KLINKE
28 Director of Diversity Mr. Gene KLINKE
30 Chief Development Officer Mr. Dan KLUG
13 Director Computing/Information Mgmt Ms. Stacey HRON
27 Chief Information Officer Ms. Becky LINDSETH
41 Athletic Director Mr. Paul PETERSON

*Northwest Technical College (E)

905 Grant Avenue, SE, Bemidji MN 56601-4907
County: Beltrami FICE Identification: 005759
Unit ID: 173115
Telephone: (218) 333-6600 Carnegie Class: Assoc/Pub-R-S
FAX Number: (218) 333-6694 Calendar System: Semester
URL: www.ntcmn.edu
Established: 1966 Annual Undergrad Tuition & Fees (In-State): $5,481
Enrollment: 1,197 Coed
Affiliation or Control: State IRS Status: 501(c)3
Highest Offering: Associate Degree
Program: Occupational; 2-Year Principally Bachelor's Creditable
Accreditation: NH, DA

05 Provost/Vice President Mr. John CENTKO
06 Registrar Ms. Heidi KIPPENHAN
10 Chief Business Officer Mr. William MAKI

*Pine Technical College (F)

900 Fourth Street, SE, Pine City MN 55063-2198
County: Pine FICE Identification: 005535
Unit ID: 174570
Telephone: (320) 629-5100 Carnegie Class: Assoc/Pub-R-S
FAX Number: (320) 629-5101 Calendar System: Semester
URL: www.pinetech.edu
Established: 1965 Annual Undergrad Tuition & Fees (In-State): $4,800
Enrollment: 1,200 Coed
Affiliation or Control: State IRS Status: 501(c)3
Highest Offering: Associate Degree
Program: Occupational; 2-Year Principally Bachelor's Creditable; Business Emphasis
Accreditation: NH

02 President Dr. Robert MUSGROVE
05 Chief Academic Officer Dr. Joan BLOEMENDAAL-GRUETT
13 Chief Information Officer Mr. Kenneth RIES
10 Chief Financial Officer Ms. Janis WEGNER
32 Dean Student Affairs Ms. Paula HOFFMAN
51 Dean of Continuing Edu/Custom Trng Mr. Jason SPAETH
103 Dean of Economic/Work Devel Ms. Stephanie SCHROEDER
88 Dir Johnson Center for Simulation Ms. Cynthia GALBRAITH
36 Exec Dir Employment/Training Ctr Mr. Tony GANTENBEIN
06 Registrar Ms. Darla CAVERLEY
15 Chief Human Resources Officer Ms. Amy KRUSE
07 Interim Director of Admissions Ms. Laureen WILLIAMS
37 Director Student Financial Aid Mr. Shawn REYNOLDS
18 Physical Plant Supervisor Mr. Steven LANGE

*Rainy River Community College (G)

1501 Highway 71, International Falls MN 56649-2187
County: Koochiching FICE Identification: 006775
Unit ID: 174604
Telephone: (218) 285-7722 Carnegie Class: Assoc/Pub-R-S
FAX Number: (218) 285-2239 Calendar System: Semester
URL: www.rrcc.mnscu.edu
Established: 1967 Annual Undergrad Tuition & Fees (In-State): $5,323
Enrollment: 300 Coed
Affiliation or Control: State IRS Status: 501(c)3
Highest Offering: Associate Degree
Program: Occupational; 2-Year Principally Bachelor's Creditable
Accreditation: NH

02 Interim College Dean Ms. Elena FAVELA
06 Registrar Ms. Berta HAGEN
37 Dir of Financial Aid/Housing Mr. Scott T. RILEY
13 Dir Information Technology Mr. James BUJOLD

*Ridgewater College (H)

PO Box 1097, 2101 15th Ave NW, Willmar MN 56201-1097
County: Kandiyohi FICE Identification: 005252
Unit ID: 175236
Telephone: (320) 222-5200 Carnegie Class: Assoc/Pub-R-M
FAX Number: (320) 222-5212 Calendar System: Semester
URL: www.ridgewater.edu
Established: 1961 Annual Undergrad Tuition & Fees (In-State): $5,408
Enrollment: 4,086 Coed
Affiliation or Control: State IRS Status: 501(c)3
Highest Offering: Associate Degree
Program: Occupational; 2-Year Principally Bachelor's Creditable
Accreditation: NH, ADNUR, CAHIIM, EMT, MAC

02 President Dr. Douglas W. ALLEN
05 Vice Pres Acad Affs/Student Svcs Dr. Betty J. STREHLOW
10 Vice President Finance & Operations Mr. Daniel F. HOLTZ
51 Dean of Cust Trng & Cont Education Mr. Sam BOWEN
20 Dean of Instruction Mr. Michael J. BOEHME
20 Dean of Instruction Mr. Mike KUTZKE
20 Dean of Instruction Dr. Ronald L. PRIBBLE
32 Dean of Student Services Ms. Heidi L. OLSON
21 Director of Business Services Ms. Cheryl A. NORLIEN
15 Chief Human Resource Officer Ms. Denise CARPENTER
66 Director of Nursing Ms. C. Lynn JOHNSON
37 Director of Financial Aid Mr. James W. RICE
07 Director of Admissions Ms. Sally KERFELD
41 Athletic Director Mr. Todd M. THORSTAD
06 Registrar Ms. Kelli S. KIENITZ
13 Chief Information Officer Mr. Timothy L. FURR
26 Director of Communication/Marketing Ms. Liz VANDERBILL
102 Foundation Executive Director Ms. Kelly J. MAGNUSON
47 Director of Management Programs Mr. James H. MOLENAAR
09 Director of Institutional Research Dr. Mary L. MYERS
28 Director of Multicultural Affairs Ms. Jehana KHAN
18 Physical Plant Director Mr. Kip R. OVESON

*Riverland Community College (I)

1900 8th Avenue, NW, Austin MN 55912-1473
County: Mower FICE Identification: 002335
Unit ID: 173063
Telephone: (507) 433-0600 Carnegie Class: Assoc/Pub-R-M
FAX Number: (507) 433-0665 Calendar System: Semester
URL: www.riverland.edu
Established: 1940 Annual Undergrad Tuition & Fees (In-State): $2,554

Enrollment: 3,519 Coed
Affiliation or Control: State IRS Status: 501(c)3
Highest Offering: Associate Degree
Program: Occupational; 2-Year Principally Bachelor's Creditable; Liberal Arts And General
Accreditation: NH, ACBSP, ADNUR, RAD

02 Interim President Dr. Adenuga ATEWOLOGUN
05 Interim VP of Acad & Stdnt Affs Dr. Mary DAVENPORT
10 Chief Financial Officer Mr. Brad DOSS
16 VP of Employee & Public Relations Ms. Celeste RUBLE
56 Dean of Extended Learning Mr. David HIETALA
76 Interim Assoc Dean of Allied Hlth Ms. Danyel HELGESON
49 Int Dean for Lib Arts & Sciences Mr. J. C TURNER
103 Dean for Workforce Education Mr. Matt BISSONETTE
32 Dean of Student Affairs Vacant
30 Dean for Institutional Advancement Mr. Steve BOWRON
06 Dir of Enrollment Svcs/Registrar Ms. Sue JECH
07 Director of Admissions Vacant
26 Director of Communications Mr. James DOUGLASS
37 Director of Financial Aid Ms. Judy ROBECK
36 Dir of Placement & K12 School Rels Ms. Mindi ASKELSON
04 Executive Assist to the President Ms. Marijo ALEXANDER
13 Director of Technology Mr. Dan HARBER
18 Facilities Supervisor Ms. Judy ENRIGHT
96 Purchasing Agent Ms. Page PETERSEN
28 Regional Diversty Trainer/Investgtr Ms. Ricki WALTERS

*Rochester Community and Technical College (A)

851 30th Avenue, SE, Rochester MN 55904-4999
County: Olmsted FICE Identification: 002373
Unit ID: 174738
Telephone: (507) 285-7210 Carnegie Class: Assoc/Pub-R-M
FAX Number: (507) 285-7496 Calendar System: Semester
URL: www.rctc.edu
Established: 1915 Annual Undergrad Tuition & Fees (In-State): $5,736
Enrollment: 6,234 Coed
Affiliation or Control: State IRS Status: 501(c)3
Highest Offering: Associate Degree
Program: Occupational; 2-Year Principally Bachelor's Creditable; Liberal Arts And General
Accreditation: NH, ADNUR, CAHIIM, DA, DH, EMT, PNUR, SURGT

02 Interim President Ms. Gail O'KANE
05 Vice President Academic Affairs Dr. Jim GROSS
10 Vice Pres Finance and Facilities Mr. Steve SCHMALL
76 Dean Allied Health Dr. Nirmala KOTAGAL
49 Dean Dr. Barbara J. MOLLBERG
75 Dean Ms. Michelle PYFFEROEN
15 Chief Human Resources Officer Mrs. Renee ENGELMEYER
13 Chief Information Technology Ofcr Mr. Scott SAHS
32 Chief Student Affairs Officer Mr. Dave N. WEBER
88 Dir of Business/Econ Development Ms. Michelle PYFFEROEN
35 Student Life Coordinator Mr. Scott KROOK
06 Registrar Ms. Nancy SHUMAKER
07 Director Admissions Ms. Holly BIGELOW
37 Director Financial Aid Ms. Beth DIEKMANN
09 Director of Institutional Research Ms. Christine MILLER
04 Assistant to President Mrs. Judy KINGSBURY
21 Business Office Supervisor Ms. Ruth SIEFERT
26 Chief Public Relations Officer Mr. Dave WEBER
19 Security Officer Mr. Andrew HAMANN
40 Bookstore Coordinator Ms. Michelle PETERSON
96 Director of Purchasing Ms. June MEITZNER
29 Dir Alumni Rels/Found Exec Dir Ms. Lisa BALDUS

*St. Cloud State University (B)

720 4th Avenue S, Saint Cloud MN 56301-4498
County: Stearns FICE Identification: 002377
Unit ID: 174783
Telephone: (320) 308-0121 Carnegie Class: Master's L
FAX Number: N/A Calendar System: Semester
URL: www.stcloudstate.edu
Established: 1869 Annual Undergrad Tuition & Fees (In-State): $7,975
Enrollment: 16,457 Coed
Affiliation or Control: State IRS Status: 501(c)3
Highest Offering: Doctorate
Program: Occupational; 2-Year Principally Bachelor's Creditable; Liberal Arts And General; Teacher Preparatory; Professional
Accreditation: NH, AAB, ART, BUS, CACREP, CORE, CS, ENG, ENGR, JOUR, MFCD, MT, MUS, NAIT, NURSE, SP, SW, TED, THEA

02 President Dr. Earl H. POTTER, III
05 Provost/Vice Pres Academic Affairs Dr. Devinder MALHOTRA
88 Assoc Provost for Org Develop Dr. John PALMER
46 Assoc Provost for Research Dr. Dan GREGORY
20 Dean/Assoc Provost Student Succes Dr. Miguel SAENZ
88 Asst Dean University College Ms. Nancy MILLS
32 Vice Pres Student Life Development Dr. Wanda OVERLAND
11 Interim Vice Pres Finance/Admin Mr. Rick DUFFETT
30 Vice Pres University Advancement Vacant
85 Assoc VP International Studies Dr. Ann B. RADWAN
10 Assoc VP Finance/Admin Mr. Patrick JACOBSON-SCHULTE
45 Assoc Provost OSPE Ms. Lisa FOSS
27 Asst VP Marketing & Communications Mr. Loren BOONE
43 Special Advisor to the President Dr. Judith P. SIMINOE
50 Dean Herberger Business School Dr. Diana LAWSON
51 Dean of Continuing Studies Dr. John BURGESON
53 Dean School of Education Dr. Osman ALAWIYE
57 Dean Liberal Arts Dr. Mark SPRINGER
72 Dean Science & Engineering Dr. David K. DEGROOTE
83 Dean School of Public Affairs Dr. Orn BODVARSSON
76 Dean Health/Human Service Dr. Monica DEVERS
08 Interim Dean Learning Resources Mr. Keith EWING
07 Director of Admissions Mr. Richard SHEARER
22 Equity and Affirmative Action Ofc Ms. Ellyn BARTGES
06 Registrar Ms. Sue BAYERL
29 Director of Constituent Engagement Ms. Terri MISCHE
41 Athletic Director Ms. Heather WEEMS
18 Facilities Management Director Mr. Tim NORTON
36 Director Career Services Ms. Addie TURKOWSKI
91 Dir Info Technology Services Mr. Phil THORSON
38 Director of Counseling Dr. John M. EGGERS
37 Director of Financial Aid Mr. Mike T. URAN
39 Director of Student Housing Mr. Daniel T. PEDERSEN
09 Institutional Research Mr. Brent DONNAY
15 Director Human Resources Ms. Holly SCHOENHERR
19 Director Public Safety Mr. Miles J. HECKENDORN
40 Bookstore Manager Mr. Ted MEARS

*Saint Cloud Technical and Community College (C)

1540 Northway Drive, Saint Cloud MN 56303-1240
County: Stearns FICE Identification: 005534
Unit ID: 174756
Telephone: (320) 308-5000 Carnegie Class: Assoc/Pub-R-M
FAX Number: (320) 308-5981 Calendar System: Semester
URL: www.sctcc.edu
Established: 1948 Annual Undergrad Tuition & Fees (In-State): $5,301
Enrollment: 3,493 Coed
Affiliation or Control: State IRS Status: 501(c)3
Highest Offering: Associate Degree
Program: 2-Year Principally Bachelor's Creditable; Technical Emphasis
Accreditation: NH, CAHIIM, CVT, DA, DH, DMS, EMT, SURGT

02 President Ms. Joyce M. HELENS
05 VP of Academic Affairs Ms. Margaret (Peg) SHROYER
04 Assistant to the President Ms. Karen A. HIEMENZ
32 Vice President of Student Affairs Mr. Phillip SCHROEDER
10 Vice Pres Admin/Chief Finan Officer Ms. Lori KLOOS
75 Dean Trade/Industry Vacant
76 Dean Health/Human Services Ms. Janet STEINKAMP
49 Dean of Liberal Arts & Sciences Mr. Jason TETZLOFF
50 Dean of Business/Comp Science Ms. Kristina KELLER
66 Dean of Nursing Ms. Carolyn OLSON
06 Registrar Ms. Lana L. FEDDEMA
15 Dir Personnel Services/Aff Action Ms. Deb A. HOLSTAD
84 Dir of Enroll Management/Admissions Ms. Jodi M. ELNESS
08 Head Librarian Ms. Patricia AKERMAN
19 Security/Safety Officer Ms. Joni AKERSON
37 Director Student Financial Aid Ms. Anita G. BAUGH
20 Curriculum/Faculty Development Ms. Margaret (Peg) SHROYER
36 Director Student Placement Ms. Jackie BAUER
40 Director Bookstore Mr. James SCHOLLA
38 Director Student Counseling Ms. Judy JACOBSON-BERG
35 Activ Dir/Chief Student Life Ofcr Mr. John R. HALLER
18 Chief Facilities/Physical Plant Mr. Jason THEISEN
27 Chief Information Officer Ms. Viola BERGQUIST
88 Director of Academic Accountability Ms. Norma KONSCHAK
21 Associate Business Officer Mr. Duane DAHLSTROM
96 Director of Purchasing Ms. Susan MEYER
13 Director Library & Info Technology Ms. Viola BERGQUIST
22 Director Affirm Action/Equal Oppty Ms. Deb HOLSTAD
30 Chief Devel/Dir Annual/Planned Giv Vacant
26 Chief Public Relations Officer Ms. Heidi EVERETT
28 Director of Diversity Mr. Phillip SCHROEDER

*Saint Paul College-A Community & Technical College (D)

235 Marshall Avenue, Saint Paul MN 55102-1800
County: Ramsey FICE Identification: 005533
Unit ID: 175041
Telephone: (651) 846-1600 Carnegie Class: Assoc/Pub-U-SC
FAX Number: (651) 846-1451 Calendar System: Semester
URL: www.saintpaul.edu
Established: 1910 Annual Undergrad Tuition & Fees (In-State): $5,198
Enrollment: 6,746 Coed
Affiliation or Control: State IRS Status: 501(c)3
Highest Offering: Associate Degree
Program: Occupational; 2-Year Principally Bachelor's Creditable
Accreditation: NH, ACBSP, ACFEI, CAHIIM, COARC, MLTAD, PNUR

02 President Dr. Rassoul DASTMOZD
05 VP Academic Affs/Chief Acad Ofcr Dr. Diane VERTIN
10 Vice President Finance & Operations Mr. Shaan HAMILTON
32 Assoc VP Student Development/Svcs Mr. Thomas MATOS
103 Dean Workforce Trng/Continuing Educ Ms. Heather MCGANNON
46 Dean Research/Planning/Effective Dr. Margie TOMSIC
84 Dean Enrollment Management Ms. Sarah CARRICO
90 Assoc Dean of Academic Services Ms. Shelley BIBEAU
20 Assoc Dean Student Develop/Svcs Ms. Molly BAHNEMAN
15 Chief Human Resources Officer Ms. Rachelle M. SCHMIDT
06 Registrar Ms. Katie YEP
18 Director Facilities/Physical Plant Mr. Tom DOODY
21 Business Manager Mr. John PALMER
37 Director of Student Financial Aid Ms. Susan PIXLEY
102 Exec Dir of Foundation/Alumni Rels Ms. Laura SAVIN
13 Chief Information Officer Mr. Najam SAEED
35 Student Life Director Mr. Andrew CLEVELAND
26 Director of Marketing Ms. Allison FRIEDLY
17 Dean of Health & Services Mr. Brendan ASHBY
49 Dean of Liberal Arts & Sciences Dr. Linda KINGSTON
50 Int Dean Business/Career Tech Educ Ms. Susan SENGER

*South Central College (E)

1920 Lee Boulevard, PO Box 1920, North Mankato MN 56002-1920
County: Nicollet FICE Identification: 005537
Unit ID: 173911
Telephone: (507) 389-7200 Carnegie Class: Assoc/Pub-R-M
FAX Number: (507) 388-9951 Calendar System: Semester
URL: www.southcentral.edu
Established: 1946 Annual Undergrad Tuition & Fees (In-District): $5,355
Enrollment: 3,904 Coed
Affiliation or Control: State/Local IRS Status: 501(c)3
Highest Offering: Associate Degree
Program: Occupational; 2-Year Principally Bachelor's Creditable
Accreditation: NH, DA, EMT, MAC, MLTAD

02 President Mr. Keith STOVER
04 Exec Assistant to the President Ms. Carol FREED
05 Int Vice Pres Academic/Stdnt Affs Dr. Mark BAAS
10 Vice President Operations/Tech Svcs Ms. Karen SNOREK
09 Assoc Vice Pres Instl Rsrch/Grants Ms. Dena COLEMER
72 Dean of Technology Dr. Mark BAAS
32 Dean of Student Affairs Ms. Linda BEER
20 Dean of Academic Affairs Dr. Suzanne NORDBLOM
20 Dean of Academic Affairs Mr. W. C. SANDERS
20 Interim Dean of Academic Affairs Dr. Jane GREATHOUSE
45 Director of Research & Planning Ms. Dena COLEMER
26 Director of Marketing Ms. Jody BLOEMKE
06 Dir of Registration/Enrollment Svcs Ms. Donna MARZOLF
28 Chief Diversity Officer Dr. Anade LONG-JACOBS
15 Dir Human Resource/Personnel Svcs Ms. Laural KUBAT
37 Director Student Financial Aid Ms. Jayne DINSE
18 Chief Facilities/Physical Plant Ms. Karen SNOREK
07 Director of Admissions/Advising Mr. John ENGQUIST
08 Director of Library/Media Services Ms. Johnna HORTON
18 Director of Safety Mr. Al KLUEVER

*Southwest Minnesota State University (F)

1501 State Street, Marshall MN 56258-1598
County: Lyon FICE Identification: 002375
Unit ID: 175078
Telephone: (507) 537-7678 Carnegie Class: Master's M
FAX Number: (507) 537-7154 Calendar System: Semester
URL: www.smsu.edu
Established: 1963 Annual Undergrad Tuition & Fees (In-State): $8,074
Enrollment: 7,012 Coed
Affiliation or Control: State IRS Status: 501(c)3
Highest Offering: Master's
Program: Liberal Arts And General; Teacher Preparatory; Professional
Accreditation: NH, MUS, SW

02 President Dr. Connie J. GORES
05 Provost Dr. Beth WEATHERBY
10 VP Finance and Admin Ms. Debra KERKAERT
32 AVP Stdnt Affairs/Dean of Students Mr. Scott CROWELL
30 VP Advance/Dir Devel/Foundation Mr. William MULSO
49 Interim Dean Arts/Letters/Sciences Dr. Jan LOFT
50 Interim Dean Bus/Ed/Grad/Prof Stud Dr. Raphael ONYEAGHALA
20 Assoc Dean Academics/Student Svcs Mr. Scott CROWELL
41 Athletic Director Mr. Christopher HMIELEWSKI
27 Chief Information Officer Mr. Dan BAUN
07 Director Admissions Mr. Gary GILLIN
14 Director of Computer Services Mr. Shawn HEDMAN
06 Registrar Ms. Patricia CARMODY
19 Director University Public Safety Mr. Michael MUNFORD
28 Director Cultural Diversity Mr. Don ROBERTSON
15 Director Human Resources Ms. Deb ALMER
29 Interim Director of Alumni Mr. Michael VANDREHLE
18 Dir of Facilities & Physical Plant Ms. Cyndi HOLM
36 Interim Director of Career Services Ms. Carrie HANSEN
35 Director of Student Center Mr. Scott CROWELL
37 Director of Student Financial Aid Mr. David VIKANDER
38 Director of Student Counseling Mr. Robert LARSEN
96 Director of Purchasing Mr. Jeff KUIPER
21 Business Manager Mr. Eric RUNESTAD

*Vermilion Community College (G)

1900 E Camp Street, Ely MN 55731-1998
County: Saint Louis FICE Identification: 002350
Unit ID: 175157
Telephone: (218) 235-2101 Carnegie Class: Assoc/Pub-R-S
FAX Number: (218) 235-2173 Calendar System: Semester
URL: www.vcc.edu
Established: 1922 Annual Undergrad Tuition & Fees (In-State): $5,180
Enrollment: 770 Coed
Affiliation or Control: State IRS Status: 501(c)3
Highest Offering: Associate Degree
Program: Occupational; 2-Year Principally Bachelor's Creditable
Accreditation: NH

02 Provost/Chief Academic Officer Mr. Shawn BINA

06 Registrar ....Ms. Nadine FORSMAN
07 Director of Admissions/Student Affs ....Mr. Jeff NELSON
09 Director of Institutional Research ....Ms. Tracey ROY
10 Business Manager ....Ms. Nicole SQUIRES
15 Director of Personnel Services ....Ms. Carmen BRADACH
32 Dir Student Life/Facil/Phy Plant ....Mr. Dave MARSHALL
36 Director of Student Placement ....Mr. Doug FURNSTAHL
37 Director of Student Financial Aid ....Ms. Kristi L'ALLIER
38 Director of Student Counseling ....Ms. Cindy ANDERSON-BINA
29 Director Alumni Relations ....Ms. Patti ZUPANCICH
28 Director of Diversity ....Ms. Patti ZUPANCICH
26 Chief Public Relations Officer ....Mr. Jeff NELSON

*Winona State University (A)

PO Box 5838, Winona MN 55987-0838
County: Winona FICE Identification: 002394
Unit ID: 175272
Telephone: (507) 457-5000 Carnegie Class: Master's M
FAX Number: (507) 457-5586 Calendar System: Quarter
URL: www.winona.edu
Established: 1858 Annual Undergrad Tuition & Fees (In-State): $7,800
Enrollment: 8,500 Coed
Affiliation or Control: State IRS Status: 501(c)3
Highest Offering: Doctorate
Program: Liberal Arts And General; Teacher Preparatory; Professional
Accreditation: NH, BUS, CACREP, ENG, MUS, NURSE, SW, TED, THEA

02 President ....Dr. Scott R. OLSON
05 Interim VP Academic Affairs ....Dr. Patricia ROGERS
10 Interim VP Finance & Administration ..Mr. Scott ELLINGHUYSEN
30 Interim VP University Advancement ....Mr. Gary EVANS
32 Vice President Student Life & Dev ....Vacant
13 Assoc Vice Pres/CIO Tech Svcs ....Mr. Kenneth JANZ
21 Assoc VP for Finance/Admin Svcs/ CFO ....Mr. Scott ELLINGHUYSEN
26 Asst VP Marketing & Communications ....Ms. Cristeen CUSTER
38 Chairperson of Counseling Services ....Ms. Elizabeth BURKE
54 Interim Dean Col of Science/Engr ....Dr. Charla MIERTSCHIN
49 Dean Liberal Arts ....Dr. Ralph TOWNSEND
50 Interim Dean of Business ....Dr. Joell BJORKE
53 Interim Dean of Education ....Dr. Janice SHERMANN
66 Dean Nursing/Health Science ....Dr. William MCBREEN
35 Dean of Students ....Ms. Karen JOHNSON
06 Registrar ....Mr. Glenn PETERSEN
09 Director Institutional Research ....Vacant
37 Director of Financial Aid ....Mr. Greg PETERSON
36 Associate Director Career Services ....Ms. Deanna GODDARD
07 Director of Admissions ....Mr. Carl STANGE
39 Residential College Program Coord ....Ms. Sarah OLCOTT
31 Director of Auxiliary Services ....Vacant
29 Interim Director Alumni Relations ....Ms. Ann MACDONALD
40 Bookstore Manager ....Ms. Karen KRAUSE
44 Director Major Gifts ....Ms. Mary ROHRER
88 Director of International Svcs ....Mr. Kemale PINAR
19 Director of Security ....Mr. Don WALSKI
41 Athletic Director ....Mr. Eric SCHOH
18 Facilities Manager ....Mr. Richard LANDE
27 Director University Communications ....Ms. Andrea MIKKELSEN
94 Director of Women's Studies ....Dr. Tamara BERG
96 Director of Purchasing ....Ms. Deborah BENZ
28 Director of Cultural Diversity ....Mr. Alexander HINES
15 Director of Human Resources ....Ms. Lori REED

*Anoka-Ramsey Community College Cambridge Campus (B)

300 Spirit River Drive South, Cambrdige MN 55008-5704
Telephone: (763) 433-1100 Identification: 770298
Accreditation: &NH

† Main campus is Anoka-Ramsey Community College in Coon Rapids, MN.

*Mesabi Range Community & Technical College-Eveleth (C)

1100 Industrial Park Drive, Eveleth MN 55734
Telephone: (218) 741-3095 Identification: 770300
Accreditation: &NH

† Main campus is Mesabi Range Community & Technical College in Virginia, MN.

*Metropolitan State University (D)

1300 Harmon Place, Minneapolis MN 55403
Telephone: (651) 793-1300 Identification: 770301
Accreditation: &NH

† Main campus is Metropolitan State University in Saint Paul, MN.

*Minnesota State College Southeast Technical Red Wing Campus (E)

308 Pioneer Road, Red Wing MN 55066
Telephone: (651) 385-6300 Identification: 770302
Accreditation: &NH

† Main campus is Minnesota State College - Southeast Technical in Winona, MN.

*Minnesota West Community and Technical College Canby Campus (F)

1011 First Street, Canby MN 56220
Telephone: (507) 223-7252 Identification: 770306
Accreditation: &NH

† Main campus is Minnesota West Community and Technical College in Worthington, MN.

*Minnesota State Community and Technical College Detroit Lakes (G)

9-- Highway 34 E, Detroit Lakes MN 56501
Telephone: (218) 846-3700 Identification: 770303
Accreditation: &NH

† Main campus is Minnesota State Community and Technical College in Fergus Falls, MN.

*Minnesota West Community and Technical College Granite Falls Campus (H)

1593 11th Avenue, Granite Falls MN 56241
Telephone: (320) 564-5000 Identification: 770307
Accreditation: &NH

† Main campus is Minnesota West Community and Technical College in Worthington, MN.

*Minnesota West Community and Technical College Jackson Campus (I)

401 West Street, Jackson MN 56143
Telephone: (547) 847-7920 Identification: 770308
Accreditation: &NH

† Main campus is Minnesota West Community and Technical College in Worthington, MN.

*Minnesota State Community and Technical College Moorhead (J)

1900 28th Avenue S, Moorhead MN 56560
Telephone: (218) 299-6500 Identification: 770304
Accreditation: &NH

† Main campus is Minnesota State Community and Technical College in Fergus Falls, MN.

*Minnesota West Community and Technical College Pipestone Campus (K)

1314 North Hiawatha Avenue, Pipestone MN 56164
Telephone: (507) 825-6800 Identification: 770309
Accreditation: &NH

† Main campus is Minnesota West Community and Technical College in Worthington, MN.

*Minnesota State Community and Technical College Wadena (L)

405 Colfax Avenue SW, Wadena MN 56482
Telephone: (213) 631-7800 Identification: 770305
Accreditation: &NH

† Main campus is Minnesota State Community and Technical College in Fergus Falls, MN.

*Minnesota West Community and Technical College Worthington Campus (M)

1450 College Way, Worthington MN 56187
Telephone: (507) 372-3400 Identification: 770310
Accreditation: &NH

† Main campus is Minnesota West Community and Technical College in Worthington, MN.

*Northland Community and Technical College East Grand Forks (N)

2022 Central Avenue NE, East Grand Forks MN 56721
Telephone: (218) 793-2800 Identification: 770311
Accreditation: &NH

† Main campus is Northland Community and Technical College in Thief River Falls, MN.

*Ridgewater College Hutchinson Campus (O)

2 Century Avenue SE, Hutchinson MN 55350
Telephone: (320) 234-8500 Identification: 770312
Accreditation: &NH

† Main campus is Ridgewater College in Willmar, MN.

*Riverland Community College Albert Lea Campus (P)

2200 Riverland Drive, Albert Lea MN 56007
Telephone: (507) 379-3300 Identification: 770313
Accreditation: &NH

† Main campus is Riverland Community College in Austin, MN.

*South Central College Faribault Campus (Q)

1225 Third Street SW, Faribault MN 55021
Telephone: (507) 332-5800 Identification: 770314
Accreditation: &NH

† Main campus is South Central College in North Mankato, MN.

*Winona State University-Rochester (R)

859 30th Avenue SE, Rochester MN 55904
Telephone: (800) 366-5418 Identification: 770317
Accreditation: &NH

† Main campus is Winona State University in Winona, MN.

National American University-Bloomington (S)

7801 Metro Pkwy, Suite 200, Bloomington MN 55425
Telephone: (952) 356-3600 Identification: 770397
Accreditation: &NH

† Main campus is National American University in Rapid City, SD.

National American University-Brooklyn Center (T)

6200 Shingle Creek Pkwy, Suite 130, Brooklyn Center MN 55430
Telephone: (763) 852-7500 Identification: 770398
Accreditation: &NH

† Main campus is National American University in Rapid City, SD.

National American University-Burnsville (U)

501 West Travelers Trail, #617, Burnsville MN 55337
Telephone: (952) 563-1250 Identification: 770399
Accreditation: &NH

† Main campus is National American University in Rapid City, SD.

National American University-Rochester (V)

3906 East Frontage Highway 52 Road, Rochester MN 55901
Telephone: (866) 628-6387 Identification: 770400
Accreditation: &NH

† Main campus is National American University in Rapid City, SD.

National American University-Roseville (W)

1550 W Highway 36, Roseville MN 55113
Telephone: (651) 855-6300 Identification: 770401
Accreditation: &NH, &MAC

† Main campus is National American University in Rapid City, SD.

North Central University (X)

910 Elliot Avenue, Minneapolis MN 55404-1391
County: Hennepin FICE Identification: 002369
Unit ID: 174437
Telephone: (612) 343-4400 Carnegie Class: Bac/Diverse
FAX Number: (612) 343-4778 Calendar System: Semester
URL: www.northcentral.edu
Established: 1930 Annual Undergrad Tuition & Fees: $19,066
Enrollment: 1,295 Coed
Affiliation or Control: Assemblies Of God Church IRS Status: 501(c)3
Highest Offering: Baccalaureate
Program: Liberal Arts And General
Accreditation: NH, @SW

01 President ....Dr. Gordon L. ANDERSON
04 Executive Assistant of President ....Mrs. Beth Ann ROCKETT
10 Vice President Finance ....Mrs. Cheryl A. BOOK
05 Vice Pres Academic Affs/Acad Dean ....Dr. Tom A. BURKMAN
30 Vice President Advancement ....Dr. Paul A. FREITAG
32 Vice President Student Development ....Mr. Mike A. NOSSER
26 VP University Rels/Enrollment ....Ms. Michael WHITE
57 Executive Director Fine Arts ....Dr. Larry C. BACH
84 Director Enrollment ....Vacant
21 Director of Accounting ....Mr. Bruce JENSEN
39 Dean of Residence Life ....Mr. Juice MONTEZON
31 Dean of Community Life ....Mr. Greg J. LEEPER
41 Athletic Director ....Mr. Jon HIGH
37 Director of Financial Aid ....Ms. Donna JAGER
08 Library Director ....Ms. Melody REEDY
13 Director of Information Technology ....Mr. Michael CAPPELLI
06 Registrar ....Mr. Cody SCHMITZ
18 Director of Plant/Operations ....Mr. Marv LANGMADE
44 Director Plannned Giving ....Mr. Wes BOOK
09 Director of Institutional Research ....Mr. Casey ROZOWSKI
07 Director of Admissions ....Mr. Joshua MARTIN
38 Director of Student Success Center ....Mr. Todd MONGER

Northwestern College (A)

3003 Snelling Avenue N, Saint Paul MN 55113-1598

County: Ramsey — FICE Identification: 002371
Unit ID: 174491
Telephone: (651) 631-5100 — Carnegie Class: Bac/Diverse
FAX Number: (651) 628-3339 — Calendar System: Semester
URL: www.nwc.edu
Established: 1902 — Annual Undergrad Tuition & Fees: $31,640
Enrollment: 3,217 — Coed
Affiliation or Control: Independent Non-Profit — IRS Status: 501(c)3
Highest Offering: Master's
Program: Liberal Arts And General; Teacher Preparatory
Accreditation: NH, MUS

01 President ... Dr. Alan S. CURETON
05 Senior Vice Pres Academic Affairs ... Dr. Janet B. SOMMERS
30 Vice President Advancement ... Mrs. Amy B. CAREY
10 Vice President Finance/CFO ... Mr. Douglas R. SCHROEDER
27 Senior Vice President Media ... Dr. Paul H. VIRTS
32 Vice Pres Student Life & Athletics ... Dr. Mathew B. HILL
00 President Emeritus ... Dr. Donald O. ERICKSEN
21 Director of Business Services ... Mrs. Marla K. DENNISON
20 Interim Dean of Faculty ... Dr. Richard C. THOMAN
88 Dean of Retention/Student Success ... Ms. Monica R. GROVES
35 Dean of Student Development ... Mr. Paul A. BRADLEY
35 Assoc Dean Student Development ... Dr. Katie J. SMITH
06 Registrar ... Mr. Andrew L. SIMPSON
09 Institutional Researcher Rprt Spec ... Mr. Russell E. ERICKSON
29 Dir of Alumni & Parent Relations ... Mr. James E. BENDER
37 Director of Financial Aid ... Mr. Richard L. BLATCHLEY
13 CIO ... Mr. David G. RICHERT
88 Controller ... Mr. Bryon D. KRUEGER
08 Director of Library Services ... Mrs. Ruth A. MCGUIRE
15 Director of Human Resources ... Mr. Timothy A. RICH
23 Director of Health Services ... Mrs. Cynthia P. REEDSTROM
42 Senior Dir of Campus Ministries ... Mr. James K. JOHNSON
18 Assoc VP Facility Ops & Planning ... Mr. Brian L. HUMPHRIES
36 Int Dir Ctr for Calling & Career ... Mrs. Linda R. ASHWORTH
26 Dir of Mktg & Communications ... Ms. Marita K. MEINERTS
40 Manager Campus Store ... Ms. Andrea R. HALVERSON
19 Director of Public Safety ... Mr. Peter L. SOLA
38 Director of Counseling/Student Svcs . Ms. Dannette C. WILFAHRT
44 Director of Planned Giving ... Mr. David D. DANIELSON
96 Purchasing Manager ... Mrs. Lindy J. STANKEY
07 Senior Director of Admissions ... Mr. Ken K. FAFFLER
88 Asst to Pres for ADA Initiatives ... Dr. Yvonne R. BANKS
88 Assoc Dean Commuter Life/Transition ... Mr. Jeff B. SNYDER
101 Exec Secy to Pres & Bd of Trustees ... Ms. Mona S. GRELLSON
39 Associate Dean for Residence Life ... Mr. Jerod L. CORNELIUS
20 Director Academic Operations ... Mr. Kevin B. MCGAUGHEY
44 Director Major Gifts ... Mr. John T. DELICH
88 Dir Dept of Support Servces ... Mr. David P. GOLIAS
106 Dir Undergrad Online Learning ... Dr. Tanya L. GROSZ

Northwestern Health Sciences University (B)

2501 W 84th Street, Bloomington MN 55431-1599

County: Hennepin — FICE Identification: 012328
Unit ID: 174507
Telephone: (952) 888-4777 — Carnegie Class: Spec/Health
FAX Number: (952) 888-6713 — Calendar System: Trimester
URL: www.nwhealth.edu
Established: 1941 — Annual Undergrad Tuition & Fees: $11,727
Enrollment: 870 — Coed
Affiliation or Control: Independent Non-Profit — IRS Status: 501(c)3
Highest Offering: First Professional Degree
Program: Professional
Accreditation: NH, ACUP, CHIRO, COMTA

01 President and CEO ... Mr. Jeff A. NELSON
03 Senior Vice President ... Dr. Charles E. SAWYER
05 Provost ... Dr. Michael WILES
11 VP Administrative Affairs/CFO ... Mr. Ross B. DUGAS
46 Vice President for Research ... Dr. Gert BRONFORT
32 Dean Student Affs/Enrollment Mgmt ... Dr. Emily J. TWEED
07 Director of Admissions ... Ms. Kate DIANA
08 Director of Library Services ... Ms. Anne MACKERETH
29 Dir Alumni Relations/Career Svcs ... Ms. Deborah A. PETERSON
06 Registrar ... Ms. Angela FREEMAN
15 Director of Human Resources ... Ms. Deborah HOGENSON
37 Director of Financial Aid ... Ms. Susan NEPPL
51 Director Continuing Education ... Ms. Diana BERG
26 Director of Marketing ... Ms. Kathryn GRIMES
30 Chief Development Officer ... Mr. Scott PALMER
13 Chief Information Systems Officer ... Mr. Steve HIDY
09 Dir Institutional Research/Planning ... Ms. Deborah HOGENSON
38 University Counselor ... Ms. Becky LAWYER
18 Director Facilities Management ... Mr. Kevin WOLPERN
96 Director Bookstore & Purchasing ... Ms. Jan HALLEEN

Oak Hills Christian College (C)

1600 Oak Hills Road, SW, Bemidji MN 56601-8826

County: Beltrami — FICE Identification: 009992
Unit ID: 174525
Telephone: (218) 751-8670 — Carnegie Class: Spec/Faith
FAX Number: (218) 751-8825 — Calendar System: Semester
URL: www.oakhills.edu
Established: 1946 — Annual Undergrad Tuition & Fees: $20,800
Enrollment: 126 — Coed
Affiliation or Control: Interdenominational — IRS Status: 501(c)3
Highest Offering: Baccalaureate
Program: Liberal Arts And General; Religious Emphasis
Accreditation: BI

01 President ... Dr. Steve J. HOSTETTER
05 Dean of the College ... Dr. Steven J. WARE
30 Vice President for Advancement ... Mrs. Joan L. BERNTSON
10 Business Manager ... Mrs. Carol NELSON
06 Registrar ... Mrs. Mary HANNAH
08 Library Director ... Mr. Keith BUSH
07 Dean of Student Enrollment ... Mr. John ENGQUIST
37 Director of Financial Aid ... Mr. Daniel HOVESTOL

Presentation College Fairmont (D)

115 S Park Street, Suite 117, Fairmont MN 56031

Telephone: (507) 235-4658 — Identification: 770418
Accreditation: &NH

† Main campus is Presentation College in Aberdeen, SD.

*Rasmussen College Corporate Office (E)

8300 Norman Center Drive, Suite 300, Bloomington MN 55437

County: Washington — Identification: 667034
Unit ID: 17501405
Telephone: (952) 806-3900 — Carnegie Class: N/A
FAX Number: (952) 831-0624
URL: www.rasmussen.edu

01 President ... Kristi WAITE

*Rasmussen College - St. Cloud (F)

226 Park Avenue South, Saint Cloud MN 56301-3713

County: Stearns — FICE Identification: 008694
Unit ID: 175014
Telephone: (320) 251-5600 — Carnegie Class: Assoc/PrivFP4
FAX Number: (320) 251-3702 — Calendar System: Quarter
URL: www.Rasmussen.edu
Established: 1902 — Annual Undergrad Tuition & Fees: $15,100
Enrollment: 1,251 — Coed
Affiliation or Control: Proprietary — IRS Status: Proprietary
Highest Offering: Baccalaureate
Program: Occupational; 2-Year Principally Bachelor's Creditable
Accreditation: NH, CAHIIM, MAAB, MLTAD, SURGT

02 Campus Director ... Ms. Mary SWINGLE

† Regional accreditation carried under the parent institution in Lake Elmo, MN.

**Rasmussen College - Blaine* (G)

3629 95th Avenue Northeast, Blaine MN 55014

Telephone: (763) 795-4720 — Identification: 667061
Accreditation: &NH, MAAB

† Main campus is Rasmussen College - St. Cloud in Saint Cloud, MN.

**Rasmussen College - Bloomington* (H)

4400 W 78th St, 6th Floor, Bloomington MN 55435

Telephone: (952) 545-2000 — FICE Identification: 011686
Accreditation: &NH, CAHIIM, MAAB

† Main campus is Rasmussen College - St. Cloud in Saint Cloud, MN.

**Rasmussen College - Brooklyn Park* (I)

8301 93rd Avenue North, Brooklyn Park MN 55445-1512

Telephone: (763) 493-4500 — Identification: 666769
Accreditation: &NH, CAHIIM, MAAB, SURGT

† Main campus is Rasmussen College - St. Cloud in Saint Cloud, MN.

**Rasmussen College - Eagan* (J)

3500 Federal Drive, Eagan MN 55122-1346

Telephone: (651) 687-9000 — FICE Identification: 004648
Accreditation: &NH, CAHIIM, MAAB

† Main campus is Rasmussen College - St. Cloud in Saint Cloud, MN.

**Rasmussen College - Lake Elmo/Woodbury* (K)

8565 Eagle Point Circle, Lake Elmo MN 55042

Telephone: (651) 259-6600 — Identification: 770486
Accreditation: &NH, CAHIIM, MAC, MLTAD

† Main campus is Rasmussen College Corporate Office in Bloomington, MN.

**Rasmussen College - Mankato* (L)

130 Saint Andrews Drive, Mankato MN 56001

Telephone: (507) 625-6556 — FICE Identification: 025033
Accreditation: &NH, CAHIIM, MAAB, MLTAD

† Main campus is Rasmussen College - St. Cloud in Saint Cloud, MN.

**Rasmussen College - Moorhead Park* (M)

1250 29th Avenue South, Moorhead MN 56560

Telephone: (218) 304-6200 — Identification: 770487
Accreditation: &NH, MAC, MLTAD, SURGT

† Main campus is Rasmussen College Corporate Office in Bloomington, MN.

St. Catherine University (N)

601 25th Avenue S, Minneapolis MN 55454

Telephone: (651) 690-6000 — Identification: 770315
Accreditation: &NH

† Main campus is St. Catherine University in Saint Paul, MN.

St. Catherine University (O)

2004 Randolph Avenue, Saint Paul MN 55105-1789

County: Ramsey — FICE Identification: 002342
Unit ID: 175005
Telephone: (651) 690-6000 — Carnegie Class: Master's L
FAX Number: (651) 690-6024 — Calendar System: 4/1/4
URL: www.stkate.edu
Established: 1905 — Annual Undergrad Tuition & Fees: $34,744
Enrollment: 5,075 — Female
Affiliation or Control: Roman Catholic — IRS Status: 501(c)3
Highest Offering: Doctorate
Program: Liberal Arts And General; Teacher Preparatory; Professional
Accreditation: NH, ADNUR, #ARCPA, CAHIIM, COARC, DIETD, DMS, EXSC, LIB, MACTE, NUR, OT, OTA, PHLEB, PTA, PTAA, RAD, SW

01 President ... Dr. Andrea J. LEE, IHM
03 Senior Vice President ... Dr. Colleen HEGRANES
10 Vice Pres Finance/Administration ... Mr. Thomas ROONEY
26 Vice Pres for External Relations ... Ms. Blanche ABDALLAH
84 VP Enrollment Mgmt/Student Affairs ... Dr. Brian BRUESS
35 Dean of Student Affairs ... Mr. Curt GALLOWAY
07 Associate Dean of Admissions ... Ms. Marlene MOHS
27 Assoc Dean Admiss/Market Devel ... Mr. Greg STEENSON
20 Associate Dean Academic Affairs ... Ms. Bonnie LADUCA
35 Associate Dean of Students ... Ms. Ellen RICHTER-NORGEL
05 Chief Academic Officer ... Dr. Colleen HEGRANES
06 Registrar ... Ms. Cynthia EGENESS
08 Library Director ... Mr. Randall SCHROEDER
30 Chief Development ... Ms. Elizabeth RIEDEL CARNEY
32 Chief Student Life Officer ... Dr. Brian BRUESS
29 Director of Alumnae Relations ... Ms. Karen G. JOTHEN
26 Dir of Marketing & Communications ... Ms. Amy GAGE
37 Director of Financial Aid ... Ms. Elizabeth STEVENS
36 Director of Career Development ... Ms. Tina WAGNER
13 Director of Computing Services ... Mr. John JERIES
15 Director of Personnel Services ... Ms. Susan SEXTON
38 Director of Student Counseling ... Ms. Heide MALAT
92 Director of Honors Program ... Dr. Gayle GASKILL
94 Director of Women's Studies ... Dr. Sharon DOHERTY
96 Director of Purchasing ... Ms. Gail BLIVEN
09 Dir Instl Rsrch/Plng/ Assessment ... Dr. Jennifer ROBINSON KLOOS
18 Chief Facilities/Physical Plant ... Mr. James MANSHIP
21 Business Manager ... Ms. Tracey GRAN
04 Exec Assistant to the President ... Ms. Stacy JACOBSON
49 AVP/Dean Sch Humanities/Arts/Sci ... Dr. Alan SILVA
76 Dean Hen Schmoll Sch Hlth/Grad Col ... Dr. Penelope MOYERS
50 Dean Sch Business/Professional Stds ... Dr. Joann BANGS

Saint John's University (P)

Box 2000, Collegeville MN 56321-2000

County: Stearns — FICE Identification: 002379
Unit ID: 174792
Telephone: (320) 363-2011 — Carnegie Class: Bac/A&S
FAX Number: (320) 363-2504 — Calendar System: Semester
URL: www.csbsju.edu
Established: 1857 — Annual Undergrad Tuition & Fees: $37,162
Enrollment: 1,854 — Coordinate
Affiliation or Control: Roman Catholic — IRS Status: 501(c)3
Highest Offering: Master's
Program: Liberal Arts And General; Teacher Preparatory; Professional
Accreditation: NH, DIETD, MUS, NURSE, TED, THEOL

01 President ... Dr. Michael HEMESATH
05 Provost Academic Affairs ... Dr. Rita KNUESEL
20 Vice Provost ... Dr. Joseph DESJARDINS
20 Academic Dean ... Dr. Richard ICE
30 Vice President for Inst Advancement ... Mr. Rob CULLIGAN
32 Vice President Student Development ... Fr. Douglas MULLIN, OSB
10 Vice Pres Finance/Admin Services ... Mr. Richard ADAMSON
46 VP Inst Plng/Research/Communication ... Mr. Jon MCGEE
07 Vice Pres Admissions/Financial Aid ... Dr. Cal MOSLEY
73 Dean School Theology ... Dr. William CAHOY
88 Dir of Center for Global Educ ... Mr. Joseph ROGERS
35 Dean of Students ... Mr. Michael CONNOLLY
45 Associate Dean Planning/Budget ... Mr. David LYNDGAARD
26 Exec Director of Comm & Marketing ... Mr. Michael HEMMESCH
08 Director of Library ... Ms. Kathleen PARKER
06 Registrar ... Ms. Julie GRUSKA
38 Director of Career Services ... Ms. Heidi HARLANDER
37 Exec Director of Financial Aid ... Mr. Stuart PERRY
13 Director of Info Technology Svcs ... Mr. Jim KOENIG
29 Director of Alumni Relations ... Mr. Adam HERBST

15 Director Human Resources .... Ms. Carol ABELL
41 Athletic Director .... Mr. Tom STOCK
19 Director Life Safety Services .... Mr. Shawn VIERZBA
42 Director of Campus Ministry .... Fr. Ian DOMMER, OSB
18 Director Facilities/Physical Plant .... Mr. Bill BOOM
40 Director Bookstore .... Mr. Donald FORBES
09 Assoc Director Inst Research .... Ms. Karen G. KNUTSON

Saint Mary's University of Minnesota (A)

700 Terrace Heights, Winona MN 55987-1399
County: Winona FICE Identification: 002380
Unit ID: 174817
Telephone: (507) 452-4430 Carnegie Class: DRU
FAX Number: (507) 457-1633 Calendar System: Semester
URL: www.smumn.edu
Established: 1912 Annual Undergrad Tuition & Fees: $29,315
Enrollment: 5,574 Coed
Affiliation or Control: Roman Catholic IRS Status: 501(c)3
Highest Offering: Doctorate
Program: Liberal Arts And General; Teacher Preparatory
Accreditation: NH, ANEST, IACBE, MFCD, MUS, NMT, NURSE, SURGT

01 President .... Bro. William MANN, FSC
18 Vice President of Facilities .... Mr. James BEDTKE
84 Vice Pres Enrollment Management .... Ms. Brandi DEFRIES
30 Vice Pres for Development .... Ms. Audrey KINTZI
32 Vice President Student Development .... Mr. Chris KENDALL
10 Vice President Financial Affairs .... Mr. Ben MURRAY
43 Exec Vice Pres/General Counsel .... Ms. Ann E. MERCHLEWITZ
05 Vice President for Academic Affairs .... Dr. Donna ARONSON
58 VP Schs of Graduate/Professnl Pgms .... Bro. Robert SMITH
26 Assoc VP Marketing & Communications .... Mr. Nick LEMMER
20 Academic Dean/Assoc Vice President .... Ms. Linka HOLEY
35 Dean of Students/Dir Resident Life .... Mr. Tim GOSSEN
04 Exec Assistant to the President .... Ms. Mary BECKER
06 Registrar .... Ms. Lori TURNER
13 Chief Information Officer .... Mr. Scott COWDREY
37 Director of Financial Aid .... Ms. Jayne WOBIG
88 Director of Toner Student Center .... Ms. Terrie LUECK
36 Dir Career Services & Internships .... Ms. Jackie BAKER
38 Director of Counseling Center .... Dr. Ruth MATTHEWS
08 Director of Library .... Ms. Laura OANES
22 Affirmative Action Officer .... Ms. Ann E. MERCHLEWITZ
21 Assistant Controller .... Mr. Paul J. WILDENBORG
19 Director of Security .... Vacant
18 Director of Buildings/Grounds .... Mr. John SCHOLLMEIER
23 Director of Health Services .... Ms. Angela WEISBROD
29 Director Alumni Relations .... Ms. Margaret RICHTMAN
41 Director of Athletics .... Ms. Nicole FENNERN
15 Director of Human Resources .... Ms. Genelle GROH BECK
09 Institutional Researcher .... Ms. Kara WENER
53 Dean School Education .... Dr. Scott SORVAAG
79 Dean School of the Arts .... Mr. Michael CHARRON

St. Olaf College (B)

1520 St. Olaf Avenue, Northfield MN 55057-1098
County: Rice FICE Identification: 002382
Unit ID: 174844
Telephone: (507) 786-2222 Carnegie Class: Bac/A&S
FAX Number: (507) 786-3549 Calendar System: 4/1/4
URL: www.stolaf.edu
Established: 1874 Annual Undergrad Tuition & Fees: $49,960
Enrollment: 3,176 Coed
Affiliation or Control: Evangelical Lutheran Church In America
IRS Status: 501(c)3
Highest Offering: Baccalaureate
Program: Liberal Arts And General; Teacher Preparatory; Professional
Accreditation: NH, DANCE, MUS, NURSE, SW, TED, THEA

01 President .... Dr. David R. ANDERSON
05 Provost & Dean of the College .... Dr. Marci J. SORTOR
10 Vice President & Treasurer .... Dr. Alan J. NORTON
30 Vice Pres for Advancement .... Mr. Enoch BLAZIS
32 Vice Pres of Student Life .... Mr. Greg KNESER
84 Vice Pres Enrollment/Col Relations .... Mr. Michael KYLE
88 Vice President for Mission .... Dr. Paula J. CARLSON
18 Asst Vice President for Facilities .... Mr. Peter SANDBERG
31 Asst to the Pres for Inst Diversity .... Mr. Bruce KING
20 Associate Provost .... Dr. Dan DRESSEN
06 Asst VP Registrar .... Dr. Mary CISAR
89 Assoc Dean Interdisciplin/Gen Stds .... Dr. Dana GROSS
81 Assoc Dean Natural Sciences & Math .... Dr. Matthew RICHEY
79 Assoc Dean Humanities .... Dr. Corliss SWAIN
57 Assoc Dean Fine Arts .... Ms. Mary GRIEP
83 Assoc Dean Social Sciences .... Dr. Dan HOFRENNING
21 Asst VP/Chief Investment Officer .... Mr. Mark GELLE
07 Dean of Admissions & Financial Aid .... Mr. Jeff MCLAUGHLIN
07 Director of Admissions .... Mr. Brad LINDBERG
35 Dean of Students .... Ms. Rosalyn EATON-NEEB
35 Assoc Dean of Students .... Mr. Justin FLEMING
35 Assoc Dean of Students .... Mr. Timothy SCHROER
42 Campus Pastor .... Dr. Matthew MAROHL
36 Sr Assoc Dir of Career Connections .... Ms. Kirsten CAHOON
13 Director of IT and Libraries .... Ms. Roberta LEMBKE
08 Director of IT and Libraries .... Ms. Roberta LEMBKE
44 Director Annual Giving .... Ms. Tracy FOSSUM
29 Dir of Engage Alum Parent Relations .... Mr. Brad HOFF
15 Director of Human Resources .... Mr. Roger LOFTUS
19 Director of Public Safety .... Mr. Fred C. BEHR
41 Director of Athletics .... Mr. Matt C. MCDONALD
38 Director of Counseling .... Dr. Stephen O'NEILL
26 Dir of Marketing & Communications .... Mr. Steve BLODGETT
75 Dir Center for Vocation and Career .... Mr. Branden GRIMMETT
108 Director of Evaluation & Assessment .... Dr. Jo M. BELD
09 Director of Institutional Research .... Ms. Susan CANON
39 Director of Residence Life .... Ms. Pamela MCDOWELL
40 Bookstore Director .... Ms. Victoria BEUSSMAN
96 Director of Auxiliary Operations .... Mr. Steve ABBOTT
37 Director of Student Financial Aid .... Ms. Sandra SUNDSTROM
102 Int Dir of Govt & Found Relations .... Dr. Matt RICHEY
104 Dir of Intl & Off Campus Studies .... Dr. Eric LUND
85 International Student Coordinator .... Ms. Kelly DEUTSCHMAN
04 Exec Assistant to the President .... Ms. Pat HESS

United Theological Seminary of the Twin Cities (C)

3000 5th Street, NW, New Brighton MN 55112-2598
County: Ramsey FICE Identification: 002386
Unit ID: 175139
Telephone: (651) 633-4311 Carnegie Class: Spec/Faith
FAX Number: (651) 633-4315 Calendar System: 4/1/4
URL: www.unitedseminary.edu
Established: 1962 Annual Graduate Tuition & Fees: $16,390
Enrollment: 132 Coed
Affiliation or Control: United Church Of Christ IRS Status: 501(c)3
Highest Offering: Doctorate; No Undergraduates
Program: Professional; Religious Emphasis
Accreditation: NH, THEOL

01 President .... Rev. Barbara A. HOLMES
05 VP for Academic Affairs/Dean .... Dr. Sharon M. TAN
10 VP for Finance and Administration .... Mr. Tom LOCKHART
30 VP for Development .... Vacant
44 Director of Development .... Vacant
07 Director of Admissions .... Rev. Glen HERRINGTON-HALL
04 Admin Assistant to the President .... Ms. Gretchen MILLOY
06 Registrar .... Ms. Susan HASTINGS
37 Director Student Financial Aid .... Ms. Michelle TURNAU
08 Librarian .... Ms. Susan EBBERS
51 Director Continuing Education .... Dr. Cindi Beth JOHNSON
42 Chaplain/Assc Prof Spirit Formation .... Rev. Martha POSTLETHWAITE
18 Director Physical Plant .... Mr. Brandon KROSCH

University of Minnesota Duluth (D)

1049 University Drive, Duluth MN 55812-3011
County: Saint Louis FICE Identification: 002388
Unit ID: 174233
Telephone: (218) 726-8000 Carnegie Class: Master's M
FAX Number: (218) 726-6254 Calendar System: Semester
URL: www.d.umn.edu
Established: 1947 Annual Undergrad Tuition & Fees (In-State): $12,815
Enrollment: 11,491 Coed
Affiliation or Control: State IRS Status: 501(c)3
Highest Offering: Doctorate
Program: Liberal Arts And General; Teacher Preparatory; Professional
Accreditation: NH, BUS, CS, ENG, MUS, SP, SW, TED

01 Chancellor .... Dr. Lendley C. BLACK
05 Exec Vice Chanc Academic Affairs .... Dr. Andrea SCHOKKER
32 Vice Chanc Stdnt Life/Dean Stdnts .... Dr. Lisa ERWIN
10 Vice Chanc Finance/Operations .... Mr. Michael SEYMOUR
84 Assoc VC Enroll/Inst Effectiveness .... Dr. Monica BRUNING
06 Registrar .... Ms. Carla L. BOYD
08 Director of Library .... Mr. Matt ROSENDAHL
37 Director Financial Aid .... Ms. Brenda H. HERZIG
36 Director Career Services .... Ms. Julie A. WESTLUND
13 Director Info Tech Systems/Services .... Dr. Linda DENEEN
09 Director Institutional Research .... Ms. Irina BEZROUKOVA
25 Senior Grant Administrator .... Ms. Janice SAKRY
51 Int Director Continuing Education .... Ms. Lynn BURBANK
41 Athletic Director .... Mr. Josh BERLO
15 Dir Human Resources/Equal Opporty .... Mr. Timothy CASKEY
07 Interim Director Admissions .... Mr. Scott SCHULZ
18 Director Facilities/Physical Plant .... Mr. John KING
29 Director Alumni Relations .... Ms. Lisa PRATT
30 Director Development .... Ms. Tricia BUNTEN
21 Director of Finance .... Ms. Susan KERRY
86 Director of External Affairs .... Ms. Gina KATZMARK
63 Associate Dean School of Medicine .... Dr. Gary DAVIS
81 Dean College Science/Engineering .... Dr. James RIEHL
49 Dean College Liberal Arts .... Dr. Susan MAHER
53 Dean Col Education/Human Svc Prof .... Dr. Jill PINKNEY-PASTRANA
50 Dean School of Business & Economics .... Dr. Amy HIETAPELTO
57 Dean School Fine Arts .... Mr. William PAYNE
58 Director of Graduate Programs .... Dr. Tim HOLST

University of Minnesota-Crookston (E)

2900 University Avenue, Crookston MN 56716-5001
County: Polk FICE Identification: 004069
Unit ID: 174075
Telephone: (218) 281-6510 Carnegie Class: Bac/Diverse
FAX Number: (218) 281-8040 Calendar System: Semester
URL: www.crk.umn.edu
Established: 1965 Annual Undergrad Tuition & Fees (In-State): $11,465
Enrollment: 1,802 Coed
Affiliation or Control: State IRS Status: 501(c)3
Highest Offering: Baccalaureate
Program: Occupational; Business Emphasis
Accreditation: NH

01 Chancellor .... Dr. Fred WOOD
05 Sr VC Academic/Student Affairs .... Dr. Thomas BALDWIN
32 Assoc VC Student Affs/Enrollment .... Dr. Peter PHAIAH
18 Director Facilities/Operations .... Mr. Rich CONNELL
10 Dir of Finance/University Services .... Ms. Tricia SANDERS
15 Director Human Resources .... Mr. Les JOHNSON
37 Director Financial Aid .... Ms. Melissa DINGMANN
26 Director of Communications .... Mr. Andrew SVEC
30 Dir Development/Alumni Relations .... Mr. Corby KEMMER
08 Director Library .... Mr. Owen WILLIAMS
36 Director Career/Counseling .... Mr. Donald R. CAVALIER
49 Head of Arts/Humanities/Soc Sci ... Dr. Soo-Yin LIM-THOMPSON
47 Head Agriculture & Nat Resources .... Dr. Ron DEL VECCHIO
72 Head Math/Science/Technology .... Dr. Bill PETERSON
50 Head Business .... Dr. Susan BRORSON
51 Director Center for Adult Learning .... Ms. Michelle CHRISTOPHERSON
06 Registrar .... Dr. Ken MYERS
07 Director of Admissions .... Ms. Carola THORSON
28 Director of Diversity .... Ms. Lorna HOLLOWELL
85 Dir of International Programs .... Dr. Kimberly GILLETTE

University of Minnesota-Morris (F)

600 E 4th Street, Morris MN 56267-2132
County: Stevens FICE Identification: 002389
Unit ID: 174251
Telephone: (320) 589-2211 Carnegie Class: Bac/A&S
FAX Number: (320) 589-6399 Calendar System: Semester
URL: www.morris.umn.edu
Established: 1959 Annual Undergrad Tuition & Fees (In-State): $12,584
Enrollment: 1,896 Coed
Affiliation or Control: State IRS Status: 501(c)3
Highest Offering: Baccalaureate
Program: Liberal Arts And General; Teacher Preparatory
Accreditation: NH, TED

01 Chancellor .... Dr. Jacqueline JOHNSON
05 Vice Chanc Academic Affs/Dean .... Dr. Bart FINZEL
32 Vice Chanc for Student Affairs .... Ms. Sandra OLSON-LOY
30 Assoc VC for External Relations .... Ms. Maddy MAXEINER
18 Assoc VC Physical Plant/Master Plng .... Mr. Lowell C. RASMUSSEN
10 Director for Finance .... Ms. Colleen MILLER
08 Head Librarian .... Ms. LeAnn DEAN
06 Registrar .... Ms. Clare DINGLEY
26 Interim Director of Communications .... Ms. Melissa WEBER
29 Director of Alumni Relations .... Ms. Carla RILEY
09 Director of Institutional Research .... Ms. Nancy HELSPER
36 Director Career Center .... Mr. Gary L. DONOVAN
14 Director of Information Technology .... Mr. James HALL
38 Director of Counseling .... Dr. Henry FULDA
37 Director of Financial Aid .... Ms. Jill BEAUREGARD
93 Dir Multi Ethnic Student Program .... Ms. Hilda LADNER
24 Director Educational Media .... Mr. Roger P. BOLEMAN
07 Director of Admissions .... Mr. Bryan HERRMANN
53 Chair of Education Division .... Dr. Gwen RUDNEY
81 Chair of Science/Math Division .... Dr. Peh Peh NG
79 Chair of Humanities Division .... Dr. Pieranno GARAVASO
83 Chair of Social Science Division .... Dr. Leslie MEEK

University of Minnesota-Twin Cities (G)

100 Church Street, SE, Minneapolis MN 55455-0213
County: Hennepin FICE Identification: 003969
Unit ID: 174066
Telephone: (612) 625-5000 Carnegie Class: RU/VH
FAX Number: (612) 624-6369 Calendar System: Semester
URL: www.umn.edu
Established: 1851 Annual Undergrad Tuition & Fees (In-State): $13,384
Enrollment: 51,853 Coed
Affiliation or Control: State IRS Status: 501(c)3
Highest Offering: Doctorate
Program: Occupational; Liberal Arts And General; Teacher Preparatory; Professional
Accreditation: NH, ANEST, AUD, BUS, CIDA, CLPSY, COARC, COPSY, DANCE, DENT, DH, DIETC, DIETD, DIETI, ENG, ENGR, FOR, FUSER, HSA, IPSY, JOUR, LAW, LSAR, MED, MFCD, MIDWF, MT, MUS, NURSE, OT, PCSAS, PH, PHAR, PLNG, PTA, RTT, #SCPSY, SP, SPAA, SW, TED, THEA, VET

01 President .... Dr. Eric W. KALER
100 Chief of Staff .... Ms. Amy PHENIX
05 Sr VP for Academic Affairs/Provost .... Dr. Karen HANSON
17 Vice President for Health Sciences .... Dr. Aaron FRIEDMAN
10 Vice President/Chief Financial Ofcr .... Mr. Richard H. PFUTZENREUTER
46 Vice President for Research .... Dr. Brian HERMAN
58 Vice Prov/Dean Graduate Education .... Dr. Henning SCHROEDER
20 Vice Prov/Dean Undergrad Education .... Dr. Robert MCMASTER
15 Vice President Human Resources .... Ms. Kathryn F. BROWN
88 Vice Pres for University Services .... Ms. Pam WHEELOCK
28 Vice Pres for Equity and Diversity .... Dr. Katrice ALBERT
27 Vice President/Chief Info Officer .... Mr. Scott STUDHAM
43 General Counsel .... Mr. William DONOHUE
102 President Univ Minnesota Foundation .... Ms. Elizabeth MALKERSON
25 Assoc VP Sponsored Projects Admin .... Ms. Frances LAWRENZ
86 Assoc Vice Pres for Govt Relations .... Mr. Jason ROHLOF

18 Associate VP/Chief of Facilities ....Mr. Mike BERTHELSEN
32 Vice Provost for Student Affairs ....Ms. Danita BROWN
19 Asst VP Pub Safety/Chief of Police ....Mr. Gregory S. HESTNESS
08 University Librarian ....Dr. Wendy P. LOUGEE
06 Registrar ....Ms. Sue N. VAN VOORHIS
07 Director of Admissions ....Vacant
09 Director of Institutional Research ....Dr. John KELLOGG
22 Director Equal Oppty/Affirm Action ..Ms. Kimberly HEWITT BOYD
37 Director of Student Finance ....Ms. Kristine A. WRIGHT
40 Director of the U of M Bookstores ....Mr. Robert J. CRABB
39 Dir of Housing & Residential Life ....Ms. Laurie L. MCLAUGHLIN
48 Dean of the College of Design ....Dr. Thomas R. FISHER
86 Director of Federal Relations ....Ms. Channing RIGGS
29 CEO Alumni Association ....Ms. Lisa LEWIS
38 Dir of Counseling & Consulting Srvc ....Dr. Glenn HIRSCH
87 Director of the Summer Session ....Michelle KOKER
21 Associate VP for Budget/Finance ....Ms. Julie A. TONNESON
36 Director of Student Placement ....Vacant
96 Interim Director of Purchasing ....Mr. Tim BRAY
49 Dean of the College of Liberal Arts ..Mr. James A. PARENTE, JR.
51 Dean College of Continuing Educ ....Dr. Mary L. NICHOLS
61 Dean of the Law School ....Mr. David WIPPMAN
74 Dean College of Veterinary Medicine ....Dr. Trevor R. AMES
63 Dean of the Medical School ....Dr. Aaron FRIEDMAN
66 Dean of the School of Nursing ....Dr. Connie J. DELANEY
53 Dean College Education/Human Devel ....Dr. Jean K. QUAM
52 Dean of the School of Dentistry ....Dr. Leon ASSAEL
69 Dean of the School Public Health ....Dr. John FINNEGAN
72 Dean College of Science/Engineering ....Dr. Steven CROUCH
67 Dean of the College Pharmacy ....Dr. Marilyn K. SPEEDIE
50 Dean Carlson School of Management ....Dr. Srilata A. ZAHEER
80 Dean Humphrey Sch of Pub Aff ....Dr. Eric SCHWARTZ
81 Dean College of Biological Science ....Dr. Robert P. ELDE
47 Dean Col Food/Agric/Nat Resourc Sci ....Dr. Allen LEVINE
41 Director Intercollegiate Athletics ....Mr. Norwood TEAGUE
26 Chief Public Relations Officer ....Mr. Chuck TOMBARGE

University of Minnesota-Twin Cities Rochester Campus (A)

111 South Broadway, Suite 300, Rochester MN 55904
Telephone: (800) 947-0117 Identification: 770316
Accreditation: &NH

† Main campus is University of Minnesota-Twin Cities in Minneapolis, MN.

University of Phoenix Minneapolis/St. Paul Campus (B)

435 Ford Road, St. Louis Park MN 55426-4915
Telephone: (952) 487-7226 Identification: 770212
Accreditation: &NH, ACBSP

† Main campus is University of Phoenix in Tempe, AZ.

University of Saint Thomas (C)

2115 Summit Avenue, Saint Paul MN 55105-1096
County: Ramsey FICE Identification: 002345
Unit ID: 174914
Telephone: (651) 962-5000 Carnegie Class: DRU
FAX Number: (651) 962-6360 Calendar System: 4/1/4
URL: www.stthomas.edu
Established: 1885 Annual Undergrad Tuition & Fees: $34,528
Enrollment: 10,316 Coed
Affiliation or Control: Roman Catholic IRS Status: 501(c)3
Highest Offering: Doctorate
Program: Liberal Arts And General; Teacher Preparatory; Professional
Accreditation: NH, BUS, COPSY, ENG, HSA, IPSY, LAW, MUS, SW, TED, THEOL

01 President ....Rev. Dennis J. DEASE
04 Executive Advisor to President ....Dr. Susan L. ALEXANDER
05 Int Exec VP/Chief Academic Officer ....Dr. Susan J. HUBER
88 Rector/Vice Pres School of Divinity ....Msgr. Aloysius R. CALLAGHAN
88 Vice President for Mission ....Fr. John MALONE
32 Vice President for Student Affairs ....Ms. Jane W. CANNEY
10 Vice Pres for Business Affairs/CFO .....Mr. Mark D. VANGSGARD
26 Vice President University Relations ....Mr. Doug E. HENNES
13 VP Information Resources & Tech ....Dr. Samuel J. LEVY
20 Assoc Vice Pres Academic Affairs ....Dr. Joseph L. KREITZER
20 Assoc Vice Pres Academic Affs ....Dr. Eleni ROULIS
84 Assoc VP Enrollment Services ....Ms. Marla J. FRIEDERICHS
15 Assoc VP Human Res/General Counsel ....Ms. Sara E. GROSS METHNER
21 Assoc VP/Finance & Controller ....Mr. Gary L. THYEN
18 Associate Vice Pres Facilities ....Mr. James M. BRUMMER
88 Associate VP for Auxiliary Services ......Mr. Gerald M. ANDERLEY
49 Dean College Arts & Sciences ....Dr. Terrence G. LANGAN
50 Dean Opus College of Business ....Dr. Christopher P. PUTO
53 Int Dean of School of Education ....Dr. Mark SALISBURY
83 Dean of School of Social Work ....Dr. Barbara W. SHANK
73 Dean St Paul Seminary School of Div ....Dr. Christopher J. THOMPSON
61 Int Dean School of Law ....Mr. Robert VISCHER
35 Dean of Student Life ....Ms. Karen M. LANGE
88 Assoc Dean Grad Prof Psychology ....Dr. Christopher VYE
58 Dir Graduate Programs/Business Comm ......Dr. Michael PORTER
88 Sr Assoc Dean College of Business ....Dr. Michael GARRISON
54 Dean School of Engineering ....Dr. Donald H. WEINKFAUF
30 Executive Director for Development ....Mr. Stephen A. HOEPPNER
06 Registrar ....Mr. Paul M. SIMMONS
07 Director Admissions & Financial Aid ....Ms. Kris A. GETTING
09 Director of Institutional Research ....Dr. Michael F. COGAN
35 Executive Director Campus Life ....Ms. Mary A. RYAN
36 Director of Career Services ....Ms. Diane G. CRIST
27 Director of the News Service ....Mr. James C. WINTERER
29 Exec Dir Alumni/Constituent Rels .....Ms. Rachel A. WOBSCHALL
41 Athletic Director ....Mr. Stephen J. FRITZ
40 Director Bookstore ....Mr. Tony W. ERICKSON
42 Director Campus Ministry ....Fr. Erich RUTTEN
19 Director Safety/Security ....Mr. Daniel J. MEUWISSEN
39 Director Campus Life ....Ms. Margaret D. CAHILL
38 Director Student Counseling ....Dr. Jeri M. ROCKETT
96 Director Purchasing Services ....Ms. Karen M. HARTHORN
88 Director Recruit/Admis MBA Pgms ....Dr. William WOODSON
28 Director of Diversity ....Dr. MariAnn GRAHAM

Walden University (D)

100 Washington Ave S, Suite 900, Minneapolis MN 55401
County: Hennepin FICE Identification: 025042
Unit ID: 125231
Telephone: (612) 338-7224 Carnegie Class: DRU
FAX Number: (612) 338-5092 Calendar System: Other
URL: www.waldenu.edu
Established: 1970 Annual Undergrad Tuition & Fees: $11,130
Enrollment: 50,208 Coed
Affiliation or Control: Proprietary IRS Status: Proprietary
Highest Offering: Doctorate
Program: Teacher Preparatory
Accreditation: NH, ACBSP, CACREP, NURSE, TED

00 Chief Executive Officer ....Mr. Jonathan A. KAPLAN
01 President ....Dr. Cynthia G. BAUM
05 Chief Academic Officer ....Dr. Eric RIEDEL
69 VP College Health Sciences ....Dr. Melanie STORMS
53 VP RWR College of Education ....Ms. Debra TERVALA
83 VP College Soc & Behav Sciences ....Dr. Melanie STORMS
50 VP College of Mgmt & Tech ....Mr. Paul THOMAS
26 VP Marketing ....Mr. Christian SCHINDLER
43 VP and Assistant General Counsel ....Ms. Deborah L. ZIMIC
20 VP of Undergraduate Programs ....Ms. Debra TERVALA
88 Div VP for Inst Quality & Integrity .....Dr. John A. SABATINI, JR.
11 COO ....Mr. Rick PATRO
10 CFO ....Mr. Roger MCKINNEY
53 Dean RWR College of Education ....Dr. Kate STEFFENS
46 Exec Dir Office of IR & Assesment ....Mr. Jim LENIO
32 Exec Dir Ctr for Student Success ....Ms. Susanna DAVIDSEN
15 Exec Dir Ctr for Fac Exc ....Dr. Kimberlee BONURA
88 Exec Dir Ctr for Research Support ....Dr. Laura LYNN
88 Exec Dir International Programs ....Ms. Lauren STONE
15 Director of Human Resources ....Ms. Sherine HIGH
13 Director of IT ....Ms. Terri THOMPSON
07 Director of Admissions ....Ms. Devon LOETZ
21 Bursar ....Ms. Linda ANTHONY
37 Director of Financial Aid ....Ms. Teresa DRZEWIECKI
06 Registrar ....Ms. Eve DAUER

White Earth Tribal and Community College (E)

PO Box 478, Mahnomen MN 56557-0478
County: Mahnomen FICE Identification: 039214
Unit ID: 434751
Telephone: (218) 935-0417 Carnegie Class: Tribal
FAX Number: (218) 936-5814 Calendar System: Semester
URL: www.wetcc.edu
Established: 1997 Annual Undergrad Tuition & Fees: $3,285
Enrollment: 87 Coed
Affiliation or Control: Tribal Control IRS Status: 501(c)3
Highest Offering: Associate Degree
Program: 2-Year Principally Bachelor's Creditable; Liberal Arts And General
Accreditation: #NH

01 President ....Dr. Vincent PELLEGRINO
05 Vice President Academic Affairs ....Dr. Ann BRUMMEL
32 Dean of Student Services ....Gene KLINKE
10 Chief Financial Officer ....Gina MURRAY
15 Vice President Human Resources ....Denise ASKELSON
37 Director Student Financial Aid ....Vacant
56 Director of Extension ....Steve DAHLBERG
06 Registrar ....Vacant

William Mitchell College of Law (F)

875 Summit Avenue, Saint Paul MN 55105-3076
County: Ramsey FICE Identification: 002391
Unit ID: 175281
Telephone: (651) 227-9171 Carnegie Class: Spec/Law
FAX Number: (651) 290-6414 Calendar System: Semester
URL: www.wmitchell.edu
Established: 1900 Annual Graduate Tuition & Fees: $37,320
Enrollment: 924 Coed
Affiliation or Control: Independent Non-Profit IRS Status: 501(c)3
Highest Offering: First Professional Degree; No Undergraduates
Program: Professional
Accreditation: LAW

01 President & Dean ....Mr. Eric S. JANUS
04 Exec Asst to President & Board ....Ms. Deb CALVERT
11 Assoc Dean for Administration ....Ms. Mary Pat BYRN
05 Assoc Dean for Faculty ....Mr. Mehmet KONAR-STEENBERG
30 VP of Institutional Advancement ....Ms. Linda K. BERG
16 Vice President Human Resources ....Ms. Mary E. GALE
13 Director of Information Technology ....Mr. Chad JOHNSON
10 Vice President Finance ....Ms. Kathy PANCIERA
32 Vice President of Student Affairs ....Mr. Daniel J. THOMPSON
08 Assoc Dean of Info Resources ....Mr. Simon CANICK
28 Assoc Dean/Multicultural Affairs ....Hon. Edward TOUSSAINT
28 Asst Dean/Dir Multicultural Affairs ......Ms. Lawrencina ORAMALU
36 Asst Dean for Career Development .Ms. Karen VANDER SANDEN
07 Asst Dean/Director of Admissions ....Ms. Julie EKKERS
06 Registrar ....Mr. Jim STEVENS
26 Director of Marketing/Alumni Rels ....Ms. Louise COPELAND
37 Director of Financial Aid ....Ms. Patty HARRIS
18 Director of Facilities ....Mr. Larry EVELAND
96 Purchasing Manager ....Ms. Paula B. MERTH

MISSISSIPPI

Alcorn State University (G)

1000 ASU Drive, #359, Alcorn State MS 39096-7500
County: Claiborne FICE Identification: 002396
Unit ID: 175342
Telephone: (601) 877-6100 Carnegie Class: Master's M
FAX Number: (601) 877-2975 Calendar System: Semester
URL: www.alcorn.edu
Established: 1871 Annual Undergrad Tuition & Fees (In-State): $6,096
Enrollment: 3,950 Coed
Affiliation or Control: State IRS Status: 501(c)3
Highest Offering: Beyond Master's But Less Than Doctorate
Program: 2-Year Principally Bachelor's Creditable; Liberal Arts And General; Teacher Preparatory; Professional
Accreditation: SC, AAFCS, ACBSP, ADNUR, #DIETD, MUS, NAIT, NUR, NURSE, SW, TED

01 President ....Dr. M.Christopher BROWN, II
05 Exec VP/Provost for Academic Affair ....Dr. Samuel L. WHITE
10 Sr VP for Univ Operations/COO ....Dr. Betty ROBERTS
04 Exec Asst to the President ....Mrs. Karen R. SHEDRICK
88 Sp Asst for Univ Initiatives ....Mr. Jeremy MASON
88 Director of Internal Audit ....Mr. Permy K. THUHA
46 Chief Research Officer ....Dr. Babu P. PATLOLLA
21 VP for Fiscal Affairs ....Ms. Carolyn DUPRE
32 VP for Student Affairs ....Vacant
30 VP Institutional Advancement ....Mr. Marcus D. WARD
27 VP for Media Relations ....Ms. Clara R. STAMPS
20 Vice Provost for Academic Affs ....Dr. Donzell LEE
35 Assoc VP for Student Life ....Mr. Juan MCCULLUM
18 Assoc VP for Facilities Management ....Mr. Jessie STEPHNEY
39 Director Housing ....Ms. Jessica L. FOXWORTH
88 Director Strategic Innovations ....Dr. Kassie FREEMAN
88 Presidential Ombudsman Admin Affs ....Mr. Charles SHORETTE
28 Dir of Educational Equity/Inclusion ....Dr. Derek GREENFIELD
21 Director of Accounting ....Mrs. Cassandra B. LEWIS
96 Purchasing Agent ....Ms. Mertha V. GEORGE
07 Director of Admissions/Recruiting ....Mr. Emanuel BARNES
37 Director Student Financial Aid ....Mrs. Juanita RUSSELL
06 Registrar ....Mr. Jimmy L. SMITH
08 Dean University Libraries ....Dr. Blanche SANDERS
47 Dean School of Agriculture ....Dr. Barry BEQUETTE
49 Int Dean School of Arts & Science ....Dr. Babu P. PATLOLLA
50 Int Dean School of Business ....Dr. Vivek BHARGAVA
53 Dean School of Education ....Dr. Robert CARR
66 Int Dean School of Nursing ....Dr. Norris EDNEY
88 Dir Academic Support Services ....Dr. Edward L. VAUGHN
13 CIO for Ctr for Info Tech Svcs ....Ms. Donna G. HAYDEN
15 Director of Human Resources ....Ms. Carla WILLIAMS
36 Director Career Services ....Vacant
23 Director of Health Services ....Ms. Dorothy G. DAVIS
41 Interm Director of Athletics ....Mr. Dwayne WHITE
40 Manager Barnes and Noble ....Mr. Domonic RABY
38 Director of Counseling & Testing ....Mrs. Dyann W. MOSES
09 Director Institutional Res/Assess ....Dr. Ramesh MADDALI
88 Dir Institutional Effectiveness ....Dr. Latoya HART
19 Chief of Campus Police ....Vacant
88 General Manager Sodexo ....Mr. Corey D. YOUNG
102 Exec Dir ASU Foundation ....Mr. Marcus D. WARD
30 Asst VP Advancement Services ....Mr. Dameon A. SHAW
31 Dir Ctr Rural Life/Econ Dev ....Dr. Samuel L. WHITE
92 Director of Pre-Prof/Honors Program ......Dr. Thomas C. STURGIS
58 Vice Provost Acad/Graduate Studies ....Dr. Donzell LEE
25 Grants/Contract Administrator ....Ms. Sallie GRIFFIN
88 Senior Dir Community Outreach ....Dr. Ruth R. NICHOLS
12 Exec Director Vicksburg Campus ....Dr. Cheryl KARIUKI

Antonelli College (H)

1500 N 31st Avenue, Hattiesburg MS 39401-3056
Telephone: (601) 583-4100 Identification: 666517
Accreditation: ACCSC

† Main campus is Antonelli College in Cincinnati, OH.

Antonelli College (I)

2323 Lakeland Drive, Jackson MS 39208-9549
Telephone: (601) 362-9991 Identification: 666518
Accreditation: ACCSC

† Main campus is Antonelli College in Cincinnati, OH.

Belhaven University (A)

1500 Peachtree, Jackson MS 39202-1798
County: Hinds FICE Identification: 002397
Unit ID: 175421
Telephone: (601) 968-5919 Carnegie Class: Master's M
FAX Number: (601) 968-9998 Calendar System: Semester
URL: www.belhaven.edu
Established: 1883 Annual Undergrad Tuition & Fees: $19,970
Enrollment: 3,507 Coed
Affiliation or Control: Presbyterian Church (U.S.A.) IRS Status: 501(c)3
Highest Offering: Master's
Program: Liberal Arts And General; Teacher Preparatory; Professional
Accreditation: SC, ART, DANCE, IACBE, MUS, THEA

01 President .... Dr. Roger PARROTT
05 Exec Vice President & Provost .... Dr. Dan FREDERICKS
30 Vice Pres Institutional Advancement .... Mr. Kevin RUSSELL
88 VP of Adult & Graduate Marketing .... Dr. Audrey KELLEHER
10 Chief Financial Officer .... Mrs. Virginia HENDERSON
32 VP for Student Affairs and Athletic .... Mr. Scott LITTLE
11 Asst Vice Pres Campus Operations .... Mr. David POTVIN
51 Asst Vice Pres of Adult Studies .... Dr. Richard HARRIS
20 Asst VP of Academics .... Dr. Lee SKINKLE
12 Academic Dean/Houston Campus .... Dr. Larry RUDDELL
12 Academic Dean/Mississippi .... Dr. Ken ELLIOTT
12 Academic Dean/Memphis Tennessee .... Dr. Paul CRISS
12 Academic Dean/Chattanooga-Atlanta .... Dr. Kym CHAVEZ
53 Dean of the School of Education .... Dr. Sandra RASBERRY
50 Dean of the School of Business .... Dr. Chip MASON
08 Librarian .... Mr. Chris CULLNANE
07 Asst VP Trad & Online Admissions .... Mrs. Suzanne SULLIVAN
06 Registrar .... Mrs. Donna WEEKS
27 Director of Integrated Marketing .... Mr. Bryant BUTLER
35 Director of Student Leadership .... Ms. JoBeth PETTY
29 Director Alumni Relations .... Mr. Michael DUKES
13 Director Institutional Technology .... Mr. Bo MILLER
19 Director Security/Safety .... Mr. Steve FARMER
40 Bookstore Manager .... Ms. Sheila LYONS
36 Dean of Student Development .... Mr. Ron PIRTLE
35 Dean of Student Life .... Mr. Greg HAWKINS

Blue Cliff College (B)

12251 Bernard Parkway, Gulfport MS 39503-5086
County: Harrison FICE Identification: 035253
Unit ID: 441502
Telephone: (228) 896-9727 Carnegie Class: Assoc/PrivFP
FAX Number: (228) 896-7238 Calendar System: Quarter
URL: www.bluecliffcollege.com
Established: 1987 Annual Undergrad Tuition & Fees: $16,148
Enrollment: 204 Coed
Affiliation or Control: Proprietary IRS Status: Proprietary
Highest Offering: Associate Degree
Program: Occupational
Accreditation: ACCSC

01 Director .... Ms. Gina QUINN

Blue Mountain College (C)

201 W Main Street, PO Box 160,
Blue Mountain MS 38610-0160
County: Tippah FICE Identification: 002398
Unit ID: 175430
Telephone: (662) 685-4771 Carnegie Class: Bac/Diverse
FAX Number: (662) 685-4776 Calendar System: Semester
URL: www.bmc.edu
Established: 1873 Annual Undergrad Tuition & Fees: $9,470
Enrollment: 513 Coed
Affiliation or Control: Southern Baptist IRS Status: 501(c)3
Highest Offering: Master's
Program: Liberal Arts And General; Teacher Preparatory; Religious Emphasis
Accreditation: SC

01 President .... Dr. Barbara C. MCMILLIN
05 Vice President for Academic Affairs .... Dr. Sharon B. ENZOR
32 VP for Enrollment/Student Services .... Mr. Jack T. MOSER
10 Chief Financial Officer .... Mrs. Joyce PETERS
04 Admin Assistant to the President .... Mrs. Pam BOWMAN
58 Dean Graduate Studies .... Dr. Jenetta WADDELL
06 Registrar .... Mrs. Sheila D. FREEMAN
08 Director of Library Services .... Dr. Derek J. CASH
37 Director of Financial Aid .... Mrs. Michelle HALL
07 Director of Admissions .... Miss Maria TEEL
40 Director Bookstore .... Mrs. Dot M. LOCKE
41 Athletic Director .... Mr. Lavon DRISKELL
42 Director Baptist Student Union .... Mrs. Tracy S. MOSER
09 Director of Institutional Research .... Mr. Robert E. RUCKER
36 Director Career Services .... Dr. Teresa R. ARRINGTON
13 Director of Information Services .... Mr. Kevin BAREFIELD
26 Dir of PR/Publications .... Ms. Emma L. AINSWORTH
29 Director of Alumni Affairs .... Mrs. Lea S. BENNETT

Coahoma Community College (D)

3240 Friars Point Road, Clarksdale MS 38614-9700
County: Coahoma FICE Identification: 002401
Unit ID: 175519
Telephone: (662) 627-2571 Carnegie Class: Assoc/Pub-R-S
FAX Number: (662) 627-9451 Calendar System: Semester
URL: www.ccc.cc.ms.us
Established: 1949 Annual Undergrad Tuition & Fees (In-District): $2,060
Enrollment: 2,317 Coed
Affiliation or Control: State/Local IRS Status: 501(c)3
Highest Offering: Associate Degree
Program: Occupational; 2-Year Principally Bachelor's Creditable
Accreditation: SC, #COARC, POLYT

01 President .... Dr. Valmadge T. TOWNER
05 Vice President for Academic Affairs .... Dr. Rosetta HOWARD
10 Vice Pres for Finance & Operations .... Ms. Deborah MCNEAL
32 Vice Pres Student Affs/Support Svcs .... Dr. Gregory HUDSON
09 VP Inst Effectiveness/SACS Liaison .... Ms. Rosemary DILL
30 VP Instnl Advance/Federal Programs .... Mrs. Marilyn STARKS
75 VP Career & Technical Education .... Mrs. Anne SHELTON-CLARK
07 Dean of Admissions/Registrar .... Mr. Michael HOUSTON
08 Dean Library/Instructionl Resources .... Mrs. Yvonne STANFORD
13 Director Computer Services .... Mr. Leandrew PRESLEY
19 Director of Safety/Transportation .... Mr. William HOUSTON
26 Director of Public Relations .... Ms. Panny MAYFIELD
37 Director of Financial Aid .... Mrs. Patricia BROOKS
15 Director Human Resources .... Mrs. Wanda HOLMES
18 Chief Facilities/Physical Plant .... Mr. Jerone SHAW
51 Director of Educational Outreach .... Ms. Cynthia WILLIAMS
29 Director Alumni Relations .... Mrs. Rita HANFOR
36 Director Student Placement .... Mr. Orlando PADEN
38 Director Student Counseling .... Vacant
96 Director of Purchasing .... Mrs. Deborah MCNEAL

Concorde Career College (E)

7900 Airways Boulevard, Suite 103, Southaven MS 38671
Telephone: (662) 429-9909 Identification: 770540
Accreditation: COE

† Main campus is Concorde Career College in Memphis, TN.

Copiah-Lincoln Community College (F)

PO Box 649, Wesson MS 39191-0649
County: Copiah FICE Identification: 002402
Unit ID: 175573
Telephone: (601) 643-5101 Carnegie Class: Assoc/Pub-R-M
FAX Number: (601) 643-8212 Calendar System: Semester
URL: www.colin.edu
Established: 1928 Annual Undergrad Tuition & Fees (In-State): $3,940
Enrollment: 3,436 Coed
Affiliation or Control: State IRS Status: 501(c)3
Highest Offering: Associate Degree
Program: Occupational; 2-Year Principally Bachelor's Creditable
Accreditation: SC, ADNUR, COARC, MLTAD, RAD

01 President .... Dr. Ronald E. NETTLES
04 Assistant to the President .... Mrs. Brenda J. PARRETT
10 Vice President Business Affairs .... Mr. Michael TANNER
05 Vice Pres of Instructional Services .... Dr. Jane HULON
12 VP of the Simpson County Center .... Dr. Dewayne MIDDLETON
12 Vice Pres of the Natchez Campus .... Ms. Teresa BUSBY
20 Academic Dean .... Dr. Jill B. LOGAN
32 Dean of Student Services .... Mrs. Brenda SMITH
75 Dean Career & Technical Educ .... Dr. Gail BALDWIN
31 Dean of Community Programs .... Dr. Brenda B. ORR
41 Athletic Director .... Mr. Gwyn YOUNG
38 Director of Counseling/Recruitment .... Mrs. Lea Ann KNIGHT
35 Assistant Dean of Students .... Mr. Bryan NOBILE
37 Director Student Financial Aid .... Mrs. Leslie SMITH
40 Director Bookstore .... Mr. Charles HART
08 Director of Library Resources .... Mr. Kendall P. CHAPMAN
26 Director of Public Relations .... Mrs. Natalie DAVIS
14 Director of Computer Center .... Mr. Danny DYKES
19 Director of Security .... Mr. Wayne ROBERTS
09 Director of Institutional Research .... Dr. Jeff POSEY
07 Director of Admissions .... Mr. Chris WARREN
102 Executive Dir Foundation/Alumni .... Mr. David CAMPBELL
18 Director of Physical Plant .... Mr. Daniel CASE
66 Director of Assoc Degree Nursing .... Mrs. Mary Ann CANTERBURY
06 Student Records Manager .... Mrs. Gay LANGHAM
57 Chair Fine Arts Division .... Mrs. Janet SMITH
50 Chair Business Division .... Mr. Richard BAKER
68 Chair Physical Education Division .... Dr. Stephanie DUGUID
81 Chair Math/Computer Science Div .... Mrs. Carol FORD
79 Chair Humanities Division .... Mrs. Pam REID
82 Chair Social Science Division .... Mr. David HIGGS
88 Chair Science Division .... Dr. Kevin MCKONE
96 Director of Purchasing .... Mrs. Erin LIKENS

Delta State University (G)

1003 W. Sunflower Rd., Cleveland MS 38733
County: Bolivar FICE Identification: 002403
Unit ID: 175616
Telephone: (662) 846-3000 Carnegie Class: Master's L
FAX Number: (662) 846-4014 Calendar System: Semester
URL: www.deltastate.edu
Established: 1924 Annual Undergrad Tuition & Fees (In-State): $6,012
Enrollment: 4,764 Coed
Affiliation or Control: State IRS Status: 501(c)3
Highest Offering: Doctorate
Program: Liberal Arts And General; Teacher Preparatory; Professional
Accreditation: SC, AAFCS, ACBSP, ART, CACREP, DIETC, MUS, NURSE, SW, TED

01 President .... Dr. William (Bill) LAFORGE
05 Provost/VP Academic Affairs .... Vacant
32 Vice President for Student Affairs .... Dr. H. Wayne BLANSETT
10 Vice President for Finance .... Vacant
11 Vice President University Relations .... Dr. Michelle A. ROBERTS
21 Assoc VP for Finance/Director HR .... Dr. Myrtis TABB
41 Director of Athletics .... Mr. Ronnie MAYERS
29 Exec Dir of Alumni/Foundation .... Mr. D. Keith FULCHER
04 Exec Assistant to the President .... Ms. Leigh S. KORB
49 Dean College of Arts & Sciences .... Vacant
50 Dean College of Business .... Dr. Billy MOORE
53 Dean College of Education .... Dr. Leslie GRIFFIN
66 Dean School of Nursing .... Dr. Libby L. CARLSON
08 Dean Library Services .... Mr. Jeff SLAGELL
58 Dean Grad/Cont Studies & Research .... Dr. Beverly MOON
07 Dean Enrollment Management .... Dr. Debbie S. HESLEP
88 Internal Auditor .... Ms. Vicki WILLIAMS
88 Associate Dean Delta Regional Devel .... Dr. Luther BROWN
13 Chief Information Officer .... Mr. Edwin CRAFT
20 Director Academic Support Services .... Mr. Doug JOHNSON
25 Director Institutional Grants .... Ms. Robin BOYLES
06 Registrar & Director Inst Research .... Ms. Suzanne SIMPSON
106 Director of E-Learning .... Dr. Angela BRIDGES
31 Director Ctr for Community/Econ Dev .... Ms. Judith WINFORD
88 Director Coahoma County Higher Educ .... Ms. Jennifer WALLER
88 Director Field Experiences .... Dr. Cheryl CUMMINS
21 Comptroller/Accounting .... Mr. James RUTLEDGE
18 Director of Facilities Management .... Mr. Robert TURNER
88 Director Student Business Services .... Ms. Teresa HOUSTON
96 Manager Procurement & Accts Payable .... Ms. Beverly LINDSEY
35 Ast to VP Stdnt Affs/Dir Stdnt Life .... Ms. Elsie L. ERVIN
38 Director Counsel/Stdnt Health Svcs .... Dr. Richard HOUSTON
37 Director Student Financial Assist .... Ms. Ann M. MULLINS
19 Director of Police Department .... Mr. N. Lynn BUFORD
36 Director Career Services/Placement .... Mr. Davlon MILLER
39 Director of Housing .... Ms. Julie JACKSON
30 Chief Development Officer .... Mr. Gary BOUSE
29 Director of Alumni Affairs .... Mr. Jeffery FARRIS
26 Director of Communications & Mktg .... Mr. Michael GANN
88 Executive Director BPAC .... Ms. Laura HOWELL
40 Manager of Bookstore .... Ms. Tina GLADDEN
84 Dean of Enrollment/Director Ad Mkt .... Ms. Debbie HESLEP
88 Director of Facilities Operations .... Mr. Ted HOCHRADEL
88 Executive Director Student Success .... Ms. Christy RIDDLE

East Central Community College (H)

PO Box 129, Decatur MS 39327-0129
County: Newton FICE Identification: 002404
Unit ID: 175643
Telephone: (601) 635-2111 Carnegie Class: Assoc/Pub-R-M
FAX Number: (601) 635-4011 Calendar System: Semester
URL: www.eccc.edu
Established: 1928 Annual Undergrad Tuition & Fees (In-District): $2,170
Enrollment: 2,638 Coed
Affiliation or Control: Local IRS Status: 501(c)3
Highest Offering: Associate Degree
Program: Occupational; 2-Year Principally Bachelor's Creditable
Accreditation: SC, ADNUR, EMT, SURGT

01 President .... Dr. Billy W. STEWART
05 Vice President for Instruction .... Dr. Teresa L. HOUSTON
10 Vice Pres for Business Operations .... Mr. Mickey VANCE
32 Vice President for Student Services .... Dr. Randall LEE
102 Vice Pres Foundation/Alumni Rels .... Vacant
26 Vice Pres for Public Information .... Mr. F. Bubby JOHNSTON
51 Director of ABE/GED .... Mr. Ryan CLARKE
75 Director of Career Tech Instruction .... Mr. Wayne EASON
07 Director Admissions and Records .... Mrs. Deanna RUSH
41 Athletic Dir/Dir of Personnel Svcs .... Mr. Chris HARRIS
18 Director of Physical Plant .... Mr. Artie FOREMAN
103 Dean Workforce Educ & Development .... Mr. Roger WHITLOCK
13 Director for Technology Management .... Mr. Derek PACE
38 Academic Counselor .... Mr. Michael D. ALEXANDER
37 Director of Financial Aid .... Mrs. Brenda B. CARSON
08 Library Director .... Mr. Leslie HUGHES
13 Assoc Director for Technology Mgmt .... Mrs. Regena BOYKIN
19 Chief of Police .... Mr. Mitch MCCLEON
39 Director of Hous/Student Activities .... Mrs. Marcie PINSON
29 Director Alumni Relations .... Dr. Stacey HOLLINGSWORTH
57 Chairperson Fine Arts Division .... Mrs. Vicki BLAYLOCK
83 Chairperson Social Sciences .... Mrs. Wanda HURLEY
81 Chrpn Mathematics/Computer Science .... Dr. Lisa MCMILLIN
66 Dean of Healthcare Education .... Mrs. Denita THOMAS
81 Chairperson Science .... Mr. Curt SKIPPER
60 Chairperson Communications/ Language .... Mrs. Carol SHACKELFORD

East Mississippi Community College (I)

PO Box 158, Scooba MS 39358-0158
County: Kemper FICE Identification: 002405
Unit ID: 175652
Telephone: (662) 476-8442 Carnegie Class: Assoc/Pub-R-M
FAX Number: (662) 476-5058 Calendar System: Semester
URL: www.eastms.edu
Established: 1927 Annual Undergrad Tuition & Fees (In-District): $3,050
Enrollment: 4,802 Coed
Affiliation or Control: State/Local IRS Status: 501(c)3
Highest Offering: Associate Degree
Program: Occupational; 2-Year Principally Bachelor's Creditable
Accreditation: SC, ADNUR, EMT, FUSER

01 President .... Dr. F. Rick YOUNG
05 Vice Pres for Instruction .... Dr. Thomas WARE
12 Vice President for GT Campus .... Dr. Paul MILLER
12 Vice President for Scooba Campus .... Dr. Andrea MAYFIELD
10 Chief Financial Officer .... Ms. Melissa MOSLEY
32 VP for SC Student Affs & Athletics .... Mr. Mickey E. STOKES
30 VP Institutional Advanc/Alumni Affs .... Mr. Nick CLARK
103 VP of Workforce & Cmty Services .... Dr. Raj SHAUNAK
37 Vice Pres for Financial Aid .... Mr. James GIBSON
04 Administrative Asst to President .... Mrs. Lauren CLAY
09 Dist Dir Instl Research/Effective .... Mrs. Diana PRUETT
08 District Librarian .... Ms. Donna BALLARD
13 Dist Director of Info Technology .... Mr. Michael TVARKUNAS
18 Physical Plant Director-Scooba .... Mr. Charles B. WILLIAMS
37 Director of Financial Aid GT .... Mr. Garry JONES
06 Registrar-Scooba .... Mrs. Melinda SCIPLE
07 Director of Admissions-SC .... Mrs. Karen BRIGGS
56 Director of MNAS Extension .... Mr. Jeff JOWERS
40 District Bookstore Manager .... Ms. Vickie TURNER
27 Director of Public Information .... Ms. Suzanne MONK
35 Dean of Student Affairs .... Mr. Tony MONTGOMERY

Hinds Community College (A)

PO Box 1100, Raymond MS 39154-1100
County: Hinds FICE Identification: 002407
Unit ID: 175786
Telephone: (601) 857-5261 Carnegie Class: Assoc/Pub-R-L
FAX Number: (601) 857-3392 Calendar System: Semester
URL: www.hindscc.edu
Established: 1917 Annual Undergrad Tuition & Fees (In-District): $2,260
Enrollment: 18,000 Coed
Affiliation or Control: State/Local IRS Status: 501(c)3
Highest Offering: Associate Degree
Program: Occupational; 2-Year Principally Bachelor's Creditable
Accreditation: SC, ADNUR, CAHIIM, COARC, DA, DMS, EMT, MAC, MLTAD, PTAA, RAD, SURGT

01 President .... Dr. Clyde MUSE
11 VP Admin Svcs/VP Utica/Vicksburg .. Dr. Debra MAYS-JACKSON
10 Vice President Business Services .... Mr. Russell SHAW
12 VP Raymond/NSG/AH/Parallel Pgm .... Dr. Theresa HAMILTON
12 VP Rankin/Jackson/Dir Occup Pgm .... Dr. Sue POWELL
31 Vice Pres Community Relations .... Ms. Colleen C. HARTFIELD
88 VP for Economic Dev & Training .... Mr. John J. WOODS
18 VP Physical Plant & Aux Services .... Mr. Thomas WASSON
30 VP for Advancement & Stdnt Success .... Ms. Jacqueline M. GRANBERRY
84 Director of Enrollment Services .... Ms. Kathryn B. COLE
32 District Dean of Student Affairs .... Dr. Tyrone JACKSON
07 Associate Vice President for Stdnts .... Mr. Randall HARRIS
08 Dean of Learning Resources .... Ms. Mary Beth APPLIN
20 Academic Dean .... Dr. Thomas KELLY
15 Director of Human Resources .... Ms. Gay Lynn CASTON
37 Dir of Financial Aid & VA Affairs .... Ms. Joy WILLIS
38 Director of Counseling Services .... Ms. Mary Lee MCDANIEL
41 Athletic Director .... Mr. Gene MURPHY
09 Director of Institutional Research .... Ms. Carley DEAR
26 Public Relations Director .... Ms. Cathy C. HAYDEN
96 Director of Purchasing .... Mr. Samuel LEMONIS

Holmes Community College (B)

Hill Street, PO Box 369, Goodman MS 39079-0369
County: Holmes FICE Identification: 002408
Unit ID: 175810
Telephone: (662) 472-2312 Carnegie Class: Assoc/Pub-R-L
FAX Number: (662) 472-9152 Calendar System: Semester
URL: www.holmescc.edu
Established: 1925 Annual Undergrad Tuition & Fees (In-District): $5,230
Enrollment: 6,246 Coed
Affiliation or Control: Local IRS Status: 501(c)3
Highest Offering: Associate Degree
Program: Occupational; 2-Year Principally Bachelor's Creditable
Accreditation: SC, ADNUR, EMT, FUSER, NAIT, OTA, SURGT

01 President .... Dr. Glenn F. BOYCE
04 Asst to President/Dir Inst Rsch .... Dr. Lindy MCCAIN
05 Vice Pres for Academic Programs .... Dr. Fran COX
12 Vice President Ridgeland Campus .... Dr. Don BURNHAM
12 Vice President Grenada Center .... Dr. Jim HAFFEY
72 Vice Pres Career/Technical Educ .... Mrs. Sherrie CHEEK
32 Dn Goodman Cam/Dist Coord Stdt Svcs .... Mr. Andy WOOD
07 Director of Admissions & Records .... Mr. Joshua GUEST
10 Director of Financial Services .... Mr. Sonny SPARKS
08 Librarian .... Mrs. Joan TIERCE
26 District Director of Communications .... Mr. Steve DIFFEY
31 Director Community/Workforce Devel .... Mr. Mike BLANKENSHIP
37 Director Student Financial Aid .... Mrs. Gail MUSE
15 Director Personnel Services .... Mrs. Julia BROWN
09 Director of Institutional Research .... Dr. Lindy MCCAIN
27 Dir Communications & Publications .... Mr. Steve DIFFEY
18 Chief Facilities/Physical Plant .... Vacant
96 Director of Purchasing .... Ms. Roxanne CHISOLM
06 Registrar .... Mr. Joshua GUEST
29 Director Alumni Relations .... Mr. Joe ADAMS
21 Business Manager .... Mr. Matt SURRELL

Itawamba Community College (C)

602 W Hill Street, Fulton MS 38843-1022
County: Itawamba FICE Identification: 002409
Unit ID: 175829
Telephone: (662) 862-8000 Carnegie Class: Assoc/Pub-R-M
FAX Number: (662) 862-8036 Calendar System: Semester
URL: www.icc.cc.ms.us
Established: 1948 Annual Undergrad Tuition & Fees (In-District): $2,100
Enrollment: 6,002 Coed
Affiliation or Control: Local IRS Status: 501(c)3
Highest Offering: Associate Degree
Program: Occupational; 2-Year Principally Bachelor's Creditable
Accreditation: SC, ADNUR, CAHIIM, COARC, EMT, OTA, PTAA, RAD, SURGT

01 President .... Mr. Michael B. EATON
05 Vice President of Instruction .... Dr. Sara JOHNSON
10 Vice President of Business Services .... Mr. Jerry SENTER
32 Vice President of Student Services .... Mr. Buddy COLLINS
30 Vice Pres Dev/Plng/Telecom/Info Svc .... Mr. Wayne SULLIVAN
07 Dir Admiss/Registration .... Ms. Cay LOLLAR
26 Dir Pub Rel/Mktg/Sports Info .... Mr. Will KOLLMEYER
37 Director of Financial Aid .... Mr. Robert WALKER
24 Director of Learning Resources .... Dr. Glenda SEGARS
08 Librarian/Tupelo .... Ms. Janet Y. ARMOUR
51 Director of Adult & Continuing Educ .... Mr. Scott BLACKLEY
41 Athletic Director .... Ms. Carrie BALL-WILLIAMSON
44 Dir of Institutional Advancement .... Mr. Jim INGRAM
18 Chief Facilities/Physical Plant .... Mr. Thomas BONDS
35 Director Stdnt Affs/Counseling .... Mr. Larry BOGGS
09 Director of Institutional Research .... Mrs. Elizabeth EDWARDS
15 Director Personnel Services .... Mr. Timothy C. SENTER

ITT Technical Institute (D)

382 Galleria Parkway, Suite 100, Madison MS 39110
Telephone: (601) 607-4500 Identification: 666701
Accreditation: ACICS

† Main campus is ITT Technical Institute in Indianapolis, IN.

Jackson State University (E)

1400 J. R. Lynch Street, Jackson MS 39217
County: Hinds FICE Identification: 002410
Unit ID: 175856
Telephone: (601) 979-2121 Carnegie Class: RU/H
FAX Number: (601) 979-2358 Calendar System: Semester
URL: www.jsums.edu
Established: 1877 Annual Undergrad Tuition & Fees (In-State): $6,348
Enrollment: 8,819 Coed
Affiliation or Control: State IRS Status: 501(c)3
Highest Offering: Doctorate
Program: Liberal Arts And General; Teacher Preparatory; Professional
Accreditation: SC, ART, BUS, CACREP, CLPSY, CORE, CS, ENG, JOUR, MUS, NAIT, PH, PLNG, SP, SPAA, SW, TED

01 President .... Dr. Carolyn MEYERS
05 Provost/VP Academic Affairs .... Dr. James RENICK
10 VP for Business & Finance .... Mr. Michael THOMAS
46 Int VP for Res Federally Relations .... Dr. Loretta A. MOORE
30 VP Institutional Advancement .... Mr. David HOARD
13 Int VP for Information Mgmt .... Dr. Deborah F. DENT
43 Legal Counsel .... Mr. Deshun T. MARTIN
21 Internal Auditor .... Ms. Ella HOLMES
18 Assoc VP for Facil/Construct/Mgmt .... Mr. Wayne GOODWIN
21 Assoc VP for Business & Finance .... Ms. Dana BROWN
20 Assoc Provost for Academic Affairs .... Dr. Thomas CALHOUN
106 Executive Dir of Distance Learning .... Dr. Debra BUCHANAN
32 VP for Student Life .... Dr. Marcus A. CHANAY
35 Assoc VP for Student Life/Dean Std .... Dr. Phillip COCKRELL
09 Asst VP Inst Research/Plng/Enr Mgt .... Dr. Nicole EDWARDS- EVANS
46 Assoc VP for Research & Development .... Vacant
53 Dean College Educ/Human Devel .... Dr. Daniel WATKINS
58 Dean Division of Graduate Studies .... Dr. Dorris R. ROBINSON-GARDNER
20 Dean Division Undergrad Studies .... Dr. Evelyn LEGGETTE
49 Dean College of Liberal Arts .... Dr. Lawrence POTTER
106 Int Dean Div of Internat Studies .... Vacant
50 Int Dean College of Business .... Dr. Jean-Claude ASSAD
80 Dean College of Public Service .... Dr. Ricardo BROWN
72 Dean College of Sci/Engr/Tech .... Dr. Richard ALO
51 Director of Lifelong Learning .... Dr. Millard BINGHAM
08 Int Dean Div of Library & Info Res .... Dr. Melissa DRUCKREY
20 Assoc Dean University College .. Dr. Marie O'BANNER-JACKSON
92 Assoc Dean Div of Honors College .. Dr. Loria BROWN GORDAN
46 Dir of JSU RTRNDTCC/Prof Chem .... Dr. Jim PERKINS
88 Director Testing & Assessment .... Dr. Arthur JEFFERSON
31 Assoc Dir Ctr Svc & Comm/Eng Lrng .... Dr. Gisele GENTRY
29 Dir Alumni/Constituency Rels .... Dr. Steven SMITH
15 Executive Director Human Resources ... Mrs. Robin SPANN-PACK
88 Asst VP of Development .... Mrs. Patricia MITCHELL
39 Director of Residence Life .... Ms. Vera JACKSON
18 Director of Facilities Operations .... Ms. Jennie GRIFFIN
37 Director of Financial Aid .... Mrs. Betty MONCURE
21 Dir Budget & Financial Analysis .... Mrs. Tammiko HARRISON
06 Registrar .... Mr. Alfred B. JACKSON
23 University Physician .... Dr. Robert SMITH
88 Dir Mississippi Learning Inst .... Vacant
89 Director of First Year Experience .... Mrs. Patricia SHERIFF-TAYLOR
07 Dir Undergrad Adm & Recruit .... Mrs. Janieth ADAMS
41 Director of Athletics .... Dr. Vivian L. FULLER
88 Director of Title III .... Dr. Mary MYLES
96 Dir Purchasing and Travel .... Ms. Claudette ANDERSON
88 Director MS Urban Research Ctr .... Dr. Melvin DAVIS
19 Director Public Safety .... Mr. Thomas ALBRIGHT
26 Director Public Relations .... Mr. Eric STRINGFELLOW
22 Asst Dir for ADA Services .... Ms. Monica WALL JONES
88 Exec Dir Auxiliary Enterprises .... Ms. Alicina PUGH
88 Director Human Capital Development .... Ms. Angela GOBAR
88 Director of Capital Improvement .... Mr. Walter JOHNSON
35 Assoc Director of Campus Life .... Mrs. Lori STEWART
40 Manager Bookstore .... Mr. Mark PERSON
88 Spec Asst to the Prov for Cyber Lrn .... Dr. Robert BLAINE
88 Spec Asst to the Prov for Cmty Col .... Dr. Priscilla SLADE
09 Int Dir of Institutional Research .... Dr. Stephen OKOYE

Jones County Junior College (F)

900 S Court Street, Ellisville MS 39437-3999
County: Jones FICE Identification: 002411
Unit ID: 175883
Telephone: (601) 477-4000 Carnegie Class: Assoc/Pub-R-M
FAX Number: (601) 477-4017 Calendar System: Semester
URL: www.jcjc.edu
Established: 1927 Annual Undergrad Tuition & Fees (In-District): $2,722
Enrollment: 4,259 Coed
Affiliation or Control: State/Local IRS Status: Exempt
Highest Offering: Associate Degree
Program: Occupational; 2-Year Principally Bachelor's Creditable
Accreditation: SC, ACBSP, ADNUR, EMT, RAD

01 President .... Dr. Jesse R. SMITH
05 VP Instructional Affrs/Assessment .... Dr. Laverne ULMER
10 Vice President of Business Affairs .... Mr. Rick YOUNGBLOOD
32 Vice President of Student Affairs .... Mr. Ed SMITH
86 Vice President of External Affairs .... Mr. Jim WALLEY
30 VP of Institutional Advancement .... Ms. Caroline RAMAGOS
13 VP of Information Technology .... Mr. Casey MERCIER
26 Director of Marketing .... Ms. Finee RUFFIN
04 Assistant to the President .... Ms. Gwen MAGEE
04 Assistant to the President .... Mr. John M. CARTER
35 Dean of Student Affairs .... Dr. Sam JONES
75 Dean of Sci/Tech/Engr & Math .... Ms. Candace WEAVER
92 Dean of Arts and Honors .... Dr. Mark TAYLOR
103 Director of the Adv Tech Center .... Mr. Greg BUTLER
07 Director of Admissions & Records .... Mr. Rick HAMILTON
38 Dir of Student Success Center .... Mr. Andrew SHARP
37 Director of Student Financial Aid .... Ms. Jennifer SUBER
39 Director of Housing-Women .... Ms. Ashley HILL
39 Director of Housing-Men .... Mr. Joseph TUGGLE
40 Bookstore Manager .... Mr. Kevin KUHN
41 Athletic Director .... Ms. Katie HERRINGTON
18 Director of Physical Plant .... Mr. Michael BRADSHAW
25 Director of External Funding .... Mr. Brian GINN
15 Human Resources Manager .... Ms. Christy HILBUN
96 Director of Purchasing .... Ms. LeAnne NIXON
106 Dean of eLearning .... Ms. Jennifer POWELL
08 Head Librarian .... Ms. Julie ATWOOD
19 Chief Campus Police .... Mr. Stan LIVINGSTON

Meridian Community College (G)

910 Highway 19 N, Meridian MS 39307-5890
County: Lauderdale FICE Identification: 002413
Unit ID: 175935
Telephone: (601) 483-8241 Carnegie Class: Assoc/Pub-R-M
FAX Number: (601) 481-1305 Calendar System: Semester
URL: www.meridiancc.edu
Established: 1937 Annual Undergrad Tuition & Fees (In-District): $2,250
Enrollment: 3,948 Coed
Affiliation or Control: Local IRS Status: 501(c)3
Highest Offering: Associate Degree
Program: Occupational; 2-Year Principally Bachelor's Creditable
Accreditation: SC, ADNUR, CAHIIM, COARC, DA, DH, MLTAD, PNUR, PTAA, RAD, SURGT

01 President .... Dr. Scott D. ELLIOTT
10 Assoc Vice President for Finance .... Mrs. Amy BRAND
03 Vice President of Operations .... Mrs. Barbara JONES
07 Director of Admissions .... Mrs. Angela PAYNE
09 Dir Institutional Effectiveness .... Mrs. Cathy PARKER
32 Dean of Students .... Mrs. Soraya WELDEN
05 Dean of Academic Affs/General Educ .... Mr. Michael THOMPSON
62 Dean of Learning Resources .... Mr. Billy BEAL
30 Assoc Vice Pres for Development .... Mrs. Kathy BROOKSHIRE
18 Director Physical Plant .... Mr. Terry WILLIAMS
37 Director Financial Aid .... Ms. Nedra BRADLEY
15 Director Human Resources .... Ms. Shellye ESPEY
41 Athletic Director .... Mr. Sander ATKINSON
19 Chief of Security .... Mr. Shane WILLIAMS
40 Bookstore Manager .... Mrs. Martha WILLIAMS
27 College Promotions Coordinator .... Mrs. Kay THOMAS
36 Career Center Development Director .... Mrs. Darlene MAYATT
103 Assoc Vice Pres for Workforce Educ .... Dr. Richie MCALISTER

Miller-Motte Technical College (H)

12121 Highway 49, Gulfport MS 39503
Telephone: (228) 273-3400 Identification: 770845
Accreditation: ACICS

† Main campus is McCann School of Business & Technology in Pottsville, PA.

Millsaps College (I)

1701 N State Street, Jackson MS 39210-0001
County: Hinds FICE Identification: 002414
Unit ID: 175980
Telephone: (601) 974-1000 Carnegie Class: Bac/A&S

FAX Number: (601) 974-1059 Calendar System: Semester
URL: www.millsaps.edu
Established: 1890 Annual Undergrad Tuition & Fees: $32,520
Enrollment: 909 Coed
Affiliation or Control: United Methodist IRS Status: 501(c)3
Highest Offering: Master's
Program: Liberal Arts And General; Teacher Preparatory
Accreditation: SC, BUS, TED

Code	Title	Name
01	President	Dr. Rob PEARIGEN
05	VP/Dean of the College	Dr. Keith DUNN
10	Vice President for Finance	Ms. Louise BURNEY
30	VP for Institutional Advancement	Mr. Michael HUTCHISON
32	VP Student Life/Dean Students	Dr. Brit KATZ
50	Dean of the School of Management	Dr. Kimberly G. BURKE
84	Vice Pres Enrollment/Communications	Dr. Robert ALEXANDER
79	Assoc Dean Arts & Letters	Dr. David DAVIS
81	Associate Dean Sciences Division	Dr. Timothy J. WARD
82	Assoc Dean International Education	Dr. George J. BEY
37	Director of Financial Aid	Mr. Patrick JAMES
20	Director Academic Support Services	Ms. Janet R. LANGLEY
51	Director of Continuing Education	Dr. Nola R. GIBSON
08	College Librarian	Mr. Thomas W. HENDERSON
36	Director of Career Center	Ms. Tonya CRAFT
41	Director of Athletics	Mr. Tim WISE
15	Dir of Payroll & Employee Services	Ms. Patricia S. BRUCE
42	Chaplain	Rev. Christopher DONALD
28	Director of Multicultural Affairs	Ms. Sherryl E. WILBURN
21	Assistant Controller	Ms. Allison ROOKER
06	Coordinator of Records	Ms. Katherine ADAMS
09	Institutional Research Analyst	Mr. Jonathan BOGGESS
18	Director of Physical Plant	Mr. W. David WILKINSON
29	Director Alumni Relations	Ms. Maribeth K. WANN

Mississippi College (A)

200 W College Street, Clinton MS 39058-0001
County: Hinds FICE Identification: 002415
Unit ID: 176053
Telephone: (601) 925-3000 Carnegie Class: Master's L
FAX Number: (601) 925-3276 Calendar System: Semester
URL: www.mc.edu
Established: 1826 Annual Undergrad Tuition & Fees: $14,868
Enrollment: 5,070 Coed
Affiliation or Control: Southern Baptist IRS Status: 501(c)3
Highest Offering: Doctorate
Program: Liberal Arts And General; Teacher Preparatory; Professional
Accreditation: SC, ACBSP, #ARCPA, CACREP, CIDA, LAW, MUS, NURSE, SW, TED

Code	Title	Name
01	President	Dr. Lee G. ROYCE
04	Sr Exec Assistant to President	Ms. Patty TADLOCK
10	Chief Financial Officer	Ms. Donna LEWIS
05	Vice President Academic Affairs	Dr. Ronald HOWARD
32	VP Enrollment Svcs/Dean of Students	Dr. Jim TURCOTTE
45	Vice President Planning/Assessment	Dr. Debbie NORRIS
42	Vice Pres Christian Development	Dr. Eric PRATT
30	VP Inst Advan/Alum/Leg Coun to Pres	Dr. Bill TOWNSEND
11	Vice Pres Admin/Government Rels	Dr. Steve STANFORD
84	Director Enrollment Services	Mr. Mark HUGHES
06	Registrar	Ms. Ginger ROBBINS
09	Director of Institutional Research	Ms. Cassandra SESSUMS
08	Librarian	Ms. Kathleen HUTCHISON
21	Comptroller	Ms. Cheryl MOBLEY
27	Chief Information Officer	Mr. Bill CRANFORD
38	Director Counseling/Testing Center	Dr. Morgan BRYANT
15	Director Human Resources	Ms. Donna SMITH
29	Interim Director Alumni Affairs	Ms. Lori BOBO
26	Director Public Relations	Ms. Tracey HARRISON
18	Director of Physical Plant	Mr. Billy THORNTON
39	Director of Residence Life	Mr. Joseph ODENWALD
37	Director Student Financial Aid	Ms. Karon MCMILLAN
07	Director of Admissions	Mr. Kyle BRANTLEY
35	Assistant Director Student Life	Ms. Dannie WOODS
19	Director of Public Safety	Mr. Steven MCCRANEY
41	Director of Athletics	Mr. Mike JONES
96	Director of Purchasing	Ms. Dana ELMORE
40	Manager Bookstore	Ms. Karen BARNES
36	Director of Career Services	Ms. Jennifer MCGILL
81	Dean School of Science/Mathematics	Dr. Stan BALDWIN
50	Dean School of Business Admin	Dr. Marcelo EDUARDO
79	Dean School of Humanities	Dr. Jonathan RANDLE
53	Dean School of Education	Dr. Don LOCKE
73	Dean Sch Christian Studies/Fine Art	Dr. Wayne VAN HORN
61	Dean School of Law	Dr. Jim ROSENBLATT
58	Dean Grad School/Special Programs	Dr. Debbie NORRIS
66	Dean School of Nursing	Dr. Mary Jean PADGETT

Mississippi Delta Community College (B)

PO Box 668, Moorhead MS 38761-0668
County: Sunflower FICE Identification: 002416
Unit ID: 176008
Telephone: (662) 246-6322 Carnegie Class: Assoc/Pub-R-M
FAX Number: (662) 246-6321 Calendar System: Semester
URL: www.msdelta.edu
Established: 1926 Annual Undergrad Tuition & Fees (In-District): $2,450
Enrollment: 3,342 Coed
Affiliation or Control: Local IRS Status: 501(c)3
Highest Offering: Associate Degree
Program: Occupational; 2-Year Principally Bachelor's Creditable
Accreditation: SC, ADNUR, DH, MLTAD, PNUR, RAD

Code	Title	Name
01	President	Dr. Larry NABORS
03	Executive Vice President	Dr. Charles BARNETT
05	Vice President of Instruction	Ms. Magdalene ABRAHAM
10	Vice President of Business Services	Mrs. Marsha LEE
32	Vice President of Student Services	Dr. Edward RICE
11	VP of GHEC Administration	Dr. Mary Jean LUSH
88	Assoc VP GHEC Operations	Dr. MaryAnne BROCATO
84	Associate Vice Pres of Enrollment	Dr. Brent GREGORY
30	Assoc VP College Advancement/PR	Mr. Reed ABRAHAM
15	Director of Human Resources	Ms. Brenda VANLANDINGHAM
37	Director of Financial Aid	Mrs. Mary P. RODGERS
07	Director of Admissions	Dr. Brent GREGORY
13	Director Computer & Info Tech Svcs	Mr. Jimmy H. FREE
08	Director of Library Services	Mrs. Kristi BARIOLA
07	Director Counseling/Recruiting	Mrs. Stacy UPTON
18	Director of Maintenance	Mr. Rick DAVIS
88	Director of Special Events	Mrs. Corey SMITH
09	Director of Institutional Research	Ms. Carmela STATEN
04	Admin Asst to the President	Mrs. Debra BAKER
41	Athletic Director	Mr. Domino BELLIPANNI

Mississippi Gulf Coast Community College (C)

PO Box 609, Perkinston MS 39573-0012
County: Stone FICE Identification: 002417
Unit ID: 176071
Telephone: (601) 928-5211 Carnegie Class: Assoc/Pub-R-L
FAX Number: (601) 928-6386 Calendar System: Semester
URL: www.mgccc.edu
Established: 1911 Annual Undergrad Tuition & Fees (In-District): $2,712
Enrollment: 10,112 Coed
Affiliation or Control: Local IRS Status: 501(c)3
Highest Offering: Associate Degree
Program: Occupational; 2-Year Principally Bachelor's Creditable
Accreditation: SC, ADNUR, EMT, FUSER, MLTAD, PNUR, RAD, SURGT

Code	Title	Name
01	President	Dr. Mary S. GRAHAM
05	VP Instruction/Community Campus	Dr. Jason PUGH
10	Vice Pres Administration/Finance	Dr. Michael J. HEINDL
12	Vice President Perkinston Campus	Dr. Jay ALLEN
12	Vice Pres Jefferson Davis Campus	Dr. Susan SCAGGS
12	Vice Pres Jackson County Campus	Dr. Carmen WALTERS
46	VP Inst Advancement/Student Svcs	Ms. Michelle SEKUL
75	AVP Cmty Campus/CareerTech Ed	Mr. John SHOWS
09	Director Inst Research & Planning	Ms. Angela BRYAN
41	College Dean for Athletics	Mr. Ladd TAYLOR
106	Director of Distance Learning	Ms. Jennifer LEIMER
50	Director of Business Services	Mr. Wayne KUNTZ
21	Comptroller	Ms. Shelly FORD
06	Records Clerk Perkinston Campus	Ms. Latrice MCDONALD
06	Records Clerk Jackson Co Campus	Ms. Linda OTIS
06	Records Clerk Jeff Davis Campus	Ms. Mary JOYCE
20	Dean Instruct Jackson Co Campus	Dr. Jonathan WOODWARD
05	Dean of Instruction Jeff Davis Camp	Mr. Larry MILLER
05	Dean of Instruction Perkinston Camp	Dr. Jan MOODY
50	Dn Business Svcs Perkinston Campus	Ms. Tracy WILSON
50	Dn Business Svcs Jackson Co Campus	Ms. Tammy FRANKS
50	Dn Business Svcs Jeff Davis Campus	Ms. Stacy CARMICHAEL
75	Dn Career Tech/Wrkfc/Cmty Ed P Camp	Mr. Bobby GHOSAL
75	Dn Career/Tech/Wrkf/Cmty Ed JD Camp	Dr. Beverly CLARK
75	Dn Career/Tech/Wrkf/Cmty Ed JC Camp	Mr. Brock CLARK
08	Librarian Perkinston Campus	Dr. Brenda RIVERO
08	Librarian Jackson County Campus	Dr. Pam LADNER
08	Librarian Jefferson Davis Campus	Mr. Charles CLARK
32	Int Dean Student Svcs Perk Campus	Ms. Kashanta JACKSON
32	Dean Student Svcs Jackson Co Campus	Vacant
32	Dean Student Svcs Jeff Davis Campus	Vacant
88	Admin Dean George County Center	Ms. Cheryl BOND
07	Dir Admissions Perkinston Campus	Ms. Nichol GREEN
07	Dir Admissions Jack County Campus	Ms. Kay ROSONET
07	Dir Admissions Jeff Davis Campus	Ms. Leana WILSON
29	Alumni Relations Coordinator	Ms. Jenifer FRERIDGE
37	Financial Aid Director Jeff Davis	Dr. Stephanie MESSER-ROY
37	Financial Aid Director Perkinston	Ms. LeighAnn HUSSEY
37	Financial Aid Dir Jackson County	Ms. LaShanda CHAMBERLAIN
15	Director Human Resources	Mr. Glen MOORE
96	Dir Purchasing/Property Control	Ms. Lynn DEEGEN
18	Construction Manager	Mr. Jason BRELAND
26	Coord Institutional Development	Ms. Brenda DAVIS
04	Special Assistant to the President	Vacant
66	College Dean Nursing/Allied Health	Dr. Joan HENDRIX

Mississippi State University (D)

Mississippi State MS 39762-5708
County: Oktibbeha FICE Identification: 002423
Unit ID: 176080
Telephone: (662) 325-2323 Carnegie Class: RU/VH
FAX Number: (662) 325-7455 Calendar System: Semester
URL: www.msstate.edu
Established: 1878 Annual Undergrad Tuition & Fees (In-State): $6,672
Enrollment: 20,365 Coed
Affiliation or Control: State IRS Status: 501(c)3
Highest Offering: Doctorate
Program: Liberal Arts And General; Teacher Preparatory; Professional
Accreditation: SC, AAFCS, ART, BUS, BUSA, CACREP, CIDA, CORE, CS, DIETD, DIETI, ENG, FOR, LSAR, MUS, SCPSY, SPAA, SW, TED, VET

Code	Title	Name
01	President	Dr. Mark E. KEENUM
05	Provost/Executive Vice President	Dr. Jerome A. GILBERT
46	Vice Pres Research & Economic Devel	Dr. David SHAW
88	Vice Pres Agricult/Forestry/Vet Med	Dr. Gregory BOHACH
10	VP for Budget and Planning	Mr. Don ZANT
32	Vice President for Student Affairs	Dr. William L. KIBLER
30	VP for Development and Alumni	Mr. John P. RUSH
18	VP for Campus Services	Ms. Amy TUCK
41	Athletic Director	Mr. Scott STRICKLIN
43	General Counsel	Ms. Joan LUCAS
28	Dir Diversity/Inclusion	Dr. Tommy STEVENSON, JR.
04	Assistant to the President	Mr. Joe R. FARRIS
16	Director Human Resources Mgmt	Ms. Judith SPENCER
26	Exec Dir External Affairs	Mr. Kyle STEWARD
27	Director University Relations	Mr. Sid SALTER
86	Director Government Relations	Mr. John A. TOMLINSON
20	Assoc Provost Academic Affairs	Dr. Peter RYAN
13	Chief Information Officer	Mr. J. Mike RACKLEY
14	Dir Enterprise Information Systems	Ms. Rene HUNT
88	Exec Dir International Institute	Dr. Benjy MIKEL
48	Dean of Architecture/Art/Design	Mr. James L. WEST
49	Dean College Arts & Sciences	Dr. Greg DUNAWAY
50	Dean College Business	Dr. Sharon OSWALD
53	Dean of Education	Dr. Richard L. BLACKBOURN
58	Dean of Graduate Studies	Dr. Lori BRUCE
54	Dean College of Engineering	Dr. Achille MESSAC
65	Dean of Forest Resources	Dr. George M. HOPPER
47	Dean College Agriculture & Life Sci	Dr. George M. HOPPER
74	Dean of Veterinary Medicine	Dr. Kent H. HOBLET
12	Dean/Assoc VP Meridian Campus	Dr. Steven F. BROWN
08	Dean of Libraries	Ms. Frances N. COLEMAN
92	Dean Honors College	Dr. Christopher SNYDER
56	Dir Univ Extension Service	Dr. Gary JACKSON
88	Dir Agricultural Experiment Station	Dr. George M. HOPPER
06	Registrar	Dr. John R. DICKERSON
51	Dir Center for Distance Learning	Dr. Steve TAYLOR
36	Director Career Services/Coop Educ	Mr. Scott MAYNARD
35	Asst Vice Pres of Student Affairs	Mr. Bill BROYLES
32	Dean of Students	Dr. Thomas BOURGEOIS
07	Exec Director Enrollment	Dr. Philip BONFANTI
38	Director of Counseling Center	Dr. Leigh JENSEN
37	Director Student Financial Aid	Mr. Paul MCKINNEY
39	Director Housing/Residence Life	Dr. Ann BAILEY
09	Director Institutional Research	Dr. Tim CHAMBLEE
23	Director Student Health Center	Dr. Robert K. CADENHEAD
29	Director of Alumni Association	Dr. John RUSH
44	Director of Planned Giving	Mr. Vance BRISTOW
25	Director Sponsored Programs	Mrs. Jennifer EASLEY
88	Director Internal Audit	Ms. Leisa ERVIN
96	Director Procurement/Contracts	Mr. Don BUFFUM
19	Police Chief	Ms. Georgia LINDLEY

Mississippi University for Women (E)

1100 College Street, Columbus MS 39701-5800
County: Lowndes FICE Identification: 002422
Unit ID: 176035
Telephone: (877) 462-8439 Carnegie Class: Master's S
FAX Number: (662) 329-7297 Calendar System: Semester
URL: www.muw.edu
Established: 1884 Annual Undergrad Tuition & Fees (In-State): $5,640
Enrollment: 2,650 Coed
Affiliation or Control: State IRS Status: 501(c)3
Highest Offering: Doctorate
Program: Liberal Arts And General; Teacher Preparatory; Professional
Accreditation: SC, ACBSP, ADNUR, ART, MUS, NURSE, SP, TED

Code	Title	Name
01	President	Dr. Jim BORSIG
05	Provost/VP Academic Affairs	Dr. Dan HEIMMERMANN
10	Sr Vice Pres Administration & CFO	Ms. Nora R. MILLER
30	Exec Dir of University Relations	Ms. Maridith GEUDER
32	Vice Pres for Student Affairs	Dr. Jennifer MILES
20	Assoc Vice Pres Academic Affairs	Dr. Martin HATTON
04	Assistant to the President	Mr. Perry SANSING
49	Dean College Arts/Sciences	Dr. Thomas C. RICHARDSON
107	Dean Business/Professional Studies	Dr. Scott TOLLISON
53	Dean College Educ/Human Sciences	Dr. Sue JOLLY-SMITH
66	Dean College Nursing/Speech	Dr. Sheila V. ADAMS
08	Dean of Library Services	Ms. Gail P. GUNTER
58	Director Graduate Studies	Dr. Martin HATTON
88	Dir Roger Wicker Ctr Creative Lrng	Ms. Katherine BROWN
06	Registrar	Ms. Tammy PRATHER
92	Dir Honors College/Study Abroad	Dr. Thomas VELEK
88	Director Sponsored Programs	Mr. James DENNEY
29	Interim Director Alumni Relations	Ms. Lyndsay CUMBERLAND
30	Int Exec Dir Develop/Alumni Rels	Ms. Andrea N. STEVENS
44	Director Annual Giving	Ms. Brandy WILLIAMS
26	Director Public Affairs	Ms. Anika M. PERKINS
105	Dir Web Development/Univ Webmaster	Mr. Rich SOBOLEWSKI
21	Director University Accounting	Ms. Susan SOBLEY
88	Internal Auditor	Mr. Kenneth WIDNER
13	Director Information Tech Services	Mr. Larry W. JONES
07	Interim Director Admissions	Ms. Shelley MOSS
37	Director Financial Aid	Ms. Nicole PATRICK
15	Director Human Resources	Ms. Melanie H. FREEMAN
09	Director Institutional Research	Ms. Carla LOWERY
19	Interim Chief of Police	Mr. Danny PATTON
18	Director of Facilities Management	Mr. Dewey BLANSETT
96	Director Resources Management	Ms. Angie S. ATKINS
28	Director Student Life	Ms. Jessica HARPOLE
39	Director Community Living	Ms. Sirena PARKER
41	Exec Director Campus Recreation	Ms. Lindsey SHELNUT
40	Director Bookstore	Ms. Helana ROBINSON

88 Coord Student Retention Initiatives ... Ms. Kimberly GATHINGS
88 Coordinator of Academic Advising ... Ms. Rhonda THOMAS
88 General Manager of MUW Dining Svcs ... Mr. Eric DAWSON
85 Coord International Student Svcs ... Ms. Taylor EUBANKS

Mississippi Valley State University (A)

14000 Highway 82 W, Itta Bena MS 38941-1400
County: Leflore　FICE Identification: 002424
Unit ID: 176044
Telephone: (662) 254-9041　Carnegie Class: Master's M
FAX Number: (662) 254-6709　Calendar System: Semester
URL: www.mvsu.edu
Established: 1950　Annual Undergrad Tuition & Fees (In-State): $6,436
Enrollment: 2,479　Coed
Affiliation or Control: State　IRS Status: 501(c)3
Highest Offering: Master's
Program: Liberal Arts And General; Teacher Preparatory; Professional
Accreditation: SC, ACBSP, ART, CS, MUS, SW, TED

01 Acting President ... Dr. Alfred RANKINS, JR.
05 Interim Provost/VP Academic Affairs ... Dr. John D. JONES
10 Vice Pres for Business and Finance ... Vacant
32 Vice Pres for Student Affairs ... Dr. Jerald ADLEY
35 Assoc VP for Student Affairs ... Vacant
20 Int Assoc Provost Academic Affairs ... Dr. Vincent VENTURINI
20 Asst Provost for IRE/Strat Planning ... Dr. Sharon FREEMAN
21 Asst Vice Pres Business & Finance ... Vacant
100 Chief of Staff/Spec Asst to Pres ... Vacant
30 Vice Pres for Univ Advancement ... Vacant
51 Director of Continuing Education ... Dr. Ronald LOVE
58 Dean of Graduate College ... Vacant
41 Interim Director of Athletics ... Mr. Lee C. SMITH
06 Director of Student Records ... Mr. Jeff LOGGINS
07 Director Admission/Recruitment ... Ms. Jacqueline A. WILLIAMS
08 Head Librarian ... Ms. Mantra HENDERSON
15 Director of Human Resources ... Mr. Frank SOWELL
14 Director of Computer Center ... Mr. Steven L. PITCHFORD
37 Director of Financial Aid ... Mrs. Margaret SHERRER
29 Director of Alumni Relations ... Ms. Latacha DAVIS
26 Interim Director of Comm/Mktg ... Ms. Jennifer FREEMAN
19 Director University Police ... Mr. Robert SANDERS
18 Director Facilities/Physical Plant ... Mr. Tommy VERDELL
39 Interim Director Residential Life ... Mr. Lugene RUCKER
36 Director Career Development ... Ms. Tiffany WALLACE
38 Director Student Counseling ... Ms. Yolanda JONES
50 Int Chair of Business Department ... Dr. Jongchai KIM
53 Chair of Education Department ... Vacant
65 Int Chair Nat Sci/Env Health Dept ... Dr. Louis J. HALL
49 Dean College of Arts & Sciences ... Vacant
88 Chair English/Foreign Language ... Dr. John ZHENG
57 Chair Fine Arts Department ... Dr. Alphonso SANDERS
68 Actg Chair Health/Phys Ed/Rec Dept ... Mr. James WILKINSON
81 Chair of Math/Computer Science Dept ... Dr. Constance BLAND
54 Actg Chair of Industrial Tech Dept ... Dr. Richard MAXWELL
60 Chair Mass Communication Dept ... Dr. Samuel OSUNDE
88 Acting Chair Criminal Justice ... Dr. Vincent VENTURINI
70 Int Chair Social Work Department ... Dr. Catherine SINGLETON-WALKER
96 Director of Purchasing ... Mr. Billy SCOTT
28 Director of Cultural Diversity ... Vacant
84 Director Enrollment Management ... Vacant

Northeast Mississippi Community College (B)

101 Cunningham Boulevard, Booneville MS 38829-1731
County: Prentiss　FICE Identification: 002426
Unit ID: 176169
Telephone: (662) 728-7751　Carnegie Class: Assoc/Pub-R-M
FAX Number: (662) 728-1165　Calendar System: Semester
URL: www.nemcc.edu
Established: 1948　Annual Undergrad Tuition & Fees (In-District): $1,920
Enrollment: 3,508　Coed
Affiliation or Control: State/Local　IRS Status: 501(c)3
Highest Offering: Associate Degree
Program: Occupational; 2-Year Principally Bachelor's Creditable
Accreditation: SC, ADNUR, COARC, DH, MAC, MLTAD, RAD

01 President ... Johnny L. ALLEN
03 Executive Vice President ... Ricky G. FORD
103 Vice Pres Wrkfrce Training/Econ Dev ... Nadara L. COLE
26 Assoc Vice Pres of Public Info ... Tony FINCH
09 Assoc Vice Pres Planning/Research ... Craig-Ellis SASSSER
05 Dean of Instruction ... Charlie BARNETT
35 Assoc Dean of Student Activities ... Angie LANGLEY
08 Director Learning Resources ... Glenice STONE
96 Director of Purchasing ... Sheila OWENS
37 Director of Financial Aid ... Greg WINDHAM
38 Director Student Counseling ... Joey WILLIFORD
14 Director Computer Center ... Gregory SMITH
18 Director Facilities/Maintenance ... Mark HATFIELD
39 Director Residential Housing ... Rod COGGIN
32 Dean of Students/Athletic Director ... Ricky FORD
75 Director of Vocational Tech Educ ... Ritchie WILLIAMS
84 Dir of Enrollment Svcs/Registrar ... Lynn GIBSON
15 Human Resources Officer ... Tammie HARDIN

Northwest Mississippi Community College (C)

4975 Highway 51 N, Senatobia MS 38668-1703
County: Tate　FICE Identification: 002427
Unit ID: 176178
Telephone: (662) 562-3200　Carnegie Class: Assoc/Pub-R-L
FAX Number: (662) 562-3911　Calendar System: Semester
URL: www.northwestms.edu
Established: 1927　Annual Undergrad Tuition & Fees (In-State): $1,125
Enrollment: 8,600　Coed
Affiliation or Control: State　IRS Status: 501(c)3
Highest Offering: Associate Degree
Program: Occupational; 2-Year Principally Bachelor's Creditable
Accreditation: SC, ADNUR, COARC, EMT, #FUSER

01 President ... Dr. Gary Lee SPEARS
10 Vice President for Fiscal Affairs ... Mr. Gary MOSLEY
32 VP Student Affairs/Chief of Staff ... Mr. Dan SMITH
05 Vice Pres for Educational Affairs ... Dr. Chuck STRONG
20 Academic Dean ... Dr. Matthew S. DOMAS
103 Dean Career Tech Ed/Wrkfce Dev Trng ... Mr. Jerry NICHOLS
51 Dir Division of Continuing Educ ... Ms. Pam WOOTEN
84 Dean Enrollment Mgmt & Registrar ... Mr. Larry SIMPSON
35 Director of Student Personnel ... Mr. Mike DOTTOREY
27 Director of Communications ... Mrs. Sarah SAPP
37 Director of Financial Aid ... Mr. Terry BLAND
36 Dir Student Development Center ... Ms. Meg ROSS
08 Director of Learning Resources ... Mrs. Maggie MORAN
13 Director Management Information Sys ... Mrs. Amy LATHAM
07 Director of Recruiting ... Mrs. Jere HERRINGTON
09 Director Planning/Inst Research ... Dr. Carolyn WARREN
18 Director of Physical Plant Building ... Mr. Mike ROBISON
19 Chief of Campus Security ... Mr. Al DODSON
30 Director of Development/Alumni Rels ... Mrs. Sybil CANON
39 Director of Campus Life and Housing ... Mrs. Aime ANDERSON
40 Director Bookstore ... Mr. Joel BOYLES
41 Director of Athletics/Intramurals ... Mr. Cameron BLOUNT
96 Director of Purchasing ... Mrs. Barbara YOUNG
15 Personnel Officer ... Mrs. Rita DOWDLE
29 Director Alumni Relations ... Mrs. Dolores WOOTEN
21 Business Manager ... Ms. Ruthie CASTLE

Pearl River Community College (D)

101 Highway 11 N, Poplarville MS 39470-2298
County: Pearl River　FICE Identification: 002430
Unit ID: 176239
Telephone: (601) 403-1200　Carnegie Class: Assoc/Pub R M
FAX Number: (601) 403-1129　Calendar System: Semester
URL: www.prcc.edu
Established: 1909　Annual Undergrad Tuition & Fees (In-District): $2,450
Enrollment: 2,200　Coed
Affiliation or Control: State/Local　IRS Status: 501(c)3
Highest Offering: Associate Degree
Program: Occupational; 2-Year Principally Bachelor's Creditable
Accreditation: SC, ADNUR, COARC, DA, DH, MLTAD, OTA, PTAA, RAD, SURGT

01 President ... Dr. William A. LEWIS
05 VP for General Education ... Dr. Martha L. SMITH
32 VP Poplarville Campus/Hancock Ctr ... Dr. Adam BREERWOOD
10 VP for Business/Admn Services ... Mr. Roger A. KNIGHT
08 Director of College Libraries ... Ms. Tracy SMITH
26 Director of Public Relations ... Mr. Chuck ABADIE
84 VP for Enrollment Management ... Mr. Dow FORD
12 VP for Forrest County Operations ... Dr. Cecil BURT
14 Chief Technology Officer ... Mr. Steve HOWARD
18 Director of Physical Plant ... Mr. Craig TYNES
30 Director Development/Alumni Rels ... Mr. Ernest L. LOVELL, JR.
37 Director Student Financial Aid ... Ms. Valerie HORNE
41 Director of Athletics ... Mr. Jason FRANCIS
07 Director of Recruitment/Orientation ... Ms. Casey RAWLS
09 VP for Planning & Research ... Dr. Rebecca ASKEW
36 Dir Student Placement/Counselor ... Dr. Ann MOORE
31 VP Econ/Comm Development ... Dr. David S. ALSOBROOKS

Reformed Theological Seminary (E)

5422 Clinton Boulevard, Jackson MS 39209-3099
County: Hinds　FICE Identification: 009193
Unit ID: 176284
Telephone: (601) 923-1600　Carnegie Class: Not Classified
FAX Number: (601) 923-1654　Calendar System: 4/1/4
URL: www.rts.edu
Established: 1965　Annual Graduate Tuition & Fees: $14,150
Enrollment: 329　Coed
Affiliation or Control: Independent Non-Profit　IRS Status: 501(c)3
Highest Offering: Doctorate; No Undergraduates
Program: Professional
Accreditation: SC, MFCD, THEOL

00 Chancellor Emeritus ... Dr. Robert C. CANNADA, JR.
01 Acting CEO/Chief Operations Ofcr ... Mr. Steve WALLACE
10 Chief Financial Officer ... Mr. Bradley TISDALE
05 Chief Academic Officer ... Dr. Robert CARA
30 Chief Development Officer ... Dr. Lynwood C. PEREZ
12 President Charlotte Campus ... Dr. Michael J. KRUGER
12 President Orlando Campus ... Dr. Don W. SWEETING
12 President Jackson Campus ... Dr. Guy L. RICHARDSON
12 President RTS Global Campus ... Dr. Andrew J. PETERSON
12 President Atlanta Campus ... Mr. John T. SOWELL
12 President Washington DC ... Mr. Scott REDD
84 Senior VP Enrollment Management ... Vacant
44 Vice President for Development ... Mr. Robert PENNY
06 Registrar Jackson Campus ... Ms. Kim LEE
08 Library Director ... Mr. John MUETHER
32 Dean of Student Affairs/Admissions ... Mr. Brian C. GAULT
29 Dir Alum Rels/Dev/Supt Svcs Jackson ... Mrs. Stephanie J. HARTLEY
04 Assistant to Pres Jackson Campus ... Mrs. Wanda RUSHING
88 Dir Marriage & Fam Ther Jackson ... Dr. James B. HURLEY
18 Maintenance Director Jackson Campus ... Mr. Joe MORRIS
26 Dir of Institutional Communications ... Dr. Lynwood C. PEREZ
09 Director of Institutional Research ... Ms. Polly STONE
15 Director Personnel Svcs Jackson ... Ms. Linda COCHRAN

Rust College (F)

150 Rust Avenue, Holly Springs MS 38635-2328
County: Marshall　FICE Identification: 002433
Unit ID: 176318
Telephone: (662) 252-8000　Carnegie Class: Bac/A&S
FAX Number: (662) 252-6107　Calendar System: Semester
URL: www.rustcollege.edu
Established: 1866　Annual Undergrad Tuition & Fees: $8,900
Enrollment: 995　Coed
Affiliation or Control: United Methodist　IRS Status: 501(c)3
Highest Offering: Baccalaureate
Program: Liberal Arts And General
Accreditation: SC, SW, @TEAC

01 President ... Dr. David L. BECKLEY
30 Vice President for College Relation ... Dr. Ishmell H. EDWARDS
10 Vice President for Finance ... Mr. Donald MANNING-MILLER
108 Asst to Pres for Assess & Accred ... Dr. Sandra VAUGHN
05 VP for Academic Affairs ... Dr. Paul C. LAMPLEY
06 Registrar ... Mr. Clarence E. SMITH
08 Library Director ... Mrs. Anita W. MOORE
14 Director Computer Center ... Ms. Barbara NAYLOR MOORE
32 Dean of Student Affairs ... Mrs. Carolyn HYMON
35 Director Student Activities ... Mrs. Priscilla FISHER
37 Director of Financial Aid ... Mrs. Helen STREET
25 Director Contracts & Grants ... Mrs. Christine L. RATCLIFF
27 Director of Public Information ... Ms. Adrienne PHILLIPS
29 Director Alumni Development ... Ms. Jo Ann SCOTT
89 Chair First Year Experience ... Dr. Kenneth E. JONES
26 Director of Public Relations ... Vacant
21 Comptroller ... Vacant
84 Director Enrollment Services ... Mr. Johnny MCDONALD
23 Director Student Health Services ... Dr. Dianna HUGHES
39 Director Student Housing ... Mrs. Dorothy DONNELL
36 Director of Career Development ... Mr. John PEACHES
18 Director Physical Plant ... Mr. Robert CURRY
83 Division Chair Social Science ... Dr. Alfred J. STOVALL
15 Director Personnel Services ... Ms. Patricia PEGUES
19 Chief of Security ... Mr. Claude GLEETON
30 Director of Development ... Ms. Jo Ann SCOTT
40 Bookstore Manager ... Mrs. Patricia HARRIS
42 College Chaplain ... Rev. Annie TRAVIS
96 Director of Purchasing ... Ms. Ollie BOWENS
28 Director of Diversity ... Miss Patricia PEGUES
50 Division Chair Business ... Mr. Richard FREDERICK
53 Division Chair Education ... Dr. Leon HOWARD
79 Division Chair Humanities ... Dr. Margaret DELASHMIT
81 Chair Division Science & Math ... Dr. Frank YEH
70 Chair Department of Social Work ... Dr. Gemma BECKLEY

Southeastern Baptist College (G)

4229 Highway 15 N, Laurel MS 39440-1096
County: Jones　FICE Identification: 002435
Unit ID: 176336
Telephone: (601) 426-6346　Carnegie Class: Spec/Faith
FAX Number: (601) 426-6347　Calendar System: Semester
URL: www.southeasternbaptist.edu
Established: 1948　Annual Undergrad Tuition & Fees: $4,000
Enrollment: 57　Coed
Affiliation or Control: Baptist　IRS Status: 501(c)3
Highest Offering: Baccalaureate
Program: 2-Year Principally Bachelor's Creditable; Liberal Arts And General; Religious Emphasis
Accreditation: BI

01 Interim President ... Vacant
03 Executive Vice President ... Vacant
05 Academic Dean ... Dr. Aaron L. PARKER
32 Dean of Student Services ... Dr. Daryle COATS
13 Director Information Technology ... Mr. Hubert DYESS
07 Director of Admissions ... Mr. Ronnie KITCHENS
06 Registrar ... Mrs. Emma BOND
37 Financial Aid Administrator ... Mr. Ronnie KITCHENS
08 Director of Library ... Mrs. Amy E. HINTON

Southwest Mississippi Community College (H)

1156 College Drive, Summit MS 39666-9029
County: Pike　FICE Identification: 002436
Unit ID: 176354
Telephone: (601) 276-2000　Carnegie Class: Assoc/Pub-R-S
FAX Number: (601) 276-3888　Calendar System: Semester
URL: www.smcc.edu
Established: 1918　Annual Undergrad Tuition & Fees (In-District): $2,090
Enrollment: 2,083　Coed

Affiliation or Control: Local IRS Status: 501(c)3
Highest Offering: Associate Degree
Program: Occupational; 2-Year Principally Bachelor's Creditable
Accreditation: SC, ADNUR, CAHIIM

01	President	Dr. Steve BISHOP
05	Vice President of Academic Affairs	Ms. Alicia SHOWS
10	Vice President of Financial Affairs	Mr. Grady SMITH
32	Vice President of Student Affairs	Mr. Bill ASHLEY
75	Vice Pres Career & Tech Education	Mr. Jeremy SMITH
06	Registrar/Vice President Admissions	Mr. Matthew CALHOUN
37	Director Student Financial Aid	Mrs. Stacey HODGES
09	Director of Institutional Research	Dr. Bill TUCKER
08	Librarian	Mrs. Natalie MCMAHON

Tougaloo College (A)

500 West County Line Road, Tougaloo MS 39174-9999
County: Madison FICE Identification: 002439
Unit ID: 176406
Telephone: (601) 977-7730 Carnegie Class: Bac/A&S
FAX Number: (601) 977-7739 Calendar System: Semester
URL: www.tougaloo.edu
Established: 1869 Annual Undergrad Tuition & Fees: $9,740
Enrollment: 934 Coed
Affiliation or Control: United Church Of Christ IRS Status: 501(c)3
Highest Offering: Baccalaureate
Program: Liberal Arts And General
Accreditation: SC

01	President	Dr. Beverly W. HOGAN
05	Provost/Vice Pres Academic Affairs	Dr. Bettye Parker SMITH
32	Vice President for Student Affairs	Mr. Fred ALEXANDER
30	Act Vice Pres Institutional Advance	Dr. Delores Bolden STAMPS
10	Vice Pres Finance Administration	Dr. Cynthia MELVIN
18	Vice Pres for Facilities Management	Mr. Kelle MENOGAN
20	Asst Provost/VP Academic Affairs	Dr. Candice Love JACKSON
84	Asst VP for Enrollment Management	Mr. Steven SMITH
35	Asst Vice Pres for Student Affairs	Mrs. Gladys J. JONES
88	Ex Dir Ntnl Transp Sec Ctr of Excel	Vacant
08	Director of Library Services	Mrs. Orthella P. MOMAN
13	Chief Information Officer	Mr. Terry J. JORDAN
37	Director of Student Financial Aid	Ms. Maria THOMAS
09	Director Inst Research/Assess/Plng	Dr. Larry JOHNSON
06	Registrar	Ms. Carolyn L. EVANS
15	Director Human Resources	Ms. Doretha PRESLEY
26	Dir Communications/Public Affairs	Mr. Danny L. JONES
29	Director of Alumni Affairs	Mrs. Doris BRIDGEMAN
07	Director of Admissions	Ms. Junoesque JACOBS
36	Director of Career Services	Mrs. Gladys J. JONES
44	Director of Advancement Services	Mrs. Sanette LANGSTON-SMITH
46	Dir of Sponsored Programs/Research	Dr. Motice BRUCE
88	Director of TRiO	Dr. Valvia WILSON
38	Director of Counseling Services	Dr. Rosie HARPER
96	Purchasing Agent	Ms. Easter COMMON
102	Dir Corporation & Foundation Rels	Vacant

University of Mississippi (B)

University MS 38677-9999
County: Lafayette FICE Identification: 002440
Unit ID: 176017
Telephone: (662) 915-7211 Carnegie Class: RU/H
FAX Number: (662) 915-7010 Calendar System: Semester
URL: www.olemiss.edu
Established: 1844 Annual Undergrad Tuition & Fees (In-State): $6,660
Enrollment: 18,794 Coed
Affiliation or Control: State IRS Status: 501(c)3
Highest Offering: Doctorate
Program: Liberal Arts And General; Teacher Preparatory; Professional
Accreditation: SC, ART, BUS, BUSA, CACREP, CLPSY, CS, @DIETC, DIETD, ENG, FEPAC, JOUR, LAW, MUS, NRPA, PHAR, SP, SW, TED, THEA

01	Chancellor	Dr. Daniel W. JONES
26	Chief Communications Officer	Mr. Thomas E. EPPES
05	Provost/Vice Chanc Academic Affairs	Dr. Morris H. STOCKS
10	Vice Chanc Finance & Administration	Mr. Larry D. SPARKS
32	Vice Chancellor Student Life	Dr. Brandi HEPHNER-LABANC
46	Vice Chanc Research/Sponsored Pgms	Dr. Alice M. CLARK
35	Asst Vice Chanc Student Affairs	Dr. Thomas J. REARDON
87	Int Asst Prov Summer Sch/Outreach	Dr. Linda CHITWOOD
20	Asst VC Academic Affairs/Registrar	Dr. Charlotte FANT
20	Associate Provost	Dr. Maurice R. EFTINK
20	Associate Provost	Dr. Noel E. WILKIN
85	Ast Prov/Ast to Chanc Multicul Affs	Dr. Donald R. COLE
08	Dean of Libraries	Ms. Julia RHOLES
13	Chief Information Officer	Dr. Kathryn F. GATES
30	Sr Executive Dir of Development	Ms. Deborah S. VAUGHN
29	Exec Director of Alumni Affairs	Mr. Timothy L. WALSH
37	Director of Financial Aid	Ms. Laura DIVEN-BROWN
36	Director Career Center	Ms. Toni D. AVANT
41	Director Intercollegiate Athletics	Mr. Ross BJORK
15	Director of Human Resources	Mr. Clayton H. JONES
18	Director of Physical Plant	Mr. Ashton PEARSON
19	Director Univ Police/Campus Safety	Chief Calvin SELLERS
38	Director of Counseling Center	Dr. Marc K. SHOWALTER
23	Director University Health Service	Vacant
39	Dir of Student Housing/Res Life	Mr. Lionel MATEN
09	Director Institutional Research	Ms. Mary M. HARRINGTON
22	Exec Dir Equal Oppty/Reg Compliance	Ms. Wilma F. WEBBER-COLBERT
04	Assistant to the Chancellor	Ms. Sue T. KEISER
43	General Counsel/Chief of Staff	Dr. Lee TYNER
96	Director of Procurement Services	Mr. James R. WINDHAM
06	Associate Registrar	Mrs. Denise KNIGHTON
21	Controller	Mr. Sam THOMAS
07	Interim Director of Admissions	Ms. Jennifer A. SIMMONS
84	Director of Enrollment Services	Mr. Whitman SMITH
50	Dean School of Business Admin	Dr. Kendall B. CYREE
49	Dean College of Liberal Arts	Dr. Glenn W. HOPKINS
81	Dean School of Applied Sciences	Dr. Velmer S. BURTON, JR.
53	Dean School of Education	Dr. David ROCK
54	Dean School of Engineering	Dr. Alex CHENG
61	Dean School of Law	Dr. I. Richard GERSHON
67	Dean of the School of Pharmacy	Dr. David D. ALLEN
88	Dean School of Accountancy	Dr. W. Mark WILDER
60	Dean Journalism & New Media	Dr. H. Will NORTON

University of Mississippi Medical Center (C)

2500 N State Street, Jackson MS 39216-4505
County: Hinds FICE Identification: 004688
Unit ID: 176026
Telephone: (601) 984-1000 Carnegie Class: Spec/Med
FAX Number: (601) 984-1013 Calendar System: Semester
URL: www.umc.edu
Established: 1955 Annual Undergrad Tuition & Fees (In-State): $3,330
Enrollment: 2,734 Coed
Affiliation or Control: State IRS Status: 501(c)3
Highest Offering: Doctorate
Program: Professional; Nursing Emphasis
Accreditation: SC, CAHIIM, CYTO, DENT, DH, IPSY, MED, MT, NMT, NURSE, OT, PTA, RAD

01	Vice Chancellor Health Affairs	Dr. James E. KEETON
63	Assoc VC Health Affs/Vice Dean SOM	Dr. LouAnn WOODWARD
100	Chief of Staff to Vice Chancellor	Dr. Brian RUTLEDGE
10	Chief Financial Officer	Mr. James WENTZ
21	Comptroller	Mr. Sam E. SMITH
11	Chief Administrative Officer	Vacant
46	Associate Vice Chanc Research	Dr. John E. HALL
05	Interim Chief Academic Officer	Dr. LouAnn WOODWARD
20	Deputy Chief Academic Officer	Dr. Robin ROCKHOLD
28	Assoc Vice Chanc Multicultural Affs	Dr. Jasmine P. TAYLOR
88	Assoc VC for Rural Hlth & Hlth Disp	Dr. Bettina BEECH
23	Assoc Vice Chanc Clinical Affairs	Vacant
17	CEO Univ Hosp & Clinics	Mr. Kevin COOK
88	Sr Advisor to VC for External Aff	Dr. Claude BRUNSON
17	Chief Medical Officer	Dr. William CLELAND
88	Sr Advisor to VC for Internal Aff	Dr. Martin H. MCMULLAN
43	Interim Chief Legal Officer	Mrs. Jamie CHRISTIAN
26	Chief Public Affs & Comm Officer	Mr. Tom FORTNER
26	Chief Marketing Officer	Ms. Rondah MARKS
27	Chief Information Officer	Mr. David CHOU
15	Chief Human Resources Officer	Mr. Michael ESTES
66	Dean School of Nursing	Dr. Kim HOOVER
58	Dean Sch Grad Stds Health Sciences	Dr. Joey GRANGER
76	Dean Sch Health Related Profess	Dr. Jessica H. BAILEY
52	Dean of School of Dentistry	Dr. Gary W. REEVES
67	Assoc Dean for Clinical Affairs	Dr. Leigh A. ROSS
63	Assoc Dean-Graduate Medical Educ	Dr. Shirley SCHLESSINGER
09	Director Institutional Research	Dr. David G. FOWLER
19	Director Police & Logistical Svcs	Mr. Arty E. GIROD
18	Director Physical Facilities	Mr. Ivory BOGAN
30	Director Development	Ms. Sara MERRICK
88	Director of Accreditation	Dr. Mitzi NORRIS
29	Assoc Director Alumni Affairs	Mr. Geoffrey MITCHELL
38	Director Academic Counseling	Dr. Natalie W. GAUGHF
37	Director Student Financial Aid	Ms. Carrie COOPER
32	Chief Student Affairs Officer	Dr. Jerry CLARK
06	Dir Student Records & Registrar	Ms. Barbara M. WESTERFIELD
08	Director Rowland Medical Library	Ms. Susan B. CLARK

University of Phoenix Jackson Campus (D)

120 Stone Creek Blvd, Suite 200,
Flowood MS 39232-8205
Telephone: (601) 664-9500 Identification: 770215
Accreditation: &NH, ACBSP

† Main campus is University of Phoenix in Tempe, AZ.

University of Southern Mississippi (E)

118 College Drive, #5001, Hattiesburg MS 39406-0001
County: Forrest FICE Identification: 002441
Unit ID: 176372
Telephone: (601) 266-1000 Carnegie Class: RU/H
FAX Number: (601) 266-5756 Calendar System: Semester
URL: www.usm.edu
Established: 1910 Annual Undergrad Tuition & Fees (In-State): $6,744
Enrollment: 16,468 Coed
Affiliation or Control: State IRS Status: 501(c)3
Highest Offering: Doctorate
Program: Liberal Arts And General; Teacher Preparatory; Professional
Accreditation: SC, AAFCS, ANEST, ART, AUD, BUS, BUSA, CIDA, CLPSY, CONST, COPSY, CS, DANCE, DIETD, DIETI, ENGT, JOUR, KIN, LIB, MFCD, MT, MUS, NRPA, NURSE, PH, PHLEB, SCPSY, SP, SW, TED, THEA

01	President	Dr. Rodney D. BENNETT
04	Assistant to the President	Vacant
05	Provost	Dr. Denis WIESENBURG
10	VP of Finance & Administration	Dr. Douglas VINZANT
12	Vice Pres for Gulf Coast Campus	Dr. Frances LUCAS
32	Vice President for Student Affairs	Dr. Joseph S. PAUL
30	Vice President Advancement	Mr. Bob PIERCE
20	Associate Provost Academic Affairs	Dr. William W. POWELL
20	Assoc Provost Academic Affairs	Dr. Cynthia EASTERLING
46	Vice President Research	Dr. Gordon CANNON
37	Asst VP Student Affs & Finan Aid	Dr. Kristi MOTTER
35	Asc Vice President Student Affairs	Mr. Sid GONSOULIN
53	Dean College Education/Psychology	Dr. Ann BLACKWELL
49	Dean College Arts & Letters	Dr. Steven MOSER
50	Dean College Business	Dr. Faye GILBERT
72	Dean College Science/Technology	Dr. Joe WHITEHEAD
92	Dean of Honors College	Dr. David DAVIES
76	Dean College Health	Dr. Michael FORSTER
58	Dean Graduate School	Dr. Susan SILTANEN
08	Dean/University Librarian	Dr. Melanie NORTON
18	Director Physical Plant	Mr. Chris CRENSHAW
14	Chief Information Technology Ofcr	Mr. David SLIMAN
41	Athletic Director	Mr. Jeff HAMMOND
06	Registrar	Mr. Greg PIERCE
25	Dir Research & Sponsored Programs	Mr. Syd CONNOR
09	Director of Institutional Research	Mrs. Michelle ARRINGTON
45	Dir of Institutional Effectiveness	Mrs. Kathryn LOWERY
29	Alumni Activities/Exec Director	Mr. Jerry DEFATTA
36	Director Career Planning/Placement	Mr. Russell ANDERSON
21	Controller	Ms. Allyson EASTERWOOD
22	Director of Affirmative Action	Ms. Rebecca WOODRICK
38	Director of Counseling Center	Dr. Deena CRAWFORD
23	Director of Health Services	Dr. Virginia CRAWFORD
39	Director of Residence Life	Dr. Scott BLACKWELL
15	Director of Human Resources	Mrs. Linda RASMUSSEN
94	Director of Women's Studies	Dr. Ellen WEINAUR
96	Director Purchasing/Procuremnt Svcs	Mr. Steve BALLEW
07	Int Director of Admissions	Ms. Amanda KING
26	Chief Public Relations Officer	Mr. James P. COLL

Virginia College (F)

920 Cedar Lake Road, Biloxi MS 39532-2107
Telephone: (228) 546-9100 Identification: 666073
Accreditation: ACICS, MAAB

† Main campus is Virginia College in Birmingham, AL.

Virginia College (G)

5841 Ridgewood Road, Jackson MS 39211
Telephone: (601) 977-0960 Identification: 666032
Accreditation: ACICS, MAAB

† Main campus is Virginia College in Birmingham, AL.

Wesley Biblical Seminary (H)

787 E Northside Drive, Jackson MS 39206-4945
County: Hinds FICE Identification: 025162
Unit ID: 176451
Telephone: (601) 366-8880 Carnegie Class: Spec/Faith
FAX Number: (601) 366-8832 Calendar System: Semester
URL: www.wbs.edu
Established: 1974 Annual Graduate Tuition & Fees: $12,700
Enrollment: 106 Coed
Affiliation or Control: Interdenominational IRS Status: 501(c)3
Highest Offering: Master's; No Undergraduates
Program: Professional; Religious Emphasis
Accreditation: THEOL

01	President	Dr. John E. NEIHOF, JR.
05	Vice President Academic Affairs	Vacant
32	VP of Business/Student Development	Vacant
08	Director of Library Services	Vacant
10	Business Officer	Vacant
18	Director of Operations	Mr. Ken MONEY

William Carey University (I)

498 Tuscan Avenue, Hattiesburg MS 39401-5461
County: Forrest FICE Identification: 002447
Unit ID: 176479
Telephone: (601) 318-6051 Carnegie Class: Master's L
FAX Number: (601) 318-6494 Calendar System: Trimester
URL: www.wmcarey.edu
Established: 1892 Annual Undergrad Tuition & Fees: $14,580
Enrollment: 4,008 Coed
Affiliation or Control: Southern Baptist IRS Status: 501(c)3
Highest Offering: Doctorate
Program: Liberal Arts And General; Teacher Preparatory; Professional
Accreditation: SC, MUS, NURSE, @OSTEO, TED

01	President/Chief Executive Officer	Dr. Tommy KING
05	Vice President of Academic Affairs	Dr. Garry M. BRELAND
10	Vice Pres Business Affs/CFO	Mr. Grant GUTHRIE
32	Dean of Student Services	Mrs. Valerie BRIDGEFORTH
46	Vice President Inst Effectiveness	Dr. Bennie R. CROCKETT
30	Assoc VP Athletics/Advancement	Mr. Richard VOGEL
63	Dean College Osteopathic Medicine	Dr. James TURNER
12	Admin Dean Tradition Campus	Mr. Gerald BRACEY
04	Executive Assistant to President	Ms. Barbara HAMILTON
50	Dean School of Business	Dr. Cheryl DALE
53	Dean School of Education	Dr. Barry MORRIS

83 Dean Sch Natural/Behavioral Science ....Dr. Frank BAUGH
66 Dean School of Nursing ....Dr. Janet WILLIAMS
49 Dean School of Arts & Letters ....Dr. Myron NOONKESTER
64 Dean Winters School of Music ....Dr. Don ODOM
73 Dean School of Missions ....Dr. Daniel CALDWELL
84 Dean of Enrollment Management ....Mr. William N. CURRY
58 Dean of Graduate Studies ....Dr. Frank BAUGH
20 Assoc Dean of Academic Services ....Dr. Les STEVERSON
09 Director Institutional Research ....Dr. William T. RIVERO
06 Registrar ....Mrs. Gayle KNIGHT
08 Director of Libraries ....Mrs. Sherry LAUGHLIN
29 Alumni Director ....Mrs. Cindy COFIELD
26 Chief Public Relations Officer ....Vacant
13 Director of Information Technology ....Mr. Jeff ANDREWS
92 Director of Honors Program ....Dr. Scott HUMMEL
21 Director of Budget Management ....Mr. Grant GUTHRIE
41 Athletic Director ....Mr. Steven H. KNIGHT
18 Dir Facilities/Grounds/Maintenance ....Mr. Robert BLEVINS
35 Dir Student Svcs Tradition Campus ....Mr. James M. HARRISON
66 Associate Dean Nursing NO Campus ....Dr. Marilyn COOKSEY
21 Dir Business Svcs Tradition Campus ....Mr. Gerald BRACEY
12 Director of Keesler Center ....Ms. Amanda KNESAL
15 Director Personnel Services ....Ms. Deidre SHOWS
19 Director Campus Security ....Mr. Bob BLEVINS
88 Coord of Instructional Technology ....Mr. David J. BROCKWAY
12 Coordinator New Orleans Campus ....Mr. LaRue HATTEN
07 Director of Admissions ....Mrs. Alissa KING

MISSOURI

A. T. Still University of Health Sciences (A)

800 W Jefferson Street, Kirksville MO 63501-1497
County: Adair FICE Identification: 002477
Unit ID: 177834
Telephone: (660) 626-2391 Carnegie Class: Spec/Med
FAX Number: (660) 626-2672 Calendar System: Semester
URL: www.atsu.edu
Established: 1892 Annual Graduate Tuition & Fees: N/A
Enrollment: 3,141 Coed
Affiliation or Control: Independent Non-Profit IRS Status: 501(c)3
Highest Offering: First Professional Degree; No Undergraduates
Program: Professional
Accreditation: NH, OSTEO

01 President ....Dr. Craig PHELPS
05 Sr VP Academic Affairs ....Dr. Norman GEVITZ
45 VP Planning and Assessment ....Dr. Michael MCMANIS
63 Dean of KCOM ....Dr. Margaret WILSON
32 VP Student Affairs ....Mrs. Lori HAXTON
30 Interim VP for Univ Advancement ....Mr. Randy ROGERS
43 VP & General Counsel ....Mr. Matthew HEEREN
46 VP Inst Res Grants & Info Systems ....Dr. John HEARD
26 Co-Interim VP Comm & Marketing ....Ms. Virginia HALTERMAN
26 Co-Interim VP Comm & Marketing ....Mr. Greg RUBENSTEIN
52 Dean MO Sch of Dentistry/Oral Hlth ....Dr. Chris HALLIDAY
88 Interim Dean School of Hlth Mgmt ....Dr. Don ALTMAN
52 Dean AZ Sch of Dentistry/Oral Hlth ....Dr. Jack DILLENBERG
76 Dean Arizona Sch of Health Sciences ....Dr. Randy DANIELSEN
63 Dean School of Osteo Med in Arizona ....Dr. Kay KALOUSEK
10 Vice President for Finance/CFO ....Mrs. Monnie HARRISON
35 Assoc VP AZ-Student Affairs ....Mrs. Beth POPPRE
13 Asst VP Info Technologies/Services ....Mr. Bryan KRUSNIAK
07 Asst VP Admissions ....Dr. David KOENECKE
88 VP Univ Strategic Partnerships ....Dr. Gary CLOUD
12 VP AZ Operations & San Diego Initia ....Dr. O.T WENDEL
88 Associate VP Sponsored Programs ....Mrs. Gaylah SUBLETTE
04 Asst to Pres & Secretary to BoT ....Mrs. Norine EITEL
06 Registrar ....Dr. Deanna HUNSAKER
08 Director of Library ....Mr. Michael KRONENFIELD
15 Director of Human Resources ....Mrs. Donna BROWN
18 Director Facilities/Plant Operation ....Mr. Robert EHRLICH
22 Affirmative Action Officer ....Mrs. Donna BROWN
37 Dir Student Financial Assistance ....Mr. Steven JORDEN
38 Director of Student Counseling ....Mr. Thomas VAN VLECK
96 Director of Purchasing ....Mr. Corey LOUDER
29 Director Alumni Relations ....Mr. Bob BASHAM

† Arizona campus accreditation includes ARPCA, AUD, DENT, OSTEO, OT, PTA.

American College of Technology (B)

2300 Frederick Avenue, Saint Joseph MO 64506
County: Buchanan FICE Identification: 041187
Unit ID: 457688
Telephone: (816) 279-7000 Carnegie Class: Not Classified
FAX Number: (888) 890-8190 Calendar System: Other
URL: www.acot.edu
Established: 2001 Annual Undergrad Tuition & Fees: $8,720
Enrollment: 480 Coed
Affiliation or Control: Proprietary IRS Status: Proprietary
Highest Offering: Master's
Program: Occupational; 2-Year Principally Bachelor's Creditable; Technical Emphasis
Accreditation: DETC

01 President ....Mr. Sam ATIEH
11 Director/Chief of Operations ....Mr. Lute ATIEH
37 Financial Aid Administrator ....Mr. Calvin HAYNES

Anthem College (C)

9001 State Line Road, Kansas City MO 64114
Telephone: (816) 444-4300 Identification: 770735
Accreditation: ACICS

† Main campus is Anthem College in Phoenix, AZ.

Anthem College (D)

13723 Riverport Drive, Suite 103,
Maryland Heights MO 63043-4819
County: Saint Louis FICE Identification: 022392
Unit ID: 176549
Telephone: (314) 595-3400 Carnegie Class: Assoc/PrivFP
FAX Number: (314) 739-5133 Calendar System: Other
URL: www.anthemcollege.edu
Established: 1981 Annual Undergrad Tuition & Fees: $24,310
Enrollment: 220 Coed
Affiliation or Control: Proprietary IRS Status: Proprietary
Highest Offering: Associate Degree
Program: Occupational
Accreditation: ABHES, SURTEC

01 Executive Director ....Mr. Jeremiah HOOD

Anthem College-Fenton (E)

645 Gravois Bluffs Boulevard, Fenton MO 63026
Telephone: (636) 326-7300 Identification: 770530
Accreditation: ABHES

† Main campus is Anthem College in Maryland Heights, MO.

Aquinas Institute of Theology (F)

23 S Spring Avenue, Saint Louis MO 63108-3323
County: City of Saint Louis FICE Identification: 001632
Unit ID: 176600
Telephone: (314) 256-8800 Carnegie Class: Spec/Faith
FAX Number: (314) 256-8888 Calendar System: Semester
URL: www.ai.edu
Established: 1951 Annual Graduate Tuition & Fees: $16,230
Enrollment: 206 Coed
Affiliation or Control: Roman Catholic IRS Status: 501(c)3
Highest Offering: Doctorate; No Undergraduates
Program: Professional; Religious Emphasis
Accreditation: NH, THEOL

01 President ....Rev. David G. CARON
05 Academic Dean ....Rev. Gregory HEILLE
10 Director of Finance ....Mr. Thomas BARBARAK
06 Registrar ....Mrs. Erin HAMMOND
30 Director of Inst Advancement ....Mrs. Barbara MAYNARD
32 Dean of Students ....Rev. George BOUDREAU
07 Director Admissions/Financial Aid ....Mr. David WERTHMANN
26 Director of Marketing ....Mr. Thomas BARBARAK

The Art Institute of St. Louis (G)

1520 South Fifth Street, Suite 107,
Saint Charles MO 63303
Telephone: (636) 688-9281 Identification: 770738
Accreditation: ACICS

† Main campus is The Art Institute of Phoenix in Phoenix, AZ.

Avila University (H)

11901 Wornall Road, Kansas City MO 64145-9990
County: Jackson FICE Identification: 002449
Unit ID: 176628
Telephone: (816) 942-8400 Carnegie Class: Master's M
FAX Number: (816) 942-3362 Calendar System: Semester
URL: www.avila.edu
Established: 1916 Annual Undergrad Tuition & Fees: $24,950
Enrollment: 1,908 Coed
Affiliation or Control: Roman Catholic IRS Status: 501(c)3
Highest Offering: Master's
Program: Liberal Arts And General; Teacher Preparatory; Professional
Accreditation: NH, IACBE, NURSE, RAD, SW

01 President ....Dr. Ron SLEPITZA
05 Provost/Vice Pres Academic Affairs ....Sr. Marie Joan HARRIS
20 Vice Provost for Academic Affairs ....Dr. Sue KING
10 Vice Pres for Finance/Admin Svcs ....Mr. Paul G. BOOKMEYER
26 Asst VP Marketing/Communication ....Mrs. Ann O'MEARA
30 Chief Development Officer ....Ms. Angela HEER
32 Dean of Students ....Ms. Darby GOUGH
07 Director of Admission ....Mr. Brandon JOHNSON
06 Registrar ....Mrs. Dana R. SHIRLEY
08 Librarian ....Ms. Kathleen FINEGAN
37 Director of Financial Aid ....Ms. Crystal BRUNTZ
42 Dir Mission Effect & Campus Ministr ....Mr. David M. ARMSTRONG
21 Controller ....Mr. Joseph H. SJUTS
29 Director Alumni & Donor Relations ....Mrs. Vanessa HERRING
41 Athletic Director ....Mr. Gary GALLUP
15 Director of Human Resources ....Ms. Janet MCMANUS
18 Chief Facilities/Physical Plant ....Mr. Mike STUCKEY
40 Bookstore Manager ....Mr. John A. TARANTO
38 Coord Counseling & Career Services ....Ms. Susan WULFF

Baptist Bible College (I)

628 E Kearney St, Springfield MO 65803-3498
County: Greene FICE Identification: 013208
Unit ID: 176664
Telephone: (417) 268-6013 Carnegie Class: Spec/Faith
FAX Number: (417) 268-6694 Calendar System: Semester
URL: www.gobbc.edu
Established: 1950 Annual Undergrad Tuition & Fees: $7,090
Enrollment: 321 Coed
Affiliation or Control: Baptist IRS Status: 501(c)3
Highest Offering: First Professional Degree
Program: Teacher Preparatory; Professional; Religious Emphasis
Accreditation: NH, BI

01 President ....Mr. Mark L. MILIONI
05 Vice President of Academic Affairs ....Dr. Greg T. CHRISTOPHER
10 Chief Financial Officer ....Vacant
32 Senior Director of Student Life ....Mr. John L. SLAYDEN
18 Chief Facilities/Physical Plant ....Mr. Chris C. WILLIAMS
88 Director of Campus Advising ....Dr. Joseph K. GLEASON
06 Registrar/Dir Enrollment Svcs ....Mr. Terry A. ALLCORN
37 Director of Financial Aid ....Mr. Bob L. KOTULSKI
38 Campus Counselor ....Mr. Bill A. PIATT
39 Director of Resident Life ....Mr. Bill J. LEVERGOOD
15 Director of Human Resources ....Vacant
19 Director Security/Safety ....Mr. Stephen J. CRANE
41 Athletic Director ....Mr. Mark HEDGER
40 Bookstore ....Mrs. Julie BECK
08 Director of Library Services ....Mr. Jon JONES
09 Director of Institutional Research ....Mrs. Lesa M. CHASTAIN
106 Dean of Online Education ....Ms. Cheryl PAGE
72 Director of Technology ....Vacant
108 Director of Campus Assessment ....Mrs. Lesa M. CHASTAIN
21 Business Officer ....Mr. Jason L. TODD
35 Executive Director of Student Svcs ....Mr. Nathaniel S. HARMON

Bolivar Technical College (J)

2001 W Broadway Street, 2nd Floor, Bolivar MO 65613
Telephone: (417) 777-5062 Identification: 667033
Accreditation: ACICS

† Main campus is Texas County Technical College in Houston, MO.

Brookes Bible Institute (K)

3465 South Grand Blvd, St. Louis MO 63118
County: St. Louis Identification: 667137
Telephone: (314) 773-0083 Carnegie Class: Not Classified
FAX Number: (314) 773-7471 Calendar System: Semester
URL: www.brookesbible.com
Established: 1909 Annual Undergrad Tuition & Fees: $2,840
Enrollment: N/A Coed
Affiliation or Control: Independent Non-Profit IRS Status: 501(c)3
Highest Offering: Associate Degree
Program: Religious Emphasis
Accreditation: @BI

01 President ....Dr. Chris STOCKTON
05 Academic/Student Dean ....Dr. James MCINTOSH

Brown Mackie College-St. Louis (L)

2 Soccer Park Road, Fenton MO 63026-2564
Telephone: (636) 651-3290 Identification: 666793
Accreditation: ACICS, OTA, SURGT, SURTEC

† Main campus is The Art Institute of Phoenix in Phoenix, AZ.

Bryan University (M)

3215 LeMone Industrial Boulevard, Columbia MO 65201
Telephone: (573) 777-5550 Identification: 770725
Accreditation: ACICS

† Main campus is Bryan University in Springfield, MO.

Bryan University (N)

4255 Nature Center Way, Springfield MO 65804
County: Greene FICE Identification: 030663
Unit ID: 369516
Telephone: (417) 862-5700 Carnegie Class: Assoc/PrivFP
FAX Number: (417) 865-7144 Calendar System: Other
URL: www.bryanu.edu
Established: 1982 Annual Undergrad Tuition & Fees: $14,371
Enrollment: 357 Coed
Affiliation or Control: Proprietary IRS Status: Proprietary
Highest Offering: Associate Degree
Program: Occupational; 2-Year Principally Bachelor's Creditable; Business Emphasis
Accreditation: ACICS

01 Executive Director ....Mr. Scott HAAR

Calvary Bible College and Theological Seminary (O)

15800 Calvary Road, Kansas City MO 64147-1341
County: Cass FICE Identification: 002450
Unit ID: 176789
Telephone: (816) 322-0110 Carnegie Class: Spec/Faith

FAX Number: (816) 331-4474 Calendar System: Semester
URL: www.calvary.edu
Established: 1932 Annual Undergrad Tuition & Fees: $13,716
Enrollment: 317 Coed
Affiliation or Control: Independent Non-Profit IRS Status: 501(c)3
Highest Offering: First Professional Degree
Program: Teacher Preparatory; Religious Emphasis
Accreditation: NH, BI

01 President .... Dr. James L. CLARK
11 Vice President of Operations .... Mr. Randy GRIMM
05 Academic Dean of the College .... Dr. Teddy BITNER
20 Seminary Academic Dean .... Dr. Thomas S. BAURAIN
32 Dean of Students .... Mr. Cory D. TROWBRIDGE
34 Dean of Women .... Mrs. Kim BAILEY
07 Dean Enrollment Mgmt/Admissions .... Mr. Mike PIBURN
06 Registrar .... Mr. Larry SPRY
08 Head Librarian .... Miss Hannah BITNER
88 Director of Non-traditional Studies .... Mr. Mike PIBURN
18 Director of Maintenance .... Mr. Willis TALLEY
41 Athletic Director .... Miss Jeanette REGIER
91 Director Administrative Computing .... Mr. Aaron HEATH
38 Director Biblical Counsel/Educ Ctr .... Mrs. Patricia A. MILLER
30 Director of Development .... Mrs. Sherry HILLEARY
19 Director of Security .... Mr. Jesse A. RIGGS
37 Director of Financial Aid .... Mr. Robert CRANK
26 Director of Public Relations/Market .... Mr. Jeff CAMPA
09 Institutional Research Coordinator .... Mr. Jesse A. RIGGS
15 Human Resources Coordinator .... Mrs. Jolayne ROGERS
29 Alumni Relations Coordinator .... Mrs. Sara KLAASSEN
88 Director of The Learning Center .... Dr. Terri STRICKER
88 Director of Christian Ministries .... Mr. Joe EVERETT
88 Director of Food Service .... Mr. Joe DAPRA

Central Christian College of the Bible (A)

911 E Urbandale Drive, Moberly MO 65270-1997
County: Randolph FICE Identification: 022664
Unit ID: 176910
Telephone: (660) 263-3900 Carnegie Class: Spec/Faith
FAX Number: (660) 263-3936 Calendar System: Semester
URL: www.cccb.edu
Established: 1957 Annual Undergrad Tuition & Fees: $13,800
Enrollment: 339 Coed
Affiliation or Control: Christian Churches And Churches of Christ
IRS Status: 501(c)3
Highest Offering: Baccalaureate
Program: 2-Year Principally Bachelor's Creditable; Liberal Arts And General; Professional; Religious Emphasis
Accreditation: @NH, BI

01 President .... Dr. Ronald L. OAKES
05 Vice President of Academics .... Dr. David B. FINCHER
84 Vice President of Enrollment .... Mr. Richard R. REXRODE
30 VP of Institutional Advancement .... Mr. Phillip MARLEY
10 VP of Business & Finance .... Mrs. Lara LAWRENCE
108 Associate Dean of Assessment .... Mr. Richard A. FORDYCE
07 Associate Director of Admissions .... Mr. Michael BUTRUM
07 Director of Admissions Services .... Mr. Rocky CHRISTENSEN
88 Director of Development .... Dr. Barry THORNTON
88 Director of Stewardship .... Mr. Alan G. WILSON
04 Executive Asst to the President .... Mrs. Loretta L. KELCHNER
33 Dean of Students/Dean of Men .... Mr. Jason LYKINS
34 Dean of Women .... Ms. Anne P. MENEAR
41 Athletic Director .... Mr. Jack DEFREITAS
08 Head Librarian .... Mrs. Patty A. AGEE
06 Registrar .... Mrs. Faith M. AXTON
37 Director of Financial Aid .... Mrs. Rhonda J. DUNHAM
13 Director of Information Technology .... Mr. David ROSADO
18 Physical Plant Manager .... Mr. Mark E. DUNHAM
40 Bookstore Manager .... Mrs. Kelly HARDING
29 Alumni Relations & Event Coord .... Mrs. Sherry WALLIS
35 Director of Student Services .... Mrs. Lori PETER
39 Residence Director - Women .... Mrs. April CHRISTENSEN
39 Residence Director - Men .... Mr. Rocky CHRISTENSEN
21 Accounting Manager .... Mrs. Theresa BARTHOLMEY
102 Foundation & Corporate Relations .... Mrs. Veronica HAMBLIN
04 Administrative Executive Assistant .... Mrs. Cindy MEYER

† Onsite students accepted into a degree or certificate program will receive Full-Tuition Scholarship which equals cost of tuition up to 18 hrs/semester. Scholarship may be reduced from deficiencies in grades, Christian service, or chapel attendance.

Central Methodist University (B)

411 Central Methodist Square, Fayette MO 65248-1198
County: Howard FICE Identification: 002453
Unit ID: 445267
Telephone: (660) 248-3391 Carnegie Class: Bac/Diverse
FAX Number: (660) 248-2287 Calendar System: 4/1/4
URL: www.centralmethodist.edu
Established: 1854 Annual Undergrad Tuition & Fees: $21,320
Enrollment: 5,616 Coed
Affiliation or Control: United Methodist IRS Status: 501(c)3
Highest Offering: Master's
Program: Liberal Arts And General; Teacher Preparatory
Accreditation: NH, MUS, NURSE

01 President .... Dr. Roger D. DRAKE
05 Vice Pres & Dean of the University .... Dr. Rita GULSTAD
10 Vice Pres Finance & Administration .... Ms. Julee SHERMAN
30 Vice Pres Advancement/Alumni Rels .... Ms. Donna MERRELL
32 VP Instl Growth/Student Engagement .... Mr. Kenneth R. OLIVER
20 Assoc Dean for Academics .... Dr. Barbara ANDERSON
27 Vice President Information Services .... Mr. Chad GAINES
09 Asst Dean Inst Research/Assessment .... Ms. Sandy PIETA
07 Director of Admission .... Mr. Larry ANDERSON
41 Athletic Director .... Mr. Kenneth R. OLIVER
29 Exec Dir Development/Alumni Pgms .... Mr. Alan G. MARSHALL
06 Registrar .... Ms. Kathryn WINEGARD
37 Director of Financial Assistance .... Ms. Kristen GIBBS
18 Chief Facilities/Physical Plant .... Mr. Derry WISWALL
26 Exec Dir Marketing Communications .... Mr. Kent PROPST
36 Director Student Placement .... Ms. Nicolette YERICH
15 Director of Human Resources .... Ms. Becky KENDRICK

Chamberlain College of Nursing-St. Louis (C)

11830 Westline Industrial, Ste 106, St. Louis MO 63146
Telephone: (314) 991-6200 Identification: 770494
Accreditation: &NH, NURSE

† Main campus is Chamberlain College of Nursing - Addison in Addison, IL.

City Vision College (D)

3101 Troost Avenue, Kansas City MO 64109
FICE Identification: 041191
Unit ID: 457697
Telephone: (816) 960-2008 Carnegie Class: Not Classified
FAX Number: (617) 825-0313 Calendar System: Other
URL: www.cityvision.edu
Established: 1998 Annual Undergrad Tuition & Fees: $6,000
Enrollment: 61 Coed
Affiliation or Control: Other IRS Status: 501(c)3
Highest Offering: Baccalaureate
Program: Professional; Religious Emphasis
Accreditation: DETC

01 Executive Director/President .... Mr. Andrew SEARS
05 Chief Academic Officer .... Rev. Michael K. LIIMATTA
10 Director of Operations .... Mrs. Harriet HODGE-HENRY

† Mail address is 31 Torrey St, Dorchester, MA 02124-3543.

College of the Ozarks (E)

PO Box 17, Point Lookout MO 65726-0017
County: Taney FICE Identification: 002500
Unit ID: 178697
Telephone: (417) 334-6411 Carnegie Class: Bac/Diverse
FAX Number: (417) 335-2618 Calendar System: Semester
URL: www.cofo.edu
Established: 1906 Annual Undergrad Tuition & Fees: $430
Enrollment: 1,374 Coed
Affiliation or Control: Independent Non-Profit IRS Status: 501(c)3
Highest Offering: Baccalaureate
Program: Liberal Arts And General
Accreditation: NH, DIETD, NURSE

01 President .... Dr. Jerry C. DAVIS
03 Vice President .... Dr. Howell W. KEETER
05 Dean of the College .... Dr. Eric BOLGER
30 Director of Development .... Mrs. Natalie RASNICK
10 Treasurer .... Mr. Charles F. HUGHES
11 Dean of Administration .... Dr. Marvin SCHOENECKE
88 Dean of Work Education .... Dr. Chris LARSEN
32 Dean of Student Services .... Mr. Nick SHARP
07 Dean of Admissions and Financial Ai .... Dr. Marci LINSON
06 Registrar .... Mrs. Fran FORMAN
29 Director of Alumni Affairs .... Mrs. Angela WILLIAMSON
36 Director of Career Placement .... Mr. Ron MARTIN
37 Director of Financial Aid .... Mrs. Kyla MCCARTY
26 Director of Public Relations .... Mrs. Elizabeth B. HUGHES
96 Director of Purchasing .... Mr. Kurt MCDONALD
38 Student Counseling .... Mrs. Pat MCLEAN

Colorado Technical University, Kansas City (F)

520 E 19th Avenue, North Kansas City MO 64116-3614
Telephone: (816) 303-7799 Identification: 666457
Accreditation: &NH, MAAB

† Main campus is Colorado Technical University in Colorado Springs, CO.

Columbia College (G)

1001 Rogers Street, Columbia MO 65216-0001
County: Boone FICE Identification: 002456
Unit ID: 177065
Telephone: (573) 875-8700 Carnegie Class: Master's M
FAX Number: (573) 875-7209 Calendar System: Semester
URL: www.ccis.edu
Established: 1851 Annual Undergrad Tuition & Fees: $19,386
Enrollment: 1,050 Coed
Affiliation or Control: Christian Church (Disciples Of Christ)
IRS Status: 501(c)3
Highest Offering: Master's
Program: Liberal Arts And General; Teacher Preparatory; Professional
Accreditation: NH

01 Interim President .... Dr. Terry B. SMITH
04 Exec Assistant to the President .... Ms. Lori K. EWING
05 Exec Vice Pres/Dean Academic Affs .... Dr. David ROEBUCK
56 Vice Pres of Adult Higher Education .... Mr. Mike RANDERSON
84 Assistant VP for Enrollment Mgmt .... Mr. Tery DONELSON
32 Dean for Student Affairs .... Ms. Faye C. BURCHARD
10 Controller/Chief Financial Officer .... Mr. Bruce E. BOYER
30 Exec Director of Devel/Alumni Svcs .... Mr. Mike KATEMAN
18 Exec Director of Admin Services .... Mr. Bob C. HUTTON
88 Executive Director of Marketing .... Ms. Lana POOLE
27 Chief Information Officer .... Mr. Kevin PALMER
07 Director of Admissions .... Ms. Samantha WHITE
06 Registrar .... Ms. Sue M. KOOPMANS
29 Senior Director of Alumni Services .... Ms. Susan Y. DAVIS
26 Senior Director of Public Relations .... Ms. Joanne TEDESCO
37 Director of Financial Aid .... Ms. Sharon A. ABERNATHY
08 Director of Stafford Library .... Ms. Janet CARUTHERS
35 Director of Student Activities .... Vacant
36 Director Career Services Center .... Mr. Don G. MALSON
16 Director Human Resources .... Ms. Patty FISCHER
23 Director of Wellness Center .... Ms. Kim J. KINYON
13 Deputy Chief Information Officer .... Mr. Gary STANOWSKI
55 Assoc Dean Adult Higher Education .... Mr. Eric CUNNINGHAM
58 Associate Dean Graduate Studies .... Dr. Steve C. WIEGENSTEIN
41 Athletic Director .... Mr. Bob P. BURCHARD
09 Institutional Research Analyst .... Ms. Misty HASKAMP
19 Director of Campus Safety .... Mr. Robert KLAUSMEYER
21 Associate Controller .... Mr. Randal SCHENEWERK
51 Dean for Adult Higher Education .... Mr. Gary MASSEY

Conception Seminary College (H)

37174 State Highway VV, PO Box 502,
Conception MO 64433-0502
County: Nodaway FICE Identification: 002467
Unit ID: 177083
Telephone: (660) 944-3105 Carnegie Class: Spec/Faith
FAX Number: (660) 944-2829 Calendar System: Semester
URL: www.conception.edu
Established: 1883 Annual Undergrad Tuition & Fees: $18,236
Enrollment: 101 Male
Affiliation or Control: Roman Catholic IRS Status: 501(c)3
Highest Offering: Baccalaureate
Program: Liberal Arts And General; Religious Emphasis
Accreditation: NH

01 Rector & President .... Rev. Samuel J. RUSSELL
11 Director of Administration .... Mrs. Amy K. SCHIEBER
32 Dean of Students .... Rev. Ralph O'DONNELL
05 Dean of Academic Affairs .... Dr. William BROWNSBERGER
10 Business Manager/Dir Auxiliary Svcs .... Rev. Benedict T. NEENAN
30 Development Director .... Rev. Benedict NEENAN
07 Director of Admissions .... Vacant
37 Director of Student Financial Aid .... Bro. Justin J. HERNANDEZ
06 Registrar .... Mrs. Jeanette SCHIEBER
29 Director of Alumni .... Rev. Daniel PETSCHE
08 Librarian .... Bro. Thomas SULLIVAN
26 Director of Communications .... Mrs. Jenny HUARD
13 Director of Information Technology .... Mr. Tony MEISTER
38 Director of Counseling Services .... Rev. Duane REINERT
41 Director of Wellness Program .... Mr. Skip SHEAR

Concorde Career College (I)

3239 Broadway Boulevard, Kansas City MO 64111-2407
County: Jackson FICE Identification: 023616
Unit ID: 155283
Telephone: (816) 531-5223 Carnegie Class: Assoc/PrivFP
FAX Number: (816) 756-3231 Calendar System: Other
URL: www.concorde.edu
Established: 1986 Annual Undergrad Tuition & Fees: $27,322
Enrollment: 611 Coed
Affiliation or Control: Proprietary IRS Status: Proprietary
Highest Offering: Baccalaureate
Program: Occupational
Accreditation: ACCSC, COARC, DH, PTAA

01 President .... Jami FRAZIER
05 Academic Dean .... James KRALICEK
07 Director Student Recruitment .... Aaron GRAY

Concordia Seminary (J)

801 Seminary Place, Saint Louis MO 63105-3168
County: Saint Louis FICE Identification: 002457
Unit ID: 177092
Telephone: (314) 505-7000 Carnegie Class: Spec/Faith
FAX Number: (314) 505-7001 Calendar System: Quarter
URL: www.csl.edu
Established: 1839 Annual Graduate Tuition & Fees: $26,043
Enrollment: 603 Coed
Affiliation or Control: Lutheran Church - Missouri Synod
IRS Status: 501(c)3
Highest Offering: Doctorate; No Undergraduates
Program: Professional; Religious Emphasis
Accreditation: NH, THEOL

01 President .... Dr. Dale A. MEYER
03 Executive Vice President .... Mr. Michael LOUIS
05 Provost .... Dr. Jeffrey KLOHA
10 Sr VP for Finance/Administration .... Mr. Chad A. CATTOOR

30 Senior VP for Advancement ... Mr. Michael VINCENT
58 Dean of Advanced Studies ... Dr. Bruce G. SCHUCHARD
06 Registrar ... Mrs. Beth R. MENNEKE
08 Director of Library Services ... Rev. Benjamin HAUPT
51 Director Continuing Education ... Dr. Anthony COOK
26 Director of Communications ... Mr. Phil EBELING
88 Director Center for Hispanic Study ... Dr. Leopoldo A. SANCHEZ
15 Director of Human Resources ... Mr. Thomas MYERS
18 Director Facilities/Physical Plant ... Mr. Stephen B. MUDD
36 Director of Placement ... Rev. Wayne KNOLHOFF
37 Director of Student Financial Aid ... Mrs. Kerry R. HALLAHAN
27 Chief Information Officer ... Mr. John KLINGER
29 Director of Alumni Relations ... Rev. Michael REDEKER

Cottey College (A)

1000 W Austin Boulevard, Nevada MO 64772-2763
County: Vernon FICE Identification: 002458
Unit ID: 177117
Telephone: (417) 667-8181 Carnegie Class: Assoc/PrivNFP
FAX Number: (417) 667-8103 Calendar System: Semester
URL: www.cottey.edu
Established: 1884 Annual Undergrad Tuition & Fees: $18,800
Enrollment: 290 Female
Affiliation or Control: Independent Non-Profit IRS Status: 501(c)3
Highest Offering: Baccalaureate
Program: 2-Year Principally Bachelor's Creditable; Liberal Arts And General
Accreditation: NH, MUS

01 President ... Dr. Judy R. ROGERS
05 Vice President for Academic Affairs ... Dr. Cathryn PRIDAL
88 Exec Dir Women's Leadership ... Ms. Sonia COWEN
36 Student Success Coordinator ... Ms. Renee HAMPTON
04 Assistant to the President ... Mrs. Tricia BOBBETT
10 VP for Administration & Finance ... Mrs. Amy RUETTEN
26 VP for Inst Advancement ... Ms. Judyth WIER
32 VP for Student Life ... Dr. Mari Anne PHILLIPS
42 Dir Spiritual Life & Diversity ... Ms. Erica SIGAUKE
84 VP for Enrollment Management ... Vacant
07 Director of Admissions ... Ms. Judi STEEGE
06 Registrar ... Ms. Marcia MORTON
21 Controller ... Vacant
08 Library Director ... Mr. Phillip JOHNSON
18 Director Physical Plant/Security ... Mr. Neal R. SWARNES
27 Director of Public Information ... Mr. Steve E. REED
15 Director of Human Resources ... Ms. Betsy A. MCREYNOLDS
91 Director Administrative Computing ... Mr. Keith J. SPENCER
37 Director of Financial Aid ... Mrs. Sherry R. PENNINGTON
90 Director Academic Computing ... Mr. Adam S. DEAN
88 Director Center Women's Leadership ... Ms. Denise C. HEDGES
39 Director of Student Housing ... Ms. Helen LODGE
41 Director of Athletics ... Mr. Dave V. KETTERMAN
30 Director of Development ... Ms. Terri FALLIN
21 Asst to VP Admin & Finance ... Mrs. Tina BUCKNER
40 Bookstore Manager ... Mrs. Lois J. WITTE
09 Coordinator Institutional Research ... Mrs. Nancy KERBS
29 Coordinator Alumnae Relations ... Ms. Courtney MAJORS
38 Coordinator of Counseling ... Ms. Jeanna BRAUER
88 Campaign Manager ... Ms. Carla FARMER
88 Director of Food Service ... Mr. Michael RICHARDSON
88 Coordinator of PEO Relations ... Ms. Tracy H. CORDOVA

Court Reporting Institute of St. Louis (B)

7730 Carondelet, Clayton MO 63105
Telephone: (713) 996-8300 Identification: 770617
Accreditation: ACICS

† Main campus is Court Reporting Institute of Dallas in Dallas, TX.

Covenant Theological Seminary (C)

12330 Conway Road, Saint Louis MO 63141-8697
County: Saint Louis FICE Identification: 004707
Unit ID: 177126
Telephone: (314) 434-4044 Carnegie Class: Spec/Faith
FAX Number: (314) 434-4819 Calendar System: 4/1/4
URL: www.covenantseminary.edu
Established: 1956 Annual Graduate Tuition & Fees: $14,700
Enrollment: 687 Coed
Affiliation or Control: Presbyterian Church In America IRS Status: 501(c)3
Highest Offering: Doctorate; No Undergraduates
Program: Professional; Religious Emphasis
Accreditation: NH, THEOL

01 President ... Dr. Mark DALBEY
05 Vice President of Academics ... Dr. Mark DALBEY
10 Vice President of Business Admin ... Mr. Al LI
20 Dean of Faculty ... Dr. Jay SKLAR
20 Dean of Academic Services ... Dr. Tasha CHAPMAN
32 Dean of Students ... Rev. Michael HIGGINS
20 Dean of Academic Administration ... Rev. Christopher FLORENCE
30 Sr Director of Development ... Mr. John RANHEIM
07 Sr Director of Admissions ... Mr. Jeremy KICKLIGHTER
21 Controller ... Vacant
13 Director of Information Technology ... Mr. Richard HIERS
18 Director Facilities & Operations ... Mr. David BROWN
08 Library Director ... Rev. James C. PAKALA
29 Dir Alumni Relations/Career Svcs ... Mr. Joel HATHAWAY
37 Director of Financial Aid ... Ms. Melinda CONN
06 Registrar ... Ms. Betsy GASOSKE

Cox College (D)

1423 N Jefferson Avenue, Springfield MO 65802-1917
County: Greene FICE Identification: 020682
Unit ID: 176770
Telephone: (417) 269-3401 Carnegie Class: Spec/Health
FAX Number: (417) 269-3581 Calendar System: Semester
URL: www.coxcollege.edu
Established: 1995 Annual Undergrad Tuition & Fees: $12,293
Enrollment: 849 Coed
Affiliation or Control: Independent Non-Profit IRS Status: 501(c)3
Highest Offering: Master's
Program: Occupational; 2-Year Principally Bachelor's Creditable; Professional
Accreditation: NH, ADNUR, DIETI, DMS, NURSE, RAD

01 Interim President ... Dr. Lance RATCLIFF
05 Vice President of Academic Affairs ... Dr. Lance RATCLIFF
32 Vice President Student Services ... Mr. David SCHOOLFIELD
08 Director Library Services ... Wilma C. BUNCH
66 Dean Department of Nursing ... Dr. Tricia WAGNER
76 Dean Health Sciences Department ... Sonya HAYTER
88 Dean Interprofess Undergrad Stds ... Sonya HAYTER
09 Director of Institutional Research ... Vacant
10 Comptroller ... Deborah ADKINS
37 Director of Financial Aid ... Steve NICHOLS
07 Director of Admissions ... Lindy BIGLIENI
29 Director of Alumni Relations & Mktg ... Todd RUTLEDGE

Crowder College (E)

601 Laclede Avenue, Neosho MO 64850-9165
County: Newton FICE Identification: 002459
Unit ID: 177135
Telephone: (417) 451-3223 Carnegie Class: Assoc/Pub-R-M
FAX Number: (417) 455-5702 Calendar System: Semester
URL: www.crowder.edu
Established: 1963 Annual Undergrad Tuition & Fees (In-District): $2,700
Enrollment: 5,590 Coed
Affiliation or Control: Local IRS Status: 501(c)3
Highest Offering: Associate Degree
Program: Occupational; 2-Year Principally Bachelor's Creditable
Accreditation: NH, EMT

01 Interim President ... Dr. Kent A. FARNSWORTH
10 Vice President of Finance ... Dr. Jim CUMMINS
05 Vice President of Academic Affairs ... Dr. Glenn COLTHARP
32 Vice President of Student Affairs ... Mrs. Tiffany SLINKARD
20 Assoc VP of Academic Affairs ... Mrs. Amy RAND
75 Assoc VP of Careers & Tech Ed ... Mr. Edward STEPHENS
07 Director of Admissions ... Mr. Jim RIGGS
09 Director of Institutional Research ... Mrs. Mickie MAHAN
08 Director of Lee Library ... Mr. Eric DEATHERAGE
27 Director of Public Information ... Mrs. Cindy BROWN
41 Athletic Director ... Mrs. Millie GILION
37 Director of Financial Aid ... Mrs. Stephanie FERGUSON
15 Director of Human Resources ... Mrs. Michelle PAUL
25 Director of Grants & Development ... Mrs. Pam HUDSON
40 Bookstore Manager ... Ms. Colleen HOLLAND
36 Career Svcs Coordinator ... Ms. Casey OWENS
13 Director of Information Technology ... Mr. Chris WOITOWITZ

Culver-Stockton College (F)

1 College Hill, Canton MO 63435-1257
County: Lewis FICE Identification: 002460
Unit ID: 177144
Telephone: (573) 288-6000 Carnegie Class: Bac/Diverse
FAX Number: (573) 288-6611 Calendar System: Semester
URL: www.culver.edu
Established: 1853 Annual Undergrad Tuition & Fees: $23,000
Enrollment: 769 Coed
Affiliation or Control: Christian Church (Disciples Of Christ)
IRS Status: 501(c)3
Highest Offering: Baccalaureate
Program: Liberal Arts And General; Teacher Preparatory; Professional
Accreditation: NH, IACBE, MUS

01 President ... Mr. Richard D. VALENTINE
05 Vice Pres Academic Affs/Dean of Col ... Dr. Daniel K. SILBER
32 Dean of Student Life ... Mr. D. Christopher GILL
07 Director of Admission ... Mrs. Misty MCBEE
30 VP for Advancement/Alumni Pgm ... Mr. Eric BARKLEY
06 Registrar/Director Inst Research ... Mrs. Chris HUEBOTTER
08 Librarian ... Mrs. Sharon K. UPCHURCH
26 Director of College Communications ... Mr. Kyle TRUDELL
37 Director Financial Aid ... Mrs. Tina WISEMAN
29 Director of Alumni Programs ... Mrs. Jennifer SOUSA
91 Exec Dir Admin Systems & Service ... Mr. Joseph LIESEN
10 Chief Financial Officer/Controller ... Mrs. Diane BOZARTH
15 Director of Human Resources ... Mrs. Amy BAKER
35 Coordinator of Student Activities ... Mr. Devon OSSORIO
42 Chaplain ... Rev. Amanda SORENSON
41 Athletic Director ... Mr. Greg MCVEY
40 Logo Shop Manager ... Mrs. Sharon FARR
04 Assistant to the President ... Mrs. Doris BRISCOE
19 Director Campus Security & Facil ... Mr. Michael BRINGER
81 Chair Natural & Math Sciences Div ... Dr. Lauren SCHELLENBERGER
50 Chair Business Division ... Dr. Kimberly GAITHER
53 Chair Education/Applied Arts Div ... Ms. Ann E. HAMMER
57 Chair Fine Arts Division ... Mr. Kent MILLER
79 Chair Humanities Division ... Dr. P. Ronald STORMER
83 Chair Social/Behavior Sciences Div ... Dr. Chad DEWAARD
88 Assoc Dean/Experiential Learning ... Dr. Dell Ann JANNEY
92 Director of Honors Program ... Mrs. Julie STRAUS
93 Director of Minority Students ... Dr. Mohamed EL-BERMAWY
24 Media Coordinator ... Mrs. Julie WRIGHT
44 Director of the Annual Fund ... Mr. Scott MCGAUGHEY
36 Coord of Career Services/Internship ... Mrs. Heather KELLER-GILTNER
39 Director of Residential Life ... Mr. Jackson SEEMAYER
20 Director of Advising/Retention/FY ... Ms. Holly ANDRESS-MARTIN
38 Dir Counseling/Student Wellness ... Ms. Susan MOON
09 Director of Institutional Research ... Mrs. Karla MCREYNOLDS
88 Director of Advancement Operations ... Mrs. Marjorie ELLISON

DeVry University - Kansas City Campus (G)

11224 Holmes Road, Kansas City MO 64131-3626
Telephone: (816) 943-7300 FICE Identification: 002455
Accreditation: &NH, ENGT

† Main campus is DeVry University - Chicago Campus in Chicago, IL.

Drury University (H)

900 N Benton Avenue, Springfield MO 65802-3791
County: Greene FICE Identification: 002461
Unit ID: 177214
Telephone: (417) 873-7879 Carnegie Class: Master's M
FAX Number: (417) 873-7529 Calendar System: Semester
URL: www.drury.edu
Established: 1873 Annual Undergrad Tuition & Fees: $21,700
Enrollment: 5,228 Coed
Affiliation or Control: Independent Non-Profit IRS Status: 501(c)3
Highest Offering: Master's
Program: Liberal Arts And General; Teacher Preparatory; Professional
Accreditation: NH, ACBSP, BUS, MUS, TED

01 President ... Dr. David MANUEL
10 Chief Financial Officer ... Mr. Rob FRIDGE
11 Vice President for Administration ... Mr. Bill SCORSE
32 Vice President for Student Services ... Dr. Tijuana S. JULIAN
18 VP Campus Oper/Sustainability ... Mr. Pete RADECKI
05 Vice President for Academic Affairs ... Dr. Charles TAYLOR
30 Interim Vice Pres Alumni & Develop ... Ms. Dawn HILES
84 Vice Pres of Enrollment Management ... Ms. Dawn HILES
58 Dean Grad & Cont Studies ... Mr. Aaron JONES
20 Associate Dean of College ... Dr. Bruce CALLEN
06 Registrar ... Mrs. Cindy M. JONES
26 Dir of Marketing & Communications ... Ms. Jann HOLLAND
37 Director of Financial Aid ... Mrs. Annette AVERY
88 Director of Facilities Services ... Mr. Ron CUSHMAN
08 Director of Library/Info Services ... Ms. Polly BORUFF-JONES
36 Director of Career Development ... Ms. Jill WIGGINS
15 Director of Human Resources ... Ms. Scotti SIEBERT
29 Director Alumni Relations ... Ms. Meleah SPENCER
09 Director of Institutional Research ... Vacant
38 Dir of Counseling/Student Devel ... Mr. Ed DERR
19 Director Safety/Security ... Ms. Sarene DEEDS
35 Director Student Affairs ... Ms. Emily GIVENS

Drury University Cabool Campus (I)

620 Peabody Avenue, Cabool MO 65689
Telephone: (417) 962-5314 Identification: 770318
Accreditation: &NH

† Main campus is Drury University in Springfield, MO.

Drury University Ft. Leonard Wood Campus (J)

268 Constitution Street, Suite 12,
Ft. Leonard Wood MO 65473
Telephone: (573) 329-4400 Identification: 770319
Accreditation: &NH

† Main campus is Drury University in Springfield, MO.

Drury University Lebanon Campus (K)

531 West Bland Road, Lebanon MO 65536
Telephone: (417) 532-9828 Identification: 770320
Accreditation: &NH

† Main campus is Drury University in Springfield, MO.

Drury University Rolla Campus (L)

1280 Forum Drive, Rolla MO 65401
Telephone: (573) 368-4959 Identification: 770321
Accreditation: &NH

† Main campus is Drury University in Springfield, MO.

East Central College (M)

1964 Prairie Dell Road, Union MO 63084-0529
County: Franklin FICE Identification: 008862
Unit ID: 177250
Telephone: (636) 584-6500 Carnegie Class: Assoc/Pub-S-MC
FAX Number: (636) 583-1897 Calendar System: Semester
URL: www.eastcentral.edu
Established: 1968 Annual Undergrad Tuition & Fees (In-District): $2,670
Enrollment: 4,043 Coed

Affiliation or Control: Local IRS Status: 501(c)3
Highest Offering: Associate Degree
Program: Occupational; 2-Year Principally Bachelor's Creditable
Accreditation: **NH**, ACFEI, NAIT, OTA

01	President	Dr. C. Jon BAUER
10	Vice Pres Finance/Administration	Mr. Phil PENA
05	Vice President Instruction	Ms. Jean A. MCCANN
32	Vice President Student Development	Ms. Ina R. HAYS
88	VP External Relations	Vacant
12	Director of Rolla Campus	Ms. Christina M. AYRES
30	Dir of Institutional Development	Ms. Shannon M. GRUS
18	Director Facilities & Grounds	Mr. Mark A. EATON
08	Director of Library Services	Ms. Lisa M. FARRELL
96	Purchasing Manager	Ms. Melissa D. POPP
83	Div Chair Educ/Business/Soc Science	Ms. Mary B. HUXEL
79	Div Chair English/For Language	Mr. John M. HARDECKE
81	Div Chair Science	Ms. Fatemeh NICHOLS
15	Director Human Resources	Ms. Wendy HARTMANN
66	Director of Nursing/Allied Health	Ms. Robyn C. WALTER
37	Director Financial Aid	Ms. Karen GRIFFIN
06	Registrar	Ms. Marcia BAILEY
21	Director Financial Svcs/Comptroller	Ms. Shirley A. HOFSTETTER
09	Director of Institutional Research	Ms. Bethany L. LOHDEN
26	Director of Public Relations	Ms. Dorothy A. SCHOWE
13	Director Information Technology	Vacant
40	Bookstore/Mail/Imaging Coordinator	Mr. Doug A. AGEE
36	Coordinator Advisement Services	Ms. Tammy A. WEINHOLD
103	Executive Director Workforce Devel	Ms. Gretchen A. PETTIT
51	Coordinator Adult Educ & Literacy	Ms. Micki D. HOFFMAN
24	Coordinator Instructional Design	Mr. R. Chad BALDWIN
35	Coordinator Student Activities	Ms. Goldie GILDEHAUS

Eden Theological Seminary (A)

475 E Lockwood Avenue,
Webster Groves MO 63119-3192
County: Saint Louis FICE Identification: 002462
Unit ID: 177278
Telephone: (314) 961-3627 Carnegie Class: Spec/Faith
FAX Number: (314) 918-2626 Calendar System: 4/1/4
URL: www.eden.edu
Established: 1850 Annual Graduate Tuition & Fees: $15,370
Enrollment: 170 Coed
Affiliation or Control: United Church Of Christ IRS Status: 501(c)3
Highest Offering: Doctorate; No Undergraduates
Program: Professional; Religious Emphasis
Accreditation: **NH**, THEOL

01	President	Dr. David M. GREENHAW
30	Vice Pres Institutional Advancement	Mr. Bryce KRUG
05	Academic Dean	Dr. Deborah KRAUSE
44	Director of Development	Ms. Jackie HAMILTON
06	Registrar	Ms. Michelle WOBBE
08	Director Eden Library	Mr. Michael BODDY
07	Director of Recruitment/Admissions	Rev. Carol SHANKS
40	Director Eden Bookstore	Ms. Hannah RICE
04	Executive Asst to the President	Ms. Denise STAUFFER

Evangel University (B)

1111 N Glenstone, Springfield MO 65802-2191
County: Greene FICE Identification: 002463
Unit ID: 177339
Telephone: (417) 865-2811 Carnegie Class: Bac/Diverse
FAX Number: (417) 865-9599 Calendar System: Semester
URL: www.evangel.edu
Established: 1955 Annual Undergrad Tuition & Fees: $20,020
Enrollment: 2,079 Coed
Affiliation or Control: Assemblies Of God Church IRS Status: 501(c)3
Highest Offering: Master's
Program: Liberal Arts And General; Teacher Preparatory
Accreditation: **NH**, MUS, SW, TED

01	President-Elect/CEO	Dr. Carol A. TAYLOR
01	President	Vacant
10	Vice President for Business/Finance	Mr. David WILLEMSEN
32	Vice Pres for Student Development	Dr. Sheri PHILLIPS
30	Vice Pres Institutional Advancement	Mr. James WILLIAMS
05	Vice President for Academic Affairs	Dr. Glenn H. BERNET
84	Vice Pres Enrollment Management	Dr. Andy DENTON
18	Director of Physical Plant	Mr. Tom KELTNER
41	Director of Athletics	Dr. David L. STAIR
06	Registrar	Mrs. Cathy WILLIAMS
14	Director Computer Svcs/Acad Comput	Mr. Brett WEIMER
08	Librarian	Mr. Dale JENSEN
19	Director of Public Safety	Mr. Gene THOMLINSON
38	Director of Counseling Services	Mr. Brian UPTON
29	Director Alumni Relations	Mr. Chuck COX
37	Dir of Student Financial Services	Mrs. Valerie SHARP
36	Career Development/Placement	Mrs. Tina MOORE
42	Campus Pastor	Rev. John PLAKE
26	Director of Public Relations	Mr. Paul LOGSDON
07	Director of Admissions	Mrs. Brittney GRANTHAM
23	Director of Health Services	Mrs. Susan BRYAN
21	Controller	Mr. John KRAUS
35	Director Student Life	Miss Gina RENTSCHLER
15	Supervisor Human Resources	Mrs. Ocki HAAS
39	Housing Coordinator	Mrs. Pamela SMALLWOOD
09	Director of Institutional Research	Dr. Linda WELLBORN

Everest College (C)

3420 Rider Trail South, Earth City MO 63045
Telephone: (314) 739-7333 Identification: 770618
Accreditation: ACICS

† Main campus is Everest College in Bremerton, WA.

Everest College (D)

1010 W Sunshine, Springfield MO 65807-2488
County: Greene FICE Identification: 022506
Unit ID: 179070
Telephone: (417) 864-7220 Carnegie Class: Bac/Assoc
FAX Number: (417) 864-5697 Calendar System: Quarter
URL: www.everestcollege.com
Established: 1976 Annual Undergrad Tuition & Fees: $13,320
Enrollment: 314 Coed
Affiliation or Control: Proprietary IRS Status: Proprietary
Highest Offering: Baccalaureate
Program: Occupational; 2-Year Principally Bachelor's Creditable; Business Emphasis
Accreditation: ACICS, MAC

01	President	Mr. Mark CROSBY
05	Academic Dean	Ms. Rachel MCCOWN
07	Director of Admissions	Ms. Wendy WOOSLEY
06	Registrar	Ms. Roxanne KUTCH
37	Financial Aid Director	Ms. Erica SEAMEN
10	Director of Student Accounts	Ms. Brendy MERRILL
07	High School Director of Admissions	Vacant
08	Librarian	Mr. Trenton TUBBS

Fontbonne University (E)

6800 Wydown Boulevard, Saint Louis MO 63105-3098
County: Saint Louis FICE Identification: 002464
Unit ID: 177418
Telephone: (314) 862-3456 Carnegie Class: Master's L
FAX Number: (314) 889-1451 Calendar System: Semester
URL: www.fontbonne.edu
Established: 1923 Annual Undergrad Tuition & Fees: $22,324
Enrollment: 2,075 Coed
Affiliation or Control: Roman Catholic IRS Status: 501(c)3
Highest Offering: Master's
Program: Liberal Arts And General; Teacher Preparatory; Professional
Accreditation: **NH**, ACBSP, DIETD, SP, SW, TED

01	President	Dr. Dennis C. GOLDEN
03	Executive Vice Pres Strat/Oper	Mr. Gregory TAYLOR
05	Vice President/Dean Acad Affairs	Vacant
30	Vice President Inst Advancement	Mr. Randy LOECHNER
32	Vice President Student Affairs	Ms. Randi WILSON
10	Vice President Finance & Admin/CFO	Dr. Gary L. ZACK
84	Vice President Enrollment Mgt	Ms. Suzanne SWOPE
13	Vice Pres Information Technology	Mr. Mark FRANZ
35	Associate Vice Pres Student Affairs	Ms. Carla HICKMAN
20	Interim Assoc VP Acad Affairs	Dr. Heather NORTON
58	Director of Graduate Studies/MAED	Vacant
53	Dean of Education	Vacant
50	Dean of Global Business & Prof Stds	Ms. Linda MAURER
88	Asst to the Pres for Mission Integ	Dr. Mary Beth GALLAGHER
06	Registrar	Ms. Mazie MOORE
15	Director of Human Resources	Ms. Linda PIPITONE
08	University Librarian	Ms. Sharon MCCASLIN
45	Director of Academic Resources	Mr. Mark POUSSON
09	Dir of Inst Research & Assessment	Dr. Laurie A. RODGERS
26	Director Communications/Marketing	Mr. Mark JOHNSON
106	Director of Online Program	Ms. Jo MATTSON
37	Director of Financial Aid	Ms. Nicole MOORE
88	Director of Academic Advising	Ms. Lee DELAET
85	Director of International Affairs	Ms. Rebecca GRANT BAHAN
29	Director of Alumni Relations	Ms. Carrie WENBERG
41	Interim Director of Athletics	Ms. Maria EFTINK
28	Director of Multicultural Affairs	Ms. Leslie DOYLE
88	Dir Ldrshp Educ & Stdnt Activities	Dr. Janelle DENSBERGER
42	Director of Campus Ministry	Ms. Sarah BOUL
19	Director of Public Safety	Mr. Bob KRAEUCHI
21	Controller	Mr. Dennis JOHNSON
07	Director of Admissions	Ms. Michelle PALUMBO
18	Director Physical Plant	Mr. Brent SPIES

Global University (F)

1211 South Glenstone Avenue,
Springfield MO 65804-1894
County: Greene Identification: 666687
Unit ID: 247296
Telephone: (800) 443-1083 Carnegie Class: Not Classified
FAX Number: (417) 865-7167 Calendar System: Other
URL: www.globaluniversity.edu
Established: 1948 Annual Undergrad Tuition & Fees: $3,870
Enrollment: 5,310 Coed
Affiliation or Control: Assemblies Of God Church IRS Status: 501(c)3
Highest Offering: Doctorate
Program: Occupational; 2-Year Principally Bachelor's Creditable; Liberal Arts And General; Professional; Religious Emphasis
Accreditation: **NH**, DETC

01	President	Dr. Gary SEEVERS, JR.
03	Executive Vice President	Rev. Keith HEERMANN
05	Provost	Dr. Jack NILL
20	Vice Provost and Dean of Berean	Dr. Randy HUDLUN
58	Graduate School Dean	Dr. Carl CHRISNER
73	UG School of Bible & Theology	Dr. Willard TEAGUE
13	VP Info Tech/Media Dept	Dr. Mark BARCLIFT
20	Dean of Education	Rev. Brad AUSBURY
07	Director of Enrollment Services	Rev. Todd WAGGONER
06	Registrar	Mrs. Lynne KROH
10	Chief Financial Officer	Mr. Mark PERRY
15	Director of Human Resources	Rev. Bob ARMONT

Goldfarb School of Nursing at Barnes-Jewish College (G)

4483 Duncan Avenue, Saint Louis MO 63110-1111
County: Saint Louis FICE Identification: 006389
Unit ID: 177719
Telephone: (314) 454-7055 Carnegie Class: Spec/Health
FAX Number: (314) 362-9250 Calendar System: Semester
URL: www.barnesjewishcollege.edu
Established: 1902 Annual Undergrad Tuition & Fees: $26,105
Enrollment: 840 Coed
Affiliation or Control: Independent Non-Profit IRS Status: 501(c)3
Highest Offering: Doctorate
Program: Professional; Nursing Emphasis
Accreditation: **NH**, ANEST, NURSE

01	Dean	Dr. Michael BLEICH
05	Vice Dean/Academic Effectiveness	Dr. Connie KOCH
11	Assoc Dean for Administration	Mr. Thomas EDLER
20	Vice Dean Stdnt Affairs/Diversity	Dr. Michael WARD
46	Associate Dean for Research	Vacant
58	Assoc Dean Graduate Programs	Dr. Gretchen DRINKARD
20	Assoc Dean Undergraduate Pgms	Dr. Gail REA
08	Library & Info Services Director	Ms. Renee GORRELL
13	Information System Director	Mr. Wade LEHDE
37	Director Enrollment Mgmnt	Mr. Jason CROWE
32	Director Student Services	Vacant

Graceland University (H)

1401 West Truman Road, Independence MO 64050-3434
Telephone: (816) 833-0524 Identification: 666262
Accreditation: &**NH**, NURSE

† Main campus is Graceland University in Lamoni, IA.

Grantham University (I)

7200 NW 86th Street, Kansas City MO 64153-2262
FICE Identification: 004283
Unit ID: 442569
Telephone: (800) 955-2527 Carnegie Class: Master's S
FAX Number: (816) 595-5757 Calendar System: Other
URL: www.grantham.edu
Established: 1951 Annual Undergrad Tuition & Fees: $7,985
Enrollment: 9,463 Coed
Affiliation or Control: Proprietary IRS Status: Proprietary
Highest Offering: Master's
Program: Occupational; Professional; Technical Emphasis
Accreditation: DETC

01	President	Joseph C. MCGRATH
05	Provost	Dr. Marilyn BARTELS
26	Vice President of Marketing	Alex BACH
07	Vice President of Admissions	Les HYDE
10	Vice President of Finance	Ed SAMMARCO
30	Vice Pres of Strategic Initiatives	Dr. Jeffrey CROPSEY
22	Vice President of Compliance	Karan KRNA
38	Vice President of Student Advising	Steve WALDRON
15	Vice President of Human Resources	Kip ESRY
37	Vice President of Financial Aid	Roman YAGNITINSKY
20	Chief Academic Officer	Dr. Cheryl HAYEK
13	Chief Information Officer	Jeff BRAMBLETT
06	Registrar	Russell PERKINS
103	Exec Director Education Outreach	George COLON

Hannibal-La Grange University (J)

2800 Palmyra Road, Hannibal MO 63401-1999
County: Marion FICE Identification: 009089
Unit ID: 177542
Telephone: (573) 221-3675 Carnegie Class: Bac/Diverse
FAX Number: (573) 221-6594 Calendar System: Semester
URL: www.hlg.edu
Established: 1858 Annual Undergrad Tuition & Fees: $18,770
Enrollment: 1,241 Coed
Affiliation or Control: Southern Baptist IRS Status: 501(c)3
Highest Offering: Master's
Program: Liberal Arts And General
Accreditation: **NH**, ADNUR

01	President	Dr. Anthony W. ALLEN
05	VP for Academic Affairs	Dr. David J. PELLETIER
84	VP for Enrollment Management	Dr. Raymond W. CARTY
30	VP for Institutional Advancement	Mr. Steve T. MILLER
32	Dean of Student Development	Mr. Kyle R. BRENNEMANN
10	Dean of Business & Finance	Mrs. Betty L. ANDERSON
26	Director Public Relations	Mrs. Carolyn A. CARPENTER
06	Director of Records/Student Accts	Mrs. Mary E. FORD
37	Director of Financial Aid	Mr. Brice D. BAUMGARDNER

29 Director Alumni Services/Devel .... Ms. Lauren YOUSE
35 Director Student Affairs .... Ms. Margaret F. STREET
36 Director Student Placement .... Dr. Karry D. RICHARDSON
08 Library Director .... Mrs. Julie A. ANDRESEN
18 Chief Facilities/Physical Plant .... Mr. James P. MILLER
19 Director Public Safety .... Mr. Albert HIGDON
39 Director Student Housing .... Mrs. Sara E. KECK
41 Athletic Director .... Mr. Jason D. NICHOLS
42 Director Campus Ministry .... Dr. Jeffrey D. BROWN
40 University Bookstore Manager .... Mrs. Susan A. BOOTH

Harris-Stowe State University (A)

3026 Laclede Avenue, Saint Louis MO 63103-2199
County: Independent City FICE Identification: 002466
Unit ID: 177551
Telephone: (314) 340-3366 Carnegie Class: Bac/Diverse
FAX Number: (314) 340-3399 Calendar System: Semester
URL: www.hssu.edu
Established: 1857 Annual Undergrad Tuition & Fees (In-State): $5,220
Enrollment: 1,484 Coed
Affiliation or Control: State IRS Status: 501(c)3
Highest Offering: Baccalaureate
Program: Liberal Arts And General; Teacher Preparatory; Professional; Business Emphasis
Accreditation: NH, ACBSP, IACBE, TED

01 President .... Dr. Albert WALKER
05 Vice President Academic Affairs .... Dr. Dwayne SMITH
10 Exec VP Business/Financial Affairs .... Mrs. Constance G. GULLY
21 Asst VP Business/Financial Affairs .... Vacant
26 Asst VP Comm/Mktg/Alumni Affs/Dev .... Ms. Courtney MCCALL
06 Registrar .... Ms. Chauvette MCELMURRY
84 Exec Director of Enrollment Mgmt .... Ms. LaShanda R. BOONE
88 Director of Academic Advisement .... Ms. Carla LEE
08 Director Library Services .... Mrs. Barbara NOBLE
37 Director of Financial Aid .... Ms. Sandra CALL
15 Director Human Resources .... Mrs. Virginia J. MALONE
38 Director Counseling Services .... Mrs. Vicki BERNARD
56 Exec Dir Title III/Sponsored Pgms .... Mrs. Heather BOSTIC
20 Director Ctr Retent/Student Success .... Mrs. Anne GRICE
41 Director of Athletics .... Mr. Don KAVERMAN
18 Director of Physical Plant .... Mr. Paul KENNON
30 Dir Development & Alumni Affairs .... Vacant
88 Director of Business Services .... Ms. Barbara A. MORROW
09 Director of Institutional Research .... Vacant
36 Director of Career Services .... Mrs. Wanda MCNEIL
21 Comptroller/Grants Officer .... Mr. Brian HUGGINS
38 Coord Student Counseling/Wellness .... Vacant
53 Dean College of Education .... Dr. LaTisha T. SMITH
50 Dean Busch School of Business .... Ms. Fatemeh ZAKERY
32 Dean Student Affairs .... Mr. Charles H. GOODEN
88 Chair Urban Specializations .... Vacant
49 Dean College of Arts & Sciences .... Dr. Lateef ADELANI
07 Director of Admissions .... Ms. Meghan SPRUNG

Heartland Christian College (B)

500 New Creation Rd, Newark MO 63458
County: Knox Identification: 667091
Telephone: (660) 284-4800 Carnegie Class: Not Classified
FAX Number: (680) 284-4098 Calendar System: Semester
URL: www.heartlandcollege.org
Established: 1992 Annual Undergrad Tuition & Fees: $1,085
Enrollment: 45 Coed
Affiliation or Control: Non-denominational IRS Status: 501(c)3
Highest Offering: Associate Degree
Program: 2-Year Principally Bachelor's Creditable; Religious Emphasis
Accreditation: @BI

01 President .... Kris R. PALMER
05 Chief Academic Officer .... Martha PALMER
10 CFO .... David BARTON
06 Registrar .... Vacant

Heritage College (C)

1200 E 104th Street, Suite 300,
Kansas City MO 64131-4557
Telephone: (816) 942-5474 Identification: 666155
Accreditation: ABHES

† Main campus is Heritage College in Denver, CO.

Hickey College (D)

940 W Port Plaza, Suite 101, Saint Louis MO 63146-3127
County: Saint Louis FICE Identification: 010279
Unit ID: 177579
Telephone: (314) 434-2212 Carnegie Class: Bac/Assoc
FAX Number: (314) 434-1974 Calendar System: Other
URL: www.hickeycollege.edu
Established: 1933 Annual Undergrad Tuition & Fees: $13,610
Enrollment: 396 Coed
Affiliation or Control: Proprietary IRS Status: Proprietary
Highest Offering: Baccalaureate
Program: Business Emphasis
Accreditation: ACICS, ACFEI

01 President .... Mr. Christopher A. GEARIN
11 Director of Operations .... Mr. Ken SIMONS
05 Director of Education .... Ms. Connie L. SCOTT
32 Director of Student Services .... Ms. Deanna L. PECORONI
07 Director of Admissions .... Mr. Bill E. LEWIS

ITT Technical Institute (E)

1930 Meyer Drury Drive, Arnold MO 63010-6004
Telephone: (636) 464-6600 Identification: 666033
Accreditation: ACICS

† Main campus is ITT Technical Institute in Indianapolis, IN.

ITT Technical Institute (F)

3640 Corporate Trail Drive, Earth City MO 63045-1122
Telephone: (314) 298-7800 FICE Identification: 007557
Accreditation: ACICS

† Main campus is ITT Technical Institute in Indianapolis, IN.

ITT Technical Institute (G)

9150 East 41st Terrace, Kansas City MO 64133-1448
Telephone: (816) 276-1400 Identification: 666380
Accreditation: ACICS

† Main campus is ITT Technical Institute in Indianapolis, IN.

ITT Technical Institute (H)

3216 South National Avenue, Springfield MO 65807
Telephone: (417) 877-4800 Identification: 666702
Accreditation: ACICS

† Main campus is ITT Technical Institute in Indianapolis, IN.

Jefferson College (I)

1000 Viking Drive, Hillsboro MO 63050-2441
County: Jefferson FICE Identification: 002468
Unit ID: 177676
Telephone: (636) 797-3000 Carnegie Class: Assoc/Pub-S-MC
FAX Number: (636) 789-4012 Calendar System: Semester
URL: www.jeffco.edu
Established: 1963 Annual Undergrad Tuition & Fees (In-District): $2,850
Enrollment: 5,494 Coed
Affiliation or Control: State/Local IRS Status: 501(c)3
Highest Offering: Associate Degree
Program: Occupational; 2-Year Principally Bachelor's Creditable
Accreditation: NH, #COARC, OTA, @PTAA

01 President .... Dr. Raymond V. CUMMISKEY
05 VP Instruction .... Dr. Melinda K. SELSOR
10 VP Finance & Administration .... Mr. Daryl GEHBAUER
32 Associate VP Student Services .... Ms. Julie FRASER
49 Dean of Arts & Sciences .... Ms. Shirley DAVENPORT
75 Interim Dean Career/Technical Ed .... Dr. Dena MCCAFFREY
30 Executive Director of Advancement .... Vacant
15 Director of Human Resources .... Ms. Tasha D. WELSH
26 Director of PR & Marketing .... Mr. Roger A. BARRENTINE
09 Director Research & Planning .... Vacant
81 Division Chair Math/Sci/Business .... Ms. Linda ABERNATHY
83 Division Chair Social Sciences .... Ms. Sandy FREY
60 Division Chair Comm/Fine Arts .... Mr. Michael BOOKER
75 Div Chair Business/Technical Educ .... Dr. Marybeth OTTINGER
35 Director Student Support Services .... Ms. Diane ARNZEN
21 Controller .... Mr. Richard H. HARDIN
41 Director Athletics .... Mr. Doug STOTLER
31 Director Business & Community Devel .... Mr. Bryan D. HERRICK
12 Director Outreach/Educational Sites .... Vacant
08 Director Library Services .... Ms. Lisa C. WOLFE
90 Dir Online Learning/Inst Tech .... Mr. Allan A. WAMSLEY
18 Director Buildings & Grounds .... Mr. Ed TOMASZKIEWICZ
96 Procurement Coordinator .... Ms. Sheree BELL
13 Director Information Technology .... Mr. Tracy JAMES
74 Director Veterinary Technology .... Ms. Dana A. NEVOIS
88 Director Child Care Center .... Ms. Sandra K. BASLER
76 Director Health Occupation Programs .... Mr. Kenny WILSON
06 Director Admissions/Student Records .... Dr. Kim M. HARVEY
37 Director Student Financial Services .... Ms. Sarah BRIGHT
66 Director of Nursing .... Ms. Linda BOEVINGLOH
38 Director Advising & Retention .... Ms. Kathy JOHNSTON
39 Director Residential & Student Life .... Ms. Anna FABATZ

Kansas City Art Institute (J)

4415 Warwick Boulevard, Kansas City MO 64111-1874
County: Jackson FICE Identification: 002473
Unit ID: 177746
Telephone: (816) 472-4852 Carnegie Class: Spec/Arts
FAX Number: (816) 472-3439 Calendar System: Semester
URL: www.kcai.edu
Established: 1885 Annual Undergrad Tuition & Fees: $33,112
Enrollment: 822 Coed
Affiliation or Control: Independent Non-Profit IRS Status: 501(c)3
Highest Offering: Baccalaureate
Program: Fine Arts Emphasis
Accreditation: NH, ART

01 President .... Dr. Jacqueline CHANDA
11 Vice Pres for Administration .... Mr. Rick RIEDER
05 Vice President for Academic Affairs .... Dr. Bambi BURGARD
30 Vice President for Advancement .... Ms. Nicolle RATLIFF
84 VP Enroll Mgt & Student Achievement .... Vacant
26 Vice President for Communications .... Ms. Anne CANFIELD
13 Vice Pres/Chief Information Officer .... Mr. Larry DICKERSON
20 Associate Academic Officer .... Mr. Milton KATZ
51 Dir Continuing/Professional Studies .... Ms. Tabitha SCHMIDT
06 Registrar .... Ms. Andrea KHAN
15 Director of Human Resources .... Ms. Barbara FINKE
18 Facilities Director/Plant Services .... Mr. Larry STUCKEY
29 Director of Alumni Relations .... Mr. Eric DOBBINS
37 Director of Financial Aid .... Ms. Darci WEBSTER
21 Controller .... Ms. Suzette NAYLOR
36 Dir of Acad Advising & Career Svcs .... Ms. Tori SINCLAIR
08 Director of Library .... Ms. M. J. POEHLER
32 Dean of Students .... Ms. Gina GOLBA
24 Director of Media Center .... Mr. Aldo BACCHETTA
19 Director of Safety & Security .... Mr. Robert BAYLESS
40 Director of Auxiliary Services .... Mr. Ed RODRIGUEZ
88 Director of Block Artspace Gallery .... Ms. Raechell SMITH
104 Study Abroad Coordinator .... Ms. Emily BRATTIN
04 Exec Admin Asst to the President .... Ms. Susan KLEIN

Kansas City University of Medicine & Biosciences (K)

1750 East Independence Avenue, Kansas City MO 64119
County: Jackson FICE Identification: 002474
Unit ID: 179812
Telephone: (816) 654-7000 Carnegie Class: Spec/Med
FAX Number: (816) 654-7101 Calendar System: Semester
URL: www.kcumb.edu
Established: 1916 Annual Graduate Tuition & Fees: $42,039
Enrollment: 1,012 Coed
Affiliation or Control: Independent Non-Profit IRS Status: 501(c)3
Highest Offering: First Professional Degree; No Undergraduates
Program: Professional
Accreditation: NH, OSTEO

01 President & CEO .... Dr. H. Danny WEAVER
05 Exec VP Acad & Med Affairs/Dean COM .... Dr. Marc B. HAHN
10 Chief Financial Officer .... Mr. Joseph MASSMAN
30 Vice Pres for Advancement .... Ms. Beth DOLLASE
10 Vice President Finance & Admin .... Mr. James E. PARK
43 Interim EVP Adm & Legal Affairs .... Mr. Nelson T. MANN
20 Assoc Dean for Clin Educ & Med Affs .... Dr. John DOUGHERTY
20 Assoc Dean for Curriculum Affairs .... Ms. Linda ADKISON
32 Assoc Dean for Student Affairs .... Dr. Maurice OELKLAUS
35 Asst Dean for Student Affairs .... Ms. LeAnn K. CARLTON
88 Exec Director University Events .... Ms. Nancy A. JONES
26 Vice Pres Marketing/Univ Relations .... Ms. Natalie LUTZ
08 Director of Libraries .... Miss Marilyn J. DEGEUS
15 Vice Pres Human Resources .... Ms. Dawn M. ROHRS
18 Director Physical Facilities .... Mr. Walter W. SNYDER
96 Director of Purchasing .... Ms. Carrie L. SIMSHEUSER
88 Director Clinical Research .... Dr. Patrick G. CLAY
27 Chief Information Officer .... Ms. Rebecca G. TALKEN
37 Director of Financial Aid .... Ms. Sharon S. HERMAN
30 Director of Development .... Ms. Christine A. WAHLERT
84 VP Enrollment & Registrar .... Ms. Heidi TERRY
88 Adm Dir Community Clin Educ .... Ms. Valorie L. MILLICAN
19 Director Security .... Mr. Freddy D. POINDEXTER
28 Director Learning Enhancement .... Mr. Stan VIEBROCK
44 Dir Alumni & Major Gift Development .... Mr. Ted P. PLACE
35 Exec Dir Comm of Student Affairs .... Ms. Sara E. SELKIRK
76 Dean of College of Biosciences .... Dr. Douglas R. RUSHING
63 Assoc Dean Basic Medical Sciences .... Dr. Alan G. GLAROS
20 Asst Dean Curricular Affairs .... Dr. Gary O. BALLAM
76 Assoc Dean College of Biosciences .... Dr. Robert E. STEPHENS
24 Instructional Tech Media Technician .... Mr. Wade W. GLOSSER
04 Assistant to the President .... Mr. Brian T. REESE
07 Director Admissions .... Ms. Patricia HARPER
36 Coordinator Placement .... Ms. Allison O. MOORE

Kenrick-Glennon Seminary-Kenrick School of Theology (L)

5200 Glennon Drive, Saint Louis MO 63119-4399
County: Saint Louis FICE Identification: 002476
Unit ID: 177816
Telephone: (314) 792-6100 Carnegie Class: Spec/Faith
FAX Number: (314) 792-6500 Calendar System: Semester
URL: www.kenrick.edu
Established: 1893 Annual Undergrad Tuition & Fees: $27,695
Enrollment: 108 Male
Affiliation or Control: Roman Catholic IRS Status: 501(c)3
Highest Offering: Master's
Program: Professional; Religious Emphasis
Accreditation: NH, THEOL

01 President/Rector .... Rev. John P. HORN, S.J.
42 Dir Pre-Theology/Vice Rector .... Msgr. Gregory MIKESCH
05 Academic Dean .... Dr. John GRESHAM
32 Dean of Students .... Rev. Kristian TEATER
08 Director of Library .... Ms. Mary Ann AUBIN
88 Director of Spiritual Formation .... Vacant
42 Director of Worship .... Rev. Jason SCHUMER
30 Director of Development .... Ms. Kate GUYOL
06 Registrar/Financial Aid .... Deacon Joseph MEIERGERD
18 Chief Facilities/Physical Plant .... Mr. Gerry KLAAS

L'Ecole Culinaire (A)

9811 South Outer Forty Drive, Saint Louis MO 63124
Telephone: (314) 587-2433 Identification: 666275
Accreditation: ACCSC, ACFEI

† Main campus is Vatterott College-Des Moines in Des Moines, IA.

L'Ecole Culinaire Kansas City (B)

310 Ward Parkway, Kansas City MO 64112
Telephone: (816) 627-0100 Identification: 770579
Accreditation: ACCSC

† Main campus is Vatterott College-Des Moines in Des Moines, IA.

Lincoln University (C)

820 Chestnut Street, Jefferson City MO 65101-3537
County: Cole FICE Identification: 002479
Unit ID: 177940
Telephone: (573) 681-5000 Carnegie Class: Master's S
FAX Number: (573) 681-5566 Calendar System: Semester
URL: www.lincolnu.edu
Established: 1866 Annual Undergrad Tuition & Fees (In-State): $6,725
Enrollment: 3,205 Coed
Affiliation or Control: State IRS Status: 501(c)3
Highest Offering: Beyond Master's But Less Than Doctorate
Program: 2-Year Principally Bachelor's Creditable; Liberal Arts And General; Teacher Preparatory; Professional; Music Emphasis
Accreditation: NH, #ACBSP, ADNUR, MUS, NUR, SURGT, @SW, TED

01 President .... Dr. Kevin ROME
05 Interim VP Academic Affairs/Provost .... Dr. Ann HARRIS
32 Vice President Student Affairs .... Mrs. Theressa FERGUSON
30 VP University Advancement .... Mrs. Benecia R. WILLIAMS
10 Vice President Administration .... Mr. Curtis CREAGH
83 Dean Col Behavioral\Technical Sci .... Dr. Ruthie STURDEVANT
107 Dean Col of Professional Studies .... Dr. Linda S. BICKEL
49 Interim Dean College of Art/Letters .... Dr. Ruthie STURDEVANT
47 Dean College of Ag/Natural Sciences .... Vacant
08 University Librarian .... Mr. Jerome OFFORD, JR.
21 Controller .... Mrs. Sandy KOETTING
51 Director Continuing Education .... Ms. Kathy PABST
15 Director Human Resources .... Mr. James MARCANTONIO
88 Director Design and Construction .... Mrs. Sheila GASSNER
19 Director Police Department .... Mr. Bill NELSON
41 Director of Athletics .... Mrs. Betty KEMNA
29 Director Alumni Affairs .... Ms. Benecia WILLIAMS
26 Director Public Info/Univ Relations .... Ms. Misty YOUNG
06 Director of Records/Registrar .... Ms. Liz MORROW
38 Director Counseling/Career Services .... Vacant
07 Director of Admissions .... Ms. Annette CROWDER
09 Director Ctr Assess/Inst Rsrch .... Mrs. Beth NOLTE
23 Director Student Health Services .... Mrs. Latoya DUCKWORTH
35 Director of Student Activities .... Ms. Tammy NOBLES
43 Director Legal Svcs/Genl Counsel .... Mr. Kent BROWN
37 Dir Financial Aid/Stdnt Employment .... Mr. Alfred L. ROBINSON
96 Director of Purchasing .... Ms. Debra KIDWELL
18 Director of Buildings and Grounds .... Mr. Mark FRIEDMAN
13 Interim Chief Information Officer .... Mr. Jerome OFFORD
39 Director of Student Housing .... Mr. Carlos GRAHAM
12 Director Fort Leonard Wood Site .... Mrs. Barbara LANE
24 Director of Innovative Instruction .... Dr. Rachel SALE
40 Manager LU Bookstore .... Mr. James HOWARD
101 Exec Asst to President & Curators .... Ms. Rose Ann ORTMEYER
85 International Student Advisor .... Mrs. Mary BEZA
105 Web Content Manager .... Vacant

Lindenwood University (D)

209 S Kingshighway, Saint Charles MO 63301-1695
County: Saint Charles FICE Identification: 002480
Unit ID: 177968
Telephone: (636) 949-2000 Carnegie Class: Master's L
FAX Number: (636) 949-4910 Calendar System: Semester
URL: www.lindenwood.edu
Established: 1827 Annual Undergrad Tuition & Fees: $14,800
Enrollment: 11,483 Coed
Affiliation or Control: Independent Non-Profit IRS Status: 501(c)3
Highest Offering: Doctorate
Program: Liberal Arts And General; Teacher Preparatory; Professional
Accreditation: NH, ACBSP, SW, @TEAC

01 President .... Dr. James D. EVANS
04 Executive Assistant .... Ms. Judy SHANAHAN
05 Provost & Vice Pres Acad Affairs .... Dr. Jann RUDD WEITZEL
11 Vice Pres Operations/Finance & COO .... Ms. Julie MUELLER
30 Vice Pres Institutional Advancement .... Dr. Susan MANGELS
32 Vice President Student Development .... Dr. John OLDANI
16 Vice Pres Human Res/Dean Faculty .... Dr. Richard A. BOYLE
12 President Belleville Campus .... Mr. Jerry BLADDICK
09 Dean of Institutional Research .... Dr. Jeannie THIES
06 Registrar .... Ms. Christine HANNAR
10 Chief Financial Officer .... Mr. David KANDEL
29 Director Alumni Relations .... Ms. Elizabeth KING
26 Dir Communications/Public Relations .... Mr. Scott QUEEN
31 Director Community Development .... Ms. Charlsie FLOYD
13 Director of Information Services .... Mr. Shawn HAGHIGHI
08 Director of Library Services .... Ms. Elizabeth MACDONALD
37 Director of Financial Aid .... Ms. Lori BODE
35 Director of Student Activites .... Ms. Angela ROYAL
39 Director of Residential Operations .... Mr. Terry RUSSELL
39 Director of Residential Life .... Ms. Michelle GIESSMAN
92 Director of Honors Program .... Dr. Michael WHALEY
44 Dir Planned Giving/Internal Counsel .... Mr. Eric STUHLER
102 Dir Corporate/Foundation Relations .... Vacant
86 Dir of Outreach & Govt Relations .... Vacant
85 Director International Programs .... Dr. Ryan GUFFEY
40 Director of Auxiliary Services .... Mr. David DICKHERBER
22 Director of Compliance .... Ms. Christine REBORI
84 Dean of Enrollment Management .... Ms. Christie RODGERS
07 Dean of Undergraduate Admissions .... Dr. Joseph PARISI
89 Dean First Year Programs .... Dr. Shane WILLIAMSON
51 Dean Distance Learning .... Dr. Ed PERANTONI
12 Dean of Boone Campus .... Dr. David KNOTTS
20 Dean of Academic Services .... Mr. Barry FINNEGAN
55 Dean Evening/Ext Campus Admissions .... Mr. Brett BARGER
36 Director of Student Placement .... Ms. Dana WEHRLI
41 Athletic Director .... Mr. John CREER
42 Chaplain .... Mr. Timothy BUTLER
15 Personnel Officer .... Ms. Joyce TOWNSEND
79 School Dean Humanities .... Dr. Michael WHALEY
81 School Dean Sciences .... Dr. Ricardo DELGADO
53 School Dean Education .... Dr. Cynthia BICE
57 School Dean Arts .... Mr. Joe ALSOBROOK
50 Sch Dean Business/Entrepreneurship .... Dr. Roger ELLIS
60 School Dean Communications .... Mr. Mike WALL
88 School Dean Human Services .... Dr. Carla MUELLER
51 School Dean LCIE(Adult Learning) .... Mr. Dan KEMPER

Linn State Technical College (E)

One Technology Drive, Linn MO 65051-0479
County: Osage FICE Identification: 004711
Unit ID: 177977
Telephone: (573) 897-5000 Carnegie Class: Assoc/Pub-R-S
FAX Number: (573) 897-4656 Calendar System: Semester
URL: www.linnstate.edu
Established: 1961 Annual Undergrad Tuition & Fees (In-State): $5,820
Enrollment: 1,212 Coed
Affiliation or Control: State IRS Status: 501(c)3
Highest Offering: Associate Degree
Program: Occupational; 2-Year Principally Bachelor's Creditable
Accreditation: NH, ENGT, NAIT, PTAA, RAD

01 President .... Dr. Donald M. CLAYCOMB
05 Dean Academic Affairs/Student Svcs .... Victoria SCHWINKE
13 Dean Information Technology .... Don LLOYD
09 Dean Institutional Research/Plng .... Dr. Rick MIHALEVICH
30 Executive Director Development .... Scott PETERS
08 Int College Librarian .... Fran STUMPF
37 Director Student Financial Aid .... Becky WHITHAUS
06 Registrar .... Elaine BRANDT
07 Director Admissions .... Kathy SCHEULEN
11 Dir of Administrative Services .... Jeff FLETCHER
20 Associate Academic Officer .... Janet CLANTON
21 Controller .... Jennifer JACOBS
29 Dir Alumni Relations/Chief PR Ofcr .... Scott PETERS
35 Director Student Affairs .... Richard PEMBERTON
36 Director Student Placement .... Glenda WHITNEY
28 Director of Diversity .... Richard PEMBERTON
15 Director Personnel Services .... Jeff FLETCHER
84 Director Enrollment Management .... Kathy SCHEULEN
18 Chief Facilities/Physical Plant .... Dennis SALLIN
38 Student Counselor .... Ronda THOMPSON

Logan College of Chiropractic (F)

1851 Schoettler Road, PO Box 1065,
Chesterfield MO 63006-1065
County: Saint Louis FICE Identification: 004703
Unit ID: 177986
Telephone: (636) 227-2100 Carnegie Class: Spec/Health
FAX Number: (636) 207-2424 Calendar System: Trimester
URL: www.logan.edu
Established: 1935 Annual Undergrad Tuition & Fees: $7,420
Enrollment: 1,015 Coed
Affiliation or Control: Independent Non-Profit IRS Status: 501(c)3
Highest Offering: First Professional Degree
Program: Professional
Accreditation: NH, CHIRO

01 President .... Dr. Clay MCDONALD
05 VP Academic Affairs .... Dr. Carl W. SAUBERT, IV
11 VP Administrative Affairs .... Ms. Sharon K. KEHRER
84 VP Enrollment Management .... Dr. Boyd BRADSHAW
30 VP Institutional Advancement .... Ms. Patricia C. JONES
17 VP Chiropractic Affairs/PostGrad Ed .... Dr. Ralph BARALLE
43 Gen Counsel/VP Strategic Perf .... Ms. Laura MCLAUGHLIN
10 Chief Financial Officer .... Mr. Adil KHAN
27 Chief Information Officer .... Dr. Bradley HOUGH
20 Associate VP Academic Affairs .... Dr. Angela R. MCCALL
88 Dean of Chiropractic .... Vacant
23 Chief of Clinical Services .... Dr. Michael WITTMER
76 Dean of Health Sciences .... Vacant
46 Dean of Research .... Dr. Cheryl HAWK
32 Dean of Student Services .... Dr. James PAINE
26 Associate VP Public Relations .... Mr. Thomas KELLER
24 Associate VP for Educational Tech .... Mr. Vince MCGEE
88 Director of Assessment Center .... Dr. Martha KAESER
07 Director of Admissions .... Ms. Stacey TILL
06 Registrar .... Mr. John-Herbert JAFFRY
37 Director Student Financial Aid .... Ms. Linda HAMAN
08 Director Learning Resource Center .... Vacant
15 Director of Human Resources .... Mr. Les LEXOW
96 Director of Purchasing .... Mr. Charles FELTMANN
18 Physical Plant Superintendent .... Mr. Bill WHARTON

Maryville University of Saint Louis (G)

650 Maryville University Drive,
Saint Louis MO 63141-7299
County: Saint Louis FICE Identification: 002482
Unit ID: 178059
Telephone: (314) 529-9300 Carnegie Class: DRU
FAX Number: (314) 542-9085 Calendar System: Semester
URL: www.maryville.edu
Established: 1872 Annual Undergrad Tuition & Fees: $23,812
Enrollment: 4,203 Coed
Affiliation or Control: Independent Non-Profit IRS Status: 501(c)3
Highest Offering: Doctorate
Program: Liberal Arts And General; Teacher Preparatory; Professional
Accreditation: NH, ACBSP, ART, CIDA, CORE, MUS, NURSE, OT, PTA, TED

01 President .... Dr. Mark LOMBARDI
05 Vice Pres Academic Affairs .... Dr. Mary Ellen FINCH
45 Exec Dir of Planning/Research/Tech .... Mr. Jerry BRISSON
10 Vice Pres Administration & Finance .... Dr. Larry HAYS
84 Vice President Enrollment .... Mr. Jeffrey MILLER
30 VP Inst Advancemnt & Chief Dev Ofcr .... Mr. Thomas ESCHEN
32 VP for Student Life & Dn of Stdnts .... Dr. Nina CALDWELL
20 Associate VP Academic Affairs .... Dr. Tammy GOCIAL
100 Chief of Staff .... Ms. Kathy LUNAN
50 Dean School of Business .... Dr. Pamela HORWITZ
53 Dean School of Education .... Dr. Sam HAUSFATHER
76 Dean School Health Professions .... Dr. Charles GULAS
49 Dean College of Arts & Sciences .... Dr. Candace CHAMBERS
08 Dean University Library .... Dr. Eugenia MCKEE
106 Dean Adult & Online Education .... Mr. Dan VIELE
06 Exec Dir Student Svcs Ctr/Registrar .... Ms. Stephanie ELFRINK
89 Assoc Dir Acad Success & FYE .... Ms. Kelly MOCK
07 Assoc VP Enrollment .... Ms. Shani LENORE-JENKINS
29 Director of Alumni Affairs .... Ms. Erin VERRY
41 Director of Athletics .... Mr. Marcus MANNING
42 Dir Campus Ministry & Comm Service .... Mr. Stephen DISALVO
35 Assoc Dean of Students .... Ms. Kathy QUINN
36 Director Career Education .... Ms. Lynn WILLITS
35 Director Student Involvement .... Mr. Brian GARDNER
21 Controller/Dir Finance & Aux Entrpr .... Mr. Steven MANDEVILLE
102 Director of Development .... Ms. Megan HOLMES
37 Dir Student Svcs Ctr/Financial Aid .... Ms. Martha HARBAUGH
23 Director of Health & Wellness .... Ms. Pamela CULLITON
15 Dir HR/Affirm Action Officer .... Ms. Jackie PLUNKETT
14 Director Technology Services .... Mr. Richard KUBB
91 Dir Enterprise Information Systems .... Mr. David SCHULTE
09 Director Institutional Research .... Ms. Mary MERRIFIELD
90 Dir Learning Design & Technology .... Ms. Julie BERGFELD
26 Exec Dir Marketing & Community Rel .... Ms. Susan DAVIS
28 Asst Dean & Dir Multicultural Pgm .... Ms. Christie CRUISE-HARPER
18 Director of Physical Plant .... Mr. Tom BENNING
44 Director of Planned Gifts .... Mr. Mark ROOCK
102 Dir Foundation/Corp Relations .... Ms. Peggy MICHELSON
19 Director of Public Safety .... Mr. Michael PARKINSON
39 Director of Residential Life .... Ms. Kimberly WATSON
88 Assoc VP/Dir Acad Success & FYE .... Dr. Jennifer MCCLUSKEY
104 Assoc VP/Dir Ctr for Global Educ .... Dr. James HARF
88 Asst Athletic Dir-Communications .... Mr. Charles YAHNG
53 Asst Dean & Dir Teacher Education .... Dr. Nancy WILLIAMS
21 Dir Student Svcs Ctr/Student Accts .... Ms. Karen SCHOLBE
88 Director Fresh Ideas Food Services .... Ms. Linda THACKER
38 Director Personal Counseling .... Ms. Jennifer HENRY
44 Director of Development .... Ms. Fay FETICK
88 Assoc VP Ctr for Civic Engage & Dem .... Dr. Alden CRADDOCK

Metro Business College (H)

2132 Tenbrook Road, Arnold MO 63010
Telephone: (636) 296-9300 Identification: 770736
Accreditation: ACICS

† Main campus is Metro Business College in Cape Girardeau, MO.

Metro Business College (I)

1732 N Kingshighway, Cape Girardeau MO 63701-2122
County: Cape FICE Identification: 021802
Unit ID: 178110
Telephone: (573) 334-9181 Carnegie Class: Assoc/PrivFP
FAX Number: (573) 334-0617 Calendar System: Quarter
URL: www.metrobusinesscollege.edu
Established: 1981 Annual Undergrad Tuition & Fees: $14,000
Enrollment: 138 Coed
Affiliation or Control: Proprietary IRS Status: Proprietary
Highest Offering: Associate Degree
Program: Occupational; 2-Year Principally Bachelor's Creditable; Business Emphasis
Accreditation: ACICS

01 President .... Ms. Mary BUCKLEY
12 Campus Director .... Mrs. Jan REIMANN
05 Education Director .... Mr. Shannon BUFORD
37 Financial Aid Director .... Mrs. Janie WARNE
36 Career Services Coordinator .... Ms. Diane JORDAN

Metro Business College (A)

210 El Mercado Plaza, Jefferson City MO 65109
Telephone: (573) 635-6600 Identification: 666454
Accreditation: ACICS

† Main campus is Metro Business College in Cape Girardeau, MO.

Metro Business College (B)

1202 E Highway 72, Rolla MO 65401-3938
Telephone: (573) 364-8464 Identification: 666455
Accreditation: ACICS

† Main campus is Metro Business College in Cape Girardeau, MO.

*Metropolitan Community College - Kansas City Administrative Center (C)

3200 Broadway, Kansas City MO 64111-2429
County: Jackson FICE Identification: 009137
Unit ID: 178129
Telephone: (816) 604-1000 Carnegie Class: N/A
FAX Number: (816) 759-1158
URL: www.mcckc.edu

01 Chancellor .... Mr. Mark S. JAMES
101 Chancellor's Asst/Board Secretary .... Ms. Cindy K. JOHNSON
05 Vice Chanc Acad Affairs/Technology .... Mr. Paul D. LONG
10 Vice Chanc Admin Svcs/Student Dev .... Dr. Tuesday L. STANLEY
100 Chief of Staff/Associate VC HR .... Ms. Kathy WALTER-MACK
88 Performance Director Resource Dev .... Vacant
45 Director Budget and Planning .... Vacant
14 Director Computer Services .... Mr. Gary W. SCHIEBER
102 Exec Director MCC Foundation .... Mr. Kent HUYSER
96 Manager Purchasing .... Ms. Diane PACHEO
18 Director Facility Services .... Mr. Douglas LIGHTFOOT
103 Exec Dir Workforce Dev/HSI .... Ms. Nancy RUSSELL
88 Director Educational Services .... Ms. Fran A. PADOW
106 Director Distance Education .... Dr. Leo J. HIRNER
09 Director Inst Research/Assessment .... Dr. Kristy A. BISHOP
88 Director of Student Success .... Ms. Sydney BEELER
37 Director Student Financial Services .... Ms. Dena NORRIS
84 Director of Enrollment Services .... Vacant
21 Director of Accounting .... Mr. Steve FROMMELT
88 Director Adm Sys & Mngment Svcs .... Ms. Patricia A. AMICK
19 Assoc Director Public Safety .... Mr. Domenick R. BROUILLETTE
88 Chief of Campus Police .... Vacant
88 Director Tech Prep .... Ms. Teresa A. LONEY
88 Director Auxiliary Services .... Mr. Bradley BRIDGES

*Metropolitan Community College - Blue River (D)

20301 E 78 Highway, Independence MO 64057-2053
County: Jackson FICE Identification: 032613
Unit ID: 440305
Telephone: (816) 604-6550 Carnegie Class: Assoc/Pub-U-MC
FAX Number: (816) 759-6582 Calendar System: Semester
URL: www.mcckc.edu
Established: 1997 Annual Undergrad Tuition & Fees (In-District): $2,580
Enrollment: 3,900 Coed
Affiliation or Control: State/Local IRS Status: 501(c)3
Highest Offering: Associate Degree
Program: Occupational; 2-Year Principally Bachelor's Creditable
Accreditation: &NH

02 President .... Dr. Michael BANKS
04 Assistant to the President .... Mrs. Kimberly A. MORICONI
05 Dean of Instruction .... Vacant
32 Dean of Student Development .... Dr. Jonathan L. BURKE
51 Assoc Dean of Instruction .... Vacant
35 Assoc Dean of Student Development .... Mr. Basil LISTER
88 Director Western Missouri PSTI .... Mr. Mike W. HENDERSHOT
08 Head Librarian .... Mr. Jared RINCK
19 Campus Police Captain .... Mr. Booker S. ARMSTRONG
18 Facilities Superintendent .... Mr. Tom COOLEY
38 Lead Counselor .... Mr. Jeff WILT
84 Enrollment Manager .... Mr. Rowdy PYLE
13 Campus Network Coordinator .... Vacant
26 Marketing Coordinator .... Mr. Bob K. FLORENCE

† Regional accreditation is carried under the parent institution Metropolitan Community College-Kansas City Administrative Center in Kansas City, MO.

*Metropolitan Community College - Business and Technology (E)

1775 Universal Avenue, Kansas City MO 64120-2429
Identification: 666295
Unit ID: 442000
Telephone: (816) 604-1000 Carnegie Class: Assoc/Pub-U-MC
FAX Number: (816) 482-5256 Calendar System: Semester
URL: www.mcckc.edu/btc
Established: 1995 Annual Undergrad Tuition & Fees (In-District): $2,208
Enrollment: 1,158 Coed
Affiliation or Control: Local IRS Status: 501(c)3
Highest Offering: Associate Degree
Program: Occupational; 2-Year Principally Bachelor's Creditable; Technical Emphasis
Accreditation: &NH

02 Provost .... Vacant
05 Dean of Instruction .... Dr. Thomas WHEELER
32 Dean of Student Development .... Ms. Karen MOORE
84 Enrollment Manager .... Ms. Rene BENNETT
04 Assistant to the Provost .... Ms. LeAnn BRADBERRY

† Regional accreditation is carried under the parent institution Metropolitan Community College-Kansas City Administrative Center in Kansas City, MO.

*Metropolitan Community College - Longview (F)

500 SW Longview Road, Lee's Summit MO 64081-2105
County: Jackson FICE Identification: 009140
Unit ID: 177995
Telephone: (816) 604-2000 Carnegie Class: Assoc/Pub-U-MC
FAX Number: (816) 672-2025 Calendar System: Semester
URL: www.mcckc.edu
Established: 1969 Annual Undergrad Tuition & Fees (In-District): $2,760
Enrollment: 7,061 Coed
Affiliation or Control: Local IRS Status: 501(c)3
Highest Offering: Associate Degree
Program: Occupational; 2-Year Principally Bachelor's Creditable
Accreditation: &NH

02 President .... Dr. Kirk A. NOOKS
05 Dean of Instruction .... Dr. Arminda MCCALLUM
32 Dean Student Devel/Support Services .... Mrs. Karen GOOS
20 Associate Dean Instruction .... Vacant
35 Assoc Dean Student Dev/Support Svcs .... Mrs. Linda NELSON
07 Director of Admissions/Registrar .... Vacant
37 Manager of Student Financial Aid .... Ms. Lisa L. FANNAN
10 Business Office Supervisor .... Ms. Dianna M. CARPENTER
18 Physical Facilities Superintendent .... Mr. Steve B. GREIFE
36 Coordinator Student Employment Svcs .... Ms. Linda S. ANDERSON
38 Director Student Counseling .... Mrs. Gretchen S. BLYTHE

† Regional accreditation is carried under the parent institution Metropolitan Community College-Kansas City Administrative Center in Kansas City, MO.

*Metropolitan Community College - Maple Woods (G)

2601 NE Barry Road, Kansas City MO 64156-1299
County: Clay FICE Identification: 009139
Unit ID: 178022
Telephone: (816) 604-3000 Carnegie Class: Assoc/Pub-U-MC
FAX Number: (816) 437-3049 Calendar System: Semester
URL: www.mcckc.edu
Established: 1968 Annual Undergrad Tuition & Fees (In-District): $2,938
Enrollment: 9,050 Coed
Affiliation or Control: Local IRS Status: 501(c)3
Highest Offering: Associate Degree
Program: Occupational; 2-Year Principally Bachelor's Creditable
Accreditation: &NH

02 President .... Dr. Utpal GOSWAMI
05 Dean Instruction .... Vacant
32 Dean Student Services .... Ms. Shelli ALLEN
20 Associate Dean .... Mrs. Dawn K. HATTERMAN
20 Associate Dean .... Dr. Brian BECHTEL
08 Librarian .... Mrs. Linda CARTER
41 Athletic Director .... Dr. Brian BECHTEL
37 Manager Student Financial Aid .... Mrs. Robin STIMAC
40 College Bookstore Manager .... Vacant
18 Physical Facilities Superintendent .... Mr. Tom HULETT
10 Business Office Supervisor .... Ms. Emily THOMPSON
31 Community Relations Coordinator .... Mrs. Heather K. PEREZ
36 Student Employment Service Coord .... Ms. Mary Lynn MUNGER
38 Lead Counselor .... Vacant

† Regional accreditation is carried under the parent institution Metropolitan Community College-Kansas City Administrative Center in Kansas City, MO.

*Metropolitan Community College - Penn Valley (H)

3201 Southwest Trafficway, Kansas City MO 64111-2764
County: Jackson FICE Identification: 002484
Unit ID: 178785
Telephone: (816) 604-1000 Carnegie Class: Assoc/Pub-U-MC
FAX Number: (816) 759-4161 Calendar System: Semester
URL: www.mcckc.edu
Established: 1915 Annual Undergrad Tuition & Fees (In-District): $3,096
Enrollment: 5,409 Coed
Affiliation or Control: Local IRS Status: 501(c)3
Highest Offering: Associate Degree
Program: Occupational; 2-Year Principally Bachelor's Creditable; Nursing Emphasis
Accreditation: &NH, ADNUR, CAHIIM, DA, OTA, PNUR, PTAA, RAD, SURGT

02 President .... Dr. Joe SEABROOKS
05 Dean of Instruction .... Dr. Cheryl CARPENTER-DAVIS
32 Dean of Student Services .... Ms. Yvette SWEENEY
76 Dean of Health Science Institute .... Dr. Lester HARDEGREE, JR.
20 Assoc Dean Instructional Svc .... Mr. Michael MCCLOUD
35 Associate Dean of Student Services .... Mrs. Mindy JOHNSON
23 Director of Health Sciences .... Ms. Sandy MCILNAY
06 Registrar/Director of Admissions .... Mr. Carlton FOWLER
08 Librarian .... Vacant
14 NUS Department Director .... Vacant
18 Facilities Services Support .... Mr. Lloyd HALE
19 Campus Police Captain .... Cpt. Gary WILSON
41 Athletic Programs Manager .... Mr. Marcus HARVEY
37 Student Financial Aid Manager .... Ms. Rossann DOWNING
40 College Bookstore Manager .... Ms. Selin GAONA
10 Business Office Supervisor .... Ms. Michele ALLEN
27 Community & Public Relations Coord .... Ms. Kimberly RILEY
36 Career Coordinator .... Vacant

† Regional accreditation is carried under the parent institution Metropolitan Community College-Kansas City Administrative Center in Kansas City, MO.

Midwest Institute (I)

964 S. Highway Drive, Fenton MO 63026
County: St. Louis FICE Identification: 021211
Unit ID: 178183
Telephone: (314) 965-8363 Carnegie Class: Assoc/PrivFP
FAX Number: (636) 326-1059 Calendar System: Other
URL: www.midwestinstitute.com
Established: 1965 Annual Undergrad Tuition & Fees: $14,680
Enrollment: 183 Coed
Affiliation or Control: Proprietary IRS Status: Proprietary
Highest Offering: Associate Degree
Program: Occupational
Accreditation: ABHES

01 Director .... Dr. Adam EPSTEIN

Midwest Institute-Earth City (J)

4260 Shoreline Drive Suite 100, Earth City MO 63045
County: Saint Louis Identification: 667074
Telephone: (314) 344-4440 Carnegie Class: Not Classified
FAX Number: (314) 344-0495 Calendar System: Other
URL: www.midwestinstitute.com
Established: 1970 Annual Undergrad Tuition & Fees: N/A
Enrollment: N/A Coed
Affiliation or Control: Proprietary IRS Status: Proprietary
Highest Offering: Associate Degree
Program: Occupational
Accreditation: ABHES

01 President .... Ms. Christine SHREFFLER

Midwest University (K)

851 Parr Road, Wentzville MO 63385-0365
County: Saint Charles FICE Identification: 035283
Unit ID: 440253
Telephone: (636) 327-4645 Carnegie Class: Spec/Faith
FAX Number: (636) 327-4715 Calendar System: Semester
URL: www.midwest.edu
Established: 1986 Annual Undergrad Tuition & Fees: $7,950
Enrollment: 228 Coed
Affiliation or Control: Non-denominational IRS Status: 501(c)3
Highest Offering: Doctorate
Program: Professional; Religious Emphasis
Accreditation: BI

01 President .... Dr. James SONG
11 Executive Assistant to President .... Ms. Taylor J. BUMILLER
05 Academic Dean .... Dr. Myeong H. OH
09 Dir of Institutional Effectiveness .... Mr. Rolfe E. KIEHNE
32 Director of Student Affairs .... Dr. Chong W. LIM
42 Chaplin .... Dr. Dae G. KIM
06 Registrar/Admission .... Mr. Jeoung H. HAM
08 Director of Library Services .... Mrs. Hyun Shim JUNG
106 Director of E-Learning .... Dr. Dong Won SON
10 Director of Finance .... Mr. Kyong S. YEOM
21 Business Office Manager .... Ms. Bok H. SONG
45 Director of Planning & Marketing .... Mr. Jae P. SONG
13 Director of Information Technology .... Mr. Hee C. LEE
12 Korea Office Regional Director .... Dr. Jae M. SONG
12 Washington DC Regional Director .... Dr. Yoo K. KO
07 Admission Counselor .... Mrs. Yoo J. HAM
85 International Student Officer .... Mr. Kyong S. YEOM
85 International Student Officer .... Mr. Kyoo W. SEO

Midwestern Baptist Theological Seminary (L)

5001 N Oak Trafficway, Kansas City MO 64118-4697
County: Clay FICE Identification: 002485
Unit ID: 178208
Telephone: (816) 414-3700 Carnegie Class: Spec/Faith
FAX Number: (816) 414-3724 Calendar System: Semester
URL: www.mbts.edu
Established: 1957 Annual Undergrad Tuition & Fees: $6,746
Enrollment: 1,500 Coed
Affiliation or Control: Southern Baptist IRS Status: 501(c)3
Highest Offering: Doctorate
Program: Professional; Religious Emphasis
Accreditation: NH, THEOL

01 President .... Dr. Jason K. ALLEN
10 Vice President for Business Svcs .... Mr. Andrew DAVEY
05 Interim VP Academic Dev & Acad Dean .... Dr. Thor MADSEN
09 Vice President Inst Effectiveness .... Dr. Rodney A. HARRISON
32 Vice President Student Development .... Dr. David M. MCALPIN
30 VP of Institutional Advancement .... Mr. Charles SMITH

13 Vice President Info Technology .... Vacant
06 Registrar .... Dr. Mike HAWKINS
08 Librarian .... Dr. Craig KUBIC
73 Director of Doctoral Studies .... Dr. Rodney A. HARRISON
21 Director Financial Services .... Mrs. Cheryl HICKS
15 Human Resources .... Mr. Gary CRUTCHER
04 Exec Assistant to the President .... Mr. Pat HUDSON
18 Director of Campus Operations .... Mr. Larry HEADLEY
37 Financial Aid Director .... Mrs. Raschelle JOHNSTON
84 Dir Student Recruitment & Admission .... Mr. Nels CARLSON
20 Associate Dean .... Dr. Rustin UMSTATTD
26 Director Communications/Public Rels .... Mr. Tim SWEETMAN

Mineral Area College (A)

5270 Flat River Drive, Park Hills MO 63601-2224
County: Saint Francois FICE Identification: 002486
Unit ID: 178217
Telephone: (573) 431-4593 Carnegie Class: Assoc/Pub-R-M
FAX Number: (573) 518-2164 Calendar System: Semester
URL: www.mineralarea.edu
Established: 1922 Annual Undergrad Tuition & Fees (In-District): $3,060
Enrollment: 3,775 Coed
Affiliation or Control: Local IRS Status: 501(c)3
Highest Offering: Associate Degree
Program: Occupational; 2-Year Principally Bachelor's Creditable
Accreditation: NH, PTAA, RAD

01 President .... Dr. Steve KURTZ
03 Vice Pres/Dean Career/Tech Educ .... Mr. John (Gil) KENNON
49 Dean of Arts & Sciences .... Ms. Carolyn CRECELIUS
32 Dean Student Services .... Ms. Jean MERRILL-DOSS
10 Business Manager .... Mr. Rusty STRAUGHAN
13 Director of Computer Services .... Mr. Chad PIPKIN
06 Registrar .... Ms. Pam REEDER
07 Director of Admissions .... Ms. Julie SHEETS
09 Director of Institutional Research .... Ms. Lisa EDBURG
18 Chief Facil/Phys Plnt/Purchasing .... Mr. Rusty STRAUGHAN
26 Chief Public Relations Officer .... Ms. Sarah HAAS
29 Director Alumni Relations .... Vacant
15 Chief Human Resource Officer .... Ms. Kathryn NEFF
37 Director Student Financial Aid .... Ms. Denise SEBASTIAN
38 Director Student Counseling .... Mr. Michael EASTER
88 General Services Supervisor .... Mr. Rodney RESINGER
21 Director Payroll .... Ms. Lisa CLAUSER

Missouri Baptist University (B)

One College Park Drive, Saint Louis MO 63141-8698
County: Saint Louis FICE Identification: 007540
Unit ID: 178244
Telephone: (314) 434-1115 Carnegie Class: Master's L
FAX Number: (314) 434-7596 Calendar System: Semester
URL: www.mobap.edu
Established: 1964 Annual Undergrad Tuition & Fees: $20,764
Enrollment: 5,212 Coed
Affiliation or Control: Baptist IRS Status: 501(c)3
Highest Offering: Doctorate
Program: Liberal Arts And General; Teacher Preparatory
Accreditation: NH, EXSC, MUS, TED

01 President .... Dr. R. Alton LACEY
04 Assistant to the President .... Mrs. Susan RUTLEDGE
05 Senior VP of Academic Affs/Provost .... Dr. Arlen R. DYKSTRA
30 Senior VP of Inst Advancement .... Mr. Keith ROSS
32 Senior VP of Student Development .... Dr. Andy CHAMBERS
10 Senior VP for Business Affairs .... Mr. Ken REVENAUGH
58 VP of Grad Stds/Academic Pgm Review .... Dr. Clark TRIPLETT
84 VP of Enrollment Services .... Vacant
29 Director for Alumni Relations .... Ms. Abigail LESLIE
85 Director of International Services .... Mrs. Kari SAUNDERS
09 Director Institutional Research .... Mrs. Heather BRASE
08 Librarian .... Ms. Nitsa HINDELEH
37 Director Financial Services .... Mr. John BRANDT
26 Director University Communications .... Mr. Bryce CHAPMAN
36 Dir Career Svcs/Assoc Dean Students .... Ms. Kimberly GREY
41 Athletic Director .... Dr. Thomas SMITH
20 Associate Academic Dean .... Vacant
18 Director Campus Operations .... Mr. Stu LINDLEY
06 Director of Records .... Mrs. Linda CHRISOPE
15 Director Personnel Services .... Mrs. Barb BURNS
14 Director of Information Systems .... Mr. Chris SANDERS
19 Director Public Safety .... Mr. Stephen HEIDKE
35 Director Student Activities .... Mrs. Lara HINES
21 Controller .... Mrs. Pam SAVAGE
44 Development Officer .... Mrs. Ashlee JOHNSON
07 Director of Admissions .... Mrs. Cynthia SUTTON

Missouri College (C)

1405 South Hanley Road, Brentwood MO 63144-2902
County: St. Louis FICE Identification: 009795
Unit ID: 178305
Telephone: (314) 768-7800 Carnegie Class: Bac/Assoc
FAX Number: (314) 768-7900 Calendar System: Semester
URL: www.missouricollege.com
Established: 1963 Annual Undergrad Tuition & Fees: $16,498
Enrollment: 502 Coed
Affiliation or Control: Proprietary IRS Status: Proprietary
Highest Offering: Baccalaureate
Program: Occupational; 2-Year Principally Bachelor's Creditable
Accreditation: ACICS, DA, DH

01 President .... Mr. Karl PETERSEN
05 Dean of Academics .... Mrs. Nicole GRAMLICH
07 Admissions Director .... Ms. Heidi HOLMES
06 Registrar .... Ms. Brandi MENKE

Missouri Southern State University (D)

3950 E Newman Road, Joplin MO 64801-1595
County: Jasper FICE Identification: 002488
Unit ID: 178341
Telephone: (417) 625-9300 Carnegie Class: Bac/Diverse
FAX Number: (417) 625-3121 Calendar System: Semester
URL: www.mssu.edu
Established: 1965 Annual Undergrad Tuition & Fees (In-State): $5,376
Enrollment: 5,271 Coed
Affiliation or Control: State IRS Status: 501(c)3
Highest Offering: Master's
Program: Liberal Arts And General; Teacher Preparatory; Professional
Accreditation: NH, ACBSP, COARC, DH, ENGT, NUR, NURSE, RAD, TED

01 Interim President .... Dr. Alan MARBLE
05 Interim Vice Pres Academic Affairs .... Dr. Pat LIPIRA
32 Vice President for Student Affairs .... Mr. Darren S. FULLERTON
10 Vice President Business Affairs .... Mr. Rob YUST
13 Dir of Information Technology Svcs .... Mr. Albert (Al) STADLER
09 Asst VP Assessment/Inst Research .... Dr. Delores HONEY
20 Int Asst Vice Pres Academic Affairs .... Dr. Crystal LEMMONS
35 Dean of Students .... Dr. Ronald S. MITCHELL
06 Registrar .... Ms. Cheryl DOBSON
84 Director of Admissions .... Mr. Derek S. SKAGGS
92 Director of Honors Program .... Dr. Michael HOWARTH
08 Library Director .... Mrs. Wendy MCGRANE
30 Vice Pres for Development .... Mrs. JoAnn K. GRAFFAM
27 Director Univ Relations & Marketing .... Ms. Cassie M. MATHES
36 Director of Career Services .... Ms. Nicole R. BROWN
29 Director Alumni Association .... Mrs. Lee Eliff POUND
37 Director Student Financial Aid .... Ms. Becca L. DISKIN
38 Director of ACTS .... Mrs. Kelly WILSON
39 Director Student Housing .... Mr. Josh DOAK
21 Treasurer .... Mrs. Linda EIS
15 Director Human Resources .... Ms. Debbie D. KELLEY
18 Director Facilities/Physical Plant .... Mr. Robert HARRINGTON
32 Director of Student Activities .... Ms. Malorie CASHEL
96 Director of Purchasing .... Ms. Hiedi CARLIN
72 Dean School Technology .... Dr. Tia STRAIT
49 Dean School of Arts & Sciences .... Dr. Richard B. MILLER
53 Dean School Education .... Dr. Alfred CADE
50 Dean School of Business Admin .... Dr. John GROESBECK

Missouri State University (E)

901 S National Avenue, Springfield MO 65897-0027
County: Greene FICE Identification: 002503
Unit ID: 179566
Telephone: (417) 836-8500 Carnegie Class: Master's L
FAX Number: (417) 836-7669 Calendar System: Semester
URL: www.missouristate.edu
Established: 1905 Annual Undergrad Tuition & Fees (In-State): $6,908
Enrollment: 21,059 Coed
Affiliation or Control: State IRS Status: 501(c)3
Highest Offering: Doctorate
Program: Liberal Arts And General; Teacher Preparatory; Professional
Accreditation: NH, ADNUR, ANEST, ARCPA, AUD, BUS, BUSA, CEA, CONST, CS, DIETD, @DIETI, MUS, NHPA, NURSE, PH, PLNG, PTA, SP, SPAA, SW, TED, THEA

01 President .... Mr. Clifton M. SMART, III
05 Provost .... Dr. Frank E. EINHELLIG
12 Chancellor West Plains Campus .... Dr. Drew A. BENNETT
46 VP for Research/Economic Devel .... Dr. James P. BAKER
11 Vice Pres Administrative/Info Svcs .... Mr. Ken MCCLURE
30 Vice Pres University Advancement .... Mr. W. Brent DUNN
32 VP Student Affairs & Dean of Stdts .... Dr. Denita SISCOE
28 Vice Pres Diversity/Inclusion .... Dr. Kenneth COOPWOOD, SR.
20 Associate Provost .... Dr. Christopher J. CRAIG
20 Associate Provost .... Dr. Rachelle DARABI
20 Associate Provost .... Dr. Joyc NORRIS
58 Dean of Grad College .... Vacant
10 Chief Financial Officer .... Mr. Steve FOUCART
84 Asst VP Stdnt Affs/Enrollment Svcs .... Mr. Donald E. SIMPSON
08 Dean Library Services .... Mr. Thomas A. PETERS
09 Director of Institutional Research .... Dr. Katherine C. COY
29 Exec Dir of Alumni Relations .... Ms. Julie A. EBERSOLD
15 Director of Human Resources .... Mr. Edward CHOATE
37 Director of Student Financial Aid .... Ms. Vicki S. MATTOCKS
19 Director of Safety & Transportation .... Mr. Donald A. CLARK
36 Director of the Career Center .... Mr. Jack M. HUNTER
14 Director of Computer Services .... Mr. Jeff P. MORRISSEY
22 Equal Opportunity Officer .... Mr. Harold W. PRATT
100 Chief of Staff .... Mr. Paul K. KINCAID
23 Director of Health & Wellness Svcs .... Mr. Burnie L. SNODGRASS
92 Director Honors College .... Dr. John F. CHUCHIAK
18 Director Facilities Management .... Mr. Robert T. ECKELS
96 Director of Procurement .... Mr. Mike WILLS
07 Director of Admissions .... Mr. Andrew WRIGHT
06 Enrollment Services Systems Coord .... Mr. Rob HORNBERGER
49 Int Dean College Arts & Letters .... Dr. Gloria GALANES
79 Dean Col Humanities/Public Affairs .... Dr. Victor MATTHEWS
76 Dean Col Health/Human Services .... Dr. Helen C. REID
81 Dean Col Natural/Applied Science .... Dr. Tamera S. JAHNKE
53 Interim Dean College of Education .... Dr. David HOUGH
50 Dean Col of Business Administration .... Dr. Stephanie BRYANT

56 Asst Provost Extended Campus .... Mr. Stephen H. ROBINETTE
105 Director of Web Services .... Ms. Sara M. CLARK

Missouri State University - West Plains (F)

128 Garfield, West Plains MO 65775-2715
County: Howell FICE Identification: 031060
Unit ID: 179344
Telephone: (417) 255-7255 Carnegie Class: Assoc/Pub2in4
FAX Number: (417) 255-7962 Calendar System: Semester
URL: www.wp.missouristate.edu
Established: 1963 Annual Undergrad Tuition & Fees (In-State): $3,720
Enrollment: 2,102 Coed
Affiliation or Control: State IRS Status: 501(c)3
Highest Offering: Associate Degree
Program: Occupational; 2-Year Principally Bachelor's Creditable
Accreditation: NH, #COARC

05 Chief Academic Officer .... Mr. Dennis LANCASTER
32 Dean of Student Services .... Dr. Herbert LUNDAY
10 Director of Business Services .... Mr. Scott SCHNEIDER
30 Director of Development .... Mr. Joe KAMMERER
27 Director of Univ Communications .... Mrs. Cheryl CALDWELL
31 Director of Univ/Community Pgms .... Mrs. Brenda MALKOWSKI
14 Director of Computer Services .... Mrs. Sue INGRAM
06 Registrar .... Ms. Lu ADAMS
07 Coordinator of Admissions .... Mrs. Melissa JETT
09 Coord of Institutional Research .... Mrs. Patricia J. WALSH
26 Chief Public Relations Officer .... Mrs. Cheryl CALDWELL
36 Coordinator of Career Services .... Ms. Alice SMITH
37 Coord of Student Financial Aid .... Mrs. Donna BASSHAM
84 Director Enrollment Management .... Dr. Herbert LUNDAY
18 Chief Facilities/Physical Plant .... Mr. Ron HENSLEY

Missouri Tech (G)

1690 Country Club Plaza Drive, Saint Charles MO 63303
County: Saint Louis FICE Identification: 023040
Unit ID: 178350
Telephone: (636) 573-9300 Carnegie Class: Spec/Tech
FAX Number: (636) 573-9398 Calendar System: Semester
URL: www.motech.edu
Established: 1932 Annual Undergrad Tuition & Fees: $14,330
Enrollment: 117 Coed
Affiliation or Control: Proprietary IRS Status: Proprietary
Highest Offering: Baccalaureate
Program: Technical Emphasis
Accreditation: ACCSC

01 President .... Ms. Cynthia DODGE
05 Dean of Education .... Dr. Mark STINSON
37 Director Financial Aid .... Ms. Cindy Ann SINNOTT

*Missouri University of Science & Technology Engineering Education Center (H)

12837 Flushing Meadows Drive, St. Louis MO 63131
Telephone: (314) 835-9822 Identification: 770323
Accreditation: &NH

† Main campus is Missouri University of Science & Technology in Rolla, MO.

Missouri Valley College (I)

500 E College, Marshall MO 65340-3197
County: Saline FICE Identification: 002489
Unit ID: 178369
Telephone: (660) 831-4000 Carnegie Class: Bac/Diverse
FAX Number: (660) 831-4039 Calendar System: Semester
URL: www.moval.edu
Established: 1889 Annual Undergrad Tuition & Fees: $18,800
Enrollment: 1,440 Coed
Affiliation or Control: Presbyterian Church (U.S.A.) IRS Status: 501(c)3
Highest Offering: Master's
Program: Liberal Arts And General; Teacher Preparatory
Accreditation: NH

01 President .... Dr. Bonnie HUMPHREY
00 Chancellor Emeritus .... Dr. Earl J. REEVES
10 Chief Financial Officer .... Mr. Greg SILVEY
30 Vice Pres Institutional Advancement .... Mr. Eric SAPPINGTON
05 Chief Academic Officer .... Dr. Sharon WEISER
07 Dean of Admissions .... Ms. Tennille LANGDON
06 Registrar .... Ms. Marsha LASHLEY
21 Business Officer .... Mrs. Tonia BARTEL
08 Head Librarian .... Mrs. Pamela K. REEDER
41 Athletic Director/Dir of Operations .... Mr. Tom FIFER
42 Director Campus Ministry .... Rev. Pam SEBASTIAN
18 Director Maintenance .... Mr. Tim SCHULTE
32 Dean of Students .... Mr. Heath MORGAN
09 Director of Institutional Research .... Ms. Marilyn BELWOOD
15 Dir Personnel Svcs/Dir Purchasing .... Mr. Greg SILVEY
37 Director Student Financial Aid .... Mrs. Rachel ROBINSON
38 Director Student Counseling .... Ms. Teresa CESELSKI
13 Director of Systems Administration .... Mr. Jason RINNE
29 Director Alumni Relations .... Mr. Eric SAPPINGTON
26 Dir of Marketing & Media Relations .... Mrs. April DEGRAFF

Missouri Western State University (A)

4525 Downs Drive, Saint Joseph MO 64507-2294
County: Buchanan FICE Identification: 002490
Unit ID: 178387
Telephone: (816) 271-4200 Carnegie Class: Bac/Diverse
FAX Number: N/A Calendar System: Semester
URL: www.missouriwestern.edu
Established: 1915 Annual Undergrad Tuition & Fees (In-State): $5,342
Enrollment: 6,074 Coed
Affiliation or Control: State IRS Status: 501(c)3
Highest Offering: Master's
Program: Liberal Arts And General; Teacher Preparatory
Accreditation: NH, BUS, CAHIIM, ENGT, MUS, NURSE, PTAA, SW, TED

01 President .... Dr. Robert A. VARTABEDIAN
05 Provost/VP Academic Affairs .... Dr. Jeanne DAFFRON
30 Vice Pres University Advancement .... Mr. Jerry PICKMAN
10 VP Financial Planning and Admin .... Mr. Cale FESSLER
32 Vice Pres for Student Affairs .... Ms. Shana MEYER
20 Assoc Vice Pres Academic Affairs .... Dr. Cindy HEIDER
21 Assoc VP Financial Plng/Admin .... Ms. Carey MCMILLIAN
35 Dean of Students .... Dr. Judith GRIMES
49 Dean Liberal Arts & Science .... Dr. Murray NABORS
107 Dean Professional Studies .... Dr. Kathleen O'CONNOR
51 Dean of Western Institute .... Dr. Gordon MAPLEY
06 Registrar .... Ms. Susan BRACCIANO
07 Director of Admissions .... Mr. Howard MCCAULEY
08 Director of Library .... Ms. Julia SCHNEIDER
37 Director Student Financial Aid .... Ms. Marilyn BAKER
13 Director of Information Technology .... Mr. Mark MABE
38 Director Student Counsel & Testing .... Mr. H. David BROWN
18 Director Physical Plant .... Mr. Lonnie JOHNSON
41 Director of Athletics .... Mr. Kurt MCGUFFIN
15 Director of Human Resources .... Ms. Sally SANDERS
24 Director of Instructional Media .... Vacant
26 Dir of Public Relations & Marketing .... Ms. Mallory MURRAY
29 Director of Alumni Services .... Ms. Colleen KOWICH
44 Director of Development .... Mr. Jerry PICKMAN
96 Director of Purchasing .... Ms. Carey MCMILLIAN

Moberly Area Community College (B)

101 College Avenue, Moberly MO 65270-1304
County: Randolph FICE Identification: 002491
Unit ID: 178448
Telephone: (660) 263-4110 Carnegie Class: Assoc/Pub-R-M
FAX Number: (660) 263-6252 Calendar System: Semester
URL: www.macc.edu
Established: 1927 Annual Undergrad Tuition & Fees (In-District): $2,790
Enrollment: 5,500 Coed
Affiliation or Control: State/Local IRS Status: 501(c)3
Highest Offering: Associate Degree
Program: Occupational; 2-Year Principally Bachelor's Creditable
Accreditation: NH, MLTAD, OTA

01 President .... Dr. Jeffery LASHLEY
10 Vice President for Finance .... Mr. Gary STEFFES
05 Vice President of Instruction .... Ms. Paula GLOVER
75 Dean of Career/Technical Educ .... Ms. Jo FEY
32 Dean of Student Services .... Dr. James GRANT
12 Dean Off-Camp Pgms/Instr Tech .... Ms. Michele MCCALL
20 Dean of Academic Affairs .... Ms. Jacqueline FISCHER
09 Director Inst Effectiveness/Plng .... Mrs. Deanne K. FESSLER
21 Director Business/Accounting Svcs .... Ms. Sandra MAREK
26 Dir of Mktg and Public Relations .... Mr. Scott MCGARVEY
18 Director of Plant Operations .... Mr. Eric ROSS
14 Chief Information Officer .... Mr. Lloyd MARCHANT
08 Director of Library Services .... Ms. Valerie DARST
15 Director of Human Resources .... Ms. Ann PARKS
40 Director of Inst Svcs/Bookstore Mgr .... Ms. Virginia GEBHARDT
37 Director of Financial Aid .... Mrs. Amy HAGER
06 Registrar .... Ms. Lynn WALKER
29 Director Alumni Services .... Mr. Chad JAECQUES
36 Dir of Career and Technical Pgms .... Ms. Susan BROUK
88 Dir of Academic Services .... Ms. Katelyn BRANDKAMP

National American University-Independence (C)

3620 Arrowhead Avenue, Independence MO 64057
Telephone: (816) 418-7700 Identification: 770402
Accreditation: &NH, &MAC

† Main campus is National American University in Rapid City, SD.

National American University-Lee's Summit (D)

401 NW Murray Road, Lee's Summit MO 64081
Telephone: (816) 600-3900 Identification: 770404
Accreditation: &NH

† Main campus is National American University in Rapid City, SD.

National American University-Weldon Spring (E)

Triad Crossing, 1030 Wolfrum Rd,
Weldon Spring MO 63304
Telephone: (623) 229-3200 Identification: 770405
Accreditation: &NH

† Main campus is National American University in Rapid City, SD.

National American University-Zona Rosa (F)

7490 NW 87th Street, Kansas City MO 64153
Telephone: (816) 412-5500 Identification: 770403
Accreditation: &NH, &MAC

† Main campus is National American University in Rapid City, SD.

Nazarene Theological Seminary (G)

1700 E Meyer Boulevard, Kansas City MO 64131-1263
County: Jackson FICE Identification: 002494
Unit ID: 178518
Telephone: (816) 268-5400 Carnegie Class: Spec/Faith
FAX Number: (816) 268-5500 Calendar System: Semester
URL: www.nts.edu
Established: 1945 Annual Graduate Tuition & Fees: $8,190
Enrollment: 282 Coed
Affiliation or Control: Church Of The Nazarene IRS Status: 501(c)3
Highest Offering: Doctorate; No Undergraduates
Program: Professional
Accreditation: THEOL

01 President .... Dr. David BUSIC
05 Dean of the Faculty .... Dr. Roger HAHN
11 Dean for Administration .... Dr. D. Martin BUTLER
08 Director Library Service .... Mrs. Debra BRADSHAW
06 Registrar & Director of Admissions .... Mrs. Pamela ASHER
37 Financial Aid Coordinator .... Mr. Derek DAVIS

North Central Missouri College (H)

1301 Main Street, Trenton MO 64683-1824
County: Grundy FICE Identification: 002514
Unit ID: 179715
Telephone: (660) 359-3948 Carnegie Class: Assoc/Pub-R-S
FAX Number: (660) 359-2211 Calendar System: Semester
URL: www.ncmissouri.edu
Established: 1925 Annual Undergrad Tuition & Fees (In-District): $3,510
Enrollment: 1,786 Coed
Affiliation or Control: Local IRS Status: 501(c)3
Highest Offering: Associate Degree
Program: Occupational; 2-Year Principally Bachelor's Creditable
Accreditation: NH, DH, OTA

01 President .... Dr. Neil NUTTALL
05 VP Instruction/Student Services .... Dr. James GARDNER
10 Chief Financial Officer .... Mr. Tyson OTTO
32 Dean of Student Services .... Dr. Kristen ALLEY
20 Dean of Instruction .... Dr. Jamie HOOYMAN
76 Dean Allied Health Sciences .... Ms. Janet VANDERPOOL
06 Registrar .... Ms. Linda BROWN
27 Chief Information Officer .... Mr. Alan BARNETT
08 Librarian .... Ms. Beth CALDARELLO
37 Director of Financial Aid .... Ms. Megan DEWITT
30 Director Development .... Ms. Teresa CROSS
40 Director Bookstore .... Ms. Cecilia MARSH
39 Director Student Housing .... Mr. Donnie HILLERMAN
41 Athletic Director .... Mr. Steve RICHMAN
18 Director of Facilities .... Mr. Randy YOUNG
15 Director Human Resources .... Ms. Lee Ann SEARCY
101 Sec of Inst/Board of Governors .... Ms. Vicki WEAVER
105 Director Web Services .... Mr. Anthony ALEXANDER
09 Director of Institutional Research .... Ms. Tara NOAH

Northwest Missouri State University (I)

800 University Drive, Maryville MO 64468-6015
County: Nodaway FICE Identification: 002496
Unit ID: 178624
Telephone: (660) 562-1212 Carnegie Class: Master's L
FAX Number: (660) 562-1900 Calendar System: Trimester
URL: www.nwmissouri.edu
Established: 1905 Annual Undergrad Tuition & Fees (In-State): $7,455
Enrollment: 6,831 Coed
Affiliation or Control: State IRS Status: 501(c)3
Highest Offering: Beyond Master's But Less Than Doctorate
Program: Liberal Arts And General; Teacher Preparatory
Accreditation: NH, ACBSP, DIETD, MUS, NRPA, TED

01 President .... Dr. John JASINSKI
05 Provost .... Dr. Doug DUNHAM
10 Vice Pres for Finance .... Ms. Stacy CARRICK
32 VP Student Affairs/Dean of Students .... Dr. Matt BAKER
13 Vice Pres for Information Systems .... Dr. Roger VON HOLZEN
26 Vice President University Relations .... Ms. Mitzi LUTZ
15 Vice Pres of Human Resources .... Ms. Nola BOND
30 VP University Advancement .... Mr. Michael JOHNSON
84 Dean Enrollment Management .... Ms. Beverly S. SCHENKEL
09 Assoc Dir Institutional Research .... Ms. Mary Ann PENNISTON
08 Dir of Academic & Library Services .... Dr. Leslie GALBREATH
06 Registrar .... Ms. Terri VOGEL
37 Director Financial Aid .... Mr. Del MORLEY
36 Director of Career Services .... Ms. Joan SCHNEIDER
29 Director Alumni Relations .... Mr. Steve SUTTON
19 Chief University Police Department .... Mr. Clarence GREEN
41 Director Athletics/HPERD .... Mr. Nel TJEERDSMA
23 Director Wellness Services .... Dr. Gerald WILMES
96 Director of Purchasing .... Ms. Ann MARTIN
18 Director Facility Services .... Mr. David BRIDGE
58 Dean of Graduate School .... Dr. Gregory HADDOCK
53 Dean Col of Education & Human Svcs .... Dr. Joyce PIVERAL
49 Dean Col of Arts & Sciences .... Dr. Charles MCADAMS
50 Int Dean Col of Business/Prof Stds .... Dr. Greg HADDOCK
38 Director Student Counseling Center .... Vacant

Ozark Christian College (J)

1111 N Main Street, Joplin MO 64801-4804
County: Jasper FICE Identification: 022027
Unit ID: 178679
Telephone: (417) 626-1234 Carnegie Class: Spec/Faith
FAX Number: (417) 624-0090 Calendar System: Semester
URL: www.occ.edu
Established: 1942 Annual Undergrad Tuition & Fees: $10,350
Enrollment: 732 Coed
Affiliation or Control: Independent Non-Profit IRS Status: 501(c)3
Highest Offering: Baccalaureate
Program: Religious Emphasis
Accreditation: BI

01 President .... Matt PROCTOR
03 Executive Vice President .... Damien SPIKEREIT
04 Assistant to the President .... Kathy BOWERS
05 Academic Dean .... Doug ALDRIDGE
06 Registrar .... Jennifer MCMILLIN
32 Exec Director of Student Devel .... Monte SHOEMAKE
10 Exec Dir of Business Operations .... David MCMILLIN
07 Executive Director Admissions .... Troy NELSON
09 Exec Dir Inst Research/Gen Counsel .... Doug MILLER
29 Exec Director Alumni .... Dru ASHWELL
30 Exec Director of Development .... David DUNCAN
20 Assistant Academic Dean .... Chad RAGSDALE
26 Assoc Dir of College Advancement .... Jim DALRYMPLE
37 Director of Student Financial Aid .... Kim BALENTINE
90 Director Academic Computing .... David FISH
07 Director of Recruitment .... Kristin WRIGHT
88 Director of Church Relations .... Travis HURLEY
08 Director of Library Services .... John HUNTER
106 Associate Dean Online Learning .... Shawn LINDSAY
64 Coordinator of Music Department .... Scott HANDLEY
38 Student Counselor .... Sharon ENGELBRECHT
88 Director of Food Services .... Danon GALE
23 Campus Nurse .... Alecia CHAFFEE
34 Dean of Women .... Lisa WHITE
42 Director Campus Ministry .... Kevin GREER
88 Director of Christian Services .... Bob WITTE
40 Director of Bookstore .... Bob HEATH
41 Director Athletics .... Chris LAHM
18 Director Physical Plant .... Tim RUNYON
13 Director of College Technology Dept .... Mitchell PIERCY
105 Web Developer/Network Admin .... Matt DICKEY
14 Coordinator of Data Processing .... Gary WHEAT

Ozarks Technical Community College (K)

1001 E Chestnut Expressway, Springfield MO 65802-3625
County: Greene FICE Identification: 030830
Unit ID: 177472
Telephone: (417) 447-7500 Carnegie Class: Assoc/Pub-R-L
FAX Number: N/A Calendar System: Semester
URL: www.otc.edu
Established: 1990 Annual Undergrad Tuition & Fees (In-District): $3,330
Enrollment: 15,123 Coed
Affiliation or Control: State/Local IRS Status: 501(c)3
Highest Offering: Associate Degree
Program: Occupational; 2-Year Principally Bachelor's Creditable
Accreditation: NH, ACFEI, ADNUR, CAHIIM, COARC, DA, DH, EMT, IFSAC, MLTAD, OTA, PTAA, SURGT

01 Chancellor .... Dr. Hal L. HIGDON
04 Exec Secretary to Chancellor .... Ms. Karen CREIGHTON
05 Vice Chancellor Academic Affairs .... Dr. Steve BISHOP
11 Vice Chancellor Admin Services .... Mr. Rob RECTOR
13 Vice Chancellor IT .... Mr. Joel LAREAU
30 Vice Chancellor Inst Advancement .... Mr. Cliff DAVIS
10 Vice Chancellor Finance .... Ms. Marla MOODY
12 President Richwood Valley Campus .... Dr. Jeff JOCHEMS
32 Assoc Chancellor Student Services .... Ms. Joan BARRETT
20 Dean of Academic Services .... Dr. Kathy PERKINS
76 Dean of Allied Health Programs .... Dr. Sherry TAYLOR
97 Interim Dean of General Education .... Mr. Richard TURNER
56 Dean Extended Campus/Col Outreach .... Mr. Steve BIERMAN
72 Dean of Technical Education .... Mr. Layton CHILDRESS
08 Dean of Learning Resources .... Mr. Mike MADDEN
103 Dir Ctr Workforce Development .... Ms. Sherry COKER
38 Director of Counseling & Advising .... Ms. Joyce BATEMAN
26 College Dir Comm & Marketing .... Mr. Joel DOEPKER
18 Director of College Facilities .... Mr. Rickie TAYLOR
13 Asst Vice Chancellor IT .... Mr. Gerald BRYANT
14 Director of Computer Services .... Mr. Jack DOZIER
28 Asst Dean Disabilities Support Svcs .... Ms. Julie EDWARDS
37 College Director of Financial Aid .... Mr. Jeff FORD
15 College Director of Human Resources .... Mr. Tim BALTES
88 Director of Learning Resources Ctr .... Mr. Corky MCCORMACK
36 Director of Career Employment Svcs .... Ms. Kathy CHRISTY
102 Exec Director of OTC Foundation .... Mr. Cliff DAVIS
09 Dir Research/Strategic Planning .... Mr. John CLAYTON
19 Director of Safety & Security .... Mr. Scott LEVEN
35 Dean of Students .... Ms. Karla GREGG
29 Director of Development .... Ms. Stephanie BROWN
56 Coord Dual Credit/Tech Prep Program .... Ms. Cindy PHILLIPS

Ozarks Technical Community College Richwood Valley (A)

3369 W Jackson Street, Nixa MO 65714
Telephone: (417) 447-7700 Identification: 770324
Accreditation: &NH

† Main campus is Ozarks Technical Community College in Springfield, MO.

Ozarks Technical Community College Table Rock Campus (B)

10698 Historic Highway 165, Hollister MO 65672
Telephone: (417) 447-7500 Identification: 770325
Accreditation: &NH

† Main campus is Ozarks Technical Community College in Springfield, MO.

Park University (C)

8700 River Park Drive, Parkville MO 64152-3795
County: Platte FICE Identification: 002498
Unit ID: 178721
Telephone: (816) 741-2000 Carnegie Class: Master's M
FAX Number: (816) 746-6423 Calendar System: Semester
URL: www.park.edu
Established: 1875 Annual Undergrad Tuition & Fees: $10,500
Enrollment: 11,787 Coed
Affiliation or Control: Independent Non-Profit IRS Status: 501(c)3
Highest Offering: Master's
Program: Liberal Arts And General; Teacher Preparatory; Professional
Accreditation: NH, ACBSP, ADNUR, SW

01 President .... Dr. Michael DROGE
05 Provost & Senior Vice President .... Dr. Jerry JORGENSEN
10 Vice President for Finance & Admin .... Ms. Dorla WATKINS
30 Vice Pres University Advancement .... Ms. Laurie MCCORMACK
84 VP Enrollment Mgt/Student Services .... Mr. Alan J. LIEBRECHT
27 VP for Communication & Marketing .... Ms. Rita WEIGHILL
43 Vice President & General Counsel .... Mr. Roger HERSHEY
20 Associate VP for Academic Affairs .... Dr. Kenneth CHRISTOPHER
11 AVP for Finance & Administration .... Mr. Dean VAKAS
32 Associate VP for Student Services .... Ms. Clarinda CREIGHTON
31 Assoc VP for Constituent Engagement .... Mr. Erik BERGRUD
35 Dean of Student Life .... Dr. Diana MCELROY
58 Dean School of Grad & Prof Studies .... Dr. Laurie DIPADOVA-STOCKS
06 Registrar .... Ms. Jody MANCHION
07 Assoc Dean Admissions and SFS .... Ms. Cathy COLAPIETRO
08 Director of Library Systems .... Mr. Glenn FERDMAN
12 Director Park Accelerated Programs .... Mr. Eric BLAIR
88 Director of Advancement Services .... Mrs. Sandra SANDERS
15 Director of Human Resources .... Mr. Roger DUSING
29 Director of Alumni Relations .... Ms. Julie MCCOLLUM
96 Dir or Budget and Purchasing .... Ms. Donna BAKER
18 Director of Environmental Services .... Mr. Paul TOHLE
41 Director of Athletics .... Mr. Claude ENGLISH
66 Director of Nursing Program .... Ms. Gerry WALKER
85 Director of Foreign Students .... Vacant
37 Director Student Financial Services .... Ms. Carla BOREN
13 CIO Technical Services .... Mr. David MONCHUSIE
09 Director Inst Research & Assessment .... Dr. John TEW, JR.
19 Director of Campus Safety .... Mr. Christopher LOOS
50 Director MBA Program .... Dr. Nick KOUDOU
96 Asst Director Purchasing Services .... Ms. Nicole WILLIAMS
04 Exec Asst to the President .... Ms. Laure CHRISTENSEN
26 Director of Marketing .... Vacant
25 Director Sponsored Programs .... Mr. Edmund BRACKETT
50 Dean School of Business/Mgmt .... Dr. Brad KLEINDL
106 Assoc VP Park Distance Learning .... Dr. Charles KATER
49 Dean Liberal Arts & Sciences .... Dr. Emily DONNELLI SALLEE
53 Dean School for Education .... Dr. Michelle MYERS
80 Associate Dean HSPA .... Dr. Rebekkah STUTEVILLE

Pinnacle Career Institute (D)

1001 E 101st Terrace, Suite 325,
Kansas City MO 64131-3368
County: Jackson FICE Identification: 010405
Unit ID: 177302
Telephone: (816) 331-5700 Carnegie Class: Assoc/PrivFP
FAX Number: (816) 331-2026 Calendar System: Quarter
URL: www.pcitraining.edu
Established: 1953 Annual Undergrad Tuition & Fees: $13,848
Enrollment: 708 Coed
Affiliation or Control: Proprietary IRS Status: Proprietary
Highest Offering: Associate Degree
Program: Occupational
Accreditation: ACICS

01 Executive Director .... Ms. Maggie FRANZ
05 Director of Education .... Greg SMEE
36 Director Student Placement .... Ms. Jenny MISCHE
07 Director of Admissions .... Maggie FRANZ

Pinnacle Career Institute (E)

11500 Ambassador Road, Suite 221,
Kansas City MO 64153
Telephone: (816) 270-5300 Identification: 770737
Accreditation: ACICS

† Main campus is Pinnacle Career Institute in Kansas City, MO.

Ranken Technical College (F)

4431 Finney Avenue, Saint Louis MO 63113-2898
County: Saint Louis FICE Identification: 012500
Unit ID: 178891
Telephone: (314) 371-0236 Carnegie Class: Assoc/PrivNFP4
FAX Number: (314) 371-0241 Calendar System: Semester
URL: www.ranken.edu
Established: 1907 Annual Undergrad Tuition & Fees: $14,232
Enrollment: 1,221 Coed
Affiliation or Control: Independent Non-Profit IRS Status: 501(c)3
Highest Offering: Baccalaureate
Program: Occupational; 2-Year Principally Bachelor's Creditable; Technical Emphasis
Accreditation: NH

01 President .... Mr. Stan SHOUN
10 Vice President for Finance & Admin .... Mr. Peter T. MURTAUGH
05 Vice President for Education .... Mr. Don POHL
32 Vice President for Student Success .... Mr. John WOOD
51 Dean of Continuing Education .... Mr. Keyvan GERAMI
20 Dean Academic Affairs .... Ms. Crystal HERRON
07 Admissions Director .... Mr. Michael E. HAWLEY
06 Registrar .... Ms. Carol J. WINKLER
08 Head Librarian .... Ms. Barbara EDWARDS
18 Director Buildings & Grounds .... Mr. David CADLE
29 Director of Alumni Relations .... Ms. Kathy T. FERN
37 Director Financial Aid .... Ms. Michelle L. WILLIAMS
21 Business Office Manager .... Ms. Seletha R. CURTIS
36 Career Services Coordinator .... Ms. Janie K. SUMMERS
15 Human Resources Coordinator .... Ms. Janice A. BOLLMANN

Research College of Nursing (G)

2525 E Meyer Boulevard, Kansas City MO 64132-1133
County: Jackson FICE Identification: 006392
Unit ID: 178989
Telephone: (816) 995-2800 Carnegie Class: Spec/Health
FAX Number: (816) 995-2817 Calendar System: Semester
URL: www.researchcollege.edu
Established: 1980 Annual Undergrad Tuition & Fees: $31,650
Enrollment: 433 Coed
Affiliation or Control: Proprietary IRS Status: Proprietary
Highest Offering: Master's
Program: Liberal Arts And General; Professional; Nursing Emphasis
Accreditation: NH, NURSE

01 President .... Dr. Nancy O. DEBASIO
05 Dean .... Dr. Julie NAUSER
07 Director Admissions .... Ms. Leslie MENDENHALL
28 Director Diversity .... Ms. Victoria HAYNES
37 Director Financial Aid .... Ms. Stacie WITHERS
24 Director LRC .... Ms. Tobey STOSBERG
32 Director Student Affairs .... Ms. Lori VITALE
105 Director Web Based Education .... Ms. Sheryl MAX
09 Senior Technology Analyst .... Mr. Will GIVENS

Rockbridge Seminary (H)

3111 E. Battlefield Street, Springfield MO 65804
County: Greene Identification: 667151
Telephone: (866) 931-4300 Carnegie Class: Not Classified
FAX Number: (866) 931-4300 Calendar System: Semester
URL: www.rockbridge.edu
Established: 2002 Annual Graduate Tuition & Fees: $6,030
Enrollment: 150 Coed
Affiliation or Control: Independent Non-Profit IRS Status: 501(c)3
Highest Offering: Master's; No Undergraduates
Program: Religious Emphasis
Accreditation: DETC

01 President .... Dr. Daryl ELDRIDGE
05 Chief Learning Officer .... Dr. Sam SIMMONS

Rockhurst University (I)

1100 Rockhurst Road, Kansas City MO 64110-2561
County: Jackson FICE Identification: 002499
Unit ID: 179043
Telephone: (816) 501-4000 Carnegie Class: Master's L
FAX Number: (816) 501-4588 Calendar System: Semester
URL: www.rockhurst.edu
Established: 1910 Annual Undergrad Tuition & Fees: $30,550
Enrollment: 2,808 Coed
Affiliation or Control: Roman Catholic IRS Status: 501(c)3
Highest Offering: Doctorate
Program: Liberal Arts And General; Teacher Preparatory; Professional; Business Emphasis
Accreditation: NH, BUS, OT, PTA, SP, TEAC

01 President .... Rev. Thomas B. CURRAN
30 Vice Pres University Advancement .... Mr. Robert GRANT
10 Vice Pres Finance & Administration .... Mr. Guy SWANSON
05 Int Vice Pres for Academic Affairs .... Dr. Jeffrey BREESE
88 Asst to Pres for Mission & Ministry .... Dr. Ellen SPAKE
32 VP Student Developmnt/Athletics .... Dr. Matthew D. QUICK
11 Assoc VP Facilities & Technology .... Mr. Matt W. HEINRICH
84 Associate Vice Pres Enrollment .... Mr. Lane RAMEY
20 Assoc VP Academic Affairs/Planning .... Dr. Paula SHORTER
35 Director of Student Life .... Ms. Angie CARR ROBINETT
88 Assistant Dean of Students .... Mrs. Sandy WADDELL
39 Associate Dean of Students .... Vacant
04 Assistant to the President .... Ms. Kathy J. SOLODUCHA
50 Dean Helzberg Sch of Management .... Dr. Cheryl M. MCCONNELL
49 Dean Arts & Sciences .... Dr. Timothy MCDONALD
58 Int Dean Sch Graduate/Prof Studies .... Dr. James MILLARD
66 Pres Research Col of Nursing .... Dr. Nancy DEBASIO
08 Director Library .... Ms. Laurie E. HATHMAN
06 Registrar .... Ms. Minda THROWER
37 Director Student Financial Aid .... Ms. Maureen MCKINNON
41 Director of Athletics .... Mr. Gary BURNS
15 Director of Human Resources .... Ms. Cheri HARLOW
14 Director of Infrastructure Services .... Mr. Michael CRAIG
36 Director of Career Center .... Mr. Michael J. THEOBALD
26 Director of Public Relations .... Ms. Katherine FROHOFF
88 Director of Marketing .... Ms. Lauren DEBIAK
29 Director Alumni Rels & Constituent .... Mrs. Mary LANDERS
42 Director of Campus Ministry .... Ms. Maureen E. HENDERSON
19 Director Security/Safety .... Mr. William G. EVANS
38 Director of Student Counseling .... Dr. Rick D. HANSON
44 Director of Gift Planning .... Vacant
31 Director Community Relations .... Ms. Alicia R. DOUGLAS
40 Director Bookstore .... Mr. James GARBARINO
92 Director Honors Program .... Dr. Mindy WALKER
108 Assessment Coordinator .... Ms. Annalisa GRAMLICH
44 Senior Development Officer .... Ms. Amy DROUIN
09 Institutional Research Coordinator .... Ms. Wendy PICKEL
28 Area & Diversity Coordinator .... Ms. Emily J. KEMPF
24 Coordinator AV and Media .... Mr. Darnell JONES
88 Controller .... Ms. Rachel LIERZ
88 Dean Research Col of Nursing .... Ms. Julie NAUSER

St. Charles Community College (J)

4601 Mid Rivers Mall Drive, Cottleville MO 63376-2865
County: Saint Charles FICE Identification: 025306
Unit ID: 262031
Telephone: (636) 922-8000 Carnegie Class: Assoc/Pub-S-SC
FAX Number: (636) 922-8352 Calendar System: Semester
URL: www.stchas.edu
Established: 1986 Annual Undergrad Tuition & Fees (In-District): $2,850
Enrollment: 7,724 Coed
Affiliation or Control: State/Local IRS Status: 501(c)3
Highest Offering: Associate Degree
Program: Occupational; 2-Year Principally Bachelor's Creditable
Accreditation: NH, ADNUR, CAHIIM, OTA

01 President .... Dr. Ronald CHESBROUGH
04 Exec Assistant to the President .... Ms. Julie PARCEL
05 Vice Pres Academic/Student Affairs .... Mr. Chris BREITMEYER
30 Vice Pres for College Advancement .... Ms. Kasey MCKEE
10 Vice Pres for Administrative Svcs .... Mr. Todd GALBIERZ
16 Vice President for Human Resources .... Ms. Donna DAVIS
26 Vice President for Marketing & Comm .... Ms. Heather MCDORMAN
18 Director of Facilities .... Mr. Al KOEHLER
20 AVP for Academic/Student Affairs .... Dr. Michael B. DOMPIERRE
62 Dean Learning Resources & Acad Sup .... Dr. Stephanie TOLSON
09 Director Institutional Research .... Dr. Ronald PENNINGTON
13 AVP for Technology/Online Learning .... Mr. William STRECKER
84 Dean of Enrollment Services .... Ms. Kathy BROCKGREITENS
19 Director of Public Safety .... Mr. Bob RONKOSKI
90 Manager of Academic Computing .... Ms. Lisa MOUSER
35 Dean of Students .... Ms. Yvette M. SWEENEY
103 Director of Workforce Development .... Ms. Amanda SIZEMORE
51 Assoc Dean Continuing Education .... Ms. Tina SIEKER
50 Dean Bus/Sci/Educ/Math & Comp Sci .... Dr. John BOOKSTAVER
57 Dean Arts/Humanities & Soc Sci .... Ms. Karen JONES
40 Director of Bookstore and Food Svcs .... Ms. Patricia A. HAYNES
41 Athletic Director .... Mr. Chris G. GOBER
96 Director of Purchasing .... Ms. Christine E. ROMER
91 Director of Admin Computing .... Ms. Floretha J. JOHNSON
07 Dean of Enrollment Services .... Ms. Kathy BROCKGREITENS
21 Director of Financial Services .... Ms. Susan RUBEMEYER
36 Job Placement Coordinator .... Ms. Martha A. TOEBBEN
51 Dean Corporate & Community Dev .... Ms. Yvonne WILLS
88 Student Activities Manager .... Ms. Kelley PFEIFFER

Saint Louis Christian College (K)

1360 Grandview Drive, Florissant MO 63033-6499
County: Saint Louis FICE Identification: 012580
Unit ID: 179256
Telephone: (314) 837-6777 Carnegie Class: Spec/Faith
FAX Number: (314) 837-8291 Calendar System: Semester
URL: www.slcconline.edu
Established: 1956 Annual Undergrad Tuition & Fees: $8,215
Enrollment: 246 Coed
Affiliation or Control: Other Protestant IRS Status: 501(c)3
Highest Offering: Baccalaureate
Program: 2-Year Principally Bachelor's Creditable; Religious Emphasis
Accreditation: BI

00 Chancellor .... Mr. Thomas W. MCGEE
01 President .... Dr. Guthrie VEECH
05 Academic Dean .... Dr. Michael CHAMBERS
10 Vice Pres of Finance/Operations .... Dr. Judy LINCOLN
32 Dean of Students .... Ms. Christine CABLE
08 Library Manager .... Mr. Matt DEWITT

41 Athletic Director .... Mr. Michael WOMBLE
06 Registrar .... Ms. Cindy BINGAMON
37 Financial Aid Director .... Ms. Cathy WILHOIT
40 Bookstore Manager .... Ms. Melissa RABIDEAU
07 Admissions Counselor .... Ms. Haley WOMBLE

Saint Louis College of Health Careers-Fenton Campus (A)

1297 N Highway Drive, Fenton MO 63026-1909
Telephone: (636) 529-0000 Identification: 666274
Accreditation: ABHES, COARC, OTA, @PTAA

† Main campus is Saint Louis College of Health Careers-South Taylor in Saint Louis, MO.

Saint Louis College of Health Careers-South Taylor (B)

909 S Taylor Avenue, Saint Louis MO 63110-1511
County: Saint Louis FICE Identification: 023405
Unit ID: 179511
Telephone: (314) 652-0300 Carnegie Class: Assoc/PrivFP
FAX Number: (314) 652-2125 Calendar System: Semester
URL: www.slchc.com
Established: 1981 Annual Undergrad Tuition & Fees: $19,650
Enrollment: 362 Coed
Affiliation or Control: Proprietary IRS Status: Proprietary
Highest Offering: Associate Degree
Program: Occupational
Accreditation: ABHES

01 Associate Dean .... Lou VIDOVIC
05 Director of Education .... Michelle YEAGER

St. Louis College of Pharmacy (C)

4588 Parkview Place, Saint Louis MO 63110-1088
County: Independent City FICE Identification: 002504
Unit ID: 179265
Telephone: (314) 367-8700 Carnegie Class: Spec/Health
FAX Number: (314) 446-8304 Calendar System: Semester
URL: www.stlcop.edu
Established: 1864 Annual Undergrad Tuition & Fees: $27,993
Enrollment: 1,299 Coed
Affiliation or Control: Independent Non-Profit IRS Status: 501(c)3
Highest Offering: First Professional Degree
Program: Professional
Accreditation: NH, PHAR

01 President .... Dr. John A. PIEPER
30 Vice Pres Devel/Alumni Relations .... Mr. Brett T. SCHOTT
10 VP Finance/Administration/CFO .... Mr. Gary G. TORRENCE
07 Vice Pres of Enrollment Services .... Ms. Gloria J. VERTREES
90 Vice Pres Info Technology & CIO .... Mr. Chad SHEPHERD
49 Dean Arts & Science/Student Affairs ...... Dr. Kimberly J. KILGORE
67 Dean of Pharmacy .... Vacant
15 Director of Human Resources .... Mr. Daniel C. BAUER
06 Registrar .... Ms. Penny J. BRYANT
08 Library Director .... Ms. Jill NISSEN
37 Director of Financial Aid .... Mr. Daniel J. STIFFLER
36 Director of Placement Services .... Vacant
18 Chief Facilities/Physical Plant .... Mr. Al FARROW
26 Vice President Mktg/Communications .... Mr. Marcus LONG
29 Director Devel/Alumni Relations .... Ms. Necole POWELL
41 Director of Athletics .... Ms. Jill JOKERST-HARTER
04 Special Assistant to the President .. Sr. Mary Louise DEGENHART

*Saint Louis Community College Center (D)

300 S Broadway, Saint Louis MO 63102-2820
County: Saint Louis FICE Identification: 002469
Unit ID: 179283
Telephone: (314) 539-5000 Carnegie Class: N/A
FAX Number: (314) 539-5170
URL: www.stlcc.edu

01 Chancellor .... Dr. Myrtle E B. DORSEY
05 Vice Chanc Academic & Stdnt Affairs .... Dr. Donna DARE
10 Vice Chanc Finance/Administration .... Mr. Kent KAY
13 Vice Chancellor Technology .... Dr. Craig KLIMCZAK
103 Vice Chanc Workforce & Cmty Develop .... Mr. Rod NUNN
102 Executive Director Foundation .... Ms. Jo-Ann DIGMAN
84 Director Enrollment Management .... Dr. Joanie FRIEND
21 Controller .... Mr. Bruce VOGELGESANG
15 Assoc Vice Chanc HR .... Mr. Bill MILLER
26 Director Communications .... Mr. DeLancey SMITH
09 Director of Institutional Research .... Ms. Kelli BURNS
20 Director Instructional Resources .... Ms. Sheila OUELLETTE
30 Director Institutional Development .... Ms. Castella HENDERSON
06 Manager Central Student Records .... Ms. Lauren ROBERDS

*Saint Louis Community College at Forest Park (E)

5600 Oakland Avenue, Saint Louis MO 63110-1393
County: Independent City FICE Identification: 002471
Unit ID: 179308
Telephone: (314) 644-9100 Carnegie Class: Assoc/Pub-U-MC
FAX Number: (314) 644-9752 Calendar System: Semester
URL: www.stlcc.edu
Established: 1962 Annual Undergrad Tuition & Fees (In-District): $2,232
Enrollment: 7,994 Coed
Affiliation or Control: Local IRS Status: 501(c)3
Highest Offering: Associate Degree
Program: Occupational; 2-Year Principally Bachelor's Creditable
Accreditation: NH, ACFEI, ADNUR, CAHIIM, COARC, DA, DH, DMS, MLTAD, RAD, SURGT

02 President .... Dr. Cindy K. HESS
05 Vice President Academic Affairs .... Dr. Tracy HALL
32 Vice President Student Affairs .... Dr. Thomas WALKER, JR.
83 Dean Hum/Social Sci/Soc Pgms ...... Mrs. Amanda MEAD-ROACH
76 Dean Allied Health/Natural Science ..... Mr. Vincent FEATHERSON
50 Dean Business/Math/Technology .... Ms. Elizabeth WILCOXSON
38 Chair of Counseling .... Ms. Marlene RHODES
27 Manager Campus Community Relations ..... Ms. Susan EDMISTON
19 College Police Chief .... Mr. Richard BANAHAN
10 Manager Campus Business Office ...... Ms. Chitra SUBRAMANIAN
36 Manager Career & Employment Svcs .... Mr. Davis MOORE
37 Manager of Student Aid .... Ms. Paulette JOHNSON
51 Manager Harrison Education Ctr .... Ms. Kim PORTER

**Saint Louis Community College at Florissant Valley* (F)

3400 Pershall Road, Saint Louis MO 63135-1499
Telephone: (314) 513-4200 FICE Identification: 002470
Accreditation: &NH, ADNUR, ART, DIETT, ENGT

† Main campus is Saint Louis Community College at Forest Park in Saint Louis, MO.

**Saint Louis Community College at Meramec* (G)

11333 Big Bend Rd., Kirkwood MO 63122-5799
Telephone: (314) 984-7500 FICE Identification: 002472
Accreditation: &NH, ADNUR, ART, OTA, PTAA

† Main campus is Saint Louis Community College at Forest Park in Saint Louis, MO.

**Saint Louis Community College at Wildwood* (H)

2645 Generations Drive, Wildwood MO 63040-1168
Telephone: (636) 422-2000 Identification: 667084
Accreditation: &NH

† Main campus is Saint Louis Community College at Forest Park in Saint Louis, MO.

Saint Louis University (I)

One Grand Boulevard, Saint Louis MO 63103-2097
County: Independent City FICE Identification: 002506
Unit ID: 179159
Telephone: (314) 977-2500 Carnegie Class: RU/H
FAX Number: (314) 977-3874 Calendar System: Semester
URL: www.slu.edu
Established: 1818 Annual Undergrad Tuition & Fees: $36,360
Enrollment: 13,981 Coed
Affiliation or Control: Roman Catholic IRS Status: 501(c)3
Highest Offering: Doctorate
Program: Liberal Arts And General; Teacher Preparatory; Professional
Accreditation: NH, AAB, ARCPA, ART, BUS, CAHIIM, CLPSY, CYTO, DENT, DIETD, DIETI, ENG, HSA, LAW, MED, MFCD, MT, NMT, NURSE, OT, PH, PTA, RTT, SP, SPAA, SW, TED

01 Interim President .... Mr. William R. KAUFFMAN
05 Vice Pres for Academic Affairs .... Dr. Ellen F. HARSHMAN
10 Vice Pres/Chief Financial Officer .... Mr. David HEIMBURGER
18 Vice Pres Facilities Management .... Ms. Kathleen BRADY
84 Vice President Enrollment & Ret .... Mr. Jay GOFF
12 Director Madrid Campus .... Dr. Paul VITA
16 Vice Pres Human Resources .... Mr. Kenneth FLEISCHMANN
30 VP Advancement/Univ Relations .... Mr. Jeffrey FOWLER
43 Vice President/General Counsel .... Mr. William R. KAUFFMAN
32 Vice President Student Development .... Dr. Kent PORTERFIELD
42 Vice President Mission & Ministry .... Rev. Paul STARK, SJ
13 Vice Pres Information Tech Svcs/CIO .... Mr. David HAKANSON
23 Vice President for Medical Affairs .... Dr. Philip O. ALDERSON
26 Asst VP for Marketing & Creat Svcs .... Ms. Laura GEISER
29 Assoc VP for Alumni Relations .... Ms. Meg CONNOLLY
21 Controller .... Mr. David GRABE
35 Associate VP and Dean of Students .... Dr. Ramona HICKS
54 Assoc Dean Parks Col Engr/Aviation ... Dr. Theodore ALEXANDER
76 Dean Doisy College of Health Scis .... Dr. Lisa DORSEY
49 Dean Arts & Sciences .... Rev. Michael BARBER, SJ
50 Int Dean Cook School of Business .... Dr. Scott SAFRANSKI
61 Dean of Law .... Mr. Michael A. WOLFF
63 Dean of Medical School .... Dr. Philip O. ALDERSON
79 Dean Philosophy & Letters .... Bro. William REHG, SJ
69 Col for Pub Health & Soc Justice .... Dr. Ed TREVATHAN
53 Dean Col of Educ & Public Svc .... Dr. Anne RULE
08 University Librarian .... David CASSENS
88 Exec Dir Ctr for Health Care Ethics .... Dr. Jeffrey BISHOP
52 Exec Dir Ctr Advanced Dental Educ .... Dr. John HATTON
46 Vice President for Research .... Dr. Raymond TAIT
19 Director Public Safety & Security .... Mr. James MORAN
06 University Registrar .... Mr. Jay HAUGEN
07 Dean of Undergraduate Admission .... Ms. Jean GILMAN
37 Director Financial Aid .... Ms. Cari S. WICKLIFFE
39 Director Housing & Res Life .... Mr. Ray QUIROLGICO
41 Athletics Director .... Mr. Christopher V. MAY
36 Director Career Services .... Ms. Kim REITTER
28 Dir Diversity/Affirmative Action .... Ms. Michelle LEWIS
85 Director International Center .... Mr. Tim HERCULES
92 Director Honors Program .... Dr. Elizabeth WHITT
23 Director Student Health Center .... Ms. Deborah M. SCHEFF
31 Pgm Mgr Leadership Community Svcs .... Dr. Bryan SOKOL
88 Director Internal Audit .... Ms. Elizabeth A. WINCHESTER
04 Assistant to the President .... Ms. Bridget FLETCHER
88 Director Univ Museums/Galleries .... Dr. Petruta LIPAN
44 Director Planned Giving .... Mr. Kent G. LEVAN
40 Manager Bookstore .... Ms. Debbie SCHNEIDER
09 Assistant Vice President .... Dr. Steven SANCHEZ
96 Director of Business Services .... Mr. Jeff HOVEY

Saint Luke's College of Health Sciences (J)

624 Westport Road, Kansas City MO 64111
County: Jackson FICE Identification: 009782
Unit ID: 179450
Telephone: (816) 932-6700 Carnegie Class: Spec/Health
FAX Number: (816) 932-6760 Calendar System: Semester
URL: www.saintlukescollege.edu
Established: 1903 Annual Undergrad Tuition & Fees: $14,305
Enrollment: 365 Coed
Affiliation or Control: Independent Non-Profit IRS Status: 501(c)3
Highest Offering: Master's
Program: Nursing Emphasis
Accreditation: NH, NURSE

01 President .... Dr. Dean L. HUBBARD
10 Exec Dir Bus Operations/Stdnt Svcs .... Ms. Marcia LADAGE
09 Exec Asst to Pres/Dir Inst Research .... Ms. Tere E. NAYLOR
05 Academic Dean .... Dr. Jim HAUSCHILDT
07 Director Admissions .... Mr. Josh RICHARDS
06 Registrar .... Ms. Jean SUMMERS

Sanford-Brown College (K)

1345 Smizer Mill Road, Fenton MO 63026-3400
County: Saint Louis FICE Identification: 022052
Unit ID: 179201
Telephone: (636) 651-1600 Carnegie Class: Bac/Assoc
FAX Number: (636) 651-1732 Calendar System: Quarter
URL: www.sanfordbrown.edu/Fenton
Established: 1866 Annual Undergrad Tuition & Fees: $15,696
Enrollment: 791 Coed
Affiliation or Control: Proprietary IRS Status: Proprietary
Highest Offering: Baccalaureate
Program: Occupational; 2-Year Principally Bachelor's Creditable; Liberal Arts And General
Accreditation: ACICS, COARC, DMS, EMT, POLYT, RAD

01 Campus President .... Ms. Melissa MANGOLD
10 Vice President of Finance .... Mr. Jim REICH
12 Campus President-Hazelwood .... Ms. Phyllis FORNEY
12 Campus President-St. Peters .... Ms. Julia LEEMAN
27 Information Technology Manager .... Mr. Wade THURMOND
37 Director Student Financial Aid .... Ms. Amy KETTS

Sanford-Brown College (L)

100 Richmond Center Boulevard,
Saint Peters MO 63376-5950
Telephone: (636) 696-2300 Identification: 666458
Accreditation: ACICS, SURTEC

† Main campus is Sanford-Brown College in Fenton, MO.

The School of Professional Psychology at Forest Institute (M)

2885 West Battlefield Road, Springfield MO 65807-1445
County: Greene FICE Identification: 021642
Unit ID: 177427
Telephone: (800) 424-7793 Carnegie Class: Spec/Health
FAX Number: (417) 823-3442 Calendar System: Semester
URL: www.forest.edu
Established: 1979 Annual Graduate Tuition & Fees: $2,800
Enrollment: 255 Coed
Affiliation or Control: Independent Non-Profit IRS Status: 501(c)3
Highest Offering: Doctorate; No Undergraduates
Program: Professional
Accreditation: NH, #CLPSY, IPSY, MFCD

01 President .... Dr. Mark SKRADE
05 Vice President of Academic Affairs .... Dr. Gerald PORTER
17 Vice Pres of Innovation/Cmty Health .... Ms. Jennifer BAKER
10 Chief Financial Officer .... Mr. Bob DAVIS
58 Dean of Doctoral Program .... Dr. Michael LEFTWICH
12 Exec Dir Forest Institute-St Louis .... Mr. Brian NEDWEK
17 Director of Clinical Training .... Mr. David MRAD
37 Director of Financial Aid .... Mr. Andrew TATE
06 Registrar .... Ms. Katrina CHAVEZ
08 Library Services Manager .... Ms. Renee MCHENRY

Southeast Missouri Hospital College of Nursing and Health Sciences (A)

2001 William Street, 2nd Floor,
Cape Girardeau MO 63703-5815
County: Cape Girardeau FICE Identification: 030709
Unit ID: 417734
Telephone: (573) 334-6825 Carnegie Class: Assoc/PrivNFP
FAX Number: (573) 339-7805 Calendar System: Other
URL: www.southeastmissourihospitalcollege.edu
Established: 1990 Annual Undergrad Tuition & Fees: $13,800
Enrollment: 207 Coed
Affiliation or Control: Independent Non-Profit IRS Status: 501(c)3
Highest Offering: Associate Degree
Program: 2-Year Principally Bachelor's Creditable; Nursing Emphasis
Accreditation: NH, ADNUR, MT, RAD, SURGT

01 President .... Dr. Tonya BUTTRY
06 Registrar .... Ms. Debbie HOWEY

Southeast Missouri State University (B)

One University Plaza, Cape Girardeau MO 63701-4799
County: Cape Girardeau FICE Identification: 002501
Unit ID: 179557
Telephone: (573) 651-2000 Carnegie Class: Master's L
FAX Number: (573) 651-2200 Calendar System: Semester
URL: www.semo.edu
Established: 1873 Annual Undergrad Tuition & Fees (In-State): $6,863
Enrollment: 11,729 Coed
Affiliation or Control: State IRS Status: 501(c)3
Highest Offering: Beyond Master's But Less Than Doctorate
Program: Liberal Arts And General; Teacher Preparatory; Professional
Accreditation: NH, BUS, CACREP, CS, DIETD, DIETI, ENG, ENGT, JOUR, MUS, NAIT, NRPA, NURSE, SP, SW, TED

01 President .... Dr. Kenneth W. DOBBINS
05 Interim Provost/Chief Academic Ofcr .... Dr. Gerald MCDOUGALL
10 VP Finance & Administration .... Mrs. Kathy M. MANGELS
84 VP Enrollment Mgmt/Student Success .... Dr. Debbie BELOW
30 Vice Pres University Advancement .... Mr. Bill HOLLAND
20 Vice Provost .... Dr. Bill EDDLEMAN
108 Asst Provost for Inst Rsch & Assess .... Vacant
04 Assistant to the President .... Ms. Diane O. SIDES
100 Sr Assoc to the President/Board Sec .... Mr. Brady L. BARKE
22 Asst to Pres for Equity & Diversity .... Vacant
13 Asst Vice Pres Information Tech .... Mr. Archie SPRENGEL
106 Associate Dean Online Lrng .... Dr. Allen GATHMAN
58 Dean Sch of Grad Studies .... Dr. Bill EDDLEMAN
89 Dean of University Studies .... Dr. Francisco BARRIOS
50 Int Dean DL Harrison College Bus .... Dr. Charles MCALLISTER
53 Dean College of Education .... Dr. Diana ROGERS-ADKINSON
76 Dean College Health & Human Svc .... Dr. Morris JENKINS
79 Dean College of Liberal Arts .... Dr. Francisco BARRIOS
72 Dean College of Science/Tech & Ag .... Dr. Chris MCGOWAN
32 Dean of Students .... Dr. Debbie BELOW
88 Dean Academic Information Svcs .... Dr. David STARRETT
07 Director of Admissions .... Ms. Lenell HAHN
39 AVP Stdnt Success & Dir Res Life .... Dr. Bruce SKINNER
35 Director of Campus Life .... Ms. Michele IRBY
26 Director Marketing & Univ Relations .... Ms. Karen GREBING
41 Director of Athletics .... Mr. Mark ALNUTT
29 Director Alumni Services .... Mr. Jay WOLZ
85 Exec Dir Intl Education & Svcs .... Mr. Zahir AHMED
51 Dir Extended & Continuing Education .... Ms. Joyce D. BECKER
12 Director Malden Campus .... Dr. Nicholas THIELE
12 Director Kennett Campus .... Ms. Marsha L. BLANCHARD
12 Director Sikeston Campus .... Mr. Stephen BORGSMILLER
18 Director of Facilities Management .... Ms. Angela MEYER
37 Director of Financial Aid .... Ms. Karen WALKER
09 Institutional Research .... Dr. Dennis HOLT
27 Director of News Bureau .... Ms. Ann K. HAYES
15 Director of Human Resources .... Mr. Jim COOK
19 Director of Public Safety/Transit .... Mr. Doug RICHARDS
06 Registrar .... Ms. Sandy L. HINKLE
88 Director of Show Me Center .... Mr. Wil GORMAN
21 Director of Business Operations .... Ms. Laura D. STOCK
92 Director University Honors Program .... Dr. Craig W. ROBERTS
38 Dir Counseling & Disability Svcs .... Mr. Bob LEFEBVRE
96 Director of Purchasing .... Ms. Sarah STEINNERD

Southwest Baptist University (C)

1600 University Avenue, Bolivar MO 65613-2597
County: Polk FICE Identification: 002502
Unit ID: 179326
Telephone: (417) 328-5281 Carnegie Class: Master's L
FAX Number: (417) 328-1514 Calendar System: Semester
URL: www.sbuniv.edu
Established: 1878 Annual Undergrad Tuition & Fees: $20,040
Enrollment: 3,864 Coed
Affiliation or Control: Southern Baptist IRS Status: 501(c)3
Highest Offering: Doctorate
Program: Liberal Arts And General; Teacher Preparatory; Professional
Accreditation: NH, ACBSP, ADNUR, MUS, NUR, PTA, @SW

01 President .... Dr. Pat TAYLOR
05 Provost .... Dr. Bill BROWN
11 Vice President Administration .... Mr. Ron MAUPIN
30 Vice President University Relations .... Dr. Brad JOHNSON
84 Vice Pres Enrollment Management .... Dr. Stephanie MILLER
32 Vice Pres for Student Development .... Dr. Rob HARRIS
56 Assc Provost Extend Lrng/Tech Svcs .... Dr. Robert MCGLASSON
20 Associate Provost .... Dr. Allison LANGFORD
44 Director Estate Planning .... Vacant
29 Director Alumni & Church Relations .... Mrs. Lindsay SCHINDLER
07 Director Admissions .... Mr. Darren CROWDER
41 Athletic Director .... Mr. Mike PITTS
06 Registrar .... Mr. John CREDILLE
35 Director Student Activities .... Mr. Nathan PENLAND
39 Director Residence Life .... Ms. Landee NEVILLS
42 Director University Ministries .... Mr. Kurt CADDY
15 Director of Human Resources .... Mr. David PIERCE
18 Director Physical Plant .... Mr. Bob GLIDWELL
19 Director Campus Security .... Mr. Mark GRABOWSKI
08 Director of Library Services .... Dr. Ed WALTON
50 Dean College Business/Computer Sci .... Vacant
73 Dean College Theology/Ministry .... Dr. Rodney REEVES
53 Dean Education/Social Sciences .... Dr. Linda WOODERSON
57 Dean Music/Arts/Letters .... Dr. Jeff WATERS
81 Dean Science/Math .... Dr. Perry TOMPKINS
36 Director of Career Services .... Mrs. Suzanne POWERS
14 Director Computer Services .... Mr. Kevin KELLEY
90 Director Institutional Computing .... Mr. Jeffery H. HOGUE
91 Director Administrative Computing .... Mr. David BOLTON
38 Director Counseling Services .... Mrs. Pearlene BRESHEARS
37 Director Student Financial Planning .... Mr. Brad GAMBLE
26 Chief Public Relations Officer .... Mrs. Charlotte MARSCH
09 Director of Institutional Research .... Mr. Jason VAUGHN
96 Director of Purchasing .... Vacant
40 Book Store Manager .... Ms. Carol SHOEMAKER

Southwest Baptist University Mountain View Center (D)

209 W First Street, Mountain View MO 65548
Telephone: (417) 934-2999 Identification: 770326
Accreditation: &NH

† Main campus is Southwest Baptist University in Bolivar, MO.

Southwest Baptist University Salem Center (E)

501 S Grand, Salem MO 65560
Telephone: (573) 729-7071 Identification: 770327
Accreditation: &NH

† Main campus is Southwest Baptist University in Bolivar, MO.

Southwest Baptist University Springfield Center (F)

4431 S Fremont, Springfield MO 65804
Telephone: (417) 820-5049 Identification: 770328
Accreditation: &NH

† Main campus is Southwest Baptist University in Bolivar, MO.

State Fair Community College (G)

3201 W 16th Street, Sedalia MO 65301-2199
County: Pettis FICE Identification: 008080
Unit ID: 179539
Telephone: (660) 596-7222 Carnegie Class: Assoc/Pub-R-M
FAX Number: (660) 596-7335 Calendar System: Semester
URL: www.sfccmo.edu
Established: 1966 Annual Undergrad Tuition & Fees (In-District): $2,940
Enrollment: 5,115 Coed
Affiliation or Control: Local IRS Status: 501(c)3
Highest Offering: Associate Degree
Program: Occupational; 2-Year Principally Bachelor's Creditable
Accreditation: NH, CONST, DH, OTA, RAD

01 President .... Dr. Joanna ANDERSON
05 VP for Educ/Student Support Svcs .... Dr. Brent BATES
10 VP for Finance/Administration & HR .... Mr. Garry SORRELL
13 CIO Information Systems & Tech .... Mr. Mark HAVERLY
20 Dean of Academic Affairs .... Mr. Steve SCHEINER
75 Dean Vocational/Technical Studies .... Mr. Mark KELCHNER
38 Dean Student Support .... Dr. Joe GILGOUR
30 Exec Director for Development .... Ms. Mary TEURNER
09 Director Institutional Planning .... Mrs. Amanda STOECKLEIN
06 Registrar .... Mrs. Jennifer WILBANKS
37 Director of Financial Aid .... Mr. John MATTHEWS
18 Chief Facilities/Physical Plant .... Mr. Steve KUCYNDA
21 Associate Business Officer .... Mrs. Diane BROCKMAN
26 Director of Marketing/Communication .... Mrs. Dana KELCHNER
07 Director of Admissions .... Mr. Mark CARTER

Stephens College (H)

1200 E Broadway, Columbia MO 65215-0001
County: Boone FICE Identification: 002512
Unit ID: 179548
Telephone: (573) 442-2211 Carnegie Class: Bac/Diverse
FAX Number: (573) 876-7248 Calendar System: Semester
URL: www.stephens.edu
Established: 1833 Annual Undergrad Tuition & Fees: $27,945
Enrollment: 903 Female
Affiliation or Control: Independent Non-Profit IRS Status: 501(c)3
Highest Offering: Master's
Program: Liberal Arts And General; Teacher Preparatory; Professional; Fine Arts Emphasis
Accreditation: NH, CAHIIM, IACBE

01 President .... Dr. Dianne LYNCH
10 Vice Pres Finance/Business/CFO .... Dr. Lindi OVERTON
05 Vice President Academic Affairs .... Dr. Annette DIGBY
30 Vice President of Philanthropy .... Ms. Meichele FOSTER
32 Vice President for Student Services .... Ms. Deborah DUREN
26 VP of Marketing/Public Relations .... Ms. Rebecca KLINE
84 Vice Pres Enrollment Management .... Ms. Suzanne SHARP
29 Director of Alumnae Relations/Phila .... Ms. Marissa TODD
06 Registrar .... Ms. Linda SHARP
13 IT Director .... Mr. Mark BRUNNER
16 Director Human Resources .... Ms. Kim SCHELLENBERGER
36 Director Career Development .... Ms. Amanda ROBERTS
41 Athletic Director .... Ms. Deborah DUREN
21 Director of Accounting .... Mr. Josh HENGGLER
37 Director of Financial Aid .... Mr. Paul GORDON
09 Dir of Institutional Research .... Mr. Isaac TUTTLE
39 Director of Residence Life .... Vacant
23 Director of Health Services .... Dr. Kathy DOISY
08 Library Dir/Tech Svcs Librarian .... Ms. Corrie HUTCHINSON

Stevens Institute of Business & Arts (I)

1521 Washington Avenue, Saint Louis MO 63103
County: Saint Louis FICE Identification: 008552
Unit ID: 178767
Telephone: (314) 421-0949 Carnegie Class: Bac/Diverse
FAX Number: (314) 421-0304 Calendar System: Quarter
URL: www.siba.edu
Established: 1947 Annual Undergrad Tuition & Fees: $16,200
Enrollment: 171 Coed
Affiliation or Control: Proprietary IRS Status: Proprietary
Highest Offering: Baccalaureate
Program: Occupational
Accreditation: ACICS

01 President .... Ms. Cynthia A. MUSTERMAN
05 Academic Dean & Registrar .... Ms. Ruth Ann HOLTMANN
37 Director of Financial Aid .... Ms. Christa SIAMPOS
07 Director of Admissions .... Vacant

Texas County Technical College (J)

6915 S Highway 63 PO Box 314, Houston MO 65483
County: Texas FICE Identification: 035793
Unit ID: 441487
Telephone: (417) 967-5466 Carnegie Class: Assoc/PrivNFP
FAX Number: (417) 967-4604 Calendar System: Semester
URL: www.texascountytech.edu
Established: 1986 Annual Undergrad Tuition & Fees: $15,590
Enrollment: 140 Coed
Affiliation or Control: Independent Non-Profit IRS Status: 501(c)3
Highest Offering: Associate Degree
Program: Occupational; 2-Year Principally Bachelor's Creditable
Accreditation: ACICS

01 President .... Ms. Charlotte GRAY
07 Director of Admissions/Registrar .... Ms. Clarice CASEBEER
37 Acting Financial Aid Director .... Ms. Clarice CASEBEER

Three Rivers Community College (K)

2080 Three Rivers Boulevard,
Poplar Bluff MO 63901-2350
County: Butler FICE Identification: 004713
Unit ID: 179645
Telephone: (573) 840-9600 Carnegie Class: Assoc/Pub-R-M
FAX Number: (573) 840-9604 Calendar System: Semester
URL: www.trcc.edu
Established: 1966 Annual Undergrad Tuition & Fees (In-State): $3,552
Enrollment: 4,652 Coed
Affiliation or Control: State IRS Status: 501(c)3
Highest Offering: Associate Degree
Program: Occupational; 2-Year Principally Bachelor's Creditable
Accreditation: NH, ACBSP, ADNUR, MLTAD, OTA

01 President .... Dr. Devin STEPHENSON
10 Chief Financial Officer .... Ms. Charlotte EUBANK
32 Vice President for Student Success .... Dr. Angela TOTTY
05 Vice President for Learning .... Dr. Wesley A. PAYNE
08 Director Library Services .... Vacant
37 Director Financial Aid .... Ms. Laura MILLIGAN
06 Registrar .... Mr. Derrick MILLER
35 Director of Student Services .... Mr. Derrick MILLER
09 Director of Institutional Research .... Ms. Melanie HAMANN
18 Chief Facilities/Physical Plant .... Mr. Rob TOMLINSON
15 Director Human Resources .... Ms. Kristina D. MCDANIEL
26 Chief Public Relations Officer .... Ms. Teresa JOHNSON
29 Director Alumni Relations .... Ms. Emily PARKS
30 Chief Development .... Ms. Emily PARKS
84 Director Enrollment Management .... Mr. Chris ADAMS
96 Dir Procurement/Risk Management .... Ms. Cambrea HALCUMB

Truman State University (L)

100 E Normal, Kirksville MO 63501-4221
County: Adair FICE Identification: 002495
Unit ID: 178615
Telephone: (660) 785-4000 Carnegie Class: Master's M
FAX Number: (660) 785-4030 Calendar System: Semester
URL: www.truman.edu

Established: 1867 Annual Undergrad Tuition & Fees (In-State): $7,368
Enrollment: 5,615 Coed
Affiliation or Control: State IRS Status: 501(c)3
Highest Offering: Master's
Program: Liberal Arts And General; Teacher Preparatory; Professional
Accreditation: NH, BUS, BUSA, MUS, NURSE, SP, TED

Code	Title	Name
01	President	Dr. Troy D. PAINO
05	Provost/VP for Academic Affairs	Dr. Joan POOR
30	Vice Pres University Advancement	Mr. Mark GAMBAIANA
11	VP for Admin Finance & Planning	Mr. David RECTOR
84	Assoc VP for Enrollment Management	Mrs. Regina MORIN
32	Dean of Student Affairs	Dr. Lou Ann GILCHRIST
43	General Counsel	Mr. Warren WELLS
21	Comptroller	Mrs. Judy MULLINS
41	Athletic Director	Mr. Jerry WOLLMERING
15	Exec Dir HR/EEO Compliance Ofcr	Ms. Sally DETWEILER
07	Director of Admissions	Mrs. Melody CHAMBERS
37	Financial Aid Director	Mrs. Kathy ELSEA
06	Registrar	Mrs. Margaret HERRON
13	Director Information Technology	Mrs. Donna LISS
26	Director of Public Relations	Mrs. Heidi TEMPLETON
88	Director of Truman Institute	Dr. Kevin MINCH
38	Dir Student Health/Counseling Svcs	Dr. Brenda HIGGINS
83	Dean of Social & Cultural Studies	Dr. Elizabeth CLARK
49	Dean School of Arts & Letters	Dr. James O'DONNELL
81	Dean Sch of Science & Mathematics	Dr. Jon GERING
53	Dean Sch of Health Sciences & Educ	Dr. Janet GOOCH
08	Dean of Libraries & Museums	Mr. Richard COUGHLIN
50	Dean School of Business	Dr. Debra KERBY

University of Central Missouri (A)

Administration Building, room 101,
Warrensburg MO 64093-5299

County: Johnson FICE Identification: 002454
Unit ID: 176965
Telephone: (660) 543-4255 Carnegie Class: Master's L
FAX Number: (660) 543-4200 Calendar System: Semester
URL: www.ucmo.edu
Established: 1871 Annual Undergrad Tuition & Fees (In-State): $7,264
Enrollment: 11,878 Coed
Affiliation or Control: State IRS Status: 501(c)3
Highest Offering: Beyond Master's But Less Than Doctorate
Program: Liberal Arts And General; Teacher Preparatory; Professional
Accreditation: NH, AAB, AAFCS, ART, BUS, BUSA, CACREP, CEA, CONST, DIETD, ENGR, MUS, NAIT, NURSE, SP, SW, TED, THEA

Code	Title	Name
01	President	Dr. Charles M. AMBROSE
101	Exec Asst to Pres/Asst Sec to Board	Ms. Monica R. HUFFMAN
45	Chief Strategy Officer	Mr. Mike RACY
05	Provost and Chief Learning Officer	Dr. Deborah J. CURTIS
32	Vice Prov Student Experience/Engage	Dr. Sharlene GARBER BAX
45	Vice Provost Institutional Effectiv	Dr. Michael GRELLE
35	Assoc Vice Prov Student Services	Dr. Corey L. BOWMAN
84	Vice Prov Recruitment & Outreach	Dr. Richard D. SLUDER
30	Vice Pres Univ Development	Mr. Jason S. DRUMMOND
08	Dean of Library Services	Ms. Mollie D. DINWIDDIE
58	Dean Graduate and Extended Studies	Dr. Joseph VAUGHN
49	Dean College of Arts/Humanities/Sci	Dr. Gersham NELSON
72	Dean College of Health/Science/Tech	Dr. Alice L. GREIFE
50	Dean Harmon Col Business/Prof Stds	Dr. Roger J. BEST
92	Dean of the Honors College	Dr. Joseph D. LEWANDOWSKI
53	Dean of College of Education	Dr. Michael D. WRIGHT
10	Vice Pres Finance/Chief Ops Ofcr	Mr. John MERRIGAN
13	Vice Provost for Technology & CIO	Dr. James F. GRAHAM
43	General Counsel	Mr. Henry R. SETSER
41	Athletic Director	Mr. Jerry M. HUGHES
06	Director of Registrar	Ms. Teri A. BOWMAN
26	Interim Chief Comm Officer	Mr. Dennis CRYDER
09	Director Testing Services	Ms. Carole NIMMER
36	Dir Career Development Services	Mr. Kenneth SCHUELLER
37	Dir Student Financial Assistance	Ms. Angela L. KARLIN
19	Director of Public Safety	Ms. Kimberly J. VANSELL
39	Asst Vice Prov Student Aux Services	Mr. Patrick J. BRADLEY
21	Director Accounting Services	Ms. Toni L. KREKE
18	Dir Facilities & Planning Op	Mr. Chris BAMMAN
96	Director Purchasing	Mr. Michael SMITH
15	Director Human Resources	Mr. Rick L. DIXON
40	Director of Univ Store & Textbooks	Mr. Charles D. RUTT
85	Director of International Center	Dr. Adalynn J. STEVENSON
07	Director Admissions	Ms. Ann A. NORDYKE
15	Asst Director of Human Resources	Ms. Cheryl D. TRELOW
29	Asst VP Resources Development	Ms. Jennifer L. VANDERBOUT
38	Director Counseling Center	Dr. Paul D. POLYCHRONIS
44	Dir of Annual Giving Program	Mr. Scott ALVESTED
24	Director CentralNET	Mr. Michael JEFFRIES

*University of Missouri System Administration (B)

321 University Hall, Columbia MO 65211-3020

County: Boone FICE Identification: 002515
Unit ID: 178439
Telephone: (573) 882-2011 Carnegie Class: N/A
FAX Number: (573) 882-2721
URL: www.umsystem.edu

Code	Title	Name
01	President	Mr. Timothy M. WOLFE
100	Chief of Staff	Dr. Robert W. SCHWARTZ
10	Interim Vice Pres Finance & Treas	Mr. Thomas F. RICHARDS
05	Exec Vice Pres Acad Affairs	Dr. Henry C. FOLEY
13	Vice President Info Technology	Dr. Gary K. ALLEN
86	Vice President Government Relations	Mr. Stephen C. KNORR
15	Vice Pres Human Resource Services	Ms. Elizabeth RODRIGUEZ
20	Sr Assoc Vice Pres Academic Affairs	Dr. Steven W. GRAHAM
43	General Counsel	Mr. Stephen J. OWENS
26	Chief Communications Officer	Mr. John FOUGERE
17	CEO/COO UM Health Care	Mr. Mitch WASDEN
23	Vice Chancellor for Health Sciences	Dr. Harold A. WILLIAMSON
21	Controller	Ms. Jane E. CLOSTERMAN

*University of Missouri - Columbia (C)

Columbia MO 65211-0001

County: Boone FICE Identification: 002516
Unit ID: 178396
Telephone: (573) 882-2121 Carnegie Class: RU/VH
FAX Number: (573) 882-9907 Calendar System: Semester
URL: www.missouri.edu
Established: 1839 Annual Undergrad Tuition & Fees (In-State): $9,415
Enrollment: 34,748 Coed
Affiliation or Control: State IRS Status: 501(c)3
Highest Offering: Doctorate
Program: Liberal Arts And General; Teacher Preparatory; Professional
Accreditation: NH, BUS, BUSA, CIDA, CLPSY, COARC, COPSY, CS, DIETC, DMS, ENG, FOR, HSA, IPSY, JOUR, LAW, #LIB, MED, MUS, NMT, NRPA, NURSE, OT, PCSAS, PH, PTA, RAD, #SCPSY, SP, SPAA, SW, @TEAC, VET

Code	Title	Name
02	Chancellor	Dr. Brady J. DEATON
03	Deputy Chancellor	Mr. Michael A. MIDDLETON
05	Provost	Dr. Brian L. FOSTER
20	Deputy Provost	Mr. Kenneth D. DEAN
20	Vice Provost Undergrad Studies	Dr. James SPAIN
32	Vice Chancellor Student Affairs	Dr. Catherine C. SCROGGS
11	VC Administrative Services	Ms. Jacquelyn K. JONES
58	VP Adv Studies/Dean Grad Sch	Mr. George JUSTICE
04	Asst to Chanc for University Affs	Ms. Christine H. KOUKOLA
30	Vice Chancellor University Advance	Dr. Tom HILES
29	Assoc VC Alumni Relations/Devel	Mr. Todd A. MCCUBBIN
17	Vice Chancellor for Health Sciences	Dr. Harold A. WILLIAMSON, JR.
57	Director School of Music	Dr. Robert SHAY
84	Vice Provost for Enrollment Mgmt	Dr. Ann J. KORSCHGEN
56	Vice Provost for Extension	Dr. Michael D. OUART
85	Vice Provost International Pgms	Dr. Handy WILLIAMSON
46	Vice Chancellor for Research	Mr. Robert DUNCAN
88	Director of Budget	Ms. Rhonda GIBLER
13	Chief Information Officer	Dr. Gary K. ALLEN
15	Asst Vice Chanc Human Resources	Ms. Karen E. TOUZEAU
18	Assoc Vice Chanc Campus Facilities	Mr. Gary L. WARD
46	Spec Asst to Vice Chanc of Research	Dr. Michael WARNOCK
35	Asst Vice Chanc Student Affairs	Dr. Jeffrey ZEILENGA
06	University Registrar	Ms. Brenda V. SELMAN
09	VProv Inst Research & Quality Impr	Dr. Mardy T. EIMERS
08	Director of Libraries	Mr. James A. COGSWELL
37	Director Student Financial Aid	Mr. Nick PREWETT
47	Vice Chanc/Dean Agric/Food/Nat Res	Dr. Thomas L. PAYNE
49	Dean Arts & Science	Dr. Michael J. O'BRIEN
50	Dean of Business	Ms. Joan GABEL
88	Director School of Accountancy	Dr. Vairam ARUNACHALAM
53	Dean of Education	Dr. Daniel CLAY
54	Dean of Engineering	Dr. James E. THOMPSON
65	Dir School of Natural Resources	Dr. Mark R. RYAN
76	Dean School of Health Professions	Dr. Richard E. OLIVER
59	Dean Human Environmental Science	Dr. Stephen R. JORGENSEN
60	Dean of Journalism	Dr. R. Dean MILLS
61	Dean of Law	Dr. Gary MYERS
63	Dean of Medicine	Dr. Robert CHURCHILL
66	Dean of Nursing	Dr. Judith FITZGERALD MILLER
70	Director School of Social Work	Dr. Marjorie SABLE
74	Dean of Veterinary Medicine	Dr. Neil OLSON
19	Director of University Police	Mr. Jack W. WATRING
27	Director News Services	Ms. Mary Jo BANKEN
41	Intercollegiate Athletic Director	Mr. Michael F. ALDEN
39	Director Residential Life	Mr. Frankie D. MINOR
25	Director Sponsored Program Admin	Ms. Jennifer DUNCAN
40	Regional Director Retail Operations	Ms. Sherry POLLARD
38	Director Counseling Services	Dr. David WALLACE
88	Assoc Vice Provost Intl Initiatives	Dr. James K. SCOTT
36	Director Career Services	Dr. Matthew REISKE
23	Director Student Health Services	Dr. Susan E. EVEN
92	Director Honors College	Dr. Stuart B. PALONSKY
94	Director Women's/Gender Studies	Dr. Jacquelyn S. LITT
88	Director Info Science Learning Tech	Dr. John WEDMAN
80	Director Truman Schl Public Affairs	Dr. Barton J. WECHSLER
07	Director of Admissions	Ms. Barbara A. RUPP
26	Assistant to Chancellor Univ Affs	Ms. Christine H. KOUKOLA
35	Director Student Life	Dr. Mark L. LUCAS
28	Chief Diversity Officer	Ms. Noor AZIZAN-GARDNER
96	Manager of Campus Procurement	Ms. Sherri L. WOOD

*University of Missouri - Kansas City (D)

5100 Rockhill Road, Kansas City MO 64110-2499

County: Jackson FICE Identification: 002518
Unit ID: 178402
Telephone: (816) 235-1000 Carnegie Class: RU/H
FAX Number: (816) 235-1717 Calendar System: Semester
URL: www.umkc.edu
Established: 1929 Annual Undergrad Tuition & Fees (In-State): $7,755
Enrollment: 16,019 Coed
Affiliation or Control: State IRS Status: 501(c)3
Highest Offering: Doctorate
Program: Liberal Arts And General; Teacher Preparatory; Professional
Accreditation: NH, AA, ANEST, BUS, CLPSY, COPSY, CS, DANCE, DENT, DH, ENG, IPSY, LAW, MED, MUS, NURSE, OTA, PHAR, SPAA, SW, TED, THEA

Code	Title	Name
02	Chancellor	Mr. Leo E. MORTON
28	Deputy Chancellor for Diversity	Vacant
05	Exec Vice Chanc and Provost	Dr. Gail HACKETT
32	Vice Chanc Stdnt Affs/Enroll Mgmt	Mr. Melvin C. TYLER
11	Vice Chanc for Admin Services	Ms. Sharon LINDENBAUM
21	Director Budgeting and Planning	Ms. Karen D. WILKERSON
102	Pres UMKC Foundation	Mr. Murray BLACKWELDER
30	Vice Chanc for Univ Advancement	Mr. Curt J. CRESPINO
41	Athletic Director	Vacant
20	CIO & Vice Prov for Acad Pgms	Dr. Mary Lou A. HINES-FRITTS
20	Vice Prov for Academic Affairs	Dr. Cynthia L. PEMBERTON
20	Vice Prov for Faculty Affairs	Dr. Denis M. MEDEIROS
49	Dean College of Arts & Sciences	Dr. Wayne VAUGHT
50	Dean Bloch School of Management	Dr. Teng-Kee TAN
81	Int Dean Sch of Biological Sciences	Dr. Theodore WHITE
64	Dean Conservatory of Music & Dance	Mr. Peter T. WITTE
52	Dean School of Dentistry	Dr. Marsha A. PYLE
53	Dean School of Education	Dr. Wanda J. BLANCHETT
54	Dean Sch of Computing/Engineering	Dr. Kevin Z. TRUMAN
61	Dean School of Law	Ms. Ellen Y. SUNI
63	Dean School of Medicine	Dr. Betty M. DREES
66	Dean Sch of Nursing & Health Stds	Dr. Lora LACEY-HAUN
67	Dean School of Pharmacy	Dr. Russell B. MELCHERT
62	Dean University Libraries	Dr. Sharon L. BOSTICK
58	Dean School of Graduate Studies	Dr. Denis M. MEDEIROS
108	Asst Vice Provost Assessment	Dr. Nathan LINDSAY
09	Director Institutional Research	Dr. Larry BUNCE
16	Assoc Vice Chanc Human Resources	Ms. Carol HINTZ
84	Assoc Vice Chanc Enrollment Mgmt	Ms. Jennifer DEHAEMERS
35	Dean of Students	Dr. Eric GROSPITCH
35	Assistant Dean of Students	Dr. Jeff TRAIGER
35	Director Student Involvement	Dr. Angela COTTRELL
88	Vice Chan Strategic Market & Comm	Ms. Anne SPENNER
26	Director Media Relations	Mr. John MARTELLARO
102	Asst VC for Development	Ms. Jenea OLIVER
29	Asst VC AlumniConstituent Relations	Ms. Lisen TAMMEUS
44	Director Planned Giving	Mr. Phil WATSON
86	Asst Vice Chanc External Relations	Mr. Troy LILLEBO
22	Director Affirmative Action	Mr. Michael D. BATES
88	Dir Acad Support and Development	Dr. Marion STONE
07	Director of Admissions	Ms. Tamara C. BYLAND
85	Director Internatl Student Affairs	Ms. Sandra GAULT
28	Director Multicultural Affairs	Ms. Tiffany S. WILLIAMS
37	Director Student Financial Aid	Ms. Nancy MERZ
06	Registrar	Mr. Doug SWINK
19	Chief Campus Police	Mr. Michael BONGARTZ
40	Director Bookstore	Mr. Pete EISENTRAGER
38	Director Counseling/Health Test Ctr	Dr. Marita BARKIS
88	Director Womens Center	Dr. Brenda BETTIMAN
36	Director Career Services	Mr. Greg HAYES
39	Director Residential Life	Mr. Sean GRUBE
96	Manager Campus Procurement	Ms. Catherine A. BARKER
25	Asst to VC for Admin Services	Mr. Colin C. GAGE
18	Assoc Vice Chanc Campus Facilities	Mr. Robert A. SIMMONS
104	Director International Acad Pgms	Dr. Linna F. PLACE

*University of Missouri - Saint Louis (E)

One University Boulevard, Saint Louis MO 63121-4400

County: Saint Louis FICE Identification: 002519
Unit ID: 178420
Telephone: (314) 516-5000 Carnegie Class: RU/H
FAX Number: (314) 516-5378 Calendar System: Semester
URL: www.umsl.edu
Established: 1963 Annual Undergrad Tuition & Fees (In-State): $9,474
Enrollment: 12,351 Coed
Affiliation or Control: State IRS Status: 501(c)3
Highest Offering: Doctorate
Program: Liberal Arts And General; Teacher Preparatory; Professional
Accreditation: NH, BUS, BUSA, CACREP, CLPSY, ENG, IPSY, MUS, NURSE, OPT, OPTR, SPAA, SW, TED

Code	Title	Name
02	Chancellor	Dr. Thomas F. GEORGE
05	Provost/Vice Chanc Academic Affairs	Dr. Glen H. COPE
10	Vice Chanc Managerial/Tech Svcs	Dr. James M. KRUEGER
30	Vice Chancellor Univ Advancement	Mr. Martin F. LEIFELD
22	Dir of Equal Opportunity/Diversity	Ms. Deborah J. BURRIS
46	Vice Provost Research Admin	Dr. Nasser ARSHADI
32	Vice Provost Student Affairs	Mr. Curtis C. COONROD
58	Vice Prov Acad Affs/Dean Grad Sch	Dr. Judith WALKER DE FELIX
13	Assoc VC Information Technology/CIO	Mr. Lawrence W. FREDERICK
88	Dir Center for Teaching & Learning	Dr. Margaret W. COHEN
85	Director International Studies	Dr. Joel N. GLASSMAN
49	Dean College Arts & Sciences	Dr. Ronald YASBIN
50	Interim Dean College Business Admin	Dr. Michael T. ELLIOTT
53	Dean College of Education	Dr. Carole G. BASILE
57	Dean College of Fine Arts/Comm	Dr. Jean M. MILLER
66	Dean College of Nursing	Dr. Susan DEAN-BAAR
92	Dean Honors College	Dr. Robert M. BLISS
88	Dean College of Optometry	Dr. Larry J. DAVIS
08	Dean of Libraries	Mr. Christopher DAMES
54	Dean Engineering Program	Dr. Joseph O'SULLIVAN
51	Dean Professional/Continuing	Dr. Wm Thomas WALKER
88	Assistant to Provost Public Affairs	Ms. Elizabeth VAN UUM
23	Asst Vice Provost Hlth/Wellness	Dr. Nancy M. MAGNUSON
88	Asst Dean of Students/Stdnt Conduct	Mr. D'Andre BRADDIX
93	Asst Dean of Stdnts/MultiCultural	Ms. Natissia SMALL

35 Asst Dean of Students/Student Life ....Ms. Miriam I. ROCCIA
41 Director of Athletics ....Ms. Lori FLANAGAN
07 Dean of Enrollment ....Mr. Alan BYRD
40 Manager Bookstore ....Ms. Stephanie EATON
36 Director Career Services ....Ms. Teresa A. BALESTRERI
38 Director Counseling Services ....Dr. M. Sharon BIEGEN
06 Registrar ....Ms. Linda C. SILMAN
39 Director Residential Life ....Mr. Jonathan A. LIDGUS
37 Director Student Financial Aid ....Dr. Anthony C. GEORGES
88 Director Ctr Nanoscience ....Dr. George W. GOKEL
88 Director Center Neurodynamics ....Dr. Sonya BAHAR
88 Dir Scientific & Computing/ITE ....Mr. William J. LEMON
88 Dir MO Institute of Mental Health ....Mr. Joseph PARKS
25 Manager Bus/Fiscal/Research Admin ....Ms. Karen O. BOYD
88 Director Business Services ....Ms. Gloria J. LEONARD
18 Special Asst Vice Chancellor ....Mr. Larry A. EISENBERG
18 Director Engr/Planning & Const ....Mr. H. Sam DARANDARI
18 Director Facilities Services ....Mr. Frank S. KOCHIN
88 Director Budget Services ....Ms. Joann F. WILKINSON
88 Director of Finance ....Mr. Ernest A. CORNFORD
15 Assoc VC Human Resources ....Mr. Peter A. HEITHAUS
19 Director Institutional Safety ....Mr. Forrest L. VAN NESS
09 Director Institutional Research ....Mr. Lawrence W. WESTERMEYER
26 Chief Marketing Officer ....Mr. Ronald H. GOSSEN
102 Assoc VC Development ....Dr. Brenda M. MCPHAIL
88 Sr Dir Development Colleges/Units ....Mr. Dan C. DIEDRIECH
88 Senior Director of Development ....Mr. Mark A. BERLYN
88 Director KWMU-FM Radio/Gen Mgr ....Mr. Tim J. EBY
29 Dir Alumni Community Engagement ....Ms. Linda CARTER
27 Chief Information Officer ....Mr. Robert D. SAMPLES
44 Director of Planned Giving ....Mr. Kent KROBER
94 Director Women's & Gender Studies ....Dr. Kathy J. GENTILE
70 Director Social Work ....Dr. Lois PIERCE
79 Director Center for the Humanities ....Dr. Diane H. TOULIATOS-MILES
88 Dir Public Policy Administration ....Dr. Deborah B. BALSER
88 Director Public Policy Research Ctr ....Dr. Mark TRANEL
88 Dir Women in Public Life ....Ms. Vivian EVELOFF
31 Director Community College Relation ....Ms. Melissa HATTMAN
88 Managing Dir Performing Arts Center ....Mr. John R. CATTANACH
88 Dir Des Lee Collaborative Vision ....Ms. Patricia ZAHN

*Missouri University of Science & Technology (A)

300 W 13th Street, Rolla MO 65409-0001

County: Phelps — FICE Identification: 002517

Unit ID: 178411

Telephone: (573) 341-4111 — Carnegie Class: RU/H

FAX Number: (573) 341-4307 — Calendar System: Semester

URL: www.mst.edu

Established: 1870 — Annual Undergrad Tuition & Fees (In-State): $10,078

Enrollment: 9,350 — Coed

Affiliation or Control: State — IRS Status: 501(c)3

Highest Offering: Doctorate

Program: Professional; Technical Emphasis

Accreditation: NH, BUS, CS, ENG

02 Chancellor ....Dr. Cheryl B. SCHRADER
05 Provost/Exec Vice Chanc Acad Affs ....Dr. Warren K. WRAY
11 Vice Chanc Administrative Services ....Vacant
30 Vice Chance University Advancement ....Ms. Joan M. NESBITT
32 Vice Chancellor Student Affairs ....Dr. Debra A G. ROBINSON
46 Vice Provost for Research Services ....Dr. K. KRISHNAMURTHY
20 Interim Vice Provost Acad Affairs ....Dr. Philip D. WHITEFIELD
20 Vice Prov Undergrad Studies ....Dr. Jeffrey CAWLFIELD
58 Vice Provost Graduate Studies ....Dr. Venkata ALLADA
56 Vice Provost of Global Learning ....Dr. Henry A. WIEBE
84 Vice Prov & Dean of Enrollment Mgmt ....Ms. Laura K. STOLL
08 Acting Director of Library ....Ms. Maggie TRISH
13 Chief Information Officer ....Mr. Greg H. SMITH
06 Registrar ....Ms. Deanne JACKSON
38 Asst Vice Chanc Stdnt Affs/Supp Svc ....Dr. Carl F. BURNS
41 Director of Athletics ....Mr. Mark E. MULLIN
15 Dir Human Resource/Affirm Action ....Ms. Shenethia MANUEL
36 Dir Career Opportunities Center ....Dr. Edna GROVER-BISKER
85 Director Intl/Cultural Affairs ....Ms. Jeanie H. HOFER
35 Director Student Life/Univ Center-R ....Mr. Mark POTRAFKA
39 Director Residential Life ....Ms. Tina F. SHEPPARD
09 Director Inst Research & Assessment ....Vacant
07 Director of Admissions ....Ms. Lynn STICHNOTE
29 Executive Dir Alumni Relations ....Ms. Darlene RAMSAY
37 Director Student Financial Aid ....Ms. Bridget K. BETZ
26 Director of Communications ....Mr. Andrew P. CAREAGA
18 Director of Physical Facilities ....Mr. James PACKARD
88 Dir of Womens Leadership Institute ....Ms. Cecilia ELMORE
40 Asst Director of Univ Bookstore ....Mr. Mark GALLARDO

University of Phoenix Kansas City Campus (B)

1310 E 104th Street, Kansas City MO 64131-4504

Telephone: (816) 943-9600 — Identification: 770213

Accreditation: &NH, ACBSP

† Main campus is University of Phoenix in Tempe, AZ.

University of Phoenix St. Louis Campus (C)

13801 Riverport Drive, St. Louis MO 63043

Telephone: (314) 298-9755 — Identification: 770214

Accreditation: &NH, ACBSP

† Main campus is University of Phoenix in Tempe, AZ.

Urshan Graduate School of Theology (D)

704 Howdershell Road, Florissant MO 63031-7526

County: St. Louis — FICE Identification: 041461

Unit ID: 455099

Telephone: (314) 921-9290 — Carnegie Class: Spec/Faith

FAX Number: (314) 921-9203 — Calendar System: Semester

URL: www.ugst.edu

Established: 2001 — Annual Undergrad Tuition & Fees: $9,775

Enrollment: 75 — Coed

Affiliation or Control: Other Protestant — IRS Status: 501(c)3

Highest Offering: Master's

Program: Professional; Religious Emphasis

Accreditation: THEOL

01 President ....Dr. David K. BERNARD
05 Academic Dean ....Dr. James A. LITTLES
11 Chief Administrative Officer ....Mrs. Jennie RUSSELL

Vatterott College-Joplin (E)

809 Illinois, Joplin MO 64801-9538

Telephone: (417) 781-5633 — Identification: 666060

Accreditation: ACCSC

† Main campus is Vatterott College-NorthPark in Berkeley, MO.

Vatterott College-Kansas City (F)

4131 N. Corrington Avenue, Kansas City MO 64117-1681

Telephone: (816) 861-1000 — Identification: 666519

Accreditation: ACCSC

† Main campus is Vatterott College-NorthPark in Berkeley, MO.

Vatterott College-NorthPark (G)

8580 Evans Avenue, Berkeley MO 63134-2900

County: Saint Louis — FICE Identification: 025997

Unit ID: 245342

Telephone: (314) 264-1000 — Carnegie Class: Assoc/PrivFP4

FAX Number: (314) 522-6174 — Calendar System: Other

URL: www.vatterott-college.edu

Established: 1969 — Annual Undergrad Tuition & Fees: $12,306

Enrollment: 1,344 — Coed

Affiliation or Control: Proprietary — IRS Status: Proprietary

Highest Offering: Baccalaureate

Program: Occupational; 2-Year Principally Bachelor's Creditable; Technical Emphasis

Accreditation: ACCSC

01 Campus Director ....Leeann EDWARDS
10 Chief Financial Officer ....Dennis BEAVERS
05 Director of Education ....Al WASHINGTON
05 Director of Education ....Samuel BOYD, III
06 Registrar ....Brenda LINCOLN-PENZEL
07 Director of Admissions ....Harvey CHAMBERLAIN

Vatterott College-St. Charles (H)

3550 West Clay Street, St. Charles MO 63301

Telephone: (636) 940-4100 — Identification: 666584

Accreditation: ACCSC

† Main campus is Vatterott College-NorthPark in Berkeley, MO.

Vatterott College-Saint Joseph (I)

3131 Frederick Avenue, Saint Joseph MO 64506

Telephone: (816) 364-5399 — Identification: 666520

Accreditation: ACCSC

† Main campus is Vatterott College-Des Moines in Des Moines, IA.

Vatterott College-Springfield (J)

3850 S Campbell Avenue, Springfield MO 65807-5340

Telephone: (417) 831-8116 — Identification: 666521

Accreditation: ACCSC

† Main campus is Vatterott College-NorthPark in Berkeley, MO.

Vatterott College-Sunset Hills (K)

12970 Maurer Industrial Drive,
Sunset Hills MO 63127-1516

Telephone: (314) 843-4200 — Identification: 666522

Accreditation: ACCSC

† Main campus is Vatterott College-NorthPark in Berkeley, MO.

Washington University in St. Louis (L)

One Brookings Drive, Saint Louis MO 63130-4899

County: Saint Louis — FICE Identification: 002520

Unit ID: 179867

Telephone: (314) 935-5000 — Carnegie Class: RU/VH

FAX Number: N/A — Calendar System: Semester

URL: www.wustl.edu

Established: 1853 — Annual Undergrad Tuition & Fees: $43,705

Enrollment: 13,952 — Coed

Affiliation or Control: Independent Non-Profit — IRS Status: 501(c)3

Highest Offering: Doctorate

Program: Liberal Arts And General; Professional

Accreditation: NH, ACAE, ART, AUD, BUS, CLPSY, ENG, LAW, MED, OT, PCSAS, PH, PTA, SW

01 Chancellor ....Dr. Mark S. WRIGHTON
05 Provost/Exec VC Academic Affairs ....Dr. Herbert Holden THORP
11 Exec VC Administration ....Mr. Henry S. WEBBER
63 Exec Vice Chanc/Dean of Medicine ....Dr. Larry J. SHAPIRO
43 Exec Vice Chanc/General Counsel ....Mr. Michael R. CANNON
30 Exec VC Alumni & Development ....Mr. David T. BLASINGAME
10 Vice Chancellor for Finance/CFO ....Ms. Barbara A. FEINER
46 Vice Chancellor for Research ....Dr. Evan D. KHARASCH
15 Vice Chanc for Human Resources ....Ms. Ann B. PRENATT
32 Vice Chancellor for Students ....Dr. Sharon STAHL
26 Vice Chanc for Public Affairs ....Ms. Jill D. FRIEDMAN
86 VC Government & Community Relations ....Ms. Pamela S. LOKKEN
88 Chief Investment Officer ....Ms. Kimberly G. WALKER
21 Assoc VC for Finance and Treasurer ....Ms. Amy B. KWESKIN
49 Dean Faculty of Arts & Sciences ....Dr. Barbara A. SCHAAL
61 Dean School of Law ....Mr. Kent D. SYVERUD
54 Dean Engineering & Applied Sciences ....Dr. Ralph S. QUATRANO
57 Dean Sam Fox Sch Design/Visual Arts ....Prof. Carmon COLANGELO
57 Dean College & Graduate Sch of Art ....Prof. Franklin SPECTOR
50 Dean Olin School of Business ....Prof. Mahendra R. GUPTA
58 Dean Graduate School of A & S ....Prof. Richard J. SMITH
70 Dean Brown School of Social Work ....Prof. Edward F. LAWLOR
55 Dean University College ....Prof. Robert E. WILTENBURG
48 Dean Architecture ....Prof. Bruce M. LINDSEY
100 Assoc Vice Chanc/Chief of Staff ....Mr. Steven J. GIVENS
101 Secretary to the Board of Trustees ....Ms. Ida H. EARLY
07 Vice Chancellor for Admissions ....Mr. John A. BERG
20 Vice Provost/Assoc VC Academic Affs ....Prof. Gerhild S. WILLIAMS
88 Assoc VC for Development ....Mr. William S. STOLL
29 Assoc VC Alumni & Development Pgm ....Ms. Pamella A. HENSON
26 Assoc VC Medical Public Affairs ....Mr. Donald E. CLAYTON
28 Vice Provost ....Prof. Adrienne D. DAVIS
85 VC for International Affairs ....Prof. James V. WERTSCH
08 University Librarian ....Mr. Jeffrey G. TRZECIAK
39 Assoc VC Students/Dean Students ....Mr. Justin X. CARROLL
35 Assoc VC Students/Dean Campus Life ....Dr. Jill E. CARNAGHI
13 Assoc VC Info Services & Tech ....Mr. Andrew D. ORTSTADT
27 Assoc VC for Public Affairs/U News ....Vacant
85 Asst VC/Dir International Students ....Ms. Kathy STEINER-LANG
96 Asst Vice Chanc Resource Management ....Mr. Alan S. KUEBLER
36 Asst VC/Director Career Center ....Mr. Mark W. SMITH
18 Asst VC Facilities Planning/Mgmt ....Mr. Arthur J. ACKERMANN
88 Asst VC Environ Health & Safety ....Mr. Bruce D. BACKUS
88 Asst VC Real Estate ....Ms. Mary B. CAMPBELL
72 Asst VC/Technology Management ....Dr. Bradley J. CASTANHO
14 Asst VC Univ Admin/Acad Computing ....Ms. Denise R. HIRSCHBECK
23 Asst VC/Dir Stdnt Hlth Counslng Svc ....Dr. Alan I. GLASS
37 Director Student Financial Services ....Mr. Michael RUNIEWICZ
41 Director of Athletics ....Mr. John M. SCHAEL
19 Director of Campus Police ....Mr. Donald STROM
07 Director of Admissions ....Ms. Julie SHIMABUKURO
06 University Registrar ....Ms. Susan E. HOSACK
38 Director of Mental Health Services ....Dr. Thomas M. BROUNK

Washington University in St. Louis-School of Medicine (M)

660 Euclid Avenue, Saint Louis MO 63110

Telephone: (314) 360-5000 — Identification: 770329

Accreditation: &NH

† Main campus is Washington University in St. Louis in Saint Louis, MO.

Webster University (N)

470 E Lockwood, Webster Groves MO 63119-3141

County: Saint Louis — FICE Identification: 002521

Unit ID: 179894

Telephone: (314) 968-6900 — Carnegie Class: Master's L

FAX Number: (314) 968-7112 — Calendar System: Semester

URL: www.webster.edu

Established: 1915 — Annual Undergrad Tuition & Fees: $23,700

Enrollment: 20,579 — Coed

Affiliation or Control: Independent Non-Profit — IRS Status: 501(c)3

Highest Offering: Doctorate

Program: Liberal Arts And General

Accreditation: NH, ACBSP, ANEST, MUS, NUR, TED

01 President ....Dr. Elizabeth J. STROBLE
04 Special Assistant to President ....Vacant
05 Provost ....Dr. Julian Z. SCHUSTER
30 Interim Chief Development Officer ....Mr. A. P PERKINSON
84 Interim Chief Enrollment Officer ....Mr. Robert PARRENT
10 VP & Chief Financial Officer ....Dr. Greg GUNDERSON
13 VP & Chief Information Officer ....Mr. Kenneth FREEMAN
20 AVP Academic Affairs ....Dr. Carol J. ADAMS
20 Asst Provost for Graduate Studies ....Dr. Elizabeth RUSSELL
32 Asst Provost Student Affairs/Athls ....Dr. Paul CARNEY
44 AVP Development/Alumni Pgms ....Mr. Matt ANDREW
32 Associate VP/Dean of Students ....Dr. Ted HOEF
106 Interim AVP/Dir OnLine Learning ....Ms. Thao DANG-WILLIAMS
82 AVP Academic Affairs/Dir Intl Pgms ....Dr. Grant CHAPMAN
15 AVP & Chief Human Resources Officer ....Ms. Betsy SCHMUTZ
84 AVP for Enrollment Management ....Ms. Anne EDMUNDS
29 AVP Alumni Programs ....Ms. Jennifer JEZEK-TAUSSIG

86 AVP Military & Government Programs .... Mr. Mike CALLAN
27 AVP & Chief Communications Officer .... Ms. Barbara O'MALLEY
46 AVP & Chief Strategic Initiatives .... Mr. Tom JOHNSON
20 Associate Provost .... Ms. Nancy HELLERUD
50 Dean School Business & Technology .... Dr. Benjamin O. AKANDE
53 Dean School of Education .... Dr. Brenda S. FYFE
57 Dean Leigh Gerdine Col of Fine Arts .... Mr. Peter E. SARGENT
49 Dean Col of Arts & Sciences .... Dr. David C. WILSON
60 Dean School of Communications .... Mr. Eric ROTHENBUHLER
08 Dean of University Library .... Ms. Laura REIN
39 Assoc Dean Stdts/Housing/Res Life .... Dr. John BUCK
20 Director of Academic Advising .... Dr. Tom NICKOLAI
21 Interim Dir Resource Plng & Budget .... Ms. Kathleen PARDO
19 Director Public Safety .... Mr. Dan PESOLD
06 Registrar .... Mr. Don MORRIS
26 Dir Public Relations/Global Mktg .... Mr. Patrick GIBLIN
24 Director of Media Services .... Mr. Dewey MARTIN
88 Director International Recruitment .... Mr. Calvin SMITH
41 Director Athletics .... Mr. Tom HART
36 Director Career Services .... Ms. Tamara GEGG-LAPLUME
23 Director Student Health Svcs .... Ms. Ann BROPHY
35 Director Student Activities .... Ms. Jennifer STEWART
37 Director Financial Aid .... Mr. James MYERS
38 Director Counsel & Life Development .... Dr. Patrick STACK
96 Director of Procurement Services .... Ms. Maria HEIN
09 Director Institutional Effectivenes .... Dr. Julie WEISSMAN
88 Senior Project Manager .... Mr. Steven STRANG
18 Director Facilities Planning .... Mr. Craig MILLER

Wentworth Military Academy and Junior College (A)

1880 Washington Avenue, Lexington MO 64067-1799

County: Lafayette
FICE Identification: 002522
Unit ID: 179919
Telephone: (800) 962-7682
Carnegie Class: Assoc/PrivNFP
FAX Number: (660) 259-2677
Calendar System: Semester
URL: www.wma.edu
Established: 1880
Annual Undergrad Tuition & Fees: $5,335
Enrollment: 860
Coed
Affiliation or Control: Independent Non-Profit
IRS Status: 501(c)3
Highest Offering: Associate Degree
Program: Occupational; 2-Year Principally Bachelor's Creditable
Accreditation: NH

01 Interim President/Superintendent .... Col. Michael LIERMAN
05 Chief Academic Officer .... Col. Timothy CASEY
11 Chief of Operations/Admin .... Col. Rick COTTRELL
30 Chief Development .... Mr. Dan RYAN
32 Commandant of Cadets .... LtCol. Darren FITZGERALD
84 Director Enrollment Managment .... Vacant
41 Athletic Director .... LtCol. Tom HUGHES
10 CFO .... LtCol. Glenn MILLER
21 Director of Business Services .... Maj. Jacque FRITCH
81 Professor of Military Science .... LtCol. Jeff PERRY
29 Alumni Director .... LtCol. Al MCCORMICK
04 Executive Assistant .... Ms. Rebecca MARKLEY
06 Registrar .... Ms. Melissa SCOTT
08 Librarian .... Capt. Linda CHRISTIAN
37 Director Student Financial Aid .... Capt. Brad FULLER
13 Director Information Technology .... Maj. Logan SEALS
85 Director Foreign Students .... Maj. Christhina STARKE
23 Director Health Services .... Capt. Barb PIERCE
35 Director Student Affairs .... LtCol. Darren FITZGERALD
09 Director of Institutional Research .... Col. Rick COTTRELL
15 Director Personal Services .... Ms. Rebecca MARKLEY
18 Chief Facilities/Physical Plant .... Mr. Wally RATLIFFE
26 Chief Public Relations Officer .... Maj. Kevin FARLEY
42 Chaplain .... Vacant
19 Director Safety and Security .... Maj. Fred FAILING
40 Director Bookstore .... Capt. Jerry MAGGERT

Westminster College (B)

501 Westminster Avenue, Fulton MO 65251-1230

County: Callaway
FICE Identification: 002523
Unit ID: 179946
Telephone: (573) 642-3361
Carnegie Class: Bac/A&S
FAX Number: (573) 592-5227
Calendar System: Semester
URL: www.westminster-mo.edu
Established: 1851
Annual Undergrad Tuition & Fees: $21,680
Enrollment: 1,080
Coed
Affiliation or Control: Independent Non-Profit
IRS Status: 501(c)3
Highest Offering: Baccalaureate
Program: Liberal Arts And General; Teacher Preparatory
Accreditation: NH

01 President .... Dr. George B. FORSYTHE
05 Sr Vice President/Dean of Faculty .... Dr. Carolyn J. PERRY
30 VP for Advancement .... Dr. William F. SHEEHAN, JR.
10 VP for Business and CFO .... Mr. Phil DANIELS
26 Director of College Relations .... Mr. Robert CROUSE
84 Dean of Enrollment Services .... Vacant
32 VP & Dean of Student Life .... Dr. Stephanie KRAUTH
20 Associate Dean .... Dr. David JONES
08 Director of Library Services .... Ms. Angela GROGAN
06 Registrar .... Mrs. Phyllis J. MASEK
13 Executive Director of IT .... Mr. Bill LOUCKS
37 Director of Financial Aid .... Ms. Aimee BRISTOW
15 Director of Human Resources .... Vacant
39 Director of Residential/Greek Life .... Ms. Jacqueline J. WEBER
41 Athletic Director .... Mr. Matt MITCHELL
23 Exec Director Wellness Center .... Dr. Kasi LACEY
88 Exec Dir Marketing/Communications .... Ms. Jennifer BONDURANT
29 Dir Alumni Engagement/Events .... Ms. Sharon MATHER
36 Director of Career Services .... Ms. Meg LANGLAND
18 Exec Dir Plant Ops/Auxiliary Svcs .... Mr. Daniel HASLAG
07 Director of Admissions .... Ms. Kelle SILVEY
09 Director of Institutional Research .... Dr. Ray BROWN
19 Dir Campus Safety & Security .... Mr. Jack BENKE
42 Chaplain .... Rev. Jamie HASKINS

William Jewell College (C)

500 College Hill, Liberty MO 64068-1896

County: Clay
FICE Identification: 002524
Unit ID: 179955
Telephone: (816) 781-7700
Carnegie Class: Bac/A&S
FAX Number: (816) 415-5027
Calendar System: Semester
URL: www.jewell.edu
Established: 1849
Annual Undergrad Tuition & Fees: $30,800
Enrollment: 1,052
Coed
Affiliation or Control: Independent Non-Profit
IRS Status: 501(c)3
Highest Offering: Master's
Program: Liberal Arts And General; Teacher Preparatory; Professional
Accreditation: NH, MUS, NURSE

01 President .... Dr. David L. SALLEE
05 Provost .... Dr. Anne C. DEMA
10 Vice Pres for Finance & Operations .... Mr. Brian CLEMONS
30 Vice Pres Institutional Advancement .... Mr. Clark MORRIS
84 Vice Pres for Enrollment .... Mr. Gary BRACKEN
42 Vice Pres for Social Responsibility .... Dr. Andrew L. PRATT
32 Dean of Student Life .... Ms. Shelly KING
07 Dean of Admissions .... Mr. Clint CHAPMAN
06 Registrar .... Dr. Edwin H. LANE
08 Director of the Library .... Ms. Stephanie DECLUE
21 Controller .... Mr. Ron DEMPSEY
13 Director of Information Services .... Ms. Lan GUO
97 Assoc Dean Core Curriculum .... Dr. Gary ARMSTRONG
37 Director of Financial Aid .... Ms. Susan J. KARNES
15 Assoc Director of Human Resources .... Ms. Penny OWENS
18 Director of Facilities Mgmt .... Mr. Steve ANDERSON
57 Executive Director Harriman-Jewell .... Mr. Clark W. MORRIS
41 Director of Athletics .... Dr. Darlene BAILEY
36 Director of Career Development .... Ms. Marissa BLAND
38 Director of Counseling Services .... Dr. Beth GENTRY-EPLEY
29 Director of Alumni Relations .... Ms. Andrea MELOAN
104 Director of International Study .... Ms. Sara ROUND

William Woods University (D)

One University Avenue, Fulton MO 65251-1098

County: Callaway
FICE Identification: 002525
Unit ID: 179964
Telephone: (573) 642-2251
Carnegie Class: Master's L
FAX Number: (573) 592-1146
Calendar System: Other
URL: www.williamwoods.edu
Established: 1870
Annual Undergrad Tuition & Fees: $19,950
Enrollment: 1,792
Coed
Affiliation or Control: Christian Church (Disciples Of Christ)
IRS Status: 501(c)3
Highest Offering: Doctorate
Program: Liberal Arts And General; Teacher Preparatory; Professional
Accreditation: NH, SW, TEAC

01 President .... Dr. Jahnae H. BARNETT
03 Vice President .... Scott GALLAGHER
05 Vice President & Academic Dean .... Dr. Sherry MCCARTHY
11 Vice President Administration .... Dr. Robert FESSLER
04 Executive Assistant to President .... Kenda E G. SHINDLER
07 Dean of Admissions .... Sarah MUNNS
58 VP and Dean of Grad Studies .... Dr. Michael W. WESTERFIELD
32 Dean of Student Life .... Venita MITCHELL
41 Director of Athletics .... Jason VITTONE
10 Chief Financial Officer .... Vacant
20 Assoc Dean Academic Services .... Tom FRANKMAN
88 Assoc Dean Assessment .... Dr. Susan JONES
44 Assoc VP of Advancement .... Dr. Carie MCCRAY
08 Director Libraries .... Erlene DUDLEY
26 Director of Marketing .... Kristina BRIGHT
18 Director of Buildings & Grounds .... Mike DILLON
06 Director of Records/Registrar .... Tara DEIERLING
15 Director Human Resources & Benefits .... Kathy GROVES
21 Controller .... Julie HOUSEWORTH
37 Director Student Financial Services .... Deana READY
27 Director of University Relations .... Mary Ann BEAHON
29 Director of Alumni Activities .... Becky STINSON
50 Chair Business & Economics Division .... David FORSTER
53 Chair Education Division .... Dr. Susan JONES
49 Chair Art Division .... Dr. Aimee SAPP
88 Chair Equestrian Studies Division .... Jennifer PETTERSON
88 Chair Human Performance Division .... Anthony LUNGSTRUM
83 Chair Behavioral/Soc Sciences Div .... Shawn HULL
88 Director Graduate Education Pgms .... Dr. E. Douglas EBERSOLD
39 Dir Residential Life/Campus Safety .... Mike WILLS
13 Director of Technology .... Jim LONG
09 Director of Institutional Research .... Dr. Paul STURGIS
36 Dir Career Svcs/Student Success .... Amy DITTMER
35 Coord Greek Life/Student Involvemnt .... Lacy SWEETEN
42 Chaplain/Faith & Service Director .... Travis TAMERIUS
88 ADA Coordinator/Interpreter .... Margie COATNEY
28 Coordinator Multicultural Affairs .... Cyndi KOONSE
38 Counselor .... Rebecca SEITZ

MONTANA

Aaniiih Nakoda College (E)

PO Box 159, Harlem MT 59526-0159

County: Blaine
FICE Identification: 025175
Unit ID: 180203
Telephone: (406) 353-2607
Carnegie Class: Tribal
FAX Number: (406) 353-2898
Calendar System: Semester
URL: www.ancollege.edu
Established: 1984
Annual Undergrad Tuition & Fees: $2,410
Enrollment: 144
Coed
Affiliation or Control: Tribal Control
IRS Status: 501(c)3
Highest Offering: Associate Degree
Program: Occupational; 2-Year Principally Bachelor's Creditable
Accreditation: NW

01 President .... Dr. Carole FALCON-CHANDLER
05 Dean of Academic Affairs .... Ms. Carmen CORNELIUS TAYLOR
32 Dean of Student Affairs .... Ms. Clarena BROCKIE
10 Comptroller .... Ms. Debra EVE
06 Registrar/Admissions Officer .... Mrs. Dixie BROCKIE
37 Financial Aid Director .... Ms. Toma CAMPBELL-HOOPS
08 Director of Library Services .... Ms. Eva ENGLISH
25 Director Sponsored Programs .... Mr. Scott FRISKICS
13 Information Systems Manager .... Mr. Harold H. HEPPNER
40 Bookstore Manager .... Ms. Kimberly BROCKIE
04 Assistant to the President .... Ms. Michele LEWIS

Blackfeet Community College (F)

Box 819, Browning MT 59417-0819

County: Glacier
FICE Identification: 025106
Unit ID: 180054
Telephone: (406) 338-5441
Carnegie Class: Tribal
FAX Number: (406) 338-3272
Calendar System: Semester
URL: www.bfcc.edu
Established: 1976
Annual Undergrad Tuition & Fees: $2,350
Enrollment: 450
Coed
Affiliation or Control: Independent Non-Profit
IRS Status: 501(c)3
Highest Offering: Associate Degree
Program: Occupational; 2-Year Principally Bachelor's Creditable
Accreditation: NW

01 President .... Dr. Billie Jo KIPP
05 Dean Academic Affs/Student Svcs .. Dr. Dorothy STILL SMOKING
10 Chief Financial Officer .... Ms. Natalie JACKSON
37 Director of Financial Aid .... Ms. Gaylene DUCHARME
06 Registrar/Admissions Officer .... Ms. Deana M. MCNABB
15 Director Human Resources .... Ms. Dana L. PEMBERTON
07 Director of Admissions .... Ms. Deana M. MCNABB
09 Director of Institutional Research .... Vacant
18 Chief Facilities/Physical Plant .... Mr. Curtis HENRIKSEN

Carroll College (G)

1601 N Benton Avenue, Helena MT 59625-0002

County: Lewis And Clark
FICE Identification: 002526
Unit ID: 180106
Telephone: (406) 447-4300
Carnegie Class: Bac/Diverse
FAX Number: (406) 447-4533
Calendar System: Semester
URL: www.carroll.edu
Established: 1909
Annual Undergrad Tuition & Fees: $27,914
Enrollment: 1,436
Coed
Affiliation or Control: Roman Catholic
IRS Status: 501(c)3
Highest Offering: Baccalaureate
Program: Occupational; Liberal Arts And General; Teacher Preparatory; Professional
Accreditation: NW, ENG, NURSE

01 President .... Dr. Thomas EVANS
05 Sr Vice President Academic Affairs .... Dr. Paula MCNUTT
10 VP for Finance & Administration .... Ms. Lori PETERSON
30 VP Institutional Advanc/Cmty Rels .... Mr. Thomas J. MCCARVEL
32 Vice President for Student Life .... Dr. James D. HARDWICK
84 Assoc Vice Pres of Enrollment Mgmt .... Ms. Nina LOCOCO
42 Chaplain/Director .... Rev. Marc LENNEMAN
26 Dir of Communications .... Vacant
26 Director of Marketing .... Ms. Patty WHITE
06 Registrar .... Ms. Cassie HALL
08 Director of Library .... Mr. Christian FRAZZA
37 Financial Aid Director .... Ms. Janet RIIS
36 Dir of Career Services/Testing .... Ms. Rosalie K. WALSH
07 Director Admissions/Enrollment Ops .... Ms. Cynthia J. THORNQUIST
15 Director of Human Res & Adm Svcs .... Ms. Renee M. MCMAHON
18 Director of Facilities .... Mr. Walter H. BISKUPIAK
39 Director of Community Living .... Mr. Bennett MACINTYRE
35 Dir Student Activities/Ldrshp .... Mr. Patrick HARRIS
38 Director of Counseling .... Mr. K. Mike FRANKLIN
21 Controller .... Ms. Kari BRUSTKERN
13 Director Information Technology .... Ms. Loretta ANDREWS
29 Director Alumni Relations .... Ms. Kathy RAMIREZ
09 Dir Research/Planing/Assess .... Dr. Dawn GALLINGER

Chief Dull Knife College (H)

One College Drive, Lame Deer MT 59043

County: Rosebud
FICE Identification: 025452
Unit ID: 180160
Telephone: (406) 477-6215
Carnegie Class: Tribal
FAX Number: (406) 477-6219
Calendar System: Semester

URL: www.cdkc.edu
Established: 1975 Annual Undergrad Tuition & Fees: $2,260
Enrollment: 361 Coed
Affiliation or Control: Independent Non-Profit IRS Status: 501(c)3
Highest Offering: Associate Degree
Program: Occupational; 2-Year Principally Bachelor's Creditable
Accreditation: NW

01 President Dr. Richard LITTLEBEAR
03 Vice President Mr. William WERTMAN
05 Dean Academic Affairs Ms. Michelle CURLEE
32 Dean Student Affairs Mr. Vince HERTIK
37 Director Student Financial Aid Mr. Devin WERTMAN
08 Head Librarian Mrs. Joan HANTZ

Dawson Community College (A)

Box 421, Glendive MT 59330-0421
County: Dawson FICE Identification: 002529
Unit ID: 180151
Telephone: (406) 377-3396 Carnegie Class: Assoc/Pub-R-S
FAX Number: (406) 377-8132 Calendar System: Semester
URL: www.dawson.edu
Established: 1940 Annual Undergrad Tuition & Fees (In-District): $3,083
Enrollment: 312 Coed
Affiliation or Control: State/Local IRS Status: 501(c)3
Highest Offering: Associate Degree
Program: Occupational; 2-Year Principally Bachelor's Creditable
Accreditation: NW

01 President Mr. Mike SIMON
05 Dean of Instructional Services Dr. Jackie SCHULTZ
32 Dean of Student Services Ms. Joyce AYRE
11 Dean of Administrative Services Mr. Justin CROSS
06 Registrar Ms. Virginia BOYSUN
88 Director Special Services Mr. Kent DION
08 Library Director Mr. Todd KNISPEL
07 Director Admissions/Financial Aid Ms. Jolene MYERS
13 Director Information Technology Mr. Shane BISHOP
26 Chief Public Relations Officer Ms. Jane WYNNE
41 Athletic Director Ms. Joyce AYRE
15 Human Resource Director Ms. Julie GRIFFITH

Flathead Valley Community College (B)

777 Grandview Drive, Kalispell MT 59901
County: Flathead FICE Identification: 006777
Unit ID: 180197
Telephone: (406) 756-3822 Carnegie Class: Assoc/Pub-R-M
FAX Number: (406) 756-3815 Calendar System: Semester
URL: www.fvcc.edu
Established: 1967 Annual Undergrad Tuition & Fees (In-District): $3,730
Enrollment: 2,395 Coed
Affiliation or Control: Local IRS Status: 501(c)3
Highest Offering: Associate Degree
Program: Occupational; 2-Year Principally Bachelor's Creditable
Accreditation: NW, EMT, MAC, @PTAA, SURGT

01 President Dr. Jane A. KARAS
05 Vice President Instruction Dr. Kristen JONES
10 Vice Pres Administration & Finance Mr. Chuck JENSEN
12 Director Lincoln County Campus Mr. Patrick PEZZELLE
20 Director Educational Services Ms. Mary JORDT
32 Dean of Students Ms. Brenda HANSON
06 Registrar/Coord/Admissions/Records Ms. Marlene STOLTZ
51 Director Economic Dev/Continuing Ed Ms. Susan BURCH
20 Director TRIO Ms. Lynn L. FARRIS
13 Director Mgmt Information Services Mr. Bill E. BOND
37 Director Student Financial Aid Ms. Cindy KIEFER
15 Director of Human Resources Mr. Warren D. TOLLEY
88 Director of Adult Basic Education Ms. Margaret L. GIRKINS
18 Director Maintenance Service Mr. Jack ROARK
21 Controller Mr. Kirk ZANDER
26 Asst Dir Marketing/Communications Ms. Tara E. ROTH
24 Coord Instructional Media Services Ms. Malinda CRAWFORD
36 Director Student Placement Ms. Karen DARROW
96 Director of Purchasing Mr. Steve LARSON
30 Director Institutional Advancement Ms. Coleen UNTERREINER
09 Director of Institutional Research Dr. Brad ELDREDGE

Fort Peck Community College (C)

PO Box 398, Poplar MT 59255-0398
County: Roosevelt FICE Identification: 023430
Unit ID: 180212
Telephone: (406) 768-6300 Carnegie Class: Tribal
FAX Number: (406) 768-6301 Calendar System: Semester
URL: www.fpcc.edu
Established: 1978 Annual Undergrad Tuition & Fees: $2,250
Enrollment: 438 Coed
Affiliation or Control: Tribal Control IRS Status: 501(c)3
Highest Offering: Associate Degree
Program: Occupational; 2-Year Principally Bachelor's Creditable; Business Emphasis
Accreditation: NW

01 President Dr. Florence GARCIA
05 Academic Vice President Mr. Wayne TWO BULLS
32 Vice President Student Services Ms. Haven GOURNEAU
09 Vice Pres Institutional Research Mr. Craig SMITH
31 Vice President Community Services Mr. Larry WETSIT
10 Business Manager Ms. Rose ATKINSON
06 Registrar/Admissions Ms. Linda L. HANSEN
37 Financial Aid Officer Ms. Lanette CLARK
40 Bookstore Manager Ms. Jackie AZURE
08 Head Librarian Mrs. Anita A. SCHEETZ

Little Big Horn College (D)

PO Box 370, Crow Agency MT 59022-0370
County: Big Horn FICE Identification: 022866
Unit ID: 180328
Telephone: (406) 638-3104 Carnegie Class: Tribal
FAX Number: (406) 638-3169 Calendar System: Semester
URL: www.lbhc.edu
Established: 1980 Annual Undergrad Tuition & Fees: $2,760
Enrollment: 325 Coed
Affiliation or Control: Tribal Control IRS Status: 501(c)3
Highest Offering: Associate Degree
Program: Occupational; 2-Year Principally Bachelor's Creditable; Business Emphasis
Accreditation: NW

01 President Dr. David YARLOTT, JR.
05 Academic Dean Miss Frederica LEFT HAND
32 Dean of Student Services Miss Te-Atta OLD BEAR
11 Dean of Administration Mr. David SMALL
08 Director of Library Mr. Tim BERNARDIS
13 Chief Information Officer Mr. Franklin COOPER
10 Chief Finance Officer Ms. Aldean GOOD LUCK
15 Director Human Resources Ms. Natalie COLLIFLOWER
97 Dept Head/General Stds/Crow Stds Dr. Tim MCCLEARY
81 Dept Head/Math/Science/Technology Dr. Dianna HOOKER

Miles Community College (E)

2715 Dickinson, Miles City MT 59301-4799
County: Custer FICE Identification: 002528
Unit ID: 180373
Telephone: (406) 874-6100 Carnegie Class: Assoc/Pub-R-S
FAX Number: (406) 874-6282 Calendar System: Semester
URL: www.milescc.edu
Established: 1939 Annual Undergrad Tuition & Fees (In-District): $3,810
Enrollment: 466 Coed
Affiliation or Control: State/Local IRS Status: 501(c)3
Highest Offering: Associate Degree
Program: Occupational; 2-Year Principally Bachelor's Creditable
Accreditation: NW, ADNUR, PHLEB

01 Interim President Ms. Lisa WATSON
11 VP Administration & Finance Ms. Lisa WATSON
05 Vice Pres of Academic Affairs Ms. Shelly WEIGHT
32 VP Student Success/Inst Research Ms. Jessie DUFNER
08 Director of Library Ms. Ann O. RUTHERFORD
13 Director Information Technology Mr. Donald D. WARNER
37 Director Student Financial Aid Mr. Loren LANCASTER
18 Chief Facilities/Physical Plant Mr. Ross LAWRENCE
21 Controller Ms. Nancy AABERGE
06 Registrar Ms. Lisa BLUNT
15 Director Human Resources Ms. Kylene PHIPPS
66 Director Nursing Ms. Karla LUND
20 Associate Academic Officer Mr. Garth SLEIGHT
40 Manager Bookstore Vacant

Montana Bible College (F)

3625 South 19th Avenue, Bozeman MT 59718-9108
County: Gallatin FICE Identification: 041403
Unit ID: 262165
Telephone: (406) 586-3585 Carnegie Class: Not Classified
FAX Number: (406) 586-3585 Calendar System: Semester
URL: www.montanabiblecollege.edu
Established: 1987 Annual Undergrad Tuition & Fees: $6,740
Enrollment: 123 Coed
Affiliation or Control: Independent Non-Profit IRS Status: 501(c)3
Highest Offering: Baccalaureate
Program: Religious Emphasis
Accreditation: BI

01 President Mr. Jim CARLSON
05 Academic Dean Dr. Gale HEIDE
06 Registrar Mrs. Louise TURNER
07 Admissions Coordinator Mrs. Susan JACKSON
08 Head Librarian Mr. Micah FORSYTHE
32 Dean of Students Mr. Scott MORNINGSTAR
10 Business Manager Mrs. Leota FRED
21 Office Manager Mrs. Jeanie TYPOLT
18 Facilities Manager Mr. Ty TYPOLT
30 Advancement Ms. Barbara HANNO
26 Recruitment Mr. Ryan WARD

*Montana University System Office (G)

2500 Broadway, Helena MT 59601-3201
County: Lewis And Clark FICE Identification: 029072
Unit ID: 180470
Telephone: (406) 444-6570 Carnegie Class: N/A
FAX Number: (406) 444-1469
URL: www.mus.edu

01 Commissioner Higher Education Mr. Clayton T. CHRISTIAN
05 Deputy Comm Academic/Student Affs Dr. Neil MOISEY
10 Assoc Comm for Fiscal Affairs Mr. Mick ROBINSON
45 Assoc Comm for Plng & Public Policy Mr. Tyler TREVOR
43 Chief Legal Counsel Ms. Viv HAMMILL
15 Director Labor Relations/Personnel Mr. Kevin MCRAE
88 Director of Benefits Mrs. Connie WELSH
37 Director Guaranteed Student Loans Vacant
21 Director Accounting & Budget Ms. Frieda HOUSER
88 Director of Work Comp Risk Mgmt Ms. Leah Jo TIETZ
103 Deputy Comm Two-Year Educ Mr. John CECH
93 Dir Minority/Amer Ind Achievement Ms. Brandi FOSTER
13 IT Manager Ms. Edwina MORRISON

*The University of Montana - Missoula (H)

32 Campus Drive, Missoula MT 59812-0001
County: Missoula FICE Identification: 002536
Unit ID: 180489
Telephone: (406) 243-0211 Carnegie Class: RU/H
FAX Number: (406) 243-2797 Calendar System: Semester
URL: www.umt.edu
Established: 1893 Annual Undergrad Tuition & Fees (In-State): $6,071
Enrollment: 14,660 Coed
Affiliation or Control: State IRS Status: 501(c)3
Highest Offering: Doctorate
Program: 2-Year Principally Bachelor's Creditable; Liberal Arts And General; Teacher Preparatory; Professional
Accreditation: NW, ART, BUS, BUSA, CACREP, CLPSY, COARC, CS, FOR, JOUR, LAW, MUS, PH, PHAR, PTA, @SP, SW, TED, THEA

02 President Dr. Royce C. ENGSTROM
88 VP for Integrated Communications Ms. Peggy KUHR
05 Provost/VP Academic Affairs Dr. Perry BROWN
10 Vice President Finance/Admin Mr. Michael REID
32 Vice President for Student Affairs Dr. Teresa S. BRANCH
46 Vice Pres Research/Development Dr. Scott WHITTENBURG
84 Asst Vice Pres Enrollment Services Mr. Jed LISTON
27 Asst Vice Pres Marketing Mr. Mario SCHULZKE
45 AVP for Plng/Budget Analysis Ms. Dawn RESSEL
15 AVP Human Resource Services Ms. Terri PHILLIPS
20 Associate Provost Dr. Arlene WALKER-ANDREWS
58 Dean of the Graduate School Dr. Sandy ROSS
35 Dean of Students Ms. Rhondie VOORHEES
43 Legal Counsel Ms. Lucy FRANCE
12 Director Mansfield Center Vacant
104 International Progams Director Mr. Paulo ZAGALO-MELO
88 Director Broadcast Media Center Mr. William MARCUS
22 Dir Equal Opportunity/Affirm Action Vacant
06 Registrar Mr. Edwin JOHNSON
18 Director Facilities Services Mr. Hugh A. JESSE
13 CIO Mr. Matt RILEY
38 Interim Director Counseling Mr. Mike FROST
36 Director Career Services Mr. Michael HEURING
37 Director of Financial Aid Mr. Kent MCGOWAN
29 Director of Alumni Relations Mr. William S. JOHNSTON
102 President & CEO/UM Foundation Mr. Shane GEISE
19 Director of Public Safety Mr. Gary TAYLOR
23 Int Director Curry Health Center Dr. Rick CURTIS
24 Director Presentation Tech Services Mr. Randy GOTTFRIED
39 Director Residence Life Ms. Sandra SCHOONOVER
41 Athletic Director Mr. Kent HASLAM
85 Dir Foreign Student & Scholar Svcs Ms. Effie F. KOEHN
21 Director Business Services Mr. Mark H. PULLIUM
07 Director Marketing Recruitment Ms. Juana J. ALCALA
40 General Manager Univ Bookstore Mr. Bryan C. THORNTON
62 Dean Library Services Dr. Sha Li ZHANG
51 Dean Continuing Education Dr. Roger MACLEAN
49 Dean College Arts & Sciences Dr. Christopher COMER
61 Dean School of Law Dr. Irma RUSSELL
65 Dean Col Forestry/Conservation Dr. James BURCHFIELD
50 Dean School of Business Admin Dr. Larry D. GIANCHETTA
76 Dean Col Health Prof & Biomed Sci Dr. David S. FORBES
60 Interim Dean School of Journalism Ms. Denise DOWLING
53 Dean College of Educ & Human Svcs Dr. Roberta EVANS
57 Dean College Visual Performing Arts Mr. Stephen KALM
75 Dean Missoula College Dr. Barry GOOD
92 Dean Honors College Dr. James MCKUSICK

*The University of Montana Western (I)

710 S Atlantic St, Dillon MT 59725-3598
County: Beaverhead FICE Identification: 002537
Unit ID: 180692
Telephone: (406) 683-7011 Carnegie Class: Bac/Diverse
FAX Number: (406) 683-7493 Calendar System: Other
URL: www.umwestern.edu
Established: 1893 Annual Undergrad Tuition & Fees (In-State): $4,111
Enrollment: 1,483 Coed
Affiliation or Control: State IRS Status: 501(c)3
Highest Offering: Baccalaureate
Program: 2-Year Principally Bachelor's Creditable; Liberal Arts And General; Teacher Preparatory
Accreditation: NW, IACBE, TED

02 Chancellor Dr. Richard D. STOREY
05 Provost/Vice Chanc Academic Affairs Dr. Karl ULRICH
10 Vice Chanc Administration/Finance Ms. Susan BRIGGS
26 Director Marketing/Univ Relations Mr. Kent J. ORD
06 Registrar Ms. Charity WALTERS
07 Director of Admissions Ms. Catherine REDHEAD
08 Librarian Mr. Michael SCHULZ

36 Director of Field Learning .... Mr. Michael MILLER
24 Director of Media Relations .... Vacant
41 Director of Athletics .... Mr. Ryan NOURSE
14 Director of Computer Center .... Mr. Scott WADE
18 Director of Facilities Services .... Mr. Dan PAYNE
32 Dean of Students .... Ms. Nicole HAZELBAKER
88 Dean School of Outreach .... Ms. Anneliese RIPLEY
30 Director of Devel/Alumni Relations .... Ms. Roxanne ENGELLANT
37 Director Student Financial Aid .... Ms. Erica JONES
38 Director Student Counseling .... Ms. Lynn MEIER WELTZIEN
15 Director Personnel Services .... Ms. Dorothy SEYMOUR

*The University of Montana - Helena College of Technology (A)

1115 N Roberts, Helena MT 59601-3098
County: Lewis and Clark FICE Identification: 007570
Unit ID: 180276
Telephone: (406) 447-6900 Carnegie Class: Assoc/Pub2in4
FAX Number: (406) 444-6892 Calendar System: Semester
URL: www.umhelena.edu
Established: 1939 Annual Undergrad Tuition & Fees (In-State): $3,061
Enrollment: 1,627 Coed
Affiliation or Control: State IRS Status: 501(c)3
Highest Offering: Associate Degree
Program: Occupational; 2-Year Principally Bachelor's Creditable; Technical Emphasis
Accreditation: NW, ADNUR

02 Dean/CEO .... Dr. Daniel BINGHAM
04 Assistant to the Dean/CEO .... Ms. Gigi BOTTENFIELD
05 Associate Dean of Academic Affairs .... Vacant
06 Director of Admissions and Records .... Ms. Sarah DELLWO
08 Director of Library Services .... Vacant
51 Director of Continuing Education .... Ms. Mary LANNERT
18 Assistant Dean of Fiscal & Plant .... Mr. Russ FILLNER
13 Director of IT Services .... Mr. Jeff BLOCK
40 Retail Services Manager .... Mr. Josh BENNETT
32 Assistant Dean of Student Services .... Ms. Elizabeth STEARNS-SIMS
26 Marketing & Comm Coordinator .... Ms. Barb MCALMOND
37 Director Student Financial Aid .... Ms. Valerie CURTIN
32 Director of Student Success .... Ms. Suzanne HUNGER
88 Dir Disability & Veterans Services .... Ms. Cindy YARBERRY
15 Director of Human Resources .... Vacant
36 Career Services Coordinator .... Mr. Alan THOMPSON

*Montana State University (B)

PO Box 172190, Bozeman MT 59717-2190
County: Gallatin FICE Identification: 002532
Unit ID: 180461
Telephone: (406) 994-2452 Carnegie Class: RU/VH
FAX Number: (406) 994-1923 Calendar System: Semester
URL: www.montana.edu
Established: 1893 Annual Undergrad Tuition & Fees (In-State): $6,752
Enrollment: 14,660 Coed
Affiliation or Control: State IRS Status: 501(c)3
Highest Offering: Doctorate
Program: Occupational; 2-Year Principally Bachelor's Creditable; Liberal Arts And General; Teacher Preparatory; Professional
Accreditation: NW, ART, BUS, CACREP, CS, DIETD, @DIETI, ENG, ENGT, IPSY, MT, MUS, NURSE, TEAC

02 President .... Dr. Waded CRUZADO
05 Provost/Vice Pres Academic Affairs .... Dr. Martha POTVIN
20 Assoc Provost .... Dr. David SINGEL
88 Assoc Provost Accreditation .... Dr. Ron LARSEN
10 Vice Pres Admin/Finance .... Mr. Terry LEIST
32 Interim Vice Pres Student Success .... Dr. Robert MARLEY
56 Interim Director Extension .... Jill MARTZ
46 Int VP Research/Creat/Tech Transf .... Dr. Anne CAMPER
04 Special Assistant to the President .... Dr. Henrietta MANN
18 Assoc Vice Pres University Services .... Mr. Robert V. LASHAWAY
88 Assoc VP Res/Creativity/Tch Trnsfer .... Dr. Lee SPANGLER
15 Chief Human Resources Officer .... Mr. Dennis DEFA
21 Asst Vice Pres Financial Services .... Ms. Laura HUMBERGER
102 President/CEO MSU Foundation .... Mr. Michael STEVENSON
104 Exec Dir International Education .... Dr. Norman PETERSON
27 Exec Director Univ Communications .... Mr. Tracy ELLIG
88 Exec Director Museum of the Rockies .... Ms. Sheldon MCKAMEY
50 Dean Business .... Dr. Kregg AYTES
53 Dean Education/Health/Human Dev .... Dr. Lynda RANSDELL
54 Acting Dean Engineering .... Dr. Brett GUNNINK
49 Dean Letters & Science .... Dr. Nicol RAE
66 Dean Nursing .... Dr. Helen MELLAND
08 Dean Libraries .... Mr. Kenning ARLITSCH
88 Dean Students .... Dr. Matthew CAIRES
58 Acting Dean Graduate School .... Dr. Ronald LARSEN
47 Dean Agriculture .... Dr. Jeffrey JACOBSEN
48 Dean Arts/Architecture .... Dr. Nancy CORNWELL
70 Dean Gallatin College Programs .... Mr. Robert HIETALA
07 Director Admissions .... Ms. Ronda RUSSELL
22 Director Institutional Equity .... Ms. Diane LETENDRE
29 Pres/CEO Alumni Foundation .... Mr. Michael STEVENSON
41 Director Athletics .... Mr. Peter FIELDS
88 Director Auxiliary Services .... Mr. Tom STUMP
36 Director Career Services .... Dr. Carina BECK
38 Director Counseling/Psych Services .... Dr. Patrick DONAHOE
88 Dir Disability/Re-ent/Veteran Svcs .... Ms. Brenda YORK
56 Exec Director Extended University .... Dr. Kim OBBINK
37 Director Financial Aid .... Ms. Brandi PAYNE
43 Legal Counsel .... Dr. Leslie TAYLOR
45 Director Planning & Analysis .... Dr. Chris FASTNOW
96 Director Purchasing .... Mr. Brian O'CONNOR
06 Registrar .... Ms. Bonnie ASHLEY
26 Director Marketing/Creative Service .... Ms. Julie KIPFER
19 Director University Police .... Mr. Robert PUTZKE

*Montana State University - Billings (C)

1500 University Drive, Billings MT 59101-0245
County: Yellowstone FICE Identification: 002530
Unit ID: 180179
Telephone: (406) 657-2011 Carnegie Class: Master's M
FAX Number: (406) 657-2302 Calendar System: Semester
URL: www.msubillings.edu
Established: 1927 Annual Undergrad Tuition & Fees (In-State): $5,745
Enrollment: 5,081 Coed
Affiliation or Control: State IRS Status: 501(c)3
Highest Offering: Master's
Program: Occupational; Liberal Arts And General; Teacher Preparatory; Business Emphasis
Accreditation: NW, ART, BUS, CORE, EMT, MUS, TED

02 Chancellor .... Dr. Rolf S. GROSETH
11 Administrative Vice Chancellor .... Ms. Terrie IVERSON
05 Academic Vice Chancellor & Provost .... Dr. Mark PAGANO
32 Vice Chancellor for Student Affairs .... Dr. Stacy KLIPPENSTEIN
20 Vice Provost Academic Affairs .... Dr. Matthew REDINGER
102 President/CEO Foundation .... Ms. Marilynn MILLER
08 Director Library Services .... Mr. Brent ROBERTS
84 Director Enrollment Management .... Dr. Stacy KLIPPENSTEIN
07 Director Admiss/Records/Registrar .... Dr. Cheri JOHANNES
15 Director Human Resources/EEO AA .... Ms. Janet SIMON
36 Director Career Services .... Ms. Patricia B. REUSS
27 Chief Information Officer .... Dr. Michael J. BARBER
56 Director Extended Campus .... Mr. Kevin NEMETH
25 Dir Grants & Sponsored Pgms .... Dr. David MCGINNIS
26 Int Director University Relations .... Mr. Aaron CLINGINGSMITH
09 Office Institutional Planning .... Vacant
18 Director Facility Services .... Mr. Jason MCGIMPSEY
58 Int Director Graduate Programs .... Dr. David CRAIG
41 Athletic Director .... Ms. Krista MONTAGUE
19 Chief of Campus Police .... Mr. Scott FORSHEE
29 Director Alumni Relations .... Ms. Sarah BROCKEL
37 Director Student Financial Aid .... Ms. Leslie WELDON
40 Director Bookstore .... Mr. Chad SCHREIER
39 Dir Stdnt Union/Housing/Res Life .... Ms. Jeannie MCISAAC-TRACY
31 Director of Community Involvement .... Ms. Kathy KOTECKI
35 City Col Dir Stdnt Svc/Asc Registr .... Dr. Rita KRATKY
21 University Budget Director .... Ms. Trudy COLLINS
96 Director of Business Services .... Mr. Jim NIELSEN
20 Dir Academic Support Center .... Mr. Benjamin BARCKHOLTZ
20 Dir Ctr for Applied Econ Research .... Dr. Scott RICKARD
28 Dir Montana Ctr for Inclusive Educ .... Ms. Marsha SAMPSON
89 Dir New Student/Retention Services .... Ms. Tammi WATSON
38 Director of Advising .... Dr. Becky LYONS
88 Director American Indian Outreach .... Ms. Reno CHARETTE
85 Exec Dir Intl Studies/Outreach .... Dr. Paul FOSTER
106 Director e-Learning .... Dr. Susan BALTER-REITZ
92 Dir of University Honors Program .... Dr. David CRAIG
104 Dir ESL Pgm/Intl Studies & Outreach .... Ms. Xia CHAO
49 Dean of Arts & Sciences .... Dr. Tasneem KHALEEL
53 Dean of Education .... Dr. Mary Susan FISHBAUGH
50 Dean College of Business .... Dr. Barbara WHEELING
12 Dean City College @ MSU Billings .... Dr. Marsha RILEY
76 Dean Col of Allied Health Prof .... Dr. Diane DUIN
88 Assoc Dean City Col @ MSU Billings .... Vacant

*Montana State University - Northern (D)

PO Box 7751, Havre MT 59501-7751
County: Hill FICE Identification: 002533
Unit ID: 180522
Telephone: (406) 265-3700 Carnegie Class: Bac/Diverse
FAX Number: N/A Calendar System: Semester
URL: www.msun.edu
Established: 1929 Annual Undergrad Tuition & Fees (In-State): $4,818
Enrollment: 1,282 Coed
Affiliation or Control: State IRS Status: 501(c)3
Highest Offering: Master's
Program: Liberal Arts And General; Teacher Preparatory; Professional; Music Emphasis
Accreditation: NW, ADNUR, ENGT, NUR

02 Chancellor .... Dr. James LIMBAUGH
05 Provost/Vice Chanc Academic Affairs .... Dr. Rosalyn TEMPLETON
10 VC Finance & Administration .... Mr. Brian SIMONSON
102 Executive Director of Foundation .... Ms. Shauna ALBRECHT
72 Dean College Technical Sciences .... Mr. Gregory KEGEL
32 Assistant Dean of Students .... Vacant
53 Dean Col Educ/Arts & Sci/Nursing .... Dr. Christine SHEARER-CREMEAN
06 Interim Registrar .... Ms. Alisha SCHROEDER
66 Director of Nursing .... Dr. Lisa O'NEIL
21 Director of Business Services .... Ms. Jamie MCBRYAN
41 Athletic Director .... Mr. Christian OBERQUELL
36 Director Career Center .... Ms. Mary HELLER
13 Dir Information Technology Svcs .... Mr. Carlo DACUMOS
37 Director of Financial Aid .... Ms. Cindy SMALL
26 Director of University Relations .... Mr. James POTTER
08 Director of Library .... Ms. Vicki GIST
38 Director Student Support Services .... Mr. John A. DONALDSON
07 Director of Admissions .... Ms. Kristi SHETTEL
15 Director Human Resources .... Ms. Kathy JAYNES
35 Sr Director Student Success .... Ms. Tracey JETTE
18 Facilities Manager .... Mr. Dan ULMEN
29 Alumni Coordinator .... Ms. Autumn ELLIOT

*Great Falls College Montana State University (E)

2100 16th Avenue South, Great Falls MT 59405-4909
County: Cascade FICE Identification: 009314
Unit ID: 180249
Telephone: (406) 771-4300 Carnegie Class: Assoc/Pub2in4
FAX Number: (406) 771-4317 Calendar System: Semester
URL: www.gfcmsu.edu
Established: 1969 Annual Undergrad Tuition & Fees (In-State): $3,077
Enrollment: 1,835 Coed
Affiliation or Control: State IRS Status: 501(c)3
Highest Offering: Associate Degree
Program: 2-Year Principally Bachelor's Creditable
Accreditation: NW, CAHIIM, COARC, DA, DH, @DIETT, EMT, MAC, PTAA, SURGT

02 CEO/Dean .... Dr. Susan J. WOLFF
04 Executive Assistant to the CEO/Dean .... Ms. Lorene JAYNES
05 Chief Academic Officer .... Dr. Heidi PASEK
10 Chief Financial Officer .... Dr. Darryl STEVENS
14 CTO .... Mr. Ken WARDINSKY
26 Exec Director Community Relations .... Ms. Pamela PARSONS
06 Registrar .... Ms. Dena WAGNER-FOSSEN
07 Director of Admissions .... Ms. Brittany BUDESKI
15 Exec Director Human Resources .... Ms. Mary Kay BONILLA
30 Director of Development .... Dr. Lisa FLOWERS
37 Director Student Financial Aid .... Ms. Leah HABEL
36 Director Advising & Career Center .... Ms. Courtney JOHNSRUD
32 Associate Dean Student Services .... Dr. Camille CONSOLVO
40 Bookstore Manager .... Mr. Steve HALSTED
96 Budget & Purchasing Officer .... Vacant
18 Director of Facilities Services .... Mr. Dennis DEVINE
08 Director of eLearning & Library .... Ms. Laura WIGHT
09 Director of Institutional Research .... Vacant

*Montana Tech of The University of Montana (F)

1300 W Park Street, Butte MT 59701-8997
County: Silver Bow FICE Identification: 002531
Unit ID: 180416
Telephone: (406) 496-4101 Carnegie Class: Bac/Diverse
FAX Number: (406) 496-4133 Calendar System: Semester
URL: www.mtech.edu
Established: 1893 Annual Undergrad Tuition & Fees (In-State): $6,722
Enrollment: 2,816 Coed
Affiliation or Control: State IRS Status: 501(c)3
Highest Offering: Master's
Program: 2-Year Principally Bachelor's Creditable; Liberal Arts And General; Professional; Technical Emphasis
Accreditation: NW, ADNUR, CS, ENG, ENGR

02 Chancellor .... Dr. Donald M. BLACKKETTER
05 Vice Chanc Acad Affs/Research .... Dr. Douglas M. ABBOTT
10 Business Officer/Controller .... Mr. John C. BADOVINAC
11 VC for Administration & Finance .... Ms. Maggie PETERSON
30 Vice Chanc Dev/Alumni Aff .... Mr. Joseph MCCLAFFERTY
32 Assoc VC for Student Affairs .... Mr. Paul V. BEATTY
46 VC Research & Dean Grad Sch .... Dr. Beverly HARTLINE
65 Director Bureau of Mines & Geology .... Dr. John J. METESH
84 Director of Enrollment Management .... Ms. Kathy WILLIAMS
31 Dir Inst of Educational Opportunity .... Ms. Amy VERLANIC
36 Director Career Services .... Ms. Sarah RAYMOND
08 Director Library .... Ms. Ann F. ST. CLAIR
37 Director of Financial Aid .... Mr. Michael W. RICHARDSON
18 Director of Physical Facilities .... Mr. Michael ALLEN
29 Director Alumni Affairs .... Ms. Peggy S. MCCOY
41 Athletic Director .... Mr. Charles BRADLEY
21 Dir Financial Planning/Analysis .... Mr. Daniel FAUGHT
72 Dean College of Technology .... Mr. John GARIC
81 Dean Col Letters/Sci/Prof Studies .... Dr. Douglas A. COE
54 Dean School of Mines & Engineering .... Dr. H. Peter KNUDSEN
44 Director of Development .... Mr. Michael BARTH
39 Director Residence Life .... Mr. Scott FORTHOFER
26 Director Public Relations .... Ms. Amanda BADOVINAC
40 Bookstore Director .... Ms. Laurie MICHALEK
09 Director Institutional Research .... Ms. Melissa HARRINGTON

*City College at Montana State University Billings (G)

3803 Central Avenue, Billings MT 59102-4398
Telephone: (406) 247-3000 FICE Identification: 010166
Accreditation: &NW

† Main campus is Montana State University - Billings in Billings, MT.

*Highlands College of Montana Tech (H)

25 Basin Creek Road, Butte MT 59701-9704
Telephone: (406) 496-3701 FICE Identification: 009282
Accreditation: &NW

† Main campus is Montana Tech of The University of Montana in Butte, MT.

* *The University of Montana - Missoula College* (A)

909 South Avenue West, Missoula MT 59801
Telephone: (406) 243-7811 FICE Identification: 007561
Accreditation: &NW, ACFEI, ADNUR, SURGT

† Main campus is The University of Montana - Missoula in Missoula, MT.

Rocky Mountain College (B)

1511 Poly Drive, Billings MT 59102-1796
County: Yellowstone FICE Identification: 002534
Unit ID: 180595
Telephone: (406) 657-1000 Carnegie Class: Bac/Diverse
FAX Number: (406) 259-9751 Calendar System: Semester
URL: www.rocky.edu
Established: 1878 Annual Undergrad Tuition & Fees: $23,718
Enrollment: 1,087 Coed
Affiliation or Control: Interdenominational IRS Status: 501(c)3
Highest Offering: Master's
Program: Liberal Arts And General; Teacher Preparatory
Accreditation: NW, AAB, ARCPA

01 President .... Dr. Robert WILMOUTH
05 Academic Vice President/Provost .... Mr. Anthony PILTZ
32 Vice President of Student Services .... Mr. Bradley A. NASON
84 Vice Pres Enrol Svcs/Dir Admissions .... Ms. Kelly EDWARDS
30 Vice President of Advancement .... Ms. Julie SEEDHOUSE
10 Chief Financial Officer .... Ms. Carol JENSEN
35 Associate Dean of Students .... Ms. Katie CARPENTER
16 Director of Human Resources .... Mr. Gregory N. KOHN
88 Director of Educational Leadership .... Dr. Stevie SCHMITZ
08 Assistant Director of the Library .... Ms. Bobbi OTTE
44 Director of Planned Giving .... Mr. Obert UNDEM
26 Director News and Information .... Mr. Dan BURKHART
91 Dir of Administrative Computing .... Ms. Kellee PIERCE
18 Director of Facilities Management .... Mr. Terry STEINER
41 Director of Athletics .... Mr. Robert BEERS
30 Director of Advancement .... Ms. Vickie DAVISON
09 Institutional Research Analyst .... Mr. Erik WILLBORG
06 Registrar .... Ms. Annalea AVERY
37 Director of Financial Assistance .... Ms. Jessica FRANCISCHETTI
39 Director of Residence Life .... Ms. Lindsay ROSSMILLER
04 Executive Assistant to the Pres .... Ms. Pam ERICKSON
29 Dir of Parent Relations and Alumni .... Ms. Kristin MULLANEY

Salish Kootenai College (C)

PO Box 70, Pablo MT 59855-0070
County: Lake FICE Identification: 021434
Unit ID: 180647
Telephone: (406) 275-4800 Carnegie Class: Tribal
FAX Number: (406) 275-4801 Calendar System: Quarter
URL: www.skc.edu
Established: 1977 Annual Undergrad Tuition & Fees: $6,549
Enrollment: 951 Coed
Affiliation or Control: Independent Non-Profit IRS Status: 501(c)3
Highest Offering: Baccalaureate
Program: Occupational; 2-Year Principally Bachelor's Creditable; Liberal Arts And General
Accreditation: NW, ADNUR, DA, NUR, SW

01 President .... Mr. Robert DEPOE
05 Interim Academic Vice President .... Mrs. Alice OECHSLI
10 Interim VP Finance/Business/Admin .... Ms. Audrey PLOUFFE
06 Registrar .... Ms. Cleo KENMILLE
37 Financial Aid Director .... Ms. Jackie SWAIN
09 Director of Institutional Research .... Dr. Robert PEREGOY
15 Director Personnel Services .... Mrs. Dawn BENSON
30 Development Director .... Ms. Angelique ALBERT
32 Chief Student Life Officer .... Mr. Juan PEREZ
13 Director of Information Technology .... Mr. Al ANDERSON
18 Facilities/Physical Plant Manager .... Mr. Michael BIGCRANE

Stone Child College (D)

8294 Upper Box Elder Road, Box Elder MT 59521-9796
County: Hill FICE Identification: 026109
Unit ID: 366340
Telephone: (406) 395-4313 Carnegie Class: Tribal
FAX Number: (406) 395-4836 Calendar System: Semester
URL: www.stonechild.edu/
Established: 1984 Annual Undergrad Tuition & Fees: $2,505
Enrollment: 501 Coed
Affiliation or Control: Tribal Control IRS Status: 501(c)3
Highest Offering: Associate Degree
Program: 2-Year Principally Bachelor's Creditable; Business Emphasis
Accreditation: NW

01 President .... Ms. Melody HENRY
05 Dean of Academics .... Ms. Cory SANGREY-BILLY
32 Dean of Student Services .... Ms. Clarice MORSETTE
10 Business Office/Finance Manager .... Ms. Jewel L. WHITFORD
04 Admin Asst to the President .... Ms. Wanda ST. MARKS
06 Registrar .... Mrs. Gaile TORRES
13 Management Information Specialist .... Mr. Jeffery HENRY
40 Bookstore Manager .... Ms. Shannon MONTEAU
37 Financial Aid Officer .... Ms. Tiffany GALBAVY
18 Facilities Manager .... Mr. Frank HENRY
08 Head Librarian .... Ms. Helen WINDY BOY

University of Great Falls (E)

1301 Twentieth Street S, Great Falls MT 59405-4996
County: Cascade FICE Identification: 002527
Unit ID: 180258
Telephone: (800) 856-9544 Carnegie Class: Bac/Diverse
FAX Number: (406) 791-5209 Calendar System: Semester
URL: www.ugf.edu
Established: 1932 Annual Undergrad Tuition & Fees: $21,930
Enrollment: 1,032 Coed
Affiliation or Control: Roman Catholic IRS Status: 501(c)3
Highest Offering: Master's
Program: Liberal Arts And General; Teacher Preparatory; Professional
Accreditation: NW, NURSE

01 President .... Dr. Eugene J. MCALLISTER
05 VP for Academic Affairs .... Dr. Timothy LAURENT
10 Vice President for Finance .... Ms. Stacey EVE
32 Dean of Student Development .... Vacant
30 VP for Philanthropy .... Vacant
84 VP for Enrollment Management .... Ms. Julie EDSTROM
20 Academic Dean .... Dr. Gregory MADSON
37 Director Financial Aid .... Ms. Kelli ENGELHARDT
06 Registrar .... Ms. Kerri KOTESKEY
14 Director Administrative Computing .... Ms. Kathryn CARBIS
26 Director of Marketing and PR .... Ms. Tara TANNER
18 Director Physical Plant .... Mr. Chet PIETRYKOWSKI
38 Director Student Counseling .... Ms. Linda FAGENSTROM
41 Director of Athletics .... Mr. Gary EHNES
21 Director of the Business Office .... Ms. Amber OBRESLEY
51 Director of Continuing Education .... Ms. Sonja BICKFORD
106 Director of Distance Learning .... Mr. Jim GRETCH
15 Director of Human Resources .... Ms. Kristen RANTZ
09 Director of Institutional Research .... Mr. Greg MADSON
40 Campus Store Manger .... Ms. Cheryl DORN
13 Operations Manager/IT Services .... Mr. John KOEHLER
88 Director Student Support Services .... Ms. LaTosha WILLIAMS

NEBRASKA

Alegent Health School of Radiologic Technology (F)

7500 Mercy Road, Omaha NE 68124
County: Douglas FICE Identification: 008492
Unit ID: 181145
Telephone: (402) 398-5527 Carnegie Class: Assoc/PrivNFP
FAX Number: (402) 398-6650 Calendar System: Semester
URL: www.alegent.com
Established: 1953 Annual Undergrad Tuition & Fees: $5,050
Enrollment: 18 Coed
Affiliation or Control: Independent Non-Profit IRS Status: 501(c)3
Highest Offering: Associate Degree
Program: Occupational; 2-Year Principally Bachelor's Creditable
Accreditation: RAD

01 Program Director .... Robert A. HUGHES

Bellevue University (G)

1000 Galvin Road S, Bellevue NE 68005-3098
County: Sarpy FICE Identification: 009743
Unit ID: 180814
Telephone: (402) 293-2000 Carnegie Class: Master's L
FAX Number: (402) 293-2020 Calendar System: Other
URL: www.bellevue.edu
Established: 1966 Annual Undergrad Tuition & Fees: $7,800
Enrollment: 9,791 Coed
Affiliation or Control: Independent Non-Profit IRS Status: 501(c)3
Highest Offering: Doctorate
Program: Liberal Arts And General
Accreditation: NH, IACBE

01 President .... Dr. Mary B. HAWKINS
00 Chancellor .... Vacant
11 Vice President Administration .... Mr. Jerry A. BLASIG
88 VP Enterprise Services .... Ms. Martyne HALLGREN
10 VP Finance .... Mr. Russ ANDERSEN
05 Vice President Academic Affairs .... Ms. Donna N. MCDANIEL
45 Exec VP Strategic Initiatives .... Dr. Mike ECHOLS
07 VP Mktg/Sales/Enrollmnt Mgmt .... Mr. Matthew DAVIS
106 Dean Ctr Learning Innovation .... Ms. Cathy ERION
72 Dean of College of Science & Tech .... Ms. Mary DOBRANSKY
50 Interim Dean College of Business .... Dr. Pamela IMPERATO
108 Dean Center for Academic Excellence .... Dr. Linda WILD
51 Dean of Continuing and Profess Educ .... Dr. Michelle EPPLER
14 Asst VP of Information Technology .... Mr. James S. VEREBELY
04 Exec Assistant to the President .... Ms. Christine DOOCY
35 Assoc VP Student Services .... Mr. Russ LANE
37 Director Student Financial Svcs .... Ms. Janet YALE
08 Sr Dir Library Services .... Ms. Robin BERNSTEIN
102 Foundation CEO .... Mr. Russ RUPIPER
41 Director of Athletics .... Mr. Ed LEHOTAK
40 Director Bookstore .... Mr. Mark RIGGERT
18 Director of Facilities .... Mr. Ralph (Sam) J. BORER
30 VP Development Programs .... Ms. Dorothy MORROW
21 Asst VP Financial Strategies .... Ms. Lori PIRSCH
15 Sr Director Human Resources .... Ms. Lora IOSSI
19 Director of Security/Safety .... Mr. Greg ALLEN
88 Quality Assurance Programs Director .... Mr. Pete HEINEMAN

85 Director International Admissions .... Mr. Lee WESTPHAL
26 Associate Dir Public Relations .... Mr. Jim MAXWELL
49 Dean College Arts & Sciences .... Vacant
105 Director Web Services .... Ms. Geri MASON
06 Registrar .... Mr. Scott BIERMAN

Bryan College of Health Sciences (H)

5035 Everett Street, Lincoln NE 68506-1315
County: Lancaster FICE Identification: 006399
Unit ID: 180878
Telephone: (402) 481-8697 Carnegie Class: Spec/Health
FAX Number: N/A Calendar System: Semester
URL: www.bryanhealth.com/CollegeofHealthSciences
Established: 2001 Annual Undergrad Tuition & Fees: $11,736
Enrollment: 714 Coed
Affiliation or Control: Independent Non-Profit IRS Status: 501(c)3
Highest Offering: Master's
Program: Professional; Nursing Emphasis
Accreditation: NH, ANEST, CVT, DMS, NUR

01 President .... Dr. Marilyn MOORE
05 Provost .... Dr. Kay MAIZE
97 Dean of General Studies .... Dr. Peter IYERE
11 Dean of Operations .... Dr. June SMITH
66 Dean of Nursing .... Dr. Theresa DELAHOYDE
76 Dean of Health Professions .... Ms. Diane KATHOL
58 Dean of Graduate Studies .... Dr. Sharon HADENFELDT
32 Dean of Students .... Ms. Debra BORDER
08 Director of Library Services .... Ms. Anne HEIMANN
84 Director of Enrollment Management .... Ms. Kelli BACKMAN
06 Registrar .... Ms. Pam MCMASTER

Central Community College (I)

PO Box 4903, Grand Island NE 68802-4903
County: Hall FICE Identification: 020995
Unit ID: 180902
Telephone: (308) 398-4222 Carnegie Class: Assoc/Pub-R-L
FAX Number: (308) 398-7398 Calendar System: Semester
URL: www.cccneb.edu
Established: 1966 Annual Undergrad Tuition & Fees (In-District): $2,700
Enrollment: 7,283 Coed
Affiliation or Control: Local IRS Status: 501(c)3
Highest Offering: Associate Degree
Program: Occupational; 2-Year Principally Bachelor's Creditable
Accreditation: NH, ADNUR, CAHIIM, DA, DH, EMT, MAC, MLTAD, OTA

01 College President .... Dr. Greg P. SMITH
05 Exec Vice Pres/Chief Academic Ofcr .... Dr. Deb BRENNAN
12 Columbus Campus President .... Dr. Matt R. GOTSCHALL
12 Grand Island Campus President .... Dr. Mike CALVERT
12 Hastings Campus President .... Mr. Bill HITESMAN
26 Public Relations/Marketing Director .... Mr. James E. STRAYER
10 College Business Officer .... Mr. Larry C. GLAZIER
13 Dir Information Technology Services .... Mr. Tom D. PETERS
102 Foundation Director .... Mr. Dean MOORS
15 Human Resource Manager .... Dr. Chris WADDLE
06 Registrar .... Ms. Barb LARSON
29 Director Alumni Relations .... Mr. Dean MOORS
37 Director Student Financial Aid .... Ms. Hylee ASCHE
84 Director Enrollment Management .... Mr. Jerry RACIOPPI
09 Director Institutional Research .... Mr. Brian MCDERMOTT
28 Director Diversity .... Dr. Chris WADDLE
32 Director Student Affairs .... Mr. Jerry RACIOPPI
96 Director of Purchasing .... Ms. Marilyn BOTTRELL
29 Alumni Coordinator .... Ms. Pat STANGE

Central Community College Columbus Campus (J)

PO Box 1027, 4500 63rd Street,
Columbus NE 68602-1027
Telephone: (402) 564-7132 Identification: 770331
Accreditation: &NH

† Main campus is Central Community College in Grand Island, NE.

Central Community College Hastings Campus (K)

550 S Technical Blvd, PO Box 1024,
Hastings NE 68902-1024
Telephone: (402) 463-9811 Identification: 770332
Accreditation: &NH

† Main campus is Central Community College in Grand Island, NE.

Clarkson College (L)

101 S 42nd Street, Omaha NE 68131-2739
County: Douglas FICE Identification: 009862
Unit ID: 180832
Telephone: (402) 552-3100 Carnegie Class: Spec/Health
FAX Number: (402) 552-3369 Calendar System: Semester
URL: www.clarksoncollege.edu
Established: 1888 Annual Undergrad Tuition & Fees: $14,010
Enrollment: 1,204 Coed
Affiliation or Control: Independent Non-Profit IRS Status: 501(c)3
Highest Offering: Doctorate
Program: Liberal Arts And General; Professional; Nursing Emphasis

Accreditation: NH, ANEST, CAHIIM, IACBE, NUR, PTAA, RAD

01 President .... Dr. Louis W. BURGHER
05 VP of Academic Affairs .... Dr. Jody WOODWORTH
84 VP of Enroll Mgt/Campus Life Ops .... Tony M. DAMEWOOD
10 Controller .... Megan WICKLESS
06 Registrar .... Michele D. STIRTZ
15 Director Human Resources .... Deb TOMEK
13 Director Technology .... Larry J. VINSON
26 Director of Marketing .... Jina PAUL
28 Director Diversity Services .... Aubray D. ORDUNA
37 Director Student Financial Services .... Margie R. HARRIS
08 Director Library Services .... Nancy M. RALSTON
38 Director Success Center .... Chuck C. MACDONELL
97 Director General Education .... Lori BACHLE
66 Dean Nursing/Dir BS & Grad Nursing .... Dr. Aubray ORDUNA
50 Dir of Business & HIM .... Carla DIRKSCHNEIDER
76 Dir Medical Imaging/Radiologic Tech .... Ellen COLLINS
76 Dir Physical Therapist Asst Pgm .... Andreia NEBEL
07 Director Admissions .... Denise WORK
51 Director of Professional Dev .... Judi B. DUNN
29 Director Alumni Relations .... Rita VANFLEET
88 Dir Basic and Advanced Life Support .... Liz A. SVATOS
106 Coordinator Online Education .... Linda A. NIETO
88 Dir Center of Teaching Excellence .... Mary BALL

College of Saint Mary (A)

7000 Mercy Road, Omaha NE 68106-2606
County: Douglas FICE Identification: 002540
Unit ID: 181604
Telephone: (402) 399-2400 Carnegie Class: Master's S
FAX Number: (402) 399-2647 Calendar System: Semester
URL: www.csm.edu
Established: 1923 Annual Undergrad Tuition & Fees: $26,934
Enrollment: 1,037 Female
Affiliation or Control: Roman Catholic IRS Status: 501(c)3
Highest Offering: Doctorate
Program: Liberal Arts And General; Teacher Preparatory; Professional
Accreditation: NH, ADNUR, IACBE, NUR, OT

01 President .... Dr. Maryanne STEVENS, RSM
32 Vice President Student Development .... Dr. Tara KNUDSON-CARL
05 Vice Pres Academic Affairs/Dean .... Dr. Christine PHARR
07 Vice President Enrollment .... Mr. Greg FRITZ
10 Vice Pres Financial Services/CFO .... Ms. Sarah KOTTICH
04 Executive Asst to the President .... Ms. Shirley GUNDERSON
06 Registrar .... Mrs. Deb NUGEN
08 Director of Library .... Ms. Sara WILLIAMS
14 Director of Computer Center .... Mr. Jason DEGN
29 Director of Alumnae .... Ms. Diane PROULX
37 Director Student Financial Aid .... Ms. Beth SISK
26 Public Relations Director .... Mr. Brittney LONG
35 Director Student Affairs .... Mrs. Katty PETAK
39 Director Student Housing .... Vacant
40 Director Bookstore .... Mr. Steve WESTENBROEK
41 Athletic Director .... Mr. Jim KRUEGER
42 Director Campus Ministry .... Ms. Vicki ZOBRIST
18 Director Physical Plant .... Mr. Dan SPARGEN
44 Director Annual Giving .... Vacant
21 Associate Business Officer .... Ms. Bridgette RENBARGER
15 Director Personnel Services .... Ms. Sarah M. LIVINGSTON

Concordia University (B)

800 N Columbia Avenue, Seward NE 68434-1599
County: Seward FICE Identification: 002541
Unit ID: 180984
Telephone: (402) 643-3651 Carnegie Class: Master's S
FAX Number: (402) 643-4073 Calendar System: Other
URL: www.cune.edu
Established: 1894 Annual Undergrad Tuition & Fees: $24,750
Enrollment: 2,091 Coed
Affiliation or Control: Lutheran Church - Missouri Synod
IRS Status: 501(c)3
Highest Offering: Master's
Program: Liberal Arts And General; Teacher Preparatory
Accreditation: NH, IACBE, MUS, TED

01 President .... Rev Dr. Brian L. FRIEDRICH
05 Provost .... Dr. Jenny MUELLER-ROEBKE
30 Vice President Inst Advancement .... Rev. Richard MADDOX
84 VP Enroll Mgt/Stdnt Svcs/Athletics .... Mr. Scott SEEVERS
20 Associate Provost .... Vacant
10 Chief Financial Officer .... Mr. David KUMM
53 Dean of College of Education .... Dr. Ronald BORK
49 Dean of Arts & Sciences .... Dr. Brent ROYUK
13 Co-Dean Information Technology .... Dr. Donald SYLWESTER
13 Co-Dean Information Technology .... Dr. Kent EINSPAHR
58 Dean College Grad Studies/Adult Ed .... Dr. Thad WARREN
08 Director of Library Services .... Mr. Philip HENDRICKSON
06 University Registrar .... Mr. Ed SIFFRING
36 Synodical & Education Placement Dir .... Mr. William SCHRANZ
29 Director Alumni/University Rels .... Mrs. Jan KOOPMAN
35 Director Student Life .... Mr. Charles GEBHARDT
36 Career Counselor .... Mr. Corey GRAY
41 Athletic Director .... Mr. Devin SMITH
42 Campus Pastor .... Rev. Ryan MATTHIAS
37 Director of Financial Aid .... Mrs. Gloria HENNIG
18 Chief Facilities/Physical Plant .... Mr. Rick IHDE
15 Director of Human Resources .... Mrs. Connie BUTLER
07 Director Undergraduate Admissions .... Mr. Aaron ROBERTS
26 Director of Marketing .... Mr. Andrew SWENSON

21 Dir Invest/Student Admin Svcs .... Mr. Curt SHERMAN
44 Coord of Resource Devel Ops .... Mrs. Janet TONJES
38 Director of Counseling .... Ms. Dina CRITEL-RATHJE

Creative Center (C)

10850 Emmet Street, Omaha NE 68164-2911
County: Douglas FICE Identification: 031643
Unit ID: 430485
Telephone: (402) 898-1000 Carnegie Class: Spec/Arts
FAX Number: (402) 898-1301 Calendar System: Semester
URL: www.creativecenter.edu
Established: 1993 Annual Undergrad Tuition & Fees: N/A
Enrollment: 105 Coed
Affiliation or Control: Proprietary IRS Status: Proprietary
Highest Offering: Baccalaureate
Program: Occupational; 2-Year Principally Bachelor's Creditable; Fine Arts Emphasis
Accreditation: ACCSC

01 President .... Mr. Ray DOTZLER
05 Director .... Ms. Kim GUYER

Creighton University (D)

2500 California Plaza, Omaha NE 68178-0001
County: Douglas FICE Identification: 002542
Unit ID: 181002
Telephone: (402) 280-2700 Carnegie Class: Master's L
FAX Number: N/A Calendar System: Semester
URL: www.creighton.edu
Established: 1878 Annual Undergrad Tuition & Fees: $34,330
Enrollment: 7,736 Coed
Affiliation or Control: Roman Catholic IRS Status: 501(c)3
Highest Offering: Doctorate
Program: Liberal Arts And General; Teacher Preparatory; Professional
Accreditation: NH, BUS, BUSA, DENT, EMT, LAW, MED, NURSE, OT, PHAR, PTA, SW, TED

01 President .... Rev. Timothy R. LANNON, SJ
05 Provost .... Dr. Edward R. O'CONNOR
32 Vice President for Student Services .... Dr. John C. CERNECH
11 Vice President for Administration .... Mr. John L. WILHELM
17 Associate Provost Health Sciences .... Dr. Donald FREY
03 Sr Vice President for Operations .... Mr. Daniel E. BURKEY
26 Vice Pres for University Relations .... Mr. Richard P. VIRGIN
13 Vice President Information Systems .... Mr. Brian A. YOUNG
42 Vice President University Ministry .... Rev. Andrew F. ALEXANDER, SJ
43 VP and General Legal Counsel .... Mr. James S. JANSEN
30 Sr Assoc VP Devel/Campaign Dir .... Vacant
39 Assoc Vice President Resident Life .... Dr. Richard E. ROSSI
22 Assoc VP Affirm Act/Divrsty Outrch .... Mr. John E. PIERCE
84 Assoc VP Enrollment Management .... Ms. Mary E. CHASE
20 Assoc VP Academic Affairs .... Ms. Tricia A. BRUNDO-SHARRAR
20 Assoc VP for Acad Excel .... Dr. Mary Ann DANIELSON
35 Assoc VP Student Services .... Vacant
27 Assoc VP Marketing & Communication .... Ms. Carol ASH
27 Asst VP Marketing/Public Relations .... Ms. Kim B. MANNING
90 Assoc VP Information Technology .... Vacant
30 Asst VP Advancement .... Vacant
46 Assoc VP for Research/Compliance .... Mrs. Kathleen J. TAGGART
29 Assistant VP for Alumni Relations .... Ms. Anna NUBEL
15 Exec Director Human Resources .... Mr. Jeffrey C. BRANSTETTER
10 Chief Business Officer .... Ms. Jan D. MADSEN
06 Registrar .... Ms. Patricia HALL
07 Director Admissions/Scholarships .... Ms. Sarah RICHARDSON
08 Director Reinert Alumni Library .... Mr. Michael J. LACROIX
85 Director International Programs .... Dr. Maria C. KRANE
18 Director Facility Planning/Mgmt .... Vacant
19 Director of Public Safety .... Mr. Richard J. MCAULIFFE
38 Director of Univ Counseling Center .... Dr. Michael KELLEY
37 Director Student Financial Aid .... Mr. Robert D. WALKER
36 Director Career Services .... Mr. Jim BRETL
41 Director Athletics .... Mr. Bruce D. RASMUSSEN
27 Director Public Relations .... Ms. Deborah DALEY
21 Budget Director .... Ms. Tara MCGUIRE
92 Director Honors Program .... Dr. Jeffrey HAUSE
96 Director of Purchasing .... Mr. Joseph J. ZABOROWSKI
87 Director of the Summer Session .... Ms. Debra DALY
28 Director of Multicultural Affairs .... Mr. Ricardo ARIZA
40 Bookstore Manager .... Mr. Calvin PETERSEN
49 Interim Dean Arts & Sciences .... Dr. Bridget M. KEEGAN
58 Dean of Graduate School .... Dr. Gail JENSEN
61 Dean of Law .... Ms. Marianne B. CULHANE
63 Interim Dean of Medicine .... Dr. Robert DUNLAY
52 Dean of Dentistry .... Dr. Mark A. LATTA
50 Dean Business Administration .... Dr. Anthony HENDRICKSON
67 Dean Pharm/Allied Health Profession .... Dr. J. Chris BRADBERRY
66 Dean of Nursing .... Dr. Eleanor V. HOWELL
51 Dean of University College .... Dr. Gail JENSEN

Doane College (E)

1014 Boswell Avenue, Crete NE 68333
County: Saline FICE Identification: 002544
Unit ID: 181020
Telephone: (402) 826-2161 Carnegie Class: Bac/A&S
FAX Number: (402) 826-8600 Calendar System: 4/1/4
URL: www.doane.edu
Established: 1872 Annual Undergrad Tuition & Fees: $25,560
Enrollment: 2,773 Coed
Affiliation or Control: United Church Of Christ IRS Status: 501(c)3
Highest Offering: Beyond Master's But Less Than Doctorate
Program: Liberal Arts And General; Teacher Preparatory
Accreditation: NH, TED

01 President .... Dr. Jacque CARTER
05 Vice President Academic Affairs .... Dr. John BURNEY
10 Vice President Financial Affairs .... Ms. Julie SCHMIDT
30 Vice President for Advancement .... Mr. Kevin C. MEYER
32 Vice President Student Leadership .... Ms. Kim JACOBS
13 VP for Information Technology .... Mr. Mike CARPENTER
07 VP for Enrollment Svcs & Marketing .... Mr. Joel WEYAND
88 Dean of Educational Leadership .... Dr. Jed JOHNSTON
20 Dean of Curriculum & Instruction .... Dr. Lyn FORESTER
58 Dean of Grad Studies in Mgmt .... Ms. Janice M. HADFIELD
51 Dean Adult Undergraduate Studies .... Ms. Janice M. HADFIELD
88 Director of Hansen Leadership Pgm .... Ms. Carrie PETR
06 Registrar .... Ms. Denise ELLIS
37 Director of Financial Aid .... Ms. Peggy TVRDY
08 Director of the Library .... Ms. Julie PINNELL
21 Controller .... Mr. Ned TUCKER
36 Director Career Development .... Ms. Carolyn ERSLAND
26 Sr Director of Strategic Comm .... Vacant
29 Director of Alumni Relation .... Ms. Anne ZIOLA
29 Director of Advancement Operation .... Ms. Jennifer JORGENSEN
15 Director of Human Resources .... Ms. Laura SEARS
18 Dir of Facilities & Constr Proj .... Mr. Wayne SPARY
58 Dean of Grad Studies in Counseling .... Dr. Thomas J. GILLIGAN
41 Athletic Director .... Mr. Greg HEIER
42 Chaplain .... Ms. Karla COOPER
40 Bookstore Manager .... Ms. Lynette NEWTON
28 Director of Multicultural Pgm & Edu .... Ms. Wilma JACKSON
23 Director of Health and Wellness .... Ms. Kelly JIROVEC
35 Director of Student Support Service .... Ms. Sherri HANIGAN
09 Director of Institutional Research .... Ms. Raja TAYEH
19 Dir of Campus Safety/Assoc Dean .... Mr. Russ HEWITT

Doane College (F)

3180 W U.S. Highway 34, Grand Island NE 68801
Telephone: (308) 398-0800 Identification: 770333
Accreditation: &NH

† Main campus is Doane College in Crete, NE.

Doane College (G)

303 North 52nd Street, Lincoln NE 68504
Telephone: (402) 466-4774 Identification: 770334
Accreditation: &NH

† Main campus is Doane College in Crete, NE.

Grace University (H)

1311 S 9th Street, Omaha NE 68108-3629
County: Douglas FICE Identification: 002547
Unit ID: 181093
Telephone: (402) 449-2800 Carnegie Class: Bac/Diverse
FAX Number: (402) 341-9587 Calendar System: Semester
URL: www.graceu.edu
Established: 1943 Annual Undergrad Tuition & Fees: $17,366
Enrollment: 439 Coed
Affiliation or Control: Independent Non-Profit IRS Status: 501(c)3
Highest Offering: Master's
Program: Liberal Arts And General; Teacher Preparatory; Religious Emphasis
Accreditation: NH, BI

01 President .... Dr. David M. BARNES
03 Executive Vice President .... Mr. Michael F. JAMES
05 Academic Dean .... Dr. John D. HOLMES
32 Student Services Dean .... Mrs. Deb OSMANSON
84 Enrollment Management Dean .... Mr. Chris PRUITT
10 Director of Finance .... Ms. Anita RODRIGUEZ
06 Registrar .... Dr. Kris J. UDD
88 Director of Adult Education .... Mr. C. James SANTORO
07 Manager TUG Admissions .... Ms. Tara KOTH
09 Dir of Assessment & Inst Research .... Dr. Ronald J. SHOPE
37 Director of Financial Aid .... Mr. Ray MILLER
15 Director Human Resources .... Mr. Steve R. WIEMEYER
26 Development & Marketing Officer .... Vacant
08 Librarian .... Mr. Harold (Ben) B. BRICK, III
04 Admin Assistant to the President .... Ms. Joanne R. FAST
11 Director of Operations .... Mrs. Deb OSMANSON
33 Dean of Men .... Mr. Jon T. MCNEEL
34 Dean of Women .... Dr. Tara RYE
41 Athletic Director .... Mr. Jon HOOD
13 Director Information Services .... Vacant
88 Director Christian Formation & SLT .... Mr. Wesley WILMER

Hastings College (I)

710 N Turner Avenue, Box 269, Hastings NE 68902-0269
County: Adams FICE Identification: 002548
Unit ID: 181127
Telephone: (402) 463-2402 Carnegie Class: Bac/Diverse
FAX Number: (402) 461-7490 Calendar System: 4/1/4
URL: www.hastings.edu
Established: 1882 Annual Undergrad Tuition & Fees: $25,520
Enrollment: 1,058 Coed
Affiliation or Control: Presbyterian Church (U.S.A.) IRS Status: 501(c)3
Highest Offering: Master's
Program: Liberal Arts And General; Teacher Preparatory

Accreditation: NH, MUS, TED

01 President .... Mr. Donald JACKSON
00 Chairman of the Board .... Mr. Harold "Hal" E. DITTMER
30 Vice President College Advancement .... Mr. Gary FREEMAN
10 Interim Vice President for Finance .... Mr. Gary FREEMAN
84 VP for Enrollment and Marketing .... Ms. Susan MEESKE
05 Vice Pres Acad Affs/Dean Faculty .... Dr. Gary C. JOHNSON
32 Vice President for Student Affairs .... Dr. Gilbert HINGA
20 Assoc VP for Academic Affairs .... Dr. Liz FROMBGEN
41 Athletic Director .... Mr. Jerry SCHMUTTE
35 Assoc VP for Student Affairs .... Rev. Joan MCCARTHY
44 VP for Planned & Major Gifts .... Mr. Michael KARLOFF
88 VP of Scholarship Development .... Ms. Patty SITORIUS
102 Assoc VP for Development .... Ms. Judee L. KONEN
06 Registrar .... Mr. Shawn BAKER
37 Director of Financial Aid .... Ms. Terri GRAHAM
39 Director of Housing .... Mrs. Lori HERGOTT
15 Director of Human Resources .... Ms. Margo BUSBOOM
105 Web Content Manager .... Mr. Michael HOWIE
08 Director of Libraries .... Mr. Robert M. NEDDERMAN
24 Director Educ Media/Librarian .... Ms. Susan FRANKLIN
29 Director of Alumni Relations .... Ms. Hauli SABATKA
27 Chief Information Officer .... Mr. Steve HUTCHINSON
105 Network Administrator .... Mr. Jim MACKIN
90 Acad Computer Support Specialist .... Mr. Erik NIELSEN
18 Director Physical Plant Services .... Mr. James RUZICKA
93 Minority Students .... Dr. Moses DOGBEVIA
28 International Studies/Diversity Pgm .... Dr. Liz FROMBGEN
36 Director of Career Services .... Ms. Kimberly K. GRAVIETTE
23 Director Campus Health Services .... Ms. Beth LITTRELL
42 Chaplain .... Rev Dr. David B. MCCARTHY
21 Director of Accounting .... Mr. Dan LAUX
35 Director of Student Life .... Mr. Colt KRAUS
19 Director of Security/Safety .... Mr. John SILVESTER
38 Director of Counseling Services .... Mr. Jon LOETTERLE
40 Bookstore Manager .... Mrs. Nikki HAYWOOD
27 News Service/Writer/Editor .... Ms. Alicia O'DONNELL
88 Graphic Designer/Publisher .... Mrs. Camille KASTL
85 Foreign Students/Student Life .... Dr. Antje ANDERSON

ITT Technical Institute (A)

1120 North 103rd Plaza, Ste. 200, Omaha NE 68114
Telephone: (402) 331-2900 Identification: 666543
Accreditation: ACICS

† Main campus is ITT Technical Institute in Indianapolis, IN.

Kaplan University (B)

1821 K Street, PO Box 82826, Lincoln NE 68501-2826
Telephone: (402) 474-5315 FICE Identification: 004721
Accreditation: &NH, ACBSP, MAC

† Main campus is Kaplan University in Davenport, IA.

Kaplan University (C)

5425 N. 103rd Street, Omaha NE 68134-1002
Telephone: (402) 431-6100 FICE Identification: 008491
Accreditation: &NH, ACBSP, DA, MAC

† Main campus is Kaplan University in Davenport, IA.

Little Priest Tribal College (D)

PO Box 270, Winnebago NE 68071-0270
County: Thurston FICE Identification: 033233
Unit ID: 434016
Telephone: (402) 878-2380 Carnegie Class: Tribal
FAX Number: (402) 878-2355 Calendar System: Semester
URL: www.littlepriest.edu
Established: 1996 Annual Undergrad Tuition & Fees: $2,985
Enrollment: 173 Coed
Affiliation or Control: Independent Non-Profit IRS Status: 501(c)3
Highest Offering: Associate Degree
Program: Occupational; 2-Year Principally Bachelor's Creditable
Accreditation: NH

01 President .... Dr. Johnny D. JONES
05 Academic Dean .... Ms. Brigid QUINN
10 Controller .... Mr. Robert BAXTER
37 Director of Financial Aid .... Vacant
13 IT Director .... Mr. Brandon STOUT
31 Coordinator of Community Education .... Ms. Tori KITCHEYAN
06 Registrar .... Ms. Janet NIELSEN

Mary Lanning Healthcare School of Radiology (E)

715 North St. Joseph Avenue, Hastings NE 68901
County: Adams FICE Identification: 004431
Unit ID: 181251
Telephone: (402) 461-5177 Carnegie Class: Not Classified
FAX Number: (402) 460-5059 Calendar System: Other
URL: www.marylanning.org
Established: 1952 Annual Undergrad Tuition & Fees: $3,457
Enrollment: 19 Coed
Affiliation or Control: Independent Non-Profit IRS Status: 501(c)3
Highest Offering: Associate Degree
Program: Occupational
Accreditation: RAD

01 Program Director .... Cristi L. ENGEL

McCook Community College (F)

1205 East Third Street, McCook NE 69001
Telephone: (308) 345-8100 Identification: 770337
Accreditation: &NH

† Main campus is Mid-Plains Community College in North Platte, NE.

Metropolitan Community College (G)

PO Box 3777, Omaha NE 68103-0777
County: Douglas FICE Identification: 012586
Unit ID: 181303
Telephone: (402) 457-2400 Carnegie Class: Assoc/Pub-U-MC
FAX Number: (402) 457-2395 Calendar System: Quarter
URL: www.mccneb.edu
Established: 1974 Annual Undergrad Tuition & Fees (In-District): $2,610
Enrollment: 17,376 Coed
Affiliation or Control: Local IRS Status: 501(c)3
Highest Offering: Associate Degree
Program: Occupational; 2-Year Principally Bachelor's Creditable
Accreditation: NH, ACBSP, ACFEI, ADNUR, COARC, DA, EMT, MAC

01 President .... Mr. Randy SCHMAILZL
03 Executive Vice President .... Mr. James GROTRIAN
05 Vice President Academic Affairs .... Dr. Kathleen CURPHY
11 VP Technology/Administrative Svcs .... Dr. Mary K. WISE
32 VP of Campuses/Student Affairs .... Dr. Arthur RICH
28 Assoc Vice Pres Equity/Diversity .... Dr. Cynthia GOOCH
16 Assoc Vice Pres of Human Resources .... Ms. Maureen MOEGLIN
30 Assoc Vice Pres of Development .... Ms. Pat CRISLER
20 Associate VP of Academic Affairs .... Mr. William OWEN
84 Asst Vice Pres for Student Affairs .... Ms. Marie VAZQUEZ
10 Executive College Business Officer .... Mr. Dave KOEBEL
26 Exec Director of Public Affairs .... Ms. Sheila O'CONNOR
18 Director Facilities Management .... Mr. Bernard SEDLACEK
37 Director of Financial Aid .... Ms. Wilma HJELLUM
13 Dir Management Information Svcs .... Mr. Mick GAHAN
96 Director Administrative Management .... Mr. Richard HANNEMAN
19 Chief of Police/Dir Emergency Mgmt .... Mr. David FRIEND
84 Dean of Enrollment Management .... Ms. Ingrid BERLIN

Metropolitan Community College Elkhorn Valley Campus (H)

204th & Way Dodge Road, Omaha NE 68022
Telephone: (402) 289-1200 Identification: 770335
Accreditation: &NH

† Main campus is Metropolitan Community College in Omaha, NE.

Metropolitan Community College South Omaha Campus (I)

2909 Edward Babe Gomez Avenue, Omaha NE 68107
Telephone: (402) 738-4500 Identification: 770336
Accreditation: &NH

† Main campus is Metropolitan Community College in Omaha, NE.

Mid-Plains Community College (J)

601 W State Farm Road, North Platte NE 69101-9491
County: Lincoln FICE Identification: 002557
Unit ID: 181312
Telephone: (800) 658-4308 Carnegie Class: Assoc/Pub-R-M
FAX Number: (308) 535-3794 Calendar System: Semester
URL: www.mpcc.edu
Established: 1926 Annual Undergrad Tuition & Fees (In-District): $2,760
Enrollment: 2,591 Coed
Affiliation or Control: State/Local IRS Status: 501(c)3
Highest Offering: Associate Degree
Program: Occupational; 2-Year Principally Bachelor's Creditable; Technical Emphasis
Accreditation: NH, ADNUR, DA, EMT, MLTAD

01 President .... Mr. Ryan PURDY
12 VP North Platte Community College .... Mr. Marcus GARSTECKI
12 Vice Pres McCook Community College .... Mr. Andrew LONG
11 Area Business Officer .... Mr. Michael STEELE
32 Area VP for Instruction .... Dr. Jody TOMANEK
09 Area Dir Instl Research & Planning .... Mr. Tad PFEIFER
32 Area Dean of Student Life .... Ms. Michele GILL
56 Area Dean of Outreach & Training .... Mr. Bruce DOWSE
36 Area Dean of Career Services .... Mr. Bill EAKINS
84 Area Dean of Enrollment Management .... Ms. Kelly RIPPEN
06 Area Registrar .... Ms. Mari Jo WIDGER
26 Area Dir Public Inform/Marketing .... Mr. Charles SALESTROM
15 Area Director of Acct & Hum Res .... Mr. Bruce BERGMAN
13 Area Director of Info Technology .... Mr. Tim HALL
37 Area Dir of Student Financial Aid .... Mr. Dale BROWN

Midland University (K)

900 N Clarkson, Fremont NE 68025-4395
County: Dodge FICE Identification: 002553
Unit ID: 181330
Telephone: (402) 721-5480 Carnegie Class: Bac/Diverse
FAX Number: (402) 721-0250 Calendar System: 4/1/4
URL: www.midlandu.edu
Established: 1883 Annual Undergrad Tuition & Fees: $26,746
Enrollment: 1,164 Coed
Affiliation or Control: Evangelical Lutheran Church In America
IRS Status: 501(c)3
Highest Offering: Master's
Program: Occupational; Liberal Arts And General; Teacher Preparatory; Professional; Business Emphasis
Accreditation: NH, COARC, NUR

01 President .... Dr. Benjamin E. SASSE
32 Vice Pres Student Affairs .... Mr. Merritt NELSON
05 Vice President of Academic Affairs .... Dr. Steven BULLOCK
10 Vice Pres for Administration & CFO .... Ms. Jodi BENJAMIN
07 VP Admissions/Enrollment Management .... Ms. Eliza FERZELY
15 Vice President Human Capital .... Mr. Erich ZIEGLER
26 Director of Communications .... Mr. Nate NEUFIND
06 Registrar & Institutional Research .... Ms. Jenifer JOST
37 Director of Financial Aid .... Mr. Doug WATSON
21 Controller .... Ms. Denise PRATT
41 Director of Athletic Operations .... Mr. Dave GILLESPIE
66 Chair of Nursing .... Ms. Linda QUINN
14 Director Information Technology .... Mr. Shane PERRIEN
18 Director of Physical Plant .... Mr. Roger SONGSTER
30 Director of Advancement .... Ms. Kari RIDDER
84 Director of Student Recruitment .... Mr. Jason BLOHM

Myotherapy Institute (L)

4001 Pioneer Woods Drive, Lincoln NE 68506-7547
County: Lancaster FICE Identification: 032793
Unit ID: 434432
Telephone: (402) 421-7410 Carnegie Class: Assoc/PrivFP
FAX Number: (402) 421-6736 Calendar System: Other
URL: www.myotherapy.edu
Established: 1992 Annual Undergrad Tuition & Fees: $15,650
Enrollment: 29 Coed
Affiliation or Control: Proprietary IRS Status: Proprietary
Highest Offering: Associate Degree
Program: Occupational
Accreditation: ACCSC

01 Director .... Ms. Sue KOZISEK

National American University-Bellevue (M)

3604 Summit Plaza Drive, Bellevue NE 68123
Telephone: (402) 972-4250 Identification: 770406
Accreditation: &NH

† Main campus is National American University in Rapid City, SD.

Nebraska Christian College (N)

12550 S 114th Street, Papillion NE 68046-4256
County: Sarpy FICE Identification: 012976
Unit ID: 181376
Telephone: (402) 935-9400 Carnegie Class: Spec/Faith
FAX Number: (402) 935-9500 Calendar System: Semester
URL: www.nechristian.edu
Established: 1945 Annual Undergrad Tuition & Fees: $11,400
Enrollment: 133 Coed
Affiliation or Control: Christian Churches And Churches of Christ
IRS Status: 501(c)3
Highest Offering: Baccalaureate
Program: Religious Emphasis
Accreditation: BI

01 President .... Mr. Richard MILLIKEN
05 Vice Pres Academics .... Dr. Mark KRAUSE
10 Vice Pres Operations .... Mr. Tony CLARK
26 Vice Pres Advancement .... Mr. David MILLER
30 Director of Development .... Mr. James HARDY
32 Dean of Students/Chief Stdnt Ofcr .... Vacant
07 Director of Admissions .... Mrs. Kristin MILLER
18 Director of Facilities .... Mr. Andrew CARLSON
08 Director of Library Services .... Mr. Christopher KELLEHER
37 Financial Aid Officer .... Mrs. Sarah NIGRO

Nebraska Indian Community College (O)

1111 Hwy 75 - PO Box 428, Macy NE 68039-0428
County: Thurston FICE Identification: 025508
Unit ID: 181419
Telephone: (402) 494-2311 Carnegie Class: Tribal
FAX Number: (402) 837-4183 Calendar System: Semester
URL: www.thenicc.edu
Established: 1973 Annual Undergrad Tuition & Fees: $4,080
Enrollment: 140 Coed
Affiliation or Control: Tribal Control IRS Status: Exempt
Highest Offering: Associate Degree
Program: Occupational; 2-Year Principally Bachelor's Creditable
Accreditation: NH

01 President .... Dr. Michael OLTROGGE
05 Academic Dean .... Don TORGERSON
10 Business Office Director .... Tiffany SPARKS
32 Student Support Services .... Dawne PRICE
30 Director of Development .... Mark GORDON
27 Chief Information Officer .... Justin KOCIAN

Nebraska Indian Community College-Santee (P)

415 North River Road, Niobrara NE 68760
Telephone: (402) 494-2311 Identification: 770339
Accreditation: &NH

† Main campus is Nebraska Indian Community College in Macy, NE.

Nebraska Indian Community College-South Sioux City (A)

2605 1/2 Dakota Avenue, South Sioux City NE 68776
Telephone: (402) 494-2311 Identification: 770340
Accreditation: &NH

† Main campus is Nebraska Indian Community College in Macy, NE.

Nebraska Methodist College (B)

720 N 87th Street, Omaha NE 68114-2852
County: Douglas FICE Identification: 006404
Unit ID: 181297
Telephone: (402) 354-7000 Carnegie Class: Spec/Health
FAX Number: (402) 354-7090 Calendar System: Semester
URL: www.methodistcollege.edu
Established: 1891 Annual Undergrad Tuition & Fees: $12,289
Enrollment: 899 Coed
Affiliation or Control: Independent Non-Profit IRS Status: 501(c)3
Highest Offering: Master's
Program: Professional; Nursing Emphasis
Accreditation: NH, COARC, DMS, MAC, NURSE, PTAA, RAD, SURGT

01 President ....Dr. Dennis A. JOSLIN
05 Vice President Academic Affairs ....Dr. Paul A. SAVORY
32 Vice President Student Affairs ....Dr. Kristine M. HESS
26 VP Business Dev & Communication ....Ms. Danielle DUBUC-PEDERSEN
45 VP Organizational Development ....Dr. Deborah CARLSON
35 Dean of Students ....Dr. Melissa HOFFMAN
66 Dean Nursing ....Dr. Linda HUGHES
58 Program Director Master's Nursing ....Dr. Linda FOLEY
66 Pgm Director Undergrad Nursing ....Dr. Karen JOHNSON
88 Director of Special Pgms Nursing ....Dr. Susie WARD
76 Dean Health Professions ....Dr. Patricia SULLIVAN
97 Dean General Education ....Dr. Mary Lee LUSBY
76 Pgm Director Phys Therapist Asst ....Ms. Shannon STRUBY
76 Program Director Respiratory Care ....Dr. John JAROSZ
88 Program Director Radiography ....Ms. Jane SIMS
88 Program Director Sonography ....Ms. Rebecca MATHIASEN
88 Pgm Director Surgical Technology ....Ms. Christy GRANT
08 Director of Library Services ....Ms. Beverly SEDLACEK
42 Dir Spiritual Dev/Campus Ministry ....Rev. Daniel JOHNSTON
29 Director Alumni Relations ....Ms. Denise M. CARLSON
07 Director Enrollment Services ....Ms. Sara HANSON
06 Director Registration & Records ....Ms. Melinda STONER
37 Director Financial Aid ....Ms. Penny JAMES
88 Exec Dir Professional Development ....Ms. Candy HOABY
10 Director Business Office ....Ms. Beth FRIEDMAN
88 Educational Compliance Officer ....Mr. Ryan PORTWOOD

*Nebraska State College System (C)

PO Box 94605, Lincoln NE 68509-4605
County: Lancaster FICE Identification: 033441
Telephone: (402) 471-2505 Carnegie Class: N/A
FAX Number: (402) 471-2669
URL: www.nscs.edu

01 Chancellor ....Mr. Stan CARPENTER
43 General Counsel & VC for Emp Rel ....Ms. Kristin PETERSEN
10 Vice Chancellor Finance/Admin ....Ms. Carolyn MURPHY
32 VC for Stdnt Aff/Mkt/Enrol/Pub Info ....Ms. Korinne TANDE
18 Vice Chanc Facil/Plng/Info Tech ....Mr. Ed HOFFMAN
05 VC Acad Planning/Partnerships ....Dr. Oren YAGIL
11 Operations Director ....Ms. Becky KOHRS
88 Director of Systemwide Accounting ....Ms. Amy HOCK

*Chadron State College (D)

1000 Main Street, Chadron NE 69337-2690
County: Dawes FICE Identification: 002539
Unit ID: 180948
Telephone: (308) 432-6000 Carnegie Class: Bac/Diverse
FAX Number: (308) 432-6464 Calendar System: Semester
URL: www.csc.edu
Established: 1911 Annual Undergrad Tuition & Fees (In-State): $5,606
Enrollment: 2,932 Coed
Affiliation or Control: State IRS Status: 501(c)3
Highest Offering: Master's
Program: Liberal Arts And General; Teacher Preparatory; Professional
Accreditation: NH, ACBSP, SW, TED

02 President ....Dr. Randy RHINE
30 Executive Director CS Foundation ... Ms. Connie A. RASMUSSEN
05 Vice President Academic Affairs ....Dr. Charles SNARE
32 Sr Director of Student Affairs ....Mr. Aaron PRESTWICH
11 Vice Pres Administration & Finance ....Mr. Dale E. GRANT
09 Director Institutional Research ....Ms. Theresa R. DAWSON
26 Assoc VP for Market Development ....Mr. Steve M. TAYLOR
06 Director of Records ....Ms. Melissa MITCHELL
07 Int Director of Admissions ....Ms. Lisa STEIN
10 Comptroller ....Ms. Julie GOODMAN
88 Dean of Professional Licensure ....Dr. Margaret CROUSE
49 Dean of Teaching and Learning ....Dr. Katharine FORSTROM
20 Dean of Curriculum & Academic Advmt ....Dr. Joel HYER
14 Chief Information Officer ....Ms. Ann M. BURK
35 Sr Exec Director Student Services ....Ms. Sherry L. DOUGLAS
15 Director Human Resources ....Ms. Shelley DUNBAR
39 Director of Housing ....Ms. Sherri J. SIMONS
41 Athletics Director ....Mr. Joel SMITH
12 Director Extended Campus Sites ....Ms. Deann BAYNE
36 Director of Internships/Career Svcs ....Ms. Deena KENNELL
21 Budget Director ....Ms. Melany HUGHES
26 Interim Marketing Coordinator ....Ms. Tena COOK
18 Coordinator of Physical Facilities ....Mr. Blair BRENNAN

*Peru State College (E)

PO Box 10, Peru NE 68421-0010
County: Nemaha FICE Identification: 002559
Unit ID: 181534
Telephone: (402) 872-3815 Carnegie Class: Master's L
FAX Number: (402) 872-2375 Calendar System: Semester
URL: www.peru.edu
Established: 1867 Annual Undergrad Tuition & Fees (In-State): $5,746
Enrollment: 2,373 Coed
Affiliation or Control: State IRS Status: 501(c)3
Highest Offering: Master's
Program: Liberal Arts And General; Teacher Preparatory
Accreditation: NH, TED

02 President ....Dr. Daniel HANSON
05 Vice Pres Academic Affairs ....Dr. Todd DREW
10 Vice Pres Administration & Finance ....Ms. Kathy CARROLL
84 VP Enrollment Mgmt/Student Services ....Ms. Michaela WILLIS
32 Dean of Student Life ....Mr. Kristiaan RAWLINGS
102 Exec Director PSC Foundations ....Mr. Todd SIMPSON
41 Athletic Director ....Mr. Steve SCHNEIDER
26 Dir of Marketing & Media Services ....Ms. Regan ANSON
06 Registrar ....Ms. Dixie TETEN
37 Director of Financial Aid ....Ms. Janice VOLKER
08 Director of Library ....Ms. Veronica MCASEY
15 Human Resources Director ....Ms. Eulanda CADE
18 Director Campus Services ....Mr. Richard HARRISON
09 Dir Student Assess & Success Svcs ....Dr. Ursula WALN
21 Director of Business Services ....Ms. Kathy TYNON
07 Director of Admissions ....Mr. Heath CHRISTIANSEN
38 Counselor ....Mr. Dan FENDER

*Wayne State College (F)

1111 Main Street, Wayne NE 68787-1172
County: Wayne FICE Identification: 002566
Unit ID: 181783
Telephone: (402) 375-7000 Carnegie Class: Master's L
FAX Number: (402) 375-7204 Calendar System: Semester
URL: www.wsc.edu
Established: 1909 Annual Undergrad Tuition & Fees (In-State): $5,574
Enrollment: 3,555 Coed
Affiliation or Control: State IRS Status: 501(c)3
Highest Offering: Beyond Master's But Less Than Doctorate
Program: Liberal Arts And General; Teacher Preparatory; Professional; Business Emphasis
Accreditation: NH, ART, IACBE, MUS, TED

02 President ....Mr. Curt FRYE
05 Vice President Academic Affairs ....Dr. Michael ANDERSON
10 Vice Pres Admin/Finance ....Ms. Jean DALE
30 Vice Pres Institutional Advancement ....Ms. Phyllis CONNER
32 Vice President & Dean Students ....Dr. Jeffrey CARSTENS
37 Director Financial Aid ....Ms. Kyle ROSE
07 Director of Admissions ....Mr. Kevin HALLE
38 Director of Counseling ....Ms. Lin BRUMMELS
39 Director Housing/Residence Life ....Mr. Matt WEEKLEY
36 Director of Career Services ....Ms. Jason BARELMAN
14 Director of Computer Center ....Ms. Janell SCARDINO
26 Director College Relations ....Mr. Jay COLLIER
41 Director of Athletics ....Mr. Mike POWICKI
18 Director of Physical Plant ....Mr. Chad ALTWINE
08 Director of Library Services ....Mr. David GRABER
06 Registrar ....Ms. Lynette LENTZ
29 Dir Development & Alumni Relations ....Ms. Deb LUNDAHL
15 Director Personnel Services ....Dr. Cheryl WADDINGTON
79 Int Dean School of Arts & Hum ....Dr. Steven ELLIOTT
50 Dean Sch of Business & Technology ....Dr. Vaughn BENSON
53 Int Dean Sch of Educ & Couns ....Dr. Dennis LICHTY
83 Int Dean Sch of Natural/Social Sci ....Dr. Tammy EVETOVICH
28 Director of Multicultural Affairs ....Dr. Leah KEINO
09 Institutional Research Analyst ....Ms. Jeannette BARRY
27 Chief Information Officer ....Mr. John DUNNING

Nebraska Wesleyan University (G)

5000 St. Paul Avenue, Lincoln NE 68504-2794
County: Lancaster FICE Identification: 002555
Unit ID: 181446
Telephone: (402) 466-2371 Carnegie Class: Bac/A&S
FAX Number: (402) 465-2179 Calendar System: Semester
URL: www.nebrwesleyan.edu
Established: 1887 Annual Undergrad Tuition & Fees: $27,191
Enrollment: 1,855 Coed
Affiliation or Control: United Methodist IRS Status: 501(c)3
Highest Offering: Master's
Program: Liberal Arts And General
Accreditation: NH, ACBSP, FEPAC, MUS, NUR, SW, TED

01 President ....Dr. Frederik OHLES
05 Provost ....Dr. Judy A. MUYSKENS
10 Vice Pres Finance/Administration ....Mr. Clark T. CHANDLER
07 Vice President Enrollment Mgmt ....Ms. Kim S. JOHNSON
30 Vice President Advancement ....Mr. John GREVING
58 Dean of University College ....Ms. Elizabeth M. WALLS
32 Dean of Students ....Mr. Peter ARMSTRONG
49 Dean College of Lib Arts & Sciences ....Dr. Katherine J. WOLFE
88 Asst Provost Integr/Exper Learning ....Dr. Jeff A. ISAACSON
28 Asst Provost Success & Diversity ....Ms. Candice HOWELL
21 Asst VP & Controller ....Mr. Greg D. MASCHMAN
06 Registrar ....Ms. Nancy SCHILZ
35 Asst Dean of Students ....Ms. Geri E. COTTER
09 Asst Dean Inst Effectiveness ....Ms. Bette OLSON
15 Asst VP Human Resources ....Ms. Nancy B. COOKSON
18 Asst VP Physical Plant ....Mr. Matthew T. KADAVY
07 Director of Enrollment ....Mr. David B. DUZIK
27 Director of Public Relations ....Ms. Sara M. OLSON
08 University Librarian ....Ms. Margaret L. EMONS
37 Director of Financial Aid ....Mr. Tom J. OCHSNER
29 Director of Alumni Relations ....Ms. Shelley MCHUGH
41 Athletic Director ....Dr. Ira A. ZEFF
13 Director of Computer Services ....Mr. Steven R. DOW
90 Director Instructional Technology ....Mr. Jay L. KAHLER
13 Director Administrative Systems ....Mr. Mark MURPHY
26 Director of Marketing ....Ms. Peggy S. HAIN
36 Director Career & Counseling Ctr ....Ms. Janelle S. ANDREINI
39 Director Residential Education ....Ms. Brandi SESTAK
104 Director of Global Engagement ....Ms. Sarah BARR
92 Director Wesleyan Honors Academy ....Dr. Marian BORGMANN-INGWERSEN
35 Dir Student Involvement & Ldrship ....Ms. Karri SANDERSON
102 Director of Foundation Relations ....Ms. Nancy WEHRBEIN
23 Director Student Health Services ....Ms. Nancy J. NEWMAN
42 University Minister ....Rev. Eduardo BOUSSON

North Platte Community College-North Campus (H)

1101 Halligan Drive, North Platte NE 69101
Telephone: (308) 535-3600 Identification: 770338
Accreditation: &NH

† Main campus is Mid-Plains Community College in North Platte, NE.

Northeast Community College (I)

801 E Benjamin, PO Box 469, Norfolk NE 68702-0469
County: Madison FICE Identification: 011667
Unit ID: 181491
Telephone: (402) 371-2020 Carnegie Class: Assoc/Pub-R-M
FAX Number: (402) 844-7400 Calendar System: Semester
URL: www.northeast.edu
Established: 1973 Annual Undergrad Tuition & Fees (In-District): $3,008
Enrollment: 5,251 Coed
Affiliation or Control: Local IRS Status: 501(c)3
Highest Offering: Associate Degree
Program: Occupational; 2-Year Principally Bachelor's Creditable; Technical Emphasis
Accreditation: NH, ADNUR, EMT, PTAA

01 President ....Dr. Michael R. CHIPPS
03 Executive Vice President ....Mrs. Mary J. HONKE
05 Vice President Educational Services ....Mr. John V. BLAYLOCK
10 Vice Pres of Administrative Svcs ....Ms. Lynne D. KOSKI
32 Vice President of Student Services ....Dr. Karen J. SEVERSON
88 Vice President of Technology ....Mr. Derek BIERMAN
14 Associate VP of Ctr for Enterprise ....Mr. Eric JOHNSON
30 Assoc VP of Development & External ....Dr. Tracy L. KRUSE
75 Dean of Applied Technology ....Mr. Lyle J. KATHOL
49 Dean Humanities/Arts/Social Sci ....Mrs. Donna A. NIEMEYER
11 Dean of Administrative Services ....Mrs. Coleen BRESSLER
30 Dean of Institutional Advancement ....Mr. Wayne ERICKSON
21 Director of Business Services ....Mrs. Mary J. MEYER
47 Dean Ag/Health/Sciences ....Mrs. Corinne MORRIS
50 Interim Dean of Business/Math/Tech ....Mr. Stephen MORTON
84 Dean of Enrollment Management ....Mrs. Amanda NIPP
37 Financial Aid Director ....Ms. Stacy DIECKMAN
06 Registrar ....Mrs. Kathy J. STOVER
12 South Sioux City College Ctr Dean ....Mrs. Pamela MILLER
18 Director of Physical Plant ....Mr. Brandon MCLEAN
36 Director of Career Services ....Mrs. Terri HEGGEMEYER
66 Director of Nursing Programs ....Mrs. Karen K. WEIDNER
21 Director of Accounting Services ....Mr. John ROBERTSON
15 Human Resources Coordinator ....Mrs. Jennifer HAPPOLD
96 Director of Purchasing ....Mrs. Nell VOTRUBA
41 Athletic Director ....Mr. Kurt PYTLESKI
105 Director of Web System Services ....Mr. Mike AUEN
39 Director Residence & Student Life ....Mr. Pete RIZZO
26 Director of Public Relations ....Mr. James CURRY
08 Director of Library Services ....Mrs. Mary Louise FOSTER
35 Director of Student Conduct ....Mrs. Maureen BAKER
40 Bookstore Manager ....Mrs. Julie CARLSON
09 Director of Institutional Research ....Ms. Julie MELNICK
88 Advisor ....Mr. Anthony FAUST
88 Advisor ....Ms. Lisa REIFENRATH
35 Student Activities Coordinator ....Ms. Carissa KOLLATH
76 Director of Allied Health Services ....Mrs. Heather CLAUSEN

Omaha School of Massage and Healthcare of Herzing University (J)

9478 Park Drive, Omaha NE 68127
Telephone: (402) 331-3694 Identification: 770432
Accreditation: &NH, MAAB

† Main campus is Herzing University in Madison, WI.

Saint Gregory the Great Seminary (A)

800 Fletcher Road, Seward NE 68434-8145
County: Seward Identification: 667027
Telephone: (402) 643-4052 Carnegie Class: Not Classified
FAX Number: (402) 643-6964 Calendar System: Semester
URL: www.stgregoryseminary.edu
Established: 1998 Annual Undergrad Tuition & Fees: $8,300
Enrollment: 46 Male
Affiliation or Control: Roman Catholic IRS Status: 501(c)3
Highest Offering: Baccalaureate
Program: Liberal Arts And General; Religious Emphasis
Accreditation: NH

01 Rector/President Msgr. John T. FOLDA

Southeast Community College (B)

4771 West Scott Road, Beatrice NE 68310-7042
Telephone: (402) 228-3468 Identification: 770341
Accreditation: &NH

† Main campus is Southeast Community College in Lincoln, NE.

Southeast Community College (C)

301 S 68 Street Place, Lincoln NE 68510-2449
County: Lancaster FICE Identification: 025083
Unit ID: 181640
Telephone: (402) 323-3400 Carnegie Class: Assoc/Pub-R-L
FAX Number: (402) 323-3420 Calendar System: Quarter
URL: www.southeast.edu
Established: 1973 Annual Undergrad Tuition & Fees (In-District): $2,486
Enrollment: 10,168 Coed
Affiliation or Control: State/Local IRS Status: 501(c)3
Highest Offering: Associate Degree
Program: Occupational; 2-Year Principally Bachelor's Creditable
Accreditation: NH, ACBSP, ACFEI, ADNUR, COARC, DA, DIETT, MAC, MLTAD, PNUR, POLYT, PTAA, RAD, SURGT

01 President Dr. Jack J. HUCK
05 Vice President Instruction Dr. Dennis HEADRICK
22 Vice Pres Access/Equity/Diversity Mr. Jose SOTO
11 VP Administrative Svcs/Res Devel Mr. Theodore G. SUHR
12 VP Student Svcs/Campus Director Ms. Jeanette VOLKER
12 VP Technology/Campus Director Mr. Lyle NEAL
15 Vice Pres Human Resources Mr. Don BYRNES
37 Dean Student Svcs/Dir Financial Aid Mr. Dave SONENBERG
35 Dean Student Svcs/Dir Stdnt Support Dr. Thomas CARDWELL
84 Dean Student Svcs/Dir Enrollment Ms. Robin MOORE
26 Dir of Public Information/Marketing Mr. Stu OSTERTHUN
90 Information Services Manager Mr. Alan BRUNKOW

Southeast Community College (D)

600 State Street, Milford NE 68405-8498
Telephone: (402) 761-2131 Identification: 770342
Accreditation: &NH

† Main campus is Southeast Community College in Lincoln, NE.

Union College (E)

3800 S 48th, Lincoln NE 68506-4300
County: Lancaster FICE Identification: 002563
Unit ID: 181738
Telephone: (402) 486-2600 Carnegie Class: Bac/Diverse
FAX Number: (402) 486-2895 Calendar System: Semester
URL: www.ucollege.edu
Established: 1891 Annual Undergrad Tuition & Fees: $20,470
Enrollment: 881 Coed
Affiliation or Control: Seventh-day Adventist IRS Status: 501(c)3
Highest Offering: Master's
Program: Liberal Arts And General; Teacher Preparatory; Professional
Accreditation: NH, ARCPA, NURSE, SW, TED

01 President Dr. John WAGNER
05 Vice President for Academic Admin Dr. Malcolm RUSSELL
10 Vice President for Financial Admin Vacant
32 Vice President Student Services Dr. Linda BECKER
30 Vice President for Advancement Ms. LuAnn DAVIS
07 Vice President Enrollment Services Ms. Nadine NELSON
42 Vice President for Spiritual Life Dr. Rich CARLSON
08 Library Director Ms. Sabrina RILEY
14 Director of Information Systems Mr. Richard HENRIQUES
34 Dean of Women Ms. Donene CASTER-BRAITHWAITE
33 Dean of Men Mr. Doug TALLMAN
06 Dir Records/Registrar Ms. Michelle YOUNKIN
26 Director of Public Relations Mr. Ryan TELLER
29 Director Alumni Relations Ms. Kenna Lee CARLSON
37 Director Student Financial Aid Ms. Taryn ROUSE
15 Director for Human Resources Mr. Jonathan SHIELDS
18 Director of Plant Services Mr. Paul JENKS
21 Associate Business Officer Mr. Harvey MEIER
36 Career Center Coordinator Ms. Teresa EDGERTON
38 Director Student Counseling Dr. Linda BECKER

Universal College of Healing Arts (F)

8702 N 30th Street, Omaha NE 68112-1810
County: Douglas FICE Identification: 038214
Unit ID: 446598
Telephone: (402) 556-4456 Carnegie Class: Assoc/PrivFP
FAX Number: (402) 561-0635 Calendar System: Semester
URL: www.ucha.com
Established: 1995 Annual Undergrad Tuition & Fees: $15,010
Enrollment: 27 Coed
Affiliation or Control: Proprietary IRS Status: Proprietary
Highest Offering: Associate Degree
Program: Occupational
Accreditation: ABHES

01 Director Ms. Paulette GENTHON

*University of Nebraska Central Administration (G)

3835 Holdrege, Lincoln NE 68583-0745
County: Lancaster FICE Identification: 008025
Unit ID: 181747
Telephone: (402) 472-2111 Carnegie Class: N/A
FAX Number: (402) 472-1237
URL: www.nebraska.edu

01 President Mr. James B. MILLIKEN
05 Int Exec Vice President & Provost Dr. Susan M. FRITZ
10 Sr Vice Pres Business & Finance Mr. David LECHNER
43 Vice President General Counsel Mr. Joel D. PEDERSEN
47 VP Agriculture/Natural Resources Dr. Ronnie GREEN
88 Vice Provost for Global Engagement Mr. Thomas FARRELL
100 Chief of Staff Ms. Dara L. TROUTMAN
13 Chief Information Officer Mr. Walter G. WEIR
101 Corporation Secretary Ms. Carmen K. MAURER
86 Assoc VP/Director Govt Relations Mr. Ron WITHEM
16 Asst VP/Dir HR/Acad Affs/Diversity Mr. Edward D. WIMES
88 Sr Assoc to Pres Innov/Econ Compet Dr. Jim LINDER
18 Asst VP/Dir Facility Plng/Mgmt Ms. Rebecca H. KOLLER
26 Vice President External Affairs Ms. Sharon R. STEPHAN
09 Asst VP/Dir Inst Research/Planning Dr. Kristin YATES

*University of Nebraska at Kearney (H)

905 W 25th Street, Kearney NE 68849
County: Buffalo FICE Identification: 002551
Unit ID: 181215
Telephone: (308) 865-8208 Carnegie Class: Master's L
FAX Number: (308) 865-8665 Calendar System: Semester
URL: www.unk.edu
Established: 1903 Annual Undergrad Tuition & Fees (In-State): $6,521
Enrollment: 7,199 Coed
Affiliation or Control: State IRS Status: 501(c)3
Highest Offering: Beyond Master's But Less Than Doctorate
Program: Liberal Arts And General; Teacher Preparatory; Professional
Accreditation: NH, BUS, CACREP, CIDA, COARC, MUS, NAIT, SP, SW, TED

02 Chancellor Dr. Douglas A. KRISTENSEN
05 Sr VC Academic & Student Affairs Dr. Charles J. BICAK
10 Vice Chanc Business & Finance Ms. Barbara L. JOHNSON
26 Asst VC Comm/Community Relations Ms. Kelly H. BARTLING
30 Vice President Development Mr. Peter KOTSIOPULOS
13 Asst Vice Chanc Info Technology Ms. Debbie SCHROEDER
21 Asst Vice Chanc Business & Finance Ms. Jane SHELDON
83 Dean Natural/Social Science Dr. John C. LA DUKE
50 Dean Business/Technology Dr. Timothy J. BURKINK
53 Dean of Education Dr. Edgar (Ed) L. SCANTLING
57 Dean Fine Arts & Humanities Dr. William JURMA
58 Dean Graduate Studies & Research Dr. Kenya S. TAYLOR
32 Dean Division of Student Affairs Dr. Joseph A. ORAVECZ
04 Exec Assistant to the Chancellor Mr. Neal H. SCHNOOR
06 Registrar Ms. Kim SCHIPPOREIT
08 Dean of the Library Ms. Janet S. WILKE
15 Director Human Resources Ms. Cheryl BRESSINGTON
36 Director Academic & Career Services Ms. Mary DAAKE
07 Director of Admissions Mr. Dusty NEWTON
18 Director Facilities Mr. Lee MCQUEEN
19 Director Police & Parking Services Ms. Michelle HAMAKER
22 Dir Affirm Action/Equal Opportunity Ms. Cheryl BRESSINGTON
09 Director Institutional Research Ms. Kathy LIVINGSTON
27 Dir News/Internal Commununication Mr. Todd GOTTULA
29 Director Alumni Services Mr. Peter KOTSIOPULOS
88 Director Student Union Ms. Sharon PELC
38 Director Counseling Center Dr. LeAnn OBRECHT
39 Director Residential Life Dr. C. Anthony EARLS
40 Director Bookstore Mr. Len J. FANGMEYER
41 Athletic Director Vacant
21 Director Finance Mr. Larry RIESSLAND
23 Director Student Health Service Dr. LeAnn OBRECHT
104 Director International Education Dr. Keith (Dallas) KENNY
21 Budget Director Ms. Jean MATTSON
96 Director Business Services Mr. Jonathan C. WATTS
37 Director Financial Aid Ms. Mary SOMMERS
28 Director of Diversity Mr. Juan GUZMAN

*University of Nebraska - Lincoln (I)

14th and R Streets, Lincoln NE 68588-0002
County: Lancaster FICE Identification: 002565
Unit ID: 181464
Telephone: (402) 472-7211 Carnegie Class: RU/VH
FAX Number: (402) 472-2410 Calendar System: Semester
URL: www.unl.edu
Established: 1869 Annual Undergrad Tuition & Fees (In-State): $7,896
Enrollment: 24,207 Coed
Affiliation or Control: State IRS Status: 501(c)3
Highest Offering: Doctorate
Program: Liberal Arts And General; Teacher Preparatory; Professional
Accreditation: NH, ART, AUD, BUS, BUSA, CIDA, CLPSY, CONST, COPSY, CS, DANCE, DIETD, DIETI, ENG, IPSY, JOUR, LAW, LSAR, MFCD, MUS, PLNG, SCPSY, SP, TEAC, THEA

02 Chancellor Mr. Harvey PERLMAN
05 Senior Vice Chanc Academic Affairs Ms. Ellen WEISSINGER
10 Vice Chanc Business & Finance Ms. Christine JACKSON
32 Vice Chancellor Student Affairs Dr. Juan FRANCO
65 Vice Chanc Agric/Nat Resources Dr. Ronnie D. GREEN
46 VC Research & Economic Development Dr. Prem S. PAUL
13 Chief Information Officer Mr. Mark ASKREN
04 Associate to Chancellor Mr. William NUNEZ
31 Asst to Chanc Community Relations Ms. Michelle WAITE
15 Asst Vice Chanc for Human Resources Mr. Bruce A. CURRIN
18 Asst VC Facilities Mgt/Planning Dr. Ted WEIDNER
07 Director Admissions Ms. Amber S. HUNTER
08 Interim Dean University Libraries Dr. Nancy BUSCH
58 Dean Graduate Studies Dr. Lance C. PEREZ
49 Dean Arts & Sciences Dr. David C. MANDERSCHEID
54 Dean Engineering Dr. Timothy WEI
61 Dean of Law Dr. Susan POSER
47 Dean Agric Scienc/Nat Resources Dr. Steven WALLER
50 Dean Business Administration Dr. Donde PLOWMAN
60 Interim Dean Journ/Mass Communic Dr. James P. O'HANLON
53 Dean Education & Human Sciences Dr. Marjorie KOSTELNIK
48 Interim Dean College Architecture Dr. Kim L. WILSON
47 Dean Agricultural Research Division Dr. Archie CLUTTER
56 Dean & Dir Cooperative Extens Dr. Charles HIBBERD
93 Director Educ Access & TRIO Pgms Ms. Catherine YAMAMOTO
57 Dean Fine & Performing Arts Dr. Charles D. O'CONNOR
37 Director Scholarships/Financial Aid Mr. Craig D. MUNIER
09 Director Inst Research & Planning Dr. William J. NUNEZ
92 Director Honors Program Dr. Patrice BERGER
94 Director Women's Studies Dr. Marie-Chantal KALISA
06 Director Registrar & Records Dr. Earl W. HAWKEY
36 Director Career Services Center Dr. Larry R. ROUTH
19 Chief University Police Services Mr. Owen YARDLEY
22 Director Affirm Action/Diversity Ms. Linda CRUMP
23 Director University Health Center Dr. James GUEST
39 Director Housing Office Ms. Susan M. GILDERSLEEVE
41 Director of Athletics Mr. Shawn EICHORST
55 Dir Distance Education Services Dr. Nancy ADEN-FOX
29 Exec Director Alumni Association Ms. Diane MENDENHALL
26 Director University Communications Dr. Meg LAUERMAN
20 Associate Academic Officer Dr. Lance C. PEREZ
30 Chief Development Mr. Brian HASTINGS
38 Director Student Counseling Dr. Robert N. PORTNOY
84 Dean Enrollment Management Dr. Alan CERVENY
96 Director of Purchasing Mr. Gary L. KRAFT
28 Director of Diversity Ms. Linda CRUMP

*University of Nebraska Medical Center (J)

987020 Nebraska Medical Center, Omaha NE 68198-7020
County: Douglas FICE Identification: 006895
Unit ID: 181428
Telephone: (402) 559-4000 Carnegie Class: Spec/Med
FAX Number: (402) 559-4396 Calendar System: Semester
URL: www.unmc.edu
Established: 1869 Annual Undergrad Tuition & Fees (In-State): $8,338
Enrollment: 3,655 Coed
Affiliation or Control: State IRS Status: 501(c)3
Highest Offering: Doctorate
Program: Professional
Accreditation: NH, ARCPA, CYTO, DENT, DH, DIETI, DMS, MED, MT, NMT, NURSE, PERF, PH, PHAR, PTA, RAD, RADMAG, RTT

02 Chancellor Dr. Harold M. MAURER
05 Vice Chancellor Acad Affairs Dr. H. Dele O. DAVIES
10 Vice Chancellor Bus & Finance Mr. Donald LEUENBERGER
46 Vice Chancellor Research Dr. Jennifer LARSEN
86 Vice Chancellor External Affairs Mr. Robert D. BARTEE
20 Assoc Vice Chanc Academic Affairs Dr. James TURPEN
20 Asst Vice Chanc Acad Affairs Dr. Cheryl THOMPSON
20 Assoc Vice Chanc Acad Affs/Reg Comp Dr. Ernest D. PRENTICE
45 Assoc Vice Chanc Basic Sci Rsch Dr. Kenneth BAYLES
45 Assoc Vice Chancellor Clinical Rsch Dr. Christopher KRATOCHVIL
21 Assoc Vice Chanc Bus & Finance Ms. Deborah THOMAS
13 Assoc Vice Chanc Bus Dev/CTO Dr. Rodney MARKIN
18 Asst Vice Chanc Facilities/Mgt/Plng Mr. Kenneth HANSEN
21 Asst Vice Chanc Budget & Planning Ms. Pamela BATAILLON
14 Asst Vice Chancellor ITS Ms. Yvette A. HOLLY
58 Dean Graduate Studies Dr. H. Dele O. DAVIES
52 Dean College of Dentistry Dr. John W. REINHARDT
63 Dean College of Medicine Dr. Bradley E. BRITIGAN
66 Dean College of Nursing Dr. Juliann SEBASTIAN
67 Dean College of Pharmacy Dr. Courtney FLETCHER
69 Dean College of Public Health Dr. Ayman EL MOHANDES
76 Assoc Dean Allied Hlth Professions Dr. Kyle MEYER
88 Dir Eppley Cancer Research Inst Dr. Kenneth H. COWAN
88 Director Munroe-Meyer Inst Dr. J. Michael LEIBOWITZ
08 Interim Director Library of Med Ms. Marie A. REIDELBACH
37 Dir Financial Aid Office Ms. Judith D. WALKER
26 Director of Public Relations Mr. William O'NEILL
15 Exec Director Human Resources Mr. John P. RUSSELL
29 Director Alumni Affairs Ms. Roxana JOKELA
38 Director Student Counseling Dr. David S. CARVER
28 Director of Diversity Vacant
96 Director Procurement & Mtrls Mgt Mr. Jeffrey ELLIOTT
09 Director Institutional Research Ms. Jeanne FERBRACHE
19 Director Campus Security Mr. Gary SVANDA

*University of Nebraska at Omaha (A)

6001 Dodge Street, Omaha NE 68182-0001
County: Douglas FICE Identification: 002554
Unit ID: 181394
Telephone: (402) 554-2200 Carnegie Class: DRU
FAX Number: (402) 554-3555 Calendar System: Semester
URL: www.unomaha.edu
Established: 1908 Annual Undergrad Tuition & Fees (In-State): $6,510
Enrollment: 14,786 Coed
Affiliation or Control: State IRS Status: 501(c)3
Highest Offering: Doctorate
Program: Liberal Arts And General; Teacher Preparatory; Professional
Accreditation: NH, AAB, ART, BUS, BUSA, CACREP, CS, MUS, SP, SPAA, SW, TED

02 Chancellor .... Dr. John E. CHRISTENSEN
05 Sr Vice Chanc Acad/Student Affs .... Dr. Burton J. REED
10 Vice Chanc Business & Finance .... Mr. Bill CONLEY
04 Exec Assistant to the Chancellor .... Ms. Nancy CASTILOW
13 Assoc Vice Chanc Information Svcs .... Mr. John L. FIENE
21 Assoc Vice Chanc Business & Finance .... Ms. Julie TOTTEN
32 Assoc Vice Chanc Student Affairs .... Dr. Daniel SHIPP
84 Asst Vice Chanc Enroll Mgmt Svcs .... Dr. Pelema I. MORRICE
58 Dean Graduate Studies .... Dr. Deb SMITH-HOWELL
57 Dean Fine Arts/Communication/Media .... Dr. Gail BAKER
53 Dean of Education .... Dr. Nancy EDICK
50 Dean of Business Administration .... Dr. Lou POL
49 Dean of Arts & Sciences .... Dr. David J. BOOCKER
82 Dean of International Studies/Pgms . Mr. Thomas E. GOUTTIERRE
72 Dean Info Science/Technology .... Dr. Hesham ALI
80 Dean Public Affairs/Community .... Dr. John R. BARTLE
62 Dean of Library Services .... Mr. Stephen SHORB
09 Dir Institutional Effectiveness .... Dr. Russell SMITH
35 Chief Student Life Officer .... Ms. Rita HENRY
15 Director Human Resources .... Ms. Mollie ANDERSON
18 Director Facilities Mgmt/Planning .... Mr. John AMEND
06 Registrar .... Mr. Mark GOLDSBERRY
07 Director of Admissions .... Vacant
37 Director Financial Aid .... Mr. Randall L. SELL
88 Director Student Testing Center .... Ms. Marion FORTIN-WAVRA
41 Director of Athletics .... Mr. Trev ALBERTS
29 President/CEO Alumni Association .... Mr. Lee DENKER
26 Director Communications .... Mr. Tim KALDAHL
96 Director of Purchasing .... Mr. Ken HULTMAN
40 Manager Book Store .... Mr. Michael E. SCHMIDT
19 Manager Campus Security .... Mr. Paul KOSEL

*University of Nebraska - Nebraska College of Technical Agriculture (B)

404 E 7th Street, Curtis NE 69025-9502
County: Frontier FICE Identification: 007358
Unit ID: 181765
Telephone: (308) 367-4124 Carnegie Class: Assoc/Pub2in4
FAX Number: (308) 367-5203 Calendar System: Semester
URL: www.ncta.unl.edu
Established: 1912 Annual Undergrad Tuition & Fees (In-State): $3,944
Enrollment: 331 Coed
Affiliation or Control: State IRS Status: 501(c)3
Highest Offering: Associate Degree
Program: Occupational; 2-Year Principally Bachelor's Creditable; Technical Emphasis
Accreditation: NH

02 Dean .... Dr. Ron ROSATI
03 Associate Dean .... Dr. Scott R. MICKELSEN
10 Business Officer .... Ms. Jan GILBERT

University of Phoenix Omaha Campus (C)

13321 California Street, Suite 200, Omaha NE 68154-5258
Telephone: (402) 334-4936 Identification: 770217
Accreditation: &NH, ACBSP

† Main campus is University of Phoenix in Tempe, AZ.

Vatterott College-Omaha (D)

11818 I Street, Omaha NE 68137-1237
County: Douglas FICE Identification: 007501
Unit ID: 181756
Telephone: (402) 891-9411 Carnegie Class: Assoc/PrivFP
FAX Number: (402) 891-9413 Calendar System: Quarter
URL: www.vatterott-college.edu
Established: 1996 Annual Undergrad Tuition & Fees: $12,262
Enrollment: 405 Coed
Affiliation or Control: Proprietary IRS Status: Proprietary
Highest Offering: Associate Degree
Program: Occupational; 2-Year Principally Bachelor's Creditable; Technical Emphasis
Accreditation: ACCSC, DA, MAAB

01 CEO & President .... Ms. Pam BELL
10 Chief Financial Officer .... Mr. Dennis BEAVERS
05 Vice President Academic Affairs .... Dr. Brandon SHEDRON
45 VP Regulatory Affs/Strategic Devel .... Mr. Aaron LACEY
43 General Counsel/Chief Administrator .... Mr. Scott CASANOVER
12 Campus Director .... Ms. Deb LENIHAN

Western Nebraska Community College (E)

1601 E 27th Street, Scottsbluff NE 69361-1815
County: Scotts Bluff FICE Identification: 002560
Unit ID: 181817
Telephone: (308) 635-3606 Carnegie Class: Assoc/Pub-R-L
FAX Number: (308) 635-6100 Calendar System: Semester
URL: www.wncc.edu
Established: 1926 Annual Undergrad Tuition & Fees (In-District): $2,985
Enrollment: 2,230 Coed
Affiliation or Control: State/Local IRS Status: 501(c)3
Highest Offering: Associate Degree
Program: Occupational; 2-Year Principally Bachelor's Creditable
Accreditation: NH, CAHIIM, PNUR

01 President .... Dr. Todd R. HOLCOMB
05 Vice President Educational Services .... Mr. Terry B. GAALSWYK
15 Vice President Human Resources .... Mr. David E. GROSHANS
32 Vice President Student Services .... Ms. Susan K. YOWELL
11 Vice Pres Administrative Services .... Mr. William D. KNAPPER
20 Dean of Instruction .... Mr. Garry R. ALKIRE
103 Dean of Workforce Development .... Mr. Jason L. STRATMAN
50 Dean Business & Individual Training .... Ms. Judith L. AMOO
35 Dean Student Services .... Dr. Michael HOUDYSHELL
12 Sidney Campus Director .... Ms. Paula J. ABBOTT
12 Ast Dn Instruct/Alliance Campus Dir .... Ms. Ellen M. DILLON
102 Foundation Executive Director .... Ms. Dayle L. WALLIEN
06 Registrar .... Mr. Roger S. HOVEY
37 Financial Aid Director .... Ms. Sheila R. JOHNS
26 Public Relations & Marketing Dir .... Ms. Erin STINNER
38 Counseling Director .... Mr. Norman J. STEPHENSON
62 Int Library Services Director .... Ms. Merrillene E. WOOD
21 Accounting Services Director .... Mr. David KOEHLER
41 Athletic Director .... Mr. Ryan C. BURGNER
51 Bus & Individual Training Director .... Ms. Lori S. STROMBERG
07 Admissions Director .... Ms. Gretchen K. FOSTER
39 Residence Life Director .... Mr. Mario J. CHAVEZ
13 Information Technology Director .... Mr. Joe W. DEER
40 Bookstore Operations Director .... Ms. Suzane KARBOWSKI
19 Safety/Environmental Mgmt Director .... Mr. Robert L. HESSLER
09 Institutional Research Director .... Mrs. Mary E. BARKELOO
88 Academic Testing & Tutoring Coord .... Ms. Tammie KLEICH
39 Residence Life/Activities Coord .... Vacant
39 Residence Life/Activities Coord .... Ms. Molly A. BONUCHI
50 Division Chair Business .... Mr. Tom ROBINSON
83 Division Chair Social Sciences .... Ms. Hallie L. FEIL
88 Division Chair Language & Arts .... Ms. Jennifer L. PEDERSEN
75 Division Chair Applied Technology .... Mr. Willie QUINDT
66 Nursing Education Director .... Ms. Melaney A. THOMAS
81 Math Coordinator .... Dr. Scott A. SCHAUB
81 Sciences Coordinator .... Mr. David NASH
68 Health-Physical Education Coord .... Ms. Maria L. WINN-RATLIFF
88 Health Info Technology Program Dir .... Ms. Peg A. WOLFF
88 Academic Enrichment Coord-Language .... Ms. Susan DICKINSON
29 Director Alumni Relations .... Ms. Tina R. DUEKER
88 Academic Enrichment Coord-Math .... Ms. Laurie A. ALKIRE
106 Online Learning/Services/Assess Dir .... Ms. Jackie S. JACOBSEN

Western Nebraska Community College Alliance Campus (F)

1750 Sweetwater Avenue, Alliance NE 69301
Telephone: (308) 763-2000 Identification: 770343
Accreditation: &NH

† Main campus is Western Nebraska Community College in Scottsbluff, NE.

Western Nebraska Community College Sidney Campus (G)

371 College Drive, Sidney NE 69162
Telephone: (308) 254-5450 Identification: 770344
Accreditation: &NH

† Main campus is Western Nebraska Community College in Scottsbluff, NE.

Wright Career College (H)

3000 South 84th Street, Omaha NE 68124
Telephone: (913) 381-2577 Identification: 770739
Accreditation: ACICS

† Main campus is Wright Career College in Overland Park, KS.

York College (I)

1125 E 8th Street, York NE 68467-2699
County: York FICE Identification: 002567
Unit ID: 181853
Telephone: (402) 363-5600 Carnegie Class: Bac/Diverse
FAX Number: (402) 363-5623 Calendar System: Semester
URL: www.york.edu
Established: 1890 Annual Undergrad Tuition & Fees: $15,600
Enrollment: 500 Coed
Affiliation or Control: Churches Of Christ IRS Status: 501(c)3
Highest Offering: Master's
Program: Liberal Arts And General; Business Emphasis
Accreditation: NH, TED

01 President .... Dr. Steven W. ECKMAN
05 Academic Dean .... Dr. Tracey L. WYATT
10 Vice President Finance & Operations .... Mr. Todd SHELDON
30 Vice Pres Advancement .... Mr. Brent MAGNER
32 Vice Pres for Student Development .... Dr. Shane MOUNTJOY
21 Business Manager .... Mr. Dan COLE
06 Registrar .... Mr. Tod J. MARTIN
07 Vice President of Admissions .... Mr. Willie SANCHEZ
08 Director of Library .... Mrs. Ruth CARLOCK
26 Director of Publications .... Mr. Steddon L. SIKES
37 Financial Aid Director .... Mr. Brien ALLEY
40 Campus Store Manager .... Mrs. Janet RUSH
41 Athletic Director .... Mr. Jared A. STARK
18 Supervisor Buildings & Grounds .... Mr. Bob GAVER
91 Director Administrative Computing .... Mr. Joel COEHOORN
36 Director Student Placement .... Vacant
42 Campus Minister .... Mr. Willie SANCHEZ
50 Chair Business .... Dr. Mark MOORE
53 Chair Education .... Mr. Robert DEHART
73 Chair Bible .... Dr. Frank E. WHEELER
88 Chair History .... Mr. Tim D. MCNEESE
50 Chair English .... Mr. Joshua FULLMAN
81 Chair Math/Sciences .... Dr. Alex WILLIAMS
57 Chair Performing Arts/Communication .... Dr. Clark A. ROUSH
29 Dir Alumni & Community Relations .... Mrs. Chrystal HOUSTON

NEVADA

The Art Institute of Las Vegas (J)

2350 Corporate Circle, Henderson NV 89074-7737
Telephone: (702) 369-9944 FICE Identification: 030846
Accreditation: ACICS, ACFEI, CIDA

† Main campus is The Art Institute of Phoenix in Phoenix, AZ.

Career College of Northern Nevada (K)

1421 Pullman Drive, Sparks NV 89434
County: Washoe FICE Identification: 026215
Unit ID: 181941
Telephone: (775) 856-2266 Carnegie Class: Assoc/PrivFP
FAX Number: (775) 856-0935 Calendar System: Quarter
URL: www.ccnn.edu
Established: 1984 Annual Undergrad Tuition & Fees: $23,973
Enrollment: 522 Coed
Affiliation or Control: Proprietary IRS Status: Proprietary
Highest Offering: Associate Degree
Program: Occupational
Accreditation: ACCSC

01 President .... Mr. L. Nathan N. CLARK

Carrington College (L)

5740 S Eastern Avenue, Suite 140, Las Vegas NV 89119
Telephone: (702) 514-3236 Identification: 770742
Accreditation: ACICS, COARC, @PTAA

† Main campus is Carrington College - Phoenix in Phoenix, AZ.

Carrington College (M)

5580 Kietzke Lane, Reno NV 89511
Telephone: (775) 335-1714 Identification: 770743
Accreditation: ACICS, ADNUR

† Main campus is Carrington College - Boise in Boise, ID.

Everest College (N)

170 North Stephanie Street, Henderson NV 89074
FICE Identification: 022375
Unit ID: 182148
Telephone: (702) 567-1920 Carnegie Class: Assoc/PrivFP
FAX Number: (702) 566-9725 Calendar System: Semester
URL: www.everest.edu
Established: 2004 Annual Undergrad Tuition & Fees: N/A
Enrollment: 934 Coed
Affiliation or Control: Proprietary IRS Status: Proprietary
Highest Offering: Associate Degree
Program: Occupational
Accreditation: ACICS, MAAB

01 President .... Mr. Dave FRITZ
03 Vice President .... Dr. Steven GUELL

International Academy of Design and Technology (O)

2495 Village View Drive, Henderson NV 89074
Telephone: (702) 990-0150 Identification: 770744
Accreditation: ACICS

† Main campus is International Academy of Design and Technology in Tampa, FL.

ITT Technical Institute (P)

168 N Gibson Road, Henderson NV 89014-6712
Telephone: (702) 558-5404 Identification: 666544

Accreditation: ACICS

† Main campus is ITT Technical Institute in Indianapolis, IN.

ITT Technical Institute (A)

3825 West Cheyenne Avenue, Ste 600,
North Las Vegas NV 89032

Telephone: (702) 240-0967 Identification: 770658
Accreditation: ACICS

† Main campus is ITT Technical Institute in Indianapolis, IN.

Kaplan College (B)

3535 West Sahara Ave, Las Vegas NV 89102

County: Clark FICE Identification: 030432
Unit ID: 374875
Telephone: (702) 368-2338 Carnegie Class: Assoc/PrivFP
FAX Number: (702) 368-3853 Calendar System: Other
URL: www.kaplancollege.com
Established: 1991 Annual Undergrad Tuition & Fees: $15,648
Enrollment: 871 Coed
Affiliation or Control: Proprietary IRS Status: Proprietary
Highest Offering: Associate Degree
Program: Occupational; 2-Year Principally Bachelor's Creditable; Technical Emphasis
Accreditation: ACCSC, ACICS, CAHIIM, MAAB, PNUR

01	Campus President	Mr. Lisia MOORE
05	Director of Education	Ms. Pam LIVINGSTON
07	Director of Admissions	Mr. Derrick PERRY
06	Registrar	Mr. Gregory NELSON
10	Director of Finance	Ms. Carmen TORRES
36	Director of Career Services	Mr. Tom WISEMAN
20	Assistant Director of Education	Mr. Jeffrey FOUNTAIN
66	Director of Nursing	Ms. Catherine CYLKE
76	Dept Chr Med Coder & Biller	Mrs. Phyllis ECKERT
67	Dept Chair Pharmacy Technician	Mr. Mark BRUNTON

Le Cordon Bleu College of Culinary Arts in Las Vegas (C)

1451 Center Crossing Road, Las Vegas NV 89144-7047

Telephone: (702) 365-7690 Identification: 666303
Accreditation: ACCSC, ACFEI, ACICS

† Main campus is Le Cordon Bleu College of Culinary Arts in Scottsdale in Scottsdale, AZ.

*Nevada System of Higher Education (D)

2601 Enterprise Road, Reno NV 89512-1666

County: Washoe FICE Identification: 008026
Unit ID: 182519
Telephone: (775) 784-4901 Carnegie Class: N/A
FAX Number: (775) 784-1127
URL: www.nevada.edu

01	Chancellor	Mr. Daniel J. KLAICH
05	VC Academic & Student Affairs	Ms. Crystal ABBA
10	Vice Chanc for Budget & Finance	Mr. Larry EARDLEY
11	Vice Chanc for for Fin and Admin	Mr. Vic REDDING
88	Chief Exec Ofcr Board of Regents	Mr. Scott WASSERMAN

*College of Southern Nevada (E)

6375 W Charleston Boulevard, Las Vegas NV 89146-1139

County: Clark FICE Identification: 010362
Unit ID: 182005
Telephone: (702) 651-5000 Carnegie Class: Assoc/Pub4
FAX Number: (702) 651-4835 Calendar System: Semester
URL: www.csn.edu
Established: 1971 Annual Undergrad Tuition & Fees (In-State): $2,850
Enrollment: 37,696 Coed
Affiliation or Control: State IRS Status: 501(c)3
Highest Offering: Baccalaureate
Program: Occupational; 2-Year Principally Bachelor's Creditable
Accreditation: NW, ACBSP, ACFEI, ADNUR, CAHIIM, CEA, COARC, DA, DH, DMS, EMT, ENGT, MAC, MLTAD, OPD, #OTA, PNUR, PTAA, SURGT

02	President	Dr. Michael D. RICHARDS
04	Exec Assistant to the President	Ms. Francine WOODHOUSE
10	Sr Vice Pres Finance & Facilities	Ms. Patricia A. CHARLTON
05	Vice Pres Academic Affairs	Dr. Darren D. DIVINE
32	Vice Pres for Student Affairs	Dr. Santos MARTINEZ
88	Sr Advisor to the President	Mr. Thomas BROWN
12	Campus Manager Charleston	Dr. Joan MCGEE
12	Campus Manager Henderson	Mr. Josh RUTER
20	Assoc VP Academic Affairs	Dr. Hyla WINTERS
21	Asst Vice Pres Fin Svcs/Controller	Ms. Mary Kaye BAILEY
18	Assoc VP Facilities/Oper/Maint	Ms. Sherri PAYNE
43	Legal Counsel	Mr. Richard HINCKLEY
88	Assistant Vice President	Dr. Bradley W. GRUNER
06	Registrar	Ms. Pat ZOZAYA
21	Exec Director Business Services	Mr. Dan MORRIS
103	Exec Dir Workforce/Economic Devel	Mr. Dan GOUKER
36	Director Student Services	Ms. Kelly WUEST
102	Exec Dir CSN Foundation	Ms. Jacque MATTHEWS
30	Operations Manager CSN Foundation	Ms. Shirley CARTON
72	Dean Adv & Applied Technologies	Dr. Michael SPANGLER
81	Dean Science & Mathematics	Ms. Sally JOHNSTON
83	Dean Social Sciences & Education	Dr. Charles OKEKE
88	Dean Arts & Letters	Dr. Wendy WEINER
76	Dean Health Sciences	Dr. Patricia CASTRO
50	Dean of Business	Dr. Marcus JOHNSON
96	Director of Purchasing	Mr. Rolando MOSQUEDA
41	Director of Athletics	Mr. Marc MORSE
27	Director of Communications	Ms. Kathryn C. BREKKEN
35	Associate Dean	Ms. Stephanie C. HILL
45	Director Resource Development	Ms. Rosemary W. WEST
88	Director of Budget Services	Ms. Lisa BAKKE
09	Director of Institutional Research	Mr. John BEARCE
62	Director Library Services	Ms. Clarissa ERWIN
37	Asst Director Student Financial Aid	Ms. Katharyn VAN DE CAR
19	Chief of Police	Mr. Darryl CARABALLO
85	Director International Student Ctr	Ms. Tammy SILVER
13	Technology CIO	Mr. Mugunth VAITHYLINGAM
105	Webmaster	Mr. Lowe ROB
15	Director of Personnel Services	Mr. Thomas BROWN
28	Director of Diversity	Ms. Maria MARINCH

*Great Basin College (F)

1500 College Parkway, Elko NV 89801-5032

County: Elko FICE Identification: 006977
Unit ID: 182306
Telephone: (775) 738-8493 Carnegie Class: Bac/Assoc
FAX Number: (775) 738-8771 Calendar System: Semester
URL: www.gbcnv.edu
Established: 1967 Annual Undergrad Tuition & Fees (In-State): $2,700
Enrollment: 3,067 Coed
Affiliation or Control: State IRS Status: 501(c)3
Highest Offering: Baccalaureate
Program: Occupational; 2-Year Principally Bachelor's Creditable
Accreditation: NW, ADNUR, NUR, RAD

02	President	Dr. Mark CURTIS
32	Vice President Student Services	Mrs. Lynn M. MAHLBERG
05	Vice President Academic Affairs	Dr. Mike MCFARLANE
10	Vice President for Business Affairs	Ms. Sonja SIBERT
04	Assistant to the President	Ms. Mardell WILKINS
07	Director of Admissions	Ms. Janice KING
09	Dir Institutional Rsrch/Effective	Vacant
30	Chief Development Officer	Dr. John RICE
08	Library Director	Vacant
37	Dir Student Financial Svcs & VA	Mr. Scott NIELSEN
84	Director Enrollment Management	Ms. Julie BYRNES
75	Dean of Applied Science	Mr. Bret MURPHY
76	Dir of Health Sciences & Human Svcs	Dr. Kris MILLER
12	Director Ely Center	Ms. Mary SWETICH
12	Director Winnemucca Center	Ms. Lisa CAMPBELL
12	Manager Pahrump Valley Center	Ms. Diane WRIGHTMAN
21	Controller	Vacant
51	Director Continuing Education	Mrs. Angie DEBRAGA
56	Dean of Extended Studies	Vacant
102	Director Foundation	Dr. John RICE
19	Director Safety and Security	Ms. Patricia ANDERSON

*Nevada State College (G)

1125 Nevada State Drive, Henderson NV 89002-9455

County: Clark FICE Identification: 041143
Unit ID: 441900
Telephone: (702) 992-2000 Carnegie Class: Bac/Diverse
FAX Number: (702) 992-2226 Calendar System: Semester
URL: www.nsc.edu
Established: 2002 Annual Undergrad Tuition & Fees (In-District): $3,870
Enrollment: 3,405 Coed
Affiliation or Control: State/Local IRS Status: 501(c)3
Highest Offering: Baccalaureate
Program: Liberal Arts And General; Teacher Preparatory; Professional; Nursing Emphasis
Accreditation: NW, NURSE

02	President	Mr. Bart PATTERSON
05	Provost	Dr. Erika BECK
10	VP Finance and Administration	Mr. Buster NEEL
26	Assoc VP for College Relations	Dr. Spencer STEWART
06	Registrar	Ms. Adelfa SULLIVAN
29	Exec Coordinator Alumni Relations	Ms. Danielle JOHNSTON
30	Assoc Vice Pres Development	Dr. Russell RAKER
100	Exec Assistant to the President	Ms. Jennifer HAFT
31	AVP Finance and Administration	Mr. Kevin BUTLER

*Truckee Meadows Community College (H)

7000 Dandini Boulevard, Reno NV 89512-3999

County: Washoe FICE Identification: 021077
Unit ID: 182500
Telephone: (775) 673-7000 Carnegie Class: Assoc/Pub-R-L
FAX Number: (775) 673-7108 Calendar System: Semester
URL: www.tmcc.edu
Established: 1971 Annual Undergrad Tuition & Fees (In-State): $2,720
Enrollment: 12,142 Coed
Affiliation or Control: State IRS Status: 501(c)3
Highest Offering: Associate Degree
Program: Occupational; 2-Year Principally Bachelor's Creditable
Accreditation: NW, ACFEI, ADNUR, DA, DH, DIETT

02	President	Dr. Maria C. SHEEHAN
04	Executive Assistant to President	Ms. Nadine J. WINSLOW
05	Vice President Academic Affairs	Dr. Jane NICHOLS
10	Vice Pres Finance & Admin Services	Dr. Rachel SOLEMSAAS
32	Dean of Student Services	Ms. Estela GUTIERREZ
81	Dean of Sciences	Mr. Ted PLAGGEMEYER
49	Dean of Liberal Arts	Dr. Armida FRUZZETTI
20	Assoc Dean Office of the President	Ms. Patricia SLAVIN
30	Exec Dir Institutional Advancement	Ms. Paula Lee HOBSON
07	Director Admissions & Records	Mr. Andrew HUGHES
21	Controller	Vacant
37	Director Financial Aid	Ms. Sharon WURM
08	Director Learning Resources Center	Ms. Michelle NOEL
15	Director Human Resources	Ms. Michele MEADOR
18	Director Facilities Services	Mr. Dave ROBERTS
102	Dir Institutional Advancement	Dr. J. Kyle DALPE
103	Dir Workforce Devel/Cont Education	Ms. Deb O'GORMAN
38	Director Counseling	Vacant
13	Exec Director Information Tech Ops	Mr. Christopher WINSLOW
19	Chief of Police/Campus Police	Mr. Randy FLOCCHINI
09	Director Institutional Research	Ms. Elena BUBNOVA
28	Director of Equity & Inclusion	Dr. Barbara WRIGHT-SANDERS
29	Donor & Alumni Coordinator	Ms. Tara HAWKINS

*University of Nevada, Las Vegas (I)

4505 S Maryland Parkway, Las Vegas NV 89154-1001

County: Clark FICE Identification: 002569
Unit ID: 182281
Telephone: (702) 895-3201 Carnegie Class: RU/H
FAX Number: (702) 895-1088 Calendar System: Semester
URL: www.unlv.edu
Established: 1957 Annual Undergrad Tuition & Fees (In-State): $6,428
Enrollment: 27,364 Coed
Affiliation or Control: State IRS Status: 501(c)3
Highest Offering: Doctorate
Program: Liberal Arts And General; Teacher Preparatory; Professional
Accreditation: NW, ART, BUS, BUSA, CACREP, CIDA, CLPSY, CONST, CS, DENT, DIETD, DIETI, ENG, ENGR, LAW, LSAR, MFCD, MUS, NMT, NURSE, PH, PTA, RAD, SPAA, SW, THEA

02	President	Dr. Neal SMATRESK
100	Chief of Staff	Dr. Fred TREDUP
05	Executive Vice President & Provost	Mr. John V. WHITE
10	Senior Vice Pres Finance & Business	Mr. Gerry BOMOTTI
41	Dir Intercollegiate Athletics	Mr. Jim LIVENGOOD
32	Vice President for Student Affairs	Dr. Juanita FAIN
58	Int VP Research & Graduate Studies	Dr. Thomas C. PIECHOTA
88	Senior Advisor to President	Vacant
30	VP Advancement	Dr. William BOLDT
86	VP Diversity & Govt Relations	Mr. Luis VALERA
43	General Counsel	Mrs. Elda SIDHU
11	Assoc Vice Pres for Administration	Dr. Mike SAUER
35	Assoc VP for Student Affairs	Ms. Karen STRONG
31	Assoc VP Alumni Relations	Mr. Jim RATIGAN
26	Assoc Vice Pres Community Relations	Ms. Lucy KLINKHAMMER
15	Chief Human Resources Officer	Mr. Larry HAMILTON
87	Int Vice Prov Educational Outreach	Dr. Margaret REES
13	Vice Provost Info Technology	Dr. Lori TEMPLE
50	Dean Business	Dr. Percy POON
49	Dean Liberal Arts	Dr. Chris HUDGINS
53	Interim Dean of Education	Dr. William SPEER
54	Dean of Engineering	Dr. Rama VENKAT
52	Dean School of Dental Medicine	Dr. Karen P. WEST
61	Dean School of Law	Ms. Nancy RAPOPORT
81	Dean of Sciences	Dr. Timothy PORTER
88	Dean Hotel Administration	Dr. Donald SNYDER
57	Dean Fine Arts	Dr. Jeffrey KOEP
08	Dean of Libraries	Ms. Patricia IANNUZZI
88	Interim Dean Urban Affairs	Dr. Lee BERNICK
92	Dean Honors College	Dr. Marta MEANA
88	Dean Academic Success Ctr	Dr. Ann MCDONOUGH
88	Founding Dean Community Health	Dr. Mary GUINAN
76	Dean Sch Allied Health Sciences	Dr. Carolyn YUCHA
06	Exec Dir of Admissions & Recruiting	Vacant
37	Financial Aid & Scholarships	Mr. Norm BEDFORD
27	Assoc VP Univ Communications	Mr. Earnest PHILLIPS
19	Director Public Safety	Mr. Jose ELIQUE
09	Director Inst Analysis/Planning	Mrs. Kari C. COBURN
39	Exec Dir Residential Life	Mr. Richard CLARK
38	AVP Student Wellness	Dr. Jamie DAVIDSON
23	Director Student Health	Ms. Kathy A. UNDERWOOD
96	Director Purchasing	Ms. Sharrie MAYDEN
85	Director Intl Students & Scholars	Ms. Kristen YOUNG
25	Director Sponsored Programs	Ms. Rochelle ATHEY
46	AVP for Research	Dr. Stan SMITH
102	Sr Assoc VP & Exec Dir UNLV Found	Ms. Nancy STROUSE
44	Assoc VP Development	Mr. Scott ROBERTS

*University of Nevada, Reno (J)

Reno NV 89557-0095

County: Washoe FICE Identification: 002568
Unit ID: 182290
Telephone: (775) 784-1110 Carnegie Class: RU/H
FAX Number: (775) 784-1300 Calendar System: Semester
URL: www.unr.edu
Established: 1874 Annual Undergrad Tuition & Fees (In-State): $6,365
Enrollment: 18,227 Coed
Affiliation or Control: State IRS Status: 501(c)3
Highest Offering: Doctorate
Program: Liberal Arts And General; Teacher Preparatory; Professional

Accreditation: NW, BUS, BUSA, CACREP, CLPSY, CS, DIETD, DIETI, ENG, JOUR, MED, MUS, NURSE, PH, SP, SW, TED

02 President .... Dr. Marc JOHNSON
05 Exec Vice Pres & Provost .... Dr. Kevin CARMAN
11 Vice Pres Administration & Finance .... Mr. Ronald M. ZUREK
63 VP Health Sci/Dean Sch of Medicine .... Dr. Thomas L. SCHWENK
30 Vice President Devel/Alumni Rels .... Mr. John CAROTHERS
32 Vice President for Student Services .... Dr. Shannon ELLIS
46 Vice President for Research .... Dr. Mridul GAUTAM
08 Dean of Libraries .... Dr. Kathlin D. RAY
20 Vice Prov Instr/Undergrad Programs .... Dr. Joseph CLINE
20 Vice Provost Faculty Affairs .... Dr. Stacy BURTON
51 Vice Provost for Extended Studies .... Dr. Fred B. HOLMAN
10 Assoc VP Business & Finance .... Mr. Thomas L. JUDY
84 Assoc VP Enrollment Services .... Dr. Melisa N. CHOROSZY
38 Assoc VP Student Success Services .... Dr. Jerry MARCZYNSKI
45 Asst VP Planning/Budget/Analysis .... Mr. Bruce L. SHIVELY
18 Int Asst Vice Pres Facilities Svcs .... Mr. John WALSH
21 Controller .... Ms. Sheri MENDEZ
41 Director Athletics .... Mr. Doug KNUTH
96 Director Purchasing .... Mr. Garth KWIECHIEN
19 Director University Police Svcs .... Mr. Adam GARCIA
22 Dir Equal Opportunity & Title IX .... Ms. Denise CORDOVA
37 Director Student Financial Svcs .... Mr. Timothy WOLFF
39 Director Resident Life & Housing . Mr. Rodney L. AESCHLIMANN
23 Director Student Health Svcs .... Dr. Cheryl HUG-ENGLISH
09 Director Institutional Analysis .... Dr. Serge HERZOG
86 Dir Govt Relations & Economic Dev .... Dr. Robert E. DICKENS
65 Dir Mackay Sch Mines/Earth Science .... Dr. Russell FIELDS
66 Director of Nursing .... Dr. Patsy L. RUCHALA
57 Director School of the Arts .... Vacant
25 Director Sponsored Projects .... Ms. Charlene HART
40 Director Wolf Shop .... Mr. Steve DUBEY
49 Dean Liberal Arts .... Dr. Heather HARDY
47 Dean Agriculture/Biotech/Nat Res .... Dr. Ron PARDINI
50 Dean Business Admininistration .... Dr. Gregory MOSIER
53 Dean of Education .... Dr. Christine CHENEY
54 Dean Engineering .... Dr. Emmanuel MARAGAKIS
60 Dean School of Journalism .... Mr. Alan STAVITSKY
81 Dean College of Science .... Dr. Jeffrey S. THOMPSON
65 Director Academy for Environment .... Dr. Jen HUNTLEY-SMITH
07 Director of Admissions .... Dr. Stephen MAPLES
29 Director Alumni Relations .... Ms. Amy CAROTHERS

*Western Nevada College (A)

2201 W College Parkway, Carson City NV 89703-7316
County: Carson FICE Identification: 010363
Unit ID: 182564
Telephone: (775) 445-3000 Carnegie Class: Assoc/Pub4
FAX Number: (775) 887-3051 Calendar System: Semester
URL: www.wnc.edu
Established: 1971 Annual Undergrad Tuition & Fees (In-State): $2,700
Enrollment: 4,167 Coed
Affiliation or Control: State IRS Status: 501(c)3
Highest Offering: Baccalaureate
Program: Occupational; 2-Year Principally Bachelor's Creditable
Accreditation: NW, ADNUR

02 President .... Dr. Carol A. LUCEY
04 Assistant to the President .... Ms. Bonnie M. BERTOCCHI
05 Vice Pres Academic/Student Affairs .... Ms. Robert WYNEGAR
15 VP Human Resources/Dir Diversity .... Mr. Mark GHAN
20 Dean of Instruction .... Vacant
32 Dean Student Services .... Mr. John KINKELLA
10 Controller .... Ms. Coral LOPEZ
88 Director Child Development Center .... Ms. Andrea DORAN
38 Director of Counseling/Advising .... Ms. Deborah CASE
18 Director Facilities Mgmt/Planning .... Mr. Dave ROLLINGS
37 Director Financial Aid .... Mr. John (Lee) HARRELL
27 Director Information & Marketing .... Ms. Anne P. HANSEN
08 Director Library & Media Services .... Mr. Kenneth A. SULLIVAN
06 Registrar/Director of Admissions .... Ms. Dianne HILLIARD
30 Director of Development .... Ms. Katie LEAO
09 Director of Institutional Research .... Ms. Cathy FULKERSON
13 Director of Computing Services .... Ms. Susan SCHOEFFLER
21 Budget Officer .... Ms. Darla DODGE
15 Asst Director Human Resources .... Ms. Irene TUCKER
51 Outreach Coordinator .... Vacant
35 Student Life Coordinator .... Ms. Shelly BALE
72 Academic Director Career & Tech Div .... Mr. Scott MORRISON
49 Academic Director Liberal Arts .... Ms. Sherry BLACK
66 Academic Dir Nursing/Allied Health .... Dr. Judith CORDIA

Northwest Career College (B)

7398 smoke Ranch Road, Las Vegas NV 89128
County: Clark FICE Identification: 038385
Unit ID: 445948
Telephone: (702) 254-7577 Carnegie Class: Not Classified
FAX Number: (702) 256-9181 Calendar System: Semester
URL: www.northwestcareercollege.edu
Established: Annual Undergrad Tuition & Fees: $11,212
Enrollment: 132 Coed
Affiliation or Control: Proprietary IRS Status: Proprietary
Highest Offering: Associate Degree
Program: Occupational
Accreditation: ABHES

01 Director .... Dr. John KENNY

Pima Medical Institute-Las Vegas (C)

3333 E Flamingo Road, Las Vegas NV 89121-4329
Telephone: (702) 458-9650 Identification: 666273
Accreditation: ABHES, COARC, PTAA, RAD

† Main campus is Pima Medical Institute-Tucson in Tucson, AZ.

Regis University Las Vegas Campus (D)

1401 N Green Valley Pkwy, Suite 100,
Henderson NV 89074
Telephone: (702) 990-0375 Identification: 770046
Accreditation: &NH

† Main campus is Regis University in Denver, CO.

Roseman University of Health Sciences (E)

11 Sunset Way, Henderson NV 89014-2333
County: Clark FICE Identification: 040653
Unit ID: 445735
Telephone: (702) 990-4433 Carnegie Class: Spec/Health
FAX Number: (702) 990-4435 Calendar System: Other
URL: www.roseman.edu
Established: 1999 Annual Undergrad Tuition & Fees: $32,317
Enrollment: 1,123 Coed
Affiliation or Control: Independent Non-Profit IRS Status: 501(c)3
Highest Offering: Doctorate
Program: Professional
Accreditation: NW, DENT, IACBE, NUR, PHAR

01 President .... Dr. Renee COFFMAN
12 Chancellor South Jordan Campus .... Dr. Mark A. PENN
12 Chancellor Henderson Campus .... Dr. Eucharia E. NNADI
10 VP for Fiscal Affairs & Treasurer .... Mr. Stuart A. WIENER
18 Vice President Facilities & Mgmt .... Ms. Marlene R. MILLER
13 Vice President Info Technologies .... Mr. Raymond PEREZ
03 Vice President Executive Affairs .... Dr. Charles F. LACY
26 Vice President Communications & PR .... Mr. Jason ROTH
09 VP Qual Assurance/Intercampus Cons .... Dr. Thomas METZGER
46 Vice President for Research .... Dr. Ronald FISCUS
67 Dean College of Pharmacy .... Dr. Scott STOLTE
67 Campus Dean College of Pharmacy UT .... Dr. Larry FANNIN
66 Dean College of Nursing Henderson .... Dr. Mable H. SMITH
66 Dean College of Nursing UT .... Dr. Marlene LUNA
52 Dean College of Dental Medicine .... Dr. Frank LICARI
52 Dean College of Dental Medicine Hen .... Dr. Jaleh POURHAMIDI
50 Director MBA Program .... Dr. Okeleke NZEOGWU
88 Assoc Dean Admissions Pharmacy .... Dr. Michael DEYOUNG
37 Director of Financial Aid .... Mr. Jesse STASHER
88 Assoc Dean Clinical Programs Pharm .... Dr. Gary M. LEVIN
51 Director of Continuing Education .... Dr. Katherine SMITH
52 Assoc Dean Academic Affairs Dental .... Dr. Victor A. SANDOVAL
52 Assoc Dean Clinical Affairs .... Dr. Leslie KARNS
07 Assoc Dean Admissions/Student Svcs .... Dr. William HARMAN
15 Director of Human Resources .... Dr. G. Benjamin WILLS
62 Director of Library Services .... Ms. Karen CANEPI
30 Director of University Relations .... Ms. Barbara WOOD
44 Director of Development .... Ms. Brenda GRIEGO
06 Registrar/Director of Student Svcs .... Ms. Angela D. BIGBY
88 Marketing Director South Jordan .... Ms. Tracy HERNANDEZ
66 Assoc Dean Nursing .... Dr. Catherine D'AMICO

Sierra Nevada College (F)

999 Tahoe Boulevard, Incline Village NV 89451-9500
County: Washoe FICE Identification: 009192
Unit ID: 182458
Telephone: (775) 831-1314 Carnegie Class: Master's M
FAX Number: (775) 832-1696 Calendar System: Semester
URL: www.sierranevada.edu
Established: 1969 Annual Undergrad Tuition & Fees: $27,654
Enrollment: 987 Coed
Affiliation or Control: Independent Non-Profit IRS Status: 501(c)3
Highest Offering: Master's
Program: Liberal Arts And General
Accreditation: NW

00 Chairman Board of Trustees .... Dr. Barry MUNITZ
01 President .... Dr. Lynn GILLETTE
05 Executive Vice President/Provost .... Dr. Shannon BEETS
30 Vice President Development .... Mr. Dino HERNANDEZ
26 Vice Pres External Relations .... Mr. Leroy HARDY
32 Dean of Students/Dir Student Act .... Mr. Will HOIDA
84 Dean Enrollment Services & Student .... Ms. Julie FOSTER
20 Associate Provost .... Mr. Dan O'BRYAN
37 Director of Financial Aid .... Ms. Nicole FERGUSON
07 Dean of Admissions .... Mr. Steve BERRY
08 Director of Library .... Dr. Elizabeth MARKLE
06 Registrar .... Ms. Rose BEENK
53 Statewide Dir Teacher Education .... Ms. Beth BOUCHARD
13 Director Information Technology .... Ms. Nicole FERGERSON
10 Chief Financial Officer .... Ms. Susan JOHNSON
15 Director Human Resources .... Mr. David WEBB
21 Controller .... Ms. Lynda ODELL
04 Executive Asst to the President .... Ms. Kristine YOUNG

University of Phoenix Las Vegas Campus (G)

3755 Breakthrough Way, Las Vegas NV 89135-3047
Telephone: (702) 638-7279 Identification: 770220
Accreditation: &NH, ACBSP

† Main campus is University of Phoenix in Tempe, AZ.

NEW HAMPSHIRE

Antioch University New England (H)

40 Avon Street, Keene NH 03431-3516
Telephone: (800) 553-8920 Identification: 666992
Accreditation: &NH, CACREP, CLPSY, MFCD

† Main campus is Antioch University in Yellow Springs, OH.

Colby-Sawyer College (I)

541 Main Street, New London NH 03257-7835
County: Merrimack FICE Identification: 002572
Unit ID: 182634
Telephone: (603) 526-3000 Carnegie Class: Bac/Diverse
FAX Number: (603) 526-2135 Calendar System: Semester
URL: www.colby-sawyer.edu
Established: 1837 Annual Undergrad Tuition & Fees: $37,300
Enrollment: 1,414 Coed
Affiliation or Control: Independent Non-Profit IRS Status: 501(c)3
Highest Offering: Baccalaureate
Program: Liberal Arts And General; Teacher Preparatory
Accreditation: EH, NURSE

01 President .... Mr. Thomas C. GALLIGAN
05 Academic Vice Pres/Dean of Faculty .... Dr. Deborah A. TAYLOR
11 Vice President Administration .... Mr. Douglas G. ATKINS
10 Vice Pres for Finance & Treasurer .... Mr. Todd C. EMMONS
32 VP Stdnt Devel/Dean of Students .... Mr. David A. SAUERWEIN
30 Vice President Advancement .... Ms. Elizabeth A. CAHILL
84 Vice Pres Enrollment Management .... Vacant
101 Secretary of the College .... Ms. Linda J. VARNUM
100 Chief of Staff/Dir Strategic Plng .... Ms. Lisa F. TEDESCHI
20 Academic Dean .... Dr. J Burton KIRKWOOD
35 Assoc Dean Stdnt/Dir Citizenship Ed .... Ms. Robin BURROUGHS-DAVIS
39 Director Residential Education .... Ms. Mary MCLAUGHLIN
37 Director of Financial Aid .... Mr. Ted W. CRAIGIE
30 Director of Development .... Ms. Kathleen A. CARROLL
88 Senior Development Officer .... Mr. Glen R. KERKIAN
08 College Librarian .... Ms. Carrie THOMAS
06 Registrar .... Ms. Carole H. PARSONS
07 Director of Admission Counseling .... Ms. Tracey G. PERKINS
13 Director Information Resources .... Mr. Kenneth G. KOCHIEN
41 Director of Athletics .... Ms. Deborah F. MCGRATH
36 Director of Career Development .... Ms. Kathy J. TAYLOR
88 Asst Dir Acad Development Ctr .... Ms. Caren BALDWIN-DIMEO
44 Dir Annual Giving .... Mr. Christopher S. REED
29 Dir Alumni Relations .... Ms. Tracey M. AUSTIN
19 Director of Campus Safety .... Mr. Peter L. BERTHIAUME
15 Director of Human Resources .... Mr. Tye A. DEINES
09 Director Institutional Research .... Dr. Yi NI
21 Controller .... Ms. Karen I. BONEWALD
40 Bookstore Manager .... Ms. Mairim KILMISTER
92 Coordinator of the Honors Program .... Ms. Ann Page STECKER

*Community College System of New Hampshire (J)

26 College Drive, Concord NH 03301-7407
County: Merrimack Identification: 666462
Telephone: (603) 230-3500 Carnegie Class: N/A
FAX Number: (603) 271-2725
URL: www.ccsnh.edu

01 Chancellor .... Dr. Ross GITTELL
03 Vice Chancellor .... Ronald RIOUX
10 Director of Financial Management .... Michael MARR
15 Director of Human Resources .... Sara SAWYER
27 Director of Communications .... Shannon REID

*Great Bay Community College (K)

320 Corporate Drive, Portsmouth NH 03801-2879
County: Rockingham FICE Identification: 002583
Unit ID: 183150
Telephone: (603) 427-7600 Carnegie Class: Assoc/Pub-R-M
FAX Number: (603) 334-6308 Calendar System: Semester
URL: www.greatbay.edu
Established: 1945 Annual Undergrad Tuition & Fees (In-State): $7,008
Enrollment: 2,172 Coed
Affiliation or Control: State IRS Status: 501(c)3
Highest Offering: Associate Degree
Program: Occupational; 2-Year Principally Bachelor's Creditable
Accreditation: EH, ACBSP, ADNUR, SURGT

02 President .... Mr. Wildolfo ARVELO
05 Int Vice President Academic Affairs .... Ms. Diane KING
84 VP Enrollment Mgmt/Student Svcs .... Dr. Bruce BAKER
06 Registrar .... Ms. Sandra HO
10 Chief Financial Officer .... Ms. Joanne BERRY

*Lakes Region Community College (L)

379 Belmont Road, Laconia NH 03246-1364
County: Belknap FICE Identification: 007555
Unit ID: 183123
Telephone: (603) 524-3207 Carnegie Class: Assoc/Pub-R-S

FAX Number: (603) 527-2042 Calendar System: Semester
URL: www.lrcc.edu
Established: 1967 Annual Undergrad Tuition & Fees (In-District): $6,840
Enrollment: 1,562 Coed
Affiliation or Control: State/Local IRS Status: 501(c)3
Highest Offering: Associate Degree
Program: Occupational; 2-Year Principally Bachelor's Creditable
Accreditation: EH

02 President .... Dr. Scott KALICKI
05 VP of Academic & Community Affairs .... Mr. Thomas GOULETTE
32 VP of Student Services & Enrollment .... Dr. Larissa BAIA
10 Chief Financial Officer .... Mr. John HARRINGTON

*Manchester Community College (A)

1066 Front Street, Manchester NH 03102-8518
County: Hillsborough FICE Identification: 002582
Unit ID: 183132
Telephone: (603) 206-8000 Carnegie Class: Assoc/Pub-R-M
FAX Number: (603) 668-5354 Calendar System: Semester
URL: www.mccnh.edu
Established: 1945 Annual Undergrad Tuition & Fees (In-State): $5,226
Enrollment: 2,918 Coed
Affiliation or Control: State IRS Status: 501(c)3
Highest Offering: Associate Degree
Program: Occupational; 2-Year Principally Bachelor's Creditable
Accreditation: EH, ACBSP, ADNUR, MAC

02 President .... Dr. Susan D. HUARD
05 Vice President Academic Affairs .... John COOK
32 VP Students/Community Development .... Kim KEEGAN
20 Associate VP Academic Affairs .... Joan ACORACE
84 Assoc VP Enrollment Management .... Vacant
26 Director of Communications .... Vacant
37 Financial Aid Officer .... Stephanie J. WELDON
06 Registrar .... Evelyn R. PERRON
08 Librarian .... Melinda MALIK
09 Director Institutional Research .... Dr. Jere TURNER
10 Chief Financial Officer .... Sarah DIVERSI
22 Human Resources Officer .... Alicia CUTTING
40 Bookstore Manager .... Vacant
66 Nursing Director .... Charlene WOLFE-STEPRO
21 Accountant I .... Carol DESPATHY
13 Director Information Technology .... Vacant
35 Director Student Life .... Aileen CLAY

*Nashua Community College (B)

505 Amherst Street, Nashua NH 03063-1092
County: Hillsborough FICE Identification: 009236
Unit ID: 183141
Telephone: (603) 882-6923 Carnegie Class: Assoc/Pub-R-M
FAX Number: (603) 882-8690 Calendar System: Semester
URL: www.nashuacc.edu
Established: 1967 Annual Undergrad Tuition & Fees (In-State): $7,232
Enrollment: 2,278 Coed
Affiliation or Control: State IRS Status: 501(c)3
Highest Offering: Associate Degree
Program: Occupational; 2-Year Principally Bachelor's Creditable
Accreditation: EH, ADNUR, ENGT

02 President .... Ms. Lucille A. JORDAN
32 Vice Pres Student Services .... Ms. Patricia GOODMAN
10 Chief Financial Officer .... Ms. Amber WHEELER
06 Registrar-Nashua .... Ms. Jennifer LEITNER
08 Librarian-Nashua .... Mr. William A. MCINTYRE
37 Financial Aid Officer .... Ms. Lizbeth GONZALEZ
09 Institutional Researcher .... Mr. Phil FRANKLAND
15 Human Resources .... Ms. Catherine BARRY
18 Plant Maintenance Engineer .... Mr. Scott BIENVENUE
26 Marketing/Public Relations .... Ms. Dawn KILCREASE

*NHTI-Concord's Community College (C)

31 College Drive, Concord NH 03301-7412
County: Merrimack FICE Identification: 002581
Unit ID: 183099
Telephone: (603) 271-6484 Carnegie Class: Assoc/Pub-R-M
FAX Number: (603) 230-9311 Calendar System: Semester
URL: www.nhti.edu
Established: 1965 Annual Undergrad Tuition & Fees (In-State): $6,890
Enrollment: 6,890 Coed
Affiliation or Control: State IRS Status: 501(c)3
Highest Offering: Associate Degree
Program: Occupational; 2-Year Principally Bachelor's Creditable
Accreditation: EH, ACBSP, ADNUR, DA, DH, DMS, EMT, ENGT, PNUR, RAD, RTT

02 President .... Ms. Lynn KILCHENSTEIN
32 Vice President Student Affairs .... Mr. Stephen P. CACCIA
35 Associate VP Student Affairs .... Dr. Charles LLOYD
05 Vice President Academic Affairs .... Dr. Pamela LANGLEY
51 Vice Pres Continuing/Corp Education .... Vacant
20 Assoc Vice Pres of Academic Affairs .... Mr. Matt WOOD
84 Assoc VP of Enrollment Management .... Vacant
10 Chief Financial Officer .... Ms. Melanie KIRBY
08 Director Learning Resources .... Mr. Stephen AMBRA
07 Director of Admissions .... Mr. Francis P. MEYER
06 Registrar .... Ms. Michele KARWOCKI
13 Director of Computer Services .... Mr. Thomas TOWLE
18 Director of Facilities Maintenance .... Mr. Michael THERRIEN
27 Director of Communications .... Mr. Alan BLAKE
36 Dir Residence Life/Career Counsel .... Ms. Trish LORING
38 Director Student Counseling .... Ms. Donna DOOLEY
37 Financial Aid Director .... Ms. Sheri GONTHIER
19 Chief of Campus Safety .... Ms. Anne L. BREEN
41 Athletic Director .... Mr. Paul HOGAN
15 Director Human Resources .... Ms. Alyssa LABELLE
28 Dir Cross-Cultural Education/ESOL .... Ms. Dawn HIGGINS
96 Director of Purchasing .... Ms. Irene AUBUT
21 Bursar .... Ms. Jessica BRYAN
105 Website Coordinator .... Ms. Christine METCALF

*River Valley Community College (D)

1 College Place, Claremont NH 03743-9707
County: Sullivan FICE Identification: 007560
Unit ID: 183114
Telephone: (603) 542-7744 Carnegie Class: Assoc/Pub-R-S
FAX Number: (603) 543-1844 Calendar System: Semester
URL: www.rivervalley.edu
Established: 1968 Annual Undergrad Tuition & Fees (In-State): $6,300
Enrollment: 1,347 Coed
Affiliation or Control: State IRS Status: 501(c)3
Highest Offering: Associate Degree
Program: Occupational; 2-Year Principally Bachelor's Creditable
Accreditation: EH, ACBSP, ADNUR, COARC, MAC, MLTAD, OTA, PTAA

02 President .... Dr. Alicia HARVEY-SMITH
05 Vice President Academic Affairs .... Ms. Andrea GORDON
32 VP Student Svcs/Cmty Relations .... Ms. Valerie MAHAR
20 Assoc Vice Pres Academic Affairs .... Dr. Lisa HAYWARD-WYZIK
37 Financial Aid Officer .... Ms. Julia DOWER
06 Registrar .... Ms. Sharon GILBERT
10 Chief Financial Officer .... Ms. Marie MARCUM

*White Mountains Community College (E)

2020 Riverside Drive, Berlin NH 03570-3799
County: Coos FICE Identification: 005291
Unit ID: 183105
Telephone: (603) 752-1113 Carnegie Class: Assoc/Pub-R-S
FAX Number: (603) 752-6335 Calendar System: Semester
URL: www.wmcc.edu
Established: 1966 Annual Undergrad Tuition & Fees (In-State): $7,664
Enrollment: 831 Coed
Affiliation or Control: State IRS Status: 501(c)3
Highest Offering: Associate Degree
Program: Occupational; 2-Year Principally Bachelor's Creditable
Accreditation: EH, MAC

02 President .... Katharine ENEGUESS
05 Vice Pres Academic Affairs .... Vacant
32 Vice President Student Affairs .... Martha LAFLAMME
37 Financial Aid Officer .... Tyler BERGMEIER
10 Business Administrator .... Lynn MOORE
06 Registrar .... Marie BLY
08 Librarian .... Meagan CARR
18 Chief Facilities/Physical Plant .... Stephen DEROSIER
14 Director Computer Center .... Jeffrey SCHALL
91 Director Administrative Computing .... Donald WEEKS
38 Director Student Counseling .... Emily ELLIOTT
22 Dir Affirmative Action/Equal Oppty .... Donna BRIERE
40 Director Bookstore .... Karen SEVIER
07 Director of Admissions .... Mark DESMARAIS

Daniel Webster College (F)

20 University Drive, Nashua NH 03063-1300
County: Hillsborough FICE Identification: 004731
Unit ID: 182661
Telephone: (603) 577-6000 Carnegie Class: Bac/Diverse
FAX Number: (603) 577-6001 Calendar System: Semester
URL: www.dwc.edu
Established: 1965 Annual Undergrad Tuition & Fees: $15,630
Enrollment: 15,090 Coed
Affiliation or Control: Proprietary IRS Status: Proprietary
Highest Offering: Master's
Program: Liberal Arts And General; Professional; Technical Emphasis
Accreditation: EH, AAB, ENG

01 President .... Dr. Michael E. DIFFILY
05 VP Academic Affairs .... Dr. Ben LATIGO
10 Director of Finance & Operations .... Ms. Darla AMMIDOWN
09 Director of Institutional Research .... Ms. Heidi CROWELL
106 Director of Online Operations .... Dr. Jeremy OWENS
04 Exec Assistant to the President .... Mrs. Dee KOUMARIANOS
49 Dean School of Arts and Sciences .... Dr. Kathleen HIPP
88 Dean School of Aviation Science .... Vacant
20 Dean of Academic Affairs Online .... Dr. Deborah JAMESON
50 Dean School of Business Management .... Vacant
54 Dean School Engineering & Comp Sci .... Mr. Nicholas BERTOZZI
07 Director of Admissions .... Ms. Jennifer O'NEILL
08 Library Director .... Ms. Marie MUELLER
06 Registrar .... Ms. Rayann FRYATT
06 Registrar Online .... Ms. Laura CLEAVES
35 Dean of Students .... Ms. Susan ELSASS
36 Director Career Planning/Placement .... Vacant
41 Director of Athletics .... Mr. Chris GILMORE
19 Director of Campus Safety .... Mr. Kevin MOORE
15 Human Resources Generalist .... Ms. Donna BAILEY

Dartmouth College (G)

Hanover NH 03755-4030
County: Grafton FICE Identification: 002573
Unit ID: 182670
Telephone: (603) 646-1110 Carnegie Class: RU/VH
FAX Number: N/A Calendar System: Quarter
URL: www.dartmouth.edu
Established: 1769 Annual Undergrad Tuition & Fees: $46,752
Enrollment: 6,277 Coed
Affiliation or Control: Independent Non-Profit IRS Status: 501(c)3
Highest Offering: Doctorate
Program: Liberal Arts And General; Professional
Accreditation: EH, BUS, ENG, IPSY, MED, PH

01 President .... Dr. Philip J. HANLON
03 Executive Vice President and CFO .... Vacant
101 Secretary to Board of Trustees .... Ms. Marcia J. KELLY
05 Interim Provost .... Dr. Martin N. WYBOURNE
30 Sr Vice President for Advancement .... Mr. Robert W. LASHER
46 Interim Vice Provost for Research .... Dr. Lindsay J. WHALEY
10 Vice Pres Finance .... Mr. Michael F. WAGNER
26 Vice Pres for Communications .... Vacant
28 Vice Pres for Inst Diversity/Equity .... Dr. Evelynn ELLIS
15 Vice Pres Human Resources .... Mr. Myron S. MCCOO
29 Vice President Alumni Relations .... Ms. Martha J. BEATTIE
63 VP Hlth Affs/Dean Geisel Sch of Med .... Dr. Wiley W. SOUBA, JR.
18 Int VP Campus Planning/Facilities .... Mr. William J. ANDERSON
43 General Counsel .... Mr. Robert B. DONIN
20 Dean of the College .... Ms. Charlotte H. JOHNSON
06 Registrar .... Ms. Meredith BRAZ
07 Dean Admiss/Finan Aid/Assoc Provost .... Ms. Maria LASKARIS
37 Director of Financial Aid .... Ms. Virginia S. HAZEN
13 Chief Information Officer .... Ms. Ellen J. WAITE-FRANZEN
08 Dean of Libraries/Librarian of Col .... Mr. Jeffrey L. HORRELL
49 Dean of Faculty of Arts & Sciences .. Dr. Michael MASTANDUNO
50 Dean of Amos Tuck School .... Dr. Paul DANOS
54 Dean of the Thayer School .... Dr. Joseph HELBLE
58 Dean of Graduate Studies .... Dr. F. Jon KULL
88 Dean of Tucker Foundation .... Vacant
41 Director of Athletics .... Mr. Harry SHEEHY
21 Director Integrated Risk Mgmt/Insur .... Ms. Catherine LARK
23 Director of Health Services .... Dr. John H. TURCO
36 Director of Career Services .... Mr. Roger W. WOOLSEY
25 Dir Office of Sponsored Projects .... Ms. Jill M. MORTALI
35 Assoc Dean Student Acad Spprt Svcs .... Dr. Inge-Lise AMEER
19 Director Safety & Security .... Mr. Harry C. KINNE, III
09 Actg Dir of Institutional Research .. Ms. Lynn FOSTER-JOHNSON
38 Dir Counseling/Human Development .... Dr. Mark H. REED
22 Dir Equal Opportunity/Affirm Action .... Dr. Evelynn ELLIS
96 Director of Procurement .... Ms. Tammy L. MOFFATT
88 Chief Investment Officer .... Ms. Pamela L. PEEDIN

Franklin Pierce University (H)

40 University Drive, Rindge NH 03461-5046
County: Cheshire FICE Identification: 002575
Unit ID: 182795
Telephone: (603) 899-4000 Carnegie Class: Master's S
FAX Number: (603) 899-6448 Calendar System: Semester
URL: www.franklinpierce.edu
Established: 1962 Annual Undergrad Tuition & Fees: $29,100
Enrollment: 2,003 Coed
Affiliation or Control: Independent Non-Profit IRS Status: 501(c)3
Highest Offering: Doctorate
Program: 2-Year Principally Bachelor's Creditable; Liberal Arts And General; Teacher Preparatory; Professional
Accreditation: EH, ARCPA, NUR, PTA

01 President .... Dr. James F. BIRGE
05 VP Academic Affairs/Provost .... Dr. Kim MOONEY
10 Vice Pres Finance & Administration .... Mr. Richard MARSHALL
32 Vice President for Student Affairs .... Dr. James P. EARLE
84 Vice Pres Enrollment Management .... Ms. Lisa BUNDERS
30 Vice Pres for Institutional Advance .... Mr. Ahmad BOURA
58 Dean Grad/Professional Studies .... Dr. Doug SOUTHARD
35 Associate Dean Student Affairs .... Mr. Jules TETREAULT
41 Athletic Director .... Mr. Bruce M. KIRSH
07 Director of Admissions .... Ms. Linda QUIMBY
15 Director of Human Resources .... Ms. Janette T. MEREDITH
06 Registrar .... Ms. Tonya B. LABROSSE
08 Director of Library Resource Center .... Ms. Carissa DELIZIO
37 Director of Financial Aid .... Mr. Ken FERREIRA
29 Director of Alumni Affairs .... Ms. Christina YOUNG
12 Academic Dean Rindge Campus .... Dr. Kerry MCKEEVER
27 Dir of Marketing & Communication .... Ms. Michelle MARRONE
36 Director of Career Development .... Ms. Rosemary NICHOLS
20 Dir Center for Academic Excellence .... Ms. Teresa DOWNING
42 Chaplain .... Rev. Bill BEARDSLEE
19 Director Campus Safety .... Ms. Maureen STURGIS
39 Director Residential Life .... Mr. Kenneth ERVIN
18 Chief Facilities/Physical Plant .... Mr. Doug LEAR
21 Director of Financial Services .... Ms. Sandra QUAYE
96 Director of Purchasing .... Mr. Robert ST. JEAN
104 Director Study Abroad .... Mrs. Stella WALLING
40 Manager Follett's Bookstore .... Ms. Kate BROWN

Lebanon College (A)

15 Hanover Street, Lebanon NH 03766-1312
County: Grafton　FICE Identification: 007025
Unit ID: 182908
Telephone: (603) 448-2445　Carnegie Class: Assoc/PrivNFP
FAX Number: (603) 448-2491　Calendar System: Trimester
URL: www.lebanoncollege.edu
Established: 1956　Annual Undergrad Tuition & Fees: $7,400
Enrollment: 315　Coed
Affiliation or Control: Independent Non-Profit　IRS Status: 501(c)3
Highest Offering: Associate Degree
Program: Occupational; 2-Year Principally Bachelor's Creditable; Business Emphasis
Accreditation: ACICS, RAD

01 President ... Dr. Ronald BIRON
05 Academic Dean ... Dr. Dan WHITAKER
06 Registrar ... Ms. Karen GOSSELIN
88 Chair Management Committee ... Mr. Arthur Z. GARDINER
37 Financial Aid ... Ms. Tina POPIELSKI

MCPHS-Manchester Campus (B)

1260 Elm Street, Manchester NH 03101
Telephone: (603) 314-0210　Identification: 770113
Accreditation: &EH

† Main campus is MCPHS University in Boston, MA.

Mount Washington College (C)

3 Sundial Avenue, Manchester NH 03103-7245
County: Hillsborough　FICE Identification: 004729
Unit ID: 182865
Telephone: (603) 668-6660　Carnegie Class: Bac/Assoc
FAX Number: (603) 666-4722　Calendar System: Semester
URL: www.mountwashington.edu
Established: 1900　Annual Undergrad Tuition & Fees: $7,986
Enrollment: 3,006　Coed
Affiliation or Control: Proprietary　IRS Status: Proprietary
Highest Offering: Baccalaureate
Program: Occupational; 2-Year Principally Bachelor's Creditable
Accreditation: EH, MAC, PTAA

01 Interim President ... Dr. Andrew TEMTE
05 Academic Vice Provost ... Dr. Jan WYATT
32 Dean of Student Services ... Vacant
10 Director of Finance ... Mr. David FAXON
37 Executive Director Financial Aid ... Ms. Elizabeth NILSSON
06 Registrar ... Ms. Susan PROVENCHER
08 Director of Library Services ... Vacant
18 Director of Operations/Security ... Mr. Russell BOYNTON
36 Director of Career Services ... Vacant
37 Director Student Financial Aid ... Vacant
04 Assistant to the President ... Mrs. Carol DEWALT

New England College (D)

98 Bridge Street, Henniker NH 03242-3244
County: Merrimack　FICE Identification: 002579
Unit ID: 182980
Telephone: (603) 428-2211　Carnegie Class: Master's M
FAX Number: (603) 428-7230　Calendar System: Semester
URL: www.nec.edu
Established: 1946　Annual Undergrad Tuition & Fees: $33,000
Enrollment: 2,017　Coed
Affiliation or Control: Independent Non-Profit　IRS Status: 501(c)3
Highest Offering: Doctorate
Program: Liberal Arts And General; Teacher Preparatory; Professional
Accreditation: EH

01 President ... Dr. Michele D. PERKINS
05 Int VP for Academic Affairs ... Mr. Mark WATMAN
84 VP of Enrollment and Marketing ... Dr. Barbara LAYNE
10 VP for Finance and Administration ... Ms. Paula A. AMATO
30 Vice President Advancement ... Mr. Morgan SMITH
08 Director of Danforth Library ... Ms. Kathy VAN WEELDEN
32 Dean of Students ... Ms. Laura PANTANO
58 Dean Graduate School ... Dr. Nelly LEJTER
07 Dean of Admissions ... Mr. Yasin ALSAIDI
20 Associate Dean of Academic Services ... Mr. Mark WATMAN
04 Admin Assistant to President ... Ms. Melissa K. STEPHENSON
91 Director of Information Technology ... Mr. Greg SCHOLZ
06 Registrar ... Mr. Frank L. HALL
37 Director Student Financial Svcs ... Ms. Kristen BLASE
21 Controller ... Ms. Betty FARR
18 Dir Campus Facilities/Planning ... Mr. Jay BURGESS
41 Athletic Director ... Ms. Lori RUNKSMEIER
36 Director Career/Life Planning ... Mr. Gene DURKEE
30 Director of Development ... Ms. Meghan HALLOCK
26 Dir of Public Rels/Communications ... Ms. Dia KALAKONAS
15 Human Resources Manager ... Ms. Holly COLE

New Hampshire Institute of Art (E)

148 Concord Street, Manchester NH 03104-4858
County: Hillsborough　FICE Identification: 031823
Unit ID: 430810
Telephone: (603) 623-0313　Carnegie Class: Spec/Arts
FAX Number: (603) 641-1832　Calendar System: Semester
URL: www.nhia.edu
Established: 1898　Annual Undergrad Tuition & Fees: $23,010
Enrollment: 541　Coed
Affiliation or Control: Independent Non-Profit　IRS Status: 501(c)3
Highest Offering: Master's
Program: Fine Arts Emphasis
Accreditation: EH, ART

01 President ... Mr. Roger WILLIAMS
03 Executive Vice President ... Mr. Richard STRAWBRIDGE
10 Vice President for Finance ... Mr. Jim CHATTERTON
30 Vice President of Development ... Ms. Suzanne LENZ
84 Vice President of Enrollment ... Mr. Bob GIELOW
12 Campus Director ... Ms. Keri WIEDERSPAHN
04 Executive Assistant to President ... Mr. Zdzislaw SIKORA
05 Dean of Academic Affairs ... Vacant
58 Associate Dean of Graduate Studies ... Ms. Alison WILLIAMS
08 Library Director ... Ms. Betsy HOLMES
88 Director of Advising ... Vacant
06 Registrar ... Ms. Gail SORA
20 Academic Affairs Administrator ... Ms. Rebecca DESROCHERS
88 Bursar ... Ms. Diane VESCI
32 Director of Student Affairs ... Ms. Paulette CHAPLIN
37 Director Financial Aid ... Ms. Cami CZOHARA
51 Continuing Education Director ... Ms. Karen FRANCIS
15 Director of Human Resources ... Vacant
21 Accounting Manager ... Ms. Mary Anne LA BRIE
21 Business Services Manager ... Ms. Kelly LEVIS
18 Facilities Manager ... Mr. Jonathan WOODCOCK
40 Retail Manager ... Mr. Joe VIVILECCHIA
13 Manager of Information Technologies ... Mr. Drew ROYER
88 IT Specialist ... Mr. Bob MASTERTON
38 Counselor ... Ms. Tanya POPOLOSKI
88 Academic Support Center Coordinator ... Ms. Liza OPPENHEIM

Rivier University (F)

420 S Main Street, Nashua NH 03060-5086
County: Hillsborough　FICE Identification: 002586
Unit ID: 183211
Telephone: (603) 888-1311　Carnegie Class: Master's L
FAX Number: (603) 897-8811　Calendar System: Semester
URL: www.rivier.edu
Established: 1933　Annual Undergrad Tuition & Fees: $27,480
Enrollment: 929　Coed
Affiliation or Control: Roman Catholic　IRS Status: 501(c)3
Highest Offering: Doctorate
Program: Liberal Arts And General; Teacher Preparatory; Professional; Nursing Emphasis
Accreditation: EH, ADNUR, NUR

01 President ... Sr. Paula Marie BULEY
05 Vice President for Academic Affairs ... Sr. Therese LAROCHELLE
10 Vice Pres Finance & Administration ... Mr. Kurt STIMELING
32 Vice Pres Student Affairs ... Mr. Kurt STIMELING
84 Vice Pres Enrollment Management ... Ms. Karen SCHEDIN
30 Vice Pres University Advancement ... Ms. Karen COOPER
35 Asst Vice Pres Student Affairs ... Ms. Paula RANDAZZA
13 Chief Information Officer ... Mr. H. William SCHLEIFER
21 Controller ... Ms. Jennifer YEOMANS
06 Registrar ... Mr. Kevin GATELY
08 Library Director ... Mr. Daniel SPEIDEL
36 Dir Career Development Center ... Ms. Marie SULLIVAN
37 Director Student Financial Aid ... Ms. Valerie PATNAUDE
15 Director Human Resources ... Ms. Diana STRANO
18 Director Facilities Management ... Mr. Richard PERRINE
14 Director Instructional Computing ... Sr. Martha VILLENEUVE
41 Athletic Director ... Ms. Joanne MERRILL
42 Chaplain Campus Ministry ... Bro. Paul DEMERS
28 Director Multicultural Affairs ... Ms. Sharron ROWLETT
29 Dir Alumni Relations/Special Events ... Ms. Mary BOLLINGER
26 Director Marketing/Communication ... Ms. Patricia GARRITY

Saint Anselm College (G)

100 Saint Anselm Drive, Manchester NH 03102-1310
County: Hillsborough　FICE Identification: 002587
Unit ID: 183239
Telephone: (603) 641-7000　Carnegie Class: Bac/A&S
FAX Number: (603) 641-7116　Calendar System: Semester
URL: www.anselm.edu
Established: 1889　Annual Undergrad Tuition & Fees: $35,634
Enrollment: 1,918　Coed
Affiliation or Control: Roman Catholic　IRS Status: 501(c)3
Highest Offering: Baccalaureate
Program: Liberal Arts And General; Teacher Preparatory
Accreditation: EH, NURSE

01 President ... Dr. Steven R. DISALVO
03 Executive Vice President ... Vacant
30 Vice President College Advancement ... Mr. James P. FLANAGAN
11 Vice President for Administration ... Ms. Patricia SHUSTER
84 VP College Mktg & Enrollment Mgmt ... Mr. Brad F. POZNANSKI
32 Vice President Student Affairs ... Dr. Joseph M. HORTON
26 Asst VP of College Comm & Mktg ... Ms. Barbara LEBLANC
05 Dean of the College ... Rev. Augustine KELLY, OSB
10 Chief Financial officer ... Dr. Harry E. DUMAY
06 Registrar ... Ms. MaryAnn ERICSON
07 Director of Admissions ... Mr. Eric NICHOLS
08 Librarian ... Dr. Charles M. GETCHELL, JR.
37 Director of Financial Aid ... Ms. Elizabeth KEUFFEL
35 Dean of Students ... Dr. Alicia A. FINN
36 Director of Career Planning ... Mr. Samuel ALLEN, JR.
20 Director of Academic Advisement ... Ms. Anne E. HARRINGTON
66 Dean of Nursing ... Dr. Sharon A. GEORGE
04 Assistant to the President ... Ms. Janet L. POIRIER
18 Director of Maintenance ... Mr. Donald MOREAU
23 Director of Health Services ... Ms. Maura MARSHALL
29 Asst VP of Alum/Advanc Programming ... Ms. Patricia GUANCI-THERRIEN
41 Director of Athletics ... Dr. Kelly HIGGINS
42 Director of Campus Ministry ... Ms. Susan S. GABERT
09 Director of Institutional Research ... Dr. Hui-Ling CHEN
27 Chief Information Officer ... Mr. Adam R. ALBINA
15 Director Human Resources ... Mr. David HARRINGTON
19 Director Security/Safety ... Mr. Donald DAVIDSON
53 Director Education Planning ... Dr. Laura WASIELEWSKI
28 Director Multicultural Center ... Ms. Oluyemi MAHONEY
39 Director Student Housing ... Ms. Susan WEINTRAUB
96 Director of Purchasing ... Mr. Jacques PLANTE

St. Joseph School of Nursing (H)

5 Woodward Avenue, Nashua NH 03060
County: Hillsborough　FICE Identification: 021404
Unit ID: 183248
Telephone: (603) 594-2567　Carnegie Class: Not Classified
FAX Number: (603) 578-5028　Calendar System: Semester
URL: www.sjhacademiccenter.org
Established: 1964　Annual Undergrad Tuition & Fees: $28,419
Enrollment: 119　Coed
Affiliation or Control: Independent Non-Profit　IRS Status: 501(c)3
Highest Offering: Associate Degree
Program: 2-Year Principally Bachelor's Creditable; Nursing Emphasis
Accreditation: ACCSC, ADNUR, PNUR

01 Executive Director ... Dr. Sherrie PALMIERI

Southern New Hampshire University (I)

2500 N River Road, Manchester NH 03106-1045
County: Hillsborough　FICE Identification: 002580
Unit ID: 183026
Telephone: (603) 668-2211　Carnegie Class: Master's L
FAX Number: (603) 645-9665　Calendar System: Semester
URL: www.snhu.edu
Established: 1932　Annual Undergrad Tuition & Fees: $28,560
Enrollment: 17,454　Coed
Affiliation or Control: Independent Non-Profit　IRS Status: 501(c)3
Highest Offering: Doctorate
Program: Liberal Arts And General; Teacher Preparatory; Professional
Accreditation: EH, ACBSP, ACFEI, @TEAC

01 President ... Dr. Paul LEBLANC
04 Special Assistant to the President ... Ms. Helen DAVIES
05 Provost/Sr VP Academic Affairs ... Dr. Patricia LYNOTT
51 CEO College of Online & Cont Educ ... Mr. Stephen HODOWNES
10 Chief Finance Officer ... Mr. Joseph SERGI
30 VP Institutional Advancement ... Mr. Donald BREZINSKI
20 VP Academic Administration COCE ... Dr. Gregory FOWLER
15 VP Human Resources & Development ... Ms. Danielle STANTON
26 VP Marketing & Communications ... Mr. Gregg MAZZOLA
13 Chief Information Officer ... Mr. John HOLLINGER
43 General Counsel/Secretary to Board ... Ms. Karen D. ABBOTT
50 Dean School of Business ... Mr. William GILLETT
08 Dean of the Library ... Ms. Kathy GROWNEY
49 Dean School of Arts & Sciences ... Dr. Karen ERICKSON
53 Dean School of Education ... Mr. Mark MCQUILLAN
32 Dean of Students ... Ms. Heather LORENZ
20 Assoc VP Academic Affairs ... Dr. Nicholas HUNT-BULL
21 Assoc VP and Controller ... Mr. Darrell KROOK
37 Assoc VP Enrolled Student Services ... Ms. Beverly COTTON
18 Assoc VP Facilities/Physical Plant ... Mr. Robert VACHON
31 Asst Dean Cmty Engaged Learning ... Vacant
88 Executive Director Innovation Lab ... Ms. Kris CLERKIN
07 Director of UG Admissions ... Ms. Bethany PERKINS
06 Registrar ... Ms. Jennifer DISTEFANO
09 Director of Institutional Research ... Mr. Thomas F. BERALDI, JR.
07 Director of Intl Admissions ... Dr. Steven HARVEY
07 Director of Transfer Admissions ... Ms. Julie CALLAHAN
28 Dir Cultural Outreach & Involvement ... Ms. Louisa MARTIN
19 Director of Public Safety ... Mr. James WINN
29 Director of Alumni Relations ... Ms. Kristi DURETTE
23 Director Wellness Center ... Ms. Jeanette GOLDBERG
36 Director of Career Development ... Ms. Beth PRIETO
35 Director of Student Life ... Mr. Scott TIERNO
39 Director of Residence Life ... Mr. Robert SCHIAVONI
41 Director of Athletics ... Mr. Anthony FALLACARO
42 Director of Campus Ministry ... Rev. Bruce COLLARD
92 Director of Univ Honors Program ... Dr. Andrew MARTINO
85 Director of Intl Student Services ... Ms. Dawn SEDUTTO
96 Director of Purchasing & Risk Mgmt ... Mr. Frank EATON
102 Director of Foundation & Corp Rel ... Vacant
14 Director of Computing Resources ... Mr. Daryl A. DREFFS
105 Director of Web Services ... Mr. Curtis KIMBALL
88 Director of Academic Advising ... Ms. Carey GLINES
88 Director of the Learning Center ... Ms. Lori DECONINCK
88 Director of Disability Services ... Ms. Hyla JAFFE
104 Director Study Abroad ... Mr. Stefano PARENTI
90 Assoc Dir of Academic Computing ... Mr. Aaron FLINT
24 AV Services Manager ... Mr. Thomas HELM

The Thomas More College of Liberal Arts (A)

6 Manchester Street, Merrimack NH 03054-4805
County: Hillsborough FICE Identification: 030431
Unit ID: 183275
Telephone: (603) 880-8308 Carnegie Class: Bac/A&S
FAX Number: (603) 880-9280 Calendar System: Semester
URL: www.thomasmorecollege.edu
Established: 1978 Annual Undergrad Tuition & Fees: $19,800
Enrollment: 94 Coed
Affiliation or Control: Independent Non-Profit IRS Status: 501(c)3
Highest Offering: Baccalaureate
Program: Liberal Arts And General; Religious Emphasis
Accreditation: EH

01 President ... Dr. William E. FAHEY
11 Vice President Administration ... Mr. Clint HANSON
30 Vice Pres Institutional Advancement ... Mr. Paul JACKSON
05 Academic Dean ... Dr. Walter THOMPSON
32 Dean of Students ... Mr. Denis KITZINGER
07 Director of Admission ... Ms. Aja COWHIG
06 Registrar ... Ms. Pamela BERNSTEIN
35 Director of Student Life ... Dr. Sara KITZINGER
04 Executive Asst President's Office ... Ms. Valerie BURGESS

*University System of New Hampshire (B)

Dunlap Center, 25 Concord Road,
Durham NH 03824-3545
County: Strafford FICE Identification: 008027
Unit ID: 183327
Telephone: (603) 862-1800 Carnegie Class: N/A
FAX Number: (603) 862-0908
URL: usnh.edu

01 Interim Chancellor ... Dr. Todd J. LEACH
03 Vice Chancellor & Treasurer ... Vacant
15 Director Human Resource Services ... Mr. Robin A. SWITZER
43 General Counsel ... Mr. Ronald F. RODGERS
04 USNH Secretary ... Mr. Ronald F. RODGERS
86 Assoc Vice Chanc Government Affs ... Vacant
05 Assoc Vice Chanc Academic & Student ... Vacant

*University of New Hampshire (C)

105 Main Street, Durham NH 03824
County: Strafford FICE Identification: 002589
Unit ID: 183044
Telephone: (603) 862-1234 Carnegie Class: RU/H
FAX Number: N/A Calendar System: Semester
URL: www.unh.edu
Established: 1866 Annual Undergrad Tuition & Fees (In-State): $16,496
Enrollment: 14,761 Coed
Affiliation or Control: State IRS Status: 501(c)3
Highest Offering: Doctorate
Program: Occupational; 2-Year Principally Bachelor's Creditable; Liberal Arts And General; Teacher Preparatory; Professional
Accreditation: EH, BUS, CS, DIETD, DIETI, DIETT, ENG, ENGT, FOR, IPSY, MFCD, MT, MUS, NRPA, NURSE, OT, PH, SP, SW, TEAC

02 President ... Dr. Mark W. HUDDLESTON
100 Chief of Staff ... Ms. Megan W. DAVIS
05 Prov & VP Academic Affairs ... Dr. Lisa MACFARLANE
10 VP Finance/Administration ... Mr. Richard J. CANNON
46 Sr Vice Provost Research ... Dr. Jane A. NISBET
32 VP Student & Academic Services ... Dr. Mark RUBINSTEIN
26 Assoc VP Univ Communications ... Mr. Justin HARMON
43 General Counsel ... Mr. Ronald F. RODGERS
88 Assoc Prov Academic Administration ... Ms. Leigh Anne MELANSON
28 Vice Prov & Chief Diversity Officer ... Dr. Christine M. SHEA
20 Sr Vice Prov Academic Affairs ... Vacant
16 Assoc VP Chief HR Officer ... Ms. Kathleen A. NEILS
20 Asst Prov AcadAff/MPA Program Dir ... Mr. James S. VARN
88 Sr VP Rsrch & Outreach Scholar ... Dr. Julie E. WILLIAMS
21 Int Assoc VP for Finance ... Ms. Joanna YOUNG
13 Assoc VP Computing/Info Svcs ... Ms. Joanna C. YOUNG
40 Manager of UNH Bookstore ... Vacant
16 Asst VP Human Resources ... Ms. Sari M. BENNETT
21 Assoc VP Business Affairs ... Mr. David J. MAY
18 Asst VP Energy & Campus Development ... Mr. Paul D. CHAMBERLIN
35 Dean of Students ... Dr. Martha A. LAWING
35 Asst VP Stdnt/Acad Svc/Dir Res Life ... Mr. Scott CHESNEY
23 Asst VP SAS/Exec Dir Health Svcs ... Dr. Kevin E. CHARLES
36 Assoc Prov Acad Achievement/Support ... Dr. Judith SPILLER
25 Dir Sponsored Programs ... Mr. Victor SOSA
30 VP Advancement ... Ms. Deborah DUTTON COX
47 Dean Life Sciences/Agriculture ... Dr. Jon M. WRAITH
49 Dean Liberal Arts ... Dr. Kenneth FULD
50 Dean Peter Paul College of Business ... Dr. Daniel E. INNIS
58 Dean Graduate School ... Dr. Harry J. RICHARDS
76 Dean Health & Human Services ... Dr. Michael FERRARA
54 Dean Engineering/Physical Sciences ... Dr. Samuel MUKASA
12 Dean UNH at Manchester ... Dr. Ali RAFIEYMEHR
08 Dean of the University Library ... Dr. Annie DONAHUE
56 Dean/Dir Cooperative Extension ... Dr. John E. PIKE
88 Dir Thompson School Appl Science ... Dr. Regina A. SMICK-ATTISANO
22 Dir Affirmative Action & Equity ... Ms. Donna Marie SORRENTINO
07 Asst VP Stdnt & Acad Svc/Dir Admiss ... Mr. Robert P H. MCGANN
06 Registrar ... Ms. Kathryn P. FORBES
37 Dir Financial Aid ... Ms. Susan K. ALLEN
41 Dir Intercollegiate Athletics ... Mr. Martin SCARANO
38 Dir Counseling Center ... Dr. David CROSS
29 Assoc VP Advance/Exec Dir Alum Assn ... Mr. Stephen J. DONOVAN
39 Dir Housing/Conf Services ... Ms. Kathy IRLA-CHESNEY
19 Exec Dir Public Safety ... Chief Paul M. DEAN
85 Dir Intl Students & Scholars ... Ms. Leila L. PAJE-MANALO
42 University Chaplain ... Pastor Larry BRICKNER-WOOD
96 Dir Purchasing & Contract Svcs ... Ms. Denise M. SMITH
92 Dir Honors Program ... Dr. Sean MOORE
09 Dir Inst Research & Assessment ... Dr. John D. KRAUS
88 Dir Writing Program ... Dr. Edward A. MUELLER
18 Director of Facility Operations ... Mr. Larry VANDESSEL
104 Dir Center International Education ... Dr. Claire L. MALARTE-FELDMAN
94 Coord Women's Studies Program ... Dr. Marla B. BRETTSCHNEIDER

*University of New Hampshire School of Law (D)

Two White Street, Concord NH 03301-4197
County: Merrimack FICE Identification: 020979
Unit ID: 182829
Telephone: (603) 228-1541 Carnegie Class: Spec/Law
FAX Number: (603) 228-1074 Calendar System: Semester
URL: www.law.unh.edu
Established: 1973 Annual Graduate Tuition & Fees: $41,190
Enrollment: 346 Coed
Affiliation or Control: Independent Non-Profit IRS Status: 501(c)3
Highest Offering: First Professional Degree; No Undergraduates
Program: Professional
Accreditation: EH, LAW

02 Dean/President ... Mr. John T. BRODERICK, JR.
04 Executive Assistant to The Dean ... Ms. Linda L. LUGG
05 Associate Dean ... Prof. Jordan BUDD
00 Chairman of the Board ... Ms. Cathy GREEN
10 Vice President Financial Affairs ... Ms. Yvonne BERRY
32 Assistant Dean for Student Affairs ... Ms. Fran CANNING
06 Assistant Dean Registration/Records ... Ms. Lory ATTALLA
84 Chair Admissions Committee ... Prof. Albert SCHERR
08 Director Law Librarian ... Ms. Susan ZAGO
88 Director of Accreditation ... Prof. Margaret S. MCCABE
88 Director of Clinical Programs ... Prof. Peter WRIGHT
36 Assistant Dean for Career Services ... Ms. Donna MILLER
58 Director of Graduate Programs ... Ms. Debbie BEAUREGARD
07 Assistant Dean for Admissions ... Ms. Robin INGLI
30 VP for Institutional Development ... Ms. Karen BORGSTROM
29 Director of Alumni Relations ... Ms. Mary SHEFFER
37 Director of Financial Aid ... Vacant
26 Director of Communications ... Mr. Peter DAVIES

*Granite State College (E)

25 Hall Street, Concord NH 03301-7317
County: Merrimack FICE Identification: 031013
Unit ID: 183257
Telephone: (603) 228-3000 Carnegie Class: Bac/A&S
FAX Number: (603) 513-1389 Calendar System: Trimester
URL: www.granite.edu
Established: 1972 Annual Undergrad Tuition & Fees (In-State): $7,065
Enrollment: 2,018 Coed
Affiliation or Control: State IRS Status: 501(c)3
Highest Offering: Master's
Program: 2-Year Principally Bachelor's Creditable; Liberal Arts And General; Teacher Preparatory; Professional
Accreditation: EH

02 President ... Dr. Todd J. LEACH
100 Chief of Staff ... Ms. Kathleen A. MULLIN
05 Provost & VP for Academic Affairs ... Dr. Laurie A. QUINN
27 Chief Information Officer ... Mr. Michael M. MOROUKIAN
10 Dean of Financial Affairs ... Ms. Lisa L. SHAWNEY
32 Dean of Students/External Engage ... Ms. Tessa H. MCDONNELL
53 Dean of the School of Education ... Dr. Mary J. FORD
20 Vice Provost ... Dr. Scott A. STANLEY
84 Dean of Enrollment Management ... Ms. Mary Beth LUFKIN
06 Registrar ... Ms. Kristin MULLANEY
13 Chief Technical Officer ... Mr. Marty CHANG
24 Director of Educational Technology ... Ms. Reta CHAFFEE
14 Director Enterprise Infrastructure ... Mr. Charles LIPORTO
26 Director of Public Affairs ... Ms. Tiffany EDDY
37 Exec Dir Financial Aid ... Dr. Barbara LAYNE
15 Director of Human Resources ... Ms. Beth DALZELL
09 Director of Institutional Research ... Mr. Jim MILLER
18 Dir of Facilities/Safety/Sustain ... Mr. Peter CONKLIN
08 College Librarian/Senior Lecturer ... Ms. Patricia ERWIN-PLOOG
07 Associate Director of Admissions ... Ms. Ruth NAWN
21 Director of Financial Operations ... Mr. Steve PERROTTA
21 Bursar ... Ms. Jodi WOLBERT
04 Exec Assistant to the President ... Ms. Mary L. YOUNG

*Keene State College (F)

229 Main Street, Keene NH 03435-0001
County: Cheshire FICE Identification: 002590
Unit ID: 183062
Telephone: (603) 352-1909 Carnegie Class: Master's S
FAX Number: (603) 358-2257 Calendar System: Semester
URL: www.keene.edu
Established: 1909 Annual Undergrad Tuition & Fees (In-State): $12,776
Enrollment: 5,060 Coed
Affiliation or Control: State IRS Status: 501(c)3
Highest Offering: Master's
Program: Liberal Arts And General; Teacher Preparatory; Professional
Accreditation: EH, DIETD, DIETI, MUS, TED

02 President ... Dr. Anne E. HUOT
05 Provost/VP Academic Affairs ... Dr. Melinda TREADWELL
32 Vice President Student Affairs ... Dr. Andrew ROBINSON
10 VP Finance & Planning ... Dr. Jay V. KAHN
30 Vice President Advancement ... Ms. Maryann LINDBERG
04 Interim Special Asst to the Pres ... Ms. Barbara HALL
04 Executive Asst to the President ... Ms. Ann M. GAGNON
20 Assoc Provost Academic Affairs ... Dr. Ann RANCOURT
35 Dean of Students ... Dr. Gail ZIMMERMAN
08 Interim Dean of Library ... Dr. Frank WOJCIK
07 Director of Admissions ... Ms. Margaret RICHMOND
06 Registrar ... Mr. Thomas RICHARD
27 Chief Information Officer ... Ms. Laura SERAICHICK
30 Director of Development ... Mr. Ken GOEBEL
15 Human Resources Director ... Ms. Kim HARKNESS
26 Director of Marketing & Comm ... Ms. Kathleen WILLIAMS
37 Director Financial Aid ... Ms. Patricia A. BLODGETT
18 Director Physical Plant ... Mr. Frank MAZZOLA
39 Director of Residential Life ... Mr. Kent DRAKE-DEESE
09 Director of Institutional Research ... Dr. Cathryn TURRENTINE
29 Alumni & Parent Relations Director ... Ms. Patricia FARMER
38 Director Student Counseling ... Dr. Brian QUIGLEY
96 Purchasing Agent ... Mr. James DRAPER
81 Dean of Sciences ... Dr. Gordon LEVERSEE
58 Interim Dean Prof/Graduate Studies ... Dr. Wayne HARTZ
79 Dean Arts & Humanities ... Dr. Andrew HARRIS
28 Chief Officer Diversity/Multicult ... Dr. Dottie MORRIS

*Plymouth State University (G)

17 High Street, Plymouth NH 03264-1595
County: Grafton FICE Identification: 002591
Unit ID: 183080
Telephone: (603) 535-5000 Carnegie Class: Master's L
FAX Number: (603) 535-2654 Calendar System: Semester
URL: www.plymouth.edu
Established: 1871 Annual Undergrad Tuition & Fees (In-State): $12,610
Enrollment: 6,755 Coed
Affiliation or Control: State IRS Status: 501(c)3
Highest Offering: Doctorate
Program: Liberal Arts And General; Teacher Preparatory; Professional; Business Emphasis
Accreditation: EH, ACBSP, ART, CACREP, SW, TED

02 President ... Dr. Sara Jayne STEEN
05 Vice Pres Academic Affairs/Provost ... Dr. Julie N. BERNIER
10 VP for Finance & Administration ... Mr. Stephen TAKSAR
32 Vice President for Student Affairs ... Dr. James HUNDRIESER
20 VP for Undergraduate Studies ... Dr. David ZEHR
30 VP for University Advancement ... Ms. Sally C. HOLLAND
20 Vice Provost Research & Engagement ... Dr. Thad GULDBRANDSEN
58 Associate VP Graduate Studies ... Dr. George F. TUTHILL
13 AVP Info Tech Svcs/Chief Info Ofcr ... Mr. Richard G. GROSSMAN
35 Dean of Students ... Mr. Timothy C. KEEFE
09 Director of Institutional Research ... Ms. Joyce LARSON
06 Registrar ... Mr. George GILMORE
08 Dean of Library & Academic Support ... Dr. David BERONA
84 Asst VP Enroll Mgmt/Dir Admissions ... Mr. Andrew B. PALUMBO
26 Exec Director University Relations ... Mr. Steve BARBA
29 Director of Alumni Relations ... Mr. Rodney EKSTROM
36 Director Career Services ... Mr. James KURAS
37 Director of Financial Aid ... Ms. June SCHLABACH
15 Director of Human Resources ... Ms. Elaine DOELL
19 Chief of Campus Police ... Mr. Creig DOYLE
41 Athletic Director ... Mr. John P. CLARK
18 Director of Physical Plant ... Ms. Ellen SHIPPEE
38 Director of Counseling ... Dr. Michael L. FISCHLER
40 Bookstore Manager ... Mr. Steve RHEAUME
39 AVP Student Affairs - Res Life ... Mr. Frank L. COCCHIARELLA
88 AVP Student Affairs - HUB ... Ms. Terri L. POTTER
96 Manager of Purchasing ... Ms. Heather HUCKINS

*University of New Hampshire at Manchester (H)

400 Commerical Street, Manchester NH 03101-1113
Telephone: (603) 641-4321 FICE Identification: 009009
Accreditation: &EH

† Main campus is University of New Hampshire in Durham, NH.

NEW JERSEY

Assumption College for Sisters (I)

350 Bernardsville Road, Mendham NJ 07945-2923
County: Morris FICE Identification: 002595
Unit ID: 183600
Telephone: (973) 543-6528 Carnegie Class: Assoc/PrivNFP
FAX Number: (973) 543-1738 Calendar System: Semester
URL: www.acs350.org
Established: 1953 Annual Undergrad Tuition & Fees: $10,609
Enrollment: 47 Female

Affiliation or Control: Roman Catholic IRS Status: 501(c)3
Highest Offering: Associate Degree
Program: 2-Year Principally Bachelor's Creditable; Religious Emphasis
Accreditation: M

01 President/Chief of Development ... Sr. Joseph SPRING, SCC
05 Academic Dean ... Sr. Mary Catherine SLATTERY, SCC
06 Dean/Registrar/Admissions ... Sr. Gerardine TANTSITS, SCC
10 Treasurer ... Mrs. Patricia MCGRADY
08 Librarian/Technology ... Sr. Theresa BOWER, SCC
32 Chief Student Life Officer ... Sr. Marie Cecelia LANDIS, SCC

Atlantic Cape Community College (A)

5100 Black Horse Pike, Mays Landing NJ 08330-2699
County: Atlantic FICE Identification: 002596
Unit ID: 183655
Telephone: (609) 343-4900 Carnegie Class: Assoc/Pub-R-L
FAX Number: (609) 343-4917 Calendar System: Semester
URL: www.atlantic.edu
Established: 1964 Annual Undergrad Tuition & Fees (In-District): $3,956
Enrollment: 7,523 Coed
Affiliation or Control: State/Local IRS Status: 501(c)3
Highest Offering: Associate Degree
Program: Occupational; 2-Year Principally Bachelor's Creditable
Accreditation: M, ACFEI, ADNUR, SURGT

01 President ... Dr. Peter L. MORA
05 Vice President Academic Affairs ... Dr. Arthur WEXLER
51 Dean Cape May Camp/Cont Ed/Res Dev ... Dr. Patricia GENTILE
46 Dean Facilities/Planning/Research ... Dr. Richard PERNICIARO
10 Dean Finance and Administration ... Ms. Catherine SKINNER
35 Dean of Students ... Vacant
14 Dean Information Tech Services ... Mr. Douglas HEDGES
15 Dean Human Resources & Compliance ... Ms. Eileen CURRISTINE
20 Dean of Instruction ... Dr. Ronald MCARTHUR
20 Dean of STEM ... Vacant
88 Dean Academy of Culinary Arts ... Ms. Kelly MCCLAY
32 Dir of Stdnt Dev & Judical Officer ... Ms. Nancy PORFIDO
88 Assoc Dean Academic Support Svcs ... Mr. Grant WILINSKI
88 Assoc Dean Aviation/Tech Inst & GIS ... Mr. Otto HERNANDEZ
09 Asst Dean Research & Assessment ... Vacant
101 Exec Asst to Pres/Dir of Board Svcs ... Mr. Sean FISCHER
21 Dean Administration and Business ... Ms. Therese SAMPSON
26 Exec Director College Relations ... Vacant
37 Director Financial Aid ... Ms. Linda DESANTIS
06 Registrar ... Ms. Heather PETERSON
07 Director of Admissions ... Vacant
18 Director Facil Plng & Capital Proj ... Mr. Mark STRECKENBEIN
38 Director of Student Counseling ... Ms. Paula DAVIS

Bais Medrash Toras Chesed (B)

910 Monmouth Avenue, Lakewood NJ 08701-1921
County: Ocean FICE Identification: 040813
Unit ID: 449658
Telephone: (732) 364-1220 Carnegie Class: Spec/Faith
FAX Number: (732) 886-2323 Calendar System: Semester
Established: 1999 Annual Undergrad Tuition & Fees: $8,800
Enrollment: 116 Male
Affiliation or Control: Independent Non-Profit IRS Status: 501(c)3
Highest Offering: Baccalaureate
Program: Professional
Accreditation: RABN

01 Dean ... Rabbi N. STEIN
37 Director of Financial Aid ... Mrs. H. WEISS
10 Bursar ... Rabbi M. GELFAND

Bergen Community College (C)

400 Paramus Road, Paramus NJ 07652-1595
County: Bergen FICE Identification: 004736
Unit ID: 183743
Telephone: (201) 447-7100 Carnegie Class: Assoc/Pub-S-SC
FAX Number: (201) 444-7036 Calendar System: Semester
URL: www.bergen.edu
Established: 1965 Annual Undergrad Tuition & Fees (In-District): $4,147
Enrollment: 17,015 Coed
Affiliation or Control: State/Local IRS Status: 501(c)3
Highest Offering: Associate Degree
Program: Occupational; 2-Year Principally Bachelor's Creditable
Accreditation: M, ADNUR, COARC, DH, DMS, MAC, RAD, RTT, SURGT

01 President ... Dr. B. Kaye WALTER
05 Vice President of Academic Affairs ... Dr. William MULLANEY
32 Vice President Student Services ... Dr. Naydeen GONZALEZ-DE JESUS
11 Vice President of Admin Services ... Dr. Ronald MILON
10 Executive Director of Finance ... Mr. Victor ANAYA
09 Vice Pres of Inst Effectiveness ... Dr. Yun KIM
50 Interim Dean Bus/Social Sci/Pub Svc ... Dr. Andrew TOMKO
79 Dean Arts/Humanities & Wellness ... Prof. Amparo CODDING
17 Dean Health Professions ... Dr. Susan BARNARD
81 Dean Math & Science ... Dr. Pascal J. RICATTO
51 Dean of Continuing Education ... Ms. Christine GILLESPIE
08 Dean Library Services ... Ms. Amy BETH
35 Dean of Student Affairs at Ciarco . Ms. Denise JERMAN LIGUORI
35 Dean of Student Support Services ... Ms. Jennifer REYES
15 Executive Director of Human Resourc ... Mr. James MILLER
18 Acting Director Physical Plant ... Mr. Samuel JOHN
19 Exec Dir of Safety/Security & Cr ... Mr. William CORCORAN
13 Executive Dir of Info Technolgy ... Ms. Sharyne MILLER
06 Mging Dir Registration & Records ... Ms. Jacqueline OTTEY
88 Mgin Dir Community/Cultural Affairs ... Mr. Peter LEDONNE
101 Exec Asst Board of Trustees/Pre ... Ms. Maria FERRARA
29 Managing Dir of Alumni Affairs ... Mr. Joseph CAVALUZZI
88 Mgr Dir Inst of Learning in Retire ... Dr. Ilene KLEINMAN
37 Mging Dir Fin Ops/Stdnt Assistance ... Ms. Caroline OFODILE
102 Exec Dir Foundation/Development ... Ms. Laurie FRANCIS
25 Mging Dir of Grants Admin/Inst Eff ... Dr. William YAKOWICZ
96 Mging Dir of Purchasing & Services ... Ms. Barbara HAMILTON-GOLDEN
26 Managing Dir of Public Relations ... Mr. Lawrence HLAVENKA
04 Exec Assistant to the President ... Dr. Ursula DANIELS

Berkeley College (D)

44 Rifle Camp Road, Woodland Park NJ 07424-3367
County: Passaic FICE Identification: 007502
Unit ID: 183789
Telephone: (973) 278-5400 Carnegie Class: Spec/Bus
FAX Number: (973) 278-0080 Calendar System: Quarter
URL: www.berkeleycollege.edu
Established: 1931 Annual Undergrad Tuition & Fees: $23,100
Enrollment: 2,878 Coed
Affiliation or Control: Proprietary IRS Status: Proprietary
Highest Offering: Baccalaureate
Program: Business Emphasis
Accreditation: M, SURGT

00 Chairman of the Board ... Mr. Kevin L. LUING
01 President ... Dr. Dario A. CORTES
100 Chief of Staff & Assoc VP Planning ... Dr. Linda LUCIANO
04 Special Assistant to the President ... Dr. Rose Mary HEALY
05 Provost ... Dr. Marianne VAKALIS
10 Sr Vice President Finance & Admin ... Mr. Donald DEVINE
84 Sr Vice Pres Enrollment Mgmt ... Ms. Diane RECINOS
26 Senior Vice President Marketing ... Mr. Don CHALLIS
32 VP Stdnt Development & Campus Life ... Dr. Edwin HUGHES
07 VP International Enrollment Svcs ... Ms. Cynthia C. MARCHESE
22 Vice Pres & Compliance Officer ... Mr. William BRANDT
08 Vice President Library Services ... Ms. Marlene DOTY
12 Woodland Park Campus Oper Ofcr ... Ms. Linda PINSKY
12 Newark Campus Operating Officer ... Mr. W. Stan HOLLAND
12 Online Campus Operating Officer ... Ms. Sharon GOLDSTEIN
09 Asst VP Assessment & Inst Research ... Dr. Ross MILLER
50 Interim Dean School of Business ... Dr. Wolfgang HINCK
49 Dean School Liberal Arts ... Dr. Don KIEFFER
107 Dean School Professional Studies ... Dr. Judith KORNBERG
106 Assistant Provost & Dean of Online ... Ms. Carol SMITH
86 Senior Vice Pres External Affairs ... Ms. Teri DUDA
84 Assoc Vice President Enrollment ... Ms. Carol ALLEN-COVINO
38 Sr Director Personal Counseling ... Ms. Sandra COPPOLA
35 Director Student Devel/Campus Life ... Ms. Nicole LUTHMAN-TURNBULL
21 Assoc VP Financial Aid ... Ms. Ursula BISCONTI
37 Senior Director Financial Aid ... Ms. Barbara SYLVESTER
09 VP Student Accts & Inst Research ... Ms. Eileen BERLIN
26 Director Media Relations ... Ms. Ilene GREENFIELD
36 VP Advisement ... Ms. Gail OKUN
41 Athletic Director ... Mr. Brian MAHER

Beth Medrash Govoha (E)

617 Sixth Street, Lakewood NJ 08701-2797
County: Ocean FICE Identification: 007947
Unit ID: 183804
Telephone: (732) 367-1060 Carnegie Class: Spec/Faith
FAX Number: (732) 367-7487 Calendar System: Semester
URL: www.bmg.edu
Established: 1943 Annual Undergrad Tuition & Fees: $17,616
Enrollment: 6,538 Male
Affiliation or Control: Independent Non-Profit IRS Status: 501(c)3
Highest Offering: Beyond Master's But Less Than Doctorate
Program: Teacher Preparatory; Professional
Accreditation: RABN

00 President ... Rabbi A. Malkiel KOTLER
01 Chief Executive Officer ... Rabbi Aaron KOTLER
10 VP Finance/Technology Compliance ... Mr. Isaac LEVINE
43 VP Finance/Corporate/Legal Affairs ... Rabbi Eli KUPERMAN
11 Vice President Admin/Campus Life ... Rabbi Yitzchok S. KOTLER
33 Dean of Students ... Rabbi Mattisyahu SALOMON
58 Dean of Graduate Studies ... Rabbi Yisroel NEUMAN
05 Executive Administrator ... Rabbi Mordechai HERSKOWITZ
86 Director Government Affairs ... Mrs. Chanie JACOBOWITZ
06 Registrar ... Rabbi Jacob BURSZTYN
07 Director of Admissions ... Rabbi Avraham FEUER
08 Director Library/Research Programs ... Rabbi Benjamin SPIEGEL
36 Director of Field Services ... Rabbi Jacob SHULMAN
39 Director Residence Halls ... Rabbi Yosef SLOMOVITS

Bloomfield College (F)

467 Franklin Street, Bloomfield NJ 07003-3425
County: Essex FICE Identification: 002597
Unit ID: 183822
Telephone: (973) 748-9000 Carnegie Class: Bac/A&S
FAX Number: (973) 743-3998 Calendar System: Semester
URL: www.bloomfield.edu
Established: 1868 Annual Undergrad Tuition & Fees: $24,680
Enrollment: 2,044 Coed
Affiliation or Control: Presbyterian Church (U.S.A.) IRS Status: 501(c)3
Highest Offering: Master's
Program: Liberal Arts And General; Teacher Preparatory; Professional
Accreditation: M, NURSE, TEAC

01 President ... Richard A. LEVAO
10 Senior Vice Pres of Admin/Finance ... Howard BUXBAUM
04 Administrative Asst to President ... Christina NOLAN
05 Vice President Academic Affairs ... Marion TERENZIO
07 Interim VP Enroll Mgmt/Admission ... Adam CASTRO
32 VP Student Affairs/Dean of Students ... Patrick J. LAMY
30 Interim VP for Advancement ... Nicole QUINN
72 VP Inst of Tech & Prof Studies ... Peter JEONG
21 AVP for Finance and Administration ... William A. MCDONALD
20 AVP for Academic Development ... Josephine COHN
06 Registrar and Director of Advising ... Eileen M. POLAZZI
09 Director Instnl Research/Assessment ... Eugene W. MULLER
20 Associate Dean for Faculty ... Carolyn I. SPIES
79 Chair Div of Humanities ... Paul GENEGA
83 Chair Div Social/Behavioral Science ... Denise DENNIS
66 Chair Div of Nursing ... Neddie SERRA
81 Chair Div of Natural Science/Math ... Jim MURPHY
57 Chair Div Creative Arts Technology ... Nancy BACCI
50 Chair Div Accounting/Business/CIS ... Robert COLLMIER
53 Chair Div of Education ... Nora KRIEGER
88 Assoc Dean Inst Educ Support Svcs ... Leonard ROBERTS
08 Library Director ... Danilo H. FIGUEREDO
13 Director of Information Services ... Erzsebet FELSOVALYI
36 Director of Career Services ... Carol RUIZ
37 Director of Financial Aid ... Vacant
06 Associate Registrar ... Annette RAYMOND
35 Associate Dean Student Development ... Rose MITCHELL
15 Assoc Director Human Resources ... Janice CECERE
18 Super of Buildings & Grounds ... Jack V. MCGRANE
07 Coordinator of Intl Admissions ... Ninah PRETTO
44 Director Annual Giving/Alumni Rels ... Janis OOLIE
38 Director Personal Counseling ... Jessica DISLA
26 Director Public Rels/Advancemnt Mkt ... Jill ALEXANDER
42 Dir Spirtual Life/Col Chaplain ... Sherry BLACKMAN
88 Director Teacher Education ... Dayna HASSELL
41 Director of Athletics ... Sheila WOOTEN
88 Director Center Academic Develop ... Patricia ARTEAGA
19 Director of Security ... Jack CORTEZ
39 Director Res Educ & Housing ... Rochelle GABRIEL
105 Webmaster ... Vacant
24 Director of Media Center ... Barbara ISACSON
88 Director Office for Instnl Tech ... Yifeng BAI
40 Store Manager ... Roberta STEVENSON

Brookdale Community College (G)

Newman Springs Road, Lincroft NJ 07738-1597
County: Monmouth FICE Identification: 008404
Unit ID: 183859
Telephone: (732) 842-1900 Carnegie Class: Assoc/Pub-S-SC
FAX Number: (732) 224-2242 Calendar System: Other
URL: www.brookdalecc.edu
Established: 1967 Annual Undergrad Tuition & Fees (In-District): $4,297
Enrollment: 14,637 Coed
Affiliation or Control: State/Local IRS Status: 501(c)3
Highest Offering: Associate Degree
Program: Occupational; 2-Year Principally Bachelor's Creditable
Accreditation: M, ADNUR, CAHIIM, COARC, MLTAD, RAD

01 President ... Dr. Maureen MURPHY
03 Executive Vice President ... Dr. Dianna PHILLIPS
10 Vice Pres Business & Finance ... Ms. Maureen LAWRENCE
04 Executive Assistant to President ... Ms. Louise M. HORGAN
46 Vice Pres Plng/Dev/Govt & Comm Rels ... Dr. Webster B. TRAMMELL
13 Executive Director/OIT ... Dr. Patricia KAHN
84 Dean Enrollment Dev/Student Affairs ... Mr. Richard PFEFFER
05 Dean of Academic Affairs ... Dr. Nancy KEGELMAN
15 Dean Human Resources ... Ms. Patricia SENSI
08 Executive Director Library ... Mr. David MURRAY
45 Exec Dir Planning/Assessment/Rsrch ... Mr. Arnold J. GELFMAN
27 Dir Communications & Public Rels ... Ms. Avis MCMILLON
102 Exec Dir Foundation/Alumni Affs ... Mr. Timothy ZEISS
18 Exec Dir Facilities Plng/Engnrng ... Mr. Richard FRANK
32 Director Stdnt Affs/Support Svcs ... Mr. Richard J. PFEFFER
88 Assoc Director/Creative Services ... Ms. Barbara PETERSON
37 Director of Financial Aid ... Ms. Stephanie FITZSIMMONS
25 Director Grants & Institutional Dev ... Ms. Laura V. QAISSAUNEE
38 Director Student Development Svcs ... Dr. Stephen A. CURTO
06 Registrar ... Ms. Kimberly TOOMEY
09 Dir of Institutional Research/Evalu ... Ms. Laura LONGO
26 Dir of Marketing/Creative Services ... Ms. Laurie BENDER
96 Director Material & Printing Svcs ... Mr. Raimondi OTTO
28 Mgr Diversity/Inclusion/Compliance ... Ms. Sondra CANNON

Brookdale Community College Western Monmouth Branch Campus (H)

3680 US Highway 9 South, Freehold NJ 07728
Telephone: (732) 780-0020 Identification: 770125
Accreditation: &M

† Main campus is Brookdale Community College in Lincroft, NJ.

Burlington County College (I)

601 Pemberton-Browns Mills Road,
Pemberton NJ 08068-1599
County: Burlington FICE Identification: 007730
Unit ID: 183877
Telephone: (609) 894-9311 Carnegie Class: Assoc/Pub-S-MC
FAX Number: (609) 894-0183 Calendar System: Semester

URL: www.bcc.edu
Established: 1966 Annual Undergrad Tuition & Fees (In-District): $3,012
Enrollment: 10,071 Coed
Affiliation or Control: State/Local IRS Status: 501(c)3
Highest Offering: Associate Degree
Program: Occupational; 2-Year Principally Bachelor's Creditable
Accreditation: M, ADNUR, CAHIIM, DH, DMS, ENGT, RAD

01 President .... Mr. David C. HESPE
05 Provost .... Dr. David I. SPANG
10 Senior VP Finance and Facilities .... Mr. Ronald BRAND
26 VP of Communications/Comm Rel .... Dr. Kris DIXON
11 VP of Administration .... Mr. Dennis HAGGERTY
88 Interim VP Special Projects .... Dr. Beverly A. RICHARDSON
30 VP Inst Advance/Exec Dir Foundation ..... Ms. Rebecca A. CORBIN
32 VP for Student Success .... Dr. Terrence HARDEE
14 Chief Information Officer .... Mr. Mark MEARA
18 Exec Dir Facilities/Construction .... Mr. Donald HUDSON
09 Exec Dir of Inst Effect & Research .... Mr. Max SLUSHER
37 Acting Exec Dir Enroll Mgmt/Dir FA .... Mr. Michael CIOCE
79 Dean of Liberal Arts .... Dr. Nichole BENNETT-BEALER
81 Dean Science Math & Technology .... Dr. Anand RAMASWAMI
103 Acting Dean Corp Col/Workforce Dev .... Mr. Frank KEITH
66 Assoc Dean of Nursing/Allied Health .... Ms. Charlotte MCCARRAHER
07 Assoc Dean Admissions/ Registration .... Ms. Nyambura M. PHILLIPS
106 Assoc Dean Dist Ed/Integ Learn Res .... Mr. Martin A. HOFFMAN, SR.
88 Assoc Dean Educational Services .... Ms. Sharon ROGERS
35 Assoc Dean Student Act/Campus Pgms .... Ms. Catherine R. BRIGGS
20 Assoc Dean Acad Adv and Programs .... Ms. Tracey THOMAS
88 Assoc Dean of Client Services .... Mr. Roy MILLER
41 Director of Athletics .... Ms. Heather CONGER
21 Director of Business Operations .... Mr. Matthew FARR
36 Director of Career Services .... Ms. Roseanne BUCKLEY
88 Director of Culinary Arts .... Ms. Elizabeth M. DINICE
88 Director of EOF Program .... Ms. Edith CORBIN
25 Director of Grants Administration .... Ms. Barbara WITKOWSKI
88 Director of Military Ed & Vet Svcs .... Ms. Christine ULCH
19 Director of Public Safety .... Mr. Hector GONZALEZ
88 Director of Transfer .... Dr. Robert ARIOSTO

Caldwell College (A)

120 Bloomfield Avenue, Caldwell NJ 07006-5310
County: Essex FICE Identification: 002598
Unit ID: 183910
Telephone: (973) 618-3000 Carnegie Class: Master's M
FAX Number: (973) 618-3300 Calendar System: Semester
URL: www.caldwell.edu
Established: 1939 Annual Undergrad Tuition & Fees: $27,900
Enrollment: 2,213 Coed
Affiliation or Control: Roman Catholic IRS Status: 501(c)3
Highest Offering: Doctorate
Program: Liberal Arts And General; Teacher Preparatory
Accreditation: M, ACBSP, CACREP, NURSE, TEAC

01 President .... Dr. Nancy BLATTNER
05 Vice President for Academic Affairs .... Dr. Patrick R. PROGAR
10 Vice President for Finance & Admin .... Mr. Jack T. RAINEY
16 VP Institutional Effectiveness .... Mrs. Sheila N. O'ROURKE
32 Vice President for Student Affairs .... Sr. Kathleen TUITE
84 Vice President for Enrollment/Comm ..... Mr. Joseph J. POSILLICO
30 Vice Pres Development/Alumni Affs .... Mr. Kevin BOYLE
50 Associate Dean Business Division .... Dr. Bernard C. O'ROURKE
53 Associate Dean Education Division .... Dr. Joan MORIARTY
35 Director International Student Svcs .... Mr. Andrew BRACKETT
88 Exec Director Student Success .... Ms. Joann GONZALEZ-GENERALS
44 Director Development .... Ms. Beth GORAB
29 Director of Gift Planning .... Ms. Kathleen BUSE
06 Registrar & Director Inst Research .... Mr. Ian K. WHITE
08 College Librarian .... Ms. Nancy BECKER
07 Asst Vice President Enrollment .... Mr. Stephen QUINN
58 Director Graduate Studies .... Ms. Vilma MUELLER
88 Assoc Dean External Partnerships .... Vacant
38 Director of Counseling .... Ms. Robin DAVENPORT
39 Director Residence Life .... Ms. Sandra GILOT
13 Exec Director Information Techn .... Mr. Donald O'HAGAN
36 Dir Career Plng & Development .... Ms. Geraldine PERRET
37 Director Financial Aid .... Mr. Hayato SUZUKI
42 Chaplain .... Fr. Albert J. BERNER
41 Executive Director of Athletics .... Mr. Mark A. CORINO
88 Director Technical Support Services . Ms. Roselle LAZA-SCHMITZ
27 Dir Media Relations and Advertising .... Ms. Colette LIDDY
19 Director Campus Safety .... Mr. William B. ORTMAN
91 Director Administrative Technology .... Mr. David BOHNY
15 Director of Human Resources .... Mrs. Michelle STAUSS
35 Director Student Activities .... Mr. Timothy KESSLER-CLEARY
20 Associate Academic Officer .... Dr. Victoria UKACHUKWU

Camden County College (B)

PO Box 200, Blackwood NJ 08012-0200
County: Camden FICE Identification: 006865
Unit ID: 183938
Telephone: (856) 227-7200 Carnegie Class: Assoc/Pub-S-MC
FAX Number: (856) 374-4894 Calendar System: Semester
URL: www.camdencc.edu
Established: 1967 Annual Undergrad Tuition & Fees (In-District): $4,140
Enrollment: 13,807 Coed
Affiliation or Control: State/Local IRS Status: 501(c)3
Highest Offering: Associate Degree
Program: Occupational; 2-Year Principally Bachelor's Creditable
Accreditation: M, CAHIIM, DA, DH, DIETT, MLTAD, OPD

01 President .... Dr. Raymond YANNUZZI
05 Vice Pres Academic Affairs .... Dr. Margaret HAMILTON
30 VP for Institutional Advancement .... Mr. William THOMPSON
41 Athletic Director .... Mr. Peter DILORENZO
15 Executive Director Human Resources .... Ms. Rose COSTON-MCHUGH
26 Dean Communications/Enroll Dev .... Ms. Rosemary SCHAMP
32 Dean Student Support Services .... Ms. Jackie BALDWIN
21 Director Business Office .... Mr. Maris KUKAINIS
08 Library Director .... Ms. Barbara LAYNOR
10 Chief Fiscal Officer .... Ms. Patricia MEEHAN
37 Director of Financial Aid .... Ms. Felicia BRYANT
36 Director Testing/Assessment .... Ms. Eve HIGHSTREET
09 Dean Inst Research/Planning/Grants .... Dr. Marilyn FEINGOLD
18 Exec Dir Safety and Facilities .... Mr. Edward CARNEY
84 Exec Dean Enrollment/Student Svcs .... Dr. James CANONICA
07 Dir Admissions/Registration Svcs .... Ms. Danielle POWERS
12 Exec Dean William G Rohrer Center ... Dr. Robert KACZOROWSKI
81 Dean of Math & Science .... Dr. Susan CHOI
66 Dean Nursing/Health Sci/Human Svcs .... Dr. Anne M. MCGINLEY
50 Dean Div Business/Comptr/Tech Stds .... Dr. Melvin ROBERTS
12 Exec Dean Camden City Campus .... Mr. Gary DIVENS

Camden County College Camden City Campus (C)

200 N Broadway, Camden NJ 08102-1185
Telephone: (856) 338-1817 Identification: 770126
Accreditation: &M

† Main campus is Camden County College in Blackwood, NJ.

Centenary College (D)

400 Jefferson Street, Hackettstown NJ 07840-2100
County: Warren FICE Identification: 002599
Unit ID: 183974
Telephone: (908) 852-1400 Carnegie Class: Master's M
FAX Number: (908) 850-9508 Calendar System: Semester
URL: www.centenarycollege.edu
Established: 1867 Annual Undergrad Tuition & Fees: $28,890
Enrollment: 2,644 Coed
Affiliation or Control: Independent Non-Profit IRS Status: 501(c)3
Highest Offering: Master's
Program: Liberal Arts And General; Teacher Preparatory
Accreditation: M, IACBE, SW, TEAC

01 President .... Dr. Barbara-Jayne LEWTHWAITE
05 Provost & Chief Academic Officer .... Dr. James PATTERSON
10 Chief Operating Officer .... Mr. Roger ANDERSON
26 Sr VP College Relations .... Ms. Diane P. FINNAN
32 Dean of Students .... Ms. Kerry MULLINS
18 Assoc Vice Pres for Operations .... Mr. Todd MILLER
31 Dean Community & College Affairs .... Ms. Nancy PAFFENDORF
07 VP for Enrollment & Sch Prof Stds .... Dr. Dierdre LETSON
09 Dean of Institutional Research .... Mr. Robert MILLER
06 Registrar/Academic Dean .... Dr. Thomas BRUNNER
08 Director Learning Services .... Ms. Suzanne MCCARTHY
36 Director Career Services .... Mr. Michael IRIS
15 Exec Director of Human Resources .... Ms. Virginia GALDIERI
23 Director of Health Services .... Ms. Jean ROBERT
41 Director of Athletics .... Ms. Billie Jo BLACKWELL
19 Director of Security .... Mr. Leonard CUNZ
38 Director of Counseling Center .... Ms. Lorna FARMER
29 Director of Alumni .... Ms. Deana CYNAR
13 Director Technology Services .... Mr. Matthew KELLY
40 Manager of the Bookstore .... Ms. Heidi MCDONNELL

The College of New Jersey (E)

2000 Pennington Road, Ewing NJ 08628-1104
County: Mercer FICE Identification: 002642
Unit ID: 187134
Telephone: (609) 771-1855 Carnegie Class: Master's L
FAX Number: (609) 637-5191 Calendar System: Semester
URL: www.tcnj.edu
Established: 1855 Annual Undergrad Tuition & Fees (In-State): $14,709
Enrollment: 7,270 Coed
Affiliation or Control: State IRS Status: 501(c)3
Highest Offering: Master's
Program: Liberal Arts And General; Teacher Preparatory; Professional
Accreditation: M, BUS, CACREP, CS, ENG, MUS, NURSE, TED

01 President .... Dr. R. Barbara GITENSTEIN
05 Provost/VP Academic Affairs .... Dr. Jacqueline TAYLOR
11 Vice Pres for Administration .... Mr. Curt HEURING
10 Treasurer .... Mr. Lloyd RICKETTS
43 General Counsel .... Mr. Thomas MAHONEY
30 Vice Pres Advancement .... Mr. John DONOHUE
32 Int Vice President Student Affairs .... Dr. Gregory POGUE
15 Vice Pres Human Resources .... Dr. Gregory POGUE
84 Vice Pres Enrollment Management .... Ms. Lisa ANGELONI
101 Exec Asst to Pres/Secy to Board .... Ms. Heather FEHN
18 Assoc VP Facilities & Admin Svcs .... Ms. Kathryn LEVERTON
44 Assoc Vice President of Development .... Mr. Pete MANETAS
35 Assoc VP Student Affs/Dn Students .... Ms. Magda MANETAS
38 AVP Stdnt Affs/Dir Couns/Psych Svc .... Dr. Marc CELENTANA
35 Asst Vice Pres Student Affairs .... Ms. Cecelia O'CALLAGHAN
26 Assoc VP for College Relations .... Ms. Stacy SCHUSTER
20 Interim Vice Provost .... Dr. William BEHRE
57 Dean School of The Arts & Comm .... Dr. John LAUGHTON
50 Dean School of Business .... Dr. John KEEP
79 Dean Sch Humanities/Social Sciences .... Dr. Benjamin RIFKIN
53 Dean School of Education .... Dr. Jeffrey PASSE
54 Dean School of Engineering .... Dr. Steven SCHREINER
66 Int Dean Nursing/Hlth/Exercise Sci .... Dr. Marcia BLICHARZ
81 Dean School of Science .... Dr. Jeffrey OSBORN
58 Dir Grad & Intersession Programs .... Dr. Susan HYDRO
21 Assistant Treasurer .... Ms. Amy MERCOGLIANO
37 Dir of Student Financial Services .... Ms. Anne MACMORRIS
09 Asst Provost Ctr for Inst Effective .... Dr. Mosen AURYAN
41 Director of Athletics .... Mr. John CASTALDO
29 Director Alumni Affairs .... Ms. Lisa MCCARTHY
102 Dir Corp & Foundation Relations .... Mr. Gregory CAIOLA
18 Director of Campus Construction .... Mr. William RUDEAU
23 Assoc Director for Health Services ...... Ms. Janice VERMEYCHUK
06 Exec Director Records/Registration .... Mr. Frank COOPER
19 Chief of Police/Dir Campus Police .... Chief John COLLINS
21 Exec Dir Procure/Fiscal Planning .... Mr. Mark MEHLER
28 Director of EEO/AA/Diversity .... Ms. Kerry TILLETT
07 Director of Admissions .... Ms. Grecia MONTERO
36 Director Career Center .... Ms. Debra KELLY
96 Director of Purchasing .... Ms. Kristine D'APOLITO

College of Saint Elizabeth (F)

2 Convent Road, Morristown NJ 07960-6989
County: Morris FICE Identification: 002600
Unit ID: 186618
Telephone: (973) 290-4000 Carnegie Class: Master's L
FAX Number: (973) 290-4488 Calendar System: Semester
URL: www.cse.edu
Established: 1899 Annual Undergrad Tuition & Fees: $31,095
Enrollment: 1,687 Coed
Affiliation or Control: Roman Catholic IRS Status: 501(c)3
Highest Offering: Doctorate
Program: Liberal Arts And General; Teacher Preparatory
Accreditation: M, DIETD, DIETI, NUR, TEAC

01 President .... Dr. Helen STREUBERT
05 Int VP Academic Affs/Dean of Stds .... Dr. Carol STROBECK
32 VP Student Affairs/Dean of Students .... Ms. Katherine BUCK
10 VP Finance/Administration/Treasurer . Ms. Maria R. CAMMARATA
30 Vice Pres Institutional Advancement .... Ms. Deborah M. MCCREERY
21 Asst VP Finance & Admin .... Mr. Anthony COLABRARO
07 Dean of Admission .... Ms. Donna TATARKA
20 Asst Dean Undergrad Programs .... Ms. Jane BOURHILL
06 Registrar .... Vacant
13 Chief Technology Officer .... Mr. Brad MORTON
09 Director Institutional Research .... Dr. Louise MURRAY
73 Dir DePaul Ctr/Mission & Values .... Ms. Carol PISANI
08 Director of Library .... Ms. Amira UNVER
42 Campus Minister .... Vacant
18 Director of Facilities .... Mr. Frank A. NEGLIA
37 Director of Financial Aid .... Vacant
27 Director Marketing/ Communications .... Ms. Donna M. LINDEMEYER
22 Director EOF Program .... Ms. Carolina E. GONZALEZ
36 Director Career Services .... Ms. Teri CORSO
39 Director of Residence Life .... Ms. Meredith NOVKOVIC
38 Director of Counseling .... Ms. Sharon MCNULTY
88 Director of Volunteer Services .... Ms. Nanette SPEDDEN
35 Director of Student Activities .... Ms. Leigh Anne WALTERS
41 Director of Athletics .... Ms. Juliene SIMPSON
90 Director of Academic Computing .... Ms. Kathy MARINO
91 Dir Application Devel & Support .... Ms. Ana M. FIGUEROA
44 Director of Annual Fund .... Ms. Tanya SORCE
24 Director Media Services .... Mr. Ronald LONEKER
29 Exec Director Alumnae Association .... Ms. Debbie MARTIN
15 Director Human Resources .... Ms. Dianna SOFO
84 Director of Enrollment Management .... Mr. Jonathan S. WHITE
85 Director Intl/Multicultural Affairs .... Ms. Lenee WOODSON
28 Asst Dir Intl/Multicultural Affairs .... Ms. Maya BLEY
19 Securitas Site Manager .... Mr. Donald GREEN
40 College Store Manager .... Ms. Amy HAUSMAN
88 Acad Advisor Intl Sisters Educ .... Sr. Gabriel M. DONAHUE
04 Spec Asst to Pres Mission/Values .... Ms. Carol PISANI

County College of Morris (G)

214 Center Grove Road, Randolph NJ 07869-2086
County: Morris FICE Identification: 007729
Unit ID: 184180
Telephone: (973) 328-5000 Carnegie Class: Assoc/Pub-S-SC
FAX Number: (973) 328-1282 Calendar System: Semester
URL: www.ccm.edu
Established: 1965 Annual Undergrad Tuition & Fees (In-District): $4,155
Enrollment: 8,679 Coed
Affiliation or Control: State/Local IRS Status: 501(c)3
Highest Offering: Associate Degree
Program: Occupational; 2-Year Principally Bachelor's Creditable
Accreditation: M, ACBSP, ADNUR, COARC, ENGT, RAD

01 President .... Dr. Edward J. YAW
05 Vice President of Academic Affairs .... Dr. Dwight L. SMITH
10 Vice President of Business/Finance .... Ms. Karen VANDERHOOF
32 VP of Student Dev/Enrollment Mgmt .... Dr. Bette M. SIMMONS
30 Exec Dir Col Advancement/Planning .... Mr. Joseph VITALE
15 Dir Human Resources & Labor Rels .... Mr. Thomas BURK

09	Director Inst Research & Planning	Ms. Phebe LACAY
21	Director Budget & Business Services	Mr. John YOUNG
25	Director Resource Development	Dr. Kevin KEEFE
07	Admissions Officer	Vacant
37	Director Financial Aid	Mr. Harvey WILLIS
06	Associate Registrar	Ms. Karen WHITMORE
06	Registrar	Ms. Michelle DUNN
26	Chief Public Relations Officer	Ms. Kathleen BRUNET EAGAN
29	Director Alumni Office	Ms. Barbara CAPSOURAS
13	Director Information Systems	Mr. Roger FLAHIVE
08	Director of Library Services	Ms. Heather CRAVEN
36	Director Career Svcs/Coop Education	Ms. Denise SCHMIDT
38	Counseling Services Coordinator	Ms. Janique CAFFIE
79	Dean Liberal Arts	Dr. Keith SMITH
76	Dean Health/Natural Sciences	Ms. Joan CUNNINGHAM
81	Dean Business/Math/Engr/Technology	Mr. Patrick ENRIGHT
31	Dean Corp & Community Programs	Dr. Jane ARMSTRONG
19	Director Security & Safety	Mr. Harvey JACKSON
41	Director Athletics	Mr. Jack SULLIVAN
23	Health Services Coordinator	Ms. Elizabeth HOBAN
18	Director of Plant & Maintenance	Mr. Joseph PONTURO
96	Director of Purchasing	Ms. Joanne KEARNS
40	Bookstore Manager	Mr. Abdelilan ENNASSEF

Cumberland County College (A)

3322 College Drive, PO Box 1500,
Vineland NJ 08362-1500

County: Cumberland — FICE Identification: 002601
Unit ID: 184205
Telephone: (856) 691-8600 — Carnegie Class: Assoc/Pub-R-M
FAX Number: (856) 691-3876 — Calendar System: Semester
URL: www.cccnj.edu
Established: 1963 — Annual Undergrad Tuition & Fees (In-District): $4,200
Enrollment: 3,944 — Coed
Affiliation or Control: State/Local — IRS Status: 501(c)3
Highest Offering: Associate Degree
Program: Occupational; 2-Year Principally Bachelor's Creditable
Accreditation: M, ADNUR, RAD

01	President	Dr. Thomas A. ISEKENEGBE
05	VP Academic Affairs/Enrollment Svcs	Dr. Jacqueline GALBIATI
10	Vice President Finance & Admin Svcs	Mr. John K. PITCHER
30	Exec Dir Grant Develop/Trustee Rels	Ms. Anne M. BERGAMO
21	Director Finance & Budget	Ms. Sherri L. WELCH
07	Director of Admissions/Registration	Ms. Anne M. DALY-EIMER
32	Sr Exec Dir Student Svcs	Mr. Joseph L. HIBBS
08	Director Library Services	Ms. Patti A. SCHMID
88	Ex Dir Ctr for Acad & Student Succ	Dr. Maud FRIED-GOODNIGHT
26	Director Comm/Marketing	Vacant
29	Exec Dir Foundation & Alumni	Ms. Sue A. PERRY
37	Director Student Financial Aid	Ms. Kim HENRY-MITCHELL
88	Acting Director University Ctr	Ms. Valerie GOUSE
50	Acting DeanBusiness/Educ/Soc Sci	Dr. Lynn LICHTENBERGER
51	Exec Dir Prof & Community Education	Ms. Vicki SIMEK
76	Dean STEM/Health	Dr. MaryAnn WESTERFIELD
57	Dean Arts & Humanities	Mr. James PICCONE
100	Assistant to the President	Ms. Anne M. BERGAMO
15	Executive Director Human Resources	Ms. Patricia N. BRINING
72	Chief Technology Officer	Mr. Douglas WHITE
18	Director Facilities & Grounds	Mr. Brian EWAN
96	Purchasing Agent	Ms. Cynthia OSTER
09	Exec Dir Assessment/Plng/Research	Ms. Rebecca SHEPPARD

DeVry University - North Brunswick Campus (B)

630 US Highway One, North Brunswick NJ 08902-3362
Telephone: (732) 729-3960 — FICE Identification: 009228
Accreditation: &NH, CAHIIM, ENGT, NDT

† Main campus is DeVry University - Chicago Campus in Chicago, IL.

Drew University (C)

36 Madison Avenue, Madison NJ 07940-1493
County: Morris — FICE Identification: 002603
Unit ID: 184348
Telephone: (973) 408-3000 — Carnegie Class: Bac/A&S
FAX Number: N/A — Calendar System: 4/1/4
URL: www.drew.edu
Established: 1866 — Annual Undergrad Tuition & Fees: $42,936
Enrollment: 2,447 — Coed
Affiliation or Control: Independent Non-Profit — IRS Status: 501(c)3
Highest Offering: Doctorate
Program: Liberal Arts And General; Professional
Accreditation: M, @TEAC, THEOL

01	Interim President	Dr. Vivian BULL
11	Vice President Admin/Univ Relations	Dr. Margaret HOWARD
30	Vice Pres Devel/Alumni Affairs	Dr. Kenneth ALEXO
10	Vice Pres Finance/Business Affairs	Mr. Michael GROENER
20	Vice President & Dean of College	Dr. Alan CANDIOTTI
73	Vice Pres/Dean Theological School	Dr. Ginny SAMUEL
08	Dean of the Libraries	Dr. Andrew SCRIMGEOUR
32	Dean Campus Life & Student Affs	Dr. Sara WALDRON
26	Chief Communications Officer	Mr. David MUHA
15	Director of Human Resources	Vacant
22	Affirmative Action Officer	Dr. George-Harold JENNINGS
90	Dir Instructional Technology Svcs	Ms. Gamin BARTLE
21	Controller	Mr. Frank MALTINO
96	Director Purchasing	Vacant
18	Director Facilities Operations	Mr. Michael KOPAS
37	Dir Finan Assistance/Col Admissions	Ms. Renee VOLAK
19	Director Public Safety	Mr. Robert LUCID
23	Director Health Services	Ms. Joyce MAGLION
39	Director Housing/Conf/Hospitality	Ms. Patricia NAYLOR
35	Director Student Activities	Ms. Michelle BRISSON
38	Director Counseling Services	Dr. Jim MANDALA
07	Director Theological Admissions	Mr. Kevin D. MILLER
07	Director Graduate Admissions	Ms. Carla BURNS
58	Dean of Casperson Sch Grad Stdy	Dr. Robert READY
42	University Chaplain	Rev. Tanya Lynn BENNETT
09	Director Institutional Research	Dr. John MUCCIGROSSO
84	Director Enrollment Management	Mr. Mark KAPENSKI
41	Director Athletics	Mr. Jason FEIN
06	Registrar	Ms. Patricia SEUNARINE
28	Special Asst to Prov for Diversity	Dr. Carlos YORDAN
40	Manager Bookstore	Ms. Liz GALLO

Eastern International College (D)

251 Washington Avenue, Belleville NJ 07109
Telephone: (973) 751-9051 — Identification: 770580
Accreditation: ACCSC

† Main campus is Eastern International College in Jersey City, NJ.

Eastern International College (E)

3000 Kennedy Blvd, Ste 310, Jersey City NJ 07306
County: Hudson — FICE Identification: 031226
Unit ID: 421878
Telephone: (201) 216-9901 — Carnegie Class: Assoc/PrivFP
FAX Number: (201) 216-9225 — Calendar System: Semester
URL: www.eicollege.edu
Established: 1990 — Annual Undergrad Tuition & Fees: $22,500
Enrollment: 7,500 — Coed
Affiliation or Control: Proprietary — IRS Status: Proprietary
Highest Offering: Associate Degree
Program: Occupational
Accreditation: ACCSC, DH

01	President	Mr. Bashir MOHSEN
05	Vice President of Academic Affairs	Dr. Mustafa MUSTAFA

Eastwick College (F)

250 Moore Street, Hackensack NJ 07601
County: Bergen — Identification: 667131
Telephone: (201) 488-9400 — Carnegie Class: Not Classified
FAX Number: (201) 488-1007 — Calendar System: Quarter
URL: www.eastwick.edu
Established: — Annual Undergrad Tuition & Fees: $24,900
Enrollment: N/A — Coed
Affiliation or Control: Proprietary — IRS Status: Proprietary
Highest Offering: Associate Degree
Program: Occupational
Accreditation: ACICS

01	President	Thomas EASTWICK

Eastwick College (G)

10 South Franklin Turnpike, Ramsey NJ 07446
FICE Identification: 020537
Unit ID: 184959
Telephone: (201) 327-8877 — Carnegie Class: Assoc/PrivFP
FAX Number: (201) 327-9054 — Calendar System: Other
URL: www.eastwick.edu
Established: 1968 — Annual Undergrad Tuition & Fees: $18,377
Enrollment: 1,119 — Coed
Affiliation or Control: Proprietary — IRS Status: Proprietary
Highest Offering: Associate Degree
Program: Occupational; 2-Year Principally Bachelor's Creditable; Nursing Emphasis
Accreditation: ACICS, SURGT

01	Corporate Systems Administrator	Antonio JEREZ
05	Vice President Academic Affairs	Joyce TRAINA
32	Dean of Students	Bobby DAVIES
37	Director of Financial Aid	Christy DELAGUERRA

Essex County College (H)

303 University Avenue, Newark NJ 07102-1798
County: Essex — FICE Identification: 007107
Unit ID: 184481
Telephone: (973) 877-3000 — Carnegie Class: Assoc/Pub-U-MC
FAX Number: (973) 877-3044 — Calendar System: Other
URL: www.essex.edu
Established: 1966 — Annual Undergrad Tuition & Fees (In-District): $3,384
Enrollment: 11,979 — Coed
Affiliation or Control: State/Local — IRS Status: 501(c)3
Highest Offering: Associate Degree
Program: Occupational; 2-Year Principally Bachelor's Creditable
Accreditation: M, ADNUR, ENGT, OPD, PTAA, RAD

01	Interim President	Dr. Gale E. GIBSON
100	Acting Exec Dir/Pres Initiatives	Mr. Courtney INNISS
101	Acting Exec Asst to the President	Mrs. NaKesha DAVIS
05	Acting VP & Chief Academic Ofcr	Dr. Edwin KNOX
49	Dean of Liberal Arts & Sciences	Dr. Stephanie STEPLIGHT-JOHNSON
50	Acting Dean Business & Government	Mr. Carlos RIVERA
81	Acting Dean STEM	Dr. Alvin WILLIAMS
10	Acting VP Administration & Finance	Dr. Joyce W. HARLEY
21	Comptroller	Mrs. Avril GEORGE-ROBINSON
43	General Counsel	Ms. Rashidah HASAN
45	Exec Dean Institutional Advancement	Dr. Susan MULLIGAN
108	Director Academic Assessment	Dr. Douglas WALCERZ
51	Exec Dean Community & Cont Ed	Mr. Charles G. LOVALLO
13	Exec Dean/CIO Admin & Learning Tech	Mr. Mohamed SEDDIKI
32	Exec Dean of Student Success	Dr. Felix LINFANTE
88	Asst Dean Academic Foundations	Dr. Leigh BELLO-DECASTRO
35	Assistant Dean Student Success	Mrs. Charlotte ATTENBOROUGH
09	Director Institutional Research	Dr. Jinsoo PARK
35	Asst Dean Recruitment & Marketing	Ms. Marva MACK
12	Assoc Dean West Essex Campus	Dr. Elvira VIEIRA
08	Director MLK Library	Mrs. Gwendolyn SLATON
35	Asst Dean Student Life & Activities	Ms. Patricia SLADE
18	Director Facilities Mgmt	Mr. Jeff SHAPIRO
19	Director Public Safety	Mr. Anthony CROMARTIE
26	Director Marketing & Communications	Mrs. Marsha MCCARTHY
30	Director of Development	Mrs. Coleen PORCHER
15	Director of Human Resources	Ms. Jeannette ROBINSON
96	Director Purchasing	Mrs. Marylyn RUTHERFORD
37	Director Financial Aid	Mrs. Mildred COFER
84	Asst Dean Registration	Ms. Zewdnesh KASSA
21	Director Bursar's Office	Ms. Darlene MILLER
36	Director Student Development	Ms. Pamela MAYNARD
88	Director Child Development Center	Ms. Deloris GRIMSLEY
41	Director Athletics	Mr. Melvin KNIGHT
24	Director Media Prod Tech	Mrs. Nadine ABRAM
55	Director College Information Cntr	Mr. Ronald ROSS
00	President Emeritus	Dr. A. Zachary YAMBA

Essex County College-West Essex Branch Campus (I)

730 West Bloomfield Avenue, West Caldwell NJ 07006
Telephone: (973) 877-6590 — Identification: 770127
Accreditation: &M

† Main campus is Essex County College in Newark, NJ.

Fairleigh Dickinson University (J)

1000 River Road, Teaneck NJ 07666-1996
County: Bergen — FICE Identification: 002607
Unit ID: 184603
Telephone: (201) 692-2000 — Carnegie Class: Master's L
FAX Number: N/A — Calendar System: Semester
URL: www.fdu.edu
Established: 1942 — Annual Undergrad Tuition & Fees: $33,920
Enrollment: 12,783 — Coed
Affiliation or Control: Independent Non-Profit — IRS Status: 501(c)3
Highest Offering: Doctorate
Program: Occupational; 2-Year Principally Bachelor's Creditable; Liberal Arts And General; Teacher Preparatory; Professional
Accreditation: M, BUS, CACREP, CLPSY, CS, ENG, ENGT, NURSE, @PHAR, TEAC

01	President	Mr. Sheldon DRUCKER
43	University Counsel/Secretary	Mr. John CODD
05	Univ Provost/VPAA	Dr. Christopher CAPUANO
30	Sr Vice Pres University Advancement	Mr. Richard REISS
03	Senior Vice President & CEO	Vacant
10	Vice Pres for Finance & Treasurer	Ms. Hania FERRARA
11	Vice President for Administration	Mr. Richard A. RICCIO
84	Vice Pres for Enrollment Management	Mr. Jon WEXLER
13	VP/Chief Information Officer	Mr. Neal M. STURM
26	Associate VP Communications	Mr. Angelo CARFAGNA
16	Associate VP Human Resources	Ms. Rose D'AMBROSIO
29	Director Alumni Affairs	Mr. Okang MCBRIDE
12	Dean Petrocelli Col of Cont Stds	Mr. Kenneth T. VEHRKENS
49	Dean Becton Col of Arts & Sci	Dr. Geoffrey WEINMAN
50	Interim Dean College Business Admin	Dr. James ALMEIDA
20	Dean University College	Dr. Patti MILLS
32	Dean of Students-Teaneck Campus	Ms. Michelle MCCROY-HEINS
32	Dean of Students-Madison Campus	Dr. Jas VEREM
08	Assoc University Librarian-Florham	Vacant
08	Associate University Librarian-Met	Ms. Kathy STEIN-SMITH
51	Director Continuing Education	Dr. Thomas SWANZEY
26	Dir Public Administration Institute	Dr. William ROBERTS
38	Director Psychology	Dr. Ronald DUMONT
21	Director Internal Audit	Mr. Peter FORMAN
53	Director School of Education	Dr. Vicki COHEN
66	Director Sch of Nurs/Allied Health	Dr. Minerva GUTTMAN
88	Director Sch Hotel/Restaurant Mgmt	Vacant
41	Director of Athletics-Teaneck	Mr. David LANGFORD
41	Director of Athletics-Madison	Mr. William KLIKA
07	Univ Dir of Undergrad Admissions	Mr. Andrew IPPOLITO
09	Director of Institutional Research	Ms. Indira GOVINDAN
37	University Director Financial Aid	Ms. Susan GROSS
19	Campus Dir Public Safety/F/M Campus	Ms. Willie THORNTON
20	Provost Metropolitan Campus	Dr. Joseph KIERNAN
12	Provost Florham/Madison Campus	Dr. Peter WOOLLEY
19	Univ Dir Public Safety/T/H Campus	Mr. David A. MILES
96	Director of Purchasing	Ms. Juliette BROOKS

Felician College (A)

262 S Main Street, Lodi NJ 07644-2198
County: Bergen FICE Identification: 002610
Unit ID: 184612
Telephone: (201) 559-6000 Carnegie Class: Master's S
FAX Number: (201) 559-6188 Calendar System: Semester
URL: www.felician.edu
Established: 1942 Annual Undergrad Tuition & Fees: $29,990
Enrollment: 2,109 Coed
Affiliation or Control: Roman Catholic IRS Status: 501(c)3
Highest Offering: Doctorate
Program: Liberal Arts And General; Teacher Preparatory; Professional
Accreditation: M, IACBE, NURSE, TEAC

01 President ... Dr. Anne PRISCO
03 Senior Exec Vice President ... Dr. Charles J. ROONEY
05 Provost/Vice Pres Acad Affairs ... Sr. Mary Rosita BRENNAN
20 Asst VP Academic Support Services ... Dr. Ann V. GUILLORY
30 Vice Pres Institutional Advancement ... Vacant
21 Vice President for Finance ... Mr. Michael FESCOE
32 Vice President for Student Affairs ... Dr. James FITZPATRICK
11 VP Administration/Enrollment/Plng ... Ms. Francine ANDREA
04 Admin Assistant to the President ... Ms. Meggan O'NEILL
06 Registrar ... Vacant
07 Assoc VP Undergrad Enroll Services ... Mr. Steven E. GOETSCH
07 Assoc VP Adult/Grad & Intl Enroll ... Mr. Michael SZAREK
08 Director of the Library ... Mr. Paul GLASSMAN
09 Director Institutional Research ... Dr. Jerry TROMBELLA
15 Director of Human Resources ... Ms. Virginia TOPOLSKI
88 Director Conferences and Event Plng ... Ms. Maria MALLIA
37 Director Student Financial Aid ... Ms. Cynthia MONTALVO
29 Director of Alumni Relations ... Ms. Lori WALKER
42 Director Campus Ministry/Chaplain ... Vacant
39 Director of Residence Life ... Ms. Laura BARRY
36 Director of Career Counseling ... Ms. Melissa FAULKNER
13 Asst VP of Information Technology ... Mr. Christopher FINCH
24 Director A-V Center ... Mr. Anthony KLYMENKO
88 Assoc Director Center for Learning ... Mr. Hamdi SHAHIN
26 Director of Institutional Communica ... Ms. Angela DAIDONE
26 Dir Inst Marketing & Publications ... Ms. Barbara PURDUE-LYNCH
40 Manager College Bookstore ... Ms. Beth LIGNOWSKI
76 Dean School of Nursing ... Dr. Muriel SHORE
53 Dean School of Education ... Dr. Rose RUDNITSKI
49 Dean School of Arts & Science ... Dr. Edward KUBERSKY
50 Dean School of Business ... Dr. Beth CASTIGLIA
88 Dean Assessment/Fac Excellence ... Dr. Dolores HENCHY
88 Director EOF Program ... Ms. Dinelia GARDNER
104 Director Study Abroad Program ... Mr. Carlo COLECCHIA
85 Director of International Programs ... Ms. Corinne SPRING
23 Director Health Services ... Ms. Carolyn LEWIS
41 Director of Athletics ... Mr. Benjamin DI NALLO
92 Director Honors Program ... Dr. Maria VECCHIO
91 Director Administrative Computing ... Mr. John PANNEGGIANTE

Georgian Court University (B)

900 Lakewood Avenue, Lakewood NJ 08701-2697
County: Ocean FICE Identification: 002608
Unit ID: 184773
Telephone: (732) 987-2200 Carnegie Class: Master's L
FAX Number: N/A Calendar System: Semester
URL: www.georgian.edu
Established: 1908 Annual Undergrad Tuition & Fees: $29,606
Enrollment: 2,313 Coed
Affiliation or Control: Roman Catholic IRS Status: 501(c)3
Highest Offering: Master's
Program: Liberal Arts And General; Teacher Preparatory; Professional
Accreditation: M, ACBSP, NURSE, SW, TEAC

01 President ... Sr. Rosemary JEFFRIES
05 Provost ... Ms. Evelyn QUINN
10 Chief Financial Officer/VP Finance ... Mr. Robert KENNY
30 Vice Pres Institutional Advancement ... Ms. Mellissia ZANJANI
20 Assoc Provost Academic Pgm Devel ... Dr. Michael GROSS
84 VP of Enrollment Management ... Mr. John MCAULIFFE
32 Dean of Students ... Ms. Karen GOFF
88 Director of Advising ... Mrs. Carol A. LIPPIN
42 Director of Campus Ministry ... Sr. Mariann MAHON
41 Director Athletics/Recreation ... Ms. Laura LIESMAN
88 Dir Academic Development Center ... Vacant
50 Dean School of Business ... Dr. Janice WARNER
53 Dean of School of Education ... Dr. Lynn DECAPUA
49 Dean School of Arts & Sciences ... Dr. Rita KIPP
09 Director of Institutional Research ... Mr. Wayne S. ARNDT
08 Int Director of Library Services ... Ms. Mary BASSO
06 Registrar ... Ms. Christina REEVES
21 Controller ... Mrs. Maureen RYAN-HOFFMAN
15 Director of Human Resources ... Ms. Linda PIERCE
13 Chief Information Officer ... Mr. Steve CAROL
07 Director Undergraduate Admissions ... Ms. Tracey HOWARD-UBELHOER
37 Director of Student Accounts ... Ms. Linda PAGAN
26 Dir Public Rels/Col Communications ... Ms. Gail TOWNS
31 Dir Conferences & Special Events ... Ms. Mary E. CRANWELL
44 Dir Devel Alumni and Annual Giving ... Ms. Alice VELEZ
36 Director Career Development ... Mrs. Catherine MOORE
38 Director of Counseling ... Dr. Robin SOLBACH
23 Director of Health Services ... Ms. Cynthia MATTIA
22 Affirmative Action Officer ... Ms. Linda PIERCE
18 Director of Facilities ... Mr. Mark BIANCHI
96 Director of Purchasing ... Mr. Thomas BARANOWSKI

19 Director of Security ... Mr. Thomas ZAMBRANO
09 Dir Ofc Assessment/Intl Research ... Dr. Pamela SCHNEIDER
07 Director Graduate Admissions ... Mr. Patrick GIVENS
39 Director of Residence Life ... Mr. Gary MILLER

Gloucester County College (C)

1400 Tanyard Road, Sewell NJ 08080-9518
County: Gloucester FICE Identification: 006901
Unit ID: 184791
Telephone: (856) 468-5000 Carnegie Class: Assoc/Pub-S-SC
FAX Number: N/A Calendar System: 4/1/4
URL: www.gccnj.edu
Established: 1966 Annual Undergrad Tuition & Fees (In-District): $3,795
Enrollment: 6,762 Coed
Affiliation or Control: State/Local IRS Status: 501(c)3
Highest Offering: Associate Degree
Program: Occupational; 2-Year Principally Bachelor's Creditable
Accreditation: M, ADNUR, DMS, NMT

01 President ... Dr. Frederick KEATING
05 VP Academic Svcs ... Vacant
03 Vice President & COO ... Mr. Dominick BURZICHELLI
32 Vice President Student Svcs ... Ms. Judith ATKINSON
10 Exec Director Financial Services ... Mrs. Elizabeth HALL
16 Exec Director Human Resource ... Ms. Danielle MORGANTI
04 Exec Assistant to the President ... Mrs. Karen SITARSKI
22 Exec Dir Diversity and Equity ... Mrs. Almarie JONES
09 Dean Inst Research & Assessment ... Ms. Karen DURKIN
13 Chief Information Officer ... Mr. Josh R. PIDDINGTON
66 Dean Nursing & Allied Health ... Dr. Susan HALL
49 Dean Liberal Arts ... Dr. Paul RUFINO
81 Dean STEM ... Dr. Brenden RICKARDS
05 Dean Curriculum & Instruction ... Ms. Barbara NIENSTEDT
68 Dean Health/Physical Educ/Rec ... Mr. Ron CASE
88 Dean Public Safety & Security ... Mr. Fred H. MADDEN
50 Dean Business Studies & CE ... Ms. Patricia CLAGHORN
07 Director Admissions/Registrar ... Ms. Sandra HOFFMAN
36 Director Advising ... Mr. Richard BROWN
35 Director Student Affairs ... Ms. Samantha VAN KOOY
08 Director Library Services ... Mrs. Jane S. CROCKER

Hudson County Community College (D)

70 Sip Avenue, Jersey City NJ 07306
County: Hudson FICE Identification: 012954
Unit ID: 184995
Telephone: (201) 714-7100 Carnegie Class: Assoc/Pub-U-SC
FAX Number: (201) 656-1799 Calendar System: Semester
URL: www.hccc.edu
Established: 1974 Annual Undergrad Tuition & Fees (In-District): $4,511
Enrollment: 9,397 Coed
Affiliation or Control: State/Local IRS Status: 501(c)3
Highest Offering: Associate Degree
Program: Occupational; 2-Year Principally Bachelor's Creditable
Accreditation: M, ACFEI, EMT

01 President ... Dr. Glen E. GABERT
05 Vice President Academic Affairs ... Dr. Eric FRIEDMAN
10 Vice President for Finance ... Mr. John SOMMER
30 VP Development/Asst to President ... Mr. Joseph SANSONE
11 Vice President College Operations ... Mr. Frank MERCADO
32 VP North Hudson Ctr/Student Affairs ... Ms. Paula PANDO
88 Dean for Non Traditional Programs ... Dr. Jennifer DUDLEY
09 Assoc Dean Institutional Rsrch/Plng ... Ms. Alexa BESHARA
20 Assistant Dean Academic Affairs ... Dr. Chanida KATKANANT
84 Assoc Dean Enrollment Services ... Mr. Peter VIDA
50 Assoc Dean Business and Science ... Ms. Catherine SIRANGELO-ELBADAWY
79 Associate Dean English/Humanities ... Ms. Mirta TEJADA
37 Assoc Dean Student Financial Asst ... Ms. Pamela F. NORRIS-LITTLES
35 Associate Dean for Student Services ... Mr. Michael REIMER
88 Assoc Dean ESL/Bilingual & Dev Educ ... Mr. Chris WAHL
06 Registrar ... Ms. Victoria ORELLANA
13 Chief Information Officer ... Mr. Vincent ZICOLELLO
07 Director of Admissions ... Mr. Jose OLIVARES
20 Dean of Arts and Sciences ... Mr. Chris WAHL
88 Director Testing & Assessment ... Ms. Darlery FRANCO
88 Director EOF ... Ms. Sabrina MAGLIULO
88 Executive Director Culinary Arts ... Mr. Paul DILLON
76 Director Health Related Programs ... Ms. Susanne SANSEVERE
88 Ex Dir Ctr Bus/Industry/Cntrct Trng ... Ms. Ana CHAPMAN
45 Director Academic Foundations ... Ms. Elizabeth NESIUS
18 Director of Facilities ... Mr. Joseph TORTURELLI
21 Controller ... Mr. Robert CRUZ
25 Director of Grants ... Mr. Ryan MARTIN
08 Librarian ... Ms. Cynthia COULTER
35 Director Student Activities ... Ms. Ophelia MORGAN
26 Director of Communications ... Ms. Jennifer CHRISTOPHER
28 Director of Diversity ... Ms. Randi MILLER
29 Director Alumni Relations/Devel ... Mr. Joseph SANSONE
15 Executive Director Human Resources ... Ms. Randi MILLER
38 Director Advisement & Counseling ... Ms. Rose CUNNINGHAM
40 Manager HCCC Bookstore ... Ms. Christine SALZMAN
96 Manager Purchasing ... Mr. Alus GREEN
88 Coordinator Medical Assisting ... Ms. Judith A. BENDER
36 Coordinator Career & Transfer Svc ... Ms. Karine PIERRE-PIERRE

ITT Technical Institute (E)

9000 Lincoln Drive E, Suite 100, Marlton NJ 08053
Telephone: (856) 396-3500 Identification: 770657
Accreditation: ACICS

† Main campus is ITT Technical Institute in Indianapolis, IN.

Kean University (F)

1000 Morris Avenue, Union NJ 07083-0411
County: Union FICE Identification: 002622
Unit ID: 185262
Telephone: (908) 737-5326 Carnegie Class: Master's L
FAX Number: (908) 737-4636 Calendar System: Semester
URL: www.kean.edu
Established: 1855 Annual Undergrad Tuition & Fees (In-State): $10,917
Enrollment: 15,391 Coed
Affiliation or Control: State IRS Status: 501(c)3
Highest Offering: Doctorate
Program: Liberal Arts And General; Teacher Preparatory
Accreditation: M, ART, CACREP, CIDA, MUS, NUR, OT, SP, SPAA, SW, TED, THEA

01 President ... Dr. Dawood FARAHI
10 Exec VP for Operations ... Mr. Philip CONNELLY
101 Exec Asst Board/Exec Dir Media/Pub ... Ms. Audrey KELLY
05 Provost/Vice Pres Academic Affairs ... Dr. Jeffrey TONEY
30 Assoc VP Institutional Advancement ... Dr. Diane SCHWARTZ
32 Vice President for Student Affairs ... Ms. Janice MURRAY-LAURY
20 Assoc VP for Academic Affairs ... Dr. Katerina ANDRIOTIS-BAITINGER
12 Assoc VP/Dean Kean Ocean ... Dr. Stephen KUBOW
58 Dean Nathan Weiss Grad Col ... Dr. Jeffrey BECK
53 Dean Col Education ... Dr. Susan POLIRSTOK
79 Actg Dean Col Humanities/Social Sci ... Dr. Suzanne BOUSQUET
81 Acting Dean Col Nat & Appl Hlth Sci ... Dr. George CHANG
50 Dean Col Business & Public Admin ... Dr. Michael COOPER
57 Dean Col Visual & Performing Arts ... Dr. George ARASIMOWICZ
15 Director Human Resources ... Mr. Faruque CHOWDHURY
07 Director for Undergrad Admissions ... Ms. Valerie WINSLOW
06 Registrar ... Mr. Ken WOLPIN
08 Interim University Librarian ... Ms. Kimberly FRAONE
27 Dir Media & Publications ... Mr. Matt CARUSO
21 Dir Student Financial Services ... Mr. Charlie XU
25 Director Research & Sponsored Pgms ... Ms. Susan GANNON
09 Director Institutional Research ... Dr. Shiji SHEN
108 Director for Accredit & Assessment ... Dr. Edward BARBONI
37 Acting Director Financial Aid ... Ms. Sherrell WATSON-HALL
39 Asst VP Residential Stdnt Services ... Ms. Maximina RIVERA
38 Dir Counseling & Disability Servs ... Dr. Andrew LEE
41 Director for Athletics ... Mr. Chris MORGAN
29 Director Alumni Relations ... Ms. Adriana BRENNAN
96 Director for Purchasing ... Mr. George THORN
18 Asst VP for Operations ... Ms. Phyllis DUKE
88 Director for Sustainability ... Dr. Nicholas SMITH-SEBASTO
23 Director for Health Services ... Ms. Lori PURWIN
22 Director Affirmative Action ... Dr. Charlie WILLIAMS
14 Dir Office for Computer/Inform Svcs ... Mr. Anthony SANTORA
35 Dir Center for Leadership & Service ... Mr. Scott SNOWDEN
36 Dir Career Development & Adv ... Dr. Sophia HOWLETT
104 Dir Center International Studies ... Dr. Stephen FERST
88 Veterans Affairs ... Ms. Lilliam BANNER
19 Acting Director of Campus Police ... Mr. Adam SHUBSDA
43 University Counsel ... Mr. Michael TRIPODI
42 Chaplain for Campus Ministry ... Ms. Jackie OESMAN

Mercer County Community College (G)

1200 Old Trenton Road, PO Box 17202,
Trenton NJ 08690-1099
County: Mercer FICE Identification: 004740
Unit ID: 185509
Telephone: (609) 586-4800 Carnegie Class: Assoc/Pub-R-L
FAX Number: (609) 570-3870 Calendar System: Semester
URL: www.mccc.edu
Established: 1966 Annual Undergrad Tuition & Fees (In-District): $4,260
Enrollment: 8,873 Coed
Affiliation or Control: State/Local IRS Status: 501(c)3
Highest Offering: Associate Degree
Program: Occupational; 2-Year Principally Bachelor's Creditable
Accreditation: M, AAB, ADNUR, FUSER, MLTAD, PTAA, RAD

01 President ... Dr. Patricia C. DONOHUE
30 Vice President College Advancement ... Vacant
05 Vice President Academic Affairs ... Dr. Donald GENERALS
11 Vice President for Admin & CBO ... Mr. Jacob EAPEN
32 Exec Dean for Student Affairs ... Dr. Diane CAMPBELL
76 Dean Sciences/Health Professions ... Dr. Linda MARTIN
49 Dean Liberal Arts ... Dr. Robin SCHORE
50 Dean Business and Technology ... Mr. Winston MADDOX
31 Ast Dean-JKC-Acad Pgm/Evening Svcs ... Mr. Edward W. FREDERICK
35 Asst Dean Student Services ... Mr. John SIMONE
13 Exec Dir for Info Technology Svcs ... Ms. Susan BOWEN
21 Exec Dir of Finance ... Mr. Walter BROOKS
26 Dir Marketing/Public Information ... Ms. Lynn HOLL
15 Exec Dir for Compliance & Human Res ... Mr. Jose FERNANDEZ
06 Registrar ... Ms. Joan GUGGENHEIM
37 Director of Financial Aid ... Mr. Jason TAYLOR
09 Director Institutional Research ... Ms. Nina MAY

18 Chief Facilities/Physical Plant .... Mr. Bryon MARSHALL
96 Director of Purchasing .... Mr. Stephen GREGOROWICZ
07 Director of Admissions & Outreach .... Ms. Savita BAMBHROLIA
38 Director Student Counseling .... Ms. Laurene JONES
84 Director Enrollment Management .. Ms. Latonya ASHFORD-LIGON
29 Manager of Alumni Relations .... Dr. Diane CAMPBELL

Mesivta Keser Torah (A)

503 Eleventh Avenue, Belmar NJ 07719-2407

County: Monmouth FICE Identification: 041803
Unit ID: 461847
Telephone: (732) 367-4259 Carnegie Class: Not Classified
FAX Number: (732) 681-7171 Calendar System: Semester
Established: 1991 Annual Undergrad Tuition & Fees: $13,400
Enrollment: 41 Male
Affiliation or Control: Independent Non-Profit IRS Status: 501(c)3
Highest Offering: Baccalaureate
Program: Liberal Arts And General; Professional; Religious Emphasis
Accreditation: RABN

01 President .... Rabbi Dovid HEINEMANN

Middlesex County College (B)

2600 Woodbridge Avenue, Edison NJ 08818-3050

County: Middlesex FICE Identification: 002615
Unit ID: 185536
Telephone: (732) 548-6000 Carnegie Class: Assoc/Pub-S-SC
FAX Number: (732) 494-8244 Calendar System: Semester
URL: www.middlesexcc.edu
Established: 1964 Annual Undergrad Tuition & Fees (In-District): $4,125
Enrollment: 12,898 Coed
Affiliation or Control: State/Local IRS Status: 501(c)3
Highest Offering: Associate Degree
Program: Occupational; 2-Year Principally Bachelor's Creditable
Accreditation: M, ADNUR, DH, DIETT, ENGT, MLTAD, RAD

01 President .... Dr. Joann LA PERLA-MORALES
05 Interim VP Academic & Sdnt Affairs .... Dr. Ronald GOLDFARB
10 Vice Pres Finance & Administration .... Ms. Susan K. PERKINS
30 VP for Institutional Advancement .... Mr. Patrick MADAMA
32 Dean Student Affairs .... Ms. Marla BRINSON
84 Interm Dean Enrollment/Student Svc .... Ms. Alice PICARDO
107 Dean Professional Studies .... Ms. Marilyn LASKOWSKI-SACHNOFF
49 Dean Arts and Sciences .... Mr. David EDWARDS
31 Dean Corporate & Commuity Education . Ms. Mary Ann CONNERS
18 Exec Director Facilities Management .... Mr. Donald DROST
14 Exec Director Information Tech .... Mr. Neil SACHNOFF
21 Controller .... Ms. Lori WILKIN
07 Asst Dean of Admissions .... Ms. Aretha WATSON
06 Registrar .... Mr. Richard COLE
36 Director of Counseling/Career Svcs .... Dr. Fannie GORDON
37 Financial Aid Director .... Vacant
08 Director Learning Resources .... Mr. Mark THOMPSON
26 Chief Public Relations Officer .... Mr. Thomas PETERSON
96 Director of Purchasing .... Mr. David FRICKE

Monmouth University (C)

400 Cedar Avenue, West Long Branch NJ 07764-1898

County: Monmouth FICE Identification: 002616
Unit ID: 185572
Telephone: (732) 571-3400 Carnegie Class: Master's L
FAX Number: (732) 571-3629 Calendar System: Semester
URL: www.monmouth.edu
Established: 1933 Annual Undergrad Tuition & Fees: $31,018
Enrollment: 6,472 Coed
Affiliation or Control: Independent Non-Profit IRS Status: 501(c)3
Highest Offering: Doctorate
Program: 2-Year Principally Bachelor's Creditable; Liberal Arts And General; Teacher Preparatory; Professional
Accreditation: M, BUS, CACREP, ENG, NURSE, SW, TED

01 President .... Dr. Paul R. BROWN
04 Executive Assistant to President .... Mrs. Annette GOUGH
101 Special Asst Board of Trustees .... Ms. Janet FELL
05 Vice Pres Academic Affs/Provost .... Dr. Thomas PEARSON
20 Vice Provost/Dean Graduate School .... Dr. Datta V. NAIK
06 Registrar .... Mrs. Lynn REYNOLDS
49 Dean Sch Humanities/Social Science .... Dr. Stanton GREEN
50 Dean Leon Hess Business Sch .... Prof. Donald MOLIVER
53 Dean School of Education .... Dr. Lynn ROMEO
81 Dean School of Science .... Dr. Michael PALLADINO
66 Dean School of Nursing/Health Stds .... Dr. Janet MAHONEY
70 Dean School of Social Work .... Dr. Robin MAMA
92 Dean Honors School .... Dr. Kevin DOOLEY
08 Interim Dean of Library .... Dr. Edward CHRISTENSEN
10 Vice President Finance .... Mr. William G. CRAIG
21 Assoc VP for Finance/Budgets .... Mr. Jack GAVIN
96 Director of Purchasing .... Mr. Mark MIRANDA
43 Vice President & General Counsel .... Mr. Grey DIMENNA
88 Dir of Compliance .... Ms. Melissa DALE
22 Dir Equity and Diversity .... Ms. Nina ANDERSON
11 Vice President Administrative Svcs .... Mrs. Patricia SWANNACK
18 Assoc VP Campus Plng/Construction .... Mr. Robert CORNERO
19 Director/Chief of Police .... Capt. William MCELRATH
15 Director of Human Resources .... Ms. Robyn SALVO
32 VP Student & Community Services .... Mrs. Mary Anne NAGY
35 Assoc VP for Student Services .... Mr. James PILLAR
35 Dir Student Activities/Student Ctr .... Ms. Amy BELLINA
26 Director of Public Affairs .... Ms. Petra LUDWIG
30 Vice Pres University Advancement .... Mr. Jason KROLL
29 Director of Alumni Affairs .... Ms. Marilynn PERRY
84 Vice Pres Enrollment Management .... Dr. Robert MC CAIG
37 Assoc VP/Director Financial Aid .... Ms. Claire ALASIO
84 Assoc VP Enrollment Mgmt .... Ms. Lauren VENTO-CIFELLI
07 Director Graduate Admission .... Mr. Kevin ROANE
41 Vice Pres & Director of Athletics .... Dr. Marilyn MCNEIL
13 Vice Pres Information Management ..... Dr. Edward CHRISTENSEN
108 Assoc VP Acad & Inst Assessment .... Dr. David STROHMETZ
09 Director of Institutional Research .... Dr. Eleanor SWANSON
20 Assoc VP Academic Admin .... Mrs. Susan O'KEEFE
38 Dean of the Center for Student Succ .... Dr. Mercy AZEKE
36 Assistant Dean for Career Services .... Mr. William HILL
20 Assoc VP for Global Initiatives .... Dr. Saliba SARSAR
86 Dir of Gov & Community Relations .... Mr. Paul DEMENT

Montclair State University (D)

1 Normal Avenue, Montclair NJ 07043-9987

County: Essex and Passaic FICE Identification: 002617
Unit ID: 185590
Telephone: (973) 655-4000 Carnegie Class: Master's L
FAX Number: N/A Calendar System: Semester
URL: www.montclair.edu
Established: 1908 Annual Undergrad Tuition & Fees (In-State): $11,318
Enrollment: 18,382 Coed
Affiliation or Control: State IRS Status: 501(c)3
Highest Offering: Doctorate
Program: Liberal Arts And General; Teacher Preparatory; Professional
Accreditation: M, ART, AUD, BUS, CACREP, CS, DANCE, DIETD, DIETI, MUS, SP, TED, THEA

01 President .... Dr. Susan A. COLE
05 Provost/Vice Pres Academic Affairs .... Dr. Willard P. GINGERICH
10 Vice President Finance & Treasurer .... Mr. Donald D. CIPULLO
32 Vice Pres Student Devel/Campus Life . Dr. Karen L. PENNINGTON
30 Vice Pres University Advancement .... Mr. John T. SHANNON
16 Vice President Human Resources .... Vacant
18 Vice Pres Univ Facilities .... Mr. Gregory W. BRESSLER
13 VP Information Technology .... Dr. Edward V. CHAPEL
43 University Counsel .... Ms. Valerie L. VAN BAAREN
86 Director Government Relations .... Ms. Shivaun P. GAINES
45 Exec Director Budget and Planning .... Mr. David JOSEPHSON
79 Dean College Humanities/Soc Scis .... Dr. Marietta MORRISSEY
81 Dean College Science & Math .... Dr. Robert S. PREZANT
53 Dean Col Education & Human Svcs .... Dr. Francine PETERMAN
57 Dean College of the Arts .... Dr. Daniel A. GURSKIS
50 Dean School of Business .... Dr. E. LaBrent CHRITE
08 Dean of Library Services .... Dr. Judith L. HUNT
20 Dean of Grad School .... Dr. Joan C. FICKE
35 Dean of Students .... Dr. Rose Mary HOWELL
84 Assoc VP Enrollment/Stdnt Acad Sup .... Dr. Bryan J. TERRY
20 Assoc Provost for Academic Affairs .... Dr. Frederick BONATO
108 Assoc Provost Acad Pgm/ Assessment .... Dr. Joanne F. COTE-BONANNO
18 Assoc Vice Pres Facilities Svcs .... Dr. Timothy CAREY
18 Assoc VP Design & Construction .... Mr. Charles SARAJIAN
18 Assoc VP Facilities Maintenance .... Mr. Shawn CONNOLLY
18 Exec Dir Facil Maintnc/Engineering .... Mr. Walter D. EDDY
91 Asso VP Enterprise Software/Dep CIO .... Ms. Carolyn M. ORTEGA
35 Assoc VP Student Dev/Campus Life .... Ms. Kathleen E. RAGAN
15 Asst VP for HR .... Mr. Gilbert RIVERA
15 Asst VP for HR Operations .... Ms. Catherine N. BONGO
64 Director School of Music .... Dr. Robert CART
09 Director Institutional Research .... Dr. Steven L. JOHNSON
06 Registrar .... Ms. Denise M. DEBLASIO
07 Director Undergraduate Admissions .... Ms. Lisa A. KASPER
30 Assoc VP Univ Advancement .... Ms. Carol A. BLAZEJOWSKI
26 Exec Dir Strategic Communications .... Ms. Deborah GAINES
26 Dir Marketing and Graphic Svcs .... Vacant
31 Exec Dir Community Relations .... Ms. Julie ADAMS
29 Exec Dir Alumni Relations .... Ms. Jeanne MARANO
19 Chief of University Police .... Mr. Paul M. CELL
22 Dir EO/Affirmative Action/Diversity .... Ms. Barbara J. MILTON
38 Director Counseling/Psych Services .... Dr. Jaclyn FRIEDMAN-LOMBARDO
39 Exec Director Residential Ed/Svcs .... Mr. Jeffrey HURRIN
40 General Mgr University Bookstore .... Mr. Richard AMMERMAN
41 Director Intercollegiate Athletics .... Ms. Holly P. GERA
37 Director Financial Aid .... Mr. James T. ANDERSON
56 Assoc Dean Extended Learning .... Mr. Jamieson A. BILELLA
36 Exec Dir Ctr Career Svcs/Coop Educ .... Ms. Carolyn D. JONES
96 Dir Procurement/Fin Div Admin .... Ms. Nancy G. CARVER
88 Exec Director Center for Advising .... Ms. Michele CAMPAGNA
92 Director Honors Program .... Dr. Gregory L. WATERS
21 Asst VP for Finance & Controller .... Ms. Catherine A. CORYAT
21 Director of Student Accounts .... Ms. Marion CAGGIANO
23 Director University Health Center .... Ms. Donna M. BARRY
104 Exec Director International Affairs .... Ms. Marina CUNNINGHAM
28 Director Equity and Diversity .... Ms. Esmilda M. ABREU-HORNBOSTEL
25 Dir Research & Sponsored Programs .... Mr. Ted RUSSO
88 Asst Dean for Student Life .... Ms. Fatima DECARVALHO
105 Dir Web Services .... Ms. Cindy L. MENEGHIN
04 Exec Asst to the President .... Ms. Phyllis L. WOOSTER
42 Chaplain .... Fr. James CHERN
88 Director Fin Systems Administration .... Ms. Catherine I. RUSH
88 Dir Construction Procurement .... Mr. Daniel ROCHE
88 Asst VP Enterprise Tech Services .... Mr. Jeff GIACOBBE
88 Exec Dir Advancement Services .... Ms. Jeanette HANLEIN
88 Dir Campus Planning .... Mr. Michael ZANKO
88 Dir Tech Training and Integration .... Ms. Yanling SUN
88 Dir Environmental Health and Safety .... Ms. Amy FERDINAND
27 Director Media Relations .... Ms. Suzanne BRONSKI
100 Chief of Staff .... Vacant

New Brunswick Theological Seminary (E)

17 Seminary Place, New Brunswick NJ 08901-1196

County: Middlesex FICE Identification: 002619
Unit ID: 185758
Telephone: (732) 247-5241 Carnegie Class: Spec/Faith
FAX Number: (732) 249-5412 Calendar System: Semester
URL: www.nbts.edu
Established: 1784 Annual Graduate Tuition & Fees: $11,440
Enrollment: 186 Coed
Affiliation or Control: Reformed Church In America IRS Status: 501(c)3
Highest Offering: Doctorate; No Undergraduates
Program: Professional; Religious Emphasis
Accreditation: THEOL

01 President .... Dr. Gregg A. MAST
04 Assistant to the President .... Ms. Yasha PEOPLE
05 Dean of the Seminary .... Dr. Willard W.C ASHLEY, SR.
10 Director Finance & Administration .... Mr. Allan BENISH
21 Controller .... Mr. Kenneth TERMOTT
30 Director of Development .... Mrs. Catherine PROCTOR
08 Director of Library .... Mr. Christopher BRENNAN
06 Registrar & Assistant Dean of AA .... Ms. Sharon A. WATTS
07 Admissions Committee Chair .... Dr. Beth L. TANNER

New Jersey City University (F)

2039 Kennedy Boulevard, Jersey City NJ 07305-1597

County: Hudson FICE Identification: 002613
Unit ID: 185129
Telephone: (201) 200-2000 Carnegie Class: Master's L
FAX Number: (201) 200-2352 Calendar System: Semester
URL: www.njcu.edu
Established: 1927 Annual Undergrad Tuition & Fees (In-State): $10,653
Enrollment: 8,492 Coed
Affiliation or Control: State IRS Status: 501(c)3
Highest Offering: Doctorate
Program: Liberal Arts And General; Teacher Preparatory; Professional
Accreditation: M, ACBSP, ART, MUS, NUR, TEAC, TED

01 President .... Dr. Sue HENDERSON
05 Vice Pres Academic Affairs .... Dr. Joanne Z. BRUNO
32 Vice Pres for Student Affairs .... Dr. John MELENDEZ
11 Vice Pres Administration/Finance .... Dr. Aaron ASKA
30 Interim VP University Advancement ...... Mr. William FELLENBERG
21 Controller .... Ms. Mary BOLOWSKI
13 Assoc VP Computer Inform Systems .... Mr. Robert MCBRIDE
18 Assoc VP Facil/Construction Mgmt .... Mr. Andrew CHRIST
25 Assoc VP AA/Director of Grants .... Mr. Ruddys ANDRADE
07 Assoc VP Admissions/Enrollment Mgmt .... Vacant
16 Assoc VP Human Resources .... Mr. Hunt BARTINE
20 Asst Vice Pres Academic Affs .... Dr. Deborah WOO
26 Asst VP Pub Info/Community Rel . Ms. Ellen WAYMAN-GORDON
14 Asst VP Information Technology .... Ms. Phyllis SZANI
88 Interim Asst VP Univ Advancement .... Mr. Michael PERNA
35 Asst Vice Pres Student Affairs .... Mr. Demond HARGROVE
04 Executive Asst to the President .... Ms. Maria COBARRUBIAS
49 Dean Arts & Sciences .... Dr. Barbara FELDMAN
58 Dean of Graduate Studies .... Vacant
53 Dean Education .... Dr. Allan DE FINA
107 Dean Professional Studies .... Dr. Sandra BLOOMBERG
35 Dean of Students .... Dr. Lyn HAMLIN
08 Interim Director of Univ Library .... Mr. Frederick SMITH
06 Registrar .... Ms. Miriam LARIA
36 Director Career Planning/Placement .... Dr. Jennifer JONES
09 Director Institutional Research .... Dr. Arthur KRAMER
15 Director Human Resources .... Mr. Robert PIASKOWSKY
19 Director Public Safety .... Mr. Bruce HARMAN
41 Director Athletics/Recreation .... Ms. Alice DE FAZIO
22 Dir Affirmative Action/Equal Oppty .... Ms. Lisa NORCIA
29 Director Alumni Relations .... Ms. Jane MCCLELLAN
78 Director Cooperative Education .... Dr. Jennifer JONES
44 Director Annual Giving .... Vacant
38 Director Student Counseling .... Dr. Abisola GALLAGHER
96 Director of Purchasing .... Ms. Edie DELVECCHIO
43 General Counsel .... Mr. Alfred RAMEY
90 Director of Academic Computing .... Dr. Charles PRATT
85 Foreign Student Advisor .... Mr. Craig KATZ
37 Director Student Financial Aid .... Mr. Frank CUOZZO
30 Director of Development .... Ms. Lori SUMMERS
58 Acting Director of Graduate Studies .... Dr. William BAJOR
88 Director of Leadership Gifts .... Mr. Alan GROSSMAN
88 Director Student Fin Svcs/Risk Mgr .... Mr. Peter LJUTIC

New Jersey Institute of Technology (G)

University Heights, Newark NJ 07102-1982

County: Essex FICE Identification: 002621
Unit ID: 185828
Telephone: (973) 596-3000 Carnegie Class: RU/H
FAX Number: (973) 642-4380 Calendar System: Semester
URL: www.njit.edu
Established: 1881 Annual Undergrad Tuition & Fees (In-State): $15,218
Enrollment: 9,944 Coed
Affiliation or Control: State IRS Status: 501(c)3

Highest Offering: Doctorate
Program: Professional
Accreditation: M, BUS, CS, ENG, ENGT, PH

01 President ....Dr. Joel BLOOM
05 Provost and Senior Executive VP ....Dr. Fadi P. DEEK
10 Senior Vice Pres Admin & Treasurer ....Mr. Henry A. MAUERMEYER
30 Vice Pres University Advancement ....Dr. Charles DEES
46 Vice President Research & Devel ....Dr. Donald H. SEBASTIAN
15 Vice President Human Resources ....Ms. Kay CLARKE-TURNER
48 Dean of Architecture ....Mr. Urs P. GAUCHAT
54 Dean of Engineering ....Dr. Basil BALTZIS
49 Interim Dean Col Sci/Liberal Arts ....Dr. Jonathan H. LUKE
50 Dean School of Management ....Dr. Pius J. EGBELU
92 Interim Dean A Dorman Honors Col ....Dr. Katia PASSERINI
77 Interim Dean Col Computing Science ....Dr. James GELLER
21 Asst Vice Pres Finance & Controller ....Mr. William GARCIA
18 Assoc VP Facilities Management ....Mr. Joseph F. TARTAGLIA
58 Interim Assoc Provost Grad Studies ....Dr. Sotirios G. ZIAVRAS
13 Assoc Provost Information Svcs Tech ....Mr. David F. ULLMAN
51 Assoc VP Cont/Distance Education ....Dr. Gale T. SPAK
07 Assoc VP Enroll Svcs/Dean Admiss ....Ms. Kathryn KELLY
88 Asst Vice Pres Pre-College Programs ....Dr. Howard S. KIMMEL
32 Dean Student Services ....Dr. Jack GENTUL
89 Assoc Dean/Ctr for First Yr Stdnts ....Dr. Sharon E. MORGAN
27 Executive Director Communications ....Ms. Jean M. LLEWELLYN
29 Exec Director of Alumni Affairs ....Mr. Robert A. BOYNTON
04 Executive Assistant to President ....Ms. Mary Jane POHERO
78 Exec Director Career Devel Svcs ....Mr. Gregory MASS
26 Director of Public Relations ....Ms. Sheryl M. WEINSTEIN
09 Director Inst Research/Planning ....Dr. Eugene P. DEESS
08 University Librarian ....Mr. Richard T. SWEENEY
06 Registrar ....Mr. Michael E. MAYSILLES
37 Director of Financial Aid ....Ms. Ivon NUNEZ
38 Director of Counseling Center ....Dr. Phyllis BOLLING
19 Director of Public Safety ....Mr. Robert G. SABATTIS
24 Dir Instructional Tech/Media Svcs ....Mr. William F. REYNOLDS
41 Sr Admin Physical Educ/Athletics ....Mr. Leonard I. KAPLAN
85 Director International Students/Fac ....Mr. Jeffrey W. GRUNDY
35 Director Student Activities ....Ms. Donna MINNICH
96 Director Purchasing/Office Services ....Ms. Eugenia REGENCIO
43 Office of General Counsel ....Ms. Holly C. STERN

Ocean County College (A)

PO Box 2001, Toms River NJ 08754-2001
County: Ocean — FICE Identification: 002624 — Unit ID: 185873
Telephone: (732) 255-0400 — Carnegie Class: Assoc/Pub-S-SC
FAX Number: (732) 255-0444 — Calendar System: Semester
URL: www.ocean.edu
Established: 1964 — Annual Undergrad Tuition & Fees (In-District): $3,970
Enrollment: 10,048 — Coed
Affiliation or Control: State/Local — IRS Status: 501(c)3
Highest Offering: Associate Degree
Program: Occupational; 2-Year Principally Bachelor's Creditable
Accreditation: M, ADNUR, EMT

01 President ....Dr. Jon H. LARSON
11 Executive VP Operational ....Dr. James J. MCGINTY
05 Executive VP Instruction ....Mr. Richard STRADA
32 VP Student Affairs ....Mr. Donald DORAN
10 VP of Finance & Administration ....Ms. Sara WINCHESTER
20 VP of Academic Affairs ....Dr. Jianping WANG
15 Asst VP Human Resources ....Mr. Leslie COHEN
84 Asst VP of Enrollment Management ....Ms. Norma BETZ
04 Senior Asst to the President ....Mr. David WOLFE
04 Asst to Pres for Inst Quality ....Ms. Janet HUBBS
20 Assoc VP of Academic Affairs ....Dr. Carolyn LAFFERTY
20 Asst VP for Instructional Services ....Dr. Antoinette M. CLAY
18 Asst VP Facilities/Planning/Constr ....Vacant
57 Interim Dean Language and the Arts ....Mr. Henry JACKSON
81 Dean Math/Science & Tech ....Dr. Yehia ELMOGAHZY
66 Dean of Nursing ....Ms. Tracy WALSH
83 Interim Dean of Soc Science ....Mr. Bradford YOUNG
106 Dean of E-learning Faculty ....Dr. Maysa HAYWARD
88 Exec Dir Acad Outreach & Sch Rel ....Ms. Eileen SCHILLING
102 Exec Dir OCC Foundation ....Ms. Sandy S. BROUGHTON
106 Exec Director of E-learning & CPE ....Ms. Patricia FENN
08 Interim Dir of Library Services ....Mr. Gary SCHMIDT
13 CIO ....Mr. Hatem AKL
37 Director of Financial Aid ....Ms. Eileen BUCKLE
88 Dir of Academic Advising Services ....Ms. Anna REGAN
19 Director of College Security ....Mr. Robert KUMPF
88 Exec Dir of Instruction Technology ....Mr. Lee KOBUS
88 Exec Director of College Relations ....Ms. Jan KIRSTEN
06 Acting Director of Admissions ....Mr. Arthur CRISS
93 Director of EOF & OMS ....Ms. Laura RICKARDS
18 Interim Exec Dir of Facilities ....Mr. Matthew KENNEDY
41 Exec Director of Athletics ....Ms. Ilene COHEN
09 Director of Institutional Research ....Dr. Mary MORLEY
40 Director of Auxiliary Services ....Ms. Carol KAUNITZ
21 Controller ....Ms. Karen PAPAKONSTANTINOU
20 Dean of Academic Services ....Ms. Maureen REUSTLE

Passaic County Community College (B)

1 College Boulevard, Paterson NJ 07509-1179
County: Passaic — FICE Identification: 009994 — Unit ID: 186034
Telephone: (973) 684-6868 — Carnegie Class: Assoc/Pub-S-SC
FAX Number: (973) 684-5843 — Calendar System: Semester
URL: www.pccc.edu
Established: 1968 — Annual Undergrad Tuition & Fees (In-District): $4,166
Enrollment: 9,782 — Coed
Affiliation or Control: State/Local — IRS Status: 501(c)3
Highest Offering: Associate Degree
Program: Occupational; 2-Year Principally Bachelor's Creditable
Accreditation: M, ADNUR, CAHIIM, ENGT, RAD

01 President ....Dr. Steven ROSE
05 Vice Pres Academic/Student Affairs ....Dr. Jacqueline KINEAVY
10 Vice Pres Finance/Administration ....Mr. Maurice FEIGENBAUM
12 Vice Pres Passaic Academic Center . Ms. Josephine HERNANDEZ
13 Vice Pres Information Technology ....Mr. Robert MONDELLI
15 Vice Pres Human Resources ....Mr. Michael SILVESTRO
20 Dean Academic Affairs ....Dr. Bassel STASSIS
08 Associate Dean Learning Resources ....Mr. Greg FALLON
66 Asst Dean Nurse Educ/Health Scis ....Ms. Donna STANKIEWICZ
88 Asst Dean for Testing & Tutoring ....Mr. Peter HYNES
09 Exec Dir Institutional Rsrch/Plng ....Mr. Alex MCCLUNG
88 Ex Dir Cultural Affs/The Poetry Ctr ....Ms. Maria GILLAN
30 Exec Dir of Institutional Devel ....Mr. Todd SORBER
84 Exec Dir of Enrollment Management ....Ms. Betsy MARINACE
18 Exec Dir Facilities Mgmt/Planning ....Mr. Brian EGAN
37 Director Financial Aid ....Ms. Linda GAYTON
06 Registrar ....Ms. Donna FISCHER
19 Director Security ....Mr. John MORGAN
35 Director Student Activities ....Mr. Takem DEAN
41 Athletic Director ....Mr. Bernard JOHNSON
07 Director of Admissions ....Ms. Stephanie DECKER
29 Director Alumni Relations ....Ms. Maria MEDINA
32 Chief Student Life Officer ....Dr. Sharon GOLDSTEIN
36 Director Student Placement ....Vacant
26 Chief Public Relations Officer ....Ms. Betsy MARINACE
96 Director of Purchasing ....Ms. Marge HOLLINGSWORTH
04 Administrative Asst to President ....Ms. Evelyn DEFEIS

Pillar College (C)

60 Park Place, Suite 701, Newark NJ 07102
County: Essex — FICE Identification: 036663 — Unit ID: 440794
Telephone: (973) 803-5000 — Carnegie Class: Spec/Faith
FAX Number: (973) 242-3282 — Calendar System: Semester
URL: www.somerset.edu
Established: 1908 — Annual Undergrad Tuition & Fees: $17,304
Enrollment: 425 — Coed
Affiliation or Control: Wesleyan Church — IRS Status: 501(c)3
Highest Offering: Baccalaureate
Program: Liberal Arts And General; Professional; Religious Emphasis
Accreditation: M, BI

01 President ....Dr. David E. SCHROEDER
03 Executive Vice President ....Mr. Daniel W. WRIGHT
05 VP Academic Affairs ....Dr. Alford H. OTTLEY
26 VP Public Relations ....Dr. Ralph T. GRANT
45 VP Strategic Initiatives ....Ms. Linda SCHMITT
10 Assistant VP of Financial Services ....Mr. Joel DAVIS
06 Asst VP of Academics & Registrar ....Mrs. Amy HUBER
07 Director of Admissions ....Ms. Amanda SIMPSON
88 Director of Adult Degree Program ....Dr. Wayne DYER
37 Director of Financial Aid ....Mrs. Betzi SCHROEDER
42 Coordinator of Spiritual Formation ....Mr. Nishanth THOMAS

Princeton Theological Seminary (D)

PO Box 821, Princeton NJ 08542-0803
County: Mercer — FICE Identification: 002626 — Unit ID: 186122
Telephone: (609) 921-8300 — Carnegie Class: Spec/Faith
FAX Number: (609) 924-2973 — Calendar System: Semester
URL: www.ptsem.edu
Established: 1812 — Annual Graduate Tuition & Fees: $11,500
Enrollment: 518 — Coed
Affiliation or Control: Presbyterian Church (U.S.A.) — IRS Status: 501(c)3
Highest Offering: Doctorate; No Undergraduates
Program: Professional; Religious Emphasis
Accreditation: M, THEOL

01 President ....Dr. M. Craig BARNES
10 Sr Vice Pres/Chief Oper Ofcr/Treas ....Mr. John W. GILMORE
26 Int Vice President Seminary Rels ....Rev. William R. SHARMAN
13 Int Vice Pres Information Tech ....Mr. William R. FRENCH
05 Dean of Academic Affairs ....Dr. James F. KAY
32 Dean of Student Life ....Rev. John E. WHITE
20 Associate Dean of Curricula ....Dr. Shawn OLIVER
35 Asc Dean Stdnt Life/Dir Sr Plcmnt ....RevDr. Catherine C. DAVIS
73 Int Dir Sch Christian/Voc/Mission ....Rev. Dayle G. ROUNDS
21 Controller ....Mr. James F. MORGAN
29 Director Alumni/ae Relations/Giving ....Rev. Jake J. KIM
06 Registrar ....Mr. David H. KIM
07 Director Admissions/Financial Aid ....Mr. Matthew R. SPINA
08 Interim Chief Librarian ....Mr. Donald M. VORP
30 Director Development ....Ms. Susannah COLEMAN
15 Director of Human Resources ....Ms. Sandra J. MALEY
27 Director Communications/Publication ....Rev. Barbara A. CHAAPEL
18 Director of Facilities ....Mr. German MARTINEZ
14 Dir Telecomm/Network/Suport Svcs ....Mr. William R. FRENCH
24 Director Educational Media ....Rev. Joicy BECKER-RICHARDS
39 Director of Housing/Auxiliary Svcs ....Mr. Stephen CARDONE
44 Director of Planned Giving ....Ms. Lisa TITUS
36 Director of Student Placement ....Dr. Catherine C. DAVIS
38 Director of Student Counseling ....Rev. Nancy L. SCHONGALLA-BOWMAN
42 Minister of the Chapel ....Rev. Janice S. AMMON
28 Director Multicultural Relations ....Rev. Victor ALOYO, JR.

Princeton University (E)

Princeton NJ 08544-1098
County: Mercer — FICE Identification: 002627 — Unit ID: 186131
Telephone: (609) 258-3000 — Carnegie Class: RU/VH
FAX Number: N/A — Calendar System: Semester
URL: www.princeton.edu
Established: 1746 — Annual Undergrad Tuition & Fees: $40,170
Enrollment: 8,010 — Coed
Affiliation or Control: Independent Non-Profit — IRS Status: 501(c)3
Highest Offering: Doctorate
Program: Liberal Arts And General; Teacher Preparatory; Professional
Accreditation: M, ENG, TEAC

01 President ....Cristopher L. EISGRUBER
03 Acting Executive Vice President ....Treby WILLIAMS
05 Provost ....David S. LEE
04 Vice President & Secretary ....Robert K. DURKEE
10 Vice Pres for Finance & Treasurer ....Carolyn N. AINSLIE
30 Vice President for Development ....Elizabeth B. WOOD
26 Vice President for Public Affairs ....Robert K. DURKEE
32 Vice President of Campus Life ....Cynthia CHERREY
18 Vice President for Facilities ....Michael E. MCKAY
13 Vice President Info Technology/CIO ....Jay DOMINICK
16 Vice President for Human Resources ....Lianne C. SULLIVAN-CROWLEY
11 VP for University Services ....Chad L. KLAUS
20 Vice Provost Academic Affairs ....Katherine ROHRER
22 Vice Provost Instl Equity/Diversity ....Michelle MINTER
09 Vice Provost Institutional Research ....Jed MARSH
25 Vice Prov Space Programming/Plan ....Paul LAMARCHE
21 Budget Dir/Vice Provost Finance ....Steven GILL
20 Vice Provost Intl Initiatives ....Diana K. DAVIES
26 Asst Vice President Communications ....Lauren D. UGORJI
29 Asst Vice President Alumni Affairs ....Margaret M. MILLER
44 Asst Vice President Annual Giving ....William M. HARDT
88 Asst VP for University Services ....Paul BREITMAN
88 AVP Facilities Design/Construction ....Anne ST. MAURO
18 Asst Vice Pres Facilities Plant ....Roger DEMARESKI
46 Chair Univ Rsrch Bd/Dean Research ....Pablo DEBENEDETTI
43 General Counsel ....Peter G. MCDONOUGH
88 President PRINCO ....Andrew K. GOLDEN
88 Dean of the Faculty ....David P. DOBKIN
58 Dean of Graduate School ....William B. RUSSEL
49 Dean of the College ....Valerie SMITH
54 Dean of School of Engineering ....H. Vincent POOR
82 Dean of WW Sch of Public/Intl Affs ....Cecilia ROUSE
48 Dean of School of Architecture ....Stanley T. ALLEN
42 Dean of Religious Life ....Alison BODEN
35 Dean of Undergraduate Students ....Kathleen DEIGNAN
07 Dean of Admission ....Janet L. RAPELYE
17 Exec Director Health Services ....John KOLLIGIAN
08 University Librarian ....Karin TRAINER
06 Registrar ....Polly WINFREY GRIFFIN
37 Dir Undergraduate Financial Aid ....Robin A. MOSCATO
86 Director Government Affairs ....Joyce A. RECHTSCHAFFEN
31 Dir Community & Regional Affairs ....Kristin APPELGET
41 Director of Athletics ....Gary D. WALTERS
96 Director of Purchasing ....Donald E. WESTON, JR.
38 Dir of Counseling & Psych Services ....Anita MCLEAN
15 Director Human Resources ....Claire JACOBS ELSON
85 Director Davis International Center ....Jackie LEIGHTON
36 Director Career Services ....Beverly HAMILTON-CHANDLER
90 Assoc CIO/Dir Academic Services OIT ....Serge J. GOLDSTEIN
14 Assoc CIO/Dir Support Services OIT ....Steven M. SATHER
91 Dir Enterprise Infrastructure OIT ....Donna E. TATRO
27 Director of News and Editorial Svcs ....Daniel DAY
105 Director of Web Communications ....Thomas J. BARTUS
88 Dir of Development Communications ....Ruth STEVENS
44 AVP for Development ....Kerstin LARSEN
104 Sr Asc Dn of Col/Dir Ofc Intl Pgms ....Nancy A. KANACH
39 Director Housing ....Andrew KANE

Rabbi Jacob Joseph School (F)

1 Plainfield Avenue, Edison NJ 08817-4494
County: Middlesex — FICE Identification: 030775 — Unit ID: 384421
Telephone: (732) 985-6533 — Carnegie Class: Spec/Faith
FAX Number: (732) 985-6553 — Calendar System: Semester
URL: www.jfgmc.org/rjjy/htm
Established: 1982 — Annual Undergrad Tuition & Fees: $10,900
Enrollment: 79 — Male
Affiliation or Control: Independent Non-Profit — IRS Status: 501(c)3
Highest Offering: Baccalaureate
Program: Teacher Preparatory; Professional
Accreditation: @RABN

01 President ....Dr. Marvin SCHICK
03 Rosh Yeshiva ....Rabbi Yaakov BUSEL
05 Rosh Yeshiva ....Rabbi Joseph EICHENSTEIN
37 Financial Aid Director ....Rabbi Yitzchok WEINTRAUB

Rabbinical College of America (G)

226 Sussex Avenue, Morristown NJ 07960-3600
County: Morris — FICE Identification: 008609 — Unit ID: 186186

Telephone: (973) 267-9404 Carnegie Class: Spec/Faith
FAX Number: (973) 267-5208 Calendar System: Trimester
URL: www.rca.edu
Established: 1956 Annual Undergrad Tuition & Fees: $10,700
Enrollment: 250 Male
Affiliation or Control: Independent Non-Profit IRS Status: 501(c)3
Highest Offering: Baccalaureate
Program: Teacher Preparatory
Accreditation: RABN

00 Chairman of the Board ... David T. CHASE
01 Dean ... Rabbi Moshe HERSON
04 Admin Assistant to the Dean ... Shoshana SOLOMON
26 Public Relations Officer ... Rabbi Mendel SOLOMON
06 Registrar ... Rabbi Yisroel GOLDBERG
20 Director New Direction Program ... Rabbi Zalman DUBINSKY
88 Advanced Talmud Program ... Rabbi Aharon GANCZ
10 Chief Business Officer ... Rabbi Hershel LIPSKIER
37 Director Student Financial Aid ... Rabbi Moshe WEISBERG
08 Chief Librarian ... Rabbi Sholom SPALTER
51 Dir Continuing Educ/Alumni Rels ... Rabbi Boruch HECHT
88 Director Semicha Program ... Rabbi Chaim SCHAPIRO

Ramapo College of New Jersey (A)

505 Ramapo Valley Road, Mahwah NJ 07430-1680
County: Bergen FICE Identification: 009344
Unit ID: 186201
Telephone: (201) 684-7500 Carnegie Class: Master's M
FAX Number: (201) 684-7508 Calendar System: Semester
URL: www.ramapo.edu
Established: 1969 Annual Undergrad Tuition & Fees (In-State): $13,388
Enrollment: 5,817 Coed
Affiliation or Control: State IRS Status: 501(c)3
Highest Offering: Master's
Program: Liberal Arts And General; Teacher Preparatory; Professional
Accreditation: M, BUS, NUR, SW, TEAC

01 President ... Dr. Peter P. MERCER
05 Provost/VP Academic Affairs ... Dr. Beth BARNETT
10 Interim VP Administration & Finance ... Ms. Maria KRUPIN
32 Assoc VP of Student Affairs ... Dr. Miki CAMMARATA
84 Assoc VP of Enrollment Mgmt ... Mr. Christopher ROMANO
46 Chief Planning Officer ... Dr. Dorothy ECHOLS TOBE
20 Vice Provost for Academic Affairs ... Dr. Eric DAFFRON
21 Assoc Vice Pres Admin/Finance ... Mr. Richard ROBERTS
08 College Librarian/Dean ... Ms. Elizabeth SIECKE
102 Exec Director Ramapo Found/VPIA ... Ms. Cathleen DAVEY
06 Registrar ... Ms. Michele DUNN
07 Director of Admissions ... Mr. Peter RICE
37 Director of Financial Aid ... Mr. Mark SINGER
21 Controller ... Mr. Lawrence FERRIER
13 Chief Information Officer ... Mr. George TABBACK
15 Director of Human Resources ... Mr. Bill STOVALL
78 Dir Exper Learning/Career Svcs ... Ms. Beth RICCA
39 Director Residence Life ... Ms. Linda DIAZ
41 Director of Athletics ... Mr. Charles J. GORDON
18 Director Campus Facilities ... Mr. Ronald MARTUCCI
19 Director Security & Safety ... Mr. Vincent MARKOWSKI
88 Director Educ Opportunity Program ... Mr. Lorne WEEMS
50 Dean Anisfield School of Business ... Dr. Lewis CHAKRIN
82 Dean Salameno Sch Amer Intl Studies ... Dr. Stephen RICE
57 Dean Sch of Contemporary Arts ... Mr. Steven PERRY
83 Dean Sch Soc Science & Human Svc ... Dr. Samuel ROSENBERG
81 Actg Dn Sch Theoretical/Applied Sci ... Dr. Edward SAIFF
53 Asst Dean for Teacher Education ... Dr. Rexton LYNN
38 Director Ctr for Health/Counseling ... Dr. Judith GREEN
29 Asst Director Alumni Relations ... Ms. Purvi PAREKH
24 Asst Manager Academic Media Svcs ... Mr. Michael SAVIANESO
04 Executive Assistant to President ... Ms. Patricia KOZAKIEWICZ
25 Dir Grants Admin/Assoc VPIA ... Dr. Ronald KASE
23 Coordinator Health Services ... Ms. Debbie LUKACSKO
09 Director of Institutional Research ... Dr. Gurvinder KHANEJA
22 Dir Affirm Action/Equal Opportunity ... Ms. Melissa VAN DER WALL
35 Assoc VP Student Affairs ... Dr. Patrick CHANG
40 Bookstore Manager ... Ms. Theresa KING
85 Exec Director of Intl Education ... Mr. Ben LEVY
36 Asst Dir Career Dev & Placement ... Ms. Debra STARK
96 Director of Purchasing ... Mr. Stephen SONDEY
04 Special Assistant to President ... Ms. Brittany WILLIAMS-GOLDSTEIN
30 Chief Develop/VP Inst Advancement ... Ms. Cathleen DAVEY
86 Government Relations Officer ... Ms. Anna FARNESKI
26 Asst VP Mktg & Web Administrator ... Ms. Melissa HORVATH-PLYMAN

Raritan Valley Community College (B)

118 Lamington Road, Branchgurg NJ 08876
County: Somerset FICE Identification: 007731
Unit ID: 186645
Telephone: (908) 526-1200 Carnegie Class: Assoc/Pub-S-SC
FAX Number: (908) 526-0253 Calendar System: Semester
URL: www.raritanval.edu
Established: 1966 Annual Undergrad Tuition & Fees (In-District): $4,694
Enrollment: 8,210 Coed
Affiliation or Control: State/Local IRS Status: 501(c)3
Highest Offering: Associate Degree
Program: Occupational; 2-Year Principally Bachelor's Creditable
Accreditation: M, ADNUR, CAHIIM, MAC, OPD

01 Interim President ... Mr. James VENTANTONIO
05 Sr Vice Pres Academic Affairs ... Dr. Eileen ABEL
10 Vice President Finance/Facilities ... Mr. John TROJAN
13 Vice Pres Technology/Assess/Plng ... Mr. Charles E. CHULVICK
15 VP Human Resources/Labor Relations ... Ms. Nancy MOORE
30 Dean of College Advancement ... Ms. Jackie BELIN
20 Dean Academic Affairs ... Dr. Patrice MARKS
45 Dean Academic Resource Development ... Ms. Nancy E. JORDAN
51 Dean of Corporate & Continuing Educ ... Vacant
20 Dean of Faculty ... Vacant
32 Dean Student Services ... Ms. Diane LEMCOE
85 Dean Multicultural Affairs ... Ms. Richeleen DASHIELD
18 Exec Director Facilities/Grounds ... Mr. Brian O'ROURKE
84 Exec Dir of Enrollment Services ... Vacant
24 Director Media Relations ... Ms. Donna STOLZER
88 Conference Services Director ... Ms. Karen VAUGHAN
72 Executive Director Inst Technology ... Mr. Michael E. MACHNIK
102 Executive Director Foundation ... Ms. Ronnie WEYL
13 Information Technology Director ... Mr. Robert PESCINSKI
21 Controller/Exec Dir of Finance ... Ms. Violet J. WILLENSKY
57 Director of Theatre ... Mr. Alan C. LIDDELL
09 Dir of Inst Research/Assessment ... Mr. Keith GUERIN
88 Director of Planetarium ... Mr. Jerome VINSKI
88 Director of Child Care Center ... Ms. Cathy GRIFFIN
37 Director of Financial Aid ... Mr. Lenny MESONAS
08 Library Director ... Ms. Julie MAGINN
06 Registrar ... Mr. Dan PALUBNIAK
96 Director of Purchasing ... Mr. Lester MILLER
35 Director of Student Life ... Mr. Russell BAREFOOT
36 Director Transfer/Career Services ... Mr. Paul MICHAUD
26 Executive Director Marketing ... Ms. Janet THOMPSON

The Richard Stockton College of New Jersey (C)

101 Vera King Farris Drive, Galloway NJ 08205-9441
County: Atlantic FICE Identification: 009345
Unit ID: 186876
Telephone: (609) 652-1776 Carnegie Class: Master's M
FAX Number: (609) 652-0275 Calendar System: Semester
URL: www.stockton.edu
Established: 1969 Annual Undergrad Tuition & Fees (In-State): $12,692
Enrollment: 8,400 Coed
Affiliation or Control: State IRS Status: 501(c)3
Highest Offering: Doctorate
Program: Liberal Arts And General; Teacher Preparatory; Professional
Accreditation: AUD, M, NURSE, OT, PTA, @SP, SW, TEAC

01 President ... Dr. Herman J. SAATKAMP, JR.
05 Provost/Exec Vice Pres of Acad Affs ... Dr. Harvey KESSELMAN
100 Chief of Staff ... Mr. Brian K. JACKSON
10 Vice Pres Administration & Finance ... Mr. Charles E. INGRAM
32 Vice President Student Affairs ... Dr. Thomasa GONZALEZ
45 Chief Planning Officer ... Vacant
20 Associate Provost ... Dr. Kris KRISHNAN
20 Assistant Provost ... Dr. Debra DAGAVARIAN
96 Asst Supervisor Purchasing ... Ms. Annette HAMM
13 Assoc Prov Computing/Communication ... Mr. James MCCARTHY
21 Assoc VP Administration & Finance ... Vacant
18 Assoc VP Facilities/Construction ... Vacant
22 Sp Ast to Pres Affirm Act/Ethcl Std ... Ms. Nancy W. HICKS
26 Chf Exec Ofcr Ext Affs/Instnl Rsch ... Ms. Sharon SCHULMAN
30 Chief Dev Ofcr/Exec Dir Foundation ... Mr. Philip T. ELLMORE
84 Dean of Enrollment Management ... Mr. John IACOVELLI
07 Associate Dean of Admissions ... Ms. Alison HENRY
35 Dean of Students ... Mr. Pedro SANTANA
06 Assoc Dean Records/Registration ... Mr. Joseph LO SASSO
53 Dean School of Education ... Dr. Claudine KEENAN
97 Dean School of General Studies ... Dr. Robert S. GREGG
79 Int Dean School Arts & Humanities ... Dr. Lisa HONAKER
50 Dean School of Business ... Dr. Janet M. WAGNER
58 Dean School of Graduate Studies ... Dr. Lewis LEITNER
81 Dean School of Natural Science/Math ... Dr. Dennis WEISS
83 Dean Sch Social/Behavioral Sciences ... Dr. Cheryl KAUS
76 Dean School of Health Sciences ... Dr. Bess KATHRINS
15 Director Human Resource Management ... Ms. Natalie M. HAVRAN
09 Director Institutional Research ... Dr. Xiangping KONG
08 Director of Library Services ... Mr. Joseph TOTH
88 Director South Regional ETTC ... Ms. Patricia WEEKS
37 Director of Financial Aid ... Ms. Jeanne LEWIS
19 Dir Campus Security/Chief of Police ... Vacant
88 Int Director Performing Arts Center ... Ms. Suze DIPIETRO-STEWART
41 Dir of Athletics and Recreations ... Mr. Lonnie FOLKS
39 Director of Residential Life ... Dr. Denise O'NEILL
36 Director of Career Services ... Mr. Walter L. TARVER, III
43 General Counsel ... Ms. Melissa HAGER
38 Dir Counseling and Health Services ... Ms. Frances H. BOTTONE
88 Director Academic Advising ... Dr. Peter HAGEN
21 Director Budget & Fiscal Planning ... Mr. Michael WOOD
29 Director Alumni Relations ... Ms. Sara FAUROT-CROWLEY
44 Assoc Chf Devel Ofcr/Campaign Mgr ... Ms. Cindy CRAGER

Rider University (D)

2083 Lawrenceville Road, Lawrenceville NJ 08648-3099
County: Mercer FICE Identification: 002628
Unit ID: 186283
Telephone: (609) 896-5000 Carnegie Class: Master's L
FAX Number: (609) 896-8029 Calendar System: Semester
URL: www.rider.edu
Established: 1865 Annual Undergrad Tuition & Fees: $35,270
Enrollment: 5,485 Coed
Affiliation or Control: Independent Non-Profit IRS Status: 501(c)3
Highest Offering: Master's
Program: Liberal Arts And General; Teacher Preparatory; Professional
Accreditation: M, BUS, BUSA, CACREP, MUS, TED

01 President ... Dr. Mordechai ROZANSKI
05 Provost/Vice Pres Academic Affairs ... Dr. DonnaJean A. FREDEEN
10 Vice President Finance/Treasurer ... Ms. Julie A. KARNS
30 Vice Pres University Advancement ... Mr. Jonathan D. MEER
32 VP Student Affairs/Dean of Students ... Dr. Anthony CAMPBELL
84 Vice Pres Enrollment Management ... Mr. James P. O'HARA
14 Assoc VP Information Technology ... Ms. Carol S. KONDRACH
21 Associate Vice President/Controller ... Ms. Jennifer M. POTTER
09 Assoc Vice Pres Institutional Rsrch ... Mr. Ronald WALKER
18 Associate Vice President ... Mr. Michael F. RECA
45 Associate Vice President Planning ... Ms. Debbie STASOLLA
26 Asst VP for Univ Comm/Marketing ... Mr. John G. LENOX
20 Associate Provost ... Dr. James O. CASTAGNERA
12 Dean Westminster ... Mr. Robert L. ANNIS
07 Dean of Enrollment ... Ms. Susan C. CHRISTIAN
51 Dean College of Cont Studies ... Mr. Boris VILIC
49 Dean Liberal Arts & Science/Educ ... Dr. Pat MOSTO
53 Dean School of Education ... Dr. Sharon SHERMAN
50 Dean Business Administration ... Dr. Steven J. LORENZET
06 Registrar ... Ms. Susan A. STEFANICK
36 Director of Career Placement ... Ms. Gwendolyn J. TYLER
08 Director of Library Services ... Mr. F. William CHICKERING
15 Dir Human Resources/Affirm Action ... Mr. Robert STOTO
19 Director of Public Safety ... Ms. Vickie L. WEAVER
29 Director of Alumni Relations ... Ms. Natalie M. POLLARD
41 Director of Athletics ... Mr. Donald P. HARNUM
37 Director Student Financial Svcs ... Mr. Drew C. AROMANDO
40 Manager College Store ... Mr. Joseph JUDGE
04 Executive Asst to the President ... Ms. Christine ZELENAK

Rowan University (E)

201 Mullica Hill Road, Glassboro NJ 08028-1700
County: Gloucester FICE Identification: 002609
Unit ID: 184782
Telephone: (856) 256-4000 Carnegie Class: Master's L
FAX Number: (856) 256-4929 Calendar System: Semester
URL: www.rowan.edu
Established: 1923 Annual Undergrad Tuition & Fees (In-State): $12,380
Enrollment: 12,183 Coed
Affiliation or Control: State IRS Status: 501(c)3
Highest Offering: Doctorate
Program: Liberal Arts And General; Teacher Preparatory; Professional
Accreditation: M, ART, BUS, CACREP, CS, ENG, #MED, MUS, NURSE, OSTEO, TED, THEA

01 President ... Dr. Ali A. HOUSHMAND
05 Provost ... Dr. James NEWELL
10 Vice Pres of Finance/CFO ... Mr. Joseph F. SCULLY
30 Vice Pres University Advancement ... Vacant
32 VP Student Life/Dean of Students ... Mr. Richard JONES
86 VP for Govt Rels/Gen Couns ... Mr. Steve WEINSTEIN
18 VP for Facilities & Operations ... Mr. Donald MOORE
44 Assoc VP University Advancement ... Mr. Ronald J. TALLARIDA
20 Assoc Provost Academic Affairs ... Dr. Roberta HARVEY
16 VP Employ & Labor Rels/Chf of Stff ... Mr. Robert ZAZZALI
46 Assoc Provost Research ... Dr. Shreekanth MANDAYAM
13 VP Info Resources/Chf Tech Officer ... Dr. Mira LALOVIC-HAND
26 VP for University Relations ... Dr. Jose CARDONA
84 VP Strategic Enroll Mgmt ... Dr. Jeffrey HAND
88 Asst VP Campus Rec/Stdnt Ctr/CES ... Ms. Tina M. PINOCCI
19 Asst VP Public Safety/Emerg Mgmt ... Mr. Michael KANTNER
15 Asst VP Labor Relations ... Mr. Kenneth KUERZI
38 Dir Counseling/Psych Services ... Dr. David RUBENSTEIN
91 Director of EIS ... Mr. James HENDERSON
37 Director of Financial Aid ... Mr. Luis A. TAVAREZ
06 Registrar ... Ms. Muriel FRIERSON
63 Dean of Cooper Medical School of RU ... Dr. Paul KATZ
08 Assoc Provost Library Info Services ... Mr. Scott MUIR
50 Dean Rohrer College of Business ... Dr. Robert BEATTY
81 Dean of Science & Mathematics ... Dr. Parviz ANSARI
53 Dean of Education ... Dr. Monika SHEALEY
57 Dean of Performing Arts ... Dr. John R. PASTIN
58 Dean Graduate & Continuing Educ ... Dr. Horacio SOSA
54 Dean of Engineering ... Dr. Tony LOWMAN
60 Dean Communication & Creative Arts ... Dr. Lorin ARNOLD
83 Dean Humanities & Social Sciences ... Dr. Cindy VITTO
12 Asst Provost/Dean Camden Campus ... Dr. Tyrone MCCOMBS
15 Assoc VP Employment/Labor Relations ... Ms. Eileen SCOTT
22 Asst VP for Equity and Diversity ... Dr. Johanna VELEZ-YELIN
41 Director of Athletics ... Mr. Dan GILMORE
29 Director Alumni Relations ... Ms. Kathy ROZANSKI
07 Director of Admissions ... Dr. Albert BETTS
36 Dir Career Management Center ... Ms. Lizziel SULLIVAN-WILLIAMS
96 Sr Dir Contracting & Procurement ... Ms. Christina BRASTETER
27 Director University Publications ... Ms. Lori MARSHALL
105 Director Web Services ... Ms. Jennifer BELL
85 Director International Center ... Mr. Timothy TORRE
28 Assoc Dean Acad Enrich/Dir EOF/MAP ... Dr. Penny MCPHERSON-BARNES
04 Exec Asst to the President ... Dr. Joanne CONNOR

Rowan University at Camden (F)

200 North Broadway, Camden NJ 08102
Telephone: (856) 361-2900 Identification: 770132
Accreditation: &M

† Main campus is Rowan University in Glassboro, NJ.

*Rutgers the State University of New Jersey Central Office (A)

83 Somerset Street, New Brunswick NJ 08901-1281
County: Middlesex FICE Identification: 002629
Unit ID: 186362
Telephone: (848) 445-4636 Carnegie Class: N/A
FAX Number: (732) 932-8060
URL: www.rutgers.edu

01 President Dr. Robert L. BARCHI
05 Exec VP for Acad Affairs Dr. Richard EDWARDS
102 Pres Rutgers Found/EVP Dev & Alum Mr. Nevin E. KESSLER
10 Senior VP for Finance & Admin Mr. Bruce C. FEHN
100 Chief of Staff Dr. Gregory S. JACKSON
21 Vice President Budgeting Dr. Nancy S. WINTERBAUER
14 Vice President Info Tech Mr. Donald E. SMITH
26 Vice President University Relations Ms. Kimberly M. MANNING
18 Vice Pres Univ Facil/Capital Plng Mr. Antonio CALCADO
88 Vice Chancellor Interprofess Ed Dr. Denise RODGERS
43 Senior VP & General Counsel Dr. John J. FARMER
29 VP for Development & Alumni Rel Vacant
04 Exec Assistant to the President Ms. Carol KONCSOL
20 VP Academic Affairs & Admin Dr. Karen R. STUBAUS
15 Vice Pres of Fac & Staff Resources Ms. Vivian FERNANDEZ
08 VP Info Services & Univ Librarian Ms. Marianne I. GAUNT
101 Secretary of the University Mrs. Leslie A. FEHRENBACH
19 Vice Pres Admin & Public Safety Mr. Jay KOHL
23 Exec Director Health Svcs Dr. Melodee S. LASKY
06 University Registrar Mr. Kenneth J. IUSO
37 University Dir Financial Aid Ms. Jean MCDONALD-RASH
41 Director Intercollegiate Athletics Ms. Julie K. HERMANN
22 Assoc VP Labor Relations Mr. Harry M. AGNOSTAK
36 Director Career Services Ms. Jennifer BROYLES
09 Exec Dir Inst Research & Planning Dr. Robert J. HEFFERNAN
86 Vice President Public Affairs Mr. Peter J. MCDONOUGH, JR.
84 Vice President Enrollment Mgmt Dr. Courtney MCANUFF
29 VP Alumni Relations Ms. Donna THORNTON
28 Dir Inst Diversity & Equity Dr. Karen R. STUBAUS
86 Asst VP Federal Relations Ms. Francine PFEIFFER
86 Senior Director State Relations Vacant
88 Assc VP Promtg Women Sci Eng Math Dr. Joan W. BENNETT
88 VP Health Science Partnerships Dr. Kenneth J. BRESLAUER
12 Interim Chancellor New Brunswick Dr. Richard EDWARDS
12 Chancellor Rutgers-Camden Dr. Wendell E. PRITCHETT
12 Interim Chancellor RU Newark Dr. Todd CLEAR
88 Int Chancellor Biomed & Health Sci Dr. Christopher MOLLOY
88 Director Cancer Institute NJ Dr. Robert S. DIPAOLA
88 Interim VP Research & Econ Dev Dr. Kenneth J. BRESLAUER
88 VP Physical Sci & Eng Partnership Dr. Leonard C. FELDMAN
11 Exec Vice Chancellor Admin Dr. Kemel W. DAWKINS
21 Vice Chancellor Admin & Finance Dr. Larry R. GAINES, JR.
20 Vice Chancellor Acad Pgms & Svcs Dr. John GUNKEL
88 University Controller Mr. Stephen J. DIPAOLO
21 VP Finance & Assoc Treasurer Ms. Delanie S. MOLER
88 VP International & Global Affairs Dr. Joanna REGULSKA
106 Interim VP Cont Stdnt & Dist Educ Dr. Richard J. NOVAK
28 VP Intl Diversity & Inclusion Dr. Jorge R. SCHEMENT

*Rutgers the State University of New Jersey New Brunswick Campus (B)

85 Somerset Street, New Brunswick NJ 08901-1281
County: Middlesex FICE Identification: 006964
Unit ID: 186380
Telephone: (848) 932-4636 Carnegie Class: RU/VH
FAX Number: (732) 932-8060 Calendar System: Semester
URL: www.rutgers.edu
Established: 1766 Annual Undergrad Tuition & Fees (In-State): $13,499
Enrollment: 40,434 Coed
Affiliation or Control: State IRS Status: 501(c)3
Highest Offering: Doctorate
Program: Liberal Arts And General; Teacher Preparatory; Professional
Accreditation: M, CACREP, CEA, CLPSY, DANCE, DIETD, ENG, LIB, LSAR, MUS, PH, PHAR, PLNG, SCPSY, SPAA, SW, TEAC

02 Interim Chancellor NB Campus Dr. Richard EDWARDS
05 Provost New Brunswick Vacant
58 Dean Graduate School Dr. Jerome J. KUKOR
80 Dean EJB School Plng/Public Policy Dr. James W. HUGHES
81 Exec Dean Sch Enviro/Biological Sci Dr. Robert M. GOODMAN
12 Dean Douglass Residential College Dr. Jacquelyn S. LITT
12 Dean Livingston Campus Dr. Lea P. STEWART
12 Dean Busch Campus Dr. Thomas V. PAPATHOMAS
49 Acting Executive Dean of SAS Dr. Richard S. FALK
12 Dean College Avenue Campus Dr. Matthew K. MATSUDA
12 Dean Cook Campus Dr. Barbara TURPIN
12 Dean Univ College Community Dr. Susan J. SCHURMAN
54 Dean School of Engineering Dr. Thomas N. FARRIS
67 Acting Dean Ernest Mario Sch Pharm Dr. Joseph BARONE
57 Dean Mason Gross School of Art Dr. George B. STAUFFER
62 Actg Dean Sch Communication & Info Dr. Claire R. MCINERNEY
83 Dean Grad School Applied/Prof Psych Dr. Stanley B. MESSER
53 Dean Grad School of Education Dr. Richard DE LISI
66 Dean College of Nursing Dr. William L. HOLZEMER
70 Actg Dean School of Social Work Dr. Kathleen J. POTTICK
69 Interim Dean Sch Public Health Dr. George G. RHOADS
50 Sr Assoc Dean Sch of Business NB Dr. Martin S. MARKOWITZ
88 Dean Sch Mgmt/Labor Relations Dr. Susan J. SCHURMAN
06 University Registrar Mr. Kenneth J. IUSO
104 Director Rutgers Study Abroad Dr. Giorgio G. DIMAURO
07 Director Graduate Admissions Ms. Linda J. COSTA
37 University Dir Financial Aid Ms. Jean MCDONALD-RASH
36 Dir Career Dev/Placement Svcs Ms. Jennifer BROYLES
27 Deputy Chief Information Officer Ms. Bernice GINDER
09 Exec Dir Institutional Rsrch & Plng Dr. Robert J. HEFFERNAN
39 Director Residence Life Mr. Michael TOLBERT
84 VP Enrollment Management Dr. Courtney O. MCANUFF
88 Provost RBHS New Brunswick Campus Vacant
63 Dean RWJ Medical School Dr. Peter S. AMENTA
88 Interim Chancellor RBHS Dr. Christopher MOLLOY

*Rutgers the State University of New Jersey Camden Campus (C)

303 Cooper Street, Camden NJ 08102-1461
County: Camden FICE Identification: 004741
Unit ID: 186371
Telephone: (856) 225-6026 Carnegie Class: Master's M
FAX Number: (856) 225-6495 Calendar System: Semester
URL: www.camden.rutgers.edu
Established: 1927 Annual Undergrad Tuition & Fees (In-State): $13,348
Enrollment: 6,343 Coed
Affiliation or Control: State IRS Status: 501(c)3
Highest Offering: Doctorate
Program: Liberal Arts And General; Teacher Preparatory; Professional
Accreditation: &M, BUS, LAW, NURSE, PTA, SPAA, TEAC

02 Chancellor Dr. Wendell E. PRITCHETT
05 Provost Vacant
11 Vice Chancellor Admin & Finance Dr. Larry R. GAINES, JR.
32 Assoc Chancellor Student Life Dr. Mary Beth B. DAISEY
20 Assoc Chancellor for UG Education Ms. Julie AMON
84 Assoc Chancellor Enrollment Mgmt Dr. Rodney MORRISON
88 Assoc Chancellor Civic Engage Mr. Andrew J. SELIGSOHN
88 Director Economic Development Mr. Gregory GAMBLE
61 Dean School of Law Dr. Rayman L. SOLOMON
58 Dean Grad School Dr. Kriste LINDENMEYER
50 Dean School of Business Dr. Jaishankar GANESH
49 Dean Fac Arts & Sci/Univ Col Dr. Kriste LINDENMEYER
66 Dean School of Nursing Dr. Joanne P. ROBINSON
26 Assoc Chancellor for Ext Relations Mr. Michael J. SEPANIC
06 Registrar Ms. Theresa R. CRISTOFARO
37 Director Financial Aid Ms. Linda J. TAYLOR-BURCH
10 Director Campus Financial Services Ms. Rosa M. RIVERA
19 Chief Campus Police Chief Guy M. STILL
29 Director Alumni Relations Mr. Charles J. MANNELLA
15 Human Resources Manager Mr. Gregory M. O'SHEA
18 Director Facilities Services Vacant
21 Business Manager FAS Camden Ms. Marlene DRUDING
41 Dir Athletics & Rec Services Mr. Jeffrey L. DEAN
36 Asst Dean/Director Stdnt Career Ctr Mr. James MARINO
38 Assoc Director Student Counseling Dr. N. Maria SERRA
30 Director of Development Ms. Akua ASIAMAH-ANDRADE
08 Director Paul Robeson Library Dr. Gary A. GOLDEN
23 Director Health Services Dr. Paul P. BROWN
39 Dir House & Resident Life Mr. Brandon CHANDLER
87 Summer Coord/Sr Program Coordinator Dr. Paul C. BUTLER
46 Director Sponsored Research Ms. Carberta A. MORRISON
13 Director Information Technology Mr. Joseph R. SANDERS
30 Asst Chancellor Development Camden Ms. Tracy E. ELLIOTT
07 Director of Admissions Ms. Victoria E. TOOMER
85 Asst Dean International Students Ms. Elizabeth A. ATKINS

† Regional accreditation is carried under Rutgers the State University of New Jersey New Brunswick.

*Rutgers the State University of New Jersey Newark Campus (D)

249 University Avenue, Newark NJ 07102-1897
County: Essex FICE Identification: 002631
Unit ID: 186399
Telephone: (973) 353-5568 Carnegie Class: RU/H
FAX Number: (973) 353-1048 Calendar System: Semester
URL: www.newark.rutgers.edu
Established: 1892 Annual Undergrad Tuition & Fees (In-State): $12,998
Enrollment: 12,011 Coed
Affiliation or Control: State IRS Status: 501(c)3
Highest Offering: Doctorate
Program: Liberal Arts And General; Teacher Preparatory; Professional
Accreditation: &M, ANEST, BUS, LAW, NURSE, SPAA, SW, TEAC

02 Interim Chancellor Dr. Todd R. CLEAR
05 Provost Vacant
10 Exec Vice Chancellor Administration Dr. Kemel W. DAWKINS
15 Director of Human Resources Ms. Susan CHAMPION-TINTORER
18 Assoc Vice Chancellor Facilities Dr. Christopher PYE
30 Vice Chancellor for Development Dr. Irene O'BRIEN
05 Vice Chancellor Acad Pgms & Svcs Dr. John GUNKEL
46 Vice Chancellor Research Dr. Alexander E. GATES
26 Assoc Chancellor External Relations Dr. Steven GOLDSTEIN
11 Asst Chanc Admin Services/Budget Dr. Mary TAMASCO
35 Asst Chancellor for Student Life Dr. Gerald MASSENBURG
88 Asst Chancellor Comm Partner Dr. Diane HILL
06 Acting Registrar Dr. Marie DIAZ-TORRES
21 Exec Dir Business& Financial Svcs Dr. Sanjana RIMAL
13 Director Information Technology Ms. Stacia A. ZELICK
07 Director of Admissions Mr. Jason HAND
19 Director Public Safety Newark Mr. Michael P. LATTIMORE
27 Director of Communications Ms. Helen S. PAXTON
08 Interim Asst Chancellor/Dir Dana L Dr. Jeanne BOYLE
37 Director Financial Aid Mr. Melvin L. BROWN
49 Interim Dean Faculty Arts & Science Dr. Jan Ellen LEWIS
61 Acting Dean of School of Law Dr. Ronald K. CHEN, JR.
50 Dean Business Newark/New Bruns Dr. Glenn R. SHAFER
66 Dean College of Nursing Dr. William L. HOLZEMER
88 Dean School Criminal Justice Dr. Todd R. CLEAR
38 Acting Director Student Counseling Dr. Polly MCLAUGHLIN
96 Director of Purchasing & Admin Svc Mr. Alvin L. COOLEY
80 Dean Sch of Public Affairs & Admin Dr. Marc HOLZER
39 Director Housing & Residence Life Dr. Angelita BONILLA
23 Director Health Services Dr. Sandra SAMUELS
41 Director of Athletics & Recreation Mr. Mark GRIFFIN
82 Director of Global Affairs Dr. Jean-Marc COICAUD
58 Dean Graduate School Newark Dr. Margaret M. SHIFFRAR
87 Director Summer Session Dr. Elizabeth C. ROWE
88 Assoc Dean/Dir Robeson Campus Ctr Dr. Clayton WALTON
28 Director Diverse Community Affairs Dr. Maren GREATHOUSE
88 Provost RBHS Newark Campus Vacant

† Regional accreditation is carried under Rutgers the State University of New Jersey New Brunswick.

*Rutgers Graduate School of Biomedical Sciences (E)

185 South Orange Avenue, MSB C-696, Newark NJ 07107-1709
Telephone: (973) 972-5332 FICE Identification: 011174
Accreditation: &M

† Main campus is Rutgers the State University of New Jersey Central Office in New Brunswick, NJ.

*Rutgers-New Jersey Medical School (F)

185 S Orange Avenue, Newark NJ 07101-1709
Telephone: (973) 972-4538 FICE Identification: 002620
Accreditation: &M, MED

† Main campus is Rutgers the State University of New Jersey Central Office in New Brunswick, NJ.

*Rutgers - Robert Wood Johnson Medical School (G)

675 Hoes Lane, Piscataway NJ 08854-5635
Telephone: (732) 235-6300 FICE Identification: 024549
Accreditation: &M, IPSY, MED

† Main campus is Rutgers the State University of New Jersey Central Office in New Brunswick, NJ.

*Rutgers School of Dental Medicine (H)

110 Bergen Street, Room B-830, Newark NJ 07101-1709
Telephone: (973) 972-4633 FICE Identification: 024635
Accreditation: &M, DENT

† Main campus is Rutgers the State University of New Jersey Central Office in New Brunswick, NJ.

*Rutgers School of Health Related Professions (I)

65 Bergen Street, Room 149, Newark NJ 07101-1709
Telephone: (973) 972-5454 FICE Identification: 020668
Accreditation: &M, ARCPA, CACREP, CAHIIM, CORE, CVT, CYTO, DA, DH, DIETC, DIETI, DMS, MT, NMT, PTA

† Main campus is Rutgers the State University of New Jersey Central Office in New Brunswick, NJ.

*Rutgers School of Nursing (J)

65 Bergen Street, Room 1126, Newark NJ 07101-1709
Telephone: (973) 972-4276 Identification: 666970
Accreditation: &M, MIDWF, NURSE

† Main campus is Rutgers the State University of New Jersey Central Office in New Brunswick, NJ.

*Rutgers-School of Public Health (K)

683 Hoes Lane W, Room 235, Piscataway NJ 08854-8021
Telephone: (732) 445-9700 Identification: 666991
Accreditation: &M, PH

† Main campus is Rutgers the State University of New Jersey Central Office in New Brunswick, NJ.

Saint Peter's University (L)

2641 Kennedy Boulevard, Jersey City NJ 07306-5997
County: Hudson FICE Identification: 002638
Unit ID: 186432
Telephone: (201) 761-6000 Carnegie Class: Master's L
FAX Number: (201) 761-7801 Calendar System: Semester
URL: www.saintpeters.edu
Established: 1872 Annual Undergrad Tuition & Fees: $32,230
Enrollment: 3,045 Coed
Affiliation or Control: Roman Catholic IRS Status: 501(c)3
Highest Offering: Doctorate
Program: Liberal Arts And General; Teacher Preparatory; Professional

Accreditation: M, NURSE, TEAC

01 President ... Dr. Eugene J. CORNACCHIA
05 Provost/Vice Pres Academic Affairs ... Dr. Marylou YAM
10 Vice Pres of Finance & Business ... Mr. Denton L. STARGEL
30 Vice President Advancement ... Mr. Michael A. FAZIO
32 Assoc VP Student Life & Develop ... Ms. Carla THARP
42 Vice Pres for Mission & Ministry ... Fr. Michael L. BRADEN, SJ
84 VP Enrollment Mgmt & Marketing ... Mr. Jeffrey HANDLER
04 Special Assistant to the President ... Dr. Virginia BENDER
20 Academic Dean Day Session ... Dr. Velda GOLDBERG
51 Assoc Dean & Director of JC SPCS ... Ms. Elizabeth KANE
78 Assoc Dean of Experiential Lrng ... Dr. Peter M. GOTLIEB
88 Associate Dean of Undergraduates ... Dr. Anna CICIRELLI
35 Dean of Students ... Mr. Anthony SKEVAKIS
26 Director University Communications ... Ms. Sarah MALINOWSKI
84 Director Enrollment/Research/Tech ... Mr. Ben SCHOLZ
07 Director of Admissions ... Ms. Elizabeth SULLIVAN
08 Director of the Libraries ... Mr. David HARDGROVE
37 Director of Student Fin Aid ... Ms. Jennifer RAGSDALE
06 Registrar & Dir of Student Accounts ... Ms. Irma WILLIAMS
27 Chief Information Officer ... Ms. Dale HOCHSTEIN
09 Director of Institutional Research ... Mr. Lamberto C. NIEVES
66 Dean of Nursing ... Dr. Ann TRITAK
19 Director of Campus Safety ... Mr. Art YOUMANS
24 Instructional Design Specialist ... Ms. Renee EVANS
15 Director of Human Resources ... Mr. Joseph A. DESCISCIO
29 Executive Director Alumni Relations ... Ms. Gloria MERCURIO
30 Director of Gift/Planning ... Ms. Ana M. CRAVO
38 Director Personal Development ... Mr. Ron BECKER
39 Director of Residence Life ... Ms. Rochelle GABRIEL
41 Director of Athletics ... Mr. Joseph QUINLAN
42 Director of Campus Ministry ... Rev. Rocco DANZI, SJ
36 Director of Career Services ... Mr. Crescenzo FONZO
13 Director of Network Services ... Mr. Bert VABRE
85 Foreign Studies Adviser ... Mr. Tushar TRIVEDI
18 Manager of College Services ... Ms. Anna DE PAULA

Saint Peter's University Englewood Cliffs Campus (A)

Hudson Terrace, Englewood Cliffs NJ 07632
Telephone: (201) 761-7480 Identification: 770133
Accreditation: &M

† Main campus is Saint Peter's University in Jersey City, NJ.

Salem Community College (B)

460 Hollywood Avenue, Carneys Point NJ 08069-2799
County: Salem FICE Identification: 005461
Unit ID: 186469
Telephone: (856) 299-2100 Carnegie Class: Assoc/Pub-S-SC
FAX Number: (856) 351-2634 Calendar System: Semester
URL: www.salemcc.edu
Established: 1972 Annual Undergrad Tuition & Fees (In-District): $4,050
Enrollment: 1,283 Coed
Affiliation or Control: State/Local IRS Status: 501(c)3
Highest Offering: Associate Degree
Program: Occupational; 2-Year Principally Bachelor's Creditable
Accreditation: M, ADNUR, PNUR

01 President ... Mrs. Joan M. BAILLIE
30 Exec Asst to Pres/Dir Advancem/Alum ... Mr. William CLARK
05 Dean of Academic Affairs/CAO ... Mr. Mark MCCORMICK
66 Director Nursing ... Mrs. Michelle O'NEAL
84 Director Enrollment/Admissions ... Mr. Kevin CATALFAMO
102 Chief Foundation Officer ... Ms. Linda P. SMITH
96 Manager of Purchasing ... Mr. John RECCHINTI
09 Director Inst Rsrch/Planning/Devel ... Ms. Denise DERSCH
10 Manager of Finance ... Ms. Catherine PRIEST
37 Director of Financial Aid ... Mr. Maurice THOMAS
06 Registrar ... Ms. Elizabeth MERCADO

Seton Hall University (C)

400 S Orange Avenue, South Orange NJ 07079-2697
County: Essex FICE Identification: 002632
Unit ID: 186584
Telephone: (973) 761-9000 Carnegie Class: DRU
FAX Number: N/A Calendar System: Semester
URL: www.shu.edu
Established: 1856 Annual Undergrad Tuition & Fees: $35,820
Enrollment: 9,357 Coed
Affiliation or Control: Roman Catholic IRS Status: 501(c)3
Highest Offering: Doctorate
Program: Liberal Arts And General; Teacher Preparatory; Professional
Accreditation: M, ARCPA, BUS, BUSA, COPSY, LAW, MFCD, NURSE, OT, PTA, SP, SPAA, SW, TED, THEOL

01 President ... Dr. A. Gabriel ESTEBAN
05 Provost & Executive Vice President ... Dr. Larry ROBINSON
10 Vice Pres for Finance/CFO ... Mr. Stephen A. GRAHAM
11 Vice President for Administration ... Mr. Dennis J. GARBINI
43 Vice President & General Counsel ... Ms. Catherine A. KIERNAN
30 Vice Pres Univ Advancement ... Mr. David BOHAN
32 Vice President Student Affairs ... Dr. Tracy T. GOTTLIEB
84 Vice President of Enrollment Mgmt ... Dr. Alyssa MCCLOUD
42 Vice Pres for Mission & Ministry ... Msgr. C. Anthony ZICCARDI
16 Assoc Vice Pres Human Resources ... Mr. David K. MCNICHOL
29 Assoc VP Alumni/Government Rels ... Mr. Matthew BOROWICK
44 Assoc Vice Pres Univ Advance ... Mr. Joseph GUASCONI
26 Assoc VP Public Relations & Mktg ... Mr. Dan P. KALMANSON
18 Assoc VP for Facilities & Operation ... Mr. John SIGNORELLO
35 Asst VP Student Affs/Dir Pub Safety ... Mr. Patrick LINFANTE
31 Asc VP/Dean of Students/Cmty Dev ... Ms. Karen VAN NORMAN
20 Senior Vice Provost ... Dr. Joan GUETTI
88 Assoc Prov Finance/Administration ... Dr. Nicholas SNOW
45 Assoc Provost/Dean Rsrch/Grad Stds ... Dr. Gregory A. BURTON
49 Dean of Arts & Sciences ... Dr. Michael S. ZAVADA
50 Dean School of Business ... Dr. Joyce A. STRAWSER
66 Dean of Nursing ... Dr. Phyllis HANSELL
53 Dean College Education Svcs ... Dr. Grace MAY
73 Dean School of Theology ... Msgr. Joseph R. REILLY
63 Dean School of Health & Med Science ... Dr. Brian SHULMAN
82 Int Dean Diplomacy/Intl Relations ... Amb. Thomas P. MELADY
61 Dean of Law School ... Mr. Patrick J. HOBBS
08 Dean of University Libraries ... Dr. John E. BUSCHMAN
51 Dean Cont Educ/Professional Studies ... Ms. Nancy LOW-HOGAN
88 Assoc Dean/Director of EOP ... Dr. Hasani CARTER
88 Assoc Dean/Exec Dir of Special Pgms ... Ms. Cassandra E. DAVIS
21 Director of Business Affairs ... Ms. Theresa L. DEEHAN
13 Chief Information Officer ... Dr. Stephen LANDRY
28 Director Compliance & Risk Mgmt ... Ms. Lori A. BROWN
37 Director for Financial Aid ... Ms. Javonda T. ASSANTE
39 Director of Housing/Residence Life ... Ms. Tara HART
06 University Registrar ... Ms. Mary Ellen FARRELL
07 Recruitment/Compensation Manager ... Ms. Jane JACOBS
36 Director of the Career Center ... Ms. Reesa GREENWALD
41 Dir Athletics/Recreational Services ... Mr. Patrick G. LYONS
18 Director of Physical Plant ... Mr. Steve KURTYKA
38 Director of Counseling ... Dr. Katherine EVANS
42 Director of Campus Ministry ... Rev. Nicholas FIGURELLI
88 Minister to Priest Community ... Msgr. James M. CAFONE
09 Dir Planning Inst Research & Asses ... Ms. Connie L. BEALE
07 Dir of Undergraduate Admissions ... Dr. Wendy W. LIN-COOK
96 Director of Procurement ... Mr. Martin E. KOELLER
23 Director Health Services ... Ms. Mary Elizabeth COSTELLO
88 Director Core Curriculum ... Dr. Anthony C. SCIGLITANO, JR.
15 Manager Employer & Labor Relations ... Vacant

Seton Hall University School of Law (D)

One Newark Center, Newark NJ 07102-5210
County: Essex FICE Identification: 009986
Telephone: (973) 642-8500 Carnegie Class: Not Classified
FAX Number: (973) 642-8031 Calendar System: Semester
URL: law.shu.edu
Established: 1951 Annual Graduate Tuition & Fees: $49,070
Enrollment: 983 Coed
Affiliation or Control: Roman Catholic IRS Status: 501(c)3
Highest Offering: First Professional Degree; No Undergraduates
Program: Professional
Accreditation: &M, LAW

01 Dean ... Patrick E. HOBBS
05 Vice Dean ... Erik R. LILLQUIST
20 Associate Dean for Curriculum ... Claudette L. ST. ROMAIN
84 Dean of Enrollment Management ... Gisele JOACHIM
32 Dean of Students ... Cara Herrick FOERST
20 Asst Dean Academic Affairs/Policy ... Gary S. BAVERO
10 Asst Dean Finance/Administration ... Terry DE ALMEIDA
30 Asst Dean Alumni/Development ... Vacant
13 Asst Dean Leg Comp/Info Tech/Comm ... Carmelo LUBRANO
09 Asst Dean for Special Projects ... Rosa ALVES-FERREIRA
36 Asst Dean of Career Services ... Jessica MILES
36 Director of Career Services ... Sonia CUNHA
08 Director Law Library ... Charles SULLIVAN
88 Director Special Programs ... Gina FONDETTO
37 Director of Financial Aid ... Karen A. SOKOL
42 Campus Minister ... Rev. Nicholas GENGARO
06 Registrar & Bursar ... Jo Ann MALDONADO
18 Director of Facilities ... John FLANAGAN
90 Director PC Support/Systems Mgmt ... Michael J. MCBRIDE
91 Director of IT Projects ... Eric D. WINCH
19 Security Manager ... Gerald LENIHAN
08 Law Librarian ... Christina L. BENNETT
102 Director Corp/Foundation Relations ... Andrea CASCARANO
43 Director Center for Social Justice ... Lori A. NESSEL
29 Director Alumni Relations ... Lori THIMMEL
44 Director of Development ... Anthony BELLUCCI
35 Director Student Services ... Molly ZLOCK
20 Director Academic Services ... Gwenda R. DAVIS
26 Exec Director of Communications ... Janet LEMONNIER
36 Assoc Director of Career Services ... Paula EDGAR
36 Assoc Director of Career Services ... Erin SCHERZER
07 Assoc Director of Admissions ... Katherine VALASEK
07 Assoc Director of Admissions ... Mimi HUANG
23 Exec Dir Center Health/Pharm/Policy ... Simone HANDLER-HUTCHINSON
58 Asst Dean of Graduate Programs ... Helen CUMMINGS
105 Manager Website Services ... Ana L. SANTOS
36 Career Development Counselor ... Joseph STEINBERG

† Regional accreditation is carried under the parent institution in South Orange, NJ.

Stevens Institute of Technology (E)

Castle Point on Hudson, Hoboken NJ 07030-5991
County: Hudson FICE Identification: 002639
Unit ID: 186867
Telephone: (201) 216-5000 Carnegie Class: RU/H
FAX Number: (201) 216-8341 Calendar System: Semester
URL: www.stevens.edu
Established: 1870 Annual Undergrad Tuition & Fees: $44,302
Enrollment: 5,649 Coed
Affiliation or Control: Independent Non-Profit IRS Status: 501(c)3
Highest Offering: Doctorate
Program: Liberal Arts And General; Technical Emphasis
Accreditation: M, CS, ENG

01 President ... Dr. Nariman FARVARDIN
04 Exec Assistant to the President ... Ms. Diana COLOMBO
03 Provost/University Vice President ... Dr. George P. KORFIATIS
30 Vice Pres Development ... Mr. Edward EICHHORN
10 Vice Pres for Finance/Treasurer ... Mr. Randy GREENE
07 VP Enrollment/Student Affairs ... Ms. Marybeth MURPHY
18 VP Facilities/Community Relations ... Mr. Henry DOBBELAAR
15 Vice President Human Resources ... Mr. Mark SAMOLEWICZ
43 Vice President General Counsel ... Ms. Kathy L. SCHULZ
32 Asst VP Stdnt Dev/Dir Coop Educ ... Mr. Joseph STAHLEY
13 VP for Information Technology & CIO ... Mr. David DODD
27 VP Communications & Marketing ... Mr. Edward STUKANE
05 Dean Undergraduate Academics ... Dr. Larry RUSS
35 Dean of Student Life ... Mr. Kenneth NILSEN
39 Dean of Residence Life ... Ms. Trina BALLANTYNE
20 Assoc Dean Undergraduate Academics ... Dr. Erol CESMEBASI
29 Exec Director Alumni Association ... Ms. Anita LANG
36 Director of Career Services ... Ms. Lynn INSLEY
19 Chief/Director of Security ... Mr. Timothy GRIFFIN
41 Athletic Director ... Mr. Russell ROGERS
85 Dir of Intl Student/Scholar Svcs ... Ms. Doris CLAUSEN
06 Registrar ... Ms. Laura Lee BOWENS
37 Director Student Financial Aid ... Mr. Shawn O'NEILL
38 Director Student Counseling ... Ms. Jodi STREICH
08 Director of Library ... Ms. Ourida OUBRAHAM
40 Manager Campus Bookstore ... Ms. Teresa TRIDENTE
25 Director Sponsored Research ... Ms. Barbara DEHAVEN
58 Dean of Graduate Academics ... Dr. Charles SUFFEL
54 Dean School of Engineering & Scienc ... Dr. Michael S. BRUNO
72 Dean Howe Sch of Technology Mgmt ... Dr. Gregory PRASTACOS
49 Dean College of Arts & Letters ... Dr. Lisa DOLLING
88 Dean School of Systems & Enterprise ... Dr. Dinesh VERMA
09 Director of Institutional Research ... Ms. Agata WOLFE
100 Chief of Staff ... Ms. Elisabeth MCGRATH
28 Director of Diversity and Inclusion ... Ms. Susan METZ
88 Vice Provost Strategic Initiatives ... Mr. Ralph G. GIFFIN
20 Vice Provost Academics ... Dr. Constantin CHASSAPIS
46 Vice Provost of Research ... Dr. Mo DEHGHANI

Sussex County Community College (F)

One College Hill Road, Newton NJ 07860-1146
County: Sussex FICE Identification: 025688
Unit ID: 247603
Telephone: (973) 300-2100 Carnegie Class: Assoc/Pub-S-SC
FAX Number: (973) 579-9351 Calendar System: Semester
URL: www.sussex.edu
Established: 1982 Annual Undergrad Tuition & Fees (In-District): $5,010
Enrollment: 3,403 Coed
Affiliation or Control: State/Local IRS Status: 501(c)3
Highest Offering: Associate Degree
Program: Occupational; 2-Year Principally Bachelor's Creditable
Accreditation: M, MAC, SURGT

01 President ... Dr. Paul MAZUR
04 Asst to President/Board of Trustees ... Wendy FULLEM
05 Interim VP of Academic Affairs ... William WAITE
10 VP of Finance and Operations ... Frank NOCELLA
32 Dean of Students ... Deborah MCFADDEN
16 Exec Dir of Human Res/Legal Matters ... Debra CARTER
26 Exec Dir of Marketing/Public Info ... Paul RICHARTZ
30 Exec Director of the Foundation ... Vacant
59 Sr Dean of Business/Law/Math/Scienc ... William WAITE
49 Interim Dean Lib Arts/Sol Sci/Educ ... Dr. Kathleen OKAY
24 Assoc Dean of Learning Resources ... Jan TENSEN
20 Asst Dean of Academic Affairs ... Alberta JAEGER
103 Asst Dean of Community Ed/Workf Dev ... Kathleen NELSON
41 Asst Dean of Athletics/Student Affs ... John KUNTZ
21 Exec Director of Finance ... Kristine PERRY
18 Dir Facilities/Campus Security ... Kenneth EVANS
13 Dir of Management Info Systems ... Craig MACKEY
88 Director of Bursar Office ... Catherine WINTERFIELD
106 Dir of Media Services/Distance Educ ... Tony SELIMO
08 Director of Library ... Stephanie COOPER
07 Director of Admissions ... Todd POLTERSDORF
88 Director of Health Sciences ... Barbara COOK
88 Director of Instructional Design ... Anthony SORRENTO
37 Director of Financial Aid ... Vacant
88 Director of Accounting ... Patricia NOBLIN
09 Dir of Institutional Research ... Susan HAYES
06 Assoc Registrar ... Solweig DIMINO
35 Assoc Dir of Student Activities ... Heidi GREGG

Talmudical Academy of New Jersey (G)

Route 524, Adelphia NJ 07710-9999
County: Monmouth FICE Identification: 011989
Unit ID: 186900
Telephone: (732) 431-1600 Carnegie Class: Spec/Faith
FAX Number: (732) 431-3951 Calendar System: Semester
Established: 1971 Annual Undergrad Tuition & Fees: $11,000
Enrollment: 58 Male
Affiliation or Control: Independent Non-Profit IRS Status: 501(c)3
Highest Offering: Baccalaureate
Program: Teacher Preparatory; Professional

Accreditation: RABN

01 President ... Mr. Charles SEMAH
05 Dean ... Rabbi Yeruchim SHAIN

Thomas Edison State College (A)

101 W State Street, Trenton NJ 08608-1176
County: Mercer FICE Identification: 021922
Unit ID: 187046
Telephone: (609) 984-1100 Carnegie Class: Master's S
FAX Number: (609) 292-9000 Calendar System: Other
URL: www.tesc.edu
Established: 1972 Annual Undergrad Tuition & Fees (In-State): $5,700
Enrollment: 20,877 Coed
Affiliation or Control: State IRS Status: 501(c)3
Highest Offering: Master's
Program: Liberal Arts And General; Professional
Accreditation: M, ENGT, NUR, NURSE, POLYT, TEAC

01 President ... Dr. George A. PRUITT
05 Vice President & Provost ... Mr. William J. SEATON
10 Vice Pres Administration & Finance ... Mr. Christopher STRINGER
26 Vice President Public Affairs ... Mr. John P. THURBER
31 Vice Pres Cmty & Govt Relations ... Ms. Robin WALTON
45 VP Institutional Planning/Research ... Mr. Dennis DEVERY
84 VP Enrollment Mgmt/Learner Services ... Dr. Mary Ellen CARO
88 Vice Prov Academic Administration ... Dr. Henry VAN ZYL
51 Vice Prov/Dean Watson Sch Cont Stds ... Dr. Joseph YOUNGBLOOD
88 Vice Prov Ctr Assessment of Lrng ... Mr. Marc SINGER
88 Assoc VP Enrollment Management ... Ms. Sylvia HAMILTON
88 Assoc VP Military/Veteran Education ... Mr. Louis MARTINI
32 Assoc VP and Dean of Learner Svcs ... Dr. Raymond YOUNG
09 Assoc VP for Planning & Research ... Dr. Ann Marie SENIOR
16 Assoc VP & Director Human Resources ... Ms. Mindi BEAVER
27 Assoc VP/Director of Communications ... Mr. Joseph GUZZARDO
88 Assoc Provost Learning Technology ... Mr. Matthew COOPER
21 Treasurer ... Mr. Stephen D. ALBANO
100 Chief of Staff ... Ms. Linda M. MEEHAN
26 Director Market Research/ Assessment ... Ms. Marie R. POWER-BARNES
43 General Counsel ... Ms. Barbara KLEVA
66 Dean School of Nursing ... Dr. Phyllis MARSHALL
49 Dean Heavin Sch of Arts & Sciences ... Vacant
50 Dean School of Business & Mgmt ... Dr. Michael WILLIAMS
06 Registrar ... Ms. Sharon SMITH
72 Dean School of Applied Sci/Tech ... Dr. John AJE
21 Controller ... Ms. Michele EVANCHIK
13 Chief Information Officer ... Mr. Drew W. HOPKINS
07 Director Admissions ... Mr. David HOFTIEZER
29 Director of Alumni Affairs ... Ms. Roxanne GLOBIS
37 Director of Financial Aid ... Mr. James OWENS
18 Director Facilities & Operations ... Ms. Mary C. HACK
21 Dir Instnl Environ/Budget Analysis ... Ms. Diane KOYE
21 Admin of Student Fees & Revenues ... Mr. Philip SANDERS
30 Director of Development ... Ms. Misty ISAK
102 Director Corporate Relations ... Mr. Frederick BRAND
08 State Librarian ... Ms. Mary CHUTE
105 Director Website & Multimedia Produ ... Mr. Jeffery LUSHBAUGH
88 Director of Advancement Services ... Ms. Erica SPIZZIRRRI
44 Asc Dir Annual Fund/Donor Relations ... Ms. Jennifer GUERRERO
88 Executive Director Watson Institute ... Ms. Barbara JOHNSON
88 Dir Learning Outcomes Assessment ... Ms. Cynthia MACMILLAN
88 ADA Coordinator ... Ms. Laura BRENNER-SCOTTI

Union County College (B)

1033 Springfield Avenue, Cranford NJ 07016-1598
County: Union FICE Identification: 002643
Unit ID: 187198
Telephone: (908) 709-7000 Carnegie Class: Assoc/Pub-S-MC
FAX Number: (908) 709-0527 Calendar System: Semester
URL: www.ucc.edu
Established: 1933 Annual Undergrad Tuition & Fees (In-District): $4,080
Enrollment: 12,146 Coed
Affiliation or Control: State/Local IRS Status: 501(c)3
Highest Offering: Associate Degree
Program: Occupational; 2-Year Principally Bachelor's Creditable
Accreditation: M, PNUR, PTAA

01 President ... Dr. Margaret M. MCMENAMIN
05 Vice President Academic Affairs ... Dr. Maris LOWN
10 Vice Pres Financial Affs/Treasurer ... Mr. Bernard LENIHAN
32 Vice President Student Services ... Dr. Ralph FORD
11 Vice Pres Administrative Services ... Dr. Stephen NACCO
12 Provost Elizabeth Campus ... Dr. Barbara GABA
12 Provost Plainfield Campus ... Dr. Negar FARAKISH
26 Exec Director College Relations ... Ms. Ellen DOTTO
13 Director of IT Operations ... Mr. Thomas CHERUBINO
06 Dir Admissions/Records/Registrar ... Ms. Nina HERNANDEZ
08 Director of Libraries ... Ms. Dena LEITER
38 Director of Counseling ... Ms. Heather KEITH
37 Director of Financial Aid ... Ms. Rebecca ROYAL
21 Director of Student Accounts ... Mr. Larry GOLDMAN
51 Dean Continuing Educ & Prof Educ ... Dr. Lisa HISCANO
108 Int Exec Dir Assess Plng & Research ... Ms. Jamie DUGGAN
15 Director of Human Resources ... Mr. Michael ESNES
18 Director Facilities ... Mr. Henry KEY
45 Director of Grants ... Ms. Cheryl SHIBER
102 Interim Exec Director Foundation ... Ms. Beth GORIN
20 Director Student Assessment Center ... Dr. Susan METTLEN
28 Director EOF ... Mr. Ruben MELENDEZ
41 Dean of College Life ... Ms. Tamalea SMITH
19 Director Public Safety ... Mr. Joseph HINES
27 Director Media Services ... Mr. Stephen KATO
88 Interim Dir Acad Learning Center ... Ms. Jacqueline LEONARD
21 Controller ... Ms. Lynne WELCH
96 Director of Purchasing ... Ms. Sandra AULD
40 Manager Bookstore ... Mr. Carl BRUSS

Union County College Elizabeth Campus (C)

40 W Jersey Street, Elizabeth NJ 07202-2314
Telephone: (908) 965-6000 Identification: 770134
Accreditation: &M

† Main campus is Union County College in Cranford, NJ.

Union County College Plainfield Campus (D)

232 E 2nd Street, Plainfield NJ 07060
Telephone: (908) 412-3599 Identification: 770135
Accreditation: &M

† Main campus is Union County College in Cranford, NJ.

Union County College Scotch Plains (E)

1776 Raritan Road, Scotch Plains NJ 07076
Telephone: (908) 889-2483 Identification: 770136
Accreditation: &M

† Main campus is Union County College in Cranford, NJ.

University of Phoenix Jersey City Campus (F)

100 Town Square Place, Jersey City NJ 07310-1756
Telephone: (201) 610-1408 Identification: 770218
Accreditation: &NH, ACBSP

† Main campus is University of Phoenix in Tempe, AZ.

Warren County Community College (G)

475 Route 57 W, Washington NJ 07882-4343
County: Warren FICE Identification: 025039
Unit ID: 245625
Telephone: (908) 835-9222 Carnegie Class: Assoc/Pub-S-SC
FAX Number: (908) 689-9262 Calendar System: Semester
URL: www.warren.edu
Established: 1981 Annual Undergrad Tuition & Fees (In-District): $3,900
Enrollment: 2,144 Coed
Affiliation or Control: State/Local IRS Status: 501(c)3
Highest Offering: Associate Degree
Program: Occupational; 2-Year Principally Bachelor's Creditable
Accreditation: M, ADNUR, MAC

01 President ... Dr. William AUSTIN
05 Vice Pres Academics/Student Svcs ... Dr. Lisa SUMMINS
10 Vice Pres Finance & Operations ... Ms. Barbara PRATT
51 Vice Pres Corporate/Continuing Educ ... Ms. Eve AZAR
11 Dean of Administration ... Mr. Dennis FLORENTINE
20 Dean of Academic Affairs ... Mr. David ORENSTEIN
37 Director of Financial Aid ... Ms. Debra WULFF
32 Asst Dean of Academic & Stdnt Svcs ... Mr. Jeremy BEELER
15 Director Human Resources ... Ms. Sharon HINTZ
35 Director Student Activities ... Ms. Rose LYNCH
21 Director Business Services ... Mr. Jay ALEXANDER
36 Director Student Success ... Ms. Fae GUERIN

Westminster Choir College (H)

101 Walnut Lane, Princeton NJ 08540
Telephone: (609) 921-7100 Identification: 770128
Accreditation: &M

† Main campus is Rider University in Lawrenceville, NJ.

William Paterson University of New Jersey (I)

300 Pompton Road, Wayne NJ 07470-2152
County: Passaic FICE Identification: 002625
Unit ID: 187444
Telephone: (973) 720-2000 Carnegie Class: Master's L
FAX Number: (973) 720-2399 Calendar System: Semester
URL: www.wpunj.edu
Established: 1855 Annual Undergrad Tuition & Fees (In-State): $11,918
Enrollment: 11,423 Coed
Affiliation or Control: State IRS Status: 501(c)3
Highest Offering: Doctorate
Program: Liberal Arts And General; Teacher Preparatory; Professional
Accreditation: M, ART, BUS, CACREP, CS, MUS, NURSE, SP, TED

01 President ... Dr. Kathleen WALDRON
05 Senior Vice President/Provost ... Dr. Warren SANDMANN
101 Chf of Staff to Pres/Board of Trust ... Dr. Robert SEAL
11 Vice Pres Administration/Finance ... Mr. Stephen BOLYAI
30 Vice Pres Institutional Advancement ... Ms. Pamela FERGUSON
32 Vice President Student Development ... Dr. John MARTONE
84 VP of Enrollment Management ... Dr. Kristin COHEN
58 Assoc VP Acad Affs/Dean Grad Stds ... Vacant
21 Assoc VP Finance Budget/Fiscal Plng ... Ms. Pamela WINSLOW
21 Assoc VP for Administration ... Mr. Richard STOMBER
26 Assoc VP Mkting & Public Relations ... Mr. Stuart GOLDSTEIN
16 Associate Vice Pres Human Resources ... Mr. John POLDING
08 Assoc VP Library Services/Info Tech ... Vacant
35 Associate VP for Campus Life ... Vacant
19 Dir Public Safety & Univ Police ... Mr. Robert FULLEMAN
35 Asst Vice Pres for Campus Life ... Mr. Francisco DIAZ
35 Assoc VP/Dean Student Development ... Dr. Glen SHERMAN
60 Dean Col Arts/Comm ... Mr. Daryl MOORE
53 Dean College of Education ... Dr. Candace BURNS
66 Dean College of Science & Health ... Dr. Kenneth WOLF
79 Dean Human & Social Science ... Dr. Kara M. RABBITT
50 Interim Dean College of Business ... Dr. Susan GODAR
08 Dean D & L Cheng Library ... Dr. Anne CILIBERTI
21 Assoc VP Finance & Comptroller ... Ms. Rosemarie GENCO
28 Dir Employment Equity & Diversity ... Mr. Richard FIELDS
46 Exec Director Academic Development ... Ms. Janet DAVIS-DUKES
51 Exec Dir Cont Educ/Distance Lrng ... Ms. Bernadette TIERNAN
20 Associate Provost ... Dr. Stephen HAHN
26 Director External Relations ... Mr. Patrick DEDEO
29 Executive Director Alumni ... Ms. Janis SCHWARTZ
45 Director Inst Research & Assessment ... Dr. Jane ZEFF
13 Chief Information Officer ... Mr. Eric ROSENBERG
43 General Counsel ... Mr. Glenn JONES
15 Director of Human Resources ... Ms. Denise ROBINSON-LEWIS
07 Director of Undergrad Admissions ... Mr. Rohan HOWELL
37 Director Financial Aid ... Mr. Michael CORSO
06 Registrar ... Ms. Nina TRELISKY
41 Director Athletics ... Ms. Sabrina GRANT
36 Director of Career Dev & Advisement ... Ms. Sharon ROSENGART
39 Director of Residence Life ... Mr. Joseph CAFFARELLI
23 Director Health & Wellness Center ... Dr. Eileen LUBECK
90 Director Instruction/Research Tech ... Dr. Sandra MILLER
09 Dir Institutional Research/Assess ... Dr. Jane ZEFF
40 Director Bookstore ... Mr. Scott DUNLAP
27 Director Public Information ... Ms. Mary Beth ZEMAN
24 Head Audio Visual-Library ... Ms. Jane HUTCHISON
18 Director Capital Plng/Design/Constr ... Vacant
85 Director International Student Svcs ... Ms. Cinzia RICHARDSON
94 Director of Women's Center ... Ms. Librada SANCHEZ
96 Director of Purchasing ... Mr. Lirse JONES
38 Director Student Counseling ... Dr. Eileen LUBECK
89 Director of Freshmen Studies ... Dr. Kim DANIEL-ROBINSON
92 Director of Honors College ... Dr. Susan DINAN

Yeshiva Gedolah Zichron Leyma (J)

1000 Orchard Terrace, Linden NJ 07036
County: Union FICE Identification: 041924
Unit ID: 476692
Telephone: (908) 587-0502 Carnegie Class: Not Classified
FAX Number: N/A Calendar System: Semester
Established: 1999 Annual Undergrad Tuition & Fees: $11,500
Enrollment: 43 Male
Affiliation or Control: Independent Non-Profit IRS Status: 501(c)3
Highest Offering: First Talmudic Degree
Program: Professional
Accreditation: RABN

Yeshiva Toras Chaim (K)

999 Ridge Avenue, Lakewood NJ 08701-2120
County: Ocean FICE Identification: 041311
Unit ID: 451398
Telephone: (732) 414-2834 Carnegie Class: Spec/Faith
FAX Number: (732) 414-2838 Calendar System: Semester
Established: 2000 Annual Undergrad Tuition & Fees: $11,800
Enrollment: 147 Male
Affiliation or Control: Independent Non-Profit IRS Status: 501(c)3
Highest Offering: Baccalaureate
Program: Teacher Preparatory; Professional
Accreditation: RABN

05 Chief Academic Officer ... Rabbi Mendel SLOMOVITS
06 Registrar ... Mrs. Devoiry DURST
21 Bookkeeper ... Mrs. Ruth GROSSMAN

Yeshiva Yesodei Hatorah (L)

2 Yesodei Court, Lakewood NJ 08701
County: Ocean Identification: 667109
Telephone: (732) 370-3360 Carnegie Class: Not Classified
FAX Number: (732) 886-2659 Calendar System: Semester
Established: 1995 Annual Undergrad Tuition & Fees: $11,000
Enrollment: 61 Male
Affiliation or Control: Independent Non-Profit IRS Status: 501(c)3
Highest Offering: First Talmudic Degree
Program: Professional
Accreditation: RABN

05 Dean ... Rabbi Shaya TREFF
10 Chief Financial/Business Officer ... Rabbi Shaya UNGAR
20 Associate Academic Officer ... Rabbi Yisroel Meir TREFF

Yeshivas Be'er Yitzchok (M)

1391 North Avenue, Elizabeth NJ 07208-2480
County: Union FICE Identification: 041234
Unit ID: 451370
Telephone: (908) 354-6057 Carnegie Class: Spec/Faith
FAX Number: (908) 820-0431 Calendar System: Semester
Established: 1999 Annual Undergrad Tuition & Fees: $12,200
Enrollment: 57 Male

Affiliation or Control: Independent Non-Profit IRS Status: 501(c)3
Highest Offering: Baccalaureate
Program: Professional; Religious Emphasis
Accreditation: **RABN**

01 Chief Executive Officer .... Rabbi Avrohom SCHULMAN
37 Director of Student Financial Aid .... Chani MILLER
11 Chief of Administration .... Shlomo PINES

NEW MEXICO

Anamarc College (A)
2660 Airport Road, Suite 780, Santa Teresa NM 88008
Telephone: (575) 589-3158 Identification: 770740
Accreditation: **ACICS**

† Main campus is Anamarc College in El Paso, TX.

Brookline College (B)
4201 Central Avenue NW Ste J,
Albuquerque NM 87105-1649
Telephone: (505) 880-2877 Identification: 666724
Accreditation: **ACICS**

† Main campus is Brookline College in Phoenix, AZ.

Brown Mackie College (C)
10500 Cooper Avenue NE, Albuquerque NM 87123
Telephone: (505) 559-5200 Identification: 770741
Accreditation: **ACICS**, OTA, SURGT, SURTEC

† Main campus is The Art Institute of Phoenix in Phoenix, AZ.

Carrington College - Albuquerque (D)
1001 Menaul Boulevard NE, Albuquerque NM 87107-1642
Telephone: (505) 254-7777 Identification: 666014
Accreditation: **ACICS**, PTAA

† Main campus is Carrington College - Phoenix in Phoenix, AZ.

Central New Mexico Community College (E)
525 Buena Vista, SE, Albuquerque NM 87106-4096
County: Bernalillo FICE Identification: 004742
Unit ID: 187532
Telephone: (505) 224-4412 Carnegie Class: Assoc/Pub-U-MC
FAX Number: (505) 224-4417 Calendar System: Semester
URL: www.cnm.edu
Established: 1965 Annual Undergrad Tuition & Fees (In-District): $1,902
Enrollment: 28,263 Coed
Affiliation or Control: State/Local IRS Status: 501(c)3
Highest Offering: Associate Degree
Program: 2-Year Principally Bachelor's Creditable
Accreditation: **NH**, ACBSP, ACFEI, ADNUR, CAHIIM, COARC, CONST, DA, DMS, EMT, MLTAD, PNUR, SURGT

01 President .... Dr. Katharine W. WINOGRAD
05 Vice President for Academic Affairs ... Dr. Sydney D. GUNTHORPE
35 Vice President for Student Services .... Mr. Phillip BUSTOS
10 Vice Pres for Finance & Operations ...... Mrs. Katherine ULIBARRI
84 Assoc Vice Pres Enrollment Mgmt .... Mr. Eugene PADILLA
08 Director Learning Resources ...... Ms. Poppy JOHNSON RENVALL
23 Director Student Health Center .... Ms. Marti BRITTENHAM
19 Director Security .... Vacant
13 Director Info Technology Services .... Mr. Joe GIERI
103 Director Workforce Training Center .... Ms. Evelyn DOW
36 Director of Job Connection Center .... Ms. Tammy STRICKLER
30 Director of Development .... Mrs. Lisa MCCULLOCH
07 Director Enrollment Services .... Mr. Glenn DAMIANI
26 Dir Marketing & Public Relations .... Mrs. Alexis KERSCHNER-TAPPAN
27 Dir Communications & Media Relation .... Mr. Brad MOORE
37 Director Student Financial Aid .... Mr. Lee CARRILLO
15 Executive Director Human Resources .... Ms. Denise MONTOYA
81 Interim Dean Sch of Math/Sci/Engr .... Mr. Philip CARMAN
50 Dean School of Bus/Info Technology .... Ms. Donna DILLER
72 Dean School of Applied Technologies .... Mr. John BRONISZ
53 Int Dean Sch of Adult & Gen Educ .... Ms. LouAnne LUNDGREN
83 Dean Comm/Humanities/Soc Sci .... Ms. Erica VOLKERS
76 Dean Health/Well/Pub Safety .... Ms. Tamra MASON
06 Registrar .... Ms. Yvonne MARTINEZ
18 Exec Dir Facilities/Physical Plant .... Mr. Luis CAMPOS
21 Comptroller .... Ms. Loretta MONTOYA
29 Director of Alumni Relations .... Mrs. Anna SANCHEZ
32 Dean of Student Services .... Mr. Rudy GARCIA
38 Director of Student Counseling .... Ms. Tammy STRICKLER
96 Director of Purchasing .... Mrs. Charlotte GENSLER
19 Chief Public Safety & Security .... Mr. William DURAN

Clovis Community College (F)
417 Schepps Boulevard, Clovis NM 88101-8381
County: Curry FICE Identification: 004743
Unit ID: 187639
Telephone: (575) 769-2811 Carnegie Class: Assoc/Pub-R-M
FAX Number: (575) 769-4190 Calendar System: Semester
URL: www.clovis.edu
Established: 1971 Annual Undergrad Tuition & Fees (In-State): $936
Enrollment: 3,900 Coed
Affiliation or Control: State IRS Status: 501(c)3
Highest Offering: Associate Degree
Program: Occupational; 2-Year Principally Bachelor's Creditable
Accreditation: **NH**, ADNUR, RAD

01 President .... Dr. Becky ROWLEY
03 Executive Vice President .... Dr. Robin JONES
10 Chief Financial Officer .... Mrs. Debbie ZURZOLO
05 Chief Academic Officer .... Dr. Robin JONES
13 Chief Information Officer .... Mr. Norman KIA
11 VP Administration/Govt Relations .... Mr. Tom DRAKE
21 Director of Business Affairs .... Ms. Jayne CRAIG
07 Dir Admissions/Records/Registrar .... Ms. Rosie CORRIE
37 Director of Financial Aid .... Ms. April CHAVEZ
08 Director Library/Learning Resources .... Ms. Kelly GRAY
35 Dir Center for Student Success .... Mrs. Mona Lee NORMAN-ARMSTRONG
38 Dir of Counseling/Testing/Advisemnt .... Mr. Marcus SMITH
15 Director of Human Resource Services .... Mrs. Rhonda JESKO
88 Director Small Business Development .... Mrs. Sandra TAYLOR-SAWYER
91 Director of Administrative Info Sys .... Ms. Teresa WHITEHEAD
56 Director Extended Learning .... Ms. Judith SPILLANE
36 Director Student Placement .... Vacant
30 Chief Development Officer .... Ms. Natalie DAGGETT
18 Director of Physical Plant .... Ms. Brenda DIXON
26 Director of Marketing/Cmty Rels .... Ms. Lisa SPENCER
76 Div Chair Allied Health Programs .... Ms. Shawna MCGILL
83 Div Chair Soc/Behav Sci/Humanities .... Mr. Paul NAGY
50 Div Chair of Business Admin & Tech . Mrs. Becky CARRUTHERS
81 Division Chair of Math/Science .... Mr. Todd KUYKENDALL

Dine College Shiprock Branch (G)
1228 Yucca St., PO Box 580, Shiprock NM 87420
Telephone: (505) 368-3500 Identification: 770007
Accreditation: **&NH**

† Main campus is Dine College in Tsaile, AZ.

Eastern New Mexico University Main Campus (H)
1500 S Avenue K, Portales NM 88130-7400
County: Roosevelt FICE Identification: 002651
Unit ID: 187648
Telephone: (575) 562-1011 Carnegie Class: Master's S
FAX Number: (575) 562-2256 Calendar System: Semester
URL: www.enmu.edu
Established: 1927 Annual Undergrad Tuition & Fees (In-State): $4,459
Enrollment: 5,814 Coed
Affiliation or Control: State IRS Status: 501(c)3
Highest Offering: Master's
Program: Liberal Arts And General; Teacher Preparatory
Accreditation: **NH**, ACBSP, MUS, NUR, SP, SW, TED

01 President .... Dr. Steven GAMBLE
05 Vice President Academic Affairs .... Dr. Jamie LAURENZ
10 Vice President Business Affairs .... Mr. Scott SMART
32 Vice President for Student Affairs .... Dr. Judith HAISLETT
26 VP University Relations/Enroll Svcs .... Ms. Ronnie BIRDSONG
45 Exec Dir Planning/Analysis/Inst Ren .... Dr. Patrice CALDWELL
20 Asst Vice Pres for Academic Affairs .... Dr. Renee NEELY
20 Asst Vice Pres Academic Affairs .... Dr. John MONTGOMERY
21 Comptroller .... Mrs. Carol FLETCHER
53 Dean Education/Technology .... Vacant
50 Dean Business .... Dr. Janet BUZZARD
57 Dean Fine Arts .... Dr. Joseph KLINE
49 Dean Liberal Arts & Science .... Dr. Mary AYALA
58 Dean Graduate School .... Dr. Linda WEEMS
22 Affirmative Action Officer .... Ms. Tammi GARDNER
08 Director of Library .... Ms. Melveta WALKER
06 Registrar .... Ms. Crystal CREEKMORE
37 Director Student Financial Aid .... Mr. Brent SMALL
07 Director Enrollment Services .... Mr. Cody SPITZ
30 Director Development .... Ms. Noelle BARTL
13 Dir Computing/Information Mgmt .... Mr. Clark ELSWICK
15 Director of Human Resources .... Ms. Julie GAWEHN
88 Director of Broadcasting .... Mr. Duane RYAN
18 Director Physical Plant .... Mr. Ted FARES
41 Athletic Director .... Dr. Jeff GEISER
19 Chief of University Police .... Mr. Brad MAULDIN
23 Director of Health Services .... Dr. Kristin KUHLMANN
36 Dir Counseling Ctr/Career Svcs .... Ms. Susan LARSON
39 Director Student Housing .... Mr. Steven ESTOCK
09 Assoc Dir Institutional Research .... Ms. Amy HOLT
96 Director of Purchasing .... Mr. Brad KEMPER
27 Director of Publications .... Vacant
29 Coordinator of Alumni .... Mr. Robert GRAHAM
56 Dir of Distance Learning/Outreach .... Ms. Trish MAGUIRE
25 Director Grant Activities .... Vacant
84 Director Enrollment Management .... Ms. Ronnie BIRDSONG
38 Director Student Counseling .... Ms. Susan LARSON
35 Director Campus Life .... Mr. Draco MILLER

Eastern New Mexico University-Roswell (I)
PO Box 6000, Roswell NM 88202-6000
County: Chaves FICE Identification: 002661
Unit ID: 187666
Telephone: (575) 624-7000 Carnegie Class: Assoc/Pub2in4
FAX Number: (575) 624-7119 Calendar System: Semester
URL: www.roswell.enmu.edu
Established: 1958 Annual Undergrad Tuition & Fees (In-State): $1,632
Enrollment: 4,195 Coed
Affiliation or Control: State IRS Status: 501(c)3
Highest Offering: Associate Degree
Program: Occupational; 2-Year Principally Bachelor's Creditable
Accreditation: **NH**, ADNUR, COARC, DH, EMT, MAC, OTA

01 President .... Dr. John MADDEN
05 VP for Academic Affairs .... Ms. Betty PATTON
10 VP for Business Affairs .... Mr. Eric JOHNSTON-ORTIZ
32 VP for Student Affairs .... Mr. Robert BOWMAN
20 Asst VP for Academic Affairs .... Vacant
21 Controller .... Ms. Karen FRANKLIN
35 Asst VP for Student Affairs .... Mr. Mike MARTINEZ
08 Director Learning Resource Center .... Mr. Rollah ASTON
37 Director Financial Aid .... Ms. Jessie SJUE
30 Director College Development .... Ms. Donna ORACION
07 Director Admissions and Records .... Ms. Linda NEEL
13 Director of Computer Services .... Mr. Tillman CROCKER
15 Director of Human Resources .... Dr. Steve CHAMBERS
18 Director of Physical Plant .... Mr. Darryl WARD
19 Director of Security .... Mr. Robert NEWBERRY
96 Director of Purchasing .... Mr. Stephen BRUCE
09 Institutional Research Professional .... Ms. Rhonda CROCKER

Institute of American Indian Arts (J)
83 Avan Nu Po Road, Santa Fe NM 87508-1300
County: Santa Fe FICE Identification: 021464
Unit ID: 187745
Telephone: (505) 424-2300 Carnegie Class: Tribal
FAX Number: (505) 424-3900 Calendar System: Semester
URL: www.iaia.edu
Established: 1962 Annual Undergrad Tuition & Fees: $3,610
Enrollment: 414 Coed
Affiliation or Control: Federal IRS Status: Exempt
Highest Offering: Master's
Program: Liberal Arts And General; Fine Arts Emphasis
Accreditation: **NH**, ART

01 President .... Dr. Robert MARTIN
05 Academic Dean .... Dr. Ann FILEMYR
10 Chief Financial Officer .... Mr. Larry MIRABAL
32 Dean of Student Life .... Ms. Carmen HENAN
84 Dir of Enrollment Management .... Ms. Nena ANAYA
30 Dir of Institutional Advancement .... Mr. Alex SHAPIRO
88 Dir of Ctr for Lifelong Education .... Mr. Ron SOLIMON
88 Dir of IAIA Museum .... Ms. Patsy PHILLIPS
88 Dir of Sponsored Programs .... Ms. Laurie BRAYSHAW
09 Dir of Institutional Research .... Dr. William SAYRE

ITT Technical Institute (K)
5100 Masthead Street NE, Albuquerque NM 87109-4366
Telephone: (505) 828-1114 Identification: 666545
Accreditation: **ACICS**, CAHIIM

† Main campus is ITT Technical Institute in Indianapolis, IN.

Luna Community College (L)
366 Luna Drive, Las Vegas NM 87701-1510
County: San Miguel FICE Identification: 009962
Unit ID: 363633
Telephone: (505) 454-2500 Carnegie Class: Assoc/Pub-R-M
FAX Number: (505) 454-2519 Calendar System: Semester
URL: www.luna.cc.nm.us
Established: 1970 Annual Undergrad Tuition & Fees (In-District): $886
Enrollment: 1,739 Coed
Affiliation or Control: State/Local IRS Status: 501(c)3
Highest Offering: Associate Degree
Program: Occupational; Liberal Arts And General; Teacher Preparatory; Professional
Accreditation: **NH**, ADNUR, DA

01 President .... Dr. Pete CAMPOS
10 Vice President of Finance .... Ms. Donna FLORES-MEDINA
09 Exec Dir Inst Research/Development .... Dr. Peter MANTHEI
05 Vice Pres Academic/Student Affairs .... Dr. Vidal MARTINEZ
07 Int Director of Admissions .... Mr. Moses MARQUEZ
06 Registrar .... Mr. Johnathan ORTIZ
18 Director Facilities/Physical Plant .... Mr. Ron GONZALES
37 Director Student Financial Aid .... Mr. Michael MONTOYA
15 Director Human Resources .... Vacant
30 Chief Development .... Ms. Mary WARD
13 Director of Computer Services .... Mr. Rick JARAMILLO

Mesalands Community College (M)
911 S 10th Street, Tucumcari NM 88401-3352
County: Quay FICE Identification: 032063
Unit ID: 188261
Telephone: (505) 461-4413 Carnegie Class: Assoc/Pub-R-S
FAX Number: (505) 461-1901 Calendar System: Semester
URL: www.mesalands.edu
Established: 1980 Annual Undergrad Tuition & Fees (In-District): $1,950
Enrollment: 1,002 Coed
Affiliation or Control: State/Local IRS Status: 501(c)3
Highest Offering: Associate Degree
Program: Occupational; 2-Year Principally Bachelor's Creditable
Accreditation: **NH**

01 President Dr. Thomas W. NEWSOM
04 Executive Asst to President Ms. Consuelo E. CHAVEZ
32 Vice President Student Affairs Dr. Aaron KENNEDY
05 Vice President of Academic Affairs Ms. Natalie GILLARD
37 Director Financial Aid Ms. Amanda HAMMER
26 Director Public Relations Ms. Kimberly HANNA
72 Director of NAWRTC Mr. Jim MORGAN
84 Director of Enrollment Management Ms. Amber MCCLURE
14 Asst Director of Inst Technology Mr. Larry WICKHAM
09 Dir Inst Research and Development Dr. Forrest KAATZ
15 Director of Personnel Vacant

National American University-Albuquerque (A)

4775 Indian School Road NE, Ste 200,
Albuquerque NM 87110
Telephone: (505) 348-3700 Identification: 770407
Accreditation: &NH, &MAC

† Main campus is National American University in Rapid City, SD.

National American University-Albuquerque West (B)

10131 Coors Blvd NW, Suite I-01, Albuquerque NM 87114
Telephone: (505) 348-3750 Identification: 770408
Accreditation: &NH

† Main campus is National American University in Rapid City, SD.

National College of Midwifery (C)

209 State Road 240, Taos NM 87571-6834
County: Taos Identification: 666251
Telephone: (575) 758-8914 Carnegie Class: Not Classified
FAX Number: (575) 758-0302 Calendar System: Other
URL: www.midwiferycollege.org
Established: 1989 Annual Undergrad Tuition & Fees: $5,000
Enrollment: 160 Coed
Affiliation or Control: Independent Non-Profit IRS Status: 501(c)3
Highest Offering: Doctorate
Program: Professional
Accreditation: MEAC

01 President Jennifer WEST

Navajo Technical College (D)

PO Box 849, Crownpoint NM 87313-0849
County: McKinley FICE Identification: 023576
Unit ID: 187596
Telephone: (505) 786-4100 Carnegie Class: Tribal
FAX Number: (505) 786-5644 Calendar System: Semester
URL: www.navajotech.edu
Established: 1979 Annual Undergrad Tuition & Fees: $2,690
Enrollment: 1,777 Coed
Affiliation or Control: Tribal Control IRS Status: 501(c)3
Highest Offering: Baccalaureate
Program: Occupational; 2-Year Principally Bachelor's Creditable; Technical Emphasis
Accreditation: NH, ACFEI

01 President Dr. Elmer GUY
05 Provost Mr. Tom DAVIS
32 Dean of Student Affairs Ms. Delores BECENTI
06 Registrar/Director of Admissions Ms. Jerlynn HENRY
09 Data Assessment Director Mr. Roy TRACY
25 Contracts & Grant Officer Ms. Thomasina GREY
37 Director of Student Financial Aid Mr. Tyrrell HARDY
15 Director Human Resources Mr. Steven BENALLY
18 Director of Operations Mr. Euegene GLASSES
21 Associate Business Officer Vacant
20 Associate Academic Officer Dr. Casmir AGBARAJI

† Tuition figure is for a student enrolled in a federally recognized Indian tribe.

New Mexico Highlands University (E)

PO Box 9000, Las Vegas NM 87701-9000
County: San Miguel FICE Identification: 002653
Unit ID: 187897
Telephone: (505) 425-7511 Carnegie Class: Master's L
FAX Number: N/A Calendar System: Semester
URL: www.nmhu.edu
Established: 1893 Annual Undergrad Tuition & Fees (In-State): $4,000
Enrollment: 3,768 Coed
Affiliation or Control: State IRS Status: 501(c)3
Highest Offering: Master's
Program: Liberal Arts And General; Teacher Preparatory
Accreditation: NH, ACBSP, CORE, NURSE, SW, TED

01 President Dr. James FRIES
05 VP for Academic Affairs Dr. Gilbert RIVERA
10 VP Finance & Administration Vacant
20 Associate VP of Academic Affairs Dr. Linda LAGRANGE
32 Dean of Students Dr. Fidel J. TRUJILLO
07 Registrar/Director of Admissions Mr. Michael RAINE
08 Library Director Mr. Ruben ARAGON
09 Dir Inst Effectiveness & Research Dr. Jean HILL
13 Director of Information Technology Mr. Max BACA
15 Director Human Resources Ms. Donna CASTRO
18 Director of Facilities Management Vacant
19 Chief Police/Security Mr. Donato SENA
21 Comptroller Vacant
26 Director of University Relations Mr. Sean WEAVER
29 Coordinator of Alumni Affairs Mr. James MANDARINO
30 Executive Dir for Advancement Dr. Sharon CABALLERO
36 Director of Career Services Mr. Ron GARCIA
37 Director of Financial Aid Ms. Eileen SEDILLO
40 Bookstore Manager Vacant
41 Athletic Director Mr. Ed MANZANARES
49 Dean College of Arts & Sci Dr. Kenneth BENTSON
50 Dean School of Business Dr. Margaret YOUNG
70 Dean School of Social Work Dr. Alfredo GARCIA
96 Director of Purchasing Mr. Michael SAAVEDRA

New Mexico Institute of Mining and Technology (F)

801 Leroy Place, Socorro NM 87801-4796
County: Socorro FICE Identification: 002654
Unit ID: 187967
Telephone: (575) 835-5434 Carnegie Class: Master's M
FAX Number: (575) 835-6329 Calendar System: Semester
URL: www.nmt.edu
Established: 1889 Annual Undergrad Tuition & Fees (In-State): $6,553
Enrollment: 2,105 Coed
Affiliation or Control: State IRS Status: 501(c)3
Highest Offering: Doctorate
Program: Professional; Technical Emphasis
Accreditation: NH, CS, ENG

01 President Dr. Daniel H. LOPEZ
10 Vice Pres Administration & Finance Mr. Lonnie G. MARQUEZ
05 Vice President Academic Affairs Dr. Peter F. GERITY
32 VP Student & Univ Rels/Dean Stdnt Ms. Melissa JARAMILLO FLEMING
46 Vice Pres Research/Economic Devel Dr. Van D. ROMERO
20 Assoc Vice Pres Academic Affairs Dr. Mary DEZEMBER
45 Asst VP Research/Econ Development Mr. Richard CERVANTES
08 Librarian Ms. Lisa BEINHOFF
15 Director of Human Resources Ms. Joann SALOME
06 Registrar Ms. Sara GRIJALVA
07 Director of Admission Mr. Michael KLOEPPEL
37 Director of Financial Aid Ms. Annette KAUS
30 Director Office for Advancement Ms. Colleen GUENGERICH
22 Director Affirm Action & Compliance Ms. Joann SALOME
14 Director Computer Center Dr. Michael L. TOPLIFF
13 Director of Information Services Mr. Joseph FRANKLIN
65 Director Bur Geology & Mineral Res Dr. Greer PRICE
12 Director Petro Recovery Res Ctr Dr. Robert L. LEE
58 Interim Dean of Graduate Studies Dr. Lorie LIEBROCK
18 Director Facilities Management Ms. Yvonne MANZANO-BROWN
21 Director of Finance Ms. Arleen VALLES
36 Director Career Services Ms. Lillian ARMIJO
38 Dir Counseling/Disabilities Svcs Ms. Janet WARD
96 Director of Purchasing Ms. Kimela MILLER
09 Institutional Researcher Ms. Stephany MOORE

New Mexico Junior College (G)

1 Thunderbird Circle, Hobbs NM 88240-9123
County: Lea FICE Identification: 002655
Unit ID: 187903
Telephone: (575) 392-4510 Carnegie Class: Assoc/Pub-R-M
FAX Number: (575) 492-2732 Calendar System: Semester
URL: www.nmjc.edu
Established: 1965 Annual Undergrad Tuition & Fees (In-District): $1,248
Enrollment: 3,450 Coed
Affiliation or Control: Local IRS Status: 501(c)3
Highest Offering: Associate Degree
Program: Occupational; 2-Year Principally Bachelor's Creditable
Accreditation: NH, ADNUR

01 President Dr. Steve MCCLEERY
05 Vice President Instruction Dr. Dennis ATHERTON
10 Vice President Finance Dan HARDIN
32 Vice President Student Services Dr. Regina ORGAN
103 Vice President Training & Outreach Dr. Robert RHODES
84 Dean Enrollment Management Dr. A. Michele CLINGMAN
14 Dir Computer Information System Bill KUNKO
26 Director PR/Marketing Vacant
04 Executive Asst to the President Jerri SHIELDS
37 Director Financial Aid Kerrie MITCHELL
09 Director of Inst Effectiveness Dr. Larry SANDERSON
66 Director of Nursing Delores THOMPSON
18 Chief Facilities/Physical Plant Dr. Charley CARROLL
81 Dean Business/Math & Sciences Kelly HOLLADAY
79 Dean Arts & Humanities Dianne MARQUEZ
40 Director of Bookstore Services Robert ADAMS
106 Dean of Training & Outreach Jeffery MCCOOL
75 Dean of Public Safety & Career Tech Dr. August FONS
08 Director of Library Services James BRITSCH
96 Coordinator of Purchasing Regina CHOATE
41 Director of Athletics Donald WORTH
102 Acct/Controller-NMJC Foundation Christina KUNKO
11 Director of Administrative Services Bill MORRILL
88 Controller Joshua MORGAN
39 Director Student Housing Sandy HARDIN
88 Executive Director WHM/LCCHF Dr. Darrell BEAUCHAMP
88 Exec Dir NMJC Research Foundation Dale GANNAWAY

New Mexico Military Institute (H)

101 W College, Roswell NM 88201-5173
County: Chaves FICE Identification: 002656
Unit ID: 187912
Telephone: (575) 622-6250 Carnegie Class: Assoc/Pub-Spec
FAX Number: (575) 624-8058 Calendar System: Semester
URL: www.nmmi.edu
Established: 1891 Annual Undergrad Tuition & Fees (In-State): $11,406
Enrollment: 490 Coed
Affiliation or Control: State IRS Status: 501(c)3
Highest Offering: Associate Degree
Program: 2-Year Principally Bachelor's Creditable
Accreditation: NH

01 Superintendent/President MGen. Jerry W. GRIZZLE
32 Commandant BGen. Richard V. GERACI
100 Chief of Staff Col. David WEST
10 Chief Financial Officer Col. Judy SCHARMER
05 Dean BGen. Douglas J. MURRAY
21 Asst Chief Financial Officer LtCol. Charles HENDRICKSON
07 Director of Admissions LtCol. Jeffery SAVAGE
41 Athletic Director/Dir Physical Educ Col. Reginald FRANKLIN
30 Director of Development LtCol. Nickie VIGIL-GARCIA
21 Internal Auditor LtCol. David GRAY
88 Professor of Military Science LtCol. Jonathan GRAFF
20 Asst Dean & High School Princ LtCol. George BRICK
35 Associate Dean Leadership Vacant
50 Assoc Dean Social Science/Business Col. Walter T. HITCHCOCK
81 Assoc Dean Science/Mathematics LtCol. John R. MCVAY
79 Associate Dean Humanities Major Joel DYKSTRA
64 Director of Music LtCol. Stephen M. THORP
08 Director of the Library Col. Jerome J. KLOPFER
26 Public Relations Officer CWO3 Carl K. HANSEN
18 Chief Facilities/Physical Plant Mr. Kent TAYLOR
06 Registrar Maj. Edwin G. PREBLE
37 Director Student Financial Aid Maj. Sonya F. RODRIGUEZ
38 Dir College Acad Advising/Placement Maj. Donald HANAK
19 Director Security/Safety Mr. Jerrold LONOWSKI
42 Chaplain/Director Campus Ministry Maj. Dan MUSGRAVE
29 Director Alumni Association LtCol. David ROMERO

New Mexico State University Main Campus (I)

Box 30001, Las Cruces NM 88003-8001
County: Dona Ana FICE Identification: 002657
Unit ID: 188030
Telephone: (575) 646-2035 Carnegie Class: RU/H
FAX Number: (575) 646-6334 Calendar System: Semester
URL: www.nmsu.edu
Established: 1888 Annual Undergrad Tuition & Fees (In-State): $6,221
Enrollment: 17,651 Coed
Affiliation or Control: State IRS Status: 501(c)3
Highest Offering: Doctorate
Program: Liberal Arts And General; Teacher Preparatory; Professional
Accreditation: NH, BUS, BUSA, CACREP, COPSY, DIETD, @DIETI, ENG, ENGT, MUS, NURSE, PH, SP, SPAA, SW, TED

01 President Dr. Garrey E. CARRUTHERS
05 Interim Provost & Exec VP Dr. Gregory FANT
10 Sr VP Administration/Finance Ms. Angela THRONEBERRY
100 Sr VP External Rel/Chief of Staff Mr. Benjamin E. WOODS
30 Int VP Univ Advance/Pres NMSU Found Ms. Tina BYFORD
85 Assoc Provost Intl & Border Program Dr. Cornell MENKING
26 Assoc VP Univ Comm/Marketing Ms. Maureen HOWARD
21 Assoc VP Admin & Finance Ms. D'Anne STUART
20 VP Student Affairs/Enroll Mgmt Dr. Bernadette MONTOYA
20 Asst VP/Deputy Provost Dr. Greg FANT
47 Dean College of Agric & Home Econ Dr. Lowell CATLETT
49 Dean College of Arts & Sciences Dr. Christa D. SLATON
50 Interim Dean Business College Dr. Kathleen BROOK
53 Dean College of Education Dr. Michael A. MOREHEAD
54 Dean College of Engineering Dr. Ricardo JACQUEZ
58 Interim Dean Graduate School Dr. Loui REYES
76 Dean Col of Health & Social Svcs Dr. Tilahuan ADERA
32 Dean of Students Dr. Michael D. JASEK
37 Dir Fin Aid/Scholarship Svcs Ms. Janie MERCHANT
27 Interim Chief Information Officer Ms. Norma GRIJALVA
06 Registrar Mr. Michael ZIMMERMAN
43 General Counsel Mr. Bruce KITE
08 Dean University Library Dr. Elizabeth TITUS
29 Director Alumni Affairs Dr. Tammie CAMPOS
25 Assoc Controller Sponsored Projects Ms. Norma NOEL
39 Director Student Housing Ms. Julie WEBER
09 Asst VP Institutional Analysis Ms. Judy BOSLAND
23 Director Student Health Center Ms. Lori MCKEE
38 Director Counseling Center Dr. Karen D. SCHAEFER
86 Asst VP Government Relations Mr. Ricardo REL
41 Director Athletics Dr. McKinley BOSTON
36 Dir Placement/Career Services Dr. Anthony S. MARIN
96 Dir Purchasing/Materials Mgt Ms. Rennette APODACA
28 Dir Institutional Equity/EEO Mr. Gerard NEVAREZ
07 Director Admissions Ms. Valerie PICKETT
15 Assoc VP Human Resources Svcs Dr. Andrew M. PENA
18 Exec Dir Facilities/Services Mr. Timothy DOBSON

New Mexico State University at Alamogordo (J)

2400 N Scenic Drive, Alamogordo NM 88310-4239
County: Otero FICE Identification: 002658
Unit ID: 187994

Telephone: (575) 439-3600 Carnegie Class: Assoc/Pub2in4
FAX Number: (575) 439-3643 Calendar System: Semester
URL: www.nmsua.edu
Established: 1958 Annual Undergrad Tuition & Fees (In-State): $1,920
Enrollment: 3,230 Coed
Affiliation or Control: State IRS Status: 501(c)3
Highest Offering: Associate Degree
Program: Occupational; 2-Year Principally Bachelor's Creditable
Accreditation: NH, ADNUR

01 President .... Dr. Cheri A. JIMENO
05 Vice President for Academic Affairs .... Dr. Debra TEACHMAN
32 Vice President for Student Services .... Mr. Juan B. GARCIA
10 Vice President for Business/Finance .... Mr. Antonio SALINAS
56 Assoc Vice Pres Extended Programs .... Mrs. Donna L. COOK
26 Campus Public Information Officer .... Ms. Hope PATTERSON
08 Librarian .... Dr. Sharon JENKINS
07 Director of Admissions/Registrar .... Mr. Jeremy PATTON
37 Director Student Financial Aid .... Dr. Vandeen MCKENZIE
09 Director of Institutional Research .... Mr. Greg HILLIS
36 Director Student Placement .... Mr. Juan B. GARCIA
15 Director Human Resources .... Mrs. Brenda W. GARCIA
18 Director Facilities/Physical Plant .... Ms. Nancy MONTGOMERY
38 Director Student Counseling .... Mr. Juan B. GARCIA
96 Buyer Specialist 1 .... Mr. Lee M. KINNEY

New Mexico State University at Carlsbad (A)

1500 University Drive, Carlsbad NM 88220-3598
County: Eddy FICE Identification: 002659
Unit ID: 188003
Telephone: (575) 234-9200 Carnegie Class: Assoc/Pub2in4
FAX Number: (575) 885-4951 Calendar System: Semester
URL: www.carlsbad.nmsu.edu
Established: 1950 Annual Undergrad Tuition & Fees (In-State): $1,608
Enrollment: 2,060 Coed
Affiliation or Control: State IRS Status: 501(c)3
Highest Offering: Associate Degree
Program: Occupational; 2-Year Principally Bachelor's Creditable
Accreditation: NH, ADNUR

01 Campus President .... Dr. John GRATTON
05 Chief Academic Officer .... Dr. Vincent W. BEACH
32 Vice Pres Student Services .... Mr. Michael J. CLEARY
10 Chief Business Officer .... Dr. Robert KEYES
38 Director Student Counseling .... Ms. Karla K. THOMPSON
37 Director Financial Aid .... Ms. Diana CAMPOS
15 Human Resources Specialist .... Ms. Bobbi Jo WILLINGHAM
09 Institutional Researcher .... Vacant
26 Director Marketing & Publications .... Mr. Khushroo GHADIALI
18 Manager Facilities Services .... Vacant

New Mexico State University Dona Ana Community College (B)

Box 30001, MSC 3DA, Las Cruces NM 88003-8001
County: Dona Ana Identification: 666649
Unit ID: 187620
Telephone: (575) 527-7500 Carnegie Class: Assoc/Pub2in4
FAX Number: (575) 527-7515 Calendar System: Semester
URL: dacc.nmsu.edu
Established: 1973 Annual Undergrad Tuition & Fees (In-State): $1,950
Enrollment: 9,270 Coed
Affiliation or Control: State IRS Status: 501(c)3
Highest Offering: Associate Degree
Program: Occupational; 2-Year Principally Bachelor's Creditable
Accreditation: NH, ACBSP, COARC, DA, DH, DMS, EMT, IFSAC, RAD

01 Interim President/CEO .... Mr. Andrew J. BURKE
05 Interim VP for Academic Affairs .... Dr. Monica TORRES
10 VP for Business & Finance .... Mr. Andrew J. BURKE
32 VP for Student Services .... Mr. Amadeo LEDESMA
20 Assoc VP for Academic Affairs .... Dr. John WALKER
50 Division Dean Business/Info Systems .... Ms. Lydia BAGWELL
97 Division Dean General Studies .... Dr. Bernard PINA
76 Div Dean Health/Public Services .... Ms. Evelyn HOBBS
72 Division Dean Technical Studies .... Ms. Saundra CASTILLO
103 Exec Director Workforce Dev/Trng .... Mr. Fred OWENSKY
62 Director Library Services .... Ms. Tammy POWERS
36 Director of Career Services .... Ms. Rosa DE LA TORRE-BURMEISTER
09 Campus Inst Effectiveness/Plng Ofcr .... Dr. Fred LILLIBRIDGE
26 Chief Public Relations/Devel Ofcr .... Vacant
31 Director Community Education .... Ms. Vickie GALINDO
40 Bookstore Manager .... Mr. Marvin PAZ
21 Business Manager .... Ms. Nancy RITTER
15 Human Resources Manager .... Mr. Mack ADAMS
90 Computer Support Manager .... Ms. Lori ALLEN
18 Facilities Manager .... Ms. Kathleen REDDINGTON
07 Coordinator Admissions & Records .... Ms. Geraldine MARTINEZ
37 Dir Financial Aid/Scholarships .... Ms. Gladys CHAIREZ
28 Coord Disabled Student Services .... Dr. Michael BANEGAR

New Mexico State University Dona Ana Community College East Mesa Campus (C)

2800 N Sonoma Ranch Boulevard, Las Cruses NM 88011
Telephone: (575) 528-7250 Identification: 770346
Accreditation: &NH

† Main campus is New Mexico State University Dona Ana Community College in Las Cruces, NM.

New Mexico State University Grants (D)

1500 Third Street, Grants NM 87020-2025
Telephone: (505) 287-6678 FICE Identification: 008854
Accreditation: &NH

† Main campus is New Mexico State University Main Campus in Las Cruces, NM.

Northern New Mexico College (E)

921 N Paseo de Onate, Espanola NM 87532-2649
County: Rio Arriba FICE Identification: 020839
Unit ID: 188058
Telephone: (505) 747-2100 Carnegie Class: Bac/Assoc
FAX Number: (505) 747-2170 Calendar System: Semester
URL: www.nnmc.edu
Established: 1909 Annual Undergrad Tuition & Fees (In-State): $4,060
Enrollment: 1,832 Coed
Affiliation or Control: State IRS Status: 501(c)3
Highest Offering: Baccalaureate
Program: Occupational; 2-Year Principally Bachelor's Creditable; Liberal Arts And General; Teacher Preparatory
Accreditation: NH, ACBSP, NURSE, #RAD

01 President .... Dr. Nancy (Rusty) BARCELO
10 Vice Pres Finance & Administration .... Mr. Domingo SANCHEZ
30 Vice Pres Institutional Advancement .... Mr. Ricky SERNA
05 Provost .... Dr. Anthony SENA
32 Dean of Student Services .... Mr. Frank ORONA
12 Director El Rito Campus .... Ms. Melissa VELASQUEZ
06 Registrar .... Ms. Kathleen SENA
08 Head Librarian .... Ms. Jessica JONES
84 Director of Recruitment .... Mr. Frank ORONA
37 Director of Financial Aid .... Mr. Jacob PACHECO
13 Director of IT .... Mr. Angelo JACQUES
15 Director of Human Resources .... Mr. Bernie PADILLA
18 Director of Facilities .... Vacant
26 Director of Public Information .... Vacant
09 Director of Inst Effectiveness .... Ms. Carmella MARTINEZ
21 Director of Business Operations .... Ms. Henrietta TRUJILLO
108 Dir Inst Advise/Coord Stdnt Advise .... Mr. Tony GALLEGOS
41 Athletic Director/Coach .... Mr. Ryan CORDOVA
51 Coordinator Continuing Education .... Ms. Virginia CATA
53 Dean College of Teacher Education .... Dr. Cathy BERRYHILL
49 Dean College of Arts and Sciences .... Dr. Mellis SCHMIDT
103 Dn Col Cmty Wrkfrce/Career Tech Ed .... Dr. Camilla BUSTAMANTE

Pima Medical Institute-Albuquerque (F)

4400 Cutler Avenue NE, Albuquerque NM 87110-3935
Telephone: (505) 881-1234 FICE Identification: 036783
Accreditation: ABHES, COARC, DH, PTAA, RAD

† Main campus is Pima Medical Institute-Tucson in Tucson, AZ.

Ruidoso Branch Community College (G)

709 Mechum Drive, Ruidoso NM 88345
Telephone: (575) 257-2120 Identification: 770345
Accreditation: &NH

† Main campus is Eastern New Mexico University Main Campus in Portales, NM.

St. John's College (H)

1160 Camino de la Cruz Blanca,
Santa Fe NM 87505-4599
County: Santa Fe FICE Identification: 002093
Unit ID: 245652
Telephone: (505) 984-6000 Carnegie Class: Master's S
FAX Number: (505) 984-6003 Calendar System: Semester
URL: www.stjohnscollege.edu
Established: 1964 Annual Undergrad Tuition & Fees: $45,004
Enrollment: 429 Coed
Affiliation or Control: Independent Non-Profit IRS Status: 501(c)3
Highest Offering: Master's
Program: Liberal Arts And General
Accreditation: NH

01 President .... Mr. Michael P. PETERS
05 Dean .... Mr. Walter J. STERLING
30 Vice President for Advancement .... Ms. Victoria MORA
10 Treasurer .... Mr. Bryan VALENTINE
06 Registrar .... Mrs. Marline MARQUEZ-SCALLY
08 Library Director .... Ms. Jennifer SPRAGUE
07 Director of Admissions .... Mr. Larry CLENDENIN
58 Director of Graduate Institute .... Mr. David CARL
09 Director of Institutional Research .... Mr. Nick GIACONA
15 Director of Human Resources .... Mr. Aaron YOUNG
18 Chief Facilities/Physical Plant .... Mr. Pat HOLMAN
26 Dir of Communications/External Rels .... Mr. Gabe GOMEZ
29 Director of Alumni Relations .... Ms. Sarah PALACIOS
36 Director Student Placement .... Ms. Margaret ODELL
37 Director Student Financial Aid .... Mr. Mike RODRIQUEZ

† Affiliated with St. John's College, Maryland.

San Juan College (I)

4601 College Boulevard, Farmington NM 87402-4699
County: San Juan FICE Identification: 002660
Unit ID: 188100
Telephone: (505) 326-3311 Carnegie Class: Assoc/Pub-R-L
FAX Number: (505) 566-3385 Calendar System: Semester
URL: www.sanjuancollege.edu
Established: 1956 Annual Undergrad Tuition & Fees (In-District): $1,338
Enrollment: 11,483 Coed
Affiliation or Control: Local IRS Status: 501(c)3
Highest Offering: Associate Degree
Program: Occupational; 2-Year Principally Bachelor's Creditable
Accreditation: NH, ACBSP, ADNUR, CAHIIM, #COARC, DH, MLTAD, PTAA, SURGT

01 President .... Dr. Toni PENDERGRASS
05 Vice Pres for Learning .... Dr. Barbara AKE
10 Vice Pres Administrative Services .... Mr. Russell LITKE
32 Vice Pres for Student Services .... Mr. David EPPICH
04 Executive Asst to President .... Ms. Jeanne NOTSON
20 Assoc VP Learning/Strategic Init .... Ms. Lisa WILSON
102 Executive Director Foundation .... Ms. Gayle DEAN
31 Chief Community Relations Officer .... Ms. Nancy SHEPHERD
21 Controller .... Mr. Scott BERKLEY
26 Director Marketing/Public Relations .... Ms. Rhonda SCHAEFER
88 Dir Ctr for Student Engagement .... Dr. Michaele BRANDON
84 Sr Dir Enrollment Management .... Mr. Jon BETZ
50 Dean Sch Business/Sciences .... Dr. Merrill ADAMS
79 Interim Dean School of Humanities .... Mr. Allan NASS
76 Dean School of Health Sciences .... Mr. Oliver BORDEN
65 Dean School of Energy .... Mr. Randy PACHECO
72 Dean School Trades & Technology .... Mr. Bill LEWIS
22 Director Affirmative Action/EEO .... Ms. Stacey ALLEN
88 Director Native American Programs .... Ms. Michele PETERSON
08 Director Library Services .... Mr. Chris SCHIPPER
37 Director of Financial Aid .... Mr. Jerry MCKEEN
18 Director Physical Plant .... Mr. Steve BIERNACKI
19 Director Security/Safety .... Mr. Billy NEWTON
35 Director Student Activities .... Ms. Marcia STERLING
96 Director Purchasing .... Mr. Frank COLE
38 Director Student Advising Center .... Vacant
74 Director Vet-Tech Program .... Dr. David WRIGHT
36 Dir Quality/Improve/Career Svcs Ctr .... Ms. Tonya NELSON
06 Registrar .... Ms. Sherri GAUGH
09 Int Dir of Institutional Research .... Mr. Ron JERNIGAN
15 Director Human Resources .... Ms. Stacey ALLEN

Santa Fe Community College (J)

6401 Richards Avenue, Santa Fe NM 87508-4887
County: Santa Fe FICE Identification: 022781
Unit ID: 188137
Telephone: (505) 428 1000 Carnegie Class: Assoc/Pub-R-L
FAX Number: (505) 428-1296 Calendar System: Semester
URL: www.sfcc.edu
Established: 1983 Annual Undergrad Tuition & Fees (In-State): $22,781
Enrollment: 6,524 Coed
Affiliation or Control: State IRS Status: 501(c)3
Highest Offering: Associate Degree
Program: Occupational; 2-Year Principally Bachelor's Creditable
Accreditation: NH, ADNUR, COARC, DA, MAC

01 President .... Dr. Ana (Cha) GUZMAN
05 Vice Pres Academic Affairs .... Dr. Randy GRISSOM
10 Vice Pres Finance & Administration .... Ms. Meridee WALTERS
09 VP Planning & Inst Effectiveness .... Dr. Jacqueline VIRGINT
32 Vice President Student Success .... Dr. Carmen GONZALES
21 Associate Vice President Finance .... Ms. Gilda ESPINOZA
20 Asst VP of Academic Support .... Ms. Jill DOUGLASS
84 Asst VP Enrollment & Student Svcs .... Dr. Cheryl DRANGMEISTER
51 Asst VP Cont Educ Customized Trng .... Mr. Randy GRISSOM
53 Asst VP for School of Education .... Ms. Michelle STOBNICKE
26 Exec Dir Marketing/Public Rels .... Ms. Janet WISE
30 Dir Devel/Exec Dir SFCC Foundation .... Ms. Deborah BOLDT
06 Registrar .... Ms. Barbara TUCCI
13 Chief Information Officer .... Dr. Christopher DELA ROSA
37 Financial Aid Director .... Mr. Scott WHITAKER
66 Interim Director of Nursing .... Ms. Carmen ANGEL
08 Library Director .... Ms. Peg JOHNSON
15 Director of Human Resources .... Ms. Karla QUINTANA
88 Director Small Business Development .... Mr. Michael MYKRIS
18 Director of Plant Operations .... Mr. Frank JOY
24 Media Technician .... Vacant
49 Dean School of Liberal & Fine Arts .... Dr. Margaret PETERS
76 Dean Health/Math/Sciences .... Dr. Jenny LANDEN
57 Int Dean School of Arts and Design .... Dr. Mechele HESBROOK
50 Dean Sch Business & Applied Tech .... Dr. Patricia EAVES FINN
101 Executive Asst to the President .... Ms. Rosemarie M. GARCIA
96 Director of Purchasing .... Mr. Michael CLOKEY

Santa Fe University of Art and Design (K)

1600 St. Michael's Drive, Santa Fe NM 87505-7634
County: Santa Fe FICE Identification: 002649
Unit ID: 188146
Telephone: (505) 473-6011 Carnegie Class: Spec/Arts
FAX Number: (505) 473-6127 Calendar System: Semester
URL: www.santafeuniversity.edu
Established: 1947 Annual Undergrad Tuition & Fees: $30,682
Enrollment: 544 Coed
Affiliation or Control: Proprietary IRS Status: Proprietary
Highest Offering: Master's
Program: Liberal Arts And General; Professional; Fine Arts Emphasis
Accreditation: NH

01 President .... Mr. Laurence A. HINZ
05 Vice President for Academic Affairs .... Mr. Gerry SNYDER
20 Associate Dean Academic Affairs .... Mr. Allen BUTT
32 Sr Director of Student Life .... Ms. Laura NUNNELLY
07 Exec Director Student Operations .... Ms. Christine GUEVARA
10 Director of Finance .... Mr. Michael BOTTRILL
18 Dir Facilities & Security .... Mr. Peter ROMERO
88 Director Campus-Based Facilities .... Mr. Thomas OLMSTEAD
13 Dir Campus Technology Services .... Mr. Jeff PEARCE
37 Director of Financial Aid .... Ms. Becky CONNOLLY
39 Director of Campus Life .... Mr. John RODRIGUEZ
06 Registrar .... Ms. Mary ANGELL
88 Dir of International Development .... Mr. Mark ASTROM
15 Director of Human Resources .... Mr. Todd SPILMAN
11 Operations Manager .... Ms. Melissa LEWIS
88 Executive Director of Marketing .... Ms. Betty CESARANO
88 Marketing Manager .... Mr. Dan MILLER
26 Public Relations Manager .... Ms. Lauren EICHMANN
105 Digital Marketing Manager .... Ms. Rachel GANTT

† Annual tuition for Graphic Design, Creative Writing, Digital Arts and Arts Management programs is $19,646.

Southwest Acupuncture College (A)

1622 Galisteo Street, Santa Fe NM 87505-6351
County: Santa Fe FICE Identification: 026220
Unit ID: 366605
Telephone: (505) 438-8884 Carnegie Class: Spec/Health
FAX Number: (505) 438-8883 Calendar System: Semester
URL: www.acupuncturecollege.edu
Established: 1980 Annual Undergrad Tuition & Fees: $14,053
Enrollment: 71 Coed
Affiliation or Control: Proprietary IRS Status: Proprietary
Highest Offering: Master's; No Lower Division
Program: Professional
Accreditation: ACUP

01 CEO .... Dr. Anthony ABBATE
03 Executive Director .... Dr. Skya ABBATE
10 Chief Fiscal Officer .... Ms. Piper KING
12 Campus Director Santa Fe .... Ms. Latricia GONZALES-MCKOSKY
17 Clinical Director Santa Fe .... Dr. Hiroki TAKEDA
05 Academic Dean Santa Fe .... Dr. Maya YU
37 Director of Financial Aid .... Ms. Angela ANAYA

Southwest Acupuncture College-Albuquerque (B)

7801 Academy Blvd N Town Bdg #1 NE,
Albuquerque NM 87109
Telephone: (505) 888-8898 Identification: 666666
Accreditation: ACUP

† Main campus is Southwest Acupuncture College in Santa Fe, NM.

Southwest University of Visual Arts (C)

5000 Marble Avenue, NE, Albuquerque NM 87110-6344
Telephone: (505) 254-7575 Identification: 666524
Accreditation: &NH, CIDA

† Main campus is Southwest University of Visual Arts in Tucson, AZ.

Southwestern College (D)

3960 San Filipe Road, Santa Fe NM 87507
County: Santa Fe FICE Identification: 030761
Unit ID: 188207
Telephone: (505) 471-5756 Carnegie Class: Assoc/PrivNFP4
FAX Number: (505) 471-4071 Calendar System: Quarter
URL: www.swc.edu
Established: 1979 Annual Graduate Tuition & Fees: $16,200
Enrollment: 145 Coed
Affiliation or Control: Independent Non-Profit IRS Status: 501(c)3
Highest Offering: Master's; No Undergraduates
Program: Professional
Accreditation: NH

01 President .... Dr. Jim NOLAN
03 Vice Pres/Dir Community Educ Pgms .... Ms. Katherine NINOS
05 Academic Dean .... Dr. Webb GARRISON
07 Director of Admissions .... Ms. Dru PHOENIX
06 Registrar .... Ms. Andrea PACHECO

Southwestern Indian Polytechnic Institute (E)

9169 Coors Blvd., NW, Albuquerque NM 87120
County: Bernalillo FICE Identification: 025110
Unit ID: 188216
Telephone: (505) 346-2347 Carnegie Class: Tribal
FAX Number: (505) 346-2343 Calendar System: Trimester
URL: www.sipi.edu
Established: 1971 Annual Undergrad Tuition & Fees: $280
Enrollment: 500 Coed
Affiliation or Control: Federal IRS Status: 501(c)3
Highest Offering: Associate Degree
Program: Occupational; 2-Year Principally Bachelor's Creditable; Technical Emphasis
Accreditation: @NH

01 President .... Dr. Sherry ALLISON
10 Acting Vice Pres College Operations .... Mr. Monte MONTEITH
05 Vice President Academic Programs .... Ms. Valerie MONTOYA
39 Director of Residential Life .... Vacant
07 Director Admissions/Registrar .... Mr. Joseph CARPIO
09 Director of Institutional Research .... Mr. Edward HUMMINGBIRD
15 Human Resources Specialist .... Ms. Bernadine FISHERMAN
18 Facilities Director .... Ms. Karlisa SHOMOUR
37 Director Student Financial Aid .... Mr. Joseph CARPIO

University of New Mexico Main Campus (F)

1 University of New Mexico, Albuquerque NM 87131-0001
County: Bernalillo FICE Identification: 002663
Unit ID: 187985
Telephone: (505) 277-0111 Carnegie Class: RU/VH
FAX Number: (505) 277-6019 Calendar System: Semester
URL: www.unm.edu
Established: 1889 Annual Undergrad Tuition & Fees (In-State): $6,447
Enrollment: 29,100 Coed
Affiliation or Control: State IRS Status: 501(c)3
Highest Offering: Doctorate
Program: Liberal Arts And General; Teacher Preparatory; Professional
Accreditation: NH, #ARCPA, BUS, BUSA, CACREP, CLPSY, CONST, CS, DANCE, DENT, DH, DIETD, DIETI, EMT, ENG, IPSY, JOUR, LAW, LSAR, MED, MIDWF, MT, MUS, NURSE, OT, PH, PHAR, PLNG, PTA, SP, SPAA, TED, THEA

01 President .... Dr. Robert G. FRANK
05 Provost/Exec VP Academic Affs .... Dr. Chaouki T. ABDALLAH
17 Chancellor of Health Sciences Ctr .... Dr. Paul B. ROTH
10 Exec Vice Pres Administration .... Dr. David W. HARRIS
100 Chief of Staff .... Duffy RODRIGUEZ
12 Special Asst for Branch Affairs .... Dr. Wynn M. GOERING
104 Special Asst for Global Initiatives .... Dr. MaryAnne SAUNDERS
20 Sr Vice Provost Academic Affairs .... Dr. Michael J. DOUGHER
106 Vice Provost Extended Learning .... Dr. Monica OROZCO
46 Interim VP Research & Econ Develop .... Dr. Michael J. DOUGHER
25 AVP Research Administration .... Carlos ROMERO
20 Assoc Provost Academic Personnel .... Dr. Jane SLAUGHTER
20 Assoc Provost Curriculum .... Dr. Gregory HEILEMAN
32 Vice President Student Affairs .... Dr. Eliseo S. TORRES
28 Vice President Equity & Inclusion .... Dr. Josephine DE LEON
28 Vice President HSC Diversity .... Dr. Valerie ROMERO-LEGGOTT
84 AVP Enrollment Management .... Dr. Terry BABBITT
15 Interim VP Human Resources .... Jewel WASHINGTON
41 Vice President for Athletics .... Paul R. KREBS
21 Interim University Controller .... Elizabeth METZGER
13 Chief Information Officer .... Gilbert GONZALES
43 University Counsel .... Elsa KIRCHER COLE
29 AVP Alumni Relations .... Karen A. ABRAHAM
20 AVP Academic Administration .... Curtis R. PORTER
21 AVP Planning/Budget & Analysis .... Andrew CULLEN
35 AVP Student Life .... Dr. Walter C. MILLER
35 AVP Student Services .... Dr. Tim GUTIERREZ
50 Dean Anderson School of Management .... Doug M. BROWN
48 Dean Sch of Architecture & Planning .... Dr. Geraldine FORBES ISAIS
49 Dean College of Arts & Sciences .... Dr. Mark PECENY
53 Interim Dean College of Education .... Dr. Viola FLOREZ
54 Dean School of Engineering .... Dr. Catalin ROMAN
57 Dean College of Fine Arts .... Dr. Kymberly PINDER
61 Dean School of Law .... David HERRING
63 Exec Vice Dean School of Medicine .... Dr. Jeffrey GRIFFITH
66 Dean College of Nursing .... Dr. Nancy A. RIDENOUR
67 Dean College of Pharmacy .... Dr. Lynda S. WELAGE
80 Dir School of Public Administration .... Dr. Amy WOHLERT
92 Dean Honors & University Colleges .... Dr. Kate KRAUSE
58 Dean Office of Graduate Studies .... Dr. Julie COONROD
51 Assoc Dean Continuing Education .... Joseph MIERA
08 Dean University Libraries .... Dr. Martha BEDARD
26 Chief Univ Marketing & Comm Officer .... Cinnamon BLAIR
26 HSC Exec Dir Comm & Marketing .... William O. SPARKS
27 Director University Communications .... Dianne ANDERSON
105 Mgr University Web Communications .... Matt CARTER
86 Director Government Affairs .... Marc SAAVEDRA
09 Acting Dir Institutional Analytics .... Terry J. TURNER
18 University Architect .... Robert DORAN
18 Director Physical Plant .... Mary VOSEVICH
19 Chief of Police .... Kathy A. GUIMOND
96 Chief Procurement Officer .... Bruce E. CHERRIN
23 Director Student Health Center .... Dr. Beverly KLOEPPEL
22 Interim Director Equal Opportunity .... Theresa RAMOS
24 Dir New Media & Extended Learning .... Debby KNOTTS
35 Dean of Students .... Dr. Thomas AGUIRRE
07 Director Admissions and Recruitment .... Matt HULETT
06 Registrar .... Alex GONZALEZ
37 Director Student Financial Aid .... Brian MALONE
36 Director Career Services .... Jenna S. CRABB
39 Director Student Housing & Res Life .... Wayne SULLIVAN
40 Director Bookstore .... Melanie SPARKS
108 Outcomes Assessment Planning Mgr .... Dr. Tom ROOT
102 UNM Foundation President and CEO .... Henry NEMCIK
30 VP University Development .... Larry RYAN
30 VP Development Health Sciences Ctr .... Bill UHER
88 CEO UNM Hospital .... Steve MCKERNAN

University of New Mexico-Gallup (G)

705 Gurley Avenue, Gallup NM 87301
Telephone: (505) 863-7500 FICE Identification: 006881
Accreditation: &NH, CAHIIM, DA, MLTAD

† Main campus is University of New Mexico Main Campus in Albuquerque, NM.

University of New Mexico-Los Alamos (H)

4000 University Drive, Los Alamos NM 87544-2233
Telephone: (505) 662-5919 Identification: 666742
Accreditation: &NH

† Main campus is University of New Mexico Main Campus in Albuquerque, NM.

University of New Mexico-Taos (I)

1157 Country Road 110, Ranchos de Taos NM 87557
Telephone: (575) 737-6200 Identification: 666743
Accreditation: &NH, ADNUR

† Main campus is University of New Mexico Main Campus in Albuquerque, NM.

University of New Mexico-Valencia (J)

280 La Entrada Road, Los Lunas NM 87031-7633
Telephone: (505) 925-8500 Identification: 666741
Accreditation: &NH

† Main campus is University of New Mexico Main Campus in Albuquerque, NM.

University of Phoenix New Mexico Campus (K)

5700 Pasadena Avenue, NE,
Albuquerque NM 87113-1570
Telephone: (505) 821-4800 Identification: 770219
Accreditation: &NH, ACBSP

† Main campus is University of Phoenix in Tempe, AZ.

University of St. Francis (L)

4401 Silver SE, Albuquerque NM 87108
Telephone: (505) 266-5565 Identification: 770099
Accreditation: &NH

† Main campus is University of St. Francis in Joliet, IL.

University of the Southwest (M)

6610 Lovington Highway, Hobbs NM 88240-9129
County: Lea FICE Identification: 002650
Unit ID: 188182
Telephone: (575) 392-6561 Carnegie Class: Bac/Diverse
FAX Number: (575) 392-6006 Calendar System: Semester
URL: www.usw.edu
Established: 1962 Annual Undergrad Tuition & Fees: $12,240
Enrollment: 719 Coed
Affiliation or Control: Independent Non-Profit IRS Status: 501(c)3
Highest Offering: Master's
Program: Liberal Arts And General; Teacher Preparatory; Professional
Accreditation: NH

01 President .... Dr. Gary A. DILL
05 Provost .... Dr. James H. SMITH
10 VP for Administration & CFO .... Dr. Dee MOONEY
13 VP of Technology .... Dr. Ryan TIPTON
41 Dean of Athletics .... Mr. Michael GALVAN
18 Campus Steward .... Mr. David ARNOLD
07 Sr Dir of Admissions & Recruitment .... Mrs. Michele GOAR
49 Dean School of Arts & Sciences .... Dr. Marianne WESTBROOK
50 Dean School of Business .... Dr. Ryan TIPTON
53 Dean School of Education .... Dr. Mary R. HARRIS
08 Dean of Library Services .... Mr. John MCCANCE
32 Associate Provost .... Mrs. Rhonda TYLER
33 Dean of Students .... Mr. Tom MULKEY
42 Campus Minister .... Dr. Randy SAVAGE
15 Director of Personnel Services .... Mrs. Melody ARNOLD
06 University Registrar .... Mrs. Rebecca WHITLEY
37 Financial Aid Director .... Ms. Anne GAGLIA
44 Director Develop/Public Relations .... Ms. Laurie DEAN
88 Maintenance Supervisor .... Mr. Lonnie HARRISON

Western New Mexico University (N)

PO Box 680, Silver City NM 88062-0680
County: Grant FICE Identification: 002664
Unit ID: 188304
Telephone: (505) 538-6011 Carnegie Class: Master's M
FAX Number: (505) 538-6364 Calendar System: Semester
URL: www.wnmu.edu
Established: 1893 Annual Undergrad Tuition & Fees (In-State): $4,330
Enrollment: 3,300 Coed
Affiliation or Control: State IRS Status: 501(c)3
Highest Offering: Beyond Master's But Less Than Doctorate
Program: Liberal Arts And General; Teacher Preparatory
Accreditation: NH, ACBSP, ADNUR, NURSE, OT, OTA, SW, TED

01 President .... Dr. Joseph SHEPARD
05 Provost/Vice Pres Academic Affairs .... Dr. Jack CROCKER
32 VP Student Affairs/Enrollment Mgmt .... Dr. Isaac BRUNDAGE
10 Vice President Business Affairs .... Ms. Sherri A. BAYS
30 VP Instl Advancement/Economic Devel .... Ms. Linda Kay JONES
20 Assoc Vice Pres Academic Affairs .... Ms. Marcia BOURDETTE
35 Assoc Vice Pres Student Affairs .... Ms. Peggy LANKFORD
06 Registrar .... Ms. Betsy MILLER

08 University Librarian .... Ms. Gilda BAEZA-ORTEGO
37 Director Student Financial Aid .... Ms. Onorina FRANCO
07 Director Admissions .... Mr. Dan TRESSLER
09 Director of Institutional Research .... Mr. Paul LANDRUM
15 Director of Human Resources .... Ms. Charlene ASHBURN
18 Chief Facilities/Physical Plant .... Mr. Stan PENA
26 Chief Public Relations Officer .... Mr. Abe VILLARREAL
29 Director of Alumni Relations .... Ms. Danielle MOFFETT
44 Chief Development Officer .... Mr. Vance REDFERN
36 Director of Career Services .... Mr. Nick GIORDANO
28 Dir Multi-Cultural Affs/Student Act .... Ms. Maria DOMINGUEZ
96 Director of Purchasing .... Ms. Amy BACA

NEW YORK

Adelphi University (A)

1 South Avenue, PO Box 701,
Garden City NY 11530-0701
County: Nassau　FICE Identification: 002666
Unit ID: 188429
Telephone: (516) 877-3000　Carnegie Class: DRU
FAX Number: (516) 877-3545　Calendar System: Semester
URL: www.adelphi.edu
Established: 1896　Annual Undergrad Tuition & Fees: $30,800
Enrollment: 7,859　Coed
Affiliation or Control: Independent Non-Profit　IRS Status: 501(c)3
Highest Offering: Doctorate
Program: Liberal Arts And General; Teacher Preparatory; Professional
Accreditation: M, AUD, BUS, CLPSY, NURSE, SP, SW, TED

01 President .... Dr. Robert A. SCOTT
03 Provost .... Dr. Gayle D. INSLER
05 Senior Assoc Provost for Acad Affs .... Dr. Audrey S. BLUMBERG
20 Assoc Provost for Academic Affairs .... Dr. Lester BALTIMORE
11 Assoc Provost for Administration .... Dr. Lawrence HOBBIE
28 Assoc Prov Fac Affairs & Diversity .... Dr. Perry GREENE
84 VP Enroll Mgmt/Student Success .... Dr. Lauren MOUNTY
10 Senior Vice President & Treasurer .... Mr. Timothy P. BURTON
30 Vice Pres University Advancement .... Mr. Chris VAUPEL
26 Vice President for Communications .... Ms. Lori DUGGAN-GOLD
18 Asst to Pres Facilities Planning .... Mr. Bill PROTO
32 Assoc VP Enroll Mgt/Student Success .... Ms. Esther GOODCUFF
21 Assoc VP for Finance & Co-Treasurer .... Mr. Robert L. DECARLO
15 Assoc VP Human Resource/Labor Rel .... Ms. Lisa ARAUJO
49 Dean of Arts & Sciences .... Dr. Sam L. GROGG
53 Dean RS Ammon School of Education .... Dr. Jane ASHDOWN
66 Dean Col of Nursing & Public Hlth .... Dr. Patrick R. COONAN
70 Dean School of Social Work .... Dr. Andrew SAFYER
58 Dean Derner Inst Advanc Psych Std .... Dr. Jacques BARBER
50 Dean RB Willumstad Schl of Business .. Dr. Anthony LIBERTELLA
92 Dean of Honors College .... Dr. Richard GARNER
88 Dean University Col/Adult Pgms .... Dr. Shawn O'RILEY
08 Dean University Libraries .... Dr. Brian LYM
35 Dean Student Affairs .... Mr. Jeffrey A. KESSLER
13 Chief Information Officer/CIO .... Mr. Jack CHEN
41 Asst VP/Director of Athletics .... Mr. Robert E. HARTWELL
56 Exec Dir Off-Campus Administration .... Mr. James MCGOWAN
19 Asst VP for Public Safety .... Mr. Eugene PALMA
18 Exec Dir Facilities/Physical Plant .... Mr. James KOSLOSKI
09 Exec Dir Research/Assessment/Plng .... Dr. Nava LERER
37 Asst VP Student Financial Aid .... Ms. Sheryl L. MIHOPULOS
07 Asst VP of Admissions .... Ms. Christine MURPHY
36 Exec Dir Career Plng & Placement .... Mr. Thomas J. WARD
06 Registrar .... Ms. Jill GLATTER
104 Director International Education .... Dr. Barry STINSON
23 Director Health Services .... Ms. Jacqueline CARTABUKE
38 Director Student Counseling Center .... Ms. Carol PHELAN
39 Director Residential Life/Housing .... Mr. Guy SENEQUE
29 Interim Director Alumni Relations .... Ms. Mary Ann MEARINI
88 Assoc Treasurer/Budget Director .... Mr. Michael J. MCLEOD
88 Director Business Affairs .... Mr. Russell A. PALMER
12 Director Manhattan Center .... Ms. June TRIZZINO-PECOR
96 Purchasing Manager .... Ms. Elizabeth F. KASH
40 Bookstore Manager .... Mr. Will GILER

Albany College of Pharmacy and Health Sciences (B)

106 New Scotland Avenue, Albany NY 12208-3492
County: Albany　FICE Identification: 002885
Unit ID: 188526
Telephone: (518) 694-7200　Carnegie Class: Spec/Health
FAX Number: (518) 694-7202　Calendar System: Semester
URL: www.acphs.edu
Established: 1881　Annual Undergrad Tuition & Fees: $28,200
Enrollment: 1,702　Coed
Affiliation or Control: Independent Non-Profit　IRS Status: 501(c)3
Highest Offering: Doctorate
Program: Professional
Accreditation: M, CYTO, MT, PHAR

01 President .... James GOZZO
05 Provost .... John DENIO
46 Vice Provost for Research .... Shaker MOUSA
88 Vice Provost Innovative Learning .... Ian DOUGLAS
49 Dean School of Arts and Sciences .... David CLARKE
67 Dean School of Pharmacy .... Angela DOMINELLI
58 Dean School of Graduate Studies .... Martha HASS
12 Associate Dean for Vermont Campus .... Robert HAMILTON
35 Associate Dean of Student Affairs .... Ronald A. DEBELLIS
43 General Counsel .... Gerald KATZMAN
10 VP of Finance .... Michele VIEN
30 VP of Institutional Advancement .... Vicki DILORENZO
84 VP of Enrollment Management .... Tiffany GUTIERREZ
13 Chief Technology Officer .... Pamela SMITH
11 AVP of Administrative Operations .... Packy MCGRAW
100 Special Assistant to the President .... Michael SASS
07 Director of Admissions .... Matthew STEVER
06 Registrar .... Craig TYNAN
08 Director of Library Services .... Sue IWANOWICZ
26 Exec Director of Marketing/Comm .... Gil CHORBAJIAN
41 Assistant Director of Athletics .... Christine KANAWADA
15 Director of Human Resources .... Casey DIMARCO

Albany Law School (C)

80 New Scotland Avenue, Albany NY 12208-3494
County: Albany　FICE Identification: 002886
Unit ID: 188535
Telephone: (518) 445-2311　Carnegie Class: Spec/Law
FAX Number: (518) 445-2315　Calendar System: Semester
URL: www.albanylaw.edu
Established: 1851　Annual Undergrad Tuition & Fees: $43,523
Enrollment: 690　Coed
Affiliation or Control: Independent Non-Profit　IRS Status: 501(c)3
Highest Offering: First Professional Degree
Program: Professional
Accreditation: LAW

01 President & Dean .... Dean Penelope ANDREWS
05 Asc Dean Acad Affs/Intellect Life .... Prof. Alicia OUELLETTE
10 Vice President Finance & Business .... Mr. Victor E. RAUSCHER
08 Assoc Dean/Director of Library .... Prof. Helane DAVIS
30 Asst Dean Institutional Advancement ... Mr. James KELLERHOUSE
32 Associate Dean for Student Affairs .... Prof. Rosemary QUEENAN
06 Assistant Dean and Registrar .... Ms. Joanne FITZSIMMONS
36 Assistant Dean Career Center .... Ms. Sandra MANS
27 Director Communications .... Mr. David SINGER
04 Executive Assistant to the Dean .... Vacant
07 Assistant Dean of Admissions .... Ms. Nadia CASTRIOTA
88 Co-Director Clinical Program .... Prof. Bridgit BURKE
88 Co-Director Clinical Program .... Prof. Nancy MAURER
13 Director Enterprise Tech Services .... Vacant
29 Director Alumni Affairs .... Ms. Kristin SHEEHAN
15 Director Human Resources .... Ms. Sherri DONNELLY
37 Director Student Financial Aid .... Ms. Andrea WEDLER
18 Facilities Manager .... Mr. Brian LAPLANTE
44 Director of Annual Giving .... Ms. Anne Marie JUDGE
36 Career Center Coordinator .... Mrs. Joanne CASEY

Albany Medical College (D)

47 New Scotland Avenue, Mail #34,
Albany NY 12208-3479
County: Albany　FICE Identification: 002887
Unit ID: 188580
Telephone: (518) 262-6008　Carnegie Class: Spec/Med
FAX Number: (518) 262-6515　Calendar System: Other
URL: www.amc.edu
Established: 1839　Annual Graduate Tuition & Fees: $56,874
Enrollment: 816　Coed
Affiliation or Control: Independent Non-Profit　IRS Status: 501(c)3
Highest Offering: Doctorate; No Undergraduates
Program: Professional
Accreditation: M, ANEST, ARCPA, IPSY, MED

01 Dean/Exec VP Health Affairs .... Dr. Vincent P. VERDILE
05 Vice Dean for Academic Admin .... Dr. Henry S. POHL
05 Vice Dean Clinical Affairs .... Dr. Ferdinand VENDITTI
32 Assoc Dean for Acad & Student Affs .... Dr. Elizabeth HIGGINS
63 Assoc Dean Graduate Medical Educ .... Dr. Joel BARTFIELD
90 Assoc Dean Info Resources & Tech .... Ms. Enid GEYER
88 Assoc Dean Medical Education .... Dr. Jonathan M. ROSEN
22 Assoc Dean Cmty Outreach/Medical Ed .... Ms. Ingrid M. ALLARD
08 Asc Dn Info Resrcs/Tech/Dir Library .... Ms. Enid GEYER
88 Asst Dean Medical Education .... Dr. Rebecca KELLER
58 Asst Dean for Graduate Studies .... Dr. Richard KELLER
06 Registrar .... Mr. Len SCHLEGEL
63 Director Graduate Medical Education .... Ms. Catherine RIDDLE
76 Director Physician Asst Program .... Mr. David IRVINE
07 Dir Admissions & Student Records .... Ms. Joanne NANOS
29 Executive Director Alumni Relations .... Ms. Maura MACK-HISGEN
26 Director Public Relations .... Mr. Jeffrey GORDON
30 Chief Development .... Ms. Terri CERVENY
51 Director Cont Medical Education .... Ms. Jennifer PRICE
15 Director Human Resources .... Ms. Cathy HALAKAN
37 Director Student Financial Aid .... Ms. Ann LOUGHMAN
96 Director of Purchasing .... Ms. Patricia MARINO

Alfred University (E)

One Saxon Drive, Alfred NY 14802-1205
County: Allegany　FICE Identification: 002668
Unit ID: 188641
Telephone: (607) 871-2111　Carnegie Class: Master's L
FAX Number: (607) 871-2339　Calendar System: Semester
URL: www.alfred.edu
Established: 1836　Annual Undergrad Tuition & Fees: $28,774
Enrollment: 2,362　Coed
Affiliation or Control: Independent Non-Profit　IRS Status: 501(c)3
Highest Offering: Doctorate
Program: Liberal Arts And General; Teacher Preparatory; Professional
Accreditation: M, ART, BUS, ENG, SCPSY, TEAC

01 President .... Dr. Charles M. EDMONDSON
05 Provost/VP for Academic Affairs .... Dr. Rick STEPHENS
10 VP for Business & Finance/Treasurer .... Ms. Giovina LLOYD
30 Acting VP for University Relations ... Mrs. Susan C. GOETSCHIUS
84 VP for Enrollment Management .... Mr. Earl E. PIERCE, JR.
32 VP for Student Affairs .... Mrs. Kathy WOUGHTER
57 Dean School of Art & Design .... Ms. Leslie BELLAVANCE
49 Dean Col of Lib Arts & Sciences .... Dr. Mary MCGEE
107 Dean College of Prof Studies .... Dr. Nancy EVANGELISTA
54 Dean School of Engineering .... Dr. Doreen EDWARDS
29 Exec Dir Annual Giv/Alum Relations .... Mr. Mark SHARDLOW
37 Director of Student Financial Aid .... Mr. Earl E. PIERCE, JR.
07 Director of Admissions .... Mr. Corry D. UNIS
06 Registrar .... Mr. Lawrence J. CASEY
19 Chief of Public Safety .... Mr. John M. DOUGHERTY
09 Dir Enrollment Operations & Rsch .... Ms. Karen L. JOHNSON
27 Acting Director of Communications .... Mrs. Deborah E. CLARK
39 Director of Residence Life .... Mrs. Brenda I. PORTER
13 Director Information Tech Svcs .... Mr. Gary O. ROBERTS
36 Director Career Development Ctr .... Mr. Mark MCFADDEN
41 Director of Athletics .... Mr. Paul VECCHIO
23 Dir Counseling & Wellness Center .... Dr. Stanley TAM
18 Director of Physical Plant .... Mr. Brian R. DODGE
08 Dir Herrick Lib/Dean of Libraries .... Mr. Stephen S. CRANDALL
08 Director of Scholes Library .... Mr. Mark SMITH
16 Director of Human Resources .... Mr. Mark A. GUINAN, JR.
21 Interim Controller .... Ms. Jodi L. HOWE
92 Director of the Honors Program .... Dr. Gordan ATLAS
94 Dir of Women's Leadership Center ... Ms. Julia OVERTON-HEALY
35 Director of Student Activities .... Mr. Daniel NAPOLITANO
96 Director of Office Services .... Ms. Susan M. PECK
43 Dir Capital Operations/Leg Affairs .. Mr. Michael A. NEIDERBACH
101 Secretary to the Corporation .... Ms. Laura J. CRAIN
104 Dir Intl Programs/Writing Ctr .... Dr. Vicky WESTACOTT
40 Bookstore Manager .... Mrs. Marcy K. BRADLEY
88 Assistant VP for Statutory Affairs .... Dr. Linda E. JONES
88 Dir of Summer/Parent Programs .... Mrs. Melody H. MCLAY

AMDA College and Conservatory of the Performing Arts (F)

211 West 61st Street, New York NY 10023-7832
County: New York　FICE Identification: 007572
Unit ID: 188854
Telephone: (212) 787-5300　Carnegie Class: Spec/Arts
FAX Number: (212) 247-0488　Calendar System: Semester
URL: www.amda.edu
Established: 1964　Annual Undergrad Tuition & Fees: $31,500
Enrollment: 1,429　Coed
Affiliation or Control: Independent Non-Profit　IRS Status: 501(c)3
Highest Offering: Baccalaureate
Program: Liberal Arts And General; Fine Arts Emphasis
Accreditation: THEA

01 President/Artistic Director .... Mr. David MARTIN
11 Executive Director .... Ms. Jan MARTIN
07 Director of Admissions .... Ms. Bridget QUINN

American Academy of Dramatic Arts (G)

120 Madison Avenue, New York NY 10016-7089
County: New York　FICE Identification: 007465
Unit ID: 188678
Telephone: (212) 686-9244　Carnegie Class: Assoc/PrivNFP
FAX Number: (212) 545-7934　Calendar System: Other
URL: www.aada.edu
Established: 1884　Annual Undergrad Tuition & Fees: $29,900
Enrollment: 211　Coed
Affiliation or Control: Independent Non-Profit　IRS Status: 501(c)3
Highest Offering: Associate Degree
Program: Occupational; 2-Year Principally Bachelor's Creditable
Accreditation: M, THEA

01 Acting President/COO .... Ms. Susan ZECH
10 Chief Financial Officer .... Mr. John POLSKY
05 Director of Instruction .... Mr. Constantine SCOPAS
07 National Director of Admissions .... Mr. Steven HONG
37 Director Financial Aid .... Mr. Roberto LOPEZ
08 Librarian .... Ms. Deborah PICONE
21 Controller .... Ms. Linda VIALA
11 Director of Operations .... Mr. Peter TUFEL
26 Director External Affairs .... Mrs. Elizabeth LAWSON
04 Assistant to the President .... Ms. Jackie REINKING

American Academy McAllister Institute of Funeral Service (H)

619 W 54th Street, 2nd Floor, New York NY 10019
County: New York　FICE Identification: 010813
Unit ID: 188687
Telephone: (212) 757-1190　Carnegie Class: Assoc/PrivNFP
FAX Number: (212) 765-5923　Calendar System: Semester
URL: www.funeraleducation.org
Established: 1926　Annual Undergrad Tuition & Fees: $12,420
Enrollment: 408　Coed
Affiliation or Control: Independent Non-Profit　IRS Status: 501(c)3
Highest Offering: Associate Degree
Program: Occupational

Accreditation: FUSER

01 President/CEO ... Ms. Meg DUNN
05 Director of Student Support ... Ms. Regina SMITH
43 Legal Counsel ... Mr. Charles MAURER
10 Bursar ... Mr. Jay TSO
06 Registrar/Director of Admissions ... Mr. Andre RAMPAUL
08 Librarian ... Ms. Mary MOON
37 Financial Aid Officer ... Ms. Natalie GIVAN
20 Academic Advisor ... Ms. Charlotte RERRICK
20 Academic Advisor ... Ms. Kerriann DENHAM
69 Div Chair Public Hlth/Technical ... Dr. Elissa DEBENEDICTS
50 Division Chair Business/Law/Ethics ... Mr. Brian KASLER

The Art Institute of New York City (A)

11 Beach Street, New York NY 10013-1917
County: New York FICE Identification: 025256
Unit ID: 365055
Telephone: (212) 625-6000 Carnegie Class: Assoc/PrivFP
FAX Number: (212) 226-5644 Calendar System: Quarter
URL: www.ainyc.aii.edu
Established: 1980 Annual Undergrad Tuition & Fees: $19,656
Enrollment: 1,480 Coed
Affiliation or Control: Proprietary IRS Status: Proprietary
Highest Offering: Associate Degree
Program: 2-Year Principally Bachelor's Creditable; Fine Arts Emphasis
Accreditation: ACICS

01 President ... Mrs. Jennifer RAMEY
05 Dean of Academic Affairs ... Mr. David MOUGHALIAN
07 Director of Admissions ... Ms. Mary Ann GRILLO
10 Campus Finance Director ... Mr. Daniel LENZO
37 Director of Student Financial Svcs ... Mr. Fred HAMILTON
36 Director of Career Services ... Ms. Emily ALLEN
32 Dean of Student Affairs ... Vacant
06 Registrar ... Mr. Giovanni PALOMO

ASA Institute of Business & Computer Technology (B)

81 Willoughby Street, Brooklyn NY 11201
County: Kings FICE Identification: 030955
Unit ID: 404994
Telephone: (718) 522-9073 Carnegie Class: Assoc/PrivFP
FAX Number: (718) 532-1433 Calendar System: Semester
URL: www.asa.edu
Established: 1985 Annual Undergrad Tuition & Fees: $14,000
Enrollment: 1,255 Coed
Affiliation or Control: Proprietary IRS Status: Proprietary
Highest Offering: Associate Degree
Program: Occupational; 2-Year Principally Bachelor's Creditable
Accreditation: M, MAC

01 President ... Mr. Alex SHCHEGOL
05 Sr Vice President Academic Affairs ... Dr. Alexander AGAFONOV
07 Vice President Marketing/Admissions ... Ms. Victoria KOSTYUKOV
36 Vice Pres Placement/Alumni Svcs ... Ms. Lesia WILLIS
86 Vice Pres Govt & Community Rels ... Mr. Roberto DUMAUAL

Bank Street College of Education (C)

610 W 112 Street, New York NY 10025-1898
County: New York FICE Identification: 002669
Unit ID: 189015
Telephone: (212) 875-4400 Carnegie Class: Spec/Other
FAX Number: (212) 875-4759 Calendar System: Semester
URL: www.bankstreet.edu
Established: 1916 Annual Graduate Tuition & Fees: $24,702
Enrollment: 929 Coed
Affiliation or Control: Independent Non-Profit IRS Status: 501(c)3
Highest Offering: Master's; No Undergraduates
Program: Teacher Preparatory; Professional
Accreditation: M

01 President ... Elizabeth D. DICKEY
10 Interim Vice President of Finance ... Norm WALKER
11 Chief Administrative Officer ... Frank NUARA
30 Vice Pres Institutional Advancement ... John S. BORDEN
05 Dean of the College ... Jon D. SNYDER
58 Dean of the Graduate School ... Virginia ROACH
88 Dean of Childrens Programs ... Alexis S. WRIGHT
88 Associate Dean for IPR ... Farhad ASGHAR
11 Associate Dean Administration ... Barbara COLEMAN
20 Associate Dean Academic Affairs ... Nancy GROPPER
07 Director of Admissions ... Amy GREENSTEIN
06 Registrar ... Sandra SCLAFANI
37 Director Student Financial Aid ... Lou PALEFSKY
29 Director of Alumni Relations ... Linda REING
15 Director of Human Resources ... Carol SAMBERG
13 Director Information Services ... Christina D'AIELLO
18 Director of Facilities ... Daniel BENCHIMOL
08 Director of Library Services ... Kristin FREDA
36 Director Student Placement ... Susan LEVINE
09 Director of Institutional Research ... Amy KLINE

Bard College (D)

PO Box 5000, Annandale-On-Hudson NY 12504-5000
County: Dutchess FICE Identification: 002671
Unit ID: 189088
Telephone: (845) 758-6822 Carnegie Class: Bac/A&S
FAX Number: (845) 758-4294 Calendar System: Semester
URL: www.bard.edu
Established: 1860 Annual Undergrad Tuition & Fees: $46,370
Enrollment: 2,322 Coed
Affiliation or Control: Independent Non-Profit IRS Status: 501(c)3
Highest Offering: Doctorate
Program: Liberal Arts And General
Accreditation: M, TEAC

01 President ... Dr. Leon BOTSTEIN
03 Executive Vice President of College ... Dr. Dimitri B. PAPADIMITRIOU
05 Vice President Academic Affairs ... Dr. Robert MARTIN
30 Vice Pres Alumni/ae Affairs/Devel ... Ms. Debra PEMSTEIN
11 Vice President for Administration ... Dr. James BRUDVIG
10 Vice President for Finance ... Mr. John FRANZINO
20 Vice President/Dean of the College ... Dr. Michele DOMINY
32 VP Student Affairs/Dir Admissions ... Ms. Mary I. BACKLUND
82 AVP/Dn Intl Aff/Civ Engmt/Dir IILE ... Dr. Jonathan BECKER
88 Associate VP & Dean of Studies ... Dr. David SHEIN
08 Dean Information Svcs/Dir Libraries ... Mr. Jeffrey KATZ
39 Dean of Campus Life ... Ms. Gretchen PERRY
32 Dean of Students ... Ms. Erin CANNAN
88 Associate Dean of the College ... Dr. Mark D. HALSEY
35 Dean of Student Affairs ... Ms. Bethany NOHLGREN
53 Dir Master of Arts in Teaching Pgm ... Mr. Ric CAMPBELL
57 Dir Milton Avery Grad Sch of Arts ... Mr. Arthur GIBBONS
88 Dir Bard Grad Ctr Decorative Arts ... Dr. Susan WEBER
88 Exec Dir Ctr Curatorial Studies ... Mr. Tom ECCLES
88 Director of Institutional Support ... Ms. Karen UNGER
88 Director Ctr Environmental Policy ... Dr. Eban GOODSTEIN
37 Director Financial Aid ... Ms. Denise ACKERMAN
06 Registrar ... Mr. Peter GADSBY
26 Director of Communications ... Mr. Mark PRIMOFF
15 Director of Human Resources ... Ms. Fiona SMARRITO
21 Controller ... Mr. Kevin PARKER
88 Director Inst Writing/Thinking ... Ms. Peg PEOPLES
18 Director of Buildings & Grounds ... Mr. Chuck SIMMONS
13 Director Mgmt Info Systems ... Mr. Michael TOMPKINS
29 Director Alumni/ae Affairs ... Ms. Jane BRIEN
36 Director Career Development ... Ms. April KINSER
19 Director Safety & Security ... Mr. Kenneth COOPER
09 Director of Institutional Research ... Mr. Joseph F. AHERN
24 Audio/Video Engineer ... Mr. Paul LABARBERA
28 Director of Multicultural Affairs ... Dr. Ann SEATON
41 Director of Athletics ... Ms. Kristin E. HALL
42 Chaplain ... Dr. Bruce D. CHILTON
40 Bookstore Manager ... Ms. Merry MEYER
23 Director Health Services ... Ms. Marsha DAVIS
38 Director Student Counseling ... Ms. Tamara TELBERG
96 Director of Purchasing ... Ms. Julie K. MYERS

Bard High School Early College Manhattan (E)

525 East Houston Street, New York NY 10002
Telephone: (212) 995-8479 Identification: 770114
Accreditation: &EH

† Main campus is Bard College at Simon's Rock in Great Barrington, MA.

Bard High School Early College Queens (F)

30-20 Thomson Avenue, Long Island City NY 11101
Telephone: (718) 361-3133 Identification: 770115
Accreditation: &EH

† Main campus is Bard College at Simon's Rock in Great Barrington, MA.

Barnard College (G)

3009 Broadway, New York NY 10027-6598
County: New York FICE Identification: 002708
Unit ID: 189097
Telephone: (212) 854-5262 Carnegie Class: Bac/A&S
FAX Number: (212) 854-6220 Calendar System: Semester
URL: www.barnard.edu
Established: 1889 Annual Undergrad Tuition & Fees: $44,790
Enrollment: 2,466 Female
Affiliation or Control: Independent Non-Profit IRS Status: 501(c)3
Highest Offering: Baccalaureate
Program: Liberal Arts And General
Accreditation: M, DANCE, @TEAC

01 President ... Debora L. SPAR
05 Provost & Dean of Faculty ... Linda BELL
11 Vice Pres Campus Services ... Gail BELTRONE
26 Vice Pres Comm/Counsel to Pres ... Joanne KWONG
30 Vice President Development ... Bret SILVER
08 Vice Pres Information Technology ... Carol KATZMAN
10 Chief Operating Officer/VP Finance ... Gregory N. BROWN
20 Dean of the College ... Avis HINKSON
32 Dean of Studies ... Natalie FRIEDMAN
07 Dean of Admissions ... Jennifer FONDILLER
39 Assoc Dean Residential Life/Housing ... Ann AVERSA
06 Registrar ... Constance BROWN
29 Director of Alumnae Affairs ... Erin FREDRICK
37 Director of Financial Aid ... Nanette DILAURO
36 Director of Career Development ... Robert EARL
15 Director of Human Resources ... Catherine GEDDIS
19 Director of Safety/Security ... Dianna PENNETTI
23 Director of Health Services ... Brenda SLADE
96 Director of Purchasing & Stores ... Douglas MAGET
21 Associate Business Officer ... Eileen M. DIBENEDETTO
09 Director of Institutional Support ... Abigail FEDER-KANE

† Affiliated with Columbia University in the City of New York.

Be'er Yaakov Talmudic Seminary (H)

12 Jefferson Avenue, Spring Valley NY 10977
County: Rockland FICE Identification: 041928
Unit ID: 476717
Telephone: (845) 362-3053 Carnegie Class: Not Classified
FAX Number: (845) 406-9699 Calendar System: Semester
Established: 1995 Annual Undergrad Tuition & Fees: $7,600
Enrollment: 261 Male
Affiliation or Control: Independent Non-Profit IRS Status: 501(c)3
Highest Offering: First Talmudic Degree
Program: Professional
Accreditation: RABN

01 CEO ... Mr. Jacob UNGAR
05 Dean ... Rabbi Israel EISENBERGER
06 Registrar/Administrator ... Rabbi Yitzchok SOIFER
37 Financial Aid Administrator ... Rabbi Yosef BRAILOFSKY

Beis Medrash Heichal Dovid (I)

211 Beach 17th Street, Far Rockaway NY 11691-4433
County: Queens FICE Identification: 037133
Unit ID: 444413
Telephone: (718) 868-2300 Carnegie Class: Spec/Faith
FAX Number: (718) 868-0517 Calendar System: Semester
Established: 1999 Annual Undergrad Tuition & Fees: $8,000
Enrollment: 111 Male
Affiliation or Control: Independent Non-Profit IRS Status: 501(c)3
Highest Offering: Second Talmudic Degree
Program: Teacher Preparatory; Professional
Accreditation: RABN

01 Dean ... Rabbi Yaakov BENDER
05 Rosh Yeshiva ... Rabbi Shlomo Avidgor ALTUSKY
37 Financial Aid Officer ... Rabbi Aaron STEINBERG

The Belanger School of Nursing (J)

650 McClellan Street, Schenectady NY 12304
County: Schenectady FICE Identification: 006448
Unit ID: 190956
Telephone: (518) 243-4471 Carnegie Class: Assoc/PrivNFP
FAX Number: (518) 243-4470 Calendar System: Other
URL: www.ellisbelangerschoolofnursing.org
Established: 1903 Annual Undergrad Tuition & Fees: $8,894
Enrollment: 120 Coed
Affiliation or Control: Independent Non-Profit IRS Status: 501(c)3
Highest Offering: Associate Degree
Program: Nursing Emphasis
Accreditation: ADNUR

01 Director ... Dr. Marilyn STAPLETON

Berkeley College (K)

3 East 43rd Street, New York NY 10017-4604
County: New York FICE Identification: 007394
Unit ID: 189228
Telephone: (212) 986-4343 Carnegie Class: Spec/Bus
FAX Number: (212) 818-1169 Calendar System: Quarter
URL: www.berkeleycollege.edu
Established: 1931 Annual Undergrad Tuition & Fees: $23,700
Enrollment: 7,742 Coed
Affiliation or Control: Proprietary IRS Status: Proprietary
Highest Offering: Baccalaureate
Program: Business Emphasis
Accreditation: M

00 Chairman of the Board ... Mr. Kevin L. LUING
01 President ... Dr. Dario A. CORTES
05 Provost ... Dr. Marianne VAKALIS
84 SVP Enrollment Management ... Ms. Diane RECINOS
10 SVP Finance & Administration/CFO ... Mr. Donald E. DEVINE
45 VP Planning & Chief of Staff ... Dr. Linda LUCIANO
04 Special Assistant to the President ... Dr. Rose Mary HEALY
26 SVP Marketing & CMO ... Mr. Don CHALLIS
86 SVP Government Relations ... Ms. Teri DUDA
43 VP & Chief Compliance Officer ... Mr. William BRANDT
13 Chief Information Officer ... Mr. Leonard DE BOTTON
08 VP Library Services ... Ms. Marlene DOTY
32 VP Student Development/Campus Life ... Dr. Edwin HUGHES
37 VP Financial Aid ... Mr. Howard LESLIE
21 VP Student Accounts ... Ms. Eileen LOFTUS-BERLIN
36 Int VP Career Svcs & Athletic Dir ... Mr. Brian MAHER
85 VP International Division ... Ms. Cynthia C. MARCHESE
07 VP Enrollment ... Ms. Catherine PALMER
86 VP Government Relations/NY ... Ms. Cynthia RUBINO
18 VP Operations ... Mr. Mark WAGENER
50 Interim Dean School of Business ... Dr. Wolfgang HINCK
49 Dean School of Liberal Arts ... Dr. Don KIEFFER
107 Dean School of Professional Studies ... Dr. Judith KORNBERG
06 Associate Provost Registrar ... Ms. Gail OKUN
20 Assistant Provost Advisement ... Ms. Kristin ROWE
106 Assistant Provost Online ... Ms. Carol SMITH
27 Director Media Relations ... Ms. Ilene GREENFIELD

Bet Medrash Gadol Ateret Torah (A)

901 Quentin Road, Brooklyn NY 11223
County: Kings Identification: 667146
Telephone: (347) 394-1036 Carnegie Class: Not Classified
FAX Number: (347) 394-1096 Calendar System: Semester
Established: 1992 Annual Undergrad Tuition & Fees: $9,000
Enrollment: 211 Male
Affiliation or Control: Independent Non-Profit IRS Status: 501(c)3
Highest Offering: Second Talmudic Degree
Program: Teacher Preparatory; Professional
Accreditation: @RABN

01 President/CEO .... Rabbi Joseph HARARI-RAFUL
10 Chief Financial/Business Officer .... Irwin SHAMAH
06 Registrar .... Eli BARAKER
11 Chief of Operations/Administration .... Zev KLEINER

Beth Hamedrash Shaarei Yosher Institute (B)

4102-10 16th Avenue, Brooklyn NY 11204-1099
County: Kings FICE Identification: 011192
Unit ID: 189273
Telephone: (718) 854-2290 Carnegie Class: Spec/Faith
FAX Number: (718) 436-9045 Calendar System: Semester
Established: 1962 Annual Undergrad Tuition & Fees: $7,500
Enrollment: 35 Male
Affiliation or Control: Independent Non-Profit IRS Status: 501(c)3
Highest Offering: Second Talmudic Degree
Program: Teacher Preparatory; Professional; Religious Emphasis
Accreditation: RABN

05 Chief Academic Officer .... Rabbi Yosef ROSENBLUM
10 Chief Business Officer .... Rabbi Pinches KAFF
29 Director Alumni Association .... Rabbi Chaim ROSENBERG
15 Director Personnel Services .... Rabbi Mordechai MARGULIES
37 Director Student Financial Aid .... Rabbi Aaron ROTTENBERG
06 Registrar .... Rabbi Sol ROSENBERG

Beth Hatalmud Rabbinical College (C)

2127 82nd Street, Brooklyn NY 11214-2594
County: Kings FICE Identification: 011922
Unit ID: 189264
Telephone: (718) 259-2525 Carnegie Class: Spec/Faith
FAX Number: (718) 256-5502 Calendar System: Semester
Established: 1950 Annual Undergrad Tuition & Fees: $7,400
Enrollment: 43 Male
Affiliation or Control: Independent Non-Profit IRS Status: 501(c)3
Highest Offering: Second Talmudic Degree
Program: Teacher Preparatory; Professional; Religious Emphasis
Accreditation: RABN

01 President .... Rabbi Chaim STEFANSKY
10 Fiscal Officer .... Rabbi C. L. PERKOWSKI
08 Librarian .... Mr. Shimon HESS

Beth Medrash Meor Yitzchok (D)

65 Dykstra's Way East, Monsey NY 10952
County: Rockland Identification: 667111
Telephone: (845) 426-3488 Carnegie Class: Not Classified
FAX Number: (845) 425-5415 Calendar System: Semester
Established: 2007 Annual Undergrad Tuition & Fees: $8,000
Enrollment: 135 Male
Affiliation or Control: Independent Non-Profit IRS Status: 501(c)3
Highest Offering: First Talmudic Degree
Program: Professional
Accreditation: RABN

Boricua College (E)

3755 Broadway, New York NY 10032-1599
County: New York FICE Identification: 013029
Unit ID: 189413
Telephone: (212) 694-1000 Carnegie Class: Bac/Diverse
FAX Number: (212) 694-1015 Calendar System: Semester
URL: www.boricuacollege.edu
Established: 1974 Annual Undergrad Tuition & Fees: $10,025
Enrollment: 1,235 Coed
Affiliation or Control: Independent Non-Profit IRS Status: 501(c)3
Highest Offering: Master's
Program: Liberal Arts And General; Professional
Accreditation: M, @TEAC

01 President .... Dr. Victor G. ALICEA
04 Admin Assistant to the President .... Ms. Sandra BELLAMY
12 VP/Dean Academic Affairs .... Dr. Maria MONTES-MORALES
05 VP/Dean & Chief Academic Officer .... Dr. Shivaji SENGUPTA
13 VP Information Technology .... Mr. Irving RAMIREZ
20 VP/Academic Planning & Programming .... Dr. John GUZMAN
43 Legal Counsel .... Mr. Jorge BATISTA
10 Director Finance .... Mr. Elias OYOLA
07 Director Admissions Northside Ctr .... Vacant
84 VP Enrollment & Managemen Bronx .... Mr. Abraham CRUZ
07 Director Admissions Graham .... Ms. Aurea MORALES
06 Director Registration & Assessment .... Ms. Beatriz AHORRIO
37 Director Financial Aid .... Ms. Rosalia CRUZ
15 Director Personnel/Human Resources .... Ms. Francia L. CASTRO
08 Director Library/Learning Resources .... Ms. Liza RIVERA
18 Director Environmental Services .... Mr. Elias RIVERA
41 Director of Athletics .... Vacant
30 Director of Development .... Vacant
20 Dean Academic Affairs Manhattan .... Mr. Moises PEREYRA
88 Dean of Generic Studies Bronx .... Mr. Jose Israel LOPEZ

Bramson O R T College (F)

69-30 Austin Street, Forest Hills NY 11375-4239
County: Queens FICE Identification: 021068
Unit ID: 189422
Telephone: (718) 261-5800 Carnegie Class: Assoc/PrivNFP
FAX Number: (718) 575-5119 Calendar System: Semester
URL: www.bramsonort.edu
Established: 1977 Annual Undergrad Tuition & Fees: $10,970
Enrollment: 690 Coed
Affiliation or Control: Independent Non-Profit IRS Status: 501(c)3
Highest Offering: Associate Degree
Program: Occupational; 2-Year Principally Bachelor's Creditable
Accreditation: NY

01 Director .... Dr. Ephraim BUHKS
05 Dean of Academic Services .... Dr. Robert ADELBERG
07 Recruitment/Admissions .... Ms. Dashia SILVA
08 Librarian .... Ms. Rivka BURKOS
21 Bursar .... Ms. Marina SHALAMOV
37 Financial Aid Coordinator .... Ms. Angelina MARRA
60 ESL/English Coordinator .... Ms. Pamela DAMBROSIA
36 Job Development Advisor .... Ms. Beth MORGANLANDER
50 Business Technology & Account Coord .... Mr. Robert ADELBERG
56 Computer Tech/Distance Learn Coord .... Mr. Damindra PERSAUD
56 Coordinator Extension Site .... Mr. Yair ROSENRAUCH
76 Medical Assistant Program Coord .... Dr. Emil ASDURIAN
96 Director of Purchasing .... Ms. Svetlana NISENBOYM
06 Registrar .... Ms. Aleksandra KAGAN
10 Controller .... Mr. Denis KOLJENOVIC

Briarcliffe College (G)

1055 Stewart Avenue, Bethpage NY 11714-3545
County: Nassau FICE Identification: 020757
Unit ID: 189459
Telephone: (516) 918-3600 Carnegie Class: Bac/Assoc
FAX Number: (516) 470-6020 Calendar System: Semester
URL: www.briarcliffe.edu
Established: 1966 Annual Undergrad Tuition & Fees: $18,720
Enrollment: 2,109 Coed
Affiliation or Control: Proprietary IRS Status: Proprietary
Highest Offering: Baccalaureate
Program: Business Emphasis
Accreditation: M, DH

01 President .... Dr. George SANTIAGO, JR.
10 VP Finance & Oper/Chief Fin Ofcr .... Mr. Louis COMMISSO
07 Vice Pres Admissions .... Mr. C. Gabriel CASTANO
32 Vice President Student Affairs .... Ms. Kathy GENUA
05 Provost .... Dr. Hubert BENITEZ
22 Director Regulatory Operations .... Ms. Helen GALLAGHER
35 Director of Student Management .... Ms. Georgette OSTROSKE
13 Director of Information Systems .... Mr. Hoober ZULUAGA
21 Business Office Manager .... Ms. Cindy ROYS
06 Registrar .... Ms. Joyce GIBSON
36 Director of Career Services .... Ms. Marieelena VULPIS
41 Athletic Director .... Ms. Gina D'AMARO
08 Librarian .... Mr. Andrew GIBSON

Brooklyn Law School (H)

250 Joralemon Street, Brooklyn NY 11201-3798
County: Kings FICE Identification: 002677
Unit ID: 189501
Telephone: (718) 625-2200 Carnegie Class: Spec/Law
FAX Number: (718) 780-0393 Calendar System: Semester
URL: www.brooklaw.edu
Established: 1901 Annual Graduate Tuition & Fees: N/A
Enrollment: 1,270 Coed
Affiliation or Control: Independent Non-Profit IRS Status: 501(c)3
Highest Offering: First Professional Degree; No Undergraduates
Program: Professional
Accreditation: LAW

01 President .... Ms. Joan G. WEXLER
00 Chairman of the Board of Trustees .... Mr. Stuart SUBOTNICK
05 Dean .... Dean Nicholas W. ALLARD
20 Assoc Dean for Academic Affairs .... Dean Michael T. CAHILL
32 Assoc Dean for Student Affairs .... Dean Beryl R. JONES-WOODIN
10 Chief Financial Officer .... Ms. Laurie H. NEWITZ
21 Treasurer .... Ms. Shoshanna M. CAMPBELL
07 Dean of Admissions & Financial Aid .... Dean Henry W. HAVERSTICK, III
08 Director of Library & Assoc Prof .... Prof. Janet SINDER
30 Director of Development .... Ms. Jean SMITH
29 Director of Alumni Relations .... Ms. Caitlin MONCK-MARCELLINO
36 Director of Career Services .... Ms. Camille CHIN KEE FATT
06 Registrar .... Ms. Suzanne DENNIS
37 Director of Financial Aid .... Ms. Nancy L. ZAHZAM
26 Asst Dean of External Affairs .... Ms. Linda HARVEY
39 Director of Residence Life .... Ms. Jennifer LANG
07 Director of Admissions .... Mr. Myron B. CHAITOVSKY
18 Facilities Manager .... Mr. Steven OLEKSIW
15 Human Resources Manager .... Ms. Christina WALLACE

Broome Community College (I)

PO Box 1017, Binghamton NY 13902-1017
County: Broome FICE Identification: 002862
Unit ID: 189547
Telephone: (607) 778-5000 Carnegie Class: Assoc/Pub-R-L
FAX Number: (607) 778-5310 Calendar System: Semester
URL: www.sunybroome.edu
Established: 1946 Annual Undergrad Tuition & Fees (In-District): $4,342
Enrollment: 6,866 Coed
Affiliation or Control: State/Local IRS Status: 501(c)3
Highest Offering: Associate Degree
Program: Occupational; 2-Year Principally Bachelor's Creditable
Accreditation: M, ADNUR, CAHIIM, DH, ENGT, MAC, MLTAD, PTAA, RAD

01 President .... Dr. Kevin DRUMM
05 Exec VP/Chief Academic Officer .... Dr. Francis BATTISTI
11 Vice Pres Admin/Financial Affairs .... Ms. Regina LOSINGER
32 VP Student and Economic Development .... Ms. Debra MORELLO
10 Associate Vice Pres & Controller .... Ms. Jeanette TILLOTSON
50 Assoc VP & Dean Bus/Public Svcs .... Ms. Elizabeth MOLLEN
76 Assoc VP & Dean of Health Sciences .... Dr. Andrea WADE
49 Assoc VP & Dean of Liberal Arts .... Dr. Michael KINNEY
51 Dir Continuing Educ & Workforce Dev .... Ms. Janet HERTZOG
81 Assoc Vice Pres & Dean STEM .... Dr. Kelli LIGEIKIS
102 Executive Director BCC Foundation .. Ms. Catherine R. WILLIAMS
08 Director Learning Resource Center .... Ms. Robin PETRUS
07 Director of Admissions .... Ms. Jenae SCHMIDT-NORRIS
15 Human Resources Officer .... Ms. Lynn FEDORCHAK
06 Registrar .... Mr. Martin GUZZI
36 Director of Placement Services .... Mr. Lawrence T. TRUILLO
09 Dean Institutional Effectiveness .... Mr. Jason ZBOCK
18 Campus Operations Director .... Mr. Phil TESTA
37 Director of Financial Aid .... Mr. Douglas S. LUKASIK
14 Dir Information Technology Services .... Mr. John PETKASH
23 Director of Health Services .... Ms. Margaret SMITH
25 Director of Sponsored Programs .... Ms. Shelli CORDISCO
41 Director of Athletics .... Mr. Brett CARTER
19 Dir of Campus Safety & Security .... Mr. Joseph O'CONNOR
29 Director Alumni Affairs .... Ms. Natalie THOMPSON
35 Director Student Activities .... Mr. David R. MASLAR
40 Director Bookstore .... Vacant
88 Dir Educational Opportunity Pgm .... Ms. Claudia CLARKE
96 Director of Purchasing .... Mr. Randy CAMPBELL
26 Public Affairs Officer .... Mr. Richard DAVID
85 Ast Dir Intl Admiss/Intl Stdnt Stds .... Ms. Angela LAROSA
104 Coordinator Study Abroad Program .... Ms. Maria BASUALDO
38 Student Counseling .... Ms. Mary MCCARTHY

*Bryant & Stratton College System Office (J)

2410 N. Forest Road, Suite 101, Getzville NY 14068-1224
County: Erie Identification: 666828
Telephone: (716) 250-7500 Carnegie Class: N/A
FAX Number: (716) 250-7510
URL: www.bryantstratton.edu

01 President & CEO .... Mr. John J. STASCHAK
03 Executive Vice President .... Dr. Francis J. FELSER
05 Vice Pres Chief Academic Officer .... Ms. Beth A. TARQUINO
10 VP/Chief Financial Ofcr/Treasurer .... Mr. David VADEN

*Bryant & Stratton College (K)

465 Main Street, Suite 400, Buffalo NY 14203-1795
County: Erie FICE Identification: 002678
Unit ID: 189583
Telephone: (716) 884-9120 Carnegie Class: Assoc/PrivFP4
FAX Number: (716) 884-0091 Calendar System: Semester
URL: www.bryantstratton.edu
Established: 1854 Annual Undergrad Tuition & Fees: $16,530
Enrollment: 865 Coed
Affiliation or Control: Proprietary IRS Status: Proprietary
Highest Offering: Associate Degree
Program: 2-Year Principally Bachelor's Creditable; Liberal Arts And General; Business Emphasis
Accreditation: M, MAC

02 Campus Director .... Dr. Marvel E. ROSS-JONES
05 Dean of Instruction .... Dr. Adiam TSEGAI
07 Director of Admissions .... Mr. Phil J. STRUEBEL
36 Director of Career Services .... Ms. Diane WESTBROOK
10 WNY Business Office Director .... Ms. Kathleen OWCZARCZAK

*_Bryant & Stratton College_ (L)

1259 Central Avenue, Albany NY 12205-5230
Telephone: (518) 437-1802 FICE Identification: 004749
Accreditation: &M, MAC

† Main campus is Bryant & Stratton College in Buffalo, NY.

*_Bryant & Stratton College_ (M)

150 Bellwood Drive, Rochester NY 14606-4227
Telephone: (585) 720-0660 FICE Identification: 012470
Accreditation: &M

† Main campus is Bryant & Stratton College in Buffalo, NY.

* *Bryant & Stratton College* (A)
953 James Street, Syracuse NY 13203-2502
Telephone: (315) 472-6603 FICE Identification: 008276
Accreditation: &M, MAC

† Main campus is Bryant & Stratton College in Buffalo, NY.

Business Informatics Center, Inc. (B)
134 S Central Avenue, Valley Stream NY 11580-5418
County: Nassau FICE Identification: 025729
Unit ID: 189653
Telephone: (516) 561-0050 Carnegie Class: Assoc/PrivFP
FAX Number: (516) 561-0074 Calendar System: Quarter
URL: www.thecollegeforbusiness.com
Established: 1983 Annual Undergrad Tuition & Fees: $11,250
Enrollment: 125 Coed
Affiliation or Control: Proprietary IRS Status: Proprietary
Highest Offering: Associate Degree
Program: Occupational
Accreditation: ACCSC

01 President .... Ms. Constance BROWN
05 Academic Dean .... Dr. Eugene ALEXANDER
07 Admissions Director .... Mr. Ira WOLK
37 Financial Aid Director .... Ms. Carolyn WIRTH

Canisius College (C)
2001 Main Street, Buffalo NY 14208-1098
County: Erie FICE Identification: 002681
Unit ID: 189705
Telephone: (716) 883-7000 Carnegie Class: Master's L
FAX Number: (716) 888-2525 Calendar System: Semester
URL: www.canisius.edu
Established: 1870 Annual Undergrad Tuition & Fees: $33,332
Enrollment: 4,908 Coed
Affiliation or Control: Roman Catholic IRS Status: 501(c)3
Highest Offering: Master's
Program: Liberal Arts And General; Teacher Preparatory; Professional; Business Emphasis
Accreditation: M, BUS, CACREP, TED

01 President .... Mr. John J. HURLEY
43 Special Counsel to President .... Mr. George M. MARTIN
05 Interim VP Academic Affairs .... Dr. Richard A. WALL
10 Vice President Business & Finance .... Mr. Patrick E. RICHEY
32 Interim VP Student Affairs .... Dr. Terri L. MANGIONE
30 VP for Institutional Advancement .... Vacant
20 Interim Assoc VP for Acad Affairs .... Dr. Margaret MCCARTHY
08 Director of Library .... Ms. Kristine E. KASBOHM
07 Director Undergrad Admissions .... Mrs. Mollie BALLARO
07 Exec Directror Grad Enrollment .... Dr. Margaret MCCARTHY
44 Director of Principal Gifts .... Mr. J. Patrick GREENWALD
06 Assoc VP of Acad Affairs/Registrar .... Mr. Blair W. FOSTER
30 Assoc VP Institutional Advancement .... Ms. Dianna CIVELLO
21 Int Assoc VP of Finance/Controller .... Mr. Ronald J. HABERER
35 Dean of Students .... Dr. Terri L. MANGIONE
87 Director of Summer Sessions .... Mr. Blair W. FOSTER
49 Dean College of Arts & Sciences .... Dr. David W. EWING
50 Interim Dean School of Business .... Dr. Richard A. SHICK
37 Director of Student Financial Aid .... Mr. Curtis C. GAUME
36 Director of Career Center .... Mr. James V. JONES
26 Assoc VP of Public Relations .... Ms. Debra S. PARK
15 Director of Human Resourses .... Ms. Deborah J. WINSLOW-SCHABER
53 Dean School Education/Human Svcs .... Dr. Michael J. PARDALES
107 Exec Dir of Professional Studies .... Dr. Khalid W. BIBI
25 Director of Sponsored Programs .... Ms. Mary Ann LANGLOIS
18 Director Facilities Management .... Mr. Thomas E. CIMINELLI
19 Director of Public Safety .... Mr. Gary M. EVERETT
23 Director Student Health Center .... Ms. Patricia H. CREAHAN
29 Interim Director Alumni Relations .... Ms. Rachel FLAMMER
38 Director Counseling Center .... Ms. Eileen A. NILAND
39 Dir Res Life/Assoc Dean of Stdnts .... Mr. Matthew H. MULVILLE
85 Director Intl/Student Programs .... Ms. Esther A. NORTHMAN
40 Manager Bookstore .... Mr. Bhagbat KARKI
41 Director Athletics .... Mr. William J. MAHER
42 Interim Director Campus Ministry .... Ms. Luanne C. FIRESTONE
88 Director of Creative Services .... Ms. Andolyn M. COURTNEY
88 Director of Advancement Services .... Ms. Francine R. MERGL
90 Director of Academic Computing .... Ms. Estelle M. SIENER
88 Associate Controller .... Mr. Ronald J. HABERER
94 Director of Women Studies .... Dr. Jane E. FISHER
92 Director of All College Honors Pgm .... Dr. Bruce J. DIERENFIELD
09 Director of Institutional Research .... Dr. Matthew HERTZ
88 Director of Multi Cultural Programs .... Mr. Sababu C. NORRIS
14 Dir Computer Infrastructure/Opers .... Mr. Frank W. KIRSTEIN
24 Director Media Center .... Mr. Daniel J. DREW
27 Interim Chief Information Officer .... Mr. Walter J. DRABEK
96 Facilities Operations Manager .... Mr. Gary B. LEW
102 Director Corp/Foundation Relations .... Vacant
105 Director of Web Services/Mkt Comm .... Mr. David H. COURTNEY
04 Assistand to the President .... Ms. Erica C. SAMMARCO
88 Director of Marketing .... Mr. Robert R. HILL
102 Asst Dir Corp/Found Relations .... Ms. Emma PERROTT

Cayuga Community College (D)
197 Franklin Street, Auburn NY 13021-3099
County: Cayuga FICE Identification: 002861
Unit ID: 189839
Telephone: (315) 255-1743 Carnegie Class: Assoc/Pub-S-SC
FAX Number: (315) 255-2117 Calendar System: Semester
URL: www.cayuga-cc.edu
Established: 1953 Annual Undergrad Tuition & Fees (In-District): $4,090
Enrollment: 4,749 Coed
Affiliation or Control: State/Local IRS Status: 501(c)3
Highest Offering: Associate Degree
Program: Occupational; 2-Year Principally Bachelor's Creditable
Accreditation: M, ADNUR

01 President .... Vacant
04 Assistant to President/Board .... Ms. Carolyn L. GUARIGLIA
05 Provost/Vice Pres Academic Affairs .... Dr. Anne J. HERRON
32 Vice President Student Affairs .... Mr. Jeffrey E. ROSENTHAL
10 Vice Pres Administration/Treasurer .... Ms. Diane L. HUTCHINSON
12 Assoc VP & Dean Fulton Campus .... Ms. Margaret A. KILLORAN
30 Executive Director Foundation .... Mr. Jeffrey L. HOFFMAN
103 Dean Cmty Educ & Workforce Develop .... Ms. Carla M. DESHAW
84 Dean Enrollment Management .... Ms. Cheryl A. LINDSAY
14 Dean Information Technology .... Mr. John M. TAYLOR
07 Director of Admissions .... Mr. Bruce M. BLODGETT
29 Director Alumni Association .... Ms. Louise B. WILSON
18 Director Buildings & Grounds .... Mr. Kevin S. DRAYER
21 Dir Business Services & Comptroller .... Ms. Marie A. NELLENBACK
106 Director Distance Learning .... Mr. Edward J. KOWALSKI, JR.
37 Director Financial Aid .... Ms. Judith G. MILADIN
09 Director Institutional Research .... Ms. Carol E. RUNGE
08 Director Library & Learn Resources .... Vacant
41 Director Athletics .... Mr. Peter E. LIDDELL
88 Director Center for Acad Success .... Ms. Terry L. KUPP
88 Director Adult Learning .... Ms. Janet A. NELSON
66 Director Nursing .... Ms. Linda L. ALFIERI
15 Director HR & Affirm Action .... Mr. Scott M. WHALEN
27 Director Public Rel & Inst Commun .... Ms. Margaret D. SPILLETT
06 Registrar .... Mr. Michael A. PASTORE
32 Director Student Development .... Dr. Julie A. WHITE
36 Director Career Services .... Ms. Margaret H. OSBORNE
19 Director Campus Safety and Security .... Mr. Scott E. SHAFT
108 Director Assessment .... Ms. Maureen N. ERICKSON

Cazenovia College (E)
Cazenovia NY 13035-1085
County: Madison FICE Identification: 002685
Unit ID: 189848
Telephone: (800) 654-3210 Carnegie Class: Bac/Diverse
FAX Number: (315) 655-4143 Calendar System: Semester
URL: www.cazenovia.edu
Established: 1824 Annual Undergrad Tuition & Fees: $28,900
Enrollment: 980 Coed
Affiliation or Control: Independent Non-Profit IRS Status: 501(c)3
Highest Offering: Baccalaureate
Program: Liberal Arts And General; Professional
Accreditation: M, IACBE, @TEAC

01 President .... Dr. Mark J. TIERNO
03 Exec Vice Pres/COO/Sec of College .... Dr. Susan A. BERGER
05 VP Academic Affs/Dean of Faculty .... Dr. Donald A. MCCRIMMON
10 VP Financial Affs/Chief Fin Officer .... Mr. Mark H. EDWARDS
84 VP Enrol Mgmt/Dean Admiss/Fin Aid .... Mr. Robert A. CROOT
30 VP for Institutional Advancement .... Ms. Carol SATCHWELL
32 VP Student Devel/Dean of Students .... Mr. C. Joseph BEHAN
20 Assoc Dean Faculty/Dn First Yr Pgm .... Dr. Timothy G. MCLAUGHLIN
51 Director of Extended Learning .... Ms. Lesley C. OWENS-PELTON
08 Int Director of Library Services .... Dr. Timothy G. MCLAUGHLIN
37 Director of Financial Aid .... Ms. Christine MANDEL
26 Director of Communications .... Mr. Wayne WESTERVELT
15 Director Human Resources .... Ms. Janice ROMAGNOLI
23 Director Health Services .... Dr. Susan A. BERGER
36 Dir Career Svcs/Internship Pgms .... Ms. Christine RICHARDSON
41 Director Athletics .... Mr. Robert F. KENNA
13 Director of Technology Development .... Vacant
06 Registrar .... Ms. Christine MANDEL
09 Dir Institutional Rsrch/Assessment .... Ms. Bridget MILLER
18 Dir of Physical Plant Operations .... Mr. Jeff SLOCUM
29 Director Alumni Relations .... Ms. Shari WHITAKER
38 Director of Counseling Services .... Dr. Todd SPANGLER
42 Chaplain .... Ms. Elizabeth BURLEW

Central Yeshiva Tomchei Tmimim Lubavitch America (F)
841-853 Ocean Parkway, Brooklyn NY 11230-2798
County: Kings FICE Identification: 004776
Unit ID: 189857
Telephone: (718) 434-0784 Carnegie Class: Spec/Faith
FAX Number: (718) 434-1519 Calendar System: Semester
Established: 1941 Annual Undergrad Tuition & Fees: $6,700
Enrollment: 695 Male
Affiliation or Control: Independent Non-Profit IRS Status: 501(c)3
Highest Offering: Second Talmudic Degree
Program: Teacher Preparatory; Professional; Music Emphasis
Accreditation: RABN

01 President .... Rabbi Shloime ZARCHI
05 Dean .... Rabbi Zalman LABKOWSKI
06 Registrar .... Rabbi Joseph WILMOWSKY
37 Financial Aid Director .... Rabbi Moshe M. GLUCKOWSKY
26 Director Public Relations .... Mr. Shaya BOYMELGREEN
10 Treasurer .... Rabbi Moshe BOGOMILSKY

Christ the King Seminary (G)
711 Knox Road, Box 607, East Aurora NY 14052-0607
County: Erie FICE Identification: 002822
Unit ID: 189981
Telephone: (716) 652-8900 Carnegie Class: Spec/Faith
FAX Number: (716) 652-8903 Calendar System: Semester
URL: www.cks.edu
Established: 1974 Annual Graduate Tuition & Fees: $9,320
Enrollment: 88 Coed
Affiliation or Control: Roman Catholic IRS Status: 501(c)3
Highest Offering: Master's; No Undergraduates
Program: Religious Emphasis
Accreditation: M, THEOL

01 Rector/President .... Rev. Peter DRILLING
03 Vice Rector .... Rev. Gregory M. FAULHABER
05 Academic Dean .... Dr. Dennis A. CASTILLO
10 Comptroller .... Mrs. Nancy M. EHLERS
11 Chief of Operations .... Mr. Michael SHERRY
30 Director Institutional Advancement .... Mr. Richard SUCHAN
18 Director of Facilities .... Vacant
08 Library Director .... Ms. Teresa LUBIENECKI
38 Director of Ministry Development .... Mr. Douglas J. GEORGE
26 Chief Public Relations Officer .... Ms. Susan LANKES

Christie's Education, Inc. (H)
11 West 42nd Street, 8th Floor, New York NY 10036
County: New York FICE Identification: 036654
Unit ID: 475510
Telephone: (212) 355-1501 Carnegie Class: Not Classified
FAX Number: (212) 355-7370 Calendar System: Other
URL: www.christieseducation.com
Established: 1996 Annual Graduate Tuition & Fees: $44,963
Enrollment: 82 Coed
Affiliation or Control: Proprietary IRS Status: Proprietary
Highest Offering: Master's; No Undergraduates
Program: Professional; Fine Arts Emphasis
Accreditation: NY

01 Director of Studies .... Dr. Veronique CHAGNON-BURKE
08 Librarian .... Ms. Karen MAGUIRE
07 Academic and Admissions Coordinator .... Ms. Hilary SMITH
04 Administrative Assistant .... Ms. Claire PRIDDY
10 Business Manager .... Ms. Margaret CONKLIN
88 Administrator .... Ms. Amanda MUSCATO
88 Administrator .... Ms. Jillian SCOTT

*City University of New York (I)
205 E. 42nd Street, New York NY 10017
County: New York FICE Identification: 025061
Unit ID: 190035
Telephone: (646) 664-9100 Carnegie Class: N/A
FAX Number: (646) 664-3868
URL: www.cuny.edu

01 Interim Chancellor .... Dr. William P. KELLY
03 Exec Vice Chanc/Chief Oper Officer .... Mr. Allan H. DOBRIN
05 Exec VC/University Provost .... Dr. Alexandra LOGUE
26 Sr Vice Chanc University Relations .... Mr. Jay HERSHENSON
43 Sr Vice Chancellor Legal Affairs .... Mr. Frederick P. SCHAFFER
10 Sr Vice Chancellor Budget/Finance .... Mr. Marc SHAW
45 Vice Chanc Facility Plng/Constr Mgt .... Ms. Iris WEINSHALL
15 Vice Chanc for Human Resources Mgmt .... Ms. Gloriana WATERS
88 Vice Chancellor for Labor Relations .... Ms. Pamela S. SILVERBLATT
09 Vice Chancellor for Research .... Dr. Gillian SMALL
32 Vice Chancellor Student Affairs .... Dr. Frank SANCHEZ
27 Assoc VC/Chief Information Officer .... Mr. Brian COHEN
21 Assoc Vice Chanc Budget/Finance .... Mr. Matthew SAPIENZA

*Baruch College/City University of New York (J)
One Bernard Baruch Way, New York NY 10010-5526
County: New York FICE Identification: 007273
Unit ID: 190512
Telephone: (646) 312-1000 Carnegie Class: Master's L
FAX Number: N/A Calendar System: Semester
URL: www.baruch.cuny.edu
Established: 1968 Annual Undergrad Tuition & Fees (In-District): $5,730
Enrollment: 17,373 Coed
Affiliation or Control: State/Local IRS Status: 501(c)3
Highest Offering: Doctorate
Program: Liberal Arts And General; Professional; Business Emphasis
Accreditation: M, BUS, BUSA, HSA, SPAA

02 President .... Dr. Mitchel B. WALLERSTEIN
05 Int Provost/SVP Academic Affairs .... Dr. John BRENKMAN
11 Vice Pres Administration/Finance .... Ms. Katharine COBB
32 Vice Pres Student Affs/Enroll Mgmt .... Dr. Ben CORPUS
30 Vice Pres for College Advancement .... Mr. Mark GIBBEL
50 Interim Dean Zicklin Sch Business .... Dr. Myung-Soo LEE
45 Asst VP Campus Facilities .... Vacant
84 Asst VP Enrollment Services .... Ms. Leslie SUTTON-SMITH
13 Asst VP Info Tech/Chief Librarian .... Mr. Arthur DOWNING
35 Asst Vice President Student Affairs .... Dr. Corlisse THOMAS
21 Asst Vice President Finance .... Ms. Mary FINNEN
102 President Baruch College Fund .... Mr. Joel J. COHEN

49 Dn Sch Arts & Sci/V Prov Glob Strat ... Dr. Jeffrey M. PECK
20 Associate Provost ... Dr. Barbara LAWRENCE
20 Associate Provost ... Dr. Dennis SLAVIN
80 Dean School Public Affairs ... Dr. David BIRDSELL
43 Executive Legal Counsel ... Ms. Stephanie VULLO
58 Executive Officer Doctoral Program ... Dr. Joseph WEINTROP
100 Chief of Staff ... Ms. Mary GORMAN
25 Director of Sponsored Programs ... Mr. Alan EVELYN
15 Exec Dir of Human Resources ... Ms. Monique GEORGE
36 Director Career Development Center ... Dr. Patricia IMBIMBO
90 Asst Dir Client Svcs/Fac Liais ... Mr. Frank WERBER
85 Director Intl Student Office ... Ms. Rosa KELLEY
19 Director Public Safety ... Mr. Henry J. MCLAUGHLIN
09 Dir Institutional Rsrch/Pgm Assess ... Mr. John CHOONOO
26 VP for Cmty/Ext Rels & Econ Dev ... Ms. Christina LATOUF
29 Director Alumni Relations ... Vacant
96 Director of Purchasing ... Dr. Diane OQUENDO
22 Acting Director Affirmative Action ... Ms. Mona JHA
41 Athletic Director ... Mr. Ray RANKIS
86 Dir of Govt and Community Relations ... Mr. Eric LUGO

*City University of New York Borough of Manhattan Community College (A)

199 Chambers Street, New York NY 10007-1047
County: New York FICE Identification: 002691
Unit ID: 190521
Telephone: (212) 220-1230 Carnegie Class: Assoc/Pub-U-MC
FAX Number: (212) 220-1244 Calendar System: Semester
URL: www.bmcc.cuny.edu
Established: 1963 Annual Undergrad Tuition & Fees (In-District): $4,518
Enrollment: 24,537 Coed
Affiliation or Control: State/Local IRS Status: 501(c)3
Highest Offering: Associate Degree
Program: Occupational; 2-Year Principally Bachelor's Creditable
Accreditation: M, ADNUR, CAHIIM, COARC, EMT

02 President ... Dr. Antonio PEREZ
05 Senior Vice Pres Academic Affairs ... Dr. Sadie BRAGG
11 Vice President Administration/Plng ... Mr. G. Scott ANDERSON
43 VP Legal Affs/Faculty & Staff Rels ... Mr. Robert DIAZ
32 Vice President of Student Affairs ... Dr. Marva CRAIG
30 Int Vice Pres of Development ... Ms. Doris HOLZ
10 Asst Vice Pres of Finance ... Ms. Elena SAMUELS
51 Dean Ctr for Cont Ed/Workforce Dev ... Dr. Sunil GUPTA
25 Dean Grants & Development ... Mr. John MONTANEZ
20 Dean for Instruction/Curriculum ... Dr. Erwin WONG
88 Assoc Dean Academic Support Svcs ... Dr. Michael GILLESPIE
37 Deputy Director Financial Aid ... Mr. Ralph W. BUXTON
15 Deputy Director Human Resources ... Ms. Gloria CHAO
07 Assoc Director of Admissions ... Ms. Antoinette MIDDLETON
84 Director Enrollment Management ... Dr. Eugenio BARRIOS
06 Senior Registrar ... Mr. Mohammad ALAM
08 Director Learning Resource Center ... Mr. James TYNES
09 Director Institutional Research ... Dr. Jane Lee DELGADO
22 Affirmative Action Officer ... Ms. Iyana TITUS
18 Campus Facilities Officer ... Vacant
26 Public Relations Officer ... Mr. Barry ROSEN
41 Director of Athletics ... Mr. Stephen KELLY
102 Dir Foundation/Corporate Relations ... Mr. Bryan HALLER
36 Dir Acad Advisement/Transfer Ctr ... Ms. Freda MCCLEAN
38 Director Counseling Center ... Dr. Lily HUNG
96 Director of Procurement ... Mr. Robert COX

*City University of New York Bronx Community College (B)

2155 University Avenue, Bronx NY 10453-2895
County: Bronx FICE Identification: 002692
Unit ID: 190530
Telephone: (718) 289-5100 Carnegie Class: Assoc/Pub-U-MC
FAX Number: (718) 289-6011 Calendar System: Semester
URL: www.bcc.cuny.edu
Established: 1957 Annual Undergrad Tuition & Fees (In-District): $3,954
Enrollment: 11,287 Coed
Affiliation or Control: State/Local IRS Status: 501(c)3
Highest Offering: Associate Degree
Program: Occupational; 2-Year Principally Bachelor's Creditable
Accreditation: M, ACBSP, ADNUR, ENGT, NMT, RAD

02 President ... Dr. Carole M. BEROTTE JOSEPH
05 Interim VP of Academic Affairs ... Dr. David HADALLER
11 SVP of Administration & Finance ... Ms. Mary E. COLEMAN
26 Government Rels and Ext Affairs ... Mr. David W. LEVERS
04 Exec Asst to the Pres ... Ms. Carmen VAZQUEZ
32 VP for Student Affairs ... Dr. Athos K. BREWER
30 Vice Pres for Strategic Initiatives ... Dr. Eddy BAYARDELLE
26 Asst VP Comm & Marketing ... Ms. Diane WEATHERS
84 Dean of Enrollment Management ... Mr. Bernard GANTT
11 Dean Administrative Services ... Mr. David A. TAYLOR
45 Dean Inst Research & Planning ... Dr. Nancy RITZE
20 Dean of Faculty & Academic Affairs ... Dr. Luis MONTENEGRO
88 Int Assoc Dn of AA for Student Svc ... Dr. Neal PHILLIP
10 Chief Business Officer ... Mr. Donovan THOMPSON
06 Registrar ... Mr. Robert DEMPSEY
14 Exec Dir of Information Technology ... Mr. Loic AUDUSSEAU
37 Director of Financial Aid ... Ms. Maria BARLAAM
07 Admissions Officer ... Vacant
15 Personnel Officer ... Mrs. Shelley LEVY
08 Chief Librarian ... Mr. Michael J. MILLER

19 Director of Security ... Mr. James VERDICCHIO
35 Director Student Life ... Ms. Melissa KIRK
41 Director of Athletics ... Mr. Michael BELFIORE
18 Chief Superintendnt Phys Plant Svcs ... Mr. Wayne MURPHY
29 Director of Alumni Relations ... Mr. Robert WHELAN
35 Assoc Dean Student Svcs ... Dr. Annecy BAEZ
88 Dir of College Discovery ... Ms. Cynthia SUAREZ-ESPINAL
43 Executive Counsel & Labor Designee ... Ms. Karla R. WILLIAMS
96 Director of Purchasing ... Ms. Sharon LUCKIE
28 Chief Diversity Officer ... Mrs. Jesenia MINIER-DELGADO

*City University of New York Brooklyn College (C)

2900 Bedford Avenue, Brooklyn NY 11210-2889
County: Kings FICE Identification: 002687
Unit ID: 190549
Telephone: (718) 951-5000 Carnegie Class: Master's L
FAX Number: N/A Calendar System: Semester
URL: www.brooklyn.cuny.edu
Established: 1930 Annual Undergrad Tuition & Fees (In-District): $5,884
Enrollment: 16,524 Coed
Affiliation or Control: State/Local IRS Status: 501(c)3
Highest Offering: Master's
Program: Liberal Arts And General; Teacher Preparatory; Professional
Accreditation: M, AUD, CACREP, DIETD, DIETI, PH, SP, TED

02 President ... Dr. Karen L. GOULD
05 Provost/Sr Vice Pres Acad Affairs . Dr. William A. TRAMONTANO
10 Sr VP for Finance & Administration .... Mr. Joseph GIOVANNELLI
30 Vice Pres Institutional Advancement ... Dr. Andrew SILLEN
84 VP for Enrollment Management ... Dr. Stephen E. JOYNER
32 VP for Student Affairs ... Dr. Milga MORALES
26 AVP of Communicat & Marketing ... Vacant
100 Chief of Staff to President ... Ms. Nicole HAAS
86 Exec Dir Govt & External Affairs ... Mr. Steven SCHECHTER
20 Associate Provost for Faculty & Adm ... Dr. Jerrold MIROTZNIK
20 Associate Provost for Acad Pgms ... Dr. Terence CHENG
45 Assistant Provost Plng & Spec Projs ... Ms. Colette WAGNER
57 Dean School Visual Media & Perf Art ... Dr. Maria A. CONELLI
50 Dean of School of Business ... Dr. Willie HOPKINS
83 Act Dean Sc Humanities & Social Sci ... Dr. Matthew MOORE
81 Dean School Natural & Behav Science ... Dr. Kleanthis PSARRIS
53 Dean School of Education ... Dr. Deborah A. SHANLEY
21 AVP Budget & Planning & CFO ... Mr. Alan GILBERT
18 Asst VP Facilities Plng/Operations ... Mr. Francis X. FITZGERALD
13 Asst VP Information Technology Svcs ... Mr. Mark GOLD
16 Asst VP Human Resource Services ... Mr. Michael HEWITT
35 Assoc Dean for Student Affairs ... Dr. Jacqueline WILLIAMS
88 Asst Dean for School of Education ... Dr. Geraldine FARIA
35 Asst Dean Student Development ... Ms. Vannessa GREEN
51 Asst Dean Enroll Advoc & Adult Lit ... Ms. Lillian O'REILLY
08 Chief Librarian ... Ms. Stephanie WALKER
88 Deputy Comptroller ... Ms. Beatrice GILLING RAYNOR
88 Bursar ... Ms. Yasmin ALI
44 Assoc Director Annual Funds ... Ms. Patricia ALLEN
108 Director Academic Assessment ... Dr. Michael ANDERSON
09 Dir Inst Plng/Research & Assess ... Dr. Michael AYERS
88 Director of Women's Center ... Ms. Sau Fong AU
88 Director of Speech & Hearing Center ... Mr. Michael BERGEN
104 Sen Dir Int Ed & Global Engagement ... Dr. Alice G. BIER
85 Actg Exec Dir Intl Student Services ... Mr. Ryan BUCK
25 Dir Research & Sponsored Programs ... Ms. Sabrina CEREZO
96 Act Dir Procurement and Support Svc .... Ms. Madonna CHARLES
40 Bookstore Manager ... Mr. Michael D'ACIERNO
37 Director Financial Aid ... Mr. Ahad FARHANG
06 Registrar ... Mr. Richard FELTMAN
41 Dir Rec Intramurals/Intercol Athl ... Mr. Bruce FILOSA
88 General Mgr Media/Perform Arts Ctr .... Mr. Richard GROSSBERG
88 Dir Scholarships & Honors Recruit ... Ms. Evelyn GUZMAN
105 Web Manager ... Ms. Leonora KISSIS
38 Director of Personal Counseling ... Dr. Gregory KUHLMAN
30 Assoc Exec Director of Development ... Ms. Beth F. LEVINE
94 Coordinator of Women's Studies ... Dr. Namita MANOHAR
22 Dir Diversity & Equity Programs . Ms. Natalie L. MASON-KINSEY
36 Dir Magner Ctr Career Dev/Intrn ... Mr. Robert OLIVA
88 Dir Academic Advise & Stdnt Success ... Mr. Jesus PEREZ
43 Legal Counsel to the President ... Ms. Pamela POLLACK
29 Director Alumni Affairs ... Ms. Marla H. SCHREIBMAN
92 Dir Scholars Pgm & Honors Academy ... Dr. Lisa SCHWEBEL
90 Dir Acad Computer & Library Systems ... Dr. Howard SPIVAK
88 Director of Testing ... Ms. Althea STERLING
88 Dir Ctr for Stdnt Disability Svcs ... Ms. Valerie M. STEWART-LOVELL
23 Director Health Clinic ... Ms. Ilene TANNENBAUM
07 Dir Undergrad Admiss & Recruitment ... Ms. Penelope TERRY
19 Director Safety & Security ... Mr. Donald A. WENZ
15 Dir Human Resource Services ... Ms. Renita WHITE SIMMONS

*City University of New York The City College (D)

160 Convent Avenue, New York NY 10031-9198
County: New York FICE Identification: 002688
Unit ID: 190567
Telephone: (212) 650-7000 Carnegie Class: Master's L
FAX Number: (212) 650-7680 Calendar System: Semester
URL: www1.ccny.cuny.edu
Established: 1847 Annual Undergrad Tuition & Fees (In-District): $6,088
Enrollment: 16,161 Coed
Affiliation or Control: State/Local IRS Status: 501(c)3
Highest Offering: Doctorate
Program: Liberal Arts And General; Teacher Preparatory; Professional
Accreditation: M, ARCPA, CLPSY, CS, ENG, LSAR, TED

02 President ... Dr. Lisa STAIANO-COICO
05 Provost/Sr VP Academic Affairs ... Dr. Maurizio TREVISAN
27 Vice Pres Communication/Marketing ... Dr. Deidra W. HILL
30 VP Development/Inst Advancement ... Mr. Jeffrey MACHI
10 Vice Pres Finance & Administration ... Mr. Jerald POSMAN
84 Asst Vice Pres Enrollment Mgmt ... Ms. Celia LLOYD
45 VP Campus Planning/Facilities Mgmt ... Mr. Robert SANTOS
26 VP Governmental/Community Affairs .. Ms. Karen WITHERSPOON
32 Vice Pres for Student Affairs ... Ms. Juana REINA
13 VP Information Technology/CIO ... Mr. Praveen PANCHAL
21 Asst VP of Finance & Management ... Mr. Felix LAM
100 Sr Advisor to Pres/Chief of Staff ... Ms. Deborah HARTNETT
63 Dean Sophie Davis Sch of BioMed Ed ... Dr. Maurizio TREVISAN
54 Dean of Engineering ... Dr. Gilda BARABINO
53 Dean of the School of Education ... Dr. Mary Erina DRISCOLL
47 Dean School of Architecture ... Dr. George RANALLI
88 Dean of CWE ... Dr. Juan Carlos MERCADO
81 Acting Dean of Science ... Dr. Christine LI
83 Acting Dean of Social Science ... Dr. Jeffrey ROSEN
79 Dean of Humanities & The Arts ... Dr. Eric WEITZ
04 Counsel to President ... Mr. Paul F. OCCHIOGROSSO
15 Asst Vice Pres of Human Resources ... Mr. John SIDERAKIS
29 Executive Director Alumni Affairs ... Mr. Donald K. JORDAN
35 Actg Dir Student Support Resources ... Ms. Teresa WALKER
06 Senior Registrar ... Mr. Daniel MATOS
35 Exec Dir of Student Affairs at CWE ... Ms. Sophia DEMETRIOU
08 Chief Librarian ... Ms. Pamela GILLESPIE
46 Director Research Administration ... Vacant
09 Director of Institutional Research ... Mr. Edward SILVERMAN
37 Director of Financial Aid ... Ms. Thelma MASON
26 Director of Public Relations ... Mr. Ellis SIMON
28 Chf Diversity Ofcr/Dean Faculty Rel ... Ms. Michele BAPTISTE
90 Director of IT & Computer Services ... Mr. Curtis RIAS
88 Director of Accessability Center ... Ms. Sarah DAMSKY
36 Director of Career Services ... Vacant
19 Director Public Safety & Security ... Vacant
11 Administrative Superintendent ... Mr. Kyle MANLEY
24 Director of Instructional Media ... Mr. Nana ABEYIE
07 Director of Admissions ... Mr. Joseph FANTOZZI
38 Director Student Counseling ... Dr. Jenev CADDELL
21 Director of Business & Finance ... Mr. Mario CRESCENZO
96 Director of Purchasing ... Mr. Mario CRESCENZO

*City University of New York College of Staten Island (E)

2800 Victory Boulevard, Staten Island NY 10314-6600
County: Richmond FICE Identification: 002698
Unit ID: 190558
Telephone: (718) 982-2000 Carnegie Class: Master's L
FAX Number: N/A Calendar System: Semester
URL: www.csi.cuny.edu
Established: 1976 Annual Undergrad Tuition & Fees (In-District): $6,158
Enrollment: 14,321 Coed
Affiliation or Control: State/Local IRS Status: 501(c)3
Highest Offering: Doctorate
Program: 2-Year Principally Bachelor's Creditable; Liberal Arts And General; Teacher Preparatory; Professional
Accreditation: M, ADNUR, CS, ENG, ENGT, MT, NUR, PTA, @SW, TED

02 Interim President ... Dr. William J. FRITZ
05 Int Sr VP Acad Affairs/Provost ... Dr. Fred NAIDER
10 VP for Finance and Administration ... Mr. Ira PERSKY
32 VP for Student Affairs ... Ms. A. Ramona BROWN
30 VP Inst Advance/External Affairs ... Dr. Kenneth BOYDEN
13 VP Tech Systems & Economic Develop ... Dr. Michael KRESS
21 AVP for Finance & Business Services ... Mr. Ed RIOS
100 Deputy to President/Chief of Staff ... Mr. Kenichi IWAMA
84 VP for Enrollment Management ... Ms. MaryBeth REILLY
35 Asst VP for Student Affairs ... Mr. Salvador B. MENA
18 AVP Campus Planing/Facilities Mgmt ... Mr. Stephen J. BRENNAN
20 Assoc Provost Inst Effectiveness ... Dr. Susan L. HOLAK
20 Assoc Provost for Undergrad Studies ... Dr. Deborah VESS
81 Dean of Science & Technology ... Dr. Alex CHIGOGIDZE
79 Int Dean Humanities & Social Sci ... Dr. Nan M. SUSSMAN
08 Chief Librarian ... Dr. Wilma JONES
43 Special Counsel and Labor Designee ... Ms. Kathleen GALVEZ
28 Director of Diversity & Compliance ... Ms. Danielle E. DIMITROV
41 Director of Athletics ... Mr. Charles GOMES

*City University of New York Graduate Center (F)

365 Fifth Avenue, New York NY 10016-4309
County: New York FICE Identification: 004765
Unit ID: 190576
Telephone: (212) 817-7000 Carnegie Class: RU/VH
FAX Number: (212) 817-1624 Calendar System: Semester
URL: www.gc.cuny.edu
Established: 1961 Annual Undergrad Tuition & Fees (In-District): $8,200
Enrollment: 4,838 Coed
Affiliation or Control: State/Local IRS Status: 501(c)3
Highest Offering: Doctorate
Program: Professional
Accreditation: M, PH, SCPSY

02 Interim President ... Dr. Chase F. ROBINSON
05 Interim Provost/Sr VP ... Dr. Louise LENNIHAN
10 Sr VP Finance and Administration ... Dr. Sebastian T. PERSICO
20 Acting Assoc Provost/Dean Human & S ... Dr. David OLAN

32 Vice President Student Affairs ... Mr. Matthew G. SCHOENGOOD
30 Vice Pres Institutional Advancement ... Vacant
13 VP Information Technology ... Mr. Robert D. CAMPBELL
21 Asst Vice President Finance ... Mr. Stuart B. SHOR
15 Asst VP for Faculty & Staff Rels .. Ms. Yosette JONES JOHNSON
88 Assoc Provost/Dean for Sciences ... Dr. Ann S. HENDERSON
46 Exec Dir Research & Sponsored Pgm ... Dr. Edith GONZALEZ DE SCOLLARD
25 Director Sponsored Research ... Ms. Hilry FISHER
26 Exec Dir Communications/Marketing ... Ms. Jane E. TROMBLEY
08 Chief Librarian ... Ms. Polly THISTLETHWAITE
07 Director Admissions ... Mr. Les GRIBBEN
06 Dir Student Svcs/Senior Registrar ... Mr. Vincent J. DELUCA
09 Dir Institutional Research & Effect ... Dr. Marie BURRAGE
88 Director Building Design/Exhibits ... Mr. Ray RING
28 Executive Officer Educ Opp/Div Pgm ... Dr. Donald ROBOTHAM
85 Director International Students ... Mr. Douglas EWING
88 Dir Well Ctr/Psy Coun Svc/Adult Dev ... Dr. Robert HATCHER
23 Director Student Health Services ... Ms. Adraenne BOWE
37 Director of Financial Aid ... Mr. John WILLIAMS
22 Chief Diversity Officer ... Ms. Edith RIVERA
16 Director of Human Resources ... Ms. Ella KISELYUK
31 Dpty Dir Special Events/Events Plng ... Vacant
18 Director Facilities/Physical Plant ... Mr. Michael BYERS
96 Director of Purchasing ... Mr. Ronald PAYNTER
35 Director Student Affairs ... Ms. Sharon LERNER
19 Dir of Security & Public Safety ... Mr. John FLAHERTY
94 Coordinator Women's Studies ... Dr. Victoria PITTS-TAYLOR

*City University of New York Herbert H. Lehman College (A)

250 Bedford Park Boulevard W, Bronx NY 10468-1589

County: Bronx | FICE Identification: 007022 | Unit ID: 190637
Telephone: (718) 960-8000 | Carnegie Class: Master's L
FAX Number: N/A | Calendar System: Semester
URL: www.lehman.cuny.edu
Established: 1968 | Annual Undergrad Tuition & Fees (In-District): $2,865
Enrollment: 11,862 | Coed
Affiliation or Control: State/Local | IRS Status: 501(c)3
Highest Offering: Master's
Program: Liberal Arts And General; Teacher Preparatory; Professional
Accreditation: M, CACREP, DIETD, DIETI, NURSE, PH, SP, SW, TED

02 President ... Dr. Ricardo R. FERNANDEZ
100 Chief of Staff/Chief Diversity Ofcr ... Ms. Dawn EWING-MORGAN
43 Sp Coun to Pres Legal Affs/Lab Rels ... Ms. Mary T. ROGAN
88 Dep to Pres/Educ Init & Spec Proj ... Ms. Sandra LERNER
05 Provost/Vice Pres Academic Affs ... Dr. Anny MORROBEL-SOSA
11 Vice President for Administration ... Mr. Vincent W. CLARK
32 Vice President Student Affairs ... Mr. Jose MAGDALENO
30 Vice President for Inst Advancement ... Mr. Mario DELLAPINA
27 Vice Pres/Chief Info Officer ... Mr. Ronald BERGMANN
84 Assoc Provost/VP Enroll Mgmt ... Dr. Robert C. TROY
20 AsscProv/AVP/UG Stdnt/Online Ed ... Dr. Robert WHITTAKER
18 Asst VP Campus Planning/Facilities ... Ms. Rene M. ROTOLO
30 Asst Vice President Inst Advance ... Mr. Fredrick GILBERT
88 Exec Asst to Vice Pres Student Affs ... Mr. Vincent ZUCCHETTO
79 Dean School of Arts/Humanities ... Dr. Deirdre PENNIPIECE
53 Dean School of Education ... Dr. Harriet FAYNE
83 Acting Dean School of Nat & Soc Sci ... Dr. Stefan BECKER
51 Dean Adult & Cont Education ... Dr. Marzie A. JAFARI
35 Dean of Student Affairs ... Mr. John HOLLOWAY
21 Business Manager ... Vacant
08 Chief Librarian ... Dr. Kenneth SCHLESINGER
06 Acting Registrar ... Ms. Yvette ROSARIO
07 Director of Admissions ... Ms. Laurie AUSTIN
29 Director of Alumni Relations ... Ms. Cristina NECULA
88 Director of the Art Gallery ... Ms. Susan HOELTZEL
36 Director Career Services ... Ms. Nancy A. CINTRON
38 Director Counseling Center ... Ms. Norma COFRESI
37 Director Financial Aid ... Mr. David MARTINEZ
89 Director Freshmen Year Initiative ... Dr. Steven WYCKOFF
46 Director Research & Spons Pgms ... Ms. Saeedah HICKMAN
92 Director of Honors College Program ... Dr. Gary SCHWARTZ
15 Director of Human Resources ... Mr. Eric WASHINGTON
14 Director Info Tech Resources ... Mr. Joseph MIDDLETON
09 Director of Institutional Research ... Dr. Susanne M. TUMELTY
38 Dir Instruct Support Services Pgm ... Ms. Althea FORDE
26 Director Comm & College Relations ... Mr. Alex BURNETT
88 Director Performing Arts Center ... Ms. Eva BORNSTEIN
19 Director of Public Safety ... Mr. Domenick LAPERUTA
96 Director of Purchasing ... Mr. Sunny VIRK
41 Athletic Director ... Dr. Martin ZWIREN
40 Bookstore Manager ... Vacant

*Hostos Community College-City University of New York (B)

500 Grand Concourse, Bronx NY 10451-5323

County: Bronx | FICE Identification: 008611 | Unit ID: 190585
Telephone: (718) 518-4300 | Carnegie Class: Assoc/Pub-U-MC
FAX Number: (718) 518-4294 | Calendar System: Semester
URL: www.hostos.cuny.edu
Established: 1970 | Annual Undergrad Tuition & Fees (In-District): $2,100
Enrollment: 6,835 | Coed
Affiliation or Control: State/Local | IRS Status: 501(c)3
Highest Offering: Associate Degree
Program: 2-Year Principally Bachelor's Creditable
Accreditation: M, DH, RAD

02 President ... Dr. Felix MATOS
05 Provost/Sr VP for Academic Affairs ... Dr. Carmen COBALLES-VEGA
10 Senior Vice Pres for Admin/ Finance ... Ms. Esther RODRIGUEZ-CHARDAVOYNE
32 Vice Pres Student Development ... Mr. Nathaniel CRUZ
100 Deputy to President ... Ms. Dolly MARTINEZ
30 Vice Pres Institutional Advancement ... Ms. Ana M. CARRION-SILVA
88 VP for Cont Educ & Workforce Dev ... Dr. Carlos MOLINA
13 Asst Vice Pres Info Technology ... Mr. Varun SEHGAL
21 Budget Director ... Ms. Fanny DUMANCELA
18 Exec Dir Facil Plng Des Mgmt ... Ms. Elizabeth FRIEDMAN
04 Associate Dean for Community Rels .. Ms. Ana I. GARCIA-REYES
20 Assoc Dean of Academic Support ... Ms. Christine MANGINO
35 Assistant Dean of Student Life ... Ms. Johanna GOMEZ
88 Executive Counsel & Labor Designee ... Ms. Glenda GRACE
27 Dir of Publications Development ... Mr. Don BRASWELL
38 Director of Counseling ... Ms. Linda ALEXANDER-WALLACE
15 College Personnel Officer ... Ms. Shirley SHEVACH
86 Director of Government Relations ... Mr. Joshua RIVERA
06 Registrar ... Ms. Nelida PASTORIZA
07 Director of Admissions ... Mr. Roland VELEZ
37 Director of Financial Aid ... Mr. Joseph ALICEA
19 Director of Campus Security ... Mr. Arnaldo BERNABE
25 Director Grants & Contracts ... Ms. Lourdes TORRES
09 Director Institutional Research ... Dr. Richard GAMPERT
08 Head Librarian ... Ms. Madeline FORD
22 Chief Diversity Officer ... Mr. Eugene SOHN
29 Director Alumni Relations ... Ms. Nydia EDGECOMBE
36 Director Career Services ... Ms. Lisanette ROSARIO
35 Director Student Activities ... Mr. Jerry ROSA
96 Director of Purchasing ... Mr. Kevin CARMINE

*City University of New York Hunter College (C)

695 Park Avenue, New York NY 10065

County: New York | FICE Identification: 002689 | Unit ID: 190594
Telephone: (212) 772-4000 | Carnegie Class: Master's L
FAX Number: N/A | Calendar System: Semester
URL: www.hunter.cuny.edu
Established: 1870 | Annual Undergrad Tuition & Fees (In-District): $6,129
Enrollment: 22,890 | Coed
Affiliation or Control: State/Local | IRS Status: 501(c)3
Highest Offering: Master's
Program: Liberal Arts And General; Teacher Preparatory; Professional
Accreditation: M, AUD, CACREP, CORE, DIETD, DIETI, ENGR, NURSE, PH, PLNG, PTA, SP, SW, TED

02 President ... Ms. Jennifer J. RAAB
100 Chief of Staff/Exec Asst to Pres ... Ms. Anne LYTLE
10 Vice President Fin & Administration ... Vacant
05 Provost/Vice Pres Academic Affairs ... Dr. Vita RABINOWITZ
32 VP Student Affs/Dean of Stdnts ... Ms. Eija AYRAVAINEN
43 Counsel to the President ... Ms. Gail A. SCOVELL
13 Asst Vice Pres Information Tech ... Mr. Mitch AHLBAUM
21 Asst Vice Pres for Budget & Finance ... Ms. Sharon NEILL
21 Asst Vice Pres Business Svcs ... Mr. Carlos SERRANO
35 Asst Vice Pres of Student Affairs ... Ms. Madlyn STOKELY
18 Asst Vice Pres of Facilities ... Mr. Rick CHANDLER
28 Dean Diversity and Compliance ... Mr. John ROSE
49 Actg Dean School of Arts & Sciences ... Dr. Andrew POLSKY
70 Dean School of Social Work ... Dr. Jacqueline MONDROS
53 Dean School of Education ... Dr. David STEINER
66 Dean School of Nursing ... Dr. Gail C. MCCAIN
69 Dean of School of Public Health ... Dr. Neal COHEN
30 Executive Director Development ... Ms. Patricia MORAN
26 Ex Dir Communication/Marketing ... Vacant
08 Chief Librarian ... Mr. Daniel CHERUBIN
06 Registrar ... Ms. Marilyn DALY-WESTON
07 Director of Admissions ... Mr. William ZLATA
09 Director of Institutional Research ... Ms. Joan LAMBE
15 Director of Human Resources ... Ms. Serafina RUTIGLIANO
35 Director Student Advising ... Mr. Bryan MAASJO
36 Director Student Placement ... Ms. Susan MCCARTY
37 Director Student Financial Aid ... Ms. Aristalia RODRIGUEZ
29 Director Alumni Relations ... Ms. Deborah DAVIS
19 College Security Director ... Mr. Louis MADER

*City University of New York John Jay College of Criminal Justice (D)

524 West 59th Street, New York NY 10019-1093

County: New York | FICE Identification: 002693 | Unit ID: 190600
Telephone: (212) 237-8600 | Carnegie Class: Master's L
FAX Number: (212) 237-8607 | Calendar System: Semester
URL: www.jjay.cuny.edu
Established: 1964 | Annual Undergrad Tuition & Fees (In-District): $5,759
Enrollment: 14,669 | Coed
Affiliation or Control: State/Local | IRS Status: 501(c)3
Highest Offering: Master's
Program: Liberal Arts And General; Professional
Accreditation: M, SPAA

02 President ... Mr. Jeremy TRAVIS
05 Prov/Sr Vice Pres Academic Affairs ... Dr. Jane BOWERS
11 Sr Vice Pres Administrative Affairs ... Mr. Robert PIGNATELLO
32 Vice Pres Student Affairs ... Ms. Lynette COOK-FRANCIS
30 Vice Pres Marketing/Dev ... Ms. Jayne ROSENGARTEN
84 Vice Pres Enrollment Management ... Dr. Richard SAULNIER
45 Assoc Provost for Effect/Assessment ... Dr. James LLANA
04 Executive Associate to President ... Ms. Nina CONROY
100 Chief of Staff ... Ms. Rulisa GALLOWAY-PERRY
58 Graduate & Professional Studies ... Dr. Jannette DOMINGO
46 Int Asc Prov/Dn Rsrch/Strat Partner ... Dr. Anthony CARPI
32 Dean of Students ... Dr. Kenneth HOLMES
15 Dean Human Resources ... Mr. Kevin HAUSS
20 Dean of Undergraduate Studies ... Dr. Anne LOPES
10 Exec Dir Financial/Business Svcs ... Ms. Patricia KETTERER
08 Chief Librarian ... Dr. Lawrence SULLIVAN
37 Director of Financial Aid ... Ms. Sylvia CRESPO-LOPEZ
44 Director of Development ... Vacant
35 Interim Director Student Activities ... Ms. Danielle OFFICER
25 Director of Funded Research ... Mr. Jacob MARINI
09 Director of Institutional Research ... Mr. Ricardo ANZALDVA
89 Director of First Year Experience ... Ms. Katalin SZUR
06 Registrar ... Mr. Adam STONE
88 Director of CRJ Research & Eval ... Dr. Jeffrey BUTTS
07 Director of Admissions ... Ms. Sandra PALLEJA
13 Interim Chief Information Officer ... Mr. Joe LAUB
19 Director of Public Safety ... Mr. Stephen HOLLOWELL
90 Director Technology Services ... Mr. William PANGBURN
22 Affirmative Action Officer ... Ms. Silvia MONTALBAN
24 Director of Media Services ... Mr. Paul BRENNER
27 Exec Dir Marketing & Communications ... Ms. Vivian TODINI
36 Director of Career Development Svcs ... Mr. Will SIMKINS
38 Director of Counseling ... Dr. Calvin CHIN
41 Athletic Director ... Mr. Daniel PALUMBO
21 Associate Business Officer ... Ms. Emily KARP
29 Director Alumni Relations ... Ms. Jerylle KEMP
96 Director of Purchasing ... Mr. Daniel DOLAN
04 Exec Associate to the President ... Ms. Raeanne DAVIS
18 Director Facilities/Physical Plant ... Mr. Elmer PHELON
43 Assistant Vice President & Counsel ... Hon. Rosemarie MALDONADO
86 Exec Dir of External Relations ... Ms. Mayra NIEVES
88 Director of Academic Advisement ... Dr. Sumaya VILLANUEVA
88 Int Dir of Accessibility Services ... Ms. Malanie CLARKE

*City University of New York Kingsborough Community College (E)

2001 Oriental Boulevard, Brooklyn NY 11235-2333

County: Kings | FICE Identification: 002694 | Unit ID: 190619
Telephone: (718) 368-5000 | Carnegie Class: Assoc/Pub-U-MC
FAX Number: (718) 368-5003 | Calendar System: Other
URL: www.kbcc.cuny.edu
Established: 1963 | Annual Undergrad Tuition & Fees (In-District): $4,900
Enrollment: 18,936 | Coed
Affiliation or Control: State/Local | IRS Status: 501(c)3
Highest Offering: Associate Degree
Program: Occupational; 2-Year Principally Bachelor's Creditable
Accreditation: M, PTAA, SURGT

02 Interim President ... Dr. Stuart SUSS
05 Vice Pres Academic Affs/Provost ... Dr. Stuart SUSS
10 Vice Pres Finance/Administration ... Mr. Bill KELLER
100 Executive Chief of Staff ... Mr. Peter POBAT
32 Dean of Student Affairs ... Mr. Peter COHEN
51 Dean Continuing Educ/Dir Cmty Rels ... Dr. Saul W. KATZ
35 Dean of Student Life ... Ms. Tasheka YOUNG
20 Vice Pres Academic Administration ... Dr. David GOMEZ
84 Dean Enrollment Management ... Mr. Thomas FRIEBEL
09 Dean Inst Effective/Strategic Plng ... Dr. Richard FOX
30 Assoc Dean College Advancement ... Dr. Elizabeth BASILE
15 Director of Human Resources ... Ms. Micheline DRISCOLL
22 Dir Affirmative Action/EO Officer ... Mr. Angel RIVERA
19 Actg Director of Security & Safety ... Mr. Pat MORENA
08 Chief Librarian ... Ms. Josephine MURPHY
06 Registrar ... Mr. Michael KLEIN
18 Campus Facilities Officer ... Mr. Anthony CORAZZA
37 Financial Aid Officer ... Mr. Wayne H. HAREWOOD
27 Chief Information Officer ... Mr. Asif HUSSAIN
36 Dir Career Couns/Placement/Transfer ... Mr. Brian MITRA
23 Director of Health Services ... Vacant
24 Director of Educational Media ... Mr. Michael ROSSON
41 Director of Athletics ... Mr. Domani THOMAS
26 Chief Public Relations Officer ... Ms. Ruby RYLES
96 Director of Purchasing ... Ms. Lyn RELAY
07 Director of Admissions ... Ms. Rosalie FAYAD
29 Director Alumni Relations ... Ms. Laura GLAZIER-SMITH
38 Director Student Counseling ... Ms. Dasha GORINSHTEYN
14 Assoc Director of Computer Center ... Vacant
21 Business Manager ... Mr. Anthony IMPERATO
88 Deputy Business Officer ... Mr. Bill CORRENTI

*La Guardia Community College/ City University of New York (F)

31-10 Thomson Avenue, Long Island City NY 11101-3083

County: Queens | FICE Identification: 010051 | Unit ID: 190628
Telephone: (718) 482-7200 | Carnegie Class: Assoc/Pub-U-SC
FAX Number: (718) 609-2000 | Calendar System: Semester
URL: www.lagcc.cuny.edu
Established: 1971 | Annual Undergrad Tuition & Fees (In-District): $4,564
Enrollment: 26,103 | Coed
Affiliation or Control: State/Local | IRS Status: 501(c)3
Highest Offering: Associate Degree
Program: Occupational; 2-Year Principally Bachelor's Creditable

Accreditation: M, ADNUR, DIETT, OTA, PTAA

02 President ... Dr. Gail O. MELLOW
05 Provost and Senior Vice President ... Dr. Paul ARCARIO
04 Executive Associate to President ... Ms. Rosemary TALMADGE
11 Vice President of Administration ... Mr. Shahir ERFAN
30 Acting VP of Inst Advancement ... Ms. Susan LYDDON
13 Vice Pres Information Technology ... Mr. Henry SALTIEL
32 Vice President Student Affairs ... Dr. Michael BASTON
51 Vice Pres Adult/Continuing Educ ... Ms. Jane SCHULMAN
88 Assoc Dean Ctr for Teaching & Lrng ... Mr. Bret EYNON
84 Asst Dean Enrollment Services ... Ms. Reine SARMIENTO
18 Exec Dir Facilities Mgmt/Planning ... Vacant
15 Exec Director of Human Resources ... Ms. Diane DARCY
10 Exec Director Finance & Business ... Mr. Thomas HLADEK
86 Government Relations Manager ... Ms. Claudia CHAN
35 Asst Dean Student Development ... Ms. Renee BUTLER
08 Chief Librarian ... Ms. Jane DEVINE
37 Director Student Financial Services ... Ms. Gail BAKSH-JARRETT
44 Director of Development ... Ms. Angela WAMBUGU-COBB
36 Assoc Dean Acad & Career Develop ... Ms. Jane MACKILLOP
103 Asst Dean of Workforce Development ... Ms. Francesca FIORE
07 Director of Admissions ... Ms. LaVora DESVIGNE
26 Dir Marketing/Communications ... Mr. Charles ELIAS
43 Legal & Labor Relations Officer .. Ms. Jemma ROBAIN LACAILLE
22 Affirmative Action Specialist ... Ms. Arlene PETERSON
09 Director of Institutional Research ... Mr. Nathan DICKMEYER
21 Associate Business Manager ... Ms. Carmen LUONG
36 Director Employment/Career Svc Ctr ... Ms. Claudia BALDONEDO
96 Director Procurement & Contracts ... Mr. Mitchell HENDERSON
20 Assoc Dean for Academic Affairs ... Ms. Ann FEIBEL

*City University of New York Medgar Evers College (A)

1650 Bedford Avenue, Brooklyn NY 11225-2010

County: Kings FICE Identification: 010097
Unit ID: 190646
Telephone: (718) 270-4900 Carnegie Class: Bac/Assoc
FAX Number: (718) 270-5126 Calendar System: Semester
URL: www.mec.cuny.edu
Established: 1970 Annual Undergrad Tuition & Fees (In-District): $5,730
Enrollment: 6,540 Coed
Affiliation or Control: State/Local IRS Status: 501(c)3
Highest Offering: Baccalaureate
Program: Liberal Arts And General; Teacher Preparatory; Professional
Accreditation: M, ACBSP, ADNUR, NUR, SW, TED

02 President ... Dr. Rudolph F. CREW
05 Int Provost/Senior Vice President ... Dr. Karrin E. WILKS
100 Interim Sr VP for Operations ... Mr. G. Scott ANDERSON
32 Interim VP of Student Affairs ... Dr. Janice M. BORLANDOE
51 Interim Dean Sch Prof & Comm Dev ... Dr. Simone RODRIGUEZ-DORESTANT
20 Interim Associate Provost ... Dr. Theresa WILLIAMS
18 Asst VP Facilities Management ... Ms. Lisa K. EDWARDS
50 Dean of the School of Business ... Dr. Byron PRICE
89 Dean College of Freshman Studies ... Vacant
49 Interim Dean Sch of Lib Arts & Educ ... Dr. Carlyle THOMPSON
72 Dean School of Science/Health/Tech ... Dr. Mohsin PATWARY
09 Exec Dean Accred/Inst Effectiveness ... Dean Richard JONES
21 Comptroller ... Mr. Donal CHRISTIAN
43 Counsel to President ... Ms. Valerie KENNEDY
04 Exec Assistant to the President ... Ms. Lisa YOUNG
22 Director of Affirmative Action ... Ms. Sylvia KINARD
06 Registrar ... Ms. Johana RIVERA
91 Chief Information Officer ... Ms. Claudia COLBERT
37 Director of Financial Aid ... Mr. Conley JAMES
38 Director of Counseling ... Dr. JoAnn JOYNER-GRAHAM
19 Director of Security ... Mr. Elvert MILLER
41 Director of Athletics ... Ms. Renee BOSTIC
25 Grants Officer ... Mr. Chi KOON
89 Dir Freshman Year Program ... Mr. Jeffrey SIGLER
55 Director Evening/Weekend Programs ... Ms. Yvette WALL
36 Director of Career Development ... Ms. Deborah YOUNG
30 Exec Director of Development ... Vacant
26 Asst VP of External Relations ... Ms. Dawn WALKER
18 Supt of Buildings & Grounds ... Mr. Cory WRIGHT
07 Director of Admissions ... Mr. Warren HEUSNER
29 Director of Alumni Relations ... Mr. Fred PRICE
21 Exec Dir for Risk Mgmt & Int Con ... Mr. Bruno DEGEN
96 Director of Purchasing ... Ms. Goldene LEWIS
84 Director Enrollment Management ... Dr. Vincent BANREY
09 Director of Institutional Research ... Dr. Eva CHAN
08 Chief Librarian ... Dr. David ORENSTEIN
66 Chair Dept of Nursing ... Dr. Jean GUMBS
50 Chair Dept of Business Admin ... Ms. Evelyn MAGGIO
53 Chair Department of Education ... Dr. Sheilah PAUL
60 Interim Chair Dept of Mass Comm ... Dr. Clinton CRAWFORD
88 Chair Department Accounting ... Dr. Rosemary WILLIAMS
81 Chair Department of Mathematics ... Dr. Umesh NAGARKATTE
77 Chair Dept Physical/Computer Sci ... Dr. Wilbert HOPE
81 Chair Department of Biology ... Dr. Anthony UDEOGALANYA
83 Chair Dept of Social/Behavioral Sci ... Dr. Henry DAVIS
88 Chair Department of Psychology ... Dr. Ethan GOLOGOR
88 Chair Dept of Public Administration ... Dr. John FLATEAU
13 Chair Computer Info Systems ... Dr. Adesina FADARIO
88 Chair Department Economics/Finance ... Dr. Emmanuel EGBE
88 Chair Department of English ... Dr. Augustine OKEREKE
88 Chair Dept of Philosophy & Religion ... Dr. Gary SEAY
88 Chair Dept of Foreign Languages ... Dr. Jesus BOTTARO
35 Director of Student Life ... Mr. Kevin ADAMS
15 Director of Human Resources ... Mr. Oswald E. FRASER

88 Director of Bursar ... Mr. George SOFTLEIGH
10 Chief Business Officer ... Vacant
28 Chief Diversity Officer ... Dr. Sylvia G. KINARD

*New York City College of Technology/City University of New York (B)

300 Jay Street, Brooklyn NY 11201-1909

County: Kings FICE Identification: 002696
Unit ID: 190655
Telephone: (718) 260-5000 Carnegie Class: Bac/Assoc
FAX Number: (718) 260-5198 Calendar System: Semester
URL: www.citytech.cuny.edu
Established: 1946 Annual Undergrad Tuition & Fees (In-District): $5,430
Enrollment: 16,208 Coed
Affiliation or Control: State/Local IRS Status: 501(c)3
Highest Offering: Baccalaureate
Program: Professional; Technical Emphasis
Accreditation: M, ADNUR, DH, DT, ENGT, NUR, OPD, RAD, TED

02 President ... Dr. Russell K. HOTZLER
05 Provost ... Dr. Bonne AUGUST
10 Vice Pres Finance/Administration ... Dr. Miguel CAIROL
84 VP Enrollment/Student Affairs ... Dr. Marcela ARMOZA
20 Associate Provost Academic Affairs ... Dr. Pamela BROWN
22 Counsel/Affirmative Action Officer ... Ms. Gilen CHAN
07 Director of Admissions ... Ms. Alexis CHACONIS
06 Registrar ... Mr. Jerry M. BERROL
37 Director of Financial Aid ... Ms. Sandra HIGGINS
08 Librarian ... Mr. Darrow WOOD
14 Director of Computer Center ... Ms. Rita UDDIN
107 Dean of Professional Studies ... Dr. Barbara GRUMET
54 Interim Dean of Technology ... Mr. Kevin HOM
49 Interim Dean of Arts & Science ... Dr. Pamela BROWN
51 Dean Continuing Education ... Dr. Carol SONNENBLICK
55 Director Evening Session ... Mr. James LAP
15 Director of Human Resources ... Ms. Sandra GORDON
25 Grants Officer ... Ms. Barbara BURKE
24 Director of Inst Tech/Media Svcs ... Ms. Karen LUNDSTREM
09 Director of Assessment ... Dr. Tammie CUMMING
26 Chief Public Relations Officer ... Ms. Michele FORSTEN
29 Director Alumni Relations ... Ms. Jessica MALAVEZ
36 Director Student Placement ... Mr. Adrian GRIFFIN
38 Director Student Counseling ... Ms. Cynthia BINK
96 Director of Purchasing ... Mr. Wayne ROBINSON
18 Chief Facilities/Physical Plant ... Mr. James VASQUEZ
30 Chief Development/Spec Asst to Pres ... Dr. Stephen SOIFFER
35 Director Student Life ... Mr. Daniel FICTUM
35 Administrator Student Affairs ... Mr. Joseph LENTO
21 Business Manager ... Mr. Wayne ROBINSON

*City University of New York Queens College (C)

65-30 Kissena Boulevard, Flushing NY 11367-1597

County: Queens FICE Identification: 002690
Unit ID: 190664
Telephone: (718) 997-5000 Carnegie Class: Master's L
FAX Number: (718) 997-5598 Calendar System: Semester
URL: www.qc.cuny.edu
Established: 1937 Annual Undergrad Tuition & Fees (In-District): $5,730
Enrollment: 20,100 Coed
Affiliation or Control: State/Local IRS Status: 501(c)3
Highest Offering: Master's
Program: Liberal Arts And General; Teacher Preparatory; Professional
Accreditation: M, AAFCS, DIETD, DIETI, LAW, #LIB, SP, TED

02 President ... Dr. James L. MUYSKENS
11 Chief Operating Officer ... Vacant
05 Provost ... Dr. Elizabeth HENDREY
10 Vice Pres Finance/Administration ... Mr. William KELLER
32 Vice President for Student Affairs ... Mr. Adam ROCKMAN
91 Asst Vice Pres Converging Tech ... Mr. Naveed HUSAIN
20 Assoc Provost Academic Plng/Pgms ... Dr. Steven SCHWARZ
43 Asst Vice Pres for Labor Relations ... Ms. Meryl KAYNARD
27 Asst Vice Pres of Communications ... Vacant
21 Assistant VP Business Affairs ... Mr. Brian MURPHY
26 Asst VP Institutional Advancement ... Ms. Laurie DORF
88 Assistant Provost ... Dr. June BOBB
57 Dean Arts & Humanities ... Dr. William MCCLURE
81 Dean Math & Natural Sciences ... Dr. Larry LIEBOVITCH
53 Dean Education ... Dr. Craig MICHAELS
58 Dean of Research/Grad Studies ... Dr. Richard BODNAR
83 Dean Social Sciences ... Dr. Elizabeth HENDREY
15 Director Human Resources/Payroll ... Ms. Reinalda MEDINA
41 Assistant Vice President Athletics ... Ms. China JUDE
88 Director of Events ... Vacant
07 Executive Director Admissions ... Mr. Vincent ANGRISANI
38 Dir of Counseling and Advisement ... Dr. Barbara MOORE
06 Director Registrar's Office ... Mr. Matthew CASANOVA
09 Director of Institutional Research ... Dr. Margaret MCAULIFFE
08 Chief Librarian ... Dr. Robert SHADDY
37 Director Financial Aid Services ... Ms. Rena SMITH-KIAWU
29 Manager Alumni Affairs ... Mr. Christopher GREAVES
19 Director Security/Safety ... Mr. Pedro PINEIRO
22 Director Affirmative Action ... Ms. Cynthia ROUNTREE
96 Director of Purchasing ... Ms. Berniesha COLEMAN

*City University of New York Queensborough Community College (D)

222-05 56th Avenue, Bayside NY 11364-1497

County: Queens FICE Identification: 002697
Unit ID: 190673
Telephone: (718) 631-6262 Carnegie Class: Assoc/Pub-U-MC
FAX Number: N/A Calendar System: Semester
URL: www.qcc.cuny.edu
Established: 1958 Annual Undergrad Tuition & Fees (In-District): $4,200
Enrollment: 15,711 Coed
Affiliation or Control: State/Local IRS Status: 501(c)3
Highest Offering: Associate Degree
Program: Occupational; 2-Year Principally Bachelor's Creditable
Accreditation: M, ACBSP, ADNUR, ENGT

02 President ... Dr. Diane CALL
05 Int Vice President Academic Affairs ... Dr. Karen B. STEELE
10 Vice Pres Finance & Administration ... Ms. Sherri NEWCOMB
30 Vice Pres Institutional Advancement ... Ms. Rosemary S. ZINS
32 Vice President Student Affairs ... Ms. Ellen HARTIGAN
15 Dean Human Resource/Labor Rels ... Ms. Liza LARIOS
51 Dean Continuing Ed/Workforce Devel ... Ms. Denise WARD
20 Assoc Dean Acad Affs/Inst Research ... Dr. Paul J. MARCHESE
35 Assoc Dean of Student Affairs ... Dr. Paul JEAN-PIERRE
20 Assoc Dean for Academic Affairs ... Ms. Michele CUOMO
88 Assoc Dean Accred Assessment ... Dr. Arthur CORRADETTI
21 Assoc Dean Bus Admin/Comptroller ... Mr. William FAULKNER
13 Chief Information Technology Ofcr ... Mr. George SHERMAN
08 Chief Librarian ... Ms. Jeanne GALVIN
06 Registrar ... Ms. Ann TULLIO
37 Financial Aid Director ... Ms. Veronica LUKAS
07 Director Admissions & Recruitment ... Ms. Laura BRUNO
09 Director of Institutional Research ... Ms. Elisabeth LACKNER
15 Personnel Officer ... Ms. Ellen ADAMS
26 Dir of Communications/Marketing ... Mr. Stephen DI DIO
19 Director of Safety & Security ... Mr. Edward LOCKE
22 Affirmative Action Officer ... Ms. Mavis HALL
04 Executive Assistant to President ... Ms. Millie CONTE
104 Dir Ctr for Intl Stds/Study Abroad ... Ms. Lampeto (Betty) EFTHYMIOU
90 Exec Dir Academic Computing Center ... Mr. Bruce NAPLES
96 Director of Purchasing ... Mr. MacArthur MARSHALL
18 Chief Facilities/Physical Plant ... Mr. Joseph CARTOLANO
36 Director of Career Services ... Ms. Constance PELUSO
38 Director of Student Counseling ... Dr. Jannette URCIUOLI
30 Chief Devel/Dir Alumni Relations ... Vacant
84 Director Enrollment Management ... Ms. Laura BRUNO
44 Director Annual Giving/Major Gifts ... Vacant

*City University of New York Stella and Charles Guttman Community College (E)

50 West 40th Street, New York NY 10018

County: New York Identification: 667126
Unit ID: 475565
Telephone: (646) 313-8000 Carnegie Class: Not Classified
FAX Number: N/A Calendar System: Semester
URL: www.guttman.cuny.edu
Established: 2011 Annual Undergrad Tuition & Fees (In-District): $3,900
Enrollment: 289 Coed
Affiliation or Control: State/Local IRS Status: 501(c)3
Highest Offering: Associate Degree
Program: Occupational; 2-Year Principally Bachelor's Creditable
Accreditation: NY

02 President ... Scott EVENBECK
05 Vice President & Provost ... Jose Luis MORIN
11 Vice Pres Admin & Finance ... Larian ANGELO
45 Dean Strategic Plng & Effectiveness ... Stuart COCHRAN

*City University of New York York College (F)

94-20 Guy Brewer Boulevard, Jamaica NY 11451-0001

County: Queens FICE Identification: 004759
Unit ID: 190691
Telephone: (718) 262-2000 Carnegie Class: Bac/Diverse
FAX Number: (718) 262-2730 Calendar System: Semester
URL: www.york.cuny.edu
Established: 1966 Annual Undergrad Tuition & Fees (In-District): $5,730
Enrollment: 8,420 Coed
Affiliation or Control: State/Local IRS Status: 501(c)3
Highest Offering: Master's
Program: Liberal Arts And General; Teacher Preparatory; Professional
Accreditation: M, ARCPA, MT, NUR, OT, SW, TED

02 President ... Dr. Marcia V. KEIZS
05 Provost & Sr VP for Academic Affs ... Dr. Panayiotis MELETIES
10 VP of Adm & Finance/COO ... Mr. Ronald C. THOMAS
32 Vice Pres for Student Development ... Dr. Geneva WALKER-JOHNSON
20 Assistant Provost ... Dr. Holger HENKE
100 Dean for the Executive Office ... Dr. William V. DINELLO
49 Dean School of Arts & Sciences ... Dr. Donna CHIRICO
83 Dean Sch of Health & Behavioral Sci ... Dr. Lynne CLARK
50 Dean Sch of Business & Info Systems ... Dr. Alfred NTOKO

35 Associate Dean Student Development ... Dr. Thomas GIBSON
43 Exec Dir Compliance & Legal Affairs ... Ms. Olga DAIS
15 Assc Exec Dir HR & Labor Design ... Ms. Barbara MANUEL
13 Chief Information Officer ... Mr. Peter TIGHE
09 Director Institutional Research ... Dr. Aghajan MOHAMMADI
06 Registrar ... Ms. Sharon DAVIDSON
08 Chief Librarian ... Ms. Njoki KINYATTI
90 Director of Academic Computing ... Dr. Che-Tsao HUANG
86 Dir of Govt and Community Relations ... Mr. Earl G. SIMONS
19 Director of Security ... Chief Tyrone FORTE
37 Director of Financial Aid ... Ms. Cathy MICHAELS
18 Director Campus Planning ... Mr. Noel GAMBOA
35 Director Student Activites ... Dr. Jean PHELPS
36 Director Career Services ... Ms. Linda H. CHESNEY
25 Dir Research/Sponsored Programs ... Ms. Dawn HEWITT
38 Director of Counseling ... Dr. Susan LINDNER
41 Athletic Director ... Mr. Ronald ST. JOHN
10 Confidential Business Manager ... Ms. Jacqueline CLARK
04 Executive Asst to the President ... Ms. Sandra BELL ADAMS
84 Executive Dir Enrollment Management ... Mr. Michel A. HODGE
96 Director of Purchasing ... Mr. Marlon TORRES

Clarkson University (A)

8 Clarkson Ave, Potsdam NY 13699
County: St. Lawrence FICE Identification: 002699
Unit ID: 190044
Telephone: (315) 268-6400 Carnegie Class: RU/H
FAX Number: (315) 268-7647 Calendar System: Semester
URL: www.clarkson.edu
Established: 1896 Annual Undergrad Tuition & Fees: $40,610
Enrollment: 3,604 Coed
Affiliation or Control: Independent Non-Profit IRS Status: 501(c)3
Highest Offering: Doctorate
Program: Liberal Arts And General; Professional; Technical Emphasis
Accreditation: M, #ARCPA, BUS, ENG, PTA

01 President ... Dr. Anthony G. COLLINS
05 Senior Vice President & Provost ... Dr. Charles E. THORPE
26 Vice Pres External Relations ... Mrs. Kelly O. CHEZUM
32 Vice Pres Outreach & Stdnt Affairs ... Mrs. Kathryn B. JOHNSON
30 Vice Pres Philanthropy & Alumni ... Mr. Richard W. JOHNSON
29 Assoc VP Alumni Relations ... Vacant
44 Assoc VP Philanthropy ... Mr. Paul JULIN
88 Assoc VP Student Success ... Mrs. Catherine CLARK
28 Asst VP Diversity Initiatives ... Mr. Warren ANDERSON
10 Chief Financial Officer ... Mr. James D. FISH
13 Chief Information Officer ... Mr. Joshua A. FISKE
54 Dean of Engineering ... Dr. Goodarz AHMADI
50 Dean of Business ... Dr. Dayle M. SMITH
49 Dean of Arts & Sciences ... Dr. Peter TURNER
07 Dean of Admissions ... Mr. Brian T. GRANT
35 Dean of Students ... Mr. Stephen NEWKOFSKY
15 Exec Director Human Resources ... Ms. Marilyn ARDITO
21 Controller ... Mrs. Donna MARTELL
41 Director Athletics & Recreation ... Mr. Steven J. YIANOUKOS
45 Director Budget & Planning ... Mrs. Allison S. ALDRICH
19 Director Campus Safety & Security ... Mr. David W. DELISLE
36 Director Career Center ... Mr. Jeffrey D. TAYLOR
102 Director Corp & Foundation Rels ... Ms. Jennifer CLARKE
38 Director Counseling & Health Svcs ... Mr. Timothy J. CORBITT
18 Director Facilities & Services ... Mr. Ian HAZEN
37 Director Financial Aid ... Mrs. Pamela NICHOLS
86 Director Government Relations ... Mr. Robert H. WOOD
92 Director Honors Program ... Mr. Jonathan D. GOSS
20 Director Institutional Assessment ... Mr. Geoffrey BROWN
85 Director Intl Students & Scholars ... Mrs. Tess C. CASLER
08 Director Libraries ... Ms. Michelle L. YOUNG
96 Dir Payroll/Purchasing/Risk Mgmt ... Mr. George GIORDANO
46 Director Research & Tech Transfer ... Mr. Gregory C. SLACK
88 Director Student Administration ... Mrs. Suzanne E. DAVIS
23 Director Student Health Services ... Mrs. Susan KNOWLES
105 Director Web Development ... Mrs. Julie DAVIS
06 Registrar ... Mrs. Karen J. BURKUM
39 Assoc Dean for Residence Life ... Mr. Mark DERITIS
09 Asst Director Institutional Rsrch ... Mrs. Jenna STONE
25 Contract & Grant Administrator ... Ms. Anna Marie DAWLEY
106 Distance Learning Coordinator ... Mrs. Laura PERRY
40 Bookstore Manager ... Ms. Sara JOHNSON

Clinton Community College (B)

136 Clinton Point Drive, Plattsburgh NY 12901-9573
County: Clinton FICE Identification: 006787
Unit ID: 190053
Telephone: (518) 562-4200 Carnegie Class: Assoc/Pub-R-M
FAX Number: (518) 561-4890 Calendar System: Semester
URL: www.clinton.edu
Established: 1966 Annual Undergrad Tuition & Fees (In-District): $3,960
Enrollment: 2,258 Coed
Affiliation or Control: State/Local IRS Status: 501(c)3
Highest Offering: Associate Degree
Program: Occupational; 2-Year Principally Bachelor's Creditable
Accreditation: M, ADNUR

01 President ... Mr. John E. JABLONSKI
05 Vice President for Academic Affairs ... Dr. Cheryl REAGAN
10 Vice Pres for Admin/Business Affs ... Mrs. Lisa SHOVAN
32 Vice President for Student Affairs ... Vacant
30 Vice Pres InstitutionalAdvancement ... Mr. Steven G. FREDERICK
08 Dean Learning Resource Center ... Vacant
84 Assoc Dean Student Retention Svcs ... Vacant

09 Assoc Dean Inst Research/Planning ... Ms. Victoria DULEY
37 Director of Financial Aid ... Mrs. Cheryl SEYMOUR
07 Director Admissions ... Mrs. Tobi MAY
06 Registrar ... Mr. Sean DERMODY
13 Mgmt Information Systems Director ... Mr. Rick BATCHELDER
15 Human Resource/Affirm Act Officer ... Vacant
26 Director of College Relations ... Ms. Jaime KAZLO WATSON
18 Chief Facilities/Physical Plant ... Mr. John CONLEY

Cochran School of Nursing (C)

967 North Broadway, Yonkers NY 10701-1399
County: Westchester FICE Identification: 006443
Unit ID: 190071
Telephone: (914) 964-4282 Carnegie Class: Assoc/PrivNFP
FAX Number: (914) 964-4266 Calendar System: Semester
URL: www.cochranschoolofnursing.us
Established: Annual Undergrad Tuition & Fees: $11,450
Enrollment: 167 Coed
Affiliation or Control: Independent Non-Profit IRS Status: 501(c)3
Highest Offering: Associate Degree
Program: 2-Year Principally Bachelor's Creditable; Nursing Emphasis
Accreditation: ADNUR

05 Dean ... Dr. Karen DAVENPORT
08 Learning Resources Director ... Ms. Allyn KULK
06 Registrar ... Ms. Janee MCCOY

Cold Spring Harbor Laboratory/ Watson School of Biological Sciences (D)

PO Box 100, One Bungtown Road,
Cold Spring Harbor NY 11724-0100
County: Suffolk FICE Identification: 034563
Unit ID: 436377
Telephone: (516) 367-6890 Carnegie Class: Not Classified
FAX Number: (516) 367-6919 Calendar System: Other
URL: www.cshl.edu
Established: 1890 Annual Graduate Tuition & Fees: N/A
Enrollment: 54 Coed
Affiliation or Control: Independent Non-Profit IRS Status: 501(c)3
Highest Offering: Doctorate; No Undergraduates
Program: Professional
Accreditation: NY

00 Chancellor Emeritis ... Dr. James D. WATSON
01 President ... Dr. Bruce STILLMAN
05 Dean ... Dr. Alexander GANN

Colgate Rochester Crozer Divinity School (E)

1100 S Goodman Street, Rochester NY 14620-2589
County: Monroe FICE Identification: 002700
Unit ID: 190080
Telephone: (585) 271-1320 Carnegie Class: Spec/Faith
FAX Number: (585) 271-8013 Calendar System: Semester
URL: www.crcds.edu
Established: 1817 Annual Graduate Tuition & Fees: $10,075
Enrollment: 87 Coed
Affiliation or Control: Independent Non-Profit IRS Status: 501(c)3
Highest Offering: Doctorate; No Undergraduates
Program: Religious Emphasis
Accreditation: THEOL

01 President ... Dr. Marvin A. MCMICKLE
05 VP Academic Life & Dean of Faculty ... Prof. Stephanie L. SAUVE
10 Chief Financial Officer ... Mr. Gerald E. VANSTRYDONCK
84 Vice Pres of Enrollment Services ... Ms. Melissa MORRAL
30 VP Institutional Advancement ... Mr. W. Thomas MCDADE-CLAY
94 Dean of Women & Gender Studies ... Dr. Barbara MOORE
06 Registrar ... Ms. Andrea MASON
18 Director of Facilities ... Mr. Mark DEVINCENTIS
08 Librarian ... Vacant
73 Dean Black Church Studies ... Vacant
40 Director Bookstore ... Ms. Margaret A. NEAD
37 Director of Financial Aid ... Ms. Andrea MASON

Colgate University (F)

13 Oak Drive, Hamilton NY 13346-1386
County: Madison FICE Identification: 002701
Unit ID: 190099
Telephone: (315) 228-1000 Carnegie Class: Bac/A&S
FAX Number: (315) 228-7798 Calendar System: Semester
URL: www.colgate.edu
Established: 1819 Annual Undergrad Tuition & Fees: $46,380
Enrollment: 2,860 Coed
Affiliation or Control: Independent Non-Profit IRS Status: 501(c)3
Highest Offering: Master's
Program: Liberal Arts And General
Accreditation: M, TEAC

01 President ... Jeffrey HERBST
101 VP/Sr Advisor/Sec Board of Trustees ... Robert L. TYBURSKI
05 Provost & Dean of Faculty ... Douglas HICKS
10 Interim VP for Finance & Admin ... Carolee WHITE
26 Interim VP Communications ... Barbara BROOKS

30 Vice President Inst Advancement ... Murray DECOCK
07 Vice President & Dean of Admissions ... Gary L. ROSS
20 Vice Pres & Dean of the College ... Suzy NELSON
21 Associate Vice Pres/Controller ... Thomas O'NEILL
18 Assoc Vice Pres for Facilities ... Paul FICK
21 Assoc VP for Finance/Asst Treasurer ... Carolee WHITE
15 Assoc VP for Human Resources ... Lori CHLAD
89 Dean of First Year Students ... Beverly LOW
20 Associate Dean of the Faculty ... Nancy PRUITT
28 Assoc Provost Equity & Diversity ... Marilyn RUGG
06 Registrar ... Gretchen HERRINGER
08 University Librarian ... Joanne SCHNEIDER
13 Chief Information Technology Offcr ... Kevin LYNCH
29 Director of Alumni Affairs ... Tim MANSFIELD
37 Director of Financial Aid ... Marcelle TYBURSKI
19 Director of Campus Safety ... William FERGUSON
36 AVP of Adv & Dir of Career Services ... Michael SCIOLA
41 Director of Athletics ... Victoria CHUN
40 Director of Bookstore ... Victoria BONDUM
42 University Chaplain ... Mark SHINER
44 Director of Planned Giving ... Andrew CODDINGTON
38 Director Counseling/Psych Services ... Mark THOMPSON
96 Director of Purchasing ... Art PUNSONI
23 Director Student Health Services ... Merrill MILLER
94 Director Women's Studies ... Meika LOE
44 Director Annual Fund Operations ... Sara GROH
39 Director of Residential Life ... Brenda ICE
09 Dir Institutional Planning/Research ... Brendt SIMPSON

College of Mount Saint Vincent (G)

6301 Riverdale Avenue, Riverdale NY 10471-1093
County: Bronx FICE Identification: 002703
Unit ID: 193399
Telephone: (718) 405-3200 Carnegie Class: Master's S
FAX Number: (718) 601-6392 Calendar System: Semester
URL: www.mountsaintvincent.edu
Established: 1847 Annual Undergrad Tuition & Fees: $30,290
Enrollment: 1,952 Coed
Affiliation or Control: Independent Non-Profit IRS Status: 501(c)3
Highest Offering: Master's
Program: Liberal Arts And General; Teacher Preparatory; Professional
Accreditation: M, ACBSP, NURSE, TEAC

01 President ... Dr. Charles L. FLYNN
05 Provost/Dean of Faculty ... Dr. Guy LOMETTI
20 Dean Undergraduate College ... Dr. Paul DOUILLARD
30 Sr VP Inst Advanc/External Rels ... Mrs. Madeleine MELKONIAN
10 Executive VP/Treasurer ... Mr. Abed ELKESHK
10 VP for Operations ... Mr. Kevin DEGROAT
32 VP Student Affs/Dean of Students ... Dr. Dianna DALE
88 Executive Director/Mission ... Dr. Jean FLANNELY, SC
108 Executive Dir Assessment & Planning ... Dr. Rachel FESTER
84 VP for Admissions/Financial Aid ... Mr. Timothy NASH
88 Assoc VP Institutional Advancement ... Sr. Kathleen TRACEY, SC
51 Dean School Professional/Cont Stds ... Dr. Edward MEYER
06 Registrar ... Mrs. Jeanette PICHARDO
20 Director of Academic Advisement ... Ms. Sandra JENNINGS
08 Director of Library ... Mr. Sebastian DERRY
13 VP Information Technology/CIO ... Mr. Adam WICHERN
09 Director of Institutional Research ... Sr. Carol M. FINEGAN, SC
36 Director Internships/Career Devel ... Mrs. Diane MACHADO
37 Director of Financial Aid ... Mrs. Monica SIMOTAS
42 Director of Campus Ministry ... Sr. Cecilia HARRIENDORF, SC
39 Director of Residence Life ... Ms. Kelli BODRATO
41 Director of Athletics ... Mr. Jay BUTLER
38 Director Counseling Services ... Ms. Vicki HALLAS
23 Director of Health Services ... Ms. Eileen MCCABE
29 Director Alumnae Relations ... Ms. Christina WESOLEK
26 Director College Relations ... Ms. Erin WALSH
31 Director Campus Events/Admin Svcs ... Vacant
19 Dir Campus Safety/Security ... Mr. Paul RUNG
66 Director of Nursing ... Dr. Justine TADDEO
44 Director of Annual Giving ... Ms. Nancy TOTINO
15 Director of Human Resources ... Ms. Annette PIECORA
21 Controller ... Ms. Barbara HURLEIGH
04 Assistant to the President ... Ms. Catherine MCKENNA
18 Director of Facilities ... Mr. Timothy DRURY
07 Director of Admissions ... Ms. Brenda NELSON
92 Director of Honors Program ... Dr. Daniel OPLER
97 Director of Core Curriculum ... Dr. Sarah STEVENSON

The College of New Rochelle (H)

29 Castle Place, New Rochelle NY 10805-2338
County: Westchester FICE Identification: 002704
Unit ID: 193645
Telephone: (914) 654-5000 Carnegie Class: Master's L
FAX Number: (914) 654-5554 Calendar System: Semester
URL: www.cnr.edu
Established: 1904 Annual Undergrad Tuition & Fees: $30,210
Enrollment: 4,206 Coed
Affiliation or Control: Independent Non-Profit IRS Status: 501(c)3
Highest Offering: Master's
Program: Liberal Arts And General; Teacher Preparatory; Professional
Accreditation: M, NURSE, SW, @TEAC

01 President ... Mrs. Judith A. HUNTINGTON
03 Executive Vice President ... Dr. Ellen R. CURRY DAMATO
05 Sr Vice Pres Acad Affairs & Provost ... Dr. Dorothy A. ESCRIBANO
10 Vice President Financial Affairs ... Mr. Keith BORGE
32 Vice President Student Services ... Dr. Colette GEARY

30 Vice President College Advancement .... Ms. Brenna S. MAYER
49 Dean School of Arts & Sciences .... Dr. Richard H. THOMPSON
58 Dean of the Graduate School .... Dr. Marie RIBARICH
51 Dean School of New Resources .... Dr. Darryl JONES
66 Acting Dean School of Nursing .... Dr. Mary MCGUINNESS
06 Registrar .... Ms. Tania QUINN
08 Dean of the Library .... Ms. Ana FONTOURA
37 Director of Financial Aid .... Ms. Anne C. PELAK
36 Director of Career Development .... Ms. Diane SPIZZIRRO
29 Associate VP College Advancement .... Dr. Kelly BRENNAN
15 Director of Human Resources .... Ms. JoEllen L. VAVASOUR
18 Director of Facilities Management .... Mr. Fred SULLO
09 Coordinator Institutional Research .... Ms. Nancy KOTONIAS
21 Controller .... Mr. Stephen J. WALKER

The College of Saint Rose (A)

432 Western Avenue, Albany NY 12203-1490
County: Albany FICE Identification: 002705
Unit ID: 195234
Telephone: (518) 454-5111 Carnegie Class: Master's L
FAX Number: (518) 438-3293 Calendar System: Semester
URL: www.strose.edu
Established: 1920 Annual Undergrad Tuition & Fees: $27,684
Enrollment: 4,698 Coed
Affiliation or Control: Independent Non-Profit IRS Status: 501(c)3
Highest Offering: Master's
Program: Liberal Arts And General; Teacher Preparatory
Accreditation: M, ACBSP, ART, MUS, SP, SW, TED

01 Interim President .... Dr. Margaret M. KIRWIN
04 Assistant to President .... Ms. Debra LIBERATORE
05 Provost/VP Academic Affairs .... Dr. Hadi SALAVITABAR
10 Chief Operating Officer .... Mr. Marcus BUCKLEY
32 Vice President Student Services .... Mr. Dennis MCDONALD
84 Vice Pres of Enroll Mgmt/Admissions . Mrs. Mary M. GRONDAHL
15 Asst Vice Pres Human Res/Risk Mgt .... Mr. Jeffrey KNAPP
07 Asst VP of Undergrad Admissions .... Mr. Jeremy BOGAN
07 Asst VP of Graduate Admissions .... Ms. Susan PATTERSON
37 Asst VP of Financial Aid .... Mr. Steven W. DWIRE
27 Asst VP of Public Information .... Mrs. Lisa HALEY-THOMSON
35 Assoc Dn Stdnt Affs/Dir Stdnt Life .... Ms. Mary R. MCLAUGHLIN
42 Dean of Spiritual Life .... Rev. Christopher DEGIOVINE
86 Exec Dir of Govt Community Affairs .... Mr. Michael D'ATTILIO
90 Exec Dir of Info Technology Service .... Mr. John ELLIS
29 Dir Alumni Relations .... Ms. Andrea LOMANTO
30 Director Development/Annual Fund .... Ms. Lisa MCKENZIE
21 Comptroller .... Ms. Debra Lee POLLEY
06 Registrar .... Ms. Judith KELLY
08 Director of Library .... Mr. Peter KOONZ
39 Director Residence Life .... Ms. Jennifer RICHARDSON
36 Director Career Development Center .... Ms. Michelle OSBORNE
38 Director Counsel/Psychological Svcs .... Mr. Ronald J. HAMER
41 Director Athletics & Recreation .... Ms. Catherine A. HAKER
91 Director Administrative Info Sys .... Mr. William TRAVER
44 Director Annual Giving .... Mr. Jason MANNING
31 Director Community Services .... Mr. Kenneth SCOTT
42 Director of Campus Ministry .... Ms. Joan HORGAN
23 Director of Health Services .... Ms. Sandra FREHSE
19 Director of Safety/Security .... Mr. Steven STELLA
09 Exec Dir Budget & Inst Research .... Ms. Gail A. GARDNER
28 Director of Diversity .... Ms. Shai BUTLER
38 Director of Advisement .... Dr. Kelly MEYER
88 Art Gallery Director .... Ms. Jeanne FLANAGAN
23 Director of Clinical Services .... Ms. Kimberly LAMPARELLI
96 Director Purchasing/Auxiliary Svcs .... Ms. Patricia BUCKLEY
26 Assoc Dir Media Relations .... Mr. Benjamin MARVIN
18 Dir of Facilities Planning & Mgmt .... Ms. Nancy MACDONALD
09 Manager of Institutional Research .... Mr. Patrick CONNELL
40 Manager of Campus Store .... Mr. Chris WILSON
24 Coord of Academic Media Technology .... Mr. Michael STRATTON
04 Exec Admin Asst to the President .... Mrs. Julie KOCHAN

The College of Westchester (B)

PO Box 710, White Plains NY 10602-0710
County: Westchester FICE Identification: 005208
Unit ID: 197285
Telephone: (914) 948-4442 Carnegie Class: Assoc/PrivFP4
FAX Number: (914) 948-5441 Calendar System: Semester
URL: www.cw.edu
Established: 1915 Annual Undergrad Tuition & Fees: $21,015
Enrollment: 1,036 Coed
Affiliation or Control: Proprietary IRS Status: Proprietary
Highest Offering: Baccalaureate
Program: Business Emphasis
Accreditation: M

00 Chairman Emeritus .... Mr. Ernest H. SUTKOWSKI
01 President .... Mrs. Karen J. SMITH
03 Vice President .... Mrs. Mary Beth DEL BALZO
26 Vice President Marketing .... Mr. Dale T. SMITH
05 Chief Academic Officer .... Dr. Joann MULQUEEN
20 Dean of Student Academic Services .... Ms. Jean CARLSON
07 Director of Admissions .... Mr. Matt CURTIS
36 Director of Career Services .... Ms. Joann SONDEY
88 Dir of Student Success/Retention .... Dr. Judith LILLESTON
37 Dir of Student Financial Services .... Mrs. Dianne PEPITONE

Columbia-Greene Community College (C)

4400 Route 23, Hudson NY 12534-9543
County: Columbia FICE Identification: 006789
Unit ID: 190169
Telephone: (518) 828-4181 Carnegie Class: Assoc/Pub-R-S
FAX Number: (518) 828-8543 Calendar System: Semester
URL: www.sunycgcc.edu
Established: 1966 Annual Undergrad Tuition & Fees (In-District): $4,290
Enrollment: 2,126 Coed
Affiliation or Control: State/Local IRS Status: 501(c)3
Highest Offering: Associate Degree
Program: Occupational; 2-Year Principally Bachelor's Creditable
Accreditation: M, ADNUR

01 President .... Mr. James R. CAMPION
05 VP & Dean of Academic Affairs .... Ms. Phyllis CARITO
11 Vice Pres & Dean of Administration .... Mr. A. Joseph MATTIES
32 VP/Dean of Students/Enrollment Mgmt .... Dr. Joseph WATSON
38 Counselor .... Ms. Diane JOHNSON
18 Director Building & Grounds .... Mr. James FOLZ
26 Director Public Information .... Mr. Allen KOVLER
37 Dir Stndt Fin Aid/Asst Dean Stdnts .... Vacant
21 Assistant Dean of Administration .... Ms. Dianne TOPPLE
06 Acting Registrar .... Ms. Gail SHADER
14 Director Information Systems .... Mr. Gino RIZZI
15 Director of Human Resources .... Ms. Melissa FANDOZZI
22 Affirmative Action Officer .... Ms. Melissa FANDOZZI
09 Director of Institutional Research .... Vacant
31 Director of Community Services .... Mr. Robert BODRATTI
41 Athletic Director .... Mr. Walter RICKARD
88 Director Academic Support Center .... Dr. Mary-Teresa HEATH
103 Director of Workforce Development .... Ms. Mary Alane WILTSE
07 Director of Admissions .... Mr. Josh HORN
30 Dir of Development & Alumni Svcs .... Ms. Joan KOWEEK
20 Assistant Dean of Academic Affairs .... Ms. Carol DOERFER
21 Bursar .... Ms. Christy DECKER
19 Director of Security .... Mr. John LEONE
96 Purchasing Officer .... Ms. Patricia DAY
62 Department Chair Library Services .... Ms. Geralynn DEMAREST
83 Div Chair Behavioral/Social Science .... Mr. Thomas GERRY
81 Div Chair Math & Science .... Ms. Siri CARLISLE
57 Division Chair Arts & Humanities .... Mr. Michael ALLARD
66 Division Chair Nursing .... Ms. Dawn WRIGLEY
72 Division Chair Technology .... Vacant

Columbia University in the City of New York (D)

615 West 131st Street, New York NY 10027-6902
County: New York FICE Identification: 002707
Unit ID: 190150
Telephone: (212) 851-0627 Carnegie Class: RU/VH
FAX Number: (212) 851-7022 Calendar System: Semester
URL: www.columbia.edu
Established: 1754 Annual Undergrad Tuition & Fees: $51,408
Enrollment: 26,471 Coed
Affiliation or Control: Independent Non-Profit IRS Status: 501(c)3
Highest Offering: Doctorate
Program: Liberal Arts And General; Professional; Business Emphasis
Accreditation: M, ANEST, BUS, DENT, ENG, HSA, IPSY, JOUR, LAW, MED, MIDWF, NURSE, OT, PH, PLNG, PTA, SPAA, SW

01 President .... Mr. Lee C. BOLLINGER
05 Provost .... Dr. John COATSWORTH
03 Senior Exec Vice President .... Mr. Robert KASDIN
10 Exec Vice President for Finance .... Ms. Anne R. SULLIVAN
76 Exec VP Health/Biomed Sciences .... Dr. Lee GOLDMAN
30 Exec VP Univ Devel/Alumni Rels ... Mr. Frederick M. VAN SICKLE
88 Special Advisor to the President .... Ms. Susan K. FEAGIN
18 Exec Vice President Facilities .... Mr. Joe A. IENUSO
32 Exec Vice Pres Student/Admin Svcs .... Mr. Jeffrey F. SCOTT
27 Exec Vice Pres Communications .... Mr. David M. STONE
09 Exec Vice President Research .... Dr. G. Michael PURDY
26 Exec Vice Pres Govt & Cmty Affairs .... Ms. Maxine F. GRIFFITH
49 Int Exec Vice Pres Arts & Sciences .... Mr. David MADIGAN
08 Vice Pres Info Svcs Univ Libraries .... Dr. James G. NEAL
88 Pres IMC Ofc of Univ Investments .... Mr. Nirmal P. NARVEKAR
15 Vice President Human Resources .... Mr. Louis BELLARDINE
37 Vice Pres Student Financial Svcs .... Ms. Cheryl A. ROSS
29 Vice Pres Alumni Relations .... Ms. Donna H. MACPHEE
96 Vice President Procurement Svcs .... Mr. Joseph M. HARNEY
43 General Counsel .... Ms. Jane E. BOOTH
06 Assoc Vice Pres & Registrar .... Mr. Barry S. KANE
20 Vice Provost Acad Administration .... Mr. Stephen A. RITTENBERG
88 Vice Provost for Academic Planning .... Dr. Andrew R. DAVIDSON
101 Secretary of the University .... Mr. Jerome DAVIS
100 Chief of Staff .... Ms. Susan GLANCY
07 Dean of Undergraduate Admissions ...... Ms. Jessica MARINACCIO
21 Treasurer .... Ms. Gail HOFFMAN
38 Exec Director Student Counseling .... Dr. Richard EICHLER
48 Dean Grad School Arch/Plng/Preserv .... Dr. Mark A. WIGLEY
57 Dean School of the Arts .... Dr. Carol BECKER
50 Dean Graduate School of Business .... Dr. R. Glenn HUBBARD
49 Dean Columbia College .... Dr. James J. VALENTINI
52 Int Dean Sch Dental & Oral Surgery .... Dr. Ronnie MYERS
54 Int Dean Sch Engr/Applied Science .... Dr. Donald GOLDFARB
97 Dean School General Studies .... Dr. Peter AWN
49 Dean Grad School of Arts & Science .... Dr. Carlos J. ALONSO
82 Int Dean School Intl/Public Affairs ...... Dr. Robert C. LIEBERMAN
60 Dean Graduate School Journalism .... Mr. Nicholas LEMANN
61 Dean School of Law .... Mr. David M. SCHIZER
63 Dean Faculty of Medicine .... Dr. Lee GOLDMAN
66 Dean School of Nursing .... Dr. Bobbie BERKOWITZ
69 Dean School of Public Health .... Dr. Linda P. FRIED
70 Dean School of Social Work .... Dr. Jeanette C. TAKAMURA

† Parent institution of Barnard College and Teachers College, Columbia University.

Concordia College (E)

171 White Plains Road, Bronxville NY 10708-1923
County: Westchester FICE Identification: 002709
Unit ID: 190248
Telephone: (914) 337-9300 Carnegie Class: Bac/Diverse
FAX Number: (914) 395-4500 Calendar System: Semester
URL: www.concordia-ny.edu
Established: 1881 Annual Undergrad Tuition & Fees: $28,180
Enrollment: 867 Coed
Affiliation or Control: Lutheran Church - Missouri Synod
IRS Status: 501(c)3
Highest Offering: Master's
Program: Liberal Arts And General; Teacher Preparatory; Professional
Accreditation: M, NURSE, SW, TED

01 President .... Dr. Viji D. GEORGE
10 Chief Financial Officer .... Mr. William W. ZAMBELLI
11 Vice Pres Administration .... Mr. Lloyd WARDLEY
30 Vice Pres Advancement .... Mr. Paul D. GRAND PRE
04 Special Assistant to the President .... Ms. Eloise L. MORGAN
05 VP/Dean of the College .... Prof. Sherry J. FRASER
20 Dean of Undergraduate Programs .... Dr. Mandana NAKHAI
66 Dean of Health & Human Services .... Dr. Susan M. APOLD
88 Dean of Adult Education & Business .... Dr. William M. SALVA
42 Campus Pastor .... Rev. Roy MINNIX
32 Assc Dean of Student Development .... Mr. Christopher S. KOUTSOVITIS
06 Registrar .... Mr. Mark E. BLANCO
08 Library Director .... Mr. William L. PERRENOD
38 Director of Counseling .... Ms. Marilyn AMES
41 Athletic Director .... Mr. Ivan MARQUEZ
23 Director Health Services .... Ms. Susan CRANE
37 Director Financial Aid .... Mr. Kenneth T. FICK
18 Director Support Services .... Mr. Paul A. SCHULZ
26 Senior Director of Marketing .... Mr. North CALLAHAN
42 Director of Church Relations .... Ms. Lorilee JOERZ
84 VP of Enrollment Management .... Mr. Donald VOX
31 Dir of Cmty Life & Judicial Affairs .... Mr. Michael KUSH
92 Director of Honors Program .... Dr. Kate E. BEHR
15 Director of Human Resources .... Ms. Terry VIDAL
13 Manager of Information Services .... Mr. Aaron J. MEYER
21 Business Manager .... Mr. Edward J. MCPARTLAN
44 Director of Development .... Mr. William MORIN
35 Director of Student Success .... Ms. Johanna L. PERRY
36 Director Student Placement .... Ms. Lois DIERLAM
88 Dean of Teacher Education .... Ms. Christine ROWE
85 Dir of Intl Stdtn Recruitment/Advis .... Ms. Claire ZHOU
29 Dir of Alumni & Church Relations .... Ms. LoriLee JOERZ
104 Dean for Pgm Dev & Intl Education .... Dr. James BURKEE

Cooper Union (F)

30 Cooper Square, New York NY 10003-7120
County: New York FICE Identification: 002710
Unit ID: 190372
Telephone: (212) 353-4100 Carnegie Class: Bac/Diverse
FAX Number: (212) 353-4244 Calendar System: Semester
URL: www.cooper.edu
Established: 1859 Annual Undergrad Tuition & Fees: $38,550
Enrollment: 990 Coed
Affiliation or Control: Independent Non-Profit IRS Status: 501(c)3
Highest Offering: Master's
Program: Liberal Arts And General; Professional
Accreditation: M, ART, ENG

01 President .... Jamshed BHARUCHA
10 Vice President Finance and Admin .... Theresa C. WESTCOTT
26 Vice President of External Affairs .... Vacant
30 Vice President Development .... Derek WITTNER
101 Chf of Staff/Secy Board of Trustees .... Lawrence CACCIATORE
07 Dean Admissions/Records/Registrar .... Mitchell LIPTON
32 Dean of Students .... Linda LEMIESZ
57 Dean of Art .... Saskia BOS
48 Dean of Architecture .... Vacant
54 Actg Dean of Engineering .... Alan WOLF
79 Dean Human & Social Sciences .... William GERMANO
08 Acting Head Librarian .... Carol SALOMON
21 Dir Budget/Personnel/Inst Research .... Vacant
44 Dir Major Gifts & Donor Relations .... Jeanne LUNIN
29 Director Alumni Affairs .... Caitlin TRAMEL
44 Director of Institutional Giving .... Vacant
37 Director Financial Aid .... Mary RUOKONEN
06 Registrar .... Ellen DORSEY
46 Director of Research .... Vacant
26 Director of Public Affairs .... Vacant
14 Chief Technology Officer .... Robert P. HOPKINS
09 Director Assessment & Innovation .... Gerardo DEL CERRO
88 Director of Off Campus Programming .... Margaret MORTON
18 Director of Facilities Management .... Jody GRAPES
51 Director of Continuing Education .... David GREENSTEIN
41 Dean of Athletics .... Stephen BAKER
36 Director of Career Services .... Robert THILL

24 Director of Audiovisual/Media .... Paul TUMMOLO
39 Residence Hall Manager .... Christopher CHAMBERLIN
91 Director of Administrative Database .... Sue MCCOY

† Every student receives a full-tuition scholarship.

Cornell University (A)

Ithaca NY 14853-2801
County: Tompkins
FICE Identification: 002711
Unit ID: 190415
Telephone: (607) 255-2000
Carnegie Class: RU/VH
FAX Number: (607) 255-5396
Calendar System: Semester
URL: www.cornell.edu
Established: 1865
Annual Undergrad Tuition & Fees: $45,358
Enrollment: 21,424
Coed
Affiliation or Control: Independent Non-Profit
IRS Status: 501(c)3
Highest Offering: Doctorate
Program: Liberal Arts And General; Professional
Accreditation: M, BUS, CIDA, DIETD, DIETI, ENG, HSA, LAW, LSAR, PLNG, @TEAC, VET

01 President .... David J. SKORTON
05 Provost .... W. Kent FUCHS
63 Prov Medical Affairs/Dean Med Col .... Laurie GLIMCHER
20 Sr Vice Provost Academic Affairs .... John A. SILICIANO
20 Sr Vice Provost Undergrad Educ .... Laura S. BROWN
46 Senior Vice Provost Research .... Robert A. BUHRMAN
58 Vice Prov & Dean Graduate School .... Barbara A. KNUTH
88 Vice Prov International Relations .... Fredrick LOGEVALL
88 Vice Provost .... Judith A. APPLETON
88 Vice Provost/Dean Cornell NYC Tech .... Daniel P. HUTTENLOCHER
45 Vice Pres Planning & Budget .... Elmira MANGUM
30 VP Alumni Affairs & Development .... Charles D. PHLEGAR
16 Vice President Human Resources .... Mary George G. OPPERMAN
32 VP Student & Academic Services .... Susan H. MURPHY
26 Vice Pres for University Relations .... Glenn C. ALTSCHULER
86 VP Government & Community Rels .... Stephen P. JOHNSON
27 Vice President Univ Communications .... Thomas W. BRUCE
88 Vice Pres Cornell NYC Tech .... Cathy S. DOVE
43 University Counsel & Secretary Corp .... James J. MINGLE
10 VP Financial Affs/CFO .... Joanne M. DESTEFANO
13 CIO and VP for Info Technology .... Thomas E. DODDS
18 Vice President Facilities/Services .... Kyu-Jung WHANG
84 Int Assoc Vice Provost Enrollment .... Jason LOCKE
21 University Controller .... Aimee L. TURNER
21 Assoc Vice President/Treasurer .... Patricia A. JOHNSON
21 University Auditor .... Michael B. DICKINSON
20 Dean of Faculty .... Joseph A. BURNS
47 Dean Col Agriculture/Life Sciences .... Kathryn J. BOOR
48 Dean College Arch/Art/Planning .... Kent KLEINMAN
49 Dean College Arts & Science .... Gretchen RITTER
54 Dean College of Engineering .... Lance R. COLLINS
88 Dean School Hotel Administration .... Michael D. JOHNSON
59 Dean College Human Ecology .... Alan D. MATHIOS
50 Dean Johnson Graduate School Mgmt .... Soumitra DUTTA
50 Dean School Industrial/Labor Rels .... Harry C. KATZ
61 Dean Law School .... Stewart J. SCHWAB
74 Dean College Veterinary Medicine .... Michael I. KOTLIKOFF
77 Dean Faculty of Computing and Info .... Haym HIRSH
51 Dean Cont Education/Summer Session .... Glenn C. ALTSCHULER
08 University Librarian .... Anne R. KENNEY
88 Director Africana Studies/Research .... Gerard L. ACHING
07 Int Dir Undergraduate Admissions .... Shawn FELTON
37 Dir Financial Aid/Student Employ .... Susan HITCHCOCK
35 Dean of Students .... Kent L. HUBBELL
06 University Registrar .... Cassandra C. DEMBOSKY
41 Director Athletics/Physical Educ .... J. Andrew NOEL, JR.
36 Director of Cornell Career Services .... Rebecca M. SPARROW
22 Assoc VP Wrkfrce Dvrsty & Inclusion .... Lynette CHAPPELL-WILLIAMS
23 Assoc Vice Pres Gannett Health Svcs .... Janet L. CORSON-RIKERT
28 Assoc Vice Provost Acad Diversity .... Andrew T. MILLER
93 Assoc Dean Intercultural Programs .... Renee T. ALEXANDER
42 Dir Cornell United Religious Works .... Kenneth I. CLARKE
25 Assoc Vice Pres Research Admin .... Catherine E. LONG
25 Sr Director Sponsored Programs Svcs .... Jeffrey A. SILBER
19 Chief Cornell Police .... Kathy R. ZONER
96 Sr Dir Supply Channel Management .... Thomas W. ROMANTIC
29 Assoc Vice Pres Alumni Affairs .... James A. MAZZA
09 Director Inst Research/Planning .... Marin E. CLARKBERG

† Parent institution of Weill Medical College of Cornell University.

Corning Community College (B)

One Academic Drive, Corning NY 14830-3297
County: Steuben
FICE Identification: 002863
Unit ID: 190442
Telephone: (607) 962-9011
Carnegie Class: Assoc/Pub-R-M
FAX Number: (607) 962-9456
Calendar System: Semester
URL: www.corning-cc.edu
Established: 1956
Annual Undergrad Tuition & Fees (In-District): $4,815
Enrollment: 4,971
Coed
Affiliation or Control: State/Local
IRS Status: 501(c)3
Highest Offering: Associate Degree
Program: Occupational; 2-Year Principally Bachelor's Creditable
Accreditation: M, ADNUR

01 President .... Dr. Katherine P. DOUGLAS
05 Vice President Academic Affairs .... Ms. Marian EBERLY
11 Vice President Administrative Svcs .... Mr. Thomas F. CARR
32 Vice Pres & Dean of Student Devel .... Mr. Donald HEINS
30 Exec Dir Institutional Advancement .... Mr. William LITTLE
08 Director Learning Resources Center .... Ms. Sarah WEISMAN
06 Registrar .... Ms. Karen BOULAS
07 Director of Admissions .... Ms. Karen BROWN
15 Director Human Resources .... Ms. Nannette NICHOLAS
10 Chief Business Officer .... Mr. Thomas F. CARR
18 Chief Facilities/Physical Plant .... Mr. Calvin WILLIAMS
37 Director Student Financial Aid .... Mrs. Barbara SNOW
09 Research Analyst .... Vacant

Crouse Hospital College of Nursing (C)

736 Irving Avenue, Syracuse NY 13210
County: Onondaga
FICE Identification: 006445
Unit ID: 190451
Telephone: (315) 470-7481
Carnegie Class: Assoc/PrivNFP
FAX Number: (315) 470-5774
Calendar System: Semester
URL: www.crouse.org/nursing
Established: 1913
Annual Undergrad Tuition & Fees: $10,583
Enrollment: 330
Coed
Affiliation or Control: Independent Non-Profit
IRS Status: 501(c)3
Highest Offering: Associate Degree
Program: 2-Year Principally Bachelor's Creditable; Nursing Emphasis
Accreditation: ADNUR

01 Interim Director .... Lynn ROUNSVILLE

Culinary Institute of America (D)

1946 Campus Drive, Hyde Park NY 12538-1499
County: Dutchess
FICE Identification: 007304
Unit ID: 190503
Telephone: (845) 452-9600
Carnegie Class: Spec/Other
FAX Number: (845) 452-0165
Calendar System: Semester
URL: www.ciachef.edu
Established: 1946
Annual Undergrad Tuition & Fees: $27,720
Enrollment: 2,827
Coed
Affiliation or Control: Independent Non-Profit
IRS Status: 501(c)3
Highest Offering: Baccalaureate
Program: Occupational; 2-Year Principally Bachelor's Creditable; Technical Emphasis
Accreditation: M

01 President .... Dr. Tim RYAN
10 Senior VP Finance/Administration .... Mr. Charles A. O'MARA
30 VP Advancement & Business Develop .... Dr. Victor GIELISSE
05 Provost .... Mr. Mark ERICKSON
07 VP Admissions & Marketing .... Mr. Bruce HILLENBRAND
11 VP Administration & Shared Svcs .... Mr. Richard MIGNAULT
88 VP Strategic Initiatives & Industry .... Mr. Greg DRESCHER
32 Assoc VP & Dean of Student Affairs .... Ms. Alice-Ann SCHUSTER
35 Assoc Dean Student Activities .... Mr. David WHALEN
38 Director Counseling Services .... Dr. Daria PAPALIA
23 Director Health Services .... Ms. Katherine MILLER
21 Director Finance & Accounting .... Mr. Steven STROM
96 Director Purchasing .... Mr. Brad MATTHEWS
88 Director Student Services .... Ms. Linda TERWILLIGER
18 Director Facilities .... Mr. Thomas M. HIRST
19 Director Safety .... Mr. Richard T. CULLEN
37 Director Financial Aid .... Ms. Kathleen GAILOR
29 Senior Alumni Relations Officer .... Ms. Denise ZANCHELLI
88 VP Academic Degree Programs .... Dr. Michael SPERLING
88 Dean Academic Support Services .... Ms. Carolyn TRAGNI
12 Assoc VP Branch Campuses .... Ms. Susan CUSSEN
88 Dean Culinary Arts .... Mr. Brendan WALSH
88 Dean Baking & Pastry Arts .... Mr. Thomas VACCARO
49 Dean of Liberal Arts & Business Mgt .... Dr. Kathleen MERGET
108 Director Academic Assessment & Accr .... Ms. Sharon ZRALY
06 Registrar .... Mr. Chester KOULIK
36 Director Career Services .... Mrs. Wendy HIGGINS
08 Director Library & Information Syst .... Mr. Eric HINSDALE
07 Director Admissions .... Ms. Rachel BIRCHWOOD
45 Assoc VP Planning & Operations Sup .... Mr. Rick TIETJEN
13 Assoc VP Information Technology .... Mr. Inder SINGH
88 Director Compliance .... Ms. Maura KING
88 Director HR Faculty Relations .... Mr. Joseph MORANO
88 Director HR Organizational Effectiv .... Ms. Vincenza MUELLER
15 Director HR Administration .... Ms. Shaynan GARRIOCH

Daemen College (E)

4380 Main Street, Amherst NY 14226-3592
County: Erie
FICE Identification: 002808
Unit ID: 190725
Telephone: (716) 839-3600
Carnegie Class: Master's L
FAX Number: (716) 839-8516
Calendar System: Semester
URL: www.daemen.edu
Established: 1947
Annual Undergrad Tuition & Fees: $24,090
Enrollment: 2,983
Coed
Affiliation or Control: Independent Non-Profit
IRS Status: 501(c)3
Highest Offering: Doctorate
Program: Liberal Arts And General; Teacher Preparatory; Professional
Accreditation: M, ARCPA, IACBE, NUR, PTA, SW, TEAC

01 President .... Dr. Gary A. OLSON
05 Vice Pres Academic Affairs/Dean .... Dr. Michael S. BROGAN
10 VP for Business Affairs & Treasurer .... Mr. Robert C. BEISWANGER
30 Vice President External Relations .... Vacant
84 VP of Enrollment Management .... Dr. Patricia R. BROWN
32 VP Student Affairs/Dean of Students .... Dr. Richanne C. MANKEY
20 Assoc VP Academic Affairs .... Dr. Kathleen C. BOONE
07 Dean of Admissions .... Mr. Frank WILLIAMS
21 Controller & Assistant Treasurer .... Mr. Michael E. LOOKER
91 Director Information Resources Mgmt .... Mr. Brian J. WILKINS
90 Director Academic Computing Service .... Ms. Kelly DURAN
09 Director of Institutional Research .... Dr. Patricia L. BEAMAN
88 Dir of Institutional Assessment .... Dr. Mimi H. STEADMAN
08 Head Librarian .... Mr. Francis J. CAREY
06 Registrar .... Ms. Paulette A. ANZELONE
88 Exec Dir for Academic Support Svcs .... Ms. Sabrina FENNELL
37 Director Financial Aid .... Mr. Jeffrey M. PAGANO
15 Director of Human Resources .... Mrs. Pamela R. NEUMANN
07 Director Grad Admissions .... Mr. Joseph PAGANO
26 Director of College Relations .... Mr. Michael G. ANDREI
44 Dir Annual Giving/Alumni Relations .... Mr. Justin JOHNSTON
78 Director of Career Services .... Ms. Maureen MILLANE
39 Director of Residence Life .... Ms. Sara C. ALEXANDERSON
35 Director of Student Activities .... Mr. Christopher P. MALIK
24 Director Instruct Technology Svcs .... Mr. James J. BACHRATY
18 Director of Physical Plant .... Mr. Frank X. SWEITZER, JR.
19 Director Security & Fire Safety .... Mr. Craig HUGHES
42 Director Campus Ministry .... Rev. Cassandra L. SALTER-SMITH
41 Director of Athletics .... Mr. Donald V. SILVERI
96 Dir of Purchasing/Central Services .... Ms. Gwendolyn M. WALKER
92 Director of Honors Program .... Dr. Matthew WARD
29 Director Alumni Relations .... Ms. Katie M. GRAF
40 Bookstore Manager .... Ms. Jaclyn HERNE
31 Coordinator Service Learning .... Ms. Susan M. MARCHIONE

Davis College (F)

400 Riverside Drive, Johnson City NY 13790-2714
County: Broome
FICE Identification: 021691
Unit ID: 194569
Telephone: (607) 729-1581
Carnegie Class: Spec/Faith
FAX Number: (607) 729-2962
Calendar System: Semester
URL: www.davisny.edu
Established: 1900
Annual Undergrad Tuition & Fees: $12,640
Enrollment: 360
Coed
Affiliation or Control: Independent Non-Profit
IRS Status: 501(c)3
Highest Offering: Baccalaureate
Program: Professional; Religious Emphasis
Accreditation: M, BI

01 Chief Executive Officer .... Dr. Dino J. PEDRONE
05 Chief Academic Officer .... Dr. Gilbert A. PARKER
84 Enrollment Management Officer .... Mr. Rick CRAMER
32 Student Development Officer .... Mrs. Nichole POST
11 Chief Operating Officer .... Rev. Jerry TRAISTER
10 Chief Financial Officer .... Mr. Larry ELLIS
04 Assistant to the President .... Mr. Daniel RATHMELL
06 Registrar .... Mr. Spencer KEY
08 Library Manager .... Mrs. Shelley BYRON
37 Director Financial Aid .... Mrs. Sandra CONKLIN
04 Executive Assistant .... Ms. Jenny GREEN

Dominican College of Blauvelt (G)

470 Western Highway, Orangeburg NY 10962-1210
County: Rockland
FICE Identification: 002713
Unit ID: 190761
Telephone: (845) 848-7800
Carnegie Class: Master's S
FAX Number: (845) 359-2313
Calendar System: Semester
URL: www.dc.edu
Established: 1952
Annual Undergrad Tuition & Fees: $24,790
Enrollment: 2,051
Coed
Affiliation or Control: Independent Non-Profit
IRS Status: 501(c)3
Highest Offering: Doctorate
Program: Liberal Arts And General; Teacher Preparatory; Professional
Accreditation: M, IACBE, NURSE, OT, PTA, SW, TEAC

01 President .... Sr Dr. Mary Eileen O'BRIEN
00 Chancellor .... Sr. Kathleen SULLIVAN
05 Vice Pres/Dean Academic Affairs .... Dr. Thomas S. NOWAK
84 Vice Pres of Enrollment Management .... Mr. Brian FERNANDES
32 Dean of Students .... Mr. John BURKE
10 Director of Fiscal Affairs .... Mr. Anthony CIPOLLA
06 Registrar .... Ms. Mary MCFADDEN
07 Director of Admissions .... Ms. Joyce ELBE
08 Librarian .... Mr. John BARRIE
30 Director of Inst Advancement .... Ms. Dorothy FILORAMO
15 Director Human Resources .... Ms. Marybeth BRODERICK
26 Chief Public Relations Officer .... Mr. Brett BEKRITSKY
29 Director Alumni Relations .... Ms. Samira ALLEN
35 Director Student Activities .... Ms. Katrina REDMOND
09 Inst Research/Plng/Assessment Ofcr .... Dr. Shao-Wei WU
37 Director Student Financial Aid .... Ms. Stacy SALINAS
36 Director Student Placement .... Ms. Evelyn FISKAA
38 Director Student Couseling .... Ms. Alise COHEN
21 Controller .... Ms. Joanne PORETTE
13 Director Information Technology .... Mr. Russell DIAZ
18 Chief Facilities/Physical Plant .... Mr. Michael DEMPSEY
20 Associate Academic Officer .... Ms. Ann VAVOLIZZA
39 Director Student Housing .... Mr. Ryan O'GORMAN
41 Athletic Director .... Mr. Joseph CLINTON
42 Director Campus Ministry .... Sr. Barbara MCENEANY
96 Director of Purchasing .... Ms. Amy BIANCO
28 Director of Diversity .... Vacant
19 Director of Security/Safety .... Mr. John LENNON
42 Chaplain .... Vacant
88 Dir Cmty Engagemt/Ldrship Develop .... Ms. Christine DILTS

Dorothea Hopfer School of Nursing at Mount Vernon Hospital (A)

53 Valentine Avenue, Mount Vernon NY 10550

County: Westchester FICE Identification: 022178
Unit ID: 193380
Telephone: (914) 361-6221 Carnegie Class: Not Classified
FAX Number: (914) 665-7047 Calendar System: Semester
URL: www.hopfer.org
Established: 1901 Annual Undergrad Tuition & Fees: $11,402
Enrollment: 129 Coed
Affiliation or Control: Independent Non-Profit IRS Status: 501(c)3
Highest Offering: Associate Degree
Program: 2-Year Principally Bachelor's Creditable; Nursing Emphasis
Accreditation: ADNUR

01 Dean ..... Joanna SCALABRINI

Dowling College (B)

Idle Hour Boulevard, Oakdale NY 11769-1999

County: Suffolk FICE Identification: 002667
Unit ID: 190770
Telephone: (631) 244-3000 Carnegie Class: Master's L
FAX Number: (631) 563-7831 Calendar System: Semester
URL: www.dowling.edu
Established: 1959 Annual Undergrad Tuition & Fees: $28,390
Enrollment: 4,047 Coed
Affiliation or Control: Independent Non-Profit IRS Status: 501(c)3
Highest Offering: Doctorate
Program: Liberal Arts And General; Teacher Preparatory; Professional
Accreditation: M, IACBE, TED

01 President ..... Dr. Norman R. SMITH
03 Senior Vice President ..... Dr. Elana ZOLFO
05 Provost ..... Dr. David MARKER
32 Vice Pres Student Affairs ..... Dr. Clyde PAYNE
84 VP Enrollment and Financial Aid ..... Mr. David BOISVERT
10 VP for Business & Finance ..... Mr. Ralph CERULLO
21 Associate VP Business and Finance ..... Ms. Jaclyn CARLO
07 Dean of Admissions ..... Mr. Richard LEBEL
41 Assoc Director of Athletics ..... Ms. Melody COPE
15 Exec Director Human Resources ..... Ms. Anne DIMOLA
18 Exec Dir Safety/Facil/Compliance ..... Mr. Robert CAMPBELL
06 Registrar ..... Ms. Cathryn MOONEY
37 Director of Financial Svcs ..... Ms. Carla GUEVARA
96 Director of Purchasing ..... Ms. Stephanie SWEET
13 Dir of Information Technology Svcs ..... Mr. Thomas FRANZA

Dutchess Community College (C)

53 Pendell Road, Poughkeepsie NY 12601-1595

County: Dutchess FICE Identification: 002864
Unit ID: 190840
Telephone: (845) 431-8000 Carnegie Class: Assoc/Pub-R-L
FAX Number: (845) 431-8984 Calendar System: Semester
URL: www.sunydutchess.edu
Established: 1957 Annual Undergrad Tuition & Fees (In-District): $3,635
Enrollment: 10,478 Coed
Affiliation or Control: State/Local IRS Status: 501(c)3
Highest Offering: Associate Degree
Program: Occupational; 2-Year Principally Bachelor's Creditable; Business Emphasis
Accreditation: M, ADNUR, EMT, MLTAD

01 President ..... Dr. D. David CONKLIN
05 Dean of Academic Affairs ..... Dr. Jose ADAMES
20 Associate Dean of Academic Affairs ..... Ms. Ellen GAMBINO
20 Associate Dean of Academic Affairs ..... Mr. Michael BODEN
32 Dean Student Svcs/Enroll Mgmt ..... Dr. Carol STEVENS
11 Dean of Administration ..... Mr. William ANDERSON
31 Dean Community Svcs/Special Pgms ..... Ms. Virginia STOEFFEL
21 Associate Dean Administration ..... Ms. Donna ROCAP
06 Registrar ..... Mr. William BENEDETTO
07 Director of Admissions ..... Mr. Michael ROE
08 Director of the Library ..... Ms. Cathy CARL
14 Director Information Systems ..... Mr. Patrick GRIFFIN
30 Director Institutional Advancement ..... Vacant
09 Director Planning/Inst Research ..... Ms. Donna JOHNSON
24 Director Telecomm/Instructnl Media ..... Vacant
37 Director Financial Aid ..... Ms. Susan MEAD
36 Director Counseling/Career Svcs ..... Mr. Michael BALABAN
15 Director Human Resources Mgmt ..... Ms. Esther COURET
18 Assoc Dean of Admin Facilities Mgmt . Ms. Bridgette ANDERSON
19 Interim Director Campus Security ..... Mr. Ed COX
13 Assoc Dean Admin Info Technology ..... Mr. Klaus GESSLER
35 Director of Student Activities ..... Mr. Michael WEIDA
26 Chief Public Relations Officer ..... Ms. Judi STOKES
88 Assoc Dir Teaching Learning Center ..... Ms. Chrisie MITCHELL
88 Director of Scheduling ..... Ms. Virginia CARRIG
12 Director DCC South Branch ..... Mr. Timothy DECKER
04 Admin Assistant to the President ..... Ms. Linda M. BEASIMER

D'Youville College (D)

320 Porter Avenue, Buffalo NY 14201-1084

County: Erie FICE Identification: 002712
Unit ID: 190716
Telephone: (716) 829-8000 Carnegie Class: Master's L
FAX Number: (716) 829-7820 Calendar System: Semester
URL: www.dyc.edu
Established: 1908 Annual Undergrad Tuition & Fees: $22,850
Enrollment: 3,204 Coed
Affiliation or Control: Independent Non-Profit IRS Status: 501(c)3
Highest Offering: Doctorate
Program: Liberal Arts And General; Teacher Preparatory; Professional; Nursing Emphasis
Accreditation: M, CHIRO, ARCPA, DIETC, IACBE, NURSE, OT, @PHAR, PTA

01 President ..... Sr. Denise A. ROCHE
05 Vice President for Academic Affairs ..... Dr. Arup SEN
10 Vice President Financal Affairs ..... Mr. Edward JOHNSON
32 VP Student Affairs & Enroll Mgmt ..... Mr. Robert P. MURPHY
30 Vice Pres Institutional Advancement ..... Ms. Kathleen CHRISTY
11 Associate Vice Pres of Operations ..... Mr. Edward P. COGAN
88 VP Admin Svcs & External Relations ..... Dr. William MARIANI
06 Registrar ..... Mr. Daryl SMITH
66 Dean School of Nursing ..... Dr. Judith LEWIS
49 Dean Sch of Arts/Sciences & Educ ..... Vacant
67 Dean School of Pharmacy ..... Dr. Gary STOEHR
76 Dean School of Health Professions ..... Dr. Anthony BILLITTIER
88 Artistic Director Kavinoky Theater ..... Mr. David LAMB
35 Associate VP for Student Affairs ..... Mr. Jeffrey PLATT
35 Assistant VP for Student Affairs ..... Mr. Anthony SPINA
21 Bursar ..... Mrs. Lisa HIGGINS
21 Controller ..... Ms. Laurie HALL
09 Dir Inst Rsrch & Assessment Support ..... Mr. Mark ECKSTEIN
90 Director Academic Computing ..... Dr. John T. MURPHY
91 Director Administrative Computing ..... Mr. Robert HALL
29 Director Alumni Relations ..... Ms. Meg RICHARDSON
44 Director Annual Giving ..... Mrs. Aimee PEARSON
41 Director Athletics ..... Mr. Brian CAVANAUGH
42 Director Campus Ministry ..... Fr. Paterick O'KEEFE
36 Director Career Services Center ..... Ms. Christine DEMCIE
88 Director College Center ..... Ms. Deborah E. OWENS
13 Director Computer & Network Svcs ..... Ms. Mary SPENCE
102 Director Foundation Relations ..... Mr. William P. MCKEEVER
25 Director Government Grants ..... Mrs. Colleen BRENNAN
23 Director Health Center ..... Mrs. Nicole CONROE
15 Director Human Resources ..... Ms. Linda MORETTI
85 Director International Stdnt Svcs ..... Mrs. Laryssa PETRYSHYN
88 Director Learning Center ..... Mrs. Karen KWANDRANS
08 Director Library Services ..... Mr. Rand BELLAVIA
44 Director Major & Planned Gifts ..... Ms. Patricia VAN DYKE
28 Director Multicultural Affairs ..... Mrs. Yolanda WOOD
38 Director Personal Counseling ..... Ms. Kimberly ZITTEL
26 Director Public Relations ..... Mr. D. John BRAY
19 Director of Security ..... Mr. Jeremy SMITH
37 Director Student Financial Aid ..... Ms. Lorraine METZ
07 Director Undergraduate Admissions ..... Dr. Steve SMITH
07 Director Graduate Admissions ..... Ms. Linda FISHER
07 Director Intl Admiss & Marketing ..... CMDR. Ronald DANNECKER
88 Director Veterans Affairs Office ..... Mr. Benjamin RANDLE
27 Chief Information Officer ..... Mr. Roozbeh TAVAKOLI
51 Director Prof Development Center ..... Vacant

The Elmezzi Graduate School of Molecular Medicine (E)

350 Community Drive, Manhasset NY 11030-3828

County: Nassau Identification: 666671
Telephone: (516) 562-3405 Carnegie Class: Not Classified
FAX Number: (516) 562-1022 Calendar System: Other
URL: www.elmezzigraduateschool.org
Established: 2003 Annual Graduate Tuition & Fees: N/A
Enrollment: 11 Coed
Affiliation or Control: Independent Non-Profit IRS Status: 501(c)3
Highest Offering: Doctorate; No Undergraduates
Program: Professional; Technical Emphasis
Accreditation: NY

01 President ..... Dr. Kevin J. TRACEY
05 Dean ..... Dr. Bettie STEINBERG

Elmira Business Institute (F)

Langdon Plaza, 303 N Main Street, Elmira NY 14901-3086

County: Chemung FICE Identification: 009043
Unit ID: 190974
Telephone: (607) 733-7177 Carnegie Class: Assoc/PrivFP
FAX Number: (607) 733-7178 Calendar System: Semester
URL: www.ebi-college.com
Established: 1858 Annual Undergrad Tuition & Fees: $18,400
Enrollment: 425 Coed
Affiliation or Control: Proprietary IRS Status: Proprietary
Highest Offering: Associate Degree
Program: Occupational
Accreditation: ACICS, MAC

01 President ..... Mr. Brad C. PHILLIPS
03 Vice President ..... Mrs. Kathleen M. HAMILTON
32 Director of Student Services ..... Mrs. Lindsay N. DULL

Elmira Business Institute (G)

4100 Old Vestal Road, Vestal NY 13850

Telephone: (607) 729-8915 Identification: 770745
Accreditation: ACICS

† Main campus is Elmira Business Institute in Elmira, NY.

Elmira College (H)

One Park Place, Elmira NY 14901-2099

County: Chemung FICE Identification: 002718
Unit ID: 190983
Telephone: (607) 735-1800 Carnegie Class: Bac/Diverse
FAX Number: (607) 735-1758 Calendar System: Other
URL: www.elmira.edu
Established: 1855 Annual Undergrad Tuition & Fees: $36,600
Enrollment: 1,530 Coed
Affiliation or Control: Independent Non-Profit IRS Status: 501(c)3
Highest Offering: Master's
Program: Liberal Arts And General; Teacher Preparatory; Professional; Business Emphasis
Accreditation: M, NUR, @TEAC

01 President ..... Dr. Ronald O. CHAMPAGNE
10 Vice President & Treasurer ..... Dr. Robert W. RUBLE
05 Academic Vice President ..... Dr. Stephen F. COLEMAN
30 Vice Pres Institutional Advancement ..... Ms. Deborah MCKINZIE
84 Vice Pres of Enrollment Management . Ms. Julianne D. BAUMANN
100 Vice President and Chief of Staff ..... Mr. Michael B. ROGERS
41 Vice President Athletics ..... Ms. Patricia A. THOMPSON
51 Dean of Continuing Education ..... Ms. Elizabeth A. LAMBERT
07 Dean of Admissions ..... Mr. Brett C. MOORE
37 Dean of Financial Aid ..... Ms. Kathleen L. COHEN
06 Registrar ..... Mr. Michael HALPERIN
08 Dean of Library ..... Ms. Elizabeth M. WAVLE
36 Director of Career Services ..... Mr. Michael D. BLASIC
50 Chair Business Programs ..... Dr. Mariam KHAWAR
57 Chair Fine Arts Program ..... Prof. George DEFALUSSY
79 Chair of Humanities ..... Dr. Heidi DIERCKX
81 Chair Math/Natural Sciences ..... Dr. Christine BEZOTTE
83 Chair Social/Behavioral Sciences ..... Dr. Charles MITCHELL
88 Chair of Professional Programs .. Dr. Maureen DONOHUE-SMITH
29 Director of Alumni Relations ..... Ms. Lindsay PETRILLOSE
66 Director Nursing Program ..... Prof. Lois SCHOENER
18 Superintendent of Buildings/Grounds ..... Mr. Donald L. BRIMMER
27 Director of Digital Media ..... Mr. Daniel A. BAROODY
39 Director of Campus Life ..... Mr. Benjamin J. CURTIS
40 Director Business Operations ..... Mrs. Shannon MOYLAN
15 Director of Human Resources ..... Ms. Carey L. IPPINECA
09 Director of Development Research ..... Ms. Ellen BURKE
20 Associate Academic Officer ..... Dr. Charles W. LINDSAY

Erie Community College City Campus (I)

121 Ellicott Street, Buffalo NY 14203-2698

County: Erie FICE Identification: 010684
Unit ID: 191083
Telephone: (716) 842-2770 Carnegie Class: Assoc/Pub-U-MC
FAX Number: (716) 851-1129 Calendar System: Semester
URL: www.ecc.edu
Established: 1971 Annual Undergrad Tuition & Fees (In-District): $4,559
Enrollment: 3,355 Coed
Affiliation or Control: State/Local IRS Status: 501(c)3
Highest Offering: Associate Degree
Program: Occupational; 2-Year Principally Bachelor's Creditable
Accreditation: M, ADNUR, RTT

01 President ..... Mr. Jack F. QUINN
05 Associate Vice President Academics ..... Dr. Edward J. HOLMES
88 Assoc VP Academic Transition Pgms ..... Vacant
32 Associate VP Student Services ..... Dr. Marsha D. JACKSON
19 Assoc Vice President Security ..... Mr. John MCDONNELL
102 Associate Vice Pres Foundation ..... Mr. Jeffrey BAGEL
10 Chief Admin & Financial Officer ..... Mr. William D. REUTER
35 Dean of Students ..... Ms. Petrina HILL-CHEATOM
103 Exec Dean Workforce Dev/Cmty Svcs ..... Ms. Carrie W. KAHN
49 Asst Academic Dean Liberal Arts ..... Dr. Marcia A. GELLIN
50 Asst Academic Dean Business ..... Dr. Kenneth J. BARNES
28 Director of Equity & Diversity ..... Ms. Darley WILLIS
06 Registrar ..... Ms. Cynthia LUDLOW
08 Librarian ..... Ms. Kathleen MCGRIFF-POWERS
40 Bookstore Manager ..... Ms. Teresa KALINOWSKI
23 Health Services Nurse ..... Ms. Frances WILLIAMS
26 Director of Public Relations ..... Mr. Lance R. KONKLE
27 Public Information Officer ..... Mr. Michael FARRELL
41 Director of Athletics ..... Mr. Peter J. JEREBKO
37 Financial Aid Coordinator ..... Ms. Charlotte M. COSTON
24 Audio Visual Coordinator ..... Mr. Gregg S. FILIPPONE
36 Career Resource Center Coordinator ..... Vacant
92 Coordinator Honors Program ..... Vacant
88 Coordinator of Corporate Training ..... Mr. John P. SLISZ
29 Coordinator of Alumni Affairs ..... Ms. Mary Jo R. DENNEE
55 Asst Coordinator Evening Activities ..... Vacant
04 Assistant to the President ..... Mr. John FOLEY
07 Admissions Counselor ..... Ms. Heather A. CRUZ
07 Admissions Counselor ..... Ms. Deborah M. MEDINA

Erie Community College North Campus (J)

6205 Main Street, Williamsville NY 14221-7095

Telephone: (716) 634-0800 FICE Identification: 002865
Accreditation: &M, ADNUR, CAHIIM, COARC, DH, DIETT, ENGT, MAC, MLTAD, OPD, OTA

† Main campus is Erie Community College City Campus in Buffalo, NY.

Erie Community College-South Campus (K)

4041 Southwestern Boulevard,
Orchard Park NY 14127-2199

Telephone: (716) 648-5400 FICE Identification: 012427
Accreditation: &M, DT

† Main campus is Erie Community College City Campus in Buffalo, NY.

Everest Institute (A)

1630 Portland Avenue, Rochester NY 14521-3007

County: Monroe
FICE Identification: 004811
Unit ID: 194967
Telephone: (585) 266-0430
Carnegie Class: Assoc/PrivFP
FAX Number: (585) 266-8243
Calendar System: Quarter
URL: www.everest.edu
Established: 1863
Annual Undergrad Tuition & Fees: $18,000
Enrollment: 572
Coed
Affiliation or Control: Proprietary
IRS Status: Proprietary
Highest Offering: Associate Degree
Program: Occupational; 2-Year Principally Bachelor's Creditable; Business Emphasis
Accreditation: ACICS, #MAC

01	President	Mr. Carl A. SILVIO
05	Academic Dean	Ms. Eva WILCOX
07	Director of Admissions	Ms. Deanna PFLUKE
37	Director Student Finance	Mrs. Kandace REID
10	Director of Student Accounts	Ms. Maureen GILMORE
36	Director of Career Services	Ms. Annette PERRIN
04	Admin Asst to the President	Ms. Karen M. BAFFORD-BUBEL
08	Librarian	Mr. Kyle DANIELS
06	Registrar	Ms. Gail BRUENGINSEN

Excelsior College (B)

7 Columbia Circle, Albany NY 12203-5156

County: Albany
FICE Identification: 002834
Unit ID: 196680
Telephone: (518) 464-8500
Carnegie Class: Master's M
FAX Number: (518) 464-8777
Calendar System: Other
URL: www.excelsior.edu
Established: 1971
Annual Undergrad Tuition & Fees: N/A
Enrollment: 39,728
Coed
Affiliation or Control: Independent Non-Profit
IRS Status: 501(c)3
Highest Offering: Master's
Program: Liberal Arts And General; Professional
Accreditation: M, ADNUR, ENGT, IACBE, NUR

01	President	Dr. John F. EBERSOLE
100	Chief of Staff	Dr. Murray BLOCK
05	Chief Academic Officer/Provost	Dr. Mary Beth HANNER
20	Vice Provost	Dr. Patrick JONES
88	VP for Innovation & Strategy	Dr. Steve ERNST
10	VP Finance & Administration	Mr. John M. PONTIUS, JR.
43	VP and General Counsel	Mr. Joseph B. PORTER
26	VP Institutional Advancement	Ms. Cathy KUSHNER
16	VP Human Resources & Facilities	Mr. Edmund MCTERNAN
84	VP Enrollment Management	Mr. Craig MASLOWSKY
13	VP Information Technology	Ms. Susan O'HERN
07	AVP for Enrollment Management	Mr. Thomas DALTON
30	AVP Institutional Advancement	Mr. William M. STEWART
15	AVP for Human Resources	Ms. Anita BURNS
86	AVP for Government Relations	Dr. Paul SHIFFMAN
21	AVP and Controller	Vacant
106	Dean Online Education/Learning Svcs	Dr. George TIMMONS
21	AVP/Dir Budgets/Financial Analysis	Mr. Todd S. THOMAS
13	AVP Information Technology	Mr. Ronald MARZITELLI
88	AVP Outcomes Assessment & Inst	Dr. Lisa DANIELS
07	Exec Director of Admissions	Mr. Roberto FIGUEROA
88	Exec Director of Outreach/Access	Ms. Lisa LAVIGNA
88	Exec Director of Outreach	Ms. Lynda HOLT
88	Exec Director of CEM	Dr. Mika HOFFMAN
88	Exec Director of Marketing	Ms. Shannon EASTON
88	Exec Director of CME	Ms. Sue DEWAN
102	Director of Grants and Research	Ms. Patricia CROOP
37	Director of Financial Aid	Ms. Donna COOPER
108	Director of Outcomes Assessment	Dr. Mohua BOSE
88	Director of Faculty Development	Dr. Joan MIKALSON
88	Director of Academic Operations	Ms. Emilsen HOLGUIN
30	Director of Development	Ms. Marcy STRYKER
06	Registrar	Ms. Lori MORANO
88	Bursar	Mr. John LEWIS
66	Dean of Nursing	Dr. Mary Lee POLLARD
50	Dean of Business & Technology	Vacant
49	Dean of Liberal Arts	Dr. Scott DALRYMPLE
76	Dean of Health Sciences	Dr. Debbie SOPCZYK
09	Director of Institutional Research	Dr. Lisa DANIELS
18	Chief Facilities/Physical Plant	Mr. Robert RANALLI
28	Diversity Coordinator	Ms. Toby HAMLIN
29	Director of Alumni Relations	Ms. Marcy STRYKER

Fashion Institute of Technology (C)

Seventh Avenue at 27 Street, New York NY 10001-5992

County: New York
FICE Identification: 002866
Unit ID: 191126
Telephone: (212) 217-7999
Carnegie Class: Master's S
FAX Number: N/A
Calendar System: Semester
URL: www.fitnyc.edu
Established: 1944
Annual Undergrad Tuition & Fees (In-District): $6,068
Enrollment: 10,052
Coed
Affiliation or Control: State/Local
IRS Status: 501(c)3
Highest Offering: Master's
Program: 2-Year Principally Bachelor's Creditable; Professional
Accreditation: M, ART, CIDA

01	President	Dr. Joyce F. BROWN
10	Treas/VP Finance/Administration	Ms. Sherry F. BRABHAM
101	Secy of College/General Counsel	Dr. Stephen TUTTLE
05	Vice President Academic Affairs	Dr. Giacomo OLIVA
26	Vice Pres Comm/External Rels	Ms. Loretta LAWRENCE KEANE
84	VP Enrollment Mgmt/Student Success	Dr. Leellen BRIGMAN
84	Assistant VP Enrollment Services	Dr. Kelly BRENNAN
15	Vice President Human Res/Labor Rels	Mr. Arthur E. BROWN
13	VP for Information Technology/CIO	Mr. Gregg CHOTTINER
30	Acting Asst VP Develop & Exec Dir	Mr. Terry CULVER
20	Assoc Vice Pres Academic Affairs	Mr. Howard DILLON
88	Asst Vice Pres Human Res/Labor Rels	Ms. Karen YUEN
21	Asst Vice Pres Finance	Mr. Mark BLAIFEDER
21	Assistant VP of Administration	Ms. Rebecca CORRADO
88	Asst VP Software Svcs/Info Access	Mr. Van Buren WINSTON
27	Asst Vice Pres for Communications	Ms. Carol LEVEN
04	Exec Asst to the President	Ms. Shari PRUSSIN
20	Dean Curriculum/Instruction	Vacant
32	Asst VP/Dean of Students	Mr. Erik KNEUBUEHL
51	Dean Continuing & Prof Studies	Vacant
57	Dean Art & Design	Ms. Joanne ARBUCKLE
58	Dean School of Graduate Studies	Dr. Mary DAVIS
49	Dean Liberal Arts	Dr. Scott F. STODDART
50	Dean Business & Technology	Mr. Steven FRUMKIN
07	Dir of Admissions/Strat Recruiting	Ms. Laura ARBOGAST
88	Director Special Events	Ms. Vicki GURANOWSKI
11	Director Operational Services	Mr. John WILSON
18	Executive Director of Facilities	Mr. George JEFREMOW
22	Affirm Action Ofcr/Dir Compliance	Ms. Griselda GONZALEZ
38	Director of the Counseling Center	Ms. Terry GINDER
37	Director of Financial Aid	Ms. Mina FRIEDMANN
08	Dir of the Gladys Marcus Library	Mr. NJ WOLFE
06	Director of Registration & Records	Ms. Rita ARMENIA
39	Director of Residental Life	Ms. Ann Marie GRAPPO
36	Director Career & Internship	Mr. Andrew CRONAN
35	Director of Student Life	Ms. Michelle VAN-ESS
23	Director of Health Services	Ms. Anne MILLER
19	Acting Director of Security	Mr. Mario CABRERA
88	Director of The Museum at FIT	Dr. Valerie STEELE
09	Director of Institutional Research	Mr. Darrell GLENN
86	Dir Government/Community Relations	Ms. Lisa WAGER
27	Exec Director of Public & Media Rel	Ms. Cheri FEIN
104	Director of International Programs	Dr. Georgianna APPIGNANI
41	Director of Athletics & Recreation	Ms. Kerri-Ann MCTIERNAN
96	Director of Budget	Ms. Nancy SU
88	Dir of Education Opportunity Pgms	Ms. Taur D. ORANGE
21	Controller/Assistant Treas	Mr. John JOHNSTON
88	Dir Envir Health/Safety Compliance	Mr. Joseph J. ARCOLEO
92	Coord Presidential Scholars Pgm	Dr. Irene BUCHMAN
96	Director of Purchasing	Dr. Robert OTTO
105	Manager of Web Communications	Ms. Donna LEHMANN
55	Dir Evening/Weekend/Pre-College	Ms. Michele NAGEL
29	Manager of Alumni Relations	Vacant
102	Dir of Corporate & Foundation Rels	Mr. Kevin HERVAS
28	Chair of Diversity Council	Ms. Griselda GONZALEZ
28	Chair of Diversity Council	Mr. Michael COKKINOS

Finger Lakes Community College (D)

3325 Marvin Sands Drive, Canandaigua NY 14424-8405

County: Ontario
FICE Identification: 007532
Unit ID: 191199
Telephone: (585) 394-3500
Carnegie Class: Assoc/Pub-S-SC
FAX Number: (585) 394-5005
Calendar System: Semester
URL: www.flcc.edu
Established: 1965
Annual Undergrad Tuition & Fees (In-District): $3,834
Enrollment: 6,539
Coed
Affiliation or Control: State/Local
IRS Status: 501(c)3
Highest Offering: Associate Degree
Program: Occupational; 2-Year Principally Bachelor's Creditable
Accreditation: M, ADNUR

01	President	Dr. Barbara G. RISSER
05	Vice Pres Academic/Student Affairs	Dr. Thomas E. TOPPING
10	Vice President of Admin/Treasurer	Mr. James R. FISHER
84	Vice Pres Enrollment Management	Ms. Carol S. URBAITIS
32	Assoc Vice Pres of Student Affairs	Ms. Sarah E. WHIFFEN
20	Assoc VP Instruction & Assessment	Dr. Karen TAYLOR
20	Assoc VP Academic Initiatives	Mr. Jacob E. AMIDON
16	Director of Human Resources	Ms. Grace H. LOOMIS
30	Director of Development	Ms. Amy I. PAULEY
19	Director Campus Security Operations	Mr. Jason R. MAITLAND
21	Controller	Mr. Joseph L. DELFORTE
18	Director of Facilities & Grounds	Ms. Jan J. JUNE
07	Director of Admissions	Ms. Bonnie B. RITTS
15	Director Personnel Services	Ms. Kathryn A. BOLLEN
25	Director of Grants Development	Ms. Karen A. VAN KEUREN
37	Director of Financial Aid	Ms. Susan M. ROMANO
35	Director of Student Life	Vacant
13	Director Information Technology	Dr. Richard W. EVANS
38	Director Career Services	Ms. Corrine M. CANOUGH
36	Career Services Coordinator	Vacant
08	Director of Library	Mr. Frank R. QUEENER
26	Director of Marketing	Ms. Heidi C. MARCIN
23	Director of Student Health Services	Ms. Karen P Z. STEIN
24	Director of Educational Technology	Mr. Daniel P. FARSACI
29	Director of Alumni Relations	Ms. Lisa L. SCOTT
96	Director of Business Services	Mr. Bruce J. TREAT
72	Chair Science & Technology	Dr. Melissa A. MILLER
50	Chair Business	Ms. Mary M. WILSEY
65	Chair Environment Conservation Hort	Ms. Ann B. SCHNELL
57	Chair Visual/Performing Arts	Mr. Richard D. COOK
66	Chair Nursing	Ms. Nancy E. CLARKSON
68	Chair Physical Education	Mr. Dennis T. MOORE
81	Chair Computer Science	Ms. April A. DEVAUX
79	Chair Humanities	Mr. Jon A. PALZER
83	Chair Social Science	Mr. Joshua W. HELLER
81	Chair Mathematics	Vacant

Finger Lakes Health College of Nursing (E)

196 North Street, Geneva NY 14456

County: Ontario
Identification: 667154
Unit ID: 475422
Telephone: (315) 787-4005
Carnegie Class: Not Classified
FAX Number: (313) 787-4770
Calendar System: Semester
URL: www.flhealth.org/nursingeducation
Established: 2008
Annual Undergrad Tuition & Fees: $8,890
Enrollment: 109
Coed
Affiliation or Control: Independent Non-Profit
IRS Status: 501(c)3
Highest Offering: Associate Degree
Program: 2-Year Principally Bachelor's Creditable; Nursing Emphasis
Accreditation: ADNUR

01	Dean	Victoria RECORD

Five Towns College (F)

305 North Service Road, Dix Hills NY 11746-6055

County: Suffolk
FICE Identification: 012561
Unit ID: 191205
Telephone: (631) 656-2157
Carnegie Class: Bac/Diverse
FAX Number: (631) 656-2172
Calendar System: Semester
URL: www.ftc.edu
Established: 1972
Annual Undergrad Tuition & Fees: $20,400
Enrollment: 952
Coed
Affiliation or Control: Proprietary
IRS Status: Proprietary
Highest Offering: Doctorate
Program: Fine Arts Emphasis
Accreditation: M, TED

01	President	Dr. Stanley G. COHEN
05	Dean of Academic Affairs/Provost	Dr. Roger H. SHERMAN
11	Dean of Administration	Dr. Martin L. COHEN
84	Dean of Enrollment	Mr. Jerry L. COHEN
32	Dean of Students	Dr. Susan BARR
06	Registrar	Ms. Mara MALTZ
21	Business Officer	Mr. Robert A. SHERMAN
07	Director of Recruitment Services	Mr. Daniel EDWARDS
08	Head Librarian	Mr. John VANSTEEN
38	College Counselor	Ms. Carolyn NEWMAN
64	Chair of Music Division	Prof. Jeffrey LIPTON
50	Chair of Business Division	Ms. Darlene DECICCO
49	Chair of Liberal Arts Division	Dr. Richard D. KELLEY
53	Chair of Education Division	Dr. Patricia SCHMIDT
88	Chair of Film/Video	Mr. Robert DIGIACOMO
88	Chair of Theatre Arts	Prof. Jeffrey LIPTON

Fordham University (G)

441 East Fordham Road, Bronx NY 10458-9993

County: Bronx
FICE Identification: 002722
Unit ID: 191241
Telephone: (718) 817-1000
Carnegie Class: RU/H
FAX Number: (718) 817-4925
Calendar System: Semester
URL: www.fordham.edu
Established: 1841
Annual Undergrad Tuition & Fees: $42,845
Enrollment: 15,170
Coed
Affiliation or Control: Independent Non-Profit
IRS Status: 501(c)3
Highest Offering: Doctorate
Program: Liberal Arts And General; Teacher Preparatory; Professional
Accreditation: M, BUS, CLPSY, COPSY, DANCE, LAW, SCPSY, SW, TED

01	President	Rev. Joseph M. MCSHANE, SJ
04	Exec Assistant to the President	Ms. Dorothy MARINUCCI
04	Assistant to the President	Dr. Rosemary A. DEJULIO
05	Provost	Dr. Stephen FREEDMAN
10	Sr VP & Chief Financial Officer	Mr. John J. LORDAN
21	Vice President for Finance	Mr. Frank SIMIO
32	Vice President Student Affairs	Mr. Jeffrey L. GRAY
13	VP for Information Technology	Dr. Frank SIRIANNI
84	Vice President for Enrollment	Dr. Peter A. STACE
12	Vice President for Lincoln Center	Dr. Brian J. BYRNE
30	Vice President for Development	Mr. Roger MILICI
88	Vice President for Mission/Ministry	Msgr. Joseph G. QUINN
86	Vice President for Government Rels	Mr. Thomas A. DUNNE
18	VP Facilities/Physical Plant	Mr. Marc VALERA
11	Vice President for Administration	Mr. Thomas A. DUNNE
20	Assoc Vice Pres Academic Affairs	Dr. Benjamin CROOKER
20	Assoc Vice Pres Academic Affairs	Dr. Ron JACOBSON
26	AVP Univ Marketing Communications	Ms. Catherine SPENCER
29	AVP/Director of Alumni Relations	Mr. Michael GRIFFIN
07	Asst Vice Pres Undgrad Enrollment	Mr. John W. BUCKLEY
06	Asst Vice Pres Enrollment/Registrar	Dr. Gene FEIN
37	Asst VP Student Financial Services	Ms. Angela VAN DEKKER
86	Assoc Vice Pres for Government Rels	Mr. Joseph P. MURIANA
101	Secretary of the University	Ms. Margaret T. BALL
43	General Counsel	Mr. Thomas E. DEJULIO
35	Dean of Students	Mr. Christopher RODGERS
35	Dean of Student Services	Mr. Gregory J. PAPPAS
12	Dean Fordham College at Rose Hill	Dr. Michael LATHAM
58	Dean Graduate Arts & Science	Dr. Nancy BUSCH
73	Dean Graduate Religious Education	Dr. C. Colt ANDERSON
50	Dean College Business Admin	Dr. Donna RAPACCIOLI
107	Dean Fordham Col of Prof Studies	Dr. Isabel FRANK

12 Dean Fordham College Lincoln Center .... Rev. Robert GRIMES
88 Dean Graduate Business Admin LC .... Dr. David GAUTSCHI
53 Dean Graduate Education LC .... Dr. James HENNESSY
61 Dean School of Law LC .... Mr. Michael MARTIN
70 Dean Graduate Social Service LC .... Vacant
15 Exec Director of Human Resources .... Mr. Michael MINEO
09 Director Institutional Research .... Vacant
42 AVP Campus Ministry .... Rev. Philip J. FLORIO, SJ
21 Controller .... Mr. Anthony GRONO
19 Director of Security .... Mr. John CARROLL
22 Administrative Policies Monitor .... Vacant
46 Dir Research/Sponsored Programs .... Dr. Nancy BUSCH
08 Director of University Libraries .... Ms. Linda LOSCHIAVO
24 Director Media Center .... Mr. Jerry GREEN
23 Director of Health Center .... Ms. Kathleen MALARA
35 Assistant Dean of Students .... Ms. Alanna NOLAN
41 AVP of Athletic Alumni Relations ... Mr. Francis X. MCLAUGHLIN
96 Director of Procurement .... Mr. Frank A. DEORIO
38 Director of Psychological Svcs .... Dr. Jennifer NEUHOF
28 Director of Multicultural Programs .... Ms. Sofia BAUSTISTA PERTUZ
36 Director Career Services .... Ms. Stefany FATTOR

Fulton-Montgomery Community College (A)

2805 State Highway 67, Johnstown NY 12095-3790
County: Montgomery FICE Identification: 002867
Unit ID: 191302
Telephone: (518) 736-3622 Carnegie Class: Assoc/Pub-R-M
FAX Number: (518) 762-4334 Calendar System: Semester
URL: www.fmcc.suny.edu
Established: 1963 Annual Undergrad Tuition & Fees (In-District): $4,108
Enrollment: 2,683 Coed
Affiliation or Control: State/Local IRS Status: 501(c)3
Highest Offering: Associate Degree
Program: Occupational; 2-Year Principally Bachelor's Creditable
Accreditation: M, RAD

01 President .... Dr. Dustin SWANGER
05 Provost/Vice Pres Academic Affairs ... Dr. Greg TRUCKENMILLER
10 Vice Pres Finance & Administration .... Mr. David M. MORROW
32 Vice President of Student Affairs .... Ms. Jane KELLEY
49 Dean of Arts & Sciences .... Vacant
75 Dean Business/Tech/Health Prof .... Ms. Diana PUTNAM
21 Controller .... Vacant
13 Director of Information Technology .... Mr. Gregg ROTH
18 Superintendent Building & Grounds .... Mr. Joshua FLEMMING
07 Director of Admissions .... Ms. Laura LAPORTE
06 Registrar .... Vacant
08 Librarian .... Mrs. Mary DONOHUE
103 Director Workforce Development .... Vacant
36 Director of Career Planning .... Ms. Andrea SCRIBNER
38 Director Advisement/Counseling/ Test .... Ms. Mary-Jo FERRAUILO-DAVIS
30 Chief Development .... Ms. Lesley LANZI
09 Director of Institutional Research .... Mr. Eric KIMMELMAN
37 Coordinator Financial Aid .... Ms. Rebecca COZZOCREA

General Theological Seminary (B)

440 West 21st Street, New York NY 10011-2981
County: New York FICE Identification: 002726
Unit ID: 191320
Telephone: (212) 243-5150 Carnegie Class: Spec/Faith
FAX Number: (212) 727-3907 Calendar System: Semester
URL: www.gts.edu
Established: 1817 Annual Graduate Tuition & Fees: $15,400
Enrollment: 118 Coed
Affiliation or Control: Protestant Episcopal IRS Status: 501(c)3
Highest Offering: Doctorate; No Undergraduates
Program: Professional; Religious Emphasis
Accreditation: THEOL

01 President and Dean .... Rev. Kurt DUNKLE
10 Executive VP and CFO .... Ms. Sandra JOHNSON
11 Vice President of Operations .... Mr. Anthony KHANI
30 VP for Institutional Advancement .... Ms. Donna ASHLEY
08 Head Librarian .... Rev. Andrew KADEL
07 Director of Admissions .... Mr. William C. WEBSTER
27 Director of Communications .... Mr. Chad RANCOURT
06 Registrar .... Ms. Emily BEEKMAN
04 Exec Asst to the President & Dean .... Ms. Kim ROBEY

Genesee Community College (C)

One College Road, Batavia NY 14020-9704
County: Genesee FICE Identification: 006782
Unit ID: 191339
Telephone: (585) 343-0055 Carnegie Class: Assoc/Pub-R-M
FAX Number: (585) 343-4541 Calendar System: Semester
URL: www.genesee.edu
Established: 1966 Annual Undergrad Tuition & Fees (In-District): $3,700
Enrollment: 6,965 Coed
Affiliation or Control: State/Local IRS Status: 501(c)3
Highest Offering: Associate Degree
Program: Occupational; 2-Year Principally Bachelor's Creditable
Accreditation: M, ADNUR, COARC, POLYT, PTAA

01 President .... Dr. James SUNSER
05 Provost/Exec VP Academic Affairs .... Dr. Kathleen SCHIEFEN
10 Vice Pres for Finance & Operations .... Mr. Kevin HAMILTON
32 VP for Student & Enrollment Svcs .... Dr. Virginia TAYLOR
45 Exec VP for Planning/Inst Effectiv .... Mr. William T. EMM
103 Exec Dir for Workforce Development .... Mr. Reid SMALLEY
15 Assoc VP for Human Resources .... Ms. Gina WEAVER
20 Asc Dean Accelerated Col Enrol Pgms ... Mr. Edward LEVINSTEIN
81 Dean Math/Science/Career Education .... Dr. Rafael ALICEA-MALDONADO
83 Dean Human Communication/ Behavior .... Dr. Katharina E. KOVACH-ALLEN
56 Dean of Distributed Learning .... Mr. Craig LAMB
35 Dean of Students .... Ms. Jennifer M. NEWELL
06 Registrar .... Mr. Terrence REDING
07 Director of Admissions .... Ms. Tanya LANE-MARTIN
14 Director of Computer Services .... Ms. Cindy DELMAR
37 Director of Financial Aid .... Mr. Joseph A. BAILEY
26 Director Devel & External Affairs .... Mr. Richard G. ENSMAN, JR.
88 Director of Student Activities .... Mr. Clifford M. SCUTELLA
21 Controller .... Ms. Kristin L. YUNKER
41 Director of Athletics .... Ms. Kristen SCHUTH
18 Director of Buildings & Grounds .... Mr. Timothy M. LANDERS
88 Director Business Skills Training .... Mr. Ramon C. CHAYA
09 Assoc Dean Inst Rsrch & Assessment .... Ms. Carol MARRIOTT
57 Director Fine & Performing Arts .... Ms. Maryanne ARENA
90 Manager of Academic Computing .... Mrs. Mary Jane HEIDER
91 Manager of Administrative Computing .... Vacant
35 Assoc Dean for Student Development .... Ms. Margaret HEATER
88 Director of Health and Phys Ed .... Ms. Rebecca DZIEKAN
88 Director Business Skills Training .... Vacant

Globe Institute of Technology (D)

500 Seventh Avenue, New York NY 10018
County: New York FICE Identification: 025408
Unit ID: 188465
Telephone: (212) 349-4330 Carnegie Class: Spec/Bus
FAX Number: (212) 227-5920 Calendar System: Semester
URL: www.globe.edu
Established: 1985 Annual Undergrad Tuition & Fees: $11,120
Enrollment: 740 Coed
Affiliation or Control: Proprietary IRS Status: Proprietary
Highest Offering: Baccalaureate
Program: Occupational
Accreditation: NY

01 President .... Mr. Martin OLINER
05 Academic Dean .... Ms. Elena ESTRIN
11 Dean of Administrative Services .... Mr. Alex OLINER
32 Dean of Student Services .... Ms. Marsanda DARCY
27 Director of Information Services .... Mr. Boris KAMENETSKIY
13 Director of Information Technology ..... Mr. Jacob KUPERSHTEYN
07 Director of Admissions .... Mr. Al GARCIA
37 Director of Financial Aid .... Ms. Tatiana NUSENBAUM
06 Registrar .... Ms. Vivian PAGAN
41 Athletic Director .... Mr. Mark MORSE
38 Coord Student Counseling/Placement .... Ms. Nellie CHEN

Hamilton College (E)

198 College Hill Road, Clinton NY 13323-1218
County: Oneida FICE Identification: 002728
Unit ID: 191515
Telephone: (315) 859-4011 Carnegie Class: Bac/A&S
FAX Number: (315) 859-4991 Calendar System: Semester
URL: www.hamilton.edu
Established: 1812 Annual Undergrad Tuition & Fees: $45,620
Enrollment: 1,884 Coed
Affiliation or Control: Independent Non-Profit IRS Status: 501(c)3
Highest Offering: Baccalaureate
Program: Liberal Arts And General
Accreditation: M

01 President .... Joan H. STEWART
05 VPAA/Dean of Faculty .... Patrick D. REYNOLDS
11 Vice Pres Administration/Finance .... Karen L. LEACH
30 Vice President Commun/Development .... Richard C. TANTILLO
13 Vice Pres Information Technology .... David L. SMALLEN
07 VP/Dean Admission & Financial Aid .... Monica C. INZER
32 Dean of Students .... Nancy R. THOMPSON
20 Associate Dean of Faculty .... Margaret GENTRY
41 Athletic Director .... Jonathan T. HIND
39 Director Residential Life .... Travis R. HILL
10 Controller .... Shari K. WHITING
08 Dir of Library/Info Technology .... David L. SMALLEN
27 Director Strategic Communications .... Stacey J. HIMMELBERGER
37 Director of Financial Aid .... Melissa ROSE
36 Exec Director Career Center .... Mary EVANS
06 Registrar .... Kristin M. FRIEDEL
15 Director of Human Resources .... Stephen STEMKOSKI
23 Director Student Health Services .... Christine C. MERRITT
18 Director Physical Plant .... Steven J. BELLONA
19 Director of Campus Safety .... Francis A. MANFREDO
38 Director Counseling/Psych Services .... Robert KAZIN
42 Newman Chaplain .... John CROGHAN
24 Director Audiovisual Services .... Timothy J. HICKS
09 Director of Institutional Research .... Gordon J. HEWITT
27 Exec Director of Communications .... Michael J. DEBRAGGIO
28 Chief Diversity Officer .... Amit TANEJA
29 Director Alumni Relations .... Sharon T. RIPPEY
96 Director of Purchasing .... Irene K. CORNISH
40 Manager College Store .... Jennifer PHILLIPS

Hartwick College (F)

One Hartwick Drive, Oneonta NY 13820-1790
County: Otsego FICE Identification: 002729
Unit ID: 191533
Telephone: (607) 431-4000 Carnegie Class: Bac/A&S
FAX Number: (607) 431-4206 Calendar System: 4/1/4
URL: www.hartwick.edu
Established: 1797 Annual Undergrad Tuition & Fees: $38,930
Enrollment: 1,558 Coed
Affiliation or Control: Independent Non-Profit IRS Status: 501(c)3
Highest Offering: Baccalaureate
Program: Liberal Arts And General; Professional
Accreditation: M, ART, MUS, NURSE, TEAC

01 President .... Dr. Margaret L. DRUGOVICH
05 Executive Vice President & Provost .... Dr. Michael TANNENBAUM
10 Vice President Finance/CFO .... Mr. George J. ELSBECK
30 Vice Pres Institutional Advancement .... Mr. Jim BROSCHART
32 Vice President for Student Life .... Dr. Meg NOWAK
84 Vice Pres for Enrollment Management .... Mr. David CONWAY
04 Exec Assistant to the President .... Ms. Ashley MCCARTHY
15 Director Human Resources .... Ms. Suzanne JANITZ
39 Director Residence Life .... Mr. Zachary BROWN
06 Registrar .... Mr. Matthew SANFORD
20 Dean of Academic Affairs .... Dr. Kim NOLING
37 Director of Financial Aid .... Ms. Melissa ALLEN
08 Director of Libraries .... Mr. F. Paul COLEMAN
88 Coord Yager Museum of Art & Culture ... Ms. Donna ANDERSON
85 Director International Pgms .... Vacant
46 Exec Dir of Info Technology .... Mr. Davis B. CONLEY
13 Director Inst Info Systems Services .... Ms. Deb B. HILTS
91 Director Technologies Services .... Ms. Suzanne GAYNOR
18 Director of Facilities Services .... Mr. Joseph MACK
41 Director of Athletics .... Dr. Kimberly FIERKE
38 Director of Counseling Services .... Mr. Gary ROBINSON
23 Director of Student Health Center .... Ms. Elizabeth MORLEY
27 Exec Dir Marketing & Communications .... Ms. Susan SALTON
26 Director of Donor Relations .... Ms. Alicia FISH
07 Director Admissions .... Ms. Lisa STARKEY-WOODS
12 Director Pine Lake Campus .... Dr. Brian HAGENBUCH
21 Director Financial Svcs/Controller .... Ms. Karen ZUILL
09 Director of Institutional Research .... Ms. Minghui WANG
29 Director of Alumni Relations .... Mr. Duncan MACDONALD
19 Director of Security .... Mr. Thomas KELLY
40 Manager of Bookstore .... Mr. Frank WERDANN
96 Manager of Purchasing .... Ms. Marilyn NIENART
44 Major Gifts Officer .... Mr. Eric SHOEN

Hebrew Union College-Jewish Institute of Religion (G)

1 West 4th Street, New York NY 10012-1186
County: New York FICE Identification: 004054
Unit ID: 203067
Telephone: (212) 674-5300 Carnegie Class: Spec/Faith
FAX Number: (212) 388-1720 Calendar System: Semester
URL: www.huc.edu
Established: 1875 Annual Graduate Tuition & Fees: $23,000
Enrollment: 372 Coed
Affiliation or Control: Jewish IRS Status: 501(c)3
Highest Offering: Doctorate; No Undergraduates
Program: Professional; Religious Emphasis
Accreditation: M

01 President .... Rabbi David ELLENSON
30 Vice President Inst Advancement .... Dr. Jane KARLIN
10 Chief Financial Officer .... Ms. Sandra M. MILLS
05 Vice President for Academic Affairs .... Rabbi Michael MARMUR
101 Admin Exec to Board of Governors .... Ms. Sylvia POSNER
26 National Dir Public Affs/Inst Plng .... Ms. Jean B. ROSENSAFT
44 Natl Dir of Institutional Giving .... Dr. Andrew GRANT
08 Director of Libraries .... Dr. David GILNER
79 Director American Jewish Archives .... Dr. Gary ZOLA
09 Acting Coordinator IR/Assessment .... Mr. Bobby COVITZ
29 Director of Alumni Relations .... Ms. Joy WASSERMAN
06 National Registrar .... Mr. Clyde PARRISH
13 Director of Information Systems .... Mr. John H. BRUGGEMAN
106 Director of eLearning .... Mr. Gregg ALPERT
16 Director of Legal Affairs & HR .... Mr. Jeremy PERLIN
07 Director of Admissions .. Rabbi Rachel SABATH BEIT-HALACHMI
37 Director of Financial Aid .... Ms. Roseanne ACKERLEY

Helene Fuld College of Nursing (H)

24 East 120th Street, New York NY 10035
County: New York FICE Identification: 010153
Unit ID: 191597
Telephone: (212) 616-7200 Carnegie Class: Assoc/PrivNFP
FAX Number: (212) 427-2453 Calendar System: Quarter
URL: www.helenefuld.edu
Established: 1945 Annual Undergrad Tuition & Fees: $16,693
Enrollment: 356 Coed
Affiliation or Control: Independent Non-Profit IRS Status: 501(c)3
Highest Offering: Baccalaureate
Program: Occupational; 2-Year Principally Bachelor's Creditable
Accreditation: M, ADNUR

01 President .... Dr. Wendy ROBINSON
05 Vice President Academic Affairs .... Ms. Wendy ROBINSON
10 Head of Finance .... Mrs. Galina VILKINA

11 Director of Administration .... Ms. Celeste WALLIN
32 Director Student Services .... Mrs. Sandra SENIOR
08 Director of Learning Center .... Mr. Indrajeet SINGH CHAUHAN
35 Associate Director Student Services .... Ms. Gladys PINEDA
26 Director of External Affairs .... Ms. Michelle HERNANDEZ
30 Development Officer .... Ms. Barbara PAXON

Herkimer County Community College (A)

100 Reservoir Road, Herkimer NY 13350-1598
County: Herkimer FICE Identification: 004788
Unit ID: 191612
Telephone: (315) 866-0300 Carnegie Class: Assoc/Pub-R-M
FAX Number: (315) 866-7253 Calendar System: Semester
URL: www.herkimer.edu
Established: 1966 Annual Undergrad Tuition & Fees (In-District): $4,350
Enrollment: 3,465 Coed
Affiliation or Control: State/Local IRS Status: 501(c)3
Highest Offering: Associate Degree
Program: Occupational; 2-Year Principally Bachelor's Creditable
Accreditation: M, EMT, PTAA

01 President .... Dr. Ann Marie MURRAY
10 Vice Pres Administration & Finance .... Mr. Nicholas LAINO
05 Dean of Academic Affairs .... Mr. Michael ORIOLO
32 Dean of Students .... Dr. Matthew HAWES
20 Associate Dean Academic Affairs BH .... Mr. Henry TESTA
27 Director of Information Services .... Mrs. AnneMarie AMBROSE
84 Assoc Dean for Enrollment .... Mr. Robert PALMIERI
83 Assoc Dean Academic Affairs Soc Sci .... Dr. Robin VOETTERL
51 Assoc Dean of Continuing Education .... Mrs. Linda LAMB
15 Director of Human Resources .... Mr. James SALAMY
41 Director of Athletics .... Mr. Donald DUTCHER
08 Director of Library Services .... Mr. Andrew URBANEK
09 Director Institutional Research .... Ms. Marie MIKNAVICH
31 Director of Community Education .... Mr. William MCDONALD
18 Int Director Facilities Operations .... Mr. Bob WOUDENBERG
37 Director Student Financial Aid .... Mrs. Susan TRIPP
26 Director of Public Relations .... Ms. Rebecca RUFFING
06 Interim Registrar .... Mr. Eric VERNOLD
36 Career Services Counselor .... Mrs. Suzanne PADDOCK
36 Transfer Counselor .... Mrs. Katie SCHWABACH
40 Bookstore Manager .... Ms. Julie LEWIS
96 Purchasing Agent .... Mr. Robert NEARY

Hilbert College (B)

5200 S Park Avenue, Hamburg NY 14075-1597
County: Erie FICE Identification: 002735
Unit ID: 191621
Telephone: (716) 649-7900 Carnegie Class: Bac/Diverse
FAX Number: (716) 649-0702 Calendar System: Semester
URL: www.hilbert.edu
Established: 1957 Annual Undergrad Tuition & Fees: $19,440
Enrollment: 1,075 Coed
Affiliation or Control: Independent Non-Profit IRS Status: 501(c)3
Highest Offering: Master's
Program: Liberal Arts And General; Professional
Accreditation: M

01 President .... Dr. Cynthia A. ZANE
05 Provost/Vice Pres Academic Affairs . Dr. Christopher L. HOLOMAN
30 Vice Pres Institutional Advancement .... Mr. Gregg FORT
10 Vice President Business/ Finance .... Mr. Richard J. PINKOWSKI, JR.
27 Vice President Information Services .... Mr. Michael MURRIN
84 VP Enrollment Mgmt/Dean of Students .... Mr. Peter S. BURNS
32 Vice Prov Leadership Development .... Mr. James P. STURM
49 Chair Arts & Sciences .... Dr. Amy E. SMITH
26 Director Public Relations .... Ms. Paula WITHERELL
92 Director Honors Program .... Dr. Amy E. SMITH
39 Dir Residence Life/Judicial Affairs .... Mr. Jason LANKER
41 Athletic Director .... Vacant
19 Director Security/Safety .... Mr. Matthew SCHAMANN
30 Director of Development .... Mr. Craig HARRIS
42 Dir Mission Intgrtn/Campus Ministry .... Ms. Barbara BONANNO
08 Director of McGrath Library .... Mr. Wilson PROUT
07 Director of Admissions .... Mr. Justin ROGERS
36 Director Placement/Career Services .... Ms. Denise HARRIS
37 Director Financial Aid .... Ms. Beverly CHUDY-SZCZUR
06 Director of Student Records .... Ms. Caprice ARABIA
38 Director Student Counseling .... Ms. Phyllis K. DEWEY
09 Director of Institutional Research .... Dr. Ron ESKEW
15 Director of Human Resources .... Ms. Maura FLYNN
28 Director of Multicultural Affairs . Ms. Tara JABBAAR-GYAMBRAH
35 Director of Student Activities .... Ms. Jean MACDONALD
96 Director of Purchasing .... Mr. Gary DILLSWORTH
21 Associate Business Officer .... Mr. Anthony WIERTEL
18 Chief Facilities/Physical Plant .... Mr. Gary DILLSWORTH

Hobart and William Smith Colleges (C)

300 Pulteney Street, Geneva NY 14456-3397
County: Ontario FICE Identification: 002731
Unit ID: 191630
Telephone: (315) 781-3000 Carnegie Class: Bac/A&S
FAX Number: (315) 781-3654 Calendar System: Semester
URL: www.hws.edu
Established: 1822 Annual Undergrad Tuition & Fees: $46,165
Enrollment: 2,216 Coordinate
Affiliation or Control: Independent Non-Profit IRS Status: 501(c)3
Highest Offering: Master's
Program: Liberal Arts And General; Teacher Preparatory; Fine Arts Emphasis
Accreditation: M, @TEAC

01 President .... Mr. Mark D. GEARAN
05 Provost and Dean of Faculty .... Dr. Titilayo UFOMATA
84 VP for Enrollment/Dean of Admission .... Mr. Robert MURPHY
32 Vice President for Student Affairs .... Mr. Robert FLOWERS
30 Vice President for Advancement .... Mr. Robert O'CONNOR
10 Vice President for Finance .... Mr. Peter POLINAK
27 VP for Strategic Initiatives/CIO .... Mr. Fred DAMIANO
16 Vice President for Human Resources .... Ms. Sandra BISSELL
26 Vice President for Communicatons .... Ms. Cathy WILLIAMS
33 Dean of Hobart College .... Dr. Eugen BAER
34 Dean of William Smith College .... Dr. Susanne MCNALLY
42 Chaplain .... Rev. Lesley ADAMS
04 Exec Assistant to the President .... Ms. Valerie VISTOCCO
100 Asst to the Pres/Chief of Staff .... Mr. Michael HOEPP
88 Associate Dean 1st Yr Seminars .... Dr. Eric KLAUS
20 Associate Dean of Faculty .... Dr. Dwayne LUCAS
20 Associate Provost .... Dr. Christine DE DENUS
35 Assistant VP for Student Affairs .... Dr. Montrose STREETER
35 Assistant VP for Student Affairs .... Mr. Jeffrey VANLONE
07 Director of Admissions .... Mr. John YOUNG
41 Director of Hobart Athletics .... Mr. Michael HANNA
41 Director of William Smith Athletics .... Ms. Deborah STEWARD
08 Director of the Library .... Mr. Vincent BOISSELLE
06 Registrar .... Mr. Peter SARRATORI
21 Controller .... Mr. Michael PAPARO
39 Director of Residential Education .... Ms. Stacey PIERCE
104 Associate Dean Global Education .... Dr. Thomas D'AGOSTINO
09 Assoc Dean Inst Research/Retent .... Mr. Don EMMONS
19 Director of Campus Safety .... Mr. Martin CORBETT
24 Director of Digital Learning .... Mr. Jeffrey WETHERILL
38 Dir Counseling Ctr/Student Wellness .... Ms. Shelly LEAR
85 Director of International Students .... Mr. David GAGE
37 Director of Financial Aid .... Ms. Beth TURNER
36 Director Center for Career Services .... Ms. Brandi FERRARA
25 Director of Grants .... Ms. Martha BOND
29 Assistant VP for Alumni Relations .... Mr. Jared WEEDEN
29 Assistant VP for Alumnae Relations .... Ms. Kathleen REGAN
40 Director of the College Store .... Ms. Lucille SMART
15 Associate Director Human Resources .... Ms. Peggy FERRAN
44 Associate VP for Advancement .... Ms. Leila RICE
23 Coordinator Health Services/NP .... Ms. Betti GREEN
108 Assoc Dean Teach Learn & Assessmen .... Dr. Susan PLINER
88 Director Academic Opportunity Pgm .... Mr. James BURRUTO
31 Dir Community Engagement .... Ms. Kathleen FLOWERS
88 Director Operations & Tech Services .... Ms. Kelly Anne MCLAUGHLIN
88 Director of Digital Learning .... Mr. Jeffrey WETHERILL
14 Dir Network/Systems Infrastructure .... Mr. Derek LUSTIG
88 Director of Intercultural Affairs .... Ms. Alejandra MOLINA

Hofstra University (D)

Hempstead NY 11549-1000
County: Nassau FICE Identification: 002732
Unit ID: 191649
Telephone: (516) 463-6600 Carnegie Class: DRU
FAX Number: (516) 463-4848 Calendar System: Semester
URL: www.hofstra.edu
Established: 1935 Annual Undergrad Tuition & Fees: $37,400
Enrollment: 11,023 Coed
Affiliation or Control: Independent Non-Profit IRS Status: 501(c)3
Highest Offering: Doctorate
Program: Liberal Arts And General; Teacher Preparatory; Professional
Accreditation: M, ARCPA, AUD, BUS, BUSA, CLPSY, CORE, ENG, JOUR, LAW, #MED, SCPSY, SP, TEAC

01 President .... Mr. Stuart RABINOWITZ
05 Provost/Sr VP for Academic Affairs .... Dr. Herman A. BERLINER
45 Sr VP for Planning and Admin .... Ms. M. Patricia ADAMSKI
10 VP Financial Affairs/Treasurer .... Ms. Catherine HENNESSY
32 Vice President for Student Affairs .... Ms. Sandra JOHNSON
30 Vice President for Development .... Mr. Alan J. KELLY
26 Vice President University Relations ..... Ms. Melissa A. CONNOLLY
43 VP Legal Affairs & General Counsel .... Ms. Dolores FREDRICH
13 Vice Pres Information Technology ..... Mr. Robert W. JUCKIEWICZ
18 VP for Facilities and Operations .... Mr. Joseph BARKWILL
84 Vice Pres Enrollment Management .... Ms. Jessica L. EADS
86 Vice President Business Dev Ctr .... Mr. Richard V. GUARDINO
91 Asst VP for Information Technology ... Ms. Linda J. HANTZSCHEL
09 VP Inst Research/Admin Assess .... Ms. Stephanie BUSHEY
20 Vice Provost for Academic Affairs .... Dr. Liora P. SCHMELKIN
21 Assoc Provost Budget & Planning .... Mr. Richard M. APOLLO
25 Assoc Provost Rsrch/Sponsored Pgms ..... Ms. Sofia KAKOULIDIS
07 Dean Admissions & Financial Aid .... Ms. Jessica L. EADS
50 Dean Frank G Zarb Sch of Business .... Dr. Patrick J. SOCCI
54 Dean School of Engineering .... Dr. Simon S. BEN-AVI
60 Dean School of Communication .... Dr. Evan W. CORNOG
53 Interim Dean School of Education .... Dr. Sean A. FANELLI
49 Dean College Liberal Arts/Science .... Dr. Bernard J. FIRESTONE
08 Acting Dean Library & Info Services .... Dr. Bernard J. FIRESTONE
88 Dean for University Advisement .... Ms. Anne M. MONGILLO
07 Dean Graduate Admissions .... Ms. Carol J. DRUMMER
61 Dean of Maurice Deane School of Law .... Mr. Eric LANE
63 Dean Medical School .... Dr. Lawrence SMITH
76 Actg Dean School of Health Sciences .... Dr. Ronald L. BLOOM
35 Dean of Students .... Mr. Peter LIBMAN
84 Asst Dean Law Sch Enrollment Mgmt .... Mr. John CHALMERS
29 Senior Director Alumni Affairs .... Mr. Robert SALTZMAN
39 Assoc Director Residential Programs .... Ms. Novia P. WHYTE
38 Dir Student Counseling Services .... Dr. John C. GUTHMAN
22 Equal Rights/Opportunity Ofcr .... Ms. Jennifer MONE
23 Director Health & Wellness Center .... Ms. Maureen B. HOUCK
41 Director Intercollegiate Athletics .... Mr. Jeffrey HATHAWAY
15 Director of Human Resources .... Ms. Evelyn V. MILLER-SUBER
90 Director Faculty Computing Services .... Ms. Judith L. TABRON
40 Manager Bookstore .... Mr. Steven BABBITT
19 Director Public Safety .... Ms. Karen O'CALLAGHAN
96 Director of Purchasing .... Mr. Richard FRANCOS
92 Dean Honors College .... Dr. Warren FRISINA
06 Registrar .... Ms. Lynne DOUGHERTY
04 Admin Assistant to the President .... Ms. Isabel D. FREY
37 Director Student Financial Aid .... Ms. Sandra FILBRY

Holy Trinity Orthodox Seminary (E)

PO Box 36, Jordanville NY 13361-0036
County: Herkimer FICE Identification: 002733
Unit ID: 191658
Telephone: (315) 858-0945 Carnegie Class: Not Classified
FAX Number: (315) 858-0945 Calendar System: Semester
URL: www.hts.edu
Established: 1948 Annual Undergrad Tuition & Fees: $3,000
Enrollment: 30 Male
Affiliation or Control: Russian Orthodox IRS Status: 501(c)3
Highest Offering: Baccalaureate
Program: Professional; Religious Emphasis
Accreditation: NY

01 Rector and Dean .... V.Rev. Luke MURIANKA
06 Registrar .... Rev. Theophylact CLAPPER-DEWELL
32 Dean of Students .... Rev. Cyprian ALEXANDROU
04 Administrative Assistant .... RevDcn. Ephraim WILLMARTH

Houghton College (F)

One Willard Avenue, Houghton NY 14744-0128
County: Allegany FICE Identification: 002734
Unit ID: 191676
Telephone: (585) 567-9200 Carnegie Class: Bac/A&S
FAX Number: (585) 567-9572 Calendar System: Semester
URL: www.houghton.edu
Established: 1883 Annual Undergrad Tuition & Fees: $27,728
Enrollment: 1,165 Coed
Affiliation or Control: Wesleyan Church IRS Status: 501(c)3
Highest Offering: Master's
Program: Liberal Arts And General; Teacher Preparatory
Accreditation: M, MUS, TEAC

01 President .... Dr. Shirley A. MULLEN
05 Vice President for Academic Affairs .. Dr. Linda MILLS WOOLSEY
32 Vice President for Student Life .... Mr. Robert POOL
10 Vice President for Finance and Plng .... Mr. David SMITH
30 Vice President for Advancement .... Mr. Rick MELSON
07 Vice President for Enrollment .... Mr. Eric CURRIE
06 Registrar .... Ms. Margery L. AVERY
37 Director of Financial Aid .... Ms. Marianne LOPER
08 Director of the Library .... Mr. David STEVICK
29 Executive Director Alumni Relations .... Mr. Daniel NOYES
09 Assoc Dean Institutional Research .... Dr. John WISE
20 Associate Academic Dean .... Dr. Mark HIJLEH
36 Coordinator of Career Services .... Mr. Brian REITNOUR
15 Director of Human Resources .... Mr. Dale F. WRIGHT
26 Dir Marketing & Communications .... Mr. Jeff BABBITT
14 Director of Technology .... Mr. Donald HAINGRAY
18 Director of Facilities .... Mr. Chad PLYMALE
19 Chief Security Officer .... Mr. Ray M. PARLETT
23 Director of Health Services .... Dr. David BRUBAKER
41 Executive Director of Athletics .... Mr. Harold W. LORD
21 Controller .... Mr. David M. MERCER
39 Director Residence Life .... Vacant
38 Director Student Counseling .... Dr. Michael D. LASTORIA
92 Director of Honors Program .... Dr. Benjamin LIPSCOMB
31 Director Community Relations .... Mrs. Phyllis E. GAERTE
35 Dean of Students .... Mr. Dennis STACK

Hudson Valley Community College (G)

80 Vandenburgh Avenue, Troy NY 12180-6096
County: Rensselaer FICE Identification: 002868
Unit ID: 191719
Telephone: (518) 629-4822 Carnegie Class: Assoc/Pub-U-SC
FAX Number: (518) 629-4576 Calendar System: Semester
URL: www.hvcc.edu
Established: 1953 Annual Undergrad Tuition & Fees (In-District): $4,734
Enrollment: 13,230 Coed
Affiliation or Control: State/Local IRS Status: 501(c)3
Highest Offering: Associate Degree
Program: Occupational; 2-Year Principally Bachelor's Creditable
Accreditation: M, ADNUR, COARC, DH, DMS, EMT, ENGT, FUSER, POLYT

01 President .... Dr. Andrew J. MATONAK
04 Exec Assistant to the President .... Dr. Michael S. GREEN
04 Assistant to the President .... Ms. Suzanne K. KALKBRENNER
11 Int Vice Pres for Administration .... Mr. James J. LAGATTA
05 Vice President for Academic Affairs .... Dr. Carolyn G. CURTIS
32 VP Enrol Mgmt/Stdnt Development .... Dr. Alexander J. POPOVICS
10 Vice President for Finance .... Mr. Joel R. FATATO
49 Dean Sch Liberal Arts/Health Sci .... Dr. Margaret M. GEEHAN
72 Dean Engr/Indus Tech/Business .... Mr. P. Phillip WHITE

51	Assoc Dean Cmty/Professional Pgms	Ms. Christine A. HELWIG
08	Director of Learning Resources Ctr	Mr. David CLICKNER
07	Director of Admissions	Ms. Mary Claire BAUER
06	Registrar	Ms. Kathleen PETLEY
14	Chief Information Officer	Dr. Steve CHEN
18	Director Physical Plant	Ms. Karen SEWARD
38	Director Student Development	Dr. Kathleen SWEENER
37	Director of Financial Aid	Ms. Lisa VAN WIE
36	Dir Center For Careers/Employment	Ms. Gayle HEALY
15	Director of Human Resources	Mr. John TIBBETTS
19	Director of Public Safety	Mr. Fred ALIBERTI
23	Coordinator Health Services	Ms. Claudine POTVIN-GIORDANO
88	Director of Disability Resources	Mr. Pablo E. NEGRON
09	Director Planning & Research	Mr. James F. MACKLIN
35	Director of Student Life	Mr. Louis COPLIN
85	International Student Advisor	Mr. Jay DEITCHMAN
40	Director of Bookstore	Mr. Stephen J. STEGMAN
41	Director of Athletics	Ms. Kristan M. PELLETIER
72	Assistant to VP of Academics	Dr. Sondra E. VALLE
88	Asoc Dean Instruct Spprt Svcs/Reten	Ms. Karen FERRER-MUNIZ
50	Director of Business Services	Ms. Mary Ellen LAJEUNESSE
21	Comptroller	Ms. Debra D. STORY
26	Exec Dir Communications/Marketing	Mr. Dennis KENNEDY
102	Exec Director Foundation	Ms. Rachel KIMMELBLATT

Icahn School of Medicine at Mount Sinai (A)

One Gustave L. Levy Place, New York NY 10029-6500
County: New York FICE Identification: 007026
Unit ID: 193405
Telephone: (212) 241-6500 Carnegie Class: Spec/Med
FAX Number: (212) 241-7146 Calendar System: Other
URL: www.icahn.mssm.edu
Established: 1968 Annual Graduate Tuition & Fees: $44,608
Enrollment: 1,064 Coed
Affiliation or Control: Independent Non-Profit IRS Status: 501(c)3
Highest Offering: Doctorate; No Undergraduates
Program: Professional
Accreditation: M, DENT, IPSY, MED, PH

01	President & CEO	Dr. Kenneth L. DAVIS
03	Exec Vice Pres/Dean Sch of Medicine	Dr. Dennis S. CHARNEY
05	Dean for Medical Education	Dr. David MULLER
11	Dean for Operations	Mr. Jeffrey SILBURSTEIN

Institute of Design and Construction (B)

141 Willoughby Street, Brooklyn NY 11201-5317
County: Kings FICE Identification: 012107
Unit ID: 191764
Telephone: (718) 855-3661 Carnegie Class: Assoc/PrivNFP
FAX Number: (718) 852-5889 Calendar System: Semester
URL: www.idc.edu
Established: 1947 Annual Undergrad Tuition & Fees: $8,775
Enrollment: 127 Coed
Affiliation or Control: Independent Non-Profit IRS Status: 501(c)3
Highest Offering: Associate Degree
Program: 2-Year Principally Bachelor's Creditable; Technical Emphasis
Accreditation: NY

01	Executive Director	Mr. Vincent C. BATTISTA
11	Administrator	Ms. Ruth DAVIS
18	Chairman Building Construction	Vacant
07	Director of Admissions	Vacant
27	Dir Communications/Inst Development	Ms. Elizabeth BATTISTA
08	Head Librarian	Mrs. Eleanor J. BROWN
37	Asst Director Financial Aid	Mr. Giovanny SANTANA

Iona College (C)

715 North Avenue, New Rochelle NY 10801-1890
County: Westchester FICE Identification: 002737
Unit ID: 191931
Telephone: (914) 633-2000 Carnegie Class: Master's L
FAX Number: (914) 633-2642 Calendar System: Semester
URL: www.iona.edu
Established: 1940 Annual Undergrad Tuition & Fees: $32,770
Enrollment: 4,241 Coed
Affiliation or Control: Independent Non-Profit IRS Status: 501(c)3
Highest Offering: Master's
Program: Liberal Arts And General; Teacher Preparatory; Professional
Accreditation: M, BUS, CS, JOUR, MFCD, SW, TED

01	President	Dr. Joseph E. NYRE
05	Provost/Sr VP Academic Affairs	Dr. Brian J. NICKERSON
10	Sr Vice President Finance & Admin	Vacant
30	Sr VP Advance/External Affairs	Mr. Paul J. SUTERA
100	Sr Policy Advisor/Chief of Staff	Ms. MaryEllen CALLAGHAN
84	VP Enrollment Management	Ms. Mary Beth CAREY
13	Vice Provost Info Technology/CIO	Ms. Joanne STEELE
32	Vice Provost Student Development	Mr. Charles CARLSON
37	Asst VP Student Financial Services	Ms. Eileen DOYLE
91	Asst Vice Provost for Info Tech	Mr. Dimitris HALARIS
20	Assistant VP Academic Affairs	Dr. Tresmaine GRIMES
29	Asst VP Advancement & Spec Projects	Ms. Nancy PATOTA
35	Asst Vice Provost Student Develop	Ms. Elizabeth OLIVIERI-LENAHAN
49	Dean School Arts & Sciences	Dr. Sibdas GHOSH
50	Dean Hagan School of Business	Dr. Vincent CALLUZZO
04	Sr Policy Advisor & Board Secretary	Sr. Patricia MCGINLEY
18	Director of Facilities Management	Mr. Mark MURPHY
39	Director Residential Life	Vacant
15	Director of Human Resources	Ms. Kathleen CLARKE
38	Director of Counseling Center	Dr. Ingrid GRIEGER
36	Director of Career Development	Ms. F. Phyllis BLAKE
08	Director of Libraries	Mr. Richard PALLADINO
42	Director of Campus Ministries	Mr. Carl PROCARIO-FOLEY
06	Registrar	Ms. Nancy MILLS
41	Director of Athletics	Mr. Richard COLE, JR.
86	Director of Govt Relations/Grants	Mr. Daniel KONOPKA
12	Director of Rockland Campus	Sr. Patricia MCGINLEY
09	Dir of Inst Effectiveness/Planning	Dr. Joseph WYCOFF
21	Director of Business Services	Ms. Joan CLARK
26	Director of Public Relations	Ms. Dawn INSANALLI
19	Dir Campus Safety and Security	Mr. Dominic LOCATELLI
23	Director of Health Services	Ms. Jacqueline AGNELLO-VAZQUEZ
44	Director of Annual Giving	Ms. Kara BRENNAN
96	Purchasing Coordinator	Ms. Kimberly MONTEMURRO
92	Director of Honors Program	Dr. James STILLWAGGON

Island Drafting and Technical Institute (D)

128 Broadway, Amityville NY 11701-2704
County: Suffolk FICE Identification: 007375
Unit ID: 191959
Telephone: (631) 691-8733 Carnegie Class: Assoc/PrivFP
FAX Number: (631) 691-8738 Calendar System: Semester
URL: www.idti.edu
Established: 1957 Annual Undergrad Tuition & Fees: $15,200
Enrollment: 128 Coed
Affiliation or Control: Proprietary IRS Status: Proprietary
Highest Offering: Associate Degree
Program: Occupational
Accreditation: ACCSC

01	President	Mr. James G. DILIBERTO
03	Vice President	Mr. John G. DILIBERTO

Ithaca College (E)

953 Danby Road, Ithaca NY 14850-7001
County: Tompkins FICE Identification: 002739
Unit ID: 191968
Telephone: (607) 274-3011 Carnegie Class: Master's L
FAX Number: N/A Calendar System: Semester
URL: www.ithaca.edu
Established: 1892 Annual Undergrad Tuition & Fees: $37,000
Enrollment: 6,759 Coed
Affiliation or Control: Independent Non-Profit IRS Status: 501(c)3
Highest Offering: Doctorate
Program: Liberal Arts And General; Teacher Preparatory; Professional
Accreditation: M, BUS, MUS, NRPA, OT, PTA, SP, THEA

01	President	Dr. Thomas R. ROCHON
04	Exec Assistant to President	Ms. Diane VERONEAU
05	Provost/Vice Pres Education Affairs	Ms. Marisa KELLY
10	VP of Finance & Administration	Mr. Gerald HECTOR
43	Vice President & General Counsel	Ms. Nancy E. PRINGLE
84	VP Enrollment Management	Mr. Eric MAGUIRE
30	Vice Pres Institutional Advancement	Mr. Christopher BIEHN
20	Asst Prov/Dean Interdis/Intl Stds	Dr. Tanya R. SAUNDERS
26	Associate Vice President	Ms. Rachel REUBEN
13	Assoc VP for Info Tech Svcs	Mr. Edwin W. FULLER
15	Assoc VP for Human Resources	Mr. Mark COLDREN
18	Assoc VP for Facilities Management	Mr. Richard COUTURE
35	Sr Assoc Vice Pres Student Affairs	Dr. Roger RICHARDSON
35	Assoc Vice Pres Student Affairs	Mr. Rory ROTHMAN
20	Associate Provost	Ms. Carol HENDERSON
20	Associate Provost	Mr. David GARCIA
58	Asst Provost Extended Studies	Mr. Rob GEARHART
88	Assistant Vice President	Mr. Anthony HOPSON
49	Dean School Humanities/Science	Dr. Leslie LEWIS
64	Dean of School of Music	Dr. Karl PAULNACK
76	Dean Sch Health Sciences/Human Perf	Ms. Linda PETROSINO
50	Dean School of Business	Ms. Mary Ellen ZUCKERMAN
60	Dean School of Communications	Ms. Diane GAYESKI
29	Director Alumni Relations	Ms. Gretchen VAN VALEN
44	Executive Director of Development	Ms. Kate LARRABEE
06	Registrar	Mr. Brian SCHOLTEN
22	Asst Counsel & Dir EO Compliance	Ms. Traevena BYRD
09	Director Institutional Research	Ms. Martha D. GRAY
07	Director of Admission	Mr. Gerard TURBIDE
12	Director London Center	Mr. William SHEASGREEN
36	Director Career Services	Mr. John P. BRADAC
38	Director for Counseling Svcs	Dr. Deborah HARPER
37	Dir of Student Financial Services	Mrs. Lisa HOSKEY
23	Director Health Center	Dr. Justine SCHAFF
39	Dir Res Life/Judicial Affairs	Ms. Bonnie S. PRUNTY
08	College Librarian	Ms. Lisabeth CHABOT
41	Dir Intercol Athletics/Rec Sports	Ms. Sally BASSETT
21	Director of Budget	Ms. Sally DIETZ
90	Dir Technology/Inst Support Svcs	Mr. Michael E. TAVES
91	Director Information Systems/Svcs	Mr. Michael E. TAVES
19	Director Public Safety	Ms. Terri STEWART
27	Assoc Dir for Campus Communication	Mr. David C. MALEY
40	Manager of College Stores	Mr. Rick WATSON
42	Coordinator of Chaplains	Fr. Carsten P. MARTENSEN
88	Director of First Year Experience	Mr. Erica SHOCKLEY
28	Director of Mulitcultural Affairs	Ms. Malinda SMITH
85	Dir International Student Services	Ms. Diana DIMITROVA
104	Director of Study Abroad	Ms. Rachel CULLENEN
88	Dir Center for Faculty Excellence	Mr. Wade PICKREN

ITT Technical Institute (F)

13 Airline Drive, Albany NY 12205-1003
Telephone: (518) 452-9300 Identification: 666138
Accreditation: ACICS

† Main campus is ITT Technical Institute in Indianapolis, IN.

ITT Technical Institute (G)

2295 Millersport Hwy, PO Box 327, Getzville NY 14068-1219
Telephone: (716) 689-2200 Identification: 666609
Accreditation: ACICS

† Main campus is ITT Technical Institute in Indianapolis, IN.

ITT Technical Institute (H)

235 Greenfield Parkway, Liverpool NY 13088-6653
Telephone: (315) 461-8000 Identification: 666137
Accreditation: ACICS

† Main campus is ITT Technical Institute in Indianapolis, IN.

Jamestown Business College (I)

7 Fairmount Avenue, Box 429, Jamestown NY 14702-0429
County: Chautauqua FICE Identification: 008495
Unit ID: 192004
Telephone: (716) 664-5100 Carnegie Class: Assoc/PrivFP4
FAX Number: (716) 664-3144 Calendar System: Quarter
URL: www.jamestownbusinesscollege.edu
Established: 1886 Annual Undergrad Tuition & Fees: $11,700
Enrollment: 294 Coed
Affiliation or Control: Proprietary IRS Status: Proprietary
Highest Offering: Baccalaureate
Program: Occupational; 2-Year Principally Bachelor's Creditable
Accreditation: M

01	President	Mr. David CONKLIN
05	Dean	Ms. Gretchen LINDELL
32	Vice Pres/Dean of Student Affairs	Ms. Rosanne JOHANSON
07	Director Admissions	Ms. Brenda SALEMME
37	Director of Financial Aid	Mrs. Diane STURZENBECKER
26	Director of Communications	Ms. Jessica GOLLEY

Jamestown Community College (J)

525 Falconer Street, Jamestown NY 14701
County: Chautauqua FICE Identification: 002869
Unit ID: 191986
Telephone: (716) 338-1000 Carnegie Class: Assoc/Pub-R-M
FAX Number: (716) 338-1466 Calendar System: Semester
URL: www.sunyjcc.edu
Established: 1950 Annual Undergrad Tuition & Fees (In-District): $4,725
Enrollment: 5,057 Coed
Affiliation or Control: State/Local IRS Status: 501(c)3
Highest Offering: Associate Degree
Program: 2-Year Principally Bachelor's Creditable
Accreditation: M, ADNUR, OTA

01	President	Dr. Cory L. DUCKWORTH
05	VP/Dean of Academic Affairs	Dr. Marilyn A. ZAGORA
32	VP/Dean of Student Development	Dr. Eileen J. GOODLING
12	VP/Dean Catt County Campus	Mr. Jean J. SAYEGH
11	VP/Dean of Administration	Mr. John R. GARFOOT
06	Registrar	Mr. Kreig ELICKER
07	Director Admission	Ms. Wendy PRESENT
26	Executive Director of Marketing	Mr. Nelson J. GARIFI
08	Library Director	Ms. Linda LARKIN
36	Placement Coordinator	Mr. Ronald A. TURAK
37	Director of Financial Aid	Ms. Laurie A. VORP
15	Director Human Resources	Ms. Susan BRONSTEIN
09	Director Institutional Research	Ms. Barbara RUSSELL
41	Athletic Director	Mr. Keith MARTIN
43	Legal Counsel	Mr. Stephen ABDELLA
18	Director Facilities/Physical Plant	Mr. David JOHNSON

Jamestown Community College Cattaraugus County Campus (K)

260 North Union Street, PO Box 5901, Olean NY 14760-5901
Telephone: (716) 376-7500 Identification: 770138
Accreditation: &M

† Main campus is Jamestown Community College in Jamestown, NY.

Jefferson Community College (L)

1220 Coffeen Street, Watertown NY 13601-1897
County: Jefferson FICE Identification: 002870
Unit ID: 192022
Telephone: (315) 786-2200 Carnegie Class: Assoc/Pub-R-M
FAX Number: (315) 786-0158 Calendar System: Semester
URL: www.sunyjefferson.edu
Established: 1961 Annual Undergrad Tuition & Fees (In-District): $4,397
Enrollment: 3,841 Coed
Affiliation or Control: State/Local IRS Status: 501(c)3

Highest Offering: Associate Degree
Program: Occupational; 2-Year Principally Bachelor's Creditable
Accreditation: M, ADNUR

01 President ... Dr. Carole A. MCCOY
05 Vice President Academic Affairs ... Mr. Thomas FINCH
10 Vice President Admin/Finance ... Mr. Daniel DUPEE
32 Vice President of Students ... Ms. Betsy S. PENROSE
20 Dean Curriculum/Instruction ... Ms. Jerilyn FAIRMAN
51 Dean for Continuing Education ... Ms. Jill PIPPIN
04 Assistant to the President ... Ms. Karen A. CARR
08 Library Director ... Ms. Connie HOLBERG
07 Director of Admissions ... Ms. Roseanne N. WEIR
37 Director Financial Aid ... Mr. James AMBROSE
06 Registrar ... Ms. Natalie M. SPOONER
88 Director Small Business Center ... Mr. Eric F. CONSTANCE
09 Director of Institutional Research ... Ms. Mary A. PERRINE
18 Chief Facilities/Physical Plant ... Mr. Bruce ALEXANDER
29 Director Alumni Relations ... Ms. Mary KINNE
35 Director Student Devel/Activities ... Mr. Frank DOLDO
36 Director Student Placement ... Ms. Michele D. GEFELL
38 Director Student Counseling ... Mr. Matthew LAMBERT
26 Chief Public Relations Officer ... Ms. Karen J. FREEMAN
15 Exec Dir Finance/Human Resources ... Ms. Kerry A. YOUNG
30 College Development Officer ... Vacant
31 Coordinator Community Services ... Ms. Andrea PEDRICK

Jewish Theological Seminary of America (A)

3080 Broadway, New York NY 10027-4649
County: New York FICE Identification: 002740
Unit ID: 192040
Telephone: (212) 678-8023 Carnegie Class: Spec/Faith
FAX Number: (212) 678-8947 Calendar System: Semester
URL: www.jtsa.edu
Established: 1886 Annual Undergrad Tuition & Fees: $18,460
Enrollment: 457 Coed
Affiliation or Control: Independent Non-Profit IRS Status: 501(c)3
Highest Offering: Doctorate
Program: Liberal Arts And General; Teacher Preparatory; Professional; Religious Emphasis
Accreditation: M

01 Chancellor ... Dr. Arnold M. EISEN
03 Exec VC/Chief Operating Officer ... Mr. Marc GARY
30 Vice Chanc/Chief Development Office ... Ms. Marilyn F. KOHN
05 Provost ... Dr. Alan COOPER
10 Chief Financial Officer ... Mr. Fred SCHNUR
43 Counsel ... Mr. Martin OPPENHEIMER
49 Dean List College Jewish Studies ... Dr. Shuly SCHWARTZ
53 Dean Davidson School of Education ... Dr. Alex SINCLAIR
58 Dean The Graduate School ... Dr. Shuly SCHWARTZ
64 Director Miller Cantorial School ... Cantor Nancy ABRAMSON
73 Dean of Religious Leadership ... Rabbi Daniel NEVINS
32 Dean of Student Life ... Ms. Sara HOROWITZ
08 Librarian ... Dr. David KRAEMER
15 Director of Human Resources ... Ms. Diana TORRES-PETRILLI
18 Director of Operations ... Mr. James ESPOSITO
13 Director Information Technology ... Mr. Hal POLLENZ
27 Chief Communications Officer ... Ms. Elise DOWELL
06 Registrar/Director Financial Aid ... Ms. Linda LEVINE
39 Director of Residence Life ... Mr. Bradley MOOT
84 Director of Enrollment Management ... Ms. Melissa PRESENT
35 Director of Student Life ... Ms. Ruth DECALO
38 Director Student Counseling ... Dr. David DAVAR
29 Director of Alumni Affairs ... Mrs. Melissa FRIEDMAN
20 Associate Provost ... Dr. Stephen GARFINKEL
26 Chief Communications Officer ... Ms. Elise DOWELL
37 Director of Financial Aid ... Ms. Linda LEVINE
88 Director of Community Engagement ... Rabbi Julia ANDELMAN

The Juilliard School (B)

60 Lincoln Center Plaza, New York NY 10023-6588
County: New York FICE Identification: 002742
Unit ID: 192110
Telephone: (212) 799-5000 Carnegie Class: Spec/Arts
FAX Number: (212) 724-0263 Calendar System: Semester
URL: www.juilliard.edu
Established: 1905 Annual Undergrad Tuition & Fees: $36,720
Enrollment: 853 Coed
Affiliation or Control: Independent Non-Profit IRS Status: 501(c)3
Highest Offering: Doctorate
Program: Professional
Accreditation: M

01 President ... Dr. Joseph W. POLISI
05 Provost & Dean ... Mr. Ara GUZELIMIAN
10 Vice Pres/Chief Operating Officer ... Mr. Jon ROSENHEIN
30 Vice Pres for Dev/Public Affairs ... Ms. Elizabeth HURLEY
20 Vice Pres/Dean Academic Affairs ... Ms. Karen WAGNER
08 VP for Library/Info Resources ... Ms. Jane GOTTLIEB
18 Vice Pres for Facilities Management ... Mr. Joseph MASTRANGELO
21 Vice Pres for Finance & Controller ... Ms. Christine TODD
84 Vice Pres for Enrollment Management ... Ms. Joan D. WARREN
88 Vice Pres for Global Initiatives ... Mr. Christopher MOSSEY
27 Associate VP for Communications ... Ms. Janet KESSIN
88 Assoc VP for Special Projects ... Ms. Tricia ROSS
07 Associate Dean for Admissions ... Ms. Lee CIOPPA
11 Assoc Dean for Administration ... Mr. Adam MEYER
64 Asst Dean/Dir of Chamber Music ... Ms. Barli NUGENT
32 Asst Dean for Student Affairs ... Ms. Sabrina TANBARA
57 Director Richard Rodgers Drama Div ... Mr. James HOUGHTON
57 Artistic Director of Dance Division ... Mr. Lawrence RHODES
88 Artistic Director of Vocal Arts ... Mr. Brian ZEGER
88 Artist in Residence/Artistic Advise ... Ms. Monica HUGGETT
88 Director of Historical Performance ... Mr. Robert MEALY
88 Artistic Dir Pre-College Division ... Ms. Yoheved KAPLINSKY
06 Registrar ... Ms. Katherine GERTSON
16 Director of Human Resources ... Ms. Caryn G. DOKTOR
38 Director of Counseling Services ... Mr. William BUSE
37 Director Student Financial Aid ... Ms. Tina GONZALEZ
88 Artistic Director of Jazz Studies ... Mr. Carl ALLEN
96 Director of Office Services ... Mr. Scott A. HOLDEN
36 Director Career Services ... Ms. Courtney BURTON
13 Director Information Technology ... Mr. Tunde GIWA

Kehilath Yakov Rabbinical Seminary (C)

638 Bedford Avenue, Brooklyn NY 11211-8007
County: Kings FICE Identification: 010549
Unit ID: 192165
Telephone: (718) 963-1212 Carnegie Class: Spec/Faith
FAX Number: (718) 387-8586 Calendar System: Semester
Established: 1948 Annual Undergrad Tuition & Fees: $8,600
Enrollment: 112 Male
Affiliation or Control: Independent Non-Profit IRS Status: 501(c)3
Highest Offering: First Talmudic Degree
Program: Teacher Preparatory; Professional
Accreditation: RABN

01 President ... Mr. Sandor SCHWARTZ

Keuka College (D)

Keuka Park NY 14478-0098
County: Yates FICE Identification: 002744
Unit ID: 192192
Telephone: (315) 279-5000 Carnegie Class: Master's S
FAX Number: (315) 279-5216 Calendar System: Semester
URL: www.keuka.edu
Established: 1890 Annual Undergrad Tuition & Fees: $27,240
Enrollment: 2,772 Coed
Affiliation or Control: Independent Non-Profit IRS Status: 501(c)3
Highest Offering: Master's
Program: Liberal Arts And General; Teacher Preparatory; Professional
Accreditation: M, IACBE, NURSE, OT, SW, @TEAC

01 President ... Dr. Jorge L. DIAZ-HERRERA
05 Vice President Academic Affairs ... Dr. Anne K. WEED
10 VP Finance/Administration ... Mr. Jerry HILLER
32 VP Student Develop/Dean of Students ... Dr. James BLACKBURN
30 Vice Pres for College Advancement ... Ms. Amy STOREY
20 Asc Vice Pres of Academic Programs ... Dr. Timothy SELLERS
58 Assoc VP for Prof & Intl Programs ... Mr. Gary SMITH
36 Asst Dean for Experiential Educ ... Dr. Anne Marie GUTHRIE
08 Director of Library ... Ms. Linda PARK
29 Director of Alumni/Family Relations ... Ms. Kathy WAYE
27 Exec Director of Communications ... Mr. Doug LIPPINCOTT
37 Director Financial Aid ... Ms. Jennifer BATES
84 Dir of Enrollment Management ... Mr. Jack FARRELL
09 Dir of Institutional Assessment ... Ms. Dorothy SCHRAMM
14 Director of Computer Services ... Mr. Brad TURNER
18 Director of Facilities ... Mr. Dennis HOINS
21 Controller ... Ms. Carol N. GROVER
19 Director of Campus Security ... Mr. Pat KASNICK
23 Director of Health Services ... Ms. Martha RICH
38 Director of Counseling Services ... Ms. Claudia WELBOURNE
35 Director of Student Life Activities ... Ms. Jennifer FURNER
07 Director of Admissions ... Mr. Gary BOYER
41 Director of Athletics ... Mr. David M. SWEET
88 Dir Administrative/Adult Learning ... Ms. Anne KILLEN
42 Chaplain ... Mr. Eric DETAR
06 Registrar ... Ms. Julia BIES
44 Asst Director Dev/Donor Relations ... Ms. Billie Jo JAYNE
44 Asst Dir Devel/Annual Giving Pgms ... Ms. Andi LIPPINCOTT
88 Marketing Manager Adult Learning ... Mr. Jack FARRELL
96 Purchasing Agent ... Ms. Audrey FAULKNER
15 Personnel Coordinator ... Ms. Susan DELYSER
76 Div Chair OT & Dir OT Grad Studies ... Ms. Victoria SMITH
83 Div Chrm Basic Social & Applied Sci ... Dr. Steve HALLAM
50 Div Chrm Business & Management ... Mr. Neil SEIBENHAR
53 Div Chrm Ed & Dir Ed Grad Studies ... Ms. Diane M. BURKE
79 Div Chrm Humanities/Fine Arts ... Dr. Alexis HAYNES
81 Div Chrm Natural Sciences/Math/PE ... Dr. Michael KECK
75 Division Chairman OT ... Ms. Vicki SMITH

The King's College (E)

56 Broadway, 5th Floor, New York NY 10004-1613
County: New York FICE Identification: 040953
Unit ID: 454184
Telephone: (212) 659-7200 Carnegie Class: Bac/A&S
FAX Number: (212) 659-7210 Calendar System: Semester
URL: www.tkc.edu
Established: 1938 Annual Undergrad Tuition & Fees: $29,750
Enrollment: 582 Coed
Affiliation or Control: Independent Non-Profit IRS Status: 501(c)3
Highest Offering: Baccalaureate
Program: Liberal Arts And General; Business Emphasis
Accreditation: M

00 Chairman of the Board of Trustees ... Mr. Andrew MILLS
01 President ... Dr. Gregory A. THORNBURRY
07 Vice Pres Admissions/Advancement ... Mr. Brian PARKER
32 Vice President Student Development ... Mr. Eric BENNETT
05 Acting Provost ... Dr. Ina KUMI
35 Dean of Students ... Mr. David LEEDY
10 Vice President Finance/CFO ... Mr. Frank TORINO
21 Controller ... Ms. Judy BARRINGER
06 Registrar ... Ms. Sue HO
37 Director of Financial Services ... Ms. Anna PETERS

Le Moyne College (F)

1419 Salt Springs Road, Syracuse NY 13214-1301
County: Onondaga FICE Identification: 002748
Unit ID: 192323
Telephone: (315) 445-4100 Carnegie Class: Master's L
FAX Number: (315) 445-4540 Calendar System: Semester
URL: www.lemoyne.edu
Established: 1946 Annual Undergrad Tuition & Fees: $30,460
Enrollment: 2,475 Coed
Affiliation or Control: Independent Non-Profit IRS Status: 501(c)3
Highest Offering: Master's
Program: Liberal Arts And General; Teacher Preparatory; Professional; Business Emphasis
Accreditation: M, ARCPA, BUS, NURSE, TEAC

01 President ... Dr. Fred P. PESTELLO
05 Provost & VP for Academic Affairs ... Dr. Linda M. LEMURA
84 Vice Pres Enrollment Management ... Dr. John F. DOLAN
10 Vice Pres Finance & Administration . Mr. Roger W. STACKPOOLE
30 Vice Pres Institutional Advancement ... Ms. Mary L. COTTER
32 Vice Pres Student Development ... Dr. Deborah M. CADY MELZER
88 Director of Mission & Identity ... Rev. David C. MCCALLUM, SJ
88 Rector of the Jesuit Community ... Rev. John P. BUCKI, SJ
22 EEO/Affirmative Action Officer ... Mr. Jack MATSON
49 Dean of Arts & Sciences ... Dr. Christopher M. JONES
50 Interim Dean School of Business . Rev. David C. MCCALLUM, SJ
58 Dean of Graduate & Prof Studies ... Mr. Dennis R. DEPERRO
20 Assoc Provost New Program Develop ... Dr. Mary K. COLLINS
51 Director of Continuing Education ... Ms. Patricia J. BLISS
08 Director of the Library ... Dr. Robert C. JOHNSTON
07 Dean of Admission ... Mr. Dennis J. NICHOLSON
07 Director of Graduate Admission ... Ms. Kristen P. TRAPASSO
07 Director of Transfer Admission ... Ms. Cathleen R. ANDERSON
37 Director of Financial Aid ... Mr. William C. CHEETHAM
06 Registrar ... Ms. Cynthia A. ALIBRANDI
21 Assoc VP for Finance & Controller ... Mr. Brian M. LOUCY
41 Asst VP & Director of Athletics ... Mr. Matthew D. BASSETT
18 Asst VP Facilities Mgmt & Planning ... Mr. Jed S. SCHNEIDER
15 Assoc VP for Human Resources ... Mr. Jack MATSON
13 Acting Director of Info Technology ... Mr. Shaun C. BLACK
09 Director of Institutional Research ... Dr. Daniel L. SKIDMORE
40 Bookstore Manager ... Ms. Jessica L. HAMMOND
26 Assoc VP for Marketing ... Mr. Peter S. KILLIAN
88 Director of Advancement Services ... Mr. Paul F. LYNCH
29 Director Alumni & Parent Programs ... Ms. Kimberly B. MCAULIFF
44 Dir of Annual Giving/Stewardship ... Ms. Katherine COGSWELL
26 Director of Communications ... Mr. Joseph B. DELLA POSTA
44 Director Development & Foundations ... Ms. Melissa R. REIDER
44 Director of Devel & Planned Giving ... Mr. Philip J. GEORGE
86 Director Govt/Foundation Relations ... Mr. Steven W. KULICK
88 Asst VP for Multicultural Programs ... Ms. Barbara M. KARPER
88 Asst Dean for Academic Advising ... Ms. Susan E. AMES
35 Asst Dean for Student Development ... Mr. Mark G. GODLESKI
88 Director Campus Life & Leadership ... Mr. John R. HALEY
42 Director of Campus Ministry ... Rev. John P. BUCKI, SJ
36 Director Career Advising/Devpment ... Ms. Patricia A. BEVANS
88 Dir Collegiate Sci Tech Entry Pgm ... Ms. Darshini ROOPNARINE
38 Director Health/Counseling Center ... Ms. Anne E. KEARNEY
88 Director of HEOP and AHANA ... Ms. Esi A. ASARE
19 Director of Security ... Mr. John P. O BRIEN
88 Director of Service Learning ... Ms. Gloria C. HEFFERNAN
28 Director of Diversity ... Ms. Barbara M. KARPER

LIM College (G)

12 E 53rd Street, New York NY 10022-5268
County: New York FICE Identification: 007466
Unit ID: 192271
Telephone: (212) 752-1530 Carnegie Class: Spec/Bus
FAX Number: (212) 832-6109 Calendar System: Semester
URL: www.limcollege.edu
Established: 1939 Annual Undergrad Tuition & Fees: $23,070
Enrollment: 1,552 Coed
Affiliation or Control: Proprietary IRS Status: Proprietary
Highest Offering: Master's
Program: Professional; Business Emphasis
Accreditation: M, ACBSP

01 President ... Elizabeth S. MARCUSE
03 Executive Vice President ... Christopher J. CYPHERS
10 Senior Vice Pres Finance/Operations ... Michael DONOHUE
88 President Emeritus ... Adrian G. MARCUSE
04 Special Assistant to the President ... Linda HARRIS PAOLILLO
04 Assistant to the President ... Jessica HODGE
05 Vice President for Academic Affairs ... Milan MILASINOVIC
58 Graduate Studies Director ... Patricia HOELTGE
20 Dean of Academic Affairs ... Michael LONDRIGAN
20 Asst Dean of Academic Affairs ... Patricia FITZMAURICE
08 Director of Library Services ... Lou ACIERNO
06 College Registrar ... Carolyn DISNEW

36 Interim Sr Dr Exper Ed & Career Mgt .... Susan BAUER
32 Dean of Student Affairs ....Charles PRYOR
88 Vice Pres for Student Development .... Michael FERRY
35 Asst Director of Student Affairs .... Lauren BAZHDARI
35 Director of Student Life ....Michael PALLADINO
38 Sr Dir Counseling & Wellness Svcs .... Jodi N. LICHT
39 Dir of Housing & Residence Life .... Jennifer K. LUCIANO
07 Assistant Dean of Admissions ....Kristina ORTIZ
07 Assoc Dir of Graduate Admissions .... Paul MUCCIARONE
09 Assoc Dean Recruit/Inst Research .... William IMBRIALE
88 Director of Data Resources .... Nikisha WILLIAMS
21 Controller .... Hubert STACHURA
96 Purchasing Agent .... Eric MARTIN
37 Sr Dir of Student Financial Svcs .... Brandon VINSON
30 Sr Dir Institutional Advancement .... Gail NARDIN
88 Sr Dir of Strategic Initiatives .... Pamela LINTON
26 Director of Communications .... Meredith FINNIN
105 Web Production Administrator .... Lola REPHANN
13 Chief Technology Officer .... Maurice MORENCY
14 Director of Information Technology .... Nelson LEON
15 Director of Human Resources .... Andrea L. GRANVILLE
18 Manager of Facilities .... Jonathan ABREU
108 VP for Planning & Assessment .... Jacqueline LEBLANC
88 Asst VP Stndt Fin/Chief Compl Ofcr .... Christopher T. BARTO

Long Island Business Institute (A)

6500 Jericho Turnpike, Commack NY 11725
Telephone: (631) 499-7100 Identification: 770746
Accreditation: ACICS

† Main campus is Long Island Business Institute in Flushing, NY.

Long Island Business Institute (B)

136-18 39th Avenue, Flushing NY 11354
County: Queens FICE Identification: 020937
Unit ID: 192509
Telephone: (718) 939-5100 Carnegie Class: Assoc/PrivFP
FAX Number: (718) 939-9235 Calendar System: Semester
URL: www.libi.edu
Established: 1968 Annual Undergrad Tuition & Fees: $14,124
Enrollment: 515 Coed
Affiliation or Control: Proprietary IRS Status: Proprietary
Highest Offering: Associate Degree
Program: Occupational; 2-Year Principally Bachelor's Creditable; Business Emphasis
Accreditation: ACICS

01 President .... Ms. Monica W. FOOTE
05 Provost .... Ms. Stacey JOHNSON
12 Asst Campus Program Director .... Ms. Michelle HOUSTON
11 Dean of Administration ....Mr. Enos CHEUNG
37 Financial Aid Director .... Mr. Nazaret KIREGIAN
08 Librarian Commack Campus .... Ms. Terry CANAVAN
08 Librarian Flushing Campus .... Ms. Adrianna ARGUELLES

*Long Island University (C)

700 Northern Boulevard, Brookville NY 11548-1326
County: Nassau FICE Identification: 002751
Unit ID: 192457
Telephone: (516) 299-1926 Carnegie Class: N/A
FAX Number: (516) 299-2072
URL: www.liu.edu

01 President ....Dr. Kimberly R. CLINE
05 Vice President Academic Affairs .... Dr. Jeffrey KANE
88 Academic Budget Officer ....Ms. M. Peggy RIGGS
10 Vice President Finance & Treasurer ... Mr. Christopher N. FEVOLA
20 Exec Asst to VP Acad Affairs .... Ms. Gabrielle TOBIN
29 VP For Alumni Relations ....Vacant
43 Vice Pres Legal Svcs/Univ Counsel .... Ms. Lynette PHILLIPS
88 Sr Advisor & Teasurer Emerita ....Mrs. Mary M. LAI
04 Exec Assistant to the President ....Ms. Kathy CAMPO
20 Deputy VP Academic Affairs ....Dr. Lori KNAPP
13 VP for Information Technology & CIO .... Mr. George BAROUDI
18 Assoc VP for Capital Projects .... Mr. Peter TYMUS
21 Assoc Vice Pres/Controller .... Mr. Mark SCHMOTZER
29 Assoc VP Delevop/Alumni Relations .... Ms. Jennifer GOODWIN
30 Assoc Vice Pres Development .... Ms. Melodee GANDIA
20 Asst VP Instr Tech/Faculty Develop .... Dr. Elizabeth CIABOCCHI
100 Asst Vice Pres Office of President ....Ms. Heather GIBBS
25 Asst Vice Pres Sponsored Research ....Ms. Kathryn S. ROCKETT
86 Assoc VP Public Policy/Govt/Found ... Mr. Christopher WILLIAMS
16 Assoc Vice Pres Human Resources .... Ms. Lisa CONZA
22 Asst VP for Employee Relations .... Ms. Gail WEINER
14 Assoc VP Information Systems ....Mr. Sal GRECO
62 Dean of University Libraries .... Ms. Valeda DENT
26 Assistant VP for Public Relations .... Mrs. Kimberly VOLPE-CASALINO
21 Assoc VP Finance and Budget Dir .... Mr. Kirk LENGA
88 Assoc Controller Accounting Svcs .... Mr. Joseph PELIO, JR.
88 Associate Counsel ....Ms. Catherine MURPHY
88 Assoc Controller Comp Operations ....Ms. Linda NOYES
21 Dir of Student Financial Services .... Ms. Lorraine CELLI
88 Director Devel Svcs/Campaign Assoc .... Ms. Linda GORNEY
16 Senior Dir of Employee Benefits .... Mr. John DORAN
09 Director of Institutional Research .... Mr. Claude CHEEK
88 Univ Director Network Services .... Mr. Carlos SIVERIO
96 Director of Purchasing .... Ms. Margaret NATALIE
37 Univ Director Financial Aid .... Mr. David MAINENTI

*Long Island University - Post Campus (D)

720 Northern Boulevard, Brookville NY 11548-1300
County: Nassau FICE Identification: 002754
Unit ID: 192448
Telephone: (516) 299-2000 Carnegie Class: Master's L
FAX Number: (516) 299-4020 Calendar System: Semester
URL: www.liu.edu/cwpost
Established: 1954 Annual Undergrad Tuition & Fees: $34,070
Enrollment: 11,012 Coed
Affiliation or Control: Independent Non-Profit IRS Status: 501(c)3
Highest Offering: Doctorate
Program: Occupational; Liberal Arts And General; Teacher Preparatory; Professional
Accreditation: M, BUS, CACREP, CAHIIM, CLPSY, DIETD, DIETI, #LIB, MT, NURSE, PERF, RAD, SP, SPAA, SW, TEAC

02 President ....Dr. Kimberly R. CLINE
100 Chief of Staff and Vice President ....Dr. Jackie NEALON
07 Dean of Admissions .... Ms. Angela DELCID
51 Dir of Hutton House Continuing Ed .... Dr. Kay SATO
88 Exec Director for Student Success .... Mr. William GUSTAFSON
37 Exec Dir of Student Financial Svcs ....Ms. Joanne GRAZIANO
30 Assoc VP of Development/Alumni Rels .... Ms. Lisa MULVEY
06 Registrar ....Ms. Beth CARSON
21 Bursar .... Mr. Edward A. BOSS, JR.
66 Dean School Health Prof/Nursing ....Dr. MaryAnn CLARK
57 Dean School Visual/Performing Arts ....Dr. Noel ZAHLER
53 Dean Col Education & Info Sciences .... Dr. Robert HANNAFIN
50 Dean College of Management .... Dr. Andrew ROSMAN
49 Dean Col of Liberal Arts & Sciences .Dr. Katherine HILL-MILLER
15 Interim Exec Dir for Human Resource ....Dr. Lee KELLY
88 Dir Higher Educ Opportunity Pgms .... Mr. William CLYDE, JR.
92 Director Honors Program ....Dr. Joan DIGBY
88 Director of Conference Services ....Ms. Theresa DUGGAN
27 Deputy Chief Information Officer .... Ms. Nancy MARKSBURY
18 Director of Facilities ....Mr. William KIRKER
19 Director of Public Safety ....Mr. Paul RAPESS
23 Dir Student Health Services ....Mr. William MILFORD
41 Director of Athletics ....Mr. Bryan COLLINS
32 Director of Student Life ....Dr. Jessica HAYES
88 Director of SCALE/ACE Programs ....Ms. Ann WALSH
88 Director of English Lang Institute .... Mr. Joseph GRANITTO
42 Director of Religious Life ....Fr. Ted BROWN
88 Dir Student Conduct/Veteran Affairs .... Mr. Adam GROHMAN
88 Dir Center for Student Information ....Ms. Jennifer POLIS
88 Director Recreational Sports ....Mr. Richard HAMILTON
44 Assoc Director of Development .... Ms. Jennifer GREISOFE
29 Director of Alumni Relations .... Ms. Katherine HOWLETT
07 Director of Graduate Admissions ....Ms. Carol ZERAH
36 Director of Career Development ....Mr. Jason CASCONE
07 Director of Transfer Admissions .... Ms. Denise SEIGEL
26 Exec Dir of Admissions Marketing ....Ms. Catherine CALAME

**LIU Riverhead* (E)

121 Speonk-Riverhead Road - LIU Bld, Riverhead NY 11901-3499
Telephone: (631) 287-8010 Identification: 666174
Accreditation: &M, TEAC

† Main campus is Long Island University - Post Campus in Brookville, NY.

**Long Island University Brentwood Campus* (F)

100 Second Avenue, Brentwood NY 11717-5300
Telephone: (631) 273-5112 Identification: 666076
Accreditation: &M

† Main campus is Long Island University - Post Campus in Brookville, NY.

**Long Island University Brooklyn Campus* (G)

1 University Plaza, Brooklyn NY 11201-5301
Telephone: (718) 488-1000 FICE Identification: 004779
Accreditation: &M, ARCPA, CLPSY, COARC, DMS, NURSE, OT, PHAR, PTA, SP, SPAA, SURGT, SW, TEAC

† Main campus is Long Island University - Post Campus in Brookville, NY.

**Long Island University Hudson Graduate Center at Rockland* (H)

70 Route 340, Orangeburg NY 10962-2219
Telephone: (845) 359-7200 Identification: 666077
Accreditation: &M

† Main campus is Long Island University - Post Campus in Brookville, NY.

**Long Island University Hudson Graduate Center at Westchester* (I)

735 Anderson Hill Road, Purchase NY 10577-1400
Telephone: (914) 831-2700 Identification: 666078
Accreditation: &M, TEAC

† Main campus is Long Island University - Post Campus in Brookville, NY.

Louis V. Gerstner Jr. Graduate School of Biomedical Sciences, Memorial Sloan-Kettering Cancer Ctr (J)

1275 York Avenue, P.O. Box 441, New York NY 10065
County: New York Identification: 666643
Unit ID: 458511
Telephone: (646) 888-6639 Carnegie Class: Not Classified
FAX Number: N/A Calendar System: Other
URL: www.sloankettering.edu
Established: 2004 Annual Graduate Tuition & Fees: $35,308
Enrollment: 60 Coed
Affiliation or Control: Independent Non-Profit IRS Status: 501(c)3
Highest Offering: Doctorate; No Undergraduates
Program: Professional
Accreditation: NY

01 President .... Dr. Craig THOMPSON
05 Provost .... Dr. Thomas J. KELLY
20 Dean .... Dr. Kenneth J. MARIANS
88 Associate Dean ....Mrs. Linda BURNLEY

Machzikei Hadath Rabbinical College (K)

5407 16th Avenue, Brooklyn NY 11204-1805
County: Kings FICE Identification: 013026
Unit ID: 192624
Telephone: (718) 854-8777 Carnegie Class: Spec/Faith
FAX Number: (718) 851-1265 Calendar System: Semester
Established: 1956 Annual Undergrad Tuition & Fees: $9,400
Enrollment: 146 Male
Affiliation or Control: Independent Non-Profit IRS Status: 501(c)3
Highest Offering: Second Talmudic Degree
Program: Teacher Preparatory
Accreditation: RABN

01 President .... Mr. Alexander SCHAECHTER

Mandl School (L)

254 W 54th Street, 9th Floor, New York NY 10019
County: New York FICE Identification: 007401
Unit ID: 192688
Telephone: (212) 247-3434 Carnegie Class: Assoc/PrivFP
FAX Number: (212) 247-3617 Calendar System: Semester
URL: www.mandl.edu
Established: 1924 Annual Undergrad Tuition & Fees: $24,675
Enrollment: 900 Coed
Affiliation or Control: Proprietary IRS Status: Proprietary
Highest Offering: Associate Degree
Program: Occupational; 2-Year Principally Bachelor's Creditable
Accreditation: ABHES, #COARC, SURTEC

01 President ....Mr. Melvyn P. WEINER
05 Vice President of Academic Affairs ....Ms. Allison WRIGHT
37 VP/Director of Financial Aid ....Mr. Stuart WEINER
88 Director of Compliance ....Ms. Maritza E M. MERCADO
36 Vice President of Career Services ....Mr. James FLANAGAN
06 Dean of Records & Registration ....Mr. Marc WEINER
84 Director of Enrollment Management ....Ms. Randie SENSER
06 Registrar ....Ms. Yana DJIN
07 Director of Recruitment ....Ms. Racquel GARCIA
08 Head Librarian ....Ms. Clover STEELE

Manhattan College (M)

Manhattan College Parkway, Bronx NY 10471-4099
County: Bronx FICE Identification: 002758
Unit ID: 192703
Telephone: (718) 862-8000 Carnegie Class: Master's M
FAX Number: (718) 862-8014 Calendar System: Semester
URL: www.manhattan.edu
Established: 1853 Annual Undergrad Tuition & Fees: $35,865
Enrollment: 3,351 Coed
Affiliation or Control: Independent Non-Profit IRS Status: 501(c)3
Highest Offering: Master's
Program: Liberal Arts And General; Teacher Preparatory; Professional
Accreditation: M, BUS, ENG, TEAC

01 President ....Dr. Brennan O'DONNELL
05 Executive Vice President & Provost .... Dr. William CLYDE
10 VP for Finance & Capital Projects ....Mr. Michael MASCH
32 Vice President Student Life .... Dr. Richard SATTERLEE
30 Vice President College Advancement ..... Mr. Thomas MAURIELLO
15 Vice President for Human Resources ....Ms. Barbara A. FABE
18 Vice President for Facilities ....Mr. Andrew RYAN
84 Vice President Enrollment Mgmt ....Mr. William J. BISSET
88 Vice President for Mission ....Br. Jack CURRAN
20 Assoc Prov Res/Fac/Computer System .. Mr. Walter F. MATYSTIK
35 Assistant VP of Student Life .... Dr. Emmanuel AGO
35 Dean of Students ....Dr. Michael CAREY
39 Director Residence Life ....Mr. Jack GORMLEY
06 Registrar ....Mrs. Luz TORRES
07 Director of Admissions .... Ms. Dana ROSE
35 Director Student Development ....Vacant
08 Director of Libraries ....Ms. Maire I. DUCHON
13 Director of Information Tech Svcs .... Mr. Jake HOLMQUIST

19 Director of Public Safety ... Mr. Juan E. CEREZO
29 Director of Alumni Relations ... Mr. Thomas MCCARTHY
26 Director of Mktg & Communications ... Mrs. Lydia E. GRAY
36 Director Ctr Career Development ... Ms. Kelly AHN
38 Dir of Counseling & Health Services ... Dr. Terence HANNIGAN
41 Director of Athletics ... Mr. Robert J. BYRNES
42 Director of Campus Ministry ... Ms. Lois HARR
44 Director of Development/Advancement ... Mr. Stephen WHITE
78 Director Academic Support Services ... Ms. Marilyn CARTER-STEVENS
40 Director of Campus Bookstore ... Vacant
22 Dir of Personnel/Affirm Action Ofcr ... Ms. Vickie M. COWAN
09 Dir Inst Research/Assessment ... Dr. David MAHAN
21 Controller ... Mr. Dennis LONERGAN
21 Business Manager ... Vacant
85 International Student Advisor ... Ms. Debra L. DAMICO
37 Director of Student Financial Svcs ... Mr. Edward KEOUGH
49 Dean of Arts ... Dr. Richard K. EMMERSON
50 Dean of Business ... Dr. Salwa AMMAR
53 Dean of Education ... Dr. William J. MERRIMAN
54 Dean of Engineering ... Dr. Tim WARD
51 Exec Dir Sch Cont & Prof Studies ... Dr. Cheryl HARRISON
88 Director Ctr for Academic Success ... Ms. Marisa PASSAFIUME
81 Dean of Science ... Dr. Constantine THEODOSIOU
88 Dir of Specialized Resource Center ... Ms. Anne VACCARO
88 Dir Grad & Fellowship Advisement ... Dr. Rani R. ROY

Manhattan School of Music (A)

120 Claremont Avenue, New York NY 10027-4698
County: New York FICE Identification: 002759
Unit ID: 192712
Telephone: (212) 749-2802 Carnegie Class: Spec/Arts
FAX Number: (212) 749-5471 Calendar System: Semester
URL: www.msmnyc.edu
Established: 1917 Annual Undergrad Tuition & Fees: $36,500
Enrollment: 933 Coed
Affiliation or Control: Independent Non-Profit IRS Status: 501(c)3
Highest Offering: Doctorate
Program: Professional; Music Emphasis
Accreditation: M

01 President ... Dr. James GANDRE
00 Vice President Emeritis ... Mr. Richard E. ADAMS
10 Exec VP Finance & Administration ... Mr. Paul D. KELLEHER
05 Vice Pres Academics & Performance ... Dr. Marjorie MERRYMAN
64 Vice Pres Instrument Performance ... Mr. David GEBER
32 Dean of Students ... Ms. Elsa Jean DAVIDSON
07 Associate Dean for Enrollment Mgt ... Ms. Amy A. ANDERSON
26 Dir Public Rel/Mrktng/Publications ... Ms. Debra KINZLER
15 Director Admin & Human Relations ... Ms. Carol MATOS
06 Registrar ... Mr. David MCDONAGH
39 Dir of Student & Residential Life ... Mr. Wadner AUGUSTE
31 Director of Educational Outreach ... Ms. Rebecca CHARNOW
18 Director of Facilities ... Mr. Luis PLAZA
29 Director Alumni Affairs ... Mr. John BLANCHARD
08 Director of Library Services ... Mr. Peter CALEB
37 Coordinator Student Financial Aid ... Mr. Daniel KELLEHER

Manhattanville College (B)

2900 Purchase Street, Purchase NY 10577-2132
County: Westchester FICE Identification: 002760
Unit ID: 192749
Telephone: (914) 694-2200 Carnegie Class: Master's L
FAX Number: (914) 694-2386 Calendar System: Semester
URL: www.mville.edu
Established: 1841 Annual Undergrad Tuition & Fees: $49,886
Enrollment: 2,856 Coed
Affiliation or Control: Independent Non-Profit IRS Status: 501(c)3
Highest Offering: Doctorate
Program: Liberal Arts And General; Teacher Preparatory
Accreditation: M, IACBE, TED

01 President ... Mr. Jon C. STRAUSS
04 Special Asst to the President ... Ms. Laura PROSTANO
04 Exec Admin Asst to the President ... Ms. Deborah A. FALLONE
05 Provost/VP of Academic Affairs ... Dr. Gail SIMMONS
10 VP Finance/Administration ... Ms. Marina VASARHELYI
84 Vice Pres Enrollment Management ... Mr. Nikhil KUMAR
30 Vice Pres Institutional Advancement ... Mr. Jose GONZALEZ
11 Vice President of Operations ... Mr. Gregory PALMER
58 Dean Graduate/Professional Studies ... Dr. Anthony DAVIDSON
53 Dean School of Education ... Dr. Shelley WEPNER
26 Mng Dir Media/PR/ Communications ... Ms. Jennifer JAMES PRYOR
06 Registrar ... Mr. Thomas MURASSO
85 Director of English Lang Institute ... Ms. Judith H. LEWIS
08 Director of the Library ... Mr. Jeff ROSEDALE
37 Director of Financial Aid ... Mr. Robert GILMORE
23 Exec Dir Hlth Svcs/Counseling Svcs ... Dr. Pamela DUNCAN
32 Dean of Students ... Vacant
41 Director of Athletics ... Mr. Keith LEVINTHAL
42 Int Catholic Chpln/Interfaith Coord ... Fr. Wil TYRRELL
36 Director Center for Career Devel ... Ms. Rosalie SHEMMER
29 Dir Alumni Relations/Annual Giving ... Ms. Teresa WEBER
19 Director of Security ... Mr. Anthony HERRMANN
30 Director of Development ... Vacant
07 Director of Undergrad Admissions ... Mr. Kevin O'SULLIVAN
09 Director of Institutional Research ... Ms. Noreen O'HARA
15 Director of Human Resources ... Mr. Don DEAN
35 Asst Director of Student Activities ... Mr. Andrew FULTON
18 Chief Facilities/Physical Plant ... Mr. Gregory PALMER
96 Director of Purchasing ... Ms. Cheryl DOBSON

Maria College of Albany (C)

700 New Scotland Avenue, Albany NY 12208-1798
County: Albany FICE Identification: 002763
Unit ID: 192785
Telephone: (518) 438-3111 Carnegie Class: Assoc/PrivNFP
FAX Number: (518) 438-7170 Calendar System: 4/1/4
URL: www.mariacollege.edu
Established: 1958 Annual Undergrad Tuition & Fees: $10,520
Enrollment: 903 Coed
Affiliation or Control: Independent Non-Profit IRS Status: 501(c)3
Highest Offering: Baccalaureate
Program: Occupational; 2-Year Principally Bachelor's Creditable
Accreditation: M, ADNUR, NUR, OTA

01 President ... Dr. Lea JOHNSON
05 Vice President for Academic Affairs ... Dr. Margie L. BYRD
10 Director of Business Affairs ... Mrs. Frances BERNARD
51 Director of Continuing Education ... Sr. Ellen BOYLE
06 Registrar ... Ms. Kari BENNETT
07 Director of Admissions ... Ms. Laurie A. GILMORE
08 Director Library ... Sr. Rose HOBBS
32 Dean Student Svcs/Dir Counsel Ctr ... Ms. Deborah CORRIGAN
13 Director of Academic Computing ... Mr. Stephen F. DELORENZO
18 Superintendent Physical Plant ... Mr. Andrew PEREZ
36 Director Placement/Alumni ... Sr. Renee M. CUDHEA
30 Chief Development/Marketing ... Mrs. Martha FASHOUER

Marist College (D)

3399 North Road, Poughkeepsie NY 12601-1387
County: Dutchess FICE Identification: 002765
Unit ID: 192819
Telephone: (845) 575-3000 Carnegie Class: Master's L
FAX Number: (845) 471-6213 Calendar System: Semester
URL: www.marist.edu
Established: 1929 Annual Undergrad Tuition & Fees: $30,950
Enrollment: 6,377 Coed
Affiliation or Control: Independent Non-Profit IRS Status: 501(c)3
Highest Offering: Master's
Program: Liberal Arts And General; Teacher Preparatory; Professional
Accreditation: M, BUS, MT, SW

01 President ... Dr. Dennis J. MURRAY
03 Executive Vice President ... Dr. Geoffrey L. BRACKETT
05 Vice President for Academic Affairs ... Dr. Thomas S. WERMUTH
84 VP Admission & Enrollment Planning ... Mr. Sean P. KAYLOR
30 Vice President College Advancement ... Mr. Christopher M. DELGIORNO
13 VP Information Technology/CIO ... Mr. William T. THIRSK
32 VP/Dean of Student Affairs ... Mrs. Deborah A. DICAPRIO
10 Vice President Business Affairs/CFO ... Mr. John P. PECCHIA
20 Assoc VP/Dean Academic Affairs ... Dr. John RITSCHDORFF
07 Dean of Undergraduate Admission ... Mr. Kenton W. RINEHART
88 Dean of Grad and Adult Enrollment ... Vacant
35 Assoc Dean of Student Affairs ... Mr. Steve SANSOLA
29 Executive Director Alumni Relations ... Ms. Amy K. WOODS
09 Director Inst Research & Planning ... Mrs. Susan H. DUNCAN
20 Assoc Dean of Academic Affairs ... Mrs. Judith IVANKOVIC
37 Exec Dir Student Financial Services ... Mr. Joseph R. WEGLARZ
08 Director Library ... Mr. Verne NEWTON
38 Director Counseling Services ... Ms. Naomi A. FERLEGER
90 Director Academic Technology ... Mr. Joshua D. BARON
18 Director of Physical Plant ... Mr. Justin BUTWELL
26 Chief Public Affairs Officer ... Mr. Gregory CANNON
15 Assoc VP for Human Resources ... Mrs. Deborah RAIKES-COLBERT
96 Director of Purchasing ... Mr. Stephen J. KOCHIS
36 Director Career Services ... Mr. Stephen W. COLE

Marymount Manhattan College (E)

221 E 71st Street, New York NY 10021-4597
County: New York FICE Identification: 002769
Unit ID: 192864
Telephone: (212) 517-0400 Carnegie Class: Bac/A&S
FAX Number: (212) 517-0541 Calendar System: Semester
URL: www.mmm.edu
Established: 1936 Annual Undergrad Tuition & Fees: $26,640
Enrollment: 1,946 Coed
Affiliation or Control: Independent Non-Profit IRS Status: 501(c)3
Highest Offering: Baccalaureate
Program: Liberal Arts And General
Accreditation: M

01 President ... Dr. Judson R. SHAVER
88 Assoc to the Pres for Operations ... Ms. Melissa G. RICHMAN
05 VP Acad Affairs/Dean of Faculty ... Dr. David PODELL
10 Exec Vice Pres Admin & Finance ... Mr. Paul CIRAULO
30 VP Institutional Advancement ... Ms. Marilyn L. WILKIE
32 VP Student Affairs/Dean of Students ... Dr. Carol JACKSON
21 Associate Vice Pres & Controller ... Mr. Wayne SANTUCCI
07 Dean of Admissions ... Mr. James ROGERS
20 Associate Dean for Academic Affairs ... Dr. Kathleen LEBESCO
06 Registrar ... Ms. Regina CHAN
15 Director of Human Resources ... Ms. Bree BULLINGHAM
08 Librarian ... Mr. Brian ROCCO
13 Director Information Technology ... Ms. Patricia HANSEN
37 Director Student Financial Svcs ... Ms. Maria DEINNOCENTIIS
38 Dir Counseling & Psychological Svcs ... Dr. Paul GRAYSON
18 Director of Facilities ... Mr. Pete ROMAIN
35 Asst Dean/Dir Student Activities ... Ms. Rosemary AMPUERO
36 Director Career Svcs & Internships ... Ms. Melissa BENCA
96 Director of Purchasing ... Ms. Maria MARZANO
88 Asst Controller ... Ms. Bree HIMMELSTEIN
29 Dir of Annual and Alumni Programs ... Ms. Carolyn BOLT

Medaille College (F)

Agassiz Circle, Buffalo NY 14214-2695
County: Erie FICE Identification: 002777
Unit ID: 192925
Telephone: (716) 880-2000 Carnegie Class: Master's L
FAX Number: (716) 884-0291 Calendar System: Semester
URL: www.medaille.edu
Established: 1875 Annual Undergrad Tuition & Fees: $23,812
Enrollment: 2,634 Coed
Affiliation or Control: Independent Non-Profit IRS Status: 501(c)3
Highest Offering: Doctorate
Program: Liberal Arts And General; Teacher Preparatory
Accreditation: M, IACBE, TEAC

01 President ... Dr. Richard T. JURASEK
05 Int Vice President Academic Affairs ... Dr. Norm MUIR
10 Vice President Business/Finance ... Mr. Matthew J. CARVER
30 Vice Pres for College Relations ... Mr. John P. CRAWFORD
07 VP Enroll Mgmt/Undergrad Admissions ... Ms. Karen P. MCGRATH
09 Asst Vice Pres Institutional Rsrch ... Mr. Patrick S. MCDONALD
32 Dean for Student Affairs ... Ms. Amy M. DEKAY
44 Dir of Major Gifts & Planned Giving ... Vacant
41 Interim Athletic Director ... Ms. Amy DEKAY
36 Director Career Planning/Placement ... Ms. Carol CULLINAN
27 Chief Information Officer ... Mr. Robert D. CHYKA
06 Registrar ... Mrs. Kathleen LAZAR
08 Library Director ... Ms. Pamela R. JONES
37 Director Financial Aid ... Ms. Catherine BUZANSKI
15 Director of Human Resources ... Ms. Barbara J. BILOTTA
20 Sr Dir Special Academic Services ... Vacant
18 Director Facilities/Physical Plant ... Mr. Nate R. MARTON
35 Director Ofc of Student Involvement ... Ms. Melisa L. WILLIAMS
38 Director Counseling Services ... Ms. Jeannine D. SUK
26 Director of Communications ... Vacant
19 Director of Campus Public Safety ... Mr. Ronald J. CHRISTOPHER
96 Manager of Purchasing ... Vacant
29 Coordinator of Alumni Relations ... Vacant

Medaille College Amherst Branch Campus (G)

30 Wilson Road, Amherst NY 14221
Telephone: (716) 631-1061 Identification: 770139
Accreditation: &M

† Main campus is Medaille College in Buffalo, NY.

Medaille College Rochester Branch Campus (H)

1880 S Winston Road, Rochester NY 14618
Telephone: (585) 272-0030 Identification: 770140
Accreditation: &M

† Main campus is Medaille College in Buffalo, NY.

Memorial Hospital School of Nursing (I)

600 Northern Boulevard, Albany NY 12204-1004
County: Albany FICE Identification: 012203
Unit ID: 192961
Telephone: (518) 471-3260 Carnegie Class: Assoc/PrivNFP
FAX Number: N/A Calendar System: Semester
URL: www.nehealth.com
Established: Annual Undergrad Tuition & Fees: $7,500
Enrollment: 115 Coed
Affiliation or Control: Independent Non-Profit IRS Status: 501(c)3
Highest Offering: Associate Degree
Program: 2-Year Principally Bachelor's Creditable; Nursing Emphasis
Accreditation: NY

01 Executive Director ... Ms. Linda D'ARCANGELIS

Mercy College (J)

555 Broadway, Dobbs Ferry NY 10522-1189
County: Westchester FICE Identification: 002772
Unit ID: 193016
Telephone: (800) 637-2969 Carnegie Class: Master's L
FAX Number: N/A Calendar System: Semester
URL: www.mercy.edu
Established: 1950 Annual Undergrad Tuition & Fees: $17,556
Enrollment: 11,454 Coed
Affiliation or Control: Independent Non-Profit IRS Status: 501(c)3
Highest Offering: Doctorate
Program: 2-Year Principally Bachelor's Creditable; Liberal Arts And General; Teacher Preparatory; Professional
Accreditation: M, ARCPA, NURSE, OT, OTA, PTA, SP, SW

01 Interim President ... Dr. Concetta STEWART
05 Provost & Vice Pres Acad Affairs ... Dr. Concetta STEWART
20 Vice Provost & Executive Dean ... Dr. Graham GLYNN

50 Dean School of Business .... Dr. Ed WEIS
53 Dean School of Education .... Dr. Alfred POSAMENTIER
83 Act Dean School Soc/Behavioral Sci .... Dr. Mary Knopp KELLY
76 Dean School Health/Natural Sci .... Dr. Joan TOGLIA
79 Dean School Liberal Arts .... Dr. Miriam GOGOL
16 Director of Human Resources/Safety .... Ms. Anne GILMARTIN
11 Chief Operating Officer .... Mr. Joseph SCHAEFER
84 Vice Pres for Enrollment Management .... Ms. Deirdre WHITMAN
10 Vice & Chief Finance/Plng Officer .... Mr. Donald AUNGST
37 AVP for Student Financial Services .... Ms. Margaret MCGRAIL
30 Exec Dir Institutional Advancement .... Mr. William MARTINOV
100 Chief of Staff .... Ms. Irene BUCKLEY
04 Staff Assistant .... Ms. Grace CREIGHTON
108 Director of Assessment .... Ms. Victoria FERRARA
88 Chief Compliance Officer .... Mr. James MCCUE
43 General Counsel .... Ms. Carolyn COTTINGHAM
07 Senior Director of Admissions .... Ms. Tara FAY-REILLY
09 Dir Institutional Research/Planning .... Ms. Victoria TYLER
88 Exec Dir of Inst Effectiveness .... Mr. Andy PERSON
39 Deputy Director PACT/Residence Life ... Ms. Patricia CHRISTIANO
36 Exec Dir Student Life & Career Svcs .... Mr. Kevin JOYCE
13 Director of Information Technology .... Mr. Todd PRATTELLA
06 Exec Director of Registrar .... Ms. Debra KENNEY
88 Associate Provost .... Ms. Jessica HABER
21 Director of Business Operations .... Vacant
21 Controller .... Ms. Narda ROMERO
45 Director of Budgets & Planning .... Mr. Bernard COSTELLO
96 Director of Purchasing .... Ms. Patricia SABATINO
08 Director of Mercy College Libraries .... Mr. Mustafa SAKARYA
41 Director of Athletics .... Ms. Patricia KENNEDY
26 Associate Director Public Relations .... Ms. Jessica BAILY
29 Director of Alumni Relations .... Vacant
102 Director of Corporate & Foundations .... Mr. Terrence HENRY
25 Dir Sponsored Programs .... Ms. Monique CAUBERE
104 Director Center Global Engagement .... Dr. Sheila GERCH
106 Director Online Learning .... Dr. Mary LOZINA
18 Director of Facilities .... Ms. Elaine TREFFILETTI

Mesivta of Eastern Parkway Rabbinical Seminary (A)

510 Dahill Road, Brooklyn NY 11218-5559
County: Kings FICE Identification: 009335
Unit ID: 193061
Telephone: (718) 438-1002 Carnegie Class: Spec/Faith
FAX Number: (718) 438-2591 Calendar System: Semester
Established: 1947 Annual Undergrad Tuition & Fees: $11,825
Enrollment: 36 Male
Affiliation or Control: Independent Non-Profit IRS Status: 501(c)3
Highest Offering: Second Talmudic Degree
Program: Teacher Preparatory; Professional
Accreditation: RABN

01 President .... Rabbi Issac HEIMOVITZ
32 Dean of Students .... Rabbi Chaim L. EPSTEIN
37 Director of Student Financial Aid .... Rabbi Ira LIBERMAN
46 Director of Research .... Rabbi Hersch BASCH
10 Chief Fiscal Officer .... Rabbi Joseph HALBERSTADT

Mesivta Tifereth Jerusalem of America (B)

141-7 E Broadway, New York NY 10002-6301
County: New York FICE Identification: 003974
Unit ID: 193070
Telephone: (212) 964-2830 Carnegie Class: Spec/Faith
FAX Number: (212) 349-5213 Calendar System: Semester
Established: 1907 Annual Undergrad Tuition & Fees: $13,500
Enrollment: 87 Male
Affiliation or Control: Independent Non-Profit IRS Status: 501(c)3
Highest Offering: Second Talmudic Degree
Program: Teacher Preparatory; Professional
Accreditation: RABN

01 President & Dean Faculties .... Rabbi David FEINSTEIN

Mesivta Torah Vodaath Seminary (C)

425 E Ninth Street, Brooklyn NY 11218-5299
County: Kings FICE Identification: 007264
Unit ID: 193052
Telephone: (718) 941-8000 Carnegie Class: Spec/Faith
FAX Number: (718) 941-8032 Calendar System: Semester
Established: 1918 Annual Undergrad Tuition & Fees: $9,750
Enrollment: 223 Male
Affiliation or Control: Independent Non-Profit IRS Status: 501(c)3
Highest Offering: Second Talmudic Degree
Program: Teacher Preparatory; Professional
Accreditation: RABN

01 Dean .... Rabbi Yisroel BELSKY
03 Executive Director .... Rabbi Yitzchok GOTTDIENER
06 Registrar .... Rabbi Yonason SHAPIRO
33 Dean of Men .... Rabbi Elya KATZ
31 Director Community Services .... Mr. Shraga WERNER

Metropolitan College of New York (D)

431 Canal Street, New York NY 10013-1919
County: New York FICE Identification: 009769
Unit ID: 190114
Telephone: (212) 343-1234 Carnegie Class: Master's L
FAX Number: (212) 343-7399 Calendar System: Semester
URL: www.metropolitan.edu
Established: 1964 Annual Undergrad Tuition & Fees: $17,530
Enrollment: 1,277 Coed
Affiliation or Control: Independent Non-Profit IRS Status: 501(c)3
Highest Offering: Master's
Program: Professional
Accreditation: M, ACBSP, TED

01 President .... Dr. Vinton THOMPSON
10 EVP Finance & Admininstration/CFO .... Vacant
84 EVP for Enrollment Management .... Mr. Terence PEAVY
07 Director of Admissions .... Ms. Patricia RAMOS
58 Dean School Public Affairs & Admin .... Dr. Humphrey CROOKENDALE
50 Dean School for Business .... Dr. Tilokie DEPOO
88 Dean Audrey Cohen School Human Svcs .... Dr. Ruth E. LUGO
35 Dean of Students .... Ms. Dona SOSA
37 Director of Financial Aid .... Ms. Andrea DAMAR
06 Registrar .... Ms. Noreen SMITH
08 Director of Library Services .... Vacant
09 Dir Institutional Rsrch/Assessment .... Mr. Anthony WILLIAMS
15 Director Human Resources .... Ms. Judith SANTIAGO
18 Chief Facilities/Physical Plant .... Ms. Mercedes MELENDEZ
30 Chief Development Officer .... Ms. Beth DUNPHE
26 Chief Public Relations Officer .... Ms. Tina GEORGIOU
13 Information Systems Manager .... Mr. Naftaly KLEINMAN

Mildred Elley (E)

855 Central Avenue, Albany NY 12206
County: Albany FICE Identification: 022195
Unit ID: 193201
Telephone: (518) 786-0855 Carnegie Class: Assoc/PrivFP
FAX Number: (518) 786-0890 Calendar System: Other
URL: www.mildred-elley.edu
Established: 1917 Annual Undergrad Tuition & Fees: $9,456
Enrollment: 826 Coed
Affiliation or Control: Proprietary IRS Status: Proprietary
Highest Offering: Associate Degree
Program: Occupational
Accreditation: ACICS

01 President .... Ms. Faith A. TAKES

Mildred Elley-New York City (F)

25 Broadway, 16th Floor, New York NY 10004
Telephone: (212) 380-9004 Identification: 770747
Accreditation: ACICS

† Main campus is Mildred Elley in Albany, NY.

Mirrer Yeshiva Central Institute (G)

1795 Ocean Parkway, Brooklyn NY 11223-2010
County: Kings FICE Identification: 004798
Unit ID: 193247
Telephone: (718) 645-0536 Carnegie Class: Spec/Faith
FAX Number: (718) 645-9251 Calendar System: Semester
Established: 1947 Annual Undergrad Tuition & Fees: $5,586
Enrollment: 248 Male
Affiliation or Control: Independent Non-Profit IRS Status: 501(c)3
Highest Offering: Second Talmudic Degree
Program: Teacher Preparatory; Professional
Accreditation: RABN

00 Chancellor .... Rabbi Avrohom Yaakov NELKENBAUM
01 President and Dean .... Rabbi Osher KALMANOWITZ
05 Vice President & Dean .... Rabbi Osher BERENBAUM
33 Dean of Men .... Rabbi Esrael ERLANGER
03 Executive Director .... Rabbi Pinchas HECHT
06 Registrar-Administrator .... Mrs. Devorah BERENBAUM
08 Director of the Library .... Rabbi Jacob FELDMANN
38 Director of Guidance .... Rabbi Yisroel FISHMAN
37 Financial Aid Director .... Mrs. Rachel BERENBAUM

Mohawk Valley Community College (H)

1101 Floyd Avenue, Rome NY 13440
Telephone: (315) 339-3470 Identification: 770141
Accreditation: &M

† Main campus is Mohawk Valley Community College in Utica, NY.

Mohawk Valley Community College (I)

1101 Sherman Drive, Utica NY 13501-5394
County: Oneida FICE Identification: 002871
Unit ID: 193283
Telephone: (315) 792-5400 Carnegie Class: Assoc/Pub-R-L
FAX Number: (315) 792-5666 Calendar System: Semester
URL: www.mvcc.edu
Established: 1946 Annual Undergrad Tuition & Fees (In-District): $4,288
Enrollment: 7,451 Coed
Affiliation or Control: State/Local IRS Status: 501(c)3
Highest Offering: Associate Degree
Program: Occupational; 2-Year Principally Bachelor's Creditable
Accreditation: M, ADNUR, CAHIIM, COARC, ENGT

01 President .... Dr. Randall J. VAN WAGONER
04 Assistant to the President .... Ms. Jill HEINTZ
88 Exec Dir Organizational Development .... Mr. David KATZ
09 Dir Institutional Research/Analysis .... Mr. Mark E. RADLOWSKI
05 Vice Pres Learning/Academic Affairs .... Dr. Maryrose EANNACE
20 Director of Academic Systems .... Mr. Richard PUCINE
79 Dean of Arts & Humanities .... Mr. Lewis KAHLER
88 Dean of Language & Learn Design .... Dr. Jennifer BOULANGER
76 Dean of Life & Health Sciences .... Dr. Terry SCHWANER
81 Dean of STEM .... Dr. Seyed AKHAVI
50 Dean of Business/Soc Sci & Info Sci .... Ms. Marianne BUTTENSCHON
08 Director College Libraries .... Mr. Stephen FRISBEE
24 Dir of Educational Technologies .... Mr. James LYNCH
11 Vice Pres Administrative Services .... Mr. Thomas SQUIRES
32 VP Student Affairs .... Ms. Stephanie C. REYNOLDS
84 Assoc Dean Enrollment & Advisement ... Mrs. Jennifer DEWEERTH
36 Assoc Dean Development & Transition .... Mr. James MAIO
39 Assoc Dean Student & Residence Life .... Mr. Dennis GIBBONS
12 Dean Rome Campus .... Dr. Richard QUEST
30 Exec Dir Institutional Advancement .... Mr. Frank DUROSS
44 Dir of Donor & Resource Development .... Ms. Deanna FERRO
96 Coord Expend/Fixed Asset Procure .... Ms. Joyce PALMER
13 Exec Dir of Information Technology .... Mr. Paul KATCHMAR
31 Exec Dir Ctr Community/Economic Dev .... Ms. Franca ARMSTRONG
15 Exec Director of Human Resources . Mrs. Kimberly EVANS-DAME
26 Director Marketing/Communications .... Mr. Matthew SNYDER
07 Director of Admissions .... Mr. Daniel IANNO
37 Director of Financial Aid .... Mrs. Annette BROSKI
06 Dir of Student Records/Registrar .... Mrs. Rosemary V. SPETKA
18 Dir of Facilities and Operations .... Mr. Michael MCHARRIS
19 Director Campus Safety & Security .... Vacant
21 Business Office Controller .... Mr. Brian MOLINARO
29 Coord Annual Funds/Alumni Relations .... Ms. Marie KOHL

Molloy College (J)

1000 Hempstead Avenue, PO Box 5002, Rockville Centre NY 11571-5002
County: Nassau FICE Identification: 002775
Unit ID: 193292
Telephone: (516) 323-3000 Carnegie Class: Master's L
FAX Number: (516) 256-2247 Calendar System: 4/1/4
URL: www.molloy.edu
Established: 1955 Annual Undergrad Tuition & Fees: $25,710
Enrollment: 4,482 Coed
Affiliation or Control: Independent Non-Profit IRS Status: 501(c)3
Highest Offering: Doctorate
Program: Liberal Arts And General; Teacher Preparatory; Professional
Accreditation: M, COARC, CVT, MUS, NMT, NURSE, @SP, SW, TED

01 President .... Dr. Drew BOGNER
05 VP Academic Affairs/Dean of Faculty .... Dr. Valerie COLLINS
10 Vice Pres for Finance & Treasurer .... Mr. Michael MC GOVERN
84 Vice Pres Enrollment Management .... Ms. Linda ALBANESE
30 Vice President for Advancement .... Mr. Edward J. THOMPSON
32 Vice President Student Affairs .... Mr. Robert HOULIHAN
45 VP Info Tech/Planning/Research .... Dr. Robert PATERSON
88 Vice President for Mission .... Sr. Dorothy FITZGIBBONS
42 Director of Campus Ministries .... Mr. Scott SALVATO
37 Director Student Financial Services .... Ms. Sharion SCOTT
36 Director of Career Development .... Ms. Theresa ACCARDI
41 Director of Athletics .... Ms. Susan CASSIDY
07 Dean of Admissions .... Ms. Marguerite LANE
37 Director of Financial Aid .... Mrs. Ana C. LOCKWARD
21 Assistant Treasurer .... Mr. Anthony PERFETTI
44 Director of Development .... Ms. Catherine MUSCENTE
06 Registrar .... Ms. Susan FORTMAN
09 Director of Institutional Research .... Mr. Michael TORRES
15 Director of Human Resources .... Ms. Lisa MILLER
18 Director of Facilities .... Mr. James MULTARI
26 Director Public Relations .... Mr. Ken YOUNG
96 Director Purchasing & Admin Service .... Ms. Lorraine JACKSON
35 Director of Campus Life .... Ms. Janine MCELROY
29 Alumni Relations Officer .... Dr. Marion FLOMENHAFT
19 Director of Public Safety .... Mr. Harry HERMAN
85 Director of International Education .... Ms. Kathleen REBA
105 Director Web Technologies .... Mr. Keith REDO
24 Director Client Services .... Mr. Nick SIMONE
20 Director Academic Support Services .... Ms. Nicolette CEO
13 Director of Management Info Systems .... Mr. Michael OLIVO
88 Director of Infrastructure & OS .... Mr. Sean LAURIE

Monroe College (K)

2501 Jerome Avenue, Bronx NY 10468-5407
County: Bronx FICE Identification: 004799
Unit ID: 193308
Telephone: (718) 933-6700 Carnegie Class: Master's S
FAX Number: (718) 295-5861 Calendar System: Semester
URL: www.monroecollege.edu
Established: 1933 Annual Undergrad Tuition & Fees: $13,236
Enrollment: 7,359 Coed
Affiliation or Control: Proprietary IRS Status: Proprietary
Highest Offering: Master's
Program: Liberal Arts And General; Teacher Preparatory; Business Emphasis
Accreditation: M, ACFEI

01 President .... Stephen J. JEROME
03 Exec VP/Director of Branch Campus .... Marc M. JEROME
05 Vice President Academics .... Dr. W. Jeff WALLIS

11 Vice President Administration .... David DIMOND
10 Vice President for Finance .... Scott COOPER
84 Vice Pres Enroll Mgmt/Campus Dean .... Anthony ALLEN
32 Vice President Student Affairs .... Roberta GREENBERG
58 Dean of Graduate Programs .... Alex CANALS
20 Assoc Vice President for Academics .... Dr. Karenann CARTY
12 Assoc Vice Pres New Rochelle Camp .... Carol GENESE
86 Asst Vice Pres Governmental Affairs .... Dr. Donald E. SIMON
09 Dean Office of the Registrar/IR ... Dr. Edward S. SCHNEIDERMAN
55 Director of Evening Division .... Allen JENKINS
26 Exec Dir of Marketing .... Craig PATRICK
06 Registrar .... Abigail THORPE
09 Dir Institutional Research .... Peter NWAKEZE
21 Bursar/Branch Campus .... Michael NIEDZWIECKI
21 Director Student Financial Services .... Daniel SHARON
35 Dean of Student Services - Branch .... Stephen SCHULTHEIS
21 Bursar .... Villan CRUZ
88 Assistant Dean for Student Services .... Mark SONNENSTEIN
31 Director Auxilliary Services .... Nivia CAMARA
07 Dean of Admissions Branch .... Gersom LOPEZ
07 Vice President Admissions .... Evan JEROME
88 Director Student Fin Aid Compliance .... Vacant
36 Exec Dir Ofc of Career Advancement .... Bary GREENE
36 Dir Ofc of Career Advancement-NR .... Vacant
08 Director of Library Services .... Christine ARTIS
08 Director of Library Services/Branch .... Angela LAURETANO
24 Director of Learning Center .... Marie LOFTUS
39 Exec Director of Residential Life .... Mark GOODMAN
29 Director of Alumni Relations .... Leslie JEROME

Monroe Community College (A)

1000 E Henrietta Road, Rochester NY 14623-5780
County: Monroe FICE Identification: 002872
Unit ID: 193326
Telephone: (585) 292-2000 Carnegie Class: Assoc/Pub-U-MC
FAX Number: (585) 427-2749 Calendar System: Semester
URL: www.monroecc.edu
Established: 1961 Annual Undergrad Tuition & Fees (In-District): $3,240
Enrollment: 17,296 Coed
Affiliation or Control: State/Local IRS Status: 501(c)3
Highest Offering: Associate Degree
Program: Occupational; 2-Year Principally Bachelor's Creditable
Accreditation: M, ADNUR, CAHIIM, DA, DH, EMT, ENGT, RAD

01 President .... Dr. Anne M. KRESS
05 Provost & VP Academic Services .... Dr. Michael J. MCDONOUGH
72 Vice President Educational Tech Svc . Dr. Jeffrey P. BARTKOVICH
32 Vice President Student Services .... Vacant
10 CFO and VP Administrative Svcs .... Mr. Hezekiah N. SIMMONS
103 VP Econ Dev/Workforce Svc .... Mr. Todd M. OLDHAM
102 Exec Director MCC Foundation .... Ms. Diane L. SHOGER
35 Assoc Vice Pres Student Services .... Mr. Richard H. RYTHER
12 Exec Dean Damon City Campus .... Dr. Emeterio M. OTERO
26 Asst to the Pres College Relations .... Ms. Cynthia L. COOPER
35 Asst Vice Pres Student Services .... Dr. Susan D. BAKER
88 Asst VP Educational Technology Svcs .... Mr. Dale E. MALLORY
18 Assistant Vice President Facilities .... Mr. Paul E. WURSTER
84 Asst Vice Pres Enroll Managment .... Mr. Randyll BOWEN
88 Asst Vice Pres ETS .... Mr. Terrance KEYS
20 Asst Vice Pres Academic Services .... Ms. Kimberley COLLINS
20 Dean Curriculum/Program Devel ...... Mrs. Charlotte M. DOWNING
37 Director Financial Aid .... Mr. Jerome S. ST. CROIX
09 Director Research .... Mr. Angel E. ANDREU
08 Interim Director ETS
Libraries .... Ms. Alice E. HARRINGTON WILSON
36 Director Career Center .... Mr. G. Christopher BELLE-ISLE
21 Asst Vice President Admin Svcs .. Mr. Darrell K. JACHIM-MOORE
06 Director Registration and Records .... Ms. Elizabeth R. RIPTON
30 Director of Development .... Mr. Mark J. PASTORELLA
38 Dir Counseling/Intern & Vet Svcs ...... Ms. Peggy A. HARVEY-LEE
19 Interim Director Public Safety .... Ms. Debra DWYER
41 Director Athletics .... Mr. Dudley (Skip) L. BAILEY
25 Director Grants .... Ms. Patricia R. WILLIAMS
35 Director of Student Life .... Ms. Elizabeth J. STEWART
23 Director of Health Services .... Ms. Donna G. MUELLER
21 Controller .... Mr. Michael G. QUINN
79 Dean Liberal Arts .... Ms. Kristen M. FRAGNOLI
50 Dean Science/Health/Business .... Ms. Laurel T. SANGER
75 Dean Career Technical Education .... Dr. Javier I. AYALA
88 Interim Dean Academic Foundations .... Ms. Catherine E. SMITH
19 Dean Public Safety Training Ctr .... Mr. Michael S. KARNES
32 Dean Student Services-DCC .... Dr. Ann V. TOPPING
88 Dean Acad Svcs DCC .... Dr. Kimberly MCKINSEY-MABRY
13 Assoc Dean/Director ETS Computing ..... Mr. Robert G. BERTRAM
16 Asst to President Human Resources .... Ms. Alberta G. LEE
40 Manager Bookstore .... Ms. Carol M. FISHER
22 Affirmative Action Officer .... Ms. Diane M. CECERO
88 Director Educ Opportunity Program .... Ms. Brenda A. SMITH
32 Assoc Director Student Svcs-DCC .... Mr. Rick F. SADWICK
78 Director Adult/Experiential Lrng .... Mr. William D. SIGISMOND
43 Legal Counsel .... Ms. Diane M. CECERO
88 Assoc Director Master Scheduling .... Dr. Kimberley D. WILLIS
96 Director of Purchasing .... Mr. Patrick M. BATES
39 Director Housing/Residence Life .... Ms. Shelitha W. WILLIAMS
88 Director of Planning .... Ms. Valarie L. AVALONE
28 Chief Diversity Officer .... Ms. Diane M. CECERO
15 Director Human Resources .... Ms. Martha MAHER-GARCIA

Mount Saint Mary College (B)

330 Powell Avenue, Newburgh NY 12550-3412
County: Orange FICE Identification: 002778
Unit ID: 193353
Telephone: (845) 561-0800 Carnegie Class: Master's L
FAX Number: (845) 562-6762 Calendar System: Semester
URL: www.msmc.edu
Established: 1959 Annual Undergrad Tuition & Fees: $25,800
Enrollment: 2,580 Coed
Affiliation or Control: Independent Non-Profit IRS Status: 501(c)3
Highest Offering: Master's
Program: Liberal Arts And General; Teacher Preparatory; Professional; Nursing Emphasis
Accreditation: M, IACBE, NURSE, TED

01 President .... Fr. Kevin MACKIN, OFM
05 Vice President Academic Affairs .... Dr. Mary D. HINTON
10 Vice Pres Finance & Admin/Treasurer .... Mrs. Cathleen KENNY
30 Vice Pres for College Advancement .... Mr. Joseph VALENTI
18 Vice Pres Facilities & Operations .... Mr. James RAIMO
07 Dean of Admissions .... Mrs. Elaine O'GRADY
35 Dean of Students .... Ms. Kelly YOUGH
38 Dir Counseling/Coord Prsns w/Disab .... Dr. Orin STRAUCHLER
20 Associate Dean for Academic Affairs .... Dr. Alice WALTERS
06 Registrar .... Mr. Carlos TONCHE, JR.
07 Director of Admissions .... Mrs. Nancy SCAFFIDI CLARKE
08 Director of the Library .... Mrs. Barbara W. PETRUZZELLI
37 Director of Financial Aid .... Ms. Barbara WINCHELL
09 Director of Planning and Researach .... Mr. Ryan WILLIAMS
15 Director of Human Resources .... Mr. Lee ZAWISTOWSKI
42 Chaplain .... Fr. Francis AMODIO
35 Director of Student Activities .... Ms. Sandra HENDERSON
39 Exec Dir of Operations and Housing .... Mr. Michael O'KEEFE
29 Director of Alumni Affairs .... Ms. Michelle A. IACUESSA
41 Director of Athletics & Recreation .... Mr. John WRIGHT
36 Exec Director of the Career Center .... Mrs. Janet ZEMAN
27 Chief Information Officer .... Mr. Dennis RUSH
96 Purchasing Manager .... Mr. Brian MOORE
106 Exec Dir Curr & Instr Online Learn ... Ms. Maria F. MINICKIELLO
39 Director of Residence Life .... Ms. Christine PUPEK
18 Director of Facilities .... Ms. Maryann PILON
26 Director of Marketing & Advertising .... Mr. Dean DIMARZO

Nassau Community College (C)

1 Education Drive, Garden City NY 11530-6793
County: Nassau FICE Identification: 002873
Unit ID: 193478
Telephone: (516) 572-7501 Carnegie Class: Assoc/Pub-S-SC
FAX Number: (516) 572-7750 Calendar System: Semester
URL: www.ncc.edu
Established: 1959 Annual Undergrad Tuition & Fees (In-District): $4,300
Enrollment: 23,206 Coed
Affiliation or Control: State/Local IRS Status: 501(c)3
Highest Offering: Associate Degree
Program: Occupational; 2-Year Principally Bachelor's Creditable
Accreditation: M, ADNUR, COARC, ENGT, FUSER, MLTAD, MUS, PTAA, RTT, SURGT

01 Acting President .... Dr. Kenneth K. SAUNDERS
03 Acting Exec Vice Pres .... Ms. Maria P. CONZATTI
05 Vice President Academic Affairs .... Vacant
11 Vice Pres Facilities Management ..... Dr. Joseph V. MUSCARELLA
10 Vice President Finance .... Mr. James BEHRENS
32 Vice Pres Academic/Student Svcs .... Ms. Maria P. CONZATTI
22 AVP Equity & Inclusion/AA Officer .... Mr. Craig J. WRIGHT
43 Spec Asst to Pres/College Counsel .... Ms. Donna M. HAUGEN
103 Asst Vice Pres Workforce Devel .... Dr. Janet CARUSO
21 Comptroller .... Ms. Inna REZNIK
13 Dean Management Info Svcs .... Vacant
18 Asst VP Maintenance/Operations .... Mr. Masoom ALI
15 Asst Vice Pres Human Resources . Ms. Deborah REED-SEGRETTI
96 Asst Vice President Procurement .... Mr. Gary HOMKOW
35 Dean of Students .... Ms. Charmian SMITH
09 Assc VP Institutional Effectiveness .... Mr. Frank BILLINGS
37 Dean Financial Aid .... Ms. Patricia NOREN
07 Dean of Admissions .... Ms. Tika ESLER
25 Resource Devel/Grants Fiscal Mgr .... Mr. Edmund KOEPPEL
86 General Counsel for Govt Relations .... Mr. Chuck CUTOLO
26 Director Marketing/Communications .... Ms. Alicia STEGER
08 Director of Library .... Ms. Nancy WILLIAMSON
41 Director Special Pgm Athletics/PED .... Mr. Michael C. PELLICCIA
06 Registrar .... Mr. Chester BARKAN
19 Director of Public Safety .... Mr. Martin RODDINI
23 Director Health Services .... Ms. Cynthia STOUDMIRE
36 Director of Placement Testing .... Ms. Noreen WADE
38 Dir Advisement/Special Programs .... Mr. John SPIEGEL
27 Chief Information Officer .... Mr. Richard LAWLESS
102 Exec Director Nassau CC Foundation .... Ms. Dawn DISTEFANO

Nazareth College of Rochester (D)

4245 East Avenue, Rochester NY 14618-3790
County: Monroe FICE Identification: 002779
Unit ID: 193584
Telephone: (585) 389-2525 Carnegie Class: Master's L
FAX Number: (585) 586-2452 Calendar System: Semester
URL: www.naz.edu
Established: 1924 Annual Undergrad Tuition & Fees: $29,424
Enrollment: 2,910 Coed
Affiliation or Control: Independent Non-Profit IRS Status: 501(c)3
Highest Offering: Doctorate
Program: Liberal Arts And General; Teacher Preparatory; Professional
Accreditation: M, IACBE, MUS, NURSE, PTA, SP, SW, TEAC

01 President .... Mr. Daan BRAVEMAN
04 Assistant to President .... Ms. Patricia GENTHNER
04 Executive Secretary to President .... Ms. Cathleen M. STEVENS
05 Vice President Academic Affairs .... Dr. Sara VARHUS
30 Vice Pres Institutional Advancement .... Ms. Kelly GAGAN
10 Vice President Finance & Treasurer ..... Ms. Maragaret C. FERBER
32 Vice President Student Development .... Mr. Kevin WORTHEN
84 Interim VP Enrollment Management .... Mr. Michael MCGWIN
29 Director of Alumni Relations .... Ms. Donna BORGUS
15 Assoc VP Human Resources .... Mrs. JoEllen PINKHAM
20 Asst VP Academic Affairs .... Dr. Robert MARINO
06 Registrar .... Mr. Andrew MORRIS
37 Director Student Financial Aid .... Ms. Samantha VEEDER
26 Director Marketing & Communications .... Ms. Kathleen PHILBIN
13 Director Information Tech Svcs .... Ms. Karen KUPPINGER
08 Director of Library .... Ms. Catherine DOYLE
19 Director of Security .... Mr. Robert MALDONADO
39 Director of Campus Life .... Ms. Carey BACKMAN
41 Director of Athletics .... Mr. Peter G. BOTHNER
38 Director of Counseling .... Vacant
42 Director Center for Spirituality .... Ms. Lynne BOUCHER
36 Director of Career Services .... Mr. Michael D. KAHL
18 Director Buildings/Grounds .... Mr. Peter LANA
09 Director of Institutional Research .... Ms. Nancy C. GREAR
23 Director of Health Services .... Ms. Donna WILLOME
20 Director of Academic Advisement .... Ms. Linda SEARING
88 Director of the Arts Center .... Ms. Susan C. LUSIGNAN
21 Bursar .... Mr. John GARBE
35 Director of Student Affairs .... Vacant
92 Director Honors Program .... Dr. Marjorie ROTH
94 Director Women's Studies Program ..... Dr. Rachel BAILEY-JONES
49 Dean of Col of Arts and Sciences .... Dr. Deborah DOOLEY
76 Dean School of Health & Human Svcs ...... Dr. Shirley SZEKERES
53 Dean School of Education .... Dr. Craig HILL
88 Dean School of Management .... Mr. Gerard ZAPPIA
88 Director of the Casa Italiana ..... Dr. Stella PLUTINO-CALABRESE
88 Exec Dir of Ctr International Educ .... Dr. George EISEN
88 Dir of Center for Service Learning .... Dr. Marie WATKINS
89 Dir Stdnt Transition/First Year Ctr .... Ms. Marrlee BURGESS
96 Director of Purchasing .... Ms. Tracy MORAN
88 Exec Dir Center 4 Civic Engagement .... Ms. Nuala BOYLE

The New School (E)

66 W 12th Street, New York NY 10011-8603
County: New York FICE Identification: 020662
Unit ID: 193654
Telephone: (212) 229-5600 Carnegie Class: DRU
FAX Number: (212) 229-5330 Calendar System: Semester
URL: www.newschool.edu
Established: 1919 Annual Undergrad Tuition & Fees: $40,761
Enrollment: 10,575 Coed
Affiliation or Control: Independent Non-Profit IRS Status: 501(c)3
Highest Offering: Doctorate
Program: 2-Year Principally Bachelor's Creditable; Liberal Arts And General
Accreditation: M, ART, CLPSY, SPAA

01 President .... Dr. David VAN ZANDT
04 Asst & Scheduler to President .... Ms. Ann WHELAN
05 Provost and Chief Academic Officer .... Mr. Tim MARSHALL
20 Dep Provost & Sr VP Academic Affs .... Dr. Bryna SANGER
13 Sr VP for Information Technology .... Vacant
16 Sr VP for HR & Labor Relations .... Ms. Carol CANTRELL
32 Sr Vice President Student Services .... Ms. Linda REIMER
84 Sr VP for Enrollment Management .... Mr. Donald RESNICK
10 VP & Treasurer .... Mr. Steve STABILE
26 VP Comm/External Affs .... Mr. Peter TABACK
43 VP/General Counsel & Sec of Corp .... Mr. Roy P. MOSKOWITZ
88 VP for Global and Distrib Education .... Mr. Andy ATZERT
88 VP Design/Construction & Facilities .... Ms. Lia GARTNER
30 VP Devel & Alumni Relations .... Vacant
51 Exec Dean School for Public Engage .... Mr. David SCOBEY
57 Exec Dean Parsons School for Design .... Mr. Joel TOWERS
49 Dean Eugene Lang College .... Ms. Stephanie BROWNER
87 Dean New School for Social Research .... Dr. William MILBERG
64 Dean Mannes College of Music .... Mr. Richard KESSLER
88 Exec Dir Jazz & Contemp Music .... Mr. Martin MUELLER
88 Director The New School for Drama .... Mr. Pippin PARKER
20 Vice Provost Acad Planning Admin .... Ms. Pat BAXTER
20 Vice Provost Acad Services Support .... Dr. Elizabeth ROSS
09 Assoc Provost Inst Rsrch/Effectiv .... Dr. Paula MAAS
20 Assoc Provost Acad Plng Admin .... Ms. Kristi ALLEN
20 Assoc Provost Curr & Learning .... Ms. Lisa DEBENEDITTIS
07 Assoc VP Strat Enrollment Mgmt .... Mr. Chris FERGUSON
35 Asst VP for Student & Campus Life .... Mr. Tom MCDONALD
21 Asst VP & Controller .... Ms. Natalie PRESSEY
06 Asst VP & University Registrar .... Mr. William KIMMEL
39 Asst VP Student Housing & Res Life .... Mr. Robert LUTOMSKI
15 Asst VP Human Resources .... Mr. Irwin KROOT
23 LCSW/Asst VP Student Health .... Ms. Tracy ROBIN
91 Asst VP Systems Network Security .... Mr. Chris BREZIL
90 Asst VP Academic Technology .... Ms. Lillian SARTORI
08 University Librarian .... Mr. Ed SCARCELLE
19 Director Security .... Mr. Thomas ILICETO
37 Director Financial Aid .... Ms. Lisa SHAHEEN
18 Director Facilities Management .... Mr. Thomas WHELAN
96 Sr Director of Business Operations .... Mr. Ed VERDI
85 Sr Dir International Student Svcs .... Ms. Monique N. NRI
38 Director Counseling Services .... Dr. Jerry FINKELSTEIN
106 Director The New School Online .... Mr. James O'CONNOR
36 Director Career Services .... Vacant
28 Director Intercultural
Support .... Ms. Keisha DAVENPORT-RAMIREZ
29 Director Alumni Relations .... Ms. Amy GARAWITZ
88 Director Student Disability Svcs .... Mr. Jason LUCHS

24 Director Media Services .... Mr. Mark FITZPATRICK
41 Director Athletics and Recreation .... Ms. Diane YEE

New York Academy of Art (A)

111 Franklin Street, New York NY 10013-2911
County: New York FICE Identification: 026001
Unit ID: 366368
Telephone: (212) 966-0300 Carnegie Class: Spec/Arts
FAX Number: (212) 966-3217 Calendar System: Semester
URL: www.nyaa.edu
Established: 1982 Annual Graduate Tuition & Fees: $32,500
Enrollment: 108 Coed
Affiliation or Control: Independent Non-Profit IRS Status: 501(c)3
Highest Offering: Master's; No Undergraduates
Program: Professional; Fine Arts Emphasis
Accreditation: NY, ART

01 President .... Mr. David KRATZ
05 Dean of Academic Affairs .... Mr. Peter DRAKE
37 Director of Student Financial Aid .... Mr. Andrew MUELLER
32 Director of Student Affairs .... Mr. Elvin R. FREYTES
08 Librarian & Archivist .... Ms. Holly FRISBEE

New York Career Institute (B)

11 Park Place, 4th Floor, New York NY 10007
County: New York FICE Identification: 021634
Unit ID: 195845
Telephone: (212) 962-0002 Carnegie Class: Assoc/PrivFP
FAX Number: (212) 385-7574 Calendar System: Trimester
URL: www.nyci.edu
Established: 1941 Annual Undergrad Tuition & Fees: $13,050
Enrollment: 723 Coed
Affiliation or Control: Proprietary IRS Status: Proprietary
Highest Offering: Associate Degree
Program: Occupational; 2-Year Principally Bachelor's Creditable
Accreditation: NY

01 CEO .... Ivan LONDA
05 Chief Academic Officer .... Lisa Therese FOWLER
32 Director of Student Services .... Cindy MCMAHON
37 Director Financial Aid .... Brenda SORIANO

New York Chiropractic College (C)

2360 State Route 89, Seneca Falls NY 13148-0800
County: Seneca FICE Identification: 012277
Unit ID: 193751
Telephone: (315) 568-3000 Carnegie Class: Spec/Health
FAX Number: (315) 568-3012 Calendar System: Trimester
URL: www.nycc.edu
Established: 1919 Annual Undergrad Tuition & Fees: N/A
Enrollment: 913 Coed
Affiliation or Control: Independent Non-Profit IRS Status: 501(c)3
Highest Offering: First Professional Degree
Program: Professional
Accreditation: M, ACUP, CHIRO

01 President .... Dr. Frank J. NICCHI
05 Exec Vice President & Provost .... Dr. Michael A. MESTAN
10 Vice Pres of Finance/Admin Svcs .... Mr. Sean ANGLIM
20 Dean Academic Programs & Services .... Dr. J. Nicolas POIRIER
20 Dean of Chiropractic Education .... Dr. Karen A. BOBAK
20 Dean Chiropractic Clinical Educ .... Dr. Wendy L. MANERI
88 Vice Pres Inst Quality/Assessment .... Dr. David R. ODIORNE
06 Registrar .... Mr. Kevin MCCARTHY
84 Vice Pres Enrollment Management .... Ms. Diane DIXON
07 Director of Admissions .... Mr. Michael LYNCH
37 Director Financial Aid .... Mr. Darrin ROOKER
88 Director of Bachelor Prof Studies .... Dr. Kristina L. PETROCCO-NAPULI
46 Dean of Research .... Dr. Jeanmarie R. BURKE
12 Depew Health Center Administrator .... Dr. Michael FLYNN
12 Levittown Health Ctr Chief of Staff .... Dr. Charles HEMSEY
17 Seneca Falls Hlth Ctr Chf of Staff .... Dr. Wendy L. MANERI
51 Dean Post Grad & Cont Educ .... Dr. Thomas VENTIMIGLIA
08 Director of the Library .... Ms. Bethyn BONI
38 Assoc Director Counseling Services .... Ms. Eve ABRAMS
88 Dir Academy Admc Excl Stdnt Success .... Dr. Jerimy BLOWERS
39 Secretary Housing .... Ms. Janette ELSTER
41 Dir Health & Fitness Education .... Mr. Anthony M. PETROCCIA
35 Director Student Life .... Ms. Holly Anne WAYE
36 Director of Career Development Ctr .... Ms. Susan D. PITTENGER
30 Exec Director Devel & Govt Rels .... Vacant
29 Director of Alumni Relations .... Ms. Diane ZINK
30 Vice President of Inst Advancement .... Mr. Peter R. VANTYLE
45 Director Accreditation .... Dr. Beth DONOHUE
09 Quality Engineer .... Ms. Patricia MERKLE
15 Human Resources Manager .... Ms. Christine MCDERMOTT
91 Information Tech Administrator .... Mr. Shane SHOWERS
19 Director Facilities/Security .... Mr. William WAYNE
96 Assoc VP Admin Svcs/Dir Purchasing ... Mr. Richard B. WORDEN
40 Bookstore Manager .... Ms. Helen STUCK
63 Dir MS Clinical Anatomy Pgm .... Dr. Karen GANA
76 Dir Applied Clinical Nutrition Pgm .... Dr. Peter NICKLESS
88 Dean of FL Sch Acup/Oriental Med .... Mr. Jason WRIGHT
88 Dir MS Diagnostic Imaging Program .... Dr. Chad WARSHEL
88 Dir Academy for Teaching Excellence .... Ms. Amy THOMPSON
12 Campus Health Ctr Chief of Staff .... Dr. Jonathon EGAN
12 Rochester Hlth Ctr Chf of Staff .... Dr. Wendy L. MANERI
90 Systems Administrator .... Ms. Shelly STUCK
24 Educational Tech Administrator .... Mr. Bernard CECCHINI
23 Executive Dir of the Hlth Ctrs .... Ms. Jennifer VONHAHMANN
21 Controller .... Ms. Karen QUEST
88 Director Academy for Prof Success .... Dr. Theresa M. HOBAN
88 Dir MS Hum Anat Phys Instructn Pgm ....Dr. Robert A. CROCKER

New York College of Health Professions (D)

6801 Jericho Turnpike, Syosset NY 11791-4413
County: Nassau FICE Identification: 025994
Unit ID: 418126
Telephone: (516) 364-0808 Carnegie Class: Spec/Health
FAX Number: (516) 364-6645 Calendar System: Trimester
URL: www.nycollege.edu
Established: 1981 Annual Undergrad Tuition & Fees: $12,786
Enrollment: 825 Coed
Affiliation or Control: Independent Non-Profit IRS Status: 501(c)3
Highest Offering: Master's
Program: Professional; Technical Emphasis
Accreditation: NY, ACUP

01 President .... Ms. Lisa PAMINTUAN
04 Administrative Asst to President .... Ms. Stefania CUFFARI
26 Sr VP Mktg/Comm/Business Oper .... Ms. Barbara CARVER
10 Chief Financial Officer .... Mr. Errol VIRASAWMI
63 Dean Grad Sch Oriental Medicine .... Dr. A. Li SONG
05 Chief Academic Officer .... Dr. Mohammad HASHEMIPOUR
88 Chair of Massage Therapy .... Ms. Genevieve REITER
06 Registrar .... Ms. Jin WU
88 Senior Admissions Counselor .... Ms. Mary RODAS
07 Interim Director of Admissions .... Ms. Sinead RODGERS
08 Dir Library/Information Services .... Ms. Cynthia CAYEA
21 Bursar .... Ms. Jacqueline MCINTYRE
13 Manager Information Technology .... Mr. Vicente CALDAS
32 Director of Student Services .... Ms. Susan SCHOEN
37 Associate Director of Financial Aid .... Mr. Bernard WALKER
88 Dean Sch of Massage Therapy NYC .... Dr. Claire CASSEUS
88 Bursar .... Ms. Jacqueline MCINTYRE

New York College of Podiatric Medicine (E)

53 E 124th Street, New York NY 10035-1815
County: New York FICE Identification: 002749
Unit ID: 194073
Telephone: (212) 410-8000 Carnegie Class: Spec/Health
FAX Number: (212) 876-7670 Calendar System: Semester
URL: www.nycpm.edu
Established: 1911 Annual Undergrad Tuition & Fees: $28,500
Enrollment: 385 Coed
Affiliation or Control: Independent Non-Profit IRS Status: 501(c)3
Highest Offering: First Professional Degree
Program: Professional
Accreditation: POD

01 President .... Mr. Louis L. LEVINE
05 Dean/Chief Academic Officer .... Dr. Michael J. TREPAL
11 Chief Operating Officer .... Mr. Joel STURM
10 Chief Financial Officer .... Mr. Greg ONAIFO
13 Vice Pres Info Systems & Technology .... Mr. Evan KOBOLAKIS
32 Dean Student Affairs .... Dr. Laurence LOWY
63 Dean Medical Education/Medical Dir .... Dr. Mark SWARTZ
81 Dean Basic Sciences .... Dr. Eileen CHUSID
51 Dean Post-Doctorate Education .... Dr. Robert ECKLES
20 Dean Clinical Educ/Dir Res Pgms .... Dr. Robert ECKLES
09 Dean Institutional Research .... Dr. Eileen CHUSID
07 Assoc Dean Admissions/Student Svcs .... Ms. Lisa LEE
30 VP of Development & Operations .... Mr. Desander MAS
26 Director Public Affairs/Development .... Mr. Roger GREENE
15 Dir Human Resources/Risk Management .... Mr. Joel STURM
08 Director of Library .... Mr. Thomas WALKER
18 Director Safety .... Mr. James WARREN
37 Director Financial Aid .... Ms. Eve TRAUBE
06 Registrar .... Ms. Vernese PANNELL

New York College of Traditional Chinese Medicine (F)

155 First Street, Mineola NY 11501-4005
County: Nassau FICE Identification: 034433
Unit ID: 439783
Telephone: (516) 739-1545 Carnegie Class: Spec/Health
FAX Number: (516) 873-9622 Calendar System: Trimester
URL: www.nyctcm.edu
Established: 1996 Annual Undergrad Tuition & Fees: $16,655
Enrollment: 140 Coed
Affiliation or Control: Independent Non-Profit IRS Status: 501(c)3
Highest Offering: Master's
Program: Professional
Accreditation: ACUP

01 President .... Dr. Yemeng CHEN
11 Administrative Dean .... Dr. James S. BARE
05 Academic Dean .... Dr. Sunny SHEN
07 Admissions Manager .... Ms. Christina CAO
23 Clinic Director .... Mr. Yongshun BEI
88 Clinic Manager .... Ms. Yiping ZHAO
06 Records Manager .... Ms. Susan SU
32 Student Services Coordinator .... Mr. Robert LUTZ
37 Financial Aid Coordinator .... Ms. Anna HSIUNG
21 Financial Manager .... Ms. Lily ZOU
08 Operations Manager .... Ms. Ling Ling CHANG
04 Executive Assistant .... Ms. Elise MA
88 Admissions Assistant .... Mr. Tony YAM

New York Graduate School of Psychoanalysis (G)

16 West Tenth Street, New York NY 10011
Telephone: (212) 260-7050 Identification: 770116
Accreditation: &EH

† Main campus is Boston Graduate School of Psychoanalysis in Brookline, MA.

New York Institute of Technology (H)

Northern Boulevard, Old Westbury NY 11568-8000
County: Nassau FICE Identification: 004804
Unit ID: 194091
Telephone: (516) 686-7516 Carnegie Class: Master's L
FAX Number: (516) 686-7613 Calendar System: Semester
URL: www.nyit.edu
Established: 1955 Annual Undergrad Tuition & Fees: $29,700
Enrollment: 7,883 Coed
Affiliation or Control: Independent Non-Profit IRS Status: 501(c)3
Highest Offering: Doctorate
Program: Liberal Arts And General; Teacher Preparatory; Professional
Accreditation: M, ARCPA, CIDA, ENG, ENGT, NURSE, OSTEO, OT, PTA, TED

01 President .... Dr. Edward GUILIANO
05 Provost/Vice Pres Academic Affairs .... Dr. Rahmat SHOURESHI
100 Chief of Staff .... Mr. Peter KINNEY
30 Vice President for Development .... Mr. John ELIZANDRO
17 Vice President Health Affairs .... Dr. Barbara ROSS-LEE
32 VP Stdnt Affs/Chief Stdnt Affs Ofcr .... Vacant
11 Vice Pres of IT & Infrastructure .... Dr. Niyazi BODUR
45 Vice Pres for Planning/Assessment .... Dr. Harriet ARNONE
84 Vice Pres Enrollment/Comm & Mktg .... Vacant
10 CFO & Treasurer .... Mr. Leonard AUBREY
21 Comptroller .... Mr. Daniel MCGOVERN
43 General Counsel .... Ms. Catherine FLICKINGER
06 Registrar .... Ms. Kristen SMITH
76 Dean School of Health Professions .... Dr. Patricia CHUTE
48 Dean Sch Architecture & Design .... Ms. Judith DIMAIO
53 Dean School of Education .... Dr. Satasha GREEN
54 Dean School of Engr & Comp Sciences .... Dr. Nada ANID
49 Dean School Arts & Sciences .... Dr. Roger YU
50 Dean School of Management .... Dr. Jess BORONICO
20 Dean Operations/Assessments & Acc .... Dr. Patricia BURLAUD
35 Dean for Campus Life .... Ms. Francy MAGEE
36 Dean of Career Services .... Mr. John HYDE
75 Dean Voc Independence Program .... Dr. Ernst VANBERGEIJK
09 Director Inst Research & Assessment .... Mr. Michael LANE
07 Associate Dean of UG Admissions .... Mr. Troy MILLER
84 Associate Dean Acad Sppt/Enroll .... Dr. Alexander OTT
88 Director Branch Services .... Dr. Gerri FLANZRAICH
27 Director Publications & Advertising .... Ms. Susan WARNER
27 Director of Communications .... Ms. Bobbie DELL'AQUILO
29 Director of Alumni Relations .... Ms. Jennifer KELLY
18 Director of Facilities Operations .... Mr. William MARCHAND
37 Associate Dean of Financial Aid .... Ms. Rosemary FERRUCCI
37 Senior Director of Financial Aid .... Ms. Karyn WRIGHT-MOORE
19 Director Security .... Mr. Denis MCGUCKIN
41 Director Athletics & Recreation .... Mr. Clyde DOUGHTY, JR.
25 Asst Provost Spnsrd Pgms & Research .... Dr. Allison ANDORS
13 Director Plng & Business Affairs .... Ms. Ajisa DERVISEVIC
96 Director Purchasing .... Mr. David UDKOW
88 Director of Internal Audit .... Vacant
38 Director Counseling & Wellness Svcs .. Ms. Alice HERON-BURKE
88 Assistant Dean Academic Enrichment .... Ms. Monika SCHUEREN
15 Director of Human Resources .... Ms. Carol JABLONSKY
90 Director Client Services .... Ms. Laurie HARVEY
91 Director Systems & Network .... Mr. Brian MAROLDO
91 Director Enterprise Systems & Svcs .... Ms. Chuqian ZHANG
35 Assoc Dean Student Development .... Ms. Zennabelle SEWELL
88 Dir Events Planning & Hospitality .... Mr. Jerry LIMONCELLI

New York Law School (I)

185 West Broadway, New York NY 10013-2959
County: New York FICE Identification: 002783
Unit ID: 193821
Telephone: (212) 431-2100 Carnegie Class: Spec/Law
FAX Number: (212) 965-8838 Calendar System: Semester
URL: www.nyls.edu
Established: 1891 Annual Graduate Tuition & Fees: $49,225
Enrollment: 1,503 Coed
Affiliation or Control: Independent Non-Profit IRS Status: 501(c)3
Highest Offering: Doctorate; No Undergraduates
Program: Professional
Accreditation: LAW

01 Dean and President .... Dean Anthony CROWELL
03 Executive VP & Chief Strategy Ofcr .... Ms. Carole POST
05 Assoc Dean of Academic Affairs .... Dean Deborah ARCHER
10 Vice President for Finance & Admin .... Dean Stuart KLEIN
45 Assoc Dean for Inst Accountability .... Dean Joan R. FISHMAN
26 Vice Pres Communications/Mrktng .... Ms. Nancy J. GUIDA
26 Vice President for Public Affairs .... Mr. Darren BLOCH

08 Director of Law Library/Assoc Dean ... Prof. Camille BROUSSARD
32 Assoc Dean of Student Development ... Dean Marianna HOGAN
88 Director Academic Publishing ... Prof. Jethro K. LIEBERMAN
84 Assoc Dean Admissions/Financial Aid ... Mr. Adam BARRETT
21 Asst VP Financial Planning & Mgmt ... Ms. Susan REDLER
18 Chief of Maintenance/Operations ... Mr. George HAYES
15 Asst Vice President Human Resources ... Ms. Jody PARIANTE
19 Assist Vice Pres Security & Safety ... Mr. George HAYES
07 Asst Dean of Admissions & Finan Aid ... Ms. Ella Mae ESTRADA
21 Asst Vice Pres Business Operations ... Ms. Catherine MACLEOD
09 Asst VP Institutional Research ... Dr. Joanne INGHAM
44 Assistant Vice Pres Development . Ms. Tara REGIST-TOMLINSON
29 Assistant Vice Pres Alumni Relation ... Mr. Travis FRASER
20 Assistant Dean Academic Affairs ... Ms. Victoria EASTUS
20 Asst Dean Academic Program Developm ... Ms. Erin BOND
06 Assistant Dean and Registrar ... Mr. Oral HOPE
58 Asst Dean for Graduate Education ... Ms. Tracey PARR
13 Chief Information Officer ... Mr. Thomas SOCASH
32 Assistant Dean for Student Services ... Ms. Helena PRIGAL
36 Asst Dean for Career Planning ... Mr. Jeffery BECHERER
35 Sr Director of Student Life ... Ms. Sally HARDING
20 Assoc Director Academic Planning ... Ms. Kiera FLAD
20 Assoc Director Academic Planning ... Ms. Jaime LANGINESTRA
96 Purchasing Coordinator ... Mr. Norman DAWKINS

New York Medical College (A)

40 Sunshine Cottage Road, Valhalla NY 10595-1690
County: Westchester FICE Identification: 002784
Unit ID: 193830
Telephone: (914) 594-4900 Carnegie Class: Spec/Med
FAX Number: (914) 594-4145 Calendar System: Other
URL: www.nymc.edu
Established: 1860 Annual Graduate Tuition & Fees: $48,000
Enrollment: 1,455 Coed
Affiliation or Control: Jewish IRS Status: 501(c)3
Highest Offering: Doctorate; No Undergraduates
Program: Professional; Business Emphasis
Accreditation: M, DENT, MED, PH, PTA, SP

01 President ... Dr. Alan H. KADISH
03 Administrator ... Ms. Vilma BORDONARO
17 CEO/Exec Dean/Chanc Health Affairs ... Dr. Edward C. HALPERIN
10 Sr VP/CFO/Vice Prov Admin & Finance ... Mr. Stephen PICCOLO, JR.
58 Dean Grad Sch Basic Medical Science ... Dr. Francis L. BELLONI
43 Vice President/General Counsel ... Mr. Waldemar A. COMAS
30 Vice President Univ Dev/Alumni Rels ... Ms. LArissa REECE
86 Vice President Government Affairs ... Dr. Robert W. AMLER
15 Assoc Vice Pres Human Resources ... Mr. Peter M. BROWN
21 Assoc Vice Pres/Controller ... Mr. George NESTLER
43 Assoc Vice Pres Legal Affairs ... Ms. Dana LEE
26 Assoc Vice Pres Communications ... Ms. Donna E. MORIARTY
11 Vice Prov/Sr Assoc Dean Acad Admin ... Mr. William A. STEADMAN, II
27 Chief Information Officer ... Dr. Sandra SHIVERS
76 Dean Sch Health Sciences & Practice ... Dr. Robert W. AMLER
63 Vice Dean Grad Med Ed/Affiliations .. Dr. Richard G. MCCARRICK
09 Assoc Dean Research Administration ... Ms. Catharine CREA
32 Sr Assoc Dean Student Affairs ... Dr. Gladys M. AYALA
37 Asc Dn Stdnt Affs/Dir Finan Plng ... Mr. Anthony M. SOZZO
88 Sr Assoc Dean Pre-Internship Pgm .. Dr. Saverio S. BENTIVEGNA
07 Sr Associate Dean Admissions ... Dr. Fern R. JUSTER
51 Assoc Dean Continuing Med Education ... Dr. Joseph F. DURSI
08 Assoc Dean/Dir Health Sci Library ... Ms. Diana J. CUNNINGHAM
07 Director of Admissions ... Ms. Robin BAUM
06 University Registrar/Assoc Provost ... Ms. Judith A. EHREN
39 Director Student Housing ... Vacant
18 Director Facilities Management ... Mr. Michael J. SHALLO
19 Director of Security ... Mr. William ALLISON
85 Intl Student/Scholar Advisor ... Ms. Elizabeth WARD
51 Director of Continuing Medical Educ ... Ms. Kathy J. KAVANAGH
101 Secretary to Board of Trustees ... Ms. Patricia J. TRAVIS
23 Director Health Services ... Dr. Joseph F. DURSI
38 Director Student Counseling ... Dr. Mark SINGER
105 Director Web Services ... Mr. Kevin R. CUMMINGS
40 Director Bookstore ... Ms. Liz REYNOLDS
24 Head Educational Media ... Mr. Michael COTTER
13 Coord of Instruct Computing Tech ... Mr. Jason DI NARDI
96 Purchasing Manager ... Mr. John STEIN

New York School of Interior Design (B)

170 East 70th Street, New York NY 10021-5110
County: New York FICE Identification: 020690
Unit ID: 194116
Telephone: (212) 472-1500 Carnegie Class: Spec/Arts
FAX Number: (212) 472-3800 Calendar System: 4/1/4
URL: www.nysid.edu
Established: 1916 Annual Undergrad Tuition & Fees: $30,996
Enrollment: 647 Coed
Affiliation or Control: Independent Non-Profit IRS Status: 501(c)3
Highest Offering: Master's
Program: Professional
Accreditation: @M, ART, CIDA

01 President ... Mr. David SPROULS
05 VP Academic Affairs/Dean ... Dr. Ellen FISHER
10 VP for Finance & Administration ... Ms. Jane CHEN
32 Dean of Students ... Ms. Karen HIGGINBOTHAM
04 Assistant to the President ... Ms. Jeanne KO
36 Academic Advisor/Dir Career Place ... Ms. Patricia ZIEGLER
06 Registrar ... Ms. Susan LOVELL
08 Director of the Library ... Ms. Sarah FALLS
07 Director of Admissions ... Ms. Celeste COLLINS
37 Financial Aid Administrator ... Ms. Rashmi WADHVANI
15 Director of Personnel Services ... Ms. Balbina CALO
18 Chief Facilities/Physical Plant ... Mr. Zeke KOLENOVIC
26 Director of External Relations ... Ms. Samantha HOOVER
29 Chief Development/Dir Alumni Rels ... Ms. Samantha FINGLETON
20 Associate Dean ... Ms. Veronica WHITLOCK
13 Dir Computing/Information Mgmt ... Mr. Tomasz SOWINSKI
90 Director Academic Computing ... Mr. Richard T. CLASS
40 Director Bookstore ... Mr. Daniel TERCHEK
38 Director Student Counseling ... Dr. Penny MORGANSTEIN
09 Director of Institutional Research ... Mr. Greg LINCOLN
30 Director Development ... Ms. Elizabeth GRAY KOGEN

New York Theological Seminary (C)

475 Riverside Drive, Suite 500, New York NY 10115-0083
County: New York FICE Identification: 002674
Unit ID: 193894
Telephone: (212) 870-1211 Carnegie Class: Not Classified
FAX Number: (212) 870-1236 Calendar System: Semester
URL: www.nyts.edu
Established: 1900 Annual Graduate Tuition & Fees: $15,750
Enrollment: 392 Coed
Affiliation or Control: Independent Non-Profit IRS Status: 501(c)3
Highest Offering: Doctorate; No Undergraduates
Program: Professional
Accreditation: THEOL

01 President ... Dr. Dale T. IRVIN
30 Dir Development/Inst Advancement ... Ms. Courtney WILEY-HARRIS
05 Academic Dean ... Mr. Kirkpatrick G. COHALL
08 Librarian ... Mr. Jerry REISIG
06 Registrar ... Ms. Lydia R. BUMGARDNER
37 Director Financial Aid ... Ms. Tamisia WHITE

New York University (D)

70 Washington Square S, New York NY 10012-1092
County: New York FICE Identification: 002785
Unit ID: 193900
Telephone: (212) 998-1212 Carnegie Class: RU/VH
FAX Number: N/A Calendar System: Semester
URL: www.nyu.edu
Established: 1831 Annual Undergrad Tuition & Fees: $43,204
Enrollment: 44,516 Coed
Affiliation or Control: Independent Non-Profit IRS Status: 501(c)3
Highest Offering: Doctorate
Program: Occupational; 2-Year Principally Bachelor's Creditable; Liberal Arts And General; Teacher Preparatory; Professional
Accreditation: M, BUS, COPSY, DENT, DH, DIETD, DIETI, HSA, IPSY, JOUR, LAW, MED, MIDWF, NURSE, OT, PH, PLNG, PTA, SCPSY, SP, SPAA, SURGT, SW, TEAC

01 President ... Dr. John SEXTON
05 Provost ... Dr. David MCLAUGHLIN
10 Executive VP for Finance/IT ... Dr. Martin DORPH
11 Executive VP for Operations ... Ms. Alison L. LEARY
17 Executive VP for Health ... Dr. Robert BERNE
100 Chief of Staff/Deputy to President ... Ms. Diane YU
26 Sr VP for Univ Rels/Pub Affairs ... Dr. Lynne BROWN
30 Sr VP Development/Alumni Relations ... Ms. Debra A. LAMORTE
43 Sr VP General Counsel & Secretary ... Ms. Bonnie BRIER
88 Vice Prov Glblztn/Multi-Cult Affs ... Dr. Ulrich C. BAER
46 Sr Vice Provost for Research ... Dr. Paul M. HORN
20 Sr Vice Provost ... Dr. Jules L. COLEMAN
20 Senior Presidential Fellow ... Dr. Michael C. ALFANO
88 Sr Vice Provost NYU Abu Dhabi ... Dr. Ron ROBIN
20 Sr Vice Prov Undrgrd Acad Affairs . Dr. Matthew S. SANTIROCCO
45 Vice Chancellor Strategic Planning ... Dr. Richard FOLEY
32 VC Global Pgms/Univ Life at NYU ... Dr. Linda G. MILLS
20 Provost Polytech Inst at NYU ... Dr. Katepalli R. SREENIVASAN
18 VP Construction Mgmt/Strategic Svcs ... Mr. David ALONSO
26 VP for Public Affairs ... Mr. John H. BECKMAN
45 VP Public Resource Admin & Devel ... Dr. Richard N. BING
15 Sr VP for HR/Global Support ... Ms. Catherine M. CASEY
84 VP Enrollment ... Dr. Randall DEIKE
88 VP Univ Enterprise Initiatives ... Dr. Richard A. MATASAR
44 VP Development and Campaigns ... Ms. Sarah P. WATERBURY
16 VP Human Resources ... Mr. Andrew R. GORDON
13 VP for Global Technology ... Mr. Thomas DELANEY
11 VP for Admin/Chief of Staff ... Mr. A. Steven DONOFRIO
86 VP Gov Affairs/Community Engagement ... Dr. Alicia HURLEY
21 VP Budget & Planning ... Mr. Anthony JIGA
40 VP for Auxiliary Services ... Dr. Robert KIVETZ
21 VP Finance Operations/Treasurer ... Ms. Stephanie PIANKA
19 VP Global Security & Crisis Mgmt ... Mr. Jules A. MARTIN
13 VP IT and CITO for NYU NY Campus ... Ms. Marilyn A. MCMILLAN
06 University Registrar ... Dr. Roger O. PRINTUP
21 Chief Investment Officer ... Ms. Tina H. SURH
35 VP for Global Student Affairs ... Dr. Marc L. WAIS
88 VP Acad/Fac/Rsrch Affairs ... Dr. C. Cybele RAVER
26 Assoc VP for Marketing Comm ... Ms. Deborah BRODERICK
29 Assoc VP for Alumni Relations ... Mr. Brian PERILLO
88 Assoc Vice Prov Rsrch Cmplnc/Admin ... Dr. Martha L. DUNNE
96 Assoc VP Purchasing & Logistics ... Mr. Charles SCHOTT
*20 Assoc Vice Prov Acad Init/Spcl Proj ... Dr. Nancy J. MORRISON
20 Assoc Provost Academic Operations ... Dr. Carol K. MORROW
07 Asst VP for Undergrad Admissions ... Mr. Shawn L. ABBOTT
20 Asst Provost Academic Pgm Review ... Mr. Barnett W. HAMBERGER
28 Asst VP Commun Outreach & Engagemnt ... Mr. Allen M. MCFARLANE
21 Asst VP/Controller ... Ms. Kerri J. TRICARICO
41 Asst VP Stdnt Affairs/Dir Athletics ... Mr. Christopher BLEDSOE
23 Assoc VP Stdnt Hlth/Exec Dir SHC ... Dr. Carlo CIOTOLI
09 Dir Institutional Research ... Dr. Randall DEIKE
37 Asst VP Financial Aid ... Ms. Lynn E. HIGINBOTHAM
102 Dir Office of Sponsored Programs ... Mr. Richard L. LOUTH
88 Dir Internal Audit ... Mr. Eugene PAWLOWSKI
22 Exec Dir Ofc of Equal Opportunity ... Ms. Mary SIGNOR
36 Asst VP Student Affairs ... Ms. Trudy G. STEINFELD

Niagara County Community College (E)

3111 Saunders Settlement Road, Sanborn NY 14132-9460
County: Niagara FICE Identification: 002874
Unit ID: 193946
Telephone: (716) 614-6200 Carnegie Class: Assoc/Pub-S-SC
FAX Number: (716) 614-6700 Calendar System: Semester
URL: www.niagaracc.suny.edu
Established: 1962 Annual Undergrad Tuition & Fees (In-District): $4,040
Enrollment: 6,743 Coed
Affiliation or Control: State/Local IRS Status: 501(c)3
Highest Offering: Associate Degree
Program: Occupational; 2-Year Principally Bachelor's Creditable
Accreditation: M, ACFEI, ADNUR, MAC, PTAA, RAD, SURGT

01 President ... Dr. James KLYCZEK
05 Vice President Academic Affairs ... Dr. Eunice BELLINGER
103 VP Workforce Development ... Vacant
10 Vice President of Finance/Info Tech ... Mr. William SCHICKLING
32 Vice President of Student Services ... Mrs. Julia PITMAN
11 Vice President of Operations ... Mr. Michael DOMBROWSKI
09 Director Planning and Research ... Dr. Mary Jane FELDMAN
20 Associate Dean ... Vacant
15 Interim Director of Human Resources ... Mr. Donald ARMSTRONG
07 Director of Admissions ... Ms. Kathy SAUNDERS
21 Director of Business Services ... Ms. Theresa DIGREGORIO
04 Assistant to President ... Ms. Barbara WALCK
06 Registrar ... Ms. Julie SPEER
35 Director of Student Development ... Mrs. Allison ARMUSEWICZ
30 Chief Development Officer ... Ms. Deborah BREWER
37 Director of Financial Aid ... Mr. James TRIMBOLI
26 Director Public Relations ... Ms. Paula SANDY
18 Assistant Director of Facilities ... Mr. James LOBDELL
28 Interim Director of Diversity ... Mr. Donald ARMSTRONG

Niagara University (F)

Niagara University NY 14109-9999
County: Niagara FICE Identification: 002788
Unit ID: 193973
Telephone: (716) 285-1212 Carnegie Class: Master's L
FAX Number: (716) 286-8710 Calendar System: Semester
URL: www.niagara.edu
Established: 1856 Annual Undergrad Tuition & Fees: $28,200
Enrollment: 4,045 Coed
Affiliation or Control: Independent Non-Profit IRS Status: 501(c)3
Highest Offering: Doctorate
Program: Liberal Arts And General; Teacher Preparatory; Professional
Accreditation: M, BUS, NURSE, SW, TED

01 President ... Rev. James MAHER, CM
03 Exec Vice President ... Dr. Bonnie ROSE
05 Vice President for Academic Affairs ... Dr. Timothy M. DOWNS
32 Vice President for Student Affairs ... Dr. Kevin HEARN
10 Vice Pres Business Aff & Treasurer ... Mr. Michael S. JASZKA
30 Vice Pres Institutional Advancement ... Mr. David CRISTANTELLO
20 Asc VP Academic Affs/Pgms & Policy ... Dr. Thomas A. CHAMBERS
20 Assoc VP Acad Affs/Ops/Outreach ... Ms. Mary E. BORGOGNONI
44 Assoc VP for Institutional Advance ... Vacant
45 Asst to the President for Planning ... Dr. Judith A. WILLARD
43 General Counsel ... Ms. Stephanie A. COLE
06 Registrar/Dean of Enrollment Mgmt ... Vacant
09 Director Institutional Research ... Ms. Catherine E. SERIANNI
07 Director of Admissions ... Mr. Mark E. WOJNOWSKI
08 Director of Libraries ... Mr. David SCHOEN
19 Director of Campus Safety ... Mr. John F. BARKER
35 Dean of Student Affairs ... Ms. Carrie MCLAUGHLIN
37 Director Student Financial Aid ... Vacant
39 Director of Residence Life ... Mr. Jason JAKUBOWSKI
26 Assoc VP of Comm/Public Relations ... Mr. Thomas BURNS
29 Exec Director Alumni Engagement ... Ms. Christine S. O'HARA
13 Director Information Technology ... Mr. Richard P. KERNIN
49 Dean College of Arts & Science ... Dr. Timothy IRELAND
53 Dean College of Education ... Dr. Debra A. COLLEY
50 Dean College Business Admin ... Dr. Shawn p. DALY
88 Dean Col Hospitality/Tourism Mgmt ... Dr. Gary D. PRAETZEL
57 Director of Art Museum ... Ms. Kate KOPERSKI
15 Director of Human Resources ... Mr. Robert PFEIL
23 Director of Health Services ... Ms. Lori SOOS
41 Director of Athletics ... Mr. Tom CROWLEY
18 Director of Facility Services ... Mr. Daniel M. GUARIGLIA
44 Director Annual Fund ... Ms. Christine S. O'HARA
42 Assoc VP of Campus Ministry ... Rev. Kevin KREAGH, CM
88 Director of Academic Support ... Mrs. Diane STOELTING

51 Dir Continuing/Community Education ..... Mr. Jon Jay STOCKSLADER
38 Director Counseling Services ..... Monica ROMEO
21 Controller ..... Mr. Donald E. SMITH
96 Director of Business Services ..... Ms. Christy FERGUSON
88 Assoc Dean for Graduate Recruitment ..... Mr. Evan F. PIERCE
88 Exec Dir Division of Academic Svcs ..... Ms. Antonia KNIGHT
85 Dir Multicultural & Intl Stdnt Affs ..... Mr. David BLACKBURN
06 Director of Records & Operations ..... Ms. Lenora ANDREWS
88 Director of Student Accounts ..... Ms. Martie HOWELL
25 Director Grants & Sponsored Program .. Ms. Adrienne LEIBOWITZ
36 Director of Career Services ..... Mr. Robert P. SWANSON
88 Director of Academic Exploration ..... Ms. Stephanie CURRIE
88 Director of Lean and Serve ..... Ms. Fran BOLTZ

North Country Community College (A)

23 Santanoni Avenue, PO Box 89,
Saranac Lake NY 12983-0089
County: Essex FICE Identification: 007111
Unit ID: 194028
Telephone: (518) 891-2915 Carnegie Class: Assoc/Pub-R-S
FAX Number: (518) 891-2915 Calendar System: Semester
URL: www.nccc.edu
Established: 1967 Annual Undergrad Tuition & Fees (In-District): $4,800
Enrollment: 2,335 Coed
Affiliation or Control: State/Local IRS Status: 501(c)3
Highest Offering: Associate Degree
Program: Occupational; 2-Year Principally Bachelor's Creditable
Accreditation: M, RAD

01 President ..... Dr. Steve J. TYRELL
05 Vice Pres of Academic Affairs ..... Dr. Patricia OWEN
10 Vice Pres for Fiscal Operations/CFO ..... Mr. William CHAPIN
84 VP Enroll/Stdnt Svcs/Asst to Pres ..... Vacant
06 Registrar/Records Officer ..... Vacant
09 Asst Dean Inst Research/Support ..... Mr. Scott HARWOOD
18 Asst Dean Facilities/Spec Projects ..... Mr. Jim JACKSON
07 Dir Admiss/Alumni Rels/Chf PR Ofcr ..... Vacant
35 Director of Campus & Student Life ..... Mrs. Roberta KARP
15 Director Personnel Services ..... Ms. Colleen DOWNS
29 Director Alumni Relations ..... Ms. Diana FORTUNE

Northeastern Seminary (B)

2265 Westside Drive, Rochester NY 14624-1932
County: Monroe FICE Identification: 034194
Unit ID: 439817
Telephone: (585) 594-6800 Carnegie Class: Spec/Faith
FAX Number: (585) 594-6801 Calendar System: Semester
URL: www.nes.edu
Established: 1998 Annual Graduate Tuition & Fees: $8,572
Enrollment: 173 Coed
Affiliation or Control: Independent Non-Profit IRS Status: 501(c)3
Highest Offering: Doctorate; No Undergraduates
Program: Professional; Religious Emphasis
Accreditation: M, NY, THEOL

01 President ..... Dr. John A. MARTIN
05 Academic Vice President and Dean ..... Dr. Douglas CULLUM

† The Seminary is affiliated with Roberts Wesleyan College.

Nyack College (C)

1 South Boulevard, Nyack NY 10960-3698
County: Rockland FICE Identification: 002790
Unit ID: 194161
Telephone: (845) 675-4400 Carnegie Class: Master's L
FAX Number: (845) 358-1751 Calendar System: Semester
URL: www.nyack.edu
Established: 1882 Annual Undergrad Tuition & Fees: $23,250
Enrollment: 3,318 Coed
Affiliation or Control: The Christian And Missionary Alliance
IRS Status: 501(c)3
Highest Offering: Doctorate
Program: 2-Year Principally Bachelor's Creditable; Liberal Arts And General; Teacher Preparatory; Professional
Accreditation: M, MUS, SW, TED, THEOL

01 President ..... Dr. Michael G. SCALES
04 Assistant to the President ..... Mrs. Carol Ann FREEMAN
05 Provost/VP for Academic Affairs ..... Dr. David F. TURK
10 Exec Vice President & Treasurer ..... Mr. David C. JENNINGS
84 Vice President for Enrollment ..... Dr. Andrea HENNESSY
30 Vice President of Advancement ..... Mr. Jeff CORY
20 Assistant Provost ..... Dr. Bennett SCHEPENS
73 Dean Seminary ..... Dr. Ronald WALBORN
50 Dean School of Business & Ldrshp ..... Dr. Anita UNDERWOOD
64 Dean School of Music ..... Dr. Glenn KOPONEN
53 Dean School of Education ..... Dr. JoAnn LOONEY
49 Assoc Dean College of Arts & Sci ..... Dr. Fernando ARZOLA
08 Dean of Library Services ..... Mrs. Linda K. POSTON
89 Assoc Dean Student Success ..... Dr. Gwen PARKER AMES
73 Assoc Dean Seminary (NYC) ..... Dr. Luis CARLO
73 Asst Dean Seminary (Puerto Rico) ..... Dr. Julio APONTE
32 Dean of Students ..... Mrs. Wanda VELEZ
06 Undergraduate Registrar ..... Ms. Evangeline COUCHEY
06 Graduate Registrar ..... Ms. Rebecca NOSS
07 Dir of Admissions Undergrad ..... Mr. Dinesh MAHTANI
07 Dir of Admissions Undergrad (NYC) ..... Vacant
07 Dir of Admissions Seminary ..... Mrs. Traci PIESCKI
21 Assistant Treasurer ..... Mrs. Dona P. SCHEPENS
37 Dir of Fin Svcs Undergrad ..... Mr. Steve PHILLIPS
37 Dir of Fin Svcs Undergrad (NYC) ..... Mr. Isaac FOSTER
31 Executive Director of Community Rel ..... Mr. Earl MILLER
41 Director of Athletics ..... Mr. Keith A. DAVIE
36 Director of Career Services ..... Ms. Tiffany AUSTIN
15 Director of Human Resources ..... Mrs. Karen DAVIE
13 Director of Information Technology ..... Mr. Kevin A. BUEL
09 Director of Institutional Research ..... Mr. Greg BEEMAN
18 Director of Operations/Aramark ..... Mr. Douglas WALKER
26 Director of Pub & Media Relations ..... Ms. Deborah WALKER
42 Director of Spiritual Formation ..... Mrs. Wanda F. WALBORN
38 Director of Wellness Services ..... Mrs. Drusila F. NIEVES
29 Coordinator of Alumni Services ..... Mrs. Melissa HICKEY
105 Webmaster ..... Mr. Joshua WAY

Nyack College Manhattan Center (D)

361 Broadway, New York NY 10013
Telephone: (212) 625-0500 Identification: 770143
Accreditation: &M

† Main campus is Nyack College in Nyack, NY.

Ohr Hameir Theological Seminary (E)

141 Furnace Woods Road,
Cortlandt Manor NY 10567-6112
County: Westchester FICE Identification: 011984
Unit ID: 194189
Telephone: (914) 736-1500 Carnegie Class: Spec/Faith
FAX Number: (914) 736-1055 Calendar System: Semester
Established: 1962 Annual Undergrad Tuition & Fees: $8,900
Enrollment: 90 Male
Affiliation or Control: Independent Non-Profit IRS Status: 501(c)3
Highest Offering: Second Talmudic Degree
Program: Teacher Preparatory; Professional
Accreditation: RABN

01 President ..... Rabbi E. KANAREK
30 Chief Devel Ofcr/Dir Financial Aid ..... Rabbi Jacob ROTHBERG
06 Registrar ..... Rabbi Berel KANAREK

Ohr Somayach Tanenbaum Educational Center (F)

244 Route 306, Monsey NY 10952-0334
County: Rockland FICE Identification: 023201
Unit ID: 243805
Telephone: (845) 425-1370 Carnegie Class: Not Classified
FAX Number: (845) 425-8865 Calendar System: Trimester
URL: www.os.edu
Established: 1979 Annual Undergrad Tuition & Fees: $7,250
Enrollment: 50 Coordinate
Affiliation or Control: Independent Non-Profit IRS Status: 501(c)3
Highest Offering: First Professional Degree
Program: Professional
Accreditation: RABN

01 Director ..... Rabbi Abraham BRAUN
05 Dean ..... Rabbi Israel ROKOWSKY
06 Registrar ..... Mrs. Miriam GROSSMAN
10 Chief Business Officer ..... Rabbi Eli ROKOWSKY

Onondaga Community College (G)

4585 West Seneca Turnpike, Syracuse NY 13215-4585
County: Onondaga FICE Identification: 002875
Unit ID: 194222
Telephone: (315) 498-2622 Carnegie Class: Assoc/Pub-U-MC
FAX Number: (315) 492-9208 Calendar System: Semester
URL: www.sunyocc.edu
Established: 1962 Annual Undergrad Tuition & Fees (In-District): $4,756
Enrollment: 13,018 Coed
Affiliation or Control: State/Local IRS Status: 501(c)3
Highest Offering: Associate Degree
Program: Occupational; 2-Year Principally Bachelor's Creditable
Accreditation: M, ADNUR, CAHIIM, COARC, ENGT, PTAA, SURGT

01 President ..... Dr. Casey CRABILL
03 VP College-affiliated Enterprises ..... Mr. Seth TUCKER
03 VP College-affiliated Enterprises ..... Ms. Anastasia URTZ
05 Provost and SVP Educational Svcs ..... Dr. Cathleen C. MCCOLGIN
10 SVP College-affltd Ent & Asset Mgmt ..... Mr. David W. MURPHY
30 Vice President Development ..... Mr. John ZACHAREK
15 VP HR & External Affairs ..... Ms. Amy KREMENEK
09 VP Inst Planning/Assess/Research ..... Dr. Agatha AWUAH
14 Chief Information Officer ..... Ms. Andrea VENUTI
11 Chief Financial Officer ..... Mr. Mark MANNING
20 Int VP Academic Svcs & Global Init ..... Dr. Emmanuel AWUAH
28 VP Curr & Instr Supp/Diversity ..... Ms. Eunice WILLIAMS
18 VP Property Management ..... Mr. John PADDOCK
32 AVP Student Development ..... Mr. William BRYAN
84 AVP Enrollment Management ..... Ms. Melissa GREEN
84 AVP Enrollment Development ..... Ms. Shannon PATRIE
37 Director Student Finance ..... Ms. Kate BELLEFEUILLE
41 Athletic Director ..... Mr. Rob EDSON
08 Chair Library ..... Ms. Pauline SHOSTACK
38 Chair Counseling Department ..... Mr. Timothy SINGER
19 VP Campus Safety & Security ..... Mr. Douglas KINNEY
88 Director Disability Services ..... Ms. Nancy CARR
06 Dir Student Certification/Records ..... Ms. Tracey GREEN
21 Bursar ..... Ms. Shawn GILLEN-CARYL
36 Director Student Life & Development ..... Ms. Lysa SIMMONS
96 Director Management Services ..... Mr. Michael MCMULLEN
39 Residence Life Director ..... Ms. Cathy DOTTERER
35 Dir Student Activities & Leadership ..... Mr. Monty FLYNN
07 Director Recruitment & Admission ..... Ms. Katherine PERRY
89 Dir Ctr Advising & 1st Year Student ..... Dr. Anne SHELLY
88 Director of Sustainability ..... Mr. Sean VORMWALD

Orange County Community College (H)

115 South Street, Middletown NY 10940-6437
County: Orange FICE Identification: 002876
Unit ID: 194240
Telephone: (845) 344-6222 Carnegie Class: Assoc/Pub-R-L
FAX Number: (845) 343-1228 Calendar System: Semester
URL: www.sunyorange.edu
Established: 1950 Annual Undergrad Tuition & Fees (In-District): $4,548
Enrollment: 7,257 Coed
Affiliation or Control: State/Local IRS Status: 501(c)3
Highest Offering: Associate Degree
Program: Occupational; 2-Year Principally Bachelor's Creditable; Business Emphasis
Accreditation: M, ACBSP, ADNUR, DH, MLTAD, OTA, PHLEB, PTAA, RAD

01 President ..... Dr. William RICHARDS
05 Vice President Academic Affairs ..... Ms. Heather PERFETTI
32 Vice President Student Services ..... Mr. Paul BROADIE, II
10 Vice Pres Administration/Finance ..... Ms. Roslyn SMITH
30 Vice Pres Institutional Advancement ..... Mr. Vinnie CAZZETTA
12 Vice President Newburgh Campus ..... Ms. Mindy ROSS
13 Vice President & Chief Info Ofcr ..... Mr. Jose BERNIER
20 Sr Assoc Vice Pres Academic Affairs ..... Mr. Peter SOSCIA
84 Assoc VP for Enrollment Management ..... Ms. Gerianne BRUSATI
76 Assoc VP Health Professions ..... Mr. Michael GAWRONSKI, JR.
49 Int Assoc Vice Pres of Liberal Arts ..... Ms. Mary WARRENER
50 Assoc VP Business/Math/Sci/Tech ..... Ms. Stacey MOEGENBURG
88 Assoc Vice Pres Newburgh Campus ..... Ms. Rosana REYES-ROSELLO
15 Assoc Vice Pres Human Resources ..... Ms. Wendy HOLMES
08 Director Learning Resource ..... Ms. Susan PARRY
51 Dir Continuing/Professional Educ ..... Mr. David KOHN
19 Director Campus Security/Safety ..... Mr. John AHERNE
09 Inst Plng/Assessment/Research Ofcr ..... Ms. Christine WORK
18 Director Administrative Services ..... Mr. Michael WORDEN
21 Comptroller ..... Ms. Jo Ann HAMBURG
37 Director of Financial Aid ..... Mr. John IVANKOVIC
06 Registrar ..... Mr. Neil FOLEY
27 Director of Communications ..... Mr. Mike ALBRIGHT
38 Director Advising and Counseling ..... Ms. Crystal SCHACHTER
07 Director of Admissions/Recruitment ..... Mr. Michael ROE
35 Director Student Activities ..... Mr. Steve HARPST
37 Asst Director of Financial Aid ..... Ms. Rosemary BARRETT

Orange County Community College Newburgh Branch Campus (I)

1 Washington Center, Newburgh NY 12550
Telephone: (845) 562-2454 Identification: 770144
Accreditation: &M

† Main campus is Orange County Community College in Middletown, NY.

Pace University (J)

1 Pace Plaza, New York NY 10038-1598
County: New York FICE Identification: 002791
Unit ID: 194310
Telephone: (212) 346-1200 Carnegie Class: DRU
FAX Number: (212) 346-1933 Calendar System: Semester
URL: www.pace.edu
Established: 1906 Annual Undergrad Tuition & Fees: $36,614
Enrollment: 12,772 Coed
Affiliation or Control: Independent Non-Profit IRS Status: 501(c)3
Highest Offering: Doctorate
Program: Liberal Arts And General; Teacher Preparatory; Professional
Accreditation: M, ARCPA, BUS, BUSA, CS, IPSY, LAW, NURSE, PSPSY, TED

01 President ..... Mr. Stephen J. FRIEDMAN
10 Exec Vice Pres/CFO/Treasurer ..... Mr. Toby R. WINER
05 Provost/Exec VP Academic Affairs ..... Dr. Uday SUKHATME
11 Sr Vice Pres/Chief Admin Ofcr ..... Mr. William MCGRATH
84 Vice Pres Enrollment/Placement ..... Ms. Robina C. SCHEPP
30 VP Development/Alumni Relations ..... Ms. Jennifer BERNSTEIN
13 VP Information Tech/Chief Info Ofcr ..... Mr. Thomas A. HULL
26 VP/Chief Marketing Ofcr Univ Rels ..... Ms. Frederica N. WALD
15 Int Vice Pres Human Resources ..... Mr. Matt RENNA
09 Asst Vice Pres Plng/Assess/Inst Res . Ms. Barbara S. PENNIPEDE
86 Asst Vice Pres Govt/Community Rels ..... Ms. Vanessa J. HERMAN
32 AVP Ofc Student Assistance ..... Mr. Matthew F. BONILLA
27 Asst VP Marketing/Communications ..... Ms. Susan W. KAYNE
21 Asst Vice Pres Academic Finance ..... Mr. Dominick BUMBACO
19 Associate VP General Services ..... Mr. Frank MCDONALD
35 Assoc Provost for Student Success ..... Dr. Mark Allen POISEL
20 Int Assoc Provost for Academic Affs ..... Dr. David N. RAHNI
50 Dean Lubin School of Business ..... Mr. Neil S. BRAUN
49 Dean Dyson College Arts/Sci ..... Dr. Nira HERRMANN
53 Dean School of Education ..... Dr. Andrea M. SPENCER
66 Dean Lienhard School of Nursing ..... Dr. Harriet R. FELDMAN

77 Dean School of CSIS .... Dr. Susan M. MERRITT
32 Dean of Students New York .... Dr. Marijo RUSSELL O'GRADY
32 Dean of Students Westchester .... Dr. Lisa BARDILL MOSCARITOLO
61 Dean School of Law .... Ms. Michelle S. SIMON
06 Assoc VP Stdnt Svcs/Univ Registrar .... Mr. Steven L. JOHNSON
06 Graduate Registrar .... Ms. Margaret JONES
06 Registrar Pleasantville .... Ms. Annmarie MCGRAIL
06 Law School Registrar .... Ms. Nilda RODRIGUEZ
88 Associate University Registrar .... Ms. Barbara MCCARTHY
36 Exec Director Career Svcs/Coop Educ .... Ms. Jody QUEEN-HUBERT
88 Asst Director Adult Education NY .... Ms. Nicola FOSTER
21 Interim Comptroller .... Mr. William VOLL
44 Manager Annual Fund .... Ms. Nicole L. SOUZA
29 Director of Alumni Relations .... Ms. Sheri GIBSON
43 University Counsel .... Mr. Stephen BRODSKY
08 Associate Director Library .... Mr. Melvin ISAACSON
21 University Bursar .... Ms. Susan WEYGANT
37 Director Financial Aid .... Mr. Steven JOHNSON
07 Dir of Admissions NY/Westchester .... Ms. Joanna BRODA
45 Director Budget/Planning/Analysis .... Mr. Len CERTA
22 Affirmative Action Officer .... Ms. Arletha MILES
14 Univ Director Computer Systems .... Mr. Gerard TARPEY
24 Univ Director Educational Media Svc .... Mr. Frank MANNLE
84 Director Adult Enroll Svcs/New York .... Ms. Janet KIRTMAN
23 Assoc Director Health Care Unit .... Ms. Jamesetta NEWLAND
27 Director of Media Relations .... Mr. Christopher CORY
88 Director Pace Adult Resource Center .... Ms. Tamra PLOTNICK
35 Director of Student Devel New York .... Dr. David CLARK
38 Director Counseling Services .... Dr. Richard SHADICK
39 Director of Residential Life .... Mr. A. Patrick ROGER-GORDON
40 Executive Director Bookstore .... Ms. Mary LIETO
85 Assoc Dir Intl Pgms & Services .... Mr. Kraig WALKUP
96 Director of Purchasing - Contracts .... Ms. Alice SEIFERT
18 Director Facilities/Physical Plant .... Mr. Abdul JABAR
28 Director of Diversity .... Ms. Shanelle HENRY ROBINSON

Pacific College of Oriental Medicine (A)

915 Broadway, Second Floor, New York NY 10107-8243
Telephone: (212) 982-3456 Identification: 666139
Accreditation: ACCSC, ACUP

† Main campus is Pacific College of Oriental Medicine in San Diego, CA.

Paul Smith's College (B)

PO Box 265, Paul Smiths NY 12970-0265
County: Franklin FICE Identification: 002795
Unit ID: 194392
Telephone: (518) 327-6000 Carnegie Class: Bac/Diverse
FAX Number: (518) 327-6060 Calendar System: Trimester
URL: www.paulsmiths.edu
Established: 1937 Annual Undergrad Tuition & Fees: $24,652
Enrollment: 1,058 Coed
Affiliation or Control: Independent Non-Profit IRS Status: 501(c)3
Highest Offering: Baccalaureate
Program: 2-Year Principally Bachelor's Creditable; Technical Emphasis
Accreditation: M, ACFEI, ENGT, FOR

01 President .... Dr. John W. MILLS
04 Assistant to the President .... Ms. Kathleen A. KECK
05 Provost .... Dr. Richard NELSON
10 Vice President Business/Finance .... Ms. Ann Marie SOMMA
30 Vice President Inst Advancement .... Mr. F. Raymond AGNEW
84 Vice Pres Enrollment Management .... Vacant
18 VP Facilities Mgmt/Capital Project ... Mr. Steven W. MCFARLAND
13 Vice Pres Information Services .... Mr. James BUYEA
29 Director of Alumni Relations .... Ms. Heather TUTTLE
38 Director of Student Development .... Ms. Cheryl C. CULOTTA
37 Director of Financial Aid .... Ms. Mary Ellen M. CHAMBERLAIN
23 Director of Health Services .... Ms. Reiko REXILIUS-TUTHILL
24 Director Education Support Services .... Mr. Neil SURPRENANT
26 Director of Communications .... Mr. Kenneth AARON
06 Registrar .... Dr. Loralyn TAYLOR
07 Director of Admissions .... Mr. Keith BRAUN
19 Lead Campus Safety Officer .... Mr. Phil FIACCO
09 Director Institutional Research .... Dr. Loralyn TAYLOR
22 Director HEOP .... Ms. Kate MULLEN
41 Dir of Athletics/Physical Educ .... Mr. James TUCKER
21 Comptroller .... Ms. Laura ROZELL
32 Chief Student Affairs Officer .... Mr. Matthew SETON-SCHUR
40 Manager of College Store .... Ms. Diana L. LYNG-GLIDDI
15 Human Resources Generalist .... Ms. Sharon VAN AUKEN
96 Purchasing Coordinator .... Ms. Cynthia LEMERY
36 Career Coordinator .... Ms. Debra DUTCHER
49 Dean Commercial/Applied/Lib Arts .... Dr. Phillip TAYLOR
65 Dean Natural Resource Mgmt/Ecology .... Dr. Jeffrey T. WALTON

Phillips Beth Israel School of Nursing (C)

776 Sixth Avenue, 4th Floor, New York NY 10001-6354
County: New York FICE Identification: 006438
Unit ID: 189282
Telephone: (212) 614-6110 Carnegie Class: Assoc/PrivNFP
FAX Number: (212) 614-6109 Calendar System: Semester
URL: www.futurenursebi.org
Established: 1904 Annual Undergrad Tuition & Fees: $21,510
Enrollment: 304 Coed
Affiliation or Control: Independent Non-Profit IRS Status: 501(c)3
Highest Offering: Associate Degree
Program: Occupational; 2-Year Principally Bachelor's Creditable; Nursing Emphasis
Accreditation: NY, ADNUR

01 Dean .... Dr. Janet MACKIN
05 Assistant Dean .... Mrs. Bernice PASS-STERN
32 Director Student Services .... Ms. Linda FABRIZIO

Plaza College (D)

74-09 37th Avenue, Jackson Heights NY 11372-6391
County: Queens FICE Identification: 012358
Unit ID: 194499
Telephone: (718) 779-1430 Carnegie Class: Bac/Assoc
FAX Number: (718) 779-7423 Calendar System: Semester
URL: www.plazacollege.edu
Established: 1916 Annual Undergrad Tuition & Fees: $12,350
Enrollment: 822 Coed
Affiliation or Control: Proprietary IRS Status: Proprietary
Highest Offering: Baccalaureate
Program: Occupational; 2-Year Principally Bachelor's Creditable
Accreditation: M, MAC

01 President .... Charles E. CALLAHAN, SR.
03 Provost .... Charles E. CALLAHAN, III
10 Vice Pres of Financial Services .... Elizabeth K. CALLAHAN
05 Academic Dean .... Marie DOLLA
06 Registrar .... Carol GARCIA
21 Comptroller .... Linda ROCKHILL
07 Dean of Admissions .... Rose Ann BLACK
20 Dean Curriculum Development .... Marianne C. ZIPF
08 College Librarian .... Eva BABALIS
23 Director Health Services .... Candice CALLAHAN
37 Financial Aid Coord/Dir Fin Svcs .... Peggy CHUNG
29 Alumni Relations/Internship Coord .... Jonathan HOWLE
100 Chief of Staff/HR Officer/Placement .... Correne CAVALIERI
09 Assoc Dean Institutional Research .... Edward DEE
27 Chief Information Officer .... Dean DEBEER
32 Director of Student Services .... Dawn VETRANO
62 Director of Library/LRC .... Kathleen D'APRIX
13 Director Information Technology .... Norman ALVARADO
45 Director Strategic Initiatives .... Charles CALLAHAN, IV
76 Program Director Medical Assisting .... Daryl ANDERSON

Polytechnic Institute of New York University (E)

6 Metrotech Center, Brooklyn NY 11201-3840
County: Kings FICE Identification: 002796
Unit ID: 194541
Telephone: (718) 260-3600 Carnegie Class: RU/H
FAX Number: (718) 260-3136 Calendar System: Semester
URL: www.poly.edu
Established: 1854 Annual Undergrad Tuition & Fees: $40,570
Enrollment: 4,652 Coed
Affiliation or Control: Independent Non-Profit IRS Status: 501(c)3
Highest Offering: Doctorate
Program: Liberal Arts And General; Professional; Technical Emphasis
Accreditation: M, ENG

01 President .... Dr. Katepalli SREENIVASAN
05 Provost .... Dr. Katepalli SREENIVASAN
10 VP Finance & Business Affairs .... Mr. Dennis DINTINO
30 VP Devel & Alumni Relations .... Ms. Erica MARKS
88 VP of Enterprise Learning .... Mr. Robert N. UBELL
100 Chief of Staff/VP Strat Initiatives .... Ms. Elizabeth LUSSKIN
88 Assc Prov Research/Tech Initiatives .... Dr. Kurt BECKER
45 Assc Provost Pgms/Plng/Development .... Dr. Mary COWMAN
54 Assoc Provost Abu Dhabi Engineering .... Dr. Sunil KUMAR
58 Assoc Provost Graduate Academics .... Dr. Walter ZURAWSKY
20 Assoc Provost Undergrad Academics .... Dr. Iraj KALKHORAN
32 Dean of Student Affairs .... Ms. Anita FARRINGTON
26 Director Marketing & Communications .. Ms. Kathleen HAMILTON
08 Director of Libraries .... Ms. Jana STEVENS-RICHMAN
06 Registrar .... Ms. Beth KIENLE-GRANZO
36 Director of Career Services .... Mr. James SILLCOX
88 Director of Special Services .... Ms. Nicole JOHNSON
37 Director Financial Aid .... Vacant
15 Director Human Resources .... Mr. Stephen WEISENHOLZ
29 Director Alumni Relations .... Ms. Valerie CABRAL
46 Director Sponsored Research .... Ms. Christine VILLANI
18 Director Facilities .... Ms. Annie CARINO
41 Director of Athletics .... Mr. Curtis SPENCE
88 Assoc Dir Student Financial Svcs .... Ms. Deborah WEBER
09 Director of Institutional Research .... Mr. Michael A. MAINIERO
84 Director Grad Enrollment Mgmt .... Mr. Raymond LUTZKY
88 Director K-12 Stem Education .... Mr. Ben ESNER
07 Dean of Admissons & New Student Svc .... Mr. Joy COLELLI
96 Director of Purchasing .... Mr. Jerry SAIEH

Pratt Institute (F)

200 Willoughby Avenue, Brooklyn NY 11205-3899
County: Kings FICE Identification: 002798
Unit ID: 194578
Telephone: (718) 636-3600 Carnegie Class: Master's L
FAX Number: (718) 636-3670 Calendar System: Semester
URL: www.pratt.edu
Established: 1887 Annual Undergrad Tuition & Fees: $41,226
Enrollment: 4,688 Coed
Affiliation or Control: Independent Non-Profit IRS Status: 501(c)3
Highest Offering: Master's
Program: 2-Year Principally Bachelor's Creditable; Liberal Arts And General; Teacher Preparatory; Professional
Accreditation: M, ART, CIDA, LIB, PLNG, @TEAC

01 President .... Dr. Thomas F. SCHUTTE
05 Provost .... Mr. Peter BARNA
32 Vice President for Student Life .... Dr. Helen MATUSOW-AYRES
10 Vice Pres Finance/Administration .... Mr. Edmund RUTKOWSKI
30 Vice President Development .... Mr. Todd GALITZ
84 Vice President for Enrollment .... Ms. Judith AARON
11 Assistant to Pres Administration .... Ms. Josie CAPORUSCIO
06 Registrar .... Mr. Lisle HENDERSON
08 Acting Director of the Library .... Mr. Russ ABELL
20 Associate Provost .... Dr. Marianthi ZIKOPOULOS
15 Director Human Resources .... Mr. Tom GREENE
51 Head Ctr for Continuing & Prof Stds .... Mr. Charles MUNSTER
21 Comptroller .... Ms. Sylvia ACUESTA
26 Executive Director Public Relations .... Ms. Mara MCGINNIS
29 Director Alumni Relations .... Mr. Michael SCLAFANI
36 Director of Career Services .... Ms. Rhonda SCHALLER
37 Director Student Financial Aid .... Mr. Nedzad GOGA
09 Exec Dir Institutional Research .... Mr. Vladimir BRILLER
07 Director of Undergraduate Admission .... Mr. William SWAN
96 Director of Purchasing .... Vacant
57 Acting Dean Art & Design .... Mr. Leighton PIERCE
49 Dean Liberal Arts/Science .... Dr. Andrew BARNES
48 Dean School of Architecture .... Mr. Thomas HANRAHAN
62 Dean Information/Library Sci .... Dr. Tula GIANNINI

Professional Business College (G)

408 Broadway, New York NY 10013
County: New York FICE Identification: 023065
Unit ID: 194611
Telephone: (212) 226-7300 Carnegie Class: Assoc/PrivNFP
FAX Number: (212) 431-8294 Calendar System: Semester
URL: www.pbcny.edu
Established: 2004 Annual Undergrad Tuition & Fees: $16,489
Enrollment: 1,090 Coed
Affiliation or Control: Independent Non-Profit IRS Status: 501(c)3
Highest Offering: Associate Degree
Program: Occupational; 2-Year Principally Bachelor's Creditable; Business Emphasis
Accreditation: ACICS

01 President .... Mr. Leon LEE
05 Academic Vice President .... Mr. Richard SLUSARCZYK
88 Chief Compliance Officer .... Mr. Nick POLISENO
36 Placement Director .... Ms. Judith RODRIGUEZ
06 Registrar .... Mr. Ken CHANG
08 Head Librarian .... Ms. Diane LEE
07 Admissions Director .... Mr. David WANG
37 Financial Aid Director .... Ms. Cheryl ZHANG
10 Director of Advising .... Ms. Taryn SHUHY

Rabbi Isaac Elchanan Theological Seminary (H)

2495 Amsterdam Avenue, New York NY 10033-9986
County: New York FICE Identification: 033104
Unit ID: 194727
Telephone: (212) 960-5310 Carnegie Class: Not Classified
FAX Number: (212) 960-0055 Calendar System: Semester
URL: riets.edu
Established: 1886 Annual Graduate Tuition & Fees: $15,200
Enrollment: 320 Male
Affiliation or Control: Jewish IRS Status: 501(c)3
Highest Offering: Beyond Master's But Less Than Doctorate; No Undergraduates
Program: Professional
Accreditation: NY

Rabbinical Academy Mesivta Rabbi Chaim Berlin (I)

1605 Coney Island Avenue, Brooklyn NY 11230-4715
County: Kings FICE Identification: 003976
Unit ID: 194657
Telephone: (718) 377-0777 Carnegie Class: Spec/Faith
FAX Number: (718) 338-5578 Calendar System: Semester
Established: 1939 Annual Undergrad Tuition & Fees: $11,900
Enrollment: 316 Male
Affiliation or Control: Independent Non-Profit IRS Status: 501(c)3
Highest Offering: Second Talmudic Degree
Program: Teacher Preparatory; Professional
Accreditation: RABN

01 Provost .... Rabbi Abraham H. FRUCHTHANDLER
05 President of the Faculty .... Rabbi Aaron M. SCHECHTER
03 Executive Director .... Rabbi Y. Mayer LASKER
29 Director of Alumni Association .... Mendel SCHECHTER
45 Chief Planning Officer .... Rabbi Tuvia M. OBERMEISTER
20 Associate Director .... Eli RABINOWITZ
37 Financial Aid Administrator .... Michael A. REISS

Rabbinical College Beth Shraga (J)

28 Saddle River Road, Monsey NY 10952-3035
County: Rockland FICE Identification: 010943
Unit ID: 194693
Telephone: (845) 356-1980 Carnegie Class: Spec/Faith
FAX Number: (845) 425-2604 Calendar System: Semester
Established: 1965 Annual Undergrad Tuition & Fees: $11,050
Enrollment: 44 Male

Affiliation or Control: Independent Non-Profit IRS Status: 501(c)3
Highest Offering: Second Talmudic Degree
Program: Teacher Preparatory; Professional
Accreditation: RABN

01 President .... Rabbi Sidney SCHIFF

Rabbinical College Bobover Yeshiva B'nei Zion (A)

1577 48th Street, Brooklyn NY 11219-3293
County: Kings FICE Identification: 008614
Unit ID: 194666
Telephone: (718) 438-2018 Carnegie Class: Spec/Faith
FAX Number: (718) 871-9031 Calendar System: Semester
Established: 1947 Annual Undergrad Tuition & Fees: $8,960
Enrollment: 320 Male
Affiliation or Control: Independent Non-Profit IRS Status: 501(c)3
Highest Offering: Second Talmudic Degree
Program: Teacher Preparatory; Professional
Accreditation: RABN

01 President .... Rabbi Boruch Avrohom HOROWITZ

Rabbinical College Ch'san Sofer (B)

1876 50th Street, Brooklyn NY 11204-0304
County: Kings FICE Identification: 003977
Unit ID: 194675
Telephone: (718) 236-1171 Carnegie Class: Spec/Faith
FAX Number: (718) 236-1119 Calendar System: Semester
Established: 1940 Annual Undergrad Tuition & Fees: $8,500
Enrollment: 39 Male
Affiliation or Control: Independent Non-Profit IRS Status: 501(c)3
Highest Offering: Second Talmudic Degree
Program: Teacher Preparatory; Professional
Accreditation: RABN

01 Executive Vice President .... Rabbi A. EHRENFELD
05 Dean of the College .... Rabbi S. B. EHRENFELD
10 Treasurer .... Mr. Mordechai STUHL
06 Registrar .... Rabbi Meyer WEINBERGER

Rabbinical College of Long Island (C)

205 W Beech Street, Long Beach NY 11561-0630
County: Nassau FICE Identification: 010378
Unit ID: 194736
Telephone: (516) 255-4700 Carnegie Class: Spec/Faith
FAX Number: (516) 255-4701 Calendar System: Semester
Established: 1965 Annual Undergrad Tuition & Fees: $13,700
Enrollment: 93 Male
Affiliation or Control: Independent Non-Profit IRS Status: 501(c)3
Highest Offering: First Talmudic Degree
Program: Teacher Preparatory; Professional
Accreditation: RABN

01 President .... Rabbi Yitzchok FEIGELSTOCK
06 Registrar .... Rabbi Dovid N. ROTHSCHILD
32 Dean of Students .... Rabbi Yeruchem PITTER
07 Director of Admissions .... Rabbi Chaim HOBERMAN
37 Financial Aid Administrator .... Rabbi Shlomo TEICHMAN

Rabbinical College Ohr Shimon Yisroel (D)

215-217 Hewes Street, Brooklyn NY 11211-8102
County: Kings FICE Identification: 031292
Unit ID: 405854
Telephone: (718) 855-4092 Carnegie Class: Spec/Faith
FAX Number: (718) 855-8479 Calendar System: Semester
Established: Annual Undergrad Tuition & Fees: $10,800
Enrollment: 147 Male
Affiliation or Control: Independent Non-Profit IRS Status: 501(c)3
Highest Offering: First Talmudic Degree
Program: Professional
Accreditation: @RABN

01 President .... Rabbi Shulem WALTER

Rabbinical College Ohr Yisroel (E)

8800 Seaview Avenue, Brooklyn NY 11236
County: Kings Identification: 667145
Telephone: (718) 633-4715 Carnegie Class: Not Classified
FAX Number: (347) 702-5436 Calendar System: Semester
Established: 2009 Annual Undergrad Tuition & Fees: $9,000
Enrollment: 80 Male
Affiliation or Control: Independent Non-Profit IRS Status: 501(c)3
Highest Offering: First Talmudic Degree
Program: Teacher Preparatory; Professional
Accreditation: @RABN

01 President .... Rabbi Daniel GELDZAHLER

Rabbinical Seminary of America (F)

76-01 147th Street, Flushing NY 11367-3148
County: Queens FICE Identification: 003978
Unit ID: 194763
Telephone: (718) 268-4700 Carnegie Class: Spec/Faith
FAX Number: (718) 268-4684 Calendar System: Semester
Established: 1933 Annual Undergrad Tuition & Fees: $8,500
Enrollment: 453 Male
Affiliation or Control: Independent Non-Profit IRS Status: 501(c)3
Highest Offering: Second Talmudic Degree
Program: Teacher Preparatory; Professional
Accreditation: RABN

01 President .... Rabbi David HARRIS
01 President .... Rabbi Akiva GRUNBLATT
03 Executive Vice President .... Rabbi Hayim SCHWARTZ
11 Director of Operation .... Rabbi Meir GLAZER
06 Registrar .... Rabbi Abraham SEMMEL
30 Director Development .... Rabbi Yossi SINGER
37 Director of Financial Aid .... Mrs. Laya EISENSTEIN
18 Chief Physical Plant .... Mr. David COHEN
88 Director of Special Projects .... Vacant
91 Director of Admin Computing .... Mr. Jonathan PLATOVSKY
39 Director Student Housing .... Rabbi Aryeh GOLDMAN
46 Director Research & Development .... Vacant

Rabbinical Seminary M'kor Chaim (G)

1571 55th Street, Brooklyn NY 11219-4300
County: Kings FICE Identification: 008617
Unit ID: 194718
Telephone: (718) 851-0183 Carnegie Class: Spec/Faith
FAX Number: (718) 853-2967 Calendar System: Semester
Established: 1965 Annual Undergrad Tuition & Fees: $6,675
Enrollment: 35 Male
Affiliation or Control: Independent Non-Profit IRS Status: 501(c)3
Highest Offering: Second Talmudic Degree
Program: Teacher Preparatory; Professional
Accreditation: RABN

01 President .... Rabbi Benjamin LEDERER

Relay Graduate School of Education (H)

40 West 20th Street, 7th Floor, New York NY 10011
County: New York Identification: 667117
Telephone: (212) 228-1888 Carnegie Class: Not Classified
FAX Number: (212) 228-1855 Calendar System: Other
URL: www.relayschool.org
Established: 2011 Annual Graduate Tuition & Fees: $17,500
Enrollment: 220 Coed
Affiliation or Control: Independent Non-Profit IRS Status: 501(c)3
Highest Offering: Master's; No Undergraduates
Program: Teacher Preparatory
Accreditation: M, TED

01 Co-Founder/President .... Mr. Norman ATKINS
05 Provost .... Dr. Brent MADDIN
10 Chief Financial Officer .... Ms. Yvonne CHAO
20 Dean .... Ms. Mayme HOSTELLER

Rensselaer Polytechnic Institute (I)

110 8th Street, Troy NY 12180-3590
County: Rensselaer FICE Identification: 002803
Unit ID: 194824
Telephone: (518) 276-6000 Carnegie Class: RU/VH
FAX Number: N/A Calendar System: Semester
URL: www.rpi.edu
Established: 1824 Annual Undergrad Tuition & Fees: $46,269
Enrollment: 6,999 Coed
Affiliation or Control: Independent Non-Profit IRS Status: 501(c)3
Highest Offering: Doctorate
Program: Liberal Arts And General; Professional
Accreditation: M, BUS, ENG

01 President .... Dr. Shirley A. JACKSON
05 Provost .... Dr. Prabhat HAJELA
11 Vice President for Administration .... Mr. Claude ROUNDS
22 Actg VP Strat Comm/External Rels .... Ms. Allison NEWMAN
10 Vice President for Finance/CFO .... Ms. Virginia GREGG
30 Vice Pres Institute Advancement .... Vacant
32 Vice President Student Life .... Dr. Timothy E. SAMS
15 Vice Pres Human Resources .... Mr. Curtis N. POWELL
45 Vice Pres for Research .... Mr. Jonathan S. DORDICK
13 Vice Pres for Info Services & CIO .... Mr. John E. KOLB
84 Vice Pres Enrollment/Dean Admiss .... Dr. Paul MARTHERS
21 Asst Vice Pres for Administration .... Mr. Paul MARTIN
26 Asst VP for Govt & Ext Relations .... Ms. Allison NEWMAN
29 Asst Vice Pres Alumni Relations .... Mr. Jeff SCHANZ
54 Dean School of Engineering .... Vacant
81 Dean School of Science .... Dr. Laurie LESHIN
79 Dean Sch of Humanities/Social Sci .... Dr. Mary SIMONI
50 Dean Lally School of Mgmt/Tech .... Dr. Thomas BEGLEY
48 Dean School of Architecture .... Mr. Evan DOUGLIS
43 Secy of the Inst/General Counsel .... Mr. Charles F. CARLETTA
20 Associate Dean for Information Tech .... Mr. David SPOONER
32 Dean of Students .... Mr. Mark SMITH
06 Dir Stdnt Records/Fin Svcs/Registr .... Ms. Sharon L. KUNKEL
37 Director Financial Aid .... Mr. Larry CHAMBERS
09 Director of Institutional Research .... Mr. Jack MAHONEY
08 Acting Director of Libraries .... Mr. Bob MAYO
25 Director Office Contracts & Grants ..... Mr. Richard E. SCAMMELL
36 Director Career Development Center .... Mr. Thomas L. TARANTELLI
07 Director of Graduate Admissions .... Mr. George ROBBINS
100 Chief of Staff .... Ms. Elisha MOZERSKY
18 Director Physical Plant .... Mr. Mark FROST
86 Director of Federal Relations .... Ms. Deborah E. ALTENBURG
23 Director Student Health Center .... Dr. Leslie LAWRENCE
38 Director Student Counseling .... Dr. Benjamin MARTE
96 Manager Purchasing Systems .... Mr. Craig MCINTOSH

Richard Gilder Graduate School at the American Museum of Natural History (J)

Central Park West at 79th Street, New York NY 10024
County: New York Identification: 667003
Unit ID: 458548
Telephone: (212) 769-5055 Carnegie Class: Not Classified
FAX Number: (212) 769-5257 Calendar System: Other
URL: rggs.amnh.org
Established: 2006 Annual Graduate Tuition & Fees: N/A
Enrollment: 20 Coed
Affiliation or Control: Independent Non-Profit IRS Status: 501(c)3
Highest Offering: Doctorate; No Undergraduates
Program: Professional
Accreditation: NY

01 Dean .... Dr. John J. FLYNN

Roberts Wesleyan College (K)

2301 Westside Drive, Rochester NY 14624-1997
County: Monroe FICE Identification: 002805
Unit ID: 194958
Telephone: (585) 594-6000 Carnegie Class: Master's L
FAX Number: (585) 594-6371 Calendar System: Semester
URL: www.roberts.edu
Established: 1866 Annual Undergrad Tuition & Fees: $27,354
Enrollment: 1,752 Coed
Affiliation or Control: Independent Non-Profit IRS Status: 501(c)3
Highest Offering: Master's
Program: Liberal Arts And General; Teacher Preparatory; Professional
Accreditation: M, ART, IACBE, MUS, NURSE, SW, @TEAC

01 President .... Dr. John A. MARTIN
05 Sr VP & Provost .... Dr. Robert ZWIER
03 Executive Vice President .... Dr. S. Jack CONNELL
10 Sr Vice President & Treasurer .... Mr. James E. CUTHBERT
05 VP for Academic & Student Support .... Dr. Nelson W. HILL
11 Vice President for Administration .... Mrs. Ruth LOGAN
07 Assoc VP for UG Admissions .... Mr. JP ANDERSON
44 Assoc VP for Major Gifts .... Mr. Maurice (Max) MCGINNIS
40 Director of Bookstore Services .... Ms. Nicole TEDESCO
41 Director of Athletics .... Mr. Michael E. FARO
37 Director of Student Financial Svcs .... Mr. Stephen G. FIELD
09 Dir Institutional Research/Assess .... Dr. Paul W. KENNEDY
42 Chaplain .... Rev. Jonathan BRATT
06 Registrar .... Mrs. Lesa J. KOHR
08 Director of Library Services .... Mr. Alfred C. KROBER
27 Chief Information Officer .... Mr. Pradeep SAXENA

† Parent institution of Northeastern Seminary.

Rochester Institute of Technology (L)

1 Lomb Memorial Drive, Rochester NY 14623-5604
County: Monroe FICE Identification: 002806
Unit ID: 195003
Telephone: (585) 475-2411 Carnegie Class: Master's L
FAX Number: (585) 475-7049 Calendar System: Quarter
URL: www.rit.edu
Established: 1829 Annual Undergrad Tuition & Fees: $34,424
Enrollment: 17,950 Coed
Affiliation or Control: Independent Non-Profit IRS Status: 501(c)3
Highest Offering: Doctorate
Program: Liberal Arts And General; Teacher Preparatory; Professional; Technical Emphasis
Accreditation: M, ARCPA, ART, BUS, CIDA, CS, DIETD, DMS, ENG, ENGR, ENGT, TEAC

01 President .... Dr. William W. DESTLER
05 Provost & Sr VP for Acad Affs .... Dr. Jeremy A. HAEFNER
100 Chief of Staff .... Mrs. Karen A. BARROWS
10 Sr Vice Pres Finance/Administration .... Dr. James H. WATTERS
84 Sr VP Enroll Mgmt/Career Svcs .... Dr. James G. MILLER
32 Sr Vice President Student Affairs .... Vacant
12 President NTID/RIT Vice Pres & Dean .... Dr. Gerard BUCKLEY
12 President RIT Dubai .... Dr. Yousef AL-ASSAF
30 VP for Development & Alumni Rels .... Ms. Lisa CAUDA
86 Vice President Govt/Cmty Relations .... Ms. Deborah M. STENDARDI
46 Vice President Research .... Dr. Ryne RAFFAELLE
28 VP for Diversity & Inclusion .... Mr. Kevin MCDONALD
12 VP AUK/Academic Dir RIT Pgms Kosovo .... Dr. Brian BOWEN
76 VP/Dean Coll Health Sciences/Tech .... Dr. Daniel B. ORNT
46 Senior Assoc Provost .... Dr. Christine M. LICATA
36 Assoc VP/Dir Coop Ed/Career Svcs .... Dr. Emanuel CONTOMANOLIS
27 Chief Communications Officer .... Mr. Robert FINNERTY
20 Asst Provost and Director CIMS .... Dr. Nabil NASR
08 Director of RIT Libraries .... Ms. Shirley BOWER
88 Assoc Provost Faculty Career Dev .... Dr. Lynn A. WILD
12 Pres/Dean Amer Col Mgt/Tech RIT .... Mr. Donald HUDSPETH

29 Asst VP Alumni Relations ... Ms. Kelly REDDER
21 Asst VP/Controller/Asst Treasurer ... Ms. Lyn KELLY
18 Asst VP Facilities Management Svs ... Mr. John MOORE
38 Ast VP Stdnt Aff/Dir Counseling Ctr ... Mr. John WEAS
06 Asst VP/Registrar ... Mr. Joe LOFFREDO
07 Asst VP/Exec Dir of Admissions ... Dr. Daniel SHELLEY
37 Asst VP & Dir Fin Aid & Scholarship ... Ms. Verna J. HAZEN
88 Asst VP and Dir Grad/PT Enroll Svc ... Ms. Diane ELLISON
44 Asst VP for Principal/Planned Gift ... Ms. Heather ENGEL
09 Asst VP Inst Rsrch/Policy Studies ... Dr. Joan E. GRAHAM
15 Asst VP/Director Human Resources ... Ms. Judy BENDER
44 Exec Dir Fund for RIT ... Ms. Marisa PSAILA
35 Sr Director Center for Campus Life ... Dr. Karey PINE
88 Sr Director Academic Support Center ... Ms. Phillippa POWERS
85 Director International Student Svcs ... Mr. Jeffrey W. COX
96 Exec Director Procurement Services ... Ms. Debra KUSSE
102 Exec Director Foundation Relations ... Ms. Susan WATSON MOLINE
102 Dir Corporate Relations ... Mr. Paul HARRIS
26 Chief Communications Officer ... Mr. Robert FINNERTY
101 Secretary of the Institute ... Mrs. Karen A. BARROWS
50 Dean of Business ... Dr. dt OGILVIE
54 Dean of Engineering ... Dr. Harvey J. PALMER
72 Dean Applied Science/Technology ... Dr. H. Fred WALKER
49 Dean of Liberal Arts ... Dr. James J. WINEBRAKE
81 Dean of Science ... Dr. Sophia MAGGELAKIS
57 Dean College Imaging Arts/Sci ... Ms. Lorraine JUSTICE
77 Dean B Golisano Col Comp/Info Sci ... Dr. Andrew L. SEARS
58 Dean Graduate Studies ... Dr. Hector FLORES

Rockefeller University (A)

1230 York Avenue, New York NY 10065-6399

County: New York FICE Identification: 002807
Unit ID: 195049

Telephone: (212) 327-8000 Carnegie Class: RU/VH
FAX Number: (212) 327-8699 Calendar System: Other
URL: www.rockefeller.edu
Established: 1901 Annual Graduate Tuition & Fees: N/A
Enrollment: 192 Coed
Affiliation or Control: Independent Non-Profit IRS Status: 501(c)3
Highest Offering: Doctorate; No Undergraduates
Program: Professional
Accreditation: NY

01 President ... Dr. Marc TESSIER-LAVIGNE
43 Vice President & General Counsel ... Ms. Harriet RABB
05 Vice President Academic Affairs ... Mr. Michael W. YOUNG
10 Vice President Finance ... Mr. James H. LAPPLE
30 Vice President Development ... Ms. Maren E. IMHOFF
17 Vice President for Medical Affairs ... Dr. Barry S. COLLER
20 Dean & Vice Pres of Educ Affairs ... Dr. Sidney STRICKLAND
100 Chief of Staff and Vice President ... Dr. Timothy O'CONNOR
16 Vice President Human Resources ... Ms. Virginia A. HUFFMAN
18 Assoc Vice Pres Plant Operations ... Mr. Alexander KOGAN
45 Assoc Vice Pres Plng & Constr ... Mr. George B. CANDLER
13 Chief Information Officer ... Mr. Gerald LATTER
25 Dir Pgm Dev & Sponsored Research ... Dr. Gila BUDESCU
08 University Librarian ... Ms. Carol FELTES
19 Director Security ... Mr. James ROGERS

Rockland Community College (B)

145 College Road, Suffern NY 10901-3699

County: Rockland FICE Identification: 002877
Unit ID: 195058

Telephone: (845) 574-4000 Carnegie Class: Assoc/Pub-S-SC
FAX Number: (845) 574-4463 Calendar System: Semester
URL: www.sunyrockland.edu
Established: 1959 Annual Undergrad Tuition & Fees (In-District): $4,176
Enrollment: 8,000 Coed
Affiliation or Control: State/Local IRS Status: 501(c)3
Highest Offering: Associate Degree
Program: Occupational; 2-Year Principally Bachelor's Creditable
Accreditation: M, ADNUR, OTA

01 President ... Dr. Cliff L. WOOD
03 VP Finance/Administration ... Mr. Nayyer HUSSAIN
05 Vice President Academic Affairs ... Dr. Susan DEER
32 Vice Pres Student Services ... Vacant
10 Assoc VP Finance/Administration ... Vacant
88 Dean Academic/Community Partnershp ... Mr. Thomas DELLA TORRE
35 Dean of Student Development ... Dr. James SIEGEL
84 Dean of Enrollment Management ... Ms. Dana STILLEY
37 Director Financial Aid ... Ms. Debra BOUABIDI
06 Registrar ... Ms. Robin CONKLIN
14 Director of Information Services ... Dr. Steven FERRES
08 Director of Library/Learning Res ... Ms. Sarah LEVY
38 Director Student Counseling ... Vacant
18 Chief Facilities/Physical Plant ... Mr. Douglas SCHMIDT
28 Dir Equity/Compliance/Affirm Act ... Ms. Melissa ROY
09 Director of Institutional Research ... Dr. Jim ROBERTSON
20 Asst to Vice Pres Academic Affairs ... Ms. Patricia KOBES
26 Chief Public Relations Officer ... Ms. Tzipora REITMAN

The Sage Colleges (C)

65 First Street, Troy NY 12180-4199

County: Rensselaer FICE Identification: 002810
Unit ID: 195128

Telephone: (518) 244-2000 Carnegie Class: Master's L
FAX Number: (518) 244-2460 Calendar System: Semester
URL: www.sage.edu
Established: 1916 Annual Undergrad Tuition & Fees: $28,000
Enrollment: 2,965 Coed
Affiliation or Control: Independent Non-Profit IRS Status: 501(c)3
Highest Offering: Doctorate
Program: Liberal Arts And General; Teacher Preparatory; Professional
Accreditation: M, ART, DIETD, DIETI, NURSE, OT, PTA, TED

01 President ... Dr. Susan C. SCRIMSHAW
05 Provost ... Dr. Terry WEINER
30 VP for Institutional Advancement ... Ms. Melissa KOMORA
12 Dean Sage College of Albany ... Dr. Joanne CURRAN
12 Dean Russell Sage College ... Dr. Donna HEALD
51 Dean Professional & Continuing Ed ... Mr. Albert ORBINATI
10 VP for Finance & Treasurer ... Dr. Peter D. HUGHES
84 VP Marketing/Enrollment Mgmt ... Mr. Daniel LUNDQUIST
32 Vice Pres for Campus Life ... Ms. Patricia CELLEMME
13 VP Administration & Planning ... Ms. Deirdre ZARRILLO
35 Dean of Students - RSC ... Mr. Michael BAUMGARDNER
35 Dean of Students - SCA ... Ms. Sharon MURRAY
76 Dean of Health Sciences ... Dr. Esther HASKVITZ
06 Registrar ... Ms. Andrea DEMAYO
07 Senior Director of UG Admission ... Mr. Thomas BREEN
88 Dean of School of Management ... Dr. Dan ROBESON
53 Dean School of Education ... Dr. Lori QUIGLEY
29 Director of Alumni Relations ... Ms. Rachel POMBO
29 Director Alumnae Relations ... Ms. Joan CLIFFORD
07 Director of Graduate & Adult Admiss ... Ms. Wendy DIEFENDORF
37 Assoc Director of Financial Aid ... Ms. Kelley ROBINSON
38 Director Student Counseling ... Vacant
15 Director of Human Resources ... Ms. Caryn KENT
09 Director of Institutional Research ... Ms. Lori PIZER
18 Director Facilities Management ... Mr. John ZAJACESKOWSKI
28 Dir Cultural Enrichment/Diversity ... Ms. Sabrina MC GINTY
36 Associate Dean of Academic Advising ... Ms. Karen SCHELL
36 Associate Dean of Academic Advising ... Ms. Stacy GONZALEZ
26 Dir of Communications & Marketing ... Ms. Shannon BALLARD GORMAN
92 Director of Honors Programs ... Dr. Julie MCINTYRE
21 Senior Director of Finance ... Mr. Thomas GIAQUINTO
96 Dir of Purchasing/Accts Payable ... Ms. Paula SELMER

Saint Bernard's School of Theology & Ministry (D)

120 French Road, Rochester NY 14618-3822

County: Monroe FICE Identification: 002815
Unit ID: 195155

Telephone: (585) 271-3657 Carnegie Class: Spec/Faith
FAX Number: (585) 271-2045 Calendar System: Semester
URL: www.stbernards.edu
Established: 1893 Annual Graduate Tuition & Fees: $3,220
Enrollment: 95 Coed
Affiliation or Control: Roman Catholic IRS Status: 501(c)3
Highest Offering: Master's; No Undergraduates
Program: Professional
Accreditation: THEOL

01 President ... Sr. Patricia A. SCHOELLES, SSJ
05 Academic Dean ... Dr. Devadasan N. PREMNATH
06 Registrar ... Mrs. Ellen MORNINGSTAR
10 Controller ... Ms. Mary MUGGLETON
07 Admissions Director ... Ms. Christina SCHMIDT
51 Dir Certification/Professional Dev ... Rev. George HEYMAN
08 Librarian ... Ms. Sheila SMYTH
30 Director of Advancement ... Ms. Laura HAMILTON

St. Bonaventure University (E)

St. Bonaventure NY 14778-9999

County: Cattaraugus FICE Identification: 002817
Unit ID: 195164

Telephone: (716) 375-2000 Carnegie Class: Master's L
FAX Number: (716) 375-2005 Calendar System: Semester
URL: www.sbu.edu
Established: 1858 Annual Undergrad Tuition & Fees: $29,589
Enrollment: 2,329 Coed
Affiliation or Control: Roman Catholic IRS Status: 501(c)3
Highest Offering: Master's
Program: Liberal Arts And General; Teacher Preparatory; Professional
Accreditation: M, BUS, CACREP, TED

01 President ... Dr. Margaret CARNEY, OSF
05 Provost and VP for Academic Affairs ... Dr. Michael J. FISCHER
32 Vice Provost for Student Life ... Mr. Richard C. TRIETLEY, JR.
10 Senior VP Finance & Administration ... Ms. Brenda L. MCGEE
26 Vice Pres University Relations ... Dr. Emily F. SINSABAUGH
42 Exec Director of Faith Formation ... Fr. Francis J. DISPIGNO, OFM
88 Vice Pres for Franciscan Mission ... Bro. F. Edward COUGHLIN, OFM
30 Vice Pres University Advancement ... Mrs. Mary C. DRISCOLL
30 Assoc VP Development ... Mr. Matthew J. TORNAMBE
84 Associate VP for Enrollment ... Ms. Kate DILLON HOGAN
25 Assc VP Ofc Grants Admn/Lflng Lrng ... Mr. Lawrence SOROKES
57 Interim Exec Dir of Q Arts Center ... Mr. Ludwig BRUNNER
20 Assoc Provost Academic Affairs ... Dr. Peggy Y. BURKE
04 Director of Operations Ofc of Pres ... Mr. Thomas BUTTAFARRO, JR.
15 Interim Director Human Resources ... Ms. Francine Z. SCHAEFER
07 Director of Admissions ... Ms. Monica EMERY
37 Director of Financial Aid ... Mr. Troy MARTIN
39 Exec Dir Res Living/Chief Judicial ... Ms. Nichole GONZALEZ
14 Director Technology Services ... Mr. Michael HOFFMAN
08 Director of Friedsam Mem Library ... Mr. Paul J. SPAETH
38 Director Counseling ... Dr. Roger E. KEENER
41 Director of Athletics ... Mr. Steve WATSON
06 Registrar & Dir of Inst Research ... Ms. Ann LEHMAN
29 Director of Alumni Services ... Ms. Monica MATTIOLI
36 Director of Career Services ... Ms. Connie F. WHITCOMB
43 University Counsel ... Mr. J. Michael SHANE
23 Director Wellness Center ... Dr. Roger E. KEENER
18 Director Physical Plant ... Mr. Philip G. WINGER
21 Controller ... Mrs. Nancy K. TAYLOR
19 Director of Safety and Security ... Mr. Vito CZYZ
40 Manager Bookstore ... Ms. Annette MCGRAW
44 Director Annual Giving Program ... Ms. Julie CUNNINGHAM
92 Director of Honors Program ... Vacant
96 Dir of Budget & Purchasing ... Ms. Lorraine SMITH
73 Director Franciscan Institute ... Bro. Gary MACIAG
49 Dean School of Arts & Sci ... Dr. Wolfgang NATTER
50 Dean School of Business ... Dr. Pierre BALTHAZARD
58 Assc Provost/Dean Sch Graduate Stds ... Dr. Peggy Y. BURKE
53 Dean School of Education ... Dr. Joseph ZIMMER
60 Dean Jandoli Sch Journ/Mass Comm ... Dr. Pauline HOFFMANN

St. Elizabeth College of Nursing (F)

2215 Genesee Street, Utica NY 13501-5998

County: Oneida FICE Identification: 006461
Unit ID: 195687

Telephone: (315) 798-8144 Carnegie Class: Assoc/PrivNFP
FAX Number: (315) 798-8271 Calendar System: Semester
URL: www.secon.edu
Established: 1904 Annual Undergrad Tuition & Fees: $15,250
Enrollment: 200 Coed
Affiliation or Control: Independent Non-Profit IRS Status: 501(c)3
Highest Offering: Associate Degree
Program: 2-Year Principally Bachelor's Creditable; Nursing Emphasis
Accreditation: M, ADNUR

01 President ... Mrs. Marian KOVATCHITCH

St. Francis College (G)

180 Remsen Street, Brooklyn NY 11201-4398

County: Kings FICE Identification: 002820
Unit ID: 195173

Telephone: (718) 522-2300 Carnegie Class: Bac/Diverse
FAX Number: (718) 522-1274 Calendar System: Semester
URL: www.sfc.edu
Established: 1859 Annual Undergrad Tuition & Fees: $20,700
Enrollment: 2,900 Coed
Affiliation or Control: Independent Non-Profit IRS Status: 501(c)3
Highest Offering: Master's
Program: Liberal Arts And General; Teacher Preparatory; Technical Emphasis
Accreditation: M, NURSE, TEAC

01 President ... Mr. Brendan J. DUGAN
03 Executive Vice President ... Ms. June MCGRISKEN
05 Provost/Vice Pres for Academic Affs ... Dr. Timothy J. HOULIHAN
26 Vice Pres Govt/Community Relations ... Ms. Linda WERBEL DASHEFSKY
30 Vice President of Development ... Mr. Thomas FLOOD
84 Asst Vice Pres Enrollment Mgmt ... Mr. Joseph CUMMINGS
15 Asst VP Human Resources/Org Dev ... Mr. Richard COLADARCI
18 Asst Vice Pres Facilities Mgmt ... Mr. Kevin O'ROURKE
21 Asst Vice President for Finance ... Mr. John RAGNO
88 Dean Academic Program Development ... Dr. Allen BURDOWSKI
20 Asst Dean of Academic Affairs ... Dr. Michele HIRSCH
89 Asst Dean of Freshmen Studies ... Ms. Monica MICHALSKI
13 Chief Information Officer ... Mr. Guy F. CARLSEN
06 Registrar ... Ms. Roxanne PERSAUD
32 Dean of Students ... Dr. Cheryl A. HOWELL
08 Director Library ... Dr. James SMITH
36 Director of Career Development ... Ms. Naomi KINLEY
29 Director of Alumni Relations ... Mr. Dennis MCDERMOTT
41 Director of Athletics ... Ms. Irma GARCIA
42 Director Campus Ministry ... Fr. Brian JORDAN
09 Director of Institutional Research ... Mr. Steven CATALANO

St. John Fisher College (H)

3690 East Avenue, Rochester NY 14618-3597

County: Monroe FICE Identification: 002821
Unit ID: 195720

Telephone: (585) 385-8000 Carnegie Class: DRU
FAX Number: (585) 899-3870 Calendar System: Semester
URL: www.sjfc.edu
Established: 1948 Annual Undergrad Tuition & Fees: $28,370
Enrollment: 4,022 Coed
Affiliation or Control: Independent Non-Profit IRS Status: 501(c)3
Highest Offering: Doctorate
Program: Liberal Arts And General; Teacher Preparatory; Professional; Business Emphasis
Accreditation: M, BUS, CACREP, NURSE, PHAR, TED

01 President ... Dr. Donald E. BAIN
04 Exec Asst to Pres/Secy to Board ... Ms. Joan R. BENULIS
05 Provost/Dean of College ... Dr. Randall KRIEG
84 Exec VP Enrollment/Advancement/Plng ... Dr. Gerard J. ROONEY
10 Vice President for Finance/CFO ... Ms. Jacqueline S. DISTEFANO
32 VP Student Affairs & Diversity ... Dr. Richard DEJESUS-RUEFF
49 Assoc VP Acad Affs/Dean Arts & Sci ... Dr. David S. PATE

50 Dean School of Business ... Dr. David G. MARTIN
53 Dean School of Education ... Dr. Michael WISCHNOWSKI
66 Dean School of Nursing ... Dr. Dianne C. COONEY MINER
67 Dean School of Pharmacy ... Dr. Scott A. SWIGART
28 Director Multicultural Affairs ... Mr. Yantee SLOBERT
06 Registrar ... Ms. Julia M. THOMAS
16 Assistant Vice Pres Human Resources .. Mr. Douglas J. STEWART
27 Director Marketing & Communications ... Ms. Anne R. GEER
06 Associate Registrar ... Ms. Cheryl O. EVANS
08 Director of the Library ... Ms. Melissa JADLOS
14 Chief Information/Computing Officer ... Mr. Stacy S. SLOCUM
15 Director of Payroll & Benefits ... Ms. Mary R. POWLEY
29 Director Alumni Relations ... Mr. Christopher B. SULLIVAN
37 Director Student Financial Aid ... Mrs. Angela B. MONNAT
42 Chaplain/Director Campus Ministry . Rev. Joseph M. LANZALACO
19 Director of Safety & Security ... Mr. David DICARO
41 Athletic Director ... Mr. Robert A. WARD
18 Director of Physical Plant ... Mr. Larry P. JACOBSON
21 Controller ... Ms. Linda M. STEINKIRCHNER
23 Director of Wellness Center ... Mrs. Mary Lou D'AMICO
31 Director of Community Service ... Mrs. Sally J. VAUGHAN
07 Director of Freshman Admissions ... Ms. Stacy A. LEDERMANN
07 Dir of Transfer/Graduate Admissions ... Mr. Jose PERALES
09 Director of Institutional Research ... Ms. Elizabeth A. LACHANCE
35 Director Student Affairs ... Mr. Thomas C. RODGERS
36 Director Career Services ... Mr. Matt CARDIN
105 Webmaster ... Ms. Jody C. BENEDICT

St. John's University (A)

8000 Utopia Parkway, Queens NY 11439-0001
County: Queens FICE Identification: 002823
Unit ID: 195809
Telephone: (718) 990-6161 Carnegie Class: DRU
FAX Number: (718) 990-5723 Calendar System: Semester
URL: www.stjohns.edu
Established: 1870 Annual Undergrad Tuition & Fees: $37,260
Enrollment: 16,438 Coed
Affiliation or Control: Roman Catholic IRS Status: 501(c)3
Highest Offering: Doctorate
Program: Liberal Arts And General; Teacher Preparatory; Professional
Accreditation: M, ARCPA, ART, AUD, BUS, BUSA, CACREP, CLPSY, EMT, LAW, LIB, MT, PHAR, RAD, SCPSY, SP, TEAC

01 Interim President ... Rev. Joseph L. LEVESQUE, CM
11 Exec VP/COO/Treasurer ... Ms. Martha K. HIRST
05 Provost ... Dr. Robert A. MANGIONE
03 Exec VP Mission ... Rev. Gerard H. LUTTENBERGER, CM
16 Sr VP Human Res/Strategic Plan/ IR ... Ms. Mary T. HARPER HAGAN
101 Vice Pres & Secretary of University ... Dr. Dorothy E. HABBEN
20 Vice Pres Academic Support Services ... Dr. Andre A. MCKENZIE
31 Vice President Community Relations ... Mr. Joseph A. SCIAME
09 VP Institutional Research/Acad Plng ... Dr. Clover W. HALL
84 Vice President Enrollment Mgmt ... Ms. Beth EVANS
18 VP Campus Facilities & Services ... Mr. Brij B. ANAND
19 Vice President Public Safety ... Mr. Thomas J. LAWRENCE
26 VP Marketing and Communications . Dr. Hallie G. SAMMARTINO
104 Vice President Global Programs ... Mr. Anthony R. PACHECO
13 Vice Pres of Info Technology/CIO ... Mr. Joseph J. TUFANO
10 VP for Business Affairs & CFO ... Ms. Sharon HEWITT WATKINS
42 VP University Ministry and Events ... Dr. Pamela G. SHEA-BYRNES
32 VP Student Affairs ... Dr. Kathryn T. HUTCHINSON
20 Vice Provost ... Dr. Derek V. OWENS
49 Dean St. John's College ... Dr. Jeffrey W. FAGEN
53 Dean Sch of Edu/Academic VP SI Camp ... Dr. Jerrold ROSS
50 Dean Tobin Col of Business ... Dr. Victoria L. SHOAF
67 Dean Pharmacy/Health Sciences ... Dr. Russell J. DIGATE
107 Dean Col of Professional Studies ... Dr. Kathleen VOUTE MACDONALD
61 Dean School of Law ... Mr. Michael A. SIMONS
08 Dean University Libraries ... Ms. Theresa M. MAYLONE
20 Assoc Provost Administration ... Ms. Linda A. SHANNON
20 Associate Provost Planning/Res Mgmt ... Dr. Diane S. HERGENROTHER
37 Assoc VP Student Financial Svcs ... Mr. Jorge L. RODRIGUEZ
35 Assoc VP & Dean of Students ... Dr. Daniel A. TRUJILLO
35 Assoc VP Student Affairs ... Dr. Douglas GEIGER
91 Assoc Vice President Info Tech ... Ms. Maura A. WOODS
26 Assoc VP External Relations ... Mr. Dominic SCIANNA
29 Assoc VP Alumni Relations ... Mr. Scott WILLIAMS
86 Asst VP Government Relations ... Mr. Brian BROWNE
88 Asst VP Campus Services ... Ms. Bernadette GROGAN LAVIN
20 Acad Asst VP - SI Campus ... Dr. Christopher CUCCIA
21 Asst VP and Exec Dir - SI Campus .. Mr. Gerard A. MCENERNEY
43 General Counsel ... Mr. Joseph E. OLIVA
21 Controller ... Mr. Anthony MACALUSO
06 University Registrar ... Ms. Joanne A. LLERANDI
90 Exec Director User Services ... Mr. Kenneth J. MAHLMEISTER
88 Exec Director Vincentian Center ... Sr. Margaret J. KELLY, DC
36 Exec Director Career Center ... Ms. Denise C. HOPKINS
15 Director Human Resources Svcs ... Ms. Cynthia F. SIMPSON
07 Director Admissions-Q ... Mr. David FOLLICK
38 Dir Ctr Counseling & Consultation ... Dr. Edward A. HATTAUER
37 Dir Financial Aid Staten Isl Campus ... Ms. Theresa C. CANTARELLA
39 Director Residence Life ... Mr. Eric M. FINKELSTEIN
44 Director Gift Planning ... Ms. Susan M. DAMIANI
23 Director Queens Health Services ... Mrs. Pauline TUMMINO
23 Director SI Health Services ... Mrs. Margaret A. TIERNEY
96 Director Purchasing ... Mr. Jeffery I. WEISS
41 Athletic Director ... Mr. Chris P. MONASCH
92 Director Honors Program ... Dr. Robert J. FORMAN
56 Director Special Programs ... Mrs. Cecelia M. RUSSO
88 Director Ctr for Teaching/Learning ... Dr. Maura C. FLANNERY
85 Dir Internatl Students/Scholar Svcs ... Ms. Krista L. GARD
88 Director Internal Audit ... Mr. Alex J. HOEHN
25 Director Grants & Research ... Mr. Jared E. LITTMAN
14 Dir Network & Comm Services ... Ms. Anne L. ROCCO
105 Director of Digital Communications ... Ms. Luci GERACI
39 Asst Dn Stdnt Life/Dir Res Life SI ... Ms. Anilsa R. NUNEZ
36 Director Career Ctr Staten Island ... Ms. Valora N. BLACKSON
07 Sr Assoc Director Admissions - SI ... Ms. Samantha R. HASTLER
40 Manager of Bookstore ... Mrs. Denise SERVIDIO

Saint Joseph's College, New York (B)

245 Clinton Avenue, Brooklyn NY 11205-3688
County: Kings FICE Identification: 002825
Unit ID: 195544
Telephone: (718) 940-5300 Carnegie Class: Master's M
FAX Number: (718) 636-7245 Calendar System: Semester
URL: www.sjcny.edu
Established: 1916 Annual Undergrad Tuition & Fees: $21,250
Enrollment: 1,477 Coed
Affiliation or Control: Independent Non-Profit IRS Status: 501(c)3
Highest Offering: Master's
Program: Liberal Arts And General; Teacher Preparatory; Professional
Accreditation: M, ADNUR, NUR, @TEAC

01 President ... Sr. Elizabeth A. HILL
05 Provost ... Sr. Loretta A. MCGRANN
30 VP Institutional Advancement ... Ms. Nancy J. CONNORS
84 VP Enrollment Management ... Mrs. Theresa LAROCCA MEYER
49 Academic Dean Arts & Sciences ... Dr. Richard GREENWALD
32 Dean of Students ... Dr. Susan HUDEC
10 Chief Financial Officer ... Mr. John C. ROTH
13 Chief Information Officer ... Mr. Kenneth MCCOLLUM
08 Director of Library ... Dr. William MENG
06 Registrar ... Mr. Robert PERGOLIS
37 Director of Financial Aid ... Ms. Amy THOMPSON
38 Exec Director Career Development ... Mr. Frank LATERRA BELLINO
35 Assistant to Dean of Students ... Mrs. Sherrie VAN ARNAM
29 AVP Alumni Relations/Stewardship ... Ms. Mary Jo B. CHIARA
21 Controller ... Mr. Matthew BRELLIS
88 Director of Child Study Center ... Dr. Susan STRAUT COLLARD
18 Director Physical Plant ... Mr. Alvin DORTA
44 Assoc VP Grants/Major Gifts ... Ms. Clare KEHOE
15 Exec Director of Human Resources ... Ms. D'adra CRUMP
28 Director of Diversity ... Mr. Rupert CAMPBELL
26 Director of Public Affairs ... Mr. Michael BANACH
13 Exec Director Network Operations ... Mr. Ted DEC
14 Exec Director Enterprise Systems ... Ms. Michelle PAPAJOHN
90 Exec Director Client Services ... Ms. Lichele ABEAR
41 Director of Athletics ... Mr. Frank CARBONE

Saint Joseph's College, New York - Suffolk Campus (C)

155 W Roe Boulevard, Patchogue NY 11772-2399
Telephone: (631) 687-5100 FICE Identification: 029081
Accreditation: &M, NRPA

† Main campus is Saint Joseph's College, New York in Brooklyn, NY.

St. Joseph's College of Nursing (D)

206 Prospect Avenue, Syracuse NY 13203-1806
County: Onondaga FICE Identification: 006467
Unit ID: 195191
Telephone: (315) 448-5040 Carnegie Class: Assoc/PrivNFP
FAX Number: (315) 448-5745 Calendar System: Semester
URL: www.sjhsyr.org/sjhhc/sjhcon
Established: 1898 Annual Undergrad Tuition & Fees: N/A
Enrollment: 294 Coed
Affiliation or Control: Independent Non-Profit IRS Status: 501(c)3
Highest Offering: Associate Degree
Program: Occupational; 2-Year Principally Bachelor's Creditable; Nursing Emphasis
Accreditation: M

01 Dean ... Mrs. Marianne MARKOWITZ

Saint Joseph's Seminary (E)

Dunwoodie, #201 Seminary Avenue, Yonkers NY 10704-1852
County: Westchester FICE Identification: 002826
Unit ID: 195571
Telephone: (914) 968-6200 Carnegie Class: Spec/Faith
FAX Number: (914) 376-2019 Calendar System: Quarter
URL: www.dunwoodie.edu
Established: 1896 Annual Graduate Tuition & Fees: $30,000
Enrollment: 104 Male
Affiliation or Control: Roman Catholic IRS Status: 501(c)3
Highest Offering: Master's; No Undergraduates
Program: Professional; Religious Emphasis
Accreditation: M, THEOL

01 Rector ... Msgr. Peter I. VACCARI
05 Academic Dean ... Rev. Kevin P. O'REILLY
32 Dean of Students/Admissions ... Rev. Nicholas A. ZIENTARSKI
08 Director Library Services ... Ms. Barbara CAREY
10 Director Finance ... Mr. Ronald TUTTLE
30 Director of Development ... Vacant
42 Director Campus Ministry ... Vacant
06 Registrar ... Ms. Kathleen M. RUSSELL
38 Director of Psychological Services ... Dr. Richard GALLAGHER
18 Director of Buildings & Grounds ... Mr. Joseph DI LELLO

St. Lawrence University (F)

23 Romoda Drive, Canton NY 13617-1423
County: St. Lawrence FICE Identification: 002829
Unit ID: 195216
Telephone: (315) 229-5011 Carnegie Class: Bac/A&S
FAX Number: (315) 229-5502 Calendar System: Other
URL: www.stlawu.edu
Established: 1856 Annual Undergrad Tuition & Fees: $46,040
Enrollment: 2,488 Coed
Affiliation or Control: Independent Non-Profit IRS Status: 501(c)3
Highest Offering: Master's
Program: Liberal Arts And General; Teacher Preparatory
Accreditation: M, TEAC

01 President ... Dr. William FOX
05 Vice Pres/Dean Academic Affairs ... Dr. Valerie D. LEHR
30 Vice Pres University Advancement ... Dr. Laura ELLIS
10 Vice President Finance & Treasurer ... Ms. Kathryn L. MULLANEY
32 Vice Pres/Dean Student Life ... Dr. Joseph TOLLIVER
07 Vice Pres/Dean Admissions/Fin Aid ... Mr. Jeffrey RICKEY
26 VP for Employee/Community Relations ... Mrs. Lisa M. CANIA
21 Assoc Vice President for Finance ... Ms. Carol GABLE
89 Associate Dean of the First-Year ... Dr. Rebecca DANIELS
35 Associate Dean of Student Life ... Mr. Rance DAVIS
06 Registrar ... Ms. Carolyn FILLIPPI
37 Director of Financial Aid ... Mrs. Patricia J B. FARMER
08 Librarian ... Mr. Justin SIPHER
36 Director of Career Planning ... Dr. Carol BATE
09 Director of Institutional Research ... Ms. Christine ZIMMERMAN
18 Chief Facilities/Physical Plant ... Mr. Daniel B. SEAMAN
20 Asst Dean of Academic Affairs ... Ms. Lorie MACKENZIE
29 Director Alumni Relations ... Ms. Kimberly HISSONG
35 Director Residence Life ... Mr. Christopher MARQUARDT
23 Director of Health & Counseling ... Ms. Pat ELLIS
84 Director Enrollment Management ... Mr. Jeffrey RICKEY
96 Director of Purchasing ... Ms. Ruta OZOLS
15 Director Personnel Services ... Mrs. Colleen MANLEY
38 Director Student Counseling ... Mr. Timothy CORBITT

St. Paul's School of Nursing (G)

97-77 Queens Blvd, Rego Park NY 11374
County: Queens FICE Identification: 012364
Unit ID: 189811
Telephone: (718) 357-0500 Carnegie Class: Assoc/PrivFP
FAX Number: (718) 357-4683 Calendar System: Semester
URL: www.stpaulsschoolofnursing.edu
Established: 1969 Annual Undergrad Tuition & Fees: $46,065
Enrollment: 365 Coed
Affiliation or Control: Proprietary IRS Status: Proprietary
Highest Offering: Associate Degree
Program: Occupational; 2-Year Principally Bachelor's Creditable; Nursing Emphasis
Accreditation: ABHES

01 President ... Dr. Carol S. ZAJAC
66 Regional Dean of Nursing Schools ... Genevieve M. JENSEN
37 Financial Aid Director ... Jennifer OSORIO
07 Asst Director of Admissions ... Nickeshia DURANT
08 Head Librarian ... Chris SCHNUPP
10 Chief Financial/Business Officer ... Eric SEDA
06 Registrar ... Claudia MENJIVAR

Saint Paul's School of Nursing-Staten Island (H)

2 Teleport Dr Ste 203, Corp Comm 2, Staten Island NY 10311
County: Richmond FICE Identification: 009479
Unit ID: 195784
Telephone: (718) 517-7700 Carnegie Class: Assoc/PrivFP
FAX Number: (718) 818-6020 Calendar System: Semester
URL: www.stpaulsschoolofnursing.edu
Established: 1904 Annual Undergrad Tuition & Fees: $21,945
Enrollment: 719 Coed
Affiliation or Control: Proprietary IRS Status: Proprietary
Highest Offering: Associate Degree
Program: Occupational; 2-Year Principally Bachelor's Creditable; Nursing Emphasis
Accreditation: ABHES

01 President ... Mr. Oleg RABINOVICH
05 Director of Education ... Dr. Ann LUBRANO
66 Dean of Nursing ... Ms. Elizabeth BRAUN
06 Registrar ... Ms. Nancy MULLER
10 Business Office Manager ... Ms. Olga FORINA
07 Director of Admissions ... Ms. Kimberly WEINSTEIN
32 Director of Career Services ... Ms. Lynn SALVAGE
37 Director of Financial Aid ... Ms. Nayamka WARD
88 LRC Manager ... Ms. Michelle MALONE

St. Thomas Aquinas College (A)

125 Route 340, Sparkill NY 10976-1050
County: Rockland FICE Identification: 002832
Unit ID: 195243
Telephone: (845) 398-4000 Carnegie Class: Master's S
FAX Number: (845) 359-8136 Calendar System: 4/1/4
URL: www.stac.edu
Established: 1952 Annual Undergrad Tuition & Fees: $25,840
Enrollment: 2,000 Coed
Affiliation or Control: Independent Non-Profit IRS Status: 501(c)3
Highest Offering: Master's
Program: Liberal Arts And General; Teacher Preparatory; Professional
Accreditation: M, IACBE, TED

01 President .... Dr. Margaret M. FITZPATRICK, SC
03 Senior Vice President .... Mr. Vincent CRAPANZANO
10 Vice Pres Administration & Finance .... Mr. Joseph DONINI
05 Provost/Vice Pres Academic Affairs .... Dr. L. John DURNEY
32 Vice Pres/Dean Student Development .... Dr. Kirk MANNING
30 Vice Pres Institutional Advancement .... Mr. Kevin DUIGNAN
15 Sr Exec Director Human Resources .... Ms. Patricia PACCHIANA
07 Director Admissions .... Ms. Danielle MACKAY
09 Dir Inst Research/Program Develop .... Dr. Renee QUINTYNE
21 Controller .... Ms. Jennifer MAZZA
44 Dir Annual Giving & Alumni Affairs .... Mrs. Joanne FAVATA
35 Director Student Activities .... Mr. Dave ENG
38 Director Student Counseling .... Dr. Louis MUGGEP
08 Librarian .... Vacant
06 Registrar .... Mrs. Mildred ALEXIOU
36 Director Placement Services .... Ms. Rachel JACKIEWICZ
37 Director Financial Aid .... Mrs. Jean Marie MOHR
13 Director of Computing Services .... Mr. Sunny ANTHWAL
18 Dir Facilities & Construction .... Mr. Patrick LAMBERT
26 Director Communications .... Ms. Danielle MACKAY
50 Dean School of Business .... Mr. Michael MURPHY
53 Dean School of Education .... Dr. Meenakshi GAJRIA
49 Dean School of Arts & Sciences .... Dr. Robert MURRAY

Saint Vladimir's Orthodox Theological Seminary (B)

575 Scarsdale Road, Crestwood NY 10707-1699
County: Westchester FICE Identification: 002833
Unit ID: 195580
Telephone: (914) 961-8313 Carnegie Class: Spec/Faith
FAX Number: (914) 961-4507 Calendar System: Semester
URL: www.svots.edu
Established: 1938 Annual Graduate Tuition & Fees: $11,200
Enrollment: 55 Coed
Affiliation or Control: Independent Non-Profit IRS Status: 501(c)3
Highest Offering: Doctorate; No Undergraduates
Program: Religious Emphasis
Accreditation: THEOL

01 Interim President .... H.E. Most Reverend NATHIEL
00 Chancellor .... V.Rev. Chad HATFIELD
05 Dean .... Rev. John BEHR
10 Assoc Chanc for Finance .... Ms. Melanie RINGA
30 Assoc Chanc for Advancement .... Mr. Theodore BAZIL
20 Assoc Dean Academic Affairs .... Dr. John BARNET
32 Assoc Dean for Student Affairs .... Rev. David MEZYNSKI
08 Librarian/Circulation .... Ms. Eleana SILK
13 Director of Computer Systems .... Mr. Georgios KOKONAS
35 Student Affairs Administrator .... Mrs. Ann SANCHEZ
07 Director Admissions/Financial Aid .... Pdn. Joseph MATUSIAK
21 Business Manager .... Mr. Ted BAZIL
40 Bookstore/Operations Manager .... Rev Dn. Gregory HATRAK

Salvation Army College for Officer Training (C)

201 Lafayette Avenue, Suffern NY 10901-4707
County: Rockland Identification: 666020
Telephone: (845) 368-7200 Carnegie Class: Not Classified
FAX Number: (845) 357-6644 Calendar System: Other
URL: www.use.salvationarmy.org
Established: 1905 Annual Undergrad Tuition & Fees: $1,070
Enrollment: 99 Coed
Affiliation or Control: Independent Non-Profit IRS Status: 501(c)3
Highest Offering: Associate Degree
Program: Professional
Accreditation: NY

01 Principal .... Major Ronald R. FOREMAN
03 Associate Principal .... Major Dorine M. FOREMAN
11 Asst Principal for Administration .... Major James B. COCKER
05 Director of Curriculum .... Major Eva R. GEDDES
06 Registrar .... Ms. Victoria DESANTIS
09 Director of Institutional Research .... Dr. Dennis VANDER WEELE
10 Chief Business Officer .... Major Wesley GEDDES
15 Director Personnel Services .... Major David B. DAVIS
20 Associate Academic Officer .... Major James GUEST
21 Associate Business Officer .... Mrs. Robin FRASER
32 Director Student Affairs .... Capt. Margaret DAVIS

Samaritan Hospital School of Nursing (D)

2215 Burdett Avenue, Troy NY 12065
County: Rensselaer FICE Identification: 009248
Unit ID: 196289
Telephone: (518) 271-3285 Carnegie Class: Not Classified
FAX Number: (518) 271-3303 Calendar System: Semester
URL: www.nehealth.com
Established: 1903 Annual Undergrad Tuition & Fees: $9,025
Enrollment: 160 Coed
Affiliation or Control: Independent Non-Profit IRS Status: 501(c)3
Highest Offering: Associate Degree
Program: 2-Year Principally Bachelor's Creditable; Nursing Emphasis
Accreditation: NY

01 Executive Director .... Ms. Linda D'ARCANGELIS

Sarah Lawrence College (E)

1 Meadway, Bronxville NY 10708-5999
County: Westchester FICE Identification: 002813
Unit ID: 195304
Telephone: (914) 337-0700 Carnegie Class: Bac/A&S
FAX Number: (914) 395-2668 Calendar System: Semester
URL: www.slc.edu
Established: 1926 Annual Undergrad Tuition & Fees: $46,924
Enrollment: 1,736 Coed
Affiliation or Control: Independent Non-Profit IRS Status: 501(c)3
Highest Offering: Master's
Program: Liberal Arts And General
Accreditation: M, @TEAC

01 President .... Dr. Karen R. LAWRENCE
05 Dean of the College .... Dr. Jerrilynn D. DODDS
10 Vice Pres Finance/Operations .... Vincent MASSARO
30 Vice President for Advancement .... Charles J. RASBERRY
26 Vice Pres Communication & Marketing .... Dr. Gerald A. SCHORIN
11 Vice President for Administration .... Thomas L. BLUM
15 VP Human Resources/Legal Affairs .... Julie AUSTER
88 Assoc VP for Advancement .... Ellen REYNOLDS
20 Associate Dean of the College .... Dr. Kanwal SINGH
32 Dean of Studies & Student Life .... Dr. Allen GREEN
35 Dean of Student Affairs .... Dr. Paige CRANDALL
07 Director of Admission .... Jennifer GAYLES
58 Dean Graduate Studies .... Susan GUMA
06 Registrar .... Daniel LICHT
08 Director of Libraries .... Charling FAGAN
13 Chief Technology Officer .... Sean JAMESON
29 Director of Alumni Relations .... Cheryl CIPRO
36 Director Career Counseling .... Angela CHERUBINI
44 Major Gifts Officer .... Elizabeth CAFFERKEY
28 Director of Diversity .... Natalie GROSS
18 Asst Vice President of Facilities .... Maureen GALLAGHER
19 Director of Public Safety .... Larry HOFFMAN

SBI Campus-An Affiliate of Sanford-Brown (F)

320 S Service Road, Melville NY 11747-3201
County: Suffolk FICE Identification: 011647
Unit ID: 192156
Telephone: (631) 370-3300 Carnegie Class: Assoc/PrivFP
FAX Number: (631) 293-5872 Calendar System: Quarter
URL: www.sbmelville.edu
Established: 2008 Annual Undergrad Tuition & Fees: $10,030
Enrollment: 300 Coed
Affiliation or Control: Proprietary IRS Status: Proprietary
Highest Offering: Associate Degree
Program: Occupational; 2-Year Principally Bachelor's Creditable
Accreditation: ACICS

01 President .... Dr. Eric RICIOPPO
05 Director of Education .... Dr. Bindu PILLAI
06 Registrar .... Ms. Manique HIGHSMITH
07 Director of Admissions .... Mr. Nicholas FERLISI

Schenectady County Community College (G)

78 Washington Avenue, Schenectady NY 12305
County: Schenectady FICE Identification: 006785
Unit ID: 195322
Telephone: (518) 381-1200 Carnegie Class: Assoc/Pub-U-SC
FAX Number: (518) 346-0379 Calendar System: Semester
URL: www.sunysccc.edu
Established: 1967 Annual Undergrad Tuition & Fees (In-District): $3,384
Enrollment: 7,142 Coed
Affiliation or Control: State/Local IRS Status: 501(c)3
Highest Offering: Associate Degree
Program: Occupational; 2-Year Principally Bachelor's Creditable
Accreditation: M, ACFEI, MUS

01 President .... Dr. Quintin B. BULLOCK
05 Vice President of Academic Affairs .... Dr. Penny A. HAYNES
10 Vice President of Administration .... Mr. Charles J. RICHARDSON
32 Vice President of Student Affairs .... Dr. Martha J. ASSELIN
103 Exec Dir of Workforce Development .... Mr. Matthew GRATTAN
37 Director of Financial Aid .... Mr. Brian F. MCGARVEY
20 Assistant VP Academic Affairs .... Ms. Angela M. PRESTIACOMO
11 Assistant VP of Administration .... Ms. Susan BEAUDOIN
35 Asst Vice President Student Affairs .... Mr. Stephen FRAGALE
108 Assistant Dean for Assessment & Int .... Dr. Leonard GAINES, JR.
45 Asst Dean for Planning/Acct/Effect .... Mr. Darren JOHNSON
30 Executive Director of Development .... Ms. Carmel PATRICK
06 Registrar .... Ms. Laurie A. HEMPSTEAD
07 Director of Admissions .... Mr. David G. SAMPSON
08 Director Library Services .... Ms. Lynne O. KING
15 Exec Director of Human Resources .... Ms. Christine PIRRI
90 Director of Academic Computing .... Mr. Nicholas G. LTAIF
18 Director of Campus Maintenance .... Mr. Alan J. YAUNEY
27 Chief Information Officer .... Mr. Antione HARRISON
44 Coordinator of Development .... Vacant
91 Manager of Administrative Computing .... Mr. Arthur PAOLELLI
26 Public Rels/Publications Specialist .... Ms. Heather L. MEANEY
36 Coordinator Career/Employment Svcs .... Mr. Robert FREDERICK
15 Coordinator Personnel Services/AAO .... Ms. Carolyn PINN
09 Coordinator Institutional Research .... Ms. Brandie DINGMAN
28 Coord Multicult/Educ/Oppty Pgms .... Ms. Angela WEST-DAVIS
21 Coordinator for Financial Services .... Ms. Aimee S. WARFIELD
04 Assistant to the President/BOT .... Ms. Paula OHLHOUS

School of Visual Arts (H)

209 E 23rd Street, New York NY 10010-3994
County: New York FICE Identification: 007468
Unit ID: 197151
Telephone: (212) 592-2000 Carnegie Class: Spec/Arts
FAX Number: (212) 725-3587 Calendar System: Semester
URL: www.sva.edu
Established: 1947 Annual Undergrad Tuition & Fees: $32,270
Enrollment: 4,323 Coed
Affiliation or Control: Proprietary IRS Status: Proprietary
Highest Offering: Master's
Program: Music Emphasis
Accreditation: M, ART, CIDA

00 Acting Chairman .... Milton GLASER
01 President .... David J. RHODES
03 Executive Vice President .... Anthony P. RHODES
05 Provost .... Jeffrey NESIN
10 Chief Financial Officer .... Gary SHILLET
32 Exec Dir of Student Affairs/Admiss .... Javier VEGA
26 Exec Director of External Relations .... Susan MODENSTEIN
13 Chief Information Officer .... Cosmin TOMESCU
06 Registrar .... Jon TODD
07 Director Admission .... Adam ROGERS
35 Director of Student Affairs .... Bill MARTINO
08 Director Visual Arts Library .... Robert LOBE
37 Director Financial Aid .... William BERRIOS
36 Director Career Development .... Angie WOJAK
30 Director Development/Alumni Affairs .... Carrie LINCOURT
19 Director Security .... Nick AGJMURATI
15 Director of Human Resources .... Frank AGOSTA
09 Director of Institutional Research .... Jerold DAVIS
27 Director of Communications .... Michael GRANT

Sh'or Yoshuv Rabbinical College (I)

1 Cedar Lawn Avenue, Lawrence NY 11559-1714
County: Nassau FICE Identification: 025059
Unit ID: 195438
Telephone: (516) 239-9002 Carnegie Class: Spec/Faith
FAX Number: (516) 239-9003 Calendar System: Semester
URL: www.shoryoshuv.org
Established: 1963 Annual Undergrad Tuition & Fees: $9,000
Enrollment: 157 Male
Affiliation or Control: Independent Non-Profit IRS Status: 501(c)3
Highest Offering: Second Talmudic Degree
Program: Teacher Preparatory; Professional
Accreditation: RABN

01 Dean .... Rabbi Naftalie JAEGER
05 Director .... Rabbi Avrohom HALPERN
32 Director of Student Affairs .... Rabbi Moshe GREENE
06 Registrar .... Mrs. Sharon JACOBOWITZ
37 Director SFA .... Mr. Moshe RUBIN

Siena College (J)

515 Loudon Road, Loudonville NY 12211-1462
County: Albany FICE Identification: 002816
Unit ID: 195474
Telephone: (518) 783-2300 Carnegie Class: Bac/A&S
FAX Number: (518) 783-4293 Calendar System: Semester
URL: www.siena.edu
Established: 1937 Annual Undergrad Tuition & Fees: $31,118
Enrollment: 3,267 Coed
Affiliation or Control: Independent Non-Profit IRS Status: 501(c)3
Highest Offering: Master's
Program: Liberal Arts And General; Teacher Preparatory
Accreditation: M, BUS, SW, TED

01 President .... Fr. Kevin J. MULLEN, OFM
05 Vice President for Academic Affairs .... Dr. Linda L. RICHARDSON
32 Vice President for Student Affairs .... Dr. Maryellen GILROY
10 Vice President for Finance & Admin .... Mr. Paul T. STEC
84 VP for Enrollment Management .... Mr. Ned J. JONES
30 VP for Development & External Affs .... Mr. David B. SMITH
100 Chief of Staff .... Fr. Kenneth P. PAULLI, OFM
13 Chief Information Officer .... Mr. Mark A. BERMAN
49 Dean of Liberal Arts .... Dr. Janet L. SHIDELER
50 Dean of Business .... Dr. Jeffrey A. MELLO
81 Dean of Science .... Dr. Allan WEATHERWAX
20 Assoc VP Acad Affs/Student Success .... Dr. Peter C. ELLARD
45 Assoc VP Acad Affs/Inst Effectivns .... Dr. Mary Lou D'ALLEGRO
15 Asst VP for Human Resources .... Ms. Cynthia B. KING-LEROY

07 Assoc VP Enrollment Mgmt .... Ms. Heather M. RENAULT
21 Asst VP for Finance & Admin .... Ms. Mary C. STRUNK
18 Asst VP for Facilities Management .... Mr. Mark FROST
19 Asst VP Stdnt Aff/Dir Public Safety .... Mr. Michael PAPADOPOULOS
86 Asst VP Acad Affs/Govt & Found Rels .. Mr. Alfredo MEDINA, JR.
06 Registrar .... Mr. James SERBALIK
37 Asst Vice Pres Financial Aid .... Ms. Mary K. LAWYER
08 Dir of Library/Audio Visual Svcs .... Mr. Gary B. THOMPSON
92 Director of Honors Program .... Dr. Lois K. DALY
35 Dean of Students .... Mr. John R. FELIO
39 Director of Residence Life .... Ms. Kathleen BRANNOCK
41 Director of Athletics .... Mr. John D'ARGENIO
36 Director of Career Center .... Ms. Debra DELBELSO
88 Director of ITS .... Mr. Rad W. TAYLOR
42 Chaplain of the College .... Fr. Gregory JAKUBOWICZ, OFM
88 Dir Franciscan Ctr/Svc & Advocacy .... Fr. Russel MURRAY, OFM
26 Dir Strategic Comm/Integrated Mktg .... Ms. Delcy FOX
38 Director of Counseling Center .... Dr. Wally B. BZBELL
29 Director of Alumni Relations .... Ms. Mary Beth FINNERTY
09 Dir of Institutional Research .... Mr. Lee ALLARD
88 Dir of Risk Analysis/Project Mgmt .... Ms. Sandy SERBALIK
94 Dir Sr Thea Bowman Ctr for Women .... Dr. Shannon O'NEILL
23 Director of Health Services .... Ms. Carrie HOGAN
40 Bookstore Manager .... Mr. Richard IVES
88 Director of Development .... Mr. Bob P. KLEIN
44 Director of Planned Giving .... Mr. Jack R. SISE
28 Dir of Damietta Cross-Cultural Ctr .... Ms. Christa J. GRANT
104 Director of Study Abroad/Intl Pgms .... Bro. Brian C. BELANGER, OFM
96 Dir of Auxiliary Svcs & Procurement .... Ms. Laura S. PARRY
09 Institutional Research Analyst .... Ms. Kai ZHOU

Skidmore College (A)

815 N Broadway, Saratoga Springs NY 12866-1632
County: Saratoga FICE Identification: 002814
Unit ID: 195526
Telephone: (518) 580-5000 Carnegie Class: Bac/A&S
FAX Number: (518) 580-5936 Calendar System: Semester
URL: www.skidmore.edu
Established: 1911 Annual Undergrad Tuition & Fees: $45,874
Enrollment: 2,643 Coed
Affiliation or Control: Independent Non-Profit IRS Status: 501(c)3
Highest Offering: Master's
Program: Liberal Arts And General; Teacher Preparatory; Professional
Accreditation: M, ART, SW, @TEAC

01 President .... Dr. Philip A. GLOTZBACH
05 VP Academic Affairs/Dean of Faculty .... Dr. Beau BRESLIN
10 Vice President Finance/Treasurer .... Mr. Michael D. WEST
30 Vice President for Advancement .... Mr. Michael T. CASEY
16 Assoc VP Bus Aff/Dir Human Res .... Ms. Barbara E. BECK
32 Dean of Student Affairs .... Ms. W. Rochelle CALHOUN
07 Dean of Admissions & Financial Aid ..... Ms. Mary Lou W. BATES
71 Dean of Special Programs .... Mr. Paul CALHOUN
06 Registrar .... Mr. David DECONNO
20 Associate Dean Academic Advising .... Dr. Corey FREEMAN-GALLANT
20 Associate Dean of Faculty .... Dr. Paty RUBIO
89 Assoc Dean/Dir of First Year Exper .... Ms. Janet CASEY
35 Int Assoc Dean Student Affairs .... Mr. David KARP
39 Asst Dean Stdnt Affs/Dir Resid Life .... Mr. Donald B. HASTINGS
88 Assoc Dean Higher Ed Oppty Pgm .... Ms. Susan LAYDEN
45 Exec Dir Strategic Initiatives .... Vacant
26 Executive Director Communications .... Mr. Dan FORBUSH
09 Director of Institutional Research .... Mr. Joseph STANKOVICH
102 Dir Foundations & Corporate Rels .... Mr. Barry PRITZKER
46 Director of Sponsored Research .... Mr. Bill TOMLINSON
13 Director Center Info Tech Services .... Vacant
105 Director of Web Development .... Mr. Andy CAMP
31 Director Community Education .... Ms. Sharon A. ARPEY
87 Dir Summer Sessions/Summer Pgms .... Dr. Auden THOMAS
41 Athletic Director .... Dr. Gail L. CUMMINGS-DANSON
28 Director for Intercultural Studies .... Vacant
22 Asst Dir EEO & Workforce Diversity .... Mr. Herb CROSSMAN
91 Director of MIS .... Mr. Jeffrey A. CLARK
104 Dir of Off-Campus Study & Exchanges .... Ms. Cori FILSON
26 Director of Community Relations .... Mr. Robert S. KIMMERLE
44 Director Donor Relations .... Ms. Mary L. SOLOMONS
30 Director of Development .... Ms. Lori EASTMAN
29 Director of Alumni Affairs/Events .... Mr. Michael SPOSILI
36 Director of Career Services .... Vacant
37 Director of Financial Aid .... Ms. Beth POST-LUNDQUIST
38 Director Counseling Center .... Dr. Julia C. ROUTBORT
21 Director of Business Services .... Ms. Christine KACZMAREK
23 Director of Health Services .... Ms. Pamela HOULE
18 Director of Facilities Services .... Mr. Daniel RODECKER
19 Director of Campus Safety .... Mr. Dennis S. CONWAY
08 College Librarian .... Ms. Ruth S. COPANS
28 Director Student Diversity Programs .... Ms. Mariel L. MARTIN
96 Director of Purchasing .... Mrs. Carol N. SCHNITZER
42 Dir of Religious & Spiritual Life .... Mr. Rick CHRISMAN
24 Director of Media Services .... Mr. T. Hunt CONARD
40 Manager Skidmore Shop .... Mr. Jon NEIL
101 Coordinator of Trustee Affairs .... Ms. Jeanne M. SISSON
04 Special Asst to the President .... Ms. Elizabeth B. BOURQUE

Sotheby's Institute of Art (B)

570 Lexington Ave, 6th Floor, New York NY 10022
County: New York Identification: 667007
Telephone: (212) 517-3929 Carnegie Class: Not Classified
FAX Number: (212) 517-6568 Calendar System: Semester
URL: www.sothebysinstitute.com
Established: Annual Graduate Tuition & Fees: $55,082
Enrollment: 139 Coed
Affiliation or Control: Proprietary IRS Status: Proprietary
Highest Offering: First Professional Degree; No Undergraduates
Program: Professional; Fine Arts Emphasis
Accreditation: ART

01 Director .... Ms. Lesley A. CADMAN

*State University of New York System Office (C)

State University Plaza, Albany NY 12246-0001
County: Albany FICE Identification: 008788
Unit ID: 195827
Telephone: (518) 320-1100 Carnegie Class: N/A
FAX Number: (518) 320-1561
URL: www.suny.edu

01 Chancellor .... Dr. Nancy L. ZIMPHER
03 Vice Chancellor & Chief of Staff .... Dr. Jim MALATRAS
05 Provost and Sr Vice Chancellor .... Dr. Elizabeth BRINGSJORD
88 Chanc's Dpty to Ed Pipeline of SUNY .... Ms. Johanna DUNCAN-POITIER
10 Chief Financial Officer .... Mr. Brian HUTZLEY
102 Senior VP Research Foundation .... Vacant
101 V Chanc for Rsrch/Pres Rsrch Found .... Dr. Timothy KILLEEN
20 Vice Chanc Academic Programs .... Dr. Jason LANE
15 Vice Chancellor Human Resources .... Mr. Curtis LLOYD
20 Associate Provost .... Dr. Robert KRAUSHAAR
18 Vice Chanc for Capital Facilities .... Mr. Robert HAELEN
85 Vice Chancellor for Global Affairs .... Dr. Mitchel LEVENTHAL
28 Assoc VC Diversity/Equity & Inclus .... Dr. Carlos MEDINA
43 Vice Chancellor & General Counsel .... Mr. William F. HOWARD
88 VP/General Counsel Charter Sch Inst .... Mr. Ralph ROSSI
20 Deputy Provost .... Vacant
27 Chief Information Officer .... Dr. Hao WANG
09 Assc Provost Inst Research/Analysis .... Dr. Rick MILLER
35 Assoc Provost Opportunity Programs .... Vacant
17 Assoc VC for Health Affairs .... Ms. Lora LEFEBVRE
19 Asst VC for University Police .... Vacant
32 Assoc VC for Student Life .... Dr. Edward ENGELBRIDE
21 University Auditor .... Mr. Michael ABBOTT
26 Director of Communications .... Mr. David DOYLE
86 Asst Vice Chanc Govt Relations .... Ms. Stacey HENGSTERMAN
45 Asst Vice Chancellor Strat Plng .... Ms. Kaitlin GAMBRILL
31 Asst Vice Chancellor External Affs .... Ms. Jennifer LOTURCO
80 Executive Director Levin Inst .... Dr. Daniel J. JULIUS

*University at Albany, SUNY (D)

1400 Washington Avenue, Albany NY 12222-1000
County: Albany FICE Identification: 002835
Unit ID: 196060
Telephone: (518) 442-3300 Carnegie Class: RU/VH
FAX Number: N/A Calendar System: Semester
URL: www.albany.edu
Established: 1844 Annual Undergrad Tuition & Fees (In-State): $9,038
Enrollment: 17,316 Coed
Affiliation or Control: State IRS Status: 501(c)3
Highest Offering: Doctorate
Program: Liberal Arts And General; Teacher Preparatory; Professional
Accreditation: M, BUS, BUSA, CLPSY, COPSY, FEPAC, IPSY, LIB, PH, PLNG, SCPSY, SPAA, SW, TEAC

02 President .... Robert J. JONES
05 Provost/Vice Pres for Academic Affs .... Susan D. PHILLIPS
46 Vice President for Research .... James DIAS
10 Int Vice Pres Finance & Business .... Stephen BEDITZ
32 Vice President Student Success .... Christine A. BOUCHARD
30 Vice Pres University Development .... Fardin SANAI
26 Vice Pres Communications/Marketing .... Catherine HERMAN
54 Sr VP/CEO Col of Nanoscale Sci/Eng .... Alain KALOYEROS
41 VP Athletic Adm/Dir Intercol Athl .... Lee MCELROY
21 Assoc Vice President & Controller .... Kevin WILCOX
35 Assoc Vice Pres for Student Affairs .... John MURPHY
45 Assoc Vice President for Research .... Robert O. WEBSTER
09 Asst VP Inst Rsrch/Plng/Effvnss .... Bruce SZELEST
18 Assistant Vice President Facilities .... John GIARRUSSO
20 Provost & Asst VP Acad Affairs .... Robert ANDREA
28 Asst VP Diversity/Inclusion .... Tamra MINOR
97 Vice Prov Undergraduate Education .... Sue S. FAERMAN
49 Dean of Arts & Sciences .... Edelgard WULFERT
53 Dean School of Education .... Robert BANGERT-DROWNS
50 Dean School of Business .... Donald S. SIEGEL
69 Dean School of Public Health .... Philip NASCA
61 Dean of Criminal Justice .... Alan J. LIZOTTE
80 Dean Rockefeller Col of Pub Affs .... David ROUSSEAU
70 Dean of Social Welfare .... Katharine BRIAR-LAWSON
77 Dean Col of Computing & Information .... Peter BLONIARZ
58 Dean of Graduate Studies .... Kevin WILLIAMS
08 Dean/Director of Libraries .... Mary F. CASSERLY
13 Chief Information Officer .... Christine E. HAILE
29 Exec Director Alumni Association .... Lee SERRAVILLO, JR.
90 Director Academic Computing .... Felix WU
100 Chief of Staff .... Vincent DELIO
38 Director Advisement Services Center .... Suzanne K. FREED
43 Senior Counsel .... John H. REILLY
38 Director of Health/Counseling Svcs .... Estela RIVERO
36 Director Career Development .... Philippe J. ABRAHAM
96 Director of Administrative Svcs .... Edward KANE, JR.

*State University of New York at Binghamton (E)

Vestal Parkway E, Box 6000, Binghamton NY 13902-6000
County: Broome FICE Identification: 002836
Unit ID: 196079
Telephone: (607) 777-2000 Carnegie Class: RU/H
FAX Number: (607) 777-4000 Calendar System: Semester
URL: www.binghamton.edu
Established: 1946 Annual Undergrad Tuition & Fees (In-State): $8,144
Enrollment: 15,308 Coed
Affiliation or Control: State IRS Status: 501(c)3
Highest Offering: Doctorate
Program: Liberal Arts And General; Professional
Accreditation: M, BUS, CLPSY, CS, ENG, MUS, NURSE, SPAA, SW, TEAC

02 President .... Dr. Harvey G. STENGER, JR.
88 University Ombudsman .... Ms. Dawn OSBORNE-ADAMS
100 Chief of Staff .... Mr. Terrence KANE
05 Exec VP for Academic Affs/Provost .... Dr. Donald NIEMAN
10 Vice President Administration .... Mr. James R. VANVOORST
32 Vice Pres Student Affairs .... Mr. Brian T. ROSE
26 Vice President External Affairs .... Vacant
09 Vice President for Research .... Dr. Bahgat SAMMAKIA
104 Vice Prov International Education .... Dr. Katharine KREBS
45 Senior Vice Provost .... Dr. Michael F. MCGOFF
84 Vice Prov Enrollment Management .... Ms. Sandra STARKE
58 Vice Prov/Dean of Graduate School .... Dr. Susan STREHLE
18 Assoc VP Facilities Management .... Mr. Lawrence J. ROMA
35 Dean of Students .... Dr. April THOMPSON
29 Assoc VP for External Affairs .... Ms. Sheila DOYLE
26 Asst Vice Pres Univ Comm/Mktg .... Mr. Gregory DELVISCIO
21 Assoc VP Computing Services .... Mr. Mark V. REED
35 Asst Vice Pres Student Life .... Mr. Terry WEBB
04 Exec Assistant to the President .... Ms. Laura L. O'NEIL
11 Assoc Vice Pres Admin Services .... Ms. JoAnn NAVARRO
15 Asst Vice Pres for Human Resources ...... Mr. Joseph P. SCHULTZ
07 Int Dir Undergraduate Admissions .... Ms. Sandra STARKE
08 Dean of Libraries .... Mr. John M. MEADOR, JR.
85 Director Intl Students/Scholar Svcs .... Vacant
86 Director of State Relations .... Mr. Terrence KANE
37 Int Dir Stdnt Financial Aid/Employ .... Mr. Dennis J. CHAVEZ
06 University Registrar .... Vacant
38 Director Health & Counseling .... Ms. Johann FIORE CONTE
36 Director Career Development Center .... Vacant
19 Director Public Safety .... Mr. Timothy FAUGHANAN
41 Director Athletics .... Mr. Patrick ELLIOTT
71 Director EOP/Spec Programs .... Mr. Randall EDOUARD
22 Director of Affirmative Action/EEO .... Ms. Valerie J. HAMPTON
28 Director Multi-Cultural Res Ctr .... Ms. Nicole SIRJU-JOHNSON
92 Director Binghamton Univ Scholars .... Mr. George CATALANO
94 Exec Director of Women's Studies ...... Ms. Dara J. SILBERSTEIN
96 Director of Purchasing .... Mr. Kenneth G. WASKIE
09 Asst Provost Institutional Research .... Ms. Nasrin FATIMA
49 Dean Arts & Science Harpur Col .... Dr. Anne MCCALL
53 Dean School of Education .... Dr. S. G GRANT
50 Dean School of Management .... Dr. Upinder S. DHILLON
54 Dn Watson Sch Engr/Applied Science .... Dr. Hari SRIHARI
66 Dean Decker School of Nursing .... Dr. Joyce A. FERRARIO
31 Int Dean Community & Public Affairs .... Dr. Laura BRONSTEIN
106 Director Continuing Educ/Outreach .... Mr. Thomas KOWALIK

*University at Buffalo-SUNY (F)

3435 Main Street, Buffalo NY 14214
County: Erie FICE Identification: 002837
Unit ID: 196088
Telephone: (716) 645-2000 Carnegie Class: RU/VH
FAX Number: N/A Calendar System: Semester
URL: www.buffalo.edu
Established: 1846 Annual Undergrad Tuition & Fees (In-State): $8,289
Enrollment: 28,199 Coed
Affiliation or Control: State IRS Status: 501(c)3
Highest Offering: Doctorate
Program: Liberal Arts And General; Professional
Accreditation: M, ANEST, AUD, BUS, BUSA, CEA, CLPSY, CORE, DA, DENT, DIETI, ENG, IPSY, LAW, #LIB, MED, MT, NMT, NURSE, OT, PH, PHAR, PLNG, PSPSY, PTA, SP, SW, TEAC

02 President .... Dr. Satish K. TRIPATHI
05 Provost/Exec VP Academic Affs .... Dr. Charles F. ZUKOSKI
10 Vice Pres Finance & Administration .... Ms. Laura E. HUBBARD
32 Vice President Student Affairs .... Mr. Dennis R. BLACK
17 Vice President Health Sciences .... Dr. Michael CAIN
30 Vice Pres Development & Alumni Rels .... Ms. Nancy L. WELLS
46 Vice President for Research/EcoDev . Dr. Alexander CARTWRIGHT
84 Vice Provost of Enrollment .... Dr. Lee H. MELVIN
15 Asst VP Human Resources .... Ms. Susan KRZYSTOFIAK
58 Vice Provost Graduate Education .... Mr. John T. HO
20 Sr Vice Provost Acad Affairs .... Dr. A. Scott WEBER
20 Vice Provost for Faculty Affairs .... Ms. Lucinda M. FINLEY
104 Vice Provost for International Educ .... Dr. Stephen C. DUNNETT
45 Vice Provost Academic Plng & Budget ..... Mr. Sean P. SULLIVAN
21 Assoc Vice President & Controller .... Vacant
18 Assoc Vice Pres Univ Facilities .... Vacant
08 Assoc VP for Univ Libraries .... Mr. Austin BOOTH
27 Int Assoc VP Information Technology .... Mr. Thomas FURLANI
37 Interim Director Financial Aid .... Ms. Cheryl TAPLIN
09 Assoc V Provost/Dir Inst Research .... Mr. Craig W. ABBEY
96 Asst Vice Pres Procurement Services .... Mr. Daniel VIVIAN
27 Assoc VP Univ Communications .... Mr. Joseph A. BRENNAN
22 Dir Equity/Diversity/Inclusion .... Ms. Sharon E. NOLAN-WEISS

41 Director of Athletics ....Mr. Danny WHITE
20 Director Academic Services CIT ....Vacant
91 Director Enterprise Application Svc ....Ms. Susan A. HUSTON
07 Director of Admissions ....Mr. Barry TAYLOR
19 Chief of Police ....Mr. Gerald W. SCHOENLE, JR.
39 Director of Campus Living ....Ms. Andrea COSTANTINO
38 Director of Counseling Services ....Dr. Sharon L. MITCHELL
23 Dir Hlth Svcs/Stdnt Wellness Coord ....Ms. Susan M. SNYDER
36 Director Career Services ....Ms. Arlene F. KAUKUS
85 Director Intl Students/Scholar Svc ....Ms. Ellen A. DUSSOURD
40 Director University Bookstores ....Mr. Gregory NEUMANN
92 Admin Dir Univ Honors College ....Ms. Krista L. HANYPSIAK
29 Sr Assoc Director Alumni Relations ....Mr. Jay R. FRIEDMAN
20 Dean of Undergraduate Educ ....Dr. Andrew M. STOTT
48 Dean School Arch & Planning ....Dr. Robert SHIBLEY
49 Dean College of Arts/Sciences ....Dr. Bruce PITMAN
52 Dean School Dental Medicine ....Dr. Michael L. GLICK
53 Dean Graduate Sch of Education ....Dr. Jaekyung LEE
54 Dean School Engr/Applied Sci ....Dr. Liesl FOLKS
61 Dean School of Law ....Prof. Makau W. MUTUA
50 Dean School of Management ....Dr. Arjang A. ASSAD
63 Dean School Medicine/Biomed Sci ....Dr. Michael E. CAIN
66 Dean School of Nursing ....Dr. Marsha L. LEWIS
67 Dean School Pharmacy/Pharm Sciences ....Dr. Wayne K. ANDERSON
76 Dean Sch Public Hlth/Hlth Prof ....Dr. Lynn T. KOZLOWSKI
70 Dean School of Social Work ....Dr. Nancy J. SMYTH

*State University of New York at Fredonia (A)

138 Fenton Hall, Fredonia NY 14063-1136
County: Chautauqua FICE Identification: 002844
Unit ID: 196158
Telephone: (716) 673-3111 Carnegie Class: Master's M
FAX Number: N/A Calendar System: Semester
URL: www.fredonia.edu
Established: 1826 Annual Undergrad Tuition & Fees (In-State): $7,400
Enrollment: 5,545 Coed
Affiliation or Control: State IRS Status: 501(c)3
Highest Offering: Master's
Program: Liberal Arts And General; Teacher Preparatory; Professional
Accreditation: M, MUS, SP, SW, TED, THEA

02 President ....Dr. Virginia S. HORVATH
05 Provost & VP for Acad Affairs ....Dr. Terry BROWN
11 VP for Administration ....Mr. Stephen SCHILLO
32 Vice President for Student Affairs ....Dr. David E. HERMAN
35 Assoc Vice Pres for Student Affairs ....Ms. Monica J. WHITE
30 Vice Pres University Advancement ....Dr. David M. TIFFANY
20 Assoc VP Curriculum & Acad Support ....Dr. Melinda Ann KARNES
49 Dean College of Liberal Arts & Sci ....Dr. John L. KIJINSKI
88 VP Engagement & Economic Dev ....Dr. Kevin KEARNS
57 Dean College of Visual & Perf Arts ....Dr. Ralph BLASTING
88 Int Assoc Provost Spec Initiatives ....Dr. Adrienne MCCORMICK
50 Dean School of Business ....Dr. Russell P. BOISJOLY
53 Dean College of Education ....Dr. Christine E. GIVNER
102 Director Corp/Univ Advancement ....Dr. David M. TIFFANY
18 Director Facilities Services ....Mr. Kevin P. CLOOS
06 Registrar ....Mr. Scott D. SAUNDERS
07 Director of Admissions ....Mr. John C. DEARTH
37 Director Financial Aid ....Mr. Daniel M. TRAMUTA
08 Director Library Services ....Mr. Randolph Lee GADIKIAN
09 Dir Institutional Research/Planning ....Dr. Xiao Y. ZHANG
36 Director of Career Development ....Ms. Tracy COLLINGWOD
84 Assoc Vice Pres for Enrollment Mgmt ....Mr. Daniel M. TRAMUTA
19 Chief University Police ....Ms. Ann K. MCCARRON-BURNS
25 Director of Sponsored Programs ....Vacant
39 Director Residence Life ....Mr. Gary L. BICE, JR.
41 Athletic Director ....Mr. Gregory D. PRECHTL
23 Director of Health Services ....Ms. Patricia A. BORIS
38 Director Counseling ....Dr. Sally J. TURNER
90 Academic Information Technology ....Mr. John MCCUNE
15 Director of Human Resources ....Mr. Michael D. DALEY
26 Director of Public Relations ....Mr. Michael BARONE
85 Director of Multicultural Affairs ....Ms. Jellema STEWART
92 Director of Honors Program ....Dr. David KINKELA
94 Director of Women's Studies ....Mr. Jeffry J. IOVANNONE
96 Director of Purchasing ....Mrs. Shari K. MILLER
28 Chief Diversity Officer ....Dr. William BOERNER
29 Director Alumni Affairs ....Ms. Patricia A. FERALDI

*State University of New York at New Paltz (B)

1 Hawk Drive, New Paltz NY 12561-2443
County: Ulster FICE Identification: 002846
Unit ID: 196176
Telephone: (845) 257-7869 Carnegie Class: Master's L
FAX Number: (845) 257-3009 Calendar System: Semester
URL: www.newpaltz.edu
Established: 1823 Annual Undergrad Tuition & Fees (In-State): $7,083
Enrollment: 7,767 Coed
Affiliation or Control: State IRS Status: 501(c)3
Highest Offering: Beyond Master's But Less Than Doctorate
Program: Liberal Arts And General; Teacher Preparatory; Professional
Accreditation: M, ART, BUS, ENG, MUS, SP, TED, THEA

02 President ....Dr. Donald P. CHRISTIAN
100 Chief of Staff/AVP Communication ....Ms. Shelly A. WRIGHT
05 Provost ....Dr. Philip MAUCERI
11 Vice Pres Administration & Finance ....Vacant
32 Student Affairs Vice President ....Dr. L. David ROONEY
84 Vice Pres Enrollment Management ....Mr. L. David EATON
13 Asst Vice Pres Tech/Info Systems ....Mr. Jonathan D. LEWIT
21 Asst Vice President Administration ....Ms. Michele HALSTEAD
09 Int Asst VP Inst Research/Planning ....Ms. Lucy WALKER
18 Asst VP Facilities Management ....Mr. John SHUPE
07 Dean of Admissions ....Ms. Lisa JONES
08 Dean Sojourner Truth Library ....Mr. W. Mark COLVSON
07 Asst Dean/Dir Freshmen Admissions ....Ms. Kimberly STRANO
30 Director of Development ....Vacant
36 Director Career Resource Center ....Ms. Tonda S. HIGHLEY
15 Director Human Resources ....Ms. Dawn BLADES
37 Director of Financial Aid ....Mr. Daniel SISTARENIK
06 Registrar ....Ms. Bernadette MORRIS
29 Director Alumni Relations ....Ms. Brenda DOW
38 Director Student Counseling ....Dr. Gweneth LLOYD
26 Dir Communication & Marketing ....Ms. Suzanne GRADY
96 Director of Purchasing/Procurement ....Mr. David FARBANIEC
19 Director Security/Safety ....Mr. David DUGATKIN
86 Ex Dir Compliance/Camp Clm/Title IX ....Ms. Tanhena PACHECO DUNN
53 Dean of Education ....Dr. Michael ROSENBERG
57 Int Dean Fine & Performing Arts ....Mr. Paul KASSEL
49 Int Dean Liberal Arts & Sciences ....Dr. Mary Stella DEEN
54 Dean Science and Engineering ....Dr. Daniel FREEDMAN
50 Interim Dean School of Business ....Dr. Chih-Yang TSAI
58 Assoc Provost/Dean Graduate School ....Dr. Laurel GARRICK DUHANEY

*State University of New York at Stony Brook (C)

310 Administration Building, Stony Brook NY 11794-0701
County: Suffolk FICE Identification: 002838
Unit ID: 196097
Telephone: (631) 632-6265 Carnegie Class: RU/VH
FAX Number: (631) 632-6621 Calendar System: Semester
URL: www.stonybrook.edu
Established: 1957 Annual Undergrad Tuition & Fees (In-State): $7,560
Enrollment: 23,946 Coed
Affiliation or Control: State IRS Status: 501(c)3
Highest Offering: Doctorate
Program: Liberal Arts And General; Teacher Preparatory; Professional
Accreditation: M, ARCPA, CLPSY, COARC, COARCP, CS, DENT, DIETI, ENG, IPSY, MED, MIDWF, MT, NURSE, OT, PCSAS, PH, POLYT, PTA, RADDOS, SW, TED

02 President ....Dr. Samuel L. STANLEY
05 Provost & Sr Vice Pres Acad Affairs ....Dr. Dennis N. ASSANIS
63 Sr VP HSC/Dean School of Medicine ....Dr. Kenneth KAUSHANSKY
46 Vice President Research ....Dr. Benjamin HSIAO
32 Vice President Student Affairs ....Dr. Peter M. BAIGENT
10 VP Finance ....Mr. Lyle GOMES
30 Vice Pres University Advancement ....Mr. Dexter BAILEY
88 VP Econ Devel/Dean Engr/Applied Sci ....Dr. Yacov SHAMASH
100 Interim Chief Deputy to President ....Ms. Yoonmi NOH
45 Asst VP for Budget ....Mr. Mark MACIULAITIS
11 Sr VP for Administration ....Ms. Barbara CHERNOW
26 Asst Vice Pres Communications ....Vacant
39 Asst Vice Pres Campus Residences ....Dr. Dallas BAUMAN
17 CEO University Hospital ....Dr. Reuven PASTERNAK
84 Assoc Prov Enrollment/Retent Mgmt ....Dr. Peter BAIGENT
13 VP Information Technology and CIO ....Mr. Cole CAMPLESE
43 Associate Counsel ....Ms. Susan BLUM
49 Dean College Arts & Sciences ....Dr. Nancy SQUIRES
54 Dean Col of Engr & Applied Science ....Dr. Yacov SHAMASH
88 Dean School of Marine & Atmos Sci ....Dr. Minghua ZHANG
52 Dean School of Dental Medicine ....Dr. Ray WILLIAMS
68 Dean Div Physical Educ & Athletics ....Mr. James FIORE
58 Interim Dean Graduate School ....Dr. Charles TABLE
51 Dean Sch Profess Devel & Cont Educ ....Dr. Paul EDELSON
07 Asst Provost Admission & Fin Aid ....Dr. Matthew WHELAN
76 Dean School Health Technology Mgmt ....Dr. Craig LEHMANN
35 Dean of Students ....Dr. Jerrold STEIN
66 Dean School of Nursing ....Dr. Lee XIPPOLITOS
70 Dean School of Social Welfare ....Dr. Frances L. BRISBANE
08 Int Director & Dean of Libraries ....Mr. Daniel KINNEY
86 Vice President External Relations ....Ms. Elaine CROSSON
88 Exec Dir LI State Vets Home ....Mr. Fred SGANGA
19 Chief of Police ....Mr. Robert LENAHAN
15 VP Human Resource Svcs ....Ms. Lynn JOHNSON
28 Dir Diversity/AA/Equal Employ Oppty ....Vacant
09 Director Planning & Inst Research ....Vacant
85 Dean International Programs ....Dr. William ARENS
102 Exec Dir of Stony Brook Foundation ....Vacant
29 Director Alumni Relations ....Mr. Matthew COLSON
23 Director University Health Services ....Dr. Rachel BERGESON
38 Director Counseling Center ....Dr. Jenny HWANG
36 Director Career Placement Center ....Ms. Marianna SAVOCA
06 Registrar ....Ms. Diane BELLO
37 Financial Aid/Scholarships ....Ms. Jacqueline PASCARIELLO
50 Dean College of Business ....Dr. Manuel LONDON
08 Director Health Sciences Library ....Mr. Spencer MARSH
27 University Media Relations Officer ....Ms. Lauren SHEPROW
96 Director of Purchasing/Procurement ....Mr. James FABIAN
60 Dean School of Journalism ....Mr. Howard SCHNEIDER

*State University of New York Health Science Center at Brooklyn (D)

450 Clarkson Avenue, Brooklyn NY 11203-2098
County: Kings FICE Identification: 002839
Unit ID: 196255
Telephone: (718) 270-1000 Carnegie Class: Spec/Med
FAX Number: (718) 270-4092 Calendar System: Semester
URL: www.downstate.edu
Established: 1860 Annual Undergrad Tuition & Fees (In-State): $6,415
Enrollment: 1,751 Coed
Affiliation or Control: State IRS Status: 501(c)3
Highest Offering: Doctorate
Program: Occupational; Liberal Arts And General; Professional
Accreditation: M, ANEST, ARCPA, DMS, MED, MIDWF, NURSE, OT, PH, PTA, RAD

02 President ....Dr. John F. WILLIAMS
03 Interim Chief Executive Officer ....Mr. George CARALIS
10 Chief Financial Officer ....Mr. Alan DZIJA
11 COO/Exec Vice Pres Administration ....Ms. Astra BAIN-DOWELL
63 Sr VP Biomed Research/Dean Col Med ....Dr. Ian L. TAYLOR
18 Interim Vice President Facilities ....Vacant
17 SVP Inst Dev/Phylthrpy/VP Acad Affs ....Dr. JoAnn BRADLEY
32 Assoc VP Student Aff/Dean of Stdnts ....Dr. Jeffrey PUTMAN
45 Assoc Vice Pres for Planning ....Ms. Dorothy R. FYFE
39 Asst Vice Pres Stdnt Life/Housing ....Ms. Meg O'SULLIVAN
16 AVP Labor Relations ....Mr. Leonzo CUIMAN
15 AVP for Personnel ....Ms. Hendrina GOELOE-ALSTON
46 Asst Provost Scientific Affairs ....Mr. John M. ALLEN
58 Dean School Graduate Studies ....Dr. Mark STEWART
66 Dean College of Nursing ....Dr. Daisy CRUZ-RICHMAN
20 Asst Dean Academic Development ....Vacant
30 Director Institutional Advancement ....Ms. Ellen WATSON
13 Interim Chief Information Officer ....Mr. John DOOLEY
17 Medical Director ....Dr. Michael LUCCHESI
08 Director of Libraries ....Dr. Richard M. WINANT
07 Director of Admissions ....Ms. Shushawana DEOLIVEIRA
06 Registrar ....Ms. Anne SHONBRUN
37 Director Student Financial Aid ....Mr. James NEWELL
21 Bursar ....Mr. Charles CONWAY
51 Director of CME ....Ms. Edeline MITTEN
23 Director of Student Health Svc ....Dr. Sigrid ULRICH
28 Director Ofc Opportunity/Diversity ....Mr. Kevin ANTOINE
29 Exec Dir Alumni Assn Col Medicine ....Ms. Jill DITCHIK
38 Director of Student Counseling ....Dr. Christine V. SAUNDERS-FIELDS
19 Chief of Police ....Mr. Thomas F. DUGAN
09 Director of Institutional Research ....Vacant
26 Chief Public Relations Officer ....Ms. Ellen WATSON
96 Director of Purchasing ....Mr. Carter LARD

*State University of New York Upstate Medical University (E)

750 E Adams Street, Syracuse NY 13210-2375
County: Onondaga FICE Identification: 002840
Unit ID: 196307
Telephone: (315) 464-5540 Carnegie Class: Spec/Med
FAX Number: (315) 464-8823 Calendar System: Semester
URL: www.upstate.edu
Established: 1834 Annual Undergrad Tuition & Fees (In-State): $6,573
Enrollment: 1,632 Coed
Affiliation or Control: State IRS Status: 501(c)3
Highest Offering: Doctorate
Program: Professional
Accreditation: M, ARCPA, COARC, DENT, DMOLS, IPSY, MED, MT, NURSE, PERF, PTA, RAD, RTT

02 President ....Dr. David R. SMITH
63 Dean College of Medicine ....Dr. David B. DUGGAN
17 CEO University Hospital ....Dr. John MCCABE
10 Vice President Finance & Management ....Mr. Steven BRADY
05 Vice President Academic Affairs ....Dr. Lynn CLEARY
46 Dean College Graduate Studies ....Dr. Mark SCHMITT
32 Dean Student Affairs ....Dr. Julie R. WHITE
102 Exec Director HSC Foundation ....Ms. Eileen PEZZI
66 Dean College of Nursing ....Dr. Joyce GRIFFIIN SOBEL
76 Dean College Health Profession ....Dr. Hugh W. BONNER
06 Registrar/Dir Inst Research ....Ms. Jennifer MARTIN TSE
25 Vice President for Research ....Dr. Rosemary ROCHFORD
29 Director of Medical Alumni Affairs ....Mr. Vincent KUSS
15 Assoc VP Human Resources ....Mr. Eric FROST
13 Chief Information Officer ....Ms. Teresa J. WAGNER
08 Director of Libraries ....Ms. Christina POPE
28 Dir Diversity & Affirmative Action ....Ms. Maxine THOMPSON
07 Assoc Dean Admissions/Financial Aid ....Ms. Jennifer C. WELCH
18 Chief Facilities/Physical Plant ....Mr. Gary KITTELL
21 Assistant Vice President Finance ....Mr. Eric SMITH
37 Director Student Financial Aid ....Mr. Michael PEDE

*State University of New York, The College at Brockport (F)

350 New Campus Drive, Brockport NY 14420-2914
County: Monroe FICE Identification: 002841
Unit ID: 196121
Telephone: (585) 395-2211 Carnegie Class: Master's L
FAX Number: (585) 395-2401 Calendar System: Semester
URL: www.brockport.edu
Established: 1867 Annual Undergrad Tuition & Fees (In-State): $7,222
Enrollment: 8,271 Coed

Affiliation or Control: State IRS Status: 501(c)3
Highest Offering: Master's
Program: Liberal Arts And General; Teacher Preparatory; Professional
Accreditation: M, BUS, CACREP, CS, DANCE, NRPA, NURSE, SPAA, SW, TED, THEA

02 President Dr. John R. HALSTEAD
05 Int Provost & VP Academic Affairs Dr. Doug SCHEIDT
10 VP Administration & Finance Dr. James A. WILLIS
32 VP Enrollment Mgmt/Student Affairs Dr. Kathryn WILSON
30 VP Advancement Ms. Roxanne JOHNSTON
20 Vice Provost Dr. P. Michael FOX
58 Asst Provost Research/Dean Grad Sch Dr. James SPILLER
28 Int Asst Provost for Diversity Dr. Susan SEEM
84 Asst VP Enroll Mgmt Mr. Randall LANGSTON
35 Asst VP Student Affairs Ms. Leah A. BARRETT
18 Asst VP Facilities & Planning Mr. Robert HENRY
21 Asst VP Finance & Management Ms. Karen M. RIOTTO
13 Int Assoc Provost & CIO Mr. Jeff SMITH
49 Dean Arts/Humanities & Social Sci Dr. Darwin PRIOLEAU
50 Dean Business Dr. Daniel PETREE
53 Int Dean Education & Human Services Dr. Thomas J. HERNANDEZ
68 Dean Health & Human Performance Dr. Frank SHORT
81 Dean Science & Mathematics Dr. Jose MALIEKAL
13 Director of Info Tech System Mr. David R. STRASENBURGH
07 Int Dir of Undergrad Admissions Mr. Randall LANGSTON
44 Asst VP for Ldrshp/Planned Giving Mr. Michael ANDRIATCH
56 Exec Dir Brockport Metro Center Dr. Karen SCHUHLE-WILLIAMS
44 Exec Dir Dev Comm & Campaign Ms. Darby KNOX
51 Exec Dir Continuing Professional Ed Ms. Kathleen H. GROVES
104 Exec Dir International Education Dr. Ralph R. TRECARTIN
26 Chief Communications Officer Mr. David MIHALYOV
37 Dir Financial Aid & Enrollment Svcs Mr. J. Scott ATKINSON
36 Director of Career Services Ms. Jill WESLEY
19 Chief of University Police Mr. Robert J. KEHOE
06 College Registrar Mr. Peter DOWE
16 Director of Human Resources Ms. Amy KAHN
22 Affirmative Action Officer Ms. Adrienne COLLIER
23 Director Student Health/Counseling Ms. Elizabeth S. CARUSO
39 Int Dir Res Life/Learning Comm Ms. Leah BARRETT
41 Director of Athletics Mr. Erick HART
25 Director of Grants Development Ms. Colleen DONALDSON
92 Director of Honors Program Dr. Donna M. KOWAL
09 Director of Inst Effectiveness Dr. Jeffrey T. LASHBROOK
96 Director of Procurement & Payment Mr. Mark W. STACY
94 Dir of Women and Gender Studies Dr. Barbara LESAVOY
29 Director Alumni Relations Mr. Kerry GOTHAM

*State University of New York College at Buffalo (A)

1300 Elmwood Avenue, Buffalo NY 14222-1091
County: Erie FICE Identification: 002842
Unit ID: 196130
Telephone: (716) 878-4000 Carnegie Class: Master's L
FAX Number: (716) 878-3039 Calendar System: Semester
URL: www.buffalostate.edu
Established: 1871 Annual Undergrad Tuition & Fees (In-State): $7,024
Enrollment: 11,781 Coed
Affiliation or Control: State IRS Status: 501(c)3
Highest Offering: Master's
Program: Liberal Arts And General; Teacher Preparatory; Professional
Accreditation: M, ART, CIDA, DIETC, DIETD, ENGT, JOUR, MUS, NAIT, SP, SW, TED, THEA

02 Interim President Dr. Howard COHEN
100 Chief of Staff Dr. Bonita R. DURAND
05 Provost Dr. Dennis K. PONTON
10 Vice President Finance & Management Mr. Michael F. LEVINE
32 Vice President Student Affairs Dr. Hal D. PAYNE
30 Vice Pres Inst Advancement & Devel Dr. Susanne P. BAIR
28 Chief Diversity Officer Dr. Karen A. CLINTON-JONES
20 Interim Assoc VP Teacher Education Dr. John F. SISKAR
84 Associate Vice Pres Enrollment Mgmt Mr. Mark J. PETRIE
21 Assoc Vice President & Comptroller Mr. James A. THOR
102 Director College & Foundation Mr. Robert L. BAUMET
35 Assoc Vice President Campus Life Dr. Timothy R. ECKLUND
35 Asc VP Student Affs/Dean Students Dr. Charles B. KENYON
14 Assoc Vice Pres Computing Services Ms. Judith B. BASINSKI
09 Assoc VP Curriculum/Assessment Dr. Rosalyn A. LINDNER
26 Assoc VP College Relations Mr. Timothy J. WALSH
08 Assoc VP Library/Instr Technology Ms. Maryruth F. GLOGOWSKI
44 Assoc VP Development Ms. Jane A. ARMBRUSTER
86 Assoc VP Government Relations Mr. William J. BENFANTI
51 Assoc VP Continuing Prof Studies Dr. Margaret A. SHAW-BURNETT
20 Dean Univ Col/AVP Undergrad Ed Dr. Scott L. JOHNSON
53 Dean School of Education Dr. Wendy A. PATERSON
49 Dean School of Arts & Humanities Mr. Benjamin C. CHRISTY
83 Dean Natural & Social Science Dr. Mark W. SEVERSON
50 Interim Dean Professions Dr. Rita M. ZIENTEK
58 Dean Graduate School Dr. Kevin J. RAILEY
36 Director of Career Development Ms. Stephanie B. ZUCKERMAN-AVILES
07 Director Admissions Dr. Carmela THOMPSON
06 Registrar Mr. Mark T. BAUSILI
37 Director of Financial Aid Ms. Connie F. COOKE
88 Director of Student Accounts Ms. Susan F. WRIGHT
38 Director Counseling Center Dr. Joan L. MCCOOL
41 Director Intercollegiate Athletics Mr. Jerry S. BOYES
39 Director of Residence Life Mr. Kris A. KAUFMAN
23 Director Student Health Center Dr. Theresa R. STEPHAN HAINS
85 Director Intl Student Affairs Dr. Jean F. GOUNARD
15 Assoc VP Human Resource Management Ms. Susan J. EARSHEN
26 Director Public Relations Mr. Jerod T. DAHLGREN
29 Director of Alumni Affairs Ms. Mary-Jo JAGORD
88 Director Research Admin/Svcs Vacant
88 Director Special Events & Protocol Ms. Pamela B. VOYER
88 Director Campus Services Mr. Terry M. HARDING
88 Director Events Management Mr. Thomas E. COATES
90 Director Budget & Internal Controls Ms. Rebecca J. SCHENK
09 Director Institutional Research Mr. Yves M. GACHETTE
19 Chief University Police Mr. Peter M. CAREY
88 Director Parking Services Ms. Jayme S. RITER
96 Purchasing Manager Mr. Steven M. OLSEN
40 Manager BSC Bookstore Ms. Lynn M. PUMA
88 Interim Director Student Life Mrs. Sarah M. VELEZ
88 Director Disability Service Ms. Lisa T. MORRISON-FRONCKOWIAK
43 Director Judicial Affairs Dr. Latonia D. GASTON-MARSH
27 Chief Information Officer Mr. Don F. ERWIN
88 Asst to the Pres for Communications Mrs. Paula A. WITHERELL

*State University of New York College at Cortland (B)

PO Box 2000, Cortland NY 13045-0900
County: Cortland FICE Identification: 002843
Unit ID: 196149
Telephone: (607) 753-2011 Carnegie Class: Master's L
FAX Number: (607) 753-5999 Calendar System: Semester
URL: www.cortland.edu
Established: 1868 Annual Undergrad Tuition & Fees (In-State): $7,357
Enrollment: 7,098 Coed
Affiliation or Control: State IRS Status: 501(c)3
Highest Offering: Master's
Program: Liberal Arts And General; Teacher Preparatory; Professional
Accreditation: M, NRPA, @SP, TED

02 President Dr. Erik J. BITTERBAUM
05 Provost Dr. Mark PRUS
32 Vice Pres Student Affairs Mr. C. Gregory SHARER
30 Vice Pres Institutional Advancement Ms. Kimberly PIETRO
10 Vice President Business/Finance Dr. William SHAUT
21 VP/Assoc Finance & Management Ms. Mary K. MURPHY
27 Assoc Provost for Info Resources Ms. Amy BERG
18 Assoc VP Facilities Management Ms. Nasrin PARVIZI
20 Assoc Prov for Academic Affairs Dr. Carol VAN DER KARR
04 Exec Assistant to the President Dr. Virginia LEVINE
07 Director of Admissions Mr. Mark YACAVONE
09 Assoc Dir Inst Rsrch/Assessment Dr. Merle CANFIELD
08 Director of Libraries Ms. Gail WOOD
06 Registrar Mr. Thomas HANFORD
36 Director of Career Services Mr. John SHIRLEY
15 Asst VP Human Resources Ms. Joanne BARRY
29 Director Alumni Affairs Mr. Michael SGRO
38 Dir Counseling/Student Devel Dr. Carolyn BERSHAD
37 Dir of Student Financial Aid Ms. Karen GALLAGHER
19 Chief of University Police Mr. Steven DANGLER
91 Director Admin Computing Svcs Mr. Daniel SIDEBOTTOM
90 Director Campus Technology Services Ms. Lisa KAHLE
107 Dean Professional Studies Dr. John COTTONE
49 Dean Arts & Sciences Dr. Bruce MATTINGLY
26 Chief Public Relations Officer Mr. Frederic PIERCE
53 Dean of Education Dr. Andrea LACHANCE
93 Director Educational Oppty Program Dr. Lewis ROSENGARTEN
92 Director of Honors Program Dr. Lisi KRALL
94 Director of Women's Studies Dr. Caroline KALTEFLEITER
96 Director of Purchasing Mr. Samuel COLOMBO
22 Affirmative Action Officer Ms. Dawn NORCROSS
28 Dir Multicultural Life/Diversity Ms. Noelle PALEY
41 Athletic Director Mr. Mike URTZ

*State University of New York College at Geneseo (C)

1 College Circle, Geneseo NY 14454-1401
County: Livingston FICE Identification: 002845
Unit ID: 196167
Telephone: (585) 245-5000 Carnegie Class: Master's S
FAX Number: (585) 245-5005 Calendar System: Semester
URL: www.geneseo.edu
Established: 1871 Annual Undergrad Tuition & Fees (In-State): $7,467
Enrollment: 5,557 Coed
Affiliation or Control: State IRS Status: 501(c)3
Highest Offering: Master's
Program: Liberal Arts And General; Teacher Preparatory; Professional
Accreditation: M, BUS, TED

02 Interim President Dr. Carol S. LONG
05 Provost Dr. Carol S. LONG
20 Associate Provost Dr. David F. GORDON
11 Vice President Administration Dr. James B. MILROY
32 Vice Pres for Student & Campus Life Dr. Robert A. BONFIGLIO
30 Vice President College Relations Mr. William BROWER
84 Assoc Vice Pres Enrollment Mgmt Dr. William L. CAREN
10 Assoc VP Administration/Controller Mr. Brice M. WEIGMAN
27 Asst Vice Pres Communications Mr. Anthony T. HOPPA
86 Asst Prov of International Affairs Dr. Rebecca LEWIS
15 Asst Vice Pres Human Resources Ms. Julie A. BRIGGS
26 Asst VP for College Advancement Vacant
29 Director of Alumni & Parent Rels Ms. Ronna BOSKO
20 Dean of Curriculum & Academic Svcs Dr. Savitri V. IYER
35 Dean of Students Dr. Leonard SANCILIO
07 Director of Admissions Ms. Kristine M. SHAY
08 Library Director Mr. Cyril OBERLANDER
13 Director Computing/Info Technology Ms. Susan E. CHICHESTER
37 Director of Financial Aid Mr. Archie L. CURETON
25 Director of Sponsored Research Dr. Anne E. BALDWIN
09 Director of Institutional Research Dr. Julie M. RAO
06 Registrar Mr. Delbert W. BROWN
36 Director of Career Development Ms. Stacey WILEY
22 Affirmative Action Officer Vacant
88 Director of Multicultural Affairs Ms. Fatima R. JOHNSON
19 Chief of University Police Mr. Salvatore J. SIMONETTI
17 Director Counseling & Health Svcs Ms. Melinda C. DUBOIS
18 Chief Facilities/Physical Plant Mr. George F. STOOKS
21 Dir of Budget & Financial Analysis Ms. Julie MORGAN
38 Clinical Dir Counseling Services Dr. Beth K. CHOLETTE
96 Director of Purchasing Ms. Rebecca E. ANCHOR

*State University of New York College at Old Westbury (D)

P.O. Box 210, 223 Store Hill Road, Old Westbury NY 11568-0210
County: Nassau FICE Identification: 007109
Unit ID: 196237
Telephone: (516) 876-3000 Carnegie Class: Bac/A&S
FAX Number: (516) 876-3209 Calendar System: Semester
URL: www.oldwestbury.edu
Established: 1965 Annual Undergrad Tuition & Fees (In-State): $6,924
Enrollment: 4,282 Coed
Affiliation or Control: State IRS Status: 501(c)3
Highest Offering: Master's
Program: Liberal Arts And General; Teacher Preparatory; Professional
Accreditation: M, TED

02 President Dr. Calvin O. BUTTS, III
03 Executive Vice President Ms. Mona G. RANKIN
05 Provost/Vice Pres Academic Affairs Dr. Patrick O'SULLIVAN
84 Vice President Enrollment Services Ms. Mary MARQUEZ BELL
32 Vice President Student Affairs Dr. Mary L. LANGLIE
10 VP Div of Business & Finance/CFO Mr. Len L. DAVIS
16 Asst to Pres for Admin/Dir HR Mr. William P. KIMMINS
30 Asst to President for Advancement Mr. Michael G. KINANE
53 Dean School of Education Dr. Ruben L. GONZALEZ
21 Assoc Vice Pres/Business Affairs Ms. Deirdre M. DOWD
21 Assoc VP of Business Compliance Mr. Arthur H. ANGST, JR.
20 Asst Vice Pres Academic Affairs Mr. Ronald J. WELTON
20 Asst Vice Pres Academic Affairs Mr. Anthony BARBERA
50 Dean School of Business Mr. Anthony BARBERA
35 Dean of Students Mr. Rollie O. BUCHANAN
49 Dean School of Arts & Sciences Dr. Barbara HILLERY
19 Chief of Police Mr. Michael C. YANNIELLO
26 Director Public & Media Relations Mr. Michael G. KINANE
13 Chief Information Officer Mr. Marc P. SEYBOLD
06 Registrar Ms. Patricia A. SMITH
96 Director of Purchasing Mr. Patrick ADAMS
89 Director First-Year Experience Dr. Laura M. ANKER
31 Director of Community Relations Ms. Carolyn BENNETT
38 Dir Counseling/Psych Wellness Svcs Dr. Trisha BILLARD
29 Director of Alumni Affairs Ms. Penny J. CHIN
88 Coordinator of Scholarships Ms. Pritpal KAINTH
09 Director of Institutional Research Ms. Sandra KAUFMANN
08 Library Director Mr. Stephen KIRKPATRICK
88 Dir Educational Opportunity Program Mr. Alonzo L. MCCOLLUM
18 Director of Facilities Mr. Timothy MCGARRY
88 Director of Student Activities Ms. Suzanne MCLOUGHLIN
23 Director of Student Health Services Ms. Susan R. MUNDY
88 Director of Sponsored Programs Mr. Thomas MURPHY
37 Director Financial Aid Ms. Mildred O'KEEFE
39 Director of Residential Life Mr. Usama SHAIKH
41 Director of Athletics Ms. Lenore J. WALSH
102 Dir Corp & Foundation Relations Vacant

*State University of New York College at Oneonta (E)

108 Ravine Parkway, Oneonta NY 13820-4015
County: Otsego FICE Identification: 002847
Unit ID: 196185
Telephone: (607) 436-3500 Carnegie Class: Master's S
FAX Number: N/A Calendar System: Semester
URL: www.oneonta.edu
Established: 1889 Annual Undergrad Tuition & Fees (In-State): $5,870
Enrollment: 5,800 Coed
Affiliation or Control: State IRS Status: 501(c)3
Highest Offering: Master's
Program: Liberal Arts And General; Teacher Preparatory; Professional
Accreditation: M, AAFCS, BUS, DIETD, DIETI, MUS, TED

02 President Dr. Nancy KLENIEWSKI
04 Senior Assistant to the President Ms. Colleen E. BRANNAN
05 Provost/Vice Pres Academic Affairs Dr. E. Maria THOMPSON
32 Vice President Student Development Dr. Steven R. PERRY
10 Vice Pres Finance/Administration Mr. Todd D. FOREMAN
30 Vice President College Advancement Mr. Paul J. ADAMO
09 Assoc Prov Inst Assessment & Eff Dr. Patricia L. FRANCIS
83 Int Dean Behavioral/Applied Science Dr. Alexander THOMAS
83 Dean Social Science Dr. Susan TURELL
58 Director of Graduate Studies Mr. Patrick J. MENTE
50 Dean Economics/Business Dr. David YEN

53 Interim Dean Education .... Dr. Richard LEE
84 Assoc Vice Pres Enrollment Mgmt .... Mr. Roger B. SULLIVAN
35 Assoc Vice President Student Life .... Dr. Jeanne C. MILLER
19 Chief of Police .... Mr. Daniel P. CHAMBERS
15 Sr Exec Employee Services Officer .... Ms. Lisa M. WENCK
18 Assoc Vice Pres Facilities/Safety .... Mr. Thomas M. RATHBONE
90 Director IT Customer Support .... Mr. Steven J. MANISCALCO
07 Director of Admissions .... Ms. Karen A. BROWN
29 Director of Alumni Affairs .... Ms. Laura MADELONE
44 Director Fund for Oneonta .... Ms. Kim NOSTROM
41 Athletic Director .... Ms. Tracey M. RANIERI
21 Budget Control Officer/Budget Dir .... Ms. Julie ROSEBOOM
25 Director Business Services .... Ms. Betty M. TIRADO
36 Dir Career Dev/Student Emp Svcs .... Dr. Amy BENEDICT-AUGUSTINE
13 Dir Computing Ctr/Chief Info Ofcr .... Dr. Karlis KAUGARS
38 Director Counseling Services .... Dr. Melissa A. FALLON
24 Director Creative Media Services .... Mr. David W. GEASEY
37 Director Financial Aid .... Mr. Bill GOODHUE
09 Assoc Dir Institutional Research .... Ms. Chunmei YAO
85 Director of International Education .... Dr. Vernon C. LARSON
89 Director Orientation/First Year Exp .... Ms. Monica C. GRAU
96 Procurement/Travel Office Manager .... Ms. Terri THOMAS
06 College Registrar .... Ms. Maureen P. ARTALE
39 Director Residential Community Life .... Ms. Michele LUETTGER
93 Director Special Programs/EOP .... Ms. Lynda D. BASSETTE
23 Int Dir Student Health Services .... Ms. Mary MANCUSO
26 Director of Communications .... Mr. Hal S. LEGG
28 Dir of Office of Equity & Inclusion .... Vacant
88 Affirmative Action Officer .... Mr. Andrew STAMMEL

*State University of New York College at Oswego (A)

7060 State Route 104, Oswego NY 13126-3501
County: Oswego FICE Identification: 002848
Unit ID: 196194
Telephone: (315) 312-2500 Carnegie Class: Master's L
FAX Number: (315) 312-5799 Calendar System: Semester
URL: www.oswego.edu
Established: 1861 Annual Undergrad Tuition & Fees (In-State): $7,181
Enrollment: 7,921 Coed
Affiliation or Control: State IRS Status: 501(c)3
Highest Offering: Master's
Program: Liberal Arts And General; Teacher Preparatory; Professional
Accreditation: M, ART, BUS, MUS, TED, THEA

02 President .... Dr. Deborah F. STANLEY
05 VP Academic Affairs/Provost .... Dr. Lorrie A. CLEMO
10 Vice President Admin/Finance .... Mr. Nicholas A. LYONS
84 Vice Pres Student Affs/Enroll Mgmt .... Vacant
30 Vice Pres Devel/Alumni Relations .... Ms. Kerry DORSEY
32 Assoc VP/Dean of Students Affs .. Dr. James SCHARFENBERGER
18 Asst VP for Facilities Services .... Mr. Mitch FIELDS
21 Asst Vice Pres for Finance & Budget .... Mr. Byron SMITH
20 Associate Provost .... Dr. Rameen MOHAMMADI
04 Ex Asst to Pres/Int Affrm Act Ofcr .... Mr. Howard GORDON
26 Director of Public Affairs .... Ms. Julie H. BLISSERT
25 Dir Research/Sponsored Pgms .... Dr. Jack GELFAND
94 Director Women's Studies .... Dr. Mary MCCUNE
06 Registrar .... Mr. Jerret LEMAY
08 Director of Libraries .... Ms. Barbara SHAFFER
91 Director Admin Computer Center .... Mr. Michael C. PISA
37 Director of Financial Aid .... Mr. Mark HUMBERT
09 Director Inst Research & Assessment .... Dr. Mehran NOJAN
36 Director Career Services .... Mr. Gary MORRIS
38 Director Counseling Services Center .... Dr. Maria GRIMSHAW-CLARK
15 Director Human Resources .... Ms. Amy PLOTNER
19 University Police Chief .... Mr. John ROSSI
23 Director of Student Health Center .... Ms. Elizabeth BURNS
56 Asst Prov Distance Lrng/Info Resour .... Dr. Michael AMEIGH
28 Assoc Prov Multicltrl Pgms & Opps .... Ms. Catherine SANTOS
39 Dir Residence Life/Housing .... Dr. Richard KOLENDA
41 Athletic Director .... Ms. Susan VISCOME
96 Director Purchasing .... Mr. Mark COLE
13 Chief Technology Officer .... Mr. Sean MORIARTY
29 Interim Director Alumni Relations .... Ms. Laura PAVLUS
07 Interim Dir of Admiss/Enroll Mgmt .... Mr. Daniel GRIFFIN
40 College Store Manager .... Ms. Susan RABY
49 Interim Dean Col Lib Arts & Science .... Dr. Richard BACK
53 Interim Dean School of Education .... Dr. Pamela MICHEL
58 Dean Graduate Studies/Research .... Dr. David KING
50 Dean School of Business .... Dr. Richard J. SKOLNIK
51 Dean of Extended Learning .... Ms. Yvonne PETRELLA
88 Dean of Comm/Media & the Arts .... Mr. Fritz MESSERE
100 Chief of Staff .... Dr. Kenneth J. CLOUGH
88 Director of Auxiliary Services .... Mr. Michael FLAHERTY

*State University of New York College at Plattsburgh (B)

101 Broad Street, Plattsburgh NY 12901-2637
County: Clinton FICE Identification: 002849
Unit ID: 196246
Telephone: (518) 564-2000 Carnegie Class: Master's L
FAX Number: (518) 564-7827 Calendar System: Semester
URL: www.plattsburgh.edu
Established: 1889 Annual Undergrad Tuition & Fees (In-State): $5,870
Enrollment: 6,167 Coed
Affiliation or Control: State IRS Status: 501(c)3
Highest Offering: Master's
Program: Liberal Arts And General; Teacher Preparatory; Professional
Accreditation: M, BUS, CACREP, DIETD, NURSE, SP, SW, TEAC

02 President .... Dr. John ETTLING
04 Exec Assistant to the President .... Mr. Keith D. TYO
05 Provost/Vice Pres Academic Affairs .... Dr. James LISZKA
10 Vice President for Administration .... Mr. John R. HOMBURGER
30 Vice Pres Institutional Advancement .... Ms. Anne WHITMORE-HANSEN
32 Vice President for Student Affairs .... Mr. Bryan G. HARTMAN
20 Assistant Provost .... Ms. Diane MERKEL
21 Assoc Vice Pres Administration .... Vacant
15 Director of Human Resource Svces .... Ms. Susan T. WELCH
39 Director of Housing .... Ms. Cathy B. MOULTON
07 Assoc VP Enroll Mgmt/Admissions .... Mr. Richard J. HIGGINS
06 Registrar .... Ms. Denise M. PHILO
49 Dean of Arts & Science .... Dr. Andrew BUCKSER
53 Dean Educ/Health/Human Services .... Dr. Michael D. MORGAN
50 Dean of Business/Economics .... Dr. Raymond M. GUYDOSH
08 Interim Dean Library/Info Services .... Ms. Holly HELLER-ROSS
12 Dean Branch Campus at ACC .... Mr. Stephen DANNA
35 Dean of Students .... Mr. Stephen P. MATTHEWS
26 Exec Dir of Marketing & Commun .... Mr. Bryce T. HOFFMAN
27 Dir for Public Rel & Publications .... Ms. Michelle M. OUELLETTE
29 Director of Alumni Relations .... Ms. Joanne E. NELSON
88 Asst VP for Institutional Advanc .... Mr. David P. GREGOIRE
30 Director of Development .... Ms. Faith LONG
44 Director of Annual Giving .... Mr. Paul D. LEDUC
37 Director of Financial Aid .... Mr. Todd A. MORAVEC
18 Director of Facilities .... Mr. Kevin W. ROBERTS
23 Dir Ctr for Stdnt Hlth & Psych Svcs .... Dr. Kathleen M. CAMELO
19 Chief University Police .... Ms. Arlene SABO
41 Director of Athletics .... Mr. Bruce W. DELVENTHAL
22 Director of Affirmative Action .... Dr. Lynda J. AMES
09 Director of Institutional Research .... Mr. Robert M. KARP
36 Director of Career Development Ctr .... Ms. Tracey CROSS BAKER
22 Budget Officer .... Mr. Clark M. FOSTER
11 Controller .... Ms. Diane A. WYAND
96 Director of Purchasing .... Mr. Joseph P. TESORIERE
88 Exec Dr/College Aux Services .... Mr. Wayne A. DUPREY
40 Director of College Store .... Mr. Jerry L. DECELLE
46 Dir Sponsored Research/Programs .... Mr. Michael E. SIMPSON
91 Programming Manager .... Mr. Thomas J. HIGGINS

*State University of New York College at Potsdam (C)

44 Pierrepont Avenue, Potsdam NY 13676-2294
County: Saint Lawrence FICE Identification: 002850
Unit ID: 196200
Telephone: (315) 267-2000 Carnegie Class: Master's L
FAX Number: (315) 267-2496 Calendar System: Semester
URL: www.potsdam.edu
Established: 1816 Annual Undergrad Tuition & Fees (In-State): $7,214
Enrollment: 4,224 Coed
Affiliation or Control: State IRS Status: 501(c)3
Highest Offering: Master's
Program: Liberal Arts And General; Teacher Preparatory; Professional; Fine Arts Emphasis
Accreditation: M, IACBE, MUS, TED, THEA

02 Interim President .... Dr. Dennis L. HEFNER
05 Provost .... Dr. Margaret E. MADDEN
10 Vice President for Business Affairs .... Ms. Natalie L. HIGLEY
32 Vice President for Student Affairs .... Vacant
30 Vice President College Advancement .... Ms. Vicki L. TEMPLETON-CORNELL
09 VP Inst Effect/Enrollment Mgmt .... Vacant
84 Assoc VP Enroll Mgmt/Inst Effect .... Dr. Bruce BRYDGES
04 Assistant to the President .... Ms. Carol M. ROURKE
90 Associate VP for Academic Affairs .... Dr. Gerald L. RATLIFF
20 Assistant Provost .... Dr. Jill R. PEARON
18 Asst Vice Pres for Facilities .... Mr. Anthony DITULLIO
88 Director of Special Programs .... Mr. Shailindar SINGH
90 Asst Vice Pres for Information Tech .... Mr. Andy A. HARRADINE
53 Dean Education & Prof Studies .... Dr. Peter S. BROUWER
49 Dean of Arts and Sciences .... Dr. Steven J. MARQUSEE
64 Dean of Music .... Dr. Michael R. SITTON
35 Dean of Students .... Mr. William G. MORRIS
51 Director of Extended Education .... Dr. Thomas W. FUHR
15 Asst VP for Human Resources .... Ms. Mary K. DOLAN
08 Director of Libraries .... Ms. Jenica P. ROGERS
06 Registrar .... Dr. Ramona M. RALSTON
07 Director of Admissions .... Mr. Thomas W. NESBITT
37 Director of Financial Aid .... Mrs. Susan C. MERCHANT
36 Director of Career Planning .... Ms. Karen L. HAM
38 Director of Counseling Center .... Mrs. Gena C. NELSON
19 Chief of University Police .... Mr. John A. KAPLAN
29 Director of Alumni Relations .... Ms. Mona O. VROMAN
31 Executive Dir of Auxiliary Corp .... Mr. Daniel J. HAYES
23 Director of Health Services .... Dr. Richard E. MOOSE
39 Director of Residence Life .... Mr. Eric D. DUCHSCHERER
40 Director of College Bookstore .... Mr. Lyndon J. LAKE
41 Athletic Director .... Mr. James A. ZALACCA
25 Director Research & Sponsored Pgms .... Dr. Nancy M. DODGE-REYOME
21 Assistant VP Business Affairs .... Vacant
28 Director of Diversity Center .... Ms. Sheila M. MARSHALL
92 Director of Honors Program .... Dr. Thomas N. BAKER
94 Director of Women's Studies .... Dr. Jacqueline K. GOODMAN
26 Asst VP Marketing/Communications .... Ms. Deborah L. DUDLEY
86 Community and Gov Rel Associate .... Mrs. Alexandra M. JACOBS-WILKE

*Purchase College, State University of New York (D)

735 Anderson Hill Road, Purchase NY 10577-1402
County: Westchester FICE Identification: 006791
Unit ID: 196219
Telephone: (914) 251-6000 Carnegie Class: Bac/A&S
FAX Number: (914) 251-6014 Calendar System: Semester
URL: www.purchase.edu
Established: 1967 Annual Undergrad Tuition & Fees (In-State): $7,230
Enrollment: 4,300 Coed
Affiliation or Control: State IRS Status: 501(c)3
Highest Offering: Master's
Program: Liberal Arts And General; Professional; Fine Arts Emphasis
Accreditation: M, ART

02 President .... Mr. Thomas J. SCHWARZ
19 Chief of University Police .... Mr. Michael BAILEY
10 CFO/VP Operations .... Ms. Judy NOLAN
05 Provost/VP Academic Affairs .... Dr. Barry PEARSON
32 Vice President Student Affairs .... Mr. Ernie PALMIERI
84 VP Enroll Mgmt/Integrated Mktg .... Mr. Dennis CRAIG
30 Vice Pres of Institutional Advance .... Ms. Jeannine STARR
57 Director Conservatory Theatre Arts .... Dr. Gregory TAYLOR
51 Exec Dir Liberal Stds/Cont Educ .... Ms. Danielle D'AGOSTO
81 Dean Sch Natural/Social Sciences .... Dr. Suzanne KESSLER
79 Chair School of Humanities .... Dr. Ross DALY
20 Associate Provost .... Dr. William BASKIN
88 Director Performing Arts Center .... Mr. Harry MCFADDEN
88 Interim Dir Neuberger Museum of Art .... Ms. Paola MORSIANI
08 Director of the Library .... Mr. Patrick F. CALLAHAN
64 Director Conservatory of Music .... Dr. Suzanne FARRIN
57 Dean School of Arts .... Mr. Ravi RAJAN
13 Director Campus Technology Services .... Mr. Bill JUNOR
37 Director Student Financial Services .... Ms. Corey YORK
38 Director of Counseling Center .... Dr. Cathie CHESTER
36 Director Career Development .... Ms. Wendy MOROSOFF
15 Director of Human Resources .... Ms. Kathleen FARRELL
41 Athletic Director .... Mr. Chris BISIGNANO
39 Interim Director Residence Life .... Mr. Denny SANTOS
96 Director of Purchasing .... Mr. Nikolaus LENTNER
06 Exec Dir Enroll Svcs/Assoc Dean Ac .... Ms. Patricia BICE
09 Director of Institutional Research .... Ms. Barbara MOORE
18 Dir Capital Facilities Planning .... Mr. Christopher GAVLICK
22 Acting Affirmative Action Officer .... Mr. Ricardo ESPINALES
88 Environmental Health/Safety Officer .... Mr. Edward MUSAL
44 Director Annual Giving .... Ms. Carla WEILAND-ZALEZNAK
27 Dir Commun & Creative Svcs .... Ms. Sandy DYLAK

*State University of New York College of Agriculture and Technology at Cobleskill (E)

Route 7, Knapp Hall, Cobleskill NY 12043
County: Schoharie FICE Identification: 002856
Unit ID: 196033
Telephone: (518) 255-5011 Carnegie Class: Bac/Assoc
FAX Number: (518) 255-5333 Calendar System: Semester
URL: www.cobleskill.edu
Established: 1911 Annual Undergrad Tuition & Fees (In-State): $7,149
Enrollment: 2,512 Coed
Affiliation or Control: State IRS Status: 501(c)3
Highest Offering: Baccalaureate
Program: Occupational; 2-Year Principally Bachelor's Creditable; Liberal Arts And General; Technical Emphasis
Accreditation: M, ACFEI, EMT, HT

02 President .... Dr. Debra THATCHER
05 Provost & Vice Pres Academic Affs .... Dr. Susan ZIMMERMANN
04 Assistant to President .... Ms. Amy HEALY
32 VP for Student Develop/Student Life .... Mr. Steven M. ACKERKNECHT
10 Vice Pres Business & Finance .... Ms. Carol BISHOP
11 Vice Pres Operations .... Ms. Bonnie MARTIN
30 VP for Institutional Advancement .... Ms. Regina LAGATTA
35 Asst VP for Student Affairs .... Mr. Edward ASSELIN
30 Asst VP Institutional Advancement .... Mrs. Lois E. GOBLET
47 Dean Agriculture/Natural Res .... Mr. Timothy MOORE
49 Dean Liberal Arts & Sciences .... Dr. Jeffrey ANDERSON
08 Dean Library/Information Svcs .... Ms. Elizabeth ORGERON
27 Director of Communications .... Dr. Diane DOBRY
06 Registrar .... Ms. Christine JOHANNESEN
21 Chief Business Officer .... Ms. Carol VOSATKA
26 VP for College Relations .... Mr. Joel SMITH
29 Director Alumni Relations .... Mrs. Lois GOBLET
07 Director of Admissions .... Mr. Robert BLANCHET
39 Director of Residential Life .... Mr. Edward E. ASSELIN
36 Director of Student Success Ctr .... Ms. Donna PESTA
23 Co-Director Wellness Center .... Ms. Mary RADLIFF
23 Co-Director Wellness Center .... Ms. Lynn ONTL
37 Director of Financial Aid .... Ms. Louise BIRON
35 Director Student Life Center .... Mr. Jeffrey C. FOOTE
41 Director of Athletics .... Mr. Kevin MCCARTHY
13 Director Information Tech Services .... Mr. James DUTCHER
19 Chief University Police Dept .... Mr. Frank LAWRENCE
09 Director of Institutional Research .... Dr. Victor J. SENSENIG
15 Director Human Resources .... Ms. Jan ELWELL
18 Director Facilities/Physical Plant .... Mr. Philip M. ARNOLD
40 Manager Bookstore .... Ms. Jeri USATCH
85 Director of International Programs .... Ms. Susan JAGENDORF
96 Director of Purchasing .... Ms. Laura GROSS

25 Dir of Grants and Sponsored Program ... Mr. Barry GELL
88 Director of EOP ... Mr. Derwin BENNETT
88 Dir of Student Accounts ... Ms. Margaret GRIPPIN
84 AVP for Enrollment Management ... Dr. Tara WINTER

*State University of New York College of Agriculture and Technology at Morrisville (A)

PO Box 901, Morrisville NY 13408-0901

County: Madison FICE Identification: 002859
Unit ID: 196051
Telephone: (315) 684-6000 Carnegie Class: Bac/Assoc
FAX Number: (315) 684-6116 Calendar System: Semester
URL: www.morrisville.edu
Established: 1908 Annual Undergrad Tuition & Fees (In-State): $7,137
Enrollment: 3,095 Coed
Affiliation or Control: State IRS Status: 501(c)3
Highest Offering: Baccalaureate
Program: Occupational; 2-Year Principally Bachelor's Creditable; Technical Emphasis
Accreditation: M, ACBSP, ADNUR, DIETT, ENGT

02 Interim President ... Dr. William J. MURABITO
05 Provost ... Dr. David E. ROGERS
11 Vice Pres for Administration ... Vacant
32 Dean of Students ... Mr. Geoffrey S. ISABELLE
47 Dean School Agriculture & Business . Dr. Christopher L. NYBERG
83 Dean School Sci/Tech & Health ... Ms. Christine A. CRING
49 Dean School of Liberal Arts ... Dr. Paul F. GRIFFIN
97 Dean School of General Studies ... Ms. Jeannette H. EVANS
30 Exec Dir Inst Advancement ... Ms. Sara A. WAY
26 Dir Public Relations/Govt Affairs ... Ms. Amy L. CORNUE
07 Director of Admissions ... Ms. Leslie V. CROSLEY
37 Director of Financial Aid ... Ms. Dacia L. BANKS
08 Director of Library ... Ms. Christine A. RUDECOFF
38 Director Student Health Center ... Ms. Nancy S. ZLOMEK
15 Dir Human Svcs/Affirmative Action ... Vacant
29 Coordinator of Alumni Relations ... Ms. Kelly E. GARDNER
96 Purchasing Assistant ... Ms. Karen H. PITTS

*State University of New York College of Environmental Science and Forestry (B)

1 Forestry Drive, Syracuse NY 13210-2778

County: Onondaga FICE Identification: 002851
Unit ID: 196103
Telephone: (315) 470-6500 Carnegie Class: DRU
FAX Number: (315) 470-6779 Calendar System: Semester
URL: www.esf.edu
Established: 1911 Annual Undergrad Tuition & Fees (In-State): $6,995
Enrollment: 2,401 Coed
Affiliation or Control: State IRS Status: 501(c)3
Highest Offering: Doctorate
Program: Liberal Arts And General; Professional
Accreditation: M, ENG, ENGT, FOR, LSAR

02 President ... Dr. Cornelius B. MURPHY, JR.
05 Vice Pres Academic Affairs/Provost ... Dr. Bruce C. BONGARTEN
11 Vice President for Administration ... Mr. Joseph RUFO
84 Vice Pres Enrollment Mgmt/Marketing ... Dr. Robert C. FRENCH
46 Vice Provost for Research ... Dr. Neil H. RINGLER
20 Assoc Prov for Instruction ... Mr. Scott S. SHANNON
32 Dean Student Life/Experiential Lrng ... Dr. Anne E. LOMBARD
10 Director of Business Affairs ... Mr. David R. DZWONKOWSKI
13 Director of Information Technology ... Mr. Yuming TUNG
15 Director Human Resources ... Ms. Marcia A. BARBER
27 Director of Communications ... Mrs. Claire B. DUNN
30 Director of Development ... Ms. Brenda T. GREENFIELD
19 Chief of University Police ... Mr. Scott M. BECKSTED
08 Director of College Libraries ... Mr. Stephen WEITER
07 Director of Admissions ... Mrs. Susan H. SANFORD
06 Registrar ... Ms. Mary CHANDLER
37 Director of Financial Aid ... Mr. John E. VIEW
29 Director of Alumni Affairs ... Ms. Debbie J. CAVINESS
09 Director of Institutional Planning ... Dr. Maureen O. FELLOWS
28 Director of Multicultural Affairs ... Dr. Raydora S. DRUMMER FRANCIS
18 Chief Facilities/Physical Plant ... Mr. Gary S. PEDEN
21 Associate Business Officer ... Ms. Danette J. DESIMONE
36 Career Planning & Devel Officer ... Mr. John TURBEVILLE
86 Director Government Relations ... Dr. Maureen O. FELLOWS
35 Director Student Activities ... Mrs. Laura CRANDALL
51 Assoc Provost for Outreach ... Dr. Charles M. SPUCHES
04 Admin Asst to the President ... Ms. Ragan A. SQUIER

*State University of New York College of Optometry (C)

33 W 42nd Street, New York NY 10036-8003

County: New York FICE Identification: 009929
Unit ID: 196228
Telephone: (212) 938-4000 Carnegie Class: Spec/Health
FAX Number: (212) 938-5696 Calendar System: Semester
URL: www.sunyopt.edu
Established: 1971 Annual Graduate Tuition & Fees: $23,569
Enrollment: 333 Coed
Affiliation or Control: State IRS Status: 501(c)3
Highest Offering: Doctorate; No Undergraduates
Program: Professional
Accreditation: M, OPT, OPTR

02 President ... Dr. David A. HEATH
05 VP Academic Affs/Academic Dean ... Dr. David TROILO
11 VP For Administration and Finance ... Mr. David A. BOWERS
32 Vice President Student Affairs ... Dr. Jeffrey L. PHILPOTT
17 Vice Pres for Clinical Affairs ... Dr. Richard SODEN
30 Vice President Advance/Public Rels ... Ms. Ann WARWICK
04 Assistant to the President ... Ms. Karen DEGAZON
09 Director Policy/Planning/Evaluation ... Dr. Steven SCHWARTZ
08 Librarian ... Ms. Elaine WELLS
16 Director of Personnel Services ... Mr. Douglas SCHADING
37 Financial Aid Officer ... Mr. Vito CAVALLARO
06 Registrar ... Mrs. Jacqueline ESTEVEZ MARTINEZ
20 Dir Inst Vision Research/Assoc Dean ... Dr. Stewart BLOOMFIELD
27 Dir of Communications ... Mr. Greg HOULE

*Alfred State College (D)

10 Upper College Drive, Alfred NY 14802-1196

County: Allegany FICE Identification: 002854
Unit ID: 196006
Telephone: (607) 587-4010 Carnegie Class: Bac/Assoc
FAX Number: N/A Calendar System: Semester
URL: www.alfredstate.edu
Established: 1908 Annual Undergrad Tuition & Fees (In-State): $7,184
Enrollment: 3,528 Coed
Affiliation or Control: State IRS Status: 501(c)3
Highest Offering: Baccalaureate
Program: 2-Year Principally Bachelor's Creditable; Nursing Emphasis
Accreditation: M, ADNUR, CAHIIM, CONST, ENGT, NURSE

02 Interim President ... Ms. Valerie NIXON
05 Int Vice Pres Academic Affairs ... Mr. Craig R. CLARK
07 Interim Director Admissions ... Ms. Kandi GEIBEL
32 Vice President Student Affairs ... Mr. Gregory S. SAMMONS
11 Int VP Administration & Enrollment ... Ms. Deborah GOODRICH
30 Vice Pres Institutional Advancement ... Dr. Derek M. WESLEY
20 Assoc Vice Pres Academic Affairs ... Mr. Charles V. NEAL
09 Dean of Research Services ... Mrs. Nancy B. SHEARER
13 Director Computer Services ... Mr. Michael A. CASE
15 Director Human Res/Affirm Action ... Ms. Wendy DRESSER-RECKTENWALD
37 Sr Dir Student Financial Services ... Mrs. Jane A. GILLILAND
29 Director Alumni Relations ... Ms. Colleen ARGENTIERI
18 Director of Physical Plant ... Mr. Glenn R. BRUBAKER
14 Asst Director of Computing Services ... Mr. Carl H. RAHR, JR.
23 Sr Director Health Svcs/Wellness ... Ms. Hollie M. HALL
38 Director Learning Center ... Ms. Janette B. THOMAS
19 Chief University Police ... Mr. Gregory S. SAMMONS
96 Director of Purchasing ... Mr. Glen E. CLINE
10 Controller ... Mr. Joseph T. GREENTHAL
26 Sr Dir Marketing/Communications ... Ms. Debra ROOT
36 Director of Career Services ... Ms. Elaine MORSMAN
88 Chief Sustainability Officer ... Mr. Julian DAUTREMONT-SMITH
49 Dean School of Arts & Sciences ... Dr. Terry W. TUCKER
54 Dean School of Mgmt & Engr Tech ... Dr. John WILLIAMS
75 Int Dean Sch Applied Technology .. Mr. George H. RICHARDSON

*SUNY Adirondack (E)

640 Bay Road, Queensbury NY 12804-1498

County: Warren FICE Identification: 002860
Unit ID: 188438
Telephone: (518) 743-2200 Carnegie Class: Assoc/Pub-R-M
FAX Number: (518) 745-1433 Calendar System: Semester
URL: www.sunyacc.edu
Established: 1960 Annual Undergrad Tuition & Fees (In-District): $3,774
Enrollment: 3,987 Coed
Affiliation or Control: State/Local IRS Status: 501(c)3
Highest Offering: Associate Degree
Program: Occupational; 2-Year Principally Bachelor's Creditable
Accreditation: M, ADNUR

02 President ... Dr. Kristine DUFFY
04 Assistant to the President ... Ms. Dari L. NORMAN
05 Vice Pres Academic/Student Affairs ... Mr. Brian DURANT
11 Vice Pres Admin Services/Treasurer ... Mr. William LONG, III
30 Exec Dir Dev/Alumni Rels/ACC Fndtn ... Ms. Rachael HUNSINGER PATTEN
20 Dean for Academic Affairs ... Dr. Martin MCCLINTON
51 Dean of Cont & External Stds ... Ms. Denise BRUCKER
20 Dean for Special Academic Svcs ... Ms. Diane DALTO
32 Dean for Student Affairs ... Mr. Jason ENSER
26 Director Marketing & Cmty Rels ... Mr. Mark PARFITT
09 Director of Inst Research/Planning ... Mr. David SMITH
27 Chief Information Officer ... Ms. Susan A. TRUMPICK
15 Director of Human Resources ... Ms. Marjorie KELLY
40 Director Bookstore ... Mr. Tom KENT
10 Chief Financial Officer ... Mr. Dan SILVEY
21 Director of Business Affairs ... Ms. Lisa DESTER
18 Director Facilities ... Mr. Anthony PALANGI
37 Director Student Financial Aid ... Ms. Maureen REILLY
06 Director of Records ... Vacant
84 Director of Enrollment Management ... Ms. Sarah J. LINEHAN
90 Director Academic Computer Services ... Ms. Roseann ANZALONE
08 Director of Library Services ... Ms. Teresa RONNING
35 Director of Student Activities ... Ms. Heather CHARPENTIER
41 Athletic Director ... Mr. John QUATTROCCHI

*SUNY Canton-College of Technology (F)

34 Cornell Drive, Canton NY 13617-1098

County: Saint Lawrence FICE Identification: 002855
Unit ID: 196015
Telephone: (315) 386-7011 Carnegie Class: Bac/Assoc
FAX Number: (315) 386-7930 Calendar System: Semester
URL: www.canton.edu
Established: 1906 Annual Undergrad Tuition & Fees (In-State): $7,171
Enrollment: 3,769 Coed
Affiliation or Control: State IRS Status: 501(c)3
Highest Offering: Baccalaureate
Program: Occupational; 2-Year Principally Bachelor's Creditable; Technical Emphasis
Accreditation: M, ADNUR, DH, ENGT, FUSER, PTAA

02 Acting President ... Dr. Joseph C. HOFFMAN
05 Interim Provost ... Ms. Karen M. SPELLACY
11 Vice Pres Business Affairs/Admin ... Ms. Natalie HIGLEY
10 Chief Business Officer ... Ms. Natalie HIGLEY
30 Vice President for Advancement ... Mr. David M. GERLACH
32 Vice Pres of Student Affairs ... Vacant
35 Dean of Students ... Ms. Courtney D. BISH
72 Int Dean Canino Sch Eng Tech ... Mr. Michael J. NEWTOWN
76 Dean Sch Sci/Health/Crim Justice ... Dr. Kenneth M. ERICKSON
50 Dean Sch Business/Liberal Arts ... Mr. Jondavid S. DELONG
88 Dean Acad Support Svcs/Instr Tech ... Dr. Molly A. MOTT
41 Director of Athletics ... Mr. Randy B. SIEMINSKI
100 Chief of Staff ... Ms. Lenore VANDERZEE
101 Acting Sec to the College Council ... Ms. Michaela J. YOUNG
04 Assistant to President ... Ms. Michaela J. YOUNG
35 Director Student Activities ... Ms. Priscilla LEGGETTE
28 Director of Diversity ... Ms. Lashawanda T. INGRAM
96 Director of Purchasing ... Ms. Bethany A. MARTIN
37 Director of Financial Aid ... Ms. Kerrie L. COOPER
88 College Accountant ... Mr. John N. MAISONNEUVE
15 Director of Human Resources ... Ms. Mary K. DOLAN
36 Director of Career Services ... Mr. David F. NORENBERG
06 Registrar ... Ms. Memorie L. SHAMPINE
08 Director of Library Services ... Ms. Michelle L. CURRIER
18 Asst Facilities Planning Coord ... Mr. Patrick G. HANSS
18 Plant Superintendent ... Mr. Martin D. AVERY
19 Chief of University Police ... Mr. John KAPLAN
23 Director of Health Services ... Ms. Patricia A. TODD
26 Int Dir Public Rels/Web Coord ... Mr. Travis SMITH
40 Manager Campus Store ... Mr. Corey JORDAN
39 Director of Residence Life ... Mr. John M. KENNEDY
09 Dir of Inst Research/Assessment ... Ms. Sarah E. TODD
13 Chief Information Officer ... Mr. Kyle BROWN
22 Director of Affirmative Action ... Ms. Elizabeth A. CONNOLLY
29 Director of Alumni Affairs ... Ms. Peggy S. LEVATO
38 Director of Counseling ... Ms. Melinda A. MILLER
07 Int Director Admissions ... Mr. Michael J. PERRY
18 Dir Facilities/Capital Improvement ... Mr. Michael R. MCCORMICK
44 Director of Development ... Ms. Peggy S. LEVATO
88 User Support Services Manager ... Ms. Theresa C. CORBINE
104 Director International Programs ... Ms. Marela FIACCO
105 Publications/Coordinator ... Mr. Matthew J. MULKIN
25 Grants Coordinator ... Ms. JoAnne M. FASSINGER

*State University of New York College of Technology at Delhi (G)

454 Delhi Drive, Delhi NY 13753-4454

County: Delaware FICE Identification: 002857
Unit ID: 196024
Telephone: (607) 746-4000 Carnegie Class: Bac/Assoc
FAX Number: (607) 746-4208 Calendar System: Semester
URL: www.delhi.edu
Established: 1913 Annual Undergrad Tuition & Fees (In-State): $7,410
Enrollment: 3,480 Coed
Affiliation or Control: State IRS Status: 501(c)3
Highest Offering: Baccalaureate
Program: Occupational; 2-Year Principally Bachelor's Creditable; Liberal Arts And General
Accreditation: M, ACFEI, ADNUR, CONST, NUR

02 President ... Dr. Candace S. VANCKO
05 Provost ... Dr. John S. NADER
32 Vice President for Student Life ... Ms. Barbara E. JONES
10 Vice Pres for Business & Finance ... Ms. Carol M. BISHOP
26 Vice Pres for College Relations ... Mr. Joel M. SMITH
30 Vice Pres for College Advancement ... Ms. Regina M. LAGATTA
11 Vice Pres for Operations ... Ms. Bonnie G. MARTIN
84 Assistant VP Enrollment Management ... Dr. Tara L. WINTER
36 Coordinator Career & Transfer Svcs ... Ms. Kristin A. DEFOREST
07 Director of Admissions ... Mr. Robert C. PIUROWSKI
27 Chief Information Officer ... Mr. Jonathan R. BRENNAN
19 Chief of University Police ... Mr. Perri D. DEFREECE
39 Director of Residence Life ... Mr. John J. PADOVANI
88 Dir Inter-Institutional Programs ... Mr. Robert W. MAZZEI
08 Director of the Resnick Library ... Ms. Pamela J. PETERS
36 Dir Career & Business Development ... Ms. Glenda V. ROBERTS
88 Director of Resnick Learning Center ... Ms. Michele T. DEFREECE
18 Director of Physical Plant ... Mr. David A. LOVELAND
41 Director of Athletics ... Mr. Robert H. BACKUS
06 Registrar/Dir of Inst Research ... Ms. Nancy L. SMITH
37 Director of Financial Aid ... Ms. Nancy B. HUGHES
38 Director Counseling & Health Svcs ... Ms. Lori B. OSTERHOUDT
29 Alumni/Annual Giving Coordinator ... Ms. Lucinda C. BRYDON

21 Controller .... Ms. Amy L. BROWN
88 Communications & New Media Manager .... Ms. Kimberly M. MACLEOD

*State University of New York Empire State College (A)

2 Union Avenue, Saratoga Springs NY 12866-4390
County: Saratoga FICE Identification: 010286
Unit ID: 196264
Telephone: (518) 587-2100 Carnegie Class: Master's M
FAX Number: (518) 587-2886 Calendar System: Other
URL: www.esc.edu
Established: 1971 Annual Undergrad Tuition & Fees (In-State): $5,870
Enrollment: 12,028 Coed
Affiliation or Control: State IRS Status: 501(c)3
Highest Offering: Master's
Program: Liberal Arts And General; Professional
Accreditation: M, IACBE, NURSE, TEAC

02 President .... Dr. Merodie HANCOCK
100 Chief of Staff .... Ms. Patrice DECOSTER
05 Acting Provost/Vice Pres AA .... Dr. Deborah AMORY
10 Vice President for Administration .... Mr. Paul TUCCI
86 VP for Communications & Govt Rels .... Ms. Mary Caroline VAN DER VEER
32 Int VP Enroll Mgmt & Stdnt Svcs .... Dr. Mitchell S. NESLER
30 VP for External Affairs .... Dr. Hugh B. HAMMETT
13 VP for Integrated Technologies .... Vacant
09 VP for Plng & Inst Effectiveness .... Dr. Mitchell S. NESLER
20 Vice Prov for Academic Development .... Dr. Marjorie W. LAVIN
106 Int Vice Prov Global/Online Lrng .... Dr. Robert CLOUGHERTY
88 Vice Prov for Reg Ctrs & Ntd Lrng .... Vacant
12 Dean Central New York Center .... Dr. Nikki SHRIMPTON
12 Dean Genesee Valley Center .... Dr. Jonathan R. FRANZ
88 Dean HVA Center for Labor Studies .... Dr. Michael MERRILL
12 Dean Hudson Valley Center .... Dr. Gary LACY
12 Dean Long Island Center .... Dr. Michael SPITZER
12 Dean Metropolitan Center .... Dr. Cynthia L. WARD
12 Dean Niagara Frontier Center .... Dr. Nan M. DIBELLO
12 Dean Northeast Center .... Dr. Gerald F. LORENTZ
106 Dean Center for Distance Lng .... Dr. Thomas MACKEY
58 Actg Dean Ctr for Graduate Programs .... Dr. Tai ARNOLD
20 Asst Vice Pres for Academic Pgms .... Vacant
21 Asst Vice Pres for Administration .... Mr. Frederick BARTHELMAS
30 Asst Vice Pres for Development .... Vacant
84 Asst VP Enrollment Mgt/Student Svcs .... Ms. Anna MIARKA-GRZELAK
14 Dir Enterprise Sys/Infrastructure .... Mr. AJ LACOMBA
72 Director Academic Technology .... Ms. Suzanne HAYES
91 Director Admin Applications .... Mr. Mark CLAVERIE
88 Director Advancement Services .... Ms. Vicki SCHAAKE
29 Dir Alumni and Student Relations .... Ms. Maureen WINNEY
44 Director Annual Giving .... Ms. Diane THOMPSON
21 Director Business Affairs .... Ms. Becky PALMIERI
88 Director of Real Estate .... Mr. Jeffrey ELLENBOGEN
88 Dir Center for Mentoring & Learning .... Dr. Katherine JELLY
20 Dir Col Acad Sppt/H V Arsdale Labor .... Ms. Sophia MAVROGIANNIS
20 Dir Col Acad Sppt/Long Island Ctr .... Ms. Mildred VAN BERGEN
20 Dir Collegewide Academic Review .... Dr. Nan TRAVERS
35 Dir Collegewide Student Services .... Ms. Patricia MYERS
27 Director of Communications .... Mr. David HENAHAN
88 Dir Cmty College Partnerships .... Mr. Brian GOODALE
88 Dir Corp & Community Partnerships .... Ms. Lisa SAX
88 Dir Environmental Sustainability .... Ms. Sadie ROSS
18 Director Facilities and Maintenance .... Mr. Rick REIMANN
37 Director Financial Aid .... Ms. Kristina DELBRIDGE
44 Director Gift Planning .... Vacant
30 Director of Development .... Mr. Toby TOBROCKE
86 Director Government Relations .... Vacant
25 Director Grants & Contracts .... Ms. Lorraine ANTHONY
16 Asst VP for Human Resources .... Ms. Mary Ellen R. KEENEY
88 Director Marketing .... Ms. Renelle SHAMPENY
88 Director Outcomes Asessment .... Vacant
88 Director Project Management .... Mr. Walter LEWIS
96 Director Procurement .... Mr. Charley SUMMERSELL
88 Director Publications .... Mr. Kirk STARCZEWSKI
19 Director Campus Safety & Security .... Mr. Thomas VUMBACO
21 Director Student Accounts .... Ms. Pamela MALONE
88 Dir Veteran & Military Education .... Ms. Linda FRANK
26 Senior Director of Marketing .... Dr. John MCKENNA
22 Affirmative Action Officer .... Ms. Mary MORTON
06 Registrar .... Ms. Mary EDINBURGH
07 Asst Director Admissions .... Ms. Tina MASSA

*Farmingdale State College (B)

2350 Broadhollow Road, Farmingdale NY 11735-1021
County: Suffolk FICE Identification: 002858
Unit ID: 196042
Telephone: (631) 420-2000 Carnegie Class: Bac/Diverse
FAX Number: N/A Calendar System: Semester
URL: www.farmingdale.edu
Established: 1912 Annual Undergrad Tuition & Fees (In-State): $6,487
Enrollment: 7,889 Coed
Affiliation or Control: State IRS Status: 501(c)3
Highest Offering: Baccalaureate
Program: Liberal Arts And General; Professional
Accreditation: M, DH, ENGT, MLTAD, NAIT, NUR, PNUR

02 President .... Dr. Hubert KEEN
05 Provost/Vice Pres for Academic Affs .... Dr. Lucia CEPRIANO
10 Senior Vice President & CFO .... Mr. George P. LAROSA
32 Vice Pres Student Affairs .... Dr. Tom CORTI
84 VP Inst Advancement/Enrollment Mgmt .... Mr. Patrick CALABRIA
30 Chief Development Officer .... Dr. Henry SIKORSKI
20 Assistant VP Academic Affairs .... Dr. Marie HAYDEN-MILES
11 Asst Vice President Admin Services .... Vacant
35 Dean of Students .... Ms. Theresa ESNES-JOHNSON
07 Director of Admissions .... Mr. Jim HALL
19 Chief University Police .... Mr. Marvin FISCHER
18 Director of Physical Plant .... Mr. John S. DZINANKA
27 Director of Communications .... Ms. Kathryn S. COLEY
06 Registrar .... Ms. Cindy MCCUE
08 Head Librarian .... Mr. Michael KNAUTH
15 Director Human Resources .... Ms. Marybeth INCANDELA
36 Director Career Development .... Ms. Dolores CIACCIO
37 Director Financial Aid .... Ms. Diane KAZANECKI-KEMPTER
09 Institutional Research Associate .... Ms. Patricia LIND-GONZALEZ
23 Director Student Health Services .... Ms. Audrey KRAPF
41 Director Athletics .... Mr. Michael HARRINGTON
39 Director of Residence Life .... Ms. Andela JASUR
102 President Farmingdale Foundation .... Mr. Richard OVERTON
24 Director Media Resources .... Mr. Martin BRANDT
29 Acting Director Alumni Affairs .... Ms. Regina VAZQUEZ
28 Director of Diversity .... Ms. Veronica HENRY
38 Director Student Success Center .... Ms. Marguerite FAGELLA-D'ALOSIO
40 Manager Bookstore .... Ms. Roberta MIRRO
21 Controller .... Mr. Richard HUME
96 Purchasing Assistant .... Ms. Lisa BRUNS
75 Director LI Educ Oppty Center .... Mr. Brian MAHER
50 Dean School of Business .... Dr. Richard VOGEL
76 Acting Dean School Health Sciences .... Dr. Mary STEDMAN
49 Dean Sch of Arts & Sciences .... Dr. Lou REINISCH
54 Dean Sch Engineer Technology .... Dr. Kamal SHAHRABI

*State University of New York Institute of Technology at Utica-Rome (C)

100 Seymour Road, Utica NY 13502
County: Oneida FICE Identification: 011678
Unit ID: 196112
Telephone: (315) 792-7100 Carnegie Class: Master's M
FAX Number: (315) 792-7222 Calendar System: Semester
URL: www.sunyit.edu
Established: 1966 Annual Undergrad Tuition & Fees (In-State): $7,090
Enrollment: 2,373 Coed
Affiliation or Control: State IRS Status: 501(c)3
Highest Offering: Master's
Program: Liberal Arts And General; Professional; Technical Emphasis
Accreditation: M, BUS, CAHIIM, ENGT, NURSE

02 Acting President .... Dr. Robert E. GEER
04 Exec Assistant to the President .... Ms. Laurie HARTMAN
05 Provost/Vice Pres Academic Affairs .... Dr. William DURGIN
11 Vice President Administration .... Mr. James LLOYD
15 Assistant VP for Human Resources .... Ms. Wendy CRANMER
84 Assoc Provost for Student Affairs .... Ms. Marybeth LYONS
79 Chair Communications/Humanities .... Dr. Mary PERRONE
83 Chair Social & Behavioral Sci .... Dr. Paul SCHULMAN
77 Chair Computer Info Sciences .... Dr. John MARSH
54 Chair Engineering Technologies .... Dr. Daniel JONES
81 Chair Engineering Science & Math .... Dr. Andrew WOLFE
66 Chair Nursing & Health Profess .... Dr. Louise DEAN-KELLY
07 Director Admissions .... Ms. Jennifer PHELAN-NINH
41 Director Athletics .... Mr. Kevin M. GRIMMER
21 Interim Director Business Affairs .... Ms. Susan HEAD
35 Director Campus Life .... Mr. John BORNER
36 Director Career Services .... Mr. Sim COVINGTON
38 Dir Counseling & Special Pgms .... Mr. David GARRETT
30 Assistant VP Foundation .... Mr. Peter PERKINS
18 Director Facilities .... Mr. Carson SORRELL
23 Director Health & Wellness Center .... Ms. Jo RUFFRAGE
09 Assistant VP Institutional Research .... Ms. Valerie FUSCO
26 Associate VP and Chief of Staff .... Mr. John SWANN
19 Chief University Police .... Mr. Gary BEAN
39 Director of College Housing .... Mrs. Jennifer ADAMS
46 Assoc Prov Spons Rsrch/Cont Prof Ed .. Ms. Deborah TYKSINSKI
37 Director Student Financial Aid .... Ms. Melissa ROSE
06 Registrar .... Mr. John LASHER
58 Coordinator Graduate Center .... Ms. Maryrose RAAB
29 Alumni & Advancement Services .... Mr. Nick GRIMMER
96 Purchasing .... Mr. Charlie SCHIRALLI

*State University of New York Maritime College (D)

6 Pennyfield Avenue, Throggs Neck NY 10465-4198
County: Bronx FICE Identification: 002853
Unit ID: 196291
Telephone: (718) 409-7200 Carnegie Class: Bac/Diverse
FAX Number: (718) 409-7392 Calendar System: Semester
URL: www.sunymaritime.edu
Established: 1874 Annual Undergrad Tuition & Fees (In-State): $6,782
Enrollment: 1,761 Coed
Affiliation or Control: State IRS Status: 501(c)3
Highest Offering: Master's
Program: Liberal Arts And General; Professional
Accreditation: M, ENG

02 President .... RADM. Wendi B. CARPENTER
04 Executive Assistant to President .... Ms. Desiree MARTIN
05 Provost/Vice Pres Academic Affairs .... Dr. Michael CAPPETO
10 Vice Pres Finance/Admin/COO .... Ms. Elizabeth PRAETORIUS
26 Vice President University Relations .... Ms. Aimee BERNSTEIN
32 Commandant of Cadets/Master TSES .... CAPT. Richard S. SMITH
20 Academic Dean .... Dr. Gilbert TRAUB
07 Dean of Admissions .... Ms. Yamiley SAINTVIL
32 Assoc Provost/Dean of Students .... Dr. Irene R. DELGADO
21 Director of Business Affairs .... Mr. Keith MURPHY
30 Director of Development .... Mr. John CONNOLLY
26 Exec Director of External Affairs .... Ms. Mary MUECKE
27 Director of Communications/PR .... Ms. Jane BARTNETT
15 Director Human Resources .... Ms. LuAnn AUGUSTINE-PLAISANCE
18 Exec Dir Phys Plant/Plant Superin .... Mr. William RUEGER
88 Company Security Officer/Maritime .... MajGen. Robert WOLF
19 Chief University Police .... Mr. Myron PRYJMAK
84 Exec Dir Enroll Svcs/Financial Aid .... Mr. Paul BAMONTE
41 Director of Athletics .... Ms. Heather MACCULLOCH
88 Director of the Waterfront .... Mr. Robert CRAFA
09 Dir of Institutional Rsrch/Asses .... Dr. Michael CAPPETO
88 Coord Institutional Effectiveness .... Ms. Iris VANKERCKHOVE
06 Registrar .... Ms. Sarah GRADY
08 Head of Library .... Ms. Constantia CONSTANTINOU
88 Dean of Maritime Educ/Training .... CAPT. Ernest FINK
07 Director of Graduate Admissions .... BGen. Robert WOLF
07 Assoc Dir Undergrad Admissions .... Mr. Matthew GAROFALOW
88 Director of Conference Services .... Ms. Nancy RUEGER
21 Director of Student Accounts .... Ms. Denise ALBERTELLI
36 Director Career Services .... Ms. Michele BERISH
40 Director of Ship's Store .... Ms. Florence MANDRACHIA
23 Director of Health Services .... Ms. Cortney WORRELL
13 Chief Information Officer .... Mr. Brian CORNELL
22 Affirmative Action Officer .. Ms. Lu-Ann AUGUSTINE-PLAISANCE
96 Manager of Purchasing/Contracts .... Vacant
88 Construction/Capital Programs Mgr .... Mr. William HERRMANN
85 Coord Intl Student Svcs .... Ms. Devon SWITZER

*Suffolk County Community College Central Administration (E)

533 College Road, Selden NY 11784-2899
County: Suffolk Identification: 666658
Unit ID: 366395
Telephone: (631) 451-4000 Carnegie Class: N/A
FAX Number: (631) 451-4715
URL: www.sunysuffolk.edu

01 President .... Dr. Shaun L. MCKAY
04 Exec Assistant to the President .... Dr. Christopher J. ADAMS
43 College General Counsel .... Mr. Louis S. PETRIZZO
05 Vice Pres Academic/Student Affairs .... Dr. Carla MAZZARELLI
10 VP Business/Financial Affairs .... Ms. Gail VIZZINI
30 Vice Pres Institutional Advancement .... Ms. Mary Lou ARANEO
45 VP Planning/Inst Effectiveness .... Dr. Nathaniel PUGH
20 Assoc VP Academic Affairs .... Dr. Maria DELONGORIA
32 Assoc VP of Student Affs/Dean Col .... Vacant
103 Assoc VP Workforce/Econ Development .... Mr. John LOMBARDO
16 Assistant VP Employee Resources .... Mr. Jeffrey L. TEMPERA
07 College Dean Enroll/Mgt .... Ms. Joanne E. BRAXTON
06 College Registrar .... Ms. Anna FLACK
37 Director of Financial Aid .... Vacant
88 Director of Publications .... Ms. Mary FEDER

*Suffolk County Community College Ammerman Campus (F)

533 College Road, Selden NY 11784-2899
County: Suffolk FICE Identification: 002878
Unit ID: 195951
Telephone: (631) 451-4000 Carnegie Class: Not Classified
FAX Number: (631) 451-4015 Calendar System: Semester
URL: www.sunysuffolk.edu
Established: 1959 Annual Undergrad Tuition & Fees (In-District): $4,820
Enrollment: 26,219 Coed
Affiliation or Control: State/Local IRS Status: 501(c)3
Highest Offering: Associate Degree
Program: Occupational; 2-Year Principally Bachelor's Creditable
Accreditation: M, ADNUR, PNUR, PTAA

02 Executive Dean/Campus CEO .... Dr. James SHERWOOD
32 Assoc Dean of Student Services .... Mr. Charles BARTOLOTTA

*Suffolk County Community College Eastern Campus (G)

121 Speonk-Riverhead Road, Riverhead NY 11901-3499
Telephone: (631) 548-2500 FICE Identification: 004816
Accreditation: &M, DIETT

† Main campus is Suffolk County Community College Ammerman Campus in Selden, NY.

*Suffolk County Community College Grant Campus (H)

1001 Crooked Hill Road, Brentwood NY 11717-1091
Telephone: (631) 851-6700 FICE Identification: 013204
Accreditation: &M, ADNUR, CAHIIM, OTA

† Main campus is Suffolk County Community College Ammerman Campus in Selden, NY.

Sullivan County Community College (A)

112 College Road, Loch Sheldrake NY 12759-5721
County: Sullivan FICE Identification: 002879
Unit ID: 195988
Telephone: (845) 434-5750 Carnegie Class: Assoc/Pub-R-S
FAX Number: (845) 434-4806 Calendar System: Semester
URL: www.sullivan.suny.edu
Established: 1962 Annual Undergrad Tuition & Fees (In-District): $4,474
Enrollment: 4,474 Coed
Affiliation or Control: State/Local IRS Status: 501(c)3
Highest Offering: Associate Degree
Program: Occupational; 2-Year Principally Bachelor's Creditable
Accreditation: M, ACBSP, COARC

01 President ....Dr. Karin M. HILGERSOM
05 Vice Pres Academic & Student Affs ....Dr. Robert SCHULTZ
30 Vice Pres for Advance/Enroll Mgmt ....Ms. Cindy KASHAN
20 Asst VP Academic/Student Affairs ....Ms. Iman ELGINBEHI
32 Dean Student Services ....Ms. Sara THOMPSON-TWEEDY
45 Assoc VP for Planning/HR & Facilit ....Dr. Stephen MITCHELL
39 Asst Dean Student Life & Housing ....Vacant
31 Dir Spec Events/Campus Activities ....Ms. Hillary EGELAND
10 Chief Business Officer ....Ms. Susan HORTON
18 Chief Facilities/Physical Plant ....Mr. Tracy HALL
07 Director Admissions/Registration ....Ms. Sari ROSENHECK
21 Controller ....Ms. Susan HORTON
30 Director Inst Development/Outreach ....Vacant
37 Director of Financial Aid ....Mr. James WINDERL
08 Director of Library Services ....Mr. Jon GRENNAN
35 Director Student Activities ....Ms. Adrianna MAYSON
88 Director Early Childhood ....Vacant
41 Director of Athletics ....Mr. Chris DEPEW
15 Asst Director of Human Resources ....Ms. Stephanie SMART
09 Director Institutional Research ....Ms. Janet HALPRIN
25 Grants Writer ....Vacant
38 Director Student Counseling ....Ms. Rose HANOFEE
96 Purchasing Agent ....Ms. Lorry IRWIN
13 Int Dir Campus Computer Services ....Ms. Cheryl WELSCH
06 Coord of Registration Services ....Mr. Frank SINIGAGLIA
26 Coord of Public & Alumni Relations ....Mr. Jason UPCHURCH
50 Chair Business/Information Tech ....Ms. Mary SUDOL
79 Chair Liberal Arts & Humanities ....Dr. Paul REIFENHEISER
107 Chair Professional Studies ....Mr. Michael FISHER
83 Chair Health/Social/Behavioral Sci ....Dr. Beverly MOORE
81 Chair Mathematics/Natural Sciences ....Ms. Debra LEWKIEWICZ

Swedish Institute--College of Health Sciences (B)

226 W 26th Street, New York NY 10001-6700
County: New York FICE Identification: 021700
Unit ID: 196389
Telephone: (212) 924-5900 Carnegie Class: Spec/Health
FAX Number: (212) 924-7600 Calendar System: Semester
URL: www.swedishinstitute.edu
Established: 1916 Annual Undergrad Tuition & Fees: $15,008
Enrollment: 600 Coed
Affiliation or Control: Proprietary IRS Status: Proprietary
Highest Offering: Master's
Program: Occupational; 2-Year Principally Bachelor's Creditable; Professional
Accreditation: ACCSC

01 President ....Mr. Peter NEIGLER
03 Executive Vice President ....Ms. Stacey JAMESON
05 Director of Education ....Dr. Joseph BALATBAT
10 Chief Financial Officer ....Mr. Bill BERNARD
46 Senior Vice President ....Ms. Paula J. ECKARDT
29 Dean of Alumni Services ....Ms. Meg DARNELL
07 Director of Admissions ....Mr. Tony PELUSO
88 Dean for Massage Therapy ....Ms. Lucy LIBEN
13 Director of Information Technology ....Mr. Benn LI
32 Director of Student Services ....Ms. Jessica FERRANTE
26 Director of Public Relations ....Ms. Barbara GOLDSCHMIDT
37 Financial Aid Director ....Mr. Alex ORMENO
08 Director of Library Services ....Ms. Jill GOLDSTEIN
06 Registrar ....Mr. Jeff NAMIAN
21 Bursar ....Ms. Beatriz ACEVEDO
51 Manager of Continuing Education ....Ms. Meg DARNELL
40 Bookstore Manager ....Mr. Dan YUEN

Syracuse University Main Campus (C)

Syracuse NY 13244-1100
County: Onondaga FICE Identification: 002882
Unit ID: 196413
Telephone: (315) 443-1870 Carnegie Class: RU/H
FAX Number: (315) 443-3503 Calendar System: Semester
URL: www.syr.edu
Established: 1870 Annual Undergrad Tuition & Fees: $40,458
Enrollment: 21,029 Coed
Affiliation or Control: Independent Non-Profit IRS Status: 501(c)3
Highest Offering: Doctorate
Program: Liberal Arts And General; Teacher Preparatory; Professional
Accreditation: M, ART, AUD, BUS, CACREP, CIDA, CLPSY, CS, DIETD, DIETI, ENG, JOUR, LAW, LIB, MFCD, MUS, SCPSY, SP, SPAA, SW, TED

01 Chancellor & President ....Dr. Nancy CANTOR
05 Vice Chanc/Prov Academic Affs ....Dr. Eric F. SPINA
10 Executive Vice President & CFO ....Dr. Louis G. MARCOCCIA
43 Sr Vice Pres General Counsel ....Mr. Dickens MATHIEU
30 Exec VP Advancement/External Affs ....Mr. Thomas J. WALSH
32 Sr Vice Pres/Dean Student Affairs ....Rev. Thomas V. WOLFE
46 Vice Pres Research ....Dr. Gina LEE-GLAUSER
41 Athletic Director ....Dr. Daryl J. GROSS
26 Sr Vice Pres Public Affairs ....Mr. Kevin C. QUINN
84 Vice Pres Enrollment Management ....Mr. Donald A. SALEH
21 Comptroller ....Ms. Rebecca L. FOOTE
88 Assoc Prov International Education ....Dr. Margaret R. HIMLEY
20 Assoc Vice Chanc Academic Opers ....Mr. Christopher M. SEDORE
08 Dean of University Libraries ....Dr. Suzanne E. THORIN
88 Senior VP Human Capital Development ....Dr. Karen ALSTON
20 Assc Provost Academic Programs ....Ms. Andria COSTELLO STANIEC
88 Assc Provost Entrep Innovation ....Dr. Bruce KINGMA
48 Dean School of Architecture ....Dr. Michael A. SPEAKS
49 Dean Col of Arts & Sciences ....Dr. George M. LANGFORD
53 Dean School of Education ....Dr. Douglas P. BIKLEN
76 Dean Col of Sport & Human Dynamics ....Dr. Diane Lyden MURPHY
54 Dean Col Engreeing & Computer Sci ....Dr. Laura J. STEINBERG
62 Dean School of Information Studies ....Dr. Elizabeth D. LIDDY
61 Dean College of Law ....Dr Hannah ARTERIAN
50 Dean Whitman School of Management ....Dr. Kenneth A. KAVAJECZ
80 Dean Maxwell Sch of Citizenship ....Dr. James B. STEINBERG
60 Dean Newhouse School of Public Comm ....Ms. Lorraine BRANHAM
57 Dean Col Visual & Performing Arts ....Ms. Ann CLARKE
58 Dean Graduate Studies ....Dr. Ben R. WARE
51 Dean University College ....Ms. Bethaida GONZALEZ
101 Secretary Board of Trustees ....Ms. Elizabeth B. O'ROURKE

Talmudical Institute of Upstate New York (D)

769 Park Avenue, Rochester NY 14607-3046
County: Monroe FICE Identification: 025506
Unit ID: 196440
Telephone: (585) 473-2810 Carnegie Class: Spec/Faith
FAX Number: (585) 442-0417 Calendar System: Semester
Established: 1974 Annual Undergrad Tuition & Fees: $5,000
Enrollment: 27 Male
Affiliation or Control: Independent Non-Profit IRS Status: 501(c)3
Highest Offering: Second Talmudic Degree
Program: Professional
Accreditation: RABN

01 Dean ....Rabbi Menachem DAVIDOWITZ
03 Executive Vice President ....Rabbi Shlomo NOBLE

Talmudical Seminary of Bobov (E)

5120 New Utrecht Avenue, Brooklyn NY 11204-1108
County: Kings FICE Identification: 041155
Unit ID: 451404
Telephone: (718) 854-8700 Carnegie Class: Spec/Faith
FAX Number: (718) 854-8707 Calendar System: Semester
Established: 2005 Annual Undergrad Tuition & Fees: $7,100
Enrollment: 253 Male
Affiliation or Control: Independent Non-Profit IRS Status: 501(c)3
Highest Offering: First Talmudic Degree
Program: Teacher Preparatory; Professional; Religious Emphasis
Accreditation: RABN

01 Dean ....Rabbi Joshua RUBIN

Talmudical Seminary Oholei Torah (F)

667 Eastern Parkway, Brooklyn NY 11213-3397
County: Kings FICE Identification: 012011
Unit ID: 196431
Telephone: (718) 774-5050 Carnegie Class: Spec/Faith
FAX Number: (718) 778-0784 Calendar System: Semester
Established: 1956 Annual Undergrad Tuition & Fees: $8,100
Enrollment: 353 Male
Affiliation or Control: Independent Non-Profit IRS Status: 501(c)3
Highest Offering: First Talmudic Degree
Program: Teacher Preparatory
Accreditation: RABN

01 Chief Executive Officer ....Mendel MARSOW
05 Dean ....Elchonon LESCHES
10 Business Officer ....Gary SUSSKIND
37 Financial Aid Officer ....Sholom ROSENFELD

Teachers College, Columbia University (G)

525 West 120th Street, New York NY 10027
County: New York FICE Identification: 003979
Unit ID: 196468
Telephone: (212) 678-3000 Carnegie Class: RU/H
FAX Number: (212) 678-4048 Calendar System: Semester
URL: www.tc.columbia.edu
Established: 1887 Annual Graduate Tuition & Fees: $36,930
Enrollment: 5,236 Coed
Affiliation or Control: Independent Non-Profit IRS Status: 501(c)3
Highest Offering: Doctorate; No Undergraduates
Program: Teacher Preparatory; Professional
Accreditation: M, CLPSY, COPSY, DIETI, SCPSY, SP, TED

01 President ....Dr. Susan H. FUHRMAN
05 Provost & VP for Academic Affairs ....Dr. Thomas JAMES
100 Secretary to College/Chief of Staff ....Mr. Scott FAHEY
10 Vice Pres Finance & Administration ....Mr. Harvey SPECTOR
30 Vice Pres Devel/External Affairs ....Ms. Suzanne MURPHY
22 Vice Pres/Dir Diversity/Cmty Affs ....Ms. Janice S. ROBINSON
88 VP/Sch/Cmty Partnshp/Spec Advis ....Dr. Nancy STREIM
20 Vice Provost ....Dr. William J. BALDWIN
21 Assoc Vice Pres/Controller ....Mr. Henry PERKOWSKI
31 Assoc VP Campus/Auxiliary Services ....Mr. James MITCHELL
85 Assoc VP of International Affairs ....Dr. Thomas B. CORCORAN
20 Deputy Vice Provost ....Dr. John P. ALLEGRANTE
84 Assoc Dean Enrollment/Student Svcs ....Dr. Thomas ROCK
06 Registrar ....Ms. Diana MAUL
13 Director Information Technology ....Ms. Ena HAINES
90 Director Academic Computing ....Mr. George SCHUESSLER
08 Library Director ....Dr. Gary NATRIELLO
09 Director of Institutional Studies ....Mr. Scott SCHNACKENBERG
36 Director Career Services/Stdnt Life ....Ms. Marianne TRAMELLI
15 Director Human Resources ....Mr. Randy GLAZER
19 Director Public Safety ....Mr. John DE ANGELIS
43 General Counsel ....Ms. Lori E. FOX
25 Director Grants/Sponsored Programs ....Mr. Paul KRAN
26 Exec Director of External Affairs ....Mr. Joe LEVINE
29 Asst Director Alumni Relations ....Ms. Lindsey BRENAN
07 Director of Admissions ....Dr. Thomas ROCK
18 Director of Facilities Operations ....Ms. Suzanne JABLONSKI
32 Dir Student Activities/Programs ....Ms. Maria HATAIER
25 Manager Contracts & Grants ....Mr. John HERNANDEZ
11 Manager Administrative Services ....Ms. Patricia WALKER
37 Director Student Financial Aid ....Ms. Melanie WILLIAMS-BETHEA
39 Director of Residential Services ....Mr. Dewayne WHITE

† Affiliated with Columbia University in the City of New York.

Technical Career Institutes (H)

320 W 31st Street, New York NY 10001-2789
County: New York FICE Identification: 011031
Unit ID: 196477
Telephone: (212) 594-4000 Carnegie Class: Assoc/PrivFP
FAX Number: (212) 330-0898 Calendar System: Semester
URL: www.tcicollege.edu
Established: 1909 Annual Undergrad Tuition & Fees: $13,240
Enrollment: 3,603 Coed
Affiliation or Control: Proprietary IRS Status: Proprietary
Highest Offering: Associate Degree
Program: Occupational; 2-Year Principally Bachelor's Creditable; Technical Emphasis
Accreditation: M, NY, ENGT, OPD

00 Chief Executive Officer ....Dr. John MCGRATH
01 President ....Mr. William TALBOT
05 Provost & VP for Academic Affairs ....Dr. Peter SLATER
11 Exec Vice Pres Administration ....Mr. Felix PRETTO
07 Actg Vice Pres for Admissions ....Mr. Bernard PRICE
37 Vice President Financial Aid ....Ms. Cynthia FEKARIS
09 Vice Pres for Research and Planning ....Ms. Susanna KUNG
10 Vice President/CFO ....Mr. Richard GOLDENBERG
20 Dean of Academic Affairs ....Ms. Pansy JAMES
49 Dean of Arts & Sciences ....Dr. John LUUKKONEN
88 Dean of Facilities Technologies ....Ms. Regina CAHILL
50 Dean of Business and New Media Tech ....Ms. Clotilde DILLON
72 Dean of Technology ....Mr. Seyed AKHAVI
76 Dean of Health Sciences and Tech ....Dr. Michael MEIR

Tompkins Cortland Community College (I)

170 North Street, PO Box 139, Dryden NY 13053-8504
County: Tompkins FICE Identification: 006788
Unit ID: 196565
Telephone: (607) 844-8211 Carnegie Class: Assoc/Pub-R-M
FAX Number: (607) 844-9665 Calendar System: Semester
URL: www.TC3.edu
Established: 1968 Annual Undergrad Tuition & Fees (In-District): $4,871
Enrollment: 5,450 Coed
Affiliation or Control: State/Local IRS Status: 501(c)3
Highest Offering: Associate Degree
Program: Occupational; 2-Year Principally Bachelor's Creditable
Accreditation: M, ADNUR

01 President ....Dr. Carl E. HAYNES
03 Provost and VP of College ....Dr. John R. CONNERS
32 Dean of Student Life ....Ms. Amy TRUEMAN
05 Dean of Instruction ....Mr. Carl PENZIUL
08 Library Director ....Mr. Gregg KIEHL
84 Dean Operations & Enrollment Mgmt ....Ms. Blixy K. TAETZSCH
20 Assoc Dean Curriculum & Acad Record ....Ms. Jane F. HAMMOND
14 Director of Technology Support ....Mr. Brian ACKLEY
88 Dean Org Success & Learning ....Ms. Kathryn WUNDERLICH
09 Assoc Dean IR and Org Learning ....Dr. Kristine ALTUCHER
38 Coordinator/Counseling & Career Svc ....Ms. Meg GARVEY
37 Director of Financial Aid ....Ms. Sharon KARWOWSKI
26 Dean of External Relations ....Dr. Bruce RYAN
15 Human Resources Administrator ....Ms. Sharon DOVI
07 Director of Admissions ....Mr. Sandy DRUMLUK
21 Director of Budget & Finance ....Ms. Susan DEWEY
13 Dean of Campus Technology ....Mr. Martin G. CHRISTOFFERSON
19 Director of Safety & Security ....Mr. J. Beau SAUL

41 Athletic Director .... Mr. Mick R. MCDANIEL
39 Director Residence Life .... Ms. Darese DOSKAL-SCAFFIDO
36 Coordinator Counseling/Career Svcs .... Ms. Joan DONOVAN
91 Manager Academic Computer Services .... Mr. Dino LEOPARDI
18 Director of Facilities .... Mr. James TURNER
23 Director of Health Services .... Ms. Shari SHAPLEIGH
28 Director of Multicultural Services .... Mr. Seth THOMPSON
101 Asst to President/Clerk of Board .... Ms. Cathy NORTHROP

Torah Temimah Talmudical Seminary (A)

507 Ocean Parkway, Brooklyn NY 11218-5913
County: Kings FICE Identification: 021916
Unit ID: 196583
Telephone: (718) 853-8500 Carnegie Class: Spec/Faith
FAX Number: (718) 438-5779 Calendar System: Semester
Established: 1978 Annual Undergrad Tuition & Fees: $10,450
Enrollment: 190 Male
Affiliation or Control: Independent Non-Profit IRS Status: 501(c)3
Highest Offering: Second Talmudic Degree
Program: Teacher Preparatory; Professional
Accreditation: RABN

01 President & Dean .... Rabbi L. MARGULIES
03 Executive Director .... Rabbi Yaakov APPLEGRAD
05 Chief Academic Officer .... Rabbi Lipa GELDWORTH
37 Financial Aid Administrator .... Mr. Mendel ROCHLITZ
38 Director of Guidance .... Rabbi Yirmiya GUGENHEIMER
11 Administrator .... Rabbi Yisroel KLEINMAN

Touro College (B)

27 W 23rd Street, 5th Floor, New York NY 10010
County: New York FICE Identification: 010142
Unit ID: 196592
Telephone: (212) 463-0400 Carnegie Class: Master's L
FAX Number: (212) 627-9144 Calendar System: Semester
URL: www.touro.edu
Established: 1970 Annual Undergrad Tuition & Fees: $15,070
Enrollment: 13,909 Coordinate
Affiliation or Control: Independent Non-Profit IRS Status: 501(c)3
Highest Offering: Doctorate
Program: Liberal Arts And General; Professional
Accreditation: M, ARCPA, LAW, OSTEO, OT, #OTA, PHAR, PTA, SP, SW, @TEAC

01 President .... Dr. Alan KADISH
03 Executive Vice President .... Mr. David RAAB
03 Executive VicePresident .... Mr. Moshe KRUPKA
10 Senior Vice President & CFO .... Mr. Melvin M. NESS
11 Sr Vice Pres/Chief Admin Officer .... Mr. Alan SCHOOR
30 Vice Pres Institutional Advancement .... Dr. Eric LEVINE
20 VP Undergrad Acad Affs/Dean of Facu .... Dr. Stanley L. BOYLAN
58 Vice Pres of Graduate Studies .... Dr. Anthony POLEMENI
13 VP of Technology .... Dr. Franklin STEEN
88 Vice Pres for National Programs .... Dr. Jay SEXTER
56 Vice President Com Ed/Ex Dn NYSCAS .... Ms. Eva SPINELLI-SEXTER
32 VP Plng & Assessment/Dean of Stdnts .... Mr. Robert GOLDSCHMIDT
106 VP Online Edu/Dean Women's Division .... Dr. Marion STOLTZ-LOIKE
09 Dean Inst Rsrch/Review/Enroll Mgmt .... Mr. Ira TYSZLER
43 General Counsel/Chief Comp Off .... Mr. Michael NEWMAN
61 Dean Jacob D Fuchsberg Law Center .... Dr. Patricia SALKIN
63 Dean Col of Osteopathic Medicine .... Dr. Robert GOLDBERG
67 Dean College of Pharmacy .... Dr. Stuart FELDMAN
70 Dean School of Social Work .... Dr. Steven HUBERMAN
76 Dean of School of Health Sciences .... Dr. Louis H. PRIMAVERA
58 Dean Grad School Jewish Studies .... Dr. Michael A. SHMIDMAN
90 Dn Grad Sch of Tech/Dir Acad Comp .... Dr. Issac HERSKOWITZ
12 Dean Lander College for Men .... Dr. Moshe Z. SOKOL
50 Acting Dean Grad School of Business .... Dr. Sabra BROCK
38 Dean of Advising & Counseling .... Dr. Avery HOROWITZ
51 Asst Dean School Lifelong Education .... Dr. Charlotte HOLZER
06 Asst Dean Enroll Mgmt/Registrar .... Mr. Vladmir ROZIN
37 Exec Dir Financial Aid/Compliance .... Mrs. Carol ROSENBAUM
08 Director of Libraries .... Ms. Bashe SIMON
07 Director of Admissions .... Mr. Arthur WIGFALL
76 Director Physician Asst Program .... Dr. Joseph TOMMASINO
75 Director of Occupational Therapy .... Dr. Stephanie DAPICE-WONG
76 Director of Physical Therapy .... Ms. Jill HORBACEWICZ
88 Pgm Dir Speech Lang Path/Grad Pgm .... Ms. Hindy LUBINSKY
13 Director of OIT .... Mr. Mark SHOR
13 Chief Info Security Officer .... Ms. Patricia CIUFFO
19 Director of Security .... Ms. Lydia PEREZ
19 Dir of Emergency Preparedness .... Ms. Shoshana YEHUDAH
15 Director of Human Resources .... Ms. Roberta JACKSON
96 Director of Purchasing .... Ms. Wanda HERNANDEZ
18 Dir of Facilities/Real Estate .... Mr. Kenneth DAVID
21 Controller .... Mr. Stuart LIPPMAN
26 Dir of Communication/External Rels .... Ms. Hedy SHULMAN
29 Director Alumni Relations .... Vacant
36 Director Student Placement .... Mr. Stuart ANSEL
108 Director of Assessment .... Dr. Eric LINDEN
25 Director Office Sponsored Pgm .... Mr. Glenn DAVIS

Touro College Bay Shore (C)

1700 Unim Boulevard, Bay Shore NY 11706
Telephone: (631) 665-1600 Identification: 770145
Accreditation: &M

† Main campus is Touro College in New York, NY.

Touro College Flatbush (D)

1602 Avenue J, Brooklyn NY 11230
Telephone: (718) 252-7800 Identification: 770146
Accreditation: &M

† Main campus is Touro College in New York, NY.

Touro Law School (E)

225 Eastview Drive, Central Islip NY 11722
Telephone: (631) 761-7000 Identification: 770148
Accreditation: &M

† Main campus is Touro College in New York, NY.

Tri-State College of Acupuncture (F)

80 Eighth Avenue, #400, New York NY 10011-0890
County: New York FICE Identification: 025460
Unit ID: 130581
Telephone: (212) 242-2255 Carnegie Class: Spec/Health
FAX Number: (212) 242-2920 Calendar System: Semester
URL: www.tsca.edu
Established: 1982 Annual Graduate Tuition & Fees: $20,850
Enrollment: 128 Coed
Affiliation or Control: Proprietary IRS Status: Proprietary
Highest Offering: Master's; No Undergraduates
Program: Professional
Accreditation: ACUP

01 President .... Dr. Mark D. SEEM
06 Registrar .... Sandra TURNER

Trocaire College (G)

360 Choate Avenue, Buffalo NY 14220-2094
County: Erie FICE Identification: 002812
Unit ID: 196653
Telephone: (716) 826-1200 Carnegie Class: Assoc/PrivNFP
FAX Number: (716) 828-6109 Calendar System: Semester
URL: www.trocaire.edu
Established: 1958 Annual Undergrad Tuition & Fees: $14,980
Enrollment: 1,406 Coed
Affiliation or Control: Independent Non-Profit IRS Status: 501(c)3
Highest Offering: Baccalaureate
Program: Occupational; 2-Year Principally Bachelor's Creditable
Accreditation: M, ADNUR, CAHIIM, @DIETT, MAC, NUR, PHLEB, PNUR, RAD, SURGT

01 President .... Dr. Bassam M. DEEB
05 Vice President of Academic Affairs .... Dr. Richard T. LINN
10 Chief Finance Officer .... Mr. John J. HUDACK
30 Vice Pres Institutional Advancement .... Mr. John VECCHIO
32 Dean Student Affairs .... Mr. Tony FUNIGIELLO
46 VP Research/Planning/Assessment .... Dr. Richard T. LINN
84 Chief Enrollment Officer .... Ms. Jacqueline MATHENY
66 Dean Catherine McAuley Sch of Nurs .... Dr. Carol FANUTTI
15 Exec Dir Human Resources .... Mrs. Rebecca BOYLE
35 Student Activities Coordinator .... Mr. Jon HUDACK
14 Sr InformationTechnology Specialist .... Ms. Robin LOOMIS
103 Sr Director Workforce Development .... Mr. Hal KINGSLEY
105 Director Data Administration .... Ms. Michele PETERS
37 Director of Financial Aid .... Ms. Janet MCGRATH
25 Director of Grants/Govt Relations .... Ms. Sandra MILLER
16 Payroll/Benefits/Human Res Coord .... Ms. Linda SANSONE
06 Registrar .... Mrs. Theresa HORNER
36 Director Career Center .... Mrs. Maureen PERNICK HUBER
42 Campus Ministry .... Sr. Marie Andre MAIN
18 Facilities Director .... Mrs. Margaret ANDRZEJEWSKI
30 Dir Development/Alumni Relations .... Mrs. Joan P. WILLIAMS
07 Director of Admissions .... Mrs. Maria POVLACK
105 Dir College Communications/Web Mgr .... Mrs. Kathy POPIELSKI
38 Director Student Counseling .... Ms. Joyce KAISER
40 Manager Bookstore .... Ms. Debbie CAMMARATA
88 Web/Social Media Editor .... Mrs. Jackie HAUSLER
76 Dean Division of Health Prof .... Dr. Linda KERWIN

Ulster County Community College (H)

491 Cottekill Road, PO Box 557, Stone Ridge NY 12484
County: Ulster FICE Identification: 002880
Unit ID: 196699
Telephone: (845) 687-5000 Carnegie Class: Assoc/Pub-R-M
FAX Number: (845) 687-5083 Calendar System: Semester
URL: www.sunyulster.edu
Established: 1961 Annual Undergrad Tuition & Fees (In-District): $4,230
Enrollment: 3,702 Coed
Affiliation or Control: State/Local IRS Status: 501(c)3
Highest Offering: Associate Degree
Program: Occupational; 2-Year Principally Bachelor's Creditable
Accreditation: M, ADNUR

01 President .... Dr. Donald C. KATT
84 Vice Pres & Dean Enrollment Mgmt .... Ms. Ann MARROTT
05 Dean of Academic Affairs .... Dr. John GANIO
30 Dean of Advancement/Continuing Educ .... Ms. Marianne COLLINS
10 Dean of Admin/Chief Business Ofcr .... Mr. Mark KOMDAT
04 Executive Assistant to President .... Ms. Jean ROSE
20 Assoc Dean of Academic Affairs .... Ms. Cornelia DENVIR
32 Assoc Dean for Student Services .... Mr. John FRAMPTON
08 Director of Library Services .... Ms. Kari MACK
37 Director of Financial Aid .... Mr. Christopher CHANG
06 Registrar .... Ms. Marion GOSS
41 Athletic Director .... Mr. James DELMAR
19 Director of Safety & Security .... Mr. Wayne FREER
07 Director of Admissions .... Mr. Matthew GREEN
26 Chief Public Relations Officer .... Ms. Ann MARROTT
36 Dir Student Plcmnt/Acad Sppt Svcs .... Ms. Jane KITHCART
35 Director Student Affairs .... Ms. Ann MARROTT
18 Director of Plant Operations .... Mr. Steven FREER
09 Director of Institutional Research .... Mr. Clarence (Hank) MILLER
103 Workforce Development .... Mr. Christopher MARX
15 Coordinator of Personnel Services .... Mrs. Debra DELANOY
21 Coordinator of Accounting .... Ms. Amy WINTERS
96 Coord Procurement/General Services .... Mr. Stephen GALLART

Unification Theological Seminary (I)

30 Seminary Drive, Barrytown NY 12507-5021
County: Dutchess FICE Identification: 032163
Unit ID: 246789
Telephone: (845) 752-3000 Carnegie Class: Spec/Faith
FAX Number: (845) 758-2156 Calendar System: Semester
URL: www.uts.edu
Established: 1975 Annual Undergrad Tuition & Fees: $11,040
Enrollment: 78 Coed
Affiliation or Control: Unification Church IRS Status: 501(c)3
Highest Offering: Doctorate
Program: Professional; Religious Emphasis
Accreditation: M

01 President .... Dr. Richard PANZER
05 Vice President for Academic Affairs .... Dr. Kathy WININGS
88 Dean of the Undergraduate Program .... Dr. Stephen MURRAY
88 Director of Field Education .... Dr. Jacob DAVID
10 Chief Financial Officer .... Mr. John REDMOND
06 Registrar .... Mrs. Ute DELANEY
07 Admissions Officer .... Mrs. Davetta Ann MORGAN-HOLDER
08 Library Director .... Dr. Keisuke NODA
32 Director of Student Life .... Mr. Paul G. RAJAN
35 Assistant Director of Student Life .... Mrs. Rachel CURRY
37 Student Financial Aid Director .... Mrs. Angie CALLWOOD
11 Chief Operations Officer .... Mr. Paul STUPPLE
18 Plant Director .... Mr. Carl VERDERBER

Union College (J)

807 Union Street, Schenectady NY 12308-3181
County: Schenectady FICE Identification: 002889
Unit ID: 196866
Telephone: (518) 388-6000 Carnegie Class: Bac/A&S
FAX Number: (518) 388-6800 Calendar System: Trimester
URL: www.union.edu
Established: 1795 Annual Undergrad Tuition & Fees: $46,785
Enrollment: 2,183 Coed
Affiliation or Control: Independent Non-Profit IRS Status: 501(c)3
Highest Offering: Baccalaureate
Program: Liberal Arts And General; Professional
Accreditation: M, ENG

01 President .... Dr. Stephen C. AINLAY
05 Dean Faculty/VP Academic Affs .... Dr. Therese A. MCCARTY
30 Vice President College Relations .... Vacant
10 Vice President for Finance & Admin .... Ms. Diane T. BLAKE
07 Vice President of Admissions/FA .... Mr. Matthew J. MALATESTA
100 Chief of Staff .... Dr. Edward SUMMERS
32 Vice President of Student Affairs .... Dr. Stephen C. LEAVITT
88 Dean of Studies .... Dr. Mark E. WUNDERLICH
13 Chief Information Officer .... Ms. Ellen Y. BORKOWSKI
06 Registrar .... Ms. Penelope S. ADEY
30 Sr Director of Development .... Mr. Dominick F. FAMULARE
08 College Librarian .... Ms. Frances J. MALOY
26 Director of Media and Public Rels .... Mr. Phillip J. WAJDA
37 Director of Financial Aid .... Ms. Linda M. PARKER
38 Director of Student Counseling .... Mr. Marcus S. HOTALING
36 Director of Career Center .... Mr. Robert C. SOULES
15 Director of Human Resources .... Mr. Eric NOLL
41 Director of Athletics .... Mr. James MCLAUGHLIN
22 Sr Director Campus Diversity/AA .... Dr. Gretchel L. HATHAWAY
19 Director Campus Safety .... Mr. Christopher HAYEN
39 Director Residence Life .... Ms. Molly MACELROY

† Tuition figure is a comprehensive fees figure.

Union Graduate College (K)

80 Nott Terrace, Schenectady NY 12308-3131
County: Schenectady FICE Identification: 038813
Unit ID: 446932
Telephone: (518) 631-9900 Carnegie Class: Master's M
FAX Number: (518) 631-9901 Calendar System: Trimester
URL: www.uniongraduatecollege.edu
Established: 2003 Annual Graduate Tuition & Fees: $2,775
Enrollment: 460 Coed
Affiliation or Control: Independent Non-Profit IRS Status: 501(c)3
Highest Offering: Master's; No Undergraduates
Program: Professional
Accreditation: M, NY, BUS, HSA, TEAC

01 President .... Dr. Laura SCHWEITZER
10 Vice President of Finance/Operation .... Joseph MCDONALD
84 VP Enrollment Mgmt/Student Svcs .... Joanne FITZGERALD
30 VP Institutional Advancement .... Dan CHRISTOPHER

06 Registrar/Director of Admissions .... Rhonda SHEEHAN
50 Dean School of Management .... Dr. Alan BOWMAN
54 Dean School of Engineering .... Bob KOZIK
53 Dean School of Education .... Dr. Patrick ALLEN
76 Director Center for Bioethics .... Dr. Robert BAKER
07 Director Student Recruitment .... Erin WHEELER
36 Coordinator of Career Services .... Jane FLEURY
09 Director Institutional Research .... Amy NEVIN
29 Coordinator of Alumni Relations .... Kim PERRONE
13 Director of Information Technology .... Robert KEENAN
37 Director Financial Aid .... Nikki GALLUCCI

Union Theological Seminary (A)

3041 Broadway, New York NY 10027-5792
County: New York FICE Identification: 002890
Unit ID: 196884
Telephone: (212) 662-7100 Carnegie Class: Spec/Faith
FAX Number: (212) 280-1416 Calendar System: Semester
URL: www.utsnyc.edu
Established: 1836 Annual Graduate Tuition & Fees: $21,890
Enrollment: 248 Coed
Affiliation or Control: Independent Non-Profit IRS Status: 501(c)3
Highest Offering: Doctorate; No Undergraduates
Program: Religious Emphasis
Accreditation: M, THEOL

01 President .... Dr. Serene JONES
03 Executive Vice President .... Mr. Fred DAVIE
10 VP Finance & Operations .... Mr. Richard A. MADONNA, JR.
30 VP for Institutional Advancement .... Mr. Bob BOMERSBACH
05 Dean of Academic Affairs .... Dr. Mary BOYS
32 Associate Dean Student Life .... Ms. Yvette WILSON
08 Director Library .... Vacant
04 Special Assistant to the President .... Ms. Tania BRUNO
06 Registrar .... Ms. Edith T. HUNTER
18 Director Facilities/Physical Plant .... Mr. Michael MALONEY
39 Director Student Housing .... Mr. Michael ORZECHOWSKI
07 Admissions Director .... Ms. Nichelle JENKINS

United Talmudical Seminary (B)

191 Rodney Street, Brooklyn NY 11211-7900
County: Kings FICE Identification: 011189
Unit ID: 197018
Telephone: (718) 963-9770 Carnegie Class: Spec/Faith
FAX Number: (718) 963-9775 Calendar System: Semester
Established: 1949 Annual Undergrad Tuition & Fees: $13,200
Enrollment: 1,956 Male
Affiliation or Control: Independent Non-Profit IRS Status: 501(c)3
Highest Offering: Second Talmudic Degree
Program: Teacher Preparatory; Professional; Religious Emphasis
Accreditation: RABN

01 Dean .... Rabbi Zalman TEITLBAUM
05 Assoc Dean Scholastic Services .... Rabbi Yeruchem DEUTSCH
37 Financial Aid Administrator .... Mr. Bernard KATZ
10 Business Officer .... Mr. Shia GREENFELD

University of Rochester (C)

Rochester NY 14627-0033
County: Monroe FICE Identification: 002894
Unit ID: 195030
Telephone: (585) 275-2121 Carnegie Class: RU/VH
FAX Number: (585) 275-0359 Calendar System: Semester
URL: www.rochester.edu
Established: 1850 Annual Undergrad Tuition & Fees: $45,342
Enrollment: 10,510 Coed
Affiliation or Control: Independent Non-Profit IRS Status: 501(c)3
Highest Offering: Doctorate
Program: Liberal Arts And General; Teacher Preparatory; Professional
Accreditation: M, BUS, CACREP, CLPSY, DENT, ENG, IPSY, MED, MFCD, MUS, NURSE, PDPSY, PH, TED

01 President .... Mr. Joel SELIGMAN
05 Provost and Dean of Arts/Sci & Engr .... Mr. Peter LENNIE
10 Sr VP Administration & Fin/CFO .... Mr. Ronald J. PAPROCKI
03 VP/University Dean .... Mr. Paul J. BURGETT
17 Sr VP Health Sciences/Med Ctr CEO .... Dr. Bradford C. BERK
45 Sr VP for Institutional Resources .... Mr. Douglas PHILLIPS
30 Sr VP/Chief Advancement Officer .... Mr. Jim THOMPSON
43 VP/General Counsel .... Ms. Gail NORRIS
46 Sr VP for Research .... Mr. Rob CLARK
26 VP for Communications .... Mr. Bill MURPHY
13 Vice President/Chief Info Officer .... Mr. David E. LEWIS
15 Assoc VP Human Resources .... Mr. Charles J. MURPHY
58 Vice Provost/Univ Dean Grad Studies ...... Ms. Margaret KEARNEY
100 General Sect/Pres Chief of Staff .... Ms. Lamar R. MURPHY
28 Vice Provost Fac Devel & Diversity .... Dr. Vivian LEWIS
08 Dean River Campus Libraries .... Ms. Mary Ann MAVRINAC
88 Vice President/Laser Lab Director .... Mr. Robert L. MCCRORY
49 Dean of School of Arts & Sciences .... Ms. Joanna OLMSTED
54 Dean of Hajim Engineering School .... Mr. Rob CLARK
84 Dean AS&E Undergrad Admis & Fin Aid .. Mr. Jonathan BURDICK
21 Assoc VP for Budgets & Planning .... Ms. Holly CRAWFORD
32 Dean of Students Arts/Sci & Engr .... Mr. Matthew BURNS
63 Dean School of Medicine & Dent .... Dr. Mark B. TAUBMAN
64 Dean Eastman School of Music .... Mr. Douglas LOWRY
66 Dean School of Nursing .... Ms. Kathy RIDEOUT
50 Dean Simon Grad Sch Business Admin .... Mr. Mark ZUPAN
53 Dean Warner Grad Sch Educ & Hum Dev ... Ms. Raffaella BORASI
89 Dean of Freshmen Arts/Sci & Engr .... Ms. Marcy KRAUS
88 Dean of Sophmores Arts/Sci & Engr .... Mr. Sean HANNA
37 Assoc Dean Enroll & Fin Aid A/S&E .... Mr. Charles PULS
35 Assoc Dean Students Arts/Sci & Engr .... Ms. Anne-Marie ALGIER
23 Strong Health Chief Medical Officer ..... Dr. Raymond MAYEWSKI
52 Dir Eastman Institute Oral Health .... Dr. Eli ELIAV
25 Assoc VP Research & Project Admin .... Ms. Gunta LIDERS
18 Assoc VP Facilities & Services .... Mr. Richard PIFER
86 Executive Director Govt Relations .... Mr. Peter J. ROBINSON
96 Director Corporate Purchasing .... Mr. Philip S. PROFETA
04 Executive Asst to the President .... Ms. Susan NIGGLI
06 Registrar .... Ms. Nancy SPECK
19 Director of University Security .... Mr. Walter MAULDIN
57 Director Memorial Art Gallery .... Mr. Grant HOLCOMB
29 Exec Director Alumni Relations .... Mr. Kevin P. WESLEY
41 Director of Athletics & Recreation ... Mr. George VANDERZWAAG
39 Dir Res Life & Housing Services ..... Ms. Laurel CONTOMANOLIS
36 Asst Dean/Director Career Center .... Mr. Burton NADLER
101 Administrator to Board of Trustees .... Ms. Jackie E. KING

USC The Business College (D)

201 Bleecker Street, Utica NY 13501-2200
County: Oneida FICE Identification: 009077
Unit ID: 197081
Telephone: (315) 733-2300 Carnegie Class: Assoc/PrivFP
FAX Number: (315) 733-9281 Calendar System: Semester
URL: www.uscny.edu
Established: 1896 Annual Undergrad Tuition & Fees: $12,865
Enrollment: 355 Coed
Affiliation or Control: Proprietary IRS Status: Proprietary
Highest Offering: Associate Degree
Program: Occupational; 2-Year Principally Bachelor's Creditable; Business Emphasis
Accreditation: NY

01 President & Treasurer .... Mr. Philip M. WILLIAMS
03 Exec Vice Pres/Asst to President .... Mr. Scott K. WILLIAMS
11 Exec Vice President Administration .... Mr. John L. CROSSLEY
05 Exec Vice President for Academics .... Vacant
103 VP Corp/Workforce Develop .... Mr. Don REESE
10 Vice President of Finance .... Mr. Richard H. HILTON
43 General Counsel .... Mr. John H. STORY, JR.
12 Director Canastota Branch .... Mrs. Wendy M. CARY
06 Registrar/Bursar .... Mrs. Marian J. NIELSON
30 Director of Development .... Mr. John CROSSLEY
08 Head Librarian .... Ms. Anne NASSAR
37 Director of Student Financial Aid .... Mr. Fred P. ZUCALLA
12 Dir Oneonta Campus/Dean Students .... Ms. Deb HADDOW
07 Director of Admissions .... Mr. Tom VERDOW
13 Director Information Technology .... Mr. Jarrod BOREK
36 Director of Career Services .... Ms. Emily TRACY
18 Facilities Manager Physical Plant .... Mr. Dave DUTCHER

U.T.A. Mesivta of Kiryas Joel (E)

PO Box 2009, Monroe NY 10949-8509
County: Orange FICE Identification: 038023
Unit ID: 446604
Telephone: (845) 783-9901 Carnegie Class: Spec/Faith
FAX Number: (845) 782-3620 Calendar System: Semester
Established: 1999 Annual Undergrad Tuition & Fees: $9,000
Enrollment: 1,450 Male
Affiliation or Control: Independent Non-Profit IRS Status: 501(c)3
Highest Offering: First Talmudic Degree
Program: Teacher Preparatory; Professional
Accreditation: RABN

01 President .... Elias HOROWITZ
05 Rosh Yeshiva .... Rabbi Aharon TEITELBAUM
37 Financial Aid Director .... David SCHWARTZ

Utica College (F)

1600 Burrstone Road, Utica NY 13502-4892
County: Oneida FICE Identification: 002883
Unit ID: 197045
Telephone: (315) 792-3111 Carnegie Class: Master's M
FAX Number: (315) 792-3292 Calendar System: Semester
URL: www.utica.edu
Established: 1946 Annual Undergrad Tuition & Fees: $32,800
Enrollment: 3,839 Coed
Affiliation or Control: Independent Non-Profit IRS Status: 501(c)3
Highest Offering: Doctorate
Program: Liberal Arts And General; Teacher Preparatory; Professional
Accreditation: M, NURSE, OT, PTA, TEAC

01 President .... Dr. Todd S. HUTTON
05 Provost & Vice Pres Academic Aff .... Dr. Judith A. KIRKPATRICK
10 Vice Pres Financial Affs/Treasurer .... Ms. Tammara RAUB
32 Vice Pres Stdnt Affs/Dean of Stdnts .... Mr. Stephen PATTARINI
04 Executive Assistant to President .... Ms. Kim D. LAMBERT
30 Senior VP & Chief Advanc Officer .... Ms. Laura CASAMENTO
09 Vice Pres for Planning & Analysis .... Ms. Carol MACKINTOSH
84 Vice President for Enrollment Mgmt .... Vacant
88 Vice President for Strategic Initiv .... Dr. James C. BROWN
20 Associate Provost .... Dr. Robert M. HALLIDAY
26 Asst VP Marketing/Communication .... Mr. Kelly L. ADAMS
76 Dean for Health Professions/Educ .... Dr. Richard RAFES
49 Dean for Arts & Sciences .... Dr. John H. JOHNSEN
50 Dean for Business & Justice Studies .... Ms. Patricia SWANN
35 Dean of Students .... Ms. Alane P. VARGA
21 Director of Student Acct Operation .... Ms. Gail TUTTLE
29 Director Alumni & Parent Relations .... Mr. Mark C. KOVACS
08 Asst VP for Library & IITS .... Ms. Beverly J. MARCOLINE
36 Director Career Services .... Ms. Halina LOTYCZEWSKI
37 Exec Dir of Student Financial Svcs .... Ms. Laura BEDFORD
06 Registrar .... Mr. Dominic PASSALACQUA
44 Director of Development .... Mr. Athony VILLANTI
41 Director of Physical Educ/Athletics .... Mr. David FONTAINE
39 Director of Residence Life .... Mr. Carl LOHMANN
13 Infrastructure Manager .... Mr. John KAFTAN
16 Director of Human Resources .... Ms. Lisa GREEN
14 Dir College Info & Application Svcs .... Mr. Scott HUMPHREY
24 Dir Computer User Svcs .... Mr. Jason LEWIN
31 Exec Dir Corp/Professional Pgms .... Ms. Joni L. PULLIAM
51 Director of Credit Programs .... Ms. Evelyn FAZEKAS
85 Dean of International Education ...... Dr. Laurence W. ROBERTS, II
18 Director Facilities Management .... Mr. Donald L. HARTER
19 Director of Campus Safety .... Mr. Wayne SULLIVAN
92 Director Honors Program .... Dr. Diane MATZA
28 Dir Office of Opportunity Programs .... Ms. Johnni F. MAHDI
96 Manager of Purchasing .... Ms. Bobbie H. SMOROL

† Utica College maintains an academic tie with Syracuse University that allows undergraduates to receive a Syracuse University degree.

Vassar College (G)

124 Raymond Avenue, Poughkeepsie NY 12604-0001
County: Dutchess FICE Identification: 002895
Unit ID: 197133
Telephone: (845) 437-7000 Carnegie Class: Bac/A&S
FAX Number: (845) 437-7187 Calendar System: Semester
URL: www.vassar.edu
Established: 1861 Annual Undergrad Tuition & Fees: $59,070
Enrollment: 2,406 Coed
Affiliation or Control: Independent Non-Profit IRS Status: 501(c)3
Highest Offering: Master's
Program: Liberal Arts And General
Accreditation: M, @TEAC

01 President .... Dr. Catharine B. HILL
05 Dean of the Faculty .... Dr. Jonathan CHENETTE
20 Dean of the College .... Dr. Christopher ROELLKE
10 Vice President for Finance & Admin .... Mr. Robert WALTON
30 Vice President for Development .... Ms. Catherine E. BAER
26 Vice Pres for College Relations .... Ms. Susan DEKREY
90 Vice Pres for Computing/Info Svcs .... Vacant
32 Dean of Students .... Dr. David H. BROWN
07 Dean Admission/Financial Aid .... Mr. David M. BORUS
49 Dean of Studies .... Dr. Joanne LONG
20 Associate Dean College .... Mr. Edward L. PITTMAN
35 Assoc Dean Col/Dir Campus Activit .... Ms. Teresa QUINN
06 Registrar .... Ms. Colleen MALLET
08 Director of the Libraries .... Ms. Sabrina PAPE
37 Director of Financial Aid .... Ms. Jessica BERNIER
36 Director Career Development Center .... Ms. Stacy Lee SCHNEIDER BINGHAM
87 Director Conferences/Summer Pgms .... Ms. Katherine BUSH
39 Director Residential Life .... Mr. Luis INOA
09 Director of Institutional Research ..... Mr. David DAVIS-VAN ATTA
15 Director Human Resources .... Ms. Ruth SPENCER
18 Exec Dir Buildings & Grounds .... Mr. Thomas ALLEN
38 Director of Psychological Services .... Dr. Sylvia BALDERRAMA
96 Director of Purchasing .... Ms. Rosaleen CARDILLO

Vaughn College of Aeronautics and Technology (H)

86-01 23rd Avenue, Flushing NY 11369
County: Queens FICE Identification: 002665
Unit ID: 188340
Telephone: (718) 429-6600 Carnegie Class: Bac/Assoc
FAX Number: (718) 429-0256 Calendar System: Semester
URL: www.vaughn.edu
Established: 1932 Annual Undergrad Tuition & Fees: $20,450
Enrollment: 1,712 Coed
Affiliation or Control: Independent Non-Profit IRS Status: 501(c)3
Highest Offering: Master's
Program: 2-Year Principally Bachelor's Creditable; Liberal Arts And General; Professional
Accreditation: M, ENGT, IACBE

01 President .... Dr. John C. FITZPATRICK
05 Sr Vice Pres Academic/Student Affs .... Dr. Sharon B. DEVIVO
10 Vice Pres for Business & Finance ...... Mr. Robert G. WALDMANN
84 Vice President Enrollment Services .... Mr. Ernie SHEPELSKY
11 Asst VP College Services/Human Res .... Mr. Paul MIRANDA
20 Asst Vice Pres of Academic Affairs .... Vacant
45 Asst VP Academic Support Svcs .... Mr. Said LAMHAOUAR
35 Asst Vice Pres/Dean Student Affairs .... Ms. Jerima DEWESE
84 Ast VP Instl Rels/New Initiatives .... Mr. Vincent PAPANDREA
37 Director of Financial Aid .... Ms. Dorothy MARTIN
06 Registrar .... Mrs. Beatriz CRUZ
08 Librarian .... Ms. Joanne JAYNE
102 Exec Dir Corp/Foundation Relations .... Ms. Kalli KOUTSOUTIS
26 Director of Public Affairs .... Ms. Maureen KIGGINS
96 Director of Purchasing .... Vacant
09 Director of Institutional Research .... Vacant
07 Director of Admissions .... Mr. David GRIFFEY, JR.
18 Director Facilities .... Mr. Michael DALY

38 Dir Student Counseling/Wellness .... Dr. Nancy ADEGOKE
13 Asst Director Computer Operations ..... Mr. Hamwant (Neil) SINGH

Villa Maria College of Buffalo (A)

240 Pine Ridge Road, Buffalo NY 14225-3999
County: Erie FICE Identification: 002896
Unit ID: 197142
Telephone: (716) 896-0700 Carnegie Class: Assoc/PrivNFP4
FAX Number: (716) 896-0705 Calendar System: Semester
URL: www.villa.edu
Established: 1960 Annual Undergrad Tuition & Fees: $17,640
Enrollment: 411 Coed
Affiliation or Control: Independent Non-Profit IRS Status: 501(c)3
Highest Offering: Baccalaureate
Program: Liberal Arts And General; Fine Arts Emphasis
Accreditation: M, CIDA, MUS, PTAA

01 President ....Sr. Marcella Marie GARUS
05 Vice President for Academic Affairs ....Dr. Matthew GIORDANO
10 Vice President for Business Affairs .... Mr. Vincent GRIZANTI
30 Vice President for Development ......Sr. Mary Marcine BOROWIAK
32 Vice President for Student Affairs .....Sr. Mary Louis RUSTOWICZ
44 Asst to Vice Pres for Development .... Ms. Kathy SEIBOLD
06 Registrar ....Ms. Melany SHIELDS
84 Director of Enrollment Management .... Mr. Kevin DONOVAN
08 Director of Library ....Sr. Mary Anna FALBO
37 Director of Financial Aid ....Ms. Laura FITZGERALD
09 Director of Institutional Research .... Sr. Mary Albertine STACHOWSKI
38 Director Student Counseling ....Ms. Palma M. ZANGHI
13 Director of Computer Services ...... Ms. Christine E. PALCZEWSKI
88 Systems Analyst .... Mr. Robert STRUBLE
18 Plant & Grounds Manager ....Mr. David WISNER
23 Director of Health Services .... Mrs. Minerva MONTIJO
25 Director of Grants .... Mrs. Mary ROBINSON
51 Instructional Design & Program Dev ....Vacant
36 Director of Career Development .... Ms. Deborah HANDZLIK
42 Director of Campus Ministry .... Mr. Frank ANTONUCCI
85 Director of Foreign Students .... Ms. Palma ZANGHI
27 Coordinator of Communications .... Ms. Jenna SMITH
35 Director of Student Life .... Ms. Ceceile PAWLOWSKI
88 Archivist ....Sr. Anita BENECKI
22 Affirmative Action Officer ....Ms. Diane M. HANDZLIK
29 Director of Alumni Relations .... Ms. Mary MERIGOLD
24 Coordinator of Educational Media .... Mrs. Barbara WETZEL
88 Coord Academic Success Center ....Ms. Elizabeth KIRCHMEYER-BATTAGLIA
76 Business/Health Science Dept ....Mr. Todd BAKER
77 Director of Computer Services ....Ms. Christine PALCZEWSKI
57 Art Department Chair ....Ms. Sandra REICIS
64 Music Department Chair .... Dr. Sylvia GRMELA
49 Liberal Arts Department Chair .... Ms. Joyce KESSEL

Wagner College (B)

1 Campus Road, Staten Island NY 10301-4479
County: Richmond FICE Identification: 002899
Unit ID: 197197
Telephone: (718) 390-3100 Carnegie Class: Master's M
FAX Number: (718) 390-3467 Calendar System: Semester
URL: www.wagner.edu
Established: 1883 Annual Undergrad Tuition & Fees: $39,220
Enrollment: 1,825 Coed
Affiliation or Control: Independent Non-Profit IRS Status: 501(c)3
Highest Offering: Master's
Program: Liberal Arts And General; Teacher Preparatory; Professional
Accreditation: M, ACBSP, ARCPA, NUR, TED

01 President .... Dr. Richard GUARASCI
11 Vice President for Administration ....Mr. David MARTIN
05 Provost/Vice Pres Academic Affairs ....Dr. Lily D. MCNAIR
10 Vice Pres Business & Finance ....Mr. William MEA
84 Vice Pres Enrollment Management ....Mr. Angelo ARAIMO
30 Int VP Instititutional Advancement ....Mr. Frank YOUNG
26 Chief of Staff/VP Communications ....Mr. Joseph ROMANO
04 Assistant to the President .... Ms. Pat FITZPATRICK
32 Vice Pres and Dean of Campus Life ....Ms. Ruta SHAH-GORDON
21 Asst Vice Pres/Controller ....Mr. John CARRESCIA
108 Dean of Assessment ....Dr. Anne LOVE
20 Associate Provost .... Dr. Jeffrey KRAUS
06 Registrar ....Mr. Jeffrey KRAUS
13 Int Director Information Technology ....Mr. Frank CAFASSO
42 Chaplain ....Vacant
29 Director Alumni Relations ....Mr. Kenneth LAM
39 Director Housing ....Ms. Jen CIACCIO
30 Director of Development .... Ms. Ashley ALEXANDER
18 Chief Facilities/Physical Plant .... Mr. Dominick FONTANO
41 Director of Athletics .... Mr. Walter HAMELINE
23 Director of Health Services .... Ms. Kathleen OBERFELDT
19 Director Security/Safety ....Mr. Anthony MARTINESI
15 Director Personnel Services .... Ms. Tania ROSSINI
37 Director Student Financial Aid .... Ms. Theresa WEIMER
58 Coordinator of Graduate Studies .... Dr. Jeffrey KRAUS
07 Dean of Admissions .... Mr. Robert HERR
09 Director of Institutional Research .... Mrs. Rosemary ANASTASIO
28 Director of Diversity ....Mr. Curtis WRIGHT
35 Director Student Affairs ....Dr. Sara KLEIN
36 Director Student Placement .... Mr. Geoffrey HEMPILL
38 Director Student Counseling .... Dr. Sharon KIUHARA

Webb Institute (C)

298 Crescent Beach Road, Glen Cove NY 11542-1398
County: Nassau FICE Identification: 002900
Unit ID: 197221
Telephone: (516) 671-2213 Carnegie Class: Spec/Engg
FAX Number: (516) 674-9838 Calendar System: Semester
URL: www.webb-institute.edu
Established: 1889 Annual Undergrad Tuition & Fees: N/A
Enrollment: 79 Coed
Affiliation or Control: Independent Non-Profit IRS Status: 501(c)3
Highest Offering: Baccalaureate
Program: Professional; Technical Emphasis
Accreditation: M, ENG

01 President ....Mr. R. Keith MICHEL
05 Dean ....Prof. Richard P. NEILSON
20 Assistant Dean ....Prof. Richard C. HARRIS
08 Librarian .... Ms. Patricia M. PRESCOTT
30 Chief Development .... Mr. Rick PARADIS
10 Director of Financial Affairs .... Ms. Margo ZOLDESSY
32 Director of Student Affairs ....Mr. David BYRNES
18 Director of Facilities ....Mr. John FERRANTE
84 Director of Enrollment Management .... Mr. William G. MURRAY
29 Director of Alumni Relations ....Ms. Gailmarie SUJECKI
26 Chief Public Relations Officer .... Mr. Rick PARADIS
13 Director of Communications and IT ....Ms. Erica L. HANSEN
06 Registrar ....Ms. Jocelyn M. WILSON
37 Director of Financial Aid .... Ms. Lauri D'AMBRA

Weill Cornell Medical College (D)

1300 York Avenue, F-113, New York NY 10065-4805
Telephone: (212) 746-5454 FICE Identification: 004762
Accreditation: &M, ARCPA, DENT, IPSY, MED

† Main campus is Cornell University in Ithaca, NY.

Wells College (E)

170 Main Street, Aurora NY 13026-0500
County: Cayuga FICE Identification: 002901
Unit ID: 197230
Telephone: (315) 364-3266 Carnegie Class: Bac/A&S
FAX Number: (315) 364-3227 Calendar System: Semester
URL: www.wells.edu
Established: 1868 Annual Undergrad Tuition & Fees: $35,900
Enrollment: 532 Coed
Affiliation or Control: Independent Non-Profit IRS Status: 501(c)3
Highest Offering: Baccalaureate
Program: Liberal Arts And General; Teacher Preparatory
Accreditation: M, @TEAC

01 Interim President .... Dr. Thomas E. DEWITT
05 Provost and Dean of the College .... Dr. Cindy SPEAKER
11 Chief Operating Officer ....Mr. Terry NEWCOMB
10 Treasurer and Controller .... Ms. Melody PONZI
30 Vice President for Advancement .... Mr. Michael MCGREEVEY
32 Dean of Students ....Ms. Jennifer MICHAEL
07 Dir of Admissions/Financial Aid .... Ms. Susan SLOAN
06 Registrar ....Mr. Andre SIAMUNDELE
08 Library Director ....Ms. Muriel GODBOUT
37 Director Financial Aid .... Ms. Cathleen PATELLA
44 Director of Annual Giving .... Ms. Pamela SHERADIN
26 Dir of Communications/Marketing ....Ms. Ann ROLLO
29 Director Alumni Relations ....Ms. Laura SANDERS
19 Director of Security .... Mr. David GARDNER
18 Chief Facilities/Physical Plant .... Mr. Brian BROWN
15 Manager of Human Resources ....Ms. Kit VAN ORMAN

Westchester Community College (F)

75 Grasslands Road, Valhalla NY 10595-1636
County: Westchester FICE Identification: 002881
Unit ID: 197294
Telephone: (914) 606-6600 Carnegie Class: Assoc/Pub-S-SC
FAX Number: (914) 606-6780 Calendar System: Semester
URL: www.sunywcc.edu
Established: 1946 Annual Undergrad Tuition & Fees (In-District): $4,704
Enrollment: 13,997 Coed
Affiliation or Control: State/Local IRS Status: 501(c)3
Highest Offering: Associate Degree
Program: Occupational; 2-Year Principally Bachelor's Creditable
Accreditation: M, COARC, DIETT, RAD

01 President ....Dr. Joseph N. HANKIN
05 Vice President Academic Affairs ....Ms. Joanne RUSSELL
32 Vice Pres Student Personnel Svcs ....Mr. Donald WEIGAND
11 Vice Pres Administrative Services ....Mr. Pat D'IMPERIO
102 VP Ext Affs/Exec Dir Found for WCC ....Mrs. Eve LARNER
51 Dean Community/Adult/Cont Educ ....Dr. Marjorie GLUSKER
81 Assoc Dean Math/Phys Engr/Tech .... Mr. Ted NYGREEN
76 Assoc Dean Natural/Health Sciences ....Mr. Michael OLIVETTE
83 Assoc Dean Bus/Behav/Soc Sci Svcs .... Mr. Jeffrey A. CONTE
79 Assoc Dean Arts/Humanities/Lrng Res .. Ms. Veronica DELCOURT
22 Associate Dean of EOC .... Ms. Renee GUY
35 Assoc Dean Student Personnel Svcs ....Mr. Kevin B. SLAVIN
08 Asc Dn Lrng Res/Dist Lrng/Inst Tech .... Ms. Pamela POLLARD
26 Director of College/Cmty Relations ....Mr. Patrick HENNESSEY
06 Registrar ....Mr. John CAPOCCI
37 Dir of Student Financial Assistance .... Mr. Alikhan MORGAN
13 Vice President of IT ....Mr. Anthony SCORDINO

07 Director of Admissions ....Ms. Gloria LEON
38 Acting Director of Counseling ....Mr. Ruben BARATO
16 Director Human Resources ....Ms. Sabrina J. CHANDLER
88 Director Faculty Student Assoc .... Mr. David SKLAR
09 Director Inst Research & Planning .... Ms. Nancy M. DERIGGI
19 Director of Security ....Mr. Brian P. DOLANSKY
24 Director Media Services ....Mr. Thomas GALA
41 Athletic Director ....Mr. Larry MASSARONI
21 Assoc Business Officer/Controller .... Mr. Mario CAVALLI
18 Director Physical Plant ....Mr. Robert CIRILLO
96 Deputy Purchasing Agent ....Mr. Richard CASHMAN
27 Publications Manager .... Mr. Craig FISCHER
23 Coordinator Student Health Services .... Ms. Janice GILROY
75 Coord of Transfer & Career Service .....Dr. Gwen D. ROUNDTREE

Wood Tobé-Coburn School (G)

Eight E 40th Street, New York NY 10016
County: New York FICE Identification: 007405
Unit ID: 197522
Telephone: (212) 686-9040 Carnegie Class: Assoc/PrivFP
FAX Number: (212) 686-9171 Calendar System: Semester
URL: www.woodtobecoburn.edu
Established: 1879 Annual Undergrad Tuition & Fees: $16,640
Enrollment: 523 Coed
Affiliation or Control: Proprietary IRS Status: Proprietary
Highest Offering: Associate Degree
Program: Occupational; 2-Year Principally Bachelor's Creditable
Accreditation: NY, MAC

01 President ....Ms. Sandra GRUNINGER
05 Director of Education .... Ms. Arlette BALRAM
07 Director of Admissions .... Ms. Sandra ANDUJAR-WENDLAND
32 Student Services Director .... Ms. Yessika GARCIA
37 Financial Aid Administrator .... Ms. Yessika GARCIA
36 Placement Director ....Ms. Lisa RINI

Yeshiva Derech Chaim (H)

1573 39th Street, Brooklyn NY 11218-4413
County: Kings FICE Identification: 022651
Unit ID: 197647
Telephone: (718) 438-5476 Carnegie Class: Spec/Faith
FAX Number: (718) 435-9285 Calendar System: Semester
Established: 1975 Annual Undergrad Tuition & Fees: $10,200
Enrollment: 156 Male
Affiliation or Control: Independent Non-Profit IRS Status: 501(c)3
Highest Offering: Second Talmudic Degree
Program: Professional; Religious Emphasis
Accreditation: RABN

01 President ....Rabbi Mordechai RENNERT
01 President ....Rabbi Yisroel PLUTCHOK

Yeshiva D'Monsey Rabbinical College (I)

2 Roman Boulevard, Monsey NY 10952-3106
County: Rockland FICE Identification: 031473
Unit ID: 420325
Telephone: (845) 426-3276 Carnegie Class: Spec/Faith
FAX Number: (845) 352-1119 Calendar System: Semester
Established: 1984 Annual Undergrad Tuition & Fees: $5,400
Enrollment: 74 Male
Affiliation or Control: Independent Non-Profit IRS Status: 501(c)3
Highest Offering: Second Talmudic Degree
Program: Teacher Preparatory; Professional
Accreditation: RABN

01 Rosh Yeshiva ....Rabbi Moishe GREEN
05 Rosh Yeshiva ....Rabbi Ruvain GREEN
37 Financial Aid Director ....Rabbi Aron BERGER

Yeshiva of Far Rockaway (J)

802 Hicksville Road, Far Rockaway NY 11691-5219
County: Queens FICE Identification: 041196
Telephone: (718) 327-7600 Carnegie Class: Not Classified
FAX Number: (718) 327-1430 Calendar System: Semester
Established: 1969 Annual Undergrad Tuition & Fees: $10,000
Enrollment: 71 Male
Affiliation or Control: Independent Non-Profit IRS Status: 501(c)3
Highest Offering: First Talmudic Degree
Program: Professional; Religious Emphasis
Accreditation: RABN

01 President ....Rabbi Yechiel I. PERR
03 Executive Director .... Rabbi Shayeh KOHN
32 Dean of Students ....Rabbi Dovid KLEINKAUFMAN

Yeshiva Gedolah Imrei Yosef D'Spinka (K)

1466 56th Street, Brooklyn NY 11219-4696
County: Kings FICE Identification: 030001
Unit ID: 375230
Telephone: (718) 851-8721 Carnegie Class: Spec/Faith
FAX Number: (718) 686-8849 Calendar System: Semester
Established: 1987 Annual Undergrad Tuition & Fees: $7,500
Enrollment: 130 Male
Affiliation or Control: Independent Non-Profit IRS Status: 501(c)3

Highest Offering: First Talmudic Degree
Program: Teacher Preparatory; Religious Emphasis
Accreditation: @RABN

01 President .... Mordechai MAJEROWITZ

Yeshiva Gedolah Kesser Torah (A)

28 Cedar Lane, Monsey NY 10952
County: Rockland Identification: 667112
Telephone: (845) 406-4308 Carnegie Class: Not Classified
FAX Number: (845) 406-4199 Calendar System: Semester
Established: 2004 Annual Undergrad Tuition & Fees: $9,300
Enrollment: 71 Male
Affiliation or Control: Independent Non-Profit IRS Status: 501(c)3
Highest Offering: First Talmudic Degree
Program: Teacher Preparatory; Professional
Accreditation: RABN

00 CEO .... Rabbi David FISHMAN
01 President .... David BERNSTEIN

Yeshiva Gedolah Ohr Yisrael (B)

2899 Nostrand Avenue, Brooklyn NY 11229
County: Kings Identification: 667077
Telephone: (718) 382-8702 Carnegie Class: Not Classified
FAX Number: (718) 382-8703 Calendar System: Semester
Established: 1999 Annual Undergrad Tuition & Fees: $6,750
Enrollment: 80 Male
Affiliation or Control: Independent Non-Profit IRS Status: 501(c)3
Highest Offering: First Talmudic Degree
Program: Professional
Accreditation: RABN

01 Rosh Yeshiva .... Avraham ZUCKER
10 Treasurer .... Avi KAHN

Yeshiva Karlin Stolin Beth Aaron V'Israel Rabbinical Institute (C)

1818 54th Street, Brooklyn NY 11204-1545
County: Kings FICE Identification: 025058
Unit ID: 197601
Telephone: (718) 232-7800 Carnegie Class: Spec/Faith
FAX Number: (718) 331-4833 Calendar System: Semester
Established: 1948 Annual Undergrad Tuition & Fees: $8,000
Enrollment: 119 Male
Affiliation or Control: Independent Non-Profit IRS Status: 501(c)3
Highest Offering: Second Talmudic Degree
Program: Teacher Preparatory; Professional
Accreditation: RABN

01 Chief Executive Officer .... Rabbi Yochanan PILCHICK
05 Dean Theology/Chief Acad Officer .... Rabbi Chaim WOLPIN
06 Registrar .... Rabbi Aryeh WOLPIN
08 Librarian .... Rabbi Yochanan GOLDHABER
10 Fiscal Officer .... Rabbi Irving PERRES
37 Financial Aid Director .... Rabbi Mayer PILCHICK
33 Dean of Men .... Rabbi Gedelyah MACHLIS

Yeshiva and Kolel Bais Medrash Elyon (D)

73 Main Street, Monsey NY 10952-3013
County: Rockland Identification: 666707
Unit ID: 245777
Telephone: (845) 356-7064 Carnegie Class: Spec/Faith
FAX Number: (845) 356-7065 Calendar System: Semester
Established: 1945 Annual Undergrad Tuition & Fees: $10,575
Enrollment: 49 Male
Affiliation or Control: Independent Non-Profit IRS Status: 501(c)3
Highest Offering: Second Talmudic Degree
Program: Professional
Accreditation: @RABN

01 President .... Rabbi Yerachmiel CENSOR
05 Dean .... Rabbi Israel FALK

Yeshiva and Kollel Harbotzas Torah (E)

1049 E 15th Street, Brooklyn NY 11230-4462
County: Kings FICE Identification: 023506
Unit ID: 245731
Telephone: (718) 692-0208 Carnegie Class: Spec/Faith
FAX Number: (718) 692-0363 Calendar System: Semester
Established: 1969 Annual Undergrad Tuition & Fees: $8,100
Enrollment: 44 Male
Affiliation or Control: Independent Non-Profit IRS Status: 501(c)3
Highest Offering: Second Talmudic Degree
Program: Professional
Accreditation: @RABN

01 President .... Rabbi Y. BITTERSFELD

Yeshiva of Machzikai Hadas (F)

1301 47th Street, Brooklyn NY 11219
County: Kings FICE Identification: 041381
Unit ID: 455257
Telephone: (718) 853-2442 Carnegie Class: Spec/Faith
FAX Number: (718) 853-2504 Calendar System: Semester
Established: 2001 Annual Undergrad Tuition & Fees: $7,100
Enrollment: 334 Male
Affiliation or Control: Independent Non-Profit IRS Status: 501(c)3
Highest Offering: First Talmudic Degree
Program: Professional
Accreditation: RABN

01 Rosh Yeshiva .... Rabbi Yidel MONHEIT

Yeshiva Mikdash Melech (G)

1326 Ocean Parkway, Brooklyn NY 11230-5655
County: Kings FICE Identification: 025068
Unit ID: 197610
Telephone: (718) 339-1090 Carnegie Class: Spec/Faith
FAX Number: (718) 998-9321 Calendar System: Semester
Established: 1972 Annual Undergrad Tuition & Fees: $15,300
Enrollment: 143 Male
Affiliation or Control: Independent Non-Profit IRS Status: 501(c)3
Highest Offering: Second Talmudic Degree
Program: Teacher Preparatory; Professional; Religious Emphasis
Accreditation: RABN

01 Dean .... Rabbi Haim BENOLIEL
05 Dean of Faculty .... Rabbi David LOPIAN
06 Registrar .... Rabbi Josh SANANES
10 Chief Business Officer .... Rabbi Amram SANANES
11 Administrator .... Rabbi Abraham BENOLIEL

Yeshiva of Nitra Rabbinical College (H)

194 Division Avenue, Brooklyn NY 11211-7199
County: Kings FICE Identification: 011670
Unit ID: 197674
Telephone: (718) 387-0422 Carnegie Class: Spec/Faith
FAX Number: (718) 387-9400 Calendar System: Semester
Established: 1946 Annual Undergrad Tuition & Fees: $7,900
Enrollment: 236 Male
Affiliation or Control: Independent Non-Profit IRS Status: 501(c)3
Highest Offering: Second Talmudic Degree
Program: Professional
Accreditation: RABN

01 President .... Mr. Alexander FISCHER
03 Vice President .... Mr. Mendel KLEIN
05 Dean .... Rabbi Samuel D. UNGAR
11 Administrative Officer .... Mr. Ernest SCHWARTZ

Yeshiva Shaar HaTorah-Grodno (I)

83-96 117th Street, Kew Gardens NY 11415
County: Queens FICE Identification: 021520
Unit ID: 197692
Telephone: (718) 846-1940 Carnegie Class: Spec/Faith
FAX Number: (718) 850-7916 Calendar System: Semester
Established: 1976 Annual Undergrad Tuition & Fees: $16,200
Enrollment: 89 Male
Affiliation or Control: Independent Non-Profit IRS Status: 501(c)3
Highest Offering: Second Talmudic Degree
Program: Professional
Accreditation: RABN

01 Administrator .... Rabbi Yoel YANKELEWITZ

Yeshiva Shaarei Torah of Rockland (J)

91 W Carlton Road, Suffern NY 10901-4013
County: Rockland FICE Identification: 034963
Unit ID: 441609
Telephone: (845) 352-3431 Carnegie Class: Spec/Faith
FAX Number: (845) 352-3433 Calendar System: Semester
Established: 1977 Annual Undergrad Tuition & Fees: $12,750
Enrollment: 109 Male
Affiliation or Control: Independent Non-Profit IRS Status: 501(c)3
Highest Offering: First Talmudic Degree
Program: Professional
Accreditation: RABN

01 President .... Rabbi Mordechai WOLMARK
30 Chief Devel Officer/Financial Aid .... Mrs. Teri SCHILLER
06 Registrar .... Rabbi Neil RATNER

Yeshiva Sholom Shachna (K)

401 Elmwood Avenue, Brooklyn NY 11230
County: Kings Identification: 667147
Telephone: (718) 252-6333 Carnegie Class: Not Classified
FAX Number: (718) 338-2536 Calendar System: Semester
Established: 2005 Annual Undergrad Tuition & Fees: $9,400
Enrollment: 57 Male
Affiliation or Control: Independent Non-Profit IRS Status: 501(c)3
Highest Offering: First Talmudic Degree
Program: Teacher Preparatory; Professional
Accreditation: @RABN

01 Chief Executive Officer .... Rabbi Meir Chaim GUTFREUND
10 Chief Financial/Business Officer .... Mrs. Dina GUTFREUND
05 Chief Academic Officer/Registrar .... Rabbi Mordechai GUTFREUND
37 Director Student Financial Aid .... Mrs. Yehudis KIRZNER

Yeshiva of the Telshe Alumni (L)

4904 Independence Avenue, Riverdale NY 10471
County: Bronx FICE Identification: 025463
Unit ID: 431983
Telephone: (718) 601-3523 Carnegie Class: Spec/Faith
FAX Number: (718) 601-2141 Calendar System: Semester
Established: 1981 Annual Undergrad Tuition & Fees: $8,800
Enrollment: 97 Male
Affiliation or Control: Independent Non-Profit IRS Status: 501(c)3
Highest Offering: First Talmudic Degree
Program: Teacher Preparatory; Professional
Accreditation: RABN

01 President .... Rabbi Avrohom AUSBAND
03 Executive Director .... Rabbi Noson JOSEPH
29 Director Alumni Relations .... Rabbi Moshe FERBER

Yeshiva University (M)

500 W 185th Street, New York NY 10033-3201
County: New York FICE Identification: 002903
Unit ID: 197708
Telephone: (212) 960-5400 Carnegie Class: RU/VH
FAX Number: (212) 960-0055 Calendar System: Semester
URL: www.yu.edu
Established: 1886 Annual Undergrad Tuition & Fees: $36,500
Enrollment: 6,740 Coordinate
Affiliation or Control: Independent Non-Profit IRS Status: 501(c)3
Highest Offering: Doctorate
Program: Liberal Arts And General; Professional
Accreditation: M, BUS, CLPSY, DENT, IPSY, LAW, MED, PSPSY, SW, @TEAC

01 President .... Mr. Richard M. JOEL
05 Provost/Sr VP Academic Affairs .... Dr. Morton LOWENGRUB
100 Sr Vice Pres/Chief of Staff .... Mr. Josh JOSEPH
17 Vice President Medical Affairs .... Dr. Allen M. SPIEGEL
10 Vice President Business Affairs/CFO .... Mr. J. Michael GOWER
30 Vice Pres Institutional Advancement .... Mr. Daniel T. FORMAN
11 Vice President University Affairs .... Dr. Herbert C. DOBRINSKY
13 VP Information Technology/CIO .... Mr. Marc MILSTEIN
43 VP Legal Affs/Secretary/Gen Counsel .... Mr. Andrew J. LAUER
32 Vice Pres Univ & Cmty Life .... Rabbi Kenneth BRANDER
26 Vice Pres Communications/Pub Affs .... Mrs. Georgia B. POLLAK
18 Vice Pres Administrative Services .... Mr. Jeffrey ROSENGARTEN
04 Assistant to President .... Ms. Cynthia PHELPS
08 Dean of University Libraries .... Mrs. Pearl BERGER
35 Dean of Students .... Mr. David HIMBER
49 Dean Yeshiva College .... Dr. Barry EICHLER
49 Dean Undergrd Jewish Stds/Mazer Sch .... Rabbi Yona REISS
49 Dean Stern College for Women .... Dr. Karen BACON
50 Dean Sy Syms School of Business .... Dr. Moses PAVA
63 Dean Albert Einstein Col Medicine .... Dr. Allen M. SPIEGEL
58 Dean Ferkauf Graduate School Psych .... Dr. Lawrence J. SIEGEL
58 Dean Bernard Revel Graduate School .... Dr. David BERGER
58 Dean Azrieli Graduate Sch Jewish Ed .... Dr. David J. SCHNALL
70 Dean Wurzweiler School Social Work .... Dr. Carmen ORTIZ HENDRICKS
58 Director Sue Golding Grad Program .... Dr. Victoria FREEDMAN
84 Director Enrollment Management .... Ms. Diana BENMERGUI
37 Director of Student Finances .... Mr. Robert FRIEDMAN
07 Director Undergraduate Admissions .... Mr. Michael KRANZLER
29 Director University Alumni Affairs .... Ms. Barbara BIRCH
06 Interim University Registrar .... Ms. Diana BENMERGUI
09 Director of Institutional Research .... Dr. Ariel FISHMAN
96 Director of Purchasing .... Mr. Jack ZENCHECK
15 Director Human Resources .... Ms. Yvonne RAMIREZ
38 Director Student Counseling .... Dr. Chaim NISSEL

Yeshiva Zichron Aryeh (N)

1213 Bay 25th Street, Far Rockaway NY 11691
County: Queens Identification: 667110
Telephone: (516) 295-5700 Carnegie Class: Not Classified
FAX Number: (516) 295-5737 Calendar System: Semester
Established: 1992 Annual Undergrad Tuition & Fees: $8,750
Enrollment: 44 Male
Affiliation or Control: Independent Non-Profit IRS Status: 501(c)3
Highest Offering: Second Talmudic Degree
Program: Teacher Preparatory; Religious Emphasis
Accreditation: RABN

03 Executive Vice President .... Rabbi Shaya COHEN
06 Registrar .... Rabbi Yosef AMSTER
07 Dir of Admiss/Financial Aid Admin .... Rabbi Avraham BURGER
10 Controller .... Mr. Shmuel BURGER
18 Chief Facilities .... Mr. Danny SCHUSTER

Yeshivas Novominsk (O)

1690 60th Street, Brooklyn NY 11204-2138
County: Kings FICE Identification: 031271
Unit ID: 405058
Telephone: (718) 438-2727 Carnegie Class: Spec/Faith
FAX Number: (718) 438-2472 Calendar System: Semester
Established: 1988 Annual Undergrad Tuition & Fees: $9,000
Enrollment: 122 Male
Affiliation or Control: Independent Non-Profit IRS Status: 501(c)3
Highest Offering: First Talmudic Degree

Program: Teacher Preparatory; Professional
Accreditation: RABN

01 Administrative Director .... Rabbi Lipa BRENNAN
32 Dean of Students .... Rabbi Yaakov PERLOW

Yeshivath Viznitz (A)

PO Box 446, Monsey NY 10952-0446
County: Rockland FICE Identification: 013027
Unit ID: 197735
Telephone: (845) 731-3700 Carnegie Class: Spec/Faith
FAX Number: (845) 356-7359 Calendar System: Semester
Established: 1946 Annual Undergrad Tuition & Fees: $7,500
Enrollment: 556 Male
Affiliation or Control: Independent Non-Profit IRS Status: 501(c)3
Highest Offering: Second Talmudic Degree
Program: Teacher Preparatory; Professional
Accreditation: RABN

01 President .... Gershon NEIMAN
10 Chief Fiscal Officer .... Rabbi J. LURIA

Yeshivath Zichron Moshe (B)

PO Box 580, South Fallsburg NY 12779-0580
County: Sullivan FICE Identification: 011821
Unit ID: 197744
Telephone: (845) 434-5240 Carnegie Class: Spec/Faith
FAX Number: (845) 434-1009 Calendar System: Semester
Established: 1969 Annual Undergrad Tuition & Fees: $10,700
Enrollment: 197 Male
Affiliation or Control: Independent Non-Profit IRS Status: 501(c)3
Highest Offering: Second Talmudic Degree
Program: Professional
Accreditation: RABN

01 President .... Rabbi Ephraim Y. SHER
37 Director Student Financial Aid .... Rabbi Dov PERECMAN
06 Registrar .... Mrs. Miryom R. MILLER

NORTH CAROLINA

Apex School of Theology (C)

1701 T. W. Alexander Drive, Durham NC 27703-8024
County: Durham FICE Identification: 035134
Unit ID: 441511
Telephone: (919) 572-1625 Carnegie Class: Spec/Faith
FAX Number: (919) 572-1762 Calendar System: Other
URL: www.apexsot.edu
Established: 1995 Annual Undergrad Tuition & Fees: $6,200
Enrollment: 815 Coed
Affiliation or Control: Independent Non-Profit IRS Status: 501(c)3
Highest Offering: Doctorate
Program: Religious Emphasis
Accreditation: TRACS

01 President .... Dr. Joseph E. PERKINS
03 Executive Vice President .... Dr. Herbert R. DAVIS
05 Academic Dean/Graduate Dean .... Dr. Lafayette MAXWELL
06 Registrar .... Ms. Juretta RUFFIN
08 Head Librarian .... Ms. Cynthia RUFFIN
106 Director of E-Learning .... Dr. John CHAPMAN
10 Director of Finance .... Mrs. Carolyn PEEBLES
20 Undergraduate Dean .... Dr. Gladys LONG
88 Dean Master of Arts Christian Couns .... Dr. John F. BRADSHAW
73 Dean Doctor of Ministry .... Vacant
32 Director Student Affairs .... Dr. Clarence BURKE
09 Dir of Institutional Effectiveness .... Dr. Henry D. WELLS, JR.

The Art Institute of Charlotte (D)

2110 Water Ridge Parkway, Charlotte NC 28217-4536
Telephone: (704) 357-8020 FICE Identification: 021105
Accreditation: &SC, ACFEI

† Main campus is South University in Savannah, GA.

The Art Institute of Raleigh-Durham (E)

410 Blackwell Street, Suite 200, Durham NC 27701
Telephone: (919) 317-3050 Identification: 770843
Accreditation: &SC

† Main campus is South University in Savannah, GA.

Barton College (F)

704-A College Street, PO Box 5000,
Wilson NC 27893-7000
County: Wilson FICE Identification: 002908
Unit ID: 197911
Telephone: (252) 399-6300 Carnegie Class: Bac/Diverse
FAX Number: (252) 399-6571 Calendar System: Semester
URL: www.barton.edu
Established: 1902 Annual Undergrad Tuition & Fees: $25,396
Enrollment: 1,130 Coed
Affiliation or Control: Christian Church (Disciples Of Christ)
IRS Status: 501(c)3
Highest Offering: Master's
Program: Liberal Arts And General; Teacher Preparatory
Accreditation: SC, NUR, SW, TED

01 President .... Dr. Norval C. KNETEN
10 Vice Pres Finance & Administration .... Mr. Kris LYNCH
05 Vice President Academic Affairs .... Dr. John MARSDEN
100 Senior Advisor to President .... Mrs. Carolyn HARMON
31 Vice President External Relations .... Dr. Kelly M. THOMPSON
32 Vice President Student Life .... Mr. George SOLAN
30 Asst VP Development .... Mr. Jason GIPE
35 Asst Vice Pres for Student Affairs .... Ms. Holly ZACHARIAS
21 Comptroller .... Ms. Adrienne SMITH
06 Registrar .... Ms. Sheila MILNE
08 Director of the Library .... Mr. George LOVELAND
42 Chaplain .... Rev. Jamie EUBANKS
36 Coordinator of Career Services .... Ms. Kimberly FLEMING
23 Director of Health Services .... Mrs. Amy BRIDGERS
26 Director of Public Relations .... Mrs. Kathy DAUGHETY
29 Director of Alumni Affairs .... Ms. Summer BROCK
07 Director of Admissions .... Ms. Amanda METTS
15 Director Human Resources .... Mrs. Linda TYSON
37 Director Student Financial Aid .... Ms. Bridget ELLIS
88 Dean of Accelerated Professional Pr .... Dr. Jackie ENNIS
14 Director Technology .... Mr. Kent WHEELESS
40 Bookstore Manager .... Ms. Candice BARNES
41 Athletic Director .... Mr. Gary HALL
13 Director of Information Technology .... Ms. Callie BISSETTE
35 Director of Student Activities .... Mr. Jared TICE
18 Director of Physical Plant .... Mr. Phil BEHE
09 Director of Institutional Research .... Vacant
50 Interim Dean School of Business .... Dr. Kevin RENSHLER
53 Dean School of Education .... Dr. Jackie ENNIS
66 Dean School of Nursing .... Dr. Sharon SARVEY
88 Dean School of Social Work .... Dr. Barbara CONKLIN

Belmont Abbey College (G)

100 Belmont Mount Holly Road, Belmont NC 28012-1802
County: Gaston FICE Identification: 002910
Unit ID: 197984
Telephone: (704) 461-6700 Carnegie Class: Bac/Diverse
FAX Number: (704) 461-6670 Calendar System: Semester
URL: www.bac.edu
Established: 1876 Annual Undergrad Tuition & Fees: $18,500
Enrollment: 1,629 Coed
Affiliation or Control: Roman Catholic IRS Status: 501(c)3
Highest Offering: Baccalaureate
Program: Liberal Arts And General; Teacher Preparatory
Accreditation: SC

01 President .... Dr. William K. THIERFELDER
05 VP Academic Affs/Dean of Faculty .... Dr. Carson DALY
11 Vice Pres Administration & Finance .... Mr. Wayne SCROGGINS
26 VP College Relations .... Mr. Gregory SWANSON
20 Assoc Dean for Academic Affairs .... Dr. Mark NEWCOMB
30 Director of Development .... Mr. Dave TARGONSKI
04 Exec Assistant to the President .... Ms. Rita F. LEWIS
29 Alumni & Community Relations Dir .... Ms. Chris Goff PEELER
08 Director of the Library .... Mr. Donald BEAGLE
06 Registrar .... Ms. Margot RHOADES
09 Director of Institutional Research .... Ms. Karen PRICE
36 Director Career Counseling/Placemnt .... Ms. Stephannie MILES
27 Director Marketing .... Vacant
37 Director of Financial Aid .... Mrs. Anne A. STEVENS
38 Wellness Center Counselor .... Vacant
41 Athletic Director .... Mr. Stephen MISS
21 Staff Accountant .... Ms. Patti PIZZANO
19 Chief of Campus Police .... Mr. Shane STARNES
42 Director of Campus Ministry .... Mr. Patrick FORD
15 Director of Human Resources .... Ms. Cheryl TROTTER
18 Chief Facilities/Physical Plant .... Mr. J. R. MARR
07 Executive Director of Admissions .... Ms. Nicole FOCARETO

Bennett College (H)

900 E Washington Street, Greensboro NC 27401-3239
County: Guilford FICE Identification: 002911
Unit ID: 197993
Telephone: (336) 273-4431 Carnegie Class: Bac/A&S
FAX Number: (336) 370-8688 Calendar System: Semester
URL: www.bennett.edu
Established: 1873 Annual Undergrad Tuition & Fees: $16,794
Enrollment: 707 Female
Affiliation or Control: United Methodist IRS Status: 501(c)3
Highest Offering: Baccalaureate
Program: Liberal Arts And General; Teacher Preparatory; Business Emphasis
Accreditation: SC, SW, TED

01 President .... Dr. Rosalind FUSE-HALL
05 Provost/Academic VP .... Dr. Joyce BLACKWELL
100 Chief of Staff .... Dr. Ralonda BURNEY
10 Interim VP Business & Finance .... Mr. LeRoy SUMMERS
39 Director of Residence Life .... Ms. Ruth DENNIS-PHILLIPS
30 Interim Vice Pres Inst Advancement .... Ms. Iris RAMEY
26 Dir Public Relations & Publication .... Ms. Wanda MOBLEY
09 Dir Institutional Effective/Rsrch .... Dr. William MYERS
32 Assoc Provost of Student Affairs .... Dr. Audrey WARD
84 Interim Director Enrollment Mgmt .... Ms. Arlene CASH
06 Registrar .... Ms. Karen GREEN
08 Director of Holgate Library .... Ms. Joan WILLIAMS
07 Interim Director of Admissions .... Ms. Taunya N. MONROE
37 Director of Financial Aid .... Ms. Keisha RAGSDALE
29 Director Alumnae Affairs .... Ms. Audrey FRANKLIN
36 Director Career Services .... Ms. Ilona MCGRIFF
38 Director of Counseling Services .... Ms. Robin CAMPBELL
23 Director of Health Services .... Vacant
15 Director of Human Resources .... Ms. Linda MACK
42 Chaplain/Director Campus Ministry .... Rev. Natalie MCLEAN
83 Chair Social Sciences/Educ Division .... Dr. Rhonda WHITE
79 Chair Humanities/Fine Arts Division .... Mr. Steven WILLIS
81 Chair Natural & Behavioral Sciences .... Dr. Susan CURTIS
97 Dean of Academic Support .... Dr. Audrey WARD

Brevard College (I)

One Brevard College Drive, Brevard NC 28712-3306
County: Transylvania FICE Identification: 002912
Unit ID: 198066
Telephone: (828) 883-8292 Carnegie Class: Bac/A&S
FAX Number: (828) 884-3790 Calendar System: Semester
URL: www.brevard.edu
Established: 1853 Annual Undergrad Tuition & Fees: $34,180
Enrollment: 633 Coed
Affiliation or Control: United Methodist IRS Status: 501(c)3
Highest Offering: Baccalaureate
Program: Liberal Arts And General
Accreditation: #SC, MUS, TEAC

01 President .... Dr. David C. JOYCE
05 VP Academic Affairs/Dean of Faculty .... Dr. Roy S. SHEFFIELD
10 Vice President for Business/Finance .... Ms. Deborah P. HALL
30 Vice Pres Institutional Advancement .... Ms. Susan L. COTHERN
07 Vice Pres Admissions/Financial Aid .... Mr. Ryan C. HOLT
04 Assistant to the President .... Mrs. Julie MCCAY
32 Dean of Students .... Mrs. Debora D'ANNA
13 Int Dir of Information Technology .... Mr. Jay TRUSSELL
06 Registrar .... Mrs. Amy HERTZ
37 Director of Financial Aid .... Mrs. Caron SURRETT
08 Director of Library .... Mr. Michael M. MCCABE
29 Director of Alumni Affairs .... Mrs. Rebecca GILL
19 Dir of Safety/Security/Risk Mgmt .... Mr. Stan JACOBSEN
41 Director of Athletics .... Mr. Juan MASCARO
18 Director of Facilities/Grounds .... Mr. James HARGIS
24 Director Academic Enrichment Ctr .... Ms. Shirley E. ARNOLD
36 Dir of Career Exploration/Develop .... Ms. Nacole POTTS
92 Director of Honors Program .... Dr. Laura L. FRANKLIN
21 Controller .... Mr. Thomas Ove ANDERSEN
38 Assoc Dean/Dir of Counseling .... Ms. Deanne DASBURG
57 Chair Division of Fine Arts .... Dr. Laura FRANKLIN
79 Chair Division of Humanities .... Dr. Mary L. BRINGLE
83 Chair Div of Social Studies .... Dr. Helen C. GIFT
81 Chair Div Env Stds/Math/Nat Science .... Dr. Kenneth DUKE

Cabarrus College of Health Sciences (J)

401 Medical Park Drive, Concord NC 28025-3959
County: Cabarrus FICE Identification: 006477
Unit ID: 198109
Telephone: (704) 403-1555 Carnegie Class: Spec/Health
FAX Number: (704) 403-2077 Calendar System: Semester
URL: www.cabarruscollege.edu
Established: 1942 Annual Undergrad Tuition & Fees: $11,330
Enrollment: 484 Coed
Affiliation or Control: Independent Non-Profit IRS Status: 501(c)3
Highest Offering: Baccalaureate
Program: Occupational; 2-Year Principally Bachelor's Creditable; Nursing Emphasis
Accreditation: SC, ADNUR, MAC, NURSE, OTA, SURGT

01 Chancellor .... Dr. Dianne O. SNYDER
05 Provost .... Dr. Margaret B. PATCHETT
32 Dean of Student Aff/Enrollment Mgt .... Ms. Christine L. CORSELLO
10 Chief Financial Officer .... Vacant
66 ADN Program Chair .... Ms. Kim PLEMMONS
66 BSN Program Chair .... Ms. Molly PATTON
88 Occupational Therapy Program Chair .... Ms. Nancy GREEN
88 Medical Assisting Program Chair .... Ms. Rachel HOUSTON
88 Surgical Technology Program Chair .... Ms. Michelle GAY
88 Medical Imagining Program Chair .... Ms. Mary HOLDER
88 Associate in Science Program Chair .... Mr. John KAPP
88 Pharmacy Technology Program Chair .... Ms. Annette SIMMONS
88 General Education Program Chair .... Ms. Stacey WILSON
88 Coord Campus & Community Outreach .... Ms. Cara LURSEN
29 Coord of Alumni Affairs .... Mrs. Melanie GASS
32 Coord of Advising & Student Succes .... Mrs. Julie E. HOLLAND
37 Director of Financial Aid .... Ms. Valerie RICHARD
06 Dir Student Records & Info Mgmt .... Mr. Todd DEESE
07 Director of Admissions .... Dr. Mark A. ELLISON

Campbell University (K)

PO Box 97, Buies Creek NC 27506-0097
County: Harnett FICE Identification: 002913
Unit ID: 198136
Telephone: (910) 893-1200 Carnegie Class: Master's L
FAX Number: (910) 893-1424 Calendar System: Semester
URL: www.campbell.edu
Established: 1887 Annual Undergrad Tuition & Fees: $26,240
Enrollment: 6,189 Coed
Affiliation or Control: Baptist IRS Status: 501(c)3
Highest Offering: Doctorate
Program: Liberal Arts And General; Teacher Preparatory; Professional
Accreditation: SC, ACBSP, #ARCPA, LAW, @OSTEO, PHAR, SW, TED, THEOL

01 President .... Dr. Jerry M. WALLACE
05 Vice Pres Academic Affs & Provost .... Vacant
10 Vice President Business/Treasurer .... Mr. Jim O. ROBERTS
30 Vice President for Advancement .... Mr. Britt DAVIS
32 Vice President for Student Life .... Dr. Dennis BAZEMORE
84 Vice Pres Enrollment Management .... Vacant
07 Asst Vice Pres of Admissions .... Mr. Jason HALL
49 Dean of College of Arts & Science .... Dr. Mark L. HAMMOND
61 Dean of the Law School .... Mr. J. Rich LEONARD
50 Dean Lundy-Fetterman Sch Business .... Dr. Ben HAWKINS
53 Dean School of Education .... Dr. Karen NERY
67 VP of Health Sciences and Dean .... Dr. Ronald W. MADDOX
63 Dean of Osteopathic Medical School .... Dr. John M. KAUFFMAN, JR.
35 Dean of Students .... Dr. Sherry L. HAEHL
51 Director Continuing Education .... Vacant
06 Registrar .... Mr. David MCGIRT
21 Assistant Treasurer .... Mr. Win QUAKENBUSH
29 Director of Alumni Relations .... Rev. Doug JONES
89 Director of Freshman Experience .... Dr. Jennifer A. LATINO
08 Dean of Library .... Mrs. Borree KWOK
37 Director of Financial Aid .... Mrs. Michelle DAY
14 Director of Computing Services .... Mr. Chris BUCKLEY
26 Director of Public Information .... Ms. Haven HOTTEL
15 Human Resources Director .... Mr. Bob COGSWELL
18 Chief Facilities/Physical Plant .... Mr. David MARTIN
38 Director Student Counseling .... Mrs. Laura RICH
96 Director of Purchasing .... Mr. James NOWELL
92 Director of Honors Program .... Dr. Ann ORTIZ
09 Director of Institutional Research .... Dr. Timothy D. METZ
56 Dean Extended Programs .... Dr. John ROBERSON

Carolina Christian College (A)

PO Box 777, Winston-Salem NC 27102

County: Forsyth — FICE Identification: 035703
Unit ID: 199971
Telephone: (336) 744-0900 — Carnegie Class: Spec/Faith
FAX Number: (336) 744-0901 — Calendar System: Semester
URL: www.carolina.edu
Established: 1945 — Annual Undergrad Tuition & Fees: $8,350
Enrollment: 74 — Coed
Affiliation or Control: Independent Non-Profit — IRS Status: 501(c)3
Highest Offering: Master's
Program: Liberal Arts And General; Religious Emphasis
Accreditation: BI

01 President .... Dr. Donald R. YOUNG
05 Academic Dean .... Ms. LaTanya V. LUCAS
32 Dean of Students .... Vacant
08 Library Director .... Ms. Laura RHODEN
37 Financial Aid Director .... Vacant

Carolina College of Biblical Studies (B)

817 S. McPherson Church Road, Fayetteville NC 28303

County: Cumberland — FICE Identification: 041542
Unit ID: 461032
Telephone: (910) 323-5614 — Carnegie Class: Not Classified
FAX Number: (910) 323-0425 — Calendar System: Quarter
URL: www.ccbs.edu
Established: 1973 — Annual Undergrad Tuition & Fees: $5,500
Enrollment: 120 — Coed
Affiliation or Control: Non-denominational — IRS Status: 501(c)3
Highest Offering: Baccalaureate
Program: Religious Emphasis
Accreditation: BI

01 President .... Dr. Bill KORVER
05 Academic Dean .... Dr. Harry GHEE
30 Vice Pres Strategic Development .... Dr. Bill BOYD
06 Registrar .... Ms. Kathy SCHULTINGKEMPER
07 Director of Admissions .... Ms. Marcia KORVER

Carolina Graduate School of Divinity (C)

2400 Old Chapman St., Greensboro NC 27403

County: Guilford — FICE Identification: 039395
Telephone: (336) 315-8660 — Carnegie Class: Not Classified
FAX Number: (336) 315-8660 — Calendar System: Semester
URL: www.carolinagrad.edu
Established: 2003 — Annual Graduate Tuition & Fees: $11,000
Enrollment: 54 — Coed
Affiliation or Control: Interdenominational — IRS Status: 501(c)3
Highest Offering: Doctorate; No Undergraduates
Program: Professional; Religious Emphasis
Accreditation: THEOL

01 President .... Dr. Frank P. SCURRY
05 Vice President for Academics .... Dr. Terry W. EDDINGER
32 Director of Student Life .... Dr. Darryl A. BODIE
06 Director of Student Records .... Mrs. Cindy H. BODIE
37 Director of Financial Aid .... Ms. Shirley P. CARTER
10 Business Manager .... Mrs. Rosalie CARR

Carolinas College of Health Sciences (D)

1200 Blythe Boulevard, Charlotte NC 28203

County: Mecklenburg — FICE Identification: 031042
Unit ID: 433174
Telephone: (704) 355-5043 — Carnegie Class: Assoc/Pub-Spec
FAX Number: (704) 355-5967 — Calendar System: Semester
URL: www.CarolinasCollege.edu
Established: 1990 — Annual Undergrad Tuition & Fees (In-District): $14,766
Enrollment: 445 — Coed
Affiliation or Control: State/Local — IRS Status: 501(c)3
Highest Offering: Associate Degree
Program: 2-Year Principally Bachelor's Creditable
Accreditation: SC, ADNUR, MT, PHLEB, RAD, SURGT

01 President .... Dr. Ellen SHEPPARD
05 Provost .... Dr. Janice TERRELL
10 Dean of Business/Finance/Technology .... Ms. Kim BRADSHAW
32 Dean Student Svcs/Enrollment Mgmt .... Dr. T. Hampton HOPKINS
66 Dean of Nursing .... Dr. Deborah BLACKWELL
97 Dean Assessment/General Studies .... Dr. Lori BEQUETTE
76 Director Surgical Technology .... Ms. Kali SIMIEN
76 Director Radiologic Technology .... Mr. Doug FRANKENBURG
76 Director Radiation Therapy .... Mr. Lee BRASWELL
76 Director Clincial Lab Sciences .... Ms. Kelly SHIRLEY
06 Registrar .... Ms. Sue ROUX
07 Admissions Coordinator .... Ms. Rhoda RILLORTA
37 Financial Aid Coordinator .... Ms. Jill POWELL
29 Director Alumni Relations .... Ms. Ruthie MIHAL
90 Instructional Tech Coordinator .... Mr. Larry TURNER
26 Chief Public Relations Officer .... Mr. Kevin MCCARTHY
36 Director Student Placement .... Ms. Nancy WATKINS
51 Director Continuing Education .... Ms. Susan THOMASSON
09 Director of Institutional Research .... Dr. Lori BEQUETTE
18 Chief Facilities/Physical Plant .... Ms. Kim BRADSHAW
30 Chief Development .... Dr. Ellen SHEPPARD

Catawba College (E)

2300 W Innes Street, Salisbury NC 28144-2488

County: Rowan — FICE Identification: 002914
Unit ID: 198215
Telephone: (704) 637-4111 — Carnegie Class: Bac/Diverse
FAX Number: (704) 637-4444 — Calendar System: Semester
URL: www.catawba.edu
Established: 1851 — Annual Undergrad Tuition & Fees: $26,820
Enrollment: 1,293 — Coed
Affiliation or Control: United Church Of Christ — IRS Status: 501(c)3
Highest Offering: Master's
Program: Liberal Arts And General; Teacher Preparatory
Accreditation: SC, TED

01 President .... Mr. Brien LEWIS
03 Senior Vice President/Chaplain .... Dr. Kenneth W. CLAPP
05 Acting Provost .... Dr. Michael BITZER
30 Vice President of Development .... Mr. Rex OTEY
84 Vice Pres of Enrollment Management .... Ms. Lois H. WILLIAMS
04 Assistant to President .... Mrs. Amy H. WILLIAMS
09 Assoc Provost/Dir Instl Research .... Dr. Steven J. COGGIN
10 Chief Financial Officer .... Mr. Charles F. WILLIAMS
15 Chief Human Resources Officer .... Mr. Larry G. FARMER
26 Chief Public Relations Officer .... Mrs. Tonia BLACK-GOLD
32 Dean of Students .... Mr. G. Ben SMITH
39 Associate Dean of Residence Life .... Ms. Kara OSTLUND
08 Head Librarian .... Dr. Steve MCKINZIE
06 Registrar .... Ms. Carol GAMBLE
07 Sr Director of Admissions .... Ms. Elaine P. HOLDEN
37 Director of Financial Assistance .... Ms. Dawn SNOOK
36 Director of Placement .... Ms. Robin PERRY
88 Director Sports Info & Promotion .... Mr. Jim D. LEWIS
40 Director Bookstore .... Mrs. Stephanie TAYLOR
41 Athletic Director .... Mr. Dennis W. DAVIDSON
18 Chief Facilities/Physical Plant .... Mr. Eric NIANOURIS
29 Director Alumni Relations .... Ms. Margaret FAUST
38 Director Student Counseling .... Dr. Nancy ZIMMERMAN

Charlotte School of Law (F)

2145 Suttle Avenue, Charlotte NC 28208

County: Mecklenburg — FICE Identification: 041435
Unit ID: 455169
Telephone: (704) 971-8500 — Carnegie Class: Spec/Law
FAX Number: (704) 971-8599 — Calendar System: Semester
URL: www.charlottelaw.edu
Established: 2008 — Annual Graduate Tuition & Fees: $40,146
Enrollment: 1,169 — Coed
Affiliation or Control: Proprietary — IRS Status: Proprietary
Highest Offering: First Professional Degree; No Undergraduates
Program: Professional
Accreditation: LAW

01 President .... Mr. Don LIVELY
07 Associate Dean of Admissions .... Vacant
15 Director of Human Resources .... Ms. Deidra HARRIS-LUMPKINS
30 Dir of Institutional Advancement .... Mr. Harry WORKMAN
13 Director of Information Technology .... Mr. Clark MACIAG
05 Dean .... Mr. Jay CONISON
20 Interim Assoc Dean for Academics .... Mr. Daniel PIAR
36 Director of Center for Prof Dev .... Ms. Aretha BLAKE
08 Associate Dean for Library Services .... Vacant
32 Assistant Dean of Students .... Mr. Michael FARLEY
10 Vice Pres of Business and Finance .... Vacant
21 Assistant Dir of Fiscal Affairs .... Ms. Tamika JACKSON
37 Assistant Director of Financial Aid .... Mr. Anthony PIZZUTI
06 Dir of Academic Svcs/Registration .... Ms. Traci FLEURY
18 Facilities Manager .... Mr. Jay BEAM
19 Director of Security .... Mr. William HARPER

The Chef's Academy (G)

2001 Carrington Mill Boulevard, Morrisville NC 27560

Telephone: (919) 246-9394 — Identification: 770101
Accreditation: &@NH, ACICS

† Main campus is Harrison College - Indianapolis Downtown Campus in Indianapolis, IN.

Chowan University (H)

One University Place, Murfreesboro NC 27855-1844

County: Hertford — FICE Identification: 002916
Unit ID: 198303
Telephone: (252) 398-6500 — Carnegie Class: Bac/Diverse
FAX Number: (252) 398-1190 — Calendar System: Semester
URL: www.chowan.edu
Established: 1848 — Annual Undergrad Tuition & Fees: $27,000
Enrollment: 1,340 — Coed
Affiliation or Control: Baptist — IRS Status: 501(c)3
Highest Offering: Master's
Program: Liberal Arts And General
Accreditation: SC, MUS, TED

01 President .... Dr. M. Chrisopher WHITE
05 Vice President Academic Affairs .... Dr. Danny B. MOORE
10 Vice President Business Affairs .... Mr. Donnie O. CLARY
32 Vice President Student Affairs .... Mr. P. Randy HARRELL
30 Vice President Advancement .... Mr. John TAYLOE
15 Vice President Human Resources .... Mr. John A. HINTON
07 Vice President Admissions .... Mr. Craig JANNEY
13 Exec Dir Info Tech/Network Svcs .... Mr. James R. HOWELL
06 Registrar .... Ms. Donna ROBBINS
26 Director of Public Relations .... Mr. Joshua BARKER
08 Head Librarian .... Mrs. Georgia E. WILLIAMS
37 Director of Financial Aid .... Mrs. Sharon ROSE
42 Campus Minister .... Ms. Mari E. WILES
18 Director Physical Plant .... Mr. Bob ROWE
19 Chief of Security .... Mr. Derek A. BURKE
35 Director Student Life .... Ms. Laurica YANCEY
38 Director Counseling/Career Services .... Mrs. Frances E. COLE
39 Director Housing & Residence Life .... Mr. Brandon ZOCH
41 Athletics Director .... Mr. Dennis HELSEL
09 Director Institutional Research .... Mr. Daniel MCCAMISH
88 Director Upward Bound .... Mr. E. Frank STEPHENSON
21 Director Business Services .... Mrs. Julie W. EMORY
29 Director Alumni Services .... Mrs. Kay M. THOMAS
49 Dean Liberal Arts .... Dr. John DILUSTRO
50 Dean Business .... Dr. Linda MILES
53 Dean Education .... Dr. Brenda S. TINKHAM
40 Bookstore Manager .... Vacant

Daoist Traditions College of Chinese Medical Arts (I)

382 Montford Ave, Asheville NC 28801

County: Buncombe — FICE Identification: 041464
Unit ID: 455178
Telephone: (828) 225-3993 — Carnegie Class: Not Classified
FAX Number: (828) 255-3306 — Calendar System: Semester
URL: www.daoisttraditions.edu
Established: 2003 — Annual Graduate Tuition & Fees: $15,750
Enrollment: 77 — Coed
Affiliation or Control: Proprietary — IRS Status: Proprietary
Highest Offering: Master's; No Undergraduates
Program: Professional
Accreditation: ACUP

01 President .... Dr. Mary Cissy MAJEBE

Davidson College (J)

PO Box 5000, Davidson NC 28035-5000

County: Mecklenburg — FICE Identification: 002918
Unit ID: 198385
Telephone: (704) 894-2000 — Carnegie Class: Bac/A&S
FAX Number: (704) 894-2005 — Calendar System: Semester
URL: www.davidson.edu
Established: 1837 — Annual Undergrad Tuition & Fees: $42,849
Enrollment: 1,790 — Coed
Affiliation or Control: Presbyterian Church (U.S.A.) — IRS Status: 501(c)3
Highest Offering: Baccalaureate
Program: Liberal Arts And General
Accreditation: SC

01 President .... Dr. Carol E. QUILLEN
05 Vice Pres Acad Affs/Dean of Faculty .... Dr. Wendy E. RAYMOND
26 Vice President College Relations .... Ms. Eileen M. KEELEY
10 Vice Pres Finance & Administration .... Mr. Edward A. KANIA
32 VP Student Life/Dean of Students .... Dr. Thomas C. SHANDLEY
07 VP & Dean Admissions/Financial Aid .... Mr. Christopher J. GRUBER
09 VP Planning/Institutional Research .... Ms. Linda M. LEFAUVE

27 Assoc VP Comm/Tech/Operations .... Ms. Cat S. NIEKRO
20 Assoc Dean Academic Administration .... Ms. Leslie M. MARSICANO
20 Assoc Dean for Curriculum .... Dr. Patrick J. SELLERS
20 Assoc Dean Teaching/Lrng/Rsrch .... Dr. Verna M. CASE
06 Registrar .... Ms. Angela B. DEWBERRY
13 Exec Director Information Tecnology .... Mr. Mur K. MUCHANE
37 Director Financial Aid .... Mr. David GELINAS
15 Director of Human Resources .... Dr. Kim BALL
41 Director of Athletics .... Mr. James E. MURPHY, III
08 Director of the Library .... Ms. Gillian (Jill) S. GREMMELS
29 Director Alumni Relations .... Ms. Marya L. HOWELL
21 Controller/Director Business Svcs .... Ms. Lori GASTON
18 Director Facilities & Engineering ...... Mr. David M. HOLTHOUSER
19 Director of Public Safety & Police .... Vacant
36 Director Career Services .... Mr. Nathan J. ELTON
35 Director of College Union .... Mr. William H. BROWN
39 Dir Resid Life/Assoc Dean Students .... Mr. Jason S. SHAFFER
42 College Chaplain .... Dr. Robert C. SPACH
71 Dir Cntr for Interdisciplinary Stds .... Dr. Peter M. KRENTZ
82 Assoc Dean Int'l Programs/ Studies .... Dr. M. Christopher ALEXANDER
25 Director of Grants & Contracts .... Dr. Mary W. MUCHANE
24 Director Instructional Support .... Ms. Diane S. STIRLING
38 Director Student Counseling Center .... Dr. Trish MURRAY
44 Director of Annual Fund .... Ms. Maria ALDRICH
96 Director of Purchasing .... Ms. Elizabeth S. CHRISTENBURY
40 Bookstore Manager .... Ms. Gwendolyn S. GARDNER

Duke University (A)

Durham NC 27706-8001
County: Durham FICE Identification: 002920
Unit ID: 198419
Telephone: (919) 684-8111 Carnegie Class: RU/VH
FAX Number: (919) 684-3200 Calendar System: Semester
URL: www.duke.edu
Established: 1838 Annual Undergrad Tuition & Fees: $45,376
Enrollment: 15,172 Coed
Affiliation or Control: Independent Non-Profit IRS Status: 501(c)3
Highest Offering: Doctorate
Program: Liberal Arts And General; Teacher Preparatory; Professional
Accreditation: SC, ANEST, ARCPA, BUS, CLPSY, ENG, FOR, IPSY, LAW, MED, NURSE, PA, PTA, TED, THEOL

01 President .... Richard H. BRODHEAD
05 Provost .... Peter LANGE
11 Exec Vice Pres for Administration .... Tallman TRASK, III
26 Vice President Public Affairs .... Michael J. SCHOENFELD
45 President/Duke Management Company .... Neal TRIPLETT
30 Vice Pres Alumni Affs/Development .... Robert S. SHEPARD
23 VP Admin Duke Univ Health Systems .... Monte BROWN
32 Vice President for Student Affairs .... Larry MONETA
22 Vice Pres for Institutional Equity .... Benjamin D. REESE
10 Vice President Financial Services .... Timothy WALSH
17 Chief Exec Officer Duke Univ Hosp .. William J. FULKERSON, JR.
88 Vice Pres - Chief Medical Officer .... Karen FRUSH
15 Vice President for Administration .... Kyle CAVANAUGH
41 Vice Pres & Director of Athletics .... Kevin WHITE
101 Vice Pres & University Secretary .... Richard RIDDELL
17 Chancellor for Health Affairs .... Victor DZAU
30 VP Duke Med Devel/Alumni Affairs .... Ellen MEDEARIS
72 Vice Chanc Science & Technology .... Vacant
31 Assoc VP Community Affairs DUHS .... Maryann BLACK
35 Asst VP Student Affs/Dean Students .... Sue WASIOLEK
19 Assoc VP Campus Safety and Security .... Aaron GRAVES
07 Dean Undergraduate Admissions .... Christoph O. GUTTENTAG
21 Exec Vice Provost Finance & Admin .... James S. ROBERTS
13 Vice Prov Information Technology .... Tracy FUTHEY
88 Vice Provost Interdisciplin Studies .... Susan ROTH
20 Vice Provost for Academic Affairs .... Keith WHITFIELD
88 Director Intl Area Studies .... Gilbert MERKX
88 Vice Prov Faculty Diversity & Dev .... Nancy ALLEN
88 Vice Provost for the Arts .... Scott A. LINDTORTH
46 Vice Provost for Research .... James N. SIEDOW
29 Executive Director Alumni Affairs .... Sterly WILDER
36 Executive Director Career Devel Ctr .... William WRIGHT-SWADEL
21 Exec Director of Internal Audits .... Michael L. SOMICH
23 Exec Dir Student Health Service .... John VAUGHN
38 Exec Director of Student Counseling .... Kelly CRACE
06 Registrar .... Bruce W. CUNNINGHAM
08 Librarian/Vice Prov Library Affairs .... Deborah JAKUBS
43 University Counsel .... Pamela BERNARD
09 Director of Institutional Research .... David JAMIESON-DRAKE
37 Asst Vice Provost/Dir Financial Aid .... Alison RABIL
87 Director of Summer Session .... Paula E. GILBERT
61 Dean of Law School .... David F. LEVI
63 Dn Sch Med/Sr Vice Chanc Acad Affs .... Nancy ANDREWS
50 Dean Fuqua School of Business .... William BOULDING
65 Dean School of the Environment .... William L. CHAMEIDES
73 Dean of the Divinity School .... Richard HAYS
58 Dean Grad School/Vice Prov Grad Ed .... Paula D. MCCLAIN
49 Dean Faculty Arts/Science .... Laurie PATTON
88 Dean of the Natural Sciences .... Dan KIEHART
49 Dean Acad Affs Trinity Col Arts/Sci .... Lee D. BAKER
66 Dean School of Nursing .... Catherine GILLISS
54 Dean of Engineering .... Thomas KATSOULEAS
83 Dean of the Humanities .... Srinivas ARAVAMUDAN
83 Dean of the Social Sciences .... Angela M. O'RAND
53 Dean and Vice Provost Undergrad Ed .... Stephen NOWICKI
94 Director of Women's Studies .... Ranjana KHANNA
93 Director Ofc of Intercultural Affs .... Li-Chen CHIN
88 Director Duke University Press .... Stephen A. COHN

18 Vice President for Facilities .... John NOONAN
27 Chief Info Ofcr/Vice Pres Duke Med .... Jeffrey FERRANTI
88 Vice Chanc for Clinical Research .... Robert M. CALIFF
88 Chief Med Ofcr .... Thomas OWENS
88 Exec Vice Dean Admin Sch Med .... Scott GIBSON
88 Vice Pres/Vice Prov Global Strategy .... Michael H. MERSON
88 Vice Chanc Corp and Venture Devel .... Robert L. TABER
45 VP Bus Devel & Chf Strat Plng Ofcr .... Molly O'NEILL

Elon University (B)

2700 Campus Box, Elon NC 27244-2010
County: Alamance FICE Identification: 002927
Unit ID: 198516
Telephone: (336) 278-2000 Carnegie Class: Master's S
FAX Number: N/A Calendar System: 4/1/4
URL: www.elon.edu
Established: 1889 Annual Undergrad Tuition & Fees: $30,149
Enrollment: 6,029 Coed
Affiliation or Control: Independent Non-Profit IRS Status: 501(c)3
Highest Offering: Doctorate
Program: Liberal Arts And General; Teacher Preparatory; Professional
Accreditation: SC, #ARCPA, BUS, JOUR, LAW, PTA, TED

01 President .... Dr. Leo M. LAMBERT
03 Executive Vice President .... Dr. Gerald L. FRANCIS
100 Chief of Staff/Sec to the Board .... Mr. Jeff STEIN
05 Provost/Vice Pres Academic Affairs .... Dr. Steven D. HOUSE
07 VP of Admissions/Financial Planning .... Mr. Greg ZAISER
10 Senior VP for Business/Finance/ Tech .... Mr. Gerald O. WHITTINGTON
30 Vice Pres Institutional Advancement .... Mr. James B. PIATT
32 Vice Pres/Dean of Student Life .... Dr. G. Smith JACKSON
27 Vice Pres University Communications ... Mr. Daniel J. ANDERSON
20 Associate VP of Academic Affairs .... Dr. Mary B. WISE
20 Associate Provost for Academic Affs .... Dr. Connie BOOK
88 Associate Provost for Faculty Affs .... Dr. Tim PEEPLES
21 Asst VP for Finance .... Ms. Susan M. KIRKLAND
49 Dean College of Arts & Sci ..... Dr. Alison MORRISON-SHETLAR
50 Dean Love School of Business .... Dr. Raghu TADEPALLI
60 Dean of School of Communications .... Dr. Paul F. PARSONS
53 Interim Dean of School of Education .... Dr. Deborah LONG
61 Dean of School of Law .... Mr. George JOHNSON
76 Dean of School of Health Sciences .... Dr. Elizabeth A. ROGERS
85 Dean of International Programs .... Mr. Woody PELTON
35 Assistant VP of Student Life .... Mrs. Jana Lynn F. PATTERSON
08 Dean and University Librarian .... Ms. Joan RUELLE
41 Director of Athletics .... Mr. Dave L. BLANK
06 Registrar .... Dr. Rodney PARKS
42 University Chaplain .... Dr. Janet FULLER
37 Director of Financial Planning .... Dr. M. Patrick MURPHY
29 Interim Dir of Alumni Engagement .... Mr. Tait AREND
88 Assoc Dean of Academic Support .... Dr. Becky OLIVE-TAYLOR
36 Exec Director of Career Services .... Dr. Tom VECCHIONE
88 Dir of Planning/Design/Construction .... Mr. Brad D. MOORE
18 Director of Physical Plant .... Mr. Robert BUCHHOLZ
15 Director of Human Resources .... Mr. Ronald A. KLEPCYK
31 Director of Auxiliary Services .... Ms. Vickie L. SOMERS
19 Director of Campus Safety & Police .... Mr. Dennis FRANKS
23 Director of Health Services .... Dr. Ginette ARCHINAL
38 Director Counseling Services .... Mr. Bruce F. NELSON
27 Assistant VP of Technology/CIO . Mr. Christopher D. FULKERSON
09 Exec Director Institutional Rsch .... Dr. Robert I. SPRINGER
13 Assistant CIO .... Mr. Christopher C. WATERS
25 Director of Sponsored Programs .... Ms. Bonnie BRUNO
93 Interim Dir of Multicultural Ctr .... Ms. Melissa JORDAN
92 Director of Honors Program .... Dr. Maureen VANDERMAAS-PEELER
94 Director Women's Stds/Gender Stds .... Dr. Mandy GALLAGHER
96 Director of Purchasing .... Mr. Jeff HENDRICKS
88 Sustainability Coordinator .... Ms. Elaine DURR

Gardner-Webb University (C)

PO Box 897 (110 South Main Street), Boiling Springs NC 28017-0897
County: Cleveland FICE Identification: 002929
Unit ID: 198561
Telephone: (704) 406-2361 Carnegie Class: Master's L
FAX Number: (704) 406-4329 Calendar System: Semester
URL: www.gardner-webb.edu
Established: 1905 Annual Undergrad Tuition & Fees: $25,440
Enrollment: 4,941 Coed
Affiliation or Control: Baptist IRS Status: 501(c)3
Highest Offering: Doctorate
Program: 2-Year Principally Bachelor's Creditable; Liberal Arts And General; Teacher Preparatory; Professional
Accreditation: SC, ACBSP, ADNUR, CACREP, MUS, NUR, TED, THEOL

01 President .... Dr. A. Frank BONNER
05 Provost & Senior Vice President .... Dr. Benjamin C. LESLIE
04 Sr Assistant to the President .... Mrs. Glenda S. CROTTS
10 Vice President for Business/Finance .... Mr. Mike W. HARDIN
26 Sr VP University Rels Marketing .... Mr. Ralph W. DIXON, JR.
30 Vice President for Advancement .... Mr. Monte WALKER
32 Vice Pres/Dean Student Development .... Dr. Delores HUNT
84 Vice Pres Enrollment Management .... Mrs. Debra HINTZ
41 Vice President for Athletics .... Mr. Chuck S. BURCH
09 VP Distance Learning/Inst Research .... Dr. Jeffrey L. TUBBS
18 Assoc Vice Pres for Operations .... Mr. Wayne E. JOHNSON
91 Assoc VP for Technology Services .... Mr. Joey BRIDGES
20 Associate Provost for Schools .... Dr. Franki BURCH

49 Assoc Provost for Arts & Sciences .... Dr. Earl LEININGER
21 Asst Vice President Business .... Mr. Jeff S. INGLE
51 Asst Provost for Distance Learning .... Dr. Bobbie COX
07 Dir of Undergraduate Admissions .... Ms. Kristen SETZER
37 Director of Financial Planning .... Ms. Summer ROBERTSON
06 Registrar .... Mrs. LouAnn P. SCATES
35 Director of Academic Advising .... Dr. Doug BRYAN
19 Chief of University Police .... Mr. Barry JOHNSON
27 Dir of University & Media Relations .... Mr. Noel T. MANNING
08 Director of the Library .... Ms. Mary ROBY
38 Dir of Counseling & Career Svcs .... Ms. Cindy WALLACE
89 Director of Freshmen Programs .... Ms. Jessica HERRNDON
58 Dean of Graduate School .... Dr. Jeffrey ROGERS
73 Dean of Divinity School .... Dr. Robert W. CANOY
66 Dean of Nursing School .... Dr. Rebecca BECK-LITTLE
50 Director of School Management .... Dr. Sue C. CAMP
92 Director of Honors Program .... Dr. Thomas H. JONES
88 Director Program for Blind/Deaf .... Mrs. Cheryl J. POTTER
21 Comptroller .... Mrs. Robin G. HAMRICK
35 Director Student Activities .... Ms. Karissa L. WEIR
42 Minister to the University .... Dr. Tracy C. JESSUP
39 Director of Residence Life .... Ms. Sherry INGRAM
50 Dean of Business School .... Dr. Anthony I. NEGBENEBOR
15 Director Human Resources .... Mr. W. Scott WHITE
09 Director of Institutional Research .... Mr. Garry MCSWAIN
29 Director Alumni Relations .... Ms. Dena SPANGLER
44 Director of Annual Campaign .... Ms. Sara MCCALL
24 Asst Dir University Media Relations .... Ms. Kathy MARTIN
40 Bookstore Manager .... Ms. Cary CALDWELL
96 Director of Operations Support .... Mr. Brian SPEER

Grace College of Divinity (D)

5117 Cliffdale Road, Fayetteville NC 28314
County: Cumberland FICE Identification: 041737
Unit ID: 461528
Telephone: (910) 221-2224 Carnegie Class: Not Classified
FAX Number: (910) 221-2226 Calendar System: Semester
URL: www.gcd.edu
Established: 2000 Annual Undergrad Tuition & Fees: $3,570
Enrollment: 144 Coed
Affiliation or Control: Other Protestant IRS Status: 501(c)3
Highest Offering: Baccalaureate
Program: Religious Emphasis
Accreditation: BI

01 President .... Dr. Steven CROWTHER
11 Vice President of Administration .... Mrs. Michelle GARAYUA
05 Academic Dean .... Mr. David CHOI
84 Dean of Enrollment Management .... Mr. Jason CROWTHER
32 Dean of Students .... Mrs. Stefanie ERTEL
106 Dean of Online Education/E-Learning .... Mr. Tom JOHNSON
10 Chief Financial Officer .... Ms. Omayra COON
08 Librarian .... Mr. David ASPINALL
108 Director of Assessment & Planning .... Ms. Sharyn J. TEAGUE
06 Registrar .... Ms. Shaila BERMUDEZ

Greensboro College (E)

815 W Market Street, Greensboro NC 27401-1875
County: Guilford FICE Identification: 002930
Unit ID: 198598
Telephone: (336) 272-7102 Carnegie Class: Bac/Diverse
FAX Number: (336) 217-6634 Calendar System: Semester
URL: www.greensboro.edu
Established: 1838 Annual Undergrad Tuition & Fees: $25,806
Enrollment: 1,200 Coed
Affiliation or Control: United Methodist IRS Status: 501(c)3
Highest Offering: Master's
Program: Liberal Arts And General; Teacher Preparatory
Accreditation: #SC, ACBSP, MUS, TED

01 President .... Dr. Lawrence D. CZARDA
10 VP for Finance .... Mr. David MCCONNELL
05 VP Academic Affairs/Dean of Faculty .... Dr. Paul L. LESLIE
11 Vice President for Operations .... Dr. Robin L. DANIEL
30 VP Inst Advancement .... Ms. Joan M. GLYNN
21 Assoc Vice President for Finance .... Mr. Chris ELMORE
20 Asst Vice President Academic Admin .... Mrs. Martha M. BUNCH
07 Director of Admissions .... Ms. Julianne SCHATZ
13 Director for IT and Network Systems .... Mr. Joshua AYLOR
37 Dir of Financial Planning Services .... Ms. Annette ORBERT
27 Dir of External Communications .... Mr. Lex ALEXANDER
06 Registrar .... Ms. Phyllis P. CHAMBERS
35 Dean of Students .... Mr. Matthew LONG
36 Director Career Exploration & Dev .... Mr. Brent ATWATER
09 Director Institutional Rsrch & SIS .... Ms. Phyllis P. CHAMBERS
88 Director Academic Success Program .... Ms. Tica D. GREEN
15 Director of Human Resources .... Ms. Sonia HOFFMAN
18 Director of Facilities .... Mr. John LANGSDORF
19 Director of Campus Security .... Mr. Calvin L. GILMORE
23 Director of Student Health .... Ms. Lauren T. CHILDREY
53 Director of Teacher Education .... Dr. Rebecca BLOMGREN
38 Director of Counseling Services .... Vacant
92 Dir George Ctr/Honors Stds .... Dr. Jessica G. SHARPE
44 Dir of Annual Giving/Alumni Engage .... Ms. Kristen C. BROWN
08 Director of Library Services .... Ms. Christine A. WHITTINGTON
41 Athletic Director .... Mr. John P. TRICE
42 Campus Chaplin .... Rev. Robert W. BREWER
40 Bookstore Manager .... Mr. Cliff BRALY, JR.

Guilford College (A)

5800 W Friendly Avenue, Greensboro NC 27410-4173
County: Guilford FICE Identification: 002931
Unit ID: 198613
Telephone: (336) 316-2000 Carnegie Class: Bac/A&S
FAX Number: (336) 316-2950 Calendar System: Semester
URL: www.guilford.edu
Established: 1837 Annual Undergrad Tuition & Fees: $32,470
Enrollment: 2,462 Coed
Affiliation or Control: Friends IRS Status: 501(c)3
Highest Offering: Baccalaureate
Program: Liberal Arts And General; Teacher Preparatory
Accreditation: SC

01 President ... Dr. Kent J. CHABOTAR
05 Vice President & Academic Dean ... Dr. Adrienne M. ISRAEL
04 Executive Assoc to the President ... Mrs. Joyce A. EATON
45 Asst to President for Planning/Mgt ... Mr. Jeff E. FAVOLISE
11 Vice President Administration ... Mr. Jonathan P. VARNELL
10 Vice President Finance ... Mr. Gregory F. BURSAVICH
30 Vice Pres Institutional Advancement ... Mr. Michael J. POSTON
32 Vice President Student Affairs ... Mr. Aaron L. FETROW
26 Assoc VP Communications & Marketing ... Mr. R. Ty BUCKNER
29 Assoc Vice Pres Alumni Relations ... Mr. Jerry W. HARRELSON
21 Associate Vice President Finance ... Mr. James WILSON
51 Assoc VP/Dean Continuing Education ... Dr. Rita S. SEROTKIN
07 Dean of Admission & Financial Aid ... Mr. Andy STRICKLER
31 Asst Dean of Career/Community Lrng ... Mr. Alan C. MUELLER
20 Assistant Academic Dean ... Ms. Erin B. DELL
20 Assistant Academic Dean ... Dr. Barbara G. BOYETTE
37 Director Student Financial Svcs ... Mr. Paul COSCIA
06 Registrar ... Mrs. Norma L. MIDDLETON
08 Director of the Library ... Ms. Suzanne BARTELS
41 Director of Athletics ... Mr. Tom J. PALOMBO
19 Director of Public Safety ... Mr. Ron M. STOWE
15 Director Human Resources ... Mr. John SANDERS
09 Dir Institutional Research/Assess ... Dr. Owen Kent GRUMBLES
90 Director Info Technology & Services ... Mr. Craig GRAY
42 Campus Ministry Coordinator ... Rev. Max L. CARTER
87 Director of Summer School ... Dr. Rita S. SEROTKIN
38 Director Student Counseling ... Ms. Gaither M. TERRELL
28 Director Multicultural Education ... Vacant
92 Director Honors Program ... Dr. Heather HAYTON
89 Director of First Year Program ... Dr. William PIZIO
96 Director of Purchasing ... Ms. Tracy A. HALL
104 Director Study Abroad ... Dr. Jack ZERBE

Heritage Bible College (B)

PO Box 1628, Dunn NC 28335-1628
County: Harnett FICE Identification: 030893
Unit ID: 198677
Telephone: (910) 892-3178 Carnegie Class: Spec/Faith
FAX Number: (910) 891-1809 Calendar System: Semester
URL: www.heritagebiblecollege.edu
Established: 1971 Annual Undergrad Tuition & Fees: $9,470
Enrollment: 70 Coed
Affiliation or Control: Other IRS Status: 501(c)3
Highest Offering: Baccalaureate
Program: Occupational; 2-Year Principally Bachelor's Creditable; Religious Emphasis
Accreditation: TRACS

01 President ... Dr. Elvin BUTTS
05 Academic Dean ... Mr. Stephen RZONCA
32 Dean Student Services ... Mr. Randy BARKER
06 Registrar ... Ms. Traci NEWTON
07 Admissions ... Ms. Peggy PARKER
08 Librarian ... Ms. Janet PARKER
10 Business Administrator ... Ms. Sandra FRAZIER
37 Director Financial Aid ... Ms. Traci NEWTON
09 Director of Inst Effectiveness ... Ms. Chrissy KRIEGBAUM
29 Director Alumni Relations ... Ms. Traci NEWTON
30 Director of Advancement ... Vacant

High Point University (C)

833 Montlieu Avenue, High Point NC 27262-3598
County: Guilford FICE Identification: 002933
Unit ID: 198695
Telephone: (336) 841-9000 Carnegie Class: Bac/Diverse
FAX Number: (336) 841-4599 Calendar System: Semester
URL: www.highpoint.edu
Established: 1924 Annual Undergrad Tuition & Fees: $41,600
Enrollment: 4,263 Coed
Affiliation or Control: United Methodist IRS Status: 501(c)3
Highest Offering: Doctorate
Program: Liberal Arts And General; Teacher Preparatory; Professional
Accreditation: SC, CIDA, TED

01 President ... Dr. Nido R. QUBEIN
05 Provost ... Dr. Dennis G. CARROLL
03 Executive Vice President ... Dr. Denny G. BOLTON
13 VP of Strategic Business Planning ... Mr. Wellington O. DESOUZA
31 VP of Community Relations ... Dr. Donald A. SCARBOROUGH
100 VP and Chief of Staff ... Mr. Christopher H. DUDLEY
32 VP of Student Life ... Mrs. Gail C. TUTTLE
84 VP of Enrollment ... Mr. Andy BILLS
27 VP of Communications ... Mr. Roger D. CLODFELTER, JR.
41 Director of Athletics ... Mr. Craig D. KEILITZ
88 Assoc VP of Inst Effectiveness ... Dr. Alberta H. HERRON
88 Asst VP of Inst Effectiveness ... Dr. Jeffrey M. ADAMS
49 Dean of College of Arts & Science ... Dr. Carole B. STONEKING
76 Dean of School of Health Sciences ... Dr. Daniel E. ERB
67 Dean of School of Pharmacy ... Dr. Ronald E. RAGAN
57 Dean of School of Art and Design ... Dr. John C. TURPIN
50 Dean of School of Business ... Dr. James B. WEHRLEY
53 Dean of School of Education ... Dr. Mariann W. TILLERY
35 Dean of Students ... Mr. Paul KITTLE
58 Assoc Dean of Graduate Admissions ... Mrs. Tracy L. COLLUM
89 Assoc Dean of Freshman Success ... Dr. Beth HOLDER
20 Assoc Dean Academic Development ... Dr. Allen GOEDEKE
88 Bishop in Residence ... Bishop Thomas B. STOCKTON
23 Medical Director ... Dr. Danielle L. MAHAFFEY
19 Chief of Security ... Mr. Jeff A. KARPOVICH
08 Director of Library Services ... Mr. David L. BRYDEN
06 Interim Registrar ... Ms. Crystal E. CRUTHIS
07 Director of Admissions ... Vacant
29 Director of Alumni Relations ... Ms. Jill E. THOMPSON
10 Chief Financial Officer ... Ms. Debi S. BUTT
37 Dir of Student Financial Planning ... Mr. Ronald ELMORE
88 Director of Sponsored Programs ... Mr. Timothy L. LINKER
15 Director of Human Resources ... Mrs. Kathy S. SMITH
88 Director of Student Accounts ... Mrs. Teresa L. KANE
38 Director of Student Counseling ... Ms. Lynda D. NOFFSINGER
18 Dir of Construction and Renovation ... Mr. Ron GUERRA
18 Director of Facility Operations ... Mr. Stephen L. POTTER
88 Director of Interactive Media ... Ms. Hillary C. KOKAJKO
88 Director of University Events ... Ms. Melissa L. ANDERSON
108 Coordinator of Inst Assessment ... Ms. Andrea KENNEDY
88 Director of Campus Enhancement ... Mr. Troy J. THOMPSON
88 Dir Athletic Facilities/Operations ... Mr. Sam PHIPPS
06 Associate Registrar ... Ms. Ann M. MILLER
40 Manager Bookstore ... Mr. William HOLSTON
85 Director of ESL/International Rells ... Ms. Marjorie R. CHURCH
36 Interim Director of Career Services ... Ms. Bridget HOLCOMBE
104 Director of Study Abroad ... Ms. Heidi FISCHER
88 Director of Service Learning ... Dr. Joseph D. BLOSSER
88 Director of Undergraduate Research ... Dr. Joanne D. ALTMAN
27 Media Relations Coordinator ... Ms. Pamela J. HAYNES
04 Admin Assistant to President ... Ms. Judy K. RAY
88 Manager of University Mail Center ... Mr. Michael R. HALL

Hood Theological Seminary (D)

1810 Lutheran Synod Drive, Salisbury NC 28144-5768
County: Rowan FICE Identification: 036633
Unit ID: 443076
Telephone: (704) 636-7611 Carnegie Class: Spec/Faith
FAX Number: (704) 636-7699 Calendar System: Semester
URL: www.hoodseminary.edu
Established: 1904 Annual Undergrad Tuition & Fees: $13,500
Enrollment: 250 Coed
Affiliation or Control: African Methodist Episcopal Zion Church
IRS Status: 501(c)3
Highest Offering: Doctorate
Program: Professional; Religious Emphasis
Accreditation: THEOL

01 President-Elect ... Dr. Vergel L. LATTIMORE
05 Academic Dean ... Dr. Trevor EPPEHIMER
20 Associate Academic Dean ... Dr. Trevor EPPEHIMER
32 Dean of Students ... Dr. Dora R. MBUWAYESANGO
10 Fiscal Officer ... Dr. Regina M. DANCY
30 Development Officer ... Mrs. Margaret KLUTTZ
06 Registrar ... Ms. Nancy BAKER

ITT Technical Institute (E)

5520 Dillard Drive, Suite 100, Cary NC 27518
Telephone: (919) 233-2520 Identification: 666704
Accreditation: ACICS

† Main campus is ITT Technical Institute in Indianapolis, IN.

ITT Technical Institute (F)

4135 S Stream Boulevard, Suite 200,
Charlotte NC 28217-4555
Telephone: (704) 423-3100 Identification: 666161
Accreditation: ACICS

† Main campus is ITT Technical Institute in Indianapolis, IN.

ITT Technical Institute (G)

10926 David Taylor Drive, Suite 100, Charlotte NC 28262
Telephone: (704) 548-2300 Identification: 666705
Accreditation: ACICS

† Main campus is ITT Technical Institute in Indianapolis, IN.

ITT Technical Institute (H)

3518 Westgate Drive, Suite 150, Durham NC 27707
Telephone: (919) 401-1400 Identification: 770656
Accreditation: ACICS

† Main campus is ITT Technical Institute in Indianapolis, IN.

ITT Technical Institute (I)

4050 Piedmont Parkway, Suite 110, High Point NC 27265
Telephone: (336) 819-5900 Identification: 666703
Accreditation: ACICS

† Main campus is ITT Technical Institute in Indianapolis, IN.

Johnson & Wales University-Charlotte (J)

801 W Trade Street, Charlotte NC 28202-1122
Telephone: (980) 598-1000 Identification: 666375
Accreditation: &EH

† Main campus is Johnson & Wales University in Providence, RI.

Johnson C. Smith University (K)

100 Beatties Ford Road, Charlotte NC 28216-5398
County: Mecklenburg FICE Identification: 002936
Unit ID: 198756
Telephone: (704) 378-1000 Carnegie Class: Bac/A&S
FAX Number: (704) 372-1242 Calendar System: Semester
URL: www.jcsu.edu
Established: 1867 Annual Undergrad Tuition & Fees: $18,236
Enrollment: 1,665 Coed
Affiliation or Control: Independent Non-Profit IRS Status: 501(c)3
Highest Offering: Baccalaureate
Program: Liberal Arts And General
Accreditation: SC, SW

01 President ... Dr. Ronald L. CARTER
03 Exec Vice Pres/Chief Operating Ofcr ... Dr. Elfred A. PINKARD
10 Vice Pres for Finance ... Mr. Greg PETZKE
30 Vice President for Inst Advancement ... Ms. Joy PAIGE
86 VP Government Sponsored Pgms ... Dr. Diane BOWLES
15 Asst VP for Human Resources ... Ms. Latrelle P. MCALLISTER
18 Asst VP for Business Operations ... Mr. Anayo EZEIGBO
30 Asst VP for Institutional Advancmnt ... Ms. Sharon HARRINGTON
05 Council of Deans Chair/Dean of STEM ... Dr. Magdy ATTIA
49 Interim Dean of Arts and Letters ... Dr. Brian JONES
107 Dean of Professional Studies ... Dr. Helen CALDWELL
84 Dean of Enrollment Services ... Ms. Cathy HURD
32 Dean of Student Development ... Mrs. Cathy JONES
51 Dean of Metropolitan College ... Dr. Zenobia EDWARDS
88 Dean of Academic Support Services ... Ms. Kelli RAINEY
08 Director of the Library ... Ms. Monika RHUE
07 Director of Admissions ... Mr. James BURRELL
14 Director Information Technology ... Mr. John NORRIS
31 Dir of App Leadership/Comm Dev ... Ms. Sherill HAMPTON
09 Dir Plng/Assess/Effect/Rsrch ... Mrs. Harriet HOBBS
26 Director of Comm and Marketing ... Ms. Sherri BELFIELD
29 Director Alumni Affairs ... Mr. Ron MATTHEWS
37 Director Financial Aid ... Vacant
38 Director Counseling ... Mr. Frederick MURPHY
19 Director of Campus Police ... Mr. Gregory C. HARRIS
35 Director of Student Activities ... Mr. Aleczander WHITFIELD
41 Athletic Director ... Mr. Stephen JOYNER, SR.
06 Registrar ... Mrs. Keisha WILSON
85 Mgr of Multi/International Stud Aff ... Mr. Rixon CAMPBELL
44 Major Gift Officer ... Mr. Alvin AUSTIN
102 Director Foundations Rel/Priv Grant ... Vacant
102 Director of Corporate Relations ... Ms. Angela MAULDIN
36 Director Career Services ... Mrs. Barbara WILKS
39 Director Residence Life ... Mr. Terry MCPHERSON
40 Manager of Bookstore ... Ms. Robin SORENSEN
96 Purchasing Manager ... Mr. Joe MAJORS
16 Manager Risk Management ... Mrs. Debra HOLLIS
88 Coordinator of Retention ... Ms. Lisa DURHAM
23 Health Center Coordinator ... Ms. Marian JONES

Kaplan College (L)

6070 East Independence Boulevard, Charlotte NC 28212
Telephone: (704) 567-3700 Identification: 770543
Accreditation: ACICS, COE

† Main campus is Kaplan Career Institute in Nashville, TN.

King's College (M)

322 Lamar Avenue, Charlotte NC 28204-2493
County: Mecklenburg FICE Identification: 002937
Unit ID: 382504
Telephone: (704) 372-0266 Carnegie Class: Assoc/PrivFP
FAX Number: (704) 348-2029 Calendar System: Semester
URL: www.kingscollege.org
Established: 1901 Annual Undergrad Tuition & Fees: $13,700
Enrollment: 501 Coed
Affiliation or Control: Proprietary IRS Status: Proprietary
Highest Offering: Associate Degree
Program: Occupational; 2-Year Principally Bachelor's Creditable
Accreditation: ACICS, MAC

01 School Director ... Mrs. Diane RYON
05 Chief Academic Officer ... Ms. Barbara ROCKECHARLIE

Laurel University (N)

1215 Eastchester Drive, High Point NC 27265-3115
County: Guilford FICE Identification: 002935
Unit ID: 198747
Telephone: (336) 887-3000 Carnegie Class: Spec/Faith
FAX Number: (336) 889-2261 Calendar System: Semester
URL: www.laureluniversity.edu
Established: 1903 Annual Undergrad Tuition & Fees: $9,230
Enrollment: 389 Coed
Affiliation or Control: Independent Non-Profit IRS Status: 501(c)3

Highest Offering: Doctorate
Program: Professional; Religious Emphasis
Accreditation: BI

01 President ... Vacant
05 Vice President for Academic Affairs ... Dr. John L. LINDSEY
88 Dean School of Management ... Dr. Owen ALLEN
06 Registrar ... Mr. Greg WORKMAN
84 Director of Enrollment Management ... Ms. Erin MURRAY
37 Director of Financial Aid ... Mrs. Shirley CARTER
18 Director of Facilities and Grounds ... Mr. Eugene ALBERTSON
08 Librarian ... Mrs. April LINDSEY
10 Chief Financial Officer ... Mr. David WHITE
15 Director of Human Resources ... Mrs. Kathy CUTRELL
32 Director of Student Life ... Mr. Kevin DUNOVANT
106 Director of Distance Education ... Mr. Marty HILL
26 Public Relations Director ... Ms. Wanda CLARK
29 Alumni Coordinator ... Mrs. April LINDSEY

Lees-McRae College (A)

PO Box 128, 191 Main Street, Banner Elk NC 28604-0128
County: Avery FICE Identification: 002939
Unit ID: 198808
Telephone: (828) 898-5241 Carnegie Class: Bac/Diverse
FAX Number: (828) 898-8814 Calendar System: Semester
URL: www.lmc.edu
Established: 1900 Annual Undergrad Tuition & Fees: $23,450
Enrollment: 800 Coed
Affiliation or Control: Presbyterian Church (U.S.A.) IRS Status: 501(c)3
Highest Offering: Baccalaureate
Program: Liberal Arts And General; Teacher Preparatory
Accreditation: SC, NURSE, @TEAC

01 President ... Dr. Barry M. BUXTON
05 Provost/Dean Faculty ... Dr. Kacy CRABTREE
10 VP Finance & Business Affairs ... Ms. Suzette FRONK
30 Vice Pres Institutional Advancement ... Ms. Caroline HART
84 Vice Pres Enrollment Management ... Ms. Ginger HANSEN
18 Vice Pres Facilities Management ... Mr. Bill MCGOWAN
32 Dean of Students ... Vacant
29 Director of Alumni Relations ... Vacant
08 Director of Libraries ... Mr. Russell TAYLOR
06 Registrar ... Ms. Lynn HINSHAW
04 Secretary to the President ... Ms. Darcy VASILAS
37 Financial Aid Director ... Ms. Cathy SHELL
44 Director of Prospect Research ... Mrs. Frankie NEEDHAM
21 Business Affairs Liaison ... Ms. Megan HALL
15 Director Human Resources/Telecomm ... Mrs. Carolyn WARD
38 Director Student Counseling ... Ms. Janice HALL
96 Dir Col Post Ofc/Purchasing Clerk ... Ms. Sandy RAMSEY
41 Athletic Director ... Mr. Craig MCPHAIL

Lenoir-Rhyne University (B)

625 7th Avenue NE, Hickory NC 28601-3984
County: Catawba FICE Identification: 002941
Unit ID: 198835
Telephone: (828) 328-1741 Carnegie Class: Bac/Diverse
FAX Number: (828) 328-7368 Calendar System: Semester
URL: www.lr.edu
Established: 1891 Annual Undergrad Tuition & Fees: $29,310
Enrollment: 1,862 Coed
Affiliation or Control: Evangelical Lutheran Church In America
IRS Status: 501(c)3
Highest Offering: Master's
Program: Liberal Arts And General; Teacher Preparatory; Professional
Accreditation: SC, ACBSP, @DIETI, NURSE, OT, TED

01 President ... Dr. Wayne POWELL
05 Provost ... Dr. Larry HALL
10 Sr Vice President Finance/Admin ... Mr. Peter KENDALL
30 Vice Pres Institutional Advancement ... Mr. Drew VAN HORN
84 Vice President for Enrollment Mgmt ... Ms. Rachel NICHOLS
32 Dean of Students ... Dr. Katie FISHER
104 Assoc Dean Global Learning ... Ms. Charlotte WILLIAMS
58 Dean Grad Studies/Lifelong Learning ... Dr. Amy WOOD
97 Assoc Dean Co-Curricular Programs ... Mr. Leonard GEDDES
06 Registrar ... Ms. Kathy HAHN
08 Librarian ... Ms. Rita JOHNSON
15 Director of Human Resources ... Mr. Rick NICHOLS
40 Director of Bookstore ... Ms. Leslie SKAFF
18 Director of Facilities/Plant ... Mr. Otis PITTS
41 Athletic Director ... Mr. Neill MCGEACHY
42 Campus Pastor ... Rev. Andrew WEISNER
19 Director of Security ... Mr. Norris YODER
92 Director of Honors Program ... Dr. Joshua RING
13 Chief Information Officer ... Ms. Melissa MULLINAX
26 Int Dir of Marketing/Communication ... Ms. Maggie GREENE
88 Director of Conferences & Events ... Ms. Janet MATTHEWS
29 Director of Alumni Relations ... Ms. Dana HAMILTON
07 Director of Admissions ... Ms. Karen FEEZOR
09 Director of Institutional Research ... Dr. Ginger BISHOP
37 Director Student Financial Aid ... Mr. Eric BRANDON
38 Dir Student Counseling/Placement ... Ms. Jenny SMITH
88 Dir Liberal Arts/Visiting Writers ... Dr. Rand BRANDES
28 Director Multicultural Affairs ... Ms. Emma SELLERS
88 Dir of Deaf/Hard-of-Hearing Svcs ... Ms. Shawn FRANK
88 Institute on Obesity ... Ms. Kimberly PENNINGTON
65 Institute on Conservation ... Dr. John BRZORAD
85 Coord of International Programs ... Dr. Duane KIRKMAN
53 College of Education/Human Services ... Dr. Hank WEDDINGTON
76 College of Health Sciences ... Dr. Katherine PASOUR
49 College of Arts & Sciences ... Dr. Dan KISER
81 Int Col Professional/Math Studies ... Dr. Mary LESSER

Living Arts College @ School of Communication Arts (C)

3000 Wakefield Crossing Drive, Raleigh NC 27614-7076
County: Wake FICE Identification: 031090
Unit ID: 421832
Telephone: (919) 488-8500 Carnegie Class: Assoc/PrivFP
FAX Number: (919) 488-8490 Calendar System: Quarter
URL: www.living-arts-college.edu
Established: 1992 Annual Undergrad Tuition & Fees: $15,325
Enrollment: 578 Coed
Affiliation or Control: Proprietary IRS Status: Proprietary
Highest Offering: Baccalaureate
Program: Occupational; Technical Emphasis
Accreditation: ACICS, MAC

01 Director ... Ms. Debra A. HOOPER

Livingstone College (D)

701 W Monroe Street, Salisbury NC 28144-5298
County: Rowan FICE Identification: 002942
Unit ID: 198862
Telephone: (704) 216-6000 Carnegie Class: Bac/Diverse
FAX Number: (704) 216-6217 Calendar System: Semester
URL: www.livingstone.edu
Established: 1879 Annual Undergrad Tuition & Fees: $16,369
Enrollment: 1,111 Coed
Affiliation or Control: African Methodist Episcopal Zion Church
IRS Status: 501(c)3
Highest Offering: Baccalaureate
Program: Liberal Arts And General; Teacher Preparatory; Professional
Accreditation: SC, SW, TED

01 President ... Dr. Jimmy R. JENKINS, SR.
04 Exec Asst to the President ... Mr. State ALEXANDER
05 Vice Pres Academic Affairs ... Dr. Lelia VICKERS
10 Vice Pres Business & Finance/Ops ... Mr. Reginald DICKENS
32 Vice President Student Affairs ... Vacant
30 Vice Pres Inst Advance/College Rels ... Dr. Herman FELTON
35 Assoc Vice Pres of Student Affairs ... Mr. Tony BALDWIN
20 Asst Vice Pres Academic Affairs ... Vacant
38 Dean of Counseling Services . Mrs. Elizabeth ALSTON-PINCKNEY
06 Registrar ... Mrs. Wendy JACKSON
08 Director Library Services ... Ms. Laura JOHNSON
26 Director of Public Relations ... Mr. State W. ALEXANDER
37 Director of Financial Aid ... Ms. Desmona BROWN-CAYRUTH
36 Dir Career Counseling/Placement ... Mrs. Melissa RIVERS
13 Director of Computer Info Systems ... Mr. Chong DAN
15 Director of Human Resources ... Mr. Donald PEARSALL
29 Director Alumni Affairs ... Ms. Carmen C. WILDER
09 Director of Institutional Research ... Mr. Robert L. MCINNIS
84 Dir Enrollment Mgmt & Admissions ... Vacant
07 Director of Admissions ... Mr. Sha-Ron JONES
40 Bookstore Director ... Mr. Jerome FUNDERBURK
41 Athletic Director ... Mr. Andre SPRINGS
96 Director of Purchasing ... Ms. Debra WOOD
18 Director of Physical Plant ... Mr. Russell SMYRE
23 Health Services Manager ... Vacant

Louisburg College (E)

501 N Main Street, Louisburg NC 27549-7705
County: Franklin FICE Identification: 002943
Unit ID: 198871
Telephone: (919) 496-2521 Carnegie Class: Assoc/PrivNFP
FAX Number: (919) 496-7141 Calendar System: Semester
URL: www.louisburg.edu
Established: 1787 Annual Undergrad Tuition & Fees: $15,540
Enrollment: 695 Coed
Affiliation or Control: United Methodist IRS Status: 501(c)3
Highest Offering: Associate Degree
Program: 2-Year Principally Bachelor's Creditable
Accreditation: SC

01 President ... Rev Dr. Mark D. LA BRANCHE
05 VP of Academic Life ... Dr. James C. ECK
11 VP of Administration/Inst Effect ... Vacant
30 Vice Pres Institutional Advancement ... Mr. Kurt CARLSON
32 Vice President of Student Life ... Mr. Jason E. MODLIN
10 Vice President of Finance ... Ms. Belinda FAULKNER
84 Vice Pres of Enrollment Management . Ms. Stephanie B. TOLBERT
29 Alumni Director ... Ms. Jamie PATRICK
06 Registrar/Dir of Inst Research ... Ms. Catherine ZIENCIK
08 Librarian ... Ms. Candace L. JONES
38 Director of Counseling Services ... Ms. Fonda PORTER
37 Director of Financial Aid ... Ms. Vickie FLEMING
26 Director of College Communications ... Ms. Melinda MCKEE
18 Chief Facilities/Physical Plant ... Mr. Nathan BIEGENZAHN

Mars Hill College (F)

PO Box 370, Mars Hill NC 28754-0370
County: Madison FICE Identification: 002944
Unit ID: 198899
Telephone: (828) 689-1307 Carnegie Class: Bac/Diverse
FAX Number: (828) 689-1478 Calendar System: Semester
URL: www.mhc.edu
Established: 1856 Annual Undergrad Tuition & Fees: $25,636
Enrollment: 1,336 Coed
Affiliation or Control: Independent Non-Profit IRS Status: 501(c)3
Highest Offering: Master's
Program: Liberal Arts And General; Teacher Preparatory; Professional
Accreditation: SC, MUS, SW, TED, THEA

01 President ... Dr. Dan G. LUNSFORD
30 Vice President for Inst Advancement ... Mr. Harold (Bud) G. CHRISTMAN
05 Exec Vice Pres Acad & Student Affs ... Dr. John W. WELLS
32 Asst Vice Pres for Student Life ... Ms. Laura WHITAKER-LEA
20 Asst Vice Pres for Academic Affairs ... Dr. Jason A. PIERCE
84 Asst Vice Pres for Enrollment Mgt ... Dr. Craig GOFORTH
06 Dean Academic Records/Resource ... Ms. Edith L. WHITT
08 Director of Library Services ... Ms. Beverly ROBERTSON
26 Director of Public Information ... Mr. Mike D. THORNHILL
10 Vice Pres for Finance ... Mr. Neil TILLEY
42 Campus Chaplain ... Rev. Stephanie MCLESKEY
41 Director of Athletics ... Mr. David W. RIGGINS
37 Director of Financial Aid ... Ms. Nichole THOMAS
29 Director of Alumni Relations ... Ms. Elizabeth HARDIN
85 Director International Education ... Mr. Gordon HINNERS
09 Director Institutional Research ... Dr. Suzanne C. KLONIS
38 Director Student Counseling ... Ms. Cassandra PAVONE
15 Director of Human Resources ... Ms. Deana K. HOLLAND
13 Director Information Technology Svc ... Mr. Gerald D. BALL
18 Director of Facilities ... Mr. Donald EDWARDS
40 Director of Bookstore ... Mr. Darryl R. NORTON
51 Dean of Adult & Graduate Studies ... Ms. Marie NICHOLSON
97 Chair of General Studies ... Ms. Cathy L. ADKINS

Meredith College (G)

3800 Hillsborough Street, Raleigh NC 27607-5298
County: Wake FICE Identification: 002945
Unit ID: 198950
Telephone: (919) 760-8600 Carnegie Class: Bac/Diverse
FAX Number: (919) 760-2828 Calendar System: Semester
URL: www.meredith.edu
Established: 1891 Annual Undergrad Tuition & Fees: $30,562
Enrollment: 1,947 Female
Affiliation or Control: Independent Non-Profit IRS Status: 501(c)3
Highest Offering: Master's
Program: Liberal Arts And General; Teacher Preparatory; Professional
Accreditation: SC, BUS, CIDA, DIETD, DIETI, MUS, SW, TED

01 President ... Dr. Jo ALLEN
05 Sr Vice Pres and Provost ... Dr. Matthew POSLUSNY
30 Vice Pres Institutional Advancement ... Dr. Charles "Lennie" BARTON
10 Vice Pres for Business & Finance ... Mr. Craig BARFIELD
32 Vice President for College Programs ... Dr. Jean JACKSON
84 Assoc Provost Enrollment Management ... Dr. Danny GREEN
35 Dean of Students ... Ms. Ann C. GLEASON
06 Registrar ... Ms. Amanda STEELE-MIDDLETON
09 Dir of Assessment & Inst Research ... Ms. Dianne RAUBENHEIMER
08 Director Library Info Services ... Ms. Laura DAVIDSON
07 Director of Admissions ... Ms. Shery BOYLES
37 Director of Financial Assistance ... Mr. Kevin MICHAELSEN
26 Executive Director of Marketing ... Ms. Kristi EAVES-MCLENNAN
35 Dir Student Activ/Leadership Devel ... Ms. Cheryl S. JENKINS
28 Dir Commuter Life/Diversity Pgms ... Ms. Tomecca SLOANE
36 Director of Career Planning ... Dr. Marie B. SUMEREL
29 Dir of Alumnae & Parent Relations ... Ms. Hilary ALLEN
38 Director of Counseling Center ... Ms. Beth A. MEIER
58 Director of Graduate Studies ... Dr. Denise ROTONDO
39 Director Resident Life/Housing ... Ms. Heidi LECOUNT
20 Director of Academic Advising ... Ms. Amy HITLIN
31 Director Campus Events ... Mr. Bill BROWN
23 Director Health Services ... Ms. Sherri HENDERSON
42 Campus Minister ... Rev. Stacy PARDUE
13 Chief Information Officer ... Mr. Jeffrey HOWLETT
19 Chief Campus Police ... Mr. David KENNEDY
15 Director of Human Resources ... Ms. Pamela DAVIS
18 Chief Facilities/Physical Plant ... Ms. Sharon CAMPBELL
21 Controller ... Ms. Lori DUKE

Methodist University (H)

5400 Ramsey Street, Fayetteville NC 28311-1498
County: Cumberland FICE Identification: 002946
Unit ID: 198969
Telephone: (910) 630-7000 Carnegie Class: Bac/Diverse
FAX Number: (910) 630-7317 Calendar System: Semester
URL: www.methodist.edu
Established: 1956 Annual Undergrad Tuition & Fees: $27,530
Enrollment: 2,359 Coed
Affiliation or Control: United Methodist IRS Status: 501(c)3
Highest Offering: Master's
Program: Liberal Arts And General; Teacher Preparatory
Accreditation: SC, ACBSP, ARCPA, SW, TED

01 President ... Dr. Ben E. HANCOCK, JR.
05 Vice Pres for Academic Affairs ... Dr. Delmas S. CRISP, JR.
10 Vice President for Business Affairs ... Mr. Gene T. CLAYTON
32 Vice President for Student Affairs ... Mr. William WALKER
30 Vice President for Development ... Mrs. Robin DAVENPORT
09 VP of Institutional Research ... Dr. Donald L. LASSITER
20 Associate VP for Academic Affairs ... Ms. Jane W. GARDINER
35 Assoc Dean Student Services ... Mr. Todd D. HARRIS

84 Director Enrollment Management .... Mr. Rick D. LOWE
42 Chaplain/Director Campus Ministry ....Rev. Michael W. SAFLEY
26 Director of Public Relations .... Mrs. Pam MCEVOY
41 Director of Athletics .... Mr. Robert T. MCEVOY
29 Director of Alumni Affairs .... Ms. Lauren C. WIKE
07 Dean of Admissions .... Mr. Jamie W. LEGG
37 Director of Financial Aid .... Ms. Bonnie J. ADAMSON
06 Registrar .... Ms. Jasmin K. BROWN
08 Head Librarian .... Ms. Tracey PEARSON
85 Director Foreign Students .... Ms. Lyle SHEPPARD
19 Director Security/Safety .... Mr. James K. PHILLIPS
15 Director Personnel Services .... Mrs. Debra YEATTS
18 Chief Facilities/Physical Plant ... Mr. Thomas W. DAUGHTREY, III
21 Associate Business Officer .... Ms. Dawn AUSBORN
36 Director Student Placement .... Ms. Antoinette P. BELLAMY
38 Director Student Counseling .... Ms. Darlene HOPKINS
96 Director of Purchasing .... Ms. Deborah DEMBOSKY
14 Director Institutional Computing .... Mr. Samuel J. CLARK, III

Mid-Atlantic Christian University (A)

715 N Poindexter, Elizabeth City NC 27909-4054
County: Pasquotank FICE Identification: 022809
Unit ID: 199458
Telephone: (252) 334-2000 Carnegie Class: Bac/Diverse
FAX Number: (252) 334-2071 Calendar System: Semester
URL: www.macuniversity.edu
Established: 1948 Annual Undergrad Tuition & Fees: $12,160
Enrollment: 170 Coed
Affiliation or Control: Churches Of Christ IRS Status: 501(c)3
Highest Offering: Baccalaureate
Program: Liberal Arts And General; Religious Emphasis
Accreditation: SC

01 President .... Dr. D. Clay PERKINS
05 Vice President Academic Affairs .... Dr. Kevin W. LARSEN
10 Vice President Finance .... Mr. Kurtis L. KIGHT
32 Vice President Student Services .... Dr. Ken S. GREENE
30 Vice President Institutional Advanc .... Vacant
09 Director of Institutional Research .... Dr. Kevin W. LARSEN
06 Registrar .... Miss Yolanda TESKE
08 Director of Library .... Mr. Ken D. GUNSELMAN
38 Counselor .... Mr. Donald W. MCKINNEY
37 Financial Aid Administrator .... Mrs. Lisa W. PIPKIN
18 Superintendent Buildings & Grounds .....Mr. Phillip N. ALLIGOOD
21 Assistant Vice President Finance .... Mrs. Carol M. STUART
42 Campus Minister .... Mr. Roger E. BURNS
49 Chair of Arts and Sciences .... Dr. Robert W. SMITH
73 Chair of Biblical Studies .... Dr. Lee M. FIELDS
88 Chair of Christian Ministry .... Dr. Robert B. REESE
88 Chair of Marketplace Ministry .... Mr. Donald W. MCKINNEY
35 Student Life Administrator ....Miss Andrea A. STRAWDERMAN

Miller-Motte College (B)

2205 Walnut Street, Cary NC 27518
Telephone: (919) 532-7171 Identification: 770726
Accreditation: ACICS, MAC, SURGT

† Main campus is Miller-Motte Technical College in Lynchburg, VA.

Miller-Motte College (C)

3725 Ramsey Street, Fayetteville NC 28311
Telephone: (910) 354-1900 Identification: 770728
Accreditation: ACICS

† Main campus is Miller-Motte Technical College in Lynchburg, VA.

Miller-Motte College (D)

1021 W.H. Smith Blvd, Suite 102, Greenville NC 27834
Telephone: (252) 215-2000 Identification: 770730
Accreditation: ACICS

† Main campus is Miller-Motte Technical College in Clarksville, TN.

Miller-Motte College (E)

1291 Hargett Street, Jacksonville NC 28540
Telephone: (910) 478-4300 Identification: 770729
Accreditation: ACICS

† Main campus is Miller-Motte Technical College in Lynchburg, VA.

Miller-Motte College (F)

3901 Capital Boulevard, Suite 151, Raleigh NC 27604
Telephone: (919) 723-2820 Identification: 770727
Accreditation: ACICS, DA, MAC

† Main campus is Miller-Motte Technical College in Lynchburg, VA.

Miller-Motte Technical College (G)

5000 Market Street, Wilmington NC 28405-3430
Telephone: (910) 392-4660 FICE Identification: 030632
Accreditation: ACICS, DA, MAC, SURGT

† Main campus is Miller-Motte Technical College in Clarksville, TN.

Montreat College (H)

PO Box 1267, 310 Gaither Circle,
Montreat NC 28757-1267
County: Buncombe FICE Identification: 002948
Unit ID: 199032
Telephone: (828) 669-8012 Carnegie Class: Master's S
FAX Number: (828) 669-9554 Calendar System: Semester
URL: www.montreat.edu
Established: 1916 Annual Undergrad Tuition & Fees: $24,348
Enrollment: 785 Coed
Affiliation or Control: Non-denominational IRS Status: 501(c)3
Highest Offering: Master's
Program: Liberal Arts And General; Teacher Preparatory
Accreditation: SC, IACBE, TED

01 Interim President .... Mr. Joe KIRKLAND
04 Interim Assistant to the President .... Ms. Kate LEDBETTER
05 Senior Vice President and Provost .... Dr. Marshall FLOWERS
10 Vice President for Finance .... Mr. Geoff BREMER
84 VP for Enrollment and Marketing .... Mr. Jonathan SHORES
32 Vice President for Student Services .... Mr. Charles A. LANCE
30 Vice President for Advancement .... Mr. Joe KIRKLAND
13 Vice President for Technology .... Vacant
42 Interim Chaplain .... Dr. John ELLINGTON
08 Library Director .... Ms. Elizabeth R. PEARSON
06 Registrar .... Vacant
37 Director of Financial Aid .... Mr. Jeff HOLLIDAY
26 Director of Communications .... Ms. Annie CARLSON
38 Director of Counseling .... Ms. Jane CARTER
41 Athletic Director .... Mr. Craig JACKSON
35 Director of Student Activities .... Mr. Jim DAHLIN
40 Bookstore Manager .... Ms. Carly BRAENDEL
09 Assoc Dean of Academics & Inst Eff .... Ms. Becky FRAWLEY
19 Chief of Campus Police .... Dr. N. Scott ADAMS
07 Director of Admissions and Outreach .... Mr. Tony ROBINSON

Mount Olive College (I)

634 Henderson Street, Mount Olive NC 28365-1263
County: Wayne FICE Identification: 002949
Unit ID: 199069
Telephone: (919) 658-2502 Carnegie Class: Bac/Diverse
FAX Number: (919) 658-7180 Calendar System: Semester
URL: www.moc.edu
Established: 1951 Annual Undergrad Tuition & Fees: $16,800
Enrollment: 3,714 Coed
Affiliation or Control: Original Free Will Baptist Church IRS Status: 501(c)3
Highest Offering: Master's
Program: Liberal Arts And General
Accreditation: SC, ACBSP

01 President .... Dr. Philip P. KERSTETTER
03 Executive Vice President .... Dr. Carol G. CARRERE
05 VP for Academic Affairs .... Dr. Ellen S. JORDAN
88 VP for Special Services .... Dr. Opey D. JEANES
10 Interim VP Finance & Treasurer .... Ms. Debra SMITH
84 VP for Enrollment .... Dr. Barbara R. KORNEGAY
32 VP for Student Affairs .... Dr. Dan SULLIVAN
30 VP for Institutional Advancement .... Mr. Kevin J. JEAN
50 Interim Dean School of Business .... Dr. Ellen JORDAN
49 Dean School of Arts and Sciences .... Dr. Kenneth D. HINES
08 Director of Library Services .... Ms. Pamela R. WOOD
12 Director of MOC New Bern .... Mr. Guy BRADBURY
12 Director of MOC Jacksonville .... Mr. Guy BRADBURY
12 Director of MOC Goldsboro .... Dr. Opey JEANES
12 Director of MOC Evening College .... Mr. Stanley J. ELLIOTT
12 Director of MOC Wilmington .... Dr. Marna R. MCMURRY
12 Director MOC Research Triangle Park .... Ms. Lisa NUESELL
07 Director of Admissions .... Mr. Timothy E. WOODARD
06 Registrar .... Mr. David L. BOURGEOIS
36 Director of Career Center .... Vacant
27 Director of Public Relations .... Ms. Rhonda E. JESSUP
102 Dir Foundations & Sponsored Program .... Vacant
29 Dir Young Alumni Relations .... Ms. Vickie S. ROBINSON
44 Director of Annual Fund .... Mr. Yeeka YAU
37 Director of Financial Aid .... Ms. Katrina K. LEE
15 Director of Human Resources .... Mr. Stephen A. SWEET
23 Student Health Services .... Ms. Joanne L. MORGAN
42 Campus Chaplain .... Ms. Carla WILLIAMSON
04 Assistant to the President .... Ms. Katherine B. GARDNER
18 Superintendent Building & Grounds .... Mr. Jeff D. BROGDEN
40 Bookstore Manager .... Mr. Brian GRIFFIN
41 Athletics Director .... Mr. Jeffrey M. EISEN
13 Director Technology Support .... Mr. Robert R. PRUETT
88 Director Technology Services .... Mr. Kenneth M. DAVIS, JR.
92 Director Honors Program .... Dr. Ellen JORDAN
09 Director Inst Research & Planning .... Vacant

Native American Bible College (J)

PO Box 248, Shannon NC 28386
County: Robeson Identification: 667092
Telephone: (910) 843-5304 Carnegie Class: Not Classified
FAX Number: N/A Calendar System: Semester
URL: nativeamericanbiblecollege.org
Established: 1968 Annual Undergrad Tuition & Fees: $1,590
Enrollment: N/A Coed
Affiliation or Control: Assemblies Of God Church IRS Status: 501(c)3
Highest Offering: Baccalaureate
Program: Religious Emphasis
Accreditation: @BI

01 President .... James A. KEYS
05 Chief Academic Officer .... Dossie MORRIS WOOD, JR.
32 Chief Student Development Officer .... Larry GILMER
10 CFO .... Michael GRIFFES
08 Chief Librarian .... T. Liisa KELLY
06 Registrar .... Michelle Rae GRIFFES

New Life Theological Seminary (K)

3117 Whting Avenue / PO Box 790106,
Charlotte NC 28206-4910
County: Mecklenburg FICE Identification: 038273
Unit ID: 444778
Telephone: (704) 334-6882 Carnegie Class: Spec/Faith
FAX Number: (704) 334-6885 Calendar System: Semester
URL: www.nlts.edu
Established: 1996 Annual Undergrad Tuition & Fees: $8,070
Enrollment: 139 Coed
Affiliation or Control: Independent Non-Profit IRS Status: 501(c)3
Highest Offering: Master's
Program: 2-Year Principally Bachelor's Creditable; Professional; Religious Emphasis
Accreditation: TRACS

01 President .... Dr. Eddie G. GRIGG
04 Executive Asst to the President .... Mr. Travis JOHNSON
05 Vice President of Academic Affairs .... Dr. Robert A. YOST
32 Vice President of Student Affairs .... Dr. Nathaniel PEARCE
30 Director of Advancement .... Vacant
06 Registrar/Dir International Student .... Ms. Anne WITT
08 Head Librarian .... Mr. Robert MCINNES
07 Director of Admissions .... Ms. Constance HEMPHILL
10 Chief Finance Officer .... Mr. Al WITT, JR.
37 Financial Aid Officer .... Mr. Kenneth ROACH

*North Carolina Community College System (L)

200 W Jones Street, 5001 MSC, Raleigh NC 27699-5001
County: Wake FICE Identification: 033445
Unit ID: 199166
Telephone: (919) 807-7100 Carnegie Class: N/A
FAX Number: (919) 807-7166
URL: www.nccommunitycolleges.edu

01 President .... Dr. R. Scott RALLS
05 Exec VP Programs/Chief Acad Ofcr ...... Dr. Sharron MORRISSEY
10 Exec VP Operation/Chief Fin Ofcr .... Ms. Jennifer HAYGOOD
103 Sr VP Tech & Workforce Development .... Dr. Saundra WILLIAMS
101 Director State Board Affairs .... Mr. Bryan JENKINS
04 Special Assistant to the President .... Ms. Pia MCKENZIE
46 VP Engagement/Strategic Innovation .... Ms. Linda WEINER

*Alamance Community College (M)

1247 Jimmie Kerr Road/PO Box 8000,
Graham NC 27253-8000
County: Alamance FICE Identification: 005463
Unit ID: 199786
Telephone: (336) 578-2002 Carnegie Class: Assoc/Pub-S-MC
FAX Number: (336) 578-1987 Calendar System: Semester
URL: www.alamancecc.edu
Established: 1958 Annual Undergrad Tuition & Fees (In-District): $1,746
Enrollment: 4,747 Coed
Affiliation or Control: State/Local IRS Status: 501(c)3
Highest Offering: Associate Degree
Program: Occupational; 2-Year Principally Bachelor's Creditable
Accreditation: SC, ACFEI, DA, MAC, MLTAD

02 President .... Dr. Martin H. NADELMAN
05 Executive Vice President .... Dr. Gene C. COUCH, JR.
10 Vice Pres Admin & Fiscal Svcs .... Mr. Mark NEWSOME
30 VP Institutional Advancement .... Ms. Carolyn RHODE
20 Dean of Curriculum Programs .... Dr. William T. MCNEILL
51 Dean of Continuing Education .... Mr. Gary SAUNDERS
32 Dean of Student Development .... Dr. Carol DISQUE
50 Assoc Dean Business Technologies .... Mr. Scott QUEEN
72 Assoc Dean Industrial/Graphics Tech .... Mr. Wally M. SHEARIN
49 Assoc Dean Arts & Sciences .... Ms. Catherine W. JOHNSON
69 Assoc Dean Health & Public Svcs .... Ms. Kelly TATE
21 Controller .... Ms. Cynthia COLLIE
11 Director Administrative Services .... Mr. Erik CONTI
16 Director Human Resources .... Ms. Lorri ALLISON
08 Director Learning Resources Center .... Ms. Sheila STREET
26 Director Public Information/Mktg .... Mr. Edward WILLIAMS
56 Director Occupational Ext Program .... Mr. David PARKER
84 Director Enrollment Management .... Ms. Elizabeth BREHLER
37 Director Financial Aid .... Ms. Sabrina DEGAIN
36 Director Counseling & Career Svcs .... Vacant
38 Special Needs/Counseling Svcs Coord .... Ms. Monica ISBELL
88 Academic Support Specialist .... Ms. Jennifer BROWNELL
09 Institutional Researcher .... Dr. Jessica HARRELL

*Asheville - Buncombe Technical Community College (N)

340 Victoria Road, Asheville NC 28801-4897
County: Buncombe FICE Identification: 004033
Unit ID: 197887
Telephone: (828) 254-1921 Carnegie Class: Assoc/Pub-R-L
FAX Number: (828) 251-6355 Calendar System: Semester
URL: www.abtech.edu

Established: 1959 Annual Undergrad Tuition & Fees (In-District): $1,998
Enrollment: 8,083 Coed
Affiliation or Control: State/Local IRS Status: 501(c)3
Highest Offering: Associate Degree
Program: Occupational; 2-Year Principally Bachelor's Creditable
Accreditation: SC, ACFEI, DA, DH, DMS, MAC, MLTAD, PHLEB, RAD, SURGT

02 President .... Dr. Hank DUNN
10 VP Business & Finance/CFO .... Mr. Scott MCKINNEY
13 Vice Pres Information Technology .... Mr. Brian WILLIS
05 VP Instructional Services .... Ms. Melissa QUINLEY
20 Associate VP Instructional Services .... Dr. Gene LOFLIN
32 VP Student Services .... Dr. Terry BRASIER
103 Sr Exec Dir Econ Wrkfrc Dev/Cont Ed .... Ms. Shelley WHITE
04 Executive Administrative Assistant .... Ms. Martha SHANKS
49 Dean Arts & Sciences .... Dr. Beth STEWART
30 Exec Director/College Advancement .... Ms. Sue OLESIUK
50 Dean Business & Hospitality Educ .... Mr. RJ CORMAN
54 Dean Engineering & Applied Tech .....Mr. Vernon D. DAUGHERTY
91 Director Info Systems Technology .... Mr. David C. MCKINNEY
84 Dir Recruitment/Student Activities .... Ms. Michele HATHCOCK
61 Director Law Enforcement Academy .... Ms. Dianne L. DAVIS
21 Director Business Services .... Ms. Lisa EVANS
37 Director of Financial Aid .... Mr. Brian CLEMMONS
06 Registrar .... Mr. Scott C. DOUGLAS
07 Director of Admissions .... Ms. Lisa F. BUSH
24 Director Library Services .... Ms. Carol FLEMING
12 Director Madison County Campus .... Vacant
18 Director Plant Operations .... Mr. Benny R. SMITH
19 Director Security .... Ms. Kara KELLER
31 Director Community Services .... Ms. Brinda W. CALDWELL
08 Librarian .... Ms. Martha DICKENS
09 Director Research & Planning .... Mr. David B. WHITE
15 Vice President Human Resources & OD .....Ms. Kaye N. WAUGH
27 Dir Community Relns & Marketing .... Vacant
28 Director of Diversity .... Vacant
40 Bookstore Manager .... Mr. Kevin MILLS
96 Coordinator of Purchasing .... Ms. Rebecca R. WATKINS
72 Coordinator Technology Services .... Mr. Cris HARSHMAN

*Beaufort County Community College (A)

Box 1069, Washington NC 27889-1069
County: Beaufort FICE Identification: 008558
Unit ID: 197966
Telephone: (252) 946-6194 Carnegie Class: Assoc/Pub-R-S
FAX Number: (252) 946-0271 Calendar System: Semester
URL: www.beaufortccc.edu
Established: 1967 Annual Undergrad Tuition & Fees (In-District): $2,352
Enrollment: 1,946 Coed
Affiliation or Control: State/Local IRS Status: 501(c)3
Highest Offering: Associate Degree
Program: Occupational; 2-Year Principally Bachelor's Creditable
Accreditation: SC, MLTAD

02 President .... Dr. Barbara TANSEY
05 VP of Academics .... Dr. Crystal ANGE
11 VP of Administrative Services .... Mr. Mark NELSON
32 VP of Student Services .... Mr. Rick ANDERSON
51 VP of Continuing Education .... Mr. Chet JARMAN
45 VP of Research & Inst Effectiveness .... Dr. Jay SULLIVAN
26 Director of Public Relations .... Mrs. Betty GRAY
55 Dir of Evening/Off Campus Svcs .... Mr. Clay CARTER
76 Dean Allied Health .... Ms. Erica SCHATZ
49 Dean Arts & Sciences .... Mr. Dixon BOYLES
50 Dean of Business .... Mr. Ben MORRIS
72 Dean Industrial Technology .... Mr. Ben MORRIS
08 Dir Learning Resources Center .... Mrs. Penny SERMONS
88 Network Administrator .... Mr. Brown MCFADDEN
91 System Administrator .... Mr. Whiting TOLER
15 Director of Human Resources .... Mrs. Emily WOOLARD
19 Director of Campus Police .... Mr. Hal SWINDELL
06 Registrar .... Mrs. Camille RICHARDSON
37 Director of Financial Aid .... Ms. Megan SOMMERS
07 Director of Admissions .... Mr. Daniel WILSON
38 Director of Counseling .... Mrs. Kimberly JACKSON
36 Director of Career Center .... Mrs. Sandy MCFADDEN
103 Dir of Business & Industry Svcs .... Mr. Lentz STOWE

*Bladen Community College (B)

PO Box 266, Dublin NC 28332-0266
County: Bladen FICE Identification: 007987
Unit ID: 198011
Telephone: (910) 879-5500 Carnegie Class: Assoc/Pub-R-S
FAX Number: (910) 879-5564 Calendar System: Semester
URL: www.bladencc.edu
Established: 1967 Annual Undergrad Tuition & Fees (In-State): $2,361
Enrollment: 1,393 Coed
Affiliation or Control: State IRS Status: 501(c)3
Highest Offering: Associate Degree
Program: Occupational; 2-Year Principally Bachelor's Creditable; Technical Emphasis
Accreditation: SC

02 President .... Dr. William FINDT
10 Vice President for Finance .... Mr. Jay STANLEY
05 VP for Instruction & Student Svcs .... Mr. Jeffrey KORNEGAY
32 Dean of Students .... Ms. Marva DINKINS
08 Director Learning Resource Ctr .... Ms. Sherwin RICE
55 Dean Distance & Evening Programs .... Ms. Ann RUSSELL
35 Assoc VP for Student Services .... Mr. Barry PRIEST
09 Dir Institutional Effect & Planning .... Ms. Harriet HOBBS
18 Director of Facilities .... Mr. Bradley TAYLOR
20 Assoc VP for Program Services .... Mr. Lynn KING
21 Director of Budgeting .... Ms. Sheila DOCKERY
37 Director of Financial Aid .... Ms. Samantha BENSON
15 Human Resources Officer .... Ms. Tiina MUNDY
26 Public Information Officer .... Mr. Jack MCDUFFIE
30 Foundation Specialist .... Ms. Linda BURNEY

*Blue Ridge Community College (C)

180 W Campus Drive, Flat Rock NC 28731-4728
County: Henderson FICE Identification: 009684
Unit ID: 198039
Telephone: (828) 694-1700 Carnegie Class: Assoc/Pub-R-M
FAX Number: (828) 694-1690 Calendar System: Semester
URL: www.blueridge.edu
Established: 1969 Annual Undergrad Tuition & Fees (In-District): $2,293
Enrollment: 2,412 Coed
Affiliation or Control: State/Local IRS Status: 501(c)3
Highest Offering: Associate Degree
Program: Occupational; 2-Year Principally Bachelor's Creditable
Accreditation: SC, EMT, SURGT

02 President .... Dr. Molly PARKHILL
05 VP for Instruction .... Dr. Alan H. STEPHENSON
10 VP for Finance and Operations .... Ms. Antonia BERBRICK
32 VP for Student Services .... Ms. Marcia L. STONEMAN
13 VP for Technology-CIO .... Mr. Ernest L. SIMONS
51 VP for Continuing Education .... Ms. Julie G. THOMPSON
100 Chief of Staff .... Dr. Chad MERRILL
49 Dean for Arts and Sciences .... Mr. David H. DAVIS
72 Dean for Applied Technology .... Mr. Chris ENGLISH
76 Dean for Allied Health Programs .... Ms. Rita D. CONNER
97 Dean for Basic Skills .... Mr. Rick MARSHALL
50 Dean for Business/Service Careers .... Ms. Kathy ALLEN
102 Executive Director Foundation .... Ms. Ann F. GREEN
44 Institutional Advance/Rsrch Coord .... Ms. Carol Ann LYDON
06 Registrar .... Ms. Kirsten H. BUNCH
08 Director for Library Services .... Ms. Susan D. WILLIAMS
21 Director Administrative Services .... Ms. Carolyn ALLEY
37 Director Financial Aid .... Ms. Lisanne MASTERSON
38 Director for Counseling .... Vacant
14 Director Information Technologies .... Mr. Steve YOUNG
18 Director of Facilities .... Mr. Peter HEMANS
26 Dir of Marketing & Communications .... Ms. Lee Anna HANEY
35 Student Activities Coordinator .... Ms. April KILLOUGH
84 Director of Enrollment Management .... Ms. Cathy STEPHENSON
15 Director of Human Resources .... Mr. Tommy OAKMAN

*Brunswick Community College (D)

PO Box 30, Supply NC 28462-0030
County: Brunswick FICE Identification: 021707
Unit ID: 198084
Telephone: (910) 755-7300 Carnegie Class: Assoc/Pub-R-S
FAX Number: (910) 754-7805 Calendar System: Semester
URL: www.brunswickcc.edu
Established: 1979 Annual Undergrad Tuition & Fees (In-State): $1,700
Enrollment: 1,600 Coed
Affiliation or Control: State IRS Status: 501(c)3
Highest Offering: Associate Degree
Program: Occupational; 2-Year Principally Bachelor's Creditable; Business Emphasis
Accreditation: SC, CAHIIM, PHLEB

02 President .... Dr. Susanne H. ADAMS
05 VP Academic Svcs & Student Affairs .... Dr. Sharon THOMPSON
10 Vice President Budget and Finance .... Dr. Benjamin A. DEBLOIS
32 Assoc VP Student Svcs & Enrollment .... Mr. Levy BROWN
11 Vice President Operations .... Mr. Jerry L. THRIFT
09 Coordinator Inst Effectiveness .... Ms. Pamela FEDERLINE
08 Director Library .... Ms. Carmen BLANTON
06 Registrar .... Mr. Lawrence PAKOWSKI
15 Director Human Resources .... Ms. Nicole WILLIAMS
19 Public Safety/Police Director .... Mr. Lindsay WALTON
18 Physical Plant Director .... Ms. Donna BAXTER
102 Executive Director Foundation .... Mr. Terry MOHR
26 Director of Marketing & Public Info .... Ms. London SCHMIDT
37 Financial Aid/Veterans Affs Coord .... Ms. Paula ALMOND
72 Dean Professional Technical Service .... Ms. Gina ROBINSON
49 Dean Arts & Sciences .... Ms. Jennifer SCHUMAKER

*Caldwell Community College and Technical Institute (E)

2855 Hickory Boulevard, Hudson NC 28638-1399
County: Caldwell FICE Identification: 004835
Unit ID: 198118
Telephone: (828) 726-2200 Carnegie Class: Assoc/Pub-R-M
FAX Number: (828) 726-2216 Calendar System: Semester
URL: www.cccti.edu
Established: 1964 Annual Undergrad Tuition & Fees (In-District): $2,326
Enrollment: 4,504 Coed
Affiliation or Control: State/Local IRS Status: 501(c)3
Highest Offering: Associate Degree
Program: Occupational; 2-Year Principally Bachelor's Creditable
Accreditation: SC, DMS, NMT, PTAA, RAD

02 President .... Dr. Kenneth A. BOHAM
03 Executive Vice President .... Mr. Mark POARCH
18 Vice President Facility Services .... Mr. Donnie BASSINGER
32 Vice President Student Services .... Mrs. Dena HOLMAN
51 VP Adult/Corp/Continuing Education .... Mrs. Elaine LOCKHART
12 Executive Director Watauga Campus .... Mr. Steve MELTON
84 Dir Enrollment Mgmt Services .... Ms. LaTosha HICKS
08 Director Learning Resources Center .... Ms. Deborah JOYNER
37 Director Financial Aid .... Mrs. Eva HARMON
36 Dir Career Planning/Job Placement .... Mr. Rick SHEW
15 Director Human Resources .... Mrs. Kathy SEITZ
26 Director Marketing & Communications .... Mrs. Sherry WILSON
10 Controller .... Mr. Scott ROGERS
09 Director Inst Effectiveness/Rsrch .... Mrs. Kate BENOIT
26 Public Relations Officer .... Mr. Edward TERRY
102 Director Foundation Office .... Mrs. Marla CHRISTIE
28 Director of Diversity .... Mrs. Alice LENTZ
38 Director Student Counseling .... Mr. Shannon BROWN
96 Director of Purchasing .... Mrs. Marcia POTTS
40 Manager Bookstore .... Mr. Michael PHILYAW

*Cape Fear Community College (F)

411 N Front Street, Wilmington NC 28401-3993
County: New Hanover FICE Identification: 005320
Unit ID: 198154
Telephone: (910) 362-7000 Carnegie Class: Assoc/Pub-R-L
FAX Number: (910) 763-2279 Calendar System: Semester
URL: www.cfcc.edu
Established: 1958 Annual Undergrad Tuition & Fees (In-District): $2,425
Enrollment: 9,154 Coed
Affiliation or Control: State/Local IRS Status: 501(c)3
Highest Offering: Associate Degree
Program: Occupational; 2-Year Principally Bachelor's Creditable
Accreditation: SC, ADNUR, DA, DH, DMS, OTA, PHLEB, RAD, SURGT

02 President .... Dr. Ted SPRING
05 Vice Pres for Instructional Service .... Dr. Amanda LEE
10 Sr VP for Business & Inst Svcs .... Ms. Camellia N. RICE
32 Vice Pres for Student Services .... Ms. Carol J. CULLUM
09 VP for Inst Effectiveness/Planning .... Ms. Kim LAWING
18 Director of Institutional Services .... Mr. Kenneth D. PEARCE
06 Registrar .... Mr. Phil FARINHOLT
102 VP for Institutional Advancement .... Ms. Margaret ROBISON
84 Director of Enrollment Management .... Ms. Linda KASYAN
08 Dean Learning Resources Center .... Ms. Catherine LEE
37 Director of Financial Aid .... Ms. Jo-Ann CRAIG
36 Director of Career & Testing .... Mr. Patrick PITTMAN
26 Dir of Marketing & Public Relations .... Mr. David M. HARDIN
13 Acting Dir Info Technology Services .... Mr. Jakim FRIANT
15 Chief Human Resources Officer .... Mr. John UPTON
41 Dir Student Activities/Athletics .... Mr. Robert MCGEE
96 Director of Purchasing & Inventory .... Mr. Brooke MESEROLE
38 Director Student Counseling .... Ms. Jacqueline FOSTER
21 Controller .... Mr. Ravi VELAUTHAPILLAI
28 Director of Diversity .... Mr. David HARDIN
07 Director of Admissions .... Ms. Linda KASYAN
44 Annual Giving Director .... Ms. Dana MCKOY
30 Chief Development Officer .... Ms. Margaret ROBISON
51 Dean of Continuing Education .... Mr. Clarence L. SMITH
75 Dean Vocational/Technical Education .... Mr. Pat HOGAN
49 Dean Arts & Sciences .... Ms. Orangel J. DANIELS
105 Web Services Analyst .... Ms. Christina HEIKKILA

*Carteret Community College (G)

3505 Arendell Street, Morehead City NC 28557-2989
County: Carteret FICE Identification: 008081
Unit ID: 198206
Telephone: (252) 222-6000 Carnegie Class: Assoc/Pub-R-S
FAX Number: (252) 222-2514 Calendar System: Semester
URL: www.carteret.edu
Established: 1963 Annual Undergrad Tuition & Fees (In-District): $2,271
Enrollment: 1,681 Coed
Affiliation or Control: State/Local IRS Status: 501(c)3
Highest Offering: Associate Degree
Program: Occupational; 2-Year Principally Bachelor's Creditable
Accreditation: SC, ADNUR, COARC, MAC, RAD

02 President .... Dr. Kerry L. YOUNGBLOOD
05 VP for Instruction/Student Support .... Dr. Fran EMORY
10 VP Finance/Administrative Services .... Ms. Madelene BROOKS
31 Vice Pres Corporate & Community .... Mr. Perry L. HARKER
04 Executive Assistant to President .... Ms. Brenda REASH
08 Director LRC .... Ms. Elizabeth BAKER
32 Senior Director Student Services .... Ms. Robie MCFARLAND
35 Director of Student Success .... Mr. Rick HILL
13 Director Information Technology .... Mr. Parker MORAN
15 Director of Human Resources .... Ms. Barbara I. COOPER
30 Director of Advancement .... Mr. David NATEMAN
49 Div Director Arts & Sciences .... Ms. Doree EVANS
76 Div Director Health Sciences .... Ms. Laurie A. FRESHWATER
75 Div Director Service Technology .... Ms. Evanglene REELS
50 Div Director Business Technologies .... Vacant
88 Director Div of Applied Science .... Ms. Susan H. MCINTYRE
37 Financial Aid Officer .... Ms. Brenda J. LONG
06 Registrar .... Ms. Tammi COBLE
07 Admissions Officer .... Mr. Martin NICHOLS
09 Dir of Institutional Effectiveness .... Vacant
18 Dir Operations/Facil Maintenance .... Mr. Steve SPARKS
26 Director of Public Affairs .... Mr. Morgan SMITH
96 Purchasing/Accts Payable Manager .... Ms. Donna L. CUMBIE
106 Director Distance Learning .... Ms. Mary WALTON

*Catawba Valley Community College (A)

2550 Highway 70, SE, Hickory NC 28602-9699
County: Catawba FICE Identification: 005318
Unit ID: 198233
Telephone: (828) 327-7000 Carnegie Class: Assoc/Pub-R-M
FAX Number: (828) 327-7276 Calendar System: Semester
URL: www.cvcc.edu
Established: 1960 Annual Undergrad Tuition & Fees (In-District): $1,560
Enrollment: 5,134 Coed
Affiliation or Control: State/Local IRS Status: 501(c)3
Highest Offering: Associate Degree
Program: Occupational; 2-Year Principally Bachelor's Creditable
Accreditation: SC, ADNUR, CAHIIM, COARC, DH, EMT, NDT, POLYT, RAD, SURGT

02 President .... Dr. Garrett D. HINSHAW
05 Vice President of Instruction .... Dr. Keith MACKIE
10 Vice President of Fiscal Affairs .... Mr. Wes BUNCH
32 Vice Pres Student Svcs/Technology .... Mr. Bill DULIN
35 CEO of of Student Services .... Mrs. Cindy COULTER
15 Director Human Resources .... Mr. Mike KIDD
06 Director of Admissions/Records .... Ms. Paula HOLLAR
21 Controller .... Ms. Robyn F. CHAPMAN
37 Director Scholarships/Financial Aid .... Ms. Debbie BARGER
09 Ofc Accountability/Efficienc/Effect .... Mr. Kevin ROUSE
88 Director Industrial Training .... Ms. Crystal GLENN
88 Director Small Business Center .... Mr. Jeff NEUVILLE
50 Director Business/Technolgy Ext .... Ms. Susan KILLIAN
88 Director Hosiery Technology Center .... Mr. Daniel C. ST. LOUIS
13 Director Information Technologies .... Mr. Ken ELLIOTT
19 Director Campus Safety/Security .... Mr. Bill DULIN
27 Director Community Relations .... Ms. Mary M. REYNOLDS
31 Director Community Education .... Ms. Chanell MORELLO
36 Counselor/Job Placement Svcs Coord .... Ms. Teresa RAY
16 Coordinator Health/Human Services .... Ms. Donna TRADO

*Central Carolina Community College (B)

1105 Kelly Drive, Sanford NC 27330-9000
County: Lee FICE Identification: 005449
Unit ID: 198251
Telephone: (919) 775-5401 Carnegie Class: Assoc/Pub-R-M
FAX Number: (919) 718-7380 Calendar System: Semester
URL: www.cccc.edu
Established: 1958 Annual Undergrad Tuition & Fees (In-District): $2,296
Enrollment: 4,900 Coed
Affiliation or Control: State/Local IRS Status: 501(c)3
Highest Offering: Associate Degree
Program: Occupational; 2-Year Principally Bachelor's Creditable; Nursing Emphasis
Accreditation: SC, DA, DH, MAC, POLYT

02 President .... Dr. T. Eston MARCHANT
05 Exec Vice Pres of Instruction .... Dr. Lisa M. CHAPMAN
11 Vice Pres for Administrative Svcs .... Mr. Wayne G. ROBINSON
32 Vice President Student Services .... Mr. Ken R. HOYLE
51 VP Economic & Community Development .... Ms. Pamela SENEGAL
30 VP of Institutional Advancement .... Mrs. Celia HURLEY
12 Provost Chatham Campus .... Dr. Karen H. ALLEN
12 Provost Harnett Campus .... Mr. William R. TYSON
08 Director of Library Services .... Ms. Tara GUTHRIE
15 Exec Human Resources Director .... Ms. Stacey CARTER-COLEY
102 Foundation Executive Director .... Ms. Diane F. GLOVER
06 Dean of Enrollment/Registrar .... Ms. Jamie CHILDRESS
07 Director of Admissions .... Ms. Jamee STIFFLER
26 Director Marketing & Public Affairs .... Ms. Marcie DISHMAN
37 Director Student Financial Aid .... Ms. Ann PEACOCK
96 Director of Purchasing .... Mrs. Starlene JACKSON
18 Physical Plant Manager .... Mr. Ronnie MEASAMER
75 Dean Vocational/Technical Programs .... Dr. Stephan ATHANS
50 Dean Business/Media Tech/Publ Srvs .... Mrs. Joni P. PAVLIK
36 Dean of College & Career Readiness .... Ms. Dawn TUCKER
51 Dean of Continuing Education .... Ms. Phyllis HUFF

*Central Piedmont Community College (C)

PO Box 35009, Charlotte NC 28235-5009
County: Mecklenburg FICE Identification: 002915
Unit ID: 198260
Telephone: (704) 330-2722 Carnegie Class: Assoc/Pub-U-MC
FAX Number: (704) 330-5045 Calendar System: Semester
URL: www.cpcc.edu
Established: 1963 Annual Undergrad Tuition & Fees (In-District): $2,617
Enrollment: 19,498 Coed
Affiliation or Control: State/Local IRS Status: 501(c)3
Highest Offering: Associate Degree
Program: Occupational; 2-Year Principally Bachelor's Creditable
Accreditation: SC, ACFEI, CAHIIM, COARC, CVT, CYTO, DA, DH, ENGT, MAC, MLTAD, PTAA, SURGT

02 President .... Dr. P. Anthony ZEISS
03 Executive Vice President .... Dr. Kathy DRUMM
05 Vice President for Learning .... Mr. Richard ZOLLINGER
84 VP Enrollment & Student Services .... Dr. Marcia CONSTON
10 VP Finance/Administrative Services .... Mr. Michael MOSS
04 Exec Assistant to the President .... Ms. Susan OLESON-BRIGGS
30 VP for Inst Advancement .... Dr. Kevin MCCARTHY
13 VP for Technology and CIO .... Mr. David KIM
11 Assoc VP Financial Svcs .... Ms. Diep TONG
20 Assoc VP Learning .... Dr. Deborah BOUTON
18 Assoc VP Facilities & Construction .... Mr. Rich ROSENTHAL
09 Assoc VP Institutional Research .... Dr. Terri MANNING
88 Assoc VP Compliance and Audit .... Dr. Brenda LEONARD
15 Assoc VP of Human Resources .... Mr. Paul SANTOS
25 Assoc VP Government Rels & Grants .... Mr. Michael HORN
26 PIO & Asst to Pres Cmty Rels/Mktg .... Mr. Jeffrey LOWRANCE
12 Dean Levine Campus .... Dr. Edith MCELROY
12 Dean Merancas Campus .... Ms. Tamara WILLIAMS
12 Dean Central Campus .... Mr. Paul KOEHNKE
12 Dean Cato Campus .... Ms. Janet MALKEMES
12 Dean Harris Campus .... Ms. Mary VICKERS-KOCH
12 Dean Harper Campus .... Mr. Jay POTTER
54 Dean STEM-S .... Mr. Chris PAYNTER
88 Dean Retention Services .... Dr. Clint MCELROY
35 Dean Student Life/Service Learning .... Mr. Mark HELMS
38 Dean Student Success Services .... Ms. Rita DAWKINS
84 Dean Enrollment Management .... Mr. Daniel MCEACHERN
08 Dean Libraries .... Ms. Gloria KELLEY
88 Dean Community Development .... Ms. Kathi MCLENDON
07 Dean Enrollment Services .... Ms. April JONES
106 Dean Profess Development/eLearning .... Ms. Karen MERRIMAN
88 General Station Manager WTVI PBS .... Ms. Amy BURKETT

*Cleveland Community College (D)

137 S Post Road, Shelby NC 28152-6296
County: Cleveland FICE Identification: 008082
Unit ID: 198321
Telephone: (704) 669-6000 Carnegie Class: Assoc/Pub-R-M
FAX Number: (704) 669-4202 Calendar System: Semester
URL: www.clevelandcc.edu
Established: 1965 Annual Undergrad Tuition & Fees (In-District): $1,750
Enrollment: 3,416 Coed
Affiliation or Control: State/Local IRS Status: 501(c)3
Highest Offering: Associate Degree
Program: Occupational; 2-Year Principally Bachelor's Creditable
Accreditation: SC, RAD, SURGT

02 President .... Dr. L. Steve THORNBURG
05 Vice President of Academic Programs .... Dr. Becky SAIN
32 Vice President of Student Services .... Dr. Andy GARDNER
10 Senior VP Finance/Admin Svcs .... Mr. Tommy GREENE
51 Vice Pres of Continuing Education .... Mr. Ken MOONEY
26 Senior Dean Cmty Relations/Devel .... Mr. Eddie HOLBROOK
84 Dean of Enrollment Management .... Vacant
20 Executive VP of Instr & Student Dev .... Dr. Shannon KENNEDY
102 Executive Director Foundation .... Mr. U. L. PATTERSON, III
09 Dir Planning/Inst Effectiveness .... Mrs. Laura BOWEN
40 Bookstore Manager .... Vacant
06 Registrar .... Vacant
88 Director CECHS Relations .... Ms. Nedra MADDOX
37 Financial Aid Coordinator .... Ms. Emily HURDT
08 Dean of Learning Resources .... Mrs. Barbara MCKIBBIN
96 Purchasing Officer .... Mrs. Kathy EVERETT
18 Director of Physical Plant .... Mr. Mark FOX
19 Director of Campus Security .... Mr. Bill NEAL
15 Human Resources & Safety Manager .... Mr. Allen KNICELEY
14 Systems Administrator .... Mr. Mike FALLS
90 Computer Network Administrator .... Mr. Robin DYER
24 Audiovisual Coordinator .... Mr. Rodger PERRY
49 Dean Arts & Sciences .... Mrs. Barbara ROMICH
50 Dean Business & Allied Health .... Dr. John LATTIMORE
75 Dean Vocational/Engrng/Public Svcs .... Mr. Michael MCSWAIN
88 Dean Basic Skills .... Dr. Chris NANNEY

*Coastal Carolina Community College (E)

444 Western Boulevard, Jacksonville NC 28546-6816
County: Onslow FICE Identification: 005316
Unit ID: 198330
Telephone: (910) 455-1221 Carnegie Class: Assoc/Pub-R-M
FAX Number: (910) 455-7027 Calendar System: Semester
URL: www.coastalcarolina.edu
Established: 1963 Annual Undergrad Tuition & Fees (In-District): $2,538
Enrollment: 4,691 Coed
Affiliation or Control: State/Local IRS Status: 501(c)3
Highest Offering: Associate Degree
Program: Occupational; 2-Year Principally Bachelor's Creditable
Accreditation: SC, DA, DH, MLTAD, SURGT

02 President .... Dr. Ronald K. LINGLE
03 Executive Vice President .... Mr. David L. HEATHERLY
05 VP Instruction/Info Resources .... Mr. Dewey H. LEWIS
09 VP Inst Eff/Research/Innovation .... Ms. Sharon R. MCGINNIS
32 Division Chair for Student Services .... Dr. Donald R. HERRING
16 Personnel Officer .... Ms. Cindy B. WOOLRIDGE
26 Pub Info Ofcr/Ex Dir Col Foundation .... Ms. Krystal PHILLIPS
06 Dir Admin/Data Mgmt Svc/Registrar .... Ms. Sue FLAHARTY
18 Dir Physical Plant & Aux Services .... Ms. Carol PHILLIPS
37 Director for Financial Aid Services .... Ms. Tammy LYON
88 Director for Veterans Services .... Mr. Christopher P. SABIN
88 Director Economic Development .... Ms. Anne C. SHAW

*College of the Albemarle (F)

1208 North Road Street, Elizabeth City NC 27906-2327
County: Pasquotank FICE Identification: 002917
Unit ID: 197814
Telephone: (252) 335-0821 Carnegie Class: Assoc/Pub-R-M
FAX Number: (252) 335-2011 Calendar System: Semester
URL: www.albemarle.edu
Established: 1960 Annual Undergrad Tuition & Fees (In-District): $2,315
Enrollment: 2,591 Coed
Affiliation or Control: State/Local IRS Status: 501(c)3
Highest Offering: Associate Degree
Program: Occupational; 2-Year Principally Bachelor's Creditable
Accreditation: SC, ADNUR, MAC, MLTAD, SURGT

02 President .... Dr. Kandi W. DEITEMEYER
10 VP Business & Admin Services .... Mr. Robert HOWARD
05 Vice President for Learning .... Dr. Evonne CARTER
32 VP for Student Suc & Enr Mgnt .... Mr. Steven WOODBURN
51 VP Workforce Dev & Cont Edu .... Ms. Suzanne ROHRBAUGH
12 Dean Dare County Campus .... Mr. Joseph T. TURNER
35 Assistant Dean SSEM .... Ms. Martha JOHNSON
26 Director Marketing & Communications .... Mrs. Lisa A. JOHNSON
07 Director Admissions & Testing .... Mr. Kenneth L. KRENTZ
37 Director Scholarship/Student Aid .... Ms. Angela R. GODFREY-DAWSON
88 Director Student Activities .... Mrs. Maenecia COLE
06 Registrar .... Ms. Andrea DANCE
88 Director Small Business Center .... Ms. Ginger H. O'NEAL
78 Director Coop Educ/Job Placement .... Mr. Charles K. CARTER
04 Exec Assistant to the President .... Ms. Sandra W. STRICKLAND
08 Director Learning Resources Center .... Mr. Robert B. SCHENCK
12 Dean Edenton-Chowan Campus .... Ms. B. Lynn HURDLE-WINSLOW
13 Director Mgmt Information Services .... Mr. Wayman WHITE
15 Director Human Resources .... Ms. Wendy W. BRICKHOUSE
18 Director Physical Facilities .... Mr. Richard R. SEYMOUR
21 Controller .... Ms. Susan GENTRY
40 Director Admin Support Services .... Ms. Lisa JONES
08 Dir Learning Resources Ctr-Dare .... Mr. George STRAWLEY
36 Director Counseling & Career Devel .... Mr. John M. WELLS
09 Director of Inst Effectiveness .... Dr. Eric LOVIK
88 Coord Prison Education Programs .... Mr. Cecil PHILPOTT
88 Director Secondary Education .... Ms. Rita O. JENNINGS
49 Division Chair Arts and Sciences .... Mr. Dean ROUGHTON
50 Divison Chair Bus & Applied Tech .... Mr. Mark FAITHFUL
76 Division Chair Health & Wellness .... Ms. Robin HARRIS
83 Department Chair Social Sciences .... Mr. Rodger ROSSMAN
60 Dept Chair English & Comm .... Mrs. Laura MORRISON
81 Dept Chair Math and Science .... Ms. Rhonda WATTS
75 Dept Chair Design Manuf & Ind Tech .... Mr. Charles PURSER
88 Director Business & Economic Devel .... Vacant
77 Dept Chair Bus & Computer Sys Tech .... Ms. Karen ALEXANDER
103 Dir Workforce & Cont Educ .... Ms. Lynda HESTER
57 Department Chair Human & Fine Arts .... Ms. Gale FLAX
88 Dept Chair Developmental Studies .... Ms. Ruth WARREN
88 Department Chair Public Services .... Mrs. Robin ZINSMEISTER
88 Div Chair Foundational Studies .... Ms. Michelle WATERS
19 Director Public Safety & Preparedns .... Mr. Joe DESTEFANO
88 Dir Basic Skills/Workforce Reading .... Mr. Timothy SWEENEY

*Craven Community College (G)

800 College Court, New Bern NC 28562-4984
County: Craven FICE Identification: 006799
Unit ID: 198367
Telephone: (252) 638-7200 Carnegie Class: Assoc/Pub-R-M
FAX Number: (252) 638-4232 Calendar System: Semester
URL: www.cravencc.edu
Established: 1965 Annual Undergrad Tuition & Fees (In-District): $1,144
Enrollment: 3,326 Coed
Affiliation or Control: State/Local IRS Status: 501(c)3
Highest Offering: Associate Degree
Program: Occupational; 2-Year Principally Bachelor's Creditable
Accreditation: SC, MAC, PTAA

02 President .... Dr. Catherine CHEW
05 Exec VP Learning/Student Success .... Dr. Daryl MINUS
12 VP Hvlck-Chry Pt/Mil Affs/Wrkfc Dev .... Dr. Layne HARPINE
11 Vice Pres of Administrative Svcs .... Ms. Karla (Page) JONES-VARNELL
20 AVP Academic Affairs/Student Engage .... Ms. Kathleen GALLMAN
49 Dean Liberal Arts & Univ Transfer .... Ms. Betty K. HATCHER
36 Dean Career Programs .... Mr. James R. MILLARD
09 Director of Institutional Effective .... Ms. Mary C. CLARK
06 Registrar .... Mr. John A. FONVILLE
30 Exec Dir Institutional Advaancement .... Ms. Judy EURICH
103 Ex Dir Ops Wrkfc Dev/Mil Aff-New Bn .... Mr. Eddie D. FOSTER
12 Dean Havelock-Cherry Point Campus .... Mr. Walter CALABRESE
37 Director Financial Aid .... Ms. Kathryn M. BANKS
103 Dir Workforce Readiness & Spec Pgms .... Mr. Mark W. BEST
88 Director Basic Skills Programs .... Ms. Zeledith BLAKELY
32 Director Student Services-Havelock .... Ms. Amy DERCK
08 Director Library Services .... Mrs. Catherine C. CAMPBELL
10 Director Financial Svcs/Purchasing .... Mrs. Cynthia A. PATTERSON
35 Director TRIO Student Support Svcs .... Ms. LaRhonda K. JOHNSON
15 Director Human Resources .... Mrs. Vickie MOSELEY-JONES
88 Dir Workforce Develop/Military Pgms .... Mr. Robin MATTHEWS
106 Dir Distance Learning/Prof Devel .... Dr. Autumn GRUBB
18 Director of Facilities .... Mr. Michael WILLIAMS
13 Director Technology Services .... Ms. Bambi EDWARDS
19 Chief Campus Security .... Mr. H. Steve CARTER
96 Procurement & Fixed Assets Officer .... Mr. Hiram Todd MURPHREY
88 Exec Dir Sustainability/Aux Svcs .... Mr. Martin GUION
76 Interim Dean Health Programs .... Ms. Belinda BARNHILL

*Davidson County Community College (A)

PO Box 1287, Lexington NC 27293-1287
County: Davidson FICE Identification: 002919
Unit ID: 198376
Telephone: (336) 249-8186 Carnegie Class: Assoc/Pub-S-SC
FAX Number: (336) 249-0379 Calendar System: Semester
URL: www.davidsonccc.edu
Established: 1958 Annual Undergrad Tuition & Fees (In-District): $1,846
Enrollment: 4,160 Coed
Affiliation or Control: State/Local IRS Status: 501(c)3
Highest Offering: Associate Degree
Program: Occupational; 2-Year Principally Bachelor's Creditable
Accreditation: SC, ADNUR, CAHIIM, HT, MAC, MLTAD

02 President ....Dr. Mary E. RITTLING
05 VP Academic Programs & Services ....Ms. Jeannine H. WOODY
32 VP Student Affairs ....Dr. Kim W. SEPICH
10 VP Financial/Administrative Svcs ....Mr. Rusty HUNT
102 VP Ext Affairs/Exec Dir Foundation ....Ms. Jenny M. VARNER
76 Dean Health/Wellness/Pub Safety ....Vacant
49 Dean Arts/Sciences/Education ....Dr. Mark BRANSON
88 Dean Foundational Stdnt/Acad Supp ....Dr. Christy FORREST
50 Dean Business Engineering Technical ....Vacant
12 Dean Davie Campus ....Ms. Teresa KINES
35 Dean Student Success ....Mr. Stephen CAMP
21 Dean Financial/Admin Svcs ....Ms. Laura L. YARBROUGH
09 Exec Dir Rsrch Planning Innovation ....Ms. Susan BURLESON
26 Exec Dir Marketing & Communications ....Ms. Terri SMITH
06 Dir Student Records/Registration ....Mr. Bryan MCCULLOUGH
07 Director Admissions & Financial Aid ....Ms. Lori BLEVINS
36 Director Career Development ....Mr. Charles MAYER
18 Director Physical Plant Services ....Mr. Keith RAKER
15 Director Personnel Services ....Ms. Denise BARNHARDT

*Durham Technical Community College (B)

1637 Lawson Street, Durham NC 27703-5023
County: Durham FICE Identification: 005448
Unit ID: 198455
Telephone: (919) 536-7200 Carnegie Class: Assoc/Pub-U-SC
FAX Number: (919) 686-3601 Calendar System: Semester
URL: www.durhamtech.edu
Established: 1961 Annual Undergrad Tuition & Fees (In-District): $1,840
Enrollment: 5,304 Coed
Affiliation or Control: State/Local IRS Status: 501(c)3
Highest Offering: Associate Degree
Program: Occupational; 2-Year Principally Bachelor's Creditable
Accreditation: SC, ADNUR, CAHIIM, COARC, DT, MAC, OPD, OTA, PNUR, SURGT

02 President ....Dr. William G. INGRAM
03 Vice President Institutional Advanc ....Mr. Tom JAYNES
05 VP Student Learning/Devel & Support ....Dr. Valarie J. EVANS
10 VP Finance and Administration ....Mr. Robert KEENEY
51 Int Corporate/Continuing Education ....Dr. Peter WOOLDRIDGE
88 Exec Dir Center for Global Learner ....Ms. Constanza GOMEZ-JOINS
04 Assistant to the President ....Vacant
04 Executive Secy to the President ....Ms. Janelle G. MONTALVO
09 Director Institutional Research ....Dr. Teri L. KAASA
07 Director of Admissions ....Ms. Iesha M. CLEVELAND
30 Director Resource Development ....Ms. Gayle SIMS
14 Executive Director Info Tech Svcs ....Mr. Patrick HINES
15 Director Human Resources ....Ms. Kathy MCKINLEY
08 Director Library & Media Services ....Ms. Irene H. LAUBE
55 Coordinator Evening College ....Ms. Martita WILLIAMS
18 Director Facility Services ....Mr. Richard A. MCKOWN
37 Director Financial Aid ....Mr. Everett M. JETER
96 Director Auxiliary Services ....Ms. Yolanda V. MOORE-JONES
49 Dean Arts & Sciences ....Dr. Thomas E. GOULD
76 Dean Health Technologies ....Ms. Melissa OAKLEY OCKERT
88 Asst Dean Applied & Public Svc ....Mr. Randall J. EGSEGIAN
06 Interim Dean Student Services ....Ms. Lisa INMAN
75 Dean Career and Technical Programs ....Vacant
77 Assoc Dean Info Systems Technology ....Ms. Charlene C. WEST
38 Int Asst Dean Student Development ....Ms. K. Leigh FORELL
19 Director Campus Police & Safety ....Ms. Sarah L. MINNIS

*Edgecombe Community College (C)

2009 W Wilson Street, Tarboro NC 27886-9399
County: Edgecombe FICE Identification: 008855
Unit ID: 198491
Telephone: (252) 823-5166 Carnegie Class: Assoc/Pub-R-M
FAX Number: (252) 823-6817 Calendar System: Semester
URL: www.edgecombe.edu
Established: 1967 Annual Undergrad Tuition & Fees (In-District): $2,400
Enrollment: 3,033 Coed
Affiliation or Control: State/Local IRS Status: 501(c)3
Highest Offering: Associate Degree
Program: Occupational; 2-Year Principally Bachelor's Creditable
Accreditation: SC, CAHIIM, COARC, MAC, RAD, SURGT

02 President ....Dr. Deborah L. LAMM
05 Vice President of Instruction ....Dr. Kristi L. SNUGGS
11 Vice Pres Administrative Services ....Mr. Charlie R. HARRELL
32 Vice President Student Services ....Mr. Michael J. JORDAN
20 Asc VP Instruct/Curriculum/Cont Ed ....Mr. Lynn CALE
84 Dean Enrollment Management ....Ms. Ginny MCLENDON
45 Director of Inst Effectiveness ....Ms. Sheila HOSKINS
26 Director of Public Information ....Ms. Mary T. BASS
08 Director of Library Services ....Ms. Deborah PARISHER
06 Registrar ....Ms. Cathy P. DUPREE
15 Director Personnel Services ....Ms. Janice TOLSON
18 Chief Facilities/Physical Plant ....Mr. Freddy WHITLEY
37 Director Student Financial Aid ....Vacant

*Fayetteville Technical Community College (D)

PO Box 35236, 2201 Hull Road, Fayetteville NC 28303-0236
County: Cumberland FICE Identification: 007640
Unit ID: 198534
Telephone: (910) 678-8400 Carnegie Class: Assoc/Pub-R-L
FAX Number: (910) 678-8269 Calendar System: Semester
URL: www.faytechcc.edu
Established: 1961 Annual Undergrad Tuition & Fees (In-State): $2,290
Enrollment: 12,127 Coed
Affiliation or Control: State IRS Status: 501(c)3
Highest Offering: Associate Degree
Program: Occupational; 2-Year Principally Bachelor's Creditable
Accreditation: SC, ADNUR, COARC, DA, DH, FUSER, PTAA, RAD, SURGT

02 President ....Dr. Larry KEEN
11 Vice Pres for Administrative Svcs ..Mr. Joseph W. LEVISTER, JR.
05 Vice Pres for Academic/Student Svcs ....Dr. David BRAND
15 VP Human Res/Inst Effect/Assessment ....Mr. Carl MITCHELL
10 Vice Pres for Business and Finance ....Mrs. Betty J. SMITH
26 Exec Dir Marketing/Public Relations ....Mr. Brent MICHAELS
72 Vice Pres Learning Technologies ....Mr. Bob J. ERVIN
51 Assoc Vice Pres for Continuing Educ ....Dr. Joe W. MULLIS
32 Assoc Vice Pres Student Services ....Dr. Rosemary KELLY
56 Assoc Vice Pres Off-Campus Programs ....Dr. Michelle SAMUELS-JONES
84 Dean Enrollment Mgmt/Financial Aid .Mr. Harper SHACKELFORD
06 Registrar ....Ms. Melissa A. JONES
21 Controller ....Mrs. Robin DEAVER
07 Director of Admissions ....Vacant
13 Director Management Information Svc ....Mr. Roderick BROWER
38 Director of Counseling Services ....Ms. DeSandra WASHINGTON
18 Director of Facility Services ....Mr. Harold WYCKOFF
96 Purchasing Agent ....Ms. Amy SAMPERTON
50 Dean of Business Programs ....Mr. William GRIFFIN
49 Dean College Transfer/Gen Educ Pgms ....Dr. Anthony HUBERT
76 Dean of Health Programs ....Ms. Mary JOHNSON
54 Dean Engr/Pub Svs/Applied Tech Pgms ....Mr. Daryle NOBLES

*Forsyth Technical Community College (E)

2100 Silas Creek Parkway, Winston-Salem NC 27103-5197
County: Forsyth FICE Identification: 005317
Unit ID: 198552
Telephone: (336) 723-0371 Carnegie Class: Assoc/Pub-U-SC
FAX Number: (336) 761-2399 Calendar System: Semester
URL: www.forsythtech.edu
Established: 1960 Annual Undergrad Tuition & Fees (In-State): $1,893
Enrollment: 9,999 Coed
Affiliation or Control: State IRS Status: 501(c)3
Highest Offering: Associate Degree
Program: Occupational; 2-Year Principally Bachelor's Creditable
Accreditation: SC, COARC, DA, DH, DMS, ENGT, MAC, NMT, RAD, RTT

02 President ....Dr. Gary M. GREEN
05 Vice Pres Instructional Services ....Dr. Conley F. WINEBARGER
13 Vice Pres of Planning & Info Svcs ....Ms. Rachel M. DESMARAIS
32 Vice President Student Services ....Ms. Jewel B. CHERRY
30 VP Inst Advancement/Exec Dir Found ....Ms. Mamie M. SUTPHIN
10 Vice President Business Services ....Ms. Wendy R. EMERSON
103 Vice Pres Economic & Workforce Dev ....Mr. Alan K. MURDOCK
100 Director Office of the President ....Ms. Sherri W. BOWEN
50 Dean Business Info Tech Div ....Mr. G. Bernard YEVIN
79 Dean of Humanities/Social Sci Div ....Ms. Yolanda S. WILSON
81 Dean Math/Science & Technologies ....Mr. Michael V. AYERS
54 Dean of Engineering Tech Div ....Mr. Leonard R. KISER
17 Dean of Health Technologies ....Dr. Bonnie G. POPE
31 Dean Community/Economic Development ....Ms. Sharon D. ANDERSON
08 Dean Learning Resources ....Mr. J. Randel CANDELARIA
88 Dean Adult Literacy ....Mr. Michael E. HARRIS
66 Director Nursing ....Ms. Linda H. LATHAM
76 Director Imaging ....Ms. Deborah D. TAYLOR
76 Director Health Services ....Ms. Jean E. MIDDLESWARTH
84 Dean Enrollment & Student Svcs ....Vacant
21 Dean Financial Services ....Ms. Melanie L. NUCKOLS
38 Dir Student Success Ctr/Counseling ....Mr. Joe E. MCINTOSH
15 Director Human Resources ....Mr. Gregory M. CHASE
09 Dir Institutional Effectiveness ....Ms. Dana L. DALTON
14 Director Information Systems ....Mr. Randall A. ROBERTSON
88 Dir Recruiting/Student Support Svcs ....Mr. Edwin B. WADDELL
37 Director Student Financial Services ....Mr. Ricky C. HODGES
06 Director Records/Registrar ....Ms. Gwen D. WHITAKER
07 Director of Admissions ....Ms. Jean M. GROOME
18 Director Physical Plant Services ....Mr. Scot R. QUESENBERRY
19 Director Campus Police ....Mr. Renarde D. EARL
88 Director Small Business Center ....Mr. Allan YOUNGER
35 Director Student Activities ....Ms. Beverly N. LEWIS
96 Director Purchasing/Equipment ....Mr. Philip L. MCCLUNG
40 Director Auxiliary Svcs/Bookstore ....Mr. Brian A. HICKS
12 Director Grady Swisher Center ....Ms. Mary B. KING
12 Director Mazie Woodruff Center ....Mr. TerCraig D. EDWARDS
12 Director Northwest Forsyth Center ....Ms. Kristie F. HENDRIX
12 Sr Dir Off-Campus/Stokes Cty Op ....Ms. Ann B. WATTS
88 Dean Educational Partnerships ....Dr. Susan Q. PHELPS
88 Dean Business and Industry ....Ms. Jennifer B. COULOMBE
88 Dean Health and Emergency Programs ....Mr. Wesley D. HUTCHINS
12 Dir Transportation Technology Ctr ....Mr. Forrest LINEBERRY
88 Dean Learning Technologies ....Mr. James COOK
44 Dir Major Gifts & Planned Giving ....Ms. Edyce ELWORTH
44 Dir Annual Giving & Special Events ....Ms. Angela BRYANT
04 Senior Administrative Associate ....Ms. Dawn P. MITCHELL
25 Director Grants and Contracts ....Mr. Mike MASSOGLIA

*Gaston College (F)

201 Highway 321 S, Dallas NC 28034-1499
County: Gaston FICE Identification: 002973
Unit ID: 198570
Telephone: (704) 922-6200 Carnegie Class: Assoc/Pub-S-SC
FAX Number: (704) 922-2323 Calendar System: Semester
URL: www.gaston.edu
Established: 1964 Annual Undergrad Tuition & Fees (In-District): $2,480
Enrollment: 5,705 Coed
Affiliation or Control: State/Local IRS Status: 501(c)3
Highest Offering: Associate Degree
Program: Occupational; 2-Year Principally Bachelor's Creditable
Accreditation: SC, ACBSP, ADNUR, DIETT, ENGT, MAC, PNUR

02 President ....Dr. Patricia A. SKINNER
10 VP Finance/Facilities/Operations ....Ms. Cynthia MCCRORY
05 Vice President of Academic Affairs ....Dr. Don AMMONS
20 Associate VP Academic Affairs ....Dr. Dewey DELLINGER
32 VP Student Services/Enrollment Mgmt ....Dr. Silvia Patricia RIOS-HUSAIN
35 Assistant VP for Student Services ....Ms. Audrey SHERRILL
103 VP Econ Workforce & Marketing/PR ....Dr. Linda L. GREER
04 Exec Admin Assistant to the Pres ....Ms. Sylvia DIXON
09 Director Insti Effectiveness ....Dr. Rex J. CLAY
08 Director Libraries ....Dr. Harry COOKE
13 Chief Technology Services Officer ....Ms. Savonne MCNEILL
38 Director of Counseling ....Ms. Jennifer NICHOLS
84 Director Enrollment Mgmt/Admission ....Vacant
06 Director of Registration/Records ....Ms. Alisa ROY
37 Director of Financial Aid ....Ms. Judy SCHNEIDER
19 Chief of Campus Police ....Mr. Billy LYTTON
15 Director Human Resources and Safety ....Mr. Todd BANEY
18 Director Facilities Management ....Mr. Wes LANDRUM
26 Director of Marketing/PR ....Ms. Stephanie MICHAEL-PICKETT
30 Chief Development Officer ....Ms. Julia ALLEN
96 Director Purchasing/Receiv/Shipping ....Mr. Chuck WRAY
21 Controller ....Mr. Bruce COLE
40 Director Bookstore ....Mr. Charles WILSON
49 Dean of Liberal Arts & Science ....Ms. Heather WOODSON
72 Dean Engr/Industrial Technologies ....Mr. Virgil COX
66 Dean Health & Human Services ....Vacant
50 Dean Business & Information Tech ....Ms. Michelle BYRD
51 Dean Cont Educ and Public Safety ....Dr. Karen LESS
12 Dean Lincoln Campus ....Dr. John MCHUGH
12 Dean Kimbrell Campus/Textile Ctr ....Dr. Joe KEITH
78 Dir Educational Partnerships ....Ms. Kimberly WYONT

*Guilford Technical Community College (G)

PO Box 309, Jamestown NC 27282-0309
County: Guilford FICE Identification: 004838
Unit ID: 198622
Telephone: (336) 334-4822 Carnegie Class: Assoc/Pub-S-MC
FAX Number: (336) 454-2745 Calendar System: Semester
URL: www.gtcc.edu
Established: 1958 Annual Undergrad Tuition & Fees (In-State): $2,314
Enrollment: 14,802 Coed
Affiliation or Control: State IRS Status: 501(c)3
Highest Offering: Associate Degree
Program: Occupational; 2-Year Principally Bachelor's Creditable; Technical Emphasis
Accreditation: SC, ACFEI, DA, DH, MAC, PTAA, RAD, SURGT

02 President ....Dr. Randy PARKER
03 Executive Vice President ....Mrs. Rae Marie SMITH
05 Vice President of Instruction ....Dr. Beth PITONZO
32 Vice Pres Student Support Services ....Dr. Quentin JOHNSON
11 Assoc Vice Pres Administrative Svcs ....Mr. Mitchell JOHNSON
10 Assoc VP of Business & Finance ....Ms. Nancy B. SOLLOSI
20 Assoc VP Student Support Services ....Dr. Alison WIERS
51 VP Corporate & Continuing Educ ....Mr. Leroy STOKES
30 Exec Dir Institutional Advancement ....Mr. Alan PIKE
12 Dean Greensboro Campus ....Mr. Manuel DUDLEY
12 Dean High Point Campus ....Ms. Janette N. MCNEILL
50 Dir Business & Industry Training ....Mr. Stephen CASTELLOE
30 Director of Development ....Vacant
15 Director of Human Resources ....Ms. Jean R. JACKSON
13 Chief Information Officer ....Mr. Rob RAMEY
18 Director of Construction ....Vacant
09 Director of Institutional Research ....Ms. Stephanie WRIGHT
07 Director of Admissions ....Mr. Jesse CROSS
35 Director of Student Life ....Ms. Berri V. CROSS

37 Director Financial Aid .... Ms. Lisa A. KORETOFF
19 Chief of Campus Police .... Ms. Dawn TEVEPAUGH
06 Registrar .... Mr. Sanjay RAMDATH
21 Controller .... Ms. Angela M. CARTER
40 Bookstore Manager .... Mr. Shawn G. DEE
36 Coordinator Career Services .... Mr. Daniel J. GRIGG
38 Director Counseling & Assessment .... Ms. Angela LEAK
29 Coord Resource Dev/Alumni Affairs .... Vacant
08 Dir of Library Services .... Ms. Mary LANE

*Halifax Community College (A)

PO Drawer 809, Weldon NC 27890-0809

County: Halifax FICE Identification: 007986

Unit ID: 198640

Telephone: (252) 536-4221 Carnegie Class: Assoc/Pub-R-S

FAX Number: (252) 536-4144 Calendar System: Semester

URL: www.halifaxcc.edu

Established: 1967 Annual Undergrad Tuition & Fees (In-District): $2,405

Enrollment: 1,556 Coed

Affiliation or Control: State/Local IRS Status: 501(c)3

Highest Offering: Associate Degree

Program: Occupational; 2-Year Principally Bachelor's Creditable; Business Emphasis

Accreditation: SC, DH, MLTAD, PHLEB

02 President .... Dr. Ervin V. GRIFFIN, SR.
04 Exec Assistant to the President .... Ms. Kimberly J. MACK
05 Vice Pres Academic Affairs .... Dr. Deryl FULMER
10 Vice President Admin Services .... Mrs. Debra SMITH
30 Vice Pres Institutional Advancement .... Dr. Dianne RHOADES
32 Dean Student Svcs & Enrollment Mgmt .... Dr. Barbara BRADLEY-HASTY
20 Dean of Curriculum Programs .... Ms. B. T. BROWN
06 Registrar .... Ms. Dawn VELIKY
07 Director of Admissions .... Mr. James Bernard WASHINGTON
08 Director Learning Resources .... Mr. Marc FINNEY
09 Dir of Institutional Effectiveness .... Dr. Adrian LECHE
26 Dir Public Relations & Marketing .... Mrs. Melanie TEMPLE
40 Bookstore Manager .... Mrs. Doris GARNER
38 Director Counseling Services .... Ms. Teresa MAYLE
18 Chief Facilities/Physical Plant .... Mr. Ray HESTER
36 Coord of Testing & Job Placement .... Ms. Angela RANOLPH
37 Director of Financial Aid .... Mrs. Tara KEETER
96 Purchasing Agent .... Mrs. Tina CURRY
15 Personnel Officer .... Mrs. Margaret MURGA
13 Computer Network Manager .... Mr. Jerry THOMPSON
49 Div Chair Arts & Sciences .... Mr. Calvin STANSBURY
50 Div Chair Business/Commercial Tech .... Mr. Lateef BALOGUN
76 Division Chair Health Sciences .... Mrs. Kelly HARVEY
88 Div Chair Public Service Technology .... Mr. Michael EARL
75 Div Chair Vocation/Industrial Tech .... Mr. Hunter TAYLOR

*Haywood Community College (B)

185 Freedlander Drive, Clyde NC 28721-9453

County: Haywood FICE Identification: 008083

Unit ID: 198668

Telephone: (828) 627-2821 Carnegie Class: Assoc/Pub-R-M

FAX Number: (828) 627-3606 Calendar System: Semester

URL: www.haywood.edu

Established: 1965 Annual Undergrad Tuition & Fees (In-State): $2,288

Enrollment: 2,279 Coed

Affiliation or Control: State IRS Status: 501(c)3

Highest Offering: Associate Degree

Program: Occupational; 2-Year Principally Bachelor's Creditable; Technical Emphasis

Accreditation: SC, MAC

02 President .... Dr. Barbara PARKER
05 Vice President of Academics .... Dr. Buddy TIGNOR
32 VP Student/Workforce Development .... Dr. Laura LEATHERWOOD
10 Vice President Business Operations .... Mrs. Karen DENNEY
18 Director of Campus Development .... Mr. Bill DECHANT
30 Dir of Institutional Advancement .... Mrs. Sherri MYERS
26 Director Marketing & Communications .... Ms. Debbie DAVIS
15 Director of Human Resources .... Mrs. Marsha STINES
84 Director of Enrollment Management .... Mrs. Jennifer HERRERA
37 Director of Financial Aid .... Vacant
36 Career Devel Specialist/Recruiter .... Ms. Meg CONNER
09 Coord of Research & Inst Research .... Dr. Marlowe MAGER

*Isothermal Community College (C)

PO Box 804, Spindale NC 28160-0804

County: Rutherford FICE Identification: 002934

Unit ID: 198710

Telephone: (828) 286-3636 Carnegie Class: Assoc/Pub-R-M

FAX Number: (828) 286-1120 Calendar System: Semester

URL: www.isothermal.edu

Established: 1964 Annual Undergrad Tuition & Fees (In-District): $2,565

Enrollment: 2,516 Coed

Affiliation or Control: State/Local IRS Status: 501(c)3

Highest Offering: Associate Degree

Program: Occupational; 2-Year Principally Bachelor's Creditable

Accreditation: SC

02 President .... Mr. Walter H. DALTON
11 Vice Pres Administrative Services .... Mr. Stephen MATHENY
05 VP Academic/Stdnt Svcs/Instl Assess .... Dr. Kim GOLD
103 VP Cmty/Workforce Educ/Inst Advance .... Mr. Thad HARRILL
32 Dean of Student Affairs .... Dr. Karen JONES
50 Dean of Business Sciences .... Ms. Kim ALEXANDER
49 Dean of Arts & Sciences .... Dr. Kathy ACKERMAN
75 Dean of Applied Science/Technology .... Dr. Amber THOMPSON
51 Dean of Continuing Education .... Mrs. Donna HOOD
12 Director of Polk Campus .... Mrs. Kate BARKSCHAT
20 Director Academic Development .... Mrs. Debbie PUETT
08 Director Library Services .... Mr. Charles WIGGINS
10 Controller .... Mrs. Amy M. PENSON
37 Financial Aid Officer .... Mr. Jeff BOYLE
26 Dir Marketing/Community Relations .... Mr. Mike GAVIN
18 Dir Plant Operations/Maintenance .... Mr. Rick EDWARDS
38 Director Student Counseling Testing .... Mr. Johnny SMITH
84 Director of Enrollment Management .... Ms. Alice MCCLUNEY
06 Registrar .... Ms. Kelly METCALF
96 Director of Purchasing .... Ms. Trish HUNTSINGER
13 Director of Information Technology .... Mr. Robby WALTERS
40 Bookstore Manager .... Mr. Nathan COLE

*James Sprunt Community College (D)

PO Box 398, Kenansville NC 28349-0398

County: Duplin FICE Identification: 007687

Unit ID: 198729

Telephone: (910) 296-2400 Carnegie Class: Assoc/Pub-R-S

FAX Number: (910) 296-1636 Calendar System: Semester

URL: www.jamessprunt.edu

Established: 1964 Annual Undergrad Tuition & Fees (In-State): $2,208

Enrollment: 1,572 Coed

Affiliation or Control: State IRS Status: 501(c)3

Highest Offering: Associate Degree

Program: Occupational; 2-Year Principally Bachelor's Creditable; Technical Emphasis

Accreditation: SC, MAC

02 Chief Executive Officer/President .... Dr. Lawrence L. ROUSE
05 VP of Curriculum Services .... Ms. June DAVIS
51 VP of Continuing Education .... Dr. Unita KNIGHT
10 VP of Admin & Fiscal Services .... Mr. John HARDISON
32 VP of Student Services .... Vacant
30 VP Coll Advance/Inst Effectiveness .... Mr. Robert TURNER
06 Registrar .... Ms. Patricia NORRIS
07 Admissions Specialist .... Ms. Lea W. MATTHEWS
37 Director Financial Aid/Vet Affairs .... Ms. Tamara GLASPIE
38 Director of Student Counseling .... Ms. Amber FERRELL
08 Director Library Services .... Ms. Patricia KLIMSCHOT
15 Dir Human Resources/Campus Safety .... Vacant
51 Director Continuing Education .... Vacant
97 Director of General Education .... Mr. Andy CAVENAUGH
09 Dir Research/Plng/Instl Effective .... Mr. William (Bill) CANUETTE, JR.
18 Chief Facilities/Physical Plant .... Mr. Arthur KORNEGAY
96 Director of Purchasing .... Ms. Toni HENDERSON
55 Instr/Coord Evening/Weekend Svcs .... Mr. James THOMAS

*Johnston Community College (E)

PO Box 2350, 245 College Road, Smithfield NC 27577-2350

County: Johnston FICE Identification: 009336

Unit ID: 198774

Telephone: (919) 934-3051 Carnegie Class: Assoc/Pub-S-SC

FAX Number: (919) 209-2142 Calendar System: Semester

URL: www.johnstoncc.edu

Established: 1969 Annual Undergrad Tuition & Fees (In-District): $1,813

Enrollment: 5,635 Coed

Affiliation or Control: State/Local IRS Status: 501(c)3

Highest Offering: Associate Degree

Program: Occupational; 2-Year Principally Bachelor's Creditable

Accreditation: SC, DMS, MAC, RAD

02 President .... Dr. David N. JOHNSON
10 VP Finance & Administrative Svcs .... Mr. Michael CROSS
05 Vice Pres Curriculum Programs .... Mrs. Dee Dee D. DAUGHTRY
32 Vice Pres of Student Services .... Dr. Pamela J. HARRELL
30 VP Institutional Effectiveness .... Mrs. Dale A. O'NEILL
102 Executive Director of Foundation .... Ms. Twyla C. WELLS
13 Executive Director Info Technology .... Mr. Hal MURY
08 Director Learning Resources Center .... Ms. Christine B. ROBERTS
105 Internet Info Systems Coordinator .... Ms. Lisa H. MCLAURIN
06 Registrar .... Ms. Deena H. HENRY
37 Financial Aid Officer .... Mrs. Betty C. WOODALL
88 Director of Auditorium .... Mr. Ken H. MITCHELL
07 Director of Admissions/Counseling .... Mrs. Joan S. MCLENDON
103 Director Workforce Development .... Mrs. Joy T. CALLAHAN
26 Chief Public Relations Officer .... Mrs. Traci D. ASHLEY
18 Manager Facilities/Physical Plant .... Mr. Michael MASSEY
96 Coordinator of Purchasing .... Mr. Doug PATE

*Lenoir Community College (F)

231 Highway 58 South, Kinston NC 28502-0188

County: Lenoir FICE Identification: 002940

Unit ID: 198817

Telephone: (252) 527-6223 Carnegie Class: Assoc/Pub-R-M

FAX Number: (252) 233-6879 Calendar System: Semester

URL: www.lenoircc.edu

Established: 1958 Annual Undergrad Tuition & Fees (In-District): $2,407

Enrollment: 2,963 Coed

Affiliation or Control: State/Local IRS Status: 501(c)3

Highest Offering: Associate Degree

Program: Occupational; 2-Year Principally Bachelor's Creditable

Accreditation: SC, ACFEI, MAC, POLYT, RAD, SURGT

02 President .... Dr. Brantley BRILEY
51 VP Continuing Education .... Dr. Jay CARRAWAY
11 VP of Administrative Services .... Ms. Deborah SUTTON
05 VP Academic & Student Services .... Dr. Deborah GRIMES
10 Chief Financial Officer .... Ms. Deborah S. SUTTON
06 Registrar .... Mrs. Shelia WIGGINS
84 Director Enrollment Mgmt/Admissions .... Vacant
32 Dean of Student Services .... Dr. John Paul BLACK
37 Director of Student Financial Aid .... Ms. Melissa WHITMAN
27 Director of Information Services .... Mr. Lee WETHERINGTON
09 Dir Planning Rsch/Inst Effective .... Mrs. Karen HILL
15 Chief Human Resources Officer .... Mrs. Tasha JOHNSON
18 Director of Maintenance .... Mr. Reed LOVICK
41 Dir Athletic Operations .... Mr. Stony WINE
21 Director of Financial Services .... Ms. Jessica MCMAHON
96 Purchasing Agent .... Mrs. Rhonda REEDER
26 Director of Mktg/Recruiting/Comm .... Mrs. Richy HUNEYCUTT
30 Director Institutional Advancement .... Mrs. Jeanne KENNEDY
36 Director Coop Ed/Job Dev/Placement .... Mrs. Frances GASKINS
08 Director of Learning Resources .... Mr. Carenado DAVIS
50 Dean of Business/Industrial/Technol .... Mr. Gary CLEMENTS
49 Dean of Arts & Sciences .... Dr. Evelyn KELLY
76 Dean of Health Sciences & Nursing .... Dr. Alexis WELCH
89 Director of Freshman Studies .... Mrs. Evelyn KELLY
92 Dean/Director of Honors Program .... Dr. John Paul BLACK
93 Dean/Director of Minority Students .... Vacant
94 Dean/Director of Women's Studies .... Dr. Deborah GRIMES
35 Director Student Activities .... Vacant

*Martin Community College (G)

1161 Kehukee Park Road, Williamston NC 27892-9988

County: Martin FICE Identification: 007988

Unit ID: 198905

Telephone: (252) 792-1521 Carnegie Class: Assoc/Pub-R-S

FAX Number: (252) 792-0826 Calendar System: Semester

URL: www.martin.cc.nc.us

Established: 1967 Annual Undergrad Tuition & Fees (In-State): $1,836

Enrollment: 778 Coed

Affiliation or Control: State IRS Status: 501(c)3

Highest Offering: Associate Degree

Program: Occupational; 2-Year Principally Bachelor's Creditable

Accreditation: SC, DA, MAC, PTAA

02 President .... Dr. Ann R. BRITT
05 Dean Curriculum Pgm/Dean Stdnt Svcs .... Ms. Dorothy CARTER
11 Dean of Administrative Services .... Vacant
04 Asst to Pres for Business/Industry .... Mr. Billy BARBER
37 Financial Aid Director .... Ms. Michelle LANE COBB
38 Counselor .... Dr. Brian BUSCH
06 Registrar .... Ms. Jennifer BALLS
07 Admissions Officer .... Mr. Michael CURRY
51 Exec Dir Continuing Education .... Mr. Walter V. WHITFIELD
14 Systems Administrator .... Ms. Donna ROGERS
18 Director of Facilities .... Mr. Walter WHEELER
15 Human Resource Officer .... Ms. Rebecca P. WOOLARD
88 Telecommunication/Network Manager .... Mr. Elijah T. FREEMAN
09 Director of Institutional Research .... Ms. Catherine CURRIN

*Mayland Community College (H)

PO Box 547, Spruce Pine NC 28777-0547

County: Avery FICE Identification: 011197

Unit ID: 198914

Telephone: (828) 765-7351 Carnegie Class: Assoc/Pub-R-S

FAX Number: (828) 765-0728 Calendar System: Semester

URL: www.mayland.edu

Established: 1971 Annual Undergrad Tuition & Fees (In-District): $2,635

Enrollment: 1,230 Coed

Affiliation or Control: State/Local IRS Status: 501(c)3

Highest Offering: Associate Degree

Program: Occupational; 2-Year Principally Bachelor's Creditable; Technical Emphasis

Accreditation: SC, MAC

02 President .... Dr. John C. BOYD
04 Assistant to the President .... Ms. Kristabell KENNEDY
05 Vice Pres Instructional Services .... Mrs. Rhia CRAWFORD
10 Vice President Administrative Svcs .... Mr. Gerald HYDE
51 Assoc VP Cont Ed Programs/Workforce .... Mrs. Rita EARLEY
32 Dean of Students .... Ms. Michelle MUSICH
76 Dean of Health Sciences Programs .... Mrs. Sheryl YOUNG
49 Dean of Arts & Sciences .... Ms. Beth MITCHELL
50 Dean of Business & Technology .... Ms. Brenda MCFEE
08 Dean Learning Resources Center .... Mr. Jon WILMESHERR
09 Institutional Effectiveness .... Mrs. Liz SILVERS
06 Registrar .... Mrs. Tracy E. WEBBER
88 Director of Basic Skills Programs .... Mr. Steve GUNTER
12 Director of Avery County Cont Ed .... Mrs. Melissa C. PHILLIPS
12 Director of Mitchell County Cont Ed .... Mr. Chris HELMS
12 Dean of Yancey County Cont Ed .... Dr. Monica S. CARPENTER
37 Director Student Financial Aid .... Mrs. Cassie FORBES
18 Director Facilities/Physical Plant .... Mr. Lee WHITTINGTON
13 Director Mgt Information Systems .... Mr. Tommy R. LEDFORD
15 Director Personnel Services .... Mr. Michael AYERS
26 Chief Public Relations Officer .... Mrs. Beth MORRIS
96 Coordinator of Purchasing/Equipment .... Mr. Sam PRESNELL

*McDowell Technical Community College (A)

54 College Drive, Marion NC 28752-8728
County: McDowell FICE Identification: 008085
Unit ID: 198923
Telephone: (828) 652-6021 Carnegie Class: Assoc/Pub-R-S
FAX Number: (828) 652-1014 Calendar System: Semester
URL: www.mcdowelltech.edu
Established: 1964 Annual Undergrad Tuition & Fees (In-District): $1,716
Enrollment: 1,316 Coed
Affiliation or Control: State/Local IRS Status: 501(c)3
Highest Offering: Associate Degree
Program: Occupational; 2-Year Principally Bachelor's Creditable
Accreditation: SC, CAHIIM

02 President .... Dr. Bryan W. WILSON
05 Vice President for Learning .... Mrs. Shirley F. BROWN
20 Dean Academic Programs .... Dr. James BENTON
09 Director of Inst Effectiveness .... Mr. Ladelle HARMON
26 Director of External Relations .... Mr. Michael K. LAVENDER
13 Director of Technology/Info Systems .... Mr. Elmer R. MACOPSON
08 Director of Library Services .... Ms. Sharon P. SMITH
88 Director of Correctional Programs .... Mr. Frank D. SILVER
88 Director of Industrial Training .... Mr. Eddie SHUFORD
76 Director of Health Sciences .... Mrs. Penny CROSS
06 Registrar .... Ms. Kelly HAMLIN
37 Dir Student Financial Aid/Counselor ...... Ms. Kim M. LEDBETTER
36 Director of Student Enrichment Ctr .... Mrs. Donna SHORT
88 Director of Adult Basic Skills .... Mrs. Teresa VALENTINO
88 Counselor/VA Director .... Mrs. Donna SHORT
51 Director of Continuing Education .... Mr. William B. LEDBETTER
88 Director Basic Law Enforcement Trng .... Mr. Stacy BUFF
07 Director of Admissions .... Mr. Wingate CAIN
30 Resource Development .... Ms. Susan BERLEY
106 Coordinator of Distance Education .... Mrs. Joan WEILER
16 Coord of Human Resources Devel .... Mrs. Mary L. LEDBETTER
18 Coord Maintenance/Custodial Svcs .... Mr. Carl COSTNER
88 Coord of Small Business Center .... Mr. H. Dean KANIPE
04 Exec Assistant to the President .... Mrs. Rhonda SILVER

*Mitchell Community College (B)

500 W Broad Street, Statesville NC 28677-5293
County: Iredell FICE Identification: 002947
Unit ID: 198987
Telephone: (704) 878-3200 Carnegie Class: Assoc/Pub-R-M
FAX Number: (704) 878-0872 Calendar System: Semester
URL: www.mitchellcc.edu
Established: 1852 Annual Undergrad Tuition & Fees (In-State): $2,356
Enrollment: 3,800 Coed
Affiliation or Control: State IRS Status: 501(c)3
Highest Offering: Associate Degree
Program: Occupational; 2-Year Principally Bachelor's Creditable
Accreditation: SC, ADNUR, MAC

02 President .... Dr. Tim BREWER
05 Vice President of Instruction .... Dr. Camille REESE
10 Vice Pres of Finance/Administration .... Mr. Richard J. LEFEVRE
103 Vice Pres Workforce Development/CEC .... Ms. Carol JOHNSON
32 Vice Pres Student Services .... Mr. Dan MANNING
09 Director Inst Effectiveness .... Ms. Mary Ellen GOLDSTEIN
08 Int Director of Learning Resources .... Ms. Vicki CALDWELL
37 Director of Financial Aid .... Ms. Candace COOPER
18 Exec Dir Facilities/Auxiliary Svcs .... Mr. Gary JOHNSON
29 Director Alumni Relations .... Vacant
26 Chief Public Relations Officer .... Ms. Kathy HOLLAND
30 Dir Development/College Relations .... Mr. Harry STILLERMAN

*Montgomery Community College (C)

1011 Page Street, Troy NC 27371-0787
County: Montgomery FICE Identification: 008087
Unit ID: 199023
Telephone: (910) 576-6222 Carnegie Class: Assoc/Pub-R-S
FAX Number: (910) 576-2176 Calendar System: Semester
URL: www.montgomery.edu
Established: 1967 Annual Undergrad Tuition & Fees (In-District): $1,830
Enrollment: 838 Coed
Affiliation or Control: State/Local IRS Status: 501(c)3
Highest Offering: Associate Degree
Program: Occupational; 2-Year Principally Bachelor's Creditable
Accreditation: SC, DA, MAC

02 President .... Dr. Mary P. KIRK
05 VP of Instruction/Continuing Ed .... Dr. Jeff HAMILTON
11 VP of Administrative Services .... Jeanette MCBRIDE
32 VP of Student Services .... Beth SMITH
97 Dean of Curriculum Programs .... Randy GUNTER
51 Dean of Continuing Education .... Robin COATES
102 Executive Director Foundation/Grant .... Gay ROATCH
26 Public Information Officer .... Michele HAYWOOD
106 Dir of Distance Learning/Prof Dev .... Julie A. KENNEDY
09 Dir Institutional Effectiveness .... Tim KENNEDY
13 Dir of Information Technology .... Mitch WALKER
04 Assistant to the President .... Korrie ERVIN
38 Counseling Services .... Natalie WINFREE
07 Admissions Officer .... Karen FRYE
37 Director of Financial Aid .... Doni S. CODY
15 Coordinator Of Human Resources .... Susan MCLEOD
10 Accountant .... Anita PRESNELL
18 Director of Facilities .... Kevin MCNEILL
35 Student Activities Coordinator .... Riley BEAMAN

*Nash Community College (D)

522 N Old Carriage Road, Rocky Mount NC 27804-0488
County: Nash FICE Identification: 008557
Unit ID: 199087
Telephone: (252) 443-4011 Carnegie Class: Assoc/Pub-R-M
FAX Number: (252) 451-8201 Calendar System: Semester
URL: www.nashcc.edu
Established: 1967 Annual Undergrad Tuition & Fees (In-District): $2,145
Enrollment: 3,355 Coed
Affiliation or Control: State/Local IRS Status: 501(c)3
Highest Offering: Associate Degree
Program: Occupational; 2-Year Principally Bachelor's Creditable; Business Emphasis
Accreditation: SC, MAC, PHLEB, PTAA

02 President .... Dr. William S. CARVER, II
05 Vice President for Instruction .... Dr. Trent L. MOHRBUTTER
10 Executive Vice President and CFO .... Ms. Annette H. DISHNER
30 Assoc VP Institutional Advancement .... Ms. Pat E. DANIELS
08 Director of Library Services .... Ms. Deana GUIDO
88 Director Small Business Center .... Mr. Fred BROOKS
86 Assoc VP Community & Govt Affairs .... Dr. Keith SMITH
32 VP Student & Enrollment Svcs .... Mr. Larry K. MITCHELL
21 Assoc VP Finance .... Ms. Stephanie B. FISHER
20 Dean of Instruction/Chief Pgm Ofcr .... Mr. Mike LATHAM
09 Assoc Dean Institutional Effective .... Ms. Farley PHILLIPS
14 Director Institutional Technology .... Mr. Jonathan VESTER
07 Director of Admissions .... Ms. Stephanie BROWN
06 Registrar .... Ms. Kathy S. ADCOX
37 Director of Financial Aid .... Ms. Tammy LESTER
15 Director Human Resources .... Ms. Susan L. BARKALOW
04 Administrative Asst to President .... Ms. Faye CAHOON
24 Dir Instructional Publ/Printing .... Mr. James M. QUIGLEY
18 Director of Facilities .... Mr. C. Ted KENNEDY
26 Sr Dir Marketing/Communication .... Ms. Kelley DEAL

*Pamlico Community College (E)

PO Box 185, Grantsboro NC 28529-0185
County: Pamlico FICE Identification: 007031
Unit ID: 199263
Telephone: (252) 249-1851 Carnegie Class: Assoc/Pub-R-S
FAX Number: (252) 249-2377 Calendar System: Semester
URL: www.pamlicocc.edu
Established: 1962 Annual Undergrad Tuition & Fees (In-District): $1,791
Enrollment: 560 Coed
Affiliation or Control: State/Local IRS Status: 501(c)3
Highest Offering: Associate Degree
Program: Occupational; 2-Year Principally Bachelor's Creditable; Technical Emphasis
Accreditation: SC, MAC, NDT

02 President .... Dr. Cleve H. COX
11 Vice Pres Administrative Svcs .... Mr. James CURRY
05 Vice Pres Instructional Svcs .... Dr. Larry W. GRACIE
32 Vice Pres of Student Services .... Mr. Jamie GIBBS

*Piedmont Community College (F)

PO Box 1197, 1715 College Drive,
Roxboro NC 27573-1197
County: Person FICE Identification: 009646
Unit ID: 199324
Telephone: (336) 599-1181 Carnegie Class: Assoc/Pub-R-M
FAX Number: (336) 597-3817 Calendar System: Semester
URL: www.piedmontcc.edu
Established: 1970 Annual Undergrad Tuition & Fees (In-District): $2,381
Enrollment: 1,750 Coed
Affiliation or Control: State/Local IRS Status: 501(c)3
Highest Offering: Associate Degree
Program: Occupational; 2-Year Principally Bachelor's Creditable; Technical Emphasis
Accreditation: SC, EMT, MAC

02 President .... Dr. Walter C. BARTLETT
05 Vice Pres Instruction/Student Devel .... Mr. Michael S. DOSSETT
51 Vice President Continuing Education .... Dr. Doris W. CARVER
11 Vice Pres Administrative Services .... Mr. Robert E. SIMONS
20 Dean Caswell Curriculum Programs .... Ms. Shelly T. STONE
32 Dean Student Development .... Mr. R. Leland PROCTOR
08 Dean LRC & Distance Education .... Ms. Gretchen M. BELL
07 Director Admissions & Records .... Mr. Eugene W. RITTER
13 Director Information Technology .... Mr. Steven C. ROCHEFORT
09 Dir Research/Inst Effectiveness .... Dr. Jeff PATON
15 Director Personnel/Payroll .... Ms. Pamelia C. HOBBS
102 Director PCC Foundation Inc .... Ms. Elizabeth R. TOWNSEND
26 Director Public Information .... Ms. Bonnie H. DAVIS
37 Dir Financial Aid/Veterans Affairs .... Vacant
40 Manager Bookstore .... Ms. Tammy H. MORRIS
25 Director Grants .... Ms. Kelly R. SCHELIN
07 Coordinator Admissions .... Vacant
18 Director Buildings and Grounds .... Mr. Bruce CHISHOLM
97 Dean General Educ/Devel Studies .... Dr. Dawn E. LANGLEY
75 Dean Technical/Occupational Pgms .... Ms. Judy S. BRADSHER
76 Dean Health Sciences and Human Svcs .... Vacant

*Pitt Community College (G)

PO Drawer 7007, Greenville NC 27835-7007
County: Pitt FICE Identification: 004062
Unit ID: 199333
Telephone: (252) 493-7200 Carnegie Class: Assoc/Pub-R-L
FAX Number: (252) 321-4458 Calendar System: Semester
URL: www.pittcc.edu
Established: 1961 Annual Undergrad Tuition & Fees (In-State): $2,294
Enrollment: 9,023 Coed
Affiliation or Control: State IRS Status: 501(c)3
Highest Offering: Associate Degree
Program: Occupational; 2-Year Principally Bachelor's Creditable
Accreditation: SC, ADNUR, CAHIIM, COARC, #DMS, MAC, OTA, POLYT, RAD, RADDOS, RTT

02 President .... Dr. Dennis MASSEY
05 Int Vice Pres Academic Affairs .... Ms. Donna NEAL
11 Vice Pres Administrative Services .... Mr. Donald HEISEY
32 Vice President Student Development .... Dr. Donald R. SPELL
30 Vice Pres Institutional Advancement .... Mrs. Susan Q. NOBLES
20 Asst Vice Pres Academic Affairs .... Ms. Maria PHARR
35 Asst Vice Pres Student Development .... Mrs. Leslie D. ROGERS
13 AVP Information Technology/Services .... Mr. Rick OWENS
10 Chief Financial Officer .... Mr. Ricky BROWN
04 Administrative Asst to President .... Mrs. Kathy M. CARNES
31 Dean Economic & Cmty Development .... Dr. David LUSK
08 Dean Learning Resources .... Mr. Xudong JIN
09 Dean of Planning & Research .... Vacant
46 Resource Development Director .... Vacant
15 Director of Human Resources .... Mr. Michael SHREVES
91 Director of Admin Computing .... Mrs. Janet MINTERN
06 Registrar .... Ms. Joanne T. CERES
38 Director of Counseling .... Dr. Kimberly WILLIAMSON
88 Director Basic Skills Program .... Vacant
18 Director of Facilities .... Mr. Timothy STRICKLAND
103 Director of JobLink Career Center .... Vacant
84 Director of Admiss & Enroll Mgmt .... Ms. Joanne T. CERES
41 Athletic Director .... Mr. William BAILEY
29 Director of Alumni Relations .... Mrs. Ashley SMITH
36 Director of Student Placement .... Ms. Sharon CERES
96 Director of Purchasing .... Mr. Wade QUINN
19 Chief-Public Safety/Campus Police .... Mr. Jay SHINGLETON
88 Director Business & Industry Svcs .... Mrs. Mary PARAMORE
104 Director Study Abroad .... Mrs. Darlene SMITH-WORTHINGTON
09 Director Planning & Analysis .... Dr. Brian MILLER
37 Director Financial Aid .... Mrs. Lisa M. REICHSTEIN
40 Manager of College Store .... Ms. Holly EDWARDS
106 Coord Instructional Tech/Dist Ed .... Mr. Mike CLENDENEN
55 Coord/Counselor Evening Programs .... Mr. Kendrick PRICE
50 Division Dean of Business .... Dr. Donald E. LEE
76 Division Dean Health Sciences .... Ms. Donna V. NEAL
49 Division Dean of Art & Sciences ... Dr. Stephanie MANLEY-ROOK
75 Div Dean Construct/Indus Tech .... Dr. Van MADRAY
61 Div Dean Legal Sci/Public Svc .... Dr. Dan MAYO

*Randolph Community College (H)

629 Industrial Park Avenue, Asheboro NC 27205
County: Randolph FICE Identification: 005447
Unit ID: 199421
Telephone: (336) 633-0200 Carnegie Class: Assoc/Pub-S-SC
FAX Number: (336) 629-4695 Calendar System: Semester
URL: www.randolph.edu
Established: 1962 Annual Undergrad Tuition & Fees (In-District): $2,296
Enrollment: 2,894 Coed
Affiliation or Control: State/Local IRS Status: 501(c)3
Highest Offering: Associate Degree
Program: Occupational; 2-Year Principally Bachelor's Creditable
Accreditation: SC, ADNUR

02 President .... Dr. Robert S. SHACKLEFORD, JR.
11 Vice Pres Administrative Services .... Ms. Daffie H. GARRIS
05 Vice Pres Instructional Services .... Ms. Anne B. HOCKETT
32 Vice President Student Services .... Mr. James W. KELLEY
30 Assoc VP Institutional Advancement .... Ms. Shelley W. GREENE
51 Dean Corporate & Continuing Educ .... Ms. Amanda P. BYRD
62 Dean Library Services .... Ms. Deborah S. LUCK
12 Director Archdale Center .... Ms. Lisa L. BOCK
21 Dir Financial Svcs/Controller .... Ms. Susan I. RICE
26 Director Marketing .... Mr. Kris N. JULIAN
18 Director Facilities Operations .... Ms. Cindi J. GOODWIN
14 Director Information Tech Svcs .... Ms. Tara A. WILLIAMS
09 Director Planning & Assessment .... Ms. Karen R. RITTER
15 Director of Human Resources .... Ms. Nancy BULLINS
37 Director Student Financial Aid .... Mr. Chad WILLIAMS
06 Director Enrollment Mgmt/Registrar .... Ms. Brandi F. HAGERMAN
106 Director Distance Education .... Mr. Devin A. SOVA
88 Director of ABE and AHS .... Ms. Ashley MOODY
88 Director ESTC/Coord Fire Services .... Vacant
96 Purchasing Agent .... Ms. Sharon P. REYNOLDS
27 Asst Dir Public Information .... Ms. Cathy D. HEFFERIN
101 Exec Asst to Pres/Board of Trustees .. Ms. Heather O. CLOUSTON

*Richmond Community College (I)

Box 1189, Hamlet NC 28345-1189
County: Richmond FICE Identification: 005464
Unit ID: 199449
Telephone: (910) 410-1700 Carnegie Class: Assoc/Pub-R-S
FAX Number: (910) 582-7028 Calendar System: Semester
URL: www.richmondcc.edu
Established: 1964 Annual Undergrad Tuition & Fees (In-District): $2,366
Enrollment: 2,063 Coed

Affiliation or Control: State/Local IRS Status: 501(c)3
Highest Offering: Associate Degree
Program: Occupational; 2-Year Principally Bachelor's Creditable; Technical Emphasis
Accreditation: SC, MAC

02 President ... Dr. W. Dale MCINNIS
32 Vice President for Student Services ... Ms. Saundra RICHARDSON
05 Vice President for Instruction/CAO ... Dr. Anthony CLARKE
03 Executive VP/VP Admin Svcs/CFO ... Mr. Brent BARBEE
103 VP for Workforce & Economic Develop ... Mr. Steve SMITH
08 Dean of Learning Resources ... Ms. Carolyn BITTLE
88 Director of Basic Skills ... Ms. Sherry BYRD
108 Dean of Inst Effectiveness & Acct ... Mr. William COUNCIL
06 Registrar ... Ms. Lori GRAHAM
09 Director of Institutional Research ... Ms. Chihoko TERRY
15 Director of Human Resources ... Ms. Gaye CLARK
26 Director of Marketing & Communic ... Mr. Andy CAGLE
21 Controller ... Ms. Debbie CASHWELL
37 Director Student Financial Aid ... Mr. Bruce BLACKMON
96 Purchasing Officer ... Mr. Martin BRIDGES
18 Director of Facility Services ... Mr. Glenn SIMS
38 Director Student Counseling ... Ms. Sharon GOODMAN

*Roanoke-Chowan Community College (A)

109 Community College Road, Ahoskie NC 27910-9522
County: Hertford FICE Identification: 008613
Unit ID: 199467
Telephone: (252) 862-1200 Carnegie Class: Assoc/Pub-R-S
FAX Number: (252) 862-1358 Calendar System: Semester
URL: www.roanokechowan.edu
Established: 1967 Annual Undergrad Tuition & Fees (In-District): $2,389
Enrollment: 890 Coed
Affiliation or Control: State/Local IRS Status: 501(c)3
Highest Offering: Associate Degree
Program: Occupational; 2-Year Principally Bachelor's Creditable
Accreditation: SC

02 President ... Dr. Michael A. ELAM
05 Dean of Curriculum Programs/CAO ... Dr. Pocahantas JONES
103 Dean Workforce & Student Devel ... Ms. Myra POOLE
88 Dean Basic Skills ... Mrs. Michelle MEISCHEID
32 Dean of Student Services ... Mrs. Wendy VANN
10 Controller ... Ms. Sheena SUGGS
08 Dean Learning Res/Info Systems ... Mrs. Monique MITCHELL
06 Registrar ... Mrs. Amy WIGGINS
18 Int Dir Facilities/Physical Plant ... Mr. Charles STRICKLAND
38 Director Student Counseling ... Ms. Sandra COPELAND
106 Director Distance Learning ... Ms. Rita ROGERS
37 Director Financial Aid ... Mrs. Crystal HARRIS
09 Compliance & Data Director ... Mr. Juan E. VAUGHAN, II
07 Director of Admissions ... Mrs. Amy F. WIGGINS
35 Director Student Support Services ... Ms. Lorraine C. MITCHELL
15 Human Resource Coordinator ... Ms. Kathleen TOURE

*Robeson Community College (B)

PO Box 1420, Lumberton NC 28359-1420
County: Robeson FICE Identification: 008612
Unit ID: 199476
Telephone: (910) 272-3700 Carnegie Class: Assoc/Pub-R-M
FAX Number: (910) 272-3328 Calendar System: Semester
URL: www.robeson.edu
Established: 1965 Annual Undergrad Tuition & Fees (In-District): $2,384
Enrollment: 2,786 Coed
Affiliation or Control: State/Local IRS Status: 501(c)3
Highest Offering: Associate Degree
Program: Occupational; 2-Year Principally Bachelor's Creditable
Accreditation: SC, COARC, SURGT

02 President ... Dr. Pamela HILBERT
05 Vice Pres Instruction/Support Svcs ... Dr. Mark O. KINLAW
51 Vice Pres Adult & Continuing Educ ... Mr. R. Channing JONES
10 Vice President Business Services ... Mrs. Tami B. GEORGE
11 VP for Institutional Services ... Mr. Alphonzo MCRAE
55 Asst VP Public Svc/Appl Tech Pgms ... Mr. William L. LOCKLEAR
88 Asst VP Univ Transfer/Bus/Hlth Pgms ... Ms. Sheila A. REGAN
32 Asst Vice Pres Student Services ... Mr. Billy L. MAUNEY
07 Director of Admissions ... Ms. Judith A. REVELS
22 Director Affirm Action/Equal Oppty ... Mr. Alphonzo MCRAE
08 Director of Learning Resource Svcs ... Mrs. Maryellen CLARKE
38 Director Counseling & Testing ... Mr. Danford F. GROVES
06 Dir Records/Registration/Registrar ... Mrs. Beth CARMICAL
37 Financial Aid Director ... Ms. Teresa TUBBS
09 Director of Institutional Research ... Mrs. Lisa O. HUNT
18 Chief Facilities/Physical Plant ... Mr. Alphonzo MCRAE
102 Director Foundation/Development ... Ms. Rebekah R. LOWRY
36 Director Counseling & Career Svcs ... Mr. Danford F. GROVES
29 Director Alumni Relations ... Ms. Rebekah LOWRY
84 Director Enrollment Management ... Mrs. Beth CARMICAL
13 Asst VP/Chief Information Officer ... Mr. James TAGLIARENI
15 Personnel Services Specialist ... Ms. Pam ROMANO
96 Purchasing Specialist ... Mr. Jason O. LEVISTER

*Rockingham Community College (C)

PO Box 38, Wentworth NC 27375-0038
County: Rockingham FICE Identification: 002958
Unit ID: 199485
Telephone: (336) 342-4261 Carnegie Class: Assoc/Pub-R-M
FAX Number: (336) 349-9986 Calendar System: Semester
URL: www.rockinghamcc.edu
Established: 1963 Annual Undergrad Tuition & Fees (In-District): $1,772
Enrollment: 2,254 Coed
Affiliation or Control: State/Local IRS Status: 501(c)3
Highest Offering: Associate Degree
Program: Occupational; 2-Year Principally Bachelor's Creditable
Accreditation: SC, COARC, PHLEB, SURGT

02 President ... Dr. Michael S. HELMICK
05 Vice President Instruction ... Dr. Jan G. OVERMAN
11 VP of Administrative Services ... Mr. Steven W. WOODRUFF
32 Vice Pres for Student Development ... Dr. Robert S. LOWDERMILK
88 Assoc VP Administrative Services ... Dr. E. Anthony GUNN
51 Dean of Continuing Education ... Ms. Laura F. COFFEE
50 Dean of Business Technologies ... Vacant
75 Dean Industrial Technologies ... Vacant
79 Dean of Humanities/Social Sciences ... Ms. Joyce W. RUSSELL
81 Dean of Sciences & Math ... Ms. Celeste H. ALLIS
76 Dean of Health Sciences ... Ms. Tiffany D. MORRIS
08 Director of Library Services ... Ms. Kimberly SHIREMAN
09 Director Inst Research/Planning ... Mr. Kevin OSBORNE
30 Director Development/Foundation ... Ms. Gaye B. CLIFTON
14 Dir Technology Support Services ... Ms. Gretchen PARRISH
37 Director of Financial Aid ... Ms. Coe Ann TRENT
84 Director of Enrollment Services ... Mr. Derick SATTERFIELD
35 Interim Director Student Life ... Mr. Chris JOHNSON
40 Bookstore Manager ... Ms. Della J. GASTON
15 Director Human Resources ... Ms. Dana K. HUSKEY
27 Director Public Information ... Ms. Kim A. PRYOR
96 Director of Purchasing ... Mr. John PARRISH

*Rowan-Cabarrus Community College (D)

1333 Jake Alexander Blvd., South, Salisbury NC 28145
County: Rowan FICE Identification: 005754
Unit ID: 199494
Telephone: (704) 216-7222 Carnegie Class: Assoc/Pub-S-MC
FAX Number: N/A Calendar System: Semester
URL: www.rccc.edu
Established: 1963 Annual Undergrad Tuition & Fees (In-State): $2,208
Enrollment: 6,697 Coed
Affiliation or Control: State IRS Status: 501(c)3
Highest Offering: Associate Degree
Program: Occupational; 2-Year Principally Bachelor's Creditable
Accreditation: SC, ADNUR, DA, PNUR, RAD

02 President ... Dr. Carol SPALDING
05 Academic Vice President ... Dr. Rod TOWNLEY
10 Chief Financial Officer ... Ms. Janet SPRIGGS
84 Vice President Student Services ... Ms. Gaye MCCONNELL
30 Vice Pres Advancement & Cont Educ ... Mrs. Jeanie MOORE
27 Chief Information Officer ... Mr. Jeremy CAMPBELL
16 Chief Human Resources Officer ... Ms. Tina HAYNES
18 Chief Facilities Officer ... Mr. Jonathan CHAMBERLIN
101 Secretary of the Institution/Board ... Ms. Carla HOWELL
20 Assoc Academic Vice President ... Mr. Ron SCOZZARI
32 Assoc VP Student Services ... Mr. Mark EBERSOLE
76 Dean Health Programs ... Mrs. Wendy BARNHARDT
50 Dean Science Bus Math & Info Tech ... Dr. Marcy CORJAY
49 Dean Liberal Arts & General Educ ... Dr. Carolyn HOLBERT
88 Dean Pre-College Stds ... Mrs. Cheryl MARSH
88 Dean Special Programs ... Ms. Claudia SWICEGOOD
103 Dean Corporate Programs ... Mrs. Ann MORRIS
106 Dean Eductional Resource Services ... Ms. Debra NEESMITH
71 Dean Public Services ... Mr. Spencer RUMMAGE
08 Director Learning Resource Center ... Mr. Rodney LIPPARD
07 Director Admissions & Recruitment ... Ms. Dina HARKEY
38 Director Counseling and Career Svs ... Ms. Misty MOLER
37 Director Fin Aid & VA Benefit ... Mrs. Lisa LEDBETTER
26 Dir College Relations Mktg & Comm ... Ms. Paula DIBLEY
35 Director Student Life & Leadership ... Ms. Natasha LIPSCOMB
102 Director RCCC Foundation ... Mrs. Celeste A. GRUNER
25 Director Grants Development ... Mrs. Daphne LEWIS
09 Director of Institutional Research ... Dr. Michael FELDSTEIN
96 Director of Purchasing ... Ms. Kathy PIPER
19 Director of Campus Security ... Mr. Tim BOST
55 Director Evening & Weekend Oper ... Mr. Mike HENSLEY
06 Director Registration & Records ... Mrs. Joan CREEGER
14 Director Computer Center ... Mr. Bill PLYLER
72 Assoc Dean Information Technology ... Mr. Ian STEVENS
21 Controller ... Ms. Kizzy LEA

*Sampson Community College (E)

PO Box 318, Clinton NC 28329-0318
County: Sampson FICE Identification: 007892
Unit ID: 199625
Telephone: (910) 592-8081 Carnegie Class: Assoc/Pub-R-S
FAX Number: (910) 592-8048 Calendar System: Semester
URL: www.sampsoncc.edu
Established: 1967 Annual Undergrad Tuition & Fees (In-District): $2,365
Enrollment: 1,524 Coed
Affiliation or Control: State/Local IRS Status: 501(c)3
Highest Offering: Associate Degree
Program: Occupational; 2-Year Principally Bachelor's Creditable
Accreditation: SC, ADNUR, PNUR

02 President ... Dr. Paul C. HUTCHINS
05 Vice President of Academic Affairs ... Dr. James GILLISPIE
10 Vice President of Finance ... Mrs. Virginia S. LUCAS
11 Vice President of Administration ... Dr. William J. STARLING
32 Dean of Student Services ... Ms. Amy NOEL
07 Director of Admissions ... Mr. Oscar RODRIGUEZ
06 Registrar ... Mrs. Delsey BREWINGTON
27 Public Information Office ... Mr. Dan GRUBB
37 Director Financial Aid ... Ms. Judye TART
08 Director Library Services ... Mr. Mark RUSHING
30 Resource Development Officer ... Mrs. Lisa TURLINGTON
15 Personnel Officer ... Mrs. Frankie K. SUTTER
35 Director Student Support Services ... Ms. Lisa DOBSON
51 Dean of Continuing Education ... Mrs. Ann BUTLER

*Sandhills Community College (F)

3395 Airport Road, Pinehurst NC 28374-8283
County: Moore FICE Identification: 002961
Unit ID: 199634
Telephone: (910) 692-6185 Carnegie Class: Assoc/Pub-R-M
FAX Number: (910) 695-1823 Calendar System: Semester
URL: www.sandhills.edu
Established: 1963 Annual Undergrad Tuition & Fees (In-State): $2,385
Enrollment: 4,192 Coed
Affiliation or Control: State IRS Status: 501(c)3
Highest Offering: Associate Degree
Program: Occupational; 2-Year Principally Bachelor's Creditable
Accreditation: SC, COARC, MLTAD, POLYT, RAD, SURGT

02 President ... Dr. John R. DEMPSEY
05 Provost ... Dr. John T. TURNER
10 Exec VP Business/Admin Svcs ... Dr. Richard GOUGH
09 Dean of Institutional Plng/Rsrch ... Mrs. Kristie SULLIVAN
32 Dean of Student Services ... Mrs. Kellie SHOEMAKE
35 Dean of Student LIfe ... Mr. David FARMER
04 Exec Assistant to the President ... Mrs. Wendy B. DODSON
10 Chief Business Officer ... Mrs. Brenda JACKSON
20 Dean of Instruction ... Dr. Rebecca ROUSH
51 Dean Continuing Education ... Ms. Andi KORTE
30 Dean of Institutional Advancement ... Mr. Rick H. SMITH
08 Dean of Learning Resources ... Dr. John STACEY
06 Director of Records & Registration ... Vacant
37 Financial Aid Officer ... Ms. Lindsey FARMER
106 Director of Distance Learning ... Ms. Wendy KAUFFMAN
14 Director of Computer Center ... Mr. Brad ROBBINS
19 Director of Security/Safety ... Vacant
18 Physical Plant Manager ... Mr. Melvin RITTER
15 Director Human Resources ... Ms. Wendy B. DODSON
21 Assistant Business Officer ... Mr. Joseph BROWN
26 Director of Marketing and PR ... Ms. Karen MANNING
40 Bookstore Manager ... Ms. Sandra DALES
07 Director of Admissions ... Ms. Cary GREENE

*South Piedmont Community College (G)

PO Box 126, Polkton NC 28135-0126
County: Anson/Union FICE Identification: 007985
Unit ID: 197850
Telephone: (704) 272-5300 Carnegie Class: Assoc/Pub-R-M
FAX Number: (704) 272-5350 Calendar System: Semester
URL: www.spcc.edu
Established: 1999 Annual Undergrad Tuition & Fees (In-District): $2,437
Enrollment: 2,596 Coed
Affiliation or Control: State/Local IRS Status: 501(c)3
Highest Offering: Associate Degree
Program: Occupational; 2-Year Principally Bachelor's Creditable; Business Emphasis
Accreditation: SC, DMS, MAC, SURGT

02 President ... Dr. Stanley M. SIDOR
10 Sr VP Finance/Administrative Svcs ... Mr. John DEVITTO
05 Vice Pres Academic Affairs/CAO ... Dr. Tiffany EVANS
51 Exec Dir Career Devel/Cont Educ ... Mr. Dan MERLE
32 VP Student Services ... Mrs. Elaine CLODFELTER
30 VP Inst Advancement/SPCC Foundation ... Ms. Hayne WHITE
04 Exec Assistant to President ... Ms. Nanci OSVAI
15 Asst VP Human Res/Payroll/Org Dev ... Ms. Susan R. FLAKE
21 Asst Vice Pres Financial Services ... Ms. Michelle BROCK
13 Asst VP Information Svcs Tech/CIO ... Mr. Dan DOMBCHEWSKYJ
18 Asst VP of Facilities ... Mr. William M. TRUETT
49 Dean Arts & Science ... Vacant
76 Dean Allied Health ... Ms. Alice BRADLEY
66 Dean Nursing ... Ms. Joyce LONG
72 Dean Applied Science & Technology ... Dr. Maria LANDER
06 Registrar ... Ms. Cathy HORNE
84 Dean of Enrollment Services ... Mr. John RATLIFF
35 Dean of Student Development ... Ms. Makena STEWART
108 Asst VP Planning/IE ... Ms. Jill MILLARD
08 Director Library Services ... Mr. Grant LEFOE
88 Director of Basic Skills ... Ms. Denise WILSON
103 Dir Human Resources Development ... Ms. Linda KAPPAUF
107 Director Professional Programs ... Ms. Geri DUNCAN
38 Director of Counseling ... Vacant
36 Director of Advising ... Vacant
35 Director Student Engagement ... Mr. Michael MAFFUCCI
44 Development Officer ... Ms. Gina RHODES
25 Dir of Grants & Community Relations ... Ms. Caroline CATE
26 Chief Public Information Officer ... Vacant
09 Director of Institutional Research ... Mr. Mark LUPTON

*Southeastern Community College (A)

4564 Chadbourn Highway, PO Box 151,
Whiteville NC 28472-0151

County: Columbus FICE Identification: 002964
Unit ID: 199722
Telephone: (910) 642-7141 Carnegie Class: Assoc/Pub-R-M
FAX Number: (910) 642-5658 Calendar System: Semester
URL: www.sccnc.edu
Established: 1964 Annual Undergrad Tuition & Fees (In-State): $2,397
Enrollment: 1,975 Coed
Affiliation or Control: State IRS Status: 501(c)3
Highest Offering: Associate Degree
Program: Occupational; 2-Year Principally Bachelor's Creditable
Accreditation: SC, MLTAD, PHLEB

02 President ... Dr. Kathy MATLOCK
10 Vice President Operations/Finance ... Ms. Betty Jo RAMSEY
05 Vice Pres Academic/Student Affairs ... Dr. Morgan A. PHILLIPS
103 VP Workforce & Cmty Development ... Ms. Beverlee S. NANCE
30 Exec Dean Institutional Advancement ... Ms. Sue W. HAWKS
32 Dean of Students ... Ms. Kelly KINGRY
57 Dean of Arts & General Education ... Dr. Kevin BRATTON
75 Dean of Business & Tech Programs ... Ms. Lauren COLE
76 Dean of Allied Health & Science ... Dr. James HUTCHERSON
103 Dean of Workforce & Comm Dev ... Ms. Teresa TRIPLETT
08 Librarian ... Ms. Kay HOUSER
15 Human Resources Administrator ... Mr. Bill MAULTSBY
106 Moodle Administrator ... Dr. Teronda MCNEIL
21 Controller/Operations/Finance ... Ms. Donna TURBEVILLE
26 Director Marketing & Public Affairs ... Mr. Justin SMITH
09 Director of Research & Reporting ... Mr. Don WHITE
13 Director of Information Technology ... Mr. Jason STRICKLAND
51 Director of Continuing Education ... Ms. Mary Ruth EDWARDS
37 Director of Financial Aid ... Mr. Glenn HANSON
06 Director of Student Records ... Ms. Sylvia MCQUEEN
20 Academic/Student Affairs Associate ... Ms. Vanessa HAWES

*Southwestern Community College (B)

447 College Drive, Sylva NC 28779-8581

County: Jackson FICE Identification: 008466
Unit ID: 199731
Telephone: (828) 339-4000 Carnegie Class: Assoc/Pub-R-M
FAX Number: (828) 586-3129 Calendar System: Semester
URL: www.southwesterncc.edu
Established: 1964 Annual Undergrad Tuition & Fees (In-District): $2,224
Enrollment: 2,612 Coed
Affiliation or Control: State/Local IRS Status: 501(c)3
Highest Offering: Associate Degree
Program: Occupational; 2-Year Principally Bachelor's Creditable
Accreditation: SC, CAHIIM, COARC, DMS, EMT, MAC, MLTAD, PHLEB, PTAA, RAD

02 President ... Dr. Don TOMAS
03 Executive Vice President ... Dr. Janet K. BURNETTE
05 Vice Pres Instructional Services ... Dr. Tom BROOKS
10 Chief Financial Officer ... Ms. Janet K. BURNETTE
13 VP Information Technology ... Mr. Ryan SCHWIEBERT
103 Dean of Workforce/Economic Devel ... Ms. Sonja HAYNES
12 Dean Macon Campus/Inst Dev ... Dr. Cheryl DAVIDS
32 Dean of Student Services ... Dr. Phil WEAST
06 Registrar ... Ms. Christy DEAVER
08 Director of Learning Resources ... Mrs. Dianne LINDGREN
09 Inst Research & Planning Officer ... Mr. Delos D. MONTEITH
37 Director of Financial Aid ... Ms. Melody L. LAWRENCE
26 Director of Public Relations ... Mr. Tyler GOODE
102 Director of SCC Foundation ... Ms. Mary SELZER

*Stanly Community College (C)

141 College Drive, Albemarle NC 28001-7458

County: Stanly FICE Identification: 011194
Unit ID: 199740
Telephone: (704) 982-0121 Carnegie Class: Assoc/Pub-R-M
FAX Number: (704) 982-0819 Calendar System: Semester
URL: www.stanly.edu
Established: 1971 Annual Undergrad Tuition & Fees (In-District): $2,328
Enrollment: 2,988 Coed
Affiliation or Control: State/Local IRS Status: 501(c)3
Highest Offering: Associate Degree
Program: Occupational; 2-Year Principally Bachelor's Creditable
Accreditation: SC, COARC, MAC, MLTAD

02 President ... Dr. Brenda KAYS
05 Exec VP of Educational Services ... Mrs. Robin MCCREE
32 Exec VP Student/Academic Affairs ... Mrs. Robin MCCREE
10 VP Administrative Services/CFO ... Mrs. Becky WALL
13 Vice Pres InfoTechnology Services ... Mr. Joel ALLEN
37 Associate Dean Financial Aid ... Ms. Petra FIELDS
51 VP Organizational Growth/Dev/Effect ... Ms. Lois SMITH
04 Exec Assistant to the President ... Mrs. Gaye WOOD
36 Dean Stdnt Outrch/Career Plng/Plcmt ... Mrs. Kathy GARDNER
76 Dean Health & Public Svcs ... Dr. Tammy CRUMP
50 Dean Business & Technology ... Mrs. Merlin AMIRTHARAJ
06 Assoc Dean of Records/Registrar ... Mrs. Kristina EUDY
26 Director Marketing & Communication ... Mrs. Michelle PEIFER
35 Director of Student Life/Learning ... Ms. Stephanie CHRISTY
07 Director of Admissions ... Ms. Jeania MARTIN
21 Controller ... Mrs. Debra HARWOOD
18 Director of Physical Plant ... Mr. David HINSON
88 Director of Learning Technologies ... Dr. Jana ULRICH
102 Foundation Director ... Mrs. Janet SISTARE
15 Director Human Resources ... Miss Donna KIMREY
08 Director Library Services ... Mrs. Erin ALLEN
88 Director Basic Skills ... Ms. Dianne COOKER
24 Dir Testing/Media Specialist Svcs ... Mr. Mark SAMPLE
96 Purchasing Agent ... Mrs. Shelley OSBORNE

*Surry Community College (D)

630 S Main Street, Dobson NC 27017-0304

County: Surry FICE Identification: 002970
Unit ID: 199768
Telephone: (336) 386-8121 Carnegie Class: Assoc/Pub-R-M
FAX Number: (336) 386-8951 Calendar System: Semester
URL: www.surry.edu
Established: 1964 Annual Undergrad Tuition & Fees (In-State): $2,419
Enrollment: 3,476 Coed
Affiliation or Control: State IRS Status: 501(c)3
Highest Offering: Associate Degree
Program: Occupational; 2-Year Principally Bachelor's Creditable; Business Emphasis
Accreditation: SC, MAC, PTAA

02 President ... Dr. David R. SHOCKLEY
05 Vice Pres Curriculum Programs ... Dr. Jami WOODS
10 Vice President for Finance ... Mr. Tony L. MARTIN
32 Vice Pres Student Development ... Mr. Randy LEDFORD
45 Vice Pres Institutional Effective ... Dr. Anne R. HENNIS
51 VP Corporate & Cont Education ... Dr. George O. SAPPENFIELD
11 Vice Pres of Administrative Svcs ... Mrs. Susan PENDERGRAFT
13 Vice President Technology Services ... Dr. Candace HOLDER
49 Dean of Arts & Sciences ... Ms. Connie WOLFE
50 Dean of Business/Tech/Hlth Sciences ... Mr. Mike B. MILLER
55 Assoc Dean Evening Operations ... Ms. Sabra L. RICE
08 Assoc Dean of Learning Resources ... Dr. David WRIGHT
84 Assoc Dean Enrollment Mgmt ... Mr. Brian WEBB
37 Director Financial Aid ... Mrs. Andrea SIMPSON
14 Director Computer Center ... Ms. Rhonda L. HAZELWOOD
18 Director of Physical Facilities ... Mr. Randy ROGERS
31 Director Auxiliary Services ... Ms. Debbie WOLFE
102 Exec Dir SCC Foundation/Pub Info ... Mrs. Marion F. VENABLE
41 Athletic Director ... Mr. Mark TUCKER
07 Director of Admissions ... Mrs. Renita HAZELWOOD
19 Chief Campus Police ... Mr. Martin W. SHROPSHIRE
96 Director of Purchasing ... Mrs. Cindy A. GALLIMORE
35 Director Student Activities ... Mr. Tony V. SEARCY
15 Human Resources Generalist ... Mrs. Melonie WEATHERS

*Tri-County Community College (E)

21 Campus Circle, Murphy NC 28906-7919

County: Cherokee FICE Identification: 009430
Unit ID: 199795
Telephone: (828) 837-6810 Carnegie Class: Assoc/Pub-R-S
FAX Number: (828) 837-0028 Calendar System: Semester
URL: www.tricountycc.edu
Established: 1964 Annual Undergrad Tuition & Fees (In-State): $2,346
Enrollment: 1,484 Coed
Affiliation or Control: State IRS Status: 501(c)3
Highest Offering: Associate Degree
Program: Occupational; 2-Year Principally Bachelor's Creditable; Technical Emphasis
Accreditation: SC, MAC

02 President ... Dr. Donna TIPTON-ROGERS
09 VP Instruction/Institution Effect ... Dr. Steve WOOD
13 Dir of Computing & Information Mgt ... Mr. Jason OUTEN
30 Coordinator of Foundation/SGA ... Ms. Samantha MAJOR
103 Dir of Economic & Workforce Develop ... Mr. Paul WORLEY
45 VP College & Community Initiatives ... Mr. Bo GRAY
12 Asst to Pres Graham Cty Operations ... Ms. Charlene WOOD
88 Dean Research & Planning/EC Liaison ... Dr. Jason CHAMBERS
10 VP for Business & Finance ... Mr. Bill VESPASIAN
15 Director of Human Resources ... Ms. Sallie BAKER
91 Systems Administrator/Data Base Mgr ... Mr. Wes CHASTAIN
08 Dean Learning Resources ... Ms. Linda KRESSAL
106 Learning Mgt Systems Administrator ... Mr. Cody ANDERSON
38 Counselor ... Ms. Linda HOWELL
26 Communications Officer ... Mr. Roarke ARROWOOD
06 Registrar Curriculum ... Ms. Holly HYDE
37 Director of Financial Aid ... Ms. Diane OWL
96 Purchasing Agent ... Ms. Judy OWENBY
32 Director of Student Success ... Ms. Sarah TATHAM
18 Coordinator of Facility Services ... Mr. Tim NICHOLSON

*Vance-Granville Community College (F)

PO Box 917, Henderson NC 27536-0917

County: Vance FICE Identification: 009903
Unit ID: 199838
Telephone: (252) 492-2061 Carnegie Class: Assoc/Pub-R-M
FAX Number: (252) 430-0460 Calendar System: Semester
URL: www.vgcc.edu
Established: 1969 Annual Undergrad Tuition & Fees (In-State): $1,826
Enrollment: 4,040 Coed
Affiliation or Control: State Related IRS Status: 501(c)3
Highest Offering: Associate Degree
Program: Occupational; 2-Year Principally Bachelor's Creditable
Accreditation: SC, MAC, RAD

02 President ... Dr. Stelfanie WILLIAMS
05 Vice Pres of Acad & Stdnt Affairs ... Dr. Angela BALLENTINE
10 Vice Pres for Finance & Operations ... Mr. Steve GRAHAM
09 VP of Institutional Research & Tech ... Dr. Kenneth A. LEWIS, JR.
26 VP of Employee & Public Relations . Ms. Stacey CARTER-COLEY
12 Dean South Campus ... Ms. Cecilia B. WHEELER
12 Dean Franklin County Campus ... Ms. Bobbie Jo C. MAY
12 Dean Warren County Campus ... Mr. George A. HENDERSON
08 Director Learning Resources Center ... Mr. Dave TRUDEAU
06 Registrar ... Ms. Kathy KTUL
15 Director of Human Resources ... Ms. Katherine WILLIAMSON
37 Director of Financial Aid ... Ms. Kali BROWN
18 Director of Plant Operations ... Mr. Jack PUCKETT
27 Director of Marketing ... Ms. Elaine STEM
38 Dir of Counseling & Student Support ... Ms. Joy TUCKER
07 Director of Admissions & Records ... Ms. Tonya WADDLE
09 Director of Planning & Research ... Dr. Rodney FOTH
40 Bookstore Manager ... Ms. Sandra NEWTON

*Wake Technical Community College (G)

9101 Fayetteville Road, Raleigh NC 27603-5696

County: Wake FICE Identification: 004844
Unit ID: 199856
Telephone: (919) 866-5000 Carnegie Class: Assoc/Pub-U-MC
FAX Number: (919) 779-3360 Calendar System: Semester
URL: www.waketech.edu
Established: 1958 Annual Undergrad Tuition & Fees (In-District): $2,380
Enrollment: 20,123 Coed
Affiliation or Control: State/Local IRS Status: 501(c)3
Highest Offering: Associate Degree
Program: Occupational; 2-Year Principally Bachelor's Creditable
Accreditation: SC, ACFEI, DA, DH, MAC, MLTAD, PHLEB, RAD, SURGT

02 President ... Dr. Stephen C. SCOTT
03 Executive Vice President ... Mr. Gerald A. MITCHELL
102 SVP College Dev/Exec Dir Foundation ... Mr. O. Mort CONGLETON
43 General Counsel/VP Legal Services ... Ms. Clay T. HINES
05 SVP Curriculum Education Svcs ... Mr. Bryan K. RYAN
32 SVP Student Services ... Ms. Rita H. JERMAN
103 SVP Econ & Workforce Development ... Mr. Samuel STRICKLAND
10 SVP of Financial & Business Svcs ... Mr. Arthur W. ANDREWS
12 SVP Northern Wake Campus & HR ... Dr. D. Gayle GREENE
51 VP Continuing Education Svcs ... Mr. Anthony CAISON
13 VP Info Tech & Dean RTP Campus ... Dr. Darryl D. MCGRAW
18 Facility Engineering Officer ... Mr. Wendell B. GOODWIN
26 AVP Communications ... Mrs. Laurie C. CLOWERS
20 AVP Arts and Sciences ... Ms. Tonya FORBES
20 AVP Career Programs ... Ms. Sandra DIETRICH
84 AVP Enrollment Management ... Mr. John W. SAPARILAS
15 Chief Human Resource Officer ... Ms. Benita I. CLARK
19 Chief of Police ... Mr. Michael A. PENRY
21 Chief Accounting Officer ... Ms. Marla L. TART
10 Chief Business Officer ... Mrs. Debra S. WALLACE
46 Dean IE/Accreditation & Research ... Dr. John B. BOONE
30 Director of Development ... Mrs. Stephanie S. LAKE
25 Interim Dean Sponsored Programs ... Mr. Richard W. SULLINS
06 Dean Enrollment/Records/Registrar ... Mrs. Amanda T. ROBERTS
06 Dean Records & Reg/Registrar CE ... Ms. Karen R. HOLDING-JORDAN
35 Dean of Student Development ... Mr. Mark T. GIBSON
72 Dean Educ Svcs & Technology ... Mr. Ray L. TIMS
37 Dean Financial Aid/Veterans Affairs ... Mrs. Regina M. HUGGINS
35 Sr Dean Stdnt Svcs Northern Campus ... Mrs. Karen B. PHINAZEE
88 Dean BioNetwork Capstone Center ... Ms. Ana M. MCCLANAHAN
38 Dean Acad Advising/Stdnt Success ... Mr. Kevin A. BROWN
07 Dean Admissions/Outreach Services .Ms. Susan R. BLOOMFIELD
08 Dean Library Services ... Ms. Jackie L. CASE
12 Campus Dean Public Safety Ed Campus ... Ms. Angela J. MIZELLE
27 Director Creative Services ... Mrs. Francie W. SANDERSON
36 Dean Career Readiness & Employment ... Vacant
76 Dean Health Sciences Campus ... Mrs. Dianne B. HINSON
81 Dean Mathematics/Sciences Div ... Dr. Cheryl L. KEETON
79 Dean Arts/Humanities/Soc Sci Div ... Dr. Diane E. LODDER
50 Dean Business Technologies ... Mr. Walter MARTIN
75 Dean Applied Technologies ... Ms. Patricia A. GODIN
88 Sr Dean Instructional Support ... Mr. James A. ROBERSON
55 Dean Evening Division ... Ms. Pamela M. LITTLE
77 Dean Computer & Engineering Tech ... Ms. Angela L. BEQUETTE
88 Dean of College & Career Readiness ... Mrs. Monica P. GEMPERLEIN

*Wayne Community College (H)

3000 Wayne Memorial Drive Box 8002,
Goldsboro NC 27533-8002

County: Wayne FICE Identification: 002980
Unit ID: 199892
Telephone: (919) 735-5151 Carnegie Class: Assoc/Pub-R-M
FAX Number: (919) 736-9425 Calendar System: Semester
URL: www.waynecc.edu
Established: 1957 Annual Undergrad Tuition & Fees (In-District): $2,300
Enrollment: 3,965 Coed
Affiliation or Control: State/Local IRS Status: 501(c)3
Highest Offering: Associate Degree
Program: Occupational; 2-Year Principally Bachelor's Creditable
Accreditation: SC, ADNUR, DA, DH, MAC, PNUR

02 President ... Dr. Kay H. ALBERTSON
05 VP Academic and Student Services ... Dr. Peggy S. TEAGUE
32 AVP Academic and Student Services ... Mr. Gene SMITH

51 VP Continuing Education Services ... Mr. Ray BURRELL
30 Assoc VP Institutional Advancement ... Mr. Bill T. THOMPSON
72 Division Head Applied Technologies ... Mr. Ernie WHITE
49 Division Head Arts & Sciences ... Dr. Tracey IVEY
50 Div Head Business & Computer Tech ... Mrs. Beth HOOKS
76 Division Head Allied Health ... Mrs. Pattie PFEIFFER
88 Division Head Public Safety ... Ms. Beverly DEANS
62 Head Librarian ... Dr. Aletha ANDREW
12 Coordinator Seymour Johnson AFB ... Mrs. Dori FRASER
92 Honors Program Coordinator ... Mr. Brandon JENKINS
45 Chief Admin Support Services ... Mr. Don MAGOON
106 Coord Distance Education ... Mr. Randall SHEARON
105 Coord Educ Tech Services/Webmaster ... Mr. Brent HOOD
13 Director Information Systems ... Ms. Katherine JONES
18 Chief Facilities/Physical Plant ... Mr. Edward E. FARRIS
19 Chief Security ... Mr. Willie L. BRINSON
40 Director Bookstore ... Mrs. Trellie HERRING
88 Ex Dir Wayne Bus/Indus Ctr & WORKS ... Mrs. Diane IVEY
07 Director Admissions & Records ... Mrs. Susan M. SASSER
37 Director Student Financial Aid ... Mrs. Brenda D. MERCER
84 Dir Student Devel/Enrollment Mgmt ... Mrs. Joanna MORRISETTE
36 Coord Coop Ed and Career Services ... Mrs. Lorie WALLER
78 Director Cooperative Programs ... Ms. Anne MILLINGTON
35 Student Activities Coordinator ... Ms. Paige HAM
10 Chief Financial Officer ... Mrs. Joy KORNEGAY
96 Accountant/Equipment Coordinator ... Mr. Mark R. JOHNSON
102 Executive Director of Foundation ... Mr. Jack KANNAN
26 Public Information Officer ... Ms. Tara HUMPHRIES
16 Director Personnel ... Mrs. Ina R. RAWLINSON
55 Evening Coord/Security Services ... Mr. James BYNUM

*Western Piedmont Community College (A)

1001 Burkemont Avenue, Morganton NC 28655-4504
County: Burke FICE Identification: 002982
Unit ID: 199908
Telephone: (828) 438-6000 Carnegie Class: Assoc/Pub-R-M
FAX Number: (828) 438-6015 Calendar System: Semester
URL: www.wpcc.edu
Established: 1964 Annual Undergrad Tuition & Fees (In-State): $2,208
Enrollment: 2,593 Coed
Affiliation or Control: State IRS Status: 501(c)3
Highest Offering: Associate Degree
Program: Occupational; 2-Year Principally Bachelor's Creditable
Accreditation: SC, ADNUR, DA, MAC, MLTAD

02 President ... Dr. Jim W. BURNETT
05 Exec Vice Pres/VP Academic Affairs ... Dr. Chad A. BLEDSOE
10 VP Admin Svcs/Chief Financial Ofcr ... Ms. Sandra K. HOILMAN
32 Vice President Student Development ... Mr. Atticus J. SIMPSON
51 Dean of Continuing Education ... Mr. Lee KISER
35 Dean of Student Services ... Ms. Susan WILLIAMS
08 Dean Learning Resources/Technology ... Mr. Daniel R. SMITH
54 Dean Science/Engineering/Math ... Mr. Michael DANIELS
79 Dean Humanities/Social Sciences ... Mrs. Mary C. SAFFORD
76 Dean Health Sciences ... Dr. Linda S. SATEY
50 Dean Business & Public Services ... Mrs. Leslie MCKESSON
21 Controller ... Mr. Michael BINGHAM
06 Director Records & Registration ... Mrs. Joan P. HOGAN
15 Director Human Resources ... Ms. Lisa H. SESSIONS
84 Director Enrollment Management ... Mrs. Jennifer PROPST
37 Director Student Financial Aid ... Mr. Keith A. CONLEY
13 Director Management Info Systems ... Ms. Nancy E. NORRIS
09 Director of Planning & Research ... Mr. William L. LEFEVERS
96 Director of Purchasing ... Ms. Linda CARSWELL
18 Director of Maintenance ... Vacant

*Wilkes Community College (B)

1328 S Collegiate Drive, Wilkesboro NC 28697-0120
County: Wilkes FICE Identification: 002983
Unit ID: 199926
Telephone: (336) 838-6100 Carnegie Class: Assoc/Pub-R-M
FAX Number: (336) 903-3219 Calendar System: Semester
URL: www.wilkescc.edu
Established: 1965 Annual Undergrad Tuition & Fees (In-State): $2,328
Enrollment: 2,660 Coed
Affiliation or Control: State IRS Status: 501(c)3
Highest Offering: Associate Degree
Program: Occupational; 2-Year Principally Bachelor's Creditable; Technical Emphasis
Accreditation: SC, COARC, DA, MAC

02 President ... Dr. Gordon G. BURNS
05 Sr VP of Instruction ... Dr. Dean E. SPRINKLE
10 Senior VP of Administration ... Mr. D. Morgan FRANCIS, JR.
20 VP of Instr Support/Student Svcs ... Ms. Kim E. FAW
103 VP Adv Industrial & Workforce Dev ... Mr. John HAUSER
13 Assoc VP Information Technology ... Mr. Mike WINGLER
12 Assoc VP Ashe Campus ... Mr. Christopher D. ROBINSON
12 Director Alleghany Center ... Ms. Jayne PHIPPS-BOGER
09 Inst Effectiveness Exec Director ... Mr. J. Kelly PIPES, III
50 Dean Business/Public Svc Tech Div ... Mrs. Robin PHILLIPS-HAUSER
76 Dean Health Sciences Division ... Mr. Billy WOODS
49 Dean Arts & Sciences Division ... Ms. Blair M. HANCOCK
18 Exec Director/Facilities Services ... Mr. Ronald DOLLYHITE
30 Exec Director/Endowment ... Ms. Allison PHILLIPS
15 Director of Human Resources ... Mr. Tracy D. MCENTIRE
06 Registrar ... Ms. Melonie KILBY
07 Director of Admissions ... Mr. Scott JOHNSON
37 Director of Financial Aid ... Ms. Vickie G. CALL
38 Director Counseling & Career Svcs ... Dr. Lynda K. BLACK
32 Director Enrollment Mgmt/Stdnt Life ... Ms. Jane BOWMAN
08 Director Learning Resources ... Ms. Christy EARP
38 Director Student Support Services ... Ms. Angela SCHEUERMANN
40 Bookstore Manager ... Ms. Lynn OSBORNE
26 PIO & Relations Officer ... Ms. Amber HERMAN
19 Safety & Security Manager ... Mr. Jamie MCGUIRE

*Wilson Community College (C)

902 Herring Avenue, Wilson NC 27893-3310
County: Wilson FICE Identification: 004845
Unit ID: 199953
Telephone: (252) 291-1195 Carnegie Class: Assoc/Pub-R-M
FAX Number: (252) 243-7148 Calendar System: Semester
URL: www.wilsoncc.edu
Established: 1958 Annual Undergrad Tuition & Fees (In-State): $1,865
Enrollment: 1,865 Coed
Affiliation or Control: State IRS Status: 501(c)3
Highest Offering: Associate Degree
Program: Occupational; 2-Year Principally Bachelor's Creditable
Accreditation: SC, SURGT

02 President ... Dr. Rusty STEPHENS
05 Vice Pres Instruction/Student Devel ... Dr. Denise L. SESSOMS
10 Vice Pres for Finance & Admin Svcs ... Mr. Hadie C. HORNE
09 Assoc VP Institutional Effective ... Ms. Debra S. HOLLEY
51 Dean of Cont Educ/Sustainability ... Mr. Robert D. HOLSTEN
32 Dean of Student Development ... Mr. Don L. BOYETTE
76 Associate Dean of Allied Health ... Ms. Glenda P. BONDURANT
88 Assoc Dean Indust Tech/Public Svcs ... Ms. NaDene TUCKER
50 Assoc Dean of Business/Comp Tech ... Vacant
15 Human Resources Manager ... Ms. Kathy WILLIAMSON
08 Head Librarian ... Mr. Gerry J. O'NEILL
45 Planning & Research Director ... Ms. Pat B. PERRY
21 Controller ... Ms. Jessica S. JONES
06 Registrar ... Mr. Jennifer DAVIS
07 Director of Admission ... Ms. Sandra LACKNER
18 Director of Facilities ... Mr. Ray OWEN
37 Dir of Financial Aid/Vet Affairs ... Ms. Lisa SHEARIN
102 Director of Foundation ... Ms. Lynn WAGNER
13 Asst Director of IT ... Ms. Molly ARMSTRONG
96 Purchasing Manager ... Ms. Donna A. TURNER
40 Bookstore Manager ... Ms. Kaschia SPELLS

North Carolina Wesleyan College (D)

3400 N Wesleyan Boulevard, Rocky Mount NC 27804-8630
County: Nash FICE Identification: 002951
Unit ID: 199209
Telephone: (252) 985-5100 Carnegie Class: Bac/Diverse
FAX Number: (252) 985-5231 Calendar System: 4/1/4
URL: www.ncwc.edu
Established: 1956 Annual Undergrad Tuition & Fees: $26,482
Enrollment: 1,522 Coed
Affiliation or Control: United Methodist IRS Status: 501(c)3
Highest Offering: Baccalaureate
Program: Liberal Arts And General; Teacher Preparatory
Accreditation: SC, TED

01 President ... Mr. James A. GRAY, III
05 Provost/Sr VP Academic Affairs ... Dr. Michael B. BROWN
10 Vice President of Finance ... Mr. Jason EDWARDS
30 Vice President of Development ... Mr. Michael PRATT
84 Vice President of Enrollment ... Mr. Bill ALLEN
32 VP Student Affairs/Dean of Students ... Dr. Randy WILLIAMS
09 Chief Planning & Research Officer ... Dr. Larry H. KELLEY
06 Registrar ... Mrs. Candace CASHWELL
08 Director of Library ... Mrs. Kathy WINSLOW
26 Director of Communications ... Mrs. Susan BEST
23 Director Health Services ... Ms. Jessica BRYS-WILSON
36 Director Internship & Career Center ... Ms. Tiffany ALEXANDER
19 Director of Campus Security ... Vacant
41 Director of Athletics ... Mr. John THOMPSON
29 Director Alumni Rels/Annual Fund ... Ms. Cricket MORRIS
21 Controller ... Vacant
37 Director of Financial Aid ... Ms. Leah HILL
15 Director of Human Resources ... Mr. Darrell S. WHITLEY
18 Chief Facilities/Physical Plant ... Mr. David KNIGHT
07 Interim Director of Admissions ... Ms. Lori MELTON
38 Director Student Counseling ... Ms. Leslie VEACH
40 Manager College Store ... Ms. Rachel T. DIX
20 Associate Academic Officer ... Dr. Molly WYATT

Pfeiffer University (E)

48380 US Highway 52 N / PO Box 960, Misenheimer NC 28109-0960
County: Stanly FICE Identification: 002955
Unit ID: 199306
Telephone: (704) 463-1360 Carnegie Class: Master's L
FAX Number: (704) 463-1363 Calendar System: Semester
URL: www.pfeiffer.edu
Established: 1885 Annual Undergrad Tuition & Fees: $24,150
Enrollment: 2,020 Coed
Affiliation or Control: United Methodist IRS Status: 501(c)3
Highest Offering: Master's
Program: Liberal Arts And General; Teacher Preparatory; Professional
Accreditation: SC, MFCD, MUS, TED

01 President ... Mr. Michael C. MILLER
04 Executive Assistant to President ... Ms. Teena P. MAULDIN
11 Chief Operations Officer ... Vacant
10 Vice President for Finance ... Vacant
05 Provost/VP Academic Affairs ... Dr. Tracy Y. ESPY
84 VP for Enrollment Mgmt/Marketing ... Vacant
32 VP for Student Devel/Dn of Students ... Dr. Russell SHARPLES
30 Spec Asst to Pres for Ldrship & Adv ... Mr. Thad HENRY
07 Director of Undergrad Admissions ... Ms. Terry PARKER-JEFFRIES
20 Associate VP for Academic Affairs ... Vacant
06 Registrar ... Ms. Lourdes SILVA
84 Director of Enrollment Operations ... Mr. Michael UTSMAN
15 Director of Human Resources ... Ms. Kathy ODELL
09 Director Institutional Rsrch/Plng ... Ms. Eva EISNAUGLE
26 Director Inst Communications ... Ms. Susan G. MESSINA
38 Director Counseling/Residence Educ ... Ms. Laura HERRICK
08 Acquisitions Librarian ... Mr. John MERCER, JR.
37 Director of Financial Aid ... Ms. Amy BROWN
13 Director of IT ... Mr. William SEWARD, II
07 Associate Director of Admissions ... Ms. Diane MARTIN
20 Dir of Academic Support Services ... Dr. Jim E. GULLEDGE
19 Dir of Campus Safety & Security ... Mr. Erik MCGINNIS
23 Director of Health Services ... Vacant
18 Director of Facilities ... Ms. Sharon K. BARD
41 Athletic Director ... Ms. Mary Ann SUNBURY
42 Minister to the University ... Rev. Dana MCKIM
36 Director of Career Services ... Vacant
35 Dir of Student Involvement ... Mr. Demond HAIRSTON
50 Dean of School of Business ... Dr. Kenneth BANDY
53 Dean of School of Education ... Dr. Dawn LUCAS
79 Dean of School of Humanities ... Dr. David HECKEL
81 Dean Sch of Natural & Health Sci ... Dr. Mark MCCALLUM
83 Dean Sch of Soc & Behav Sciences ... Dr. Donald POE, JR.
51 Director of School of Adult Studies ... Dr. Paulita BROOKER
88 Director of MHA Program ... Ms. Vernease MILLER
88 Exec Director Intl Business Studies ... Vacant
58 Director MS Org Leadership & Change ... Vacant
58 Director of MCE Program ... Rev. Kathleen KILBOURNE
102 Assoc VP Adv/Dir Corp & Found Rels ... Vacant
44 Director of Alumni & Annual Giving ... Vacant
39 Director of Residence Life ... Ms. Rebecca MCQUEEN
40 Bookstore Manager ... Ms. Dechelle ELLIS
12 Director of Triangle Campus ... Mr. Bennie L. FELTS

Piedmont International University (F)

420 S Broad Street, Winston-Salem NC 27101-5197
County: Forsyth FICE Identification: 002956
Unit ID: 199315
Telephone: (336) 725-8344 Carnegie Class: Spec/Faith
FAX Number: (336) 725-5522 Calendar System: Semester
URL: www.piedmontu.edu
Established: 1945 Annual Undergrad Tuition & Fees: $12,340
Enrollment: 530 Coed
Affiliation or Control: Independent Non-Profit IRS Status: 501(c)3
Highest Offering: Doctorate
Program: 2-Year Principally Bachelor's Creditable; Liberal Arts And General; Teacher Preparatory; Professional; Religious Emphasis
Accreditation: TRACS

01 President ... Dr. Charles W. PETITT
00 Chancellor ... Dr. Howard L. WILBURN
05 Provost ... Dr. Beth D. ASHBURN
11 Vice President of Operations ... Dr. Alan COX
58 Vice Pres of Graduate Studies ... Dr. Barkev TRACHIAN
06 Registrar ... Mr. Jeremy PATISSAL
08 Librarian ... Dr. Catherine CHATMON
32 Director of Student Services ... Mr. Paul SMELTZER
34 Dean of Women ... Mrs. Rebecca BOTTOMS

Queens University of Charlotte (G)

1900 Selwyn Avenue, Charlotte NC 28274-0001
County: Mecklenburg FICE Identification: 002957
Unit ID: 199412
Telephone: (704) 337-2200 Carnegie Class: Master's M
FAX Number: (704) 337-2517 Calendar System: Semester
URL: www.queens.edu
Established: 1857 Annual Undergrad Tuition & Fees: $28,800
Enrollment: 2,386 Coed
Affiliation or Control: Presbyterian Church (U.S.A.) IRS Status: 501(c)3
Highest Offering: Master's
Program: Liberal Arts And General; Teacher Preparatory; Professional; Business Emphasis
Accreditation: SC, ACBSP, ADNUR, BUS, MUS, NURSE, TED

01 President ... Dr. Pamela L. DAVIES
05 VP Academic Affairs & Provost ... Dr. Abiodun GOKE-PARIOLA
30 Vice Pres University Advancement ... Mr. James BULLOCK
84 Vice Pres Enrollment Management ... Dr. Brian RALPH
26 Vice Pres Marketing & Cmty Rels ... Mrs. Rebecca ANDERSON
45 VP Campus Planning and Services ... Mr. Bill NICHOLS
11 CFO & VP for Administration ... Mr. Matthew PACKEY
19 AVP Campus Safety & Security ... Vacant
29 Exec Director Alumni Relations ... Ms. Sara BLAKENEY
32 Dean of Students ... Dr. John DOWNEY
06 Registrar ... Ms. Linda FLEISCHMAN
07 Dir Undergraduate Admissions ... Mr. Woody O'CAIN
09 Director of Inst Research & Assess ... Vacant
39 Director Residence Life ... Mr. Edward YOUNG
13 Chief Information Officer ... Mr. John CHAMPION
15 Director of Human Resources ... Ms. Teri ORSINI, SPHR

08 University Librarian ..... Dr. Carol W. JORDAN
36 Dir Internships/Career Pgm ..... Ms. Angela TSUEI-STRAUSE
42 Chaplain/Director Campus Ministry ..... Rev. J. Diane MOWREY
19 Chief of Campus Police ..... Vacant
41 Director of Athletics ..... Ms. Jeannie KING
20 Dir of International Programs ..... Ms. Angie EDWARDS
04 Exec Director Pres Affairs ..... Mrs. Tamara BURRELL
37 AVP Student Financial Services ..... Mrs. Christy MAJORS
18 Facilities Manager ..... Mr. Tim ESTEP
50 Dean of McColl School of Business ..... Mr. Ronald SHIFFLER
49 Dean College of Arts & Sciences ..... Dr. Lynn MORTON
53 Int Dean Cato School of Education ..... Dr. Lynn MORTON
76 Dean Blair College of Health ..... Dr. Kevin L. BURKE
60 Dean Knight School of Communication ..... Dr. Eric FREEDMAN
55 Dean of Hayworth College Adult Stds ..... Dr. Kevin BUTLER

Reformed Theological Seminary (A)

2101 Carmel Road, Charlotte NC 28226-6399
Telephone: (704) 366-5066 Identification: 666785
Accreditation: &SC, &THEOL

† Main campus is Reformed Theological Seminary in Jackson, MS.

St. Andrews University (B)

1700 Dogwood Mile, Laurinburg NC 28352-5598
Telephone: (910) 277-5000 FICE Identification: 002967
Accreditation: &SC, TED

† Main campus is Webber International University in Babson Park, FL.

Saint Augustine's University (C)

1315 Oakwood Avenue, Raleigh NC 27610-2298
County: Wake FICE Identification: 002968
Unit ID: 199582
Telephone: (919) 516-4000 Carnegie Class: Bac/Diverse
FAX Number: (919) 828-0817 Calendar System: Semester
URL: www.st-aug.edu
Established: 1867 Annual Undergrad Tuition & Fees: $17,890
Enrollment: 1,442 Coed
Affiliation or Control: Protestant Episcopal IRS Status: 501(c)3
Highest Offering: Master's
Program: Liberal Arts And General; Teacher Preparatory
Accreditation: SC

01 President ..... Dr. Dianne BOARDLEY SUBER
04 Exec Assistant to the President ..... Mrs. Gloria T. ROWLAND
31 AVP External Relations ..... Mrs. Doris BULLOCK
10 Interim VP for Business & Finance ..... Ms. Angela N. HAYNES
05 Provost ..... Dr. B. Connie ALLEN
30 VP for Inst Advancement & Dev ..... Mr. Marc A. NEWMAN
32 VP Student Development & Services .. Dr. Roland N. BULLARD, II
45 VP Strategic Initiatives ..... Dr. Ronald H. BROWN
21 Asst Vice Pres for Business/Finance ..... Vacant
20 Asst VP Academic Affairs ..... Dr. Orlando E. HANKINS
21 Asst Vice President/Comptroller ..... Vacant
26 Assoc VP Marketing & Communication ..... Mrs. Shelley M. WILLINGHAM-HINTON
09 Asst VP Institutional Research ..... Dr. Tammalyn M. THOMAS-GOLDEN
35 Dean of Students & Residential Life ..... Vacant
42 Chaplain ..... Ms. Nita BYRD
13 Chief Information Officer ..... Mr. Harod C. DEMBY
15 AVP Human Resources ..... Dr. Sadie CARTER
41 Director Athletics ..... Mr. George D. WILLIAMS
06 Registrar ..... Ms. Crystal G. WILLIAMS
50 Dean Business & Technology ..... Dr. F. Perna CARTER
83 Dean Social and Behavorial Sciences ..... Dr. Zaphon WILSON
81 Dean Natural Sciences/Mathematics ..... Dr. Mark A. MELTON
76 Dean Allied Health ..... Dr. Hengameh G. ALLEN
49 Interim Dean Liberal Arts & Educ ..... Dr. M. Iyailu MOSES
51 Dean Extended Studies ..... Mrs. Dekhasta B. ROZIER
07 Director Admissions ..... Ms. Vonda EASTERLING
37 Director Financial Aid/Scholarships ..... Ms. Nadine Y. FORD
08 Dean of Library Services ..... Mr. Clevell S. ROSEBORO
36 Director Career Services ..... Ms. Nichole R. LEWIS
19 Chief of Police ..... Mr. George H. BOYKIN, III
18 Director Physical Plant ..... Ms. Sonya Y. CANNADY
29 Director Alumni Affairs ..... Ms. Sheryl H. XIMINES

Salem College (D)

601 South Church Street, Winston-Salem NC 27101
County: Forsyth FICE Identification: 002960
Unit ID: 199607
Telephone: (336) 721-2600 Carnegie Class: Bac/A&S
FAX Number: (336) 917-5339 Calendar System: 4/1/4
URL: www.salem.edu
Established: 1772 Annual Undergrad Tuition & Fees: $24,566
Enrollment: 1,165 Female
Affiliation or Control: Moravian Church IRS Status: 501(c)3
Highest Offering: Master's
Program: Liberal Arts And General; Teacher Preparatory; Professional
Accreditation: SC, MUS, TED

01 President ..... Dr. Susan E. PAULY
05 VP Acad & Stdnt Affs/Dn of College ..... Dr. Susan CALOVINI
30 VP for Institutional Advancement ..... Ms. Vicki SHEPPARD
07 Dean Admissions & Financial Aid ..... Ms. Katherine K. WATTS
32 Dean of Students ..... Ms. Krispin W. BARR
58 Dean of Graduate Studies ..... Ms. Mary Ann DAVIS
51 Dean of Continuing Studies ..... Ms. Suzanne WILLIAMS
20 Dean Undergraduate Studies ..... Dr. Richard VINSON
11 Director of Administration ..... Ms. Anna GALLIMORE
08 Librarian ..... Ms. Elizabeth NOVICKI
44 Director Annual Giving ..... Ms. Laura SLAWTER
13 Director Information Technology ..... Mr. Paul BENNINGER
15 Director of Payroll & Benefits ..... Ms. Cheryl HAMILTON
10 Chief Financial Officer ..... Mr. Derek BRYAN
38 Director Counseling Services ..... Mr. Jack LOCICERO
37 Director Student Financial Aid ..... Ms. Lori LEWIS
27 Director of Communications ..... Ms. Michelle MELTON
26 Assistant Director Public Relations ..... Ms. Jennifer HANDY
36 Director Career Devel/Internships ..... Ms. Esther GONZALEZ
06 Registrar/Dir Inst Research ..... Ms. Jeannette RORK
18 Chief Facilities/Physical Plant ..... Mr. George MORALES
29 Director Alumnae Relations ..... Ms. Karla GORT
21 Accounts Receivable Manager ..... Ms. Nikki BROCK
21 Accounts Payable Manager ..... Ms. Judy SIGMON
19 Coordinator Institutional Services ..... Mr. Tommy WILLIAMSON

Shaw University (E)

118 E South Street, Raleigh NC 27601
County: Wake FICE Identification: 002962
Unit ID: 199643
Telephone: (919) 546-8200 Carnegie Class: Bac/Diverse
FAX Number: (919) 546-8301 Calendar System: Semester
URL: www.shawuniversity.edu
Established: 1865 Annual Undergrad Tuition & Fees: $16,480
Enrollment: 2,183 Coed
Affiliation or Control: Baptist IRS Status: 501(c)3
Highest Offering: Master's
Program: Liberal Arts And General
Accreditation: SC, KIN, SW, TED, THEOL

01 President ..... Dr. Dorothy COWSER YANCY
32 Vice Pres Student Affairs/Admin ..... Dr. Jeffrey SMITH
05 Vice Pres Academic Affairs ..... Dr. Marilyn SUTTON-HAYWOOD
10 VP for Fiscal Affairs ..... Ms. Debra LATIMORE
30 VP for Institutional Advancement ..... Ms. Evelyn LEATHERS
20 Int Assoc VP for Academic Affairs ..... Dr. Renata DUSENBURY
20 Asst VP for Academic Affairs ..... Dr. Cynthia BEAMON
25 Spec Asst/Dir of Special Programs ..... Ms. Paula "Tendai" JOHNSON
27 Chief Information Officer ..... Mr. Hooshang FOROUDASTAN
21 Controller ..... Ms. Gwendolyn WEBB
21 Bursar ..... Ms. Shirley FENNELL
06 Registrar ..... Ms. Jody HAMILTON-DAVIS
32 Dean of Students ..... Mr. Alfonza CARTER
84 Dean of Enrollment Management ..... Ms. Rochelle KING
49 Dean Col of Arts and Sciences ..... Dr. Renata DUSENBURY
58 Dean Col of Grad/Prof Studies ..... Dr. Gaddis FAULCON
73 Dean Shaw Univ Divinity School ..... Dr. Bruce GRADY
39 Assoc Dean of Students ..... Vacant
15 Director of Human Resources ..... Ms. Diane CRAWFORD
26 Director of Public Relations ..... Ms. Odessa HINES
08 Director of Library Services ..... Ms. Carolyn PETERSON
07 Director of Admissions/Recruitment ... Mr. Sherlock MCDOUGALD
37 Director of Financial Aid ..... Ms. Rochelle KING
29 Director Alumni Affairs ..... Mr. Seddrick HILL
45 Dir of Stratetic Planning/Inst Res ..... Dr. Cecil MCMANUS
41 Director of Athletics ..... Mr. Marcus CLARKE
19 Chief of Campus Police & Security ..... Mr. Wayne JOINER
96 Manager of Procurement & Contracts ..... Ms. Gwendolyn PERRY
18 Facilities Manager ..... Mr. Cleon PIERCE
25 Int Dir Inst for HSC Research ..... Dr. Moses GOLDMAN
38 Director of Counseling Center ..... Ms. Jerelene CARVER
88 Director of Judicial Affairs ..... Ms. Agnes BAXTER
36 Dir Experiential Lrng/Career Devel ..... Dr. Denise VAUGHN
50 Chair Dept Business/Public Admin ..... Dr. Mma KALU
53 Chair Dept Education ..... Dr. Paula MOTEN-TOLSON
81 Chair Dept Natural Science/Math ..... Dr. Tashni DUBROY
76 Chair Dept Allied Health ..... Dr. James MCCALLUM
79 Chair Dept Humanities ..... Dr. Desire' BALOUBI
60 Chair Dept Mass Comm ..... Dr. Cassandra MITCHELL
57 Chair Dept Visual/Performing Arts ..... Mr. George HATCHER
83 Int Chair Dept Social Sciences ..... Dr. Beau NILES
77 Int Chair Dept Computer Info Sci ..... Dr. Lloyd WILLIAMS
88 Chair Dept Religion/Philosophy ..... Dr. James KIRKLEY

Shepherds Theological Seminary (F)

6051 Tryon Road, Cary NC 27518-9316
County: Wake FICE Identification: 041730
Unit ID: 461485
Telephone: (800) 672-3060 Carnegie Class: Not Classified
FAX Number: (919) 459-0022 Calendar System: Semester
URL: www.shepherds.edu
Established: 2003 Annual Graduate Tuition & Fees: $6,060
Enrollment: 81 Coed
Affiliation or Control: Independent Non-Profit IRS Status: 501(c)3
Highest Offering: Master's; No Undergraduates
Program: Professional; Religious Emphasis
Accreditation: TRACS

01 President ..... Dr. Stephen DAVEY
05 Provost/Dean ..... Dr. Larry PETTEGREW
06 Vice President of Academic Affairs ..... Dr. Randall L. MCKINION
30 Vice President of Advancement ..... Dr. Alan POTTER
07 Director of Recruitment ..... Dr. Douglas BOOKMAN
18 Chief Facilities/Physical Plant ..... Dr. Samuel WINCHESTER
06 Registrar/Financial Aid Officer ..... Mrs. Lucy BURGGRAFF

South College-Asheville (G)

140 Sweeten Creek Road, Asheville NC 28803
County: Buncombe FICE Identification: 010264
Unit ID: 198242
Telephone: (828) 398-2500 Carnegie Class: Assoc/PrivFP4
FAX Number: (828) 277-6151 Calendar System: Quarter
URL: www.southcollegenc.edu
Established: 1905 Annual Undergrad Tuition & Fees: $17,000
Enrollment: 259 Coed
Affiliation or Control: Proprietary IRS Status: Proprietary
Highest Offering: Baccalaureate
Program: Occupational; 2-Year Principally Bachelor's Creditable; Nursing Emphasis
Accreditation: ACICS, MAC, PTAA, RAD, SURGT

00 President/Owner ..... Mr. Stephen A. SOUTH
01 Executive Director ..... Mr. Nick SOUTH
05 Dean of Academic Affairs ..... Mr. Patrick S. LAROSE
10 Business Manager ..... Ms. Christine CHANCEY
07 Director of Admissions ..... Ms. Elisa JACOBS
37 Financial Aid Officer ..... Ms. Ronda BLACKMAN
08 Head Librarian ..... Ms. Jennifer FINLEY

South University (H)

3975 Premier Drive, High Point NC 27265
Telephone: (336) 812-7200 Identification: 770915
Accreditation: &SC

† Main campus is South University in Savannah, GA.

Southeastern Baptist Theological Seminary (I)

Box 1889, Wake Forest NC 27588-1889
County: Wake FICE Identification: 002963
Unit ID: 199759
Telephone: (919) 761-2100 Carnegie Class: Not Classified
FAX Number: N/A Calendar System: Semester
URL: www.sebts.edu
Established: 1950 Annual Undergrad Tuition & Fees: $9,150
Enrollment: 2,595 Coed
Affiliation or Control: Southern Baptist IRS Status: 501(c)3
Highest Offering: Doctorate
Program: Professional
Accreditation: SC, THEOL

01 President ..... Dr. Daniel L. AKIN
05 Provost/Dean of Faculty ..... Dr. Bruce R. ASHFORD
10 Sr VP for Business Administration ..... Mr. Ryan HUTCHINSON
20 Associate Academic Officer ..... Mr. Sheldon H. ALEXANDER
06 Registrar ..... Mr. Shane BAKER
07 Director of Admissions ..... Mr. Larry LYON
09 Asst VP Institutional Effectiveness ..... Dr. Michael E. TRAVERS
29 Director of Alumni Development ..... Mr. Albie BRICE
30 Vice Pres Institutional Advancement ..... Mr. Dennis DARVILLE
37 Director of Financial Aid ..... Dr. Don ALLARD

Southern Evangelical Seminary (J)

3000 Tilley Morris Road, Matthews NC 28105-8635
County: Union FICE Identification: 036115
Unit ID: 438522
Telephone: (704) 847-5600 Carnegie Class: Not Classified
FAX Number: (704) 845-1747 Calendar System: Semester
URL: www.ses.edu
Established: 1992 Annual Undergrad Tuition & Fees: $5,970
Enrollment: 350 Coed
Affiliation or Control: Independent Non-Profit IRS Status: 501(c)3
Highest Offering: Doctorate
Program: Professional; Religious Emphasis
Accreditation: TRACS

01 President & COO ..... Dr. Richard D. LAND
05 Academic Dean ..... Dr. Floyd ELMORE
07 Director of Admissions ..... Mr. Duke HALE
10 Business Manager ..... Mrs. Joan C. SOLHEIM
08 Librarian ..... Mr. Ronald I. JORDAHL
06 Registrar ..... Dr. Douglas E. POTTER
29 Director Alumni Rels/Student Svcs ..... Mrs. Jill JOYNER
13 Dir of Information Technology ..... Mr. Timothy BURKETT
30 Director of Development ..... Mr. Eric T. GUSTAFSON
04 Executive Asst to President ..... Mrs. Christina S. WOODSIDE
33 Dean of Men ..... Mr. Duke HALE
34 Dean of Women ..... Mrs. Nora M. HALE
88 Director Missions ..... Mr. Simon BRACE
106 Dir Online Education/E-learning ..... Dr. Daniel JANOSIK

*University of North Carolina General Administration (K)

Box 2688, 910 Raleigh Road, Chapel Hill NC 27515-2688
County: Orange FICE Identification: 002971
Unit ID: 199175
Telephone: (919) 962-1000 Carnegie Class: N/A
FAX Number: (919) 962-2751
URL: www.northcarolina.edu

01 President ..... Mr. Thomas W. ROSS

100 Chief of Staff ... Mr. Kevin FITZGERALD
05 Sr Vice Pres Academic Affairs ... Dr. Suzanne ORTEGA
10 Vice President for Finance ... Mr. Charles E. PERUSSE
45 Vice Pres for Academic Planning ... Vacant
13 Vice Pres Information Resources/CIO ... Mr. John LEYDON
43 Int VP Legal Affs/General Counsel ... Mr. Thomas SHANAHAN
46 VP Research/Graduate Education ... Dr. Christopher BROWN
101 Secretary of the University ... Ms. Ann LEMMON
86 Vice President for Govt Relations ... Mr. Drew MORETZ
86 Vice President for Federal Rels ... Ms. Kimrey RHINEHARDT
26 Vice President for Communications ... Ms. Joni WORTHINGTON
15 Vice Pres for Human Resources ... Mr. William FLEMING

*Appalachian State University (A)

Boone NC 28608-0001
County: Watauga FICE Identification: 002906
Unit ID: 197869
Telephone: (828) 262-2000 Carnegie Class: Master's L
FAX Number: (828) 262-2347 Calendar System: Semester
URL: www.appstate.edu
Established: 1899 Annual Undergrad Tuition & Fees (In-State): $6,492
Enrollment: 17,589 Coed
Affiliation or Control: State IRS Status: 501(c)3
Highest Offering: Doctorate
Program: Liberal Arts And General; Teacher Preparatory; Professional
Accreditation: SC, AAFCS, ART, BUS, CACREP, CIDA, CS, DIETD, DIETI, IPSY, MFCD, MUS, NRPA, NURSE, SP, SPAA, SW, TED, THEA

02 Chancellor ... Dr. Kenneth E. PEACOCK
05 Provost/Exec Vice Chancellor ... Dr. Lori S. GONZALEZ
10 Vice Chanc Business Affairs ... Mr. Greg M. LOVINS
32 Vice Chanc Student Development ... Ms. Cindy A. WALLACE
30 Vice Chanc Univ Advancement ... Mrs. Susan H. PETTYJOHN
20 Vice Provost for Undergrad Educ ... Dr. Mike W. MAYFIELD
45 Vice Provost for Resource Mgmt ... Dr. Tim H. BURWELL
26 Assc VC Univ Comm/Cultural Affairs ... Mr. Hank T. FOREMAN
84 Assoc VC for Enrollment Management ... Mrs. Susan DAVIES
22 Dir of Equity/Diversity/Compliance ... Ms. Linda M. FOULSHAM
29 Exec Director of Alumni Affairs ... Mr. Patrick K. SETZER
43 General Counsel ... Mr. Dayton T. COLE
13 Chief Information Officer ... Mrs. Cathy J. BATES
06 University Registrar ... Ms. Andrea C. WAWRZUSIN
38 Dir Counseling/Psychological Svcs ... Dr. Dan L. JONES
37 Director of Financial Aid ... Ms. Esther M. MANOGIN
15 Director of Human Resources ... Mr. Patrick J. MCCOY
36 Director of Career Development Ctr ... Ms. Marjorie N. ELLIS
09 Director Inst Research & Planning ... Dr. Bobby H. SHARP
51 Int Exec Dir of Distance Education ... Dr. Mary F. ENGLEBERT
41 Director of Athletics ... Mr. Charles G. COBB
49 Dean for College of Arts & Sciences ... Dr. Anthony G. CALAMAI
50 Dean for College of Business ... Dr. Randy K. EDWARDS
53 Dean for College of Education ... Dr. Charles R. DUKE
57 Dean for College Fine/Applied Arts ... Dr. Glenda J. TREADAWAY
64 Dean for the School of Music ... Dr. William L. PELTO
58 Dean of Research/Graduate Studies ... Dr. Edelma D. HUNTLEY
08 Dean of Libraries ... Dr. Mary L. REICHEL
18 Director of the Physical Plant ... Mr. Mike J. O'CONNOR
21 Budget Director ... Ms. Betsy P. PAYNE
35 Dean of Students/Assoc VC Stdnt Dev ... Mr. J.J BROWN
07 Director of Admissions ... Mr. Lloyd M. SCOTT
96 Director of Materials Management ... Mr. Dwayne E. ODVODY
28 Dir Multicultural Student Develop ... Mr. Augusto E. PENA

*East Carolina University (B)

1000 East Fifth Street, Greenville NC 27858-4353
County: Pitt FICE Identification: 002923
Unit ID: 198464
Telephone: (252) 328-6212 Carnegie Class: DRU
FAX Number: (252) 328-4155 Calendar System: Semester
URL: www.ecu.edu
Established: 1907 Annual Undergrad Tuition & Fees (In-State): $6,143
Enrollment: 26,947 Coed
Affiliation or Control: State IRS Status: 501(c)3
Highest Offering: Doctorate
Program: Liberal Arts And General; Teacher Preparatory; Professional
Accreditation: SC, AAFCS, ANEST, ARCPA, ART, AUD, BUS, CAHIIM, CIDA, CLPSY, CONST, CORE, DENT, DIETD, DIETI, ENG, MED, MFCD, MIDWF, MT, MUS, NAIT, NRPA, NURSE, OT, PH, PLNG, PTA, SP, SPAA, SW, TED, THEA

02 Chancellor ... Dr. Steve BALLARD
100 Chief of Staff ... Mr. Chris LOCKLEAR
05 Provost & Sr Vice Chanc Acad Affs ... Dr. Marilyn SHEERER
32 Vice Chancellor for Student Affairs ... Dr. Virginia HARDY
17 Vice Chanc Health Sciences ... Dr. Phyllis N. HORNS
10 Vice Chanc Administration & Finance ... Dr. Frederick NISWANDER
30 Int Vice Chanc Univ Advancement ... Dr. Glen GILBERT
46 Int VC Research/Graduate Studies ... Dr. Ron MITCHELSON
29 Assoc VC for Alumni Relations ... Mr. Paul CLIFFORD
39 Assoc VC Camp Liv/Dining ... Mr. William L. MCCARTNEY, JR.
38 Assoc Vice Chanc & Dean of Stdnts ... Dr. Lynn M. ROEDER
35 Assoc Dean of Students ... Dr. Lathan E. TURNER
22 Assoc Provost Equity/Diversity ... Ms. Lakesha ALSTON
43 Vice Chancellor for Legal Affairs ... Ms. Donna G. PAYNE
09 Associate Provost IPRE ... Vacant
41 Athletic Director ... Mr. Jeff COMPHER
13 CIO and Assoc Vice Chanc ITCS ... Mr. Don SWEET
15 Int Assoc Vice Chanc Human Resource ... Mr. Jim MULLEN
18 Assoc VC for Campus Opers ... Mr. William BAGNELL
21 Assoc VC for Business Services ... Mr. A. Scott BUCK
19 Assoc VC Environ Health & Safety ... Mr. Bill KOCH
82 Assoc VC of International Affairs ... Dr. Jim GEHLHAR
88 Assoc VC for Academic Outreach ... Dr. Elmer POE
20 Assoc VC for Academic Programs ... Dr. Linner GRIFFIN
88 Asst VC Recreational/Wellness Svcs ... Ms. Nancy MIZE
84 Assoc Provost for Enrollment Svcs ... Dr. John FLETCHER
07 Director of Admissions ... Vacant
06 Registrar ... Ms. Angela R. ANDERSON
08 Int Dean Library Services ... Ms. Jan LEWIS
88 Director Health Sciences Library ... Dr. Dorothy A. SPENCER
101 Asst Secretary to Board of Trustees ... Dr. Steve DUNCAN
37 Director of Financial Aid ... Ms. Julie POORMAN
19 Director/Chief of Police ... Vacant
51 Director of Continuing Studies ... Dr. F. Clayton SESSOMS
27 Director of Publications ... Mr. Jimmy ROSTAR
88 Director of Military Programs ... Dr. Steve DUNCAN
96 Director of Purchasing ... Mr. Kevin CARRAWAY
36 Director Career Center ... Ms. Karen S. THOMPSON
26 Director of University Marketing ... Mr. Clint BAILEY
21 Director of Internal Audit ... Ms. Stacie TRONTO
21 Associate VC for Financial Services ... Ms. Anne JENKINS
26 Ex Dir Communication/Pub Affs/Mktg ... Ms. Mary C. SHULKEN
49 Dean College of Arts & Sciences ... Dr. John SUTHERLAND
76 Dean Sch Allied Health Sciences ... Dr. Stephen W. THOMAS
68 Dean Col Health/Human Performance ... Dr. Glen G. GILBERT
59 Dean College of Human Ecology ... Dr. Judy SIGUAW
66 Dean College of Nursing ... Dr. Sylvia BROWN
50 Dean College of Business ... Dr. Stanley G. EAKINS
57 Interim Dean Col Fine Arts/Comm ... Dr. Michael DORSEY
53 Dean College of Education ... Dr. Linda PATRIARCA
72 Dean of Col Tech/Computer Sci ... Dr. David WHITE
58 Dean Graduate School ... Dr. Paul GEMPERLINE
92 Interim Dean Honors College ... Vacant
63 Dean Brody School of Medicine ... Dr. Paul R G. CUNNINGHAM
52 Dean School of Dental Medicine ... Dr. Gregory CHADWICK

*Elizabeth City State University (C)

1704 Weeksville Road, Elizabeth City NC 27909-7806
County: Pasquotank FICE Identification: 002926
Unit ID: 198507
Telephone: (252) 335-3400 Carnegie Class: Bac/Diverse
FAX Number: (252) 335-3731 Calendar System: Semester
URL: www.ecsu.edu
Established: 1891 Annual Undergrad Tuition & Fees (In-State): $6,145
Enrollment: 2,713 Coed
Affiliation or Control: State IRS Status: 501(c)3
Highest Offering: Master's
Program: Liberal Arts And General; Teacher Preparatory; Fine Arts Emphasis
Accreditation: SC, BUS, MUS, NAIT, SW, TED

02 Chancellor ... Mr. Charles L. BECTON
100 Chief of Staff ... Ms. Gwendolyn SANDERS
05 Provost/VC Academic Affairs ... Dr. Ali A. KHAN
10 VC for Business & Finance ... Mr. Benjamin DURANT
32 VC for Student Affairs ... Dr. Anthony BROWN
30 VC for Institutional Advancemnt ... Mr. William G. SMITH
43 General Counsel ... Ms. Bernetta H. BROWN
35 Assoc VC for Student Affairs ... Mrs. Deborah G. BRANCH
35 Assoc VC for Student Affairs ... Ms. Barbaina M. HOUSTON-BLACK
20 Assoc VC Academic Affs/Acad Support ... Dr. W. E. THOMAS
13 Director of Information Systems ... Mr. Matthew SIMPSON
38 Dir Counsel/Test Student Affairs ... Ms. Felicia BROWN
27 Interim Chief Information Officer ... Ms. Kim STAHL
06 Registrar ... Mr. Vincent L. BEAMON
84 Director Enrollment Management ... Dr. Monette WILLIAMS
09 Dir Institutional Effectiveness/Res ... Dr. Damon R. WADE
08 Director of Library Services ... Dr. Juanita MIDGETTE
07 Director of Admissions ... Mr. Darius EURE
37 Director Student Financial Aid ... Ms. Tracie N. HUNTER
36 Director of Career Services ... Ms. Makitta WHITEHURST-MCLEAN
15 Director Human Resources ... Mrs. Donna JAMES-WHIDBEE
29 Director of Alumni Relations ... Ms. Barbara B. SUTTON
18 Director Facilities/Physical Plant ... Mr. Dennis LEARY
26 Director of Marketing ... Ms. Rhonda M. HAYES
87 Director of Summer School ... Mr. Warren E. POOLE
41 Interim Athletic Director ... Ms. Angelia J. NELSON
21 Director of Budgets ... Mrs. Sharnita L. WILSON-PARKER
92 Director of Honors Program ... Dr. Velma B. BLACKMON
96 Director of Purchasing ... Ms. Rachel HAINES
53 Dean Sch Education & Psychology ... Dr. Charles D. CHERRY
49 Dean Sch of Arts & Humanities ... Dr. Murel M. JONES
50 Dean Sch of Business & Economics ... Dr. Kingsley NWALA
81 Dean Sch of Math/Science/Technology ... Dr. Harry S. BASS

*Fayetteville State University (D)

1200 Murchison Road, Fayetteville NC 28301-4298
County: Cumberland FICE Identification: 002928
Unit ID: 198543
Telephone: (910) 672-1111 Carnegie Class: Master's M
FAX Number: (910) 672-1769 Calendar System: Semester
URL: www.uncfsu.edu
Established: 1867 Annual Undergrad Tuition & Fees (In-State): $6,330
Enrollment: 6,060 Coed
Affiliation or Control: State IRS Status: 501(c)3
Highest Offering: Doctorate
Program: Liberal Arts And General; Teacher Preparatory
Accreditation: SC, BUS, CS, MUS, NURSE, SW, TED

02 Chancellor ... Dr. James A. ANDERSON
100 Vice Chancellor and Chief of Staff ... Dr. Thomas CONWAY
05 Provost & Vice Chanc Academic Affs ... Dr. Jon YOUNG
10 Vice Chancellor Business/Finance ... Mr. Robert L. BOTLEY
32 Vice Chancellor Student Affairs ... Dr. Janice HAYNIE
30 Vice Chancellor Inst Advancement ... Mr. Getchel CALDWELL
13 Vice Chanc Info Technology/CIO ... Mr. Arasu GANESAN
44 Asst Vice Chanc for Advancement ... Ms. Mary H. BAILEY
35 Assoc Vice Chanc Student Affairs ... Ms. Juanette COUNCIL
18 Assoc Vice Chanc Facilities Mgmt ... Mr. Rudolph CARDENAS
21 Asst VC Business/Financ/Comptroller ... Ms. Lisa BLAUSER
88 Senior Assoc Vice Chanc Inst Transf ... Dr. Curtis CHARLES
15 Assoc Vice Chanc Human Resources ... Ms. Denise BROWN-HART
88 AVC Inst Research/Testing/Title III ... Vacant
85 Asst VC Acad Affs/Interntl Studies ... Dr. Chen YUNKAI
88 Senior Assoc Vice Chancellor ... Dr. Perry A. MASSEY
45 Assoc VC Pgms/Plng/Assessment ... Vacant
84 Assoc VC for Enrollment Management ... Ms. Roxie SHABAZZ
36 Director Career Svcs & Bus Mgr SA ... Ms. Helene CAMERON
92 Acting Program Director Honors ... Dr. Erin WHITE
06 Registrar ... Ms. Sarah BAKER
29 Director of Alumni Affairs ... Mrs. Michaela BROWN
26 Director Public Relations ... Mr. Jeff WOMBLE
08 Director of Library Services ... Mr. Bobby C. WYNN
07 Director of Admissions ... Ms. Ulisa BOWLES
90 Director of IT Operations ... Ms. Michelle WHITAKER
09 Director Institutional Research ... Mr. Ivan WALKER
39 Director of Residence Life ... Mr. Greg MOYD
37 Director Student Financial Aid ... Ms. Kamesia EWING
43 General Counsel ... Mrs. Wanda LESSANE JENKINS
41 Athletic Director ... Dr. Edward MCLEAN
96 Director of Purchasing ... Ms. Willie MCINTYRE
38 Dir Center Personal Development ... Mr. Fred SAPP
28 Director of Diversity ... Vacant
88 Dean University College ... Dr. John I. BROOKS
66 Department Chair Nursing ... Dr. Afua ARHIN
50 Dean School Business/Economics ... Dr. Assad TAVAKOLI
53 Dean School of Education ... Dr. Leontye LEWIS
58 Dean Graduate Stds/Sponsored Rsrch ... Dr. LaDelle OLION
49 Dean College of Arts and Sciences ... Dr. David BARLOW

*North Carolina Agricultural and Technical State University (E)

1601 E Market Street, Greensboro NC 27411-0001
County: Guilford FICE Identification: 002905
Unit ID: 199102
Telephone: (336) 334-7500 Carnegie Class: DRU
FAX Number: (336) 334-7136 Calendar System: Semester
URL: www.ncat.edu
Established: 1891 Annual Undergrad Tuition & Fees (In-State): $6,797
Enrollment: 10,561 Coed
Affiliation or Control: State IRS Status: 501(c)3
Highest Offering: Doctorate
Program: Liberal Arts And General; Teacher Preparatory; Professional
Accreditation: SC, AAFCS, BUS, BUSA, CACREP, CONST, CORE, CS, DIETD, ENG, JOUR, LSAR, MUS, NAIT, NUR, SW, TED, THEA

02 Chancellor ... Dr. Harold L. MARTIN
05 Provost/Vice Chanc Academic Aff ... Dr. Joe B. WHITEHEAD, JR.
10 Vice Chanc Business & Finance ... Mr. Robert POMPEY, JR.
30 Interim Vice Chanc Univ Advancement ... Nicole PRIDE
46 Vice Chanc Research/Economic Dev ... Dr. Barry L. BURKS
32 Vice Chancellor of Student Affairs ... Dr. Melody C. PIERCE
15 Vice Chancellor for Human Resources ... Ms. Linda R. MCABEE
13 Vice Chanc Info Tech & Telecom/CIO ... Ms. Barbara J. ELLIS
43 General Counsel for Legal Affairs ... Dr. J. Charles WALDRUP
20 Assoc VC for Undergraduate Pgm ... Vacant
27 Assoc Vice Chanc for Univ Relations ... Ms. Nicole PRIDE
84 Int Asst Vice Chanc Enrollment Mgmt ... Mrs. Tracy SMITH
88 Vice Prov Rsrch Grad Pgm/Extnd Lrng ... Dr. Sanjiv SARIN
18 Asst VC for Bus/Finance/Facilities ... Mr. Andrew M. PERKINS, JR.
19 Asst VC Police/Public Safety ... Mr. Glen C. NEWELL
08 Dean of Library Services ... Ms. Vicki COLEMAN
47 Dean Agric/Environmental Sci ... Dr. William M. RANDLE
49 Dean Arts & Sciences ... Dr. Goldie S. BYRD
53 Dean School of Education ... Dr. William B. HARVEY
54 Dean of Engineering ... Dr. Robin N. COGER
58 Dean of Graduate School ... Dr. Sanjiv SARIN
66 Dean of Nursing ... Dr. Inez TUCK
50 Int Dean of Business & Economics ... Dr. Patrick R. LIVERPOOL
72 Dean School of Technology ... Dr. Benjamin O. UWAKWEH
88 Dean Joint Sch Nanoscience/Nanoengr ... Dr. James G. RYAN
09 Director Inst Research/Planning ... Dr. G. Scott JENKINS
06 University Registrar ... Mr. Lester LUGO
07 Interim Director of Admissions ... Ms. Cheryl POLLARD-BURNS
37 Director Financial Aid ... Mrs. Sherri M. AVENT
36 Director Career Services ... Ms. Joyce P. EDWARDS
91 Dir Info Systems/Data Center Ops ... Vacant
29 Director of Alumni Affairs ... Vacant
85 Dir International Student Affairs ... Ms. Loreatha D. GRAVES
88 Dir Multicultural Student Center ... Mr. Gerald SPATES
41 Director of Athletics ... Mr. Earl M. HILTON, III
39 Dir Student Housing/Residence Life ... Ms. Linda D. INMAN
23 Director Student Health Services ... Mrs. Linda WILSON
38 Director of Counseling Service ... Dr. Vivian D. BARNETTE
25 Director of Contracts/Grants ... Ms. Lavonne MATTHEWS
92 Director of Honors Program ... Dr. Michael CUNDALL, JR.
96 Director of Purchasing ... Mr. Ted A. LITTLE
26 Director of Media Relations ... Ms. Samantha V. HARGROVE
40 Manager of Bookstore ... Ms. Catrina JACKSON

*North Carolina Central University (A)

1801 Fayetteville Street, Durham NC 27707-3129
County: Durham FICE Identification: 002950
Unit ID: 199157
Telephone: (919) 530-6100 Carnegie Class: Master's L
FAX Number: (919) 530-5014 Calendar System: Semester
URL: www.nccu.edu
Established: 1910 Annual Undergrad Tuition & Fees (In-State): $5,444
Enrollment: 8,761 Coed
Affiliation or Control: State IRS Status: 501(c)3
Highest Offering: Doctorate
Program: Liberal Arts And General; Teacher Preparatory; Professional
Accreditation: SC, ACBSP, BUS, CACREP, DIETD, DIETI, LAW, LIB, NRPA, NUR, SP, SW, TED, THEA

02 Chancellor ...... Dr. Debra SAUNDERS-WHITE
05 Provost/Vice Chanc Academic Affairs ...... Dr. Bernice JOHNSON
100 Vice Chanc/Chief of Staff ...... Dr. Kimberly LUSE
43 General Counsel ...... Ms. Melissa JACKSON HOLLOWAY
46 Vice Chanc Research/Economic Devel ...... Dr. Hazell REED
11 Vice Chanc Admin & Finance ...... Mr. Wendell M. DAVIS
32 Vice Chanc Student Affs/Enroll Mgt ...... Dr. Jennifer A. WILDER
30 Vice Chanc Inst Advancement ...... Dr. Kenneth CHANDLER
20 Assoc Provost/Assoc VC ...... Vacant
10 Assoc VC Administration/Finance ...... Ms. Yolanda E. BANKS-DEAVER
20 Assoc Vice Chanc Academic Affairs ...... Dr. Frances D. GRAHAM
15 Assoc Vice Chanc Human Resources ...... Ms. Sharon LAISURE
88 Asst VC for University Programs ...... Dr. Janice A. HARPER
88 Ast Dean of Stdnts/Dir Stdnt Union ...... Mr. Kevin M. JONES
45 Director Strategic Planning ...... Mr. Johnnie SOUTHERLAND
35 Dir Student Rights/Responsibilities ...... Mr. Gary L. BROWN
13 Chief Information Officer ...... Mr. John SMITH
07 Admissions Director ...... Mr. Anthony M. BROOKS
31 Dir Govt & Community Relations ...... Ms. Starla H. TANNER
88 Dir JLC Biomed/Biotech Rsrch Inst ...... Dr. K. Sean KIMBRO
44 Director Major Gifts ...... Mr. Randal V. CHILDS
88 Dir Biomanfct Rsch Inst/Tech Ent ...... Dr. Li-An YEH
44 Director Annual Giving ...... Vacant
06 Registrar ...... Dr. Jerome GOODWIN
91 Dir Enterprise Information System ...... Mr. Donald R. NOLEN
29 Director of Alumni Affairs ...... Ms. Anita B. WALTON
26 Director of Public Relations ...... Ms. Ayana D. HERNANDEZ
37 Director of Student Financial Aid ...... Ms. Sharon J. OLIVER
08 Director Library Services ...... Dr. Theodosia T. SHIELDS
19 Chief of Campus Police & Security ...... Mr. Timothy R. BELLAMY
88 Director Academic Advising ...... Dr. Jennifer SCHUM
88 Director Art Museum ...... Dr. Kenneth G. RODGERS
18 Director Facilities Services ...... Mr. Phillip POWELL
39 Director Residential Life ...... Vacant
41 Director Athletics ...... Dr. Ingrid L. WICKER-MCCREE
09 Dir Research/Evaluation/Planning ...... Mr. Shawn STEWART
96 Director of Purchasing ...... Mr. Godfrey B. HERNDON
92 Director of Honors Program ...... Dr. Ansel E. BROWN
38 Director of Counseling Center ...... Dr. Carolyn D. MOORE-ASSEM
22 Dir Equal Opportunity/Affirm Act ...... Vacant
84 Director Enrollment Management ...... Ms. Sharon J. OLIVER
88 Asst Dir Greek Life/Special Pgms ...... Mrs. Robin FEATHERSTONE-HANES
21 Dir Auxiliaries/Business Services ...... Mr. Timothy J. MOORE
40 Manager Bookstore ...... Ms. Stephanie L. GETCHELL
58 Dean Sch Grad Stds/Asc VC Grad Rsch ...... Dr. Caesar R. JACKSON
61 Dean of the Law School ...... Ms. Phyliss V. CRAIG-TAYLOR
62 Dean School of Library/Info Science ...... Dr. Irene OWENS
50 Dean School of Business ...... Mr. D. Keith PIGUES
88 Dean of University College ...... Dr. Ontario S. WOODEN
49 Dean College of Arts and Sciences ...... Dr. Carlton E. WILSON
72 Dean College of Science/Technology ...... Dr. Abdul K. MOHAMMED
83 Dean College Behavioral/Social Scis ...... Dr. Debra O. PARKER
53 Dean School of Education ...... Dr. Wynetta LEE

*North Carolina State University (B)

20 Watauga Club Drive, Raleigh NC 27695-0001
County: Wake FICE Identification: 002972
Unit ID: 199193
Telephone: (919) 515-2011 Carnegie Class: RU/VH
FAX Number: (919) 515-7740 Calendar System: Semester
URL: www.ncsu.edu
Established: 1887 Annual Undergrad Tuition & Fees (In-State): $8,206
Enrollment: 34,340 Coed
Affiliation or Control: State IRS Status: 501(c)3
Highest Offering: Doctorate
Program: Occupational; Liberal Arts And General; Teacher Preparatory; Professional; Technical Emphasis
Accreditation: SC, ART, BUS, BUSA, CACREP, CS, ENG, FOR, LSAR, NRPA, SCPSY, SPAA, SW, TED, VET

02 Chancellor ...... Dr. William Randy WOODSON
05 Provost/Exec Vice Chancellor ...... Dr. Warwick A. ARDEN
43 Vice Chanc & General Counsel ...... Ms. Eileen GOLDGEIER
10 Vice Chanc Finance & Business ...... Mr. Charles D. LEFFLER
46 Vice Chanc Research/Grad Studies ...... Dr. Terri L. LOMAX
32 Vice Chan/Dean Div Acad & Stdnt Aff ...... Dr. Michael D. MULLEN
30 Vice Chanc Univ Advancement ...... Vacant
13 Vice Chanc Information Technology ...... Dr. Marc I. HOIT
100 Secretary of the University ...... Ms. P. J. TEAL
26 Asst to Chanc External Affairs ...... Mr. Kevin HOWELL
88 Sr Vice Provost for Acad Strategy ...... Dr. Duane K. LARICK
106 Sr Vice Prov Acad Outreach/Entrepre ...... Dr. Thomas K. MILLER
08 Vice Provost/Director of Libraries ...... Ms. Susan K. NUTTER
22 Vice Prov Inst Equity & Diversity ...... Ms. Joanne G. WOODARD
21 Assoc Vice Chanc Finance/Res Mgt ...... Mr. Stephen W. KETO
18 Assoc Vice Chanc Facilities ...... Mr. Kevin J. MACNAUGHTON
39 Vice Provost for Residential Life ...... Dr. Timothy R. LUCKADOO
29 Assoc Vice Chanc Alumni Relations ...... Mr. Benny SUGGS
15 Assoc Vice Chanc Human Resources ...... Ms. Barbara L. CARROLL
19 Director Public Safety ...... Mr. Jack W. MOORMAN
09 Director Univ Planning/Analysis ...... Ms. Karen P. HELM
07 Director Undergrad Admissions ...... Mr. Thomas H. GRIFFIN
06 Registrar ...... Dr. Louis D. HUNT
25 Director Contracts & Grants ...... Ms. Julie A. BRASFIELD
27 Director News Services ...... Mr. Fred W. HARTMAN
37 Director of Financial Aid ...... Ms. Krista R. DOMNICK
38 Director of Counseling Center ...... Dr. Monica OSBURN
41 Director Athletics ...... Ms. Deborah YOW
21 Treasurer ...... Ms. Mary T. PELOQUIN-DODD
88 Director of Materials Management ...... Mrs. Sharon LOOSMAN
79 Dean Humanities/Social Sciences ...... Dr. Jeffery P. BRADEN
48 Dean of Design ...... Dr. Marvin J. MALECHA
54 Dean of Engineering ...... Dr. Louis A. MARTIN-VEGA
47 Dean Agriculture/Life Sciences ...... Dr. Richard H. LINTON
65 Dean of Natural Resources ...... Dr. Mary WATZIN
53 Dean of Education ...... Dr. Jayne FLEENER
50 Dean of Management ...... Dr. Ira R. WEISS
81 Dean College of Sciences ...... Dr. Daniel L. SOLOMON
88 Dean of Textiles ...... Dr. Blanton GODFREY
74 Dean of Veterinary Medicine ...... Dr. D. Paul LUNN
58 Interim Dean of Graduate School ...... Dr. Rebeca C. RUFTY

*University of North Carolina at Asheville (C)

1 University Heights, Asheville NC 28804-8503
County: Buncombe FICE Identification: 002907
Unit ID: 199111
Telephone: (828) 251-6600 Carnegie Class: Bac/A&S
FAX Number: (828) 251-6495 Calendar System: Semester
URL: www.unca.edu
Established: 1927 Annual Undergrad Tuition & Fees (In-State): $5,916
Enrollment: 3,751 Coed
Affiliation or Control: State IRS Status: 501(c)3
Highest Offering: Master's
Program: Liberal Arts And General; Teacher Preparatory
Accreditation: SC, BUS, ENG, TED

02 Chancellor ...... Dr. Anne PONDER
100 Chief of Staff ...... Ms. Christine RILEY
05 Provost/VC Academic Affairs ...... Dr. Jane K. FERNANDES
10 Vice Chancellor Finance/Operations ...... Mr. John PIERCE
30 Vice Chancellor Advancement ...... Ms. Elizabeth BAGWELL
32 Vice Chanc for Student Affairs ...... Dr. Bill HAGGARD
41 Director of Athletics ...... Ms. Janet R. CONE
43 University General Counsel ...... Mr. Lucien CAPONE
15 Interim Dir HR/Affirmative Act ...... Ms. Christy WILLIAMS
09 Director of Institutional Research ...... Dr. Archer R. GRAVELY
20 Asst Provost Academic Admin ...... Ms. Patricia MCCLELLAN
81 Dean Natural Science ...... Dr. Keith KRUMPE
79 Dean Humanities ...... Dr. Gwen ASHBURN
83 Dean Social Science ...... Dr. Jeff KONZ
88 Dean University Programs ...... Dr. Edward J. KATZ
08 University Librarian ...... Ms. Leah DUNN
13 Chief Information Officer ...... Mr. Jeff BROWN
07 Director Admissions ...... Ms. Shannon EARLE
25 Director Contracts & Grants ...... Dr. Gerard VOOS
06 Registrar ...... Ms. Debbie RACE
21 Assoc Vice Chancellor of Finance ...... Ms. Suzanne BRYSON
21 Controller ...... Ms. Karen SHAW
19 Director of Public Safety ...... Mr. Eric BOYCE
96 Senior Buyer ...... Mr. Joel KNISLEY
29 Assoc VC Alumni Relations ...... Mr. Kevan FRAZIER
26 Assoc VC Communication & Mktg ...... Ms. Debbie GRIFFITH
27 Asst Director News Services ...... Mr. Steve PLEVER
23 Dir Student Health/Counseling ...... Mr. John CUTSPEC
39 Director Residential Education ...... Ms. Melanie RHODARMER
39 Director Housing Operations ...... Mr. Vollie BARNWELL
36 Director of Career Center ...... Ms. Marlane MOWITZ
35 Dean of Students ...... Ms. Jackie MCHARGUE
37 Assoc Director Financial Aid ...... Vacant
04 Exec Asst to Chancellor ...... Ms. Lynn SPAIGHT

*University of North Carolina at Chapel Hill (D)

Chapel Hill NC 27599-0001
County: Orange FICE Identification: 002974
Unit ID: 199120
Telephone: (919) 962-2211 Carnegie Class: RU/VH
FAX Number: (919) 962-5604 Calendar System: Semester
URL: www.unc.edu
Established: 1789 Annual Undergrad Tuition & Fees (In-State): $8,340
Enrollment: 29,278 Coed
Affiliation or Control: State IRS Status: 501(c)3
Highest Offering: Doctorate
Program: Occupational; Liberal Arts And General; Teacher Preparatory; Professional
Accreditation: SC, ACAE, AUD, BUS, CACREP, CLPSY, CORE, DA, DENT, DH, DIETC, DMOLS, HSA, IPSY, JOUR, LAW, LIB, MED, MT, NMT, NUR, NURSE, OT, PH, PHAR, PLNG, PTA, RAD, RADDOS, RTT, SCPSY, SP, SPAA, SW, TED

02 Chancellor ...... Dr. Carol L. FOLT
03 Exec Vice Chancellor & Provost ...... Dr. James W. DEAN, JR.
05 Exec Vice Provost/Chief Intl Ofcr ...... Dr. Ronald STRAUSS
43 Vice Chancellor/General Counsel ...... Ms. Leslie CHAMBERS STROHM
11 Vice Chancellor Finance & Admin ...... Ms. Karol KAIN GRAY
32 Vice Chancellor Student Affairs ...... Mr. Winston B. CRISP
30 Interim Vice Chanc Univ Advancememt ...... Ms. Julia SPRUNT GRUMBLES
16 Vice Chancellor Human Resources ...... Ms. Brenda R. MALONE
13 VC Info Technology/Chief Info Ofcr ...... Mr. Chris KIELT
04 Secretary of the University ...... Vacant
46 Vice Chancellor for Research ...... Dr. Barbara ENTWISLE
26 Assoc Vice Chanc Univ Relations ...... Vacant
24 Asst VC Rsch Computing/Learng Tech ...... Dr. Michael BARKER
08 Assoc Prov/University Librarian ...... Ms. Sarah MICHALAK
10 Vice Prov Finance & Acad Planning ...... Dr. Dwayne PINKNEY
20 Vice Provost Academic Initiatives ...... Dr. Carol TRESOLINI
18 Assoc Vice Chanc Facilities Plng ...... Mr. Bruce L. RUNBERG
31 Director Community Relations ...... Ms. Linda DOUGLAS
28 Vice Prov Diversity/Multicultural ...... Dr. Taffye B. CLAYTON
09 Asst Prov Inst Research/Assessment ...... Dr. Lynn E. WILLIFORD
39 Dir Housing & Residential Education ...... Dr. Larry HICKS
41 Director of Athletics ...... Mr. Lawrence (Bubba) R. CUNNINGHAM
06 Asst Prov/University Registrar ...... Mr. Christopher DERICKSON
07 Vice Prov Enrollment & Ugrad Admiss ...... Dr. Stephen M. FARMER
29 Pres/Director General Alumni Assoc ...... Mr. Douglas S. DIBBERT
37 Assoc Prov/Dir Scholar/Student Aid ...... Ms. Shirley A. ORT
36 Director University Career Services ...... Mr. Ray ANGLE
38 Dir Counseling & Psychological Svcs ...... Dr. Allen H. O'BARR
44 Director of Annual Giving ...... Ms. Rebecca BRAMLETT
22 Equal Opportunity/ADA Officer ...... Ms. Ann E. PENN
19 Dir Public Safety/Chief of Police ...... Chief Jeff B. MCCRACKEN
51 Director Center for Cont Education ...... Mr. Rob BRUCE
27 Director Univ Communications ...... Mr. Mike MCFARLAND
96 Director Procurement Services ...... Ms. Martha PENDERGRASS
35 Assoc Vice Chanc Student Affairs ...... Dr. Bettina SHUFORD
87 Dean of the Summer School ...... Ms. Jan YOPP
49 Dean College Arts & Sciences ...... Dr. Karen GIL
61 Dean School of Law ...... Mr. John C. BOGER
17 V Chanc Med Affs/CEO UNC HlthCare ...... Dr. William L. ROPER
66 Dean School of Nursing ...... Dr. Kristen M. SWANSON
52 Dean School of Dentistry ...... Dr. Jane WEINTRAUB
58 Dean of Graduate School ...... Dr. Steven W. MATSON
50 Dean Kenan-Flagler Business School ...... Vacant
70 Dean School of Social Work ...... Dr. Jack M. RICHMAN
67 Dean School of Pharmacy ...... Dr. Robert A. BLOUIN
60 Dean School of Journalism/Mass Comm ...... Ms. Susan KING
62 Dean School of Info/Library Science ...... Dr. Gary MARCHIONINI
69 Dean School of Public Health ...... Dr. Barbara K. RIMER
53 Dean School of Education ...... Dr. Bill MCDIARMID
80 Dean School of Government ...... Dr. Michael R. SMITH
23 Exec Dir Campus Health Services ...... Dr. Mary COVINGTON
92 Associate Dean for Honors ...... Dr. James L. LELOUDIS

*University of North Carolina at Charlotte (E)

9201 University City Boulevard, Charlotte NC 28223-0001
County: Mecklenburg FICE Identification: 002975
Unit ID: 199139
Telephone: (704) 687-2000 Carnegie Class: DRU
FAX Number: (704) 687-2144 Calendar System: Semester
URL: www.uncc.edu
Established: 1946 Annual Undergrad Tuition & Fees (In-State): $6,107
Enrollment: 26,232 Coed
Affiliation or Control: State IRS Status: 501(c)3
Highest Offering: Doctorate
Program: Liberal Arts And General; Teacher Preparatory; Professional
Accreditation: SC, ANEST, BUS, BUSA, CACREP, CLPSY, ENG, ENGT, EXSC, HSA, IPSY, NURSE, PH, SPAA, SW, TED

02 Chancellor ...... Dr. Philip L. DUBOIS
100 Chief of Staff ...... Ms. Krista L. NEWKIRK
05 Vice Chanc Academic Affs/Provost ...... Dr. Joan F. LORDEN
20 Senior Associate Provost ...... Dr. Jay RAJA
88 Assoc Provost/Academic Services ...... Dr. Cynthia WOLF JOHNSON
88 Assoc Provost Metro Studies/Ext Pgm ...... Dr. Owen J. FURUSETH
10 Vice Chancellor Business Affairs ...... Ms. Elizabeth A. HARDIN
30 Vice Chancellor Univ Advancement ...... Mr. Niles F. SORENSEN
86 Spec Asst for Constituent Relations ...... Ms. Betty DOSTER
32 Vice Chancellor Student Affairs ...... Dr. Arthur R. JACKSON
46 Vice Chanc Research/Econ Dev ...... Dr. Robert W. WILHELM
13 Vice Chanc Info Tech Svcs/CIO ...... Dr. Michael CARLIN
18 Assoc Vice Chanc Facilities Mgmt ...... Mr. Philip M. JONES, JR.
08 University Librarian ...... Mr. Stanley J. WILDER
82 Asst Provost for Intl Programs ...... Mr. Joel A. GALLEGOS
27 Exec Dir Univ Communications ...... Mr. Stephen P. WARD
56 Dir Credit Programs/Extended Acad ...... Dr. Dennis MCELHOE
51 Dir Continuing Education ...... Ms. Lesley A. SNYDER
26 Director of Public Relations ...... Mr. John D. BLAND
31 Director Community Affairs ...... Ms. Jeanette SIMS
39 Assoc Vice Chanc/Dir Residence Life ...... Ms. Jacklyn A. SIMPSON
21 Assoc Vice Chancellor for Finance ...... Ms. Susan H. BROOKS
21 Assoc Vice Chanc Business Svcs ...... Ms. Keith N. WASSUM
58 Assoc Provost/Dean Graduate School ...... Dr. Thomas L. REYNOLDS
84 Assoc Provost for Enrollment Mgmt ...... Ms. Tina M. MCENTIRE
43 General Counsel ...... Mr. David E. BROOME, JR.
07 Director Undergraduate Admissions ...... Ms. Claire J. KIRBY
35 Dean of Students/Assoc VC Stdnt Aff ...... Vacant
37 Director of Financial Aid ...... Vacant
38 Assoc VC Health Programs & Services ...... Dr. David B. SPANO
36 Director University Career Center ...... Ms. Denise DWIGHT SMITH
40 Bookstore and Licensing Mgr ...... Mr. Greg MCCAMBRIDGE
29 Exec Director Alumni Affairs ...... Ms. Jenny JONES

88 Assoc VC Risk Mgmt/Safety/Security .... Mr. Henry D. JAMES
19 Chief/Dir Police & Public Safety .... Mr. Jeffrey A. BAKER
09 Asst Provost Institutional Reseach .... Mr. Stephen A. COPPOLA
41 Director of Athletics .... Ms. Judy W. ROSE
96 Director of Purchasing .... Mr. Randy DUNCAN
93 Dir Multicultural Academic Services .... Dr. Sam T. LOPEZ
23 Admin Director Student Health Svcs .... Mr. David ROUSMANIERE
15 Assoc Vice Chanc HumanRes/Aff Act .... Mr. Gary W. STINNETT
85 Int Dir Intl Student/Scholar Svcs .... Ms. Denise V. MEDEIROS
104 Director Study Abroad .... Mr. Brad SEKULICH
48 Dean College of Arts/Architecture .... Mr. Kenneth A. LAMBLA
50 Dean College of Business .... Dr. Steven H. OTT
54 Dean College of Engineering .... Dr. Robert E. JOHNSON
53 Dean College of Education .... Dr. Ellen C. MCINTYRE
49 Dean Col of Liberal Arts & Sciences .... Dr. Nancy A. GUTIERREZ
88 Dean College Health & Human Svcs .... Dr. Nancy FEY-YENSAN
72 Dean College Computing/Informatics .... Dr. Yi DENG
97 Dean University College .... Dr. John SMAIL
92 Exec Director of Honors College .... Dr. Malin PEREIRA
06 University Registrar .... Mr. Christopher B. KNAUER
44 Director of Planning Giving .... Dr. Carl E. JOHNSON

*University of North Carolina at Greensboro (A)

PO Box 26170,1000 Spring Garden St,
Greensboro NC 27402-6170

County: Guilford
FICE Identification: 002976
Unit ID: 199148
Telephone: (336) 334-5000
Carnegie Class: RU/H
FAX Number: (336) 256-0408
Calendar System: Semester
URL: www.uncg.edu
Established: 1891
Annual Undergrad Tuition & Fees (In-State): $6,388
Enrollment: 18,516
Coed
Affiliation or Control: State
IRS Status: 501(c)3
Highest Offering: Doctorate
Program: Liberal Arts And General; Teacher Preparatory; Professional
Accreditation: SC, ANEST, BUS, BUSA, CACREP, CIDA, CLPSY, CS, DANCE, DIETD, DIETI, LIB, MUS, NRPA, NUR, NURSE, PH, SP, SPAA, SW, TED, THEA

02 Chancellor .... Dr. Linda P. BRADY
100 Chief of Staff .... Ms. Bonita J. BROWN
05 Provost and VC for Academic Affairs .... Dr. David H. PERRIN
10 Vice Chancellor Business Affairs .... Mr. Reade TAYLOR
11 Vice Chanc Info Tech Services .... Dr. James H. CLOTFELTER
32 Vice Chanc for Student Affairs .... Dr. Cheryl M. CALLAHAN
30 Sr Assoc Vice Chanc Univ Advncemnt .... Ms. Judy PIPER
43 University Counsel .... Vacant
20 Vice Provost .... Dr. Alan J. BOYETTE
97 Dean of Undergraduate Studies .... Dr. Steve ROBERSON
46 Vice Chanc Research & Econ Devel .... Dr. Terri L. SHELTON
104 Assoc Provost Intl Programs .... Dr. Penelope J. PYNES
15 Assoc VC Human Resource Services .... Dr. Edna CHUN
21 Associate VC Financial Services .... Mr. Steven W. RHEW
18 Associate Vice Chanc for Facilities .... Mr. Jorge QUINTAL
88 Associate VC for Campus Enterprises .... Mr. Michael T. BYERS
09 Director of Institutional Research .... Dr. Sarah D. CARRIGAN
26 Associate VC University Relations .... Ms. Helen D. HEBERT
91 Associate VC for Administrative Sys .... Mr. Joel DUNN
35 Assistant VC for Student Affairs .... Dr. Vickie J. MCNEIL
88 Assoc VC for Enterprise Admin Appl .... Ms. Laura R. YOUNG
44 Asst VC for Central Develop Pgms .... Ms. Lynn BRESKO
88 Asst VC for Foundation Finance .... Ms. Jill HILLYER
58 Dean of Graduate School .... Dr. William R. WIENER
49 Dean of Arts & Sciences .... Dr. Timothy D. JOHNSTON
50 Dean of Business & Economics .... Dr. McRae BANKS
53 Dean of Education .... Dr. Karen WIXSON
68 Dean of Health & Human Sciences .... Dr. Celia R. HOOPER
64 Dean of Music/Theatre & Dance .... Dr. Peter ALEXANDER
66 Dean of Nursing .... Dr. Robin E. REMSBURG
08 Dean of University Libraries .... Ms. Rosann V. BAZIJIAN
06 University Registrar .... Dr. Kelly A. ROWETT-JAMES
108 Dir Assessment and Accreditation .... Dr. Jodi E. PETTAZZONI
07 Director of Admissions .... Ms. Lise K. KELLER
29 Director of Alumni Relations .... Vacant
88 Director of Campus Recreation .... Ms. Jill BEVILLE
23 Director Student Health Services .... Dr. Tresa M. SAXTON
36 Director Career Services Center .... Mr. Patrick O. MADSEN
51 Int Dean Division of Continual Lrng .... Dr. James M. EDDY
25 Dir Contracts and Grants .... Mr. William D. WALTERS
38 Director Counseling/Testing Center .... Dr. Bruce G. LYNCH
37 Director of Financial Aid .... Ms. Deborah TOLLEFSON
39 Director Housing & Residence Life .... Mr. Timothy JOHNSON
41 Director Intercollegiate Athletics .... Ms. Kim RECORD
88 Director of Orientation .... Dr. Kim SOUSA-PEOPLES
19 Assoc VC for Safety and Emergency .... Mr. Rollin DONELSON
28 Director Multicultural Affairs .... Ms. Audrey O. LUCAS
96 Dir Purchasing and Warehouse Svcs .... Mr. Trace LITTLE
40 University Bookstore Manager .... Mr. Brad LIGHT

*University of North Carolina at Pembroke (B)

One University Drive, PO Box 1510,
Pembroke NC 28372-1510

County: Robeson
FICE Identification: 002954
Unit ID: 199281
Telephone: (910) 521-6000
Carnegie Class: Master's M
FAX Number: (910) 521-6176
Calendar System: Semester
URL: www.uncp.edu
Established: 1887
Annual Undergrad Tuition & Fees (In-State): $5,144
Enrollment: 6,269
Coed
Affiliation or Control: State
IRS Status: 501(c)3
Highest Offering: Master's
Program: Liberal Arts And General; Teacher Preparatory
Accreditation: SC, ART, BUS, CACREP, MUS, NURSE, SW, TED

02 Chancellor .... Dr. Kyle R. CARTER
05 Provost/Vice Chanc Academic Affairs .... Dr. Kenneth D. KITTS
10 Vice Chanc Finance & Administration .... Dr. Richard E. COSENTINO
32 Vice Chanc Student Affairs .... Dr. John R. JONES
30 Vice Chancellor for Advancement .... Ms. Wendy LOWERY
84 Interim Exec Dir Enroll Plan .... Ms. Lela C. CLARK
26 Special Asst for Constituent Rels .... Dr. Glen G. BURNETTE, JR.
41 Chief of Staff .... Mr. Daniel KENNEY
20 Assoc Vice Chanc Planning and Acred .... Dr. Elizabeth NORMANDY
35 Assoc Vice Chanc Student Affairs .... Dr. Lisa SCHAEFFER
13 Int Assoc VC Info Res/Chf Info Ofcr .... Mr. Henry JACKSON
85 Director of International Pgms .... Vacant
43 General Counsel .... Mr. Joshua MALCOLM
39 Dir Housing and Resident Life .... Mr. R. Preston SWINEY
49 Dean of Arts & Sciences .... Dr. Mark CANADA
08 Interim Dean of Library Services .... Ms. Susan WHITT
58 Dean of Grad Studies & Research .... Dr. Rebecca BULLARD-DILLARD
92 Dean of Honors College .... Dr. Mark MILEWICZ
53 Dean of School of Education .... Dr. Zoe LOCKLEAR
50 Dean of School of Business .... Dr. Ramin MAYSAMI
29 Director Alumni Relations .... Ms. Renee STEELE
09 Asst VC Institutional Effectiveness .... Dr. Beverly KING
36 Director Career Services Center .... Dr. Karen PRUETT
38 Director Counseling/Testing Center .... Dr. Mary-Jeanne RALEIGH
06 Registrar .... Ms. Sharon KISSICK
37 Director Financial Aid .... Ms. Jenelle HANDCOX
96 Director of Business Services .... Ms. Denise CARROLL
15 Director of Human Resources .... Ms. Debbie BURGESS
44 Assistant Director of Annual Fund .... Ms. Morgan WARRIAX
25 Dir Ofc of Sponsored Rsrch & Pgms .... Vacant
88 Director Public Administration Pgm .... Dr. Michael PENNINGTON
27 Public Communications Specialist .... Mr. Scott BIGELOW
21 Asst Vice Chancellor for Finance .... Mr. Ray OXENDINE
40 Director of Bookstore .... Ms. Karen SWINEY
88 Sports Information Director .... Mr. Todd ANDERSON
07 Director of Admissions .... Ms. Natalya FREEMAN
18 Director of Physical Plant .... Mr. Larry FREEMAN
28 Dir Multicultural/Minority Affairs .... Mr. Robert L. CANIDA, II
88 Dir Fac Plng/Construction/Univ Engr .... Mr. Michael CLARK
88 Dir Ctr for Academic Excellence .... Mr. Steven HUNT
88 Administrative Associate-Chancellor .... Ms. Marla K. LOCKLEAR
88 Internal Auditor .... Ms. Kelley R. HORTON
41 Director of Athletics .... Mr. Dick CHRISTY
88 Faculty Senate Chair .... Dr. Judy CURTIS
23 Director of Student Health Services .... Ms. Cora BULLARD
04 Executive Asst to the Chancellor .... Ms. Lisa CANADA
04 Executive Asst to the Chancellor .... Ms. Kindra LOCKLEAR
88 Director of Disability Support Svcs .... Ms. Mary WALKER

*University of North Carolina Wilmington (C)

601 S College Road, Wilmington NC 28403-3297

County: New Hanover
FICE Identification: 002984
Unit ID: 199218
Telephone: (910) 962-3000
Carnegie Class: Master's L
FAX Number: (910) 962-4050
Calendar System: Semester
URL: www.uncw.edu
Established: 1947
Annual Undergrad Tuition & Fees (In-State): $6,343
Enrollment: 13,733
Coed
Affiliation or Control: State
IRS Status: 501(c)3
Highest Offering: Doctorate
Program: Liberal Arts And General; Teacher Preparatory; Professional
Accreditation: SC, BUS, CS, MUS, NRPA, NURSE, SPAA, SW, TED

02 Chancellor .... Dr. Gary L. MILLER
05 Provost/Vice Chanc Acad Affs .... Dr. Denise BATTLES
10 Vice Chancellor Business Affairs .... Dr. Charles MAIMONE
32 Vice Chanc for Student Affairs .... Ms. Patricia L. LEONARD
30 Vice Chanc University Advancement .... Mrs. Mary M. GORNTO
21 Sr Assoc Vice Chanc Finance .... Mr. Rick N. WHITFIELD
20 Assoc Vice Chanc Academic Affairs .... Dr. Johnson O. AKINLEYE
44 Assoc Vice Chanc Univ Advancement .... Ms. Marla D. RICE-EVANS
20 Vice Provost .... Dr. Stephen L. MCFARLAND
21 Assoc Vice Chanc Business Services .... Ms. Sharon H. BOYD
21 Int Assoc VC Bus Affs Facilities .... Vacant
28 Assoc Provost/Diversity & Inclusion .... Dr. Jose E. HERNANDEZ
26 Exec Dir of University Relations .... Ms. Janine IAMUNNO
09 Asst VC Institutional Rsrch/Assess .... Ms. Lisa CASTELLINO
35 Dean of Students .... Dr. Michael A. WALKER
84 Assoc Provost for Enrollment Mgmt .... Dr. Terrence M. CURRAN
85 Asst Provost International Programs .... Dr. Denise DIPUCCIO
15 Int VC for Human Resources .... Ms. Joann MCDOWELL
100 Chief of Staff .... Mr. Max ALLEN
22 Int Assoc VC for HR .... Ms. Joann MCDOWELL
06 Registrar .... Mr. Jonathan REECE
08 University Librarian .... Ms. Sarah WATSTEIN
37 Director Fin Aid/Veterans Svcs .... Dr. Ixchel BAKER-TATE
18 Director of Physical Plant .... Mr. Thomas A. FRESHWATER
19 Director Envir Health & Safety .... Mr. Stanley H. HARTS
23 Dir Student Health/Wellness Center .... Ms. Katrin WESNER
31 Director of Auxiliary Services .... Mr. Brian DAILEY
41 Director of Athletics .... Mr. Jimmy BASS
36 Director Career Services .... Mr. Thomas D. RAKES
29 Director of Alumni Relations .... Mr. Rob MCINTURF
96 Director of Purchasing .... Ms. Mary E. FORSYTHE
38 Director Student Counseling Center .... Dr. Lynne REEDER
40 Manager Bookstore .... Ms. Stephanie GARAY
49 Interim Dean Col Arts & Sciences .... Dr. Stephen MCNAMEE
50 Dean Cameron School of Business .... Dr. Lawrence S. CLARK
53 Dean Watson School of Education .... Dr. Kenneth TEITELBAUM
66 Director School of Nursing .... Dr. James D. MCCANN
58 Interim Dean of Graduate School .... Dr. Ron VETTER
76 Dean Col Health & Human Svcs .... Dr. Charles HARDY

*University of North Carolina School of the Arts (D)

1533 S Main Street, Winston-Salem NC 27127-2738

County: Forsyth
FICE Identification: 003981
Unit ID: 199184
Telephone: (336) 770-3399
Carnegie Class: Spec/Arts
FAX Number: (336) 770-3375
Calendar System: Semester
URL: www.uncsa.edu
Established: 1963
Annual Undergrad Tuition & Fees (In-State): $8,271
Enrollment: 880
Coed
Affiliation or Control: State
IRS Status: 501(c)3
Highest Offering: Master's
Program: Fine Arts Emphasis
Accreditation: SC

02 Interim Chancellor .... Dr. James MOESER
05 Provost .... Dr. David P. NELSON
10 Senior Director of Business Affairs .... Ms. Carin IOANNOU
11 Chief Operating Officer .... Mr. George BURNETTE
31 Director Econ Devel/External Affs .... Mr. James DECRISTO
18 Assoc VC Facilities/Services .... Mr. Chrispher BOYD
09 Director of Institutional Research .... Dr. Xiaoyun YANG
07 Director of Admissions .... Ms. Sheeler LAWSON
08 Librarian .... Ms. Vicki WEAVIL
26 Director Communications/Marketing .... Ms. Marla CARPENTER
06 Registrar .... Ms. Erin MORIN
15 Director Human Resources .... Mr. James LUCAS
37 Director Financial Aid .... Mrs. Jane KAMIAB
49 Dean of Liberal Arts .... Mr. Dean WILCOX
64 Dean School of Music .... Dr. Wade WEAST
57 Dean School of Dance .... Ms. Susan JAFFE
88 Dean School of Design/Production .... Mr. Joseph TILFORD
88 Dean School of Drama .... Mr. Carl FORSMAN
13 Chief Information Officer .... Ms. Lisa HARDEN SMITH
19 Chief of Police .... Ms. Deb CHEESEBRO
38 Dir of Counseling & Testing Svcs .... Dr. Thomas MURRAY
58 Assoc Provost & Dean Grad Studies .... Dr. David ENGLISH
30 Chief Advancement Officer .... Mr. Mark HOUGH
29 Director of Alumni Affairs .... Mr. Jonas SILVER
32 Dean of Students .... Mr. Ward CALDWELL
96 Interim Director of Purchasing .... Mr. Allen CARNES
44 Dir of Individual & Planned Giving .... Ms. Paula PRESSLEY
88 Dir Center for Design Innovation .... Dr. Carol STROHECKER
88 Int Ex Dir Kenan Inst for the Arts .... Ms. Lynda LOTICH

*Western Carolina University (E)

65 West University Way, HFR 501,
Cullowhee NC 28723-9646

County: Jackson
FICE Identification: 002981
Unit ID: 200004
Telephone: (828) 227-7211
Carnegie Class: Master's L
FAX Number: (828) 227-7202
Calendar System: Semester
URL: www.wcu.edu
Established: 1889
Annual Undergrad Tuition & Fees (In-State): $7,384
Enrollment: 9,608
Coed
Affiliation or Control: State
IRS Status: 501(c)3
Highest Offering: Doctorate
Program: Liberal Arts And General; Teacher Preparatory; Professional
Accreditation: SC, ANEST, ART, BUS, CACREP, CAHIIM, CIDA, CONST, DIETD, DIETI, EMT, ENG, ENGT, MUS, NURSE, PTA, SP, SW, TED, THEA

02 Chancellor .... Dr. David O. BELCHER
05 Interim Provost .... Dr. Beth LOFQUIST
10 Vice Chanc/Admin & Finance .... Mr. Robert EDWARDS
32 Vice Chancellor/Student Affairs .... Dr. H. Samuel MILLER
35 Asst Vice Chanc Student Affairs .... Mrs. Jane ADAMS-DUNFORD
35 Asst Vice Chanc/Student Affairs .... Ms. Kellie MONTEITH
30 Assoc Vice Chancellor Development .... Mr. Jim MILLER
20 Interim Associate Provost .... Dr. Mark LORD
18 Assoc VC for Facilities Management .... Mr. Joe WALKER
100 Chief of Staff .... Dr. Melissa WARGO
04 Executive Asst to the Chancellor .... Ms. Terry WELCH
44 Sr Director Development .... Mr. Brett WOODS
43 Legal Counsel .... Ms. Mary Ann LOCHNER
88 Director Student Support Services .... Mr. David GOSS
38 Director of Counseling Services .... Dr. Kimberly GORMAN
06 Registrar .... Mr. Larry HAMMER
07 Director of Student Recruitment .... Mr. Phil CAULEY
09 Interim Asst Vice Chancellor OIPE .... Ms. Kay TURPIN
37 Director of Financial Aid .... Ms. Trina ORR
15 Director of Human Resources .... Ms. Kathy WONG
27 Chief Information Officer .... Mr. Craig FOWLER
29 Director of Alumni Affairs .... Mr. Marty RAMSEY
08 Dean of Library Services .... Dr. Dana SALLY
19 Director University Police .... Mr. Earnest HUDSON
88 Dean Educational Outreach .... Vacant
31 Director Auxiliary Services .... Mr. Jeff BEWSEY
41 Athletic Director .... Mr. Randy EATON
23 Director University Health Services .... Ms. Pamela BUCHANAN
28 Director of Intercultural Affairs .... Mr. James FELTON
96 Director of Purchasing .... Mr. Arthur STEPHENS
40 Director Book & Supply Store .... Ms. Pamela DEGRAFFENREID

88 Director of Orientation .... Ms. Tammy HASKETT
38 Director of Undergraduate Advising .... Mr. David GOSS
36 Director of Career Services .... Ms. Mardy ASHE
26 Sr Director Comm & Public Relations .... Mr. Bill STUDENC
57 Dean of Fine & Performing Arts .... Dr. Robert KEHRBERG
58 Dean Grad School & Research .... Dr. Mimi FENTON
49 Dean Arts & Sciences .... Dr. Richard STARNES
72 Dean Kimmel School Constr Mgmt/Tech .... Dr. James ZHANG
50 Dean College of Business .... Dr. Darrell PARKER
53 Int Dean Educ & Allied Professions .... Dr. Dale CARPENTER
76 Associate Dean Health/Human Science .... Dr. Marie HUFF
76 Dean Health & Human Sciences .... Dr. Douglas R. KESKULA
92 Dean of Honors College .... Dr. Brian RAILSBACK
88 Director of Marketing .... Vacant

*Winston-Salem State University (A)

601 MLK Jr. Drive, 200 Blair Hall,
Winston-Salem NC 27110-0001
County: Forsyth FICE Identification: 002986
Unit ID: 199999
Telephone: (336) 750-2000 Carnegie Class: Master's M
FAX Number: (336) 750-2049 Calendar System: Semester
URL: www.wssu.edu
Established: 1892 Annual Undergrad Tuition & Fees (In-State): $4,941
Enrollment: 6,000 Coed
Affiliation or Control: State IRS Status: 501(c)3
Highest Offering: Doctorate
Program: Liberal Arts And General; Teacher Preparatory; Professional
Accreditation: SC, BUS, CORE, CS, MT, MUS, NRPA, NURSE, OT, PTA, SW, TED

02 Chancellor .... Dr. Donald J. REAVES
05 Provost/VC Academic Affairs .... Dr. Brenda ALLEN
32 Vice Chancellor Student Affairs .... Dr. Trae COTTON
09 Asst Prov Plng/Assessment/Research .... Dr. Jamie B. SLATER
45 Int Asst Prov Administration/Plng .... Ms. Letitia CORNISH
10 Vice Chanc Finance & Administration .... Mr. Gerald E. HUNTER
21 Assoc VC Financial Plng & Budget .... Dr. Randy W. MILLS
30 Vice Chanc University Advance .... Mrs. Michelle COOK
18 Assoc Vice Chanc Facilities Mgmt .... Mr. Owen J. COOKS
27 Assoc Provost Info Resources/CIO .... Dr. Justin D. MCKENZIE
51 Assoc Dir Cont Educ/Summer Sessions ... Mr. W. Kenneth BULLS
88 Director Internal Audit/Compliance .... Ms. Shannon B. HENRY
53 Dean Sch Educ/Human Performance .... Dr. Manuel VARGAS
19 Chief of Campus Police .... Mrs. Patricia D. NORRIS
08 Librarian .... Dr. Mae L. RODNEY
39 Director Hous/Residence Life .... Mrs. Abeer MUSTAFA
37 Director of Financial Aid .... Mr. Robert MUHAMMED
15 Asst Vice Chanc Human Resources .... Mr. Ivan V. FOSTER
36 Asst Director of Career Services .... Mrs. LaMonica SLOAN
27 Director Public & Media Relations .... Ms. Nancy N. YOUNG
26 Director Marketing/Publications .... Ms. Sigrid HALL
88 Dir Enrollment Communications .... Ms. Cathy HOOTS
29 Director of Alumni Affairs .... Mr. Gregory G. HAIRSTON
44 Director Institutional Annual Fund .... Mrs. Kimberly REESE
35 Assoc Director Student Activities .... Ms. Heather DAVIS
23 Int Dir of Student Health Center .... Dr. Philadelphia ANTHONY
41 Athletic Director .... Mr. William HAYES
101 Asst to the Chancellor/Sec of Univ .... Mrs. RaVonda DALTON-RANN
07 Int Asst VC Enrollment Services .... Ms. Joycelyn FOY
43 General Legal Counsel .... Mrs. Camille KLUTTZ-LEACH
96 Director Purchasing .... Mr. Alan IRELAND
90 Director Academic Computer Center .... Mr. Cuthrell JOHNSON
50 Dean School Business/Economics .... Dr. Jessica M. BAILEY
88 Assoc Provost Life Long Learning .... Dr. Doria K. STITTS
49 Dean College Arts & Sciences .... Vacant
76 Dean School of Health Sciences .... Dr. Peggy VALENTINE
89 Dean of University College .... Dr. Michele RELEFORD
92 Int Director of Honors College .... Dr. Soncerey L. MONTGOMERY
88 Director of Title III .... Dr. Everette L. WITHERSPOON
88 Asst Provost Faculty Affairs .... Dr. Denise PEARSON

University of Phoenix Charlotte Campus (B)

3800 Arco Corporate Drive, Charlotte NC 28273-3409
Telephone: (704) 504-5409 Identification: 770216
Accreditation: &NH, ACBSP

† Main campus is University of Phoenix in Tempe, AZ.

Virginia College (C)

3740 South Holden Road, Greensboro NC 27406
Telephone: (336) 398-5400 Identification: 770619
Accreditation: ACICS

† Main campus is Virginia College in Birmingham, AL.

Wake Forest University (D)

1834 Wake Forest Road, Winston-Salem NC 27109-8758
County: Forsyth FICE Identification: 002978
Unit ID: 199847
Telephone: (336) 758-5000 Carnegie Class: RU/H
FAX Number: (336) 758-6074 Calendar System: Semester
URL: www.wfu.edu
Established: 1834 Annual Undergrad Tuition & Fees: $44,200
Enrollment: 7,351 Coed
Affiliation or Control: Independent Non-Profit IRS Status: 501(c)3
Highest Offering: Doctorate
Program: Liberal Arts And General; Teacher Preparatory; Professional
Accreditation: SC, ANEST, ARCPA, BUS, BUSA, CACREP, DENT, LAW, MED, MT, TED, THEOL

01 President .... Dr. Nathan O. HATCH
43 VP Gen Counsel/Sec Board of Trust .... Mr. J. Reid MORGAN
03 Sr Vice Pres/Chief Financial Ofcr .... Mr. B. Hofler MILAM
05 Provost .... Mr. Rogan KERSH
10 Exec VP Finance/Admin/Chf Oper Ofcr .... Vacant
17 Sr Vice Pres Health Affairs .... Vacant
11 Vice President for Administration .... Vacant
30 Vice Pres University Advancement .... Mr. Mark A. PETERSEN
32 Vice Pres Campus Life .... Ms. Penny RUE
88 Vice Pres/Chief Investment Officer .... Mr. James J. DUNN
20 Assoc Provost Academic Initiatives .... Ms. Jennifer COLLINS
04 Senior Advisor to the President .... Ms. Sandra C. BOYETTE
35 Assoc VP/Dean of Student Services .... Mr. Harold R. HOLMES
44 Ast VP/Dir Parent/Donor Relations .... Ms. Minta A. MCNALLY
30 Asst VP/Director of Development .... Mr. Robert T. BAKER
13 CIO/Assoc Provost for Tech/IS .... Dr. George E. MATTHEWS, JR.
46 Assoc Provost for Research .... Dr. S. Bruce KING
49 Dean of the College .... Dr. Jacquelyn FETROW
63 Dean School Med/Int Health Sci Pres .... Dr. Edward ABRAHAM
58 Dean Graduate School Arts/Sciences .... Dr. Lorna G. MOORE
61 Dean School of Law .... Mr. Blake MORANT
50 Dean of Business .... Mr. Steven REINEMUND
73 Dean of Divinity .... Dr. Gail R. O'DAY
89 Assoc Dean & Dean of Freshmen .... Dr. Paul N. ORSER
09 Dir Inst Research/Academic Admin .... Mr. Ross A. GRIFFITH
08 Dir of the Z Smith Reynolds Library .... Dr. Lynn SUTTON
85 Director of International Studies .... Steven DUKE
07 Director of Admissions .... Ms. Martha B. ALLMAN
37 Director of Financial Aid .... Mr. William T. WELLS
36 VP/Office of Personal & Career Dev .... Mr. Andy CHAN
06 Registrar .... Mr. Harold PACE
41 Director of Athletics .... Mr. Ronald D. WELLMAN
15 Chief Human Resources Officer .... Ms. Carmen I. CANALES
18 Director Facilities Management .... Vacant
38 Dir University Counseling Center ...... Dr. Marianne A. SCHUBERT
84 Director Enrollment Management .... Vacant
23 Director Student Health Service .... Dr. Cecil D. PRICE
39 Exec Dir of Residential Services .... Vacant
40 Exec Director Business Services .... Mr. Donald J. MOSER
42 Chaplain .... Rev. Timothy L. AUMAN
19 Chief University Police .... Ms. Regina G. LAWSON
22 EEO Mgr/Diversity & Compliance Dir .... Ms. Angela CULLER
96 Director Purchasing .... Vacant
94 Director Women's & Gender Studies .... Dr. Wanda BALZANO

Warren Wilson College (E)

PO Box 9000, Asheville NC 28815-9000
County: Buncombe FICE Identification: 002979
Unit ID: 199865
Telephone: (828) 298-3325 Carnegie Class: Bac/A&S
FAX Number: (828) 771-7097 Calendar System: Semester
URL: www.warren-wilson.edu
Established: 1894 Annual Undergrad Tuition & Fees: $27,740
Enrollment: 924 Coed
Affiliation or Control: Presbyterian Church (U.S.A.) IRS Status: 501(c)3
Highest Offering: Master's
Program: Liberal Arts And General; Teacher Preparatory
Accreditation: SC, SW

01 President .... Dr. Steven L. SOLNICK
05 VP Academic Affairs/Dean of College .... Dr. Paula K. GARRETT
11 VP for Administration/Finance .... Mr. Jonathan D. EHRLICH
30 Vice Pres for Advancement .... Mr. Richard BLOMGREN
84 VP Enrollment Mgmt/Marketing .... Ms. Dawn MEDLEY
32 Dean of Student Life .... Mr. Paul PERRINE
88 Dean of Work .... Mr. Ian ROBERTSON
88 Dean of Service .... Ms. Cathy KRAMER
20 Assoc Dean for Faculty .... Ms. Carol HOWARD
06 Registrar .... Miss Christa L. BRIDGMAN
09 Director Institutional Research .... Ms. Allyson HETTRICK
08 Director Library .... Dr. Christine R. NUGENT
37 Director Financial Aid .... Ms. Kathy P. PACK
21 Controller .... Ms. Mary DAVIS
29 Director Alumni Relations .... Mr. Rodney LYTLE
26 Director of Media Relations .... Mr. Benjamin J. ANDERSON
88 Director Community Relations .... Ms. Ally WILSON
20 Director Academic Support Service .... Ms. Lyn O'HARE
88 Director of Service Leaning .... Ms. Brooke MILLSAPS
35 Director of Student Activities .... Mr. Daniel SEEGER
38 Director of Counseling .... Mr. Arthur SHUSTER
36 Director Career Services .... Ms. Wendy SELIGMANN
42 Dir of Spiritual Life & Chaplain .... Rev. Brian AMMONS
41 Director of Athletics .... Ms. Stacey ENOS
91 Dir Admin Data Processing .... Ms. Omega HODGES
40 Campus Store Manager .... Ms. Keller Anne KNIGHT
15 Director Human Resources .... Ms. Gail BAYLOR
18 Acting Dir Facil Mgmt/Tech Svcs .... Ms. Deborah ANSTROM
19 Director Public Safety .... Mr. Terry PAYNE
88 Int Dir Environment Leadership Ctr .... Mr. Stan CROSS
88 Director Swannanoa Gathering .... Mr. Jim MAGILL
104 Director of International Programs .... Ms. Naomi OTTERNESS
42 Minister of WW Pres Church .... Mr. Steve RUNHOLT
96 Director of Purchasing .... Ms. Deborah ANSTROM
13 Manager Computing Services .... Mr. David HARPER
85 Dir Diversity/Intercultural Init .... Ms. Lorrie JAYNE
88 Conference Coordinator .... Ms. Liz BRACE

William Peace University (formerly Peace College) (F)

15 E Peace Street, Raleigh NC 27604-1194
County: Wake FICE Identification: 002953
Unit ID: 199272
Telephone: (919) 508-2000 Carnegie Class: Bac/A&S
FAX Number: (919) 508-2326 Calendar System: Semester
URL: www.peace.edu
Established: 1857 Annual Undergrad Tuition & Fees: $23,700
Enrollment: 791 Coed
Affiliation or Control: Presbyterian Church (U.S.A.) IRS Status: 501(c)3
Highest Offering: Baccalaureate
Program: Liberal Arts And General
Accreditation: SC

01 President .... Dr. Debra M. TOWNSLEY
04 Executive Secretary to President ... Ms. Patricia L. LUKASZEWSKI
05 Vice President for Academic Affairs .... Vacant
32 Vice President for Student Services .... Mr. Frank RIZZO
30 Vice President for Engagement .... Ms. Julie E. RICCIARDI
09 Director of Institutional Research .... Ms. Vanessa TINSLEY
10 Vice Pres Finance & Administration ... Mr. George A. YEARWOOD
84 Vice Pres Enrollment Mgmt/Admission . Ms. Amber L. STENBECK
15 Asst Vice Pres for Human Resources ...... Ms. Amber M. KIMBALL
107 Dean Wm Peace School of Prof Stds .... Ms. Laurie ALBERT
20 Dean of Academic Services .... Mr. Jerry J. NUESELL
18 Asst VP for Buildings and Grounds .... Mr. John B. CRANHAM
37 Director of Financial Aid .... Vacant
41 Director of Athletics .... Mr. P. Kelly JOHNSON, JR.
26 VP for Communications and Marketing .... Mr. Justin G. ROY

Wingate University (G)

220 N. Camden Street, Wingate NC 28174-0157
County: Union FICE Identification: 002985
Unit ID: 199962
Telephone: (704) 233-8000 Carnegie Class: Master's S
FAX Number: (704) 233-8192 Calendar System: Semester
URL: www.wingate.edu
Established: 1896 Annual Undergrad Tuition & Fees: $25,040
Enrollment: 2,648 Coed
Affiliation or Control: Southern Baptist IRS Status: 501(c)3
Highest Offering: Doctorate
Program: Liberal Arts And General; Teacher Preparatory; Professional; Business Emphasis
Accreditation: SC, ACBSP, ARCPA, MUS, PHAR, TED

01 President .... Dr. Jerry E. MCGEE
05 Senior VP Academic Affairs .... Dr. Martha S. ASTI
10 VP Business/Chief Financial Ofcr .... Mr. William H. DURHAM
30 Vice President Resource Development .... Mr. E. Vincent TILSON
41 Vice Pres & Director of Athletics .... Mr. R. Stephen POSTON
32 VP for Student Life/Enrollment Mgmt .... Mr. T. Rhett BROWN
58 VP for Grad & Prof Programs .... Dr. Robert B. SUPERNAW
11 VP for Operations .... Mr. Scott E. HUNSUCKER
23 Asst VP for Health Sciences Div .... Mr. Roy Lee RAGSDALE, JR.
58 Asst VP Grad & Cont Educ .... Mr. Greg CLEMMER
32 Dean of Student Affairs .... Mrs. Glenda H. BEBBER
49 Dean School Arts & Sciences .... Dr. H. Donald MERRILL
50 Dean School of Business .... Mr. Joe M. GRAHAM
53 Dean School of Education .... Dr. Sarah H. BURNS
08 Director of Library .... Mrs. Amee M. ODOM
35 Director of Involvement .... Ms. Brandy SHOTT
30 Director of Development .... Dr. Wayne D. WIKE
09 Director Inst Research/Registrar .... Mrs. Nicci C. BROWN
37 Director Student Financial Planning .... Ms. Teresa G. WILLIAMS
26 Dir of Marketing/Communications .... Mr. Jeffrey ATKINSON
91 Director Administrative Computing .... Mr. Timothy D. HERRIN
29 Director of Alumni Development .... Mrs. Suzanne B. PHILEMON
42 Minstr to Stdnts/Asst Dn Stdnt Affs .... Rev. A. Dane JORDAN
40 Director of Campus Store .... Mrs. Sherri SHANK
19 Campus Safety Chief .... Mr. Mike EASLEY
44 Director of Annual Fund .... Dr. Wayne D. WIKE
44 Dir of Major Gifts & Planned Giving ... Mr. J. Theodore JOHNSON
27 Asst Dir Marketing & Communications .... Vacant
38 Director of Counseling Services .... Ms. Jessica HYLTON
13 Director of Information Technology .... Ms. Jeanette K. BUJAK
36 Dir of Internships and Career Svcs .... Ms. Sharon ROBINSON
15 Human Resources Coordinator .... Mrs. Lisa B. RAGSDALE
39 Dir Resid Life/Asst Dn Stdnt Affs .... Mr. Patrick BIGGERSTAFF
35 Dir of Retention/Asst Dn Stdnt Affs .... Ms. Kristin WHARTON
06 Registrar .... Mrs. Nicci C. BROWN
07 Director of Admissions .... Mr. Gabe HOLLINGSWORTH

NORTH DAKOTA

Cankdeska Cikana Community College (H)

PO Box 269, 214 First Avenue,
Fort Totten ND 58335-0269
County: Benson FICE Identification: 022365
Unit ID: 200208
Telephone: (701) 766-4415 Carnegie Class: Tribal
FAX Number: (701) 766-4077 Calendar System: Semester
URL: www.littlehoop.edu
Established: 1974 Annual Undergrad Tuition & Fees: $638,150
Enrollment: 223 Coed
Affiliation or Control: Independent Non-Profit IRS Status: 501(c)3
Highest Offering: Associate Degree

Program: Occupational; 2-Year Principally Bachelor's Creditable
Accreditation: NH

01 President ....Dr. Cynthia A. LINDQUIST
05 Vice President Academics ....Dr. Leander MCDONALD
10 Vice President for Finance ....Ms. Chelly MERKEL-VEER
32 Vice Pres Student Services ....Ms. Erica CAVANAUGH
06 Registrar ....Mr. Ermen BROWN, JR.

Ft. Berthold Community College (A)

PO Box 490, New Town ND 58763-0490
County: Mountrail FICE Identification: 025537
Unit ID: 200086
Telephone: (701) 627-4738 Carnegie Class: Tribal
FAX Number: (701) 627-3609 Calendar System: Semester
URL: www.fortbertholdcc.edu
Established: 1973 Annual Undergrad Tuition & Fees: $4,210
Enrollment: 211 Coed
Affiliation or Control: Independent Non-Profit IRS Status: 501(c)3
Highest Offering: Baccalaureate
Program: Occupational; 2-Year Principally Bachelor's Creditable
Accreditation: NH

01 President ....Mr. Russell D. MASON, JR.
05 Academic Dean ....Dr. Stacey MORTENSON
32 Dean of Students ....Ms. Twila BAKER
10 Chief Finance Manager ....Mr. Kim CONNOLE
37 Financial Aid Administration ....Ms. Kathleen FREDERICKS
06 Registrar ....Mr. Garrett TITUS
08 Librarian ....Mrs. Quincee BAKER
38 Counselor ....Vacant
40 Bookstore Manager ....Ms. Iona LITTLE WHITEMAN

*North Dakota University System Office (B)

600 E Boulevard Avenue, Dept 215,
Bismarck ND 58505-0230
County: Burleigh FICE Identification: 033434
Telephone: (701) 328-2960 Carnegie Class: N/A
FAX Number: (701) 328-2961
URL: www.ndus.edu

01 Acting Chancellor ....Larry C. SKOGEN
05 Vice Chanc Academic Affairs ....William LESCH
10 Vice Chanc Administrative Affairs ....Laura GLATT
45 Vice Chancellor Strategic Planning ....Vacant
13 Chief Information Officer ....Lisa FELDNER
24 Director Interactive Video Network ....Jerry ROSTAD
37 Director Financial Aid ....Brenda ZASTOUPIL
16 Human Resources ....Kirsten FRANZEN
20 Associate Vice Chan for Acad Affair ....John GIRARD
88 Dir State Approving Agency ....Rhonda SCHAUER
21 Director of Finance ....Cathy MCDONALD
88 Research Analyst ....Michelle OLSEN
43 General Counsel ....Claire HOLLOWAY
26 Dir of Communications & Media Rels ....Linda DONLIN
88 Director Financial Reporting ....Robin PUTNAM
106 Exec Dir Acad Tech/Dist Ed & K-12 ....Tanya SPILOVOY
88 Articulation & Transfer ....Lisa JOHNSON
88 Compliance Officer ....Kirsten FRANZEN

*University of North Dakota Main Campus (C)

264 Centennial Drive, Grand Forks ND 58202
County: Grand Forks FICE Identification: 003005
Unit ID: 200280
Telephone: (701) 777-2011 Carnegie Class: RU/H
FAX Number: (701) 777-2696 Calendar System: Semester
URL: www.und.edu
Established: 1883 Annual Undergrad Tuition & Fees (In-State): $7,508
Enrollment: 15,250 Coed
Affiliation or Control: State IRS Status: 501(c)3
Highest Offering: Doctorate
Program: Liberal Arts And General; Teacher Preparatory; Professional
Accreditation: NH, AAB, ANEST, ARCPA, ART, BUS, CLPSY, COPSY, CS, CYTO, DIETC, ENG, HT, IPSY, LAW, MED, MT, MUS, NAIT, NURSE, OT, PTA, SP, SPAA, SW, TED, THEA

02 President ....Dr. Robert O. KELLEY
29 Exec Vice Pres & CEO Alumni Assoc ....Mr. Tim O'KEEFE
05 Vice Pres Academic Affairs/Provost ....Dr. Thomas DILORENZO
10 Vice President Operations/Finance ....Ms. Alice BREKKE
32 Vice Pres Student Affairs ....Dr. Lori REESOR
17 Vice President Health Affairs ....Dr. Joshua WYNNE
46 Vice Pres Research/Economic Devel ....Dr. Phyllis E. JOHNSON
26 VP for University & Public Affairs ....Ms. Susan WALTON
26 Exec Assoc VP University Rels ....Mr. Peter B. JOHNSON
30 Assoc Exec VP/Chief Devel Officer ..Ms. DeAnna CARLSON ZINK
35 Associate VP & Dean of Students ....Dr. Cara HALGREN
21 Assoc VP Finance/Operations ....Ms. Peggy LUCKE
21 Assoc VP Finance/Operations ....Ms. Margaret MYERS
45 Assoc Vice Pres Research/Econ Dev ....Dr. Barry MILAVETZ
25 Assoc VP Research/Capacity Building ....Dr. Mark HOFFMANN
25 AVP Intellectual Prop Comm/Econ Dev ....Mr. Michael MOORE
88 Assoc VP for Health & Wellness ....Dr. Laurie BETTING
25 AVP Res & Econ Dev/Grants/Contracts ....Mr. David O. SCHMIDT
20 Asst VP Student Academic Services ....Ms. Lisa BURGER
07 Asst VP Admissions/Financial Aid ....Mr. Sol JENSEN
08 Director of Libraries ....Mr. Wilbur STOLT
27 Chief Information Officer ....Vacant
06 Registrar ....Dr. Suzanne ANDERSON
15 Dir Human Resources/Payroll Svcs ....Ms. Patricia HANSON
19 Chief of University Police ....Mr. Eric PLUMMER
38 Director Counseling Center ....Dr. Myron VEENSTRA
36 Dir Career Services/Coop Education ....Ms. Ilene ODEGARD
87 Director Summer Sessions ....Ms. Diane HADDEN
20 Director Instructional Development ....Dr. Anne KELSCH
22 Acting Affirmative Action Officer ....Ms. Julie EVANS
37 Director Student Financial Aid ....Ms. Janelle KILGORE
39 Director Residence Services ....Ms. Judy L. SARGENT
23 Director of Student Health ....Ms. Michelle D. ESLINGER
43 General Counsel ....Ms. Julie EVANS
41 Director Athletics ....Mr. Brian FAISON
18 Director of Facilities Management ....Mr. Larry L. ZITZOW
85 Director International Programs ....Mr. Ray LAGASSE
21 Controller ....Ms. Sharon LOILAND
88 Director Judicial Affs/Crisis Pgm ....Vacant
09 Director of Institutional Research ....Ms. Carmen WILLIAMS
94 Director Women's Center ....Ms. Kay MENDICK
96 Director Purchasing ....Mr. Scott SCHREINER
92 Director Honors Program ....Dr. Sally PYLE
28 Dir Multicultural Student Services ....Ms. Malika CARTER
19 Dir Emergency Mgmt & Public Safety ....Vacant
13 Deputy CIO IT Systems & Services ....Mr. Rick ANDERSON
21 Budget Manager ....Ms. Cindy FETSCH
40 Manager University Bookstore ....Ms. Marie MACK
49 Dean of Arts & Sciences ....Dr. Debbie STORRS
58 Int Dean of Graduate School ....Dr. Wayne SWISHER
61 Dean School of Law ....Ms. Kathryn RAND
66 Dean Col Nursing/Profess Discipl ....Dr. Denise KORNIEWICZ
50 Dean Business/Public Administration ....Dr. Dennis J. ELBERT
54 Dean College of Engr/Mines ....Dr. Hesham EL-REWINI
53 Dean Col Education/Human Devel ....Dr. Robert HILL
88 Dean of Aerospace Sciences ....Dr. Bruce SMITH
63 Dean Sch Medicine/Health Science ....Dr. Joshua WYNNE

*Dickinson State University (D)

291 Campus Drive, Dickinson ND 58601-4896
County: Stark FICE Identification: 002989
Unit ID: 200059
Telephone: (701) 483-2507 Carnegie Class: Bac/Diverse
FAX Number: (701) 483-2006 Calendar System: Semester
URL: www.dickinsonstate.edu
Established: 1918 Annual Undergrad Tuition & Fees (In-State): $5,540
Enrollment: 1,837 Coed
Affiliation or Control: State IRS Status: 501(c)3
Highest Offering: Baccalaureate
Program: Liberal Arts And General; Teacher Preparatory
Accreditation: NH, IACBE, MUS, NUR, PNUR, TED

02 President ....Dr. D.C COSTON
05 Provost/Vice Pres Academic Affairs ....Dr. Cynthia PEMBERTON
10 VP for Finance & Administration ....Mr. Tad TORGERSON
32 Interim VP for Student Development ....Ms. Pattie CARR
49 Dean of Arts & Sciences ....Dr. Kenneth HAUGHT
53 Dean of Educ/Business/Applied Sci ....Dr. Dawn OLSON
102 Exec Dir Alumni Assoc/Foundation ....Mr. Kevin J. THOMPSON
07 Exec Dir Enrollment & Communication ....Ms. Marie MOE
41 Director of Intercollege Athletics ....Mr. Tim DANIEL
88 Strom Ctr for Entrpshp & Ino ....Ms. Ray Ann KILEN
56 Asst Director of Extended Learning ....Mr. Anthony WILLER
12 Asst Director of DSU Bismarck ....Ms. Chris HERINGER
06 Director of Academic Records ....Ms. Kathy MEYER
08 Director of Library Services ....Ms. Rita ENNEN
13 Director of Information Technology ....Mr. Todd HAUF
37 Director of Financial Aid ....Ms. Sandy L. KLEIN
88 Director Academic Success Center ....Dr. Stacie VARNSON
88 Director of Food Service ....Mr. Charles DORSA
40 Manager University Store ....Ms. Loretta A. HEIDT
21 Controller ....Mr. Mark S. LOWE
36 Director of Career Services ....Ms. Tara BUCK ELK
09 Coordinator of Institutional Rsrch ....Dr. Chris P. BELCHER
85 Associate Dir International Program ....Mr. Nicholas MAHAN
39 Housing Coordinator ....Ms. Lydia DWORSHAK
15 Coordinator of Human Resources ....Ms. Gail EBELTOFT

*Mayville State University (E)

330 3rd Street, NE, Mayville ND 58257-1299
County: Traill FICE Identification: 002993
Unit ID: 200226
Telephone: (701) 788-2301 Carnegie Class: Bac/Diverse
FAX Number: (701) 788-4748 Calendar System: Semester
URL: www.mayvillestate.edu
Established: 1889 Annual Undergrad Tuition & Fees (In-State): $6,354
Enrollment: 1,020 Coed
Affiliation or Control: State IRS Status: 501(c)3
Highest Offering: Baccalaureate
Program: 2-Year Principally Bachelor's Creditable; Liberal Arts And General; Teacher Preparatory; Business Emphasis
Accreditation: NH, TED

02 President ....Dr. Gary D. HAGEN
04 Exec Assistant to the President ....Ms. Mary L. TRUDEAU
05 Vice President for Academic Affairs ....Dr. Keith A. STENEHJEM
10 Vice President for Business Affairs ....Mr. Steven P. BENSEN
32 VP for Student Affairs/Inst Researc ....Dr. Raymond H. GERSZEWSKI
08 Director of Library Services ....Ms. Kelly KORNKVEN
37 Director of Financial Aid ....Mrs. Shirley M. HANSON
06 Registrar ....Mrs. Pamela K. BRAATEN
84 Director of Enrollment Services ....Mr. James MOROWSKI
36 Dir Career Services & Internships ....Mr. Jay A. HENRICKSON
39 Director of Student Housing ....Mr. Richard SMITH
40 Director of Bookstore ....Mrs. Pam B. SOHOLT
41 Athletic Director ....Mr. Mike K. MOORE
18 Physical Plant Director ....Vacant
26 Chief Public Relations Officer ....Ms. Beth I. SWENSON
18 Director of Facilities Services ....Mr. Bob J. KOZOJED
15 Director of Human Resources ....Mr. Noah M. FISCHER
13 Director of Information Technology ....Mr. Patrick W. STEELE
14 Director of Computer Center ....Mr. Shawn D. OGBURN
07 Director of Admissions & Ext Learn ....Ms. Misti L. WUORI
96 Business Office Accountant ....Mrs. Janice E. JORGENSEN
30 Director of Development ....Mr. John J. KLOCKE
38 Director of Counseling ....Ms. Kristi L. LENTZ

*Minot State University (F)

500 University Avenue W, Minot ND 58707-0001
County: Ward FICE Identification: 002994
Unit ID: 200253
Telephone: (701) 858-3000 Carnegie Class: Master's M
FAX Number: (701) 839-6933 Calendar System: Semester
URL: www.minotstateu.edu
Established: 1913 Annual Undergrad Tuition & Fees (In-State): $6,086
Enrollment: 3,560 Coed
Affiliation or Control: State IRS Status: 501(c)3
Highest Offering: Beyond Master's But Less Than Doctorate
Program: Liberal Arts And General; Teacher Preparatory; Professional; Business Emphasis
Accreditation: NH, IACBE, MUS, NUR, SP, SW, TED

02 President ....Dr. David FULLER
05 VP for Academic Affairs ....Dr. Lenore KOCZON
10 Vice President for Finance/Admin ....Mr. Brian FOISY
30 Vice President for Advancement ....Mr. Marv SEMRAU
32 Vice President for Student Affairs ....Dr. Richard J. JENKINS
21 AVP Business Services/Controller ....Ms. Jonelle WATSON
07 AVP Admissions ....Mr. Kevin HARMON
18 AVP Facilities Management ....Vacant
06 Registrar ....Ms. Rebecca PORTER
08 Director of the Library ....Mr. Stephen BANISTER
35 Director of Student Life ....Ms. Lisa ERIKSMOEN
37 Director of Financial Aid ....Ms. Laurie WEBER
58 Dean of Graduate School ....Vacant
50 Dean College of Business ....Dr. Jacek MROZIK
49 Dean College Arts & Science ....Dr. Conrad DAVIDSON
53 Dean Col Education/Health Sci ....Dr. Neil NORDQUIST
51 Dean Continuing Education ....Dr. Kristin WARMOTH
29 Director Alumni Relations ....Ms. Janna MCKECHNIE
14 Director Computer Services ....Ms. Cathy HORVATH
40 Director Bookstore ....Ms. Gerri KUNA
41 Athletic Director ....Mr. Rick HEDBERG
27 Director of Public Information ....Ms. Susan NESS
15 Director of Human Resources ....Mr. Wesley MATTHEWS
12 Dean of Dakota College at Bottineau ....Dr. Kenneth GROSZ
36 Director of Campus Career Services ....Ms. Lynda BERTSCH
25 Grants & Contracts Accountant ....Ms. Sheila LATHAM
09 Director of Institutional Research ....Ms. Cari OLSON

*North Dakota State University Main Campus (G)

P.O. Box 6050, Fargo ND 58108-6050
County: Cass FICE Identification: 002997
Unit ID: 200332
Telephone: (701) 231-8011 Carnegie Class: RU/VH
FAX Number: (701) 231-8722 Calendar System: Semester
URL: www.ndsu.edu
Established: 1890 Annual Undergrad Tuition & Fees (In-State): $7,539
Enrollment: 14,443 Coed
Affiliation or Control: State IRS Status: 501(c)3
Highest Offering: Doctorate
Program: Liberal Arts And General; Teacher Preparatory; Professional
Accreditation: NH, ART, BUS, CACREP, CIDA, COARC, CONST, DIETC, DIETD, ENG, EXSC, #LSAR, MFCD, MUS, NURSE, PHAR, TED, THEA

02 President ....Dr. Dean BRESCIANI
05 Provost/Vice Pres Academic Affairs ....Dr. J. Bruce RAFERT
10 Vice President Business & Finance ....Mr. Bruce BOLLINGER
32 Vice President for Student Affairs ....Mr. Prakash C. MATHEW
46 Vice Pres Research Crea Act & Tech ....Dr. Philip BOUDJOUK
88 Vice President Ag/Univ Extension ....Dr. Ken GRAFTON
30 President/CEO Dev Found/Alumni Assn ....Mr. Doug MAYO
13 Interim VP Information Technology ....Mr. Marc WALLMAN
22 VP Equity/Diversity/Global Outreach ....Mrs. Eveadean MYERS
35 Associate Vice Pres Student Affairs . Dr. Catherine (Kate) HAUGEN
88 Assoc VP Sponsored Programs Admin ....Ms. Valrey V. KETTNER
06 University Registrar ....Dr. Kristi D. WOLD-MCCORMICK
84 Coordinator Enrollment Management ....Mr. Viet DOAN
08 Dean of Libraries ....Dr. Michelle REID
35 Dean Student Life ....Ms. Janna M. STOSKOPF
51 Dir Distance/Continuing Education ....Ms. Lisa NORDICK
37 Director Student Financial Services ....Ms. Jeanette E. ENEBO
36 Director Career Center ....Ms. Jill J. WILKEY
27 Communication Coordinator ....Ms. Ann ROBINSON-PAUL
88 Asst VP University Relations ....Ms. Laura MCDANIEL
56 Director Extension Service ....Mr. Chris BOERBOOM
50 Dean Business Administration ....Dr. Ronald D. JOHNSON
54 Dean Engineering/Architecture ....Dr. Gary R. SMITH

59 Dean Human Development & Education ... Dr. Virginia L. CLARK JOHNSON
49 Dean Arts/Humanities/Social Science ... Dr. Kent SANDSTROM
81 Dean of Science & Math ... Dr. Scott WOOD
67 Dean of Pharmacy/Nursing/Allied Sci ... Dr. Charles D. PETERSON
58 Dean Col of Grad/Inter Studies ... Dr. David A. WITTROCK
89 Assoc Dean University Studies ... Dr. Carolyn A. SCHNELL
21 Director of Budget ... Ms. Cynthia ROTT
25 Manager Grant & Contract Acctng ... Mrs. Karen HENDRICKSON
18 Director Facilities Management ... Mr. Mike ELLINGSON
19 Dir of Univ Police/Safety Officer ... Mr. Raymond E. BOYER
38 Director Counseling/Disability Svcs ... Dr. William BURNS
23 Director Wellness Center ... Mr. Gary T. FISHER
39 Director of Residence Life ... Mr. Rian NOSTRUM
40 Director Bookstore ... Ms. Carol J. MILLER
41 Director of Athletics ... Mr. Gene F. TAYLOR
43 General Counsel ... Mr. Chris WILSON
57 Director Fine Arts ... Dr. E. John MILLER
09 Director Inst Research/Analysis ... Dr. William D. SLANGER
96 Director of Purchasing ... Ms. Stacey O. WINTER
07 Director of Admissions ... Mr. Jobey L. LICHTBLAU

*Valley City State University (A)

101 College Street, SW, Valley City ND 58072-4098
County: Barnes
FICE Identification: 003008
Unit ID: 200572
Telephone: (701) 845-7990
Carnegie Class: Bac/Diverse
FAX Number: (701) 845-7253
Calendar System: Semester
URL: www.vcsu.edu
Established: 1889
Annual Undergrad Tuition & Fees (In-State): $6,516
Enrollment: 1,362
Coed
Affiliation or Control: State
IRS Status: 501(c)3
Highest Offering: Master's
Program: Liberal Arts And General; Teacher Preparatory
Accreditation: NH, MUS, TED

02 President ... Dr. Steven W. SHIRLEY
05 Vice President Academic Affairs ... Dr. Margaret DAHLBERG
10 Vice President Business Affairs ... Mr. Doug DAWES
32 Vice President Student Affairs ... Dr. Vitaliano FIGUEROA
53 Dean Sch of Educ/Graduate Stds ... Dr. Gary THOMPSON
08 Library Director ... Ms. Donna JAMES
20 Director Student Academic Services ... Ms. Janet M. DRAKE
37 Director Student Financial Aid ... Ms. Betty A. SCHUMACHER
36 Director Career Services ... Ms. Marcia J. FOSS
14 Chief Information Officer ... Mr. Joseph TYKWINSKI
41 Athletic Director ... Mr. Jack DENHOLM
84 Director of Enrollment Services ... Ms. Charlene STENSON
30 Director of University Advancement ... Mr. Larry J. ROBINSON
18 Director of Facilities Services ... Mr. Ron POMMERER
07 Director of Admissions & Records ... Ms. Charlene STENSON
15 Director of Human Resources ... Ms. Jennifer LARSON
44 Asst Dir University Advancement ... Ms. Kim HESCH
38 Director of Student Counseling ... Ms. Erin KLINGENBERG
26 Director Marketing/Communications ... Mr. Greg VANNEY
40 Director Bookstore ... Mr. Todd ROGELSTAD
06 Registrar ... Ms. Jody KLIER
09 Dir Institutional Rsch/Assessment ... Mr. Gregory CARLSON
29 Director Alumni Relations ... Mr. Larry ROBINSON
28 Diversity/Retention/Inclusion Coord ... Dr. Nadja JOHNSON

*Bismarck State College (B)

PO Box 5587, Bismarck ND 58506-5587
County: Burleigh
FICE Identification: 002988
Unit ID: 200022
Telephone: (701) 224-5400
Carnegie Class: Assoc/Pub4
FAX Number: (701) 224-5550
Calendar System: Semester
URL: www.bismarckstate.edu
Established: 1939
Annual Undergrad Tuition & Fees (In-State): $3,715
Enrollment: 4,109
Coed
Affiliation or Control: State
IRS Status: 501(c)3
Highest Offering: Baccalaureate
Program: Occupational; 2-Year Principally Bachelor's Creditable; Liberal Arts And General
Accreditation: NH, EMT, ENGT, MLTAD, PHLEB, SURGT

02 President ... Dr. Larry C. SKOGEN
03 Executive Vice President ... Mr. David CLARK
05 Provost/VP Academic Affairs ... Dr. Drake CARTER
30 VP College Advance/Exec Dir Found ... Mr. Gordy BINEK
88 VP National Energy Ctr of Excellenc ... Ms. Kari KNUDSON
32 Associate VP for Student Affairs ... Dr. Donna FISHBECK
10 Assoc VP for Finance & Operations ... Mrs. Tamara BARBER
88 Assoc VP Nat Energy Ctr of Excell ... Mr. Bruce EMMIL
51 Assoc VP Cont Educ/Training & Innov ... Mrs. Carla HIXSON
20 Dean of Academic Affairs ... Dr. Janelle MASTERS
16 Chief Human Resources Officer ... Mrs. Rita LINDGREN
13 Chief Information Officer ... Mr. Elmer WEIGEL
09 Chief Inst Effect/Strat Plan Office ... Dr. Stacie IKEN
106 Chief Dist Learning/Military Affair ... Mr. Lane HUBER
18 Chief Buildings/Grounds Officer ... Mr. Don ROETHLER
08 Director of Library Services ... Ms. Marlene ANDERSON
26 Director of College Relations ... Mrs. Mary FRIESZ
41 Director of Athletics ... Mr. Buster GILLISS
37 Director of Financial Aid ... Mr. Jeff JACOBS
51 Dir of Cont Educ/Trng & Innovation ... Ms. Lori HEINSOHN
07 Dir Admissions/Enrollment Services ... Ms. Karen ERICKSON
88 Dir Great Plains Energy Corridor ... Ms. Emily MCKAY
35 Director Student & Residence Life ... Ms. Heather SHEEHAN
06 Director Academic Records/Registrar ... Mr. Tom LENO

36 Dir Couseling and Advising Services ... Mr. Jay MEIER
88 Program Manager NECE ... Mr. Dan SCHMIDT
88 Project Manager NECE ... Mr. Zachery ALLEN
88 Program Manager NECE ... Mr. Scott AGNEW
88 Training & Program Manager NECE ... Mrs. Alicia UHDE
46 Resource Development Manager ... Mrs. Janet DIXON
44 Development Manager ... Mrs. Gina BUCHHOLTZ
29 Alumni Coordinator ... Mrs. Rita NODLAND
40 Bookstore Manager/Purchasing Coord ... Ms. Debra SANDNESS
04 Executive Assistant to President ... Mrs. Debbie VAN BERKOM

*Dakota College at Bottineau (C)

105 Simrall Boulevard, Bottineau ND 58318-1198
County: Bottineau
FICE Identification: 002995
Unit ID: 200314
Telephone: (701) 228-2277
Carnegie Class: Assoc/Pub2in4
FAX Number: (701) 228-5468
Calendar System: Semester
URL: www.dakotacollege.edu
Established: 1907
Annual Undergrad Tuition & Fees (In-State): $4,019
Enrollment: 774
Coed
Affiliation or Control: State
IRS Status: 501(c)3
Highest Offering: Associate Degree
Program: Occupational; 2-Year Principally Bachelor's Creditable
Accreditation: NH

02 Campus Dean ... Dr. Ken GROSZ
10 Director of Business Affairs ... Ms. Kara BOWEN
32 Assoc Dean for Student Affairs ... Mr. Dennis ZIEGLER
05 Assoc Dean for Academic Affairs ... Mr. Larry BROOKS
08 Librarian ... Dr. Debra SYVERTSON
07 Director of Admissions ... Vacant
06 Registrar ... Mr. Dennis ZIEGLER
37 Director Financial Aid ... Ms. Valerie HEILMAN
41 Athletic Director ... Mr. Scott JOHNSON
29 Director Alumni Relations ... Ms. Brandy SIMPSON
18 Chief Facilities/Physical Plant ... Ms. Kara BOWEN
39 Housing Director ... Mr. Dan DAVIS
28 Director of Diversity ... Ms. Colette SCHIMETZ
40 Bookstore Manager ... Ms. Janeen POLLMAN

*Lake Region State College (D)

1801 College Drive N, Devils Lake ND 58301-1598
County: Ramsey
FICE Identification: 002991
Unit ID: 200192
Telephone: (701) 662-1600
Carnegie Class: Assoc/Pub-R-M
FAX Number: (701) 662-1570
Calendar System: Semester
URL: www.lrsc.edu
Established: 1941
Annual Undergrad Tuition & Fees (In-State): $4,037
Enrollment: 1,974
Coed
Affiliation or Control: State
IRS Status: 501(c)3
Highest Offering: Associate Degree
Program: Occupational; 2-Year Principally Bachelor's Creditable
Accreditation: NH

02 President ... Dr. Douglas D. DARLING
05 Vice Pres of Academic Affairs ... Mr. Lloyd HALVORSON
10 Vice Pres Administrative Affairs ... Mr. Corry G. KENNER
32 Vice Pres Student Affairs ... Dr. Randall FIXEN
12 Director of Branch Campus ... Mr. John COWGER
30 Vice Pres Advancment/Foundation ... Ms. Laurel GOULDING
84 Director of Enrollment Management ... Ms. Stephanie SHOCK
37 Dir Student Finan Aid/Placemnt Svcs ... Ms. Katie NETTELL
88 Director Food Service ... Mr. Steve HARISH
18 Superintendent Buildings/Grounds ... Mr. Donald JORGENSON
08 Librarian ... Ms. Celeste ERTELT
41 Director Athletics ... Mr. Duane SCHWAB
13 Chief Information Officer ... Ms. Toofawn SIMHAI
15 Chief of Personnel ... Mr. Corry G. KENNER
40 Director of Bookstore ... Ms. Melissa STOTTS
06 Registrar ... Mr. Daniel JOHNSON
26 Director of Public Relations/Mktg ... Ms. Erin WOOD
31 Director Community Education ... Ms. Edith ARMEY
09 Director of Institutional Research ... Ms. Brandi NELSON
28 Director of Diversity ... Mrs. Nicole CLAUSSEN
38 Director Counseling Services ... Ms. Brigitte FRESCHETTE
07 Director of Admissions ... Ms. Stephanie SHOCK
21 Controller ... Ms. Joann KITCHENS

*North Dakota State College of Science (E)

800 N Sixth Street, Wahpeton ND 58076-0002
County: Richland
FICE Identification: 002996
Unit ID: 200305
Telephone: (800) 342-4325
Carnegie Class: Assoc/Pub-R-M
FAX Number: (701) 671-2145
Calendar System: Semester
URL: www.ndscs.edu
Established: 1903
Annual Undergrad Tuition & Fees (In-State): $4,325
Enrollment: 3,066
Coed
Affiliation or Control: State
IRS Status: 501(c)3
Highest Offering: Associate Degree
Program: Occupational; 2-Year Principally Bachelor's Creditable
Accreditation: NH, CAHIIM, DA, DH, EMT, OTA, PNUR

02 President ... Dr. John RICHMAN
05 VP Academic & Student Affairs ... Mr. Harvey LINK
11 Vice Pres Administrative Affairs ... Mr. Dennis GLADEN
09 Assoc Vice Pres Institutional Rsrch ... Mrs. Gloria DOHMAN
32 Assoc Vice Pres Acad/Student Affs ... Mr. Philip PARNELL

84 Dir Enroll Svcs/Finan Aid/Placement ... Vacant
08 Director Library ... Ms. Karen M. CHOBOT
26 Dir Marketing/Communications/PR ... Mrs. Barbara SPAETH-BAUM
29 Director of Alumni Foundation ... Mr. Brad BARTH
41 Athletic Director ... Mr. Stuart ENGEN
15 Human Resource Director ... Mrs. Ann HIEDEMAN
18 Director Facilities/Physical Plant ... Mr. Dallas FOSSUM
20 Academic Services Director ... Ms. Maria KADUC
39 Director of Residence Life ... Mrs. Melissa JOHNSON
96 Director of Purchasing ... Mr. David MEYER
06 Associate Registrar ... Mrs. Barb MUND
21 Business Manager ... Mr. Keith JOHNSON
24 Instructional Technology Coord ... Mr. Tom HICKMAN
07 Admissions Counselor ... Mr. Dale GROSZ
38 Counseling Center ... Mr. Vince PLUMMER
49 Dean Arts Sciences/Business ... Mr. Ken KOMPELIEN
72 Dean Technology/Services Division ... Mrs. Barbara BANG
64 Director of Music ... Ms. Laurie LEKANG
56 Dean of Extended Learning ... Mrs. Patricia SCHROM
88 Dean of College Outreach ... Mrs. Patricia KLINE

*Williston State College (F)

1410 University Avenue, Williston ND 58801-1326
County: Williams
FICE Identification: 003007
Unit ID: 200341
Telephone: (701) 774-4200
Carnegie Class: Assoc/Pub-R-S
FAX Number: (701) 774-4275
Calendar System: Semester
URL: www.willistonstate.nodak.edu
Established: 1961
Annual Undergrad Tuition & Fees (In-State): $4,542
Enrollment: 808
Coed
Affiliation or Control: State
IRS Status: 501(c)3
Highest Offering: Associate Degree
Program: Occupational; 2-Year Principally Bachelor's Creditable
Accreditation: NH

02 President ... Raymond NADOLNY
05 Provost/VP Instructn & Student Svcs ... Wanda MEYER
103 CEO of Workforce Education Train ... Deanette PIESIK
10 Exec Director for Business Services ... James FOERTSCH
26 VP College Advancement ... Terry OLSON

Rasmussen College - Bismarck (G)

1701 East Century Avenue, Bismarck ND 58503
Telephone: (701) 530-9600
Identification: 666301
Accreditation: &NH

† Main campus is Rasmussen College - St. Cloud in Saint Cloud, MN.

Rasmussen College - Fargo/Moorhead (H)

4012 19th Avenue, SW, Fargo ND 58103-7196
Telephone: (701) 277-3889
FICE Identification: 004846
Accreditation: &NH

† Main campus is Rasmussen College - St. Cloud in Saint Cloud, MN.

Sanford College of Nursing (I)

512 N 7th Street, Bismarck ND 58501-4494
County: Burleigh
FICE Identification: 009354
Unit ID: 200244
Telephone: (701) 323-6271
Carnegie Class: Spec/Health
FAX Number: (701) 323-6289
Calendar System: Semester
URL: www.bismarck.sanfordhealth.org/collegeofnursing
Established: 1988
Annual Undergrad Tuition & Fees: $11,579
Enrollment: 109
Coed
Affiliation or Control: Independent Non-Profit
IRS Status: 501(c)3
Highest Offering: Baccalaureate
Program: Nursing Emphasis
Accreditation: NH, NURSE, RAD

01 President ... Dr. Karen K. LATHAM
05 Associate Dean ... Dr. Wanda F. ROSE
32 Director Student Services ... Ms. Mary J. SMITH
37 Dir Student Financial Aid ... Ms. Janell D. THOMAS
08 Head Librarian ... Mr. Travis SCHULTZ
10 Chief Business Officer ... Ms. Candy RIFFEY
06 Registrar ... Ms. Ardys PFAFF

Sitting Bull College (J)

9299 Highway 24, Fort Yates ND 58538-9706
County: Sioux
FICE Identification: 021882
Unit ID: 200466
Telephone: (701) 854-8000
Carnegie Class: Tribal
FAX Number: (701) 854-8197
Calendar System: Semester
URL: www.sittingbull.edu
Established: 1971
Annual Undergrad Tuition & Fees: $3,910
Enrollment: 273
Coed
Affiliation or Control: Tribal Control
IRS Status: 501(c)3
Highest Offering: Baccalaureate
Program: Occupational; 2-Year Principally Bachelor's Creditable
Accreditation: NH

01 President ... Dr. Laurel VERMILLION
05 Vice President of Academic Affairs ... Dr. Koreen RESSLER
10 Vice President of Finance ... Ms. Leonica ALKIRE
37 Director Financial Student Aid ... Ms. Donna SEABOY
06 Registrar ... Ms. Melody AZURE
08 Head Librarian ... Mr. Mark HOLMAN
40 Director of Bookstore ... Mrs. Tracy MAHER

Trinity Bible College (A)

50 S 6th Avenue, Ellendale ND 58436-7150
County: Dickey FICE Identification: 012059
Unit ID: 200484
Telephone: (701) 349-3621 Carnegie Class: Spec/Faith
FAX Number: (701) 349-5443 Calendar System: Semester
URL: www.trinitybiblecollege.edu
Established: 1948 Annual Undergrad Tuition & Fees: $13,900
Enrollment: 227 Coed
Affiliation or Control: Assemblies Of God Church IRS Status: 501(c)3
Highest Offering: Baccalaureate
Program: 2-Year Principally Bachelor's Creditable; Liberal Arts And General; Teacher Preparatory; Professional; Religious Emphasis
Accreditation: #BI

01 President .... Dr. Paul ALEXANDER
05 Vice President of Academic Affairs .... Dr. Stephen CHANDLER
10 Vice President of Administration .... Rev. Winston TITUS
32 Vice President of Student Life .... Rev. Ian O'BRIEN
30 Vice President of Development .... Mr. Dan KUNO
58 Director of Graduate Studies .... Mrs. Carol ALEXANDER
07 Academic Registrar External Studies .... Ms. Sara BEST
06 Academic Registrar .... Mrs. Luanne CHANDLER
84 Director of Enrollment .... Mrs. Kerri FRANSISCO
08 Librarian .... Mrs. Phyllis KUNO
106 Director of Distance Education .... Mr. John FRANSISCO
37 Director Student Financial Aid .... Ms. Nicole MCINTOSH
13 Director of Computer Services .... Mr. Matthew JOHNSON

Turtle Mountain Community College (B)

Box 340, Belcourt ND 58316-0340
County: Rolette FICE Identification: 023011
Unit ID: 200527
Telephone: (701) 477-7862 Carnegie Class: Tribal
FAX Number: (701) 477-7807 Calendar System: Semester
URL: www.tm.edu
Established: 1972 Annual Undergrad Tuition & Fees: $1,125
Enrollment: 532 Coed
Affiliation or Control: Independent Non-Profit IRS Status: 501(c)3
Highest Offering: Baccalaureate
Program: Occupational; 2-Year Principally Bachelor's Creditable; Technical Emphasis
Accreditation: NH, PHLEB

01 President .... Jim L. DAVIS
03 Executive Vice President .... Kellie HALL
05 Academic Dean .... Larry HENRY
32 Dean Student Affairs .... Anita FREDERICK
37 Director Financial Aid .... Wanda LADUCER
10 Comptroller .... Tracy AZURE
75 Director Vocational/Education .... Sheila TROTTIER
06 Registrar .... Angel GLADUE
36 Career Ladder Coordinator .... Vacant
31 Dir of Community/Adult Education .... Sandra LAROCQUE
07 Director of Admissions .... Joni LAFONTAINE
15 Director Personnel Services .... Holly CAHILL
37 Financial Aid Officer .... Alexsis MARCELLAIS
40 Director of Bookstore .... Kathe ZASTE
18 Chief Facilities/Physical Plant .... Wesley DAVIS
30 Chief Development .... Dave RIPLEY
13 Chief Informational Officer .... Vacant
25 Sponsored Programs Officer .... Larretta HALL
35 Student Support Services Coord .... Steve DECOTEAU

United Tribes Technical College (C)

3315 University Drive, Bismarck ND 58504-7596
County: Burleigh FICE Identification: 022429
Unit ID: 200554
Telephone: (701) 255-3285 Carnegie Class: Tribal
FAX Number: (701) 530-0605 Calendar System: Semester
URL: www.uttc.edu
Established: 1969 Annual Undergrad Tuition & Fees: $3,840
Enrollment: 505 Coed
Affiliation or Control: Independent Non-Profit IRS Status: 501(c)3
Highest Offering: Baccalaureate
Program: Occupational; 2-Year Principally Bachelor's Creditable
Accreditation: NH, CAHIIM, PNUR

01 President .... Dr. David GIPP
05 Vice Pres Academic Career/Tech Educ .... Dr. Phil BAIRD
32 Vice Pres Student & Campus Services .... Dr. Russell SWAGGER
10 Dean Finance & Business Services .... Ms. Shirley BORDEAUX
07 Director of Admissions .... Mr. Donovan LAMBERT
06 Registrar .... Vacant
46 Director Research .... Vacant
15 Director Human Resources .... Ms. Barbara LITTLE OWL
20 Director Academic Support Services .... Vacant
84 Director Enrollment Management .... Vacant
19 Supervisor Security .... Mr. James REDTOMAHAWK
37 Director Financial Aid .... Vacant
41 Athletic Director .... Mr. Hunter BERG
13 Director of IT/Jenzabar Coordinator .... Mr. Monty SCHASS
19 Director of Safety .... Mr. Joely HEAVY RUNNER

University of Jamestown (D)

6000 College Lane, Jamestown ND 58405-0001
County: Stutsman FICE Identification: 002990
Unit ID: 200156
Telephone: (701) 252-3467 Carnegie Class: Bac/Diverse
FAX Number: (701) 253-4318 Calendar System: Semester
URL: www.jc.edu
Established: 1883 Annual Undergrad Tuition & Fees: $24,668
Enrollment: 946 Coed
Affiliation or Control: Presbyterian Church (U.S.A.) IRS Status: 501(c)3
Highest Offering: Doctorate
Program: Liberal Arts And General; Teacher Preparatory; Professional
Accreditation: NH, IACBE, NUR, @PTA

01 President .... Dr. Robert S. BADAL
05 Vice Pres/Dean Academic Affairs .... Dr. Gary WATTS
32 Dean of Students .... Mr. Gary VAN ZINDEREN
11 VP Planning/Administrative Services .... Mr. Thomas R. HECK
30 VP Inst Advancement/Business Affs .... Ms. Polly J. PETERSON
84 Vice President of Enrollment Mgmt .... Mr. Scott GOPLIN
26 VP for Marketing/Public Relations .... Ms. Tena LAWRENCE
101 Asst to Pres/Secy to Bd of Trustees .... Ms. Liz HUNT
06 Registrar .... Mr. Michael P. WOODLEY
37 Director of Financial Aid .... Mrs. Marge M. MICHAEL
08 Librarian .... Mrs. Phyllis K. BRATTON
36 Director Experiential Education .... Ms. Pat J. RINDE
27 Director Information Office .... Ms. Donna SCHMITZ
41 Athletic Director .... Mr. Lawrie PAULSON
14 Director Computer Center .... Mr. Tim KACHEL
18 Chief Facilities/Physical Plant .... Mr. Mark KOEPKE

University of Mary (E)

7500 University Drive, Bismarck ND 58504-9652
County: Burleigh FICE Identification: 002992
Unit ID: 200217
Telephone: (701) 255-7500 Carnegie Class: Master's L
FAX Number: (701) 255-7687 Calendar System: Other
URL: www.umary.edu
Established: 1959 Annual Undergrad Tuition & Fees: $14,000
Enrollment: 2,893 Coed
Affiliation or Control: Roman Catholic IRS Status: 501(c)3
Highest Offering: Doctorate
Program: Liberal Arts And General; Professional
Accreditation: NH, COARC, EXSC, IACBE, MUS, NURSE, OT, PTA, SW

01 President .... Fr. James P. SHEA
03 Executive Vice President .... Mr. Gregory A. VETTER
05 Vice President for Academic Affairs .... Dr. Diane FLADELAND
10 Vice President Financial Affairs .... Ms. Elizabeth S. CONDIC
32 Vice President Student Development .... Dr. Timothy SEAWORTH
84 Vice President Enrollment Services .... Mr. Michael S. MCMAHON
26 Vice President for Public Affairs .... Mr. Neal KALBERER
06 Registrar .... Mr. Rod SCHEETT
08 Librarian .... Mrs. Cheryl BAILEY
37 Director of Financial Aid .... Mr. David K. HANSON
07 Director of Admissions .... Vacant
09 Director of Institutional Research .... Mr. Scott J. STAUDINGER
15 Director Human Resources .... Ms. Mary A. BRANDT
20 Associate Academic Officer .... Dr. Kimberly MCDOWALL-LONG
18 Chief Facilities/Physical Plant .... Mr. Mark R. STEPHENS

OHIO

Allegheny Wesleyan College (F)

2161 Woodsdale Road, Salem OH 44460-8920
County: Columbiana FICE Identification: 034573
Unit ID: 200873
Telephone: (330) 337-6403 Carnegie Class: Spec/Faith
FAX Number: (424) 228-3006 Calendar System: Semester
URL: www.awc.edu
Established: 1956 Annual Undergrad Tuition & Fees: $8,400
Enrollment: 46 Coed
Affiliation or Control: Wesleyan Church IRS Status: 501(c)3
Highest Offering: Baccalaureate
Program: Liberal Arts And General; Religious Emphasis
Accreditation: BI

01 President .... Rev. Daniel R. HARDY, SR.
05 Academic Dean .... Vacant
10 Business Manager .... Mr. Troy MUIR
32 Dean of Students .... Rev. Timothy FORRIDER
26 Director of Public Relations .... Mr. Tom SANDERS
06 Registrar & Director Admissions .... Mrs. Jeanne ZVARITCH
08 Head Librarian .... Mrs. Alice WEINGARD
37 Financial Aid Administrator .... Mrs. Esther PHELPS
09 Dir of Institutional Effectiveness .... Mrs. Jeanne ZVARITCH
40 Bookstore Manager .... Rev. Daniel R. HARDY
33 Dean of Men .... Rev. Timothy FORRIDER
34 Dean of Women .... Mrs. Holly FORRIDER
07 Director of Admissions .... Mrs. Jeanne ZVARITCH
18 Chief Facilities/Physical Plant .... Mr. Darrin PATTERSON
21 Associate Business Officer .... Mrs. Linda SAY
29 Director Alumni Relations .... Rev. John DYE
35 Director Student Affairs .... Rev. Timothy FORRIDER
38 Director Student Counseling .... Mrs. Kimberly FORD

American Institute of Alternative Medicine (G)

6685 Doubletree Avenue, Columbus OH 43229-1113
County: Franklin FICE Identification: 035344
Unit ID: 441636
Telephone: (614) 825-6255 Carnegie Class: Not Classified
FAX Number: (614) 825-6279 Calendar System: Quarter
URL: www.aiam.edu
Established: 1994 Annual Undergrad Tuition & Fees: $33,880
Enrollment: 302 Coed
Affiliation or Control: Proprietary IRS Status: Proprietary
Highest Offering: Master's
Program: 2-Year Principally Bachelor's Creditable; Professional; Nursing Emphasis
Accreditation: ACCSC, ACUP

01 Campus Director .... Mark SULLIVAN
05 Academic Dean .... Dr. Elaine HIATT
32 Dir of Student & Graduate Services .... Linda FLEMING-WILLIS
10 Director of Finance .... Ray WINDISCH
06 Registrar .... Danielle ANDREWS
37 Financial Aid Officer .... Ulrike ROSSER

*Antioch University (H)

900 Dayton Street, Yellow Springs OH 45387-1635
County: Greene FICE Identification: 003010
Unit ID: 442392
Telephone: (937) 769-1351 Carnegie Class: N/A
FAX Number: (937) 769-1350
URL: www.antioch.edu

01 Chancellor .... Ms. Felice NUDELMAN
10 Vice Chanc/Chief Financial Officer .... Mr. Tim JORDAN
05 Vice Chanc Univ Academic Affairs .... Dr. Iris WEISMAN
13 Vice Chancellor CIO .... Mr. Bob DEWITT
15 Director HR Systems/Payroll Svcs .... Ms. Suzette CASTONGUAY
91 Dir Administrative Info Systems .... Ms. Candice SANTELL
04 Executive Asst to the Chancellor .... Ms. Michelle WARD

† Parent institution of Antioch University Midwest in OH; Antioch University Seattle in WA; Antioch University New England in NH; and Antioch University Los Angeles and Antioch University Santa Barbara in CA.

*Antioch University Midwest (I)

900 Dayton Street, Yellow Springs OH 45387-1745
County: Greene Identification: 666811
Unit ID: 245892
Telephone: (937) 769-1800 Carnegie Class: Master's M
FAX Number: (937) 769-1805 Calendar System: Semester
URL: midwest.antioch.edu/
Established: 1988 Annual Undergrad Tuition & Fees: $13,043
Enrollment: 364 Coed
Affiliation or Control: Independent Non-Profit IRS Status: 501(c)3
Highest Offering: Master's
Program: Liberal Arts And General; Teacher Preparatory; Professional
Accreditation: NH, TED

02 President .... Dr. Ellen W. HALL
10 Regional CFO .... Ms. Barbara STEWART
04 Executive Assistant to President .... Ms. Jennifer MAYNARD
37 Director Student Financial Aid .... Ms. Kathy JOHN
15 Director Personnel Services .... Ms. Suzette CASTONGUAY
21 Associate Business Officer .... Ms. Deborah CARAWAY
62 Library Director .... Dr. Stephen SHAW
06 Registrar .... Dr. Maureen HEACOCK
18 Director Facility Management .... Mr. Ray SIMONELLI
84 Director Outreach Services .... Mr. Oscar ROBINSON
30 Dir Development/Alumni Relations .... Ms. Kimberly HORTON
49 Chair of Undergraduate Studies .... Dr. Mary Ann SHORT
88 Chair Management Leadership & Chang .... Vacant
53 Director School of Education .... Dr. Marian GLANCY
88 Chair Conflict Analysis & Engagemnt .... Vacant

Antonelli College (J)

124 E Seventh Street, Cincinnati OH 45202-2592
County: Hamilton FICE Identification: 012891
Unit ID: 201016
Telephone: (800) 505-4338 Carnegie Class: Assoc/PrivFP
FAX Number: (513) 241-9396 Calendar System: Quarter
URL: www.antonellicollege.edu
Established: 1947 Annual Undergrad Tuition & Fees: $15,426
Enrollment: 266 Coed
Affiliation or Control: Proprietary IRS Status: Proprietary
Highest Offering: Associate Degree
Program: Occupational
Accreditation: ACCSC

01 Campus President .... Mr. Edward RITO
05 Director of Education .... Ms. Frances CARROLL
32 Director Student Services .... Ms. Leah ELKINS
06 Registrar .... Ms. Angela BARCLAY
36 Career Services Coordinator .... Ms. Charlene SMITH

Art Academy of Cincinnati (K)

1212 Jackson Street, Cincinnati OH 45202-7106
County: Hamilton FICE Identification: 003011
Unit ID: 201061
Telephone: (513) 562-6262 Carnegie Class: Spec/Arts
FAX Number: (513) 562-8778 Calendar System: Semester
URL: www.artacademy.edu
Established: 1869 Annual Undergrad Tuition & Fees: $24,330
Enrollment: 197 Coed
Affiliation or Control: Independent Non-Profit IRS Status: 501(c)3
Highest Offering: Master's
Program: Fine Arts Emphasis

Accreditation: NH, ART

01 President ... John M. SULLIVAN
10 Director of Finance ... Jean SPOHR
07 Director of Admissions ... Joseph FISHER
05 Academic Dean ... Diane K. SMITH
37 Director of Financial Aid ... Kristina OLBERDING
06 Registrar ... Sue HUTCHENS
31 Director of Community Education ... Jennifer SPURLOCK
18 Director of Facilities ... Jack HENNEN
32 Director of Student Services ... Galen CRAWFORD

The Art Institute of Cincinnati (A)

1171 East Kemper Road, Cincinnati OH 45246-3322
County: Hamilton FICE Identification: 021286
Unit ID: 200624
Telephone: (513) 751-1206 Carnegie Class: Assoc/PrivFP
FAX Number: (513) 751-1209 Calendar System: Semester
URL: www.aic-arts.edu
Established: 1976 Annual Undergrad Tuition & Fees: $2,300
Enrollment: 50 Coed
Affiliation or Control: Proprietary IRS Status: Proprietary
Highest Offering: Baccalaureate
Program: Occupational
Accreditation: ACCSC

00 CEO ... Ms. Marion K. ALLMAN
01 President ... Mr. Sean M. MENDELL

The Art Institute of Ohio-Cincinnati (B)

8845 Governors Hill Drive, Cincinnati OH 45249
Telephone: (513) 833-2400 Identification: 666693
Accreditation: &NH, ACFEI

† Main campus is The Illinois Institute of Art in Chicago, IL.

Ashland University (C)

401 College Avenue, Ashland OH 44805-3799
County: Ashland FICE Identification: 003012
Unit ID: 201104
Telephone: (419) 289-4142 Carnegie Class: DRU
FAX Number: (419) 289-5333 Calendar System: Semester
URL: www.ashland.edu
Established: 1878 Annual Undergrad Tuition & Fees: $28,858
Enrollment: 5,901 Coed
Affiliation or Control: Brethren Church IRS Status: 501(c)3
Highest Offering: Doctorate
Program: 2-Year Principally Bachelor's Creditable; Liberal Arts And General; Teacher Preparatory; Professional
Accreditation: NH, ACBSP, CACREP, @DIETD, MUS, NURSE, SW, TED, THEOL

01 President ... Dr. Frederick J. FINKS
73 President Theological Seminary ... Dr. John C. SHULTZ
05 Provost ... Dr. Frank E. PETTIGREW
32 VP Student Affairs/Dean of Students ... Mrs. B. Sue HEIMANN
84 Vice Pres Enroll Mgt & Marketing ... Dr. Scott D. VAN LOO
13 Vice Pres Information Technology ... Mr. Curtis WHITE
18 Vice Pres Facilities/Mgmt & Plng ... Mr. Rick M. EWING, II
21 Vice President Business Opers ... Vacant
42 Dean of Religious Life ... Dr. Dan L. LAWSON
06 Registrar ... Ms. Kathleen HALL
08 Director of the Library ... Mr. Edward M. KRAKORA
37 Director Student Financial Aid ... Mr. Stephen C. HOWELL
29 Director Alumni/Parent Relations ... Mr. Jeff ALIX
15 Director of Human Resources ... Mr. John R. BRANDON
36 Executive Director Career Services ... Ms. Karen HAGANS
26 Director of Public Relations ... Mr. Steven M. HANNAN
41 Director of Athletics ... Mr. William J. GOLDRING
88 Exec Dir Ashbrook Ctr ... Dr. Peter W. SCHRAMM
09 Director of Institutional Research ... Mrs. Karen A. LITTLE
07 Director of Admissions ... Mr. W.C VANCE
49 Dean College of Arts & Sciences ... Dr. Dawn WEBER
73 Dean Theological Seminary ... Dr. Paul CHILCOTE
50 Dean College Business/Econ ... Dr. Jeffery RUSSELL
53 Dean College of Education ... Dr. James P. VANKEUREN
58 Dean Graduate School ... Vacant
66 Int Dean Col Nursing & Health Sci ... Ms. Faye GRUND
51 Dean School of Continuing Educ ... Mr. Dwight MCELFRESH
28 Director of Diversity ... Vacant
28 Dir Multicultural Stdnt Svcs & Stds ... Mr. Jonathan E. LOCUST, JR.
88 Director of Marketing ... Ms. Jan BOND

Athenaeum of Ohio (D)

6616 Beechmont Avenue, Cincinnati OH 45230-5900
County: Hamilton FICE Identification: 003013
Unit ID: 201140
Telephone: (513) 231-2223 Carnegie Class: Spec/Faith
FAX Number: (513) 231-3254 Calendar System: Semester
URL: www.athenaeum.edu
Established: 1829 Annual Graduate Tuition & Fees: $20,400
Enrollment: 213 Coed
Affiliation or Control: Roman Catholic IRS Status: 501(c)3
Highest Offering: Master's; No Undergraduates
Program: Professional; Religious Emphasis
Accreditation: NH, THEOL

01 President & Rector ... Rev. Benedict O'CINNSEALAIGH
10 Vice President for Finance ... Mr. Dennis K. EAGAN
30 Vice President for Advancement ... Mr. James RICE
05 Dean of Athenaeum ... Rev. Earl K. FERNANDES
08 Librarian ... Mrs. Connie SONG
06 Registrar ... Mr. Michael E. SWEENEY
88 Dir Lay Pastoral Ministry Program ... Dr. Susan MCGURGAN
108 Director of Assessment ... Dr. Terrance D. CALLAN

Aultman College of Nursing and Health Sciences (E)

2600 6th Street SW, Canton OH 44710-1702
County: Stark FICE Identification: 006487
Unit ID: 201177
Telephone: (330) 363-6347 Carnegie Class: Assoc/PrivNFP
FAX Number: (330) 580-6654 Calendar System: Semester
URL: www.aultmancollege.edu
Established: 2004 Annual Undergrad Tuition & Fees: $17,424
Enrollment: 343 Coed
Affiliation or Control: Independent Non-Profit IRS Status: 501(c)3
Highest Offering: Baccalaureate
Program: 2-Year Principally Bachelor's Creditable; Nursing Emphasis
Accreditation: NH, ADNUR, RAD

01 President ... Ms. Rebecca R. CROWL
11 VP Administrative & Student Affairs .. Ms. Jeannine SHAMBAUGH
26 Vice President Community Engagement ... Ms. Vi LEGGETT
05 Vice President Academic Affairs ... Dr. Jean PADDOCK
09 Director Inst Effectiveness ... Ms. Lyn SABINO
13 Director Information Technology ... Ms. Jacquelyn SCHMOTZER

Baldwin Wallace University (F)

275 Eastland Road, Berea OH 44017-2088
County: Cuyahoga FICE Identification: 003014
Unit ID: 201195
Telephone: (440) 826-2900 Carnegie Class: Master's L
FAX Number: (440) 826-2329 Calendar System: Semester
URL: www.bw.edu/
Established: 1845 Annual Undergrad Tuition & Fees: $36,980
Enrollment: 4,173 Coed
Affiliation or Control: United Methodist IRS Status: 501(c)3
Highest Offering: Master's
Program: Liberal Arts And General; Teacher Preparatory; Professional
Accreditation: NH, #ARCPA, MUS, TED

01 President ... Dr. Robert C. HELMER
03 Senior Vice President ... Mr. Richard L. FLETCHER
05 Int Vice Pres Academic Affairs/Dean ... Dr. Stephen D. STAHL
30 Vice President for Advancement ... Mr. William J. SPIKER
10 Vice President for Finance & Admin ... Mr. William M. RENIFF
32 VP Student Affairs/Dean of Students ... Dr. Trina DOBBERSTEIN
84 Vice Pres of Enrollment Management ... Ms. Susan DILENO
26 Asst VP/Director College Relations ... Mr. George RICHARD
20 Associate Academic Dean ... Dr. Guy E. FARISH
35 Director of Student Success ... Mr. Marc ADKINS
51 Director of Adult Learning ... Ms. Nancy JIROUSEK
08 Director of Ritter Library ... Mr. John DIGENNARO
13 Chief Information Officer ... Mr. Greg G. FLANIK
44 Director Annual Giving ... Ms. Aimee BELL
29 Director Alumni Relations ... Mr. Terry J. KURTZ
44 Director Development Gift Plng ... Mr. Thomas H. KONKOLY
37 Director of Financial Aid ... Dr. George ROLLESTON
15 Asst VP for Human Resources ... Mr. Sam RAMIREZ
38 Director of Counseling Services ... Ms. Joy D. WYATT
36 Director of Academic Advising ... Ms. Margaret STINER
06 Registrar ... Ms. Linda L. YOUNG
07 Director of Undergraduate Admission ... Ms. Pattie SKRHA
88 Dir of Adult/Cont Educ Admission ... Ms. Winifred GERHARDT
18 Director of Buildings & Grounds ... Mr. William KERBUSCH
88 Director of Intercultural Education ... Dr. Judith B. KRUTKY
96 Director of Purchasing ... Ms. Karen STENGER
28 Director Campus Diversity Affairs ... Mr. Charles HARKNESS

Beckfield College (G)

225 Pictoria Drive Suite 200, Cincinnati OH 45246
Telephone: (513) 671-1920 Identification: 666673
Accreditation: ACICS

† Main campus is Beckfield College in Florence, KY.

Belmont College (H)

120 Fox Shannon Place, Saint Clairsville OH 43950-9766
County: Belmont FICE Identification: 009941
Unit ID: 201283
Telephone: (740) 695-9500 Carnegie Class: Assoc/Pub-R-M
FAX Number: (740) 695-2247 Calendar System: Semester
URL: www.belmontcollege.edu
Established: 1969 Annual Undergrad Tuition & Fees (In-State): $4,310
Enrollment: 1,652 Coed
Affiliation or Control: State IRS Status: 501(c)3
Highest Offering: Associate Degree
Program: Occupational; 2-Year Principally Bachelor's Creditable
Accreditation: NH, MAC

01 President ... Dr. Joseph E. BUKOWSKI
05 VP of Learning & Student Success ... Dr. Rebecca KURTZ
11 Vice Pres of Administrative Affairs .. Mr. John S. KOUCOUMARIS
20 Exec Dean of Academic Affairs ... Dr. Brenda LOHRI-POSEY
09 Dean Institutional Research/Plng ... Dr. Jane EVANS
08 Assoc Dean Lrng/Info Svcs/Tech ... Mrs. Cathy BENNETT
103 Director Workforce/Econ Devel ... Mr. Robert GUENTTER
32 Dean of Student Services ... Mr. Tim HOUSTON
18 Director of Facilities Management ... Mr. Steve MORGAN
06 Registrar ... Mrs. Colleen SECKMAN
15 Exec Director of HR & Org Dev ... Mr. Matt KENDALL
37 Assoc Dean of Financial Aid ... Mr. Jody PEELER
20 Director of Educational Services ... Mrs. Elayne STUPAK
24 Dir Library/Info/Lrng Commons Svcs ... Ms. Joyce BAKER
54 Faculty Admin Industrial Trades Pgm ... Mr. Dirk DECOY
07 Exec Dir Enroll Svcs/Strat Comm ... Mrs. Laura DOTY
29 Coordinator of Development ... Ms. Erin NEELY
36 Transfer/Articulat/Academic Advisor ... Ms. Jane BLACK
27 Exec Dir of Information Services ... Mr. Matthew TARBETT
30 Dir of Dev & External Affairs ... Mr. RJ KONKOLESKI

Bexley Seabury (I)

583 Sheridan Avenue, Columbus OH 43209
County: Franklin FICE Identification: 037473
Unit ID: 443702
Telephone: (614) 231-3095 Carnegie Class: Spec/Faith
FAX Number: (614) 231-3236 Calendar System: Semester
URL: www.bexley.edu
Established: Annual Graduate Tuition & Fees: $14,890
Enrollment: 17 Coed
Affiliation or Control: Independent Non-Profit IRS Status: 501(c)3
Highest Offering: Master's; No Undergraduates
Program: Religious Emphasis
Accreditation: THEOL

01 President ... Rev. Roger FERLO
05 Dean ... Mr. Thomas FERGUSON

Bluffton University (J)

1 University Drive, Bluffton OH 45817-2104
County: Allen FICE Identification: 003016
Unit ID: 201371
Telephone: (419) 358-3000 Carnegie Class: Bac/Diverse
FAX Number: (419) 358-3323 Calendar System: Semester
URL: www.bluffton.edu
Established: 1899 Annual Undergrad Tuition & Fees: $28,504
Enrollment: 1,198 Coed
Affiliation or Control: Mennonite Church IRS Status: 501(c)3
Highest Offering: Master's
Program: Liberal Arts And General; Teacher Preparatory; Business Emphasis
Accreditation: NH, DIETD, MUS, SW, TED

01 President ... Dr. James M. HARDER
10 Vice President for Fiscal Affairs ... Mr. Kevin A. NICKEL
30 Vice President for Inst Advancement ... Dr. Hans HOUSHOWER
05 Vice Pres & Dean Academic Affairs ... Dr. Sally W. SOMMER
84 VP for Enrollment Management/Mktg ... Mr. Ronald HEADINGS
32 VP for Student Life/Dean of Stdnts ... Dr. Julie DEGRAW
21 Chief Business Officer ... Mr. Richard LICHTLE
08 Director of Libraries ... Ms. Mary Jean JOHNSON
06 Registrar ... Ms. Iris NEUFELD
26 Chief Public Relations Officer ... Mrs. Robin BOWLUS
29 Dir of Alumni Relations/Annual Giv ... Mrs. Julia SZABO
37 Director of Student Financial Aid ... Mr. Lawrence MATTHEWS
07 Director of UG Admissions ... Mr. Derek STEMEN
18 Director Building/Grounds ... Mr. Mustaq AHMED
15 Director Human Resources ... Vacant

Bowling Green State University (K)

220 McFall Center, Bowling Green OH 43403-0001
County: Wood FICE Identification: 003018
Unit ID: 201441
Telephone: (419) 372-2531 Carnegie Class: RU/H
FAX Number: (419) 372-8446 Calendar System: Semester
URL: www.bgsu.edu
Established: 1910 Annual Undergrad Tuition & Fees (In-State): $10,590
Enrollment: 19,697 Coed
Affiliation or Control: State IRS Status: 501(c)3
Highest Offering: Doctorate
Program: Liberal Arts And General; Teacher Preparatory; Professional
Accreditation: NH, ART, BUS, BUSA, CACREP, CLPSY, CONST, DIETD, DIETI, EXSC, IPSY, JOUR, MT, MUS, NAIT, NRPA, NURSE, PH, SP, SW, TED, THEA

01 President ... Dr. Mary Ellen MAZEY
05 Sr VP Academic Affairs/Provost ... Dr. Rodney K. ROGERS
10 CFO/VP Finance & Admin ... Ms. Sherideen S. STOLL
100 Chief of Staff ... Ms. Lisa C. MATTIACE
32 Vice President Student Affairs ... Vacant
04 Asst to President ... Ms. Laurel E. ZAWODNY
30 VP Univ Advancement ... Mr. Shea MCGREW
84 VP Enrollment Management ... Mr. Albert N. COLOM
20 Vice Provost Undergraduate Educ ... Dr. M. Sue HOUSTON
35 Asst VP Student Affs/Dean of Stdnts ... Ms. Jill CARR
11 Assoc VP for Campus Operations ... Mr. Bruce MEYER
27 Chief Communications Officer ... Ms. Robin GERROW
29 Director Alumni Affairs ... Ms. Montique R. COTTON KELLY
46 VP Research & Econ Dev ... Dr. Michael Y. OGAWA
41 Asst VP Student Affs/Dir Rec Sports ... Dr. Stephen KAMPF
41 Director of Athletics ... Mr. Chris KINGSTON
16 Chief Human Resources Officer ... Ms. Rebecca C. FERGUSON
39 Director of Residence Life ... Ms. Sarah WATERS

88	Assoc VP Capital Planning & Design	Mr. Steve P. KRAKOFF
13	Chief Information Officer	Mr. John M. ELLINGER
43	General Counsel	Mr. Sean P. FITZGERALD
22	Director Equity & Diversity	Ms. Barbara WADDELL
58	Interim Dean Graduate College	Dr. Michael OGAWA
49	Dean College Arts/Sciences	Dr. Simon N. MORGAN-RUSSELL
50	Dean College Business Admin	Mr. Raymond BRAUN
51	Exec Director University Outreach	Dr. Marcia SALAZAR-VALENTINE
53	Dean College Educ/Human Development	Dr. Brad COLWELL
12	Dean Firelands College	Dr. William BALZER
69	Int Dean College Hlth/Human Svcs	Dr. Chris DUNN
08	Dean University Libraries	Ms. Sara BUSHONG
64	Dean College of Musical Arts	Dr. Jeffrey A. SHOWELL
72	Dean College of Technology	Dr. Faris A. MALHAS
57	Director of School of Art	Dr. Katerina R. RAY
60	Dir Sch of Media & Communication	Dr. Laura STAFFORD
88	Dir Sch Human Move/Sport/Leisure	Dr. Philip F. XIE
88	Dir Sch Family & Consumer Sciences	Dr. Deborah G. WOOLDRIDGE
53	Dir Sch Educ Fnds/Leadership/Policy	Dr. Sherri HORNER
53	Dir Sch of Teaching and Learning	Dr. Dawn SHINEW
92	Director Honors Program	Dr. Simon MORGAN-RUSSELL
106	Exec Director On-line Programs	Dr. Marcia SALAZAR-VALENTINE
85	Exec Dir International Student Svcs	Dr. Marcia SALAZAR-VALENTINE
21	Exec Dir of Business Operations	Mr. Bradley K. LEIGH
07	Asst VP/Director Admissions	Mr. Gary D. SWEGAN
21	Dir Budgeting & Resource Planning	Mr. Geofrey L. TRACY
09	Director of Institutional Research	Vacant
06	University Registrar	Mr. Christopher P. COX
40	Director Bookstore	Mr. Jeffrey D. NELSON
19	Director Public Safety	Ms. Monica M. MOLL
36	Director Career Center	Mr. Jeff JACKSON
23	Exec Director Center for Health	Mr. Richard G. SIPP
38	Director Counseling Center	Dr. Garrett GILMER
37	Director Student Financial Aid	Ms. Laura EMCH
23	Asst Director Center for Health	Ms. Marlene REYNOLDS
44	Director of Annual Giving	Ms. Shannon SPENCER
101	Secretary to the Board	Dr. Patrick PAUKEN
88	Co-Gen Manager WBGU Public Media	Mr. Anthony E. SHORT
88	Co-Gen Manager WBGU Public Media	Ms. Tina L. SIMON
35	Director TRIO Collegiate Services	Mr. Sidney CHILDS
21	Internal Auditing & Adv Svcs	Mr. James LAMBERT
88	Director Women's Center	Dr. Mary M. KRUEGER
88	Assoc Director Disability Services	Ms. Peggy DENNIS
88	Dir President's Leadership Acad	Dr. Julie A. SNYDER
88	Director Dining Services	Mr. Michael L. PAULUS
96	Director of Business Operations	Mr. Andrew D. GRANT
88	Director Student Employment	Ms. Dawn CHONG
88	Director Learning Commons	Mr. Mark NELSON
88	Director Advising Services	Mr. Dermot M. FORDE
88	Asst VP Non-Trad & Transfer Svcs	Dr. Barbara L. HENRY
20	Vice Provost Academic Operations	Dr. Joseph FRIZADO
65	Dir Sch Earth/Environ & Society	Dr. Charles ONASCH

Bowling Green State University Firelands College (A)

One University Drive, Huron OH 44839-9719
Telephone: (419) 433-5560 FICE Identification: 007856
Accreditation: &NH, CAHIIM, COARC

† Main campus is Bowling Green State University in Bowling Green, OH.

Bradford School (B)

2469 Stelzer Road, Columbus OH 43219-3129
County: Franklin FICE Identification: 004853
Unit ID: 202161
Telephone: (614) 416-6200 Carnegie Class: Assoc/PrivFP
FAX Number: (614) 416-6210 Calendar System: Semester
URL: www.bradfordschoolcolumbus.edu
Established: 1985 Annual Undergrad Tuition & Fees: $13,980
Enrollment: 543 Coed
Affiliation or Control: Proprietary IRS Status: Proprietary
Highest Offering: Associate Degree
Program: Occupational
Accreditation: ACICS, MAC, @PTAA

01	President	Mr. Dennis BARTELS
05	Director of Education	Ms. Barbara ELLISON
07	Director of Admissions	Ms. Raeann LEE

Brown Mackie College-Akron (C)

755 White Pond Drive, Suite 101, Akron OH 44320-4221
Telephone: (330) 869-3600 Identification: 666470
Accreditation: ACICS, OTA, SURGT

† Main campus is The Art Institute of Phoenix in Phoenix, AZ.

Brown Mackie College-Cincinnati (D)

1011 Glendale-Milford Road, Cincinnati OH 45215-1107
Telephone: (513) 771-2424 FICE Identification: 005127
Accreditation: ACICS, MAC, SURGT

† Main campus is The Art Institute of Phoenix in Phoenix, AZ.

Brown Mackie College-Findlay (E)

1700 Fostoria Avenue, Suite 100, Findlay OH 45840-6857
Telephone: (419) 423-2211 FICE Identification: 026162
Accreditation: ACICS, OTA, SURGT

† Main campus is The Art Institute of Phoenix in Phoenix, AZ.

Brown Mackie College-North Canton (F)

4300 Munson Street, NW, Canton OH 44718-3674
Telephone: (330) 494-1214 FICE Identification: 030778
Accreditation: ACICS, SURTEC

† Main campus is The Art Institute of Phoenix in Phoenix, AZ.

Bryant & Stratton College (G)

12955 Snow Road, Parma OH 44130-1013
Telephone: (216) 265-3151 FICE Identification: 022744
Accreditation: &M, MAC

† Main campus is Bryant & Stratton College in Buffalo, NY.

Capital University (H)

1 College and Main Street, Columbus OH 43209-2394
County: Franklin FICE Identification: 003023
Unit ID: 201548
Telephone: (614) 236-6011 Carnegie Class: Master's M
FAX Number: (614) 236-6820 Calendar System: Semester
URL: www.capital.edu
Established: 1850 Annual Undergrad Tuition & Fees: $31,990
Enrollment: 3,584 Coed
Affiliation or Control: Evangelical Lutheran Church In America
IRS Status: 501(c)3
Highest Offering: First Professional Degree
Program: Liberal Arts And General; Teacher Preparatory; Professional
Accreditation: NH, ACBSP, LAW, MUS, NURSE, SW, TED

01	President	Dr. Denvy A. BOWMAN
05	Vice Pres Academic/Student Affairs	Dr. Richard M. ASHBROOK
10	Vice President Business & Finance	Ms. Susan E. TATE
45	Exec VP Planning & Advancement	Dr. Kevin W. SAYERS
32	Assoc VP for Student Affairs	Dr. Betty M. LOVELACE-ROSS
30	Assoc Vice Pres Advancement	Ms. Jennifer PATTERSON
84	Assoc VP Enrollment Services	Dr. Amy ADAMS
26	Asst Vice Pres External Relations	Ms. Patricia CRAMER
21	Associate VP Business & Finance	Ms. Lori MCKIRNAN
44	Asst Vice President Major Gifts	Ms. April NOVOTNY
43	University Counsel	Dr. Tanya J. POTEET
20	Associate Provost	Dr. Terry D. LAHM
100	Chief of Staff	Ms. Susan MERRYMAN
101	Dir Pres Ofc/Liaison to Board Trust	Ms. Nona S. MCGUIRE
27	Dir Communications/Media Relations	Ms. D. Nichole JOHNSON
09	Director of Institutional Research	Dr. Larry T. HUNTER
06	Registrar	Mr. Brent KOERBER
37	Director of Financial Aid	Ms. Susan E. KANNENWISCHER
07	Director of Admissions	Ms. Amanda SOHL
29	Director Alumni/Parent Relations	Ms. Diane LOESER
36	Director of Career Services	Mr. Eric R. ANDERSON
08	University Librarian/Director IMC	Vacant
87	Director of Summer Programs	Dr. Jerry P. THOMAS
88	Academic Service Coordinator	Mr. Bruce EPPS
26	Director Public Relations	Ms. Denise RUSSELL
41	Athletic Director	Dr. Steve BRUNING
13	Int Director Information Technology	Mr. Jeff GUILER
85	Director Intl Education & ESL Pgm	Ms. Jennifer ADAMS
35	Director Student Activities	Vacant
18	Director Facilities Management	Ms. Beth Anne CARMAN
15	Director of Human Resources	Ms. Theresa FELDMEIER
38	Dir Univ Counseling/Health Svcs	Dr. Cathy MCDANIELS WILSON
28	Dir Diversity/Multicultural Affairs	Ms. Cynthia DUNCAN JOSEPH
92	Honors Program	Dr. Dina LENTSNER
40	Manager Bookstore	Mr. Joseph AMBUSKE
42	Dean of the Chapel	Mr. Gary SANDBERG
61	Dean of Law School	Mr. Richard SIMPSON
49	Dean Unified College	Dr. Cedric ADDERLEY
64	Ast Dn Conservtry of Music/Sch Comm	Dr. Lynn ROSEBERRY
50	Asst Dean Sch Management/Leadership	Dr. Keirsten MOORE
66	Asst Dean Sch Nat Sci/Nursing/Hlth	Dr. Jens HEMMINGSEN
83	Asst Dean Sch Social Sciences/Educ	Dr. Jody FOURNIER
79	Assistant Dean School of Humanities	Vacant

Capital University Law School (I)

303 East Broad Street, Columbus OH 43215
Telephone: (614) 236-6500 Identification: 770347
Accreditation: &NH

† Main campus is Capital University in Columbus, OH.

Case Western Reserve University (J)

10900 Euclid Avenue, Cleveland OH 44106-7001
County: Cuyahoga FICE Identification: 003024
Unit ID: 201645
Telephone: (216) 368-2000 Carnegie Class: RU/VH
FAX Number: N/A Calendar System: Semester
URL: www.case.edu
Established: 1826 Annual Undergrad Tuition & Fees: $41,800
Enrollment: 10,026 Coed
Affiliation or Control: Independent Non-Profit IRS Status: 501(c)3
Highest Offering: Doctorate
Program: Liberal Arts And General; Professional
Accreditation: NH, AA, ANEST, BUS, BUSA, CLPSY, CS, DENT, DIETD, DIETI, ENG, LAW, MED, MIDWF, MUS, NUR, NURSE, PH, SP, SW, TEAC

01	President	Ms. Barbara R. SNYDER
05	Provost/Executive Vice President	Dr. William A. BAESLACK, III
20	Deputy Provost/VP Academic Affairs	Dr. Lynn T. SINGER
10	Senior Vice Pres for Finance & CFO	Mr. John F. SIDERAS
11	Senior Vice Pres for Administration	Mr. John D. WHEELER
30	Sr VP for Univ Rels & Development	Mr. Bruce A. LOESSIN
17	Vice President Medical Affairs	Dr. Pamela B. DAVIS
46	Vice President for Research	Dr. Robert H. MILLER
13	Interim VP for Information Services	Mr. Mark HENDERSON
32	Vice President for Student Affairs	Mr. Louis W. STARK
18	VP Campus Planning/Facilities Mgmt	Mr. Stephen CAMPBELL
16	Vice President for Human Resources	Ms. Carolyn GREGORY
43	Vice President/General Counsel	Ms. Elizabeth KEEFER
19	Vice President for Campus Services	Mr. Richard J. JAMIESON
26	Vice Pres for University Relations	Ms. Lara A. KALAFATIS
86	Asso VP Govt & Foundation Relations	Dr. Julie M. REHM
86	Exec Director Government Relations	Ms. Jennifer RUGGLES
31	Sr Director Local Govt and Comm Rel	Ms. Latisha JAMES
45	Vice Pres for University Planning	Ms. Christine A. ASH
84	Vice Pres for Enrollment Management	Mr. Richard W. BISCHOFF
28	VP Inclusion/Diversity/Equal Opptny	Dr. Marilyn S. MOBLEY
26	VP Univ Marketing/Communications	Ms. Chris SHERIDAN
88	Treasurer	Mr. Robert C. BROWN
88	Chief Investment Officer	Ms. Sally STALEY
20	Vice Provost Undergrad Education	Dr. Donald L. FEKE
88	Assoc Prov for International Affs	Mr. David FLESHLER
100	Chief of Staff	Ms. Jennifer CIMPERMAN
88	Dean of Undergraduate Studies	Mr. Jeffrey WOLCOWITZ
21	Controller	Mr. Bradley W. FRALIC
06	Registrar	Ms. Amy S. HAMMETT
29	Associate VP for Alumni Relations	Mr. Christopher J. VLAHOS
37	Director of Financial Aid	Ms. Venus PULIAFICO
07	Director Undergraduate Admissions	Mr. Robert R. MCCULLOUGH
08	University Librarian	Mr. Arnold HIRSHON
36	Director Career Center	Dr. Thomas MATTHEWS
85	Dir International Student Svcs	Ms. Marielena MAGGIO
38	Director University Counseling Svcs	Dr. James E. SELLERS
09	Director of Institutional Research	Ms. Jean E. GUBBINS
96	Dir Procurement/Distribution Svcs	Ms. Melinda BOYKIN
41	Athletic Director	Dr. David DILES
61	Dean of Law	Mr. Lawrence E. MITCHELL
49	Dean of Arts & Sciences	Dr. Cyrus C. TAYLOR
63	Dean of Medicine	Dr. Pamela B. DAVIS
66	Dean of Nursing	Dr. Mary E. KERR
52	Dean of Dental Medicine	Dr. Jerold S. GOLDBERG
50	Dean of Management	Dr. Robert E. WIDING, II
70	Dean Applied Social Science	Dr. Grover C. GILMORE
54	Dean of Engineering	Dr. Jeffrey DUERK
58	Dean of Graduate Studies	Dr. Charles E. ROZEK

Cedarville University (K)

251 N Main Street, Cedarville OH 45314-0601
County: Greene FICE Identification: 003025
Unit ID: 201654
Telephone: (937) 766-2211 Carnegie Class: Bac/Diverse
FAX Number: (937) 766-2760 Calendar System: Semester
URL: www.cedarville.edu
Established: 1887 Annual Undergrad Tuition & Fees: $28,536
Enrollment: 3,038 Coed
Affiliation or Control: Baptist IRS Status: 501(c)3
Highest Offering: Doctorate
Program: Liberal Arts And General; Teacher Preparatory; Professional
Accreditation: NH, ACBSP, CS, ENG, MUS, NURSE, @PHAR, SW, TED

01	President	Dr. William E. BROWN
03	Provost	Dr. John W. GREDY
05	Academic Vice President	Dr. Thomas H. CORNMAN
10	Sr Vice President for Business	Mr. Christopher SOHN
30	Vice President for Advancement	Mr. William L. BIGHAM
32	Vice President for Student Life	Dr. Carl A. RUBY
42	Vice Pres for Christian Ministry	Rev. Robert K. ROHM
84	Vice Pres Enrollment Management	Mrs. Janice SUPPLEE
43	General Counsel	Mr. John HART
11	Assoc VP for Operations	Mr. Rodney JOHNSON
06	Asst Acad VP Stdnt Success/Registr	Mrs. Frances CAMPBELL
106	Sr Assoc Acad VP Col Extended Lrng	Dr. Andy RUNYAN
16	Assoc VP of Human Resources	Mrs. Lisa TODD
13	Assoc VP Information Technology/CIO	Dr. David L. ROTMAN
09	Associate VP for Strategic Planning	Mr. David ORMSBEE
69	Assoc VP Col of Health Professions	Dr. Pamela D. JOHNSON
49	Assoc Acad VP Col of Arts & Sci	Dr. Steven WINTEREGG
107	Assoc Acad VP Col of Professions	Dr. Mark MCCLAIN
08	Asst Acad VP of Library Services	Mr. Lynn A. BROCK
67	Dean School of Pharmacy	Dr. Marc SWEENEY
32	Dean of Students	Miss Kirsten GIBBS
34	Assoc Dean Women	Miss Rebecca STOWERS
35	Associate Dean Campus Life	Mr. Brad D. SMITH
37	Executive Director of Financial Aid	Mr. Kim JENERETTE
07	Director of Admissions	Miss Amy HOLDERBY
38	Director of Counseling Services	Mr. John M. POTTER
29	Director of Alumni Relations	Mr. Jeff BESTE
36	Director Career Services	Mr. Jeff REEP
87	Director Summer School/Cont Educ	Dr. Jewerl MAXWELL
92	Director Honors Program	Dr. David MILLS
96	Director of Purchasing/Inventory	Mr. Tim P. JOHNSON
04	Executive Asst to the President	Mrs. Carol S. GEORGE

41 Athletic Director .... Dr. Alan GEIST
26 Exec Director of Public Relations .... Mr. Mark WEINSTEIN
19 Director of Campus Safety .... Mr. Douglas W. CHISHOLM
40 Manager of Retail Services .... Mrs. Tammy L. SLONE

Central Ohio Technical College (A)

1179 University Drive, Newark OH 43055-1767

County: Licking FICE Identification: 011046
Unit ID: 201672
Telephone: (740) 366-1351 Carnegie Class: Assoc/Pub-S-SC
FAX Number: (740) 366-5047 Calendar System: Semester
URL: www.cotc.edu
Established: 1971 Annual Undergrad Tuition & Fees (In-State): $6,300
Enrollment: 3,718 Coed
Affiliation or Control: State IRS Status: 501(c)3
Highest Offering: Associate Degree
Program: Occupational; 2-Year Principally Bachelor's Creditable; Technical Emphasis
Accreditation: NH, ADNUR, DMS, RAD, SURGT

01 President .... Dr. Bonnie L. COE
10 Vice President Business & Finance .... Mr. David BRILLHART
05 Chief Academic Officer .... Dr. Mark KNUTSEN
32 Director of Student Life .... Dr. John BERRY
15 VP for Instnl Planning & HR Develop .... Ms. Jacqueline PARRILL
08 Director of Library .... Ms. Susan SCOTT
06 Records Manager/Registrar .... Ms. Veronica RINE
07 Director of Enrollment Management .... Ms. Tara HOUDESHELL
88 Director Child Development Center .... Vacant
27 Director Marketing/Public Relations .... Ms. Alice HUTZEL-BATESON
37 Director Financial Aid/Veteran Affs .... Ms. Faith PHILLIPS
19 Director Public Safety .... Mr. Denny HOLLERN
29 Dir Alumni Rels/Development Officer .... Mr. Matthew KELLY
35 Asst Director of Student Affairs .... Ms. Holly MASON
13 Chief Information Officer .... Mr. Howard IMHOF
38 Program Mgr Learn Asst Ctr Disabled .... Ms. Connie ZANG
11 Director of Academic Operations .... Ms. Cathie CLIPPINGER
96 Manager of Purchasing .... Ms. Kimberley SIBERT
18 Manager Facilities .... Mr. Brian BOEHMER
51 Coord of Community Svc/Learning .... Ms. Vorley TAYLOR
36 Dir Career Dev & Experiential Lrng .... Mr. Derek THATCHER
12 Coshocton Campus Administrator .... Vacant
12 Knox Campus Administrator .... Vacant
12 Pataskala Campus Administrator .... Vacant
04 Assistant to the President .... Ms. Jan TOMLINSON

Central Ohio Technical College Coshoctin Campus (B)

200 North Whitewoman Street, Coshoctin OH 43812
Telephone: (740) 622-1408 Identification: 770348
Accreditation: &NH

† Main campus is Central Ohio Technical College in Newark, OH.

Central Ohio Technical College Knox Campus (C)

236 South Main Street, Mount Vernon OH 43050
Telephone: (740) 392-2526 Identification: 770350
Accreditation: &NH

† Main campus is Central Ohio Technical College in Newark, OH.

Central Ohio Technical College Pataskala Campus (D)

8660 East Broad Street, Reynoldsburg OH 43068
Telephone: (740) 964-7090 Identification: 770351
Accreditation: &NH

† Main campus is Central Ohio Technical College in Newark, OH.

Central State University (E)

PO Box 1004, 1400 Brush Row Road,
Wilberforce OH 45384-1004
County: Greene FICE Identification: 003026
Unit ID: 201690
Telephone: (937) 376-6332 Carnegie Class: Bac/Diverse
FAX Number: (937) 376-6138 Calendar System: Semester
URL: www.centralstate.edu
Established: 1887 Annual Undergrad Tuition & Fees (In-State): $5,870
Enrollment: 2,152 Coed
Affiliation or Control: State IRS Status: 501(c)3
Highest Offering: Master's
Program: Liberal Arts And General; Teacher Preparatory; Business Emphasis
Accreditation: NH, ART, ENG, MUS, TED

01 President .... Dr. Cynthia JACKSON-HAMMOND
04 Exec Asst to the President .... Mrs. Wendy HAYES
05 Provost/VP Academic Affairs .... Dr. Charles WESLEY FORD
10 Vice President Admin & Finance .... Mrs. Daarel BURNETTE
30 Vice Pres Institutional Advancement .... Mr. Anthony FAIRBANKS
11 Asst VP Administration & Finance .... Vacant
32 Vice President for Student Affairs .... Mr. Jerryl BRIGGS
13 Vice Pres/Chief Information Officer .... Dr. Donald STEWARD
20 Assoc Vice Pres Academic Affairs .... Dr. Willie HOUSTON
06 Registrar .... Mrs. LaTonya BRANHAM
07 Director of Admissions .... Ms. Robin RUCKER
08 Director of Hallie Q Brown Library .... Mr. Johnny JACKSON
89 Int Dean Ctr Stdnt Academic Success .... Dr. LaKeysha CATRON
12 Dean CSU Dayton Campus .... Dr. Kaye JETER
09 Director Assessment/Inst Research .... Mr. Mohammad ALI
19 Chief of Police .... Chief Anthony PETTIFORD
26 Director Public Relations .... Dr. Gayle BARGE
23 Medical Director .... Dr. Karen MATHEWS
29 Director Alumni Relations .... Mr. Keith PERKINS
88 Director Career Services .... Ms. Elizabeth BEEMER
37 Director Student Financial Aid .... Ms. Sonia SLOMBIA
39 Director Residence Life .... Mr. Raynaldo GILLUS
41 Athletic Director .... Mr. Jahan CULBREATH
42 Director Campus Ministry .... Rev. Nigel FELDER
46 Director Sponsored Pgms/Research .... Mr. Morakinyo KUTI
49 Int Dean Coll Humanities/Arts & Sci .... Dr. Lovette CHINWAH
50 Dean College Business & Industry .... Dr. Charles SHOWELL, JR.
53 Dean College of Education .... Dr. Reginald NNAZOR
15 Director of Human Resources .... Ms. Kimberly MANIGAULT
21 Director Business Svcs/Capital Dev .... Mr. Harlan HENDERSON
25 Director Grants Accounting .... Vacant
92 Director Honors Program .... Vacant
21 Controller .... Ms. Beth ANDERSON
21 Budget Director .... Mr. Curtis PETTIS
38 Director Student Counseling .... Mr. Frank PORTER

Chamberlain College of Nursing-Cleveland (F)

6700 Euclid Avenue, Suite 201, Cleveland OH 44103
Telephone: (216) 361-6005 Identification: 770505
Accreditation: &NH, NURSE

† Main campus is Chamberlain College of Nursing - Addison in Addison, IL.

Chamberlain College of Nursing-Columbus Campus (G)

1350 Alum Creek Drive, Columbus OH 43209
Telephone: (614) 252-8890 Identification: 770499
Accreditation: &NH, ADNUR, NURSE

† Main campus is Chamberlain College of Nursing - Addison in Addison, IL.

Chatfield College (H)

20918 State Route 251, Saint Martin OH 45118-9059
County: Brown FICE Identification: 010880
Unit ID: 201751
Telephone: (513) 875-3344 Carnegie Class: Assoc/PrivNFP
FAX Number: (513) 875-3912 Calendar System: Semester
URL: www.chatfield.edu
Established: 1971 Annual Undergrad Tuition & Fees: $10,815
Enrollment: 424 Coed
Affiliation or Control: Independent Non-Profit IRS Status: 501(c)3
Highest Offering: Associate Degree
Program: 2-Year Principally Bachelor's Creditable; Fine Arts Emphasis
Accreditation: NH

01 President .... Mr. John P. TAFARO
11 Vice President & COO .... Mr. David J. LAUB
05 Chief Academic Officer/Dean .... Mr. Alan D. SIMMONS
10 Director of Finance .... Ms. Mary R. JACOBS
30 Director of Advancement .... Mr. Steve RANIERI
07 Director of Admissions .... Mr. John PENROSE
20 Associate Dean/Site Director .... Ms. Wanda HILL
20 Associate Dean/Site Director .... Sr. Patricia HOMAN
26 Director of Marketing Communication .... Ms. Pamela SPENCER

The Christ College of Nursing and Health Sciences (I)

2139 Auburn Avenue, Cincinnati OH 45219
County: Hamilton FICE Identification: 006489
Unit ID: 201821
Telephone: (513) 585-2401 Carnegie Class: Assoc/PrivNFP
FAX Number: (513) 585-3540 Calendar System: Semester
URL: www.thechristcollege.edu
Established: 2006 Annual Undergrad Tuition & Fees: $16,700
Enrollment: 357 Coed
Affiliation or Control: Independent Non-Profit IRS Status: 501(c)3
Highest Offering: Associate Degree
Program: 2-Year Principally Bachelor's Creditable; Nursing Emphasis
Accreditation: NH, ADNUR

01 President .... Dr. Nathan A. LONG
05 Provost and Chief Academic Officer .... Dr. Michael SMITH
09 Dean Inst Planning & Research .... Ms. Carolyn A. HUNTER
24 Dean Educational Technology .... Dr. Meghan E. HOLLOWELL
88 Dir Inst Clinical Learning Excelle .... Ms. Linda TURPIN
88 Dir Inst Organizational Excellence .... Ms. Regina TROXELL
08 Director Library Services .... Ms. Regina HARTMAN
06 Registrar .... Mr. Perry CARROLL

Cincinnati Christian University (J)

2700 Glenway Avenue, Cincinnati OH 45204-3200
County: Hamilton FICE Identification: 003029
Unit ID: 201858
Telephone: (513) 244-8100 Carnegie Class: Spec/Faith
FAX Number: (513) 244-8140 Calendar System: Semester
URL: www.ccuniversity.edu
Established: 1924 Annual Undergrad Tuition & Fees: $14,766
Enrollment: 1,112 Coed
Affiliation or Control: Christian Churches And Churches of Christ
IRS Status: 501(c)3
Highest Offering: First Professional Degree
Program: Liberal Arts And General; Professional; Religious Emphasis
Accreditation: NH, BI, MUS, TEAC, THEOL

01 President .... Dr. David M. FAUST
05 Chief Academic Officer .... Dr. Tom THATCHER
32 Vice Pres Leadership Development .... Vacant
30 Vice President for Advancement .... Vacant
10 Vice President Finance & Operations .... Mr. Chuck ABBOTT
20 Dean of Seminary .... Dr. David RAY
51 Dean of College of Adult Learning .... Ms. Judy PRATT
73 Dean of Russell School of Ministry .... Mr. Mike SHANNON
49 Dean Biblical Studies/Arts & Sci .... Mr. Paul FRISKNEY
53 Dean Education/Behavioral Sciences .... Mrs. Jodie EDWARDS
50 Dean of School of Business .... Mr. Aaron BURGESS
108 Dean of Institutional Effectiveness .... Mrs. Sara FUDGE
09 Dean of Dist Educ & Inst Research .... Vacant
06 Registrar .... Mr. Don A. THOMASON
08 Director of Libraries .... Mr. James H. LLOYD
35 Dean of Students .... Mrs. Kristin MERRILL
33 Dean of Men/Campus Minister .... Mr. Dan BURTON
37 Director of Financial Aid .... Mrs. Linda WAUGH
84 Director of Enrollment Services .... Mr. Jeffrey DERICO
07 Director Undergraduate Admissions .... Mr. David BRUNNER
29 Director of Alumni Ministries .... Vacant
21 Accounting Manager .... Mr. Randy KOEHLER
88 Dir Center for Church Advancement .... Vacant
41 Director of Athletics .... Mr. Joshua SNYDER
18 Director of Operations .... Vacant
15 Human Resources Director .... Mrs. Nancy HARTMAN
14 Director of Computer Services .... Mr. James MCINTYRE
19 Director of Security .... Mrs. Karen LITTLE
40 Manager of Bookstore .... Miss Beth ROGERS
07 Director of Graduate Admissions .... Mr. Alex EDDY
38 Director Student Counseling .... Dr. Tim BARBER
28 Director of Urban/Global Outreach .... Mr. Steve SKAGGS
105 Digital Strategist .... Mr. Steve CARR
04 Assistant to the President .... Mrs. Wendy SPALDING

Cincinnati College of Mortuary Science (K)

645 W North Bend Road, Cincinnati OH 45224-1462
County: Hamilton FICE Identification: 010906
Unit ID: 201867
Telephone: (513) 761-2020 Carnegie Class: Spec/Other
FAX Number: (513) 761-3333 Calendar System: Quarter
URL: www.ccms.edu
Established: 1882 Annual Undergrad Tuition & Fees: $20,750
Enrollment: 111 Coed
Affiliation or Control: Independent Non-Profit IRS Status: 501(c)3
Highest Offering: Baccalaureate
Program: Occupational; Liberal Arts And General
Accreditation: NH, FUSER

01 President .... Mr. Gene KRAMER
07 Admissions/Registrar .... Ms. Blanche KABENGELE
37 Financial Aid Director .... Mr. Russ ROMANDINI

Cincinnati State Technical and Community College (L)

3520 Central Parkway, Cincinnati OH 45223-2690
County: Hamilton FICE Identification: 010345
Unit ID: 201928
Telephone: (513) 569-1500 Carnegie Class: Assoc/Pub-U-SC
FAX Number: (513) 569-1495 Calendar System: Other
URL: www.cincinnatistate.edu
Established: 1966 Annual Undergrad Tuition & Fees (In-State): $4,523
Enrollment: 10,614 Coed
Affiliation or Control: State IRS Status: 501(c)3
Highest Offering: Associate Degree
Program: Occupational; 2-Year Principally Bachelor's Creditable; Business Emphasis
Accreditation: NH, ACFEI, ADNUR, CAHIIM, COARC, CONST, DIETT, DMS, ENGT, IFSAC, MAC, MLTAD, OTA, SURGT

01 President .... Dr. O'dell OWENS
03 Executive Vice President .... Ms. Carla CHANCE
05 Academic Vice President .... Dr. Monica POSEY
13 Vice President of IT/CIO .... Dr. David HICKEY
10 Vice President Finance/Treasurer .... Mr. Michael GEOGHEGAN
26 Vice Pres Marketing/Communications .... Ms. Jean MANNING
72 Dean of Engineering Technology .... Mr. Doug BOWLING
50 Dean of Business Technologies .... Dr. Nick NISSLEY
76 Dean Health/Public Safety .... Dr. Jean CHAPPELL
81 Dean Humanities/Sciences .... Ms. Robbin HOOPES
84 Dean Enrollment/Student Development .... Dr. Wendy BOLT
06 Registrar .... Mr. Ryan HUNT
08 Library Director .... Mrs. Cindy SEFTON
41 Dir Athletics/Student Activities .... Mr. Tom HATHAWAY
18 Director of Facilities .... Mr. Rob EPLING
103 Exec Director Workforce Development .... Dr. Dennis ULRICH
09 Director of Institutional Research .... Ms. Anne FOSTER
07 Director of Admissions .... Ms. Gabriele BOECKERMANN
15 Director of Human Resources .... Ms. Lisa EVANS
32 Chief Student Life Officer .... Ms. Brenda MAPLES-STERRY

35 Director of Student Affairs .... Mrs. Sharon DAVIS
96 Director of Purchasing .... Mr. Brian FRANK
92 Coordinator Honors Program .... Dr. Andrea LESLIE
30 Director of Development .... Ms. Dawn PERRIN
86 Director of Government Affairs .... Ms. Nan KOHNEN-CAHALL
04 Executive Administrative Associate ....Mrs. Michelle GRIFFIN-DONALDSON
19 Director of Public Safety ....Mr. Michael WYLIE
37 Director of Financial Aid .... Mrs. La Saundra CRAIG
101 Secretary to the Board of Trustees .... Mrs. Nancy STUBBEMAN
88 Director of Student Success ....Mr. Martino HARMON
25 Contract Administrator .... Mrs. Ann JAMES

Clark State Community College (A)

570 E Leffel Lane, PO Box 570,
Springfield OH 45501-0570
County: Clark FICE Identification: 004852
Unit ID: 201973
Telephone: (937) 325-0691 Carnegie Class: Assoc/Pub-U-SC
FAX Number: (937) 328-6142 Calendar System: Quarter
URL: www.clarkstate.edu
Established: 1966 Annual Undergrad Tuition & Fees (In-State): $5,640
Enrollment: 5,168 Coed
Affiliation or Control: State IRS Status: 501(c)3
Highest Offering: Associate Degree
Program: Occupational; 2-Year Principally Bachelor's Creditable
Accreditation: NH, ADNUR, MAC, MLTAD, PTAA

01 President .... Dr. Jo A. BLONDIN
05 Vice Pres Academic/Student Affairs .... Dr. David H. DEVIER
10 Vice President Business Affairs .... Joseph R. JACKSON
30 Vice President of Advancement ....Kristin J. CULP
21 Controller ....Dixie A. DEPEW
12 Interim Dean Greene Center ....Dr. Edward J. BUSHER
08 Director Library Services .... Beth DEGER
32 Dean of Stdnt Affs/Enrollment Mgmt ....Dr. Edward J. BUSHER
49 Dean Arts & Sciences/Public Svcs .... Martha CRAWMER
50 Dean Business/Applied Technologies .... Jane A. CAPE
76 Dean Health and Human Services .... Kathleen J. WILCOX
37 Financial Aid Director ....Kathy A. KLAY
06 Registrar ....Diane SEAMAN
07 Director of Admissions ....Corey HOLLIDAY
13 Exec Dir Information Technology ....Matt FRANZ
102 Foundation/Executive Director ....Kristin J. CULP
45 Dir of Inst Research and Planning .... Cynthia APPLIN
15 Director of Human Resources ....Marvin NEPHEW
57 Director of Performing Arts Center ....Stuart A. SECTTOR
18 Dir Facilities/Oper/Maintenance ....Randall CONOVER
41 Dir Athletics/Act & Evening Svcs .... Ronald GORDON
51 Program Mgr Continuing Education ....Vacant
09 Institutional Research Technician .... Leeann PERKINS

Clark State Community College Greene Center (B)

3775 Pentagon Boulevard, Beavercreek OH 45431
Telephone: (937) 429-8819 Identification: 770352
Accreditation: &NH

† Main campus is Clark State Community College in Springfield, OH.

Cleveland Institute of Art (C)

11141 East Boulevard, Cleveland OH 44106-1710
County: Cuyahoga FICE Identification: 003982
Unit ID: 202046
Telephone: (216) 421-7000 Carnegie Class: Spec/Arts
FAX Number: (216) 421-7438 Calendar System: Semester
URL: www.cia.edu
Established: 1882 Annual Undergrad Tuition & Fees: $34,270
Enrollment: 556 Coed
Affiliation or Control: Independent Non-Profit IRS Status: 501(c)3
Highest Offering: Baccalaureate
Program: Professional; Fine Arts Emphasis
Accreditation: NH, ART

01 President a& CEO .... Mr. Grafton J. NUNES
05 VP Academic & Faculty Affairs .... Mr. Chris WHITTEY
30 Sr Vice Pres Inst Advancement ....Mr. Michael COLE
10 Vice President Business Affairs/CFO .... Mrs. Almut ZVOSEC
26 Vice President Mktg & Communication .... Mr. Mark INGLIS
07 Exec Dir Enrollment & Financial Aid ....Mr. Robert BORDEN
37 Asst Director of Financial Aid ....Ms. Delores HALL
06 Registrar ....Mrs. Karen HUDY
08 Librarian .... Ms. Cristine ROM
07 Director of Admissions .... Ms. Joanne LANDERS
18 Director Safety & Facility Mgmt ....Mr. Howard D. WEINER
29 Director Annual Giving/Alumni Rels .... Mr. Michael KINSELLA
20 Director of Academic Services .... Ms. Anne GATES
44 Director Major Gifts/Planned Giving ....Ms. Margaret GUDBRANSON
15 Exec Dir of HR & Inclusion .... Mr. Raymond SCRAGG
32 Dean of Student Affairs ....Ms. Nancy NEVILLE
37 Director of Financial Aid ....Mr. Martin CARNEY
26 Director of Mktg & Communications ....Ms. Ann MCGUIRE
57 Art Director ....Mr. Richard SARIAN

Cleveland Institute of Electronics (D)

1776 E 17th Street, Cleveland OH 44114-3679
County: Cuyahoga FICE Identification: 005210
Unit ID: 202064
Telephone: (216) 781-9400 Carnegie Class: Assoc/PrivFP
FAX Number: (216) 781-0331 Calendar System: Other
URL: www.cie-wc.edu
Established: 1934 Annual Undergrad Tuition & Fees: $4,150
Enrollment: 1,648 Coed
Affiliation or Control: Proprietary IRS Status: Proprietary
Highest Offering: Associate Degree
Program: Occupational
Accreditation: DETC

01 President .... Mr. J. Randall DRINKO
37 Director of Financial Aid .... Mr. Scott KATZENMEYER
88 Coordinator Veteran Affairs .... Mrs. Marites CAPISTRANO

Cleveland Institute of Music (E)

11021 East Boulevard, Cleveland OH 44106-1776
County: Cuyahoga FICE Identification: 003031
Unit ID: 202073
Telephone: (216) 791-5000 Carnegie Class: Spec/Arts
FAX Number: (216) 791-3063 Calendar System: Semester
URL: www.cim.edu
Established: 1920 Annual Undergrad Tuition & Fees: $44,039
Enrollment: 450 Coed
Affiliation or Control: Independent Non-Profit IRS Status: 501(c)3
Highest Offering: Doctorate
Program: Professional; Music Emphasis
Accreditation: NH, MUS

01 President/CEO ....Mr. Joel SMIRNOFF
03 Vice President/COO/Asst Treasurer ....Mr. Eric BOWER
30 VP for Institutional Advancement ....Ms. Karin STONE
51 Dean Prep/Continuing Education .... Ms. Sandra SHAPIRO
05 Dean of Conservatory ....Dr. Adrian DALY
26 Director Marketing & Communications .... Ms. Susan ILER
13 Director Systems Management ....Ms. Aimee BARTON
07 Director Admission & Enrollment Mgt ....Ms. Lynn JOHNSON
32 Associate Dean of Student Affairs ....Mr. David GILSON
37 Director Financial Aid ....Ms. Kristine GRIPP
21 Chief Financial Office .... Ms. Kristen KOLLAR
06 Registrar ....Mrs. Hallie MOORE
15 Director Human Resources .... Mrs. Megan SWERBINSKY
08 Director of the Library ....Ms. Jean TOOMBS
18 Director Buildings & Grounds ....Mr. Alan VALEK
88 Director of Concerts & Events ....Ms. Lori WRIGHT
40 Bookstore Manager ....Ms. Antoinette MILLER
106 Director of Distance Learning ....Mr. Gregory HOWE

Cleveland State University (F)

2121 Euclid Avenue, Cleveland OH 44115-2214
County: Cuyahoga FICE Identification: 003032
Unit ID: 202134
Telephone: (216) 687-2000 Carnegie Class: RU/H
FAX Number: (216) 687-9366 Calendar System: Semester
URL: www.csuohio.edu
Established: 1964 Annual Undergrad Tuition & Fees (In-State): $9,449
Enrollment: 17,525 Coed
Affiliation or Control: State IRS Status: 501(c)3
Highest Offering: Doctorate
Program: Liberal Arts And General; Teacher Preparatory; Professional
Accreditation: NH, ARCPA, BUS, BUSA, CACREP, COPSY, ENG, ENGT, LAW, MUS, NURSE, OT, PH, PLNG, PTA, SP, SPAA, SW, TED

01 President .... Dr. Ronald M. BERKMAN
100 Chief of Staff .... Mr. Michael ARTBAUER
05 Provost ....Dr. Deirdre MAGEEAN
10 Vice President Business Affairs ....Ms. Stephanie MCHENRY
84 VP Enrollment/Student Affairs ..... Ms. Carmen ALVAREZ BROWN
09 VP Research & Graduate Studies .... Dr. Jerzy SAWICKI
31 Vice Pres University Engagement .... Dr. Byron WHITE
30 VP Univ Advancement/Exec Dir Found .... Ms. Berinthia LEVINE
45 Vice Provost for Academic Planning ....Dr. Teresa LAGRANGE
20 Vice Provost for Academic Affairs ....Dr. Vijaya KONANGI
26 Asst VP University Mktg/Admissions .... Mr. Robert SPADEMAN
15 Asst VP Human Resources ....Mr. Jesse DRUCKER
88 Asst VP Campus Support Services ....Ms. Clare RAHM
21 Controller/Assoc VP Finance .... Ms. Kathleen MURPHY
32 Dean of Student Life ....Dr. James DRNEK
49 Dean Coll Liberal Arts/Soc Sci ....Dr. Gregory M. SADLEK
81 Dean College of Science .... Dr. Meredith R. BOND
50 Dean Ahuja College Business Admin .... Dr. Joseph MAZZOLA
53 Dean College Education & Human Svcs ......Dr. Sajit ZACHARIAH
54 Dean Fenn College of Engineering .... Dr. Anette KARLSSON
58 Dean College Graduate Studies ....Dr. Jianping ZHU
61 Dean of College of Law ....Mr. Craig BOISE
80 Dean of College of Urban Affairs ....Dr. Edward HILL
43 General Counsel ....Ms. Sonali B. WILSON
86 Sr Advisor to Pres Government Rels ....Dr. William NAPIER
08 Director of Libraries ....Dr. Glenda THORNTON
22 Affirmative Affairs Officer .... Ms. Yulanda MCCARTY-HARRIS
07 Director Undergraduate Admissions .... Ms. Heike HEINRICH
09 Director Institutional Research ....Mr. Tom GEAGHAN
85 Director International Programs .... Mr. Harlan SMITH
36 Director Career Services .... Ms. Yolanda BURT
38 Director Counseling Services .... Dr. Janilee B. WHEATON
19 Asst VP Facilities & Safety ....Dr. Joseph HAN
37 Director Student Financial Aid .... Ms. Rachel SCHMIDT
06 Registrar ....Ms. Janet STIMPLE
41 Director of Athletics ....Mr. John PARRY
29 Director Alumni Affairs ....Mr. Brian BREITHOLZ
18 Chief Facilities/Physical Plant ....Mr. Shehadeh ABDELKARIM
96 Director of Purchasing ....Ms. Laurie MCCOMBS
92 Director Honors Program .... Dr. Peter MEIKSINS
28 Chief Diversity Officer .... Dr. Byron WHITE

College of Mount St. Joseph (G)

5701 Delhi Road, Cincinnati OH 45233-1670
County: Hamilton FICE Identification: 003033
Unit ID: 204200
Telephone: (513) 244-4200 Carnegie Class: Master's M
FAX Number: (513) 244-4654 Calendar System: Semester
URL: www.msj.edu
Established: 1920 Annual Undergrad Tuition & Fees: $25,800
Enrollment: 2,294 Coed
Affiliation or Control: Roman Catholic IRS Status: 501(c)3
Highest Offering: Doctorate
Program: Liberal Arts And General; Teacher Preparatory; Professional
Accreditation: NH, MUS, NURSE, PTA, SW, TEAC

01 President ....Dr. Anthony J. ARETZ
05 Vice President for Academic Affairs ....Dr. Alan DECOURCY
30 Vice Pres Institutional Advancement .... Ms. Patricia L. RAGIO
32 Vice President for Student Affairs ....Dr. Douglas K. FRIZZELL
10 Chief Financial Officer .... Ms. Anne Marie WAGNER
13 Chief Information Officer ....Mr. Keith A. WEBER
88 Chief Compliance and Risk Officer .... Ms. Linda PANZECA
58 Dean of Adult & Graduate Studies ....Dr. Darla VALE
20 Associate Academic Dean .... Ms. Maggie DAVIS
15 Assoc Director of Human Resources ....Ms. Ashley LITTON
35 Dean of Students ....Ms. Janet COX
06 Registrar .... Ms. Irene RICHARDSON
29 Director of Alumni Relations .... Ms. Jenny KAEPPNER
37 Director Student Admin Services ....Ms. Kathy KELLY
36 Interim Dir Career/Experi Educ ....Ms. Judi HEILE
25 Director Corporate & Found Rels ....Ms. Linda B. LIEBAU
18 Director Buildings & Grounds ....Mr. Dennis YOUNG
09 Director Institutional/Market Rsrch ... Mr. Joseph S. SPORTSMAN
07 Director of Admission ....Ms. Peggy MINNICH
21 Controller Fiscal Operations ....Ms. Liane BARBER
38 Director Wellness Center ....Ms. Patsy SCHWAIGER
08 Director Library ....Mr. Paul JENKINS
14 Director Instructional Technology ....Ms. Kim HUNTER
19 Director of Campus Police ....Mr. Tim CARNEY
41 Director of Athletics ....Mr. Steve RADCLIFFE
88 Director Learning Center ....Dr. Dana FREER
42 Director of Campus Ministry ....Sr. Nancy BRAMLAGE, SC
44 Director of Development ....Ms. Lisa ODENBECK
40 Manager of Bookstore ....Mr. Brad HOFFMAN
66 Interim Dean Div of Health Science ....Dr. Darla VALE
79 Interim Dean of Div of Arts & Hum ....Dr. Michael SONTAG
50 Dean of Business .... Dr. Jamal RASHED
53 Dean of Education ....Dr. Mary WEST
81 Dean Div of Behav/Natural Sci .... Dr. Diana DAVIS
26 Director of Marketing .... Ms. Kathleen LUNDRIGAN
91 Director Administrative Computing ....Mr. Dan LUKAC
88 Director of Online Initiatives .... Dr. Lynn BERTSCH
105 Webmaster ....Ms. Carolyn BOLAND
102 Director Donor Corporate Relations .... Ms. Susan BALLARD
88 Exec Dir Ethical Leadership Devel .... Dr. Tim BRYANT
44 Coordinator Annual Giving .... Ms. Alissa BECK
89 Coordinator First Year Experience .... Dr. Patty MILLS
23 Coordinator Health Services ....Ms. Linda PRUSS
39 Coordinator of Residence Life ....Mr. Warren GROVE
04 Admin Asst to the President .... Ms. Tina MERSMANN

The College of Wooster (H)

1189 Beall Avenue, Wooster OH 44691-2363
County: Wayne FICE Identification: 003037
Unit ID: 206589
Telephone: (330) 263-2000 Carnegie Class: Bac/A&S
FAX Number: (330) 263-2427 Calendar System: Semester
URL: www.wooster.edu
Established: 1866 Annual Undergrad Tuition & Fees: $41,680
Enrollment: 2,043 Coed
Affiliation or Control: Independent Non-Profit IRS Status: 501(c)3
Highest Offering: Baccalaureate
Program: Liberal Arts And General; Teacher Preparatory
Accreditation: NH, MUS, TED

01 President ....Dr. Grant H. CORNWELL
05 Provost ....Dr. Carolyn NEWTON
10 Vice Pres Finance/Bus/Treasurer ....Vacant
30 Vice President for Development ....Ms. Laurie HOUCK
84 Vice Pres Enrollment/College Rels .... Dr. Scott FRIEDHOFF
04 Administrative Asst to President ....Ms. Lynette ARNER
26 Assoc VP College Rels & Marketing ....Mr. John HOPKINS
18 Assc VP Facilities & Auxiliaries .... Ms. Jacqueline MIDDLETON
32 Dean of Students ....Mr. Kurt HOLMES
20 Dean Curriculum/Academic Engagement .... Dr. Henry B. KREUZMAN
20 Dean for Faculty Development ....Dr. Heather M. FITZGIBBON
07 Dean of Admissions ....Ms. Jennifer D. WINGE
35 Senior Associate Dean of Students ....Ms. Carolyn BUXTON
35 Assoc Dean of Students ....Ms. Robyn LADITKA
35 Assoc Dean of Students .... Ms. Christie KRACKER
28 Asst Dn Stdnts/Co-Dir Ctr for D&GE ....Ms. Susan LEE
85 Dir Office of Intl Student Affairs ....Mr. Yorgun MARCEL
09 Chief Information Planning Officer ....Dr. Ellen FALDUTO
06 Registrar ....Ms. Suzanne BATES
08 Director of Libraries ....Mr. Mark A. CHRISTEL
37 Director of Financial Aid ....Mr. Joseph WINGE
27 Director Office Public Information ....Mr. John FINN

29 Dir of Alumni Rels & Wooster Fund ...Ms. Heidi A. MCCORMICK
36 Director Career Services ....Ms. Lisa KASTOR
35 Dir Student Center/Stdnt Activities ....Vacant
41 Dir Phys Educ/Athletics/Recreat ....Dr. Keith BECKETT
18 Director Physical Plant Operations ....Mr. Doug LADITKA
19 Director Security/Protective Svcs ....Mr. Steven GLICK
16 Director of Human Resources ....Ms. Marcia BEASLEY
39 Director of Residence Life ....Ms. Krista KRONSTEIN
42 Camp Chaplain/Dir Intfth Camp Mins ....Rev. Linda MORGAN-CLEMENT
101 Secretary of College/Chief Staff ....Ms. Angela JOHNSTON

Columbus College of Art & Design (A)

60 Cleveland Avenue, Columbus OH 43215-1758
County: Franklin FICE Identification: 003039
Unit ID: 202170
Telephone: (614) 224-9101 Carnegie Class: Spec/Arts
FAX Number: (614) 222-4040 Calendar System: Semester
URL: www.ccad.edu
Established: 1879 Annual Undergrad Tuition & Fees: $28,872
Enrollment: 1,356 Coed
Affiliation or Control: Independent Non-Profit IRS Status: 501(c)3
Highest Offering: Master's
Program: Professional; Fine Arts Emphasis
Accreditation: NH, ART, CIDA

01 President ....Mr. Dennison W. GRIFFITH
04 Exec Assistant to the President ....Ms. Sheri LUCAS
05 Provost ....Mr. Kevin J. CONLON
10 Senior Vice President/CFO ....Mr. Jeffrey A. FISHER
30 Vice President for Advancement ....Ms. Laurie Beth SWEENEY
84 VP Enrollment Mgmt & Communications . Mr. Jonathan LINDSAY
32 Vice President for Student Affairs ....Mr. Dwayne TODD
20 Dean of Faculty ....Ms. Char NORMAN
60 Dean School of Design Arts ....Mr. Tom GATTIS
57 Dean School of Studio Arts ....Ms. Julie TAGGART
58 Director Graduate Studies ....Mr. Ric PETRY
06 Registrar ....Ms. Michele KIBLER
13 Chief Information Officer ....Mr. Jeffrey BROTHERTON
15 Director of Human Resources ....Ms. Barbara DAVIS
08 Director of Library Services ....Ms. Gail STORER
19 Director of Safety & Security ....Mr. Wallace TANKSLEY
18 Director of Facilities ....Mr. Joseph SPYBEY
27 Director Communications & Marketing ....Ms. Robin HEPLER
38 Director of Counseling & Wellness ....Ms. Erin VLACH
37 Director Student Financial Aid ....Ms. Anna M. SCHOFIELD
36 Director Career Resources ....Ms. Tiffany SPERRING
21 Controller ....Mr. Roger ESCOLAS
35 Dir of Student Involvement ....Ms. Heather BRAY
51 Dir Continuing/Professional Study ....Ms. Catherine SHERIDAN
39 Director of Residence Life ....Mr. Mickey HART
88 Director of Special Projects ....Mr. Dave STOCKWELL
40 Supply Store Manager ....Mr. Danny HINTY

Columbus State Community College (B)

Box 1609, Columbus OH 43216-1609
County: Franklin FICE Identification: 006867
Unit ID: 202222
Telephone: (614) 287-5353 Carnegie Class: Assoc/Pub-U-SC
FAX Number: (614) 287-5113 Calendar System: Semester
URL: www.cscc.edu
Established: 1963 Annual Undergrad Tuition & Fees (In-State): $3,978
Enrollment: 25,970 Coed
Affiliation or Control: State IRS Status: 501(c)3
Highest Offering: Associate Degree
Program: Occupational
Accreditation: NH, ACBSP, ACFEI, ADNUR, CAHIIM, COARC, CONST, DH, DIETT, EMT, ENGT, MAC, MLTAD, PHLEB, RAD, SURGT

01 President ....Dr. David T. HARRISON
100 Chief of Staff ....Ms. Kimberly HALL
05 Senior Vice Pres Academic Affairs ....Dr. John COOLEY
10 Sr Vice President & CFO ....Ms. Theresa GEHR
26 Vice Pres Marketing/Communications ....Mr. Will KOPP
13 Int Vice President Info Technology ....Ms. Carol THOMAS
15 Vice President for Human Resources ....Ms. Deborah HEATER
32 Vice Pres for Student Affairs ....Dr. Janet ROGERS
84 Dean of Enrollment Services ....Mr. Martin MALIWESKY
12 Dean of Delaware Campus ....Mr. Angelo FROLE
49 Interim Dean of Arts & Sciences ....Ms. Karen MUIR
50 Int Dean Technical/Career Programs ....Ms. Mokie STEISKAL
35 Dean Student Life ....Ms. Rene HAMPTON
30 Executive Director for Development ....Ms. Pamela BISHOP
14 Director of Data Center ....Mr. Etienne MARTIN
21 Director of Business Services ....Ms. Aletha SHIPLEY
06 Director of Records & Registration ....Dr. Regina A. PEAL
37 Dir Enroll/Fin Aid/Veterans Svcs ....Mr. David METZ
19 Director of Public Safety ....Dr. John NESTOR
18 Director of Facilities Planning ....Mr. Mark FRENCH
28 Director of Diversity ....Ms. Renee HAMPTON
09 Dir Institutional Effectiveness ....Ms. Jennifer ANDERSON
08 Director Educational Resources Ctr ....Mr. Bruce MASSIS
07 Director of Admissions ....Ms. Tari BLANEY
40 Director of Operations/Bookstore ....Ms. Stacy MULINEX
96 Director of Purchasing ....Mr. Bradley FARMER

Columbus State Community College-Delaware (C)

5100 Cornerstone Drive, Delaware OH 43015
Telephone: (742) 203-8000 Identification: 770353
Accreditation: &NH

† Main campus is Columbus State Community College in Columbus, OH.

Cuyahoga Community College (D)

700 Carnegie Avenue, Cleveland OH 44115-2878
County: Cuyahoga FICE Identification: 003040
Unit ID: 202356
Telephone: (216) 987-4000 Carnegie Class: Assoc/Pub-U-MC
FAX Number: (216) 566-5977 Calendar System: Semester
URL: www.tri-c.edu
Established: 1963 Annual Undergrad Tuition & Fees (In-District): $3,036
Enrollment: 30,065 Coed
Affiliation or Control: State/Local IRS Status: 501(c)3
Highest Offering: Associate Degree
Program: Occupational; 2-Year Principally Bachelor's Creditable
Accreditation: NH, ACFEI, ADNUR, ARCPA, CAHIIM, COARC, DH, DIETT, DMS, ENGT, MAC, MLTAD, NDT, NMT, OTA, POLYT, PTAA, RAD, SURGT

01 President ....Dr. Alex JOHNSON
05 Provost/EVP Acad & Stdnt Affairs ....Dr. Belinda MILES
10 Exec Vice Pres Admin and Finance ....Dr. Craig FOLTIN
103 Exec Vice Pres Workforce & Econ Dev ....Ms. Susan MUHA
13 Vice Pres Advanced Technology/Admin ....Dr. Michael BANKEY
12 Campus President/VP Westshore ....Dr. J. M. THOMSON
12 Corporate College President ....Mr. Robert PETERSON
12 Campus President/VP West ....Dr. Ron LISS
12 Campus President/VP Metro ....Dr. Michael SCHOOP
12 Campus President/VP East ....Dr. Paul GASPARRO
21 Vice Pres Finance & Admin ....Mr. Mike ABOUSERHAL
15 Vice Pres/Chief Human Res Ofcr ....Ms. Judith MCMULLEN
31 Vice Pres College Pathway Programs ....Dr. JaNice MARSHALL
30 Vice Pres Development Office ....Ms. Gloria MOOSMANN
27 Vice Pres/Chief Info Officer ....Mr. Gerard HOURIGAN
09 VP Inst Planning/Effectiveness ....Dr. Jennifer SPIELVOGEL
86 Vice Pres Govt Affair/Comm Outreach ....Ms. Claire ROSACCO
18 Vice Pres Facilities Devel & Opers ....Mr. Peter MAC EWAN
84 Vice Pres Enroll Mgmt/Stdnt Affairs ....Ms. Karen MILLER
26 Vice Pres Marketing/Communications ....Mr. Alan MORAN
43 Vice President Legal Services ....Ms. Renee RICHARD
20 Vice Pres Academic Affairs ....Dr. Sandy ROBINSON
103 Vice Pres CC/WEDD ....Dr. Linda WOODARD
17 Vice Pres Health Care Educ ....Ms. Patricia REID
19 Vice Pres Public Safety & Security ....Chief Clayton HARRIS
88 Associate VP Faculty Affairs & Prof ....Ms. Sandra MCKNIGHT
106 Associate VP eLearning/Innovation ....Dr. Kelvin BENTLEY
88 Exec Dir Business Continuity ....Mr. Marvin RICHARDS
88 Exec Director Media Engineering ....Mr. Robert BRYAN
13 Int Exec Dir Info Technology Svc ....Mr. Jon DELINAR
07 Executive Director Enrollment Opers ....Ms. Angela JOHNSON
06 Registrar ....Ms. Mary Kay WEIS
21 Exec Director Plant Operations ....Mr. Blair BOSWORTH
88 Exec Dir Veteran Services/Programs ....Mr. Richard DE CHANT
26 Executive Director Marketing ....Ms. Kimberly PLEASANT
88 Exec Dir College Svcs & Retail ....Mr. Chris MOIR
51 Program Coordinator Cmty Cont Educ ....Ms. Fran TOMBA
88 Exec Dir College Pathway Programs ....Mr. Kenneth HALE
96 Executive Dir Supplier Manage Svcs ....Ms. Cynthia LEITSON
36 Exec Dir Career Dev & Trng Center ....Ms. Treacy CROWLEY
20 Dean Academic Affairs East ....Dr. John W. MARR, JR.
20 Dean Academic Affairs West ....Dr. Amit SINGH
35 Dean Student Affairs ....Ms. Denise MCCORY
32 Dean Student Affairs West ....Ms. Diana DEL ROSARIO
32 Dean Student Affairs East ....Dr. Mel A. MAY
66 Dean Nursing Metro ....Dr. Vivian M. YATES
88 Dean & GM Hospitality Mgmt ....Mr. Gregory FORTE
20 Dean Academic Affairs-Metro ....Mr. Lindsay ENGLISH
20 Dean Academic Affairs-Westshore ....Mr. Robert SEARSON
32 Dean Student Affairs Westshore ....Ms. Ann PROUDFIT
88 Dean Developmental Education ....Vacant
88 Assoc Dean Creative Arts ....Ms. Amy PARKS
76 Assoc Dean Medical Assisting ....Ms. Barbara MIKUSZEWSKI
76 Assoc Dean Health & Science ....Mr. Daniel MCDERMOTT
81 Assoc Dean Math & Applied Tech West ....Dr. Guy HUTT
83 Assoc Dean Social Sciences West ....Dr. Carol FRANKLIN
49 Assoc Dean Liberal Arts East ....Mr. Raymond IRWIN
49 Assoc Dean Liberal Arts Metro ....Dr. Jocelyn LADNER-MATHIS
49 Assoc Dean Liberal Arts West ....Vacant
50 Assoc Dean Business/Math Tech Metro ....Dr. Pamela ELLISON
72 Assoc Dean Business & Technology ....Dr. Lorraine HARTLEY
54 Assoc Dean Engineering ....Mr. Lam WONG
50 Assoc Dean Business & IT ....Dr. Donald SMITH
76 Assoc Dean Health Careers ....Mr. David FRAZEE
66 Assoc Dean Nursing ....Ms. Irene MEYER
23 Exec Dir Healthcare Ind Solutions ....Mrs. Kimberly BABICH-SPECK
16 Exec Dir HR Ops & Employee Svcs ....Ms. Cristine BOARD
100 Chief of Staff/Exec Asst President ....Mr. David HOOVLER
28 Director of Diversity ....Dr. Deborale RICHARDSON-BOUIE
37 District Dir Student Financial Aid ....Ms. Kimberly NASH-YORE
38 Campus Dir Student Counseling-Metro ....Ms. Brenda PAYNE-RILEY
38 Campus Dir Student Counseling-East ....Ms. Johanna BACIK
38 Campus Dir Student Counseling-West ....Mr. Marcos RIVERA

Cuyahoga Community College Eastern Campus (E)

4250 Richmond Road, Highland Hills OH 44122
Telephone: (800) 954-8742 Identification: 770355
Accreditation: &NH

† Main campus is Cuyahoga Community College in Cleveland, OH.

Cuyahoga Community College Metropolitan Campus (F)

2900 Community College Avenue, Cleveland OH 44115
Telephone: (800) 954-8742 Identification: 770354
Accreditation: &NH, PHLEB

† Main campus is Cuyahoga Community College in Cleveland, OH.

Cuyahoga Community College Western Campus (G)

11000 Pleasant Valley Road, Parma OH 44130
Telephone: (800) 954-8742 Identification: 770356
Accreditation: &NH

† Main campus is Cuyahoga Community College in Cleveland, OH.

Cuyahoga Community College Westshore (H)

31001 Clemens Road, Westlake OH 44145
Telephone: (800) 954-8742 Identification: 770357
Accreditation: &NH

† Main campus is Cuyahoga Community College in Cleveland, OH.

Davis College (I)

4747 Monroe Street, Toledo OH 43623-4389
County: Lucas FICE Identification: 004855
Unit ID: 202435
Telephone: (419) 473-2700 Carnegie Class: Assoc/PrivFP
FAX Number: (419) 473-2472 Calendar System: Quarter
URL: www.daviscollege.edu
Established: 1858 Annual Undergrad Tuition & Fees: $12,600
Enrollment: 284 Coed
Affiliation or Control: Proprietary IRS Status: Proprietary
Highest Offering: Associate Degree
Program: Occupational; 2-Year Principally Bachelor's Creditable; Business Emphasis
Accreditation: NH, MAC

01 President ....Diane BRUNNER
05 Vice President Academic Affairs ....Vicky RYAN
32 Vice President of Student Services ....Mary RYAN BULONE
06 Registrar ....Marsha KLINGBEIL
37 Director Student Financial Aid ....Melissa DODSWORTH
07 Director of Admissions ....Dana STERN
36 Director of Student Placement ....Nick NIGRO
04 Assistant to the President ....Jane MULLIKIN
13 Information Services Director ....Vacant
26 Chief Public Relations Officer ....Tim BRUNNER
18 Chief Facilities/Physical Plant ....Greg RIPPKE
08 Librarian ....Peggy PETERSON-SENIUK
96 Purchasing ....Marilyn BOVIA
13 Director of Information Technology ....Aaron COWELL
31 Chief Community Relations Officer ....Dan BRUNNER, JR.
40 Director Bookstore ....Michael LAMBERT
108 Director Institutional Assessment ....Marsha KLINGBEIL
50 Business Admin & IT Chair ....Mary DELOE
57 Design Dept Chair ....Janet WEBER
97 General Education Dept Chair ....Kathleen FRANCE
76 Admin Prof & Allied Health Chair ....Terry DIPPMAN

Daymar College-Chillicothe (J)

1410 Industrial Drive, Chillicothe OH 45601-3977
County: Ross FICE Identification: 020568
Unit ID: 205568
Telephone: (740) 774-6300 Carnegie Class: Assoc/PrivFP
FAX Number: (740) 774-6317 Calendar System: Quarter
URL: www.daymarcollege.edu
Established: 1962 Annual Undergrad Tuition & Fees: $24,000
Enrollment: 92 Coed
Affiliation or Control: Proprietary IRS Status: Proprietary
Highest Offering: Associate Degree
Program: Occupational; 2-Year Principally Bachelor's Creditable; Technical Emphasis
Accreditation: ACICS

01 President ....Mr. Dan INMAN
12 Campus President ....Ms. Elizabeth SANDMAN
07 Senior Director of Admissions ....Vacant
36 Dir of Career Svc & Cmty Relations ....Mr. Robert ARCHER
37 Director Financial Services ....Vacant
05 Director of Education ....Ms. Heather MORRIS

Daymar College-Jackson (K)

980 East Main, Jackson OH 45640
Telephone: (740) 286-1554 Identification: 666468
Accreditation: ACICS

† Main campus is Daymar College-Chillicothe in Chillicothe, OH.

Daymar College-Lancaster (A)

1579 Victor Road, Lancaster OH 43130-8039
Telephone: (740) 687-6126 Identification: 666469
Accreditation: ACICS

† Main campus is Daymar College-Chillicothe in Chillicothe, OH.

Daymar College-New Boston (B)

3879 Rhodes Avenue, Suite A,
New Boston OH 45662-4900
Telephone: (740) 456-4124 Identification: 667082
Accreditation: ACICS

† Main campus is Daymar College-Chillicothe in Chillicothe, OH.

The Defiance College (C)

701 N Clinton Street, Defiance OH 43512-1695
County: Defiance FICE Identification: 003041
Unit ID: 202514
Telephone: (419) 784-4010 Carnegie Class: Bac/Diverse
FAX Number: (419) 784-0426 Calendar System: Semester
URL: www.defiance.edu
Established: 1850 Annual Undergrad Tuition & Fees: $28,700
Enrollment: 1,021 Coed
Affiliation or Control: United Church Of Christ IRS Status: 501(c)3
Highest Offering: Master's
Program: Liberal Arts And General; Teacher Preparatory
Accreditation: NH, IACBE, NURSE, SW, TED

01 President ... Mr. Mark C. GORDON
05 Provost/VP for Academic Affairs ... Dr. Barbara SCHIRMER
30 Vice Pres Institutional Advancement ... Mrs. Wendy PESTRUE
10 Vice Pres for Finance & Management ... Mrs. Lois N. MCCULLOUGH
32 VP Stdnt Engagement/Dean of Stdnts ... Dr. Kenneth A. WETSTEIN
84 Vice Pres for Enrollment Management ... Mr. Michael SUZO
88 Dean McMaster Sch Adv Hum ... Mrs. Mary Ann STUDER
20 Associate Academic Dean ... Dr. Donald S. KNUEVE
07 Director of Admissions ... Mr. Brad HARSHA
15 Director of Human Resources ... Ms. Mary E. BURKHOLDER
29 Director Alumni and Parent Relation ... Mrs. Lorie RATH
08 Dir of Library and Instr Resource ... Mrs. Michelle BLANK
26 Director Public Relations/Marketing ... Mrs. Kathy M. PUNCHES
14 Director of Computer Services ... Mr. Jeremy KENNEDY
06 Registrar ... Mrs. Mariah ORZOLEK
36 Director of Career Development ... Mrs. Lisa MARSALEK
37 Director of Financial Aid ... Mrs. Amy FRANCIS
41 Athletic Director ... Ms. Jenni MORRISON
42 Campus Minister/Church Relations ... Rev. Janice L. BECHTEL
28 Director Intercultural Relations ... Ms. Mercedes CLAY
39 Director of Residence Life ... Ms. Kim LAMMERS
18 Director of Physical Plant ... Mr. James CORESSEL
21 Director of Accounting ... Mrs. Kristine BOLAND

Denison University (D)

100 W College Street, Granville OH 43023-1359
County: Licking FICE Identification: 003042
Unit ID: 202523
Telephone: (740) 587-0810 Carnegie Class: Bac/A&S
FAX Number: (740) 587-6417 Calendar System: Semester
URL: www.denison.edu
Established: 1831 Annual Undergrad Tuition & Fees: $43,910
Enrollment: 2,185 Coed
Affiliation or Control: Independent Non-Profit IRS Status: 501(c)3
Highest Offering: Baccalaureate
Program: Liberal Arts And General
Accreditation: NH

01 President ... Dr. Adam S. WEINBERG
05 Interim Provost ... Dr. Kimberly A. COPLIN
20 Associate Provost ... Dr. Susan P. GARCIA
20 Associate Provost ... Dr. James PLETCHER
20 Associate Provost ... Dr. Toni C. KING
10 Vice President Finance & Management ... Mr. Seth H. PATTON
30 VP Institutional Advancement ... Ms. Julia BEYER HOUPT
32 Vice President Student Affairs ... Dr. Laurel B. KENNEDY
07 Vice Pres/Director of Admissions ... Mr. Perry H. ROBINSON
89 Dean of First-Year Students ... Dr. Mark MOLLER
35 Dean of Students ... Mr. William A. FOX
06 Registrar ... Ms. Yadigar COLLINS
08 Director of Libraries ... Ms. BethAnn ZAMBELLA
37 Dir of Financial Aid & Student Empl ... Ms. Nancy Z. HOOVER
14 Dir Information Technology Services ... Ms. Lisa BAZLEY
15 Director of Human Resources ... Mr. Jim ABLES
18 Director of Facilities Services ... Mr. Arthur J. CHONKO
19 Dir Security/Safety/Risk Mgmt ... Mr. Garret MOORE
26 Admin Dir of Univ Communications ... Mr. Jack HIRE
88 Creative Dir of Univ Communications ... Mr. Paul A. PEGHER
29 Director of Alumni Relations ... Mr. Steven R. CRAWFORD
36 Dir Career Exploration & Dev ... Ms. Kathleen I. POWELL
38 Interim Director of Counseling Svc ... Mr. Timothy DURHAM
23 Interim Director of Health Services ... Ms. Mary THURLOW-COLLEN
40 Manager of Bookstore/Business Svc ... Mr. Joseph E. WARMKE
42 Chaplain/Director of Religious Life ... Rev. Mark ORTEN
100 Special Asst to Pres/Chief of Staff ... Dr. Joyce MEREDITH
93 Dir Multicultural Stdnt Affs/Ast Dn ... Mr. Erik S. FARLEY
11 Director of Administrative Services ... Ms. Jenna MCDEVITT
09 Director of Institutional Research ... Dr. Todd M. JAMISON
41 Director of Athletics ... Ms. Nan CARNEY-DEBORD
88 Chief Investment Officer ... Ms. Adele N. GORRILLA

DeVry University - Columbus Campus (E)

1350 Alum Creek Drive, Columbus OH 43209-2705
Telephone: (614) 253-7291 FICE Identification: 003099
Accreditation: &NH, CAHIIM, ENGT

† Main campus is DeVry University - Chicago Campus in Chicago, IL.

Eastern Gateway Community College - Jefferson County Campus (F)

4000 Sunset Boulevard, Steubenville OH 43952-3594
County: Jefferson FICE Identification: 007275
Unit ID: 203331
Telephone: (740) 264-5591 Carnegie Class: Assoc/Pub-R-M
FAX Number: (740) 264-1338 Calendar System: Semester
URL: www.egcc.edu
Established: 1966 Annual Undergrad Tuition & Fees (In-District): $3,420
Enrollment: 2,561 Coed
Affiliation or Control: State/Local IRS Status: 501(c)3
Highest Offering: Associate Degree
Program: Occupational; 2-Year Principally Bachelor's Creditable; Technical Emphasis
Accreditation: NH, CAHIIM, COARC, DA, MAC, MLTAD, RAD

01 President ... Dr. Laura M. MEEKS
05 Exec Vice Pres Academic/Stdnt Affs ... Dr. James BABER
10 Vice Pres Business Services/Treas ... Mr. James J. MCGRAIL, III
11 Vice Pres Administrative Services ... Ms. Sherri VANTASSEL
46 Vice Pres Strategic Initiatives ... Mr. Dante ZAMBRINI
84 Dean Enrollment Management ... Ms. Patty Jo STURCH
76 Dean Health & Biological Sciences ... Dr. Robin FLOHR
50 Dean Business/Engineering & Info ... Mr. Jerry KLINESMITH
21 Controller ... Mr. C. Michael PAYNE
07 Director of Admissions ... Mrs. Marlana FEATNER
26 Dir Public Information/Web Coord ... Mrs. Ann M. KOON
37 Director Student Info/Financial Aid ... Ms. Kelly WILSON
103 Dir Workforce/Community Outreach ... Mr. Mark CICCARELLI
14 Director Technology Services ... Ms. Karen L. TUCCI
36 Director Career Services/Alumni ... Vacant
40 Director of Bookstore ... Mrs. Judith LUDE
21 Director Student Billing/Payroll ... Ms. Tonya LOGAN
10 Director Building & Grounds ... Mr. Julius J. DZIEWATKOSKI
08 Int Dean/Library Services ... Mrs. Lois T. REKOWSKI
06 Registrar ... Mrs. Patty J. STURCH
29 Director of Alumni Relations ... Mr. John O'BRIEN

Edison State Community College (G)

1973 Edison Drive, Piqua OH 45356-9239
County: Miami FICE Identification: 012750
Unit ID: 202648
Telephone: (937) 778-8600 Carnegie Class: Assoc/Pub-S-SC
FAX Number: (937) 778-1920 Calendar System: Semester
URL: www.edisonohio.edu
Established: 1973 Annual Undergrad Tuition & Fees (In-State): $4,149
Enrollment: 3,171 Coed
Affiliation or Control: State IRS Status: 501(c)3
Highest Offering: Associate Degree
Program: Occupational; 2-Year Principally Bachelor's Creditable
Accreditation: NH, ADNUR, MAC, MLTAD, PHLEB, PTAA

01 President ... Dr. Cristobal O. VALDEZ
04 Executive Asst to the President ... Ms. Heather LANHAM
05 Interim Sr VP of Academic Affairs ... Ms. Patricia A. ROSS
11 VP of Administration & Finance ... Mr. John W. SHISHOFF
90 VP of Information Technology ... Mr. David GANSZ
30 VP for Institutional Advancement ... Ms. Kimberly HORTON
15 VP of Strategic Human Resources ... Mrs. Linda M. PELTIER
32 Vice President of Student Affairs ... Mr. Scott M. BURNAM
07 Director of Admissions ... Ms. Teresa ROTH
49 Dean of Arts and Science ... Ms. Naomi LOUIS
50 Dean of Business/Workforce Develop ... Ms. Shirley MOORE
69 Dean of Health/Public Services ... Ms. Gwendolyn A. STEVENSON
09 Director of Institutional Research ... Ms. Rebecca P. TELFORD
38 Dean of Student Success ... Vacant
72 Dean of IT and Engineering ... Ms. Patricia A. ROSS
21 Controller ... Mr. Thomas FRYMAN
41 Interim Director of Athletics ... Mr. Kim RANK
37 Director of Financial Aid ... Ms. Kathi S. RICHARDS
26 Dir of Mktg/Community Relations ... Vacant
07 Coord of Admissions ... Mr. Trevor STUTZ

Edison State Community College Darke County Campus (H)

601 Wagner Avenue, Greenville OH 45331
Telephone: (937) 548-5546 Identification: 770358
Accreditation: &NH

† Main campus is Edison State Community College in Piqua, OH.

ETI Technical College of Niles (I)

2076-86 Youngstown-Warren Road, Niles OH 44446-4398
County: Trumbull FICE Identification: 030790
Unit ID: 200590
Telephone: (330) 652-9919 Carnegie Class: Assoc/PrivFP
FAX Number: (330) 652-4399 Calendar System: Semester
URL: www.eticollege.edu
Established: 1989 Annual Undergrad Tuition & Fees: $8,620
Enrollment: 190 Coed
Affiliation or Control: Proprietary IRS Status: Proprietary
Highest Offering: Associate Degree
Program: Occupational; 2-Year Principally Bachelor's Creditable
Accreditation: ACCSC

01 Director ... Mrs. Renee ZUZOLO
07 Director of Admissions ... Mrs. Diane MARSTELLER
37 Director Financial Aid ... Ms. Kay MADIGAN

Fortis College (J)

555 E Alex-Bell Road, Centerville OH 45459-6120
County: Montgomery FICE Identification: 021907
Unit ID: 205179
Telephone: (937) 433-3410 Carnegie Class: Assoc/PrivFP
FAX Number: (937) 435-6516 Calendar System: Semester
URL: www.fortiscollege.edu
Established: 1970 Annual Undergrad Tuition & Fees: $13,030
Enrollment: 915 Coed
Affiliation or Control: Proprietary IRS Status: Proprietary
Highest Offering: Baccalaureate
Program: Occupational; 2-Year Principally Bachelor's Creditable
Accreditation: ACCSC, ADNUR, EMT, MAC

01 President ... Richard RUCKER
11 Director of Administration ... Vacant
05 Director Education ... Claude SMITH
07 Director Admissions ... Sean KUHN
37 Director Financial Aid ... Tom BARKER

Fortis College (K)

2545 Bailey Road, Cuyahoga Falls OH 44221-2949
County: Summit FICE Identification: 009412
Unit ID: 204307
Telephone: (330) 923-9959 Carnegie Class: Assoc/PrivFP
FAX Number: (330) 923-0886 Calendar System: Other
URL: www.fortis.edu
Established: 1922 Annual Undergrad Tuition & Fees: $18,600
Enrollment: 530 Coed
Affiliation or Control: Proprietary IRS Status: Proprietary
Highest Offering: Associate Degree
Program: Occupational
Accreditation: ACCSC, DA

01 Director ... Ms. Carson BURKE

Fortis College (L)

653 Enterprise Parkway, Ravenna OH 44266-8058
Telephone: (330) 297-7319 FICE Identification: 023036
Accreditation: ACICS, CAHIIM

† Main campus is Fortis College in Norfolk, VA.

Fortis College (M)

4151 Executive Parkway, Suite 120,
Westerville OH 43081-3860
County: Franklin Identification: 666602
Unit ID: 450058
Telephone: (614) 882-2551 Carnegie Class: Assoc/PrivFP
FAX Number: (614) 882-2914 Calendar System: Other
URL: www.fortis.edu
Established: 2010 Annual Undergrad Tuition & Fees: $12,308
Enrollment: 748 Coed
Affiliation or Control: Proprietary IRS Status: Proprietary
Highest Offering: Associate Degree
Program: Occupational; 2-Year Principally Bachelor's Creditable; Music Emphasis
Accreditation: ABHES, RAD, SURGT

01 President ... Mr. Wynn BLANTON

Franciscan University of Steubenville (N)

1235 University Boulevard, Steubenville OH 43952-1763
County: Jefferson FICE Identification: 003036
Unit ID: 205957
Telephone: (740) 283-3771 Carnegie Class: Master's M
FAX Number: (740) 283-6472 Calendar System: Semester
URL: www.franciscan.edu
Established: 1946 Annual Undergrad Tuition & Fees: $22,720
Enrollment: 2,351 Coed
Affiliation or Control: Roman Catholic IRS Status: 501(c)3
Highest Offering: Master's
Program: Liberal Arts And General; Religious Emphasis
Accreditation: NH, NUR, SW, TED

01 President ... Rev. Sean SHERIDAN, TOR
00 Chancellor ... Rev. Terence HENRY, TOR
03 Executive Vice President ... Dr. Robert G. FILBY
05 Vice President for Academic Affairs ... Dr. Daniel KEMPTON
10 Vice President for Finance ... Mr. David M. SKIVIAT

30 Vice President for Advancement ... Mr. Michael HERNON
31 Vice Pres for Community Relations ... Rev. Nathan MALAVOLTI, TOR
46 Vice Pres for Mission Effectiveness ... Vacant
15 VP of Human Resources/Legal Counsel ... Mr. Adam SCURTI
32 Vice President of Student Life ... Mr. David A. SCHMIESING
84 Vice Pres of Enrollment Management ... Mr. Joel S. RECZNIK
88 Religious Administrator ... Rev. Terence HENRY, TOR
42 University Chaplain ... Rev. Dominic SCOTTO, TOR
20 Dir of Advising & Acad Operations ... Ms. Ann DULANY
13 Exec Dir of Information Technology ... Mr. Kevin G. SEBOLT
35 Asst Vice Pres of Student Life ... Ms. Catherine J. HECK
08 Director of Library ... Mr. William JAKUB
88 Exec Director Christian Outreach ... Mr. Mark JOSEPH
44 Director of Planned Giving ... Dr. Mark E. RECZNIK
30 Director of Development ... Mr. Mark NEHRBAS
29 Director of Alumni Relations ... Mr. Timothy J. DELANEY
26 Director of Public Relations ... Miss Lisa M. FERGUSON
07 Director of Admissions ... Mrs. Margaret WEBER
07 Director of Graduate Enrollment ... Mr. Mark T. MCGUIRE
06 Registrar ... Mrs. Kathryn REEHL
37 Dir of Financial Aid/Student Accts ... Mr. John L. HERRMANN
09 Institutional Research Manager ... Mr. Mark A. ERSTE
21 Controller ... Mr. John A. STEITZ
96 Director of Business Services ... Ms. Marlene K. TERPENNING
40 Bookstore Manager ... Mr. John RECZNIK
91 Data Processing Manager ... Mr. Vince E. CARTLEDGE
16 Director of Human Resources ... Mr. Brenan PERGI
18 Director Physical Plant Services ... Mr. Joseph P. MCGURN
88 Director of Missionary Outreach ... Mr. Rhett YOUNG
88 Director of Chapel Ministries ... Mr. Robert PALLADINO
88 Director of JCW Center/Planning ... Mrs. Kathy L. MATTIOLI
104 Director of Study Abroad ... Mr. Mark HANRAHAN
38 Director of Counseling ... Mr. Joseph A. LOIZZO
41 Director of Athletics ... Mr. Christopher L. LEDYARD
36 Director Career Planning/Placement ... Mrs. Nancy S. RONEVICH
73 Director MA Theology Program ... Rev. Daniel J. PATTEE, TOR
50 Director MBA Program ... Mr. Joseph ZORIC
83 Director MA Counseling Program ... Dr. Milo C. MILBURN
53 Director MS Education Program ... Dr. Charles JOYCE
88 Director MA Philosophy Program ... Dr. Mark ROBERTS
90 Coord Academic Computer Services ... Ms. Sandy M. RADVANSKY
28 Director of Diversity ... Vacant
66 Director MS Nursing ... Dr. Carolyn MILLER

Franklin University (A)

201 S Grant Avenue, Columbus OH 43215-5399
County: Franklin — FICE Identification: 003046
Unit ID: 202806
Telephone: (614) 797-4700 — Carnegie Class: Spec/Bus
FAX Number: N/A — Calendar System: Trimester
URL: www.franklin.edu
Established: 1902 — Annual Undergrad Tuition & Fees: $13,320
Enrollment: 6,886 — Coed
Affiliation or Control: Independent Non-Profit — IRS Status: 501(c)3
Highest Offering: Master's
Program: Professional; Business Emphasis
Accreditation: NH, IACBE, NURSE

01 President ... Dr. David R. DECKER
11 Sr VP Adminstration/Chief of Staff ... Ms. Christi L. CABUNGCAL
05 Provost/Sr VP for Academic Affairs ... Dr. Christopher L. WASHINGTON
12 Director Indianapolis Location ... Ms. Marnie GLANNER
45 Sr Vice Pres Planning/Global Pgms ... Mr. Klaus HABERICH
07 VP Enrollment & Student Affairs ... Ms. Linda M. STEELE
30 Vice Pres University Advancement ... Ms. Bonnie SMITH QUIST
16 VP fo Human Resources & Campus Svcs ... Ms. Christi CABUNGCAL
09 VP Accred/Institutional Effective ... Dr. Pamela SHAY
22 VP Planning & University Services ... Ms. Evelyn LEVINO
20 Assistant Provost Academic Quality ... Mr. Ross WIRTH
04 Executive Assistant to President ... Ms. Bonnie MCCANN
32 Dean of Students ... Vacant
108 Dean/Exec Dir of Accreditation ... Mr. Wayne C. MILLER
88 Assoc Dean Ctr Professional Trng ... Vacant
10 Chief Financial Officer ... Mr. Marvin BRISKEY
13 Chief Information Officer ... Mr. Rick SUNDERMAN
20 Dir of Academic Support Services ... Ms. Susanne SMITH
06 Registrar ... Mr. Frank YANCHAK
08 Director of Library Services ... Ms. Tiffany LIPSTREU
37 Director of Financial Aid ... Ms. Goldie LANGLEY
46 Director of Strategic Relations ... Ms. Jody NOREEN
35 Dir Student Development ... Ms. Wendi ROBINSON
35 Dir Graduate Stdnt Svcs/Operations ... Vacant
88 VP Franklin Learning Systems ... Mr. Patrick BENNETT
84 Exec Director of Marketing & Enroll ... Mr. Scott BOOTH
12 Exec Dir Domestic Expan/Reg Cmps ... Mr. Bill CHAN
18 Director of Facilities ... Mr. Carl BROWN
26 Director of Public Relations ... Ms. Sherry MERCURIO
29 Director of Alumni Engagement & Dev ... Mr. Kevin GREENWOOD
96 Director of Purchasing ... Mr. Bob DONAHUE
44 Director of Development ... Ms. Nana WATSON
28 Director of Benefits ... Ms. Brenda LISTON
24 Director of Student Learning Center ... Mr. Christopher FIELDS
88 Director of Teaching Effectiveness ... Dr. Fawn WINTERWOOD
49 Dean Arts/Science & Technology ... Dr. Keith GROFF
50 Dean College of Business ... Dr. Tom SEILER
69 Dean College of Health & Public Adm ... Dr. Robert CURTIS
88 Dean Global Programs ... Dr. Godfrey MENDES
15 Director of Human Resources ... Ms. Randi MOLDOVAN
88 Director of Accounting ... Mr. Jeffrey GERBERRY
88 Exec Dir of Financial Services ... Mr. Randolph SNYDER

Galen College of Nursing (B)

100 E Business Way, Suite 200, Cincinnati OH 45241
Telephone: (210) 733-3600 — Identification: 770537
Accreditation: &SC, COE

† Main campus is Galen College of Nursing in Louisville, KY.

Gallipolis Career College (C)

1176 Jackson Pike, Suite 312, Gallipolis OH 45631-2600
County: Gallia — FICE Identification: 030079
Unit ID: 205513
Telephone: (740) 446-4367 — Carnegie Class: Assoc/PrivFP
FAX Number: (740) 446-4124 — Calendar System: Quarter
URL: www.gallipoliscareercollege.edu
Established: 1962 — Annual Undergrad Tuition & Fees: $11,570
Enrollment: 136 — Coed
Affiliation or Control: Proprietary — IRS Status: Proprietary
Highest Offering: Associate Degree
Program: 2-Year Principally Bachelor's Creditable; Business Emphasis
Accreditation: ACICS

01 President ... Mr. Robert L. SHIREY, JR.
05 Director of Education ... Mr. Wes YOUNG
07 Director of Admissions ... Mr. Bo SHIREY, III
37 Director Student Financial Aid ... Mrs. Jeanette SHIREY

God's Bible School and College (D)

1810 Young Street, Cincinnati OH 45202-6838
County: Hamilton — FICE Identification: 022205
Unit ID: 202903
Telephone: (513) 721-7944 — Carnegie Class: Spec/Faith
FAX Number: (513) 763-6649 — Calendar System: Semester
URL: www.gbs.edu
Established: 1900 — Annual Undergrad Tuition & Fees: $7,000
Enrollment: 310 — Coed
Affiliation or Control: Interdenominational — IRS Status: 501(c)3
Highest Offering: Baccalaureate
Program: Religious Emphasis
Accreditation: NH, BI

01 President ... Dr. Michael R. AVERY
05 Vice President Academic Affairs ... Mr. Aaron PROFITT
32 Vice President Student Development ... Mr. Richard MILES
30 Director Institutional Advancement ... Mrs. Faith AVERY
06 Registrar ... Mr. Christopher LAMBETH
08 Head Librarian ... Mr. Joshua AVERY
10 Director of Finance ... Mr. David FREDERICK
37 Director of Financial Aid ... Mr. Stephen BUCKLAND
11 Campus Administrator ... Mr. Harry CROUSE
26 Director of Public Relations ... Mr. Don DAVISON
13 Coordinator Information Services ... Mr. Steve HARMS
07 Student Recruiter ... Mr. Adam PROFITT

Good Samaritan College of Nursing and Health Science (E)

375 Dixmyth Avenue, Cincinnati OH 45220-2489
County: Hamilton — FICE Identification: 006494
Unit ID: 202912
Telephone: (513) 862-2743 — Carnegie Class: Assoc/PrivNFP
FAX Number: (513) 862-3572 — Calendar System: Semester
URL: www.gscollege.edu
Established: 2001 — Annual Undergrad Tuition & Fees: $20,202
Enrollment: 335 — Coed
Affiliation or Control: Independent Non-Profit — IRS Status: 501(c)3
Highest Offering: Baccalaureate
Program: 2-Year Principally Bachelor's Creditable; Nursing Emphasis
Accreditation: NH, ADNUR

01 President ... Mr. Morris COHEN
05 Dean of Academic Affairs ... Ms. Patricia MCMAHON
32 Dean of Students/Alumni ... Ms. Mary Jo KATHMAN
09 Dir of Inst Research/Assessment ... Ms. Sherry DOWNING
84 Dean of Enrollment Management ... Ms. Linda HAYES

Harrison College (F)

3880 Jackpot Road, Grove City OH 43123
Telephone: (260) 471-7667 — Identification: 770748
Accreditation: ACICS, MAC

† Main campus is Harrison College - Indianapolis Downtown Campus in Indianapolis, IN.

Heidelberg University (G)

310 E Market Street, Tiffin OH 44883-2462
County: Seneca — FICE Identification: 003048
Unit ID: 203085
Telephone: (419) 448-2000 — Carnegie Class: Master's S
FAX Number: (419) 448-2124 — Calendar System: Semester
URL: www.heidelberg.edu
Established: 1850 — Annual Undergrad Tuition & Fees: $25,600
Enrollment: 1,368 — Coed
Affiliation or Control: United Church Of Christ — IRS Status: 501(c)3
Highest Offering: Master's
Program: Liberal Arts And General; Teacher Preparatory
Accreditation: NH, CACREP, MUS, TED

01 President ... Dr. Robert HUNTINGTON
05 VP for Academic Affairs & Provost ... Dr. David WEININGER
10 VP for Admin & Business Affairs ... Mr. John WILKIN
84 VP for Enrollment Mgmt ... Mr. Doug KELLAR
30 VP Inst Advancement & Univ Relation ... Ms. Connie L. HARRIS
20 Assoc VP Acad Affs/Dean Undergr Fac ... Dr. Vicki OHL
44 Assoc VP for Institutional Advance ... Dr. Kathryn VENEMA
13 Assoc VP for Information Resources ... Mr. Kurt HUENEMANN
18 Assoc VP for Facilities & Engrng ... Mr. Rodney MORRISON
50 Dean of the School of Business ... Dr. Haseeb AHMED
06 Registrar ... Ms. Cindy SUTER
88 Director MA in Counseling Pgm ... Dr. Jo-Ann SANDERS
53 Director of School of Education ... Dr. Robert SWANSON
64 Director of School of Music ... Dr. John OWEN
92 Assoc Dean for Honors Program ... Dr. Doug COLLAR
104 Director Intl Affairs & Studies ... Ms. Julie ARNOLD
36 Asst Dean Stdnt Affs for Stdnt Succ ... Ms. Kristen LINDSAY
12 Director of Heidelberg at Arrowhead ... Mr. Allen UNDERWOOD
88 Dir Faculty Student Advising & Supp ... Dr. Ellen NAGY
08 Director of Library ... Dr. Nainsi HOUSTON
41 Athletic Director ... Mr. Matt PALM
21 Business Officer ... Ms. Barb GABEL
37 Director Student Financial Aid ... Mrs. Juli WEININGER
30 Director of Development ... Mr. Lee MARTIN
29 Director of Alumni Relations ... Dr. Kathryn VENEMA
32 Dean of Student Affairs ... Mr. Dustin BRENTLINGER
39 Asst Dn Stdnt Affs for Campus Life ... Mr. Mark ZENO
88 Dir Student Engagement ... Ms. Andrea WENSOWITCH
15 Director of Human Resources ... Ms. Margaret RUDOLPH
21 Controller ... Ms. Kelly WARNKE
04 Exec Assistant to President ... Ms. Monica VERHOFF
40 Director of University Bookstore ... Ms. Gail ROBERTS
42 Director of Campus Ministry ... Rev. Paul STARK

Herzing University Toledo Campus (H)

5212 Hill Avenue, Toledo OH 43615
Telephone: (419) 776-0030 — Identification: 770434
Accreditation: &NH, MAAB, SURTEC

† Main campus is Herzing University in Madison, WI.

Hiram College (I)

Box 67, Hiram OH 44234-0067
County: Portage — FICE Identification: 003049
Unit ID: 203128
Telephone: (330) 569-3211 — Carnegie Class: Bac/A&S
FAX Number: (330) 569-5494 — Calendar System: Semester
URL: www.hiram.edu
Established: 1850 — Annual Undergrad Tuition & Fees: $40,150
Enrollment: 1,324 — Coed
Affiliation or Control: Independent Non-Profit — IRS Status: 501(c)3
Highest Offering: Master's
Program: Liberal Arts And General; Teacher Preparatory
Accreditation: NH, MUS, NURSE, TED

01 President ... Mr. Thomas V. CHEMA
05 Vice President & Dean of College ... Dr. Robert HAAK
10 Vice President Business & Finance ... Mr. Stephen W. JONES
30 Vice Pres Development & Alumni Rels ... Mr. Patrick S. ROBERTS
32 Vice President & Dean of Students ... Mr. Eric R. RIEDEL
07 Vice Pres Admission/Financial Aid ... Mr. James M. ABBUHL
20 Associate Dean of the College ... Ms. Ellen L. WALKER
107 Assc Dean Professional/Grad Studies ... Ms. Jennifer N. MCDONOUGH
06 Registrar ... Ms. Virginia L. TAYLOR
08 Head Librarian ... Mr. David D. EVERETT
29 Director Alumni Relations ... Mr. John B. COYNE
37 Director Student Financial Services ... Ms. Andrea L. CAPUTO
36 Director of Career Services ... Ms. Kathryn M. CRAIG
14 Director of Computer Center ... Mr. Frank J. VENTURA
100 Chief of Staff ... Mr. Timothy B. BRYAN
107 Dean Professional/Grad Studies ... Mr. Paul E. BOWERS
09 Director of Institutional Research ... Dr. Michael A. GRAJEK
41 Director of Athletics ... Ms. Ellen E. DEMPSEY
42 Chaplain ... Mr. Jason A. BRICKER-THOMPSON
15 Director of Human Resources ... Ms. Lynn M. KOSTRAB
18 Director of the Physical Plant ... Mr. Andy J. BIHL
21 Controller/Director of Accounting ... Ms. Susan A. BOYLE
35 Director of Student Involvement ... Mr. Alexandra K. ULBRICHT
38 Director Student Counseling ... Dr. Kevin P. FEISTHAMEL
28 Director Ethnic Diversity Affairs ... Ms. Detra E. WEST
96 Director of Purchasing ... Ms. Martha A. SCHETTLER

Herzing University-Akron (J)

1600 S Arlington Street, Suite 100, Akron OH 44306-3958
Telephone: (330) 724-1600 — FICE Identification: 020695
Accreditation: &NH, ADNUR, MAC

† Main campus is Herzing University in Madison, WI.

Hocking College (K)

3301 Hocking Parkway, Nelsonville OH 45764-9704
County: Athens — FICE Identification: 007598
Unit ID: 203155
Telephone: (740) 753-3591 — Carnegie Class: Assoc/Pub-R-L
FAX Number: (740) 753-7039 — Calendar System: Semester
URL: www.hocking.edu
Established: 1968 — Annual Undergrad Tuition & Fees (In-State): $6,435
Enrollment: 4,581 — Coed
Affiliation or Control: State — IRS Status: 501(c)3

Highest Offering: Associate Degree
Program: Occupational; 2-Year Principally Bachelor's Creditable; Technical Emphasis
Accreditation: NH, ACBSP, ACFEI, ADNUR, CAHIIM, MAC, PNUR, PTAA

01	President	Dr. Ron ERICKSON
10	Vice President & Treasurer	Ms. Gina FETTY
05	Provost/VP Acad & Student Affairs	Dr. Carl BRIDGES
11	Vice Pres Administrative Services	Dr. Myriah DAVIS
20	Associate Provost	Mr. Joe WAKEMAN
04	Executive Assistant to President	Ms. Nancy VANDEMAN
20	Dean of Reg Campuses/Industry Tech	Mr. Neil HINTON
66	Dean School of Health & Nursing	Ms. Tammy KEITH
13	Chief Technology Officer	Mr. Ben DALTON
19	Director Public Safety Services	Ms. Scott MONG
08	Director Learning Resource Center	Ms. Jeff GRAFFIUS
15	Director Human Resources	Mr. John SANDERS
26	Director Public Relations	Ms. Laura ALLOWAY
19	Director Campus Safety	Mr. Al MATTHEWS
06	Registrar	Ms. Roxana HERDLITZKA
18	Director Building/Grounds	Mr. Ron MASH
29	Director Alumni Relations	Ms. Libby VILLAVICENCIO
09	Director of Institutional Research	Ms. Kensey LOVE
30	Director Marketing & Advancement	Ms. Laura ALLOWAY
21	Controller/Assistant Treasurer	Mrs. Anna JOHNSON

Hocking College Perry Campus (A)

5454 State Route 37, New Lexington OH 43764
Telephone: (740) 342-3337 Identification: 770359
Accreditation: &NH

† Main campus is Hocking College in Nelsonville, OH.

Hondros College (B)

1810 Successful Drive, Fairborn OH 45324
Telephone: (937) 879-1940 Identification: 770751
Accreditation: ACICS

† Main campus is Hondros College in Westerville, OH.

Hondros College (C)

4100 Rockside Road, Second Floor, Independence OH 44131
Telephone: (216) 524-1143 Identification: 770750
Accreditation: ACICS

† Main campus is Hondros College in Westerville, OH.

Hondros College (D)

7600 Tyler's Place Boulevard, West Chester OH 45069
Telephone: (513) 508-3005 Identification: 770749
Accreditation: ACICS

† Main campus is Hondros College in Westerville, OH.

Hondros College (E)

4140 Executive Parkway, Westerville OH 43081-3855
County: Franklin FICE Identification: 040743
Unit ID: 203386
Telephone: (614) 508-7277 Carnegie Class: Assoc/PrivFP
FAX Number: (614) 508-7280 Calendar System: Quarter
URL: www.hondros.edu
Established: 1981 Annual Undergrad Tuition & Fees: $20,622
Enrollment: 1,415 Coed
Affiliation or Control: Proprietary IRS Status: Proprietary
Highest Offering: Associate Degree
Program: Occupational; 2-Year Principally Bachelor's Creditable; Nursing Emphasis
Accreditation: ACICS, NURSE

01	President	Ms. Linda HONDROS
66	President Nursing Programs	Ms. Carol THOMAS
07	Director of Admission	Mr. Brent STARK
06	Registrar	Ms. Michelle HARDEN

International College of Broadcasting (F)

6 S Smithville Road, Dayton OH 45431-1898
County: Montgomery FICE Identification: 013132
Unit ID: 203289
Telephone: (937) 258-8251 Carnegie Class: Assoc/PrivFP
FAX Number: (937) 258-8714 Calendar System: Semester
URL: www.icb.edu
Established: 1968 Annual Undergrad Tuition & Fees: $14,950
Enrollment: 66 Coed
Affiliation or Control: Proprietary IRS Status: Proprietary
Highest Offering: Associate Degree
Program: Occupational
Accreditation: ACCSC

01	President	J. Michael LEMASTER
05	School Director	Eric CLARK

ITT Technical Institute (G)

3428 W Market Street, Akron OH 44333
Telephone: (330) 865-8600 Identification: 770660
Accreditation: ACICS

† Main campus is ITT Technical Institute in Indianapolis, IN.

ITT Technical Institute (H)

4717 Hilton Corporate Drive, Columbus OH 43232
Telephone: (614) 868-2000 Identification: 666706
Accreditation: ACICS

† Main campus is ITT Technical Institute in Indianapolis, IN.

ITT Technical Institute (I)

3325 Stop Eight Road, Dayton OH 45414-3456
Telephone: (937) 264-7700 FICE Identification: 009088
Accreditation: ACICS

† Main campus is ITT Technical Institute in Indianapolis, IN.

ITT Technical Institute (J)

3781 Park Mill Run Drive, Hilliard OH 43026-8110
Telephone: (614) 771-4888 Identification: 666318
Accreditation: ACICS

† Main campus is ITT Technical Institute in Indianapolis, IN.

ITT Technical Institute (K)

1656 Henthorne Boulevard, Suite B, Maumee OH 43537-3920
Telephone: (419) 861-6500 Identification: 666160
Accreditation: ACICS

† Main campus is ITT Technical Institute in Indianapolis, IN.

ITT Technical Institute (L)

4750 Wesley Avenue, Norwood OH 45212-2244
Telephone: (513) 531-8300 Identification: 666546
Accreditation: ACICS

† Main campus is ITT Technical Institute in Indianapolis, IN.

ITT Technical Institute (M)

14955 Sprague Road, Strongsville OH 44136-1758
Telephone: (440) 234-9091 Identification: 666547
Accreditation: ACICS

† Main campus is ITT Technical Institute in Indianapolis, IN.

ITT Technical Institute (N)

4700 Richmond Road, Warrensville Heights OH 44128-5984
Telephone: (216) 896-6500 Identification: 666379
Accreditation: ACICS

† Main campus is ITT Technical Institute in Indianapolis, IN.

ITT Technical Institute (O)

7116 Office Pard Drive, West Chester OH 45069
Telephone: (513) 644-0600 Identification: 770659
Accreditation: ACICS

† Main campus is ITT Technical Institute in Indianapolis, IN.

ITT Technical Institute (P)

1030 N Meridian Road, Youngstown OH 44509-4098
Telephone: (330) 270-1600 FICE Identification: 009837
Accreditation: ACICS

† Main campus is ITT Technical Institute in Indianapolis, IN.

James A. Rhodes State College (Q)

4240 Campus Drive, Lima OH 45804-3597
County: Allen FICE Identification: 010027
Unit ID: 203678
Telephone: (419) 995-8200 Carnegie Class: Assoc/Pub-R-M
FAX Number: (419) 221-0450 Calendar System: Semester
URL: www.rhodesstate.edu
Established: 1971 Annual Undergrad Tuition & Fees (In-State): $4,705
Enrollment: 3,883 Coed
Affiliation or Control: State IRS Status: 501(c)3
Highest Offering: Associate Degree
Program: Occupational; 2-Year Principally Bachelor's Creditable
Accreditation: NH, ACBSP, ADNUR, COARC, DH, ENGT, MAC, OTA, PTAA, RAD

01	President	Dr. Debra L. MCCURDY
10	Vice President Business & Treasurer	Mr. Chris R. SCHMIDT
05	Interim VP Academic Affairs	Mr. Richard WOODFIELD
32	Vice President Student Affairs	Dr. Cynthia E. SPIERS
35	Associate Dean for Student Services	Ms. Judi MAZZARELLLI
30	Executive Director of Development	Mr. Kevin L. REEKS
20	Interim Associate Vice President	Dr. Antoinette BALDIN
07	Director of Admissions	Ms. Traci R. COX
37	Director Student Financial Aid	Ms. Cathy L. KOHLI
09	Director Institutional Research	Mr. Steve S. MILLER
36	Director of Career Services	Ms. Krista RICHARDSON
08	Head Librarian	Ms. Tina SCHNEIDER
103	Exec Dir for Workforce & Econ Dev	Dr. Matthew J. KINKLEY
15	Director Human Resources	Mr. Jonathon HORN
50	Dean Div Business & Public Services	Ms. Brenda RIZOR
54	Dean Div Info Tech/Engr Tech	Ms. Antoinette BALDIN
49	Dean Division of Arts & Sciences	Mr. William C. WELLS
66	Dean Division of Nursing	Ms. Carol SCHMIDT
76	Dean Div of AH/Sciences	Ms. Tish HATFIELD
45	Vice President Inst Effect/Planning	Ms. Becky BURRELL
18	Chief Facilities/Physical Plant	Mr. Chris R. SCHMIDT
21	Assistant Treasurer/Controller	Ms. Beverly REX-COOK
26	Coordinator Public Relations	Ms. Paula J. SIEBENECK
06	Registrar	Dr. Rose REINHART
38	Director Advising & Counseling	Mr. Chris JEBSEN

John Carroll University (R)

1 John Carroll Boulevard, University Heights OH 44118-4581
County: Cuyahoga FICE Identification: 003050
Unit ID: 203368
Telephone: (216) 397-1886 Carnegie Class: Master's L
FAX Number: (216) 397-4256 Calendar System: Semester
URL: www.jcu.edu
Established: 1886 Annual Undergrad Tuition & Fees: $34,480
Enrollment: 3,583 Coed
Affiliation or Control: Roman Catholic IRS Status: 501(c)3
Highest Offering: Beyond Master's But Less Than Doctorate
Program: Liberal Arts And General; Teacher Preparatory; Professional
Accreditation: NH, BUS, BUSA, CACREP, TED

01	President	Rev. Robert L. NIEHOFF, SJ
43	Director of Legal Affairs	Mr. James P. CROSBY
04	VP and Exec Asst to the President	Dr. Jonathan E. SMITH
88	VP for Univ Mission & Identity	Dr. Paul V. MURPHY
101	Interim Secretary to Board of Dir	Ms. Dora PRUCE
05	Provost & Academic Vice President	Dr. John T. DAY
32	Vice President for Student Affairs	Dr. Mark D. MCCARTHY
84	Vice President for Enrollment	Mr. Brian G. WILLIAMS
10	Vice President for Finance	Mr. Richard F. MAUSSER
30	Vice President for Univ Advancement	Ms. Doreen K. RILEY
20	Assoc Academic Vice President	Dr. James H. KRUKONES
20	AAVP Stdnt Lrng Initiat & Diversity	Dr. Lauren L. BOWEN
45	Chief Planning Officer	Vacant
108	Asst Provost for Inst Effectiveness	Dr. Kathleen L. DEAN
21	Exec Dir Administrative Finance	Mr. David W. WONG
49	Dean College of Arts & Sciences	Dr. Jeanne COLLERAN
50	Dean Boler School of Business	Dr. Karen SCHUELE
35	Dean of Students	Dr. Sherri A. CRAHEN
13	Chief Information Officer	Mr. Michael J. BESTUL
26	Asst VP Intg Mktg & Communications	Mr. John CARFAGNA
18	Assoc Vice Pres for Facilities	Ms. Carol P. DIETZ
16	Director of Human Resources	Mr. Charles STUPPY
08	Director of the Library	Ms. Michelle MILLET
36	Acting Director Ctr for Career Svcs	Dr. Cynthia MARCO SCANLON
28	Director Ctr Stdnt Diversty/Inclusn	Ms. Danielle J. CARTER
104	Dir Center for Global Education	Dr. Andreas SOBISCH
06	Registrar	Vacant
88	Bursar & Dir of Student Accounts	Ms. Diane M. WARD
39	Director of Residence Life	Ms. Lisa M. BROWN
92	Director Honors Program	Dr. Julia KAROLLE-BERG
07	Executive Director of Enrollment	Mr. Steven P. VITATOE
88	Executive Director of Development	Ms. Molly MCARDLE
37	Director of Financial Aid	Ms. Claudia WENZEL
31	Dir Ctr for Service & Social Action	Dr. Margaret O. FINUCANE
42	Director of Campus Ministry	Mr. John SCARANO
38	Director Univ Counseling Center	Dr. Mary Beth E. JAVOREK
24	Dir Instructional Tech Services	Dr. Jay TARBY
23	Director Student Health Center	Ms. Janet M. KREVH
41	Sr Director Athletics & Recreation	Ms. Laurie MASSA
29	Director Alumni Relations	Mr. David A. VITATOE
44	Director Planned Giving	Mr. Peter R. BERNARDO
102	Dir Corp Relations and Major Gifts	Ms. Christina BEG
25	Director Fdn Rels & Grant Writing	Ms. Pamela GEORGE
86	Dir Government & Community Rels	Ms. Dora PRUCE
96	Director Purchasing & Aux Services	Mr. Andrew F. FRONCZEK
19	Director Campus Safety Services	Mr. Timothy PEPPARD
105	Dir Marketing Services (Web)	Mr. Michael RICHWALSKY
88	Coordinator Institutional Effective	Ms. Marilyn F. VALENCIA

Kaplan Career Institute (S)

8720 Brookpark Road, Brooklyn OH 44129
County: Cuyahoga FICE Identification: 025829
Unit ID: 206093
Telephone: (216) 485-0900 Carnegie Class: Assoc/PrivFP
FAX Number: (216) 661-6842 Calendar System: Other
URL: cleveland.kaplancareerinstitute.com
Established: 1980 Annual Undergrad Tuition & Fees: $15,100
Enrollment: 301 Coed
Affiliation or Control: Proprietary IRS Status: Proprietary
Highest Offering: Associate Degree
Program: Occupational; 2-Year Principally Bachelor's Creditable; Technical Emphasis
Accreditation: ACCSC, ACICS

01	Campus Director	Anthony HIBBS

Kaplan College (T)

801 Linn Street, Cincinnati OH 45203
Telephone: (513) 421-9900 Identification: 770581

Accreditation: ACCSC, ACICS

† Main campus is Kaplan Career Institute in Philadelphia, PA.

Kaplan College (A)

2800 East River Road, Dayton OH 45439
County: Montgomery FICE Identification: 020520
Unit ID: 204626
Telephone: (937) 294-6155 Carnegie Class: Assoc/PrivFP
FAX Number: (937) 294-2259 Calendar System: Quarter
URL: dayton.kaplancollege.com
Established: 1971 Annual Undergrad Tuition & Fees: $15,195
Enrollment: 492 Coed
Affiliation or Control: Proprietary IRS Status: Proprietary
Highest Offering: Associate Degree
Program: Occupational; Technical Emphasis
Accreditation: ACCSC, MAC

01 President ... Mr. Robert ELMOORE
05 Director of Education ... Ms. Kelly GRAMLING

Kent State University Main Campus (B)

PO Box 5190, Kent OH 44242-0001
County: Portage FICE Identification: 003051
Unit ID: 203517
Telephone: (330) 672-2121 Carnegie Class: RU/H
FAX Number: (330) 672-2190 Calendar System: Semester
URL: www.kent.edu
Established: 1910 Annual Undergrad Tuition & Fees (In-State): $9,846
Enrollment: 27,706 Coed
Affiliation or Control: State IRS Status: 501(c)3
Highest Offering: Doctorate
Program: Liberal Arts And General; Teacher Preparatory; Professional
Accreditation: NH, AAB, ART, AUD, BUS, BUSA, CACREP, CIDA, CLPSY, CORE, DANCE, DIETD, DIETI, EXSC, JOUR, LIB, MUS, NAIT, NRPA, NURSE, POD, SCPSY, SP, SPAA, TED, THEA

01 President ... Dr. Lester A. LEFTON
05 Provost/Sr VP Academic Affairs ... Dr. Todd DIACON
10 Vice Pres Finance & Administration ... Mr. Gregg S. FLOYD
16 Interim Vice Pres Human Resources ... Mr. Joseph VITALE
30 Vice Pres Institutional Advancement ... Mr. Eugene J. FINN
26 Vice Pres Univ Relations ... Ms. Iris E. HARVEY
32 VP Enrollment Mgmt/Student Affairs ... Mr. Greg I. JARVIE
46 Vice President Research ... Dr. W. Grant MCGIMPSEY
27 Vice Pres Information Services/CIO ... Mr. Edward G. MAHON
22 VP Diversity/Equity/Inclusion ... Dr. Alfreda BROWN
20 Interim Dean Undergraduate Studies ... Ms. Eboni PRINGLE
35 Student Ombuds ... Dr. Jennifer KULICS
45 Sr Assoc Provost ... Dr. Melondy TANKERSLEY
20 Assoc Provost Faculty Affairs ... Ms. Sue AVERILL
44 Sr Assoc VP Institutional Adv ... Mr. Stephen G. SOKANY
84 Assoc Vice Pres Enrollment Services ... Mr. David GARCIA
29 Exec Director of Alumni Affairs ... Mrs. Lori RANDORF
07 Director of Admissions ... Ms. Nancy J. DELLAVECCHIA
06 Registrar ... Mr. Glenn DAVIS
43 Vice Pres University Counsel ... Mr. Willis WALKER
100 Sec Bd Trustees/Chief of Staff ... Ms. Charlene K. REED
41 Director Intercollegiate Athletics ... Mr. Joel NIELSON
22 Director of Compliance & Benefits ... Ms. Loretta SHIELDS
37 Director Student Financial Aid ... Mr. Mark EVANS
19 Director of Public Safety ... Mr. John PEACH
12 Assoc Provost/Dean Trumbull Campus ... Dr. Wanda THOMAS
96 Director of Procurement ... Mr. Timothy J. KONCZAL
49 Interim Dean Arts & Sciences ... Dr. James BLANK
50 Dean of Business Administration ... Dr. Deborah F. SPAKE
53 Dean of Education ... Dr. Daniel F. MAHONY
57 Dean of the Arts ... Dr. John CRAWFORD
66 Dean College of Nursing ... Dr. Laura DZUREC
51 Exec Director Continuing Studies ... Ms. Deborah C. HUNTSMAN
92 Dean Honors College ... Dr. Donald F. PALMER
08 Dean Library & Media Services ... Dr. James BRACKEN
48 Dean Architect/Environ Design ... Mr. Douglas STEIDL
27 Dean Communication & Information ... Dr. Stanley T. WEARDEN
72 Dean Col of Applied Engr/Sust/Tech . Dr. Shin-Min (Simon) SONG
58 Dean of Graduate Studies ... Dr. Mary Ann STEPHENS
88 CEO College of Podiatric Medicine ... Dr. Thomas V. MELILLO, SR.

Kent State University at Ashtabula (C)

3300 Lake Road W, Ashtabula OH 44004-2299
Telephone: (440) 964-3322 FICE Identification: 003052
Accreditation: &NH, ADNUR, COARC, OTA, PTAA, RAD

† Main campus is Kent State University Main Campus in Kent, OH.

Kent State University East Liverpool Campus (D)

400 E Fourth Street, East Liverpool OH 43920-3497
Telephone: (330) 385-3805 FICE Identification: 003056
Accreditation: &NH, ADNUR, OTA, PTAA

† Main campus is Kent State University Main Campus in Kent, OH.

Kent State University Geauga Campus (E)

14111 Claridon-Troy Road,
Burton Township OH 44021-9500
Telephone: (440) 834-4187 FICE Identification: 003059
Accreditation: &NH

† Main campus is Kent State University Main Campus in Kent, OH.

Kent State University Salem Campus (F)

2491 State Road 45 South, Salem OH 44460-9412
Telephone: (330) 332-0361 FICE Identification: 003061
Accreditation: &NH, NMT, RAD, RTT

† Main campus is Kent State University Main Campus in Kent, OH.

Kent State University Stark Campus (G)

6000 Frank Avenue NW, North Canton OH 44720-9988
Telephone: (330) 499-9600 FICE Identification: 003054
Accreditation: &NH

† Main campus is Kent State University Main Campus in Kent, OH.

Kent State University Trumbull Campus (H)

4314 Mahoning Avenue, NW, Warren OH 44483-1998
Telephone: (330) 847-0571 FICE Identification: 003064
Accreditation: &NH

† Main campus is Kent State University Main Campus in Kent, OH.

Kent State University Tuscarawas Campus (I)

330 University Drive, NE,
New Philadelphia OH 44663-9403
Telephone: (330) 339-3391 FICE Identification: 003062
Accreditation: &NH, ADNUR, ENGT

† Main campus is Kent State University Main Campus in Kent, OH.

Kenyon College (J)

Gambier OH 43022-9623
County: Knox FICE Identification: 003065
Unit ID: 203535
Telephone: (740) 427-5000 Carnegie Class: Bac/A&S
FAX Number: (740) 427-3077 Calendar System: Semester
URL: www.kenyon.edu
Established: 1824 Annual Undergrad Tuition & Fees: $45,640
Enrollment: 1,667 Coed
Affiliation or Control: Independent Non-Profit IRS Status: 501(c)3
Highest Offering: Baccalaureate
Program: Liberal Arts And General
Accreditation: NH

01 President ... Dr. Sean DECATUR
05 Provost ... Vacant
30 Vice President College Relations ... Ms. Sarah H. KAHRL
10 Vice President for Finance ... Mr. Joseph G. NELSON
08 Vice Pres Library & Info Svcs ... Mr. Ronald K. GRIGGS
100 Advisor to President ... Mr. Jesse E. MATZ
21 Assoc Vice President for Finance ... Ms. Teri L. BLANCHARD
44 Assoc VP College Relations ... Mr. Kyle W. HENDERSON
32 Dean of Students ... Dr. Henry P. TOUTAIN
07 Dean of Admissions/Fin Aid ... Ms. Jennifer DELAHUNTY
20 Associate Provost ... Dr. Ric S. SHEFFIELD
08 Director of Information Resources ... Mr. Joseph M. MURPHY
06 Registrar/Dean Academic Support ... Ms. Ellen K. HARBOUT
26 Director of Public Affairs ... Mr. Shawn PRESLEY
13 Director Systems Design/Consulting ... Mr. Ronald K. GRIGGS
29 Dir Alumni/Parent Rels ... Mr. Scott R. BAKER
37 Director of Financial Aid ... Mr. Craig A. DAUGHERTY
38 Director of Counseling Services ... Dr. Patrick K. GILLIGAN
15 Director of Human Resources ... Ms. Jennifer G. CADRAL
42 Director Board College Ministries ... Rev. Karl P B. STEVENS
21 Chief Business Officer ... Mr. Mark KOLMAN
22 Equal Opportunity Officer ... Ms. Mariam N. EL-SHAMAA
19 Director of Campus Safety ... Mr. Robert D. HOOPER
09 Director of Institutional Research ... Ms. Erika M. FARFAN
21 Manager of Business Services ... Mr. Frederick S. LINGER
28 Director of Multicultural Affairs ... Mr. A. Chris KENNERLY

Kettering College (K)

3737 Southern Boulevard, Kettering OH 45429-1299
County: Montgomery FICE Identification: 007035
Unit ID: 203544
Telephone: (937) 395-8601 Carnegie Class: Spec/Health
FAX Number: (937) 395-8106 Calendar System: Semester
URL: www.kc.edu
Established: 1967 Annual Undergrad Tuition & Fees: $12,540
Enrollment: 981 Coed
Affiliation or Control: Seventh-day Adventist IRS Status: 501(c)3
Highest Offering: Master's
Program: Occupational; 2-Year Principally Bachelor's Creditable; Professional; Nursing Emphasis
Accreditation: NH, ADNUR, ARCPA, COARC, DMS, NUR, RAD

00 Chairman of the Board ... Dr. Roy CHEW
01 President ... Dr. Alexander BRYAN
15 Vice President Human Resources ... Mrs. Beverly MORRIS
05 Dean for Academic Affairs ... Dr. William G. NELSON
102 President Foundation ... Dr. Martin CLARK
84 Dean for Enrollment Services ... Mr. Victor BROWN
10 Chief Business Officer ... Vacant
06 Registrar ... Mrs. Robin VANDERBILT
88 Dean Assessment & Learning Support ... Dr. Beverly COBB
37 Director Student Financial Aid ... Mrs. Kim SNELL
40 Manager Bookstore ... Mrs. Stella FREEMAN
42 Chaplain Director Campus Ministry ... Mr. Clive WILSON
32 Director Student Life/Residence ... Mr. Jerry MAHN
26 Public Relations Officer ... Ms. Mindy CLAGGETT
08 Director of Library ... Mr. John KISSINGER
29 Director Alumni Relations ... Mrs. Amy ORTIZ-MORETTA
07 Director of Admissions ... Mrs. Becky MCDONALD
27 Senior Information Officer ... Mr. Jim NESBIT

Lake Erie College (L)

391 W Washington Street, Painesville OH 44077-3389
County: Lake FICE Identification: 003066
Unit ID: 203580
Telephone: (440) 375-7000 Carnegie Class: Master's S
FAX Number: (440) 375-7005 Calendar System: Semester
URL: www.lec.edu
Established: 1856 Annual Undergrad Tuition & Fees: $27,368
Enrollment: 1,202 Coed
Affiliation or Control: Independent Non-Profit IRS Status: 501(c)3
Highest Offering: Master's
Program: Liberal Arts And General; Teacher Preparatory; Professional; Business Emphasis
Accreditation: NH, IACBE, @TEAC

01 President ... Michael T. VICTOR
05 Vice Pres for Academic Affairs/CAO ... Dr. Jana HOLWICK
10 Vice Pres Administration & Finance ... Brian DIRK
84 VP Enroll Mgmt & Student Affairs ... Robin JOHNSON
26 VP for Institutional Advancement ... Vacant
20 Assoc VP for Academic Admin ... Dr. Jennifer COLLIS
53 Dean School of Educ & Prof Studies ... Prof. Dale SHEPTAK
50 Dean School of Business ... Prof. Robert TREBAR
88 Dean School of Equine Studies ... Dr. Pam HESS
88 Dean School of Arts/Human & SS ... Dr. Tom DAVIS
81 Dean School of Natural Sci & Math .. Dr. Steven REYNOLDS, JR.
06 Registrar ... Barbara ARILSON
107 Director Prof Development & ADCP ... Lisa STRAUSBAUGH
58 Director Parker MBA Program ... Donna BARES
88 Director Physician Assistant Pgm ... Joe WEBER
36 Director Career Services ... Erin NUNN
13 Director of Information Technology ... Vacant
38 Director Student Success Center ... Dr. John SPIESMAN
37 Director Financial Aid ... Patricia PANGONIS
15 Assistant Director Human Resources ... Andrea MYERS
32 Dean of Students ... Billie DUNN
07 Dean Admissions/Financial Aid ... Chris HARRIS
18 Director Physical Plant ... Herb DILL
30 Director Development ... Ed MAYER
29 Director Alumni & Community Rels ... Debra REMINGTON
41 Director Athletics ... Vacant
08 Director Lincoln Library ... Christopher BENNETT
19 Director Security ... Richard KLINE
39 Director Residence Life ... Megan MCKENNA
09 Institutional Research Specialist ... Amanda ZINNI
40 Bookstore Manager ... Natalie SCALA

Lakeland Community College (M)

7700 Clocktower Drive, Kirtland OH 44094-5198
County: Lake FICE Identification: 006804
Unit ID: 203599
Telephone: (440) 525-7000 Carnegie Class: Assoc/Pub-S-SC
FAX Number: (440) 525-7651 Calendar System: Semester
URL: www.lakelandcc.edu
Established: 1967 Annual Undergrad Tuition & Fees (In-District): $3,188
Enrollment: 9,307 Coed
Affiliation or Control: State/Local IRS Status: 501(c)3
Highest Offering: Associate Degree
Program: Occupational; 2-Year Principally Bachelor's Creditable
Accreditation: NH, ADNUR, CAHIIM, COARC, DH, ENGT, HT, IFSAC, MAC, MLTAD, RAD, SURGT

01 President ... Dr. Morris W. BEVERAGE, JR.
05 Exec VP & Provost/Dean Faculty ... Dr. Margaret BARTOW
10 Sr Vice Pres Admin Svcs/Treasurer ... Mr. Michael E. MAYHER
100 Chief of Staff/Sr VP Inst Effectiv ... Ms. Mary Ann BLAKELEY
26 Chief Commun Ofcr/VP College Rels ... Ms. Dawn M. PLANTE
20 Assoc Provost Teach & Lrng Effectiv ... Dr. Deborah L. HARDY
84 Assoc Provost for Enrollment Mgmt ... Mr. William KRAUS
20 Assoc VP Student Development ... Mr. Richard J. NOVOTNY
83 Dean Math/Soc Science/Public Svcs ... Dr. Steven OLUIC
76 Dean of Health Technologies ... Dr. Deborah L. HARDY
79 Dean Arts/Humanities ... Dr. Donald KILLEEN
50 Dean Business/Engineering ... Dr. Gary L. EITH
88 Dean of Learning Technologies ... Mr. William KNAPP
21 Assoc VP Bus Svcs/Deputy Treasurer ... Mr. Brian COOK
13 Dir Administrative Technologies ... Mr. Rick PENNY
31 Director Community Learning ... Vacant
21 Controller & Bursar ... Mr. Paul D. HENSCHEL
15 Director Hum Res/Organizational Dev ... Ms. Cathy BUSH
18 Director for Facilities Management ... Mr. Bert DIEHL
19 Chief of Police/Director of Safety ... Mr. Gerald JENKINS
07 Director for Admissions/Registrar ... Ms. Tracey L. COOPER

37 Dir Financial Aid/Enroll Support ....Ms. Melissa A. AMSPAUGH
35 Director of Student Activities ....Mr. Mario PETITTI
30 Dir Development/Alumni Relations ....Dr. Robert CAHEN
96 Director of Purchasing ....Mr. Tom A. KIRCHNER
09 Director of Institutional Research ....Mrs. Lisa DURST

Lakewood College (A)

12900 Lake Avenue, Lakewood OH 44107-1558
County: Cuyahoga Identification: 666715
Telephone: (800) 517-0857 Carnegie Class: Not Classified
FAX Number: (216) 803-9899 Calendar System: Other
URL: www.lakewoodcollege.edu
Established: 1998 Annual Undergrad Tuition & Fees: $4,950
Enrollment: N/A Coed
Affiliation or Control: Independent Non-Profit IRS Status: 501(c)3
Highest Offering: Associate Degree
Program: Occupational
Accreditation: DETC

01 CEO and Founder ....Ms. Tanya HAGGINS
11 Vice President of Operations ....Ms. Aleia EVANS
21 Vice President of Administration ....Ms. Summer HAGGINS
30 Vice President of Business Develop ....Mr. Isaac HAGGINS

Lorain County Community College (B)

1005 N Abbe Road, Elyria OH 44035-1691
County: Lorain FICE Identification: 003068
Unit ID: 203748
Telephone: (440) 365-5222 Carnegie Class: Assoc/Pub-U-SC
FAX Number: (440) 365-6519 Calendar System: Semester
URL: www.lorainccc.edu
Established: 1963 Annual Undergrad Tuition & Fees (In-District): $2,977
Enrollment: 12,637 Coed
Affiliation or Control: State/Local IRS Status: 501(c)3
Highest Offering: Associate Degree
Program: Occupational; 2-Year Principally Bachelor's Creditable
Accreditation: NH, ADNUR, ART, DH, DMS, EMT, ENGT, MAC, MLTAD, OTA, PHLEB, PNUR, PTAA, RAD, SURGT

01 President ....Dr. Roy A. CHURCH
46 VP Strategic & Institutional Devel ....Ms. Tracy A. GREEN
05 Provost/VP for Acad & Student Svcs ... Dr. Marcia J. BALLINGER
10 Vice President Admin Svcs/Treasurer ....Mr. Quentin J. POTTER
88 Assoc Prov University Partnership ....Dr. John R. CROOKS
08 Int Dean Library/Instruction Media ....Ms. Susan PAUL
84 Dean Enroll Svcs/Fin Aid/Registrar ....Ms. Stephanie SUTTON
09 Dean Rsch/Inst Effect/Public Svcs ....Ms. Shara DAVIS
13 Director Information Systems ....Mr. Lou KOMPARE
15 Director Human Resources ....Mrs. Sydney LANCASTER
88 Dir Entrepreneurship Innov Inst ....Ms. Terri B. SANDU
19 Director of Campus Security ....Mr. Keith BROWN
18 Director of Physical Plant ....Mr. Robert FLYER
51 Director Public Services ....Ms. Shara DAVIS
88 Interim Dean Academic Foundations ....Mr. Jeff KOLENO
57 Dir Stocker Humanit/Fine Arts Ctr .Ms. Janet HERMAN-BARLOW
96 Dir Purchasing/Facilities Planning ....Ms. Laura K. CARISSIMI
50 Dean of Business ....Dr. Robert B. YOUNG
54 Dean Engineering Tech ....Ms. Kelly ZELESNIK
76 Int Dean Allied Health & Nursing ....Ms. Hope MOON
79 Dean Arts/Humanities ....Dr. Robert A. BECKSTROM
81 Dean Science/Math ....Dr. Rosa HAINAJ
83 Int Dean Social Science/Human Svc ......Dr. Jonathan N. DRYDEN
68 Int Dean Health/PE/Recreation ....Ms. Lisa AUGUSTINE

Lourdes University (C)

6832 Convent Boulevard, Sylvania OH 43560-2898
County: Lucas FICE Identification: 003069
Unit ID: 203757
Telephone: (419) 885-3211 Carnegie Class: Master's S
FAX Number: (419) 882-3987 Calendar System: Semester
URL: www.lourdes.edu
Established: 1958 Annual Undergrad Tuition & Fees: $17,456
Enrollment: 2,047 Coed
Affiliation or Control: Roman Catholic IRS Status: 501(c)3
Highest Offering: Master's
Program: Liberal Arts And General; Professional
Accreditation: NH, ANEST, IACBE, NURSE, SW, TEAC

01 President ....Dr. David J. LIVINGSTON
00 President Emerita ....Sr. Ann Francis KLIMKOWSKI
05 Provost ....Dr. Geoffrey GRUBB
32 Vice Pres for Student Life ....Ms. Roseanne GILL-JACOBSON
10 Vice Pres Finance & Administration ....Mr. Michael KILLIAN
42 Vice Pres for Mission & Ministry .Sr. Ann Carmen BARONE, OSF
30 Vice President for Inst Advancement ....Ms. Mary ARQUETTE
49 Dean College of Arts & Sciences ....Dr. Holly J. BAUMGARTNER
53 Dean Coll of Education & Human Svcs ......Dr. Michael J. SMITH
66 Dean College of Nursing ....Dr. Judy DIDION
50 Dean College Business & Leadership ....Dr. Dean LUDWIG
58 Dean of Graduate School ....Sr. Shannon SCHREIN OSF
07 Dean of Admissions ....Ms. Amy MERGEN
35 Assoc Dean of Students & Retention ....Ms. Rachel DUFF-ANDERSON
37 Interim Director Financial Aid ....Ms. Deb LAJEUNESSE
26 Director of University Relations ....Ms. Helene SHEETS
08 Director of Library Services ....Sr. Sandra RUTKOWSKI
06 Registrar ....Ms. Michelle A. RABLE
13 Director of Information Technology ....Dr. LeRoy BUTLER

15 Director of Human Resources ....Mr. Scott SIMON
85 Director Foreign Students ....Vacant
36 Director of Career Counseling ....Vacant
11 Director of Administrative Systems .....Ms. Laurie ORZECHOWSKI
21 Director of Finance ....Ms. Melissa RICHBERG
88 Director Academic Advising ....Dr. Robert DETWILER
44 Dir Development/Annual Fund Officer ....Mr. Michael GEORGE
18 Director of Facilities & Grounds ....Mr. Michael CRAVENS
09 Director of Institutional Research ....Ms. Pam CURAVO
29 Alumni Relations Officer ....Ms. Erin HAFNER
40 Manager of Bookstore ....Ms. Ann MORRIS

Malone University (D)

2600 Cleveland Avenue NW, Canton OH 44709-3897
County: Stark FICE Identification: 003072
Unit ID: 203775
Telephone: (330) 471-8100 Carnegie Class: Master's M
FAX Number: (330) 471-8478 Calendar System: Semester
URL: www.malone.edu
Established: 1892 Annual Undergrad Tuition & Fees: $25,678
Enrollment: 2,373 Coed
Affiliation or Control: Friends IRS Status: 501(c)3
Highest Offering: Master's
Program: Liberal Arts And General; Teacher Preparatory; Professional
Accreditation: NH, ACBSP, CACREP, NURSE, SW, TED

01 President ....Dr. David A. KING
10 Vice President for Finance/CFO ....Mrs. Joy E. BRATHWAITE
05 Provost ....Dr. Donald L. TUCKER
30 Vice Pres for Univ Advancement ....Mr. Howard E. TAYLOR
84 Interim Vice Pres for Enrollment ....Dr. Christopher T. ABRAMS
32 Vice Pres for Student Development ... Dr. Christopher T. ABRAMS
49 Dean Col of Theol/Arts & Sciences ....Dr. D. Nathan PHINNEY
51 Dean Sch of Business & Leadership ....Dr. Marjorie F. CARLSON HURST
53 Dean Sch of Education & Human Devel ....Dr. Rhoda C. SOMMERS
66 Dean Sch of Nursing & Health Sci ....Dr. Debra A. LEE
21 Finance Manager ....Mr. Tracy L. MILLER
06 Registrar ....Mr. Gary L. PHELPS
07 Director of Admissions ....Mrs. Linda K. HOFFMAN
29 Dir of Alumni & Parent Relations .... Mrs. Deborah M. ROBINSON
44 Director of The Malone Fund ....Mr. F. Allen FRALEY
36 Director of Alumni Career Services ....Mr. Douglas C. REICHENBERGER
27 Director of University Relations ....Mrs. Suzanne W. THOMAS
30 Senior Dev Officer for Intercol Ath ....Mr. John C. FEHLMAN
105 Web Administrator ....Mr. Michael R. MILLER
37 Director of Financial Aid ....Mrs. Pamela S. PUSTAY
15 Director of Human Resources ....Mr. Michael J. FAIRLESS
41 Athletic Director ....Mr. Charles R. GRIMES
08 Acting Director of Library Services ....Ms. Rebecca L. FORT
93 Director of Multicultural Services ....Mrs. Brenda D. STEVENS
18 Director of Physical Plant ....Mr. James E. PALONE
88 Dir of Center for Student Success ....Mrs. Patricia L. LITTLE
108 Dir of Inst Effectiveness/Assesmnt ....Dr. Charles R. LARTEY
91 Enterprise Systems Manager ....Mr. John D. RIVERS
24 Support and Infrastructure Manager ....Mr. M. Adam KLEMANN
90 Senior Systems Engineer ....Mr. Alexander YU
42 University Chaplain ....Rev. L. Randall HECKERT
40 Bookstore Manager ....Mr. Derek R. MYERS
09 Assistant to the Provost ....Ms. Karen R. WARNER
92 Director of Honors Programs ....Dr. Diane M. CHAMBERS
89 Dir of the College Experience Pgm ....Dr. Marcia K. EVERETT
38 Director of Counseling Center ....Mr. Timothy T. MORBER
23 Health Center Nurse ....Mrs. Janet A. PERKO

Marietta College (E)

215 Fifth Street, Marietta OH 45750-4033
County: Washington FICE Identification: 003073
Unit ID: 203845
Telephone: (740) 376-4000 Carnegie Class: Bac/Diverse
FAX Number: (740) 376-4896 Calendar System: Semester
URL: www.marietta.edu
Established: 1835 Annual Undergrad Tuition & Fees: $31,940
Enrollment: 1,629 Coed
Affiliation or Control: Independent Non-Profit IRS Status: 501(c)3
Highest Offering: Master's
Program: Liberal Arts And General; Teacher Preparatory; Professional
Accreditation: NH, ARCPA, ENG, MUS, TED

01 President ....Dr. Joseph W. BRUNO
05 Provost/Dean of Faculty ....Dr. Karyn Z. SPROLES
10 Vice President for Admin & Finance ....Mr. Daniel C. BRYANT
30 VP for College Advancement ....Dr. Joseph G. SANDMAN
28 VP for Diversity & Inclusion ....Dr. Richard K. DANFORD
32 Vice President for Student Life ....Dr. Robert A. PASTOOR
29 Assoc VP Alumni/College Relations ....Mr. Crompton (Hub) B. BURTON
88 Dean McDonough Ctr for Leadership ....Dr. Gamaliel (Gama) PERRUCI
101 Secretary Board of Trustees ....Mr. William H. DONNELLY
08 Director of Library ....Dr. N. Douglas ANDERSON
21 Controller ....Mr. Dan HUNGERFORD
37 Director Student Financial Services ....Mr. Kevin D. LAMB
18 Director of Physical Plant ....Mr. Fred R. SMITH
38 Director of Counseling Services ....Dr. Eric LIMEGROVER
06 Registrar ....Mrs. Tina K. PERDUE
15 Director of Human Resources ....Mr. Debra C. EVANS
19 Chief of Campus Police ....Mr. Thomas M. SACCENTI

26 Executive Dir of College Relations ....Mr. Thomas D. PERRY
07 Dean of Admissions ....Mr. Jason J. TURLEY
09 Director of Institutional Research ...Dr. Gregory J. DELEMEESTER
36 Career Center Director ....Ms. B. Hilles HUGHES
41 Director of Athletics ....Mr. Larry R. HISER
27 Chief Information Officer ....Mr. John R. DAVIS
63 Dir Physician Assistant Programs ....Dr. Gloria STEWART
85 Director of Education Abroad ....Ms. Christy BURKE
105 Webmaster ....Mr. Chris J. CRAIG
25 Grants Officer ....Ms. Elizabeth B. MCNALLY
51 Continuing Education ....Ms. Tina K. PERDUE
35 Dean of Students ....Mr. Bruce E. PETERSON
20 Associate Provost ....Dr. Mark A. MILLER

Marion Technical College (F)

1467 Mount Vernon Avenue, Marion OH 43302-5694
County: Marion FICE Identification: 010736
Unit ID: 203881
Telephone: (740) 389-4636 Carnegie Class: Assoc/Pub-R-M
FAX Number: (740) 389-6136 Calendar System: Semester
URL: www.mtc.edu
Established: 1971 Annual Undergrad Tuition & Fees (In-State): $4,282
Enrollment: 2,740 Coed
Affiliation or Control: State IRS Status: 501(c)3
Highest Offering: Associate Degree
Program: Occupational; 2-Year Principally Bachelor's Creditable
Accreditation: NH, ADNUR, CAHIIM, MAC, MLTAD, OTA, PTAA, RAD

01 President ....Dr. J. Richard BRYSON
05 Vice Pres Instructional Services ....Mr. Dennis BUDKOWSKI
32 VP of Student Svcs & Inst Advance ....Vacant
84 Dean of Enrollment Services ....Mr. Joel O. LILES
06 Registrar ....Mr. Jim LAVERY
13 Director Mgmt Information Systems ....Ms. Joy A. MOORE
26 Director of Public Relations ....Ms. Nikki WORKMAN
66 Dean of Nursing Technology ....Ms. Mary MCWILLIAMS
103 Director Ctr Workforce Development ....Ms. Tami GALLOWAY
15 Director Human Resources ....Ms. Brenda MCKINNON
88 Dir Physical Therapist Asst Pgm ....Ms. Susan COTTERMAN
88 Dir Occupational Therapy ....Mr. Chad SCHNEIDER
04 Assistant to Pres for Research/Plng ....Ms. Teresa PARKER
18 Coord Facil Improvements/Operations ....Ms. Leeann GRAU
37 Coordinator Student Financial Aid ....Ms. Deb LANGDON
54 Dean of Engineering Technology ....Mr. Dave WAGNER
50 Dean of Business/Information Tech ....Ms. Vicky WOOD
49 Dean of Arts and Sciences ....Mr. Scott POTTER
76 Dean of Allied Health ....Mr. Chris GASE

Mercy College of Ohio (G)

2221 Madison Avenue, Toledo OH 43604
County: Lucas FICE Identification: 030970
Unit ID: 203960
Telephone: (419) 251-1313 Carnegie Class: Spec/Health
FAX Number: (419) 251-1570 Calendar System: Semester
URL: www.mercycollege.edu
Established: 1993 Annual Undergrad Tuition & Fees: $9,144
Enrollment: 1,210 Coed
Affiliation or Control: Roman Catholic IRS Status: 501(c)3
Highest Offering: Baccalaureate
Program: Occupational; 2-Year Principally Bachelor's Creditable; Professional; Nursing Emphasis
Accreditation: NH, ADNUR, CAHIIM, CVT, NUR, NURSE, POLYT, RAD

01 President ....Mr. John HAYWARD
05 VP Acad Affs/Dean of Faculty ....Dr. Anne LOOCHTAN
11 Vice Pres Administrative Services ....Mr. James L. HARTER
66 Associate Dean Nursing ....Dr. Susan BERNHEISEL
81 Associate Dean Scimatics Division ....Dr. Barbara STOOS
97 Assoc Dean Humanities/Social Scis ....Dr. Regan BROCK
76 Assoc Dean Allied Health/Dist Ed ....Dr. Kimberly WATSON
10 Director College Finances/Res Plng ..Ms. Joan M. RUTHERFORD
30 Director College Advancement ....Mr. Michael WHALEN
84 Dir Enroll Svcs/Chief Admiss Ofcr ..Ms. Aimee BISHOP-STUART
08 Director Library/Resource Services ....Ms. Deborah JOHNSON
91 Manager College Admin Info Systems ....Mr. Gary BROCK
06 Registrar ....Ms. Heather HOPPE
37 Financial Aid Director ....Ms. Julie LESLIE
26 Director of Communications ....Ms. Denise HUDGIN
42 Dir Campus Ministry/Coord Ser Learn ....Sr. Sally BOHNETT
21 Business Officer ....Ms. Diane RAHN
103 Director Short Term Educ Programs ....Ms. Cheryl NUTTER
09 Director of Institutional Research ....Ms. Heather HOPPE
15 Director Personnel Services ....Ms. Joan BUNCH
18 Chief Facilities/Physical Plant ....Mr. James HARTER
29 Director Alumni Relations ....Sr. Barbara DAVIS
32 Chief Student Life Officer ....Ms. Megan GRAY
35 Assoc Dean Student Affs/Placement ....Ms. Jennifer PIZIO
38 Director Student Counseling ....Ms. Wendy NATHAN
108 Dir Inst Assessment & Planning ....Ms. Lori EDGEWORTH
07 Director of Admissions ....Ms. Aimee BISHOP STUART
36 Director of Career & Prof Develop ....Ms. Megan GRAY

Methodist Theological School in Ohio (H)

3081 Columbus Pike, Delaware OH 43015-3211
County: Delaware FICE Identification: 003075
Unit ID: 203997
Telephone: (740) 363-1146 Carnegie Class: Spec/Faith
FAX Number: (740) 362-3135 Calendar System: 4/1/4
URL: www.mtso.edu

Established: 1958 Annual Graduate Tuition & Fees: $15,990
Enrollment: 193 Coed
Affiliation or Control: United Methodist IRS Status: 501(c)3
Highest Offering: Doctorate; No Undergraduates
Program: Professional; Religious Emphasis
Accreditation: NH, THEOL

01 President .... Rev. Jay A. RUNDELL
05 Academic Dean .... Dr. Randy I. LITCHFIELD
11 VP for Administrative Services .... Mr. Jonathan D. JUMP
04 Executive Asst to the President .... Ms. Linda J. OGDEN
30 Sp Asst to Pres for Advancement .... Mr. Stan LING
27 Director of Communications .... Mr. Danny RUSSELL
07 Director of Admissions .... Ms. April CASPERSON
06 Registrar .... Ms. Sue LAMPHERE
08 Director of the Library .... Mr. Paul BURNAM
10 Controller .... Mrs. Carolyn ROTHERMEL
18 Director Buildings/Grounds .... Mr. James ROHLER
32 Director of Student Services .... Rev. Leslie TAYLOR
13 Director Information Technology .... Mr. Matthew REHM
37 Financial Aid Officer .... Ms. Molly HOFFMAN

Miami-Jacobs Career College (A)

150 E Gay Street, 1st Floor, Columbus OH 43215-3227
Telephone: (614) 221-7770 Identification: 666465
Accreditation: ACICS, MAC

† Main campus is McCann School of Business & Technology in Pottsville, PA.

Miami-Jacobs Career College (B)

110 N Patterson Boulevard, Dayton OH 45402-1771
Telephone: (937) 222-7337 FICE Identification: 003076
Accreditation: ACICS, MAC, SURGT

† Main campus is McCann School of Business & Technology in Pottsville, PA.

Miami-Jacobs Career College (C)

6400 Rockside Road, Independence OH 44131
Telephone: (216) 834-1400 FICE Identification: 021521
Accreditation: ACICS

† Main campus is McCann School of Business & Technology in Pottsville, PA.

Miami-Jacobs Career College (D)

2 Crowne Point Court, Suite 100, Sharonville OH 45241
Telephone: (513) 693-4400 Identification: 770755
Accreditation: ACICS

† Main campus is McCann School of Business & Technology in Pottsville, PA.

Miami-Jacobs Career College (E)

875 Central Avenue, Springboro OH 45066
Telephone: (937) 746-1830 Identification: 770757
Accreditation: ACICS, COMTA, DA

† Main campus is McCann School of Business & Technology in Pottsville, PA.

Miami-Jacobs Career College (F)

865 West Market Street, Troy OH 45373
Telephone: (937) 332-8585 Identification: 770756
Accreditation: ACICS, COMTA

† Main campus is McCann School of Business & Technology in Pottsville, PA.

Miami University (G)

501 E High Street, Oxford OH 45056-1846
County: Butler FICE Identification: 003077
Unit ID: 204024
Telephone: (513) 529-1809 Carnegie Class: RU/H
FAX Number: (513) 529-3841 Calendar System: Semester
URL: www.miamioh.edu
Established: 1809 Annual Undergrad Tuition & Fees (In-State): $13,266
Enrollment: 23,390 Coed
Affiliation or Control: State IRS Status: 501(c)3
Highest Offering: Doctorate
Program: Liberal Arts And General; Teacher Preparatory; Professional
Accreditation: NH, ART, BUS, BUSA, CIDA, CLPSY, CS, DIETD, ENG, ENGT, IPSY, MUS, NURSE, SP, SW, TED, THEA

01 President .... Dr. David HODGE
05 Exec Vice Pres Academic Affs/Prov .... Dr. Bobby GEMPESAW
10 VP Finance & Bus Svcs/Treasurer .... Dr. David CREAMER
32 Vice President Student Affairs .... Vacant
30 VP University Advancement .... Mr. Tom HERBERT
13 VP Information Technology .... Mr. J. Peter NATALE
15 Ast Prov Personnel/Dir Acad Per Svc .... Dr. Janet L. COX
21 Assoc VP Finance/Business Svcs .... Dr. David A. ELLIS
20 Int Assoc Provost for Ugrad Studies .... Dr. Carolyn A. HAYNES
35 Interim Dean of Students .... Dr. Michael A. CURME
27 Assoc VP Comm/Marketing .... Ms. Deedie Kay DOWDLE
18 Assoc VP Facilities Planning & Op .... Mr. Cody J. POWELL
84 Assoc VP Enrollment Mgmt .... Mr. Michael S. KABBAZ
28 Assoc VP Inst Diversity .... Dr. Ronald B. SCOTT
29 Asst Vice Pres Alumni Relations .... Mr. Raymond F. MOCK
26 Director Institutional Relations .... Mr. Randi Malcolm THOMAS
100 Secy Board/Exec Asst to President .... Mr. Ted O. PICKERILL
49 Dean College Arts & Science .... Dr. Phyllis CALLAHAN
76 Dean Education/Health & Society .... Dr. Carine FEYTEN
50 Interim Dean Farmer Sch of Business .... Dr. Raymond F. GORMAN
57 Int Dean College of Creative Arts .... Dr. Elizabeth R. MULLENIX
54 Dean College of Engr & Computing .... Dr. Marek DOLLAR
08 Interim Dean University Libraries .... Mr. Jerome CONLEY
58 Dean Graduate School .... Dr. James T. ORIS
107 Dean College of Prof Studies/App Sc .... Dr. G. Michael PRATT
88 Assoc Provost/Assoc Vice Pres .... Vacant
07 Director of Admission .... Ms. Ann LARSON
88 Asst Provost Global Initiatives .... Ms. Cheryl D. YOUNG
88 Univ Dir/Teach Effectiveness Pgm .... Dr. Cecilia M. SHORE
88 Univ Dir Liberal Educ/Assessment .... Dr. John P. TASSONI
92 Univ Dir Honors & Scholars Program .... Dr. Cynthia KLESTINEC
15 Sr Director Human Resources .... Ms. Carol HAUSER
88 Dir Center American/World Cultures .... Dr. Mary Jane BERMAN
23 Medical Director Student Health Svc .... Dr. Gregory CALKINS
104 Director Intl Education Services .... Dr. David KEITGES
06 University Registrar .... Mr. David M. SAUTER
36 Interim Director Career Services .... Mr. Michael GOLDMAN
38 Director Student Counseling Service .... Dr. Kip C. ALISHIO
09 Director Institutional Research .... Ms. Denise A. KRALLMAN
27 Assoc Dir Univ Communications .... Ms. Claire M. WAGNER
19 Chief of Police/Dir Public Safety .... Mr. John MCCANDLESS
96 Sr Director Purchasing/Central Svcs .... Mr. William G. SHAWVER
43 University General Counsel .... Ms. Robin L. PARKER
22 Director Equity & Equal Opportunity .... Ms. Kenya D. ASH
41 Director Intercollegiate Athletics .... Mr. David A. SAYLER
23 Asst VP Student Health & Wellness .... Ms. Gail A. WALENGA
04 Assistant to the President .... Ms. Deborah P. MASON

Miami University Hamilton Campus (H)

1601 University Boulevard, Hamilton OH 45011-3399
Telephone: (513) 785-3000 FICE Identification: 003079
Accreditation: &NH

† Main campus is Miami University in Oxford, OH.

Miami University Middletown (I)

4200 E University Boulevard, Middletown OH 45042-3497
Telephone: (513) 727-3200 FICE Identification: 003080
Accreditation: &NH

† Main campus is Miami University in Oxford, OH.

Mount Carmel College of Nursing (J)

127 S Davis Avenue, Columbus OH 43222-1504
County: Franklin FICE Identification: 030719
Unit ID: 204176
Telephone: (614) 234-5800 Carnegie Class: Spec/Health
FAX Number: (614) 234-2875 Calendar System: Semester
URL: www.mccn.edu
Established: 1990 Annual Undergrad Tuition & Fees: $17,691
Enrollment: 1,056 Coed
Affiliation or Control: Roman Catholic IRS Status: 501(c)3
Highest Offering: Master's
Program: Professional; Nursing Emphasis
Accreditation: NH, NURSE

01 President .... Dr. Ann E. SCHIELE
05 Associate Dean Undergrad Nsg Pgm .... Dr. Barbara BARTA
05 Associate Dean Graduate Nursing Pgm .... Dr. Angela PHILLIPS
106 Associate Dean Distance Education .... Dr. Tara SPALLA
06 Director of Records & Registration .... Ms. Karen L. GREENE
10 Director Business Affairs .... Ms. Kathy SMITH
07 Director Recruitment & Admissions .... Ms. Kim CAMPBELL
13 Systems Administrator .... Mr. Tim TABOL
37 Director Financial Aid .... Dr. Alyncia BOWEN
32 Director Student Life .... Ms. Colleen CIPRIANI
28 Director Diversity/Comm Initiative .... Ms. Kathlynne D. ESPY
04 CON Administrator .... Ms. Robin L. SHOCKLEY
29 Coordinator Alumni Affairs .... Ms. Phylis CROOK
26 Director College Relations .... Ms. Robin HUTCHINSON BELL
08 Director Library Services .... Mr. Stevo ROKSANDIC

Mount Vernon Nazarene University (K)

800 Martinsburg Road, Mount Vernon OH 43050-9500
County: Knox FICE Identification: 007085
Unit ID: 204194
Telephone: (740) 392-6868 Carnegie Class: Master's M
FAX Number: (740) 397-2769 Calendar System: 4/1/4
URL: www.mvnu.edu
Established: 1968 Annual Undergrad Tuition & Fees: $23,690
Enrollment: 2,267 Coed
Affiliation or Control: Church Of The Nazarene IRS Status: 501(c)3
Highest Offering: Master's
Program: Liberal Arts And General; Teacher Preparatory
Accreditation: NH, ACBSP, MUS, NURSE, SW, TED

01 President/CEO .... Dr. Henry W. SPAULDING, II
10 Interim Vice Pres for Finance/CFO .... Dr. Robert P. HAMILL
05 Vice Pres for Academic Affairs/CAO .... Dr. B.Barnett COCHRAN
84 Vice President for GPS & Enrollment .... Dr. Brock SCHROEDER
32 Vice President Student Life .... Dr. Lanette SESSINK
42 University Chaplain .... Rev. Joe NOONEN
20 Assoc VP for Academic Affairs .... Vacant
26 VP for University Relations .... Rev. Scott PETERSON
30 Managing Dir of Advancement .... Mrs. Laura M. SHORT
21 Director of Business Services .... Mr. Alan D. SHAFFER
06 University Registrar .... Mr. Mel SEVERNS
24 Educational Resource Ctr Specialist .... Ms. Amy HAMILL
15 Director of Human Resources .... Mrs. Tricia POKOSH
38 Director Counseling and Wellness .... Mr. Eric BROWNING
91 Director of Information Technology .... Mr. Chris MILLER
19 Director of Campus Safety .... Mr. Patrick RHOTON
29 Director of Alumni Relations .... Mr. Thomas H. WEST
40 Director of the Bookstore .... Mrs. Gina A. BLANCHARD
41 Athletic Director .... Vacant
27 Director of Communications .... Mr. Jeffrey SCOTT
53 Dir Teacher Education/ Certification .... Dr. Debbie SHEPHERD-GREGG
37 Dir of Student Financial Services .... Mrs. Mary CANNON
18 Director of Facilities Management .... Mr. Dennis D. TAYLOR
21 Controller .... Mr. Steven JENKINS
35 Director of Student Life .... Mr. Travis KELLER
39 Director of Residence Life .... Vacant
28 Director Intercultural Affairs .... Mr. James M. SINGLETARY
09 Director Inst Research & Reporting .... Mrs. Kathy GRIFFITH

Muskingum University (L)

163 Stormont Street, New Concord OH 43762-1199
County: Muskingum FICE Identification: 003084
Unit ID: 204264
Telephone: (740) 826-8211 Carnegie Class: Master's M
FAX Number: (740) 826-8404 Calendar System: Semester
URL: www.muskingum.edu
Established: 1837 Annual Undergrad Tuition & Fees: $23,662
Enrollment: 2,304 Coed
Affiliation or Control: Presbyterian Church (U.S.A.) IRS Status: 501(c)3
Highest Offering: Beyond Master's But Less Than Doctorate
Program: Liberal Arts And General; Teacher Preparatory
Accreditation: NH, ENG, MUS, NURSE, TED

01 President .... Dr. Anne C. STEELE
05 Vice President Academic Affairs .... Dr. James CALLAGHAN
10 Vice President Business & Finance .... Mr. James R. WILSON
30 Vice President of Inst Advancement .... Ms. Kathy FITZGERALD
32 Dean of Student Life .... Mrs. Janet A. HEETER-BASS
84 Dean Enrollment/Dir Financial Aid .... Mr. Jeff W. ZELLERS
20 Associate Academic Dean .... Vacant
08 Director of Library .... Dr. Sheila J. ELLENBERGER
06 Registrar .... Mr. Daniel B. WILSON
36 Assistant Director Career Services .... Mrs. Jacquelyn L. VASCURA
13 Director of Computing Services .... Mr. Lewis M. DREBLOW
26 Director Public Relations .... Ms. Janice TUCKER-MCCLOUD
29 Director Alumni Relations .... Ms. Jennifer BRONNER
07 Director of Admissions .... Mrs. Beth DALONZO
19 Director of Public Safety .... Mr. Danny VINCENT
42 College Minister .... Rev. William MULLINS
18 Supt of Building & Grounds .... Mr. Kevin J. WAGNER
41 Director of Athletics .... Mr. Larry SHANK
21 Associate Business Officer .... Mr. Philip LAUBE
35 Director of Student Affairs .... Ms. Susan HOGLUND
37 Director of Student Financial Aid .... Mrs. Janet VEJSICKY
38 Director of Student Counseling .... Mrs. Tracy BUGGLIN
40 Manager of Bookstore .... Ms. Jessica FRENCH
15 Coordinator of Human Resources .... Ms. Kathy J. MOORE

National College (M)

4736 Dressler Road NW, Canton OH 44718
Telephone: (330) 492-5300 Identification: 770698
Accreditation: ACICS

† Main campus is American National University in Salem, VA.

National College (N)

6871 Steger Drive, Cincinnati OH 45237
Telephone: (513) 761-1291 Identification: 770699
Accreditation: ACICS, MAC, SURGT

† Main campus is American National University in Salem, VA.

National College (O)

5665 Forest Hills Boulevard, Columbus OH 43231
Telephone: (614) 212-2800 Identification: 770700
Accreditation: ACICS, MAC

† Main campus is American National University in Salem, VA.

National College (P)

1837 Woodman Center Drive, Kettering OH 45420
Telephone: (937) 299-9450 Identification: 770697
Accreditation: ACICS, CAHIIM, MAC, SURGT

† Main campus is American National University in Salem, VA.

National College (Q)

3855 Fishcreek Road, Stow OH 44224
Telephone: (330) 676-1351 Identification: 770702
Accreditation: ACICS, MAC, SURGT

† Main campus is National College of Business and Technology in Nashville, TN.

National College (A)

27557 Chardon Road, Willoughby Hills OH 44092
Telephone: (440) 944-0825 Identification: 770703
Accreditation: ACICS, MAC

† Main campus is National College of Business and Technology in Nashville, TN.

National College (B)

3487 Belmont Avenue, Youngstown OH 44505
Telephone: (330) 759-0205 Identification: 770701
Accreditation: ACICS, MAC, SURGT

† Main campus is American National University in Salem, VA.

National Institute of Massotherapy (C)

3681 Manchester Road, Suite 304, Akron OH 44319
County: Summit FICE Identification: 034684
Unit ID: 412003
Telephone: (330) 867-1996 Carnegie Class: Assoc/PrivFP
FAX Number: (330) 867-6422 Calendar System: Other
URL: www.nim.edu
Established: 1991 Annual Undergrad Tuition & Fees: $15,540
Enrollment: 68 Coed
Affiliation or Control: Proprietary IRS Status: Proprietary
Highest Offering: Associate Degree
Program: Occupational; 2-Year Principally Bachelor's Creditable; Technical Emphasis
Accreditation: CNCE

01 President ... Mr. Stephen PERKINSON

North Central State College (D)

2441 Kenwood Circle, Mansfield OH 44906
County: Richland FICE Identification: 005313
Unit ID: 204422
Telephone: (419) 755-4800 Carnegie Class: Assoc/Pub-R-M
FAX Number: (419) 755-4750 Calendar System: Semester
URL: www.ncstatecollege.edu
Established: 1961 Annual Undergrad Tuition & Fees (In-State): $4,389
Enrollment: 2,886 Coed
Affiliation or Control: State IRS Status: 501(c)3
Highest Offering: Associate Degree
Program: Occupational; 2-Year Principally Bachelor's Creditable
Accreditation: NH, ACBSP, ADNUR, COARC, OTA, PTAA, RAD

01 President ... Dr. Dorey DIAB
04 Exec Assistant to the President ... Mr. Stephen R. WILLIAMS
10 VP Business Svcs ... Mr. Koffi AKAKPO
05 Vice President Academic Services ... Dr. Karen A. REED
26 Chief Public Affairs Officer ... Ms. Betty E. PRESTON
32 Interim Dean of Students ... Ms. Cheryl CARTER
15 Director of Human Resources ... Mr. R. Douglas HANUSCIN
37 Director of Financial Aid ... Mr. James PHINNEY
08 Director Library ... Ms. Beth BURNS
22 Counselor/Coord Disability Services ... Ms. Sandra LUCKIE
50 Dean of Business/Lib Arts/Public Sv ... Mr. Gregory BUSCH
103 Dean of Tech/Workforce Develop ... Dr. Gregory TIMBERLAKE
76 Dean Health & Public Services ... Mr. James L. HULL
13 Director Information Technology ... Mr. Jim TURNER
06 Registrar ... Mr. Mark J. MONNES
18 Chief Facilities/Physical Plant ... Mr. Dean SCHAAD
96 Director of Purchasing ... Ms. Renee NUSSBAUM
102 Foundation Director ... Ms. Chriss HARRIS
09 Director of Institutional Research ... Mr. Thomas M. PRENDERGAST
88 Director of Retention Services ... Ms. Bev WALKER
88 Phi Theta Kappa Advisor ... Ms. Barb KEENER
66 Director of Nursing Programs ... Ms. Kelly GRAY
40 Campus Bookstore Manager ... Ms. Carla BUTDORFF
21 Controller ... Ms. Lori MCKEE
26 Director Marketing/Creative Design ... Mr. Keith STONER
105 Web Master ... Mr. Mark HUPP
88 Director of Tech Prep ... Mr. Tom KLUDING
51 Continuing Education Director ... Ms. Gina KAMWITHI
32 Coord Student Life Activities ... Ms. Elise RIGGLE
41 Coord Recreation/Intra Sports ... Mr. Mike LACROIX
29 Coord of Alumni/Employer Relations ... Ms. Mary J. RODRIGUEZ
36 Coordinator of Career Development ... Mr. Troy SHUTLER
103 Exec Dir Workforce Partnerships ... Ms. Marybeth BUSCH

Northeast Ohio Medical University (E)

PO Box 95, State Route 44, Rootstown OH 44272-0095
County: Portage FICE Identification: 024544
Unit ID: 204477
Telephone: (330) 325-2511 Carnegie Class: Spec/Med
FAX Number: (330) 325-7943 Calendar System: Other
URL: www.neomed.edu
Established: 1973 Annual Graduate Tuition & Fees: $35,617
Enrollment: 860 Coed
Affiliation or Control: State IRS Status: 501(c)3
Highest Offering: First Professional Degree; No Undergraduates
Program: Professional
Accreditation: NH, IPSY, MED, PH, PHAR

01 President ... Dr. Jay A. GERSHEN
100 Chief of Staff ... Mr. Sergio GARCIA
10 VP Administration/Finance ... Mr. John WRAY
30 VP Advancement ... Mr. Daniel BLAIN
46 VP Research ... Dr. Walter E. HORTON, JR.
67 Dean College of Pharmacy ... Dr. Charles TAYLOR
63 Dean College of Medicine ... Dr. Jeffrey L. SUSMAN
58 Dean College of Graduate Studies ... Dr. Walter E. HORTON, JR.
43 General Counsel ... Ms. Maria R. SCHIMER
32 Chief Student Affairs Officer ... Ms. Sandra EMERICK
88 Executive Director Wasson Center ... Ms. Holly GERZINA
84 Executive Director Enrollment ... Ms. Heidi TERRY
88 Executive Director Research ... Ms. Elizabeth CLINE
88 Executive Director Ind Relations ... Dr. Walter HORNE
88 Executive Director Faculty ... Dr. Robert EAGLEN
09 Executive Director Inst Research ... Dr. Margarita D. KOKINOVA
26 Director Public Relations ... Ms. Cristine BOYD
14 Director of Diversity Affairs ... Mr. Andre BURTON
13 Director Information Technology ... Mr. Ronald L. MCGRADY
24 Dir Academic Technology Svcs ... Mr. Rey T. NOTARESCHI
86 Dir Government Relations/Sec BOT ... Mr. Richard LEWIS
21 Director Budget and Business Svcs ... Ms. Carrie BAST
18 Director Physical Plant ... Mr. Blaine M. WYCKOFF
15 Director Human Resources ... Ms. Barbara TOBIAS
35 Dir Career Development & Advising ... Ms. Anita R. POKORNY
36 Director Academic Support ... Ms. Amanda YOCUM
40 Supervisor Bookstore ... Ms. Christine KOVACICH
19 Supervisor Public Safety ... Ms. Kali MEONSKE
04 Assistant to the President ... Ms. Michelle MULHERN

Northwest State Community College (F)

22-600 State Route 34, Archbold OH 43502-9542
County: Henry FICE Identification: 008677
Unit ID: 204440
Telephone: (419) 267-5511 Carnegie Class: Assoc/Pub-R-M
FAX Number: (419) 267-3688 Calendar System: Semester
URL: www.northweststate.edu
Established: 1968 Annual Undergrad Tuition & Fees (In-State): $4,300
Enrollment: 4,079 Coed
Affiliation or Control: State IRS Status: 501(c)3
Highest Offering: Associate Degree
Program: Occupational; 2-Year Principally Bachelor's Creditable
Accreditation: NH, ACBSP, ADNUR, MAC, OTA

01 President ... Dr. Thomas L. STUCKEY
05 VP for Academics ... Ms. Cindy KRUEGER
30 VP for Institutional Advancement ... Ms. Mari YODER
88 VP for Innovation ... Mr. Todd HERNANDEZ
50 Int Dean of Business Technologies ... Mrs. Lori ROBISON
69 Dean of Allied Health & Public Svcs ... Mrs. Lori ROBISON
49 Dean of Arts & Science ... Ms. Lana EVANS
66 Dean of Nursing ... Mrs. Lori BIRD
06 Registrar ... Ms. Connie KLINGSHIRN
40 Bookstore Manager ... Mr. Kemp STAPLETON
08 Director of Student Resources ... Ms. Kristi ROTROFF
18 Director of Plant Operations ... Mr. Timothy NELSON
15 Director of Human Resources ... Mr. Denis CIACIUCH
21 Director of Business Services ... Ms. Lynn SPEISER
07 Director of Admissions ... Mr. Dennis GIACOMINO
10 Chief Fiscal Officer ... Ms. Kathy SOARDS
44 Chief Development ... Ms. Robbin WILCOX
37 Director Student Financial Aid ... Ms. Charlotte SORG
32 Coordinator Student Activities ... Mr. Keith F. VAN HORN

Notre Dame College (G)

4545 College Road, South Euclid OH 44121-4293
County: Cuyahoga FICE Identification: 003085
Unit ID: 204468
Telephone: (216) 381-1680 Carnegie Class: Bac/Diverse
FAX Number: (216) 381-3802 Calendar System: Semester
URL: www.notredamecollege.edu
Established: 1922 Annual Undergrad Tuition & Fees: $26,344
Enrollment: 2,096 Coed
Affiliation or Control: Roman Catholic IRS Status: 501(c)3
Highest Offering: Master's
Program: Liberal Arts And General; Teacher Preparatory
Accreditation: NH, NURSE, TED

01 President ... Dr. Andrew P. ROTH
05 Vice Pres Student/Academic Affairs ... Dr. Nick SANTILLI
10 Sr Vice Pres Finance/Administration ... Ms. Janet ASHE
45 Vice Pres for Assessment Planning ... Vacant
30 Director of Development ... Ms. Maureen ISCHAY
31 Vice Pres for Board/Community Rels ... Ms. Karen L. POELKING
20 Assoc Dean of Academic Affairs ... Vacant
66 Nursing Division Chair ... Vacant
53 Education Division Chair ... Dr. Yvonne ALLEN
81 Math & Science Division Chair ... Mr. David OROSZ
50 Business Division Chair ... Ms. Karen PENLER
57 Fine Arts Division Chair ... Ms. Rachel MORRIS
26 Director of Public Relations ... Vacant
07 Director of Traditional Admissions ... Ms. Beth FORD
88 Director of the Finn Center (Adult) ... Vacant
32 Dean for Student Affairs ... Vacant
06 Registrar ... Ms. Jameka WINDHAM
37 Dir Student Financial Assistance ... Ms. Mary MCCRYSTAL
88 Director of Student Accounts ... Mr. Jason LAPINSKI
19 Director Security/Safety ... Vacant
18 Director Physical Plant ... Mr. Tom MEEKS
13 Director Information Technology ... Mr. Michael KIEC
15 Director Personnel Services ... Ms. Susan ANDERSON
08 Director of Library ... Ms. Karen ZOLLER
42 Director Ctr Campus Theol/Ministry ... Mr. Ted STERLING
78 Director Coop Educ & Career Devel ... Ms. Kimberly LANE
38 Director of Counseling Center ... Ms. Susan LIPIEC
39 Director of Residence Life ... Ms. Tera JOHNSON
29 Dir Alumni Rels/Asc Dir Development ... Mrs. Mary Elizabeth COTLEUR
04 Admin Assistant to the President ... Ms. April KENNEDY
27 Chief Information Officer ... Ms. Deborah SHEREN
26 Chief Communications Officer ... Mr. Brian JOHNSTON
106 Online Education/E-learning ... Ms. Mary Ann SCHNEIDER

Oberlin College (H)

173 West Lorain Street, Oberlin OH 44074-1057
County: Lorain FICE Identification: 003086
Unit ID: 204501
Telephone: (440) 775-8121 Carnegie Class: Bac/A&S
FAX Number: (440) 775-8886 Calendar System: 4/1/4
URL: www.oberlin.edu
Established: 1833 Annual Undergrad Tuition & Fees: $46,870
Enrollment: 2,889 Coed
Affiliation or Control: Independent Non-Profit IRS Status: 501(c)3
Highest Offering: Master's
Program: Liberal Arts And General; Teacher Preparatory; Professional
Accreditation: NH, MUS

01 President ... Mr. Marvin KRISLOV
10 Vice President for Finance ... Mr. Ronald R. WATTS
30 VP Development/Alumni Affair ... Mr. William BARLOW
26 Vice President College Relations ... Mr. Ben JONES
49 Interim Dean of Arts & Sciences ... Dr. Joyce BABYAK
64 Interim Dean Conservatory Music ... Ms. Andrea KALYN
32 Dean of Student Life ... Dr. Eric ESTES
35 Dean of Studies/VP Strategic Init ... Dr. Kathryn STUART
07 Dean Admissions/Financial Aid ... Ms. Debra J. CHERMONTE
43 VP General Counsel and Secretary ... Ms. Sandhya SUBRAMANIAN
86 Spec Asst Community/Govt Relations ... Ms. Tita REED
21 Assoc Vice Pres Finance/Controller ... Mr. Mark R. BATES
29 Exec Director Alumni Assoc ... Ms. Danielle YOUNG
20 Assoc Dean of College Arts & Sci ... Ms. Joyce BABYAK
20 Assoc Dean of College Arts & Sci ... Dr. Heather HOGAN
14 Chief Tech Ofcr/Dir Computing Ctr ... Dr. John E. BUCHER
08 Director of Libraries ... Dr. Raymond A. ENGLISH
07 Director Admissions Conservatory ... Mr. Michael C. MANDEREN
38 Director of Counseling Center ... Mr. John HARSHBARGER
57 Director of Allen Art Museums ... Dr. Andria DERSTINE
06 Registrar ... Ms. Elizabeth CLERKIN
37 Director of Financial Aid ... Mr. Robert A. REDDY, JR.
09 Director of Institutional Research ... Mr. Ross PEACOCK
18 Asst VP for Facilities ... Mr. Tom PICCORELLI
36 Director Career Devel/Placement ... Mr. Richard T. BERMAN
42 Director Religious Life ... Mr. Gregory MCGONIGLE
39 Dir Residential/Dining Services ... Mr. Adrian BATISTA
41 Director of Physical Educ/Athletics ... Ms. Natalie WINKELFOOS
19 Director of Safety & Security ... Ms. Marjorie BURTON
28 Director Multicultural Affairs ... Dr. Alison WILLIAMS
96 Director of Purchasing ... Mr. James S. KLAIBER
15 Manager of Employee Relations ... Ms. Sharon JOHNSON

Ohio Business College (I)

4525 Trueman Boulevard, Hillard OH 43026
Telephone: (614) 891-5030 FICE Identification: 030658
Accreditation: ACICS, MAC

† Main campus is Ohio Business College, Lorain Branch in Sheffield Village, OH.

Ohio Business College (J)

5202 Timber Commons Drive, Sandusky OH 44870-5894
Telephone: (419) 627-8345 Identification: 666467
Accreditation: ACICS

† Main campus is Ohio Business College, Lorain Branch in Sheffield Village, OH.

Ohio Business College, Lorain Branch (K)

5095 Waterford Drive, Sheffield Village OH 44035-0701
County: Lorain FICE Identification: 021585
Unit ID: 203720
Telephone: (440) 934-3101 Carnegie Class: Assoc/PrivFP
FAX Number: (440) 934-3105 Calendar System: Quarter
URL: www.ohiobusinesscollege.edu
Established: 1903 Annual Undergrad Tuition & Fees: $14,500
Enrollment: 375 Coed
Affiliation or Control: Proprietary IRS Status: Proprietary
Highest Offering: Associate Degree
Program: Occupational; 2-Year Principally Bachelor's Creditable
Accreditation: ACICS, MAC

01 Executive Director ... Mrs. Rosanne CATELLA
07 Admissions Director ... Mrs. Rosemerry NICKELS
10 Financial Manager ... Mrs. Christine TODD
36 Career Services ... Ms. Cheryl JANKOWSKI

Ohio Christian University (L)

1476 Lancaster Pike, Circleville OH 43113-0458
County: Pickaway FICE Identification: 003030
Unit ID: 201964

Telephone: (740) 474-8896 Carnegie Class: Bac/Diverse
FAX Number: (740) 477-7755 Calendar System: Semester
URL: www.ohiochristian.edu
Established: 1948 Annual Undergrad Tuition & Fees: $17,720
Enrollment: 3,146 Coed
Affiliation or Control: Other Protestant IRS Status: 501(c)3
Highest Offering: Master's
Program: 2-Year Principally Bachelor's Creditable; Teacher Preparatory; Professional; Religious Emphasis
Accreditation: NH, BI, TEAC

01 President .... Dr. Mark A. SMITH
03 Provost .... Dr. Hank KELLY
05 Vice President of Academics .... Vacant
10 Vice President of Finance .... Mr. Robert HARTMAN
30 Vice President for Advancement .... Mr. Mark TAYLOR
32 Vice President Student Development .... Dr. Rick CHRISTMAN
11 Vice President of Operations .... Mr. Curtis CHRISTOPHER
13 Assistant VP for IT .... Mr. Ryan WHISLER
09 Director of Institutional Research .... Mr. David PENNINGTON
06 Registrar .... Dr. Rodney SONES
84 Associate Vice Pres Enrollment .... Mr. Michael EGENREIDER
55 VP College of Adult & Graduate Stds .... Dr. Tim EADES
08 Director of Library Services .... Mrs. Barbara MEISTER
37 Director Student Financial Services .... Mr. Wes BROTHERS
41 Athletic Director .... Mr. Ben BELLEMAN
29 Director Alumni Relations .... Vacant

Ohio College of Massotherapy (A)

225 Heritage Woods Drive, Akron OH 44321-1363
County: Summit FICE Identification: 031163
Unit ID: 204592
Telephone: (330) 665-1084 Carnegie Class: Assoc/PrivNFP
FAX Number: (330) 319-7733 Calendar System: Semester
URL: www.ocm.edu
Established: 1973 Annual Undergrad Tuition & Fees: $16,333
Enrollment: 110 Coed
Affiliation or Control: Proprietary IRS Status: Proprietary
Highest Offering: Associate Degree
Program: 2-Year Principally Bachelor's Creditable; Technical Emphasis
Accreditation: ACCSC

01 President .... Mr. Jeffrey S. MORROW
11 Director of Administration .... Mrs. Debra M. SMITH

Ohio Dominican University (B)

1216 Sunbury Road, Columbus OH 43219-2099
County: Franklin FICE Identification: 003035
Unit ID: 204617
Telephone: (614) 251-4500 Carnegie Class: Master's L
FAX Number: (614) 251-4634 Calendar System: Semester
URL: www.ohiodominican.edu
Established: 1911 Annual Undergrad Tuition & Fees: $28,932
Enrollment: 2,663 Coed
Affiliation or Control: Roman Catholic IRS Status: 501(c)3
Highest Offering: Master's
Program: Liberal Arts And General; Teacher Preparatory; Professional
Accreditation: NH, ACBSP, #ARCPA, SW, TED

01 President .... Dr. Peter CIMBOLIC
05 Vice President Academic Affairs .... Dr. Theresa HOLLERAN
32 Vice President Student Development .... Dr. James A. CARIDI
10 Vice President Finance & Admin .... Mr. David KOSANOVIC
04 Executive Asst to the President .... Ms. Candie LESTER
35 Asst Vice Pres Student Development .... Ms. Sharon REED
20 Assoc Vice Pres Academic Affairs .... Dr. Linda SCHOEN
58 Dean Graduate/Professional Studies .... Dr. Jay YOUNG
06 Registrar .... Ms. Christine GROVES
07 Director of Admissions .... Ms. Nicole EVANS
08 Director of the Library .... Mr. James E. LAYDEN
37 Director of Financial Aid .... Ms. Laura MEEK
36 Director Career Services .... Mr. Gary SWISHER
38 Director of Counseling Services .... Mr. Michael LEWIS
85 Director of Intercultural Office .... Ms. Deanna SHINE
26 Vice President for Marketing & PR .... Mr. Mark COOPER
42 Director of Campus Ministry .... Rev. Thomas BLAU
27 Chief Information Officer .... Mr. Fred LASSITER
15 Director of Human Resources .... Ms. Michelle GEIMAN
18 Director of Physical Facilities .... Mr. Darrel PLUMLEE
29 Director of Alumni/AE Relations .... Ms. Ann SNIDER
39 Director of Resident Life .... Ms. Kerry SOLLER
41 Athletic Director .... Mr. Jeff BLAIR
24 Dir Center for Instruct Technology .... Vacant
96 Director of Purchasing .... Sr. Margaret WALSH
19 Director of Safety & Security .... Mr. John RACE
92 Director of Honors Program .... Mr. Matthew PONESSE
88 Dean Learning Enhanced Adult Degree .... Vacant
09 Director of Institutional Research .... Vacant

Ohio Mid-Western College (Formerly Temple Baptist College) (C)

19 Triangle Park Drive, Sharonville OH 45246
County: Hamilton FICE Identification: 037263
Unit ID: 206002
Telephone: (513) 772-9888 Carnegie Class: Spec/Faith
FAX Number: (513) 771-0702 Calendar System: Quarter
URL: www.omw.edu
Established: 1972 Annual Undergrad Tuition & Fees: $10,944
Enrollment: 151 Coed
Affiliation or Control: Baptist IRS Status: 501(c)3
Highest Offering: Baccalaureate
Program: Liberal Arts And General; Religious Emphasis
Accreditation: TRACS

01 Chancellor .... Dr. Darrell HORSLEY
10 Chief Financial Officer .... Mr. Tyler CLEM
05 VP/Dean of Academic Affairs .... Dr. Bill G. DYKES
37 Director of Financial Aid .... Mrs. Gail GOODE
06 Registrar .... Mrs. Pauline GRUNDEN
32 Director of Student Success .... Mrs. Susan SICKLES
07 Director of Recruiting .... Mr. Ricardo HILL

Ohio Northern University (D)

525 S Main Street, Ada OH 45810-1599
County: Hardin FICE Identification: 003089
Unit ID: 204635
Telephone: (419) 772-2000 Carnegie Class: Bac/Diverse
FAX Number: (419) 772-1932 Calendar System: Quarter
URL: www.onu.edu
Established: 1871 Annual Undergrad Tuition & Fees: $36,704
Enrollment: 3,557 Coed
Affiliation or Control: United Methodist IRS Status: 501(c)3
Highest Offering: First Professional Degree
Program: Liberal Arts And General; Teacher Preparatory; Professional; Business Emphasis
Accreditation: NH, BUS, CS, ENG, EXSC, LAW, MT, MUS, NAIT, NURSE, PHAR, TED

01 President .... Dr. Daniel A. DIBIASIO
05 Provost/Vice Pres Academic Affairs .... Dr. David C. CRAGO
10 Vice President Financial Affairs .... Mr. William H. BALLARD
30 Vice Pres of University Advancement .... Mr. Ken W. BLOCK
84 Vice Pres Enrollment Management .... Dr. Lawrence T. LESICK
32 VP Student Affairs/Dean of Students .... Dean Adriane THOMPSON-BRADSHAW
49 Dean of Arts & Sciences .... Dr. Catherine ALBRECHT
54 Dean of Engineering .... Dr. Eric T. BAUMGARTNER
67 Dean of Pharmacy .... Dr. Jon E. SPRAGUE
50 Dean Business Administration .... Dr. James W. FENTON
61 Dean of Law .... Dr. Richard C. BALES
35 Dean of Students .... Vacant
30 Senior Director of Development .... Mr. Scott D. WILLS
06 Registrar .... Mrs. Melanie HOUGH
08 Librarian .... Mr. Paul M. LOGSDON
14 Director of Computer Center .... Mr. C. Lawrence BUSCH
36 Interim Director Career Services .... Mr. Justin COURTNEY
61 Dir Law Ext Affs/Career Strategies .... Mrs. Cheryl KITCHEN
38 Director of Counseling .... Dr. Michael SCHAFER
29 Director of Alumni Relations .... Ms. Sarah PRASHER
08 Law Librarian .... Dr. Nancy A. ARMSTRONG
42 University Chaplain .... Rev. David MACDONALD
18 Director of Physical Plant .... Mr. Marc STALEY
13 Director of Technology .... Mr. Jef RIEMAN
09 Director of Institutional Research .... Dr. Omer MINHAS
15 Director of Human Resources .... Ms. Tonya PAUL
20 Associate Academic Officer .... Dr. Juliet K. HURTIG
37 Director of Student Financial Aid .... Mrs. Melanie WEAVER
92 Director of Honors Program .... Dr. Patrick T. CROSKERY
21 Bursar .... Mrs. Amber L. CARPENTER
26 Dir of Communications & Marketing .... Mrs. Amy PRIGGE
07 Director of Admissions .... Ms. Deborah MILLER
06 Asst Registrar .... Mrs. Andrea RICHARDSON
28 Director Multicultural Development .... Ms. LaShonda GURLEY
41 Athletic Director .... Mr. Thomas SIMMONS
27 Assoc Dir Communications/Marketing .... Ms. Portia ASH
44 Director of Annual Giving .... Ms. Kelly ANDERSON
96 Manager of Purchasing .... Ms. Vicki J. NIESE

The Ohio State University Main Campus (E)

281 W. Lane Ave., Columbus OH 43210-1358
County: Franklin FICE Identification: 003090
Unit ID: 204796
Telephone: (614) 292-6446 Carnegie Class: RU/VH
FAX Number: (614) 292-9180 Calendar System: Semester
URL: www.osu.edu
Established: 1870 Annual Undergrad Tuition & Fees (In-State): $10,036
Enrollment: 56,387 Coed
Affiliation or Control: State IRS Status: 501(c)3
Highest Offering: Doctorate
Program: Liberal Arts And General; Teacher Preparatory; Professional
Accreditation: NH, ART, AUD, BUS, BUSA, CAHIIM, CIDA, CLPSY, COARC, CS, DANCE, DENT, DH, DIETC, DIETD, DIETI, ENG, FOR, HSA, IPSY, LAW, LSAR, MED, MFCD, MIDWF, MT, MUS, NMT, NURSE, OPT, OPTR, OT, PH, PHAR, PLNG, PTA, RTT, SP, SPAA, SW, TED, THEA, VET

01 Interim President .... Dr. Joseph A. ALUTTO
05 Executive Vice Pres/Provost .... Dr. Joseph E. STEINMETZ
10 Senior VP Business & Finance & CFO .... Mr. Geoffrey CHATAS
43 Sr VP & General Counsel .... Mr. Christopher M. CULLEY
32 Vice President for Student Life .... Dr. Javaune ADAMS-GASTON
20 Vice Provost for Academic Planning .... Mr. Michael J. BOEHM
26 VP University Relations .... Ms. Melinda CHURCH
15 VP Talent/Cult & Human Resources .... Ms. Andraea DOUGLASS
46 Vice Pres for Research .... Dr. Caroline WHITACRE
86 Sr Vice Pres of Govt Relations .... Mr. Herb ASHER
23 Sr Vice Pres Health Sci .... Dr. Steve G. GABBE
47 Vice Pres & Dean FAES .... Dr. Bruce MCPHERON
30 Sr Vice President for Advancement .... Mr. Michael EICHER
28 Vice Prov Div & Incl & VP O & E .... Dr. Valerie LEE
88 Vice Provost UG Stds & Dean UG Ed .... Dr. Wayne E. CARLSON
58 Vice Provost/Dean Grad School .... Dr. Patrick S. OSMER
18 Assoc VP Facilities Op/Dev .... Ms. Mary L. READEY
07 Assoc VP UG Admissions/First-Yr Exp .... Mr. Vern GRANGER
13 Int Chief Information Officer .... Mr. Michael HOFHERR
08 Director of Libraries .... Ms. Carol P. DIEDRCHS
101 Secretary Board of Trustees .... Dr. David G. HORN
17 VP Health Svcs .... Dr. Peter E. GEIER
85 Vice Prov Global Strat/Intl Affs .... Dr. William I. BRUSTEIN
90 Int Exec Dir Ohio Supercomputr Ctr .... Mr. Steve GORDON
29 Sr VP for Alumni Relations .... Mr. Archie GRIFFIN
41 Director Athletics .... Mr. Gene SMITH
12 Executive Dean of Reg Campuses .... Dr. William L. MACDONALD
49 Vice Prov & Exec Dean Arts & Sci .... Dr. David C. MANDERSCHEID
50 Dean Fisher Col of Business .... Dr. Christine A. POON
52 Dean College of Dentistry .... Dr. Patrick M. LLOYD
53 Dean College of Educ & Hum Ecology .... Dr. Cheryl L. ACHTERBERG
54 Dean College of Engineering .... Dr. David B. WILLIAMS
61 Dean College of Law .... Dr. Alan C. MICHAELS
63 Dean College of Medicine .... Dr. Charles J. LOCKWOOD
88 Dean College of Optometry .... Dr. Melvin D. SHIPP
67 Dean College of Pharmacy .... Dr. Robert W. BRUEGGEMEIER
69 Int Dean College of Public Health .... Dr. Michael S. BISESI
70 Dean College of Social Work .... Dr. Tom GREGOIRE
74 Dean Col Veterinary Medicine .... Dr. Lonnie KING
66 Dean College of Nursing .... Dr. Bernadette MELNYK
84 VP Strategic Enrollment Planning .... Mr. Dolan EVANOVICH
09 Asst VP Inst Research/Planning .... Ms. Julie CARPENTER-HUBIN
37 Director Student Financial Aid .... Ms. Diane L. STEMPER
88 Director of OES Analysis & Reporting .... Ms. Gail C. STEPHENOFF
35 Sr Assoc VP Student Life .... Dr. Gretchen METZELAARS
06 University Registrar .... Mr. Bradley A. MYERS
38 Asst VP & Dir Younkin Success Ctr .... Ms. Louise A. DOUCE
96 Director of Purchasing .... Mr. Russell CHUNG
11 Sr Vice Pres Admin & Planning .... Mr. Jay D. KASEY
40 General Manager OSU Bookstores .... Ms. Kathy SMITH

The Ohio State University Agricultural Technical Institute (F)

1328 Dover Road, Wooster OH 44691-4000
County: Wayne FICE Identification: 010687
Unit ID: 204662
Telephone: (330) 264-3911 Carnegie Class: Assoc/Pub2in4
FAX Number: (330) 287-1333 Calendar System: Semester
URL: ati.osu.edu/
Established: 1971 Annual Undergrad Tuition & Fees (In-State): $6,744
Enrollment: 612 Coed
Affiliation or Control: State IRS Status: 501(c)3
Highest Offering: Associate Degree
Program: Occupational; 2-Year Principally Bachelor's Creditable
Accreditation: NH

01 Interim Director .... Dr. Jim KINDER
05 Associate Director .... Dr. Steven M. NEAL
26 Public Relations Coordinator .... Ms. Frances P. WHITED
03 Assistant Director .... Dr. Rhonda BILLMAN
37 Coordinator Student Financial Aid .... Ms. Barbara LAMOREAUX
07 Manager of Enrollment .... Mr. David DIETRICH
21 Business Manager 2 .... Ms. Rita M. SMOLKO
32 Coordinator Student Programs .... Ms. Kathy E. MAKSYMICZ
40 Bookstore Manager .... Ms. Patricia A. PAXTON
08 Library Director .... Vacant
19 Assistant Chief Campus Police .... Mr. Gregory K. FERRELL
13 Systems Manager .... Mr. Rick L. MITCHELL
23 Registered Nurse .... Mr. Lenni HOWELL
50 Director Business Trng & Educ Svcs .... Ms. Kimberly J. SAYERS
39 Housing Coordinator .... Mr. Michael STEINER
88 Coordinator Disability Services .... Ms. Silvia H. HENRISS
88 Program Director Program EXCEL .... Ms. Dee Dee SNYDER
06 Academic Records Manager .... Ms. Peggy E. LAMBERT
29 Assistant to Director .... Ms. Helen THOMPSON
38 SOAR Coordinator Stdnt Success Svcs .... Ms. Ruth MONTZ

The Ohio State University at Lima Campus (G)

4240 Campus Drive, Lima OH 45804-3597
Telephone: (419) 995-8600 FICE Identification: 003092
Accreditation: &NH

† Main campus is The Ohio State University Main Campus in Columbus, OH.

The Ohio State University Mansfield Campus (H)

1760 University Drive, Mansfield OH 44906-1599
Telephone: (419) 755-4011 FICE Identification: 003093
Accreditation: &NH

† Main campus is The Ohio State University Main Campus in Columbus, OH.

The Ohio State University at Marion (I)

1465 Mount Vernon Avenue, Marion OH 43302-5628
Telephone: (740) 389-6786 FICE Identification: 003094
Accreditation: &NH

† Main campus is The Ohio State University Main Campus in Columbus, OH.

The Ohio State University Newark Campus (A)

1179 University Drive, Newark OH 43055-9990
Telephone: (740) 366-3321 FICE Identification: 003095
Accreditation: &NH

† Main campus is The Ohio State University Main Campus in Columbus, OH.

Ohio Technical College (B)

1374 E 51st Street, Cleveland OH 44103-1269
County: Cuyahoga FICE Identification: 011745
Unit ID: 204608
Telephone: (216) 881-1700 Carnegie Class: Assoc/PrivFP
FAX Number: (216) 881-9145 Calendar System: Quarter
URL: www.ohiotech.edu
Established: 1969 Annual Undergrad Tuition & Fees: $26,600
Enrollment: 1,163 Coed
Affiliation or Control: Proprietary IRS Status: Proprietary
Highest Offering: Associate Degree
Program: Occupational
Accreditation: ACCSC

01 Director ... Mr. Tom KING

Ohio University Main Campus (C)

Athens OH 45701-2979
County: Athens FICE Identification: 003100
Unit ID: 204857
Telephone: (740) 593-1000 Carnegie Class: RU/H
FAX Number: N/A Calendar System: Quarter
URL: www.ohiou.edu
Established: 1804 Annual Undergrad Tuition & Fees (In-State): $10,928
Enrollment: 37,452 Coed
Affiliation or Control: State IRS Status: 501(c)3
Highest Offering: Doctorate
Program: Liberal Arts And General; Teacher Preparatory; Professional
Accreditation: NH, AAFCS, ADNUR, AUD, BUS, BUSA, CACREP, CIDA, CLPSY, CORE, CS, DANCE, DIETD, ENG, FEPAC, JOUR, MUS, NAIT, NRPA, NURSE, OSTEO, PH, PTA, SP, SW, TED, THEA

01 President ... Dr. Roderick J. MCDAVIS
100 Chief of Staff ... Ms. Jennifer KIRKSEY
05 Executive Vice President & Provost ... Dr. Pam BENOIT
10 VP for Finance & Administration ... Mr. Stephen T. GOLDING
32 VP for Student Affairs ... Dr. Ryan LOMBARDI
30 VP Univ Advance/Pres/CEO OU Fdn ... Mr. Bryan BENCHOFF
27 Chief Information Officer ... Mr. J. Brice BIBLE
46 VP Research & Dean Grad College ... Dr. Joseph SHIELDS
84 Vice Provost Enrollment Management ... Mr. Craig CORNELL
43 General Counsel ... Mr. John J. BIANCAMANO
26 Exec Dir Comm/Marketing ... Ms. Renea MORRIS
80 Director of Government Relations ... Mr. Eric BURCHARD
88 Exec Vice Provost/Dean Univ Col ... Dr. David N. DESCUTNER
49 Dean College of Arts & Sciences ... Dr. Robert FRANK
50 Dean College of Business ... Dr. Hugh SHERMAN
60 Dean Scripps Col Communication ... Dr. Scott TITSWORTH
53 Dean Patton College of Education ... Dr. Renee A. MIDDLETON
54 Dean Russ Col Engineering/Tech ... Dr. Dennis IRWIN
57 Dean College of Fine Arts ... Dr. Margaret KENNEDY-DYGAS
69 Dean Col Health/Human Services ... Dr. Randy LEITE
92 Dean Honors Tutorial College ... Dr. Jeremy WEBSTER
63 Dean Heritage Col Osteopathic Med ... Dr. Kenneth JOHNSON
62 Dean University Libraries ... Mr. Scott H. SEAMAN
35 Dean of Students ... Dr. Jenny HALL-JONES
12 Exec Dean Regional Campuses ... Dr. William WILLAN
12 Dean Eastern Campus ... Dr. Paul ABRAHAM
12 Int Dean Southern Campus ... Dr. Dan EVANS
12 Dean Chillicothe Campus ... Dr. Martin TUCK
12 Dean Lancaster Campus ... Dr. James SMITH
12 Int Dean Zanesville Campus ... Vacant
20 Associate Provost Academic Affairs ... Dr. Howard DEWALD
58 Director Graduate Student Services ... Dr. Katherine TADLOCK
88 Int Exec Dir Ctr for Intl Studies ... Dr. Ming LI
28 Int Vice Prov Diversity & Inclusion ... Dr. David DESCUTNER
09 Assoc Prov Inst Rsrch/Assessment ... Dr. A. Michael WILLIFORD
41 Director of Athletics ... Mr. Jim SCHAUS
06 University Registrar ... Mrs. Debra M. BENTON
18 Assoc VP Finance/Admin/Facilities ... Mr. Harry WYATT
15 Assoc VP for Human Resources ... Ms. Linda LONSINGER
22 Director Institutional Equity ... Dr. Laura MYERS
29 Int Exec Director Alumni Relations ... Ms. Connie ROMINE
36 Asst Dean for Career Services ... Mr. Imants JAUNARAJS
07 Asst Vice Provost/Dir Ungrad Admiss ... Ms. Candice BOENINGER
38 Director Counseling Services ... Dr. Alfred B. WEINER
44 Exec Dir of Develop Planned Giving ... Ms. Kelli BELL
37 Director Student Financial Aid ... Ms. Valerie MILLER
23 Medical Dir of Campus Care ... Dr. John J. KEMERER
106 Vice Provost for eLearning/Str Prtn ... Dr. Deb GEARHART
96 Director of Procurement Services ... Ms. Laura NOWICKI
19 Chief of Police/Dir Campus Safety ... Mr. Andrew POWERS
85 Assoc Dir Intl Students/Fac Svcs ... Dr. Krista MCCALLUM-BEATTY
39 Asst Vice Pres Auxiliary Services ... Ms. Christine SHEETS
88 Asst VP for Economic & Tech Devel ... Vacant
25 Asst VP Res & Sponsored Programs ... Mr. Shane L. GILKEY
24 Media Library Manager ... Ms. Robin KRIVESTI

Ohio University Chillicothe Campus (D)

PO Box 629, 101 University Drive,
Chillicothe OH 45601-0629
Telephone: (740) 774-7200 FICE Identification: 003102
Accreditation: &NH

† Main campus is Ohio University Main Campus in Athens, OH.

Ohio University Eastern Campus (E)

45425 National Road, Saint Clairsville OH 43950-9724
Telephone: (740) 695-1720 FICE Identification: 003101
Accreditation: &NH

† Main campus is Ohio University Main Campus in Athens, OH.

Ohio University Lancaster Campus (F)

1570 Granville Pike, Lancaster OH 43130-1097
Telephone: (740) 654-6711 FICE Identification: 003104
Accreditation: &NH, MAC

† Main campus is Ohio University Main Campus in Athens, OH.

Ohio University Southern Campus (G)

1804 Liberty Avenue, Ironton OH 45638-2279
Telephone: (740) 533-4600 Identification: 666000
Accreditation: &NH

† Main campus is Ohio University Main Campus in Athens, OH.

Ohio University Zanesville Branch (H)

1425 Newark Road, Zanesville OH 43701-2695
Telephone: (740) 453-0762 FICE Identification: 003108
Accreditation: &NH

† Main campus is Ohio University Main Campus in Athens, OH.

Ohio Valley College of Technology (I)

15258 State Route 170, East Liverpool OH 43920
County: Columbiana FICE Identification: 023014
Unit ID: 204884
Telephone: (330) 385-1070 Carnegie Class: Assoc/PrivFP
FAX Number: (330) 385-4606 Calendar System: Semester
URL: www.ovct.edu
Established: 1886 Annual Undergrad Tuition & Fees: $11,180
Enrollment: 213 Coed
Affiliation or Control: Proprietary IRS Status: Proprietary
Highest Offering: Associate Degree
Program: Occupational; 2-Year Principally Bachelor's Creditable; Technical Emphasis
Accreditation: ACICS, MAC

01 President/Executive Director ... Mr. Scott S. ROGERS

Ohio Wesleyan University (J)

61 S Sandusky Street, Delaware OH 43015-2398
County: Delaware FICE Identification: 003109
Unit ID: 204909
Telephone: (740) 368-2000 Carnegie Class: Bac/A&S
FAX Number: (740) 368-3299 Calendar System: Semester
URL: www.owu.edu
Established: 1842 Annual Undergrad Tuition & Fees: $40,250
Enrollment: 1,825 Coed
Affiliation or Control: United Methodist IRS Status: 501(c)3
Highest Offering: Baccalaureate
Program: Liberal Arts And General
Accreditation: NH, MUS, TED

01 President ... Dr. Rockwell F. JONES
05 Provost ... Dr. Charles L. STINEMETZ
10 Vice Pres for Fin/Admin/Treas ... Mr. Dan J. HITCHELL
26 VP for University Advancement ... Ms. Colleen C. GARLAND
84 Vice Pres for Enrollment ... Ms. Rebecca R. ECKSTEIN
32 Vice President for Student Affairs ... Dr. Craig E. ULLOM
30 Asst VP for University Advancement .. Mr. Christopher J. DELISIO
20 Dean of Academic Affairs ... Dr. Martin J. EISENBERG
09 Assoc Provost for Inst Research ... Dr. Dale E. SWARTZENTRUBER
108 Asst Provost Assmt/Accreditation ... Dr. Barbara S. ANDERECK
37 Director Student Financial Aid ... Mr. Kevin F. PASKVAN
36 Director of Career Services ... Ms. Leslie J. DELERME
08 Chief Info Officer/Dir of Libraries ... Ms. Cathi A. CARDWELL
06 Registrar ... Ms. Shelly A. MCMAHON
14 Director of Computer Center ... Mr. Harold D. WIEBE
13 Exec Director Information Tech ... Mr. Brian A. RELLINGER
19 Director of Public Safety ... Mr. Robert A. WOOD
29 Director Alumni Relations ... Ms. Brenda E. DEWITT
26 Director Marketing/Communications ... Mr. Mark E. COOPER
85 Director International Student Svcs ... Mr. Darrell J. ALBON
18 Director Physical Plant ... Mr. Peter K. SCHANTZ
15 Director Human Resources ... Ms. Debra A. GUILBERT
31 Director Community Svc Learning ... Ms. Sally S. LEBER
11 Director of Administrative Services ... Ms. Susan K. WIEL
04 Asst to President/Board Secy ... Ms. Lisa D. JACKSON
23 Director Wellness Center ... Ms. Marsha A. TILDEN
35 Dean of Students ... Dr. Kimberlie L. GOLDSBERRY
39 Director Residential Life ... Ms. Wendy L. PIPER
41 Director of Athletics ... Mr. Roger D. INGLES
42 Chaplain ... Rev. Jon R. POWERS
89 Dean First Year Students ... Vacant
92 Honors Program Codirector ... Dr. Edward H. BURTT
92 Honors Program Codirector ... Dr. Amy MCCLURE
93 Dir Multicultural Student Affairs ... Ms. Terree L. STEVENSON
102 Dir Foundation/Corp/Govt Relations ... Ms. Karen CROSMAN
07 Associate Director of Admissions ... Ms. Alisha M. COUCH
88 Special Assistant to the President ... Mr. Mark H. SHIPPS
40 Bookstore Manager ... Mr. Kevin U. STITH
38 Coord Counseling/Mental Health Svcs ... Vacant
96 Purchasing Coordinator ... Ms. Melanie T. KALB

Otterbein University (K)

1 South Grove Street, Westerville OH 43081-2006
County: Franklin FICE Identification: 003110
Unit ID: 204936
Telephone: (614) 890-3000 Carnegie Class: Master's M
FAX Number: (614) 823-3114 Calendar System: Semester
URL: www.otterbein.edu
Established: 1847 Annual Undergrad Tuition & Fees: $31,424
Enrollment: 2,537 Coed
Affiliation or Control: United Methodist IRS Status: 501(c)3
Highest Offering: Doctorate
Program: Liberal Arts And General; Teacher Preparatory; Professional
Accreditation: NH, ANEST, MUS, NURSE, TED, THEA

01 President ... Dr. Kathy A. KRENDL
100 Chief of Staff ... Ms. Kristine ROBBINS
05 Vice President Academic Affairs ... Dr. Victoria MCGILLIN
32 Vice President Student Affairs ... Mr. Robert M. GATTI
10 Vice President for Business Affairs ... Mrs. Rebecca D. VAZQUEZ-SKILLINGS
30 VP Institutional Advancement ... Ms. Heidi L. TRACY
84 Vice President for Enrollment ... Mr. Jefferson BLACKBURN-SMITH
20 Assoc VP AA/Dean Academic Services ... Vacant
91 Exec Director of Information Tech ... Vacant
08 Director of the Library ... Mrs. Lois F. SZUDY
06 Registrar ... Mr. Donald W. FOSTER
26 Exec Dir Marketing/Communications ... Mrs. Jennifer PEARCE
36 Director Career Planning/Placement ... Mr. Ryan BRECHBILL
37 Director of Financial Aid ... Mr. Thomas V. YARNELL
41 Athletic Director ... Ms. Dawn STEWART
42 Chaplain ... Vacant
51 Assoc Dean Adult & Transfer Office ... Ms. Kate CAREY
107 Dean School of Prof Studies ... Dr. Barbara H. SCHAFFNER
49 Dean School of Arts/Sciences ... Dr. Paul EISENSTEIN
85 Exec Director Intl Programs ... Mr. Chris MUSICK
07 Director of Admissions ... Mr. Ben SHOEMAKER
15 Director Human Resources ... Vacant
18 Director/Physical Plant ... Mr. David D. BELL
29 Director Alumni Relations ... Ms. Rebecca F. SMITH
28 Director of Diversity ... Dr. Lisa PATTERSON
96 Director of Purchasing ... Mr. Steven H. ROSENBERGER
21 Inst Rsrch Spec/Financial Analyst ... Mr. Christopher A. HAYTER
09 Asst VP for Institutional Planning ... Dr. Barbara I. WHARTON
19 Director of Security ... Mr. Larry BANASZAK
04 Executive Assistant to President ... Vacant

Owens Community College (L)

30335 Oregon, PO Box 10000, Toledo OH 43699-1947
County: Wood FICE Identification: 005753
Unit ID: 204945
Telephone: (567) 661-7000 Carnegie Class: Assoc/Pub-U-MC
FAX Number: N/A Calendar System: Semester
URL: www.owens.edu
Established: 1965 Annual Undergrad Tuition & Fees (In-State): $3,504
Enrollment: 16,996 Coed
Affiliation or Control: State IRS Status: 501(c)3
Highest Offering: Associate Degree
Program: Occupational; 2-Year Principally Bachelor's Creditable; Technical Emphasis
Accreditation: NH, ACBSP, ADNUR, CAHIIM, DH, DIETT, DMS, EMT, MAC, NAIT, OTA, PTAA, RAD, SURGT

01 President ... Dr. Mike BOWER
101 Secretary to the Board of Trustees ... Ms. Patricia JEZAK
04 Executive Assistant to President ... Ms. Vicki DUPKE
05 Vice President/Provost ... Dr. Renay SCOTT
10 Vice President/Treasurer ... Ms. Laurie SABIN
16 VP Human Resources ... Mr. Jack WITT
108 Assoc VP Assessment/Accreditation ... Mr. Thomas PERIN
20 Vice Provost Academic Services ... Ms. Denise SMITH
30 Development Officer ... Mr. John SATKOWSKI
103 Executive Dir Wrkfrce/Comm Service ... Dr. Brian PASKVAN
12 Associate VP Findlay Campus ... Dr. Melissa GREEN
32 Assoc VP Student Services ... Vacant
21 Assoc VP Business Affs/Controller ... Ms. Pam BECK
13 Chief Information Officer ... Dr. Connie SCHAFFER
19 Chief of Police ... Mr. John BETORI
37 Director Financial Aid ... Ms. Donna HOLUBIK
18 Director Operations ... Mr. Michael MCDONALD
09 Inst Research Associate ... Ms. Debra RATHKE
72 Dean School of Technology ... Mr. Randy WHARTON
84 Dean Student Enrollment ... Dr. Betsy JOHNSON
76 Dean School of Health Sciences ... Dr. Doug MEAD
66 Dean School of Nursing ... Ms. Dawn WETMORE
50 Dean School of Business ... Dr. Ann THEIS

49 Dean School of Arts & Sciences .... Vacant
62 Dean Library .... Mr. Tom SINK
106 Director eLearning .... Mr. Mark KARAMOL
43 In-House Legal Counsel .... Dr. Natalie JACKSON
22 Equal Opp/Inclusiveness Officer .... Ms. Lisa DUBOSE
06 Registrar .... Ms. Juliette QUINONEZ
26 Exec Dir Marketing/Communications .... Ms. Jennifer FEHNRICH
29 Director Alumni Affairs .... Ms. Laura MOORE
35 Director Student Life .... Mr. Chris GIORDANO
07 Manager Dual Enrollment Prtnrshps .... Mr. Joseph CARONE
36 Specialist Admiss/Career Services .... Ms. Gentry DIXON
40 Manager Auxiliary Services .... Mr. David WAHR
85 Director International Programs .... Ms. Deborah GAVLIK
41 Director Athletics .... Mr. Rudy YOUVICH

Owens Community College Findlay Campus (A)
3200 Bright Road, Findlay OH 45840
Telephone: (567) 429-3500 Identification: 770360
Accreditation: &NH

† Main campus is Owens Community College in Toledo, OH.

Payne Theological Seminary (B)
PO Box 474, Wilberforce OH 45384-0474
County: Greene FICE Identification: 010017
Unit ID: 204990
Telephone: (937) 376-2946 Carnegie Class: Spec/Faith
FAX Number: (937) 376-3330 Calendar System: 4/1/4
URL: www.payne.edu
Established: 1844 Annual Graduate Tuition & Fees: $7,240
Enrollment: 132 Coed
Affiliation or Control: African Methodist Episcopal IRS Status: 501(c)3
Highest Offering: Master's; No Undergraduates
Program: Professional; Business Emphasis
Accreditation: THEOL

01 President .... Rev Dr. Leah GASKIN-FITCHUE
05 Interim Academic Dean .... Dr. William J. AUGMAN, JR.
30 Director of Development .... Rev. Jules DUNHAM HOWIE
10 Finance Director .... Mr. Alan COSTNER
37 Financial Aid Officer .... Ms. Pat COPELY
08 Head Librarian .... Mr. George JOHNSON

Pontifical College Josephinum (C)
7625 N High Street, Columbus OH 43235-1498
County: Franklin FICE Identification: 003113
Unit ID: 205027
Telephone: (614) 885-5585 Carnegie Class: Spec/Faith
FAX Number: (614) 885-2307 Calendar System: Semester
URL: www.pcj.edu
Established: 1888 Annual Undergrad Tuition & Fees: $19,985
Enrollment: 197 Male
Affiliation or Control: Roman Catholic IRS Status: 501(c)3
Highest Offering: Beyond Master's But Less Than Doctorate
Program: Liberal Arts And General; Professional; Religious Emphasis
Accreditation: NH, THEOL

01 Rector/President .... R.Msgr. Christopher J. SCHRECK
10 VP for Administration/Treasurer .... Mr. John O. ERWIN
03 Vice Rector School of Theology .... Rev. Walter R. OXLEY
05 Provost .... Dr. Michael D. ROSS
30 Vice President for Advancement .... Rev. John A. ALLEN
49 Vice Rector College Liberal Arts .... Rev. John F. HEISLER
73 Academic Dean School of Theology .... Dr. Perry J. CAHALL
20 Academic Dean College Liberal Arts .... Dr. David J. DE LEONARDIS
06 Registrar .... Mr. Samuel J. DEAN
08 Librarian .... Mr. Peter G. VERACKA
33 Dean of Men In Theology .... Rev. Joseph A. MURPHY, SJ
33 Dean of Men In College .... Rev. John ROZEMBAJGIER
07 Co-Director of Admissions .... Rev. John F. HEISLER
07 Co-Director of Admissions .... Rev. Walter R. OXLEY
37 Financial Aid Director .... Mrs. Marky LEICHTNAM

PowerSport Institute (D)
21210 Emery Road, North Randall OH 44128
Telephone: (216) 587-5000 Identification: 770582
Accreditation: ACCSC

† Main campus is Ohio Technical College in Cleveland, OH.

Professional Skills Institute (E)
1505 Holland Road, Maumee OH 43537
County: Lucas FICE Identification: 023377
Unit ID: 205054
Telephone: (419) 720-6670 Carnegie Class: Assoc/PrivFP
FAX Number: (419) 720-6674 Calendar System: Quarter
URL: www.proskills.edu
Established: 1984 Annual Undergrad Tuition & Fees: $11,550
Enrollment: 400 Coed
Affiliation or Control: Proprietary IRS Status: Proprietary
Highest Offering: Associate Degree
Program: Occupational; 2-Year Principally Bachelor's Creditable; Nursing Emphasis
Accreditation: ABHES, PTAA

01 CEO .... Mr. Daniel FINCH
07 Admissions Coordinator .... Mr. Tony DICKENS

Rabbinical College of Telshe (F)
28400 Euclid Avenue, Wickliffe OH 44092-2584
County: Lake FICE Identification: 003115
Unit ID: 205124
Telephone: (440) 943-5300 Carnegie Class: Spec/Faith
FAX Number: (440) 943-5303 Calendar System: Quarter
Established: 1941 Annual Undergrad Tuition & Fees: $9,600
Enrollment: 80 Male
Affiliation or Control: Independent Non-Profit IRS Status: 501(c)3
Highest Offering: Doctorate
Program: Teacher Preparatory; Professional
Accreditation: RABN

01 President .... Rabbi Shlomo EISENBERGER
06 Registrar .... Rabbi Abraham MATITIA

Remington College Cleveland Campus (G)
14445 Broadway Avenue, Cleveland OH 44125-1900
County: Cuyahoga FICE Identification: 007777
Unit ID: 375416
Telephone: (216) 475-7520 Carnegie Class: Assoc/PrivFP
FAX Number: (216) 475-6055 Calendar System: Other
URL: www.remingtoncollege.edu
Established: 1990 Annual Undergrad Tuition & Fees: $16,686
Enrollment: 487 Coed
Affiliation or Control: Independent Non-Profit IRS Status: 501(c)3
Highest Offering: Associate Degree
Program: Occupational
Accreditation: ACCSC

01 President .... Mr. Gary A. AZOTEA

Remington College-Cleveland West Campus (H)
26350 Brookpark Road, North Olmstead OH 44070-5905
Telephone: (440) 777-2560 Identification: 770583
Accreditation: ACCSC, @PTAA

† Main campus is Remington College Cleveland Campus in Cleveland, OH.

Rosedale Bible College (I)
2270 Rosedale Road, Irwin OH 43029-9517
County: Madison FICE Identification: 034253
Unit ID: 439899
Telephone: (740) 857-1311 Carnegie Class: Assoc/PrivNFP
FAX Number: (877) 857-1312 Calendar System: Semester
URL: www.rosedale.edu
Established: 1952 Annual Undergrad Tuition & Fees: $8,401
Enrollment: 56 Coed
Affiliation or Control: Mennonite Church IRS Status: 501(c)3
Highest Offering: Associate Degree
Program: 2-Year Principally Bachelor's Creditable; Religious Emphasis
Accreditation: BI

01 President .... Mr. Daniel ZIEGLER
05 Academic Dean .... Mr. Phil WEBER
32 Dean of Students .... Mr. Matthew SHOWALTER
84 Director of Enrollment Services .... Mr. Darnell BRENNEMAN
08 Director of Library Services .... Mr. Reuben SAIRS
06 Registrar .... Ms. Bethany GEIB
10 Chief Financial Officer .... Mr. Lynford SCHROCK
26 Chief Public Relations Officer .... Mr. Kenneth MILLER

Saint Mary Seminary and Graduate School of Theology (J)
28700 Euclid Avenue, Wickliffe OH 44092-2585
County: Lake FICE Identification: 004061
Unit ID: 205319
Telephone: (440) 943-7600 Carnegie Class: Not Classified
FAX Number: (440) 943-7577 Calendar System: Semester
URL: www.stmarysem.edu
Established: 1848 Annual Graduate Tuition & Fees: $10,120
Enrollment: 131 Coed
Affiliation or Control: Roman Catholic IRS Status: 501(c)3
Highest Offering: Doctorate; No Undergraduates
Program: Professional; Religious Emphasis
Accreditation: NH, THEOL

01 President/Rector .... Rev. Mark A. LATCOVICH
03 Vice President/Vice Rector .... Rev. Gerald J. BEDAR
05 Academic Dean .... Sr. Mary MCCORMICK, OSU
33 Student Dean .... Rev. Michael G. WOOST
42 Spiritual Director .... Rev. Mark HOLLIS
06 Registrar/Assistant Dean .... Sr. Brendon ZAJAC, SND
08 Librarian .... Mr. Alan K. ROME
10 Treasurer .... Mr. Philip GUBAN

Sandford-Brown College (K)
2800 Corporate Exchange Parkway, Columbus OH 43231
Telephone: (614) 948-0130 Identification: 770758
Accreditation: ACICS

† Main campus is Sanford-Brown College in Atlanta, GA.

Sandford-Brown College (L)
17535 Rosbough Drive, Suite 100, Middleburg Heights OH 44130
Telephone: (440) 202-3232 Identification: 770759
Accreditation: ACICS, CVT, RAD

† Main campus is Sanford-Brown College in Atlanta, GA.

School of Advertising Art (M)
1725 E David Road, Dayton OH 45440-1612
County: Montgomery FICE Identification: 025530
Unit ID: 205391
Telephone: (877) 300-9866 Carnegie Class: Assoc/PrivFP
FAX Number: (937) 294-5869 Calendar System: Semester
URL: www.saa.edu
Established: 1983 Annual Undergrad Tuition & Fees: $27,440
Enrollment: 110 Coed
Affiliation or Control: Proprietary IRS Status: Proprietary
Highest Offering: Associate Degree
Program: Occupational; 2-Year Principally Bachelor's Creditable; Technical Emphasis
Accreditation: ACCSC

01 Owner/President/Creative Director .... Ms. Jessica BARRY
03 Vice President .... Mr. Matt FLICK
06 Vice President/HR/Registrar .... Mr. Nathan SUMMERS
05 Director of Education .... Ms. Karen ABNEY KORN
36 Director of Career Services & PR .... Ms. Roxann PATRICK
37 Director of Financial Aid .... Ms. Tracy GARDNER

Shawnee State University (N)
940 Second Street, Portsmouth OH 45662-4344
County: Scioto FICE Identification: 009942
Unit ID: 205443
Telephone: (740) 351-3205 Carnegie Class: Bac/A&S
FAX Number: (740) 351-3470 Calendar System: Semester
URL: www.shawnee.edu
Established: 1975 Annual Undergrad Tuition & Fees (In-State): $6,988
Enrollment: 4,620 Coed
Affiliation or Control: State IRS Status: 501(c)3
Highest Offering: Master's
Program: Occupational; Liberal Arts And General; Teacher Preparatory
Accreditation: NH, ADNUR, COARC, DH, MLTAD, NUR, OT, OTA, PTAA, RAD, TED

01 President .... Dr. Rita R. MORRIS
05 Provost/VP Academic Affairs .... Dr. David TODT
10 Vice President for Finance & Admin .... Ms. Elinda C. BOYLES
32 Vice President for Student Affairs .... Vacant
43 General Counsel/Asst to the Pres .... Ms. Cheryl HACKER
84 Assoc Vice Pres Enrollment Mgmt .... Mr. Robert J. TRUSZ
20 Associate Provost .... Dr. Paul MADDEN
26 Director Communications .... Ms. Elizabeth BLEVINS
107 Dean Professional Studies .... Dr. Jim KADEL
49 Dean College Arts & Sciences .... Dr. Jeffery BAUER
08 Director Library .... Ms. Rebekah KILZER
13 Director Univ Information Systems .... Mr. Charles WARNER
30 Director of Development .... Mr. Eric BRAUN
07 Director of Admission & Retention .... Mr. Robert J. TRUSZ
06 Registrar .... Mr. Mark MOORE
15 Director of Human Resources/Payroll .... Mr. Dave ZINDER
41 Athletic Director .... Mr. Jeff HAMILTON
37 Director of Financial Aid .... Dr. Nicole NEAL
36 Director Career Services .... Vacant
38 Director of Counseling & Psych Svcs .... Dr. Michael J. HUGHES
21 Assoc VP for Finance & Admin .... Ms. Joanne CHARLES
88 Dean University College .... Dr. Brenda HAAS
86 Director of Government Relations .... Vacant
85 Director for International Pgms .... Ms. Rita HAIDER
24 Director Instructional Technology .... Mr. Pete DUNCAN
96 Dir of Purchasing & Mail Services .... Ms. Pat CARSON
29 Coordinator Alumni & Retirees .... Ms. Denise GREGORY
18 Director of Facilities .... Mr. Butch KOTCAMP
97 Director General Education Program .... Dr. Phil BLAU
09 Dir of Institutional Effectiveness .... Mr. Christopher SHAFFER
21 Controller .... Mr. Greg A. BALLENGEE
35 Dean of Students .... Ms. Marcie SIMMS
19 Chief of Police .... Mr. David THOROUGHMAN

Sinclair Community College (O)
444 W Third Street, Dayton OH 45402-1460
County: Montgomery FICE Identification: 003119
Unit ID: 205470
Telephone: (937) 512-2500 Carnegie Class: Assoc/Pub-U-SC
FAX Number: (937) 512-5192 Calendar System: Semester
URL: www.sinclair.edu
Established: 1887 Annual Undergrad Tuition & Fees (In-District): $2,871
Enrollment: 23,563 Coed
Affiliation or Control: State/Local IRS Status: 501(c)3
Highest Offering: Associate Degree
Program: Occupational; 2-Year Principally Bachelor's Creditable
Accreditation: NH, ACBSP, ACFEI, ADNUR, ART, CAHIIM, COARC, DH, DIETT, ENGT, MAC, MUS, OTA, PTAA, RAD, SURGT, THEA

00 President Emeritus .... Dr. Ned J. SIFFERLEN
01 President .... Dr. Steven L. JOHNSON
05 Provost .... Dr. Dave COLLINS
20 Associate Provost .... Dr. Kathleen CLEARY
20 Assistant Provost .... Mr. Jared CUTLER
10 Vice Pres Business Operations .... Dr. Ty STONE
103 VP Workforce Develop/Corporate Svcs .... Ms. Deb NORRIS
88 Assistant VP for Workforce Develop .... Mr. Jeff MILLER
88 Superintendent-School Partnerships .... Mr. Michael CARTER
100 Chief of Staff .... Mr. Mitchell BAILEY
30 Vice President Advancement .... Ms. Madeline ISELI
10 VP and CFO .... Mr. Jeff BOUDOURIS
37 Chief Student Financial Svcs Ofcr .... Dr. Annesa CHEEK
45 Vice Pres Organizational Dev .... Dr. Mary GAIER
84 VP of Enrollment Management .... Dr. Anthony CRUZ
12 VP for Regional Centers .... Dr. Scott MARKLAND
81 Dean of Science/Math/Engineering .... Mr. Anthony PONDER
76 Dean Life & Health Sciences .... Ms. Rena SHUCHAT
105 Dean Distance Learning/Inst Support .... Dr. Nancy THIBEAULT
83 Dean Liberal Arts/Comm/Soc Sci .... Dr. Lori ZAKEL
50 Dean Business & Public Services .... Dr. Sue MERRELL
26 Director of Public Relations .... Mr. Adam MURKA
88 Dir Learning Resources Center .... Mr. Dawayne KIRKMAN
09 Dir Research/Analytics/Reporting .... Ms. Laura MERCER
15 Director Human Resources .... Ms. Janet JONES
13 Chief Information Officer .... Mr. Scott MCCOLLUM
25 Director Grants Development .... Ms. Karla HIBBERT-JONES
18 Director Facilities Management .... Mr. Robert WOODRUFF
84 Dir Strategic Enrollment Management .... Ms. Melissa TOLLE
19 Director of Public Safety .... Mr. Charles GIFT
28 Diversity Officer .... Ms. Gwen JONES
32 Director Student Affairs .... Ms. LaRue PIERCE
43 General Counsel .... Ms. Lauren ROSS
88 Director School Linkages .... Mr. Michael GAINES
06 Registrar .... Ms. Tina HUMMONS
96 Dir Budget and Analysis .... Mr. Michael BARHORST
08 Director Library .... Mr. Doug KAYLOR
37 Director Financial Aid .... Mr. Matthew MOORE
21 Director Business Services .... Mr. Paul MURPHY
21 Director Accounting .... Mr. Mike PLOURDE
104 Director International Education .... Ms. Allison RHEA
20 Director Academic Advising .... Ms. Phyllis SALTER

South University (A)

4743 Richmond Road, Cleveland OH 44128
Telephone: (216) 755-5000 Identification: 770916
Accreditation: &SC, NURSE, @PTAA

† Main campus is South University in Savannah, GA.

Southern State Community College (B)

100 Hobart Drive, Hillsboro OH 45133-9488
County: Highland FICE Identification: 012870
Unit ID: 205966
Telephone: (937) 393-3431 Carnegie Class: Assoc/Pub-R-M
FAX Number: (937) 393-9370 Calendar System: Semester
URL: www.sscc.edu
Established: 1975 Annual Undergrad Tuition & Fees (In-State): $3,988
Enrollment: 2,856 Coed
Affiliation or Control: State IRS Status: 501(c)3
Highest Offering: Associate Degree
Program: Occupational; 2-Year Principally Bachelor's Creditable
Accreditation: NH, ADNUR, MAC

01 President .... Dr. Kevin S. BOYS
05 Vice President Academic Affairs .... Dr. Ryan MCCALL
10 Vice President Business & Finance .... Mr. James E. BUCK
32 Vice Pres Student Svcs/Enroll Mgmt .... Mr. James BLAND
30 Vice Pres Instl Advancement .... Ms. Nicole ROADES
12 Director of Fayette Campus .... Ms. Jessica WISE
12 Director of South Campus .... Dr. Peggy CHALKER
12 Director of North Campus .... Vacant
20 Dean Instruction .... Ms. Karen S. DAVIS
103 Dean Workforce Dev/Community Svcs .... Mr. John JOY
15 Director of Human Resources .... Ms. Mindy MARKEY-GRABILL
88 Dean of Adult Opportunity Center .... Ms. Karyn EVANS
88 Dean of Course Studies .... Mr. JR ROUSH
102 Executive Director Foundation .... Vacant
91 Computer System/Communication Mgr .... Ms. Shirley A. CORNWELL
26 Director of Public Relations .... Ms. Kris CROSS
06 Registrar .... Ms. Sharon PURVIS
66 Director of Nursing .... Dr. Julianne KREBS
08 Librarian .... Vacant
37 Director Financial Aid .... Ms. Janeen S. DEATLEY
07 Dir Admission/Student Activities .... Ms. Wendy JOHNSON
41 Athletic Director .... Mr. Adam HOLBROOK
40 Bookstore Manager .... Ms. Jessica STEADMAN
13 Director Information Tech .... Mr. Dennis R. GRIFFITH
36 Director of Recruitment .... Mr. Tom PAYTON
84 Coordinator Enrollment Management .... Ms. Lisa COPAS

Southern State Community College Fayette Campus (C)

1270 US Route 62 SW,
Washington Court House OH 43160
Telephone: (740) 333-5115 Identification: 770362
Accreditation: &NH, COARC

† Main campus is Southern State Community College in Hillsboro, OH.

Southern State Community College North Campus (D)

1850 Davids Drive, Wilmington OH 45177
Telephone: (937) 382-6645 Identification: 770363
Accreditation: &NH

† Main campus is Southern State Community College in Hillsboro, OH.

Southern State Community College South Campus (E)

12681 U.S. Route 62, Sardinia OH 45171
Telephone: (937) 695-0307 Identification: 770361
Accreditation: &NH

† Main campus is Southern State Community College in Hillsboro, OH.

Stark State College (F)

6200 Frank Avenue, NW, North Canton OH 44720-7299
County: Stark FICE Identification: 010881
Unit ID: 205841
Telephone: (330) 494-6170 Carnegie Class: Assoc/Pub-R-L
FAX Number: (330) 497-6313 Calendar System: Semester
URL: www.starkstate.edu
Established: 1960 Annual Undergrad Tuition & Fees (In-District): $4,509
Enrollment: 15,672 Coed
Affiliation or Control: State/Local IRS Status: 501(c)3
Highest Offering: Associate Degree
Program: 2-Year Principally Bachelor's Creditable; Technical Emphasis
Accreditation: NH, ACBSP, ADNUR, CAHIIM, COARC, DH, @DIETT, ENGT, MAC, MLTAD, OTA, PTAA

01 President .... Dr. Para M. JONES
05 Provost and Chief Academic Officer .... Vacant
10 VP for Business and Finance .... Mr. Thomas A. CHIAPPINI
27 Chief Information Officer .... Mr. Michael DRONEY
32 VP Student Services/Enrollment Mgmt .... Mrs. Cheryl RICE
15 Director of Human Resources .... Ms. Melissa A. GLANZ
49 Dean Liberal Arts .... Dr. Lada GIBSON-SHREVE
81 Dean Sciences .... Mr. James TREACLE
81 Dean Mathematics .... Mr. Andrew STEPHAN
50 Dean Business and Entrep Studies .... Dr. Glenda ZINK
76 Interim Dean Health Technologies .... Mrs. Donna ALEXANDER
07 Dean Admissions/Student Services .... Mr. Wallace C. HOFFER
21 Controller .... Mr. David A. JOHNSON
14 Director Computer Services .... Mr. Greg LANKA
88 Sr Dir Strategic Grant .... Ms. Rebecca PRIEST
36 Director of Career Development .... Ms. Kristin HANNON
37 Dean Financial Aid and Registration .... Ms. Amy SMUCKER
51 Director Continuing Education .... Mr. Russ O'NEILL
18 Director of Physical Plant and Cons .... Mr. Steve SPRADLING
90 Director Academic Computing .... Mr. Jeff LASH
40 Bookstore Manager .... Ms. Kathryn FEICHTER
06 Registrar .... Ms. Pam ARRINGTON
26 Director Marketing & Communications .... Ms. Irene LEWIS-MOTTS
21 Director of Budget .... Mr. Bruce WYDER
09 Director of Institutional Research .... Mr. Peter TRUMPOWER
54 Dean Eng/Indus and Emerg Tech .... Mr. Don BALL
72 Dean Information Technology Div .... Vacant
38 Dean Advising & Student Engagement .... Ms. Renee LILLY
106 Director eStarkState .... Ms. Linda MOROSKO
53 Dean Education and Human Services .... Vacant

Stautzenberger College (G)

8001 Katherine Boulevard, Brecksville OH 44141
Telephone: (440) 838-1999 Identification: 770760
Accreditation: ACICS

† Main campus is Stautzenberger College in Maumee, OH.

Stautzenberger College (H)

1796 Indian Wood Circle, Maumee OH 43537-4007
County: Lucas FICE Identification: 004866
Unit ID: 205887
Telephone: (419) 866-0261 Carnegie Class: Assoc/PrivFP
FAX Number: (419) 867-9821 Calendar System: Quarter
URL: www.sctoday.edu
Established: 1926 Annual Undergrad Tuition & Fees: $11,304
Enrollment: 848 Coed
Affiliation or Control: Proprietary IRS Status: Proprietary
Highest Offering: Associate Degree
Program: Occupational; 2-Year Principally Bachelor's Creditable; Technical Emphasis
Accreditation: ACICS, MAC

01 President/Director .... Mr. James T. ROYSTER
03 Vice President .... Mr. Brian E. NIEDZWIECKI
07 Director of Admissions .... Ms. Amanda L. BOYD
05 Dean of Academics .... Ms. Susan M. LIPPENS
37 Financial Aid Director .... Mrs. Mari L. HUFFMAN
36 Career Services Director .... Mr. Robert A. GARVER

Terra State Community College (I)

2830 Napoleon Road, Fremont OH 43420-9670
County: Sandusky FICE Identification: 008278
Unit ID: 206011
Telephone: (419) 334-8400 Carnegie Class: Assoc/Pub-R-M
FAX Number: (419) 334-3719 Calendar System: Semester
URL: www.terra.edu
Established: 1968 Annual Undergrad Tuition & Fees (In-State): $3,395
Enrollment: 3,192 Coed
Affiliation or Control: State IRS Status: 501(c)3
Highest Offering: Associate Degree
Program: Occupational; 2-Year Principally Bachelor's Creditable; Technical Emphasis
Accreditation: NH, ADNUR, CAHIIM, @PTAA

01 President .... Dr. Jerome WEBSTER
30 Senior VP Inst Advancement .... Ms. Lisa WILLIAMS
05 VP for Academic Affairs .... Mr. John FATICA
10 VP for Financial Affairs .... Mr. Randy MCCULLOUGH
32 VP Student Success/Dean of Students .... Ms. Lisa KIRCHNER
54 Dean Engineering Technology/Math .... Mr. Andrew G. CARROLL
50 Dean Business and Creative Arts .... Mr. Michael SHIRTZ
66 Dean Allied Health/Nursing/Science .... Ms. Cindy HALL
49 Dean Liberal Arts and Public Svcs .... Ms. Lynette SULLIVAN
37 Director Financial Aid .... Ms. Christina BRATTON
102 Interim Exec Dir of Foundation .... Ms. Lisa WILLIAMS
09 Interim Registrar .... Dr. Julianna BORDERS
13 Director Information Technology .... Mr. Tim KINCAID
21 Director of Finance .... Ms. Renee D. BROWN
18 Director Facilities/Plant Ops .... Ms. Elaine ROSENGARTEN
08 Librarian .... Vacant
26 Dir Mktg Public Rels/Enroll Svcs .... Ms. Mary E. MCCUE
36 Coordinator Career Services .... Ms. Joan GAMBLE
19 Coord Campus Safety/Evening Svcs .... Mr. Jeffery HUFFMAN

Tiffin University (J)

155 Miami Street, Tiffin OH 44883-2161
County: Seneca FICE Identification: 003121
Unit ID: 206048
Telephone: (419) 447-6442 Carnegie Class: Master's L
FAX Number: (419) 443-5022 Calendar System: Semester
URL: www.tiffin.edu
Established: 1888 Annual Undergrad Tuition & Fees: $20,700
Enrollment: 6,920 Coed
Affiliation or Control: Independent Non-Profit IRS Status: 501(c)3
Highest Offering: Master's
Program: 2-Year Principally Bachelor's Creditable; Liberal Arts And General
Accreditation: NH, ACBSP

01 President .... Dr. Paul MARION
05 Vice President for Academic Affairs .... Dr. Charles CHRISTENSEN
30 Vice Pres Development/Pub Affairs .... Mr. Ron SCHUMACHER
10 Vice Pres Finance/Administration .... Mr. Leon WYDEN
16 VP Human Resources/Campus Services .... Ms. Lori HALL
07 Dean of Admissions/Financial Aid .... Mr. Jeremy MARINIS
58 Dean Sch Grad/Degree Completion .... Dr. Jason SLONE
88 Dean of Academic Support Programs .... Ms. Annette STAUNTON
04 Assistant to the President .... Ms. Nancy GILBERT
32 Dean of Students .... Mr. Mike HERDLICK
13 Chief Information Officer .... Mr. John HALLIS
07 Director Undergrad Admissions .... Mr. Joe BORICH
26 Exec Dir Media Rels/Publications .... Ms. Lisa WILLIAMS
38 Director of Academic Advising .... Ms. Judith GARDNER
06 Registrar .... Ms. Alice NICHOLS
41 Director Athletics .... Mr. Lonny ALLEN
21 Controller .... Mr. Robert WATSON
08 Head Librarian .... Ms. Frances FLEET
09 Director of Institutional Research .... Mr. Michael HERDLICK
29 Director Alumni Relations .... Ms. Vickie GALASKA
36 Director of Career Development .... Ms. Celinda SCHERGER
18 Director of Facilities .... Mr. Harold KINN
22 Equal Opportunity Officer .... Ms. Lori HALL
39 Director of Residence Life .... Ms. Mandi HUMMEL
44 Director of Annual Fund .... Ms. Colleen LAZAR
28 Director of Institutional Diversity .... Dr. Sharon PERRY-NAUSE
37 Director Student Financial Aid .... Ms. Andrea FABER
40 Bookstore Manager .... Mr. Charles LUTZ
49 Dean of Arts & Sciences .... Ms. Joyce HALL-YATES
50 Dean of Business .... Dr. Lillian SCHUMACHER
88 Dean Criminal Justice/Social Sci .... Dr. Jaimie ORR
92 Chair of Freshman Honors Program .... Dr. John MILLAR

Tri-State Bible College (K)

506 Margaret Street, PO Box 445,
South Point OH 45680-8402
County: Lawrence FICE Identification: 034754
Unit ID: 206154
Telephone: (740) 377-2520 Carnegie Class: Spec/Faith
FAX Number: (740) 377-0001 Calendar System: Semester
URL: www.tsbc.edu
Established: 1970 Annual Undergrad Tuition & Fees: $7,700
Enrollment: 75 Coed
Affiliation or Control: Independent Non-Profit IRS Status: 501(c)3
Highest Offering: Baccalaureate
Program: 2-Year Principally Bachelor's Creditable; Professional; Religious Emphasis
Accreditation: BI

00 Chancellor .... Dr. Clifford L. MARQUARDT
01 President .... Dr. Jack R. FINCH
05 Vice President Academic Affairs .... Mr. Phillip KINNEY
10 Vice President Finance .... Ms. Clyda HESTER
11 Vice President Administrative Affs .... Ms. Bobby MERCER

Trinity Lutheran Seminary (A)

2199 E Main Street, Columbus OH 43209-2334
County: Franklin FICE Identification: 003044
Unit ID: 206215
Telephone: (614) 235-4136 Carnegie Class: Spec/Faith
FAX Number: (614) 238-0263 Calendar System: Semester
URL: www.TLSohio.edu
Established: 1830 Annual Graduate Tuition & Fees: $14,754
Enrollment: 116 Coed
Affiliation or Control: Evangelical Lutheran Church In America
IRS Status: 501(c)3
Highest Offering: Doctorate; No Undergraduates
Program: Professional; Religious Emphasis
Accreditation: NH, THEOL

01 President ... Rev. Robert C. BARGER
05 Academic Dean ... Dr. Brad A. BINAU
20 Associate Academic Dean ... Dr. Diane J. HYMANS
88 Dean of Leadership Formation ... Rev. Emlyn A. OTT
84 Director Vocation and Enrollment ... Rev. Shari L. AYERS
06 Registrar ... Mrs. Carol M. DIXON
08 Director Hamma Library ... Mr. Ray A. OLSON
26 Director Communications/Marketing ... Ms. Margaret L. FARNHAM
37 Director Financial Aid ... Mrs. Melissa CURTIS POWELL
88 Director Contextual Education ... Rev. Jane E. JENKINS
88 Director MA in Church Music Program ... Ms. May L. SCHWARZ
58 Director Graduate Studies ... Dr. Walter F. TAYLOR, JR.
88 Director MACE/MAYFM/MTS Programs ... Dr. Mary E. HUGHES
21 Controller ... Mrs. Patricia A. FORK
18 Director Facilities Management ... Ms. Laura K. PETERSON

Trumbull Business College (B)

3200 Ridge Road, Warren OH 44484-3272
County: Trumbull FICE Identification: 020543
Unit ID: 206224
Telephone: (330) 369-3200 Carnegie Class: Assoc/PrivFP
FAX Number: (330) 369-6792 Calendar System: Quarter
URL: www.tbc-trumbullbusiness.com
Established: 1972 Annual Undergrad Tuition & Fees: $11,671
Enrollment: 229 Coed
Affiliation or Control: Proprietary IRS Status: Proprietary
Highest Offering: Associate Degree
Program: Occupational
Accreditation: ACICS

01 President ... Mr. Dennis J. GRIFFITH
37 Director of Financial Aid ... Ms. Florence HENNING
36 Director of Student Placement ... Ms. Kimberly STRANIAK
12 Director of Branch Campus ... Mr. Kimberly STRANIAK
06 Registrar ... Ms. Teresa SHAMBACH

Union Institute & University (C)

440 E McMillan Street, Cincinnati OH 45206-1947
County: Hamilton FICE Identification: 010923
Unit ID: 206279
Telephone: (513) 861-6400 Carnegie Class: DRU
FAX Number: (513) 861-0779 Calendar System: Semester
URL: www.myunion.edu
Established: 1964 Annual Undergrad Tuition & Fees: $11,760
Enrollment: 1,666 Coed
Affiliation or Control: Independent Non-Profit IRS Status: 501(c)3
Highest Offering: Doctorate
Program: Liberal Arts And General; Teacher Preparatory; Professional
Accreditation: NH, @SW

01 President ... Dr. Roger H. SUBLETT
05 VP Academic Affairs ... Dr. Nelson SOTO
04 Executive Assistant to President ... Ms. Carolyn KRAUSE
10 Chief Fiscal Officer ... Mr. Tom CUNNINGHAM
15 Vice President Human Resources ... Ms. Deborah EAMOE
84 VP Enrollment Management ... Mr. Jon MAYS
46 Assoc VP Inst Effectiveness ... Dr. Elizabeth PRUDEN
88 Assoc VP Special Projects ... Dr. James ROCHELEAU
58 Dean PhD Pgm ... Dr. Arlene SACKS
58 Dean Graduate Studies in Education ... Dr. Arlene SACKS
58 Dean Graduate Studies in Psychology ... Dr. William LAX
21 Controller ... Vacant
06 Registrar ... Ms. Lew Rita MOORE
09 Director Institutional Research ... Ms. Linda C. VAN VOLKENBURGH
13 Asst VP Information Technology ... Mr. Greg THOMPSON
18 Director Building Management ... Ms. Janet DAY
26 Assoc VP Communications ... Ms. Carolyn KRAUSE
96 Director of Purchasing ... Vacant
12 Dean Undergrad Studies Miami Center ... Dr. Beryl WATNICK
12 Dean Undergrad Studies LA Center ... Dr. Elizabeth PASTORRES-PALFFY
12 Dean Undergrad Studies Cincinnati ... Dr. Carolyn TURNER
12 Dean Undergrad Studies Sacramento ... Dr. Chuck PIAZZA
08 Director Gary Library ... Mr. Matthew PAPPATHAN
37 Director Financial Aid ... Mr. Edward WALTON
29 Director Alumni Relations ... Dr. Neal MEIER

United Theological Seminary (D)

4501 Denlinger Road, Dayton OH 45426-2308
County: Montgomery FICE Identification: 003122
Unit ID: 206288
Telephone: (937) 529-2201 Carnegie Class: Spec/Faith
FAX Number: (866) 433-8235 Calendar System: Semester
URL: www.united.edu
Established: 1871 Annual Graduate Tuition & Fees: $16,556
Enrollment: 573 Coed
Affiliation or Control: United Methodist IRS Status: 501(c)3
Highest Offering: Doctorate; No Undergraduates
Program: Professional; Religious Emphasis
Accreditation: NH, THEOL

01 President & CEO ... Dr. Wendy J. DEICHMANN
05 Vice Pres Academic Affairs & Dean ... Dr. David WATSON
10 Vice Pres Finance/Treasurer ... Mr. Ronald KUKER
30 Vice Pres Development ... Rev. Timothy FORBESS
84 VP Enrollment/Dir Doctoral Studies ... Dr. Harold HUDSON
101 Corporate Secretary/Exec Assistant ... Ms. Pat LODGE
06 Registrar ... Mr. Stephen KLEINER
13 Director of Information Technology ... Mr. Rick MOHR
106 Dir Distance Learning/Educ Tech ... Ms. Phyllis ENNIST
08 Librarian ... Ms. Sarah D. BROOKS BLAIR
88 Director of Contextual Ministries ... Rev. Gary EUBANK
26 Director of Communications ... Ms. JoAnn WAGNER
37 Director Financial Aid ... Ms. Marcia BYRD
29 Assoc Dir Alumni/ae Services ... Rev. Brice THOMAS
18 Facility Manager ... Mr. Roger BOWYER

The University of Akron, Main Campus (E)

302 Buchtel Common, Akron OH 44325
County: Summit FICE Identification: 003123
Unit ID: 200800
Telephone: (330) 972-7111 Carnegie Class: RU/H
FAX Number: (330) 972-6990 Calendar System: Semester
URL: www.uakron.edu
Established: 1870 Annual Undergrad Tuition & Fees (In-State): $9,734
Enrollment: 28,771 Coed
Affiliation or Control: State IRS Status: 501(c)3
Highest Offering: Doctorate
Program: 2-Year Principally Bachelor's Creditable; Liberal Arts And General; Teacher Preparatory; Professional
Accreditation: NH, AAFCS, ACBSP, ANEST, ART, AUD, BUS, BUSA, CACREP, CIDA, COARC, COPSY, DANCE, DIETC, DIETD, ENG, ENGR, ENGT, IFSAC, IPSY, LAW, MAC, MFCD, MUS, NURSE, PH, SP, SURGT, SW, TED

01 President ... Dr. Luis M. PROENZA
05 Senior Vice President & Provost ... Dr. Mike SHERMAN
46 Vice Pres Research/Dean of Grad Sch .. Dr. George R. NEWKOME
10 VP Finance & Administration/CFO ... Mr. David J. CUMMINS
43 Vice President & General Counsel ... Mr. Ted A. MALLO
44 Vice Pres Public Affs/Development ... Mr. John A. LAGUARDIA
13 VP Information Technology/CIO ... Mr. James L. SAGE
18 Vice Pres Capital Plng/Facil Mgmt ... Mr. Ted CURTIS
88 VP of Strategic Engagement ... Mr. James P. TRESSEL
88 Assistant Secretary of the BOT ... Mr. Paul A. HEROLD
100 Vice President/Chief of Staff ... Mrs. Candace CAMPBELL JACKSON
101 Secretary Board of Trustees ... Mr. Ted A. MALLO
32 Assoc VP & Dean of Student Life ... Ms. Denine M. ROCCO
30 Assoc Vice Pres Development ... Mr. Timothy R. DUFORE
44 Special Assistant to the President ... Mr. Paul A. HEROLD
31 Assoc VP Community Relations ... Mr. David NYPAVER
21 Assc VP Treasury/Financial Planning ... Mr. Brian E. DAVIS
46 Assoc Vice President for Research ... Mr. Kenneth G. PRESTON
46 Assoc Vice President for Research ... Mr. Wayne H. WATKINS
21 Assoc Vice President & Controller ... Mr. John E. KOVATCH
38 Associate Vice Pres for Campus Life ... Vacant
88 Assoc VP Strategic Init & Engage ... Mrs. Holly HARRIS BANE
22 Assoc VP Inclusion & Equity ... Mr. Lee A. GILL
27 Assoc Vice Pres/Chief Comm Officer ... Ms. Eileen KOREY
15 Assoc VP Talent Dev/Human Resources ... Mr. Bill J. VIAU
26 Assoc VP/Chief Marketing Officer ... Mr. Wayne R. HILL
35 Assoc VP for Student Services ... Mrs. Karla MUGLER
88 Assoc VP for Student Success ... Dr. Stacey MOORE
20 Asst VP for Academic Affairs ... Mrs. Julie BURDICK
88 Asst VP for Student Success ... Mr. Adam A. SMITH
19 Ast VP Camp Safety/Chf Univ Police ... Mr. Paul J. CALLAHAN
43 Asst VP & Assoc General Counsel ... Mr. Sidney C. FOSTER, JR.
29 Asst VP Alumni/College Cen Programs ... Mrs. Kimberly M. KARSON
88 Asst VP for Student Success ... Mrs. Nancy L. ROADRUCK
88 Asst VP for Student Success ... Ms. Fedearia A. NICHOLSON
06 Registrar ... Mrs. Debra L. HAYES
07 Director of Admissions ... Ms. Diane R. RAYBUCK
09 Director Institutional Research ... Ms. Sabrina L. ANDREWS
13 Director Technology Transfer ... Mr. Kenneth G. PRESTON
08 Dean of University Libraries ... Mr. Mark WINSTON
49 Dean Buchtel College of Arts & Sci ... Dr. Chand MIDHA
54 Dean College of Engineering ... Dr. George K. HARITOS
53 Interim Dean College of Education ... Dr. Susan G. CLARK
50 Dean College of Business Admin ... Dr. Ravi KROVI
76 Int Dean College Health Professions ... Dr. Roberta A. DEPOMPEI
72 Dean Summit College ... Mr. Stanley B. SILVERMAN
61 Interim Dean School of Law ... Ms. Elizabeth H. REILLY
54 Dean of Polymer Science/Engineering ... Dr. Stephen Z D. CHENG
12 Interim Dean Wayne College ... Dr. Daniel B. DECKLER
37 Director Student Financial Aid ... Mrs. Michelle ELLIS
96 Director of Purchasing ... Mr. Andrew W. ROTH
88 Director of Internal Communications ... Mr. Robert KROPFF
105 Director of Web Services ... Mr. Eric W. KRIEDER
92 Dean Honors College ... Dr. Dale H. MUGLER
88 Director UA Adult Focus ... Mrs. Laura H. CONLEY
41 Director Athletics ... Mr. Tom WISTRCILL
36 Director Counseling/Test/Career Ctr ... Dr. Juanita K. MARTIN
39 Asst VP & Chief Housing Officer ... Mr. John A. MESSINA
25 Director Rsrch Svcs/Sponsored Pgms ... Ms. Katie WATKINS-WENDELL
85 Director International Programs ... Mr. Peter B. LI
23 Director Health Services ... Ms. Diane J. FASHINPAUR
14 Dir Hardware Opers/Oper Sys Svcs ... Mr. Thomas R. BEITL
21 Spec Asst to VP/IT & Spec Proj Mgr ... Mr. David G. WASIK
88 Exec Dir University Park Alliance ... Vacant
88 Information Security Officer ... Mrs. Deborah WHITE
88 Director of Media Relations ... Ms. Laura MASSIE

The University of Akron-Wayne College (F)

1901 Smucker Road, Orrville OH 44667-9758
County: Wayne FICE Identification: 010818
Unit ID: 200846
Telephone: (330) 683-2010 Carnegie Class: Assoc/Pub2in4
FAX Number: (330) 684-8989 Calendar System: Semester
URL: www.wayne.uakron.edu
Established: 1972 Annual Undergrad Tuition & Fees (In-State): $6,185
Enrollment: 2,450 Coed
Affiliation or Control: State IRS Status: 501(c)3
Highest Offering: Associate Degree
Program: Occupational; 2-Year Principally Bachelor's Creditable
Accreditation: NH

01 Interim Dean ... Dr. Dan DECKLER
04 Senior Administrative Assistant ... Ms. Lindsie B. WEBB
05 Associate Dean of Instruction ... Dr. Denise UITTO
10 Sr Dir Business Operations/Finance ... Mrs. Tamara A. LOWE
32 Sr Dir Student Life/Enroll Mgmt ... Mr. Gordon K. HOLLY
18 Chief Facilities/Physical Plant ... Mr. W. Russ PUGH
26 Chief Public Relations Officer ... Mrs. Regina L. SCHWARTZ
08 Manager Library Services ... Mrs. Maureen T. LERCH
06 Registrar ... Mrs. Charlene LANCE
07 Director of Admissions ... Mrs. Alicia BROADUS
09 Director of Institutional Research ... Mr. William CLARK
15 Director Personnel Services ... Ms. Kathy BATCHELDER
20 Associate Academic Officer ... Mr. Garth D. SCHOFFMAN
88 Assistant to the Dean ... Mr. Kevin E. ENGLE
35 Student Activities Coordinator ... Ms. Jackie E. ASHBAUGH
36 Coord Career and Assessment Svcs ... Ms. Carol J. PLEUSS
37 Manager Student Svcs/Financial Aid ... Ms. Barb CAILLET
38 Coordinator of Academic Advising ... Ms. Wendy CUNDIFF
96 Accounting Clerk Sr ... Ms. Amy M. HAYNES
13 Manager Technical Support Services ... Ms. Cher DEEDS
19 University Police ... Lt. Tom WYKOFF
40 Director Bookstore ... Ms. Pat PAXTON
41 Athletic Director ... Mr. Patrick S. RUFENER
103 Dir Cont Ed & Workforce Development ... Ms. Amy H. MAST

University of Cincinnati Main Campus (G)

2624 Clifton Avenue, Cincinnati OH 45221-0001
County: Hamilton FICE Identification: 003125
Unit ID: 201885
Telephone: (513) 556-6000 Carnegie Class: RU/VH
FAX Number: (513) 556-3237 Calendar System: Quarter
URL: www.uc.edu
Established: 1819 Annual Undergrad Tuition & Fees (In-State): $10,784
Enrollment: 41,970 Coed
Affiliation or Control: State IRS Status: 501(c)3
Highest Offering: Doctorate
Program: 2-Year Principally Bachelor's Creditable; Liberal Arts And General; Teacher Preparatory; Professional
Accreditation: NH, ANEST, ART, AUD, BBT, BUS, CACREP, CAHIIM, CIDA, CLPSY, CONST, CS, DANCE, DENT, DIETC, DIETD, ENG, ENGR, ENGT, LAW, MED, MIDWF, MT, MUS, NMT, NURSE, PH, PHAR, PLNG, PTA, PTAA, SP, SURGA, SW, TED, THEA

01 President ... Dr. Santa J. ONO
05 Sr VP/Provost Academic Affairs ... Dr. Beverly DAVENPORT SYPHER
11 Sr VP for Administration & Finance ... Mr. Robert AMBACH
03 Executive VP ... Dr. Ryan HAYS
46 Vice President for Research ... Dr. William S. BALL
63 Dean Medicine/VP for Health Affairs ... Dr. Thomas F. BOAT
30 VP Development/Alumni Rels ... Mr. Rod M. GRABOWSKI
86 Vice Pres Govt Rels/University Comm ... Mr. Gregory J. VEHR
32 Vice Pres Student Affairs & Svcs ... Ms. Debra S. MERCHANT
10 Vice President for Finance ... Mr. James D. PLUMMER
13 VP & CIO for Information Technology ... Dr. Nelson C. VINCENT
43 Interim General Counsel ... Mr. Gregory D. MOHAR
88 Special Assistant to President ... Ms. Kenya MANN FAULKNER
15 Chief Human Resources Officer ... Ms. Erin E. ASCHER
84 Sr Assoc Vice President Enrollment ... Dr. Caroline B. MILLER
21 Assoc VP Community Development ... Mr. Gerald A. SIEGERT
27 Assoc VP PR/Univ Spokesperson ... Mr. Greg HAND
07 Assoc Vice Pres for Admissions ... Dr. Thomas CANEPA
76 Dean Allied Health Sciences ... Dr. Elizabeth C. KING
49 Dean Arts & Sciences ... Dr. Ronald JACKSON
50 Dean Business Administration ... Dr. David M. SZYMANSKI
64 Dean College Conservatory of Music ... Mr. Peter LANDGREN
48 Dean Design/Architecture/Art & Plng ... Dr. Robert PROBST
53 Dean Education ... Dr. Lawrence J. JOHNSON
54 Int Dean Engineering & Appld Sci ... Dr. Teik C. LIM
61 Dean Law ... Mr. Louis D. BILIONIS
66 Dean Nursing ... Dr. Greer L. GLAZER
67 Dean Pharmacy ... Dr. Neil J. MACKINNON

70 Director School Social Work .... Mr. James CLARK
08 Dean Library .... Mr. Xuemao WANG
29 Executive Director Alumni Affairs .... Mr. Myron HUGHES
41 Director Athletics .... Mr. Whit BABCOCK
40 Director Bookstore .... Ms. Linda K. GINDELE
36 Director Career Development .... Dr. Katrina JORDAN
38 Director Counseling Center .... Dr. Tow Y. YAU
22 Director Equal Opportunity .... Mr. Matthew L. BOAZ
39 Director Housing/Food Service .... Mr. Todd DUNCAN
37 Director Student Financial Aid .... Ms. Connie WILLIAMS
09 Director Institutional Research .... Mr. Lee E. MORTIMER
19 Director Public Safety .... Mr. Michael CURETON
06 Registrar .... Dr. Douglas BURGESS
96 Director of Purchasing .... Mr. Thomas B. GUERIN
45 CoDir Institute for Policy Research .... Dr. Eric RADEMACHER
45 CoDir Institute for Policy Research .... Dr. Kimberly DOWNING

University of Cincinnati-Blue Ash College (A)

9555 Plainfield Road, Blue Ash OH 45236-1096

County: Hamilton FICE Identification: 004868
Unit ID: 201955
Telephone: (513) 745-5600 Carnegie Class: Assoc/Pub2in4
FAX Number: (513) 745-5780 Calendar System: Semester
URL: www.ucblueash.edu
Established: 1967 Annual Undergrad Tuition & Fees (In-State): $5,890
Enrollment: 4,971 Coed
Affiliation or Control: State IRS Status: 501(c)3
Highest Offering: Baccalaureate
Program: Occupational; 2-Year Principally Bachelor's Creditable
Accreditation: NH, ADNUR, ART, DH, EMT, MAC, RAD, RTT

01 Dean .... Dr. Cady SHORT-THOMPSON
05 Assoc Dean Academic Affairs .... Dr. Marlene R. MINER
10 Director of Business Affairs .... Mr. Marc WATSON
20 Asst Dean Academic Affairs .... Ms. Gregory METZ
18 Int Director Facilities .... Mr. Tom CRUSE
13 Director Information Technology .... Mr. Dale HOFSTETTER
84 Director Enrollment Services .... Mr. Christopher POWERS
09 Director Institutional Research .... Ms. Sandra PARKER
06 Asst Director of Regist & Sch .... Ms. Kyla TEUFEL
08 Library Director .... Ms. Heather MALONEY
26 Director of Communication .... Mr. Peter GEMMER
36 Career Development Specialist .... Ms. Carly DENNIS
32 Director of Student Life .... Mr. Marcus LANGSFORD

University of Cincinnati-Clermont College (B)

4200 Clermont College Drive, Batavia OH 45103-1785

County: Clermont FICE Identification: 010805
Unit ID: 201946
Telephone: (513) 732-5200 Carnegie Class: Assoc/Pub2in4
FAX Number: (513) 732-5275 Calendar System: Quarter
URL: www.ucclermont.edu
Established: 1972 Annual Undergrad Tuition & Fees (In-State): $5,210
Enrollment: 3,652 Coed
Affiliation or Control: State IRS Status: 501(c)3
Highest Offering: Baccalaureate
Program: Occupational; 2-Year Principally Bachelor's Creditable; Technical Emphasis
Accreditation: NH, COARC, MAC, SURGT

01 Dean .... Dr. Gregory S. SOJKA
05 Assoc Dean Academic Affairs .... Dr. Rajiv S. SOMAN
20 Sr Assistant Dean Academic Affairs .... Ms. Mary F. STEARNS
08 Senior Librarian .... Ms. Rosemary YOUNG
24 Dir Learning Center .... Ms. Pam MAVI
76 Director Allied Health .... Ms. Sharman WILLMORE
09 Director of Institutional Research .... Ms. Susan RILEY
10 Director Business Affairs .... Ms. Maria KERR
32 Int Asst Dean Enroll & Student Svcs .... Ms. Jennifer RADT
84 Director Advising & Registration .... Mr. Ryan HALL
84 Director of Enrollment Services .... Vacant
06 Asst Dir Registration & Scheduling .... Ms. Kristine LOUGHRAN
88 Director Disability Services .... Ms. Jennifer RADT
35 Director of Student Life .... Ms. Kimberly ELLISON
41 Program Coord/Athletic Director .... Mr. Brian SULLIVAN
18 Asst Dean Facilities & Tech Svcs .... Mr. Stephen W. YOUNG
30 Director of Development .... Ms. Dana PARKER
26 Asst Dean Communications & Mktg .... Ms. Mae HANNA

University of Dayton (C)

300 College Park, Dayton OH 45469-0001

County: Montgomery FICE Identification: 003127
Unit ID: 202480
Telephone: (937) 229-1000 Carnegie Class: RU/H
FAX Number: (937) 229-4000 Calendar System: Semester
URL: www.udayton.edu
Established: 1850 Annual Undergrad Tuition & Fees: $35,800
Enrollment: 11,186 Coed
Affiliation or Control: Roman Catholic IRS Status: 501(c)3
Highest Offering: Doctorate
Program: Liberal Arts And General; Teacher Preparatory; Professional
Accreditation: NH, ART, BUS, BUSA, CACREP, DIETD, ENG, ENGT, LAW, MUS, PTA, SPAA, TED

01 President .... Dr. Daniel J. CURRAN
05 Provost .... Dr. Joseph E. SALIBA
32 VP Student Development .... Mr. William M. FISCHER
10 VP Finance & Admin Services .... Mr. Thomas E. BURKHARDT
30 VP Univ Advancement .... Mr. David HARPER
41 VP/Director of Athletics .... Mr. Timothy J. WABLER
15 VP Human Resources .... Ms. Joyce M. CARTER
84 VP for Enrollment Mgmt .... Mr. Sundar KUMARASAMY
46 VP of Research/Exec Dir UDRI .... Dr. Michael V. MCCABE
26 Assoc VP University Communications .... Ms. Teresa J. RIZVI
44 Sr Development Officer .... Mr. James F. BROTHERS
42 Director Campus Ministry .... Ms. Crystal C. SULLIVAN
88 VP for Mission and Rector .... Rev. James F. FITZ, SM
88 Univ Prof Faith and Culture .... Dr. Miquel H. DIAZ
31 Dir Ctr for Leadership in Community .. Mr. Richard T. FERGUSON
20 Assoc Provost Faculty & Admin Affs .... Dr. Patrick G. DONNELLY
88 Asc Prov Lrng Spprt/Dir Rch Tch Ctr .. Dr. Deborah J. BICKFORD
90 Assoc Prov/Chief Information Ofcr .... Dr. Thomas D. SKILL
06 Registrar .... Mr. Thomas J. WESTENDORF
07 Asst VP/Dean of Admission .... Mr. Robert F. DURKLE
19 Director Public Safety .... Mr. Bruce E. BURT
09 Director Institutional Studies .... Ms. Susan K. SEXTON
21 Comptroller .... Ms. Angela K. BUECHELE
88 Assoc VP/Dean of Students .... Ms. Christine M. SCHRAMM
36 Director Career Services .... Mr. Jason C. ECKERT
38 Asst VP Student Dev/Dir Counseling .... Dr. Steven D. MUELLER
18 VP for Facilities Management .... Ms. Beth H. KEYES
23 Medical Director Univ Health Ctr .... Dr. Mary P. BUCHWALDER
62 Dean University Libraries .... Ms. Kathleen M. WEBB
49 Dean College Arts & Sciences .... Dr. Paul H. BENSON
61 Dean School of Law .... Mr. Paul E. MCGREAL
50 Dean Sch of Business Admin .... Dr. Paul BOBROWSKI
58 Assoc Prov Graduate Acad Affairs .... Dr. Paul M. VANDERBURGH
53 Dean School of Educ & Allied Prof .... Dr. Kevin R. KELLY
54 Dean School of Engineering .... Dr. Tony E. SALIBA
29 Sr Development Officer .... Mr. Todd W. IMWALLE
35 Dir Student Life & Kennedy Union .... Ms. Amy L. LOPEZ-MATTHEWS
37 Dean of Admission/Dir of Fin Aid .... Ms. Kathy M. HARMON
39 Asst Dean Students & Dir Res Life .... Mr. Steven T. HERNDON
40 Manager UD Bookstore .... Ms. Julie M. BANKS
43 Director Legal Affairs/Univ Counsel .... Ms. Mary A. POIRIER
96 Director of Purchasing .... Mr. Ken R. SOUCY
92 Dir University Honors/Scholars Pgm .... Dr. David W. DARROW
94 Director of Women's Studies .... Dr. Rebecca S. WHISNANT
22 Dir Affirmative Action & Compliance .... Ms. Patricia BERNAL-OLSON
86 Government/Regional Relations Dir .... Mr. S. Ted BUCARO
28 Exe Dir Inst Diversity & Inclusion .... Dr. Jack T. LING

The University of Findlay (D)

1000 North Main Street, Findlay OH 45840-3653

County: Hancock FICE Identification: 003045
Unit ID: 202763
Telephone: (419) 422-8313 Carnegie Class: Master's L
FAX Number: (419) 434-4822 Calendar System: Semester
URL: www.findlay.edu
Established: 1882 Annual Undergrad Tuition & Fees: $29,346
Enrollment: 4,858 Coed
Affiliation or Control: Church Of God IRS Status: 501(c)3
Highest Offering: Doctorate
Program: Occupational; Liberal Arts And General; Teacher Preparatory; Professional
Accreditation: NH, ARCPA, ENGR, NMT, OT, PHAR, PTA, SW, TED

01 President .... Dr. Katherine R. FELL
05 Vice President for Academic Affairs .... Dr. Darin FIELDS
10 Vice President for Business Affairs .... Mr. Martin L. TERRY
84 Vice President Enrollment Mgmt .... Ms. Rebecca A. BUTLER
20 Asst Vice President Instruction .... Dr. Thomas DILLON
30 Vice Pres University Advancement .... Vacant
32 Vice President for Student Affairs .... Mr. David W. EMSWELLER
04 Assistant to the President .... Ms. Meg FLEMION
81 Interim Dean College of Sciences .... Dr. Jeffrey FRYE
50 Dean College of Business .... Dr. Paul SEARS
49 Interim Dean College of Liberal Art .... Dr. Nicole DIEDERICH
76 Dean College of Health Sciences .... Dr. Andrea KOEPKE
67 Dean College of Pharmacy .... Dr. Donald STANSLOSKI
53 Dean College of Education .... Dr. Julie MCINTOSH
18 Director of Physical Plant .... Mr. Myreon K. COBB
09 Director of Institutional Research .... Mr. Tony G. GOEDDE
06 Registrar .... Mr. Tony G. GOEDDE
41 Athletic Director .... Mr. Steven P. RACKLEY
08 Director of Shafer Library .... Mr. Andrew WHITIS
37 Director of Financial Aid .... Mr. Edward R. RECKER
13 Director of Computer Services .... Dr. Raymond MCCANDLESS
29 Director of Alumni Affairs .... Ms. Deanna SPRAW
26 Dir Public Relations/Media Rels .... Ms. Rebecca JENKINS
36 Director of Career Placement .... Mr. Bradley C. HAMMER
15 Director of Human Resources .... Mr. Robert LINK
23 Director of Health Services .... Ms. Julie R. YINGLING
38 Director Counseling Services .... Ms. Karyn J. WESTRICK
40 Manager of Bookstore .... Mr. Jay CANTERBURY
42 Director Christian Ministries .... Rev. William D. MILLER
19 Director of Security/Safety .... Mr. Kenneth WALERIUS
93 Dir Intercultural Student Services .... Mr. Almar WALTER
21 Business Manager .... Mr. Robert LINK
28 Director of Diversity .... Mr. Almar WALTER
35 Chief Student Life Officer .... Mr. David W. EMSWELLER
85 Dir Intl Student Admissions & Svcs .... Ms. Penny GERDEMAN
101 Secretary to the Board of Trustees .... Ms. C. Sue PIRSCHEL
25 Financial Dir Projects & Grants .... Mr. Gregory BUDDELMEYER
07 Director of Admissions .... Vacant
21 Associate Business Officer .... Mr. Dane ERFORD
22 Director Affirmative Action/Equal .... Mr. Robert LINE
35 Director of Student Affairs .... Mr. Brian TREECE

University of Mount Union (E)

1972 Clark Avenue, Alliance OH 44601-3993

County: Stark FICE Identification: 003083
Unit ID: 204185
Telephone: (330) 821-5320 Carnegie Class: Bac/Diverse
FAX Number: (330) 823-3457 Calendar System: Semester
URL: www.mountunion.edu
Established: 1846 Annual Undergrad Tuition & Fees: $27,380
Enrollment: 2,253 Coed
Affiliation or Control: United Methodist IRS Status: 501(c)3
Highest Offering: Master's
Program: Liberal Arts And General; Teacher Preparatory
Accreditation: NH, ARCPA, MUS, TED

01 President .... Dr. Richard F. GIESE
05 Vice Pres Acad Affs/Dean of Univ .... Dr. Patricia H. DRAVES
10 Vice Pres Business Affs/Treasurer ... Mr. Patrick D. HEDDLESTON
30 Vice President Univ Advancement .... Mr. Gregory KING
32 Vice Pres Student Affs/Dean Stdnts .... Mr. John FRAZIER
84 Vice President for Enrollment Mgmt .... Ms. Amy A. TOMKO
26 Vice President for Marketing .... Ms. Melissa GARDNER
08 Librarian .... Mr. Robert R. GARLAND
06 Registrar .... Ms. Wendy LEWIS
29 Exec Dir Alumni Relations/MU Fund .... Ms. Anne GRAFFICE
07 Director of Admissions .... Ms. Jessie CANAVAN
44 Director Annual Fund .... Ms. Elizabeth JOHNSON
44 Director of Planned Giving .... Mr. David WOLPERT
14 Director Computer Information Sys .... Ms. Tina STUCHELL
88 Director of Advance for Major Gifts .... Mr. Matt STINSON
09 Director Assesment/Program Develop .... Dr. Fang DU
29 Director Alumni/College Activities .... Ms. Tiffany HOGYA
85 Director Center for Global Educ .... Dr. Jennifer HALL
18 Director of Physical Plant .... Mr. Blaine D. LEWIS
16 Director of Human Resources .... Ms. Pamela NEWBOLD
39 Director of Housing .... Ms. Michelle GAFFNEY
42 Chaplain .... Rev. Martha D. CASHBURLESS
36 Director of Career Services .... Ms. Rebecca DOAK
37 Director of Student Financial Svcs .... Ms. Emily SWAIN
40 Manager of College Bookstore .... Mr. Rod PETERSON
41 Athletic Director .... Mr. Larry T. KEHRES
04 Exec Assistant to the President .... Ms. Laura E. GOOD
21 Assoc VP for Business Affairs .... Mr. Ronald CROWL
20 Associate Academic Officer .... Dr. William CUNION
35 Associate Dean of Students .... Ms. Michelle GAFFNEY
96 Purchasing Agent .... Mr. Shawn BAGLEY

University of Northwestern Ohio (F)

1441 N Cable Road, Lima OH 45805-1498

County: Allen FICE Identification: 004861
Unit ID: 204486
Telephone: (419) 227-3141 Carnegie Class: Assoc/PrivNFP4
FAX Number: (419) 229-6926 Calendar System: Quarter
URL: www.unoh.edu
Established: 1920 Annual Undergrad Tuition & Fees: $13,940
Enrollment: 4,136 Coed
Affiliation or Control: Independent Non-Profit IRS Status: 501(c)3
Highest Offering: Master's
Program: 2-Year Principally Bachelor's Creditable; Business Emphasis
Accreditation: NH, ACBSP, MAC

01 President .... Dr. Jeffrey A. JARVIS
05 Vice Pres Academic Affairs/Provost .... Dr. Cheryl MUELLER
10 Vice President Finance .... Mrs. Marcia EICKHOLT
84 Vice Pres Enrollment Management .... Mr. Ricky MORRISON
18 Vice Pres of Property Management .... Mr. Don RICKER
26 Vice Pres Public Relations/Mktg .... Mrs. Cheryl STEINWEDEL
30 Vice President Development .... Mr. Steve FARMER
32 Vice President Campus Life .... Mr. Bob FRICKE
39 Director of Housing .... Mr. Pat FINNERTY
15 Exec Director of Human Resources .... Ms. Geri MORRIS
10 Controller/Chief Financial Officer .... Mr. James S. BRONDER
06 Director of Registration & Advising .... Mr. Loren KORZAN
37 Director of Financial Aid .... Mr. Wendell SCHICK
88 Director MBA Program .... Mr. Michael CALLAHAN
36 Co-Director Career Services .... Mr. Justin FLANAGAN
36 Co-Director Career Services .... Mrs. Nicole NEIMEYER
25 Coordinator of Grant Writing .... Mrs. Jessica SPIERS
04 Executive Assistant to President .... Mrs. Jennifer BENDELE
50 Dean College of Business .... Mr. Dean HOBLER
72 Dean College of Technologies .... Mr. Andy O'NEAL
07 Director of Admissions .... Mr. Don LOWDEN
38 Director Student Counseling .... Mrs. Danielle MCCLURE
96 Director of Purchasing .... Mrs. Angela DENNISON

University of Phoenix Cleveland Main Campus (G)

3401 Enterprise Parkway, Suite 115,
Beechwood OH 44122-7343

Telephone: (216) 378-0473 Identification: 770238
Accreditation: &NH

† Main campus is University of Phoenix in Tempe, AZ.

University of Rio Grande (A)

218 N College Avenue, PO BOX 500,
Rio Grande OH 45674-3100
County: Gallia FICE Identification: 003116
Unit ID: 205203
Telephone: (740) 245-5353 Carnegie Class: Master's M
FAX Number: (740) 245-5266 Calendar System: Semester
URL: www.rio.edu
Established: 1876 Annual Undergrad Tuition & Fees: $20,300
Enrollment: 2,278 Coed
Affiliation or Control: Independent Non-Profit IRS Status: 501(c)3
Highest Offering: Master's
Program: 2-Year Principally Bachelor's Creditable; Liberal Arts And General; Teacher Preparatory; Professional
Accreditation: NH, ADNUR, COARC, DMS, IACBE, NUR, RAD, SW, TED

01 President ... Dr. Barbara GELLMAN-DANLEY
05 Provost/VP of Academic Affairs ... Vacant
30 Executive VP & VP for Inst Advance ... Mr. Paul D. HARRISON
10 Vice President for Finance/CFO ... Mr. Tim PRUETT
11 Vice President for Administration ... Mrs. Rebecca LONG
15 Director of Human Resources ... Mr. Chris NOURSE
88 Chief Compliance Officer ... Ms. Sophia CHIOU
49 Dean Col of Arts & Sciences ... Dr. David LAWRENCE
76 Dean Col of Health & Behav Science ... Dr. Donna MITCHELL
107 Dean Col of Professional Studies ... Dr. Zaki SHARIF
84 Dean of Enrollment Management ... Mr. Mark ABELL
07 Director Admissions ... Mr. Thomas MANSPERGER
25 Exec to Provost & Dir of Grants ... Dr. Yasmin SHARIF
32 Dean of Students ... Mr. Aaron QUINN
41 Athletics Director ... Mr. Jeff LANHAM
08 Director of the Library ... Mr. J. David MAUER
14 Dir Campus Computing & Networking ... Mr. Kingsley MEYER
13 MIS Director ... Dr. Steve COX
06 Registrar ... Mrs. Debbie BROWNING
29 Director of Alumni Relations ... Mrs. Annette P. WARD
04 Exec Assistant to the President ... Mrs. Lori TAYLOR

University of Toledo (B)

2801 W Bancroft, Toledo OH 43606-3390
County: Lucas FICE Identification: 003131
Unit ID: 206084
Telephone: (419) 530-4636 Carnegie Class: RU/H
FAX Number: (419) 530-4984 Calendar System: Semester
URL: www.utoledo.edu
Established: 1872 Annual Undergrad Tuition & Fees (In-State): $9,192
Enrollment: 21,501 Coed
Affiliation or Control: State IRS Status: 501(c)3
Highest Offering: Doctorate
Program: Liberal Arts And General; Teacher Preparatory; Professional
Accreditation: NH, ARCPA, ART, BUS, CACREP, CAHIIM, CLPSY, COARC, CS, DENT, ENG, ENGR, ENGT, LAW, MED, MUS, NRPA, NURSE, OT, PH, PHAR, PTA, SP, SPAA, SW, TED

01 President ... Dr. Lloyd A. JACOBS
17 Exec VP/Chancellor Health Affairs ... Dr. Jeffrey P. GOLD
05 Exec VP/Provost Academic Affairs ... Dr. Scott L. SCARBOROUGH
17 Interim Exec Director of UTMC ... Ms. Norma J. TOMLINSON
10 CFO and VP for Finance ... Mr. David O. DABNEY
43 Vice President General Counsel ... Mr. Peter J. PAPADIMOS
32 Vice President for Student Affairs ... Dr. Kaye PATTEN WALLACE
30 Vice Pres Institutional Advancement ... Mr. C. Vernon SNYDER
26 Vice President External Affairs ... Mr. Lawrence J. BURNS
86 Vice President Government Relations ... Dr. Frank J. CALZONETTI
46 Vice President Research ... Dr. James P. TREMPE
11 Vice President Administration ... Mr. Charles LEHNERT
13 Vice President for Info Tech/CIO ... Dr. Godfrey ORWIGHO
41 Vice Pres and Director of Athletics ... Mr. Michael E. O'BRIEN
09 VP Institutional Research and Stats ... Dr. Geoffrey MARTIN
06 Interim University Registrar ... Mr. Terence ROMER
58 Dean College of Graduate Studies ... Dr. Patricia R. KOMUNIECKI
50 Interim Dean Business & Innovation ... Dr. Thomas W. SHARKEY
88 Dean Communication and the Arts ... Ms. Debra DAVIS
53 Int Dean J Herb College of Educ ... Dr. Penny POPLIN GOSETTI
54 Dean Engineering ... Dr. Nagi NAGANATHAN
76 Dean Health Sciences ... Dr. Beverly J. SCHMOLL
83 Dean Languages/Lit & Soc Sciences ... Dr. Jamie BARLOWE
61 Dean Law ... Mr. Daniel STEINBOCK
63 Dean Medicine & Life Sciences ... Dr. Jeffrey GOLD
81 Dean Natural Sciences & Mathematics ... Dr. Karen BJORKMAN
66 Dean Nursing ... Dr. Timothy GASPAR
67 Dean Pharmacy & Pharm Sciences ... Dr. Johnnie EARLY
83 Int Dean Social Justice/Human Svcs ... Dr. Thomas GUTTERIDGE
88 Dean Adult & Lifelong Learning ... Dr. Dennis LETTMAN
92 Dean Jesup Scott Honors College ... Dr. Lakeesha RANSOM
88 Interim Dean YouCollege ... Dr. D'Naie JACOBS
35 Dean of Students ... Ms. Tamika DOBBINS
39 Assoc Director Residence Life ... Ms. Virginia SPEIGHT
37 Director Student Financial Aid ... Ms. Carolyn G. BAUMGARTNER
15 Sr Director Faculty Labor Relations ... Mr. Kevin WEST
102 President Foundation ... Ms. Brenda LEE
29 Assoc Vice Pres Alumni Relations ... Mr. Daniel J. SAEVIG
36 Sr Dir Exp Lrng and Career Svcs ... Mr. Peter THOMAS
85 Director Immigration Services ... Ms. Christy RAKNESS
21 Director Internal Audit ... Mr. David CUTRI
19 Chief of Police ... Mr. Jeff NEWTON
101 Secretary to Brd of Trustees ... Ms. Joan STASA
25 Contract Compliance Specialist HSC ... Ms. Colleen MILLER
40 General Manager Bookstore SU ... Ms. Colleen STRAYER

Urbana University (C)

579 College Way, Urbana OH 43078-2091
County: Champaign FICE Identification: 003133
Unit ID: 206330
Telephone: (937) 484-1400 Carnegie Class: Bac/Diverse
FAX Number: (937) 484-1322 Calendar System: Semester
URL: www.urbana.edu
Established: 1850 Annual Undergrad Tuition & Fees: $20,984
Enrollment: 1,586 Coed
Affiliation or Control: Independent Non-Profit IRS Status: 501(c)3
Highest Offering: Master's
Program: Liberal Arts And General; Teacher Preparatory
Accreditation: NH, IACBE, NURSE

01 Interim President ... Dr. Kirk PETERSON
05 Interim Provost/Chief Academic Ofcr ... Dr. Charles HODGE
30 Vice Pres Institutional Advancement ... Mr. James THORNTON
32 VP Student & Enrollment Services ... Dr. James (Chip) WEISGERBER
06 Registrar ... Dr. Hedwig (Hedy) FRICK
37 Director of Financial Aid ... Vacant
09 Dean of Institutional Research ... Dr. Denise BOLDMAN
08 University Librarian ... Ms. Julie MCDANIEL
39 Director of Residence Life ... Mr. Mitch JOSEPH
14 Director Computer Center ... Vacant
26 Director of University Relations ... Mrs. Christina BRUUN-HORRIGAN
29 Director of Alumni Relations ... Ms. Kat STEINER
15 Director of Human Resources/Payroll ... Mrs. Audrey STEVENS
19 Director of Security/Safety ... Mr. Larry GLEESON
10 Interim Vice Pres Admin Svcs/CFO ... Mr. John ANGLEA
41 Athletic Director ... Mr. Doug YOUNG
40 Bookstore Manager ... Mr. Eric LATHAM

Ursuline College (D)

2550 Lander Road, Cleveland OH 44124-4398
County: Cuyahoga FICE Identification: 003134
Unit ID: 206349
Telephone: (440) 449-4200 Carnegie Class: Master's S
FAX Number: (440) 646-8318 Calendar System: Semester
URL: www.ursuline.edu
Established: 1871 Annual Undergrad Tuition & Fees: $26,490
Enrollment: 1,494 Female
Affiliation or Control: Roman Catholic IRS Status: 501(c)3
Highest Offering: Doctorate
Program: Liberal Arts And General; Teacher Preparatory; Professional; Technical Emphasis
Accreditation: NH, IACBE, NURSE, SW, TED

01 President ... Sr. Diana STANO
05 Vice President Academic Affairs ... Dr. JoAnne PODIS
10 Vice Pres & Chief Financial Officer ... Mr. David STEINER
30 Vice Pres Institutional Advancement ... Mr. Kevin GLADSTONE
18 Vice Pres of Facility Management ... Ms. June GRACYK
32 Vice President of Student Affairs ... Ms. Deanne HURLEY
84 Vice Pres of Enrollment Management ... Ms. Deanne HURLEY
58 Dean of Graduate Studies ... Dr. Gina MESSINA-DYSERT
49 Dean of Arts & Sciences ... Dr. Elizabeth KAVRAN
66 Dean Division of Nursing ... Dr. Christine WYND
88 Exec Director Accelerated Program ... Ms. JoAnne MAZUR
08 Director of Library ... Ms. Betsey BELKIN
06 Registrar ... Ms. Leah SULLIVAN
21 Accounting Manager ... Mr. Timothy REARDON
44 Director of Development ... Dr. Patrick RILEY
07 Director of Admissions ... Ms. Carolyn NOLL SORG
37 Director of Financial Aid ... Ms. Mary Lynn PERRI
29 Dir Alumae Relations/Dev Specialist ... Ms. Tiffany MUSHRUSH
26 Dir of Marketing/Communications ... Ms. Angela DELPRETE
38 Director Counseling & Career Svcs ... Ms. Geraldine M. JENKINS
15 Director of Personnel ... Ms. Kelli KNAUS
13 Dir of Computer Information Svcs ... Mr. Tim FARRIS
09 Director of Institutional Research ... Ms. Amber COVINGTON
102 Dir of Corp & Foundation Relations ... Vacant
39 Acting Director of Residence Life ... Ms. Gina DEMART-KRAUS
42 Director Campus Ministry ... Ms. Joann PIOTRKOWSKI
28 Asst Dean of Inclusion ... Ms. Tina ROAN
93 Director of Wellness Program ... Vacant
24 Library Electronic & Media Services ... Ms. Suzanna SCHROEDER-GREEN
40 Manager Bookstore ... Ms. Casey DUNN
41 Athletic Director ... Ms. Cynthia MCKNIGHT

Valor Christian College (E)

PO Box 800, Columbus OH 43216
County: Franklin Identification: 667093
Telephone: (614) 837-4088 Carnegie Class: Not Classified
FAX Number: (614) 837-6904 Calendar System: Semester
URL: www.valorcollege.com
Established: 1990 Annual Undergrad Tuition & Fees: $4,017
Enrollment: 174 Coed
Affiliation or Control: Independent Non-Profit IRS Status: 501(c)3
Highest Offering: Associate Degree
Program: Religious Emphasis
Accreditation: @BI

01 President ... Jimmy DUPREE
05 Chief Academic Officer ... Ronald JEWETT
10 CFO ... Andrew STURDON
30 Chief Development Officer ... Horace SIMONS
07 Director of Enrollment ... Tiffany VICE
06 Registrar ... Horace SIMONS

Vatterott College-Cleveland (F)

5025 E Royalton Road,
Broadview Heights OH 44147-3502
Telephone: (440) 526-1660 Identification: 666156
Accreditation: ACCSC

† Main campus is Vatterott College-NorthPark in Berkeley, MO.

Virginia Marti College of Art & Design (G)

11724 Detroit Avenue, Lakewood OH 44107-3002
County: Cuyahoga FICE Identification: 012896
Unit ID: 206394
Telephone: (216) 221-8584 Carnegie Class: Assoc/PrivFP
FAX Number: (216) 221-2311 Calendar System: Quarter
URL: www.vmcad.edu
Established: 1966 Annual Undergrad Tuition & Fees: $16,940
Enrollment: 202 Coed
Affiliation or Control: Proprietary IRS Status: Proprietary
Highest Offering: Associate Degree
Program: Occupational
Accreditation: ACCSC

01 Director ... Mrs. Virginia MARTI-VEITH
03 Assistant Director ... Mr. Dennis N. MARTI
05 Director of Education ... Mr. Joseph GUSTIN
37 Financial Aid Administrator ... Mrs. Jennifer V. MINKIEWICZ
06 Registrar ... Mrs. Lisa ALESSANDRO
07 Director of Admissions ... Mr. Quinn E. MARTI
36 Director of Career Services ... Ms. Diane NAHRA

Walsh University (H)

2020 East Maple Street, North Canton OH 44720
County: Stark FICE Identification: 003135
Unit ID: 206437
Telephone: (330) 490-7090 Carnegie Class: Master's M
FAX Number: (330) 499-7165 Calendar System: Semester
URL: www.walsh.edu
Established: 1958 Annual Undergrad Tuition & Fees: $24,610
Enrollment: 2,903 Coed
Affiliation or Control: Roman Catholic IRS Status: 501(c)3
Highest Offering: Doctorate
Program: Liberal Arts And General; Teacher Preparatory; Professional
Accreditation: NH, CACREP, NUR, PTA, TED

01 President ... Mr. Richard JUSSEAUME
05 Provost/VP Academic Affairs ... Dr. Laurence BOVE
10 Vice Pres Finance/Business Affairs ... Ms. Shelley BROWN
32 VP Student Affairs/Dean of Students ... Ms. Amy MALASKA
30 Vice Pres of Advancement/Univ Rels ... Mr. Eric BELDEN
84 Vice Pres of Enrollment Management ... Mr. Brett FRESHOUR
41 Vice Pres for Athletics ... Mr. Dale S. HOWARD
20 Dean for Academic Affairs ... Dr. Andrew GRANT
35 Dean of Students ... Ms. Amy K. MALASKA
09 Dean Inst Effectiveness/Lib Svcs ... Mr. Daniel S. SUVAK
43 Assoc Dean Stdt Life/Judicial Affs ... Ms. Amy MALASKA
13 Director of Information Systems ... Mr. Timothy OBERSCHLAKE
18 Director of Facilities & Grounds ... Mr. John SCHISSLER
26 Director University Relations ... Ms. Kelly CAMPBELL
91 Director Administrative Computing ... Ms. Hope STANCIU
22 Director of Compliance ... Mrs. Ellen M. KUTZ
36 Director of Career Services ... Mrs. Shaanette FOWLER
38 Director Counseling Services ... Ms. Frances MORROW
42 Director of Campus Ministry ... Mr. Miguel CHAVEZ
06 University Registrar ... Mrs. Edna MCCULLOH
31 Dir Campus & Community Programs ... Ms. Jacqueline M. MANSER
37 Director Financial Aid ... Mrs. Holly VAN GILDER
15 Director of Human Resources ... Mr. Frank MCKNIGHT
29 Director of Alumni Relations ... Mr. Daniel GRAVO

Washington State Community College (I)

710 Colegate Drive, Marietta OH 45750-9225
County: Washington FICE Identification: 010453
Unit ID: 206446
Telephone: (740) 374-8716 Carnegie Class: Assoc/Pub-R-M
FAX Number: (740) 374-9562 Calendar System: Semester
URL: www.wscc.edu
Established: 1971 Annual Undergrad Tuition & Fees (In-State): $1,140
Enrollment: 1,864 Coed
Affiliation or Control: State IRS Status: 501(c)3
Highest Offering: Associate Degree
Program: Occupational; 2-Year Principally Bachelor's Creditable; Technical Emphasis
Accreditation: NH, COARC, MLTAD, PTAA

01 President ... Dr. Bradley J. EBERSOLE
10 Chief Financial Officer & Treasurer ... Mr. Jess N. RAINES
84 Chief Enrollment Management Officer ... Ms. Amanda K. HERB
27 Chief Information Officer ... Vacant
05 Vice President for Academic Affairs ... Dr. John W. TIGUE
102 Exec Dir Foundation & Business Dev ... Ms. Laurene K. HUFFMAN

76 Dean of Health Sciences .... Dr. Dixie L. VAUGHAN
49 Interim Dean of Arts and Sciences .... Mr. Ben RUTHERFORD
50 Dean of Bus/Engr/Industrial Tech .... Ms. Brenda L. KORNMILLER
30 Director of Development .... Ms. Gail REYNOLDS
36 Director of Advising & Transfer .... Ms. Deb GOINS
06 Interim Registrar .... Ms. Terry SEEBER
07 Senior Director of Admissions .... Vacant
15 Director Human Resources .... Vacant
26 Dir of Marketing & Communications .... Ms. Claudia OWENS
37 Director of Financial Aid .... Ms. Emily G. SCHUCK
18 Director Plant Opers & Maintenance .... Mr. Eric LANKFORD
38 Director of Student Development .... Vacant
08 Head Librarian .... Ms. Lindsay MCVEY
40 Bookstore Operations Director .... Ms. Jennifer L. DAVIS
91 Interim Dir Manage Inform Systems .... Mr. Mike HOWERTON
37 Assistant Director of Financial Aid .... Ms. Noell DETTORRE
88 Business Intelligence Specialist .... Mr. Michael P. HOWERTON
25 Exec Dir of Inst Advan/Grant Writer .... Vacant
88 Director of Outreach .... Mr. Gary WILLIAMS

Wilberforce University (A)

PO Box 1001, Wilberforce OH 45384-1001

County: Greene | FICE Identification: 003141
Unit ID: 206491
Telephone: (937) 376-2911 | Carnegie Class: Bac/Diverse
FAX Number: (937) 376-2627 | Calendar System: Semester
URL: www.wilberforce.edu
Established: 1856 | Annual Undergrad Tuition & Fees: $13,250
Enrollment: 549 | Coed
Affiliation or Control: African Methodist Episcopal | IRS Status: 501(c)3
Highest Offering: Master's
Program: Liberal Arts And General
Accreditation: NH, CORE

01 President .... Dr. Patricia L. HARDAWAY
05 Interim VP Academic Affairs .... Dr. Norman JOHNSON
10 Vice Pres Financial/Admin Affairs .... Ms. Mary MORALE
30 Vice President Devel/Univ Relations .... Mr. Eppechal T. SMALLS
51 Vice Pres Adult/Continuing Educ .... Dr. Emeka O. MORAH
84 VP Student Devel/Enrollment Mgmt .... Dr. Jo-Ann ROBINSON
04 Executive Assistant to President .... Vacant
32 Interim Dean of Students .... Ms. Jackie THURMAN
07 Director of Admissions .... Mr. John JOHNSON
06 Registrar .... Mrs. Gail D. LASH
08 Chief Librarian .... Dr. Willette STINSON
29 Dir Alumni Relations/Development .... Ms. Sonseeahray ROSS
36 Director Coop Education/Career Svcs .... Mrs. Hila WILLIAMS
14 Interim Director IT .... Mr. Michael JUDGE
19 Campus Police Chief .... Chief David FOX
37 Director of Financial Services .... Mr. Lloyd DIXON
41 Athletic Director .... Mr. Terry FUTRELL
18 Chief Facilities/Physical Plant .... Vacant
15 Human Resources Manager .... Ms. Anita SCOTT
40 Bookstore Manager .... Ms. Denise WILLIAMS
09 Director Institutional Research .... Dr. T. HAGUE-PALMER
21 Assistant Bursar .... Ms. Debra OLIVER
90 Director of Academic Technology .... Mr. Michael JUDGE
88 Director of Master's Rehab Counslng .... Dr. Sonya WARE
25 Director of Title III & Spons Pgms .... Ms. Lisa SWINT
88 Director of CLIMB Program .... Ms. Toni PRESTON
88 Controller .... Ms. Terri CHAMBERS
39 Director of Residence Life .... Vacant

Wilmington College (B)

1870 Quaker Way, Wilmington OH 45177-2499

County: Clinton | FICE Identification: 003142
Unit ID: 206507
Telephone: (937) 382-6661 | Carnegie Class: Bac/Diverse
FAX Number: (937) 383-8583 | Calendar System: Semester
URL: www.wilmington.edu
Established: 1870 | Annual Undergrad Tuition & Fees: $28,490
Enrollment: 1,299 | Coed
Affiliation or Control: Friends | IRS Status: 501(c)3
Highest Offering: Master's
Program: Liberal Arts And General; Teacher Preparatory
Accreditation: NH, TEAC

01 President .... Dr. James M. REYNOLDS
04 Assistant to the President .... Ms. Leslie A. NICHOLS
05 Vice Pres Academic Affairs .... Dr. Erika A. GOODWIN
10 Vice Pres Business/Finance .... Mr. Bradley J. MITCHELL
30 Vice President College Advancement .... Mr. Robert C. HARROD
84 Vice Pres Enrollment Management .... Mr. Mark DENNISTON
12 Vice President External Programs .... Ms. Iris KELSEN
32 Vice President for Student Affairs .... Ms. Sigrid B. SOLOMON
41 Vice President Athletic Admin .... Dr. Terry A. RUPERT
20 Interim Assoc VP Academic Affairs .... Dr. Martha S. HENDRICKS
35 Assoc Vice Pres Student Affairs .... Mr. Kenneth A. LYDY
26 Director of Public Relations .... Mr. Randall F. SARVIS
06 Registrar/Asst Dean Acad Affairs .... Ms. Karen M. GARMAN
08 Director of Watson Library .... Dr. Jean K. MULHERN
15 Director of Human Resources .... Mr. Scott M. FARKAS
36 Director of Career Services .... Ms. Tammy FRASER
18 Director of Physical Plant .... Mr. Terry L. JOHNSON
29 Dir Alumni and Parent Relations .... Ms. Kathy L. MILAM
37 Director Student One Stop Center .... Ms. Cheryl LOUALLEN
07 Director of Admission .... Ms. Tina M. GARLAND
09 Director of Institutional Research .... Ms. Tammy SHADLEY-HUTTON
28 Director of Multicultural Affairs .... Ms. Bennyce HAMILTON
96 Purchasing Manager .... Ms. Laura BAESSLER

Wilmington College Blue Ash Branch (C)

9987 Carver Road, Blue Ash OH 45242

Telephone: (513) 793-1337 | Identification: 770364
Accreditation: &NH

† Main campus is Wilmington College in Wilmington, OH.

Winebrenner Theological Seminary (D)

950 N Main Street, Findlay OH 45840-3652

County: Hancock | FICE Identification: 004060
Unit ID: 206516
Telephone: (419) 434-4200 | Carnegie Class: Spec/Faith
FAX Number: (419) 434-4267 | Calendar System: Trimester
URL: www.winebrenner.edu
Established: 1942 | Annual Graduate Tuition & Fees: $13,125
Enrollment: 131 | Coed
Affiliation or Control: Independent Non-Profit | IRS Status: 501(c)3
Highest Offering: Doctorate; No Undergraduates
Program: Professional; Religious Emphasis
Accreditation: NH, THEOL

01 President/CEO .... Dr. David E. DRAPER
30 VP of Institutional Advancement .... Mr. Jim ALLEN
05 VP of Academic Advancement .... Rev. Joel COCKLIN
07 Regional Coordinator Admiss/Devel .... Mr. Jim WILDER
08 Director of Library Services .... Mrs. Margaret HIRSCHY
06 Registrar .... Mrs. Shari BRANDEBERRY
04 Assistant to the President .... Ms. Marilynn C. DUNN

Wittenberg University (E)

PO Box 720, Springfield OH 45501-0720

County: Clark | FICE Identification: 003143
Unit ID: 206525
Telephone: (937) 327-6231 | Carnegie Class: Bac/A&S
FAX Number: (937) 327-6340 | Calendar System: Semester
URL: www.wittenberg.edu
Established: 1845 | Annual Undergrad Tuition & Fees: $47,766
Enrollment: 1,894 | Coed
Affiliation or Control: Evangelical Lutheran Church In America
IRS Status: 501(c)3
Highest Offering: Master's
Program: Liberal Arts And General; Teacher Preparatory
Accreditation: NH, MUS, TED

01 President .... Dr. Laurie M. JOYNER
05 Provost .... Dr. Christopher M. DUNCAN
10 Vice President Business & Finance .... Mr. Darrell B. KITCHEN
32 Vice Pres Stdnt Devel/Dean Students .... Dr. Sarah M. KELLLY
20 Assistant Provost Academic Svcs .... Ms. Mary Jo ZEMBAR
89 Associate Provost/Undergraduate Aff .... Dr. Ty BUCKMAN
31 Dean of Community Education .... Dr. Thomas T. TAYLOR
35 Dean of Students .... Mr. Casey GILL
88 Assoc Dean Student Success/Retent .... Mr. Jonathan DURAJ
85 Director International Education .... Ms. JoAnn BENNETT
42 Director of Church Relations .... Mr. Robert L. WHITE
30 Director University Advancement .... Ms. Aimee LUNDE MARUYAMA
42 Pastor to the University .... Rev. Rachel SANDUM TUNE
08 Director of the Library .... Mr. Douglas K. LEHMAN
13 Chief Information Officer .... Mr. Richard MICKOOL
26 Chief Marketing & Communications Of .... Mr. Mark SULLIVAN
31 Director Community Service .... Ms. Kristen L. COLLIER
06 Registrar .... Mr. Jack M. CAMPBELL
24 Director Audio-Visual Services .... Mr. Lyndon C. MCCURDY
41 Int Director Athletics/Recreation .... Mr. Jeff ANKROM
58 Director Graduate Studies in Educ .... Dr. Regina POST
92 Director of Honors Program .... Dr. J. Fitz SMITH
94 Director of Women's Studies .... Dr. Lori J. ASKELAND
09 Director Institutional Research .... Dr. Jeff A. ANKROM
44 Exec Dir Major & Planned Giving .... Mr. Richard W. STENBERG
102 Dir Govt/Corporate & Found Rels .... Vacant
29 Director of Alumni Relations .... Ms. Linda M. BEALS
26 Director of Univ Communications .... Ms. Karen L. GERBOTH
27 Dir of News Services/Sports Info .... Mr. Ryan S. MAURER
105 Webmaster .... Vacant
39 Associate Dean for Residence Life .... Mr. Mark B. DEVILBISS
38 Director Student Counseling .... Ms. Linda M. LAUFFENBURGER
88 Director of Greek Life .... Ms. Kasey STEVENS
28 Director Multicultural Stdnt Pgms .... Mr. John YOUNG
23 Physician/Dir Health Services .... Dr. Kathrine MCKEE
07 Exec Director of Admission .... Ms. Karen HUNT
37 Director of Financial Aid .... Mr. Jonathan RANDY GREEN
21 Director Budget .... Ms. Deborah S. DEWITT
18 Director Plant/Safety & Environment .... Mr. John E. PAULSEN
96 Director of Business Services .... Mrs. Donna M. PICKLESIMER
15 Director Human Resources .... Mr. Kevin EVANS
19 Chief of Police .... Mr. Carl E. LONEY
40 Manager of Bookstore .... Mr. Tim GOGNAT

Wright State University Lake Campus (F)

7600 Lake Campus Drive, Celina OH 45822-2952

Telephone: (419) 586-0300 | FICE Identification: 009169
Accreditation: &NH

† Main campus is Wright State University Main Campus in Dayton, OH.

Wright State University Main Campus (G)

3640 Colonel Glenn Highway, Dayton OH 45435-0001

County: Greene | FICE Identification: 003078
Unit ID: 206604
Telephone: (937) 775-3333 | Carnegie Class: RU/H
FAX Number: (937) 775-3301 | Calendar System: Quarter
URL: www.wright.edu
Established: 1964 | Annual Undergrad Tuition & Fees (In-State): $8,354
Enrollment: 17,789 | Coed
Affiliation or Control: State | IRS Status: 501(c)3
Highest Offering: Doctorate
Program: Liberal Arts And General; Teacher Preparatory; Professional
Accreditation: NH, BUS, BUSA, CACREP, CLPSY, CORE, CS, ENG, IPSY, MED, MT, MUS, NURSE, PH, SPAA, SW, TED

01 President .... Dr. David R. HOPKINS
05 Provost .... Dr. S. NARAYANAN
10 Vice Pres Business/Fiscal Affairs .... Dr. Mark M. POLATAJKO
32 Vice President Student Affairs .... Dr. Dan ABRAHAMOWICZ
46 Vice Pres Research/Graduate Studies .... Dr. Robert FYFFE
30 Vice President Univ Advancement .... Ms. Rebecca S. COLE
84 Vice Pres Enrollment Management .... Dr. Jacqueline MCMILLAN
20 VP Instruction & Curriculum .... Dr. Thomas A. SUDKAMP
58 Dean Sch Graduate Studies .... Vacant
45 Exec Vice President for Planning .... Dr. Robert J. SWEENEY
08 University Librarian .... Dr. Stephen P. FOSTER
26 Assoc VP Mktg/Communications .... Mr. George HEDDLESTON
15 Asst Vice Pres for Human Resources .... Mr. Allan BOGGS
18 Assc VP Facilities Plng/Development .... Ms. Vicky L. DAVIDSON
35 Associate Vice Pres Student Affairs .... Ms. Katherine W. MORRIS
50 Dean Raj Soin College of Business .... Dr. Joanne LI
53 Dean Education/Human Services .... Dr. Charlotte HARRIS
54 Dean Engineering/Computer Science .... Dr. Nathan W. KLINGBEIL
12 Dean WSU Lake Campus .... Dr. Bonnie MATHIES
49 Dean Liberal Arts .... Dr. Kristin SOBOLIK
66 Dean College of Nursing & Health .... Dr. Rosalie O'DELL MAINOUS
63 Dean Boonshaft School of Medicine .... Dr. Marjorie BOWMAN
83 Dean Sch of Professional Psychology .... Dr. Larry C. JAMES
81 Dean Science/Mathematics .... Dr. Yi LI
06 Registrar .... Ms. Marian J. BRAINERD
07 Director Undergraduate Admissions .... Ms. Cathleen M. DAVIS
13 Director Computing/Telecomm Svcs .... Mr. Paul R. HERNANDEZ
46 Asst VP Research/Sponsored Pgms .... Ms. Ellen REINSCH FRIESE
36 Director Career Services .... Ms. Cheryl KRUEGER
37 Director of Financial Aid .... Ms. Amy BARNHART
38 Director Counsel/Wellness Svcs .... Dr. Robert A. RANDO
29 Exec Dir Alumni Relations .... Mr. Gregory SCHARER
22 Interim Dir Affirmative Action Pgm .... Ms. Hazel G. ROUNDTREE
31 Assoc Director Event Svcs .... Ms. Jane SHELB
88 Director Disability Services .... Mr. Jeffrey A. VERNOOY
86 Assoc VP Public Affairs .... Mr. Robert E. HICKEY, JR.
41 Director of Athletics .... Mr. Bob GRANT
43 General Counsel .... Ms. Gwen M. MATTISON
24 Director CTR Teaching/Learning .... Dr. Sarah TWILL
40 Store Manager .... Ms. Jennifer L. GEBHART
85 Director Intl Student/Scholar Svcs .... Mr. Steven J. LYONS
39 Director Residence Services .... Mr. Daniel BERTSOS
19 Chief Police Department .... Mr. Michael MARTINSEN
96 Dir Strategic Procurement & Contr .... Mr. Jerry D. BLACK
92 Director Honors Program .... Dr. Susan CARRAFIELLO
94 Director Womens Studies Program .... Dr. Hope JENNINGS
09 Asst VP Institutional Research .... Mrs. Barbara J. BULLOCK
28 VP Multicultural Affairs & Comm Eng .... Dr. Kimberly BARRETT

Xavier University (H)

3800 Victory Parkway, Cincinnati OH 45207-1096

County: Hamilton | FICE Identification: 003144
Unit ID: 206622
Telephone: (513) 745-3000 | Carnegie Class: Master's L
FAX Number: (513) 745-4223 | Calendar System: Semester
URL: www.xavier.edu
Established: 1831 | Annual Undergrad Tuition & Fees: $33,000
Enrollment: 6,650 | Coed
Affiliation or Control: Roman Catholic | IRS Status: 501(c)3
Highest Offering: Doctorate
Program: Liberal Arts And General; Teacher Preparatory; Professional
Accreditation: NH, BUS, CACREP, CEA, CLPSY, HSA, MACTE, MUS, NURSE, OT, RAD, SW, TEAC

01 President .... Rev. Michael J. GRAHAM, SJ
11 Administrative Vice President .... Dr. John F. KUCIA
05 Provost & Chief Academic Officer .... Dr. Scott CHADWICK
10 Sr VP Financial Administration/CFO .... Ms. Maribeth AMYOT
26 Vice Pres for University Relations .... Mr. Gary R. MASSA
88 Asst to Pres for Mission & Identity .... Dr. Debra MOONEY
13 Assoc Provost Information Resources .... Ms. Annette MARKSBERRY
84 Vice Pres for Student Enrollment .... Mr. Terry RICHARDS
28 Asst to Pres Diversity/Inclusion .... Ms. Cheryl L. NUNEZ
26 Director for Public Relations .... Ms. Deb DEL VALLE
30 Assoc VP for University Relations .... Ms. Susan ABEL
32 Assoc Provost for Student Affairs .... Mr. David J. JOHNSON
18 Asc VP Facility Mgt/Capital Project .... Mr. Robert M. SHEERAN
41 Director Athletics .... Mr. Greg CHRISTOPHER
15 Assoc Vice Pres for Human Resources .... Mrs. Shari MICKEY-BOGGS
07 Dean Undergraduate Admission .... Mr. Aaron MEIS
12 Director Cintas Center .... Mr. Michael DUNN

44 Exec Dir Gifts & Estate Planning ....Mr. Mark MCLAUGHLIN
42 Dir Center for Mission/Identity ....Mr. Joseph SHADLE
06 Registrar ....Vacant
88 Director of Scholarships ....Mr. Paul H. CALME
85 Director for Internatl Student Svcs ....Ms. Lea MINNITI
105 Exec Dir Ofc University Commun ....Mr. Doug RUSCHMAN
39 Senior Director of Residence Life ....Ms. Lori A. LAMBERT
40 Director of Bookstore ....Ms. Susan GRIFFIN
86 Dir of Comm & Government Relations ...Dr. Eugene L. BEAUPRE'
83 Dean College Social Sci/Health/Educ ....Dr. Mark MEYERS
36 Senior Director Student Involvement ....Ms. Leah BUSAM
23 Director for Health Services ....Ms. Mary ROSENFELDT
49 Dean College Arts & Sciences ....Dr. Janice B. WALKER
19 Director of Campus Police/Security ....Mr. Michael COUCH
37 Director of Financial Aid ....Mr. Todd EVERETT
43 General Counsel ....Mr. Joseph H. FELDHAUS
29 Dir Alumni Rels/Ex Dir Athletic Dev ....Mr. Brian MALEY
09 Dir Office Institutional Research ....Ms. Susana LUZURIAGA
50 Dean Williams College of Business ....Dr. Brian TILL
51 Director Center Adults/PT Students ....Ms. Patricia MEYER
96 Director of Purchasing ....Mr. John MERCER

Youngstown State University (A)

One University Plaza, Youngstown OH 44555-0001
County: Mahoning FICE Identification: 003145
Unit ID: 206695
Telephone: (330) 941-3001 Carnegie Class: Master's L
FAX Number: (330) 941-7169 Calendar System: Semester
URL: www.ysu.edu
Established: 1908 Annual Undergrad Tuition & Fees (In-State): $7,451
Enrollment: 13,380 Coed
Affiliation or Control: State IRS Status: 501(c)3
Highest Offering: Doctorate
Program: Occupational; Liberal Arts And General; Teacher Preparatory; Professional; Technical Emphasis
Accreditation: NH, AAFCS, ANEST, ART, BUS, CACREP, COARC, COARCP, DH, DIETC, DIETD, DIETT, EMT, ENG, ENGT, HT, MAC, MLTAD, MUS, NUR, PH, PTA, SW, TED, THEA

01 President ....Dr. Randy J. DUNN
05 Provost ....Dr. Ikram KHAWAJA
11 Vice President for Finance/Admin ....Mr. Eugene P. GRILLI
100 Chief of Staff ....Ms. Shannon TIRONE
32 VP for Student Affairs ....Mr. Jack FAHEY
30 VP for University Advancement ....Mr. R. Scott EVANS
43 Univ General Counsel ....Ms. Holly A. JACOBS
49 Dean of Liberal Arts/Social Science ....Dr. Shearle FURNISH
50 Dean of Business Administration ....Dr. Betty Jo LICATA
53 Dean of Education ....Dr. Charles HOWELL
54 Dean of Science/Tech/Eng/Math ....Dr. Martin A. ABRAHAM
57 Dean Fine & Performing Arts ....Mr. Byran DEPOY
76 Dean Health & Human Services ....Dr. Joseph L. MOSCA
58 Interim Dean Grad Studies/Research ....Dr. Sal SANDERS
45 Assoc Provost Acad Pgms/Planning ....Dr. Kevin BALL
20 Int Assoc Prov Acad Admin/Info Svcs ....Dr. Teri RILEY
15 Chief Human Resources Officer ....Mr. Kevin W. REYNOLDS
13 Director Computer Services ....Mr. Richard J. MARSICO
41 Exec Director of Athletics ....Mr. Ronald A. STROLLO
26 Exec Dir of Mktg/Communications ....Mr. Mark W. VANTILBURG
35 Exec Director of Student Services ....Mr. Matthew NOVOTNY
84 Exec Dir Enrollment Mgmt ....Vacant
08 Manager Library Operations ....Ms. Anna BOBBY
29 Dir Alumni and Events Mgmt ....Ms. Jacquelyn LEVISEUR
28 Int Director Diversity & Multic Aff ....Dr. Sylvia IMLER
07 Director Undergrad Recruit/Admiss ....Ms. Sue E. DAVIS
06 Registrar ....Ms. Jeanne HERMAN
19 Chief of University Police ....Mr. John BESHARA
18 Executive Director Facilities ....Mr. John P. HYDEN
21 Director Student Accts/Receivables ....Ms. Gloria KOBUS
23 Dir Environ/Occup Health & Safety ....Mr. Daniel SAHLI
37 Director Financial/Scholarships ....Ms. Elaine RUSE
21 Director General Accounting ....Ms. Katrena J. DAVIDSON
45 Int VP Budget Planning ....Mr. Neal P. MCNALLY
21 Cash Management Officer ....Ms. Akhande KHAN
25 Director Grants & Sponsored Pgms ....Mr. Edward ORONA
09 Exec Dir Institutional Research ....Vacant
39 Director Housing Services ....Ms. Danielle MEYER
85 Director International Studies ....Mr. Jef C. DAVIS
14 Director Computer Services ....Mr. Richard J. MARSICO
30 Director of Development ....Ms. Catherine CALA
28 Director Student Diversity Programs ....Mr. William J. BLAKE
88 Dir Assoc Degree/Tech Prep Pgms ....Ms. Arlene FLOYD
40 Director of Bookstore ....Mr. Charles A. SABATINO
88 Director Support Services ....Mr. Danny J. O'CONNELL
88 Dir Electronic Maintenance Svcs ....Mr. Michael REPETSKI
90 Director Media/Acad Computing ....Mr. Michael S. HRISHENKO
92 Director Univ Scholars/Honors Pgm ....Dr. Ronald SHAKLEE
36 Director of Career Services ....Ms. Jennifer JOHNSON
96 Director Procurement Services ....Mr. William WHEELOCK
88 Director Degree Audit ....Vacant
91 Director Network Telecomm & Secur ....Mr. Jason T. RAKERS
35 Executive Director Student Life ....Ms. Jonelle BEATRICE
35 Dir Campus Rec/Intramural Sports ...Ms. Joy POLKABLA-BYERS
88 Director WYSU-FM ....Mr. Gary SEXTON
04 Exec Admin to President ....Ms. Cynthia M. BELL

Zane State College (B)

9900 Brick Church Road, Cambridge OH 43725
Telephone: (740) 432-6568 Identification: 770365
Accreditation: &NH

† Main campus is Zane State College in Zanesville, OH.

Zane State College (C)

1555 Newark Road, Zanesville OH 43701-2626
County: Muskingum FICE Identification: 008133
Unit ID: 204255
Telephone: (740) 454-2501 Carnegie Class: Assoc/Pub-R-M
FAX Number: (740) 454-0035 Calendar System: Semester
URL: www.zanestate.edu
Established: 1969 Annual Undergrad Tuition & Fees (In-State): $4,470
Enrollment: 2,325 Coed
Affiliation or Control: State IRS Status: 501(c)3
Highest Offering: Associate Degree
Program: 2-Year Principally Bachelor's Creditable; Technical Emphasis
Accreditation: NH, ACFEI, CAHIIM, ENGT, MAC, MLTAD, OTA, PHLEB, PTAA, RAD

01 President ....Dr. Paul R. BROWN
102 Exec Dir Inst Advancemnt/Foundation ....Ms. Pamela A. JIRA
05 Provost/Executive Vice President ....Dr. Chad BROWN
10 Vice Pres for Business Services ....Mr. Albert F. BROWN
32 Vice Pres for Student Svcs/Registra ....Mr. Greg DART
54 Acad Dean Business & Engineering ....Mr. George HICKS
12 Exec Dean Cambridge Campus ....Mr. Mike WITSON
15 Director of Human Resources ....Dr. James KEMPER
13 Interim Exec Chief Info Officer ....Dr. Terry HERMAN
08 Library Director ....Mr. Tony HOPKINS
09 Dir of Inst Effectiveness & Plng ....Dr. Tricia LEGGETT
25 Director of Grants & Contracts ....Mrs. Larisa HARPER
07 Director of Admissions ....Mr. Paul J. YOUNG
37 Director Student Financial Aid ....Ms. Amanda B. REISINGER
36 Director Career/Employment Services ....Ms. Jamie K. CLARK
26 Director Marketing & Communications ....Mr. Nick WELCH
20 Dean of Dev Ed & First Year ....Ms. Rebecca R. AMENT
38 Interim Dir of Student Success Ctr ....Ms. Jamie K. CLARK
21 Controller ....Ms. Tammy S. HUFFMAN
40 Director of Bookstore Operations ....Ms. Linda D. METZ
19 Director of Safety and Security ....Ms. Bethany HAYES
49 Dean of Arts and Sciences ....Mrs. Susan HOLDREN
76 Int Dean of Educ Hlth & Hum Svcs ....Ms. Peg EARHART
06 Registrar/Veteran Services ....Ms. Cindi SWOPE
18 Director Facilities Management ....Mr. Joseph KEATING
28 Coordinator-Multi Cultural ....Ms. Keisha NORRIS

OKLAHOMA

Bacone College (D)

2299 Old Bacone Road, Muskogee OK 74403-1568
County: Muskogee FICE Identification: 003147
Unit ID: 206817
Telephone: (918) 683-4581 Carnegie Class: Bac/Assoc
FAX Number: (918) 781-7422 Calendar System: Semester
URL: www.bacone.edu
Established: 1880 Annual Undergrad Tuition & Fees: $14,050
Enrollment: 1,040 Coed
Affiliation or Control: American Baptist IRS Status: 501(c)3
Highest Offering: Baccalaureate
Program: 2-Year Principally Bachelor's Creditable; Liberal Arts And General; Teacher Preparatory
Accreditation: NH, IACBE, NUR, RAD

01 President ....Rev Dr. Robert J. DUNCAN, JR.
03 Exec Vice Pres & Dean of Faculty ....Dr. Robert K. BROWN
88 Director Center for American Indian ....Rev. Wilfred BROWN
30 VP Institutional Advancement ....Mr. Mike MILLER
84 AVP of Enrollment Management ....Mr. Darin MCDUGLE
42 VP Christian Ministry ....Rev Dr. Leroy THOMPSON
10 VP Finance ....Mr. Mustafa YUNDEM
32 Asst VP Student Life ....Ms. Shelli HOPKINS
06 Registrar ....Mrs. Virginia THOMPSON
40 Bookstore Manager ....Ms. Christin SWAGERS
41 Asst VP Athletics ....Mr. Alan FOSTER
39 Dir Residential Life & Hospitality ....Ms. Denise WILCOX
37 Asst Director Financial Aid ....Ms. Misty OLESON
15 Director Human Resources ....Ms. Tammy MCDANIELS
18 Chief Facilities/Physical Plant ....Vacant
35 Director of Student Services ....Mr. Dustin HOPKINS
29 Asst Director Alumni Relations ....Vacant
09 Coord Institutional Assessment Data ....Ms. Linda MILAM
26 Director of External Relations ....Ms. Susie CAGLE
21 Controller ....Vacant
36 Director of Career Services ....Vacant
105 Dir Web/Video Design Studio ....Mr. Dwayne PARTON
08 Dir Betts Library/Head Librarian ....Ms. Faye DAVIS
13 Director of Network Systems ....Mr. Chris EHLERS

Brown Mackie College-Oklahoma City (E)

7101 Northwest Expy, Suite 800,
Oklahoma City OK 73132
Telephone: (405) 261-8000 Identification: 770252
Accreditation: &NH

† Main campus is Brown Mackie College-Salina in Salina, KS.

Brown Mackie College-Tulsa (F)

4608 South Garnett Road, Ste. 110, Tulsa OK 74146
Telephone: (918) 628-3700 Identification: 666783
Accreditation: ACICS, OTA, SURGT, SURTEC

† Main campus is The Art Institute of Phoenix in Phoenix, AZ.

Cameron University (G)

2800 W Gore Boulevard, Lawton OK 73505-6377
County: Comanche FICE Identification: 003150
Unit ID: 206914
Telephone: (580) 581-2200 Carnegie Class: Master's S
FAX Number: (580) 581-2867 Calendar System: Semester
URL: www.cameron.edu
Established: 1908 Annual Undergrad Tuition & Fees (In-State): $5,055
Enrollment: 6,115 Coed
Affiliation or Control: State IRS Status: 501(c)3
Highest Offering: Master's
Program: Liberal Arts And General; Teacher Preparatory
Accreditation: NH, ACBSP, MUS, TED

01 President ....Dr. John M. MCARTHUR
05 Vice President for Academic Affairs ..Dr. Ronna J. VANDERSLICE
10 Vice Pres for Business & Finance ....Mr. Glen P. PINKSTON
30 Vice Pres University Advancement ...Mr. Albert D. JOHNSON, JR.
32 Vice President for Student Services ....Ms. Jennifer L. HOLLAND
84 Assoc Vice Pres Enrollment Mgmt ....Mrs. Jamie L. GLOVER
20 Assoc Vice Pres Academic Affairs ....Dr. Sylvia BURGESS
20 Asst Vice Pres Academic Affairs ....Dr. Margery KINGSLEY
50 Dean School of Business ....Dr. John CAMEY
79 Dean School of Liberal Arts ....Dr. Von E. UNDERWOOD
53 Dean Sch of Educ/Behav Science ....Vacant
81 Dean School Science/Tech ....Dr. Terry CONLEY
12 Director Duncan Campus ....Ms. Susan CAMP
21 Controller ....Ms. Ninette CARTER
104 Director Academic Enrichment ....Dr. Anton WOHLERS
31 Director of Public Affairs ....Mr. Josh LEHMAN
08 Librarian ....Dr. Sheridan YOUNG
29 Director Alumni Relations ....Ms. Jennifer MCGRAIL
41 Director Athletic Administration ....Mr. Jim C. JACKSON
07 Director of Admissions ....Ms. Zoe W. DURANT
06 Registrar ....Mrs. Linda PHILLIPS
09 Dir Inst Rsrch/Assess/Accountabity ....Dr. Karla OTY
37 Director of Financial Assistance ....Mr. Donald HALL
13 Director Information Tech Services ....Ms. Debbie GOODE
15 Director of Human Resources ....Mr. Chase MASSIE
38 Director Student Development ....Dr. Jennifer PRUCHNICKI
35 Director Student Activities ....Mr. Zeak NAIFEH
19 Director Public Safety ....Mr. John DEBOARD
18 Director Physical Facilities ....Mr. Robert HANEFIELD
96 Director of Purchasing ....Mr. Richard MCCOMAS

Career Point College (H)

3138 South Garnett Road, Tulsa OK 74146-1933
Telephone: (918) 627-8074 Identification: 770761
Accreditation: ACICS

† Main campus is Career Point College in San Antonio, TX.

Carl Albert State College (I)

1507 S McKenna, Poteau OK 74953-5208
County: Le Flore FICE Identification: 003176
Unit ID: 206923
Telephone: (918) 647-1200 Carnegie Class: Assoc/Pub-R-M
FAX Number: (918) 647-1201 Calendar System: Semester
URL: www.carlalbert.edu
Established: 1933 Annual Undergrad Tuition & Fees (In-State): $2,807
Enrollment: 2,613 Coed
Affiliation or Control: State IRS Status: 501(c)3
Highest Offering: Associate Degree
Program: Occupational; 2-Year Principally Bachelor's Creditable
Accreditation: NH, ACBSP, ADNUR, PTAA, RAD

01 President ....Mr. Garry M. IVEY
32 Vice President for Student Affairs ....Ms. Leah MCLAUGHLIN
05 Vice President of Academic Affairs ....Dr. James YATES
10 Vice Pres for Business Operations ....Ms. Ramona BUCKNER
13 Information Technology Director ....Mr. Michael MARTIN
04 Assistant to the President ....Vacant
26 Public Relations Director ....Ms. Judi WHITE
06 Registrar/Director Admissions ....Ms. Dee Ann DICKERSON
37 Director of Financial Aid ....Ms. Robin BENSON
86 Director Federal Programs ....Ms. Michelle WHITE
18 Director of Physical Plant ....Mr. Chuck LEWIS
15 Director Personnel Services ....Ms. Vicki HILL
21 Assistant Finance Officer ....Ms. Melinda PIERCE

Carl Albert State College Sallisaw Campus (J)

1601 S Opdyke, Sallisaw OK 74953
Telephone: (918) 775-6977 Identification: 770366
Accreditation: &NH

† Main campus is Carl Albert State College in Poteau, OK.

Clary Sage College (K)

3131 South Sheridan Road, Tulsa OK 74145-1102
Telephone: (918) 298-8200 Identification: 666368
Accreditation: ACICS

† Main campus is Community Care College in Tulsa, OK.

College of the Muscogee Nation (A)

PO Box 917, 1200 Highway Loop 56,
Okmulgee OK 74447

County: Okmulgee | Identification: 667122
Telephone: (918) 549-2800 | Carnegie Class: Not Classified
FAX Number: (918) 549-2880 | Calendar System: Semester
URL: www.mvsktc.org
Established: | Annual Undergrad Tuition & Fees: $3,795
Enrollment: N/A | Coed
Affiliation or Control: Tribal Control | IRS Status: 501(c)3
Highest Offering: Associate Degree
Program: Occupational
Accreditation: @NH

01 President .... Mr. Robert BIBLE

Comanche Nation College (B)

1608 SW 9th Street, Lawton OK 73501

County: Comanche | Identification: 667123
Telephone: (580) 591-0203 | Carnegie Class: Not Classified
FAX Number: N/A | Calendar System: Semester
URL: www.cnc.cc.ok.us
Established: 2002 | Annual Undergrad Tuition & Fees: N/A
Enrollment: N/A | Coed
Affiliation or Control: Tribal Control | IRS Status: 501(c)3
Highest Offering: Associate Degree
Program: Occupational
Accreditation: @NH

01 President .... Dr. Consuelo G. LOPEZ

Community Care College (C)

4242 S Sheridan Road, Tulsa OK 74145-1119

County: Tulsa | FICE Identification: 033674
Unit ID: 439570
Telephone: (918) 610-0027 | Carnegie Class: Assoc/PrivFP
FAX Number: (918) 610-0029 | Calendar System: Other
URL: www.communitycarecollege.edu
Established: 1995 | Annual Undergrad Tuition & Fees: $21,071
Enrollment: 700 | Coed
Affiliation or Control: Proprietary | IRS Status: Proprietary
Highest Offering: Associate Degree
Program: Occupational; 2-Year Principally Bachelor's Creditable; Technical Emphasis
Accreditation: ACICS, MAAB, SURGT

00 CEO .... Ms. Teresa L. KNOX
01 President .... Mr. Kevin L. KIRK

Connors State College (D)

Route 1, Box 1000, Warner OK 74469-9700

County: Muskogee | FICE Identification: 003153
Unit ID: 206996
Telephone: (918) 463-2931 | Carnegie Class: Assoc/Pub-R-M
FAX Number: (918) 463-2233 | Calendar System: Semester
URL: www.connorsstate.edu
Established: 1908 | Annual Undergrad Tuition & Fees (In-State): $3,292
Enrollment: 2,336 | Coed
Affiliation or Control: State | IRS Status: 501(c)3
Highest Offering: Associate Degree
Program: Occupational; 2-Year Principally Bachelor's Creditable
Accreditation: NH, ADNUR

01 President .... Dr. Timothy W. FALTYN
05 Vice Pres Academic Svcs/Stdnt Affs .... Dr. Ron RAMMING
10 Vice President of Fiscal Services .... Mrs. Shirley TWILLEY
37 Director of Financial Aid .... Ms. Jennifer WATKINS
08 Director of Learning Center .... Vacant
13 Director Information Technology .... Mr. Heath HODGES
06 Registrar .... Ms. Kwanna KING
07 Director of Recruitment .... Ms. Logan KNAPPER
26 Director of Public Information .... Mr. Ami MADDOCKS
15 Director Human Resources .... Mr. Nate WALKER
09 Int Dir of Institutional Research .... Vacant
30 Dir of Development Foundation .... Mr. Ryan BLANTON

Connors State College Muskogee Port Branch Campus (E)

2501 N 41st Street East, Muskogee OK 74403

Telephone: (918) 687-6747 | Identification: 770367
Accreditation: &NH

† Main campus is Connors State College in Warner, OK.

East Central University (F)

1100 E 14th Street, Ada OK 74820-6899

County: Pontotoc | FICE Identification: 003154
Unit ID: 207041
Telephone: (580) 332-8000 | Carnegie Class: Master's L
FAX Number: (580) 332-1623 | Calendar System: Semester
URL: www.ecok.edu
Established: 1909 | Annual Undergrad Tuition & Fees (In-State): $4,957
Enrollment: 4,819 | Coed
Affiliation or Control: State | IRS Status: 501(c)3
Highest Offering: Master's
Program: Liberal Arts And General; Teacher Preparatory; Professional
Accreditation: NH, ACBSP, CORE, MUS, NUR, SW, TED

01 President .... Dr. John R. HARGRAVE
05 Provost/Vice Pres Academic Affairs .... Dr. Duane C. ANDERSON
32 Vice President Student Development .... Dr. Gerald FORBES
10 Vice Pres Administration/Finance .... Ms. Jessica BOLES
20 Asst VP Academic Affairs .... Dr. Katricia PIERSON
53 Dean of Education .... Dr. Brenda WALLING
50 Dean of Business .... Mr. Wendell GODWIN
51 Director Continuing Education .... Dr. G. Richard WETHERILL
35 Dean of Students .... Mr. Bramer APPLEMAN
37 Director of Financial Aid .... Ms. Becky ISAACS
09 Director of Institutional Research .... Dr. Sheilynda STEWART
08 Librarian .... Dr. Adrianna LANCASTER
06 Registrar .... Ms. Pamla ARMSTRONG
14 Director Computer Center .... Mr. Frank WILLIAMS
41 Athletic Director .... Mr. Brian DEANGELIS
15 Director of Human Resources .... Mr. Lynn LOFTIN
19 Chief of Police .... Mr. Henry MILLER
18 Director Physical Plant .... Mr. Robert CASTLEBERRY
26 Dir of Marketing & Communication .... Ms. Amy FORD
29 Director Alumni Relations .... Ms. Buffy LOVELIS
84 Director Enrollment Management .... Mr. B. J ECHARD
96 Director of Purchasing .... Ms. Jo Ann JOHNSON

Eastern Oklahoma State College (G)

1301 W Main Street, Wilburton OK 74578-4999

County: Latimer | FICE Identification: 003155
Unit ID: 207050
Telephone: (918) 465-2361 | Carnegie Class: Assoc/Pub-R-S
FAX Number: (918) 465-2431 | Calendar System: Semester
URL: www.eosc.edu
Established: 1909 | Annual Undergrad Tuition & Fees (In-State): $3,528
Enrollment: 1,941 | Coed
Affiliation or Control: State | IRS Status: 501(c)3
Highest Offering: Associate Degree
Program: Occupational; 2-Year Principally Bachelor's Creditable
Accreditation: NH, ADNUR, MLTAD

01 President .... Dr. Stephen E. SMITH
05 Vice President of Academic Affairs .... Dr. Karen D. HARRISON
10 Vice Pres of Business Affairs .... Ms. La Donna HOWELL
32 Vice Pres for Student Affairs .... Dr. Steve G. GLAZIER
12 Director of McAlester Campus .... Dr. Janet WANSICK
35 Dean of Students/Athletic Director .... Mr. Greg WARREN
30 Exec Dir Development/Alumni Rels .... Mrs. Treva KENNEDY
27 Director Public Information .... Mrs. Trish MCBEATH
09 Director of Institutional Research .... Dr. Janet WANSICK
20 Associate Academic Officer .... Dr. Janet WANSICK
84 Dir Enrollment Mgmt/Financial Aid .... Dr. Steve GLAZIER
13 Chief Technical Officer .... Mr. Jeff WEEMS
08 Director Library & Media Services .... Ms. Maria MARTINEZ
15 Director Personnel Services .... Mrs. Joyce BILLS
06 Registrar .... Mrs. Jennifer LABOR
18 Chief Facilities/Physical Plant .... Mr. Rich LYNES
44 Dir of Institutional Advancement .... Mrs. Treva KENNEDY
37 Financial Aid Officer .... Ms. Patricia RECTOR

Eastern Oklahoma State College McAlester Campus (H)

1802 E College Avenue, McAlester OK 74501

Telephone: (918) 426-5272 | Identification: 770368
Accreditation: &NH

† Main campus is Eastern Oklahoma State College in Wilburton, OK.

Family of Faith College (I)

PO Box 1805, Shawnee OK 74802-1805

County: Pottawatomie | FICE Identification: 036763
Unit ID: 443058
Telephone: (405) 273-5331 | Carnegie Class: Spec/Faith
FAX Number: (405) 273-8535 | Calendar System: Semester
URL: www.familyoffaithcollege.edu
Established: 1992 | Annual Undergrad Tuition & Fees: $5,760
Enrollment: 25 | Coed
Affiliation or Control: Independent Non-Profit | IRS Status: 501(c)3
Highest Offering: Baccalaureate
Program: Professional; Religious Emphasis
Accreditation: BI

01 President .... Dr. Samuel W. MATTHEWS
05 Vice President Academic Affairs .... Mrs. Elaine W. PHILLIPS
10 Vice President Operations/Finance .... Mr. Daniel MATTHEWS
32 Vice Pres Student Affs/Dir Fin Aid .... Mrs. Dara GILLIAM
46 Director of Resource Development .... Vacant
42 Director of Spiritual Life .... Mr. Daniel J. MATTHEWS
108 Dir of Accreditation/Assessment .... Mrs. Elaine W. PHILLIPS

Heritage College (J)

7100 I-35 Services Road, Suite 7118,
Oklahoma City OK 73149-2740

County: Oklahoma | FICE Identification: 031151
Unit ID: 410070
Telephone: (405) 631-3399 | Carnegie Class: Assoc/PrivFP
FAX Number: (405) 631-6711 | Calendar System: Quarter
URL: www.heritage-education.com
Established: 2002 | Annual Undergrad Tuition & Fees: $24,550
Enrollment: 1,194 | Coed
Affiliation or Control: Proprietary | IRS Status: Proprietary
Highest Offering: Associate Degree
Program: Occupational
Accreditation: ABHES, SURTEC

01 Director .... Ms. Andrea RILEY

Hillsdale Free Will Baptist College (K)

PO Box 7208, Moore OK 73153-1208

County: Cleveland | FICE Identification: 010266
Unit ID: 207157
Telephone: (405) 912-9000 | Carnegie Class: Spec/Faith
FAX Number: (405) 912-9050 | Calendar System: Semester
URL: www.hc.edu
Established: 1959 | Annual Undergrad Tuition & Fees: $13,600
Enrollment: 267 | Coed
Affiliation or Control: Free Will Baptist | IRS Status: 501(c)3
Highest Offering: Master's
Program: Liberal Arts And General; Religious Emphasis
Accreditation: TRACS

01 President .... Dr. Timothy W. EATON
05 Chief Academic Officer .... Dr. Thomas L. MARBERRY
03 Executive Vice President .... Dr. Mark H. BRAISHER
30 Director Institutional Advancement .... Mr. Bob THOMPSON
07 Admissions Coordinator .... Ms. Lyndsey BRAISHER
37 Financial Aid Coordinator .... Ms. Denise CONKLIN
08 LRC Director .... Ms. Nancy J. DRAPER
13 Director of MIS .... Mr. Quentin C. LOOP
06 Registrar .... Ms. Patti ASHBY
58 Dean of Graduate Studies .... Dr. Mark H. BRAISHER
39 Resident Life Coordinator .... Mr. Sam CRILLY
41 Athletic Director .... Ms. Autumn DRAKE
35 Dean of Students .... Rev. Curt HOLLAND
40 Bookstore Manager .... Mr. Lee BAUDER
106 Director of Online Learning .... Dr. Paulette JONES

ITT Technical Institute (L)

50 Penn Place Ofc Tower, Ste 305R,
Oklahoma City OK 73118

Telephone: (405) 810-4100 | Identification: 666159
Accreditation: ACICS

† Main campus is ITT Technical Institute in Indianapolis, IN.

ITT Technical Institute (M)

4500 S. 129th East Avenue, Ste. 152, Tulsa OK 74134

Telephone: (918) 615-3900 | Identification: 666147
Accreditation: ACICS

† Main campus is ITT Technical Institute in Indianapolis, IN.

Langston University (N)

PO Box 1500, Langston OK 73050

County: Logan | FICE Identification: 003157
Unit ID: 207209
Telephone: (405) 466-2231 | Carnegie Class: Master's S
FAX Number: N/A | Calendar System: Semester
URL: www.langston.edu
Established: 1897 | Annual Undergrad Tuition & Fees (In-State): $4,255
Enrollment: 2,518 | Coed
Affiliation or Control: State | IRS Status: 501(c)3
Highest Offering: Doctorate
Program: Liberal Arts And General; Teacher Preparatory; Professional
Accreditation: NH, ACBSP, CORE, NUR, PTA, TED

01 President .... Dr. Kent J. SMITH, JR.
05 Vice President Academic Affairs .... Dr. Clyde MONTGOMERY
10 Interim VP Fiscal/Admin Affairs .... Dr. James MOSLEY
32 VP Student Affairs/Enrollment Mgmt .... Dr. Rafael MOFFETT
30 Interim VP Inst Devel/Advance .... Mr. James R. DUNAVANT
100 Chief of Staff .... Mrs. Cynthia S. BUCKLEY
13 Chief Information Officer .... Mr. Pritchard MONCRIFFE
20 Assoc VP Academic Affairs LU/OKC .... Dr. Blayne E. HINDS
20 COO/Assoc VP Academic Affs LU/Tulsa .... Dr. Bruce W. MCGOWAN
21 Asst VP of Fiscal Affairs .... Ms. Debra G. MASTERS
44 Asst VP Inst Advanc/Campaign Dir .... Mr. James R. DUNAVANT
35 Assistant VP of Student Affairs .... Dr. Natasha M. BILLIE
29 Director Alumni Affairs .... Mrs. Vonnie W. ROBERTS
36 Dir Assessment/Career Placement .... Mr. James A. WALLACE
26 Director Public Relations .... Vacant
07 Interim Director of Admissions .... Mr. Chauncey J. JACKSON
37 Director Financial Aid .... Ms. Shelia MCGILL
15 Director of Human Resources .... Mrs. Beverly H. SMITH
22 Dir LCDC Affirm Action/EEO Ofc .... Vacant
18 Director Facilities/Physical Plant .... Mr. Ruben D. OLIVER
38 Dir Professional Counseling Center .... Vacant
09 Director Inst Research & Planning .... Dr. Carol CAWYER
08 Director of Libraries .... Ms. Bettye R. BLACK
06 Registrar .... Mrs. Kathy SIMMONS
41 Athletic Director .... Mr. Mike GARRETT
21 Comptroller .... Mr. J.I JOHNSON
58 Director of Graduate Programs .... Dr. Alex O. LEWIS
19 Chief of Police .... Mr. Frank ATKINSON
96 Director of Purchasing .... Mrs. Deirdra M. STEVENSON
49 Dean School of Arts & Sciences .... Dr. Clarence A. HEDGE
50 Dean School of Business .... Dr. Solomon S. SMITH

46 Dean School Agric/Applied Science .... Dr. Marvin BURNS
66 Interim Dean Sch Nurs/Hlth Profess .... Dr. Teressa HUNTER
53 Acting Dean Sch Educ/Behav Sci .... Dr. Joe N. HORNBEAK
92 Dean Honors Program .... Dr. Joanne CLARK
88 Dean Physical Therapy Program .... Dr. Aliya CHAUDRY
88 Dean Entrepreneurial Studies .... Dr. Surya P. SINGH
84 Interim Dir Enrollment Mgmt .... Mr. Chauncey J. JACKSON

Langston University Oklahoma City Campus (A)

4205 N Lincoln, Oklahoma City OK 73105
Telephone: (405) 962-1620 Identification: 770370
Accreditation: &NH

† Main campus is Langston University in Langston, OK.

Langston University Tulsa Campus (B)

914 North Greenwood, Tulsa OK 74106
Telephone: (918) 877-8100 Identification: 770371
Accreditation: &NH

† Main campus is Langston University in Langston, OK.

McCurtain County Higher Education Center (C)

2805 NE Lincoln Road, Idabel OK 74745
Telephone: (580) 286-9431 Identification: 770369
Accreditation: &NH

† Main campus is Eastern Oklahoma State College in Wilburton, OK.

Mid-America Christian University (D)

3500 SW 119th Street, Oklahoma City OK 73170-4500
County: Cleveland FICE Identification: 006942
Unit ID: 245953
Telephone: (405) 691-3800 Carnegie Class: Bac/Diverse
FAX Number: (405) 692-3165 Calendar System: Semester
URL: www.macu.edu
Established: 1953 Annual Undergrad Tuition & Fees: $15,688
Enrollment: 2,606 Coed
Affiliation or Control: Church Of God IRS Status: 501(c)3
Highest Offering: Master's
Program: Liberal Arts And General; Teacher Preparatory; Religious Emphasis
Accreditation: NH

01 President .... Dr. John D. FOZARD
05 Provost .... Dr. Kathaleen REID-MARTINEZ
30 Vice Pres for Univ Advancement .... Mr. Steven SEATON
84 Assoc VP Student Affairs/Enrollment .... Mrs. Jessica RIMMER
88 Dean Academic Scholarship .... Dr. Shirley RODDY
10 Chief Financial Officer .... Ms. Mici SARTIN
15 Chief Administration Officer (HR) .... Mr. Owen SEVIER
20 Chief Academic Assessment Officer .... Mrs. Julia CARPENTER
88 Exec Director of Church Relations .... Rev. Morgan ALSIP
06 Registrar .... Mrs. Bobbie SPURGEON-HARRIS
37 Director Student Financial Services .... Mrs. Christina PADILLA
07 Director of Admissions .... Mr. Mike WILKINSON
18 Director Facilities/Physical Plant .... Mr. Clark BAREFOOT
29 Director Alumni Relations .... Vacant

Murray State College (E)

One Murray Campus, Tishomingo OK 73460-3130
County: Johnston FICE Identification: 003158
Unit ID: 207236
Telephone: (580) 371-2371 Carnegie Class: Assoc/Pub-R-M
FAX Number: (580) 371-9844 Calendar System: Semester
URL: www.mscok.edu
Established: 1908 Annual Undergrad Tuition & Fees (In-State): $4,036
Enrollment: 2,646 Coed
Affiliation or Control: State IRS Status: 501(c)3
Highest Offering: Associate Degree
Program: Occupational; 2-Year Principally Bachelor's Creditable
Accreditation: NH, ADNUR, OTA, PTAA

01 President .... Ms. Joy MCDANIEL
04 Exec Assistant to President/Board .... Mrs. Malynda COBB
10 AVP for Administration and Finance .... Mr. Dennis WESTMAN
05 VP for Academic Affairs .... Dr. Roger STACY
32 VP of Student Affairs .... Ms. Michaelle GRAY
20 AVP Learing and Student Success .... Ms. Becky HENTHORN
37 Assoc Financial Aid Director .... Ms. Machelle ELLIS
08 Director of Library .... Ms. Mary RIXEN
74 Veterinary Tech Program Director .... Dr. Carey FLOYD
66 Director of Nursing .... Ms. Robin COPPEDGE
30 Dir of Development/External Rels .... Vacant
88 Director of Academic Advisement .... Ms. Amanda BALDRIDGE
07 Registrar/Director of Admissions .... Ms. Pam WARD
15 Director of Human Resources .... Mr. Joe Pat HUGHES
35 Director of Student Life .... Ms. Linda ROBINS
18 Assistant VP of Facilities .... Mr. Gary COOK
26 Public Information Officer .... Ms. Erin KNIGHT
21 Comptroller .... Ms. Sherry GRAY-DEVINE

National American University-Tulsa (F)

8040 S Sheridan Road, Tulsa OK 74133
Telephone: (918) 879-8400 Identification: 770409
Accreditation: &NH

† Main campus is National American University in Rapid City, SD.

Northeastern Oklahoma Agricultural and Mechanical College (G)

200 I Street, NE, Miami OK 74354-6434
County: Ottawa FICE Identification: 003160
Unit ID: 207290
Telephone: (918) 542-8441 Carnegie Class: Assoc/Pub-R-M
FAX Number: (918) 542-9759 Calendar System: Semester
URL: www.neo.edu
Established: 1919 Annual Undergrad Tuition & Fees (In-State): $3,435
Enrollment: 2,519 Coed
Affiliation or Control: State IRS Status: 501(c)3
Highest Offering: Associate Degree
Program: Occupational; 2-Year Principally Bachelor's Creditable
Accreditation: NH, ADNUR, MLTAD, PTAA

01 President .... Dr. Jeffery L. HALE
05 Vice President Academic Affairs .... Dr. Bethene FAHNESTOCK
10 Vice President for Fiscal Affairs .... Mr. Mark RASOR
32 VP Student Affairs/Enrollment Svcs .... Mrs. Amy ISHMAEL
20 Asst VP for Academic Affairs .... Dr. Shannon CUNNINGHAM
37 Director of Financial Aid .... Mr. David FISHER
26 Chief Public Relations Officer .... Mrs. Katie DEWEY
15 Director Human Resources .... Mr. Evan JEWSBURY
18 Director Facilities/Physical Plant .... Mr. Steve GRIMES
27 Dir Public Information/Relations .... Mrs. Katie DEWEY
14 Coord InstructionalTechnology .... Mr. Matt WESTPHAL
30 Dir Devel/Alumni Rels/Foundation .... Ms. Jennifer HESSEE
38 Director Academic Advising Center .... Mrs. Rachel LLOYD
41 Athletic Director .... Mr. Dale PATTERSON
88 Economic Development Coordinator .... Vacant
105 Webmaster .... Mr. Jeremiah FRENCH
06 Registrar .... Mrs. Michelle SHACKELFORD
21 Asst Vice Pres for Fiscal Affairs .... Mr. Matthew GLEASON
40 Bookstore Manager .... Mrs. Kathryn VANOVER
36 Dir Ctr for Academic Success & Adv .... Ms. Rachel LLOYD
08 Coordinator Library Services .... Ms. Sloane BROWN
47 Department Chair Agriculture .... Mrs. Shannon CUNNINGHAM
83 Department Chair Social Science .... Dr. Jeff BIRDSONG
57 Dept Chair Commun/Performing Arts .... Mr. Steve MCCURLEY
81 Dept Chair Mathematics/Science .... Dr. Mark GRIGSBY
66 Dept Chr Nursing/Allied Hlth/Phy Ed .... Mrs. Deborah MORGAN
50 Dept Chair Business and Technology .... Mrs. Pat CREECH

Northeastern State University (H)

601 N Grand Avenue, Tahlequah OK 74464-2399
County: Cherokee FICE Identification: 003161
Unit ID: 207263
Telephone: (918) 456-5511 Carnegie Class: Master's L
FAX Number: (918) 458-2193 Calendar System: Semester
URL: www.nsuok.edu
Established: 1851 Annual Undergrad Tuition & Fees (In-State): $4,992
Enrollment: 8,721 Coed
Affiliation or Control: State IRS Status: 501(c)3
Highest Offering: First Professional Degree
Program: Liberal Arts And General; Teacher Preparatory; Professional; Business Emphasis
Accreditation: NH, ACBSP, DIETD, MT, MUS, NUR, OPT, OPTR, SP, SW, TED

01 President .... Dr. Steve TURNER
05 Provost & Vice Pres Academic Affs .... Dr. William RUGG
11 Vice President for Administration .... Mr. David KOEHN
31 Dir Community/Government Relations .... Mr. Jerry COOK
21 Vice Pres for Operations .... Mr. Tim FOUTCH
32 Vice President Student Affairs .... Ms. Laura BOREN
58 Asst VP Acad Affs/Dean Grad College .... Dr. Tom JACKSON
30 Asst VP Educ Foundation Leadership .... Dr. Pam FLY
12 Dean Broken Arrow Campus .... Dr. Christee JENLINK
12 Dean Muskogee Campus .... Dr. Tim MCELROY
49 Dean College of Liberal Arts .... Dr. Phillip BRIDGMON
50 Dean College of Business/Technology .... Dr. Roger COLLIER
53 Dean College of Education .... Dr. Debbie LANDRY
81 Dean Science & Health Professions .... Dr. Martin VENNEMAN
88 Dean Optometry .... Dr. Douglas PENISTEN
10 Director Business Affairs .... Ms. Sue CATRON
08 Exec Director of NSU Libraries .... Mr. Steven EDSCORN
21 Director of Budget .... Ms. Christy LANDSAW
30 Director of Development .... Ms. Peggy GLENN-SUMMITT
15 Director of Human Resources .... Dr. Martha ALBIN
37 Director Student Financial Services .... Dr. Teri COCHRAN
06 Assc Registrar/Veterans Coordinator .... Ms. Janet KELLEY
26 Director High School & College Rels .... Mr. Jason JESSIE
84 Int Exec Dir Enrollment Management .... Mr. Jerrett PHILLIPS
18 Interim Director of Physical Plant .... Mr. Jonathan ASBILL
41 Director of Athletics .... Mr. Tony DUCKWORTH
27 Director of Communications .... Vacant
19 Director of Campus Police .... Ms. Patti BUHL
29 Director Alumni Services .... Mr. Daniel JOHNSON
07 Director of Admission .... Vacant
06 Registrar .... Dr. Julie SAWYER
88 Director of Auxiliary Services .... Mr. Todd ENLOW
39 Director of Housing .... Mr. E. Thayne KING
38 Director Student Counseling .... Ms. Sheila SELF
96 Director of Purchasing .... Mr. Joseph WILLIAMS
44 Stewards/Annual Giving Coordinator .... Ms. Tina FRAZIER
09 Coordinator Institutional Research .... Vacant

Northeastern State University at Broken Arrow (I)

3100 E New Orleans, Broken Arrow OK 74014
Telephone: (918) 449-6000 Identification: 770372
Accreditation: &NH

† Main campus is Northeastern State University in Tahlequah, OK.

Northeastern State University at Muskogee (J)

2400 W Shawnee, Muskogee OK 74401
Telephone: (918) 683-0040 Identification: 770373
Accreditation: &NH

† Main campus is Northeastern State University in Tahlequah, OK.

Northern Oklahoma College (K)

PO Box 2300, Enid OK 73702
Telephone: (580) 242-6300 Identification: 770374
Accreditation: &NH

† Main campus is Northern Oklahoma College in Tonkawa, OK.

Northern Oklahoma College (L)

PO Box 1869, Stillwater OK 74076
Telephone: (405) 744-2246 Identification: 770375
Accreditation: &NH

† Main campus is Northern Oklahoma College in Tonkawa, OK.

Northern Oklahoma College (M)

1220 E Grand Avenue, PO Box 310,
Tonkawa OK 74653-0310
County: Kay FICE Identification: 003162
Unit ID: 207281
Telephone: (580) 628-6200 Carnegie Class: Assoc/Pub-R-M
FAX Number: (580) 628-6209 Calendar System: Semester
URL: www.noc.edu
Established: 1901 Annual Undergrad Tuition & Fees (In-State): $2,845
Enrollment: 5,006 Coed
Affiliation or Control: State IRS Status: 501(c)3
Highest Offering: Associate Degree
Program: Occupational; 2-Year Principally Bachelor's Creditable
Accreditation: NH, ACBSP, ADNUR, COARC

01 President .... Dr. Cheryl EVANS
05 Vice President for Academic Affairs .... Dr. Judy COLWELL
10 Vice President Financial Affairs .... Mrs. Anita SIMPSON
12 Vice President for Enid Campus .... Dr. Ed VINEYARD
32 Vice President for Student Affairs .... Dr. Mark EDWARDS
26 Vice Pres for Devel/Cmty Rels .... Mrs. Sheri SNYDER
14 Director Information Technology .... Mr. Michael MACHIA
15 Director Human Resources .... Ms. Shannon CRANFORD
20 Dean of Instruction .... Dr. Pamela STINSON
35 Dean of Students-Enid .... Mr. Ronald SHIDEMANTLE
35 Dean of Students-Tonkawa .... Mr. Jason JOHNSON
12 Assoc Vice Pres Stillwater Campus .... Ms. Debbie QUIREY
06 Assoc Vice Pres Enroll Mgt/Registr .... Dr. Rick EDGINGTON
08 Director of Library Services .... Mr. Benjamin HAINLINE
18 Assoc Vice Pres of Physical Plant .... Mr. Larry DYE
41 Athletic Director .... Vacant
29 Director Alumni Relations .... Ms. Kirby HILL
37 Director Student Financial Aid .... Ms. Holly LEE
40 Manager Student Bookstore .... Mrs. Jimilea JANSSON
96 Purchasing Agent .... Ms. Anita BARTLETT

Northwestern Oklahoma State University (N)

709 Oklahoma Boulevard, Alva OK 73717-2799
County: Woods FICE Identification: 003163
Unit ID: 207306
Telephone: (580) 327-1700 Carnegie Class: Master's S
FAX Number: (580) 327-1881 Calendar System: Semester
URL: www.nwosu.edu
Established: 1897 Annual Undergrad Tuition & Fees (In-State): $5,460
Enrollment: 2,299 Coed
Affiliation or Control: State IRS Status: 501(c)3
Highest Offering: Master's
Program: Liberal Arts And General; Teacher Preparatory; Professional
Accreditation: NH, ACBSP, NUR, SW, TED

01 President .... Dr. Janet L. CUNNINGHAM
05 Exec Vice Pres/Chief Acad Affairs .... Dr. Steven L. LOHMANN
11 Vice President for Administration .... Mr. David M. PECHA
26 Assoc VP for University Relations .... Mr. Steven J. VALENCIA
32 Dean of Student Affairs .... Mr. Calleb N. MOSBURG
41 Athletic Director .... Mr. Andrew V. CARTER
06 Registrar .... Mrs. Sheri K. LAHR
37 Director Financial Aid .... Vacant
21 Bursar .... Mrs. Fawn M. KINGCADE
07 Director of Recruitment .... Mrs. Carly WILLIAMS
18 Chief Facilities/Physical Plant .... Mr. Jim DETGEN
15 Human Resource Director .... Mrs. Tami L. COOPER
39 Director of Students/Housing .... Mr. Marcus L. WALLACE
29 Director Alumni Relations .... Mrs. Lizabeth R. RICHEY
38 Director of Student Life/Counselor .... Mrs. Kaylyn L. HANSEN
58 Assoc Dean of Graduate Studies .... Dr. Shawn P. HOLLIDAY

08 Director of Libraries ... Mrs. Susan K. JEFFRIES
09 Institutional Research Specialist ... Ms. Tara D. HALL

Northwestern Oklahoma State University (A)

2929 E Randolph, Enid OK 73701
Telephone: (580) 237-0334 Identification: 770376
Accreditation: &NH

† Main campus is Northwestern Oklahoma State University in Alva, OK.

Northwestern Oklahoma State University (B)

2007 34th Street, Woodward OK 73801
Telephone: (580) 256-0047 Identification: 770377
Accreditation: &NH

† Main campus is Northwestern Oklahoma State University in Alva, OK.

Oklahoma Baptist University (C)

500 W University, Shawnee OK 74804-2590
County: Pottawatomie FICE Identification: 003164
Unit ID: 207403
Telephone: (405) 585-4000 Carnegie Class: Bac/Diverse
FAX Number: N/A Calendar System: Semester
URL: www.okbu.edu
Established: 1910 Annual Undergrad Tuition & Fees: $28,202
Enrollment: 1,979 Coed
Affiliation or Control: Southern Baptist IRS Status: 501(c)3
Highest Offering: Master's
Program: Liberal Arts And General; Teacher Preparatory; Professional
Accreditation: NH, ACBSP, MUS, NURSE, TED

01 President ... Dr. David W. WHITLOCK
05 Provost/Exec Vice Pres Campus Life ... Dr. Robert S. NORMAN
10 Exec VP Business Affs/Admin Svcs ... Mr. Randy L. SMITH
30 Vice Pres University Advancement ... Mr. Will SMALLWOOD
42 Campus Minister ... Mr. Dale M. GRIFFIN
26 Assoc VP University Advancement ... Mrs. Paula GOWER
79 Asst Provost/Dn Humanities/Soc Sci ... Dr. Pam ROBINSON
13 Asst Vice Pres Info Sys/Services ... Mr. Gary NICKERSON
08 Dean Library Services ... Mr. Paul ROBERTS
32 Dean of Students ... Mr. Brandon SKAGGS
29 Exec Director OBU Alumni Assn ... Mrs. Lori R. HAGANS
11 Director of Executive Offices ... Mrs. Tonia KELLOGG
37 Director Student Financial Services ... Mrs. Jonna G. RANEY
12 Director Geiger Center ... Ms. Cynthia K. GATES
06 Dir Academic Records/Registrar ... Ms. Marcia MCQUERRY
20 Academic Director/Asst Registrar ... Mrs. Teri F. WALKER
21 Asst VP Finance/Admin Svcs ... Mrs. Lauri A. FLUKE
21 Controller ... Mr. Steven FLOYD
15 Director of Human Resources ... Mr. Mike JOHNSON
35 Director of Campus Services ... Mr. Larry A. WALKER
19 Chief of University Police ... Mr. David SHANNON
41 Athletic Director ... Mr. Robert DAVENPORT
18 Dir Facilities Mgt & Services ... Mr. George HAINES
96 Director of Purchasing ... Mr. Larry WALKER
84 Dean Enrollment Management ... Mr. Bruce PERKINS
58 Director OBU Graduate School ... Mrs. Shelly FRANCKA
36 Career Planning Counselor ... Vacant
38 Counselor ... Ms. Rilda SMITH
57 Dean of Fine Arts ... Dr. Ken GABRIELSE
81 Dean College of Math and Science ... Dr. Debbie BLUE
73 Dean School Christian Service ... Dr. Mack MCCLELLAN
50 Dean School of Business ... Dr. David C. HOUGHTON
66 Dean School of Nursing ... Mrs. Lepaine MCHENRY
108 Director of Assessment ... Mr. Blake DECKER

Oklahoma Christian University (D)

PO Box 11000, Oklahoma City OK 73136-1100
County: Oklahoma FICE Identification: 003165
Unit ID: 207324
Telephone: (405) 425-5000 Carnegie Class: Master's M
FAX Number: (405) 425-5090 Calendar System: Semester
URL: www.oc.edu
Established: 1950 Annual Undergrad Tuition & Fees: $18,800
Enrollment: 2,271 Coed
Affiliation or Control: Independent Non-Profit IRS Status: 501(c)3
Highest Offering: Master's
Program: Liberal Arts And General; Teacher Preparatory; Professional
Accreditation: NH, ACBSP, CIDA, ENG, MUS, NURSE, TED

01 President ... Mr. John DESTEIGUER
03 Executive Vice President ... Dr. William GOAD
05 Vice Pres for Academic Affairs ... Dr. Scott LAMASCUS
20 Associate VP for Academic Affairs ... Dr. Don DREW
11 Exec Dir of University Services ... Mr. Kinney BRYANT
10 Vice President for Finance ... Mr. Jeff BINGHAM
27 VP for Marketing ... Mrs. Risa FORRESTER
29 Exec Dir for Alumni Relations ... Mr. Bob LASHLEY
44 Vice Pres Estate/Planned Giving ... Mr. Stephen ECK
32 Vice Pres and Dean of Student Life ... Mr. Neil ARTER
35 Assoc Dean of Students ... Mr. Jeff BENNETT
84 Vice President for Admissions ... Mrs. Risa FORRESTER
14 Vice President for Information Tech ... Mr. John HERMES
43 Vice President & General Counsel ... Mr. Stephen ECK
30 Vice President for Advancement ... Mr. Kent ALLEN
58 Dean of Graduate Programs ... Dr. Don DREW
107 Dean Col of Professional Studies ... Dr. Phil LEWIS
73 Dean College of Biblical Studies ... Dr. Alan MARTIN
49 Dean College Arts & Sciences ... Dr. David LOWRY
06 Registrar ... Dr. Mickey D. BANISTER
08 Library Director ... Mrs. Tamie L. WILLIS
19 Chief of Police Dept ... Mr. John MATLOCK
41 Athletic Director ... Mr. Curtis JANZ
18 Director of Building Maintenance ... Mr. Cary FALLING
26 Assoc Director Marketing Services ... Mr. Wes MCKINZIE
37 Dir Student Financial Services ... Mr. Clint LARUE
104 Director of International Programs ... Mr. John OSBORNE
15 Human Resources Director ... Mr. Lynn HOOPER
31 Director of Church Relations ... Mr. Bob ROWLEY
42 Assoc Dean for Spiritual Life ... Mr. Chance VANOVER
89 Dir of Freshman Programs ... Mrs. Amy ROBERTS
88 Director of Creative Services ... Mr. Judson COPELAND
40 Manager of Bookstore ... Mr. James MENCER
21 Exec Dir of Accounting & Budgets ... Mr. Rory WAIDE
21 Controller ... Mr. Chris BOWMAN
07 Director of Admissions ... Mr. Michael MITCHELL
36 Director of Career Services ... Mr. Mark CHAN
85 International Student Adviser ... Mrs. Tamara J. NEWELL
38 Director of Counseling Services ... Dr. Sheldon ADKINS
88 Director of Student Services ... Mrs. Amy JANZEN
28 Multicultural & Service Learning ... Mr. Gary JONES

Oklahoma City Community College (E)

7777 S May Avenue, Oklahoma City OK 73159-4444
County: Oklahoma FICE Identification: 010391
Unit ID: 207449
Telephone: (405) 682-1611 Carnegie Class: Assoc/Pub-U-SC
FAX Number: (405) 682-7585 Calendar System: Other
URL: www.occc.edu
Established: 1972 Annual Undergrad Tuition & Fees (In-District): $3,090
Enrollment: 14,199 Coed
Affiliation or Control: State/Local IRS Status: 501(c)3
Highest Offering: Associate Degree
Program: Occupational; 2-Year Principally Bachelor's Creditable
Accreditation: NH, ACBSP, ADNUR, EMT, OTA, PTAA

01 President ... Dr. Paul W. SECHRIST
03 Executive Vice President ... Dr. Jerry STEWARD
43 Legal Counsel ... Dr. Nancy GERRITY
05 Vice President Academic Affairs ... Dr. Felix J. AQUINO
32 VP Enrollment/Student Services ... Dr. Marion PADEN
15 Vice Pres Human Resources ... Vacant
10 Vice President Business & Finance ... Dr. John BOYD
31 Vice Pres Community Development ... Mr. Steven BLOOMBERG
20 Associate VP Academic Affairs ... Mr. Greg GARDNER
37 Dean Student Financial Support Svcs ... Mr. Harold CASE
38 Dean of Student Development ... Dr. Liz LARGENT
06 Registrar ... Mr. Alan STRINGFELLOW
30 Exec Director Inst Advancement ... Mr. Lealon TAYLOR
45 Executive Director of Planning ... Mr. Stu HARVEY
13 Dir Info Tech Infrastructure ... Mr. David ANDERSON
88 Director Recreation and Fitness ... Ms. Roxanna BUTLER
44 Director of Development ... Ms. Jennifer HARDT
88 Director Students Support Svcs ... Ms. Lisa FISHER
07 Dir of Recruitment & Admissions ... Mr. Jon HORINEK
35 Director of Student Life ... Ms. Erin LOGAN
18 Director of Facilities Management ... Mr. J. B. MESSER
40 Director of Student Store ... Ms. Brenda REINKE
88 The Professional Development Inst ... Mr. John VANHOOK
26 Dir of Marketing & Public Relations ... Mr. Cordell JORDAN
25 Director of Grants & Contracts ... Mr. Joe SWALWELL
12 Director OKC Downtown College ... Dr. Gus PEKARA
36 Director Career Transitions Program ... Ms. Nora PUGH-SEEMSTER
88 Dir Child Development/Lab School ... Dr. Mary MCCOY
21 Bursar ... Ms. Cynthia GARY
08 Director of Library Services ... Ms. Barbara KING
09 Dir Institutional Effectiveness ... Dr. Janet PERRY
88 Director Cooperative Alliances ... Ms. Alexa MASHLAN
22 EEO/AA Compliance Officer ... Ms. Jana LEGAKO
31 Dir Community Outreach & Education ... Ms. Jessica MARTINEZ-BROOKS
88 Coord OCCC Capitol Hill Center ... Mr. Sergio GALLEGOS
96 Director of Purchasing ... Ms. Lori WALKER
19 Dir Emergency Planning/Risk Mgmt ... Vacant

Oklahoma City University (F)

2501 N Blackwelder, Oklahoma City OK 73106-1493
County: Oklahoma FICE Identification: 003166
Unit ID: 207458
Telephone: (405) 208-5000 Carnegie Class: Master's L
FAX Number: (405) 208-5916 Calendar System: Semester
URL: www.okcu.edu
Established: 1904 Annual Undergrad Tuition & Fees: $28,438
Enrollment: 3,300 Coed
Affiliation or Control: United Methodist IRS Status: 501(c)3
Highest Offering: First Professional Degree
Program: Liberal Arts And General; Teacher Preparatory; Professional
Accreditation: NH, ACBSP, LAW, MACTE, MUS, NUR, TED

01 President ... Mr. Robert H. HENRY
05 Provost/Vice Pres Academic Affairs ... Dr. Susan C. BARBER
30 Vice Pres University Advancement ... Mr. Marty O'GWYNN
26 Vice Pres Univ/Church Relations ... Rev. Margaret A. BALL
10 Chief Financial Officer ... Ms. Donna S. NANCE
32 Vice President for Student Affairs ... Dr. Richard HALL
84 Asst VP/Dean Enrollment Services ... Mr. Kevin WINDHOLZ
35 Dean of Students ... Dr. Liz DONNELLY
06 Registrar ... Mr. Charles MONNOT
09 Director of Institutional Research ... Dr. Kelly MEREDITH
08 Director Dulaney-Browne Library ... Dr. Victoria SWINNEY
37 Director of Financial Aid ... Ms. Denise FLIS
27 Director of Communications ... Ms. Sandy PANTLIK
15 Chief Human Resources Officer ... Ms. Joey CROSLIN
92 Director of Honors Program ... Vacant
07 Director of Undergrad Admissions ... Ms. Michelle COOK
18 Chief Facilities/Physical Plant ... Mr. Jeff CASTLEBERRY
29 Director Alumni Relations ... Mr. Cary PIRRONG
36 Director Career Planning/Placement ... Mr. Josh WADDELL
49 Dean College of Arts & Sciences ... Dr. Mark Y. DAVIES
50 Dean School of Business ... Dr. Steve AGEE
61 Dean School of Law ... Dr. Valerie COUCH
64 Dean School of Music ... Mr. Mark PARKER
66 Dean of School of Nursing ... Vacant
73 Dean School of Religion ... Dr. Mark DAVIES
88 Dean School of Amer Dance/Arts Mgt ... Mr. John BEDFORD
100 Chief of Staff ... Mr. Craig KNUTSON

Oklahoma Panhandle State University (G)

Box 430, Goodwell OK 73939-0430
County: Texas FICE Identification: 003174
Unit ID: 207351
Telephone: (580) 349-2611 Carnegie Class: Bac/Diverse
FAX Number: (580) 349-2302 Calendar System: Semester
URL: www.opsu.edu
Established: 1909 Annual Undergrad Tuition & Fees (In-State): $6,099
Enrollment: 1,382 Coed
Affiliation or Control: State IRS Status: 501(c)3
Highest Offering: Baccalaureate
Program: Liberal Arts And General
Accreditation: NH, NUR, TED

01 President ... Dr. David A. BRYANT
05 Vice Pres Academic Affairs/Outreach ... Dr. Wayne MANNING
10 Vice Pres Business & Fiscal Affairs ... Mr. Larry PETERS
47 Dean Agriculture ... Dr. Peter CAMFIELD
50 Dean Business & Technology ... Ms. Diane MURPHEY
53 Dean Education ... Dr. R. Wayne STEWART
57 Dean Liberal Arts ... Dr. Sara RICHTER
66 Dean Science/Mathematics/Nursing ... Dr. Justin COLLINS
32 Dean of Student Affairs ... Ms. Jessica LOFLAND
06 Registrar/Director of Admissions ... Mr. Bobby JENKINS
37 Director Student Financial Aid ... Ms. Lori FERGUSON
09 Director Institutional Research ... Mr. Nick TUTTLE
13 Director of Technology ... Mr. Howard HENDERSON
15 Director Personnel Services ... Ms. Dana COLLINS
08 Director of Library ... Ms. Alton (Tony) HARDMAN
21 Comptroller ... Mr. Benny DAIN
38 Director Counseling/Career Services ... Ms. Christi HALE
26 Campus Communications Director ... Ms. Danae MOORE
41 Athletic Officer ... Dr. R. Wayne STEWART
40 Bookstore Manager ... Ms. Mandy BATENHORST
18 Director Physical Plant ... Mr. Bob SCOTT
29 Director Alumni Relations ... Mr. Nick TUTTLE
96 Director of Purchasing ... Ms. Elizabeth MCMURPHY

Oklahoma State University (H)

Stillwater OK 74078
County: Payne FICE Identification: 003170
Unit ID: 207388
Telephone: (405) 744-5000 Carnegie Class: RU/H
FAX Number: N/A Calendar System: Semester
URL: osu.okstate.edu/
Established: 1890 Annual Undergrad Tuition & Fees (In-State): $7,442
Enrollment: 25,544 Coed
Affiliation or Control: State IRS Status: 501(c)3
Highest Offering: Doctorate
Program: Liberal Arts And General; Teacher Preparatory; Professional
Accreditation: NH, AAB, BUS, BUSA, CACREP, CIDA, CLPSY, COPSY, DIETD, DIETI, ENG, ENGT, FOR, JOUR, LSAR, MFCD, MUS, NRPA, SCPSY, SP, TED, THEA, VET

01 President ... Dr. V. Burns HARGIS
04 Exec Assistant to the President ... Ms. Deborah LANE
05 Interim Provost & Sr Vice Pres ... Dr. Pamela FRY
10 Vice Pres Administration & Finance ... Mr. Joseph B. WEAVER, JR.
03 Vice President for Univ Relations ... Mr. Gary C. CLARK
32 Vice President Student Affairs ... Dr. Lee E. BIRD
46 Vice Pres Research/Tech Transfer ... Dr. Stephen W. MCKEEVER
28 Assoc VP Institutional Diversity ... Dr. Jason KIRKSEY
47 Interim VP Agric Programs & Dean ... Dr. Mike WOODS
41 Vice President Athletic Programs ... Mr. Mike HOLDER
20 Interim Assoc Provost & Sr VP ... Dr. Brenda MASTERS
21 Assoc Vice President & Controller ... Ms. Kathy ELLIOTT
15 Asst Vice Pres Human Resources ... Ms. Jamie A. PAYNE
102 President & CEO OSU Foundation ... Mr. Kirk JEWELL
29 President & CEO OSU Alumni Assoc ... Mr. Larry SHELL
88 Pres Ctr for Innovation & Econ Dev ... Vacant
54 Dean Engineering ... Dr. Paul J. TIKALSKY
49 Dean Arts & Sciences ... Dr. Bret DANILOWICZ
50 Dean Spears School of Business ... Vacant
53 Dean Education ... Dr. Pamela CARROLL
59 Dean College of Human Sciences ... Dr. Stephan M. WILSON
74 Dean Veterinary Medicine ... Dr. Jean E. SANDER
58 Assoc Provost/Dean Graduate College ... Dr. Sheryl TUCKER
08 Dean Library ... Ms. Sheila G. JOHNSON

23 Director University Health Services ....Mr. Stephen K. ROGERS
27 Director Communication Services ....Mr. Gary SHUTT
26 Vice Pres Enroll Mgmt/Univ Mktg ....Mr. Kyle WRAY
07 Director Undergraduate Admissions .... Ms. Christine CRENSHAW
13 Chief Information Officer ....Ms. Darlene HIGHTOWER
43 Board of Regents Legal Counsel ....Mr. Charles E. DRAKE
06 Registrar ....Dr. K. Celeste CAMPBELL
39 Director University Housing ....Dr. Matthew S. BROWN
38 Director University Counseling Svcs ....Dr. Suzanne M. BURKS
37 Sr Director Financial Aid ....Dr. Charles W. BRUCE
92 Director Honors College ....Dr. Robert L. SPURRIER
36 Director Career Services ....Ms. Pam EHLERS
19 Chief Public Safety Officer ....Mr. Michael ROBINSON
25 Dir Grants/Contracts/Financial Admn ....Dr. Robert DIXON
22 Director Equal Opportunity ....Dr. John P. FULLER
24 Asst Prov/Dir Inst Tch/Lrng Excel ....Ms. Christine ORMSBEE
09 Director Inst Research & Info Mgmt ....Dr. Christie HAWKINS
96 Director of Purchasing ....Ms. Sharon S. TOY
18 Chief Facilities Officer ....Mr. Richard KRYSIAK
88 Asst VP/Director Student Union ....Mr. Mitch KILCREASE
40 Asst Dir Student Union Bookstore ....Mr. Lance HINKLE
85 Manager Intl Students & Scholars ....Mr. Tim T. HUFF

Oklahoma State University Center for Health Sciences College of Osteopathic Medicine (A)

1111 W 17th Street, Tulsa OK 74107-1898
Telephone: (918) 582-1972 FICE Identification: 011282
Accreditation: &NH, FEPAC, OSTEO

† Main campus is Oklahoma State University in Stillwater, OK.

Oklahoma State University Institute of Technology-Okmulgee (B)

1801 E Fourth Street, Okmulgee OK 74447-3901
County: Okmulgee FICE Identification: 003172
Unit ID: 207564
Telephone: (918) 293-4678 Carnegie Class: Assoc/Pub4
FAX Number: (918) 293-4644 Calendar System: Trimester
URL: www.osuit.edu
Established: 1946 Annual Undergrad Tuition & Fees (In-State): $4,216
Enrollment: 2,990 Coed
Affiliation or Control: State IRS Status: 501(c)3
Highest Offering: Baccalaureate
Program: Occupational; 2-Year Principally Bachelor's Creditable; Technical Emphasis
Accreditation: NH, ADNUR, CS

01 President ....Dr. Bill PATH
03 Executive VP ....Dr. Linda AVANT
10 VP Fiscal Services ....Mr. Jim SMITH
05 VP Academic Affairs ....Dr. Greg MOSIER
84 VP Enrollment Management ....Ms. Ina AGNEW
26 VP University & External Relations ..Ms. Anita GORDY-WATKINS
76 Allied Health Sciences ....Ms. Jana MARTIN
49 Arts & Sciences ....Dr. Mark ALLEN
72 Automotive Technologies ....Mr. Bill VOORHEES
72 Construction Technologies ....Mr. Steve OLMSTEAD
88 Culinary Arts ....Mr. Rene JUNGO
54 Engineering Technologies ....Mr. Dolph HAYDEN
88 Heavy Equipment & Vehicle Institute ....Mr. Roy ACHEMIRE
77 Information Technologies ....Dr. Scott NEWMAN
88 Visual Communications ....Mr. James MCCULLOUGH
37 Dir Student Financial Services ....Ms. Diana SANDERS
45 Dir Inst Assessment & Research ....Vacant
13 Dir Computer Information Systems ....Mr. Kevin HULETT
07 Dir Admissions & Records ....Ms. Genie TRAMMELL
15 Dir Human Resources ....Ms. Paula NORTH
18 Dir Physical Plant Services ....Mr. Mark PITCHER
88 Dir Student Union & Auxiliary Svcs ....Mr. James BYRD
32 Director Student Life ....Mr. Bruce FORCE
39 Director Residential Life ....Mr. Devin DEBOCK
08 Dir Learning Resource Center ....Ms. Jenny DUNCAN
96 Director Purchasing ....Mrs. Chandra MILLER
12 Dir MAIP-Pryor Campus ....Mr. Scott FRY
06 Registrar ....Ms. Crystal BOWLES
38 Counselor ....Ms. Kathy AVERY
40 Manager Bookstore ....Ms. Barbara WRIGHT
27 Public Relations Officer ....Ms. Shari ERWIN
19 Campus Police Chief ....Mr. Matt WOOLIVER
04 Admin Asst to President ....Ms. Claudette BUTCHER
103 Dir Econ Dev & Training Ctr ....Mr. Mark HAYS
26 Director of Marketing ....Ms. Shari ERWIN
09 Director of Institutional Research ....Ms. Michelle CANAN
106 Director of Distance Learning ....Ms. Kari CHANCEY
88 Dir Tutorial Ctr/Acad Accommodation ....Mr. Chad SPURLOCK

Oklahoma State University - Oklahoma City (C)

900 N Portland Ave, Oklahoma City OK 73107-6195
County: Oklahoma FICE Identification: 009647
Unit ID: 207397
Telephone: (405) 947-4421 Carnegie Class: Assoc/Pub4
FAX Number: (405) 945-3289 Calendar System: Semester
URL: www.osuokc.edu
Established: 1961 Annual Undergrad Tuition & Fees (In-State): $3,308
Enrollment: 7,590 Coed
Affiliation or Control: State IRS Status: 501(c)3
Highest Offering: Baccalaureate
Program: Occupational; 2-Year Principally Bachelor's Creditable; Technical Emphasis
Accreditation: NH, ADNUR, @DIETT, DMS

01 President ....Ms. Natalie SHIRLEY
05 Vice President Academic Affairs ....Dr. Bill PINK
10 Vice President Finance & Operations ....Ms. Ronda REECE
32 Vice President Student Services ....Mr. Brad WILLIAMS
50 Vice Pres for Business and Industry ....Ms. Robin ROBERTS KRIEGER
20 Associate VP Academic Affairs ....Ms. Kim PEARSALL
84 Director Enrollment Management ....Mr. Kyle WILLIAMS
30 Associate Dir Development OSU-OKC ....Ms. Sara FURR
13 Sr Dir Information Services ....Mr. Jonathan FOZARD
08 Director Library Services ....Mr. David ROBINSON
37 Director Financial Aid ....Ms. Bessie CARTER
15 Director Human Resources ....Ms. Melissa HERREN
18 Dir of Building Maint/Energy Mgr ....Mr. Mickey FULLER
26 Sr Dir of Marketing/Communications ....Mr. David JOPLIN
07 Assistant Director of Admissions ....Ms. Melissa GARNER
103 Director Workforce Development ....Ms. Adrianne COVINGTON-GRAHAM
29 Director Alumni Relations ....Dr. JoElla FLINTON
96 Director of Purchasing ....Ms. Sharon FITZPATRICK
06 Registrar ....Ms. Keila WHITAKER
25 Sr Dir Institutional Grants ....Ms. Amber COLE

Oklahoma State University - Tulsa (D)

700 N Greenwood Avenue, Tulsa OK 74106-0702
Telephone: (918) 594-8000 Identification: 666053
Accreditation: &NH

† Main campus is Oklahoma State University in Stillwater, OK.

Oklahoma Technical College (E)

4444 South Sheridan, Tulsa OK 74145-1122
Telephone: (918) 895-7500 Identification: 666718
Accreditation: ACICS

† Main campus is Community Care College in Tulsa, OK.

Oklahoma Wesleyan University (F)

2201 Silver Lake Road, Bartlesville OK 74006-6299
County: Washington FICE Identification: 003151
Unit ID: 206835
Telephone: (918) 333-6151 Carnegie Class: Bac/Diverse
FAX Number: (918) 335-6228 Calendar System: Semester
URL: www.okwu.edu
Established: 1910 Annual Undergrad Tuition & Fees: $22,252
Enrollment: 1,243 Coed
Affiliation or Control: Wesleyan Church IRS Status: 501(c)3
Highest Offering: Master's
Program: 2-Year Principally Bachelor's Creditable; Liberal Arts And General; Teacher Preparatory; Professional
Accreditation: NH, IACBE, NURSE, TED

01 President ....Dr. Everett G. PIPER
05 Exec Vice Pres for Academic Affairs ....Vacant
10 Vice President for Business Affairs ....Mrs. Andrea ZEPEDA
30 Vice President for Development ....Vacant
32 Vice President for Student Life ....Mr. Kyle WHITE
88 VP for Academic Program Development ....Dr. Brett ANDREWS
07 Vice President Admissions ....Mr. John MEANS
20 Assoc VP for Academic Affairs ....Dr. Mark WEETER
42 Assoc VP for Student Dev ....Rev. Ben ROTZ
53 Dean of School of Education ....Dr. Sheldon BUXTON
73 Dean of School of Religion & Phil ....Dr. Mark WEETER
49 Dean of School of Arts & Sciences ....Mrs. Gail RICHARDSON
50 Dean of School of Business ....Dr. Brett ANDREWS
66 Dean School of Nursing ....Mrs. Rebecca LE
07 Director Adult/Grad Admissions ....Mrs. Samantha PETERSON
106 Director of Online Learning ....Dr. Devon SMITH
108 Director of Assessment ....Mrs. Julia CROUCH
21 Director of Accounting ....Mrs. Margaret FRIEND
14 Director of Computer Services ....Mr. Eric GOINGS
37 Director of Financial Aid ....Mrs. Kandi MOLDER
41 Athletic Director ....Mr. Mark MOLDER
29 Director of Alumni ....Mrs. Janet ODDEN
06 Registrar ....Mrs. Cindy RIFFE
04 Executive Assistant to President ....Mrs. Kathy LINDQUIST
15 Human Resources Administrator ....Mrs. Jessica MORROW
33 Men's Resident Director ....Mr. Chris BREILAND
34 Women's Resident Director ....Ms. Sheresa GRATE
23 Director Student Health ....Mrs. Debra COOK
18 Director of Buildings and Grounds ....Mr. Dalton HIGGINS
40 Bookstore Manager ....Mrs. Jessica JARRETT

Oklahoma Wesleyan University (G)

10810 E 45th Street, Tulsa OK 74146
Telephone: (918) 728-6143 Identification: 770378
Accreditation: &NH

† Main campus is Oklahoma Wesleyan University in Bartlesville, OK.

Oral Roberts University (H)

7777 S Lewis Avenue, Tulsa OK 74171-0003
County: Tulsa FICE Identification: 003985
Unit ID: 207582
Telephone: (918) 495-6161 Carnegie Class: Master's S
FAX Number: (918) 495-6033 Calendar System: Semester
URL: www.oru.edu
Established: 1965 Annual Undergrad Tuition & Fees: $22,508
Enrollment: 3,335 Coed
Affiliation or Control: Independent Non-Profit IRS Status: 501(c)3
Highest Offering: Doctorate
Program: Liberal Arts And General; Teacher Preparatory; Professional
Accreditation: NH, ACBSP, ENG, MUS, NURSE, SW, TED, THEOL

01 President ....Dr. William M. WILSON
03 Provost ....Vacant
10 EVP and Chief Financial Officer ....Vacant
11 EVP and Chief Operations Officer ....Mr. Tim PHILLEY
30 EVP for University Advancement ....Mr. Ossie MILLS
05 VP Academic Affairs/Acting Provost ....Dr. Debra SOWELL
84 VP for Enrollment Management ....Dr. Nancy BRAINARD
43 VP and General Counsel ....Mr. Terry KOLLMORGEN
32 Vice President Student Life ....Dr. Dan GUAJARDO
13 Chief Information Officer ....Vacant
21 Controller ....Ms. Michelle MCMILLAN
42 Dean of Spiritual Formation ....Dr. Clarence BOYD
08 Dean Learning Resources ....Dr. William JERNIGAN
54 Dean Col of Science & Engineering ....Dr. Kenneth WEED
49 Dean Col of Arts & Cultural Studies ....Dr. Mark HALL
73 Dean College Theology/Ministry ....Dr. Thomson MATHEW
50 Dean College of Business ....Dr. Steve GREENE
66 Dean & Chairman College of Nursing ....Dr. Kenda JEZEK
53 Dean College of Education ....Dr. Kim BOYD
33 Dean of Men ....Mr. Matthew OLSEN
34 Dean of Women ....Ms. Lori SYLVESTER
09 Director of Institutional Research ....Dr. Cal EASTERLING
41 Director for Athletics ....Mr. Mike CARTER
25 Director of Sponsored Programs ....Ms. Kim FALCON
38 Director of Student Counseling ....Ms. Michelle TAYLOR
89 Director of Freshmen Studies ....Mr. Tom BELLATTI
92 Director of Honors Program ....Dr. John KORSTAD
88 Director Student Accounts ....Mr. Steve THANNICKAL
96 Director of Purchasing ....Ms. Jeannine HORTON
06 Registrar ....Mr. David FULMER
07 Director of Admissions ....Mr. Chris BELCHER
37 Director of Financial Aid ....Mr. William WOMACK
29 Director of Alumni Relations ....Mr. Jesse PISORS
19 Director of Security/Safety ....Mr. Jerry ISAACS
15 Director Human Resources/Risk Mgmt ....Dr. Karen ADAMS
36 Director of Student Placement ....Ms. Allison JONES
26 Director of Public Relations ....Mr. Jeremy BURTON

Phillips Theological Seminary (I)

901 N Mingo Road, Tulsa OK 74116-5612
County: Tulsa FICE Identification: 025602
Unit ID: 414966
Telephone: (918) 610-8303 Carnegie Class: Spec/Faith
FAX Number: (918) 610-8404 Calendar System: Semester
URL: www.ptstulsa.edu
Established: 1907 Annual Graduate Tuition & Fees: $10,080
Enrollment: 150 Coed
Affiliation or Control: Christian Church (Disciples Of Christ)
IRS Status: 501(c)3
Highest Offering: Doctorate; No Undergraduates
Program: Professional; Religious Emphasis
Accreditation: NH, THEOL

01 President ....Gary PELUSO-VERDEND
51 Special Assistant to the President ....John M. IMBLER
05 Vice Pres Academic Affairs & Dean ....Nancy Claire PITTMAN
11 Vice President Administration ....Lora CONGER
108 Assoc Dean Assessment and Faculty ....Joseph BESSLER
07 Assoc Dean Admissions/Student Svcs ....Belva Brown JORDAN
20 Assoc Dn Contextual Ed/Church Rels ....John THOMAS, JR.
10 Chief Financial Officer ....Lora CONGER
88 Director Doctor of Ministry Program ....Kathleen D. MCCALLIE
07 Director of Recruitment ....Josh LINTON
37 Director Student Financial Aid ....Katrina MORRISON
08 Director of Library ....Sandy SHAPOVAL
44 Director of Planned Giving ....Virginia WALKER
29 Director of Alumni Relations ....Geoffrey BREWSTER
44 Annual Fund Program Directcor ....Malisa PIERCE
26 Dir Communications/Public Relations ....Sara E. SMITH
06 Registrar ....Toni WINE IMBLER
04 Executive Assistant to President ....Mary E. MCGILVRAY

Platt College (J)

201 N Eastern Avenue, Moore OK 73160
Telephone: (405) 912-3260 Identification: 770585
Accreditation: ACCSC, COARC

† Main campus is Platt College in Tulsa, OK.

Platt College (K)

2727 W Memorial Road, Oklahoma City OK 73134
Telephone: (405) 749-2433 Identification: 770584
Accreditation: ACCSC

† Main campus is Platt College in Tulsa, OK.

Platt College (L)

3801 S Sheridan, Tulsa OK 74145-1132
County: Tulsa FICE Identification: 023068
Unit ID: 245962
Telephone: (918) 663-9000 Carnegie Class: Assoc/PrivFP
FAX Number: (918) 622-1240 Calendar System: Other
URL: www.plattcolleges.edu
Established: 1979 Annual Undergrad Tuition & Fees: $29,900

Enrollment: 528 Coed
Affiliation or Control: Proprietary IRS Status: Proprietary
Highest Offering: Baccalaureate
Program: Occupational
Accreditation: ACCSC, ACFEI

01 President Mr. Mike A. PUGLIESE
05 Director of Campus Mr. Jeremy COOPER
66 Director of Nursing LPN Program Ms. Ella ABELA
07 Director of Admission & Marketing Mr. Richard DIXON

Platt College-OKC Central (A)

309 South Ann Arbor Avenue,
Oklahoma City OK 73128-1112
Telephone: (405) 946-7799 Identification: 666341
Accreditation: ACCSC, ACFEI, SURGT

† Main campus is Platt College in Tulsa, OK.

Redlands Community College (B)

1300 S Country Club Road, El Reno OK 73036-5304
County: Canadian FICE Identification: 003156
Unit ID: 207069
Telephone: (405) 262-2552 Carnegie Class: Assoc/Pub-S-SC
FAX Number: (405) 422-1200 Calendar System: Semester
URL: www.redlandscc.edu
Established: 1938 Annual Undergrad Tuition & Fees (In-District): $3,330
Enrollment: 2,560 Coed
Affiliation or Control: State/Local IRS Status: 501(c)3
Highest Offering: Associate Degree
Program: Occupational; 2-Year Principally Bachelor's Creditable
Accreditation: NH, ADNUR

01 President Dr. Larry F. DEVANE
05 Vice President Instruction Mr. Bill BAKER
103 VP Workforce/Economic Development Mr. Jack BRYANT
10 Vice Pres Finance/Campus Services Ms. Jena MARR
30 VP Inst Advancement/Student Svcs Mr. Joel DRURY
46 VP Undergrad Research/Strat Plng Dr. Amanda EVERT
18 Director Physical Plant Mr. Richard BUCHHOLZ
66 Director Nursing/Allied Health Mrs. Cathy SALES
72 Dir Liberal Studies/Mgmt Science Dr. Laura GRUNTMEIR
81 Dir Math/Science/Developmental Stds Ms. Barbara KNOP-COX
08 Director Learning Resource Center Mrs. Christine DETTLAFF
06 Registrar/Director Student Records Mr. Dennis HARRIS
37 Director Financial Aid Ms. Paris PRZEKURAT
41 Athletic Director Mr. Matt NEWGENT
14 Director Administrative Computing Mr. Troy MILLIGAN
22 Director of Upward Bound Mrs. Linda MCDOWN
09 Director of Institutional Research Mr. Troy MILLIGAN
84 Director Enrollment Management Mrs. Tricia HOBSON
21 Associate Business Officer Mrs. Maxine CALVERT
56 Coordinator Alternative Education Ms. Arlie SCHRODER
36 Coordinator Career Services Ms. Jackie HARROL
15 Coordinator Personnel/Payroll Mrs. Kim ANDRADE
26 Coordinator Public Information Ms. Carlee NICKLOS
29 Coordinator Alumni Relations Mrs. Jill WORTHINGTON
39 Coordinator of Resident Life Ms. Margie MOORE

Rogers State University (C)

1701 W Will Rogers Boulevard,
Claremore OK 74017-2099
County: Rogers FICE Identification: 003168
Unit ID: 207661
Telephone: (918) 343-7777 Carnegie Class: Bac/Assoc
FAX Number: (918) 343-7898 Calendar System: Semester
URL: www.rsu.edu
Established: 1909 Annual Undergrad Tuition & Fees (In-State): $5,351
Enrollment: 4,774 Coed
Affiliation or Control: State IRS Status: 501(c)3
Highest Offering: Baccalaureate
Program: 2-Year Principally Bachelor's Creditable; Liberal Arts And General; Business Emphasis
Accreditation: NH, ADNUR, EMT, NUR

01 President Dr. Larry D. RICE
05 Vice President for Academic Affairs Dr. Richard BECK
03 Exec VP for Admin & Finance Mr. Tom VOLTURO
30 Vice President for Development Dr. Maynard PHILLIPS
32 Vice Pres for Student Affairs Dr. Tobie TITSWORTH
09 Asst VP Accountability & Academics Dr. Mary MILLIKIN
31 Director of Innovation Center Ms. Jeri KOEHLER
12 Director Pryor Campus Ms. Sherry ALEXANDER
12 Provost Bartlesville Campus Mr. Bill BEIERSCHMITT
50 Dean School of Business & Tech Dr. Bruce GARRISON
83 Dean School of Liberal Arts Dr. Frank ELWELL
81 Dean Sch of Math/Sci/Hlth Sci Dr. Keith MARTIN
04 Assistant to the President Vacant
35 Director of Student Development Ms. Misty SMITH
08 Director of the Library Mr. J. Alan LAWLESS
07 Director of Admissions Ms. Joy Lin HUSTED
06 Registrar Mr. David BARRON
29 Director Alumni & Special Events Ms. Marisa LITTLEFIELD
21 Comptroller/Asst Vice Pres Bus Affs Mr. Mark MEADORS
04 Exec Assistant to the President Ms. Rhonda SPURLOCK
18 Director Physical Plant Mr. Leonard SZOPINSKI
19 Director Campus Public Safety Mr. Gary BOERGERMANN
27 Director Public Relations Mr. David HAMBY
37 Director of Financial Aid Ms. Kelly HICKS
91 Director Administrative Computing Ms. Cathy BURNS
90 Director Information Technology Mr. Brian REEVES
15 Employment & Benefits Coordinator Ms. Kristi MALLETT
41 Director of Athletics Vacant
39 Director Residential Life Ms. Kyla SHORT
23 Director Student Health Clinic Ms. Lisa MARTIN

Rogers State University-Bartlesville (D)

401 South Dewey Avenue, Bartlesville OK 74003
Telephone: (918) 338-8000 Identification: 770379
Accreditation: &NH

† Main campus is Rogers State University in Claremore, OK.

Rogers State University-Pryor (E)

421 South Elliot, Pryor OK 74361
Telephone: (918) 825-6117 Identification: 770380
Accreditation: &NH

† Main campus is Rogers State University in Claremore, OK.

Rose State College (F)

6420 SE 15th, Midwest City OK 73110-2799
County: Oklahoma FICE Identification: 009185
Unit ID: 207670
Telephone: (405) 733-7311 Carnegie Class: Assoc/Pub-S-SC
FAX Number: (405) 733-7399 Calendar System: Semester
URL: www.rose.edu
Established: 1970 Annual Undergrad Tuition & Fees (In-District): $2,955
Enrollment: 7,956 Coed
Affiliation or Control: State/Local IRS Status: 501(c)3
Highest Offering: Associate Degree
Program: Occupational; 2-Year Principally Bachelor's Creditable
Accreditation: NH, ADNUR, CAHIIM, COARC, DA, DH, MLTAD, RAD

01 President Dr. Jeanie WEBB
05 Vice President for Academic Affairs Dr. Frances HENDRIX
10 Vice President for Business Affairs Mr. Keith OGANS
32 Vice President for Student Affairs Dr. Jeanie WEBB
14 Vice President for Info Technology Mr. John PRIMO
103 Vice President for Workforce Devel Mr. Stan GREIL
84 Asoc Vice Pres Enrollment Mgmt Mr. Dean FISHER
20 Associate VP Academic Affairs Dr. Jeff CALDWELL
35 Assoc Vice Pres for Student Life Dr. Kent LASHLEY
30 Exec Dir Institutional Advancement Ms. Lisa PITSIRI
15 Exec Dir Human Res/Affirm Act Ofcr Ms. Kim DELK
06 Registrar/Dir Admissions & Records Ms. Mechelle AITSON-ROESSLER
37 Director Financial Aid Mr. Steve DAFFER
26 Director Marketing/Public Relations Mr. John CAIN
31 Director Community Learning Center Mr. Joey DAVAULT
18 Director Operations Mr. Ardie RODGERS
41 Dir Health & Wellness Activities Mr. Chris LELAND
09 Dir Information Sys/Inst Research Ms. Isabelle BILLEN
21 Director of Finance Mr. Raymond BLANKE
36 Director Spec Svcs/Student Outreach Dr. Joanne STAFFORD
25 Dir Grants and Contracts Dr. Alan NEITZEL
29 Director Alumni Relations Ms. Lindsay LANCASTER
08 Dean Learning Resources Center Mr. Chris MEYER
50 Dean Business & Info Tech Division Mr. Art ZENNER
54 Dean Engineering & Science Division Dr. Wayne JONES
79 Dean Humanities Division Dr. Claudia BUCKMASTER
76 Dean Health Sciences Division Mr. Dan POINTS
83 Dean Social Sciences Division Dr. Bret WOOD

St. Gregory's University (G)

1900 W MacArthur, Shawnee OK 74804-2499
County: Pottawatomie FICE Identification: 003183
Unit ID: 207689
Telephone: (405) 878-5100 Carnegie Class: Bac/Diverse
FAX Number: (405) 878-5198 Calendar System: Semester
URL: www.stgregorys.edu
Established: 1875 Annual Undergrad Tuition & Fees: $20,765
Enrollment: 711 Coed
Affiliation or Control: Roman Catholic IRS Status: 501(c)3
Highest Offering: Master's
Program: Liberal Arts And General; Technical Emphasis
Accreditation: NH

01 President Mr. Gregory MAIN
03 Executive Vice President Mr. Harley W. LINGERFELT
05 Provost Dr. Richard L. MCDOWELL
26 Vice Pres Marketing & Development Ms. Becky M. BEAUCHAMP
10 Chief Financial Officer Ms. Catherine MANINGER
88 VP for Mission & Identity Rev. Nicholas AST
84 Vice Pres for Enrollment Management Mr. William KUEHL
55 Dean College for Working Adults Dr. Jean THORNBRUGH
49 Dean College of Arts & Sciences Dr. Ron H. FAULK
32 Dean of Student Life Mr. TC VEIT
06 Registrar Mrs. Kay K. STITH
08 Library Director Mrs. Anita SEMTNER
26 Director of Public Relations Ms. Breanne HILL
38 Director Student Counseling Mrs. Melody HARRINGTON
37 Director Student Financial Aid Vacant
41 Athletic Director Dr. Jeff POTTER
85 Director of International Office Mr. Spencer RYAN
15 Director of Human Resources Mrs. Cheri L. BOYD
18 Director Facilities/Physical Plant Mr. Mark SAUNDERS
13 Director of Information Systems Mr. Douglas D. MCCULLAR

St. Gregory's University Tulsa Campus (H)

5801 E 41st Street, Suite 900, Tulsa OK 74135
Telephone: (918) 610-8888 Identification: 770381
Accreditation: &NH

† Main campus is St. Gregory's University in Shawnee, OK.

Seminole State College (I)

PO Box 351, Seminole OK 74818-0351
County: Seminole FICE Identification: 003178
Unit ID: 207740
Telephone: (405) 382-9950 Carnegie Class: Assoc/Pub-R-M
FAX Number: (405) 382-3122 Calendar System: Semester
URL: www.sscok.edu
Established: 1931 Annual Undergrad Tuition & Fees (In-District): $3,330
Enrollment: 2,187 Coed
Affiliation or Control: State/Local IRS Status: 501(c)3
Highest Offering: Associate Degree
Program: Occupational; 2-Year Principally Bachelor's Creditable
Accreditation: NH, ADNUR, MLTAD, PHLEB

01 President Dr. Jim W. UTTERBACK
05 Vice President Academic Affairs Dr. Melanie CROY
32 Vice President for Student Affairs Dr. Brad WALCK
10 Vice President Fiscal Affairs Mrs. Katherine BENTON
30 Vice Pres Institutional Advancement Ms. Lana REYNOLDS
84 Director of Enrollment Management Dr. Mark AMES
13 Director Mgmt Information Systems Mr. Jack WHISENNAND
08 Librarian/Director Education Media Mrs. Marguerite HEAROD
66 Director of Nursing Mrs. Donna CHAMBERS
06 Registrar Mrs. Debbie ROBERTSON
15 Director Personnel Services Mrs. Courtney JONES
18 Chief Facilities/Physical Plant Mr. Braden BROWN
20 Associate Academic Officer Dr. Tom MILLS
26 Coordinator of Media Relations Ms. Dustie BUTNER

Southeastern Oklahoma State University (J)

1405 N 4th Avenue, Durant OK 74701-3330
County: Bryan FICE Identification: 003179
Unit ID: 207847
Telephone: (580) 745-2000 Carnegie Class: Master's M
FAX Number: N/A Calendar System: Semester
URL: www.se.edu
Established: 1909 Annual Undergrad Tuition & Fees (In-State): $5,314
Enrollment: 4,120 Coed
Affiliation or Control: State IRS Status: 501(c)3
Highest Offering: Master's
Program: Liberal Arts And General; Teacher Preparatory; Professional
Accreditation: NH, AAB, BUS, MUS, TED

01 President Dr. Larry MINKS
05 Vice Pres Acad Affairs Dr. Douglas MCMILLAN
10 Vice President Business Affairs Mr. Ross WALKUP
32 Vice President Student Affairs Ms. Sharon ROBINSON
20 AVP Acad Aff/Supprt/Dn Grad Studies Dr. William Jerry POLSON
20 Asst VP Academic Affs/Instruction Dr. Bryon CLARK
04 Exec Asst to President Ms. Michele CAMPBELL
35 Dean of Students Dr. Camille PHELPS
49 Dean of Instruction Dr. Lucretia SCOUFOS
07 Assoc Dean Admissions/Registrar Ms. Kristie LUKE
88 Assoc Dean Academic Services Mr. Tim BOATMUN
13 Exec Dir of Information Technology Mr. Dan MOORE
30 Exec Director of Univ Advancement Mr. Kyle STAFFORD
37 Director Student Financial Aid Mr. Tony LEHRLING
36 Director of Career Management Ctr Mr. Scott HENSLEY
08 Library Director Ms. Sharon MORRISON
51 Director Continuing Education Mr. Scott HENSLEY
41 Director of Athletics Mr. Keith BAXTER
26 Director University Communications Mr. Alan BURTON
15 Director Human Resources Ms. Cathy CONWAY
21 Director Finance/Controller Ms. Kay Lynn ROBERTS
38 Director Student Counseling Ms. Jane MCMILLAN
18 Director Facilities/Physical Plant Mr. Eddie HARBIN
28 Special Asst to the Pres/Diversity Dr. Claire STUBBLEFIELD
96 Purchasing Agent Mrs. Carol COATS
40 Book Store Manager Ms. Jackie CODNER
29 Director Alumni Relations Ms. Stephanie SHADE-DAVISON

Southern Nazarene University (K)

6729 NW 39 Expressway, Bethany OK 73008-2694
County: Oklahoma FICE Identification: 003149
Unit ID: 206862
Telephone: (405) 789-6400 Carnegie Class: Master's L
FAX Number: (405) 491-6381 Calendar System: Semester
URL: www.snu.edu
Established: 1899 Annual Undergrad Tuition & Fees: $22,182
Enrollment: 2,184 Coed
Affiliation or Control: Church Of The Nazarene IRS Status: 501(c)3
Highest Offering: Master's
Program: Liberal Arts And General; Teacher Preparatory; Professional; Business Emphasis
Accreditation: NH, ACBSP, MUS, NURSE, TED

01 President Dr. Loren P. GRESHAM
03 Provost Vacant
05 Acting Vice Pres Academic Affairs Vacant

10 Vice President Financial Affairs .... Dr. Scott STRAWN
30 VP of Univ Advance & Church Rels .... Dr. Terry TOLER
32 Vice President Student Development .... Dr. Mike REDWINE
42 University Pastor .... Dr. Blair SPINDLE
84 Vice Pres of Enrollment Management .... Dr. Linda CANTWELL
20 Dean College of Humanities .... Dr. Melany KYZER
81 Dean College of Sci & Health .... Dr. Mark WINSLOW
06 Registrar .... Mr. Charles CHITWOOD
07 Director Admissions .... Dr. Linda CANTWELL
37 Director Student Financial Aid .... Ms. Diana LEE
35 Director Student Affairs .... Mrs. Marian REDWINE
38 Director Student Counseling .... Mrs. Kimberly CAMPBELL
36 Director Career Planning/Placement .... Mrs. Angela RHODES
08 Director Learning Resources Center .... Prof. Katie KING
29 Director Alumni Relations .... Ms. Kendra THOMSON
14 Director Information Technology .... Mrs. Laureen SPRINGER
88 Director Academic Services .... Mr. Wes LEE
09 Director Institutional Research .... Dr. Randy ZABEL
58 Dean Col of Grad & Prof Study .... Dr. Davis BERRYMAN
66 Director of Nursing .... Dr. Katie SIGLER
15 Director Human Resources .... Mr. Chris PETERSON
18 Director of Physical Plant .... Mr. Ron LESTER
24 Director Network .... Mrs. Chichi FREELANDER
26 Director Communications & Marketing .... Mrs. Sarah ROBERTS
40 Bookstore Manager .... Mr. Reggie COLEMAN
41 Athletic Director .... Mr. Bobby MARTIN
88 Dean College of Teach & Learn .... Dr. Dennis WILLIAMS
50 Dean Col of Bus/Educ & KSM .... Dr. Sylvia GOODMAN

Southwestern Christian University (A)

PO Box 340, 7210 NW 39th Expressway,
Bethany OK 73008-0340

County: Oklahoma FICE Identification: 003180
Unit ID: 207856
Telephone: (405) 789-7661 Carnegie Class: Bac/Diverse
FAX Number: (405) 495-0078 Calendar System: Semester
URL: www.swcu.edu
Established: 1946 Annual Undergrad Tuition & Fees: $13,750
Enrollment: 691 Coed
Affiliation or Control: Pentecostal Holiness Church IRS Status: 501(c)3
Highest Offering: Master's
Program: Liberal Arts And General
Accreditation: NH

01 President .... Dr. Ed HUCKEBY
05 Provost & VP Academic Affairs .... Dr. Reggies WENYIKA
10 Vice President for Fiscal Affairs .... Mr. Wallace O. HAMILTON
30 Vice President for Advance/Develop .... Mr. Kevin JEAN
32 Vice President for Student Life .... Mr. Brad DAVIS
41 Athletic Director .... Mr. Mark ARTHUR
37 Director of Financial Aid .... Mrs. Kellye JOHNSON
07 Director of Admissions & Enrollment .... Mr. Joe BLACKWELL
08 Director of Library Services .... Dr. Jon SPARKS
06 Registrar .... Mrs. Sherri HENDRIX
58 Dean of Adult & Graduate Studies .... Dr. Spencer LEDBETTER
107 Dean of Professional Studies .... Mrs. Adrian HINKLE
49 Dean of Arts & Sciences .... Mrs. Shelley GROVES
18 Director of Plant/Property Mgmt .... Mr. Greg DAVALT
26 Director of Sports Information/PR .... Ms. Allison MCINTOSH
13 Director of Information Technology .... Mr. David WIGGINS
12 Director of Tulsa Campus Branch .... Mrs. Lorena RAY
42 Director of Campus Spiritual Life .... Dr. Mark CULHAM
106 Director of Online Education .... Mr. Julian COWART
108 Director of Institution Assessment .... Dr. James BOWEN

Southwestern Oklahoma State University (B)

100 Campus Drive, Weatherford OK 73096-3098

County: Custer FICE Identification: 003181
Unit ID: 207865
Telephone: (580) 772-6611 Carnegie Class: Master's M
FAX Number: (580) 774-3795 Calendar System: Semester
URL: www.swosu.edu
Established: 1901 Annual Undergrad Tuition & Fees (In-State): $5,190
Enrollment: 5,169 Coed
Affiliation or Control: State IRS Status: 501(c)3
Highest Offering: First Professional Degree
Program: Liberal Arts And General; Teacher Preparatory; Professional
Accreditation: NH, CAHIIM, ENGT, IACBE, MUS, NAIT, NUR, OTA, PHAR, PTAA, TED

01 President .... Dr. Randy L. BEUTLER
03 Executive Vice President .... Mr. Thomas W. FAGAN
05 VP for Academic Affairs/Provost .... Dr. James D. SOUTH
32 VP Student Affairs/Assoc Provost .... Dr. Cynthia R. FOUST
26 VP for Marketing/Public Relations .... Mr. Brian D. ADLER
30 Asst to Pres for Inst Advancement .... Ms. Lynne F. THURMAN
96 Dir Business Affairs/Comptroller .... Ms. Brenda K. BURGESS
35 Dean of Students/Dir Student Act .... Ms. Cynthia R. DOUGHERTY
13 Dir Information Technology Services .... Mr. Mark D. ENGELMAN
06 Registrar .... Mr. Daniel R. ARCHER
08 Interim Library Director .... Mr. Jason M. DUPREE
37 Director Student Financial Services .... Mr. Jerome L. WICHERT
15 Dir Human Resources/Affirm Action .... Mr. M. David MISAK
84 Dir Enrollment Mgmt/Career Svcs .... Mr. Todd T. BOYD
41 Athletic Director .... Mr. Todd A. THURMAN
09 Director Institutional Research .... Ms. Denisa A. ENGELMAN
06 Registrar Sayre Campus .... Ms. Terry L. BILLEY
37 Dir Financial Svcs/Sayre Campus .... Mr. Ron KISTLER
38 Director Counseling Services .... Ms. Kim K. LIEBSCHER
18 Director Physical Plant .... Mr. Rick SKINNER
57 Manager Fine Arts Center .... Mr. Kyle J. BARTEL
36 Career Services Coordinator .... Ms. Jonna MYERS
58 Dean College of Prof/Grad Studies .... Dr. Ken G. ROSE
49 Actg Dean College of Arts/Sciences .... Dr. Joseph D. MANESS
67 Dean College of Pharmacy .... Dr. Dennis F. THOMPSON
12 Dean College of Assoc/Applied Prog .... Ms. Sherron K. MANNING
76 Associate Dean Sch of Allied Health .... Ms. Marion L. PRICHARD
53 Assoc Dean Sch of Behavioral Sci .... Dr. L. Chad KINDER
50 Assoc Dean School of Business/Tech .... Dr. Leslie D. CRALL
66 Associate Dean School of Nursing .... Dr. Barbara A. PATTERSON

† Campus at Sayre offers a two-year degree and is regionally accredited (NH) under parent institution.

Southwestern Oklahoma State University-Sayre (C)

409 E Mississippi, Sayre OK 73662

Telephone: (580) 928-5533 Identification: 770382
Accreditation: &NH, MLTAB, RAD

† Main campus is Southwestern Oklahoma State University in Weatherford, OK.

Spartan College of Aeronautics and Technology (D)

8820 E Pine Street, Tulsa OK 74115

County: Tulsa FICE Identification: 007678
Unit ID: 207254
Telephone: (918) 836-6886 Carnegie Class: Spec/Tech
FAX Number: (918) 831-5287 Calendar System: Other
URL: www.spartan.edu
Established: 1928 Annual Undergrad Tuition & Fees: $15,700
Enrollment: 996 Coed
Affiliation or Control: Proprietary IRS Status: Proprietary
Highest Offering: Baccalaureate
Program: Occupational; 2-Year Principally Bachelor's Creditable; Technical Emphasis
Accreditation: ACCSC

01 CEO/President .... Mr. Jeremy GIBSON
10 CFO/Vice President Finance .... Mr. Jason LICAR
05 Vice Pres Educ/Lic/Accreditation .... Mr. Ryan GOERTZEN
11 Vice President Administration .... Mr. Dean RILING

Tulsa Community College (E)

6111 E Skelly Drive, Tulsa OK 74135-6198

County: Tulsa FICE Identification: 009763
Unit ID: 207935
Telephone: (918) 595-7000 Carnegie Class: Assoc/Pub-U-MC
FAX Number: (918) 595-7910 Calendar System: Semester
URL: www.tulsacc.edu
Established: 1968 Annual Undergrad Tuition & Fees (In-State): $3,255
Enrollment: 26,494 Coed
Affiliation or Control: State IRS Status: 501(c)3
Highest Offering: Associate Degree
Program: Occupational; 2-Year Principally Bachelor's Creditable
Accreditation: NH, ADNUR, CAHIIM, COARC, DH, MAC, MLTAD, OTA, PHLEB, PTAA, RAD

01 President .... Dr. Thomas K. MCKEON
04 Assistant to the President .... Ms. Norma L. RODGERS
10 Comptroller & CFO .... Mr. Shane NETHERTON
05 Vice President for Academic Affairs .... Dr. Ric N. BASER
13 VP Administration/Chief Tech Ofcr .... Mr. Sean A. WEINS
32 Assoc Vice Pres Student Affairs .... Dr. Jan L. CLAYTON
20 Assoc Vice Pres Academic Affairs .... Dr. Donna G. WOOD
15 Asst Vice Pres for Human Resources .... Ms. Patricia L. FISCHER
12 Provost Southeast Campus .... Dr. Brett S. CAMPBELL
12 Provost Northeast Campus .... Dr. John GIBSON
12 Provost Metro Campus .... Dr. Flo E. POTTS
12 Provost West Campus .... Dr. Peggy D. DYER
26 Vice President External Affairs .... Ms. Lauren F. BROOKEY
08 Dean Libraries .... Ms. Paula SETTOON
28 Dean of Diversity/Civic Engagement .... Mr. Tony J. ALONSO
51 Dean Continuing Educ & Wrkfrc Devel .... Mr. Anthony BRETTI
84 Dean Enrollment Management .... Ms. Traci HECK
18 Director Physical Facilities .... Vacant
37 Director Financial Aid .... Ms. Karen JEFFERS
96 Dir Purch & Inventory Control .... Mr. Bill CREECH
09 Dir Planning/Institutional Research .... Dr. Kevin DAVID
19 Director Campus Police .... Mr. Gene WIDEMAN
40 Director Campus Store Operations .... Mr. Ken A. JONES
27 Dir Communication/Production .... Ms. Susie A. BROWN
21 Director Administrative Services .... Dr. Frederick D. ARTIS
92 Director of Honors Program .... Ms. Susan ONEAL
30 Director Development .... Mr. Calvin MOORE

Tulsa Community College Metro Campus (F)

909 South Boston Avenue, Tulsa OK 74119

Telephone: (918) 595-7224 Identification: 770383
Accreditation: &NH

† Main campus is Tulsa Community College in Tulsa, OK.

Tulsa Community College Northeast Campus (G)

3727 East Apache Street, Tulsa OK 74115

Telephone: (918) 595-7529 Identification: 770384
Accreditation: &NH

† Main campus is Tulsa Community College in Tulsa, OK.

Tulsa Community College Southeast Campus (H)

10300 East 81st Street, Tulsa OK 74133

Telephone: (918) 595-7724 Identification: 770385
Accreditation: &NH

† Main campus is Tulsa Community College in Tulsa, OK.

Tulsa Community College West Campus (I)

7505 W 41st Street South, Tulsa OK 74102

Telephone: (918) 595-8100 Identification: 770386
Accreditation: &NH

† Main campus is Tulsa Community College in Tulsa, OK.

Tulsa Welding School (J)

2545 E 11th Street, Tulsa OK 74104-3909

County: Tulsa FICE Identification: 009618
Unit ID: 207962
Telephone: (918) 587-6789 Carnegie Class: Assoc/PrivFP
FAX Number: (918) 587-8170 Calendar System: Other
URL: www.weldingschool.com
Established: 1949 Annual Undergrad Tuition & Fees: $16,250
Enrollment: 989 Coed
Affiliation or Control: Proprietary IRS Status: Proprietary
Highest Offering: Associate Degree
Program: Occupational
Accreditation: ACCSC

01 President .... Mr. Mark STAATS
05 Academic Dean .... Mr. Stephen JORDAN
07 Director of Admissions .... Mr. Gabe ZAMBRANO
37 Director of Financial Aid .... Mrs. Teresa FRANKLIN
36 Director of Employment .... Ms. Tiffany JORDAN

University of Central Oklahoma (K)

100 N University Drive, Edmond OK 73034-5209

County: Oklahoma FICE Identification: 003152
Unit ID: 206941
Telephone: (405) 974-2000 Carnegie Class: Master's L
FAX Number: (405) 341-4964 Calendar System: Semester
URL: www.uco.edu
Established: 1890 Annual Undergrad Tuition & Fees (In-State): $5,092
Enrollment: 17,211 Coed
Affiliation or Control: State IRS Status: 501(c)3
Highest Offering: Master's
Program: Liberal Arts And General; Teacher Preparatory; Professional
Accreditation: NH, ACBSP, CIDA, CS, DIETD, DIETI, ENG, EXSC, FUSER, MUS, NUR, SP, TED

01 President .... Dr. Don BETZ
03 Executive Vice President .... Mr. Steve KREIDLER
05 Provost/Vice Pres Academic Affairs .... Dr. John BARTHELL
32 Vice President Student Affairs .... Dr. Myron POPE
13 Vice President Information Tech .... Dr. Cynthia ROLFE
26 Vice Pres University Relations .... Mr. Charlie JOHNSON
88 Vice Pres Public Affairs .... Mr. Mark KINDERS
102 Vice President UCO Foundation .... Mrs. Anne HOLZBERLEIN
11 Assoc VP Administration .... Mr. Mark MOORE
06 Associate Vice President/Registrar .... Mr. Adam JOHNSON
20 Vice Prov/Assoc VP Academic Affairs .... Dr. Patricia LAGROW
20 Asst Vice Pres Academic Affairs .... Dr. Lori BEASLEY
10 Asst VP Admin Financial Operations .... Ms. Lisa HARPER
18 Asst Vice Pres Admin/Facilities Mgt .... Mr. Mark RODOLF
35 Asst Vice Pres Student Affairs .... Mr. Cole STANLEY
23 Asst VP/Director Wellness Center .... Mr. Mark HERRIN
04 Special Assistant to Vice President .... Ms. Amy ROGALSKY
41 Athletic Director .... Mr. Joe MULLER
09 Exec Dir Institutional Research .... Ms. Cindy BOLING
08 Exec Director University Libraries .... Dr. Bonnie MCNEELY
37 Director Student Financial Services .... Ms. Susan PRATER
29 Int Director Alumni Relations .... Ms. Brenda KNOTT
85 Director International Student Svcs .... Dr. Dennis DUNHAM
39 Director Housing & Dining .... Mr. Josh OVEROCKER
19 Exec Dir Public Safety/Trans .... Mr. Jeff HARP
15 Dir Employment Rels/Development .... Ms. Diane FEINBERG
88 Exec Director Leadership Central .... Dr. Jarrett JOBE
07 Dir of Undergraduate Admissions .... Ms. Stephanie KAHNE
28 Director of Diversity & Inclusion .... Ms. MeShawn CONLEY
96 Director of Purchasing .... Mrs. Denise RODOLF
43 Senior Legal Counsel .... Dr. Brad MORELLI
50 Dean of Business Administration .... Dr. Mickey HEPNER
53 Dean College Education .... Dr. James MACHELL
49 Dean College of Liberal Arts .... Dr. Gary STEWARD
81 Int Dean College Math/Science .... Dr. Charlotte SIMMONS
58 Dean Graduate Studies .... Dr. Richard BERNARD
57 Dean College Fine Arts & Design .... Vacant

University of Oklahoma Health Sciences Center (A)

1000 Stanton L. Young Boulevard,
Oklahoma City OK 73117
Telephone: (405) 271-4000 FICE Identification: 005889
Accreditation: &NH, ARCPA, AUD, DENT, DH, DIETC, DIETD, DIETI, DMS, ENGR, HSA, IPSY, MED, NMT, NUR, OT, PDPSY, PH, PHAR, PTA, RAD, RADDOS, RTT, SP

† Main campus is University of Oklahoma Norman Campus in Norman, OK.

University of Oklahoma Norman Campus (B)

660 Parrington Oval, Norman OK 73019-3070
County: Cleveland FICE Identification: 003184
Unit ID: 207500
Telephone: (405) 325-0311 Carnegie Class: RU/VH
FAX Number: (405) 325-7605 Calendar System: Semester
URL: www.ou.edu
Established: 1890 Annual Undergrad Tuition & Fees (In-State): $7,340
Enrollment: 27,507 Coed
Affiliation or Control: State IRS Status: 501(c)3
Highest Offering: Doctorate
Program: Liberal Arts And General; Teacher Preparatory; Professional
Accreditation: NH, AAB, BUS, BUSA, CIDA, CONST, COPSY, CS, ENG, JOUR, LAW, LIB, LSAR, MUS, SW, TED, THEA

01 President ....Mr. David L. BOREN
10 VP Administration & Finance ....Mr. Nick HATHAWAY
101 VP Univ Gov/Exec Secy Bd of Regents ....Dr. Chris PURCELL
05 Senior Vice President/Provost ....Dr. Nancy L. MERGLER
05 Senior Vice Provost ....Dr. Kyle HARPER
43 VP of Univ/General Counsel ....Mr. Anil GOLLAHALLI
32 Vice President for Student Affairs ....Mr. Clarke STROUD
30 Vice Pres for University Devel ....Mr. Jim HALL, III
51 VP Univ Outreach/Dn Col Lib Std ....Dr. James P. PAPPAS
58 Dean Grad College ....Dr. T. H. Lee WILLIAMS
46 Vice President for Research ....Dr. Kelvin DROEGEMEIER
26 Vice President for Public Affairs ....Ms. Catherine BISHOP
13 Assoc VP/Chief Information Ofcr ....Ms. Loretta EARLY
86 Vice Pres for Governmental Relation ....Mr. Danny C. HILLIARD
20 Associate Provost/Dir of Acad Integ ....Dr. Gregory M. HEISER
20 Assoc Provost for Academic Advising ....Dr. Joyce L. ALLMAN
09 Assoc Provost/Dir Inst Research ....Ms. Susannah B. LIVINGOOD
06 Registrar/VP Enroll/Stdnt Fin Svcs ....Mr. Matt HAMILTON
35 Director Student Life ....Ms. Kristen PARTRIDGE
21 Assoc VP Administration & Finance ....Mr. Byron MILLSAP
21 Assoc VP Admin & Finance ....Mr. Chris KUWITZKY
29 Assoc VP Alum & Dev/Ex Dir Alum Asn ....Mr. Jean Paul AUDAS
18 Director Facilities Management ....Mr. Brian ELLIS
39 Director of Housing & Food Services ....Mr. David L. ANNIS
41 Director of Athletics ....Mr. Joe CASTIGLIONE
21 Controller ....Ms. Terri B. PINKSTON
23 AVP/Director Goddard Health Center ....Dr. William WAYNE
36 Director Career Services ....Ms. Bette J. SCOTT
19 Chief of Police ....Ms. Liz WOOLLEN
15 AVP/Director of Human Resources ....Mr. Julius HILBURN
22 Equal Opportunity Officer ....Dr. Shad B. SATTERTHWAITE
22 Inst Eq Ofcr & Title IX Coordinator ....Ms. Laura PALK
07 Director of Admissions ....Vacant
25 Assoc VP for Research Services ....Ms. Andrea D. DEATON
85 Director Internatl Student Services ....Ms. Monica A. SHARP
104 Director Education Abroad ....Vacant
37 Director of Financial Aid ....Ms. Caryn L. PACHECO
48 Dean College of Architecture ....Dr. Charles W. GRAHAM
49 VP/Dean College Arts & Sciences ....Dr. Paul BELL
53 Dn Jeannine Rainbolt Col of Educ ....Dr. Gregg GARN
54 Dean College of Engineering ....Dr. Thomas L. LANDERS
57 Dn Weitzenhoffer Col of Fine Arts ....Mr. Rich TAYLOR
61 VP/Dean College of Law ....Mr. Joseph HARROZ, JR.
62 Dean University Libraries ....Mr. Richard E. LUCE
65 VP/Dn Col Atmospheric/Geographic Sc ....Dr. Berrien MOORE, III
50 Interim Dn Price Col of Business ....Mr. Daniel PULLIN
92 Dean McClendon Honors College ....Dr. David H. RAY
60 Dn Gaylord Col Journ/Mass Comm ....Dr. Joe S. FOOTE
89 Dean University College ....Dr. Nicole J. CAMPBELL
88 Dean Mewborne Col of Earth & Energy ....Dr. Larry R. GRILLOT
82 Dean Col Intl Studies ....Dr. Suzette R. GRILLOT

† Tuition is now based on 30 credit hour per year.

University of Oklahoma Schusterman Center (C)

4502 E 41st Street, Tulsa OK 74135-2512
Telephone: (918) 660-3000 Identification: 770387
Accreditation: &NH

† Main campus is University of Oklahoma Norman Campus in Norman, OK.

University of Phoenix Oklahoma City Campus (D)

3 Broadway Exec Pk, 6501 N Broadway,
Oklahoma City OK 73116-8244
Telephone: (405) 842-8007 Identification: 770221
Accreditation: &NH, ACBSP

† Main campus is University of Phoenix in Tempe, AZ.

University of Science and Arts of Oklahoma (E)

1727 W Alabama, Chickasha OK 73018-5322
County: Grady FICE Identification: 003167
Unit ID: 207722
Telephone: (405) 224-3140 Carnegie Class: Bac/A&S
FAX Number: (405) 574-1220 Calendar System: Trimester
URL: www.usao.edu
Established: 1908 Annual Undergrad Tuition & Fees (In-State): $5,790
Enrollment: 985 Coed
Affiliation or Control: State IRS Status: 501(c)3
Highest Offering: Baccalaureate
Program: Liberal Arts And General; Teacher Preparatory
Accreditation: NH, MUS, TED

01 President ....Dr. John H. FEAVER
05 VP for Academic Affairs ....Dr. Dexter MARBLE
10 Vice Pres for Business & Finance ....Mr. Mike D. COPONITI
84 Vice Pres for Enrollment Management ....Ms. Monica TREVINO
30 Vice Pres University Advancement ....Dr. Michael NEALEIGH
13 VP for Information Services & Tech ....Ms. Lynn BOYCE
06 Registrar/Dir of Enrollment/Records ....Mr. Joe W. EVANS
08 Director of Nash Library ....Ms. Kelly BROWN
37 Director of Financial Aid ....Ms. Nancy I. MOATS
32 Dean of Students/Dir Student Svcs ....Ms. Nancy HUGHES
26 Director Media/Community Relations ....Ms. Kelly ARNOLD
29 Director of Alumni Development ....Mr. Eric FEUERBORN
18 Director of Physical Plant ....Mr. Mike COPONITI
14 Director of Data Processing ....Mr. Jim HOPKINS
09 Director of Institutional Research ....Mr. George GUAJARDO
15 Director Personnel Services ....Mr. Mike COPONITI
07 Acting Director of Admissions ....Ms. Monica TREVINO
35 Director Student Affairs ....Ms. Nancy HUGHES
38 Director Student Counseling ....Ms. Misty STEELE
49 Chair Div of Arts & Humanities ....Dr. Stephen WEBER
50 Chair Div of Business & Social Sci ....Dr. Christopher WALKER
53 Chair Division of Education ....Dr. Vicki FERGUSON
81 Chair Div of Science/Physical Educ ....Dr. JC SANDERS
88 Chair Interdisciplinary Studies ....Dr. Jennifer LONG

University of Tulsa (F)

800 S Tucker, Tulsa OK 74104
County: Tulsa FICE Identification: 003185
Unit ID: 207971
Telephone: (918) 631-2000 Carnegie Class: DRU
FAX Number: (918) 631-2033 Calendar System: Semester
URL: www.utulsa.edu
Established: 1894 Annual Undergrad Tuition & Fees: $45,261
Enrollment: 4,326 Coed
Affiliation or Control: Independent Non-Profit IRS Status: 501(c)3
Highest Offering: Doctorate
Program: Liberal Arts And General; Teacher Preparatory; Professional
Accreditation: NH, BUS, CLPSY, CS, ENG, LAW, MUS, NUR, SP, TEAC

01 President ....Dr. Steadman UPHAM
03 Exec Vice President & Treasurer ....Mr. Kevan C. BUCK
05 Provost/Vice Pres Academic Affairs ....Dr. Roger N. BLAIS
30 Vice Pres Institutional Advancement ....Dr. Kayla ACEBO
84 Int VP Enrollment & Stdnt Svcs ....Mr. Earl JOHNSON
41 VP & Athletic Director ....Dr. Derrick GRAGG
13 VP Info Services & CIO ....Dr. Dale A. SCHOENEFELD
88 VP Museum Affs/Exec Dir Gilcrease ....Dr. Duane KING
26 VP Public Affairs/Econ Devel ....Ms. Susan NEAL
20 Sr Vice Provost & Assoc VP ....Ms. Winona M. TANAKA
46 Vice Prov Research/Dean Grad School ....Dr. Janet A. HAGGERTY
100 Assoc VP Office of President ....Ms. Jacqueline H. CALDWELL
104 Vice Provost Intl Studies ....Dr. Cheryl MATHERLY
09 Director Inst Research & Records ....Dr. Michael W. BARNES
42 University Chaplain ....Dr. Jeffrey FRANCIS
49 Dean Arts & Sciences ....Dr. Kalpana MISRA
50 Dean Business Administration ....Dr. A. Gale SULLENBERGER
54 Dean Engineering/Natural Sciences ....Dr. James R. SOREM, JR.
61 Dean Law ....Ms. Janet LEVIT
08 RM & Ida McFarlin Dean of Library ....Mr. Adrian W. ALEXANDER
88 Assoc VP Institutional Advancement ....Ms. Amy BERRY
06 Registrar ....Ms. Ginna V. LANGSTON
15 Associate VP Human Resources ....Mr. Wayne PAULISON
18 Assoc VP Operations/Physical Plant ....Mr. Robert SHIPLEY
21 Assoc VP & Controller ....Mr. Michael D. THESENVITZ
07 Assoc VP Enrollment Dean Admission ....Mr. Earl JOHNSON
32 Assoc VP Enrollment Dean Students ....Ms. Yolanda D. TAYLOR
39 Assoc VP Director Housing ....Ms. Melissa H. FRANCE
85 Dean International Students ....Ms. Pamela A. SMITH
51 Dean Lifelong Learning ....Dr. J. Phillip APPLEGATE
62 Assoc Dean McFarlin Library ....Ms. Francine J. FISK
23 Director Health Center ....Ms. Stephanie FELL
38 Director Student Counseling ....Dr. Thomas J. BRIAN
19 Director Campus Security ....Mr. Joseph F. TIMMONS
29 Director Alumni Relations ....Ms. Amy M. FREIBERGER
36 Director Career Services ....Ms. Shelly HOLLY
37 Director Student Financial Svcs ....Ms. Vicki A. HENDRICKSON
96 Director Purchasing ....Mr. Jerry R. HOLLOWAY
90 Dir Academic Tech Services ....Ms. Janet CAIRNS
91 Dir Admin Computing ....Mr. Martin PAGE
31 Assoc Dean Community Relations ....Mr. Michael MILLS
27 Assoc Dir News & Public Rels ....Ms. Mona CHAMBERLIN
105 Director Web Communications ....Mr. Matt CASTEEL
101 Secretary Board of Trustees ....Ms. June E. BROWN
04 Sr Admin Associate to President ....Ms. Susan LAYMAN

Vatterott College-Oklahoma City (G)

5537 NW Expressway, Warr Acres OK 73132-5230
Telephone: (405) 945-0088 Identification: 666061
Accreditation: ACCSC

† Main campus is Vatterott College-Des Moines in Des Moines, IA.

Vatterott College-Tulsa (H)

4343 S 118th E Avenue, Ste A, Tulsa OK 74146-4406
Telephone: (918) 835-8288 Identification: 666102
Accreditation: ACCSC

† Main campus is Vatterott College-NorthPark in Berkeley, MO.

Virginia College (I)

5124 South Peoria Avenue, Tulsa OK 74105
Telephone: (225) 236-3900 Identification: 770825
Accreditation: ACICS

† Main campus is Virginia College in Birmingham, AL.

Western Oklahoma State College (J)

2801 N Main Street, Altus OK 73521-1397
County: Jackson FICE Identification: 003146
Unit ID: 208035
Telephone: (580) 477-2000 Carnegie Class: Assoc/Pub-R-M
FAX Number: (580) 477-7777 Calendar System: Semester
URL: www.wosc.edu
Established: 1926 Annual Undergrad Tuition & Fees (In-State): $3,148
Enrollment: 5,268 Coed
Affiliation or Control: State IRS Status: 501(c)3
Highest Offering: Associate Degree
Program: Occupational; 2-Year Principally Bachelor's Creditable
Accreditation: #NH, ADNUR, RAD

01 President ....Dr. Phil BIRDINE
04 Admin Secretary to the President ....Ms. Briar JENKINS
05 VP for Academic & Student Supp Svcs ....Ms. Lisa GREENLEE
10 Vice President for Business Affairs ....Ms. Tricia LATHAM
30 Vice Pres Development & Alumni Rels ....Mr. Larry K. DUFFY
49 Dean Arts & Sciences ....Vacant
20 Dean of Student Support Services ....Mr. Chad WIGINTON
72 Dean of Technical Programs ....Ms. Chrystal OVERTON
09 Director of Institutional Research ....Mr. Justin SMITH
13 Dir of Information Technology ....Mr. Steve PRATER
27 Director Public Information ....Ms. Judith NORTON
07 Director of Admissions & Registrar ....Ms. Lana SCOTT
37 Director of Student Financial Aid ....Ms. Myrna J. CROSS
29 Dir Development/Alumni Relations ....Ms. Haley THOMPSON
68 Dir Physical Educ/Athletic Devel ....Mr. Bob PEARSON
62 Director of Learning Resources ....Ms. Suzanne ROOKER
15 Director Personnel Services ....Ms. April NELSON
18 Director Physical Plant & Safety ....Mr. Doyle JENCKS
40 Bookstore Manager ....Ms. Kass DEWEESE
38 Counselor ....Ms. April DILL
96 Asst Director of Purchasing ....Vacant
81 Science Instructor ....Dr. Toni COAKLEY
79 Art Instructor ....Vacant
88 History Instructor ....Mr. Mickey GRAHAM

Wright Career College (K)

2219 W 1240 Service Road, Suite 124,
Oklahoma City OK 73159
Telephone: (405) 681-2300 Identification: 770763
Accreditation: ACICS

† Main campus is Wright Career College in Overland Park, KS.

Wright Career College (L)

4908 S Sheridan Road, Tulsa OK 74135
Telephone: (918) 628-7700 Identification: 770762
Accreditation: ACICS

† Main campus is Wright Career College in Overland Park, KS.

OREGON

American College of Healthcare Sciences (M)

5940 SW Hood Avenue, Portland OR 97239-3719
County: Multnomah FICE Identification: 041944
Unit ID: 443599
Telephone: (503) 244-0726 Carnegie Class: Not Classified
FAX Number: (503) 244-0727 Calendar System: Semester
URL: www.achs.edu
Established: 1978 Annual Undergrad Tuition & Fees: $500
Enrollment: 500 Coed
Affiliation or Control: Proprietary IRS Status: Proprietary
Highest Offering: Master's
Program: Occupational; 2-Year Principally Bachelor's Creditable; Professional
Accreditation: DETC

01 President ....Dorene PETERSEN

11 Director of Operations .... Tracey ABELL
03 Chief Institutional Officer .... Erika YIGZAW
06 Assistant Registrar .... Brooke PILLSBURY-GUYOT
26 Director of Marketing .... Kate HARMON

The Art Institute of Portland (A)

1122 NW Davis Street, Portland OR 97209-2911
County: Multnomah FICE Identification: 007819
Unit ID: 208239
Telephone: (503) 228-6528 Carnegie Class: Spec/Arts
FAX Number: (503) 228-4227 Calendar System: Quarter
URL: www.artinstitutes.edu/portland
Established: 1963 Annual Undergrad Tuition & Fees: $17,850
Enrollment: 1,550 Coed
Affiliation or Control: Proprietary IRS Status: Proprietary
Highest Offering: Baccalaureate
Program: Occupational; Liberal Arts And General
Accreditation: NW, CIDA

01 President .... Dr. Emily HILL
05 Dean of Academic Affairs .... Dr. Jason CLARY
06 Registrar .... Ms. Kristin MCGILLIVRAY
07 Director of Admission .... Mr. Jose SAEZ
08 Head Librarian .... Ms. Jennifer COX
37 Financial Aid Director .... Ms. Carmen SAYRE

† Granted candidacy at the Master's level.

Birthingway College of Midwifery (B)

12113 SE Foster Road, Portland OR 97266-4042
County: Multnomah FICE Identification: 036683
Unit ID: 442949
Telephone: (503) 760-3131 Carnegie Class: Spec/Health
FAX Number: (503) 760-3332 Calendar System: Quarter
URL: www.birthingway.edu
Established: 1993 Annual Undergrad Tuition & Fees: $18,034
Enrollment: 91 Coed
Affiliation or Control: Independent Non-Profit IRS Status: 501(c)3
Highest Offering: Baccalaureate
Program: 2-Year Principally Bachelor's Creditable; Professional
Accreditation: MEAC

01 President .... Ms. Holly SCHOLLES
03 Faculty Coordinator .... Ms. Nancy LONGATAN
05 Academic Coordinator .... Ms. Nichole REDING
10 Finance Coordinator .... Ms. Nina THOMPSON
37 Financial Aid Coordinator .... Ms. Amari FAUNA
06 Registrar .... Ms. Dawn BAKER
88 Midwifery Program Coordinator .... Ms. Rhonda RAY
88 Lactation Program Coordinator .... Ms. Stacey MARSHALL
88 Administrative Programs Coordinator .... Ms. Julia REID

Blue Mountain Community College (C)

PO Box 100, Pendleton OR 97801-0100
County: Umatilla/Morrow/Baker FICE Identification: 003186
Unit ID: 208275
Telephone: (541) 276-1260 Carnegie Class: Assoc/Pub-R-M
FAX Number: (541) 278-5886 Calendar System: Quarter
URL: www.bluecc.edu
Established: 1962 Annual Undergrad Tuition & Fees (In-District): $4,425
Enrollment: 2,910 Coed
Affiliation or Control: State/Local IRS Status: 501(c)3
Highest Offering: Associate Degree
Program: Occupational; 2-Year Principally Bachelor's Creditable; Business Emphasis
Accreditation: NW, DA

01 President .... Ms. Camille PREUS
05 Vice President of Instruction .... Mr. Dan LANGE
10 Vice President of Operations .... Mr. Clark WILLIAMS
20 Vice Pres of Economic Development .... Mr. Art HILL
15 Director for Human Resources .... Ms. Tammie PARKER
08 Director of Library & Media Svcs .... Ms. Shannon VAN KIRK
07 Registrar/Dir of Admiss & Records .... Ms. Theresa BOSWORTH
18 Supervisor Facilities/Phy Plant .... Mr. Steve PLATT
102 Director Foundation .... Ms. Margaret GIANOTTI
29 Director Alumni Relations .... Ms. Stacey SIMPSON
25 Director of Grants .... Mr. Casey BEARD
37 Director of Student Financial Aid .... Ms. Cristina SWEEK

Central Oregon Community College (D)

2600 NW College Way, Bend OR 97701-5998
County: Deschutes FICE Identification: 003188
Unit ID: 208318
Telephone: (541) 383-7700 Carnegie Class: Assoc/Pub-R-M
FAX Number: (541) 383-7506 Calendar System: Quarter
URL: www.cocc.edu
Established: 1949 Annual Undergrad Tuition & Fees (In-District): $3,195
Enrollment: 7,132 Coed
Affiliation or Control: Local IRS Status: 501(c)3
Highest Offering: Associate Degree
Program: Occupational; 2-Year Principally Bachelor's Creditable
Accreditation: NW, CAHIIM, DA, EMT, MAC

01 President .... Dr. James E. MIDDLETON
05 Vice President for Instruction .... Dr. Charles ABASA-NYARKO
11 Vice Pres for Administration .... Mr. Matthew J. MCCOY
10 Chief Financial Officer .... Mr. Kevin KIMBALL
51 Dean of Extended Learning .... Dr. Shirley METCALF
20 Instructional Dean .... Dr. Michael FISHER
20 Instructional Dean .... Ms. Jennifer NEWBY
84 Dean of Student/Enrollment Svcs .... Ms. Alicia MOORE
07 Director of Admissions & Records .... Ms. Courtney FORD
08 Int Director Library .... Dr. Tina HOVEKAMP
26 Director College Relations .... Mr. Ronald S. PARADIS
14 Director Information Technology .... Mr. Dan CECCHINI
18 Director Campus Services .... Mr. Joe VIOLA
15 Director Human Resources .... Ms. Sally SORENSON
22 Affirmative Action Officer .... Mrs. Sharla ANDRESEN
37 Director Student Financial Aid .... Mr. Kevin MULTOP
28 Dir of Multicultural Activities .... Ms. Karen ROTH
32 Director of Student Life .... Mr. Gordon PRICE
09 Dir Institutional Effectiveness .... Ms. Brynn PIERCE
21 Assoc Chief Financial Officer .... Mr. David DONA
38 Director Student Counseling .... Ms. Vickery VILES
96 Director of Purchasing .... Ms. Julie MOSIER
40 Bookstore Director .... Ms. Lori A. WILLIS
36 Coordinator of Career Services .... Ms. Vickery VILES

Chemeketa Community College (E)

PO Box 14007, Salem OR 97309-7070
County: Marion FICE Identification: 003218
Unit ID: 208390
Telephone: (503) 399-5000 Carnegie Class: Assoc/Pub-R-L
FAX Number: (503) 399-5214 Calendar System: Quarter
URL: www.chemeka.edu/
Established: 1962 Annual Undergrad Tuition & Fees (In-District): $3,384
Enrollment: 4,006 Coed
Affiliation or Control: Local IRS Status: 501(c)3
Highest Offering: Associate Degree
Program: Occupational; 2-Year Principally Bachelor's Creditable
Accreditation: NW, ADNUR, DA, EMT, IFSAC

01 President/Chief Executive Officer .... Dr. Cheryl ROBERTS
05 Chief Academic Officer .... Dr. Patrick LANNING
10 Chief Financial Officer .... Ms. Julie A. HUCKESTEIN
12 Campus President Yamhill Valley .... Dr. Patrick LANNING
20 Dean General Education/Trans Stds .... Dr. David HALLETT
16 Executive Dean .... Mr. Andrew BONE
32 Ex Dean Student Devel/Learning Res .... Mr. Jim EUSTROM
88 Exec Dean Academic Advancement .... Dr. Susan MURRAY
68 Dean Life Sci/Health/PE/Athletics .... Mr. Johnny MACK
79 Dean Humanities & Communications .... Mr. Don BRASE
66 Dean Dental Asst/Med Asst/Nursing .... Ms. Kay CARNEGIE
37 Dean Financial Aid/Enrollment Svcs .... Ms. Kathy CAMPBELL
38 Dean Counseling/Career Services .... Ms. Sue ORCHARD
72 Dean Applied Technologies .... Mr. Glen MILLER
81 Dean Math/Science/Technologies .... Mr. Michael MILHAUSEN
83 Dean Early Chld/Hum Svc/Soc Sci/Ed .... Ms. R. TAYLOR
84 Dean Marketing/Student Recruitment .... Mr. Greg HARRIS
45 Dean Curriculum Resource Center .... Ms. Deborah SIPE
65 Dean Natural Resources .... Mr. Joel KEEBLER
102 Executive Director Foundation .... Mr. Andrew BONE
08 Director Learning Resource Center .... Ms. Natalie BEACH
88 Director Enterprise Services .... Mr. Brian RADER
21 Director Business Services .... Ms. Miriam ROZIN
18 Director Facilities & Operations .... Mr. Phil WRIGHT
15 Director Human Resources .... Ms. Peggy BORJESSON
19 Director Public Safety .... Mr. Bill KOHLMEYER
40 Director Auxiliary Services .... Ms. Meredith SCHREIBER
06 Registrar .... Ms. Minna GELDER
41 Athletic Director .... Ms. Cassie BELMODIS
50 Dir Chemeketa Ctr for Bus/Industry .... Ms. Diane MCLARAN
88 Director Reg Prof Tech Educ .... Vacant
28 Director of Diversity & Equity .... Ms. Linda HERRERA
35 Director Student Life/Retention .... Mr. Manuel GUERRA
07 Director of Admissions .... Ms. Melissa FREY
96 Director of Purchasing .... Ms. Connie LELACK
27 Chief Information Officer .... Mr. Tim ROGERS
30 Development .... Ms. Nancy DUNCAN
25 Grants Coordinator .... Ms. Diane SCHMITZ
09 Coord of Institutional Research .... Mr. Fauzi NAAS

Clackamas Community College (F)

19600 Molalla Avenue, Oregon City OR 97045-7998
County: Clackamas FICE Identification: 004878
Unit ID: 208406
Telephone: (503) 594-6000 Carnegie Class: Assoc/Pub-S-MC
FAX Number: N/A Calendar System: Quarter
URL: www.clackamas.edu
Established: 1966 Annual Undergrad Tuition & Fees (In-District): $3,360
Enrollment: 2,258 Coed
Affiliation or Control: Local IRS Status: 501(c)3
Highest Offering: Associate Degree
Program: Occupational; 2-Year Principally Bachelor's Creditable
Accreditation: NW, CA, MAC

01 President .... Dr. Joanne TRUESDELL
05 VP Instruct & Stdnt Svcs/Provost .... Ms. Elizabeth LUNDY
11 Vice President of College Services .... Mr. Courtney WILTON
04 Executive Asst to the President .... Mr. Sean POLLACK
30 Dn Col Advanc/Chf Govt/Cmty Rel Dir .... Ms. Shelly PARINI
102 Executive Director Foundation .... Mr. Greg FITZGERALD
27 Public Information Officer .... Ms. Janet PAULSON
88 Dean Acad Found/Connections Div .... Mr. Phillip KING
06 Registrar .... Ms. Tara SPREHE
32 Assoc Dean Acad Found/Connect Div .... Mr. Jim MARTINEAU
13 Dean/CIO Information Technology .... Ms. Kim CAREY
49 Dean Arts & Sciences .... Mr. Bill BRIARE
46 Dean Curriculum/Planning/Research .... Mr. Steffen MOLLER
88 Director Educational Partnerships .... Ms. Cyndi ANDREWS
72 Dean Tech/Hlth Occup/Workforce Div .... Mr. Scott GILTZ
15 Dean Human Resources .... Ms. Marsha EDWARDS
21 Director Business Services .... Ms. Chris ROBUCK
11 Dean Campus Services .... Mr. Bob COCHRAN
18 Director Campus Services .... Mr. Lloyd HELM
37 Director Student Financial Svcs .... Ms. Chippi BELLO
41 Director Athletics/Health/PE .... Mr. Jim MARTINEAU

Clatsop Community College (G)

1651 Lexington Avenue, Astoria OR 97103
County: Clatsop FICE Identification: 003189
Unit ID: 208415
Telephone: (503) 325-0910 Carnegie Class: Assoc/Pub-R-M
FAX Number: (503) 325-5738 Calendar System: Quarter
URL: www.clatsopcc.edu
Established: 1958 Annual Undergrad Tuition & Fees (In-District): $3,978
Enrollment: 1,071 Coed
Affiliation or Control: State/Local IRS Status: 501(c)3
Highest Offering: Associate Degree
Program: Occupational; 2-Year Principally Bachelor's Creditable
Accreditation: NW

01 President .... Dr. Larry GALIZIO
05 VP Academic & Student Affairs .... Dr. Donna LARSON
10 Vice President Finance & Operations .... Ms. JoAnn ZAHN
84 Assoc Dean Enrollment Management .... Mr. Chris OUSLEY
06 Registrar .... Dr. Chris OUSLEY
26 Chief Public Rels Officer/Marketing .... Ms. Patricia WARREN
78 Dir Co-op Educ & Special Project .... Ms. Joanie WEATHERLY
51 Director Distance Education .... Mrs. Kirsten HORNING
15 Director Personnel Services .... Ms. Leslie LIPE
37 Director Student Financial Aid .... Mr. Lloyd MUELLER
09 Director of Institutional Research .... Mr. Tom GILL
18 Chief Facilities/Physical Plant .... Mr. Greg DORCHEUS
21 Associate Business Officer .... Ms. Margaret ANTILLA
29 Director of Alumni Relations/Devel .... Ms. Patricia WARREN

Columbia Gorge Community College (H)

400 East Scenic Drive, The Dalles OR 97058
County: Wasco FICE Identification: 041519
Unit ID: 420556
Telephone: (541) 506-6000 Carnegie Class: Assoc/Pub-R-S
FAX Number: N/A Calendar System: Quarter
URL: www.cgcc.cc.or.us/
Established: 1977 Annual Undergrad Tuition & Fees (In-District): $4,545
Enrollment: 1,100 Coed
Affiliation or Control: State/Local IRS Status: 501(c)3
Highest Offering: Associate Degree
Program: 2-Year Principally Bachelor's Creditable
Accreditation: NW, MAC

01 President .... Dr. Frank TODA
05 Interim Chief Academic Officer .... Brian GREENE
10 Interim Chief Financial Officer .... Lisa DESWERT
11 Chief Operating Officer .... Robb VAN CLEAVE
32 Chief Student Services Officer .... Lori UFFORD
30 Chief Inst Advancement Officer .... Dan SPATZ
13 Chief Technology Officer .... Bill BOHN

Concorde Career College (I)

1425 NE Irving Street, Suite 300, Portland OR 97232
County: Multnomah FICE Identification: 008887
Unit ID: 208479
Telephone: (503) 281-4181 Carnegie Class: Assoc/PrivFP
FAX Number: (503) 281-6739 Calendar System: Other
URL: www.concorde.edu/campus/portland
Established: Annual Undergrad Tuition & Fees: N/A
Enrollment: 912 Coed
Affiliation or Control: Proprietary IRS Status: Proprietary
Highest Offering: Associate Degree
Program: Occupational
Accreditation: ACCSC, COARC, MAC, SURGT

01 Campus President .... Kim IERIEN

Concordia University (J)

2811 NE Holman Ave, Portland OR 97211-6099
County: Multnomah FICE Identification: 003191
Unit ID: 208488
Telephone: (503) 288-9371 Carnegie Class: Master's L
FAX Number: (503) 280-8518 Calendar System: Quarter
URL: www.cu-portland.edu
Established: 1905 Annual Undergrad Tuition & Fees: $26,500
Enrollment: 3,500 Coed
Affiliation or Control: Lutheran Church - Missouri Synod
IRS Status: 501(c)3
Highest Offering: Doctorate
Program: Liberal Arts And General; Teacher Preparatory
Accreditation: NW, SW

01 President ... Dr. Charles E. SCHLIMPERT
26 Exec Vice Pres External Affairs ... Dr. Gary WITHERS
102 Exec Vice Pres Strategic Planning ... Mr. Johnnie DRIESSNER
05 Provost/Chief Academic Officer ... Dr. Mark E. WAHLERS
10 Chief Financial Officer ... Mr. Dennis J. STOECKLIN
32 VP Student Svcs/Enrollment Mgmt ... Dr. Glenn C. SMITH
04 Executive Administrator ... Ms. Nicole LAM
30 Chief Development Officer ... Mr. Kevin MATHENY
06 Registrar ... Vacant
07 Director Admissions & Enroll Mgmt ... Ms. Bobi SWAN
09 Director of Institutional Research ... Mr. Ron FONGER
15 Director of Human Resources ... Ms. Andrea STEN
18 Chief Facilities/Physical Plant ... Mr. Doug MEYER
20 Associate Academic Officer ... Vacant
88 Chief Public Relations Officer ... Ms. Madeline TURNOCK
29 Director Alumni Relations ... Vacant
35 Dean of Students ... Mr. Steve DEKLOTZ
08 Librarian ... Mr. Brent MAI
37 Director Student Financial Aid ... Ms. Rhoda RESEBURG
41 Athletic Director ... Dr. Matthew ENGLISH
38 Director Student Counseling ... Ms. Jaklin PEAKE
85 Director of International Studies ... Ms. Linda ROUNTREE
42 Campus Pastor ... Rev. Greg FAIROW
13 Chief Information Officer ... Dr. Joe MANNION
50 Dean School of Management ... Dr. Candace PETERSON
53 Interim Dean College of Education ... Dr. Sheryl REINISCH
49 Dean Theol Studies/Arts/Sciences ... Dr. David KLUTH
76 Dean Col of Health/Human Service ... Vacant
61 Dean School of Law ... Ms. Cathy SILAK

Corban University (A)

5000 Deer Park Drive, SE, Salem OR 97317
County: Marion FICE Identification: 001339
Unit ID: 210331
Telephone: (503) 581-8600 Carnegie Class: Bac/Diverse
FAX Number: (503) 585-4316 Calendar System: Semester
URL: www.corban.edu
Established: 1935 Annual Undergrad Tuition & Fees: $26,431
Enrollment: 1,161 Coed
Affiliation or Control: Independent Non-Profit IRS Status: 501(c)3
Highest Offering: Master's
Program: Liberal Arts And General; Teacher Preparatory; Professional
Accreditation: NW

01 President ... Dr. Reno R. HOFF
88 President Elect ... Dr. Sheldon NORD
05 Provost/Executive Vice President ... Dr. Matthew LUCAS
10 Vice President For Business ... Mr. Kevin BRUBAKER
32 Vice President For Student Life ... Dr. Brenda ROTH
26 Vice President for Marketing ... Mr. J. Steven HUNT
30 Vice President for Advancement ... Mr. Mike BATES
84 Vice Pres for Enrollment Management ... Mr. Marty ZIESEMER
35 Dean of Students ... Miss Brenda ROTH
11 Campus Administrator ... Dr. Leroy GOERTZEN
53 Dean of Counseling/Education ... Dr. Janine ALLEN
51 Dean of Adult Degree Programs ... Miss Nancy MARTYN
50 Dean of Business ... Mr. P. Griffith LINDELL
91 Chief Information Systems Officer ... Mr. Brian SCHMIDT
18 Director of Campus Care ... Mr. Tom SAMEK
06 Assoc Provost/Enrollment Management ... Dr. Chris VETTER
08 Librarian ... Mr. Floyd VOTAW
07 Director of Admissions ... Ms. Heidi STOWMAN
39 Director of Residential Life ... Mr. Nathan GEER
42 Director of Campus Ministries ... Dr. Gregory TRULL
41 Athletic Director ... Mr. Greg EIDE
36 Director Academic & Career Services ... Mr. Daren MILIONIS
37 Director Student Financial Aid ... Mr. Nathan WARTHAN
29 Director Alumni Relations ... Mrs. Deleen WILLS
38 Director Student Counseling ... Mrs. Stephanie HUSK
21 Associate Business Officer ... Mr. Brian ELLIOTT
40 Bookstore Manager ... Ms. Heather ULBRIGHT

Everest College (B)

425 Southwest Washington, Portland OR 97204-2296
County: Multnomah FICE Identification: 009079
Unit ID: 210359
Telephone: (503) 222-3225 Carnegie Class: Assoc/PrivFP
FAX Number: (503) 228-6926 Calendar System: Quarter
URL: www.everest-college.com
Established: 1955 Annual Undergrad Tuition & Fees: $15,612
Enrollment: 238 Coed
Affiliation or Control: Proprietary IRS Status: Proprietary
Highest Offering: Associate Degree
Program: Occupational; 2-Year Principally Bachelor's Creditable
Accreditation: ACICS, #MAC

01 President ... Ms. Siri DIXON
05 Chief Academic Officer ... Ms. Elaine SEYMAN
07 Director of Admissions ... Ms. Nancy AURAND
06 Registrar ... Mrs. Renee HATFIELD
37 Director Student Financial Aid ... Ms. Nicole TONE
36 Director of Student Placement ... Mr. Bryan JONES

George Fox University (C)

414 N Meridian, Newberg OR 97132-2697
County: Yamhill FICE Identification: 003194
Unit ID: 208822
Telephone: (503) 538-8383 Carnegie Class: Master's L
FAX Number: (503) 554-3834 Calendar System: Semester
URL: www.georgefox.edu
Established: 1891 Annual Undergrad Tuition & Fees: $30,770
Enrollment: 3,491 Coed
Affiliation or Control: Friends IRS Status: 501(c)3
Highest Offering: Doctorate
Program: Liberal Arts And General; Teacher Preparatory; Business Emphasis
Accreditation: NW, ACBSP, CACREP, CLPSY, ENG, MUS, NURSE, @PTA, SW, TED, THEOL

01 President ... Dr. Robin E. BAKER
03 Vice President/Dean of Seminary ... Dr. Charles J. CONNIRY, JR.
05 Provost ... Dr. Linda SAMEK
10 Exec VP Finance/Business Operations ... Mr. Ted ALLEN
30 Vice President Advancement ... Dr. Brian GARDNER
32 Vice President Student Life ... Dr. Bradley A. LAU
26 Exec VP Marketing/Enrollment Svcs ... Mr. Robert K. WESTERVELT
04 Executive Assistant to President ... Ms. Missy D. TERRY
21 Asst VP Financial Affairs ... Ms. Cris BANTON
08 University Librarian ... Mr. Merrill L. JOHNSON
07 Executive Director of Admissions ... Mr. Ryan DOUGHERTY
06 Registrar ... Ms. Melissa THOMAS
29 Director Alumni & Parent Relations ... Ms. Evangeline PATTISON
36 Director of Career Services ... Vacant
18 Director of Plant Services ... Mr. Clyde G. THOMAS
37 Director of Financial Aid ... Mr. James OSHIRO
96 Director Purchasing/Admin Services ... Mr. Andy DUNN
41 Director of Athletics ... Mr. Craig B. TAYLOR
105 Director of Web Development ... Mr. Peter CRACKENBERG
15 Director Human Resources ... Ms. Peggy L. KILBURG
42 University Pastor ... Ms. Sarah BALDWIN
27 Director Marketing/Communications ... Mr. Rob FELTON
13 Chief Information Officer ... Vacant
19 Director Security Services ... Mr. Ed GIEROK
38 Dir Health and Counseling Services ... Dr. William C. BUHROW
49 Dean School of Arts & Sciences ... Ms. Laura HARTLEY
83 Dean Sch Behavioral/Health Sci ... Dr. James E. FOSTER
53 Dean School of Education ... Dr. Scot HEADLEY
50 Dean School of Business ... Dr. Dirk BARRAM
88 Dean of Transitions & Inclusion ... Mr. Joel PEREZ

Gutenberg College (D)

1883 University Street, Eugene OR 97403-1368
County: Lane FICE Identification: 039324
Unit ID: 420510
Telephone: (541) 683-5141 Carnegie Class: Not Classified
FAX Number: (541) 683-6997 Calendar System: Quarter
URL: www.gutenberg.edu
Established: 1994 Annual Undergrad Tuition & Fees: $12,650
Enrollment: 22 Coed
Affiliation or Control: Independent Non-Profit IRS Status: 501(c)3
Highest Offering: Baccalaureate
Program: Liberal Arts And General; Religious Emphasis
Accreditation: #TRACS

01 President ... David CRABTREE
03 Vice President ... Richard BOOSTER
05 Dean ... Thomas DEWBERRY
07 Admissions Director ... Tim MCINTOSH
06 Registrar ... Chris SWANSON

Heald College, Portland (E)

6035 NE 78th Court, Portland OR 97218
Telephone: (503) 229-0492 FICE Identification: 037454
Accreditation: &WC, MAC

† Main campus is Heald College, San Francisco in San Francisco, CA.

ITT Technical Institute (F)

9500 NE Cascades Parkway, Portland OR 97220
Telephone: (503) 255-6500 FICE Identification: 011852
Accreditation: ACICS

† Main campus is ITT Technical Institute in Indianapolis, IN.

ITT Technical Institute (G)

4825 Commercial Street SE, Ste 100, Salem OR 97306
Telephone: (503) 576-2300 Identification: 770637
Accreditation: ACICS

† Main campus is ITT Technical Institute in Indianapolis, IN.

Klamath Community College (H)

7390 S 6th Street, Klamath Falls OR 97603-7121
County: Klamath FICE Identification: 034283
Unit ID: 428392
Telephone: (541) 882-3521 Carnegie Class: Assoc/Pub-R-S
FAX Number: (541) 885-7758 Calendar System: Quarter
URL: www.klamathcc.edu
Established: 1996 Annual Undergrad Tuition & Fees (In-District): $3,097
Enrollment: 1,172 Coed
Affiliation or Control: State/Local IRS Status: 501(c)3
Highest Offering: Associate Degree
Program: Occupational; 2-Year Principally Bachelor's Creditable
Accreditation: NW

01 President ... Dr. Roberto GUTIERREZ
11 Vice Pres Administrative Svcs ... Mr. Eric STASAK
05 Vice Pres of Academic Affairs ... Ms. Terri ARMSTRONG
32 Vice Pres of Student Services ... Ms. Julie MURRAY-JENSEN
13 Director Information Services ... Mr. Paul BREEDLOVE
15 Exec Director Human Resources ... Ms. Karren ANDREWS
06 Registrar ... Mr. John DUARTE
27 Chief Public Information Officer ... Mr. Ryan BROWN
18 Chief Facilities/Physical Plant ... Mr. Mike HOMFELDT
10 Senior Accountant ... Mr. Jack NOWAK
37 Financial Aid Specialist ... Ms. Allison BRYSON

Lane Community College (I)

4000 E 30th Avenue, Eugene OR 97405-0640
County: Lane FICE Identification: 003196
Unit ID: 209038
Telephone: (541) 463-3000 Carnegie Class: Assoc/Pub-R-L
FAX Number: (541) 463-5201 Calendar System: Quarter
URL: www.lanecc.edu
Established: 1964 Annual Undergrad Tuition & Fees (In-District): $3,682
Enrollment: 12,192 Coed
Affiliation or Control: Local IRS Status: 501(c)3
Highest Offering: Associate Degree
Program: Occupational; 2-Year Principally Bachelor's Creditable
Accreditation: NW, ACFEI, COARC, DA, DH, EMT, MAC, PTAA

01 President ... Dr. Mary SPILDE
05 Exec Vice President/CAO ... Vacant
11 Vice President College Operations ... Vacant
20 Exec Dean Academic/Student Affs/CAO ... Ms. Kerry LEVETT
20 Exec Dean Academic Affs/Career Tech ... Ms. Dawn DEWOLF
20 Exec Dean Academic Affs/Transfer ... Mr. Maurice HARRINGTON
35 Div Dean Student Life/Leadership ... Dr. Barbara DELANSKY
68 Div Dean Health/Physical Education ... Mr. Chris HAWKIN
28 Interim Chief Diversity Officer ... Dr. Donna KOECHIG
13 Chief Information Officer ... Mr. Bill SCHUETZ
10 Chief Financial Officer ... Mr. Greg MORGAN
35 Executive Dean/Student Affairs ... Ms. Helen GARRETT
15 Chief Human Resources Officer ... Mr. Dennis CARR
09 Dir Inst Research/Assess/Planning ... Dr. Craig TAYLOR
84 Director Enrollment Services ... Vacant
18 Director Facilities Mgmt/Planning ... Mr. Dave WILLIS
19 Director Public Safety ... Mr. Jace SMITH
08 Interim Library Director ... Ms. Marika PINEDA
38 Dir Counseling/Student Placement ... Mr. Jerry DELEON
37 Director of Financial Aid ... Ms. Helen FAITH
96 Director of Finance/Purchasing ... Mr. Stan BARKER
26 Public Information Officer ... Ms. Joan ASCHIM
102 Foundation Director ... Ms. Janet ANDERSON

Le Cordon Bleu College of Culinary Arts in Portland (J)

600 SW 10th Avenue, Suite 500, Portland OR 97205-2793
County: Multnomah FICE Identification: 030226
Unit ID: 375841
Telephone: (503) 223-2245 Carnegie Class: Assoc/PrivFP
FAX Number: (503) 223-0126 Calendar System: Other
URL: www.chefs.edu/portland
Established: 1983 Annual Undergrad Tuition & Fees: $17,950
Enrollment: 654 Coed
Affiliation or Control: Proprietary IRS Status: Proprietary
Highest Offering: Associate Degree
Program: Occupational
Accreditation: ACICS, ACFEI

01 Campus President ... Julia BROOKS
05 Vice President Academic Affairs ... Matt KUERBIS
07 Vice President of Admissions ... Tom BARKER
10 Business Operations Manager ... Katie STONE
32 Vice President Student Services ... Marsha PARMER
13 Director of IT & Facilities ... Bryan LEVINE
06 Registrar ... John ELIASSEN
37 Director Student Finances ... Katie STONE

Lewis and Clark College (K)

0615 SW Palatine Hill, Portland OR 97219-7899
County: Multnomah FICE Identification: 003197
Unit ID: 209056
Telephone: (503) 768-7000 Carnegie Class: Bac/A&S
FAX Number: (503) 768-7055 Calendar System: Semester
URL: www.lclark.edu
Established: 1867 Annual Undergrad Tuition & Fees: $40,330
Enrollment: 3,702 Coed
Affiliation or Control: Independent Non-Profit IRS Status: 501(c)3
Highest Offering: Doctorate
Program: Liberal Arts And General; Teacher Preparatory; Professional
Accreditation: NW, CACREP, LAW, MFCD, TED

01 President ... Dr. Barry GLASSNER
03 Vice President & Provost ... Dr. Jane M. ATKINSON
43 VP General Counsel/Secy of College ... Mr. David ELLIS
53 Dean Grad Sch Education/Counseling ... Dr. Scott FLETCHER
05 Dean of College of Arts & Sciences ... Dr. Tuajuanda C. JORDAN
61 Dean of the Law School ... Mr. Robert KLONOFF
10 Vice Pres Business/Finance/Treas ... Mr. Carl VANCE
30 Vice Pres Institutional Advancement ... Mr. Hal ABRAMS
32 Dean of Students ... Dr. Anna GONZALEZ
09 Assoc Provost Research & Planning ... Dr. Mark FIGUEROA
26 Assoc VP Public Affs/ Communications ... Mr. Tom KRATTENMAKER
07 Dean for Enrollment & Communication ... Ms. Lisa MEYER

21 Associate Vice Pres for Finance/Con .... Mr. George BATTISTEL
13 Assoc Vice Pres & Chief Info Ofcr .... Mr. Adam BUCHWALD
15 Assoc VP/Director Human Resources .... Mr. Isaac DIXON
18 Assoc Vice Pres Facilities .... Mr. Michel GEORGE
88 Assoc Vice President Campus Life .... Dr. Michael B. FORD
49 Assoc Dean College of Arts/Science .... Dr. Jim GRANT
49 Assoc Dean College of Arts/Science .... Dr. Gary REINESS
06 Registrar College of Arts/Sciences .... Ms. Judy FINCH
06 Registrar Law School .... Mr. Seneca GRAY
06 Registrar Graduate School .... Mr. Curt LUTTRELL
37 Director of Financial Aid .... Ms. Anastacia DILLON
08 Director of Library .... Mr. Mark DAHL
28 Assoc Dean Students .... Ms. Latricia BRAND
85 Assoc Dean Intl Stdnts & Scholars .... Mr. Brian WHITE
44 Director of Annual Giving & Develop .... Mr. Aaron WHITEFORD
29 Director Alumni/Parent Pgms .... Mr. Andrew MCPHEETERS
27 Senior Communications Officer .... Ms. Shelly MEYER
19 Director of Campus Safety .... Mr. Timothy O'DWYER
42 Dean of the Chapel .... Dr. Mark DUNTLEY
41 Acting Director of Athletics .... Mr. Mark PIETROK
39 Director of Residential Services .... Ms. Sandi BOTTEMILLER
24 Dir of Instructional Media Svcs .... Mr. Patrick RYALL
17 Asc Dean Stdnts/Wellness Svcs/Psych .... Dr. John HANCOCK

Linfield College (A)

900 SE Baker Street, McMinnville OR 97128-6894
County: Yamhill FICE Identification: 003198
Unit ID: 209065
Telephone: (503) 883-2200 Carnegie Class: Bac/A&S
FAX Number: (503) 883-2472 Calendar System: 4/1/4
URL: www.linfield.edu
Established: 1858 Annual Undergrad Tuition & Fees: $34,328
Enrollment: 1,663 Coed
Affiliation or Control: American Baptist IRS Status: 501(c)3
Highest Offering: Baccalaureate
Program: Liberal Arts And General; Teacher Preparatory; Professional
Accreditation: NW, MUS, NURSE

01 President .... Dr. Thomas HELLIE
05 Vice Pres Acad Affs/Dean of Faculty .... Ms. Susan AGRE-KIPPENHAN
10 Vice Pres Finance/Administration .... Mr. W. Glenn FORD
26 Vice Pres for College Relations .... Mr. Bruce WYATT
84 Vice Pres for Enrollment Management .... Mr. Daniel PRESTON
32 VP Student Svcs/Dean of Students .... Ms. Susan HOPP
43 Advisor to the Pres & General Couns .... Mr. John MCKEEGAN
66 Interim Dean of Nursing .... Dr. Pamela WHEELER
20 Associate Dean of Faculty .... Dr. Nancy DRICKEY
20 Associate Dean of Faculty .... Dr. Martha VAN CLEAVE
35 Associate Dean of Students .... Mr. Jeff MACKAY
15 Senior Director of Human Resources .... Ms. Linda POWELL
18 Director Facilities & Auxiliary Svc .... Ms. Allison HORN
28 Director Multicultural Programs .... Mr. Jason RODRIQUEZ
06 Registrar .... Dr. Eileen BOURASSA
07 Director of Admission .... Ms. Lisa KNODLE-BRAGIEL
08 Library Director .... Ms. Susan BARNES WHYTE
09 Director of Institutional Research .... Ms. Jennifer BALLARD
37 Director of Financial Aid .... Ms. Keri BURKE
13 Chief Technology Officer .... Mr. Irv WISWALL
91 Assoc Director Integrated Tech Svcs .... Mr. Phil SETH
105 Webmaster .... Mr. Jonathan PIERCE
85 Director of International Programs .... Dr. Shaik ISMAIL
51 Int Dean of Continuing Education .... Dr. Martha VAN CLEAVE
19 Director of Security .... Ms. Rebecca WALE
38 Director of Counseling Services .... Dr. John F. KERRIGAN, JR.
26 Director of Public Relations .... Ms. Mardi MILEHAM
44 Director of Annual Giving .... Ms. Christina DISS
44 Director of Planned Giving .... Mr. Craig HAISCH
102 Dir Corp & Foundation Relations .... Ms. Catherine JARMIN MILLER
29 Director of Alumni Relations .... Ms. Debbie HARMON
36 Director Career & Community Svcs .... Mr. Michael HAMPTON
42 Chaplain .... Dr. David MASSEY
41 Athletic Director .... Mr. Scott CARNAHAN
40 Bookstore Manager .... Mr. Chad COTTRILL

Linn-Benton Community College (B)

6500 SW Pacific Boulevard, Albany OR 97321-3774
County: Linn FICE Identification: 006938
Unit ID: 209074
Telephone: (541) 917-4999 Carnegie Class: Assoc/Pub-R-L
FAX Number: (541) 917-4445 Calendar System: Quarter
URL: www.linnbenton.edu
Established: 1966 Annual Undergrad Tuition & Fees (In-District): $4,032
Enrollment: 5,974 Coed
Affiliation or Control: State/Local IRS Status: 501(c)3
Highest Offering: Associate Degree
Program: Occupational; 2-Year Principally Bachelor's Creditable; Business Emphasis
Accreditation: NW, DA, MAC, OTA, POLYT

01 President .... Dr. Gregory J. HAMANN
05 Vice Pres Academic Affs/Wrkfce Dev .... Ms. Beth HOGELAND
10 Vice Pres Finance & Operations .... Mr. Jim HUCKESTEIN
32 Vice President Student Services .... Dr. Bruce CLEMETSEN
35 Assoc Dean Student Affairs .... Ms. Lynne COX
15 Dir Human Resources/Affirm Act Ofcr .... Mr. Scott ROLEN
37 Director of Student Financial Aid .... Ms. Bev GERIG
12 Director Albany Community Education .... Mr. Joel WHITE
12 Regional Director Linn County .... Mr. Gary PRICE
12 Regional Director Benton County .... Mr. Jeff DAVIS
84 Director Enrollment Services .... Mr. Danny AYNES
50 Dean Business/Applied Technology .... Vacant
41 Director of Athletics .... Mr. Randy FALK
81 Dean Science/Engr & Tech .... Mr. Andrew FELDMAN
49 Dean Arts/Soc Sci/Humanities Div .... Ms. Katie WINDER
76 Dean Health Care/E-Learning/Med Div .... Ms. Ann MALOSH
20 Dean Instruction .... Mr. Jonathan PAVER
30 Exec Dir Institutional Advancement .... Mr. Dale STOWELL
21 Budget Officer .... Ms. Betty NIELSEN
35 Director Student Life & Leadership .... Vacant
36 Dir Career Svcs/Stdnt Counseling .... Mr. Mark WEISS
13 Director Information Services .... Ms. Ann ADAMS
26 Director College Advancement .... Ms. Marlene PROPST
06 Registrar .... Vacant
18 Chief Facilities/Physical Plant .... Mr. Scott KRAMBUHL
44 Chief Development Officer .... Mr. John MCARDLE
08 Dean Academic Devel/Library Svcs .... Vacant

Marylhurst University (C)

PO Box 261, 17600 Pacific Highway, Marylhurst OR 97036-0261
County: Clackamas FICE Identification: 003199
Unit ID: 209108
Telephone: (503) 636-8141 Carnegie Class: Master's L
FAX Number: (503) 636-9526 Calendar System: Quarter
URL: www.marylhurst.edu
Established: 1893 Annual Undergrad Tuition & Fees: $19,665
Enrollment: 1,612 Coed
Affiliation or Control: Independent Non-Profit IRS Status: 501(c)3
Highest Offering: Master's
Program: Liberal Arts And General
Accreditation: NW, CIDA, IACBE, MUS

01 Interim President .... Mr. Jerry HUDSON
05 Provost/VP Academic Affairs .... Dr. David PLOTKIN
10 CFO/Exec VP Finance & Admin .... Mr. Michael LAMMERS
30 Vice Pres Institutional Advancement .... Ms. Lynn ANDREWS
15 Vice President for Human Resources .... Ms. Celina RATLIFFE
27 Vice President Info Tech/CIO .... Dr. Ethan BENATAN
84 VP Enrollment Mgmt .... Ms. Beth WOODWARD
04 Assistant to the President .... Ms. Judy MILLENBACH
32 Dean of Students .... Mr. Bill ZUELKE
07 Director of Admissions .... Mr. Chris SWEET
108 Dean of Assessment .... Vacant
06 Registrar .... Ms. Gwen HYATT
08 University Librarian .... Ms. Nancy HOOVER
26 Director Marketing & Communications .... Ms. Shirley SKIDMORE
44 Manager Annual Giving .... Vacant
25 Director of University Events .... Ms. Cheryl HANSEN
37 Director of Financial Aid .... Ms. Tracy REISINGER
88 Director Art Therapy Graduate Pgm .... Ms. Christine TURNER
72 Director Center for Learning Tech .... Dr. Vicki SUTER
13 Director of Information Systems .... Vacant
18 Director of Facilities .... Mr. Mark STRULOEFF
50 Dean School of Business .... Ms. Mary BRADBURY JONES
58 Dean School of Graduate Studies .... Dr. Debrah BOKOWSKI
49 Dean College of Arts & Sciences .... Dr. Jan DABROWSKI
88 Director Music Therapy .... Dr. Laura BEER
64 Chairperson Music Department .... Dr. John PAUL
57 Co-Chairperson & Dir Art Department .... Mr. Paul SUTINEN
57 Co-Chrpn Art Dpt/Dir Int Design Dpt .... Ms. Nancy HISS
73 Chrpsn Religious Studies & Phil .... Dr. Jeroid ROUSSELL
88 Chrpsn Grad Interdisciplinary Stds .... Dr. Susan CARTER
88 Chrpsn Interdisciplinary Studies .... Mr. Simeon DREYFUSS
79 Chrpsn Culture & Media .... Dr. David DENNY
81 Chair Science & Math .... Mr. Greg DARDIS
83 Chairperson Human Sciences .... Dr. Jennifer SASSER
88 Chairperson Real Estate Studies .... Mr. Sunny LISTON
88 Chrpsn English Literature/Writing .... Dr. Meg ROLAND
60 Chairperson Communication Studies .... Mr. Jeff SWEENEY
88 Chair Sustainable Business .... Mr. Paul VENTURA
88 Chair Food Systems & Society .... Dr. Patricia ALLEN

Mount Angel Seminary (D)

1 Abbey Drive, Saint Benedict OR 97373-0505
County: Marion FICE Identification: 003203
Unit ID: 209241
Telephone: (503) 845-3951 Carnegie Class: Spec/Faith
FAX Number: (503) 845-3128 Calendar System: Semester
URL: www.mountangelabbey.org
Established: 1887 Annual Undergrad Tuition & Fees: $29,784
Enrollment: 187 Coed
Affiliation or Control: Roman Catholic IRS Status: 501(c)3
Highest Offering: Master's
Program: Liberal Arts And General; Professional
Accreditation: NW, THEOL

01 President/Rector .... Rev. Joseph V. BETSCHART
05 Vice President/Academic Dean .... Dr. Owen CUMMINGS
08 Librarian .... Ms. Victoria ERTELT
10 Business Manager .... Fr. Martin GRASSEL, OSB
06 Registrar & Student Financial Aid .... Ms. Marina KEYS
32 Dean of Students College .... Rev. Paschal CHELINE, OSB
32 Dean of Students Theology .... Abbot Peter EBERLE, OSB
20 Academic Dean College .... Dr. Creighton LINDSAY
85 Director of Foreign Students .... Ms. Tamara SWANSON-ORR
07 Director of Admissions .... Fr. Ralph RECKER, OSB
04 Admin Assistant to the President .... Ms. Graciela CORTES
13 Director of Information Technology .... Mr. Francisco MORA
40 Director of Bookstore .... Mrs. Beth WELLS
20 Academic Dean Theology .... Dr. Seymour HOUSE

Mt. Hood Community College (E)

26000 SE Stark, Gresham OR 97030-3300
County: Multnomah FICE Identification: 003204
Unit ID: 209250
Telephone: (503) 491-6422 Carnegie Class: Assoc/Pub-S-SC
FAX Number: (503) 491-7389 Calendar System: Quarter
URL: www.mhcc.edu
Established: 1965 Annual Undergrad Tuition & Fees (In-District): $4,601
Enrollment: 9,847 Coed
Affiliation or Control: Local IRS Status: 501(c)3
Highest Offering: Associate Degree
Program: Occupational; 2-Year Principally Bachelor's Creditable
Accreditation: NW, COARC, DH, FUSER, PTAA, SURGT

01 President .... Dr. Debra DERR
11 Int VP of Administrative Services .... Mr. Bill FARVER
05 Vice Pres Instruction/Student Svcs .... Ms. Christie PLINSKI
20 Assoc Vice President of Instruction .... Dr. Ursula IRWIN
32 Assoc Vice Pres Success Services .... Mr. Robert COX
15 Director Human Resources .... Ms. Gale BLESSING
26 Chief Public Relations Officer .... Ms. Maggie HUFFMAN
88 Dir Child Dev/Family Support Pgms .... Ms. Jean WAGNER
18 Director Facilities Management .... Mr. Richard BYERS
30 Dir Comm Devel/College Advancement ... Ms. Michelle GREGORY
21 Director Auxiliary Services .... Ms. Sue ASCHIM
10 Director of Finance .... Ms. Jennifer DEMENT
06 Registrar .... Vacant
37 Director Student Financial Aid .... Ms. Christi HART
07 Director of Admissions .... Mr. John HAMBLIN
13 Chief Information Officer .... Ms. Linda VIGESAA
08 Dean Information Resources .... Vacant
76 Dean Health Professions & Nursing .... Ms. Janie GRIFFIN
81 Dean Soc Science/Perf/Visual Arts .... Ms. Janet MCINTYRE
79 Dean Humanities .... Mr. Eric TSCHUY
72 Dean Sciences .... Dr. Steve GOLDSMITH
50 Dean Bus/Info Sys/Integrated Media .... Mr. Rod BARKER
88 Dean Adult Basic Skills/Econ WF Dev .... Mr. Marc GOLDBERG
08 Dean Learning Commons .... Mr. Jeff RING

Multnomah University (F)

8435 NE Glisan Street, Portland OR 97220-5898
County: Multnomah FICE Identification: 003206
Unit ID: 209287
Telephone: (503) 255-0332 Carnegie Class: Spec/Faith
FAX Number: (503) 254-1268 Calendar System: Semester
URL: www.multnomah.edu
Established: 1936 Annual Undergrad Tuition & Fees: $21,850
Enrollment: 861 Coed
Affiliation or Control: Independent Non-Profit IRS Status: 501(c)3
Highest Offering: Master's
Program: Teacher Preparatory; Professional; Religious Emphasis
Accreditation: NW, BI, THEOL

01 President .... Dr. Daniel R. LOCKWOOD
05 Chief Academic Officer/Provost .... Dr. Wayne G. STRICKLAND
11 Chief Administrative Officer .... Ms. Gina BERQUIST
10 Chief Financial Officer .... Mr. Russell LACY
20 Academic Dean for College and Grad .... Dr. Rex KOIVISTO
73 VP/Academic Dean Biblical Seminary .... Dr. Robert R. REDMAN
32 Director/Dean of Students .... Mr. Jon MATHIS
30 Executive Director of Advancement .... Mr. John ZAREVA
39 Dean of Resident & Commuter Life .... Mr. David GROOM
35 Dean of Seminary Students .... Dr. Karen J. FANCHER
108 Dir of Institutional Effectiveness .... Dr. David FUNK
20 Associate Academic Dean .... Mr. David W. JONGEWARD
06 Registrar .... Ms. Amy M. STEPHENS
08 Librarian .... Dr. Philip M. JOHNSON
37 Director Student Financial Aid .... Mrs. Mary MCGLOTHLAN
36 Seminary Director of Placement .... Dr. Roger TRAUTMANN
13 Director Information Technology .... Mrs. Brenda GIBSON
15 Director of Human Resources .... Ms. Tracy L. MORESCHI
23 Director Health Services .... Mrs. Jana POLING
41 Athletic Director .... Ms. Lois VOS
26 Director of Marketing .... Mr. Tom MORLAN
07 Director of Admissions .... Mr. Palmer MUNTZ
29 Director Alumni Relations .... Mrs. Michelle UNDERWOOD
04 Assistant to the President .... Mrs. Denise STONE

† Granted candidacy at the Doctorate level.

National American University-Tigard (G)

1333 SW 68th Parkway, Tigard OR 97223
Telephone: (503) 403-3500 Identification: 770410
Accreditation: &NH

† Main campus is National American University in Rapid City, SD.

National College of Natural Medicine (H)

049 SW Porter Street, Portland OR 97201-4878
County: Multnomah FICE Identification: 025340
Unit ID: 209296
Telephone: (503) 552-1555 Carnegie Class: Spec/Health
FAX Number: (503) 499-0022 Calendar System: Quarter
URL: www.ncnm.edu
Established: 1956 Annual Graduate Tuition & Fees: $22,460
Enrollment: 542 Coed

Affiliation or Control: Independent Non-Profit IRS Status: 501(c)3
Highest Offering: Doctorate; No Undergraduates
Program: Professional
Accreditation: NW, ACUP, NATUR

01 President ....Dr. David J. SCHLEICH
05 Provost/VP Academic ....Dr. Andrea SMITH
10 Chief Financial Officer/VP Finances ....Mr. Gerald BORES
30 VP of Advancement ....Ms. Susan HUNTER
26 VP Marketing ....Ms. Sandra SNYDER
09 Dir of Inst Research & Compliance ....Ms. Laurie MCGRATH
17 Dean of Naturopathic Medicine ....Dr. Melanie HENRICKSEN
88 Dean Classical Chinese Medicine ....Dr. Laurie REGAN
32 Dean of Student Affairs ....Ms. Cheryl MILLER
46 Dean Helfgott Research Inst ....Dr. Heather ZWICKEY
23 Dean of Clinical Operations ....Dr. Jill SANDERS
88 Assoc Dean Naturopathic Medicine ....Dr. MaryK GEYER
20 Associate Dean Academic Progress ....Ms. Catherine DOWNEY
15 Director of Human Resources ....Mr. Steve JOHNSON
07 Director of Admissions ....Mr. Brandon HAMILTON
37 Director of Financial Aid ....Ms. Laurie RADFORD
06 Registrar ....Ms. Kelly GAREY
04 Executive Asst to the President ....Ms. Colleen CORDER
40 Dir Retail Operations ....Ms. Nora SANDE
88 Director of Professional Formation ....Dr. Marnie LOOMIS
08 Director of Library ....Dr. Rick SEVERSON
38 Director Student Counseling ....Ms. Adrienne WOLMARK

National College of Technical Instruction-College of Emergency Services (A)

9800 SE McBrod Ave, Ste 200, Milwaukie OR 97222
County: Clackamas Identification: 667128
Telephone: (971) 236-9231 Carnegie Class: Not Classified
FAX Number: (971) 653-9239 Calendar System: Semester
URL: www.ncti.edu
Established: 1995 Annual Undergrad Tuition & Fees: N/A
Enrollment: N/A Coed
Affiliation or Control: Proprietary IRS Status: Proprietary
Highest Offering: Associate Degree
Program: Occupational
Accreditation: ABHES, EMT

01 Interim Director ....Mr. David SCHAPPE

New Hope Christian College (B)

2155 Bailey Hill Road, Eugene OR 97405-1194
County: Lane FICE Identification: 021597
Unit ID: 208725
Telephone: (541) 485-1780 Carnegie Class: Spec/Faith
FAX Number: (541) 343-5801 Calendar System: Semester
URL: www.newhope.edu
Established: 1925 Annual Undergrad Tuition & Fees: $14,750
Enrollment: 200 Coed
Affiliation or Control: Other IRS Status: 501(c)3
Highest Offering: Baccalaureate
Program: Religious Emphasis
Accreditation: BI

00 Chancellor ....Mr. Wayne CORDEIRO
01 President/Dir College Advancement ....Dr. Guy HIGASHI
04 Executive Assistant to President ....Mrs. Lori HIGASHI
05 Academic Dean ....Dr. Mark KELLEY
29 Director of Alumni Relations ....Mrs. Jan HORNSHUH KENT
32 Director of Student Life ....Mr. Steven POETZL
10 Business Administrator ....Mr. David KELLEY
06 Registrar ....Ms. Mary Ellen PEREIRA
07 Enrollment Management ....Mr. Brendan LELACHEUR
37 Director of Financial Aid ....Mr. Nathan ICENHOWER
08 Head Librarian ....Ms. Jan KELLEY
38 Director of Christian Counseling ....Mr. David F. ORTEGA

Northwest Christian University (C)

828 E 11th Avenue, Eugene OR 97401-3745
County: Lane FICE Identification: 003208
Unit ID: 209409
Telephone: (541) 343-1641 Carnegie Class: Bac/Diverse
FAX Number: (541) 343-9159 Calendar System: Semester
URL: www.nwcu.edu
Established: 1895 Annual Undergrad Tuition & Fees: $24,780
Enrollment: 635 Coed
Affiliation or Control: Christian Church (Disciples Of Christ)
IRS Status: 501(c)3
Highest Offering: Master's
Program: Liberal Arts And General; Teacher Preparatory
Accreditation: NW, IACBE

01 President ....Dr. Joseph WOMACK
05 VP Academic Affairs/Dean of Faculty ....Dr. Dennis LINDSAY
10 Vice Pres Finance/Administration ....Mr. Gene DE YOUNG
30 Vice President Advancement ....Dr. Greg STRAUSBAUGH
32 VP Student Development/Enrollment ....Mr. Michael FULLER
49 Dean Arts & Sciences ....Vacant
50 Dean Business & Management ....Vacant
53 Dean School Education & Counseling ....Dr. Jim HOWARD
26 Director University Relations ....Ms. Jeannine JONES
39 Dir Residence Life/Asst Dean Stdnts ....Ms. Jocelyn HUBBS
08 Director Kellenberger Library ....Mr. Steve SILVER
06 Registrar ....Mr. Aaron PRUITT
42 Campus Pastor ....Mr. Troy DEAN
37 Director Financial Aid ....Mr. Scott PALMER
07 Director Admissions ....Ms. Kacie GERDRUM
35 Director Student Activities ....Ms. Sarah HALSTEAD
18 Plant Manager ....Mr. Oskar BUCHER
40 Bookstore Manager ....Vacant
41 Athletic Director ....Mr. Corey R. ANDERSON
36 Dir Career Dev & Disability Service ....Ms. Angela DOTY
24 Media/Computer Lab Supervisor ....Mr. Doug VERMILYEA
04 Administrative Assistant ....Ms. Carla AYDELOTT
29 Director Alumni & Church Relations ....Ms. Shannon BALMER
44 Director Annual Fund ....Ms. Glenda GORDON

Oregon College of Art and Craft (D)

8245 SW Barnes Road, Portland OR 97225-6349
County: Washington FICE Identification: 030073
Unit ID: 209533
Telephone: (503) 297-5554 Carnegie Class: Spec/Arts
FAX Number: (503) 297-3155 Calendar System: Semester
URL: www.ocac.edu
Established: 1907 Annual Undergrad Tuition & Fees: $25,500
Enrollment: 164 Coed
Affiliation or Control: Independent Non-Profit IRS Status: 501(c)3
Highest Offering: Baccalaureate
Program: Fine Arts Emphasis
Accreditation: NW, ART

01 President ....Ms. Denise MULLEN
10 Chief Financial Officer ....Vacant
05 Interim Dean for Programmatic Dev ....Ms. Jiseon LEE ISBARA
30 Chief Advanc/Marketing & CP Officer ....Ms. Roma PEYSER
07 Chief Enroll Officer/Dir of Admiss ....Ms. Anne BOERNER
06 Registrar ....Ms. Anna VARGAS
08 Head of Library Services ....Vacant
32 Coordinator of Student Services ....Ms. Meaghen PORTE
31 Interim Manager Community Programs ....Ms. Melissa LAIRD
37 Director of Financial Aid ....Ms. Linda ANDERSON
29 Dir of Exhibitions/Alumni Affairs ....Mr. Arthur DEBOW
04 Exec Assistant to the President ....Ms. Kris KEBISEK

Oregon College of Oriental Medicine (E)

75 NW Couch Street, Portland OR 97209-4018
County: Multnomah FICE Identification: 026037
Unit ID: 369659
Telephone: (503) 253-3443 Carnegie Class: Spec/Health
FAX Number: (503) 253-2701 Calendar System: Quarter
URL: www.ocom.edu
Established: 1983 Annual Graduate Tuition & Fees: $25,176
Enrollment: 274 Coed
Affiliation or Control: Independent Non-Profit IRS Status: 501(c)3
Highest Offering: Doctorate; No Undergraduates
Program: Professional
Accreditation: @NW, ACUP

01 President ....Dr. Michael GAETA
05 Vice President for Academic Affairs ....Dr. Tim CHAPMAN
10 Vice President for Finance ....Susan SLOAN
32 Dean of Academic & Student Affairs ....Carol TAUB
88 Dean of Doctoral Studies ....Dr. Beth BURCH
46 Associate Dean of Research ....Dr. Deborah ACKERMAN
17 Dean of Clinical Education ....Dr. Martin KIDWELL
30 Development Officer ....Glenn FEE
09 Planning & Inst Assessment Officer ....Shelley STUMP
15 Director of Human Resources ....Michelle VALINTIS
26 Director of Community Relations ....Gretchen HORTON
06 Registrar ....Carol ACHESON
13 Director of Operations & Technology ....Chris CHIACCHIERINI

Oregon Culinary Institute (F)

1701 SW Jefferson Street, Portland OR 97201-2571
Telephone: (503) 961-6200 Identification: 666177
Accreditation: ACICS

† Main campus is Pioneer Pacific College in Wilsonville, OR.

*Oregon University System (G)

PO Box 751, Portland OR 97207-0751
County: Multnomah FICE Identification: 009190
Unit ID: 209445
Telephone: (503) 725-5700 Carnegie Class: N/A
FAX Number: (503) 725-5709
URL: www.ous.edu

01 Interim Chancellor ....Dr. Melody ROSE
10 VC Finance & Administration ....Dr. Jay KENTON
05 Interim VC Academic Strategies ....Dr. Karen MARRONGELLE
21 Asst VC Budget/Operations ....Ms. Jan LEWIS
15 Assoc Gen Counsel Labor/Employment ....Mr. Brian CAUFIELD
43 Legal Counsel ....Mr. Ryan HAGEMANN
86 Director Government Relations ....Vacant
09 Director Institutional Research ....Mr. Robert KIERAN
100 Chief of Staff/Board Secretary ....Mr. Charles TRIPLETT III

*Eastern Oregon University (H)

One University Boulevard, La Grande OR 97850-2807
County: Union FICE Identification: 003193
Unit ID: 208646
Telephone: (541) 962-3672 Carnegie Class: Master's S
FAX Number: (541) 962-3493 Calendar System: Quarter
URL: www.eou.edu
Established: 1929 Annual Undergrad Tuition & Fees (In-State): $7,238
Enrollment: 4,208 Coed
Affiliation or Control: State IRS Status: 501(c)3
Highest Offering: Master's
Program: Liberal Arts And General; Teacher Preparatory; Professional
Accreditation: NW, IACBE

02 President ....Dr. Robert DAVIES
05 Provost/Senior VP Academic Affairs ....Dr. Stephen ADKISON
32 Vice President for Student Affairs ....Dr. Camille CONSOLVO
10 Actg Vice President Finance & Admin ....Ms. Lara MOORE
30 Vice Pres UA & Admissions ....Mr. Tim SEYDEL
20 Associate VP for Academic Affairs ....Dr. Sarah WITTE
49 Dean College Arts & Science ....Dr. Steven GAMMON
50 Interim Dean College of Bus & Educ ....Dr. Dan MIELKE
37 Director of Financial Aid ....Ms. Lara MOORE
08 Director of Pierce Library ....Ms. Karen CLAY
07 Director of Admissions ....Mr. Arlyn LOVE
06 Registrar ....Ms. Carolyn BLOYED
15 Director of Human Resources ....Mr. Art DOHERTY
29 Dir of Annual Giving and Alumni Rel ....Mr. Jon LARKIN
41 Interim Director of Athletics ....Ms. Anji WEISSENFLUH
39 Director of Residence Life ....Mr. Stephen JENKINS
18 Director of Facilities & Planning ....Mr. David LAGESON
38 Director Counseling Center ....Vacant
04 Exec Assistant to the President ....Ms. Kristen KRUSE
21 Director of Business Affairs ....Ms. Lara MOORE
36 Director of Acad & Career Advising ....Ms. Liz BURTON
88 Director of Learning Center ....Ms. Anna Maria DILL
35 Director of Student Relations ....Ms. Colleen DUNNE-CASCIO
19 Campus Security/Public Safety Ofcr ....Mr. Bill BENSON

*Oregon Health & Science University (I)

3181 SW Sam Jackson, Portland OR 97201-3098
County: Multnomah FICE Identification: 004882
Unit ID: 209490
Telephone: (503) 494-8311 Carnegie Class: Spec/Med
FAX Number: (503) 494-5738 Calendar System: Quarter
URL: www.ohsu.edu
Established: 1974 Annual Undergrad Tuition & Fees (In-State): $17,611
Enrollment: 2,849 Coed
Affiliation or Control: State IRS Status: 501(c)3
Highest Offering: Doctorate
Program: Professional
Accreditation: NW, ANEST, ARCPA, CAHIIM, DENT, DIETI, EMT, IPSY, MED, MIDWF, MT, NURSE, PH, RTT

02 President ....Dr. Joseph E. ROBERTSON
03 Executive Vice Provost ....Dr. David W. ROBINSON
05 Provost Education & Research ....Dr. Jeanette MLADENOVIC
18 Assoc VP Facilities/Physical Plant ....Mr. Scott PAGE
32 Vice Provost for Student Affairs ....Dr. Robert VIEIRA
63 Dean School of Medicine ....Dr. Mark RICHARDSON
52 Dean School of Dentistry ....Dr. Phillip T. MARUCHA
66 Dean School of Nursing ....Dr. Susan BAKEWELL-SACHS
06 Registrar/Director of Financial Aid ....Ms. Cherie HONNELL
17 Director University Hospital ....Mr. Peter RAPP
88 Director Vollum Inst Adv Biomed Res ....Dr. Richard H. GOODMAN
15 Director of Human Resources ....Vacant
08 Director Health Sciences Libraries ....Mr. Chris SHAFFER
46 Director of Research Services ....Dr. Daniel DORSA
27 Director Corporate Communications ....Ms. Lora L. CUYKENDALL
88 Director Child Devel/Rehab Center ....Dr. Brian ROGERS
37 Director Student Financial Aid ....Ms. Rachel DURBIN
28 Director of Diversity ....Ms. Leslie GARCIA

*Oregon Institute of Technology (J)

3201 Campus Drive, Klamath Falls OR 97601-8801
County: Klamath FICE Identification: 003211
Unit ID: 209506
Telephone: (541) 885-1000 Carnegie Class: Bac/Diverse
FAX Number: (541) 885-1101 Calendar System: Quarter
URL: www.oit.edu
Established: 1947 Annual Undergrad Tuition & Fees (In-State): $8,890
Enrollment: 4,001 Coed
Affiliation or Control: State IRS Status: 501(c)3
Highest Offering: Master's
Program: Liberal Arts And General; Technical Emphasis
Accreditation: NW, COARC, DH, ENG, ENGR, ENGT, IACBE, MT, POLYT

02 President ....Dr. Christopher MAPLES
05 Provost/Vice Pres Academic Affairs ....Mr. Bradley BURDA
10 Int VP Finance/Administration ....Ms. Mary Ann ZEMKE
32 VP Student Affairs/Enrollment Mgmt ....Dr. Erin FOLEY
30 Vice Pres of Development ....Vacant
35 Dean of Students ....Dr. Erin FOLEY
37 Director of Financial Aid ....Ms. Tracey A. LEHMAN
15 Director of Human Resources ....Mr. Ron MCCUTCHEON
07 Director of Admissions ....Mr. Carl THOMAS
06 Registrar ....Ms. Wendy IVIE

38 Director of Counseling ... Vacant
21 Director of Business Affairs ... Ms. Sara REUTER
13 Chief Information Officer ... Mr. Andy ABBOTT
23 Director Student Health Services ... Mr. James PITTMAN
18 Director Facilities Services ... Mr. Eric RULOFSON
41 Athletic Director ... Mr. Michael J. SCHELL
35 Director Campus Life ... Mr. Joseph MAURER
36 Director of Career Services ... Vacant
09 Director of Institutional Research ... Mr. David WAITE
29 Director Alumni Relations ... Mr. Tracy RICKETTS

*Oregon State University (A)

Corvallis OR 97331-8507

County: Benton | FICE Identification: 003210
Unit ID: 209542
Telephone: (541) 737-0123 | Carnegie Class: RU/VH
FAX Number: (541) 737-3033 | Calendar System: Quarter
URL: www.oregonstate.edu
Established: 1868 | Annual Undergrad Tuition & Fees (In-State): $8,538
Enrollment: 27,000 | Coed
Affiliation or Control: State | IRS Status: 501(c)3
Highest Offering: Doctorate
Program: Liberal Arts And General; Teacher Preparatory; Professional
Accreditation: NW, BUS, BUSA, CACREP, CONST, CS, DIETD, DIETI, ENG, ENGR, FOR, IPSY, PH, PHAR, TED, VET

02 President ... Dr. Edward J. RAY
05 Provost/Executive Vice President ... Dr. Sabah U. RANDHAWA
10 Vice Pres Finance/Administration ... Mr. Glenn FORD
30 Vice Pres University Advancement ... Mr. Steve CLARK
46 Vice President for Research ... Mr. Rick SPINRAD
20 Vice Prov Academic Affs/Intl Pgms ... Dr. Rebecca WARNER
13 Vice Prov for Information Svcs/CIO ... Ms. Lois BROOKS
32 Vice Prov for Student Affairs ... Dr. Larry D. ROPER
56 Vice Prov Univ Outreach/Engagement ... Dr. Scott REED
12 V Prov/Campus Ex Ofcr OSU-Cascades ... Dr. Rebecca JOHNSON
84 Asst Provost Enrollment Management ... Ms. Kate M. PETERSON
102 President & CEO OSU Foundation ... Mr. Mike GOODWIN
47 Dean of Agricultural Sciences ... Dr. Dan ARP
50 Dean of Business ... Dr. Ilene K. KLEINSORGE
54 Dean of Engineering ... Dr. Sandra WOODS
65 Dean of Forestry ... Dr. Thomas MANESS
68 Dean of Health & Human Sciences ... Dr. Tammy BRAY
49 Interim Dean of Liberal Arts ... Dr. Larry RODGERS
88 Dean of Oceanic & Atmos Science ... Dr. Mark R. ABBOTT
67 Dean of Pharmacy ... Dr. Mark ZABRISKIE
81 Dean of Science ... Dr. Vince REMCHO
74 Dean of Veterinary Medicine ... Vacant
51 Assoc Provost Extended Campus ... Dr. David A. KING
58 Dean of Graduate School ... Dr. Brenda MCCOMB
35 Dean of Student Life ... Dr. Mamta ACCAPADI
92 Dean University Honors College ... Dr. Toni DOOLEN
53 Dean of Education ... Dr. Larry FLICK
08 University Librarian ... Ms. Faye CHADWELL
22 Dir Affirmative Action/Equal Oppty ... Mr. Angelo GOMEZ
43 General Counsel ... Ms. Meg REEVES
41 Director Intecollegiate Athletics ... Mr. Robert J. DE CAROLIS
88 Director Intl Education & Outreach ... Vacant
36 Director of Career Services ... Mr. Douglas COCHRAN
37 Dir of Financial Aid/Scholarship ... Mr. Doug SEVERS
31 Director Memorial Union ... Mr. Michael HENTHORNE
23 Director Student Health Services ... Dr. Phillip C. HISTAND
38 Dir Univ Counseling/Psych Svcs ... Dr. Mariette BROUWERS
39 Director Univ Housing/Dining Svcs ... Mr. Thomas A. SCHEUERMANN
06 Registrar ... Ms. Rebecca MATHERN
07 Director of Admissions ... Mr. Noah BUCKLEY
24 Director Media & Outreach Services ... Mr. John GREYDANUS
14 Dir of Enterprise Computing Service ... Ms. Catherine M. WILLIAMS
21 Director of Business Affairs ... Mr. Aaron D. HOWELL
88 Director Business Services ... Mr. Brian K. THORSNESS
15 Director of Human Resources ... Mr. David BLAKE
18 Director Facility Services ... Mr. Brian THORSNES
19 Director Public Safety ... Mr. Jack T. ROGERS
29 Exec Dir of Alumni Association ... Ms. Kathy BICKEL
86 Director Government Relations ... Mr. Jock S. MILLS
44 Director of Annual Giving ... Ms. Lacie LA RUE
27 Dir News/Comm Svcs/Asst Vice Pres ... Mr. Mark FLOYD
26 Director of University Marketing ... Ms. Melody K. OLDFIELD
105 Asst Director Web Communications ... Mr. David A. BAKER
20 Dir Academic Planning/Assessment ... Mr. Gary BEACH
28 Director of Equity and Inclusion ... Mr. Angelo GOMEZ
09 Director of Institutional Research ... Mr. Salvador CASTILLO
40 General Mgr & CEO OSU Bookstores ... Mr. Steve E. ECKRICH
96 Manager Procurement/Contract Svcs ... Ms. Kelly L. KOZISEK

*Portland State University (B)

PO Box 751, Portland OR 97207-0751

County: Multnomah | FICE Identification: 003216
Unit ID: 209807
Telephone: (503) 725-3000 | Carnegie Class: RU/H
FAX Number: (503) 725-4882 | Calendar System: Quarter
URL: www.pdx.edu
Established: 1946 | Annual Undergrad Tuition & Fees (In-State): $7,653
Enrollment: 29,524 | Coed
Affiliation or Control: State | IRS Status: 501(c)3
Highest Offering: Doctorate
Program: Liberal Arts And General; Teacher Preparatory; Professional
Accreditation: NW, BUS, BUSA, CACREP, CORE, CS, ENG, HSA, MUS, PH, PLNG, SP, SPAA, SW, TED, THEA

02 President ... Dr. Wim WIEWEL
43 General Counsel ... Mr. David REESE
05 Provost ... Dr. Sona ANDREWS
10 Vice President Finance/Admin ... Dr. Monica RIMAI
30 VP for University Advancement ... Ms. Francoise AYLMER
100 Chief of Staff ... Ms. Lois DAVIS
32 VP Enroll Mgmt & Student Affairs ... Dr. Jackie BALZER
46 VP Rsrch & Strategic Partnerships ... Dr. Jonathan FINK
45 Vice Provost Budget/Planning & Int ... Mr. Kevin REYNOLDS
20 Vice Provost Acad Personnel ... Dr. Carol MACK
21 Assoc VP Budget & Finance ... Mr. Alan FINN
15 Assc VP HR & Univ Policy/Practice ... Ms. Shana SECHRIST
20 Assoc Vice Prov Academic Services ... Mr. Dan FORTMILLER
84 Assoc VP Enrollment Management ... Ms. Cindy SKARUPPA
22 Chief Diversity Officer ... Dr. Jilma MENESES
26 Assoc Vice Pres Communications ... Mr. Christopher BRODERICK
09 Dir Inst Research/Planning ... Dr. Kathi A. KETCHESON
19 Director Campus Public Safety ... Mr. Phil ZERZAN
13 AVP Strategic Plng/Prtnrshps/Tech ... Mr. Erin FLYNN
08 Dean University Librarian ... Dr. Marilyn MOODY
41 Athletics Director ... Mr. Michael T. CHISHOLM
89 AVP Acad Innov & Stdnt Success ... Mr. Sukhwant S. JHAJ
49 Dean Col of Liberal Arts/Sciences ... Dr. Susan BEATTY
50 Dean School Business Administration ... Dr. Scott DAWSON
53 Dean Graduate Sch of Education ... Dr. Randy HITZ
54 Dean Col Engr/Computer Science ... Dr. Renjeng SU
57 Dean College of the Arts ... Ms. Barbara SESTAK
70 Dean School of Social Work ... Dr. Nancy KOROLOFF
80 Dean College Urban/Public Affairs ... Dr. Lawrence WALLACK
35 Dean Student Life ... Ms. Michele TOPPE
27 AVP/Chief Information Officer ... Mr. Kirk KELLT
88 Dir Diversity & Mult Student Svcs ... Ms. Cece RIDDER
86 Dir Local & Fed Govt Relations ... Ms. Mary MOLLER
86 Dir State Govt Relations ... Ms. Debbie KORESKI
23 Exec Dir Stdnt Health & Counseling ... Dr. Dana TASSON
58 AVP & Dean Graduate Studies ... Ms. Margaret EVERETT
44 AVP Development ... Ms. Kristin COPPOLA
28 Exec Dir Diversity & Inclusion ... Mr. Chas LOPEZ
88 AVP Research ... Mr. Mark SYTSMA
100 Chief of Staff ... Ms. Debbie KIRKLAND
21 Exec Dir Financial Svcs & Contr ... Ms. Sandra BURRIS

*Southern Oregon University (C)

1250 Siskiyou Boulevard, Ashland OR 97520-5001

County: Jackson | FICE Identification: 003219
Unit ID: 210146
Telephone: (541) 552-7672 | Carnegie Class: Master's L
FAX Number: (541) 552-6329 | Calendar System: Quarter
URL: www.sou.edu
Established: 1872 | Annual Undergrad Tuition & Fees (In-State): $7,897
Enrollment: 6,572 | Coed
Affiliation or Control: State | IRS Status: 501(c)3
Highest Offering: Master's
Program: Liberal Arts And General; Professional
Accreditation: NW, ACBSP, CACREP, MUS

02 President ... Dr. Mary CULLINAN
05 Prov & VP for Acad & Student Affs ... Dr. James KLEIN
11 VP for Administration & Finance ... Mr. Craig MORRIS
30 Vice President Development ... Ms. Sylvia KELLEY
15 Director for Human Resource Svcs ... Mr. Jay STEPHENS
100 Chief of Staff/Dir Governmt Rels ... Ms. Liz SHELBY
84 Asst VP of Enrollment ... Mr. Rick WEEMS
26 Ex Dir Interactive Mktg/Media Rels ... Mr. Mark TRAMONTE
18 Dir for Facilities Mgmt & Planning ... Mr. Drew GILLILAND
58 Assoc Provost/Dean Graduate Stds ... Dr. Susan WALSH
21 Director of Business Services ... Mr. Steve LARVICK
08 Dean of Library ... Mr. Paul ADALIAN
35 Director for Student Life ... Ms. Jennifer FOUNTAIN
51 Exec Dir Division of Continuing Edu ... Ms. Jeanne STALLMAN
49 Dean College of Arts & Sciences ... Dr. Alissa ARP
19 Co-Director of Campus Public Safety ... Mr. Stephen ROSS
19 Co-Director of Campus Public Safety ... Mr. Richard WALSH
14 Director of Information Technology ... Mr. Brad CHRIST
29 Director of Alumni Affairs ... Mr. Mike BEAGLE
21 Assoc Director of Business Services ... Ms. Debbie MICHAELS
106 Director of Distance Education ... Ms. Hart WILSON
88 Director of Schneider Museum of Art ... Ms. Erika LEPPMAN
88 Dir of Accelerated Baccalureate Pgm ... Mr. Curt BACON
28 Director of Diversity ... Ms. Marjorie TRUEBLOOD-GAMBLE
44 Annual Fund Coordinator ... Ms. Chava FLORENDO
88 Director of Performing Arts ... Mr. Noel KORAN

*University of Oregon (D)

Eugene OR 97403-1226

County: Lane | FICE Identification: 003223
Unit ID: 209551
Telephone: (541) 346-1000 | Carnegie Class: RU/VH
FAX Number: (541) 346-3017 | Calendar System: Quarter
URL: www.uoregon.edu
Established: 1876 | Annual Undergrad Tuition & Fees (In-State): $9,853
Enrollment: 24,591 | Coed
Affiliation or Control: State | IRS Status: 501(c)3
Highest Offering: Doctorate
Program: Liberal Arts And General; Professional
Accreditation: NW, ART, BUS, BUSA, CEA, CIDA, CLPSY, COPSY, IPSY, JOUR, LAW, LSAR, MFCD, MUS, PCSAS, PLNG, SCPSY, SP, SPAA

02 President ... Dr. Michael R. GOTTFREDSON
04 Senior Assistant to the President ... Dr. David R. HUBIN
100 Assistant VP/Chief of Staff ... Mr. Gregory S. RIKHOFF
05 Interim Senior VP & Provost ... Dr. Scott L. COLTRANE
10 VP Finance & Admin & CFO ... Ms. Jamie H. MOFFITT
32 Vice President for Student Affairs ... Dr. Robin H. HOLMES
30 Vice Pres University Advancement ... Mr. Michael C. ANDREASEN
46 VP Research/Dean Graduate School ... Dr. Kimberly A. ESPY
20 Vice Provost Undergraduate Studies ... Dr. Karen U. SPRAGUE
28 Vice Pres Inst Equity/Diversity ... Dr. Yvette ALEX-ASSENSOH
13 Vice Prov Information Services/CIO ... Dr. Melissa Z. WOO
85 Vice Provost International Affairs ... Dr. Dennis GALVAN
30 Asst VP Campaign Initiatives ... Vacant
21 Assoc Vice Pres Budget & Finance ... Vacant
86 Assoc Vice Pres Public/Govt Affairs ... Ms. Betsy A. BOYD
29 AVP Alumni Affairs/Exec Dir UOAA ... Mr. Timothy R. CLEVENGER
43 General Counsel to the University ... Mr. L. Randy GELLER
102 Chief Investment Officer Foundation ... Mr. Jay NAMYET
06 University Registrar ... Ms. Susan M. EVELAND
07 Director of Admissions ... Mr. Jim RAWLINS
08 Philip H Knight Dean of Libraries ... Ms. Deborah A. CARVER
21 Dir Business Affairs and Controller ... Mr. Kelly B. WOLF
37 Director Student Financial Aid ... Mr. James J. BROOKS
36 Director of Career Center ... Dr. Daniel PASCOE AGUILAR
15 Assoc VP Human Resources ... Ms. Linda L. KING
18 Assoc VP Campus Operations ... Mr. George E. HECHT
22 Director Affirmative Action ... Ms. Penny J. DAUGHERTY
41 Director Intercollegiate Athletics ... Mr. Rob A. MULLENS
56 Senior Dir UO Academic Extension ... Mr. Curt D. LIND
49 Int Dean College Arts & Sciences ... Dr. W. Andrew MARCUS
48 Dean Architecture & Allied Arts ... Ms. Frances BRONET
50 Dean College of Business ... Dr. Cornelis A. DE KLUYVER
53 Dean College of Education ... Dr. Michael D. BULLIS
60 Dean School of Journalism & Comm ... Dr. Timothy W. GLEASON
58 Vice Prov Grad Studies & Assoc Dean ... Dr. Sandra MORGEN
61 Dean School of Law ... Mr. Michael L. MOFFITT
64 Dean School of Music & Dance ... Dr. C. Brad FOLEY
92 Dean Clark Honors College ... Dr. David FRANK
09 Director of Institutional Research ... Dr. J.P MONROE
35 Associate VP for Student Affairs ... Mr. Michael E. EYSTER
38 Dir Counseling & Testing Center ... Dr. Shelly K. KERR
84 Vice Provost Enrollment Management ... Mr. Roger J. THOMPSON
96 Dir Purchasing & Contracting Svcs ... Ms. Catherine D. SUSMAN

*Western Oregon University (E)

345 N Monmouth Avenue, Monmouth OR 97361-1394

County: Polk | FICE Identification: 003209
Unit ID: 210429
Telephone: (503) 838-8000 | Carnegie Class: Master's M
FAX Number: (503) 838-8474 | Calendar System: Quarter
URL: www.wou.edu
Established: 1856 | Annual Undergrad Tuition & Fees (In-State): $7,818
Enrollment: 6,187 | Coed
Affiliation or Control: State | IRS Status: 501(c)3
Highest Offering: Beyond Master's But Less Than Doctorate
Program: Liberal Arts And General; Teacher Preparatory
Accreditation: NW, CORE, MUS, TED

02 President ... Mr. Mark D. WEISS
05 Vice Pres Academic Affairs ... Dr. Stephen SCHECK
32 Vice President Student Affairs ... Dr. Gary DUKES
10 Vice President Business & Finance ... Mr. Eric YAHNKE
35 Dean of Students ... Ms. Tina M. FUCHS
49 Dean Col Liberal Arts & Sciences ... Dr. Susanne MONAHAN
53 Dean College of Education ... Dr. Mark GIROD
07 Asc Prov Admiss Retent/Enroll Mgmt ... Mr. David MCDONALD
56 Exec Dir Division Extended Pgms ... Mr. Dan CLARK
06 Registrar ... Ms. Nancy FRANCE
30 Director of Development ... Mr. Tommy LOVE
08 Director Hamersly Library ... Dr. Allen MCKIEL
13 Director University Computing Svcs ... Mr. William KERNAN
15 Director Human Resources ... Ms. Judy J. VANDERBURG
18 Director Physical Plant ... Mr. Tom NEAL
19 Director University Public Safety ... Mr. Jay CAREY
23 Dir Student Health/Counseling Ctr ... Vacant
26 Dir Public Relations/Communications ... Ms. Denise VISUANO
32 Director Student Life ... Mr. Don BODERMAN
37 Director Financial Aid ... Ms. Donna KIRK
41 Athletic Director ... Ms. Barbara DEARING
46 Dir of Teaching Research Institute ... Dr. Ella TAYLOR
85 Dir Intl Students/Scholars Affairs ... Mr. Neng YANG
88 Dir Multicultural Student Svcs/Pgms ... Ms. Anna HERNANDEZ-HUNTER
22 Director AAEO ... Ms. Judy J. VANDERBURG
29 Dir Leadership Giving/Athletic Dev ... Mr. Michael FEULING
25 Project & Contract Officer ... Mr. Stan HAGEN

Pacific Northwest College of Art (F)

1241 NW Johnson Street, Portland OR 97209-3023

County: Multnomah | FICE Identification: 003207
Unit ID: 209603
Telephone: (503) 226-4391 | Carnegie Class: Spec/Arts
FAX Number: (503) 226-3587 | Calendar System: Semester
URL: www.pnca.edu
Established: 1909 | Annual Undergrad Tuition & Fees: $30,730
Enrollment: 551 | Coed
Affiliation or Control: Independent Non-Profit | IRS Status: 501(c)3
Highest Offering: Master's
Program: Fine Arts Emphasis
Accreditation: NW, ART

01 President ... Dr. Thomas MANLEY

05 Dean of Academic Affairs ... Mr. Mark TAKIGUCHI
10 Chief Financial Officer/HR Dir ... Mr. Larry HUDSPETH
84 Vice Pres Enrollment Services ... Mr. Kavin BUCK
04 Assistant to the President ... Ms. Elizabeth CAMPBELL
51 Director of Continuing Education ... Mr. Patrick FORSTER
37 Director Financial Aid ... Ms. Heidi LOCKE
26 Director of Communications ... Mrs. Becca BIGGS
06 Registrar ... Ms. Jenifer DE KALB
08 Director of Library Services ... Mr. Dan MCCLURE
07 Director of Admissions ... Ms. D. Jean HESTER

Pacific University (A)

2043 College Way, Forest Grove OR 97116-1797
County: Washington — FICE Identification: 003212
Unit ID: 209612
Telephone: (503) 357-6151 — Carnegie Class: Master's L
FAX Number: (503) 352-2242 — Calendar System: Semester
URL: www.pacificu.edu
Established: 1849 — Annual Undergrad Tuition & Fees: $37,024
Enrollment: 3,433 — Coed
Affiliation or Control: Independent Non-Profit — IRS Status: 501(c)3
Highest Offering: Doctorate
Program: Liberal Arts And General; Teacher Preparatory; Professional
Accreditation: NW, ARCPA, @AUD, CLPSY, DH, IPSY, MUS, OPT, OPTR, OT, PHAR, PTA, @SP, SW, TED

01 President ... Dr. Lesley M. HALLICK
05 Vice Pres Academic Affairs/Provost ... Dr. John MILLER
10 Vice Pres Finance & Administration ... Mr. Mike MALLERY
30 Vice Pres University Advancement ... Ms. Cassie MCVEETY
32 Vice Pres Enrollment/Student Affs ... Dr. Mark ANKENY
35 Assoc Vice Pres Student Affairs ... Mr. Will PERKINS
46 Vice Provost for Research ... Dr. Chris WILKES
21 Assistant Vice Pres for Finance ... Mr. William RAY
26 Assoc VP for University Relations ... Ms. Jan STRICKLIN
18 Dir of Facilities/Safety Management ... Mr. Harold ROARK
07 Executive Director of Admissions ... Ms. Karen DUNSTON
06 Registrar ... Ms. Anne HERMAN
37 Director Financial Aid ... Mr. Mike JOHNSON
27 Chief Information Officer ... Mr. James FLEMING
88 Director of Conference Services ... Ms. Lois HORNBERGER
88 Director University Events ... Ms. Paula THATCHER
76 Exec Dean Col of Health Professions ... Dr. Ann BARR
49 Dean of Arts & Sciences ... Dr. Lisa CARSTENS
63 Dean of Optometry ... Dr. Jennifer SMYTHE
67 Dean of Pharmacy ... Dr. Sue STEIN
53 Dean College of Education ... Dr. Mark ANKENY
83 Dean Sch Professional Psychology ... Dr. Christiane BREMS
41 Athletic Director ... Mr. Kenneth SCHUMANN
76 Director School Physical Therapy ... Dr. Richard RUTT
76 Dir School Occupational Therapy ... Dr. John WHITE
15 Director of Human Resources ... Mr. Troy STRASS
23 Director of Health Services ... Ms. Kathryn L. EISENBARTH
88 Acad Coord/English Language Inst ... Ms. Monique GRINDELL
44 Director of Annual Giving ... Ms. Kristin STORFA
07 Exec Director of Grad/Prof Admiss ... Mr. Jon-Erik LARSEN
76 Director Physician Asst Studies ... Ms. Judy ORTIZ
29 Director Alumni Relations ... Ms. Martha CALUS-MCLAIN
88 Dir External Relations Optometry ... Ms. Jeanne OLIVER
08 Library Director ... Ms. Marita KUNKEL
88 Senior Editor/Writer ... Ms. Jenni LUCKETT
32 Dir Univ Center/Student Activities ... Mr. Steve KLEIN
36 Director Career Development ... Mr. Brian O'DRISCOLL
52 Program Director-Dental ... Ms. Lisa ROWLEY
40 Manager Bookstore ... Ms. Stacie BLANKENHORN
38 Director Counseling Center ... Ms. Robin KEILLOR
09 Director of Institutional Research ... Mr. William O'SHEA

Pioneer Pacific College (B)

27501 SW Parkway Avenue, Wilsonville OR 97070-9296
County: Clackamas — FICE Identification: 023301
Unit ID: 210076
Telephone: (503) 682-3903 — Carnegie Class: Assoc/PrivFP4
FAX Number: (503) 682-1514 — Calendar System: Other
URL: www.pioneerpacific.edu
Established: 1981 — Annual Undergrad Tuition & Fees: $13,186
Enrollment: 1,688 — Coed
Affiliation or Control: Proprietary — IRS Status: Proprietary
Highest Offering: Baccalaureate
Program: Occupational
Accreditation: ACICS

01 President ... Mr. Don MOUTOS
00 Board Chairman ... Mr. Raymond C. GAUTHIER
12 Portland Metro Campus President ... Mr. Don MOUTOS
12 OCI Campus President ... Mr. Eric STROMQUIST
12 Springfield Campus President ... Mr. Eric ARMSTRONG
10 Chief Financial Officer ... Mr. Mark MORELAND
05 Vice President of Academic Affairs ... Ms. Sandra WIGGINS
07 Vice President of Admissions ... Ms. Vicki CHURCH
37 Executive Director of Financial Aid ... Mr. Michael HARGRAVE
22 Compliance Officer ... Mr. Andrew BERNHARD
21 Controller ... Mr. Don ECK
26 Director of Marketing ... Ms. Basia PETRI
06 Lead Registrar ... Ms. Etta SCHWAB
50 Program Director Business-WLS ... Ms. Carin DYKZEUL
50 Program Director Business-CLK ... Mr. David WILHOYTE
50 Program Director Business-SPR ... Ms. Linda FARMER
61 Program Director Legal-WLS ... Ms. Vanesa PANCIC-MEIER
61 Program Director Legal-CLK ... Mr. Warren MOE
76 Program Director Medical-HCI ... Ms. Jennifer SCHILLING
76 Program Director Health-WLS & HCI ... Ms. Roxanne STEVENS
76 Program Director Massage-HCI ... Dr. Kim SCHMALTZ
76 Program Director Limited Xray ... Ms. Monica QUINTERO-DEVLAEMINCK
76 Program Director Limited X-Ray-SPR ... Ms. Katheryn MADISON
76 Program Director Medical-SPR ... Ms. Jody WEARIN
77 Program Director IT-WLS ... Mr. Rob MORRISON
77 Program Director IT-SPR ... Mr. Ed MCLAUGHLIN
66 Program Director Nursing ... Ms. Kim VOGEL
80 Program Director Criminal Just-WLS ... Mr. James FORD
80 Program Director Criminal Just-SPR ... Ms. Pamela MOORE
67 Program Director Pharmacy-HCI ... Dr. Kim SCHMALTZ
67 Program Director Pharmacy- SPR ... Ms. Lisa RUSSELL
08 Librarian ... Ms. Jill SLED

Pioneer Pacific College-Eugene Branch (C)

3800 Sports way, Springfield OR 97447
Telephone: (541) 684-4644 — Identification: 770764
Accreditation: ACICS

† Main campus is Pioneer Pacific College in Wilsonville, OR.

Portland Community College (D)

PO Box 19000, Portland OR 97280-0990
County: Multnomah — FICE Identification: 003213
Unit ID: 209746
Telephone: (971) 722-6111 — Carnegie Class: Assoc/Pub-U-MC
FAX Number: (971) 722-4960 — Calendar System: Quarter
URL: www.pcc.edu
Established: 1961 — Annual Undergrad Tuition & Fees (In-District): $4,448
Enrollment: 10,104 — Coed
Affiliation or Control: Local — IRS Status: 501(c)3
Highest Offering: Associate Degree
Program: Occupational; 2-Year Principally Bachelor's Creditable
Accreditation: NW, ADNUR, CAHIIM, DA, DH, DT, EMT, MAC, MLTAD, RAD

01 District President ... Dr. Jeremy BROWN
03 District Vice President ... Mr. Randy MCEWEN
05 VP Academic & Student Affairs ... Dr. Christine CHAIRSELL
11 Vice Pres Administrative Services ... Mr. Wing-Kit CHUNG
10 Assoc VP Financial Services ... Mr. Jim Langstraat CHEVALIER
91 Assoc VP Information Tech Svcs ... Ms. Leslie RIESTER
26 Assoc VP Institutional Advancement ... Ms. Kristin WATKINS
12 Campus President Sylvania ... Dr. Linda GERBER
12 Campus President Cascade ... Vacant
12 Int Campus President Rock Creek ... Dr. Birgitte RYSLINGE
12 Campus President Extended Lrng ... Dr. Jessica HOWARD
20 Dean Instruction Sylvania Campus ... Mr. Jeff TRIPLET
20 Dean Instruction Cascade Campus ... Mr. Kurt SIMONDS
20 Int Dean Instr Rock Creek Campus ... Dr. Cheryl SCOTT
20 Dean Instr Ext Lrng Camp ... Dr. Craig KOLINS
32 Dean Student Dev Sylvania Campus ... Ms. Heather LANG
32 Dean Stdnt Dev Rock Creek Campus ... Ms. Narce RODRIGUEZ
32 Dean Student Dev Cascade Campus ... Dr. Linda REISSER
32 Dean Student Affairs ... Ms. Veronica GARCIA
15 Interim Director Human Resources ... Ms. Lisa BLEDSOE
18 Int Director Facilities Management ... Mr. Jon MARCHETTA
08 Director Libraries ... Dr. Donna REED
09 Dir Institutional Effectiveness ... Ms. Laura MASSEY
19 Director Public Safety ... Mr. Ken GOODWIN
37 Director Financial Aid ... Mr. Bert LOGAN
22 Director Affirmative Action ... Vacant
30 Director of Development ... Ms. Kim KONO

Reed College (E)

3203 SE Woodstock Boulevard, Portland OR 97202-8199
County: Multnomah — FICE Identification: 003217
Unit ID: 209922
Telephone: (503) 771-1112 — Carnegie Class: Bac/A&S
FAX Number: (503) 777-7769 — Calendar System: Semester
URL: www.reed.edu
Established: 1908 — Annual Undergrad Tuition & Fees: $46,010
Enrollment: 1,455 — Coed
Affiliation or Control: Independent Non-Profit — IRS Status: 501(c)3
Highest Offering: Master's
Program: Liberal Arts And General
Accreditation: NW

01 President ... Mr. John KROGER
05 Dean of the Faculty ... Dr. Nigel NICHOLSON
26 Vice President College Relations ... Dr. Hugh PORTER
10 Vice President & Treasurer ... Mr. Edwin O. MCFARLANE
32 Vice Pres/Dean Student Services ... Dr. Michael BRODY
04 Exec Asst to the President ... Ms. Dawn THOMPSON
28 Dean Institutional Diversity ... Ms. Crystal WILLIAMS
35 Assoc Dean of Stdnts for Acad Supp ... Ms. Lily COPENAGLE
39 Assoc Dean Student & Campus Life ... Mr. Bruce SMITH
23 Director Health & Counseling ... Ms. Kathryn SMITH
07 Dean of Admission ... Mr. Keith TODD
06 Registrar ... Ms. Nora MCLAUGHLIN
08 College Librarian ... Ms. Dena HUTTO
30 Director of Development ... Ms. Jan KURTZ
37 Director of Financial Aid ... Ms. Leslie LIMPER
09 Director of Institutional Research ... Mr. Mike TAMADA
26 Director of Public Affairs ... Ms. Stacey KIM
29 Director of Alumni Relations ... Mr. Michael TESKEY
13 Chief Technology Officer ... Dr. Martin D. RINGLE
27 Deputy CIO/Dir Web Support Svcs ... Ms. Marianne COLGROVE
91 Director Administrative Computing ... Mr. Gary D. NORBRATEN
21 Controller ... Ms. Tracy L. FRANTEL
15 Director of Human Resources ... Ms. Michelle VALINTIS
44 Dir Annual Funds/Special Gifts ... Ms. Mary ASKELSON
102 Dir Corporate/Foundation Support ... Ms. Diane GUMZ
104 Director International Programs ... Dr. Paul DEYOUNG
36 Director of Career Services ... Mr. Ron ALBERTSON
88 Director of Special Programs ... Ms. Barbara A. AMEN
18 Director Facilities Operations ... Mr. Townsend ANGELL
19 Director Community Safety ... Mr. Gary GRANGER
68 Director of Physical Education ... Mr. Michael LOMBARDO
40 Manager of the Bookstore ... Mr. Ueli STADLER

Rogue Community College (F)

3345 Redwood Highway, Grants Pass OR 97527-9298
County: Josephine — FICE Identification: 010182
Unit ID: 209940
Telephone: (541) 956-7500 — Carnegie Class: Assoc/Pub-R-L
FAX Number: (541) 471-3591 — Calendar System: Quarter
URL: www.roguecc.edu
Established: 1970 — Annual Undergrad Tuition & Fees (In-District): $3,825
Enrollment: 7,466 — Coed
Affiliation or Control: Local — IRS Status: 501(c)3
Highest Offering: Associate Degree
Program: Occupational; 2-Year Principally Bachelor's Creditable; Technical Emphasis
Accreditation: NW

01 President ... Dr. Peter ANGSTADT
05 VP of Instrution/CAO ... Mr. Kirk GIBSON
10 VP of College Services/CFO/AA ... Mr. Curtis SOMMERFELD
103 Dean School of Workforce/Col Prep ... Ms. Linda RENFRO
72 Dean School of Arts and Technology ... Ms. Rena DENHAM
76 Dean School of Health/Public Svcs ... Mr. John OSBOURN
88 Director SBDC ... Mr. Ronald GOSS
81 Dean School of Science and Tech ... Mr. Jacob JACKSON
13 Chief Information Office/CIO ... Mr. Curtis SOMMERFELD
08 Head Librarian ... Mr. Thomas MILLER
18 Facilities and Project Manager ... Mr. Pat HUEBSCH
32 VP of Student Services/CSSO ... Ms. Kori BIEBER
102 Executive Director Foundation ... Ms. Jennifer WHEATLEY
15 Director of Human Resources ... Ms. Julie BAUMER
84 Director Enrollment Services ... Ms. Claudia SULLIVAN
24 Director Instructional Media ... Mr. Rich KIRK
21 Dir Budget & Financial Services/CFO ... Ms. Lisa STANTON
40 Director Auxiliary Services ... Ms. Shani HULST
26 Dir Marketing & Recruitment ... Ms. Margaret BRADFORD
37 Director Student Financial Aid ... Ms. Anna MANLEY
13 Director I/T Network & User Support ... Mr. Mike MCCLURE
105 Director Internet & Telecommunic ... Ms. Susie ASHBRIDGE
71 Director TRiO-EOC ... Mr. Jason FIANO
71 Director TRiO-SSS ... Ms. Colletta YOUNG
51 Apprenticeship Coordinator ... Ms. Cathy PIERSON
96 Contract and Procurment Manager ... Ms. Jodie FULTON
25 Grants and Planning Coordinator ... Ms. Mary O'KIEF
91 Coordinator of IT Programming Svcs ... Mr. Jeff MILLER
91 Applications Programmer/Analyst II ... Mr. Grant HUBLER

Sanford-Brown College (G)

600 SW 10th Avenue, Portland OR 97205
Telephone: (503) 265-1700 — Identification: 770765
Accreditation: ACICS

† Main campus is International Academy of Design and Technology in Tampa, FL.

Southwestern Oregon Community College (H)

1988 Newmark Avenue, Coos Bay OR 97420-2911
County: Coos — FICE Identification: 003220
Unit ID: 210155
Telephone: (541) 888-2525 — Carnegie Class: Assoc/Pub-R-M
FAX Number: (541) 888-7285 — Calendar System: Quarter
URL: www.socc.edu
Established: 1961 — Annual Undergrad Tuition & Fees (In-District): $5,274
Enrollment: 4,793 — Coed
Affiliation or Control: Local — IRS Status: 501(c)3
Highest Offering: Associate Degree
Program: Occupational; 2-Year Principally Bachelor's Creditable
Accreditation: NW, ACFEI, EMT

01 President ... Dr. Patty SCOTT
11 VP Administrative Services ... Ms. Linda KRIDELBAUGH
05 VP Instructional Services ... Mr. Ross TOMLIN
12 Dean Curry County ... Ms. Janet PRETTI
72 Dean of Technical & Professional Ed ... Ms. Diana SCHAB
56 Dean of Extended Learning ... Ms. Karen DOMINE
32 Dean Student Services ... Mr. Tim DAILEY
84 Exec Director Enrollment Management ... Mr. Tom NICHOLLS
102 Exec Director Foundation ... Ms. Karen PRINGLE
13 Director Integrated Technology ... Mr. Rocky LAVOIE
88 Exec Director OCCI (Culinary) ... Mr. Shawn HANLIN
20 Associate Dean of LDC & Devel Ed ... Mr. Rod KELLER
41 Director Athletics ... Mr. Mike HERBERT
07 Director of Admissions ... Mr. Tom NICHOLLS
19 Director Campus Safety ... Mr. Joe THOMAS
30 Director College Advancement ... Ms. Karen PRINGLE
18 Director Facilities Services ... Vacant
29 Director of Alumni Relations ... Ms. Karen PRINGLE

06 Registrar ... Ms. Shawn LIGGETT
37 Director Financial Aid ... Ms. Avena SINGH
15 Exec Director Human Resources ... Ms. Rachele SUMMERVILLE
08 Director Learning Resources ... Ms. Karen MATSON
66 Director Nursing ... Ms. Susan WALKER
39 Director Residence Life ... Mr. Jeff WHITEY
88 Director SOCC Business Dev Center ... Ms. Arlene SOTO
38 Director Student Support Srvcs ... Ms. Michele BENOIT
40 Manager Bookstore ... Ms. Dede CLEMENTS
09 Institutional Researcher ... Ms. Robin BUNNELL
35 Coordinator Student Life and Events ... Vacant
04 Exec Asst to the Pres/Board of Educ ... Ms. Deb NICHOLLS

Sumner College (A)

8909 SW Barbur Blvd., Ste 100, Portland OR 97219
County: Multnomah | FICE Identification: 021049 | Unit ID: 208512
Telephone: (503) 223-5100 | Carnegie Class: Not Classified
FAX Number: (503) 952-0010 | Calendar System: Other
URL: www.sumnercollege.edu
Established: 1974 | Annual Undergrad Tuition & Fees: $27,010
Enrollment: 249 | Coed
Affiliation or Control: Proprietary | IRS Status: Proprietary
Highest Offering: Associate Degree
Program: Occupational
Accreditation: ACICS

01 President ... Joanna S. RUSSELL

Tillamook Bay Community College (B)

4301 3rd Street, Tillamook OR 97141
County: Tillamook | Identification: 666647 | Unit ID: 420723
Telephone: (503) 842-8222 | Carnegie Class: Assoc/Pub-R-S
FAX Number: (503) 842-8336 | Calendar System: Quarter
URL: www.tillamookbay.cc
Established: 1981 | Annual Undergrad Tuition & Fees (In-District): $4,545
Enrollment: 559 | Coed
Affiliation or Control: State/Local | IRS Status: 501(c)3
Highest Offering: Associate Degree
Program: 2-Year Principally Bachelor's Creditable
Accreditation: @NW

01 President ... Dr. Constance C. GREEN
05 Chief Academic Officer ... Dr. Lori GATES
10 Comptroller/Budget Officer ... Ms. Kyra WILLIAMS
30 Chief Development ... Mr. Jon CARNAHAN
35 Dir Student Services & Registrar ... Ms. Michele BURTON
15 Dir Personnel Services/Facilities ... Mr. Pat RYAN
09 Coordinator Institutional Research ... Ms. Cindy ROWE

Treasure Valley Community College (C)

650 College Boulevard, Ontario OR 97914-3423
County: Malheur | FICE Identification: 003221 | Unit ID: 210234
Telephone: (541) 881-8822 | Carnegie Class: Assoc/Pub-R-M
FAX Number: (541) 881-2717 | Calendar System: Quarter
URL: www.tvcc.cc
Established: 1961 | Annual Undergrad Tuition & Fees (In-District): $4,950
Enrollment: 2,975 | Coed
Affiliation or Control: Local | IRS Status: 501(c)3
Highest Offering: Associate Degree
Program: Occupational; 2-Year Principally Bachelor's Creditable
Accreditation: NW, ADNUR, PNUR

01 President ... Ms. Dana YOUNG
05 Vice President of Academic Affairs ... Dr. Rachel ANDERSON
11 Vice Pres Administrative Services ... Mr. Randy R. GRIFFIN
08 Librarian ... Mr. Dennis GILL
32 Vice President Student Services ... Dr. Paul KRAFT
37 Financial Aid Director ... Mr. Keith RAAB
14 Director Data Processing ... Mr. Scott CARPENTER
07 Director of Admissions ... Ms. Stephanie OESTER
15 Director of Human Resources ... Ms. Gerri FLOYD
51 Director of Continuing Education ... Ms. Andrea TESTI
18 Dir of Housing/Building & Grounds ... Mr. Bernie BABCOCK
10 Comptroller ... Mr. Jonathan GILLEN
35 Director of Student Activities ... Mr. Justin CORE
41 Athletic Director ... Mr. Ed ARONSON
88 Corrections Education Director ... Ms. Carol FITZGERALD
06 Registrar ... Dr. Paul KRAFT
09 Director of Institutional Research ... Dr. Michelle LANDA
28 Director of Diversity ... Dr. Paul KRAFT
30 Chief Development ... Ms. Cathy YASUDA
40 Bookstore Manager ... Mr. Kjetil ROM
38 Vocational Counselor ... Vacant

Umpqua Community College (D)

PO Box 967, Roseburg OR 97470-0226
County: Douglas | FICE Identification: 003222 | Unit ID: 210270
Telephone: (541) 440-4600 | Carnegie Class: Assoc/Pub-R-M
FAX Number: (541) 440-4637 | Calendar System: Quarter
URL: www.umpqua.edu
Established: 1964 | Annual Undergrad Tuition & Fees (In-District): $4,796
Enrollment: 3,172 | Coed
Affiliation or Control: Local | IRS Status: 501(c)3
Highest Offering: Associate Degree
Program: Occupational; 2-Year Principally Bachelor's Creditable
Accreditation: NW, ADNUR

01 President ... Dr. Joe OLSON
05 Vice President Instruction Services ... Dr. Roxanne KELLY
10 Chief Financial Officer ... Ms. Rebecca REDELL
32 Vice President Student Development ... Dr. Rick AMAN
84 Director Enrollment Management ... Mr. David FARRINGTON
38 Director Counseling Services ... Ms. Mandie PRITCHARD
37 Director of Financial Aid ... Ms. Michelle BERGMANN
14 Director Instructional Technology ... Vacant
08 Director of Library Services ... Mr. David HUTCHISON
18 Director of Facilities ... Mr. Jess MILLER
31 Director of Community Education ... Ms. Robynne VAN WINKLE
09 Director Inst Research/Assess/Plng ... Mr. Dan YODER
15 Director Personnel Services ... Ms. Jan BAXTER
26 Chief Public Rel/Dir Community Rel ... Mr. Bentley GILBERT
96 Director of Purchasing ... Ms. Cathy VAUGHN

University of Phoenix Oregon Campus (E)

13221 SW 68th Parkway, Tigard OR 97223-8328
Telephone: (503) 403-2900 | Identification: 770222
Accreditation: &NH, ACBSP

† Main campus is University of Phoenix in Tempe, AZ.

University of Portland (F)

5000 N Willamette Boulevard, Portland OR 97203-5798
County: Multnomah | FICE Identification: 003224 | Unit ID: 209825
Telephone: (503) 943-8000 | Carnegie Class: Master's L
FAX Number: (503) 943-7491 | Calendar System: Semester
URL: www.up.edu
Established: 1901 | Annual Undergrad Tuition & Fees: $36,700
Enrollment: 3,911 | Coed
Affiliation or Control: Independent Non-Profit | IRS Status: 501(c)3
Highest Offering: Doctorate
Program: Liberal Arts And General; Teacher Preparatory; Professional
Accreditation: NW, BUS, CS, ENG, MUS, NURSE, SW, TED, THEA

01 President ... Rev. E. William BEAUCHAMP, CSC
05 Provost ... Dr. Thomas G. GREENE
03 Executive Vice President ... Rev. Mark L. POORMAN, CSC
26 Vice Pres for University Relations ... Vacant
11 Vice Pres for Univeristy Operations ... Mr. James B. RAVELLI
10 Vice Pres for Financial Affairs ... Mr. Alan P. TIMMINS
32 Vice President for Student Affairs .. Rev. Gerard J. OLINGER, CSC
100 Executive Asst to the Pres ... Ms. Danielle E. HERMANNY
35 Assoc VP for Student Development ... Rev. John J. DONATO, CSC
07 Dean of Admissions ... Mr. Jason MCDONALD
21 Controller ... Mr. Eric BARGER
06 Registrar ... Ms. Roberta LINDAHL
30 Assoc Vice President Development ... Mr. Bryce STRANG
36 Director Career Services ... Ms. Amy CAVANAUGH
15 Director for Human Resources ... Ms. Bryn SOPKO
37 Director Student Financial Aid ... Ms. Janet TURNER
27 Assoc VP of Univ Relations/CMO ... Ms. Laurie C. KELLEY
49 Dean of Arts & Sciences ... Dr. Michael F. ANDREWS
50 Dean of the Business School ... Dr. Robin ANDERSON
66 Dean of Nursing ... Dr. Joanne WARNER
54 Dean of Engineering ... Dr. Sharon JONES
53 Dean of Education ... Dr. John WATZKE
23 Director University Health Services ... Dr. Paul MYERS
19 Director of Public Safety ... Mr. Gerald A. GREGG
29 Director Alumni Relations ... Ms. Carmen GASTON
39 Director Residence Life ... Mr. Christopher HAUG
41 Athletic Director ... Mr. Scott LEYKAM
42 Director Campus Ministry ... Rev. Gary S. CHAMBERLAND, CSC
102 Director Foundation Development ... Ms. Kathy A. KENDALL-JOHNSTON
18 Director Facilities Planning Constr ... Mr. Paul J. LUTY
18 Director Physical Plant ... Mr. Andre HUTCHINSON
40 Director Bookstore ... Ms. Erin SCHUMACHER-BRIGHT
88 Director University Events ... Mr. William O. REED
09 Director of Institutional Research ... Ms. Karen NELSON
35 Director Student Activities ... Mr. Jeromy KOFFLER

University of Western States (G)

2900 NE 132nd Avenue, Portland OR 97230-3099
County: Multnomah | FICE Identification: 012309 | Unit ID: 210438
Telephone: (503) 256-3180 | Carnegie Class: Spec/Health
FAX Number: (503) 251-5723 | Calendar System: Quarter
URL: www.uws.edu
Established: 1904 | Annual Undergrad Tuition & Fees: $8,935
Enrollment: 589 | Coed
Affiliation or Control: Independent Non-Profit | IRS Status: 501(c)3
Highest Offering: Doctorate
Program: Professional
Accreditation: NW, CHIRO, COMTA

01 President ... Dr. Joseph BRIMHALL
10 Vice Pres Finance & Administration ... Mr. Eric BLUMENTHAL
05 Provost ... Ms. Laura LAMM
26 Vice Pres University Relations ... Dr. Clyde JENSEN
84 VP Enrollment & Student Affairs ... Dr. Patrick BROWNE
23 Vice President of Clinics ... Dr. Joseph PFEIFER
46 Assoc Vice President of Research ... Dr. Mitch HAAS
13 Chief Information Officer ... Mr. Kris ROSENBERG
04 Assistant to the President ... Ms. Bonnie FLATT
27 Director of Communications ... Mr. Todd LOGGAN
15 Int Director Human Resources ... Ms. Kathleen CANNON
37 Director Financial Aid ... Mr. Peter GROSS
06 Registrar ... Ms. Michelle DODGE
07 Director of Admissions ... Ms. Mary STAFFORD
08 University Librarian ... Ms. Janet TAPPER
18 Director Campus Facilities ... Mr. Todd BENSON

Warner Pacific College (H)

2219 SE 68th Avenue, Portland OR 97215
County: Multnomah | FICE Identification: 003225 | Unit ID: 210304
Telephone: (503) 517-1000 | Carnegie Class: Bac/Diverse
FAX Number: (503) 517-1350 | Calendar System: Semester
URL: www.warnerpacific.edu
Established: 1937 | Annual Undergrad Tuition & Fees: $19,030
Enrollment: 1,616 | Coed
Affiliation or Control: Church Of God | IRS Status: 501(c)3
Highest Offering: Master's
Program: 2-Year Principally Bachelor's Creditable; Liberal Arts And General; Teacher Preparatory; Professional
Accreditation: NW

01 President ... Dr. Andrea P. COOK
03 Executive Vice President ... Vacant
05 Vice Pres Acad Affs/Dean of Faculty ... Dr. Cole DAWSON
10 Vice Pres of Operations ... Mr. Steve STENBERG
30 Vice President for Inst Advancement ... Mr. Aaron MCMURRAY
32 Vice President for Community Life ... Dr. Daymond GLENN
20 Assoc VP for Acad Affairs/Dean ADP ... Dr. Lori K. JASS
84 VP for Enrollment and Marketing ... Mr. Dale SEIPP
37 Dir of Student Financial Services ... Vacant
41 Director of Athletics ... Mr. Jamie JOSS
08 Director of Library Services ... Ms. Sue KOPP
06 Registrar ... Ms. Victoria CUMINGS
13 Director of Information Technology ... Ms. Linda RUDAWITZ
29 Director of Alumni/Church Relations ... Mrs. Cindy POLLARD
27 Director of College Communications ... Vacant
88 Dir of Contextualized Ministries ... Mr. Jess BIELMAN
42 Associate Dir Campus Ministries ... Ms. Michelle LANG
39 Dir of Res Life & Judicial Affairs ... Mr. Jared VALENTINE
18 Director of Facilities ... Mr. Dean JENKS
15 Dir of Human Resources/Prof Devel ... Mrs. Bev FITTS
09 Dir of Institutional Effectiveness ... Dr. Warren J. BEAMAN
40 Director Bookstore ... Mrs. Mimi FONSECA
26 Marketing/College Relations ... Ms. Shirell HENNESSY
38 Director Student Counseling ... Dr. Denise LOPEZ HAUGEN
21 Associate Business Officer ... Mr. Nathan DUNBAR
35 Dir Leadership Dev and Stdnt Pgm ... Vacant
36 Director of Academic Success ... Mr. Rod JOHANSON
28 Urban Recruitment Coordinator ... Vacant

Western Seminary (I)

5511 SE Hawthorne Boulevard, Portland OR 97215-3399
County: Multnomah | FICE Identification: 007178 | Unit ID: 210368
Telephone: (503) 517-1800 | Carnegie Class: Spec/Faith
FAX Number: (503) 517-1801 | Calendar System: Semester
URL: www.westernseminary.edu
Established: 1927 | Annual Graduate Tuition & Fees: $11,280
Enrollment: 754 | Coed
Affiliation or Control: Independent Non-Profit | IRS Status: 501(c)3
Highest Offering: Doctorate; No Undergraduates
Program: Professional; Religious Emphasis
Accreditation: NW, THEOL

01 President ... Dr. Randal R. ROBERTS
10 Administrative Vice President/CFO ... Mr. Steve MANSDOERFER
05 Academic Dean ... Dr. Rob WIGGINS
30 Vice President for Advancement ... Mr. Greg MOON
20 Associate Academic Dean ... Vacant
06 Dean Student Devel/Registrar ... Dr. Reid KISLING
21 Controller ... Ms. Patricia A. PRICHARD
32 Dean of Students ... Mr. Andy PELOQUIN
36 Director of Student Placement ... Dr. Larry MCCRACKEN
13 Director of Information Services ... Mrs. Valerie MAINRIDGE
37 Financial Aid Director ... Ms. Shelle RIEHL
56 Asst Director of Distance Education ... Mr. Jon RAIBLEY
88 Assistant Controller ... Mrs. Sandy FOSTER
15 Human Resources Dir/Dir Communic ... Miss Julia EIDENBERG
08 Library Director ... Dr. Robert A. KRUPP
84 Director Enrollment Services/Mktg ... Mr. P.J OSWALD
29 Director Alumni Relations ... Dr. Larry MCCRACKEN
18 Chief Facilities/Physical Plant ... Mr. Cliff STEIN
106 Director of Distance Education ... Mr. James STEWART

Willamette University (J)

900 State Street, Salem OR 97301-3930
County: Marion | FICE Identification: 003227 | Unit ID: 210401
Telephone: (503) 370-6300 | Carnegie Class: Bac/A&S
FAX Number: (503) 370-6148 | Calendar System: Semester
URL: www.willamette.edu
Established: 1842 | Annual Undergrad Tuition & Fees: $42,305
Enrollment: 2,794 | Coed
Affiliation or Control: Independent Non-Profit | IRS Status: 501(c)3
Highest Offering: Doctorate
Program: Liberal Arts And General; Professional

Accreditation: NW, BUS, LAW, MUS, SPAA, TED

01 President ... Dr. Stephen THORSETT
10 Vice President Financial Affs ... Mr. W. Arnold YASINSKI
30 Vice President for Advancement ... Mr. Dennis BERGVALL
07 Vice President Enrollment ... Mr. James SUMNER
13 Vice President Integrated Tech ... Dr. John D. BALLING
11 Vice President Administrative Svcs ... Mr. James R. BAUER
04 Exec Admin Assistant to President ... Ms. Kristen GRAINGER
32 Dean of Campus Life ... Dr. David A. DOUGLASS
49 Dean of Liberal Arts ... Dr. Marlene MOORE
61 Dean of Law ... Mr. Curtis BRIDGEMAN
50 Dean Graduate School Management ... Ms. Debra RINGOLD
42 Chaplain ... Dr. Karen WOOD
23 Director of Bishop Welllness Center ... Ms. Margaret TROUT
88 Director Center Dispute Resolution ... Dr. Richard BIRKE
91 Director Administrative Computing .. Mr. Harvey J. PRUDHOMME
37 Director Student Financial Aid ... Ms. Patricia K. HOBAN
09 Director of Institutional Research ... Dr. Michael J. MOON
06 University Registrar ... Ms. Laura JACOBS ANDERSON
08 University Librarian ... Ms. Deborah B. DANCIK
21 Controller ... Mr. Kenneth PIFER
40 Bookstore Director ... Mr. Donald C. BECKMAN
104 Director of International Education ... Mr. Kris LOU
41 Interim Athletic Director ... Mr. Dave RIGSBY
29 Assistant VP Alumni Relations ... Mr. James LIPPINCOTT
44 Director of Planned Giving ... Mr. Stephen F. BRIER
15 Director of Human Resources ... Mr. Keith GRIMM
35 Director of Student Activities ... Ms. Lisa C. HOLLIDAY
36 Director Career Services ... Dr. Gerald B. HOUSER
28 Director of Multicultural Affairs ... Mr. Gordon K. TOYAMA
18 Manager Operations/Energy ... Mr. Gary GRIMM
96 Purchasing Coordinator ... Mr. Micheal K. SERAPHIN
26 Int Director Marketing Communic ... Mr. Adam TORGERSON

PENNSYLVANIA

Albright College (A)

13th & Bern Streets, PO Box 15234,
Reading PA 19612-5234

County: Berks — FICE Identification: 003229
Unit ID: 210571
Telephone: (610) 921-2381 — Carnegie Class: Bac/A&S
FAX Number: (610) 921-7530 — Calendar System: 4/1/4
URL: www.albright.edu
Established: 1856 — Annual Undergrad Tuition & Fees: $36,660
Enrollment: 2,264 — Coed
Affiliation or Control: United Methodist — IRS Status: 501(c)3
Highest Offering: Master's
Program: Liberal Arts And General; Teacher Preparatory; Professional
Accreditation: M

01 President ... Dr. Lex O. MCMILLAN, III
05 Provost/Vice Pres Academic Affairs . Dr. Andrea E. CHAPDELAINE
10 Vice President Finance & Admin ... Mr. William W. WOOD
30 Vice President Advancement ... Dr. Timothy A. MCELWEE
84 VP Enrollment Mgt/Dean Admission ... Mr. Gregory E. EICHHORN
32 VP Student Affairs/Dean of Students ... Dr. Gina-Lyn CRANCE
26 Assoc VP College Relations/Mktg ... Mr. Thomas W. DURSO
13 Chief Technology Officer ... Vacant
04 Executive Assistant to President ... Mrs. Kathy L. CAFONCELLI
20 Dean of Undergraduate Studies ... Dr. Joseph M. THOMAS
08 Library Director ... Ms. Rosemary L. DEEGAN
44 Assoc VP for Development ... Mr. John SHORT
14 Director of Core Technologies ... Mr. Hoerr U. JASON
91 Dir of Enterprise Applications ... Ms. Gena HOWARD
21 Controller ... Mr. Rick W. MELCHER
37 Director of Financial Aid ... Mr. Christopher HANLON
58 Dean of Graduate & Professional Div ... Dr. Joseph YARWORTH
35 Assistant Dean of Students ... Ms. Amanda HANINCIK
06 Registrar ... Mr. David C. BALLABAN
36 Director Career Development Center ... Ms. Karen V. EVANS
39 Director of Residential Life ... Ms. Rebecca PEAL MORROW
38 Director of Counseling Center ... Dr. Brenda J. INGRAM-WALLACE
29 Dir of Alumni Relations ... Mrs. Megan BERMUDEZ
18 Director Facilities/Operations/Svcs ... Mr. Kevin GAFFNEY
41 Co-Athletic Director ... Mr. Richard E. FERRY
41 Co-Athletic Director ... Ms. Janice J. LUCK
19 Director of Safety & Security ... Mr. Thomas MCDANIEL
40 Book Store Manager ... Ms. Coreen MCCAFFERTY
23 Director of Gable Health Center ... Ms. Samantha WESNER
42 Chaplain ... Rev. Paul E. CLARK
22 Affirmative Action Coord/Dir HR ... Vacant
85 Asst Dir Multi-Ethnic Student Affs ... Ms. Tiffany CLAYTON
88 Dir of Accelerated Degree Pgm ... Mr. Kevin EZZELL
09 Director of Institutional Research ... Mr. Jack LAFAYETTE
35 Director of Student Activities ... Mr. Bradley A. SMITH
25 Director of Grants ... Ms. Darlene ROTH
92 Director Honors Program ... Dr. Julia F. HEBERLE
07 Director of Admission ... Mr. Christopher H. BOEHM
107 Dean of Adult & Prof Studies ... Dr. Andra M. BASU
88 Director of Conferences ... Ms. Lois A. KUBINAK

Allegany College of Maryland Bedford County Campus (B)

18 North River Lane, Everett PA 15337-1410
Telephone: (814) 652-9528 — Identification: 770124
Accreditation: &M

† Main campus is Allegany College of Maryland in Cumberland, MD.

Allegany College of Maryland Somerset County Campus (C)

6022 Glades Pike, Suite 100, Somerset PA 15501-4300
Telephone: (814) 445-9848 — Identification: 770123
Accreditation: &M

† Main campus is Allegany College of Maryland in Cumberland, MD.

Allegheny College (D)

520 N Main, Meadville PA 16335-3902

County: Crawford — FICE Identification: 003230
Unit ID: 210669
Telephone: (814) 332-3100 — Carnegie Class: Bac/A&S
FAX Number: (814) 724-6032 — Calendar System: Semester
URL: www.allegheny.edu
Established: 1815 — Annual Undergrad Tuition & Fees: $38,710
Enrollment: 2,140 — Coed
Affiliation or Control: Independent Non-Profit — IRS Status: 501(c)3
Highest Offering: Baccalaureate
Program: Liberal Arts And General
Accreditation: M

01 President ... Dr. James H. MULLEN
03 Exec Vice President ... Ms. Susan GAYLOR
30 Vice Pres Devel & Alumni Affairs ... Ms. Marjorie S. KLEIN
84 Vice Pres Enrollment/Communication ... Dr. Brian F. DALTON
04 Assistant to the President ... Ms. Pamela S. HIGHAM
28 Chief Diversity Ofce/Asc Dn of Col ... Vacant
21 Senior Associate Vice President ... Vacant
45 Assoc Vice Pres for Advancement ... Mr. Bruce WHITEHAIR
29 AVP Development & Alumni Affairs ... Mr. Philip R. FOXMAN
26 Assoc VP Marketing/Communications ... Ms. Rachel GARZA
05 Provost & Dean of the College ... Dr. Linda C. DEMERITT
32 Dean of Students ... Mr. Joseph J. DICHRISTINA
28 Dean Diversity Affairs ... Dr. Kazi JOSHUA
20 Associate Dean of the College ... Dr. Terry BENSEL
37 Interim Director Financial Aid ... Mr. Jonathan BOLERATZ
88 Ex Dir Learning Info/Tech Svcs ... Dr. Richard A. HOLMGREN
06 Registrar ... Dr. Ann D. SHEFFIELD
08 Library Director ... Ms. Linda G. BILLS
15 Director of Human Resources ... Ms. Patricia A. FERREY
19 Director Campus Safety & Security ... Dr. Jeffrey A. SCHNEIDER
44 Director of Annual Giving ... Ms. Sara PINEO
18 Director Physical Plant ... Mr. Cliff K. WILLIS
91 Director Administrative Computing ... Mr. Richard A. METZGER
41 Director of Athletics ... Ms. Portia HOEG
31 Director Community Service ... Dr. David RONCOLATO
14 Dir Tech Computer & Networking Svcs ... Mr. Tim W. HUNTER
100 Chief of Staff ... Ms. Gillian F. FORD
38 Director of Counseling Center ... Ms. Yvonne M. EATON-STULL
102 Director of Found/Corporate Rels ... Dr. Ann H. ARESON
09 Director of Institutional Research ... Ms. Marian D. SHERWOOD
36 Director Career Services ... Ms. Michaeline M. SHUMAN
35 Director Student Involvement ... Ms. Gretchen A. SYMONS
21 Associate Vice President of Finance ... Ms. Linda S. WETSELL
42 Chaplain ... Dr. Jane Ellen NICKELL
88 Dir Center Political Participation ... Dr. Brian HARWARD
88 Assoc Director Learning Commons ... Mr. John J. MANGINE
84 Assoc Dir Enrollment/Communication ... Ms. Penny M. FRANK
40 Manager of Bookstore ... Mr. Peter M. LEBAR
96 Purchasing Coordinator ... Ms. Kathleen M. CONAWAY

Alvernia University (E)

400 Saint Bernardine Street, Reading PA 19607-1799

County: Berks — FICE Identification: 003233
Unit ID: 210775
Telephone: (610) 796-8200 — Carnegie Class: Master's M
FAX Number: (610) 777-6632 — Calendar System: Semester
URL: www.alvernia.edu
Established: 1958 — Annual Undergrad Tuition & Fees: $30,035
Enrollment: 2,891 — Coed
Affiliation or Control: Roman Catholic — IRS Status: 501(c)3
Highest Offering: Doctorate
Program: Liberal Arts And General; Teacher Preparatory; Professional
Accreditation: M, ACBSP, NURSE, OT, SW

01 President ... Dr. Thomas F. FLYNN
05 Provost ... Dr. Shirley J. WILLIAMS
10 VP for Finance & Administration ... Mr. Douglas F. SMITH
30 Vice Pres for Advancement ... Mr. J. Michael PRESSIMONE
32 Vice Pres Univ Life/Dean of Stdnts .. Dr. Joseph J. CICALA, RSM
84 Vice Pres for Enrollment Management ... Mr. John R. MCCLOSKEY, JR.
42 Asst to the President For Mission ... Sr. Roberta MCKELVIE, OSF
26 VP Mktg & Comms/Chief PR Ofcr ... Mr. Brad DREXLER
35 Dean of Students ... Vacant
35 Director of Student Activities ... Ms. Abby SWATCHICK
39 Director Residence Life ... Ms. Karolina DREHER
06 Registrar ... Ms. Beki STEIN
21 Controller ... Ms. Jada D. CAMPBELL
29 Director Alumni Donor Relations ... Thomas MINICK
08 Grad Program Librarian/Archivist ... Vacant
92 Director Honors Program ... Dr. Victoria WILLIAMS
41 Director Athletics & Recreation ... Bill STILES
07 Director of Admissions ... Ms. Stacy ADAMSPERRY
09 Director of Institutional Research ... Dr. Evelina PANAYOTOVA
15 Director Human Resources ... Ms. Laurel CLINE
18 Chief Facilities/Physical Plant ... Mr. David REPPERT
36 Director of Career Services ... Mrs. Megan ADUKAITIS
37 Int Dir Student Financial Planning ... Ms. Christine SAADL
96 Director of Purchasing ... Ms. Cynthia URICK
28 Director of Diversity ... Ms. Wanda COPELAND
21 Associate Business Officer ... Ms. Gwynne KOLODZIEJSKI
31 Dir Ctr for Community Engagement ... Mr. Jay WORRALL
58 Dean of Graduate & Cont Studies ... Ms. Daria LATORRE
49 Dean of Arts & Sciences ... Dr. Beth ARACENA
76 Dean Professional Programs ... Ms. Karen S. THACKER

The American College (F)

270 S Bryn Mawr Avenue, Bryn Mawr PA 19010-2196

County: Delaware — FICE Identification: 033173
Unit ID: 210809
Telephone: (610) 526-1000 — Carnegie Class: Spec/Bus
FAX Number: (610) 526-1310 — Calendar System: Quarter
URL: www.theamericancollege.edu
Established: 1927 — Annual Graduate Tuition & Fees: $5,040
Enrollment: 533 — Coed
Affiliation or Control: Independent Non-Profit — IRS Status: 501(c)3
Highest Offering: Doctorate; No Undergraduates
Program: Professional; Business Emphasis
Accreditation: M

01 President & CEO ... Dr. Laurence BARTON
03 Senior Vice President ... Mr. Steven TARR
05 Vice Pres Academic Affairs & Dean ... Dr. Walter J. WOERHEIDE
30 Sr Vice President Advancement ... Mr. Charles CRONIN
11 Chief Operating Officer ... Mr. Neal R. FEGELY
26 Chief Marketing Officer ... Mr. Jack HONDROS
13 Chief Technology Officer ... Mr. Ed M. MCEVOY
15 Vice Pres Human Resources ... Ms. Amy DEWEY
04 Assistant to the President ... Ms. Mary C. VARNER
06 Registrar ... Ms. Antoinette CHRISTALDI
08 Librarian ... Mr. John H. WHITHAM
88 Managing Director Exam Systems ... Ms. Diane M. HAMMONDS

Antonelli Institute of Art and Photography (G)

300 Montgomery Avenue, Erdenheim PA 19038-8242

County: Montgomery — FICE Identification: 007430
Unit ID: 210890
Telephone: (215) 836-2222 — Carnegie Class: Assoc/PrivFP
FAX Number: (215) 836-2794 — Calendar System: Semester
URL: www.antonelli.edu
Established: 1938 — Annual Undergrad Tuition & Fees: $19,830
Enrollment: 176 — Coed
Affiliation or Control: Proprietary — IRS Status: Proprietary
Highest Offering: Associate Degree
Program: Occupational
Accreditation: ACCSC

01 President ... Dr. John D. HAYDEN
05 Director of Education/Student Svcs ... Ms. Trish FLEMING
37 Financial Aid Officer ... Ms. Stephanie SHOWALTER

Arcadia University (H)

450 S Easton Road, Glenside PA 19038-3295

County: Montgomery — FICE Identification: 003235
Unit ID: 211088
Telephone: (215) 572-2900 — Carnegie Class: Master's L
FAX Number: (215) 572-0240 — Calendar System: Semester
URL: www.arcadia.edu
Established: 1853 — Annual Undergrad Tuition & Fees: $35,620
Enrollment: 4,027 — Coed
Affiliation or Control: Independent Non-Profit — IRS Status: 501(c)3
Highest Offering: Doctorate
Program: Liberal Arts And General; Teacher Preparatory; Professional
Accreditation: M, ACBSP, ARCPA, ART, FEPAC, PH, PTA

01 President ... Vacant
05 Provost & VP Academic Affairs ... Dr. Steve O. MICHAEL
11 COO & VP College of Global Studies ... Dr. Nicolette D. CHRISTENSEN
30 VP Development ... Dr. Janet E. WALBERT
84 VP Enrollment Management ... Mr. Mark LAPREZIOSA
10 VP Finance & Treasurer ... Mr. Len SIPPEL
27 VP Global Info Svcs & CIO ... Mr. Steven ALTER
43 VP Legal Affairs & Univ Counsel ... Ms. Valerie HARRISON
30 VP University Advancement ... Ms. Mary MCRAE
32 Assoc VP Student Affairs/Dean ... Mr. Joshua STERN
07 Assoc VP Enrollment Management ... Vacant
18 Assoc VP Facilities/Capital Plng ... Mr. Thomas J. MACCHI
21 Assoc VP Finance & COO TCGS ... Ms. Colleen BURKE
88 Assoc VP & Dir Strategic Dev TCGS .. Ms. Lorna STERN LANIAK
26 Chief Mktg & Communications Officer ... Ms. Laura BALDWIN
15 Asst VP Human Resources/AAO ... Ms. Lynette ALLEN-PERRY
44 Asst VP University Advancement ... Ms. Diana FRAZIER
21 Controller ... Ms. Julie A. ROSNER-LENGELE
06 Registrar ... Mr. William ELNICK
06 Associate Registrar ... Mrs. Nicole M. ZUCKER
49 Dean College of Arts and Sciences ... Dr. John R. HOFFMAN
88 Academic Dean TCGS ... Dr. Dennis DUTSCHKE
76 Dean College of Health Sciences ... Dr. Archie J. VOMACHKA
51 Dean School of Continuing Studies ... Dr. Erik NELSON
50 Dean School of Global Business ... Dr. N.J DELENER
58 Dean Graduate & Undergraduate Pgms ... Ms. Nancy ROSOFF
88 Dean International Affairs ... Dr. Warren HAFFAR
88 Assoc Prov Fac Advance & Stdnt Lrng ... Dr. John A. NOAKES

28 Assoc Dean Institutional Diversity .... Ms. Judith DALTON
35 Assoc Dean of Students .... Ms. Dian TAYLOR-ALLEYNE
20 Assoc Dean Undergraduate Studies .... Mr. Bruce KELLER
88 Asst Dean Graduate Studies .... Ms. Mary Kate MCNULTY
37 Exec Dir Financial Aid Systems ... Ms. Elizabeth RIHL-LEWINSKY
08 Exec Dir Program Excellence .... Mr. Eric MCCLOY
88 Director Administrative Services .... Ms. Mimi BASSETTI
29 Director Alumni Relations .... Mr. Kevin BROWN
44 Director Annual Fund .... Vacant
88 Director Art Gallery .... Mr. Richard TORCHIA
41 Director Athletics & Recreation .... Mr. Brian GRANATA
88 Director Campus Visits and EM .... Ms. Kathleen BEARDSLEY
36 Director Career Education .... Mr. Mark GRESS, JR.
38 Director Counseling Services .... Ms. Cynthia RUTHERFORD
88 Director EM & Financial Aid .... Ms. Holly R. KIRKPATRICK
91 Director Enterprise Applications .... Mr. Scott GRABUS
25 Research Compliance Officer .... Ms. Nataliia SHABLIA
09 Director Institutional Research .... Mr. Will PADDOCK
88 Assoc Dean Library & Instr Tech .... Dr. Jeanne BUCKLEY
88 Dir Network & Info Security Systems .... Mr. Marc ROCQUE
96 Payroll and Purchasing Manager .... Ms. Sharon ANTHONY
19 Director of Public Safety .... Mr. James BONNER
39 Director Residence & Commuter Life . Ms. Catherine MATTINGLY
25 Director Sponsored Research Pgms .... Vacant
60 Director Communications .... Dr. Shekhar DESHPANDE
79 Director MA in English/Humanities .... Dr. Richard A. WERTIME
69 Director Public Health/Health Educ .... Dr. Andrea COVELLI-KOVACH
88 Director EdD in Special Educ .... Dr. Christina AGER
88 Director Theater Arts .... Mr. Mark WADE

Art Institute of Philadelphia (A)

1622 Chestnut Street, Philadelphia PA 19103-5198

County: Philadelphia — FICE Identification: 008350 — Unit ID: 210942
Telephone: (215) 567-7080 — Carnegie Class: Spec/Arts
FAX Number: (215) 405-6398 — Calendar System: Quarter
URL: www.aiph.aii.edu
Established: 1971 — Annual Undergrad Tuition & Fees: $22,275
Enrollment: 2,820 — Coed
Affiliation or Control: Proprietary — IRS Status: Proprietary
Highest Offering: Baccalaureate
Program: Occupational
Accreditation: M, ACFEI, CIDA

01 President .... Ms. Lisa NUCCI
05 Dean of Academic Affairs .... Dr. Raymond BECKER
10 Director Admin & Financial Services .... Mr. James MORETTI
07 Director of Admissions .... Mr. Steven COHEN
36 Director of Career Services .... Ms. Kimberly BURNS
04 Exec Assistant to the President .... Vacant
09 Dir of Institutional Effectiveness .... Ms. Heather RAMSEY
20 Assoc Dean of Academic Affairs .... Mr. Harry COSTIGAN
32 Dean of Students .... Ms. Ashley FORSYTH
37 Director Student Financial Services .... Ms. Fatisha STRICKLAND
06 Registrar .... Ms. Adriane MEDFORD
08 Library Director .... Ms. Ruth SCHACHTER
38 Counselor .... Ms. Eileen MCMULLEN
40 Manager-Supply Store .... Ms. Sharon MASULLO
85 Regional Internatl Student Advisor .... Vacant

Art Institute of Pittsburgh (B)

420 Boulevard of the Allies, Pittsburgh PA 15219-1301

County: Allegheny — FICE Identification: 007470 — Unit ID: 210960
Telephone: (412) 263-6600 — Carnegie Class: Spec/Arts
FAX Number: (412) 263-3715 — Calendar System: Quarter
URL: www.artinstitutes.edu/pittsburgh
Established: 1921 — Annual Undergrad Tuition & Fees: $21,915
Enrollment: 16,000 — Coed
Affiliation or Control: Proprietary — IRS Status: Proprietary
Highest Offering: Baccalaureate
Program: Occupational; Fine Arts Emphasis
Accreditation: M, ACFEI, CIDA

01 President .... Mr. George W. SEBOLT
10 Vice Pres/Dir Admin/Financial Svcs .... Vacant
05 VP/Dean Academic Affairs .... Mr. Daniel GARLAND
32 Vice Pres/Director Student Affairs .... Ms. Nadine W. JOSEPHS
36 VP/Director Career Services .... Vacant
07 Director of Admissions .... Ms. Kimbra BROWNING
37 Director Student Financial Aid .... Ms. Lara HEMWALL
15 Director Human Resources .... Ms. Jacquie DEMIANCZYK
97 Director General Education .... Ms. Katie TALERICO
88 Dir Graphic/Dig Design/Web Design .... Ms. Tamara PAVLOCK
72 Director of Technology .... Mr. George ALBERT
88 Dir Indust Dsgn Tech/Entertnmt Dsgn .... Ms. Kelly SPEWOCK
88 Dir Media Animation/Game Design .... Mr. Hans WESTMAN
88 Director of Photography .... Mr. Andrew ENGLISH
88 Dir Interior Design/Residential Pln .... Ms. Kelly J K. SPEWOCK
06 Registrar .... Ms. Diane E. CARNEY
84 Enrollment Management Supervisor .... Ms. Lara SEBOLT
88 Director Culinary .... Mr. Michael ZAPPONE
88 Dir Fashion/Retail Mktng/Fashn Dsgn .... Ms. Stephanie TAYLOR
88 Dir Video Production/Visual Effects .... Mr. Andres TAPIA URZUA
88 College Affiliate/HS Articulation .... Ms. Michele BAMBURAK

The Art Institute of York - Pennsylvania (C)

1409 Williams Road, York PA 17402-9012

County: York — FICE Identification: 025578 — Unit ID: 210906
Telephone: (717) 755-2300 — Carnegie Class: Assoc/PrivFP
FAX Number: (717) 757-5552 — Calendar System: Other
URL: www.artinstitutes.edu/york
Established: 1952 — Annual Undergrad Tuition & Fees: $25,500
Enrollment: 554 — Coed
Affiliation or Control: Proprietary — IRS Status: Proprietary
Highest Offering: Baccalaureate
Program: Liberal Arts And General; Professional
Accreditation: ACICS

01 President .... Mr. Tim HOWARD
05 Dean of Academic Affairs .... Ms. Marla PRICE
07 Senior Director of Admissions .... Mr. Scott VUKODER
32 Director of Student Affairs .... Ms. Laura RYDER

Baptist Bible College and Seminary (D)

538 Venard Road, Clarks Summit PA 18411-1297

County: Lackawanna — FICE Identification: 002670 — Unit ID: 211024
Telephone: (570) 586-2400 — Carnegie Class: Spec/Faith
FAX Number: (570) 586-1753 — Calendar System: Semester
URL: www.bbc.edu
Established: 1932 — Annual Undergrad Tuition & Fees: $19,710
Enrollment: 1,107 — Coed
Affiliation or Control: Baptist — IRS Status: 501(c)3
Highest Offering: Doctorate
Program: Teacher Preparatory; Professional; Religious Emphasis
Accreditation: M, BI

01 President .... Mr. James E. JEFFERY
05 Vice President & Provost .... Dr. James R. LYTLE
10 Vice President Business/Finance .... Mr. Hal G. CROSS
30 Vice Pres Inst Advancement .... Mr. Don PATTEN
84 Vice Pres Enrollment/External Rels .... Mr. Mel WALKER
20 Seminary Dean .... Dr. Michael STALLARD
32 Dean of Students .... Mr. Roddy HANNAH
33 Associate Dean of Men .... Mr. Ted BOYKIN
34 Assoc Dean/Dir Women Ministries .... Mrs. Faye MOORE
04 President's Assistant .... Mrs. Amy HEINTER
06 Registrar .... Mr. Allen R. DREYER
08 Librarian .... Mr. Jeremy MCGINNISS
09 Director of Institutional Research .... Dr. Barry C. SMITH
37 Director of Financial Aid .... Mr. Steve BROWN
26 Exec Dir Communications/Marketing .... Mr. Ken KNELLY
19 Director Safety/Security .... Mr. Tom MORRIS
84 Director of Enrollment .... Mr. Sean MCPHERSON
18 Chief Facilities/Physical Plant .... Mr. Wayne STEVENS
13 Manager of Information/Technology .... Mr. Douglas HEITNER
73 Dean School of Bible and Theology .... Dr. David A. LACKEY
53 Dean of School of Education .... Dr. Ritch KELLEY
49 Dean of School of Arts & Sciences .... Dr. Steve A. SHUMAKER
88 Dean of School of Global Ministries .... Dr. Dennis WILHITE
15 Director Personnel Services .... Mrs. Rennelle THEODORE
29 Coordinator Alumni Relations .... Ms. Michelle HAMMAKER
36 Director Student Placement .... Mr. Roddy HANNAH

Berks Technical Institute (E)

2205 Ridgewood Road, Wyomissing PA 19610-1168

County: Berks — FICE Identification: 022539 — Unit ID: 213534
Telephone: (610) 372-1722 — Carnegie Class: Assoc/PrivFP
FAX Number: (610) 376-4684 — Calendar System: Other
URL: www.berks.edu
Established: 1974 — Annual Undergrad Tuition & Fees: $14,400
Enrollment: 1,051 — Coed
Affiliation or Control: Proprietary — IRS Status: Proprietary
Highest Offering: Associate Degree
Program: Occupational; Technical Emphasis
Accreditation: ACCSC, ACICS, MAC

01 President .... Mr. Joseph F. REICHARD
05 Dean .... Mr. Jon SCHNEIDER

Biblical Theological Seminary (F)

200 N Main Street, Hatfield PA 19440-2499

County: Montgomery — FICE Identification: 023230 — Unit ID: 211130
Telephone: (215) 368-5000 — Carnegie Class: Spec/Faith
FAX Number: (215) 368-2301 — Calendar System: Semester
URL: www.biblical.edu
Established: 1971 — Annual Graduate Tuition & Fees: $14,140
Enrollment: 337 — Coed
Affiliation or Control: Independent Non-Profit — IRS Status: 501(c)3
Highest Offering: Doctorate; No Undergraduates
Program: Professional; Religious Emphasis
Accreditation: M, THEOL

01 President .... Dr. Frank JAMES, III
32 VP for Student Advancement .... Mrs. Pamela J. SMITH
05 Academic Dean .... Dr. R. Todd MANGUM
10 Controller .... Mr. Wayne A. DAVIDSON
20 Director of Academic Services .... Mr. Rick HOUSEKNECHT
08 Director of Library Services .... Mr. Daniel N. LAVALLA
13 Director of Information Technology .... Mr. Kelly PFLEIGER
18 Director of Physical Plant .... Mr. Anthony W. PLETSCHER
88 Director of Urban Initiatives .... Dr. Dan WILLIAMS
88 Director of DMin Program .... Dr. Derek COOPER
30 Director of Development .... Mr. Thom SKINNER

Bidwell Training Center (G)

1815 Metropolitan Street, Pittsburgh PA 15233-2200

County: Allegheny — FICE Identification: 031015 — Unit ID: 211149
Telephone: (412) 323-4000 — Carnegie Class: Assoc/PrivNFP
FAX Number: (412) 325-7378 — Calendar System: Semester
URL: www.bidwell-training.org
Established: 1968 — Annual Undergrad Tuition & Fees: $14,000
Enrollment: 175 — Coed
Affiliation or Control: Independent Non-Profit — IRS Status: 501(c)3
Highest Offering: Associate Degree
Program: Occupational
Accreditation: ACCSC

01 Exec Director/Sr Vice President .... Ms. Valerie NJIE
11 Senior Director/Operations .... Mr. Ken HUSELTON

Bradford School (H)

125 W Station Square Dr, Ste 129, Pittsburgh PA 15219-2602

County: Allegheny — FICE Identification: 009721 — Unit ID: 211200
Telephone: (412) 391-6710 — Carnegie Class: Assoc/PrivFP
FAX Number: (412) 471-6714 — Calendar System: Semester
URL: www.bradfordpittsburgh.edu
Established: 1968 — Annual Undergrad Tuition & Fees: $15,300
Enrollment: 387 — Coed
Affiliation or Control: Proprietary — IRS Status: Proprietary
Highest Offering: Associate Degree
Program: Occupational; Business Emphasis
Accreditation: ACICS, DA, MAC

01 President .... Mr. Vincent S. GRAZIANO

Bryn Athyn College of the New Church (I)

PO Box 717, Bryn Athyn PA 19009-0717

County: Montgomery — FICE Identification: 003228 — Unit ID: 210492
Telephone: (267) 502-2400 — Carnegie Class: Bac/A&S
FAX Number: (215) 938-2658 — Calendar System: Trimester
URL: www.brynathyn.edu
Established: 1876 — Annual Undergrad Tuition & Fees: $16,878
Enrollment: 256 — Coed
Affiliation or Control: Church of New Jerusalem — IRS Status: 501(c)3
Highest Offering: Master's
Program: Liberal Arts And General; Teacher Preparatory; Professional
Accreditation: M

01 President .... Dr. Kristin KING
10 Chief Finance Officer .... Mr. Daniel T. ALLEN
05 Dean of Academic Affairs .... Dr. Allen BEDFORD
73 Dean of Theological School .... Rev. Andrew M T. DIBB
32 Dean of Student Affairs .... Ms. Kiri ROGERS
07 Dean of Admissions .... Mr. Matthew MCCAFFREY
08 Director of Swedenborg Library .... Mrs. Carroll C. ODHNER
41 Director of Athletics .... Mr. Matthew KENNEDY
13 Director of Information Technology .... Ms. Lelia HOWARD
15 Director of Human Resources .... Ms. T. Muriel ALLEN
19 Director of Security & Safety .... Mr. R. Scott COOPER
42 Chaplain .... Rev. Thane GLENN

Bryn Mawr College (J)

101 N Merion Avenue, Bryn Mawr PA 19010-2899

County: Montgomery — FICE Identification: 003237 — Unit ID: 211273
Telephone: (610) 526-5000 — Carnegie Class: Bac/A&S
FAX Number: (610) 526-7450 — Calendar System: Semester
URL: www.brynmawr.edu
Established: 1885 — Annual Undergrad Tuition & Fees: $43,590
Enrollment: 1,774 — Female
Affiliation or Control: Independent Non-Profit — IRS Status: 501(c)3
Highest Offering: Doctorate
Program: Liberal Arts And General
Accreditation: M, SW

01 Interim President .... Kim E. CASSIDY
05 Interim Provost .... Mary J. OSIRIM
49 Interim Dean Undergraduate College .... Judith BALTHAZAR
11 Chief Administrative Officer .... Jerry A. BERENSON
10 Chief Financial Officer & Treasurer .... John GRIFFITH
30 Interim Chief Development Officer .... Bob MILLER
07 Interim Dean of Enrollment .... Chuck RICKARD
08 Director Libraries/Chief Info Ofcr .... Elliott SHORE
58 Interim Dean of Graduate Studies .... Sharon BURGMAYER
28 Asst Dean/Dir Intercultural Affairs .... Vanessa CHRISTMAN
06 Registrar .... Kirsten O'BEIRNE

37 Director of Financial Aid .... Ethel M. DESMARAIS
19 Director of Public Safety .... Tom KING
29 Exec Director Alumnae Association .... Wendy M. GREENFIELD
68 Director of Athletics & Physical Ed .... Kathleen TIERNEY
21 Controller .... Ms. Betsy STEWART
09 Director of Institutional Research .... Richard BARRY
18 Chief Facilities/Physical Plant .... Glenn R. SMITH

Bucknell University (A)

1 Dent Drive, Lewisburg PA 17837

County: Union FICE Identification: 003238
Unit ID: 211291
Telephone: (570) 577-2000 Carnegie Class: Bac/A&S
FAX Number: (570) 577-3760 Calendar System: Semester
URL: www.bucknell.edu
Established: 1846 Annual Undergrad Tuition & Fees: $46,902
Enrollment: 3,618 Coed
Affiliation or Control: Independent Non-Profit IRS Status: 501(c)3
Highest Offering: Master's
Program: Liberal Arts And General; Teacher Preparatory; Professional
Accreditation: M, CS, ENG, MUS

01 President .... Dr. John C. BRAVMAN
05 Provost .... Dr. Michael A. SMYER
10 VP Finance & Administration .... Mr. David J. SURGALA
30 VP Development & Alumni Rels .... Dr. Scott G. ROSEVEAR
43 General Counsel .... Ms. Amy C. FOERSTER
43 Sr Legal Advisor to President .... Mr. Wayne A. BROMFIELD
84 VP Enrollment Management .... Mr. William T. CONLEY
41 Director Athletics & Recreation .... Mr. John P. HARDT
13 VP Library & Information Technology .... Mr. Param S. BEDI
27 VP Communications & Cmty Rels .... Dr. Peter F. MACKEY
88 Chief Investment Officer .... Mr. Christopher D. BROWN
49 Dean of Arts & Sciences .... Dr. George C. SHIELDS
54 Dean of Engineering .... Dr. Keith W. BUFFINTON
32 Dean of Students .... Ms. Susan L. LANTZ
20 Assoc Provost/Dean of Grad Studies .... Dr. James P. RICE
20 Assoc Prov/Dean Summer Sch/ Registr .... Dr. Robert M. MIDKIFF, JR.
50 Director School of Management .... Dr. Michael E. JOHNSON-CRAMER
21 Associate VP Finance .... Mr. Dennis W. SWANK
29 Assoc VP Development & Alumni Rels .... Ms. Kathleen GRAHAM
21 Treasurer and Controller .... Mr. Michael S. COVER
28 Assoc Provost for Diversity .... Ms. Bridget M. NEWELL
46 Assistant Provost for Research .... Ms. Carol A. BURDSAL
18 Associate VP Facilities .... Mr. Dennis W. HAWLEY
16 Executive Director Human Resources .... Ms. Marcia K. HOFFMAN
88 Executive Dir Leadership Gifts .... Mr. Robert D. RATHBUN
88 Exec Dir Alumni Relations .... Mr. Joshua L. GRILL
88 Exec Dir Donor/Volunteer Relations .... Ms. Cindy BELKNAP
88 Director of Principal Gifts .... Mr. Kenneth C. HALL
102 Dir Corporate & Foundation Rels .... Mr. David M. FOREMAN
88 Dir Parents Fund & Family Programs .... Ms. Ann L. DISTEFANO
44 Director of Gift Planning .... Ms. Melissa M. DIEHL
44 Director of the Annual Fund .... Ms. Loni N. KLINE
88 Dir Dev Research & Prospect Mgmt .... Ms. Cynthia D. JANESCH
88 Deputy Director Athletics .... Mr. Timothy N. PAVLECHKO
88 Director of Internal Audit .... Mr. Robert L. HOSTER
88 Chief Information Security Officer .... Mr. Eric J. SMITH
45 Director Business Planning .... Mr. Edward J. LOFTUS
08 Dir Library Services & Inst Tech .... Ms. Carrie E. RAMPP
14 Dir Tech Infrastructure & User Svcs .... Mr. J. Christopher WEBER
91 Dir Enterprise Systems .... Mr. Mark E. YERGER
07 Dean of Admissions .... Mr. Robert G. SPRINGALL
84 Asst VP Enroll Mgmt/Dir Partnershps .... Mr. Mark D. DAVIES
04 Dir President Ofc & Univ Secretary .... Ms. Carol M. KENNEDY
19 Chief of Public Safety .... Mr. Stephen J. BARILAR
88 Director of Business Services .... Ms. Lori J. WILSON
88 Assoc Controller Financial Services .... Mr. Ronald E. STAUFFER, II
88 Assoc Controller Accounting Svcs .... Mr. William D. GEORGE
88 Dir of Investments .... Mr. John R. LUTHI
88 Asst Controller .... Ms. Michelle M. JONES
88 Associate Budget Director .... Ms. Judy S. STABOLEPSZY
88 Director of Financial Services .... Ms. Kathy M. GUYER
36 Exec Director Career Services .... Ms. Pamela G. KEISER
09 Director of Institutional Research .... Mr. Kevork T. HORISSIAN
88 Director of Facility Services .... Mr. Michael J. PATTERSON
88 Director of Construction & Design .... Mr. James D. HOSTETLER
15 Dir Compensation & Employment Svcs .... Ms. Marcia J. COONEY
15 Director of Benefits & HRIS .... Ms. Cindy L. BILGER
88 Exec Director Events Mgmt Office .... Ms. Judith L. MICKANIS
37 Director Financial Aid .... Ms. Andrea C. LEITHNER STAUFFER
38 Director of Psychological Services .... Dr. Linda L. LOCHER
06 Associate Registrar .... Mr. Dennis M. HOPPLE
06 Associate Registrar .... Ms. Melissa A. WEBER
35 Associate Dean of Students .... Ms. Kari M. CONRAD
88 Associate Dean Student Diversity .... Mr. Thomas L. ALEXANDER
35 Associate Dean of Students .... Ms. Amy A. BADAL
35 Associate Dean of Students .... Mr. Daniel C. REMLEY
42 University Chaplain .... Mr. John P. COLATCH
104 Director of International Education .... Mr. Stephen K. APPIAH-PADI
105 Dir Digital Communications .... Ms. Roberta L. DIEHL
88 Director Media Communications .... Mr. Andrew H. HIRSCH
88 Dir Publications/Print & Mail .... Ms. Lisa D. HOOVER
88 Exec Dir Weis Center Perform Arts .... Ms. Kathryn L. MAGUET
88 Dir of Samek Art Gallery .... Mr. Richard J. RINEHART
96 Director of Procurement Services .... Mr. Donald A. KRECH
22 Affirmative Action Officer .... Ms. Linda L. BENNETT
88 Director Events Technology Services .... Mr. George A. LINCOLN, III
88 Director SBDC .... Mr. Steven V. STUMBRIS
88 Dir Univ Marketing & Web Content .... Ms. Molly E. O'BRIEN-FOELSCH
88 Dir Card Services & Student Transit .... Mr. Glenn R. FISHER
88 Dir Financial Information Systems .... Ms. Pamela K. NOONE
88 Dir Civic Engagement & Service Lrng .... Ms. Janice R. BUTLER
88 Director of Events .... Ms. Patricia M. RINGKAMP
85 Dir International Student Services .... Ms. Jennifer E. FIGUEROA
93 Director Multicultural Student Svcs .... Mr. Vincent L. STEPHENS
88 Director Office of LGBT Awareness .... Mr. William K. MCCOY
88 Director of Women's Resource Center .... Ms. Tracy E. RUSSELL
92 Honors Council Chair .... Dr. Erin L. JABLONSKI
88 Director of Writing Center .... Ms. Deirdre M. O'CONNOR

Bucks County Community College (B)

275 Swamp Road, Newtown PA 18940-4106

County: Bucks FICE Identification: 003239
Unit ID: 211307
Telephone: (215) 968-8000 Carnegie Class: Assoc/Pub-S-MC
FAX Number: (215) 968-8129 Calendar System: Semester
URL: www.bucks.edu
Established: 1964 Annual Undergrad Tuition & Fees (In-District): $3,722
Enrollment: 10,252 Coed
Affiliation or Control: Local IRS Status: 501(c)3
Highest Offering: Associate Degree
Program: Occupational; 2-Year Principally Bachelor's Creditable
Accreditation: M, ACBSP, ADNUR, ART, MUS, RAD

01 President .... Dr. Stephanie SHANBLATT
05 Int Provost/Dean of Academic Affs .... Ms. Catherine MCELROY
10 VP for Administrative Affairs & CFO .... Mr. Dennis W. MATTHEWS
32 VP Student Affairs/Dean of Students .... Ms. Barbara H. YETMAN
51 Vice Pres Cont Educ/Workforce Devel .... Ms. Barbara A. MILLER
13 Vice Pres/Chief Info Technology .... Dr. Andrew LAWLOR
20 Dean Academic & Curricular Svcs .... Ms. Catherine C. MCELROY
88 Dean Learning Resources .... Dr. Maureen MCCREADIE
84 Asst Dean for Enrollment Services .... Ms. Liz M. KULICK
38 Asst Dean Advising & Stdnt Planning .... Ms. Christine HAGEDORN
102 Exec Director of the Foundation .... Mr. Tobias BRUHN
21 Exec Dir Budget & Internal Audit .... Ms. Nancy PRUSKOWSKI
09 Exec Dir Inst Research & Assessment .... Dr. Christine BOYLE
12 Exec Dir Upper Bucks Campus .... Dr. Rodney H. ALTEMOSE
88 Exec Dir Public Safety Training .... Mr. Fred HUNSINGER
103 Exec Dir Workforce Development .... Ms. Lauren LOEFFLER
18 Exec Director Physical Plant .... Mr. Mark P. GRISI
26 Exec Dir Marketing/Public Relations .... Ms. Marta KAUFMANN
12 Exec Director Upper County Campus .... Dr. Rodney E. ALTEMOSE
04 Exec Assistant to President .... Ms. Kathleen C. FEDORKO
15 Exec Director Human Resources .... Ms. Tracey DONALDSON
96 Director of Purchasing .... Mr. James F. LOUGHERY
106 Director Online Learning .... Ms. Georglyn L. DAVIDSON
37 Director Financial Aid .... Ms. Donna M. WILKOSKI
36 Director Career Services .... Ms. Sharon STEPHENS
35 Director of Student Life Programs .... Mr. Matt J. CIPRIANO
19 Director of Security/Safety .... Mr. Dennis MCCAULEY
08 Director Library Services .... Ms. Linda MCCANN
41 Athletic Director .... Dr. Priscilla RICE
20 Executive Assistant to Provost .... Dr. William FORD
07 Director of Admissions .... Ms. Marlene T. BARLOW
06 Director Registration .... Mr. Robert MALEY
29 Alumni Relations Manager .... Ms. Jackie GEAR

Butler County Community College (C)

107 College Drive, Butler PA 16002

County: Butler FICE Identification: 003240
Unit ID: 211343
Telephone: (724) 287-8711 Carnegie Class: Assoc/Pub-S-SC
FAX Number: (724) 285-6047 Calendar System: Semester
URL: www.bc3.edu
Established: 1965 Annual Undergrad Tuition & Fees (In-District): $3,534
Enrollment: 3,873 Coed
Affiliation or Control: Local IRS Status: 501(c)3
Highest Offering: Associate Degree
Program: Occupational; 2-Year Principally Bachelor's Creditable
Accreditation: M, ACBSP, ADNUR, MAC, PTAA

01 President .... Dr. Nicholas C. NEUPAUER
05 Vice President for Academic Affairs .... Dr. Francie P. SPIGELMYER
11 VP for Administration & Finance .... Mr. James A. HRABOSKY
32 Vice President for Student Services .... Dr. Gordon C. WILLOUGHBY
51 VP Continuing Ed Off-Campus Centers .... Mr. William T. O'BRIEN
10 Chief Business Officer .... Mr. Wm. Jake FRIEL
50 Dean of Business .... Ms. Rosemary C. KEASEY
83 Dean of Social Science/Humanities .... Mr. William L. MILLER
66 Dean of Nursing/Allied Health .... Dr. Patricia MIHALCIN
72 Interim Dean of Nat Science/Tech .... Mr. Matt KOVAC
106 Dean of Education Technology .... Ms. Ann MCCANDLESS
08 Dean of Library Services .... Mr. Stephen M. JOSEPH
35 Dean of Students .... Mr. Joshua NOVAK
103 Exec Dir Workforce Dev Training .... Dr. Stephen R. CATT
16 Exec Director Human Resources .... Ms. Linda M. DODD
26 Exec Director of Comm & Mktg .... Ms. Susan J. CHANGNON
51 Director Adult/Continuing Education .... Mr. Paul M. LUCAS
06 Director of Records & Registration .... Ms. Ruth A. SCOTT
13 Director Telecommunications & MIS .... Mr. Rick H. MICHELINI
32 Director of Student Life .... Mr. Rob A. SNYDER
09 Dir Instl Research/Strategic Plng .... Ms. Sharla M. ANKE
18 Exec Director of Operations .... Mr. Brian R. OPITZ
07 Director of Admissions .... Ms. Pattie A. BAJUSZIK
12 Director of BC3 @ Lawrence Crossing .... Ms. Diane M. DECARBO
12 Director of BC3 @ Cranberry .... Mr. Alex J. GLADIS
12 Director of BC3 @ LindenPointe .... Mr. John P. SUESSER
12 Director of BC3 @ Brockway .... Ms. Jill MARTIN-REND
37 Financial Aid Director .... Ms. Julianne E. LOUTTIT
41 Athletic Director .... Mr. Rob A. SNYDER
21 Director of College Services .... Vacant
50 Director of Business/Industry Trng .... Ms. Lisa M. CAMPBELL
38 Director Student Counseling .... Vacant
29 Director Alumni Relations .... Ms. Michelle E. JAMIESON
30 Exec Director of Advancement .... Ms. Ruth PURCELL
19 Exec Dir of Campus Police/Security .... Mr. Patrick W. MASSARO
88 Director of Cultural Center .... Mr. Lawrence E. STOCK
88 Director of Children's Center .... Ms. Judith A. ZUZACK
88 Associate Director Admissions .... Mr. Sean M. CARROLL
40 Bookstore Manager .... Ms. Donna L. PALLONE

Byzantine Catholic Seminary of SS. Cyril and Methodius (D)

3605 Perrysville Avenue, Pittsburgh PA 15214-2229

County: Allegheny FICE Identification: 041180
Unit ID: 444103
Telephone: (412) 321-8383 Carnegie Class: Spec/Faith
FAX Number: (412) 321-9936 Calendar System: Semester
URL: www.bcs.edu
Established: 1950 Annual Graduate Tuition & Fees: $19,200
Enrollment: 14 Coed
Affiliation or Control: Other IRS Status: 501(c)3
Highest Offering: Master's; No Undergraduates
Program: Liberal Arts And General; Religious Emphasis
Accreditation: THEOL

01 Rector .... Rev. Kurt BURNETTE
05 Academic Dean .... Rev. Joseph RAPTOSH

Cabrini College (E)

610 King of Prussia Road, Radnor PA 19087-3698

County: Delaware FICE Identification: 003241
Unit ID: 211352
Telephone: (610) 902-8100 Carnegie Class: Master's L
FAX Number: (610) 902-8309 Calendar System: Semester
URL: www.cabrini.edu
Established: 1957 Annual Undergrad Tuition & Fees: $29,000
Enrollment: 3,290 Coed
Affiliation or Control: Roman Catholic IRS Status: 501(c)3
Highest Offering: Master's
Program: Liberal Arts And General
Accreditation: M, SW

01 Interim President .... Ms. Deb TAKES
05 Provost/Vice Pres Academic Affairs .... Dr. Anne SKLEDER
10 Vice Pres Finance/Admin & Treasurer .... Dr. Robert ALLISON
30 VP Advancement/External Relations .... Mr. Gene CASTELLANO
32 Vice Pres for Student Development .... Dr. Christine LYSIONEK
84 Vice Pres of Enrollment Management .... Mr. Robert REESE
20 Vice Provost/Dean Academic Affairs .... Dr. Jeffrey GINGERICH
35 Dean of Students .... Mr. George STROUD
58 Associate Dean of Education .... Dr. Beverly BRYDE
04 Exec Assistant to the President .... Ms. Sherry PETERS
06 Assistant Registrar .... Ms. M. Frances HARKNESS
08 Library Director .... Dr. Roberta JACQUET
14 Director of Info Tech & Resources .... Ms. Marlayne DUNOVICH
19 Director of Public Safety .... Mr. Creig DOYLE
18 Dir Construction/Plng/Facilities .... Mr. Howard HOLDEN
29 Dir of Alumni Engagement and Giving .... Ms. Rachel MCCARTER
37 Director of Financial Aid .... Ms. Elizabeth STILES
36 Dir of Cooperative Educ/Career Svcs .... Ms. Nancy HUTCHISON
41 Director of Athletics .... Mr. Bradley KOCH
15 Director of Human Resources .... Ms. Susan ROHANNA
21 Controller .... Ms. Diane SCUTTI
24 Coord of Education Resources Center .... Ms. Mary BUDZILOWICZ
40 Bookstore Manager .... Ms. Michele CONROY
105 Web Master .... Mr. Matthew HOLMES
09 Director of Institutional Research .... Ms. Lisa PLUMMER
35 Dir Student Engagement & Leadership .... Ms. Anne FILIPPONE
92 Co-Director of the Honors Program .... Dr. Paul WRIGHT
92 Co-Director of the Honors Program .... Dr. Leonard PRIMIANO
28 Dir Student Diversity Initiatives .... Ms. Stephanie REED
38 Director Counseling/Psych Service .... Dr. Sara MAGGITTI
39 Director of Residence Life .... Ms. Sue KRAMER

Cairn University (F)

200 Manor Avenue, Langhorne Manor PA 19047-2990

County: Bucks FICE Identification: 003351
Unit ID: 215114
Telephone: (215) 752-5800 Carnegie Class: Master's S
FAX Number: (215) 702-4341 Calendar System: Semester
URL: www.cairn.edu
Established: 1913 Annual Undergrad Tuition & Fees: $22,455
Enrollment: 1,216 Coed
Affiliation or Control: Independent Non-Profit IRS Status: 501(c)3
Highest Offering: Master's
Program: Liberal Arts And General; Teacher Preparatory; Professional; Religious Emphasis
Accreditation: M, BI, IACBE, MUS, SW

01 President .... Dr. Todd J. WILLIAMS
05 Provost .... Dr. Brian G. TOEWS
84 Sr VP Enrollment & Student Affairs .... Mr. J. Scott CAWOOD

10 Sr VP Finance & Administration .... Mr. Jan M. HAAS
30 Sr VP Univ Advancement .... Mr. Russell T. NIXON
15 VP Human Resources .... Ms. Mary BOYER
06 Registrar .... Dr. Steven SCHLENKER
08 Dean Educational Resources .... Dr. Timothy K. HUI
32 Dean Student Life .... Mr. Tom SHERF
49 Dean School of Lib Arts & Sciences .... Dr. Jason VANBILLIARD
50 Dean Sch of Business & Leadership .... Mr. Ronald FERNER
53 Dean School of Education .... Dr. Deborah MACCULLOUGH
64 Dean School of Music .... Dr. Paul ISENSEE
73 Dean School of Divinity .... Dr. Jonathan L. MASTER
07 Director Admissions .... Mr. Eric RIVERA
29 Director Alumni Relations .... Mr. Jamie GLEASON
18 Director Campus Services .... Mr. Robert WATSON
40 Director Campus Store .... Ms. Dana JALOVICK
36 Director Career Center .... Ms. Teri T. CANTANIO
26 Director Comm & Marketing .... Ms. Laura PENLEY
37 Director Financial Aid .... Mr. Stephen CASSEL
23 Director Health Services .... Ms. Alison KIKENDALL
09 Director Institutional Research .... Dr. Lynn H. WALLACE
42 Director Recruitment .... Ms. Brooke MCDOWELL
39 Director Resident Life .... Mr. Evan CURRY
19 Director Safety & Security .... Mr. Chris LLOYD
38 Director Student Counseling .... Mr. Baron KING
13 Director Technology Services .... Mr. Curt D. WINTERS
11 Controller .... Mr. Jeff EUBANK
21 Asst Director Business Services .... Dr. Andrew HUI

Calvary Baptist Theological Seminary (A)

1380 S Valley Forge Road, Lansdale PA 19446-4797
County: Montgomery FICE Identification: 038993
Unit ID: 211370
Telephone: (215) 368-7538 Carnegie Class: Spec/Faith
FAX Number: (215) 368-1003 Calendar System: Semester
URL: www.cbs.edu
Established: 1976 Annual Graduate Tuition & Fees: $8,940
Enrollment: 58 Coed
Affiliation or Control: Independent Non-Profit IRS Status: 501(c)3
Highest Offering: Doctorate; No Undergraduates
Program: Professional; Religious Emphasis
Accreditation: M

01 President .... Dr. Samuel L. HARBIN
05 Seminary Dean .... Dr. Charles MCLAIN
06 Registrar .... Mr. Clint J. BANZ
08 Director of Library Services .... Mr. Clint J. BANZ
10 Director of Finance .... Mr. Nicholas Y. YZZI

Cambria-Rowe Business College (B)

422 S 13th Street, Indiana PA 15701-2804
Telephone: (724) 463-0222 Identification: 666476
Accreditation: ACICS

† Main campus is Cambria-Rowe Business College in Johnstown, PA.

Cambria-Rowe Business College (C)

221 Central Avenue, Johnstown PA 15902-2494
County: Cambria FICE Identification: 004889
Unit ID: 211398
Telephone: (814) 536-5168 Carnegie Class: Assoc/PrivFP
FAX Number: (814) 536-5160 Calendar System: Quarter
URL: www.crbc.net
Established: 1891 Annual Undergrad Tuition & Fees: $13,380
Enrollment: 133 Coed
Affiliation or Control: Proprietary IRS Status: Proprietary
Highest Offering: Associate Degree
Program: Occupational; 2-Year Principally Bachelor's Creditable; Business Emphasis
Accreditation: ACICS

01 President .... Mr. William COWARD
03 Executive Director .... Mr. Michael ARTIM
88 Director of Compliance .... Mr. Jeffrey ALLEN
05 Director of Education .... Dr. Jonathon WOLF
36 Campus Director .... Mrs. Amy HORWATH
37 Director of Financial Aid Services .... Mrs. Linda WESS
07 Director of Admission .... Mrs. Amanda ARTIM
10 Business Manager .... Mrs. LeAnna BRKOVICH
07 Admissions Representative .... Ms. Riley MCDONALD

Career Training Academy (D)

4314 Old William Penn Hwy, Ste 103, Monroeville PA 15146-1455
Telephone: (412) 372-3900 Identification: 666051
Accreditation: ACCSC

† Main campus is Career Training Academy in New Kensington, PA.

Career Training Academy (E)

950 Fifth Avenue, New Kensington PA 15068-6308
County: Westmoreland FICE Identification: 026095
Unit ID: 210951
Telephone: (724) 337-1000 Carnegie Class: Assoc/PrivFP
FAX Number: (724) 335-7140 Calendar System: Other
URL: www.careerta.edu
Established: 1986 Annual Undergrad Tuition & Fees: $8,945
Enrollment: 100 Coed
Affiliation or Control: Proprietary IRS Status: Proprietary
Highest Offering: Associate Degree
Program: Occupational; 2-Year Principally Bachelor's Creditable; Technical Emphasis
Accreditation: ACCSC

01 Acting Campus Director .... Ms. Rachel ROCK

Career Training Academy (F)

1500 Shoppes at Northway, Pittsburgh PA 15237-3015
Telephone: (412) 367-4000 Identification: 666100
Accreditation: ACCSC

† Main campus is Career Training Academy in New Kensington, PA.

Carlow University (G)

3333 Fifth Avenue, Pittsburgh PA 15213-3165
County: Allegheny FICE Identification: 003303
Unit ID: 211431
Telephone: (412) 578-6000 Carnegie Class: Master's M
FAX Number: (412) 578-6668 Calendar System: Semester
URL: www.carlow.edu
Established: 1929 Annual Undergrad Tuition & Fees: $25,416
Enrollment: 2,310 Coed
Affiliation or Control: Roman Catholic IRS Status: 501(c)3
Highest Offering: Doctorate
Program: Liberal Arts And General; Teacher Preparatory; Professional
Accreditation: M, COPSY, NURSE, SW

01 President .... Dr. Suzanne K. MELLON
05 Provost/VP Academic Affairs .... Dr. Margaret K. MCLAUGHLIN
10 CFO/VP Finance and Operations .... Mr. Patrick J. CUNNINGHAM
30 VP Advancement .... Ms. Karen E. GALENTINE
26 VP Communications & External Rels .... Ms. Amy E. NEIL
88 Special Asst to Pres/Mercy Heritage .... Sr. Sheila A. CARNEY
32 Dean Student Affairs .... Ms. Jennifer CARLO
04 Asst to the President .... Ms. Barbara L. GILLES
15 Director Human Resources .... Ms. Andra M. TOKARSKY
42 Campus Minister .... Ms. Siobhan K. DEWITT
58 Interim Dean Graduate School .... Dr. Robert A. REED
06 Registrar .... Mr. Jason KRALL
88 Exec Dir & Principal Campus School .... Ms. Michelle A. PEDUTO
58 Sr Dir Adult & Graduate Admissions .... Mr. James V. SHANKEL
07 Director Admissions .... Ms. Susan M. WINSTEL
12 Dir Cranberry Education Center .... Mr. James V. SHANKEL
12 Dir Greensburg Education Center .... Ms. Wendy S. PHILLIPS
36 Director Career Development .... Ms. Erin R. BRIDGEN
08 Director Library Services .... Ms. Elaine J. MISKO
85 Coordinator Center for Global Lrng .... Mr. Garrett D. MARGLIOTTI
09 Sr Dir Inst Research & Effective .... Ms. Anne M. CANDREVA
35 Director Campus Life .... Mr. Christopher M. MEANER
39 Asst Director Campus Life .... Ms. Carrie R. BENSON
23 Director Health Services .... Ms. Mary Frances REIDELL
41 Director Athletics .... Mr. George S. SLIMAN
88 Director Wellness & Fitness Svcs .... Ms. Julie M. GAUL
28 Director Diversity Initiative .... Ms. Barbara G. JOHNSON
21 Controller .... Ms. Dorothy M. ANTONUCCI
13 Chief Technology Officer .... Mr. Jeff P. DEVLIN
18 Director Facilities .... Vacant
19 Chief of Police .... Vacant
37 Director Financial Aid .... Ms. Natalie L. WILSON
88 Director Student Accounts .... Ms. Linda C. ROOT
40 Manager Bookstore .... Ms. Athena KITCHENFLINT
44 Exec Director Advancement .... Ms. Anita S. DACAL
29 Director Alumnae/i Relations .... Ms. Rose M. WOOLLEY
44 Senior Director of Major Gifts .... Ms. Marcia M. WALLANDER
102 Director of Corp & Found Relations .... Ms. Marjorie P. BERNARD
27 Asst Dir Media & Public Rels .... Mr. Andrew G. WILSON
105 Manager Web Communications .... Ms. Kristin A. RAUP

Carnegie Mellon University (H)

5000 Forbes Avenue, Pittsburgh PA 15213-3890
County: Allegheny FICE Identification: 003242
Unit ID: 211440
Telephone: (412) 268-2000 Carnegie Class: RU/VH
FAX Number: (412) 268-2330 Calendar System: Semester
URL: www.cmu.edu
Established: 1900 Annual Undergrad Tuition & Fees: $47,412
Enrollment: 12,569 Coed
Affiliation or Control: Independent Non-Profit IRS Status: 501(c)3
Highest Offering: Doctorate
Program: Liberal Arts And General; Teacher Preparatory; Professional
Accreditation: M, BUS, ENG, MUS, SPAA

01 President .... Dr. Subra SURESH
05 Provost/Executive Vice President .... Dr. Mark S. KAMLET
10 Vice President and CFO .... Dr. Amir RAHNAMAY-AZAR
30 Vice President for Univ Advancement .... Mrs. Robbee KOSAK
46 Interim VP of Sponsored Programs .... Dr. David DZOMBAK
43 Vice President/General Counsel .... Ms. Mary Jo DIVELY
101 Secretary Board of Trustees .... Ms. Cheryl M. HAYS
04 Exec Asst to Pres & Office Mgr .... Ms. Cathy A. LIGHT
20 Vice Provost for Education .... Dr. Amy L. BURKERT
11 Vice President for Campus Affairs .... Dr. Michael C. MURPHY
13 Vice Provost for Comp Svcs/CIO .... Mr. Steven K. HUTH
15 Assoc VP Chief Human Resources Ofcr .... Ms. Dianne KENNEY
29 Assoc Vice Pres Alumni Relations .... Mr. Andrew SHAINDLIN
18 Asc VP Campus Design/Facility Devel .... Mr. Ralph R. HORGAN
26 Acting Exec Dir For Media Relations .... Mr. Kenneth WALTERS
28 Asst Vice Pres for Diversity & EOS .... Mr. Everett L. TADAMY
102 Exec Director Foundation Relations .... Dr. Peter F. COHEN
45 Director University Planning .... Mr. Russell D. O'LARE
41 Interim Dir Athletics & Physical Ed .... Mr. Josh CENTOR
19 Director Security/Chief Univ Police .... Mr. Thomas A. OGDEN
84 Co-Director of Enrollment Services .... Mr. John R. PAPINCHAK
84 Co-Director of Enrollment Services .... Mrs. Linda M. ANDERSON
14 Director Software Engr Inst .... Dr. Paul D. NIELSEN
07 Director of Admission .... Mr. Michael STEIDEL
08 Dean of University Libraries .... Mr. Keith WEBSTER
96 Director of Procurement .... Mr. Shawn G. FRONZAGLIA
06 Registrar .... Mr. John R. PAPINCHAK
09 Director of Institutional Research .... Ms. Janel SUTKUS
36 Director of Career Center .... Mr. Farouk DEY
38 Dir Counseling & Psychological Svcs .... Dr. Kurt KUMLER
32 Dean Student Affairs .... Ms. Gina CASALEGNO
54 Dean Carnegie Inst of Technology .... Dr. James GARRETT
57 Dean College Fine Arts .... Dr. Dan J. MARTIN
49 Dean Human & Social Science .... Dr. John P. LEHOCZKY
50 Dean Tepper School of Business .... Dr. Robert DAMMON
81 Dean Mellon College of Science .... Dr. Frederick J. GILMAN
80 Dean Heinz Sch Publ Policy/Mgmt .... Dr. Ramayya KRISHNAN
77 Dean School of Computer Science .... Dr. Randal E. BRYANT
35 Asst Dean of Student Affairs .... Ms. Anne WITCHNER

Cedar Crest College (I)

100 College Drive, Allentown PA 18104-6196
County: Lehigh FICE Identification: 003243
Unit ID: 211468
Telephone: (610) 437-4471 Carnegie Class: Bac/Diverse
FAX Number: (610) 437-5955 Calendar System: Semester
URL: www.cedarcrest.edu
Established: 1867 Annual Undergrad Tuition & Fees: $32,600
Enrollment: 1,567 Female
Affiliation or Control: Non-denominational IRS Status: 501(c)3
Highest Offering: Master's
Program: Liberal Arts And General; Teacher Preparatory; Professional
Accreditation: M, ACBSP, DIETD, @DIETI, FEPAC, NUR, SW

01 President .... Ms. Carmen T. AMBAR
05 Provost .... Dr. Elizabeth MEADE
10 Chief Financial Officer .... Ms. Audra KAHR
07 Director of Admissions .... Ms. Germel CLARKE
30 VP of Development/Alumnae Relation .... Ms. Susan ARNOLD
32 Dean of Student Affairs .... Ms. Mary-Alice OZECHOSKI
06 Registrar .... Ms. Janet BAKER
29 Exec Director for Alumnae Affairs .... Mrs. Susan S. COX
19 Chief of Campus Safety and Security .... Mr. Mark VITALOS
18 Director of Facilities .... Mr. Matthew YENCHA
08 Library Director .... Ms. Mary Beth FREEH
91 Director Administrative Technology .... Mrs. Kathleen CUNNINGHAM
09 Dir of Institutional Research .... Ms. Lyn WILLIAMS
04 Assistant to the President .... Ms. Meghan GRADY
37 Dir Student Financial Services .... Ms. Valerie KREISER
22 Director Health/Counseling Services .... Ms. Nancy ROBERTS
27 Chief Marketing Officer .... Mr. Gaetan GIANNINI
96 Purchasing Coordinator .... Ms. Karen KHATTARI
40 Manager Bookstore .... Ms. Maureen YOACHIM

Central Penn College (J)

College Hill Road, Summerdale PA 17093-0309
County: Cumberland FICE Identification: 004890
Unit ID: 211477
Telephone: (800) 759-2727 Carnegie Class: Bac/Diverse
FAX Number: (717) 732-5254 Calendar System: Quarter
URL: www.centralpenn.edu
Established: 1881 Annual Undergrad Tuition & Fees: $21,556
Enrollment: 1,342 Coed
Affiliation or Control: Proprietary IRS Status: Proprietary
Highest Offering: Master's
Program: Occupational; 2-Year Principally Bachelor's Creditable; Professional; Business Emphasis
Accreditation: M, MAC, PTAA

01 President .... Dr. Karen SCOLFORO
05 Vice Pres/Chief Academic Officer .... Dr. Melissa M. VAYDA
06 Director Records & Registration .... Mr. Jen CORRELL
03 Provost .... Ms. Janice MOORE
20 Academic Dean .... Ms. Kathy ANDERSEN
26 Marketing Services Manager .... Mrs. Mary E. WETZEL
07 Enrollment Director .... Ms. Kristin HORN
51 Dir Continuing Education Admissions .... Ms. Michelle MEISER
18 Facilities Director .... Mr. Rodney GROFF
37 Financial Aid Director .... Ms. Kathy J. SHEPARD
32 Asst Dean Student Services .... Mr. Ed LIESCH
09 Institutional Research Director .... Col. Wilbur E. GRAY
36 Career Services Coordinator .... Mr. Steven HASSINGER

Chatham University (K)

Woodland Road, Pittsburgh PA 15232-2826
County: Allegheny FICE Identification: 003244
Unit ID: 211556
Telephone: (412) 365-1100 Carnegie Class: Master's L
FAX Number: (412) 365-1505 Calendar System: Other
URL: www.chatham.edu
Established: 1869 Annual Undergrad Tuition & Fees: $31,532
Enrollment: 2,178 Female
Affiliation or Control: Independent Non-Profit IRS Status: 501(c)3
Highest Offering: Doctorate

Program: Liberal Arts And General; Teacher Preparatory; Professional
Accreditation: M, #ARCPA, CIDA, LSAR, NURSE, OT, PTA, SW

01 President ....Dr. Esther L. BARAZZONE
94 Dean College for Women ....Dr. Karol DEAN
10 Vice Pres Finance/Administration ....Mr. Walter B. FOWLER
05 Vice President Academic Affairs ....Dr. Wenying XU
84 Vice Pres Enrollment Management ....Ms. Wendy BECKEMEYER
32 VP Student Affairs/Dean of Stdnts ....Dr. Zauyah WAITE
27 Vice Pres for Mktg & Communications ....Mr. Bill CAMPBELL
30 Vice Pres University Advancement ....Ms. Ann BOYD-STEWART
51 Dean Continuing/Prof Studies ....Vacant
88 Dean Sch Sustainability/Environment ....Dr. David HASSENZAHL
21 Asst VP Finance/Administration ....Ms. Jennifer LUNDY
45 AVP Plng/Asst to President ....Mr. Sean COLEMAN
20 Asst VP of Academic Affairs ....Vacant
58 Dean College of Graduate Studies ....Vacant
09 Director of Institutional Research ....Dr. Robert ZHANG
06 Registrar ....Ms. Jennifer BRONSON
37 Director of Financial Aid ....Ms. Jennifer A. BURNS
08 Director of Library ....Ms. Jill AUSEL
29 Director Alumnae Affairs ....Vacant
44 Director of Annual Giving ....Ms. Donna HOLMES
102 Director of Foundation/Corp Support ....Ms. Kate FREED
15 Director of Human Resources ....Mr. Frank M. GRECO
18 Director of Facilities Management ....Mr. Robert R. DUBRAY
19 Director of Safety & Security ....Mr. Bernard D. MERRICK
41 Director of Athletics ....Ms. Terlynn OLDS
36 Director Career Development ....Ms. Monica RITTER
38 Director of Student Counseling ....Dr. Elsa M. ARCE
35 Dir Student Affs/Residence Life ....Ms. Heather BLACK

Chestnut Hill College (A)

9601 Germantown Avenue, Philadelphia PA 19118-2693
County: Philadelphia FICE Identification: 003245
Unit ID: 211583
Telephone: (215) 248-7000 Carnegie Class: Master's L
FAX Number: (215) 248-7155 Calendar System: Semester
URL: www.chc.edu
Established: 1924 Annual Undergrad Tuition & Fees: $31,270
Enrollment: 2,310 Coed
Affiliation or Control: Roman Catholic IRS Status: 501(c)3
Highest Offering: Doctorate
Program: Liberal Arts And General; Teacher Preparatory
Accreditation: M, CLPSY, MACTE

01 President ....Sr. Carol Jean VALE, SSJ
05 Vice Pres for Academic Affairs ....Dr. Steven GUERRIERO
09 Vice Pres Admin Instl Svcs & Events ....Vacant
10 Sr Vice Pres for Financial Affairs ....Ms. Lauri STRIMKOVSKY
30 Vice President for Inst Advancement ....Mr. Kenneth HICKS
32 Vice President for Student Life ....Dr. Lynn ORTALE
90 Executive Dir for Technical Svcs ....Vacant
11 Asst to Pres for Administration ....Sr. Kathryn MILLER, SSJ
42 Asst to Pres for Mission & Ministry ....Sr. Mary DARRAH, SSJ
58 Dean School of Graduate Studies ....Dr. Barbara HOGAN
97 Dean School of Undergrad Studies ....Sr. Merilyn RYAN, SSJ
51 Dean of Continuing Studies ....Dr. Elaine GREEN
08 Dean Library/Information Resources ....Sr. Mary Josephine LARKIN, SSJ
07 Vice President for Admissions ....Ms. Jodie KING
20 Assoc Dir Acad Adv Student Svcs ....Ms. Clare DOYLE
20 Assoc Dir Acad Adv Tech Support ....Mr. Michael PETERSON
06 Registrar ....Ms. Deborah EBBERT
35 Director of Student Activities ....Ms. Emily SCHADEMAN
38 Director Counseling Center ....Sr. Sheila KENNEDY, SSJ
85 Foreign Student Advisor ....Ms. Trachanda BROWN
28 Dir Cultural Diversity Initiatives ....Vacant
92 Director of Honors Programs ....Vacant
23 Director Health Services ....Ms. Shannon ROBERTS
36 Director of Career Services ....Ms. Nancy DACHILLE
07 Dir Admission/Sch Graduate Studies ....Ms. Jayne MASHETT
07 Director Accelerated Admissions ....Sr. Mary Esther LEE, SSJ
21 Controller ....Ms. Ellen MCGUINN
37 Director Financial Aid ....Ms. Kristina WILHELM-NELSON
44 Sr Director of Development ....Ms. Patricia CANNING
09 Director of Institutional Research ....Sr. Patricia O'DONNELL, SSJ
102 Dir Corporate/Found/Govt Relations ....Vacant
29 Director of Alumnae/i Affairs ....Ms. Catherine QUINN
41 Director of Athletics ....Ms. Lynn TUBMAN
15 Director Human Resources ....Ms. Michelle MOCARSKY
19 Dir Security/Safety/Bldgs/Grounds ....Ms. Polly TETI
18 Director of Physical Plant ....Mr. Mark MCGRATH
91 Administrative Software Manager ....Ms. Darlene BROWN
24 Audio Visual Manager ....Vacant
26 Public Relations Director ....Ms. Kathleen SPIGELMYER
40 Manager of Campus Store ....Vacant

The Commonwealth Medical College (B)

525 Pine Street, Scranton PA 18509
County: Lackawanna FICE Identification: 041672
Unit ID: 456542
Telephone: (570) 504-7000 Carnegie Class: Assoc/PrivNFP4
FAX Number: (570) 504-7289 Calendar System: Semester
URL: www.thecommonwealthmedical.com
Established: 2009 Annual Graduate Tuition & Fees: $41,318
Enrollment: 325 Coed
Affiliation or Control: Independent Non-Profit IRS Status: 501(c)3
Highest Offering: Doctorate; No Undergraduates
Program: Professional
Accreditation: @M, #MED

01 President and Dean ....Dr. Steven J. SCHEINMAN
10 VP for Finance & Admin/CFO ....Ms. Anna RUSNAK NOON
45 Vice Pres & Assoc Dean for Planning ....Ms. Virginia HUNT
30 VP Institutional Advancement ....Ms. Marise GAROFALO
31 VP Cmty & Government Relations ....Ms. Ida L. CASTRO
05 Senior Assoc Dean Academic Affairs ....Dr. Maurice CLIFTON
32 Assoc Dean Student Affs/ Admissions ....Ms. Linda BERARDI-DEMO
88 Assoc Dean of Fac Affairs/Fac Devel ....Ms. Andrea DIMATTIA
15 Director of Human Resources ....Mr. Joseph CORTESE
21 Dir Budgeting & Financial Services ....Mr. Sam DIAZ
105 Director of Web Services ....Mr. Jay FORTIN
35 Director of Student Affairs ....Ms. Julia KOLCHARNO
06 Registrar ....Mr. Edward LAHART
37 Director of Financial Aid ....Ms. Ellen MCGUIRE
91 Director of Administrative Systems ....Mr. John KEARNEY
08 Director of Library ....Ms. Joanne MUELLENBACH
18 Director Facility/Public Safety ....Mr. Joe ROSS
09 Dir Alumni Relations/Annual Giving ....Ms. Nina Cecelia DEI TOS

Commonwealth Technical Institute at the Hiram G. Andrews Center (C)

727 Goucher Street, Johnstown PA 15905-3092
County: Cambria FICE Identification: 025366
Unit ID: 212975
Telephone: (814) 255-8200 Carnegie Class: Assoc/PrivNFP
FAX Number: (814) 255-5709 Calendar System: Semester
URL: www.hgac.org
Established: 1959 Annual Undergrad Tuition & Fees: $11,224
Enrollment: 255 Coed
Affiliation or Control: Proprietary IRS Status: Proprietary
Highest Offering: Associate Degree
Program: Occupational
Accreditation: ACCSC

01 President ....Carol MACKEL
03 Executive Vice President ....Jill MORICONI
05 Chief Academic Officer ....Barbara PETERSEN
07 Director of Admissions ....Jason GIES
32 Chief Student Life Officer ....Stacie ANDREWS
37 Director Student Financial Aid ....Sylvia SABO
38 Director Student Counseling ....Keith RAGER

Community College of Allegheny County (D)

800 Allegheny Avenue, Pittsburgh PA 15233-1895
County: Allegheny FICE Identification: 003231
Unit ID: 210605
Telephone: (412) 323-2323 Carnegie Class: Assoc/Pub-U-MC
FAX Number: (412) 237-3037 Calendar System: Semester
URL: www.ccac.edu
Established: 1966 Annual Undergrad Tuition & Fees (In-District): $3,591
Enrollment: 18,896 Coed
Affiliation or Control: State/Local IRS Status: 501(c)3
Highest Offering: Associate Degree
Program: Occupational; 2-Year Principally Bachelor's Creditable
Accreditation: M, ADNUR, CA, CAHIIM, COARC, DIETT, DMS, EMT, MAC, MLTAD, NMT, OTA, PTAA, RAD, RTT, SURGT

01 Interim President ....Dr. Michael MURPHY
05 VP Learning & Student Development ....Dr. Mary Frances ARCHEY
10 VP Business & Admin/CFO ....Ms. Joyce BRECKENRIDGE
12 Campus President Allegheny ....Dr. Donna IMHOFF
12 Campus President Boyce ....Hon. Charles MARTONI
12 Campus President North ....Vacant
12 Campus President South ....Dr. Charlene NEWKIRK
30 VP Inst Advance/External Relations ....Ms. Nancilee BURZACHECHI
103 VP Workforce Development ....Ms. Alicia BOOKER
16 VP Human Resources ....Mr. Paul SCHWARZMILLER
102 Exec Director of Foundation ....Ms. Rose Ann DICOLA
13 Exec Dir Information Tech Svcs ....Mr. Ibrahim GARBIOGLU
20 Assistant Dean Academic Management ....Ms. Frances DICE
06 Registrar ....Ms. Frances DICE
51 Exec Dir Center Professional Dev ....Mr. Reginald OVERTON
09 Exec Dir of Strategic Planning ....Mr. Kevin SMAY
18 Director of Facilities Management ....Mr. Bob HAMILTON
21 Controller ....Mr. Paul SWEARENGIN
25 Director Contracts & Grants ....Dr. Carol YOANNONE
96 Director Purchasing/Contracts Admin ....Vacant
28 Special Asst to Pres for Diversity ....Mr. Clyde PICKETT
100 Assistant to the President ....Ms. Bonita L. RICHARDSON
22 Human Resources Generalist ....Mr. Paul SCHWARZMILLER
86 Exec Dir Gov Relations ....Dr. Charles BLOCKSIDGE
29 Dir Alumni Affairs ....Vacant
04 Exec Assistant to the President ....Vacant

Community College of Allegheny County Boyce Campus (E)

595 Beatty Road, Monroeville PA 15146-1348
Telephone: (724) 325-6614 Identification: 770150
Accreditation: &M

† Main campus is Community College of Allegheny County in Pittsburgh, PA.

Community College of Allegheny County North Campus (F)

8701 Perry Highway, Pittsburgh PA 15237-5353
Telephone: (412) 366-7000 Identification: 770151
Accreditation: &M

† Main campus is Community College of Allegheny County in Pittsburgh, PA.

Community College of Allegheny County South Campus (G)

1750 Clairton Road, West Mifflin PA 15122-3029
Telephone: (412) 469-1100 Identification: 770152
Accreditation: &M

† Main campus is Community College of Allegheny County in Pittsburgh, PA.

Community College of Beaver County (H)

1 Campus Drive, Monaca PA 15061-2588
County: Beaver FICE Identification: 006807
Unit ID: 211079
Telephone: (724) 480-2222 Carnegie Class: Assoc/Pub-S-SC
FAX Number: (724) 480-3573 Calendar System: Semester
URL: www.ccbc.edu
Established: 1966 Annual Undergrad Tuition & Fees (In-District): $4,380
Enrollment: 2,596 Coed
Affiliation or Control: State/Local IRS Status: 501(c)3
Highest Offering: Associate Degree
Program: Occupational; 2-Year Principally Bachelor's Creditable
Accreditation: M, ADNUR, PHLEB

01 President ....Dr. Joe D. FORRESTER
05 Provost/VP Learning/Student Success ....Mrs. Melissa D. DENARDO
10 Vice President Finance & Operations ....Mr. Stephen R. DANIK
15 Vice Pres Human Resource Dev ....Mr. Jeff A. FARLEY
26 VP Community Relations/Development ....Ms. Nancy A. DICKSON
13 Vice Pres Information Technology ....Mr. Walter P. LUKHAUP
38 Dean Academic Support Services ....Ms. Janice M. KAMINSKI
06 Dean of Enrollment Services ....Ms. Angela M. VEDRO
103 Dean Workforce Dev/Continuing Educ ....Mr. John S. GOBERISH
09 Director Institutional Research ....Mr. Brian HAYDEN
18 Director Physical Plant Ops ....Mr. Robert MOLLENKOPF
37 Director Student Financial Svcs ....Ms. Janet DAVIDSON
04 Assistant to President ....Ms. Jo Ann COATES
76 Division Dir Health Sciences ....Mrs. Linda A. GALLAGHER
50 Division Dir Business/Technologies ....Ms. Deborah MICHEALS
49 Division Dir Liberal Arts & Science ....Dr. John GALL
88 Division Dir Aviation ....Vacant

Community College of Philadelphia (I)

1700 Spring Garden Street, Philadelphia PA 19130-3991
County: Philadelphia FICE Identification: 003249
Unit ID: 215239
Telephone: (215) 751-8000 Carnegie Class: Assoc/Pub-U-SC
FAX Number: (215) 751-8762 Calendar System: Semester
URL: www.ccp.edu
Established: 1965 Annual Undergrad Tuition & Fees (In-District): $4,440
Enrollment: 18,923 Coed
Affiliation or Control: State/Local IRS Status: 501(c)3
Highest Offering: Associate Degree
Program: Occupational; 2-Year Principally Bachelor's Creditable
Accreditation: M, ADNUR, COARC, DH, MAC, MLTAD, PHLEB, RAD

01 Interim President ....Dr. Judith R. GAY
10 Vice President Finance/Planning ....Dr. Thomas R. HAWK
05 Act Vice President Academic Affairs ....Dr. Sharon THOMPSON
30 Vice Pres Institutional Advancement ....Ms. Marsha M. RAY
32 Vice President Student Affairs ....Dr. Samuel HIRSCH
86 Vice Pres Marketing/Government Rels ....Ms. Lynette BROWN-SOW
43 General Counsel/VP Human Resources ....Ms. Jill GARFINKLE-WEITZ
13 Chief Information Officer ....Ms. Jody BAUER
35 Dean of Students ....Mr. Ronald C. JACKSON
84 Dean Div of Enrollment Services ....Mr. Daniel ROBB
49 Dean Liberal Studies ....Dr. Sharon THOMPSON
51 Dean Div Adult/Community Education ....Dr. David E. THOMAS
72 Div Dean of Business/Technology ....Dr. Wayne WORMLEY
09 Director Institutional Research ....Dr. Jane M. GROSSET
06 Director Stdnt Records/Registration ....Ms. Bonnie HARRINGTON
18 Chief Facilities/Physical Plant ....Mr. Harry MOORE
28 Affirmative Action Director ....Mr. Simon BROWN
07 Director of Recruitment/Admissions ....Ms. Jeri DRAPER
37 Director Financial Aid ....Mr. Gim LIM
96 Director of Purchasing ....Ms. Marsia HENLEY
38 Dept Head Student Counseling ....Mr. Todd JONES
36 Coord Career Info/Placement Svcs ....Ms. Tarsha SCOVENS
29 Coord Alumni Rels/Annual Giving ....Ms. Lyvette BROOKS
25 Coord Grants/Prospect Research ....Ms. Anne GRECO

Consolidated School of Business (J)

2124 Ambassador Circle, Lancaster PA 17603-2389
County: Lancaster FICE Identification: 030299
Unit ID: 260354
Telephone: (717) 394-6211 Carnegie Class: Assoc/PrivFP
FAX Number: (717) 394-6213 Calendar System: Other

URL: www.csb.edu
Established: 1981 — Annual Undergrad Tuition & Fees: $27,300
Enrollment: 110 — Coed
Affiliation or Control: Proprietary — IRS Status: Proprietary
Highest Offering: Associate Degree
Program: Occupational
Accreditation: ACICS

01 CEO/President — Mr. Robert L. SAFRAN
11 Vice President for Administration — Mr. William HOYT
10 Vice President for Finance — Mr. Craig D. ELLIS
05 School Director — Ms. Linda CLYMAR
37 Financial Aid Director — Ms. Gail DOUGHERTY
36 Placement Director — Ms. Derena CEDENO
13 Data Systems Director — Mr. Gholamereza SALARI
21 Bursar — Mrs. Diane GRANT
23 Medical Coordinator — Ms. Joan COPP

Consolidated School of Business (A)

1605 Clugston Road, York PA 17404-1798
County: York — FICE Identification: 022896
Unit ID: 211820
Telephone: (717) 764-9550 — Carnegie Class: Assoc/PrivFP
FAX Number: (717) 764-9469 — Calendar System: Other
URL: www.csb.edu
Established: 1981 — Annual Undergrad Tuition & Fees: $14,250
Enrollment: 120 — Coed
Affiliation or Control: Proprietary — IRS Status: Proprietary
Highest Offering: Associate Degree
Program: Occupational
Accreditation: ACICS

01 CEO/President — Mr. Robert L. SAFRAN
10 Vice President of Finance — Mr. Craig D. ELLIS
11 Vice President of Administration — Mr. Bill HOYT
37 Financial Aid Director — Mrs. Gail E. DOUGHERTY
32 School Director — Ms. Jennifer HATCH

Curtis Institute of Music (B)

1726 Locust Street, Philadelphia PA 19103-6187
County: Philadelphia — FICE Identification: 003251
Unit ID: 211893
Telephone: (215) 893-5252 — Carnegie Class: Spec/Arts
FAX Number: (215) 893-9065 — Calendar System: Semester
URL: www.curtis.edu
Established: 1924 — Annual Undergrad Tuition & Fees: $2,350
Enrollment: 166 — Coed
Affiliation or Control: Independent Non-Profit — IRS Status: 501(c)3
Highest Offering: Master's
Program: Professional; Music Emphasis
Accreditation: M, MUS

01 President & Director — Mr. Roberto DIAZ
03 Executive Vice President/COO — Ms. Elizabeth WARSHAWER
05 Dean of Faculty/Students — Mr. Paul BRYAN
10 Controller — Mr. Joe SLATER
06 Registrar — Ms. Makiko FREEMAN
07 Admissions Officer — Mr. Christopher HODGES
08 Dir Music Library Info Resources — Ms. Michelle OSWELL
29 Director Alumni/Parent Relations — Ms. Anne O'DONNELL

Dean Institute of Technology (C)

1501 W Liberty Avenue, Pittsburgh PA 15226-1197
County: Allegheny — FICE Identification: 009186
Unit ID: 211909
Telephone: (412) 531-4433 — Carnegie Class: Assoc/PrivFP
FAX Number: (412) 531-4435 — Calendar System: Quarter
URL: www.deantech.edu
Established: 1947 — Annual Undergrad Tuition & Fees: $12,800
Enrollment: 185 — Coed
Affiliation or Control: Proprietary — IRS Status: Proprietary
Highest Offering: Associate Degree
Program: Occupational; Technical Emphasis
Accreditation: ACCSC

01 President/Director — Mr. James S. DEAN
05 Director of Education/Asst Director — Mr. Richard D. ALI
07 Director of Admissions — Mr. Nicholas D. ALI
37 Director Student Financial Aid — Ms. Valerie L. VELTRI
36 Placement Director — Ms. Valerie A. HAGEDORN
27 Director Information Office — Mr. Nicholas D. ALI

Delaware County Community College (D)

901 S Media Line Road, Media PA 19063-1094
County: Delaware — FICE Identification: 007110
Unit ID: 211927
Telephone: (610) 359-5000 — Carnegie Class: Assoc/Pub-S-SC
FAX Number: (610) 359-5343 — Calendar System: Semester
URL: www.dccc.edu
Established: 1967 — Annual Undergrad Tuition & Fees (In-District): $6,192
Enrollment: 13,051 — Coed
Affiliation or Control: State/Local — IRS Status: 501(c)3
Highest Offering: Associate Degree
Program: Occupational; 2-Year Principally Bachelor's Creditable
Accreditation: M, ADNUR, COARC, MAC, SURGT

01 President — Dr. Jerome S. PARKER
10 Vice Pres Administration/Treasurer — Mr. John A. GLAVIN, JR.
05 Provost — Dr. Virginia M. CARTER
30 Vice President for Advancement — Ms. Kathleen A. BRESLIN
12 Vice Provost & Vice Pres Chester Co — Dr. Mary Jo BOYER
15 Vice President of Human Resources — Ms. Connie L. MCCALLA
84 Vice President of Enrollment Mgmt — Ms. Frances M. CUBBERLEY
13 VP & CIO Information Technology — Mr. George J. SULLIVAN
32 Vice Provost Student/Instr Support — Dr. Grant S. SNYDER
96 Assoc VP Admin & Facilities Plng — Mr. Jeffrey S. BAUN
88 Director Learning Centers — Ms. Dawn M. MOSCARIELLO
88 Director Municipal Police Academy — Mr. William DAVIS
106 Director Distance Learning Services — Mr. Alexander PLUCHUTA
37 Director of Financial Aid — Mr. Raymond L. TOOLE
08 Director of Library Services — Dr. Karen M. REGE
07 Dir Admissions/Enrollment Services — Ms. Hope L. DIEHL
36 Director Career/Counseling Center — Ms. Christine M. DOYLE
06 Registrar — Mr. Thomas W. LUGG
09 Assoc Vice Prov Inst Effectiveness — Dr. Christopher TOKPAH
21 Associate VP Finance — Mr. William J. MARKLE
103 Director Workforce Entry Center — Ms. Susan E. BOND
85 Director International Student Svs — Ms. Lydia J. DELL'OSA
15 Director Human Resources — Mr. Christopher M. DICKERMAN
14 Director OIT/Technical Services — Ms. Bianca VALENTE
91 Director Admin Computing — Mr. Bob HARDCASTLE
29 Director Alumni Programs — Mr. Douglas J. FERGUSON
25 Director Grants Management — Ms. Susan M. SHISLER-RAPP
31 Director Community Education — Ms. Nan L. SMITH
35 Director Campus Life — Ms. Amy WILLIAMS-GAUDIOSO
19 Director Safety & Security — Mr. Raymond VISCUSI
12 Director Pennocks Bridge Campus — Ms. Mychell SNEED-JACOBS
88 Director Southeast & UD Centers — Ms. Jane SCHURMAN
89 Director First Year Experiences — Dr. Kendrick MICKENS
88 Director Assessment Center — Ms. Carol MULLIN
96 Director Purchasing — Ms. Jenny M. RARIG
18 Dir Plant Oper/Construction Svcs — Mr. Tony DELUCA
103 Dean Workforce Dev & Cmty Educ — Ms. Karen KOZACHYN
80 Acting Dean Public Svcs & Soc Svcs — Dr. Clayton RAILEY, III
72 Dean Tech/Engineering & Math — Dr. John R. AGAR
88 Acting Dean Learning Support Svcs — Ms. Dolores E. MARTINO
50 Dean Business & Computer Info Sys — Dr. Eric R. WELLINGTON
79 Dean Comm/Arts & Humanities — Dr. Clayton A. RAILEY III
40 Manager Bookstore — Mr. Kris STACHOWIAK

Delaware Valley College (E)

700 E Butler Avenue, Doylestown PA 18901-2697
County: Bucks — FICE Identification: 003252
Unit ID: 211981
Telephone: (215) 345-1500 — Carnegie Class: Bac/Diverse
FAX Number: (215) 345-5277 — Calendar System: Semester
URL: www.delval.edu
Established: 1896 — Annual Undergrad Tuition & Fees: $32,890
Enrollment: 1,713 — Coed
Affiliation or Control: Independent Non-Profit — IRS Status: 501(c)3
Highest Offering: Master's
Program: 2-Year Principally Bachelor's Creditable; Liberal Arts And General; Business Emphasis
Accreditation: M

01 President — Dr. Joseph S. BROSNAN
04 Exec Assistant to the President — Ms. Angela T. RECKNER
05 VP Acad Affairs/Dean of the Faculty — Dr. Bashar W. HANNA
32 VP Student Affairs/Dean of Students — Dr. April VARI
10 VP for Finance & Administration — Mr. Arthur GLASS
30 Vice President for Inst Advancement — Mr. Joseph ERCKERT
09 Assoc VP for Research/Plng & Accr — Ms. Deborah DAILEY
84 Interim VP for Enrollment Mgmt — Mr. Dwayne WALKER
81 Dean of Life & Physical Sciences — Dr. Benjamin RUSILOSKI
47 Dean of Agriculture & Environ Sci — Mr. Russell REDDING
50 Dean of Business & Humanities — Dr. Kim LONG
58 Interim Dean of Grad/Prof & Entr — Dr. James MORYAN
06 Registrar — Mr. James SLIZEWSKI
41 Athletic Director — Mr. Steve CANTRELL
26 Chief Marketing Officer — Ms. Laurie WARD
07 Director of Admissions — Mr. Dwayne WALKER
36 Director Ctr for Student Prof Dev — Ms. Tracy DEPEDRO
08 Librarian — Mr. Peter A. KUPERSMITH
37 Director Student Financial Aid — Mrs. Joan HOCK
51 Director Continuing Education — Ms. Linda LEFEVRE
38 Director Counseling/Learn Support — Ms. Sharon DONNELLY
23 Director Health Services — Ms. Miriam TORRES
14 Director of Client Services — Mr. James LINDEN
39 Director of Residence Life — Mr. Derek SMITH
19 Director Security/Public Safety — Mr. Steven JOHNSON
09 Director Institutional Research — Ms. Elisabeth ERVIN-BLANKENHEIM
15 Director Human Resources — Ms. Elaine SPIRO
18 Director Physical Plant — Mr. Theodore STANIEWICZ
44 Director Annual Fund — Ms. Jennifer ROCK
96 Director of Purchasing — Mr. William LYLE
04 Special Assistant to President — Mr. Donald FELDSCHER

DeSales University (F)

2755 Station Avenue, Center Valley PA 18034-9568
County: Lehigh — FICE Identification: 003986
Unit ID: 210739
Telephone: (610) 282-1100 — Carnegie Class: Master's L
FAX Number: (610) 282-2254 — Calendar System: Semester
URL: www.desales.edu
Established: 1965 — Annual Undergrad Tuition & Fees: $31,250
Enrollment: 3,245 — Coed
Affiliation or Control: Roman Catholic — IRS Status: 501(c)3
Highest Offering: Doctorate
Program: Liberal Arts And General; Teacher Preparatory; Professional
Accreditation: M, ACBSP, ARCPA, NUR

01 President — Dr. Bernard F. O'CONNOR, OSFS
04 Admin Assistant to the President — Ms. Mary A. GOTZON
05 Provost/Vice Pres Academic Affairs — Dr. Karen WALTON
06 Registrar — Mr. Thomas MANTONI
08 Librarian — Ms. Deborah MALONE
51 Dean of Lifelong Learning — Ms. Deborah BOOROS
88 Dean of Undergraduate Education — Dr. Robert BLUMENSTEIN
36 Director Career Svcs & Internships — Ms. Kristin EICHOLTZ
30 Vice Pres Institutional Advancement — Mr. Thomas L. CAMPBELL
86 Director of Government Relations — Dr. Bernard F. O'CONNOR, OSFS
102 Director Corp/Foundation Relations — Mrs. Judith BARBERICH
26 Executive Director of Communication — Mr. Thomas MCNAMARA
44 Executive Dir of Annual Giving — Ms. Lina BARBIERI
29 Director of Alumni Relations — Mr. Dug SALLEY
10 VP for Admin/Finance & Campus Env — Mr. Robert J. SNYDER
45 Assoc VP for Admin & Planning — Mr. Peter RAUTZHAN
21 Director of Finance/Treasurer — Mr. Michael SWEETANA
19 Chief of Police — Chief Steven MARSHALL
09 Director of Institutional Research — Deacon George KELLY
88 Assoc VP of Campus Environment — Mr. Marc ALBANESE
18 Director of Facilities — Mr. Jim MOLCHANY
40 Campus Store Manager — Mr. Robert BREEN
16 Director of Human Resources — Mr. Joseph TRELLA
15 Employment Benefits Coordinator — Ms. Elizabeth GARCIA
13 Director of Information Technology — Mr. Jim MAHACHEK
32 Vice President Student Life — Dr. Gerard JOYCE
84 Dean of Enrollment Mgmt — Mrs. Mary BIRKHEAD
35 Dean of Students — Mrs. Linda ZERBE
39 Interim Director of Residence Life — Mrs. Linda ZERBE
07 Director of Admissions — Mr. Derrick WETZEL
37 Director of Student Financial Aid — Mrs. Joyce FARMER
42 Chaplain — Fr. Timothy MCINTIRE, OSFS
38 Director of Counseling Center — Ms. Wendy KRISAK
41 Athletic Director — Mr. Scott COVAL
28 Director Multicultural/Intl Affairs — Vacant
58 Dean of Graduate Education — Dr. Peter LEONARD, OSFS
96 Campus Environment/Dir Purchasing — Mr. Michael DUFFY

DeVry University - Fort Washington Campus (G)

1140 Virginia Drive, Fort Washington PA 19034-3204
Telephone: (215) 591-5700 — Identification: 666218
Accreditation: &NH, ENGT

† Main campus is DeVry University - Chicago Campus in Chicago, IL.

Dickinson College (H)

Box 1773, College & Louther Street,
Carlisle PA 17013-2896
County: Cumberland — FICE Identification: 003253
Unit ID: 212009
Telephone: (717) 243-5121 — Carnegie Class: Bac/A&S
FAX Number: N/A — Calendar System: Semester
URL: www.dickinson.edu
Established: 1783 — Annual Undergrad Tuition & Fees: $46,094
Enrollment: 2,386 — Coed
Affiliation or Control: Independent Non-Profit — IRS Status: 501(c)3
Highest Offering: Baccalaureate
Program: Liberal Arts And General; Teacher Preparatory
Accreditation: M

01 President — Dr. Nancy A. ROSEMAN
05 Provost and Dean of the College — Dr. Neil B. WEISSMAN
84 VP Enroll/Comm & Dean Admissions — Ms. Stephanie BALMER
32 VP Student Development — Vacant
10 VP Finance & Administration — Vacant
30 Int VP College Advancement — Ms. Carolyn YEAGER
88 VP & Chief Information Officer — Mr. Robert E. RENAUD
15 VP Human Resource Services — Mr. John A. WEIS
43 General Counsel — Ms. Dana E. SCADUTO
100 Chief of Staff/Secretary of College — Ms. Karen N. FARYNIAK
18 Assoc VP Campus Operations — Mr. Kenneth E. SHULTES
20 Associate Provost — Dr. Robert P. WINSTON
30 Assoc VP Advancement/Assoc Provost — Ms. Christina P. VAN BUSKIRK
88 Associate Provost for Curriculum — Dr. Brenda K. BRETZ
28 Spcl Asst Pres Inst & Divrsty Init — Ms. Joyce A. BYLANDER
21 Assoc VP Financial Op & Aux Svcs — Mr. Stephen C. HIETSCH
26 Exec Dir Marketing & Communications — Ms. Connie MCNAMARA
06 Registrar/Summer School — Ms. Karen A. WEIKEL
09 Director Institutional Research — Dr. Michael J. JOHNSON
37 Director of Financial Aid — Mr. Richard A. HECKMAN
104 Exec Dir Ctr Global Stdy & Engagmnt — Mr. Michael D. MONAHAN
94 Professor American Studies — Dr. Amy E. FARRELL
38 Exec Dir Wellness-Counseling Center — Dr. Alecia D. SUNDSMO
36 Dean Career Dev/Asst VP Student Dev — Mr. Philip JONES
35 Dean of Students/Assoc VP — Mr. Leonard E. BROWN, JR.
90 Director Academic Computing — Ms. Patricia A. PEHLMAN
27 Director of Media Relations — Ms. Christine M. DUGAN
44 Exec Dir Annual Fund/Alum & Prnt — Ms. Kathleen A. MARCELLO
41 Dir Physical Education & Athletics — Dr. Leslie J. POOLMAN
23 Director Wellness-Health Center — Ms. Mary E. POLSON
40 Dir College Bookstore/Central Svcs — Mr. David A. NELSON
19 Director of Public Safety — Ms. Dolores A. DANSER
91 Assoc VP Enterprise Systems — Ms. Jill M. FORRESTER
29 Director Alumni & Parent Relations — Vacant

42 Director Religious Life/Cmty Svcs .... Vacant
28 Director of Diversity Initiatives .... Ms. Paula M. LIMA-JONES

Douglas Education Center (A)

130 Seventh Street, Monessen PA 15062-1097
County: Westmoreland | FICE Identification: 020683
Unit ID: 212045
Telephone: (724) 684-3684 | Carnegie Class: Assoc/PrivFP
FAX Number: (724) 684-7463 | Calendar System: Semester
URL: www.dec.edu
Established: 1904 | Annual Undergrad Tuition & Fees: $20,627
Enrollment: 258 | Coed
Affiliation or Control: Proprietary | IRS Status: Proprietary
Highest Offering: Associate Degree
Program: Occupational; 2-Year Principally Bachelor's Creditable; Fine Arts Emphasis
Accreditation: ACICS

01 President .... Mr. Jeffrey D. IMBRESCIA
05 Vice President of Academic Affairs ... Ms. Patricia A. DECONCILIS
10 Chief Financial Officer .... Mr. Jay B. CLAYTON
20 Director of Academic Progress .... Ms. Susan F. WEAVER
20 Academic Affairs Coordinator .... Ms. N. Renee MCDOWELL
07 Director of Admissions .... Mr. Tony BAEZ MILAN
37 Director of Financial Aid .... Ms. Amanda PHILLIPS
26 Director of Marketing .... Mr. Kevin G. FEAR
88 Director of Cosmetology .... Ms. Karen S. NELSON
36 Manager of Career Services .... Mrs. Donna STAIRS
27 Public Relations Coordinator .... Ms. Katharine E. KELLAR
13 Information Technology Coordinator .... Mr. Wayne NAGLE

Drexel University (B)

3141 Chestnut Street, Philadelphia PA 19104-2875
County: Philadelphia | FICE Identification: 003256
Unit ID: 212054
Telephone: (215) 895-2000 | Carnegie Class: RU/H
FAX Number: (215) 895-1414 | Calendar System: Quarter
URL: www.drexel.edu
Established: 1891 | Annual Undergrad Tuition & Fees: $35,135
Enrollment: 25,500 | Coed
Affiliation or Control: Independent Non-Profit | IRS Status: 501(c)3
Highest Offering: Doctorate
Program: Liberal Arts And General; Professional
Accreditation: M, ANEST, ARCPA, ART, BUS, CEA, CIDA, CLPSY, CONST, CS, DENT, DIETD, ENG, ENGT, HT, LAW, LIB, MED, MFCD, NURSE, PA, PH, PTA, RAD

01 President .... Mr. John A. FRY
05 Provost/Sr Vice Pres Acad Affairs .... Dr. Mark L. GREENBERG
30 Sr VP Institutional Advancement .... Dr. Elizabeth DALE
10 Sr Vice Pres Finance/Treasurer/CFO .... Mrs. Helen Y. BOWMAN
32 Sr VP Admin Services/Student Life .... Mr. James R. TUCKER
84 Senior VP Enrollment Management .... Ms. Joan T. MCDONALD
26 Sr VP University Communications .... Ms. Lori DOYLE
11 Sr Vice Provost Budget Plng/Admin .... Dr. Janice BIROS
43 Sr VP & General Counsel .... Mr. Michael J. EXLER
03 Sr VP & Executive Director .... Mr. Brian KEECH
20 Sr Vice Provost Academic Affairs .... Dr. N. John DINARDO
13 Vice Pres Info Resources/Technology .... Dr. John BIELEC
88 Vice President Internal Audit .... Mr. James SEAMAN
21 Vice Pres & Assoc Treasurer .... Vacant
86 VP Govt & Community Relations .... Mr. David E. WILSON
88 VP of Institutional Advancement .... Mr. Peter FRISKO
100 VP & Exec Dir Office of President .... Dr. Rosalind REMER
100 Senior VP President's Office .... Mr. Keith ORRIS
46 Senior Vice Provost of Research .... Dr. Deborah CRAWFORD
09 Vice Provost Institutional Research .... Dr. Mark FREEMAN
88 Vice Provost Partnerships .... Dr. Lucy E. KERMAN
18 Vice Pres Univ Facilities .... Dr. Robert FRANCIS
16 Vice President Human Resources .... Vacant
88 Assoc Vice President & Comptroller .... Mr. John CORR
108 Associate Vice Provost Assessment .... Mr. Stephen DIPIETRO
49 Dean College Arts & Sciences .... Dr. Donna MURASKO
50 Dean LeBow College of Business .... Dr. Francis LINNEHAN
54 Dean College of Engineering .... Dr. Joseph B. HUGHES
107 Dean Goodwin Col Professional Stds .... Dr. William F. LYNCH
72 Dean Col Info Science & Technology .... Dr. David E. FENSKE
92 Dean of Pennoni Honors College .... Dr. D.B JONES
62 Dean of Libraries .... Dr. Danuta NITECKI
88 Dean of Close School .... Dr. Donna DECAROLIS
58 Exec Dir Center for Grad Studies .... Dr. Sandra G. KIRSCHENMANN
61 Dean Earle Mack School of Law .... Mr. Roger J. DENNIS
60 Dean Col of Media Arts & Design .... Mr. Allen SABINSON
17 Sr VP & Dean College of Medicine .... Dr. Daniel SCHIDLOW
66 Dean College of Nursing/Health Prof .... Dr. Gloria DONNELLY
69 Interim Dean Sch of Public Health .... Dr. John RICH
88 Pres & CEO Acad of Natural Sciences .... Mr. George W. GEPHART, JR.
88 Dir Sch Biomed Engr/Sci/Hlth Sys .... Dr. Banu ONARAL
19 Vice President Public Safety .... Mr. Domenic CECCANECCHIO
88 Senior Assoc Vice President .... Ms. Rita LARUE
25 Sr Assoc Vice Provost for Research .... Mr. Michael EDWARDS
41 Athletic Director .... Dr. Eric A. ZILLMER
45 VP Fin Planning & Student Srvcs .... Ms. Amy BOSIO
14 Assoc VP Info Resources & Tech .... Mr. Kenneth BLACKNEY
90 Assoc VP Info Resources & Tech .... Dr. Michael SCHEUERMANN
29 Associate VP Alumni Relations .... Ms. Cristina A. GESO
102 Assoc Vice Pres Corp & Found Rels .... Ms. Patricia DAVIS AUSTIN
35 Assoc Vice Pres/Dean of Students .... Mr. David A. RUTH
96 Sr Assoc VP Stdnt Life/Admin Svcs .... Dr. Joseph A. CAMPBELL
44 Assoc VP Planned Giving .... Mr. David J. TOLL
36 Vice Prov Career Development Ctr .... Mr. Peter FRANKS
93 Assoc Vice Provost AARD .... Ms. Antoinette TORRES
22 Asst Vice Pres Equality & Diversity .... Ms. Michele ROVINSKY
88 Asst Vice Pres Recruitment .... Dr. Lois "Casey" TURNER
07 Asst Vice Pres Admissions .... Ms. Erin FINN
35 Assoc Dean of Students .... Dr. Rebecca L. WEIDENSAUL
23 Assoc Dean Counseling and Health .... Dr. Annette MOLYNEUX
06 Registrar .... Mr. Joseph J. SALOMONE
24 Director Instructional Media Svcs .... Mr. Christopher GIBSON
37 Asst VP EM Planning/Financial Aid .... Ms. Melissa M. ENGLUND
38 Assoc Director of Counseling .... Dr. Amy HENNING
39 Exec Director University Housing .... Mr. Christopher HEASLEY
104 Asst Vice Provost Study Abroad .... Ms. Daniela ASCARELLI
105 Director of Web Development .... Mr. James MERGENTHAL
04 Executive Asst President's Office .... Ms. Anita MCEVOY
40 Manager Bookstore .... Mr. John RORER
106 President Drexel e-Learning .... Vacant
88 Ombuds .... Dr. David FLOOD
88 Vice Provost Strategic Dev & Init .... Dr. Janet FLEETWOOD
85 Vice Provost Global Initatives .... Dr. Julie MOSTOV

DuBois Business College (C)

One Beaver Drive, DuBois PA 15801-2401
County: Clearfield | FICE Identification: 004893
Unit ID: 212072
Telephone: (814) 371-6920 | Carnegie Class: Assoc/PrivFP
FAX Number: (814) 371-3974 | Calendar System: Quarter
URL: www.dbcollege.edu
Established: 1885 | Annual Undergrad Tuition & Fees: $11,205
Enrollment: 214 | Coed
Affiliation or Control: Proprietary | IRS Status: Proprietary
Highest Offering: Associate Degree
Program: Occupational
Accreditation: ACICS

01 President and Director .... Ms. Jackie D. SYKTICH
05 Academic Dean .... Ms. Mary O. JONES
37 Financial Aid Director .... Ms. Karen S. ALDERTON
07 Director of Admissions .... Ms. Terry L. KHOURY
36 Career Services .... Ms. Barbara M. MARTINI
12 Director Huntingdon Campus .... Mrs. Susan RAMEY
12 Director Oil City Campus .... Mrs. Colleen W. COUDRIET

DuBois Business College (D)

1001 Moore Street, Huntingdon PA 16652-1800
Telephone: (814) 641-0440 | Identification: 666479
Accreditation: ACICS

† Main campus is DuBois Business College in DuBois, PA.

DuBois Business College (E)

701 E Third Street, Oil City PA 16301-2407
Telephone: (814) 677-1322 | Identification: 666480
Accreditation: ACICS

† Main campus is DuBois Business College in DuBois, PA.

Duquesne University (F)

600 Forbes Avenue, Pittsburgh PA 15282-0001
County: Allegheny | FICE Identification: 003258
Unit ID: 212106
Telephone: (412) 396-6000 | Carnegie Class: RU/H
FAX Number: (412) 396-4186 | Calendar System: Semester
URL: www.duq.edu
Established: 1878 | Annual Undergrad Tuition & Fees: $31,385
Enrollment: 10,045 | Coed
Affiliation or Control: Roman Catholic | IRS Status: 501(c)3
Highest Offering: Doctorate
Program: Liberal Arts And General; Teacher Preparatory; Professional
Accreditation: M, ARCPA, BUS, CACREP, CEA, CLPSY, FEPAC, LAW, MUS, NURSE, OT, PHAR, PTA, SCPSY, SP, TED

01 President .... Dr. Charles J. DOUGHERTY
04 Assistant to President .... Ms. Mary F. MCINTYRE
05 Provost/Academic Vice President .... Dr. Timothy R. AUSTIN
10 Vice President Management Business .... Mr. David R. BEAUPRE
32 Exec Vice Pres for Student Life .... Rev. Sean HOGAN, CSSP
30 VP for University Advancement .... Mr. John J. PLANTE
88 Vice President Mission & Identity .... Rev. Raymond FRENCH, CSSP
43 VP Legal Affairs & General Counsel .... Ms. Linda S. DRAGO
20 Assoc Academic Vice Pres Research .... Dr. Alan W. SEADLER
20 Assoc Academic Vice President .... Dr. Jeffrey A. MILLER
21 Assoc Vice Pres Financial Affairs .... Mr. David P. GROUSOSKY
13 Executive Director CTS .... Dr. John H. ZIEGLER
31 Exec Director Auxiliary Services .... Mr. David DIPETRO
85 Exec Director Intl Programs .... Dr. Roberta C. ARONSON
84 Assoc Vice Pres Enrollment Mgmt .... Mr. Paul-James CUKANNA
06 Registrar .... Ms. Kim HOERITZ
08 Librarian .... Dr. Laverna M. SAUNDERS
29 Director Alumni Relations .... Ms. Sarah SPERRY
35 Director Student Affairs .... Rev. Sean HOGAN, CSSP
09 Director of Institutional Research .... Mr. Matthew NORTH
37 Director Financial Aid .... Mr. Richard C. ESPOSITO
15 Director of Human Resource Mgmt .... Ms. Mary Ellen BANEY
19 Director of Security .... Mr. Thomas HART
88 Dir Environmental Health/Safety .... Mr. George BENDER
18 Director of Facilities Management .... Mr. Rodney W. DOBISH
36 Director of Career Services .... Ms. Nicole FELDHUES
41 Director of Athletics .... Mr. Greg J. AMODIO
26 Assoc Vice Pres of Public Affairs .... Ms. Bridget M. FARE
22 Director Affirmative Action .... Dr. Judith R. GRIGGS
23 Director Health Service .... Ms. Dessa MRVOS
38 Director Univ Counseling Center .... Dr. Ian C. EDWARDS
39 Director Residence Life .... Mrs. Sharon G. OELSCHLAGER
42 Director Campus Ministry .... Rev. Daniel WALSH, CSSP
28 Director of Multicultural Affairs .... Dr. Rahmon HART
50 Dean Business & Administration .... Dr. Dean B. MCFARLIN
66 Dean of Nursing .... Dr. Mary Ellen S. GLASGOW
67 Dean of Pharmacy .... Dr. J. Douglas BRICKER
64 Dean of Music .... Dr. Edward W. KOCHER
53 Dean of Education .... Dr. Olga M. WELCH
76 Dean of Health Sciences .... Dr. Gregory H. FRAZER
61 Dean of Law .... Mr. Ken GORMLEY
49 Dean of Liberal Arts/Graduate .... Dr. James SWINDAL
65 Dean of Natural/Environment Sci .... Dr. Philip P. REEDER
88 Dean Leadership & Profess Advanc .... Dr. Dorothy E. BASSETT
40 Bookstore Manager .... Mr. John KACHUR
88 Internal Auditor .... Mr. Aaron MITCHAM

Eastern University (G)

1300 Eagle Road, Saint Davids PA 19087-3696
County: Delaware | FICE Identification: 003259
Unit ID: 212133
Telephone: (610) 341-5800 | Carnegie Class: Master's L
FAX Number: (610) 341-1377 | Calendar System: Semester
URL: www.eastern.edu
Established: 1925 | Annual Undergrad Tuition & Fees: $27,900
Enrollment: 4,263 | Coed
Affiliation or Control: American Baptist | IRS Status: 501(c)3
Highest Offering: Doctorate
Program: 2-Year Principally Bachelor's Creditable; Liberal Arts And General; Teacher Preparatory; Professional
Accreditation: M, EXSC, NURSE, SW

01 President .... Dr. Robert DUFFETT
73 Interim Dean of the Seminary .... Dr. Diane CHEN
10 Vice Pres for Finance/Operations .... Mr. J. Pernell JONES
03 Senior Vice President/Chief Mkt Ofc . Dr. M. Thomas RIDINGTON
05 Interim Provost .... Dr. Kenton SPARKS
32 Vice Pres for Student Development .... Dr. Bettie Ann BRIGHAM
30 Vice President Development .... Mr. Derek RITCHIE
84 Exec Director Enrollment (CAS) .... Mr. Michael DZIEDZIAK
84 Dir of Enrollment(CCGPS) .... Mr. Casey MALONE
84 Dir of Seminary Admissions .... Ms. Tiffany MURPHY
15 Senior Director of Human Resources .... Mrs. Kacey BERNARD
06 Registrar/VP Administration .... Mrs. Diana S. BACCI
04 Exec Asst to the President .... Mrs. Heather NORCINI
35 Dean of Students .... Mr. Daryl HAWKINS
12 Dean Esperanza College .... Dr. Elizabeth CONDE-FRAZIER
49 Dean Arts and Sciences .... Dr. John PAULEY, II
58 Exec Dean Grad/Professional Studies .... Dr. Debra HEATH-THORNTON
53 Assoc Dean Education .... Dr. Harry GUTELIUS
66 Chair Department of Nursing .... Dr. MaryAnne PETERS
18 Exec Director Campus Services .... Mr. Carl ALTOMARE
91 Exec Director Admin Computing .... Mr. Dwight FOWLER
105 Webmaster .... Mr. Mark HOFFMAN
09 Director Institutional Research .... Mr. Thomas A. DAHLSTROM
09 Assoc Provost Inst Effectiveness .... Dr. Christine P. MAHAN
27 Exec Director of Communications .... Mrs. Linda OLSON
88 Senior Director Student Accounts .... Ms. Lisa WELLER
08 Library Director .... Mr. James L. SAUER
42 University Chaplain .... Rev Dr. Joseph B. MODICA
42 Seminary Chaplain .... Rev. Willette BURGIE-BRYANT
37 Director of Financial Aid .... Ms. Christal JENNINGS
90 Director of Academic Computing .... Mr. Philip MUGRIDGE
36 Director of Career Development .... Ms. Tess BRADLEY
29 Director Alumni Relations .... Mrs. Mary GARDNER
41 Interim Director of Athletics .... Mrs. Heidi BIRTWISTLE
19 Director of Campus Security .... Mr. Jim MAGEE
88 Director of Conferences .... Ms. Meggin CAPERS
38 Dir Counseling/Academic Support .... Dr. Lisa M. HEMLICK
23 Director College Health Center .... Mrs. Janet TOPPER
96 Manager of Purchasing .... Ms. Patricia G. ROOT
85 Dir Intl Student & Scholar Services .... Rev. Kathy KAUTZ DE ARANGO
39 Coordinator of Housing .... Mr. Anthony HARRIS
40 Bookstore Manager .... Mr. Frank MARTINEZ, JR.
88 Chair Urban Studies .... Dr. Kimberlee JOHNSON
28 Dir Multicultural Stdnt Initiatives .... Ms. Jacqueline IRVING
89 Director Advising/1st Yr Programs .... Mrs. Amy PEREZ
92 Dean Honors College .... Dr. Jonathan YONAN

† Parent institution of Palmer Theological Seminary.

Elizabethtown College (H)

1 Alpha Drive, Elizabethtown PA 17022-2298
County: Lancaster | FICE Identification: 003262
Unit ID: 212197
Telephone: (717) 361-1000 | Carnegie Class: Bac/Diverse
FAX Number: (717) 361-1207 | Calendar System: Semester
URL: www.etown.edu
Established: 1899 | Annual Undergrad Tuition & Fees: $36,550
Enrollment: 1,910 | Coed
Affiliation or Control: Church Of The Brethren | IRS Status: 501(c)3
Highest Offering: Master's

Program: Liberal Arts And General; Teacher Preparatory; Professional
Accreditation: M, ACBSP, ENG, MUS, OT, SW

01 President .... Dr. Carl J. STRIKWERDA
05 Provost & Sr Vice President .... Dr. Susan TRAVERSO
10 Vice President for Finance .... Mr. Richard L. BAILEY
30 Vice President Advancement/Cmty Rel . Mr. David C. BEIDLEMAN
11 Int Vice President Administration .... Mr. Ronald PECK
84 Vice Pres Enrollment Mgmt .... Mr. Paul CRAMER
15 Associate VP for Human Resources .... Ms. Nancy E. FLOREY
32 Dean of Students .... Ms. Marianne CALENDA
20 Dean of Faculty .... Dr. Fletcher MCCLELLAN
51 Dean Ctr Continuing Educ/Dist Lrng .... Mr. John KOKOLUS
06 Registrar/Associate Academic Dean .... Dr. Elizabeth A. RIDER
07 Assoc Dean Admissions/Enroll Mgmt .... Ms. Debra H. MURRAY
35 Asst Dean of Students & Dir of CSS .... Ms. Stephanie A. RANKIN
26 Exec Dir Marketing/ Communications .... Ms. Elizabeth A. BRAUNGARD
13 Exec Director Information/Tech Svcs .... Mr. Ronald P. HEASLEY
102 Exec Dir Foundation/Govt Relations .... Ms. Lesley M. FINNEY
46 Director Research & Planning .... Dr. Richard BASOM
27 Director of Communications .... Ms. Amy MOUNTAIN
37 Director of Financial Aid .... Ms. Elizabeth K. MCCLOUD
08 Int Director The High Library .... Ms. Sylvia MORRA
29 Director Alumni Devel & Programs .... Mr. Mark A. CLAPPER
19 Director of Campus Security .... Mr. Jack R. LONGENECKER
41 Director of Athletics .... Ms. Nancy J. LATIMORE
23 Dir Health Promotion/Campus Health .... Ms. Alexandra SPAYD
40 Director of Business Services .... Vacant
88 Director of Food Services .... Mr. Eric C. TURZAI
42 Chaplain of the College .... Dr. Tracy SADD
92 Director Honor Program .... Dr. Dana G. MEAD
18 Dir of Facilities Mgmt/Construction .... Mr. Joseph METRO
28 Director of Diversity .... Ms. Diane ELLIOTT
21 Business Office Support .... Vacant

Erie Business Center, Main (A)

246 W Ninth Street, Erie PA 16501-1392
County: Erie FICE Identification: 004894
Unit ID: 212425
Telephone: (814) 456-7504 Carnegie Class: Assoc/PrivFP
FAX Number: (814) 456-6015 Calendar System: Trimester
URL: www.eriebc.edu
Established: 1884 Annual Undergrad Tuition & Fees: $11,800
Enrollment: 295 Coed
Affiliation or Control: Proprietary IRS Status: Proprietary
Highest Offering: Associate Degree
Program: Occupational; 2-Year Principally Bachelor's Creditable
Accreditation: ACICS

01 Chief Executive Officer .... Mr. Samuel L. MCCAUGHTRY
12 Executive Director .... Ms. Donna B. PERINO
07 Admissions Director .... Ms. Gretchen M. REINARD

Erie Business Center South (B)

170 Cascade Galleria, New Castle PA 16101-3900
Telephone: (724) 658-9066 FICE Identification: 003305
Accreditation: ACICS

† Main campus is Erie Business Center, Main in Erie, PA.

Erie Institute of Technology (C)

940 Millcreek Mall, Erie PA 16565-1002
County: Erie FICE Identification: 022039
Unit ID: 212434
Telephone: (814) 868-9900 Carnegie Class: Assoc/PrivFP
FAX Number: (814) 868-9977 Calendar System: Semester
URL: www.erieit.edu
Established: 1958 Annual Undergrad Tuition & Fees: $18,400
Enrollment: 232 Coed
Affiliation or Control: Proprietary IRS Status: Proprietary
Highest Offering: Associate Degree
Program: Occupational; Technical Emphasis
Accreditation: ACCSC

01 Director .... Mr. Paul FITZGERALD
05 Director of Education .... Ms. Kate HUSHON
37 Financial Aid Officer .... Ms. Kelly SCHULTZ
07 Admissions Director .... Ms. Barb BOLT
36 Placement Director .... Mr. Bill BURCHFIELD

Esperanza College (D)

4261 North 5th Street, Philadelphia PA 19140
Telephone: (215) 324-0746 Identification: 770153
Accreditation: &M

† Main campus is Eastern University in Saint Davids, PA.

Evangelical Theological Seminary (E)

121 S College Street, Myerstown PA 17067-1222
County: Lebanon FICE Identification: 003263
Unit ID: 212443
Telephone: (717) 866-5775 Carnegie Class: Spec/Faith
FAX Number: (717) 866-4667 Calendar System: 4/1/4
URL: www.evangelical.edu
Established: 1953 Annual Graduate Tuition & Fees: $11,500
Enrollment: 125 Coed
Affiliation or Control: Evangelical Congregational Church
IRS Status: 501(c)3
Highest Offering: Master's; No Undergraduates
Program: Professional; Religious Emphasis
Accreditation: M, MFCD, THEOL

01 President .... Dr. Anothony L. BLAIR
30 Vice Pres Institutional Advancement .... Rev. Ann E. STEEL
10 Vice President Finance & Operations .... Mr. Kevin C. HENRY
05 Dean of Academic Programs .... Dr. Laurie A. MELLINGER
84 Director of Enrollment Management .... Mr. George DAVIS
08 Head Librarian .... Dr. Terry M. HEISEY
18 Director of Buildings & Grounds .... Mr. William J. ROBERTSON
88 Database Manager .... Mrs. Marsha A. CONLEY
06 Registrar/Financial Aid Admin .... Mr. Ellis I. KIRK

Everest Institute (F)

100 Forbes Avenue, Suite 1200,
Pittsburgh PA 15222-3618
County: Allegheny FICE Identification: 007091
Unit ID: 212090
Telephone: (412) 261-4520 Carnegie Class: Assoc/PrivFP
FAX Number: (412) 261-4546 Calendar System: Quarter
URL: www.everest.edu
Established: 1840 Annual Undergrad Tuition & Fees: $13,202
Enrollment: 587 Coed
Affiliation or Control: Proprietary IRS Status: Proprietary
Highest Offering: Associate Degree
Program: Occupational; 2-Year Principally Bachelor's Creditable; Business Emphasis
Accreditation: ACICS, MAC

01 President .... Mr. Steven NELSON
05 Academic Dean .... Ms. Jennifer RICHMOND
07 Director of Admissions .... Ms. Lynn FISCHER
36 Director of Career Services .... Ms. Dana MELVIN
37 Director of Student Finance .... Mrs. Annette VOSE

Fortis Institute (G)

5757 West Ridge Road, Erie PA 16506-1013
County: Erie FICE Identification: 030108
Unit ID: 216418
Telephone: (814) 838-7673 Carnegie Class: Assoc/PrivFP
FAX Number: (814) 838-8642 Calendar System: Quarter
URL: www.fortis.edu
Established: 1984 Annual Undergrad Tuition & Fees: $12,750
Enrollment: 1,090 Coed
Affiliation or Control: Proprietary IRS Status: Proprietary
Highest Offering: Associate Degree
Program: Occupational; 2-Year Principally Bachelor's Creditable
Accreditation: ACICS, DH, EMT, MAAB, MAC, RAD

01 President .... Mr. Peter CORREA
05 Director of Education .... Ms. Amy THOMPSON SMITH
10 Business Officer .... Ms. Shelley FAYTAK
07 Admissions .... Ms. Karen LAPAGLIA
06 Registrar .... Mr. Dale CHATEAU
37 Financial Aid .... Ms. Renee WRIGHT
36 Placement .... Ms. Wendy FUGATE

Fortis Institute (H)

166 Slocum Street, Forty Fort PA 18704-2347
County: Luzerne FICE Identification: 030115
Unit ID: 249609
Telephone: (570) 288-8400 Carnegie Class: Assoc/PrivFP
FAX Number: (570) 287-7936 Calendar System: Other
URL: www.fortis.edu
Established: 1984 Annual Undergrad Tuition & Fees: $14,930
Enrollment: 238 Coed
Affiliation or Control: Proprietary IRS Status: Proprietary
Highest Offering: Associate Degree
Program: Occupational
Accreditation: ACCSC

01 Campus President .... Ruth BRUMAGIN
05 Director of Education .... Joanne GIOVANNINI
07 Director of Admissions .... Jane AUSTIN

Fortis Institute (I)

517 Ash Street, Scranton PA 18509
County: Lackawanna FICE Identification: 030116
Unit ID: 385503
Telephone: (570) 558-1818 Carnegie Class: Assoc/PrivFP
FAX Number: (570) 342-4537 Calendar System: Other
URL: www.fortis.edu/scranton-pennsylvania.php
Established: 1922 Annual Undergrad Tuition & Fees: N/A
Enrollment: 500 Coed
Affiliation or Control: Proprietary IRS Status: Proprietary
Highest Offering: Associate Degree
Program: Occupational
Accreditation: ACCSC, DH

01 Campus President .... Ms. Madeline LEVY CRUZ

† Tuition varies by degree program.

Franklin & Marshall College (J)

PO Box 3003, Lancaster PA 17604-3003
County: Lancaster FICE Identification: 003265
Unit ID: 212577
Telephone: (717) 291-3911 Carnegie Class: Bac/A&S
FAX Number: (717) 291-4183 Calendar System: Semester
URL: www.fandm.edu
Established: 1787 Annual Undergrad Tuition & Fees: $46,185
Enrollment: 2,365 Coed
Affiliation or Control: Independent Non-Profit IRS Status: 501(c)3
Highest Offering: Baccalaureate
Program: Liberal Arts And General
Accreditation: M

01 President .... Dr. Daniel R. PORTERFIELD
10 Vice Pres for Finance and Treasurer .... Mr. David R. PROULX
30 Vice Pres for College Advancement .... Mr. Matthew EYNON
84 VP Enroll Mgmt & Dean of Admission .... Mr. Daniel G. LUGO
27 Vice Pres for College Communication .... Ms. Cass CLIATT
05 Provost/Dean of Faculty .... Dr. Ann STEINER
20 Dean of the College .... Dr. Kent C. TRACHTE
88 Assoc Dean of Col & Dir Klehr Ctr .... Dr. Ralph TABER
21 Assoc Vice President for Finance .... Mr. Gregory L. FULMER
11 Associate VP for Administration .... Mr. Barry BOSLEY
88 Associate VP of Development .... Ms. Mary D. WOOLSON
45 Sr Asc Dean Fac/VP Plng & Inst Res .... Dr. Alan S. CANIGLIA
100 Chief of Staff .... Dr. Samuel HOUSER
08 College Librarian .... Ms. Pamela SNELSON
44 Major Gifts Officer .... Ms. Catherine T. FERRY
85 Assoc Dean International Programs .... Ms. Sue MENNICKE
20 Associate Dean of Faculty .... Dr. Michael BILLIG
20 Associate Dean of Faculty .... Dr. Carmen TISNADO
32 Associate Dean of Students .... Dr. Marion A. COLEMAN
88 Associate Dean/House Prefect .... Dr. Roger A. GODIN
88 Associate Dean/House Prefect .... Ms. Katharine J. SNIDER
88 Associate Dean/House Prefect .... Dr. Suzanna L. RICHTER
88 Associate Dean/House Prefect .... Dr. Beth PROFFITT
88 Associate Dean/House Prefect .... Dr. Amy R. MORENO
88 Associate Dean/Senior Prefect .... Dr. Todd DEKAY
21 Assistant Controller .... Ms. Kathryn ELLIEHAUSEN-SLOBOZIEN
15 Director Human Resources .... Ms. Nancy ESHLEMAN
18 Director Facilities & Operations .... Mr. Mike WETZEL
19 Director Public Safety .... Vacant
23 Director Health Services .... Dr. Amy A. MYERS
13 Assoc Provost & Chief Info Officer .... Dr. Jonathan C. ENOS
37 Director Financial Aid .... Mr. Clarke C. PAINE
38 Clinical Dir Counseling Services .... Dr. Christine G. CONWAY
90 Dir Instructional & Emerg Technol .... Vacant
09 Director of Institutional Research .... Dr. Alan CANIGLIA
06 Registrar & Assoc Director Inst Res .... Ms. Christine D. ALEXANDER
29 Director of Alumni Programs .... Ms. Cathy ROMAN
07 Director of Admission .... Ms. Julie A. KERICH

Gannon University (K)

University Square, Erie PA 16541-0001
County: Erie FICE Identification: 003266
Unit ID: 212601
Telephone: (814) 871-7000 Carnegie Class: Master's L
FAX Number: (814) 871-7338 Calendar System: Other
URL: www.gannon.edu
Established: 1925 Annual Undergrad Tuition & Fees: $27,546
Enrollment: 4,008 Coed
Affiliation or Control: Roman Catholic IRS Status: 501(c)3
Highest Offering: Doctorate
Program: Liberal Arts And General; Teacher Preparatory; Professional
Accreditation: M, ACBSP, ANEST, ARCPA, CACREP, COARC, COARCP, CS, ENG, NURSE, OT, PTA, RAD, SW

01 President .... Dr. Keith TAYLOR
05 Provost/VP Academic Affairs .... Dr. Carolynn B. MASTERS
10 Vice President Finance/Admin .... Mrs. Linda L. WAGNER
30 Vice Pres University Advancement .... Mr. Jack SIMS
88 Assoc Vice President for Mission .... Rev. Michael KESICKI
84 Vice President for Enrollment .... Mr. William EDMONDSON
32 VP Student Development & Engagement .... Mr. Brian NICHOLS
04 Assistant to the President .... Mrs. Darlene A. THEISEN
79 Dean Col Humanities/Educ/Soc Sci .... Dr. Linda FLEMING
54 Dean College Engineering/Business .... Dr. William L. SCHELLER
76 Dean Morosky Col Health Profess/Sci .... Dr. Steven A. MAURO
49 Director of Liberal Studies .... Dr. Penny L. SMITH
08 Director Nash Library .... Mr. Ken BRUNDAGE
37 Director of Financial Aid .... Ms. Sharon A. KRAHE
06 Registrar .... Ms. Marilyn A. MOORE
36 Dir Career Develop/Employment Svcs .... Mr. James M. FINEGAN
39 Director of Residence Life .... Ms. Denise GOLDEN
23 Head Nurse .... Ms. Ali SCHNEIDER
88 Dir Student Organiz/Leadership Dev .... Ms. Beth Ann SCHICK
29 Director Development & Alumni Rels .... Ms. Cathy FRESCH
27 Dir Marketing & Communications .... Ms. Melanie A. WHALEY
44 Dir of Research/Foundation Rels .... Ms. Anita L. MILLER
21 Controller .... Mr. Jeffrey S. TAYLOR
45 Director of Budgeting .... Ms. Mary Kathleen DRAGHI
16 Director of Human Resources .... Mr. Robert J. CLINE
41 Director of Athletics .... Mr. Mark RICHARD
19 Director Campus Police & Safety .... Mr. Ted MARNEN
14 Director of Computing/Telecomm .... Mr. Mark JORDANO
42 University Chaplain .... Rev. George STROHMEYER
07 Director of Admissions .... Mr. Terrence R. KIZINA
09 Director of Institutional Research .... Ms. Margaret JAMES
15 Director Human Resources .... Mr. Robert J. CLINE
18 Chief Facilities/Physical Plant .... Mr. Gary G. GARNIC
26 Chief Media Relations Officer .... Vacant
38 Director Student Counseling .... Mr. James M. FINEGAN
86 Dir Community/Government Relations .... Ms. Erika A. RAMALHO
96 Director of Purchasing .... Mr. Andrew TEETS
40 Bookstore Manager .... Ms. Amber COOK

Geneva College (A)

3200 College Avenue, Beaver Falls PA 15010-3557
County: Beaver FICE Identification: 003267
Unit ID: 212656
Telephone: (724) 846-5100 Carnegie Class: Bac/Diverse
FAX Number: (724) 847-6687 Calendar System: Semester
URL: www.geneva.edu
Established: 1848 Annual Undergrad Tuition & Fees: $25,220
Enrollment: 1,843 Coed
Affiliation or Control: Reformed Presbyterian Church IRS Status: 501(c)3
Highest Offering: Master's
Program: Liberal Arts And General; Teacher Preparatory; Professional
Accreditation: M, ACBSP, CACREP, CVT, ENG

01 President .... Dr. Kenneth A. SMITH
03 Executive Vice President .... Mr. Larry K. GRIFFITH
05 Provost .... Dr. Kenneth P. CARSON
30 Vice Pres of Advancement .... Dr. Jeffrey A. JONES
10 Assoc Vice Pres & Controller .... Mr. Stephen C. ROSS
15 Assoc Vice Pres & Director of HR .... Mr. Timothy R. BAIRD
32 Dean of Students .... Dr. Michael J. LOOMIS
20 Dean of Faculty and Administration .... Dr. Terri B. WILLIAMS
07 Assoc VP for Enrollment .... Mr. David B. LAYTON
35 Associate Dean of Students .... Vacant
51 Director of Adult Education .... Dr. Ralph N. PHILLIPS
06 Registrar .... Mrs. Jennifer L. CARTER
37 Director of Financial Aid .... Mr. Steven K. BELL
08 Librarian .... Dr. John G. DONCEVIC
26 Director Public Relations .... Mrs. Cheryl L. JOHNSTON
29 Director of Alumni Relations .... Mr. Daniel R. WILLIAMS
88 Assoc Dir Parent & Church Relations .. Mrs. Rebecca J. PHILLIPS
14 Director of Computer Services .... Mr. Larry R. WINGARD
41 Interim Director of Athletics .... Mr. Van G. ZANIC
18 Director of Physical Plant .... Mr. R. Jeffrey LYDIC
36 Director of Career Development .... Mrs. Joy E. DOYLE
85 International Admissions Counselor .... Mr. Joel A. BRUBAKER
88 Director International Student Svcs .... Ms. Ann E. BURKHEAD
40 Campus Store Manager .... Ms. Rachael E. VAN DERVEER
19 Director of Security .... Mr. Dennis E. DAMAZO
44 Director of Planned Giving .... Mrs. Wendy B. SMITH
93 Dir Multiethnic Student Services .... Miss Kathy Y. KINZER
92 Director Honors Program .... Dr. David S. GUTHRIE
39 Director of Residence Life .... Mr. Neil A. BEST
23 Health Services Director .... Mrs. Connie I. ERWIN
96 Director of Purchasing .... Mrs. Nancy D. GRAHAM
21 Accounting and Payroll Manager .... Ms. Ruth Ann HARTZEL
38 ACCESS Director .... Miss Christy M. COULTER

Gettysburg College (B)

300 N Washington Street, Gettysburg PA 17325-1486
County: Adams FICE Identification: 003268
Unit ID: 212674
Telephone: (717) 337-6000 Carnegie Class: Bac/A&S
FAX Number: (717) 337-6008 Calendar System: Semester
URL: www.gettysburg.edu
Established: 1832 Annual Undergrad Tuition & Fees: $45,870
Enrollment: 2,700 Coed
Affiliation or Control: Evangelical Lutheran Church In America
IRS Status: 501(c)3
Highest Offering: Baccalaureate
Program: Liberal Arts And General
Accreditation: M, MUS

01 President .... Dr. Janet MORGAN RIGGS
03 Executive Vice President .... Ms. Jane D. NORTH
05 Provost .... Dr. Christopher ZAPPE
30 Vice Pres Dev & Alumni/Parent Rels .... Mr. Robert KALLIN
10 Vice President Finance/Treasurer .... Mr. Daniel T. KONSTALID
32 Vice President for College Life .... Dr. Julie L. RAMSEY
84 Vice Pres Enrollment/Education Svcs .... Ms. Barbara B. FRITZE
13 Vice President Information Tech .... Dr. Rod TOSTEN
45 Assoc Provost for Planning .... Mrs. Rhonda GOOD
20 Assoc Provost for Faculty .... Mr. Robert E. BOHRER
21 Associate Vice President/Treasurer .... Mr. Christopher DELANEY
26 Exec Dir of Comm & Marketing .... Mr. Paul W. REDFERN
35 Associate Dean of College Life .... Mr. James P. DUFFY
44 Assistant Vice Pres for Development .... Ms. Susan PYRON
93 Dean Intercultural Advancement .... Mr. H. Pete CURRY, JR.
06 Registrar .... Mr. Brian REESE
37 Director of Financial Aid .... Ms. Christina L. GORMLEY
07 Director Admissions .... Ms. Gail M. SWEEZEY
42 Chaplain .... Rev. Joseph A. DONNELLA, II
09 Director for Institutional Analysis .... Ms. Suhua DONG
38 Exec Dir of Health & Counseling .... Ms. Kathy BRADLEY
36 Director of Career Services .... Ms. Kathleen L. WILLIAMS
08 Head Librarian .... Ms. Robin WAGNER
44 Director of Annual Giving .... Mr. Christopher HARMON
29 Director of Alumni Relations .... Mr. Joe LYNCH
41 Athletic Director .... Mr. David W. WRIGHT
19 Director of Campus Safety/Security .... Mr. William J. LAFFERTY
18 Director Facilities Planning & Mgmt .... Mr. James BIESECKER
21 Controller .... Ms. Christine M. HARTMAN
80 Director Center for Public Service .... Ms. Gretchen NATTER
39 Director Residence Life .... Mr. Victor ARCELUS
20 Director of Academic Advising .... Ms. Gail Ann RICKERT
23 Director Health Services .... Mr. Frederick W. KINSELLA
35 Director Student Activities .... Ms. Morgan A. STOCKER
40 Director of College Bookstore .... Mr. Michael J. KOTLINSKI
94 Coord Women/Gender/Sexuality Stds .... Ms. Nathalie LEBON
96 Director of Procurement .... Ms. Patricia K. VERDEROSA
15 Co-Director Human Resources .... Ms. Jennifer R. LUCAS
15 Co-Director Human Resources .... Ms. Regina Z. CAMPO
25 Director of Found/Govt Grant .... Mr. Richard M. ROSENBERG
31 Assoc VP for Govt & Comm Relatio .... Ms. Patricia A. LAWSON
104 Director of Off-Campus Studies .... Ms. Rebecca A. BERGREN

Gratz College (C)

7605 Old York Road, Melrose Park PA 19027-3010
County: Montgomery FICE Identification: 004058
Unit ID: 212771
Telephone: (215) 635-7300 Carnegie Class: Master's L
FAX Number: (215) 635-1046 Calendar System: Semester
URL: www.gratz.edu
Established: 1895 Annual Undergrad Tuition & Fees: $13,464
Enrollment: 1,277 Coed
Affiliation or Control: Independent Non-Profit IRS Status: 501(c)3
Highest Offering: Doctorate
Program: Liberal Arts And General; Teacher Preparatory; Professional
Accreditation: M

01 President .... Ms. Joy W. GOLDSTEIN
05 Int Dean Academic Affs/Dir Cont Ed .... Dr. Richard SCALDINI
04 Executive Asst to President .... Ms. Dodi KLIMOFF
26 Chief Public Relations Officer .... Ms. Dodi KLIMOFF
08 Director of Tuttleman Library .... Mr. Eliezer WISE
10 Director of Finance .... Mr. Michael FOLENSBEE
06 Director of Student Records .... Ms. Lovisa WOODSON
15 Director Personnel Services .... Ms. Yaffa HOWARD
30 Dir of Institutional Advancement .... Ms. Beth SCHONBERGER
09 Director of Institutional Research .... Mr. Joseph HENDERSON
84 Director Enrollment Management .... Ms. Maria SILVESTER
88 Actg Dir Jewish Community High Sch .... Ms. Ruth SCHAPIRA
37 Student Financial Services Advisor .... Mr. Joseph HENDERSON

Great Lakes Institute of Technology (D)

5100 Peach Street, Erie PA 16509
County: Erie FICE Identification: 021122
Unit ID: 213181
Telephone: (814) 864-6666 Carnegie Class: Not Classified
FAX Number: (814) 868-1717 Calendar System: Other
URL: www.glit.edu
Established: 1965 Annual Undergrad Tuition & Fees: $15,940
Enrollment: 488 Coed
Affiliation or Control: Proprietary IRS Status: Proprietary
Highest Offering: Associate Degree
Program: Occupational
Accreditation: ACCSC, DMS, SURGT

01 Executive Director .... Tony PICCIRILLO

Grove City College (E)

100 Campus Drive, Grove City PA 16127-2104
County: Mercer FICE Identification: 003269
Unit ID: 212805
Telephone: (724) 458-2000 Carnegie Class: Bac/A&S
FAX Number: (724) 458-2190 Calendar System: Semester
URL: www.gcc.edu
Established: 1876 Annual Undergrad Tuition & Fees: $14,880
Enrollment: 2,501 Coed
Affiliation or Control: Presbyterian Church (U.S.A.) IRS Status: 501(c)3
Highest Offering: Baccalaureate
Program: Liberal Arts And General; Teacher Preparatory; Professional
Accreditation: M, ENG

01 President .... Dr. Richard G. JEWELL
05 Provost & VP for Academic Affairs .... Dr. Robert J. GRAHAM
10 Vice Pres for Financial Affairs .... Mr. Roger K. TOWLE
32 Vice Pres For Student Life/Learning .... Mr. Larry E. HARDESTY
30 Vice President for Inst Advancement .. Mr. Jeffrey D. PROKOVICH
11 Vice President for Operations .... Mr. Thomas W. GREGG
13 Vice Pres/Chief Information Officer .... Dr. Vincent F. DISTASI
84 VP of Enrollment Svcs & Registrar .... Dr. John G. INMAN
04 Assistant to the President .... Ms. Betty L. TALLERICO
49 Dean of School of Arts/Letters .... Dr. David J. AYERS
81 Dean of School of Sci/Engr/Math .... Dr. Stacy G. BIRMINGHAM
35 Assistant Dean of Students .... Mr. John M. COYNE
15 Dir of HR & Business Operations .... Mrs. Marci K. WAGNER
07 Director of Admissions .... Mrs. Sarah E. GIBBS
88 Admn Dir For Ctr For Vision/Values .... Mr. Lee S. WISHING, III
36 Director of Career Services .... Dr. James T. THRASHER
08 Librarian .... Mrs. Barbra M. MUNNELL
37 Director of Financial Aid .... Mr. Thomas G. BALL
88 Dir Std Rec/Club Sports/Frat Life .... Mr. Andrew A. TONCIC, JR.
35 Director Stdnt Activities/Programs .... Mr. T. Scott GORDON
19 Director of Campus Safety .... Mr. Seth J. VAN TIL
23 Director of Health & Wellness Ctr .... Mrs. Amy E. PAGANO
40 Bookstore Manager .... Mrs. Carrie J. GAULT
41 Athletic Director .... Dr. Donald L. LYLE
42 Dean of the Chapel .... Rev. F. Stanley KEEHLWETTER
29 Sr Dir Alumni & College Relations .... Ms. Melissa A. MACLEOD
38 Director of College Counseling .... Dr. Suzanne N. HOUK
39 Director of Residence Life .... Ms. Jamie R. SWANK

Gwynedd-Mercy University (F)

1325 Sumneytown Pike, PO Box 901,
Gwynedd Valley PA 19437-0901
County: Montgomery FICE Identification: 003270
Unit ID: 212832
Telephone: (215) 646-7300 Carnegie Class: Master's M
FAX Number: (215) 641-5596 Calendar System: Semester
URL: www.gmc.edu
Established: 1948 Annual Undergrad Tuition & Fees: $29,600
Enrollment: 2,572 Coed
Affiliation or Control: Roman Catholic IRS Status: 501(c)3
Highest Offering: Doctorate
Program: Occupational; Liberal Arts And General; Teacher Preparatory; Nursing Emphasis
Accreditation: M, ADNUR, CAHIIM, COARC, CVT, IACBE, NUR, RTT

01 President .... Dr. Kathleen C. OWENS
05 VP Academic Affairs .... Dr. Frank E. SCULLY, JR.
10 Vice President Finance .... Mr. Kevin O'FLAHERTY
30 Vice Pres Institutional Advancement .... Mr. Gerald MCLAUGHLIN
84 Vice Pres for Enrollment & SS .... Dr. Cheryl HORSEY
101 Secretary of the Institution/Board .... Ms. Barbara MCHALE
108 AVP for Assessment & Compliance .... Dr. Dawn HAYWARD
88 AVP for Enrollment & Marketing .... Mr. Jamison KRAVCAK
06 Associate Registrar .... Ms. Joanna VACCHIANO
08 Director of Library .... Mr. Daniel SCHABERT
37 Director of Student Financial Aid .... Ms. Elizabeth HOWARD
13 Chief Information Officer .... Dr. Karl HORVATH
88 Dean of Students .... Dr. Carol GRUBER
29 Director Alumni Relations .... Ms. Gianna QUINN
35 Director Student Activities ... Ms. Rouseline EMMANUEL-FRENEL
09 Director of Institutional Research .... Dr. Jing GAO
15 Director Human Resources .... Ms. Donna HAWKINS
18 Director of Physical Plant .... Mr. Joseph MOLL
21 Controller .... Ms. Mary GILBERT
38 Director Counseling .... Ms. Jeanne MCGOWAN
07 Director of Undergrad Admissions .... Ms. Michele DIEHL
07 Dir Undergrad Adult Accel Enroll .... Ms. Christine GEIB
07 Director of Graduate Admissions .... Ms. Michele VITELLI
96 Director of Purchasing/Payables .... Ms. Joyce SCHARLE

Gwynedd-Mercy University Plymouth Meeting at East Norriton (G)

480 E Germantown Pike, East Norriton PA 19462
Telephone: (215) 643-8458 Identification: 770155
Accreditation: &M

† Main campus is Gwynedd-Mercy University in Gwynedd Valley, PA.

Harcum College (H)

750 Montgomery Avenue, Bryn Mawr PA 19010-3476
County: Montgomery FICE Identification: 003272
Unit ID: 212869
Telephone: (610) 525-4100 Carnegie Class: Assoc/PrivNFP
FAX Number: (610) 526-6009 Calendar System: Semester
URL: www.harcum.edu
Established: 1915 Annual Undergrad Tuition & Fees: $20,500
Enrollment: 1,589 Coed
Affiliation or Control: Independent Non-Profit IRS Status: 501(c)3
Highest Offering: Associate Degree
Program: Occupational; 2-Year Principally Bachelor's Creditable; Technical Emphasis
Accreditation: M, ADNUR, DA, DH, HT, MLTAD, OTA, PTAA, RAD

01 President .... Dr. Jon Jay DETEMPLE
05 VP of Academic & Legal Affairs .... Ms. Julia INGERSOLL
10 Vice Pres of Finance & Operations .... Ms. Patricia BENSON
32 Dean of Student Affairs .... Dr. George THORNTON
07 Director of Admissions .... Ms. Rachel BOWEN
30 VP of College Advancement .... Ms. Sachi MALLACH
20 Asst VP for Academic Affairs .... Ms. Heather RAMSEY
35 Assistant Dean of Student Life .... Mr. Urick LEWIS
51 Exec Director of Contining Studies .... Dr. Denise BEAUCHAMP
18 Facilities Director .... Mr. Nikolay KARPALO
15 Director of Human Resources .... Ms. Claudine VITA
06 Registrar .... Ms. Madeleine V. WRIGHTSON
08 Director of Library Services .... Ms. Ann E. RANIERI
85 Director International Student Pgms .... Ms. Debra L. YOUNG-YASSINE
26 Chief Public Relations Officer .... Mr. Andy BACK
29 Director of Alumni Relations .... Ms. Melissa SAMANGO
38 Director of Student Counseling .... Ms. Kathy ANTHONY
36 Dir of Career & Transfer Services .... Ms. Danyele DOVE
37 Director of Student Financial Aid .... Mr. Eli MOINESTER
39 Director of Residence Life .... Mr. Jameel TUCKER
35 Director of Campus Activities .... Ms. Laurie PLAZA
21 Director of Business Affairs .... Mr. Stephen KLEPONIS
19 Director of Campus Safety .... Mr. Rick SANFILIPPO
41 Director of Athletics .... Mr. Drew KELLY

Harrisburg Area Community College (I)

1 HACC Drive, Harrisburg PA 17110-2999
County: Dauphin FICE Identification: 003273
Unit ID: 212878
Telephone: (717) 780-2300 Carnegie Class: Assoc/Pub-U-MC
FAX Number: (717) 780-2551 Calendar System: Semester
URL: www.hacc.edu
Established: 1964 Annual Undergrad Tuition & Fees (In-District): $4,116
Enrollment: 21,945 Coed
Affiliation or Control: State/Local IRS Status: 501(c)3
Highest Offering: Associate Degree
Program: Occupational; 2-Year Principally Bachelor's Creditable

Accreditation: M, ACBSP, ACFEI, ADNUR, COARC, CVT, DA, DH, DMS, EMT, MAC, MLTAD, PNUR, RAD, SURGT

01 President/CEO .... Dr. John J. SYGIELSKI
05 Interim Provost/VP Academic Affairs .... Dr. Suzanne E. O'HOP
32 VP Student Affairs/Enrollment Mgmt .... Dr. Rob R. STEINMETZ
10 VP Finance/College .... Mr. John M. EBERLY
30 VP College Advancement .... Dr. Linnie S. CARTER
16 Interim Chief HR Officer .... Mr. Dennis P. HEINLE
12 Interim Campus VP Lancaster/Lebanon .... Ms. Lois A. SCHAFFER
12 Executive Director Lebanon Campus .... Vacant
12 Campus VP Gettysburg .... Ms. Shannon S. HARVEY
12 Campus VP York .... Ms. Jean M. TREUTHART
106 Dir Virtual Advancement & Outreach .... Ms. Amy S. WITHROW
08 Executive Director HACC Libraries .... Ms. Beth A. EVITTS
20 Interim Dean Student/Acad Success .... Mr. David SATTERLEE
84 Interim Registrar .... Ms. Tisa R. RILEY
27 Chief Information Officer .... Mr. Robert H. MESSNER
96 Interim Director Purchasing .... Mr. Charles G. CRIDER
88 Director Performing Artist Series .... Ms. Theresa L. GUERRISI
19 Interim Director Security .... Mr. Edwin DOMINGUEZ
29 Director Alumni Relations .... Ms. Maureen G. HOEPFER
40 Director College Bookstores .... Mr. Kyle J. DIBRITO
21 Director Budget/Financial Analysis .... Ms. Kathy W. GREEN
104 Director Global Education .... Mr. Michael B. SANDY
09 Interim Dir Institutional Research .... Ms. Kimberly R. KELSEY
37 Director Financial Aid .... Mr. James J. CARIDEO
07 Dir Enrollment Services .... Ms. Tisa R. RILEY
102 Board Manager HACC Foundation .... Ms. Bonny R. ELLIS

Harrisburg Area Community College Gettysburg Campus (A)

731 Old Harrisburg Road, Gettysburg PA 17325
Telephone: (717) 337-3855 Identification: 770156
Accreditation: &M

† Main campus is Harrisburg Area Community College in Harrisburg, PA.

Harrisburg Area Community College Lancaster Campus (B)

1641 Old Philadelphia Pike, Lancaster PA 17602
Telephone: (717) 293-5000 Identification: 770157
Accreditation: &M

† Main campus is Harrisburg Area Community College in Harrisburg, PA.

Harrisburg Area Community College Lebanon Campus (C)

735 Cumberland Street, Lebanon PA 17042
Telephone: (717) 270-4222 Identification: 770158
Accreditation: &M

† Main campus is Harrisburg Area Community College in Harrisburg, PA.

Harrisburg Area Community College York Campus (D)

2010 Pennsylvania Avenue, York PA 17404
Telephone: (717) 718-0328 Identification: 770159
Accreditation: &M

† Main campus is Harrisburg Area Community College in Harrisburg, PA.

Harrisburg University of Science and Technology (E)

326 Market Street, Harrisburg PA 17101-2116
County: Dauphin FICE Identification: 039483
Unit ID: 446640
Telephone: (717) 901-5100 Carnegie Class: Bac/A&S
FAX Number: (717) 901-3152 Calendar System: Trimester
URL: www.harrisburgu.edu
Established: 2001 Annual Undergrad Tuition & Fees: $23,900
Enrollment: 354 Coed
Affiliation or Control: Independent Non-Profit IRS Status: 501(c)3
Highest Offering: Master's
Program: Professional; Technical Emphasis
Accreditation: M

01 President .... Dr. Eric D. DARR
05 Interim Provost/Chief Academic Ofcr .... Ms. Bili S. MATTES
10 Vice Pres Finance & Chief Fin Ofcr .... Mr. Duane F. MAUN
30 Assoc VP Devel & Alumni Relations .... Vacant
26 Associate VP Comm & Marketing .... Mr. Steven M. INFANTI
15 Dir Human Resources/Administration .... Ms. Pam CRUEY
88 Assoc VP for University Centers .... Mr. Dale HAMBY
32 Director of Student Services .... Dr. Laura DIMINO
13 Director of Technology Services .... Mr. Alex C. PITZNER
09 Director Compliance & Research .... Mr. Keith A. GREEN
37 Director Financial Aid .... Mr. Vincent P. FRANK
06 Director Records & Registration .... Ms. Jeanne A. WAGNER
84 Director Enrollment Mgmt/Admissions .... Mr. Timothy DAWSON
08 University Librarian .... Mr. David RUNYON

Haverford College (F)

370 Lancaster Avenue, Haverford PA 19041-1392
County: Delaware & Montgomery FICE Identification: 003274
Unit ID: 212911
Telephone: (610) 896-1000 Carnegie Class: Bac/A&S
FAX Number: (610) 896-4202 Calendar System: Semester
URL: www.haverford.edu
Established: 1833 Annual Undergrad Tuition & Fees: $45,426
Enrollment: 1,205 Coed
Affiliation or Control: Independent Non-Profit IRS Status: 501(c)3
Highest Offering: Master's
Program: Liberal Arts And General
Accreditation: M

01 President .... Dr. Daniel H. WEISS
05 Interim Provost .... Kimberly BENSTON
10 Vice Pres Finance & Administration .... G. Richard WYNN
30 VP of Advancement .... Michael KIEFER
20 Dean of the College .... Martha DENNEY
07 Dean of Admission .... Jess LORD
85 Dean of Intl Academic Programs .... Donna MANCINI
89 Dean of Freshmen Students .... Michael MARTINEZ
21 Asst VP for Budgeting and Finance .... Michael CASEL
88 Assistant VP of Inst Advancement .... Diane WILDER
100 Chief of Staff .... Jesse LYTLE
41 Director of Athletics .... Wendall SMITH
26 Exec Dir Marketing & Communication .... Chris MILLS
09 Director of Institutional Research .... Catherine FENNELL
08 Librarian .... Terry SNYDER
15 Director of Human Resources .... Christopher CHANDLER
21 Controller & Assistant Treasurer .... Michael GAVANUS
96 Director of Purchasing .... Samuel WILLIAMS
18 Director of Physical Plant .... Donald CAMPBELL
19 Director of Safety & Security .... Thomas KING
88 Director Conferences/Dir Campus Ctr .... Vacant
88 Director of Dining Services .... Bernie CHUNG
40 Bookstore Manager .... Lydia WHITELAW
39 Director of Student Housing .... Marianne SMITH
34 Director of Women's Center .... Mary Louise ALLEN
23 Director of Health Services .... Catherine SHARBAUGH
38 Director Counseling/Disability Svcs .... Richard E. WEBB
36 Dean for Career and Prof Develop .... Kelly CLEARY
06 Registrar .... Lee WATKINS
37 Director of Financial Aid .... David HOY
88 Director Leadership Gifts .... Ann WEST FIGUEREDO
44 Director of Annual Giving .... Deborah STRECKER
88 Director of Gift Planning .... Steven KAVANAUGH
102 Dir Foundation/Corporate Relations .... John MOSTELLER
28 Director of Multicultural Affairs .... Theresa TENSUAN
29 Director of Alumni Relations .... Deborah STRECKER
32 Coordinator of Student Activities .... Lilly LAVNER
27 Chief Information Officer .... Joseph SPADARO

Holy Family University (G)

9801 Frankford Avenue, Philadelphia PA 19114-2009
County: Philadelphia FICE Identification: 003275
Unit ID: 212984
Telephone: (215) 637-7700 Carnegie Class: Master's L
FAX Number: (215) 637-3787 Calendar System: Semester
URL: www.holyfamily.edu
Established: 1954 Annual Undergrad Tuition & Fees: $27,100
Enrollment: 3,094 Coed
Affiliation or Control: Roman Catholic IRS Status: 501(c)3
Highest Offering: Doctorate
Program: Liberal Arts And General; Teacher Preparatory; Professional
Accreditation: M, ACBSP, IFSAC, NURSE, RAD, @TEAC

01 President .... Sr. Francesca ONLEY
05 Provost .... Sr. Maureen MCGARRITY
10 Vice Pres Finance & Administration .... Vacant
30 Vice Pres Mission .... Ms. Margaret S. KELLY
13 Vice Pres Information Technology .... Vacant
32 Vice President for Student Life .... Sr. Marcella BINKOWSKI
30 Vice Pres for Development .... Mr. Robert WETZEL
21 Assistant VP Finance & Budget .... Mr. Michael E. VAN THUYNE
84 Assoc VP for Enrollment Services .... Mr. Arthur GOON
06 Assoc VP Academic Svcs/Registrar .... Ms. Ann Marie VICKERY
12 Assoc VP for Newtown and Planning .... Ms. Karen GALARDI
37 Director of Student Financial Aid .... Mrs. Janice HETRICK
21 Treasurer .... Vacant
15 Asst Vice Pres Human Resources .... Ms. Renee ROSENFELD
08 Director of Library Services .... Vacant
36 Director of the Career Center .... Mr. Donald BROM
26 Senior Dir Marketing-Communications .... Vacant
38 Director Counseling Center .... Dr. Diana PIPERATA
42 Chaplain/Campus Minister .... Rev. James MACNEW
07 Director of Undergraduate Admission .... Ms. Lauren CAMPBELL
41 Athletic Director .... Mrs. Sandra MICHAEL
58 Dean of the School of Education .... Dr. Kevin ZOOK
66 Dean Sch Nursing/Allied Hlth Profns .... Dr. Ana CATENZARO
49 Dean of School of Arts & Sciences .... Dr. Shelly ROBBINS
50 Dean of School of Business Admin .... Dr. J. Barry DICKENSON
58 Assoc Dean School of Education .... Dr. Antoinette SCHIAVO
29 Director Alumni & Parent Giving .... Ms. Marie ZECCA
09 Dir of Inst Research & Assessment .... Mr. Chad L. MAY
18 Chief Facilities/Physical Plant .... Mr. Mike SHANE
96 Director of Purchasing .... Mrs. Marie MELNICK
28 Coordinator Diversity .... Dr. Gloria KERSEY-MATUSIAK
39 Director of Residence Life .... Mr. Brett BUCKRIDGE

Hussian School of Art (H)

111 S Independence Mall East, #300, Philadelphia PA 19106-2521
County: Philadelphia FICE Identification: 007469
Unit ID: 212993
Telephone: (215) 574-9600 Carnegie Class: Assoc/PrivFP
FAX Number: (215) 574-9800 Calendar System: Semester
URL: www.hussianart.edu
Established: 1946 Annual Undergrad Tuition & Fees: $14,800
Enrollment: 98 Coed
Affiliation or Control: Proprietary IRS Status: Proprietary
Highest Offering: Associate Degree
Program: Occupational; Technical Emphasis
Accreditation: ACCSC

01 President .... Ms. Melissa MORGAN
03 Vice President .... Vacant
06 Dir of Student Services/Registrar .... Ms. Maureen P. FLANAGAN
37 Director Financial Aid .... Ms. Susan J. COHEN
07 Admissions Representative .... Ms. Melissa WASSERMAN
10 Director of Finance .... Mr. Eric STRUBEL
11 Administrative Coordinator .... Ms. Jodi BRABAZON

Immaculata University (I)

1145 King Road, Immaculata PA 19345-0654
County: Chester FICE Identification: 003276
Unit ID: 213011
Telephone: (610) 647-4400 Carnegie Class: DRU
FAX Number: (610) 251-1668 Calendar System: Semester
URL: www.immaculata.edu
Established: 1920 Annual Undergrad Tuition & Fees: $30,740
Enrollment: 4,117 Coed
Affiliation or Control: Roman Catholic IRS Status: 501(c)3
Highest Offering: Doctorate
Program: 2-Year Principally Bachelor's Creditable; Liberal Arts And General; Teacher Preparatory; Professional
Accreditation: M, ACBSP, CLPSY, DIETD, DIETI, MUS, NURSE

01 President .... Sr. R. Patricia FADDEN
05 Vice President Academic Affairs .... Sr. Ann HEATH
10 Vice Pres Finance/Administration .... Ms. Jenni SAUER
30 Vice Pres University Advancement .... Mr. Kevin QUINN
32 Vice President Student Development .... Dr. Stephen PUGLIESE
27 VP of University Communications .... Mr. Robert COLE
20 Assistant VP of Academic Affairs .... Dr. Janet KANE
06 Registrar .... Ms. Janice BATES
09 Director Inst Research/Assessment .... Ms. Erin R. EBERSOLE
08 Executive Director of Library .... Dr. Jeffrey D. ROLLISON
37 Director Student Financial Aid .... Mr. Robert FOREST
44 Senior Director of Gift Planning .... Sr. Rita O'LEARY
91 Director Administrative Computing .... Mr. Grant DAVIS
26 Director Public Relations .... Ms. Marie MOUGHAN
29 Alumni Director .... Ms. Karen MATWEYCHUK
36 Director Career Development .... Ms. Diane MASSEY
41 Athletic Director .... Ms. Patricia CANTERINO
85 International Student Advisor .... Sr. Catarin CONJAR
90 Director Academic Technology .... Ms. Sharon AINSLEY
42 Chaplain .... Fr. Christopher ROGERS
58 Dean Graduate Division .... Dr. Janet KANE
34 Dean College of Undergrad Studies .... Sr. Jo CARTER
51 Dean College of Lifelong Learning .... Dr. Angela TEKELY
19 Director Campus Safety .... Mr. Eugene BIAGIOTTI
15 Director of Personnel Services .... Mrs. Cathey PASSIN
18 Director of Administrative Services .... Mr. Dennis SHORES
44 Director of the Annual Fund .... Ms. Melissa HENRY
42 Director of Mission and Ministry .... Sr. Cathy NALLY
07 Director of Admissions .... Dr. Nicola DIFRONZO-HEITZER
20 Dean of Academic Affairs .... Ms. Mary Kate BOLAND
38 Director Counseling Services .... Dr. Jamie HAGENBAUGH

International Institute for Restorative Practices (J)

P.O. Box 229, Bethlehem PA 18016-0229
County: Northampton FICE Identification: 042061
Unit ID: 448691
Telephone: (610) 807-9221 Carnegie Class: Assoc/PrivNFP4
FAX Number: (610) 807-0423 Calendar System: Trimester
URL: www.iirp.edu
Established: Annual Graduate Tuition & Fees: $9,042
Enrollment: 49 Coed
Affiliation or Control: Independent Non-Profit IRS Status: 501(c)3
Highest Offering: Master's; No Undergraduates
Program: Professional
Accreditation: M

01 President .... Mr. Theodore WACHTEL
05 Vice President for Academic Affairs .... Dr. Patrick MCDONOUGH

ITT Technical Institute (K)

1000 Meade Street, Dunmore PA 18512-3195
Telephone: (570) 330-0600 Identification: 666150
Accreditation: ACICS

† Main campus is ITT Technical Institute in Indianapolis, IN.

ITT Technical Institute (L)

449 Eisenhower Blvd., Suite 100, Harrisburg PA 17111-2302
Telephone: (717) 565-1700 Identification: 666548
Accreditation: ACICS

† Main campus is ITT Technical Institute in Indianapolis, IN.

ITT Technical Institute (A)

311 Veteran's Highway, Suite 100E, Levittown PA 19056
Telephone: (215) 702-6300 Identification: 667161
Accreditation: ACICS

† Main campus is ITT Technical Institute in Indianapolis, IN.

ITT Technical Institute (B)

105 South 7th Street, Philadelphia PA 19106
Telephone: (215) 413-4300 Identification: 770620
Accreditation: ACICS

† Main campus is ITT Technical Institute in Indianapolis, IN.

ITT Technical Institute (C)

5460 Campbells Run Road, Pittsburgh PA 15205
Telephone: (412) 446-2900 Identification: 666483
Accreditation: ACICS

† Main campus is ITT Technical Institute in Indianapolis, IN.

ITT Technical Institute (D)

220 W Germantown Pike, Suilte 100,
Plymouth Meeting PA 19462
Telephone: (610) 832-3400 Identification: 667162
Accreditation: ACICS

† Main campus is ITT Technical Institute in Indianapolis, IN.

ITT Technical Institute (E)

100 Pittsburgh Mills Cir, Ste 100, Tarentum PA 15084
Telephone: (724) 274-1400 Identification: 666482
Accreditation: ACICS

† Main campus is ITT Technical Institute in Indianapolis, IN.

JNA Institute of Culinary Arts (F)

1212 S Broad Street, Philadelphia PA 19146-3119
County: Philadelphia FICE Identification: 031033
Unit ID: 419341
Telephone: (215) 468-8800 Carnegie Class: Assoc/PrivFP
FAX Number: (215) 468-8838 Calendar System: Quarter
URL: www.culinaryarts.edu
Established: 1988 Annual Undergrad Tuition & Fees: $22,075
Enrollment: 94 Coed
Affiliation or Control: Proprietary IRS Status: Proprietary
Highest Offering: Associate Degree
Program: Occupational; 2-Year Principally Bachelor's Creditable; Technical Emphasis
Accreditation: ACCSC

01 Director .... Mr. Joseph DIGIRONIMO
07 Director of Admission .... Mr. Robert FOX

Johnson College (G)

3427 N Main Avenue, Scranton PA 18508-1495
County: Lackawanna FICE Identification: 021142
Unit ID: 213233
Telephone: (570) 342-6404 Carnegie Class: Assoc/PrivNFP
FAX Number: (570) 348-2181 Calendar System: Semester
URL: www.johnson.edu
Established: 1916 Annual Undergrad Tuition & Fees: $17,095
Enrollment: 452 Coed
Affiliation or Control: Independent Non-Profit IRS Status: 501(c)3
Highest Offering: Associate Degree
Program: 2-Year Principally Bachelor's Creditable; Technical Emphasis
Accreditation: ACCSC, RAD

01 President & CEO .... Dr. Ann L. PIPINSKI
05 Vice President Academic Affairs .... Mr. Dominick A. CARACHILO
13 Director of Information Services .... Ms. Sue PHILLIPS
37 Financial Aid Director .... Mr. Matthew PETERS
84 Vice Pres of Enrollment Services .... Ms. Melissa IDE
88 Student Support Coordinator .... Ms. Lynn KRUSHINSKI
10 Chief Financial Officer .... Mr. Jeffrey NOVAK
08 Head Librarian .... Mrs. Michele M. SREBRO
04 Assistant to the President .... Ms. Lisa TOOLE
06 Associate Registrar .... Ms. Danielle CEBUKLO
38 Asst Dir Student Support Services .... Ms. Linda LEARN
51 Director of Continuing Education .... Vacant
39 Residence/Student Life Coordinator .... Ms. Tara RHODES
30 Sr VP of Institutional Advancement .... Ms. Katie LEONARD
15 Human Resources Assistant .... Ms. Diane DOLINSKY
36 Sr Assoc Dir of Career Services .... Ms. Roseann MARTINETTI
32 Director of Student Life .... Ms. Sara WILLIAMS
07 Assoc Director of Admissions .... Ms. Rita MUNIFO
18 Facilities Manager .... Mr. Bill KELLY
09 Dir of Program & Research .... Mrs. Shirley HELBING

Juniata College (H)

1700 Moore Street, Huntingdon PA 16652-2119
County: Huntingdon FICE Identification: 003279
Unit ID: 213251
Telephone: (814) 641-3000 Carnegie Class: Bac/A&S
FAX Number: (814) 641-3199 Calendar System: Semester
URL: www.juniata.edu
Established: 1876 Annual Undergrad Tuition & Fees: $1,600
Enrollment: 1,565 Coed
Affiliation or Control: Independent Non-Profit IRS Status: 501(c)3
Highest Offering: Master's
Program: Liberal Arts And General; Teacher Preparatory
Accreditation: M, SW

01 President .... Dr. James A. TROHA
05 Interim Provost .... Dr. Kathy M. WESTCOTT
84 Exec VP Enrollment and Retention .... Vacant
10 Vice President Finance/Operations .... Mr. Robert E. YELNOSKY
26 Vice President Advancement/Mkt .... Mr. Gabriel WELSCH
27 Assoc Vice President & CIO .... Mr. David J. FUSCO
30 Exec Director of Development .... Ms. Kimberly KITCHEN
26 Exec Director of Marketing .... Ms. Rosann BROWN
07 Dean of Enrollment .... Ms. Michelle M. BARTOL
85 Dean International Programs .... Ms. Jenifer S. CUSHMAN
06 Registrar .... Ms. Athena D. FREDERICK
36 Director Career Services .... Dr. Darwin V. KYSOR
37 Enrollment Mgr/Dir Student Fin Plng .... Mr. Shane D. HIMES
08 Library Director .... Mr. John W. MUMFORD
91 Director Admin Information Svcs .... Ms. Barbara J. HUGHES
15 Director of Human Resources .... Ms. Gail L. ULRICH
32 Dean of Students .... Mr. Kris R. CLARKSON
09 Dir Institutional Planning/Research .... Ms. Carlee K. RANALLI
18 Director of Facilities Services .... Mr. Tristan S. DEL GIUDICE
19 Director Public Safety .... Mr. Jesse W. LEONARD
41 Athletic Director .... Mr. Greg M. CURLEY
90 Dir Technology Solutions Center .... Mr. Joel C. PHEASANT
21 Budget Director & Bursar .... Ms. Susan F. SHONTZ
21 Controller .... Mr. Jeffrey L. SAVINO
44 Exec Dir Constituent Relations .... Mrs. Linda M. CARPENTER
35 Assistant Dean of Students .... Mr. Daniel J. COOK-HUFFMAN
42 College Chaplain .... Mr. Lowell D. WITKOVSKY
20 Director of Academic Support Svcs .... Ms. Sarah M. CLARKSON
88 Director of Student Activities .... Ms. Jessica JACKSON
88 Assoc Dir Conferences & Events .... Ms. Lorri P. SHIDELER
07 Director of Enrollment Operations .... Ms. Terri L. BOLLMAN-DALANSKY
38 College Counselor .... Ms. Mary B. WILLIAMS
28 Asst to Pres Diversity & Inclusion .... Ms. Rosalie M. RODRIGUEZ
29 Director Alumni Relations .... Mr. David D. MEADOWS
39 Director of Residential Life .... Mr. John D. CUTRIGHT

Kaplan Career Institute (I)

5650 Derry Street, Harrisburg PA 17111-4112
County: Dauphin FICE Identification: 004910
Unit ID: 251075
Telephone: (717) 564-4112 Carnegie Class: Assoc/PrivFP
FAX Number: (717) 564-3779 Calendar System: Quarter
URL: www.kci-harrisburg.com
Established: 1918 Annual Undergrad Tuition & Fees: N/A
Enrollment: 371 Coed
Affiliation or Control: Proprietary IRS Status: Proprietary
Highest Offering: Associate Degree
Program: Occupational
Accreditation: ACICS, MAC

01 Executive Director .... Adrienne SCOTT
07 Director Admissions .... Mark HALE
36 Director Student Placement .... Jennifer RIORDAN
05 Director of Education .... Sherry ERNEY
37 Director Student Financial Aid .... Sarah BROOKER

Kaplan Career Institute (J)

177 Franklin Mills Boulevard, Philadelphia PA 19154-3140
County: Bucks FICE Identification: 022898
Unit ID: 211617
Telephone: (215) 612-6600 Carnegie Class: Assoc/PrivFP
FAX Number: (215) 612-6695 Calendar System: Quarter
URL: www.chitraining.com
Established: 1982 Annual Undergrad Tuition & Fees: $15,585
Enrollment: 750 Coed
Affiliation or Control: Proprietary IRS Status: Proprietary
Highest Offering: Associate Degree
Program: Occupational
Accreditation: ACCSC, ACICS, COARC

01 President .... Ms. Jamie PEAK
07 Director of Admissions .... Mr. Dan WATKINS
05 Education Department Head .... Mrs. Dorothy MCCADEN
36 Director of Placement .... Ms. Cheryl BRAIDES
37 Director Financial Aid .... Ms. Nina BALAGOUR

Kaplan Career Institute (K)

3010 Market Street, Philadelphia PA 19104
Telephone: (215) 594-4000 Identification: 770766
Accreditation: ACICS

† Main campus is Kaplan Career Institute in Harrisburg, PA.

Kaplan Career Institute/Broomall Campus (L)

1991 Sproul Road, Suite 42, Broomall PA 19008-3516
County: Delaware FICE Identification: 007781
Unit ID: 215646
Telephone: (610) 353-7630 Carnegie Class: Assoc/PrivFP
FAX Number: (610) 359-1370 Calendar System: Quarter
URL: broomall.kaplancareerinstitute.com
Established: 1958 Annual Undergrad Tuition & Fees: $15,585
Enrollment: 559 Coed
Affiliation or Control: Proprietary IRS Status: Proprietary
Highest Offering: Associate Degree
Program: Occupational; 2-Year Principally Bachelor's Creditable; Technical Emphasis
Accreditation: ACCSC, ACICS

01 President .... Ms. Sylvia MCCARY
05 Director of Education .... Ms. Tynara CHAPELLE
36 Placement Director .... Mr. James LINCKE
07 Director of Admissions .... Vacant

Kaplan Career Institute - ICM Campus (M)

933 Penn Avenue, Pittsburgh PA 15222-3802
County: Allegheny FICE Identification: 007436
Unit ID: 213002
Telephone: (412) 338-4770 Carnegie Class: Assoc/PrivFP
FAX Number: (412) 261-0998 Calendar System: Quarter
URL: www.kcipittsburgh.com
Established: 1963 Annual Undergrad Tuition & Fees: $17,800
Enrollment: 631 Coed
Affiliation or Control: Proprietary IRS Status: Proprietary
Highest Offering: Associate Degree
Program: Occupational; 2-Year Principally Bachelor's Creditable; Technical Emphasis
Accreditation: ACICS, MAC, OTA

01 President .... Mr. Hunter H. HOPKINS
05 Director of Education .... Mr. Thomas E. ROCKS, JR.
37 Director of Financial Aid .... Mr. Chris FOX
89 Director of New Students .... Ms. Rebekah SABO
07 Director of Admissions .... Ms. Lori MILLER
10 Director of Finance .... Ms. Denise RINGER-FISHER
36 Director of Career Services .... Ms. Jennifer KELLY

Keystone College (N)

One College Green, P.O. Box 50,
La Plume PA 18440-0200
County: Lackawanna FICE Identification: 003280
Unit ID: 213303
Telephone: (570) 945-8000 Carnegie Class: Bac/Diverse
FAX Number: (570) 945-8962 Calendar System: Semester
URL: www.keystone.edu
Established: 1868 Annual Undergrad Tuition & Fees: $21,200
Enrollment: 1,683 Coed
Affiliation or Control: Independent Non-Profit IRS Status: 501(c)3
Highest Offering: Baccalaureate
Program: Liberal Arts And General
Accreditation: M

01 President .... Dr. David L. COPPOLA
05 VP Academic Affairs/Dean of College .... Dr. Thea HARRINGTON
32 VP Student Affairs/Dean Students .... Dr. Robert J. PERKINS
10 Vice Pres Finance & Administration .... Mr. Kevin WILSON
84 Vice Pres Enrollment .... Ms. Sarah KEATING
30 Interim Exec Dir Univ Advancement .... Ms. Charlotte RAVAIOLI
08 Director Miller Library .... Ms. Mari FLYNN
06 Registrar .... Ms. Kate OWENS
07 Director of Admissions .... Ms. Kathryn REILLY
37 Dir Financial Assistance & Planning .... Mr. Brian WEBER
91 Director Information Technology .... Mr. Charles L. PROTHERO
15 Director of Human Resources .... Ms. Alberta GRUSHINSKI
26 Senior Director College Relations .... Mr. Fran CALPIN
29 Director of Alumni Outreach .... Ms. Christina FENTON-MACE
36 Director Career Development .... Ms. Rhea V. ELLIS DUKE
09 Director Institutional Research .... Mr. Curtis BAUMAN

Keystone Technical Institute (O)

2301 Academy Drive, Harrisburg PA 17112-1012
County: Dauphin FICE Identification: 022342
Unit ID: 210483
Telephone: (717) 545-4747 Carnegie Class: Assoc/PrivFP
FAX Number: (717) 901-9090 Calendar System: Semester
URL: www.kti.edu
Established: 1980 Annual Undergrad Tuition & Fees: $24,420
Enrollment: 314 Coed
Affiliation or Control: Proprietary IRS Status: Proprietary
Highest Offering: Associate Degree
Program: Occupational; 2-Year Principally Bachelor's Creditable; Technical Emphasis
Accreditation: ACCSC

01 President .... Mr. David W. SNYDER
03 Vice President .... Mrs. Andrea SNYDER
05 Dean of Education .... Mr. Jason KARMANN
06 Registrar/Dir Stdnt Financial Aid .... Ms. Tracy STEWART
10 Chief Business Officer .... Mr. Dennis FIELDS
07 Admissions Officer .... Mr. Mark DYKEMA

King's College (P)

133 N River Street, Wilkes-Barre PA 18711-0801
County: Luzerne FICE Identification: 003282
Unit ID: 213321
Telephone: (570) 208-5900 Carnegie Class: Master's S
FAX Number: (570) 825-9049 Calendar System: Semester
URL: www.kings.edu

Established: 1946 Annual Undergrad Tuition & Fees: $30,310
Enrollment: 2,494 Coed
Affiliation or Control: Roman Catholic IRS Status: 501(c)3
Highest Offering: Master's
Program: Liberal Arts And General; Teacher Preparatory; Professional; Business Emphasis
Accreditation: M, ARCPA, BUS, TED

01 President .... Rev. John RYAN, CSC
05 Vice President for Academic Affairs .....Dr. Nicholas A. HOLODICK
10 Vice President for Business Affairs .... Mr. John LOYACK
30 Vice President for Inst Advancement ....Mr. Frederick PETTIT
32 Vice President for Student Affairs ..Ms. Janet E. MERCINCAVAGE
04 Assistant to the President .... Vacant
20 Assoc VP for Academic Affairs ....Dr. Joseph EVAN
13 Exec Dir Info & Tech Svc Div ....Mr. Paul J. MORAN
08 Director of Library ....Dr. Terrence F. MECH
84 Assoc VP Enroll/Academic Svcs ....Ms. Teresa M. PECK
35 Assoc Vice Pres Student Affairs .... Mr. Robert B. MCGONIGLE
07 Director of Admissions ....Mr. James ANDERSON
50 Dean Wm G McGowan Sch Business ....Dr. Barry WILLIAMS
06 Registrar ....Mr. Daniel T. CEBRICK
37 Director of Financial Aid ....Ms. Donna CERZA
42 Chaplain/Director Campus Ministry ...Rev. Thomas LOONEY, CSC
36 Director Career Planning & Placemnt ..... Mr. Christopher SUTZKO
16 Director of Human Resources ....Ms. Lita PIEKARA
26 Director of Public Relations ....Mr. John MCANDREW
29 Director of Alumni Relations ....Ms. Patrice PERSICO
18 Executive Director of Facilities ....Mr. Thomas BUTCHKO
19 Director of Security/Safety ....Mr. Francis HACKEN
41 Dir of Intercollegiate Athletics ....Ms. Cheryl J. ISH
21 Associate VP/Controller & CAO ....Mr. Thomas GRABER
39 Director of Residence Life ....Ms. Megan SELLICK
58 Dean of Graduate Programs .... Vacant
09 Director of Institutional Research ....Ms. Marian K. PALMERI
28 Director of College Diversity ....Mr. Nathan WARD
92 Director of the Honors Program ....Dr. Cristofer SCARBORO
90 Managing Dir of User Services ....Mr. Raymond G. PRYOR
91 Managing Director for MIS ....Mr. William M. CORCORAN
44 Dir Major Gifts & Planned Giving ....Mr. William LYNN

La Roche College (A)

9000 Babcock Boulevard, Pittsburgh PA 15237-5898
County: Allegheny FICE Identification: 003987
Unit ID: 213358
Telephone: (412) 367-9300 Carnegie Class: Bac/Diverse
FAX Number: (412) 536-1062 Calendar System: Semester
URL: www.laroche.edu
Established: 1963 Annual Undergrad Tuition & Fees: $24,778
Enrollment: 1,465 Coed
Affiliation or Control: Roman Catholic IRS Status: 501(c)3
Highest Offering: Master's
Program: Liberal Arts And General; Professional
Accreditation: M, ACBSP, ADNUR, ANEST, ART, CIDA, NUR

01 President ....Sr. Candace INTROCASO, CDP
04 Admin Asst to the President .... Ms. Karen P. WILLOUGHBY
05 Vice President Academic Affairs ....Dr. Howard J. ISHIYAMA
84 VP for Enrollment Mgmt & Mktg .....Mr. William H. FIRMAN, JR.
10 Vice President for Finance ....Mr. Robert VOGEL
32 Vice Pres Student Life/Dean Stdnts .... Ms. Colleen RUEFLE
11 Vice Pres Administrative Services ....Mr. George T. ZAFFUTO
30 VP for Institutional Advancement ....Mr. Michael ANDREOLA
43 General Counsel ....Ms. Mary Beth FETCHKO
20 Assoc VP Academic Affairs ....Dr. Rosemary MCCARTHY
20 Assoc Vice Pres Academic Affairs ....Dr. Thomas G. SCHAEFER
36 Assoc Dean Academic/Student Support ....Ms. Marie DEEM
35 Director of Student Development ....Mr. David DAY
84 Div Chair Natural & Behavioral Sci ....Ms. Jane ARNOLD
79 Div Chair Humanities ....Sr. Michele BISBEY, CDP
50 Div Chair Business .... Vacant
57 Div Chair Design ....Ms. Maria RIPEPI
53 Div Chair Education & Nursing ....Dr. Kathleen A. SULLIVAN
06 Registrar ....Ms. Joan CUTONE
08 Director Library/Learning Center ....Ms. Laverne COLLINS
07 Director of Admissions ....Mr. Stephen STEPPE
26 Director of Mktg & Media Relations ...Ms. Mary Gray DELBUONO
37 Director of Financial Aid ....Ms. Sharon PLATT
41 Director of Athletics ....Mr. Jim TINKEY
42 Director of Campus Ministry ....Fr. Peter HORTON
07 Director Grad Studies/Adult Ed ....Ms. Hope SCHIFFGENS
39 Director Residence Life ....Mr. Christopher WILLIS
14 Director Information Technology ....Ms. Terri BALLARD
85 Director International Student Svcs ....Dr. Natasha GARRETT
29 Director Alumni Relations ....Ms. Gina MILLER
88 Director of Special Events ....Ms. Bobbi LAPLACE
21 Director Budget & Finance ....Mr. John PETRUS
09 Director of Institutional Research ....Ms. Patricia A. CONNOLLY
18 Director of Facilities Management ....Mr. J.R YOUNG
38 Director Counseling Services ....Ms. Lori AREND
19 Director Public Safety ....Mr. David HILKE
15 Director Human Resources ....Ms. Melissa KIM
40 Bookstore Manager ....Mr. Tim JONES
88 Director of Student Accounts ....Ms. Danya TINKEY

La Salle University (B)

1900 W Olney Avenue, Philadelphia PA 19141-1199
County: Philadelphia FICE Identification: 003287
Unit ID: 213367
Telephone: (215) 951-1000 Carnegie Class: Master's L
FAX Number: (215) 951-1488 Calendar System: Semester
URL: www.lasalle.edu
Established: 1863 Annual Undergrad Tuition & Fees: $38,100
Enrollment: 6,567 Coed
Affiliation or Control: Roman Catholic IRS Status: 501(c)3
Highest Offering: Doctorate
Program: 2-Year Principally Bachelor's Creditable; Liberal Arts And General; Professional
Accreditation: M, ANEST, BUS, CLPSY, DIETC, DIETD, MFCD, NURSE, SP, SW

01 President .... Bro. Michael J. MCGINNISS
05 Vice Pres Academic Affairs/Provost ....Dr. Joseph R. MARBACH
04 Exec Assistant to the President ....Dr. Alice L. HOERSCH
04 Exec Assistant to the President ....Bro. Joseph WILLARD
30 Vice Pres University Advancement ....Mr. R. Brian ELDERTON
84 Vice Pres Enrollment Services ....Dr. George J. WALTER
10 VP Finance and Admin and Treasurer ....Mr. Matthew MCMANNESS
32 VP Student Affairs/Dean of Students ....Dr. James E. MOORE
20 Assistant Provost ....Bro. John MCGOLDRICK
49 Dean School of Arts & Sciences ....Dr. Thomas A. KEAGY
50 Dean Sch of Business Administration .. Dr. Gary A. GIAMARTINO
51 Dean Col of Professional/Cont Stds ....Dr. Joseph Y. UGRAS
66 Dean Sch of Nursing/Health Sciences ....Dr. Brian GOLDSTEIN
22 Asst VP Admin/Plng/Affirm Action ....Ms. Rose Lee PAULINE
26 Asst VP Mktg & Communication ..... Ms. Karen MULDOON GEUS
29 Asst Vice Pres of Alumni Relations ....Mr. Trey P. ULRICH
86 Asst Vice Pres Government Affairs ..... Mr. Edward A. TURZANSKI
21 Asst VP Finance & Asst Treasurer ....Ms. Rebecca L. HORVATH
88 Director Advancement Services ....Ms. Elizabeth LOCHNER
88 Director Economic Development ....Mr. William J. DEVITO
82 CoDirector Grad Ctr/East Eur Stds ....Dr. Luis GOMEZ
82 CoDirector Grad Ctr/East Eur Stds ....Dr. Leo RUDNYTZKY
77 Director Grad Computer Info Science .... Ms. Margaret MCCOEY
53 Co Director Graduate Education Pgm ......Dr. Greer RICHARDSON
53 CoDir Graduate Education Prgm .... Dr. Deborah YOST
83 Dir Grad Pgm Counsel-Fam Therapy ....Dr. Donna A. TONREY
73 Director Doctorate in Theology ....Fr. Francis J. BERNA
60 Director Grad Prof Communication .... Dr. Pamela LANNUTTI
66 Director Undergraduate Nursing .... Dr. Barbara HOERST
66 Director Graduate Nursing ....Dr. Patricia DILLON
69 Director Master Public Health Pgm .... Dr. Holly M. HARNER
88 Director Grad Econ Crime Forensics .... Ms. Margaret MCCOEY
58 Dir Grad Pgm Human Capital Develop ....Mr. Stanley A. BRAVERMAN
58 Dir Grad Pgms Nonprofit Leadership ....Dr. Laura OTTEN
25 Director Grants/Research ....Dr. Fred J. FOLEY
35 Senior Assoc Dean of Students ....Mr. Alan B. WENDALL
35 Associate Dean of Students ....Dr. Lane B. NEUBAUER
35 Associate Dean of Students ....Ms. Anna M. ALLEN
51 Asst Dean Prof/Continuing Studies ....Ms. Elizabeth A. HEENAN
42 Director Univ Ministry & Service ....Bro. Robert J. KINZLER
92 Director University Honors Program ....Dr. Richard A. NIGRO
13 Chief Information Officer .... Mr. Edward NICKERSON
08 Director of the Library ....Mr. John S. BAKY
18 Asst VP Facilities Mgmt/Capital Dev ......Mr. Robert C. KROH, JR.
19 Asst VP for Safety & Security ....Mr. Arthur GROVER
16 Asst VP for Human Resources ....Dr. Margurete WALSH
41 Athletic Director ....Dr. Thomas BRENNAN
44 Director of Major Gifts ....Bro. Charles E. GRESH
30 Director of Development .... Bro. John MCDONNELL
102 Director of The La Salle Fund .... Ms. Helene HOLMES BACZKOWSKI
30 Director of Prospect Development ....Ms. Sarah PARNUM CADBURY
36 Director of Career Services ....Mr. Louis A. LAMORTE, JR.
36 Exec Dir Career & Employ Svcs ....Mr. Steve MCGONIGLE
07 Executive Director of Admission .... Mr. James C. PLUNKETT
37 Director Student Financial Services ......Mr. Michael WISNIEWSKI
06 Registrar .... Mr. Dominic J. GALANTE
09 Dir Inst Research & Asst Provost ... Dr. Michael J. ROSZKOWSKI
88 Dir Doctorate in Psychology Program .... Dr. Kelly MCCLURE
88 Director Graduate English Studies ....Dr. Stephen P. SMITH
88 Grad Director Instr Technology Mgt .... Dr. Bobbe G. BAGGIO
88 Director Part-time MBA Program .... Ms. Denise SAURENNANN
88 Director Full-time MBA Program ....Ms. Elizabeth A. SCOFIELD
40 Manager Campus Store ....Mr. Mark ALLAN
28 Multicultural Education Coordinator .... Ms. Cherlyn L. RUSH
105 Director of Web Communication .... Mr. Gregory FALA

Lackawanna College (C)

501 Vine Street, Scranton PA 18509-3206
County: Lackawanna FICE Identification: 003283
Unit ID: 213376
Telephone: (570) 961-7810 Carnegie Class: Assoc/PrivNFP
FAX Number: (570) 961-7858 Calendar System: 4/1/4
URL: www.lackawanna.edu
Established: 1894 Annual Undergrad Tuition & Fees: $12,850
Enrollment: 1,454 Coed
Affiliation or Control: Independent Non-Profit IRS Status: 501(c)3
Highest Offering: Associate Degree
Program: Occupational; 2-Year Principally Bachelor's Creditable; Business Emphasis
Accreditation: M, DMS, PTAA, SURGT

01 President ....Mr. Mark VOLK
03 Exec Vice President/CAO .... Dr. Jill MURRAY
10 Vice Pres Finance/Administration ....Ms. Alycia SCHWARTZ
05 Associate VP Academic Affairs .... Dr. Erica PRICCI
32 Assoc VP Student Affairs ....Mrs. Suellen MUSEWICZ
35 Dean of Students ....Mr. Mark DUDA
84 Assoc VP of Enrollment Management .... Mr. Brian COSTANZO
20 Associate Dean of Faculty .... Vacant
29 Director Alumni Relations .... Ms. Ashley FETTERMAN
09 Director Institutional Research ....Mrs. Laura DUDA
88 Dir Programming & Special Events ....Mr. Jim CULLEN
31 Director of External Relations ....Ms. Wendy EVANS
51 Director of Continuing Education ....Mrs. Anita COLA
41 Director of Athletics ....Mrs. Kim MECCA
88 Director of Advising & Transfer Svc .Mrs. Barbara NOWOGORSKI
06 Registrar ....Mrs. Theresa SCOPELLITI
19 Director of Public Safety ....Mr. Gary SHOENER
12 Director of Hazleton Center ....Ms. Mary Ann DZIAK
12 Director of Center Operations .... Ms. Kim VANGARELLI
12 Exec Director School of PNGT .... Mr. Richard MARQUARDT
91 Director Admin Computing Svcs ....Mr. Edward WARGO
08 Library Director ....Mrs. Mary Beth ROCHE
102 Director of Grant Support Services ....Ms. Michelle WILLIAMS
39 Director Housing & Residence Life ....Mr. Stephen DUDA
15 Director of Human Resources ....Mrs. Sharon EBERT
18 Director of Facilities ....Mr. Joseph ERRICO
37 Director of Financial Aid .... Mrs. Barbara HAPEMAN
12 Director Towanda Center ....Ms. Kim MAPES
13 Director of MIS ....Mrs. Melanie KOWALSKI
35 Director of Student Life .... Ms. Karen LEGGE
88 Director of Health Club Facilities ....Mr. Joseph LUCIANO
07 Asst Director of Admissions ....Ms. Stacey MUCHAL
88 Service Learning Coordinator ....Ms. Jo-Ann ORCUTT

Lafayette College (D)

316 Markle Hall, Easton PA 18042-1798
County: Northampton FICE Identification: 003284
Unit ID: 213385
Telephone: (610) 330-5000 Carnegie Class: Bac/A&S
FAX Number: (610) 330-5127 Calendar System: Semester
URL: www.lafayette.edu
Established: 1826 Annual Undergrad Tuition & Fees: $43,970
Enrollment: 2,456 Coed
Affiliation or Control: Independent Non-Profit IRS Status: 501(c)3
Highest Offering: Baccalaureate
Program: Liberal Arts And General; Professional
Accreditation: M, CS, ENG

01 President .... Dr. Alison R. BYERLY
05 Provost ....Dr. Wendy L. HILL
30 Vice Pres Devel/College Relations .... Mr. James W. DICKER
10 Vice Pres Business Affairs/Treas ....Mr. Mitchell L. WEIN
32 VP Campus Life/Sr Diversity Officer ....Dr. Annette DIORIO
16 Vice President Human Resources ..... Ms. Leslie F. MUHLFELDER
27 Vice President for Communications ....Mr. Robert J. MASSA
13 VP and Chief Information Officer ....Mr. John L. O'KEEFE
21 Assoc VP Finance & Admin/Controller .... Mr. Stephen A. SCHAFER
54 Director of Engineering ....Dr. Scott R. HUMMEL
04 Executive Assistant ....Dr. James F. KRIVOSKI
84 Dean Admissions & Financial Aid .... Mr. Gregory MACDONALD
20 Dean of the College .... Dr. Hannah W. STEWART-GAMBINO
08 Dean of Libraries ....Mr. Neil J. MCELROY
35 Dean of Students ....Dr. Paul J. MCLOUGHLIN, II
07 Director of Admissions ....Mr. Matthew HYDE
37 Director of Student Financial Aid .... Ms. Ashley BIANCHI
09 Director of Institutional Research ....Dr. James P. SCHAFFER
06 Registrar ....Mr. Francis A. BENGINIA
41 Director of Athletics ....Dr. Bruce E. MCCUTCHEON
36 Director Career Services .... Ms. Linda N. ARRA
23 Director Health Services ....Dr. Jeffrey E. GOLDSTEIN
38 Director Counseling Center ....Dr. Karen J. FORBES
19 Director of Public Safety .... Mr. Hugh W. HARRIS
18 Dir Physical Planning & Plant Oper ....Mr. Bruce S. FERRETTI
29 Executive Director Alumni Relations .... Ms. Rachel NELSON MOELLER
15 Director Employment ....Ms. Lisa Youngkin REX
96 Manager of Procurement ....Ms. Linda L. JROSKI

Lake Erie College of Osteopathic Medicine (E)

1858 W Grandview Boulevard, Erie PA 16509-1025
County: Erie FICE Identification: 030908
Unit ID: 407629
Telephone: (814) 866-6641 Carnegie Class: Spec/Med
FAX Number: (814) 866-8123 Calendar System: Semester
URL: www.lecom.edu
Established: 1993 Annual Graduate Tuition & Fees: $30,570
Enrollment: 3,333 Coed
Affiliation or Control: Independent Non-Profit IRS Status: 501(c)3
Highest Offering: First Professional Degree; No Undergraduates
Program: Professional
Accreditation: M, DENT, OSTEO, PHAR

01 President/CEO ....Dr. John M. FERRETTI
05 Provost/Sr Vice Pres/Dean Acad Affs ....Dr. Silvia M. FERRETTI
10 Vice Pres of Fiscal Affairs/CFO ....Mr. Richard P. OLINGER
67 VP Acad Affs/Dn LECOM Sch Pharmacy ....Dr. Hershey BELL
12 Vice Pres for LECOM at Seton Hill ....Dr. Irving FREEMAN
52 Dean School of Dental Medicine ....Dr. Robert HIRSCH
05 Assoc Dean Acad Affairs Bradenton ....Dr. Robert GEORGE
12 Assc Dn Ops/Dist Ed Pharm Bradenton .... Dr. Sunil JAMBHEKAR
88 Asst Dean of Clinical Education .... Dr. Regan SHABLOSKI
88 Assoc Dean of Preclinical Educ .... Dr. Christine KELL
88 Asst Dean Clinical Educ Bradenton ....Dr. Anthony J. FERRETTI
88 Asst Dean Preclinical Ed Bradenton ....Dr. Mark COTY
20 Asst Dean Acad Affairs Bradenton ....Dr. Ronald BEREZNIAK
20 Assoc Dean of Accelerataed Pathway ....Dr. Rachel OGDEN
20 Assoc Dean for Traditional Pathway .... Dr. Julie WILKINSON
108 Assistant Dean for Assessment ....Dr. Theresa SCHWEIGER

20 Asst Dean of Curr & Fac Eval .... Dr. Mathew BATEMAN
32 Director of Student Affairs .... Dr. David FRIED
30 Vice President of Institutional Dev .... Dr. James K. MOORE
26 Inst Dir Communications/Marketing .... Mr. Pierre A. BELLICINI
08 Dir of Learning Resources .... Mr. Dan WELCH
72 Director of Information Technology .... Mr. Michael E. LEE
46 Director of Research .... Dr. Bertalan DUDAS
15 Director of Human Resources .... Ms. JoAnn I. JEWELL
38 Director Behavioral Health .... Dr. Richard HAHN
20 Director of Faculty Development .... Dr. Mark TERRELL
27 Asst Dir Communications/Marketing .... Mr. Michael POLIN
18 Building Operations Supervisor .... Mr. Brian KING
37 Associate Director of Financial Aid .... Ms. Bonnie CRILLEY
06 Registrar .... Mr. Jeremy SIVILLO
07 Admissions Coordinator .... Ms. Amy W. ROWE
40 Bookstore Manager .... Ms. Alice PUZAROWSKI

Lancaster Bible College (A)

901 Eden Road, Lancaster PA 17601-5036
County: Lancaster FICE Identification: 003285
Unit ID: 213400
Telephone: (717) 569-7071 Carnegie Class: Spec/Faith
FAX Number: (717) 560-8260 Calendar System: Semester
URL: www.lbc.edu
Established: 1933 Annual Undergrad Tuition & Fees: $18,270
Enrollment: 1,131 Coed
Affiliation or Control: Independent Non-Profit IRS Status: 501(c)3
Highest Offering: Doctorate
Program: Religious Emphasis
Accreditation: M, BI

01 President .... Dr. Peter W. TEAGUE
04 Assistant to the President .... Mrs. Judith M. HECKAMAN
05 Vice President for Academic Affairs .... Dr. Philip E. DEARBORN
84 VP for Enrollment Management .... Mr. Josh BEERS
30 VP of Advancement .... Mr. Tim HEITZ
10 Director of Finance .... Mr. Matthew MASON
09 AVP of Institutional Effectiveness .... Dr. Dale MORT
20 Dean of iLEAD Center .... Dr. Gary BREDFELDT
06 Associate VP & Registrar .... Mr. Jeffrey HOOVER
32 Associate VP for Student Services .... Mr. Robert MCMICHAEL
26 Director of Marketing .... Mr. Peter CASTOR
07 Director of Admissions .... Mr. Scott BOYER
38 Dean of Student Development .... Ms. Annette HERNANDEZ
08 Interm Director of Library Services .... Dr. Philip E. DEARBORN
37 Director of Financial Aid .... Mrs. Karen L. FOX
21 Controller .... Mr. Lonnie MARTIN
18 Director of Plant Operations .... Mr. Steve MUSSER
23 Director of Health Services .... Mrs. Mary Lou JOLINE
29 Dir of Alumni & Career Services .... Mr. Cameron MARTIN
41 Athletic Director .... Mr. Peter BEERS
15 Director of People Development & HR .... Mrs. Paula POOLE

Lancaster County Career and Technology Center (B)

1730 Hans Herr Drive, Willow Street PA 17584
County: Lancaster FICE Identification: 023108
Unit ID: 418533
Telephone: (717) 464-7050 Carnegie Class: Not Classified
FAX Number: (717) 464-9518 Calendar System: Semester
URL: lcctc.org
Established: 1970 Annual Undergrad Tuition & Fees (In-District): $11,275
Enrollment: 394 Coed
Affiliation or Control: State/Local IRS Status: 501(c)3
Highest Offering: Associate Degree
Program: Occupational
Accreditation: COE

01 Executive Director .... David WARREN
10 Business Manager .... Thomas BIGLER

Lancaster General College of Nursing and Health Sciences (C)

410 N Lime Street, Lancaster PA 17602-2337
County: Lancaster FICE Identification: 009863
Unit ID: 442356
Telephone: (717) 544-4912 Carnegie Class: Assoc/PrivNFP
FAX Number: (717) 544-5970 Calendar System: Semester
URL: www.lancastergeneralcollege.edu
Established: 1903 Annual Undergrad Tuition & Fees: $20,150
Enrollment: 1,375 Coed
Affiliation or Control: Independent Non-Profit IRS Status: 501(c)3
Highest Offering: Baccalaureate
Program: 2-Year Principally Bachelor's Creditable; Nursing Emphasis
Accreditation: M, ADNUR, COARC, CVT, DMS, EMT, MT, NMT, NURSE, RAD, SURGT

01 President .... Dr. Mary Grace SIMCOX
05 Vice Pres of Admin/Academic Affairs .... Ms. Penni LONGENECKER
10 Vice President of Finance & Admin .... Mr. Thomas HULSTINE
20 Vice President Learning Development .... Ms. Donna WILLIAMSON
06 Registrar .... Mr. James DONOHUE
84 Director of Enrollment Management .... Mr. Lyn LONGENECKER

Lancaster Theological Seminary (D)

555 W James Street, Lancaster PA 17603-2812
County: Lancaster FICE Identification: 003286
Unit ID: 213446
Telephone: (717) 393-0654 Carnegie Class: Spec/Faith
FAX Number: (717) 393-4254 Calendar System: Semester
URL: www.lancasterseminary.edu
Established: 1825 Annual Graduate Tuition & Fees: $14,900
Enrollment: 134 Coed
Affiliation or Control: United Church Of Christ IRS Status: 501(c)3
Highest Offering: Doctorate; No Undergraduates
Program: Professional; Religious Emphasis
Accreditation: M, THEOL

01 President .... Dr. Carol E. LYTCH
10 Vice President Business & Finance .... Ms. Valerie A. CALHOUN
05 Vice Pres Academic Affairs & Dean .... Dr. David M. MELLOTT
07 Director of Admissions .... Rev. Kendal N. BROWN
08 Director Library Services .... Rev. Richard R. BERG
06 Registrar .... Mrs. Judith G. HUMMER
29 Director Alumni Relations .... Rev. Paul EYER
13 Director Computing/Information Mgmt .... Rev. Chris BELDAN
30 Exec Director of Advancement .... Ms. Crystal MILLS
04 Assistant to the President .... Vacant

Lansdale School of Business (E)

290 Wissahickon Ave, North Wales PA 19454-4114
County: Montgomery FICE Identification: 007779
Unit ID: 213473
Telephone: (215) 699-5700 Carnegie Class: Assoc/PrivFP
FAX Number: (215) 699-8770 Calendar System: Semester
URL: www.LSB.edu
Established: 1918 Annual Undergrad Tuition & Fees: $10,850
Enrollment: 535 Coed
Affiliation or Control: Proprietary IRS Status: Proprietary
Highest Offering: Associate Degree
Program: Occupational; 2-Year Principally Bachelor's Creditable; Business Emphasis
Accreditation: ACICS

01 President .... Mr. Marlon D. KELLER
03 Executive Director .... Mrs. Marianne H. JOHNSON
05 Academic Dean .... Mr. David P. HEFFLEY
32 Student Services Coordinator .... Ms. Debora GAHMAN
08 Librarian .... Mrs. Marie B. WALCROFT
10 Director of Student Finance .... Mr. Robert RUSSO
36 Career Services Coordinator .... Ms. Jodi L. TASHMAN

Laurel Business Institute (F)

11 East Penn Street, Uniontown PA 15401-3453
County: Fayette FICE Identification: 025462
Unit ID: 250027
Telephone: (724) 439-4900 Carnegie Class: Assoc/PrivFP
FAX Number: (724) 439-3607 Calendar System: Semester
URL: www.laurel.edu
Established: 1985 Annual Undergrad Tuition & Fees: $12,591
Enrollment: 185 Coed
Affiliation or Control: Proprietary IRS Status: Proprietary
Highest Offering: Associate Degree
Program: Occupational; Technical Emphasis
Accreditation: ACICS, COARC, MLTAD

01 President .... Mrs. Nancy M. DECKER
05 Vice President of Education .... Mrs. Valerie S. BACHARACH
10 Vice President of Finance .... Ms. Vicki M. JOLLIFFE
15 Vice President of Human Resources .... Mr. Chuck SANTORE, JR.
12 Campus Director .... Mrs. Bonnie Jean MARSH
13 Network Administrator .... Mrs. JoAnna MEESE
37 Director of Financial Aid .... Ms. Stephanie M. MIGYANKO
07 Director of Admission/Marketing .... Mr. Douglas S. DECKER

Laurel Technical Institute (G)

200 Sterling Avenue, Sharon PA 16146
County: Mercer FICE Identification: 020925
Unit ID: 215992
Telephone: (724) 983-0700 Carnegie Class: Assoc/PrivFP
FAX Number: (724) 983-8355 Calendar System: Semester
URL: www.laurel.edu
Established: 1925 Annual Undergrad Tuition & Fees: $9,294
Enrollment: 284 Coed
Affiliation or Control: Proprietary IRS Status: Proprietary
Highest Offering: Associate Degree
Program: Occupational; 2-Year Principally Bachelor's Creditable
Accreditation: ACICS, COARC

01 President .... Ms. Nancy DECKER
05 Director .... Mr. Douglas DECKER
07 Director of Admission .... Ms. Maria CLYDE

Lebanon Valley College (H)

101 N College Avenue, Annville PA 17003-1400
County: Lebanon FICE Identification: 003288
Unit ID: 213507
Telephone: (717) 867-6161 Carnegie Class: Bac/Diverse
FAX Number: (717) 867-6124 Calendar System: Semester
URL: www.lvc.edu
Established: 1866 Annual Undergrad Tuition & Fees: $35,700
Enrollment: 1,984 Coed
Affiliation or Control: United Methodist IRS Status: 501(c)3
Highest Offering: Doctorate
Program: Liberal Arts And General; Teacher Preparatory; Professional
Accreditation: M, ACBSP, MUS, PTA

01 President .... Dr. Lewis E. THAYNE
05 Vice Pres Acad Affs/Dean of Faculty .... Dr. Michael R. GREEN
30 Vice President of Advancement .... Ms. Janet WILEY
11 Vice President Administration/IT .... Mr. Robert A. RILEY
10 Vice President of Finance .... Vacant
84 Vice President of Enrollment .... Mr. William J. BROWN
32 VP Student Affairs/Dean of Students .... Mr. Gregory H. KRIKORIAN
04 Exec Assistant to the President .... Ms. Beth ESLER
20 Associate Dean of the Faculty .... Dr. Ann E. DAMIANO
58 Assoc Dean of Grad Stds/Cont Educ .... Dr. Gregory A. BUCKLEY
06 Registrar .... Mr. Jeremy A. MAISTO
08 Librarian .... Mr. Frank MOLS
42 Chaplain .... Rev. Paul FULLMER
35 Associate Dean Student Services .... Mr. Robert L. MIKUS
37 Director of Financial Aid .... Mrs. Kendra M. FEIGERT
36 Director of Career Services .... Ms. Sharon M. GIVLER
41 Director of Athletics .... Mr. Richard L. BEARD
29 Director Alumni/Parent Engagement .... Ms. Jayanne HAYWARD
44 Director of Development .... Mrs. Jamie N. CECIL
26 Exec Dir Marketing/Communications .... Mr. Martin J. PARKES
27 Dir Editorial Standards/Brand Msgng .... Dr. Thomas M. HANRAHAN
21 Controller .... Ms. Eleanor LEWIS
18 Sr Director of Facilities Services .... Mr. Donald SANTOSTEFANO
19 Director of Public Safety .... Mr. Brent OBERHOLTZER
15 Director of Human Resources .... Mrs. Ann C. HAYES
28 Director of Multicultural Affairs .... Ms. Venus RICKS
35 Director of Student Activities .... Mrs. Jennifer M. EVANS
104 Director of Study Abroad .... Ms. Jill T. RUSSELL
90 Director Technology/User Support .... Mr. Michael C. ZEIGLER
91 Dir Enterprise Information Systems .... Mr. Robert J. DILLANE
39 Director of Residential Life .... Mr. Michael R. DIESNER
38 Director of Counseling .... Dr. Stephanie A. FALK
38 Director of Disability Services .... Ms. Yvonne FOSTER
09 Director of Institutional Research .... Vacant
50 Director of the MBA Program .... Vacant
96 Director of Business Services .... Mr. Todd M. LATSHAW
88 Spec Asst to Pres Innovative Pgms .... Mr. Steven P. O'DAY

Lehigh Carbon Community College (I)

4525 Education Park Drive, Schnecksville PA 18078-2598
County: Lehigh FICE Identification: 006810
Unit ID: 213525
Telephone: (610) 799-2121 Carnegie Class: Assoc/Pub-S-SC
FAX Number: (610) 799-1527 Calendar System: Semester
URL: www.lccc.edu
Established: 1966 Annual Undergrad Tuition & Fees (In-District): $3,450
Enrollment: 7,323 Coed
Affiliation or Control: Local IRS Status: 501(c)3
Highest Offering: Associate Degree
Program: Occupational; 2-Year Principally Bachelor's Creditable
Accreditation: M, ACBSP, ADNUR, CAHIIM, MAC, OTA, PNUR, PTAA

01 President .... Dr. Donald W. SNYDER
05 VP Academic/Student Dev .... Dr. Thomas C. LEAMER
11 Sr VP Administrative Services .... Dr. Ann D. BIEBER
10 VP Finance & Facilities .... Mr. James A. MORETTI
04 Admin Secy to President and Board .... Mrs. Cindy L. BROOKS
32 Dean of Students .... Ms. Peggy M. HEIM
62 Dean Library & Ed Support Services .... Dr. Richard W. WILT
88 Dean of Academic Services .... Dr. Barry L. SPRIGGS
13 Exec Dir Information Technology .... Mr. Ervin J. MEASE
106 Assoc Dean Distance Education .... Mr. Dominic CHRISTISON
20 Associate Academic Dean .... Vacant
20 Associate Academic Dean .... Ms. Larissa M. VERTA
103 Ex Dir Workforce/Community Ed .... Ms. Terri K. KEEFE
26 Ex Dir Marketing & Communications .... Mr. Sean A. DALLAS
09 Assoc Dean Inst Research/Planning .... Dr. Glynis A. DANIELS
45 Assoc Dean Planning & Assessment .... Dr. Cecelia A. CONNELLY-WEIDA
21 Assistant Controller-Accounting .... Ms. Shannon HELMER
102 Executive Director of Foundation .... Mr. Timothy J. HERRLINGER
38 Director Advising and Counseling .... Ms. Susan J. FREAD
07 Director of Recruitment/Admissions .... Mr. Louis L. HEGYES
88 Dir of Application Support Services .... Ms. Shirley DELONG
36 Director Career Development .... Ms. Christina L. MOYER
88 Assoc Dean Prof Accred/Curriculum .... Mr. Scott W. AQUILA
88 Director of High School Connections .... Ms. Jennifer K. AQUILA
15 Director of Human Resources .... Ms. Donna M. WILLIAMS
88 Dir Infrastructure Svcs/Client Sol .... Mr. Frank D. MROZ
88 Dir Fac Dev/Student Retention .... Ms. Cheryl A. DOLL
103 Director Workforce Training .... Ms. Lois M. YEAKEL
66 Director Nursing/Healthcare Science .... Ms. Barbara H. LUPOLE
35 Director of Student Life .... Ms. Gene F. EDEN
14 Director IT Support Services .... Mr. George C. HEGEDUS
18 Director of Facilities Management .... Mr. Carl S. PECKITT, JR.
37 Director of Financial Aid .... Ms. Marian L. SNYDER
25 Director of Academic Grants .... Ms. Linda L. MESICS
106 Dir of Distance Lrng/Instruct Tech .... Ms. Beverly J. BENFER
41 Director of Athletics .... Ms. Jocelyn M. BECK
88 Director of Early Learning Center .... Ms. Mary G. SALINGER
96 Purchasing Manager .... Ms. Susan E. LINDENMUTH
12 Dir Carbon/Schuylkill Cty Ed Svcs .... Ms. Jeanne Y. MILLER
88 Dir of Literacy and Job Training .... Ms. Mary KOVALCHICK
88 Controller .... Ms. Connie BURNS
88 ESC Lab Supervisor .... Ms. Debra A. CONDON
25 Dir Institutional Advancement Grant .... Mr. Thomas J. MULDERICK
74 Dir Veterinary Tech Program .... Ms. Samantha FRIEDENBERG
27 Director Marketing and Publications .... Ms. Paula A. HANNAM
06 Registrar .... Ms. Sandra L. MOSSER
19 Supervisor of Security & Safety .... Mr. Kevin J. MILES

40 Bookstore Manager .... Ms. Jennifer ERB
88 Assoc Dean Student Success .... Mr. Brian C. DELONG
19 Director of Public Safety .... Mr. Dennis PETERS

Lehigh University (A)

27 Memorial Drive W, Bethlehem PA 18015-3094
County: Northampton FICE Identification: 003289
Unit ID: 213543
Telephone: (610) 758-3000 Carnegie Class: RU/H
FAX Number: (610) 691-5420 Calendar System: Semester
URL: www.lehigh.edu
Established: 1865 Annual Undergrad Tuition & Fees: $55,080
Enrollment: 7,069 Coed
Affiliation or Control: Independent Non-Profit IRS Status: 501(c)3
Highest Offering: Doctorate
Program: Liberal Arts And General; Teacher Preparatory; Professional
Accreditation: M, BUS, BUSA, COPSY, CS, ENG, SCPSY, THEA

01 President .... Dr. Alice P. GAST
05 Provost & VP for Academic Affairs .... Dr. Patrick V. FARRELL
10 Vice Pres Finance & Administration .. Ms. Margaret F. PLYMPTON
88 VP for International Affairs .... Dr. Mohamed S. EL-AASSER
30 Vice President Advancement .... Mr. Joseph P. KENDER, JR.
46 VP & Assoc Prov Research/Graduate .... Dr. Alan J. SNYDER
26 VP Communications & Public Affairs ... Mr. Frederick J. MCGRAIL
88 Chief Investment Officer .... Mr. Peter M. GILBERT
09 Vice Provost Institutional Research .... Dr. J. Gary LUTZ
32 Vice Provost Student Affairs .... Dr. John W. SMEATON
13 Vice Provost Library & Tech Svcs .... Dr. Bruce M. TAGGART
86 Assoc VP for Govt Relations .... Mr. William D. MICHALERYA
21 Assoc VP Finance/Asst Secy Board .... Ms. Denise M. BLEW
15 Assoc Vice Pres for Human Resources .... Ms. Jacqueline MATTHEWS
18 Assoc Vice Pres Facilities Services .. Mr. Henry (Van) V. DOBSON
20 Deputy Provost Academic Affairs .... Mr. Gerald P. LENNON
35 Assoc Vice Provost Dean of Students .... Ms. Sharon K. BASSO
29 Asst Vice Pres of Alumni Relations ... Mr. Robert W. WOLFENDEN
31 Asst VP Community & Regional Affs .... Mr. Dale A. KOCHARD
54 Dean Engineering & Applied Science .... Dr. S. David WU
49 Dean Arts & Sciences .... Dr. Donald E. HALL
50 Interim Dean of Business/Economics .... Dr. Thomas J. HYCLAK
53 Dean of Education .... Dr. Gary M. SASSO
07 Dean of Admissions/Financial Aid .... Mr. J. Leon WASHINGTON
41 Murray H Goodman Dean of Athletics ... Mr. Joseph D. STERRETT
06 Registrar .... Mr. Emil A. GNASSO
37 Director Financial Aid .... Ms. Jennifer L. MERTZ
106 Director Distance Education .... Ms. Margaret A. PORTZ
36 Interim Director Career Services .... Mr. Richard C. FREED
23 Director Health Center .... Dr. Susan C. KITEI
39 Director Residential Services .... Mr. Ozzie BREINER
40 Director Bookstore .... Mr. Brian ADLER
19 Chief University Police .... Mr. Edward K. SHUPP
38 Director of Counseling Services .... Dr. Ian T. BIRKY
42 Chaplain .... Rev. Lloyd H. STEFFEN
43 General Counsel .... Mr. Frank A. ROTH
21 Director of Budget .... Mr. Stephen J. GUTTMAN
28 Director of Diversity .... Mr. Henry U. ODI
96 Manager Strategic Sourcing .... Ms. Jane ALTEMOSE
84 Director Enrollment Management .... Ms. Jennifer E. O'BRIEN

Lincoln Technical Institute (B)

5151 Tilghman Street, Allentown PA 18104-3298
County: Lehigh FICE Identification: 007759
Unit ID: 213570
Telephone: (610) 398-5300 Carnegie Class: Assoc/PrivFP
FAX Number: (610) 395-2706 Calendar System: Semester
URL: www.lincolntech.com
Established: 1946 Annual Undergrad Tuition & Fees: N/A
Enrollment: 637 Coed
Affiliation or Control: Proprietary IRS Status: Proprietary
Highest Offering: Associate Degree
Program: Occupational
Accreditation: ACCSC

01 Executive Director .... Mrs. Lisa M. KUNTZ
05 Director of Education .... Ms. Anne CONNELY
11 Director of Administrative Services .... Mrs. Angela REPPERT
37 Director of Financial Aid .... Ms. Erica BETZ
07 Director of Admissions .... Mr. Mark GARNER
36 Director of Career Services .... Mrs. Charmain BRODY

Lincoln Technical Institute (C)

9191 Torresdale Avenue, Philadelphia PA 19136-1595
County: Philadelphia FICE Identification: 007832
Unit ID: 213589
Telephone: (215) 335-0800 Carnegie Class: Assoc/PrivFP
FAX Number: (215) 335-1443 Calendar System: Other
URL: www.lincolntech.com
Established: 1946 Annual Undergrad Tuition & Fees: $32,070
Enrollment: 364 Coed
Affiliation or Control: Proprietary IRS Status: Proprietary
Highest Offering: Associate Degree
Program: Occupational
Accreditation: ACCSC

01 Executive Director .... Mr. John WILLI
07 Dir Admiss High School/Adult Educ .... Ms. Nicole ZUCCHERI
32 Director of Student Services .... Mr. John FALLOWS
05 Director of Education .... Mr. Michael CONCILIO
11 Director Administrative Services .... Ms. Gina ALTSHULER
36 Director of Career Services .... Ms. TaJuan BUSH

Lincoln University (D)

PO Box 179, 1570 Baltimore Pike, Lincoln University PA 19352-0999
County: Chester FICE Identification: 003290
Unit ID: 213598
Telephone: (484) 365-8000 Carnegie Class: Master's L
FAX Number: (484) 365-7316 Calendar System: Semester
URL: www.lincoln.edu
Established: 1854 Annual Undergrad Tuition & Fees (In-State): $11,351
Enrollment: 1,450 Coed
Affiliation or Control: State Related IRS Status: 501(c)3
Highest Offering: Master's
Program: Liberal Arts And General
Accreditation: M

01 President .... Dr. Robert R. JENNINGS
30 Interim VP for Institutional Advanc .... Ms. Cheryl THOMAS
100 Chief of Staf/Mgr Board of Trustees .... Ms. Diane M. BROWN
05 Sr VP Academic Affairs .... Dr. Kenoye K. EKE
10 Vice Pres Fiscal Affairs/Treasurer .... Mr. Charles GRADOWSKI
32 Vice Pres for Student Affairs .... Dr. F. Carl WALTON
20 Int Asst VP Academic Affs/Info Tech ..... Mr. Harry WASHINGTON
09 Asst VP Institutional Effectiveness .... Dr. Renford A B. BREVETT
07 Director Admissions .... Vacant
08 Director of Library .... Mr. Clevell S. ROSEBORO II
26 Director of Communications .... Mr. Eric C. WEBB
29 Director of Alumni Relations .... Ms. Rita DIBBLE
06 Registrar .... Ms. Catherine RUTLEDGE
30 Director Development & Major Gifts .... Vacant
15 Interim Human Resources Officer .... Mr. James LEWIS
19 Director of Public Safety/Security .... Mr. Larry WOODS
102 Dir Foundation/Corporate Relations .... Vacant
36 Director Counseling/Career Svcs Ctr .... Mr. Ralph SIMPSON
41 Director of Athletics .... Ms. Dianthia FORD-KEE
42 Chaplain .... Mr. Frederick FAISON
21 Controller .... Vacant
18 Chief Facilities/Physical Plant .... Mr. Matt MUSCELLA
39 Int Dean Students and Campus Life .... Dr. Lenetta LEE
85 Director International Services .... Ms. Constance L. LUNDY
23 Director Health Services .... Ms. Velva GREENE-RAINEY
58 Dir Graduate Student Svcs/Admission .... Ms. Jernice LEA
37 Interim Director Financial Aid .... Ms. Kim ANDERSON
96 Director of Purchasing .... Ms. Sue REED
81 Dean Sch of Natural Sciences & Math .... Dr. John O. CHIKWEM
83 Int Dean Sch Soc Sci/Behavioral Std .... Dr. Patricia A. JOSEPH
79 Dean School of Humanities/Grad Stds ... Dr. Cheryl Renee GOOCH
35 Director of Student Life & Develop .... Mr. Ihsan R. MUJAHID
84 Int AVP for Enrollment Management .... Dr. D. Zizwe POE

Lutheran Theological Seminary at Gettysburg (E)

61 Seminary Ridge, Gettysburg PA 17325-1795
County: Adams FICE Identification: 003291
Unit ID: 213631
Telephone: (717) 334-6286 Carnegie Class: Spec/Faith
FAX Number: (717) 334-3469 Calendar System: 4/1/4
URL: www.ltsg.edu
Established: 1826 Annual Graduate Tuition & Fees: $13,650
Enrollment: 123 Coed
Affiliation or Control: Evangelical Lutheran Church In America
IRS Status: 501(c)3
Highest Offering: Doctorate; No Undergraduates
Program: Professional; Religious Emphasis
Accreditation: M, THEOL

01 President .... Rev. Michael L. COOPER-WHITE
30 Chief Advancement Officer .... Rev. Glenn LUDWIG
10 Chief Financial Officer .... Dr. Marty STEVENS
05 Dean of the Seminary .... Dr. Robin J. STEINKE
08 Library Director and Archivist .... Dr. Briant BOHLEKE
06 Registrar .... Dr. Marty STEVENS
26 Exec Asst to Pres for Comm/Plng .... Rev. John R. SPANGLER
91 Director of Info Systems/Ed Tech .... Mr. Donald L. REDMAN
15 Asst to the Pres/Personnel Officer .... Mrs. Carol A. TROYER
07 Director of Admissions .... Rev. Virginia PRICE
21 Staff Accountant .... Ms. Lindsey HANN

Lutheran Theological Seminary at Philadelphia (F)

7301 Germantown Avenue, Philadelphia PA 19119-1794
County: Philadelphia FICE Identification: 003292
Unit ID: 213640
Telephone: (215) 248-4616 Carnegie Class: Spec/Faith
FAX Number: (215) 248-4577 Calendar System: Other
URL: www.ltsp.edu
Established: 1864 Annual Graduate Tuition & Fees: $15,600
Enrollment: 313 Coed
Affiliation or Control: Evangelical Lutheran Church In America
IRS Status: 501(c)3
Highest Offering: Doctorate; No Undergraduates
Program: Professional; Religious Emphasis
Accreditation: M, THEOL

01 President .... Dr. Philip D. KREY
05 Dean .... Dr. J. Jayakiran SEBASTIAN
10 Vice President Finance & Operation .... Vacant
30 Vice President LTSP Foundation .... Rev. John V. PUOTINEN
58 Director of Graduate Studies .... Dr. David GRAFTON
08 Director of the Library .... Dr. Karl KRUEGER
07 VP of Student Development .... Mr. Don JOHNSON
21 Business Office Manager .... Mr. Martin J. SCHWAB
15 Human Resources Manager .... Ms. Lisa HUTCHINSON
32 Coordinator of Student Services .... Rev. Heidi RODRICK-SCHNAATH
06 Registrar .... Ms. Rene DIEMER
37 Director of Financial Aid .... Ms. Elizabeth BRUNTON
39 Coordinator of Housing .... Ms. Sara CALDERON
19 Director of Security/Safety .... Mr. Vincent FERGUSON
13 Director Information Technology .... Mr. Kyle BARGER
27 Director of Communications .... Ms. Merri BROWN
42 Chaplain .... Dr. Nelson RIVERA
108 Vice Pres for Mission Advancement .... Rev. Louise JOHNSON
04 Admin Assist to the President .... Ms. Carrie L. SCHWAB
18 Operations Manager .... Mr. Robert EAGAN

Luzerne County Community College (G)

1333 S Prospect Street, Nanticoke PA 18634-3899
County: Luzerne FICE Identification: 006811
Unit ID: 213659
Telephone: (570) 740-0200 Carnegie Class: Assoc/Pub-S-SC
FAX Number: (570) 740-0386 Calendar System: Semester
URL: www.luzerne.edu
Established: 1966 Annual Undergrad Tuition & Fees (In-District): $3,600
Enrollment: 6,579 Coed
Affiliation or Control: Local IRS Status: 501(c)3
Highest Offering: Associate Degree
Program: Occupational; 2-Year Principally Bachelor's Creditable
Accreditation: M, ACBSP, ADNUR, COARC, DA, DH, SURGT

01 President .... Mr. Thomas P. LEARY
04 Spec Ast to Pres Policy/Staff Devel .... Ms. Laura KATRENICZ
05 Vice Pres Academic Affairs/Provost .... Dr. Dana CLARK
32 Dean Enrollment Mgmt/Student Dev .... Ms. Rosana REYES
103 VP Workforce/Community Development .... Ms. Susan SPRY
16 Dean Human Resources .... Mr. John SEDLAK
66 Dean of Nursing/Health Sciences ... Ms. Deborah VILEGI-PETERS
50 Dean of Business/Technologies .... Vacant
49 Dean of Arts & Sciences .... Vacant
10 Dean Finance .... Mr. Joseph GASPER
13 Chief Technology Office .... Mr. Don NELSON
07 Director Admissions & Recruiting .... Mr. James DOMZALSKI
37 Director of Student Financial Aid .... Ms. Mary KOSIN
08 Director of Library Services .... Mrs. Mia W. BASSHAM
38 Dir Counseling/Stdnt Support Svcs .... Mrs. Linda WALTERS
35 Dir Student Activities/Athletics .... Ms. Mary SULLIVAN
09 Director Inst Research/Planning .... Ms. Graceann PLATUKUS
36 Director Career Services .... Ms. Mary GHILANI
18 Director of Physical Plant .... Mr. Keith GRAHAM
30 Exec Dir of Institutional Advance .... Ms. Sandra NICHOLAS
84 Director Enrollment Management .... Mr. Jim DOMZALSKI
26 Chief Public Relations Officer .... Mrs. Lisa NELSON
29 Director Alumni Relations .... Ms. Bonnie LAUER
96 Director of Purchasing .... Mr. Len OLZINSKI

Lycoming College (H)

700 College Place, Williamsport PA 17701-5192
County: Lycoming FICE Identification: 003293
Unit ID: 213668
Telephone: (570) 321-4000 Carnegie Class: Bac/A&S
FAX Number: (570) 321-4337 Calendar System: Semester
URL: www.lycoming.edu
Established: 1812 Annual Undergrad Tuition & Fees: $33,756
Enrollment: 1,365 Coed
Affiliation or Control: United Methodist IRS Status: 501(c)3
Highest Offering: Baccalaureate
Program: Liberal Arts And General; Fine Arts Emphasis
Accreditation: M

01 President .... Dr. Kent C. TRACHTE
05 Provost and Dean of the College .... Dr. Philip W. SPRUNGER
10 Acting VP Administration/Planning .... Mr. Jeffrey L. BENNETT
30 Vice President for Advancement .... Mr. Charles W. EDMONDS
07 Vice Pres Admissions/Financial Aid .... Mr. James D. SPENCER
21 Controller/Chf Financial Ofcr/Treas .... Mr. Jeffrey L. BENNETT
32 Vice President for Student Life .... Dr. Daniel P. MILLER
89 Assistant Dean for Freshmen .... Mr. Andrew W. KILPATRICK
08 Director of Snowden Library .... Ms. Alison GREGORY
06 Registrar .... Ms. Whitney A. MERINAR
26 Director of College Relations .... Mr. Jerry T. RASHID
37 Director of Financial Aid .... Mr. James LAKIS
14 Assoc Dean/Chief Information Ofcr .... Mr. David B. HEFFNER
36 Director of Career Services .... Ms. MaryJo CAMPANA
29 Director Alumni Relations .... Ms. Amy S. DOWLING
44 Planned Giving Officer .... Ms. Karen M. SHEAFFER
19 Director of Safety & Security .... Mr. Donald TROUTMAN
35 Director of Student Programs ... Mr. Lawrence P. MANNOLINI, III
39 Director Residence Life .... Ms. Mary C. HEISER
41 Director of Athletics .... Mr. Michael CLARK
30 Senior Major Gift Officer .... Mr. Gregory J. BELL
44 Director of Annual Giving .... Ms. Erin MILLER
42 Campus Minister .... Rev. Jeffrey L. LECRONE
16 Director of Human Resources .... Ms. Jackie BILGER

18 Chief Facilities/Physical Plant .... Mr. F. Douglas KUNTZ
23 Director of Health Services .... Ms. Sondra L. STIPCAK
38 Director Student Counseling .... Mr. Townsend VELKOFF
40 Campus Store Manager .... Ms. Patricia E. BAUSINGER
92 Lycoming Scholars .... Dr. Michelle A. BRIGGS
94 Women's Studies .... Dr. N. J. STANLEY
15 Human Resources Coordinator .... Mrs. Cathleen A. LUTZ

Manor College (A)

700 Fox Chase Road, Jenkintown PA 19046-3399
County: Montgomery FICE Identification: 003294
Unit ID: 213774
Telephone: (215) 885-2360 Carnegie Class: Assoc/PrivNFP
FAX Number: (215) 576-6564 Calendar System: Semester
URL: www.manor.edu
Established: 1947 Annual Undergrad Tuition & Fees: $14,620
Enrollment: 926 Coed
Affiliation or Control: Independent Non-Profit IRS Status: 501(c)3
Highest Offering: Associate Degree
Program: Occupational; 2-Year Principally Bachelor's Creditable; Business Emphasis
Accreditation: M, ACBSP, DA, DH

Marywood University (B)

2300 Adams Avenue, Scranton PA 18509-1598
County: Lackawanna FICE Identification: 003296
Unit ID: 213826
Telephone: (570) 348-6211 Carnegie Class: Master's L
FAX Number: (570) 961-4769 Calendar System: Semester
URL: www.marywood.edu
Established: 1915 Annual Undergrad Tuition & Fees: $30,690
Enrollment: 3,267 Coed
Affiliation or Control: Roman Catholic IRS Status: 501(c)3
Highest Offering: Doctorate
Program: Liberal Arts And General; Teacher Preparatory; Professional
Accreditation: M, ACBSP, ARCPA, ART, CACREP, CLPSY, DIETC, DIETD, DIETI, MUS, NUR, SP, SW, TED

01 President .... Sr. Anne MUNLEY
05 Vice Pres Academic Affairs .... Dr. Alan M. LEVINE
10 VP Business Affairs/Treasurer .... Mr. Joseph X. GARVEY, JR.
30 Vice Pres University Advancement .... Ms. Renee G. ZEHEL
32 Vice President Student Life .... Dr. Raymond P. HEATH
84 Vice Pres Enrollment Management .... Ms. Ann BOLAND-CHASE
101 Secretary Univ & General Counsel .... Ms. Mary T. GARDIER PATERSON
15 Assoc Vice Pres for Human Resources .... Dr. Patricia E. DUNLEAVY
26 Assoc VP Marketing/Communication .... Mr. Peter KILCULLEN
18 Asst VP for Buildings & Grounds .... Mrs. Wendy YANKELITIS
44 Asst Vice Pres for Development .... Vacant
35 Dean of Students .... Dr. Amy PACIEJ-WOODRUFF
49 Dean College Liberal Arts/Sciences .... Dr. Frances M. ZAUHAR
53 Int Dean Reap College Ed/Human Dev .... Dr. Alan M. LEVINE
76 Dean Col of Health/Human Svcs .... Dr. Mark E. RODGERS
88 Dn Col of Creative Performing Arts .... Mr. Collier B. PARKER
48 Dean School of Architecture .... Mr. Gregory K. HUNT
90 Director User Support Services .... Dr. Michael MIRABITO
70 Director School of Social Work .... Dr. Diane W. KELLER
08 Director of Library Services .... Mr. David G. SCHAPPERT
06 Registrar .... Ms. Rosemary BURGER
07 Dir of University Admissions .... Mr. Christian DIGREGORIO
21 Controller/Asst Treasurer .... Mr. Patrick E. CASTELLANI
21 Senior Accountant .... Ms. Melissa A. SADDLEMIRE
13 Director of Enterprise Systems .... Mr. Michael P. GIBBONS
88 Asst Director Buildings & Grounds .... Mr. Myron MARCINEK
37 Director of Financial Aid .... Ms. Barbara L. SCHMITT
102 Corporate Foundation Officer .... Ms. Tina L. MCGOVERN
44 Director of Planned Giving .... Ms. Elizabeth A. CONNERY
26 Communications Director .... Ms. Juneann GRECO
44 Director of Capital Resources .... Vacant
29 Assoc Director of Alumni Engagement .... Mr. Leon JOHN, JR.
42 Chaplain/Asst Dir Campus Ministry .... Rev. Joseph P. ELSTON
39 Director Housing/Residence Life .... Mr. Ross NOVAK
41 Director Athletics/Recreation .... Dr. Mary Jo GUNNING
36 Director of Career Services .... Dr. Carole R. GUSTITUS
42 Director of Campus Ministry .... Sr. Catherine LUXNER
88 Director of Dining Services .... Mr. Thomas K. NOTCHICK
27 Chief Information Officer .... Mr. Anthony SPINILLO
27 Telecommunications Manager .... Mr. Martin O'CONNOR
19 Sr Dir Sec/Safety/Environ Complnce .... Mr. David R. ELLIOTT
23 Director of Student Health Services .... Ms. Linda MCDADE
38 Director Counseling & Student Devel .... Dr. Robert S. SHAW
40 Bookstore Manager .... Ms. Joan DIEHL
104 Assoc Dir International Affairs .... Mr. David A. CRISCI
14 Director of Operations .... Mr. John B. PORTER
30 Dir Advance Svcs/Scholar/Stewardshp .... Ms. Gretchen FRITZ
29 Director of Alumni Engagement .... Vacant
35 Dir of Student Act/Leadership Devel .... Ms. Callie FRIELER
28 Director of Diversity Services .... Dr. Lia Richards PALMITER
88 Director Human Physiology Lab .... Vacant
09 Dir of Planning & Inst Research .... Dr. Ellen BOYLAN
45 Chief Planning Officer .... Vacant
90 Asst Director of User Support .... Ms. Katherine P. LEWIS

McCann School of Business & Technology (C)

2200 North Irving Street, Allentown PA 18109
Telephone: (484) 223-4601 Identification: 770768
Accreditation: ACICS, SURGT

† Main campus is McCann School of Business & Technology in Pottsville, PA.

McCann School of Business & Technology (D)

346 York Road, Carlisle PA 17013
Telephone: (714) 218-3400 Identification: 770767
Accreditation: ACICS

† Main campus is McCann School of Business & Technology in Pottsville, PA.

McCann School of Business & Technology (E)

2227 Scranton Carbondale Highway, Dickson City PA 18519
Telephone: (570) 969-4330 Identification: 770769
Accreditation: ACICS, MAC

† Main campus is McCann School of Business & Technology in Pottsville, PA.

McCann School of Business & Technology (F)

370 Maplewood Drive, Humbolt Ind Pk, Hazleton PA 18202-9790
Telephone: (570) 454-6172 Identification: 666484
Accreditation: ACICS, MAC, SURGT

† Main campus is McCann School of Business & Technology in Pottsville, PA.

McCann School of Business & Technology (G)

2650 Woodglen Road, Pottsville PA 17901-1335
County: Schuylkill FICE Identification: 004898
Unit ID: 438212
Telephone: (570) 622-7622 Carnegie Class: Assoc/PrivFP
FAX Number: (570) 622-7770 Calendar System: Quarter
URL: www.mccann.edu
Established: 1897 Annual Undergrad Tuition & Fees: $9,820
Enrollment: 2,994 Coed
Affiliation or Control: Proprietary IRS Status: Proprietary
Highest Offering: Associate Degree
Program: Occupational
Accreditation: ACICS, MAC

01 Director Pottsville Campus .... Ms. Shannon BRENNAN
05 Director of Education .... Ms. MaryLou ORAM
36 Director of Career Services .... Ms. Michelle SCRIBBICK

McCann School of Business & Technology (H)

1147 N Fourth Street, Sunbury PA 17801-3413
Telephone: (570) 286-3058 Identification: 666485
Accreditation: ACICS, COARC, MAC, SURGT

† Main campus is McCann School of Business & Technology in Pottsville, PA.

McCann School of Business & Technology (I)

264 Highland Park Boulevard, Wilkes Barre PA 18702
Telephone: (570) 235-2200 Identification: 770770
Accreditation: ACICS

† Main campus is McCann School of Business & Technology in Pottsville, PA.

Mercyhurst University (J)

501 E 38th Street, Erie PA 16546-0001
County: Erie FICE Identification: 003297
Unit ID: 213987
Telephone: (814) 824-2000 Carnegie Class: Master's S
FAX Number: (814) 824-2438 Calendar System: 4/1/4
URL: www.mercyhurst.edu
Established: 1926 Annual Undergrad Tuition & Fees: $30,300
Enrollment: 4,323 Coed
Affiliation or Control: Roman Catholic IRS Status: 501(c)3
Highest Offering: Doctorate
Program: Occupational; 2-Year Principally Bachelor's Creditable; Liberal Arts And General; Teacher Preparatory; Professional
Accreditation: M, ADNUR, DANCE, IACBE, MUS, OTA, PTAA, SW

01 President .... Dr. Thomas J. GAMBLE
03 Provost/Sr Counselor to President .... Dr. James M. ADOVASIO
05 Vice Pres Acad Affs/Dean of College .... Dr. Phil J. BELFIORE
10 Exec Vice Pres and CFO .... Dr. Gary BROWN
84 VP Enrollment & Adult/Grad Pgm .... Dr. Michael P. LYDEN
10 Vice Pres of Finance & Treasurer .... Ms. Jane M. KELSEY
12 Exec VP Mercyhurst - NE/West .... Dr. Kenneth ZIRKLE
30 Vice Pres Development/Alumni Rels .... Dr. David RUBINO
32 Vice Pres of Student Development .... Dr. Gerry A. TOBIN
21 Associate Business Officer .... Mr. James F. LIEB
14 Chief Information Officer .... Ms. Jeanette BRITT
18 Director Facilities/Physical Plant .... Mr. Kenneth STEPHERSON
38 Director Student Counseling Service .... Ms. Judy SMITH
07 Director of Undergrad Admissions .... Mr. Christopher COONS
06 Registrar .... Sr. Patricia WHALEN
08 Director of Libraries .... Ms. Darcy JONES
39 Dir Residential Life/Stdnt Conduct .... Ms. Alice AGNEW
19 Director of Public Safety Programs .... Mr. Robert KUHN
29 Director of Alumni Services .... Mr. Ryan PALM
42 Director of Campus Ministry .... Fr. James PISZKER
37 Director of Student Financial Svcs .... Ms. Carrie NEWMAN
41 Director of Athletics .... Mr. Joseph KIMBALL
09 Director of Institutional Research .... Mrs. Sheila W. RICHTER
15 Director Human Resources .... Mr. Jim TOMETSKO
28 Director Multicultural Affairs .... Ms. Petrina WILLIAMS

Mercyhurst University Northeast (K)

16 W Division Street, North East PA 16428
Telephone: (814) 725-6100 Identification: 770161
Accreditation: &M, COARC, MLTAD

† Main campus is Mercyhurst University in Erie, PA.

Messiah College (L)

One College Avenue, Mechanicsburg PA 17055
County: Cumberland FICE Identification: 003298
Unit ID: 213996
Telephone: (717) 766-2511 Carnegie Class: Bac/Diverse
FAX Number: (717) 691-6025 Calendar System: Semester
URL: www.messiah.edu
Established: 1909 Annual Undergrad Tuition & Fees: $30,470
Enrollment: 2,798 Coed
Affiliation or Control: Interdenominational IRS Status: 501(c)3
Highest Offering: Master's
Program: Liberal Arts And General; Teacher Preparatory; Professional
Accreditation: M, ACBSP, ART, CACREP, DIETD, ENG, MUS, NURSE, SW, THEA

01 President .... Dr. Kim S. PHIPPS
05 Provost .... Dr. Randall G. BASINGER
30 Vice President for Advancement .... Mr. Barry G. GOODLING
84 Vice Pres for Enrollment Management .... Mr. John A. CHOPKA
10 Vice Pres for Finance & Planning .... Mr. David S. WALKER
15 VP for Human Res & Compliance .... Ms. Amanda A. COFFEY
27 VP Info Technology/Assoc Provost .... Dr. William G. STRAUSBAUGH
11 Vice President for Operations .... Mrs. Kathrynne G. SHAFER
32 Vice Provost & Dean of Students .... Dr. Kristin M. HANSEN-KIEFFER
58 Assoc Provost Grad & Nontrad Pgms .... Dr. John ADDLEMAN
28 Spec Asst Prov & Pres Div Affairs .... Dr. Bernardo A. MICHAEL
57 Dean School of the Arts .... Dr. Richard E. ROBERSON
53 Dean Sch Bus/Educ/Soc Sci .... Dr. Carolyn MAURER
79 Dean School of Humanities .... Dr. Peter K. POWERS
81 Dean School of Sci/Engr/Health .... Dr. W. Ray NORMAN
35 Associate Dean of Students .... Mr. Douglas M. WOOD
104 Director of Education Abroad .... Mrs. Wendy S. LIPPERT
85 Director Intl Student Programs .... Mr. Kevin J. VILLEGAS
07 Director of Admissions .... Mrs. Dana J. BRITTON
37 Director of Financial Aid .... Mr. Gregory L. GEARHART
39 Director of Housing .... Ms. Rhonda L. GOOD
21 Dir Financial Operations/Controller .... Mrs. Wendy S. STARNER
96 Director of Procurement .... Vacant
06 Registrar .... Mr. James J. SOTHERDEN
08 Director of the Murray Library .... Mr. Jonathan D. LAUER
91 Director Information Services .... Mr. John P. LUFT
90 Dir Learning Technology Services .... Mrs. Susan K. SHANNON
09 Assoc Dir Institutional Research .... Ms. Laura M. MILLER
42 College Pastor .... Rev. Eldon E. FRY
30 Director of Development .... Dr. Jon C. STUCKEY
26 Dir of Marketing & Public Relations .... Mrs. Carla E. GROSS
29 Director Alumni & Parent Relations .... Mr. Jay W. MCCLYMONT
44 Director of Annual Giving .... Ms. Beth TROTT CLARK
38 Director Counseling/Health Services .... Dr. Philip J. LAWLIS
23 Coordinator of Health Services .... Mrs. Judith M. GROOP
12 Program Dir Philadelphia Campus .... Mr. Ryan R. GLADWIN
41 Director of Athletics .... Mr. Jack T. COLE
92 Dir of the College Honors Program .... Dr. Dean C. CURRY
18 Director of Facility Services .... Mr. Bradley A. MARKLEY
36 Director of Career Development .... Mrs. Christina R. HANSON
40 Director of Campus Store .... Ms. Mindy W. LANGE
19 Director Safety/Dispatch Services .... Ms. Cindy L. BURGER

Metropolitan Career Center Computer Technology Institute (M)

100 S Broad Street, Suite 830, Philadelphia PA 19110-1018
County: Philadelphia FICE Identification: 031091
Unit ID: 214023
Telephone: (215) 568-9215 Carnegie Class: Assoc/PrivNFP
FAX Number: (215) 568-3511 Calendar System: Semester
URL: www.CareersInIT.org
Established: 1974 Annual Undergrad Tuition & Fees: $24,194
Enrollment: 82 Coed
Affiliation or Control: Independent Non-Profit IRS Status: 501(c)3
Highest Offering: Associate Degree
Program: Occupational; Technical Emphasis
Accreditation: ACCSC

01 President .... Dr. Richard COHEN
03 Executive Director .... Ms. Amy MILLER
10 Controller .... Mr. Timothy DONOHUE
88 School Director .... Ms. Amy MILLER
05 Director of Education .... Ms. Josanne FORD
37 Financial Aid Director .... Ms. Madeline SARGENT
07 Admissions Representative .... Mr. Samuel JOHNSON
07 Admissions Representative .... Ms. Judith STRAFFE
36 Relationship Manager .... Ms. Christina HARRIS

Misericordia University (A)

301 Lake Street, Dallas PA 18612-1098
County: Luzerne FICE Identification: 003247
Unit ID: 214069
Telephone: (570) 674-6400 Carnegie Class: Master's M
FAX Number: (570) 675-2441 Calendar System: Semester
URL: www.misericordia.edu
Established: 1924 Annual Undergrad Tuition & Fees: $26,670
Enrollment: 2,261 Coed
Affiliation or Control: Roman Catholic IRS Status: 501(c)3
Highest Offering: Doctorate
Program: Liberal Arts And General; Teacher Preparatory; Professional
Accreditation: M, #ARCPA, DMS, IACBE, NMT, NURSE, OT, PTA, RAD, SP, SW

01 President .... Dr. Thomas J. BOTZMAN
10 Vice Pres Finance & Administration .... Mr. Eric NELSON
05 Vice President Academic Affairs .... Dr. Mari P. KING
30 VP of Institutional Advancement .... Ms. Susan M. HELWIG
32 Vice President of Student Affairs .... Sr. Jean MESSAROS
45 VP of Planning/Assessment & Rsrch .... Dr. Barbara SAMUEL LOFTUS
45 Chief Information/Planning Officer .... Vacant
21 Controller .... Mr. Ronald S. HROMISIN
06 Registrar .... Mr. Joseph REDINGTON
84 Director Enrollment Management .... Ms. Jane F. DESSOYE
29 Director Alumni Relations .... Ms. Denise MISCAVAGE
08 Librarian .... Ms. Martha STEVENSON
04 Admin Assistant to the President .... Ms. Carol FAHNESTOCK
96 Director of Purchasing .... Mr. Thomas F. KANE
38 Exec Dir Learning Resource Ctr .... Ms. Amy LAHART
42 Director Campus Ministry .... Ms. Christine SOMERS
41 Director of Athletics .... Mr. David MARTIN
39 Director of Residents .... Ms. Donna ELLIS
13 Director of Management Info Systems .... Mr. Joseph J. MACK
14 Director of Information Technology .... Mr. Val APANOVICH
35 Director of Student Activities .... Ms. Darcy BRODMERKEL
36 Dir Insalaco Ctr Career Development .... Ms. Bernadette RUSHMER
102 Dir Foundation/Government Relations .... Mr. Larry PELLEGRINI
51 Director of Adult Education .... Mrs. Barbara LEGGAT
16 Director of Human Resources .... Ms. Pamela PARSNIK
07 Director of Admissions .... Mr. Glenn BOZINSKI
26 Dir of Public Relations/Marketing .... Mr. James ROBERTS
37 Director of Financial Aid .... Ms. Susan FRONZONI
28 Director of Multicultural Initiativ .... Dr. Scott RICHARDSON
19 Assoc Director Security/Safety .... Mr. Robert ZAVADA
18 Director of Facilities .... Mr. Paul MURPHY
09 Asst Dir of Institutional Research .... Ms. Sharon HUDAK
90 Manager of User Services .... Mr. David A. JOHNDROW

Montgomery County Community College (B)

340 Dekalb Pike, Blue Bell PA 19422-1400
County: Montgomery FICE Identification: 004452
Unit ID: 214111
Telephone: (215) 641-6300 Carnegie Class: Assoc/Pub-S-MC
FAX Number: (215) 461-1460 Calendar System: Semester
URL: www.mc3.edu
Established: 1964 Annual Undergrad Tuition & Fees (In-District): $3,672
Enrollment: 13,645 Coed
Affiliation or Control: State/Local IRS Status: 501(c)3
Highest Offering: Associate Degree
Program: Occupational; 2-Year Principally Bachelor's Creditable
Accreditation: M, ADNUR, DH, IFSAC, MAC, MLTAD, PHLEB, RAD, SURGT

01 President .... Dr. Karen A. STOUT
04 Exec Assistant to the President .... Mr. Joshua SCHWARTZ
101 Exec Asst to the Board of Trustees .... Ms. Deborah ROGERS
12 VP of the West Campus .... Dr. Steady MOONO
27 VP for Information Technology .... Ms. Celeste M. SCHWARTZ
10 VP for Finance & Administration .... Mr. Thomas FREITAG
26 Vice Pres of Devel & External Rels .... Ms. Sharon BEALES
84 VP for Student Affairs & Enrol Mgt .... Dr. Kathrine SWANSON
05 VP for Academic Affairs & Provost .... Dr. Victoria BASTECKI-PEREZ
06 Registrar .... Ms. Cynthia MCCABE
15 Executive Director Human Resources .... Ms. Diane O'CONNOR
21 Assoc VP for Finance & Admin .... Mr. Brent PARKER
21 Controller .... Ms. Kathleen MCGIRR
44 Dir of Annual Giving & Adv Services .... Ms. Megan SNEERINGER
19 Director of Campus Safety .... Mr. Joseph MCGURIMAN
07 Director of Admissions .... Vacant
08 Director of Library Services .... Vacant
37 Director of Financial Aid .... Ms. Tracey RICHARDS
09 Director of Institutional Research .... Mr. Leon HILL
28 Dir Equity & Diversity Initiatives .... Ms. Rose MAKOFSKE
29 Director of Major Gifts and Alumni .... Ms. Leslie BLUESTONE
27 Director Media/Public Relations .... Ms. Alana MAUGER
103 Dean Workforce Development & CE .... Ms. Suzanne HOLLOMAN
86 Exec Dir of Govt Relations .... Ms. Margaret LEE-CLARK
41 Dir of Athletics & Campus Rec .... Mr. Bruce BACH
44 Sr Dir of Major and Planned Gifts .... Ms. Arline STEPHAN

Montgomery County Community College West Campus (C)

101 College Drive, Pottstown PA 19464
Telephone: (610) 718-1800 Identification: 770162
Accreditation: &M

† Main campus is Montgomery County Community College in Blue Bell, PA.

Moore College of Art and Design (D)

20th and The Parkway, Philadelphia PA 19103-1179
County: Philadelphia FICE Identification: 003300
Unit ID: 214148
Telephone: (215) 568-4515 Carnegie Class: Spec/Arts
FAX Number: (215) 568-8017 Calendar System: Semester
URL: www.moore.edu
Established: 1848 Annual Undergrad Tuition & Fees: $31,895
Enrollment: 529 Female
Affiliation or Control: Independent Non-Profit IRS Status: 501(c)3
Highest Offering: Master's
Program: Religious Emphasis
Accreditation: M, ART, CIDA

01 President .... Dr. Cecelia FITZGIBBON
10 Vice Pres Finance & Administration .... Mr. William L. HILL, II
05 Academic Dean .... Ms. Dona LANTZ
32 Dean of Students .... Ms. Ruth ROBBINS
20 Assoc Dean Educational Support Svcs .... Mrs. Claudine R. THOMAS
39 Director Residence Life/Housing .... Ms. Carienne MYSLINSKI
88 Executive Director of Galleries .... Ms. Kaytie JOHNSON
51 Co-Director of Continuing Education .... Ms. Judith WOODWORTH
51 Co-Director of Continuing Education .... Mrs. Natalie PAYNE
26 Dir of Marketing/Communications .... Mr. Roy WILBUR
30 Director of Development .... Ms. Linda PORCH
29 Director Alumnae Affairs .... Ms. Doris CHORNEY
08 Library Director .... Ms. Sharon WATSON-MAURO
07 Exec Director of Admissions .... Ms. Elizabeth MATHIS
37 Director of Financial Aid .... Ms. Melissa WALSH
06 Registrar .... Ms. Cynthia VIOLET
18 Director of Operations .... Mr. Kenneth M. FERRETTI
15 Director Human Resources .... Ms. Rachel PHILLIPS
36 Director Career Services .... Ms. Belena CHAPP
58 Director of Graduate Studies .... Ms. Mechele MANNO
38 Director Student Counseling .... Ms. Ruth R. GAYLE
90 Academic Computing Manager .... Mr. Dennis DAWTON

Moravian College (E)

1200 Main Street, Bethlehem PA 18018-6650
County: Northampton FICE Identification: 003301
Unit ID: 214157
Telephone: (610) 861-1300 Carnegie Class: Bac/A&S
FAX Number: (610) 625-7918 Calendar System: Semester
URL: www.moravian.edu
Established: 1742 Annual Undergrad Tuition & Fees: $35,518
Enrollment: 1,907 Coed
Affiliation or Control: Moravian Church IRS Status: 501(c)3
Highest Offering: Master's
Program: Liberal Arts And General; Teacher Preparatory; Professional; Nursing Emphasis
Accreditation: M, MUS, NURSE, THEOL

01 President .... Dr. Bryon L. GRIGSBY
04 Assistant to the President .... Vacant
05 Vice President Academic Affairs .... Dr. Gordon WEIL
10 Vice President Finance & Admin .... Mr. Mark F. REED
21 Treasurer .... Ms. Anne M. REID
30 Vice Pres Institutional Advancement .... Mr. Gary CARNEY
32 Vice President Student Affairs .... Dr. Nicole L. LOYD
73 Vice Pres/Dean of the Seminary .... Dr. Frank CROUCH
84 Vice President for Enrollment .... Ms. Carole A. REESE
35 Dean of Students .... Dr. Nicole L. LOYD
88 Director of Leadership Development .... Ms. Catherine DANTSIN
20 Assoc Dean for Academic Affairs .... Dr. Carol TRAUPMAN-CARR
24 Director of Learning Services .... Ms. Laurie ROTH
88 Director of Event Management .... Mrs. Ann E. CLAUSSEN
21 Dir Business/Financial Operations .... Ms. Amy JOHNSON
21 Bursar .... Ms. Susan O'HARE
96 Assoc Director of Business Affairs .... Mr. Brian G. BLENIS
15 Chief Human Resources Officer .... Mr. Jon B. CONRAD
44 Director of Leadership Giving .... Ms. Bertie KNISELY
18 Dir Facilities Mgt Plng/Construct .... Mr. Douglas J. PLOTTS
19 Director of Campus Safety .... Mr. George BOKSAN
26 Director of Public Relations .... Mr. Michael P. WILSON
08 Library Director .... Vacant
06 Registrar .... Ms. Alexandra HAY
88 Director of Sports Information .... Mr. Mark J. FLEMING
27 Director of Publications .... Mrs. Susan O. WOOLLEY
29 Director of Alumni Relations .... Ms. Marsha STILES
37 Director of Financial Aid .... Ms. Colby MCCARTHY
36 Director Career Development Svcs .... Ms. Amy SAUL
38 Director of Counseling .... Dr. Ronald J. KLINE
58 Dean Continuing/Graduate Studies .... Dr. Donna SMITH
13 Director Information Technology .... Mr. Stephen MCKINNEY
40 Director of Bookstore .... Mrs. Sandra M. GIORDANO
41 Director of Athletics .... Mr. Scot DAPP
42 College Chaplain .... Rev. Jennika BORGER
88 Director of the Payne Gallery .... Dr. Diane C. RADYCKI
88 Director of Constituent Relations .... Ms. Deborah L. EVANS
23 Health Services Coordinator .... Mrs. Mary S. SEK
88 Director of International Studies .... Mr. Kerry SETHI
28 Dir Instl Diversity/Multicul Affs .... Ms. Sharon A. BROWN
24 Media Center Manager .... Mr. Craig UNDERWOOD
09 Director Institutional Research .... Ms. Carole A. REESE

Moravian Theological Seminary (F)

60 W Locust Street, Bethlehem PA 18018
Telephone: (610) 861-1516 Identification: 770163
Accreditation: &M

† Main campus is Moravian College in Bethlehem, PA.

Mount Aloysius College (G)

7373 Admiral Peary Highway, Cresson PA 16630-1999
County: Cambria FICE Identification: 003302
Unit ID: 214166
Telephone: (814) 886-6300 Carnegie Class: Bac/Assoc
FAX Number: (814) 886-2978 Calendar System: Semester
URL: www.mtaloy.edu
Established: 1853 Annual Undergrad Tuition & Fees: $19,520
Enrollment: 1,768 Coed
Affiliation or Control: Independent Non-Profit IRS Status: 501(c)3
Highest Offering: Master's
Program: Occupational; 2-Year Principally Bachelor's Creditable; Liberal Arts And General
Accreditation: M, ADNUR, DMS, MAC, MLTAD, NUR, PTAA, SURGT

01 President .... Dr. Thomas P. FOLEY
05 Sr VP Academic Affs/Dean of Faculty .... Dr. Timothy FULOP
11 Sr VP Administrative Services .... Ms. Suzanne P. CAMPBELL
32 VP Student Affs/Dean Students .... Dr. Jane M. GRASSADONIA
84 VP Enrollment Mgmt/Dean Admissions .... Mr. Francis C. CROUSE, JR.
07 Director of Freshmen Admissions .... Mr. Andrew D. CLOUSE
07 Director of Transfer Admissions .... Mr. Richard MISHLER
30 VP Institutional Advancement .... Ms. Jennifer DUBUQUE
10 Controller/CFO .... Ms. Donna K. YODER
06 Registrar .... Mr. Christopher M. LOVETT
08 Director of Library Services .... Vacant
37 Director of Financial Aid .... Ms. Stacy L. SCHENK
15 Director of Human Resources .... Ms. Tonia J. GORDON
26 Director of Communications .... Mr. John COYLE
44 Major Gifts Officer .... Mr. Michael A. GREER
13 Director of Information Technology .... Mr. Rich J. SHEA
23 Director of Health Services .... Ms. Shannon D. GROVE
40 Director of Bookstore .... Ms. Christine M. CLINTON
41 Director of Athletics .... Mr. Ryan M. SMITH
19 Director of Safety & Security .... Mr. William H. TREXLER
18 Director of Physical Plant .... Mr. Gerald RUBRITZ
09 Institutional Researcher .... Mr. Bryan J. PEARSON
36 Director Career Services .... Vacant
38 Dir Student Counseling/Disabilities .... Ms. Marisa L. EVANS
39 Director of Residence Life .... Ms. Christina KOREN
42 Director Campus Ministry .... Sr. Nancy E. DONOVAN, RSM
44 Director Annual Giving .... Ms. Sally GORDON

Muhlenberg College (H)

2400 West Chew Street, Allentown PA 18104-5586
County: Lehigh FICE Identification: 003304
Unit ID: 214175
Telephone: (484) 664-3100 Carnegie Class: Bac/A&S
FAX Number: (484) 664-3234 Calendar System: Semester
URL: www.muhlenberg.edu
Established: 1848 Annual Undergrad Tuition & Fees: $42,755
Enrollment: 2,242 Coed
Affiliation or Control: Evangelical Lutheran Church In America
IRS Status: 501(c)3
Highest Offering: Baccalaureate
Program: Liberal Arts And General; Teacher Preparatory
Accreditation: M

01 President .... Dr. Peyton R. HELM
05 Provost .... Dr. John G. RAMSAY
10 Treasurer & Vice Pres for Finance .... Mr. Kent DYER
26 Vice President of Public Relations .... Mr. Michael S. BRUCKNER
30 VP Development & Alumni Relations .... Ms. Rebekkah L. BROWN
15 Vice President of Human Resources .... Ms. Anne SPECK
04 Exec Assistant to the President .... Mr. Ken BUTLER
102 Asst VP Corporate/Found & Govt Rels .... Ms. Deborah J. KIPP
32 Dean of Students .... Ms. Karen GREEN
88 Dean of College for Academic Life .... Dr. Michael HUBER
20 Assoc Dean Institutional Assessment .... Dr. Kathleen E. HARRING
86 Assoc Dean International Programs .... Dr. Donna M. KISH-GOODLING
37 Associate Dean Financial Aid .... Mr. Gregory S. MITTON
88 Assistant Dean of Academic Life .... Ms. Wendy P. COLE
29 Alumni Relations Director .... Ms. Natalie HAND
55 Dean Wescoe Sch Muhlenberg College .... Ms. Jane E. HUDAK
07 Dean Admissions/Financial Aid .... Mr. Christopher HOOKER-HARING
08 Director of Trexler Library .... Ms. Tina L. HERTEL
06 Registrar .... Ms. Deborah TAMTE-HORAN
13 Director Information Technology .... Mr. Harry E. MILLER
19 Director of Campus Safety/Security .... Mr. Robert GERKEN
39 Director of Residence Life .... Ms. Janette SCHUMACHER
36 Director of the Career Center .... Ms. Alana M. ALBUS
21 Assistant Treasurer .... Mr. Jason FEIERTAG
23 Director of Student Health Services .... Ms. Brynnmarie DORSEY
38 Director Counseling Services .... Ms. Anita KELLY
42 Chaplain .... Rev. Callista S. ISABELLE
09 Director of Institutional Research .... Ms. Nicole HAMMEL
18 Chief Facilities/Physical Plant .... Mr. Michael H. BREWER
96 Director of Purchasing .... Ms. Elizabeth M. LEES
40 Bookstore Manager .... Ms. Karen R. NORMANN

Neumann University (I)

One Neumann Drive, Aston PA 19014-1298
County: Delaware FICE Identification: 003988
Unit ID: 214272
Telephone: (610) 459-0905 Carnegie Class: Master's M
FAX Number: (610) 459-1370 Calendar System: Semester
URL: www.neumann.edu
Established: 1965 Annual Undergrad Tuition & Fees: $24,948

Enrollment: 3,100 Coed
Affiliation or Control: Roman Catholic IRS Status: 501(c)3
Highest Offering: Doctorate
Program: Liberal Arts And General; Teacher Preparatory; Professional
Accreditation: M, ACBSP, CACREP, MT, NUR, PTA

01 President ... Dr. Rosalie M. MIRENDA
05 Vice President Academic Affairs ... Dr. Gerard P. O'SULLIVAN
43 Vice President and General Counsel ... Mr. Jonathan PERI
10 Vice Pres Finance/Administration ... Mr. Joseph GORMAN
42 Vice President Mission/Ministry ... Sr. Marguerite O'BEIRNE, OSF
30 Vice Pres Inst Advance/Univ Rels ... Mr. Henry A. SUMNER
84 Vice Pres Enrollment/Student Affs ... Mr. Dennis J. MURPHY
15 Vice President HR & Risk Management ... Mr. David W. BROWNLEE
49 Dean Division of Arts & Science ... Dr. Alfred G. MUELLER, II
50 Dean Div of Business & Info Mgmt ... Ms. Janet MASSEY
53 Dean Div of Education/Human Svcs ... Dr. Joseph E. GILLESPIE
51 Int Dean of Cont Adult/Prof Stds ... Dr. Robert D. BUNNELL
66 Dean Div Nursing/Health Sciences ... Dr. Kathleen HOOVER
04 Assistant to President ... Ms. Danielle WAGNER
06 Registrar ... Mr. Larry S. FRIEDMAN
18 Facilities Director ... Mr. Earl WORSHAM
19 Director Safety & Security ... Mr. Leon FRANCIS
08 Director Library ... Ms. Tiffany MCGREGOR
26 Exec Director Mktg/Communications ... Mr. Stephen BELL
09 Director Institutional Research ... Ms. Melissa THORPE
42 Chaplain ... Rev. Philip J. LOWE, OFM
44 Director Annual Giving/Prospect Mgt ... Ms. Christina FARRELL
29 Dir Alumni Rels/Special Programs ... Ms. Judi STANAITIS
88 Director Inst Gifts/Donor Rels ... Ms. Josephina E. BANNER
38 Director Counseling ... Mr. Fritz HAAS
39 Director Residence Life ... Mr. Michael WEBSTER
13 Exec Director University Computing ... Mr. David O'LEARY
24 Director Academic Resource Center ... Ms. Theresa HUKE
41 Director Athletics ... Mr. Chuck SACK
36 Director Career Services ... Vacant
88 Director of Academic Advising ... Mr. Michael MULLEN
88 Director Child Development Center ... Ms. Mary Ann MELISI
21 Controller ... Mr. John YOUHOUSE
37 Director Financial Assistance ... Ms. Deborah CRAWLEY
23 Director Health Services ... Ms. Janet GEDDIS
96 Director of Purchasing ... Ms. Elena BARRAR
88 Director Physical Therapy Program ... Dr. Robert POST
07 Director of Admissions ... Ms. Kidesti TEKLEGIORGIS
88 VPMM/Dir Ctr for Sprt/Spir/Char Dev ... Sr. Marguerite O'BEIRNE, OSF
90 Director Instructional Technology ... Mr. Scott BEADENKOPF
88 Director Conference/Scheduling Svcs ... Ms. Alexis SINKOW
40 Director University Bookstore ... Ms. Natalie VAN WYK
108 Assistant VP for Assessmen/Learning ... Dr. Janet THIEL, OSF
88 Director Development Education ... Ms. Lori PELLESCKI
104 Coord International Studies Educ ... Mr. Scott KELLER
88 Coord Student Retention Services ... Ms. Coleen NEDBALSKI

New Castle School of Trades (A)

4117 Pulaski Road, New Castle PA 16101
County: Lawrence FICE Identification: 007780
Unit ID: 214290
Telephone: (724) 964-8811 Carnegie Class: Assoc/PrivFP
FAX Number: (724) 202-6147 Calendar System: Other
URL: www.ncstrades.edu
Established: 1945 Annual Undergrad Tuition & Fees: $16,650
Enrollment: 664 Coed
Affiliation or Control: Proprietary IRS Status: Proprietary
Highest Offering: Associate Degree
Program: Occupational; 2-Year Principally Bachelor's Creditable; Technical Emphasis
Accreditation: ACCSC

01 Director ... Mr. Jim BUTTERMORE
05 Director of Education ... Mr. Tony GIOVANNELLI
07 Director Admiss/Veterans Affs Ofcr ... Mr. Jim CATHELINE
10 Fiscal Director ... Mrs. JoAnn MELNIK
36 Director Student Placement ... Ms. Carrie KRAYNAK
37 Director Student Financial Aid ... Miss Trudy SOTTER

Newport Business Institute (B)

945 Greensburg Road, Lower Burrell PA 15068-3929
County: Westmoreland FICE Identification: 004901
Unit ID: 214315
Telephone: (724) 339-7542 Carnegie Class: Assoc/PrivFP
FAX Number: (724) 339-2950 Calendar System: Quarter
URL: www.nbi.edu
Established: 1895 Annual Undergrad Tuition & Fees: $12,450
Enrollment: 72 Coed
Affiliation or Control: Proprietary IRS Status: Proprietary
Highest Offering: Associate Degree
Program: Occupational
Accreditation: ACICS

01 Director ... Ms. Janie GATTY
05 Dean of Academic Affairs ... Mr. Michael CHOMA
58 Director of Graduate Services ... Mrs. Nancy DONATUCCI
37 Director of Financial Aid ... Mrs. Rosemary LEIPERTZ
07 Admissions Coordinator ... Mr. Don ACKER

Newport Business Institute (C)

941 W Third Street, Williamsport PA 17701-5855
County: Lycoming FICE Identification: 004914
Unit ID: 216986
Telephone: (570) 326-2869 Carnegie Class: Assoc/PrivFP
FAX Number: (570) 326-2136 Calendar System: Quarter
URL: www.nbi.edu
Established: 1955 Annual Undergrad Tuition & Fees: $12,675
Enrollment: 54 Coed
Affiliation or Control: Proprietary IRS Status: Proprietary
Highest Offering: Associate Degree
Program: Occupational
Accreditation: ACICS

01 Director ... Mrs. Janie GATTY

Northampton Community College (D)

3835 Green Pond Road, Bethlehem PA 18020-7599
County: Northampton FICE Identification: 007191
Unit ID: 214379
Telephone: (610) 861-5300 Carnegie Class: Assoc/Pub-S-MC
FAX Number: (610) 861-5070 Calendar System: Semester
URL: www.northampton.edu
Established: 1966 Annual Undergrad Tuition & Fees (In-District): $3,690
Enrollment: 11,018 Coed
Affiliation or Control: State/Local IRS Status: 170(c)1
Highest Offering: Associate Degree
Program: Occupational; 2-Year Principally Bachelor's Creditable
Accreditation: M, ACBSP, ADNUR, DH, DMS, FUSER, PNUR, RAD

01 President ... Dr. Mark H. ERICKSON
05 Vice President Academic Affairs ... Dr. Jeffrey W. FOCHT
11 Vice Pres Administrative Affairs ... Ms. Helene M. WHITAKER
10 Vice President Finance & Operations ... Mr. James F. DUNLEAVY
30 Vice Pres Institutional Advancement ... Ms. Sheri JONES
32 Vice President Student Affairs ... Ms. Margaret MCGUIRE-CLOSSON
31 Vice President Community Education ... Dr. Paul E. PIERPOINT
12 Dean Monroe Campus ... Dr. Matthew J. CONNELL
79 Dean Humanities & Social Sciences ... Dr. Christine PENSE
53 Dean Education/Academic Success ... Dr. Elizabeth BUGAIGHIS
50 Interim Dean Business & Technology ... Ms. Denise FRANCOIS-SEENY
76 Dean Allied Health & Sciences ... Ms. Carolyn BORTZ
13 Dean & Chief Information Officer ... Dr. Deborah BURAK
27 Director Public Info/Community Rels ... Ms. Heidi BUTLER
06 Registrar ... Ms. Carolyn H. MOYER
07 Director Admissions ... Mr. James MCCARTHY
37 Director Financial Aid ... Ms. Cynthia L. KING
45 Dir Plng/Assessment/Instl Effective ... Dr. E. Jill HIRT
15 Director of Human Resources ... Ms. Kathy SIEGFRIED
09 Director of Institutional Research ... Ms. Kathy KAPCSOS
18 Director Buildings & Grounds ... Mr. Mark K. CULP
29 Director Alumni Relations ... Ms. Melissa STARACE
36 Director Career Services ... Ms. Karen VERES
38 Director Counseling & Support Svcs ... Ms. Carolyn M. BRADY
96 Director of Purchasing ... Vacant

Northampton Community College Monroe County Branch Campus (E)

205 Old Mill Road, Tannersville PA 18372
Telephone: (570) 620-9221 Identification: 770164
Accreditation: &M

† Main campus is Northampton Community College in Bethlehem, PA.

Oakbridge Academy of Arts (F)

1250 Greensburg Road, Lower Burrell PA 15068-3843
County: Westmoreland FICE Identification: 021535
Unit ID: 376039
Telephone: (724) 335-5336 Carnegie Class: Assoc/PrivFP
FAX Number: (724) 335-3367 Calendar System: Quarter
URL: www.oaa.edu
Established: 1972 Annual Undergrad Tuition & Fees: $17,300
Enrollment: 50 Coed
Affiliation or Control: Proprietary IRS Status: Proprietary
Highest Offering: Associate Degree
Program: 2-Year Principally Bachelor's Creditable; Fine Arts Emphasis
Accreditation: ACCSC

01 Director ... Ms. Janie GATTY
07 Admissions Coordinator ... Ms. Sharon PANAIA
06 Registrar ... Ms. Debra WELLS

Orleans Technical Institute (G)

2770 Red Lion Road, Philadelphia PA 19114-1014
County: Philadelphia FICE Identification: 021830
Unit ID: 214528
Telephone: (215) 728-4700 Carnegie Class: Assoc/PrivNFP
FAX Number: (215) 745-1689 Calendar System: Semester
URL: www.orleanstech.edu
Established: 1986 Annual Undergrad Tuition & Fees: $10,600
Enrollment: 501 Coed
Affiliation or Control: Independent Non-Profit IRS Status: Exempt
Highest Offering: Associate Degree
Program: Occupational; 2-Year Principally Bachelor's Creditable; Technical Emphasis
Accreditation: ACCSC

01 Campus Director ... Ms. Jayne SINIARI
88 Director Court Reporting Program ... Ms. Carol CRAWFORD

Pace Institute (H)

606 Court Street, Reading PA 19601-3542
County: Berks FICE Identification: 022895
Unit ID: 214838
Telephone: (610) 375-1212 Carnegie Class: Assoc/PrivFP
FAX Number: (610) 375-1924 Calendar System: Semester
URL: www.paceinstitute.com
Established: 1980 Annual Undergrad Tuition & Fees: $8,240
Enrollment: 251 Coed
Affiliation or Control: Proprietary IRS Status: Proprietary
Highest Offering: Associate Degree
Program: Occupational
Accreditation: ACICS

01 President ... Ms. Rhoda E. DERSH
05 School Director ... Ms. Elizabeth MATSON

Palmer Theological Seminary of Eastern University (I)

588 North Gulph Road, King of Prussia PA 19406
County: Montgomery FICE Identification: 003260
Unit ID: 212124
Telephone: (610) 896-5000 Carnegie Class: Not Classified
FAX Number: (610) 649-3834 Calendar System: 4/1/4
URL: www.palmerseminary.edu
Established: 1925 Annual Graduate Tuition & Fees: $24,500
Enrollment: 438 Coed
Affiliation or Control: American Baptist IRS Status: 501(c)3
Highest Offering: Doctorate; No Undergraduates
Program: Professional
Accreditation: THEOL

01 University President ... Dr. Robert G. DUFFETT
05 Interim Dean ... Dr. Diane CHEN
10 Chief Operating Officer ... Mr. Anup KAPUR
04 President's Assistant ... Ms. Ruth E. MCFARLAND
20 Associate Dean ... Dr. Colleen DIRADDO
15 Director of Human Resources ... Ms. Kacey BERNARD
29 Director Alumni & Church Relations ... Ms. Mary GARDNER
42 Dir Stdnt Form/Seminary Chaplain ... Rev. Willette A. BURGIE-BRYANT
88 Director D Min Marriage & Family ... Dr. Peter SCHRECK
08 Director University Libraries ... Mr. James SAUER
09 Director of Institutional Research ... Dr. Thomas DAHLSTROM
06 Associate Registrar ... Mr. Craig MILLER
07 Director Admissions ... Ms. Tiffany S. MURPHY
26 Exec Dir Marketing & Communications ... Mr. Randall L. FRAME
18 Manager Plant Operations ... Mr. Carmen ANUZZI
24 Educational Technologist ... Ms. Masego KEBAETSE

† Affiliated with Eastern University, Saint Davids, PA.

Peirce College (J)

1420 Pine Street, Philadelphia PA 19102-4699
County: Philadelphia FICE Identification: 003309
Unit ID: 214883
Telephone: (215) 545-6400 Carnegie Class: Bac/Diverse
FAX Number: (215) 670-9366 Calendar System: Semester
URL: www.peirce.edu
Established: 1865 Annual Undergrad Tuition & Fees: $17,040
Enrollment: 2,261 Coed
Affiliation or Control: Independent Non-Profit IRS Status: 501(c)3
Highest Offering: Master's
Program: Occupational; Business Emphasis
Accreditation: M, ACBSP, CAHIIM

01 President & CEO ... Mr. James J. MERGIOTTI
10 VP Finance ... Mr. Brad K. HODGE
05 VP Academic Advancement ... Dr. Rita J. TOLIVER-ROBERTS
26 VP Marketing & Admissions ... Ms. Lisa PARIS
32 VP Student Services ... Ms. Uva C. COLES
27 Chief Information Officer ... Mr. James T. BURNS
18 Chief Auxiliary Services Officer ... Mr. Vito R. CHIMENTI
16 Asst VP Human Resources ... Ms. Harriet S. GOLEN
20 Assoc Dean Academic Ops/Faculty Sup ... Mr. Jon LENROW
07 Dean Admissions ... Ms. Nadine M. MAHER
09 Dean Academic Programs & Research ... Ms. Debra S. SCHRAMMEL
21 Controller ... Ms. Karen M. BRIGGS
88 Program Manager Inst Support ... Ms. Amy A. CALIENDO

Penn Commercial Business/ Technical School (K)

242 Oak Spring Road, Washington PA 15301-6822
County: Washington FICE Identification: 004902
Unit ID: 214892
Telephone: (724) 222-5330 Carnegie Class: Assoc/PrivFP
FAX Number: (724) 222-4722 Calendar System: Quarter
URL: www.penncommercial.edu
Established: 1929 Annual Undergrad Tuition & Fees: $19,000
Enrollment: 335 Coed
Affiliation or Control: Proprietary IRS Status: Proprietary
Highest Offering: Associate Degree
Program: Occupational; Technical Emphasis
Accreditation: ACICS, MAC

01 Director .... Mr. Robert S. BAZANT
11 Vice President of Operations .... Ms. Marianne ALBERT
04 Assistant to the President .... Ms. Jennifer POLAND
07 Director of Admissions .... Ms. Jayme TUITE
32 Director of Student Affairs .... Ms. Betty SHINGLE
37 Director of Financial Aid .... Ms. Cyndi MASON
88 Director of Education .... Ms. Nicole LANE
05 Director of Academic Affairs .... Ms. Sandy PHILLIPS
09 Dir of Reports & Statistics .... Mrs. Melissa PAPSON
36 Director of Career Services .... Mrs. Kristin WISSINGER

Penn State University Park (A)

201 Old Main, University Park PA 16802-1503
County: Centre FICE Identification: 003329
Unit ID: 214777
Telephone: (814) 865-4700 Carnegie Class: RU/VH
FAX Number: N/A Calendar System: Semester
URL: www.psu.edu/
Established: 1855 Annual Undergrad Tuition & Fees (In-State): $16,992
Enrollment: 44,679 Coed
Affiliation or Control: State Related IRS Status: 501(c)3
Highest Offering: Doctorate
Program: 2-Year Principally Bachelor's Creditable; Liberal Arts And General; Teacher Preparatory; Professional
Accreditation: M, ADNUR, ART, BUS, CACREP, CEA, CLPSY, COPSY, CORE, DIETD, DIETI, ENG, FEPAC, FOR, HSA, IPSY, JOUR, LSAR, MUS, NUR, NURSE, SCPSY, SP, TED, THEA

01 President .... Dr. Rodney A. ERICKSON
05 Executive Vice President & Provost .... Dr. Nicholas P. JONES
46 Int VP Research/Dean Grad School .... Dr. Neil SHARKEY
32 Vice President Student Affairs .... Dr. Damon SIMS
26 Int Vice Pres Univ Relations .... Ms. Cynthia B. HALL
30 Sr Vice Pres Devel/Alumni Relations .... Mr. Rodney P. KIRSCH
10 Sr Vice Pres Finance & Business .... Mr. David J. GRAY
31 Vice President Outreach .... Dr. Craig D. WEIDEMANN
11 VP for Administration .... Dr. Thomas G. POOLE
104 Vice Provost for Global Programs .... Dr. Michael A. ADEWUMI
43 Vice President & General Counsel .... Mr. Stephen S. DUNHAM
49 Vice Pres & Dean Undergrad Educ .... Dr. Robert N. PANGBORN
20 Vice Provost Academic Affairs .... Dr. Blannie E. BOWEN
28 Vice Provost Educational Equity .... Dr. W. Terrell JONES
12 Vice Pres Commonwealth Campuses .... Dr. Madlyn HANES
13 Vice Provost Information Tech .... Mr. Kevin M. MOROONEY
108 Exec Dir Ofc Plng/Inst Assessment .... Dr. Michael J. DOORIS
22 Vice Provost for Affirmative Action . Dr. Kenneth F. LEHRMAN, III
45 University Budget Officer .... Ms. Rachel E. SMITH
21 Corporate Controller .... Mr. Joseph J. DONCSECZ
21 Assoc VP Finance/Business Comm Oper .... Mr. Daniel W. SIEMINSKI
16 Vice President Human Resources .... Dr. Susan BASSO
18 Assoc Vice Pres Physical Plant .... Mr. H. Ford STRYKER
21 Assoc Vice Pres Aux & Business Svcs .... Ms. Gail A. HURLEY
51 Associate Vice President Outreach .... Mr. Wayne D. SMUTZ
27 Director of Public Information .... Ms. Lisa M. POWERS
39 Asst Vice President HFS & Res Life .... Dr. Stanley LATTA
37 Exec Director for Student Aid .... Ms. Anna M. GRISWOLD
29 Exec Director Alumni Association .... Mr. Roger L. WILLIAMS
21 Exec Director Investment Management .... Mr. David BRANIGAN
07 Exec Dir of Undergrad Admissions .... Ms. Anne L. ROHRBACH
38 Sr Director Counseling/Psych Svcs .... Dr. Dennis E. HEITZMANN
41 Athletic Director .... Mr. David M. JOYNER
86 Special Asst for Government Affairs .... Mr. Michael J. DIRAIMO
06 University Registrar .... Mr. Robert A. KUBAT
36 Director Career Services .... Dr. Jeffrey W. GARIS
17 Sr VP for Health Affairs & Dean .... Dr. Harold L. PAZ
08 Dean of Univ Libraries/Scholar Comm .... Ms. Barbara I. DEWEY
47 Int Dean of Ag Sciences .... Dr. Barbara J. CHRIST
48 Dean Arts & Architecture .... Dr. Barbara O. KORNER
50 Dean of Business .... Dr. Charles H. WHITEMAN
60 Dean of Communications .... Dr. Douglas A. ANDERSON
65 Dean Earth & Mineral Sciences .. Dr. William E. EASTERLING, III
53 Dean of Education .... Dr. David H. MONK
54 Dean of Engineering .... Dr. David N. WORMLEY
58 Int Dean of the Graduate School .... Dr. Neil SHARKEY
76 Dean Health & Human Development .... Dr. Ann C. CROUTER
66 Director School of Nursing .... Dr. Paula F. MILONE-NUZZO
56 Assoc Dean Cooperative Extension .... Dr. Dennis D. CALVIN
83 Dean of Liberal Arts .... Dr. Susan WELCH
81 Dean of Science .... Dr. Daniel J. LARSON
72 Dean Info Sciences/Technology .... Dr. David L. HALL
92 Dean of Honors College .... Dr. Christian BRADY
61 Int Dean School of Law .... Mr. James W. HOUCK
63 Dean College of Medicine .... Dr. Harold L. PAZ
75 Chief College of Technology .... Dr. Davie J. GILMOUR
44 Director of Annual Giving .... Ms. Ann LEHMAN
25 Sr Assoc Dir Sponsored Programs .... Dr. John W. HANOLD
19 Director University Police .... Mr. Stephen G. SHELOW
23 Dir University Health Services .... Dr. Margaret E. SPEAR
96 Director of Procurement Services .... Ms. Joyce A. HANEY
31 Director Campus & Comm Affairs .... Ms. Barbara ETTARO
102 Director Corp/Foundation Relations .... Mr. Mark S. ARMAGOST
04 Exec Admin Asst to President .... Mrs. Carmella MULROY-DEGENHART
40 General Manager Bookstore .... Mr. Steve J. FALKE
25 Contract Coordinator .... Mr. Richel PERRETTI
15 Director Human Resources .... Mr. Robert L. MANEY
21 Director of Internal Audit .... Mr. Daniel P. HEIST

† The legal name of Penn State and all its campuses is The Pennsylvania State University. For communication purposes, the name is shortened to Penn State followed by the name of the campus.

Penn State Abington (B)

1600 Woodland Road, Abington PA 19001-3990
Telephone: (215) 881-7300 FICE Identification: 003342
Accreditation: &M

† Main campus is Penn State University Park in University Park, PA.

Penn State Altoona (C)

3000 Ivyside Park, Altoona PA 16601-3777
Telephone: (814) 949-5000 FICE Identification: 003331
Accreditation: &M, ENGT

† Main campus is Penn State University Park in University Park, PA.

Penn State Beaver (D)

100 University Drive, Monaca PA 15061-2799
Telephone: (724) 773-3800 FICE Identification: 003332
Accreditation: &M

† Main campus is Penn State University Park in University Park, PA.

Penn State Berks (E)

Tulpehocken Road, PO Box 7009,
Reading PA 19610-6009
Telephone: (610) 396-6000 FICE Identification: 003334
Accreditation: &M, ENGT, OTA

† Main campus is Penn State University Park in University Park, PA.

Penn State Brandywine (F)

25 Yearsley Mill Road, Media PA 19063-5596
Telephone: (610) 892-1200 FICE Identification: 006922
Accreditation: &M

† Main campus is Penn State University Park in University Park, PA.

The Penn State Dickinson School of Law (G)

Lewis Katz Building, University Park PA 16802-1503
Telephone: (814) 865-8900 FICE Identification: 003254
Accreditation: &M, LAW

† Main campus is Penn State University Park in University Park, PA.

Penn State DuBois (H)

One College Place, DuBois PA 15801-3199
Telephone: (800) 346-7627 FICE Identification: 003335
Accreditation: &M, ENGT, OTA

† Main campus is Penn State University Park in University Park, PA.

Penn State Erie, The Behrend College (I)

4701 College Drive, Erie PA 16563-0001
Telephone: (814) 898-6000 FICE Identification: 003333
Accreditation: &M, BUS, ENG, ENGT

† Main campus is Penn State University Park in University Park, PA.

Penn State Fayette, The Eberly Campus (J)

2201 University Drive, Lemont Furnace PA 15456-1025
Telephone: (724) 430-4100 FICE Identification: 003336
Accreditation: &M, ENGT, PTAA

† Main campus is Penn State University Park in University Park, PA.

Penn State Great Valley School of Graduate Professional Studies (K)

30 E Swedesford Road, Malvern PA 19355-1488
Telephone: (610) 648-3200 FICE Identification: 003348
Accreditation: &M, BUS

† Main campus is Penn State University Park in University Park, PA.

Penn State Greater Allegheny (L)

4000 University Drive, McKeesport PA 15132-7698
Telephone: (412) 675-9000 FICE Identification: 003339
Accreditation: &M

† Main campus is Penn State University Park in University Park, PA.

Penn State Harrisburg (M)

777 W Harrisburg Pike, Middletown PA 17057-4898
Telephone: (717) 948-6452 FICE Identification: 006814
Accreditation: &M, BUS, ENG, ENGT, SPAA, TED

† Main campus is Penn State University Park in University Park, PA.

Penn State Hazleton (N)

76 University Drive, Hazleton PA 18202-1291
Telephone: (570) 450-3000 FICE Identification: 003338
Accreditation: &M, ENGT, MLTAD, PTAA

† Main campus is Penn State University Park in University Park, PA.

Penn State Lehigh Valley (O)

2809 Saucon Valley Road, Center Valley PA 18034-8447
Telephone: (610) 285-5000 FICE Identification: 003330
Accreditation: &M

† Main campus is Penn State University Park in University Park, PA.

Penn State Milton S. Hershey Medical Center College of Medicine (P)

500 University Drive, Hershey PA 17033-2360
Telephone: (717) 531-8521 FICE Identification: 006813
Accreditation: &M, MED

† Main campus is Penn State University Park in University Park, PA.

Penn State Mont Alto (Q)

One Campus Drive, Mont Alto PA 17237-9703
Telephone: (717) 749-6000 FICE Identification: 003340
Accreditation: &M, OTA, PTAA

† Main campus is Penn State University Park in University Park, PA.

Penn State New Kensington (R)

3550 Seventh Street Road,
New Kensington PA 15068-1798
Telephone: (724) 334-5466 FICE Identification: 003341
Accreditation: &M, ENGT, RAD

† Main campus is Penn State University Park in University Park, PA.

Penn State Schuylkill (S)

200 University Drive, Schuylkill Haven PA 17972-2208
Telephone: (570) 385-6000 FICE Identification: 003343
Accreditation: &M, RAD

† Main campus is Penn State University Park in University Park, PA.

Penn State Shenango (T)

147 Shenango Avenue, Sharon PA 16146-1597
Telephone: (724) 983-2803 FICE Identification: 003345
Accreditation: &M, PTAA

† Main campus is Penn State University Park in University Park, PA.

Penn State Wilkes-Barre (U)

Old Route 115, PO Box PSU, Lehman PA 18627-0217
Telephone: (570) 675-2171 FICE Identification: 003346
Accreditation: &M, ENG, ENGT

† Main campus is Penn State University Park in University Park, PA.

Penn State Worthington-Scranton (V)

120 Ridge View Drive, Dunmore PA 18512-1602
Telephone: (570) 963-2500 FICE Identification: 003344
Accreditation: &M, ENGT

† Main campus is Penn State University Park in University Park, PA.

Penn State York (W)

1031 Edgecomb Avenue, York PA 17403-3326
Telephone: (717) 771-4000 FICE Identification: 003347
Accreditation: &M, ENGT

† Main campus is Penn State University Park in University Park, PA.

Pennco Tech (X)

3815 Otter Street, Bristol PA 19007-3696
County: Bucks FICE Identification: 009449
Unit ID: 214944
Telephone: (215) 785-0111 Carnegie Class: Assoc/PrivFP
FAX Number: (215) 785-1945 Calendar System: Other
URL: www.penncotech.edu
Established: 1973 Annual Undergrad Tuition & Fees: $21,095
Enrollment: 468 Coed
Affiliation or Control: Proprietary IRS Status: Proprietary
Highest Offering: Associate Degree
Program: Occupational; Technical Emphasis
Accreditation: ACCSC

01 CEO .... Michael S. HOBYAK
03 School Director .... Fred PARCELLS
05 Director of Education .... Vern LUCAS
07 Director of Admissions .... Glenn SLATER
07 Director of Admissions .... Joe GIEBEL
06 Registrar .... Sondra KOOB
35 Director Student Services .... Todd JANZER
37 Director Student Financial Aid .... Robin TOLLEY
36 Director Student Placement .... Teresa SCHEERER

Pennsylvania Academy of the Fine Arts (Y)

128 N Broad St, Philadelphia PA 19102-1424
County: Philadelphia FICE Identification: 021073
Unit ID: 214971

Telephone: (215) 972-7600 Carnegie Class: Spec/Arts
FAX Number: (215) 569-0153 Calendar System: Semester
URL: www.pafa.edu
Established: 1805 Annual Undergrad Tuition & Fees: $30,380
Enrollment: 309 Coed
Affiliation or Control: Independent Non-Profit IRS Status: 501(c)3
Highest Offering: Master's
Program: Liberal Arts And General; Professional; Fine Arts Emphasis
Accreditation: M, ART

01 President & CEO .... Dr. David R. BRIGHAM
30 Exec Vice President Development .... Ms. Melissa D. KAISER
26 Exec Vice President of Marketing .... Ms. Heike RASS
05 Dean of the School of Fine Arts .... Mr. Jeffrey CARR
10 Exec Vice Pres of Finance/Operation .... Mr. John BERG
07 Dean of Enrollment .... Mr. André S.F. VAN DE PUTTE
32 Dean of Students .... Ms. Anne K. STASSEN
18 Director of Operations and Safety .... Mr. Ed POLETTI
19 Director of Security .... Mr. Jimmie GREENO
37 Director of Financial Aid .... Ms. Dana MOORE
06 Registrar .... Mr. Peter MEDWICK
08 Director of Library Services .... Mr. Brian DUFFY
36 Director of Career Services .... Mr. Gregory MARTINO
21 Director of Finance .... Mr. Kevin MCCARTER
13 Director of Information Technology .... Mr. Kevin MARTIN

Pennsylvania College of Art & Design (A)

204 N Prince Street, Box 59, Lancaster PA 17608-0059
County: Lancaster FICE Identification: 022699
Unit ID: 215053
Telephone: (717) 396-7833 Carnegie Class: Spec/Arts
FAX Number: (717) 396-1339 Calendar System: Semester
URL: www.pcad.edu
Established: 1982 Annual Undergrad Tuition & Fees: $20,680
Enrollment: 242 Coed
Affiliation or Control: Independent Non-Profit IRS Status: 501(c)3
Highest Offering: Baccalaureate
Program: Professional; Fine Arts Emphasis
Accreditation: M, ART

01 President .... Ms. Mary Colleen HEIL
05 Academic Dean .... Mr. Marc TORICK
32 Dean of Students .... Ms. Pamela RICHARDSON
26 Director of Public Relations .... Mrs. Mary STADDEN
10 Director of Finance .... Mrs. Patricia ERNST
84 Dir of Admiss/Mktg & Recruitment .... Ms. Natalie LASCEK-SPEAKMAN
88 Director of Enrollment Planning .... Ms. Barbara ELLIOTT
37 Director Financial Aid .... Mr. J. David HERSHEY
08 Library Director .... Ms. Karen HUTCHISON
30 Director of Development .... Ms. Angela SPICKLER
51 Director of Continuing Education .... Ms. Valerie PAIGE
18 Director of Physical Plant .... Mr. Dan FREILER
06 Registrar .... Ms. Faith GADDIE

Pennsylvania College of Technology (B)

One College Avenue, Williamsport PA 17701-5799
County: Lycoming FICE Identification: 003395
Unit ID: 366252
Telephone: (570) 326-3761 Carnegie Class: Bac/Assoc
FAX Number: (570) 327-4503 Calendar System: Semester
URL: www.pct.edu
Established: 1941 Annual Undergrad Tuition & Fees (In-State): $14,940
Enrollment: 5,671 Coed
Affiliation or Control: State IRS Status: 501(c)3
Highest Offering: Baccalaureate
Program: Occupational; 2-Year Principally Bachelor's Creditable; Technical Emphasis
Accreditation: M, ACBSP, ACFEI, ADNUR, ARCPA, CAHIIM, CONST, DH, EMT, ENGT, NAIT, NUR, OTA, PNUR, RAD, SURGT

01 President .... Dr. Davie Jane GILMOUR
05 VP for Academic Affairs/Provost .... Dr. Paul L. STARKEY
108 VP Assessment/Research/Planning .... Vacant
10 VP for Finance/CFO .... Ms. Suzanne T. STOPPER
30 Vice Pres Institutional Advancement .... Mr. Barry R. STIGER
13 VP for Info Tech and Business .... Mr. Michael M. CUNNINGHAM
22 VP Human Resources/Employees/EEO .... Vacant
15 VP for College Services .... Mr. R. David KAY
20 Assistant VP for Academic Services .... Mrs. Carolyn R. STRICKLAND
20 Associate VP for Instruction .... Mr. Tom F. GREGORY
04 Administrative Asst to President .... Mrs. Valerie A. BAIER
88 Spec Asst to the President ITS .... Mr. James E. CUNNINGHAM
32 Chief Student Affairs Officer .... Mr. Elliott STRICKLAND, JR.
103 Asst VP for Workforce Develop .... Dr. Tracy L. BRUNDAGE
76 Dean of Health Sciences .... Dr. Edward A. HENNINGER
88 Dean Construction & Design Tech .... Mr. Marc E. BRIDGENS
54 Dean Industrial/Comp/Engineering .... Mr. Bill MACK
81 Dean of Sciences/Human/Visual Comm .... Dr. Clifford P. COPPERSMITH
88 Dean Transportation/Natl Resources .. Mr. Colin W. WILLIAMSON
50 Dean of Business/Hospitality .... Mr. Frederick W. BECKER
37 Assoc Dean of Admissions & Fin Aid ..... Mr. Dennis L. CORRELL
102 Exec Dir of Penn College Foundation ..... Mr. Robert C. DIETRICH
08 Director of the Madigan Library .... Ms. Tracey AMEY
56 Director Instruc Tech/Distance Lrng .... Mr. Walter J. SHULTZ
18 Director of General Services .... Mr. Walter D. NYMAN
09 Exec Dir Assessment/Research/Plng .... Mr. Brian CYGAN
06 Registrar .... Mr. Dennis L. DUNKLEBERGER
38 Director of Advisement Center .... Vacant
36 Dir Counsel/Career & Disability Svc .... Dr. Jennifer MCLEAN
39 Director Residence Life .... Vacant
19 Chief of Police .... Mr. Chris E. MILLER
27 Director College Info/Cmty Rels .... Mrs. Elaine J. LAMBERT
88 Director Academic Support Services .... Dr. Kimberly L. BOLIG
35 Director Student Activities .... Mrs. Kimberly R. CASSEL
29 Director Alumni Relations .... Ms. Valerie L. FESSLER
26 Director of Corporate Relations .... Ms. Debra M. MILLER
88 Director Children Learning Center .... Ms. Barbara J. ALBERT
40 Director of College Store .... Mr. Matthew P. BRANCA
41 Director of Athletics .... Mr. Scott E. KENNELL
90 Director Network Services .... Mr. Mike E. RAE
91 Director Administrative Info Sys .... Mr. Randall L. MONROE
23 Student Health Center Director .... Mr. Carl L. SHANER
28 Asst Dir Student Act/Diversity .... Mrs. Malinda C. LOVE
88 Coordinator of Disability Services ... Ms. Kay E. DUNKLEBERGER
85 International Programs Specialist .... Ms. Shanin L. DOUGHERTY
96 Director/Procurement Services .... Ms. Karen P. FESSLER

† Affiliate of Pennsylvania State University.

Pennsylvania Highlands Community College (C)

101 Community College Way, Johnstown PA 15904-2949
County: Cambria FICE Identification: 031804
Unit ID: 414911
Telephone: (814) 262-6400 Carnegie Class: Assoc/Pub-R-M
FAX Number: (814) 269-9700 Calendar System: Semester
URL: www.pennhighlands.edu
Established: 1994 Annual Undergrad Tuition & Fees (In-District): $4,460
Enrollment: 3,043 Coed
Affiliation or Control: State/Local IRS Status: 501(c)3
Highest Offering: Associate Degree
Program: Occupational; 2-Year Principally Bachelor's Creditable
Accreditation: M

01 President .... Dr. Walter J. ASONEVICH
05 VP Academic Affairs/Student Svcs .... Dr. Edward NICHOLS
10 Vice Pres Finance & Admin Services .... Lorraine DONAHUE
26 AVP for External Relations .... Trish CORLE
51 AVP for Continuing Education .... Grace MARKUM
20 Dean of Faculty .... Erica REIGHARD
20 Dean Teaching/Learning/Assessment .... Michele RICE
84 Dean Enrollment Services/Registrar .... Michelle STUMPF
08 Assoc Dean for Learning Resources .... Dr. Barbara ZABOROWSKI
07 Director of Admissions .... Jeffrey MAUL
15 Director of Human Resources .... April RENZI
21 Director of Finance/Admin Services .... Christopher PRIBULSKY
37 Director Student Financial Aid .... Brenda COUGHENOUR
26 Director of Marketing .... Raymond WEIBLE, JR.
35 Director of Student Activities .... Suzanne BRUGH
18 Director of Facilities Operation .... Reb BROWNLEE
13 Director of IT .... Danielle GERKO
09 Director of Institutional Research .... Kate DEATER
36 Dir Career Planning/Employer Svcs .... Larry BRUGH
04 Exec Asst to the President's Office .... Michelle MAKSYMIK

Pennsylvania Institute of Health and Technology (D)

PO Box 278, Mount Braddock PA 15465-0278
Telephone: (724) 437-4600 Identification: 666035
Accreditation: ACICS

† Main campus is West Virginia Junior College in Morgantown, WV.

Pennsylvania Institute of Technology (E)

800 Manchester Avenue, Media PA 19063-4098
County: Delaware FICE Identification: 010998
Unit ID: 214582
Telephone: (610) 892-1500 Carnegie Class: Assoc/PrivNFP
FAX Number: (610) 892-1510 Calendar System: Semester
URL: www.pit.edu
Established: 1953 Annual Undergrad Tuition & Fees: $12,300
Enrollment: 717 Coed
Affiliation or Control: Independent Non-Profit IRS Status: 501(c)3
Highest Offering: Associate Degree
Program: Occupational; 2-Year Principally Bachelor's Creditable; Technical Emphasis
Accreditation: M

01 President .... Mr. Walter GARRISON
05 Dean of Academic Affairs .... Dr. Robert E. HANCOX
32 Dean Student Services .... Dr. Dona M. FABRIZIO
20 Asst Dean of Academic Affairs .... Ms. Rachelle CHAYKIN
13 Chief Information Officer .... Mr. Jack BACON
10 Chief Financial Officer .... Ms. Annamarie CASSIDY
06 Registrar .... Mr. Craig M. JACOBS
08 Director of the Library .... Ms. Lynea ANDERMAN
18 Director of Facilities .... Mr. Frederick FIVECOAT
36 Director Career Placement/Transfer .... Ms. Adina TAYAR
36 Dir Career Plct/Extrn Sch Prof Pgms .... Ms. Kamira EVANS
37 Financial Aid Director .... Ms. Kristina FRIPPS
07 Director of Admissions .... Mr. John DETURRIS

Pennsylvania School of Business (F)

265 Lehigh Street, Allentown PA 18102
County: Lehigh FICE Identification: 022552
Unit ID: 213057
Telephone: (610) 841-3333 Carnegie Class: Assoc/PrivFP
FAX Number: (610) 841-3334 Calendar System: Semester
URL: www.psb.edu
Established: 1980 Annual Undergrad Tuition & Fees: $9,275
Enrollment: 259 Coed
Affiliation or Control: Proprietary IRS Status: Proprietary
Highest Offering: Associate Degree
Program: Occupational
Accreditation: ACCSC

01 President .... Mr. Michael J. O'BRIEN
10 Controller .... Ms. Michele TAYLOR
05 Dean of Education .... Ms. Dani J. PHELPS
07 Director of Admissions .... Mr. Sam JARVIS
37 Director of Financial Aid .... Ms. Megan BAUDER
36 Director of Career Services .... Ms. Jessica MELENDEZ

*Pennsylvania State System of Higher Education, Office of the Chancellor (G)

Dixon University Ctr, 2986 N 2nd St, Harrisburg PA 17110-1201
County: Dauphin FICE Identification: 029371
Unit ID: 214661
Telephone: (717) 720-4010 Carnegie Class: N/A
FAX Number: (717) 720-4011
URL: www.passhe.edu

01 Acting Chancellor .... Dr. Peter H. GARLAND
10 Vice Chancellor Admin/Finance .... Mr. James S. DILLON
21 Assoc Vice Chancellor Admin/Finance ...... Ms. Lois M. JOHNSON
18 Asst Vice Chancellor Facilities .... Mr. Steven DUPES
05 Vice Chanc Academic/Student Affairs .... Dr. James D. MORAN, III
20 Sr Assoc Vice Chanc A/S Affairs .... Dr. Kathleen HOWLEY
16 Vice Chancellor HR/LR .... Mr. Gary K. DENT
15 Asst Vice Chancellor LR .... Mr. Michael A. MOTTOLA
86 Vice Chancellor External Relations .... Ms. Karen BALL
43 Chief Legal Counsel .... Mr. Leo PANDELADIS

*Bloomsburg University of Pennsylvania (H)

400 E Second Street, Bloomsburg PA 17815-1399
County: Columbia FICE Identification: 003315
Unit ID: 211158
Telephone: (570) 389-4000 Carnegie Class: Master's L
FAX Number: (570) 389-3700 Calendar System: Semester
URL: www.bloomu.edu
Established: 1839 Annual Undergrad Tuition & Fees (In-State): $8,582
Enrollment: 9,950 Coed
Affiliation or Control: State IRS Status: 501(c)3
Highest Offering: Doctorate
Program: Liberal Arts And General; Teacher Preparatory; Professional
Accreditation: M, ANEST, ART, AUD, BUS, CS, ENGT, EXSC, MUS, NURSE, SP, SW, TED, THEA

02 President .... Dr. David L. SOLTZ
05 Sr VP/Provost Academic Affairs .... Dr. Ira BLAKE
10 Vice Pres Finance/Administration .... Mr. John F. LOONAN
32 Vice Pres Student Affairs .... Dr. Dionne D. SOMERVILLE
30 Vice Pres University Advancement .... Mr. Erik EVANS
22 Deputy to Pres for Equity .... Dr. Robert WISLOCK
04 Exec Asst to the President .... Ms. Brenda CROMLEY
20 Asst Provost Strat Init/Dean UG Ed .... Dr. Robert P. MARANDE
58 Interim Assoc VP/Dean Grad Studies .... Dr. Robert GATES
13 Assoc VP Technology & Library Serv .... Mr. Wayne C. MOHR
51 Assoc VP/Dean Extended Programs .... Mr. Thomas FLETCHER
18 Asst VP for Facilities Management .... Mr. Eric NESS
21 Asst VP Finance/Budget & Bus Svcs .... Ms. Claudia THRUSH
35 Asst VP Student Affairs/Comm Act .... Dr. Jeff C. LONG
39 Asst VP Student Affairs/Campus Life .... Mr. Thomas KRESCH
26 Asst VP External Relations .... Mr. Jim HOLLISTER
27 AVP Marketing/Communications .... Ms. Rosalee RUSH
29 AVP Alumni/Professional Engagement .... Ms. Lynda MICHAELS
49 Dean College of Liberal Arts .... Dr. James BROWN
50 Interim Dean College of Business .... Dr. George EBBS
81 Acting Dean College of Science/Tech .... Dr. Jonathan LINCOLN
53 Dean College of Education .... Dr. Elizabeth MAUCH
88 Acting Assoc Dean Acad Achievement .... Dr. Irvin WRIGHT
15 Director Human Resources/Labor Rel .... Mr. Jerry REED
46 Interim Dir Research/Sponsored Pgms .... Dr. John M. HRANITZ
06 Registrar .... Mr. Joseph KISSELL
07 Interim Director of Admissions .... Mr. Christopher LAPOS
36 Director Career Development .... Mr. Christopher KELLER
38 Director of Counsel & Human Devel .... Dr. William R. HARRAR
37 Director Financial Aid .... Mr. John BIERYLA
90 Manager Technology Support Services .... Mr. David S. CELLI
40 Manager University Store .... Ms. Beth CHRISTIAN
41 Director of Athletics .... Mr. Michael S. MCFARLAND
85 Director International Education .... Dr. Madhav P. SHARMA
42 Director Protestant Campus Ministry .... Vacant
42 Director Catholic Campus Ministry .... Rev. Timothy MARCOE
19 Dir Univ Safety & Police .... Mr. Tom PHILLIPS
92 Director University Honors Program .... Dr. Stephen KOKOSKA

96 Director of Purchasing & Operations ... Mr. Jeffrey MANDEL
08 Director Library Services ... Ms. Charlotte DROLL
91 Dir Applications Develop/Operations ... Mr. James C. GESSNER
09 Director of Institutional Research ... Ms. Karen L. SLUSSER
108 AVP Planning & Assessment ... Dr. Sheila Dove JONES
104 Director Global & Multicultural Ed ... Dr. Doreen JOWI
102 Exec Dir BU Foundation ... Mr. Jerome DVORAK

*California University of Pennsylvania (A)

250 University Avenue, California PA 15419-1394
County: Washington FICE Identification: 003316
Unit ID: 211361
Telephone: (724) 938-4000 Carnegie Class: Master's L
FAX Number: (724) 938-4138 Calendar System: Semester
URL: www.calu.edu
Established: 1852 Annual Undergrad Tuition & Fees (In-State): $9,305
Enrollment: 8,608 Coed
Affiliation or Control: State IRS Status: 501(c)3
Highest Offering: Master's
Program: 2-Year Principally Bachelor's Creditable; Liberal Arts And General; Teacher Preparatory; Professional
Accreditation: M, ART, CACREP, CS, ENGT, NAIT, NRPA, NURSE, PTAA, SP, SW, TED, THEA

02 Acting President ... Ms. Geraldine JONES
05 Provost/Vice Pres Academic Affairs ... Dr. Bruce BARNHART
10 Interim VP Administration & Finance ... Mr. Robert THORN
32 VP Student Development & Services ... Dr. Lenora ANGELONE
30 VP for University Development ... Mr. Ron HUIATT
13 VP Information Technology ... Dr. Charles MANCE
04 Special Assistant to the President ... Mr. Norman G. HASBROUCK
09 Director Institutional Research ... Mr. Richard L. KLINE
88 Executive Dir Special Initiatives ... Mr. Timothy M. BUCHANAN
58 Dean of Graduate Studies ... Dr. Stan KOMACEK
20 Assoc Provost/Student Retent Ofcr ... Dr. Dan M. ENGSTROM
30 Assoc Vice Pres for Development ... Mr. Howard GOLDSTEIN
30 Assoc Vice Pres for Development ... Mr. Mitch KOZIKOWSKI
56 Exec Director Southpointe Center ... Ms. Ellen NESSER
72 Dean of Science/Technology ... Dr. Leonard A. COLELLI
49 Interim Dean of Liberal Arts ... Dr. Mohamed YAMBA
53 Act Dean Col Education/Human Svcs ... Dr. Kevin A. KOURY
62 Dean of Library Services ... Mr. Douglas HOOVER
07 Dean of Admissions ... Dr. William A. EDMONDS
37 Director of Financial Aid ... Mrs. Jill FERNANDES
37 Sr Assoc Director of Financial Aid ... Mr. Jeff DERUBBO
06 Registrar ... Ms. Heidi WILLIAMS
36 Director of Career Services ... Ms. Rhonda GIFFORD
92 Director Honors Program ... Dr. Donald S. LAWSON
29 Director of Alumni Relations ... Ms. Amy LOMBARD
88 Director of University Exhibitions ... Mr. Walter P. CZEKAJ
44 Director of Planned Giving ... Mr. Gordon CORE
38 Assoc VP Student Development & Svcs ... Dr. Timothy SUSICK
14 Computer Systems Manager ... Ms. Rebecca NICHOLS
39 Director of Housing ... Mr. Shawn URBINE
94 Director Women's Studies ... Dr. Marta MCCLINTOCK
85 International Student Advisor ... Mr. John WATKINS
41 Athletic Director ... Dr. Tom PUCCI
88 Assoc VP of Athletic Development ... Mr. Frank BAUER
15 Interim Director of Personnel ... Ms. Pamela MURPHY
22 Special Assistant to President EEEO ... Dr. Lisa MCBRIDE
19 Chief of Police ... Mr. Robert F. DOWNEY
18 Director of Physical Plant ... Mr. Michael PEPLINSKI
26 Director of Communications & PR ... Mrs. Christine KINDL
27 Director of Publications ... Mr. Greg SOFRANKO
40 Book Store Manager ... Mr. David ALBERTS
96 Director of Purchasing ... Ms. Judith LAUGHLIN
26 Interim Vice Pres Marketing ... Mr. Craig S. BUTZINE

*Cheyney University of Pennsylvania (B)

Cheyney and Creek Roads, Cheyney PA 19319-0200
County: Delaware FICE Identification: 003317
Unit ID: 211608
Telephone: (610) 399-2000 Carnegie Class: Master's S
FAX Number: (610) 399-2415 Calendar System: Semester
URL: www.cheyney.edu
Established: 1837 Annual Undergrad Tuition & Fees (In-State): $8,602
Enrollment: 1,284 Coed
Affiliation or Control: State IRS Status: 501(c)3
Highest Offering: Master's
Program: Liberal Arts And General; Teacher Preparatory
Accreditation: M

02 President ... Dr. Michelle R. HOWARD-VITAL
03 Chief of Staff/Deputy to President ... Ms. Sheilah VANCE
05 Provost/VP Academic Affairs ... Dr. Bernadette CARTER
10 Vice Pres Finance & Administration ... Mr. Al SKUDZINSKAS
30 Asst Vice Pres Univ Advancement ... Mr. Lawrence GREEN
32 VP Student Affairs/Student Life ... Dr. Susanne D. PHILLIPS
08 Dean Library Services ... Dr. Lut NERO
49 Dean of Faculty & Academic Schools ... Dr. Donna PARKER
38 Chairperson Guidance & Counseling ... Ms. Jolly RAMAKRISHNAN
06 Registrar ... Ms. Brenda SHIELDS
37 Director Financial Aid ... Ms. Michelle BURWELL
13 Director of Information Technology ... Mr. Sheng YAO
07 Director of Enrollment Management ... Dr. Eric HILTON
09 Director Institutional Research ... Dr. Sesime ADANU
15 Director Human Resources ... Ms. Jo-Anne HARRIS
18 Deputy Dir Facilities Management ... Mr. Carl M. WILLIAMS
19 Director Public Safety ... Mr. Lawrence RICHARDS
36 Director Career Services ... Ms. Ruth BRICE
41 Athletic Director ... Mr. Ruffin BELL
17 College Physician ... Dr. Pamela HADLEY
43 University Legal Counsel ... Ms. Jacqualine BARNETT
35 Director Student Affairs ... Ms. Sharon THORN
21 Dir Business Support Service ... Vacant
25 Contract Compliance Officer ... Mr. Michael FLANAGAN
22 Social Equity ... Vacant
29 Director Alumni Relations ... Mr. Gregory BENJAMIN
39 Mg Housing Ops & Auxiliary Services ... Ms. Elizabeth BURTON
103 Dir Economic/Workforce Devel ... Ms. Sharon CANNON
24 Director Telecommunications ... Mr. Phil PAGLIARO

*Clarion University of Pennsylvania (C)

840 Wood Street, Clarion PA 16214-1232
County: Clarion FICE Identification: 003318
Unit ID: 211644
Telephone: (814) 393-2000 Carnegie Class: Master's L
FAX Number: (814) 393-1826 Calendar System: Semester
URL: www.clarion.edu
Established: 1867 Annual Undergrad Tuition & Fees (In-State): $9,545
Enrollment: 6,520 Coed
Affiliation or Control: State IRS Status: 501(c)3
Highest Offering: Master's
Program: 2-Year Principally Bachelor's Creditable; Liberal Arts And General; Teacher Preparatory; Professional
Accreditation: M, ART, BUS, CORE, LIB, MUS, NUR, SP, TED

02 President ... Dr. Karen M. WHITNEY
05 Provost/Academic Vice President ... Dr. Ronald NOWACZYK
32 Vice Pres Student & University Affs ... Mr. Harry E. TRIPP
10 Vice Pres Finance/Administration ... Mr. Pete FACKLER
20 Associate Provost ... Vacant
102 Chief Exec Officer Foundation ... Mr. Michael R. KEEFER
30 Director of Development ... Mr. John CATONE
21 Assoc VP for Finance/Administration ... Mr. Timothy P. FOGARTY
22 Asst to President for Social Equity ... Dr. Jocelind E. GANT
12 Executive Dean Venango College ... Dr. Christopher M. REBER
84 Dean of Enrollment Management ... Mr. William D. BAILEY
08 Dean of Libraries ... Dr. Terry S. LATOUR
49 Dean of Arts & Sciences ... Dr. James A. FOSTER
50 Dean of Business Administration ... Dr. Phil FRESE
66 Director Nursing & Allied Health ... Vacant
58 Assistant Dir for Graduate Studies ... Ms. Susan STAUB
09 Director Info Mgmt & Inst Research ... Dr. Raymond J. MONETA
06 Registrar ... Ms. Lisa L. HEPLER
21 Comptroller ... Ms. Tamara B. VARSEK
14 Assoc VP for Information Technology ... Mr. Samuel T. PULEIO
46 Director Faculty Research ... Dr. Brenda S. DEDE
26 Dir of Marketing & Communications ... Mr. David LOVE
35 Int Director of Student Services ... Ms. Ragan GRIFFIN
18 Director of Facilities Mgmt & Plng ... Mr. Richard TAYLOR
88 Exec Dir Programming & Devel Ctr ... Ms. Carol A. ROTH
29 Director of Alumni Relations ... Ms. Laura C. KING
36 Int Director Career Services ... Ms. Diana BRUSH
39 Director of Residence Life ... Ms. Michelle L. KEALEY
19 Int Director of Public Safety ... Ms. Marcy TROMBETTA
41 Athletic Director ... Mr. David J. KATIS
96 Director of Purchasing ... Mr. Rein A. POLD

*East Stroudsburg University of Pennsylvania (D)

200 Prospect Street, East Stroudsburg PA 18301-2999
County: Monroe FICE Identification: 003320
Unit ID: 212115
Telephone: (570) 422-3211 Carnegie Class: Master's L
FAX Number: (570) 422-3777 Calendar System: Semester
URL: www.esu.edu
Established: 1893 Annual Undergrad Tuition & Fees (In-State): $9,004
Enrollment: 6,943 Coed
Affiliation or Control: State IRS Status: 501(c)3
Highest Offering: Master's
Program: Liberal Arts And General; Teacher Preparatory; Professional
Accreditation: M, CS, EXSC, NRPA, NUR, PH, SP, @SW, TED

02 President ... Dr. Marcia G. WELSH
05 Provost ... Dr. Van A. REIDHEAD
32 Vice President Student Affairs ... Dr. Doreen TOBIN
10 Vice Pres Finance & Administration ... Mr. Kenneth A. LONG
46 Vice Pres Econ Dev & Research Supp ... Ms. Mary Frances POSTUPACK
102 President & CEO ESU Foundation ... Mr. Frank FALSO
84 Vice Pres Enrollment Management ... Vacant
58 Vice Provost & Graduate Dean ... Vacant
49 Dean of Arts & Sciences ... Dr. Peter HAWKES
76 Interim Dean of Health Sciences ... Dr. Alberto CARDELLE
53 Dean of Education ... Dr. Pamela KRAMER-ERTEL
50 Interim Dean of Business & Mgmt ... Dr. Robert FLEISCHMAN
08 Dean of Library & Univ Collections ... Dr. Edward OWUSU-ANSAH
20 Associate Provost ... Vacant
35 Asst Vice President Student Affairs ... Vacant
100 Interim Chief of Staff ... Mr. Miguel BARBOSA
88 Asst Vice Pres Instruct Supp & Outr ... Mr. Michael SOUTHWELL
07 Director of Admissions ... Mr. Jeffrey JONES
06 Registrar/Dir Enrollment Services ... Ms. Kizzy MORRIS
37 Assoc Dir Enroll Svcs/Financial Aid ... Ms. Phyllis SWINSON
36 Director of Career Services ... Ms. Daria WIELEBINSKI
38 Director Counseling Center ... Dr. John A. ABBRUZZESE
41 Director Intercollegiate Athletics ... Dr. Thomas GIOGLIO
39 Director of Residence Life ... Mr. Robert M. MOSES
88 Dir of Student Activity Association ... Vacant
21 Controller ... Ms. Donna R. BULZONI
14 Director of Computing Services ... Mr. Robert D'AVERSA
15 Director of Human Resources ... Ms. Teresa FRITSCHE
18 Director Facilities Management ... Mr. Syed S. ZAIDI
96 Director of Procurement/Contracting ... Ms. Patricia REICH
29 Director of Alumni Relations ... Ms. Brooke DONOVAN
26 Director University Relations ... Dr. Brenda FRIDAY
108 Dir Institutional Research & Assess ... Ms. Joann STRYKER

*Edinboro University of Pennsylvania (E)

219 Meadville Street, Edinboro PA 16444-0001
County: Erie FICE Identification: 003321
Unit ID: 212160
Telephone: (814) 732-2000 Carnegie Class: Master's L
FAX Number: (814) 732-2880 Calendar System: Semester
URL: www.edinboro.edu
Established: 1857 Annual Undergrad Tuition & Fees (In-State): $8,849
Enrollment: 7,462 Coed
Affiliation or Control: State IRS Status: 501(c)3
Highest Offering: Beyond Master's But Less Than Doctorate
Program: Occupational; 2-Year Principally Bachelor's Creditable; Liberal Arts And General; Teacher Preparatory; Professional
Accreditation: M, ART, ACBSP, CACREP, CORE, CS, MUS, NURSE, SP, SW, TED

02 President ... Dr. Julie E. WOLLMAN
05 Interim Provost/VP Acad Affairs ... Dr. Michael HANNAN
10 Vice Pres Finance & Administration ... Mr. Gordon J. HERBST
32 Vice President for Student Affairs ... Dr. Kahan SABLO
30 Vice Pres University Advancement ... Ms. Tina MENGINE
84 Assoc VP Enroll Mgmt/Student Succes ... Dr. Amber SCHULTZ
04 Special Assistant to the President ... Mr. Sean BLILEY
20 Sr Exec Associate to the Provost ... Ms. Judy KUBEJA
15 Assoc VP Human Res/Fac Rels ... Mr. Sid BOOKER
08 Assoc Vice President Univ Libraries ... Dr. Donald H. DILMORE
18 Director of Facilities Management ... Mr. James MILLER
27 Director of Communications ... Mr. Jeffrey HILEMAN
26 Director of Marketing ... Mr. William BERGER
37 Director of Financial Aid ... Ms. Alyssa DOBSON
07 Director of Undergrad Admissions ... Mr. Craig GROOMS
92 Director Honors Program ... Dr. Jean JONES
22 Dir of Social Equity/Ombudsperson ... Ms. Valerie O. HAYES
49 Dean College of Arts and Sciences ... Dr. Terry L. SMITH
79 Dean Arts/Humanities/Soc Sci ... Dr. Steven COMBS
81 Dean Science & Health Prof ... Dr. Nathan RITCHEY
58 Dean of Graduate Studies/Research ... Dr. Alan BIEL
53 Dean School of Education ... Dr. Nomsa GELETA
50 Acting Dean School of Business ... Dr. Scott MILLER
06 Registrar ... Mr. Tim W. PILEWSKI
36 Dir Ctr for Career Develop ... Dr. Jody GALLAGHER
29 Director Alumni Relations ... Mr. Jon PULICE
41 Athletic Director ... Mr. Bruce BAUMGARTNER
38 Dir Counseling/Psychological Svcs ... Dr. Michael BUCELL
19 Chief University Police ... Mr. Clark PETERS
39 Dir Residence Life & Orientation ... Ms. Kim KENNEDY
12 Dir & Outreach Coord EUP in Erie ... Ms. Janet L. BOWKER
23 Medical Dir Student Health Services ... Dr. Ronald C. MARTIN
40 Director Auxiliary Operations ... Mr. Paul R. KIGHTLINGER
85 Director Intl Student Svcs ... Ms. Linda KIGHTLINGER
25 Director Sponsored Programs ... Ms. Rene HEARNS
88 Dir Networks & Telecommunications ... Ms. Karen MURDZAK
90 Dir Desktop Systems/Learning Tech ... Mr. Dennis J. BRADLEY
13 Director Enterprise Systems ... Ms. Sallie A. TERPACK
96 Director Purchasing & Contract ... Ms. Darla SPAID
102 Director of Major Gifts ... Ms. Julie A. CHACONA
44 Dir of Annual Fund & Stewardship ... Ms. Marilyn GOELLNER
88 Director of Budget and Payroll ... Ms. Theresa VILLELLA
21 Controller ... Mr. Wayne T. OCHS
88 Bursar ... Mr. Mark MATLOCK
35 Director of Campus Life ... Ms. Michelle BARBICH
17 Director of Health & Wellness Ctr ... Ms. Darla ELDER
106 Manager of Online Programs ... Dr. James BOULDER
24 Learning Technology Svcs Manager ... Mr. Randall MCCASLIN
88 Coordinator Non-Credit Programs ... Ms. Beth ZEWE

*Indiana University of Pennsylvania (F)

1011 South Drive, Indiana PA 15705-0001
County: Indiana FICE Identification: 003277
Unit ID: 213020
Telephone: (724) 357-2100 Carnegie Class: DRU
FAX Number: (724) 357-6213 Calendar System: Semester
URL: www.iup.edu
Established: 1875 Annual Undergrad Tuition & Fees (In-State): $9,080
Enrollment: 15,379 Coed
Affiliation or Control: State IRS Status: 501(c)3
Highest Offering: Doctorate
Program: Liberal Arts And General; Teacher Preparatory; Professional
Accreditation: M, ACFEI, ART, BUS, CACREP, CLPSY, COARC, CS, DIETD, DIETI, ENGR, EXSC, MUS, NURSE, PLNG, SP, TED, THEA

02 President ... Dr. Michael DRISCOLL
05 Provost & VP Academic Affairs ... Dr. Timothy S. MOERLAND
11 Vice Pres Administration/Finance ... Dr. Cornelius WOOTEN
32 Vice President Student Affairs ... Dr. Rhonda H. LUCKEY
30 Vice Pres University Advancement ... Mr. William SPEIDEL

20 Assoc VP Academic Administration ....Dr. John N. KILMARX
58 Dean Graduate Studies & Research ....Dr. Timothy P. MACK
16 Assoc Vice Pres Human Resources ....Ms. Helen KENNEDY
79 Dean College Humanities & Soc Sci ....Dr. Yaw A. ASAMOAH
50 Dean Eberly Col Bus/Inform Tech ....Dr. Robert C. CAMP
20 Assoc Provost for Acad Pgms & Plng ....Vacant
53 Dean College Educ/Educ Tech ....Dr. Lara LUETKEHANS
81 Dean Col Natural Science & Math ....Dr. Deanne SNAVELY
57 Dean College of Fine Arts ....Mr. Michael J. HOOD
66 Dean College Health & Human Svcs ....Dr. Mark E. CORREIA
84 VP Enrollment Mgmt & Communications ....Mr. James BEGANY
08 Dean of Libraries ....Dr. Luis GONZALEZ
35 Dean of Students ....Vacant
06 Registrar ....Mr. Robert SIMON
38 Counseling Center ....Dr. Patti SHAFFER
27 Chief Information Officer ....Mr. Bill BALINT
04 Inst Research Planning & Assessment ....Mrs. Barbe MOORE
14 Exec Dir of Technology Services Ctr ......Mr. Todd CUNNINGHAM
28 Dir Social Equity/Civic Engagement ....Mr. Pablo MENDOZA
19 Director of Public Safety ....Mr. Sam CLUTTER
36 Director Career Development Ctr ....Ms. Tammy MANKO
29 Exec Director Alumni Association ....Mrs. Mary Jo LYTTLE
44 Director Annual Giving ....Ms. Emily SMELTZ
85 Asst VP Intl Education & Global ....Ms. Michele PETRUCCI
46 Assistant Dean for Research ....Dr. Hilliary CREELY
39 Exec Director Housing/Resid Living ......Mr. Michael LEMASTERS
40 Bookstore Director ....Mr. Tim SHARBAUGH
41 Director Athletics ....Dr. Francis CONDINO
23 Director Health Services ....Vacant
12 Dean Northpointe Campus ....Mr. Richard MUTH
12 Dean Punxsutawney Campus ....Dr. Terry APPOLONIA
43 Staff Attorney ....Ms. Jacqueline R. MORROW
26 Exec Dir Commun & Media Relations ....Ms. Michelle SHAFFER FRYLING
96 Director of Purchasing ....Mr. Robert BOWSER
10 Assoc Vice President for Finance ....Mrs. Susanna C. SINK
04 Exec Assistant to the President ....Ms. Robin GORMAN
37 Director of Financial Aid ....Ms. Stacy HOPKINS
23 Exec Dir Health & Well-Being ....Mrs. Malinda COWLES
88 Dir Admin Services Culinary Arts ....Ms. Enid RESENIC

*Kutztown University of Pennsylvania (A)

15200 Kutztown Road, Kutztown PA 19530-0730

County: Berks FICE Identification: 003322
Unit ID: 213349
Telephone: (610) 683-4000 Carnegie Class: Master's L
FAX Number: (610) 683-4693 Calendar System: Semester
URL: www.kutztown.edu
Established: 1866 Annual Undergrad Tuition & Fees (In-State): $8,819
Enrollment: 9,543 Coed
Affiliation or Control: State IRS Status: 501(c)3
Highest Offering: Master's
Program: Liberal Arts And General; Teacher Preparatory; Professional
Accreditation: M, ART, MUS, SW, TED

02 President ....Dr. F. Javier CEVALLOS
05 Vice Pres Academic & Stdnt Affairs ....Dr. Carlos VARGAS-ABURTO
10 VP Administration & Finance ....Mr. Gerald L. SILBERMAN
84 VP for Enrollment Management ....Vacant
100 Chief of Staff to the President ....Ms. Elsa G. COLLINS
102 Executive Director KU Foundation ....Vacant
30 Associate Vice Pres Comm/Mktg & Ext Aff ....Mr. John C. GREEN
22 Assoc Vice Pres Equity & Compliance ....Mr. Jesus PENA
20 Vice Provost Academic Affairs ....Dr. Carole WELLS
21 Asst Vice Pres Admin & Finance ....Vacant
32 Assoc Vice Provost/Dean of Students ....Mr. Robert WATROUS
27 Asst Vice Provost/Info Technology ....Mr. Mitchell FREED
15 Executive Director Human Resources ....Ms. Sharon M. PICUS
18 Asst Vice President for Facilities ....Mr. Robert J. GRIMM
88 Dean College Visual/Performing Arts ......Dr. William J. MOWDER
49 Dean College Liberal Arts/Sci ....Dr. Anne E. ZAYAITZ
50 Dean College of Business ....Dr. William DEMPSEY
53 Dean College Education ....Dr. Darrell GARBER
62 Dean Library Services ....Vacant
26 Director of University Relations ....Mr. Matthew SANTOS
09 Director Institutional Research ....Ms. Natalie SNOW
06 Registrar ....Ms. Michelle HUGHES
37 Director of Financial Aid ....Mr. Bernard L. MCCREE
39 Director Housing/Residential Svcs ....Mr. Kent R. DAHLQUIST
41 Director of Athletics ....Mr. Gregory BAMBERGER
38 Director Counseling & Psych Svcs ....Dr. Bruce SHARKIN
96 Assistant Director of Purchasing ....Ms. Barbara REITZ
07 Director of Admissions ....Ms. Nancy WUNDERLY
19 Acting Chief of Police ....Mr. John DILLON
36 Director Career/Community Services ....Ms. Kerri GARDI
29 Director Alumni Engagement ....Mr. Alex OGEKA

*Lock Haven University (B)

401 N Fairview Street, Lock Haven PA 17745-2390

County: Clinton FICE Identification: 003323
Unit ID: 213613
Telephone: (570) 484-2001 Carnegie Class: Master's S
FAX Number: (570) 484-2432 Calendar System: Semester
URL: www.lhup.edu
Established: 1870 Annual Undergrad Tuition & Fees (In-State): $8,238
Enrollment: 5,328 Coed
Affiliation or Control: State IRS Status: 170(c)1
Highest Offering: Master's
Program: Liberal Arts And General; Teacher Preparatory
Accreditation: M, ACBSP, ADNUR, ARCPA, NRPA, NUR, SW, TED

02 President ....Dr. Michael FIORENTINO, JR.
05 Provost/Vice Pres Academic Affs ....Dr. Donna WILSON
10 Vice Pres Finance & Administraton ....Mr. William HANELLY
32 Vice President for Student Affairs ....Vacant
84 Asst VP for Enrollment Management ....Ms. Tyana LANGE
49 Dean of Liberal Arts & Education ....Dr. Susan RIMBY
83 Dean Natural/Behavioral/Health Sci ....Dr. Jonathan LINDZEY
50 Dean Business/Info Sys/Human Svcs ....Dr. Stephen NEUN
12 Director Clearfield Branch Campus ....Dr. William CURLEY
85 Director of International Studies ....Ms. Rosana CAMPBELL
09 Director Institutional Research ....Mr. Mike ABPLANALP
15 Associate VP of Human Resources ....Ms. Deana HILL
07 Director of Admissions ....Ms. Robin ROCKEY
06 Registrar ....Mrs. Jill MITCHLEY
28 Director of Diversity ....Mr. Albert W. JONES
37 Director of Financial Aid ... Ms. Heidi HUNTER-GOLDSWORTHY
36 Director of Career Services ....Ms. Joan C. WELKER
26 Exec Asst to Pres for External Rels ....Mr. Rodney JENKINS
19 Director of Public Safety ....Mr. Paul ALTIERI
18 Director of Facilities ....Mr. Keith ROUSH
41 Director of Athletics ....Mr. Mark SHERBURNE
66 Director of Nursing Program ....Ms. Kimberly OWENS
38 Director of Counseling ....Dr. Dan E. TESS
90 Dir Computing/Instructional Tech ......Mr. Donald W. PATTERSON
88 Director of Physician Asst Program ....Mr. Walt EISENHAUER
92 Director Honors Program ....Dr. Jacqueline WHITLING
94 Director Women's Studies ....Dr. Kimberly ALEXANDER
93 Director Minority Students ....Mr. Kenneth L. HALL
40 Manager University Bookstore ....Mr. James KOWNACKI
29 Director Alumni Relations ....Ms. Tammy RICH

*Mansfield University of Pennsylvania (C)

Academy Street, Mansfield PA 16933-1697

County: Tioga FICE Identification: 003324
Unit ID: 213783
Telephone: (570) 662-4000 Carnegie Class: Master's M
FAX Number: (570) 662-4995 Calendar System: Semester
URL: www.mansfield.edu
Established: 1857 Annual Undergrad Tuition & Fees (In-State): $8,926
Enrollment: 3,131 Coed
Affiliation or Control: State IRS Status: 501(c)3
Highest Offering: Master's
Program: Liberal Arts And General; Teacher Preparatory
Accreditation: M, COARC, DIETD, MUS, NUR, RAD, SW, TED

02 President ....Gen. Francis L. HENDRICKS
05 Provost/Vice Pres Academic Affairs ....Dr. Peter KELLER
10 Vice Pres Finance/Administration ....Mr. John ADAMS
30 Vice Pres for Univ Advancement ....Vacant
32 Vice President of Student Affairs ....Vacant
35 Assoc Vice Pres/Dean of Students ....Dr. Christopher BRIDGES
39 Assoc Vice Pres Stdnt Affairs & Aux ....Mr. Chuck COLBY
49 Interim Assoc Prov/Dean Arts/Scienc ....Dr. David STINEBECK
53 Assoc Provost/Dean of Education ....Dr. Joy BURKE
15 Exec Dir Employee & Leadership Svs ......Ms. Dia M. CARLETON
08 Director Library/Info Resource Svcs ....Mr. Scott R. DIMARCO
18 Assoc Vice Pres F&A (Facilities) ....Mr. Scott WILLIAMS
84 Exec Director Enrollment Management ....Vacant
26 Director Public Rels/Publications ....Mr. Dennis R. MILLER
37 Director of Student Financial Aid ....Mr. Charles SCHEETZ
19 Director University Police & Safety ....Ms. Christine SHEGAN
41 Director of Athletics ....Mr. Roger N. MAISNER
85 Social Equity/Multicultural Affairs ....Mr. Alan ZELLNER
25 Director of Grants Development ....Ms. Anne LOUDENSLAGER
09 Dir Institutional Rsrch/Assess Data ....Dr. John COSGROVE
29 Director of Alumni Relations ....Ms. Denise BERG
96 Director of Purchasing ....Mr. Tekeste B. ABRAHAM
06 Registrar ....Ms. Lori CASS
38 Director of Counseling Center ....Vacant
07 Dir of Admissions Tactical/Enroll ....Ms. Rachel GREEN
07 Dir of Admissions Marketing ....Ms. Casey WOOD

*Millersville University of Pennsylvania (D)

PO Box 1002, Millersville PA 17551-0302

County: Lancaster FICE Identification: 003325
Unit ID: 214041
Telephone: (717) 872-3024 Carnegie Class: Master's L
FAX Number: (717) 872-3968 Calendar System: 4/1/4
URL: www.millersville.edu
Established: 1855 Annual Undergrad Tuition & Fees (In-State): $8,803
Enrollment: 8,368 Coed
Affiliation or Control: State IRS Status: 501(c)3
Highest Offering: Master's
Program: Liberal Arts And General; Teacher Preparatory; Professional
Accreditation: M, ACBSP, ART, COARC, CS, ENGR, MUS, NAIT, NUR, SW, TED

02 President ....Dr. John M. ANDERSON
05 Vice Pres Academic Affs/Provost ....Dr. Vilas A. PRABHU
10 Vice Pres Finance & Administration ....Mr. Roger BRUSZEWSKI
32 Vice President for Student Affairs ....Dr. Aminta H. BREAUX
30 Vice Pres University Advancement ....Mr. Gerald C. ECKERT
84 Vice Pres Enrollment Management ....Vacant
22 Asst to Pres Soc Equity/Div ....Mr. Hiram G. MARTINEZ
20 Associate Provost Academic Admin ....Dr. Jeffrey R. ADAMS
20 Asst Vice President Academic Svc .....Dr. Minor (Will) REDMOND
45 Asst VP Plng Assessment/Analysis ....Dr. Lisa R. SHIBLEY
21 Assoc Vice Pres Finance/Admin ....Vacant
35 Assoc VP Student Affairs ....Ms. Michelle PEREZ
15 Associate Vice Pres Human Resources ....Mr. Louis P. DESOL
26 Asst Vice Pres for Advancement ....Vacant
37 Asst VP Stdnt Affs/Dir Fin Aid ....Mr. Dwight G. HORSEY
39 Asst VP Stdnt Affs/Dir Housing ......Mr. Thomas J. RICHARDSON
25 Asst Vice President Development ....Vacant
18 Asst VP Facilities ....Mr. Thomas A. WALTZ, JR.
53 Interim Dean of Education ....Dr. Helena TULEYA-PAYNE
79 Dean Humanities/Social Sciences ....Dr. Diane UMBLE
81 Dean of Science & Mathematics ....Dr. Robert T. SMITH
58 Dean Graduate Studies ....Dr. Victor DESANTIS
84 Int Assoc Provost Enrollment Mgmt ....Dr. Brian HAZLETT
06 Registrar ....Ms. Candace DEEN
07 Director of Admissions ....Mr. Brian HAZLETT
36 Director Career Services ....Ms. Margo J. SASSAMAN
18 Dir Capital Const/Contract/Design ....Vacant
38 Director Counseling/Human Devel ....Dr. Kelsey K. BACKELS
19 Chief of University Police ....Mr. Peter J. ANDERS
23 Director of Univ Health Service ....Dr. Susan F. NORTHWALL
41 Dir of Intercollegiate Athletics ....Ms. Peg KAUFFMAN
40 Manager University Bookstore ....Ms. Audrey HERR
42 Minister-Campus ....Rev. Kirstin SHROM-RHOADS
42 Minister-Catholic ....Fr. Pang TCHEOU
44 Director of Planned Giving ....Mr. Francis SCHODOWSKI
29 Exec Dir for Alumni/Cmty Rels ....Mr. Steven A. DIGUISEPPE
44 Asst Director Major Gifts ....Ms. Alice MCMURRY
44 Asst Dir Advancement Services ....Mr. Derek M. HOFFMAN
09 Director Institutional Research ....Mr. Joseph E. REVELT
30 Director of Development ....Ms. Martha P. MACADAM
30 Dir of Major Gifts ....Ms. Linda ROUSH
102 Dir of Foundation & Govt Support ....Mr. Rene MUNOZ
96 Director of Purchasing ....Mr. David C. ERRICKSON
18 Dir of Maint Operations ....Vacant
100 Executive Deputy/Chief of Staff ....Dr. James MCCOLLUM
12 Dir The Ware Center ....Mr. Harvey OWEN
12 Director The Winter Center ....Ms. Laura KENDALL

*Shippensburg University of Pennsylvania (E)

1871 Old Main Drive, Shippensburg PA 17257-2200

County: Cumberland FICE Identification: 003326
Unit ID: 216010
Telephone: (717) 477-7447 Carnegie Class: Master's L
FAX Number: (717) 477-1273 Calendar System: Semester
URL: www.ship.edu
Established: 1871 Annual Undergrad Tuition & Fees (In-State): $9,448
Enrollment: 8,253 Coed
Affiliation or Control: State IRS Status: 501(c)3
Highest Offering: Master's
Program: Liberal Arts And General; Teacher Preparatory; Professional; Fine Arts Emphasis
Accreditation: M, BUS, CACREP, CS, JOUR, SW, TED

02 Interim President ....Dr. George F. HARPSTER
03 Exec VP Ext & University Relations ...Dr. G. F. (Jody) HARPSTER
05 Provost & Sr VP Academic Affairs ....Dr. Barbara G. LYMAN
10 Vice Pres Administration/Finance ....Dr. Jan (Denny) TERRELL
102 Pres Shippensburg Univ Foundation ....Mr. John CLINTON
32 Vice Pres for Student Affairs ....Dr. Roger L. SERR
13 Vice Pres Information Tech/Services ....Dr. Rick RUTH
20 Associate Provost/Dean of Graduate .Dr. Tracy A. SCHOOLCRAFT
20 Assoc Provost/Dean of Acad Outreach ....Dr. Christina SAX
20 Assoc VP for Enrollment Management ..Dr. William E. SOMMERS
84 Dean of Admiss/Dir of Enroll Mgmt ....Vacant
35 Dean of Students ....Dr. David L. LOVETT
06 Registrar ....Ms. Cathy J. SPRENGER
36 Director Career Development ....Vacant
37 Director Financial Aid ....Dr. Sandra TARBOX
29 Exec Dir University/AlumniRelations ....Dr. Tim EBERSOLE
27 Director Publications & Advertising ....Ms. Laura LUDLAM
88 Exec Dir Univ Communications/Mrktg ....Dr. Peter GIGLIOTTI
08 Dean Library & Multi-Media Services ....Dr. Dennis MATHES
22 Director Social Equity ....Dr. Melodye WEHRUNG
88 Director Womens Center ....Ms. Stephanie ERDICE
09 Director Inst Research & Planning ....Mr. Mark PILGRIM
25 Dir Spons Pgm/Inst Public Svc ....Mr. Christopher WONDERS
15 Director Human Resources ....Dr. David TOPPER
38 Director Counseling Services ....Dr. Philip W. HENRY
88 Director of Conferences ....Mr. Randy HAMMOND
53 Dean College Education & Human Svcs ..Dr. James R. JOHNSON
49 Dean College Arts & Science ....Dr. James MIKE
50 Dean College of Business ....Dr. John KOOTI
88 Dean Academic Engagement & Student ....Dr. Sarah STOKELY
18 Chief Facilities/Physical Plant ....Mr. Lance BRYSON
96 Director of Purchasing/Contracting ....Ms. Deborah MARTIN
19 Director Public Safety ....Ms. Cytha D. GRISSOM
41 Athletic Director ....Mr. Jeff A. MICHAELS
04 Exec Asst to the President ....Ms. Robin MAUN

*Slippery Rock University of Pennsylvania (F)

1 Morrow Way, Slippery Rock PA 16057-1326

County: Butler FICE Identification: 003327
Unit ID: 216038
Telephone: (724) 738-9000 Carnegie Class: Master's L
FAX Number: (724) 738-2169 Calendar System: Semester
URL: www.sru.edu
Established: 1889 Annual Undergrad Tuition & Fees (In-State): $9,057
Enrollment: 8,559 Coed
Affiliation or Control: State IRS Status: 501(c)3

Highest Offering: Doctorate
Program: Liberal Arts And General; Professional
Accreditation: M, ART, ACBSP, CACREP, CS, DANCE, EXSC, MUS, NRPA, NUR, PTA, SW, TED, THEA

02 President ... Dr. Cheryl NORTON
05 Provost/Vice Pres Academic Affairs ... Dr. Philip WAY
10 Interim Vice Pres Finance/Admin ... Ms. Molly MERCER
32 Interim Vice Pres Student Affairs ... Dr. Robert WATSON
30 Vice President for Univ Advancement ... Ms. Barbara A. ENDER
21 Asst Vice Pres for Finance ... Ms. Molly MERCER
18 Asst Vice Pres for Facilities ... Mr. Herbert F. CARLSON
35 Asst Vice Pres for Student Services ... Dr. John S. BONANDO
38 Asst Vice Pres for Student Devel ... Dr. Paula OLIVERO
15 Asst Vice Pres Human Resources ... Ms. Lynne M. MOTYL
28 Asst VP Diversity & Equal Oppty ... Ms. Holly M. MCCOY
04 Assistant to the President ... Ms. Tina L. MOSER
13 Assoc Prov Acad Fin Mgt & Inst Res ... Ms. Carrie BIRCKBICHLER
84 Assoc Provost Enrollment Services ... Dr. Amanda A. YALE
30 Exec Director Univ Advancement ... Dr. Edward R. BUCHA
26 Exec Director Public Relations ... Ms. Rita E. ABENT
37 Director Student Financial Aid ... Ms. Patricia A. HLADIO
19 Director Public Safety ... Mr. Paul NOVAK
19 Director University Police ... Mr. Michael SIMMONS
09 Assoc Prov Inst Rsrch/Acad Fin Mgmt ... Ms. Carrie J. BIRCKBICHLER
08 Director of Library Services ... Mr. Philip J. TRAMDACK
14 Director Computer Services ... Vacant
06 Director Acad Records/Summer School ... Mr. Eliott G. BAKER
07 Director Undergraduate Admissions ... Mr. Michael MAY
23 Director Health Services ... Ms. Kristina B. CHIPREAN
36 Associate Director Career Services ... Mr. John F. SNYDER
29 Director Alumni Affairs ... Ms. Kelly BAILEY
76 Dean Col Health Environment/Sci ... Dr. Susan E. HANNAM
07 Int Director Graduate Admissions ... Ms. Rebecca TRINCHESE
41 Athletic Director ... Mr. Paul A. LUEKEN
39 Director Housing/Residence Life ... Mr. Kevin D. CURRIE
85 Director International Services ... Ms. Pamela J. FRIGOT
25 Director Grants & Sponsored Rsrch ... Ms. Nancy L. CRUIKSHANK
38 Director of Student Counseling ... Dr. Carol L. HOLLAND
93 Director of Minority Students ... Ms. Corinne J. GIBSON
96 Director of Purchasing ... Mr. Mark S. COMBINE
92 Director of Honors Program ... Dr. Bradley WILSON
57 Dean Col of Hum/Fine/Perf Arts ... Dr. Eva TSUQUIASHI-DADDESIO
50 Dean Col Business/Info/Social Scs ... Dr. Kurt SHIMMEL
53 Dean College of Education ... Dr. Keith DILS

*West Chester University of Pennsylvania (A)

University & High Street, West Chester PA 19383-0001
County: Chester — FICE Identification: 003328
Unit ID: 216764
Telephone: (610) 436-1000 — Carnegie Class: Master's L
FAX Number: (610) 436-3115 — Calendar System: Semester
URL: www.wcupa.edu
Established: 1871 — Annual Undergrad Tuition & Fees (In-State): $6,990
Enrollment: 15,411 — Coed
Affiliation or Control: State — IRS Status: 501(c)3
Highest Offering: Doctorate
Program: Liberal Arts And General; Teacher Preparatory; Professional
Accreditation: M, ART, BUS, CACREP, COARC, CS, DIETD, EXSC, MUS, NURSE, PH, SP, SW, TED, THEA

02 President ... Dr. Greg R. WEISENSTEIN
86 Executive Deputy/Govt Relations Ofc ... Mr. Lawrence A. DOWDY
04 Sr Assoc to the President ... Ms. Rebecca HOOK
22 Director Social Equity ... Ms. Barbara SCHNELLER
05 Vice Pres Academic Affairs/Provost ... Dr. Linda L. LAMWERS
11 Vice President Admin/Finance ... Mr. Mark P. MIXNER
13 Vice Pres Information Services ... Mr. Adel BARIMANI
30 Vice President Advancement ... Dr. Mark G. PAVLOVICH
03 VP for External Operations ... Dr. Christopher M. FIORENTINO
32 VP Student Affs/Dean of Students ... Dr. Matthew M. BRICKETTO
88 AVP Planning/Academic Admin ... Mr. Vernon HARPER
64 Dean College Visual/Performing Arts ... Dr. Timothy V. BLAIR
76 Dean College Health Science ... Dr. Linda ADAMS
53 Dean College Education ... Dr. Kenneth D. WITMER
50 Interim Dean College of BPA ... Dr. Michelle PATRICK
49 Dean College Arts/Sciences ... Dr. Lori A. VERMEULEN
20 Dean Undergrad Stds/Stdt Suppt Svcs ... Dr. Idna M. CORBETT
23 Asst Dean Stdnts/Dir Health Center ... Ms. Mary Ann HAMMOND
88 Assoc VP Sponsored Research ... Dr. Gautam PILLAY
58 Interim AVP AA/Dean Grad Studies ... Dr. Lorraine BERNOTSKY
15 Assoc Vice Pres Human Resources ... Mr. Michael T. MALOY
35 Asst Vice Pres Student Affairs ... Ms. Diane DEVESTERN
35 Asst Vice Pres Student Affairs ... Dr. Thomas J. PURCE
10 Asst VP Finance/Business Svcs ... Ms. Bernadette HINKLE
06 Asst VP Enrollment Mgmt/Registrar ... Mr. Joseph SANTIVASCI
85 Asst VP International Programs ... Dr. David A. WRIGHT
102 Exec Director WCU Foundation ... Mr. Richard T. PRZYWARA
18 Exec Director Facilities Management ... Mr. Greg CUPRAK
18 Exec Direct Facilities Design/Const ... Ms. Dolores GIARDINA
106 Exec Director Distance Education ... Dr. Rui LI
21 Dir Accounting/Financial Reporting ... Mr. Kevin MCCADDEN
07 Director Admissions ... Ms. Marsha L. HAUG
09 Director Institutional Research ... Ms. Lisa YANNICK
21 Bursar/Director Student Finan Svcs ... Mr. Daniel PAULETTI
88 Director Budget/Financial Planning ... Ms. Colleen BRADLEY
26 Director Public Relations/Marketing ... Ms. Pamela SHERIDAN
88 Director Publications/Printing Svcs ... Ms. Cynthia BEDNAR
31 Director Cultural/Community Affairs ... Mr. John RHEIN
88 Director Conference Services ... Ms. Mary Beth KURIMAY
08 Director Library Services ... Mr. Richard SWAIN
88 Director Teacher Education Center ... Dr. James B. PRICE
36 Director Career Devel Center ... Ms. Rebecca ROSS
88 Dir Academic Development Pgm ... Dr. Allan HILL
88 Dir Learning Asst/Resource ... Ms. Gerardina MARTIN
37 Director Financial Aid ... Mr. Dana C. PARKER
38 Director Counseling Center ... Dr. Julie PERONE
29 Director Alumni Relations ... Ms. Tracey DUKERT
41 Director Athletics ... Dr. Edward M. MATEJKOVIC
88 Director Sports Information ... Mr. James ZUHLKE
28 Director Multicultural Affairs ... Mr. Jerome HUTSON
94 Director Women's Center ... Dr. Adale SHOLOCK
19 Director Public Safety ... Mr. Michael D. BICKING
96 Director Purchasing/Contract Svcs ... Ms. Marianne PEFFALL
88 Dir Environmental Health/Safety ... Ms. Gail FELLOWS
88 Dir Facilities Finance/Support Svcs ... Ms. Susan MILLER
91 Dir Administrative Computing Systms ... Mr. Patrick LENZI
88 Dir IT Strategic Sourcing/Planning ... Ms. Chaw-ye CHANG
105 Director Content and Web Svcs ... Ms. Kimberly SLATTERY
90 Spec Asst to VP Information Svcs ... Dr. James FABREY
88 Director Comm/Infrastructure Svcs ... Mr. Joseph SINCAVAGE
39 Director Housing Services ... Mr. Peter GALLOWAY
39 Director Residence Life ... Ms. Marion MCKINNEY
88 Dir Judicial Affairs/Student Assist ... Ms. Lynn KLINGENSMITH
88 Director Campus Recreation ... Dr. Stephen GAMBINO
88 Dir Student Leadership/Involve ... Mr. Charles WARNER
88 Director Sykes Student Union ... Mr. David TIMMANN
88 Director New Student Programs ... Mr. Jared BROWN
88 Dir Fraternity & Sorority Life ... Ms. Cara JENKINS
88 Dir Service Lrng & Volunteer Pgm ... Ms. Jodi ROTH
88 Dir Pre-major Academic Advising ... Dr. Joanne CONLON
92 Director Honors College ... Dr. Kevin DEAN
88 Exec Dir Student Service Inc ... Ms. Mell JOSEPHS
40 Student Svcs Inc Bookstore Manager ... Mr. Stephen MANNELLA

*Lock Haven University Clearfield Branch Campus (B)

201 University Drive, Clearfield PA 16830
Telephone: (814) 768-3405 — Identification: 770186
Accreditation: &M

† Main campus is Lock Haven University in Lock Haven, PA.

*Venango College of Clarion University (C)

1801 W First Street, Oil City PA 16301-3297
Telephone: (814) 676-6591 — FICE Identification: 003319
Accreditation: &M, ADNUR, COARC, NAIT, NUR

† Main campus is Clarion University of Pennsylvania in Clarion, PA.

Philadelphia College of Osteopathic Medicine (D)

4170 City Avenue, Philadelphia PA 19131-1694
County: Philadelphia — FICE Identification: 003352
Unit ID: 215123
Telephone: (215) 871-6100 — Carnegie Class: Spec/Med
FAX Number: (215) 871-6719 — Calendar System: Semester
URL: www.pcom.edu
Established: 1899 — Annual Graduate Tuition & Fees: $43,621
Enrollment: 2,580 — Coed
Affiliation or Control: Independent Non-Profit — IRS Status: 501(c)3
Highest Offering: Doctorate; No Undergraduates
Program: Professional
Accreditation: M, ARCPA, CLPSY, OSTEO

01 President & CEO ... Dr. Matthew SCHURE
05 Provost/Senior VP Acad Affairs/Dean ... Dr. Kenneth J. VEIT
10 Vice Pres Finance/Treasurer/CFO ... Mr. Peter DOULIS
58 Vice Pres Grad Pgms/Academic Plng ... Dr. Robert G. CUZZOLINO
63 Dean Osteopathic Med Pgm-GA Campus ... Dr. William CRAVER
67 Dean School of Pharmacy ... Dr. Mark OKAMOTO
17 Vice Dean Osteopathic Clinical Educ ... Dr. Richard A. PASCUCCI
20 Asst Dean Graduate Medical Educ ... Dr. David KUO
20 Asst Dean Clinical Education ... Dr. Paula GREGORY
88 Asst Dean Clinical Education ... Dr. Joseph KACZMARCZYK
35 Asst Dean Pharmacy Student Affairs ... Dr. Michael LEE
20 Asst Dean Curriculum ... Dr. Kerin FRESA-DILLON
20 Asst Dean Curriculum ... Dr. Bonnie BUXTON
12 Campus Exec Ofcr-Georgia Campus ... Mr. Bryan GINN
46 Chief Science Officer ... Dr. Kenneth SLAVIK
32 Chief Student Affair Officer ... Dr. Tina WOODRUFF
26 Chief Marketing/Communications Ofcr ... Ms. Wendy ROMANO
37 Chief Student Financial Aid Officer ... Mr. Samuel MATHENY
15 Chief Human Resources Officer ... Mr. Edward POTTS
07 Chief Admissions Officer ... Ms. Deborah A. BENVENGER
28 Chief Diversity Officer ... Dr. Lisa MCBRIDE
13 Chief Technology Officer ... Mr. James WILLIAMS
88 Chief Compliance Officer ... Dr. Allan MCLEOD
88 Chief Risk Management Officer ... Ms. Laura BELL
18 Chief Facilities/Plant Operations ... Mr. Frank H. WINDLE
08 Chair of Library/Exec Director ... Ms. Etheldra TEMPLETON
06 Registrar ... Ms. Deborah CASTELLANO
29 Dir Alumni Relations/Development ... Ms. Pamela J. RUOFF
96 Director of Purchasing ... Ms. Natalie COOPER

Philadelphia University (E)

4201 Henry Avenue, Philadelphia PA 19144
County: Philadelphia — FICE Identification: 003354
Unit ID: 215099
Telephone: (215) 951-2700 — Carnegie Class: Master's L
FAX Number: (215) 951-2615 — Calendar System: Semester
URL: www.philau.edu
Established: 1884 — Annual Undergrad Tuition & Fees: $32,990
Enrollment: 3,540 — Coed
Affiliation or Control: Independent Non-Profit — IRS Status: 501(c)3
Highest Offering: Doctorate
Program: Professional
Accreditation: M, ARCPA, ART, CIDA, ENG, LSAR, MIDWF, OT, OTA

01 President ... Dr. Stephen SPINELLI, JR.
11 VP for Administration/COO ... Dr. Geoffrey CROMARTY
10 Chief Financial Officer/Treasurer ... Mr. James P. HARTMAN
05 Provost ... Dr. Randy SWEARER
30 VP Development & Alumni Relations ... Mr. Jesse SHAFER
26 Vice Pres Marketing/Public Rels ... Ms. Patricia M. BALDRIDGE
13 Vice President/CIO ... Mr. Jeff CEPULL
84 Dean of Enrollment Management ... Ms. Christine GREB
32 Dean of Students ... Dr. Mark GOVONI
18 Asst Vice Pres for Operations ... Mr. J. Thomas BECKER
15 Asst Vice Pres Human Resources ... Ms. Katherine FLANNERY
48 Dean College of Architecture ... Vacant
81 Dean Col of Science & Health ... Dr. Matt BAKER
54 Dean College of Design Engineering ... Dr. Michael LEONARD
50 Dean School of Business Admin ... Dr. Sue LEHRMAN
58 Director Acad Pgm Continuing Stds ... Ms. Susan CALDER
08 Director of Library Services ... Ms. Karen ALBERT
38 Director Advising/Counseling ... Dr. Patricia THATCHER
41 Athletic Director ... Mr. Thomas R. SHIRLEY, JR.
29 Director Alumni Relations ... Ms. Elona LAKURIQI
36 Director of Career Services ... Ms. Tracy DEPEDRO
40 Director College Store ... Ms. Shirley A. LANDIS
37 Director Financial Aid ... Ms. Lisa J. COOPER
23 Director Health Services ... Ms. Kirstin PATRAGNONI-SAUTER
06 Registrar ... Ms. Julia AGGREH
39 Director of Residence Life Educ ... Ms. Laurie YUHNKE
19 Director Safety & Security ... Mr. Jeffrey BAIRD
35 Director Student Activities ... Mr. Timothy J. BUTLER
09 Director of Institutional Research ... Mr. Mark PALLADINO

Pittsburgh Institute of Aeronautics (F)

5 Allegheny County Airport, West Mifflin PA 15122-2674
County: Allegheny — FICE Identification: 005310
Unit ID: 215381
Telephone: (412) 346-2100 — Carnegie Class: Assoc/PrivNFP
FAX Number: (412) 466-0513 — Calendar System: Quarter
URL: www.pia.edu
Established: 1929 — Annual Undergrad Tuition & Fees: $20,400
Enrollment: 348 — Coed
Affiliation or Control: Independent Non-Profit — IRS Status: 501(c)3
Highest Offering: Associate Degree
Program: Occupational; 2-Year Principally Bachelor's Creditable; Technical Emphasis
Accreditation: ACCSC

01 President/CFO ... Mr. John GRAHAM, III
03 Executive Vice President/Director ... Ms. Suzanne MARKLE
05 Director of Education ... Mr. Greg NULL
07 Director of Admissions ... Mr. Steven SABOLD

Pittsburgh Institute of Mortuary Science (G)

5808 Baum Boulevard, Pittsburgh PA 15206-3706
County: Allegheny — FICE Identification: 010814
Unit ID: 215390
Telephone: (412) 362-8500 — Carnegie Class: Assoc/PrivNFP
FAX Number: (412) 362-1684 — Calendar System: Trimester
URL: www.pims.edu
Established: 1939 — Annual Undergrad Tuition & Fees: $16,200
Enrollment: 213 — Coed
Affiliation or Control: Independent Non-Profit — IRS Status: 501(c)3
Highest Offering: Associate Degree
Program: Occupational; 2-Year Principally Bachelor's Creditable
Accreditation: FUSER

01 President & CEO ... Eugene C. OGRODNIK
06 Registrar ... Karen S. ROCCO

Pittsburgh Technical Institute (H)

1111 McKee Road, Oakdale PA 15071-3205
County: Allegheny — FICE Identification: 007437
Unit ID: 215415
Telephone: (412) 809-5100 — Carnegie Class: Assoc/PrivFP
FAX Number: (412) 809-5320 — Calendar System: Quarter
URL: www.pti.edu
Established: 1946 — Annual Undergrad Tuition & Fees: $15,524
Enrollment: 1,794 — Coed
Affiliation or Control: Proprietary — IRS Status: Proprietary
Highest Offering: Associate Degree
Program: Occupational; 2-Year Principally Bachelor's Creditable; Technical Emphasis
Accreditation: M, MAC, SURGT

01 President ....Mr. Gregory DEFEO
03 Executive Vice President ....Mr. George PRY
05 Sr Vice Pres Academic Affairs ....Mr. Mark SCOTT
10 Sr Vice Pres Financial Affairs ....Mr. Terry FARRELL
26 Vice President of Marketing ....Mr. Bart LEVITT
10 Vice President of Business Affairs ....Mr. Chuck CUBELIC
21 Vice President Financial Services ....Mrs. Connie FRIEDBERG
32 Vice President Student Services ....Mr. Keith MERLINO
20 Vice President Education ....Ms. Eileen RILEY
30 Vice President of Inst Advancement ....Mrs. Ruth DELACH
09 Vice Pres of Strategic Initiatives ....Mr. Jeff BELSKY
43 General Counsel ....Mr. Jack MCGINTY
06 Registrar ....Mrs. Patricia TARVIN
08 Library Director ....Mrs. Ruth WALTER
36 Director of Career Services ....Mrs. Josephine SMITH
26 Director of Public Relations ....Mrs. Linda ALLAN
16 Director of Human Resources ....Ms. Nancy SHEPPARD
13 IT Department Director ....Mr. Bill SHOWERS
19 Director of Public Safety ....Dr. James LAURIA
39 Director of Resident Life ....Ms. Gloria RITCHIE
88 Director of Compliance ....Ms. Melissa BROWN
40 Campus Store Manager ....Mrs. Cynthia KLEIN
29 Alumni Coordinator ....Mrs. Christine IOLI

Pittsburgh Theological Seminary (A)

616 N. Highland Avenue, Pittsburgh PA 15206-2596

County: Allegheny FICE Identification: 003356
Unit ID: 215424
Telephone: (412) 362-5610 Carnegie Class: Spec/Faith
FAX Number: (412) 363-3260 Calendar System: Quarter
URL: www.pts.edu
Established: 1794 Annual Graduate Tuition & Fees: $11,520
Enrollment: 276 Coed
Affiliation or Control: Presbyterian Church (U.S.A.) IRS Status: 501(c)3
Highest Offering: Doctorate; No Undergraduates
Program: Professional; Religious Emphasis
Accreditation: M, THEOL

01 President ....Dr. William J. CARL, III
05 VP Academic Affs/Dean of Faculty ....Dr. Byron H. JACKSON
30 VP Strategic Advance/Mktg ....Mr. Thomas J. PAPPALARDO
32 VP Student Svcs/Dean of Students ....Mr. John WELCH
45 VP Planning/Inst Effectiveness ....Dr. James DOWNEY
06 Registrar ....Ms. Anne B. MALONE
08 Director of the Library ....Dr. Sharon TAYLOR
88 Director of Field Education ....Dr. Carolyn J. JONES
29 Director of Alumni/ae Services ....Ms. Carolyn CRANSTON
88 Director Doctor of Ministry Program ....Dr. Susan KENDALL
51 Director Cont Educ/Special Events ....Dr. James DAVISON
37 Dir Financial Aid/Admissions Ofcr ....Ms. Cheryl DEPAOLIS
07 Director of Admissions ....Vacant

Point Park University (B)

201 Wood Street, Pittsburgh PA 15222-1984

County: Allegheny FICE Identification: 003357
Unit ID: 215442
Telephone: (412) 391-4100 Carnegie Class: Master's L
FAX Number: (412) 392-3998 Calendar System: Semester
URL: www.pointpark.edu
Established: 1960 Annual Undergrad Tuition & Fees: $26,170
Enrollment: 3,827 Coed
Affiliation or Control: Independent Non-Profit IRS Status: 501(c)3
Highest Offering: Master's
Program: Liberal Arts And General; Teacher Preparatory; Professional
Accreditation: M, DANCE, ENGT, IACBE

01 President ....Dr. Paul HENNIGAN
03 VP and Artistic Director ....Mr. Ronald ALLAN-LINDBLOM
05 Sr VP Academic and Student Affairs ....Dr. Karen MCINTYRE
10 Sr VP Finance and Operations ....Ms. Bridget MANCOSH
26 VP of External Affairs ....Ms. Mariann GEYER
18 Vice Pres for Operations ....Mr. William D. CAMERON
30 Vice Pres Development/AlumniAffairs ....Mr. Richard HASKINS
84 Asst VP Strategic Plng/Enrollment ....Ms. Trudy WILLIAMS
96 Asst VP Procurement/Business Svcs ....Ms. Ruth RAULUK
32 Dean of Student Affairs ....Mr. Keith PAYLO
53 Chair Education ....Dr. Darlene MARNICH
79 Actg Chair Humanities/Human Science ....Mr. William PURCELL
88 Chair of Faculty ....Dr. Heather STARR FIEDLER
54 Act Chair Natural Science/Engr Tech ....Dr. Mark FARRELL
88 Chair Criminal Justice/Intell Stds ....Mr. Greg ROGERS
88 Chair Management ....Ms. Margaret GILFILLAN
88 Chair Theatre ....Ms. Sheila MCKENNA
88 Chair Dance ....Ms. Susan STOWE
88 Chair Cinema ....Mr. Nelson CHIPMAN
57 Dean Conservatory of Perform Arts ....Mr. Frederick JOHNSON
49 Actg Dean School Arts and Sciences ....Dr. Robert FESSLER
60 Dean School of Communication ....Vacant
50 Dean School of Business ....Vacant
04 Exec Assistant to the President ....Ms. Nina CAMPBELL
06 Registrar ....Ms. Jennifer FEDELE
15 Director Human Resources ....Mr. Guy CATANIA
21 Director of Finance/Controller ....Mr. Jim HARDT
29 Director/Alumni Relations ....Ms. Kristen BAGINSKI
08 Director/Librarian/Academic Svcs ....Ms. Liz EVANS
37 Director of Financial Aid ....Ms. Sheila NELSON-HENSLEY
26 Sr Dir Marketing & Communications ....Vacant
39 Director of Campus Life ....Ms. Janet D. EVANS
07 Director of Admissions ....Ms. Joell MINFORD
36 Director of Career Services ....Mr. Jan-Mitchell SHERRILL

41 Director of Athletics ....Mr. Dan SWALGA
09 Director Institutional Research ....Mr. Christopher CHONCEK
54 Dir of Sciences/Engineering Mgmt ....Dr. John KUDLAC
88 Dir Conference & Event Services ....Ms. Terri SNOE
38 Student Counseling ....Ms. Patti SCHWARTZ

Prism Career Institute-Upper Darby Campus (C)

6800 Market Street, Upper Darby PA 19082-1926

County: Delaware FICE Identification: 023013
Unit ID: 215433
Telephone: (610) 789-6700 Carnegie Class: Assoc/PrivFP
FAX Number: (610) 789-5208 Calendar System: Semester
URL: www.prismcareerinstitute.edu
Established: 1981 Annual Undergrad Tuition & Fees: $10,897
Enrollment: 325 Coed
Affiliation or Control: Proprietary IRS Status: Proprietary
Highest Offering: Associate Degree
Program: Occupational
Accreditation: #ACCSC

01 Campus Director ....Mr. Jeffery MANN
05 Director of Education ....Mr. Ken LEWANDOWSKI
07 Director of Admissions ....Ms. Dawn CLARK

Reading Area Community College (D)

PO Box 1706, Reading PA 19603-1706

County: Berks FICE Identification: 010388
Unit ID: 215585
Telephone: (610) 372-4721 Carnegie Class: Assoc/Pub-R-M
FAX Number: (610) 372-4264 Calendar System: Semester
URL: www.racc.edu
Established: 1971 Annual Undergrad Tuition & Fees (In-District): $4,650
Enrollment: 4,791 Coed
Affiliation or Control: State/Local IRS Status: 501(c)3
Highest Offering: Associate Degree
Program: Occupational; 2-Year Principally Bachelor's Creditable
Accreditation: M, ADNUR, COARC, MLTAD, PNUR

01 President ....Dr. Anna D. WEITZ
05 Sr VP of Academic Affairs/Provost ....Dr. A. Wade DAVENPORT
10 Sr VP Business Svcs/Treasurer ....Mr. Kenneth DEARSTYNE
103 VP Workforce Dev/Community Educ ....Dr. Robert VAUGHN
30 VP of Institutional Advancement ....Mr. Michael NAGEL
84 VP Enrollment Management ....Ms. Maria MITCHELL
21 Assoc VP for Business/Controller ....Ms. Dolores PETERSON
62 Asst Dean Library Svcs/Learning Res ....Ms. Mary Ellen HECKMAN
15 Director Human Resources ....Mr. Scott HEFFELFINGER
26 Director of Public Relations ....Ms. Melissa KUSHNER
13 Director Information Technology ....Mr. Chet WINTERS
09 Dir of Asessment/Research/Planning ....Ms. Mary FLAGG
37 Director Financial Aid/Registrar ....Mr. Benjamin ROSENBERGER
88 Dir of Miller Center for the Arts ....Ms. Cathleen STEPHEN
84 Director of Enrollment Services ....Ms. Calley STEVENS-TAYLOR
96 Purchasing Manager ....Mr. Michael HODOWANEC
19 Director of Safety & Security ....Mr. James SURGEONER
35 Coordinator of Student Activities ....Ms. Sue GELSINGER
04 Sr Admin Asst to the President ....Ms. Sandra STRAUSE
50 Asst Dean of Business Division ....Ms. Linda BELL
76 Asst Dean of Health Professions ....Dr. Amelia CAPOTOSTA
79 Assistant Dean of Humanities ....Dr. Karen JACOBSON
81 Asst Dean of Science/Math ....Dr. Steve WALLER
83 Asst Dean of Social Sci/Human Svcs ....Ms. Cynthia SEAMAN

Reconstructionist Rabbinical College (E)

1299 Church Road, Wyncote PA 19095-1898

County: Montgomery FICE Identification: 022734
Unit ID: 215619
Telephone: (215) 576-0800 Carnegie Class: Spec/Faith
FAX Number: (215) 576-6143 Calendar System: Semester
URL: www.rrc.edu
Established: 1968 Annual Graduate Tuition & Fees: $21,000
Enrollment: 52 Coed
Affiliation or Control: Jewish IRS Status: 501(c)3
Highest Offering: Doctorate; No Undergraduates
Program: Professional
Accreditation: M

01 President ....Rabbi Dan EHRENKRANTZ
05 Chief Academic Officer/Dean ....Dr. Tamar KAMIONKOWSKI
11 Vice President Administration ....Mrs. Jennifer S. ABRAHAM
10 Controller ....Ms. Lisa COHEN
20 Dean Academic Administration ....Ms. Barbara HIRSH
07 Asst VP Rabbinic Formation/Admiss ....Rabbi Amber POWERS
08 Director of the Library ....Ms. Deborah STERN

Reformed Episcopal Seminary (F)

826 Second Avenue, Blue Bell PA 19422-1257

County: Montgomery Identification: 667050
Unit ID: 216348
Telephone: (610) 292-9852 Carnegie Class: Not Classified
FAX Number: (610) 292-9853 Calendar System: Quarter
URL: www.reseminary.edu
Established: 1887 Annual Graduate Tuition & Fees: $6,650
Enrollment: 20 Coed
Affiliation or Control: Reformed Episcopal Church IRS Status: 501(c)3
Highest Offering: Master's; No Undergraduates
Program: Professional; Religious Emphasis
Accreditation: @THEOL

01 Chancellor and President ....Rt Rev. David L. HICKS
05 Dean ....Rev Dr. Jonathan S. RICHES
90 Director Information & Technology ....Mr. Gregory R. WRIGHT

Reformed Presbyterian Theological Seminary (G)

7418 Penn Avenue, Pittsburgh PA 15208-2594

County: Allegheny FICE Identification: 003358
Unit ID: 215628
Telephone: (412) 731-6000 Carnegie Class: Spec/Faith
FAX Number: (412) 731-4834 Calendar System: Quarter
URL: www.rpts.edu
Established: 1810 Annual Graduate Tuition & Fees: $10,692
Enrollment: 93 Coed
Affiliation or Control: Reformed Presbyterian Church IRS Status: 501(c)3
Highest Offering: Master's; No Undergraduates
Program: Professional; Religious Emphasis
Accreditation: THEOL

01 President ....Dr. Jerry F. O'NEILL
05 Dean of the Faculty ....Mr. Barry YORK
06 Registrar/Head Librarian ....Mr. Thomas G. REID, JR.
40 Bookstore Manager ....Ms. Sharon SAMPSON
10 Treasurer ....Mr. James MCFARLAND
07 Director of Admissions ....Mr. Aaron SAMS
37 Director of Financial Aid ....Mrs. Sharon SAMPSON
30 Director of Development ....Mr. Mark SAMPSON

The Restaurant School at Walnut Hill College (H)

4207 Walnut Street, Philadelphia PA 19104-3518

County: Philadelphia FICE Identification: 021928
Unit ID: 215637
Telephone: (215) 222-4200 Carnegie Class: Spec/Other
FAX Number: (215) 222-4219 Calendar System: Other
URL: www.walnuthillcollege.edu
Established: 1974 Annual Undergrad Tuition & Fees: $22,575
Enrollment: 376 Coed
Affiliation or Control: Proprietary IRS Status: Proprietary
Highest Offering: Baccalaureate
Program: 2-Year Principally Bachelor's Creditable
Accreditation: ACCSC

01 President ....Mr. Daniel LIBERATOSCIOLI
30 Vice President College Advancement ....Mr. Karl D. BECKER
11 Vice President Administrative Svcs ....Ms. Peggy LIBERATOSCIOLI
07 Director of Admissions ....Vacant
05 Dean of Academic Affairs ....Ms. Lenore BOCCIA
10 Chief Business Officer ....Mr. Chris MOLZ
32 Chf Student Life Ofcr/Stdnt Plcmnt ....Ms. Meghan BICKEL
51 Director Continuing Education ....Ms. Jocelyn WOOD
88 Director of Culinary Arts ....Chef Tom DELCAMP
88 Director School of Management ....Mr. David MORROW

Robert Morris University (I)

6001 University Boulevard,
Moon Township PA 15108-1189

County: Allegheny FICE Identification: 003359
Unit ID: 215655
Telephone: (412) 397-6400 Carnegie Class: Master's L
FAX Number: (412) 397-5958 Calendar System: Semester
URL: www.rmu.edu
Established: 1921 Annual Undergrad Tuition & Fees: $25,114
Enrollment: 5,181 Coed
Affiliation or Control: Independent Non-Profit IRS Status: 501(c)3
Highest Offering: Doctorate
Program: Teacher Preparatory; Professional
Accreditation: M, BUS, CS, ENG, NMT, NURSE, TEAC

01 President ....Dr. Gregory G. DELL'OMO
10 Sr Vice Pres for Business Affairs ....Mr. Dan W. KIENER
05 Provost/Sr VP Academic Affairs ....Mr. David L. JAMISON
30 Sr VP Institutional Advancement ....Mr. Jay T. CARSON
43 Vice President & General Counsel ....Ms. Renee CAVALOVITCH
21 Vice President Financial Operations ....Mr. Jeffrey A. LISTWAK
15 Vice President of Human Resources ....Mr. Peter K. FAIX
106 VP Online and Off-Campus Programs ....Dr. Darcy B. TANNEHILL
84 VP Enrollment Management ....Ms. Wendy C. BECKEMEYER
32 Vice President for Student Life ....Mr. John MICHALENKO
30 Vice President for Development ....Ms. Kimberley HAMMER
13 Vice Pres Information Technology ....Ms. Ellen G. WIECKOWSKI
18 Vice Pres for Facilities ....Mr. Perry F. ROOFNER
26 Vice Pres Public Rels/Marketing ....Ms. Kyle FISHER
20 Vice Provost for Academic Affairs ....Dr. Lawrence A. TOMEI
46 Vice Provost Research/Grad Study ....Dr. Derya JACOBS
09 Vice Provost Institutional Research ....Dr. David R. MAJKA
60 Dean School Comm/Info Systems ....Dr. Barbara J. LEVINE
50 Dean School of Business ....Dr. John BEEHLER
54 Dean School of Engr/Math/Science ....Dr. Maria V. KALEVITCH
53 Dean Sch Education/Social Sciences ....Dr. Mary Ann RAFOTH
66 Dean School Nursing/Health Sciences ....Dr. Lynda J. DAVIDSON
88 Dir Univ Sponsorships/Athletic Fund ....Mr. Matthew B. MILLET
07 Dean of Admissions ....Ms. Kellie L. LAURENZI
88 Exec Dir Bayer Ctr Nonprofit Mgmt ....Ms. Peggy M. OUTON
35 Assistant Dean of Students ....Mrs. Maureen H. KEEFER

41 Director of Athletics .... Dr. Craig S. COLEMAN
08 Interim Director University Library .... Mr. Christopher F. DEVINE
21 Controller .... Ms. Melissa A. MICCO
06 Registrar .... Mr. Frank E. PERRY
19 Director Public Safety .... Mr. Randy L. MINK
36 Director Career Center .... Ms. Kishma DECASTRO-SALLIS
39 Director Residence Life .... Mrs. Anne L. LAHODA
38 Director Center for Student Success .... Ms. Cassandra L. ODEN
28 Chief Diversity/Inclusion Officer .... Dr. Yasmin S. PUROHIT
27 Senior Director Public Relations .... Mr. Jonathan POTTS
96 Senior Director Business Operations .... Mr. Neal F. BINSTOCK
37 Director Student Financial Aid .... Ms. Stephanie N. HENDERSHOT
29 Dir Development/Alumni Relations .... Mr. Warner O. JOHNSON
88 Dean Engaged Learning .... Dr. Shari L. PAYNE

Rosedale Technical Institute (A)

215 Beecham Drive, Suite 2, Pittsburgh PA 15205-9791
County: Allegheny FICE Identification: 012050
Unit ID: 215682
Telephone: (412) 521-6200 Carnegie Class: Assoc/PrivNFP
FAX Number: (412) 521-2520 Calendar System: Semester
URL: www.rosedaletech.org
Established: 1949 Annual Undergrad Tuition & Fees: $13,310
Enrollment: 388 Coed
Affiliation or Control: Independent Non-Profit IRS Status: 501(c)3
Highest Offering: Associate Degree
Program: Occupational; 2-Year Principally Bachelor's Creditable; Technical Emphasis
Accreditation: ACCSC

01 President .... Dennis F. WILKE
05 Director of Education .... Jim SHORE
07 Director of Admissions .... Debbie BIER

Rosemont College (B)

1400 Montgomery Avenue, Rosemont PA 19010-1699
County: Montgomery FICE Identification: 003360
Unit ID: 215691
Telephone: (610) 527-0200 Carnegie Class: Master's M
FAX Number: (610) 527-0341 Calendar System: Semester
URL: www.rosemont.edu
Established: 1921 Annual Undergrad Tuition & Fees: $30,950
Enrollment: 908 Coed
Affiliation or Control: Roman Catholic IRS Status: 501(c)3
Highest Offering: Master's
Program: Liberal Arts And General; Teacher Preparatory
Accreditation: M

01 President .... Dr. Sharon LATCHAW HIRSH
05 Provost/VP Academic/Student Affairs .... Dr. B. Christopher DOUGHERTY
10 VP for Finance & Administration .... Mr. Randy ELDRIDGE
37 Director of Financial Aid .... Ms. Laverne GLENN
30 Vice Pres College Relations .... Ms. Christyn MORAN
32 Dean of Students .... Mr. Troy CHIDDICK
84 Vice President for Enrollment Mgmt .... Mr. Kevin M. MCINTYRE
88 Vice President for Mission .... Sr. Jeanne Marie HATCH, SHCJ
08 Exec Director of Library Services .... Mrs. Catherine FENNELL
58 Dean School Graduate/Prof Studies .... Dr. Dennis R. DOUGHERTY
20 Academic Dean Undergrad College .... Mrs. Paulette HUTCHINSON
29 Director of Alumni Relations .... Ms. Lauren MCDONNELL
26 Director of Public Relations .... Ms. Roberta PERRY
06 Registrar/Dir of Inst Research .... Mr. Joseph T. ROGERS
41 Director of Athletics .... Ms. Lynn S. ROTHENHOEFER
15 Director of Human Resources .... Ms. Jane FEDEROWICZ
42 Director of Campus Ministry .... Mr. Jay VERZOSA
40 Store Manager Campus Bookstore .... Mr. Rick HORNER
18 Chief Facil/Phys Plant/Pub Safety .... Mr. Raymond A. BROWN
38 Director Student Counseling .... Ms. Bonnie MARSHALL
39 Director of Res Life/Asst Dean .... Ms. Dianne VILLAR
19 Director of Public Safety .... Mr. Chuck LORENZ
21 Controller .... Ms. Renee M. WILLIAMS

Saint Charles Borromeo Seminary (C)

100 E Wynnewood Road, Wynnewood PA 19096-3099
County: Montgomery FICE Identification: 003364
Unit ID: 216047
Telephone: (610) 667-3394 Carnegie Class: Spec/Faith
FAX Number: (610) 667-7635 Calendar System: Semester
URL: www.scs.edu
Established: 1832 Annual Undergrad Tuition & Fees: $19,150
Enrollment: 208 Male
Affiliation or Control: Roman Catholic IRS Status: 501(c)3
Highest Offering: Master's
Program: Liberal Arts And General; Professional
Accreditation: M, THEOL

01 Rector & President .... M.Rev. Timothy C. SENIOR
03 Vice Rector .... Rev. Joseph W. BONGARD
10 Vice Pres of Finance & Operations .... Vacant
73 Academic Dean Theology Division .... Rev. Robert A. PESARCHICK
49 Academic Dean College Division .... Mr. James F. GROWDON
73 Director of Religious Studies .... Dr. Jared HASELBARTH
33 Dean of Men College .... Rev. Sean BRANSFIELD
33 Dean of Men Theol/Dir of Liturgy .... Rev. Patrick J. WELSH
06 Registrar .... Sr. Gilmary KAY
08 Director of Library Services .... Mrs. Cait KOKOLUS
42 Director Spiritual Formation Col .... Fr. Herb SPERGER
42 Director Spiritual Formation Theol .... Fr. Ned SHLESINGER
88 Director Pastoral/Apostolic Form .... Rev. Joseph T. SHENOSKY
64 Director of Music .... Dr. Theodore E. KIEFER
21 Director of Financial Services .... Ms. Mary D. D'URSO
37 Director Student Financial Aid .... Ms. Nora DOWNEY
19 Director of Safety and Security .... Mr. Nicholas MANCINI

Saint Francis University (D)

PO Box 600, Loretto PA 15940-0600
County: Cambria FICE Identification: 003366
Unit ID: 215743
Telephone: (814) 472-3000 Carnegie Class: Master's L
FAX Number: (814) 472-3003 Calendar System: Semester
URL: www.francis.edu
Established: 1847 Annual Undergrad Tuition & Fees: $29,992
Enrollment: 2,451 Coed
Affiliation or Control: Roman Catholic IRS Status: 501(c)3
Highest Offering: Doctorate
Program: Liberal Arts And General; Teacher Preparatory; Professional
Accreditation: M, ARCPA, IACBE, NURSE, OT, PTA, SW, @TEAC

01 President .... Rev. Gabriel ZEIS, TOR
05 Provost .... Dr. Wayne POWEL
10 Vice President for Finance .... Mr. Robert G. DATSKO
32 Vice Pres for Student Development .... Dr. Frank MONTECALVO
42 Director of Mission Integration .... Rev. Joseph LEHMAN
45 Vice Pres for Strategic Initiatives .... Ms. Patricia SEROTKIN
30 Vice President for Advancement .... Mr. Robert CRUSCIEL
84 Vice Pres for Enrollment Management .... Ms. Erin E. MCCLOSKEY
08 Dean of Library Services .... Ms. Sandra A. BALOUGH
97 Assoc Dean of General Education .... Vacant
06 Registrar .... Dr. Stephen R. ROMBOUTS
09 Director of Institutional Research .... Mr. Daniel KOSHUTE
37 Financial Aid Director .... Mr. Jamie KOSH
26 Director Marketing & Public Affairs .... Ms. Marie YOUNG
44 Director of Development .... Ms. Marie B. MELUSKY
38 Director of Counseling Center .... Mr. David P. WILSON
14 Director Computer Services .... Mr. George F. PYO
29 Director of Alumni Relations .... Ms. Anita M. BAUMANN
51 Director Continuing Education .... Ms. Julie BARRIS
18 Director of Physical Plant .... Mr. Doug EPPLEY
21 Controller .... Mr. Thomas R. FRITZ
41 Director of Athletics .... Mr. Bob S. KRIMMEL
88 Dir Small Business Devel Center .... Mr. Edward R. HUTTENHOWER
19 Director Security & Safety .... Mr. Donald MILES
39 Director of Residence Life .... Mr. Donald MILES
42 Director of Campus Ministry .... Rev. John Mark KLAUS
88 Dir Center for Academic Success .... Ms. Renee BERNARD
35 Assoc Dean of Student Life .... Mr. Dominick F. PERUSO
15 Director of Human Resources .... Ms. Heather J. MECK
28 Director of Multicultural Affairs .... Ms. Lynne BANKS
96 Director of Purchasing .... Mr. William AGOSTA
20 Associate Provost .... Dr. Peter R. SKONER
40 Manager of Bookstore .... Ms. Barbara SHINGLE

Saint Joseph's University (E)

5600 City Avenue, Philadelphia PA 19131-1376
County: Philadelphia FICE Identification: 003367
Unit ID: 215770
Telephone: (610) 660-1000 Carnegie Class: Master's L
FAX Number: (610) 660-3300 Calendar System: Semester
URL: www.sju.edu
Established: 1851 Annual Undergrad Tuition & Fees: $38,880
Enrollment: 8,805 Coed
Affiliation or Control: Roman Catholic IRS Status: 501(c)3
Highest Offering: Doctorate
Program: Liberal Arts And General; Teacher Preparatory; Professional
Accreditation: M, ANEST, BUS, BUSA

01 President .... Rev. C. Kevin GILLESPIE, SJ
05 Provost .... Dr. Brice R. WACHTERHAUSER
03 Senior Vice President .... Mr. John W. SMITHSON
88 Vice President Mission & Identity .... Dr. E. Springs STEELE
32 VP Student Life/Assoc Provost .... Dr. Cary M. ANDERSON
11 Vice Pres Administrative Services .... Mr. Kevin W. ROBINSON
30 VP Dev/Alumni Relations .... Mr. Martin F. FARRELL
26 Vice President External Affairs .... Ms. Joan F. CHRESTAY
10 Vice President Financial Affairs .... Dr. Louis J. MAYER
45 Vice President Planning .... Dr. Kathleen D. GAVAL
43 General Counsel .... Ms. Marianne SCHIMELFINIG
04 Assistant Vice President .... Ms. Sarah F. QUINN
20 Vice Provost .... Vacant
49 Interim Dean Col Arts & Sciences .... Dr. Jeanne BRADY
50 Dean Haub School of Business .... Dr. Joseph A. DIANGELO, JR.
41 Assoc VP/Director Athletics .... Mr. Dominick J. DIJULIA
107 Assoc Dean Col Prof & Liberal Stds .... Ms. Patricia GRIFFIN
58 Assoc Dean & Exec Dir Grad A&S .... Dr. Sabrina DETURK
84 Assoc Provost Enrollment Mgmt .... Mr. John G. HALLER
06 Director Student Records/Fin Svcs .... Mr. Paul KLESCHICK
08 University Librarian Drexel Library .... Ms. Evelyn MINICK
21 Assoc VP Fin Planning & Analysis .... Ms. Stephanie PRICKEN
21 Asst VP & Controller .... Mr. Joseph CASSIDY
86 Asst VP Govt & Community Rels .... Mr. Wadell RIDLEY, JR.
15 VP Human Resources .... Ms. Sharon O'GRADY EISENMANN
13 Asst VP Information Technology .... Mr. Joseph F. PETRAGNANI
13 Chief Information Officer .... Mr. Francis J. DISANTI
27 Assoc VP Marketing & Communications .... Mr. Joseph M. LUNARDI
108 Asst VP Planning & Assessment .... Ms. Dawn M. BURDSALL
88 Asst VP Student Development .... Dr. Mary Elaine PERRY
88 Asst VP Student Ed Support Services .... Ms. Jacqueline M. STARKS
26 Asst VP Univ Communications .... Ms. Harriet K. GOODHEART
29 Exec Dir Saint Joseph's Fund .... Mr. Douglas KLEINTOP
24 Exec Dir Acad Tech/Dist Learning .... Dr. David LEES
07 Exec Director UG Admissions .... Ms. Maureen MATHIS
105 Exec Dir Web & Support Services .... Mr. Jeffery J. BACHOVCHIN
22 Director Benefits and Wellness .... Mr. James MOLNAR
42 Director Campus Ministry .... Mr. Thomas J. SHEIBLEY
36 Exec Director Career Dev Center .... Ms. Trish SHAFER
38 Director Counseling/Pers Dev Ctr .... Dr. Gregory NICHOLLS
18 Director Facilities Management .... Mr. Kevin M. KANE
37 Director Financial Assistance .... Ms. Eileen TUCKER
92 Director Honors Program .... Dr. Maria S. MARSILIO
28 Director Institutional Diversity .... Dr. Valerie DUDLEY
88 Director Multicultural Life .... Dr. Shoshanna EDWARDS-ALEXANDER
19 Director Public Safety & Security .... Vacant
96 Director Purchasing .... Mr. William O. ANDERSON
39 Director Residence Life .... Mr. John A. JEFFERY
23 Director Student Health Center .... Ms. Laura HURST
35 Dir Student Leadership/Activities .... Dr. Beth HAGOVSKY
09 Dir Inst Research & Decision Supp .... Ms. Annemarie M. BARTLETT

St. Tikhon's Orthodox Theological Seminary (F)

PO Box 130, South Canaan PA 18459-0130
County: Wayne FICE Identification: 039193
Unit ID: 216180
Telephone: (570) 561-1818 Carnegie Class: Not Classified
FAX Number: (570) 937-3100 Calendar System: Semester
URL: www.stots.edu
Established: 1938 Annual Undergrad Tuition & Fees: $5,250
Enrollment: 96 Male
Affiliation or Control: Other IRS Status: 501(c)3
Highest Offering: First Professional Degree
Program: Religious Emphasis
Accreditation: THEOL

01 President .... ABP. Tikhon MOLLARD
03 Rector .... Rt Rev. Michael DAHULICH
05 Dean/COO .... V.Rev. Steven A. VOYTOVICH

Saint Vincent College (G)

300 Fraser Purchase Road, Latrobe PA 15650-2690
County: Westmoreland FICE Identification: 003368
Unit ID: 215798
Telephone: (724) 805-2500 Carnegie Class: Bac/A&S
FAX Number: (724) 805-2019 Calendar System: Semester
URL: www.stvincent.edu
Established: 1846 Annual Undergrad Tuition & Fees: $30,350
Enrollment: 1,766 Coed
Affiliation or Control: Roman Catholic IRS Status: 501(c)3
Highest Offering: Doctorate
Program: Liberal Arts And General; Professional
Accreditation: M, ACBSP, ANEST

01 President .... Br. Norman W. HIPPS, OSB
03 Executive Vice President .... Rev. Paul TAYLOR, OSB
05 VP Academic Affairs .... Dr. John SMETANKA
10 VP/Chief Finance/Admin Officer .... Mr. Richard WILLIAMS
32 VP Student Affairs .... Ms. Mary COLLINS
26 VP Marketing and Communication .... Ms. Suzanne ENGLISH
07 Asst Vice Pres Admission .... Mr. David A. COLLINS
13 Chief Information Officer .... Mr. Peter E. MAHONEY
20 Dean of Studies .... Ms. Alice J. KAYLOR
50 Dean McKenna Sch Bus/Econ/Govt .... Dr. Gary QUINLIVAN
60 Dean Sch Soc Sci/Communication/Educ .... Dr. MaryBeth SPORE
79 Dean Humanities & Fine Arts .... Rev. Rene KOLLAR, OSB
81 Dean Science/Math & Computing .... Dr. Stephen M. JODIS
06 Registrar .... Ms. Celine R. BRUDNOK
08 Librarian .... Bro. David KELLY, OSB
29 Director of Alumni Affairs .... Mr. Michael GERDICH
26 Director of Public Relations .... Mr. Donald A. ORLANDO
36 Director Career Services .... Ms. Courtney BAUM
15 Director of Human Resources .... Ms. Judith MAHER
42 Director of Campus Ministry .... Rev. Killian LOCH, OSB
23 Director Wellness Center .... Ms. Mary Alice ARMOUR
19 Director Public Safety .... Mr. Steve BROWN
41 Athletic Director .... Rev. Myron KIRSCH, OSB
39 Director Resident Life .... Mr. Robert BAUM
96 Dir of Purchasing/Chief Fire Dept .... Mr. Terry NOEL
09 Director of Institutional Research .... Vacant
18 Director of Facility Management .... Mr. Larry HENDRICK
40 Manager Book Center .... Rev. Anthony GROSSI, OSB
88 Exec Dir Fred Rogers Center .... Ms. Rita CATALANO
88 Coord of Grad Admission & Cont Educ .... Ms. Lisa GLESSNER

Saint Vincent Seminary (H)

300 Fraser Purchase Road, Latrobe PA 15650-2690
County: Westmoreland Identification: 666018
Unit ID: 215813
Telephone: (724) 805-2592 Carnegie Class: Spec/Faith
FAX Number: (724) 532-5052 Calendar System: Semester
URL: www.saintvincentseminary.edu
Established: 1846 Annual Undergrad Tuition & Fees: $24,086
Enrollment: 62 Coed
Affiliation or Control: Roman Catholic IRS Status: 501(c)3
Highest Offering: Master's

Program: Religious Emphasis
Accreditation: THEOL

01 Rector .... V.Rev. Timothy F. WHALEN
88 Director of Spiritual Formation ..... Rev. Aaron N. BUZZELLI, OSB
05 Academic Dean .... Rev. Patrick T. CRONAUER, OSB
20 Director of Human Formation .... Rev. Edward MAZICH, OSB
03 Vice-Rector .... Rev. John-Mary TOMPKINS, OSB
42 Director of Liturgy .... Rev. Cyprian G. CONSTANTINE, OSB

Salus University (A)

8360 Old York Road, Elkins Park PA 19027-1516
County: Philadelphia FICE Identification: 003311
Unit ID: 214564
Telephone: (215) 780-1400 Carnegie Class: Spec/Health
FAX Number: (215) 780-1325 Calendar System: Quarter
URL: www.salus.edu
Established: 1919 Annual Undergrad Tuition & Fees: $35,150
Enrollment: 1,080 Coed
Affiliation or Control: Independent Non-Profit IRS Status: 501(c)3
Highest Offering: Doctorate
Program: Professional
Accreditation: M, ARCPA, AUD, OPT, OPTR

01 President .... Dr. Michael H. MITTLEMAN
05 Vice President Faculty Affairs .... Dr. Anthony F. DISTEFANO
10 Vice Pres Finance/Business Affairs .... Mr. Donald KATES
17 VP/Exec Director The Eye Institute .... Dr. Susan OLESZEWSKI
45 Vice President for Inst Planning .... Dr. Lawrence MCCLURE
35 Dean Student Affairs .... Dr. James CALDWELL
20 Exec Assistant to the Dean .... Ms. Karen BOYKIN
09 Asst Dir Research Admin .... Ms. Lydia PARKE
06 Registrar .... Ms. Shannon BOSS
13 Chief Information Officer .... Mr. William BRICHTA
38 Director Personal/Prof Development .... Ms. Susan PLATT
37 Assoc Dean Student Financial Affs ..... Dr. H. Lawrence MCCLURE
18 Director Physical Plant .... Mr. Richard ECHEVARRI
30 Director of Development .... Ms. Lynne CORBOY
27 Director Publications/Communication .... Ms. Peggy SHELLY
29 Director Alumni Relations/Giving .... Ms. Jamie LEMISCH
51 Coord Continuing/Post-Graduate Educ .... Mrs. Melissa PADILLA
58 Chairperson Graduate Studies .... Vacant
40 Bookstore Manager .... Mr. Joe NOCE
24 Director Instructional Media .... Mr. Glenn ROEDEL
36 Director Student Placement .... Ms. Janice MIGNOGNA
84 Director Enrollment Management .... Dr. Tim CALDWELL
88 Exec Dir Inst Visually Impaired .... Dr. Audrey SMITH
08 Head Librarian .... Mr. Keith LAMMERS
19 Director of Security .... Mr. Wayne PANCZA
15 Dir Human Resources/Affirm Action .... Ms. Maura KEENAN
96 Director of Purchasing .... Ms. Lydia FRIEL

Sanford-Brown Institute-Pittsburgh (B)

421 Seventh Avenue, Pittsburgh PA 15219-1907
County: Allegheny FICE Identification: 022023
Unit ID: 216782
Telephone: (412) 281-2600 Carnegie Class: Assoc/PrivFP
FAX Number: (412) 281-0319 Calendar System: Other
URL: www.sanfordbrown.edu/Pittsburgh
Established: 1979 Annual Undergrad Tuition & Fees: N/A
Enrollment: 733 Coed
Affiliation or Control: Proprietary IRS Status: Proprietary
Highest Offering: Associate Degree
Program: Occupational
Accreditation: ACICS, DMS, RAD

01 President-Pittsburgh .... Patti L. YAKSHE
12 President-Monroeville .... R. Thomas CONTRELLA
05 Director of Education .... Charles LONG
07 Director of Admissions .... George MORE
06 Registrar .... Cynthia SMITH
13 Director of Information Technology .... Mark MARCI
36 Director of Career Services .... Danette ROCCO
10 Business Manager .... Lisa KOSKO

Sanford-Brown Institute (C)

3600 Horizon Boulevard, Suite GL-1, Trevose PA 19053
Telephone: (215) 436-6973 Identification: 770771
Accreditation: ACICS

† Main campus is Sanford-Brown College in Atlanta, GA.

Sanford-Brown Institute-Wilkins Township (D)

777 Penn Center Boulevard, Bldg 7, Pittsburgh PA 15235
Telephone: (412) 373-6400 Identification: 666526
Accreditation: ACICS, COARC, SURGT

† Main campus is Sanford-Brown Institute-Pittsburgh in Pittsburgh, PA.

Seton Hill University (E)

Seton Hill Drive, Greensburg PA 15601-1599
County: Westmoreland FICE Identification: 003362
Unit ID: 215947
Telephone: (724) 834-2200 Carnegie Class: Bac/Diverse
FAX Number: (724) 830-4611 Calendar System: Semester
URL: www.setonhill.edu
Established: 1883 Annual Undergrad Tuition & Fees: $29,400
Enrollment: 2,162 Coed
Affiliation or Control: Roman Catholic IRS Status: 501(c)3
Highest Offering: Master's
Program: Liberal Arts And General; Teacher Preparatory; Professional
Accreditation: M, ARCPA, DENT, DIETC, IACBE, MFCD, MUS, SW

01 Interim President .... Ms. Bibiana BOERIO
32 VP Mission/Identity/Student Life .... Dr. Lois SCULCO, SC
05 Provost & Dean of the Faculty .... Dr. Mary Ann GAWELEK
10 Vice Pres Finance & Business .... Mr. Paul ROMAN
11 Vice Pres Administration .... Mrs. Barbara C. HINKLE
44 Vice Pres Institutional Advancement ...... Ms. Christine MUESELER
13 Vice Pres Computers & Technology .... Mr. Phil KOMARNY
84 Vice Pres Enrollment Management .... Mr. Michael POLL
21 Controller .... Mr. Paul EDSALL
35 Dean of Student Services .... Dr. Charmaine R. STRONG
07 Director Admissions .... Ms. Ashley JOSAY
08 Director of Library .... Mr. David STANLEY
30 Director Development .... Ms. Molly ROBB SHIMKO
29 Director of Alumni Relations .... Ms. Mary COX
37 Director of Financial Aid .... Ms. Maryann DUDAS
36 Director of Career Development .... Ms. Renee STAREK
15 Director Personnel Services .... Mrs. Darlene SAUERS
18 Director Facilities .... Mr. Bill VOKES
41 Executive Athletic Director .... Mr. Chris SNYDER
42 Director Campus Ministry .... Sr. Maureen O'BRIEN
88 Dir Natl Educ Ctr Women in Business .... Mrs. Jayne HUSTON
04 Assistant to the President .... Mrs. Carol ZOLA
06 Registrar .... Ms. Barbara HINKLE
38 Director Student Counseling .... Ms. Teresa BASSI-COOK
09 Director of Institutional Research .... Mrs. Edith COOK
26 Chief Public Relations Officer .... Ms. Jennifer REEGER
96 Director of Purchasing .... Mr. Charles O'NEILL

South Hills School of Business and Technology (F)

508 58th Street, Altoona PA 16602
Telephone: (814) 944-6134 Identification: 770772
Accreditation: ACICS, CAHIIM

† Main campus is South Hills School of Business and Technology in State College, PA.

South Hills School of Business and Technology (G)

480 Waupelani Drive, State College PA 16801-4516
County: Centre FICE Identification: 013263
Unit ID: 216083
Telephone: (814) 234-7755 Carnegie Class: Assoc/PrivFP
FAX Number: (814) 234-0926 Calendar System: Quarter
URL: www.southhills.edu
Established: 1970 Annual Undergrad Tuition & Fees: $14,991
Enrollment: 689 Coed
Affiliation or Control: Proprietary IRS Status: Proprietary
Highest Offering: Associate Degree
Program: Occupational
Accreditation: ACICS, CAHIIM, DMS, MAAB

01 President & Owner .... Mrs. Maralyn MAZZA
05 Director .... Mr. Mark MAGGS

Susquehanna University (H)

514 University Avenue, Selinsgrove PA 17870-1025
County: Snyder FICE Identification: 003369
Unit ID: 216278
Telephone: (570) 374-0101 Carnegie Class: Bac/A&S
FAX Number: (570) 372-4040 Calendar System: Semester
URL: www.susqu.edu
Established: 1858 Annual Undergrad Tuition & Fees: $38,780
Enrollment: 2,215 Coed
Affiliation or Control: Evangelical Lutheran Church In America
IRS Status: 501(c)3
Highest Offering: Baccalaureate
Program: Liberal Arts And General; Teacher Preparatory
Accreditation: M, BUS, MUS

01 President .... Dr. L. Jay LEMONS
03 Senior Vice President .... Ms. Sara G. KIRKLAND
05 Provost .... Dr. Carl O. MOSES
10 Vice Pres for Finance .... Mr. Michael COYNE
26 Vice President for Univ Relations .... Mr. Ronald A. COHEN
84 Vice Pres Enrollment Management .... Vacant
32 Vice Pres of Student Life & Dean .... Dr. Philip E. WINGER
27 Chief Communications Officer .... Ms. Angie BURROWS
30 Asst Vice President Gift Planning .... Mr. Doug SEABERG
28 Chief Div Officer/Asst Provost .... Ms. Lisa M. SCOTT
04 Assistant to the President .... Ms. Joann B. ANTES
04 Senior Admin Asst to the President .... Ms. Sharon POPE
57 Dean Sch Arts/Humanities/Comm .... Dr. Valerie G. MARTIN
50 Dean Weis School of Business .... Dr. Marsha KELLIHER
38 Assoc Dean & Director of Counseling .... Ms. Anna Beth PAYNE
89 Asst Dean/First Year Programs .... Ms. Caroline MERCADO
28 Dir Center for Diversity & Soc Just .... Ms. Dena SALERNO
07 Director of Admissions .... Mr. Chris A. MARKLE
08 Interim Director of the Library .... Ms. Christine BOMBARO
37 Director of Financial Aid .... Ms. Helen S. NUNN
06 Registrar .... Mr. Alex G H. SMITH
42 University Chaplain .... Rev. Mark Wm RADECKE
13 Chief Information Officer .... Mr. Mark D. HUBER
41 Director of Athletics .... Ms. Pamela SAMUELSON
18 Director of Facilities Management .... Mr. Chris C. BAILEY
36 Director of Career Services .... Ms. Brenda FABIAN
88 Director of Event Management .... Ms. Brenda MULL
29 Director of Alumni Relations .... Ms. Becky DEITRICK
09 Dir Institut Research/Asst Provost .... Dr. Colleen FLEWELLING
102 Dir Corp/Found Supprt/Asst Provost .... Mr. Ed CLARKE
104 Dir Cross Cultural Off-Campus Pgm .... Dr. Scott MANNING
15 Director Human Resources/Risk Mgmt .... Ms. Maureen N. PUGH
19 Director of Public Safety .... Mr. Tom RAMBO
44 Director of the Annual Fund .... Mr. Jason MCCAHAN
92 Director of Honors Program .... Dr. Doug POWERS
20 Dir of Inst Research & Asst Provost ..... Dr. Colleen FLEWELLING

Swarthmore College (I)

500 College Avenue, Swarthmore PA 19081-1390
County: Delaware FICE Identification: 003370
Unit ID: 216287
Telephone: (610) 328-8000 Carnegie Class: Bac/A&S
FAX Number: (610) 328-8673 Calendar System: Semester
URL: www.swarthmore.edu
Established: 1864 Annual Undergrad Tuition & Fees: $44,718
Enrollment: 1,552 Coed
Affiliation or Control: Independent Non-Profit IRS Status: 501(c)3
Highest Offering: Baccalaureate
Program: Liberal Arts And General
Accreditation: M, ENG

01 President .... Rebecca S. CHOPP
05 Provost .... Thomas STEPHENSON
10 Vice President Finance/Treasurer .... Suzanne P. WELSH
30 Vice President Alumni/Development .... Karl CLAUSS
04 VP Col/Cmty Rels/Exec Asst to Pres .... Maurice G. ELDRIDGE
18 Vice Pres Facilities & Services .... C. Stuart HAIN
16 Vice Pres for Human Resources .... Pamela PRESCOD-CAESAR
26 VP/Communications & Secretary/Col .... Nancy NICELY
07 Vice Pres & Dean of Admissions .... Jim BOCK
21 Asst Vice Pres Finance & Controller .... Eileen E. PETULA
32 Dean of Students .... H. Elizabeth BRAUN
28 Assoc Dean of Diversity/Inclusion .... Liliana RODRIGUEZ
06 Registrar .... Martin O. WARNER
08 College Librarian .... Peggy SEIDEN
09 Director Institutional Research .... Robin H. SHORES
29 Director of Alumni Relations .... Lisa LEE
37 Director of Financial Aid .... Laura TALBOT
36 Director Career Services .... Nancy BURKETT
19 Director of Public Safety .... Michael HILL
22 VP Risk Mgmt/Legal & Director EOO .... Sharmaine LAMAR
23 Director Worth Health Center .... Beth KOTARSKI
38 Director Psychological Services .... David RAMIREZ
41 Director Physical Educ/Athletics .... Adam HERTZ
44 Director Annual and Parent Giving .... Lisa SHAFER
13 Chief Info Technology Officer .... Joel COOPER
35 Interim Student Activities Coord .... Michael ELIAS

Talmudical Yeshiva of Philadelphia (J)

6063 Drexel Road, Philadelphia PA 19131-1296
County: Philadelphia FICE Identification: 012523
Unit ID: 216311
Telephone: (215) 473-1212 Carnegie Class: Spec/Faith
FAX Number: (215) 477-5065 Calendar System: Semester
Established: 1953 Annual Undergrad Tuition & Fees: $8,550
Enrollment: 233 Male
Affiliation or Control: Independent Non-Profit IRS Status: 501(c)3
Highest Offering: Second Talmudic Degree
Program: Teacher Preparatory; Professional; Religious Emphasis
Accreditation: RABN

05 Dean .... Rabbi Shmuel KAMENETSKY
05 Dean .... Rabbi Yehuda SVEI
05 Dean .... Rabbi Sholom KAMENETSKY

Temple University (K)

1801 N. Broad Street, Philadelphia PA 19122-6072
County: Philadelphia FICE Identification: 003371
Unit ID: 216339
Telephone: (215) 204-7000 Carnegie Class: RU/H
FAX Number: (215) 204-5694 Calendar System: Semester
URL: www.temple.edu
Established: 1884 Annual Undergrad Tuition & Fees (In-State): $13,406
Enrollment: 36,744 Coed
Affiliation or Control: State Related IRS Status: 501(c)3
Highest Offering: Doctorate
Program: 2-Year Principally Bachelor's Creditable; Liberal Arts And General; Teacher Preparatory; Professional
Accreditation: M, ART, BUS, CAHIIM, CLPSY, DANCE, DENT, ENG, ENGT, HSA, IPSY, JOUR, LAW, LSAR, MED, MUS, NRPA, NURSE, OT, PH, PHAR, PLNG, POD, PTA, SCPSY, SP, SW, TEAC, THEA

01 President .... Dr. Neil D. THEOBALD
03 Vice President .... Mr. William T. BERGMAN, JR.
05 Provost/Sr VP Academic Affairs .... Dr. Hai-Lung DAI
43 Univ Counsel/Univ Secretary/Sr VP .... Mr. George E. MOORE
32 VP for Student Affairs .... Dr. Theresa A. POWELL
27 VP Computer/Financial Svcs/CIO .... Mr. Timothy C. O'ROURKE
17 Sr EVP Health Sci/CEO Health System .... Dr. Larry R. KAISER
03 Sr Vice Provost Strategic Init/
Comm .... Dr. Elizabeth LEEBRON TUTELMAN

10 Interim CFO & Treasurer ... Mr. Kenneth H. KAISER
86 Sr VP Govt & Community ... Mr. Kenneth LAWERENCE, JR.
26 VP Strategic Marketing & Communic ... Ms. Karen B. CLARKE
35 Assoc VP/Dean of Students ... Dr. Stephanie IVES
30 Interim Sr VP Inst Advancement ... Mr. Tilghman MOYER, IV
46 Interim Vice Provost Research ... Ms. Michele MASUCCI
18 Sr VP Construction & Facilities ... Mr. James CREEDON
16 Sr Assoc VP Finance/HR ... Mr. Kenneth H. KAISER
21 Assoc VP Finance ... Mr. William J. WILKINSON
39 Assoc VP Student Affairs/Housing ... Mr. Michael SCALES
15 Interim Assoc VP HR ... Ms. Sharon A. BOYLE
21 Assoc VP/Controller ... Mr. Frank ANNUNZIATO
88 Assoc VP Business Services ... Mr. Richard RUMER
22 Assoc VP Multicultural Affairs ... Ms. Rhonda L. BROWN
11 Asst VP Administration/Planning ... Ms. Kathryn P. D'ANGELO
29 Asst Vice Pres Alumni Relations ... Ms. Audrey SCHNEIDER
88 Sr Vice Provost Faculty Dev/Affairs ... Dr. Diane C. MAELSON
84 Senior Vice Provost Enrollment ... Mr. William N. BLACK
20 Vice Provost Undergraduate Programs ... Dr. Peter JONES
20 Vice Prov Acad Affairs/ Assessment ... Dr. Jodi LEVINE LAUFGRABEN
08 Dean for University Libraries ... Mr. Joseph LUCIA
06 Registrar ... Ms. Kim BUCKWALTER
41 Int Dir Intercollegiate Athletics ... Mr. Kevin CLARK
38 Director Tuttleman Counseling Svcs ... Dr. John L. DIMINO
36 Sr Dir Student Svcs/Career Services ... Ms. Rachel BROWN
09 Sr Director Measurement/Research ... Dr. James W. DEGNAN
85 Sr Vice Provost Intl Affairs ... Dr. Hai-Lung DAI
88 Sr Dir International Student Svcs ... Dr. Martyn J. MILLER
88 Asst VP International Affairs ... Ms. Denise A. CONNERTY
23 Assoc Director Health Services ... Dr. Mark DENYS
37 Director Student Financial Services ... Mr. Craig FENNELL
88 Vice Provost University College ... Dr. Vicki Lewis MCGARVEY
96 Director of Purchasing ... Ms. Theresa E. BURT
88 Bursar ... Mr. David R. GLEZERMAN
97 Director General Education ... Mr. Istvan L. VARKONYI
12 Exec Dir Ambler/Ctr City Campuses ... Mr. William PARSHALL
40 Bookstore Manager ... Mr. Jim HANLEY
49 Dean Liberal Arts ... Dr. Teresa SCOTT SOUFAS
53 Dean of Education ... Dr. Greg ANDERSON
61 Dean Law School ... Dr. Joanne A. EPPS
64 Dean Center for the Arts ... Dr. Robert STROKER
50 Dean Business/Management ... Dr. Moshe PORAT
52 Dean of Dentistry ... Dr. Amid ISMAIL
63 Dean of Medicine ... Dr. Larry KAISER
67 Dean of Pharmacy ... Dr. Peter H. DOUKAS
54 Dean Engineering ... Dr. Keya SADEGHIPOUR
88 Dean Podiatric Medicine ... Dr. John A. MATTIACCI
72 Dean Science & Technology ... Dr. Michael KLEIN
60 Dean Media & Communications ... Mr. David BOARDMAN
76 Int Dean Health Prof & Social Wk ... Dr. Catherine COYLE
88 Dean of Tourism/Hospitality Mgmt ... Dr. Moshe PORAT
88 Dean Environmental Design ... Dr. Teresa SCOTT SOUFAS
88 Dean Temple Japan ... Dr. Bruce STRONACH
88 Dean Temple Rome ... Mr. Kim STROMMEN

Thaddeus Stevens College of Technology (A)

750 E King Street, Lancaster PA 17602-3198
County: Lancaster FICE Identification: 007912
Unit ID: 216296
Telephone: (717) 299-7730 Carnegie Class: Assoc/Pub-R-S
FAX Number: (717) 299-7748 Calendar System: Semester
URL: www.stevenscollege.edu
Established: 1905 Annual Undergrad Tuition & Fees (In-State): $7,200
Enrollment: 870 Coed
Affiliation or Control: State IRS Status: 501(c)3
Highest Offering: Associate Degree
Program: Occupational; 2-Year Principally Bachelor's Creditable
Accreditation: M

01 President ... Dr. William E. GRISCOM
05 Vice President Academic Affairs ... Dr. William R. THOMPSON
10 Vice President Finance and Admin ... Mrs. Betty TOMPOS
32 Director for Student Services ... Mr. Christopher METZLER
84 Dir Enrollment Services/Admissions ... Dr. Erin NELSEN
08 Learning Resources Center Director ... Ms. Diane AMBRUSO
09 Director of Research & Planning ... Vacant
15 Director of Personnel Services ... Ms. Sue EMSWILER
26 Dir of Marketing/Public Information ... Mr. Chad BAKER
38 Director of Student Counseling ... Ms. Debra SCHUCH
28 Director Multicultural Affairs ... Mr. Paul CULBRETH
29 Alumni Foundation Exec Director ... Mr. Alex MUNRO
37 Director Financial Aid/Registrar ... Mr. Michael DEGROFT
41 Athletic Director ... Mr. Christopher METZLER
30 Director of Development ... Mr. Allen TATE
36 Director of Career Services ... Ms. Laurie GROVE
39 Director Residence Life ... Mr. Jason KUNTZ
18 Facilities Maintenance Manager ... Mr. Gene DUNCAN, JR.

† Qualified individuals are eligible for full scholarships based on family/financial status.

Thiel College (B)

75 College Avenue, Greenville PA 16125-2181
County: Mercer FICE Identification: 003376
Unit ID: 216357
Telephone: (724) 589-2000 Carnegie Class: Bac/Diverse
FAX Number: (724) 589-2850 Calendar System: Semester
URL: www.thiel.edu
Established: 1866 Annual Undergrad Tuition & Fees: $27,102
Enrollment: 1,056 Coed
Affiliation or Control: Evangelical Lutheran Church In America IRS Status: 501(c)3
Highest Offering: Baccalaureate
Program: Liberal Arts And General; Teacher Preparatory
Accreditation: M

01 President ... Dr. Troy D. VAN AKEN
05 VP Academic Affairs/Dean of College ... Dr. Lynn FRANKEN
30 Vice President College Advancement ... Mr. Samuel D. SIPLE
10 Vice President Finance/Management ... Mr. Robert SCHMOLL
13 Chief Information Officer ... Mr. Kurt ASHLEY
04 Administrative Asst to President ... Mrs. Linda NOCHTA
32 Dean of Students ... Mr. Michael MCKINNEY
84 Dean of Enrollment ... Ms. Amy BECHER
20 Asst Academic Dean/Prof of Psych ... Dr. Jennifer S. GRIFFIN
41 Director of Athletics ... Mr. Jack LEIPHEIMER
44 Dir of Special & Planned Giving ... Mr. Mario MARINI
44 Exec Director of Donor Services ... Mrs. Robert LEONARD
18 Exec Dir of Facilities Management ... Mr. Michael R. BROWN
08 Library Director ... Mr. Allen MORRILL
26 Director Public Relations ... Vacant
15 Director Human Resources ... Mrs. Jennifer CLARK
36 Career Service Director ... Mrs. Heather BALAS
19 Chief of Police ... Mr. Eric ALLEN
06 Registrar ... Ms. Denise UREY
29 Director of Alumni Relations ... Mrs. Stephanie WILSON
42 Campus Pastor ... Vacant
07 Assoc Director Admissions ... Mrs. Sonya L. LAPIKAS
07 Assoc Director Admissions ... Mr. Jeffrey S. LINN
37 Financial Aid Director ... Ms. Cynthia H. FARRELL
44 Coordinator of Annual Giving ... Mrs. Leta JEFFERS
23 Coordinator Health Services ... Mrs. Pamela M. DESPO

Thomas Jefferson University (C)

11th and Walnut Streets, Philadelphia PA 19107-5083
County: Philadelphia FICE Identification: 012393
Unit ID: 216366
Telephone: (215) 955-6000 Carnegie Class: Spec/Med
FAX Number: (215) 955-5587 Calendar System: Quarter
URL: www.jefferson.edu
Established: 1824 Annual Undergrad Tuition & Fees: $34,610
Enrollment: 3,666 Coed
Affiliation or Control: Independent Non-Profit IRS Status: 501(c)3
Highest Offering: Doctorate
Program: Liberal Arts And General; Professional
Accreditation: M, ANEST, CYTO, DENT, DMS, MED, MT, #NMT, NURSE, OT, PH, PHAR, PTA, RAD, RADDOS, RADMAG, RTT

01 President ... Mr. Richard C. GOZON
63 Dean Jefferson Medicial College ... Dr. Mark L. TYKOCINSKI
05 Sr VP Academic Affairs ... Dr. Michael J. VERGARE
26 Senior VP Univ Marketing/Relations ... Vacant
10 Sr Vice President for Finance ... Mr. Alfred SALVATO
30 Sr VP for Development ... Mr. Frederick E. RUCCIUS
43 Sr VP & University Counsel ... Ms. Cristina G. CAVALIERI
46 Interim Vice President for Research ... Dr. Theodore TARASCHI
18 Vice Pres for Facilities Mgmt ... Mr. Ronald E. BOWLAN
15 VP Human Resources ... Ms. Pamela TEUFEL
100 Chief of Staff ... Ms. Janice K. MARINI
58 Dean Jeff Grad Sch of Biomed Sci ... Dr. Gerald GRUNWALD
20 Assoc Sr VP Academic Affairs ... Dr. James ERDMANN
66 Dean Jefferson School of Nursing ... Dr. Beth Ann SWAN
67 Dean Jefferson School of Pharmacy ... Dr. Rebecca FINLEY
76 Dean Jefferson Sch Hlth Professions ... Dr. Janice P. BURKE
69 Dean Jefferson Sch of Pop Health ... Dr. David NASH
32 Dean of Student & Admissions JMC ... Dr. Clara A. CALLAHAN
07 Asst Dean of Admissions ... Dr. Karen JACOBS ASTLE
06 University Registrar ... Dr. Raelynn COOTER
29 Exec Director of Alumni Assoc JMC ... Dr. Phillip J. MARONE
08 University Librarian ... Mr. Anthony FRISBY
22 Univ Affirmative Action Officer ... Dr. Karen GLASER
23 Medical Director Univ Health Svcs ... Dr. Ellen M. O'CONNOR
24 Director Medical Media Services ... Mr. Pejman MAKARECHI
35 Assoc VP Student Affairs ... Dr. James ERDMANN
39 Manager Housing/Residence Life ... Ms. Patricia CRISTIANO KELLY
37 Univ Director Student Financial Aid ... Ms. Susan BATCHELOR
40 Director Bookstore ... Ms. Patricia HAAS
91 Chief Information Officer ... Mr. P. Douglas HERRICK
19 Director of Security ... Mr. Robert B. HENDRICK
85 Dir International Exchange Services ... Ms. Janice M. BOGEN
07 Dir Admission/Recruitment/Grad Stds ... Mr. Marc STEARNS
28 Asst Dean Diversity/Minority Affs ... Ms. Luz M. ORTIZ
96 Director of Purchasing ... Mr. Robert C. BURKHOLDER
35 Associate Dean Student Affairs ... Dr. Charles A. POHL

Triangle Tech (D)

191 Performance Road, Sunbury PA 17801
Telephone: (570) 988-0700 Identification: 770586
Accreditation: ACCSC

† Main campus is Triangle Tech, Dubois in Dubois, PA.

Triangle Tech, Bethlehem (E)

3184 Airport Road, Bethlehem PA 18017
Telephone: (610) 691-1300 Identification: 770587
Accreditation: ACCSC

† Main campus is Triangle Tech, Greensburg in Greensburg, PA.

Triangle Tech, Dubois (F)

PO Box 551, Dubois PA 15801-0551
County: Clearfield FICE Identification: 021744
Unit ID: 216454
Telephone: (814) 371-2090 Carnegie Class: Assoc/PrivFP
FAX Number: (814) 371-9227 Calendar System: Semester
URL: www.triangle-tech.edu
Established: 1982 Annual Undergrad Tuition & Fees: $15,744
Enrollment: 166 Coed
Affiliation or Control: Proprietary IRS Status: Proprietary
Highest Offering: Associate Degree
Program: Occupational; 2-Year Principally Bachelor's Creditable; Technical Emphasis
Accreditation: ACCSC

01 Director ... Mrs. Stephanie A. CRAIG
03 Assistant Director ... Mr. Steve CURLL
05 Academic Affairs Advisor ... Mrs. Joan HOCKMAN
07 Admiss/Recruiting/Training Coord ... Mrs. Peggy SHILK
07 Admiss/Recruiting/Training Coord ... Mr. Bill KHAMIS
36 Career Advisor ... Mrs. Dori FORDOSKI
37 Financial Aid Administrator ... Ms. Michelle L. JASHINSKI

Triangle Tech, Erie (G)

2000 Liberty Street, Erie PA 16502-2594
County: Erie FICE Identification: 020902
Unit ID: 216427
Telephone: (814) 453-6016 Carnegie Class: Assoc/PrivFP
FAX Number: (814) 454-2818 Calendar System: Semester
URL: www.triangle-tech.edu
Established: 1976 Annual Undergrad Tuition & Fees: $15,744
Enrollment: 81 Coed
Affiliation or Control: Proprietary IRS Status: Proprietary
Highest Offering: Associate Degree
Program: Occupational
Accreditation: ACCSC

00 CEO ... Mr. James R. AGRAS
01 Campus Director ... Mr. Ken ADAMS
03 Executive Vice President ... Mr. Rudy K. AGRAS
07 Vice President of Admissions ... Vacant

Triangle Tech, Greensburg (H)

222 E Pittsburgh Street, Suite A, Greensburg PA 15601-3304
County: Westmoreland FICE Identification: 021290
Unit ID: 216445
Telephone: (724) 832-1050 Carnegie Class: Assoc/PrivFP
FAX Number: (724) 834-0325 Calendar System: Semester
URL: www.triangle-tech.edu
Established: 1944 Annual Undergrad Tuition & Fees: $15,960
Enrollment: 165 Coed
Affiliation or Control: Proprietary IRS Status: Proprietary
Highest Offering: Associate Degree
Program: Occupational; 2-Year Principally Bachelor's Creditable; Technical Emphasis
Accreditation: ACCSC

00 Chairman/CEO ... James R. AGRAS
01 President ... Timothy J. MCMAHON
07 Director of Admissions ... John A. MAZZARESE
05 Senior Director ... Deborah G. HEPBURN
12 Director of Branch Campus/CEO ... Paul BEADLE

Triangle Tech, Pittsburgh (I)

1940 Perrysville Avenue, Pittsburgh PA 15214-3897
County: Allegheny FICE Identification: 007839
Unit ID: 216436
Telephone: (412) 359-1000 Carnegie Class: Assoc/PrivFP
FAX Number: (412) 359-1012 Calendar System: Semester
URL: www.triangle-tech.edu
Established: 1944 Annual Undergrad Tuition & Fees: $16,581
Enrollment: 266 Coed
Affiliation or Control: Proprietary IRS Status: Proprietary
Highest Offering: Associate Degree
Program: Occupational; 2-Year Principally Bachelor's Creditable; Technical Emphasis
Accreditation: ACCSC

00 Chairman/CEO ... James R. AGRAS
01 President ... Timothy J. MCMAHON
07 Director of Admissions ... Jason VALLOZZI
05 Senior Director ... Deborah G. HEPBURN
12 School Director ... Anthony VARGO

Trinity Episcopal School for Ministry (J)

311 11th Street, Ambridge PA 15003-2397
County: Beaver FICE Identification: 022993
Unit ID: 216463
Telephone: (724) 266-3838 Carnegie Class: Spec/Faith
FAX Number: (724) 266-4617 Calendar System: Semester
URL: www.tsm.edu
Established: 1976 Annual Graduate Tuition & Fees: $11,140
Enrollment: 141 Coed
Affiliation or Control: Protestant Episcopal IRS Status: 501(c)3

Highest Offering: Doctorate; No Undergraduates
Program: Professional; Religious Emphasis
Accreditation: THEOL

01 Dean/President .... V.Rev. Justyn TERRY
05 Academic Dean .... Rev Dr. Mark STEVENSON
30 Dean Advancement/Dir DMin Degree .... Rev Dr. H. Lawrence THOMPSON, III
32 Dean of Students .... Rev. Tina LOCKETT
37 Financial Aid Director .... Ms. Stacey WILLIARD
06 Registrar .... Rev. William STARKE
07 Director of Admissions .... Rev. Tina LOCKETT
08 Library Director .... Ms. Susanah HANSON
11 Dean of Administration .... Mrs. Karen GETZ
44 Director of Development .... Mr. Jerry MOTE

The University of the Arts (A)

320 S Broad Street, Philadelphia PA 19102-4944
County: Philadelphia FICE Identification: 003350
Unit ID: 215105
Telephone: (215) 717-6000 Carnegie Class: Spec/Arts
FAX Number: (215) 717-6045 Calendar System: Semester
URL: www.uarts.edu
Established: 1876 Annual Undergrad Tuition & Fees: $36,582
Enrollment: 2,126 Coed
Affiliation or Control: Independent Non-Profit IRS Status: 501(c)3
Highest Offering: Master's
Program: Liberal Arts And General; Teacher Preparatory; Fine Arts Emphasis
Accreditation: M, ART, MUS

01 President .... Mr. Sean T. BUFFINGTON
05 Provost .... Dr. Kirk E. PILLOW
26 Director University Communications .... Mr. Paul F. HEALY
32 Asst VP Stdnt Affs/Dean of Students .... Dr. Gregory NAYOR
20 Assistant Provost .... Mr. James SAVOIE
30 Vice Pres Advancement .... Ms. Lucille HUGHES
04 Exec Assistant to the President .... Ms. Pamela SHROPSHIRE
10 Vice Pres Finance/Administration .... Mr. Stephen LIGHTCAP
15 Director of Personnel Services .... Ms. Jennifer EDWARDS
08 Assoc Provost/Director of Libraries .... Ms. Carol GRANEY
19 Director of Public Safety .... Mr. Randolph MERCED
27 Vice Pres Technology & Info Svcs .... Mr. Thomas CARNWATH
90 Director Academic Computing .... Vacant
91 Director of Information Systems .... Mr. Jack POST
91 Director Network Services .... Mr. Kevin BRENNAN
07 VP Enroll Mgmt/Dean of Admissions .... Vacant
06 Registrar .... Ms. Margaret KIP
37 VP Enroll Mgmt/Dean of Fin Aid .... Ms. Chris PESOTSKI
57 Dean College Art/Media & Design ... Mr. Christopher SHARROCK
79 Dean of Liberal Arts .... Dr. Catherine KODAT
51 Dean of Continuing Studies .... Ms. Erin ELMAN
35 Director of Student Life .... Ms. Kathleen EMBLETON
36 Director of Career Services .... Ms. Elisa SEEHERMAN
38 Director Student Counseling .... Mr. Brian HAINSTOCK
09 Director of Institutional Research .... Ms. Beth E. FREDERICK
85 Dir International Student Services .... Ms. Mara FLAMM
29 Director Alumni & Parent Relations .... Ms. Lauren VILLANUEVE

University of Pennsylvania (B)

1 College Hall, Room 100, Philadelphia PA 19104-6830
County: Philadelphia FICE Identification: 003378
Unit ID: 215062
Telephone: (215) 898-5000 Carnegie Class: RU/VH
FAX Number: (215) 898-5756 Calendar System: Semester
URL: www.upenn.edu
Established: 1740 Annual Undergrad Tuition & Fees: $45,890
Enrollment: 24,725 Coed
Affiliation or Control: Independent Non-Profit IRS Status: 501(c)3
Highest Offering: Doctorate
Program: Liberal Arts And General; Teacher Preparatory; Professional
Accreditation: M, ANEST, BUS, CEA, CS, DENT, ENG, IPSY, LAW, LSAR, MED, MIDWF, NURSE, PCSAS, PH, PLNG, SW, VET

01 President .... Dr. Amy GUTMANN
03 Executive Vice President .... Mr. Craig CARNAROLI
05 Provost .... Dr. Vincent PRICE
06 Registrar .... Vacant
07 Dean of Admissions .... Mr. Eric J. FURDA
32 Vice Provost University Life .... Dr. Valarie S. MCCOULLUM
10 Vice Pres Finance & Treasurer .... Mr. Stephen D. GOLDING
18 Vice Pres Facil/Real Est Svcs .... Ms. Anne PAPAGEORGE
17 CEO Univ of PA Health System .... Dr. Ralph W. MULLER
08 Vice Provost/Dir of Libraries .... Mr. Harry C. ROGERS
13 Vice Pres Info Technology/CIO .... Mr. Thomas H. MURPHY
100 Vice Pres & Chief of Staff .... Mr. Gregory S. ROST
88 Vice Pres Institutional Affairs .... Ms. Joann MITCHELL
30 Vice Pres Dev/Alumni Relations .... Mr. John H. ZELLER
16 Vice Pres Human Resources .... Dr. John J. HEUER
86 Vice Pres Govt & Comm Relations .... Mr. Jeffrey COOPER
19 Vice President Public Safety .... Ms. Maureen RUSH
26 Vice Pres for Univ Communications .... Mr. Stephen J. MACCARTHY
88 Vice Pres Business Services .... Ms. Marie D. WITT
45 Vice Pres Budget Mgmt Analysis .... Ms. Bonnie C. GIBSON
43 Senior Vice Pres/General Counsel .... Ms. Wendy S. WHITE
101 VP & Secretary of the University .... Ms. Leslie L. KRUHLY
20 Vice Provost for Education .... Dr. Andrew N. BINNS
20 Vice Provost Faculty Affairs .... Dr. Anita L. ALLEN
29 Asst Vice Pres Alumni Relations .... Mr. Fredrick H. WAMPLER
88 Vice Provost for Research .... Dr. Steven J. FLUHARTY
88 Assoc Vice Provost Rsrch Svcs .... Ms. Elizabeth D. PELOSO
14 Assoc Vice Pres Networking/Telecom .... Mr. Michael A. PALLADINO
88 Assoc VP Audit Compl & Privacy .... Ms. Mary Lee BROWN
31 Assoc VP/Dir Ctr Cmty Partnerships .... Dr. Ira HARKAVY
28 Assoc Vice Prov Equity & Access .... Rev. William GIPSON
21 Comptroller .... Mr. John F. HORN
63 Exec Vice Pres/Dean Sch of Medicine .... Dr. J. L. JAMESON
49 Dean School Arts & Sciences .... Dr. Rebecca W. BUSHNELL
54 Dean School of Engr/Applied Science .... Dr. Eduardo D. GLANDT
66 Dean School of Nursing .... Dr. Afaf I. MELEIS
50 Dean Wharton School .... Dr. Thomas S. ROBERTSON
60 Dean Annenberg Sch Communications .... Dr. Michael X. DELLI CARPINI
52 Dean School of Dental Medicine .... Dr. Denis F. KINANE
57 Dean PennDesign .... Ms. Marilyn J. TAYLOR
53 Dean Graduate School Education .... Dr. Andrew C. PORTER
61 Dean School of Law .... Mr. Michael A. FITTS
70 Dean School Social Policy/Practice .... Dr. Richard J. GELLES
74 Dean School of Veterinary Medicine .... Dr. Joan C. HENDRICKS
107 Vice Dean Liberal & Prof Studies .... Ms. Nora E. LEWIS
35 Assoc VP Student Services ..... Ms. Michelle H. BROWN-NEVERS
09 Asst VP Inst Research & Analysis .... Ms. Stacey J. LOPEZ
85 Dir Intl Student & Scholar Svcs .... Dr. Rodolfo R. ALTAMIRANO
36 Dir of Career Services .... Ms. Patricia L. ROSE
37 Dir Student Financial Aid .... Mr. Joel B. CARSTENS
35 Assoc Vice Prov for Student Affairs .... Mr. Hikaru KOZUMA
38 Int Dir Counseling/Psych Services .... Dr. William B. ALEXANDER
102 Exec Dir Corp Rels/Int Dir Fnd Rels .... Dr. Don BONE
22 Exec Dir Affirm Action & Equal Op .... Mr. Sam B. STARKS
23 Dir Student Health Services .... Dr. Evelyn WIENER
88 Mgng Dir Annenberg Cr/Penn Presents .... Dr. Michael J. ROSE
88 Dir Morris Arboretum .... Mr. Paul W. MEYER
88 Dir Institute of Contempory Art .... Ms. Amy SADAO
88 Dir Museum of Archlgy/Anthrplgy .... Mr. Julian F. SIGGERS
88 Director Research Services .... Ms. Deborah M. FISHER
41 Dir Intercollegiate Athletics .... Mr. Steven BILSKY
24 IT Director .... Mr. James F. JOHNSON
91 IT Exec Dir Admin Info Tech .... Ms. Jeanne F. CURTIS
39 Dir College Houses & Academic Svcs .... Dr. Leslie J. DELAUTER
96 Chief Procurement Officer .... Vacant
42 University Chaplain .... Rev. Charles L. HOWARD
104 Dir Study Abroad .... Ms. Barbara C. GORKA
106 Online Learning Director .... Ms. Jacqueline P. CANDIDO

University of Pittsburgh (C)

4200 Fifth Avenue, Pittsburgh PA 15260-3583
County: Allegheny FICE Identification: 003379
Unit ID: 215293
Telephone: (412) 624-4141 Carnegie Class: RU/VH
FAX Number: N/A Calendar System: Semester
URL: www.pitt.edu
Established: 1787 Annual Undergrad Tuition & Fees (In-State): $17,100
Enrollment: 28,769 Coed
Affiliation or Control: State Related IRS Status: 501(c)3
Highest Offering: Doctorate
Program: Occupational; Liberal Arts And General; Teacher Preparatory; Professional
Accreditation: M, ANEST, ARCPA, AUD, BUS, CAHIIM, CEA, CLPSY, CORE, DENT, DH, DIETC, DIETD, EMT, ENG, HSA, HT, IPSY, LAW, LIB, MED, NURSE, OPE, OT, PCSAS, PERF, PH, PHAR, PTA, SP, SPAA, SW, @TEAC, THEA

01 Chancellor and Chief Exec Officer .... Mr. Mark A. NORDENBERG
05 Sr Vice Chancellor & Provost .... Dr. Patricia E. BEESON
63 Sr VC Health Sci/Dean Sch of Med .... Dr. Arthur S. LEVINE
03 Exec Vice Chancellor .... Mr. Jerome COCHRAN
101 Secy of Brd of Trustees/Asst Chanc .... Dr. B. Jean FERKETISH
88 Associate Chancellor .... Dr. Vijai P. SINGH
10 Chief Financial Officer .... Mr. Arthur G. RAMICONE
30 Vice Chancellor Inst Advancement .... Mr. Albert J. NOVAK, JR.
43 General Counsel .... Mr. P. Jerome RICHEY
22 Dir Aff Action/Diversity & Inclus .... Ms. Carol W. MOHAMED
26 Vice Chancellor Public Affairs .... Vacant
100 Chief of Staff and VC for Ext Rel .... Mr. G. Reynolds CLARK
86 Vice Chanc Community and Gov Rel .... Mr. Paul A. SUPOWITZ
18 Assoc Vice Chanc Facilities Mgmt .... Mr. Joseph W. FINK
15 Assoc Vice Chanc Human Resources .... Mr. Ronald W. FRISCH
88 Assoc Vice Chanc Mgmt Info & Analy .. Ms. Jane W. THOMPSON
27 Sr Assoc Vice Chanc Univ News/Mag .... Mr. John HARVITH
20 Vice Provost Undergraduate Studies .... Dr. Juan J. MAFREDI
58 Vice Provost Graduate Studies .... Dr. Alberta M. SBRAGIA
45 Vice Prov Acad Plng/Resource Mgmt .... Dr. David N. DEJONG
46 Vice Provost for Research .... Dr. Mark S. REDFERN
20 Vice Provost for Faculty Affairs .... Dr. Carey D. BALABAN
29 Assoc Vice Chanc Alumni Relations .... Mr. Jeffery T. GLEIM
39 Associate Vice Chancellor Business .... Mr. James V. EARLE
06 University Registrar .... Ms. Patti J. MATHAY
41 Athletic Director .... Mr. Steven C. PEDERSON
07 Chief Enrollment Officer .... Mr. Marc L. HARDING
32 Vice Provost and Dean of Students .... Dr. Kathy W. HUMPHREY
49 Dean Deitrich Sch Arts & Sci/CGS .... Dr. N. John COOPER
92 Dean University Honors College .... Dr. Edward M. STRICKER
50 Dean Jos M Katz Gr Sch Bus .... Dr. John T. DELANEY
53 Dean of School of Education .... Dr. Alan M. LESGOLD
54 Dean Swanson School of Engineering .... Dr. Gerald D. HOLDER
61 Dean of School of Law .... Mr. William M. CARTER
80 Dean Grad Sch Public/Intl Affs .... Dr. John T. KEELER
70 Dean School of Social Work .... Dr. Larry E. DAVIS
62 Dean School Information Sciences .... Dr. Ronald L. LARSEN
52 Dean School of Dental Medicine .... Dr. Thomas W. BRAUN
66 Dean of School of Nursing .... Dr. Jaqueline DUNBAR-JACOB
67 Dean School of Pharmacy .... Dr. Patricia D. KROBOTH
69 Dean Grad School Public Health .... Dr. Donald S. BURKE
76 Dean School Health & Rehab Science . Dr. Clifford E. BRUBAKER
40 Director Book Centers .... Ms. Debra R. FYOCK
24 Dir Ctr Instruct Dev/Distance Educ .... Ms. Cynthia GOLDEN
13 Dir Computer Svcs/Systems Devel .... Ms. Jinx P. WALTON
85 Dir International Services .... Dr. Charles L. NIEMAN
09 Director Institutional Research .... Ms. Cynthia A. ROBERTS
21 Director Internal Audit .... Mr. John P. ELLIOTT
36 Dir Career Dev/St Empl/Place Asst .... Ms. Cheryl S. FINLAY
25 Director Research .... Mr. Allen A. DIPALMA
38 Director of Counseling Center .... Dr. Tevya ZUKOR
08 Director Univ Library System .... Mr. Rush G. MILLER
19 Chief University Police .... Mr. Timothy R. DELANEY
23 Director Student Health Svcs .... Dr. Elizabeth WETTICK
96 Manager Purchasing Services .... Mr. Thomas E. YOUNGS, JR.
44 Sr Exec Director Planned Giving .... Mr. Walter E. BROWN
102 Exec Dir Corp & Found Relations .... Mr. Andrew B. KOVALCIK
04 Exec Asst to the Chancellor .... Ms. Mary Jo RACE

University of Pittsburgh at Bradford (D)

300 Campus Drive, Bradford PA 16701-2812
Telephone: (814) 362-7500 FICE Identification: 003380
Accreditation: &M, ADNUR, NUR

† Main campus is University of Pittsburgh in Pittsburgh, PA.

University of Pittsburgh at Greensburg (E)

150 Finoli Drive, Greensburg PA 15601-5898
Telephone: (724) 837-7040 FICE Identification: 003381
Accreditation: &M

† Main campus is University of Pittsburgh in Pittsburgh, PA.

University of Pittsburgh at Johnstown (F)

450 Schoolhouse Road, Johnstown PA 15904-2990
Telephone: (814) 269-7000 FICE Identification: 003382
Accreditation: &M, COARC, ENGT, SURGT

† Main campus is University of Pittsburgh in Pittsburgh, PA.

University of Pittsburgh at Titusville (G)

504 E Main, Titusville PA 16354-2097
Telephone: (814) 827-4400 FICE Identification: 003383
Accreditation: &M, ADNUR, PTAA

† Main campus is University of Pittsburgh in Pittsburgh, PA.

University of the Sciences in Philadelphia (H)

600 S 43rd Street, Philadelphia PA 19104-4495
County: Philadelphia FICE Identification: 003353
Unit ID: 215132
Telephone: (215) 596-8800 Carnegie Class: Spec/Health
FAX Number: (215) 895-1100 Calendar System: Semester
URL: www.usciences.edu
Established: 1821 Annual Undergrad Tuition & Fees: $33,046
Enrollment: 2,770 Coed
Affiliation or Control: Independent Non-Profit IRS Status: 501(c)3
Highest Offering: Doctorate
Program: Professional
Accreditation: M, #ARCPA, OT, PHAR, PTA

01 President .... Dr. Helen GILES-GEE
05 Provost .... Dr. Heidi ANDERSON
10 VP Finance and Administration .... Mr. John VITALI
88 Senior VP for Div External Affairs .... Vacant
30 VP for Institutional Advancement .... Ms. Carrie COLLINS
86 Director Govt and Cmty Affairs .... Ms. Mary Kate MCGINTY
26 Director Marketing and Comm .... Mr. Michael SCHWARTZMAN
102 Dir of Corporate & Foundation Rels .... Ms. Amy HOLVEY
100 Interim Chief of Staff .... Dr. Elisabeth MORLINO
13 Exec Dir Information Technology .... Mr. John MASCIANTONIO
84 Assoc Provost for Enrollment Mgmt .... Vacant
27 Associate Provost/CIO .... Dr. Mark NESTOR
37 Director of Financial Aid .... Ms. Paula LEHRBERGER
06 Registrar .... Ms. Therese ANDERSON
07 Executive Director of Admissions .... Ms. Diana COLLINS
29 Director of Alumni Relations .... Ms. Nancy SHILS
08 Director of Library Services .... Mr. Charles MYERS
58 Dean Graduate Studies .... Dr. Rodney WIGENT
32 Dean of Students .... Dr. William J. CUNNINGHAM
67 Dean of Pharmacy .... Dr. Lisa LAWSON
49 Dean Misher College Arts & Sci .... Dr. Suzanne K. MURPHY
76 Dean Samson College of Health Sci .... Dr. Laurie SHERWEN
88 Dean of Mayes College .... Dr. Andrew PETERSON
15 Exec Director Human Resources .... Ms. Rosalie I. JONES
19 Director Public Safety .... Mr. James WALDON
41 Athletic Director .... Mr. Paul KLIMITAS
88 Director of Student Engagement .... Mr. Ross RADISH
35 Director of Student Life .... Ms. Susanne E. FERRIN
39 Associate Director of Student Life .... Mr. Jay TIFONE
85 Director of Multicultural Affairs .... Mr. Walter PERRY
09 Director of Institutional Research .... Ms. Anne B. HOROWITZ
21 Controller/Asst VP Finance .... Ms. Brigid K. ISACKMAN
36 Director Career Services .... Ms. Kimberly BRYANT
38 Director Student Counseling .... Vacant
96 Manager University Purchasing .... Mr. Thomas MOIANI

88 Assistant Provost Spec Projects .... Dr. John CONNORS
88 Director Academic Advising .... Mr. Joseph CANADAY
18 Director of Facilities .... Mr. Dan SEVERINO

The University of Scranton (A)

800 Linden St, Scranton PA 18510-4622
County: Lackawanna FICE Identification: 003384
Unit ID: 215929
Telephone: (570) 941-7400 Carnegie Class: Master's L
FAX Number: (570) 941-6369 Calendar System: Semester
URL: www.scranton.edu
Established: 1888 Annual Undergrad Tuition & Fees: $38,754
Enrollment: 5,898 Coed
Affiliation or Control: Roman Catholic IRS Status: 501(c)3
Highest Offering: Doctorate
Program: Liberal Arts And General; Teacher Preparatory; Professional
Accreditation: M, ANEST, BUS, CACREP, CORE, CS, ENG, HSA, NURSE, OT, PTA, TEAC, TED

01 President .... Rev. Kevin P. QUINN, SJ
05 Sr VP Academic Affairs & Provost .... Dr. Harold W. BAILLIE
10 Sr VP Finance & Administration .. Mr. Edward J. STEINMETZ, JR.
32 Vice President Student Affairs .... Dr. Vincent CARILLI
45 Vice President Planning/CIO .... Dr. Jerome P. DESANTO
26 Vice President for External Affairs .... Mr. Gerald C. ZABOSKI
16 Vice President Human Resources .... Ms. Patricia A. DAY
42 VP for Mission and Ministry .... Rev. Richard G. MALLOY, SJ
30 VP for University Advancement .... Mr. Gary R. OLSEN
43 General Counsel .... Mr. Robert B. FARRELL
49 Dean Arts & Sciences .... Dr. Brian P. CONNIFF
50 Dean Kania School Management .... Dr. Michael O. MENSAH
58 Dean Grad School/Continuing Educ .... Dr. William J. WELSH
88 Dean Panuska Col of Prof Studies ...... Dr. Debra A. PELLEGRINO
35 Asst VP Stdnt Affs/Dean of Students .... Dr. Anitra M. MCSHEA
08 Dean of the Library/Info Fluency .... Mr. Charles E. KRATZ, JR.
51 Asst Dean of OL/Off Campus Program ..... Mrs. Lisa M. LOBASSO
21 Assistant Vice President Finance .... Vacant
20 Assoc Provost for Academic Affairs ..... Dr. Joseph H. DREISBACH
07 Assoc VP Admiss & Undergrad Enroll ..... Mr. Joseph M. ROBACK
84 Asst VP Admissions & Enrollment .... Ms. Mary Kay ASTON
21 Assistant Provost for Operations .... Vacant
06 Registrar .... Ms. Helen H. STAGER
37 Director of Financial Aid .... Mr. William R. BURKE
36 Director of Career Services .... Mrs. Constance F. MCDONNELL
29 Dir of Alumni and Parent Relations .... Ms. Maryjane S. ROONEY
28 Director of Equity/Diversity Office .... Ms. Rosette B. ADERA
09 Director of Institutional Research .... Ms. Valerie A. TAYLOR
38 Director of Counseling Center .... Mr. Thomas P. SMITH
96 Director of Purchasing .... Mr. Gary S. ZAMPANO
100 Chief of Staff .... Mr. Robert W. DAVIS, JR.
18 Asst VP Facilities Operations .... Mr. James DEVERS

Ursinus College (B)

PO Box 1000, 601 E Main Street,
Collegeville PA 19426-1000
County: Montgomery FICE Identification: 003385
Unit ID: 216524
Telephone: (610) 409-3000 Carnegie Class: Bac/A&S
FAX Number: (610) 489-0627 Calendar System: Semester
URL: www.ursinus.edu
Established: 1869 Annual Undergrad Tuition & Fees: $44,350
Enrollment: 1,661 Coed
Affiliation or Control: Independent Non-Profit IRS Status: 501(c)3
Highest Offering: Baccalaureate
Program: Liberal Arts And General; Teacher Preparatory
Accreditation: M

01 President .... Dr. Bobby FONG
05 Vice Pres Acad Affs/Dean of College .... Dr. Lucien T. WINEGAR
10 Vice Pres Finance & Administration .. Mr. Winfield L. GUILMETTE
30 Senior Vice Pres for Advancement .... Ms. Jill A. MARSTELLER
84 Vice President for Enrollment . Mr. Richard G. DIFELICIANTONIO
32 Vice Pres of Student Affairs/Dean .... Ms. Deborah O. NOLAN
21 Associate Vice Pres/Controller .... Mr. James COOPER
07 Director of Admissions .... Ms. Dana MATASSINO
44 Exec Director of Planned Giving .... Mr. Mark P. GADSON
08 Library Director .... Mr. Charles JAMISON
36 Director of Career Services .... Mrs. Carla M. RINDE
18 Director of Physical Facilities .... Mr. Andrew FEICK
41 Director of Athletics .... Mrs. Laura MOLIKEN
27 Director College Communications .... Ms. Wendy GREENBERG
37 Director Student Financial Services .... Mrs. Suzanne SPARROW
06 Registrar .... Ms. Barbara A. BORIS
29 Director of Alumni Relations .... Ms. Pamela PANARELLA
20 Associate Dean of the College .... Dr. Jay MILLER
15 Director Human Resources .... Ms. Kelly WILLIAMS
09 Director of Institutional Research .... Mr. Angelo SORRENTINO

Valley Forge Christian College (C)

1401 Charlestown Road, Phoenixville PA 19460-2399
County: Chester FICE Identification: 003306
Unit ID: 216542
Telephone: (610) 935-0450 Carnegie Class: Bac/Diverse
FAX Number: (610) 935-9353 Calendar System: Semester
URL: www.vfcc.edu
Established: 1939 Annual Undergrad Tuition & Fees: $19,264
Enrollment: 1,040 Coed
Affiliation or Control: Assemblies Of God Church IRS Status: 501(c)3
Highest Offering: Master's
Program: Liberal Arts And General; Teacher Preparatory; Professional; Religious Emphasis
Accreditation: M, SW

01 President .... Dr. Donald G. MEYER
05 VP of Academic Affairs .... Dr. Kevin E. BEERY
10 VP of Finance .... Mr. Jonathan CAPECI
32 VP of Student Life .... Rev. Jennifer D. GALE
30 Executive Director of Development .... Vacant
108 Dean Inst Assessment/Online Educ .... Vacant
21 Comptroller .... Vacant
84 Exec Director Enrollment Management .... Mrs. Evie MEYER
49 Arts & Sciences Dept Chair .... Dr. Michael DI GIACOMO
83 Behavioral Sciences Dept Chair .... Dr. David SCOLFORO
50 Business Dept Chair .... Dr. William CLARKSON
73 Church Ministry Dept Chair .... Vacant
73 Deaf Pastoral Minstries Dept Chair .... Dr. JoAnn SMITH
72 Digital Media/Commun Dept Chair .... Mr. Leone BILOTTA
53 Education Dept Chair .... Dr. A. Glann MCCLURE
88 Intercultural Studies Dept Chair .... Rev. Jennifer DUNCAN
64 Music Dept Chair .... Dr. William DESANTLO
88 Director of Accounting .... Mrs. Betty SMITH
07 Director of Admissions .... Rev. William CHENCO
29 Director Parent & Alumni Services .... Mrs. Alicia DESROSIERS
41 Director of Athletics .... Mr. Jon MACK
36 Director Career Services .... Mrs. Amy THURSTON
37 Director of Financial Aid .... Mrs. Linda STEIN
15 Director Human Resources .... Mrs. Veronica BIRD
14 Director of Information Technology .... Mr. Brian SWOMLEY
08 Librarian/Dir Storms Research Ctr .... Mrs. Deborah HIRNEISEN
26 Director of Marketing .... Mrs. Michelle MALONEY
06 Registrar .... Mr. Russell CAMBRIA
35 Campus Director .... Mrs. Wendy BEERY
35 Campus Director .... Mr. Anthony ROSS
39 Residence Director .... Ms. Trinidad ANDINO
39 Residence Director .... Mr. Yung Won PARK

Valley Forge Military College (D)

1001 Eagle Road, Wayne PA 19087-3695
County: Delaware FICE Identification: 003386
Unit ID: 216551
Telephone: (610) 989-1451 Carnegie Class: Not Classified
FAX Number: (610) 975-9642 Calendar System: Semester
URL: www.vfmac.edu
Established: 1935 Annual Undergrad Tuition & Fees: $35,000
Enrollment: 235 Coed
Affiliation or Control: Independent Non-Profit IRS Status: 501(c)3
Highest Offering: Associate Degree
Program: 2-Year Principally Bachelor's Creditable
Accreditation: M

00 President Military Academy/College .... Dr. Stacey SAUCHUK
01 President of the College .... Dr. Kathleen M. ANDERSON
32 Commandant of Cadets .... Col. Richard PISCAL
30 Vice President for Development .... Vacant
05 Chief Academic Officer .... Col. Nan S. HOOD
10 Chief Financial Officer/COO .... Mr. Vincent VUONO
18 Director of Facilities .... Mr. Bryan K. GEILING
07 Director of College Admissions .... Ms. Kristen ROSE
08 Director of Library Services .... LTC. Jean L. SMITH
37 Financial Aid .... Mr. Edward FLUOCCO
15 Director of Human Resources .... Ms. Marianne MEADE
13 Director Information Technology .... Mr. Michael BROCK
41 Director of Athletics .... Mr. Richard CASEY
35 Dean Student Services .... Maj. Robert WOOD
09 Institutional Research & Assessment .... Ms. Gloria OIKELOME
06 Assistant Dean/Registrar .... Ms. Maureen MALONE
88 Transfer Advisor .... Ms. Joann MCCRACKEN

Vet Tech Institute (E)

125 Seventh Street, Pittsburgh PA 15222-3400
County: Allegheny FICE Identification: 008568
Unit ID: 213914
Telephone: (412) 391-7021 Carnegie Class: Assoc/PrivFP
FAX Number: (412) 232-4348 Calendar System: Semester
URL: www.vettechinstitute.edu
Established: 1958 Annual Undergrad Tuition & Fees: $15,080
Enrollment: 337 Coed
Affiliation or Control: Proprietary IRS Status: Proprietary
Highest Offering: Associate Degree
Program: Occupational; Technical Emphasis
Accreditation: ACCSC

01 Director .... Jackie FLYNN

Villanova University (F)

800 Lancaster Avenue, Villanova PA 19085-1699
County: Delaware FICE Identification: 003388
Unit ID: 216597
Telephone: (610) 519-4500 Carnegie Class: Master's L
FAX Number: (610) 519-5000 Calendar System: Semester
URL: www.villanova.edu
Established: 1842 Annual Undergrad Tuition & Fees: $43,840
Enrollment: 10,379 Coed
Affiliation or Control: Roman Catholic IRS Status: 501(c)3
Highest Offering: Doctorate
Program: Liberal Arts And General; Teacher Preparatory; Professional
Accreditation: M, ANEST, BUS, BUSA, CS, ENG, LAW, NURSE, SPAA

01 President .... Rev. Peter M. DONOHUE, OSA
43 Vice President & General Counsel .... Ms. Debra FICKLER
05 Vice President for Academic Affairs .... Rev. Kail C. ELLIS, OSA
30 Vice Pres University Advancement .... Mr. Michael O'NEILL
11 Vice Pres Administration/Finance .... Mr. Kenneth G. VALOSKY
13 Vice Pres/Chief Information Officer .... Mr. Stephen FUGALE
32 Vice President for Student Life .... Rev. John P. STACK, OSA
27 Vice Pres University Communication .... Ms. Ann DIEBOLD
42 Vice Pres for Mission & Ministry .... Dr. Barbara E. WALL
20 Assoc Vice Pres Academic Affairs .... Dr. Craig WHEELAND
35 Assoc Vice Pres for Student Life .... Ms. Kathleen J. BYRNES
15 AVP Human Res/Affirm Action Ofcr .... Ms. Ellen KRUTZ
45 Assoc Vice Pres for Auxiliary Svcs .... Mr. Frederick C. SIEBER
42 Assoc Vice Pres Mission & Ministry .... Rev. Joseph L. FARRELL, OSA
29 Assoc Vice Pres Alumni Relations .... Mr. George R. KOLB
46 Asst Vice Pres for Research .... Dr. Milton T. COLE
51 Asst Vice Pres for Academic Affairs .... Dr. Robert D. STOKES
28 Asst VP Multicultural Affairs .... Dr. Teresa A. NANCE
84 Dean Enrollment Management .... Mr. Stephen R. MERRITT
09 Exec Dir Planning/Inst Research .... Dr. James F. TRAINER
18 Exec Director Facilities Management .... Mr. Robert MORRO
88 Asoc Dean Enrol Mgt For Stdnt Info ... Ms. Catherine H. CONNOR
07 Director University Admission .... Mr. Michael GAYNOR
08 Interim Director of Falvey Library .... Mr. Darren POLEY
35 Dean of Students .... Mr. Paul F. PUGH
49 Dean Liberal Arts & Sciences .... Dr. Jean A. LINNEY
50 Dean Villanova School of Business .... Dr. Patrick G. MAGGITTI
58 Dean Graduate Studies LA&S .... Dr. Adele LINDENMEYR
61 Dean School of Law .... Mr. John GOTANDA
66 Dean of Nursing .... Dr. M. Louise FITZPATRICK
54 Dean of Engineering .... Dr. Gary A. GABRIELE
88 Dir Ctr Spirituality/Discernment .... Ms. Linda JACZYNSKI
88 Dir Ctr Service/Social Justice .... Ms. Irene KING
88 Director Center for Worship .... Rev. Joseph MOSTARDI, OSA
88 Dir Ctr Grad Pastoral Ministry Educ .... Ms. Joyce ZAVARICH
55 Director Part Time Studies .... Ms. Mary BUSTAMANTE
85 Director Intl/Human Services .... Mr. Stephen T. MCWILLIAMS
37 Director Financial Assistance .... Ms. Bonnie Lee BEHM
19 Director of Public Safety .... Mr. David TEDJESKE
36 Director Career Services .... Ms. Nancy J. DUDAK
92 Director of the Honors Program .... Dr. Thomas W. SMITH
38 Director of Univ Counseling Center .... Dr. Joan G. WHITNEY
94 Co-Dir Women's Studies Programming .... Dr. Lisa SEWELL
94 Co-Dir Women's Studies Academics .... Dr. Jean LUTES
39 Director Office of Residence Life .... Mr. Thomas DE MARCO
96 Director of Procurement .... Mr. John R. DURHAM
26 Director of Media Relations .... Mr. Jonathan GUST
41 Director of Athletics .... Mr. Vincent P. NICASTRO
23 Medical Director Student Health Ctr .... Dr. Brian BULLOCK
23 Director Student Health Center .... Dr. Mary MCGONIGLE
06 Associate Registrar .... Ms. Melissa D. GERDING
22 Asc Dir Center Multicultural Affs .... Ms. Linda COLEMAN
04 Special Asst to President/Ext Rels ...... Rev. George F. RILEY, OSA

Washington & Jefferson College (G)

60 S Lincoln Street, Washington PA 15301-4801
County: Washington FICE Identification: 003389
Unit ID: 216667
Telephone: (724) 222-4400 Carnegie Class: Bac/A&S
FAX Number: (724) 223-6534 Calendar System: 4/1/4
URL: www.washjeff.edu
Established: 1781 Annual Undergrad Tuition & Fees: $39,250
Enrollment: 1,429 Coed
Affiliation or Control: Independent Non-Profit IRS Status: 501(c)3
Highest Offering: Baccalaureate
Program: Liberal Arts And General; Teacher Preparatory
Accreditation: M

01 President .... Dr. Tori HARING-SMITH
05 VP Academic Affairs/Dean of Faculty ... Dr. John E. ZIMMERMAN
10 CFO/VP Business/Finance .... Mr. Dennis MCMASTER
30 VP Development/Alumni Relations .... Mr. Michael P. GRZESIAK
84 Vice President for Enrollment .... Mr. Alton E. NEWELL
21 Assoc VP for Business & Finance .... Mr. Thomas SZEJKO
32 VP and Dean of Student Life ..... Ms. Eva CHATTERJEE-SUTTON
44 Exec Dir Campaigns/Advancement Oper ... Ms. Karen CRENSHAW
20 Associate Dean of the Faculty .... Dr. Charles HANNON
58 Assoc Dean Grad/Continuing Studies .... Dr. Michael SHAUGHNESSY
28 Asst Dean Stdnt Life/Dir Diver Pgm .... Ms. Ketwana SCHOOS
20 Asst Dean for Academic Affairs .... Dr. Kathleen MCEVOY
18 Director of Facilities and Planning .... Mr. Troy BONTE
26 Dir Comm/Special Asst to President .... Ms. Karen OOSTERHOUS
06 Registrar .... Ms. Leslie MAXIN
29 Assoc VP Alumni Relations & Dev .... Ms. Michele HUFNAGEL
07 Director of Admission .... Mr. Robert ADKINS
37 Director Financial Aid .... Ms. Michelle ANDERSON
13 Dir of Information/Technology Svcs .... Mr. Daniel FAULK
15 Director Human Resources .... Mr. Robert ALLISON
19 Director Protection Services .... Mr. Edward E. COCHRAN
36 Director Career Services .... Ms. Roberta CROSS
40 Bookstore Manager .... Ms. Cynthia BRICELAND
41 Director of Athletics .... Mr. William DUKETT
08 Director of Library Services .... Ms. Alexis RITTENBERGER
102 Foundation & Corp Relations Officer .... Ms. Julie THROCKMORTON
35 Associate Dean Student Life .... Mr. Steven ANDERSON
91 Assoc Director for Admin Computing .... Mr. Michael A. TIMKO
104 Dir of Global Education .... Ms. Tracie SEBASTIAN-FRUEHAUF
108 Dir of Assessment & Inst Research .... Dr. Chaun STORES
88 Asst Dean for Academic Advising .... Ms. Catherine SHERMAN
88 Director Conferences and Events .... Ms. Maureen VALENTINE
38 Director of Counseling Services .... Ms. Lisa HAMILTON

Waynesburg University (A)

51 W College Street, Waynesburg PA 15370-1222
County: Greene FICE Identification: 003391
Unit ID: 216694
Telephone: (724) 627-8191 Carnegie Class: Master's L
FAX Number: (724) 627-6416 Calendar System: Semester
URL: www.waynesburg.edu
Established: 1849 Annual Undergrad Tuition & Fees: $20,540
Enrollment: 2,270 Coed
Affiliation or Control: Presbyterian Church (U.S.A.) IRS Status: 501(c)3
Highest Offering: Doctorate
Program: Liberal Arts And General; Teacher Preparatory; Professional
Accreditation: M, CACREP, NURSE

00 Chancellor .... Dr. Timothy R. THYREEN
01 President .... Mr. Doug LEE
05 Vice Pres Academic Affairs/Provost .... Dr. Jaqueline CORE
10 Sr VP Business & Finance .... Mr. Roy R. BARNHART
07 Sr VP Enrollment & Univ Relations .... Mrs. Robin L. KING
32 VP of Student Services .... Mrs. Mary CUMMINGS
06 Registrar .... Mrs. Vicki WILSON
41 Athletic Director .... Mr. Larry MARSHALL
13 Interim Dir Information Technology .... Mr. Josh STARSICK
08 Director Eberly Library .... Mr. Rea REDD
18 Director of Facilites Management .... Mr. John BURKE
26 Communication Specialist .... Ms. Ashley WISE
36 Director of Placement .... Mrs. Marie E. COFFMAN
38 Student Counselor .... Mrs. Jane S. OWEN
21 Business Ofc Supervisor/Controller .... Mr. Dave MARTIN
23 Director of Health Services .... Ms. Jennifer SHIRING
42 Chaplain .... Mr. Tom RIBAR
15 Director Human Resources .... Mr. Tom HELMICK
37 Director Student Financial Aid .... Mr. Matthew STOKAN

Westminster College (B)

319 South Market Street, New Wilmington PA 16172-0001
County: Lawrence FICE Identification: 003392
Unit ID: 216807
Telephone: (724) 946-8761 Carnegie Class: Bac/A&S
FAX Number: (724) 946-7132 Calendar System: Semester
URL: www.westminster.edu
Established: 1852 Annual Undergrad Tuition & Fees: $32,445
Enrollment: 1,463 Coed
Affiliation or Control: Presbyterian Church (U.S.A.) IRS Status: 501(c)3
Highest Offering: Master's
Program: Liberal Arts And General; Teacher Preparatory
Accreditation: M, MUS

01 President .... Dr. Richard H. DORMAN
05 Vice Pres Academic Affs/Dean of Col .... Dr. Jane M. WOOD
30 VP Inst Advancement/Chief Dev Ofcr .... Mr. Grady B. JONES
10 Vice Pres Finance/Mgmt Services .... Mr. Kenneth J. ROMIG
06 Registrar .... Ms. June PIERCE
07 Vice President for Enrollment .... Mr. David J. RHODES
42 Dean of the Chapel .... Rev. James R. MOHR
32 VP Student Affairs/Dean of Students .... Dr. Neal A. EDMAN
35 Assoc Dean of Student Affairs .... Ms. Gina M. VANCE
37 Director Student Financial Aid .... Ms. Cheryl GERBER
08 Head Librarian .... Ms. Erin T. SMITH
36 Director of Career Center .... Ms. Linda B. MEADE
29 Director of Alumni Relations .... Vacant
27 Sr Dir Marketing/Communications .... Mr. Mark A. MEIGHEN
13 Director of Information Systems .... Mr. Paul N. WALLACE
51 Dir Cont Educ/Lifelong Learning .... Dr. Jamie G. MCMINN
58 Director Graduate Programs .... Dr. Robert L. ZORN
41 Athletic Director .... Mr. James E. DAFLER
18 Director of Physical Plant .... Mr. Owen W. WAGNER
21 Business Manager .... Ms. Janet M. SMITH
24 Director of Audio-Visual Aids .... Mr. Gary L. SWANSON
19 Director of Public Safety .... Mr. William A. BRANDT
09 Director of Institutional Research .... Dr. Gary D. LILLY
23 Director Health Services .... Ms. Melissa M. BARON
40 Bookstore Manager .... Ms. Kay A. GALANSKI
21 Controller .... Ms. Christine A. MILLER
15 Director of Human Resources .... Ms. Kimberlee K. CHRISTOFFERSON
38 Counselor .... Ms. Barbara I. QUINCY
28 Director of Diversity Services .... Ms. Jeannette HUBBARD

Westminster Theological Seminary (C)

2960 Church Road, Glenside PA 19038
County: Montgomery FICE Identification: 003393
Unit ID: 216816
Telephone: (215) 887-5511 Carnegie Class: Spec/Faith
FAX Number: (215) 887-5404 Calendar System: 4/1/4
URL: www.wts.edu
Established: 1929 Annual Graduate Tuition & Fees: $13,925
Enrollment: 601 Coed
Affiliation or Control: Independent Non-Profit IRS Status: 501(c)3
Highest Offering: Doctorate; No Undergraduates
Program: Liberal Arts And General; Professional; Religious Emphasis
Accreditation: M, THEOL

01 President .... Dr. Peter A. LILLBACK
30 Vice Pres Development .... Mr. William B. VINCENT
05 Provost/Executive Vice President .... Dr. Jeffrey K. JUE
45 Vice Pres Institutional Projects .... Dr. David GARNER
10 Chief Financial Officer .... Mr. Mark WILSON
11 Chief Administrative Officer .... Mr. Steven CARTER
88 Dean Student/Ministerial Formation .... Rev. Greg HOBAUGH
06 Registrar .... Ms. Melinda E. DUGAN
07 Director of Admissions .... Mr. Jonathan M. BRACK
08 Director of Library Services .... Mr. Alexander (Sandy) FINLAYSON
73 Director D.Min/Supervised Ministry .... Mr. Timothy Z. WITMER
40 Director Bookstore .... Mr. Chun LAI
37 Financial Aid Officer .... Ms. Fiona E. DAVENPORT
15 Director Human Resources .... Ms. Karin DEUSSING
13 Director Information Technology .... Mr. Matt HOGG
18 Physical Plant Manager .... Mr. Robert M. SEXTON
29 Dir Student Develop/Alumni Rels .... Rev. John CURRIE
09 Dir Institutional Assess/Accred .... Ms. Rebecca M. LIPPERT

Westmoreland County Community College (D)

145 Pavilion Lane, Youngwood PA 15697-1895
County: Westmoreland FICE Identification: 010176
Unit ID: 216825
Telephone: (724) 925-4000 Carnegie Class: Assoc/Pub-S-SC
FAX Number: (724) 925-1150 Calendar System: Semester
URL: www.wccc.edu
Established: 1970 Annual Undergrad Tuition & Fees (In-District): $3,330
Enrollment: 6,571 Coed
Affiliation or Control: Local IRS Status: 501(c)3
Highest Offering: Associate Degree
Program: Occupational; 2-Year Principally Bachelor's Creditable
Accreditation: M, ACFEI, ADNUR, DA, DH, DMS, MAC

01 President .... Dr. Daniel J. OBARA
05 Vice Pres Academic Affs/Stdnt Svcs .... Dr. Nicole REAVES
11 Vice Pres Administrative Services .... Mr. Ronald E. EBERHARDT
51 VP Cont Educ/Workforce & Cmty Devel .... Dr. Patrick E. GERITY
20 Assoc VP Academic Affairs .... Vacant
10 Chief Business Officer .... Mr. Ronald E. EBERHARDT
25 Director of Grants .... Ms. Debra J. WILLIAMS
15 Director Human Resources .... Ms. Lauren M. FARRELL
08 Director Learning Res & Sp Projects .... Ms. Kathleen A. KEEFE
77 Dean Computer Tech/Business .... Mr. Edwin C. NELSON
76 Dean Health Profess/Biology .... Dr. Kathleen A. MALLOY
81 Dean Mathematics/Sciences .... Vacant
79 Dean Public Svc/Human/Soc Science .... Dr. Andrew BARNETTE
32 Dean of Students .... Ms. Diane D. HIGHTOWER
103 Dean Workforce Development .... Mr. Douglas J. JENSEN
84 Director Enrollment Management .... Vacant
102 Exec Director Education Foundation .... Ms. Debra D. WOODS
37 Director Financial Aid .... Mr. Gary A. MEANS
18 Director Facilities .... Mr. John C. DETISCH
21 Controller .... Mr. Timothy W. STAHL
14 Director Information Technology .... Mr. Patrick R. MCKULA
88 Director College Services .... Mr. Ronald A. KRIVDA
26 Director Public Relations .... Ms. Anna Marie PALATELLA
07 Director Admissions .... Ms. Janice T. GRABOWSKI
41 Director Student Life/Athletics .... Mr. Richard G. HOLLER
09 Dir Institutional Research/Data Svc .... Mr. Randal M. FINFROCK
96 Coordinator of Purchasing .... Ms. Kim A. HIMLER
36 Coord Student Placement/Coop Ed .... Ms. Cheryl A. NOEL

Widener University (E)

One University Place, Chester PA 19013-5792
County: Delaware FICE Identification: 003313
Unit ID: 216852
Telephone: (610) 499-4000 Carnegie Class: DRU
FAX Number: (610) 876-9751 Calendar System: Semester
URL: www.widener.edu
Established: 1821 Annual Undergrad Tuition & Fees: $38,028
Enrollment: 6,238 Coed
Affiliation or Control: Independent Non-Profit IRS Status: 501(c)3
Highest Offering: Doctorate
Program: Liberal Arts And General; Teacher Preparatory; Professional
Accreditation: M, BUS, CLPSY, ENG, HSA, IPSY, LAW, NURSE, PTA, SW, TED

01 President .... Dr. James T. HARRIS, III
05 Provost/Sr Vice Pres Academic Affs .... Dr. Stephen C. WILHITE
10 Sr Vice Pres Administration/Finance .... Mr. Joseph J. BAKER
30 Vice Pres University Advancement .... Ms. Linda S. DURANT
13 Chief Information Officer .... Mr. Peter D. SHOUDY
21 Associate VP & Controller .... Ms. Catherine MCGEEHAN
11 Associate VP of Administration .... Mr. George E. HASSEL
26 Asst Vice Pres University Relations .... Ms. Lou Anne BULIK
18 Director of Operations .... Mr. Carl G. PIERCE
58 Assoc Provost Grad Studies .... Dr. Penelope S. GREENBERG
20 Associate Provost Undergraduate .... Dr. Geraldine A. BLOEMKER
32 Assoc Provost/Dean of Students .... Dr. Denise D. GIFFORD
54 Dean School of Engineering .... Dr. Fred A. AKL
49 Int Dean College Arts & Sciences .... Dr. Harry AUGENSEN
50 Dean School of Business Admin .... Dr. Savas OZATALAY
66 Dean School of Nursing .... Dr. Deborah R. GARRISON
51 Dean Sch of Educ/Innov/Cont Studies .... Dr. Brenda R. GILIO
88 Dean Sch of Hospitality Management .... Mr. Nicholas J. HADGIS
88 Dean Sch Human Svc Professions .... Dr. Paula SILVER
21 Bursar .... Ms. Diana BARRACLOUGH
08 Librarian .... Dr. Robert E. DANFORD
37 Exec Dir Student Financial Services .... Mr. Thomas K. MALLOY
06 Director of Records/Registration .... Ms. Kristen CHANDO
29 Director of Alumni Engagement .... Ms. Tina A. PHILLIPS
09 Dir of Inst Res & Effectiveness .... Dr. Stephen W. THORPE
36 Placement Director .... Ms. Jan MOPPERT
41 Director of Athletics .... Mr. Jack L. SHAFER
85 Director International Student Svcs .... Vacant
19 Director of Campus Safety .... Mr. Patrick SULLIVAN
23 Director of Health Services .... Ms. Lynn A. NELSON-RUSSOM
24 Head of Multimedia/Classroom Spprt .... Mr. Eric WOEBKENBERG
40 Manager Campus Bookstore .... Mr. Chester HENSEL
91 Director Information Systems .... Mrs. Linda TAYLOR
88 Director Technical Resources .... Mr. Perry M. DRAYFAHL
15 Director of Human Resources .... Ms. Christine M. LLOYD
96 Director of Purchasing .... Vacant
07 Exec Director of Admissions .... Mr. Edwin R. WRIGHT
89 Dir Student Success/Retention .... Mr. Timothy J. CAIRY
97 Dir Honors Program in General Educ .... Dr. Ilene LIEBERMAN
94 Director of Women's Studies .... Dr. Annalisa CASTALDO

† See Delaware listing of Widener University School of Law.

Wilkes University (F)

84 W South Street, Wilkes-Barre PA 18766-0001
County: Luzerne FICE Identification: 003394
Unit ID: 216931
Telephone: (570) 408-5000 Carnegie Class: Master's L
FAX Number: (570) 408-2934 Calendar System: Semester
URL: www.wilkes.edu
Established: 1933 Annual Undergrad Tuition & Fees: $30,353
Enrollment: 5,030 Coed
Affiliation or Control: Independent Non-Profit IRS Status: 501(c)3
Highest Offering: Doctorate
Program: Liberal Arts And General; Teacher Preparatory; Professional
Accreditation: M, ACBSP, CEA, ENG, NURSE, PHAR

01 President .... Dr. Patrick F. LEAHY
05 Provost .... Vacant
30 Vice Pres University Advancement .... Mr. Michael WOOD
10 Vice President & General Counsel .... Mr. Loren D. PRESCOTT
21 Controller .... Ms. Janet KOBYLSKI
84 Vice President Enrollment Services .... Ms. Melanie WADE
32 Vice President Student Affairs .... Dr. Paul S. ADAMS
16 Vice President Human Resources Dev .... Vacant
20 Associate Provost .... Vacant
35 Dean of Students .... Mr. Mark R. ALLEN
35 Associate Dean Student Affairs .... Ms. Barbara E. KING
54 Dean Col of Science & Engineering .... Dr. Dale BRUNS
49 Dean College of Arts & Humanities .... Dr. Linda WINKLER
67 Dean Nesbitt Col Pharm/Nursing .... Dr. Bernard GRAHAM
58 Dean Grad/Prof Studies/Sch of Educ .... Dr. Michael SPEZIALE
50 Int Dean Sidh School of Business .... Dr. Jeffrey ALVES
62 Dean Library .... Mr. John STACHACZ
09 Exec Director Info/Analysis/Plng .... Mr. Brian BOGERT
29 Director Alumni Relations .... Vacant
41 Director of Athletics .... Ms. Addy MALATESTA
23 Director Health Services .... Ms. Diane E. O'BRIEN
36 Director Career Services .... Mrs. Carol A. BOSACK-KOSEK
39 Director Residence Life .... Ms. Elizabeth ROVEDA
58 Director Graduate Teach Education .... Ms. Kristine PRUETT
06 Registrar .... Mrs. Susan A. HRITZAK
37 Dir of Financial Aid/Stdnt Services .... Mr. Joseph ALAIMO
26 Dir Mktg/Com/Sp Ast to Pres Gov Rel .... Mr. Jack A. CHIELLI
18 Director Facilities Services .... Mr. John PESTA
14 Chief Information Officer .... Ms. Gloria BARLOW
07 Assoc Director of Admissions .... Ms. Amy PATTON
07 Assoc Director of Admissions .... Mr. Alex SPERAZZA
28 Spec Asst to Pres for Multicul Affs .... Vacant
96 Director Procurement & Finan Svcs .... Ms. Alicia BOND
15 Director Human Resource Services .... Mr. Joseph HOUSENICK
38 Campus Counselor .... Ms. Melissa GAUDIO
38 Campus Counselor .... Ms. Susan BISKUP
102 Director of Corp/Found/Govt Rels .... Mrs. Anne PELAK
35 Dir Student Svc Ctr/Student Svcs .... Ms. Janine BECKER
04 Admin Asst to the President .... Ms. Susan DIBONIFAZIO

Williamson Free School of Mechanical Trades (G)

106 S New Middletown Road, Media PA 19063-5299
County: Delaware FICE Identification: 041238
Unit ID: 216940
Telephone: (610) 566-1776 Carnegie Class: Not Classified
FAX Number: (610) 566-6502 Calendar System: Semester
URL: www.williamson.edu
Established: 1888 Annual Undergrad Tuition & Fees: N/A
Enrollment: 270 Male
Affiliation or Control: Independent Non-Profit IRS Status: 501(c)3
Highest Offering: Associate Degree
Program: Occupational
Accreditation: ACCSC

01 President .... Mr. Guy S. GARDNER
05 Vice President of Education & CAO .... Mr. Thomas E. WISNESKI
10 Vice President of Finance & CFO .... Mr. Gregory L. LINDEMUTH
30 Vice President of Inst Advancement .... Mr. Peter D'ORAZIO
11 Vice Pres of Plans & Operations .... Mr. Jim HANNIGAN
32 Dean of Students .... Mr. Thomas J. MOFFITT
84 Director of Enrollments .... Mr. Jason C. MERILLAT
41 Director of Athletics .... Mr. Dale H. PLUMMER
42 Chaplain/Counselor .... Rev. Mark A. SPECHT
06 Registrar .... Ms. Anne M. HAYES
36 Director of Placement .... Ms. Margaret T. KINGHAM
26 Director of Public Relations .... Mr. Carl A. VAIRO

Wilson College (H)

1015 Philadelphia Avenue, Chambersburg PA 17201-1285
County: Franklin FICE Identification: 003396
Unit ID: 217013
Telephone: (717) 262-4141 Carnegie Class: Bac/Diverse

FAX Number: (717) 264-1578 Calendar System: 4/1/4
URL: www.wilson.edu
Established: 1869 Annual Undergrad Tuition & Fees: $29,370
Enrollment: 695 Coed
Affiliation or Control: Presbyterian Church (U.S.A.) IRS Status: 501(c)3
Highest Offering: Master's
Program: Liberal Arts And General; Teacher Preparatory
Accreditation: M

01 President .... Dr. Barbara K. MISTICK
05 VP for Academic Affairs/Dean of Fac .... Dr. Mary HENDRICKSON
30 VP for Institutional Advancement .... Ms. Camilla B. RAWLEIGH
10 Vice Pres Finance & Administration .... Mr. Brian ECKER
84 Vice President/Dean of Enrollment .... Ms. Mary Ann NASO
32 Vice President for Student Dev/Dean .... Ms. Carolyn PERKINS
26 VP for Marketing and Communications .... Mr. Brian SPEER
100 Chief of Staff .... Ms. Melissa IMES
06 Registrar .... Ms. Jean B. HOOVER
37 Dean of Financial Aid .... Ms. Linda D. BRITTAIN
09 Asst Dean IR and Assesment .... Dr. Elizabeth ANDERSON
08 Director of Library .... Ms. Kathleen MURPHY
18 Director of Physical Plant .... Mr. Jack KELLY
27 Communications Associate .... Ms. Cathy MENTZER
40 Director of Bookstore .... Ms. Deborah GAYNOR
41 Athletic Director .... Ms. Lori FREY
51 Director of Conferences .... Mr. Joel PAGLIARO
29 Director of Alumnae Programs .... Ms. Marybeth FAMULARE
44 Director of Annual Fund .... Ms. Carolyn WOODS
15 Director Human Resources .... Vacant
20 Assoc Dean of Academic Advising .... Dr. Deborah AUSTIN
21 Assoc VP for Finance/Admin .... Ms. Lori TOSTEN
26 Chief Public Relations Officer .... Ms. Debra COLLINS
36 Director of Career Development .... Vacant
38 Director of Student Counseling .... Ms. Cindy SHOEMAKER
88 Director of Women With Children Pgm .... Ms. Katherine KOUGH
37 Coordinator of Financial Aid .... Ms. Christine KNOUSE
28 Coordinator of Diversity .... Vacant
42 Chaplain .... Rev. Rosie MAGEE
39 Director of Residence Life .... Ms. Sherri SADOWSKI

Won Institute of Graduate Studies (A)

137 S Easton Road, Glenside PA 19038
County: Montgomery FICE Identification: 039493
Unit ID: 442064
Telephone: (215) 884-8942 Carnegie Class: Spec/Health
FAX Number: (215) 884-9002 Calendar System: Trimester
URL: www.woninstitute.edu
Established: 2002 Annual Graduate Tuition & Fees: $17,500
Enrollment: 73 Coed
Affiliation or Control: Independent Non-Profit IRS Status: 501(c)3
Highest Offering: Master's; No Undergraduates
Program: Professional; Religious Emphasis
Accreditation: M, ACUP

01 President .... Dr. Bokin KIM
11 Chief Administrative Officer .... Ms. Colleen O'CONNELL
10 Chief Financial Officer .... Mr. Walter SINGER
05 Chief Academic Officer .... Ms. Lynn MITCHELL
06 Registrar .... Mr. Thomas WHITMIRE
08 Librarian .... Mrs. Pat KING
07 Admissions Officer .... Rev. Hojin PARK

WyoTech-Blairsville (B)

500 Innovation Drive, Blairsville PA 15717-8060
Telephone: (724) 459-9500 Identification: 666305
Accreditation: ACCSC

† Main campus is WyoTech in Laramie, WY.

Yeshiva Beth Moshe (C)

930 Hickory Street, Scranton PA 18505-2196
County: Lackawanna FICE Identification: 013134
Unit ID: 217040
Telephone: (570) 346-1747 Carnegie Class: Spec/Faith
FAX Number: (570) 346-2251 Calendar System: Semester
Established: 1965 Annual Undergrad Tuition & Fees: $8,600
Enrollment: 53 Male
Affiliation or Control: Independent Non-Profit IRS Status: 501(c)3
Highest Offering: Second Talmudic Degree
Program: Teacher Preparatory; Professional; Religious Emphasis
Accreditation: RABN

01 Chief Executive Officer .... Rabbi Yaakov SCHNAIDMAN
03 Executive Director .... Rabbi Avraham PRESSMAN

York College of Pennsylvania (D)

Country Club Road, York PA 17405-7199
County: York FICE Identification: 003399
Unit ID: 217059
Telephone: (717) 846-7788 Carnegie Class: Master's S
FAX Number: (717) 849-1607 Calendar System: Semester
URL: www.ycp.edu
Established: 1787 Annual Undergrad Tuition & Fees: $17,010
Enrollment: 5,439 Coed
Affiliation or Control: Independent Non-Profit IRS Status: 501(c)3
Highest Offering: Doctorate
Program: Liberal Arts And General; Teacher Preparatory; Professional
Accreditation: M, ACBSP, ANEST, COARC, CS, ENG, MUS, NRPA, NURSE

01 President .... Dr. Pamela J. GUNTER-SMITH
05 Dean of Academic Affairs .... Dr. Dominic DELLICARPINI
10 Chief Financial Officer .... Mr. Matthew SMITH
20 Dean of Academic Services .... Dr. Deborah D. RICKER
32 Dean of Student Affairs .... Mr. Joseph F. MERKLE
18 Dean of Campus Operations .... Dr. Kenneth M. MARTIN
44 Dean of College Advancement .... Mr. Daniel S. HELWIG
41 Asst Dean Athletics & Recreation .... Mr. Paul SAIKIA
84 Assoc Dean Enrollment Management .... Mr. Stephen NEITZ
26 Asst Dean Institutional Advancement .... Ms. Mary E. DOLHEIMER
30 Asst Dean Development .... Mr. Zane GIZZI
07 Director of Admissions .... Ms. Ines C. RAMIREZ
06 Registrar .... Ms. Rebecca C. LINK
08 Librarian .... Ms. Denise SHOREY
37 Director of Financial Aid .... Mr. Calvin H. WILLIAMS
13 Assoc Dean Information Technology .... Mr. Robert L. ROBINSON
29 Director Alumni Relations .... Mr. Bruce WALL
36 Director of Career Services .... Ms. Beverly A. EVANS
06 Assoc Registrar/Director of Records .... Mr. William BENTON
19 Director of Public Safety .... Mr. Edward C. BRUDER
39 Director of Residence Life .... Mr. Kevin D. FEIL
31 Director Community Education .... Mr. Leroy M. KEENEY
15 Director Human Resources .... Mrs. Vicki L. STEWART
38 Director Counseling Services .... Mrs. Karen JONES
91 Dir Administrative Computer Center .... Mr. Brian K. SMELTZER
23 Director Health Services .... Mrs. Rita CLAYTON
40 Director Bookstore .... Mrs. Lynn P. FERRO
88 Director College & Special Events .... Ms. Sherry HEFLIN
102 Dir Corporate/Foundation/Govt Rels .... Mr. Chad LINDER
27 College Editor .... Mrs. Alicia BRUMBACH
42 Director of Religious Activities .... Mrs. Louise WORLEY
31 Dir Center for Community Engagement .... Vacant
09 Director of Institutional Research .... Ms. Elizabeth CARROLL
28 Director of Multicultural Affairs .... Mr. Darrien DAVENPORT
24 Learning Center Coordinator .... Mrs. Cindy CRIMMINS
44 Sr Dir Principal & Planned Gifts .... Mr. Mark RANK

Yorktowne Business Institute (E)

West Seventh Avenue, York PA 17404-9946
County: York FICE Identification: 021208
Unit ID: 217086
Telephone: (717) 846-5000 Carnegie Class: Assoc/PrivFP
FAX Number: (717) 848-4584 Calendar System: Other
URL: www.ybi.edu
Established: 1977 Annual Undergrad Tuition & Fees: $12,120
Enrollment: 218 Coed
Affiliation or Control: Proprietary IRS Status: Proprietary
Highest Offering: Associate Degree
Program: Occupational
Accreditation: ACICS

01 President .... Dr. James P. MURPHY
03 Executive Director .... Ms. Elizabeth M. DREIBELBIS
50 Business Department Chair .... Ms. Lynda R. MEYERS
06 Registrar .... Ms. Lisa MCGOWAN
37 Director Student Financial Aid .... Ms. Deborah BOSTIC
08 Director Library Services .... Ms. Lynda MEYERS
36 Director Student Placement .... Mrs. Pam STOVER
18 Chief Facilities/Physical Plant .... Mr. Frederick WEIBLE
10 Business Officer .... Vacant
26 Marketing Director .... Mr. John A. DREIBELBIS
88 Teaching Kitchen Manager .... Ms. Kim CRIM

YTI Career Institute (F)

2900 Fairway Drive, Altoona PA 16602
County: Blair FICE Identification: 030819
Unit ID: 375939
Telephone: (814) 944-5643 Carnegie Class: Not Classified
FAX Number: (814) 944-5309 Calendar System: Quarter
URL: www.yti.edu
Established: 2006 Annual Undergrad Tuition & Fees: N/A
Enrollment: 381 Coed
Affiliation or Control: Proprietary IRS Status: Proprietary
Highest Offering: Associate Degree
Program: Occupational
Accreditation: ACCSC, #COARC, MAC

01 Campus President .... Ms. Natalie LOMBARDO
05 Director of Education .... Mr. Jack MARGUIS

YTI Career Institute (G)

3050 Hempland Road, Lancaster PA 17601
Telephone: (717) 295-1100 Identification: 770588
Accreditation: ACCSC, MAC

† Main campus is YTI Career Institute in York, PA.

YTI Career Institute (H)

1405 Williams Road, York PA 17402-9017
County: York FICE Identification: 021274
Unit ID: 217077
Telephone: (717) 757-1100 Carnegie Class: Assoc/PrivFP
FAX Number: (717) 757-4964 Calendar System: Quarter
URL: www.yti.edu
Established: 1967 Annual Undergrad Tuition & Fees: $23,414
Enrollment: 1,750 Coed
Affiliation or Control: Proprietary IRS Status: Proprietary
Highest Offering: Associate Degree
Program: Occupational
Accreditation: ACCSC, ACFEI, MAC

01 Chairman and CEO .... Mr. Timothy FOSTER
12 President - York .... Ms. Carla HORN
12 President - Capital Region .... Mr. Erin CARLIN
12 President - Lancaster .... Mr. Michael MARINO
12 President - Altoona .... Mrs. Natalie LOMBARDO
12 President - MTC .... Mr. Michael MARINO
05 Sr VP Education & Regulatory .... Mrs. Sherry BOMBERGER
10 CFO .... Mr. Andrew EMMERLING
13 Director of Technology .... Mr. Andrew HIPPLE

YTI Career Institute-Capital Region (I)

401 East Winding Hill Rd, Mechanicsburg PA 17055
County: Cumberland FICE Identification: 023044
Unit ID: 211750
Telephone: (717) 761-1481 Carnegie Class: Not Classified
FAX Number: (717) 761-0558 Calendar System: Quarter
URL: www.yti.edu
Established: Annual Undergrad Tuition & Fees: $23,296
Enrollment: 290 Coed
Affiliation or Control: Proprietary IRS Status: Proprietary
Highest Offering: Associate Degree
Program: Occupational
Accreditation: ACCSC, #COARC, MAC

RHODE ISLAND

Brown University (J)

Providence RI 02912
County: Providence FICE Identification: 003401
Unit ID: 217156
Telephone: (401) 863-1000 Carnegie Class: RU/VH
FAX Number: (401) 863-3700 Calendar System: Semester
URL: www.brown.edu
Established: 1764 Annual Undergrad Tuition & Fees: $43,758
Enrollment: 8,885 Coed
Affiliation or Control: Independent Non-Profit IRS Status: 501(c)3
Highest Offering: Doctorate
Program: Liberal Arts And General; Professional
Accreditation: EH, ENG, IPSY, MED, PDPSY, PH

01 President .... Christina H. PAXSON
05 Provost .... Mark S. SCHLISSEL
30 Sr Vice Pres for Univ Advancement .... Patricia WATSON
102 Exec Vice Pres Planning & Policy .... Russell C. CAREY
10 Exec VP Finance/Administration .... Elizabeth HUIDEKOPER
26 VP Public Affairs/Univ Relations .... Marisa A. QUINN
43 Vice President/General Counsel .... Beverly E. LEDBETTER
13 Vice Pres Computing/Info Services .... Ravindra PENDSE
29 Vice President Alumni Relations .... Todd G. ANDREWS
18 Vice Pres for Facilities Management .... Stephen M. MAIORISI
46 Vice President for Research .... Clyde L. BRIANT
15 Vice Pres for Human Resources .... Karen DAVIS
35 Vice Pres Campus Life/Student Svcs .... Margaret M. KLAWUNN
20 Deputy Provost .... Joseph S. MEISEL
28 Assoc Provost Acad Devel/Diversity .... Liza CARIAGA-LO
63 Dean Medicine & Biological Sciences .... Edward WING
58 Dean of Graduate School .... Peter M. WEBER
20 Dean of the Faculty .... Kevin MCLAUGHLIN
20 Dean of the College .... Katherine BERGERON
07 Dean of Admission .... James S. MILLER
31 Director State/Community Relations .... Albert A. DAHLBERG
08 University Librarian .... Harriette HEMMASI
21 University Controller/Assistant VP .... Donald S. SCHANCK
41 Director of Athletics .... Jack HAYES
06 Registrar .... Robert F. FITZGERALD
37 Director of Financial Aid .... James TILTON
19 Dir Public Safety/Chief of Police .... Mark J. PORTER
38 Director Psychological Services .... Sherri NELSON
09 Director of Institutional Research .... Katharine T. BARNES
96 Director of Procurement .... Jeanne HEBERT

Bryant University (K)

1150 Douglas Pike, Smithfield RI 02917-1291
County: Providence FICE Identification: 003402
Unit ID: 217165
Telephone: (401) 232-6000 Carnegie Class: Master's M
FAX Number: (401) 232-6319 Calendar System: Semester
URL: www.bryant.edu
Established: 1863 Annual Undergrad Tuition & Fees: $36,300
Enrollment: 3,418 Coed
Affiliation or Control: Independent Non-Profit IRS Status: 501(c)3
Highest Offering: Beyond Master's But Less Than Doctorate
Program: Liberal Arts And General; Business Emphasis
Accreditation: EH, BUS

00 Chairman Board of Trustees .... Mr. Michael FISHER
01 President .... Mr. Ronald K. MACHTLEY
04 Exec Asst to the President .... Dr. James PATTI
05 VP Academic Affairs .... Dr. Jose-Marie GRIFFITHS
32 VP & Dean Student Affairs .... Dr. J. Thomas EAKIN
82 VP International Affairs .... Dr. Hong YANG
10 VP Business Affairs .... Mr. Barry F. MORRISON
30 VP University Advancement .... Mr. James DAMRON
13 VP Information Services/CIO .... Mr. Chuck LOCURTO
16 Assoc VP Human Resources .... Ms. Linda S. LULLI

18 Asst VP Campus Management ... Mr. Brian J. BRITTON
21 Asst VP Business & Controller ... Mr. Farokh BHADA
49 Dean College of Arts & Sciences ... Dr. David LUX
50 Int Dean College of Business ... Dr. V. K. UNNI
58 Asst Dean Graduate School ... Mr. Kristopher T. SULLIVAN
07 Dean of Admission ... Ms. Michelle BEAUREGARD
51 Dir Exec Development Center ... Ms. Annette CERILLI
88 Exec Dir Inst for Family Enterprise ... Dr. William T. O'HARA
88 Dir RI Export Assistance Center ... Mr. Raymond FOGARTY
89 Dir Academic Center for Excellence ... Dr. Laurie L. HAZARD
20 Asst to VP Academic & Dir Advising ... Vacant
06 Registrar ... Ms. Susan MCLACKEN
20 Asst to VP Academic Affairs ... Ms. Elizabeth A. POWERS
35 Assoc Dean of Students ... Mr. Robert E. SLOSS
39 Assoc Dean Residence Life ... Mr. John DENIO
35 Assoc Dean Student Life ... Ms. Judy KAWAMOTO
88 Dir Bryant Center Operations ... Mr. Richard DANKEL
36 Dir Career Services ... Ms. Judith CLARE
42 Chaplain Campus Ministry ... Rev. Philip DEVENS
38 Dir Counseling Services ... Mr. William PHILLIPS
23 Dir Health Services ... Ms. Susan CURRAN
28 Dir Intercultural Center ... Ms. Shontay DELALUE-KING
19 Dir Public Safety ... Mr. Stephen BANNON
31 Dir Student Involvement Center ... Mr. John LINDSAY
88 Dir Women's Center ... Ms. Toby SIMON
07 Dir Transfer Admission ... Ms. Brenda DORAN
07 Sr Assoc Dir Mulitcult Admission ... Ms. Priscilla ALICEA
07 Assoc Dir International Admission ... Mr. John ERIKSEN
37 Dir Financial Aid ... Mr. John B. CANNING
88 Dir Conferences & Special Events ... Ms. Sheila GUAY
96 Dir Purchasing & Support Services ... Ms. Paulette RATTIGAN
44 Exec Dir Development ... Ms. Robin MAREK
29 Dir Alumni Relations ... Ms. Robin T. WARDE
90 Dir Acad Computing & Media Svcs ... Mr. Phillip LOMBARDI
91 Dir Admin Systems ... Ms. Janice FAGAN
14 Dir Computer & Telecomm Svcs ... Mr. Richard SIEDZIK
08 Dir Library Services ... Ms. Mary F. MORONEY
15 Assoc Dir Human Resources ... Ms. Catherine CURRIE
41 Dir Athletics ... Mr. Bill SMITH
09 Dir Planning & Inst Research ... Mr. Robert JONES
88 Exec Dir US-China Institute ... Dr. Hong YANG
40 Manager Bookstore ... Mr. Stanley STOWIK

Community College of Rhode Island (A)

400 East Avenue, Warwick RI 02886-1807
County: Kent — FICE Identification: 003408
Unit ID: 217476
Telephone: (401) 825-1000 — Carnegie Class: Assoc/Pub-U-MC
FAX Number: (401) 825-2365 — Calendar System: Semester
URL: www.ccri.edu
Established: 1964 — Annual Undergrad Tuition & Fees (In-State): $3,950
Enrollment: 17,884 — Coed
Affiliation or Control: State — IRS Status: 501(c)3
Highest Offering: Associate Degree
Program: Occupational; 2-Year Principally Bachelor's Creditable
Accreditation: EH, ACBSP, ADNUR, COARC, COMTA, DA, DH, DMS, HT, MLTAD, MUS, OTA, PNUR, PTAA, RAD

01 President ... Mr. Ray DI PASQUALE
05 Vice President for Academic Affairs ... Dr. Gregory A. LAMONTAGNE
10 Vice President for Business Affairs ... Mr. David B. PATTEN
30 Int VP Institutional Advancement ... Ms. Laurie A. BOSIO
32 Assoc VP for Student Services ... Dr. Ronald L. SCHERTZ
84 Dean of Enrollment Services ... Ms. Deborah J. AIKEN
11 Director of Administration ... Mr. William R. FERLAND
49 Dean Arts/Humanities/Soc Sciences ... Dr. Lois A. WIMS
66 Dean of Nursing/Allied Health ... Dr. Maureen MCGARRY
50 Dean Business/Science/Technology ... Dr. Peter N. WOODBERRY
51 Dean of CWCE ... Ms. Robin Ann SMITH
08 Dean Library ... Ms. Ruth D. SULLIVAN
35 Dean of Students ... Mr. Michael J. CUNNINGHAM, II
21 Interim Controller ... Ms. Sharon A. PICARD
35 Associate Dean of Students ... Dr. Rebecca H. YOUNT
15 Director of Human Resources ... Ms. Sheri L. NORTON
12 Dir Ctr Advanced Tech & Careers ... Mr. Vincent BALASCO
13 Chief Information Officer ... Mr. Stephen A. VIEIRA
19 Director of Safety & Security ... Mr. Dale R. WETHERELL
26 Director Marketing & Communications ... Mr. Richard H. COREN
41 Director of Athletics ... Mr. Joseph PAVONE
09 Director Inst Research/Planning ... Dr. William LEBLANC
21 Bursar ... Mr. Dennis J. GRASSINI
88 Director Access to Opportunity ... Ms. Tracy KARASINSKI
40 Director Bookstore Operations ... Mr. Donald B. BAKER
29 Director of Alumni Affairs ... Ms. Marisa ALBINI
18 Chief Facilities/Physical Plant ... Mr. Kenneth MCCABE
96 Director of Purchasing ... Ms. Lisa M. CONSIVINE-FONTES
21 Business Manager ... Ms. Ruth A. BARRINGTON
36 Coordinator Career Services ... Ms. Camille NUMRICH
37 Director of Financial Aid ... Mr. Joel FRIEDMAN

Johnson & Wales University (B)

8 Abbott Park Place, Providence RI 02903-3703
County: Providence — FICE Identification: 003404
Unit ID: 217235
Telephone: (401) 598-1000 — Carnegie Class: Master's L
FAX Number: (401) 598-2880 — Calendar System: Quarter
URL: www.jwu.edu
Established: 1914 — Annual Undergrad Tuition & Fees: $27,156
Enrollment: 10,622 — Coed
Affiliation or Control: Independent Non-Profit — IRS Status: 501(c)3
Highest Offering: Doctorate
Program: Occupational; 2-Year Principally Bachelor's Creditable; Teacher Preparatory; Professional
Accreditation: EH, DIETD

00 Chairman of the Board ... Mr. John A. YENA
01 Chancellor ... Mr. John J. BOWEN
12 Providence Campus President/COO ... Ms. Mim L. RUNEY
32 Vice President of Student Affairs ... Mr. Ronald MARTEL
05 Interim University Provost ... Mr. Frank A. SARGENT
30 Exec Dir of University Advancement ... Ms. Page C. SCIOTTO
85 Senior VP of Special Projects ... Mr. Kenneth R. LEVY
10 Treasurer and CFO ... Mr. William F. MCARDLE
18 Sr Vice Pres Facilities Management ... Mr. Merlin A. DECONTI
43 Sr VP and General Counsel ... Mr. Wayne M. KEZIRIAN
10 Vice Chancellor & Executive VP ... Mr. Thomas L. DWYER, JR.
36 VP of Experiential Ed & Career Svc ... Ms. Maureen DUMAS
84 Sr VP of Enrollment Management ... Mr. Kenneth F. DISAIA
15 Vice President of Human Resources ... Ms. Diane D'AMBRA
21 Asst Treasurer & VP of Finance ... Mr. Joseph J. GREENE
58 Dean of Graduate School ... Mr. Michael PETRILLOSE
50 Int Dean of the College of Business ... Mr. Richard L. BRUSH
49 Dean of Arts & Sciences ... Ms. Angela RENAUD
72 Dean of the School of Technology ... Mr. Frank TWEEDIE
88 Vice President of Auxiliary Service ... Mr. Michael DOWNING
18 Vice President of Facilities Mgmt ... Mr. Christopher PLACCO
13 Chief Information Officer ... Ms. Marianne DORAN COLLINS
32 Sr VP of Student Services ... Ms. Marie BERNARDO-SOUSA
43 Sr VP of Law & Policy & Corp Secret ... Ms. Barbara L. BENNETT
96 Director of Procurement ... Mr. Michael GILLARDI
36 Director of Ext Educ & Career Svcs ... Ms. Sheri ISPIR
09 Director of Institutional Research ... Mr. George REZENDES
19 Exec Dir of Campus Safety/Security ... Major Michael P. QUINN
21 University Budget Director ... Ms. Eileen T. HASKINS
88 University Dean of Culinary Educ ... Mr. Karl J. GUGGENMOS
88 Director of Student Communications ... Ms. Kristine E. MCNAMARA
88 Dean of Academic Program Develop ... Mr. Paul J. MCVETY
106 Online Learning & Continuing Ed ... Ms. Cynthia L. PARKER
51 Director of Continuing Education ... Mr. Ian CANNING

Mater Ecclesiae College (C)

60 Austin Avenue, Greenville RI 02828-1440
County: Providence — FICE Identification: 041449
Telephone: (401) 949-2820 — Carnegie Class: Not Classified
FAX Number: (401) 949-0291 — Calendar System: Semester
URL: www.mecollege.org
Established: 1991 — Annual Undergrad Tuition & Fees: N/A
Enrollment: 70 — Female
Affiliation or Control: Independent Non-Profit — IRS Status: 501(c)3
Highest Offering: Baccalaureate
Program: Liberal Arts And General; Religious Emphasis
Accreditation: EH

01 President ... Ms. Deb BAUER
32 Vice Pres/Dir Student Affairs ... Ms. Cecilia AZCUNAGA
05 Dean of Academic Affairs ... Dr. Patricia CAMARERO
06 Registrar ... Ms. Jennifer RISTINE
07 Director of Admissions ... Ms. Katelyn MORONY
21 Business Manager ... Ms. Maritza SILVA

New England Institute of Technology (D)

One New England Tech Blvd., East Greenwich RI 02818
County: Kent — FICE Identification: 007845
Unit ID: 217305
Telephone: (401) 467-7744 — Carnegie Class: Bac/Assoc
FAX Number: (401) 886-0859 — Calendar System: Quarter
URL: www.neit.edu
Established: 1940 — Annual Undergrad Tuition & Fees: $21,330
Enrollment: 2,764 — Coed
Affiliation or Control: Independent Non-Profit — IRS Status: 501(c)3
Highest Offering: Master's
Program: Occupational; 2-Year Principally Bachelor's Creditable; Liberal Arts And General; Technical Emphasis
Accreditation: EH, ADNUR, #COARC, ENGT, OT, OTA, PTAA, SURGT

01 President ... Dr. Richard I. GOUSE
03 Executive Vice President ... Mr. Seth A. KURN
05 Senior Vice President and Provost ... Mr. Douglas H. SHERMAN
10 Sr VP Financial Affs & Endowment ... Ms. Cheryl C. CONNORS
32 Vice Pres Student Support Services ... Ms. Catherine B. KENNEDY
21 VP of Finance & Business Admin ... Mr. Robert R. THEROUX
20 Associate Provost ... Vacant
07 Director of Admissions ... Mr. James JESSUP
37 Director Financial Aid ... Ms. Anna KELLY
04 Assoc Provost & Spec Asst to Pres ... Vacant
08 Director Library ... Ms. Susan WARTHMAN
36 Director of Career Services ... Ms. Patricia BLAKEMORE
31 Director Auxiliary Services ... Mr. Patrick TRACEY
06 Registrar ... Ms. Doreen LASIEWSKI
35 Director Student Affairs ... Ms. Lee PEEBLES
29 Dir Institutional Dev & Alumni Rels ... Ms. Joan SEGERSON

Providence College (E)

1 Cunningham Square, Providence RI 02918-0001
County: Providence — FICE Identification: 003406
Unit ID: 217402
Telephone: (401) 865-1000 — Carnegie Class: Master's L
FAX Number: (401) 865-2057 — Calendar System: Semester
URL: www.providence.edu
Established: 1917 — Annual Undergrad Tuition & Fees: $43,115
Enrollment: 4,753 — Coed
Affiliation or Control: Roman Catholic — IRS Status: 501(c)3
Highest Offering: Master's
Program: Liberal Arts And General; Teacher Preparatory
Accreditation: EH, BUS, MUS, SW

01 President ... Rev. Brian J. SHANLEY, OP
03 Executive Vice President ... Rev. Kenneth R. SICARD, OP
03 Asst to Pres & Exec Vice President ... Ms. Ann MANCHESTER-MOLAK
05 Sr Vice President Academic Affairs ... Dr. Hugh F. LENA
10 Sr VP for Finance & Business/CFO ... Mr. John M. SWEENEY
30 Sr VP for Institutional Advancement ... Vacant
32 Vice Pres Student Affairs Admin ... Ms. Kristine C. GOODWIN
43 Vice President/General Counsel ... Ms. Marifrances MCGINN
42 Vice Pres for Mission & Ministry ... Rev. R. Gabriel PIVARNIK, OP
04 Special Asst to Pres for Devel Proj ... Mr. Joseph P. BRUM
21 Assoc VP for Finance/Asst Treasurer ... Ms. Jacqueline M. WHITE
35 Assoc VP for Student Affairs Admin ... Dr. Steven A. SEARS
32 Associate VP for Academic Affairs ... Dr. Brian J. BARTOLINI
41 Assoc Vice Pres for Athletics ... Mr. Robert G. DRISCOLL, JR.
15 Assoc Vice Pres for Human Resources ... Ms. Kathleen M. ALVINO
43 Assoc VP/Assoc General Counsel ... Ms. Gail A. DYER
28 Assoc VP/Chief Diversity Officer ... Mr. Rafael A. ZAPATA
26 Ast VP for Public Affairs/Cmty Rels ... Mr. Steven J. MAURANO
20 Asst Vice Pres for Academic Affairs ... Mr. Charles J. HABERLE
21 Asst Vice Pres for Business Svcs ... Mr. Warren S. GRAY
29 Asst Vice Pres for Alumni Relations ... Mr. Robert FERREIRA
30 Asst Vice Pres for Development ... Ms. Lynne FRASER
13 Asst VP for Information Technology ... Ms. Rebecca RAMOS
46 Asst VP Capital Projects & Fac Plng ... Mr. Mark F. RAPOZA
58 Dean of Undergrad & Grad Studies ... Rev. Mark D. NOWEL, OP
49 Dean School of Arts & Sciences ... Dr. Sheila M. ADAMUS LIOTTA
107 Dean School of Professional Studies ... Dr. Brian M. MCCADDEN
07 Dean of Admissions/Financial Aid ... Mr. Raul A. FONTS
50 Dean School of Business ... Dr. Sylvia MAXFIELD
51 Dean School of Continuing Education ... Dr. Janet L. CASTLEMAN
39 Dean of Residence Life ... Ms. Tiffany D. GAFFNEY
84 Dean of Enrollment Services ... Ms. Yvonne D. ARRUDA
104 Dean of International Studies ... Mr. Adrian G. BEAULIEU
88 Dean of Student Programming ... Ms. Sharon L. HAY
51 Assoc Dean Sch of Continuing Educ ... Ms. Madeleine A. METZLER
37 Exec Director of Financial Aid ... Ms. Sandra J. OLIVEIRA
19 Exec Director Safety & Security ... Mr. John J. LEYDEN
36 Director Career Education Center ... Ms. Patricia A. GOFF
18 Exec Director of Physical Plant ... Mr. William J. HARTIGAN
08 Director Library ... Dr. Donald Russell BAILEY
21 Treasurer ... Rev. Kenneth R. SICARD, OP
09 Director of Institutional Research ... Mr. Thomas E. FRANK
22 Dir Student Multicultural Affairs ... Ms. Elena T. YEE
88 Director of Telecommunications ... Mr. Carmine R. PISCOPO
92 Program Dir Liberal Arts Honors ... Dr. Stephen J. LYNCH
96 Director Cntrl Purchasing/Receiving ... Mr. Mark S. MCGOVERN
88 Director of Academic Services ... Mr. Bryan D. MARINELLI
38 Exec Director Personal Counseling ... Dr. John T. HOGAN

Rhode Island College (F)

600 Mount Pleasant Avenue, Providence RI 02908-1991
County: Providence — FICE Identification: 003407
Unit ID: 217420
Telephone: (401) 456-8000 — Carnegie Class: Master's L
FAX Number: (401) 456-8379 — Calendar System: Semester
URL: www.ric.edu
Established: 1854 — Annual Undergrad Tuition & Fees (In-State): $7,602
Enrollment: 8,869 — Coed
Affiliation or Control: State — IRS Status: 501(c)3
Highest Offering: Doctorate
Program: Liberal Arts And General; Teacher Preparatory; Professional
Accreditation: EH, ART, MUS, NURSE, SW, TED

01 President ... Dr. Nancy CARRIUOLO
05 Vice President Academic Affairs ... Dr. Ronald E. PITT
10 Vice Pres Administration & Finance ... Mr. William H. GEARHART
32 Vice President Student Affairs ... Dr. Gary M. PENFIELD
30 Int VP College Advancement & Plng ... Ms. Nanci MARTIN
107 Int Assoc VP Prof Studies & Cont Ed ... Ms. Jennifer GIROUX
20 Int Asst Vice Pres Academic Affairs ... Dr. Holly L. SHADOIAN
21 Asst Vice Pres Finance/Controller ... Mr. Paul D. FORTE
14 Int Asst VP Information Services ... Ms. Pamela CHRISTMAN
15 Int Director of Human Resources ... Ms. Maggie SULLIVAN
49 Dean Faculty Arts & Sciences ... Dr. Earl L. SIMSON
53 Int Dean Sch Education & Human Dev ... Dr. Karen CASTAGNO
66 Dean School of Nursing ... Dr. Jane WILLIAMS
50 Dean School of Management ... Dr. David M. BLANCHETTE
70 Dean School of Social Work ... Dr. Roberta S. PEARLMUTTER
58 Int Dean of Graduate Studies ... Dr. Leslie SCHUSTER
08 Director of the Library ... Mr. Hedi BENAICHA
35 Dean of Students ... Dr. Scott D. KANE
100 Assistant to the President ... Vacant
26 Director of News & Public Relations ... Vacant
105 Director Web Services ... Ms. Karen M. RUBINO
07 Director of Admissions ... Mr. John MCLAUGHLIN
06 Director of Records ... Mr. James C. DORIAN
37 Director Student Financial Aid ... Mr. James T. HANBURY
25 Director of Research & Grants ... Ms. Lisa SMOLSKI
18 Director Facilities & Operations ... Vacant
90 Director User Support Services ... Vacant
91 Director MIS ... Dr. Bin YU

13 Director Network/Telecommunications .... Mr. Henk E. SONDER
19 Director of Security .... Mr. Frederick W. GHIO
09 Dir Inst Research/Planning .... Dr. Christopher P. HOURIGAN
96 Director of Purchasing .... Ms. Jessica L. SILVA
41 Director of Athletics .... Mr. Donald E. TENCHER
39 Director Residential Life/Housing .... Ms. Teresa L. BROWN
36 Director Career Development Center ... Ms. Linda S. KENT-DAVIS
23 Director College Health Services .... Ms. Lynn A. WACHTEL
38 Director Counseling Center .... Dr. Thomas J. LAVIN
29 Director Alumni Affairs .... Ms. Kate BREZINA
04 Admin Assistant to the President .... Ms. Donna NARODOWY
40 Bookstore Manager .... Mr. Steven PLATT
104 Director of Study Abroad .... Dr. Gale GOODWIN-GOMEZ

Rhode Island School of Design (A)

2 College Street, Providence RI 02903-2784

County: Providence FICE Identification: 003409
Unit ID: 217493
Telephone: (401) 454-6100 Carnegie Class: Spec/Arts
FAX Number: (401) 454-6320 Calendar System: 4/1/4
URL: www.risd.edu
Established: 1877 Annual Undergrad Tuition & Fees: $42,932
Enrollment: 2,386 Coed
Affiliation or Control: Independent Non-Profit IRS Status: 501(c)3
Highest Offering: Master's
Program: Liberal Arts And General; Professional; Fine Arts Emphasis
Accreditation: EH, ART, LSAR

01 President .... Dr. John MAEDA
04 Executive Assistant to President .... Ms. Marina MIHALAKIS
05 Provost .... Ms. Rosanne SOMERSON
10 Exec Vice Pres Admin/Finance .... Mr. William DECATUR
32 Senior VP for Students & Enrollment .... Ms. Jean EDDY
30 Vice Pres Institutional Engagement .... Mr. Eric GRAAGE
26 Exec Dir Marketing & Communications .... Vacant
16 Vice Pres Human Resources .... Ms. Candace BAER
88 Director RISD Museum of Art .... Mr. John W. SMITH
20 Vice Provost Acad Affairs .... Vacant
48 Dean Architecture & Design .... Mr. Pradeep SHARMA
57 Interim Dean of Fine Arts .... Ms. Anais MISSAKIAN
58 Dean of Graduate Studies .... Ms. Patricia PHILLIPS
89 Dean of Foundation Studies .... Ms. Joanne STRYKER
79 Interim Dean of Liberal Arts .... Dr. Daniel CAVICCHI
51 Dean Continuing Education .... Dr. Brian K. SMITH
62 Director Library Services .... Ms. Carol S. TERRY
21 Assoc VP Finance & Business Svcs .... Mr. Richard RUMMEL
13 Interim Assoc VP Info Technology .... Mr. Joseph BERNIER
18 Assoc VP Facilities & EHS .... Mr. Jack SILVA
07 Director of Admissions .... Mr. Edward NEWHALL, JR.
35 Dean of Students .... Ms. Jerri DRUMMOND
105 Assistant VP Communications .... Mr. Brian CLARK
43 General Counsel .... Mr. Steven MCDONALD
31 Director of Media Relations .... Ms. Jaime MARLAND
19 Director Public Safety .... Vacant
09 Director Institutional Research .... Ms. Jennifer DUNSEATH
45 Director Budget .... Mr. Robert HANKE
86 Director Government Relations .... Ms. Babette ALLINA
29 Director of Alumni Relations .... Ms. Christina HARTLEY
102 Dir Corp & Foundation Relations .... Ms. Pamela HARRINGTON
44 Director of Leadership Giving .... Ms. Louise OLSON
44 Director Annual Fund .... Vacant
06 Registrar .... Mr. Steven BERENBACK
96 Director Procurement Services .... Mr. James NEWMAN
14 Director Network Services .... Mr. Steven BOUDREAU
27 Director Editorial Services/Media .... Ms. Liisa SILANDER
23 Director Health Services .... Ms. Catherine VOLTAS
39 Director of Residence Life .... Mr. Brian JANES
38 Dir Student Development/Counseling .... Mr. Wayne ASSING
37 Director Financial Aid .... Mr. Anthony GALLONIO
36 Director of Career Center .... Mr. Gregory J. VICTORY
40 Director risd:store .... Ms. Tila ADAMS
85 Dir Intercultural StdntEngagement .... Mr. Anthony JOHNSON

Roger Williams University (B)

One Old Ferry Road, Bristol RI 02809-2921

County: Bristol FICE Identification: 003410
Unit ID: 217518
Telephone: (401) 253-1040 Carnegie Class: Master's S
FAX Number: N/A Calendar System: Semester
URL: www.rwu.edu
Established: 1956 Annual Undergrad Tuition & Fees: $31,618
Enrollment: 4,768 Coed
Affiliation or Control: Independent Non-Profit IRS Status: 501(c)3
Highest Offering: First Professional Degree
Program: Liberal Arts And General; Teacher Preparatory; Professional
Accreditation: EH, BUS, CONST, ENG, LAW

01 President .... Dr. Donald J. FARISH
05 Provost/Sr VP Academic Affairs .... Dr. Andrew WORKMAN
10 EVP Finance/Administration .... Mr. Jerome WILLIAMS
43 Sr VP Legal Affs/General Counsel .... Mr. Robert H. AVERY
84 Sr VP Enrollment Mgmt/Retention .... Ms. Catherine CAPOLUPO
21 VP for Accounting/Treasury Mgmt .... Mr. David GILMORE
32 Vice President for Student Affairs .... Mr. John J. KING
30 Acting VP University Advancement .... Ms. Lisa RAIOLA
08 Asc Dn Univ Lib Svcs/Dir Honors Pgm .... Ms. Betsy P. LEARNED
32 Dean of Students .... Dr. Kathleen N. MCMAHON
88 Asst VP Enrollment Mgmt/Retenton .... Ms. Tracy M. DACOSTA
28 Assoc Dean/Dir Intercultural Center .... Ms. Andrea DIAZ
61 Dean School of Law .... Mr. David A. LOGAN
48 Dean Sch Arch/Art & Hist Preserv .... Mr. Stephen E. WHITE
50 Dean Gabelli School of Business .... Dr. Jerry DAUTERIVE
54 Dean Sch Engrng/Comput/Constr Mgmt ..... Dr. Robert A. POTTER
61 Dean School of Justice Studies ...... Dr. Stephanie PICOLO MANZI
53 Assoc Provost/Dean School Education .... Dr. Robert A. COLE
51 Dir Cont Studies/Grad Admiss .... Ms. Jamie GRENON
49 Dean Feinstein Col Arts & Sciences .... Dr. Robert EISINGER
55 Dean Instruct Sys Dev/Spec Projects .... Mr. Kenneth T. OSBORNE
07 Dir Admissions Operations/Outreach .... Ms. Amanda MARSILI
96 Director of Purchasing .... Mr. Thomas KANE
29 Assoc Dean/Dir of Conferences .... Ms. Allison CHASE PADULA
06 Interim Registrar .... Ms. Joan ROMANO
45 Assoc VP University Relations .... Mr. Peter WILBUR
19 Director of Public Safety .... Mr. Steven MELARAGNO
41 Director of Athletics .... Mr. Dave KEMMY
18 Director of Facilities Management .... Mr. John TAMEO
36 Director of Career Center .... Ms. Robin L. BEAUCHAMP
38 Director Counseling & Student Devel .... Dr. James A. AZAR
23 Director Health Services .... Ms. Anne M. ANDRADE
39 Director of Housing .... Mr. Anthony MONTEFUSCO
46 Director of Prospect Research .... Ms. Nancy L. RAMOS
39 Director Residence Life/Women's Ctr .... Ms. Jennifer STANLEY
09 Int Director Institutional Research .... Mr. Eric SPONSELLER
37 Int Director Student Financial Aid .... Ms. Tracy M. DACOSTA
40 Manager Bookstore .... Vacant

Salve Regina University (C)

100 Ochre Point Avenue, Newport RI 02840-4192

County: Newport FICE Identification: 003411
Unit ID: 217536
Telephone: (401) 847-6650 Carnegie Class: Master's M
FAX Number: (401) 341-2925 Calendar System: Semester
URL: www.salve.edu
Established: 1947 Annual Undergrad Tuition & Fees: $33,950
Enrollment: 2,613 Coed
Affiliation or Control: Roman Catholic IRS Status: 501(c)3
Highest Offering: Doctorate
Program: Liberal Arts And General; Teacher Preparatory; Professional
Accreditation: EH, ART, CORE, IACBE, NURSE, SW

01 President .... Dr. Jane GERETY, RSM
05 Vice President Academic Affairs .... Dr. Dean DE LA MOTTE
32 Vice President Student Affairs .... Dr. Margaret HIGGINS
30 VP University Rels/Advancement .... Mr. Michael L. SEMENZA
10 Vice President Administration & CFO .... Mr. William B. HALL
84 Vice President Enrollment Services .... Dr. Laura E. MCPHIE-OLIVEIRA
88 Vice Pres Mission Integration .... Sr. Leona MISTO, RSM
27 Assoc Vice Pres Univ Rels/CCO .... Ms. Kristine HENDRICKSON
21 Assoc Vice Pres Finance/ Controller .... Mr. Michael N. GRANDCHAMP
13 Assoc Vice Pres Info Technology/CIO .. Mr. Thomas H. BRENNAN
15 Assoc Vice Pres Human Resources/ AAO .... Mrs. Diane F. BLANCHETTE
20 Asst Vice Pres Deans & Registrar .... Dr. Donna M. COOK
07 Dean of Undergraduate Admissions .... Ms. Colleen EMERSON
35 Dean of Students .... Mr. J. Malcolm SMITH
49 Dean of Art & Sciences .... Dr. Laura L. O'TOOLE
20 Dean of Professional Studies .... Dr. Traci WARRINGTON
06 Registrar .... Ms. Louise MONAST
37 Director of Financial Aid .... Ms. Aida MIRANTE
29 Assoc Director Alumni & Parent Pgms .... Mr. John RISTAINO
41 Athletic Director .... Mr. Colin SULLIVAN
09 Director Institutional Research .... Dr. Frederick C. PROMADES
08 Director of Library Services .... Ms. Kathleen BOYD
39 Assoc Dean Students/Dir Campus Life .... Dr. Gerry WILLIS
90 Director Academic Computing .... Mr. Brian A. MCDONNELL
18 Director of Facilities .... Mr. Eric MILNER
19 Director of Security/Safety .... Mr. John MIXTER
40 Director of Bookstore .... Mr. Michael LEDDY
44 Assoc Director of Annual Giving .... Ms. Victoria DUCLOS-BARRETT
23 Director of Health Services .... Mrs. Mary Kay CONNELL
35 Director of Student Activities .... Ms. Heather BARBOUR
36 Director of Career Development .... Mr. Michael WISNEWSKI
96 Director of Purchasing .... Ms. Francine MONFETTE
104 Director of International Programs .... Ms. Erin FITZGERALD
38 Dir of Student Counseling Services .... Mr. David BRYANT DAWSON

University of Rhode Island (D)

Kingston RI 02881-0806

County: Washington FICE Identification: 003414
Unit ID: 217484
Telephone: (401) 874-1000 Carnegie Class: RU/H
FAX Number: (401) 874-7149 Calendar System: Semester
URL: www.uri.edu
Established: 1892 Annual Undergrad Tuition & Fees (In-State): $12,450
Enrollment: 16,451 Coed
Affiliation or Control: State IRS Status: 501(c)3
Highest Offering: Doctorate
Program: Liberal Arts And General; Teacher Preparatory; Professional
Accreditation: EH, BUS, BUSA, CLPSY, CYTO, DIETD, DIETI, ENG, LIB, LSAR, MFCD, MUS, NURSE, PHAR, PTA, SCPSY, SP, TED

01 President .... Dr. David M. DOOLEY
100 Chief-of-Staff President's Office .... Ms. Michelle S. CURRERI
88 Dir Public Programming/Events .... Ms. Diane M. BLANDA
05 Provost/Vice Pres Academic Affairs .... Dr. Donald H. DEHAYES
46 Vice Pres Research/Economic Devel .... Dr. Peter ALFONSO
88 Assoc VP Res/Int Prop Mgmt/Comm .... Mr. James PETELL
88 Dir Univ Res External Relations .... Ms. Melissa MCCARTHY
88 Dir Research Development .... Ms. Karen MARKIN
88 Dir Sponsored Projects .... Ms. Mary DEMARCO
88 Dir Research Compliance .... Vacant
29 Exec Dir Alumni Relations/Secy Assn .... Ms. Michele NOTA
31 Interim Exec Dir Comm & Cmty Rel .... Ms. Kerrie BENNETT
26 Dir of Communications & Marketing .... Ms. Linda A. ACCIARDO
88 Dir Publications and Creative Svcs .... Mr. Russell KOLTON
10 Vice Pres for Admin & Finance .... Mr. Robert A. WEYGAND
21 Dir Budget & Financial Planning .... Ms. Linda BARRETT
21 Controller .... Ms. Sharon B. BELL
16 Asst Vice Pres Human Resource Admin .... Ms. Anne Marie COLEMAN
15 Director Personnel Services .... Ms. Laura KENERSON
18 Asst Vice Pres Business Services .... Mr. J. Vernon WYMAN
19 Int Director Public Safety .... Mr. Stephen N. BAKER
12 Dir W.A. Jones Campus .... Mr. Thomas MITCHELL
88 Dir RI Transportation Res Center .... Dr. K. W. LEE
88 Dir Capital Projects .... Mr. Paul DEPACE
88 Dir Campus Planning and Design . Mr. Thomas FRISBIE-FULTON
88 Dir Facility Services .... Mr. Jerome SIDIO
88 Dir Property & Support Svc .... Mr. Bill MATTESON
96 Director Purchasing & Univ Stores .... Ms. Betty GIL
28 Assoc VP Comm/Equity/Diversity .... Ms. Naomi THOMPSON
86 Director Legislative and Government .... Ms. Kerrie BENNETT
43 General Counsel .... Mr. Louis J. SACCOCCIO
32 Vice President Student Affairs .... Dr. Thomas R. DOUGAN
41 Director of Athletics .... Mr. Thorr D. BJORN
36 Interim Director Career Services .... Ms. Carolyn THOMAS
38 Director Counseling Center .... Dr. Robert SAMUELS
88 Dir Recreational Services .... Ms. Jodi HAWKINS
35 Asst VP Stdnt Affs & Dean of Stdnts .... Dr. Mary J. GONZALES
39 Interim Dir Housing & Res Life .... Dr. Jeffrey PLOUFFE
23 Director Health Services .... Mr. Charles M. HENDERSON, III
40 Administrator Bookstore .... Mr. Paul WHITNEY
88 Spec Asst to the Prov for Acad Plng .... Ms. Ann M. MORRISSEY
88 Vice Prov Acad Finance/Personnel .... Dr. Clifford H. KATZ
108 Dir Institutional Research .... Vacant
84 Vice Provost Enrollment Management .... Mr. Dean LIBUTTI
07 Dean of Admissions .... Ms. Cynthia L. BONN
06 Dir Enrollment Services .... Dr. Carnell JONES
88 Vice Provost Faculty Affairs .... Dr. Laura BEAUVAIS
27 Chief Information Officer .... Mr. Garrett A. BOZYLINSKY
90 Dir Media & Technology Services .... Mr. David S. PORTER
91 Dir University Computing Systems .... Mr. Charlie SCHIFINO
51 V Prov Urban Pgms/Dn Col Cont Educ .... Dr. John H. MCCRAY, JR.
49 Dean of Arts & Sciences .... Dr. Winifred E. BROWNELL
50 Dean Business Administration .... Dr. Mark M. HIGGINS
54 Dean of Engineering .... Dr. Raymond M. WRIGHT
88 Dean Univ Col & Spec Acad Pgms .... Dr. Jayne E. RICHMOND
58 Dean of Graduate School .... Dr. Nasser H. ZAWIA
66 Interim Dean of Nursing .... Dr. M. SULLIVAN
67 Interim Dean of Pharmacy .... Dr. Paul LARRAT
69 Int Dean Human Sciences & Services .. Dr. Lori CICCOMOSCOLO
53 Director School of Education .... Dr. David BYRD
88 Dean Grad School Oceanography .... Dr. Bruce CORLISS
88 Dean of Environment & Life Sciences .... Dr. John KIRBY
08 Dean University Libraries .... Mr. Dave MASLYN
22 Director Affirm Act/Equal Oppty/Div .... Ms. Roxanne GOMES
37 Sr Assoc Dir Enrol Svcs/Fin Aid .... Mr. Paul LANGHAMMER
92 Director Honors Program .... Dr. Richard MCINTYRE
102 President RIU Foundation .... Mr. Michael J. SMITH
85 Dir Intl Students and Scholars .... Dr. Dania BRANDFORD-CALVO
106 Dir Learning/Assessment & Online .... Dr. Diane GOLDSMITH
94 Dir Gender and Women Studies .... Dr. Jody LISBERGER

University of Rhode Island Feinstein Providence Campus (E)

80 Washington Street, Providence RI 02903

Telephone: (401) 277-5000 Identification: 770118
Accreditation: &EH

† Main campus is University of Rhode Island in Kingston, RI.

University of Rhode Island Narragansett Bay Campus (F)

215 South Ferry Road, Narragansett RI 02882-1197

Telephone: (401) 874-6222 Identification: 770129
Accreditation: &EH

† Main campus is University of Rhode Island in Kingston, RI.

SOUTH CAROLINA

Aiken Technical College (G)

PO Drawer 696, Aiken SC 29802-0696

County: Aiken FICE Identification: 010056
Unit ID: 217615
Telephone: (803) 593-9231 Carnegie Class: Assoc/Pub-R-M
FAX Number: (803) 593-6641 Calendar System: Semester
URL: www.atc.edu
Established: 1972 Annual Undergrad Tuition & Fees (In-District): $3,972
Enrollment: 2,902 Coed
Affiliation or Control: State/Local IRS Status: 501(c)3
Highest Offering: Associate Degree
Program: Occupational; 2-Year Principally Bachelor's Creditable; Technical Emphasis
Accreditation: SC, ACBSP, ADNUR, DA, MAC, RAD, SURGT

01 President .... Dr. Susan A. WINSOR
04 Executive Assistant to President .... Mrs. Chavon THOMPSON
30 Director Foundation & Alumni .... Ms. Mary COMMONS
05 Vice President Education & Training .... Dr. Gemma FROCK
76 Dean of Health Sciences .... Ms. Hermecender WALTON
72 Dean of Technology .... Vacant
97 Dean of General Education .... Fr. Frederick ROGERS
51 Dean Training & Business Develop .... Mr. Steven SIMMONS
10 Vice Pres Administrative Services .... Mr. Andy JORDAN
37 Director of Financial Aid .... Ms. Sue SIMS
13 Director of Info Systems Mgmt .... Mr. Walter BUSBEE
16 Director of Human Resources .... Ms. Sylvia BYRD
21 Director of Financial Accounting .... Mr. Don TRUE
96 Director of Purchasing .... Ms. Toni MARSHALL
18 Campus Engineer .... Mr. Mike DUNCAN
26 Assoc VP Marketing & Enroll Mgmt .... Mr. Bryan NEWTON
07 Director of Admissions .... Mrs. Jessica MOON
06 Registrar .... Mrs. Dawn BUTTS
32 Dean of Student Development .... Dr. Vinson BURDETTE
38 Director Counseling/Disabilities .... Mr. Rich WELDON

Allen University (A)

1530 Harden Street, Columbia SC 29204-1085
County: Richland FICE Identification: 003417
Unit ID: 217624
Telephone: (803) 376-5700 Carnegie Class: Bac/A&S
FAX Number: N/A Calendar System: Semester
URL: www.allenuniversity.edu
Established: 1870 Annual Undergrad Tuition & Fees: $11,740
Enrollment: 672 Coed
Affiliation or Control: African Methodist Episcopal IRS Status: 501(c)3
Highest Offering: Baccalaureate
Program: Liberal Arts And General; Business Emphasis
Accreditation: SC

01 President .... Dr. Pamela M. WILSON
10 Vice President for Fiscal Affairs .... Ms. Brenda WALKER
21 Assoc Vice Pres Fiscal Affairs .... Mrs. Lavinia TEJADA
30 Vice Pres Institutional Advancement .... Vacant
32 Vice Pres Student Life .... Ms. Cynthia EUBANKS
45 VP Planning/Research/Sponsored Pgms .... Mr. Marcus V. BELL
06 Registrar .... Ms. Marilyn DEBERRY
07 Director of Admissions .... Mr. Brandon BYRD
15 Director of Human Resources .... Mrs. Paige MOORE
18 Facilities/Physical Plant Director .... Mr. Timothy TAYLOR
23 Director Health Services .... Mrs. Stephanie BRANTLEY
09 Director of Institutional Research .... Ms. Marilyn C. DEBERRY
29 Director of Alumni Relations .... Vacant
37 Director of Student Financial Aid .... Mrs. Shelline WARRENS
38 Director Counseling Services .... Vacant

Anderson University (B)

316 Boulevard, Anderson SC 29621-4035
County: Anderson FICE Identification: 003418
Unit ID: 217633
Telephone: (864) 231-2000 Carnegie Class: Bac/Diverse
FAX Number: (864) 231-2004 Calendar System: Semester
URL: www.andersonuniversity.edu
Established: 1911 Annual Undergrad Tuition & Fees: $22,790
Enrollment: 2,922 Coed
Affiliation or Control: Other IRS Status: 501(c)3
Highest Offering: Doctorate
Program: Liberal Arts And General; Teacher Preparatory
Accreditation: SC, ACBSP, ART, MUS, TED

01 President .... Dr. Evans P. WHITAKER
05 Provost .... Dr. Danny M. PARKER
10 VP for Finance and Operations .... Mr. James A. WRIGHT, JR.
30 VP for Institutional Advancement .... Mr. R. Dean WOODS
84 VP for Enrollment Mgt & Marketing .... Mr. D. Omar RASHED
42 VP for Christian Life .... Dr. J. Robert CLINE
32 VP for Student Development .... Dr. James A. FEREIRA
14 Chief Information Officer .... Mr. Peter B. HARVIN
28 VP for Presidential Affairs .... Dr. Beverly R. MCADAMS
20 Associate Provost .... Mrs. Susan B. WOOTEN
18 Assoc VP for Facil & Procurement .... Mr. Dane S. SLAUGHTER
06 Dean of Enrollment Svcs & Registrar .... Mrs. Carol A. PARKER
07 Dean of Admissions .... Ms. Pam ROSS
32 Dean of Student Life .... Mr. Jonathan GROPP
41 Director of Athletics .... Mrs. Nancy P. SIMPSON
09 Dir of Enrollment Mgt Sys & Ext Rpt .... Mr. Daryl A. IVERSON
08 Director of Library Services .... Mr. Kent A. MILLWOOD
26 Director Marketing & Communications .... Mr. Barry D. RAY
37 Dir Financial Aid Planning .... Mr. Michael E. YOHE
15 Director of Human Resources .... Mrs. Rose Mariee ALLISON
38 Director of Counseling Services .... Ms. Erin C. MAURER
29 Director of Alumni Relations .... Mr. Chad NELMS
36 Director Career Services .... Ms. Kelly A. BELL
23 Director Health Services .... Mrs. Deb A. TAYLOR
88 Dir of The Ctr for Student Success .... Ms. L. Dianne KING
21 Controller .... Ms. Kristie C. COLE
39 Assoc Director of Residence Life .... Mr. Tim JARED
35 Director of Student Activities .... Ms. Sara MUDD

Benedict College (C)

Harden and Bland Streets, Columbia SC 29204-1086
County: Richland FICE Identification: 003420
Unit ID: 217721
Telephone: (803) 253-5000 Carnegie Class: Bac/Diverse
FAX Number: (803) 253-5059 Calendar System: Semester
URL: www.benedict.edu
Established: 1870 Annual Undergrad Tuition & Fees: $18,286
Enrollment: 2,921 Coed
Affiliation or Control: Independent Non-Profit IRS Status: 501(c)3
Highest Offering: Baccalaureate
Program: Liberal Arts And General; Teacher Preparatory
Accreditation: #SC, ACBSP, ART, NRPA, SW, TED

01 President .... Dr. David H. SWINTON
05 Senior Vice Pres Academic Affairs .... Dr. Janeen WITTY
03 Executive Vice President .... Dr. Ruby W. WATTS
10 Vice President Business/Finance .... Mr. Nathaniel WILLIAMS
32 Vice President Student Affairs .... Mr. Gary E. KNIGHT
44 Vice Pres Institutional Advancement .... Mrs. Barbara C. MOORE
35 Dean of Students .... Mr. Rufus C. WATTS
20 Assoc Vice Pres Academic Affairs .... Dr. George A. DEVLIN
21 Asst VP for Business & Finance .... Ms. Kathryn JONES
26 Asst VP for Comm & Marketing .... Ms. Kymm HUNTER
07 Director of Admissions/Student Mktg .... Mrs. Phyllis THOMPSON
29 Assistant VP for Alumni Relations .... Mrs. Ada A. BELTON
13 Dir Management Information Systems .... Mr. Robert SQUIREWELL
15 Director of Human Resources .... Mrs. Betty A. JENKINS
06 Registrar/Director Student Records .... Mrs. Wanda A. SCOTT-KINNEY
41 Athletics Director .... Mr. Willie WASHINGTON
38 Director Service Learning & Leaders .... Ms. Tondaleya JACKSON
39 Director Community Life .... Mr. Michael REBIMBUS
42 Dir Campus Ministry/Dean of Chapel .... Mr. Thomas DAVIS
19 Director Campus Safety .... Mr. Haywood M. BAZEMORE
36 Director Career Services .... Ms. Karen W. RUTHERFORD
37 Director Financial Aid .... Ms. Sul BLACK
18 Director Physical Plant .... Ms. Chonte' MARTIN
08 Director of Library .... Mrs. Darlene ZINNERMAN-BETHEA
09 Director Institutional Research .... Mr. Jesse BELLINGER
108 Director Institutional Assessment .... Dr. Corey R. AMAKER
25 Coordinator Title III .... Mrs. Doris W. JOHNSON
96 Manager Procurement Services .... Ms. Sharling THOMPSON
49 Dean Sch Human/Arts/Soc Sci .... Dr. Charles AUSTIN
50 Dean School of Business/Econ .... Mr. Gerald SMALLS
53 Acting Dean School of Education .... Dr. David WHALEY
72 Dean Sch Science/Tech/Engrng/Math .... Dr. Samir S. RAYCHOUDHURY
92 Dean School of Honors .... Dr. Warren ROBINSON
57 Int Chair Fine Arts .... Ms. Gina MOORE
50 Chair Business Admin/Mgmt/Mktg .... Dr. Tracy H. DUNN
88 Chair Education and Family Stds .... Dr. Mona THORNTON
70 Int Chair Social Work .... Mrs. Brenda CLARK
88 Chair English/Foreign Language Dept .... Dr. Herman HOWARD
88 Chair Bio/Chem/Enviroment Hlth Sci .... Dr. Helene TAMBOUE
81 Chair Math/Computer Science .... Ms. Fereshtah ZAHED
54 Int Chair Physics/Engineering .... Dr. Fouzi H. ARAMMASH
88 Int Chair Economics/Finance/Acctg .... Dr. Syed MAHDI

Bob Jones University (D)

1700 Wade Hampton Boulevard, Greenville SC 29614-0001
County: Greenville FICE Identification: 003421
Unit ID: 217749
Telephone: (864) 242-5100 Carnegie Class: Spec/Faith
FAX Number: (864) 235-6661 Calendar System: Semester
URL: www.bju.edu
Established: 1927 Annual Undergrad Tuition & Fees: $13,430
Enrollment: 3,469 Coed
Affiliation or Control: Proprietary IRS Status: Proprietary
Highest Offering: Doctorate
Program: Liberal Arts And General
Accreditation: TRACS

00 Chancellor .... Dr. Bob JONES, III
01 President .... Dr. Stephen JONES
05 Exec Vice Pres for Academic Affairs .... Dr. Gary M. WEIER
11 Executive Vice Pres for Operations .... Mr. Marshall E. FRANKLIN
30 VP Advancement & Alumni Relations .... Mr. John D. MATTHEWS
05 Chief Academic Officer/Provost .... Dr. David A. FISHER
10 Chief Financial Officer .... Mr. Kennie M. STILL
27 Chief Communication Officer .... Ms. Carol A. KEIRSTEAD
32 Dean of Students/Chief SLO .... Dr. Eric D. NEWTON
27 Chief Branding Officer .... Vacant
15 Chief Human Resources Officer .... Mr. Kevin TAYLOR
18 Chief Facilities Management Officer .... Mr. Steve L. HENSLEY
26 Chief Publications Officer .... Mr. Bill APELIAN
13 Chief Information Officer .... Mr. Marvin P. REEM
49 Dean College of Arts and Science .... Dr. Renae WENTWORTH
73 Dean School of Religion .... Dr. Royce B. SHORT
73 Dean Seminary/Grad Sch of Religion .... Dr. Stephen J. HANKINS
57 Dean Sch Fine Arts & Communication .... Dr. Darren P. LAWSON
53 Dean School of Education .... Dr. Brian A. CARRUTHERS
50 Dean School of Business .... Mr. Mike BUITER
88 Director of Ministerial Training .... Dr. Bruce MCALLISTER
06 Registrar .... Dr. Daniel SMITH
84 Director of Enrollment Planning .... Dr. Jeffrey D. HEATH
33 Dean of Men .... Mr. Jonathan G. DAULTON
34 Dean of Women .... Ms. Deneen LAWSON
07 Director of Admission .... Mr. Gary A. DEEDRICK
41 Athletic Director .... Mr. Neal RING
37 Director of Financial Aid .... Mr. Kevin DELP
08 Libraries Manager .... Mr. Joseph L. ALLEN
09 Dir of Institutional Effectiveness .... Dr. Doug GARLAND

Brown Mackie College-Greenville (E)

75 Beattie Place, Ste. 100, Greenville SC 29601-2155
Telephone: (864) 239-5301 Identification: 666781
Accreditation: ACICS, OTA, SURGT, SURTEC

† Main campus is The Art Institute of Phoenix in Phoenix, AZ.

Central Carolina Technical College (F)

506 N Guignard Drive, Sumter SC 29150-2499
County: Sumter FICE Identification: 003995
Unit ID: 218858
Telephone: (803) 778-1961 Carnegie Class: Assoc/Pub-R-M
FAX Number: (803) 778-7880 Calendar System: Semester
URL: www.cctech.edu
Established: 1962 Annual Undergrad Tuition & Fees (In-State): $3,695
Enrollment: 4,456 Coed
Affiliation or Control: State IRS Status: 501(c)3
Highest Offering: Associate Degree
Program: Occupational; 2-Year Principally Bachelor's Creditable; Technical Emphasis
Accreditation: SC, ADNUR, MAC, PNUR, SURGT

01 President .... Dr. Tim HARDEE
05 Vice Pres Academics .... Mr. David WATSON
11 VP for Administration & Planning .... Mrs. Ann A. COOPER
10 Vice President for Business Affairs .... Ms. Terry L. BOOTH
32 Vice President for Student Affairs .... Ms. Lisa BRACKEN
04 Assistant to the President .... Ms. Emma Lee RICKARD
51 Director Cont Educ/Workforce Devel .... Ms. Elizabeth WILLIAMS
08 Dean of Learning Resources .... Ms. Nancy BISHOP
102 Director Foundation .... Ms. Meree MCALISTER
26 Director Public Relations .... Mr. Neal CROTTS
15 Director of Personnel .... Mrs. Ronalda S. STOVER
13 Director Information Systems .... Dr. Vicky G. MALONEY
06 Registrar .... Ms. Henrietta SCOTT
37 Director Student Financial Aid .... Ms. Tiffany WILSON
09 Dir Research/Institutional Effect .... Mr. Bryan MAY
07 Director of Admissions & Counseling .... Mrs. Barbara WRIGHT
54 Dean of Industrial and Engineering .... Mr. Brent RUSSELL
76 Dean of Health Sciences .... Ms. Miriam LANEY
53 Dean of General Education .... Mr. Myles WILLIAMS

Charleston School of Law (G)

81 Mary Street, PO Box 535, Charleston SC 29402
County: Charleston FICE Identification: 040963
Unit ID: 451510
Telephone: (843) 329-1000 Carnegie Class: Spec/Law
FAX Number: N/A Calendar System: Semester
URL: www.charlestonlaw.edu
Established: 2003 Annual Graduate Tuition & Fees: $37,874
Enrollment: 631 Coed
Affiliation or Control: Proprietary IRS Status: Proprietary
Highest Offering: First Professional Degree; No Undergraduates
Program: Professional
Accreditation: LAW

01 Dean .... Mr. Andrew L. ABRAMS
05 Associate Dean Academic Affairs .... Ms. Margaret M. LAWTON
07 Associate Dean Admissions .... Mr. John S. BENFIELD
32 Associate Dean of Students .... Ms. Abby EDWARDS SAUNDERS
08 Assoc Dean of Library/Tech Svcs .... Ms. Lisa SMITH-BUTLER
10 Chief Financial Officer .... Ms. Wende WOOD

Charleston Southern University (H)

PO Box 118087, Charleston SC 29423-8087
County: Charleston FICE Identification: 003419
Unit ID: 217688
Telephone: (843) 863-7000 Carnegie Class: Master's M
FAX Number: (843) 863-8074 Calendar System: Semester
URL: www.csuniv.edu
Established: 1964 Annual Undergrad Tuition & Fees: $22,050
Enrollment: 3,130 Coed
Affiliation or Control: Southern Baptist IRS Status: 501(c)3
Highest Offering: Master's
Program: Liberal Arts And General; Teacher Preparatory; Professional
Accreditation: SC, IACBE, MUS, NUR, TED

01 President .... Dr. Jairy C. HUNTER, JR.
05 Vice President Academic Affairs .... Dr. Jacqueline FISH
10 Vice President for Business Affairs .... Mr. Luke BLACKMON
04 Exec Assistant to the President .... Mrs. Faye WOOD
84 Vice Pres Enrollment Management .... Mrs. Debbie WILLIAMSON
45 Vice Pres Planning/Athletics .... Dr. Rick BREWER
26 Vice Pres Advancement & Marketing .... Mr. David BAGGS
88 Asst to the VP for Retention .... Dr. Scott YARBROUGH
30 Executive Director of Development .... Mr. Bill WARD
32 Dean of Students .... Mr. Clark CARTER
91 Director of Administrative Services .... Mr. Shannon PHILLIPS
08 Director of the Library .... Mrs. Sandra HUGHES
06 Registrar .... Mrs. Amanda SISSION
29 Director of BUC Club .... Ms. Cathryn BRODERHAUSEN
21 Associate Business Officer .... Mrs. Janet MIMS
26 Director of Integrated Marketing .... Mr. John STRUBEL
09 Dir of Institutional Effectiveness .... Mr. Jeffrey BABETZ
58 Director MBA Program .... Dr. Darin GERDES
41 Athletic Director .... Mr. Hank SMALL
42 Director Campus Ministry .... Mr. Jon DAVIS
19 Director Security .... Mr. Guy VAN HORN
90 Director Computing & Info Science .... Mr. James ROBERTS
18 Director Physical & Auxiliary Svcs .... Mr. Nick CIMORELLI
29 Director of Alumni Relations .... Mrs. Beth MYERS
07 Director of Admission .... Mr. James M. RHOTON
15 Director of Personnel Services .... Mrs. Lindsey WALKE
36 Director Career Planning .... Mrs. Hester YOUNG
38 Director Student Counseling .... Mr. Rufus WOFFORD

96 Director of Purchasing ...... Mrs. Nicole WALLENFELSZ
37 Director Student Financial Aid ...... Mrs. Teri KARGES
39 Director Residence Life ...... Mr. Tyler DAVIS
50 Dean of Business ...... Dr. John B. DUNCAN
50 Dean Education ...... Dr. George METZ
83 Dean Humanities/Social Sciences ...... Dr. Keith CALLIS
81 Dean Science & Mathematics ...... Dr. Jeryl JOHNSON
66 Dean of Nursing ...... Dr. Tara HULSEY
51 College of Adult Professional Stds ...... Mr. Gary VANCE

The Citadel, The Military College of South Carolina (A)

171 Moultrie Street, Charleston SC 29409-0001
County: Charleston FICE Identification: 003423
Unit ID: 217864
Telephone: (843) 225-3294 Carnegie Class: Master's L
FAX Number: (843) 953-5287 Calendar System: Semester
URL: www.citadel.edu
Established: 1842 Annual Undergrad Tuition & Fees (In-State): $10,838
Enrollment: 3,499 Coed
Affiliation or Control: State IRS Status: 501(c)3
Highest Offering: Beyond Master's But Less Than Doctorate
Program: Liberal Arts And General; Teacher Preparatory; Professional
Accreditation: SC, BUS, CACREP, CS, ENG, TED

01 President ...... LtGen. John W. ROSA
05 Provost/Dean of College ...... BGen. Samuel M. HINES, JR.
26 Vice President for External Affairs ...... Col. L. Jeffrey PEREZ
30 VP Inst Advanc/Citadel Fndtn Ex Dir ...... Mr. Jay DOWD
11 Vice Pres for Operations ...... Col. Thomas G. PHILIPKOSKY
10 Interim Vice President of Finance ...... Col. James N. OPENSHAW
41 Director Intercollegiate Athletics ...... Mr. Larry W. LECKONBY
32 Commandant of Cadets ...... Col. Leo A. MERCADO
04 Executive Assistant to President ...... Capt. Taylor SHARDON
88 Interim Assoc VP/Facilities & Engr ...... Mr. James J. GRIGG
43 General Counsel ...... Mr. Mark C. BRANDENBURG
20 Assoc Provost Academic Affairs ...... Col. Mark A. BEBENSEE
20 Assoc Prov Plng/Assess/Evaluation ...... LtCol. Tara F. MCNEALY
58 Assoc Provost/Citadel Graduate ...... LtCol. Bob H. MCNAMARA
07 Director of Admissions ...... LtCol. John W. POWELL, JR.
06 Registrar ...... LtCol. Sylvia L. NESMITH
29 Director Alumni Affairs/Placement ...... Mr. Michael F. ROGERS
08 Director of Library ...... LtCol. David S. GOBLE
13 Director Info Technology Services ...... Mr. Richard NELSON
37 Director Financial Aid/ Scholarships ...... LtCol. Henry M. FULLER, JR.
15 Interim Director of Human Resources ...... Ms. Leah S. SCHONFELD
36 Director of Student Placement ...... Mr. Brent A. STEWART
38 Director of Student Counseling ...... Dr. Suzanne BUFANO
09 Institutional Research Coordinator ...... Mrs. Lisa L. PACE
19 Director Security/Safety ...... Maj. William A. FLETCHER
23 College Physician ...... Dr. Carey M. CAPELL
40 Director of the Cadet Store ...... Mr. Kenneth A. WOODRUFF
42 Chaplain/Dir Religious Activities ...... LtCol. Joel C. HARRIS
92 Director Honors Program ...... Col. Jack W. RHODES
86 Director Govt & Community Affairs ...... Col. Cardon B. CRAWFORD
96 Director of Purchasing ...... Mr. James P. DE LUCA
28 Chief Diversity Officer ...... Ms. Emma BENNETT-WILLIAMS
50 Dean of the School of Bus Admin ...... Col. William N. TRUMBULL
53 Dean of the School of Education ...... Col. John J. WHEELER
54 Dean of the School of Engineering ...... Col. Ronald W. WELCH
81 Dean of the School of Science/ Math ...... Col. Lok C. LEW YAN VOON
79 Dean Sch Humanities/Social Sciences ...... Col. Winifred B. MOORE
101 Spec Asst to President/Brd Matters ...... Ms. Patricia M. KINARD
85 Director Multicultural Affairs ...... LtCol. Robert P. PICKERING

Claflin University (B)

400 Magnolia Street, Orangeburg SC 29115-4477
County: Orangeburg FICE Identification: 003424
Unit ID: 217873
Telephone: (803) 535-5000 Carnegie Class: Bac/A&S
FAX Number: (803) 531-2860 Calendar System: Semester
URL: www.claflin.edu
Established: 1869 Annual Undergrad Tuition & Fees: $15,010
Enrollment: 1,946 Coed
Affiliation or Control: United Methodist IRS Status: 501(c)3
Highest Offering: Master's
Program: Liberal Arts And General
Accreditation: SC, MUS, ACBSP, TED

01 President ...... Dr. Henry N. TISDALE
11 Vice President for Administration ...... Mr. Drexel B. BALL
05 Provost/Chief Academic Officer ...... Dr. Karl S. WRIGHT
10 Vice President for Fiscal Affairs ...... Mrs. Tijuana R. HUDSON
30 Vice Pres Institutional Advancement ...... Rev. Whittaker V. MIDDLETON
32 Vice Pres Student Devel & Services ...... Dr. Leroy A. DURANT
45 VP Plng/Assessment/Information Svcs ...... Dr. Zia HASAN
88 Dean of Visionary Leadership ...... Dr. Kenneth M. STOKES
20 Associate VP for Academic Affairs ...... Vacant
21 Associate VP for Fiscal Affairs ...... Vacant
26 Asst VP Communications & Marketing ...... Ms. Sonja BENNETT
35 Asst VP Student Devel & Services ...... Mr. Devin L. RANDOLPH
07 Director of Admissions ...... Mr. Michael ZEIGLER
79 Dean Sch Humanities & Soc Science ...... Dr. Peggy STEVENSON-RATLIFF
50 Dean School of Business ...... Dr. Harpal S. GREWAL
53 Dean School of Education ...... Dr. Valerie E. HARRISON
81 Dean Sch Natural Sciences & Math ...... Dr. Verlie A. TISDALE
13 Asst VP Information Tech Svcs ...... Mr. James E. BRENN
51 Interim Dir of Prof & Cont Studies ...... Dr. Gloria SEABROOK
88 Director of Special Events ...... Ms. Franette BOYD
08 Library Director ...... Ms. Marilyn Y. GIBBS
37 Director of Financial Aid ...... Ms. Terria C. WILLIAMS
36 Director of Career Development ...... Mrs. Carolyn R. SNELL
18 Director Plant Operations ...... Mr. Adrian PARKS
41 Athletic Director ...... Dr. Jerome H. FITCH
15 Director of Human Resources ...... Ms. Shirley A. BIGGS
06 Registrar ...... Mrs. Roe B. HUNT
29 Director Alumni Affairs/Annual Fund ...... Mr. Allen M. JACKSON
19 Chief of Campus Public Safety ...... Mr. Steven A. PEARSON
96 Director of Auxiliary Services ...... Mr. Rodeny B. HUDSON
88 Director of Sponsored Programs ...... Ms. Veronica GOODMAN
09 Dir of Institutional Effectiveness ...... Mrs. Bridget DEWEES
04 Executive Admin Asst to President ...... Ms. Melvenia WILLIAMS

Clemson University (C)

201 Sikes Hall, Clemson SC 29634-0001
County: Pickens FICE Identification: 003425
Unit ID: 217882
Telephone: (864) 656-3311 Carnegie Class: RU/H
FAX Number: (864) 656-4040 Calendar System: Semester
URL: www.clemson.edu
Established: 1889 Annual Undergrad Tuition & Fees (In-State): $13,054
Enrollment: 20,768 Coed
Affiliation or Control: State IRS Status: 501(c)3
Highest Offering: Doctorate
Program: Liberal Arts And General; Teacher Preparatory; Professional
Accreditation: SC, ART, BUS, BUSA, CACREP, CONST, CS, DIETD, ENG, ENGR, FOR, IPSY, LSAR, NRPA, NURSE, PLNG, TED

01 President ...... Mr. James F. BARKER
43 General Counsel ...... Mr. W.C. (Chip) HOOD
05 Vice President Acad Affairs/Provost ...... Dr. Doris R. HELMS
10 Chief Financial Officer ...... Mr. Brett A. DALTON
32 Vice President Student Affairs ...... Ms. Gail DISABATINO
101 Executive Secretary to the Board ...... Ms. Angie LEIDINGER
30 Vice President for Advancement ...... Mr. A. Neill CAMERON, JR.
88 Vice Pres Public Svc/Agriculture ...... Dr. John W. KELLY, JR.
46 Vice President for Research ...... Dr. Larry DOOLEY
27 Vice Prov Computer/Info Technology ...... Mr. James R. BOTTUM
20 Vice Prov/Dean Undergrad Studies ...... Dr. Janice W. MURDOCH
88 Vice Provost for International Affs ...... Ms. Sharon NAGY
29 Chief Alumni Officer ...... Mr. Brian J. O'ROURKE
18 Chief Facilities Officer ...... Mr. Robert J. WELLS, JR.
35 Associate VP/Dean of Students ...... Dr. Joy S. SMITH
88 Associate Provost for Faculty Devel ...... Dr. Nadim AZIZ
26 Chief Public Affairs Officer ...... Ms. Catherine T. SAMS
08 Dean of Libraries ...... Ms. Kay WALL
07 Director of Admissions ...... Mr. Robert S. BARKLEY
06 Registrar ...... Mr. Stanley B. SMITH
37 Director of Financial Aid ...... Mr. Chuck KNEPFLE
36 Director of Career Center ...... Mr. Burton O'NEIL
38 Director Counseling/Psych Services ...... Dr. Raquel J. CONTRERAS
47 Dean Col Agric/Forestry/Life Sci ...... Dr. Thomas R. SCOTT
58 Interim Dean Grad School/Vice Prov ...... Dr. Karen BURG
48 Dean Col Arch/Arts/Humanities ...... Dr. Richard E. GOODSTEIN
54 Dean Col Engr/Sciences ...... Dr. Anand GRAMOPADHYE
50 Int Dn Col Business/Behavioral Sci ...... Dr. Charles K. WATT
53 Dean Col Health/Educ/Human Dev ...... Dr. Lawrence R. ALLEN
09 Director Institutional Research ...... Dr. S. Wickes WESTCOTT, III
39 Executive Director of Housing ...... Ms. Verna G. HOWELL
41 Director of Athletics ...... Mr. Dan RADAKOVICH
44 Director of Estate & Planned Giving ...... Ms. Jovanna J. KING
22 Director Access & Equity ...... Mr. Byron A. WILEY
23 Director Student Health Services ...... Mr. George W. CLAY
15 Interim Chief Human Resources ...... Ms. Michelle PIEKUTOWSKI
91 Executive Director Enterprise Appl ...... Mr. Barrett KENDJORIA
25 Director Sponsored Programs ...... Ms. Sheila T. LISCHWE
19 Director Law Enforcement & Safety ...... Chief Johnson LINK
96 Director of Purchasing ...... Mr. Michael NEBESKY
04 Asst to the President/Vice Prov ...... Ms. Debra JACKSON
88 Dir Teaching Effectiveness & Innova ...... Ms. Linda TILSON
88 Director of Bridge to Clemson Pgm ...... Ms. Susan WHORTON
106 Director of Online Education ...... Mr. DeWitt SALLEY, JR.
87 Director of Summer School ...... Mr. Blake SNIDER

Clinton College (D)

1029 Crawford Road, Rock Hill SC 29730-5152
County: York FICE Identification: 004923
Unit ID: 217891
Telephone: (803) 327-7402 Carnegie Class: Assoc/PrivNFP
FAX Number: (803) 327-3261 Calendar System: Semester
URL: www.clintonjuniorcollege.edu
Established: 1894 Annual Undergrad Tuition & Fees: $13,200
Enrollment: 143 Coed
Affiliation or Control: African Methodist Episcopal Zion Church
IRS Status: 501(c)3
Highest Offering: Associate Degree
Program: Liberal Arts And General
Accreditation: TRACS

01 President ...... Dr. Elaine J. COPELAND
04 Assistant to the President ...... Ms. Cheryl A. WEBB
05 VP for Academic Affairs/Dean ...... Ms. Janis S. PENDLETON
30 VP for Development ...... Mr. William TABOR
32 VP for Student Affairs ...... Dr. Robert M. COPELAND, JR.
10 VP of Business & Finance ...... Ms. Archinya INGRAM
09 VP for Institutional Effectiveness ...... Ms. Judith COWAN
06 Registrar ...... Mrs. Altavese HUNT
37 Financial Aid ...... Ms. Sadie PYE-JUMPER
08 Librarian ...... Ms. Minora HICKS
41 Athletic Director ...... Mr. Roderick WOODS
18 Director Facilities/Bldgs/Grounds ...... Rev. Lloyd SNIPES
07 Admissions Director ...... Dr. Robert COPELAND
35 Coord Student Support Services ...... Ms. Omega HONEYWOOD

Coastal Carolina University (E)

PO Box 261954, Conway SC 29528-6054
County: Horry FICE Identification: 003451
Unit ID: 218724
Telephone: (843) 347-3161 Carnegie Class: Master's S
FAX Number: (843) 349-2990 Calendar System: Semester
URL: www.coastal.edu
Established: 1954 Annual Undergrad Tuition & Fees (In-State): $9,760
Enrollment: 9,335 Coed
Affiliation or Control: State IRS Status: 501(c)3
Highest Offering: Master's
Program: Liberal Arts And General
Accreditation: SC, ART, BUS, CS, MUS, NUR, TED, THEA

01 President ...... Dr. David A. DECENZO
05 Int Provost/Sr VP Acad/Student Affs ...... Dr. J. Ralph BYINGTON
03 Executive Vice President ...... Dr. Edgar L. DYER
10 Vice Pres Finance/Administration ...... Ms. Staci A. BOWIE
84 Interim Vice Pres Enrollment Svcs ...... Mr. Gregory W. THORNBURG
30 Vice Pres Philanthropy ...... Mr. Lawson HOLLAND
32 Vice President Student Affairs ...... Dr. Deborah CONNER
27 Assoc Vice Pres Univ Communications ...... Mr. William PLATE
50 Int Dean Business Administration ...... Dr. Barbara RITTER
53 Dean of Education ...... Dr. Edward JADALLAH
79 Dean of Humanities & Fine Arts ...... Dr. Daniel ENNIS
81 Dean of Science ...... Dr. Michael H. ROBERTS
08 Dean Library Services ...... Dr. Barbara BURD
11 Asst Vice Pres Administrative Svcs ...... Ms. Pat WEST
13 Exec Director Info Technology Svcs ...... Mr. Abdallah HADDAD
20 Assoc Provost Admin/Academic ...... Ms. Sallie CLARKSON
108 Assoc Prov Assessment/Accreditation ...... Dr. John P. BEARD
58 Assoc Provost/Dir Graduate Studies ...... Dr. James O. LUKEN
20 Assoc Provost/QEP ...... Dr. Michael RUSE
09 Director of Inst Rsrch/Assessment ...... Ms. Christine L. MEE
06 University Registrar ...... Mr. Daniel M. LAWLESS
19 Director Public Safety ...... Mr. David ROPER
21 Controller ...... Ms. Lori CHURCH
28 Dir Multicultural Student Services ...... Ms. Patricia SINGLETON-YOUNG
41 Director of Athletics ...... Mr. Hunter R. YURACHEK
38 Director of Counseling Services ...... Dr. Jennie M. CASSIDY
85 Director of International Programs ...... Mr. Geoffrey J. PARSONS
39 Director of Housing/Residence Life ...... Mr. Steve HARRISON
37 Director of Financial Aid ...... Mr. Gregory W. THORNBURG
92 Interim Director Honors Program ...... Dr. Michael RUSE
36 Director Career Services ...... Dr. Tom WOODLE
96 Dir Procurement/Business Services ...... Mr. Dean P. HUDSON
18 Dir University Projects & Planning ...... Mr. T. Rein MUNGO
26 Chief Public Relations Officer ...... Ms. Martha S. HUNN
29 Director Alumni Relations ...... Ms. Jean Ann BRAKEFIELD
104 Exec Dir Global Initiatives ...... Dr. Darla J. DOMKE-DAMONTE

Coker College (F)

300 E College Avenue, Hartsville SC 29550-3797
County: Darlington FICE Identification: 003427
Unit ID: 217907
Telephone: (843) 383-8000 Carnegie Class: Bac/Diverse
FAX Number: (843) 383-8048 Calendar System: Semester
URL: www.coker.edu
Established: 1908 Annual Undergrad Tuition & Fees: $24,576
Enrollment: 1,163 Coed
Affiliation or Control: Independent Non-Profit IRS Status: 501(c)3
Highest Offering: Master's
Program: Liberal Arts And General; Teacher Preparatory
Accreditation: SC, MUS, SW, TED

01 President ...... Dr. Robert L. WYATT
04 Exec Assistant to the President ...... Ms. Bonnie WILCOX
05 Provost & Dean of the Faculty ...... Dr. Tracy PARKINSON
30 VP Institutional Advancement ...... Ms. Patricia MEINHOLD
10 VP Administration and Legal Counsel ...... Mr. Tony FLOYD
84 VP Enrollment/Student Services ...... Dr. Stephen B. TERRY
32 Dean of Students ...... Dr. Jason UMFRESS
55 Assoc Dean Adult Learner Pgm ...... Dr. Barbara JACKOWSKI
78 Asst Dean/Dir CTR Engaged Learning ...... Ms. Darlene SMALL
26 Exec Dir Marketing/Communication ...... Mr. R. Kyle SAVERANCE
39 Director of Residence Life ...... Ms. Whitney WATTS
41 VP of Athletics and Facilities ...... Dr. Lynn GRIFFIN
07 Director of Admissions ...... Mr. Adam CONNOLLY
06 Registrar ...... Ms. Stacy R. ATKINSON
18 Director of Facilities ...... Mr. Jim WELCH
21 Director of Accounting ...... Mrs. Robin A. PERDUE
37 Director of Financial Aid ...... Mrs. Betty B. WILLIAMS
44 Director of Major Gifts ...... Ms. Tiletha LANE
29 Dir of Alumni & Advancement Svcs ...... Ms. Pat DAMPIER
38 Director Counseling Services ...... Vacant
35 Dir Student Activities/Leadership ...... Mr. Tyler MICEK
15 Director of Human Resources ...... Ms. Brianna DOUGLAS
38 Director of Career Services ...... Vacant
08 Director of Library ...... Ms. Alexa BARTEL
13 Director of Information Technology ...... Mr. Wally BOATWRIGHT
19 Director of Campus Safety ...... Mr. Michael WILLIAMSON

College of Charleston (A)

66 George Street, Charleston SC 29424-0100
County: Charleston FICE Identification: 003428
Unit ID: 217819
Telephone: (843) 953-5507 Carnegie Class: Master's M
FAX Number: (843) 953-5811 Calendar System: Semester
URL: www.cofc.edu
Established: 1770 Annual Undergrad Tuition & Fees (In-State): $10,230
Enrollment: 11,723 Coed
Affiliation or Control: State IRS Status: 501(c)3
Highest Offering: Master's
Program: Liberal Arts And General
Accreditation: SC, BUS, BUSA, CS, MUS, SPAA, TED, THEA

01 President .... Dr. George BENSON
101 Exec Secretary Board of Trustees . Ms. Elizabeth W. KASSEBAUM
10 Exec VP Business Affairs .... Mr. Steven C. OSBORNE
26 Exec VP External Relations .... Mr. Michael R. HASKINS
30 Exec VP Institutional Advancement .... Mr. George P. WATT, JR.
32 Exec VP Student Affairs .... Dr. Victor K. WILSON
05 Provost & Exec VP Academic Affairs .... Mr. George W. HYND
43 Senior VP Legal Affairs .... Ms. Kathryn BENDER
100 Chief of Staff & Sr Policy Advisor .... Dr. Brian MCGEE
88 Director Executive Communications .... Mr. Ron MENCHACA
20 Sr Vice Provost Academic Affairs .... Dr. Beverly E. DIAMOND
20 Associate Provost of Academic Admin .... Dr. Lynne E. FORD
20 Assoc Provost for Faculty Affairs .... Dr. Deanna M. CAVENY
104 Assoc Provost for Intl Education .... Dr. Andrew M. SOBIESUO
27 Senior VP Technology .... Dr. Robert E. CAPE
30 Senior VP Economic Development .... Mr. Robert W. MARLOWE
19 VP Facilities Planning .... Ms. Monica R. SCOTT
21 VP Fiscal Services .... Ms. Priscilla D. BURBAGE
30 Vice President Development .... Mr. Christopher TOBIN
15 VP of Human Resources .... Mr. Edward POPE
84 Assoc Vice Pres Enrollment Planning .... Dr. Donald C. BURKARD
20 Assoc VP Academic Experience .... Dr. Kay H. SMITH
88 Assoc VP Institutional Effectivenes ..... Dr. Penelope W. BRUNNER
09 Assoc VP Institutional Research .... Dr. James T. POSEY
30 Associate VP Development .... Ms. Cathryn A. MAHON
28 Associate VP Diversity .... Dr. John BELLO-OGUNU
35 Assistant VP Student Affairs .... Ms. Marjorie S. THOMAS
88 Asst VP New Student Programs .... Ms. Melinda MILEY
06 Registrar .... Ms. Catherine C. BOYD
21 Controller .... Ms. Dawn E. WILLAN
21 Treasurer .... Mr. David G. KATZ
58 Dean Graduate School .... Dr. Amy T. MCCANDLESS
08 Dean Libraries .... Dr. David J. COHEN
57 Dean School of the Arts .... Ms. Valerie B. MORRIS
50 Dean School of Business .... Dr. Alan T. SHAO
53 Dean School of Education .... Dr. Frances C. WELCH
79 Dean Sch of Humanities/Social Sci ... Dr. Cynthia J. LOWENTHAL
82 Dean School of Languages .... Dr. David J. COHEN
81 Dean School of Science & Math .... Dr. Michael AUERBACH
88 Dean College of Charleston North .... Dr. Godfrey GIBBISON
92 Dean Honors College .... Dr. John H. NEWELL
35 Dean of Students .... Dr. Jeri O. CABOT
39 Dean Residence Life and Housing .... Mr. John T. CAMPBELL
87 Director Summer School Programs .... Mr. Michael C. PHILLIPS
41 Director Athletics .... Mr. Joe HULL, JR.
25 Director Research and Grants Admin ...... Ms. Susan A. RIVALEAU
37 Dir Financial Asst/Veteran Affairs .... Dr. Donald R. GRIGGS
07 Director Admissions .... Ms. Suzette STILLE
88 Director First Year Experience .... Dr. Christopher A. KOREY
88 Dir Center for Academic Advising .... Ms. Karen HAUSCHILD
88 Dir Center for Student Learning .... Mr. Steve T. GIBSON
88 Dir Undergraduate Academic Services .... Ms. Deborah VAUGHN
108 Dir Academic Assessment & Planning .... Dr. Karin ROOF
88 Director Strategic Initiatives .... Ms. Denise MITCHELL
85 Dir Multicultural Student Programs .... Ms. Teresa SMITH
88 Dir Ctr for Disabilities Services .... Ms. Deborah F. MIHAL
35 Director Student Life .... Ms. Susan PAYMENT
36 Director Career Services .... Mr. Denny D. CIGANOVIC
38 Dir Counseling & Substance Abuse .... Mr. Frank C. BUDD
23 Director Health Services .... Ms. Jane RENO-MUNRO
39 Director Residence Life .... Ms. Melantha ARDREY
19 Director Public Safety .... Chief Paul V. VERRECCHIA
13 Director Information Services .... Ms. Jie ZHU
105 Director Web Strategies .... Mr. Andrew BERGSTROM
21 Assoc VP Budgeting & Payroll Svcs .... Mr. Samuel B. JONES
86 Director Government Relations .... Ms. Shirley R. HINSON
18 Director Physical Plant .... Mr. John CORDRAY
44 Director Annual Giving Programs .... Mr. Laurie A. SOENEN
44 Director of Gift Planning .... Mr. David MASICH
102 Director Corporate Relations .... Ms. Denise CICCARELLI
29 Director Alumni Relations .... Mr. John HUGULEY
40 Manager Bookstore .... Ms. Rebecca GRAY

Columbia College (B)

1301 Columbia College Drive, Columbia SC 29203-5998
County: Richland FICE Identification: 003430
Unit ID: 217934
Telephone: (803) 786-3012 Carnegie Class: Master's M
FAX Number: (803) 754-3178 Calendar System: Semester
URL: www.columbiasc.edu
Established: 1854 Annual Undergrad Tuition & Fees: $26,800
Enrollment: 1,145 Female
Affiliation or Control: United Methodist IRS Status: 501(c)3
Highest Offering: Master's
Program: Liberal Arts And General; Teacher Preparatory
Accreditation: SC, ART, DANCE, MUS, SW, TED

01 President .... Ms. Elizabeth A. DINNDORF
05 Provost/VP for Academic Affairs .... Dr. Laurie B. HOPKINS
10 Vice President for Finance .... Vacant
84 Vice Pres for Enrollment Management .... Vacant
88 Ex Dir Inst Lship & Prof Excellenc .... Ms. Chris LACOLA
30 VP for Advancement .... Ms. Amy S. LANIER
32 Dean Student Affairs .... Ms. LaNae R. BRIGGS
29 Exec Director of Alumnae Relations .... Ms. Sara S. JOHNSON
06 Registrar/Dir Institutional Rsrch .... Dr. Scott A. SMITH
08 Dir of Library & Info Tech Services .... Mr. Dan MURPHY
19 Chief of Police .... Chief Howard M. COOK
37 Director of Financial Aid .... Ms. Donna QUICK
36 Director of Ctr for Career Coaching .... Ms. Kenetta PIERCE
14 Director of Info Technology .... Mr. Dave MEDEIROS
18 Director of Facilities Management .... Mr. Lowell CUPPS
26 Exec Director Mktg & Communications .... Ms. Tracy BENDER
41 Director of Athletics .... Ms. Kelly COX
40 Director Bookstore .... Mr. Chris FREEMAN
38 Director Counseling Services .... Ms. Jessica WILLARD
04 Executive Assistant to President .... Ms. Joye G. HIPP
07 Director of Admissions .... Ms. Julie A. KING
92 Director Honors Program/Faculty Dev ..... Dr. John ZUBIZARRETA

Columbia International University (C)

PO Box 3122, Columbia SC 29230-3122
County: Richland FICE Identification: 003429
Unit ID: 217925
Telephone: (803) 754-4100 Carnegie Class: Master's S
FAX Number: (803) 786-4209 Calendar System: Semester
URL: www.ciu.edu
Established: 1923 Annual Undergrad Tuition & Fees: $25,630
Enrollment: 1,171 Coed
Affiliation or Control: Independent Non-Profit IRS Status: 501(c)3
Highest Offering: Doctorate
Program: Liberal Arts And General; Professional
Accreditation: SC, BI, THEOL

01 President .... Dr. William H. JONES
00 Chancellor .... Dr. George W. MURRAY
05 Senior Vice President/Provost .... Dr. Jim LANPHER
30 Sr Vice Pres Development/Operations .... Mr. D. Keith MARION
84 VP Marketing/Enrollment Management .... Mr. Jeff WHEELER
27 VP Communications .... Mr. Mike BLACKWELL
73 Dean Seminary & School of Ministry .... Dr. John HARVEY
49 Dean College of Arts and Sciences .... Dr. Bryan BEYER
53 Dean College of Education .... Dr. Connie MITCHELL
38 Dean College of Counselling .... Dr. Harvey PAYNE
104 Dean College Intercultural Studies .... Dr. Michael BARNETT
09 Dir Institutional Research/Assess .... Mr. Jeff MILLER
56 Director of CEID .... Mr. Rob MCDOLE
08 Director of Library .... Ms. Stephanie SOLOMON
06 University Registrar .... Mrs. Jennifer BOOTH
15 Director Human Resources .... Mr. Donald E. JONES
29 Int Director of Alumni .... Mrs. Diane MULL
32 Dean of Students .... Mr. Rick SWIFT
07 Director University Admissions .... Vacant
14 Director Computer Services .... Vacant
18 Director Physical Plant .... Mr. Phil MILLER
40 Director of Business Services .... Mr. Roger L. TILTON
21 Controller .... Mr. Larry F. HUSS
30 Director Development .... Mr. Frank BEDELL
37 Director Financial Aid .... Mrs. Patty HIX
26 Chief Public Relations Officer .... Mrs. Polly SHOEMAKER
88 General Mgr WMHK/WRCM Radio .... Mr. Joseph PAULO
36 Director Student Placement .... Mrs. Stephanie BRYANT

Converse College (D)

580 E Main, Spartanburg SC 29302-0006
County: Spartanburg FICE Identification: 003431
Unit ID: 217961
Telephone: (864) 596-9000 Carnegie Class: Master's M
FAX Number: (864) 596-9158 Calendar System: 4/1/4
URL: www.converse.edu
Established: 1889 Annual Undergrad Tuition & Fees: $29,124
Enrollment: 1,089 Female
Affiliation or Control: Independent Non-Profit IRS Status: 501(c)3
Highest Offering: Beyond Master's But Less Than Doctorate
Program: Liberal Arts And General; Teacher Preparatory; Professional; Business Emphasis
Accreditation: SC, ART, CIDA, MFCD, MUS, TED

01 President .... Dr. Elizabeth A. FLEMING
03 Senior Vice President .... Dr. Thomas MCDANIEL
05 VP Academic Affs/Dean Sch Human/Sci .... Dr. Jeffrey H. BARKER
10 Vice Pres Finance/Administration .... Vacant
84 Vice Pres Enrollment Management .... Ms. Sally J. HAMMOND
30 Vice Pres Institutional Advancement .... Mr. Robert STEWART
32 Vice Pres Student life/Dn Students .... Dr. Molly DUESTERHAUS
58 Dean Graduate Educ/Special Programs .... Dr. Kathy GOOD
64 Dean School of the Arts .... Mr. Richard HIGGS
35 Asst Dean Students for Engage/Lrng .... Ms. Rhonda MINGO
08 Librarian .... Mr. Wade WOODWARD
37 Director of Financial Assistance .... Mrs. Peggy P. COLLINS
06 Registrar .... Mrs. Mary L. BROWN
15 Human Resources Director .... Mrs. Sandy GORDIN
29 Director of Alumnae/Donor Rels .... Mrs. Carrie COLEMAN
13 Chief Information Officer .... Mr. Zach CORBITT
36 Director of Career Services .... Ms. Witney FISHER
26 Director of Media/Communications .... Mrs. Beth LANCASTER
04 Admin Assistant to the President .... Mrs. Stacey BREWER
38 Director Student Counseling .... Dr. Carol EPPS
09 Director Institutional Research .... Mr. Trevor PITTMAN
07 Director of Admissions .... Ms. April LEWIS
18 Chief Facilities/Physical Plant .... Mr. Hayden HUTCHINGS
18 Facilities Planner .... Mr. Mark L. OSINGA

Denmark Technical College (E)

PO Box 327, Denmark SC 29042-0327
County: Bamberg FICE Identification: 005363
Unit ID: 217989
Telephone: (803) 793-5176 Carnegie Class: Assoc/Pub-R-S
FAX Number: (803) 793-5942 Calendar System: Semester
URL: www.denmarktech.edu
Established: 1948 Annual Undergrad Tuition & Fees (In-State): $2,662
Enrollment: 1,867 Coed
Affiliation or Control: State IRS Status: 501(c)3
Highest Offering: Associate Degree
Program: Occupational; 2-Year Principally Bachelor's Creditable
Accreditation: SC, ACBSP, ENGT

01 President .... Dr. Joann BOYD-SCOTLAND
05 VP Academic Affairs .... Mrs. Carolyn FENNELL-MCGAY
09 Vice Pres Inst Research/Plng/Dev .... Dr. Ashok KABISATPATHY
10 VP Fiscal Affairs .... Mr. Clarence BONNETTE
16 Human Resources Director .... Ms. Tonya OTTS
32 Exec Dean Student Svcs & Arts/Sci .... Mrs. Avis GATHERS
08 Actg Dean of Learning Resources Ctr .... Mr. Louis MAYO
13 Information Technology Director .... Mr. Derrick STEWARD
19 Chief of Public Safety .... Mrs. Judy HALMON
25 Director of Grants & Contracts .... Mrs. Teresa MACK
36 Director Career Plng/Placement .... Mr. Jay FIELDS
37 Financial Aid Director .... Mrs. Connie WILLIAMS
40 Dean of Public Service .... Ms. Bijayalaxmi KABISATPATHY
49 Acting Dean of Arts & Sciences .... Ms. Yvette MCDANIEL
54 Dean Industrial/Related Technology .... Dr. Ambrish LAVANIA
50 Dean Business/Computer/Related Tech ...... Ms. Antonia ROBERTS
60 Dean of Transitional Studies .... Vacant
07 Director of Recruitment .... Ms. Margaree BONNETTE
103 AVP Economic/Workforce Develpoment .... Mr. Stephen MASON

Erskine College (F)

PO Box 338, 2 Washington Street,
Due West SC 29639-0338
County: Abbeville FICE Identification: 003432
Unit ID: 217998
Telephone: (864) 379-2131 Carnegie Class: Bac/A&S
FAX Number: (864) 379-2167 Calendar System: 4/1/4
URL: www.erskine.edu
Established: 1837 Annual Undergrad Tuition & Fees: $31,280
Enrollment: 780 Coed
Affiliation or Control: Other IRS Status: 501(c)3
Highest Offering: Doctorate
Program: Liberal Arts And General; Professional
Accreditation: SC, TED, THEOL

01 President .... Vacant
05 Sr VP of Academic Affairs .... Dr. N. Bradley CHRISTIE
10 Sr VP for Finance & Operations .... Mr. Gregory W. HASELDEN
32 Vice President Student Services .... Dr. Robyn R. AGNEW
30 Vice President for Advancement .... Mr. David EARLE
06 Registrar .... Mrs. Tracy M. SPIRES
37 Director of Student Financial Aid .... Mrs. Michelle LODATO
08 Librarian .... Mr. John F. KENNERLY
13 Director of Information Technology ...... Mr. Robert S. CLARKE, III
09 Director of Institutional Research .... Mr. Buck F. BROWN, JR.
41 Athletic Director .... Mr. Mark L. PEELER
42 Chaplain .... Mr. Paul G. PATRICK
21 Controller .... Mr. Christian M. HABEGER
15 Director Human Resources .... Ms. Hope S. HARRISON
19 Chief of Erskine Police .... Mr. Charles R. ESTEP
35 Dean of Students .... Dr. S. Bryan RUSH
36 Director Career Services .... Vacant
26 Vice President for Communications .... Mr. Cliff L. SMITH
29 Director of Alumni Affairs .... Mr. William L. FERGUSON
73 Dean Theological Seminary .... Dr. James A. MEEK

Florence - Darlington Technical College (G)

PO Box 100548, Florence SC 29502-0548
County: Florence FICE Identification: 003990
Unit ID: 218025
Telephone: (843) 661-8324 Carnegie Class: Assoc/Pub-R-M
FAX Number: (843) 661-8011 Calendar System: Semester
URL: www.fdtc.edu
Established: 1964 Annual Undergrad Tuition & Fees (In-District): $3,766
Enrollment: 6,002 Coed
Affiliation or Control: State/Local IRS Status: 501(c)3
Highest Offering: Associate Degree
Program: Occupational; 2-Year Principally Bachelor's Creditable
Accreditation: SC, ACBSP, ADNUR, CAHIIM, COARC, DA, DH, MLTAD, RAD, SURGT

01 President .... Dr. Ben P. DILLARD, III
05 Vice President Academic Affairs .... Dr. Dale DOTY
10 Vice President Business Affairs .... Mr. Tim O'DELL
32 Vice President Student Services .... Dr. Shelley FORTIN
30 Vice Pres Institutional Advancement .... Ms. Jill LEWIS
72 Assoc VP Technical & General Educ .... Ms. Suzanne JENNINGS

76 Assoc VP Health & Sciences .... Dr. Lynn BROWN-BULLOCH
13 Assoc Vice Pres Info Tech/CIO .... Mr. Bill GRIFFENBERG
15 Director Internal Relations .... Ms. Terry DINGLE
09 Director Institutional Research .... Ms. Melissa MILLER
26 Assoc VP Marketing/Public Affs .... Mr. Edward BETHEA
72 Director Manufacturing/Technology .... Mr. Jack ROACH
06 Registrar .... Ms. Abby VILLAR
37 Director Financial Aid .... Mr. Joseph DURANT
18 Chief Facilities/Physical Plant .... Mr. Harrison FORD, III
40 Director Bookstore .... Mr. Bob GARAND
96 Director of Purchasing .... Ms. Angela JORDAN
07 Director of Admissions .... Ms. Elaine HODGES

Forrest College (A)

601 E River Street, Anderson SC 29624-2405

County: Anderson | FICE Identification: 004924 | Unit ID: 218043
Telephone: (864) 225-7653 | Carnegie Class: Assoc/PrivFP
FAX Number: (864) 261-7471 | Calendar System: 4/1/4
URL: www.forrestcollege.edu
Established: 1946 | Annual Undergrad Tuition & Fees: $9,420
Enrollment: 134 | Coed
Affiliation or Control: Proprietary | IRS Status: Proprietary
Highest Offering: Associate Degree
Program: Occupational; 2-Year Principally Bachelor's Creditable
Accreditation: ACICS, MAC

00 Chairman Board of Directors .... Dr. John RE
01 Acting President .... Dr. Cosmo J. RE
11 Administrative Dean .... Jim RUSH
05 Academic Dean .... Linda REEVES
101 Secy/Treasurer Board of Directors .... Charles PALMER
06 Fin Records Coordinator/Registrar .... Elizabeth FLOYD
08 Librarian .... Darlene MCKAY
76 Medical Assistng Program Coord .... Alica SWANEY
07 Admissions Rep .... Janie TURMON
07 Admissions Rep .... Linda PERRYMAN
07 Admissions Rep .... Mandy JOYNER
07 Admissions Rep .... Scott LOCKARD
36 Job Placement Asst Coordinator .... Genny ELLIS
37 Finance & Records Office Coord .... Elizabeth FLOYD

Francis Marion University (B)

PO Box 100547, Florence SC 29501-0547

County: Florence | FICE Identification: 009226 | Unit ID: 218061
Telephone: (843) 661-1362 | Carnegie Class: Master's S
FAX Number: (843) 661-1202 | Calendar System: Semester
URL: www.fmarion.edu
Established: 1970 | Annual Undergrad Tuition & Fees (In-State): $9,066
Enrollment: 4,096 | Coed
Affiliation or Control: State | IRS Status: 501(c)3
Highest Offering: Master's
Program: Liberal Arts And General; Teacher Preparatory; Professional
Accreditation: SC, ART, BUS, NUR, TED, THEA

01 President .... Dr. Luther F. CARTER
05 Provost/Dean Col of Liberal Arts .... Dr. Richard N. CHAPMAN
10 Vice President Business Affairs .... Mr. John J. KISPERT
11 Vice President Administration .... Dr. Charlene WAGES
30 Vice President Devel/Exec Dir .... Mr. Darryl BRIDGES
26 VP Public & Community Affairs .... Mr. Tucker MITCHELL
32 Vice President for Student Affairs .... Mrs. Teresa RAMEY
84 Assoc Provost For Academic Affiars .... Dr. Peter KING
21 Asst Vice Pres for Accounting .... Mr. M. Augustus MCDILL
88 Asst Vice Pres Financial Services .... Mrs. Brinda A. JONES
53 Dean School of Educaion .... Dr. Ron FAULKENBERRY
08 Dean of the Library .... Mrs. Joyce M. DURANT
20 Asst Provost/Dir Graduate Programs .... Dr. Jeannette MYERS
37 Financial Assistance Director .... Ms. Kimberly M. ELLISOR
41 Athletic Director .... Mr. Murray G. HARTZLER
06 Registrar .... Ms. Dollie NEWHOUSE
38 Director Counseling and Testing .... Dr. Rebecca L. LAWSON
18 Director of Facilities Management .... Mr. Ralph U. DAVIS
36 Director Career Development .... Vacant
07 Director of Admissions .... Mrs. Perry T. WILSON
35 Asst Dean of Students .... Ms. R. Daphne CARTER
29 Director of Alumni Affairs .... Mr. Julian M. YOUNG
96 Director of Purchasing .... Mr. Eric L. GARRIS
92 Director of Honors Program .... Dr. Pamela A. ROOKS
27 Chief Information Officer .... Mr. John DIXON

Furman University (C)

3300 Poinsett Highway, Greenville SC 29613-0001

County: Greenville | FICE Identification: 003434 | Unit ID: 218070
Telephone: (864) 294-2000 | Carnegie Class: Bac/A&S
FAX Number: (864) 294-3001 | Calendar System: Semester
URL: www.furman.edu
Established: 1826 | Annual Undergrad Tuition & Fees: $43,164
Enrollment: 3,051 | Coed
Affiliation or Control: Independent Non-Profit | IRS Status: 501(c)3
Highest Offering: Master's
Program: Liberal Arts And General; Teacher Preparatory; Professional
Accreditation: SC, MUS, TED

01 Interim President .... Dr. Carl F. KOHRT
03 VP Academic Affairs & Dean .... Dr. John S. BECKFORD
10 VP for Finance & Administration .... Ms. Mary Lou MERKT
32 Vice President for Student Life .... Ms. Connie L. CARSON
30 Vice President for Development .... Mr. Michael D. GATCHELL
26 VP Marketing/Public Relations .... Mr. Mark L. KELLY
20 Sr Associate Academic Dean .... Dr. Marianne PIERCE
20 Associate Academic Dean .... Dr. Paula S. GADDERT
06 University Registrar .... Mr. Brad E. BARRON
58 Director Graduate Studies .... Dr. Troy M. TERRY
08 Director Libraries .... Dr. Janis M. BANDELIN
19 Chief of Police .... Mr. Tom SACCENTI
108 Director Assessment & Inst Research .... Mr. Donald E. PIERCE
37 Assoc Vice Pres of Financial Aid .... Mr. Forrest M. STUART
29 Director of Alumni Association .... Mr. Tom A. TRIPLITT
07 Assoc Vice President of Admissions .... Mr. Brad POCHARD
44 Director of Annual Giving .... Mr. John KEMP
44 Director of Planned Giving .... Mr. Steve PERRY
25 Grants Administrator .... Ms. Judith J. ROMANO
28 Director of Multicultural Affairs .... Ms. Idella G. GLENN
94 Dir Women's/Gender/Sexuality Study .... Dr. Karni BHATI
15 Asst VP Human Resources/AAO .... Ms. Pamela BARKETT
27 Chief Information Officer .... Mr. Fred MILLER
85 Asst Dean Intl Educ/Study Away .... Dr. Kailash KHANDKE
36 Director Career Services .... Mr. John D. BARKER
88 Aux Services Director .... Ms. Rebecca VUKSTA
18 Asst VP for Facilities Services .... Mr. Jeff P. REDDERSON
51 Director Continuing Education .... Dr. Brad BECHTOLD
41 VP & Director of Athletics .... Dr. Gary E. CLARK
88 Director UG Research & Internships .... Dr. Tim G. FEHLER
88 Director CTL .... Dr. Jane LOVE
17 Director Student Health Services .... Dr. Paul V. CATALANA
38 Director Counseling Center .... Dr. Stephen DAWES
39 Director University Housing .... Mr. Ronald C. THOMPSON
88 Director Disability Services .... Ms. Gina PARRIS
42 Chaplain .... Dr. Vaughn CROWETIPTON
40 Director Bookstore .... Ms. K. C ROBINSON
04 Assistant to President .... Ms. Cindy ALEXANDER
21 Budget Director .... Ms. Amy BLACKWELL
96 Director of Purchasing .... Ms. Lishan YAU
35 Director Student Activities .... Mr. Scott DERRICK

Golf Academy of America (D)

3268 Waccamaw Boulevard, Myrtle Beach SC 29579-9451

Telephone: (800) 342-7342 | Identification: 666490
Accreditation: ACICS

† Main campus is Virginia College in Birmingham, AL.

Greenville Technical College (E)

PO Box 5616, Greenville SC 29606-5616

County: Greenville | FICE Identification: 003991 | Unit ID: 218113
Telephone: (864) 250-8000 | Carnegie Class: Assoc/Pub-U-MC
FAX Number: (864) 250-8507 | Calendar System: Semester
URL: www.gvltec.edu
Established: 1962 | Annual Undergrad Tuition & Fees (In-State): $1,987
Enrollment: 13,967 | Coed
Affiliation or Control: State | IRS Status: 501(c)3
Highest Offering: Associate Degree
Program: Occupational; 2-Year Principally Bachelor's Creditable; Technical Emphasis
Accreditation: SC, ACBSP, ACFEI, ADNUR, CAHIIM, COARC, DA, DH, DMS, EMT, ENGT, MAC, MLTAD, OTA, PNUR, PTAA, RAD, SURGT

01 President .... Dr. Keith MILLER
05 Vice President for Academic Affairs .... Dr. Lenna YOUNG
10 Vice President for Finance .... Mrs. Jacqueline R. DIMAGGIO
32 Vice President Student Services .... Dr. Matteel JONES
51 Vice Pres Corp & Economic Devel .... Mrs. Cynthia G. EASON
45 VP Institutional Effectiveness .... Mrs. Lauren SIMER

Horry-Georgetown Technical College (F)

2050 Highway 501 E, Conway SC 29526-9521

County: Horry | FICE Identification: 004925 | Unit ID: 218140
Telephone: (843) 347-3186 | Carnegie Class: Assoc/Pub-R-M
FAX Number: (843) 347-4207 | Calendar System: Semester
URL: www.hgtc.edu
Established: 1966 | Annual Undergrad Tuition & Fees (In-District): $1,795
Enrollment: 7,685 | Coed
Affiliation or Control: State/Local | IRS Status: 501(c)3
Highest Offering: Associate Degree
Program: Occupational; 2-Year Principally Bachelor's Creditable
Accreditation: SC, ACBSP, ACFEI, ADNUR, DA, DH, DMS, EMT, ENGT, PNUR, PTAA, RAD, SURGT

01 President .... Mr. Neyle WILSON
05 Senior VP .... Dr. Marilyn FORE
10 Vice President for Business Affairs .... Mr. Harold HAWLEY
13 VP for Tech/Institutional Planning .... Mr. Ralph SELANDER
103 VP Wrkfc Dev/Prov GS/Georgetwn Camp . Mr. Gregory MITCHELL
84 AVP Enrollment Dev/Registration .... Mr. George SWINDOLL
32 Asc VP Student Affs/Campus Life .... Mr. Greg THOMPSON
20 AVP Acad Affs/Dean Academic Support .... Ms. Rene SMITH
20 AVP Acad Affs/Dn Univ Paral/Bus/Leg .... Dr. Shirley BUTLER
15 AVP Human Res/Employee Relations .... Ms. Judy WOOTEN
08 AVP/Dn Library/Stdnt Succ/Tech Ctr .... Ms. Peggy SMITH
20 AVP Acad Affs/Dn Allied Hlth/Agri .... Dr. Philip RENDER
21 AVP/Controller .... Ms. Ellen BLACK
38 AVP Student Success .... Ms. Melissa BATTEN
26 Chief Public Relations Officer .... Ms. Mary EADDY
18 Superintendent Bulidings & Grounds .... Mr. Kevin BROWN
37 Dir of Financial Aid/Veterans Affs .... Ms. Susan THOMPSON
07 Dir Stdnt Recruitment/Admissions .... Ms. Thyssene FREDERICK
36 Career Resource Ctr Coordinator .... Ms. April GARNER
09 Dir Institutional Rsrch/Assessment .... Ms. Lori HEAFNER
96 Procurement Manager .... Ms. Dianna CECALA

ITT Technical Institute (G)

1628 Browning Road, Suite 180, Columbia SC 29210

Telephone: (803) 216-6000 | Identification: 666162
Accreditation: ACICS

† Main campus is ITT Technical Institute in Indianapolis, IN.

ITT Technical Institute (H)

6 Independence Pointe, Greenville SC 29615-4506

Telephone: (864) 288-0777 | Identification: 666549
Accreditation: ACICS

† Main campus is ITT Technical Institute in Indianapolis, IN.

ITT Technical Institute (I)

9654 N Kings Highway, Suite 101, Myrtle Beach SC 29752

Telephone: (843) 497-7820 | Identification: 770661
Accreditation: ACICS

† Main campus is ITT Technical Institute in Indianapolis, IN.

ITT Technical Institute (J)

2431 W Aviation Avenue, North Charleston SC 29406

Telephone: (843) 745-5700 | Identification: 770662
Accreditation: ACICS

† Main campus is ITT Technical Institute in Indianapolis, IN.

Lander University (K)

320 Stanley Avenue, Greenwood SC 29649-2099

County: Greenwood | FICE Identification: 003435 | Unit ID: 218229
Telephone: (864) 388-8000 | Carnegie Class: Bac/Diverse
FAX Number: (864) 388-8890 | Calendar System: Semester
URL: www.lander.edu
Established: 1872 | Annual Undergrad Tuition & Fees (In-State): $10,100
Enrollment: 3,049 | Coed
Affiliation or Control: State | IRS Status: 501(c)3
Highest Offering: Master's
Program: Liberal Arts And General; Teacher Preparatory; Professional; Business Emphasis
Accreditation: SC, ART, BUS, MACTE, MUS, NURSE, TED

01 President .... Dr. Daniel W. BALL
05 Provost/Vice Pres Academic Affairs .... Dr. David MASH
10 Vice Pres Business/Administration .... Mr. Gary MCCOMBS
32 Vice President for Student Affairs ...... Mr. H. Randall BOUKNIGHT
30 Vice President for Univ Advancement .... Mr. Ralph PATTERSON
84 Dean of Enrollment Services .... Vacant
07 Director of Admissions .... Mrs. Jennifer M. MATHIS
08 Librarian .... Ms. Lisa WIECKI
38 Director Counseling .... Ms. Debra J. FRANKS
41 Athletic Director .... Mr. Jefferson J. MAY
15 Director Human Resources .... Ms. Jeannie MCCALLUM
19 Director University Police .... Mr. Eddie BRIGGS
26 Director of Public Information .... Mrs. Megan PRICE
37 Director of Financial Aid .... Mr. Fred HARDIN
36 Director of Career Services .... Vacant
21 Controller .... Mr. Tom COVAR
40 Dir Bookstore/Procurement/Print Svc .... Mrs. Mary W. MCDANIEL
13 Dir Office Inform Tech Services .... Ms. Robin P. LAWRENCE
18 Director Physical Plant/Engr Svcs .... Mr. Jeff S. BEAVER
09 Dir Institutional Rsrch/Registrar .... Ms. Kelly PROCTOR
29 Director Alumni Relations .... Ms. Myra GREENE

Limestone College (L)

1115 College Drive, Gaffney SC 29340-3799

County: Cherokee | FICE Identification: 003436 | Unit ID: 218238
Telephone: (864) 489-7151 | Carnegie Class: Bac/Diverse
FAX Number: (864) 487-8706 | Calendar System: Semester
URL: www.limestone.edu
Established: 1845 | Annual Undergrad Tuition & Fees: $22,080
Enrollment: 3,445 | Coed
Affiliation or Control: Independent Non-Profit | IRS Status: 501(c)3
Highest Offering: Master's
Program: Liberal Arts And General; Teacher Preparatory; Professional
Accreditation: SC, MUS, SW, TED

01 President .... Dr. Walt R. GRIFFIN
03 Exec Vice Pres/VP Academic Affairs .... Dr. Karen W. GAINEY
10 Vice President Financial Affairs .... Mr. David S. RILLING
30 Int VP Institutional Advancement .... Ms. Kelly T. CURTIS
84 Vice President Enrollment Services . Mr. Christopher N. PHENICIE
32 Vice President Student Services .... Mr. Robert A. OVERTON
13 Vice Pres Information Technology .... Mr. C. R. HORTON
41 Vice Pres Intercollegiate Athletics .... Mr. Michael H. CERINO

14 Assoc VP Information Technology .... Mr. C. Adam LONG
20 Assoc Vice Pres Academic Affairs .... Dr. Mark A. REGER
45 Assoc Vice Pres Planning/Assessment ...... Dr. Bonnie M. WRIGHT
88 Dean of Academic Success .... Dr. Charles J. CUNNING
106 Dean of Extended Campus Program .... Dr. Mark A. REGER
04 Administrative Asst to President .... Mrs. Nani Lou S. COOPER
56 Dir Extended Campus Classroom Pgm ... Mrs. Patricia L. SOKOLS
06 Registrar .... Ms. Pennie D. HUGHES
37 Director Financial Aid .... Mr. Bobby T. GREER
44 Director of Development .... Ms. Tisha L. POTEAT
08 Director Library .... Ms. Lizah ISMAIL
26 Director Communications .... Mr. Eric L. LAWSON
35 Director Student Services .... Ms. Jessica D. GOINS
36 Director Career Services .... Ms. Ileka L. LEAKS
90 Director Network Services .... Dr. Scott D. BERRY
18 Director Physical Plant .... Mr. R. Lynn LAWHON
09 Dir Institutional Rsrch/Effective .... Mr. Franklin L. MITCHELL
92 Director Academic Honors Program ...... Dr. Thomas J. THOMSON
83 Assoc Dean/Director Social Work .... Mr. Jackie A. PUCKETT
19 Chief of Public Safety .... Mr. Richard E. SIMMONS
21 Controller .... Mr. L. Wayde DAWSON
23 Campus Nurse .... Mrs. Sandy B. GREEN
44 Director Advancement Services .... Mrs. Brandi P. HARTMAN
20 Director of Academic Advising .... Ms. Pennie D. HUGHES
29 Director Alumni/Parent Programs ..... Mr. Kristopher C. BARNHILL
88 Dir Christian Ed/Leadership Program ...... Rev. J. Ron SINGLETON
88 Director of Food Services .... Mr. Joe FIELDS
88 Director of Sports Information .... Mr. Joshua J. DARLING
42 College Chaplain .... Rev. J. Ron SINGLETON
88 Dir Accessibility Services/PALS .... Ms. Tina E. VIRES
15 Dir Human Resources/AAEEO Officer ...... Ms. Brenda F. WATKINS
50 Director of MBA Program .... Mr. Brandon J. GIBSON
88 Sr Assoc Athletics Dir Compliance .... Mr. Dennis L. BLOOMER
88 Asst Athletics Dir for Media Rels .... Mr. Ernest G. MEYERS
88 Asst Athletics Dir Sports Perform .... Mr. Curtis S. LAMB
88 Assc Dir Extend Campus Internet Pgm .... Mrs. Katie P. JONES
88 Director Extended Internet Program .. Ms. Diana L. BEDENBAUGH
88 Assoc Business Manager .... Mr. Franklin L. MITCHELL
40 Campus Store Manager .... Mrs. Patti H. MCCRAW
38 College Counselor .... Mrs. Mary B. CAMPBELL
107 Chair Div of Professional Studies .... Dr. Paul R. LEFRANCOIS
88 Chair Div of Natural Sciences .... Mr. Brian F. AMELING
49 Chair Div of Arts & Letters .... Dr. Gena E. POOVEY
83 Chair Div Social & Behav Sciences .... Dr. Betsy A. WITT
53 Chair Div Educ/Phys Ed/Teacher Educ .... Dr. Shelly A. MEYERS

Lutheran Theological Southern Seminary of Lenoir-Rhyne University (A)

4201 N Main Street, Columbia SC 29203-5898

County: Richland | FICE Identification: 003437 | Unit ID: 218265

Telephone: (803) 786-5150 | Carnegie Class: Spec/Faith

FAX Number: (803) 786-6499 | Calendar System: Semester

URL: ltss.lr.edu

Established: 1830 | Annual Graduate Tuition & Fees: $15,347

Enrollment: 110 | Coed

Affiliation or Control: Evangelical Lutheran Church In America | IRS Status: 501(c)3

Highest Offering: Master's; No Undergraduates

Program: Professional; Religious Emphasis

Accreditation: THEOL

01 Provost .... Rev Dr. Clayton J. SCHMIT
05 Associate Dean .... Rev Dr. Virginia C. BARFIELD
10 Dir of Administration and Finance .... Mr. Andrew D. SMITH
30 Director of Development .... Mr. Ron WALRATH
84 Director Enrollment/Communications .... Mr. Andrew BOOZER
88 Asst Director Enrollment Services .... Ms. Jenn CASEY

Medical University of South Carolina (B)

179 Ashley Avenue, Charleston SC 29425

County: Charleston | FICE Identification: 003438 | Unit ID: 218335

Telephone: (843) 792-2300 | Carnegie Class: Spec/Med

FAX Number: N/A | Calendar System: Semester

URL: www.musc.edu

Established: 1824 | Annual Undergrad Tuition & Fees (In-State): $14,750

Enrollment: 2,731 | Coed

Affiliation or Control: State | IRS Status: Exempt

Highest Offering: Doctorate

Program: Professional

Accreditation: SC, ANEST, ARCPA, DENT, DIETI, HSA, HT, IPSY, MED, NURSE, OT, PERF, PHAR, PTA

01 Interim President .... Dr. Mark S. SOTHMANN
100 Chief of Staff .... Dr. Sabra C. SLAUGHTER
05 VP Academic Affairs & Provost .... Dr. Mark S. SOTHMANN
17 Vice Pres & Dean Col of Medicine .... Dr. Etta D. PISANO
10 Exec Vice President Finance & Admin .... Ms. Lisa P. MONTGOMERY
30 Vice President Development .... Mr. William J. FISHER
17 VP Clinical Opers/CEO Medical Ctr .... Mr. W. Stuart SMITH
13 VP Information Technology/CIO .... Dr. Frank C. CLARK
20 Assoc Prov Education/Student Life .... Dr. Darlene L. SHAW
46 Associate Provost Research .... Dr. Stephen M. LANIER
52 Dean of Dental Medicine .... Dr. John J. SANDERS
76 Interim Dean of Health Professions .... Dr. Lisa SALADIN
58 Dean of Graduate Studies .... Dr. Perry V. HALUSHKA
66 Dean of Nursing .... Dr. Gail W. STUART
67 Exec Dean SC College of Pharmacy .... Dr. Joseph T. DIPIRO
67 Int Campus Dean SC Col of Pharmacy .... Dr. Philip D. HALL
88 Exec Dir SC Area Hlth Ed Consortium .... Dr. David R. GARR
08 Director of Libraries .... Dr. Thomas G. BASLER
84 Director Enrollment Management .... Mr. George W. OHLANDT
28 Exec Director Student Programs .... Dr. Willette S. BURNHAM
43 General Counsel .... Mr. Joseph C. GOOD
26 Director Public Relations .... Dr. Sarah KING
22 Dir Affirm Act/Equal Opportunity ...... Mr. Wallace T. BONAPARTE
07 Director of Admissions .... Ms. Lyla HUDSON
18 Chief Facilities/Physical Plant .... Mr. John MALMROSE
06 Registrar .... Ms. Sandra L. MORRIS
15 Director Personnel Services .... Ms. Susan H. CARULLO
38 Director Student Counseling .... Dr. Alice Q. LIBET
29 Director Alumni Affairs .... Ms. Jean M. GROOMS
37 Director Student Financial Aid .... Dr. Cecile E. KAMATH
96 Director of Purchasing .... Ms. Betty SANDIFER

Midlands Technical College (C)

PO Box 2408, Columbia SC 29202-2408

County: Richland | FICE Identification: 003993 | Unit ID: 218353

Telephone: (803) 738-8324 | Carnegie Class: Assoc/Pub-U-MC

FAX Number: (803) 738-7784 | Calendar System: Semester

URL: www.midlandstech.edu

Established: 1974 | Annual Undergrad Tuition & Fees (In-District): $5,757

Enrollment: 11,949 | Coed

Affiliation or Control: State/Local | IRS Status: 501(c)3

Highest Offering: Associate Degree

Program: Occupational; 2-Year Principally Bachelor's Creditable

Accreditation: SC, ACBSP, ADNUR, CAHIIM, COARC, DA, DH, ENGT, MAC, MLTAD, NMT, PNUR, PTAA, RAD, SURGT

01 President .... Dr. Marshall Sonny WHITE, JR.
04 Exec Assistant to the President .... Ms. Deborah TIRADO
05 Vice President Academic Affairs .... Dr. Ronald DRAYTON
10 Sr Vice Pres .... Dr. Ronald RHAMES
49 Assoc Vice Pres Arts & Sciences .... Dr. Diane CARR
32 Vice Pres Student Development Svcs .... Ms. Sandi OLIVER
30 VP for Institutional Support .... Ms. Starnell BATES
51 VP Economic Devel & Continuing Educ .... Dr. Barrie KIRK
21 Assoc Vice Pres for Business Affs .... Ms. Debbie WALKER
88 AVP SDS: Trio Cmty Support Pgms .... Ms. Mary HOLLOWAY
43 General Counsel .... Ms. Crystal ROOKARD
06 Registrar .... Ms. Susan HOUCK
13 Director Information Resource Mgmt .... Mr. Tony HOUGH
25 Director of Resource Development .... Ms. Alice APPLEBY
37 Director of Student Financial Aid .... Mrs. Angela WILLIAMS
08 Interim Director of Library .... Ms. Florence MAYES
09 Dir Assessment/Research/Planning ...... Ms. Dorcas A. KITCHINGS
18 Director of Operations .... Mr. Craig E. HESS
35 Director of Campus Life .... Mr. Hart HAYDEN
31 Director of Auxiliary Services .... Mr. Stanley BOLTON
38 Director of Counseling .... Mr. Phil MORRIS
50 Dept Chair of Business Department .... Vacant
54 Dept Chair of Engineering Tech .... Dr. Clint CHANDLER
76 Director of Health Science Dept .... Ms. Martha HANKS
84 Director of Enrollment Services .... Ms. Sylvia LITTLEJOHN
27 Director of Public Affairs .... Mr. Todd GAVIN
44 Director of Development .... Mr. Tim NELSON
36 Director Student Employment Service .... Ms. Sarah TRICE
96 Procurement Manager .... Ms. Rochelle DANIELS
14 Manager Tech Support .... Mr. Carl CARRAWAY
15 Human Resourse Director .... Mrs. Mary Beth LAMPE
07 Director of Admissions .... Mr. Derrah CASSIDY

Miller-Motte Technical College (D)

2451 Highway 501 East, Conway SC 29526

Telephone: (843) 591-1101 | Identification: 770778

Accreditation: ACICS

† Main campus is Miller-Motte Technical College in Lynchburg, VA.

Miller-Motte Technical College (E)

8085 Rivers Avenue, Suite E, North Charleston SC 29406

Telephone: (843) 574-0101 | Identification: 666256

Accreditation: ACICS, MAC, SURGT

† Main campus is Miller-Motte Technical College in Clarksville, TN.

Morris College (F)

100 W College Street, Sumter SC 29150-3599

County: Sumter | FICE Identification: 003439 | Unit ID: 218399

Telephone: (803) 934-3200 | Carnegie Class: Bac/Diverse

FAX Number: (803) 773-3687 | Calendar System: Semester

URL: www.morris.edu

Established: 1908 | Annual Undergrad Tuition & Fees: $11,087

Enrollment: 874 | Coed

Affiliation or Control: Baptist | IRS Status: 501(c)3

Highest Offering: Baccalaureate

Program: Liberal Arts And General; Teacher Preparatory

Accreditation: SC, ACBSP, TED

01 President .... Dr. Luns C. RICHARDSON
05 Academic Dean .... Dr. Leroy STAGGERS
10 Director of Business Affairs .... Mr. Robert EAVES
86 Director Planning/Govt Relations .... Mrs. Dorothy S. CHEAGLE
32 Interim Dean Student Affairs .... Rev. Eliza E. BLACK
15 Personnel Officer .... Mr. Roy GRAHAM
42 College Minister .... Dr. Charles M. PEE
07 Director Admissions & Records .... Ms. Deborah C. CALHOUN
08 Director Learning Resources Ctr .... Mrs. Janet S. CLAYTON
37 Director of Financial Aid .... Mrs. Sandra S. GIBSON
13 Director MIS/Computer Center .... Mr. Rodney JOHNSON
36 Director Career Services Center .... Ms. Margaret A. BAILEY
108 Director of Assessment .... Dr. Lewis P. GRAHAM, JR.
29 Alumni Affairs Officer .... Mrs. Altoya A. FELDER-DEAS
38 Director Counseling & Testing Ctr .... Dr. Juana L. DAVIS-FREEMAN
39 Director Residential Life .... Mrs. Venessa F. JEFFERSON
23 Director of Health Services .... Mrs. Johnell ROGERS
41 Director of Athletics .... Mr. Clarence M. HOUCK
26 Director Public Relations .... Ms. Vicky L. SUTTON-JACKSON
30 Director Inst Advanc/Church Rels .... Rev. Melvin MACK
96 Director of Purchasing .... Mr. Robert EAVES
89 Acting Director of Freshmen Studies .... Mr. Robert ZALIMAS
92 Director of Honors Program .... Dr. Joseph K. POPOOLA
06 Registrar .... Ms. Deborah C. CALHOUN
18 Chief Facilities/Physical Plant .... Mr. Roy GRAHAM
20 Associate Academic Officer .... Dr. Kay M. RHOADS
21 Associate Business Officer .... Vacant
40 Bookstore Manager .... Ms. Jeanette MOSES-HOLMES
35 Coordinator Student Activities .... Mr. Alston FREEMAN
19 Coordinator Campus Safety Services .... Ms. Lucille W. WILLIAMS

Newberry College (G)

2100 College, Newberry SC 29108-2126

County: Newberry | FICE Identification: 003440 | Unit ID: 218414

Telephone: (800) 845-4955 | Carnegie Class: Bac/Diverse

FAX Number: (803) 321-5627 | Calendar System: Semester

URL: www.newberry.edu

Established: 1856 | Annual Undergrad Tuition & Fees: $23,800

Enrollment: 1,029 | Coed

Affiliation or Control: Evangelical Lutheran Church In America | IRS Status: 501(c)3

Highest Offering: Baccalaureate

Program: Liberal Arts And General; Teacher Preparatory

Accreditation: SC, MUS, NURSE, TED

01 President .... Dr. Maurice W. SCHERRENS
05 VP Academic Affairs & Dean .... Dr. Timothy G. ELSTON
10 CFO & Exec VP for Admin Affs .... Ms. Kathy WORSTER
30 VP for Institutional Advancement .... Mr. Scott JOYNER
84 Acting Dir of Enroll Management .... Ms. Delsie PHILLIPS
32 Dean of Students .... Dr. Kay BANKS
41 Director of Athletics .... Mr. Matt FINLEY
15 Director of Human Resources .... Mrs. Peggy SHULER
09 Exec Dir of Inst Effectiveness ...... Dr. Don W. JOHNSON-TAYLOR
06 Registrar .... Mrs. Carol A. BICKLEY
29 Assoc Dir of Alumni Relations .... Mr. Jeff WICKER
08 Librarian .... Ms. Nancy ROSENWALD
18 Director of Facilities .... Mr. Fred ERRIGO
26 Director of Public Relations .... Ms. Sharon LACKEY
42 Chaplain .... Rev. Ernie WORMAN
21 Director of Accounting .... Mrs. Landee BUZHARDT
38 Director of Wellness Services .... Mrs. Martha DORRELL
37 Director Student Financial Aid .... Mrs. Danielle BELL

North Greenville University (H)

PO Box 1892, Tigerville SC 29688-1892

County: Greenville | FICE Identification: 003441 | Unit ID: 218441

Telephone: (864) 977-7000 | Carnegie Class: Bac/Diverse

FAX Number: (864) 977-7021 | Calendar System: Semester

URL: www.ngu.edu

Established: 1892 | Annual Undergrad Tuition & Fees: $14,772

Enrollment: 2,428 | Coed

Affiliation or Control: Southern Baptist | IRS Status: 501(c)3

Highest Offering: Doctorate

Program: Liberal Arts And General; Religious Emphasis

Accreditation: SC, MUS, TED

01 President/CEO .... Dr. James B. EPTING
04 Admin Assistant for President .... Ms. Elise STYLES
05 Vice President Academics .... Dr. Randall PANNELL
32 Vice President Student Services .... Dr. Tony BEAM
58 Vice Pres/Dean Graduate Studies .... Dr. J. Samuel ISGETT
10 Vice President Business Affairs .... Ms. Michelle L. SABOU
07 VP Admissions/Financial Planning .... Ms. Keli SEWELL
30 Vice President Advancement .... Mr. Alex MILLER
88 Vice Pres Denominational Relations .... Rev. Mayson EASTERLING
42 Vice President Campus Ministries .... Dr. Steve CROUSE
44 VP Crusader Club/Corp Found Giving ... Mr. J. Wayne LANDRITH
35 Director Student Services .... Mr. Billy WATSON
09 Director of Institutional Research .... Dr. George A. HOPSON
06 Registrar .... Ms. Pam FARMER
18 Director of College Properties .... Mr. Larry BARNWELL
41 Athletic Director .... Ms. Jan MCDONALD
34 Director Residential Living Women .... Ms. Lorry GREEN
33 Director Residential Living Men .... Mr. Donald LILLY
08 Director Learning Center .... Ms. Carla MCMAHAN
19 Director Public Safety .... Mr. Rick MORRIS
88 Dean of Graduate Enrollment .... Mrs. Tawana SCOTT
26 Director Public Rels/Stewardship .... Mr. LaVerne B. HOWELL

29 Director Alumni Affairs/Annual Fund ... Mr. Jason ROSS
15 Human Resource Manager ... Mrs. Lindi FOWLER
40 Bookstore Manager ... Mrs. Cindy COWAN
38 Personal Counselor ... Dr. Bill MCMANUS
36 Career Services Coordinator ... Ms. Lisa SNYDER
23 Director Health Services ... Ms. Kathy BAILEY
30 Executive Director Development ... Rev. Joe F. HAYES
14 Director Computer Services ... Mr. Paul GARRETT
37 Financial Aid Director ... Mr. Michael JORDAN
53 Dean Education ... Dr. Constance WRIGHT
79 Dean Humanities ... Dr. Cathy SEPKO
57 Dean Fine Arts ... Dr. Jacquelyn H. GRIFFIN
81 Dean Sciences ... Dr. Tom ALLEN
73 Dean Christian Studies ... Dr. Walter JOHNSON
50 Dean Business ... Dr. Ralph JOHNSON

Northeastern Technical College (A)

1201 Chesterfield Hwy, Cheraw SC 29520
County: Chesterfield FICE Identification: 007602
Unit ID: 217837
Telephone: (843) 921-6900 Carnegie Class: Assoc/Pub-R-S
FAX Number: (843) 537-6148 Calendar System: Semester
URL: www.netc.edu
Established: 1969 Annual Undergrad Tuition & Fees (In-State): $6,390
Enrollment: 1,134 Coed
Affiliation or Control: State IRS Status: 501(c)3
Highest Offering: Associate Degree
Program: Occupational; 2-Year Principally Bachelor's Creditable
Accreditation: SC

01 President ... Dr. Ron BARTLEY
05 Vice Pres Instruction/Student Svcs ... Dr. Forest MAHAN
10 Vice Pres Administration & Finance ... Mrs. Debbie Q. CHEEK
30 Director for Inst Advancement ... Vacant
15 Director for Human Resources ... Mrs. Donna CHAVIS

Orangeburg-Calhoun Technical College (B)

3250 Saint Matthews Road, Orangeburg SC 29118-8299
County: Orangeburg FICE Identification: 006815
Unit ID: 218487
Telephone: (803) 536-0311 Carnegie Class: Assoc/Pub-R-M
FAX Number: (803) 535-1388 Calendar System: Semester
URL: www.octech.edu
Established: 1966 Annual Undergrad Tuition & Fees (In-State): $3,770
Enrollment: 3,052 Coed
Affiliation or Control: State IRS Status: 501(c)3
Highest Offering: Associate Degree
Program: Occupational; 2-Year Principally Bachelor's Creditable
Accreditation: SC, ACBSP, ADNUR, COARC, ENGT, MAC, PNUR, RAD

01 President ... Dr. Walt TOBIN, JR.
05 Vice Pres Academic Affairs ... Mrs. Donna ELMORE
10 Vice President Business Affairs ... Mr. Kim HUFF
32 Vice President of Student Services ... Mrs. Sandra S. DAVIS
11 Assoc VP of Administration ... Mr. Mike HAMMOND
36 Assoc VP Corp Trng/Econ Develop ... Mrs. Sandra MOORE
21 Assoc Vice Pres of Business Affairs ... Mr. Kim R. HUFF
46 Dean Planning/Research/Development ... Ms. Faith MCCURRY
13 Director Information Technology ... Mr. Gary A. FOLEY
62 Dean Learning Resource Center ... Mrs. Harris MURRAY
18 Chief Facilities/Physical Plant ... Mr. James S. BRYANT, III
37 Director Student Financial Aid ... Mr. Chris DOOLEY
08 Director Library Services ... Mrs. Harris MURRAY
07 Director of Recruiting ... Ms. Semetta QUICK
19 Chief of Safety/Security ... Mr. Douglas STOKES
09 Dir Acad Spprt/Institutional Effect ... Mr. Cleveland WILSON
15 Human Resource Director ... Ms. Marie HOWELL
96 Procurement Manager ... Mrs. Scarlet GEDDINGS

Piedmont Technical College (C)

620 N. Emerald Road, Greenwood SC 29646
County: Greenwood FICE Identification: 003992
Unit ID: 218520
Telephone: (864) 941-8324 Carnegie Class: Assoc/Pub-R-M
FAX Number: (864) 941-8555 Calendar System: Semester
URL: www.ptc.edu
Established: 1966 Annual Undergrad Tuition & Fees (In-District): $3,664
Enrollment: 6,541 Coed
Affiliation or Control: State/Local IRS Status: 501(c)3
Highest Offering: Associate Degree
Program: Occupational; 2-Year Principally Bachelor's Creditable
Accreditation: SC, ADNUR, COARC, CVT, ENGT, FUSER, MAC, RAD, SURGT

01 President ... Dr. L. Rayburn BROOKS
10 Vice Pres Business & Finance ... Ms. Paige K. CHILDS
05 Vice President Educational Affairs ... Dr. Susan G. TIMMONS
32 Vice Pres Student Development ... Ms. Becky R. MCINTOSH
51 Assoc Vice Pres Cont Educ/Econ Dev ... Mr. Rusty DENNING
24 Assoc VP Instructional Technology ... Dr. Joel GRIFFIN
108 Assoc VP Institutional Assessment ... Ms. Donna FOSTER
84 Dean of Enrollment Mgmt ... Ms. Tanisha LATIMER
12 Dean County Centers ... Dr. Jennifer WILBANKS
76 Dean Health Sciences ... Mr. Jerry ALEWINE
54 Dean Engr/Industrial Technologies ... Mr. Keith LASURE
66 Dean Nursing Education ... Ms. Rosalie STEVENSON
35 Dean Student Services ... Mr. J. Andrew OMUNDSON
09 Director of Inst Effectiveness ... Ms. Zeolean F. KINARD

26 Director Marketing/Public Relations ... Mr. Joshua BLACK
88 Director College Outreach ... Mr. Steve B. COLEMAN
18 Director Facilities/Management ... Mr. S. Dale WILSON
102 Foundation Exec Dir/Alumni Affairs ... Ms. Fran K. WILEY
08 Librarian ... Mr. Daniel MEREDITH
19 Director Public Safety ... Mr. Torry LEDFORD
36 Assoc Dean Student Services ... Mr. David R. ROSENBAUM
37 Director of Financial Aid ... Ms. Missy PERRY
06 Registrar ... Ms. Tamatha SELLS
21 Controller ... Ms. Paige CHILDS
15 Human Resource Manager ... Ms. Debbie THARPE
21 Manager Business Office ... Ms. Crystal PITTMAN

Presbyterian College (D)

503 S Broad Street, Clinton SC 29325-2865
County: Laurens FICE Identification: 003445
Unit ID: 218539
Telephone: (864) 833-2820 Carnegie Class: Bac/A&S
FAX Number: (864) 833-8481 Calendar System: Semester
URL: www.presby.edu
Established: 1880 Annual Undergrad Tuition & Fees: $33,650
Enrollment: 1,382 Coed
Affiliation or Control: Presbyterian Church (U.S.A.) IRS Status: 501(c)3
Highest Offering: Doctorate
Program: Liberal Arts And General; Teacher Preparatory; Professional
Accreditation: SC, MUS, @PHAR, TED

01 President ... Dr. Claude C. LILLY
04 Executive Asst to the President ... Ms. Christie L. MUELLER
05 Provost ... Dr. Donald R. RABER, II
84 VP of Enrollment/Communications ... Ms. Deborah J. THOMPSON
10 VP Finance/Administration ... Mrs. Susan A. MADDUX
30 Vice President for Advancement ... Ms. Elizabeth G. BRAXTON
15 VP of Human Resources ... Ms. Barbara H. FAYAD
32 VP for Campus Life ... Dr. Joy S. SMITH
41 Director of Athletics ... Mr. Brian P. REESE
42 Dean of Religious Life ... Dr. Jeri Parris PERKINS
67 Dean School of Pharmacy ... Dr. L. Clifton FUHRMAN, JR.
21 Controller ... Mrs. Dawn W. DURHAM
35 Dean of Community Life ... Mrs. Leni N. PATTERSON
06 Registrar ... Mr. W. Keith KARRIKER
13 Dir Information Technology ... Vacant
08 Director of Thomason Library ... Mr. David W. CHATHAM
09 Director of Institutional Research ... Dr. Norman B. BRYAN, JR.
29 Director Alumni Relations ... Vacant
30 Dir of Grants/Pharmacy Fundraising ... Ms. M. Genevra KELLY
18 Exec Director Business Operations ... Mr. L. David WALKER
19 Director of Campus Police ... Mr. Lawrence P. MULHALL
37 Director of Financial Aid ... Mrs. Rebecca D. PRESSLEY
38 Director Counseling Services ... Mrs. Susan C. GENTRY-WRIGHT

Professional Golfers Career College (E)

4454 Bluffton Pk Crescent, Ste 200, Bluffton SC 29910
Telephone: (843) 759-9611 Identification: 770779
Accreditation: ACICS

† Main campus is Professional Golfers Career College in Temecula, CA.

Sherman College of Chiropractic (F)

PO Box 1452, Spartanburg SC 29304-1452
County: Spartanburg FICE Identification: 020637
Unit ID: 218751
Telephone: (864) 578-8770 Carnegie Class: Spec/Health
FAX Number: (864) 599-4860 Calendar System: Quarter
URL: www.sherman.edu
Established: 1973 Annual Graduate Tuition & Fees: $27,752
Enrollment: 237 Coed
Affiliation or Control: Independent Non-Profit IRS Status: 501(c)3
Highest Offering: Doctorate; No Undergraduates
Program: Professional; Technical Emphasis
Accreditation: SC, CHIRO

01 President ... Dr. Edwin CORDERO
05 Vice Pres for Academic Affairs ... Dr. Robert IRWIN
84 Vice Pres for Enrollment Services ... Mrs. Kelley ASHCRAFT
10 Vice Pres for Business & Finance ... Mrs. Karen CANUP
32 Dean of Student Affairs ... Mrs. LaShanda HUTTO-HARRIS
29 Dir Alumni Rels/Instl Advancement ... Ms. Marggi ROLDAN
06 Registrar ... Ms. Melody SABIN
08 Librarian ... Mrs. Crissy LEWIS
37 Director of Financial Aid ... Mrs. Kathy WILSON
45 Dir Institutional Effectiveness ... Mrs. Crissy LEWIS

South Carolina State University (G)

300 College Street, NE, Orangeburg SC 29117-0001
County: Orangeburg FICE Identification: 003446
Unit ID: 218733
Telephone: (803) 536-7000 Carnegie Class: DRU
FAX Number: (803) 533-3622 Calendar System: Semester
URL: www.scsu.edu
Established: 1896 Annual Undergrad Tuition & Fees (In-State): $9,258
Enrollment: 3,807 Coed
Affiliation or Control: State IRS Status: 501(c)3
Highest Offering: Doctorate
Program: Liberal Arts And General; Teacher Preparatory; Professional; Business Emphasis
Accreditation: SC, AAFCS, ART, BUS, CACREP, CORE, CS, DIETD, ENG, ENGT, MUS, NURSE, SP, SW, TED

01 President ... Mr. Thomas J. ELZEY
04 Exec Asst to the President ... Mrs. Shondra N. ABRAHAM
05 Vice President Academic Affairs ... Dr. W. Franklin EVANS
10 Asst Vice Pres Business/Finance ... Mr. Eric R. EATON
32 Asst Vice President Student Affairs ... Dr. Tamara J. HUGHES
30 Vice Pres Inst Advancement ... Vacant
46 Acting VP Research/EconDevel ... Mr. Delbert T. FOSTER
43 Gen Counsel ... Mr. Craig E. BURGESS
20 Int Assoc Vice Pres Academic Affs ... Dr. M. Evelyn FIELDS
20 Int Assoc Vice Pres Academic Affs ... Dr. Learie B. LUKE
26 VP External Affairs/Communications ... Ms. Sonja A. BENNETT
84 VP Enrollment Management ... Vacant
46 Int Asst VP Sponsored Programs ... Mr. Elbert R. MALONE
72 Dean Col Sci/Math/Engineering Tech . Dr. Stanley N. IHEKWEAZU
53 Dean Col Educ/Humanities/Soc Sci ... Dr. Leonard A. MCINTYRE
58 Int Dean School of Graduate Studies ... Dr. Frederick M G. EVANS
50 Dean Col Business/Applied Prof Sci ... Dr. Robert T. BARRETT
08 Dean Library & Information Services ... Ms. Mary L. SMALLS
09 Exec Dir Institutional Effectivenes ... Dr. Rita J. TEAL
88 Asst Exec Dir Stdnt Success Retent ... Mr. Terrence M. CUMMINGS
06 Registrar ... Mrs. Annie R. BELTON
07 Director Admissions/Recruitment ... Mr. Antonio BOYLE
13 Dir Univ Computing/Info Tech Svcs ... Dr. James L. MYERS
37 Director Financial Aid to Students ... Mrs. Sandra DAVIS
38 Director Counsel/Hlth/Psycmtrc Svcs ... Dr. Cherilyn Y. TAYLOR
21 Controller ... Mr. Ernie M. TORRES
09 Director Institutional Research ... Ms. Betty R. BOATWRIGHT
26 Director Univ Relations & Mktg ... Ms. Erica PRIOLEAU-TAYLOR
36 Int Director of Career Placement ... Mr. Joseph THOMAS
15 Director Human Resource Mgmt ... Ms. Anna D. HAIGLER
41 Director Athletics ... Mrs. Charlene M. JOHNSON
18 Director of Facilities Mgmt ... Mr. Charles ALEXANDER
96 Director Procurement Services ... Mrs. Mary L. SIMS
39 Asst Director of Residential Life ... Ms. Jennifer TOWNSEND-GAMBLE
19 Chief of Campus Police ... Mr. Gregory HARRIS
92 Dir Honors Exchange/intl Program ... Dr. Harriet A. ROLAND
88 Director Sports Information ... Mr. William P. HAMILTON
35 Director of Student Life ... Mr. Terrance ALDRIDGE
88 Int Director of Internal Audit ... Mr. Kelvin WASHINGTON
25 Dir Grants & Contract Accounting ... Ms. Mildred L. DANIELS
88 Director of Title III ... Ms. Gloria D. PYLES
88 Director of Staff Development ... Ms. Patricia GIBSON-HAIGLER
28 Director of Multicultural Affairs ... Ms. Carolyn G. FREE
88 Asst Dir Educational Technology Svc ... Dr. Frederick M. EVANS
88 Station Manager WSSB-FM ... Mr. Milton E. MCKISSICK
88 Athletics Compliance Coordinator ... Mr. Robert CHATMAN

South University Columbia Campus (H)

9 Science Court, Columbia SC 29203-6400
Telephone: (803) 799-9082 FICE Identification: 004922
Accreditation: &SC, MAC, NURSE, PHAR

† Main campus is South University in Savannah, GA.

Southern Wesleyan University (I)

907 Wesleyan Drive, PO Box 1020,
Central SC 29630-1020
County: Pickens FICE Identification: 003422
Unit ID: 217776
Telephone: (864) 644-5000 Carnegie Class: Master's L
FAX Number: (864) 644-5900 Calendar System: Semester
URL: www.swu.edu
Established: 1906 Annual Undergrad Tuition & Fees: $21,600
Enrollment: 1,710 Coed
Affiliation or Control: Wesleyan Church IRS Status: 501(c)3
Highest Offering: Master's
Program: Liberal Arts And General; Teacher Preparatory; Professional
Accreditation: SC, MUS, TED

01 President ... Dr. Todd S. VOSS
04 Admin Assistant to the President ... Mrs. Andrea PILGRIM
10 Sr VP for Finance & Treasurer ... Mr. Marshall L. ATCHESON
37 Assoc VP of Student Financial Svcs ... Mr. Jeff DENNIS
13 Director Information Technology ... Mr. Mike PREUSZ
37 Director of Financial Aid ... Mrs. Melanie GILLESPIE
18 Director of Physical Plant ... Mr. Jonathan CATRON
40 Bookstore Manager ... Mrs. Darlene STANCIL
05 Provost ... Dr. Keith IDDINGS
09 Assoc VP for Planning & Assessment ... Dr. Daryl D. COUCH
20 AVP for Curriculum & Instruction ... Dr. Laurie HILLSTOCK
06 Registrar ... Mr. Rock MCCASKILL
08 Director of Library Services ... Mr. Robert E. SEARS
84 VP for Enrollment Management ... Mr. Chad PETERS
07 Dir of Admissions & Enrollment Mgmt ... Mrs. Amanda YOUNG
32 Vice President for Student Life ... Dr. W. Joseph BROCKINTON
42 AVP Spiritual Life/Univ Chaplain ... Rev. Ken DILL
35 Assoc Vice Pres for Student Life ... Dr. Justin CARTER
41 Athletic Director ... Mr. Chris WILLIAMS
38 Director of Counseling & Health Svc ... Ms. Monica PEREZ
30 Vice President for Development ... Dr. Lisa MCWHERTER
29 Exec Dir of Alumni/Constituent Rels ... Mrs. Joy L. BRYANT
49 Dean College of Arts & Sciences ... Dr. Walt SINNAMON
57 Chair Fine Arts ... Mrs. Jane P. DILL
73 Chair Religion ... Dr. Mari GONLAG
79 Chair Humanities ... Dr. Ken MYERS
83 Chair Social Sciences ... Dr. Chris ACCORNERO
50 Dean School of Business ... Dr. Jeannie TRUDEL
53 Dean of School of Education ... Dr. Sandra MCLENDON
16 Director of Human Resources ... Mrs. Dana L. FROST

Spartanburg Community College (A)

PO Box 4386, Spartanburg SC 29305-4386

County: Spartanburg | FICE Identification: 003994
Unit ID: 218830
Telephone: (864) 592-4600 | Carnegie Class: Assoc/Pub-U-SC
FAX Number: (864) 592-4642 | Calendar System: Semester
URL: www.sccsc.edu
Established: 1963 | Annual Undergrad Tuition & Fees (In-State): $3,820
Enrollment: 6,036 | Coed
Affiliation or Control: State | IRS Status: 501(c)3
Highest Offering: Associate Degree
Program: Occupational; 2-Year Principally Bachelor's Creditable
Accreditation: SC, ACBSP, ACFEI, ADNUR, COARC, DA, ENGT, MAC, MLTAD, RAD, SURGT

01 President ... Mr. Henry C. GILES, JR.
03 Executive Vice President ... Mr. Henry C. GILES, JR.
05 Sr Vice President Academic Affairs ... Dr. Cheryl COX
10 Vice Pres for Business Affairs ... Mr. Ray SWITZER
45 Vice President for Planning & Info ... Vacant
32 Vice President for Student Affairs ... Mr. Ron JACKSON
12 Asc Vice Pres Enroll Mgt/Retention ... Mrs. Lynn F. DALE
20 Assoc Vice Pres of Instruction ... Dr. Keith POMAKOY
51 Exec Asst to Pres/Dir Economic Dev . Mr. Michael P. FORRESTER
12 Executive Director Cherokee Campus ... Mr. Daryl SMITH
102 Exec Dir Advancement/SCC Foundation ... Mr. Samuel S. HOOK
08 Dean of Learning Resources ... Mr. Mark ROSEVEARE
46 Dean of Assessment/Cont Improvement ... Vacant
76 Dean Health & Human Services ... Dr. Rita A. MELTON
15 Director of Human Resources ... Mr. Rick TEAL
13 Director Information Technologies ... Mr. Peter C. GALLEN
84 Int Director Enrollment Services ... Ms. Lynn F. DALE
09 Director of Institutional Research ... Mr. Jack R. BOURGEOIS
26 Chief Public Relations Officer ... Mrs. Cheri A. HUCKS
29 Director Alumni Relations ... Vacant
38 Director Student Counseling ... Mrs. Phyllis ROGERS
14 Director Computer Center ... Mrs. Tina S. REID
19 Director Security/Safety ... Mr. Andre KERR
96 Director of Procurement ... Vacant
06 Registrar ... Ms. Celia N. BAUSS
21 Business Manager ... Mr. Cecil L. HUTCHERSON
37 Director of Financial Aid ... Mrs. Nancy T. GARMROTH

Spartanburg Methodist College (B)

1000 Powell Mill Road, Spartanburg SC 29301-5899

County: Spartanburg | FICE Identification: 003447
Unit ID: 218821
Telephone: (864) 587-4000 | Carnegie Class: Assoc/PrivNFP
FAX Number: (864) 587-4355 | Calendar System: Semester
URL: www.smcsc.edu
Established: 1911 | Annual Undergrad Tuition & Fees: $16,205
Enrollment: 803 | Coed
Affiliation or Control: United Methodist | IRS Status: 501(c)3
Highest Offering: Associate Degree
Program: 2-Year Principally Bachelor's Creditable
Accreditation: SC

01 President ... Dr. Colleen P. KEITH
05 Vice President for Academic Affairs ... Dr. Anita K. BOWLES
10 Vice President for Business Affairs ... Mr. Eric MCDONALD
84 Vice Pres for Enrollment Management ... Mr. Daniel L. PHILBECK
30 Vice President for Inst Advancement ... Mr. Bob FUZY
32 Dean of Students ... Mr. Ron LAFFITTE
06 Registrar ... Ms. Jill R. JOHNSON
08 Librarian ... Mrs. Erin WASHINGTON
04 Admin Assistant to the President ... Ms. Vicki D. KENNEDY
20 Exec Dir of Academic Services ... Vacant
14 Exec Dir Info Tech/Campus Svcs ... Mr. Bill ROACH
27 Dir Public Information/Webmaster ... Mrs. Yvonne HARPER
44 Director of Development ... Mr. Don TATE
37 Director of Financial Aid ... Ms. Kendra BURNETTE
38 Director of Student Counseling ... Mr. Pete AYLOR
42 Chaplain/Director of Church Rels ... Rev. Candice Y. SLOAN
41 Athletic Director ... Mr. Tim WALLACE
18 Director Facilities Mgmt/Purchasing ... Mr. Rick JOLLEY
29 Director Alumni Relations ... Mrs. Leah L. PRUITT
15 Dir of Human Resources/College Acct ... Mrs. Jeanette R. DUNN
35 Director of Student Support Svcs ... Ms. Sharon PORTER
44 Director Gift Planning ... Rev. Michael E. BOWERS
19 Chief of Campus Safety ... Ms. Teresa D. FERGUSON
07 Director of Admissions ... Mr. Michael QUEEN
09 Director of Assessment Activities ... Mr. Robert W. ISENHOWER

Technical College of the Lowcountry (C)

921 S Ribaut Road, PO Box 1288,
Beaufort SC 29901-1288

County: Beaufort | FICE Identification: 009910
Unit ID: 217712
Telephone: (843) 525-8211 | Carnegie Class: Assoc/Pub-R-M
FAX Number: (843) 525-8330 | Calendar System: Semester
URL: www.tcl.edu
Established: 1972 | Annual Undergrad Tuition & Fees (In-State): $3,890
Enrollment: 2,056 | Coed
Affiliation or Control: State | IRS Status: 501(c)3
Highest Offering: Associate Degree
Program: Occupational; 2-Year Principally Bachelor's Creditable
Accreditation: SC, ACBSP, ADNUR, COMTA, PNUR, PTAA, RAD, SURGT

01 Interim President ... Dr. Gina C. MOUNFIELD
10 Vice President for Finance ... Mr. Hayes WISER
05 Vice President for Academic Affairs ... Dr. Gina MOUNFIELD
26 VP Marketing/Enrollment Management ... Ms. Nancy WEBER
32 Vice President for Student Affairs ... Ms. Nancy WEBER
09 Director for Research ... Ms. Camille MYERS
15 Director for Human Resources ... Ms. Sonya LYTTLE
20 Director for Learning Resources ... Ms. Cindy HALSEY
50 Div Dean Business Technologies ... Dr. Kenneth FLICK
49 Div Dean Arts & Sciences ... Dr. Wesla FLETCHER
76 Division Dean Health Sciences ... Ms. Marge SAPP
86 Dir Retention & Federal Programs ... Mr. Rodney ADAMS
14 Director of Information Technology ... Mr. Floyd HENDERSON
37 Director Financial Aid ... Ms. Cleo MARTIN
45 Director of Inst Effectiveness ... Vacant
26 Public Relations Director ... Ms. Leigh COPELAND
21 Fiscal Manager ... Ms. Stacey DYER
40 Director for the Bookstore ... Ms. Louise RENNIX
18 Director of Facility Management ... Mr. Larry BECKLER
38 Campus Life Manager ... Ms. Mackenzie MCGREW
96 Director of Purchasing ... Ms. Carol MACK
06 Registrar ... Dr. Debralee MCCLELLAN
36 Career & Transfer Services Manager ... Ms. Melanie GALLION

Tri-County Technical College (D)

PO Box 587, Pendleton SC 29670-0587

County: Anderson | FICE Identification: 004926
Unit ID: 218885
Telephone: (864) 646-8361 | Carnegie Class: Assoc/Pub-S-SC
FAX Number: (864) 646-1895 | Calendar System: Semester
URL: www.tctc.edu
Established: 1962 | Annual Undergrad Tuition & Fees (In-District): $3,744
Enrollment: 6,616 | Coed
Affiliation or Control: State/Local | IRS Status: 501(c)3
Highest Offering: Associate Degree
Program: Occupational; 2-Year Principally Bachelor's Creditable
Accreditation: SC, ACBSP, ADNUR, DA, MAC, MLTAD, PNUR, SURGT

01 President ... Dr. Ronnie L. BOOTH
05 Provost & VP Academic Affairs ... Vacant
10 Vice Pres Business Affairs ... Mr. Gregg STAPLETON
30 VP Economic & Institutional Advance ... Mr. John LUMMUS
20 Asst Vice Pres Academic Affairs ... Mr. Galen DEHAY
51 Dean of Continuing Education ... Mr. Rick COTHRAN
88 Dean of Transition to College ... Vacant
88 Dean of Student Development ... Mr. Dan HOLLAND
49 Dean Arts & Sciences Division ... Mr. Don AVERETTE
72 Dean Engineering Technology Div ... Vacant
50 Dean Business/Human Services Div ... Mrs. Jackie BLAKLEY
76 Dean Health Education Division ... Dr. Lynn LEWIS
08 Head Librarian ... Ms. Marla ROBERSON
37 Student Financial Aid Director ... Mrs. Sarah DOWD
13 Director Computer Operations ... Mr. Lee TENNENT
26 Dir Public Relations/Communication ... Mrs. Rebecca W. EIDSON
44 Director of Development ... Mrs. Elisabeth GADD
29 Manager of Donor Relations & Alumni ... Mrs. Courtney WHITE
15 Director of Personnel Services ... Mrs. Sharon COLCOLOUGH
07 Director of Admissions ... Ms. Renae FRAZIER
06 Registrar ... Mr. Scott HARVEY
09 Director of Institutional Research ... Mr. Chris MARINO
18 Chief Facilities/Physical Plant ... Mr. Ken KOPERA
21 Director of Fiscal Affairs ... Mrs. Cara HAMILTON
96 Director of Purchasing ... Ms. Kristal DOHERTY
38 Director of Student Life/Counseling ... Ms. Croslena JOHNSON

Trident Technical College (E)

PO Box 118067, Charleston SC 29423-8067

County: Charleston | FICE Identification: 004920
Unit ID: 218894
Telephone: (843) 574-6111 | Carnegie Class: Assoc/Pub-U-MC
FAX Number: (843) 574-6541 | Calendar System: Semester
URL: www.tridenttech.edu
Established: 1964 | Annual Undergrad Tuition & Fees (In-District): $3,822
Enrollment: 17,244 | Coed
Affiliation or Control: State/Local | IRS Status: 501(c)3
Highest Offering: Associate Degree
Program: Occupational; 2-Year Principally Bachelor's Creditable
Accreditation: SC, ACBSP, ACFEI, ADNUR, COARC, DA, DH, EMT, MAC, MLTAD, OTA, PNUR, PTAA, RAD

01 President ... Dr. Mary THORNLEY
10 Vice Pres Finance & Administration ... Mr. Scott POELKER
05 Vice President Academic Affairs ... Dr. Patricia ROBERTSON
32 Vice President Student Services ... Dr. Patrice MITCHELL
30 Vice President Advancement ... Ms. Meg HOWLE
51 Vice Pres Continuing Educ/Econ Dev ... Mr. Robert WALKER
13 Vice Pres Information Technology ... Mr. Bernie STRAUB
45 Assoc VP Planning/Accreditation ... Ms. Suzy BARR
20 Asst Vice Pres Academic Programs ... Ms. Susan NORTON
51 Asst Vice Pres Continuing Education ... Ms. Yvonne NOISETTE
72 Asst Vice Pres Info Technology ... Mr. Henry COPE
35 Asst Vice Pres for Student Svcs ... Ms. Lynne ANKERSEN
20 Asst Vice President Instruction ... Mr. Eddie SIMMONS
15 Director Human Resources ... Ms. DeVetta HUGHES
96 Dir Procurement/Risk Management ... Ms. Carol BELCHER
40 Dir Auxiliary Enterprises/Bookstore ... Ms. Jloundia PINCKNEY
18 Director Facilities ... Mr. Eric HAMILTON
21 Director Finance ... Ms. Melody TAYLOR
26 Director Marketing ... Ms. Tina AHLEMANN
27 Director Public Info ... Mr. David HANSEN
88 Director High School Programs ... Ms. Melissa STOWASSER
30 Associate VP Development ... Ms. Kimberley STURGEON
14 Dir Information Technology Training ... Mr. Joseph GIBSON
36 Director Career Employment Services ... Mr. Brian ALMQUIST
81 Dean Science & Mathematics ... Mr. Bill LANDRY
79 Dean Humanities & Social Sciences ... Dr. Tim BROWN
88 Dean The Learning Center ... Ms. Pamela LEONARD-RAY
50 Dean Business Technology ... Ms. Connie JOLLY
76 Dean Allied Health Sciences ... Dr. Richard HERNANDEZ
57 Dean Film Media and Visual Arts ... Ms. Pat FOX
54 Dean Industrial/Engineering Tech ... Ms. Christine LANG
88 Dean Culinary Inst of Charleston ... Mr. Mike SABOE
61 Dean Law-Related Studies ... Mr. John UNGARO
66 Dean Nursing ... Ms. Muriel HORTON
38 Dean Student Development ... Ms. Pamela BROWN
88 Dean Comm/Family/Child Studies ... Ms. Stephany HEWITT
84 Dean Enrollment Management ... Mr. John JAMROGOWICZ
75 Dean Aeronautical Studies ... Dr. Barry FRANCO
12 Dean Berkeley Campus ... Ms. Karen WRIGHTEN
12 Dean Mount Pleasant Campus ... Mr. Michael PATTERSON
12 Dean Palmer Campus ... Dr. Louester ROBINSON
19 Director Public Safety ... Mr. Lawrence SAVIDGE
06 Registrar ... Ms. Pamela DROSTE
07 Director of Admissions ... Ms. Clara MARTIN
09 Director of Institutional Research ... Ms. Cathy ALMQUIST
37 Director Student Financial Aid ... Ms. Ellen GREEN

University of Phoenix Columbia SC Campus (F)

1001 Pinnacle Point Drive, Columbia SC 29223-5727

Telephone: (803) 699-5096 | Identification: 770223
Accreditation: &NH, ACBSP

† Main campus is University of Phoenix in Tempe, AZ.

University of South Carolina Columbia (G)

Columbia SC 29208-0001

County: Richland | FICE Identification: 003448
Unit ID: 218663
Telephone: (803) 777-7000 | Carnegie Class: RU/VH
FAX Number: (803) 777-0101 | Calendar System: Semester
URL: www.sc.edu
Established: 1801 | Annual Undergrad Tuition & Fees (In-State): $10,088
Enrollment: 31,288 | Coed
Affiliation or Control: State | IRS Status: 501(c)3
Highest Offering: Doctorate
Program: Liberal Arts And General; Teacher Preparatory; Professional
Accreditation: SC, ANEST, ART, BUS, BUSA, CACREP, CEA, CLPSY, CORE, CS, ENG, HSA, IPSY, JOUR, LAW, LIB, MED, MUS, NURSE, PH, PHAR, PTA, SCPSY, SP, SPAA, SW, TED, THEA

01 President ... Dr. Harris PASTIDES
03 Vice President & CIO ... Dr. William F. HOGUE
05 Exec VP Academic Affs/Provost ... Dr. Michael AMIRIDIS
45 Sr Vice Prov/Dir Strategic Planning ... Dr. Christine W. CURTIS
10 Vice President Finance & Planning ... Mr. Edward I. WALTON
32 VP Student Affairs/VProv Acad Suppt ... Dr. Dennis A. PRUITT
16 Vice President Human Resources ... Mr. Christopher D. BYRD
30 VP Development & Alumni Relations . Mrs. Michelle DODENHOFF
12 VP/Exec Dean Regional Campuses ... Dr. Chris P. PLYLER
46 VP Research & Grad Education ... Dr. Prakash NAGARKATTI
26 Interim VP Communications ... Mr. Wesley HICKMAN
101 Secretary to Board of Trustees ... Ms. Amy E. STONE
20 Vice Provost & Dean Undergrad Stds ... Dr. Helen I. DOERPINGHAUS
58 Vice Provost & Dean Graduate School ... Dr. Lacy K. FORD
84 Asst Vice Provost Enrollment Mgmt ... Mr. Scott VERZYL
08 Dean of Libraries ... Dr. Tom MCNALLY
43 General Counsel ... Mr. Walter H. PARHAM
09 Dir Inst Assessment & Compliance ... Dr. Philip S. MOORE
18 Assoc VP for Facilities ... Mr. Thomas D. QUASNEY
27 Director University Creative Servic ... Mr. Laurence W. PEARCE
19 Director Law Enforcement & Safety ... Mr. Christopher L. WUCHENICH
37 Dir Stdnt Financial Aid/Scholarshp ... Dr. Edgar MILLER
36 Director Career Center ... Mr. Thomas HALASZ
06 University Registrar ... Mr. Aaron C. MARTERER
22 Exec Asst to Pres Equal Oppty Pgm ... Mr. Bobby D. GIST
21 Budget Director ... Mrs. Leslie G. BRUNELLI
07 Director of Admissions ... Dr. Mary WAGNER
39 Director Housing & Residential Svcs ... Dr. Gene LUNA
38 Dir Counseling/Human Devel Center ... Dr. Deborah C. BECK
41 Director of Athletics ... Mr. Ray TANNER
35 Assoc VP for Student Life ... Mr. Jerry T. BREWER
23 Director of Student Health Services ... Ms. Deborah BECK
27 Director News & Internal Relations ... Mr. Wesley T. HICKMAN
96 Director of Purchasing ... Mrs. Venis MANIGO
29 Exec Dir Alumni Association ... Mr. Jack CLAYPOOLE
49 Dean College Arts & Sciences ... Dr. Mary Anne FITZPATRICK
88 Dean Hospitality/Retail/Sport Mgt ... Mr. Brian MIHALIK
50 Int Moore School of Business ... Dr. John MCDERMOTTE
53 Dean College of Education ... Dr. Lemuel WATSON
54 Dean Col Engineering & Computing ... Dr. Anthony P. AMBLER
69 Dean Arnold School of Public Health .. Dr. G. Thomas CHANDLER
60 Dn College of Mass Comm/Infor Stdys . Mr. Charles BIERBAUER
61 Dean School of Law ... Dr. Robert M. WILCOX
63 Dean School of Medicine ... Dr. Richard A. HOPPMANN
63 Dean Greenville School of Medicine ... Dr. Jerry R. YOUKEY
64 Dean School of Music ... Dr. Tayloe HARDING
66 Dean College of Nursing ... Jeannette ANDREWS
67 Exec Dean College of Pharmacy ... Dr. Joseph T. DIPIRO

67 Dean College of Pharmacy ... Dr. Randall C. ROWEN
70 Dean College of Social Work ... Dr. Anna M. SCHEYETTE
92 Dir Fellowships & Scholar Programs ... Ms. Novella BESKID
88 Director of Academic Programs ... Dr. Kristia H. FINNIGAN
88 Executive Director USC Connect ... Dr. Irma J. VANSCOY

University of South Carolina Aiken (A)

471 University Parkway, Aiken SC 29801-6399
County: Aiken FICE Identification: 003449
Unit ID: 218645
Telephone: (803) 648-6851 Carnegie Class: Bac/Diverse
FAX Number: (803) 641-3362 Calendar System: Semester
URL: www.usca.edu
Established: 1961 Annual Undergrad Tuition & Fees (In-State): $9,018
Enrollment: 3,211 Coed
Affiliation or Control: State IRS Status: 501(c)3
Highest Offering: Master's
Program: Liberal Arts And General; Teacher Preparatory
Accreditation: SC, BUS, MUS, NURSE, TED

01 Chancellor ... Dr. Sandra JORDAN
05 Exec Vice Chanc Academic Affairs ... Dr. Jeffrey M. PRIEST
30 Vice Chancellor Advancement ... Dr. Deidre MARTIN
32 Vice Chancellor Student Life & Svcs ... Dr. Deborah KLADIVKO
27 Vice Chancellor Information Tech ... Mr. Ernest PRINGLE
84 Vice Chancellor Enrollment Services ... Mr. Randy R. DUCKETT
18 Asst Chanc Facilities Management ... Vacant
79 College Coordinator Hum & Soc Sci ... Dr. Tom MACK
83 College Coordinator Sciences ... Dr. Edward CALLEN
50 Dean of the School of Business ... Dr. Clifton JONES
53 Dean of the School of Education ... Dr. Wendy SCHWEDER
66 Dean of the School of Nursing ... Dr. Sara CAMPBELL
88 Dir Academic Success Center ... Dr. Stacie WILLIAMS
09 Dir Institutional Effectiveness ... Dr. Lloyd A. DAWE
08 Dir of Library ... Ms. Jane TUTEN
88 Dir Ruth Patrick Sci Ed Center ... Dr. Gary SENN
25 Dir Sponsored Research ... Dr. Bill PIRKLE
24 Dir Center for Teaching Excellence ... Mr. Chad LEVERETTE
10 Vice Chanc Business & Finance ... Mr. Joe SOBIERALSKI
40 Dir Bookstore ... Ms. Heidi DIFRANCO
88 Dir Campus Support Services ... Mr. Jeff JENIK
88 Dir Children's Center ... Ms. Lynn WILLIAMS
88 Dir Convocation Center ... Mr. Josh SMALL
88 Dir Dining Services ... Mr. Brent WUSTMAN
12 Dir of Etherredge Center ... Ms. Jane SCHUMACHER
21 Controller ... Ms. Gwen ASHLEY
15 Dir Human Resources & Affirm Action ... Ms. Maria CHANDLER
17 Dir Wellness Center ... Ms. Mila PADGETT
07 Dir of Admissions ... Mr. Andrew HENDRIX
58 Coord Citizenshp Residenc Grad Stds ... Ms. Karen MORRIS
36 Dir of Career Services ... Mr. Corey FERALDI
37 Dir Financial Aid ... Mr. Glenn SHUMPERT
06 Registrar ... Ms. Vivian D. GRICE
14 Director of Client Services ... Mr. Chris SPIRES
90 Dir Communications & Hardware ... Mr. Bob WIESNER
105 Dir Network Sys/Infrastructure/Arch ... Ms. Joann WILLIAMSON
41 Dir of Athletics ... Mr. Douglas R. WARRICK, JR.
38 Dir Counseling & Disabilities ... Ms. Cynthia B. GELINAS
23 Dir Student Health Center ... Ms. Cynthia B. GELINAS
39 Dir Housing & Univ Police ... Mr. Deri WILLS
28 Dir International Programs ... Dr. Maria ANASTASIOU
35 Asst Vice Chanc Student Life ... Mr. Ahmed SAMAHA
19 Chief of Police ... Mr. Kevin LILES
29 Dir of Alumni Relations/Annual Fund ... Mr. Randy DUCKETT
51 Dir Conferences & Continuing Ed ... Ms. Mary Anne CAVANAUGH
44 Dir Major Gifts ... Ms. Linda EVANS
26 Dir Marketing & Community Relations ... Ms. Patti MCGRATH
105 Dir Visual Comm & Web Development ... Mr. Jeff MASTROMONICO
88 Director Instructional Svcs ... Mr. Keith PIERCE

University of South Carolina Beaufort (B)

1 University Boulevard, Bluffton SC 29909-6085
County: Beaufort FICE Identification: 003450
Unit ID: 218654
Telephone: (843) 208-8000 Carnegie Class: Bac/Diverse
FAX Number: (843) 208-8299 Calendar System: Semester
URL: www.uscb.edu
Established: 1959 Annual Undergrad Tuition & Fees (In-State): $8,586
Enrollment: 1,828 Coed
Affiliation or Control: State IRS Status: 501(c)3
Highest Offering: Baccalaureate
Program: Liberal Arts And General; Teacher Preparatory; Professional
Accreditation: SC, NURSE, TED

01 Chancellor ... Dr. Jane UPSHAW
05 Exec Vice Chanc Academic Affairs ... Dr. Harvey VARNET
32 Vice Chanc for Student Development ... Dr. Douglas OBLANDER
10 Vice Chancellor Finance/Operations ... Mr. Earle HOLLEY
26 Vice Chanc University Advancement ... Dr. Lynn MCGEE
18 Director of Facilities ... Mr. Mike PARROTT
13 Chief Information Officer ... Mr. Eddie KING
08 Director of Library ... Dr. Harvey VARNET
06 Registrar ... Dr. James TISDALE
84 Assoc VP Enrollment Mgmt ... Vacant
37 Director of Financial Aid ... Ms. Patricia GREENE
30 Director of Development ... Ms. Colleen CALLAHAN
09 Dir Inst Effectiveness/Research ... Ms. Jodi HERRIN
19 Director Public Safety ... Dr. Henry GARBADE
35 Director of Student Life ... Ms. Kate TORBORG
15 Director of Human Resources ... Dr. Sue GOLABEK

University of South Carolina Lancaster (C)

PO Box 889, Lancaster SC 29721-0889
Telephone: (803) 313-7000 FICE Identification: 003453
Accreditation: &SC, ACBSP, ADNUR, PNUR

† Main campus is University of South Carolina Columbia in Columbia, SC.

University of South Carolina Salkehatchie (D)

PO Box 617, Allendale SC 29810-0617
County: Allendale FICE Identification: 003454
Unit ID: 218681
Telephone: (803) 584-3446 Carnegie Class: Assoc/Pub2in4
FAX Number: (803) 584-5038 Calendar System: Semester
URL: uscsalkehatchie.sc.edu
Established: 1965 Annual Undergrad Tuition & Fees (In-State): $3,090
Enrollment: 1,173 Coed
Affiliation or Control: State IRS Status: 501(c)3
Highest Offering: Associate Degree
Program: 2-Year Principally Bachelor's Creditable
Accreditation: &SC

01 Dean ... Dr. Ann C. CARMICHAEL
05 Assoc Dean Academic Affairs ... Dr. Roberto REFINETTI
32 Asc Dean Student Svcs/Dir Athletics ... Ms. Jane T. BREWER
08 Head Librarian ... Mr. Daniel JOHNSON
37 Director Financial Aid ... Ms. Julie HADWIN
18 Director Facilities/Safety ... Dr. William A. SANDIFER
40 Bookstore Manager ... Mr. Lamar HEWETT
15 Director of Human Resources ... Dr. William A. SANDIFER
07 Director of Admissions ... Ms. Carmen BROWN
30 Chief Development ... Dr. Ann C. CARMICHAEL
84 Director Enrollment Mgmt Svcs ... Mr. Mike SMITH
88 Director Leadership Center ... Ms. Ann RICE
88 Dir Opportunity Scholars Program ... Ms. Carolyn BANNER
88 Dir Ctr Leadership Development ... Mr. Warren CHAVOUS
88 Sports Information Director ... Mr. Trent KINARD

† Regional accreditation is carried under University of South Carolina - Columbia.

University of South Carolina School of Medicine-Greenville (E)

607 Grove Road, Greenville SC 29605
County: Greenville Identification: 667114
Telephone: (864) 455-7992 Carnegie Class: Not Classified
FAX Number: (864) 455-8404 Calendar System: Semester
URL: greenvillemed.sc.edu
Established: 2010 Annual Graduate Tuition & Fees: $35,498
Enrollment: 54 Coed
Affiliation or Control: State IRS Status: 501(c)3
Highest Offering: Doctorate; No Undergraduates
Program: Professional
Accreditation: #MED

01 Dean ... Dr. Jerry R. YOUKEY
05 Sr Assc Dean Academic Affs/Diverity ... Dr. Spence TAYLOR
20 Assoc Dean for Faculty Affairs ... Dr. Robert BEST
32 Assoc Dean Student Affairs/Admiss ... Dr. James BUGGY
53 Assoc Dean for Education ... Dr. Lynn CRESPO
07 Assoc Dean for Admissions ... Dr. Paul CATALANA

University of South Carolina Sumter (F)

200 Miller Road, Sumter SC 29150-2498
County: Sumter FICE Identification: 003426
Unit ID: 218690
Telephone: (803) 775-8727 Carnegie Class: Assoc/Pub2in4
FAX Number: (803) 775-2180 Calendar System: Semester
URL: www.uscsumter.edu
Established: 1966 Annual Undergrad Tuition & Fees (In-State): $3,090
Enrollment: 898 Coed
Affiliation or Control: State IRS Status: 501(c)3
Highest Offering: Associate Degree
Program: 2-Year Principally Bachelor's Creditable
Accreditation: &SC

01 Interim Dean of the University ... Mr. Lynwood WATTS
05 Assoc Dean Academic Affairs ... Dr. Anthony M. COYNE
30 Asst Dean University Advancement ... Mr. Carl R. MCINTOSH
32 Assoc Dean for Student Affairs ... Vacant
10 Assoc Dean for Admin/Financial Svcs ... Mr. Bruce K. BLUMBERG
79 Chr Div of Hum/Social Science/Educ ... Dr. Richard S. BELL
49 Chair Division of Arts & Letters ... Dr. Hayes D. HAMPTON
81 Chr Div of Science/Math & Engr ... Dr. James E. PRIVETT
50 Chr Div of Business/Admin/ Economics ... Dr. Kay OLDHOUSER DAVIS
09 Director of Institutional Research ... Mr. Charles W. WRIGHT
08 Head Librarian ... Ms. Sharon H. CHAPMAN
07 Director of Admissions ... Mr. Keith E. BRITTON
38 Director Advisement/Counseling ... Ms. C. Gail PACK
56 Director of Distance Education ... Ms. Jean B. CARRANO
51 Director of Continuing Education ... Ms. Susan S. BRABHAM
35 Director Student Life ... Vacant
14 Director of Computer Services ... Mr. George R. THOMPSON, III
26 Dir of Public Relations/Marketing ... Ms. Misty HATFIELD
40 Bookstore Manager ... Ms. Julie MCCOY
15 Human Resources Officer ... Ms. Marchetta L. WILLIAMS
21 Budget/Planning/Grants Director ... Ms. Joann V. GROOVER
29 Director of Alumni Relations ... Ms. Erica G. CHRISTMAS
37 Coord Fin Aid/Scholarships/Vet Affs ... Ms. Sue A. SIMS
06 Records & Registration Coordinator ... Ms. Alicia CURTIS
36 Career Planning & Placement Coord ... Ms. Toni J. WILLIAMS
88 Director Opportunity Scholars ... Ms. Lisa ROSDAIL
88 Director Upstate Education Programs ... Ms. Marilyn IZZARD
18 Superintendent Buildings & Grounds ... Mr. Jeff LINGEFELT

† Regional accreditation is carried under University of South Carolina - Columbia.

University of South Carolina Union (G)

PO Drawer 729, Union SC 29379-0729
County: Union FICE Identification: 004927
Unit ID: 218706
Telephone: (864) 429-8728 Carnegie Class: Assoc/Pub2in4
FAX Number: (864) 427-3682 Calendar System: Semester
URL: uscunion.sc.edu
Established: 1965 Annual Undergrad Tuition & Fees (In-State): $3,090
Enrollment: 473 Coed
Affiliation or Control: State IRS Status: 501(c)3
Highest Offering: Associate Degree
Program: Occupational; 2-Year Principally Bachelor's Creditable
Accreditation: &SC

01 Dean ... Dr. Alice TAYLOR-COLBERT
84 Director Enrollment Services ... Mr. M. Bradley GREER
37 Director Financial Aid ... Mr. Robert HOLCOMBE
15 Human Resources ... Ms. Susan P. JETT
10 Business Manager ... Ms. Michele S. LEE
40 Bookstore Manager ... Ms. Tanja BLACK
14 Director of Information Technology ... Mr. Wesley C. BELK
108 Inst Effectiveness Officer ... Mr. Thomas W. SIMPSON
08 Library Manager ... Ms. Sharon L. RUPP

† Regional accreditation is carried under University of South Carolina - Columbia.

University of South Carolina Upstate (H)

800 University Way, Spartanburg SC 29303-4996
County: Spartanburg FICE Identification: 006951
Unit ID: 218742
Telephone: (864) 503-5000 Carnegie Class: Bac/Diverse
FAX Number: (864) 503-5375 Calendar System: Semester
URL: www.uscupstate.edu
Established: 1967 Annual Undergrad Tuition & Fees (In-State): $9,748
Enrollment: 5,561 Coed
Affiliation or Control: State IRS Status: 501(c)3
Highest Offering: Master's
Program: Liberal Arts And General; Teacher Preparatory
Accreditation: SC, ART, BUS, CAHIIM, CS, ENGT, NURSE, TED

01 Chancellor ... Dr. Thomas MOORE
05 Sr Vice Chanc for Acad Affair ... Dr. Charles HARRINGTON
13 Vice Chanc Information Technology ... Ms. Jeanne SKUL
11 Vice Chanc Admin & Business Affs ... Ms. Sheryl TURNER-WATTS
30 Vice Chanc University Advancement ... Mr. Michael E. IRVIN
12 Vice Chanc Greenville Campus ... Dr. Judith PRINCE
88 Asst Vice Chanc Student Success ... Dr. Mary THEOKAS
32 Dean of Students ... Mrs. Laura PUCKETT-BOLER
06 Registrar ... Ms. Mary David FOX
84 Asst Vice Chanc Enrollment Services ... Ms. Donette STEWART
38 Director of Counseling Services ... Ms. Frances L. JARRETT-HORTIS
08 Dean of the Library ... Ms. Frieda M. DAVISON
37 Director Financial Aid ... Ms. Allison SULLIVAN
49 Dean of Arts & Sciences ... Dr. Dirk SCHLINGMANN
50 Dean Johnson Col Business & Econ ... Dr. Frank RUDISILL
53 Interim Dean of Education ... Dr. Jim CHARLES
66 Interim Dean of Nursing ... Dr. Katharine GIBB
58 Director of Graduate Education ... Dr. Tina HERZBERG
29 Dir Alumni Relations/Ann Giv/Event ... Ms. Leah ANDERSON
102 Director Dev & Found Scholarships ... Mrs. Bea W. SMITH
40 Director of the Bookstore ... Mr. Jerry CARROLL
41 Director of Athletics ... Mr. H. Michael HALL
18 Director of Facilities Management ... Mr. Frederick D. PUNCKE
108 Dir of Inst Assessment & Planning ... Mr. C. Sam BINGHAM
96 Director of Purchasing ... Ms. Janice DELLINGER
26 Director University Communications ... Ms. Tammey E. WHALEY
19 Chief of Police ... Mr. Klay PETERSON
35 Director of Student Life ... Ms. Khrystal SMITH
39 Director of Housing ... Ms. Mandy WHITTEN
23 Director of Health Services ... Ms. Lou Anne WEBER
88 Exec Dir Univ Boards & Public Affs ... Mr. John F. PERRY
09 Dir Inst Effectiveness & Compliance ... Mr. Brian MALLORY
88 Dir Campus Fitness & Recreation ... Mr. Mark RITTER
88 Dir Disability Services ... Ms. Margaret CAMP

Virginia College (I)

7201 Two Notch Road, Columbia SC 29223
Telephone: (803) 509-7100 Identification: 770829

Accreditation: ACICS, MAAB, SURGT

† Main campus is Virginia College in Birmingham, AL.

Virginia College **(A)**

2400 David H. McLeod Blvd, Suite F, Florence SC 29501
Telephone: (843) 407-2200 Identification: 770832
Accreditation: ACICS

† Main campus is Virginia College in Birmingham, AL.

Virginia College **(B)**

78 Global Drive, Suite 200, Greenville SC 29607
Telephone: (864) 679-4900 Identification: 770838
Accreditation: ACICS, MAAB, SURGT

† Main campus is Virginia College in Birmingham, AL.

Virginia College **(C)**

6185 Rivers Avenue, North Charleston SC 29406-4999
Telephone: (843) 614-4300 Identification: 770830
Accreditation: ACICS, SURGT

† Main campus is Virginia College in Birmingham, AL.

Virginia College **(D)**

8150 Warren H. Abernathy Highway,
Spartanburg SC 29301-2450
Telephone: (864) 504-3200 Identification: 770831
Accreditation: ACICS, MAAB

† Main campus is Virginia College in Birmingham, AL.

Voorhees College (E)

PO Box 678, Denmark SC 29042-0678
County: Bamberg FICE Identification: 003455
Unit ID: 218919
Telephone: (803) 780-1234 Carnegie Class: Bac/Diverse
FAX Number: (803) 780-1015 Calendar System: Semester
URL: www.voorhees.edu
Established: 1897 Annual Undergrad Tuition & Fees: $18,126
Enrollment: 642 Coed
Affiliation or Control: Protestant Episcopal IRS Status: 501(c)3
Highest Offering: Baccalaureate
Program: Liberal Arts And General
Accreditation: SC, ACBSP

01 President ....Dr. Cleveland L. SELLERS, JR.
32 Vice President Student Affairs ....Mr. Willie JEFFERSON
10 VP Fiscal/Admin Affairs/CFO ....Mrs. V. Diane O'BERRY
30 Vice Pres Institutional Advancement ....Mr. Marcus BURGESS
09 VP Planning & Information Mgmt ....Mr. Samuel BLACKWELL
35 Director of Student Life/Counseling ....Mr. Benjamin O. WATSON
08 Administrative Librarian ....Dr. Marie MARTIN
37 Director of Financial Aid ....Mr. Augusta KITCHEN
18 Director of Physical Plant ....Mr. Eddie PATTERSON
29 Director Alumni Affairs ....Ms. Dorothy PATTERSON
36 Director Career Planning & Outreach ....Mr. Gerald DEVAUGHN
42 Chaplain ....Rev. James YARSIAH
41 Director of Athletics ....Mr. Willie JEFFERSON
19 Director of Security ....Mr. James WELDON
23 Director of Health Services ....Ms. Sheila CUNNINGHAM
06 Registrar ....Ms. Melika JACKSON
07 Director of Admissions ....Mrs. Paula PAYTON
15 Interim Director of Human Resources ....Mrs. Constance COLTER-BRABHAM
13 Chief Technology Officer ....Mr. Timothy KENTOPP
21 Internal Auditor ....Vacant
40 Bookstore Manager ....Mrs. Shanda RUFFIN
26 Coordinator Media Rels/Marketing ....Mrs. Teesa BRUNSON
04 Exec Assistant to the President ....Ms. Sandra GLOSTER
50 Division Chair Business ....Dr. Victor OYINBO
81 Div Chair Natural Sciences/Math ....Dr. Doris WARD

Williamsburg Technical College (F)

601 Martin Luther King, Jr. Avenue,
Kingstree SC 29556-4103
County: Williamsburg FICE Identification: 009322
Unit ID: 218955
Telephone: (843) 355-4110 Carnegie Class: Assoc/Pub-R-S
FAX Number: (843) 355-4296 Calendar System: Semester
URL: www.wiltech.edu
Established: 1969 Annual Undergrad Tuition & Fees (In-District): $5,538
Enrollment: 642 Coed
Affiliation or Control: State/Local IRS Status: 501(c)3
Highest Offering: Associate Degree
Program: Occupational; 2-Year Principally Bachelor's Creditable
Accreditation: SC, ACBSP

01 President ....Dr. Patricia A. LEE
05 Vice Pres for Academic Affairs ....Mr. Clifton R. ELLIOTT
10 Vice Pres for Business Affairs ....Ms. Melissa A. COKER
32 Vice Pres for Student Affairs ....Dr. Eric A. BROWN
46 Dir Planning/Research/Grants ....Mr. Andrew MULLER
08 Library Director ....Vacant
07 Admissions Counselor ....Ms. Cheryl DUBOSE
30 Director of Development/Public Rels ....Mrs. Mona B. DUKES
37 Financial Aid Officer ....Mrs. Jean BOOS
09 Research/Systems Analyst ....Mr. T. Kent COKER
06 Director Enrollment and Record Svcs ....Dr. Alexis WRIGHT-DUBOSE
18 Director of Facilities Maintenance ....Mr. Tyrone THOMAS
15 Director Human Resources ....Mrs. Jennifer STRONG
26 Dir Development & Public Relations ....Mrs. Mona B. DUKES

Winthrop University (G)

Oakland Avenue, Rock Hill SC 29733-0001
County: York FICE Identification: 003456
Unit ID: 218964
Telephone: (803) 323-2211 Carnegie Class: Master's L
FAX Number: (803) 323-3001 Calendar System: Semester
URL: www.winthrop.edu
Established: 1886 Annual Undergrad Tuition & Fees (In-State): $13,430
Enrollment: 6,170 Coed
Affiliation or Control: State IRS Status: 501(c)3
Highest Offering: Beyond Master's But Less Than Doctorate
Program: Liberal Arts And General; Teacher Preparatory; Professional
Accreditation: SC, ART, BUS, CACREP, CIDA, CS, DANCE, DIETD, DIETI, JOUR, MUS, SW, TED, THEA

01 President ....Dr. Jane Marie COMSTOCK
05 Vice Pres Academic Affairs ....Dr. Debra C. BOYD
10 Vice President Finance & Business ....Mr. J. P. MCKEE
30 Vice Pres University Advancement ....Dr. Kathryn HOLTEN
32 Vice President of Student Life ....Dr. Frank P. ARDAIOLO
29 Vice Pres Development and Alumni ....Ms. Kimberly KEEL
21 Associate VP Finance/Business ....Ms. Amanda F. MAGHSOUD
18 Assoc VP Facilities Management ....Mr. Walter A. HARDIN
15 Associate VP Human Resource ....Ms. Lisa COWART
29 Assoc Vice Pres Alumni Relations ....Ms. Debbie GARRICK
13 Assoc VP Information Technology ....Mr. James HAMMOND
26 Assoc VP/Exec Dir University Rels ..Ms. Ellen M. WILDER-BYRD
04 Exec Assistant to President ....Dr. Kimberly A. FAUST
26 Asst to President Public Affairs ....Ms. Rebecca MASTERS
20 Asst to Pres University Events ....Ms. DeeAnna BROOKS
20 Asst VP Acad Affs/Dir Summer Sess ....Mr. Tim DRUEKE
58 Dean of Graduate School ....Dr. Jack DEROCHI
49 Interim Dean College Arts & Science ....Dr. Peter JUDGE
50 Dean Col of Business Administration ....Dr. Roger D. WEIKLE
53 Dean College of Education ....Dr. Jennie RAKESTRAW
64 Dean College of Visual/Perf ....Dr. David WOHL
08 Dean Library Services ....Dr. Mark Y. HERRING
88 Dean University College ....Dr. Gloria JONES
35 Dean of Students ....Ms. Bethany MARLOWE
41 Athletic Director ....Mr. Thomas N. HICKMAN
25 Director Sponsored Pgms/Research ....Ms. Teresa R. JUSTICE
90 Director Academic Computing ....Mr. Patrice BRUNEAU
91 Director Admin System/Programming ....Mr. Larry W. FERGUSON
06 Registrar ....Ms. Gina G. JONES
07 Director of Admissions ....Ms. Deborah G. BARBER
37 Director of Financial Aid ....Ms. Leah STURGIS
19 Chief of Campus Police ....Chief Frank J. ZEBEDIS
38 Interim Director Health/Counseling ....Ms. Mary Jo BARRETO
39 Director of Residence Life ....Ms. Cynthia A. CASSENS
36 Director Career Development/Svcs ....Ms. Amy SULLIVAN
96 Director Procurement/Risk Mgmt ....Mr. Bob REID
53 Director Teaching/Learning Ctr ....Dr. John BRYD

W.L. Bonner College (H)

4430 Argent Court, Columbia SC 29203-5901
County: Richland FICE Identification: 038564
Unit ID: 446613
Telephone: (803) 754-3950 Carnegie Class: Spec/Faith
FAX Number: (803) 754-9700 Calendar System: Semester
URL: www.wlbc.edu
Established: 1995 Annual Undergrad Tuition & Fees: $7,152
Enrollment: 60 Coed
Affiliation or Control: Independent Non-Profit IRS Status: 501(c)3
Highest Offering: Baccalaureate
Program: Liberal Arts And General; Technical Emphasis
Accreditation: #BI

01 President and Founder ....Bishop William L. BONNER
05 College Dean/Chief Admin Officer ....Ms. Elaine MCQUEEN
07 Dir Ofc of Enrollment Mgt/Registrar ....Mrs. Sannie M. WRIGHT

Wofford College (I)

429 N Church Street, Spartanburg SC 29303-3663
County: Spartanburg FICE Identification: 003457
Unit ID: 218973
Telephone: (864) 597-4000 Carnegie Class: Bac/A&S
FAX Number: (864) 597-4018 Calendar System: 4/1/4
URL: www.wofford.edu
Established: 1854 Annual Undergrad Tuition & Fees: $34,555
Enrollment: 2,005 Coed
Affiliation or Control: United Methodist IRS Status: 501(c)3
Highest Offering: Baccalaureate
Program: Liberal Arts And General; Teacher Preparatory
Accreditation: SC

01 President ....Dr. Nayef H. SAMHAT
10 Chief Financial Officer ....Ms. Barbie F. JEFFERSON
05 Sr VP Academic Affs/Dean of College ....Dr. David S. WOOD
30 Sr VP Development/College Relations ....Mr. Marion B. PEAVEY
11 Sr Vice Pres for Administration ....Mr. David M. BEACHAM
32 Vice President Student Affairs ....Ms. Roberta H. BIGGER
46 Vice Pres Education Technology ....Dr. David M. WHISNANT
84 Vice President for Enrollment ....Mr. Brand R. STILLE
09 Vice Pres Academic Admin & Planning ....Dr. Boyce M. LAWTON, III
27 Assoc VP Communications/Marketing ....Dr. Doyle W. BOGGS
18 Assoc VP Facilities/Cap Projects ....Mr. Jason H. BURR
36 Dean Ctr for Professional Excellnce ....Mr. Scott COCHRAN
08 Dean of Library/Dir Cultural Events ....Mr. Oakley H. COBURN
82 Dean of International Programs ....Dr. Ana Maria WISEMAN
23 Assoc Dean Students/Dir Health Svcs ....Ms. Beth D. WALLACE
04 Exec Assistant to the President ....Ms. Mary A. GILMAN
41 Director of Athletics ....Mr. Richard A. JOHNSON
06 College Registrar ....Ms. Jennifer R. ALLISON
42 Chaplain ....Dr. Ronald R. ROBINSON
29 Dir of Alumni Affairs/Parent Assn ....Mrs. Debbi N. THOMPSON
19 Campus Safety Director ....Mr. Randy HALL
15 Human Resources Director ....Ms. Carole B. LISTER

York Technical College (J)

452 S Anderson Road, Rock Hill SC 29730-3395
County: York FICE Identification: 003996
Unit ID: 218991
Telephone: (803) 327-8000 Carnegie Class: Assoc/Pub-S-SC
FAX Number: (803) 327-8059 Calendar System: Semester
URL: www.yorktech.edu
Established: 1964 Annual Undergrad Tuition & Fees (In-State): $3,712
Enrollment: 4,849 Coed
Affiliation or Control: State IRS Status: 501(c)3
Highest Offering: Associate Degree
Program: Occupational; 2-Year Principally Bachelor's Creditable
Accreditation: SC, ACBSP, ADNUR, DA, DH, ENGT, MLTAD, PNUR, RAD, SURGT

01 President ....Dr. Greg F. RUTHERFORD
05 Exec Vice Pres Acad/Student Affs ....Dr. Carolyn G. STEWART
10 VP Business & Support Svcs ....Dr. Marc TARPLEE
32 Assoc VP Academic/Student Affairs ....Ms. Bridgett GOLMAN
30 Vice President for Advancement ....Ms. Melanie E. JONES
50 Assoc VP Business/Computer/AA/AS ....Dr. Jack BAGWELL
76 Assoc VP Health & Human Services ....Ms. Linda WEAVER-GRIGGS
54 Assoc VP Industry/Engineering Tech ....Dr. Sidney VALENTINE
103 Interim AVP Economic/Workforce Dev ....Dr. Sidney VALENTINE
08 Librarian ....Ms. Erinnae BAKER
35 Dean of Students ....Ms. Kelly T. DAWKINS
88 Dean Center for Teaching/Learning ....Ms. Kathy L. HOELLEN
71 ReadySC Area Director ....Ms. Marianne BORDERS
09 Director of Institutional Research ....Ms. Mary Beth SCHWARTZ
15 Director of Human Resources . Ms. Edwina ROSEBORO-BARNES
37 Director Student Financial Aid ....Vacant
13 Information Services Director ....Vacant
18 Facilities Management Director ....Mr. Robert L. BROWN
45 Director of Planning ....Mrs. Jacquelyn H. NESBITT
06 Registrar ....Mrs. Brandy PINER
07 Director of Admissions ....Vacant

SOUTH DAKOTA

Augustana College (K)

2001 S Summit, Sioux Falls SD 57197-0001
County: Minnehaha FICE Identification: 003458
Unit ID: 219000
Telephone: (605) 274-0770 Carnegie Class: Bac/Diverse
FAX Number: (605) 274-5299 Calendar System: 4/1/4
URL: www.augie.edu
Established: 1860 Annual Undergrad Tuition & Fees: $28,200
Enrollment: 1,839 Coed
Affiliation or Control: Evangelical Lutheran Church In America
IRS Status: 501(c)3
Highest Offering: Master's
Program: Liberal Arts And General; Teacher Preparatory; Professional
Accreditation: NH, MUS, NURSE, TED

01 President ....Mr. Robert C. OLIVER
05 Sr Vice Pres Academic Affairs ....Dr. Susan S. HASSELER
32 Vice President Student Services ....Dr. James B. BIES
10 Vice Pres Finance/Administration ....Mr. Thomas MEYER
30 Vice President for Advancement ....Mr. Robert PRELOGER
07 Vice President for Admission ....Ms. Nancy DAVIDSON
15 Vice President of Human Resources ....Ms. Jane T. KUPER
11 Assoc VP Admin/Chief Info Officer ....Mr. Daniel D. DRENKOW
21 Assoc Vice President for Finance ....Ms. Carol SPILLUM
20 Associate Academic Dean ....Dr. Mike WANOUS
32 Associate Dean of Students ....Vacant
37 Director of Financial Aid ....Ms. Brenda MURTHA
08 Director of Library ....Ms. Ronelle THOMPSON
36 Director Career Center ....Ms. Sandi VIETOR
13 Director Mgmt Information Systems ....Ms. Debra FREDERICK
18 Chief Facilities/Physical Plant ....Mr. Frank HUGHES
29 Director of Alumni Relations ....Ms. Mary TOSO
41 Athletic Director ....Mr. Bill GROSS
06 Registrar ....Ms. Joni KRUEGER

Colorado Technical University **(L)**

3901 W 59th Street, Sioux Falls SD 57108-2272
Telephone: (605) 361-0200 Identification: 666731
Accreditation: &NH, MAC

† Main campus is Colorado Technical University in Colorado Springs, CO.

Dakota Wesleyan University (A)

1200 W University, Mitchell SD 57301-4398
County: Davison | FICE Identification: 003461
Unit ID: 219091
Telephone: (605) 995-2600 | Carnegie Class: Bac/Diverse
FAX Number: (605) 995-2699 | Calendar System: Semester
URL: www.dwu.edu
Established: 1885 | Annual Undergrad Tuition & Fees: $22,700
Enrollment: 759 | Coed
Affiliation or Control: United Methodist | IRS Status: 501(c)3
Highest Offering: Master's
Program: Liberal Arts And General; Teacher Preparatory
Accreditation: NH, ADNUR

Code	Title	Name
01	President	Ms. Amy C. NOVAK
03	Provost	Ms. Rochelle VON EYE
10	Executive Vice President	Ms. Theresa KRIESE
26	Vice Pres of University Relations	Ms. Lori ESSIG
06	Registrar	Ms. Karen KNOELL
08	Chief Info Ofcr/Dir Lrng Resources	Mr. Kevin KENKEL
88	Dir Kelley Ctr for Entrepreneurship	Ms. Fredel THOMAS
88	Executive Director McGovern Center	Ms. Alisha VINCENT
81	Dean Col Health/Fitness & Science	Dr. Rochelle VON EYE
79	Dean College Arts & Humanities	Dr. Vince REDDER
30	Development Officer	Ms. Kitty ALLEN
29	Director of Alumni Relations	Ms. Jackie WENTWORTH
37	Director of Financial Aid	Ms. Kristy O'KIEF
13	Director of Information Technology	Mr. Matt MOORE
15	Director of Human Resources	Mr. Corey MELLEGAARD
42	Campus Pastor	Rev. Brandon VETTER
66	Administrative Chair Nursing Dept	Dr. Adele JACOBSON
41	Athletic Director	Mr. Curt HART
18	Director of Physical Plant	Mr. Louis SCHOENFELDER
32	Director of Student Life	Ms. Diana GOLDAMMER
35	Director Student Support Services	Ms. Kate MILLER
07	Director of Recruitment	Ms. Melissa HERR-VALBURG
38	Student Support Services Counselor	Ms. Linda CIMPL
40	Director of University Services	Ms. Lori SOLBERG
88	Day Care Director/Teacher	Ms. Linda HOFER
88	Dean Col Ldrshp & Pub Service	Dr. W. Jesse WEINS
58	Dean of Grad Stds & New Ventures	Dr. Ed PLASTOW

Globe University (B)

5101 South Broadband Lane, Sioux Falls SD 57108
Telephone: (605) 977-0705 | Identification: 770780
Accreditation: ACICS

† Main campus is Globe University in Woodbury, MN.

Kilian Community College (C)

300 E 6th Street, Sioux Falls SD 57103-7020
County: Minnehaha | FICE Identification: 021446
Unit ID: 219055
Telephone: (605) 221-3100 | Carnegie Class: Assoc/PrivNFP
FAX Number: (605) 336-2606 | Calendar System: Trimester
URL: www.kilian.edu
Established: 1976 | Annual Undergrad Tuition & Fees: $9,150
Enrollment: 294 | Coed
Affiliation or Control: Independent Non-Profit | IRS Status: 501(c)3
Highest Offering: Associate Degree
Program: Occupational; 2-Year Principally Bachelor's Creditable
Accreditation: NH

Code	Title	Name
01	President	Mr. Mark MILLAGE
11	Dean of Institutional Services	Mr. Craig JUCHT
37	Financial Aid Director	Ms. Carolyn HELGERSON
06	Academic Dean/Registrar	Ms. Janet K. GARCIA
26	Director of Marketing	Vacant
88	Director Student Success Center	Ms. Rose TOERING
07	Director of Admissions	Ms. Mary KLOCKMAN
30	Director of Development	Ms. Wendy MCDONNEL
04	Assistant to the President	Ms. Joyce HUBREGTSE
08	Librarian	Vacant
10	Manager Business Office	Vacant
18	Chief Facilities/Physical Plant	Mr. Herb ROE
49	Instruction Liberal Arts Division	Ms. Cheryl J. HARTMAN
50	Instruction Business Division	Ms. Wendy JANSEN

Lake Area Technical Institute (D)

1201 Arrow Avenue, PO Box 730,
Watertown SD 57201-2869
County: Codington | FICE Identification: 005309
Unit ID: 219143
Telephone: (605) 882-5284 | Carnegie Class: Assoc/Pub-R-S
FAX Number: (605) 882-6299 | Calendar System: Semester
URL: www.lakeareatech.edu
Established: 1965 | Annual Undergrad Tuition & Fees (In-District): $6,000
Enrollment: 1,799 | Coed
Affiliation or Control: Local | IRS Status: 501(c)3
Highest Offering: Associate Degree
Program: Occupational; 2-Year Principally Bachelor's Creditable; Technical Emphasis
Accreditation: NH, DA, EMT, MAC, MLTAD, OTA, PNUR, PTAA

Code	Title	Name
01	President	Ms. Debra SHEPHARD
03	Executive Vice President	Mr. Michael CARTNEY
84	Director of Enrollment	Mr. Eric SHULTZ
05	Dean of Instruction	Ms. Kim BELLUM
26	Chief Public Relations Officer	Ms. LuAnn STRAIT
31	Business/Industry Coordinator	Mr. Steven HAUCK
32	Student Services Coordinator	Mr. Shane ORTMEIER
37	Financial Aid Coordinator	Ms. Marlene SEEKLANDER
38	Academic Counselor	Ms. Megan HOWARD

Mitchell Technical Institute (E)

1800 E Spruce, Mitchell SD 57301-2002
County: Davison | FICE Identification: 008284
Unit ID: 219189
Telephone: (605) 995-3025 | Carnegie Class: Assoc/Pub-R-S
FAX Number: (605) 995-3083 | Calendar System: Semester
URL: www.mitchelltech.edu
Established: 1968 | Annual Undergrad Tuition & Fees (In-District): $6,000
Enrollment: 1,091 | Coed
Affiliation or Control: Local | IRS Status: 501(c)3
Highest Offering: Associate Degree
Program: Occupational; 2-Year Principally Bachelor's Creditable; Technical Emphasis
Accreditation: NH, MAC, MLTAD, RAD

Code	Title	Name
01	President	Mr. Greg VON WALD
05	Vice President for Academic Affairs	Ms. Vicki WIESE
11	Vice Pres for Admin Svcs/CFO	Vacant
13	Vice President for Technology	Mr. Dan MUCK
88	Vice Pres for Industrial Relations	Mr. Mark GERHARDT
84	Dean of Enrollment	Mr. Scott FOSSUM
06	Registrar	Ms. Janet GREENWAY
37	Director Student Financial Aid	Mr. Grant UECKER
07	Admissions Coordinator	Mr. Clayton DEUTER
38	Learning Services Coordinator	Ms. Julie HART-SCHUTTE
09	Director of Institutional Research	Ms. Marla SMITH
20	Associate Academic Officer	Ms. Carol GRODE-HANKS
26	Director of Marketing	Ms. Julie BROOKBANK
102	Foundation Director	Ms. Heather LENTZ

Mount Marty College (F)

1105 W 8th, Yankton SD 57078-3724
County: Yankton | FICE Identification: 003465
Unit ID: 219198
Telephone: (605) 668-1011 | Carnegie Class: Bac/Diverse
FAX Number: (605) 668-1607 | Calendar System: Semester
URL: www.mtmc.edu
Established: 1936 | Annual Undergrad Tuition & Fees: $22,892
Enrollment: 1,178 | Coed
Affiliation or Control: Roman Catholic | IRS Status: 501(c)3
Highest Offering: Master's
Program: Liberal Arts And General; Teacher Preparatory; Professional; Nursing Emphasis
Accreditation: NH, ANEST, NURSE

Code	Title	Name
01	President	Dr. Joseph N. BENOIT
04	Asst to the Pres/Asst Sec to Board	Ms. Carla ENG
05	VP for Academic Affairs	Dr. Susan KALSOW
10	VP for Finance/Administration	Ms. Ginger MOELLER
32	VP of Student Affairs	Ms. Sarah CARDA
84	VP for Marketing & Admissions	Ms. Paula TACKE
30	Chief Advancement Officer	Ms. Barb REZAC
27	Chief Information Officer	Mr. Ed KOSTER
11	Chief Operations Officer	Mr. Greg HEINE
09	Director of Institutional Research	Ms. Kristen WELKER
58	Director of Nurse Anesthesia	Dr. Alfred LUPIEN
42	Director of Campus Ministry	Sr. Maribeth WENTZLAFF
12	Director of Watertown Campus	Dr. Linda SCHURMANN
37	Director Student Financial Aid	Mr. Ken KOCER
06	Registrar	Ms. Jonna SUPURGECI
13	Director Information Support Servic	Mr. Paul LAMMERS
08	Director of Library	Ms. Sandra BROWN
40	Dir Bookstore/Central Scheduling	Ms. Mary ABBOTT
38	Dir Student Counseling	Ms. Tracy TAYLOR
41	Athletic Director	Mr. Chuck IVERSON
36	Director Student Placement	Ms. Estelle JOHNSON
07	Director of Admissions	Ms. Jill PAULSON
15	Human Resources Specialist	Ms. Julie DATHER
31	Director of Media Relations	Ms. Kristi TACKE
44	Director of Annual/Planned Giving	Ms. Shannon VIERECK

National American University (G)

5301 S Highway 16, Rapid City SD 57701-8932
County: Pennington | FICE Identification: 004057
Unit ID: 219204
Telephone: (605) 721-5200 | Carnegie Class: Master's S
FAX Number: (605) 721-5241 | Calendar System: Quarter
URL: www.national.edu
Established: 1941 | Annual Undergrad Tuition & Fees: $30,384
Enrollment: 11,685 | Coed
Affiliation or Control: Proprietary | IRS Status: Proprietary
Highest Offering: Master's
Program: Occupational; Professional
Accreditation: NH, CAHIIM, IACBE, MAC, NURSE

Code	Title	Name
01	University President	Dr. Jerry L. GALLENTINE
11	COO	Dr. Samuel KERR
58	System VP Grad Stds/Dean Grad Sch	Dr. Coral NOONAN-TERRY
12	President of Campus Operations	Ms. Michaelle HOLLAND
20	Assoc Provost/Sys VP Curricul/Instr	Ms. Marilyn HOLMGREN
10	Chief Executive Officer	Dr. Ronald SHAPE
06	Registrar	Mr. Tom MAHON
37	Director of Financial Aid	Ms. Cheryl BULLINGER
29	Director Alumni Relations	Mr. Guy TILLETT
21	Director of Student Accounts	Ms. Linda POTTORFF
08	System Librarian	Ms. Pat HAMILTON
12	Campus Exec Ofcr-Ellsworth AFB	Mr. Carlos MOORE
12	Campus Exec Ofcr-Rapid City	Dr. John TERRY
12	Campus Exec Ofcr-Albuquerque	Ms. Jessica CARR
12	Campus Exec Ofcr-Bloomington	Mr. Roger SAGE
12	Campus Exec Ofcr-Brooklyn Center	Mr. Travis JENSEN
12	Campus Exec Ofcr-Colorado Springs	Ms. Courtney HANSEN
12	Campus Exec Ofcr-Overland Park KS	Ms. Kerry NORBURY
12	Campus Exec Ofcr-Roseville	Ms. Samantha THOMPSON
12	Campus Exec Ofcr-Sioux Falls	Ms. Lisa HOUTSMA
12	Campus Exec Ofcr-Independence	Mr. Tyre SMITH
12	Campus Exec Ofcr-Zona Rosa	Mr. Tim DZUBAY
12	Campus Exec Ofcr-Austin	Mr. Brooke JOECKEL
12	Campus Exec Ofcr-Denver	Mr. Brian DEBOSKEY
12	Director-Watertown Education Center	Ms. Traci MAAG
12	Campus Exec Ofcr-Wichita West	Ms. Amber FROST
12	Campus Exec Ofcr-Burnsville MN	Ms. Karli GROSS
12	Campus Exec Ofcr-Minnetonka MN	Mr. Aaron ZELLMER
12	Campus Exec Ofcr-Rochester MN	Mr. Grant NUSTAD
12	Campus Exec Ofcr-Bellevue NE	Mr. Trevor MISCHKE
12	Campus Exec Ofcr-Wichita (East) KS	Ms. Colleen SCHNEIDER
12	Campus Exec Ofcr-Lee's Summit MO	Ms. Tunya CARR
12	Campus Exec Ofcr-Weldon Spring MO	Mr. Jonathan DANIELS
12	Campus Exec Ofcr-Tulsa OK	Ms. Nakia TROUTMAN
12	Campus Exec Ofcr-Centennial CO	Ms. Joanna HANSARD
12	Camp Ex Ofcr-Col Springs (South) CO	Mr. Mark HULL
12	Camp Ex Ofcr-Albuquerque (West) NM	Mr. Steve RIGNEY
12	Campus Exec Ofcr-Austin (South) TX	Dr. Mark WINKLEMAN
12	Campus Exec Ofcr-Lewinsville TX	Mr. Dan IRVIN
12	Campus Exec Ofcr-Mesquite TX	Ms. Amanda OPPEL
12	Campus Exec Ofcr-Richardson TX	Ms. Shalonda JONES
12	Campus Exec Ofcr-Georgetown TX	Mr. Joel LEE

National American University-Sioux Falls (H)

5801 S Corporate Place, Sioux Falls SD 57108
Telephone: (605) 336-5430 | Identification: 770388
Accreditation: &NH

† Main campus is National American University in Rapid City, SD.

Oglala Lakota College (I)

Box 490, Kyle SD 57752-0490
County: Shannon | FICE Identification: 014659
Unit ID: 219277
Telephone: (605) 455-6000 | Carnegie Class: Tribal
FAX Number: (605) 455-2787 | Calendar System: Semester
URL: www.olc.edu
Established: 1971 | Annual Undergrad Tuition & Fees: $2,825
Enrollment: 1,589 | Coed
Affiliation or Control: Tribal Control | IRS Status: 501(c)3
Highest Offering: Master's
Program: Liberal Arts And General
Accreditation: NH, SW

Code	Title	Name
01	President	Mr. Thomas H. SHORTBULL
05	Vice President for Instruction	Dr. Dawn FRANK
10	Vice President for Business	Mr. Thomas SHORTBULL
06	Registrar	Ms. Leslie MESTETH
08	Director Learning Resources	Ms. Michelle MAY
15	Personnel Director	Ms. Faith RICHARDS
37	Financial Aid Director	Ms. Billi HORNBECK
84	Director Enrollment Management	Ms. Leslie MESTETH
07	Director of Admissions	Ms. Leslie MESTETH
09	Director of Institutional Research	Mr. John JOHNSON
21	Assoc Business Ofcr/Dir Purchasing	Ms. Mia ALBERS
29	Director Alumni Relations	Ms. Marilyn POURIER
89	Director of Freshman Studies	Vacant
13	MIS Director	Mr. Cliff DELONG
35	Director Student Affairs	Ms. Leslie HEATHERSHAW
30	Inst Development Coordinator	Ms. Marilyn POURIER
51	Community/Cont Education Coord	Ms. Susan KOLB
88	Applied Science Department Chair	Mr. Andrew THOMPSON
81	Math & Science Department Chair	Mr. Jason TINANT
49	Art & History Department Chair	Ms. Kim BETTELYOUN
53	Education Department Chair	Mr. Thomas RAYMOND
66	Nursing Department Chair	Vacant
83	Human Services Department Chair	Dr. Jeffrey OLSON
88	LAKOTA Studies Department Chair	Ms. Karen LONE HILL
18	Chief Facilities/Physical Plant	Mr. Leonard FERGUSON

Presentation College (J)

1500 N Main Street, Aberdeen SD 57401-1280
County: Brown | FICE Identification: 003467
Unit ID: 219295
Telephone: (605) 225-1634 | Carnegie Class: Bac/Diverse
FAX Number: (605) 229-8330 | Calendar System: Semester
URL: www.presentation.edu
Established: 1951 | Annual Undergrad Tuition & Fees: $25,000
Enrollment: 759 | Coed
Affiliation or Control: Roman Catholic | IRS Status: 501(c)3
Highest Offering: Baccalaureate
Program: Occupational; Professional; Nursing Emphasis
Accreditation: NH, ADNUR, IACBE, MAC, NUR, RAD, SURGT, SW

01 President ....Dr. Margaret HUBER
05 Vice Pres for Academics ....Dr. Michelle METZINGER
10 Vice Pres for Finance ....Ms. Cathy HALL
84 Vice Pres for Enrollment ....Vacant
32 Vice Pres for Student Services ....Mr. Bob SCHUCHARDT
30 Vice President for Advancement ....Ms. Lori HARMEL
06 Registrar ....Ms. Maureen SCHUCHARDT
08 Librarian ....Vacant
37 Director Student Financial Aid ....Ms. Janel WAGNER
108 Assessment Coordinator ....Ms. Nancy VANDER HOEK
15 Director of Human Resources ....Mr. Jason PETTIGREW
26 Coord Marketing/Graphic Design ....Mr. Mark ZOELLNER

Presentation College Lakota (A)

PO Box 1070, Eagle Butte SD 57625
Telephone: (605) 964-4671 Identification: 770417
Accreditation: &NH

† Main campus is Presentation College in Aberdeen, SD.

Sinte Gleska University (B)

Antelope Lake Circle, PO Box 105, Mission SD 57555-0105
County: Todd FICE Identification: 021437
Unit ID: 219374
Telephone: (605) 856-5880 Carnegie Class: Tribal
FAX Number: (605) 856-5401 Calendar System: Semester
URL: www.sintegleska.edu
Established: 1970 Annual Undergrad Tuition & Fees: $3,154
Enrollment: 728 Coed
Affiliation or Control: Independent Non-Profit IRS Status: 501(c)3
Highest Offering: Master's
Program: Liberal Arts And General; Teacher Preparatory; Professional
Accreditation: NH

01 President ....Mr. Lionel BORDEAUX
11 Vice Pres Admin/Dean Student Svcs ....Ms. Cheryl MEDEARIS
06 Registrar ....Mr. Harvey HERMAN
08 Librarian ....Ms. Diana DILLION
10 Fiscal Officer ....Ms. Alisa BARLETT
37 Director Financial Aid ....Mr. William HAY
55 Director Adult Education ....Mr. James SHERMAN, III
15 Director Personnel Dept ....Ms. Lynette BORDEAUX

Sioux Falls Seminary (C)

2100 S Summit Ave, Sioux Falls SD 57105-2729
County: Minnehaha FICE Identification: 004056
Unit ID: 219240
Telephone: (605) 336-6588 Carnegie Class: Spec/Faith
FAX Number: (605) 335-9090 Calendar System: 4/1/4
URL: www.sfseminary.edu
Established: 1858 Annual Graduate Tuition & Fees: $15,974
Enrollment: 167 Coed
Affiliation or Control: North American Baptist IRS Status: 501(c)3
Highest Offering: Doctorate; No Undergraduates
Program: Professional; Religious Emphasis
Accreditation: NH, THEOL

01 President ....Dr. G. Michael HAGAN
05 Academic Vice President & Dean ....Dr. Ronald D. SISK
58 Director of Doctoral Studies ....Dr. Gary E. STRICKLAND
06 Registrar ....Ms. Brenda L. MEDALEN
26 Director Public Relations/Marketing ....Ms. Shanda L. STRICHERZ
84 Director of Enrollment & Fin Aid ....Mr. Nathan M. HELLING

Sisseton-Wahpeton College (D)

PO Box 689, Sisseton SD 57262-0689
County: Roberts FICE Identification: 022773
Unit ID: 219408
Telephone: (605) 698-3966 Carnegie Class: Tribal
FAX Number: (605) 698-3132 Calendar System: Semester
URL: www.swc.tc
Established: 1979 Annual Undergrad Tuition & Fees (In-District): $3,960
Enrollment: 175 Coed
Affiliation or Control: Local IRS Status: 501(c)3
Highest Offering: Associate Degree
Program: Occupational; 2-Year Principally Bachelor's Creditable
Accreditation: NH

01 President ....Dr. Harvey MARCE
05 Vice President of Academic Affairs ....Dr. Jeanette GRAVDAHL
10 Chief Financial Officer ....Ms. Tanya LAFROMEOISE
37 Financial Aid Officer ....Ms. Janel MANY LIGHTNINGS
07 Director of Admissions ....Mrs. Darlene REDDAY
66 Director Nursing ....Ms. Nola RAGAN

*South Dakota State Board of Regents System Office (E)

306 E Capitol Avenue, Suite 200, Pierre SD 57501-2545
County: Hughes FICE Identification: 033438
Telephone: (605) 773-3455 Carnegie Class: N/A
FAX Number: (605) 773-5320
URL: www.sdbor.edu

01 Executive Director ....Dr. Jack R. WARNER
10 System VP Finance & Administration ....Dr. Monte KRAMER
05 System Vice Pres Academic Affairs ....Dr. Samuel GINGERICH
46 System VP Research and Economic Dev ....Dr. Paul TURMAN
43 General Counsel ....Dr. James F. SHEKLETON
15 Director of Human Resources ....Ms. Barbara BASEL
09 Director of Communications ....Dr. Janelle TOMAN
45 Director of Policy & Planning ....Dr. Paul GOUGH
09 Director of Institutional Research ....Dr. Daniel PALMER
21 Director of Finance ....Ms. Heather FORNEY
13 System CIO ....Mr. David HANSEN

*The University of South Dakota (F)

414 E Clark, Vermillion SD 57069-2390
County: Clay FICE Identification: 003474
Unit ID: 219471
Telephone: (605) 677-5011 Carnegie Class: RU/H
FAX Number: (605) 677-5073 Calendar System: Semester
URL: www.usd.edu
Established: 1862 Annual Undergrad Tuition & Fees (In-State): $8,022
Enrollment: 10,284 Coed
Affiliation or Control: State IRS Status: 501(c)3
Highest Offering: Doctorate
Program: Liberal Arts And General; Teacher Preparatory; Professional
Accreditation: NH, ADNUR, ARCPA, ART, AUD, BUS, CACREP, CLPSY, DH, DIETI, JOUR, LAW, MED, MUS, NURSE, OT, PTA, SP, SPAA, SW, TED, THEA

02 President ....Mr. James W. ABBOTT
05 Provost/Vice Pres Academic Affairs ....Dr. Charles A. STABEN
17 Vice President Health Affairs ....Dr. Mary DEKKER NETTLEMAN
10 Vice Pres Finance - CFO ....Ms. Sheila GESTRING
46 Vice President for Research ....Dr. Laura J. JENSKI
26 VP of Marketing/Enrollment Svcs ....Mr. Jeffrey S. BAYLOR
11 Vice Pres Administration & ITS ....Ms. Roberta S. AMBUR
20 Assoc Vice Pres Academic Affairs ....Dr. Kurt B. HACKEMER
28 Associate VP of Diversity ....Dr. Jesus TREVINIO
08 Dean of Libraries ....Mr. Daniel R. DAILY
32 Dean of Students ....Dr. Kimberly GRIEVE
29 Exec Dir Alumni Association ....Ms. Kersten JOHNSON
96 Director of Purchasing ....Mr. Darby GANSCHOW
15 Director Human Resources ....Ms. Diane S. ZAK
22 Affirmative Action Officer ....Ms. Roberta H. HAKL
18 Acting Dir Facilities Management ....Mr. John DAVIS
37 Director of Financial Aid ....Ms. Julie H. PIER
09 Director of Institutional Research ....Dr. Biao ZHANG
36 Dir Ctr for Academic & Career Plng ....Mr. Steve WARD
06 Registrar ....Ms. Jennifer THOMPSON
41 Athletic Director ....Mr. David HERBSTER
30 Director Student Counseling ....Vacant
19 Director Public Safety ....Mr. Peter E. JENSEN
84 Dean of Enrollment ....Mr. Mark PETTY
49 Dean College Arts & Sciences ....Dr. Matthew C. MOEN
50 Dean School of Business ....Mr. Michael J. KELLER
51 Int Director Continuing Education ....Dr. Michael CARD
53 Interim Dean School of Education ....Dr. Hee-Sook CHOI
57 Dean College Fine Arts ....Dr. Larry SCHOU
58 Interim Dean of Graduate Education ....Dr. Laura JENSKI
63 Dean Sanford School of Medicine ....Dr. Mary DEKKER NETTLEMAN
61 Dean chool of Law ....Mr. Thomas GEU

*Black Hills State University (G)

1200 University Street, Spearfish SD 57799-9500
County: Lawrence FICE Identification: 003459
Unit ID: 219046
Telephone: (605) 642-6011 Carnegie Class: Master's S
FAX Number: (605) 642-6214 Calendar System: Semester
URL: www.bhsu.edu
Established: 1883 Annual Undergrad Tuition & Fees (In-State): $7,617
Enrollment: 4,407 Coed
Affiliation or Control: State IRS Status: 501(c)3
Highest Offering: Master's
Program: 2-Year Principally Bachelor's Creditable; Liberal Arts And General; Teacher Preparatory
Accreditation: NH, MUS, TED

02 President ....Dr. Kay SCHALLENKAMP
05 Provost/Vice Pres Academic Affairs ....Dr. Rodney CUSTER
10 Vice President Finance/Admin ....Ms. Kathy J. JOHNSON
30 Vice Pres University Advancement ....Mr. Steve L. MEEKER
32 Vice President for Student Life ....Dr. Lois FLAGSTAD
20 Assoc Vice Pres Academic Affairs ....Dr. Curtis CARD
26 Director Marketing & Communications ....Ms. Corinne HANSEN
27 Chief Information Officer ....Dr. Warren WILSON
37 Director Student Financial Aid ....Ms. Deb HENRIKSEN
38 Director Counseling Center ....Dr. James FLEMING
39 Director Residence Life ....Dr. Michael L. ISAACSON
35 Director Student Services ....Dr. Jane KLUG
15 Director of Human Resources ....Ms. Nancy GRASSEL
06 Registrar ....Ms. April M. MEEKER
07 Director of Admissions ....Ms. Beth OAKS
21 Director of Business Services ....Mr. Rob HOUDEK
18 Director Facilities/Physical Plant ....Mr. Art JONES
29 Director Alumni Relations ....Mr. Tom WHEATON
09 Director of Institutional Research ....Mr. Maxwell KWENDA
08 Director Library Operations ....Mr. Scott AHOLA
104 Director International Studies ....Dr. James FLEMING
30 Director of Development ....Mr. Dwight HANSEN
19 Director Security/Safety ....Mr. Myron SULLIVAN
40 Director University Bookstore ....Mr. Michael JASTORFF
41 Director of Athletics ....Mr. Jhett ALBERS
13 Director Network & Computer Svcs ....Mr. Fred NELSON
49 Dean College of Liberal Arts ....Dr. David WOLFF
50 Dean Col of Business & Natural Sci ....Dr. Priscilla ROMKEMA
53 Dean Col of Educ & Behavioral Sci ....Dr. Patricia SIMPSON
106 Educational Outreach ....Mr. Mitch HOPEWELL
36 Career Development Specialist ....Ms. Sara ELIAS

*Dakota State University (H)

820 N Washington Avenue, Madison SD 57042-1799
County: Lake FICE Identification: 003463
Unit ID: 219082
Telephone: (605) 256-5111 Carnegie Class: Master's S
FAX Number: (605) 256-5316 Calendar System: Semester
URL: www.dsu.edu
Established: 1881 Annual Undergrad Tuition & Fees (In-State): $7,506
Enrollment: 3,110 Coed
Affiliation or Control: State IRS Status: 501(c)3
Highest Offering: Doctorate
Program: 2-Year Principally Bachelor's Creditable; Liberal Arts And General; Teacher Preparatory; Professional; Technical Emphasis
Accreditation: NH, ACBSP, CAHIIM, COARC, TED

02 President ....Dr. David B. BOROFSKY
05 Interim VP for Academic Affairs ....Dr. Judith L. DITTMAN
10 Vice Pres for Business & Admin Svcs ....Mr. Stacy L. KRUSEMARK
32 Vice Pres/Dean Student Affairs ....Mr. Jesse KANE
50 Dean College Business/Info Systems ....Dr. Tom L. HALVERSON
53 Interim Dean College of Education ....Dr. Gale WIEDOW
49 Dean College of Arts and Sciences ....Dr. Benjamin F. JONES
58 Dean of Graduate Studies/Research ....Dr. Omar F. EL-GAYAR
102 Exec Director DSU Foundation ....Vacant
41 Director of Athletics ....Mr. Jeff L. DITTMAN
36 Asst VP Stdnt Affs/Dir Career Svcs ....Dr. Marie A. LOHSANDT
08 Director of Library ....Ms. Ethelle S. BEAN
13 Director of Computing Services ....Mr. David B. OVERBY
29 Director of Alumni ....Ms. Jona M. SCHMIDT
18 Director of Physical Plant ....Mr. Patrick C. KEATING
06 Registrar ....Ms. Sandra E. ANDERSON
37 Director Financial Aid ....Ms. Denise R. GRAYSON
38 Asst Dean for Student Development ....Mr. O. Keith BUNDY
39 Dir of Student Union/Residence Life ....Mr. Steven J. BARTEL
35 Director of Student Activities ....Ms. Amanda L. PARPART
04 Admin Assistant to the President ....Ms. Kacie M. FODNESS
16 Director Human Resources ....Ms. Maria D. HARDER
88 Director Extended Programs ....Dr. Margaret A. O'BRIEN
84 Assoc VP of Enr Mgmt & Marketing ....Ms. Amy S. CRISSINGER
92 Dir Ctr Excell Computer Info Sys ....Dr. Wayne E. PAULI
09 Director of Assessment ....Ms. Carrie A. AHERN
21 Comptroller ....Ms. Amy L. DOCKENDORF
25 Dir of Ctr for Adv of HIT ....Mr. Dan FRIEDRICH
85 International Programs Coordinator ....Ms. Jacy FRY
40 Director of Bookstore ....Mr. Dale P. DAVIS
25 Director of Budget & Grants Admin ....Ms. Sara HARE
25 Director of Sponsored Programs ....Dr. Mickie L. KREIDLER
28 Diversity Coordinator ....Ms. Jennifer ARANDA
26 Assoc Dir of Marketing ....Ms. Erica CLEMENTS

*Northern State University (I)

1200 S Jay Street, Aberdeen SD 57401-7198
County: Brown FICE Identification: 003466
Unit ID: 219259
Telephone: (605) 626-3011 Carnegie Class: Bac/Diverse
FAX Number: (605) 626-3022 Calendar System: Semester
URL: www.northern.edu
Established: 1901 Annual Undergrad Tuition & Fees (In-State): $8,067
Enrollment: 3,622 Coed
Affiliation or Control: State IRS Status: 501(c)3
Highest Offering: Master's
Program: Liberal Arts And General; Teacher Preparatory; Business Emphasis
Accreditation: NH, MUS, TED

02 President ....Dr. James M. SMITH
05 Vice Pres Academic Affs/Provost ....Dr. Thomas HAWLEY
10 Vice Pres Finance/Administration ....Ms. Veronica PAULSON
32 Vice President for Student Affairs ....Dr. Calvin PHILLIPS
29 Vice Pres Alumni Relations ....Mr. Mike BIRGEN
102 President/CEO of Foundation ....Mr. Todd JORDRE
06 Registrar ....Ms. Peggy HALLSTROM
07 Director of Admissions ....Mr. Allan VOGEL
08 Director of Library ....Mr. Robert RUSSELL
36 Director Counsel/Service Learning ....Ms. Deb THORSTENSON
09 Institutional Research Officer ....Mr. Ross NORMAN
25 Director Grants Sponsored Research ....Ms. Karen MARCHANT
13 Director of Computer Services ....Ms. Joann POMPLUN
37 Dir Student Financial Assistance ....Ms. Sharon KIENOW
39 Asst Director of Residence Life ....Mr. Salesi MOUNGA
21 Controller ....Ms. Kay FREDRICK
15 Director of Human Resources ....Ms. Susan BOSTIAN
26 Director of University Relations ....Ms. Brenda DREYER
43 General Counsel ....Mr. John MEYER
18 Director of Facilities Management ....Mr. Monte MEHLHOFF
49 Dean College of Arts & Science ....Dr. Celestino MENDEZ
50 Dean School of Business ....Dr. Willard BROUCEK
53 Dean School of Education ....Dr. Connie GEIER
57 Dean School of Fine Arts ....Dr. Alan LAFAVE
56 Director of Extended Studies ....Mr. Ronald BROWNIE
41 Director of Athletics ....Mr. Joshua MOON
40 Director of Bookstore ....Ms. Beth RASMUSSON
38 Director Student Counseling ....Ms. Deb THORSTENSON

96 Director of Purchasing .... Mr. Earl WEISENBURGER
92 Director Honors Program .... Dr. Erin FOUBERG
28 Multicultural Advisor .... Mr. Peni MOUNGA
35 Director Student Activities .... Vacant

*South Dakota School of Mines and Technology (A)

501 E Saint Joseph, Rapid City SD 57701-3995
County: Pennington FICE Identification: 003470
Unit ID: 219347
Telephone: (605) 394-2511 Carnegie Class: Spec/Engg
FAX Number: (605) 394-6131 Calendar System: Semester
URL: www.sdsmt.edu
Established: 1885 Annual Undergrad Tuition & Fees (In-State): $10,040
Enrollment: 2,424 Coed
Affiliation or Control: State IRS Status: 501(c)3
Highest Offering: Doctorate
Program: Professional; Technical Emphasis
Accreditation: NH, CS, ENG

02 President .... Dr. Heather WILSON
05 Provost/Vice Pres Academic Affs .... Dr. Duane HRNCIR
10 Vice Pres Business/Administration .. Mr. Timothy G. HENDERSON
46 Vice President of Research .... Dr. Ronald J. WHITE
32 VP Student Affs/Dean of Students .... Dr. Patricia G. MAHON
30 VP University Relations .... Ms. Christy A. HORN
20 Associate Provost Academic Affairs .... Dr. Kathryn E. ALLEY
84 Assoc Provost for Enrollment Mgmt .... Dr. Michael C. GUNN
96 Purchasing Manager .... Ms. Barbara MUSTARD
07 Director of Admissions .... Ms. Molly E. FRANKL
29 Director of Alumni Association .... Mr. Timothy J. VOTTERO
90 Director Information Tech Svcs .... Mr. Bryan J. SCHUMACHER
08 Director Devereaux Library .... Ms. Patricia M. ANDERSEN
36 Director Career Services .... Dr. Darrell R. SAWYER
37 Director of Financial Aid .... Mr. David W. MARTIN
88 Dir Inst Atmospheric Sciences .... Dr. Andrew G. DETWILER
41 Interim Director of Athletics .... Ms. Tiffany MCCAMPBELL
102 President SDSM&T Foundation .... Mr. Michael M. SELZER
15 Director Human Resources .... Ms. Kelli R. SHUMAN
18 Director of Facilities Services .... Mr. Clay NOBLE
11 Director of Administrative Services .... Ms. Terry H. GRANT
39 Dir Residence Life/Student Conduct .... Dr. Daniel SEPION
85 Director Ivanhoe International Ctr .... Ms. Susan R. AADLAND
58 Dean of Graduate Education .... Dr. Douglas WELLS
38 Director Student Counseling Svcs .... Ms. Jolie A. MCCOY
84 Registrar and Dir Academic Services .... Ms. Barbara DOLAN
09 Director of Retention & Testing .... Dr. Pat BEU
06 Registration Officer .... Mrs. Diana O'TOOLE
40 Manager College Bookstore .... Mr. Marlin L. KINZER
35 Student Activities Coordinator .... Mr. Michael KEEGAN

*South Dakota State University (B)

Brookings SD 57007-2298
County: Brookings FICE Identification: 003471
Unit ID: 219356
Telephone: (605) 688-4151 Carnegie Class: RU/H
FAX Number: (605) 688-5822 Calendar System: Semester
URL: www.sdstate.edu
Established: 1881 Annual Undergrad Tuition & Fees (In-State): $7,713
Enrollment: 12,583 Coed
Affiliation or Control: State IRS Status: 501(c)3
Highest Offering: Doctorate
Program: Liberal Arts And General; Teacher Preparatory; Professional
Accreditation: NH, AAB, AAFCS, CACREP, CIDA, CONST, CS, DIETD, ENG, ENGT, EXSC, JOUR, MT, MUS, NURSE, PHAR, TED

02 President .... Dr. David L. CHICOINE
05 Provost/Vice Pres Academic Affairs .... Dr. Laurie NICHOLS
32 Vice President Student Affairs .... Dr. Marysz RAMES
45 Vice President of Research .... Dr. Kevin KEPHART
13 VP for Information Technology .... Dr. Michael ADELAINE
10 Vice Pres Finance & Budget .... Mr. Wesley G. TSCHETTER
20 Assoc Vice Pres for Academic Affs .... Dr. Mary Kay HELLING
18 Asst Vice Pres Facilities Services .... Mr. Dean KATTELMANN
88 Asst VP AA Intl Affairs/Outreach .... Dr. Kathleen FAIRFAX
15 Asst Vice Pres Human Resources .... Mr. Marc SERRETT
04 Executive Asst to the President .... Mr. Robert OTTERSON
08 Dean of the Library .... Dr. Kristi TORNQUIST
97 Dean of University College .... Dr. Keith CORBETT
07 Director of Admissions .... Ms. Tracy WELSH
06 Registrar .... Dr. Aaron AURE
38 Director Wellness .... Mr. Jeffrey HUSKEY
37 Financial Aid Officer .... Mr. Jay A. LARSEN
102 President & CEO of Foundation .... Mr. Steve ERPENBACH
29 President & CEO Alumni Affairs .... Mr. Matt FUKS
14 Director Admin & Information Svcs .... Mr. William (Joe) MOORE
19 Chief Security/Safety .... Mr. Tim HEATON
39 Director of Residential Life .... Mr. Jeffrey HALE
40 Director of Bookstore .... Mr. Derek PETERSON
41 Director of Athletics .... Mr. Justin SELL
28 Dir of Diversity/Equal Opportunity .... Ms. Jennifer (Jaime) NOLAN
56 Interim Director of Extension .... Dr. Barry DUNN
26 Dir Marketing/Image/Communications .... Mr. Michael LOCKREM
24 Mgr Instructional Design Services .... Dr. Shouhong ZHANG
85 International Students Manager .... Mr. Greg WYMER
47 Dean Agriculture/Biological Sci .... Dr. Barry DUNN
49 Dean of Arts & Sciences .... Dr. Dennis PAPINI
54 Dean of Engineering .... Dr. Lewis BROWN
53 Dean Education & Human Science .... Dr. Jill THORNGREN
66 Dean of Nursing .... Dr. Roberta K. OLSON

67 Dean of Pharmacy .... Dr. Dennis HEDGE
58 Dean of Graduate School .... Dr. Kinchel DOERNER
92 Dean Honors College .... Dr. Timothy NICHOLS
51 Dean Continuing & Extended Educ .... Vacant

Southeast Technical Institute (C)

2320 N Career Avenue, Sioux Falls SD 57107-1302
County: Minnehaha FICE Identification: 007764
Unit ID: 219426
Telephone: (605) 367-7624 Carnegie Class: Assoc/Pub-R-M
FAX Number: (605) 367-8305 Calendar System: Semester
URL: www.southeasttech.edu
Established: 1968 Annual Undergrad Tuition & Fees (In-District): $4,176
Enrollment: 2,632 Coed
Affiliation or Control: Local IRS Status: 501(c)3
Highest Offering: Associate Degree
Program: Occupational
Accreditation: NH, CVT, DMS, NDT, NMT, SURGT

01 President .... Mr. Jeffrey R. HOLCOMB
05 Vice President of Academics .... Mr. Jim JACOBSEN
10 Vice President Finance & Operations .... Mr. Rich KLUIN
32 Vice Pres Student Affs/Inst Rsrch .... Mr. Tracy NOLDNER
35 Director of Students .... Mr. Jim ROKUSEK
50 Training Solutions Institute .... Mr. Lon HIRD
06 Registrar .... Ms. Kristie VORTHERMS
15 Human Resources Specialist .... Ms. Kathy STRUCK
20 Director of Academic Support .... Dr. Craig PETERS
26 Marketing Coordinator .... Ms. Margaret PENNOCK
102 Foundation Director .... Ms. Nancee STURDEVANT
37 Financial Aid Officer .... Ms. Lynette GRABOWSKA
21 Business Manager .... Mr. James WESTCOTT
38 Personal Counselor .... Ms. Nicole MCMILLIN

University of Sioux Falls (D)

1101 W 22nd Street, Sioux Falls SD 57105-1699
County: Minnehaha FICE Identification: 003469
Unit ID: 219383
Telephone: (605) 331-5000 Carnegie Class: Bac/Diverse
FAX Number: (605) 331-6615 Calendar System: 4/1/4
URL: www.usiouxfalls.edu
Established: 1883 Annual Undergrad Tuition & Fees: $24,550
Enrollment: 1,241 Coed
Affiliation or Control: American Baptist IRS Status: 501(c)3
Highest Offering: Beyond Master's But Less Than Doctorate
Program: Liberal Arts And General; Teacher Preparatory; Professional
Accreditation: NH, IACBE, NURSE, SW, TED

01 President .... Dr. Mark BENEDETTO
04 Exec Assistant to the President .... Ms. Karen BANGASSER
10 VP for Business and Finance .... Ms. Marsha DENNISTON
05 Provost/Vice Pres Academic Affairs .... Dr. Brett BRADFIELD
30 VP Institutional Advancement .... Mr. Jon HIATT
15 VP of Human Resources .... Ms. Julie GEDNALSKE
32 VP of Student Development .... Mr. Gene BROOKS
13 AVP Information Tech .... Mr. William BARTELL
42 Dean of the Chapel .... Rev. Dennis L. THUM
06 Registrar .... Ms. Anna HECKENLAIBLE
21 Controller .... Ms. Susan THIE
37 Director of Financial Aid .... Ms. Karrie MORGAN
07 Director of Admissions .... Ms. Aimee VANDER FEEN
08 Director of Library Services .... Ms. Rachel CROWLEY
84 Director of Academic Success Center .... Ms. Billie STREUFERT
18 Director Buildings/Grounds .... Mr. Chris NAEDELE
41 Athletic Director .... Mr. Kevin HESSER
88 Dir of Degree Completion Program .... Ms. LuAnn GROSSMAN
40 Bookstore Manager .... Ms. Lesley GORBY
58 Chair Business/Dir of MBA/Asst Prof .... Ms. Rebecca MURDOCK
53 Chair Fredrikson School Education .... Ms. Julie MCAREAVEY
57 Chair Fine Arts/Associate Professor .... Ms. Nancy OLIVE
81 Chair Natural Sciences/Assoc Prof .... Dr. William SOEFFING
79 Chair Humanities/Asst Professor .... Ms. Nicholle SCHUELKE
66 Director School of Nursing .... Ms. Jessica CHERENEGAR
83 Chair Social Sciences .... Dr. Sharon COOL

Western Dakota Technical Institute (E)

800 Mickelson Drive, Rapid City SD 57703-4018
County: Pennington FICE Identification: 010170
Unit ID: 219480
Telephone: (605) 394-4034 Carnegie Class: Assoc/Pub-R-S
FAX Number: (605) 394-1789 Calendar System: Semester
URL: www.wdt.edu
Established: 1968 Annual Undergrad Tuition & Fees (In-District): $5,490
Enrollment: 1,019 Coed
Affiliation or Control: Local IRS Status: 501(c)3
Highest Offering: Associate Degree
Program: Occupational; 2-Year Principally Bachelor's Creditable
Accreditation: NH, SURGT

01 President .... Mr. Mark WILSON
05 Dean of Academics .... Ms. Kelly OEHLERKING
10 Dean of Fiscal Operations .... Ms. Heidi ANDERSON
30 Dean of Accreditation & Advancement .... Mr. Stephen BUCHHOLZ
84 Dean of Enrollment Services .... Mr. Brad HENRICH
20 Associate Dean of Academics .... Ms. Jennifer SEALS
13 Information Technology Director .... Mr. Travis LUNDQUIST
37 Manager of Financial Aid .... Ms. Starla RUSSELL
15 Human Resources Manager .... Ms. Theresa SCHARN

36 Career Services Coordinator .... Mr. Curt LAUINGER
07 Admissions Coordinator .... Ms. Jill ELDER

TENNESSEE

All Saints Bible College (F)

930 Mason Street, Memphis TN 38126
County: Shelby Identification: 667014
Telephone: (901) 322-0120 Carnegie Class: Not Classified
FAX Number: (901) 947-3504 Calendar System: Semester
URL: www.allsaintsonline.info
Established: 2002 Annual Undergrad Tuition & Fees: N/A
Enrollment: 76 Coed
Affiliation or Control: Church of God in Christ IRS Status: 501(c)3
Highest Offering: Baccalaureate
Program: Religious Emphasis
Accreditation: @BI

01 Chancellor .... Bishop Charles E. BLAKE
11 Administrator .... Dr. Granville SCRUGGS

American Baptist College (G)

1800 Baptist World Center Drive, Nashville TN 37207
County: Davidson FICE Identification: 010460
Unit ID: 219505
Telephone: (615) 256-1463 Carnegie Class: Spec/Faith
FAX Number: (615) 226-7855 Calendar System: Semester
URL: www.abcnash.edu
Established: 1924 Annual Undergrad Tuition & Fees: $8,688
Enrollment: 121 Coed
Affiliation or Control: Baptist IRS Status: 501(c)3
Highest Offering: Baccalaureate
Program: Liberal Arts And General
Accreditation: BI

01 President .... Dr. Forrest E. HARRIS, SR.
05 Vice President Academic Affairs .... Dr. Renita WEEMS
06 Registrar .... Ms. Pamela TABOR
10 Chief Financial Officer .... Ms. Clara A. WILLIAMS
11 Chief of Campus Operations .... Dr. Vincent CAMPBELL
08 Director Library Services .... Ms. Nicole WHITE
04 Executive Assistant to President .... Mr. Robert HASSELL
32 Dir of Student Success Services .... Ms. LaShante WALKER
09 Director of Institutional Research .... Dr. Regina PRUDE
07 Admissions/Recruiter .... Ms. Brandi TAYLOR

Anthem Career College (H)

560 Royal Parkway, Nashville TN 37214
Telephone: (615) 232-3700 Identification: 770672
Accreditation: ACICS

† Main campus is Anthem College in Phoenix, AZ.

Anthem College (I)

5865 Shelby Oaks Circle, Memphis TN 38134-7345
Telephone: (901) 432-3800 Identification: 770668
Accreditation: ACICS

† Main campus is The Bryman School in Phoenix, AZ.

Aquinas College (J)

4210 Harding Road, Nashville TN 37205-2005
County: Davidson FICE Identification: 003477
Unit ID: 219578
Telephone: (615) 297-7545 Carnegie Class: Bac/Assoc
FAX Number: (615) 279-3892 Calendar System: Semester
URL: www.aquinascollege.edu
Established: 1961 Annual Undergrad Tuition & Fees: $20,550
Enrollment: 618 Coed
Affiliation or Control: Roman Catholic IRS Status: 501(c)3
Highest Offering: Master's
Program: 2-Year Principally Bachelor's Creditable; Liberal Arts And General; Teacher Preparatory; Nursing Emphasis
Accreditation: SC, ADNUR, NUR

01 President .... Sr. Mary Sarah GALBRAITH, OP
11 Vice Pres for Administration .... Mr. Daniel DONNELLY
05 Provost and Vice Pres for Academics .... Sr. Mary BENDYNA, OP
30 Vice Pres Institutional Advancement .... Sr. Mary Sarah GALBRAITH, OP
32 Vice Pres for Student Life .... Sr. Mary Cecilia GOODRUM, OP
20 Associate Provost .... Dr. William SMART
27 Director of Communications .... Mr. Ron KERMAN
07 Director of Admissions .... Ms. Connie HANSOM
06 Registrar .... Ms. Michele PRIDDY
08 Librarian .... Mr. Mark HALL
30 Director of Development .... Vacant
40 Bookstore Manager .... Mr. Alan BRADLEY
66 Dean School of Nursing .... Bro. Ignatius PERKINS, OP
66 Director of ASN Nursing Program .... Mrs. Margaret DANIEL
53 Dean School of Education .... Sr. Mary Anne ZUBERBUELER, OP
37 Director of Financial Aid .... Ms. Martha MARTINEZ
10 Business Manager .... Ms. Deb WELSH
32 Director of Student Affairs .... Mrs. Suzette TELLI
09 Director of Institutional Research .... Dr. William SMART
29 Director of Alumni Relations .... Ms. Rachel LEACH

18 Chief of Facilities/Physical Plant .... Mr. John WALL
15 Director Personnel Services .... Mr. Ron HAZEN
88 Director of Student Learning Svcs .... Ms. Nancy ARNOLD
88 Director of Catechetics .... Sr. Mary Rose BINGHAM, OP
49 Dean School of Arts and Sciences .... Dr. Aaron URBANCZYK
50 Dean School of Business .... Dr. Daniel DONNELLY
88 Dir Center for Catholic Education ... Sr. Elizabeth Anne ALLEN, OP

Argosy University, Nashville (A)

100 Centerview Drive, Suite 225,
Nashville TN 37214-3438
Telephone: (615) 525-2800 Identification: 666668
Accreditation: &WC

† Main campus is Argosy University, Orange County in Orange, CA.

Baptist College of Health Sciences (B)

1003 Monroe Avenue, Memphis TN 38104-3199
County: Shelby FICE Identification: 034403
Unit ID: 219639
Telephone: (901) 575-2247 Carnegie Class: Spec/Health
FAX Number: (901) 572-2461 Calendar System: Trimester
URL: www.bchs.edu
Established: 1994 Annual Undergrad Tuition & Fees: $11,520
Enrollment: 1,004 Coed
Affiliation or Control: Independent Non-Profit IRS Status: 501(c)3
Highest Offering: Baccalaureate
Program: Occupational; Professional
Accreditation: SC, COARC, DMS, NMT, NURSE, RAD, RTT

01 President .... Dr. Betty S. MCGARVEY
10 Vice President Business/Admin Svcs .... Ms. Leanne SMITH
11 Vice President Admin Svcs .... Dr. Adonna CALDWELL
05 Chief Academic Officer/Provost .... Dr. Loredana C. HAEGER
97 Dean General & Health Studies .... Dr. Barry SCHULTZ
66 Dean Nursing .... Dr. Anne M. PLUMB
76 Dean Allied Health .... Dr. Linda REED
32 Dean Student Services .... Ms. Nancy REED
06 Registrar .... Mrs. Denise BOWMAN
07 Director of Admissions .... Ms. Lissa MORGAN
09 Dir of Institutional Effectiveness .... Vacant
29 Director Alumni Relations .... Mrs. Bamby COUNCE
35 Director Student Services & Housing .... Mr. Jeremy WILKES
37 Director Financial Aid .... Ms. April TYSON
84 Dean Enrollment Management .... Ms. Jana TURNER

Belmont University (C)

1900 Belmont Boulevard, Nashville TN 37212-3757
County: Davidson FICE Identification: 003479
Unit ID: 219709
Telephone: (615) 460-6000 Carnegie Class: Master's L
FAX Number: (615) 460-6446 Calendar System: Semester
URL: www.belmont.edu
Established: 1890 Annual Undergrad Tuition & Fees: $27,380
Enrollment: 6,665 Coed
Affiliation or Control: Christian Churches And Churches of Christ
IRS Status: 501(c)3
Highest Offering: Doctorate
Program: Liberal Arts And General; Teacher Preparatory; Professional
Accreditation: SC, ART, BUS, BUSA, ENGT, #LAW, MACTE, MUS, NURSE, OT, PHAR, PTA, SW, TED

01 President .... Dr. Robert C. FISHER
05 Provost .... Dr. Thomas D. BURNS
07 Director of Admissions .... Ms. Brooke DAILEY
11 Vice Pres for Admin & Univ Counsel .... Dr. Jason ROGERS
30 Vice Pres University Advancement .... Dr. Bethel THOMAS
10 Vice President Finance & Operations .... Mr. Steven T. LASLEY
100 Vice President/Chief of Staff .... Dr. Susan H. WEST
42 Vice Pres Spiritual Development .... Dr. Todd LAKE
32 Assoc Provost/Dean of Students .... Vacant
84 Assoc Provost/Dean Enrollment Svcs .... Dr. David MEE
09 Asst Provost/Assess/Instl Research .... Dr. Tracy ROKAS
50 Dean College of Business .... Dr. Patrick RAINES
88 Dean College Visual/Performing Arts .... Dr. Cynthia A. CURTIS
49 Dean College Arts & Sciences .... Dr. Bryce SULLIVAN
76 Dean Col Health Sciences/Nursing .... Dr. Cathy TAYLOR
73 Dean School of Religion .... Dr. Darrell GWALTNEY
61 Dean College of Law .... Mr. Jeffrey S. KINSLER
85 Director of International Education .... Ms. Katherine SKINNER
15 Director of Human Resources .... Mrs. Sally MCKAY
37 Director of Financial Aid .... Mrs. Patricia SMEDLEY
29 Director of Alumni Relations .... Ms. Debbie COPPINGER
18 Director of Facilities Management .... Mr. Henry LACHER
19 Director of Safety & Security .... Mr. Terry A. WHITE
90 Director Technology Services .... Mr. Randall REYNOLDS
06 University Registrar .... Mr. Steven REED
08 Director of Library Services .... Dr. Ernest W. HEARD, JR.
41 Athletic Director .... Mr. Michael D. STRICKLAND
40 Manager Bookstore .... Mrs. Catherine MURPHY
36 Dir Career Svcs/Cooperative Educ .... Mrs. Patricia JACOBS
27 Director of Communications .... Mr. Greg S. PILLON
20 Associate Provost .... Dr. Jimmy DAVIS
38 Director Student Counseling .... Ms. Peg LEONARD-MARTIN

Bethel University (D)

325 Cherry Avenue, McKenzie TN 38201-1705
County: Carroll FICE Identification: 003480
Unit ID: 219718
Telephone: (731) 352-4000 Carnegie Class: Master's M
FAX Number: (731) 352-4069 Calendar System: Semester
URL: www.bethelu.edu
Established: 1842 Annual Undergrad Tuition & Fees: $15,714
Enrollment: 5,836 Coed
Affiliation or Control: Cumberland Presbyterian IRS Status: 501(c)3
Highest Offering: Master's
Program: 2-Year Principally Bachelor's Creditable; Liberal Arts And General; Teacher Preparatory; Professional; Business Emphasis
Accreditation: SC, #ARCPA, NURSE

01 Interim President .... Mr. Walter BUTLER
05 Chief Academic Officer .... Dr. Phyllis CAMPBELL
49 VP College of Arts and Sciences .... Ms. Nancy BEAN
107 VP College of Prof Studies .... Ms. Kelly SANDERS-KELLEY
06 University Registrar .... Ms. Becky HAMES
10 Business Manager .... Mr. Walter BUTLER
07 Dean of Enrollment CLA .... Mrs. Tina HODGES
30 Director of Development .... Mr. Mike PARKER
32 Dean of Student Development .... Mr. James STEWART
37 Director of Financial Aid .... Ms. Janie BURNS
26 Director of Public Relations .... Ms. Jennifer GLASS
38 Director Student Counseling .... Mrs. Sandy LOUDEN
42 Chaplain .... Rev. Anne HAMES
08 Library Director .... Ms. Jill WHITFILL
15 Human Resource Director .... Ms. Carolyn FLOOD
41 Athletic Director .... Mr. Dale KELLEY
09 Director of Institutional Effective .... Dr. Randy CROMWELL
29 Director Alumni Relations .... Mrs. Myra CARLOCK
76 Director of Col of Health Sciences .... Dr. Joe HAMES
88 Dir Sch of Conflict Resolution .... Mr. Clay PHILLIPS

Bryan College (E)

PO Box 7000, Dayton TN 37321-7000
County: Rhea FICE Identification: 003536
Unit ID: 219790
Telephone: (423) 775-2041 Carnegie Class: Bac/Diverse
FAX Number: (423) 775-7330 Calendar System: Semester
URL: www.bryan.edu
Established: 1930 Annual Undergrad Tuition & Fees: $21,150
Enrollment: 1,307 Coed
Affiliation or Control: Independent Non-Profit IRS Status: 501(c)3
Highest Offering: Master's
Program: Liberal Arts And General; Teacher Preparatory
Accreditation: SC, IACBE

01 President .... Dr. Stephen D. LIVESAY
04 Exec Assistant to the President .... Ms. Margaret A. LEGG
05 Academic Vice President .... Dr. Bradford W. SAMPLE
10 Vice President of Finance .... Mr. Vance J. BERGER
30 Vice Pres of College Advancement .... Mr. Blake W. HUDSON
11 Vice President of Operations .... Mr. Timothy J. HOSTETLER
13 Vice Pres Information Systems .... Mr. Rick TAPHORN
84 Vice Pres of Enrollment Management .... Mr. Michael C. SAPIENZA
42 Vice Pres of Spiritual Formation .... Dr. Matt A. BENSON
58 Dean Sch of Adult & Graduate Stds .... Dr. Michael K. CHASE
32 Dean of Students .... Mr. Bruce MORGAN
37 Director of Financial Aid .... Mr. David L. HAGGARD
13 Director of Information Systems .... Mr. Stephen M. PAULSON
06 Registrar .... Ms. Janet M. PIATT
08 Director of Library Sciences .... Dr. Gary N. FITSIMMONS
26 Director of Public Information .... Vacant
15 Director Personnel Services .... Mrs. Angie C. PRICE
41 Athletic Director .... Dr. Sanford ZENSEN
18 Director of Physical Plant .... Mr. David MORGAN
29 Director of Alumni Affairs .... Mrs. Paulakay HALL
07 Director of Admissions .... Mr. Aaron K. PORTER
88 Accreditation Liaison .... Mr. Bill HARLE

Carson-Newman University (F)

1646 Russell Avenue, PO Box 557,
Jefferson City TN 37760-2204
County: Jefferson FICE Identification: 003481
Unit ID: 219806
Telephone: (865) 471-2000 Carnegie Class: Bac/Diverse
FAX Number: (865) 471-3502 Calendar System: Semester
URL: www.cn.edu
Established: 1851 Annual Undergrad Tuition & Fees: $24,207
Enrollment: 2,100 Coed
Affiliation or Control: Southern Baptist IRS Status: 501(c)3
Highest Offering: Doctorate
Program: Liberal Arts And General; Teacher Preparatory; Professional
Accreditation: SC, AAFCS, ART, DIETD, MUS, NURSE, TED

01 President .... Dr. J. Randall O'BRIEN
05 Executive Vice President/Provost .... Dr. Kina S. MALLARD
30 Vice President for Advancement .... Dr. Danny NICHOLSON
32 Vice President Student Affairs .... Dr. Ross BRUMMETT
35 Dean of Student Affairs .... Mrs. Shelley BALL
08 Dean of Library Services .... Mr. Bruce KOCOUR
27 Exec Dir University Relations .... Mrs. Mary LEIDIG
37 Director Financial Aid .... Mrs. Danette SEALE
38 Director Counseling Services .... Mrs. Jennifer CATLETT
07 Director of Admissions .... Mrs. Melanie REDDING
44 Dir Charitable Gift Plan/Annual Fnd .... Mr. Chris CATES
13 Chief Information Officer/IT .... Mrs. Valerie STEPHENS
18 Chief Facilities/Physical Plant .... Mr. Ondes WEBSTER
84 Director of Enrollment Services .... Mrs. Sheryl GRAY
92 Director of Honors Program .... Dr. Brian AUSTIN
20 Associate Provost .... Dr. Naomi LARSEN
15 Director of Human Resources .... Mr. Jimmy WYATT

41 Athletic Director .... Mr. Allen MORGAN
10 Chief Financial/Business Officer .... Mrs. Martha CHAMBERS
85 Dean of Global Education .... Dr. Danny HINSON

Chattanooga College (G)

3805 Brainerd Road, Chattanooga TN 37411-3798
County: Hamilton FICE Identification: 022042
Unit ID: 220118
Telephone: (423) 624-0077 Carnegie Class: Assoc/PrivFP
FAX Number: (423) 624-1575 Calendar System: Quarter
URL: www.chattanoogacollege.edu
Established: 1968 Annual Undergrad Tuition & Fees: $9,825
Enrollment: 326 Coed
Affiliation or Control: Proprietary IRS Status: Proprietary
Highest Offering: Associate Degree
Program: Occupational
Accreditation: ACCSC

01 President .... Mr. William G. FAOUR
03 Vice President .... Mr. Toney C. MCFADDEN
37 Director Financial Aid .... Mrs. Evelyn DAVIS

Christian Brothers University (H)

650 East Parkway S, Memphis TN 38104-5581
County: Shelby FICE Identification: 003482
Unit ID: 219833
Telephone: (901) 321-3000 Carnegie Class: Master's M
FAX Number: (901) 321-3494 Calendar System: Semester
URL: www.cbu.edu
Established: 1871 Annual Undergrad Tuition & Fees: $27,600
Enrollment: 1,302 Coed
Affiliation or Control: Roman Catholic IRS Status: 501(c)3
Highest Offering: Master's
Program: Liberal Arts And General; Teacher Preparatory; Professional
Accreditation: SC, #ARCPA, ENG, NURSE, TED

01 President .... Dr. John SMARRELLI, JR.
05 Vice President Academic Affairs .... Dr. Frank BUSCHER
11 Vice Pres Administration & Finance .... Mr. Dan WORTHAM
30 Vice Pres Institutional Advancement .... Mr. Steve CRISMAN
84 VP for Enrollment Management .... Dr. Anne KENWORTHY
32 Dean of Students .... Ms. Karen CONWAY
13 Dean Information Technology .... Mr. David PALMER
26 Vice Pres Communications/Marketing .... Ms. Elisa MARUS
06 Registrar .... Mrs. Melody L. NABORS
36 Director Career Center .... Mrs. Amy WARE
08 Director of Plough Library .... Ms. Kay CUNNINGHAM
07 Director of Admissions .... Mrs. Rebecca JOHNSON
38 Director of Counseling .... Mrs. Sadie LISENBY
37 Director Financial Resources .... Mr. John LEWIS
09 Dir Inst Research/Effectiveness .... Ms. Melissa S. HANSON
39 Director Residence Life .... Mr. Alton WADE
35 Associate VP for Student Life .... Dr. Timothy DOYLE
42 Director of Ministry and Mission .... Br. Dominic EHRMANTRAUT
92 Director Honors Program .... Dr. Tracie L. BURKE
41 Athletic Director .... Mr. Joseph P. NADICKSBERND
44 Director Development .... Mr. Stephen KIRKPATRICK
29 Director Alumni .... Ms. Karen VIOTTI
21 Controller .... Mr. Thomas COCHRAN
15 Director of Personnel .... Mr. Greg ELLER
18 Chief Facility/Physical Plant .... Mr. Philip R. YELVINGTON
19 Director of Security .... Mr. John D. LOTRIONTE
40 Director Bookstore .... Vacant
50 Dean School of Business .... Dr. Jack HARGETT
54 Dean School of Engineering .... Dr. Eric WELCH
49 Dean School of Arts .... Dr. Paul A. HAUGHT
81 Dean School of Science .... Dr. Johnny B. HOLMES
107 Dir Graduate/Professional Stds Pgms .... Ms. Toni ROSS
58 Director Graduate Education Program .... Dr. Samantha ALPERIN
58 Director MBA Program .... Dr. Scott LAWYER
58 Director Engineering Management Pgm .... Vacant
66 Director Nursing Program .... Dr. Margaret I. VEESER
88 Director Physician Assistant Stds .... Mr. Mark J. SCOTT

Concorde Career College (I)

5100 Poplar Avenue, Suite 132, Memphis TN 38137-0132
County: Shelby FICE Identification: 021571
Unit ID: 219903
Telephone: (901) 761-9494 Carnegie Class: Assoc/PrivFP
FAX Number: (901) 761-3293 Calendar System: Semester
URL: www.concorde.edu
Established: 1967 Annual Undergrad Tuition & Fees: $8,045
Enrollment: 804 Coed
Affiliation or Control: Proprietary IRS Status: Proprietary
Highest Offering: Associate Degree
Program: Occupational
Accreditation: COE, COARC, DA, DH, OTA, PTAA, RAD, SURGT

01 Executive Campus Director .... Mr. Tommy STEWART

The Crown College of the Bible (J)

2307 W. Beaver Creek Dr, Powell TN 37849
County: Knox Identification: 667141
Telephone: (865) 938-8186 Carnegie Class: Not Classified
FAX Number: N/A Calendar System: Semester
URL: thecrowncollege.com
Established: 1991 Annual Undergrad Tuition & Fees: N/A
Enrollment: 3,800 Coed
Affiliation or Control: Baptist IRS Status: 501(c)3

Highest Offering: Master's
Program: Religious Emphasis
Accreditation: @TRACS

01 Founder & President .... Clarence SEXTON
05 Vice President of Academics .... Tim TOMLINSON

Cumberland University (A)

1 Cumberland Square, Lebanon TN 37087-3554
County: Wilson FICE Identification: 003485
Unit ID: 219949
Telephone: (615) 444-2562 Carnegie Class: Master's M
FAX Number: (615) 444-2569 Calendar System: Semester
URL: www.cumberland.edu
Established: 1842 Annual Undergrad Tuition & Fees: $20,200
Enrollment: 1,502 Coed
Affiliation or Control: Independent Non-Profit IRS Status: 501(c)3
Highest Offering: Master's
Program: Liberal Arts And General; Teacher Preparatory; Professional; Nursing Emphasis
Accreditation: SC, ACBSP, NUR, TED

01 President .... Dr. Harvill C. EATON
03 Executive Vice President .... Mr. Eddie PAWLAWSKI
05 Vice President for Academic Affairs . Dr. Wilbur (Pete) PETERSON
11 Director for Administration .... Dr. Joe GRAY
10 Vice President of Finance .... Ms. Judy G. JORDAN
106 Vice President Online Professional .... Ms. Stacey A. GARRETT
30 Vice President of Advancement .... Mr. Rusty RICHARDSON
45 Associate VP for Strategic Affairs .... Ms. Stephanie WALKER
53 Dean Education .... Dr. Eric CUMMINGS
50 Dean Labry School/Technology .... Dr. Paul STUMB
66 Dean Nursing .... Dr. Carol Anne BACH
101 Sec to President/Board of Trustees .... Ms. Leslie STEELE
29 Exec Dir Development/Alumni Rels .... Mr. Jonathan HAWKINS
08 Director Library Services .... Ms. Eloise HITCHCOCK
07 Exec Director Enrollment Services .... Ms. Beatrice LACHANCE
41 Athletic Director .... Mr. Ron PAVAN
06 Registrar .... Ms. Tammi PAVAN
15 Human Resources Director .... Ms. Vickie RICKARD
38 Director of Counseling .... Ms. Juanita KISSELL
13 Chief Information Officer .... Mr. Tony DEDMAN
09 Director of Institutional Research .... Mr. Larry F. VAUGHAN
26 Chief Public Relations Officer .... Mr. Phillip CARTER
40 Manager Bookstore .... Ms. Stephani DE ROUEN
36 Dir of Career Services/Internships .... Mrs. Ronie MCPEAK
39 Director of Residence Life .... Mr. Eddie LOVIN

Daymar Institute (B)

1860 Wilma Rudolph Boulevard,
Clarksville TN 37040-6718
Telephone: (931) 552-7600 Identification: 666492
Accreditation: ACICS, PTAA

† Main campus is Daymar Institute in Nashville, TN.

Daymar Institute (C)

415 Golden Bear Court, Murfreesboro TN 37128-5508
Telephone: (615) 217-9347 Identification: 666392
Accreditation: ACICS

† Main campus is Daymar Institute in Nashville, TN.

Daymar Institute (D)

340 Plus Park Boulevard, Nashville TN 37217-1056
County: Davidson FICE Identification: 004934
Unit ID: 220002
Telephone: (615) 361-7555 Carnegie Class: Assoc/PrivFP
FAX Number: (615) 367-2736 Calendar System: Quarter
URL: www.daymarinstitute.edu
Established: 1884 Annual Undergrad Tuition & Fees: $18,000
Enrollment: 233 Coed
Affiliation or Control: Proprietary IRS Status: Proprietary
Highest Offering: Baccalaureate
Program: Technical Emphasis
Accreditation: ACICS

01 President .... Mr. Mark A. GABIS
12 Campus Director .... Ms. Donna CLARKIN
05 Director of Education .... Mr. Lance WESTBROOKS
07 Director of Admissions .... Mr. Blake BANCROFT
10 Director of Financial Services .... Mr. Gregory DRUESEDOW
36 Director of Career Services .... Vacant
06 Registrar .... Vacant

Emmanuel Christian Seminary (E)

1 Walker Drive, Johnson City TN 37601-9989
County: Carter FICE Identification: 012547
Unit ID: 220136
Telephone: (423) 926-1186 Carnegie Class: Spec/Faith
FAX Number: (423) 926-6198 Calendar System: Semester
URL: www.ecs.edu
Established: 1961 Annual Graduate Tuition & Fees: $11,568
Enrollment: 139 Coed
Affiliation or Control: Christian Churches And Churches of Christ
IRS Status: 501(c)3
Highest Offering: Doctorate; No Undergraduates
Program: Professional
Accreditation: SC, THEOL

01 President .... Dr. Michael L. SWEENEY
05 Dean .... Dr. Rollin RAMSARAN
10 Director of Finance .... Ms. Jacqui R. STEADMAN
30 Executive Director of Development .... Mr. Dan R. LAWSON
08 Librarian .... Mr. John M. WADE
07 Director of Admissions & Recruitmen .... Ms. Erin C. LAYTON
42 Chaplain .... Mrs. Heather E. HOLLAND

Fisk University (F)

1000 17th Avenue N, Nashville TN 37208-3051
County: Davidson FICE Identification: 003490
Unit ID: 220181
Telephone: (615) 329-8500 Carnegie Class: Bac/A&S
FAX Number: N/A Calendar System: Semester
URL: www.fisk.edu
Established: 1866 Annual Undergrad Tuition & Fees: $20,001
Enrollment: 533 Coed
Affiliation or Control: Independent Non-Profit IRS Status: 501(c)3
Highest Offering: Master's
Program: Liberal Arts And General; Teacher Preparatory
Accreditation: #SC, MUS

01 President .... Dr. H. James WILLIAMS
05 Executive Vice President & Provost .... Dr. Princilla E. MORRIS
10 Vice President for Finance and CFO .... Mr. Gary MOORE
04 Exec Assistant to the President .... Mrs. Sherri B. RUCKER
30 Vice President of Inst Advancement .... Mrs. Edwina H. HAMBY
09 VP of Inst Assessment & Research .... Dr. Michael SELF
32 VP of Student Engagement & Enroll .... Mr. Jason MERIWETHER
20 Vice Provost for Acad Initiatives .... Dr. Arnold BURGER
13 Dir Information Technology Svcs .... Mr. LaMetrius DANIELS
29 Exec Director of Alumni Affairs .... Mrs. Adrienne LATHAM
07 Int Dir Recruitment & Admission .... Ms. Loretta MCDONALD
37 Director of Financial Aid .... Mrs. Mary CHAMBLISS
06 Registrar .... Ms. Stephanie CAGE
08 University Librarian .... Dr. Jessie C. SMITH
81 Dean Sch Natural Science/Math/Bus .... Dr. Lee LIMBIRD
41 Dir of Athletics & Intramural Pgms .... Mr. Anthony OWENS
42 Dean of the Chapel .... Dr. Jason CURRY
25 Dir Sponsored Research & Programs .... Ms. Amelia HUNTER
44 Director of Planned Giving .... Ms. Sheila SMITH
18 Director of Facilities .... Mr. Norman RAPP
19 Chief/Director of Campus Safety .... Mr. Mickey WEST
96 Director of Purchasing .... Vacant
36 Director Career Development . Ms. Tashaye BYRDSONG-WOODS
38 Coordinator of Student Counseling .... Dr. Sheila PETERS
15 Director of Human Resources .... Dr. JaCenda DAVIDSON
21 Comptroller .... Vacant

Fortis Institute (G)

1025 Highway 111, Cookeville TN 38501-4305
County: Putnam FICE Identification: 023263
Unit ID: 418870
Telephone: (931) 526-3660 Carnegie Class: Assoc/PrivFP
FAX Number: (931) 372-2603 Calendar System: Quarter
URL: www.fortis.edu/cookeville-tennessee.php
Established: 1970 Annual Undergrad Tuition & Fees: $14,490
Enrollment: 231 Coed
Affiliation or Control: Proprietary IRS Status: Proprietary
Highest Offering: Associate Degree
Program: Occupational
Accreditation: COE, MLTAD, RAD, SURGT

01 Campus Director .... Mr. Bill STRADLEY
05 Dean of Education .... Mr. James WILLIAMSON

Fortis Institute-Nashville (H)

3354 Perimeter Hill Drive, Nashville TN 37211
Telephone: (615) 320-5917 Identification: 770509
Accreditation: ABHES, CVT, MLTAD, RAD

† Main campus is Fortis College in Baton Rouge, LA.

Fountainhead College of Technology (I)

10208 Technology Drive, Knoxville TN 37932
County: Knox FICE Identification: 007439
Unit ID: 221795
Telephone: (865) 688-9422 Carnegie Class: Spec/Tech
FAX Number: (865) 688-2419 Calendar System: Semester
URL: www.fountainheadcollege.edu
Established: 1947 Annual Undergrad Tuition & Fees: $14,550
Enrollment: 180 Coed
Affiliation or Control: Proprietary IRS Status: Proprietary
Highest Offering: Baccalaureate
Program: Occupational; 2-Year Principally Bachelor's Creditable; Technical Emphasis
Accreditation: ACCSC

01 President .... Mr. Richard W. RACKLEY

Freed-Hardeman University (J)

158 E Main, Henderson TN 38340-2398
County: Chester FICE Identification: 003492
Unit ID: 220215
Telephone: (731) 989-6000 Carnegie Class: Master's M
FAX Number: (731) 989-6065 Calendar System: Semester
URL: www.fhu.edu
Established: 1869 Annual Undergrad Tuition & Fees: $20,468
Enrollment: 1,904 Coed
Affiliation or Control: Churches Of Christ IRS Status: 501(c)3
Highest Offering: Beyond Master's But Less Than Doctorate
Program: Liberal Arts And General; Teacher Preparatory
Accreditation: SC, ACBSP, SW, TED

01 President .... Dr. Joe WILEY
04 Executive Assistant to President .... Mrs. Donna STEELE
10 Exec VP and CFO .... Dr. Dwayne WILSON
30 VP for Univ Advancement .... Mr. Dave CLOUSE
05 VP Academics/Enrollment Mgmt .... Dr. Charles VIRES
88 VP for Spiritual Development .... Dr. Samuel JONES
32 VP Student Services .... Dr. Wayne SCOTT
13 VP for Innovation and Technology .... Mr. Mark SCOTT
20 Associate VP for Academics .... Dr. Vicki JOHNSON
41 Director of Athletics .... Mr. Michael MCCUTCHEN
29 Director of Alumni Relations .... Vacant
07 Director of Admissions .... Mr. Joseph ASKEW
35 Dean of Students .... Dr. Wayne SCOTT
35 Dean of Student Life .... Mr. Tony ALLEN
06 Registrar .... Mr. Larry OLDHAM
37 Director Student Financial Services .... Mrs. Summer JUDD
40 University Book Store Manager .... Mr. Logan HAWLEY
08 Interim Library Director .... Mr. Wade OSBURN
70 Director of Social Work Program .... Mrs. Nadine MCNEAL
24 A-V Supervisor .... Mrs. Gail NASH
21 Controller .... Mr. Barry V. SMITH
45 Director of Instnl Effectiveness .... Dr. Jason BRASHIER
09 Director of Institutional Research .... Mr. Micah SMITH
15 Human Resources Coordinator .... Mr. Jay SATTERFIELD
18 Director of Facilities .... Mr. Jeff BARKMAN
26 Director Marketing & Univ Relations .... Mr. Jud DAVIS
73 Dean College of Biblical Studies .... Dr. Billy R. SMITH
50 Dean College of Business .... Mr. Mark STEINER
53 Dean College of Educ & Behav Sci .... Dr. Sharen CYPRESS
49 Dean College of Arts & Sciences .... Dr. LeAnn SELF-DAVIS
92 Dean of Honors College .... Dr. Jenny JOHNSON
23 Campus Physician .... Dr. Kenneth R. CARGILE
104 Dir of International Studies .... Dr. Jenny JOHNSON
38 Director of Counseling .... Mrs. Nicole YOUNG
36 Director of Univ Career Center .... Mr. Jim BROWN
96 Director of Purchasing .... Mr. Barry V. SMITH

Harding School of Theology (K)

1000 Cherry Road, Memphis TN 38117-5499
Telephone: (901) 761-1350 FICE Identification: 004081
Accreditation: &NH, THEOL

† Main campus is Harding University Main Campus in Searcy, AR.

Hiwassee College (L)

225 Hiwassee College Drive, Madisonville TN 37354
County: Monroe FICE Identification: 003494
Unit ID: 220312
Telephone: (423) 442-2001 Carnegie Class: Assoc/PrivNFP
FAX Number: (423) 420-1929 Calendar System: Semester
URL: www.hiwassee.edu
Established: 1850 Annual Undergrad Tuition & Fees: $17,500
Enrollment: 385 Coed
Affiliation or Control: United Methodist IRS Status: 501(c)3
Highest Offering: Baccalaureate
Program: Liberal Arts And General
Accreditation: @TRACS, DH

01 President .... Dr. Robin J. TRICOLI
05 Vice President/Academic Dean .... Dr. Alan JACKSON
10 VP Business Affairs & Treasurer .... D. D THOMPSON
37 Director of Financial Aid .... Ronda MCCLANAHAN

Huntington College of Health Sciences (M)

117 Legacy View Way, Knoxville TN 37918
County: Knox Identification: 666971
Unit ID: 371274
Telephone: (800) 290-4226 Carnegie Class: Not Classified
FAX Number: (865) 524-8339 Calendar System: Semester
URL: www.hchs.edu
Established: 1985 Annual Undergrad Tuition & Fees: $5,051
Enrollment: 250 Coed
Affiliation or Control: Proprietary IRS Status: Proprietary
Highest Offering: Doctorate
Program: Occupational
Accreditation: DETC

01 Chief Executive Officer .... Dr. Art PRESSER
05 Dean of Academics .... Mr. Gene BRUNO
10 Director of Finance .... Mr. Robert SCHMAEF
07 Director of Admissions .... Ms. Kim GALYON

International Academy of Design and Technology (N)

1 Bridgestone Park, Nashville TN 37214-2428
Telephone: (615) 232-7384 Identification: 666347
Accreditation: ACICS, CIDA

† Main campus is International Academy of Design and Technology in Chicago, IL.

ITT Technical Institute (A)

5600 Brainerd Road, Suite G-1, Chattanooga TN 37411
Telephone: (423) 510-6800 Identification: 666708
Accreditation: ACICS

† Main campus is ITT Technical Institute in Indianapolis, IN.

ITT Technical Institute (B)

7260 Goodlett Farms Parkway, Cordova TN 38016-4908
Telephone: (901) 381-0200 Identification: 666550
Accreditation: ACICS

† Main campus is ITT Technical Institute in Indianapolis, IN.

ITT Technical Institute (C)

4721 Lake Park Drive, Suite 100, Johnson City TN 37615
Telephone: (423) 952-4400 Identification: 770663
Accreditation: ACICS

† Main campus is ITT Technical Institute in Indianapolis, IN.

ITT Technical Institute (D)

9123 Executive Park Drive, Knoxville TN 37923
Telephone: (865) 342-2300 FICE Identification: 030734
Accreditation: ACICS

† Main campus is ITT Technical Institute in Indianapolis, IN.

ITT Technical Institute (E)

2845 Elm Hill Pike, Nashville TN 37214-3717
Telephone: (615) 889-8700 FICE Identification: 023598
Accreditation: ACICS

† Main campus is ITT Technical Institute in Indianapolis, IN.

John A. Gupton College (F)

1616 Church Street, Nashville TN 37203-2920
County: Davidson FICE Identification: 008859
Unit ID: 220464
Telephone: (615) 327-3927 Carnegie Class: Assoc/PrivNFP
FAX Number: (615) 321-4518 Calendar System: Semester
URL: www.guptoncollege.edu
Established: 1946 Annual Undergrad Tuition & Fees: $9,440
Enrollment: 133 Coed
Affiliation or Control: Independent Non-Profit IRS Status: 501(c)3
Highest Offering: Associate Degree
Program: Occupational; 2-Year Principally Bachelor's Creditable
Accreditation: SC, FUSER

01 President ....Mr. B. Steven SPANN
08 Library Director ....Mr. William P. BRUCE
06 Registrar ....Ms. Lisa MOFFITT

Johnson University (G)

7900 Johnson Drive, Knoxville TN 37998-0001
County: Knox FICE Identification: 003495
Unit ID: 220473
Telephone: (865) 573-4517 Carnegie Class: Spec/Faith
FAX Number: (865) 251-2337 Calendar System: Semester
URL: www.johnsonu.edu
Established: 1893 Annual Undergrad Tuition & Fees: $16,250
Enrollment: 900 Coed
Affiliation or Control: Christian Churches And Churches of Christ
IRS Status: 501(c)3
Highest Offering: Doctorate
Program: Occupational; 2-Year Principally Bachelor's Creditable; Liberal Arts And General; Teacher Preparatory; Professional; Religious Emphasis
Accreditation: SC, BI

01 President ....Dr. Gary E. WEEDMAN
00 President Emeritus ....Dr. David L. EUBANKS
05 Vice President for Academics ....Dr. Christopher DAVIS
10 Vice Pres for Business and Finance ....Mr. Chris ROLPH
32 Vice President for Student Services ....Mr. David LEGG
30 Vice President for Advancement ....Mr. Philip A. EUBANKS
08 Librarian ....Miss Carrie B. LOWE
06 Registrar ....Mrs. Deborah LANE
07 Deanof Enrollment Services ....Dr. Tim WINGFIELD
37 Financial Aid Director ....Mr. Larry RECTOR
45 Dir Institutional Effectiveness ....Dr. Mark PIERCE
41 Athletic Director ....Mr. Ken UNDERWOOD
18 Director of Plant Services ....Mr. Ben LUTZ, JR.
92 Director of Honors Program ....Dr. Gerald L. MATTINGLY
15 Director Human Resources ....Mrs. Ruthanne BEAM
26 Director of Public Relations ....Mr. Kevin O'BRIEN
38 Director Student Counseling ....Dr. Sean RIDGE

Kaplan Career Institute (H)

750 Envious Lane, Nashville TN 37217-1342
County: Davidson FICE Identification: 023262
Unit ID: 246202
Telephone: (615) 279-8300 Carnegie Class: Assoc/PrivFP
FAX Number: (615) 297-6678 Calendar System: Other
URL: www.kci-nashville.com
Established: 1981 Annual Undergrad Tuition & Fees: $15,577
Enrollment: 345 Coed
Affiliation or Control: Proprietary IRS Status: Proprietary
Highest Offering: Associate Degree
Program: Occupational
Accreditation: ACICS, COE, DA

01 Executive Director ....Ms. Piper FLY

King University (I)

1350 King College Road, Bristol TN 37620-2699
County: Sullivan FICE Identification: 003496
Unit ID: 220516
Telephone: (423) 968-1187 Carnegie Class: Master's M
FAX Number: (423) 968-4456 Calendar System: Other
URL: www.king.edu
Established: 1867 Annual Undergrad Tuition & Fees: $24,052
Enrollment: 2,189 Coed
Affiliation or Control: Presbyterian Church (U.S.A.) IRS Status: 501(c)3
Highest Offering: Master's
Program: Liberal Arts And General; Teacher Preparatory; Professional; Nursing Emphasis
Accreditation: SC, NURSE

01 President ....Dr. Gregory D. JORDAN
05 Dean of Academic Affairs/CAO ....Dr. Matthew ROBERTS
10 Vice President Finance/Operations ....Mr. James P. DONAHUE
32 Vice President for Student Affairs ....Dr. Robert A. LITTLETON
84 Assoc VP of Enrollment Mgmt ....Mr. Micah R. CREWS
26 Vice Pres Marketing & Enrollment ....Mrs. A. LeAnn HUGHES
08 Dean of Library Services ....Ms. Erika BRAMMER
35 Assoc VP/Dean of Student Success ....Mr. Matthew S. PELTIER
04 Executive Assistant to President ....Mrs. Laralee F. HARKLEROAD
06 Registrar/Dir Regist & Records ....Mrs. Sarah L. DILLOW
30 Chief Development Officer ....Mr. John W. KING
09 Director of Institutional Research ....Dr. J. Kevin DEFORD
29 Director of Alumni Relations ....Mrs. Denise ASBURY
42 Chaplain ....Dr. Fred F. STRANG
21 Director of Business Operations ....Mr. Thomas R. LARSON
36 Director of Career Development ....Ms. Donna H. FELTY
41 Athletic Director ....Mr. J. David HICKS
38 Director of Counseling ....Mr. Charles S. THOMPSON
88 Sports Information Director ....Mr. Travis L. CHELL
40 Bookstore Manager ....Ms. Susan D. MARSHALL
37 Director Student Financial Aid ....Vacant
84 Assoc VP Undergrad Enrollment ....Mr. Charles G. KING
18 Chief Facilities/Physical Plant ....Mr. Todd THOMAS
92 Director of Honors Program ....Dr. Craig STREETMAN
26 Director Marketing & Communications ..Ms. Sarah CLEVENTURE
27 Assoc Director of Communication ....Mrs. Laura K. BOGGAN

Lane College (J)

545 Lane Avenue, Jackson TN 38301-4598
County: Madison FICE Identification: 003499
Unit ID: 220598
Telephone: (731) 426-7500 Carnegie Class: Bac/A&S
FAX Number: (731) 427-3987 Calendar System: Semester
URL: www.lanecollege.edu
Established: 1882 Annual Undergrad Tuition & Fees: $9,180
Enrollment: 1,512 Coed
Affiliation or Control: Christian Methodist Episcopal IRS Status: 501(c)3
Highest Offering: Baccalaureate
Program: Liberal Arts And General
Accreditation: SC, @TEAC

01 President ....Dr. Wesley C. MCCLURE
03 Executive Vice President ....Ms. Sharron T. BURNETT
05 Vice President Academic Affairs ....Dr. Deborah B. BUCHANAN
10 Vice President Business & Finance ....Mr. Melvin R. HAMLETT
32 Vice President Student Affairs ....Ms. Sherrill B. SCOTT
30 Vice Pres Inst Advance/Dir Alum Aff .....Mr. Richard H. DONNELL
04 Exec Assistant to the President ....Ms. Darlette C. SAMUELS
18 Chief Facilities/Physical Plant ....Mr. Michael BATES
26 Chief Public Relations Officer ....Ms. Darlette C. SAMUELS
09 Director Institutional Research ....Dr. Fred OKANDA
08 Librarian ....Ms. Lan WANG
07 Director of Admissions ....Ms. Evelyn BROWN
06 Registrar ....Mr. Terry W. BLACKMON
37 Director of Financial Aid ....Mr. Tony CALHOUN
20 Director Academic Assessment ....Dr. Juanita MORRIS
84 Director Enrollment Management ....Dr. Juanita MORRIS
89 Director of Freshman Studies ....Ms. Charlise ANDERSON
96 Director of Purchasing ....Ms. Tammy MCDOUGAL
36 Director Placement Services ....Ms. Virginia S. CRUMP
13 Director Information Technology ......Mr. Earnest L. MITCHELL, III
15 Director of Personnel ....Ms. Juanita MARSHALL
19 Director Security ....Mr. Ernest BOYD
40 Director Bookstore ....Mr. Jeremy MORRIS
19 Director of Safety ....Ms. Aleshia COX
20 Associate Academic Officer ....Dr. Virginia S. CRUMP
21 Associate Business Officer ....Mr. Duan ROBINSON
41 Director of Athletics ....Ms. Penny MINTER
29 Director Alumni Relations ....Ms. Monica CLAYBORNE SCOTT
35 Director Student Affairs ....Mr. Reginald CLEVELAND
27 Chief Information Officer ....Ms. Tori L. HALIBURTON
38 Director Student Counseling ....Dr. April SMITH

L'Ecole Culinaire Memphis (K)

1245 North Germantown Parkway, Cordova TN 38016
Telephone: (901) 754-7115 Identification: 770841
Accreditation: ACCSC

† Main campus is Vatterott College-Des Moines in Des Moines, IA.

Lee University (L)

1120 N Ocoee Street, Cleveland TN 37320-3450
County: Bradley FICE Identification: 003500
Unit ID: 220613
Telephone: (423) 614-8100 Carnegie Class: Master's M
FAX Number: (423) 614-8083 Calendar System: Semester
URL: www.leeuniversity.edu
Established: 1918 Annual Undergrad Tuition & Fees: $13,750
Enrollment: 4,954 Coed
Affiliation or Control: Church Of God IRS Status: 501(c)3
Highest Offering: Beyond Master's But Less Than Doctorate
Program: Liberal Arts And General; Teacher Preparatory
Accreditation: SC, ACBSP, MUS, TED

01 President ....Dr. C. Paul CONN
04 Executive Assistant to President ....Mrs. Stephanie TAYLOR
10 Vice President Business & Finance ....Mr. Chris CONINE
05 Vice President for Academic Affairs ....Dr. Deborah MURRAY
11 Vice President for Administration ....Dr. Walter MAULDIN
84 Vice President for Enrollment ....Mr. Phil COOK
26 VP for University Relations ....Dr. Jerome HAMMOND
32 VP for Student Development ....Mr. Mike HAYES
27 VP for Information Services ....Dr. Jayson VAN HOOK
21 Comptroller ....Mr. Duane PACE
37 Director of Student Aid ....Mrs. Marian DILL
35 Dean of Students ....Mr. Alan MCCLUNG
15 Director of Human Resources ....Mrs. Ann MCELRATH
14 Director of IT Operations ....Mr. Chris GOLDEN
13 Director of IT Systems ....Mr. Nate TUCKER
29 Director of Alumni Relations ....Mrs. Patti CAWOOD
39 Director of Residential Life ....Ms. Tracey CARLSON
06 Registrar ....Ms. Cathy THOMPSOM
21 Bursar ....Ms. Kristy HARNER
08 Librarian ....Ms. Barbara MCCULLOUGH
42 Director of Campus Ministries ....Rev. Jimmy HARPER
25 Director of Grants ....Mrs. Vanessa HAMMOND
19 Director of Campus Safety ....Mr. Ashley MEW
23 Director of Health Services ....Mr. Mickey MOORE
27 Director of Public Information ....Mr. Brian CONN
73 Dean School of Religion ....Dr. Terry CROSS
49 Dean College of Arts & Sciences ....Dr. Matthew MELTON
53 Dean College of Education ....Dr. William ESTES
64 Dean School of Music ....Dr. William GREEN
51 Exec Dir of Div of Adult Learning ....Dr. Joshua BLACK
07 Director of Graduate Enrollment ....Ms. Vicki GLASSCOCK
38 Director Counseling & Testing ....Mr. David QUAGLIANA
18 Director of Physical Plant ....Mr. Larry BERRY
41 Athletic Director ....Mr. Larry CARPENTER
104 Director of Global Perspectives ....Mrs. Angeline MCMULLIN
36 Director of Calling and Career ....Ms. Stacy BALLINGER
09 Director of Institutional Research ....Dr. Stacey TUCKER

LeMoyne-Owen College (M)

807 Walker Avenue, Memphis TN 38126-6595
County: Shelby FICE Identification: 003501
Unit ID: 220604
Telephone: (901) 435-1000 Carnegie Class: Bac/Diverse
FAX Number: (901) 435-1699 Calendar System: Semester
URL: www.loc.edu
Established: 1862 Annual Undergrad Tuition & Fees: $10,460
Enrollment: 1,078 Coed
Affiliation or Control: Multiple Protestant Denominations
IRS Status: 501(c)3
Highest Offering: Baccalaureate
Program: Liberal Arts And General; Teacher Preparatory
Accreditation: SC, TED

01 President ....Mr. Johnnie B. WATSON
05 VP/Chief Academic Officer ....Dr. Cheryl GOLDEN
10 Chief Financial Officer ....Mr. Jim DUGGER
88 Director Title III Administration ....Ms. Shirley HILL
32 Dean of Students ....Ms. Edythe COBB
30 Exec Dir Institutional Advancement ....Mr. Roger BROWN
84 Exec Dir Enrollment Management ......Mrs. June CHINN-JOINTER
16 Director of Human Resources ....Mr. Michael WASHINGTON
08 Librarian ....Ms. Annette BERHE
37 Director Student Financial Services ....Ms. Phyllis TORRY
06 Registrar ....Mr. Addie HARVEY
36 Director Career Services/Placement ....Dr. Denita HEDGEMAN
29 Director of Alumni Relations ....Ms. Frankie JEFFRIES
14 Director Information Technology ....Vacant
21 Controller ....Ms. Colleen GIBSON
09 Director Institutional Research ......Mr. Reoungeneria MCFARLAND
92 Director Dubois Honors Program ....Dr. Elton WEAVER, III
35 Director Student Activities ....Ms. Felecia FOSTER
50 Chair Div Business & Econ Devel ....Dr. Katherine CAUSEY
53 Chair Education Division ....Dr. Ralph CALHOUN
57 Chair Div Fine Arts & Humanities ....Mr. Claybourne FOSTER
65 Chair Div Natural & Math Science ....Dr. Delphia HARRIS
83 Chair Div Social & Behavioral Sci ....Mr. Michael ROBINSON
38 Director Student Counseling ....Mr. Tony WHITSON
26 Dir Public Relations & Marketing ....Ms. Daphne J. THOMAS
41 Director of Athletics ....Mr. William ANDERSON
11 Director Administrative Services ....Mr. Jesse CHATMAN
88 Exec Director Engaged Student Learn ....Dr. Linda WHITE

Lincoln College of Technology Nashville (N)

1524 Gallatin Road, Nashville TN 37206-3298
County: Davidson FICE Identification: 007440
Unit ID: 221148

Telephone: (615) 226-3990 Carnegie Class: Assoc/PrivFP
FAX Number: (615) 262-8466 Calendar System: Other
URL: www.lincolncollegeoftechnology.com
Established: 1919 Annual Undergrad Tuition & Fees: $25,800
Enrollment: 2,200 Coed
Affiliation or Control: Proprietary IRS Status: Proprietary
Highest Offering: Associate Degree
Program: Occupational
Accreditation: ACCSC

01 President Mr. Jim COAKLEY
05 Academic Dean Mr. Raymond BAUHS
07 Vice President of Admissions Mr. Shayne PULVER
37 Director of Financial Aid Mr. Chris BIDDLE
06 Registrar Mr. Gary WHITE

Lincoln Memorial University (A)

6965 Cumberland Gap Parkway,
Harrogate TN 37752-1901
County: Claiborne FICE Identification: 003502
Unit ID: 220631
Telephone: (423) 869-3611 Carnegie Class: Master's L
FAX Number: (423) 869-6250 Calendar System: Semester
URL: www.lmunet.edu
Established: 1897 Annual Undergrad Tuition & Fees: $18,960
Enrollment: 4,338 Coed
Affiliation or Control: Independent Non-Profit IRS Status: 501(c)3
Highest Offering: Doctorate
Program: 2-Year Principally Bachelor's Creditable; Liberal Arts And General; Teacher Preparatory; Professional
Accreditation: SC, ACBSP, ADNUR, ANEST, ARCPA, CACREP, MT, NUR, OSTEO, SW, @VET

01 President Dr. B. James DAWSON
11 Dean for Administration Ms. Lisa COX
30 VP University Advancement Ms. Cynthia L. WHITT
05 Vice President for Academic Affairs Dr. Clayton HESS
10 Vice President of Finance Ms. Kimberlee BONTRAGER
61 Interim VP/Dean School of Law Mr. Parham WILLIAMS
07 Director of Admission Ms. Sherry MCCREARY
53 Dean of School of Education Dr. Michael CLYBURN
81 Dean of Mathematics & Sciences Dr. Amiel JARSTFER
66 Dean School of Nursing Dr. Mary Anne MODRCIN
50 Dean School of Business Dr. Jack MCCANN
32 Dean of Students Mr. Robert SABBATINI
04 Exec Assistant to the President Mrs. Janet SMITH
37 Executive Director of Financial Aid Mr. Bryan ERSLAN
09 Director of Institutional Research Vacant
41 Athletic Director Mr. Roger VANNOY
18 Director Properties/Physical Plant Mr. Rodney COCHRAN
15 Director of Human Resources Ms. Libby KING
96 Director Purchasing/Accts Payable Ms. Pat TENNYSON
06 Registrar Ms. Helen BAILEY
90 Director of Acad Computing Support Vacant
42 University Chaplain Dr. Ray PENN
43 Legal Counsel Ms. Martha MCCAMPBELL
13 Chief Information Officer Mr. Jason MCCONNELL
26 Senior Director of Marketing Mrs. Kate M. REAGAN
29 Director Alumni Services Mr. Donnie LIPSCOMB
40 Bookstore Manager Mr. Rick CROWDER
49 Dean of Arts & Humanities Dr. Martin SELLERS
108 Director of Assessment Mr. Salim MCDOWELL

Lipscomb University (B)

One University Park Dr., Nashville TN 37204-3951
County: Davidson FICE Identification: 003486
Unit ID: 219976
Telephone: (615) 966-1000 Carnegie Class: Master's L
FAX Number: (615) 966-1798 Calendar System: Semester
URL: www.lipscomb.edu
Established: 1891 Annual Undergrad Tuition & Fees: $26,094
Enrollment: 4,254 Coed
Affiliation or Control: Churches Of Christ IRS Status: 501(c)3
Highest Offering: Doctorate
Program: Liberal Arts And General; Teacher Preparatory; Professional
Accreditation: SC, ACBSP, DIETD, DIETI, ENG, MUS, NUR, PHAR, SW, TED, THEOL

01 President Dr. L. Randolph LOWRY, III
05 Provost Dr. W. Craig BLEDSOE
45 Senior VP Strategic Initiatives Dr. Nancy MAGNUSSON DURHAM
10 Senior VP Finance & Administration Mr. Danny TAYLOR
26 VP University Relations Mr. Walt LEAVER
30 VP Development & Alumni Relations Dr. Bennie L. HARRIS
32 VP Student Develop/Dean Campus Life Dr. Scott MCDOWELL
26 VP Communications & Marketing Ms. Deby K. SAMUELS
42 Vice President for Church Services Dr. Scott SAGER
13 Vice President Info Technology/CIO Mr. Mike GREEN
20 Assoc Prov Acad Admin & Strat Init Dr. Susan C. GALBREATH
43 General Counsel Vacant
41 Director of Athletics Mr. Philip HUTCHESON
20 Associate Provost Academic Support Mr. Steve PREWITT
20 Assoc Provost for Grad Studies Dr. Randy BOULDIN
88 Assoc Prov for Inst Effectiveness Dr. Elaine GRIFFIN
88 Assoc Provost Sponsored Programs Dr. Jeff MCCORMACK
79 Dean College of Arts & Sciences Dr. Norma BURGESS
73 Dean College of Bible & Ministry Vacant
50 Dean College of Business Mr. Turney STEVENS
53 Dean College of Education Dr. Candice MCQUEEN
81 Dean College of Engineering Dr. Justin MYRICK
67 Dean College of Pharmacy Dr. Roger DAVIS
107 Dean College of Prof Studies Dr. Charla LONG
55 Dir School of Computing/Informatics Dr. Fortune MHLANGA
39 Associate Dean & Dir Residence Life Dr. Sam SMITH
35 Associate Dean of Campus Life Ms. Sarah GAMBLE
21 Associate VP Finance Mr. Darrell DUNCAN
102 Associate VP Advancement Mr. David ENGLAND
29 Asst VP Develop & Alumni Relations Mrs. Carrie THOMPSON
44 Senior Director of Development Mr. Mark MEADOR
07 Senior Director of Admissions Mr. Rick HOLAWAY
06 Registrar Mrs. Janet CATES
37 Director of Financial Aid Ms. Tiffany SUMMERS
08 Director of Library Services Ms. Carolyn WILSON
19 Director of Campus Safety Mr. Jim HUMPHREY
36 Director of Career Development Ctr Mrs. Monica WENTWORTH
88 Senior Director of Student Success Mr. Brian MAST
88 Director of Student Advocacy Ms. Teresa WILLIAMS
55 Director Adult Degree Program Dr. Teresa CLARK
73 Dir of Hazelip School of Theology Dr. Mark BLACK
88 Dir of Grad Exercise & Nutrition Dr. Karen ROBICHAUD
58 Director of Graduate Education Dr. Deborah BOYD
83 Dir of Grad Studies in Psychology Dr. Jake MORRIS
58 Associate Dean of Graduate Business Dr. Mike KENDRICK
88 Asst Dean of Executive Education Dr. John LOWRY
88 Dir Inst for Conflict Management Dr. Steve JOINER
88 Dir Inst for Chistian Spirituality Dr. Earl LAVENDER
88 Dir Inst for Law Justice & Society Dr. Randy SPIVEY
88 Exec Dir Inst for Civic Leadership Dr. Linda SCHACHT
88 Exec Dir Inst for Sustain Practice Mr. Dodd GALBREATH
38 Director Counseling Center Vacant
88 Director of Spiritual Outreach Mr. Steve DAVIDSON
28 Asst Dean Intercultural Development Mrs. Tenielle BUCHANAN
28 Asst Dean Intercultural Engagement Mrs. Jessica GARCIA VAN DE GRIEK
09 Director of Institutional Research Mr. Matt REHBEIN
15 Director Human Resources Mr. Matt TILLER
88 Director of Campus Enhancement Mr. Tom WOOD
18 Director of Campus & Retail Ops Mr. Jeff WILSON
91 Director of Admin Computing Mr. Joe TRIMBLE
105 Director of Information Security Mr. Dave WAGNER

Martin Methodist College (C)

433 W Madison Street, Pulaski TN 38478-2799
County: Giles FICE Identification: 003504
Unit ID: 220701
Telephone: (931) 363-9800 Carnegie Class: Bac/Diverse
FAX Number: (931) 363-9818 Calendar System: Semester
URL: www.martinmethodist.edu
Established: 1870 Annual Undergrad Tuition & Fees: $21,422
Enrollment: 1,070 Coed
Affiliation or Control: United Methodist IRS Status: 501(c)3
Highest Offering: Baccalaureate
Program: Liberal Arts And General
Accreditation: SC, NURSE

01 President Dr. Ted R. BROWN
05 Vice President of Academic Affairs Dr. James T. MURRELL
10 VP for Finance & Administration Mr. David J. STEPHENS
32 VP Campus Life/Enrollment Mgmt Mr. Robby C. SHELTON
30 Vice Pres for College Advancement Mr. David JONES
06 Registrar Mrs. Casey CAPPS
41 Athletic Director Mr. Jeff N. BAIN
42 Chaplain Rev. Laura KIRKPATRICK
08 Librarian Mr. Richard MADDEN
40 Director of Bookstore Mrs. Margaret W. JACKSON
29 Alumni Affairs Director Mrs. Edna LUNA
04 Assistant to the President Mrs. Kim W. HARRISON
07 Director of Admissions Mrs. Lisa SMITH
15 Director Personnel Services Mr. James R. HLUBB
21 Controller Ms. Rhonda CLINARD
37 Director Student Financial Aid Mrs. Emma HLUBB
18 Chief Facilities/Physical Plant Mr. Fred HYDE
26 Director of Public Relations Mr. Grant VOSBURGH
38 Dir Student Counseling/Career/Svcs Ms. Doris F. WOSSUM
85 Director Foreign Students Mrs. Robin HOOD
13 Director of Technology Mr. Edward MARTIN
09 Director of Institutional Research Dr. Dennis HASKINS

Maryville College (D)

502 E Lamar Alexander Parkway,
Maryville TN 37804-5907
County: Blount FICE Identification: 003505
Unit ID: 220710
Telephone: (865) 981-8000 Carnegie Class: Bac/A&S
FAX Number: (865) 981-8010 Calendar System: Semester
URL: www.maryvillecollege.edu
Established: 1819 Annual Undergrad Tuition & Fees: $31,132
Enrollment: 1,093 Coed
Affiliation or Control: Presbyterian Church (U.S.A.) IRS Status: 501(c)3
Highest Offering: Baccalaureate
Program: Liberal Arts And General; Teacher Preparatory; Professional
Accreditation: SC, MUS

01 President Dr. William T. BOGART
05 Vice President & Dean of College Dr. Barbara WELLS
10 Vice President & Treasurer Mr. Dana SMITH
32 Vice President & Dean of Students Ms. Vandy KEMP
84 Vice President for Enrollment Dr. Dolph HENRY
30 VP of Advancement & Cmty Rels Vacant
09 Associate Dean & Dir of IR Dr. Martha P. CRAIG
07 Director of Admissions Ms. Cyndi SWEET
35 Assistant Dean of Students Ms. Allison NORRIS
21 Controller Ms. Julie RAMSEY
39 Director Residence Life Ms. Kristin GOURLEY
26 Director of Marketing Vacant
104 Director of International Education Ms. Kirsten SHEPPARD
27 Director of Communications Ms. Karen ELDRIDGE
06 Registrar Ms. Kathi WILSON
13 Director of Information Technology Mr. Mark FUGATE
90 Dir of Instructional Technology Dr. Steven JAMES
88 Director of Academic Support Center Ms. Lori HUNTER
36 Director of Career Resources Ms. Thema MCCOWAN
37 Director of Financial Aid Mr. Richard BRAND
41 Athletic Director Ms. Kandis SCHRAM
08 Director of the Library Ms. Angela QUICK
18 Director of Physical Plant Mr. Andy K. MCCALL
42 Campus Minister Rev. Anne MCKEE
04 Assistant to President Ms. Laura M. CASE
15 Director of Human Resources Ms. Keni LANAGAN
38 Director of Counseling Mr. Bruce HOLT
44 Director of Annual Giving Mr. Eric BELLAH
22 Director of Minority Services Mr. Larry ERVIN
29 Dir of Stewardship & Alumni Bd Rels Ms. Diana CANACARIS

Meharry Medical College (E)

1005 Dr. D. B. Todd Jr. Boulevard,
Nashville TN 37208-3501
County: Davidson FICE Identification: 003506
Unit ID: 220792
Telephone: (615) 327-6111 Carnegie Class: Spec/Med
FAX Number: (615) 327-6540 Calendar System: Semester
URL: www.mmc.edu
Established: 1876 Annual Graduate Tuition & Fees: $48,173
Enrollment: 782 Coed
Affiliation or Control: Independent Non-Profit IRS Status: 501(c)3
Highest Offering: Doctorate; No Undergraduates
Program: Professional
Accreditation: SC, DENT, MED, PH

01 President/Chief Executive Ofcr Dr. Anna Cherrie EPPS
11 Exec Vice Pres & COO Dr. Frank ROYAL, JR.
63 Sr VP & Dean School of Medicine Dr. Charles P. MOUTON
32 Int Assoc Dean Student/Academic Aff Dr. Mildred D. COLLINS
17 Sr Vice President Health Affairs Dr. Charles P. MOUTON
30 Sr VP Institutional Advancement Mr. Robert S. POOLE
10 Senior Vice President & CFO Mrs. LaMel BANDY-NEAL
35 Sr VP Student Svcs/Faculty Affairs Dr. Barbara JOHNSON
45 Vice President for Research Dr. Russell POLAND
31 VP External Affs/Business Develop Mr. Osei MEVS
13 Assoc VP Information Technology Mr. Andrew JACKSON
18 Asc Vice Pres Facilities/Securities Dr. Bernard RAY
16 Int Assoc Vice Pres Human Resources Mr. Mark SMITH
26 Assoc VP Marketing/Communications Ms. Janet CALDWELL
21 Assoc Vice Pres Financial Systems Mr. Larry HOLDEN
46 Assoc VP for Research-Grants Mgmt Vacant
25 Asst Vice Pres Grants & Contracts Mr. George WILLIAMS
43 Int General Counsel/Corp Sec/Sr VP Mrs. Ivanetta DAVIS-SAMUELS
58 Dean Graduate Studies and Research Dr. Maria DE FATIMA LIMA
51 Director Lifelong Learning Dr. Allyson FLEMING
76 Dean Allied Health Professions Vacant
52 Interim Dean School of Dentistry Dr. Cherae FARMER-DIXON
29 Executive Director Alumni Affairs Dr. Henry MOSES
07 Director Admissions & Recruitment Mr. Angelo C. LEE
08 Director of Library Dr. Fatima MNCUBE-BARNES
19 Director Campus Safety & Security Ms. Theresa MCKINNON
37 Director Student Financial Aid Ms. Barbara THARPE
09 Director Institutional Research Dr. Chau-Kuang CHEN
100 Chief of Staff Ms. Amber DUVENTRE
18 Director Facilities Mr. George N. KELLY
38 Director Counseling Center Ms. Sharda D. MISHRA
06 Registrar Ms. Shanita BROWN

Memphis College of Art (F)

1930 Poplar Avenue, Overton Park,
Memphis TN 38104-2764
County: Shelby FICE Identification: 003507
Unit ID: 220808
Telephone: (901) 272-5100 Carnegie Class: Spec/Arts
FAX Number: (901) 272-5104 Calendar System: Semester
URL: www.mca.edu
Established: 1936 Annual Undergrad Tuition & Fees: $26,250
Enrollment: 401 Coed
Affiliation or Control: Independent Non-Profit IRS Status: 501(c)3
Highest Offering: Master's
Program: Professional; Fine Arts Emphasis
Accreditation: SC, ART

01 President Dr. Ronald L. JONES
05 Dean of Faculty Mr. Remy MILLER
10 Vice Pres Finance & Administration Ms. Sherry YELVINGTON
30 Vice President College Advancement Ms. Shawna ENGEL
32 Vice Pres Student Affairs Ms. Susan S. MILLER
21 Assoc Vice Pres Finance & Admin Mr. Jonathan WELDEN
08 Librarian Ms. Leslie HOLLAND
04 Assistant to President Ms. Becky RUPE
07 Director Admissions Ms. Annette JAMES-MOORE

32 Director Student Life .... Ms. Carla RUFFER
37 Director Financial Aid .... Mr. Aaron WHITE
06 Registrar .... Mr. Sean SCOTT
13 Director Institutional Technology .... Mr. Gordon DOVER
26 Director College Communications .... Ms. Carrie CORBETT
29 Director Alumni & Donor Relations .... Ms. LeeAnn WARNER
36 Director Career Services .... Ms. Carrie Allison BROOKS
19 Campus Safety & Operations Manager .... Mr. Donald KELLY
88 Business Office Manager .... Ms. Heather RAGLAND
31 Director Community Education .... Ms. Cecelia PALAZOLA

Memphis Theological Seminary (A)

168 East Parkway S at Union, Memphis TN 38104-4395
County: Shelby FICE Identification: 010529
Unit ID: 220871
Telephone: (901) 458-8232 Carnegie Class: Spec/Faith
FAX Number: (901) 452-4051 Calendar System: Semester
URL: www.memphisseminary.edu
Established: 1852 Annual Graduate Tuition & Fees: $14,000
Enrollment: 300 Coed
Affiliation or Control: Cumberland Presbyterian IRS Status: 501(c)3
Highest Offering: Doctorate; No Undergraduates
Program: Professional; Religious Emphasis
Accreditation: SC, THEOL

01 President .... Dr. Daniel J. EARHEART-BROWN
05 Vice President Academic Affs & Dean .... Dr. Robert S. WOOD
30 Vice President of Advancement .... Mrs. Cathi JOHNSON
08 Librarian .... Ms. Jane K. WILLIAMSON
51 Assoc Dean Continuing Education .... Mr. Pete GATHJE
10 Vice President of Operations/ CFO .... Mrs. Cassandra F. PRICE-PERRY
32 Director of Student Services .... Dr. Barry L. ANDERSON
06 Dir Acad Rec/Regist & Accreditation .... Dr. Gail D. ROBINSON

Mid-America Baptist Theological Seminary (B)

2095 Appling Road, Cordova TN 38016-4911
County: Shelby FICE Identification: 029172
Unit ID: 220914
Telephone: (901) 751-8453 Carnegie Class: Not Classified
FAX Number: (901) 751-8454 Calendar System: Semester
URL: www.mabts.edu
Established: 1972 Annual Undergrad Tuition & Fees: $5,290
Enrollment: 498 Coed
Affiliation or Control: Independent Non-Profit IRS Status: 501(c)3
Highest Offering: Doctorate
Program: 2-Year Principally Bachelor's Creditable; Teacher Preparatory; Professional
Accreditation: SC

01 President .... Dr. Michael R. SPRADLIN
03 Executive Vice President .... Dr. Bradley THOMPSON
05 Academic Vice President .... Dr. Timothy SEAL
10 Vice Pres for Finance & Operations .... Mr. Randy REDD
30 Chief Development Officer .... Mr. Duffy GUYTON
20 Dean of Masters & Associate Pgm .... Dr. Kirk KILPATRICK
12 Director NE Branch .... Dr. Tim CHRISTIAN
06 Registrar .... Mrs. Rose MINK
08 Director of Library Services .... Mr. Terrence BROWN
42 Director of Practical Missions .... Dr. Jeff BRAWNER
07 Director of Admissions .... Dr. Andy HYNES
04 Admin Assistant to the President .... Mrs. Maria WOOTEN
18 Supt of Buildings & Grounds .... Mr. Gene APPLEBURY
40 Manager Bookstore .... Mr. Brad JOHNSON

Mid-South Christian College (C)

PO Box 181056, Memphis TN 38181
County: Shelby Identification: 667046
Telephone: (901) 375-4400 Carnegie Class: Not Classified
FAX Number: (901) 375-4085 Calendar System: Semester
URL: www.midsouthcc.org
Established: 1959 Annual Undergrad Tuition & Fees: $5,900
Enrollment: 24 Coed
Affiliation or Control: Independent Non-Profit IRS Status: 501(c)3
Highest Offering: Baccalaureate
Program: Religious Emphasis
Accreditation: @BI

01 President .... Mr. Larry GRIFFIN
05 Academic Dean .... Mr. Wray GRAHAM
32 Director of Student Services .... Mr. Brent LINN
30 Chief Development Officer .... Mr. John BLIFFEN
88 Director Institutional Improvement .... Mr. Greg WADDELL

Middle Tennessee School of Anesthesia (D)

PO Box 417, 315 Hospital Drive, Madison TN 37116-6414
County: Davidson FICE Identification: 007783
Unit ID: 220996
Telephone: (615) 868-6503 Carnegie Class: Spec/Health
FAX Number: (615) 868-9885 Calendar System: Quarter
URL: www.mtsa.edu
Established: 1950 Annual Graduate Tuition & Fees: $30,891
Enrollment: 204 Coed
Affiliation or Control: Independent Non-Profit IRS Status: 501(c)3
Highest Offering: Doctorate; No Undergraduates
Program: Professional
Accreditation: SC, ANEST

01 President .... Dr. Kenneth L. SCHWAB
05 Dean/Program Administrator .... Dr. Christopher P. HULIN
10 VP for Finance & Administration .... Sam L. MINTEN
26 VP for Advancement & Alumni .... James B. CLOSSER
20 Assistant Program Administrator .... Dr. Rachel M. BROWN
88 Dir of Inst Effectiveness & LR .... Dr. Amy C. GIDEON

Miller-Motte Technical College (E)

6020 Shallowford Road, Suite 100, Chattanooga TN 37421
Telephone: (423) 510-9675 Identification: 770781
Accreditation: ACICS, MAC, SURGT

† Main campus is Miller-Motte Technical College in Clarksville, TN.

Miller-Motte Technical College (F)

1820 Business Park Drive, Clarksville TN 37040-6023
County: Montgomery FICE Identification: 026142
Unit ID: 382771
Telephone: (931) 553-0071 Carnegie Class: Assoc/PrivFP
FAX Number: (931) 552-2916 Calendar System: Quarter
URL: www.miller-motte.edu
Established: 1916 Annual Undergrad Tuition & Fees: $9,900
Enrollment: 548 Coed
Affiliation or Control: Proprietary IRS Status: Proprietary
Highest Offering: Associate Degree
Program: Occupational
Accreditation: ACICS, COARC, MAC, POLYT, SURGT

01 Director .... Ms. Gina CASTLEBERRY
05 Director of Education .... Ms. Kala MATHIS
37 Financial Aid Director .... Ms. Debbie STRATMAN
06 Registrar .... Ms. Patricia CLINE
36 Director of Career Development .... Mr. John MCCASLIN
07 Director of Admissions .... Mr. Nicholas DESHAZOR
72 CIS/Technology Division .... Mr. Bruce LIVESAY

Miller-Motte Technical College (G)

1515 North Gallatin Pike, Madison TN 37115
Telephone: (615) 859-8090 Identification: 770782
Accreditation: ACICS

† Main campus is Miller-Motte Technical College in Clarksville, TN.

Milligan College (H)

2010 Milligan College PO Box 500, Milligan College TN 37682-4000
County: Carter FICE Identification: 003511
Unit ID: 221014
Telephone: (423) 461-8700 Carnegie Class: Bac/Diverse
FAX Number: (423) 461-8755 Calendar System: Semester
URL: www.milligan.edu
Established: 1866 Annual Undergrad Tuition & Fees: $26,890
Enrollment: 1,164 Coed
Affiliation or Control: Independent Non-Profit IRS Status: 501(c)3
Highest Offering: Master's
Program: Liberal Arts And General; Teacher Preparatory; Professional
Accreditation: SC, NURSE, OT, TED

01 President .... Dr. William B. GREER
05 Vice Pres Academic Affairs/Dean .... Dr. Garland YOUNG
32 Vice President Student Affairs .... Mr. Mark FOX
30 Vice Pres Institutional Advancement .... Mr. Jack SIMPSON
84 Vice Pres Enrollment Management .... Dr. Lee FIERBAUGH
21 Vice Pres Business & Finance .... Mrs. Jacqui STEADMAN
06 Registrar .... Mrs. Sue SKIDMORE
07 Director of Admissions .... Ms. Tracy BRINN
08 Director of Library Services .... Mr. Gary DAUGHT
35 Director of Student Activities .... Mrs. Krystal DOVE
29 Director of Alumni Relations .... Ms. Theresa GARBE
15 Director Personnel Services .... Ms. Linda LAWSON
09 Director of Institutional Research .... Ms. Sue SKIDMORE
37 Coordinator of Financial Aid .... Ms. Diane KEASLING
26 Director of Church Relations .... Mrs. Phyllis FOX
36 Director Student Placement .... Ms. Beth ANDERSON
18 Service Manager Facilities .... Mr. Ken BROYLES
28 Director of Diversity .... Vacant

National College of Business and Technology (I)

5760 Stage Road, Bartlett TN 38134
Telephone: (901) 213-1681 Identification: 770783
Accreditation: ACICS, MAC

† Main campus is National College of Business and Technology in Nashville, TN.

National College of Business and Technology (J)

1328 Highway 11 W, Bristol TN 37620-8530
Telephone: (423) 878-4440 Identification: 666500
Accreditation: ACICS, MAC

† Main campus is National College of Business and Technology in Nashville, TN.

National College of Business and Technology (K)

8415 Kingston Pike, Knoxville TN 37919
Telephone: (865) 539-2011 Identification: 770786
Accreditation: ACICS, MAC

† Main campus is National College of Business and Technology in Nashville, TN.

National College of Business and Technology (L)

900 Madison Square, Madison TN 37115
Telephone: (615) 612-3015 Identification: 770784
Accreditation: ACICS, CAHIIM, MAC

† Main campus is National College of Business and Technology in Nashville, TN.

National College of Business and Technology (M)

2526 Thousand Oaks Cove, Memphis TN 38118
Telephone: (901) 363-9046 Identification: 770785
Accreditation: ACICS, CAHIIM, MAC, SURGT

† Main campus is National College of Business and Technology in Nashville, TN.

National College of Business and Technology (N)

1638 Bell Road, Nashville TN 37211
County: Davidson FICE Identification: 004617
Unit ID: 388043
Telephone: (615) 333-3344 Carnegie Class: Assoc/PrivFP
FAX Number: (615) 333-3429 Calendar System: Quarter
URL: www.national-college.edu
Established: 1991 Annual Undergrad Tuition & Fees: $11,436
Enrollment: 627 Coed
Affiliation or Control: Proprietary IRS Status: Proprietary
Highest Offering: Baccalaureate
Program: Occupational
Accreditation: ACICS, MAC

01 Director .... Mr. Gary ADCOX

North Central Institute (O)

168 Jack Miller Boulevard, Clarksville TN 37042-4810
County: Montgomery FICE Identification: 030791
Unit ID: 418889
Telephone: (931) 431-9700 Carnegie Class: Assoc/PrivFP
FAX Number: (931) 431-9771 Calendar System: Semester
URL: www.nci.edu
Established: 1988 Annual Undergrad Tuition & Fees: $13,770
Enrollment: 384 Coed
Affiliation or Control: Proprietary IRS Status: Proprietary
Highest Offering: Associate Degree
Program: Occupational; 2-Year Principally Bachelor's Creditable; Technical Emphasis
Accreditation: COE

01 President .... Ms. Tamela K. TALIENTO

Nossi College of Art (P)

590 Cheron Road, Nashville TN 37115
County: Davidson FICE Identification: 025782
Unit ID: 368452
Telephone: (615) 514-2787 Carnegie Class: Spec/Arts
FAX Number: (615) 514-2788 Calendar System: Trimester
URL: www.nossi.edu
Established: 1973 Annual Undergrad Tuition & Fees: $14,100
Enrollment: 375 Coed
Affiliation or Control: Proprietary IRS Status: Proprietary
Highest Offering: Baccalaureate
Program: Occupational
Accreditation: ACCSC

01 President .... Ms. Nossi VATANDOOST
07 Admissions Director .... Ms. Mary ALEXANDER
37 Financial Aid Director .... Ms. Mary KIDD

O'More College of Design (Q)

423 S Margin Street, Franklin TN 37064
County: Williamson FICE Identification: 021064
Unit ID: 221254
Telephone: (615) 794-4254 Carnegie Class: Spec/Arts
FAX Number: (615) 790-1662 Calendar System: Semester
URL: www.omorecollege.edu
Established: 1970 Annual Undergrad Tuition & Fees: $26,000
Enrollment: 210 Coed
Affiliation or Control: Independent Non-Profit IRS Status: 501(c)3
Highest Offering: Baccalaureate
Program: Occupational; Liberal Arts And General; Fine Arts Emphasis
Accreditation: ACCSC, CIDA

01	Interim President	Ms. Rebecca STILWELL
03	Executive Vice President	Ms. Shari FOX
06	Registrar/VP Student Affairs	Ms. Amy SHELTON
10	Director of Business Affairs	Ms. Teresa CORLEY
19	Director of Security	Mr. DeWayne PULLIAM
07	Director of Admissions	Ms. Melinda DABBS
08	Librarian and Bookstore Manager	Ms. Allison CRAWFORD
88	Chair Visual Communications	Mr. Josh LOMELINO
88	Chair Fashion Design/Merch	Ms. Jamie ATLAS
88	Chair Interior Design	Mr. David KOELLEIN
57	Fine Arts Curator	Mr. John WATTS

Oxford Graduate School (A)

500 Oxford Drive, Dayton TN 37321-6736

County: Rhea — FICE Identification: 038403

Unit ID: 461120

Telephone: (423) 775-6596 — Carnegie Class: Not Classified

FAX Number: (423) 775-6599 — Calendar System: Trimester

URL: www.ogs.edu

Established: 1981 — Annual Graduate Tuition & Fees: $31,500

Enrollment: 98 — Coed

Affiliation or Control: Independent Non-Profit — IRS Status: 501(c)3

Highest Offering: Doctorate; No Undergraduates

Program: Professional

Accreditation: TRACS

01	President	Dr. Richard A. HUMPHREY
00	Chancellor	Dr. Rollin VAN BROEKHOVEN
05	Vice President Acadmic Affairs	Dr. Richard P. WALTERS
07	Vice President of Recruitment	Vacant
08	Head Librarian	Mr. David WAND
09	Director Institutional Research	Dr. Joshua REICHARD
10	Chief Business Officer	Ms. Sharlene DANIEL
29	Director Alumni Relations	Dr. Jimmilea BERRYHILL
37	Director Financial Aid/Admissions	Mr. Michael FARRAND
42	Chaplain	Mr. Curtis MCCLANE
06	Registrar	Mr. Gary BOLDEN

Pentecostal Theological Seminary (B)

900 Walker Street, NE, Cleveland TN 37311

County: Bradley — FICE Identification: 021883

Unit ID: 219842

Telephone: (423) 478-1131 — Carnegie Class: Spec/Faith

FAX Number: (423) 478-7711 — Calendar System: 4/1/4

URL: www.ptseminary.edu

Established: 1975 — Annual Graduate Tuition & Fees: $10,628

Enrollment: 192 — Coed

Affiliation or Control: Church Of God — IRS Status: 501(c)3

Highest Offering: Doctorate; No Undergraduates

Program: Professional

Accreditation: SC, THEOL

01	President	Dr. Steven J. LAND
05	VP for Academics	Dr. Sang-Ehil HAN
42	VP for Ministry Formation	Dr. Oliver L. MCMAHAN
10	VP for Finance	Mr. Robert E. BUXTON
30	VP for Institutional Advancement	Rev. Ken R. DAVIS
04	Exec Assistant to the President	Mrs. Teresa GILBERT
27	Director Recruitment/Communications	Dr. J. Anthony LOMBARD
06	Director of Acad Records/Registrar	Ms. Anita F. BLEVINS
15	Director of Administrative Services	Mrs. Alanna L. HENRY
18	Dir of Facilities/Support Services	Mr. Phillip WOODS
29	Dir Donor and Alumni Relations	Mrs. Joylita TERPSTRA
32	Director of Student Services	Dr. Welton WRISTON
37	Director of Financial Aid	Mrs. Robin SLUDER
38	Director of Counseling/Testing	Dr. Douglas SLOCUMB

Remington College (C)

2710 Nonconnah Boulevard, Memphis TN 38132-2110

Telephone: (901) 345-1000 — Identification: 666062

Accreditation: ACCSC

† Main campus is Remington College, Mobile Campus in Mobile, AL.

Remington College (D)

441 Donelson Pike, Suite 150, Nashville TN 37214-3558

Telephone: (615) 889-5520 — Identification: 666307

Accreditation: ACCSC, DH

† Main campus is Remington College, Mobile Campus in Mobile, AL.

Rhodes College (E)

2000 North Parkway, Memphis TN 38112-1690

County: Shelby — FICE Identification: 003519

Unit ID: 221351

Telephone: (901) 843-3000 — Carnegie Class: Bac/A&S

FAX Number: N/A — Calendar System: Semester

URL: www.rhodes.edu

Established: 1848 — Annual Undergrad Tuition & Fees: $39,484

Enrollment: 1,927 — Coed

Affiliation or Control: Presbyterian Church (U.S.A.) — IRS Status: 501(c)3

Highest Offering: Master's

Program: Liberal Arts And General

Accreditation: SC, MUS

01	President	Dr. William E. TROUTT
05	Provost	Dr. Michael R. DROMPP
10	VP for Finance & Business Affairs	Mr. J. Allen BOONE
13	Vice Pres for Information Services	Dr. Robert M. JOHNSON, JR.
30	Vice President for Development	Ms. Jennifer G. WADE
84	Vice Pres Enrollment/Communications	Mr. Carey THOMPSON
32	Dean of Students	Ms. Carol E. CASEY
35	Associate Dean of Students	Ms. Kathleen LAAKSO
20	Assoc Dean of Academic Affairs	Dr. Brian W. SHAFFER
20	Assoc Dean of Academic Affairs	Dr. John S. OLSEN
20	Assoc Dean of Academic Affairs	Dr. Anita A. DAVIS
06	Registrar	Ms. DeAnna ADAMS
37	Director of Financial Aid	Ms. Ashley BIANCHI
08	Librarian	Ms. Darlene D. BROOKS
21	Comptroller	Mr. Kyle WEBB
29	Director of Alumni Relations	Mr. Warren A. RICHEY
15	Director of Human Resources	Ms. Claire R. SHAPIRO
14	Director of Info Tech Services	Dr. Charles LEMOND
19	Director of Campus Safety	Mr. Ike SLOAS
41	Director of Athletics	Mr. Michael T. CLARY
36	Director of Career Services	Ms. Sandra G. TRACY
38	Director of Counseling Services	Mr. Robert B. DOVE
18	Director of Physical Plant	Mr. Brian E. FOSHEE
44	Director of Planned Giving	Mr. Jim DUNCAN
27	Director of Communications	Mr. Ken WOODMANSEE
09	Director of Institutional Research	Vacant
04	Exec Assistant to the President	Ms. Melody H. RICHEY
96	Physical Plant Business Manager	Ms. Amy J. RADFORD

Richmont Graduate University (F)

1815 McCallie Avenue, Chattanooga TN 37404

FICE Identification: 033554

Unit ID: 441104

Telephone: (423) 266-4574 — Carnegie Class: Spec/Health

FAX Number: (423) 265-7375 — Calendar System: Semester

URL: www.richmont.edu

Established: 1973 — Annual Graduate Tuition & Fees: $13,200

Enrollment: 256 — Coed

Affiliation or Control: Independent Non-Profit — IRS Status: 501(c)3

Highest Offering: Master's; No Undergraduates

Program: Professional

Accreditation: SC

01	Interim President	Dr. Bob RODGERS, JR.
03	Vice Pres/Chair of Integration	Dr. Gary W. MOON
30	Vice President for Advancement	Mr. George DEMPSEY
84	Vice President Enrollment	Mr. Trent R. GILBERT
04	Assistant to the President	Ms. Jennifer COOPER
05	Academic Dean	Dr. Philip A. COYLE
10	Chief Financial Officer	Mr. William J. MUELLER

SAE Institute of Technology Nashville (G)

7 Music Circle North, Nashville TN 37203

County: Davidson — FICE Identification: 038303

Unit ID: 446525

Telephone: (615) 244-5848 — Carnegie Class: Not Classified

FAX Number: (615) 244-3192 — Calendar System: Semester

URL: www.sae.edu

Established: — Annual Undergrad Tuition & Fees: $18,500

Enrollment: 122 — Coed

Affiliation or Control: Proprietary — IRS Status: Proprietary

Highest Offering: Associate Degree

Program: Occupational

Accreditation: ACCSC

Sewanee: The University of the South (H)

735 University Avenue, Sewanee TN 37383-1000

County: Franklin — FICE Identification: 003534

Unit ID: 221519

Telephone: (931) 598-1000 — Carnegie Class: Bac/A&S

FAX Number: (931) 598-1145 — Calendar System: Semester

URL: www.sewanee.edu

Established: 1857 — Annual Undergrad Tuition & Fees: $35,756

Enrollment: 1,588 — Coed

Affiliation or Control: Protestant Episcopal — IRS Status: 501(c)3

Highest Offering: Doctorate

Program: Liberal Arts And General; Professional

Accreditation: SC, THEOL

01	Vice Chancellor & President	Dr. John M. MCCARDELL, JR.
05	Provost	Dr. John R. SWALLOW
30	Vice President for Advancement	Mr. Jay FISHER
13	Assoc Provost Info Tech/Librarian	Dr. Vicki G. SELLS
20	Associate Provost Academic Affairs	Dr. Nancy BERNER
49	Dean College of Arts & Sciences	Dr. John J. GATTA
73	Dean School of Theology	Rt Rev. J Neil ALEXANDER
32	Dean of Students	Mr. Eric G. HARTMAN
09	Director of Institutional Research	Dr. Robert A. LESTER, III
06	Registrar	Mr. Paul G. WILEY
07	Dean of Admission & Financial Aid	Ms. Lee Ann M. AFTON-BACKLUND
37	Assoc Dean Student Financial Aid	Ms. Beth CRAGAR
26	Exec Dir Marketing/Communications	Mr. Parker OLIVER
15	Director of Human Resources	Ms. Mary WILSON
41	Director of Athletics	Mr. Mark F. WEBB
29	Director of Alumni Relations	Ms. Susan S. ASKEW
36	Director of Career Services	Ms. Kim D. HEITZENRATER
38	Director of University Counseling	Dr. David L. SPAULDING
93	Director of Minority Affairs	Mr. Eric V. BENJAMIN
18	Director of Physical Plant Services	Mr. John P. VINEYARD
43	University Legal Counsel	Ms. Donna L. PIERCE
35	Associate Dean of Students	Dr. Alex M. BRUCE
19	Chief of Police	Ms. Marie ELDRIDGE
21	Treasurer	Ms. Sarah R. SUTHERLAND
23	Director of Univ Health Services	Ms. Karen THARP
24	Director of Media Services	Mr. Larry E. WOOD
42	University Chaplain & Dean	V.Rev. Thomas E. MACFIE
11	Assoc Vice President for Admin	Mr. Frank GLADU

South College (I)

3904 Lonas Drive, Knoxville TN 37909-3323

County: Knox — FICE Identification: 004938

Unit ID: 220552

Telephone: (865) 251-1800 — Carnegie Class: Bac/Assoc

FAX Number: (865) 584-7335 — Calendar System: Quarter

URL: www.southcollegetn.edu

Established: 1882 — Annual Undergrad Tuition & Fees: $18,425

Enrollment: 1,066 — Coed

Affiliation or Control: Proprietary — IRS Status: Proprietary

Highest Offering: Doctorate

Program: Occupational; Teacher Preparatory; Professional

Accreditation: SC, ARCPA, MAC, NMT, NUR, @PHAR, PTAA, RAD

01	President	Mr. Stephen A. SOUTH
05	Executive VP and Provost	Dr. Kim B. HALL
11	VP Admin & Regulatory Compliance	Mr. Steve WOODFORD
13	VP Information Tech/Facilities	Mr. Ron HALL
09	VP Inst Effective/Student Svcs	Ms. Barbara BRIMI
84	VP Enrollment Management	Mr. Walter HOSEA
10	Chief Financial Officer	Mr. Mark HAUB
26	Public Relations Coordinator	Mr. Norman HAMMITT
36	Job Placement Coordinator	Mr. Gary TAYLOR
06	Registrar	Ms. Kim WOOD
37	Director of Financial Aid	Mr. Larry BROADWATER
08	Head Librarian	Ms. Mary MCHUGH
72	Director Instructional Technology	Dr. Jennifer GRAMLING

Southern Adventist University (J)

Box 370, 5010 University Drive, Collegedale TN 37315-0370

County: Hamilton — FICE Identification: 003518

Unit ID: 221661

Telephone: (423) 236-2000 — Carnegie Class: Bac/Diverse

FAX Number: (423) 236-1000 — Calendar System: Semester

URL: www.southern.edu

Established: 1892 — Annual Undergrad Tuition & Fees: $19,790

Enrollment: 3,319 — Coed

Affiliation or Control: Seventh-day Adventist — IRS Status: 501(c)3

Highest Offering: Doctorate

Program: Liberal Arts And General; Teacher Preparatory

Accreditation: SC, ADNUR, CS, IACBE, MUS, NUR, SW, TED

01	President	Dr. Gordon BIETZ
05	Vice Pres Academic Administration	Dr. Robert YOUNG
10	Vice President Finance	Mr. Tom VERRILL
32	Vice President Student Services	Dr. William R. WOHLERS
45	Vice Pres Strategic Initiatives	Mrs. Vinita R. SAUDER
30	Vice President Advancement	Mr. Chris CAREY
84	Vice Pres Enrollment Services	Mr. Marc A. GRUNDY
20	Associate VP Academic Admin	Dr. Volker HENNING
21	Associate VP Financial Admin	Mr. Marty HAMILTON
13	Assoc VP Information Systems	Mr. Gary SEWELL
09	Director Inst Research/Planning	Dr. Hollis JAMES
08	Director of Libraries	Vacant
06	Director Records & Advisement	Mrs. Joni I. ZIER
15	Director Personnel Services	Mrs. Pat COVERDALE
26	Chief Public Relations Officer	Ms. Ingrid SKANTZ
29	Director Alumni Relations	Ms. Evonne CROOK
38	Director Student Counseling	Dr. Jim WAMPLER
33	Dean of Men	Mr. Dwight E. MAGERS
34	Dean of Women	Ms. Kassy KRAUSE
50	Dean School of Business/Mgmt	Dr. Mark HYDER
53	Dean School of Education/Psych	Dr. John MCCOY
57	Dean School of Visual Art/Design	Mr. Randy CRAVEN
60	Dean School of Journalism/Comm	Dr. Greg RUMSEY
64	Dean School of Music	Dr. Scott BALL
66	Dean School of Nursing	Dr. Barbara JAMES
68	Dean Sch of Phys Ed/Health/Wellness	Dr. Robert BENGE
73	Dean School of Religion	Dr. Greg KING
77	Dean School of Computing	Dr. Rick HALTERMAN
70	Chair Social Work/Family Studies	Dr. Rene' DRUMM
72	Chair Technology	Mr. Dale WALTERS
81	Chair Mathematics	Dr. Kevin BROWN
76	Chair Biology/Allied Health	Dr. Keith SNYDER
88	Chair Chemistry	Dr. Rhonda J. SCOTT
88	Chair English	Dr. Jan HALUSKA
88	Chair History	Dr. Lisa C. DILLER
88	Chair Modern Languages	Dr. Carlos P. PARRA
88	Chair Physics	Dr. Chris HANSEN
18	Chief Facilities/Physical Plant	Mr. Eric SCHOONARD
35	Director Student Affairs	Ms. Kari SHULTZ
37	Director Student Financial Aid	Mrs. Paula WALTERS
96	Director of Purchasing	Mr. Russell ORRISON

Southern College of Optometry (K)

1245 Madison Avenue, Memphis TN 38104-2222

County: Shelby — FICE Identification: 003517

Unit ID: 221670

Telephone: (901) 722-3200 Carnegie Class: Spec/Health
FAX Number: (901) 722-3279 Calendar System: Trimester
URL: www.sco.edu
Established: 1932 Annual Graduate Tuition & Fees: $29,496
Enrollment: 498 Coed
Affiliation or Control: Independent Non-Profit IRS Status: 501(c)3
Highest Offering: Doctorate; No Undergraduates
Program: Professional
Accreditation: SC, OPT, OPTR

01 President ...Dr. Richard W. PHILLIPS
04 Executive Admin Assistant to Pres ...Ms. Sandra S. STEPHENS
05 Vice President for Academic Affairs ...Dr. Lewis REICH
30 Vice President for Inst Advancement ...Dr. Kristin K. ANDERSON
102 Dir of Corp & Foundation Relations ...Ms. Christine M. WEINREICH
10 Vice President for Finance & Admin ...Mr. David L. WEST
13 Director of Information Services ...Mr. Dean SWICK
18 Director of Physical Plant ...Mr. Danny ANDERSON
17 Vice Pres for Clinical Programs ...Dr. James E. VENABLE
23 Director of Clinic Operations ...Mr. Gary SNUFFIN
06 Vice President for Student Services ...Mr. Joseph H. HAUSER
07 Dir of Admissions/Enrollment Svcs ...Mr. Michael N. ROBERTSON
07 Director of Student Recruitment ...Ms. Sunnie EWING
08 Director of Library ...Dr. Sharon E. TABACHNICK
27 Dir of Communications/Media Svcs ...Mr. Jim HOLLIFIELD
16 Vice President for Human Resources ...Ms. Ann Z. FIELDS
37 Director of Financial Aid ...Ms. Cindy GARNER

*Tennessee Board of Regents Office (A)

1415 Murfreesboro Road, Nashville TN 37217-2833
County: Davidson FICE Identification: 029031
Unit ID: 409379
Telephone: (615) 366-4400 Carnegie Class: N/A
FAX Number: (615) 366-3922
URL: www.tbr.edu

01 Chancellor ...Mr. John G. MORGAN
05 Vice Chanc Academic Affairs ...Dr. Tristan DENLEY
10 Vice Chanc Business & Finance ...Mr. Dale SIMS
11 Vice Chanc Admin & Fac Mgmt ...Mr. David B. GREGORY
12 VC TN Colleges Applied Technology ...Mr. James KING
13 Vice Chanc Information Systems ...Mr. Tom DANFORD
88 Vice Chanc for Community Colleges ...Dr. Warren NICHOLS
43 General Counsel ...Ms. Mary MOODY
09 Asst Vice Chanc Research/Assess ...Mr. Greg SCHUTZ
20 Assoc Vice Chanc Academic Affairs ...Dr. Treva G. BERRYMAN
20 Assoc Vice Chanc Academic Affairs ...Dr. S. Kay CLARK
20 Assoc Vice Chance Academic Affairs ...Dr. Pamela KNOX
21 Assistant Vice Chancellor Business ...Vacant
15 Asst Vice Chanc for Human Resources ...Ms. April PRESTON
21 Assistant Vice Chancellor Business ...Ms. Renee STEWART
88 Int Exec Dir of Operations for ROCC ...Dr. Patrick WILSON
26 Director of Communications ...Ms. Monica GREPPIN

*Austin Peay State University (B)

601 College Street, Clarksville TN 37044-0002
County: Montgomery FICE Identification: 003478
Unit ID: 219602
Telephone: (931) 221-7011 Carnegie Class: Master's L
FAX Number: (931) 221-7475 Calendar System: Semester
URL: www.apsu.edu
Established: 1927 Annual Undergrad Tuition & Fees (In-State): $6,876
Enrollment: 10,597 Coed
Affiliation or Control: State IRS Status: 501(c)3
Highest Offering: Beyond Master's But Less Than Doctorate
Program: Liberal Arts And General; Teacher Preparatory; Professional; Fine Arts Emphasis
Accreditation: SC, ART, ENGT, MT, MUS, NUR, RAD, SW, TED

02 President ...Mr. Timothy L. HALL
04 Exec Asst to the President ...Ms. Carol D. CLARK
05 Provost/VP Acad Affairs ...Vacant
10 Vice President for Finance & Admin ...Mr. Mitch ROBINSON
43 University Attorney ...Ms. Stephanie REEVERS
20 Assistant VP Academic Affairs ...Mr. Brian JOHNSON
32 VP for Student Affairs ...Dr. Sherryl BYRD
21 Asst Vice Pres for Finance ...Mr. Timothy HURST
84 Assoc Provost for Enrollment Mgmt ...Dr. Beverly BOGGS
30 Exec Director Univ Advancement ...Mr. J. Roy GREGORY
31 Dir Community/Business Rels ...Ms. Carol CLARK
26 Exec Dir Marketing/Public Rels ...Mr. Bill PERSINGER
12 Exec Dir APSU Fort Campbell ...Dr. William COX
29 Dir Alumni and Annual Giving ...Ms. Nicole PETERSON
21 Director Budgets ...Ms. Sonja STEWART
08 Director Library ...Mr. Joe WEBER
13 Director of Information Technology ...Mr. Charles B. WALL
09 Dir Inst Research & Effectiveness ...Ms. Melissa HUNTER
07 Director of Admissions ...Ms. Amy DEATON
06 Registrar ...Ms. Telaina WRIGLEY
18 Director of Plant Administration ...Mr. Thomas HUTCHINS
45 Dir Facilities Planning & Projects ...Mr. Al WESTERMAN
41 Athletics Director ...Mr. Derek VAN DER MERWE
27 Director of Athletic Information ...Mr. Brad J. KIRTLEY
37 Director of Student Financial Aid ...Ms. Donna PRICE
36 Director Academic Advisement ...Ms. Barbara BLACKSTON
38 Dir of Student Counseling Services ...Dr. Lowell RODDY
35 Dean of Students ...Mr. Gregory SINGLETON
88 Dir African Amer Cultural Ctr ...Mr. Henderson HILL
15 Director Human Resources ...Mr. Michael HAMLET
19 Director Public Safety ...Vacant
39 Director Housing/Resident Life ...Mr. F. Joe MILLS
21 Director Internal Audit ...Ms. Jacqueline STRUCKMEYER
25 Director of Grants ...Mr. Andrew SHEPARD-SMITH
96 Director of Purchasing ...Ms. Judy BLAIN
22 Dir Affirmative Action ...Ms. Sheila M. BRYANT
49 Dean College Arts & Letters ...Dr. Dixie WEBB
81 Dean Col Science & Math ...Dr. Jaime TAYLOR
53 Dean Col Behav Health Science ...Dr. David DENTON
58 Dean College Graduate Studies ...Dr. Dixie DENNIS
51 Exec Dir Extended & Distance Educ ...Mr. Dana WILLETT

*East Tennessee State University (C)

807 University Parkway, Johnson City TN 37614-6500
County: Washington FICE Identification: 003487
Unit ID: 220075
Telephone: (423) 439-1000 Carnegie Class: DRU
FAX Number: (423) 439-5770 Calendar System: Semester
URL: www.etsu.edu
Established: 1911 Annual Undergrad Tuition & Fees (In-State): $7,249
Enrollment: 14,536 Coed
Affiliation or Control: State IRS Status: 501(c)3
Highest Offering: Doctorate
Program: Occupational; Liberal Arts And General; Teacher Preparatory; Professional; Business Emphasis
Accreditation: SC, ART, AUD, BUS, BUSA, CACREP, CLPSY, COARC, CS, DH, DIETD, DIETI, ENGR, ENGT, MED, MUS, NURSE, PH, PHAR, POLYT, PTA, RAD, SP, SW, TED

02 President ...Dr. Brian E. NOLAND
100 Chief of Staff/Assoc VP Health Affs ...Dr. Jane M. JONES
100 Chief of Staff External Operations ...Mr. Jeremy B. ROSS
05 Provost/Vice Pres Academic Affairs ...Dr. Bert C. BACH
10 Vice Pres Finance & Administration ...Dr. David D. COLLINS
17 Vice President Health Affairs/COO ...Dr. Wilsie S. BISHOP
30 Interim VP University Advancement ...Mr. Jeffrey W. ANDERSON
41 Athletic Director ...Dr. Richard L. SANDER
28 Spec Asst to Pres Equity/Diversity ...Ms. Mary V. JORDAN
88 Director of Internal Audit ...Ms. Rebecca B. LEWIS
43 University Counsel ...Mr. Edward J. KELLY
26 Exec Director of Univ Relations ...Mr. Joseph E. SMITH
84 Vice Provost Enrollment Services ...Dr. Ramona A. WILLIAMS
51 Dean Cont Studies & Acad Outreach ...Dr. Richard E. OSBORN
46 Vice Prov Research/Sponsored Pgms ...Dr. William R. DUNCAN
32 Vice Pres Student Affairs ...Dr. Joe H. SHERLIN
20 Vice Provost Academic Affairs ...Dr. M. Marshall GRUBE
20 VProv Ugrad Ed/Dir Plan & Analysis ...Dr. William G. KIRKWOOD
18 Assoc VP for Facilities Management ...Mr. William B. RASNICK, JR.
35 Associate Vice Pres Student Affairs ...Dr. Sally LEE
13 Assoc VP/Chief Information Officer ...Mr. Mark S. BRAGG
96 Assoc VP Procurement/Contract Svcs ...Dr. Katherine M. KELLEY
21 Sr Assoc VP Finance & Admin ...Dr. B. J. KING
44 Assoc VP Univ Adv/Planned Giving ...Mr. Jeffrey W. ANDERSON
29 Assoc VP Univ Adv/Exec Dir Alumni ...Mr. Robert M. PLUMMER
106 AVP/Ex Dir E-Learning & Online Ed ...Dr. Karen D. KING
09 Director of Institutional Research ...Dr. Michael B. HOFF
86 Exec Asst to Pres Cmty & Govt Rels ...Ms. Bridget R. BAIRD
49 Dean College Arts & Science ...Dr. Gordon K. ANDERSON
50 Dean College of Business/Technology ...Dr. Linda R. GARCEAU
76 Int Dean College of Clin/Rehab Sci ...Dr. Donald A. SAMPLES
53 Dean College of Education ...Dr. W. Hal KNIGHT
92 Dean Honors College ...Dr. Rebecca A. PYLES
63 Interim Dean College of Medicine ...Dr. Kenneth E. OLIVE
67 Dean College of Pharmacy ...Dr. Larry D. CALHOUN
66 Dean College of Nursing ...Dr. Wendy M. NEHRING
69 Dean College of Public Health ...Dr. Randolph F. WYKOFF
58 Dean School of Graduate Studies ...Dr. Cecilia A. MCINTOSH
08 Dean of Libraries ...Ms. Patricia R. VAN ZANDT
06 University Registrar ...Ms. Sheryl L. BURNETTE
07 Director of Admissions ...Mr. Brian L. HENLEY
36 Director University Career Services ...Dr. David E. MAGEE, JR.
38 Director Counseling Center ...Dr. Steve D. BROWN
12 Director of ETSU at Kingsport ...Vacant
37 Director of Financial Aid ...Ms. Margaret L. MILLER
92 Director University Honors Program ...Dr. Joy E. WACHS
39 Director Student Housing ...Dr. Bonnie L. BURCHETT
85 Dir International Programs/Services ...Ms. Maria D. COSTA
93 Multicultural Director ...Ms. Laura C. TERRY
19 Director Public Safety ...Chief Jack R. COTREL
25 Director of Sponsored Programs ...Dr. Louise C. NUTTLE
87 Director Summer & Winter Sessions ...Dr. Sarah E. BRADFORD
94 Director of Women's Studies ...Dr. Phyllis A. THOMPSON
105 Web Manager ...Ms. Michaele D. LAWS
15 Dir Empl Relations/Compensation/Dev ...Ms. Diana D. MCCLAY
15 Director Benefits/Retirement/HRIS ...Ms. Tammy S. HAMM

*Middle Tennessee State University (D)

1301 E Main Street, Murfreesboro TN 37132-0001
County: Rutherford FICE Identification: 003510
Unit ID: 220978
Telephone: (615) 898-2300 Carnegie Class: DRU
FAX Number: (615) 898-5538 Calendar System: Semester
URL: www.mtsu.edu
Established: 1911 Annual Undergrad Tuition & Fees (In-State): $7,471
Enrollment: 25,394 Coed
Affiliation or Control: State IRS Status: 501(c)3
Highest Offering: Doctorate
Program: Liberal Arts And General; Teacher Preparatory
Accreditation: SC, AAB, AAFCS, ART, BUS, BUSA, CACREP, CIDA, CS, DIETD, ENGT, EXSC, JOUR, MUS, NAIT, NRPA, NURSE, SW, TED

02 President ...Dr. Sidney A. MCPHEE
03 University Provost ...Dr. Brad N. BARTEL
10 Senior Vice Pres Business & Finance ...Dr. John W. COTHERN
30 Vice President Devel/Univ Relations ...Mr. William J. BALES
32 VP Stdnt Affs/V Prov Enroll Mgmt ...Dr. Debra K. SELLS
14 VP Info Tech/Chief Info Officer ...Mr. Bruce PETRYSHAK
05 Vice Prov for Academic Affairs ...Dr. John O. OMACHONU
58 Vice Provost Rsrch/Dean Grad Stds ...Dr. Michael D. ALLEN
43 Univ Counsel & Asst to the Pres ...Ms. Heidi ZIMMERMAN
04 Exec Assistant to the President ...Ms. Kimberly S. EDGAR
22 Exec Dir Institutional Equity/Com ...Ms. Barbara L. PATTON
31 Community Engagement/Asst to Pres ...Dr. Gloria L. BONNER
07 Assoc Vice Prov Admis & Enroll Svcs ...Dr. Laurie B. WITHEROW
13 Assoc Vice Pres Info Technology ...Mr. Tom WALLACE
21 Assoc Vice Pres Business Office ...Mr. Michael E. GOWER
35 Assoc Vice Pres/Dean Student Life ...Ms. Sarah SUDAK
27 Assoc Vice Pres Mktg/Communications ...Mr. Andrew OPPMANN
15 Asst Vice Pres Human Resource Svcs ...Ms. Kathy I. MUSSELMAN
18 Asst Vice Pres Facilities Services ...Mr. David W. GRAY
11 Asst Vice Pres Admin/Business Svcs ...Ms. Kathryn CRISP
45 Asst Vice Pres Entrprse Rsrce Plng ...Mrs. Lisa C. ROGERS
90 Asst Vice Pres Acad & Instruct Tech ...Ms. Barbara J. DRAUDE
81 Dean Col Basic/Applied Science ...Dr. Robert U. FISCHER, JR.
83 Dean College Behavioral & Hlth Sci ...Dr. Harold D. WHITESIDE
60 Dean College Mass Communication ...Dr. Ken A. PAULSON
50 Dean College of Business ...Dr. David J. URBAN
53 Dean College of Education ...Dr. Lana C. SEIVERS
49 Dean College of Liberal Arts ...Dr. Mark E. BYRNES
51 Dean University College ...Dr. Mike A. BOYLE
92 Dean University Honors College ...Dr. John R. VILE
08 Dean University Library ...Ms. Bonnie J. ALLEN
09 Asst Vice Provost for IEPR ...Dr. Jeff E. HOYT
36 Dir Career & Employment Center ...Mr. Bill FLETCHER
93 Dir Intercultural/Diversity Affairs ...Mr. Vincent WINDROW
37 Dir of Financial Aid & Scholarship ...Mr. Stephen F. WHITE
25 Dir Research & Sponsored Programs ...Dr. Myra K. NORMAN
29 Director Alumni Relations ...Ms. Ginger C. FREEMAN
40 Director Bookstore ...Mr. Jeff WHITWELL
24 Director Center for Educational Med ...Dr. Tracey R. HUDDLESTON
38 Director Counseling Services ...Dr. Jane TIPPS
44 Director Development Office ...Mr. Nick PERLICK
06 Director Enrollment Technical Sys ...Ms. Teresa W. THOMAS
26 Director News & Media Relations ...Mr. Jimmy W. HART
41 Director of Athletics ...Mr. Chris J. MASSARO
23 Director of Health Services ...Mr. Richard L. CHAPMAN
94 Director Women's and Gender Studies ...Dr. Ida F. LEGGETT
06 Registrar ...Ms. Ann S. REEVES
19 Chief of Police/Dir Public Safety ...Mr. Carl S. PEASTER

*Tennessee State University (E)

3500 John A Merritt Boulevard, Nashville TN 37209-1561
County: Davidson FICE Identification: 003522
Unit ID: 221838
Telephone: (615) 963-5000 Carnegie Class: DRU
FAX Number: (615) 963-7412 Calendar System: Semester
URL: www.tnstate.edu
Established: 1912 Annual Undergrad Tuition & Fees (In-State): $6,700
Enrollment: 8,740 Coed
Affiliation or Control: State IRS Status: 501(c)3
Highest Offering: Doctorate
Program: Occupational; Liberal Arts And General; Teacher Preparatory; Professional
Accreditation: SC, AAFCS, ADNUR, ART, BUS, CAHIIM, COARC, COPSY, CS, DH, DIETD, ENG, MUS, NAIT, NUR, OT, PTA, SP, SPAA, SW, TED

02 President ...Dr. Portia H. SHIELDS
05 Vice President Academic Affairs ...Dr. Mark G. HARDY
04 Exec Ast to Pres/Chf Diversity Ofcr ...Dr. Arlene NICHOLS
10 VP Business & Finance ...Mrs. Cynthia BROOKS
32 VP Student Affairs ...Dr. A. Dexter SAMUELS
30 VP Institutional Advancement ...Ms. Robin WATSON
41 Athletic Director ...Mrs. Teresa LAWRENCE-PHILLIPS
43 University Legal Counsel ...Mr. Laurence PENDLETON
84 Assoc Provost Enrollment Mgmt ...Dr. John CADE
20 Assoc VP Academic Affairs ...Dr. Patricia CROOK
20 Assoc VP Academic Affairs Ext Ed ...Dr. Evelyn NETTLES
20 Assoc VP Academic Affairs ...Dr. Ken LOONEY
20 Assoc VP Academic Planning/Assess ...Dr. Peter NWOSU
15 Assoc VP/Dir Human Resources ...Ms. Linda C. SPEARS
46 Int Assoc VP Research/Sponsored Pgm ...Dr. Michael BUSBY
21 Assoc VP Finance/Accounting ...Mr. Robert HUGHES
18 Assoc VP Facilities/Physical Plant ...Mr. Ronnie BROOKS
35 Asst VP Student Affairs ...Ms. Michelle VIERA
88 Asst VP Budget/Travel ...Mr. Bradley WHITE
09 Dir Inst Effectiveness & Research ...Dr. G. Pamela BURCH-SIMS
28 Dir Equity Diversity & Compliance ...Ms. Tiffa COX
37 Director Financial Aid ...Ms. Amy B. WOOD
06 Registrar ...Mrs. Thelria HARDAWAY
27 Director Media Relations ...Mr. Richard DELAHAYA
19 Chief TSU Police Department ...Mr. Richard BRIGGANCE
08 Dean Libraries & Media Centers ...Dr. Murle KENERSON
49 Int Dean College of Liberal Arts ...Dr. Gloria JOHNSON
50 Int Dean College of Business ...Dr. James ELLZY
53 Interim Dean College of Education ...Dr. Heraldo RICHARDS
54 Dean College of Engr/Tech/Comp Sci ...Dr. S. Keith HARGROVE
47 Dean Agriculture/Human & Nat Sci ...Dr. Chandra REDDY
58 Dean School of Graduate Studies ...Dr. Michael OROK

88 Int Dean Coll Public Svcs/Urban Aff ... Dr. Stephanie BAILEY
76 Dean College of Health Sciences ... Dr. Kathleen MCENERNEY
66 Assoc Dean/Dir of Nursing ... Dr. Kathy MARTIN

*Tennessee Technological University (A)

1000 N Dixie Avenue, Cookeville TN 38505-0001
County: Putnam FICE Identification: 003523
Unit ID: 221847
Telephone: (931) 372-3101 Carnegie Class: Master's L
FAX Number: (931) 372-3898 Calendar System: Semester
URL: www.tntech.edu
Established: 1915 Annual Undergrad Tuition & Fees (In-State): $7,095
Enrollment: 11,469 Coed
Affiliation or Control: State IRS Status: 501(c)3
Highest Offering: Doctorate
Program: Liberal Arts And General; Teacher Preparatory; Professional
Accreditation: SC, AAFCS, ART, BUS, BUSA, CS, DIETD, EMT, ENG, MUS, NAIT, NURSE, TED

02 President ... Dr. Philip B. OLDHAM
05 Provost/Vice President Acad Affairs ... Dr. Bahman GHORASHI
10 Vice Pres Planning & Finance ... Dr. Claire STINSON
32 Vice President Student Affairs ... Mr. Marc BURNETT
32 Dean of Students ... Mr. Ed BOUCHER
46 VP Research & Economic Development ... Dr. Bharat SONI
46 Assoc VP for Research ... Dr. Francis O. OTUONYE
30 Vice President Univ Advancement ... Mr. Mark HUTCHINS
20 Sr Assoc VP Academic Affairs ... Dr. Mark STEPHENS
20 Assoc Provost/Vice Pres Acad Affs ... Dr. Xiaoming (Sharon) HUO
13 CIO Info Tech Svcs ... Mr. Reid CHRISTENBERRY
37 Director Financial Aid ... Mr. Lester MCKENZIE
08 Director Library & Learning Assist ... Dr. Doug BATES
09 Director Institutional Research ... Dr. Glenn W. JAMES
45 Director of Institutional Planning ... Vacant
15 Director of Human Resources ... Vacant
19 Director of University Police ... Ms. Gay SHEPHERD
39 Director of Housing ... Mr. Charles MACKE
41 Director of Athletics ... Mr. Mark WILSON
18 Director of Physical Plant ... Mr. Jack BUTLER
38 Director Counseling Center ... Ms. Patricia SMITH
23 Director of Health Svcs ... Ms. Leigh A. RAY
36 Director Career Services ... Ms. Alice CAMUTI
26 Assoc VP Communications & Mkting ... Ms. Karen LYKINS
85 Director Intl Student Affairs ... Mr. Charles WILKERSON
06 Director Records & Registrar ... Ms. Elizabeth ROGERS
92 Director Honors Program ... Dr. Rita BARNES
93 Director Minority Affairs ... Dr. Robert OWENS
96 Director of Purchasing ... Ms. Judy M. HULL
21 Associate Business Officer ... Mr. Jeff YOUNG
43 Director University Counsel ... Ms. Kae CARPENTER
29 Director Alumni Relations ... Ms. Tracey DUNCAN
88 Director of Internal Audit ... Ms. Deanna METTS
28 Director of Diversity/Legal Affairs ... Ms. Rachel RADER
07 Director of Admissions ... Mr. Alexis POPE
19 Dir Campus Safety & Environment ... Mr. James COBB
84 Assoc VP Enr Mgmt & Student Success ... Dr. Robert HODUM
49 Dean of Arts & Sciences ... Dr. Paul SEMMES
54 Dean of Engineering ... Dr. Joseph RENCIS
47 Dean of Agriculture & Human Ecology ... Vacant
50 Dean of Business Administration ... Dr. James JORDAN WAGNER
53 Dean College of Education ... Dr. Matt SMITH
66 Dean School of Nursing ... Vacant
88 Dean of Interdisciplinary Studies ... Vacant

*The University of Memphis (B)

Memphis TN 38152
County: Shelby FICE Identification: 003509
Unit ID: 220862
Telephone: (901) 678-2000 Carnegie Class: RU/H
FAX Number: N/A Calendar System: Semester
URL: www.memphis.edu
Established: 1912 Annual Undergrad Tuition & Fees (In-State): $8,312
Enrollment: 22,139 Coed
Affiliation or Control: State IRS Status: 501(c)3
Highest Offering: Doctorate
Program: Liberal Arts And General; Teacher Preparatory; Professional
Accreditation: SC, ART, AUD, BUS, BUSA, CACREP, CIDA, CLPSY, COPSY, CORE, CS, DIETD, DIETI, ENG, ENGT, HSA, IPSY, JOUR, LAW, MUS, NURSE, PLNG, SP, SPAA, SW, TED, THEA

02 Interim President ... R. Brad MARTIN
05 Provost ... Dr. M. David RUDD
10 Vice President Business & Finance ... Mr. David G. ZETTERGREN
86 Exec Asst Pres Govt Relations ... Mr. Kevin F. ROPER
30 Vice President Advancement ... Mrs. Julie A. JOHNSON
32 Vice President Student Affairs ... Dr. Rosie P. BINGHAM
26 VP Marketing & Communications ... Ms. Linda BONNIN
41 Director of Athletics ... Mr. Tom BOWEN
43 Pres Chief of Staff Univ Counsel ... Ms. Sheryl H. LIPMAN
04 Exec Assistant to the President ... Dr. David N. COX
46 Vice Provost for Research ... Dr. Andrew W. MEYERS
45 VP Assessment/Inst Rsrch/Reporting ... Dr. Thomas J. NENON
13 CIO/Vice Provost for Info Tech ... Dr. Ellen WATSON
84 Asst Vice Provost Enrollment Svcs ... Ms. Betty HUFF
58 Vice Prov/Dean Graduate School ... Dr. Karen D. WEDDLE-WEST
88 VP Undergrad Programs ... Dr. Shannon BLANTON
35 Asst VP Student Affs/Stdnt Dev ... Dr. Stephen H. PETERSEN
18 Asst Vice Pres Physical Plant ... Vacant
21 Assistant Vice President Finance ... Ms. Jeannie SMITH
15 Asst Vice Pres Human Resources ... Ms. Maria ALAM
44 Assoc Vice Pres Development ... Mr. Bobby A. PRINCE
08 Dean U of M Libraries ... Dr. Sylverna V. FORD
09 Director Institutional Research ... Dr. Gary L. DONHARDT
36 Director Career & Employment Svcs ... Ms. Alisha D. ROSE
06 Registrar ... Ms. Donna S. VAN CANNEYT
37 Director of Student Aid ... Mr. Richard RITZMAN
96 Director of Purchasing ... Ms. Canty ROBBINS
29 Assoc Vice President Alumni Pgm ... Ms. Tammy L. HEDGES
92 Director University Honors Program ... Dr. Melinda L. JONES
07 Director of Admissions ... Mr. Stephen MCKELLIPS
22 Office for Institutional Equity ... Mr. Carson C. COOK
88 Dn Communication Sciences Disorders ... Dr. Maurice I. MENDEL
49 Interim Dean of Arts & Science ... Dr. Thomas J. NENON
50 Dean Business & Economics ... Dr. Rajiv GROVER
53 Dean of Educ Health and Human Sci ... Dr. Donald I. WAGNER
54 Dean of Engineering ... Dr. Richard J. SWEIGARD
55 Vice Provost Extended Programs ... Dr. Dan L. LATTIMORE
57 Dean Communication & Fine Arts ... Dr. Richard R. RANTA
61 Dean School of Law ... Mr. Peter V. LETSOU
66 Dean School of Nursing ... Dr. Lin ZHAN
69 Dean School of Public Health ... Dr. Lisa M. KLESGES

*Chattanooga State Community College (C)

4501 Amnicola Highway, Chattanooga TN 37406-1097
County: Hamilton FICE Identification: 003998
Unit ID: 219824
Telephone: (423) 697-4400 Carnegie Class: Assoc/Pub-R-L
FAX Number: N/A Calendar System: Semester
URL: www.chattanoogastate.edu
Established: 1963 Annual Undergrad Tuition & Fees (In-State): $3,792
Enrollment: 11,501 Coed
Affiliation or Control: State IRS Status: 501(c)3
Highest Offering: Associate Degree
Program: Occupational; 2-Year Principally Bachelor's Creditable
Accreditation: SC, ACBSP, ADNUR, CAHIIM, COARC, DA, DH, DMS, EMT, ENGR, ENGT, MAC, NMT, OTA, PTAA, RAD, RTT, SURGT

02 President ... Dr. James L. CATANZARO
04 Special Assistant to the President ... Mr. Joe HELSETH
09 Asc VP Institutional Effectiveness ... Ms. Eva LEWIS
05 Provost/Vice Pres Academic Affairs ... Dr. Fannie HEWLETT
10 Exec Vice Pres Business & Finance ... Ms. Tammy SWENSON
32 Vice President Student Services ... Ms. Debbie ADAMS
31 Vice President Economic & Comm Dev ... Mr. Ben UBAMADU
72 Vice President for Technology ... Dr. Jim BARROTT
44 Assoc Vice Pres Fund Development ... Ms. Nancy PATTERSON
20 Assoc Vice Pres Academic Affairs ... Ms. Kimberly MCCORMICK
21 Assistant VP Business & Finance ... Ms. Susan JOSEPH
35 Asst Vice Pres Student Affairs ... Mr. Brad MCCORMICK
18 Asst VP Plant Operations/Facil Plng ... Mr. Steve HUSKINS
56 Asst VP Distributed Education ... Ms. Judy LOWE
25 Asst VP Grants/Contracts/Stdnt Acct ... Ms. Debbie MAILEN
51 Director Continuing Education ... Ms. Ju-Hsin LUSK
09 Director of Institutional Research ... Ms. Bonnie RIGGS
26 Director of Marketing ... Ms. Patty BROWN
15 Director Human Resources ... Mr. Tom CRUM
06 Registrar ... Ms. Norma LEE
36 Director Student Placement ... Ms. Sheila ALBRITTON
37 Director Student Financial Aid ... Ms. Jeanne HINCHEE
28 Director of Diversity ... Ms. Mary KNAFF
41 Athletic Director ... Ms. Kimberly SMITH
08 Dean Library Services ... Ms. Susan JENNINGS
76 Dean Allied Health & Nursing ... Dr. Howard YARBROUGH
79 Dean Humanities & Fine Arts ... Mr. Darrin HASSEVOORT
83 Dean Social/Behavioral Sciences ... Ms. Anne CARROLL
81 Dean Math & Sciences ... Dr. Mosunmola GEORGE-TAYLOR
50 Dean Business/Info Tech ... Mr. Barry JENNISON
32 Dean Student Life/Judicial Affairs ... Ms. Sandy KLUTTZ
75 Dean Tennessee Technology Center ... Dr. Mike RICKETTS
54 Dean Engineering Technology ... Mr. Tim MCGHEE

*Cleveland State Community College (D)

PO Box 3570, Cleveland TN 37320-3570
County: Bradley FICE Identification: 003999
Unit ID: 219879
Telephone: (423) 472-7141 Carnegie Class: Assoc/Pub-R-M
FAX Number: (423) 478-6255 Calendar System: Semester
URL: www.clevelandstatecc.edu
Established: 1967 Annual Undergrad Tuition & Fees (In-State): $3,773
Enrollment: 3,640 Coed
Affiliation or Control: State IRS Status: 501(c)3
Highest Offering: Associate Degree
Program: Occupational; 2-Year Principally Bachelor's Creditable
Accreditation: SC, ACBSP, ADNUR, MAC, NAIT, OTA

02 President ... Dr. Carl HITE
05 Vice President for Academic Affairs ... Dr. Denise KING
32 Vice President for Student Services ... Dr. Michael STOKES
11 Vice President Admin & Finance ... Dr. Thomas WRIGHT
09 Director of Institutional Research ... Mrs. Marcia O'CONNOR
37 Director of Financial Aid ... Mrs. Brenda DISORBO
30 Director of Inst Advancement ... Mr. Adam LOWE
26 Director Marketing & Promotions ... Mr. Tony BARTOLO
06 Asst Dir Enrollment Svcs/Registrar ... Mrs. Gail GREENWOOD
15 Director of Human Resources ... Mrs. Joan BATES
08 Director of the Library ... Ms. Sarah COPELAND
14 Director of College Computing ... Mr. Chris MOWERY
19 Coordinator Campus Security ... Mr. Mike HODGES
50 Dean of Business & Technology ... Ms. Sherra WITT
66 Dean of Health & Wellness ... Mrs. Nancy LABINE
79 Int Dean Humanities/Social Sciences ... Mr. Fred WOOD
81 Dean of Math/Science ... Dr. Mitchell RHEA
38 Dir Student Development/ACCESS Ctr ... Mr. Mark WILSON
103 Dir Workforce Development ... Mr. Rick CREASY
18 Director of Plant Operations ... Vacant
21 Business Manager ... Ms. Gena WILSON
84 Director of Enrollment Services ... Mr. Jason SEWELL
07 Asst Dir Enrollment Services Admiss ... Mrs. Suzanne BAYNE
41 Athletic Director ... Mr. Mike POLICASTRO

*Columbia State Community College (E)

1665 Hampshire Pike, Columbia TN 38401-5653
County: Maury FICE Identification: 003483
Unit ID: 219888
Telephone: (931) 540-2722 Carnegie Class: Assoc/Pub-R-M
FAX Number: (931) 540-2535 Calendar System: Semester
URL: www.columbiastate.edu
Established: 1966 Annual Undergrad Tuition & Fees (In-State): $3,617
Enrollment: 5,322 Coed
Affiliation or Control: State IRS Status: 501(c)3
Highest Offering: Associate Degree
Program: Occupational; 2-Year Principally Bachelor's Creditable
Accreditation: SC, ACBSP, ADNUR, COARC, EMT, RAD

02 President ... Dr. Janet F. SMITH
03 Executive Vice President/Provost ... Dr. Margaret D. SMITH
10 Vice Pres Financial/Admin Services ... Mr. Kenneth R. HORNER
30 Executive for Advancement ... Ms. Bethany LAY
20 Assoc VP Faculty/Curric & Programs ... Ms. Joni L. LENIG
32 Assoc VP Student Services ... Ms. Cecelia JOHNSON
13 Assoc VP Info Technology ... Ms. Emily SICIENSKY
21 Assoc VP Business Services ... Ms. Elaine CURTIS
27 Interim Dir Marketing & Public Rels ... Ms. Amy SPEARS-BOYD
28 Asst to Pres for Access & Diversity ... Ms. Christa S. MARTIN
07 Director Recruitment & Admissions ... Mr. David OGDEN
06 Director Records ... Ms. Sharon G. BOWEN
15 Director Human Resources ... Mr. Randy L. ELSTON
08 Director Library ... Ms. Kathy BREEDEN
38 Coord Counseling & Student Succ Svc ... Dr. Paula J. PETTY-WARD
09 Interim Dir Inst Effect and Plng ... Ms. Tammy BORREN
37 Director Financial Aid ... Ms. Brenda D. BURNEY
41 Director Athletics ... Mr. Louis M. CONNER
18 Director Facility Services ... Mr. David HALL
56 Dean Extended Svcs & Will Campus ... Dr. Shanna JACKSON
35 Director Student Success ... Vacant
96 Coordinator Purchasing ... Ms. Jerri H. GROOMS
84 Chief Enrollment Svcs Officer ... Ms. Patsy REYNOLDS

*Dyersburg State Community College (F)

1510 Lake Road, Dyersburg TN 38024-2450
County: Dyer FICE Identification: 006835
Unit ID: 220057
Telephone: (731) 286-3200 Carnegie Class: Assoc/Pub-R-M
FAX Number: (731) 286-3333 Calendar System: Semester
URL: www.dscc.edu
Established: 1967 Annual Undergrad Tuition & Fees (In-State): $3,627
Enrollment: 3,590 Coed
Affiliation or Control: State IRS Status: 501(c)3
Highest Offering: Associate Degree
Program: Occupational; 2-Year Principally Bachelor's Creditable
Accreditation: SC, ACBSP, ADNUR, CAHIIM

02 President ... Dr. Karen A. BOWYER
05 Vice President for the College ... Vacant
10 Vice President Finance/Admin Svcs ... Mr. Lowell HOFFMANN
30 Vice Pres Institutional Advancement ... Ms. Youlanda JONES-WILCOX
13 Vice President Technology ... Ms. Diane CAMPER
32 Asst VP for Acad & Student Affairs ... Vacant
20 Int Assistant VP for Learning ... Dr. Brian WELLS
35 Dean of Student Services ... Ms. Larenda FULTZ
08 Int Dean Learning Resources Center ... Ms. Susan CHARLEY
37 Director of Financial Aid ... Mrs. Sandra ROCKETT
09 Director of Institutional Research ... Ms. Youlanda JONES-WILCOX
15 Director Personnel Services ... Ms. Sheilah GILLAHAN
103 Director of Workforce Development ... Ms. Margaret PRATER
29 Director of Alumni Relations ... Ms. Amy FINCH
38 Director Student Counseling ... Ms. Sherry BAKER
41 Director of Athletics ... Mr. Alan BARNETT
18 Director of Physical Plant ... Mr. Kent JETTON
07 Director of Admissions ... Ms. Patricia WALKER
26 Chief Public Relations Officer ... Ms. Amy FINCH
96 Director of Purchasing ... Ms. Amy WATTS
21 Business & Student Fin Svcs Manager ... Ms. Donna MEALER
72 Coord Business/Technology Div ... Mr. James BARHAM
66 Int Dean Nursing/Allied Health Div ... Ms. Amy JOHNSON
51 Dean of Continuing Education ... Ms. Youlanda JONES-WILCOX

*Jackson State Community College (G)

2046 North Parkway, Jackson TN 38301-3797
County: Madison FICE Identification: 004937
Unit ID: 220400
Telephone: (731) 424-3520 Carnegie Class: Assoc/Pub-R-M

FAX Number: (731) 425-2647 Calendar System: Semester
URL: www.jscc.edu
Established: 1965 Annual Undergrad Tuition & Fees (In-State): $3,781
Enrollment: 4,494 Coed
Affiliation or Control: State IRS Status: 501(c)3
Highest Offering: Associate Degree
Program: Occupational; 2-Year Principally Bachelor's Creditable
Accreditation: SC, ACBSP, ADNUR, COARC, EMT, MLTAD, NAIT, PTAA, RAD

02 President ... Dr. Bruce BLANDING
05 Interim VP of Academic Affairs ... Mr. Bobby SMITH
10 Vice Pres of Finance & Admin Affs ... Mr. Horace W. CHASE
30 Dir of Development/Alumni Relations ... Ms. Dee HENDERSON
32 Interim VP of Student Services ... Ms. Linda NICKELL
30 Int VP Institutional Advancement ... Dr. William SEYMOUR
88 Internal Auditor ... Mrs. Angela P. BROWN
15 Dir Human Resources/Affirm Action ... Mrs. Amy WEST
09 Dir Inst Research & Accountability ... Mr. Scott WOODS
31 Dir of Community Education ... Ms. Leah GRAY
13 Director of Information Technology ... Ms. Dana NAILS
21 Director of Business Services ... Mr. Tim DELLINGER
18 Director of Physical Plant ... Mr. Gerald BATCHELOR
96 Director of Purchasing ... Mr. Robert D. HEMRICK
12 Director Lexington Campus ... Ms. Sandy STANFILL
12 Director Savannah Campus ... Mrs. Meda FALLS
12 Director Humboldt Campus ... Ms. Lisa BARKER
07 Director Admissions ... Mrs. Andrea WINCHESTER
26 Director Public Relations ... Vacant
37 Director Student Financial Aid ... Ms. Dewana LATIMER
06 Director of Records ... Ms. Robin MAREK

*Motlow State Community College (A)

PO Box 8500, Lynchburg TN 37352-8500
County: Moore FICE Identification: 006836
Unit ID: 221096
Telephone: (931) 393-1500 Carnegie Class: Assoc/Pub-R-M
FAX Number: (931) 393-1681 Calendar System: Semester
URL: www.mscc.edu
Established: 1969 Annual Undergrad Tuition & Fees (In-State): $3,612
Enrollment: 4,592 Coed
Affiliation or Control: State IRS Status: 501(c)3
Highest Offering: Associate Degree
Program: Occupational; 2-Year Principally Bachelor's Creditable
Accreditation: SC, ACBSP, ADNUR

02 President ... Dr. MaryLou APPLE
05 Interim VP for Academic Affairs ... Ms. Dawn COPELAND
10 Vice Pres for Business Affairs ... Ms. Hilda TUNSTILL
13 VP for Technology & Admin Services ... Dr. Eddie STONE
20 Asst Vice Pres for Academic Affair ... Vacant
32 VP for Student Affairs ... Mr. Jerry TUNSTILL
18 Director of Facilities ... Mr. Billy GARNER
14 Director of Technical Operations ... Mr. Matt HULVEY
31 Director Student & Campus Relations ... Ms. Brenda CANNON
35 Asst Vice President Student Affairs ... Ms. Regina BURDEN
08 Director of Libraries ... Mr. Stuart GAETJENS
37 Executive Director of Financial Aid ... Mr. Joe MYERS
38 Director of Disability & Testing ... Ms. Sonya HOOD
07 Director of Admissions & Records ... Ms. Greer ALSUP
66 Director of Nursing ... Ms. Amy HUFF
41 Interim Director of Athletics ... Ms. Tori RABY-GENTRY
09 Dir of Research/Planning & Comm ... Ms. Sylvia COLLINS
90 Director Center for Academic Tech ... Dr. Shelly MCCOY
12 Director McMinnville Center ... Ms. Melody EDMONDS
12 Director Fayetteville Center ... Ms. Laura MONKS
12 Director Smyrna Site ... Ms. Cheryl HYLAND
36 Dir of Career Placement & Extended ... Mr. Tom DILLINGHAM
15 Director of Human Resources ... Ms. Laura JENT
96 Director of Purchasing ... Ms. Sandy SCHAFFER
04 Admin Assistant to the President ... Ms. Christy GLENN

*Nashville State Community College (B)

120 White Bridge Road, Nashville TN 37209-4515
County: Davidson FICE Identification: 008145
Unit ID: 221184
Telephone: (615) 353-3333 Carnegie Class: Assoc/Pub-U-MC
FAX Number: (615) 353-3713 Calendar System: Semester
URL: www.nscc.edu
Established: 1969 Annual Undergrad Tuition & Fees (In-State): $3,729
Enrollment: 9,884 Coed
Affiliation or Control: State IRS Status: 501(c)3
Highest Offering: Associate Degree
Program: Occupational; 2-Year Principally Bachelor's Creditable; Business Emphasis
Accreditation: SC, ACBSP, ACFEI, ADNUR, NAIT, OTA, SURGT

02 President ... Dr. George H. VAN ALLEN
05 Vice President of Academic Affairs ... Dr. Kimberly K. ESTEP
10 Vice Pres Finance & Administration ... Mrs. Mary M. CROSS
09 Assoc VP Planning/Assessment ... Mr. Ted M. WASHINGTON
20 Assoc VP for Academic Affairs ... Dr. Jennifer A. KNAPP
30 Exec Dir of Devel/Dir Public Affs ... Mr. Keith D. FERGUSON
32 Dean of Students ... Dr. Carol J. MARTIN-OSORIO
21 Internal Auditor ... Vacant
06 Registrar ... Mr. Lance L. WOODARD
07 Director of Admissions ... Ms. Laura L. POTTER
14 Director of Computer Services ... Vacant
19 Director of Safety and Security ... Mr. Derrek G. SHEUCRAFT
37 Director of Financial Aid ... Mr. James J. MORAN
15 Dir Human Res/Affirm Act/Diversity ... Ms. Lori B. MADDOX
18 Director of Operations/Maintenance ... Mr. Jim T. DAWSON
103 Dir Workforce and Community Dev ... Ms. Gail G. PHILLIPS
27 Manager of Publications ... Ms. Ellen L. ZINK
106 Director of Online Learning ... Ms. Kathy S. EMERY
51 Coord Special Interest/CEUs ... Vacant
83 Dean of Social and Life Sciences ... Dr. Charles B. DEWITT
72 Dean of Info/Eng Technologies ... Ms. Karen L. STEVENSON
81 Dean Math & Natural Sciences ... Dr. Lisa COBB
79 Dean English/Humanities & Arts ... Ms. Valerie S. BELEW
62 Dean Lrng Resources & Distance Educ ... Dr. Faye JONES
50 Dean Bus Technology & Applied Arts .. Ms. Karen L. STEVENSON
96 Director of Purchasing ... Ms. Jo SMITH
29 Director Alumni Relations ... Mr. Keith D. FERGUSON
66 Director of Nursing ... Dr. Cynthia G. WALLER

*Northeast State Community College (C)

PO Box 246, 2425 Highway 75, Blountville TN 37617-0246
County: Sullivan FICE Identification: 005378
Unit ID: 221908
Telephone: (423) 323-3191 Carnegie Class: Assoc/Pub-R-M
FAX Number: (423) 279-7636 Calendar System: Semester
URL: www.northeaststate.edu
Established: 1965 Annual Undergrad Tuition & Fees (In-State): $3,627
Enrollment: 6,446 Coed
Affiliation or Control: State IRS Status: 501(c)3
Highest Offering: Associate Degree
Program: Occupational; 2-Year Principally Bachelor's Creditable
Accreditation: SC, ACBSP, ADNUR, CVT, DA, EMT, MLTAD, NAIT, SURGT

02 President ... Dr. Janice H. GILLIAM
04 Exec Assistant to the President ... Ms. Megan JONES
05 Vice Pres Academic Affairs ... Dr. Allana R. HAMILTON
10 Vice President Business Affairs ... Dr. Steven CAMPBELL
11 Int Vice Pres Administrative Svcs ... Mr. Fred LEWIS
32 Int Vice President Student Affairs ... Mr. Matt DELOZIER
12 VP for Northeast State at Kingsport ... Mr. Jeff D. MCCORD
56 Asst VP Evening/Distance Educ ... Dr. James C. LEFLER
20 Asst Vice Pres Academic Affairs ... Mr. Don COLEMAN
15 Director Human Resources ... Ms. Gerri S. BROCKWELL
31 Director Community Relations ... Mr. Robert CARPENTER
09 Institutional Effectiveness Officer ... Dr. Susan E. GRAYBEAL
08 Dean Library ... Mr. Duncan A. PARSONS
79 Dean Humanities ... Mr. William WILSON
81 Dean Math ... Ms. Nancy FORRESTER
76 Dean Health Related Profession ... Ms. Connie MARSHALL
72 Dean Advance Technologies ... Mr. Sam S. ROWELL
83 Dean Behavior/Social Sciences ... Dr. Xiaoping WANG
81 Dean Science ... Dr. Carolyn MCCRACKEN
50 Dean Business Technologies ... Mr. Danny L. LAWSON
66 Dean Nursing ... Dr. Melessia D. WEBB

*Pellissippi State Community College (D)

PO Box 22990, Knoxville TN 37933-0990
County: Knox FICE Identification: 012693
Unit ID: 221643
Telephone: (865) 694-6400 Carnegie Class: Assoc/Pub-U-MC
FAX Number: (865) 694-6435 Calendar System: Semester
URL: www.pstcc.edu
Established: 1974 Annual Undergrad Tuition & Fees (In-State): $3,659
Enrollment: 10,588 Coed
Affiliation or Control: State IRS Status: 501(c)3
Highest Offering: Associate Degree
Program: Occupational; 2-Year Principally Bachelor's Creditable
Accreditation: SC, ACBSP, ADNUR

02 President ... Dr. L. Anthony WISE
05 Vice President of Academic Affairs ... Dr. Ted A. LEWIS
13 Vice President Information Services ... Mr. Robert G. BRYAN
10 Vice President Business & Finance ... Mr. Ronald L. KESTERSON
30 VP College Advancement/Exec Dir Fdn ... Ms. Peggy M. WILSON
32 Vice President of Student Affairs ... Dr. Rebecca L. ASHFORD
103 Exec Dir Business/Workforce Dev ... Ms. Teri T. BRAHAMS
20 Dean Instructional Programs ... Dr. Dennis R. ADAMS
12 Campus Dean Blount County Programs ... Ms. Holly L. BURKETT
12 Campus Dean Strawberry Pl Program ... Dr. Mike NORTH
12 Campus Dean Magnolia Ave Programs .. Ms. Rosalyn P. TILLMAN
12 Campus Dean Division Street Program ... Ms. Esther L. DYER
35 Asst Vice President Dean of Student ... Ms. Mary C. BLEDSOE
35 Dir of Student Life & Recreation ... Ms. Kim THOMAS-LARUE
20 Asst VP of Academic Affairs ... Ms. Lois G. REYNOLDS
84 Asst VP Enrollment Services ... Ms. Leigh A. TOUZEAU
36 Director of Placement ... Ms. Carolyn N. CARSON
88 Dir Svc for Students w/Disabilities ... Ms. Ann E. SATKOWIAK
38 Director Counseling Department ... Dr. Elizabeth E. FIRESTONE
26 Director Marketing & Communications ... Ms. Julia H. WOOD
06 Registrar ... Ms. Melanie PARADISE
08 Director of Library Services ... Mr. J. Peter NERZAK
24 Dir Educ Technology Svcs ... Ms. Audrey WILLIAMS
37 Director of Financial Aid ... Mr. Dick SMELSER
09 Dir Inst Effectiveness/Res/Plan ... Vacant
18 Director of Facilities ... Ms. Regina MCNEW
19 Director Safety/Security ... Mr. Fred BREINER
21 Director/Budget & Payroll ... Ms. Nancy DONAHUE
96 Director of Purchasing ... Mr. John S. CLARK
15 Exec Director HR/Affirm Action ... Ms. Karen D. QUEENER
104 Exec Dir TnCIS/International Educ ... Ms. Tracey BRADLEY
21 Asst VP Business Services ... Ms. Renee R. MOORE
44 Director Major Gift Development ... Dr. Leslie G. FOUT
29 Dir Alum Relations & Annual Giving ... Ms. Patricia T. MYERS
91 Dir Applications Programming Sup ... Mr. James "Dean" COPPLE
90 Dir Network & Technical Services ... Ms. Linda C. PETERSON
07 Director of Admissions & Com Ctr ... Ms. Heather HATFIELD
28 Director of Access & Diversity ... Ms. Gayle E. WOOD
88 Director Acad Testing/Adult Ed ... Ms. Joan NEWMAN
88 Dir Curriculum & New Programs ... Ms. Judy GOSCH
88 Director of Advising ... Ms. Rachael C. CRAGLE
88 Dir Academic Support Programs ... Ms. Marilyn A. HARPER
88 Bursar ... Ms. Mandy BENTZ

*Roane State Community College (E)

276 Patton Lane, Harriman TN 37748-5011
County: Roane FICE Identification: 009914
Unit ID: 221397
Telephone: (865) 354-3000 Carnegie Class: Assoc/Pub-R-M
FAX Number: (865) 882-4585 Calendar System: Semester
URL: www.roanestate.edu
Established: 1971 Annual Undergrad Tuition & Fees (In-State): $3,733
Enrollment: 6,508 Coed
Affiliation or Control: State IRS Status: 501(c)3
Highest Offering: Associate Degree
Program: Occupational; 2-Year Principally Bachelor's Creditable
Accreditation: SC, ACBSP, ADNUR, CAHIIM, COARC, COMTA, DH, EMT, OPD, OTA, POLYT, PTAA, RAD

02 President ... Dr. Chris WHALEY
05 Vice Pres for Student Learning ... Dr. Diane WARD
10 Exec Vice Pres Business & Finance ... Mr. Danny C. GIBBS
103 VP Workforce Develop/Student Affs ... Ms. Teresa S. DUNCAN
30 VP Inst Advancement & Cmty Rels ... Ms. Melinda HILLMAN
21 Asst VP Fiscal/Auxiliary Services ... Ms. Jamie WILMOTH
32 Asst VP Student Services ... Ms. Beverly J. BONNER
13 Asst Vice Pres of Info Technology ... Mr. Timothy D. CARROLL
09 Asst VP Institutional Research ... Ms. Karen L. BRUNNER
22 Coordinator Affirmative Action ... Mr. Odell FEARN
08 Director of Library Services ... Mr. Robert M. BENSON
06 Director of Records & Registration ... Ms. Brenda RECTOR
18 Director Physical Plant & Expo Ctr ... Mr. Stan R. STARKEY
29 Director Alumni Relations ... Ms. Tamsin MILLER
96 Director of Purchasing ... Mr. Jack WALKER
36 Workforce Placement & Job Placement ... Ms. Kim HARRIS

*Southwest Tennessee Community College (F)

PO Box 780, Memphis TN 38101-0780
County: Shelby FICE Identification: 010439
Unit ID: 221485
Telephone: (901) 333-5020 Carnegie Class: Assoc/Pub-U-MC
FAX Number: (901) 333-5024 Calendar System: Semester
URL: www.southwest.tn.edu
Established: 2000 Annual Undergrad Tuition & Fees (In-State): $3,641
Enrollment: 12,220 Coed
Affiliation or Control: State IRS Status: 501(c)3
Highest Offering: Associate Degree
Program: Occupational; 2-Year Principally Bachelor's Creditable
Accreditation: SC, ACBSP, ADNUR, DIETT, EMT, ENGT, MLTAD, PHLEB, PTAA, RAD

02 President ... Dr. Nathan L. ESSEX
04 Assistant to the President ... Ms. Carol BROWN
05 Provost/Executive Vice President ... Dr. Joanne BASSETT
41 Athletic Director ... Mr. Sherman D. GREER
30 Vice Pres Institutional Advancement ... Ms. Karen F. NIPPERT
10 Vice Pres Finance & Admin Services ... Mr. Ronald G. PARR
32 Vice Pres Student Svcs/Enroll Mgmt ... Dr. Dwayne SCOTT
84 Exec Director Enrollment Management ... Ms. Thalia WILSON
26 Exec Director of Comm & Marketing ... Mr. Robert G. MILLER
15 Exec Director Hum Res/Affirm Action ... Mr. Paul THOMAS
06 Registrar ... Ms. Barbara WELLS
18 Director Physical Plant ... Vacant
96 Director of Purchasing ... Ms. Michelle NEWMAN
37 Dir Student Financial Aid ... Ms. Lechelle DAVENPORT
09 Institutional Research Analyst ... Mr. Donald C. MYERS

*Volunteer State Community College (G)

1480 Nashville Pike, Gallatin TN 37066-3188
County: Sumner FICE Identification: 009912
Unit ID: 222053
Telephone: (615) 452-8600 Carnegie Class: Assoc/Pub-S-SC
FAX Number: (615) 230-3577 Calendar System: Semester
URL: www.volstate.edu
Established: 1970 Annual Undergrad Tuition & Fees (In-State): $3,607
Enrollment: 8,177 Coed
Affiliation or Control: State IRS Status: 501(c)3
Highest Offering: Associate Degree
Program: Occupational; 2-Year Principally Bachelor's Creditable
Accreditation: SC, ACBSP, CAHIIM, COARC, DA, DMS, EMT, MLTAD, POLYT, PTAA, RAD

02 President ... Dr. Jerry FAULKNER
04 Exec Assistant to the President ... Vacant
05 Vice President Academic Affairs ... Dr. Bruce SCISM

10 Vice President Business & Finance ... Ms. Beth COOKSEY
32 Vice President Student Services ... Ms. Patty T. POWELL
30 Vice Pres for Resource Development ... Ms. Karen MITCHELL
45 Vice Pres Inst Planning/Research ... Ms. Jane MCGUIRE
20 Asst VP of Academic Affairs ... Dr. Michael TORRENCE
21 Asst Vice Pres Business & Finance ... Ms. Kathy Y. JOHNSON
35 Asst VP Student Svcs/Enrollment Mgt ... Ms. Emily SHORT
51 Asst VP/Dean Continuing Education ... Mrs. Hilary B. MARABETI
76 Assoc Vice Pres/Dean Allied Health ... Mr. Elvis BRANDON
79 Dean Humanities ... Dr. Alycia EHLERT
53 Dean Social Science/Education ... Ms. Phyllis FOLEY
81 Dean Math & Science ... Ms. Nancy MORRIS
50 Dean Business ... Dr. John ESPEY
88 Director of Development Studies Pgm ... Ms. Kay DAYTON
15 Dir Personnel/Affirm Act/Human Res ... Ms. Lori CUTRELL
08 Director Library Services ... Ms. Louise KELLY
07 Dir Admissions & College Registrar ... Mr. Tim AMYX
13 Director Information Technology ... Mr. Brian KRAUS
37 Director Student Financial Aid ... Mrs. Sue H. PEDIGO
26 Director Public Relations ... Mrs. Tami WALLACE
18 Senior Director Physical Plant ... Vacant
19 Chief Security & Safety ... Mr. William D. ROGAN
41 Director of Athletics ... Mr. Bobby HUDSON
106 Director Distance Learning ... Dr. Christine MAYER
88 Special Adult Programs/ADA Director ... Ms. Kathy SOWELL
55 Director of Evening Services ... Ms. Brenda BUFFINGTON
09 Director of Institutional Research ... Mrs. Ann Marie CALDERON
96 Director Purchasing ... Mr. Terry MCGOVERN
24 Director Media Services ... Mr. Terry HEINEN
88 Director Retention Support Services ... Ms. Heather HARPER
36 Director of Career Placement ... Dr. Rick PARRENT
38 Director Counseling & Testing ... Mrs. Teresa BROWN
28 Director Student Life & Diversity ... Mr. Kenny YARBROUGH
45 Specialist Resource Development ... Ms. Lori JOHNSON
88 Dir Health Sciences Ctr of Emphasis ... Ms. Terri CRUTCHER
29 Director Alumni Relations ... Ms. Lori JOHNSON

*Walters State Community College (A)

500 S Davy Crockett Parkway, Morristown TN 37813-6899
County: Hamblen FICE Identification: 008863
Unit ID: 222062
Telephone: (423) 585-2600 Carnegie Class: Assoc/Pub-R-L
FAX Number: (423) 585-6853 Calendar System: Semester
URL: www.ws.edu
Established: 1969 Annual Undergrad Tuition & Fees (In-State): $3,625
Enrollment: 6,576 Coed
Affiliation or Control: State IRS Status: 501(c)3
Highest Offering: Associate Degree
Program: Occupational; 2-Year Principally Bachelor's Creditable
Accreditation: **SC**, ACBSP, ACFEI, ADNUR, CAHIIM, COARC, EMT, NAIT, PTAA

02 President ... Dr. Wade B. MCCAMEY
04 Exec Director to the President ... Ms. Brenda L. SMALL
05 Vice President Academic Affairs ... Dr. Lori CAMPBELL
10 Vice President Business Affairs ... Dr. Rosemary JACKSON
32 Vice President Student Affairs ... Dr. Foster CHASON
30 Vice Pres for College Advancement ... Dr. Mark HURST
45 VP for Planning/Research/Assessment . Dr. Debbie L. MCCARTER
20 Asst Vice Pres for Academic Affairs ... Ms. Carla TODARO
35 Asst Vice Pres Student Affairs ... Mr. Michael A. CAMPBELL
18 Ast Vice Pres Facilities Management ... Mr. Max E. WILLIAMS
21 Asst Vice Pres Business Affairs ... Mr. Roger D. BEVERLY
28 Spec Asst to Pres for Diversity ... Ms. W. Ann BOWEN
08 Dean of Library ... Dr. Douglas D. CROSS
31 Dean/Dir Cmty & Economic Devel ... Mr. Joseph L. COMBS
19 Dean of Public Safety Division ... Mr. Thomas STRANGE
17 Dean Health Programs ... Ms. Marty K. RUCKER
12 Dean Greenville/Greene Co Center ... Ms. Drucilla W. MILLER
12 Dean Sevier County Campus ... Ms. Sue FRAZIER
83 Dean of Behavioral/Social Sciences ... Dr. Marilyn R. BOWERS
50 Dean of Business ... Dr. Evelyn J. HONAKER
79 Dean of Humanities ... Ms. Carla TODARO
81 Dean of Mathematics ... Dr. John P. LAPRISE
49 Dean of Natural Science ... Dr. Jeffrey T. HORNER
75 Dean of Technical Education ... Mr. Thomas R. SEWELL
06 Dean Student Info System/Records ... Ms. Linda MASON
103 Dean Ctr for Workforce Development ... Dr. Nancy B. BROWN
37 Dean of Financial Aid ... Ms. Terri STANSBERRY
38 Exec Director Counseling/Testing ... Mr. Andy HALL
15 Exec Dir of Human Resources ... Ms. Tammy GOODE
26 Vice President Public Information ... Mr. James B. PECTOL
13 Exec Director for Information ... Mr. Joe E. SARGENT
41 Director of Athletics ... Dr. Foster CHASON
07 Director of Admissions ... Ms. Mary A. RUSH
19 Chief of Campus Police ... Ms. Sarah ROSE
89 Director Freshmen Studies ... Dr. Marilyn R. BOWERS
36 Director Student Placement ... Mr. Andy HALL
92 Director Honors Program ... Ms. Janice M. DONAHUE
96 Director of Purchasing ... Mr. Shawn A. WILLIAMS
105 Director of Network Services ... Mr. Bill R. MOREFIELD
29 Coordinator of Alumni Relations ... Ms. Wanda HARRELL
84 Coordinator Enrollment Development ... Mr. Marlin R. CURNUTT
93 Coord Minority Student Recruit ... Ms. Roxanne BOWEN
108 Exec Dir of Planning & Assessment ... Dr. Deanna GARMAN

Tennessee Temple University (B)

1815 Union Avenue, Chattanooga TN 37404-3587
County: Hamilton FICE Identification: 003524
Unit ID: 221856
Telephone: (423) 493-4100 Carnegie Class: Spec/Faith
FAX Number: (423) 493-4497 Calendar System: Semester
URL: www.tntemple.edu
Established: 1946 Annual Undergrad Tuition & Fees: $17,640
Enrollment: 968 Coed
Affiliation or Control: Baptist IRS Status: 501(c)3
Highest Offering: Doctorate
Program: Liberal Arts And General; Teacher Preparatory; Professional; Business Emphasis
Accreditation: **TRACS**

00 Chancellor ... Dr. David E. BOULER
01 President ... Dr. Steve ECHOLS
05 Vice President of Academic Services ... Dr. Francis KIMMITT
73 Interim Dean of Seminary ... Dr. Howard OWENS
11 Chief Operations Officer ... Dr. Pam FREJOSKY
106 Director of Online Learning ... Mr. Jeff FARMER
06 Registrar ... Dr. Arnold ARREDONDO
08 Librarian ... Mr. Kevin WOODRUFF
32 Director of Student Services ... Mrs. Pam FREJOSKY
41 Interim Athletic Director ... Mr. Kenrick LIBURD
19 Director of Security ... Mr. Donny BEAM
13 Director of Information Technology ... Mr. Darwin BLANDON
20 Director of Academic Support ... Ms. Tina LIBURD
35 Director Student Development ... Mr. Joe FREJOSKY
37 Director Student Financial Aid ... Mr. Jeff DAVIS
26 Dir of Mktg/Strategic Initiatives ... Vacant

Tennessee Wesleyan College (C)

204 East College St., Athens TN 37303
County: McMinn FICE Identification: 003525
Unit ID: 221731
Telephone: (423) 745-7504 Carnegie Class: Bac/Diverse
FAX Number: (423) 744-9968 Calendar System: Semester
URL: www.twcnet.edu
Established: 1857 Annual Undergrad Tuition & Fees: $21,000
Enrollment: 1,080 Coed
Affiliation or Control: United Methodist IRS Status: 501(c)3
Highest Offering: Master's
Program: Liberal Arts And General; Teacher Preparatory; Professional
Accreditation: **SC**, NURSE

01 President ... Dr. Harley KNOWLES
05 Vice President for Academic Affairs ... Dr. Suzanne A. HINE
11 Vice Pres Administration ... Mr. Larry WALLACE
10 Vice Pres Financial/Business Affs ... Mrs. Gail HARRIS
32 Vice President for Student Life ... Dr. Scott MASHBURN
84 Vice President for Enrollment ... Dr. Jerry JACKSON
09 Asst VP Inst Research & Retention ... Mrs. Traci N. WILLIAMS
04 Admin Assistant to President ... Mrs. Gail ROGERS
08 Assoc Dean of Library Svcs ... Mrs. Sandra CLARIDAY
06 Registrar ... Mrs. Julie MCCASLIN
37 Director of Financial Aid ... Mr. Robert K. PERRY
29 Director of Alumni Relations ... Ms. Jessica EDWARDS
41 Athletic Director ... Mr. Donny MAYFIELD
15 Human Resources Director ... Mrs. Melody LANTZ
18 Chief of Facilities/Physical Plant ... Mr. Mike INGRAM
26 Director Public Relations ... Mr. Bridgette RAPER
35 Director of Student Activities ... Ms. Kerrie LYNN
13 Director of Information Technoloy ... Mr. Joe PASSMORE

Trevecca Nazarene University (D)

333 Murfreesboro Road, Nashville TN 37210-2877
County: Davidson FICE Identification: 003526
Unit ID: 221892
Telephone: (615) 248-1200 Carnegie Class: DRU
FAX Number: (615) 248-7728 Calendar System: Semester
URL: www.trevecca.edu
Established: 1901 Annual Undergrad Tuition & Fees: $21,830
Enrollment: 2,472 Coed
Affiliation or Control: Church Of The Nazarene IRS Status: 501(c)3
Highest Offering: Doctorate
Program: Liberal Arts And General; Teacher Preparatory; Professional
Accreditation: **SC**, ARCPA, MUS, NURSE, @SW, TED

01 President ... Dr. Dan BOONE
05 University Provost ... Dr. Stephen M. PUSEY
10 Exec Vice Pres Finance & Admin ... Mr. David CALDWELL
26 Vice President External Relations ... Mrs. Peggy J. COONING
20 Assoc Provost/Dean Academic Affairs ... Dr. Carol MAXSON
32 Assoc Provost/Dean of Student Dev ... Mr. Stephen A. HARRIS
84 Assoc Provost/Dean of Enroll Mgmt ... Dr. Kathy BAUGHER
73 Dean of School of Religion ... Dr. Timothy M. GREEN
50 Dean of Business and Technology ... Dr. Jim HIATT
51 Dean of College Lifelong Learning ... Dr. Dave PHILLIPS
35 Assoc Dean Student Community Life ... Mr. Matt SPRAKER
39 Asc Dean Students Residential Life ... Mrs. Ronda LILIENTHAL
53 Dean of the School of Education ... Dr. Suzann HARRIS
49 Dean of School of Arts & Science ... Dr. Lena WELCH
13 Chief Information Officer/ITS ... Mr. Jeff TURNER
08 Director Library Services ... Mrs. Ruth KINNERSLEY
09 Director Institutional Research ... Ms. Donna K. TUDOR
06 Registrar ... Mrs. Becky NIECE
19 Director of Security ... Mr. Norm ROBINSON
07 Director of Admissions ... Ms. Melinda MILLER
41 Athletic Director ... Mr. Mark ELLIOTT
88 Director Ctr/Ldrshp Calling Service ... Mr. Tom MIDDENDORF
36 Director Counseling Services ... Dr. Sara HOPKINS
88 Coordinator of Sophomore Year Pgm ... Ms. Jennifer NEELY
88 Coordinator of Senior Year Programs ... Ms. Nicole RABALAIS
106 Director Online Learning ... Vacant
21 Director of Financial Services ... Mr. Chuck SEAMAN
15 Director Human Resources ... Mr. Steve SEXTON
37 Financial Aid Director ... Mr. Eddie WHITE
76 Director Physician Asst Pgm ... Ms. Robin JEWETT
18 Director Plant Operations ... Mr. Glen LINTHICUM
44 Sr Stewardship Ofcr/Dir Plan Giving ... Mr. Richard UNDERWOOD
29 Director of Alumni Services ... Mrs. Nancy DUNLAP
26 Director of Public Relations ... Mrs. Jan GREATHOUSE
88 Director of Marketing & Comm ... Mr. Matthew TOY

Tusculum College (E)

60 Shiloh Road, Greeneville TN 37743-9997
County: Greene FICE Identification: 003527
Unit ID: 221953
Telephone: (423) 636-7300 Carnegie Class: Master's S
FAX Number: (423) 638-7166 Calendar System: Other
URL: www.tusculum.edu
Established: 1794 Annual Undergrad Tuition & Fees: $22,250
Enrollment: 2,199 Coed
Affiliation or Control: Presbyterian Church (U.S.A.) IRS Status: 501(c)3
Highest Offering: Master's
Program: Liberal Arts And General; Teacher Preparatory
Accreditation: **SC**

01 President ... Dr. Nancy B. MOODY
05 VP Academic Affairs ... Dr. Melinda DUKES
30 VP Institutional Advancement ... Ms. Heather PATCHETT
10 Vice Pres/Chief Financial Officer ... Mr. Steve GEHRET
84 VP for Enrollment Management ... Dr. Tom STEIN
20 Int Assoc VP for Academic Affairs ... Dr. Lisa JOHNSON
32 Dean of Students ... Dr. David MCMAHAN
35 Associate Dean of Students ... Ms. Jonita ASHLEY-PAULEY
29 Assoc VP Institutional Advancement ... Ms. Susan VANCE
06 Registrar ... Ms. Bobbie CLARKSON
21 Controller ... Ms. Tracey JULIAN
07 Director of Operations/Admissions ... Ms. Melissa RIPLEY
45 Asst to Pres Inst Plng/Effectivenes ... Dr. Carl LARSEN
15 Director Human Resources ... Ms. Mary SONNER
36 Director Career Counseling ... Ms. Robin LAY
08 Librarian ... Mr. Myron J. SMITH, JR.
42 College Minister ... Mr. Mark STOKES
37 Director of Financial Aid ... Ms. Melena VERITY
41 Athletic Director ... Mr. Frankie DEBUSK
27 Director of Communications ... Ms. Suzanne RICHEY
13 Director of Information Systems ... Dr. Blair HENLEY
18 Director Facilities Management ... Mr. David MARTIN
92 Director of Honors Program ... Dr. Angela KEATON
40 Bookstore Manager ... Mr. Cliff HOY

Union University (F)

1050 Union University Drive, Jackson TN 38305-3697
County: Madison FICE Identification: 003528
Unit ID: 221971
Telephone: (731) 668-1818 Carnegie Class: Master's L
FAX Number: (731) 661-5175 Calendar System: 4/1/4
URL: www.uu.edu
Established: 1823 Annual Undergrad Tuition & Fees: $26,880
Enrollment: 4,262 Coed
Affiliation or Control: Southern Baptist IRS Status: 501(c)3
Highest Offering: Doctorate
Program: Liberal Arts And General
Accreditation: **SC**, ANEST, ART, BUS, ENG, MUS, NURSE, PHAR, SW, TED

01 President ... Dr. David S. DOCKERY
05 Exec Vice Pres Acad Administration ... Dr. Gene FANT
10 Sr Vice Pres Business Services ... Mr. Gary L. CARTER
30 Sr Vice Pres University Relations ... Dr. Jerry TIDWELL
84 Sr Vice Pres Enrollment Services ... Mr. Rich GRIMM
32 Sr VP Student Svcs/Dean of Students . Dr. Kimberly THORNBURY
26 Vice Pres for Church Relations ... Dr. Todd BRADY
108 Vice Pres Institutional Assessment ... Dr. Jimmy H. DAVIS
42 Vice President for Spiritual Life ... Dr. Gregory THORNBURY
04 Exec Assistant to the President ... Mrs. Cynthia L. MEREDITH
21 Assoc Vice Pres Business Svcs ... Mr. Robert SIMPSON
08 Assoc VP Academic Res/Dir Library ... Ms. Anna B. MORGAN
27 Assoc VP University Communications ... Mr. Mark KAHLER
90 Assoc VP Information Technology ... Mr. James AVERY
15 Assoc VP Business Svcs/Human Res ... Mr. John CARBONELL
07 Asst VP for Undergraduate Admiss ... Mr. Robbie GRAVES
37 Director Student Financial Planning ... Mr. John WINDHAM
49 Dean College Arts & Sciences ... Dr. John NETLAND
46 Exec Vice Pres Strategic Initiative ... Dr. Carla D. SANDERSON
50 Dean School of Business ... Dr. Keith ABSHER
66 Dean School of Nursing ... Dr. Timothy SMITH
53 Exec Dean Col Educ/Human Studies ... Dr. Tom ROSEBROUGH
88 Dean School of Theology Missions ... Vacant
67 Dean School of Pharmacy ... Dr. Sheila MITCHELL
91 Assoc Dir Information Technology ... Miss Karen MCWHERTER
36 Asst Dean Students/Dir Career Svcs ... Mrs. Jackie TAYLOR
29 Director of Alumni Relations ... Mr. Josh CLARKE
13 Director of Data Management ... Mr. David PORTER
46 Director of Development Services ... Mrs. Katrina BRADFIELD
06 Registrar ... Mrs. Susan HOPPER
19 Director of Security/Safety ... Mr. Carson HAWKINS
41 Director of Athletics ... Mr. Tommy SADLER
18 Chief Facilities/Physical Plant ... Mr. David MCBRIDE

University of Phoenix Memphis Campus (G)

65 Germantown Court, Cordova TN 38018-7290
Telephone: (901) 751-1086 Identification: 770224
Accreditation: **&NH**, ACBSP

† Main campus is University of Phoenix in Tempe, AZ.

University of Phoenix Nashville Campus (A)

616 Marriott Drive, Nashville TN 37214-5048
Telephone: (615) 872-0188 Identification: 770225
Accreditation: &NH, ACBSP

† Main campus is University of Phoenix in Tempe, AZ.

*University of Tennessee System Office (B)

800 Andy Holt Tower, Knoxville TN 37996-0180
County: Knox FICE Identification: 008051
Unit ID: 221722
Telephone: (865) 974-1000 Carnegie Class: N/A
FAX Number: (865) 974-3753
URL: www.tennessee.edu

01 President .... Dr. Joe DIPIETRO
03 Executive Vice President .... Dr. David E. MILLHORN
05 VP Academic Affairs/Student Success .... Dr. Katherine N. HIGH
30 CEO UT Found/VP Develop & Alumni .... Mr. Johnnie RAY
86 VP for Government Relations .... Mr. Anthony HAYNES
45 Vice President for Research .... Dr. David E. MILLHORN
10 Treasurer & CIO/Acting CFO .... Mr. Charles (Butch) M. PECCOLO, JR.
43 VP/General Counsel/Secretary .... Ms. Catherine S. MIZELL
16 Vice President for Human Resources .... Ms. Linda HENDRICKS
86 Vice President of Public Service .... Dr. Mary JINKS
28 VP for Equity and Diversity .... Mr. Theotis ROBINSON
04 Exec Assistant to the President .... Mr. Keith CARVER
21 Exec Dir Auditing/Consulting Svcs .... Ms. Sandy JANSEN
29 Exec Dir UT Natl Alumni Assn .... Mr. Lofton K. STUART
26 VP Communications & Marketing .... Dr. Tonjanita JOHNSON

*University of Tennessee, Knoxville (C)

1331 Circle Park, Andy Holt Tower,
Knoxville TN 37996-0184
County: Knox FICE Identification: 003530
Unit ID: 221759
Telephone: (865) 974-1000 Carnegie Class: RU/VH
FAX Number: (865) 974-1182 Calendar System: Semester
URL: www.utk.edu
Established: 1794 Annual Undergrad Tuition & Fees (In-State): $11,194
Enrollment: 27,918 Coed
Affiliation or Control: State IRS Status: 501(c)3
Highest Offering: Doctorate
Program: Liberal Arts And General; Teacher Preparatory; Professional
Accreditation: SC, ANEST, ART, AUD, BUS, BUSA, CACREP, CIDA, CLPSY, COPSY, CORE, CS, DENT, DIETD, DIETI, ENG, FOR, IPSY, JOUR, LAW, LIB, LSAR, MT, MUS, NRPA, NURSE, PH, RAD, SCPSY, SP, SW, VET

02 Chancellor .... Dr. Jimmy G. CHEEK
100 Chancellor's Chief of Staff .... Vacant
05 Provost/Senior VC for Acad Affairs .... Dr. Susan D. MARTIN
32 Vice Chancellor for Student Affairs .... Mr. W. Timothy ROGERS
46 Vice Chancellor Research/Engagement .... Dr. Taylor EIGHMY
10 Vice Chanc Finance & Administration .... Mr. Chris CIMINO
27 Vice Chanc for Communications .... Ms. Margie NICHOLS
30 Vice Chanc Development/Alumni Affs .... Mr. Scott RABENOLD
20 Vice Provost for Academic Affairs .... Ms. Sally J. MCMILLAN
20 Vice Provost Academic Operations .... Vacant
58 Vice Provost/Dean Graduate School .... Dr. Carolyn R. HODGES
39 Asst VC/Exec Dir Univ Housing .... Mr. Ken STONER
51 Asst Provost Univ Outrch/Cont Educ .... Dr. Norvel BURKETT
07 Asst Provost Enrollment Svcs .... Mr. Richard L. BAYER
18 Assoc Vice Chanc Facilities Svcs .... Mr. Dave IRVIN
41 Vice Chancellor/Dir Athletics .... Mr. Dave HART
28 Director Equity/Diversity Office .... Dr. Marva RUDOLPH
37 Director of Financial Aid .... Mr. Jeffrey G. GERKIN
09 Dir Inst Research/Assessmt .... Ms. Denise GARDNER
38 Director of Student Counseling .... Dr. Victor BARR
06 Registrar .... Ms. Monique W. ANDERSON
47 Dean Ag Sciences/Natural Resources .... Dr. Caula BEYL
48 Dean of Architecture and Design .... Dr. Scott POOLE
50 Dean Business Administration .... Dr. Steve MANGUM
60 Dean Communication/Information .... Dr. Michael WIRTH
53 Dean Educ/Health/Human Sciences .... Dr. Robert RIDER
54 Dean of Engineering .... Dr. Wayne DAVIS
61 Dean of Law .... Prof. Douglas BLAZE
49 Dean of Arts & Sciences .... Dr. Theresa LEE
66 Dean of Nursing .... Dr. Joan L. CREASIA
70 Dean of Social Work .... Dr. Karen SOWERS
74 Dean of Veterinary Medicine .... Dr. James P. THOMPSON
47 Dean of Agricultural Extension Svc .... Dr. Tim L. CROSS
08 Dean of Libraries .... Dr. Steve SMITH

*University of Tennessee at Chattanooga (D)

615 McCallie Avenue, Chattanooga TN 37403-2504
County: Hamilton FICE Identification: 003529
Unit ID: 221740
Telephone: (423) 425-4111 Carnegie Class: Master's L
FAX Number: (423) 425-2200 Calendar System: Semester
URL: www.utc.edu
Established: 1886 Annual Undergrad Tuition & Fees (In-State): $3,777
Enrollment: 11,660 Coed
Affiliation or Control: State IRS Status: 501(c)3
Highest Offering: Doctorate
Program: Liberal Arts And General; Teacher Preparatory; Professional
Accreditation: SC, ANEST, ART, BUS, BUSA, CACREP, CIDA, CS, DIETD, ENG, JOUR, MUS, NURSE, PTA, SPAA, SW, TED, THEA

02 Chancellor .... Dr. Steven ANGLE
05 Provost & Sr Vice Chancellor .... Dr. Jerald AINSWORTH
30 Vice Chanc University Advancement .... Mr. Bob LYON
10 Sr Vice Chanc Fin/Operations & IT .... Dr. Richard BROWN
32 Vice Chanc Student Development .... Dr. John DELANEY
20 Assoc Provost for Academic Affairs .... Dr. Jocelyn SANDERS
21 Assoc Vice Chanc Business/Fin Affs .... Ms. Vanasia Conley PARKS
26 Assoc VC University Relations .... Mr. Chuck CANTRELL
18 Asst VC Operations/Fac Plng & Mgt .... Mr. Tom M. ELLIS
91 Assoc VC & CIO .... Mr. Tom HOOVER
35 Asst VC Student Development .... Dr. Dee Dee ANDERSON
100 Chief of Staff .... Ms. Terry DENNISTON
08 Dean of Lupton Library .... Ms. Theresa LIEDTKA
88 Assoc Dean of Student Life .... Mr. Jim HICKS
07 Asst VC Enrollment Services .... Mr. Yancy FREEMAN
06 Director of Records and Registrar .... Ms. Linda ORTH
13 Director of Information Systems .... Mr. Richard GAMBRELL
09 Dir of Planning/Eval/Inst Research .... Dr. Richard R. GRUETZEMACHER
36 Dir of Placement/Student Employment .... Mrs. Jean DAKE
15 Director of Human Resources .... Mr. Dan WEBB
38 Director of Counseling .... Dr. Nancy BADGER
37 Director of Financial Aid .... Ms. Dianne COX
41 Vice Chanc & Dir of Athletics .... Mr. David BLACKBURN
49 Dean of Arts & Sciences .... Dr. Herbert BURHENN
50 Dean of Business Administration .... Dr. Robert DOOLEY
53 Dean of Health/Educ/Prof Studies .... Dr. Mary TANNER
54 Dean of Engineering/Comp Science .... Dr. William SUTTON
58 Dean of Graduate School .... Dr. Jerald AINSWORTH
66 Director of Nursing .... Dr. Katherine S. LINDGREN
22 Director of Equity & Diversity .... Dr. Bryan SAMUEL
78 Director of Cooperative Education .... Mr. Hugh L. PREVOST, JR.
46 Director of Grants/Research .... Ms. Meredith PERRY
29 Director of Alumni Affairs .... Ms. Jayne HOLDER
14 Director of Admin Computing .... Ms. Glenda F. SULLIVAN
96 Mgr of Business Svcs (Purchasing) .... Mr. Charles SCOTT

*University of Tennessee at Martin (E)

544 University Street, Martin TN 38238-0001
County: Weakley FICE Identification: 003531
Unit ID: 221768
Telephone: (731) 881-7000 Carnegie Class: Master's M
FAX Number: (731) 881-7019 Calendar System: Semester
URL: www.utm.edu
Established: 1900 Annual Undergrad Tuition & Fees (In-State): $3,528
Enrollment: 7,751 Coed
Affiliation or Control: State IRS Status: 501(c)3
Highest Offering: Master's
Program: Liberal Arts And General; Teacher Preparatory; Professional
Accreditation: SC, AAFCS, BUS, DIETD, #DIETI, ENG, JOUR, MUS, NUR, SW, TED

02 Chancellor .... Dr. Thomas A. RAKES
05 Provost & Vice Chanc for Acad Affs .... Dr. E. Jerald OGG
10 Int Vice Chanc for Finance & Admin .... Ms. Nancy J. YARBROUGH
32 Vice Chancellor for Student Affairs .... Dr. Margarêt Y. TOSTON
30 Vice Chancellor for Univ Advancemnt .... Vacant
20 Assoc Vice Chanc for Academic Affr .... Dr. Victoria S. SENG
27 CIO .... Mr. Terry W. LEWIS
21 Int Dir of Budget & Mgmt Reporting .... Ms. Petra R. MCPHEARSON
35 Asst Vice Chanc for Student Affairs .... Mr. David J. BELOTE
44 Asst VChanc Devel & Planned Giving .... Ms. Jeanna C. SWAFFORD
04 Exec Assistant to the Chancellor .... Ms. Edie B. GIBSON
29 Asst Vice Chanc for Alumni Rels .... Mr. Charley T. DEAL
06 Dir of Acad Records & Registrar .... Ms. Brandy D. CARTMELL
07 Director of Admissions .... Ms. Judy M. RAYBURN
28 Equity and Diversity Officer .... Vacant
15 Director of Human Resources .... Mr. James (Phillip) BRIGHT
09 Int Dir Institutional Research .... Dr. Desiree A. MCCULLOUGH
41 Director Intercollegiate Athletics .... Mr. Phil W. DANE
08 Director of Library .... Ms. Mary V. CARPENTER
18 Director of Physical Plant Opers .... Mr. Tim J. NIPP
19 Director of Public Safety .... Mr. Scott D. ROBBINS
96 Purchasing Agent .... Ms. Lori A. DONAVANT
37 Int Dir Financial Aid & Scholarship .... Ms. Sheryl FRAZIER
38 Dir Student Health & Counseling Svc .... Ms. Shannon DEAL
39 Director of Student Housing .... Mr. Earl WRIGHT
26 Director of University Relations .... Mr. Robert (Bud) D. GRIMES
85 Int Dir Tenn Intensive English Pgm .... Mr. Charles (Gary) WILSON
47 Int Dean Col Agri & App Sciences .... Dr. Jerry GRESHAM
50 Dean Col Business & Global Affairs .... Dr. Ernest R. MOSER
53 Dean Col Educ/Health & Behav Sci .... Dr. Mary Lee HALL
79 Dean Col Humanities/Fine Arts .... Dr. Lynn M. ALEXANDER
54 Interim Dean Col Engr & Natural Sci .... Dr. Richard J. HELGESON

**University of Tennessee Health Science Center* (F)

800 Madison Avenue, Memphis TN 38163-0002
Telephone: (901) 448-5500 FICE Identification: 006725
Accreditation: &SC, ANEST, CAHIIM, CYTO, DENT, DH, HT, IPSY, MED, MT, NURSE, OT, PHAR, PTA

† Main campus is University of Tennessee, Knoxville in Knoxville, TN.

Vanderbilt University (G)

2201 West End Avenue, Nashville TN 37240-0002
County: Davidson FICE Identification: 003535
Unit ID: 221999
Telephone: (615) 322-7311 Carnegie Class: RU/VH
FAX Number: (615) 343-5555 Calendar System: Semester
URL: www.vanderbilt.edu
Established: 1873 Annual Undergrad Tuition & Fees: $42,978
Enrollment: 12,710 Coed
Affiliation or Control: Independent Non-Profit IRS Status: 501(c)3
Highest Offering: Doctorate
Program: Liberal Arts And General; Teacher Preparatory; Professional
Accreditation: SC, AUD, BUS, CACREP, CLPSY, DENT, DIETI, DMS, ENG, IPSY, LAW, MED, MIDWF, MT, MUS, NDT, NMT, NUR, PERF, PH, SP, TED, THEOL

01 Chancellor .... Dr. Nicholas ZEPPOS
05 Provost/Vice Chancellor .... Dr. Richard C. MCCARTY
17 Vice Chancellor Health Affairs .... Dr. Jeffrey R. BALSER
10 Vice Chanc/Chief Financial Officer .... Mr. Brett SWEET
11 Vice Chanc Administration .... Mr. Jerry FIFE
30 Vice Chanc Dev & Alumni Relations .... Ms. Susie STALCUP
15 Assoc VC/Chief Human Resource Ofcr .... Ms. Traci NORDBERG
26 VC Univ Affs/Gen Counsel/Univ Secy .... Dr. David WILLIAMS
29 Exec Asc VC Development/Alumni Rels .... Mr. Robert EARLY
20 Assoc Vice Chanc Academic Affairs .... Ms. Susan HART
18 Deputy VC Facilities & Environment .... Mr. Judson NEWBERN
27 Vice Chancellor for Public Affairs .... Ms. Beth FORTUNE
09 Director Institutional Research .... Dr. Roberta BELL
88 Int VC for Investments .... Mr. Brett SWEET
20 Assoc Provost Undergrad Education .... Ms. Cynthia J. CYRUS
58 Vice Prov Research/Dean Grad Sch .... Dr. Dennis G. HALL
84 Vice Provost Enrollment .... Dr. Douglas CHRISTIANSEN
13 Dean Student Info Tech Support .... Mr. F. Clark WILLIAMS
21 Interim Asst VC Finance/Controller .... Ms. Dalana ROBERTSON
06 Registrar .... Vacant
07 Dean of Admissions .... Dr. Douglas CHRISTIANSEN
07 Dir Undergraduate Admissions .... Mr. John GAINES
37 Exec Director of Financial Aid .... Dr. David D. MOHNING
38 Director Counseling Center .... Dr. Catherine FUCHS
36 Dir Center for Student Prof Devel .... Ms. Cynthia FUNK
46 Director Contract & Research Adm .... Dr. John CHILDRESS
14 Assoc Vice Chancellor ITS .... Vacant
32 Dean of Students/Assoc Provost .... Mr. Mark BANDAS
49 Dean College Arts & Science .... Dr. Carolyn DEVER
63 Dean School of Medicine .... Dr. Jeffrey R. BALSER
54 Dean School of Engineering .... Dr. Philippe M. FAUCHET
66 Dean School of Nursing .... Dr. Colleen CONWAY-WELCH
53 Dean Education & Human Development .... Dr. Camilla P. BENBOW
64 Dean Blair School of Music .... Dr. Mark WAIT
73 Dean of the Divinity School .... Dr. James HUDNUT-BEUMLER
61 Dean of the School of Law .... Dr. Chris GUTHRIE
50 Dean Owen Grad School of Mgmt .... Dr. James BRADFORD
88 Dean of the Ingram Commons .... Dr. Frank WCISLO
42 University Chaplain .... Rev. Gretchen PERSON
19 Chief of Police/Asst Vice Chanc .... Mr. August J. WASHINGTON
22 Dir EO/AA & Disability Svcs .... Ms. Anita JENIOUS
23 Assoc Dean Health & Wellness .... Dr. John W. GREENE
41 Director of Sport Operations .... Mr. Brockton WILLIAMS

Vatterot Career College (H)

6991 Appling Farms Parkway, Memphis TN 38133
Telephone: (901) 372-2399 Identification: 770592
Accreditation: ACCSC

† Main campus is Vatterott College-Des Moines in Des Moines, IA.

Vatterott College-Memphis (I)

2655 Dividend Drive, Memphis TN 38132-1713
Telephone: (901) 761-5730 Identification: 666308
Accreditation: ACCSC

† Main campus is Vatterott College-NorthPark in Berkeley, MO.

Victory University (formerly Crichton College) (J)

255 N Highland Street, Memphis TN 38111-1375
County: Shelby FICE Identification: 009982
Unit ID: 220941
Telephone: (901) 320-9700 Carnegie Class: Bac/Diverse
FAX Number: (901) 320-9709 Calendar System: Semester
URL: www.victory.edu
Established: 1941 Annual Undergrad Tuition & Fees: $10,800
Enrollment: 1,943 Coed
Affiliation or Control: Proprietary IRS Status: Proprietary
Highest Offering: Master's
Program: Occupational; 2-Year Principally Bachelor's Creditable; Liberal Arts And General; Teacher Preparatory; Professional; Business Emphasis
Accreditation: SC

01 President .... Dr. Shirley ROBINSON PIPPINS
04 Exec Asst to CEO/President .... Ms. Shirley MARTIN
10 Chief Financial Officer .... Mr. Thomas MAREK
37 AVP Financial Aid & Business Svcs .... Ms. Marie FORD
13 AVP IT & Enterprise Systems .... Mr. Todd WILLIAMS
15 Director Human Resources .... Mrs. Julie TYLER
21 Director Financial Planning .... Ms. Marie RYCZYWOT
05 Provost .... Dr. Sherryl D. WEEMS
09 Dir Inst Effectiveness & Research .... Vacant

41 Athletic Director .... Mr. Scott ROBINSON
106 VP Online Academic & Faculty Svcs .... Dr. Melissa HARTMAN
84 Sr VP Enollment Mgmt/Ops & Ent Sys .... Vacant
07 Assoc Vice President of Admissions .... Ms. Shelley KEMP
88 Exec Dir Online Enrollment .... Mr. Marcos ALONSO
06 Registrar .... Mr. Michael STALKER
20 Interim Vice Pres Academic Affairs .... Dr. Sherryl D. WEEMS
73 Chair Bible & Theology .... Dr. Troy MILLER
50 Chair Business .... Dr. Brodie I. JOHNSON
79 Chair Arts and Science .... Dr. Donna BRACKIN
08 Director Library .... Ms. Pamela B. WALKER
32 Director Student Development .... Mr. Brian DUFFY
11 Dir Operations & Public Safety .... Mr. Thomas MAREK

Virginia College School of Business and Health (A)

721 Eastgate Loop, Chattanooga TN 37411-5600
Telephone: (423) 893-2000 Identification: 666136
Accreditation: ACICS, MAAB

† Main campus is Virginia College in Birmingham, AL.

Virginia College School of Business and Health (B)

5003 North Broadway Street, Knoxville TN 37918
Telephone: (865) 745-4500 Identification: 770828
Accreditation: ACICS

† Main campus is Virginia College in Birmingham, AL.

Visible Music College (C)

200 Madison Avenue, Memphis TN 38103
County: Shelby FICE Identification: 039823
Unit ID: 449764
Telephone: (901) 381-3939 Carnegie Class: Spec/Arts
FAX Number: (901) 377-0544 Calendar System: Semester
URL: www.visible.edu
Established: 2000 Annual Undergrad Tuition & Fees: $25,800
Enrollment: 126 Coed
Affiliation or Control: Independent Non-Profit IRS Status: 501(c)3
Highest Offering: Baccalaureate
Program: Professional; Music Emphasis
Accreditation: TRACS

01 President .... Ken STEORTS
05 Vice President of Academics .... Dr. Pete SANCHEZ
32 Vice President of Students .... Nathan CARICO
10 Vice President of Business .... Ben RAWLEY
07 Director of Admissions .... Susan HARRIS
08 Librarian .... Christy NINI
37 Director of Financial Aid .... LaKeisha MURRY
06 Registrar .... Vincent LEE

Watkins College of Art, Design & Film (D)

2298 Rosa L. Parks Boulevard, Nashville TN 37228-1306
County: Davidson FICE Identification: 030888
Unit ID: 392840
Telephone: (615) 383-4848 Carnegie Class: Spec/Arts
FAX Number: (615) 383-4849 Calendar System: Semester
URL: www.watkins.edu
Established: 1885 Annual Undergrad Tuition & Fees: $21,900
Enrollment: 378 Coed
Affiliation or Control: Independent Non-Profit IRS Status: 501(c)3
Highest Offering: Baccalaureate
Program: Fine Arts Emphasis
Accreditation: SC, ART, CIDA

01 President .... Ms. Ellen MEYER
30 Vice Pres Institutional Advancement .... Ms. Hilrie BROWN
05 Vice President for Academic Affairs .... Ms. Joy MCKENZIE
10 Vice Pres Finance and Operations ..... Ms. Mary Ellen LOTHAMER
07 Director Admissions .... Ms. Linda SCHWAB
26 Director External Relations .... Ms. Caroline DAVIS
06 Registrar .... Ms. Tracie JOHNSON
37 Director Financial Aid .... Ms. Regina GILBERT
08 Library Director .... Ms. Lisa WILLIAMS
13 Director Information Technology .... Mr. Chris MCQUISTION
18 Director of Facilities .... Mr. Martin DILLINGHAM
88 Chair Film School .... Mr. Van FLESHER
57 Chair Fine Art Department .... Ms. Kristi HARGROVE
88 Chair Graphic Design Department .... Mr. Dan BRAWNER
88 Chair Interior Design Department .... Ms. Cheryl GULLEY
88 Chair Photography Department .... Ms. Robin PARIS
97 Director General Education .... Ms. Cary Beth MILLER
51 Director Community Education .... Ms. Meredith EASTBURN
32 Director Student Life .... Ms. Samantha BRZOZOWSKI

Welch College (E)

3606 West End Avenue, Nashville TN 37205-2498
County: Davidson FICE Identification: 030018
Unit ID: 220206
Telephone: (615) 844-5000 Carnegie Class: Bac/Diverse
FAX Number: (615) 844-5004 Calendar System: Semester
URL: www.welch.edu
Established: 1942 Annual Undergrad Tuition & Fees: $22,696
Enrollment: 319 Coed
Affiliation or Control: Free Will Baptist IRS Status: 501(c)3
Highest Offering: Baccalaureate
Program: Liberal Arts And General; Teacher Preparatory; Religious Emphasis
Accreditation: SC, BI

01 President .... Dr. J. Matthew PINSON
05 Provost .... Dr. Paul G. KETTEMAN
10 Vice President Financial Affairs .... Mr. Craig MAHLER
45 Dir Institutional Planning/Assess .... Dr. Kevin HESTER
30 Vice Pres Institutional Advancement .... Mr. David WILLIFORD
32 VP Student Svcs/Dean of Students .... Dr. Jon FORLINES
34 Dean of Women .... Mrs. Susan FORLINES
21 Comptroller .... Vacant
08 Librarian .... Mrs. Carol REID
18 Director of Plant Operations .... Mr. Sandy GOODFELLOW
26 Director of Public Relations .... Dr. Jack WILLIAMS
84 Dir of Enrollment Svcs/Fin Aid .... Mrs. Debbie MOUSER
106 Dir of Online and Adult Studies .... Mr. Allan CROWSON
09 Director of Institutional Research .... Mr. Wayne SPRUILL
41 Athletic Director .... Mr. Gary TURNER

West Tennessee Business College (F)

1186 Highway 45 Bypass, Jackson TN 38301
County: Madison FICE Identification: 004947
Unit ID: 222099
Telephone: (731) 668-7240 Carnegie Class: Assoc/PrivFP
FAX Number: (731) 668-3824 Calendar System: Other
URL: www.wtbc.edu
Established: 1888 Annual Undergrad Tuition & Fees: $15,605
Enrollment: 264 Coed
Affiliation or Control: Proprietary IRS Status: Proprietary
Highest Offering: Associate Degree
Program: Occupational
Accreditation: ACICS

01 Executive Director .... C. Vicki BURCH
05 Academic Dean .... LaVerne ADAMS
10 Chief Fiscal Officer .... Kim JONES
06 Registrar .... Sheila JOHNSON
07 Admissions Director .... Ann RECORD

† Tuition for each program includes books.

Williamson Christian College (G)

200 Seaboard Lane, Franklin TN 37067-8237
County: Williamson FICE Identification: 035135
Unit ID: 443340
Telephone: (615) 771-7821 Carnegie Class: Spec/Faith
FAX Number: (615) 771-7810 Calendar System: Semester
URL: www.williamsoncc.edu
Established: 1996 Annual Undergrad Tuition & Fees: $9,810
Enrollment: 84 Coed
Affiliation or Control: Non-denominational IRS Status: 501(c)3
Highest Offering: Baccalaureate
Program: Professional; Religious Emphasis
Accreditation: BI

01 President .... Dr. Ed SMITH
05 Exec Vice Pres Academic Affairs .... Dr. Sharon LANDERS
30 Int Vice President Advancement .... Dr. Ed SMITH
11 Vice President for Operations .... Vacant
06 Registrar .... Ms. Karen HUDSON
09 Dir Institutional Effectiveness .... Dr. Tony BUCHANAN
08 Librarian .... Ms. Elizabeth HUTCHISON
07 Dir of Admissions/Enrollment Mgmt .... Ms. Susan MAYS
37 Manager of Financial Aid .... Ms. Laura FLOWERS

TEXAS

Abilene Christian University (H)

ACU Box 29100, Abilene TX 79699-9100
County: Taylor FICE Identification: 003537
Unit ID: 222178
Telephone: (325) 674-2000 Carnegie Class: Master's L
FAX Number: (325) 674-2202 Calendar System: Semester
URL: www.acu.edu
Established: 1906 Annual Undergrad Tuition & Fees: $28,350
Enrollment: 4,367 Coed
Affiliation or Control: Churches Of Christ IRS Status: 501(c)3
Highest Offering: Doctorate
Program: Liberal Arts And General; Teacher Preparatory; Professional
Accreditation: SC, BUS, CIDA, DIETD, #JOUR, MFCD, MUS, NURSE, SP, SW, TEAC, THEOL

01 President .... Dr. Phil SCHUBERT
100 Senior Advisor to the President .... Ms. Suzanne ALLMON
05 Provost .... Dr. Robert RHODES
03 Vice President of the University .... Dr. Gary D. MCCALEB
30 Vice President for Advancement .... Mr. Phil BOONE
32 Interim VP for Student Life .... Dr. Jan MEYER
88 Chief Investment Ofcr/Pres ACIMCO .... Mr. Jack W. RICH
43 General Counsel .... Mr. Slade SULLIVAN
00 Chancellor .... Dr. Royce MONEY
88 Exec Assistant to the Chancellor .... Mr. Jim HOLMANS
102 Vice Chancellor/Pres ACU Foundation .... Mr. Dan T. GARRETT
88 Senior Vice President Emeritus .... Dr. Robert D. HUNTER
20 Vice Provost .... Dr. Susan LEWIS
97 Asst Provost for General Educ .... Dr. Nancy SHANKLE
49 Dean College of Arts & Sciences .... Dr. Greg STRAUGHN
73 Dean College of Biblical Studies .... Dr. Ken R. CUKROWSKI
50 Dean College of Business Admin .... Dr. Rick S. LYTLE
53 Dean College of Educ & Human Svcs .... Dr. Donnie SNIDER
92 Dean Honors College .... Dr. Stephen JOHNSON
58 Dean Graduate School .... Dr. Carley DODD
66 Dean School of Nursing .... Dr. Becky HAMMACK
08 Dean Library/Information Resources .... Dr. John WEAVER
104 Director of the Ctr Intl Educ .... Dr. Stephen SHEWMAKER
106 Managing Director Online Programs .... Mr. Corey PATTERSON
42 Assistant Dean for Spiritual Life .... Mr. Mark LEWIS
36 Director Career Center .... Ms. MaryEllen OLSON
06 Registrar & Dir of First Yr Program .... Dr. Eric GUMM
37 Director Student Financial Services .... Mr. Ed KERESTLY
84 Chief Enrollment Officer .... Mr. Kevin CAMPBELL
26 Chief Marketing Officer .... Mr. Jason GROVES
23 Director of Medical Clinic .... Dr. Ellen B. LITTLE
39 Co-Interim Director Residence Life .... Mrs. Shannon KAZMAREK
39 Co-Interim Director Residence Life .... Mr. Curtis SMITH
38 Director Univ Counseling Center .... Mr. Steve ROWLANDS
31 Director Ministery & Service .... Mr. Bob A. STRADER
45 VP of Planning & Operations .... Mr. Kevin J. ROBERTS
18 Exec Dir Facilities/Campus Develop .... Mr. Corey RUFF
10 Interim Chief Financial Officer .... Mrs. Stacey MCGEE
13 Exec Dir of Information Technology .... Mrs. Kay REEVES
24 Exec Dir Adams Ctr Teaching/Lrng .... Dr. Lesa BREEDING
105 Director of Educational Technology .... Dr. James D. LANGFORD
29 Dir of Alumni Rels & Annual Project .... Mr. Craig FISHER
19 Chief of ACU Police .... Mr. Jimmy ELLISON
44 Director of Major Gifts .... Mr. Don GARRETT
41 Director of Athletics .... Mr. Jared MOSLEY
15 Director of Human Resources .... Mrs. Wendy JONES
88 Director of Faculty Enrichment .... Dr. Jennifer SHEWMAKER
09 Asst Prov Dir Inst Research/Assess .... Dr. Tom A. MILHOLLAND
96 University Purchasing Manager .... Ms. Sandy HALL
40 Chief Business Services Officer .... Mr. Anthony T. WILLIAMS
101 Secretary to the Board of Trustees .... Mr. Slade SULLIVAN
04 Exec Assistant Office of President ... Mrs. Stephanie A. WOODLEE

*Alamo Community College District Central Office (I)

201 W Sheridan, San Antonio TX 78204-1429
County: Bexar FICE Identification: 003607
Unit ID: 222497
Telephone: (210) 485-0020 Carnegie Class: N/A
FAX Number: (210) 486-9166
URL: www.alamo.edu

01 Chancellor .... Dr. Bruce LESLIE
05 Vice Chanc for Academic Success .... Vacant
11 Vice Chanc for Finance & Admin .... Ms. Diane E. SNYDER
32 Vice Chancellor for Student Success .... Dr. Adelina SILVA
103 Vice Chanc Economic/Workforce Devel ... Dr. Federico ZARAGOZA
44 VC Plng/Performance/Inform/Systems .... Dr. Thomas CLEARY
15 Assoc Vice Chanc Human Resources . Ms. Linda BOYER-OWENS
27 Assoc Vice Chanc Communications .... Mr. Leo ZUNIGA
18 Assoc Vice Chanc Facilities .... Mr. John STRYBOS
20 Assoc VC Acad Partnershp/Initatives .... Vacant
10 Assoc VC Finance & Fiscal Services ...... Ms. Pamela ANSBOURY
04 Deputy to the Chancellor .... Dr. Adriana CONTRERAS
30 Exec Director Inst Advancement .... Mr. Jim ESKIN
21 Director of Internal Audit .... Ms. Patricia MAJOR
96 Director Acquisitions & Admin Svcs .... Mr. Gary O'BAR
41 Athletic Director .... Vacant
19 Chief Department of Public Safety .... Mr. Don ADAMS
21 Comptroller .... Ms. Angelia DEBARROS
12 President Northwest Vista College .... Dr. Jacqueline CLAUNCH
12 President San Antonio College .... Dr. Robert ZEIGLER
12 President St Philip's College .... Dr. Adena WILLIAMS LOSTON
12 President Palo Alto College .... Dr. Michael FLORES
12 President Northeast College .... Dr. Eric RENO

*Northwest Vista College (J)

3535 N Ellison Drive, San Antonio TX 78251-4217
County: Bexar FICE Identification: 033723
Unit ID: 420398
Telephone: (210) 486-4000 Carnegie Class: Assoc/Pub-U-MC
FAX Number: (210) 486-9105 Calendar System: Semester
URL: www.alamo.edu/nvc
Established: 1995 Annual Undergrad Tuition & Fees (In-District): $1,854
Enrollment: 15,992 Coed
Affiliation or Control: Local IRS Status: 501(c)3
Highest Offering: Associate Degree
Program: 2-Year Principally Bachelor's Creditable
Accreditation: SC

02 President .... Dr. Jacqueline CLAUNCH
03 Vice President for College Services .... Mrs. Julie PACE
05 Vice President for Academic Success .... Dr. Jimmie BRUCE
32 Vice President of Student Success .... Mrs. Deborah GAITAN
30 Director Institutional Advancement .... Mrs. Lynne DEAN
08 Learning Resources Chair .... Ms. Judy MCMILLAN
35 Dean of Student Success .... Mrs. Jennifer COMEDY-HOLMES
26 Dir of Public Relations & Marketing .... Mrs. Renata SERAFIN
27 Director Info/Communications Tech .... Mr. Felix SALINAS
37 Associate Director of Financial Aid .... Mrs. Rosalinda ENCINA
21 Assistant Bursar .... Ms. Jennifer ORTIZ
39 Assoc Director of Residency/Reports .... Ms. Cynthia ZAMUDIO
15 Sr Human Resources Generalist .... Mr. Manuel CERDA
45 Director of Resources & College Dev .... Mr. Carlos AGUIRRE
18 Superintendent NVC .... Mr. Bernie ZERTUCHE

103 Dean of Workforce Development ... Mr. Patrick FONTENOT
88 Dean of Interdisciplinary Programs ... Dr. Mary DIXSON
09 Director of Institutional Research ... Dr. Eliza HERNANDEZ
88 Coordinator Scholarship ... Mrs. Lucy GAUNA
84 Director of Enrollment Management ... Mrs. Robin CARRILLO

*Palo Alto College (A)

1400 W Villaret, San Antonio TX 78224-2499
County: Bexar FICE Identification: 023413
Unit ID: 246354
Telephone: (210) 486-3000 Carnegie Class: Assoc/Pub-U-MC
FAX Number: (210) 921-5005 Calendar System: Semester
URL: www.alamo.edu
Established: 1985 Annual Undergrad Tuition & Fees (In-District): $2,008
Enrollment: 8,568 Coed
Affiliation or Control: Local IRS Status: 501(c)3
Highest Offering: Associate Degree
Program: Occupational; 2-Year Principally Bachelor's Creditable
Accreditation: SC

02 President ... Dr. Michael FLORES
05 Vice President Academic Affairs ... Ms. Elizabeth TANNER
10 Vice Pres College Services ... Dr. Beatriz JOSEPH
32 Int Vice President Student Success ... Dr. Robert GARZA
49 Int Dean Arts & Sciences ... Dr. Mary Ellen JACOBS
49 Dean Science/Advanced/Applied Tech ... Mr. Gary SHELMAN
08 Dean of Learning Resources ... Ms. Tina MESA
26 Director of Public Relations ... Ms. Ginger HALL CARNES
21 Bursar ... Mr. Daniel ROCHA
84 Director of Enrollment Management ... Ms. Elizabeth VILLARUAL
37 Director Student Financial Services ... Mr. Lamar DUARTE
41 Athletic Director ... Mr. Adrian MONTOYA
35 Int Dean of Student Success ... Ms. Rosie CASTRO
18 Chief Facilities/Physical Plant ... Mr. Sergio RIVERA
38 Director Student Counseling ... Ms. Yolanda REYNA
29 Director Alumni Relations ... Ms. Danielle ESPINOZA
09 Dir Inst Rsrch/Plng/Effectiveness ... Ms. Lanette GARZA
30 Chief Development ... Ms. Christina ALDRETE

*St. Philip's College (B)

1801 Martin Luther King, San Antonio TX 78203-2098
County: Bexar FICE Identification: 003608
Unit ID: 227854
Telephone: (210) 486-2000 Carnegie Class: Assoc/Pub-U-MC
FAX Number: N/A Calendar System: Semester
URL: www.alamo.edu/spc/
Established: 1898 Annual Undergrad Tuition & Fees (In-District): $1,952
Enrollment: 10,710 Coed
Affiliation or Control: Local IRS Status: 501(c)3
Highest Offering: Associate Degree
Program: Occupational; 2-Year Principally Bachelor's Creditable
Accreditation: SC, ACFEI, CAHIIM, COARC, HT, MLTAD, OTA, PTAA, RAD, SURGT

02 President ... Dr. Adena WILLIAMS LOSTON
05 Vice Pres for Academic Affairs ... Ms. Ruth DALRYMPLE
32 Vice Pres of Student Success ... Dr. Sherrie LANG
11 Vice President for College Svcs ... Ms. Lacy HAMPTON
12 Vice Pres Admin Southwest Campus ... Dr. Karlene FENTON
35 Dean Student Success ... Mr. Paul MACHEN
08 Dean Interdisciplinary Programs ... Dr. Karen SIDES
75 Dean Applied Science & Tech ... Ms. Maureen CARTLEDGE
49 Dean Arts & Science ... Ms. Mary COTTIER
76 Dean of Health Sciences ... Ms. Rose SPRUILL
51 Director Continuing Ed/Extend Svcs ... Mr. Erick AKINS
37 Asst Director of Financial Aid ... Ms. Grace ZAPATA
45 Director Planning & Research ... Ms. Mecca SALAHUDDIN
10 Bursar ... Ms. Sophia GONZALEZ
26 Dir Community & Public Relations ... Ms. Tracy ROSS-GARCIA
30 Director Institutional Advancement ... Dr. Sharon CROCKETT-BELL
72 Director Instructional Technology ... Mr. John ORONA
18 Chief Facilities/Physical Plant ... Ms. Sherry TOLIVER
29 Director Alumni Relations ... Dr. Sharon CROCKETT-BELL
84 Director Enrollment Management ... Ms. Beatrice BUTLER
09 Director of Institutional Research ... Ms. Mecca SALAHUDDIN
96 Chief Budget Manager ... Mr. Paul BORREGO

*San Antonio College (C)

1300 San Pedro Avenue, San Antonio TX 78212-4299
County: Bexar FICE Identification: 009163
Unit ID: 227924
Telephone: (210) 486-0000 Carnegie Class: Assoc/Pub-U-MC
FAX Number: N/A Calendar System: Semester
URL: www.alamo.edu/sac
Established: 1925 Annual Undergrad Tuition & Fees (In-District): $2,568
Enrollment: 23,135 Coed
Affiliation or Control: Local IRS Status: 501(c)3
Highest Offering: Associate Degree
Program: Occupational; 2-Year Principally Bachelor's Creditable
Accreditation: SC, ADNUR, DA, DT, EMT, FUSER, MAC

02 President ... Dr. Robert E. ZEIGLER
05 Vice Pres Student/Academic Success ... Dr. Robert H. VELA
11 Vice President of College Services ... Mr. David E. MRIZEK
32 Dean of Student Affairs ... Ms. Emma MENDIOLA
72 Dean Professional & Tech Educ ... Ms. Vernell E. WALKER
49 Dean of Arts & Sciences ... Dr. Conrad KRUEGER
51 Dean Cont Educ/Training Network ... Mr. Tim ROCKEY
08 Dean of Learning Resources ... Dr. Alice JOHNSON
88 Dean of Performance Excellence ... Dr. David WOOD
84 Director of Enrollment Services ... Mr. J. Martin ORTEGA
35 Director of Student Activities ... Mr. Richard FARIAS
85 Coordinator International Students ... Vacant
26 Director Public Relations ... Ms. Vanessa TORRES
45 Director Resource & College Devel ... Ms. Susan B. ESPINOZA
18 Chief Facilities/Physical Plant ... Mr. David ORTEGA
23 Director Health Services ... Ms. Paula DAGGETT
37 Coordinator of Financial Aid ... Mr. Tom CAMPOS
29 Coordinator of Alumni and Friends ... Vacant

Alvin Community College (D)

3110 Mustang Road, Alvin TX 77511-4898
County: Brazoria FICE Identification: 003539
Unit ID: 222567
Telephone: (281) 756-3500 Carnegie Class: Assoc/Pub-R-L
FAX Number: (281) 756-3854 Calendar System: Semester
URL: www.alvincollege.edu
Established: 1948 Annual Undergrad Tuition & Fees (In-District): $1,510
Enrollment: 5,190 Coed
Affiliation or Control: Local IRS Status: 501(c)3
Highest Offering: Associate Degree
Program: Occupational; 2-Year Principally Bachelor's Creditable
Accreditation: SC, ADNUR, COARC, DMS, NDT, POLYT

01 President ... Dr. A. Rodney ALLBRIGHT
05 Dean Instruction/Provost ... Dr. John BETHSCHEIDER
10 Dean Financial/Admin Services ... Mr. Karl STAGER
20 Dean of Academic Programs ... Dr. Drew NELSON
32 Dean of Students ... Ms. JoAn ANDERSON
51 Dean Cont Educ/Pearland Center ... Dr. Patricia HERTENBERGER
06 Registrar ... Ms. Irene M. ROBINSON
08 Director Library Services ... Mr. Tom BATES
21 Director Fiscal Affairs/Controller ... Ms. Deborah KRAFT
13 Director Information Technology ... Mr. Jeff CERNOCH
37 Dir Student Financial Aid Placement ... Ms. Dora SIMS
45 Dir Institutional Effectiveness ... Mr. Patrick SANGER
15 Director Human Resources ... Ms. Lang WINDSOR
18 Director Physical Plant ... Mr. Mark PUTNAM
29 Director Alumni Relations ... Ms. Wendy DEL BELLO
07 Dir Admissions/Acad Advising Svcs ... Ms. Stephanie STOCKSTILL
09 Director of Inst Effective/Research ... Mr. Patrick SANGER
30 Chief Development ... Ms. Wendy DEL BELLO
26 Chief Public Relations Officer ... Ms. Wendy DEL BELLO
88 Assistant Director Fiscal Affairs ... Ms. Laurel JOSEPH
35 Coordinator Student Activities ... Ms. Amanda SMITHSON

Amarillo College (E)

PO Box 447, Amarillo TX 79178-0001
County: Potter FICE Identification: 003540
Unit ID: 222576
Telephone: (806) 371-5000 Carnegie Class: Assoc/Pub-R-L
FAX Number: (806) 371-5370 Calendar System: Semester
URL: www.actx.edu
Established: 1929 Annual Undergrad Tuition & Fees (In-District): $2,248
Enrollment: 11,426 Coed
Affiliation or Control: State/Local IRS Status: 501(c)3
Highest Offering: Associate Degree
Program: Occupational; 2-Year Principally Bachelor's Creditable
Accreditation: SC, ADNUR, COARC, DH, EMT, FUSER, MLTAD, MUS, NMT, OTA, PTAA, RAD, RTT, SURGT

01 President ... Dr. Paul MATNEY
05 VP of Academic Affairs ... Dr. Russell LOWERY-HART
10 VP of Business Affairs ... Mr. Terry BERG
51 Dean of Continuing Education ... Mrs. Kim D. DAVIS
32 VP of Student Affairs ... Mr. Robert C. AUSTIN
13 Chief Information Officer ... Mr. Lee M. COLAW
46 Chief of Planning/Advancement ... Ms. Danita L. MCANALLY
102 Dir AC Foundation/Development ... Mrs. Kathleen B. DOWDY
76 Director Ctr Cont Health Care Educ ... Mrs. Kimberly A. CROWLEY
18 Director Physical Plant ... Mr. Bruce COTGREAVE
37 Director Financial Aid ... Mrs. Mary K. MOONEY
08 Director AC Library Network ... Mr. Mark HANNA
06 Registrar ... Mrs. Diane BRICE
27 Chief of Communication/Mktg ... Mrs. Ellen R. GREEN
15 Director of Admin Svcs/Human Res ... Mr. Lynn L. THORNTON
19 Chief of Police ... Mr. Steve L. CHANCE
26 Director Found Mktg/Special Events ... Mrs. Tracy D. DOUGHERTY
35 Assoc VP of Student Affairs ... Mrs. April L. SESSLER
38 Director Advising & Counseling ... Mr. Jason A. NORMAN
88 Director Amarillo Museum of Art ... Mrs. Kim B. MAHAN
88 Director Criminal Justice Program ... Ms. Toni GRAY
96 Director of Purchasing ... Mrs. Vickie SHELTON
88 Dean of Academic Transfer Pgms ... Mr. Jerry E. MOLLER
76 Dean of Health Sciences ... Mr. Mark E. ROWH
72 Dean of Technology Education ... Mrs. Lyndy D. WILKINSON
88 Dean of Academic Success ... Dr. Tamara T. CLUNIS

Amberton University (F)

1700 Eastgate Drive, Garland TX 75041
County: Dallas FICE Identification: 022594
Unit ID: 222628
Telephone: (972) 279-6511 Carnegie Class: Master's L
FAX Number: (972) 279-9773 Calendar System: Quarter
URL: www.amberton.edu
Established: 1971 Annual Undergrad Tuition & Fees: $5,767
Enrollment: 1,381 Coed
Affiliation or Control: Independent Non-Profit IRS Status: 501(c)3
Highest Offering: Master's
Program: Professional; Business Emphasis
Accreditation: SC

01 President ... Dr. Melinda REAGAN
05 Academic Dean ... Dr. Don HEBBARD
30 Dean Univ Advance/VP Strategic Svcs ... Dr. Jo Lynn LOYD
10 Chief Business Officer ... Mr. Brent BRADSHAW
06 Registrar ... Ms. Marge MASSEY
32 Director Student Services ... Mr. Bill GILBREATH
84 Director for Recruiting ... Mr. Glenn SORRELLS
08 Head Librarian ... Ms. Judy GIBSON
29 Dir Alumni Relations & Inst Rsch ... Dr. Jo Lynn LOYD
07 Director of Admissions ... Dr. Don HEBBARD

American College of Acupuncture and Oriental Medicine (G)

9100 Park West Drive, Houston TX 77063-4104
County: Harris FICE Identification: 031533
Unit ID: 429085
Telephone: (713) 780-9777 Carnegie Class: Spec/Health
FAX Number: (713) 781-5781 Calendar System: Trimester
URL: www.acaom.edu
Established: 1991 Annual Graduate Tuition & Fees: $14,850
Enrollment: 116 Coed
Affiliation or Control: Proprietary IRS Status: Proprietary
Highest Offering: Master's; No Undergraduates
Program: Professional
Accreditation: SC, ACUP

01 President ... Dr. John Paul LIANG
11 Vice President of Operations ... Ms. Angel GUINARA
05 Dean of Academic Affairs ... Dr. Wen HUANG
20 Dean of Clinical Training ... Dr. Baisong ZHONG

American InterContinental University-Houston Campus (H)

9999 Richmond Avenue, Houston TX 77042-4516
Telephone: (832) 201-3600 Identification: 666335
Accreditation: &NH, ACBSP

† Main campus is American InterContinental University in Schaumburg, IL.

Anamarc College (I)

8720 Gateway East Boulevard, El Paso TX 79936
County: El Paso FICE Identification: 037563
Unit ID: 444389
Telephone: (915) 351-8100 Carnegie Class: Assoc/PrivFP
FAX Number: (915) 351-8300 Calendar System: Other
URL: www.anamarc.edu
Established: Annual Undergrad Tuition & Fees: $24,048
Enrollment: 234 Coed
Affiliation or Control: Proprietary IRS Status: Proprietary
Highest Offering: Associate Degree
Program: Occupational
Accreditation: ACICS, OTA

01 President/Campus Director ... Mr. Pablo FUENTES
03 Chief Executive Officer ... Dr. Ana Maria PINA HOUDE
10 Vice President of Finance ... Mr. Jaime LOWENBERG
15 Vice President of Human Resources ... Ms. Elena LIGGINGS
46 VP of Educ Research & Technology ... Mr. Sergio ZAPATA
06 Registrar ... Ms. Elsa PINA
37 Financial Aid Director ... Mr. Rick AMBRIZ

Angelina College (J)

PO Box 1768, Lufkin TX 75902-1768
County: Angelina FICE Identification: 006661
Unit ID: 222822
Telephone: (936) 639-1301 Carnegie Class: Assoc/Pub-R-M
FAX Number: (936) 639-4299 Calendar System: Semester
URL: www.angelina.edu
Established: 1966 Annual Undergrad Tuition & Fees (In-District): $2,040
Enrollment: 5,444 Coed
Affiliation or Control: State/Local IRS Status: 501(c)3
Highest Offering: Associate Degree
Program: Occupational; 2-Year Principally Bachelor's Creditable
Accreditation: SC, COARC, DMS, RAD, SURGT

01 President ... Dr. Larry M. PHILLIPS
05 Vice President/Dean of Instruction ... Dr. Patricia M. MCKENZIE
10 Vice President Business Services ... Mr. Joe MADDEN
31 Vice Pres of Community Services ... Dr. Frederick W. KANKE
32 Dean of Student Services ... Vacant
13 Dir Management Information Systems ... Mr. Kenneth STREET
37 Director Student Financial Aid ... Mrs. Sue JONES
18 Chief Facilities/Physical Plant ... Mr. Steve CAPPS
84 Director Enrollment Services ... Mr. Jeremy THOMAS
09 Coord Instnl Effectiveness & Q.E.P. ... Dr. Monica PETERS
26 Coordinator Marketing/Development ... Mr. Gary STALLARD
15 Coord of Human Resources ... Mrs. Tifini WHIDDON
06 Registrar & Records Coordinator ... Mrs. Sandra COX

Angelo State University (K)

2601 West Avenue N, San Angelo TX 76909-0001
County: Tom Green FICE Identification: 003541
Unit ID: 222831

Telephone: (325) 942-2555 Carnegie Class: Master's M
FAX Number: (325) 942-2038 Calendar System: Semester
URL: www.angelo.edu
Established: 1928 Annual Undergrad Tuition & Fees (In-State): $6,559
Enrollment: 6,888 Coed
Affiliation or Control: State IRS Status: 501(c)3
Highest Offering: Doctorate
Program: Liberal Arts And General; Teacher Preparatory; Professional; Business Emphasis
Accreditation: SC, ACBSP, ADNUR, MUS, NUR, PTA, @SW, TED

01 President Dr. Brian J. MAY
05 Provost/Vice Pres Academic Affairs Dr. Nancy ALLEN
30 Executive Dir of Dev & Alumni Rels Ms. Jamie AKIN
10 VP for Finance and Administration Ms. Angelina WRIGHT
32 VP for Student Affs & Enroll Mgmt Dr. Javier FLORES
20 Vice Provost Vacant
58 Dean College of Graduate Studies Dr. June SMITH
49 Dean of College of Arts & Sciences Dr. Paul SWETS
50 Dean College Business Dr. Corbett F. GAULDEN, JR.
53 Dean College of Education Dr. John MIAZGA
66 Dean College Health & Human Service Dr. Leslie MAYRAND
06 Director of Registrar Services Ms. Cindy WEEAKS
09 Director of Accountability Ms. Crystal BRADEN
08 Exec Director of Library Dr. Maurice G. FORTIN
36 Director Career Development Ms. Julie J. RUTHENBECK
15 Director of Human Resources Mr. Kurtis R. NEAL
14 Director Process/Integ Tech Archite Mr. Jeff SEFCIK
37 Director of Student Financial Aid Vacant
27 Director of Communications & Mktg Mr. Preston LEWIS
29 Director of Alumni Assoc Ms. Kimberly ADAMS
35 Exec Dir of Student Affairs Dr. Bradley PETTY
18 Director of Facilities Management Mr. Jay HALBERT
39 Dir of Housing & Residential Pgm Mr. Peter RIVERA
40 Manager Bookstore Ms. Margaret BOX
41 Athletic Director Mr. Sean JOHNSON
19 Chief of University Police Mr. James E. ADAMS
13 Assoc VP Information Technology/CIO Mr. Douglas FOX
21 Exec Director of Business Services Mr. Greg PECINA
96 Director Purchasing and Operations Ms. Margaret MATA
92 Director of Honors Program Dr. Shirley EOFF
04 Executive Asst to the President Ms. Adelina C. MORALES
104 Director Center International Stds Dr. Sharynn TOMLIN

† Affiliated with Texas Tech University in Lubbock, TX

Anthem College (A)

4250 N Belt Line Road, Irving TX 75038
Telephone: (972) 871-2824 Identification: 770669
Accreditation: ACICS

† Main campus is The Bryman School in Phoenix, AZ.

AOMA Graduate School of Integrative Medicine (B)

4701 West Gate Boulevard, Austin TX 78745
County: Travis FICE Identification: 031564
Unit ID: 429094
Telephone: (512) 454-1188 Carnegie Class: Spec/Health
FAX Number: (512) 454-7001 Calendar System: Quarter
URL: www.aoma.edu
Established: 1993 Annual Graduate Tuition & Fees: $12,036
Enrollment: 201 Coed
Affiliation or Control: Proprietary IRS Status: Proprietary
Highest Offering: Doctorate; No Undergraduates
Program: Professional
Accreditation: SC, ACUP

01 President Dr. William R. MORRIS
11 VP Student Svcs/Operations Ms. Anne PROVINCE
05 Vice President of Faculty Dr. Qianzhi WU
32 Dean of Students Mr. Robert LAGUNA
20 Program Director Ms. Lesley HAMILTON
08 Head Librarian Mr. David YORK
07 Dir Admissions & Student Services Ms. Hannah THORNTON
06 Registrar Ms. Kristen BORTHWICK
58 Dean of Academics Dr. Yuxin HE
88 Director of Herbal Studies Dr. Dongxin MA
88 Director of Biomedical Sciences Dr. Raja MANDYAM
45 Director of Research Dr. Yuxing LIU
88 Director Acupuncture Dr. Zheng ZENG
23 Clinic Business Director Ms. Laura COFFEY
18 Facilities Manager Mr. Stuart A. BAILEY
20 Academic Advisor Mr. Robert LAGUNA
31 Community Services Coordinator Ms. Sarah BENTLEY

Argosy University, Dallas (C)

5001 Lyndon B. Johnson Freeway, Farmers Branch TX 75244
Telephone: (214) 890-9900 Identification: 666181
Accreditation: &WC

† Main campus is Argosy University, Orange County in Orange, CA.

Arlington Baptist College (D)

3001 W Division, Arlington TX 76012-3497
County: Tarrant FICE Identification: 020814
Unit ID: 222877
Telephone: (817) 461-8741 Carnegie Class: Spec/Faith
FAX Number: (817) 274-1138 Calendar System: Semester
URL: www.arlingtonbaptistcollege.edu
Established: 1939 Annual Undergrad Tuition & Fees: $7,500
Enrollment: 265 Coed
Affiliation or Control: Baptist IRS Status: 501(c)3
Highest Offering: Master's
Program: Teacher Preparatory; Professional; Religious Emphasis
Accreditation: BI

01 President Dr. D. L MOODY
05 Academic Dean Dr. Ergun CANER
32 Dean of Students Mr. Josh MOODY
10 Business Manager/Dir Financial Aid Mr. Gerald SMITH
20 *Associate Dean of Academic Affairs Mr. Colt TURNER
06 Registrar/Director Admissions Ms. Janie TAYLOR
08 Head Librarian Ms. Jill BOTTICELLI
18 Director Physical Plant Mr. Stan SPENCE
21 Office Manager Mrs. Kim MARVIN
40 Director Bookstore Mrs. Vickie BRYANT
30 Director Institutional Advancement Rev. Michael EVANS
41 Athletic Director Mr. Cliff MCDANIEL

Art Institute of Dallas (E)

8080 Park Lane, Suite 100, Dallas TX 75231-5900
Telephone: (214) 692-8080 FICE Identification: 025396
Accreditation: &SC, ACFEI, CIDA

† Main campus is South University in Savannah, GA.

The Art Institute of Fort Worth (F)

7000 Calmont Ave, Ste 150, Fort Worth TX 76116
Telephone: (817) 210-0808 Identification: 770918
Accreditation: &SC

† Main campus is South University in Savannah, GA.

The Art Institute of Houston (G)

4140 Southwest Freeway, Houston TX 77027
County: Harris FICE Identification: 021171
Unit ID: 222938
Telephone: (713) 623-2040 Carnegie Class: Spec/Arts
FAX Number: (713) 966-2700 Calendar System: Quarter
URL: www.aih.aii.edu
Established: 1978 Annual Undergrad Tuition & Fees: $29,880
Enrollment: 1,862 Coed
Affiliation or Control: Proprietary IRS Status: Proprietary
Highest Offering: Baccalaureate
Program: Occupational
Accreditation: SC, ACFEI, CIDA

01 President Susanne BEHRENS
05 Dean of Academic Affairs Dr. Kenneth C. PASCAL
32 Dean of Student Affairs Tom WILBECK
11 Director of Finance Tom KUPER
07 Senior Director of Admissions Jane CHASTANT
15 Human Resources Generalist Elizabeth WHITTINGTON
36 Director of Career Services Mary Kate ROBINSON
37 Dir of Student Financial Services Shanika GEORGE

Austin College (H)

900 N Grand Avenue, Sherman TX 75090-4400
County: Grayson FICE Identification: 003543
Unit ID: 222983
Telephone: (903) 813-2000 Carnegie Class: Bac/A&S
FAX Number: (903) 813-3199 Calendar System: 4/1/4
URL: www.austincollege.edu
Established: 1849 Annual Undergrad Tuition & Fees: $33,830
Enrollment: 1,260 Coed
Affiliation or Control: Presbyterian Church (U.S.A.) IRS Status: 501(c)3
Highest Offering: Master's
Program: Liberal Arts And General; Teacher Preparatory
Accreditation: SC

01 President Dr. Marjorie HASS
05 VP Academic Affairs/Dean of Faculty Dr. Sheila A. PINERES
32 Vice Pres Student Affairs/Athletics Mr. Timothy P. MILLERICK
30 Vice Pres Institutional Advancement Mr. Brooks A. HULL
10 Vice President for Business Affairs Ms. Heidi B. ELLIS
84 Vice President for Inst Enrollment Ms. Nan M. DAVIS
45 Assoc VP Inst Effectiveness/Assess Dr. Jill SCHURR
21 Assoc VP Business Affairs Ms. Sheryl BRADSHAW
07 Asst VP Institutional Enrollment Mr. Matthew KROV
44 Sr Assoc VP for Inst Advancement Ms. Cary E. WACKER
29 AVP Inst Adv/Exec Dir Alumni Rels Ms. Paula JONSE
37 AVP/Exec Director Financial Aid Ms. Laurie COULTER
88 Exec Dir Transfer/Intrntl Admission Mr. David DILLMAN
42 Chaplain/Dir of Church Relations Dr. John D. WILLIAMS
35 Director of Student Life Mr. Michael DEEN
06 Registrar Mr. Texas RUEGG
08 College Librarian/Library Director Mr. John R. WEST
79 Dean of Humanities Dr. Patrick DUFFEY
81 Dean of Sciences Dr. Steve GOLDSMITH
83 Dean of Social Sciences Dr. David GRIFFITH
15 Director of Human Resources Mr. Keith L. LAREY
88 Dean of Student Services Dr. Rosemarie ROTHMEIER
36 Director Career Services Ms. Margie A. NORMAN
13 Exec Director Information Tech Mr. Bill EDGETTE
58 Director of Graduate Program Dr. Barbara N. SYLVESTER
104 Director Study Abroad Dr. Truett CATES
26 Director of Public Affairs Dr. Lynn Z. WOMBLE
25 Director of Stewardship Ms. Dara MCCOY
19 Chief of Police Mr. James PERRY
40 Manager of Campus Store Ms. Linda FRANZEO
27 Sr Dir Editorial Communications Ms. Vickie S. KIRBY
18 Exec Director of Facilities Mr. John L. JENNINGS
51 Coordinator of Continuing Education Ms. Carolyn CRANFORD
96 Purchasing Representative Ms. Jeannean SMITH

Austin Community College District (I)

5930 Middle Fiskville Road, Austin TX 78752-4390
County: Travis FICE Identification: 012015
Unit ID: 222992
Telephone: (512) 223-7000 Carnegie Class: Assoc/Pub-U-MC
FAX Number: (512) 223-7185 Calendar System: Semester
URL: www.austincc.edu
Established: 1972 Annual Undergrad Tuition & Fees (In-District): $2,490
Enrollment: 43,315 Coed
Affiliation or Control: State/Local IRS Status: 501(c)3
Highest Offering: Associate Degree
Program: Occupational; 2-Year Principally Bachelor's Creditable
Accreditation: SC, ACBSP, ACFEI, ADNUR, CAHIIM, DH, DMS, EMT, MLTAD, OTA, PHLEB, PNUR, PTAA, RAD, SURGT

01 President/CEO Dr. Richard M. RHODES
05 Interim Exec Vice Pres & Provost Dr. Enrique SOLIS
03 Exec Vice Pres College Operations Dr. Mary HENSLEY
10 Exec VP Finance & Administration Mr. Ben B. FERRELL
05 VP Instruction Mr. Michael T. MIDGLEY
32 VP Student Support/Success Systems Dr. Kathleen E. CHRISTENSEN
16 VP Human Resources Dr. Geraldine TUCKER
09 VP Effectiveness & Accountability Ms. Soon O. MERZ
20 AVP College Access Programs Dr. Stephanie HAWLEY
24 AVP Instructional Resources/Tech Dr. Richard L. SMITH
13 AVP Information Technology Mr. Stanley T. GUNN
21 VP Finance & Budget Mr. Neil W. VICKERS
88 AVP Student Success Dr. Richard R. ARMENTA
17 Executive Dean Health Sciences Dr. Eileen KLEIN
51 Executive Dean Continuing Education Dr. Hector AGUILAR
88 Dean Appl Tech/Multimedia/Pub Svc Dr. Gary W. HAMPTON
50 Dean Business Studies Mr. Charles C. QUINN
72 Dean Computer Studies/Adv Tech Ms. Linda S. SMARZIK
57 Dean Arts & Humanities Mr. Lyman W. GRANT
60 Dean Communications Dr. Hazel WARD
81 Dean Math & Science Dr. David FONKEN
83 Dean Social & Behavioral Sciences Ms. Gaye Lynn SCOTT
62 Dean Library Services Dr. Julie B. TODARO
35 Dean Student Services-South Austin Ms. Yolanda M. CHAPA
35 Dean Student Services-Riverside Dr. Virginia M. FRAIRE
35 Dean Student Services-Cypress Creek Ms. Amber L. KELLEY
35 Dean Student Services-Eastview Mr. Dorado M. KINNEY
35 Dean Student Services-Elgin Ms. Sylvia GALVAN-GONZALEZ
35 Dean Student Services-Northridge Mr. Robert W. BRADFUTE
35 Dean Student Services-Pinnacle Mr. George R. REYES
35 Dean Student Services-Round Rock Dr. Louella H. TATE
35 Dean Student Services-Rio Grande Dr. Voncille T. WRIGHT
88 Executive Director Adult Education Mr. David S. BORDEN
88 Exec Director School Relations Mr. Patrick W. ABBOTT
25 Exec Dir Grant Development Ms. Mary E. HARRIS
88 Exec Dir College & Career Prep Pgm Ms. Annette K. GREGORY
18 Exec Dir Facilities & Construction Mr. William S. MULLANE
27 Exec Dir Public Info & College Mktg Ms. Brette E. LEA
102 Executive Director ACC Foundation Ms. Stephanie C. DIINA-DEMPSEY
88 Executive Director Ms. Susan P. DAWSON
88 Exec Dir EHS & Insurance Ms. Rebecca S. COLE
12 Executive Director HILC Ms. Stacey GUNEY
07 Director Admissions/Records Ms. Linda A. KLUCK
80 Dir Ctr for Pub Policy & Pol Stds Mr. William R. YOUNG
37 Director Student Asst/Veterans Ms. Teresita BAZAN
88 Director P-16 Initiatives Mr. Gary L. MADSEN
04 Spec Asst to Pres External Affairs Ms. Linda K. YOUNG
04 Special Asst to VP Instruction Mr. Joe M. LOSTRACCO
19 Chief District Police Mr. Chester L. DIXON

Austin Graduate School of Theology (J)

7640 Guadalupe Street, Austin TX 78752
County: Travis FICE Identification: 023628
Unit ID: 247825
Telephone: (512) 476-2772 Carnegie Class: Spec/Faith
FAX Number: (512) 476-3919 Calendar System: Semester
URL: www.austingrad.edu
Established: 1976 Annual Undergrad Tuition & Fees: $8,410
Enrollment: 67 Coed
Affiliation or Control: Independent Non-Profit IRS Status: 501(c)3
Highest Offering: Master's
Program: Liberal Arts And General; Professional; Religious Emphasis
Accreditation: SC

01 President Dr. Stanley G. REID
37 Vice President/Dir Financial Aid Mr. Dave ARTHUR
07 Director Recruiting & Admissions Mrs. Lauren PORTER
30 Director of Development Mr. Neil HANEY

Austin Presbyterian Theological Seminary (A)

100 E 27th Street, Austin TX 78705-5797

County: Travis — FICE Identification: 003544 — Unit ID: 223001
Telephone: (512) 472-6736 — Carnegie Class: Spec/Faith
FAX Number: (512) 479-0738 — Calendar System: Semester
URL: www.austinseminary.edu
Established: 1902 — Annual Graduate Tuition & Fees: $7,500
Enrollment: 134 — Coed
Affiliation or Control: Presbyterian Church (U.S.A.) — IRS Status: 501(c)3
Highest Offering: Doctorate; No Undergraduates
Program: Professional
Accreditation: SC, THEOL

- 01 President ... Rev. Theodore J. WARDLAW
- 05 Academic Dean ... Dr. Allan COLE, JR.
- 10 Vice President for Business Affairs ... Mr. Kurt A. GABBARD
- 26 Vice Pres Institutional Advancement ... Ms. Donna SCOTT
- 32 Vice Pres Student Affairs/Vocation ... Rev. Jackie SAXON
- 07 Vice President for Admissions ... Rev. John H. BARDEN
- 51 VP Education Beyond the Walls ... Ms. Melissa WIGINTON
- 29 Director Alumni & Church Relations ... Rev. Lemuel GARCIA-ANOYO
- 30 Sr Dir of Development/Instl Advance ... Ms. Lisa HOLLERAN
- 08 Director of the Stitt Library ... Dr. Timothy LINCOLN
- 06 Registrar ... Ms. Jacqueline D. HEFLEY
- 37 Director of Financial Aid ... Ms. Glenna BALCH

Baptist Health System School of Health Professions (B)

8400 Datapoint Drive, San Antonio TX 78229

County: Bexar — FICE Identification: 006606 — Unit ID: 223083
Telephone: (210) 297-9636 — Carnegie Class: Assoc/PrivFP
FAX Number: (210) 297-0075 — Calendar System: Semester
URL: www.bshp.edu
Established: 1903 — Annual Undergrad Tuition & Fees: N/A
Enrollment: 525 — Coed
Affiliation or Control: Proprietary — IRS Status: Proprietary
Highest Offering: Baccalaureate
Program: Nursing Emphasis
Accreditation: ABHES, ADNUR, RAD, SURGT, SURTEC

- 01 Interim Dean ... Dr. Marion JEWEL

† Tuition varies by degree program.

Baptist Hospitals of Southeast Texas School of Radiologic Technology (C)

3030 Fannin Ste A, Beaumont TX 77704

County: Jefferson — Identification: 667153
Telephone: (409) 212-5724 — Carnegie Class: Not Classified
FAX Number: N/A — Calendar System: Semester
URL: www.bhset.net
Established: — Annual Undergrad Tuition & Fees: $6,000
Enrollment: N/A — Coed
Affiliation or Control: Independent Non-Profit — IRS Status: 501(c)3
Highest Offering: Associate Degree
Program: Occupational
Accreditation: RAD

- 01 Program Director ... Deborah SMITH

Baptist Missionary Association Theological Seminary (D)

P.O. Box 670, 1530 East Pine Street, Jacksonville TX 75766-5407

County: Cherokee — FICE Identification: 023312 — Unit ID: 223117
Telephone: (903) 586-2501 — Carnegie Class: Spec/Faith
FAX Number: (903) 586-0378 — Calendar System: Semester
URL: www.bmats.edu
Established: 1957 — Annual Undergrad Tuition & Fees: $4,200
Enrollment: 120 — Coed
Affiliation or Control: Baptist — IRS Status: 501(c)3
Highest Offering: Master's
Program: Professional
Accreditation: SC, THEOL

- 01 President ... Dr. Charley HOLMES
- 06 Registrar ... Dr. Philip ATTEBERY

Baptist University of the Americas (E)

8019 S Pan Am Expressway, San Antonio TX 78224-1336

County: Bexar — FICE Identification: 037333 — Unit ID: 444398
Telephone: (210) 924-4338 — Carnegie Class: Spec/Faith
FAX Number: (210) 924-2701 — Calendar System: Semester
URL: www.bua.edu
Established: 1947 — Annual Undergrad Tuition & Fees: $7,080
Enrollment: 241 — Coed
Affiliation or Control: Baptist — IRS Status: 501(c)3
Highest Offering: Baccalaureate
Program: 2-Year Principally Bachelor's Creditable; Liberal Arts And General; Professional; Religious Emphasis
Accreditation: BI

- 01 President ... Mr. Rene MACIEL
- 10 Chief Financial Officer ... Mr. Barry TYLER
- 30 Vice President for Development ... Rev. Teo CISNEROS
- 05 Provost & Dean of Academic Affairs ... Dr. F. Marconi MONTEIRO
- 32 VP for Student Affairs & Enrollment ... Ms. Mary RANJEL
- 37 Financial Aid Administrator ... Mrs. Araceli ACOSTA
- 88 VP for External Affairs-Dean BBI ... Dr. Moises RODRIGUEZ

Baylor College of Medicine (F)

One Baylor Plaza, Houston TX 77030-3411

County: Harris — FICE Identification: 004949 — Unit ID: 223223
Telephone: (713) 798-4951 — Carnegie Class: Spec/Med
FAX Number: (713) 798-3692 — Calendar System: Quarter
URL: www.bcm.edu/
Established: 1900 — Annual Graduate Tuition & Fees: $25,739
Enrollment: 1,525 — Coed
Affiliation or Control: Independent Non-Profit — IRS Status: 501(c)3
Highest Offering: Doctorate; No Undergraduates
Program: Professional
Accreditation: SC, ANEST, ARCPA, DIETI, IPSY, MED

- 00 Chancellor ... Dr. Bobby R. ALFORD
- 01 President and CEO ... Dr. Paul KLOTMAN
- 88 Dean Natl Sch Tropical Medicine ... Dr. Peter J. HOTEZ
- 17 Vice Pres/Chief Medical Officer ... Dr. Steve SIGWORTH
- 10 Sr Vice Pres/Chief Financial Ofcr ... Mrs. Kimberly C. DAVID
- 30 Vice Pres Development ... Ms. Kristi SHERWOOD COOPER
- 43 Sr Vice Pres/General Counsel ... Mr. Robert F. CORRIGAN, JR.
- 27 VP Communications & Marketing ... Ms. Claire M. BASSETT
- 15 Vice President Human Resources ... Mr. Dane FRIEND
- 46 Sr Vice President for Research ... Dr. Adam KUSPA
- 13 VP/Chief Technology Officer ... Dr. Alexander IZAGUIRRE
- 86 Vice Pres Government Relations ... Mr. Tom KLEINWORTH
- 63 Dean of Medical School ... Dr. Stephen B. GREENBERG
- 58 Dean Grad School of Biomed Sciences ... Dr. Deborah JOHNSON
- 76 Dean School Allied Health Programs ... Dr. J. David HOLCOMB
- 88 Senior Associate Dean ... Dr. James L. PHILLIPS
- 07 Senior Associate Dean Admissions ... Dr. Lloyd H. MICHAEL
- 51 Sr Assoc Dean Continuing Education ... Dr. C. Michael FORDIS, JR.
- 32 Sr Associate Dean Student Affairs ... Dr. Donald T. DONOVAN
- 88 Associate Dean Graduate School ... Dr. Scott F. BASINGER
- 63 Sr Assoc Dean Grad Medical Educ ... Dr. Linda ANDREWS
- 88 Associate Dean Res Assurances ... Dr. Stacey L. BERG
- 88 Associate Dean Medical Education ... Dr. Elizabeth A. NELSON
- 88 Asst Dean Graduate Education ... Dr. Gayle R. SLAUGHTER
- 88 Asst Dean Graduate Medical Educ ... Dr. Jacqueline LEVESQUE
- 88 Associate Dean for Admissions ... Dr. Graciela B. VILLARREAL
- 35 Assoc Dean Student Affairs & Admin ... Dr. Florence F. EDDINS-FOLENSBEE
- 09 Associate Dean for Research ... Dr. Placido GRINO
- 88 Associate Dean Clinical Affairs ... Dr. John W. BURRUSS
- 88 Assoc Dean Undergrad Med Education ... Dr. Jerry C. GOODMAN
- 21 Controller ... Mr. Douglas R. SPADE
- 88 Chief Performance Improvement Ofcr ... Mr. Navneet KATHURIA
- 37 Director Student Financial Planning ... Ms. Hilda DELEON
- 06 Registrar/Dir of Student Affairs ... Mr. John RAPP
- 88 Director Environmental Safety ... Mr. Paul MURACA
- 23 Director Occupational Medicine ... Dr. James E. KELAHER
- 29 Sr Director Alumni Affairs ... Ms. Barbara WALKER
- 19 Director of Security ... Vacant
- 85 Director Center for Globalization ... Dr. Bobby KAPUR
- 22 Sr Director Employee Relations ... Mr. Dane K. FRIEND
- 96 Director Supply Chain Management ... Mr. Bud BOCCHINO
- 28 Co-Chair Diversity Council ... Dr. Gayle R. SLAUGHTER

Baylor University (G)

One Bear Place #97096, Waco TX 76798-7096

County: McLennan — FICE Identification: 003545 — Unit ID: 223232
Telephone: (254) 710-1011 — Carnegie Class: RU/H
FAX Number: (254) 710-3557 — Calendar System: Semester
URL: www.baylor.edu
Established: 1845 — Annual Undergrad Tuition & Fees: $35,972
Enrollment: 15,364 — Coed
Affiliation or Control: Baptist — IRS Status: 501(c)3
Highest Offering: Doctorate
Program: Liberal Arts And General; Teacher Preparatory; Professional
Accreditation: SC, AAFCS, BUS, BUSA, CIDA, CLPSY, CS, DIETD, ENG, HSA, JOUR, LAW, MIDWF, MUS, NURSE, PTA, SP, SW, TED, THEA, THEOL

- 01 President & CEO ... Judge Kenneth W. STARR
- 05 Executive Vice President & Provost ... Dr. Elizabeth DAVIS
- 100 Chief of Staff/VP Executive Affairs ... Dr. Karla LEEPER
- 10 Senior VP for Operations & CFO ... Dr. Reagan RAMSOWER
- 30 Sr VP for Univ Dev/Strategic Initia ... Dr. Ken HALL
- 32 Vice President Student Life ... Dr. Kevin JACKSON
- 29 Exec Vice President of Alumni Assoc ... Mr. Jeffrey L. KILGORE
- 26 Vice President Marketing & Comm ... Mr. John BARRY
- 13 VP for IT & Dean of Libraries ... Ms. Pattie ORR
- 31 Vice Pres Constituent Engagement ... Ms. Tommye Lou DAVIS
- 43 General Counsel ... Mr. Charles D. BECKENHAUER
- 41 Director of Athletics ... Mr. Ian J. MCCAW
- 88 Dir Internal Audit & Mgmt Anlys ... Dr. Juan ALEJANDRO
- 09 Director Inst Research/Testing ... Dr. Kathleen MORLEY
- 84 Assoc Vice Pres Enrollment Mgmt ... Mrs. Diana M. RAMEY
- 21 Assoc VP Financial Svcs & Treasurer ... Mr. Bob C. SPENCE
- 21 Assoc VP Oper Plng & Budget Dir ... Mr. Wilson E. MCGREGOR
- 18 Assoc VP Fac Plng & Construction ... Mr. Brian W. NICHOLSON
- 15 Associate Vice Pres Human Resources ... Mr. John WHELAN
- 91 Assoc VP Info Sys/Svcs & Dpty CIO ... Mrs. Becky L. KING
- 08 Assoc Dean of the Libraries ... Mr. Jeffrey STEELY
- 35 Associate Vice Pres Student Life ... Dr. Martha Lou SCOTT
- 06 Registrar ... Mr. Jonathan C. HELM
- 88 Assoc VP Strategic Initiatives ... Mr. Chris KRAUSE
- 90 Assoc Vice Pres Electronic Library ... Mr. Timothy M. LOGAN
- 108 Vice Provost Inst Effectiveness ... Dr. Michael MATIER
- 97 Vice Provost Undergrad Education ... Dr. Wesley NULL
- 20 Vice Provost of Academic Affairs ... Dr. James BENNIGHOFF
- 46 Vice Provost for Research ... Dr. Truell HYDE
- 07 Asst Vice Pres Admissions Svcs ... Ms. Jennifer CARRON
- 88 Asst Vice President & Controller ... Ms. Susan ANZ
- 37 Asst VP Student Financial Svcs ... Mrs. Jackie DIAZ
- 88 Chief Investment Officer ... Mr. R. Brian WEBB
- 19 Chief of Police ... Mr. James W. DOAK
- 93 Director Multiculture Affairs ... Mrs. Pearlie BEVERLY
- 20 Director Academic Support Programs ... Ms. Sally E. FIRMIN
- 23 Medical Director Health Center ... Dr. Sharon STERN
- 36 Exec Dr Career & Professional Dev ... Dr. Marjorie N. ELLIS
- 25 Director Sponsored Programs ... Ms. Lisa H. MCKETHAN
- 38 Director Counseling Svcs ... Dr. James G. MARSH
- 40 Director Baylor Bookstore ... Mr. Billy NORS
- 86 Director Governmental Relations ... Ms. Rochonda FARMER-NEAL
- 96 Director Procurement Services ... Mr. Tom HOFFMEYER
- 31 Director Community Relations ... Ms. Jana HIXSON
- 49 Dean College of Arts/Sciences ... Dr. Lee C. NORDT
- 50 Dean School of Business ... Dr. Terry S. MANESS
- 53 Dean School of Education ... Dr. Jon ENGELHARDT
- 61 Dean School of Law ... Mr. Bradley J B. TOBEN
- 64 Dean School of Music ... Dr. William V. MAY
- 66 Dean School of Nursing ... Dr. Shelley F. CONROY
- 58 Dean Graduate School ... Dr. Larry LYON
- 73 Dean Truett Theological Sem ... Dr. David GARLAND
- 54 Dean Engineering & Computer Science ... Dr. Dennis O'NEAL
- 92 Dean Honors College ... Dr. Thomas S. HIBBS
- 85 Interim Dir Ctr International Educ ... Mr. Naymond KEATHLEY
- 35 Dean Student Development ... Dr. Elizabeth PALACIOS
- 39 Dean Student Learning & Engagement ... Dr. Jeff DOYLE
- 42 University Chaplain ... Dr. Burt BURLESON
- 88 Assoc Dean Student Conduct Admin ... Ms. Bethany J. MCCRAW

B.H. Carroll Theological Institute (H)

301 South Center Street, Suite 100, Arlington TX 76010-7140

County: Tarrant — Identification: 667089
Telephone: (817) 274-4284 — Carnegie Class: Not Classified
FAX Number: (817) 274-2226 — Calendar System: Semester
URL: www.bhcarroll.edu
Established: 2004 — Annual Graduate Tuition & Fees: $4,300
Enrollment: 302 — Coed
Affiliation or Control: Southern Baptist — IRS Status: 501(c)3
Highest Offering: Doctorate; No Undergraduates
Program: Religious Emphasis
Accreditation: BI

- 01 President ... Dr. Bruce CORLEY
- 10 CFO ... Dr. Bruce MUSKRAT
- 06 Registrar ... Dr. Stan MOORE
- 07 Director of Enrollment ... Mrs. Fran WILSON
- 08 Chief Librarian ... Mr. Don DAY

Blinn College (I)

902 College Avenue, Brenham TX 77833-4098

County: Washington — FICE Identification: 003549 — Unit ID: 223427
Telephone: (979) 830-4000 — Carnegie Class: Assoc/Pub-R-L
FAX Number: (979) 830-4030 — Calendar System: Semester
URL: www.blinn.edu
Established: 1883 — Annual Undergrad Tuition & Fees (In-District): $1,968
Enrollment: 17,945 — Coed
Affiliation or Control: State/Local — IRS Status: 501(c)3
Highest Offering: Associate Degree
Program: Occupational; 2-Year Principally Bachelor's Creditable
Accreditation: SC, ADNUR, DH, EMT, IFSAC, PTAA, RAD

- 01 District President ... Dr. Harold NOLTE
- 05 Int Vice President Academic Affairs ... Dr. John BEAVER
- 32 Vice Pres Student Services ... Dr. Dennis CROWSON
- 10 CFO/Sr VP Finance/Admin Svcs ... Ms. Kelli SHOMAKER
- 76 Vice Pres Allied Health ... Dr. Cynthia GRIFFITH
- 12 Int President Brazos Cty Campuses ... Ms. Sylvia MCMULLEN
- 30 Assoc VP Instl Advance/Govt Affairs ... Ms. Cathy BOEKER
- 20 Dean Academic Affairs ... Dr. John BEAVER
- 09 Dean Inst Effectiveness/Enroll Mgt ... Mr. Joe BAUMANN
- 06 Dean Admissions/Records/Regstrar ... Ms. Andrea LINER
- 35 Judicial Officer ... Mr. Keith THOMAS
- 35 Associate Dean Student Affairs ... Vacant
- 11 Exec Dir Operations Brazos County ... Mr. Ted HAJOVSKY
- 102 Executive Director Foundation ... Ms. Susan MYERS
- 18 Exec Dir Facilities/Planning/Constr ... Mr. Richard O'MALLEY
- 12 Director Schulenburg Campus ... Ms. Rebecca GARLICK
- 12 Interim Director Sealy Campus ... Ms. Joe Al PICONE
- 103 Dir Technical Education Center ... Mr. David YEAGER
- 88 Director Disability Services (Bre) ... Ms. Patricia MORAN
- 88 Dir Disability Services (Bryan) ... Ms. Brenda JONES-WILKINS

04 Admin Asst to District President ... Ms. Becky KREBS
21 Director Accounting ... Mr. Thomas BRAZZEL
08 Dean Library Services ... Ms. Linda FLYNN
38 Director of Counseling ... Mr. Robert LOVELIDGE
13 Dir Administrative Computing Svcs ... Ms. Christine WIED
37 Director Financial Aid ... Ms. Melanie MORGAN
15 Director Human Resources ... Ms. Marie KIRBY
41 Athletic Dir/Mens Head Bsktbl Coach ... Mr. Scott SCHUMACHER
19 Chief College Police Department ... Vacant
96 Director Purchasing/Transportation ... Mr. Ross SCHROEDER
07 Director Admissions & Records ... Ms. Kristi URBAN
27 Dir Prospective Student Relations ... Ms. Jennifer BYNUM
26 Dir Marketing/Media Relations ... Mr. Jeff TILLEY
35 Dir Student Leadership/Activities ... Mr. Mordecai BROWNLEE
27 Asst Dir Marketing/Media Relations ... Mr. Brandon WEBB
29 Coordinator of Campus Events ... Mr. Glen VIERUS

Brazosport College (A)

500 College Drive, Lake Jackson TX 77566-3199
County: Brazoria FICE Identification: 007287
Unit ID: 223506
Telephone: (979) 230-3000 Carnegie Class: Assoc/Pub4
FAX Number: (979) 230-3443 Calendar System: Semester
URL: www.brazosport.edu
Established: 1968 Annual Undergrad Tuition & Fees (In-District): $2,295
Enrollment: 4,033 Coed
Affiliation or Control: Local IRS Status: 501(c)3
Highest Offering: Baccalaureate
Program: Occupational; 2-Year Principally Bachelor's Creditable
Accreditation: SC, EMT

01 President ... Dr. Millicent M. VALEK
05 VP Academic & Sutdent Affairs ... Dr. Lynda VILLANUEVA
31 AVP Industry & Community Res ... Ms. Anne BARTLETT
30 AVP Institutional Advancement ... Ms. Serena ANDREWS
10 VP Administrative Services & CFO ... Mr. Fred SCOTT
16 VP Human Resources ... Dr. Herb E. MILES
32 Dean of Student Services ... Mr. David SHAW
09 Director Institutional Research ... Dr. David PRESTON
07 Director Admissions/Registrar ... Ms. Carrie STREETER
38 Director Student Counseling ... Mr. Arnold RAMIREZ
21 Internal Auditor ... Mr. Christopher BAHR
27 Director Marketing & Communications ... Mr. Kyle SMITH
13 Director Information Technology ... Mr. Ron PARKER
37 Director of Financial Aid ... Ms. Kay WRIGHT
08 Director Library Services ... Ms. Tami WISOFSKY
24 Director Learning Services ... Mr. Terry COMINGORE
19 Director College Services ... Mr. Gary DICKS
18 Director Facility Services ... Mr. Frank HICKL
88 Director Health Professions & ADN ... Dr. Susan MCCORMICK
88 Director Small Business Dev Center ... Dr. Janice GOINES
51 Director Community Education ... Ms. Catherine HANSON
88 Director Children's Center ... Ms. Julie LITTLEFIELD
25 Director Grant Administration ... Ms. Rebecca SHAWVER
88 Director Business Services ... Ms. Ginger WOOSTER

Brite Divinity School (B)

2925 Princeton Street, Fort Worth TX 76129-0001
County: Tarrant Identification: 666228
Unit ID: 450304
Telephone: (817) 257-7575 Carnegie Class: Spec/Faith
FAX Number: (817) 257-6932 Calendar System: Semester
URL: www.brite.tcu.edu
Established: 1873 Annual Graduate Tuition & Fees: $18,200
Enrollment: 212 Coed
Affiliation or Control: Independent Non-Profit IRS Status: 501(c)3
Highest Offering: Doctorate; No Undergraduates
Program: Professional; Religious Emphasis
Accreditation: SC, THEOL

01 President & Chief Executive Officer ... Dr. D. Newell WILLIAMS
10 Vice President Business/Finance ... Beverly COTTON
07 Director of Admission ... Dr. Valerie FROSTMAN

Brown Mackie College (C)

2200 North Hwy 121, Sulite 250, Bedford TX 76021
Telephone: (817) 799-0500 Identification: 770798
Accreditation: ACICS

† Main campus is The Art Institute of Phoenix in Phoenix, AZ.

Brown Mackie College (D)

4715 Fredericksburg Road, Suite 100,
San Antonio TX 78229
Telephone: (877) 460-1714 Identification: 770799
Accreditation: #ACICS, SURTEC

† Main campus is The Art Institute of Phoenix in Phoenix, AZ.

Career Point College (E)

4522 Fredericksburg Rd, Suite A-18,
San Antonio TX 78201
County: Bexar FICE Identification: 025911
Unit ID: 224439
Telephone: (210) 732-3000 Carnegie Class: Assoc/PrivFP
FAX Number: (210) 734-9225 Calendar System: Other
URL: www.careerpointcollege.edu
Established: 1921 Annual Undergrad Tuition & Fees: $17,300
Enrollment: 1,208 Coed
Affiliation or Control: Proprietary IRS Status: Proprietary
Highest Offering: Baccalaureate
Program: Occupational; 2-Year Principally Bachelor's Creditable
Accreditation: ACICS

01 Director ... Ms. Kim MURGUIA

Center for Advanced Legal Studies (F)

3910 Kirby Drive, Suite 200, Houston TX 77098-4151
County: Harris FICE Identification: 026047
Unit ID: 379782
Telephone: (713) 529-2778 Carnegie Class: Assoc/PrivFP4
FAX Number: (713) 523-2715 Calendar System: Other
URL: www.paralegal.edu
Established: 1987 Annual Undergrad Tuition & Fees: $11,150
Enrollment: 180 Coed
Affiliation or Control: Proprietary IRS Status: Proprietary
Highest Offering: Associate Degree
Program: Occupational; Technical Emphasis
Accreditation: COE

01 President/CEO ... Mr. Doyle HAPPE

Central Texas College (G)

PO Box 1800, Killeen TX 76540-9990
County: Bell FICE Identification: 004003
Unit ID: 223816
Telephone: (254) 526-7161 Carnegie Class: Assoc/Pub-Spec
FAX Number: (254) 526-0817 Calendar System: Semester
URL: www.ctcd.edu
Established: 1965 Annual Undergrad Tuition & Fees (In-District): $1,512
Enrollment: 30,054 Coed
Affiliation or Control: Local IRS Status: 501(c)3
Highest Offering: Associate Degree
Program: Occupational; 2-Year Principally Bachelor's Creditable
Accreditation: SC, ADNUR, EMT, MLTAD

01 Chancellor ... Dr. Thomas D. KLINCAR
03 Deputy Chanc Resource Management ... Mr. Al ERDMAN
03 Deputy Chanc International/Navy Op ... Mr. Jim YEONOPOLUS
03 Deputy Chanc DL/TX Campus Op ... Mr. John HUNT
05 Deputy Chanc Educ Pgm/Supp Svcs ... Dr. Dana WATSON
12 Dean Ft Hood/Service Area Campus ... Dr. Tina ADY
12 Dean Central Campus ... Ms. Janice ANDERSON
32 Dean Student Services ... Dr. Johnelle WELSH
08 Dean Library Services ... Ms. Deba SWAN
38 Associate Dean Guidance/Counseling ... Mr. David MCCLURE
06 Systems Registrar ... Ms. Lillian KROEGER
10 Comptroller ... Mr. Bob LIBERTY
15 Director Human Resource Mgmt ... Ms. Holly JORDAN
88 Director Risk Management ... Ms. Deborah SHIBLEY
106 Director Distance Education/Ed Tech ... Ms. Sharon DAVIS
18 Director Facilities Management ... Mr. Mark HARMSEN
21 Director Business Services ... Ms. Michele CARTER
30 Director College Development ... Ms. Judy HEARTFIELD
09 Director Institutional Effectivenes ... Ms. Amy BAWCOM
13 Director Information Technology ... Mr. Bruce KENDALL
07 Director Admissions/Recruitment ... Mr. Stephen O'DONOVAN
88 Director Testing ... Mr. George ERSKINE
85 Director International Student Svcs ... Ms. Marta GRANT
88 Director Student Support Services ... Ms. Denise PERGL
88 Director Substance Abuse Resource . Dr. Gerald MAHONE-LEIWS
36 Director Career Planning/Placement ... Ms. Elaine RILEY
27 Dir Community Relations/Marketing ... Ms. Barbara MERLO
88 Liaison Military Programs ... Ms. Diana CASTILLO
19 Chief Police/Security Services ... Ms. Mary WHEELER
40 Manager Bookstore ... Mr. Gary FUDA
37 Director Student Financial Aid ... Ms. Annabelle SMITH
96 Director of Purchasing ... Ms. Michele CARTER

Chamberlain College of Nursing-Houston (H)

11025 Equity Drive, Houston TX 77041
Telephone: (713) 277-9800 Identification: 770500
Accreditation: &NH, NURSE

† Main campus is Chamberlain College of Nursing - Addison in Addison, IL.

Cisco College (I)

101 College Heights, Cisco TX 76437-1900
County: Eastland FICE Identification: 003553
Unit ID: 223898
Telephone: (254) 442-5000 Carnegie Class: Assoc/Pub-R-M
FAX Number: (254) 442-5100 Calendar System: Semester
URL: www.cisco.edu
Established: 1940 Annual Undergrad Tuition & Fees (In-State): $2,640
Enrollment: 3,839 Coed
Affiliation or Control: State IRS Status: 501(c)3
Highest Offering: Associate Degree
Program: Occupational; 2-Year Principally Bachelor's Creditable
Accreditation: SC, COARC, MAC, SURGT

01 President ... Mr. Bobby SMITH
05 Vice Pres of Instruction ... Mr. Randy GOLSON
32 Vice President for Student Services ... Dr. Jerry DODSON
13 Executive Dir of IT ... Mr. Steve POWELL
09 Executive Dir of IR ... Mr. Joe CARTER
12 Provost Abilene Education Center ... Dr. Carol DUPREE
84 Dean of Enrollment Management ... Mr. Olin O. ODOM, III
38 Dean of Counseling ... Mr. Randy LEATH
30 Director of Development ... Ms. Martha MONTGOMERY
37 Director of Financial Aid ... Ms. Dianne PHARR
15 Director Human Resources ... Ms. Pamela PAGE
35 Director New Student Services ... Ms. Shae WHITE
08 Director of Libraries ... Ms. Heather WILLIAMSON

Clarendon College (J)

PO Box 968, Clarendon TX 79226-0968
County: Donley FICE Identification: 003554
Unit ID: 223922
Telephone: (806) 874-3571 Carnegie Class: Assoc/Pub-R-S
FAX Number: (806) 874-3201 Calendar System: Semester
URL: www.clarendoncollege.edu
Established: 1898 Annual Undergrad Tuition & Fees (In-District): $2,730
Enrollment: 1,253 Coed
Affiliation or Control: State/Local IRS Status: 501(c)3
Highest Offering: Associate Degree
Program: Occupational; 2-Year Principally Bachelor's Creditable
Accreditation: SC

01 President ... Dr. Phil E. SHIRLEY
05 Dean of Instruction ... Dr. Patricia WESTERGAARD
11 Vice Pres Off Campus Affairs ... Mr. Ray JARAMILLO
32 Dean of Student Services ... Mr. Tex BUCKHAULTS
08 Librarian ... Ms. Pamela REED
07 Dean of Admission Services ... Ms. Annette FERGUSON
37 Director of Financial Aid ... Vacant
06 Registrar ... Ms. Brandi HAVENS
81 Div Chr Science/Health/Liberal Arts ... Mrs. Scarlet ESTLACK

Coastal Bend College (K)

3800 Charco Road, Beeville TX 78102-2197
County: Bee FICE Identification: 003546
Unit ID: 223320
Telephone: (361) 358-2838 Carnegie Class: Assoc/Pub-R-M
FAX Number: (361) 358-3971 Calendar System: Semester
URL: www.coastalbend.edu
Established: 1965 Annual Undergrad Tuition & Fees (In-District): $2,696
Enrollment: 3,745 Coed
Affiliation or Control: State/Local IRS Status: 501(c)3
Highest Offering: Associate Degree
Program: Occupational; 2-Year Principally Bachelor's Creditable
Accreditation: SC, DH, RAD

01 President ... Dr. Beatriz T. ESPINOZA
32 Dean of Student Services ... Ms. Velma ELIZALDE
11 Dean of Administrative Services ... Ms. Ruth CUDE
07 Director of Admissions/Registrar ... Ms. Alicia ULLOA
30 Dir Institutional Advancement/PR ... Ms. Susan SMEDLEY
05 Director of Academic Programs ... Vacant
25 Director of Grants/Special Projects ... Mrs. Velma ELIZALDE
37 Director of Financial Aid ... Ms. Nora MORALES
12 Director of Alice Campus ... Dr. Patricia CANDIA
12 Director of Kingsville Campus ... Vacant
12 Coordinator Pleasanton Campus ... Ms. Teresa VILLANUEVA
09 Institutional Research Director ... Mr. Randy LINDEMAN
08 Director Library Services ... Ms. Sarah MILNARICH
15 Personnel Director ... Ms. Kathlyn PATTON
18 Chief Facilities/Physical Plant ... Mr. Michael SLAUGHTER
26 Chief Public Relations Officer ... Ms. Monica CRUZ

College of Biblical Studies-Houston (L)

7000 Regency Square Boulevard, Houston TX 77036-3298
County: Harris FICE Identification: 034224
Unit ID: 388520
Telephone: (713) 785-5995 Carnegie Class: Spec/Faith
FAX Number: (713) 785-5998 Calendar System: Trimester
URL: www.cbshouston.edu
Established: 1976 Annual Undergrad Tuition & Fees: $9,846
Enrollment: 498 Coed
Affiliation or Control: Independent Non-Profit IRS Status: 501(c)3
Highest Offering: Baccalaureate
Program: Religious Emphasis
Accreditation: @SC, BI

01 President ... Dr. Bill BLOCKER
04 Exec Administrative Assistant ... Mrs. Vicki PATTERSON
05 VP Academic Affairs/Acad Dean ... Mr. Joseph D. PARLE
10 VP Finance & Business Affairs ... Mr. Richard CAMPBELL
30 Vice President Advancement ... Dr. John R. BOAL
84 VP Enrollment and Marketing ... Mr. John E. KNIGHT
09 VP for Institutional Effectiveness ... Mr. Paul KEITH
08 Director of Library Services ... Mr. Artis LOVELADY, III
88 Assoc VP Institutionl Effectiveness ... Dr. Beverly R. LUCAS
13 Director Information Technology ... Mr. M. Shane BOOTHE
06 Registrar ... Ms. Laura Y. HAMILTON
88 Dir Christian Service Program ... Dr. Andre MORGAN
21 Controller ... Mrs. Betty-Ann W. MCNAIR
37 Director Student Financial Aid ... Ms. Roshanna HARDISON
40 Director Bookstore ... Mr. Terry BRYAN
26 Director of Marketing and PR ... Ms. Meliinda MERILAT

The College of Health Care Professions (A)

6505 Airport Blvd, Suite 102, Austin TX 78752
County: Travis FICE Identification: 034263
Unit ID: 437635
Telephone: (512) 892-2835 Carnegie Class: Not Classified
FAX Number: (512) 892-6643 Calendar System: Other
URL: www.chcp.edu
Established: Annual Undergrad Tuition & Fees: N/A
Enrollment: 196 Coed
Affiliation or Control: Proprietary IRS Status: Proprietary
Highest Offering: Associate Degree
Program: Occupational
Accreditation: ABHES

01 Director ...Ms. Sue MAGUS

The College of Health Care Professions (B)

240 Northwest Mall, Houston TX 77092
County: Harris FICE Identification: 031281
Unit ID: 392257
Telephone: (713) 425-3100 Carnegie Class: Assoc/PrivFP
FAX Number: (713) 425-3192 Calendar System: Other
URL: www.chcp.edu
Established: 1988 Annual Undergrad Tuition & Fees: $25,000
Enrollment: 425 Coed
Affiliation or Control: Proprietary IRS Status: Proprietary
Highest Offering: Associate Degree
Program: Occupational; 2-Year Principally Bachelor's Creditable
Accreditation: ABHES, SURGT, SURTEC

The College of Health Care Professions-Dallas (C)

8390 Lyndon B. Johnson Fwy, Ste 300, Dallas TX 75243
Telephone: (214) 420-3400 Identification: 770531
Accreditation: ABHES

† Main campus is The College of Health Care Professions in Austin, TX.

The College of Health Care Professions-Fort Worth (D)

4248 North Freeway, Fort Worth TX 76137
Telephone: (817) 632-5900 Identification: 770532
Accreditation: ABHES

† Main campus is The College of Health Care Professions in Houston, TX.

College of the Mainland (E)

1200 Amburn Road, Texas City TX 77591-2499
County: Galveston FICE Identification: 007096
Unit ID: 226408
Telephone: (409) 933-8271 Carnegie Class: Assoc/Pub-R-M
FAX Number: (409) 933-8010 Calendar System: Semester
URL: www.com.edu
Established: 1966 Annual Undergrad Tuition & Fees (In-District): $1,773
Enrollment: 4,010 Coed
Affiliation or Control: Local IRS Status: 501(c)3
Highest Offering: Associate Degree
Program: Occupational; 2-Year Principally Bachelor's Creditable
Accreditation: SC, ADNUR, CAHIIM, EMT, MAC

01 President ...Dr. Beth LEWIS
05 Vice President for Instruction ...Dr. Amy LOCKLEAR
10 VP College & Financial Services ...Ms. Lisa TEMPLER
32 Vice President for Student Servies ...Dr. Vicki STANFIELD
20 Dean Gen Education Programs ...Dr. Pam MILLSAP
35 Assoc VP Student Success & Conduct ...Ms. Kris KIMBARK
06 Assoc VP for Enrollment/Registrar ...Mrs. Kelly MUSICK
18 Assoc VP Facility Services ...Mr. Peter EARLY
08 Director Library Services ...Ms. Kathryn PARK
27 Chief Information Officer ...Mr. David DIVINE
37 Director of Student Financial Svcs ...Mr. Carl GORDON
28 Director of Diversity & Equity ...Ms. Lonica BUSH
96 Director of Purchasing ...Ms. Sonja BLINKA
09 Int Dir of Inst Research & Effec ...Ms. Anita GARCIA
21 Controller ...Ms. Laurie ALEXANDER

The College of Saints John Fisher & Thomas More (F)

801 W. Shaw St., Fort Worth TX 76110-4075
County: Tarrant FICE Identification: 031894
Unit ID: 420352
Telephone: (817) 923-8459 Carnegie Class: Bac/A&S
FAX Number: (817) 394-2340 Calendar System: Semester
URL: www.fishermorecollege.edu
Established: 1981 Annual Undergrad Tuition & Fees: $10,000
Enrollment: 21 Coed
Affiliation or Control: Roman Catholic IRS Status: 501(c)3
Highest Offering: Baccalaureate
Program: Liberal Arts And General
Accreditation: SC

01 President ...Mr. Michael KING
11 Director of Operations ...Mr. Matthew GRAHEK
84 Dir Enrollment Management ...Mr. Peter CAPANI
08 Head Librarian ...Ms. Marilyn ANKENBAUER
10 Bursar ...Mr. Joe MARSHALL
88 Office Manager ...Ms. Marilyn ANKENBAUER
32 Director Student Life ...Mr. Philip ONOCHIE
30 Dir Development ...Mr. Jason FABAZ
26 Director of Media Relations ...Ms. Rachel SHRADER

Collin County Community College District (G)

3452 Spur 399, McKinney TX 75069
County: Collin FICE Identification: 023614
Unit ID: 247834
Telephone: (972) 758-3800 Carnegie Class: Assoc/Pub-S-MC
FAX Number: (972) 758-3807 Calendar System: Semester
URL: www.collin.edu
Established: 1985 Annual Undergrad Tuition & Fees (In-District): $1,024
Enrollment: 27,424 Coed
Affiliation or Control: State/Local IRS Status: 501(c)3
Highest Offering: Associate Degree
Program: Occupational; 2-Year Principally Bachelor's Creditable
Accreditation: SC, ACFEI, ADNUR, CAHIIM, COARC, DH, EMT, POLYT, SURGT

01 District President ...Dr. Cary A. ISRAEL
05 Sr VP Acad Affairs/Student Dev ...Dr. Colleen SMITH
12 VP/Provost Spring Creek Campus ...Dr. Mary MCRAE
12 VP/Provost Preston Ridge Campus ...Dr. Brenda K. KIHL
12 VP/Provost Central Park Campus ...Dr. Sherry SCHUMANN
32 Vice President Student Development ...Dr. Barbara MONEY
10 Vice President Admin Svcs & CFO ...Mr. Ralph G. HALL
16 Vice Pres Org Effectiveness & HR ...Ms. Kim K. DAVISON
26 VP/PR & College Development ...Ms. Lisa R. VASQUEZ
09 Assoc VP Rsrch & Inst Effectiveness ...Dr. Thomas K. MARTIN
20 Assoc VP Teaching & Learning ...Ms. Dani DAY
106 Assoc VP Academic Outreach ...Mr. Joe BUTLER
20 Dean Acad Affs-STEM Preston Ridge ...Mr. Jon HARDESTY
20 Dean Acad Affs-Preston Ridge ...Vacant
20 Dean Acad Affs Central Park Campus ...Ms. Brenda C. CARTER
57 Dean Fine Arts ...Ms. Gaye M. COOKSEY
50 Dean Business/Computer Systems ...Mr. William J. BLITT
79 Dean Communications/Humanities ...Dr. Donald WEASENFORTH
83 Dean Social/Behavioral Sciences ...Mr. Gary B. HODGE
81 Dean Mathematics/Natural Science ...Dr. L. Cameron NEAL, JR.
76 Dean Health Sciences/Emergency Svcs ...Mr. Abe JOHNSON
88 Dean Developmental Education ...Vacant
51 Assoc VP Cont Educ/Workforce Dev ...Mr. Stephen R. HARDY
102 Executive Director of Foundation ...Ms. Amy M. EVANS
35 Dean Student Dev Spring Creek ...Mr. Terrence BRENNAN
35 Dean Student Dev Preston Ridge ...Ms. Stephanie MEINHARDT
35 Dean Student Dev Central Park ...Mr. Douglas WILLIS
06 Registrar/Director Admissions ...Mr. Todd E. FIELDS
84 Dean Enroll & Student Succss ...Dr. Alicia L. HUPPE
38 Assoc Dean Counseling/Career Svcs ...Dr. Linda R. QUALIA
37 Director Financial Aid/Vets Affairs ...Vacant
85 International Student Coordinator ...Ms. Rebecca C. CROWELL
13 Chief Information Systems Officer ...Mr. David R. HOYT
21 Assoc VP/Controller ...Ms. Julie BRADLEY
21 Assoc VP Financial Svcs & Reporting ...Ms. Barbara JINDRA
18 Dist Dir Safety/Sec/Fac/Construct ...Mr. Ed C. LEATHERS
96 Director Purchasing ...Ms. Cynthia L. WHITE
40 Director Auxiliary Services ...Mr. David S. HUSTED
15 AVP Human Resources/Org Dev ...Ms. Norma SMITH
08 Exec Dir Library Preston Ridge Cam ...Mr. John MULLIN
08 Exec Dir Library Central Park Cam ...Ms. Bobbie LONG
08 Exec Dir Library Spring Creek Cam ...Ms. Linda KYPRIOS

Commonwealth Institute of Funeral Service (H)

415 Barren Springs, Houston TX 77090-5913
County: Harris FICE Identification: 003556
Unit ID: 366261
Telephone: (281) 873-0262 Carnegie Class: Assoc/PrivNFP
FAX Number: (281) 873-5232 Calendar System: Quarter
URL: www.commonwealth.edu
Established: 1936 Annual Undergrad Tuition & Fees: $10,904
Enrollment: 237 Coed
Affiliation or Control: Independent Non-Profit IRS Status: 501(c)3
Highest Offering: Associate Degree
Program: Occupational
Accreditation: FUSER

01 President ...Mr. Jason C. ALTIERI
05 Chief Academic Officer ...Mr. Stuart MOEN
20 Associate Academic Officer ...Mr. Christopher LAYTON
37 Director Student Financial Aid ...Ms. Jessika JENKINS
06 Registrar ...Ms. Patricia MORENO
08 Head Librarian ...Ms. Therisa MASSEY

Concorde Career College (I)

12606 Greenville Avenue, Dallas TX 75243
Telephone: (469) 221-3411 Identification: 770593
Accreditation: ACCSC, #COARC, DH, SURGT

† Main campus is Concorde Career College in Aurora, CO.

Concorde Career College (J)

4803 NW Loop 410, Suite 200, San Antonio TX 78229
Telephone: (210) 428-2000 Identification: 770594
Accreditation: ACCSC, #COARC, DH, SURGT

† Main campus is Concorde Career College in Kansas City, MO.

Concorde Career Institute (K)

600 East Lamar Blvd Ste 200, Arlington TX 76011
County: Tarrant FICE Identification: 035423
Unit ID: 441742
Telephone: (817) 261-1594 Carnegie Class: Not Classified
FAX Number: (817) 261-3443 Calendar System: Semester
URL: www.concorde.edu
Established: Annual Undergrad Tuition & Fees: $23,625
Enrollment: 701 Coed
Affiliation or Control: Proprietary IRS Status: Proprietary
Highest Offering: Associate Degree
Program: Occupational
Accreditation: ACCSC, ABHES, SURTEC

01 Interim Campus President ...Ms. Kimberly RANFT

Concordia University Texas (L)

11400 Concordia University Drive, Austin TX 78726
County: Travis FICE Identification: 003557
Unit ID: 224004
Telephone: (512) 313-3000 Carnegie Class: Master's L
FAX Number: (512) 313-3339 Calendar System: Semester
URL: www.concordia.edu
Established: 1926 Annual Undergrad Tuition & Fees: $25,400
Enrollment: 2,568 Coed
Affiliation or Control: Lutheran Church - Missouri Synod
IRS Status: 501(c)3
Highest Offering: Master's
Program: Liberal Arts And General; Teacher Preparatory; Professional
Accreditation: SC, IACBE, NURSE

01 President & CEO ...Dr. Thomas CEDEL
05 Provost ...Dr. Alan RUNGE
10 Vice President Business Services ...Ms. Pamela LEE
11 Vice President University Services ...Mr. C. Gary BELCHER
03 Vice President External Relations ...Mr. Don ADAM
20 Asst Provost Quality Enhancement ...Dr. Trey BUCHANAN
84 Vice Prov Enrollmnt/Student Support ...Ms. Kristi KIRK
55 Vice Provost for Remote Operations ...Ms. Tammy STEWART
30 Associate VP External Relations ...Mr. Chris BECK
42 Campus Pastor ...Rev. Bruce PEFFER
50 Dean College of Business ...Dr. Donald CHRISTIAN
53 Dean College of Education ...Dr. Gayle GROTJAN
49 Dean College of Liberal Arts ...Dr. Carl TROVALL
81 Dean College of Science ...Dr. Janet WHITSON
12 Center Dean Austin ...Dr. DeEadra ALBERT-GREEN
106 Center Online Dean ...Ms. Alex FITTERER
12 Center Dean Ft Worth ...Dr. Rebecca BURTON
12 Center Dean Houston ...Ms. Renae LISTER
12 Center Dean San Antonio ...Dr. Mary DARDEN
06 Registrar ...Ms. Connie BERAN
41 Athletic Director ...Mr. Stan BONEWITZ
21 Director of Finance ...Ms. Sarah LOGHIN
32 Director of Student Services ...Mr. Richard POWERS
08 Director of Library Services ...Ms. Mikail MCINTOSH-DOTY
58 Director MED Graduate Program ...Dr. Chris WINKLER
58 Director MBA Graduate Program ...Dr. Elise BRAZIER
37 Director Student Financial Services ...Mr. Russell JEFFREY
07 Director of Admissions ...Ms. Kristin COULTER
13 Director of Information Systems ...Mr. DeWayne MANGAN
19 Chief of Police ...Mr. H.E JENKINS
15 Human Resources Manager ...Ms. Holly JUNG
40 Bookstore Manager ...Ms. Jessica BRIGHT
09 Director of Institutional Research ...Vacant
29 Director Alumni Relations ...Mr. John ADAMS
18 Director Facilities Management ...Mr. Eric BOOTH
38 Director Student Success Center ...Ms. Ruth COOPER
36 Director Career Center ...Ms. Joyce SINCLAIR
26 Associate VP Communications ...Ms. Melinda BRASHER
39 Director of Residential Life ...Ms. Sarah EBERLE
27 Chief Information Officer ...Ms. Linda Beth BRADY

Court Reporting Institute of Dallas (M)

1341 W Mockingbird Lane, Suite 200E,
Dallas TX 75247-4968
County: Dallas FICE Identification: 021192
Unit ID: 224183
Telephone: (214) 350-9722 Carnegie Class: Assoc/PrivFP
FAX Number: (214) 631-0143 Calendar System: Quarter
URL: www.cri.edu
Established: 1978 Annual Undergrad Tuition & Fees: $13,950
Enrollment: 472 Coed
Affiliation or Control: Proprietary IRS Status: Proprietary
Highest Offering: Associate Degree
Program: Occupational; 2-Year Principally Bachelor's Creditable; Technical Emphasis
Accreditation: ACICS

01 Campus Director ...Mr. Larry P. PAIZ

Criswell College (A)

4010 Gaston Avenue, Dallas TX 75246-1537
County: Dallas FICE Identification: 041218
Unit ID: 224208
Telephone: (214) 821-5433 Carnegie Class: Not Classified
FAX Number: (214) 370-0497 Calendar System: Semester
URL: www.criswell.edu
Established: 1970 Annual Undergrad Tuition & Fees: $14,400
Enrollment: 322 Coed
Affiliation or Control: Independent Non-Profit IRS Status: 501(c)3
Highest Offering: Master's
Program: Religious Emphasis
Accreditation: SC

01 President .... Jerry JOHNSON
05 Vice President Academic Affairs .... Barry CREAMER
10 Vice President Business & Finance .... Mike RODGERS
84 Assoc Vice Pres Enrollment Services .... Russell MARRIOTT
30 Director of Development .... Mike GOFF

Culinary Institute LeNotre (B)

7070 Allensby Street, Houston TX 77022-4322
County: Harris FICE Identification: 037233
Unit ID: 444565
Telephone: (713) 692-0077 Carnegie Class: Assoc/PrivFP
FAX Number: (713) 692-7399 Calendar System: Other
URL: www.culinaryinstitute.edu
Established: 1998 Annual Undergrad Tuition & Fees: N/A
Enrollment: 403 Coed
Affiliation or Control: Proprietary IRS Status: Proprietary
Highest Offering: Associate Degree
Program: Occupational
Accreditation: ACCSC, ACFEI

01 School Director .... Mark STROEH

Culinary Institute of America San Antonio (C)

312 Pearl Parkway, Bldg 3, San Antonio TX 78215
Telephone: (210) 554-6400 Identification: 770131
Accreditation: &M

† Main campus is Culinary Institute of America in Hyde Park, NY.

Dallas Baptist University (D)

3000 Mountain Creek Parkway, Dallas TX 75211-9299
County: Dallas FICE Identification: 003560
Unit ID: 224226
Telephone: (214) 333-7100 Carnegie Class: Master's L
FAX Number: (214) 333-6863 Calendar System: 4/1/4
URL: www.dbu.edu
Established: 1898 Annual Undergrad Tuition & Fees: $22,350
Enrollment: 5,622 Coed
Affiliation or Control: Baptist IRS Status: 501(c)3
Highest Offering: Doctorate
Program: Liberal Arts And General; Teacher Preparatory; Professional
Accreditation: SC, ACBSP, MUS

01 President .... Dr. Gary R. COOK
04 Assistant to the President .... Mr. Mitchell BENNETT
03 Executive Vice President .... Dr. J. Blair BLACKBURN
05 Provost .... Dr. Denny DOWD
10 Vice President Financial Affairs .... Mr. Eric BRUNTMYER
30 Vice Pres Advancement and Ext Affs .... Dr. Cory HINES
58 Vice Pres/Dean Cook School of Ldshp .... Dr. Adam WRIGHT
32 Dean of Students and Spiritual Life .... Mr. Jay HARLEY
13 Vice Pres for Technology .... Mr. Matt MURRAH
27 Vice Pres for Communications .... Dr. Blake KILLINGSWORTH
11 Assoc Vice Pres for Admin Affairs .... Dr. Ozzie INGRAM
20 Associate Provost .... Mrs. Deemie J. NAUGLE
50 Acting Dean College of Business .... Dr. Dale SIMS
81 Dean College Natural Science & Math .... Dr. Dionisio FLEITAS
53 Dean College of Education .... Dr. Neil DUGGER
57 Dean College of Fine Arts .... Mr. Ronald BOWLES
73 Dean College Christian Faith .... Dr. Steven K. MULLEN
79 Dean Col Humanities/Social Sciences .... Dr. Jack GOODYEAR
107 Dean College Professional Studies ... Dr. Donovan FREDRICKSEN
06 Registrar .... Mrs. Linda M. RONEY
07 Director Undergrad Admissions .... Mr. Bobby SOTO
08 Director of Library .... Ms. Debra COLLINS
37 Director of Financial Aid .... Mr. Lee FERGUSON
15 Director of Human Resources .... Mrs. Tamy ROGERS
56 Director Weekend College .... Ms. Joyce WALLACE
41 Director of Athletics .... Mr. Ryan ERWIN
19 Director of Security .... Mr. Donald KABETZKE
85 Director of International Students .... Mrs. Rebecca BROWN
38 Director Student Counseling Center .... Mrs. Joan DAVIS
18 Asst Vice Pres for Admin Affairs .... Mr. Jonathan TEAT
36 Director of Career Services .... Ms. Marion A. HILL
35 Associate Dean of Students .... Dr. Heather HADLOCK
42 Dir Intercessory Prayer Ministry .... Ms. Cyndi PETTIT
88 Academic Projects Administrator .... Ms. Lou ESPARZA
58 Director of Graduate Programs .... Mrs. Kit P. MONTGOMERY
43 General Counsel .... Mr. Dan MALONE
21 Controller .... Mrs. Mendi M. MCMAHAN
96 Accounts Payable Administrator .... Mrs. Becky BUTLER
40 Manager Bookstore .... Mr. Jason SMITH
09 Coordinator Institutional Reporting .... Mrs. Valerie FERGUSON
24 Coordinator Media Services .... Mr. Jonathan HOOVER

Dallas Christian College (E)

2700 Christian Parkway, Dallas TX 75234-7299
County: Dallas FICE Identification: 006941
Unit ID: 224244
Telephone: (972) 241-3371 Carnegie Class: Spec/Faith
FAX Number: (972) 241-8021 Calendar System: 4/1/4
URL: www.dallas.edu
Established: 1950 Annual Undergrad Tuition & Fees: $14,788
Enrollment: 329 Coed
Affiliation or Control: Christian Churches And Churches of Christ
IRS Status: 501(c)3
Highest Offering: Baccalaureate
Program: Occupational; Teacher Preparatory; Professional; Religious Emphasis
Accreditation: BI

01 President .... Mr. Dustin D. RUBECK
05 Vice President for Academic Affairs .... Dr. Perry STEPP
30 Vice Pres Institutional Advancement .... Vacant
31 Vice President for Community .... Mr. Mark WORLEY
10 Chief Financial Officer .... Dr. Jay REIMER
06 Registrar .... Mrs. Crystal LAIDACKER
37 Director of Financial Aid .... Ms. Becky AKIN-SITKA
07 Director of Admissions .... Mr. Matthew MEEKS
18 Director of Facilities .... Mr. Gary ADAMS

*Dallas County Community College District Office (F)

1601 South Lamar, Dallas TX 75215
County: Dallas FICE Identification: 009331
Unit ID: 224253
Telephone: (214) 378-1601 Carnegie Class: N/A
FAX Number: (214) 378-1810
URL: www.dcccd.edu

01 Chancellor .... Dr. Wright L. LASSITER, JR.
05 Provost Educational Affairs .... Dr. Sharon L. BLACKMAN
10 Exec Vice Chanc Business Affairs .... Mr. Ed DESPLAS
20 Exec Dist Dir WF Educ & Compliance .... Mr. Don PERRY
18 Asc Vice Chanc Facil Mgmt/Architect .... Mr. Clyde PORTER
43 District Legal Counsel .... Mr. Robert J. YOUNG
26 Vice Chanc Public & Govt Affairs .... Mr. Justin H. LONON
102 Assoc Vice Chanc Foundation .... Vacant
101 Executive Director Board Relations .... Mrs. Susan HALL
30 Assoc Vice Chanc Resource Develop .... Vacant
96 Director of Purchasing .... Mr. Steve PARK
62 Director of Technical Services .... Mr. John CRISWELL

*Brookhaven College (G)

3939 Valley View, Dallas TX 75244-4997
County: Dallas FICE Identification: 021002
Unit ID: 223524
Telephone: (972) 860-4700 Carnegie Class: Assoc/Pub-U-MC
FAX Number: (972) 860-4897 Calendar System: Semester
URL: www.brookhavencollege.edu
Established: 1978 Annual Undergrad Tuition & Fees (In-District): $1,350
Enrollment: 12,790 Coed
Affiliation or Control: State/Local IRS Status: 501(c)3
Highest Offering: Associate Degree
Program: Occupational; 2-Year Principally Bachelor's Creditable
Accreditation: SC, ADNUR, ART, EMT, RAD

02 President .... Dr. Thom D. CHESNEY
05 Vice President of Academic Affairs .... Mr. Rodger BENNETT
10 Vice President of Business Services .... Mr. George HERRING
32 Vice Pres of Student Services .... Mr. Oscar LOPEZ
50 Exec Dean Business Studies .... Mr. Sandy WYCHE
36 Assoc VP Career & Program Resources .... Ms. Marilyn K. KOLESAR-LYNCH
103 Assoc VP Workforce/Continuing Educ .... Mr. Vernon L. HAWKINS
45 Exec Dean Educational Resources .... Ms. Sarah FERGUSON
57 Exec Dean Fine Arts/Phys Ed .... Mr. Rick MAXWELL
81 Executive Dean Science/Math .... Ms. Doris ROUSEY
23 Exec Dean of Health/Human Svcs .... Dr. Juanita FLINT
09 AVP Plng/Rsrch/Inst Effectiveness .... Dr. Michael DENNEHY
90 Director of Info Tech .... Mr. Michael DEASON
83 Exec Dean Social Sci/Distance Lrng .... Mr. Sam GOVEA
27 Executive Dean Communications .... Ms. Kendra VAGLIENTI
88 Dean of Student Success .... Ms. Brenda DALTON
26 Asst Dir Marketing & Public Info .... Ms. Meridith DANFORTH
07 Director of Admissions/Registrar .... Ms. Thoa Hoang VO
41 Director of Athletics .... Ms. Lynne LEVESQUE
21 Director of Business Operations .... Vacant
36 Director Career Development Center .... Ms. Annette WILSON
88 Dir Ellison Miles Geotech Institute .... Vacant
18 Director of Facilities Services .... Mr. Tommy GALLEGOS
15 Exec Dir of Human Resources .... Ms. Terri EDRICH
85 Director of Multicultural Center .... Vacant
35 Dir Office of Student Life .... Mr. Brian BORSKI
19 Captain of College Police .... Mr. John KLINGENSMITH
23 Nurse Health Services .... Ms. Mildred KELLEY
04 Assistant to President .... Ms. Carrie SCHWEITZER

*Cedar Valley College (H)

3030 N Dallas Avenue, Lancaster TX 75134-3799
County: Dallas FICE Identification: 003561
Unit ID: 223773
Telephone: (972) 860-8201 Carnegie Class: Assoc/Pub-U-MC
FAX Number: (972) 682-7075 Calendar System: Semester
URL: www.cedarvalleycollege.edu
Established: 1974 Annual Undergrad Tuition & Fees (In-District): $1,350
Enrollment: 6,403 Coed
Affiliation or Control: State/Local IRS Status: 501(c)3
Highest Offering: Associate Degree
Program: Occupational; 2-Year Principally Bachelor's Creditable; Business Emphasis
Accreditation: SC

02 President .... Dr. Jennifer L. WIMBISH
05 Vice President for Instruction .... Dr. Nancy CURE
32 Vice Pres Student Svcs/Enroll Mgmt .... Ms. Anna MAYS
10 Vice President Business Services .... Mr. Huan LUONG
81 Director Dean Math/Science/Health .... Vacant
09 Dir Inst Research/Effectiveness .... Mr. Marlon MOTE
49 Division Dean Liberal Arts .... Dr. Mickey BEST
50 Div Dean Bus/Science/Technology .... Dr. Ruben JOHNSON
20 Dean Instructional SupportDist Ed .... Mrs. Lisa NIGHTINGALE
51 Executive Dean Cmty & Resource Dev .... Mrs. Patricia DAVIS
08 Assoc Dean Educ Resource/ Librarian .... Ms. Vidya KRISHNASWAMY
07 Director of Admissions/Registrar .... Ms. Lucia JOHNSON
18 Director Facilities Management .... Mrs. Cindy A. ROGERS
26 Dir Marketing & Public Relations .... Mrs. Megan PALSA
15 Int Director Human Resources .... Mr. Willie NEAL
37 Director of Financial Aid .... Ms. Cathryn ADAMS
88 Director of Upward Bound .... Ms. Olivia GUERRA
88 Director of Independent Study .... Vacant
35 Coordinator Office Student Life .... Ms. Myioshi U. HOLMES
36 Senior Placement Coordinator .... Mr. Mike J. ALFORD

*Eastfield College (I)

3737 Motley Drive, Mesquite TX 75150-2099
County: Dallas FICE Identification: 008510
Unit ID: 224572
Telephone: (972) 860-7100 Carnegie Class: Assoc/Pub-U-MC
FAX Number: (972) 860-8373 Calendar System: Semester
URL: www.eastfieldcollege.edu
Established: 1970 Annual Undergrad Tuition & Fees (In-District): $1,350
Enrollment: 14,383 Coed
Affiliation or Control: State/Local IRS Status: 170(c)1
Highest Offering: Associate Degree
Program: Occupational; 2-Year Principally Bachelor's Creditable
Accreditation: SC

02 President .... Dr. Jean L. CONWAY
05 Exec VP Academic Affairs .... Mr. Michael J. GUTIERREZ
45 VP Organizational Development .... Dr. Thomas J. GRACA
10 VP Business Services .... Dr. Adrian H. DOUGLAS
35 Dean Outreach & Student Development .... Ms. Dina M. SOSA-HEGARTY
26 Assistant to the President .... Ms. Sharon L. COOK
15 Executive Director Human Resources .... Mr. Larry L. WILSON
12 Exec Dir Pleasant Grove Campus .... Mr. Javier E. OLGUIN
45 Associate Vice President .... Mr. Donald BAYNHAM
04 Admin Assistant to the President .... Ms. Gloria M. JOHNSON
88 Director Decision Support .... Dr. Richard K. PLOTT
57 Executive Dean Arts & Literature .... Ms. Rachel B. WOLF
72 Executive Dean Career Technologies ... Mr. Gerald F. KOZLOWSKI
81 Executive Dean College Readiness .... Mr. Ricardo S. RODRIGUEZ
81 Executive Dean Science .... Dr. Gretchen K. RIEHL
83 Interim Dean Social Sciences .... Dr. Michael D. WALKER
103 Executive Dean Workforce Devel .... Dr. Lindle D. GRIGSBY
51 Dean Continuing Education .... Mr. Roy L. BOND
08 Dean Educational Resources .... Ms. Karla J. GREER
88 Director Advising .... Ms. Kimberly M. MOORE
37 Director Financial Aid .... Ms. Susan M. GROVE
35 Director Student Life .... Ms. Judy A. SCHWARTZ
41 Director Intercollegiate Athletics .... Mr. Anthony S. FLETCHER
23 Director Health Center .... Ms. Cynthia S. TAYLOR
38 Professional Counselor .... Mr. Jeff QUAN
88 Director Disability Services .... Ms. Barbara L. WHITE
21 Financial Manager .... Ms. Heidi M. BASSETT
21 Director Business Operations .... Ms. Linda S. ZABOJNIK
18 Director Facilities Services .... Mr. Michael BRANTLEY
90 Interim Dean Information Tech .... Mr. Jack O. THIEHOFF
91 Manager Administrative Computing .... Ms. Dana R. HASKINS
46 Dean Resource Development .... Ms. Whitney C. HOUSTON
19 Director College Police .... Chief Michael D. HORAK

*El Centro College (J)

801 Main Street, Dallas TX 75202-3604
County: Dallas FICE Identification: 004453
Unit ID: 224615
Telephone: (214) 860-2000 Carnegie Class: Assoc/Pub-U-MC
FAX Number: (214) 860-2335 Calendar System: Semester
URL: www.elcentrocollege.edu
Established: 1966 Annual Undergrad Tuition & Fees (In-District): $1,872
Enrollment: 11,381 Coed
Affiliation or Control: State/Local IRS Status: 501(c)3
Highest Offering: Associate Degree
Program: Occupational; 2-Year Principally Bachelor's Creditable
Accreditation: SC, ACFEI, ADNUR, COARC, CVT, DMS, MAC, MLTAD, PNUR, RAD, SURGT

02 President .... Dr. Paul J. MCCARTHY
05 VP Academic Affairs/Economic Dev .... Ms. Sondra G. FLEMMING
32 Int VP of Student Success .... Ms. Fela ALFARO
10 VP Business Services .... Mr. David A. BROWNING
50 Exec Dean Bus/Pub Svc/Info Tech .... Mr. Howard H. FINNEY

60 Exec Dean Communications/Math .... Ms. Lisa M. THERIOT
49 Exec Dean Arts & Sciences .... Dr. Charles MORRIS
76 Exec Dean Health Occupations .... Dr. Mary L. MCPHERSON
32 Exec Dean Student Dev/Support Svcs .... Mr. James L. HANDY
12 Executive Dean BJP Campus .... Ms. Pyeper L. WILKINS
12 Executive Director West Campus .... Ms. Ana-Maria RAMOS
108 Dean Curriculum Assessment .... Ms. Karen MONGO
09 Dean Institutional Effectiveness .... Ms. Teresa S. ISBELL
08 Asst Dean Educational Resources .... Dr. Norman HOWDEN
06 Director Admissions/Registrar .... Ms. Rebecca J. GARZA
37 Dir Student Financial Support/Svcs .... Ms. Pam A. LUCAS
19 College Director College Police .... Mr. Calvin R. RICHARDS
26 Director Marketing/Communications .... Ms. Priscilla A. STALEY
15 Exec Director Human Resources .... Ms. Dawn M. SEGROVES
38 Director Testing Center .... Mr. Monty E. FRANCIS
18 Director Facilities Services .... Mr. William E. BUTLER
21 College Director Business Operation .... Ms. Susan G. PIERCE
85 Coordinator International Center .... Mr. Robert G. REYES
35 Director Ofc of Student Life .... Ms. Shanee' S. MOORE
23 College Nurse .... Mr. Ken L. JOHNSON
91 Director Information Technology .... Mr. Michael C. JOHNSON
40 Manager Bookstore .... Mr. Richard SCHLEIFFER

*Mountain View College (A)

4849 W Illinois, Dallas TX 75211-6599
County: Dallas FICE Identification: 008503
Unit ID: 226930
Telephone: (214) 860-8680 Carnegie Class: Assoc/Pub-U-MC
FAX Number: (214) 860-8521 Calendar System: Semester
URL: www.mountainviewcollege.edu
Established: 1970 Annual Undergrad Tuition & Fees (In-District): $1,248
Enrollment: 9,065 Coed
Affiliation or Control: State/Local IRS Status: 501(c)3
Highest Offering: Associate Degree
Program: Occupational; 2-Year Principally Bachelor's Creditable
Accreditation: SC

02 President .... Mr. Felix A. ZAMORA
05 VP Academic Affairs & Student Succ .... Dr. John DELEON
32 VP Student Svcs/Enrollment Mgmt .... Dr. Leonard GARRETT
10 Vice President of Business Services .... Ms. Sharon DAVIS
84 Exec Dean Student Support Svcs .... Vacant
90 Exec Dean Curriculum & Instruction .... Dr. Karen VALENCIA
45 Dean Education Center/Dir Title V .... Mr. Moises ALMENDARIZ
06 Assoc Dean Student Support Svcs .... Ms. Glenda GARRETT
18 Director Facilities Services .... Mr. Allan KNOTT
09 Dir of Planning/Research & IE .... Ms. Iva BERGERON
37 Director Financial Aid .... Mr. James HUBENER
35 Director of Student Life .... Ms. Cathy EDWARDS
103 Associate Dean of Workforce Develop .... Ms. Vonice CHAMP
26 Director Public Info/Marketing .... Ms. Marci GARROTT
21 Director of Business Operations .... Mr. Tim SOYARS
07 Asst Director of Admissions .... Ms. Linda OSAGIE
38 Director of Advising .... Vacant
15 Director Human Resources .... Mr. Willie NEAL
36 Director Career Development .... Ms. Regina GARNER
45 Dean Resource Development .... Ms. Heather A. MARSH

*North Lake College (B)

5001 N MacArthur Boulevard, Irving TX 75038-3899
County: Dallas FICE Identification: 020774
Unit ID: 227191
Telephone: (972) 273-3000 Carnegie Class: Assoc/Pub-U-MC
FAX Number: (972) 273-3014 Calendar System: Semester
URL: www.dcccd.edu
Established: 1977 Annual Undergrad Tuition & Fees (In-District): $1,560
Enrollment: 10,932 Coed
Affiliation or Control: State/Local IRS Status: 501(c)3
Highest Offering: Associate Degree
Program: Occupational; 2-Year Principally Bachelor's Creditable; Technical Emphasis
Accreditation: SC, CONST

02 Interim President .... Ms. Christa SLEJKO
05 Vice President Academic Affairs .... Dr. Martha HUGHES
31 VP Community and Economic Develop .... Dr. Paul KELEMEN
10 Interim Vice Pres Business Services .... Ms. Shannon WEAVER
45 Vice Pres Planning & Development .... Ms. Candace CASTILLO
84 VP Stdnt Svcs/Enrollment Mgmt .... Ms. Mary CIMINELLI
88 Director of Learning Resources .... Mr. Kent SEAVER
07 Director Admissions & Registration .... Ms. Francyenne MAYNARD
26 Director Marketing & Public Info .... Ms. Gina FEDERER
12 Ex Director North and South Campus .... Mr. Arthur JAMES
08 Head Librarian .... Dr. Enrique CHAMBERLAIN
18 Director Facilities Services .... Mr. John WATSON
19 Director Campus Police .... Mr. Chris DRAKE
09 Director of Institutional Research .... Vacant
15 Director Human Resources .... Ms. Ella BARBER
21 Interim Associate Business Officer .... Ms. Pamela MAYS
32 Dir Stdnt Prog/Resources/Hlth Svcs .... Ms. Virginia JONES
103 Interim Director Workforce Dev/CE .... Ms. Lynn SMITH-BRUSH
38 Dir Acad Advising Career Edu Pl .... Ms. DeAira HOLLOWAY
83 Executive Dean Liberal Arts .... Dr. Zena JACKSON
81 Exec Dean Math/Science .... Dr. Marilyn MAYS
50 Exe Dean Arts/Bus/Sports Sci Tech .... Dr. David EVANS
12 Exec Dean West Campus .... Mr. Mike COOLEY

*Richland College (C)

12800 Abrams Road, Dallas TX 75243-2199
County: Dallas FICE Identification: 008504
Unit ID: 227766
Telephone: (972) 238-6194 Carnegie Class: Assoc/Pub-U-MC
FAX Number: (972) 238-6978 Calendar System: Semester
URL: www.rlc.dcccd.edu
Established: 1972 Annual Undergrad Tuition & Fees (In-District): $1,248
Enrollment: 19,552 Coed
Affiliation or Control: State/Local IRS Status: 501(c)3
Highest Offering: Associate Degree
Program: Occupational; 2-Year Principally Bachelor's Creditable
Accreditation: SC, MAC

02 President .... Dr. Kathryn K. EGGLESTON
04 Dean/Exec Assistant to President .... Ms. Janet C. JAMES
05 VP Teaching & Learning .... Dr. Zarina BLANKENBAKER
32 VP for Student Development .... Dr. Tony E. SUMMERS
10 VP for Business Services .... Mr. Ron M. CLARK
50 Exec Dean Sch of Engr/Business/Tech .... Ms. Martha A. HOGAN
79 Exec Dean Human/Fine & Perf Arts .... Ms. Diane HILBERT
81 Exec Dean of Math/Science/Hlth Prof .... Dr. Raymond P. CANHAM
09 Exec Dean Plng/Rsrch/Inst Effect .... Ms. Fonda L. VERA
60 Exec Dean World Lang/Cultures/Comm .... Ms. Susan E. BARKLEY
88 Exec Dean Lrng Enrich & Acad Dev .... Ms. Mary K. DARIN
41 Director Athletic Programs .... Mr. Guy SIMMONS
35 Director of Student Life .... Ms. Bobbie J. HARRISON
08 Director of Library Services .... Ms. Lennijo HENDERSON
26 Dir College Comm and Marketing .... Ms. Whitney ROSENBALM
18 Director of Facilities Services .... Mr. Kenneth DUNSON
15 Executive Director Human Resources .... Vacant
19 Chief of College Police .... Mr. Robert D. BAKER
12 Principal Richland Collegiate HS .... Dr. Kristyn EDNEY
84 Assoc VP Enrollment/Supt RCHS .... Ms. Donna WALKER

Dallas Institute of Funeral Service (D)

3909 S Buckner Boulevard, Dallas TX 75227-4314
County: Dallas FICE Identification: 010761
Unit ID: 224271
Telephone: (214) 388-5466 Carnegie Class: Assoc/PrivNFP
FAX Number: (214) 388-0316 Calendar System: Quarter
URL: www.dallasinstitute.edu
Established: 1945 Annual Undergrad Tuition & Fees: $17,500
Enrollment: 146 Coed
Affiliation or Control: Independent Non-Profit IRS Status: 501(c)3
Highest Offering: Associate Degree
Program: Occupational; 2-Year Principally Bachelor's Creditable; Technical Emphasis
Accreditation: FUSER

01 President .... Mr. James M. SHOEMAKE

Dallas Nursing Institute (E)

12170 North Abrams Rd, Ste 200, Dallas TX 75243
County: Dallas FICE Identification: 034165
Unit ID: 437732
Telephone: (214) 613-3770 Carnegie Class: Not Classified
FAX Number: (214) 593-0975 Calendar System: Semester
URL: www.dni.edu
Established: Annual Undergrad Tuition & Fees: $27,300
Enrollment: 653 Coed
Affiliation or Control: Proprietary IRS Status: Proprietary
Highest Offering: Associate Degree
Program: Occupational
Accreditation: ABHES

01 Executive Director .... Dr. Patricia PERRYMAN

Dallas Theological Seminary (F)

3909 Swiss Avenue, Dallas TX 75204-6493
County: Dallas FICE Identification: 003562
Unit ID: 224305
Telephone: (214) 887-5000 Carnegie Class: Spec/Faith
FAX Number: (214) 887-5532 Calendar System: Semester
URL: www.dts.edu
Established: 1924 Annual Graduate Tuition & Fees: $14,020
Enrollment: 2,007 Coordinate
Affiliation or Control: Independent Non-Profit IRS Status: 501(c)3
Highest Offering: Doctorate; No Undergraduates
Program: Professional; Religious Emphasis
Accreditation: SC, THEOL

01 President .... Dr. Mark L. BAILEY
05 Vice Pres Academic Affs/Acad Dean .... Dr. Mark M. YARBROUGH
32 VP Dean Stdnt Svcs/Dean of Students .... Dr. Robert J. GARIPPA
10 Vice President Business & Finance .... Mr. Dale C. LARSON
30 Vice President for Advancement .... Ms. Kimberly B. TILL
11 Vice President Campus Operations .... Mr. Robert F. RIGGS
100 Exec Assistant to the President .... Mr. Robert F. RIGGS
26 Exec Dir Communications/Ed Tech .... Mr. John C. DYER
102 President Dallas Sem Foundation .... Mr. Stephen M. GOLDING
108 Dean of Assessment .... Dr. Eugene W. POND
20 Dean of Academic Administration .... Dr. James H. THAMES
12 Dean of DTS Houston .... Dr. Bruce W. FONG
37 Dir of Employee/Stdnt Support Svcs .... Ms. Karen G. HOLDER
58 Director of Ph.D. Studies .... Dr. Richard A. TAYLOR
58 Director of D.Min. Studies .... Dr. D. Scott BARFOOT
09 Director of Inst Research/Effective .... Dr. Eugene W. POND
06 Registrar .... Mr. Billy R. TODD, JR.
88 Exec Dir of Leadership Center .... Dr. Andrew B. SEIDEL
88 Exec Dir of Cultural Engagement .... Dr. Darrell L. BOCK
07 Director of Admissions .... Mr. Joshua J. BLEEKER

08 Library Director .... Mr. Marvin T. HUNN, II
29 Director of Alumni .... Mr. Gregory A. HATTEBERG
36 Director of Placement .... Dr. Paul E. PETTIT
24 Director of Media Support .... Mr. James W. HOOVER
42 Chaplain .... Rev. G. William BRYAN
34 Adviser to Women Students .... Ms. Lynn Etta G. MANNING
93 Adviser to African-American Studnts .... Dr. Terrance S. WOODSON
18 Dir Facilities & Plant Operations .... Mr. B. Kevin FOLSOM
13 Director of Information Technology .... Mr. Richard D. BLAKE
19 Chief of Campus Police .... Mr. John S. BLOOM
39 Director of Housing & Food Services .... Mr. Drew H. WILLIAMS
106 Dir Online and External Studies .... Mr. Robert M. ABEGG
88 Director of Online Chinese Studies .... Dr. Samuel CHIA
38 Director of Counseling Services .... Dr. J. Lee JAGERS
21 Controller .... Ms. Patricia MAYABB
40 Bookstore Manager .... Mr. Kevin D. STERN
85 International Student Adviser .... Ms. Jenny MCGILL

Del Mar College (G)

101 Baldwin, Corpus Christi TX 78404-3897
County: Nueces FICE Identification: 003563
Unit ID: 224350
Telephone: (361) 698-1200 Carnegie Class: Assoc/Pub-R-L
FAX Number: (361) 698-1559 Calendar System: Semester
URL: www.delmar.edu
Established: 1935 Annual Undergrad Tuition & Fees (In-District): $2,884
Enrollment: 11,030 Coed
Affiliation or Control: Local IRS Status: 501(c)3
Highest Offering: Associate Degree
Program: Occupational; 2-Year Principally Bachelor's Creditable
Accreditation: SC, ACFEI, ADNUR, ART, CAHIIM, COARC, DA, DH, DMS, MLTAD, MUS, NMT, OTA, PTAA, RAD, SURGT, THEA

01 President .... Dr. Mark ESCAMILLA
05 Provost/VP/Instruction/Student Svcs .... Dr. Fernando FIGUEROA
10 VP Administration/Finance .... Dr. Lee SLOAN
45 Exec Dir Strategic Plng/Wkfrce Init .... Ms. Lenora KEAS
26 Exec Dir Community & Legal Rels .... Ms. Claudia JACKSON
30 Exec Director of Development .... Ms. Mary MCQUEEN
07 Dean Student Outreach & Enroll Svcs .... Mr. Gilbert BECERRA
35 Dean Student Engagement & Retention .... Ms. Cheryl GARNER
49 Dean Division Arts & Sciences .... Dr. Jonda HALCOMB
50 Dean Div Business/Prof/Tech Ed .... Dr. Larry LEE
15 Exec Director Human Resources/Admin .... Ms. Tammy MCDONALD
21 Comptroller .... Mr. John J. JOHNSON
96 Director of Purchasing/Business Svc .... Mr. James ROBERTSON
13 Chief Information Officer .... Mr. August ALFONSO
19 Dir Environ/Health/Safety/Risk Mgmt .... Mr. Kelly L. WHITE
37 Interim Director of Financial Aid .... Ms. Nancy M. BRISENO
06 Registrar .... Ms. Angalynn BISHOP
32 Dir Student Leadership/Campus Life .... Ms. Beverly CAGE
88 Director of Accounting .... Ms. Cathy WEST
88 Dir of Financial Services/Bursar .... Ms. D'Ann POLAND
08 Director of Libraries .... Ms. Chris M. TETZLAFF-BELHASEN
09 Director of Institutional Research .... Mr. Sushil PALLEMONI

DeVry University - Houston Campus (H)

11125 Equity Drive, Houston TX 77041-8217
Telephone: (713) 973-3000 Identification: 666219
Accreditation: &NH, CAHIIM, ENGT

† Main campus is DeVry University - Chicago Campus in Chicago, IL.

DeVry University - Irving Campus (I)

4800 Regent Boulevard, Irving TX 75063-2439
Telephone: (972) 929-6777 FICE Identification: 010139
Accreditation: &NH, CAHIIM, ENGT

† Main campus is DeVry University - Chicago Campus in Chicago, IL.

East Texas Baptist University (J)

One Tiger Drive, Marshall TX 75670-1498
County: Harrison FICE Identification: 003564
Unit ID: 224527
Telephone: (903) 935-7963 Carnegie Class: Bac/Diverse
FAX Number: (903) 938-1705 Calendar System: Semester
URL: www.etbu.edu
Established: 1912 Annual Undergrad Tuition & Fees: $21,144
Enrollment: 1,290 Coed
Affiliation or Control: Southern Baptist IRS Status: 501(c)3
Highest Offering: Master's
Program: Liberal Arts And General
Accreditation: SC, MUS, NURSE

01 President .... Dr. Samuel W. "Dub" OLIVER
05 Provost/Vice Pres Academic Affairs .... Vacant
20 Assistant Provost .... Dr. Tommy SANDERS
30 Vice Pres University Advancement .... Mrs. Catherine CRAWFORD
42 Vice Pres Spiritual Development .... Dr. Scott BRYANT
10 Vice Pres Administration & Finance .... Mr. Ned CALVERT
32 Vice President for Student Affairs .... Mr. Xavier WHITAKER
84 Vice Pres for Enrollment Mgmt/Mktg .... Mr. Vince BLANKENSHIP
35 Dean of Students .... Mr. Tyler SELLERS
09 Dir Inst Research/Effectiveness .... Mrs. Karen WILEY
07 Director of Admissions .... Mr. Jason SOLES
13 Director of Inst Technology .... Mr. Barry HALE
06 University Registrar .... Mr. Chris WOOD
29 Director of Alumni Relations .... Mrs. Allison PETEET

66 Dean School of Nursing .... Dr. Ellen FINEOUT-OVERHOLT
08 Director of Library .... Ms. Cynthia PETERSON
26 Director of Public Relations .... Mr. Mike MIDKIFF
37 Director of Financial Aid .... Mr. Tommy YOUNG
41 Director of Athletics .... Mr. Kent REEVES
88 Director Baptist Student Ministry .... Mr. Mark YATES
40 Director of Bookstore .... Mr. Bill WARDEN
44 Director of Alumni Development .... Mr. Paul TAPP
18 Director of Physical Facilities .... Mr. Eric WILBURN
88 Director Rec & Athletic Facilities .... Mr. Randy PRINGLE
35 Director of Student Activities .... Mr. Blair PREVOST
88 Director Great Commission Center .... Dr. Melody MAXWELL
53 Dean School of Education .... Dr. Donna LUBCKER
53 Associate Dean of Education .... Dr. Joseph D. BROWN
88 Dean School of Christian Studies .... Dr. John HARRIS
83 Dean School of Nat/Soc Sciences .... Dr. Lynn NEW
50 Dean School of Business .... Dr. Scott RAY
79 Dean School of Humanities .... Dr. Jerry SUMMERS
85 Director of International Education .... Mr. Alan HUESING
21 Director of Financial Services .... Mr. Richard HUTSELL
88 Director of Student Success .... Mrs. Kelley PAUL
57 Dean School of Fine Arts .... Dr. Tom WEBSTER
102 Director of Major Gifts .... Dr. Dane FOWLKES

Ecotech Institute (A)

14200 North IH 35, Austin TX 78728
Telephone: (877) 368-1071 Identification: 770632
Accreditation: ACICS

† Main campus is Virginia College in Birmingham, AL.

El Paso Community College (B)

PO Box 20500, El Paso TX 79998-0500
County: El Paso FICE Identification: 010387
Unit ID: 224642
Telephone: (915) 831-2000 Carnegie Class: Assoc/Pub-U-MC
FAX Number: (915) 831-6507 Calendar System: Semester
URL: www.epcc.edu
Established: 1969 Annual Undergrad Tuition & Fees (In-District): $2,580
Enrollment: 30,394 Coed
Affiliation or Control: Local IRS Status: 501(c)3
Highest Offering: Associate Degree
Program: Occupational; 2-Year Principally Bachelor's Creditable
Accreditation: SC, ADNUR, CAHIIM, COARC, DA, DH, DMS, MAC, MLTAD, PTAA, RAD, SURGT

01 President .... Dr. William SERRATA
05 Interim Vice President Instruction .... Mr. Steve SMITH
10 Vice Pres Admin & Fin Operations .... Dr. Ernst E. ROBERTS
13 Vice Pres Information Tech/CIO .... Dr. Jenny GIRON
103 Vice Pres Wrkfc/Economic Dev & CE .... Ms. Yolanda AHNER
32 Vice President Student Services .... Ms. Linda GONZALEZ
46 Vice Pres Research & Accountability .... Mr. Saul C. CANDELAS
10 Assoc VP Budget & Financial Svcs .. Ms. Josette SHAUGHNESSY
88 Assoc VP Employee Relations .... Ms. Nancy N. NELSON
26 Dir Marketing & Community Rels .... Ms. Joyce CORDELL
12 Dean Instruct Programs-MDP Campus .... Dr. Julie PENLEY
76 Dean Health Occupations/Math/Sci .... Dr. Paula MITCHELL
50 Dean Arts/Bask/Comp/Oc Educ/Soc Sci .... Dr. Eileen CONKLIN
49 Dean Arts/Bask/Comm & Soc Sci .... Ms. Janet EVELER
79 Dean ESL Reading Social Science .... Ms. Susana RODARTE
81 Dean Arch/Arts/Math/Science .... Ms. Toni BADILLO
88 Dean American Lang/BS/Comm/PA .... Mr. Claude MATHIS
53 Dean Education & Occ Programs .... Dr. Jaime D. FARIAS
66 Dean Nursing .... Ms. Paula G. MEAGHER
12 Dean Instructional Pgms-NW Campus .... Dr. Lydia TENA
81 Int Dean Math/Sci/Career Tech Ed .... Mr. Ernest R. WEBB, II
37 Exec Director Student Fin Aid .... Mr. Raul H. LERMA
45 Director Inst Effectiveness .... Dr. Ron STROUD
08 Director Library Technical Services .... Mr. Luis CHAPARRO
21 Comptroller .... Mr. Fernando FLORES
36 Director Career Services .... Ms. Carla CARDOZA
18 Executive Director Physical Plant .... Mr. Richard L. LOBATO
19 Chief of Police .... Chief Jose L. RAMIREZ
15 Exec Dir Human Resources/RM & S .... Ms. Elizabeth OLGUIN-RYAN
07 Exec Director Admissions/Registrar .... Mr. Daryle HENDRY
96 Dir Purchasing & Contract Mgmt .... Mr. Ruben C. GALLARDO
09 Director Institutional Research .... Dr. Carol KAY
88 Director Human Resources Devel .... Mr. Alex HERNANDEZ
31 Director Inst & Community Planning .... Ms. Dolores GROSS
21 Director Budget .... Ms. Laura TELLEZ
88 Director Workplace Literacy Prgm .... Mrs. Sara MARTINEZ
85 Director International Education .... Dr. Miguel A. MARTINEZ-LASSO
102 Exec Dir Foundation/Development .... Dr. Christy PONCE
88 Dir Ctr for Students w/Disabilities .... Ms. Janet M. LOCKHART
88 Director Recruitment/School Rels .... Ms. Nita CORRAL-NAVA
88 Director Testing Service .... Ms. Marisa PIERCE
25 Director Grants Management .... Mr. Alfred C. LAWRENCE
103 Director Workforce Development .... Ms. Luz E. TABOADA
56 Director Distance Education .... Mr. Robert P. JONES
88 Director Student Success .... Ms. Irma G. CAMACHO
88 Dir Law Enforcement Trng Academy .... Mr. Barry J. BOGLE
28 Director of Diversity Programs .... Mrs. Olga CHAVEZ

Everest College (C)

300 Six Flags Drive, Suite 100, Arlington TX 76011
Telephone: (817) 652-7790 Identification: 770788
Accreditation: ACICS

† Main campus is Everest Institute in Rochester, NY.

Everest College (D)

6080 N Central Expressway, Dallas TX 75206-5202
Telephone: (214) 234-4850 Identification: 666254
Accreditation: ACICS, MAAB

† Main campus is Everest College in Portland, OR.

Everest College (E)

4200 South Freeway, Suite 1940, Fort Worth TX 76115
Telephone: (817) 566-7700 Identification: 770790
Accreditation: ACICS

† Main campus is Everest College in Colorado Springs, CO.

Everest College (F)

5237 North Riverside Dr, Suite 100, Fort Worth TX 76137
Telephone: (817) 838-3000 Identification: 770789
Accreditation: ACICS

† Main campus is Everest College in West Valley City, UT.

Frank Phillips College (G)

PO Box 5118, Borger TX 79008-5118
County: Hutchinson FICE Identification: 003568
Unit ID: 224891
Telephone: (806) 457-4200 Carnegie Class: Assoc/Pub-R-S
FAX Number: (806) 457-4224 Calendar System: Semester
URL: www.fpctx.edu
Established: 1948 Annual Undergrad Tuition & Fees (In-District): $1,023
Enrollment: 1,227 Coed
Affiliation or Control: Local IRS Status: 501(c)3
Highest Offering: Associate Degree
Program: Occupational; 2-Year Principally Bachelor's Creditable
Accreditation: SC

01 President .... Dr. Jud HICKS
11 Vice Pres Administrative Services .... Dr. Jud HICKS
05 Vice President of Academic Affairs .... Ms. Shannon CARROLL
12 Dean of FPC Allen Campus .... Dr. Lew HUNNICUTT
08 Director of the Library .... Mr. Jason PRICE
06 Registrar .... Vacant
09 Director of Institutional Research .... Vacant
18 Director Physical Plant .... Ms. Regina HANEY
26 Col Advancement/Community Rels Ofcr .... Ms. Jerri AYLOR
103 Dean of Career & Technical Educ .... Mr. Jack STANLEY
37 Co-Dir Student Financial Services .... Ms. Beverly FIELDS
38 Director Student Counseling/Testing .... Mr. Kurt BILLUPS
07 Director Admissions & Records .... Ms. Michele STEVENS
56 Director of Extended Education .... Ms. Angela GRIFFIN
10 Director of Accounting .... Ms. Bridey MCCORMACK

Galen College of Nursing (H)

7411 John Smith Drive, Suite 300, San Antonio TX 78229
Telephone: (210) 733-3056 Identification: 770538
Accreditation: &SC, COE

† Main campus is Galen College of Nursing in Louisville, KY.

Galveston College (I)

4015 Avenue Q, Galveston TX 77550-7496
County: Galveston FICE Identification: 004972
Unit ID: 224961
Telephone: (409) 944-4242 Carnegie Class: Assoc/Pub-R-M
FAX Number: (409) 944-1500 Calendar System: Semester
URL: www.gc.edu
Established: 1966 Annual Undergrad Tuition & Fees (In-District): $1,558
Enrollment: 2,197 Coed
Affiliation or Control: State/Local IRS Status: 501(c)3
Highest Offering: Associate Degree
Program: Occupational; 2-Year Principally Bachelor's Creditable; Business Emphasis
Accreditation: SC, ADNUR, EMT, NMT, RAD, RTT

01 President .... Dr. Myles SHELTON
05 Vice President of Instruction .... Dr. Cissy MATTHEWS
11 Vice President for Administration .... Dr. Gaynelle H. HAYES
32 Acting VP of Student Svcs/Dir of FA .... Mr. Ron C. CRUMEDY
75 Dean of Tech & Prof Education .... Ms. Vera LEWIS-JASPER
30 Dir of Development/GC Foundation .... Ms. Maria TRIPOVICH
10 Director of Business Services .... Mr. M. Jeff ENGBROCK
14 Dir of Information Technology .... Mr. Kelly KLIMPT
26 Dir of Public Affairs .... Mr. Joseph E. HUFF, III
15 Dir Human Resources/Risk Management .... Ms. Mary Jan LANTZ
41 Athletic Director/Head Coach .... Mr. Ken DELCAMBRE
07 Director Admissions/Registrar .... Dr. Kimberly ELLIS
66 Director of Nursing .... Ms. Elaine RENOLA
09 Director Inst Effectiveness/Rsrch .... Dr. Larry ROOT
18 Director of Facilities/Security .... Mr. Tim W. SETZER
62 Dir of Library/Learning Resources .... Dr. Alan M. UYEHARA
04 Executive Assistant .... Ms. Carla D. BIGGERS

Golf Academy of America (J)

1861 Valley View Lane, Suite 100,
Farmers Branch TX 75234
Telephone: (972) 763-8100 Identification: 770621
Accreditation: ACICS

† Main campus is Virginia College in Birmingham, AL.

Grace School of Theology (K)

PO Box 7477, The Woodlands TX 77387
County: Montgomery Identification: 667100
Telephone: (877) 476-8674 Carnegie Class: Not Classified
FAX Number: (281) 602-8009 Calendar System: Semester
URL: www.gsot.edu
Established: 2002 Annual Undergrad Tuition & Fees: N/A
Enrollment: N/A Coed
Affiliation or Control: Independent Non-Profit IRS Status: 501(c)3
Highest Offering: Master's
Program: Religious Emphasis
Accreditation: TRACS

01 President .... Dr. Dave ANDERSON

Graduate Institute of Applied Linguistics (L)

7500 W Camp Wisdom Road, Dallas TX 75236-5629
County: Dallas FICE Identification: 038513
Telephone: (972) 708-7340 Carnegie Class: Not Classified
FAX Number: (972) 708-7396 Calendar System: Other
URL: www.gial.edu
Established: 1999 Annual Graduate Tuition & Fees: $13,831
Enrollment: 100 Coed
Affiliation or Control: Independent Non-Profit IRS Status: 501(c)3
Highest Offering: Master's; No Undergraduates
Program: Professional; Religious Emphasis
Accreditation: SC

01 President .... Dr. David A. ROSS
05 Chief Academic Officer .... Dr. Doug TIFFIN
10 Chief Financial Officer .... Mr. Rod JENKINS
101 Board Secretary .... Mr. James W. WALTON
32 Dean of Students .... Ms. Ruth E. SCHILBERG
06 Registrar .... Mrs. Lynne LAMIMAN
07 Director of Admissions .... Mrs. Maggie JOHNSON
08 Librarian .... Ms. Ferne L. WEIMER
30 Director of Development .... Ms. Judy POLLOCK
09 Director of Inst Research/Svcs .... Mr. Richard E. LYNCH
13 Director of Computing Services .... Mr. Chuck WALEK
26 Chief Public Relations Officer .... Vacant
21 Business Manager .... Mr. Paul W. SETTER

Grayson College (M)

6101 Grayson Drive, Denison TX 75020-8299
County: Grayson FICE Identification: 003570
Unit ID: 225070
Telephone: (903) 465-6030 Carnegie Class: Assoc/Pub-R-M
FAX Number: (903) 463-5284 Calendar System: Semester
URL: www.grayson.edu
Established: 1963 Annual Undergrad Tuition & Fees (In-District): $1,950
Enrollment: 4,973 Coed
Affiliation or Control: State/Local IRS Status: 501(c)3
Highest Offering: Associate Degree
Program: Occupational; 2-Year Principally Bachelor's Creditable
Accreditation: SC, ADNUR, DA, EMT, MLTAD

01 President .... Dr. Jeremy P. MCMILLEN
05 Vice President of Instruction .... Dr. Jeanie HARDIN
10 Vice President of Business Services .... Mr. Giles BROWN
13 Vice Pres of Information Technology .... Mr. Gary PAIKOWSKI
32 Vice President Student Services .... Vacant
31 Vice Pres Resource/Community Devel .... Dr. Roy E. RENFRO
07 Director of Admissions/Records .... Vacant
37 Director of Financial Aid .... Ms. Donna KING
14 Director of Computer Center .... Mr. Mike BROWN
19 Director Campus Police .... Mr. Andy MACPHERSON
26 Dir of Public Information/Marketing .... Mrs. Shelle R. CASSELL
21 Director of Fiscal Services .... Mr. Danny HYATT
40 Bookstore Manager .... Ms. Brenda FOX
41 Athletic Director .... Ms. Theresa BARNETT

Hallmark College of Technology (N)

10401 IH-10 W, San Antonio TX 78230-1737
County: Bexar FICE Identification: 010509
Unit ID: 225201
Telephone: (210) 690-9000 Carnegie Class: Assoc/PrivFP
FAX Number: (210) 697-8225 Calendar System: Other
URL: www.hallmarkcollege.edu
Established: 1969 Annual Undergrad Tuition & Fees: $27,681
Enrollment: 729 Coed
Affiliation or Control: Proprietary IRS Status: 501(c)3
Highest Offering: Master's
Program: Occupational; Technical Emphasis
Accreditation: ACCSC, MAC

00 College Systems President .... Mr. Joseph B. FISHER
01 Campus President .... Mr. Brent FESSLER
12 Campus President-Aeronautics .... Mr. Douglas DUNN
05 Dean of Academics .... Dr. Eric SMITH
05 Vice Pres of Academics .... Mr. Sal ROSS
26 Vice President of Marketing .... Ms. Sonia ROSS

Hardin-Simmons University (O)

2200 Hickory, Abilene TX 79698-0001
County: Taylor FICE Identification: 003571
Unit ID: 225247

Telephone: (325) 670-1000 Carnegie Class: Master's M
FAX Number: (325) 670-1267 Calendar System: Semester
URL: www.hsutx.edu
Established: 1891 Annual Undergrad Tuition & Fees: $23,465
Enrollment: 2,301 Coed
Affiliation or Control: Baptist IRS Status: 501(c)3
Highest Offering: Doctorate
Program: Liberal Arts And General; Teacher Preparatory; Professional
Accreditation: SC, ACBSP, MUS, NURSE, PTA, SW, THEOL

01 President ....Dr. Lanny HALL
05 Provost & Chief Academic Officer ....Dr. Thomas V. BRISCO
10 Sr VP for Finance & Management ....Mr. Harold R. PRESTON
30 VP for Institutional Advancement ....Mr. Mike HAMMACK
32 Vice Pres for Student Development ....Dr. Dave ROZEBOOM
84 Interim VP for Enrollment Mgmt ....Mrs. Vicki HOUSE
07 Assoc VP for Enrollment Svcs ....Mr. Jim JONES
04 Exec Assistant to the President ....Ms. Vicki D. HOUSE
53 Dean Irvin School of Education ....Dr. Pamela K. WILLIFORD
49 Dean College of Liberal Arts ....Dr. Alan STAFFORD
50 Dean Kelley College of Business ....Mr. Michael MONHOLLON
64 Dean College of Fine Arts ....Dr. Robert TUCKER
73 Dean Logsdon School of Theology ....Dr. Don WILLIFORD
58 Dean of Graduate Studies ....Dr. Nancy KUCINSKI
66 Dean School of Nursing ....Dr. Nina OUIMETTE
81 Dean School Sciences/Mathematics ....Dr. Christopher L. MCNAIR
14 Assoc Vice Pres Technical Services ....Mr. Travis P. SEEKINS
21 Assoc VP/Controller for Finance/Mgt ....Mr. Don P. ASHMORE
38 Assoc VP Academic Advising/Retent ....Mrs. Gracie CARROLL
08 Dean/Dir of University Libraries ....Mrs. Alice W. SPECHT
09 Director of Institutional Research ....Mrs. Lori BLAKE
06 Registrar ....Mrs. Kacey HIGGINS
35 Dean of Students ....Mr. Forrest MCMILLAN
29 Director of Alumni Relations ....Mrs. Britt E. JONES
19 Chief of Police ....Mr. Frank LOZA
23 University Nurse ....Mrs. Sue A. BIGGS
42 Chaplain ....Dr. Kelly PIGOTT
39 Director of Housing ....Mr. Caleb STEED
36 Director of Career Services ....Mrs. Kelley WOOD
15 Director of Human Resources ....Mr. John SNAPP
27 Interim Dir of Univ Communications ....Mr. James STONE
37 Dir Student Fin Aid & Scholarships ....Mrs. Bridget MOORE
18 Facilities Services Director ....Mr. Tim MCCARRY
41 Athletic Director ....Mr. John M. NEESE
85 Director of International Studies ....Dr. Allan J. LANDWER
26 Public Relations Director ....Mrs. Janlyn THAXTON
93 Coordinator of Minority Studies ....Dr. Joe H. ALCORTA
28 Coord of Student Diversity Programs ....Dr. Kelvin J. KELLEY

Hill College (A)

112 Lamar Drive, Hillsboro TX 76645-2711
County: Hill FICE Identification: 003573
Unit ID: 225371
Telephone: (254) 659-7500 Carnegie Class: Assoc/Pub-R-M
FAX Number: (254) 582-7591 Calendar System: Semester
URL: www.hillcollege.edu
Established: 1923 Annual Undergrad Tuition & Fees (In-District): $1,710
Enrollment: 4,381 Coed
Affiliation or Control: Local IRS Status: 501(c)3
Highest Offering: Associate Degree
Program: Occupational; 2-Year Principally Bachelor's Creditable
Accreditation: SC

01 President ....Dr. Sheryl S. KAPPUS
04 Executive Asst to the President ....Ms. Sharon MIDDLEBROOK
05 Vice President Instruction ....Mr. Rex PARCELLS
11 Vice Pres Administrative Services ....Mr. Billy D. CURBO
32 Vice President Student Services ....Dr. Robert RIZA
13 Vice Pres Information Technology ....Mrs. Jessie WHITE
84 Exec Dean of Enrollment Services ....Ms. Lizza TRENKLE
35 Exec Dean Student Success ....Ms. Leslie CANNON
09 Dean Inst Research/Effectiveness ....Dr. Teri WALKER
21 Dean Financial Services ....Mrs. Debbie GERIK
08 Librarian ....Mr. Joseph SHAUGHNESSY
08 Librarian - Cleburne Campus ....Mr. Kevin HENARD
15 Human Resources Executive Director ....Dr. Heather KISSACK
12 Exec Dir JCC/Dean of Students ....Mr. Bill GILKER
41 Athletic Director ....Mr. Paul BROWN
26 Director of Marketing & Public Rels ....Mr. Jim DALGLISH
06 Dir Student Records & Registration ....Ms. Sherry DAVIS
37 Director of Financial Aid ....Ms. Susan RUSSELL
18 Facilities Coordinator ....Ms. Wendie HERNANDEZ

Houston Baptist University (B)

7502 Fondren Road, Houston TX 77074-3298
County: Harris FICE Identification: 003576
Unit ID: 225399
Telephone: (281) 649-3000 Carnegie Class: Master's M
FAX Number: (281) 649-3012 Calendar System: Semester
URL: www.hbu.edu
Established: 1960 Annual Undergrad Tuition & Fees: $27,930
Enrollment: 2,589 Coed
Affiliation or Control: Southern Baptist IRS Status: 501(c)3
Highest Offering: Master's
Program: Liberal Arts And General; Teacher Preparatory; Professional
Accreditation: SC, ACBSP, NUR

01 President ....Dr. Robert B. SLOAN
05 Provost ....Dr. John Mark REYNOLDS
10 Vice President Financial Operations ....Ms. Sandra N. MOONEY
26 Vice Pres University Communication ....Mr. Kimberly GAYNOR
30 Vice President for Advancement ....Mr. Charles BACARISSE
26 Vice Pres University Relations ....Mrs. Sharon E. SAUNDERS
84 Vice Pres Enrollment Management ....Mr. James STEEN
20 Associate Provost ....Ms. Ritamarie TAUER
20 Associate Provost ....Dr. Robert D. STACEY
21 Asst VP for Treasury Operations ....Mr. Hugh MCCLUNG
79 Dean College Arts & Humanities ....Dr. Chris HAMMONS
50 Dean School of Business ....Dr. Mohan KURUVILLA
81 Dean College of Science & Math ....Dr. Doris C. WARREN
92 Director Honors College ....Dr. Gary HARTENBURG
53 Dean School of Education ....Dr. Cynthia SIMPSON
66 Dean Sch Nursing & Allied Hlth ....Dr. Renae SCHUMANN
41 Athletic Director ....Mr. Steve C. MONIACI
06 University Registrar ....Ms. Erinn HUGHES
40 Director of University Store ....Mr. Anthony MARTIN
07 Director of Admissions ....Mr. Eduardo BORGES
08 Director of Libraries ....Ms. Ann NOBLE
42 University Minister ....Mr. Tom MOSLEY
21 Financial Analyst ....Ms. Loree WATSON
88 Assoc Director Scholarships ....Ms. Janet FENG
29 Dir of Alumni Relations & Advance ....Ms. Amy YOUNGBLOOD
39 Director Housing Operations ....Mr. Mark ENDRASKE
13 Dir of Information Technology ....Mr. Trent CARROLL
19 Interim Chief of Police ....Mr. Charles RAGAIN
09 Sr Director Institutional Research ....Dr. Phil RHODES
32 Vice President Student Life ....Mr. Whittington GOODWIN
88 SACS Liaison ....Ms. Ritamarie TAUER
04 Sr Admin Asst to the President ....Ms. Judy FERGUSON
04 Admin Asst to the President ....Ms. Karen FRANCIES
15 Director of Human Resources ....Ms. Jennifer BOATWRIGHT
18 Dir of Maintenance & Operations ....Mr. Gary DYKE
36 Dir of Career & Calling ....Ms. Colette CROSS
37 Sr Dir Financial Aid & Scholarships ....Ms. Veronica GABBARD
96 Cost Control Analyst ....Ms. Jody WILDING-FARRELL

Houston Community College (C)

3100 Main Street, Houston TX 77002
County: Harris FICE Identification: 010633
Unit ID: 225423
Telephone: (713) 718-2000 Carnegie Class: Assoc/Pub-U-MC
FAX Number: N/A Calendar System: Semester
URL: www.hccs.edu
Established: 1971 Annual Undergrad Tuition & Fees (In-State): $813
Enrollment: 58,908 Coed
Affiliation or Control: State IRS Status: 501(c)3
Highest Offering: Associate Degree
Program: Occupational; 2-Year Principally Bachelor's Creditable
Accreditation: SC, CAHIIM, COARC, DA, DH, DMS, EMT, ENGT, HT, MAC, MLTAD, NMT, OTA, PTAA, RAD, SURGT

01 Acting Chancellor ....Dr. Renee BYAS
04 Executive Officer to the Chancellor ....Ms. Shantay GRAYS
43 Acting General Counsel ....Ms. Destinee WAITERS
05 Vice Chancellor of Academic Affairs ....Dr. Charles M. COOK
32 Vice Chancellor Student Success ....Dr. Diana PINO
14 Vice Chancellor Information Tech ....Dr. William E. CARTER
45 VC Planning and Inst Effectiveness ....Vacant
11 Chief Administration Officer ....Mr. Winston DAHSE
15 Chief Human Resource Officer ....Ms. Janet MAY
22 Director EEO/Compliance ....Mr. David CROSS
10 Controller/Chief Financial Officer ....Mr. Ron E. DEFALCO
26 Chief Communications Officer ....Mr. Daniel ARGUIJO, JR.
76 Dean Health Science Programs ....Dr. Michael EDWARDS
66 Department Chair Vocational Nursing ....Ms. Deborah SIMMONS-JOHNSON
07 Director of Admissions & Registrar ....Ms. Mary LEMBURG
09 Exec Dir of Inst Research & Innov ....Dr. Martha OBURN
46 Director of Resource Development ....Vacant
102 Interim Exec Director Foundation ....Ms. Cydney PETERS
19 Environmental Safety Manager ....Mr. Oscar GONZALES
12 President-Northeast College ....Dr. Margaret FORD FISHER
12 President-Southwest College ....Dr. Fena GARZA
12 President-Central College ....Dr. William HARMON
12 President-Southeast College ....Dr. Irene PORCARELLO
12 President-Northwest College ....Dr. Zachary HODGES
12 President-Coleman College ....Dr. Betty K. YOUNG
85 Int Dir International Initiatives ....Mr. Ricardo SOLIS
18 Dir Bldg Operations/Property Mgmt ....Ms. Jackquline SWINDLE
29 Alumni Relations Officer ....Ms. Andrea STOLLER
96 Ex Dir Purchasing/Procurement Oper ....Mr. Rogelio ANASAGASTI
35 Director Student/Financial Services ....Mr. Hernando BALDONADO
37 Ex Director Student Financial Aid ....Ms. JoEllen SOUCIER
20 Assoc VC of Academic Instruction ....Dr. Steve LEVEY
21 Ex Dir Financial & Budget Control ....Dr. Karla BENDER
06 Registrar ....Ms. Mary LEMBURG

Houston Graduate School of Theology (D)

2501 Central Parkway, Suite A19, Houston TX 77092-7726
County: Harris FICE Identification: 023202
Unit ID: 246345
Telephone: (713) 942-9505 Carnegie Class: Spec/Faith
FAX Number: (713) 942-9506 Calendar System: Semester
URL: www.hgst.edu
Established: 1983 Annual Graduate Tuition & Fees: $10,600
Enrollment: 185 Coed
Affiliation or Control: Independent Non-Profit IRS Status: 501(c)3
Highest Offering: Doctorate; No Undergraduates
Program: Professional; Religious Emphasis
Accreditation: THEOL

01 President ....Dr. James FURR
05 Assoc Dean-Curriculum & Instruction ....Dr. Chuck PITTS
73 Dir of D.Min Program ....Dr. Becky L. TOWNE
10 Chief Financial Officer ....Ms. Janell RAY
06 Registrar ....Ms. Kristin DOMERACKI
08 Director of Library Services ....Ms. Janet KENNARD

Howard College (E)

1001 Birdwell Lane, Big Spring TX 79720-3799
County: Howard FICE Identification: 003574
Unit ID: 225520
Telephone: (432) 264-5000 Carnegie Class: Assoc/Pub-R-M
FAX Number: (432) 264-5082 Calendar System: Semester
URL: www.howardcollege.edu
Established: 1945 Annual Undergrad Tuition & Fees (In-District): $2,222
Enrollment: 4,637 Coed
Affiliation or Control: State/Local IRS Status: 501(c)3
Highest Offering: Associate Degree
Program: Occupational; 2-Year Principally Bachelor's Creditable
Accreditation: SC, ADNUR, CAHIIM, COARC, DH, EMT, RAD, SURGT

01 President ....Dr. Cheryl T. SPARKS
03 Executive Vice President ....Mr. Terry HANSEN
05 Vice President Academic Affairs ....Dr. Amy BURCHETT
12 Campus Dean Academic Affairs SWCID ....Mr. Danny CAMPBELL
12 Campus Dean Student Affairs SWCID ....Mrs. Nancy BONURA
12 Provost San Angelo ....Ms. LeAnne BYRD
12 Executive Dean Big Spring ....Mrs. Kinsey HANSEN
103 Campus Dean for Workforce Devel ....Vacant
04 Executive Asst to the President ....Ms. Julie BAILEY
06 Registrar ....Mr. Scott RAINES
08 Dean of Libararies ....Mr. Luis KINCADE
14 Director of Computer Services ....Mr. Ed ROBERTS
56 Distance Learning Coordinator ....Ms. Kym CLARK
18 Director of Physical Plant ....Mr. Terry HANSON
27 Director Effectiveness/Information ....Ms. Cindy SMITH
41 Athletic Director ....Mr. Britt SMITH
10 Director of Finance ....Ms. Brenda CLAXTON
15 Director Human Resources/Payroll ....Ms. Rhonda KERNICK
96 Director Business Services ....Mr. Jason MIMS
37 Director of Financial Aid ....Ms. Liz ADAMSON
35 Director Student Affairs ....Ms. Lorinda HERROD
21 Assistant Controller-Student Acct ....Ms. Margaret CERVANTES
21 Assistant Controller-Fiscal Acct ....Mrs. Cherry FURQUERON
30 Director Institutional Advancement ....Mrs. Jan FORESYTH

Howard Payne University (F)

1000 Fisk Street, Brownwood TX 76801-2794
County: Brown FICE Identification: 003575
Unit ID: 225548
Telephone: (325) 646-2502 Carnegie Class: Bac/Diverse
FAX Number: (325) 649-8975 Calendar System: Semester
URL: www.hputx.edu
Established: 1889 Annual Undergrad Tuition & Fees: $23,200
Enrollment: 1,130 Coed
Affiliation or Control: Baptist IRS Status: 501(c)3
Highest Offering: Master's
Program: Liberal Arts And General; Teacher Preparatory
Accreditation: SC, IACBE, MUS, SW

01 President ....Dr. William N. ELLIS
05 Provost/Chief Academic Officer ....Dr. Mark TEW
10 Sr Vice Pres Finance/Administration ....Mrs. Brenda ALEXANDER
32 Vice Pres Stdnt Life/Dean Stdnts ....Dr. Brent A. MARSH
44 Vice President Development ....Mr. Randy YEAKLEY
84 Assoc VP for Enrollment Management ....Mr. Kevin KIRK
15 Asst VP for Bus & Hum Resources ....Mr. Bill FISHBACK
06 Registrar ....Mrs. Lana WAGNER
37 Director Financial Aid ....Mrs. Glenda HUFF
07 Director of Admission ....Mrs. P.J GRAMLING
36 Dir Academic Testing/Career Svcs ....Ms. Wendy MCNEELEY
27 Director of Publications ....Mr. Kyle C. MIZE
09 Director Institutional Research ....Ms. Shannon PITTMAN
41 Athletic Director ....Mr. Mike JONES
91 Database Administrator ....Mr. Randy GINTHER
90 Computer Network Administrator ....Mr. Russell EZZELL
29 Coordinator of Alumni Relations ....Ms. Nancy HEADY
18 Facilities Coordinator ....Ms. Debbie CHILDS
88 Alumni and Media Relations Asst ....Ms. Kathy JAMES
04 Executive Assistant to President ....Ms. Susan HAYNES
38 University Counselor ....Dr. Athena BEAN
56 Dean Extended Education ....Dr. Robert TUCKER
08 Dean of Libraries ....Mrs. Nancy K. ANDERSON
81 Dean School of Science & Math ....Dr. Pam BRYANT
50 Dean School of Business ....Dr. Leslie F. PLAGENS
53 Dean School of Ecucation ....Dr. Mike ROSATO
64 Dean Sch Music/Fine Arts/Extend Ed ....Dr. Robert TUCKER
73 Dean School of Christian Studies ....Dr. Donnie AUVENSHINE
79 Dean School of Humanities ....Dr. Justin MURPHY

Huston-Tillotson University (G)

900 Chicon Street, Austin TX 78702-2795
County: Travis FICE Identification: 003577
Unit ID: 225575
Telephone: (512) 505-3000 Carnegie Class: Bac/A&S
FAX Number: (512) 505-3190 Calendar System: Semester
URL: www.htu.edu
Established: 1875 Annual Undergrad Tuition & Fees: $13,494
Enrollment: 918 Coed

Affiliation or Control: Multiple Protestant Denominations
IRS Status: 501(c)3
Highest Offering: Baccalaureate
Program: Liberal Arts And General
Accreditation: **SC**, ACBSP

01 President & CEO .... Dr. Larry L. EARVIN
04 Executive Assistant to President .... Dr. Terry S. SMITH
05 Provost/VP Academic & Student Affs .... Dr. Vicki V. LOTT
32 Dean of Student Affairs .... Dr. LaTanya LOWERY
30 VP for Institutional Advancement .... Dr. Roderick L. SMOTHERA
10 VP for Administration & Finance .... Mrs. Valerie D. HILL
20 Associate Provost .... Dr. Archibald W. VANDERPUYE
08 Director Library & Media Services .... Ms. Patricia A. WILKINS
36 Director Career & Grad Development .... Mr. Paul LEVERINGTON
41 Director of Athletics .... Vacant
84 Dean Enrollment Management .... Vacant
06 Registrar .... Mrs. Earnestine J. STRICKLAND
25 Dir Sponsored PRGs/Title III Coord .... Vacant
09 Director Inst Plng/Research/Assess .... Ms. Jaya K. SONI
13 Dir Information Technology .... Vacant
26 Dir Public Relations & Marketing .... Mrs. Linda Y. JACKSON
18 Director of Facilities .... Mr. William S. GRIMES
30 Director of Development/Major Gifts .... Mr. John A. SIMPSON
29 Director of Alumni Affairs .... Ms. LaJuana R. NAPIER
35 Director of Campus Life .... Ms. Destiny S. MCKINNEY
88 Dir of Ctr for Academic Excellence .... Ms. Ericka D. JONES
15 Director of Human Resources .... Ms. Joy S. KING
37 Director Student Financial Aid .... Mr. Antonio HOLLOWAY
38 Dir Counseling & Consultation Ctr .... Vacant
42 University Chaplain .... Rev. Donald E. BREWINGTON
07 Interim Director of Admission .... Mr. Dwayne R. SHORTER
49 Dean of Arts & Sciences .... Vacant
50 Dean of Business & Technology .... Dr. Steven EDMOND
88 Director of Disability Services .... Vacant
23 University Nurse .... Ms. Ebony S. BEST

International Academy of Design and Technology (A)
4511 Horizon Hill Boulevard, San Antonio TX 78229
Telephone: (210) 530-9449 Identification: 666733
Accreditation: **ACICS**

† Main campus is International Academy of Design and Technology in Tampa, FL.

International Business College (B)
5700 Cromo Drive, El Paso TX 79912
County: El Paso FICE Identification: 009082
Unit ID: 225779
Telephone: (915) 842-0422 Carnegie Class: Assoc/PrivFP
FAX Number: (915) 584-5325 Calendar System: Other
URL: www.icbelpaso.edu
Established: Annual Undergrad Tuition & Fees: $12,762
Enrollment: 323 Coed
Affiliation or Control: Proprietary IRS Status: Proprietary
Highest Offering: Associate Degree
Program: Occupational
Accreditation: **ACICS**

01 President .... Margie AGUILAR

International Business College-East Campus (C)
1155 North Zaragosa Road, El Paso TX 79907
Telephone: (915) 859-0422 Identification: 770622
Accreditation: **ACICS**

† Main campus is International Business College in El Paso, TX.

ITT Technical Institute (D)
551 Ryan Plaza Drive, Arlington TX 76011-3919
Telephone: (817) 794-5100 FICE Identification: 023286
Accreditation: **ACICS**

† Main campus is ITT Technical Institute in Indianapolis, IN.

ITT Technical Institute (E)
6330 Highway 290 E, Suite 150, Austin TX 78723-1035
Telephone: (512) 467-6800 Identification: 666551
Accreditation: **ACICS**

† Main campus is ITT Technical Institute in Indianapolis, IN.

ITT Technical Institute (F)
921 West Belt Line Road, Desoto TX 75115
Telephone: (972) 274-8600 Identification: 770633
Accreditation: **ACICS**

† Main campus is ITT Technical Institute in Indianapolis, IN.

ITT Technical Institute (G)
2950 South Gessner, Houston TX 77063-3751
Telephone: (713) 952-2294 FICE Identification: 023287
Accreditation: **ACICS**

† Main campus is ITT Technical Institute in Indianapolis, IN.

ITT Technical Institute (H)
15651 North Freeway, Houston TX 77090-5903
Telephone: (281) 873-0512 Identification: 666554
Accreditation: **ACICS**

† Main campus is ITT Technical Institute in Indianapolis, IN.

ITT Technical Institute (I)
2101 Waterview Parkway, Richardson TX 75080-2208
Telephone: (972) 690-9100 Identification: 666327
Accreditation: **ACICS**

† Main campus is ITT Technical Institute in Indianapolis, IN.

ITT Technical Institute (J)
5700 Northwest Parkway, San Antonio TX 78249-3303
Telephone: (210) 694-4612 FICE Identification: 030714
Accreditation: **ACICS**

† Main campus is ITT Technical Institute in Indianapolis, IN.

ITT Technical Institute (K)
2895 NE Loop 410, San Antonio TX 78218
Telephone: (210) 651-8500 Identification: 770635
Accreditation: **ACICS**

† Main campus is ITT Technical Institute in Indianapolis, IN.

ITT Technical Institute (L)
3700 S Jack Kultgen Expy, Suite 100, Waco TX 76706
Telephone: (254) 881-2200 Identification: 770634
Accreditation: **ACICS**

† Main campus is ITT Technical Institute in Indianapolis, IN.

ITT Technical Institute (M)
1001 Magnolia Avenue, Webster TX 77598-5418
Telephone: (281) 316-4700 Identification: 666552
Accreditation: **ACICS**

† Main campus is ITT Technical Institute in Indianapolis, IN.

Jacksonville College (N)
105 B. J. Albritton Drive, Jacksonville TX 75766-4759
County: Cherokee FICE Identification: 003579
Unit ID: 225876
Telephone: (903) 586-2518 Carnegie Class: Assoc/PrivNFP
FAX Number: (903) 586-0743 Calendar System: Semester
URL: www.jacksonville-college.edu
Established: 1899 Annual Undergrad Tuition & Fees: $8,170
Enrollment: 560 Coed
Affiliation or Control: Baptist IRS Status: 501(c)3
Highest Offering: Associate Degree
Program: 2-Year Principally Bachelor's Creditable
Accreditation: **SC**

01 President .... Dr. Mike SMITH
05 Academic Dean/Registrar .... Mr. Lynn NABI
32 Dean of Students .... Mr. Ken RAWSON
10 Business Officer .... Mr. David PITTMAN
41 Athletic Director .... Mr. Lynn NABI

Jarvis Christian College (O)
Highway 80 E, PR 7631, Hawkins TX 75765-1470
County: Wood FICE Identification: 003637
Unit ID: 225885
Telephone: (903) 730-4890 Carnegie Class: Bac/Diverse
FAX Number: (903) 769-4852 Calendar System: Semester
URL: www.jarvis.edu
Established: 1912 Annual Undergrad Tuition & Fees: $11,369
Enrollment: 603 Coed
Affiliation or Control: Christian Church (Disciples Of Christ)
IRS Status: 501(c)3
Highest Offering: Baccalaureate
Program: Liberal Arts And General; Teacher Preparatory
Accreditation: **#SC**, ACBSP

01 President .... Dr. Lester C. NEWMAN
05 Provost/Vice Pres Academic Affairs .... Dr. Glenell PRUITT
11 Vice Pres Administration & Finance .... Vacant
32 Vice President Student Affairs .... Dr. Orlando LEWIS
30 VP Institutional Advancement/Devel .... Dr. William SMIALEK
45 Vice Pres for Inst Effectiveness .... Dr. Tequecie MEEK
13 Director Information Technology .... Mr. Quinton LATIN
06 Registrar .... Mr. Autry ACREY
35 Dean of Students/Dir of Housing .... Mr. William HAMPTON
29 Director of Alumni Affairs .... Mr. Chris WOOTEN
07 Dir Admissions & Enrollment Svcs .... Ms. Michelin LAMBERT
26 Director Public Relations/Publicity .... Vacant
19 Chief of Security .... Mr. Reginald DICKENS
04 Exec Asst to the President .... Mrs. Cynthia HOLLMAN-STANCIL
88 Dir Title III and Sponsored Program .... Ms. Connie HANNAH-BENNETT
08 Head Librarian .... Mr. Rodney ATKINS
38 Director Career Services .... Mr. Chestley TALLEY
37 Director of Financial Aid .... Ms. Alice COPELAND
41 Athletic Director .... Mrs. Elissia BURWELL
42 College Pastor .... Mr. Olin FREGIA
18 Physical Plant Director .... Mr. Reginald DICKENS
15 Dir HR/Prof Dev & Compliance .... Mrs. Dorothy LANGLEY
09 Dir Institutional Research .... Vacant
108 Dir Assessment .... Vacant

Kaplan College (P)
2241 South Watson Road, Arlington TX 76010
Telephone: (972) 623-4700 Identification: 770544
Accreditation: **ACICS**, COE

† Main campus is Kaplan College in Dallas, TX.

Kaplan College (Q)
6115 Eastex Freeway, Suite A-142, Beaumont TX 77706
Telephone: (409) 833-2722 Identification: 770545
Accreditation: **ACICS**, COE

† Main campus is Kaplan College in San Antonio, TX.

Kaplan College (R)
1900 North Expressway, Brownsville TX 78521
Telephone: (956) 547-8200 Identification: 770595
Accreditation: **ACCSC**, ACICS

† Main campus is Kaplan College in El Paso, TX.

Kaplan College (S)
1620 S Padre Island Drive, Ste 600, Corpus Christi TX 78416
Telephone: (361) 852-2900 Identification: 770597
Accreditation: **ACCSC**, ACICS

† Main campus is Kaplan College in San Antonio, TX.

Kaplan College (T)
12005 Ford Road, Suite 100, Dallas TX 75234
County: Dallas FICE Identification: 032723
Unit ID: 382896
Telephone: (972) 385-1446 Carnegie Class: Assoc/PrivFP
FAX Number: (972) 385-0641 Calendar System: Other
URL: dallas.kaplancollege.com
Established: Annual Undergrad Tuition & Fees: $14,780
Enrollment: 320 Coed
Affiliation or Control: Proprietary IRS Status: Proprietary
Highest Offering: Associate Degree
Program: Occupational; Technical Emphasis
Accreditation: **ACICS**, COE, @PTAA

01 Campus Director .... Mr. Jeffrey THORUD

Kaplan College (U)
8360 Burnham Road, Ste 100, El Paso TX 79907
County: El Paso FICE Identification: 025919
Unit ID: 246266
Telephone: (915) 595-1935 Carnegie Class: Not Classified
FAX Number: N/A Calendar System: Other
URL: www.kaplan.edu
Established: Annual Undergrad Tuition & Fees: $14,982
Enrollment: 743 Coed
Affiliation or Control: Proprietary IRS Status: Proprietary
Highest Offering: Associate Degree
Program: Occupational
Accreditation: **ACCSC**, ACICS, MAC

01 President .... Vacant
05 Director of Education .... Ms. Nova PENA

Kaplan College (V)
2001 Beach Street, Suite 201, Fort Worth TX 76103
Telephone: (817) 413-2000 Identification: 770598
Accreditation: **ACCSC**, ACICS

† Main campus is Kaplan College in San Antonio, TX.

Kaplan College (W)
6410 McPherson, Laredo TX 78041
Telephone: (956) 717-5909 Identification: 770546
Accreditation: **ACICS**, COE

† Main campus is Kaplan College in San Antonio, TX.

Kaplan College (X)
1421 9th Street, Lubbock TX 79401
Telephone: (806) 765-7051 Identification: 770547
Accreditation: **ACICS**, COE

† Main campus is Kaplan College in San Antonio, TX.

Kaplan College (A)

1500 S Jackson Road, McAllen TX 78503
Telephone: (956) 630-1499 Identification: 770596
Accreditation: ACCSC

† Main campus is Kaplan College in San Antonio, TX.

Kaplan College (B)

7142 San Pedro Avenue, Suite 100,
San Antonio TX 78216
County: Bexar FICE Identification: 009466
Unit ID: 364955
Telephone: (210) 733-0777 Carnegie Class: Assoc/PrivFP
FAX Number: (210) 340-6603 Calendar System: Other
URL: nsan-antonio.kaplancollege.com
Established: Annual Undergrad Tuition & Fees: $15,879
Enrollment: 730 Coed
Affiliation or Control: Proprietary IRS Status: Proprietary
Highest Offering: Associate Degree
Program: Occupational; 2-Year Principally Bachelor's Creditable; Technical Emphasis
Accreditation: ACCSC, ACICS, MAC

01 Executive Director .... Rene CANDELARIA

Kaplan College (C)

6441 NW Loop 410, San Antonio TX 78238
County: Bexar FICE Identification: 031158
Unit ID: 431886
Telephone: (210) 308-8584 Carnegie Class: Not Classified
FAX Number: (210) 308-8985 Calendar System: Other
URL: www.kaplancollege.com
Established: Annual Undergrad Tuition & Fees: $15,879
Enrollment: 548 Coed
Affiliation or Control: Proprietary IRS Status: Proprietary
Highest Offering: Associate Degree
Program: Occupational
Accreditation: ACICS, CAHIIM, COE

01 President .... Ms. Liza RINCONES

KD Studio-Actors Conservatory (D)

2600 N Stemmons Fwy, Suite 117, Dallas TX 75207-2111
County: Dallas FICE Identification: 023182
Unit ID: 225991
Telephone: (214) 638-0484 Carnegie Class: Assoc/PrivFP
FAX Number: (214) 630-5140 Calendar System: Semester
URL: www.kdstudio.com
Established: 1979 Annual Undergrad Tuition & Fees: $13,554
Enrollment: 164 Coed
Affiliation or Control: Proprietary IRS Status: Proprietary
Highest Offering: Associate Degree
Program: 2-Year Principally Bachelor's Creditable; Fine Arts Emphasis
Accreditation: THEA

00 Chief Executive Officer .... Ms. Kathy TYNER
01 President .... Mr. Gary TYNER, JR.
05 Director/CAO .... Mr. T. A TAYLOR

Kilgore College (E)

1100 Broadway, Kilgore TX 75662-3299
County: Gregg FICE Identification: 003580
Unit ID: 226019
Telephone: (903) 984-8531 Carnegie Class: Assoc/Pub-R-M
FAX Number: (903) 983-8600 Calendar System: Semester
URL: www.kilgore.edu
Established: 1935 Annual Undergrad Tuition & Fees (In-District): $1,368
Enrollment: 6,231 Coed
Affiliation or Control: Local IRS Status: 501(c)3
Highest Offering: Associate Degree
Program: Occupational; 2-Year Principally Bachelor's Creditable
Accreditation: SC, ADNUR, PTAA, SURGT

01 President .... Dr. William M. HOLDA
05 Vice President of Instruction .... Dr. Gerald M. STANGLIN
11 Vice Pres Administrative Services .... Mr. Duane MCNANEY
32 Vice President Student Development .... Dr. Mike JENKINS
57 Div Dean Liberal & Fine Arts .... Dr. Richard HARRISON
81 Div Dean Science/Math/Health Sci .... Mrs. Louise WILEY
50 Div Dean Business/Tech/Lang Devel/ .... Mr. Randy LEWELLEN
88 Div Dean of Public Services .... Mr. Randy LEWELLEN
72 Dir of Adult Voc Educ .... Ms. Martha WOODRUFF
12 Div Dean of Longview Center .... Dr. Julie H. FOWLER
06 Registrar .... Mrs. Staci MARTIN
15 Director of Human Resources .... Mr. Tony JOHNSON
13 Director of Information Technology .... Mr. John COLVILLE
08 Director Library .... Ms. Kathy FAIR
40 Manager of Bookstore .... Ms. Carolyn WILLIAMS
18 Director Physical Plant .... Mr. Dalton SMITH
19 Chief of Police .... Chief Martin PESSINK
84 Dir of Marketing & Enrollment Mgmt .... Mr. Trey HATTAWAY
04 Assistant to the President .... Mrs. Nancy LAW
30 Director of Development .... Mrs. Leah GORMAN
37 Financial Aid Officer .... Mrs. Annette MORGAN
85 International Student Advisor .... Mrs. Brenda THORNHILL
27 Coordinator of Public & Sports Info .... Mr. Chris CRADDOCK
09 Coord of Institutional Research .... Ms. Robin HUSKEY
36 Coordinator of Career Services .... Ms. Patty BELL
29 Coordinator of Alumni Relations .... Mrs. Paula JAMERSON
38 Coordinator of Counseling .... Mrs. Pam GATTON
96 Purchasing Agent .... Ms. Tammie PASCOE

Laredo Community College (F)

West End Washington Street, Laredo TX 78040-4395
County: Webb FICE Identification: 003582
Unit ID: 226134
Telephone: (956) 722-0521 Carnegie Class: Assoc/Pub-R-L
FAX Number: (956) 721-5381 Calendar System: Semester
URL: www.laredo.edu
Established: 1946 Annual Undergrad Tuition & Fees (In-District): $3,330
Enrollment: 9,334 Coed
Affiliation or Control: Local IRS Status: 501(c)3
Highest Offering: Associate Degree
Program: Occupational; 2-Year Principally Bachelor's Creditable; Technical Emphasis
Accreditation: SC, ADNUR, OTA, PTAA, RAD

01 President .... Dr. Juan L. MALDONADO
05 Vice President for Instruction .... Dr. Dianna L. MILLER
32 Vice President for Student Services .... Dr. Vincent R. SOLIS
25 Vice President for Resource Develop .... Dr. Nora R. GARZA
10 Chief Admin & Financial Officer .... Mr. Eleazar GONZALEZ
88 Institutional Effectiveness Officer .... Dr. Federico SOLIS, JR.
26 Communications & Outreach Officer .... Ms. Deirdre REYNA
49 Dean Arts & Humanities .... Ms. Marissa GUERRERO-LONGORIA
12 Dean - LCC South .... Mr. Luciano RAMON
103 Dean of Workforce Education .... Ms. Roxanne VEDIA
81 Dean of Sciences .... Mr. J. Alfredo INIGUEZ-JIMENEZ
35 Dean of Student Affairs .... Mr. Robert L. OCHOA
84 Dean of Enrollment & Reg Services .... Dr. Alberto SALINAS
09 Dir Institutional Research & Plng .... Mrs. Maria Luisa RAMIREZ
08 Director of Library .... Ms. Rachel C. BOHMFALK
13 Director Information Technology .... Mr. Jose A. PENA, JR.
21 Comptroller .... Mr. Cesar E. VELA, JR.
18 Director Physical Plant .... Mr. Jacob C. FLORES
26 Dir Marketing/Public Relations .... Mr. Esteban TREVINO, JR.
37 Director of Financial Aid .... Mr. Steven AGUILAR
07 Director Enrollment & Registration .... Mr. Carlos G. PEREZ
51 Director of Continuing Education .... Ms. Sandra L. CORTEZ
41 Athletic Director .... Mr. Troy G. VAN BRUNT
06 Registrar .... Ms. Olga D. RUBIO
15 Director of Human Resources .... Ms. Veronica CARDENAS
102 Dir Donor Relations & Spec Proj .... Ms. Millicent SLAUGHTER
38 Director of Student Success Ctr .... Mr. Carmelino CASTILLO, JR.
96 Director of Purchasing .... Mr. Ramiro V. MARTINEZ
19 Chief of Campus Police .... Mr. Ray CORTEZ
23 Director of Health Services .... Ms. Melissa GARCIA
24 Associate Director of Media Center .... Mr. Ceferino IZAGUIRRE

Le Cordon Bleu College of Culinary Arts in Austin (G)

3110 Esperanza Crossing Suite 100, Austin TX 78758
County: Travis FICE Identification: 025693
Unit ID: 364973
Telephone: (512) 837-2665 Carnegie Class: Assoc/PrivFP
FAX Number: (512) 977-9753 Calendar System: Other
URL: www.chefs.edu/austin
Established: 1981 Annual Undergrad Tuition & Fees: $12,567
Enrollment: 835 Coed
Affiliation or Control: Proprietary IRS Status: Proprietary
Highest Offering: Associate Degree
Program: Occupational; Technical Emphasis
Accreditation: ACICS, ACFEI

01 President .... Steve SMITH

Le Cordon Bleu College of Culinary Arts in Dallas (H)

11830 Webb Chapel Road, Suite 1200, Dallas TX 75234
Telephone: (214) 647-8505 Identification: 666728
Accreditation: ACICS

† Main campus is Le Cordon Bleu College of Culinary Arts in Austin in Austin, TX.

Lee College (I)

511 S Whiting, PO Box 818, Baytown TX 77522-0818
County: Harris FICE Identification: 003583
Unit ID: 226204
Telephone: (281) 427-5611 Carnegie Class: Assoc/Pub-S-MC
FAX Number: (281) 425-6555 Calendar System: Semester
URL: www.lee.edu
Established: 1934 Annual Undergrad Tuition & Fees (In-District): $1,518
Enrollment: 6,207 Coed
Affiliation or Control: State/Local IRS Status: 501(c)3
Highest Offering: Associate Degree
Program: Occupational; 2-Year Principally Bachelor's Creditable; Technical Emphasis
Accreditation: SC, ADNUR, CAHIIM

01 President .... Dr. Dennis BROWN
04 Executive Assistant to President .... Ms. Leslie D. GALLAGHER
05 VP Instruction .... Dr. Cathy KEMPER
32 VP Student Affairs .... Dr. Donnetta SUCHON
10 VP Finance & Administration .... Mr. Steve EVANS
21 Executive Dir Accounting .... Mr. Keith SCHEFFLER
12 Dean of Huntsville Center at TDCJ .... Ms. Donna P. ZUNIGA
30 Exec Dir Institutional Advancement .... Ms. Mary Ann AMELANG
14 Exec Dir Tech/Research/Planning .... Dr. Carolyn A. LIGHTFOOT
18 Director of Physical Plant .... Mr. Mark JAIME
06 Registrar .... Ms. Becki S. GRIFFITH
07 Director College Relations .... Mr. Steve LESTARJETTE
96 Director Purchasing .... Mr. Mike SPARKES
31 Director of Community Education .... Ms. Kimberly WHITTINGTON
15 Director Human Resources .... Ms. Amanda SUMMERS
37 Director Financial Aid .... Ms. Sharon MULLINS
41 Director Athletics .... Mr. Roy CHAMPAGNE
102 Director of Foundation & Donor Dev .... Ms. Pam WARFORD
26 Public Relations Manager .... Vacant
29 Director of Grant Dev & Alumni Rel .... Mrs. Virgina "Ginni" WHITTEN
103 Exec Dir Center for Workforce .... Ms. Debi JORDAN

LeTourneau University (J)

PO Box 7001, 2100 S Mobberly Ave,
Longview TX 75607-7001
County: Gregg FICE Identification: 003584
Unit ID: 226231
Telephone: (903) 233-3000 Carnegie Class: Master's M
FAX Number: (903) 233-3101 Calendar System: Semester
URL: www.letu.edu
Established: 1946 Annual Undergrad Tuition & Fees: $25,740
Enrollment: 2,843 Coed
Affiliation or Control: Independent Non-Profit IRS Status: 501(c)3
Highest Offering: Master's
Program: Liberal Arts And General; Teacher Preparatory; Professional
Accreditation: SC, ENG, ENGT, IACBE

01 President .... Dr. Dale A. LUNSFORD
05 Provost & Executive Vice President .... Dr. Philip COYLE
30 Executive Director Development .... Mr. Eric MCCRORY
10 VP Finance/Administration .... Mr. Mike HOOD
32 Dean of Students .... Mr. Corey ROSS
84 VP Enrollment Services .... Dr. Terry CRUSE
20 Assoc VP Provost Office .... Dr. Steven D. MASON
26 Asst VP Enroll Mgmt/Mkt Research .... Mr. Christopher W. FONTAINE
18 Asst VP of Facilities Services .... Mr. Daniel FIEDLER
53 Dean School of Education .... Dr. Wayne JACOBS
50 Dean School of Business .... Dr. Bruce BOWMAN
54 Dean Sch Engineering & Engr Tech .... Dr. Ronald DELAP
49 Dean School of Arts & Sciences .... Dr. Larry FRAZIER
88 Dean School of Aeronautical Science .... Mr. Fred L. RITCHEY
35 Assoc Dean Student Life .... Vacant
08 Director Learning Resource Center .... Mrs. Leslie BOWMAN
41 Director of Athletics .... Ms. Terri DEIKE
46 Director Office of Sponsored Pgms .... Mr. Paul R. BOGGS
106 Director Distance Lrng .... Vacant
13 Chief Information Officer .... Mr. Matthew HENRY
15 Director of Human Resources .... Mr. Sam PALOMARIA
23 Director Health Services .... Ms. Shela B. DAWSON
42 University Chaplain .... Dr. Harold F. CARL
19 Chief of Police .... Mr. Terrance A. TURNER
36 Director of Career Development .... Mr. Steven J. GATTON
06 University Registrar .... Ms. Kathy MAJZNER
07 Director of Admissions .... Mr. Michael VANBROCKLIN
29 Director of Alumni & Parent Rels .... Mrs. Martha STEED
26 Director of Univ Relations .... Ms. Janet RAGLAND
44 Dir of Gift Planning and Endowed .... Mr. Bryan E. BENSON
88 Dir Curriculum/Academic Resources .... Vacant
21 Controller .... Ms. Vikki KEILERS
09 Asst VP for Quality Assurance .... Dr. Pamela JOHNSON
88 Development Officer .... Dr. Tim WATSON
96 Purchasing Agent .... Mrs. Jana CAMPBELL
88 Executive Dir Ctr for Faith & Work .... Mr. Bill PEEL
04 Administrative Asst to President .... Ms. Vanessa HUTCHINSON
84 Exec Dir of Enrollment Services .... Mr. Carl ARNOLD
27 Director Marketing & Communication .... Ms. Kate GRONEWALD
28 Director of Diversity .... Vacant
37 Director Student Financial Aid .... Ms. Tracy WATKINS
38 Director Student Counseling .... Vacant

Lighthouse College (K)

9400 North Central Expwy., Ste. 200, Dallas TX 75231
County: Dallas Identification: 667106
Telephone: (214) 368-3680 Carnegie Class: Not Classified
FAX Number: (214) 368-3682 Calendar System: Other
URL: www.lhc.edu
Established: Annual Undergrad Tuition & Fees: $13,450
Enrollment: N/A Coed
Affiliation or Control: Proprietary IRS Status: Proprietary
Highest Offering: Associate Degree
Program: Occupational
Accreditation: ACICS

01 Campus Director .... Ms. Michelle TURNER

Lincoln College of Technology (L)

2915 Alouette Drive, Grand Praire TX 75052
County: Tarrant FICE Identification: 008353
Unit ID: 226277
Telephone: (972) 660-5701 Carnegie Class: Assoc/PrivFP
FAX Number: (972) 660-6148 Calendar System: Other

URL: www.lincolntech.com
Established: Annual Undergrad Tuition & Fees: $24,342
Enrollment: 730 Coed
Affiliation or Control: Proprietary IRS Status: Proprietary
Highest Offering: Associate Degree
Program: Occupational
Accreditation: ACCSC

Code	Title	Name
01	Executive Director	Mr. Paul MCGURIK

Lone Star College System (A)

5000 Research Forest Drive,
The Woodlands TX 77381-4356
County: Harris FICE Identification: 011145
Unit ID: 227182
Telephone: (832) 813-6500 Carnegie Class: Assoc/Pub-S-MC
FAX Number: N/A Calendar System: Semester
URL: www.lonestar.edu
Established: 1972 Annual Undergrad Tuition & Fees (In-District): $1,600
Enrollment: 77,877 Coed
Affiliation or Control: State/Local IRS Status: 501(c)3
Highest Offering: Associate Degree
Program: Occupational; 2-Year Principally Bachelor's Creditable
Accreditation: SC, ADNUR, CAHIIM, CEA, COARC, DH, DMS, EMT, MAC, OTA, PTAA, RAD, SURGT

Code	Title	Name
01	Chancellor	Dr. Richard CARPENTER
03	Senior Executive Vice Chancellor	Dr. Rand KEY
05	Vice Chanc Academic Affairs	Dr. Keri ROGERS
32	Vice Chanc Student Success	Ms. Juanita CHRYSANTHOU
10	Vice Chanc for Admin & Finance	Ms. Cynthia GILLIAM
27	Vice Chanc/Chief Info Officer	Mr. Link ALANDER
26	Vice Chancellor External Affairs	Mr. Ray LAUGHTER
43	General Counsel	Mr. Brian NELSON
101	Special Asst to Chancellor/Board	Ms. Helen CLOUGHERTY
12	President of LSC-Kingwood	Dr. Katherine PERSSON
12	President of LSC-Tomball	Dr. Susan KARR
12	President of LSC-North Harris	Dr. Steve HEAD
12	President of LSC-Montgomery	Dr. Austin LANE
12	President of LSC-CyFair	Dr. Audre LEVY
12	President of LSC-University Park	Mr. Shah ARDALAN
27	AVC Marketing & Comm	Ms. Laura MORRIS
18	Chief Fac/Construction Officer	Mr. Jimmy MARTIN
28	HR Dir Equal Employ Relations	Mr. William HERRERA
15	AVC Total Comp/Payroll/HRIS	Ms. Lisa COWART
105	Director Portal Services	Mr. Harry KHEHRA
21	AVC Admin & Finance	Ms. Tammy CORTES
21	AVC Business Services	Ms. Carin HUTCHINS
21	AVC Accounting	Ms. Diane NOVAK
16	Chief Human Resources Officer	Ms. Ronda ROTELLI
106	Exec Director/LSC-Online	Mr. Marwin BRITTO
103	AVC Workforce & Econ Dev	Ms. Linda HEAD
86	AVC Govt Affairs & Inst Adv	Mr. Jonathan DURFIELD
09	Exec Director ORIE	Dr. Christopher TKACH
13	AVC Office Tech Services	Mr. Mario BERRY
08	Director Library/LSC-Kingwood	Mr. Anthony MCMILLIAN
08	Director Library/LSC-Tomball	Ms. Pamela SHAFER
08	Director Library/LSC-North Harris	Ms. Pradeep LELE
08	Director Library/LSC-Cy Fair	Mr. Michael STAFFORD
08	Director Library/LSC-Montgomery	Dr. Janice PEYTON
08	Director Library/LSC-Univ Park	Ms. Shannon HAUSINGER
37	System Exec Dir Financial Aid	Ms. Paula JACKSON
21	Director Internal Audit	Vacant
19	Chief of Police/Dir Pub Safety	Mr. Richard GREGORY
96	Director of Purchasing	Ms. Laura RIVERA

Lubbock Christian University (B)

5601 19th Street, Lubbock TX 79407-2099
County: Lubbock FICE Identification: 003586
Unit ID: 226383
Telephone: (806) 796-8800 Carnegie Class: Master's S
FAX Number: (806) 720-7255 Calendar System: Semester
URL: www.lcu.edu
Established: 1957 Annual Undergrad Tuition & Fees: $18,740
Enrollment: 2,135 Coed
Affiliation or Control: Churches Of Christ IRS Status: 501(c)3
Highest Offering: Master's
Program: Liberal Arts And General; Teacher Preparatory; Professional
Accreditation: SC, NUR, SW

Code	Title	Name
01	President	Mr. L. Timothy PERRIN
03	Executive Vice President	Dr. Brian STARR
05	Provost & Chief Academic Officer	Dr. Rodney B. BLACKWOOD
43	General Counsel	Mrs. Monica BARNARD
26	Vice President University Relations	Mr. John C. KING
10	Vice Pres for Financial Services	Mrs. Tia CLARY
13	Vice President for Technology	Dr. Karl MAHAN
107	Dean Col of Professional Studies	Dr. Gary ESTEP
49	Dean College Liberal Arts/Education	Dr. Susan BLASSINGAME
73	Dean Col Biblical Stds/Behavior Sci	Dr. Jesse LONG
09	Asst VP for Instl Effectiveness	Mr. Randy SELLERS
41	Athletic Director	Mr. Paul HISE
06	Registrar	Mrs. Janice STONE
37	Director of Financial Assistance	Mrs. Amy HARDESTY
35	Dean of Students	Mr. Josh STEPHENS
08	Director of Library Services	Ms. Paula GANNAWAY
18	Director of Campus Facilities	Mr. Mike SELLECK
38	Director Student Counseling	Ms. Janelle M. BUCHANAN
92	Director of Honors Program	Dr. Stacy PATTY
23	Director of Medical Clinic	Dr. Jeff SMITH
13	Director of Technology Services	Mr. Robert SMITH
88	Director of Disability Services	Mrs. Elizabeth JACKSON
39	Director of Residental Life	Mrs. Sunny PARK
07	Director of Admissions	Mr. Charlie WEBB
15	Human Resources Director	Mrs. Brenda LOWE
29	Director Alumni Relations	Dr. Matt PADEN
19	Director of Security	Mr. Michael SMITH
40	Bookstore Manager	Mrs. Denise MCNEILL

Lutheran Seminary Program of the Southwest (C)

PO Box 4790, Austin TX 78765
Telephone: (512) 477-2666 Identification: 770081
Accreditation: &NH

† Main campus is Lutheran School of Theology at Chicago in Chicago, IL.

McLennan Community College (D)

1400 College Drive, Waco TX 76708-1498
County: McLennan FICE Identification: 003590
Unit ID: 226578
Telephone: (254) 299-8000 Carnegie Class: Assoc/Pub-R-L
FAX Number: (254) 299-8654 Calendar System: Semester
URL: www.mclennan.edu
Established: 1965 Annual Undergrad Tuition & Fees (In-District): $2,760
Enrollment: 9,301 Coed
Affiliation or Control: State/Local IRS Status: 501(c)3
Highest Offering: Associate Degree
Program: Occupational; 2-Year Principally Bachelor's Creditable; Nursing Emphasis
Accreditation: SC, ADNUR, CAHIIM, COARC, MLTAD, PTAA, RAD, SURGT

Code	Title	Name
01	President	Dr. Johnette MCKOWN
10	Vice Pres Finance & Administration	Mr. Gene GOOCH
05	Vice President Instruction	Dr. Donald BALMOS
46	Vice President Program Development	Mr. Al POLLARD
32	Vice President Student Services	Dr. Drew CANHAM
09	Vice Pres Research/Plng & Info Tech	Dr. Paul ILLICH
102	Exec Director McLennan CC Found	Mr. Harry HARELIK
11	Director of Administrative Services	Ms. Lori SOUTHERN
37	Director of Financial Aid	Mr. James KUBACAK
26	Director Community Relations	Ms. Lisa WILHELMI
41	Director Athletics	Mrs. Shawn TROCHIM
06	Director Records & Registration	Mr. Herman V. TUCKER
07	Director Admissions & Recruitment	Mrs. Karen CLARK
08	Director Library Services	Mr. Daniel MARTINSEN
15	Director Human Resources	Mrs. Phyllis BLACKWOOD
18	Director Physical Plant	Mrs. Dianne E. FEYERHERM
21	Director Financial Services	Mrs. Terry LECHLER
103	Dean of Workforce Education	Dr. Ronald EPPS
49	Dean of Arts & Sciences	Dr. Fred HILLS
51	Dean of Continuing Education	Mr. Frank GRAVES

McMurry University (E)

1400 Sayles Boulevard, Abilene TX 79697-0002
County: Taylor FICE Identification: 003591
Unit ID: 226587
Telephone: (325) 793-3800 Carnegie Class: Bac/Diverse
FAX Number: (325) 793-6800 Calendar System: Semester
URL: www.mcm.edu
Established: 1923 Annual Undergrad Tuition & Fees: $24,121
Enrollment: 1,368 Coed
Affiliation or Control: United Methodist IRS Status: 501(c)3
Highest Offering: Master's
Program: Liberal Arts And General; Teacher Preparatory
Accreditation: SC, NURSE

Code	Title	Name
01	President	Dr. Sandra HARPER
05	Vice President for Academic Affairs	Dr. Paul FABRIZIO
10	Vice Pres for Financial Affairs	Mrs. Lisa L. WILLIAMS
30	Vice Pres Institutional Advancement	Ms. Debra HULSE
11	Vice Pres for Info & Support Svcs	Mr. Brad POORMAN
105	Webmaster	Mr. Jim QUINNETT
14	Director of Customer Services	Mr. Freddie FAMBLE, JR.
13	Director of Administrative Systems	Ms. Kathy DENSLOW
06	Registrar	Mrs. Carolyn A. CALVERT
08	Director Jay-Rollins Library	Ms. Terry YOUNG
32	Dean of Student Affairs	Ms. Vanessa ROBERTS-BRYAN
81	Dean Sch Natural/Computational Sci	Dr. Alicia WYATT
83	Dean Sch Social Sciences/Religion	Dr. Phil LEMASTERS
57	Dean School of Arts & Letters	Dr. Christina WILSON
50	Dean School of Business	Dr. K. O. LONG
53	Dean School of Education	Dr. Perry Kay HALEY-BROWN
66	Dean School of Nursing	Dr. Nina OUIMETTE
07	Director of Admission	Mr. Jon CROOK
35	Director of Student Activities	Ms. Megan BALDREE
37	Director of Financial Aid	Mrs. Rachel ATKINS
18	Director Physical Plant	Mr. John HARVEY
21	Controller	Mrs. Carole RICKETTS
15	Director of Human Resources	Ms. Lecia HUGHES
108	Dir of Institutional Effectiveness	Dr. Thomas BENOIT
09	Director of Institutional Research	Ms. Terry NIXON
29	Director Alumni/Church Relations	Vacant
38	Director Counseling & Career Svcs	Mr. James GREER
41	Director of Athletics	Mr. Ron HOLMES
42	Dir of Religious Life/Univ Chaplain	Rev. Tim KENNEDY
19	Director of Campus Security	Mr. Mark R. ODOM
23	Director of Health Services	Ms. Ronda HOELSCHER
39	Director of Residence Life	Mr. Jason FELTZ
102	Executive Director Donor Relations	Ms. Nancy SMITH
92	Director Honors Program	Dr. Philip LE MASTERS
106	Director of Online Education	Ms. Vicki DUNNAM

Messenger College (F)

PO Box 1207, Euless TX 76039-1207
FICE Identification: 030926
Unit ID: 417752
Telephone: (417) 624-7070 Carnegie Class: Spec/Faith
FAX Number: (417) 624-5070 Calendar System: Semester
URL: www.messengercollege.edu
Established: 1987 Annual Undergrad Tuition & Fees: $7,285
Enrollment: 60 Coed
Affiliation or Control: Pentecostal Church of God IRS Status: 501(c)3
Highest Offering: Baccalaureate
Program: Liberal Arts And General; Religious Emphasis
Accreditation: TRACS

Code	Title	Name
01	President	Dr. Daniel P. DAVIS
05	Vice President Academic Affairs	Dr. Vernell INGLE
10	Vice President Business Affairs	Ms. Angela HEPPNER
32	Vice President of Student Life	Ms. Rhonda DAVIS
07	Dir of Admissions/Recruitment Coord	Ms. Kayli PRICE
08	Director of Library Services	Ms. Pam INGLE
06	Registrar	Mr. Jose MARTINEZ

Midland College (G)

3600 N Garfield, Midland TX 79705-6397
County: Midland FICE Identification: 009797
Unit ID: 226806
Telephone: (432) 685-4500 Carnegie Class: Assoc/Pub4
FAX Number: (432) 685-4714 Calendar System: Semester
URL: www.midland.edu
Established: 1969 Annual Undergrad Tuition & Fees (In-District): $2,862
Enrollment: 5,530 Coed
Affiliation or Control: Local IRS Status: 501(c)3
Highest Offering: Baccalaureate
Program: Occupational; 2-Year Principally Bachelor's Creditable
Accreditation: SC, CAHIIM, COARC, DMS, EMT

Code	Title	Name
01	President	Dr. Steve THOMAS
03	Executive Vice President	Dr. Richard C. JOLLY
88	Special Advisor to President	Dr. Deana SAVAGE
05	Vice President of Instruction	Dr. Rex PEEBLES
10	Vice Pres Administrative Services	Mr. Rick BENDER
32	Vice President Student Services	Ms. Rita Nell DIFFIE
13	Vice Pres Info Tech/Facilities	Mr. Dennis SEVER
101	Asst to President/Sec to Board	Mrs. Bahola EDWARDS
106	Dean of Distance Learning/Cont Educ	Mr. Dale BEIKIRCH
57	Dean of Fine Arts/Communication	Mr. William FEELER
72	Dean of Applied Technology	Mr. Curt PERVIER
76	Dean of Health Sciences	Ms. Carmen EDWARDS
81	Dean of Math/Natural Sciences	Dr. Margaret WADE
83	Dean Adult/Developmental Education	Dr. Lynda WEBB
30	Exec Dir Inst Advancement/Col Fndn	Ms. Kathy FLETCHER
06	Registrar	Mrs. Angela BALCH
08	Head Librarian	Mr. John DEATS
15	Director of Human Services	Ms. Zaira VALERIANO
18	Director Physical Plant	Mr. Ken RILEY
19	Chief of Police	Mr. Richard MCKEE
27	Dean of Public Information	Ms. Rebecca BELL
35	Director Student Affairs	Vacant
41	Athletic Director	Mr. Forrest ALLEN
09	Dir Institutional Effect/Planning	Mr. Thomas CORLL
37	Director Student Financial Aid	Ms. Yolanda RAMOS
96	Purchasing Agent	Ms. Barbara FENNELL
84	Dean of Enrollment Management	Dr. Michael CHAVEZ
07	Director of Admissions/Recruitment	Mr. Jeremy MARTINEZ

Midwestern State University (H)

3410 Taft Boulevard, Wichita Falls TX 76308-2095
County: Wichita FICE Identification: 003592
Unit ID: 226833
Telephone: (940) 397-4000 Carnegie Class: Master's M
FAX Number: (940) 397-4042 Calendar System: Semester
URL: www.mwsu.edu
Established: 1922 Annual Undergrad Tuition & Fees (In-State): $7,254
Enrollment: 5,916 Coed
Affiliation or Control: State IRS Status: 501(c)3
Highest Offering: Master's
Program: Liberal Arts And General; Teacher Preparatory; Professional
Accreditation: SC, ART, BUS, COARC, DH, ENG, MUS, NURSE, RAD, SW, TED, THEA

Code	Title	Name
01	President	Dr. Jesse W. ROGERS
05	Provost	Dr. Betty STEWART
46	VP Inst Effectiveness	Dr. Robert E. CLARK
10	VP Business Affairs & Finance	Dr. Marilyn FOWLE
30	VP Univ Advncmnt & Stdnt Affairs	Dr. Howard M. FARRELL
32	VP Student Affairs/Enrollment Mgmt	Dr. Keith LAMB
18	Assoc VP Facilities Services	Mr. Kyle OWEN
35	Assoc VP Student Affairs/Enrol Mgmt	Mr. Matthew PARK
14	Director Information Systems	Mr. Randy KIRKPATRICK
06	Registrar	Ms. Darla INGLISH
08	University Librarian	Dr. Clara LATHAM
37	Director of Student Financial Aid	Ms. Kathy PENNARTZ
38	Director of Counseling Center	Dr. Pam MIDGETT

51 Director of Extended Education ..... Dr. Pamela MORGAN
07 Director of Admissions ..... Vacant
19 Chief of Police ..... Mr. Dan WILLIAMS
27 Director Public Info/Marketing ..... Ms. Julie GAYNOR
30 Dir Donor Services and Scholarships ..... Ms. Laura PETERSON
36 Director Career Management Center ..... Mr. Dirk WELCH
41 Director of Athletics ..... Mr. Charles CARR
15 Director of Human Resources ..... Vacant
09 Director Inst Research & Planning ..... Mr. Mark MCCLENDON
21 Controller ..... Ms. Gail FERGUSON
23 Director Vinson Health Center ..... Dr. Keith WILLIAMSON
20 Associate VP Academic Affairs ..... Vacant
50 Dean College Business Admin ..... Dr. Terry PATTON
53 Dean College of Education ..... Dr. Matthew CAPPS
57 Dean College of Fine Arts ..... Vacant
76 Dean Col Health Sci/Human Svcs ..... Dr. James JOHNSTON
79 Dean College Humanities/Social Sci .. Dr. Samuel E. WATSON, III
81 Dean College of Science & Math ..... Dr. Lynn LITTLE
86 Director Board & Govt Relations ..... Ms. Deborah L. BARROW
29 Director of Alumni Relations ..... Ms. Leslee PONDER
88 Director of Academic Success Center ..... Ms. Naoma CLARK
105 Webmaster ..... Mr. Jonathan SHIREY
96 Director of Purchasing ..... Mr. Stephen SHELLEY
88 Dir Disability Support Services ..... Ms. Debra HIGGINBOTHAM
39 Director Housing & Residence Life ..... Mr. Michael MILLS
30 Director University Development ..... Mr. Steve SHIPP
85 Director of International Education ..... Vacant
88 Director Testing Center ..... Ms. Lynn DUCIOAME
88 Director International Services ..... Dr. Randy GLEAN
88 Director Budget & Management ..... Ms. Valarie MAXWELL
88 Director Museum ..... Mrs. Francine CARRARO
88 Director Student Support Services .... Ms. Lisa ESTRADA-HAMBY
88 Campus Postal Supervisor ..... Vacant
92 Coordinator Honors Program ..... Mrs. Juliana LEHMAN-FELTS

National American University-Austin (A)

13801 Burnet Road, Suite 300, Austin TX 78727
Telephone: (512) 651-4700 Identification: 770411
Accreditation: &NH

† Main campus is National American University in Rapid City, SD.

National American University-Georgetown (B)

1015 W University Avenue, Suite 700, Georgetown TX 78628
Telephone: (512) 942-6750 Identification: 770413
Accreditation: &NH

† Main campus is National American University in Rapid City, SD.

National American University-Lewisville (C)

475 State Hwy 121 Bypass #150, Lewisville TX 75067
Telephone: (972) 829-2150 Identification: 770415
Accreditation: &NH

† Main campus is National American University in Rapid City, SD.

National American University-Mesquite (D)

18600 LBJ Freeway, Mesquite TX 75150
Telephone: (972) 773-8800 Identification: 770416
Accreditation: &NH

† Main campus is National American University in Rapid City, SD.

National American University-Richardson (E)

300 N Coit Road, Suite 225, Richardson TX 75080
Telephone: (972) 773-8650 Identification: 770414
Accreditation: &NH

† Main campus is National American University in Rapid City, SD.

National American University-South Austin (F)

6800 Westgate Boulevard, #102, Austin TX 78945
Telephone: (512) 651-4750 Identification: 770412
Accreditation: &NH

† Main campus is National American University in Rapid City, SD.

Navarro College (G)

3200 W Seventh Avenue, Corsicana TX 75110-4899
County: Navarro FICE Identification: 003593
Unit ID: 227146
Telephone: (903) 874-6501 Carnegie Class: Assoc/Pub-R-L
FAX Number: (903) 874-4636 Calendar System: Semester
URL: www.navarrocollege.edu
Established: 1946 Annual Undergrad Tuition & Fees (In-District): $1,424
Enrollment: 10,098 Coed
Affiliation or Control: Local IRS Status: 501(c)3
Highest Offering: Associate Degree
Program: Occupational; 2-Year Principally Bachelor's Creditable
Accreditation: SC, ADNUR, EMT, MLTAD, OTA

01 District President ..... Dr. Barbara KAVALIER
12 President Ellis Co Campuses ..... Dr. Kenneth MARTIN
05 Vice President Academic Affairs ..... Dr. Harold HOUSLEY
10 Vice President Finance & Admin ..... Ms. Gertrud MORENO
30 Vice Pres Institutional Advancement ..... Dr. Tommy STRINGER
32 Vice President Student Services ..... Ms. Maryann HAILEY
84 VP Enroll Mgmt/Stdnt Succ/Inst Stds ..... Mr. T. Dewayne GRAGG
15 Director Human Resources ..... Ms. Marcy BALLEW
26 Director Marketing Relations ..... Mr. Matthew CATES
41 Athletic Director ..... Mr. Roark MONTGOMERY
49 Dean of Arts/Sciences/Humanities ..... Ms. Carol HANES
50 Dean of Business/Prof & Tech Educ ..... Ms. Judy CUTTING
12 Dean of Midlothian Campus ..... Mr. Guy FEATHERSTON
12 Dean of Mexia Campus ..... Ms. Linda DAVIS
21 Comptroller ..... Mr. Aaron YORK-LANGSTON
51 Director Continuing Education ..... Ms. Kristin WALKER
08 Director of Libraries ..... Mr. Tim KEVIL
06 Registrar ..... Mr. David EDWARDS
18 Chief Facilities/Physical Plant ..... Mr. Karl HUMPHRIES
14 Director of Computer Center ..... Ms. Dana HOLLAND
37 Director Student Financial Aid ..... Ms. Kristal NICHOLSON
40 College Store Coordinator ..... Ms. Nancy JOHNSON

North American College (H)

3203 North Sam Houston Pkwy West, Houston TX 77038
County: Harris FICE Identification: 041795
Unit ID: 461795
Telephone: (832) 230-5555 Carnegie Class: Not Classified
FAX Number: (832) 230-5546 Calendar System: Semester
URL: www.northamerican.edu
Established: 2010 Annual Undergrad Tuition & Fees: $11,900
Enrollment: 296 Coed
Affiliation or Control: Non-denominational IRS Status: 501(c)3
Highest Offering: Baccalaureate
Program: Occupational
Accreditation: ACICS

01 President ..... Dr. Reg R. PECEN
05 Vice Pres Academic Affairs-Provost ..... Dr. John C. TOPUZ
11 Vice Pres Administrative Affairs ..... Dr. Can DOGAN

North Central Texas College (I)

1525 W California Street, Gainesville TX 76240-4699
County: Cooke FICE Identification: 003558
Unit ID: 224110
Telephone: (940) 668-7731 Carnegie Class: Assoc/Pub-R-L
FAX Number: (940) 668-6049 Calendar System: Semester
URL: www.nctc.edu
Established: 1924 Annual Undergrad Tuition & Fees (In-District): $1,680
Enrollment: 10,234 Coed
Affiliation or Control: State/Local IRS Status: 501(c)3
Highest Offering: Associate Degree
Program: Occupational; 2-Year Principally Bachelor's Creditable
Accreditation: SC, ADNUR, EMT, SURGT

01 President ..... Dr. Eddie L. HADLOCK
05 Vice President of Instruction ..... Dr. Brent WALLACE
32 Vice President of Student Services ..... Dr. Billy ROESSLER
11 Dean of Administrative Services ..... Dr. Stephen BROYLES
10 Vice President Financial Services ..... Dr. Janie NEIGHBORS
30 Vice Pres Institutional Advancement ..... Ms. Debbie SHARP
12 Dean of Denton County Campuses ..... Mr. Roy CULBERSON
18 Sr Dir of Campus Operations ..... Mr. Robbie BAUGH
12 Dean of Bowie & Graham Campuses ..... Dr. Emily KLEMENT
09 Dir Inst Research & Effectiveness ..... Mr. David BROWN
06 Registrar/Director of Admission ..... Ms. Kari FORD
08 Librarian ..... Ms. Diane ROETHER
37 Financial Aid Director ..... Ms. Ashley TATUM
38 Director of Advisement ..... Mrs. Tracey FLENIKEN
26 Dir Marketing and Public Relations ..... Mrs. Dianne WALTERSCHEID
41 Athletic Director ..... Mr. Van HEDRICK
66 Dean of Nursing Program ..... Ms. Gie ARCHER
32 Director of Student Life ..... Ms. Daisy GARCIA
72 Dean of Instruction Gainesville ..... Mrs. Debbie HUFFMAN
49 Dean of Instruction Corinth ..... Dr. Larry GILBERT
49 Dean of Instruction Flower Mound ..... Mrs. Sara ALFORD

Northeast Texas Community College (J)

PO Box 1307, Mount Pleasant TX 75456-1307
County: Titus FICE Identification: 023154
Unit ID: 227225
Telephone: (903) 434-8100 Carnegie Class: Assoc/Pub-R-M
FAX Number: (903) 572-6712 Calendar System: Semester
URL: www.ntcc.edu
Established: 1984 Annual Undergrad Tuition & Fees (In-District): $1,798
Enrollment: 3,318 Coed
Affiliation or Control: Local IRS Status: 501(c)3
Highest Offering: Associate Degree
Program: Occupational; 2-Year Principally Bachelor's Creditable; Teacher Preparatory
Accreditation: SC, DH, MAC, MLTAD, PTAA

01 President ..... Dr. Brad W. JOHNSON
04 Executive Asst to the President ..... Ms. Pat L. TALLANT
05 Executive Vice Pres for Instruction ..... Dr. Ron CLINTON
11 Vice Pres Administrative Services ..... Ms. Beth THOMPSON
30 Vice Pres Institutional Advancement ..... Dr. Jonathan W. MCCULLOUGH
32 VP for Student & Outreach Services ..... Dr. Judy G. TRAYLOR
103 Assoc VP for Workforce Development ..... Mr. Kevin ROSE
37 Dean Enroll/Dir Student Fin Assist ..... Ms. Kim LAWRENCE
76 Dean of Allied Health Professions ..... Dr. Jena HAMRA
84 Associate Dean of Outreach Services ..... Ms. Melody HENRY
18 Director of Plant Services ..... Mr. Tim JOHNSTON
51 Director of Continuing Education ..... Vacant
08 Director Learning Resource Center ..... Mr. Ron BOWDEN
91 Director of Computer Services ..... Mr. Kenneth GOODSON
26 Director Marketing/Public Relations ..... Ms. Jodi WEBER
06 Registrar ..... Ms. Betsy GOODING
15 Director Human Resources ..... Ms. Diana HALL
10 Controller ..... Ms. Jaci M. MERRITT
09 Dir Institutional Effectiveness ..... Ms. Toni LABEFF
88 Advisor/Retention Specialist ..... Mr. Miles YOUNG
36 Career Development/Advisor ..... Ms. Lynda WATSON

Northwood University (K)

1114 West FM 1382, Cedar Hill TX 75104
Telephone: (972) 293-5400 Identification: 770280
Accreditation: &NH

† Main campus is Northwood University in Midland, MI.

Oblate School of Theology (L)

285 Oblate Drive, San Antonio TX 78216-6693
County: Bexar FICE Identification: 003595
Unit ID: 227289
Telephone: (210) 341-1366 Carnegie Class: Spec/Faith
FAX Number: (210) 341-4519 Calendar System: Semester
URL: www.ost.edu
Established: 1903 Annual Graduate Tuition & Fees: $13,520
Enrollment: 126 Coed
Affiliation or Control: Roman Catholic IRS Status: 501(c)3
Highest Offering: Doctorate; No Undergraduates
Program: Professional; Religious Emphasis
Accreditation: SC, THEOL

01 President ..... Rev. Ronald ROLHEISER
05 Vice Pres Academic Affairs/Dean ..... Dr. Scott WOODWARD
10 Vice Pres Finance/Human Resources ..... Mr. Rene ESPINOSA
11 Vice Pres Administrative Affairs ..... Rev. David KALERT
30 Vice Pres Institutional Advancement ..... Mrs. Lea KOCHANEK
20 Associate Dean ..... Sr. Linda GIBLER
51 Assoc Dean of Continuing Educ ..... Mrs. Rose MARDEN
88 Director Oblate Renewal Center ..... Mr. Brian WALLACE
18 Director of Physical Plant ..... Mr. Morris LIM
08 Director of the Library ..... Ms. Maria GARCIA
06 Registrar & Director of Admissions ..... Mr. Mario PORTER
88 Director Lay Ministry Institute ..... Mrs. Bonnie ABADIE
88 Director Ministry to Ministers Pgm ..... Rev. Vincent LOUWAGIE
09 Dir Instl Research/Plng/Assessment ..... Rev. David KALERT
88 Director DMin Program ..... Rev. John MARKEY

Odessa College (M)

201 W University Boulevard, Odessa TX 79764-7127
County: Ector FICE Identification: 003596
Unit ID: 227304
Telephone: (432) 335-6400 Carnegie Class: Assoc/Pub-R-M
FAX Number: (432) 335-6860 Calendar System: Semester
URL: www.odessa.edu
Established: 1946 Annual Undergrad Tuition & Fees (In-District): $2,460
Enrollment: 5,120 Coed
Affiliation or Control: Local IRS Status: 501(c)3
Highest Offering: Associate Degree
Program: Occupational; 2-Year Principally Bachelor's Creditable
Accreditation: SC, ADNUR, MUS, PTAA, RAD

01 President ..... Dr. Gregory D. WILLIAMS
05 Vice President for Instruction ..... Vacant
10 Vice President Business Affairs ..... Ms. Virginia E. CHISUM
32 Int VP Student Svcs/Enrollment Mgmt ..... Ms. Kimberly MCKAY
100 Chief of Staff ..... Dr. Tanya G. HUGHES
09 VP for Institutional Effectiveness ..... Dr. Donald WOOD
30 Exec Dir of Resource Development ..... Vacant
11 Exec Dir of Administration & HR ..... Mr. Ken ZARTERN
75 Dean of Career/Tech & Wrkforce Educ ..... Mr. Ian ROARK
49 Dean of Arts & Sciences ..... Ms. Valerie JONES
84 Exec Director Enrollment Services ..... Mr. Louis GONZALES
06 Registrar ..... Ms. Karen DOUGHTY
41 Director Intercollegiate Athletics ..... Mr. Wayne BAKER
37 Director Student Financial Svcs ..... Ms. Dee NESMITH
18 Director Facilities & Construction ..... Mr. Bryan HEIFNER
26 Exec Director of Marketing ..... Ms. Rhonda LEWALLEN
38 Exec Director Student Completion ..... Vacant
96 Dir of Purchasing/Business Services ..... Ms. Cindy CURNUTT

Our Lady of the Lake University (N)

411 SW 24th Street, San Antonio TX 78207-4689
County: Bexar FICE Identification: 003598
Unit ID: 227331
Telephone: (210) 434-6711 Carnegie Class: DRU
FAX Number: (210) 431-3928 Calendar System: Semester
URL: www.ollusa.edu
Established: 1895 Annual Undergrad Tuition & Fees: $23,588
Enrollment: 2,811 Coed
Affiliation or Control: Roman Catholic IRS Status: 501(c)3
Highest Offering: Doctorate
Program: Liberal Arts And General; Teacher Preparatory
Accreditation: SC, ACBSP, COPSY, SP, SW

01 Interim President ... Sr. Jane Ann SLATER
05 Exec Vice Pres & Chief Acad Ofcr ... Dr. Robert BISKING
32 Vice President of Student Life ... Mr. Jack L. HANK
10 Vice President Finance & Facilities ... Mr. Allen R. KLAUS
30 Vice Pres Institutional Advancement ... Mr. Daniel YOXALL
84 Vice Pres of Enrollment Management ... Vacant
26 Vice Pres Communications/Marketing ... Mr. Daniel YOXALL
42 Vice President of Mission/Ministry ... Ms. Gloria URRABAZO
13 Chief Technology Officer ... Mr. Joseph G. DECK
20 Chief Strategy & Research Officer ... Dr. Jeffrey KANTOR
35 Asst Vice Pres Student Life ... Ms. Mary F. SCOTKA
44 Exec Director Inst Advancement ... Ms. Paula PARISH
18 Director Physical Plant ... Mr. Darrell R. GLASSCOCK
15 Director Human Resources ... Mr. Phillip VARGAS
06 Registrar ... Mrs. Norma J. ANDERSON
14 Director Network & Telecomm ... Mr. David LYTLE
45 Dir Institutional/Effectiveness ... Ms. Kara LARKAN-SKINNER
19 Chief of Police/Dir Campus Safety ... Mr. David JUAREZ
39 Director Residence Life ... Mr. Mark R. CENTER
36 Director Career Counsel/Placement ... Ms. Rhonda J. BOYLES
38 Director of Counseling Services ... Dr. Rosa ESPINOSA
23 Director Student Health Services ... Ms. Julie STUCKEY
40 Director Bookstore ... Mr. Edward CROCE
102 Corporate Relations Officer ... Ms. Roxanne SANCHEZ
46 Director of Advancement Services ... Mr. John SANCHEZ
30 Dir of Stewardship/Constituent Rels ... Ms. Asia CIARAVINO
37 Director of Financial Aid ... Ms. Karla VARGAS
29 Asst Dir Stewrdshp/Constituent Rels ... Ms. Alexandra GARCIA
88 Asst Dir of Advancement Services ... Ms. Cyndi CAVAZOS

Panola College (A)

1109 West Panola Street, Carthage TX 75633-2397
County: Panola FICE Identification: 003600
Unit ID: 227386
Telephone: (903) 693-2000 Carnegie Class: Assoc/Pub-R-M
FAX Number: (903) 693-5588 Calendar System: Semester
URL: www.panola.edu
Established: 1947 Annual Undergrad Tuition & Fees (In-District): $1,608
Enrollment: 2,581 Coed
Affiliation or Control: Local IRS Status: 501(c)3
Highest Offering: Associate Degree
Program: Occupational; 2-Year Principally Bachelor's Creditable
Accreditation: SC, ADNUR, CAHIIM, EMT, OTA

01 President ... Dr. Gregory S. POWELL
05 Vice President of Instruction ... Dr. Joe SHANNON
32 Vice President of Student Services ... Mr. Don CLINTON
10 Vice President of Fiscal Services ... Mr. Steve WILLIAMS
76 Dean of Health Sciences ... Dr. Barbara CORDELL
08 Director of Library ... Mrs. Cristie FERGUSON
07 Director of Admissions/Registrar ... Mr. Jeremy DORMAN
26 Director Recruiting/College Rels ... Mr. Charles WORLEY
103 Dir of Workforce & Economic Devel ... Mrs. Whitney EDENS
30 Dir Institutional Advancement ... Mr. Charles WORLEY
09 Director of Institutional Research ... Mrs. Christine BLAIR
106 Dean Distance Education/Webmaster ... Mrs. Ann MORRIS
12 Director of Shelby County Operation ... Mrs. Natalie OSWALT
12 Director of Marshall Operations ... Mrs. Laura WOOD
14 Computer Services Director ... Mr. Allen WEST
11 Director of Administrative Services ... Mr. Mike EDENS
19 Campus Police Chief ... Mr. Ernie DAVIS
37 Director Student Financial Aid ... Mrs. Denise WELCH

Paris Junior College (B)

2400 Clarksville Street, Paris TX 75460-6298
County: Lamar FICE Identification: 003601
Unit ID: 227401
Telephone: (903) 785-7661 Carnegie Class: Assoc/Pub-R-M
FAX Number: (903) 782-0370 Calendar System: Semester
URL: www.parisjc.edu
Established: 1924 Annual Undergrad Tuition & Fees (In-District): $1,740
Enrollment: 5,522 Coed
Affiliation or Control: State/Local IRS Status: 501(c)3
Highest Offering: Associate Degree
Program: Occupational; 2-Year Principally Bachelor's Creditable
Accreditation: SC, ADNUR, EMT, RAD, SURGT

01 President ... Dr. Pamela D. ANGLIN
05 VP Instruction ... Dr. Barbara BUCHANAN
32 VP Student Services ... Dr. Curtis HILL
35 Assoc VP Student Access/Success ... Mrs. Sheila REECE
81 Dean Math/Social Sciences ... Mr. Ed MCCRAW
60 Dean Communications/Arts ... Dr. Ken HALEY
103 Dean Workforce Education ... Mr. John SPRADLING
07 Director of Admissions ... Mrs. Amie CATO
06 Registrar ... Mrs. Rita TAPP
10 Controller ... Mrs. Keitha CARLTON
37 Director Student Financial Aid ... Mrs. Linda SLAWSON
38 Director Counseling ... Mrs. Barbara THOMAS
09 Director Institutional Research ... Mrs. Beverly MATTHEWS
30 Director Institutional Advancement ... Mr. Derald BULLS
35 Director Student Life ... Mr. Kenneth WEBB
14 Director Information Technology ... Mr. David NICHOLS
26 Chief Public Relations Officer ... Ms. Margaret RUFF
18 Manager Plant Operations ... Mr. Randall COX

Parker University (C)

2540 Walnut Hill Lane, Dallas TX 75229-5609
County: Dallas FICE Identification: 023053
Unit ID: 243823
Telephone: (972) 438-6932 Carnegie Class: Spec/Health
FAX Number: (214) 902-2496 Calendar System: Trimester
URL: www.parker.edu
Established: 1982 Annual Undergrad Tuition & Fees: $29,319
Enrollment: 866 Coed
Affiliation or Control: Independent Non-Profit IRS Status: 501(c)3
Highest Offering: Doctorate
Program: Professional
Accreditation: SC, CHIRO, COMTA

01 President ... Dr. Brian J. MCAULAY
05 Provost ... Dr. Gery HOCHANADEL
20 Vice President of Academics ... Dr. Kenneth C. THOMAS
10 Vice President Business Affairs ... Mr. David GARAFOLA
20 Academic Dean ... Dr. Gene GIGGLEMAN
46 Dean of Research ... Dr. Ronald RUPPERT
84 Dean of Enrollment ... Ms. Valory HEMPHILL
32 Dean of Student Affairs ... Mr. Victor BALLESTEROS
51 Director Continuing Education ... Ms. Michelle YUNGBLUT
06 Registrar ... Ms. Paula BROWN
37 Director Financial Aid ... Vacant
08 Head Librarian ... Mrs. Becky SULLIVAN
38 Student Counseling Director ... Dr. Jacqueline ELBEL
16 Chief Human Resources Officer ... Ms. Sandra MCLEAN
19 Director Safety/Security ... Mr. Scott CHRISTENSEN
41 Athletic Director ... Mr. Steve WELLER
29 Director Alumni Relations ... Mr. Tim GUNN
26 Chief Marketing Officer ... Vacant
13 Chief Information Officer ... Vacant
18 Dir of Facilities/Procurement ... Mr. Philip CERVANTES
35 Director Student Activities ... Mrs. Wendy NULPH
17 Asst Dean of Clinic ... Vacant

Paul Quinn College (D)

3837 Simpson Stuart Road, Dallas TX 75241-4398
County: Dallas FICE Identification: 003602
Unit ID: 227429
Telephone: (214) 376-1000 Carnegie Class: Bac/Diverse
FAX Number: (214) 379-5559 Calendar System: Semester
URL: www.pqc.edu
Established: 1872 Annual Undergrad Tuition & Fees: $16,040
Enrollment: 237 Coed
Affiliation or Control: African Methodist Episcopal IRS Status: 501(c)3
Highest Offering: Baccalaureate
Program: Liberal Arts And General; Teacher Preparatory
Accreditation: TRACS

01 President ... Mr. Michael J. SORRELL
05 Vice Pres Academic Affairs ... Dr. Kizuwanda GRANT
27 Communications Coordinator ... Ms. Ashley DALY
32 Dean of Students ... Ms. Kelsel THOMPSON
06 Registrar ... Dr. Karen JARRELL
08 Librarian/Director LRC ... Ms. Clarice MEDLEY-WEEKS
13 Director of Technology ... Vacant
41 Dir Athletics/Intramural Sports ... Vacant
37 Director of Financial Aid ... Ms. Bianca MATLOCK
35 Director Student Support Svcs ... Dr. Tiffany GURLEY-ALLOWAY
18 Director of Facilities ... Vacant
09 Director of Institutional Research ... Dr. Karen JARRELL
30 Director of Development ... Mr. Dennis COLEMAN
23 Nurse ... Ms. Glenda DAVIS
107 Div Chair Professional Studies ... Mr. Reginald GRAY
53 Division Chair Education ... Dr. Kizuwanda GRANT
100 Chief of Staff ... Ms. Lori PRICE
88 Director of Service Learning ... Vacant
07 Director of Recruiting ... Mrs. Jessika LARA

Pima Medical Institute-Houston (E)

10201-C Katy Freeway, Houston TX 77024
Telephone: (713) 778-0778 Identification: 770510
Accreditation: ABHES, COARC, DH, RAD

† Main campus is Pima Medical Institute-Tucson in Tucson, AZ.

Platt College (F)

2974 LBJ Freeway, Dallas TX 75234
Telephone: (972) 243-0900 Identification: 770599
Accreditation: ACCSC

† Main campus is Platt College in Tulsa, OK.

Quest College (G)

5430 Fredericksburg Rd, Ste 310, San Antonio TX 78229
County: Bexar FICE Identification: 034003
Unit ID: 439507
Telephone: (210) 366-2701 Carnegie Class: Not Classified
FAX Number: (210) 366-0738 Calendar System: Semester
URL: www.questcollege.edu
Established: 1995 Annual Undergrad Tuition & Fees: $14,811
Enrollment: 369 Coed
Affiliation or Control: Proprietary IRS Status: Proprietary
Highest Offering: Associate Degree
Program: Occupational
Accreditation: COE

01 Owner/Administrator ... Jeanne MARTIN

Ranger College (H)

1100 College Circle, Ranger TX 76470-3298
County: Eastland FICE Identification: 003603
Unit ID: 227687
Telephone: (254) 647-3234 Carnegie Class: Assoc/Pub-R-S
FAX Number: (254) 647-1656 Calendar System: Semester
URL: www.rangercollege.edu
Established: 1926 Annual Undergrad Tuition & Fees (In-District): $2,256
Enrollment: 1,936 Coed
Affiliation or Control: Local IRS Status: 501(c)3
Highest Offering: Associate Degree
Program: Occupational; 2-Year Principally Bachelor's Creditable; Technical Emphasis
Accreditation: SC

01 President ... Dr. William J. CAMPION
12 Executive VP Brownwood ... Dr. Don BOSTIC
12 Vice President Erath County ... Dr. Kerry SCHINDLER
84 Dean of Enrollment Management ... Mr. John SLAUGHTER
10 Chief Financial Officer ... Mrs. Tammy ADAMS
32 Dean of Students ... Mr. Johnny GANN
05 Dean of Student Learning ... Mr. Billy ADAMS
11 Dean of Administration ... Dr. Dava WASHBURN
06 Registrar ... Mr. John SLAUGHTER
08 Director of Learning Resources ... Mrs. Cherie BELTRAN
18 Director of Maintenance & Grounds ... Mr. Charles LEMASTER
37 Director of Financial Aid ... Mr. Don HILTON
41 Athletic Director ... Mr. David DEAVER
15 Director of Personnel ... Miss Laura YECK
36 Director Student Placement ... Ms. Vicki LOWRANCE
38 Dir Academic Counseling & Testing ... Ms. Vicki LOWRANCE
21 Bursar ... Ms. Evonne CHERRY
40 Director Bookstore ... Miss Cindy STRINGER

Redeemer Theological Seminary (I)

6060 N Central Expressway, Ste. 700, Dallas TX 75206
County: Dallas Identification: 667055
Telephone: (214) 528-8600 Carnegie Class: Not Classified
FAX Number: N/A Calendar System: Semester
URL: www.redeemerseminary.org
Established: 1999 Annual Graduate Tuition & Fees: $12,000
Enrollment: 136 Coed
Affiliation or Control: Independent Non-Profit IRS Status: 501(c)3
Highest Offering: Master's; No Undergraduates
Program: Professional; Religious Emphasis
Accreditation: @THEOL

01 President ... Dr. Steven T. VANDERHILL
05 Academic Dean ... Dr. Douglas M. GROPP

Remington College (J)

3110 Hayes Road, Suite 380, Houston TX 77082-2782
County: Harris FICE Identification: 030265
Unit ID: 380094
Telephone: (281) 899-1240 Carnegie Class: Assoc/PrivFP
FAX Number: (281) 597-8466 Calendar System: Quarter
URL: www.remingtoncollege.edu
Established: 1981 Annual Undergrad Tuition & Fees: $15,995
Enrollment: 367 Coed
Affiliation or Control: Independent Non-Profit IRS Status: 501(c)3
Highest Offering: Baccalaureate
Program: Occupational
Accreditation: ACCSC

01 President ... Ms. Lori BANKY
05 Director of Education ... Vacant
07 Director of Admissions ... Mr. Michael HOLMES
37 Director of Financial Aid ... Mrs. Rhoda HAMILTON

Remington College-Dallas Campus (K)

1800 Eastgate Drive, Garland TX 75041-5513
Telephone: (972) 686-7878 Identification: 666037
Accreditation: ACCSC

† Main campus is Remington College in Houston, TX.

Remington College-Fort Worth Campus (L)

300 E Loop 820, Fort Worth TX 76112-1225
Telephone: (817) 451-0017 Identification: 666063
Accreditation: ACCSC

† Main campus is Remington College in Houston, TX.

Remington College-Houston Southeast Campus (M)

20985 Interstate 45 South, Webster TX 77598
Telephone: (281) 554-1700 Identification: 770601
Accreditation: ACCSC

† Main campus is Remington College in Houston, TX.

Remington College-North Houston Campus (N)

11310 Greens Crossing, Suite 300, Houston TX 77067
Telephone: (281) 885-4450 Identification: 770600
Accreditation: ACCSC

† Main campus is Remington College in Houston, TX.

Rice University (A)

PO Box 1892, Houston TX 77251-1892
County: Harris FICE Identification: 003604
Unit ID: 227757
Telephone: (713) 348-0000 Carnegie Class: RU/VH
FAX Number: N/A Calendar System: Semester
URL: www.rice.edu
Established: 1891 Annual Undergrad Tuition & Fees: $38,941
Enrollment: 6,484 Coed
Affiliation or Control: Independent Non-Profit IRS Status: 501(c)3
Highest Offering: Doctorate
Program: Liberal Arts And General; Professional
Accreditation: SC, BUS, ENG, @TEAC

01 President Mr. David W. LEEBRON
101 Deputy Sec to Board of Trustees Ms. Cynthia L. WILSON
05 Provost Dr. George L. MCLENDON
11 Vice President Administration Dr. Kevin KIRBY
10 Vice President Finance Ms. Kathy COLLINS
30 Vice President Resource Development Mr. Darrow ZEIDENSTEIN
88 Vice Pres Investments/Treasurer Ms. Allison THACKER
84 Vice President for Enrollment Mr. Chris MUNOZ
26 Vice President for Public Affairs Ms. Linda THRANE
13 Vice Provost Information Technology Dr. Kamran KHAN
46 Vice Provost Research Dr. Vicki L. COLVIN
20 Vice Provost for Academic Affairs Dr. Paula SANDERS
88 Vice Provost Interdisciplinary Init Dr. Caroline LEVANDER
88 Vice Provost Translational Biosci Dr. Cindy FARACH-CARSON
15 Associate Vice Pres Human Resources Ms. Mary A. CRONIN
91 Assoc Vice Pres for Admin Systems Mr. Randy CASTIGLIONI
18 Assoc VP Facil Engr & Planning Ms. Barbara BRYSON
04 Sr Asst to the President Dr. David K. VASSAR
43 General Counsel Mr. Richard A. ZANSITIS
06 Registrar Mr. David TENNEY
07 Dean for Undergraduate Enrollment Ms. Julie BROWNING
29 Director Alumni Affairs/Univ Events Vacant
88 Director International Opportunity Ms. Erika P. ZANETTI
37 Director Student Financial Services Ms. Anne E. WALKER
13 Director Enterprise Application Ms. Andrea MARTIN
25 Director of Sponsored Research Ms. Melinda COTTEN
41 Director of Athletics Vacant
85 Director Intl Students/Scholars Dr. Adria BAKER
31 Dir of Community Involvement Ctr Mr. Mac GRISWOLD
39 Director of Housing & Dining Mr. Mark DITMAN
23 Director Student Health Services Dr. Mark JENKINS
09 Director of Institutional Research Dr. Ratna SARKAR
21 University Controller Vacant
21 Director of Internal Audit Ms. Janet COVINGTON
19 Chief of Campus Police Mr. Johnny WHITEHEAD
22 Director of Affirmative Action Mr. Russell BARNES
27 Director of News & Media Relations Mr. B.J ALMOND
21 Director Administrative Services Mr. Eugen RADULESCU
28 Director of Diversity Dr. Roland B. SMITH
36 Dir Center for Career Development Ms. Nicole VAN DEN HEUVEL
96 Director of Purchasing Mr. Brian SOIKA
40 Manager Bookstore Mr. Tim JACKSON
79 Dean of School of Humanities Dr. Nicolas SHUMWAY
58 Dean Graduate/Postdoctoral Stds Vacant
20 Dean of Undergraduate Education Dr. John S. HUTCHINSON
48 Dean of Architecture Dr. Sarah M. WHITING
64 Dean of Shepherd School of Music Dr. Robert YEKOVICH
54 Dean GR Brown School Engineering Dr. Ned THOMAS
50 Dean JH Jones Graduate Sch Business Dr. William H. GLICK
83 Dean of Social Sciences Dr. Lyn RAGSDALE
81 Dean of Wiess Sch Natural Science Dr. Daniel CARSON
51 Dean Glasscock Sch Continuing Stds Dr. Mary MCINTIRE
88 Asst Dean Student Judicial Pgms Dr. Donald OSTDIEK
38 Asst Dean Student Counseling Dr. Donald OSTDIEK

Rio Grande Bible Institute (B)

4300 South Business 281, Edinburg TX 78539-9650
County: Hidalgo Identification: 666395
Unit ID: 475185
Telephone: (956) 380-8100 Carnegie Class: Not Classified
FAX Number: (956) 380-8256 Calendar System: Semester
URL: www.riogrande.edu
Established: 1946 Annual Undergrad Tuition & Fees: $2,179
Enrollment: 142 Coed
Affiliation or Control: Independent Non-Profit IRS Status: 501(c)3
Highest Offering: Baccalaureate
Program: Professional; Religious Emphasis
Accreditation: BI

01 President Dr. Lawrence B. WINDLE
04 Administrative Assistant to Pres Mrs. Ruth M. WINDLE
05 Vice President of Education Mr. David LOYOLA
32 Dean of Students Mr. David LOYOLA
10 Vice President of Administration Mr. Larry DICK
21 Comptroller Mr. Jonathan WHITE
08 Chief Librarian Miss Mary CANO
06 Registrar Mr. Keith SWARTZBAUGH
15 Personnel Director Mr. Larry DICK
18 Vice President of Campus Services Mr. Gary WILLIAMS
26 Vice Pres Ministerial Advancement Dr. Robert CRANE

St. Edward's University (C)

3001 S Congress Avenue, Austin TX 78704-6489
County: Travis FICE Identification: 003621
Unit ID: 227845
Telephone: (512) 448-8400 Carnegie Class: Master's L
FAX Number: (512) 448-8492 Calendar System: Semester
URL: www.stedwards.edu
Established: 1885 Annual Undergrad Tuition & Fees: $33,720
Enrollment: 5,095 Coed
Affiliation or Control: Independent Non-Profit IRS Status: 501(c)3
Highest Offering: Master's
Program: Liberal Arts And General; Teacher Preparatory; Professional; Business Emphasis
Accreditation: SC, SW

01 President Dr. George E. MARTIN
03 Executive Vice President Sr. Donna M. JURICK
10 Vice President Financial Affairs Ms. Rhonda D. CARTWRIGHT
05 Vice President for Academic Affairs Dr. Mary K. BOYD
30 Vice President for Advancement Mr. Michael F. LARKIN
26 Vice Pres Marketing/Enrollment Mgmt Ms. Paige BOOTH
32 Vice President for Student Affairs Dr. Sandra L. PACHECO
13 Vice President Information Tech Mr. David E. WALDRON
42 Director of Campus Ministry Fr. Peter J. WALSH
09 Assoc VP Inst Effectiveness/Rsrch Mr. Bhuban R. PANDEY
21 Assoc Vice Pres Financial Affairs Mr. Barton G. GLASER
88 Assoc VP for Global Initiatives Mr. William J. CLABBY
20 Assoc VP for Academic Affairs Dr. Molly F. MINUS
07 Assoc VP/Dean of Admission Ms. Tracy L. MANIER
37 Assoc VP Student Financial Services Ms. Doris F. CONSTANTINE
32 Assoc VP/Dean of Students Ms. Lisa L. KIRKPATRICK
29 Assoc VP Alumni/Parent Programs Vacant
27 Assoc VP for Marketing Ms. Christie CAMPBELL
88 Asst to Pres/Sustainability Coord Ms. Cristina L. BORDIN
04 Executive Assistant to President Ms. Lorraine M. PAGAN
83 Dean Behavioral & Social Sciences Dr. Brenda J. VALLANCE
50 Interim Dean Management & Business Dr. Thomas L. SECHREST
53 Dean School of Education Dr. Grant W. SIMPSON, JR.
79 Dean School of Humanities Dr. Sharon D. NELL
81 Interim Dean Sch of Natural Science Dr. Patricia J. BAYNHAM
88 Dean of New College Dr. Helene L. CAUDILL
88 Interim Dean University Programs Dr. Cory LOCK
08 Director of Munday Library Mr. Pongracz SENNYEY
06 Registrar Dr. Lance R. HAYES
36 Director Career Services Ms. Barbara J. HENDERSON
108 Dir of Institutional Assessment Mr. David A. BLAIR
44 Associate VP Development Mr. Joe DEMEDEIROS
104 Director Ofc of International Educ Ms. Holly R. CARTER
90 Dir Instructional & Emerging Tech Ms. Rebecca F. DAVIS
18 Assoc VP Facilities Mr. Michael W. PETERSON
91 Tech Lead Enterprise Info Systems Mr. Raymond J. SPINHIRNE
88 Director Digital Infrastructure Mr. Benjamin R. HOCKENHULL
88 Dir of Enterprise Info Systems Ms. Angela M. SVOBODA
88 Director Info Technology Resources Mr. Mark D. JACAMAN
19 Chief of Police Mr. Rudolph L. RENDON
27 Director of Communications Ms. Mischelle R. DIAZ
15 Director Human Resources Ms. Rosemary RUDNICKI
88 Assoc Dean Dir Retention Programs Ms. Nicole G. TREVINO
38 Interim Dir Health & Counseling Ctr Dr. Elizabeth H. CHARRIER
41 Athletic Director Ms. Debora W. TAYLOR
35 Director of Student Life Mr. Thomas B. SULLIVAN
39 Director Residence Life Ms. Alicia L. VELA
31 Director Auxiliary Services Mr. Michael C. STONE
88 Risk Manager Ms. Rebekah M. NAGY
21 Controller Mr. Paul R. SINTEF
102 Director Foundation Relations Ms. Carol A. JANUSZESKI
89 Director Freshman Studies Ms. Alexandra L. BARRON
92 Director Honors Program Dr. Barbara FILIPPIDIS
88 Director Capstone Course Dr. Todd D. ONDERDONK
40 Campus Stores Director Ms. Melanie FOSTER

St. Mary's University (D)

One Camino Santa Maria, San Antonio TX 78228-8572
County: Bexar FICE Identification: 003623
Unit ID: 228149
Telephone: (210) 436-3011 Carnegie Class: Master's L
FAX Number: (210) 436-3500 Calendar System: Semester
URL: www.stmarytx.edu
Established: 1852 Annual Undergrad Tuition & Fees: $25,188
Enrollment: 3,988 Coed
Affiliation or Control: Roman Catholic IRS Status: 501(c)3
Highest Offering: Doctorate
Program: Liberal Arts And General; Teacher Preparatory; Professional
Accreditation: SC, BUS, CACREP, ENG, LAW, MFCD, MUS

01 President Mr. Thomas M. MENGLER
05 Provost/Vice Pres Academic Affairs Mr. Andre HAMPTON
10 Vice Pres Administration & Finance Ms. Rebeckah J. DAY
84 Vice Pres Enrollment Management Ms. Suzanne M. PETRUSCH
32 Vice President Student Development Ms. Katherine SISOIAN
30 Vice Pres University Advancement Vacant
88 Vice President Mission & Identity Rev. Rudy VELA, SM
50 Dean/Prof Bill Greehey Sch Business Dr. Tanuja SINGH
79 Dean/Assoc Prof Hum & Social Sci Dr. Janet B. DIZINNO
54 Dean/Prof Science/Engrng/Technology Dr. Winston EREVELLES
58 Dean & Professor Graduate School Vacant
61 Dean of Law Mr. Charles CANTU
39 Director Residence Life Mr. James VILLARREAL
09 Director of Institutional Research Mr. Christopher M. ANTONS
100 Chief of Staff/Office of President Ms. Dianne L. PIPES
06 Registrar Ms. Christina VILLANUEVA
07 Director of Admissions Vacant
08 Director Louis J Blume Library Vacant
37 Director Financial Assistance Mr. David R. KRAUSE
38 Director Student Counseling Dr. Barbara HARDIN
36 Director of Career Services Ms. Amy DIEPENBROCK
90 Exec Director Academic Technology Mr. Daxing (Michael) CHEN
15 Director Human Resources Ms. Elsa YBANEZ
72 Exec Dir Tech Operations/Info Tech Vacant
91 Ex Dir Resource Mgt/Plng/Info/Tech Ms. Louisa A. MARTIN
13 Dir Network Tech Services/Info Tech Mr. Robert STOOKSBERRY
88 Director Tech User Support Vacant
42 Director University Ministry Mr. Wayne ROMO
30 Director University Advancement Mr. Peter HANSEN
21 Director of Finance Ms. Mei-Lin LEE
21 Director of Accounting Operations Ms. Sheila NIX
26 Dir Media Relations/Communications Mrs. Gina FARRELL
18 Exec Dir Facilities Administration Mr. Aaron HANNA

*San Jacinto College District (E)

4624 Fairmont Parkway, Pasadena TX 77504-3323
County: Harris FICE Identification: 029137
Unit ID: 227988
Telephone: (281) 998-6150 Carnegie Class: N/A
FAX Number: (281) 479-8127
URL: www.sanjac.edu

00 Chancellor Dr. Brenda HELLYER
01 Deputy Chancellor and President Dr. Laurel WILLIAMSON
05 Provost Dr. Brenda JONES
10 Vice Chancellor Fiscal Affairs Mr. Ken LYNN
16 Vice Chanc Human Resources Mr. Stephen TRNCAK
27 Interim CIO Mr. Rob STANICIC
26 Vice Chanc Marketing/Govt Rels Mrs. Teri CRAWFORD
108 Vice President for Accreditation Dr. Richard BAILEY
45 Vice Chanc Strategic Initiatives Dr. Allatia HARRIS
92 Director Honors Program Dr. Eddie WELLER

*San Jacinto College Central (F)

8060 Spencer Highway, Pasadena TX 77505-5903
County: Harris FICE Identification: 003609
Unit ID: 227979
Telephone: (281) 476-1501 Carnegie Class: Assoc/Pub-S-MC
FAX Number: (281) 476-1892 Calendar System: Semester
URL: www.sanjac.edu
Established: 1960 Annual Undergrad Tuition & Fees (In-District): $1,312
Enrollment: 14,732 Coed
Affiliation or Control: Local IRS Status: 501(c)3
Highest Offering: Associate Degree
Program: Occupational; 2-Year Principally Bachelor's Creditable
Accreditation: &SC, ADNUR, COARC, EMT, MLTAD, RAD, SURGT

02 President Dr. Laurel WILLIAMSON
05 Provost Dr. Van WIGGINTON
32 Vice President of Student Services Ms. Joanna ZIMMERMAN
49 Interim Dean of Lib Arts and Sci Mr. Stephen LOPEZ
75 Dean of Industrial and Applied Tech Mr. Jeffrey PARKS
76 Dean of Health Sciences Ms. Veronica JAMMER
50 Dean of Business and Prof Svcs Mr. Michael KANE
11 Dean of Administration Dr. James BRASWELL
84 Dean of Enrollment Services Mr. Kevin MCKISSON
35 Dean of Student Development Dr. Deborah MYLES
62 Director of Library Ms. Karen BLANKENSHIP
88 Director of Campus Services Mr. Christopher CRUMLEY
41 Athletic Director Ms. Sharon NELSON
06 College Registrar Dr. Wanda MUNSON

† Regional accreditation is carried under the parent institution (district office) in Pasadena, TX.

*San Jacinto College North (G)

5800 Uvalde Road, Houston TX 77049-4599
County: Harris Identification: 666747
Unit ID: 227997
Telephone: (281) 458-4050 Carnegie Class: Not Classified
FAX Number: (281) 459-7125 Calendar System: Semester
URL: www.sanjac.edu
Established: 1974 Annual Undergrad Tuition & Fees (In-District): $1,312
Enrollment: 7,381 Coed
Affiliation or Control: Local IRS Status: 501(c)3
Highest Offering: Associate Degree
Program: Occupational; 2-Year Principally Bachelor's Creditable
Accreditation: &SC, ACFEI, CAHIIM, EMT, MAC

02 President Dr. Laurel WILLIAMSON
05 Interim Provost Dr. Richard BAILEY
32 Vice President of Student Services Ms. Joanna ZIMMERMAN
88 Assoc Vice Chanc for College Prep Dr. Rebecca GOOSEN
07 Dean of Enrollment Services Ms. Amy AMMERMAN
76 Dean of Allied Health Ms. Serita DICKEY
90 Dean Educational Technology Dr. Gary FRIERY
32 Dean of Student Development Ms. Clare IANNELLI
62 Director of Library Ms. Jan CRENSHAW
49 Dean of Liberal Arts Mr. Shawn SILMAN
06 College Registrar Dr. Wanda MUNSON
41 Athletic Director Mr. Tom ARRINGTON
88 Dual Credit Director Ms. Jennifer MOWDY
55 Evening Department Chair Mr. Michael VARNELL

† Regional accreditation is carried under the parent institution (district office) in Pasadena, TX.

*San Jacinto College South (H)

13735 Beamer Road, Houston TX 77089-6099
County: Harris Identification: 666748
Unit ID: 228006

Telephone: (281) 484-1900 Carnegie Class: Not Classified
FAX Number: (281) 922-3401 Calendar System: Semester
URL: www.sanjac.edu
Established: 1979 Annual Undergrad Tuition & Fees (In-District): $1,312
Enrollment: 10,909 Coed
Affiliation or Control: Local IRS Status: 501(c)3
Highest Offering: Associate Degree
Program: Occupational; 2-Year Principally Bachelor's Creditable
Accreditation: &SC, ADNUR, PTAA

02 Deputy Chancellor and President .... Dr. Laurel WILLIAMSON
05 Provost .... Dr. Brenda JONES
49 Dean of Liberal Arts .... Ms. Kathryn ROOSA
50 Dean Business & Technology .... Mr. Kevin MORRIS
11 Dean of Administration .... Mr. Joseph HEBERT
84 Dean of Enrollment Mgmt .... Dr. Kerry MIX
32 Vice President of Student Services .... Ms. Joanna ZIMMERMANN
55 Director of Evening Division .... Mr. John BOGGS
62 Director of Library .... Mr. Richard MCKAY
88 Interim Dean of Student Development ....Ms. Shelley RINEHART
41 Interim Athletic Director .... Ms. Kelly SAENZ
88 Dual Credit Director .... Ms. Kate GRAHAM
06 College Registrar .... Dr. Wanda MUNSON

† Regional accreditation is carried under the parent institution (district office) in Pasadena, TX.

Sanford-Brown College (A)

9001 N IH-35, #105, Austin TX 78753
Telephone: (512) 582-6800 Identification: 770797
Accreditation: ACICS

† Main campus is Sanford-Brown College in Atlanta, GA.

Sanford-Brown College (B)

1250 W. Mockingbird Lane, Ste 150, Dallas TX 75247
County: Dallas FICE Identification: 026150
Unit ID: 404514
Telephone: (214) 459-8490 Carnegie Class: Assoc/PrivFP
FAX Number: (214) 638-6401 Calendar System: Other
URL: www.sanfordbrown.edu
Established: Annual Undergrad Tuition & Fees: $14,600
Enrollment: 606 Coed
Affiliation or Control: Proprietary IRS Status: Proprietary
Highest Offering: Associate Degree
Program: Occupational
Accreditation: ACICS, CVT, DH, DMS, SURTEC

01 Campus President .... David B. BOWMAN

Sanford-Brown College (C)

2627 North Loop West, Suite 100, Houston TX 77008
Telephone: (713) 863-9429 Identification: 770795
Accreditation: ACICS, RAD, SURTEC

† Main campus is Sanford-Brown College in Atlanta, GA.

Sanford-Brown College (D)

4511 Horizon Hill Boulevard, San Antonio TX 78229
Telephone: (210) 246-7700 Identification: 770796
Accreditation: ACICS, CVT

† Main campus is Sanford-Brown College in Dallas, TX.

Sanford-Brown College-Houston (E)

9999 Richmond Avenue, Houston TX 77042
Telephone: (713) 779-1110 Identification: 666382
Accreditation: ACICS, DMS, MLTAD, SURTEC

† Main campus is Sanford-Brown College in Atlanta, GA.

Schreiner University (F)

2100 Memorial Boulevard, Kerrville TX 78028-5697
County: Kerr FICE Identification: 003610
Unit ID: 228042
Telephone: (830) 896-5411 Carnegie Class: Bac/Diverse
FAX Number: (830) 896-3232 Calendar System: Semester
URL: www.schreiner.edu
Established: 1923 Annual Undergrad Tuition & Fees: $21,884
Enrollment: 1,126 Coed
Affiliation or Control: Presbyterian Church (U.S.A.) IRS Status: 501(c)3
Highest Offering: Master's
Program: Liberal Arts And General; Teacher Preparatory; Professional
Accreditation: SC

01 President .... Dr. Timothy SUMMERLIN
05 Provost/Vice Pres Acad Affairs .... Dr. Charlie T. MCCORMICK
10 Vice Pres Administration & Finance .... Mr. Bill MUSE
30 Vice Pres Advancement/Public Rels .... Mr. Mark TUSCHAK
84 Interim Vice Pres Enrollment .... Ms. Peg A. LAYTON
06 Assistant Provost & Registrar .... Ms. Darlene BANNISTER
20 Assoc Vice Pres Academic Affairs .... Dr. Candice SCOTT
26 Assistant Vice President Marketing .... Ms. Lane H. TAIT
21 Asst Vice Pres Finance/Controller .... Ms. Barbara SIEMERS
84 Asst Vice Pres Enrollment Services .... Mr. Larry J. CANTU
42 Campus Minister .... Rev. Virginia NORRIS-LANE
37 Director Student Financial Aid .... Ms. Toni BRYANT
32 Dean of Students .... Dr. Charlie HUEBER
26 Director of University Relations .... Ms. Amy ARMSTRONG
41 Athletic Director .... Mr. Ron MACOSKO
16 Director of Human Resources .... Ms. Mary WOODS
18 Director Environment Management .... Mr. Dale MYERS
29 Director Alumni Relations .... Mr. Paul CAMFIELD
38 Director Student Counseling .... Ms. Kimberly J. WOODS
36 Director Career Development .... Ms. Cristina MARTINEZ
09 Director of Institutional Research .... Dr. Gloria STEWART

Seminary of the Southwest (G)

Box 2247, Austin TX 78768-2247
County: Travis FICE Identification: 003566
Unit ID: 224712
Telephone: (512) 472-4133 Carnegie Class: Spec/Faith
FAX Number: (512) 472-3098 Calendar System: 4/1/4
URL: www.ssw.edu
Established: 1952 Annual Graduate Tuition & Fees: $13,227
Enrollment: 124 Coed
Affiliation or Control: Protestant Episcopal IRS Status: 501(c)3
Highest Offering: Master's; No Undergraduates
Program: Professional
Accreditation: SC, THEOL

01 Dean & President .... V.Rev. Douglas B. TRAVIS
05 Academic Dean .... Rev Dr. Cynthia BRIGGS KITTREDGE
03 Executive Vice President .... Mr. Fred CLEMENT
11 Exec VP Administration & Finance .... Mr. John B. WATERS
27 Exec VP of Communications .... Ms. Nancy SPRINGER-BALDWIN
30 Vice Pres Institutional Advancement .... Ms. Tara HOLLEY
84 Vice Pres Enrollment Management .... Ms. Jennielle STROTHER
21 Accounting Director .... Ms. Kathy LEBRUN
06 Registrar/Inst Research Officer .... Mrs. Madelyn SNODGRASS
08 Director of the Booher Library .... Dr. Donald KEENEY
18 Director of Facilities Management .... Mr. Tigh WALTERS
13 Director Instructional Technology .... Mr. Fito KAHN
44 Sr Dir Annual Giving/Alumni Rels .... Mr. Andrew WEST

South Plains College (H)

1401 College Avenue, Levelland TX 79336-6595
County: Hockley FICE Identification: 003611
Unit ID: 228158
Telephone: (806) 894-9611 Carnegie Class: Assoc/Pub-R-L
FAX Number: (806) 894-5274 Calendar System: Semester
URL: www.southplainscollege.edu
Established: 1957 Annual Undergrad Tuition & Fees (In-State): $2,654
Enrollment: 9,444 Coed
Affiliation or Control: State IRS Status: 501(c)3
Highest Offering: Associate Degree
Program: Occupational; 2-Year Principally Bachelor's Creditable
Accreditation: SC, ADNUR, CAHIIM, COARC, EMT, PTAA, SURGT

01 President .... Dr. Kelvin W. SHARP
05 Vice President Academic Affairs .... Mr. Jim WALKER
10 Vice Pres Finance & Administration .... Mr. Anthony G. RILEY
32 Vice President of Student Affairs .... Mrs. Cathy MITCHELL
30 Vice Pres Institutional Advancement .... Mr. Stephen S. JOHN
76 Dean of Health Occupations .... Ms. Sue Ann LOPEZ
49 Dean of Arts & Sciences .... Mr. Yancy NUNEZ
75 Dean of Technical Education .... Mr. Rob M. BLAIR
51 Dean Continuing & Distance Educ .... Mr. Ronald SPEARS
07 Dean of Admissions & Records .... Mrs. Andrea RANGEL
35 Dean of Students .... Mr. David CONNER
12 Dean of Reese Center .... Ms. Kara MARTINEZ
09 Assoc Dean of Research & Reports .... Mr. Jack WARDLOW
26 Assoc Dean of College Relations .... Mr. Dane DEWBRE
13 Assoc Dean Information Technology .... Mr. Tim WINDERS
88 Assoc Dean Dual Credit .... Mr. Ron SPEARS
103 Assoc Dean Workforce Development .... Mr. Rafael AGUILERA
20 Assoc Dean of Students .... Ms. Ursonya FLUNDER
38 Director of Counseling & Guidance .... Mrs. Christi ANDERSON
37 Director of Financial Aid .... Ms. Jim Ann BATENHORST
08 Director of Libraries .... Ms. Fran COTTON
44 Director of Development .... Mr. Russell HALL
15 Director of Human Resources .... Mrs. Jeri Ann DEWBRE
41 Director of Athletics .... Mr. Joe TUBB
06 Registrar .... Mr. Andrew RUIZ
18 Director of Physical Plant .... Mr. Cary MARROW
84 Director of Enrollment Management .... Mrs. Kimbra QUINN
21 Controller .... Ms. Teresa GREEN
40 Bookstore Manager .... Mr. Roger SHULL
28 Diversity Coord/Career Counselor ..... Ms. Maria LOPEZ-STRONG

South Texas College (I)

3201 W Pecan, McAllen TX 78501-6699
County: Hidalgo FICE Identification: 031034
Unit ID: 409315
Telephone: (956) 872-5051 Carnegie Class: Assoc/Pub4
FAX Number: (956) 971-3739 Calendar System: Semester
URL: www.southtexascollege.edu
Established: 1993 Annual Undergrad Tuition & Fees (In-District): $2,460
Enrollment: 30,558 Coed
Affiliation or Control: State/Local IRS Status: 501(c)3
Highest Offering: Baccalaureate
Program: 2-Year Principally Bachelor's Creditable
Accreditation: SC, ACBSP, CAHIIM, COARC, OTA, PTAA

01 President .... Dr. Shirley A. REED
05 Int Vice Pres Academic Affs/CAO .... Mr. Anahid PETROSIAN
10 VP Financial/Administrative Svcs .... Ms. Maria G. ELIZONDO
32 Vice Pres Stdnt Affairs/Enroll Mgmt .... Vacant
13 Vice Pres Info Services/Planning .... Mr. Jose CRUZ
30 Vice Pres Institutional Advancement .... Vacant
88 Exec Officer for NAAMRIE .... Ms. Wanda GARZA
83 Dean Liberal Arts/Soc Sci .... Dr. Margaretha BISCHOFF
50 Dean Business/Technology .... Mr. Mario REYNA
76 Int Dean Nursing/Allied Health .... Ms. Melba TREVINO
81 Interim Dean Math/Science .... Dr. Ali ESMAEILI
88 Dean Bach Deg Prog/Univ Rels .... Dr. Ali ESMAEILI
84 Interim Dean Enrollment Svcs .... Ms. Kimberly MCKAY
24 Dir Instructional Technologies .... Mr. Cody GREGG
37 Assoc Dean Student Financial Svcs .... Mr. Mike CARRANZA
21 Comptroller .... Ms. Maria ELIZONDO
16 Director Human Resources .... Ms. Shirley M. INGRAM
51 Dir Continuing/Prof & Workforce Ed .... Mr. Juan Carlos AGUIRRE
96 Director Purchasing .... Ms. Rebecca CAVAZOS
09 Dir Research/Analytical Svcs .... Mr. Serkan CELTEK
38 Dean Student Support Svcs .... Mr. Paul HERNANDEZ, JR.
18 Director Operations .... Mr. George MCCALEB
18 Director Facilities Plan/Construct .. Mr. Gerardo RODRIGUEZ, JR.
25 Dir Gr Dev/Accountability/Mgmt Svcs .... Vacant
12 Campus Administrator Starr Cty .... Dr. Arthuro MONTIEL
12 Campus Administrator Mid-Valley .... Mr. Monte CHURCHILL
88 Employee Relations Officer .... Vacant
106 Interim Director Distance Education .... Dr. Brett MILLAN
26 Director Public Rels/Marketing .... Mr. Daniel RAMIREZ
88 Dir Outreach/Orient/Wel Centers .... Ms. Kimberly MCKAY
07 Director Admissions/Registrar .... Mr. Matthew HEBBARD
88 Dir of Professional Development .... Ms. Lee GRIMES
20 Asst to VP Instructional Svcs .... Dr. Anahid PETROSIAN
19 Director Security .... Mr. Paul VARVILLE
09 Dir Inst Effectiveness/Assessment .... Vacant
62 Dean Library Services/Instr Tech .... Mr. Cody GREGG
103 Int Assc Dean Cmty Engage/Wkfrc Dev .... Vacant
14 Director for IT Services .... Mr. Daniel DE LEON
08 Director Library Technical Services .... Mr. Jesus CAMPOS
08 Director Library Public Services .... Ms. Noemi GARZA
88 Dir Student Lrg Outcomes/Achievemnt ..... Mr. Oscar HERNANDEZ
88 Int Dir Centers for Lrg Excellence .... Ms. Jennifer KNECHT
88 Director High School Programs .... Mr. Guadalupe CHAVEZ
90 Dir Info Commons Open Labs .... Dr. Lelia SALINAS
35 Int Assoc Dean Stdnt Life/Wellness .... Mr. Mike SHANNON
27 Chief Information Officer .... Ms. Alicia GOMEZ
88 Asst Chief Information Officer .... Vacant
88 Chief Information Security Officer .... Mr. Steve BOURDON
88 Curriculum/Accreditation Officer .... Ms. Laura TALBOT

South Texas College of Law (J)

1303 San Jacinto Street, Houston TX 77002-7000
County: Harris FICE Identification: 004977
Unit ID: 228194
Telephone: (713) 659-8040 Carnegie Class: Spec/Law
FAX Number: (713) 646-2909 Calendar System: Semester
URL: www.stcl.edu
Established: 1923 Annual Graduate Tuition & Fees: $28,110
Enrollment: 1,225 Coed
Affiliation or Control: Independent Non-Profit IRS Status: 501(c)3
Highest Offering: First Professional Degree; No Undergraduates
Program: Professional
Accreditation: LAW

01 President & Dean .... Mr. Donald J. GUTER
03 Executive Vice President .... Ms. Helen JENKINS
101 Sr Exec Assistant to President/Dean ...... Ms. Jennifer M. HUDSON
10 Senior Vice President & CFO .... Mr. Gregory A. BROTHERS
09 Vice Pres Strategic Plng/Inst Rsrch .. Mr. Jeffrey L. RENSBERGER
30 VP Development/Alumni Relations .... Ms. Kim PARKER
08 Vice Pres & Director Library Svcs .... Mr. David G. COWAN
20 Vice President & Associate Dean .... Mr. Bruce MCGOVERN
20 Vice President & Associate Dean .... Mr. T. Gerald TREECE
20 Vice President & Associate Dean .... Ms. Catherine G. BURNETT
13 Vice President Technology .... Mr. Randy MARAK
15 Vice President Human Resources .... Mr. Steve ALDERMAN
38 Asst Dean for Academic Assistance .... Ms. Gena L. SINGLETON
06 Registrar .... Ms. Mandi GIBSON
51 Assoc Director of Cont Legal Educ .... Vacant
36 Director of Career Resources .... Ms. Ginna PASTRANO
07 Assistant Dean for Admissions .... Ms. Alicia CRAMER
21 Controller .... Ms. Nancy N. JOHNSON
37 Director of Financial Aid .... Ms. Pat HOLLENBECK
26 Dir Marketing/Communications .... Ms. Cheryl MCENTIRE
32 Assistant Dean .... Ms. Wanda MORROW
19 Director Security & Office Services .... Ms. Debbie GIBBINS
51 Director of Cont Legal Education .... Ms. Lisa DAHM
09 Exec Dir of Institutional Research .... Ms. Julie SAUNDERS
24 Dir Instructional Technology Svcs .... Mr. Terry SMITH
27 Director Information Services .... Mr. George MILZ
43 General Counsel .... Mr. Harry REED
29 Mgr of Alumni Communications/Events ..... Ms. Christina TRUNZO
26 Manager of Public Relations .... Ms. Laura TOLLEY
44 Director of Development Services .... Ms. Veronica CANTU
44 Director of Major Gifts .... Ms. Jennifer FARMER

South University (K)

7700 West Parmer Ln Bldg A Ste A100, Austin TX 78729
Telephone: (512) 516-8800 Identification: 770917
Accreditation: &SC

† Main campus is South University in Savannah, GA.

Southern Methodist University (A)

6425 Boaz Lane, Dallas TX 75205-0100
County: Dallas FICE Identification: 003613
Unit ID: 228246
Telephone: (214) 768-2000 Carnegie Class: RU/H
FAX Number: (214) 768-1001 Calendar System: Semester
URL: www.smu.edu
Established: 1911 Annual Undergrad Tuition & Fees: $43,800
Enrollment: 10,893 Coed
Affiliation or Control: United Methodist IRS Status: 501(c)3
Highest Offering: Doctorate
Program: Liberal Arts And General; Professional
Accreditation: SC, ART, BUS, CLPSY, CS, DANCE, ENG, LAW, MUS, THEA, THEOL

01 President .... Dr. R. Gerald TURNER
05 Provost/Vice Pres Academic Affairs .... Dr. Paul W. LUDDEN
10 Vice President Business & Finance .... Ms. Chris C. REGIS
32 Vice President for Student Affairs .... Dr. Lori S. WHITE
30 Vice Pres Devel & External Affairs .... Mr. Brad E. CHEVES
43 Gen Counsel/VP Leg Affs/Govt Rels .... Mr. Paul J. WARD
11 Vice President Executive Affairs .... Dr. Thomas E. BARRY
49 Dean Dedman College .... Dr. William M. TSUTSUI
35 Interim Assoc VP/Dean Student Life .... Dr. Stephen RANKIN
21 Associate Vice President/Controller .... Mr. John O'CONNOR
45 Associate Vice President/Budgets .... Mr. Ernie BARRY
26 Assoc Vice President/Public Affairs .... Ms. Patti LASALLE
44 Asst Vice Pres Univ Development .... Ms. Pam CONLIN
15 Assoc VP Human Res & Business Svcs .... Dr. William DETWILER
84 Assoc Vice Pres Enrollment Mgmt .... Dr. Stephanie DUPAUL
88 Exec Dir of Program Services .... Ms. Dana AYRES
57 Dean Meadows School of the Arts .... Dr. Jose A. BOWEN
61 Interim Dean Dedman Schl of Law .... Ms. Julia P. FORRESTER
54 Dean Lyle School of Engr .... Dr. Marc CHRISTENSEN
73 Dean Perkins School of Theology .... Dr. William B. LAWRENCE
50 Dean Cox School of Business .... Dr. Albert W. NIEMI, JR.
58 Assoc VP Research & Grad Studies .... Dr. James E. QUICK
53 Dean Sch of Educ/Human Devel .... Dr. David J. CHARD
08 Dean/Dir Central Univ Libraries .... Ms. Gillian M. MCCOMBS
20 Assoc Provost .... Dr. Harold W. STANLEY
20 Assoc Provost .... Ms. Linda S. EADS
25 Asst VP for Research Administration .... Ms. Alicia BROSSETTE
41 Director of Athletics .... Mr. Richard L. HART
06 Registrar .... Mr. John A. HALL
07 Dean Admiss/Exec Dir Enroll Mgmt .... Mr. Wes K. WAGGONER
37 Exec Director Financial Aid .... Mr. Marc PETERSON
36 Asst VP/Exec Dir Career Center .... Dr. Troy T. BEHRENS
27 Chief Information Officer .... Mr. Joe GARGIULO
38 Director Counseling & Testing .... Dr. Karen SETTLE
23 Exec Director Health Services .... Mr. Patrick HITE
39 Dean Residence Life/Student Housing .... Vacant
04 Ex Ast to Pres/Ex Dir Inst Acc/Eqt .... Ms. Samantha THOMAS
09 Director of Institutional Research .... Dr. Michael D. TUMEO
21 Treasurer/Chief Investment Officer .... Mr. Michael A. CONDON
96 Director of Procurement .... Mr. Terrence CONNOR
42 University Chaplain .... Dr. Stephen RANKIN
24 Asst Dean Central Univ Libraries .... Dr. Bill DWORACZYK
29 Exec Dir Alumni Relations .... Ms. Marianne B. PIEPENBURG

Southwest Institute of Technology (B)

5424 Highway 290 W, Suite 200, Austin TX 78735-8890
County: Travis FICE Identification: 020936
Unit ID: 228291
Telephone: (512) 892-2640 Carnegie Class: Assoc/PrivFP
FAX Number: (512) 892-1045 Calendar System: Quarter
URL: www.swse.net
Established: 1958 Annual Undergrad Tuition & Fees: $36,892
Enrollment: 16 Coed
Affiliation or Control: Proprietary IRS Status: Proprietary
Highest Offering: Associate Degree
Program: Occupational; Technical Emphasis
Accreditation: ACCSC

01 Director .... Ms. Natasha NASH
32 Director of Student Services .... Ms. Dahlia DE LEON

Southwest Texas Junior College (C)

2401 Garner Field Road, Uvalde TX 78801-6221
County: Uvalde FICE Identification: 003614
Unit ID: 228316
Telephone: (830) 278-4401 Carnegie Class: Assoc/Pub-R-M
FAX Number: (830) 591-7354 Calendar System: Semester
URL: www.swtjc.net
Established: 1946 Annual Undergrad Tuition & Fees (In-District): $2,617
Enrollment: 5,920 Coed
Affiliation or Control: Local IRS Status: 501(c)3
Highest Offering: Associate Degree
Program: Occupational; 2-Year Principally Bachelor's Creditable; Teacher Preparatory
Accreditation: SC

01 President .... Dr. Hector GONZALES
11 Vice President Administrative Svcs .... Mr. Joe BARKER
32 Vice President Student Services .... Dr. Blaine BENNETT
10 Vice President Finance .... Ms. Anne TARSKI
05 Vice President Academic Services .... Dr. Mark UNDERWOOD
30 AVP Institutional Advancement .... Mr. Richard Dick WHIPPLE
88 Associate Vice President Outreach .... Ms. Margot MATA
12 Associate Vice President Del Rio .... Mr. Derek M. SANDOVAL
12 Associate Vice President Del Rio .... Mr. Gilbert S. BERMEA
88 Dean of College of Applied Science .... Mr. Juan Johnny C. GUZMAN
103 Dean of Workforce Education .... Ms. Romelia ARANDA
49 Dean of College of Liberal Arts .... Ms. Cheryl L. SANCHEZ
35 Director of Student Services .... Ms. Lorena LOPEZ
37 Director of Financial Aid .... Ms. Yvette HERNANDEZ
13 Director of Information Technology .... Mr. Agustin C. ALEJANDRO
18 Physical Plant Director .... Mr. Jesus J. MARTINEZ
35 Director Student Activities .... Ms. Jessica NUNEZ
15 Human Resources Coordinator .... Mr. Oscar S. GARCIA
09 Director of Institutional Research .... Ms. Carol LARUE
06 Registrar .... Mr. Luis FERNANDEZ

Southwest University at El Paso (D)

1414 Geronimo Drive, El Paso TX 79925
County: El Paso FICE Identification: 041317
Unit ID: 451556
Telephone: (915) 778-4001 Carnegie Class: Assoc/PrivFP
FAX Number: (915) 778-1575 Calendar System: Other
URL: www.southwestuniversity.edu
Established: 2001 Annual Undergrad Tuition & Fees: N/A
Enrollment: 1,155 Coed
Affiliation or Control: Proprietary IRS Status: Proprietary
Highest Offering: Associate Degree
Program: Occupational
Accreditation: ABHES, RADMAG

01 School Director .... Mr. Benjamin ARRIOLA

Southwestern Adventist University (E)

PO Box 567, 100 W Hillcrest St, Keene TX 76059-0567
County: Johnson FICE Identification: 003619
Unit ID: 228468
Telephone: (817) 645-3921 Carnegie Class: Bac/Diverse
FAX Number: (817) 202-6744 Calendar System: Semester
URL: www.swau.edu
Established: 1893 Annual Undergrad Tuition & Fees: $18,640
Enrollment: 807 Coed
Affiliation or Control: Seventh-day Adventist IRS Status: 501(c)3
Highest Offering: Master's
Program: Liberal Arts And General; Teacher Preparatory; Professional
Accreditation: SC, IACBE, NURSE

01 President .... Dr. Eric D. ANDERSON
05 VP for Academic Administration .... Dr. Amy ROSENTHAL
10 VP for Financial Administration .... Mr. Joel WALLACE
30 VP for University Advancement .... Vacant
84 VP for Enrollment .... Ms. Enga ALMEIDA
32 VP for Student Services .... Mr. James THE
42 VP for Spiritual Development .... Mr. Russ LAUGHLIN
09 Director of Institutional Research .... Dr. Thomas G. BUNCH
37 Asst VP for Student Finance .... Ms. Patricia A. NORWOOD
21 Asst VP Financial Administration .... Mr. Greg A. WICKLUND
06 Registrar .... Dr. Robert GARDNER
08 Librarian .... Ms. Cristina M. THOMSEN
34 Dean of Women .... Mrs. Janelle D. WILLIAMS
33 Dean of Men .... Mr. William IVERSON
13 Dir Information Technology Svcs .... Mr. E. Charles LEWIS
18 Plant Engineer .... Mr. Dale E. HAINEY
26 Director of Marketing .... Ms. Darcy FORCE
29 Director of Alumni Relations .... Ms. Beverly A. MENDENHALL
38 Director of Counseling & Testing .... Dr. R. Mark ALDRIDGE

Southwestern Assemblies of God University (F)

1200 Sycamore, Waxahachie TX 75165-2397
County: Ellis FICE Identification: 003616
Unit ID: 228325
Telephone: (972) 937-4010 Carnegie Class: Master's S
FAX Number: (972) 923-0488 Calendar System: Semester
URL: www.sagu.edu
Established: 1927 Annual Undergrad Tuition & Fees: $17,830
Enrollment: 2,032 Coed
Affiliation or Control: Assemblies Of God Church IRS Status: 501(c)3
Highest Offering: Master's
Program: Liberal Arts And General; Teacher Preparatory; Religious Emphasis
Accreditation: SC

01 President .... Dr. Kermit S. BRIDGES
05 Vice President for Academics .... Dr. Paul BROOKS
32 Vice President for Student Services .... Rev. Terry PHIPPS
10 Vice Pres for Business & Finance .... Vacant
30 Vice President for Univ Advancement .... Rev. Irby MCKNIGHT
84 Vice Pres Enrollment & Retention .... Rev. Eddie DAVIS
20 Dean of Academic Services .... Rev. Donny LUTRICK
58 Dean of Graduate Studies .... Dr. Robert HARDEN
73 Dean Col Bible & Church Ministries .... Dr. LeRoy BARTEL
50 Dean Col of Business & Education .... Dr. Larry GOODRICH
64 Dean Col of Music & Comm Arts .... Mr. Del GUYNES
09 Assoc Dean of Inst Effectiveness .... Dr. Kim BERNECKER
106 Asst Dean for Distance Education .... Rev. Joseph HARTMAN
06 Registrar .... Ms. Heather FRANCIS
35 Dean of Students .... Rev. Lance MECHE
89 Asst Dean for Student Success .... Rev. Rob BLAKNEY
88 Director of Achievement Center .... Mr. Nolan JONES
14 Sr Dir Information Technology .... Rev. David BUSH
29 Director of Alumni Relations .... Mr. Devin FERGUSON
08 Director of Learning Resources .... Mr. Eugene HOLDER
13 Director of Campus Software .... Mr. Mark WALKER
21 Sr Dir of Business Services .... Mr. Jimmie LAMB
88 Senior Director of Accounting .... Ms. Candee LUTRICK
37 Sr Director of Financial Aid .... Mr. Jeff FRANCIS
19 Director of Security .... Mr. Ron CRANE
07 Assistant Dean of Admissions .... Rev. Bryan BROOKS
24 Director of Media Services .... Mr. John COOKMAN
88 Director of Accounts Receivable .... Ms. Joan BUTLER
44 Sr Dir of Dev & Planned Giving .... Mr. Craig RINAS
36 Director of Career Services .... Ms. Beverly ROBINSON
41 Athletic Director .... Mr. Jesse GODDING
26 Director of University Marketing .... Mr. Ryan MCELHANY
15 Director of Human Resources .... Mrs. Ruth ROBERTS
88 Director of Educator Cert .... Ms. Janice WHITAKER
18 Projects Manager .... Mr. James DAVIS
38 Counselor .... Dr. Tim MYERS
88 Admissions Counselor .... Ms. Pat THOMPSON
88 Director of On Campus Admissions .... Ms. Sara ESCAMILLA
88 Director of Online Admissions .... Ms. Valerie FITZWATER

Southwestern Baptist Theological Seminary (G)

PO Box 22607, Fort Worth TX 76122-0150
County: Tarrant FICE Identification: 003617
Unit ID: 228477
Telephone: (817) 923-1921 Carnegie Class: Spec/Faith
FAX Number: (817) 921-8766 Calendar System: Semester
URL: www.swbts.edu
Established: 1908 Annual Undergrad Tuition & Fees: $7,586
Enrollment: 2,808 Coed
Affiliation or Control: Southern Baptist IRS Status: 501(c)3
Highest Offering: Doctorate
Program: Professional; Religious Emphasis
Accreditation: SC, MUS, THEOL

01 President .... Dr. Paige PATTERSON
05 Executive Vice President/Provost .... Dr. Craig A. BLAISING
10 Vice Pres Business Administration .... Mr. Kevin ENSLEY
30 Vice Pres Institutional Advancement .... Mr. Mike C. HUGHES
32 Vice Pres for Student Services/Comm .... Dr. Steven SMITH
88 Vice Pres of Strategic Initiatives .... Dr. Jason G. DUESING
06 Registrar & Assoc VP Inst Assessmnt .... Dr. Mark LEEDS
08 Dean of Libraries .... Dr. C. Berry DRIVER
73 Dean of the School of Theology .... Dr. David ALLEN
53 Dean Sch of Church & Fam Ministries .... Dr. Waylan OWENS
64 Dean School of Church Music .... Dr. Leo DAY
12 Dean Havard Sch for Theol Studies .... Dr. Denny AUTREY
73 Dean Sch of Evangelism & Missions .... Dr. Keith EITEL
49 Dean College at Southwestern .... Dr. Mike WILKINSON
94 Dean of Women's Programs .... Dr. Terri STOVALL
56 Dean Center for Extension Education .... Dr. Deron BILES
07 Director of Admissions .... Mr. Kyle WALKER

Southwestern Christian College (H)

Box 10, Terrell TX 75160-9002
County: Kaufman FICE Identification: 003618
Unit ID: 228486
Telephone: (972) 524-3341 Carnegie Class: Bac/Assoc
FAX Number: (972) 563-7133 Calendar System: Semester
URL: www.swcc.edu
Established: 1949 Annual Undergrad Tuition & Fees: $7,546
Enrollment: 206 Coed
Affiliation or Control: Churches Of Christ IRS Status: 501(c)3
Highest Offering: Baccalaureate
Program: Liberal Arts And General
Accreditation: SC

01 President .... Dr. Jack EVANS, SR.
30 Vice President for Instl Expansion .... Dr. James MAXWELL
05 Vice President Academic Affairs .... Mrs. Zoa Ann TURNER
10 Vice President Fiscal Affairs .... Mr. Douglas HOWIE
32 Vice President Student Affairs .... Mr. Ben FOSTER
08 Librarian .... Mrs. Doris JOHNSON
07 Director of Admissions .... Mr. Walter PRICE
37 Director of Financial Aid .... Ms. Tanya DEAN
44 Director of Development .... Mr. Jack EVANS, JR.

Southwestern University (I)

1001 E University Avenue, Georgetown TX 78626-6144
County: Williamson FICE Identification: 003620
Unit ID: 228343
Telephone: (512) 863-6511 Carnegie Class: Bac/A&S
FAX Number: (512) 863-5788 Calendar System: Semester
URL: www.southwestern.edu
Established: 1840 Annual Undergrad Tuition & Fees: $35,240
Enrollment: 1,394 Coed
Affiliation or Control: United Methodist IRS Status: 501(c)3
Highest Offering: Baccalaureate
Program: Liberal Arts And General; Teacher Preparatory
Accreditation: SC, MUS

01 President .... Dr. Edward B. BURGER
42 University Chaplain .... Ms. Beverly JONES
04 Executive Asst to the President .... Ms. Francie SCHROEDER
04 Sr Advisor Strategic Plng/Assess .... Dr. Ronald L. SWAIN

05 Provost/Dean of Faculty .... Dr. James W. HUNT
84 Vice Pres for Enrollment Services .... Mr. Dave VOSKUIL
30 Vice Pres University Relations .... Mr. C. Richard MCKELVEY
10 Vice President for Fiscal Affairs .... Mr. Richard L. ANDERSON
32 Vice President for Student Life .... Mr. Gerald D. BRODY
27 VP for Information Services and CIO .... Dr. Pam MCQUESTEN
57 Dean of Sarofim School of Fine Arts .... Dr. Paul J. GAFFNEY
08 Dean of Library Services .... Vacant
20 Assoc VP Academic Administration .... Ms. Julie A. COWLEY
26 Assoc VP for University Relations .... Ms. Cindy LOCKE
21 Assoc Vice President for Finance .... Mr. Craig ERWIN
18 Assoc VP for Facility/Campus Svcs .... Mr. Bob D. MATHIS
13 Assoc VP for Information Tech Svcs .... Vacant
15 Assoc VP for Human Resources .... Ms. Elma F. BENAVIDES
39 Assoc VP and Dean of Students .... Ms. Jaime WOODY
07 Assoc VP for Enrollment Services .... Vacant
29 Assoc VP for Alumni & Parents .... Ms. Megan FRISQUE
44 Associate Vice Pres for Development .... Mr. Kent HUNTSMAN
41 Assoc VP/Dir Intercollegiate Athl .... Dr. Glada C. MUNT
35 Associate Dean for Student Life .... Vacant
88 Asst Dean Faculty Dev & Spons Pgms .... Dr. John MCCANN
06 Assoc Director Records .... Ms. Adrienne EMBREE
21 Controller .... Ms. Brenda THOMPSON
19 Chief of Police .... Ms. Deborah BROWN
37 Director of Financial Aid .... Mr. James GAETA
36 Director Career Services .... Vacant
20 Assoc Dir Academic Success .... Mr. David SEILER
88 Dir Paideia Program/Assoc Professor .... Dr. David J. GAINES
85 Director Intercultural Learning .... Ms. Tisha TEMPLE
27 Director of Communications .... Ms. Ellen DAVIS
38 Director Counseling/Health Services .... Dr. Judith SONNENBERG
18 Director Physical Plant .... Mr. Joe LEPAGE
09 Director Institutional Research .... Vacant
28 Asst Dean Multicultural Affairs .... Ms. Terri JOHNSON
31 Director Civic Engagement .... Dr. Sarah BRACKMAN

Stephen F. Austin State University (A)

2008 Alumni Drive, Rusk 206,
Nacogdoches TX 75961-3940

County: Nacogdoches | FICE Identification: 003624
Unit ID: 228431
Telephone: (936) 468-2011 | Carnegie Class: Master's L
FAX Number: (936) 468-2202 | Calendar System: Semester
URL: www.sfasu.edu
Established: 1921 | Annual Undergrad Tuition & Fees (In-State): $8,412
Enrollment: 12,999 | Coed
Affiliation or Control: State | IRS Status: 501(c)3
Highest Offering: Doctorate
Program: Liberal Arts And General; Teacher Preparatory; Professional
Accreditation: SC, AAFCS, ART, BUS, CACREP, CIDA, CORE, CS, DIETD, DIETI, FOR, MUS, NUR, SP, SW, TED, THEA

01 President .... Dr. Baker PATTILLO
05 Provost/Vice Pres Academic Affairs .... Dr. Richard A. BERRY
10 Vice Pres Finance/Administration .... Mr. Danny R. GALLANT
32 Vice Pres for University Affairs .... Dr. Steve WESTBROOK
30 Vice Pres University Advancement .... Mrs. Jill STILL
29 Exec Director SFA Alumni Affairs .... Mr. Jeff DAVIS
20 Assoc Provost/VP Academic Affairs .... Dr. Mary Nelle BRUNSON
84 Exec Dir of Enrollment Management .... Ms. Monique COSSICH
26 Inr Exec Dir Public Affs/Marketing .... Mrs. Shirley LUNA
43 General Counsel .... Mr. Damon DERRICK
06 Registrar .... Ms. Lynda LANGHAM
09 Director Institutional Research .... Ms. Karyn HALL
08 Library Director .... Ms. Shirley DICKERSON
39 Director of Residence Life .... Mr. Winston BAKER
18 Director of Physical Plant .... Mr. Lee BRITTAIN
37 Director of Financial Aid .... Vacant
22 Director Affirmative Action .... Ms. Glenda HERRINGTON
13 Dir Computer/Communication Svcs .... Mr. Paul DAVIS
15 Personnel Director .... Ms. Glenda HERRINGTON
19 Chief of University Police .... Mr. Marc COSSICH
23 Director Health Services .... Dr. Penny JEFFERY
41 Director of Intercol Athletics .... Mr. Robert W. HILL
35 Dean Student Affairs .... Dr. Adam PECK
36 Director Counsel/Career Services .... Mrs. Jill MILEM
96 Director of Procurement .... Ms. Diana BOUBEL
45 Dir Research/Sponsored Programs .... Dr. Carrie BROWN
28 Director Multicultural Affairs .... Dr. Osaro AIREN
58 Dean Graduate School .... Dr. Mary Nelle BRUNSON
49 Dean College Liberal/Applied Arts .... Dr. Brian MURPHY
47 Dean College Forestry/Agriculture .... Dr. Steven BULLARD
53 Dean of College of Education .... Dr. Judy A. ABBOTT
57 Dean College Fine Arts .... Dr. A.C. (Buddy) HIMES
50 Int Dean College of Business .... Dr. Geralyn FRANKLIN
81 Dean College Sciences & Math .... Dr. Kimberly M. CHILDS

Tarrant County College District (B)

1500 Houston Street, Fort Worth TX 76102-6599

County: Tarrant | FICE Identification: 003626
Unit ID: 228547
Telephone: (817) 515-5100 | Carnegie Class: Assoc/Pub-U-MC
FAX Number: (817) 515-5350 | Calendar System: Semester
URL: www.tccd.edu
Established: 1965 | Annual Undergrad Tuition & Fees (In-District): $1,248
Enrollment: 50,467 | Coed
Affiliation or Control: State/Local | IRS Status: 501(c)3
Highest Offering: Associate Degree
Program: Occupational; 2-Year Principally Bachelor's Creditable
Accreditation: SC, ACFEI, ADNUR, CAHIIM, COARC, DH, DIETT, EMT, PTAA, RAD, SURGT

01 Chancellor .... Mrs. Erma C. JOHNSON HADLEY
05 Vice Chancellor Academic Affairs .... Dr. David A. WELLS
11 Vice Chanc Admin and Gen Counsel .... Mrs. Angela ROBINSON
10 Vice Chancellor for Finance .... Mr. Mark MCCLENDON
13 Vice Chanc Info/Technical Services .... Mr. Timothy (Tim) MARSHALL
88 Vice Chancellor for Student Success .... Dr. Joy GATES BLACK
18 Vice Chanc Real Estate/Facilities .... Ms. Nina PETTY
27 VC Communications/External Affairs .... Mr. Reginald GATES
20 VP Academic Affairs/SO Campus .... Vacant
20 VP Academic Affairs/NE Campus .... Mr. Gary SMITH
20 VP Academic Affairs/NW Campus .... Dr. Leann ELLIS
20 VP Academic Affairs/SE .... Vacant
20 VP Academic Affairs/TR .... Dr. Bryan STEWART
32 VP Student Dev Services/NE Campus .... Dr. Magdalena DELA TEJA
32 VP Student Dev Services/SE Campus .... Mr. Rusty FOX
32 VP Student Dev Services/So Campus .... Dr. Larry RIDEAUX
32 VP Student Dev Services/TR Campus .... Mr. Adrian RODRIGUEZ
32 VP Student Dev Services/NW .... Dr. Joe RODE
12 President South Campus .... Dr. Peter JORDAN
12 President Northwest Campus .... Dr. Elva C. LEBLANC
12 President Northeast Campus .... Dr. Larry J. DARLAGE
12 President Southeast Campus .... Dr. William COPPOLA
12 President Trinity River Campus .... Dr. Tahita M. FULKERSON
12 President TCC Connect .... Dr. Carlos MORALES
84 Assoc Vice Chanc Enrollment Svcs .... Mr. David XIMENEZ
88 Assoc Vice Chanc Student Success .... Dr. Kimberly A. BEATTY
15 Assoc Vice Chanc Human Resources .... Dr. Ricardo CORONADO
25 Assoc Vice Chanc Grants Dev/Compl .... Ms. Jackie MAKI
21 Assoc Vice Chancellor Finance .... Mrs. Nancy H. CHANG
20 Assoc Vice Chanc Academic Affairs .... Dr. Jane HARPER
51 Assoc Vice Chanc Cont Ed Svcs .... Mr. Troy VAUGHN
88 AVC Col Readiness Educ Foundations .... Mr. Rick GARCIA
30 Executive Director of Development .... Dr. Joe MCINTOSH
09 Dir Inst Rsrch/Plng/Effect .... Dr. Steven W. HAGSTROM
09 Exec Dir Inst Rsrch/Plng/Effect .... Dr. Terri L. DAY
26 Director Public Rels/Marketing .... Ms. Suzanne COTTRAUX
18 Dir of Physical Plant Operations .... Mr. Gary PREATHER
19 Chief of Police .... Mr. Shaun WILLIAMS
56 Director Distance Learning .... Vacant
08 Dir Library Svcs Northeast Campus .... Mr. Mark DOLIVE
08 Director Library Svcs South Campus .... Ms. Linda JENSON
08 Dir Library Svcs Northwest Campus .... Ms. Sandra MCGORDY
08 Dir Library Svcs Southeast Campus .... Mr. Mark DOLIVE
06 Registrar South Campus .... Mr. John D. SPENCER
06 Registrar Northeast Campus .... Mr. Brian D. BARRETT
06 Registrar Northwest Campus .... Dr. Aubra J. GANTT
06 Registrar Southeast Campus .... Mr. Juan C. TORRES
06 Registrar Trinity Campus .... Mr. Vikas RAJPUROHIT
38 Director Counseling South Campus .... Dr. Jade BORNE
38 Dir Counseling Northeast Campus .... Dr. Condoa PARRENT
38 Director Counseling Northwest Campu .... Dr. Charles (Ricks) EDMONDSON
38 Dir Counseling Southeast Campus .... Mr. Steve RAKOFF
38 Director Counseling Trinity River C .... Dr. Louann T. SCHULZE
37 Director Financial Aid South Campus .... Ms. JoLynn F. SPROLE
37 Dir Financial Aid Northeast Campus .... Vacant
37 Dir Financial Aid Northwest Campus .... Ms. Trina SMITH-PATTERSON
37 Dir Financial Aid Southeast Campus .... Ms. Erika T. WILLIAMS
37 Dir Financial Aid Trinity Campus .... Mr. William MCMULLEN
23 Dir Student Devel Svcs NE Campus .... Dr. Paula VASTINE-NORMAN
24 Dir Instruction Media South Campus .... Ms. Sue E. SANDERS
24 Dir Instruction Media NE Campus .... Mr. David B. MEAD
24 Dir Learning Resources NW Campus .... Dr. John R. MARTIN, JR.
35 Dir Student Activities So Campus .... Mr. Bobby (BJ) A. SULLIVAN
35 Dir Student Activities NW Campus .... Ms. Vesta M. MARTINEZ
35 Dir Student Devel Svcs SE Campus .... Mr. Douglas C. PEAK
96 Director of Business Svcs .... Mrs. Kathy CRUSTO-WAY
96 Director of Procurement .... Mr. Michael (Mike) HERNDON
36 Coord Student Career/Employmnt Svcs .... Ms. Sandra L. WALKER

Temple College (C)

2600 S First Street, Temple TX 76504-7435

County: Bell | FICE Identification: 003627
Unit ID: 228608
Telephone: (254) 298-8282 | Carnegie Class: Assoc/Pub-R-M
FAX Number: (254) 298-8266 | Calendar System: Semester
URL: www.templejc.edu
Established: 1926 | Annual Undergrad Tuition & Fees (In-District): $2,112
Enrollment: 5,303 | Coed
Affiliation or Control: Local | IRS Status: 501(c)3
Highest Offering: Associate Degree
Program: Occupational; 2-Year Principally Bachelor's Creditable
Accreditation: SC, ADNUR, COARC, DH, DMS, EMT, SURGT

01 President .... Dr. Glenda O. BARRON
10 AVP Finance/Info Tech Svcs .... Dr. Van MILLER
05 Vice Pres of Educational Services .... Dr. Mark A. SMITH
31 AVP Acad Outreach & Ext Programs .... Dr. Dan SPENCER
13 Senior Dir IT Services .... Vacant
15 Director Div of Resource Management .... Dr. Randy BACA
04 Div Dir Student & Enrollment Svcs .... Mrs. Carey ROSE
08 Div Director of Learning Resources .... Mrs. Kathy FULTON
102 Exec Dir Temple College Foundation .... Mrs. Jennifer GRAHAM
09 AVP Comm Init & Spec Programs .... Dr. Jimmy ROBERTS
38 Director Student Advising .... Ms. Amy FLINN
04 Assistant to the President & Board .... Mrs. Judith DOHNALIK
37 Director of Financial Aid .... Ms. Patricia GOODMAN
26 Director Marketing & Media Relation .... Ms. Erin SPENCER
18 Dir Facilities/Physical Plant .... Mr. Skeet POWELL
96 Director of Purchasing .... Mrs. Deborah SVAJDA
32 Chief Student Life Officer .... Mrs. Ruth BRIDGES
07 Assoc Dir Admission & Records .... Mrs. Toni CUELLAR
41 Athletic Director .... Mr. Craig MCMURTRY
19 Chief of Police .... Mr. Michael MARKUM

Texarkana College (D)

2500 N Robison Road, Texarkana TX 75501-3099

County: Bowie | FICE Identification: 003628
Unit ID: 228699
Telephone: (903) 823-3456 | Carnegie Class: Assoc/Pub-R-M
FAX Number: (903) 823-3451 | Calendar System: Semester
URL: www.texarkanacollege.edu
Established: 1927 | Annual Undergrad Tuition & Fees (In-District): $2,330
Enrollment: 4,111 | Coed
Affiliation or Control: Local | IRS Status: 501(c)3
Highest Offering: Associate Degree
Program: Occupational; 2-Year Principally Bachelor's Creditable
Accreditation: SC, ADNUR

01 President .... Mr. James H. RUSSELL
05 Dean of Academics .... Mr. Vernon WILDER
51 Dean Workforce & Cont Education .... Mrs. Ronda DOZIER
10 Chief Finance Officer .... Mrs. Kim JONES
32 Dean of Students .... Mr. Robert JONES
27 Chief Information Officer .... Mrs. Donna MCDANIEL
45 Dir of Institutional Effectiveness .... Mrs. Jamie ASHBY
07 Director of Admissions .... Mr. Lee WILLIAMS
06 Registrar .... Mrs. Kristi COBB
09 Director of Institutional Research .... Mrs. Jamie ASHBY
15 Director Human Resources .... Mrs. Phyllis DEESE
37 Director Student Financial Aid .... Mr. Martin HERNANDEZ
38 Director Advising .... Mr. Larry ANDREWS
18 Chief Facilities/Physical Plant .... Mr. Rick BOYETTE
30 Inst Advancement & Public Rels .... Mrs. Suzy IRWIN
84 Recruitment Coordinator .... Ms. Rebecca MILES

*The Texas A & M University System Office (E)

301 Tarrow Street, 7th Floor, College Station TX 77840

County: Brazos | FICE Identification: 003629
Unit ID: 228732
Telephone: (979) 458-6000 | Carnegie Class: N/A
FAX Number: (979) 458-6044
URL: www.tamus.edu

01 Chancellor .... Mr. John SHARP
05 Vice Chanc for Academic Affairs .... Dr. James HALLMARK
86 Vice Chanc for Federal & State Rels .... Dr. Guy DIEDRICH
09 Vice Chanc for Strategic Initiative .... Dr. Brett GIROIR
10 Chief Financial Officer .... Vacant
26 Vice Chanc Marketing/Communications .... Mr. Steve MOORE
30 Vice Chanc for Glob & Corp Partner .... Dr. Theresa FOSSUM
88 Chief Auditor .... Ms. Cathy SMOCK
43 General Counsel .... Mr. Ray BONILLA
46 Vice Chancellor for Research .... Dr. Jon MOGFORD
45 Chief Business Development Officer .... Mr. Phillip RAY
13 Chief Information Officer .... Mr. Mark STONE
22 Vice Chanc Recruitment & Diversity .... Vacant
21 Treasurer .... Ms. Maria ROBINSON

*Prairie View A & M University (F)

P.O. Box 519, Prairie View TX 77446-0519

County: Waller | FICE Identification: 003630
Unit ID: 227526
Telephone: (936) 261-3311 | Carnegie Class: Master's L
FAX Number: (936) 261-2115 | Calendar System: Semester
URL: www.pvamu.edu
Established: 1876 | Annual Undergrad Tuition & Fees (In-State): $6,764
Enrollment: 8,336 | Coed
Affiliation or Control: State | IRS Status: 501(c)3
Highest Offering: Doctorate
Program: Liberal Arts And General; Teacher Preparatory; Professional
Accreditation: SC, BUS, CS, DIETD, DIETI, ENG, ENGT, MUS, NUR, NURSE, SW, TED

02 President .... Dr. George C. WRIGHT
05 Provost/SR VP Academic Affairs .... Dr. E. Joahanne THOMAS-SMITH
20 Assoc Prov & Assoc VP Acad Afairs .... Dr. James J. WILSON, JR.
20 Assoc Prov & Assoc VP Acad Affairs .... Dr. Felicia M. NAVE
92 Director of Honors Program .... Dr. James J. WILSON, JR.
10 Sr Vice President Business Affairs .... Dr. Corey S. BRADFORD, SR.
32 VP for Student Affs/Inst Relations .... Dr. Lauretta F. BYARS
46 Vice President Research/Development .... Dr. Willie F. TROTTY
35 Vice Pres Student/Enrollment Svcs .... Mr. Don BYARS
10 Vice Pres Administration/Aux Svcs .... Mr. Fred E. WASHINGTON
20 Vice President of Business Admin .... Dr. Michael L. MCFRAZIER
84 Assoc Provost Enrollment Mgmt .... Mr. Don BYARS
21 Asst VP for Financial Accounting .... Mr. Rod MIRELES
21 Asst VP for Financial Services .... Ms. Patricia BAUGHMAN
30 Director of Development .... Mr. Nelson E. BOWMAN
09 Director Institutional Research .... Mr. Dean WILLIAMSON
07 Int Dir of Undergraduate Admissions .... Ms. Lenice BROWN
18 Int Assistant VP of Physical Plant .... Mr. Charles MUSE
08 Director of Library .... Dr. Rosie L. ALBRITTON
15 Asst VP for Human Resources .... Mr. Albert R. GEE
37 Director of Financial Aid .... Mr. K. Michael FRANCOIS

36 Program Coord Residence Life .... Mr. Charles E. CROCKETT
63 Director Undergrad Med Acad .... Dr. Dennis E. DANIELS
41 Director of Athletics .... Mr. Ashley N. ROBINSON
14 Chief Information Officer .... Mr. Rodney MOORE
58 Dean of the Graduate School .... Dr. Willie F. TROTTY
50 Dean College of Business .... Dr. Munir QUDDUS
53 Dean College of Education .... Dr. Terence HICKS
54 Dean College of Engineering .... Dr. Kendall T. HARRIS
47 Dean Col Agriculture/Human Sci .... Dr. Alton B. JOHNSON
66 Dean College of Nursing .... Dr. Betty ADAMS
49 Dean College of Arts & Sciences .... Dr. Danny R. KELLEY
48 Dean School of Architecture .... Dr. Ikhlas SABOUNI
88 Dean Col of Juv Just/Psychology .... Dr. Tamara L. BROWN
21 Director of Treasury Services .... Ms. Equilla JACKSON
23 Director Health Center .... Ms. Thelma J. PIERRE
56 Administrator Coop Extension .... Dr. Carolyn J. WILLIAMS
19 Chief of Police .... Ms. Zena A. STEPHENS
31 Asst VP Auxiliary Enterprises .... Ms. Tressey D. WILSON
29 Executive Dir for Comm/Alumni Affs .... Mrs. Sheleah D. REED
06 Registrar/Records .... Ms. Deborah J. DUNGEY
12 Exec Dir University College .... Ms. Lettie M. RAAB
28 Director of Diversity .... Ms. Elma D. GONZALEZ
85 Immigration Services Coord .... Mrs. Evelyn J. MCGINTY
26 Executive Dir for Communications .... Mrs. Sheleah D. REED
96 Procurement Sup/HUB Coordinator .... Mr. Jim A. NELMS
88 Director Budget & Reconciliation .... Mrs. Diane T. EVANS

*Tarleton State University (A)

1333 W Washington, Box T-0001,
Stephenville TX 76402-0001

County: Erath FICE Identification: 003631
Unit ID: 228529
Telephone: (254) 968-9000 Carnegie Class: Master's L
FAX Number: (254) 968-9920 Calendar System: Semester
URL: www.tarleton.edu
Established: 1899 Annual Undergrad Tuition & Fees (In-State): $7,212
Enrollment: 10,300 Coed
Affiliation or Control: State IRS Status: 501(c)3
Highest Offering: Doctorate
Program: Liberal Arts And General; Teacher Preparatory
Accreditation: SC, ACBSP, ENG, HT, MLTAD, MT, MUS, NURSE, SW

02 President .... Dr. F. Dominic DOTTAVIO
100 Chief of Staff .... Dr. Kyle W. MCGREGOR
05 Provost/Exec VPAA .... Dr. Karen MURRAY
30 Vice Pres Inst Advancement .... Dr. Rick RICHARDSON
10 Vice Pres Finance/Administration .... Mr. Tye MINCKLER
32 VP Student Life/Dean Students .... Mr. Rusty JERGINS
84 Assoc VP Enrollment/Inform Mgmt . Dr. David WEISSENBURGER
20 Assoc VP for Academic Affairs .... Dr. Dwayne SNIDER
38 Asst VP Wellness/Career Devel .... Vacant
46 Assoc VP Academic Research/Grants .... Dr. Bert LITTLE
18 Assoc Vice Pres Physical Facilities .... Mr. Joe STANDRIDGE
21 Asst VP Finance/Administration .... Ms. Cynthia CARTER
35 AVP Student Success/Multicul Init .... Dr. Jennifer T. EDWARDS
26 Assoc VP Marketing/Communications .... Ms. Janice HORAK
35 Asst VP Student Life Studies .... Dr. Ashley TULL
21 Asst VP Business Svcs/Controller .... Mr. Mike TATE
49 Dean College Science & Technology .... Dr. James PIERCE
50 Dean Col of Business Administration .... Vacant
47 Dean Col Agricul & Environ Sciences .... Dr. Donald L. CAWTHON
53 Dean College of Education .... Dr. Jill BURK
57 Dean College Liberal/Fine Arts .... Ms. Kelli STYRON
58 Dean College of Graduate Studies .... Dr. Linda M. JONES
07 Director Undergraduate Admissions .... Ms. Cynthia HESS
29 Dir Student Disability Services .... Ms. Trina GEYE
08 University Librarian .... Mrs. Donna SAVAGE
31 Asst VP External Relations .... Ms. Janice HORAK
37 Director Student Financial Aid .... Vacant
09 Director Institutional Research .... Dr. Mike HAYNES
13 CIO/Exec Dir Information Tech Svcs .... Ms. Rebecca GRAY
15 Asst VP Employee Services .... Ms. Angela C. BROWN
35 Asst VP for Student Life .... Ms. Darla DOTY
41 Athletic Director .... Mr. Lonn REISMAN
23 Director Student Health Center .... Ms. Bridgette BEDNARZ
19 University Police Chief .... Mr. Justin WILLIAMS
88 Exec Dir of Student Engagement .... Mr. Darrell BROWN
28 Dir Ofc Diversity/Inclusion .... Dr. Lora HELVIE-MASON
24 Dir Center for Instr Innovation .... Dr. Kelli SHAFFER
44 Asst VP of Development .... Ms. Sabra GUERRA
104 Dir International Academic Programs ...... Dr. Marilyn ROBITAILLE
06 Registrar .... Ms. Susan STOKER
96 Director of Purchasing/HUB .... Ms. Elaine CHEW
25 Accounts/Contracts Administrator .... Ms. Lori BEATY
40 Manager Campus Store .... Ms. Christina STRADLEY
105 Web Administrator .... Ms. Daphne HUNT

*Texas A & M International University (B)

5201 University Boulevard, Laredo TX 78041-1900

County: Webb FICE Identification: 009651
Unit ID: 226152
Telephone: (956) 326-2001 Carnegie Class: Master's L
FAX Number: (956) 326-2348 Calendar System: Semester
URL: www.tamiu.edu
Established: 1969 Annual Undergrad Tuition & Fees (In-State): $6,991
Enrollment: 7,213 Coed
Affiliation or Control: State IRS Status: 501(c)3
Highest Offering: Doctorate
Program: Liberal Arts And General; Teacher Preparatory
Accreditation: SC, BUS, NUR, SPAA

02 President .... Dr. Ray M. KECK, III
05 Provost/Vice Pres Academic Affs .... Dr. Pablo ARENAZ
10 Vice Pres Finance & Administration ... Mr. Juan J. CASTILLO, JR.
30 Vice Pres Institutional Advancement .... Mrs. Candy HEIN
32 Vice Pres for Student Success .... Dr. Minita RAMIREZ
20 Assoc Vice Pres Academic Affairs .... Mrs. Mary T. TREVINO
11 Assoc Vice Pres for Administration .. Mrs. Elizabeth N. MARTINEZ
88 Compliance Officer .... Mrs. Lisa M. PAUL
13 Assoc VP Information Technology/CIO ... Dr. Leebrian E. GASKINS
88 Regents Professor/Associate Provost .... Dr. Kevin D. LINDBERG
49 Dean College Arts & Sciences .... Dr. Thomas R. MITCHELL
50 Dean AR Sanchez Jr Sch of Business .... Dr. Steve R. SEARS
66 Dean Canseco School of Nursing .... Dr. Glenda WALKER
08 Dir Sue & Radcliffe Killam Library .... Mr. Douglas M. FERRIER
07 Director Admissions .... Mrs. Rosie A. DICKINSON
06 University Registrar .... Vacant
15 Director of Human Resources .... Mrs. Sandra V. PENA
26 Director Public Rels Mktg/Info Svcs .... Mr. Steve K. HARMON
37 Director Financial Aid .... Mrs. Laura M. ELIZONDO
88 Director of Athletics .... Mr. Gilbert ZIMMERMANN
18 Director Physical Plant .... Mr. Richard E. GENTRY
29 Director Alumni Relations .... Mrs. Yolitza Maric HOWARD
36 Director Career Services .... Mrs. Cassandra L. WHEELER
23 Assoc Director Student Health .... Ms. Elizabeth DODIER
39 Director of Residence Life/Housing .... Mr. Trevor C. LIDDLE
88 Assoc Dir Student Couns/Disb Svcs .... Ms. Aracely C. HERNANDEZ
96 Dir Purchasing & Support Services .... Mr. Carlos BELLA
92 Director Honors Program .... Vacant
21 Comptroller .... Ms. Elena M. MARTINEZ
32 Director Student Affairs .... Mr. Gerardo ALVA
88 Dir Recruitment/School Relations .... Mr. Juan G. GARCIA, JR.
35 Assoc Director Student Affairs .... Mr. Miguel A. TREVINO
09 Director of Institutional Research .... Ms. Elizabeth MARTINEZ

*Texas A & M University (C)

1246 TAMU, College Station TX 77843-1246

County: Brazos FICE Identification: 003632
Unit ID: 228723
Telephone: (979) 845-2217 Carnegie Class: RU/VH
FAX Number: (979) 845-5027 Calendar System: Semester
URL: www.tamu.edu
Established: 1876 Annual Undergrad Tuition & Fees (In-State): $9,006
Enrollment: 53,187 Coed
Affiliation or Control: State IRS Status: 501(c)3
Highest Offering: Doctorate
Program: Liberal Arts And General; Teacher Preparatory; Professional
Accreditation: SC, BUS, BUSA, CEA, CLPSY, CONST, COPSY, CS, DIETD, DIETI, ENG, ENGT, FEPAC, FOR, HSA, IPSY, LAW, LSAR, MED, NRPA, NURSE, PH, PLNG, SCPSY, SPAA, VET

02 President .... Dr. R. Bowen LOFTIN
05 Provost/Exec VP Academic Affairs .... Dr. Karan L. WATSON
11 VP Administration .... Dr. Rodney P. MCCLENDON
10 VP Finance/CFO .... Mr. B. J. CRAIN
32 VP Student Affairs .... LtGen. Joseph F. WEBER
46 Interim VP Research .... Dr. Glen A. LAINE
27 Int VP Marketing/Communications .... Mr. Shane HINCKLEY
86 VP Governmental Relations .... Mr. Michael O'QUINN
12 VP TAMU/Pres TAMU-Galveston .... RAdm. Robert SMITH, III
13 Vice Pres/Assoc Prov IT .... Dr. Pierce E. CANTRELL, JR.
28 Vice Pres/Assoc Prov Diversity .... Dr. Christine STANLEY
20 Vice Provost for Academic Affairs .... Dr. Pamela R. MATTHEWS
43 Deputy General Counsel .... Mr. Scott A. KELLY
47 Dean Agriculture & Life Science .... Dr. Mark A. HUSSEY
48 Dean Architecture .... Dr. Jorge VANEGAS
50 Dean Business .... Dr. Jerry STRAWSER
53 Dean Educ & Human Dev .... Dr. Douglas J. PALMER
54 Dean Engineering .... Dr. M. Katherine BANKS
65 Dean Geosciences .... Dr. Kate C. MILLER
80 Dean Govt & Public Policy .... Mr. Ryan C. CROCKER
49 Dean Liberal Arts .... Dr. Jose Luis BERMUDEZ
81 Dean Science .... Dr. H. Joseph NEWTON
74 Dean Vet Med & Biomed Sciences .... Dr. Eleanor M. GREEN
61 Interim Dean School of Law .... Mr. Aric SHORT
08 Dean/Director Libraries .... Mr. David H. CARLSON
12 Dean & CEO Texas A&M at Qatar .... Dr. Mark H. WEICHOLD
20 Dean of Faculties/Associate Provost .... Dr. Michael BENEDIK
20 Assoc Prov Undergrad Studies .... Dr. Ann KENIMER
20 Assoc Prov Graduate Studies .... Dr. Karen L. BUTLER-PURRY
07 Asst VP Acad Services/Admissions .... Mr. Scott MCDONALD
37 Exec Dir Student Financial Aid .... Ms. Delisa F. FALKS
06 Registrar .... Ms. Venesa A. HEIDICK
41 Athletic Director .... Mr. Eric C. HYMAN
15 Chief Human Resources Officer .... Ms. Kathryn B. SYMANK
14 Exec Dir Computing & Info Svcs .... Mr. Pete MARCHBANKS
19 Int Chief University Police .... Mr. J Michael E. REAGAN
36 Exec Dir Career Center .... Dr. J. Leigh TURNER
23 Director Student Health Center .... Dr. Martha C. DANNENBAUM
38 Exec Dir Student Counseling Svcs .... Dr. Maggie GARTNER
39 Director Residence Life/Housing .... Ms. Chareny L. RYDL
92 Exec Dir Honors Programs .... Dr. Sumana DATTA
104 Dir Study Abroad .... Dr. Jane FLAHERTY
96 Exec Dir Strategic Sourcing .... Mr. Rex JANNE
09 Exec Dir for Data & Research Svcs .... Dr. David J. MARTIN
30 Sr Executive Development .... Dr. Robert L. WALKER
102 Pres Texas A&M Foundation .... Dr. Eddie J. DAVIS
29 Pres Assoc of Former Students .... Mr. Porter GARNER
100 Chief of Staff to President .... Mr. Matt FRY

*Texas A & M University - Central Texas (D)

1001 Leadership Place, Killeen TX 76549

County: Bell Identification: 667086
Telephone: (245) 519-5400 Carnegie Class: Not Classified
FAX Number: (245) 519-5482 Calendar System: Semester
URL: www.ct.tamus.edu
Established: 1999 Annual Undergrad Tuition & Fees (In-State): $6,420
Enrollment: 2,253 Coed
Affiliation or Control: State IRS Status: 501(c)3
Highest Offering: Master's
Program: Liberal Arts And General
Accreditation: SC, ACBSP

02 President .... Dr. Marc A. NIGLIAZZO

*Texas A & M University - Commerce (E)

PO Box 3011, Commerce TX 75429-3011

County: Hunt FICE Identification: 003565
Unit ID: 224554
Telephone: (903) 886-5102 Carnegie Class: DRU
FAX Number: (903) 886-5888 Calendar System: Semester
URL: www.tamu-commerce.edu
Established: 1889 Annual Undergrad Tuition & Fees (In-State): $5,470
Enrollment: 11,187 Coed
Affiliation or Control: State IRS Status: 501(c)3
Highest Offering: Doctorate
Program: Liberal Arts And General; Teacher Preparatory; Professional
Accreditation: SC, ART, BUS, CACREP, ENG, MUS, SW

02 President .... Dr. Dan JONES
05 Provost/VP Academic Affairs .... Dr. Adolfo BENAVIDES
10 Vice Pres Business & Administration .... Mr. Bob BROWN
35 VP for Student Access & Success .... Mrs. Mary HENDRIX
30 Vice Pres Institutional Advancement .... Mr. Randy VAN DEVEN
100 Chief of Staff .... Ms. Alicia CURRIN
31 Dir Media Relations & Cmty Engage .... Mr. Noah NELSON
26 Exec Director Mktg Communications .... Ms. Lisa MARTINEZ
26 Assoc Provost for Academic Affs .... Dr. Dan EDLEMAN
20 Assoc VP Student Access & Success .... Dr. Sharon JOHNSON
09 Assoc Prov of Inst Effectiveness .... Dr. Marila PALMER
84 Dean of Enrollment Management .... Mrs. Stephanie HOLLEY
21 Assoc VP & Dir of Financial Svcs .... Ms. Paula HANSON
21 Executive Dir of Budget .... Ms. Tina LIVINGSTON
06 Registrar .... Ms. Paige BUSSELL
88 Comptroller/Director of Accounting .... Ms. Kim LAIRD
08 Library Director .... Dr. Gregory MITCHELL
27 Chief Information Officer .... Mr. Tim MURPHY
37 Director of Financial Aid .... Ms. Maria RAMOS
36 Director of Career Development .... Mrs. Tina BOITNOTT
58 Vice Prov of Research/Dean of Grad .... Mrs. Arlene HORNE
53 Int Dean Education & Human Services .... Dr. Gail JOHNSON
79 Dean of Humanities/Soc Sci & Art .... Dr. Salvatore ATTARDO
92 Dean of the Honors College .... Dr. Ray GREEN
81 Dean Science/Engr & Agric .... Dr. Grady PRICE BLOUNT
50 Int Dean Bus & Entrepreneurship .... Dr. Dale FUNDERBURK
88 Dean of University College .... Dr. Ricky DOBBS
07 Director of Undergraduate Admiss .... Mr. Jody TODHUNTER
108 Director of Student Assessment .... Ms. Wendy GRUVER
32 Asst VP/Dean Campus Life/Stdnt Dev .... Mr. John KAULFUS
29 Director of Alumni Relations .... Mr. Derryle PEACE
19 University Police Chief .... Mrs. Donna SPINATO
12 Director Metroplex Center .... Mr. Russell BLANCHETT
38 Director Counseling Center .... Dr. Linda T. CLINTON
39 Residential Living & Learning .... Mr. Dennis KOCH
41 Athletic Director .... Mr. Ryan IVEY
88 Dir of Risk Management .... Mr. Jeffrey MCMURRAY
23 Director Student Health Services .... Ms. Maxine MENDOZA-WELCH
85 Dir International Student Services .... Mr. John MARK JONES
96 Director of Purchasing/HUB Coord .... Mr. Travis BALL
28 Dir of Diversity & Cultural Affair .... Mr. Robert DOTSON
88 Safety Manager .... Mr. Derek PREAS

*Texas A & M University - Corpus Christi (F)

6300 Ocean Drive, Unit 5756,
Corpus Christi TX 78412-5756

County: Nueces FICE Identification: 011161
Unit ID: 224147
Telephone: (361) 825-5700 Carnegie Class: DRU
FAX Number: (361) 825-5887 Calendar System: Semester
URL: www.tamucc.edu
Established: 1947 Annual Undergrad Tuition & Fees (In-State): $7,779
Enrollment: 10,508 Coed
Affiliation or Control: State IRS Status: 501(c)3
Highest Offering: Doctorate
Program: Liberal Arts And General; Teacher Preparatory; Professional
Accreditation: SC, BUS, BUSA, CACREP, CS, ENGR, ENGT, MT, MUS, NURSE

02 President .... Dr. Flavius C. KILLEBREW
05 Provost/VP for Academic Affairs . Dr. Christopher L. MARKWOOD
10 Exec VP for Finance/Administration ... Ms. Kathryn FUNK-BAXTER
30 Vice Pres Institutional Advancement .... Dr. S. Trent HILL
32 VP Student Engagement & Success .... Dr. Don ALBRECHT
46 VP Rsrch/Commercialization/Outreach .... Dr. Luis CIFUENTES

20 Vice Provost Academic Affairs ....Dr. Paul MEYER
100 Chief of Staff ....Dr. Mary SHERWOOD
13 Assoc Vice Pres Info Technology/CIO ....Mr. Terry TATUM
20 Assoc VP for Academic Affairs ....Dr. David BILLEAUX
84 Assoc VP Enrollment Management ....Ms. Margaret DECHANT
35 Assoc Vice Pres/Dean of Students ....Ms. Ann DEGAISH
08 Assoc VP Acad Affs/Dir Bell Library .... Ms. Christine SHUPALA
09 Dir Planning & Instl Research ....Mr. Jerry SCHEERER
26 Dir Communications/Public Affairs ....Ms. Gloria GALLARDO
29 Dir Development/Alumni Relations ....Ms. Kimberly DEVISSER
06 Univ Registrar/Dir Veterans Affrs ....Mr. Michael RENDON
07 Exec Director of Admissions ....Mr. Oscar REYNA
37 Director of Financial Assistance ....Ms. Jeannie GAGE
31 Director Community Outreach ....Dr. James NEEDHAM
15 Director Human Resources ....Ms. Debra CORTINAS
44 Director Annual Giving ....Ms. Evon ENGLISH
36 Director Career Services ....Ms. Joanna BENAVIDES-FRANKE
38 Dir Student Counseling/Development ....Dr. Carla BERKICH
28 Dir Employee Develop/Compliance Svc ....Mr. Sam RAMIREZ
11 Exec Dir Administrative Services ....Ms. Judy HARRAL
96 Dir Procurement & Disbursements ....Mr. David DAVILA
21 Bursar ....Ms. Christina HOLZHEUSER
58 Dean College of Grad Studies ....Dr. Jo Ann CANALES
49 Dean College of Liberal Arts ....Dr. Kelly QUINTANILLA
50 Dean College of Business ....Dr. John E. GAMBLE
53 Dean College of Education ....Dr. Arthur HERNANDEZ
54 Dean College of Science & Engrng ....Dr. Frank PEZOLD
66 Dean College of Nursing/Health Sci .....Dr. Mary Jane HAMILTON

*Texas A & M University - Kingsville (A)

700 University Boulevard, Kingsville TX 78363-8202
County: Kleberg FICE Identification: 003639
Unit ID: 228705
Telephone: (361) 593-2111 Carnegie Class: DRU
FAX Number: (361) 593-3107 Calendar System: Semester
URL: www.tamuk.edu
Established: 1925 Annual Undergrad Tuition & Fees (In-State): $6,940
Enrollment: 7,234 Coed
Affiliation or Control: State IRS Status: 501(c)3
Highest Offering: Doctorate
Program: Liberal Arts And General; Teacher Preparatory; Fine Arts Emphasis
Accreditation: SC, #ACBSP, DIETD, DIETI, ENG, MUS, NAIT, PHAR, #SP, SW

02 President ....Dr. Steven H. TALLANT
100 Chief of Staff ....Mr. Randy HUGHES
88 Interim Dir of Compliance ....Ms. Antonia ALVAREZ
05 Provost & Vice Pres Acad Affs ....Dr. Rex F. GANDY
10 Sr VP Fiscal Affairs ....Dr. Terisa RILEY
88 Assistant Director of Budgets ....Ms. Jennifer ALEXANDER
88 Comptroller ....Ms. Lallah M. HOWARD
88 Risk Management ....Dr. Shane CREEL
30 Vice Pres Institutional Advancement ....Mr. Scott GINES
36 Exec Director of Career Services ....Mr. Christian FERRIS
32 Vice President Student Affairs ....Dr. Terisa C. RILEY
88 Assoc Dir MSUB ....Mr. Crispin TREVINO
88 Dir of Campus Rec & Fitness ....Mr. Charles ESPINOSA
84 VP Enrollment Management ....Mr. Manuel LUJAN
27 Chief Information Officer ....Mr. Robert PAULSON
88 Assoc CIO ....Mr. Lonnie NAGEL
88 Dir Enterprise Applications ....Mr. Lee MOORE
88 Dir IT Client Support Services ....Mr. Val RAMIREZ
35 Dean of Students ....Ms. Kristin COMPARY
20 Associate VP Academic Affairs ....Dr. Duane GARDINER
85 Ex Dir International Studies ....Ms. Marilu SALAZAR
88 Dir Center Teaching Effectiveness ....Dr. Jaya GOSWAMI
58 Assoc VP Research & Grad Studies ....Dr. Mohamed ABDELRAHMAN
88 Asst VP Student Access ....Dr. Mary GONZALEZ
47 Dean Agriculture/Nat Res/Human Sci ....Dr. George A. RASMUSSEN
49 Dean Arts & Sciences ....Dr. Abbey ZINK
50 Dean Business Administration ....Dr. Natalya DELCOURE
53 Dean Education & Human Performance ....Dr. Alberto RUIZ
54 Dean Engineering ....Dr. Stephan NIX
92 Dean Ofc Academic Affairs ....Dr. Dolores GUERRERO
89 Assoc VP for Student Success ....Dr. Nancy KING SANDERS
26 Exec Dir Mktg & Comm ....Ms. Cheryl CAIN
08 Librarian ....Mr. Bruce R. SCHUENAMAN
108 Dir Planning & Assessment ....Mr. Oscar HERNANDEZ
88 Director Citrus Center ....Dr. John DA GRACA
88 Director King Ranch Institute ....Dr. Clay P. MATHIS
88 Exec Director CKWRI ....Dr. Fred BRYANT
88 Interim Dir Nat Toxins Res Ctr ....Dr. Elda E. SANCHEZ
88 Director Inst Sust Energy & Env ....Dr. Kim JONES
06 Registrar ....Mr. George WEIR
07 Director of Admission ....Mr. Ramon BLAKLEY
29 Director Development and Alumni Rel ....Ms. Yvonne TRACHTA
41 Director Athletics ....Vacant
40 Director Bookstore ....Ms. Mary GUTIERREZ
106 Director Distance Learning ....Ms. Michelle DURAN
44 Exec Dir Development & Alumni ....Ms. Lori RUSSEK
88 Interim Dir Health and Wellness . Ms. Jo Elda CASTILLO-ALANIZ
09 Director Institutional Research ....Ms. Miao ZHUANG
88 Director John E. Conner Museum ....Mr. Jonathan PLANT
16 Exec Dir HR & Payroll ....Mr. Leon BAZAR
18 Director Physical Plant ....Mr. Roberto RAMIREZ
96 Assoc VP Support Services ....Mr. Ralph STEPHENS
25 Contract Administrator ....Ms. Rachel L. BUENTELLO
39 Director Residence Life ....Mr. Tom MARTIN
46 Exec Dir Research & Sponsored Pgms ....Dr. Rebecca DAVIS

35 Interim Director Student Activities ....Ms. Erin MCCLURE
19 Director of University Police ....Mr. Felipe GARZA
37 Director Student Financial Aid ....Mr. Ralph PERRI
38 Director Student Counseling ....Vacant
21 Supervisor Business Services ....Ms. Janet L. POLLARD
88 Advisor Pre-profession Programs ....Ms. Amanda MUNIZ
88 Bible Chair Baptist ....Mr. Mike CERVANTES
88 Bible Chair Catholic ....Mr. Victor RODRIGUEZ

*Texas A & M University System Health Science Center (B)

8441 State HWY 47, CB1 Suite 3100, Bryan TX 77807
County: Brazos FICE Identification: 004948
Unit ID: 223214
Telephone: (979) 436-9100 Carnegie Class: Spec/Med
FAX Number: (979) 436-0072 Calendar System: Semester
URL: www.tamhsc.edu
Established: 1999 Annual Undergrad Tuition & Fees (In-State): $10,010
Enrollment: 2,286 Coed
Affiliation or Control: State IRS Status: 501(c)3
Highest Offering: Doctorate
Program: Professional
Accreditation: SC

02 Interim Executive VP & CEO ....Mr. E.J. (Jere) PEDERSON
05 Int VP for Academic Affairs ....Dr. Vernon L. TESH
10 Vice Pres Finance & Administration ....Dr. Barry C. NELSON
86 Vice President Governmental Affairs ....Ms. Jenny E. JONES
46 Vice Pres Research/Graduate Studies ....Dr. David S. CARLSON
13 Assistant Vice President/CIO ....Mr. Scott HONEA
52 Dean Baylor College of Dentistry ....Dr. Lawrence E. WOLINSKY
63 Int Dean Col of Med/VP Clin Affs ....Dr. Paul E. OGDEN
66 Dean College of Nursing ....Dr. Sharon A. WILKERSON
67 Dean College of Pharmacy ....Dr. Indra K. REDDY
69 Int Dean Sch of Rural Public Health ....Dr. James N. BURDINE
88 Dir Inst for Biosciences & Tech ....Dr. Cheryl WALKER
100 Chief of Staff ....Dr. Lee Ann RAY

† Tuition varies by program.

*Texas A & M University - Texarkana (C)

7101 University Avenue, Texarkana TX 75503
County: Bowie FICE Identification: 031703
Unit ID: 224545
Telephone: (903) 223-3000 Carnegie Class: Master's L
FAX Number: (903) 832-8890 Calendar System: Semester
URL: www.tamut.edu
Established: 1971 Annual Undergrad Tuition & Fees (In-State): $5,568
Enrollment: 1,995 Coed
Affiliation or Control: State IRS Status: 501(c)3
Highest Offering: Doctorate
Program: Liberal Arts And General; Professional
Accreditation: SC, NURSE

02 President ....Dr. Emily FOURMY CUTRER
05 Provost/Vice Pres Academic Affairs ....Dr. James SCOGIN
10 Int VP Finance & Administration ....Mr. Randy RIKEL
32 VP Student Engagement & Success ....Dr. Kent KELSO
88 Dean College of STEM ....Dr. Arthur LINKINS
53 Dean College Education/Liberal Art ....Dr. Glenda BALLARD
50 Dean College of Business ....Dr. Larry DAVIS
21 Controller ....Mr. James SCOGIN
07 Exec Dir Enrollment Services ....Mr. Richard BOLLINGER
37 Dir Financial Aid & Veteran Svcs ....Ms. Alyssa HALEY
15 Director Human Resources & EEO ....Mr. Ricky NORTON
30 Asst VP University Advancement ....Mrs. LeAnne WRIGHT
09 AVP Institutional Effectiveness ....Vacant
08 Director Library ....Mrs. Teri STOVER
18 Director Physical Plant ....Mr. Jeff ALLEN
18 Director of Security ....Mr. John GANN
96 Director Purchasing ....Mrs. Cynthia HENDERSON
13 Int AVP of Information Technology ....Mr. Scott LENT
88 Director Payroll ....Mrs. Ramona GREEN
35 Director Student & Career Services ....Mr. Carl GREIG
84 Director Enrollment Management ....Mr. Toney FAVORS
27 Mgr Communications/Alumni Relation ...... Mr. Bob BRUGGEMAN

*West Texas A & M University (D)

2403 Russell C. Long Blvd., Canyon TX 79015
County: Randall FICE Identification: 003665
Unit ID: 229814
Telephone: (806) 651-0000 Carnegie Class: Master's L
FAX Number: (806) 651-2126 Calendar System: Semester
URL: www.wtamu.edu
Established: 1910 Annual Undergrad Tuition & Fees (In-State): $6,970
Enrollment: 7,955 Coed
Affiliation or Control: State IRS Status: 501(c)3
Highest Offering: Doctorate
Program: Liberal Arts And General; Teacher Preparatory; Professional
Accreditation: SC, BUS, ENG, MUS, NURSE, SP, SW

02 President ....Dr. J. Patrick O'BRIEN
05 Provost/Vice Pres Acad Affairs ....Dr. Wade SHAFFER
10 Vice Pres for Business & Finance ....Mr. Gary W. BARNES
32 Int Vice Pres for Student Affairs ....Ms. Denese SKINNER
26 Vice Pres Institutional Advancement ....Dr. Neal WEAVER
84 Vice Pres of Enrollment Management ....Mr. Dan D. GARCIA

30 Executive Director of Development ....Dr. Neal WEAVER
06 Registrar ....Ms. Tana J. MILLER
07 Director of Admissions ....Mr. Kyle MOORE
08 Dir Information/Library Resources ....Ms. Shawna J. KENNEDY-WITTHAR
36 Int Dir Career Planning & Placement ....Ms. Kim MULLER
37 Director Student Financial Aid ....Mr. James D. REED
51 Dir Education on Demand ....Ms. Andrea PORTER
23 Director Medical Service ....Dr. Jim GIBBS
18 Director Physical Plant ....Mr. Dan K. SMITH
19 Police Chief ....Chief Shawn G. BURNS
27 Director Communication Services ....Ms. Ann UNDERWOOD
29 Director of Alumni Relations ....Ms. Becky STOGNER
38 Int Director Counseling Services ....Mr. Orvie NIX
41 Director of Athletics ....Mr. Michael MCBROOM
09 Director Institutional Research ....Mr. Jarvis D. HAMPTON
13 Chief Information Officer ....Mr. James D. WEBB
96 Director of Purchasing ....Mr. Brian GLENN
40 Manager Bookstore ....Mr. Terry S. NEPPER
15 Director Personnel Services ....Mr. Harvey L. HUDSPETH
47 Dean Col Agr/Science/Engineering ....Dr. Don TOPLIFF
50 Dean College of Business ....Dr. Neil W. TERRY
53 Dean Col Education & Social Science ....Dr. Eddie W. HENDERSON
57 Dean College Fine Arts/Humanities ....Dr. Jessica MALLARD
58 Dean Graduate School & Research ....Dr. Angela SPAULDING
66 Dean College of Nursing/Health Sci ....Dr. Dirk NELSON
21 Controller ....Mr. Rick JOHNSON

*Texas A & M University Baylor College of Dentistry (E)

3302 Gaston Avenue, Dallas TX 75246-2098
Telephone: (214) 828-8100 Identification: 666240
Accreditation: &SC, DENT, DH

† Main campus is Texas A & M University System Health Science Center in Bryan, TX.

*Texas A & M University at Galveston (F)

PO Box 1675, Galveston TX 77553-1675
Telephone: (409) 740-4400 FICE Identification: 010298
Accreditation: &SC, ENG, ENGT

† Main campus is Texas A & M University in College Station, TX.

*Texas A & M University-San Antonio (G)

One University Way, San Antonio TX 78224
Telephone: (210) 784-1000 Identification: 666689
Accreditation: &SC

† Main campus is Texas A & M University - Kingsville in Kingsville, TX.

Texas Chiropractic College (H)

5912 Spencer Highway, Pasadena TX 77505-1699
County: Harris FICE Identification: 003635
Unit ID: 228866
Telephone: (281) 487-1170 Carnegie Class: Spec/Health
FAX Number: (281) 487-2009 Calendar System: Trimester
URL: www.txchiro.edu
Established: 1908 Annual Undergrad Tuition & Fees: N/A
Enrollment: 240 Coed
Affiliation or Control: Independent Non-Profit IRS Status: 501(c)3
Highest Offering: Doctorate
Program: Professional
Accreditation: SC, CHIRO

01 Interim President/CEO ....Dr. Fred ZUKER
05 Vice President/Provost ....Vacant
10 Chief Financial Officer ....Mr. Bill QUINN
20 VP Academic & Program Development ....Dr. Steve FOSTER
20 Dean of Academic Affairs ....Dr. John MROZEK
84 VP of Enrollment Management ....Dr. Fred ZUKER
23 Dean of Clinics ....Dr. Barry WIESE
06 Registrar ....Dr. Karlene DENBY
46 Director Research ....Vacant
15 Director of Human Resources ....Mrs. Sue ARNOLD
26 Director of Communications ....Ms. Melissa TREVIZO
09 Director Institutional Research ....Dr. Lee VANDUSEN
51 Director of Postgraduate ....Ms. Kristi BAILEY
08 Director of Library Services ....Ms. Carol WEBB
37 Director Financial Aid ....Mr. Arthur GOUDEAU
29 Director of Alumni Relations ....Ms. Gabrielle GREENWADE
07 Associate Director of Admissions ....Ms. Kristina HANSON
04 Admin Asst to President ....Ms. Glenda RAMIREZ
18 Physical Plant Supervisor ....Mr. Perry LATIOLAIS
18 Director of Facillities ....Mr. Joe HERNANDEZ

Texas Christian University (I)

2800 S University Drive, Fort Worth TX 76129-2800
County: Tarrant FICE Identification: 003636
Unit ID: 228875
Telephone: (817) 257-7000 Carnegie Class: DRU
FAX Number: (817) 257-7333 Calendar System: Semester
URL: www.tcu.edu
Established: 1873 Annual Undergrad Tuition & Fees: $36,590
Enrollment: 9,727 Coed
Affiliation or Control: Christian Church (Disciples Of Christ) IRS Status: 501(c)3
Highest Offering: Doctorate

Program: Liberal Arts And General; Teacher Preparatory; Professional
Accreditation: SC, ANEST, ART, BUS, BUSA, CIDA, CS, DANCE, DIETC, DIETD, ENG, JOUR, MUS, NURSE, SP, SW

01 Chancellor Dr. Victor J. BOSCHINI, JR.
05 Provost/Vice Chanc Academic Affairs Dr. R. Nowell DONOVAN
10 Vice Chanc Finance & Administration Mr. Brian G. GUTIERREZ
30 Vice Chanc University Advancement Mr. Donald J. WHELAN, JR.
32 Vice Chancellor Student Affairs Dr. Kathryn CAVINS-TULL
26 Vice Chanc Mktg & Communication Ms. Tracy SYLER-JONES
86 Vice Chanc Government Affairs Mr. Larry D. LAUER
35 Assoc Vice Chanc Student Affairs Dr. Barbara B. HERMAN
35 Assoc Vice Chanc/Dean Campus Life Ms. Susan B. ADAMS
88 Assoc Vice Chanc Advancement Ops Dr. Roby V. KEY
29 Assoc Vice Chanc Alumni Relations Ms. Kristi M. HOBAN
16 Assoc Vice Chanc HR/Risk Mgmt Ms. Jill L. LASTER
21 Assoc Vice Chanc & Controller Ms. Cheryl L. WILSON
18 Assoc Vice Chanc for Facilities Mr. Todd S. WALDVOGEL
44 Asst Vice Chanc College & Reg Devel Mr. Adam BAGGS
35 Asst VC of Student Affairs Mr. Darron TURNER
88 Chief Investment Officer Mr. Jim HILLE
41 Director Athletics Mr. Christopher DEL CONTE
100 Chief of Staff Ms. Karen M. BAKER
20 Assoc Provost Academic Affairs Dr. Bonnie MELHART
20 Assoc Provost Academic Support Dr. Leo W. MUNSON
20 Assoc Provost Academic Plan/Budget Dr. Ann C. SEWELL
20 Assoc Provost Technology Support Mr. Ruben D. CHANLATTE
20 Asst Provost Inst Effectiveness Dr. Catherine WEHLBURG
49 Dean Addran College of Liberal Arts Dr. Andrew SCHOOLMASTER
50 Dean Neeley School of Business Dr. Homer EREKSON
60 Dean College of Communication Dr. David WHILLOCK
53 Dean College of Education Dr. Mary PATTON
57 Dean College of Fine Arts Dr. Scott SULLIVAN
66 Dean Harris Col Nurs/Hlth Science Dr. Paulette BURNS
54 Dean Col of Science & Engineering Dr. Phil HARTMAN
92 Dean John V Roach Honors College Dr. Peggy WATSON
08 Dean of the Library Dr. June KOELKER
07 Dean of Admission Mr. Raymond A. BROWN
13 Director Information Technology Mr. Bryan LUCAS
88 Exec Dir Acad Resource Mgmt & Compl Ms. Susan G. CAMPBELL
22 Affirmative Action Officer Mr. Darron TURNER
06 Registrar/Dir Enrollment Management Mr. Patrick MILLER
19 Chief TCU Police Mr. Steve G. MCGEE
42 Minister to the University Rev. Angela KAUFMAN
21 Asst Vice Chanc Finance Mr. Kenneth JANAK
85 Director Center for Intl Studies Dr. Jane KUCKO
15 Director Compensation Ms. Dindy ROBINSON
25 Director Contract Administration Mr. Matthew WALLIS
15 Director Employee Relations Ms. Sharon E. BARNES
51 Director Extended Education Mr. David A. GREBEL
88 Director Freshman Admission Mr. Heath EINSTEIN
23 Director Health Center Dr. Jane TORGERSON
09 Director Institutional Research Dr. Cathan COGHLAN
24 Director Instructional Services Mr. Larry E. KITCHENS
85 Director International Student Svcs Mr. John L. SINGLETON
38 Director Mental Health Services Dr. Linda WOLSZON
96 Director Purchasing Mr. Roger D. FULLER
39 Director Housing & Residential Life Mr. Craig ALLEN
37 Director Student Aid Mr. Michael H. SCOTT
88 Assoc Dean Student Development Svc Dr. Thomas STUDDERT
25 Director Sponsored Programs Ms. Linda FREED
36 Exec Director Univ Career Svcs Dr. John THOMPSON

Texas College (A)

2404 N Grand Avenue, Tyler TX 75702-1962
County: Smith FICE Identification: 003638
Unit ID: 228884
Telephone: (903) 593-8311 Carnegie Class: Bac/Diverse
FAX Number: (903) 593-0588 Calendar System: Semester
URL: www.texascollege.edu
Established: 1894 Annual Undergrad Tuition & Fees: $10,008
Enrollment: 842 Coed
Affiliation or Control: Christian Methodist Episcopal IRS Status: 501(c)3
Highest Offering: Baccalaureate
Program: 2-Year Principally Bachelor's Creditable; Liberal Arts And General; Teacher Preparatory
Accreditation: SC

01 President Dr. Dwight FENNELL
05 Vice President Academic Affairs Mrs. Cynthia MARSHALL-BIGGINS
10 Vice Pres Business & Finance Mr. James HARRIS
32 Vice Pres Student Affairs Dr. Willie CHAMPION
30 Director of Development Mrs. Diane STEPHENSON
07 Dean of Enrollment Services Mr. John ROBERTS
35 Dean of Students Mr. Isaac WILLIAMS
06 Registrar Mr. John ROBERTS
09 Dir Inst Research/Effectiveness Mrs. Cynthia MARSHALL-BIGGINS
08 Director of Library Services Mr. Otis ALEXANDER
13 Director of Information Technology Mr. Dave PICKINS
15 Director Human Resources Ms. Lois BOWIE
21 Comptroller Mr. Walter MOSLEY
36 Coord Counseling & Career Services Vacant
41 Athletic Director Mr. Freddy RODRIGUEZ
37 Director Financial Aid Ms. Cecelia K. JONES
18 Director Physical Plant Mr. Roland BRACKENS
26 Coordinator Public Relations Ms. Christie HOWARD
29 Coordinator Alumni Affairs Ms. Orenthia MASON
88 Coordinator of Special Projects Mrs. Angelia FENNELL
88 Asst to VP for AA/Dean Lower Col Dr. Robert HARPER

Texas Health and Science University (B)

4005 Manchaca Road, Austin TX 78704-6737
County: Travis FICE Identification: 031795
Unit ID: 430704
Telephone: (512) 444-8082 Carnegie Class: Spec/Health
FAX Number: (512) 444-6345 Calendar System: Trimester
URL: www.thsu.edu
Established: 1990 Annual Undergrad Tuition & Fees: $15,304
Enrollment: 97 Coordinate
Affiliation or Control: Proprietary IRS Status: Proprietary
Highest Offering: Master's; No Lower Division
Program: Professional
Accreditation: ACICS, ACUP

01 President Ms. Lisa LIN
05 Academic Dean Dr. Maoyi CAI
20 Vice Pres of Academics/Assessment Dr. Joseph MCMILLAN
11 Sr Administrator/Program Director Dr. Floyd QUINN
88 Administrator Ms. Wai-Lan KUO
37 Financial Aid Officer Mr. Tim SPAHN
07 Director of Admissions Mr. Orlando PEREZ
17 Clinic Director Mr. Dragon CHU
88 Director Herbal Deparment Dr. Hai Tao CAO
88 Director of Acupuncture Department Dr. Shaozhi LI
88 Director Bio-Med Dept/Dean Students Dr. Maoyi CAI
08 Librarian/Systems Administrator Mr. Ryan HAECKER
46 Director of Research Department Dr. Lin-Ying TAN
10 Opers Dir Budget/Human Resources Mr. Paul LIN
06 Registrar/Administrator Ms. Paola VALLADARES
32 Dean of Students/Assoc Dir Ms. Marty CALLIHAM

Texas Lutheran University (C)

1000 W Court Street, Seguin TX 78155-5999
County: Guadalupe FICE Identification: 003641
Unit ID: 228981
Telephone: (830) 372-8000 Carnegie Class: Bac/Diverse
FAX Number: (830) 372-8096 Calendar System: Semester
URL: www.tlu.edu
Established: 1891 Annual Undergrad Tuition & Fees: $25,890
Enrollment: 1,318 Coed
Affiliation or Control: Evangelical Lutheran Church In America
IRS Status: 501(c)3
Highest Offering: Master's
Program: Liberal Arts And General; Teacher Preparatory
Accreditation: SC, ACBSP, MUS, TEAC

01 President Dr. Stuart B. DORSEY
05 Vice Pres for Academic Affairs Dr. Debbie COTTRELL
11 Asst to Pres Admin/Public Affairs Mr. Stephen P. ANDERSON
10 Vice President Finance Mr. Andrew NELSON
84 Vice President Enrollment Services Mr. Thomas OLIVER
30 VP for Development/Alumni Relations Mr. Rick ROBERTS
32 VP/Dean of Student Life & Learning Ms. Kristi QUIROS
06 Director of Records & Registration Mr. Glenn YOCKEY
08 Library Director Ms. Martha RINN
37 Director of Financial Aid Ms. Cathleen WRIGHT
42 Campus Pastor Rev. Greg RONNING
36 Director Career Services Ms. Kimberly WATTS
38 Director Counseling Services Ms. Terry WEERS
07 Director of Admissions Mr. Adam NAVARRO-JUSINO
15 Director Personnel Services Mr. Andrew VASQUEZ
41 Director of Athletics Mr. Bill MILLER
09 Director of Institutional Research Ms. Jean CONSTABLE
04 Exec Assistant to the President Ms. Susan RINN

Texas School of Business (D)

711 Airtex Drive, Houston TX 77073
County: Harris FICE Identification: 023122
Unit ID: 229036
Telephone: (281) 443-8900 Carnegie Class: Assoc/PrivFP
FAX Number: (281) 443-0777 Calendar System: Other
URL: www.tsb.edu
Established: 1983 Annual Undergrad Tuition & Fees: $15,984
Enrollment: 473 Coed
Affiliation or Control: Proprietary IRS Status: Proprietary
Highest Offering: Associate Degree
Program: Occupational
Accreditation: ACICS, MAC

01 Campus Director Mr. Greg GARRETT

Texas School of Business-Friendswood (E)

3208 FM 528, Friendswood TX 77546
Telephone: (281) 648-0880 Identification: 667051
Accreditation: ACICS, MAC

† Main campus is Texas School of Business in Houston, TX.

Texas Southern University (F)

3100 Cleburne Street, Houston TX 77004-4584
County: Harris FICE Identification: 003642
Unit ID: 229063
Telephone: (713) 313-7011 Carnegie Class: DRU
FAX Number: (713) 313-1092 Calendar System: Semester
URL: www.tsu.edu
Established: 1927 Annual Undergrad Tuition & Fees (In-State): $7,012
Enrollment: 9,600 Coed
Affiliation or Control: State IRS Status: 170(c)1
Highest Offering: Doctorate
Program: Liberal Arts And General; Teacher Preparatory; Professional
Accreditation: SC, BUS, CAHIIM, COARC, DIETD, ENGT, LAW, MT, NAIT, PHAR, PLNG, SPAA, SW

01 President Dr. John M. RUDLEY
05 Provost/VP Academic Affs & Research Dr. Sunny E. OHIA
10 Vice President for Admin & Finance Mr. Jim C. MCSHAN
30 Vice Pres University Advancement Ms. Wendy H. ADAIR
100 Chief of Staff Ms. Janis J. NEWMAN
43 General Counsel Mr. Andrew C. HUGHEY
41 Athletic Director Dr. Charles F. MCCLELLAND
32 VP Student Svcs/Dean of Students Dr. William T. SAUNDERS
09 Int Assoc Provost/Assoc VP Research Dr. Adebayo O. OYEKAN
88 Dir Title III & Ofc of Sponsored Pr Ms. Demetria JOHNSON-WEEKS
15 Assoc VP of Human Resources Mr. Brian K. DICKENS
26 Assoc VP of Communications Ms. Eva K. PICKENS
84 Executive Director Enrollment Svc Mr. Hasan JAMIL
06 University Registrar Ms. Marilyn C. SQUARE
08 Int Exec Dir Libraries/Museums Ms. Norma P. BEAN
50 Dean School of Business Dr. Ronald A. JOHNSON
51 Dean Col of Cont Educ/Asst Provost Dr. Kingston NYAMAPFENE
53 Dean College of Education Dr. Lillian B. POATS
80 Dean School of Public Affairs Dr. Robert D. BULLARD
61 Dean School of Law Dr. Dannye HOLLEY
67 Int Dean Col Pharmacy & Health Sci Dr. Shirlette G. MILTON
88 Int Assoc Prov/VP Stdt Acad Enh Svc Dr. Betty B. COX
72 Dean College of Science/Technology Dr. Lei YU
60 Dean School of Communications Dr. James W. WARD
19 Chief of Police Chief Roger D. BYARS
35 Associate Dean of Students Dr. William A. THOMAS
21 Exec Dir of Business Affairs Ms. Beverly W. RUFFIN
92 Dean Freeman Honors College Dr. Humphrey A. REGIS
96 Exec Dir Procurement Services Mr. Gregory G. WILLIAMS
102 Executive Director of Development Ms. Carolyne B. OLIVER
18 Exec Director Facilities & Maint Mr. Tim RYCHLEC
13 CIO/Information Technology Mr. Billy C. RECTOR
20 Assoc Provost/Assoc VP Acad Affairs Dr. Elizabeth BROWN-GUILLORY
58 Dean Graduate School Dr. Gregory H. MADDOX
21 Exec Dir Provost of Business Svcs Mr. Charles E. HENRY
88 Dir Acad Ret Svcs Spec Asst/Provost Ms. Lori A. LABRIE
35 Associate Dean of Students Ms. Najla F. NAJIEB
88 Exec Director Budget Mr. Elias HAILU
88 Treasurer Mr. Louis W. EDWARDS
45 Director of Marketing Mr. Gregory K. HOLLAND
108 Int Ex Dir Inst Assess Plng & Effec Dr. Chander S. MEHTA
29 Dir Alumni Relations/Special Event Ms. Connie L. COCHRAN
88 Coordinator Academic Services Ms. Michara N. MAYES
88 Director of Scholarships Ms. Jeanette J. OLIVER
88 Int Dir Teaching & Learning Center Dr. Kimberly R. MCLEOD
88 Program Director Urban Academic Vil Dr. Isiah D. BROWN
88 Associate Director of QEP Office Dr. Arbolina L. JENNINGS

*Texas State Technical College System (G)

3801 Campus Drive, Waco TX 76705-1607
County: McLennan FICE Identification: 009642
Unit ID: 228671
Telephone: (254) 867-4891 Carnegie Class: N/A
FAX Number: (254) 867-3973
URL: www.tstc.edu

01 Chancellor Mr. Michael L. REESER
100 Vice Chancellor & Chief of Staff Mr. Jonathan HOEKSTRA
10 VC Financial Svcs & CFO Dr. J. Gary HENDRICKS
09 VC of IR & Commercialization Dr. Cesar MALDONADO
26 VC of Business Development Mr. Randall WOOTEN
05 VC of Instructional Services Dr. Elton E. STUCKLY, JR.
16 VC of Human Organizational Dev Mrs. Gail LAWERENCE
13 VC & Chief Technology Officer Mr. Rick HERRERA
30 VC of Institutional Advancement Mr. Jeff KILGORE
101 Board of Regents Secretary/Ofc Mgr Ms. Lillian MACIK
04 Admin Asst Office of Chancellor Ms. Beverly E. CLARK
102 Executive Director Foundation Mr. Mike HARDER

*Texas State Technical College Harlingen (H)

1902 North Loop 499, Harlingen TX 78550-3697
County: Cameron FICE Identification: 009225
Unit ID: 229319
Telephone: (956) 364-4000 Carnegie Class: Assoc/Pub-R-M
FAX Number: (965) 364-5100 Calendar System: Trimester
URL: www.harlingen.tstc.edu
Established: 1969 Annual Undergrad Tuition & Fees (In-State): $6,099
Enrollment: 5,807 Coed
Affiliation or Control: State IRS Status: 501(c)3
Highest Offering: Associate Degree
Program: Occupational; 2-Year Principally Bachelor's Creditable; Technical Emphasis
Accreditation: SC, CAHIIM, DH, MAC, SURGT

02 President Dr. Cesar MALDONADO
05 Provost Mr. Adam HUTCHISON
10 Exec Vice Pres Financial/Admin Svcs Ms. Teri ZAMORA
09 VP Institutional Effectiveness Ms. Stella GARCIA

32 Vice Pres for Student Develoment ....Mrs. Cathy MAPLES
20 Associate VP of Academic Affairs ....Mrs. Barbara BENNETT
20 Assoc Vice Pres Student Learning .Dr. Regina GARZA-MITCHELL
88 Assoc VP Col Readiness & Advancmnt ....Mr. Javier DELEON
18 Assoc VP for Administrative Svcs ....Mr. Chuck SMITH
31 Assoc VP Corp/Community Education ... Ms. Cledia HERNANDEZ
13 Chief Technology Officer ....Mr. Rick HERRERA
30 Director Institutional Advancement ....Ms. Amy LYNCH
26 Executive Director of Marketing ....Ms. Lynda LOPEZ
09 Exec Dir for Institutional Complian ....Ms. Lisa CAVAZOS
15 Director Human/Organizational Dev ....Mrs. Mary PREPEJCHAL
19 Chief of Public Safety ....Mr. Aurelio TORRES
18 Director of Physical Plant ....Mr. Juan LOPEZ
51 Director of Continuing Education ....Mr. Juan LEAL
38 Director Student Counseling ....Ms. Liz SILVA
37 Director of Financial Aid ....Mr. Fred PENA
35 Director of Student Success ....Ms. Norma SALAZAR
41 Supervisor of Intramurals ....Mr. Joe DOMINGUEZ
08 Director of the Library ....Ms. Nancy HENDRICKS
96 Director of Procurement Management ....Ms. Linda RODRIGUEZ-GUILLEN
36 Director Career Services ....Ms. Susan HOLMES
40 Supervisor Bookstore ....Ms. Susan FLORES
39 Supervisor Housing/Dormitories ....Mr. Carlos PEREZ
88 Director Staff Professional Dev ....Mrs. Cindy MATA
106 Director Distance Education ....Dr. Gina CANO-MONREAL
27 Director College Information ....Ms. Dora COLVIN
22 Director Support Services ....Ms. Edda URREA
88 Director Instructional Support Svcs ....Mr. Steve SZYMONIAK
88 Director of Curriculum ....Mr. Juan GARCIA

*Texas State Technical College Marshall (A)

2650 East End Boulevard S, Marshall TX 75672-7402
County: Harrison FICE Identification: 033965
Unit ID: 408394
Telephone: (903) 935-1010 Carnegie Class: Assoc/Pub-R-S
FAX Number: (903) 935-9554 Calendar System: Semester
URL: www.marshall.tstc.edu
Established: 1993 Annual Undergrad Tuition & Fees (In-District): $4,200
Enrollment: 836 Coed
Affiliation or Control: State/Local IRS Status: 501(c)3
Highest Offering: Associate Degree
Program: Occupational; 2-Year Principally Bachelor's Creditable; Technical Emphasis
Accreditation: SC

02 President ....Mr. Randall E. WOOTEN
05 Vice Pres of Student Learning ....Mr. Barton DAY
10 Vice Pres of Financial Services ....Mrs. Deborah L. SANDERS
84 Dean of Enrollment Management ....Vacant
32 Vice Pres of Student Services ....Mr. Brett O. BRIGHT
102 Assoc Vice Pres Corporate College ....Vacant
20 Associate Dean Learning Community ....Ms. Annette M. ELLIS
04 Exec Assistant to the President ....Ms. Deborah COLEMAN
06 Registrar ....Ms. Patricia A. ROBBINS
09 Dir of Inst Effect/Rsrch & Planning ....Mrs. Mittie D. HUTCHINS
15 Human & Organ Develop Executive ....Mr. Jeff W. BELL
36 Coordinator of Placement ....Mr. Benjamin CANTU
37 Financial Aid Specialist ....Mrs. Susan F. WINGATE
103 Director Workforce & Economic Dev ....Mr. Bryan MAERTINS
13 Dir Network/Telecommunications Svcs ......Mr. Dennis J. BURRER
26 Chief Public Relations Officer ....Mr. Baily BRIGGS
96 Director of Purchasing ....Mrs. Eloise REED
18 Director of Physical Plant ....Mr. Doug COLEMAN

*Texas State Technical College Waco (B)

3801 Campus Drive, Waco TX 76705-1695
County: McLennan FICE Identification: 003634
Unit ID: 228680
Telephone: (254) 799-3611 Carnegie Class: Assoc/Pub-R-M
FAX Number: (254) 867-2006 Calendar System: Semester
URL: www.tstc.edu
Established: 1965 Annual Undergrad Tuition & Fees (In-State): $3,342
Enrollment: 4,277 Coed
Affiliation or Control: State IRS Status: 501(c)3
Highest Offering: Associate Degree
Program: Occupational; 2-Year Principally Bachelor's Creditable; Technical Emphasis
Accreditation: SC, DA

00 Chancellor ....Mr. Mike REESER
02 President ....Mr. Elton E. STUCKLY, JR.
03 Executive Vice President ....Mr. Rob WOLAVER
05 VP Student Learning ....Mr. Ron SANDERS
05 AVC Instructional Operations ....Ms. Kristi GILBEAUX
88 VP Off-Site-Locations ....Dr. Irene CRAVEY
30 VP Institutional Advancement ....Ms. Carliss HYDE
27 Director of Marketing ....Ms. Jan OSBURN
10 VP Financial Services ....Mr. David KOFNOVEC
09 Exec Dir Inst Effect Rsrch/Plng ....Dr. Ben COX
15 AVC/Dir Human & Org Dev ....Ms. Angela BALL
20 VP Student Development ....Ms. Sarah PATTERSON
11 VP Administrative Services ....Mr. Kevin DORTON
37 Director of Financial Aid ....Ms. Jackie ADLER
06 Registrar/Dir of Adm & Records ....Ms. Mary DANIEL

*Texas State Technical College West Texas (C)

300 Homer K. Taylor Drive, Sweetwater TX 79556-4108
County: Nolan FICE Identification: 009932
Unit ID: 229328
Telephone: (325) 235-7300 Carnegie Class: Assoc/Pub-R-S
FAX Number: (325) 235-7320 Calendar System: Semester
URL: www.tstc.edu
Established: 1970 Annual Undergrad Tuition & Fees (In-State): $6,435
Enrollment: 843 Coed
Affiliation or Control: State IRS Status: 170(c)1
Highest Offering: Associate Degree
Program: Occupational; 2-Year Principally Bachelor's Creditable; Technical Emphasis
Accreditation: SC, CAHIIM, EMT

02 President/Vice Chancellor ....Ms. Gail LAWRENCE
05 Vice President Student Learning ....Mr. Kyle SMITH
32 Vice President Student Development .....Mrs. Kathleen P. BUTLER
88 Vice Pres Corporate College ....Mr. Dixon BAILEY
10 Vice President Financial Services ....Ms. Karen WALLER
11 Vice President Admin Svcs ....Mr. Ray FRIED
35 Assoc VP Student Development ....Mr. Jeff HOWARD
20 Associate VP Student Learning ....Mrs. Debbie KARL
84 Associate VP Enrollment Management ....Mrs. Janyth USSERY
84 Associate VP Enrollment Management ....Mrs. Maria AGUIRRE-ACUNA
84 Associate VP Enrollment Management ....Mr. Brian KIGHT
84 Associate VP Enrollment Management .Mrs. Sherry STRICKLAND
21 Assistant CFO ....Mr. Kevin SHIPP
19 Chief of Police ....Mr. Mike KELLER
15 Director Human Resources ....Ms. Hannah LOVE
37 Director of Financial Aid ....Mrs. Connie CHANCE
08 Director Library ....Mr. Steven PERRY
96 Director of Purchasing ....Ms. Jessica CHAVIRA
45 Staff Development Officer ....Vacant
46 Manager Inst Planning & Research ....Mr. Stanley V. SCOTT
38 Coordinator Counseling & Testing ....Mrs. Christi SHAW
36 Coord Career Planning & Placement ....Mr. Nick ALVARADO
35 Coordinator Student Activities ....Mr. Tod RYDEN
26 Chief Public Relations Officer ....Mrs. Julie CROMEENS
39 Housing Supervisor ....Mr. Lupe NAVARRETTE
40 Bookstore Manager ....Mrs. Sherrie PARKS
13 Dir Network & Telecommunications ....Mrs. Shelli SCHERWITZ
46 Exec Director Strategic Initiatives ....Ms. Hannah LOVE

*The Texas State University System (D)

208 E 10th Street, Suite 600, Austin TX 78701-2407
County: Travis FICE Identification: 033442
Telephone: (512) 463-1808 Carnegie Class: N/A
FAX Number: (512) 463-1816
URL: www.tsus.edu

01 Chancellor ....Brian MCCALL
05 Vice Chanc for Academic Affairs ....Perry MOORE
43 Vice Chanc & General Counsel ....Fernando C. GOMEZ
10 Vice Chancellor for Finance ....Roland K. SMITH
86 VC Governmental Rels/Educ Policy ....Sean CUNNINGHAM
25 Vice Chanc Contract Administration ....Peter E. GRAVES
88 Associate General Counsel ....Diane CORLEY
18 Assoc Vice Chanc Facilities ....Rob Roy PARNELL
27 Assoc VC Govt Rels/Dir of Communic ....Mike WINTEMUTE
21 Director of Audits & Analysis ....Carole M. FOX
11 Director of Administration ....Kelly WINTEMUTE

*Lamar Institute of Technology (E)

PO Box 10043, Beaumont TX 77710-0043
County: Jefferson FICE Identification: 036273
Unit ID: 441760
Telephone: (409) 880-8321 Carnegie Class: Assoc/Pub-S-SC
FAX Number: (409) 880-1711 Calendar System: Semester
URL: www.lit.edu
Established: 1995 Annual Undergrad Tuition & Fees (In-State): $4,066
Enrollment: 2,834 Coed
Affiliation or Control: State IRS Status: 501(c)3
Highest Offering: Associate Degree
Program: Occupational; 2-Year Principally Bachelor's Creditable; Technical Emphasis
Accreditation: SC, CAHIIM, COARC, DH, DMS, RAD

02 President ....Dr. Paul SZUCH
05 Vice President for Academic Affairs ....Dr. Betty REYNARD
10 Vice President Finance & Operations ....Mr. Jonathan WOLFE
32 Vice President of Student Services ....Dr. Vivian JEFFERSON
15 Vice President for Human Resources ....Ms. Bertha FREGIA
20 Dean of Instruction ....Ms. Melissa ARMENTOR
103 Dean Workforce Development ....Dr. Jimmy ADAMS
37 Director of Student Financial Aid ....Ms. Lisa SCHROEDER
13 Director of Technology Services ....Mr. Isaac BARBOSA
30 Dir of Development/Alumni Relations ....Ms. Joanne BROWN
26 Director of Marketing/Public Info ....Ms. Beth MILLER
18 Facilities Coordinator ....Mr. Jack WIGGINS
36 Job Plcmnt/Student Activities Coord ....Vacant
09 Coord Inst Effectiveness and Grants ....Mr. David MOSLEY

*Lamar University (F)

PO Box 10009, Beaumont TX 77710-0009
County: Jefferson FICE Identification: 003581
Unit ID: 226091
Telephone: (409) 880-7011 Carnegie Class: DRU
FAX Number: (409) 880-8404 Calendar System: Semester
URL: www.lamar.edu
Established: 1923 Annual Undergrad Tuition & Fees (In-State): $9,010
Enrollment: 14,467 Coed
Affiliation or Control: State IRS Status: 501(c)3
Highest Offering: Doctorate
Program: Liberal Arts And General; Teacher Preparatory; Professional
Accreditation: SC, ACFEI, ADNUR, AUD, BUS, CS, DIETD, DIETI, ENG, MUS, NUR, SP, SW, TED

02 President ....Dr. Kenneth R. EVANS
05 Provost/Vice Pres Academic Affairs ....Dr. Stephen A. DOBLIN
10 Int Vice Pres Finance/Operations ....Dr. Cruse MELVIN
30 Vice President for Inst Advancement ....Ms. Camille MOUTON
58 Dean of Graduate Studies ....Dr. William HARN
20 Sr Assoc Provost for Academic Affs ....Dr. Kevin B. SMITH
16 Assoc Vice Pres Human Resources ....Ms. Bertha FREGIA
18 Int Assoc VP Facilities/Maint ....Mr. Gerald MCCAIG
21 Associate Vice President Finance/Co ....Ms. Vicki WARD
13 Assoc Vice Pres for Information Sys ....Ms. Priscilla PARSONS
84 Assoc VP Strategic Enrollment Mgmt ....Ms. Sherry WELLS
49 Dean College Arts & Sciences ....Dr. Brenda NICHOLS
50 Dean College of Business ....Dr. Henry VENTA
53 Dean College of Education ....Dr. Hollis LOWERY-MOORE
54 Dean College of Engineering ....Dr. Jack HOPPER
57 Dean Col Fine Arts & Communication ....Dr. Russ SCHULTZ
08 Director Library Services ....Mr. David J. CARROLL
06 Registrar ....Mr. David SHORT, JR.
106 Dir Division of Distance Learning ....Dr. Paula NICHOLS
35 Director of Academic Services ....Mr. James C. RUSH
44 Director of Development ....Ms. Laurie RITCHEL
09 Director Institutional Research ....Dr. Gregory MARSH
36 Dir Career Development/Placement ....Ms. Teresa SIMPSON
23 Director Health Services ....Ms. Shawn GRAY
19 Chief University Police ....Mr. Curtis Jason GOODRICH
26 Public Relations Director ....Mr. Brian SATTLER
29 Director Alumni Relations ....Ms. Linda LEBLANC
37 Director Student Financial Aid ....Ms. Jill ROWLEY
96 Director of Purchasing ....Vacant

*Lamar State College-Orange (G)

410 Front Street, Orange TX 77630-5802
County: Orange FICE Identification: 023582
Unit ID: 226107
Telephone: (409) 883-7750 Carnegie Class: Assoc/Pub-R-M
FAX Number: (409) 882-3374 Calendar System: Semester
URL: www.lsco.edu
Established: 1969 Annual Undergrad Tuition & Fees (In-State): $4,240
Enrollment: 2,648 Coed
Affiliation or Control: State IRS Status: 501(c)3
Highest Offering: Associate Degree
Program: Occupational; 2-Year Principally Bachelor's Creditable
Accreditation: SC

02 President ....Dr. J. Michael SHAHAN
05 Vice President Academic Affairs ....Dr. Joseph KIRKLAND
10 Vice President Finance & Operations ....Mrs. Dana ROGERS
32 Vice Pres Student Svcs & Aux Ent ....Mr. Michael YEATER
08 Director of Library Services ....Ms. Mary MCCOY
06 Registrar ....Mrs. Becky J. MCANELLEY
37 Director Student Financial Aid ....Mr. Kerry J. OLSON
15 Human Resources Director ....Mrs. Alicia GRAY
18 Director of Physical Plant ....Mr. David GOINS
13 Coord Information Resources ....Ms. Linda G. BURNETT
09 Coordinator Institutional Research ....Mr. Bishar M. SETHNA
25 Contracts/Grants Administrator ....Mrs. Dana N. ROGERS
76 Director of Allied Health ....Ms. Gina A. SIMAR
72 Director of Business/Technology ....Ms. Jacqueline A. SPEARS
96 Director of Purchasing ....Ms. Tabitha EVANS
49 Division Chair Arts & Science ....Ms. Gwen WHITEHEAD

*Lamar State College-Port Arthur (H)

1500 Procter Street, Port Arthur TX 77640-6604
County: Jefferson FICE Identification: 023485
Unit ID: 226116
Telephone: (409) 983-4921 Carnegie Class: Assoc/Pub-R-M
FAX Number: (409) 984-6032 Calendar System: Semester
URL: www.lamarpa.edu
Established: 1909 Annual Undergrad Tuition & Fees (In-State): $5,090
Enrollment: 2,708 Coed
Affiliation or Control: State IRS Status: 501(c)3
Highest Offering: Associate Degree
Program: Occupational; 2-Year Principally Bachelor's Creditable
Accreditation: SC, SURGT

02 President ....Dr. W. Sam MONROE
05 Vice President Academic Affairs ....Dr. Gary D. STRETCHER
10 Vice President for Finance ....Mrs. Mary WICKLAND
32 Vice President Student Services ....Mr. Thomas G. NEAL
04 Admin Assistant to the President ....Mrs. Donna SCHION
08 Dean Library Services ....Mr. Peter B. KAATRUDE
06 Registrar ....Ms. Connie NICHOLAS
37 Director Financial Aid ....Vacant

45 Director Inst Effectiveness .... Dr. Ben STAFFORD
18 Director of Physical Plant .... Mr. Stephen ARNOLD
27 Public Information Officer .... Mr. Gerry DICKERT
36 Career Placement Counselor .... Vacant
56 Dir Inmate Instructional Program .... Dr. Barbara HUVAL
13 Dir Information Technology Services .... Mr. Samir GHORAYEB
15 Director Human Resources .... Ms. Linda MCGEE
07 Director of Admissions .... Ms. Connie NICHOLAS
09 Director of Institutional Research .... Mrs. Petra UZORUO
51 Dean Academic/Continuing Educ Pgms .... Dr. Charles GONGRE
72 Dean Technical Programs .... Dr. Nancy CAMMACK
81 Department Head Science & Math .... Dr. Percy JORDAN
50 Dept Head Business/CIS Technology .... Mrs. Sheila GUILLOT
83 Department Head Liberal Arts .... Dr. Barbara HUVAL
76 Department Head Allied Health .... Dr. Ben STAFFORD

*Sam Houston State University (A)

1806 Avenue J, Suite 303, Huntsville TX 77341-0001
County: Walker FICE Identification: 003606
Unit ID: 227881
Telephone: (936) 294-1111 Carnegie Class: DRU
FAX Number: (936) 294-1465 Calendar System: Semester
URL: www.shsu.edu
Established: 1879 Annual Undergrad Tuition & Fees (In-State): $8,594
Enrollment: 18,461 Coed
Affiliation or Control: State IRS Status: 501(c)3
Highest Offering: Doctorate
Program: Liberal Arts And General; Teacher Preparatory; Professional
Accreditation: SC, BUS, CACREP, CIDA, CLPSY, CS, DIETD, DIETI, FEPAC, MUS, NUR, TED

02 President .... Dr. Dana L. GIBSON
05 Provost/Vice Pres Academic Affairs .... Dr. Jaimie HEBERT
10 Vice President Finance & Operations .... Mr. Al HOOTEN
84 Vice Pres Enrollment Management .... Dr. Heather THIELEMANN
32 Vice President Student Services .... Mr. Frank PARKER
30 Vice President of Univ Advancement .... Mr. Frank R. HOLMES
13 VP for Information Technology .... Mr. Mark ADAMS
41 Athletic Director .... Mr. Bobby WILLIAMS
20 Assoc Provost Academic Affairs .... Dr. Richard EGLSAER
20 Assoc VP Academic Affairs .... Dr. Kandi TAYEBI
21 Assoc VP Financial Services .... Ms. Paige SMITH
18 Assoc VP Facilities Management .... Mr. Doug J. GREENING
16 Assoc VP for HR & Risk Mgmt .... Mr. Dave HAMMONDS
44 Assoc VP for Development .... Ms. Thelma MOONEY
96 Assoc VP Business Svcs .... Mr. John HITZEMAN
26 Assoc VP Marketing & Comm .... Ms. Kris RUIZ
100 Chief of Staff .... Ms. Kathy J. GILCREASE
06 Registrar .... Ms. Teresa T. RINGO
07 Director of Undergrad Admissions .... Mr. Trevor THORN
08 Director of Library Services .... Ms. Ann H. HOLDER
29 Director of Alumni Relations .... Mr. Charlie VIENNE
09 Asst VP Inst Effectiveness .... Ms. Donna ARTHO
37 Director Student Financial Aid .... Vacant
26 Director Marketing & Communications .... Mr. Bruce O'NEAL
38 Director Counseling Services .... Dr. Drew MILLER
39 Director Residence Life .... Ms. Joellen N. TIPTON
19 Director Public Safety Services .... Mr. Kevin MORRIS
92 Dean of Honors College .... Dr. Gene YOUNG
21 Controller .... Mr. Aaron LEMAY
50 Dean of Business Administration .... Dr. Mitchell MUEHSAM
81 Dean of Sciences .... Dr. John PASCARELLA
57 Dean of Fine Arts/Mass Comm .... Dr. Ronald SHIELDS
61 Dean of Criminal Justice .... Dr. Vincent WEBB
53 Interim Dean of Education .... Dr. Jerry BRUCE
58 Dean of Graduate Studies .... Dr. Kandi TAYEBI
83 Dean Humanities/Social Sciences .... Vacant

*Sul Ross State University (B)

PO Box C-114, Alpine TX 79832-0001
County: Brewster FICE Identification: 003625
Unit ID: 228501
Telephone: (432) 837-8032 Carnegie Class: Master's L
FAX Number: (432) 837-8334 Calendar System: Semester
URL: www.sulross.edu
Established: 1917 Annual Undergrad Tuition & Fees (In-State): $6,600
Enrollment: 2,700 Coed
Affiliation or Control: State IRS Status: 501(c)3
Highest Offering: Master's
Program: Occupational; Liberal Arts And General; Teacher Preparatory; Professional
Accreditation: SC

02 President .... Dr. Ricardo MAESTAS
05 Provost/VP Acad & Student Affs .... Dr. Clifton Q. THURMAN
10 Vice Pres for Finance & Operations .... Mr. Cesario E. VALENZUELA
12 Vice President Rio Grande College .... Vacant
84 Vice Pres Enrollment Management .... Ms. Denise GROVES
11 Assoc VP Fac/Plng/Construct/Ops .... Mr. Jim W. CLOUSE
30 Assoc Vice President Advancement .... Mr. Leo G. DOMINGUEZ
12 Associate Provost & Dean RGC .... Dr. Paul SORRELS
04 Special Assistant to President .... Vacant
04 Executive Assistant to President .... Ms. Yvonne REALIVASQUEZ
06 Registrar .... Vacant
08 Dean Library & Info Technology .... Mr. Don DOWDEY
32 Dean of Student Life .... Mr. Leo DOMINGUEZ
92 Dir Honors Prog/Acad Ctr Excellence .... Dr. Kathy STEIN
27 Director News & Publications .... Mr. Stephen W. LANG
37 Dir Financial Assistance .... Mr. Mickey CORBETT
49 Dean Arts & Science .... Dr. Jimmy CASE
107 Dean Professional Studies .... Dr. Larry M. GUERRERO
47 Dean Agricult/Natural Resource Sci .... Dr. Robert J. KINUCAN
15 Director of Human Resources .... Mrs. Judy A. PERRY
18 Asst Director of Physical Plant .... Mr. Edmundo NATERA
19 Director Dept of Public Safety .... Mr. Johnnie L. HOLBROOKS
21 Senior Manager of Accounting .... Mr. Oscar JIMENEZ
39 Director Residential Living .... Mr. Mark CHASZAR
41 Interim Athletic Director .... Mr. John K. TYREE
38 Director of Counseling Ctr .... Vacant
13 Chief Information Officer .... Mr. Chandragupta GUDENA
96 Director of Purchasing .... Mr. Noe HERNANDEZ
88 Dir Center for Big Bend Studies .... Mr. Andy CLOUD
29 Director Alumni Affairs .... Ms. Karen BROWN
66 Director of Vocational Nursing .... Ms. Donna KUENSTLER
88 Director Museum of the Big Bend .... Ms. Elizabeth JACKSON
88 Director of Upward Bound .... Ms. Barbara VEGA
88 Director of University Archives .... Ms. Melleta BELL
88 Director Small Business Devel Ctr .... Mr. David WILSON
88 Director Law Enforcement Academy .... Mr. Lloyd DRAGOO
88 Dir Publication Services Coord .... Ms. Lauren MENDIAS
07 Director Admissions & Records .... Ms. Claudia WRIGHT
88 Mail Service Supervisor .... Ms. Leticia GONZALES
88 Internal Auditor .... Mrs. Stephanie NELSON
36 Coord Career Services & Testing .... Ms. Susan FOX-FORRESTER
09 Director of Institutional Research .... Dr. John D. JONES

*Texas State University-San Marcos (C)

601 University Drive, San Marcos TX 78666-4615
County: Hays FICE Identification: 003615
Unit ID: 228459
Telephone: (512) 245-2111 Carnegie Class: Master's L
FAX Number: (512) 245-3040 Calendar System: Semester
URL: www.txstate.edu
Established: 1899 Annual Undergrad Tuition & Fees (In-State): $9,150
Enrollment: 34,225 Coed
Affiliation or Control: State IRS Status: 501(c)3
Highest Offering: Doctorate
Program: Liberal Arts And General; Teacher Preparatory; Professional
Accreditation: SC, BUS, BUSA, CACREP, CAHIIM, CIDA, COARC, COARCP, CONST, CS, DIETD, DIETI, ENG, HSA, IPSY, JOUR, MT, MUS, NRPA, NURSE, PTA, RTT, SP, SPAA, SW, TEAC

02 President .... Dr. Denise M. TRAUTH
05 Provost/Vice Pres Academic Affairs .... Dr. Gene BOURGEOIS
100 Special Assistant to the President .... Dr. Robert D. GRATZ
32 Vice President Student Affairs .... Dr. Joanne H. SMITH
10 Vice Pres Finance/Support Services .... Mr. William A. NANCE
30 Vice President Univ Advancement .... Dr. Barbara BREIER
13 Vice Pres Information Technology .... Dr. Carl V. WYATT
83 Dean College of Applied Arts .... Dr. T. Jaime CHAHIN
50 Dean McCoy Col of Business Admin .... Dr. Denise T. SMART
57 Dean Col Fine Arts & Communication .... Dr. Timothy MOTTET
53 Dean College of Education .... Dr. Stan CARPENTER
76 Dean College Health Professions .... Dr. Ruth B. WELBORN
83 Dean College Liberal Arts .... Dr. Michael HENNESSY
81 Dean Col of Science & Engineering .... Dr. Stephen B. SEIDMAN
58 Dean The Graduate College .... Dr. Andrea GOLATO
97 Dean Univ Col & Dir PACE Center .... Dr. Daniel BROWN
92 Dean Honors College .... Dr. Heather GALLOWAY
20 Assoc Vice Pres Academic Affairs .... Dr. Debbie M. THORNE
20 Associate Provost .... Dr. Cynthia L. OPHEIM
18 Associate VP of Facilities .... Mr. Juan M. GUERRA
86 Assoc VP Research & Dir of Fed Rels .... Dr. Bill C. COVINGTON
35 Assoc VP Stdnt Affs/Dean of Stdnt .... Dr. Margarita M. ARELLANO
20 Assoc Vice Pres for Inst Effective .... Dr. Beth E. WUEST
21 Assoc VP Financial Services .... Mr. Darryl BORGONAH
84 Assoc VP Enrollment Mgmt/Marketing .... Dr. Michael R. HEINTZE
08 Associate VP University Library .... Ms. Joan L. HEATH
20 Assistant VP for Academic Services .... Dr. Ronald C. BROWN
38 Asst VP/Director Counseling Center .... Dr. Gregory SNODGRASS
07 Asst VP Enroll Mgmt/Dir Ug Admiss .... Ms. Stephanie ANDERSON
88 Asst VP/Dir of Multicul Stdnt Affs .... Dr. Sherri BENN
88 Asst VP for Development .... Mr. Ted M. MCKINNON
88 Asst VP University Advancement .... Mr. Matt FLORES
89 Asst Dean of University College .... Dr. Pam J. WUESTENBERG
88 Assoc VP Finance/Support Svcs Plng .... Ms. Nancy NUSBAUM
14 Assoc VP for Technology Resources .... Mr. Mark HUGHES
90 Assoc VP Instructional Tech Support .... Dr. Milton C. NIELSEN
106 Interim Dir Disatnce/Extended Lrng .... Dr. Debbie M. THORNE
06 Registrar .... Ms. Lloydean M. ECKLEY
91 Director Enterprise Systems .... Mr. Bill RAMPY
37 Director of Fin Aid & Scholarships .... Dr. Christopher MURR
36 Director Career Services .... Ms. Norma GUERRA GAIER
41 Director of Athletics .... Dr. Lawrence B. TEIS
29 Director of Alumni Affairs .... Ms. Kim GANNON
27 Director News Services .... Mr. Mark S. HENDRICKS
31 Chief Community Relations .... Ms. Kim PORTERFIELD
15 Director of Human Resources .... Mr. John E. MCBRIDE
12 Director Round Rock Higher Educ Ctr .... Dr. Edna REHBEIN
25 Director of Sponsored Programs .... Mr. W. Scott ERWIN
19 Director University Police .... Mr. Ralph MEYER
23 Director Student Health Center .... Dr. Emilio CARRANCO
39 Director Housing & Residential Life .... Dr. Rosanne PROITE
85 Director International Office .... Dr. Debbie THORNE
40 Manager University Bookstore .... Ms. Jacqueline SLAUGHTER
24 Director Education Technology Ctr .... Mr. Michael W. FARRIS
09 Director of Institutional Research .... Mr. Joseph M. MEYER
22 Chief Divsty Offc/Dir Equity & Acce .... Mr. Herman HORN
93 Dir Center for Multicul/Gender Stds .... Dr. Sandra MAYO
96 Director Purchasing .... Ms. Jacque ALLBRIGHT
26 Director of University Marketing .... Ms. Diana HARRELL
88 Director of Audit & Compliance .... Mr. Steve R. MCGEE
88 Director Campus Recreation .... Dr. Glenn HANLEY
88 Interim Director LBJ Student Center .... Dr. Margarita ARELLANO
88 Director Retention Mgmt & Planning .... Dr. Jen BECK
88 Interim Directr Disability Services .... Dr. Sherri BENN

Texas Tech University (D)

2500 Broadway Avenue, Lubbock TX 79409-2005
County: Lubbock FICE Identification: 003644
Unit ID: 229115
Telephone: (806) 742-2121 Carnegie Class: RU/H
FAX Number: (806) 742-2138 Calendar System: Semester
URL: www.ttu.edu
Established: 1923 Annual Undergrad Tuition & Fees (In-State): $4,921
Enrollment: 32,611 Coed
Affiliation or Control: State IRS Status: 170(c)1
Highest Offering: Doctorate
Program: Liberal Arts And General; Teacher Preparatory; Professional
Accreditation: SC, AAFCS, ARCPA, ART, BUS, BUSA, CACREP, CIDA, CLPSY, COPSY, DIETD, DIETI, ENG, ENGT, HSA, IPSY, LAW, LSAR, MED, MFCD, MIDWF, MUS, SPAA, SW, TED, THEA

00 Chancellor .... Mr. Kent HANCE
01 President .... Dr. M. Duane NELLIS
101 Sec Board Regents/Ex Asst to Chanc .... Mr. Ben W. LOCK
03 Provost and Sr VP .... Dr. Lawrence SCHOVANEC
05 Vice Chancellor for Academic Affair .... Dr. Joseph RALLO
10 Chief Operating Ofcr/SVP Admin/Fin .... Mr. Kyle CLARK
30 Vice Chancellor Inst Advancement .... Dr. Kelly CRONIN
46 Vice Chancellor for Research .... Mr. Jodey ARRINGTON
86 Vice Chancellor Govt Relations .... Mr. J. Michael SANDERS
43 Vice Chanc & General Counsel .... Mr. John HUFFAKER
18 VC Facilities Planning Construction .... Mr. Michael MOLINA
26 Assoc Vice Chancellor Communicatios .... Mr. Robert GIOVANNETTI
20 Vice Provost Academic Affairs .... Dr. Peggy MILLER
100 President's Chief of Staff .... Ms. Grace HERNANDEZ
29 EVP & CEO Texas Tech Alumni Assoc .... Dr. Bill DEAN
46 Interim Vice President for Research .... Dr. Michael SAN FRANCISCO
28 VP Inst Diversity & Vice Provost .... Dr. Juan S. MUNOZ
84 Sr Assoc VP Enrollment Management .... Dr. James BURKHALTER
20 Assoc Vice Provost Academic Affairs .... Dr. Gary ELBOW
20 Sr Vice Provost .... Dr. Rob STEWART
88 Director of External Relations .... Ms. Suzanne TAYLOR
21 Interim Asst Vice Pres & Controller .... Ms. Sharon WILLIAMSON
82 Assoc Vice Prov International Affs .... Mr. Tibor P. NAGY
13 Assoc VP Information Technology .... Mr. Sam SEGRAN
88 Asst VP & Dir Hospitality Services .... Vacant
08 Dean of Libraries .... Dr. Donald DYAL
60 Dean Media & Communications .... Dr. David PERLMUTTER
35 Int Dean Stdnts/Dir Campus Life .... Ms. Amy L. MURPHY
37 Managing Dir Financial Aid .... Ms. Becky WILSON
27 Chief Information Officer .... Ms. Kay RHODES
06 Registrar .... Ms. Bobbie BROWN
07 Managing Director of Admissions .... Dr. Ethan LOGAN
26 Managing Dir Comms & Marketing .... Mr. Chris COOK
104 Director Study Abroad .... Ms. Sandy CROSIER
04 Executive Asst to President .... Ms. Jessica CARRILLO
31 Assoc Dir Community Engagment .... Dr. Heather MARTINEZ
44 Senior Dir Annual Giving Programs .... Ms. Deborah FINLAYSON
23 Director Student Health Services .... Ms. Evelyn MCPHERSON
39 Managing Dir Student Housing .... Mr. Sean DUGGAN
36 Managing Director Career Center .... Mr. Jay KILLOUGH
15 Managing Director of HR Management .... Ms. Jodie BILLINGSLEY
22 Asst Vice Chanc Admin/Dir EEO .... Ms. Charlotte BINGHAM
38 Managing Dir Student Counseling .... Dr. Eileen NATHAN
41 Director of Athletics .... Mr. Kirby HOCUTT
47 Dean Agriculture Sci/Natural Res .... Dr. Michael GALYEAN
49 Interim Dean of Arts & Sciences .... Dr. Jeff WILLIAMS
48 Dean of Architecture .... Mr. Andrew VERNOOY
50 Dean Business Administration .... Dr. Lance NAIL
53 Dean of Education .... Dr. Scott RIDLEY
54 Dean of Engineering .... Dr. Albert SACCO
88 Dean of Human Sciences .... Dr. Linda HOOVER
61 Dean School of Law .... Ms. Darby DICKERSON
58 Interim Dean of Graduate School .... Dr. Dominick CASADONTE
92 Interim Dean Honors College .... Dr. Stephen FRITZ
57 Dean Visual & Performing Arts .... Dr. Carol EDWARDS
19 Chief of Police .... Mr. Ronald SEACRIST
09 Managing Dir Institutional Research .... Ms. Vicki WEST
96 Dir Purchasing & Contracting .... Ms. Jennifer ADLING

Texas Tech University Health Sciences Center (E)

3601 4th Street, Lubbock TX 79430-0001
County: Lubbock FICE Identification: 010674
Unit ID: 229337
Telephone: (806) 743-1000 Carnegie Class: Spec/Med
FAX Number: (806) 743-3027 Calendar System: Semester
URL: www.ttuhsc.edu
Established: 1969 Annual Undergrad Tuition & Fees (In-State): $7,606
Enrollment: 4,391 Coed
Affiliation or Control: State IRS Status: 501(c)3
Highest Offering: Doctorate
Program: Professional
Accreditation: SC, AUD, CORE, DMOLS, MED, MT, NURSE, OT, PHAR, PTA, SP

01 President .... Dr. Tedd MITCHELL
10 Exec Vice Pres for Finance Admin .... Mr. Elmo M. CAVIN, JR.

05 Sr Vice Pres Academic Affairs ..... Dr. Rial D. ROLFE
26 Exec Dir Communications & Mktg ..... Ms. Mary CROYLE
17 Exec Vice Pres Rural/Community Hlth .. Dr. Billy U. PHILIPS, JR.
13 Vice Pres Info Tech/Chief Info Ofcr ..... Dr. Chip SHAW
100 Chief of Staff ..... Ms. Didit MARTINEZ
43 Senior Assoc General Counsel ..... Ms. Glenda HELFRICH
21 Assoc Vice Pres Business Affairs ..... Mr. Mike CROWDER
46 Interim Vice President for Research ..... Dr. Jim HUTSON
19 Information Security Officer ..... Mr. Andrew HOWARD
15 Asst Vice Pres of Human Resources ..... Dr. Gena JONES
18 Asst Vice Pres of Physical Plant ..... Mr. George MORALES
63 Dean of Medical School ..... Dr. Steven L. BERK
58 Dean Grad Sch Biomed Sciences ..... Dr. Brandt L. SCHNEIDER
66 Dean of Nursing School ..... Dr. Michael L. EVANS
76 Dean of Allied Health Sciences Sch ..... Dr. Robin SATTERWHITE
67 Dean of Pharmacy School ..... Dr. Quentin R. SMITH
66 Dean GGH Nursing School ..... Dr. Jeanne M. NOVOTNY
12 Reg Dean Medicine Amarillo Campus ..... Dr. Richard JORDAN
12 Found Dean Medicine El Paso Campus ..... Dr. J. Manuel DE LA ROSA
12 Reg Dean Medicine Odessa Campus ..... Dr. Gary VENTOLINI
66 Reg Dean Nursing Odessa Campus ..... Dr. Sharon CANNON
76 Reg Dean Allied Health Amarillo ..... Dr. Michael HOOTEN
76 Reg Dean Allied Health Odessa ..... Dr. Tony DOMENECH
06 Registrar ..... Ms. Tamara N. LANE
08 Exec Director of HSC Libraries ..... Mr. Richard C. WOOD
21 Director of Accounting Services ..... Vacant
22 Director of Equal Employment ..... Ms. Charlotte BINGHAM
25 Director of Sponsored Programs ..... Ms. Victoria RIVERA
37 Director of Financial Aid ..... Mr. Marcus WILSON
25 Sr Director of Contracting ..... Mr. Jim LEWIS
96 Managing Director of Purchasing ..... Mr. John G. HAYNES
09 Chief Analyst Inst Research ..... Mr. Kevin MCINTYRE
35 AVP Student Services ..... Ms. Margret DURAN
29 Director of Alumni Relations ..... Ms. Danette BAKER
21 Asst Vice Pres of Budget ..... Ms. Penny HARKEY
30 Asst VC Development ..... Ms. Kendra BURRIS

Texas Wesleyan University (A)

1201 Wesleyan, Fort Worth TX 76105-1536
County: Tarrant FICE Identification: 003645
Unit ID: 229160
Telephone: (817) 531-4444 Carnegie Class: Master's L
FAX Number: (817) 531-4425 Calendar System: Semester
URL: www.txwes.edu
Established: 1890 Annual Undergrad Tuition & Fees: $22,082
Enrollment: 3,204 Coed
Affiliation or Control: United Methodist IRS Status: 501(c)3
Highest Offering: Doctorate
Program: Liberal Arts And General; Teacher Preparatory; Professional
Accreditation: SC, ACBSP, ANEST, MUS

01 President ..... Mr. Frederick G. SLABACH
05 Provost ..... Dr. Allen HENDERSON
10 Sr VP Finance & Administration ..... Ms. Karen L. MONTGOMERY
30 VP University Advancement ..... Ms. Joan CANTY
84 VP for Enrollment & Student Svcs ..... Ms. Pati ALEXANDER
26 Vice Pres Marketing/Communications ..... Mr. John VEILLEUX
11 Assoc VP Admin Svcs/Human Resources ..... Mr. Steve ROBERTS
26 Director of Marketing/Communication ..... Mr. Darren WHITE
20 Associate Provost ..... Dr. Helena BUSSELL
41 Athletic Director ..... Mr. Steven TRACHIER
53 Dean School of Education ..... Dr. Carlos MARTINEZ
50 Dean of School of Business ..... Dr. Hector QUINTANILLA
49 Dean School Arts & Letters ..... Dr. Steven DANIELL
83 Dean School of Natural & Social Sci ..... Dr. Marcel S. KERR
35 Dean of Students ..... Mr. Cary POOLE
39 Director of Residence Life ..... Ms. Sharon MANSON
06 Registrar ..... Ms. Kay VANTOORN
08 Library Science Assoc Professor ..... Ms. Cindy POTTER
21 Controller ..... Ms. Caron PATTON
07 Director of Admissions ..... Ms. Holly KISER
37 Director Financial Aid ..... Ms. Laurie ROSENKRANTZ
42 Chaplain ..... Dr. Robert FLOWERS
38 Director of Counseling ..... Dr. Michael ELLISON
29 Director Alumni Relations ..... Ms. Gina PHILLIPS
15 Human Resources Director ..... Ms. Kristi TAYLOR
96 Director of Purchasing ..... Ms. Deborah CAVITT
36 Director of Career Services ..... Ms. Robyn BONE
18 Director of Facilities/Security ..... Mr. Brian FRANKS
45 Director Institutional Research ..... Ms. Sherri CARABALLO
25 Director of Grants & Research ..... Ms. Deborah ROARK
13 CIO/Info & Communications Tech ..... Mr. Marcus KERR

Texas Woman's University (B)

Box 425589, Denton TX 76204-5587
County: Denton FICE Identification: 003646
Unit ID: 229179
Telephone: (940) 898-2000 Carnegie Class: DRU
FAX Number: (940) 898-3198 Calendar System: Semester
URL: www.twu.edu
Established: 1901 Annual Undergrad Tuition & Fees (In-State): $7,300
Enrollment: 15,168 Coed
Affiliation or Control: State IRS Status: 501(c)3
Highest Offering: Doctorate
Program: Liberal Arts And General; Teacher Preparatory; Professional
Accreditation: SC, ACBSP, CACREP, COPSY, DANCE, DH, DIETD, DIETI, HSA, IPSY, LIB, MUS, NURSE, OT, PTA, SCPSY, SP, SW

01 President ..... Dr. Ann STUART
05 Provost & VP Academic Affairs ..... Dr. Robert NEELY
10 Vice Pres Finance/Administration ..... Dr. Brenda L. FLOYD
32 Vice President Student Life ..... Dr. Richard A. NICHOLAS
13 Chief Information Officer ..... Mr. Rob PLACIDO
20 Assoc Provost ..... Dr. Michael STANKEY
26 Assoc Vice Pres Mktg/Communication ..... Ms. Carolyn BARNES
58 Sr Assoc Provost ..... Dr. Jennifer MARTIN
84 Assoc Vice Pres Enrollment Services ..... Mr. Gary RAY
21 Associate Vice President Finance ..... Ms. Pam WILSON
18 Assoc Vice Pres Facilities ..... Mr. Harold JOHNSON
15 Assoc Vice Pres Human Resources ..... Mr. Lewis BENAVIDES
49 Dean College Arts & Sciences ..... Dr. Ann STATON
69 Dean College Health Sciences ..... Dr. Jimmy ISHEE
62 Dean College Professional Education ..... Dr. Nan RESTINE
58 Interim Dean Graduate School ..... Dr. Larry LEFLORE
07 Director of Admissions ..... Ms. Erma M. NIETO
09 Director of Institutional Research ..... Dr. Mark HAMNER
43 General Counsel ..... Mr. John LAWHON
08 Director of Libraries ..... Ms. Sherilyn BYRD
37 Director Student Financial Aid ..... Mr. Governor E. JACKSON
36 Director Career & Employment Svcs ..... Ms. Deidre Lynn LESLIE
38 Director Counseling Center ..... Dr. Denise LUCERO-MILLER
27 Director News & Information ..... Ms. Amanda SIMPSON
19 Director of Public Safety ..... Ms. Liz PAWLEY
06 Registrar ..... Mr. Bobby LOTHRINGER
41 Athletic Director ..... Ms. Chalese CONNORS
23 Director Student Health Services ..... Dr. Connie MENARD
39 Director University Housing ..... Dr. Joe BERTHIAUME
28 Director of Diversity ..... Mr. Lewis BENAVIDES
29 Director Alumni Relations ..... Ms. Anne SCOTT
30 Director Development ..... Mr. Phil TRAMMELL
40 Bookstore Manager ..... Ms. Jennifer MADISON
96 Procurement Services ..... Ms. Vanna PARR

Trinity University (C)

One Trinity Place, San Antonio TX 78212-7200
County: Bexar FICE Identification: 003647
Unit ID: 229267
Telephone: (210) 999-7011 Carnegie Class: Master's M
FAX Number: (210) 999-7696 Calendar System: Semester
URL: www.trinity.edu
Established: 1869 Annual Undergrad Tuition & Fees: $34,678
Enrollment: 2,525 Coed
Affiliation or Control: Independent Non-Profit IRS Status: 501(c)3
Highest Offering: Master's
Program: Liberal Arts And General; Teacher Preparatory; Professional
Accreditation: SC, BUS, ENG, HSA, TED

01 President ..... Dr. Dennis A. AHLBURG
05 VP Faculty and Student Affairs ..... Dr. Michael R. FISCHER
10 VP Finance and Administration ..... Mr. Gary LOGAN
30 VP Alumni Relations & Develop ..... Ms. Lisa BARONIO
27 VP Info Resources/Marketing & Comm ..... Dr. Charles B. WHITE
20 Assoc VP Student Academic Issues ..... Dr. Sheryl R. TYNES
20 Assoc VP Faculty Recruitment & Dev ..... Dr. Duane COLTHARP
20 Assoc VP Budget & Research ..... Dr. Mark BRODL
21 Assoc VP Budget/Business Ops ..... Ms. Ana M. WINDHAM
07 Assoc VP Enrollment & Student Reten ..... Mr. Christopher J. ELLERTSON
08 University Librarian ..... Ms. Diane J. GRAVES
06 Registrar ..... Mr. Alfred RODRIGUEZ
37 Asst VP Student Financial Svcs ..... Ms. Glendi GADDIS
38 Director Counseling/Health Svcs ..... Dr. Gary W. NEAL
32 Assoc VP Stdnt Affs/Dean of Stdnt ..... Mr. David M. TUTTLE
31 Dir Campus/Community Involvement ..... Ms. Jamie THOMPSON
36 Director of Career Services ..... Ms. Twyla HOUGH
15 Assistant VP Human Resources ..... Ms. Pamela JOHNSTON
13 Dir/Chief Info Technology Officer ..... Mr. Fred ZAPATA
26 Asst VP External Relations ..... Ms. Sharon JONES SCHWEITZER
30 Asst VP Alumni Relations & Dev ..... Ms. Amy NEW
44 Director of Planned Giving ..... Ms. Kristine HOWLAND
29 Senior Director of Alumni Relations ..... Dr. MaryKay COOPER
51 AVP Conferences/Special Pgms ..... Ms. Ann G. KNOEBEL
04 Assistant to the President ..... Ms. Claire SMITH
19 Asst VP Public Safety/Ent Risk Mgmt ..... Mr. Paul CHAPA
18 Director Facility Services ..... Mr. Mike SCHWEITZER
40 Director of Bookstore ..... Ms. Dora AMADOR
42 Chaplain ..... Rev. Stephen R. NICKLE
09 Assoc VP & Director Inst'l Research ..... Dr. Diane G. SAPHIRE
96 Director of Purchasing ..... Ms. Cynthia LARA
28 Director Diversity ..... Ms. Jamie THOMPSON

Trinity Valley Community College (D)

100 Cardinal Drive, Athens TX 75751-2734
County: Henderson FICE Identification: 003572
Unit ID: 225308
Telephone: (903) 677-8822 Carnegie Class: Assoc/Pub-S-MC
FAX Number: (903) 675-6316 Calendar System: Semester
URL: www.tvcc.edu
Established: 1946 Annual Undergrad Tuition & Fees (In-District): $2,160
Enrollment: 7,175 Coed
Affiliation or Control: State/Local IRS Status: 501(c)3
Highest Offering: Associate Degree
Program: Occupational; 2-Year Principally Bachelor's Creditable
Accreditation: SC, ADNUR, EMT, SURGT

01 President ..... Dr. Glendon S. FORGEY
05 Vice President for Instruction ..... Dr. Jerry KING
30 VP of Institutional Advancement ..... Ms. Mary NICHOLSON
32 Vice President Student Services ..... Dr. Jay KINZER
13 VP of Information Technology ..... Mr. Mike ABBOTT
10 Vice Pres Administrative Services ..... Mrs. Jean MCSPADDEN
20 Assoc VP Instruction Academic Educ ..... Mrs. Wendy MAYS
103 Associate VP of Workforce Education ..... Mr. David MCANALLY
91 Assoc VP of Information Technology ..... Mr. Brett DANIEL
12 Assoc VP of TDCJ Programs ..... Dr. Sam HURLEY
46 Asst VP of Institutional Research ..... Ms. Kay PULLEY
18 Asst VP of Facilities Management ..... Mr. David GRAEM
76 Provost Health Occupations ..... Dr. Helen REID
12 Provost Kaufman County Campus ..... Dr. Algia ALLEN
12 Provost Anderson County Campus ..... Dr. Jeff WATSON
06 Registrar/Dean Enrollment Mgmt ..... Dr. Colette HILLIARD
09 Director of Institutional Research ..... Ms. Tina RUMMEL
08 Director Learning Resource Center ..... Ms. Janice SUTTON
38 Director Guidance Center ..... Ms. Linda DANIEL
27 Public Information Officer ..... Mrs. Jennifer HANNIGAN
07 Director School Relations ..... Ms. Audrey HAWKINS
37 Dir Student Finan Aid/Veteran's Svc ..... Ms. Julie LIVELY
41 Athletic Director ..... Mr. Brad SMILEY
19 Director of Campus Police ..... Mr. Heath CARIKER
12 Placement Officer ..... Mr. Dennis NOLLEY
40 Bookstore Manager ..... Mr. James QUATTLEBAUM
35 Director Student Activities ..... Mr. Harold JONES
31 Director Community Services ..... Ms. Gayla ROBERTS
15 Director of Human Resources ..... Ms. Jennifer ROBERTSON

Tyler Junior College (E)

PO Box 9020, Tyler TX 75711-9020
County: Smith FICE Identification: 003648
Unit ID: 229355
Telephone: (903) 510-2200 Carnegie Class: Assoc/Pub-R-L
FAX Number: (903) 510-2632 Calendar System: Semester
URL: www.tjc.edu
Established: 1926 Annual Undergrad Tuition & Fees (In-District): $1,928
Enrollment: 11,374 Coed
Affiliation or Control: State/Local IRS Status: 501(c)3
Highest Offering: Associate Degree
Program: Occupational; 2-Year Principally Bachelor's Creditable; Business Emphasis
Accreditation: SC, CAHIIM, COARC, DH, DMS, EMT, MLTAD, OPD, RAD, SURGT

01 President ..... Dr. L. Michael METKE
10 Vice President Business Affairs ..... Ms. Sarah E. VAN CLEEF
30 VP Advancement/External Affairs ..... Dr. Kimberly A. RUSSELL
32 Vice President Student Affairs ..... Vacant
05 Provost ..... Dr. Homer M. HAYES
79 Dean Humanities/Comm/Fine Arts ..... Vacant
81 Dean Engineering/Math and Sciences ..... Dr. Kenneth R. MURPHY
76 Dean Nursing & Health Professions ..... Mr. Paul R. MONAGAN
72 Dean Prof & Tech Programs ..... Dr. W. Clayton ALLEN
84 Dean Enrollment Mgmt ..... Mrs. Janna L. CHANCEY
09 Exec Dir Inst Effect/Plng & Rsrch ..... Dr. Cheryl L. ROGERS
62 Director Library Services ..... Ms. Marian D. JACKSON
51 Dean Continuing Studies ..... Dr. Aubrey D. SHARPE
21 Controller ..... Ms. Carol A. HUTSON
06 Dir Academic Svcs/Registrar ..... Mr. Thomas ELDER
37 Director Financial Aid ..... Ms. Devon WIGGINS
26 Dir Public Affairs and Grant Dev ..... Mr. Fred M. PETERS
35 Director Student Activities ..... Mrs. Lauren TYLER
29 Interim Dir Alumni Relations ..... Mrs. Ruth FLYNN
36 Coordinator Career Services ..... Mrs. Felecia NEELY-MORRIS
07 Director Admissions ..... Mrs. Nidia HASSAN
16 Exec Dir Human Resources ..... Mr. S. Kevin FOWLER
41 Director Intercol Athletics ..... Dr. Timothy S. DRAIN
09 Dir Institutional Research ..... Ms. Jacquelyn MESSINGER
18 Exec Dir Facilities & Construction ..... Mr. William L. KING
96 Director Purchasing & Contracts ..... Mr. Michael CARUSO
19 Exec Director Campus Safety ..... Dr. Thomas A. JOHNSON
13 Chief Information Officer ..... Mr. Larry MENDEZ
39 Director Auxiliary Svcs ..... Ms. Diana KAROL
44 Exec Dir Advance & Alum Engagement ..... Mr. Mitch ANDREWS
36 Director Testing/Career Services ..... Mr. Paul GOERTEMILLER
88 Director Academic Advising ..... Mrs. Jan ADAMS
88 Dean Academic Foundations ..... Ms. Lisa M. HARPER
88 Director SBDC ..... Mr. Donald W. PROUDFOOT

University of Dallas (F)

1845 E Northgate Drive, Irving TX 75062-4736
County: Dallas FICE Identification: 003651
Unit ID: 224323
Telephone: (972) 721-5000 Carnegie Class: Master's L
FAX Number: (972) 721-5017 Calendar System: Semester
URL: www.udallas.edu
Established: 1956 Annual Undergrad Tuition & Fees: $33,010
Enrollment: 2,576 Coed
Affiliation or Control: Roman Catholic IRS Status: 501(c)3
Highest Offering: Doctorate
Program: Liberal Arts And General; Teacher Preparatory
Accreditation: SC, BUS

01 President ..... Mr. Thomas W. KEEFE
04 Exec Admin Asst to the President ..... Ms. Cathy MCCALEB
05 Executive VP & Provost ..... Dr. J. William BERRY
20 Associate Provost ..... Dr. Brian MURRAY
10 Executive VP for Fince/Admin ..... Mr. Robert M. GALECKE
11 Assoc VP for Administration ..... Mr. Patrick DALY
50 Dean College of Business ..... Dr. Robert SCHERER
20 Dean of Undergraduate College ..... Dr. C. W. EAKER
58 Dean Grad School of Liberal Arts ..... Dr. David SWEET

73 Dean School of Ministry ....Dr. Mark GOODWIN
84 VP of Enroll Mgmt & Student Affairs ....Dr. John PLOTTS
38 Assoc Dean for Constantin College ....Dr. Margaret BROWN MARSDEN
06 Registrar ....Mrs. Jan BURK
19 Campus Safety Supervisor ....Mr. Charles STEADMAN
90 Director of IT User Support Service ....Mr. Sabyasachi SANYAL
91 Director Information Technology ....Mr. Richard HAYTER
44 Director of Annual Giving ....Mr. Jim LIVERNOIS
41 Director of Athletics ....Mr. Richard STROCKBINE
42 Director of Campus Ministry ....Mrs. Denise PHILLIPS
18 Director of Facilities ....Mr. Jerry HABA
21 Director of Finance ....Mr. Leonard A. ROBERTSON
15 Director of Human Resources ....Mrs. Janis TOWNSEND
09 Director of Institutional Research ....Dr. Leslie R. ODOM
08 Director of Library ....Dr. Robert S. DUPREE
27 Director of Marketing & Comm ....Mr. William HARTLEY
96 Director of Purchasing ....Mr. Alan STERLING
104 Director for Rome/Summer Programs ....Mrs. Becky DAVIES
23 Director of Student Health ....Dr. Laurie KUGELMANN DEKAT
36 Director of Career Services ....Ms. Julie JANIK

*University of Houston System (A)

212 Ezekiel Cullen Building, Houston TX 77204-2018
County: Harris FICE Identification: 011721
Unit ID: 229407
Telephone: (713) 743-1000 Carnegie Class: N/A
FAX Number: (713) 743-8837
URL: www.uhsa.uh.edu

01 Chancellor ....Dr. Renu KHATOR
05 Sr VC for Academic Affairs/Provost ....Dr. Paula SHORT
43 Vice Chancellor/General Counsel ....Ms. Dona G. CORNELL
10 Exec VC Administration/Finance ....Dr. Carl P. CARLUCCI
32 Vice Chancellor Student Affairs ....Dr. Richard WALKER
30 VC University Advancement ....Ms. Eloise D. STUHR
26 AVC University Relations ....Mr. Richard BONNIN
13 Assoc VC CIO/Information Technology ....Dr. Dennis FOUTY
21 Associate Vice Chancellor Finance ....Mr. Thomas EHARDT
11 Assoc VC Administration ....Ms. Emily MESSA
44 Assoc VC University Advancement ....Mr. Eli CIPRIANO
86 Asst Vice Chanc Govt Relations ....Ms. Laura CALFEE
88 Asst VC for Planning & Policy ....Mr. Chris STANICH
15 Exec Director Human Resources ....Ms. Joan M. NELSON
21 Director Internal Auditing ....Mr. Don GUYTON
88 Treasurer ....Mr. Raymond BARTLETT
86 Exec Director for Govt Relations ....Mr. Darrin HALL

*University of Houston (B)

4800 Calhoun Road, Houston TX 77004
County: Harris FICE Identification: 003652
Unit ID: 225511
Telephone: (713) 743-1000 Carnegie Class: RU/VH
FAX Number: (713) 743-8837 Calendar System: Semester
URL: www.uh.edu
Established: 1927 Annual Undergrad Tuition & Fees (In-State): $9,678
Enrollment: 40,747 Coed
Affiliation or Control: State IRS Status: Exempt
Highest Offering: Doctorate
Program: Liberal Arts And General; Teacher Preparatory; Professional
Accreditation: SC, AAFCS, BUS, BUSA, CEA, CLPSY, CONST, COPSY, CS, DIETD, DIETI, ENG, ENGT, IPSY, LAW, MUS, OPT, OPTR, PHAR, SCPSY, SP, SW, TED

02 President ....Dr. Renu KHATOR
05 Sr VC/VP Academic Affs/Provost ....Dr. Paula SHORT
10 Exec VP Administration/Finance ....Dr. Carl CARLUCCI
30 Vice Pres University Advancement ....Dr. Eloise D. STUHR
32 Vice President Student Affairs ....Dr. Richard WALKER
86 Exec Dir Governmental Relations ....Mr. Darrin HALL
43 VP Legal Affairs & General Counsel ....Ms. Dona G. CORNELL
31 VP for Community Rels & Inst Access ....Dr. Elwyn C. LEE
29 President/CEO Alumni Association ....Mr. Mike PEDE
13 Assoc VP Information Tech/CIO ....Dr. Dennis FOUTY
26 Interim VP for UH Mkt & Comm ....Mr. Richard BONNIN
20 Int Vice Provost & Dean UG Stdnts ....Ms. Teri E. LONGACRE
58 Int Vice Provost & Dean UH Grad ....Mr. Dimitri LITVINOV
88 Interim Assoc Provost Faculty Dev ....Mr. Richard OLENCHAK
21 Assoc Provost Finance & Admin ....Mr. Craig NESS
30 Assoc VP for Univ Development ....Mr. Cliff REDD
84 Assoc VP for Stdnt Access/Success ....Mr. Stephen C. SOUTULLO
35 Assoc VP for Student Affairs ....Mr. Daniel MAXWELL
88 Assoc VP Stdnt Affs/Dean of Stdnts ....Dr. William MUNSON
91 Assoc VP Enterprise Sys Adm ....Dr. Arun JAIN
21 Associate Vice President Finance ....Mr. Tom EHARDT
88 Interim Assoc Provost Educ Innovat ....Mr. Jeff MORGAN
22 Asst VP Equal Opportunity Services ....Dr. Richard A. BAKER
45 Asst VP Planning & Policy ....Mr. Chris M. STANICH
41 VP Intercollegiate Athletics ....Mr. Mack B. RHOADES, IV
37 Exec Dir Scholarships & Fin Aid ....Mr. Sal LORIA
16 Exec Director Human Resources ....Ms. Joan NELSON
18 Exec Dir Facilities Management ....Ms. Melissa ROCKWELL-HOPKINS
51 Director Continuing Education ....Ms. Mercedes SURATY-CLARKE
06 Registrar ....Ms. Debbie HENRY
07 Executive Director of Admissions ....Ms. Djuana YOUNG
19 Asst VP for Univ Safety & Security ....Mr. Malcolm DAVIS
96 Director of Purchasing & HUB ....Mr. Jack TENNER
79 Dean Col Liberal Arts/Soc Sci ....Dr. John ROBERTS
81 Interim Dean Col Natural Sci & Math ....Dr. Dan WELLS
88 Dean College of Optometry ....Dr. Earl SMITH, III
72 Dean College of Technology ....Dr. William E. FITZGIBBON, III
54 Dean Cullen College of Engineering ....Dr. Joseph W. TEDESCO
48 Dean College of Architecture ....Ms. Patricia Belton OLIVER
70 Dean Graduate Coll of Social Work ....Dr. Ira COLBY
67 Dean College of Pharmacy ....Dr. Lamar PRITCHARD
53 Dean College of Education ....Dr. Robert MCPHERSON
50 Dean Bauer Col Business Admin ....Dr. Latha RAMCHAND
88 Dean Hilton Col Htl/Restaurant Mgt ....Dr. John BOWEN
92 Dean Honors College ....Dr. William MONROE
61 Interim Dean UH Law Center ....Dr. Richard ALDERMAN
08 Dean University Libraries ....Ms. Dana C. ROOKS
88 Assoc VP for Administration ....Ms. Emily MESSA
44 Assoc VP for Univ Advancement ....Mr. Eli D. CIPRIANO
88 Chief Energy Officer ....Mr. Ramanan KRISHNAMOORTI

*University of Houston - Clear Lake (C)

Houston TX 77058-1098
County: Harris FICE Identification: 011711
Unit ID: 225414
Telephone: (281) 283-7600 Carnegie Class: Master's L
FAX Number: (281) 283-2219 Calendar System: Semester
URL: www.uhcl.edu
Established: 1971 Annual Undergrad Tuition & Fees (In-State): $6,514
Enrollment: 8,153 Coed
Affiliation or Control: State IRS Status: 501(c)3
Highest Offering: Doctorate
Program: Liberal Arts And General; Teacher Preparatory; Professional
Accreditation: SC, BUS, BUSA, CS, ENG, ENGR, #MFCD, SW, TED

02 President ....Dr. William A. STAPLES
05 Sr Vice Pres for Academic Affairs ....Dr. Carl A. STOCKTON
10 Vice Pres Administration & Finance ....Ms. Michelle DOTTER
04 Executive Assoc to the President ....Ms. Mary Ann H. SHALLBERG
13 Assoc VP Information Resources ....Dr. A. Glen HOUSTON
20 Assoc Vice Pres Academic Affairs ....Dr. Mrinal Mugdh VARMA
30 Assoc VP University Advancement ....Mr. Dion MCINNIS
32 Assoc Vice Pres Student Services ....Dr. Darlene BIGGERS
21 Associate Vice President Finance ....Mr. Usha MATHEW
84 Assoc Vice Pres Enrollment Mgmt ....Dr. Yvette BENDECK
18 Assoc VP Facilities Mgmt/Construct ....Mr. Ward MARTAINDALE
50 Dean School Business ....Dr. Wm. Theodore CUMMINGS
81 Dean School Science/Computer Engr ....Dr. Zbigniew CZAJKIEWICZ
79 Dean Sch Human Sci/Humanities ....Dr. Rick SHORT
53 Dean School Education ....Dr. Dennis W. SPUCK
35 Interim Dean of Students ....Mr. David A. RACHITA
28 Asst Dean Student Diversity ....Ms. Linda C. BULLOCK
08 Exec Director Neumann Library ....Ms. Karen WIELHORSKI
85 Exec Director Intl Initiatives ....Dr. Sameer PANDE
45 Exec Director Planning & Assessment ....Mr. Kevin BARLOW
15 Executive Director Human Resources ....Ms. Katherine JUSTICE
14 Exec Director University Computing ....Mr. Rodger CARR
21 Exec Dir of Procurement & Payables ....Ms. Debra CARPENTER
25 Exec Dir Sponsored Programs ....Mr. Paul MEYERS
37 Executive Director Financial Aid ....Mr. Billy SATTERFIELD
88 Exec Dir Environment Inst Houston ....Dr. George GUILLEN
06 Registrar/Director Academic Records ....Mr. Billy SATTERFIELD
56 Director Distance/Off-Campus Educ ....Ms. Lisa GABRIEL
27 Exec Director Communications ....Ms. Theresa PRESSWOOD
29 Director Alumni & Cmty Relations ....Vacant
19 Director Police ....Mr. Paul WILLINGHAM
36 Director Career/Counseling Services ....Dr. Alfred KAHN
09 Assoc Dir Institutional Research ....Vacant
12 Dir Camp Operat/UHCL Pearland Camp ....Ms. Kathy DUPREE
23 Dir Health & Disability Services ....Ms. Regina PICKETT
07 Exec Director of Admissions ....Ms. Rauchelle JONES
40 Manager Bookstore ....Ms. Trinita TOLER

*University of Houston - Downtown (D)

One Main Street, Houston TX 77002-1014
County: Harris FICE Identification: 003612
Unit ID: 225432
Telephone: (713) 221-8001 Carnegie Class: Bac/Diverse
FAX Number: (713) 221-8075 Calendar System: Semester
URL: www.uhd.edu
Established: 1974 Annual Undergrad Tuition & Fees (In-State): $5,238
Enrollment: 13,916 Coed
Affiliation or Control: State IRS Status: Exempt
Highest Offering: Master's
Program: Liberal Arts And General
Accreditation: SC, BUS, ENGT, SW

02 President ....Dr. William V. FLORES
04 Director Presidential Affairs ....Ms. Gilda PARKER
05 Provost/Sr VP Acad & Student Affrs ....Mr. Edward HUGETZ
20 Asst VP Acad Affairs/Dean Ungrad ....Dr. Gary L. STADING
108 Assoc VP Plng & Inst Effectiveness ....Dr. Patrick S. WILLIAMS
50 Dean College of Business ....Dr. Michael FIELDS
79 Dean Col Humanities/Social Sci ....Dr. DoVeanna FULTON
88 Dean College of Public Service ....Dr. Beth PELZ
81 Interim Dean Col Sciences & Tech ....Dr. Akif UZMAN
97 Dean University College ....Dr. Chris BIRCHAK
88 Dean Academic Advising & Mentoring ....Dr. Robert JARRETT
08 Executive Director WI Dykes Library ....Ms. Pat ENSOR
88 Exec Dir Distance Education ....Mr. Louis D. EVANS, III
09 Director of Institutional Research ....Ms. Carol M. TUCKER
88 Asst VP Research & Spon Programs ....Ms. Sandra GARCIA
88 Dir Ofc Research & Sponsored Pgm ....Ms. Carolyn IVEY
108 Director of Academic Assessment ....Dr. Lea CAMPBELL
88 Dir Co-Curricular & Oper Assessment ....Dr. Angela KOPONEN
88 Director Creative Services ....Mr. Joe WYNNE
88 Ex Dir Ctr Public Svc & Family Str ....Dr. Noel BEZETTE-FLORES
88 Director O'Kane Gallery ....Mr. Mark CERVENKA
88 Director International Programs ....Vacant
92 Director of Scholars Academy ....Dr. Mary Jo PARKER
88 Director Advising Center ....Ms. Jemma SYLVESTER-CAESAR
88 Director of Advising Services ....Ms. Reyna ROMERO
88 Director of Academic Support Center ....Dr. Isidro GRAU
88 Director Academic Services ....Mr. David MORALES
88 Dir Academic Budgets & Operations ....Ms. Elaine PEARSON
88 Director Academic Projects ....Ms. Lucy BOWEN
11 Dir College Admin & Operation ....Ms. Paulette PURDY
72 Dir Applied Business/Technology Ctr ....Mr. G. V. KRISHNAN
88 Director English Language Institute ....Dr. Gail KELLERSBERGER
88 Director Criminal Justice Center ....Mr. Rex WHITE
51 Director Continuing Education ....Ms. Clara ROJAS ALVAREZ LOPEREN
88 Director Energy Management ....Vacant
88 Dir Center for Entrepreneurship ....Mr. William DUDLEY
88 Director Insurance & Risk Mgmt Ctr ....Dr. Wendall BRANIFF
10 VP Administration & Finance ....Mr. David M. BRADLEY
13 Assoc VP Information Technology ....Mr. Hossein SHAHROKHI
88 Executive Director IT ....Ms. Erin MAYER
91 Director Enterprise Systems ....Mr. Kong YIN
88 Dir Technology Learning Services ....Mr. John LANE
88 Dir User Support Services ....Mr. Said FATTOUH
88 Director Technical Services ....Ms. Grace DAVILA
88 Dir Comp/Telecom & Video Networks ....Mr. Miguel RUIZ
88 Dir IT Business Services ....Ms. Jacqueline SMITH
21 Asst VP Business Affairs ....Mr. George W. ANDERSON
25 Director Risk Mgmt & Compliance ....Ms. Mary COOK
18 Asst VP Facilities Management ....Mr. Chris MCCALL
19 Chief of Police ....Mr. Richard BOYLE
16 VP Employment Svcs & Operations ....Ms. Ivonne MONTALBANO
15 Asst VP Employee Svcs/Records Mgmt ....Ms. Betty POWELL
22 Asst VP Talent Mgr/AA Ofcr ....Dr. Doug TEDUITS
84 Dean Enrollment Management ....Ms. Tomikia P. LEGRANDE
35 Dean of Students ....Vacant
06 Registrar ....Ms. Cynthia SANTOS
07 Director of Admissions ....Mr. Spencer LIGHTSY
37 Director of Scholarships & Fin Aid ....Ms. LaTasha GOUDEAU
41 Director Sports & Fitness ....Mr. Richard SEBASTIANI
36 Director Career Development Center ....Mr. Stephen MARKERT
88 Director of Testing Services ....Dr. Shakila M. FARMER
88 Director Disability Services ....Dr. Christopher KAIO
88 Director Veterans Services ....Vacant
88 Dir University Business Services ....Ms. Mary TORRES
88 Exec Director Talent Search ....Ms. Jennifer HIGHTOWER
88 Director Upward Bound ....Ms. Dawanna LEWIS
88 Pgm Dir Title V Stud Success Grant ....Ms. Katrina BORDERS
30 VP Advancement & External Rels ....Ms. Johanna WOLFE
26 Executive Dir University Relations ....Ms. Diane SUMMERS
88 Dir Constituent Events & Operations ....Ms. Karen P. RIVERA
88 Director Communications ....Ms. Mary Ann COZZA
102 Director Corporate Relations ....Mr. Jacob LIPP
88 Director Individual Giving ....Ms. Jaha WILLIAMS
88 Director Media Relations ....Ms. Claire CATON

*University of Houston - Victoria (E)

3007 N Ben Wilson, Victoria TX 77901-4450
County: Victoria FICE Identification: 013231
Unit ID: 225502
Telephone: (361) 570-4848 Carnegie Class: Master's L
FAX Number: (361) 580-5534 Calendar System: Semester
URL: www.uhv.edu
Established: 1973 Annual Undergrad Tuition & Fees (In-State): $5,194
Enrollment: 4,335 Coed
Affiliation or Control: State IRS Status: 501(c)3
Highest Offering: Master's
Program: Liberal Arts And General; Teacher Preparatory; Professional
Accreditation: SC, BUS, CACREP, NURSE, @TEAC

02 President ....Dr. Philip D. CASTILLE
11 Vice Pres Administration & Finance ....Mr. Wayne B. BERAN
05 Provost/Vice Pres Academic Affairs ....Dr. Jeffrey CASS
100 Chief of Staff ....Vacant
32 Associate Vice Pres Student Affairs ....Dr. Jay LAMBERT
49 Dean Arts & Sciences ....Dr. Jeffrey DILEO
50 Dean Business Administration ....Dr. Farhang NIROOMAND
53 Dean Education & Human Development ....Dr. Freddie LITTON
66 Dean Nursing ....Dr. Kathryn TART
30 AVP University Advancement ....Vacant
08 Senior Director of Library ....Dr. Joe F. DAHLSTROM
14 Sr Dir Academic & Student Tech Svcs ....Mr. Joseph S. FERGUSON
15 Dir Human Resource/Affirmative Act ....Ms. Laura L. SMITH
84 Sr Director of Enrollment Mgmt ....Dr. Denee THOMAS
88 Dir Small Business Development Ctr ....Mr. Joe HUMPHREYS
06 Registrar ....Ms. Trudy WORTHAM
37 Director Financial Aid ....Ms. Carolyn R. MALLORY
18 Director Facilities ....Mr. Kevin MYERS
10 Director Business Services ....Mr. Tim MICHALSKI
21 Comptroller ....Ms. Valerie WALDEN
41 Director Athletics ....Mr. Ashley WALYUCHOW
44 Director Stewardship/Planned Giving ....Vacant
102 Dir Corp & Foundation Relations ....Dr. Charles ALCORN
26 Director Marketing & Communications ....Ms. Paula COBLER
38 Director of Counseling Center ....Vacant
35 Director of Student Life & Services ....Ms. Lindsey KOCH
09 Director Institutional Research ....Dr. Tong-Ai ZHANG
88 Director Retention & Student Succ ....Ms. Sandra HEINOLD
88 Director of Budget ....Ms. Darlene PULLIN

University of the Incarnate Word (A)

4301 Broadway, San Antonio TX 78209-6397
County: Bexar FICE Identification: 003578
Unit ID: 225627
Telephone: (210) 829-6000 Carnegie Class: Master's L
FAX Number: (210) 829-1220 Calendar System: Semester
URL: www.uiw.edu
Established: 1881 Annual Undergrad Tuition & Fees: $24,790
Enrollment: 8,442 Coed
Affiliation or Control: Roman Catholic IRS Status: 501(c)3
Highest Offering: Doctorate
Program: Liberal Arts And General; Teacher Preparatory; Professional
Accreditation: SC, ACBSP, CIDA, DIETD, DIETI, HSA, NMT, NURSE, OPT, PHAR, @PTA, THEA

01 President .... Dr. Louis J. AGNESE, JR.
00 Chancellor .... Dr. Denise DOYLE
88 Mission Effectiveness .... Sr. Walter MAHER
04 Executive Assistant to President .... Ms. Yvonne BURNS
26 Asst to the President/Communication .... Mr. Vincent RODRIGUEZ
43 General Counsel .... Ms. Cindy ESCAMILLA
05 Provost .... Dr. Kathleen LIGHT
84 Vice Pres Enrollment Mgt/Stdnt Svcs . Dr. David M. JURENOVICH
30 Vice Pres Institutional Advancement .... Sr. Kathleen COUGHLIN
10 Vice Pres for Business & Finance .... Mr. Douglas ENDSLEY
104 Vice Pres International Programs .... Mr. Marcos FRAGOSO
56 Vice Pres of Ext Academic Programs .... Dr. Cyndi WILSON-PORTER
13 Vice Pres Information Resources .... Mr. Marshall EIDSON
21 Comptroller .... Ms. Edith COGDELL
50 Dean H-E-B Sch Business & Admin .... Vacant
57 Dean Humanities Arts & Social Sci .... Dr. John HEALY
66 Dean Nursing & Health Professions .... Dr. Mary HOKE
53 Dean Dreeben School of Education .... Dr. Denise STAUDT
54 Dean Math Science Engineering .... Dr. Carlos GARCIA
88 Dean Interactive Media & Design .... Dr. Sharon WELKEY
67 Dean Feik School of Pharmacy ..... Dr. Arcelia JOHNSON-FANNIN
88 Acting Dean School of Optometry .... Dr. Andrew BUZZELLI
58 Dean of Grad Studies/Research .... Dr. Kevin VICHCALES
62 Dean of Library Services .... Dr. Cheryl ANDERSON
108 Assoc Provost/Dir of Assessment .... Dr. Glenn JAMES
55 Dean Sch of Extended Studies .... Mr. Vincent PORTER
106 Dean of Virtual University .... Vacant
88 Dean Univ Preparatory Programs .... Mr. Daniel OCHOA
29 Director of Alumni Relations .... Ms. Lisa SCHULTZ
26 Director of Public Relations .... Ms. Debra DEL TORO
84 Dean of Enrollment .... Ms. Andrea CYTERSKI-ACOSTA
32 Dean of Student Success .... Ms. Sandy MCMAKIN
38 Director of Counseling .... Dr. Keith TUCKER
20 Director of Academic Advising .... Mr. Moises TORRESCANO
88 Director Learning Assistance Center .... Ms. Cristina ARIZA
06 Registrar .... Dr. Bobbye G. FRY
37 Director of Financial Aid .... Ms. Amy CARCANAGUES
32 Dean of Campus Life .... Dr. Renee MOORE
39 Director of Residence Life .... Ms. Diane SANCHEZ
35 Dir University Events/Student Pgms .... Mr. Paul AYALA
23 Director of Health Services .... Ms. Marveen MAHON
42 Chaplain .... Fr. Tom DYMOWSKI
42 Director of Campus Ministry .... Ms. Elisabeth VILLARREAL
15 Director of Human Resources .... Ms. Annette THOMPSON
96 Director of Purchasing .... Mr. Sam WAGES
18 Director Facilities Mgmt & Services .... Mr. Steve HEYING
41 Director of Athletics .... Mr. Mark PAPICH
88 Director of Infrastructure Support .... Mr. Carl HAYWOOD
88 Director of Enterprise Applications .... Ms. Iris SOLCHER
88 Director Instructional Technology .... Ms. Ana GONZALES
72 Director of Technology Support .... Mr. Anthony RAMOS
09 Director of Institutional Research .... Ms. Robin LOGAN
07 Director of Admissions .... Ms. Heather RODRIGUEZ
36 Coordinator of Career Services .... Mr. Juan ALMENDAREZ

University of Mary Hardin-Baylor (B)

900 College Street, Belton TX 76513-2578
County: Bell FICE Identification: 003588
Unit ID: 226471
Telephone: (254) 295-8642 Carnegie Class: Master's S
FAX Number: (254) 295-4535 Calendar System: Semester
URL: www.umhb.edu
Established: 1845 Annual Undergrad Tuition & Fees: $23,620
Enrollment: 3,287 Coed
Affiliation or Control: Southern Baptist IRS Status: 501(c)3
Highest Offering: Doctorate
Program: Liberal Arts And General; Teacher Preparatory; Professional
Accreditation: SC, CACREP, MUS, NURSE, SW

01 President/CEO .... Dr. Randy G. O'REAR
03 Sr Vice Pres Admin/COO .... Dr. Steve THEODORE
05 Provost/Sr Vice Pres Academics .... Dr. Steve OLDHAM
45 Sr Vice Pres Campus Planning .... Mr. Edd MARTIN
00 President Emeritus .... Dr. Jerry G. BAWCOM
30 Vice Pres for Development .... Mr. Brent DAVISON
102 Vice Pres Communication/Spec Proj .... Dr. Paula TANNER
32 Vice Pres for Student Life .... Dr. Byron WEATHERSBEE
41 Vice Pres Athletics .... Mr. Randy MANN
10 Vice Pres Business/Finance/CFO .... Mrs. Jennifer RAMM
15 Assoc Vice Pres Human Resources .... Mrs. Susan OWENS
13 Assoc Vice Pres Information Tech .... Mr. Brent HARRIS
84 Assoc Vice Pres Enrollment Mgmt .... Dr. Gary LAMM
18 Assoc Vice Pres for Facilities .... Mr. Bob PATTEE
20 Asst Provost .... Dr. Tammi COOPER
21 Controller .... Mrs. Charla KAHLIG
49 Dean of Sciences .... Dr. Carl GILBERT
66 Dean of Nursing .... Dr. Sharon SOUTER
53 Dean of Education .... Dr. Marlene ZIPPERLEN
50 Dean Global Engagmnt/Dir Global Ctr .... Vacant
58 Dean Graduate School .... Dr. Colin WILBORN
88 Dean of Christian Studies .... Dr. Tim CRAWFORD
57 Dean Visual/Performing Arts .... Mr. Ted BARNES
35 Dean of Students .... Mr. Ray MARTIN
39 Assoc Dean Students/Dir Residence .... Ms. Donna PLANK
04 Executive Assistant to President .... Mrs. Phyllis ROGERS
06 Registrar .... Mrs. Amy MCGILVRAY
07 Director of Admissions & Recruiting .... Mr. Brent BURKS
08 Director Learning Resources .... Ms. Denise KARIMKHANI
26 Director Marketing/Public Relations .... Mr. James STAFFORD
09 Director Institutional Research .... Ms. Bethany CHAPMAN
37 Director Financial Aid .... Mr. Ron BROWN
92 Director Honors Program .... Dr. David HOLCOMB
19 Director Campus Police .... Mr. Gary SARGENT
96 Director of Purchasing .... Mr. Mike FRAZIER
29 Director Alumni Relations .... Ms. Rebecca O'BANION
42 University Chaplain .... Dr. George LOUTHERBACK
36 Director Career Services .... Mr. Don OWENS
38 Director Couns Testing & Health .... Mr. Nate WILLIAMS
85 Dir International Student Services .... Mrs. Elizabeth TANAKA
44 Director Planned Giving .... Mrs. Melissa BRAGG
40 Bookstore Manager .... Ms. Debbie COTTRELL

University of North Texas (C)

1155 Union Circle #311277, Denton TX 76203-5013
County: Denton FICE Identification: 003594
Unit ID: 227216
Telephone: (940) 565-2000 Carnegie Class: RU/H
FAX Number: (940) 565-7600 Calendar System: Semester
URL: www.unt.edu
Established: 1890 Annual Undergrad Tuition & Fees (In-State): $8,745
Enrollment: 35,778 Coed
Affiliation or Control: State IRS Status: 501(c)3
Highest Offering: Doctorate
Program: Liberal Arts And General; Teacher Preparatory; Professional
Accreditation: SC, ART, AUD, BUS, BUSA, CACREP, CEA, CIDA, CLPSY, COPSY, CORE, CS, ENG, ENGT, FEPAC, JOUR, LIB, MUS, NRPA, SP, SPAA, SW, TED

00 Chancellor .... Mr. Lee F. JACKSON
01 President .... Dr. V. Lane RAWLINS
05 Provost/Vice Pres Academic Affairs .... Dr. Warren W. BURGGREN
10 Vice Pres Finance/Administration .... Mr. Andrew M. HARRIS
46 VP Research/Economic Development .... Dr. Thomas J. MCCOY
32 Vice President Student Affairs .... Dr. Elizabeth WITH
43 Vice Chancellor/General Counsel .... Ms. Nancy FOOTER
26 Vice President University Relations .... Ms. Deborah S. LELIAERT
30 VP for Advancement/Dir of Develop .... Dr. Michael MONTICINO
20 Senior Vice Provost .... Dr. Yolanda Flores NIEMANN
20 Vice Provost for Academic Resources .... Dr. Allen CLARK
20 Vice Provost for Faculty Success .... Dr. Christy CRUTSINGER
41 Athletic Director .... Mr. Rick VILLARREAL
35 Dean Students .... Dr. Maureen MCGUINNESS
13 Vice President for Information Tech .... Mr. John HOOPER
21 Senior Assoc VP for Finance .... Ms. Jean BUSH
21 Assoc VP Finance & Cont .... Vacant
28 VP Institutional Equity & Diversity .... Dr. Gilda GARCIA
88 Vice Provost for College Transfer .... Dr. Celia WILLIAMSON
18 Asst Vice President for Facilities .... Mr. Charles JACKSON
08 Dean of Libraries .... Dr. Martin HALBERT
37 Director Financial Aid .... Ms. Zelma DELEON
49 Dean College of Arts/Sciences .... Dr. Arthur GOVEN
50 Dean College Business .... Dr. Finley GRAVES
53 Dean College of Education .... Dr. Jerry R. THOMAS
57 Dean Col Visual Arts & Design .... Dr. Robert W. MILNES
88 Dean Col Public Affs/Community Svc .... Dr. Thomas L. EVENSON
64 Dean College of Music .... Dr. James C. SCOTT
59 Dean Col of Merch/Hosp & Tourism .... Dr. Judith FORNEY
62 Dean College of Information .... Dr. Herman L. TOTTEN
58 Dean Toulouse Grad School .... Dr. Mark WARDELL
92 Dean Honors College .... Dr. Gloria COX
60 Dean Mayborn Sch of Journalism .... Dr. Dorothy BLAND
54 Dean College of Engineering .... Dr. Costas TSATSOULIS
90 Director Acad Computing/User Svcs .... Dr. Philip C. BACZEWSKI
09 Director Institutional Research .... Dr. Mary BARTON
108 Director Institutional Assessment .... Dr. Jason F. SIMON
88 Dir Institutional Effectiveness .... Ms. Elizabeth FISHER
07 Director of Admissions .... Dr. Rebecca LOTHRINGER
51 Dir Ctr for Achvmnt & Lifelng Lrng .... Ms. Marilyn D. WAGNER
06 Registrar .... Ms. Lynn MCCREARY
15 Asst Vice Pres Human Resources .... Vacant
36 Dir Career & Counseling Svcs .... Mr. Dan NAEGELI
38 Director of Counseling & Testing .... Dr. Judy A. MCCONNELL
19 Director/Chief of Police .... Mr. Richard S. DETER
39 Director Housing .... Dr. Elisabeth B. WARREN
85 Vice Provost International Affairs .... Dr. Richard NADER
40 Director UNT Bookstore .... Mr. Rodney DAVISON
23 Dir Stdnt Health Ctr/Wellness Svcs .... Dr. Herschel VOORHEES
29 Exec Dir Alum Rels/N Texas Exes .... Vacant

University of North Texas at Dallas (D)

7300 University Hills Blvd, Dallas TX 75241
County: Dallas Identification: 667124
Telephone: (972) 780-3600 Carnegie Class: Not Classified
FAX Number: (972) 780-3636 Calendar System: Semester
URL: dallas.unt.edu
Established: 2000 Annual Undergrad Tuition & Fees (In-State): $7,650
Enrollment: N/A Coed
Affiliation or Control: State IRS Status: 501(c)3
Highest Offering: Master's
Program: Liberal Arts And General
Accreditation: SC

01 President .... Dr. John ELLIS
10 Chief Financial Officer .... Mr. Carlos HERNANDEZ

University of North Texas Health Science Center at Fort Worth (E)

3500 Camp Bowie Boulevard, Fort Worth TX 76107-2699
County: Tarrant FICE Identification: 009768
Unit ID: 228909
Telephone: (817) 735-2000 Carnegie Class: Spec/Med
FAX Number: (817) 735-2486 Calendar System: Semester
URL: www.hsc.unt.edu
Established: 1966 Annual Graduate Tuition & Fees: $16,330
Enrollment: 1,760 Coed
Affiliation or Control: State IRS Status: 501(c)3
Highest Offering: Doctorate; No Undergraduates
Program: Professional
Accreditation: SC, ARCPA, FEPAC, OSTEO, PH, @PHAR, PTA

01 President .... Dr. Scott B. RANSOM
10 VP for Finance and CFO .... Mr. Michael R. MUELLER
86 Vice President Governmental Affairs .... Mr. Dan JENSEN
63 Dean Texas Col of Osteopathic Med .... Dr. Don PESKA
32 Vice Pres Student Affairs .... Dr. Thomas D. MOORMAN
08 VP Information Resources & Technolo .... Dr. Renee DRABIER
15 Vice Pres Human Resource Svcs .... Vacant
81 VP Research & Biotechnology .... Vacant
51 Assoc VP for Professional/Cont Edu .... Ms. Pam MCFADDEN
58 Dean Grad Sch Biomedical Sciences .... Dr. Jamboor K. VISHWANATHA
76 Dean School of Health Professions .... Vacant
69 Dean of School of Public Health .... Dr. Richard KURZ
37 Director Student Financial Aid .... Mr. Joseph SANCHEZ
84 Executive Director Enrollment Svcs .... Mr. A.J RANDOLPH
19 Chief of Police .... Mr. Gary GAILLIARD
30 VP Institutional Advancement .... Vacant
09 VP Strategy & Measurement .... Dr. Thomas FAIRCHILD
21 Controller & Chief Budget Officer .... Mr. Geoff SCARPELLI
07 Asst Dean of Admissions & Outreach .... Mr. Joel DABOUB
18 Vice President for Operations .... Mr. Stephen BARRETT
26 VP Marketing & Communications .... Ms. Jean TIPS
96 Dir Of Contract Administration .... Mrs. Lane NESTMAN

University of Phoenix Austin Campus (F)

10801-2 MoPac Expressway, Suite 300, Austin TX 78759-5459
Telephone: (512) 344-1400 Identification: 770226
Accreditation: &NH, ACBSP

† Main campus is University of Phoenix in Tempe, AZ.

University of Phoenix Dallas Campus (G)

12400 Coit Road, Dallas TX 75251-2004
Telephone: (972) 385-1055 Identification: 770227
Accreditation: &NH, ACBSP

† Main campus is University of Phoenix in Tempe, AZ.

University of Phoenix El Paso Campus (H)

1340 Adabel Drive, El Paso TX 79936-5900
Telephone: (915) 599-5900 Identification: 770228
Accreditation: &NH, ACBSP

† Main campus is University of Phoenix in Tempe, AZ.

University of Phoenix Houston Campus (I)

11451 Katy Freeway, Houston TX 77079-2004
Telephone: (713) 465-9966 Identification: 770229
Accreditation: &NH, ACBSP

† Main campus is University of Phoenix in Tempe, AZ.

University of Phoenix McAllen Campus (J)

4201 South Shary Road, Mission TX 78572-1578
Telephone: (956) 519-5800 Identification: 770230
Accreditation: &NH, ACBSP

† Main campus is University of Phoenix in Tempe, AZ.

University of Phoenix San Antonio Campus (K)

8200 IH-10 West, Suite 1000, San Antonio TX 78230-3876
Telephone: (210) 524-2100 Identification: 770231
Accreditation: &NH

† Main campus is University of Phoenix in Tempe, AZ.

University of St. Thomas (L)

3800 Montrose Boulevard, Houston TX 77006-4696
County: Harris FICE Identification: 003654
Unit ID: 227863
Telephone: (713) 522-7911 Carnegie Class: Master's L

FAX Number: (713) 525-2125 Calendar System: Semester
URL: www.stthom.edu
Established: 1947 Annual Undergrad Tuition & Fees: $27,900
Enrollment: 3,681 Coed
Affiliation or Control: Roman Catholic IRS Status: 501(c)3
Highest Offering: Doctorate
Program: Liberal Arts And General; Teacher Preparatory; Professional
Accreditation: SC, BUS, TEAC, THEOL

01 President ... Dr. Robert IVANY
04 Exec Assistant to the President ... Ms. Sandra CACKOWSKI
04 Admin Assistant to the President ... Ms. Cindy VIAUD
10 Vice President for Finance ... Mr. James M. BOOTH
05 Vice President Academic Affairs ... Dr. Dominic AQUILA
11 Assoc VP of Administrative Svcs ... Mr. John MEUSER
20 Associate VP Academic Affairs ... Dr. John PALASOTA
49 Dean Arts & Sciences ... Fr. Joseph PILSNER
73 Dean School of Theology ... Dr. Sandra C. MAGIE, CM
50 Int Dean Cameron School of Business ... Dr. Barry WILBRATTE
53 Dean School of Education ... Dr. Robert LEBLANC
08 Dean of Libraries ... Mr. James PICCININNI
58 Dir Center for Thomistic Studies ... Dr. Mary C. SOMMERS
88 Director Center for Business Ethics ... Dr. Michele SIMMS
82 Director Center for Intl Studies ... Dr. Hans STOCKTON
88 Director Center for Irish Studies ... Ms. Lori GALLAGHER
13 Vice Pres Information Technology ... Mr. Gary MCCORMACK
30 Vice President for Inst Advancement ... Ms. Cynthia COLBERT RILEY
84 Vice Pres Marketing & Enroll Mgmt ... Ms. Vickie ALLEMAN
88 Director Center for Faith & Culture ... Fr. Donald NESTI, CSSP
06 Registrar ... Ms. Kimberly SANDERS
90 Dir of Network & Campus Computing ... Mr. Tony REYNA
90 Director Technology Support Svcs ... Mr. Mark HENDERSON
91 Dir Administrative Computing Svcs ... Ms. Joanna E. PALASOTA
88 Director Central Computing Services ... Ms. Christine BARRY
32 Vice Pres Student Affairs ... Ms. Patricia MCKINLEY
35 Dean of Students ... Ms. Lindsey MCPHERSON
38 Exec Dir Counseling & Disability ... Dr. Rose SIGNORELLO
35 Assistant VP of Campus Life ... Mr. Matthew PRASIFKA
42 Dir of Campus Ministry/Chaplain ... Fr. Michael BUENTELLO
39 Director Residence Life ... Ms. Yolanda NORMAN
88 Director of Student Activities ... Ms. Angie MONTELONGO
88 Director of Recreational Sports ... Ms. Jessica DOMANN
18 Asst VP Facilities Operations ... Mr. Howard A. ROSE
21 Controller ... Ms. Karen S. BURNS
88 Treasurer ... Ms. Susan ROSE
44 Exec Dir Institutional Advancement ... Ms. Susan E. BRADFORD
44 Director of Development/Major Gifts ... Ms. Deborah CROFOOT-MORLEY
29 Director of Major Constitutents ... Ms. Kia WISSMILLER
07 Director Admissions ... Mr. Phil BUTCHER
37 Dean of Scholarships/Financial Aid ... Ms. Lynda MCKENDREE
26 Dir of Marketing Communications ... Ms. Sandra SOLIZ
27 Director Publications ... Ms. Marionette MITCHELL

*University of Texas System Administration (A)

601 Colorado Street, Austin TX 78701-2982
County: Travis FICE Identification: 003655
Unit ID: 229090
Telephone: (512) 499-4201 Carnegie Class: N/A
FAX Number: (512) 499-4215
URL: www.utsystem.edu

01 Chancellor ... Dr. Francisco G. CIGARROA
05 Exec VC Academic Affairs ... Dr. Pedro REYES
17 Exec Vice Chanc Health Affairs ... Dr. Raymond S. GREENBERG
10 Exec Vice Chanc Business Affairs ... Dr. Scott C. KELLEY
43 Int Vice Chanc & General Counsel ... Mr. Dan SHARPHORN
86 Vice Chanc for Govt Relations ... Mr. Barry MCBEE
26 Vice Chanc for External Relations ... Dr. Randa S. SAFADY
86 Vice Chanc Federal Relations ... Mr. William SHUTE
45 Vice Chanc Strategic Initiatives ... Ms. Stephanie A. BOND-HUIE
18 Assoc VC Facil Plng/Construction ... Mr. Michael O'DONNELL
13 Assoc VC & Chief Info Officer ... Mrs. Marg KNOX
21 Asst VC/Controller/Chief Budget Ofc ... Mr. Randy WALLACE
15 Assist Vice Chanc Employee Services ... Mr. Dan STEWART
27 Director Public Affairs ... Mr. Anthony P. DE BRUYN
88 Executive Director Real Estate ... Ms. Florence P. MAYNE
30 Dir Development/Gift Planning Svcs ... Ms. Julie LYNCH
19 Director of Police ... Mr. Michael J. HEIDINGSFIELD

*The University of Texas at Arlington (B)

701 S Nedderman Drive, Arlington TX 76013
County: Tarrant FICE Identification: 003656
Unit ID: 228769
Telephone: (817) 272-2101 Carnegie Class: RU/H
FAX Number: (817) 272-5656 Calendar System: Semester
URL: www.uta.edu
Established: 1895 Annual Undergrad Tuition & Fees (In-State): $8,878
Enrollment: 33,239 Coed
Affiliation or Control: State IRS Status: 170(c)1
Highest Offering: Doctorate
Program: Liberal Arts And General; Teacher Preparatory; Business Emphasis
Accreditation: SC, ART, BUS, BUSA, CEA, CIDA, CS, ENG, LSAR, MUS, NURSE, PLNG, SPAA, SW, TED

02 President ... Dr. Vistasp M. KARBHARI
05 Provost & Vice Pres Acad Affairs ... Dr. Ronald L. ELSENBAUMER
10 Vice Pres Business Affs/Controller ... Ms. Kelly DAVIS
32 Vice President Student Affairs ... Dr. Frank LAMAS
30 Vice President Development ... Mr. Jim LEWIS
46 Vice President Research ... Dr. Carolyn CASON
13 Vice Pres Information Technology ... Mr. Jim BRADLEY
11 Vice Pres Admin & Campus Operations ... Mr. John D. HALL
27 Vice President of Communications ... Mr. Jerry LEWIS
16 Vice President for Human Resources ... Ms. Jean HOOD
84 Sr Assoc VP Student Enrollment Svcs ... Dr. Dale WASSON
45 Assoc VP & Dir Inst Research/Plng ... Dr. Pamela M. HAWS
15 Asst Vice Pres Human Resources ... Ms. Eunice M. CURRIE
26 Asst Vice President Media Services ... Ms. Kristin SULLIVAN
18 Asst VP Campus Operation/Facilities ... Mr. Bill POOLE
88 Executive Dir University College ... Dr. Dawn REMMERS
04 Exec Associate to the President ... Ms. Marcy SANDERS
58 Assoc Dean of Graduate Studies ... Mr. Raymond L. JACKSON
48 Dean of Architecture ... Mr. Donald GATZKE
50 Dean Business Administration ... Dr. Rachel CROSON
54 Dean of Engineering ... Dr. Khosrow BEHBEHANI
49 Dean of Liberal Arts ... Dr. Beth WRIGHT
66 Interim Dean of Nursing ... Dr. Jennifer GRAY
81 Dean of Science ... Dr. Pamela JANSMA
70 Dean School of Social Work ... Dr. Scott RYAN
71 Dean Urban & Public Affairs ... Dr. Barbara BECKER
53 Dean College of Education ... Dr. Jeanne M. GERLACH
92 Dean Honors College ... Dr. Karl PETRUSO
08 Dean of Libraries ... Dr. Rebecca BICHEL
07 Exec Director Admissions & Records ... Dr. Hans GATTERDAM
29 Exec Director Alumni Association ... Ms. Lora MALONE
12 Exec Dir of UTA Ft Worth Center ... Mr. Mike WEST
37 Director of Financial Aid ... Dr. Karen KRAUSE
23 Director Student Health Center ... Mr. Robert BLUM
22 Director Equal Opportunity Services ... Mr. Eddie FREEMAN
24 Director of Art Services ... Mr. Joel QUINTANS
41 Athletic Director ... Mr. Jim BAKER
19 Dir Environmental Health Safety ... Ms. Leah HOY
85 Executive Director Intl Education ... Mr. Jay HORN
88 Director Multicultural Outreach ... Mr. Casey GONZALES
88 Director Multicultural Affairs ... Ms. Leticia MARTINEZ

*University of Texas at Austin (C)

Austin TX 78712-1111
County: Travis FICE Identification: 003658
Unit ID: 228778
Telephone: (512) 471-3434 Carnegie Class: RU/VH
FAX Number: (512) 471-2942 Calendar System: Semester
URL: www.utexas.edu
Established: 1883 Annual Undergrad Tuition & Fees (In-State): $9,790
Enrollment: 52,186 Coed
Affiliation or Control: State IRS Status: 170(c)1
Highest Offering: Doctorate
Program: Liberal Arts And General; Teacher Preparatory; Professional
Accreditation: SC, ART, AUD, BUS, BUSA, CIDA, CLPSY, COPSY, CORE, DANCE, DIETC, DIETD, ENG, IPSY, JOUR, LAW, LIB, LSAR, MUS, NURSE, PHAR, PLNG, SCPSY, SP, SPAA, SW

02 President ... Dr. William C. POWERS, JR.
05 Executive Vice Pres & Provost ... Dr. Steven W. LESLIE
10 Vice Pres & Chief Financial Officer ... Mr. Kevin P. HEGARTY
28 VP Diversity & Community Engagement ... Dr. Gregory J. VINCENT
11 Vice Pres for University Operations ... Dr. Patricia L. CLUBB
46 Vice President Research ... Dr. Juan M. SANCHEZ
13 Chief Information Officer ... Mr. Bradley G. ENGLERT
27 Chief Communications Officer ... Mr. Geoff M. LEAVENWORTH
43 Vice President Legal Affairs ... Dr. Patricia A. OHLENDORF
26 Director University Media Relations ... Mr. Gary J. SUSSWEIN
04 Deputy to the President ... Dr. Charles A. ROECKLE
04 Deputy to the President ... Ms. Nancy A. BRAZZIL
04 Executive Assistant to President ... Ms. Mari "Beth" EDWARDS
88 Sr Vice Prov Resource Management ... Dr. Daniel T. SLESNICK
88 Sr Vice Provost Enroll/Grad Mgmt ... Dr. David A. LAUDE
32 Vice President Student Affairs ... Dr. Gage PAINE
07 Vice Provost & Dir Admissions ... Dr. Kedra B. ISHOP
20 Vice Provost for Faculty Affairs ... Dr. Neal E. ARMSTRONG
88 Vice Provost for Biomed Sciences ... Dr. Robert O. MESSING
88 Vice Provost for Health Affairs ... Dr. William M. SAGE
46 Assoc VP Rsrch/Dir Spnsrd Projects ... Dr. Susan W. SEDWICK
08 Vice Provost/Director UT Libraries ... Dr. Fred M. HEATH
06 Vice Provost & Registrar ... Mr. Vincent (Shelby) STANFIELD
104 Vice Provost International Programs ... Dr. Janet L. ELLZEY
58 Vice Provost/Interim Dean Grad Stds ... Dr. Judith H. LANGLOIS
20 V Prov UG Educ & Faculty Governance ... Dr. Gretchen RITTER
88 Vice Provost for Higher Ed Policy ... Dr. Harrison KELLER
21 Associate Vice President ... Ms. Mary E. KNIGHT
21 Budget Director ... Ms. Elvia H. ROSALES
09 Assoc V Prov/Dir Info Mgmt/Analysis ... Ms. Kristi D. FISHER
88 Associate Vice Provost ... Ms. Kathy FOSTER
88 Associate Vice Provost ... Ms. Carolyn K. CONNERAT
88 Associate Vice Provost ... Dr. R. Michael KERKER
88 Associate Vice President ... Ms. Renee L. WALLACE
30 Associate Vice Pres Development ... Ms. Julie HOOPER
19 Assoc VP Campus Safety/Security ... Dr. Gerald "Bob" R. HARKINS
18 Sr Assoc VP Facilities Management ... Dr. Steven A. KRAAL
15 Associate Vice Pres Human Resources ... Dr. Debra G. KRESS
22 Assoc VP/ADA Coordinator ... Ms. Linda H. MILLSTONE
23 Director University Health Services ... Ms. Jamie L. SHUTTER
37 Director Student Financial Svcs ... Dr. Thomas G. MELECKI
35 Sr Assoc Vice Pres/Dean of Students ... Dr. Soncia R. REAGINS-LILLY
39 Director Housing & Food Service ... Dr. Floyd B. HOELTING

41 Men's Athletics Director ... Mr. DeLoss DODDS
41 Women's Athletics Director ... Ms. Christine A. PLONSKY
29 CEO/Exec Director Ex-Students Assn ... Ms. Leslie CEDAR
19 Chief University Police ... Mr. David CARTER
48 Dean of Architecture ... Dr. Frederick R. STEINER
50 Dean McCombs School of Business ... Dr. Thomas W. GILLIGAN
60 Dean of Communication ... Dr. Roderick P. HART
53 Dean of Education ... Dr. Manuel J. JUSTIZ
54 Dean of Engineering ... Dr. Gregory L. FENVES
57 Dean of Fine Arts ... Dr. Douglas J. DEMPSTER
62 Dean School of Information ... Dr. Andrew P. DILLON
65 Dean Jackson School of Geosciences ... Dr. Sharon MOSHER
61 Dean School of Law ... Mr. Ward FARNSWORTH
49 Dean of Liberal Arts ... Dr. Randy L. DIEHL
81 Dean of Natural Sciences ... Dr. Linda A. HICKE
66 Dean of Nursing ... Dr. Alexa M. STUIFBERGEN
67 Dean of Pharmacy ... Dr. M. Lynn CRISMON
80 Dean LBJ School Public Affs ... Mr. Robert L. HUTCHINGS
70 Dean Social Work ... Dr. Luis H. ZAYAS
97 Interim Dean of Undergrad Studies ... Dr. Lawrence D. ABRAHAM
51 Interim Ex Dir Contin/Innovative Ed ... Mr. Jeff D. TREICHEL
88 Director Internal Audits ... Mr. Michael W. VANDERVORT
18 Director Facilities Services ... Mr. Michael A. MILLER
88 Executive Director Univ Union ... Mr. Andy SMITH
27 Dir Univ of Texas Press ... Mr. David S. HAMRICK
88 Assoc Athl Dir/Dir Spec Events Ctr ... Mr. John M. GRAHAM
96 Assistant VP/Dir of Procurement ... Mr. Jerry A. FULLER

*The University of Texas at Brownsville and Texas Southmost College (D)

One West University Boulevard, Brownsville TX 78520-4993
County: Cameron FICE Identification: 030646
Unit ID: 227377
Telephone: (956) 882-8200 Carnegie Class: Master's M
FAX Number: (956) 548-0020 Calendar System: Semester
URL: www.utb.edu
Established: 1991 Annual Undergrad Tuition & Fees (In-State): $5,930
Enrollment: 13,636 Coed
Affiliation or Control: State IRS Status: 501(c)3
Highest Offering: Doctorate
Program: Liberal Arts And General; Teacher Preparatory
Accreditation: SC, ADNUR, BUS, CACREP, COARC, CS, DMS, ENG, MLTAD, MUS, NUR

02 President ... Dr. Juliet V. GARCIA
05 Provost/VP for Academic Affairs ... Dr. Alan ARTIBISE
10 Vice President of Business Affairs ... Ms. Rosemary MARTINEZ
32 Vice President Student Affairs ... Dr. Hilda SILVA
13 Vice Pres Information Tech/CIO ... Dr. Clair GOLDSMITH
26 Vice Pres Economic Dev/Cmty Svcs ... Dr. Irvine DOWNING
04 Special Assistant to the Provost ... Dr. Wayne MOORE
84 Vice Pres Enrollment Management ... Dr. Sylvia LEAL
100 Chief of Staff ... Dr. Marilyn J. WOODS
35 Dean of Students ... Dr. Beatriz BARCKHOLTZ
58 Dean Graduate Studies ... Dr. Charles LACKEY
50 Dean School of Business ... Dr. Mark KROLL
76 Int Dean Biomed Scis/Health Profess ... Dr. Eldon NELSON
81 Dean College Science/Math/Tech ... Dr. Mikhail BOUNIAEV
53 Dean School of Education ... Dr. Miguel ESCOTET
49 Dean College Liberal Arts ... Dr. Javier MARTINEZ
06 Registrar ... Vacant
07 Director of Admissions/New Student ... Mr. Carlo TAMAYO
09 Director of Institutional Research ... Ms. Blanca TREVINO BAUER
18 Director Physical Plant ... Mr. Abraham HERNANDEZ
37 Director Student Financial Aid ... Vacant
38 Director of Student Success ... Vacant
15 Director Human Resources ... Ms. Trini YUNES
21 Director Business Office ... Ms. Yolanda DE LA RIVA
96 Director of Purchasing ... Mr. William M. DODD
89 Dir New Student Relations/Admission ... Mr. Carlo TAMAYO
29 Director of Alumni Relations ... Ms. Marisa CAMPIRANO

*The University of Texas at Dallas (E)

800 West Campbell Road, Richardson TX 75080
County: Collin FICE Identification: 009741
Unit ID: 228787
Telephone: (972) 883-2111 Carnegie Class: RU/H
FAX Number: (972) 883-2237 Calendar System: Semester
URL: www.utdallas.edu
Established: 1969 Annual Undergrad Tuition & Fees (In-State): $11,806
Enrollment: 19,727 Coed
Affiliation or Control: State IRS Status: 501(c)3
Highest Offering: Doctorate
Program: Liberal Arts And General; Professional
Accreditation: SC, AUD, BUS, BUSA, CS, ENG, IPSY, SP, SPAA

02 President ... Dr. David E. DANIEL
03 Provost/Exec VP Academic Affairs ... Dr. B. Hobson WILDENTHAL
10 Vice President for Business Affairs ... Dr. Calvin D. JAMISON
32 Vice President Student Affairs ... Dr. Darrelene RACHAVONG
30 VP Development/Alumni Relations ... Dr. Aaron CONLEY
46 VP Research/Economic Development ... Dr. Bruce GNADE
20 Vice Provost ... Dr. John WIORKOWSKI
26 Vice President for Communications ... Ms. Susan ROGERS
27 VP/Chief Info Officer ... Vacant
28 Vice President of Diversity ... Dr. Magaly SPECTOR
45 Asst Dir Budget/Resource Plng ... Mr. David K. GAARDER

Code	Title	Name
21	VP Finance & Controller	Mr. Terry PANKRATZ
09	Exec Director Strategic Planning	Dr. Lawrence J. REDLINGER
35	Dean of Students	Dr. Gene FITCH
58	Dean Graduate Studies	Dr. Austin J. CUNNINGHAM
53	Dean Undergraduate Education	Dr. Andrew BLANCHARD
79	Dean School Arts & Humanities	Dr. Dennis KRATZ
50	Dean School of Management	Dr. Hasan PIRKUL
81	Dean Sch of Natural Science/Math	Dr. Bruce NOVAK
83	Dean School of Econ/Pol/Policy Sci	Dr. Denis J. DEAN
76	Dean Sch Behavioral/Brain Science	Dr. Bert S. MOORE
97	Dean School General Studies	Dr. George W. FAIR
54	Dean EJ Sch of Engr/Computer Sci	Dr. Mark W. SPONG
08	Director of Libraries	Dr. Ellen SAFLEY
06	Registrar	Ms. Jennifer MCDOWELL
12	Exec Director of Callier Center	Dr. Thomas F. CAMPBELL
25	Assoc VP Research Administration	Mr. Rafael MARTIN
18	Assoc VP Facilities Management	Mr. Richard DEMPSEY
16	Asst VP Human Resource Management	Ms. Colleen DUTTON
96	Asst VP Procurement Management	Mr. Peter BOND
91	Asst VP Information Resources	Dr. Sue TAYLOR
19	Chief of Police	Mr. Larry ZACHARIAS
36	Director Career Services	Ms. Lisa GARZA
38	Director Student Counseling	Mr. James P. CANNICI
88	Director of Audit and Compliance	Ms. Toni STEPHENS
41	Athletics Director	Mr. Chris GAGE
78	Director Co-operative Education	Mr. Michael J. CHOATE
90	Director Tech Customer Services	Mr. Donald L. DAVIS
29	Director of Alumni Relations	Ms. Erin DOUGHERTY

*University of Texas at El Paso (A)

500 W University Avenue, El Paso TX 79968-8900

County: El Paso FICE Identification: 003661

Unit ID: 228796

Telephone: (915) 747-5000 Carnegie Class: RU/H

FAX Number: (915) 747-5111 Calendar System: Semester

URL: www.utep.edu

Established: 1914 Annual Undergrad Tuition & Fees (In-State): $7,170

Enrollment: 22,749 Coed

Affiliation or Control: State IRS Status: 501(c)3

Highest Offering: Doctorate

Program: Liberal Arts And General; Teacher Preparatory; Professional

Accreditation: SC, BUS, BUSA, CS, ENG, MT, MUS, NURSE, OT, PH, PTA, SP, SPAA, SW

Code	Title	Name
02	President	Dr. Diana S. NATALICIO
03	Sr Executive Vice President	Dr. Howard DAUDISTEL
03	Executive Vice President	Mr. Ricardo ADAUTO, III
04	Assistant to the President	Ms. Estrella ESCOBAR
05	Provost/Vice Pres Academic Affairs	Dr. Junius GONZALES
10	Vice President for Business Affairs	Ms. Cindy VILLA
46	Vice President for Research	Dr. Roberto OSEGUEDA
09	Vice Pres Info Resources & Planning	Dr. Steve RITER
20	Vice Provost	Dr. Michael R. SMITH
58	Dean of Graduate School	Dr. Ben FLORES
32	Vice President Student Affairs	Dr. Gary EDENS
50	Dean of Business Administration	Dr. Robert NACHTMANN
53	Dean of Education	Dr. Josefina V. TINAJERO
54	Dean of Engineering	Dr. Richard T. SCHOEPHOERSTER
49	Dean of Liberal Arts	Dr. Patricia WITHERSPOON
66	Dean of Health Sciences	Dr. Kathleen A. CURTIS
81	Dean of Science	Dr. Robert KIRKEN
66	Dean of School of Nursing	Dr. Elias PROVENCIO-VASQUEZ
18	Assoc VP Business Affs/Facilities	Mr. Greg L. MCNICOL
08	Assoc Vice President/Library	Mr. Robert L. STAKES
26	Asst Vice Pres University Relations	Mr. Beto LOPEZ
27	Assoc VP University Communications	Mr. Chris LOPEZ
22	Asst Vice Pres EO/AA Dept	Ms. Sandy VASQUEZ
29	Asst VP Development/Alumni Rels	Dr. Richard DANIEL
46	Assoc Provost for Resource Mgmt	Ms. Elizabeth FLORES
84	Assoc Vice Provost Enrollment Mgmt	Dr. Craig E. WESTMAN
06	Registrar	Mr. Miguel SIFUENTES
15	Interim Dir of Human Resources Svcs	Mr. Jesse MANCIAZ
19	Chief Campus Police	Mr. Clifton WALSH
37	Assoc Dir of Student Fin Aid	Mr. Ron WILLIAMS
23	Dir of Student Health Ctr	Ms. Louise P. CASTRO
36	Director of Career Services	Vacant
35	Associate VP/Dean of Students	Ms. Catherine M. MCCORRY-ANDALIS
46	Assoc VP Inst Eval/Rsrch & Planning	Dr. Roy MATHEW
39	Director of Housing Services	Mr. Charlie E. GIBBENS
40	Director of University Bookstore	Mr. Fernando PADULA
41	Athletics Director	Mr. Robert W. STULL
38	Director Counseling Services	Ms. Sherri I. TERRELL
96	Dir Purchasing/General Services	Ms. Diane N. DEHOYOS
07	Dir Admissions/Recruitment	Dr. Cassandra M. LACHICA-CHAVEZ
21	Assoc VP Business Affairs	Mr. Anthony TURRIETTA
30	Assoc VP Institutional Advancement	Dr. Sylvia Y. ACOSTA

*University of Texas - Pan American (B)

1201 W University Drive, Edinburg TX 78539-2970

County: Hidalgo FICE Identification: 003599

Unit ID: 227368

Telephone: (956) 665-2011 Carnegie Class: Master's L

FAX Number: (956) 665-2150 Calendar System: Semester

URL: www.utpa.edu

Established: 1927 Annual Undergrad Tuition & Fees (In-State): $6,124

Enrollment: 19,302 Coed

Affiliation or Control: State IRS Status: 501(c)3

Highest Offering: Doctorate

Program: Liberal Arts And General; Teacher Preparatory; Professional

Accreditation: SC, ARCPA, BUS, CORE, CS, DIETC, ENG, MT, MUS, NURSE, OT, SP, SW, THEA

Code	Title	Name
02	President	Dr. Robert S. NELSEN
100	Chief of Staff	Ms. Lisa CARDOZA
05	Provost/VP Academic Affairs	Dr. Havidan RODRIGUEZ
20	Associate Provost	Dr. Kenneth BUCKMAN
88	Vice Provost for Faculty Affairs	Dr. Ala QUBBAJ
10	Vice President for Business Affairs	Mr. Martin BAYLOR
30	VP for University Advancement	Ms. Veronica GONZALES
32	Vice President for Student Affairs	Dr. Martha CANTU
13	CIO for Information Technology	Dr. Jeffrey GRAHAM
20	Vice Prov for Undergraduate Stds	Dr. Kristin CROYLE
21	Assoc Vice Pres BA & Comptroller	Mr. Esequiel GRANADO
07	Sr Assoc VP for Enrollment Services	Dr. Maggie HINOJOSA
31	Exec Dir Ofc Ctr Oper/Community Svc	Ms. Jessica SALINAS
08	Dean of the University Library	Dr. Farzaneh RAZZAGHI
06	University Registrar	Dr. Jeff RHODES
14	Executive Director for IT Services	Mr. Frank ZECCA
15	Director of Human Resources	Ms. Francisca RIOS
19	Chief University Police	Mr. Roger STEARNS
26	Director University Relations	Ms. Sandra Q. GUZMAN
36	Director Career Placement Services	Ms. Lourdes SERVANTES
37	Director Student Financial Services	Mrs. Elaine RIVERA
29	Director Alumni Rels/Special Events	Mrs. Debby GRANT
41	Director Intercollegiate Athletics	Mr. Christopher KING
09	Exec Dir Inst Rsrch Effectiveness	Dr. S.J SETHI
53	Dean College of Education	Dr. Salvador H. OCHOA
35	Dean of Students	Dr. Mari FUENTES-MARTIN
50	Dean Col Business Admin	Dr. Teofilo OZUNA
38	Director of Couseling/Advisement	Vacant
81	Dean College of Science and Math	Dr. John M. TRANT
54	Dean College Engr/Computer Science	Dr. Miguel GONZALEZ
84	Director of Recruitment	Ms. Debbie GILCHRIST
76	Dean Col Health Sci/Human Svcs	Dr. John RONNAU
49	Dean College Arts & Humanities	Dr. Dahlia GUERRA
83	Dean Social/Behavioral Sciences	Dr. Walter DIAZ
18	Dir for Facilities & Physical Plant	Mr. Oscar VILLARREAL
96	Director Materials Management	Mr. Alex VALDEZ
25	Supervisor for Grants & Contracts	Mr. Donald MELE
22	EEO ADA Coordinator	Ms. Esmeralda GUERRA

*University of Texas at San Antonio (C)

One UTSA Circle, San Antonio TX 78249-0169

County: Bexar FICE Identification: 010115

Unit ID: 229027

Telephone: (210) 458-4011 Carnegie Class: RU/H

FAX Number: (210) 458-4187 Calendar System: Semester

URL: www.utsa.edu

Established: 1969 Annual Undergrad Tuition & Fees (In-State): $8,737

Enrollment: 30,474 Coed

Affiliation or Control: State IRS Status: 501(c)3

Highest Offering: Doctorate

Program: Liberal Arts And General; Teacher Preparatory; Professional

Accreditation: SC, ART, BUS, BUSA, CACREP, CIDA, ENG, MUS, SPAA, SW

Code	Title	Name
02	President	Dr. Ricardo ROMO
05	Provost/Vice Pres Academic Affairs	Dr. John FREDERICK
10	Vice President for Business Affairs	Mr. Kerry L. KENNEDY
46	Interim Vice President for Research	Dr. C. Mauli AGRAWAL
32	Interim VP Student Affairs	Mr. Samuel GONZALES
31	Vice President Community Services	Dr. Jude VALDEZ
30	Vice Pres for External Relations	Ms. Marjie M. FRENCH
11	Assoc Vice Pres for Administration	Ms. Pamela BACON
20	Executive Vice Provost	Mr. Julius M. GRIBOU
09	V Prov Acad Compliance/Inst Effect	Dr. Sandra T. WELCH
12	Vice Provost for Downtown Campus	Dr. Jesse T. ZAPATA
14	Vice Provost Information Officer	Mr. Kenneth PIERCE
20	V Prov Acad Supt/Dean UGrad Studies	Dr. Lawrence R. WILLIAMS
21	Interim Assoc VP Financial Affairs	Ms. Lenora CHAPMAN
15	Assoc VP Human Resources	Ms. Barbara CENTENO
08	Dean of Libraries	Dr. Krisellen MALONEY
92	Dean Honors College	Dr. Richard A. DIEM
58	Dean Graduate School	Dr. Dorothy A. FLANNAGAN
50	Dean College of Business	Dr. Wm Gerard (Gerry) Y. SANDERS
57	Dean College of Liberal & Fine Arts	Dr. Daniel J. GELO
54	Interim Dean College of Engineering	Dr. Mehdi SHADARAM
83	Dean College of Sciences	Dr. George PERRY
48	Dean School of Architecture	Prof. John MURPHY
53	Dean College Educ/Human Development	Dr. Betty MERCHANT
80	Dean College of Public Policy	Dr. Rogelio SAENZ
19	Chief of Police	Mr. Steve V. BARRERA
41	Director Intercol Athletics	Ms. Lynn HICKEY
29	Director Alumni Program Mkt	Ms. Anne ENGLERT
43	Chief Legal Officer	Ms. Gail JENSEN
26	Assoc VP Comm & Mktg	Mr. Joe IZBRAND
86	Director External Affairs	Mr. Albert A. CARRISALEZ

*University of Texas at Tyler (D)

3900 University Boulevard, Tyler TX 75799-6699

County: Smith FICE Identification: 011163

Unit ID: 228802

Telephone: (903) 566-7000 Carnegie Class: Master's L

FAX Number: (903) 566-7068 Calendar System: Semester

URL: www.uttyler.edu

Established: 1971 Annual Undergrad Tuition & Fees (In-State): $6,740

Enrollment: 6,858 Coed

Affiliation or Control: State IRS Status: 501(c)3

Highest Offering: Doctorate

Program: Liberal Arts And General; Teacher Preparatory; Professional

Accreditation: SC, BUS, ENG, NAIT, NURSE, TEAC

Code	Title	Name
02	President	Dr. Rodney H. MABRY
05	Provost/Sr VP Academic Affairs	Dr. Alisa WHITE
10	Vice President for Business Affairs	Vacant
30	Vice President Univ Advancement	Mr. Jerre IVERSEN
32	Vice Pres for Student Affairs	Dr. Howard PATTERSON
13	Vice President & CIO IT	Dr. Sherri WHATLEY
20	Vice Provost AA/Grad Studies	Dr. William GEIGER
20	Associate Provost UG Programs	Vacant
46	Assoc Vice President for Research	Vacant
21	Associate VP for Business Affairs	Ms. Sheryl DENNIS
11	Interim VP for Adminstration	Mr. Jesse ACOSTA
15	Assoc VP/Director Human Resources	Mr. Joe VORSAS
84	Interim VP for Enrollment Mgmt	Ms. Sarah BOWDIN
88	Asst Vice Pres for Assessment/IE	Dr. Lou Ann BERMAN
32	Asst VP Student Affs/Dean Students	Ms. Ona TOLLIVER
49	Dean College of Arts & Sciences	Dr. Martin SLANN
50	Dean College Business & Technology	Dr. Harold DOTY
53	Dean College Education & Psychology	Dr. Ross SHERMAN
54	Dean College Engineering & Comp Sci	Dr. James NELSON
66	Dean College Nursing & Health Sci	Dr. Pam MARTIN
08	Director of the Library	Ms. Jeanne PYLE
21	Director of Financial Services	Ms. Carrie CLAYTON
18	Dir Facility/Plng/Construct/Oper	Mr. Chip CLARK
29	Coordinator of Alumni Relations	Ms. Derrith BONDURANT
100	Chief of Staff	Vacant
27	Director Mktg & Communiation	Ms. Beverley GOLDEN
38	Dir Stdnt Svc/Stdnt Couns/Test Ctr	Ms. Ida MACDONALD
39	Director of Residence Life	Mr. David R. HILL
96	Asst Dir Financial Services	Mrs. Cindy TROYER
06	Registrar	Ms. Sonja MORALE
09	Director of Institutional Analysis	Dr. Sherri WHATLEY
19	Chief University Police	Mr. Mike W. MEDDERS

*The University of Texas Health Science Center at Houston (UTHealth) (E)

PO Box 20036, Houston TX 77225-0036

County: Harris FICE Identification: 004951

Unit ID: 229300

Telephone: (713) 500-4472 Carnegie Class: Spec/Med

FAX Number: (713) 500-3026 Calendar System: Semester

URL: www.uthouston.edu

Established: 1972 Annual Undergrad Tuition & Fees (In-State): $9,000

Enrollment: 4,489 Coed

Affiliation or Control: State IRS Status: 501(c)3

Highest Offering: Doctorate

Program: Professional

Accreditation: SC, ANEST, DENT, DH, DIETI, ENGR, MED, NURSE, PH

Code	Title	Name
02	President	Dr. Giuseppe N. COLASURDO
03	CFO/COO & Exec VP for Admin	Mr. T. Kevin DILLON
63	Dean Medical School	Dr. Giuseppe N. COLASURDO
69	Dean School of Public Health	Dr. Roberta B. NESS
52	Dean School of Dentistry	Dr. John A. VALENZA
58	Dean Grad Sch Biomedical Sciences	Dr. Michael BLACKBURN
66	Dean School of Nursing	Dr. Patricia L. STARCK
88	Dean Sch of Biomed Informatics	Dr. Jiajie W. ZHANG
05	Exec VP Acad & Res Affs	Dr. George M. STANCEL
45	Senior VP for Strategic Planning	Dr. Osama I. MIKHAIL
10	Sr VP Finance & Business Svcs	Mr. Michael TRAMONTE
46	Vice Dn Rsrch/Dir Molecular Med	Dr. John HANCOCK
30	Vice Pres Development	Mr. Kevin J. FOYLE
15	VP/Chief Human Resources Officer	Mr. Eric FERNETTE
43	VP/Chief Legal & Compliance Officer	Ms. Arlene D. STALLER
86	Interim VP Govt Relations	Mr. Scott FORBES
88	VP Research & Technology	Dr. Bruce D. BUTLER
31	VP Auxiliary Enterprises	Mr. Charles A. FIGARI
13	VP/Chief Information Officer	Mr. Richard L. MILLER
18	VP Facilities Planning & Engr	Mr. Richard L. MCDERMOTT
44	Asst VP for Principal Gifts	Ms. Betsy C. FRANTZ
90	Asst VP Academic Technology	Dr. William A. WEEMS
21	Asst VP & Chief Audit Officer	Mr. Daniel SHERMAN
06	Registrar	Mr. Robert JENKINS
19	Chief of Police	Mr. William ADCOX
17	Exec Vice Dean Clinical Affairs	Vacant
41	Director Recreation/Intramural Pgms	Ms. Pauline M. HABETZ
85	Director International Affairs	Vacant
39	Director University Housing	Mr. Billy C. HINTON
26	Asst VP for Public Affairs	Ms. Karen K. KAPLAN
88	Director of Media Relations	Ms. Meredith RAINE
37	Director Student Financial Svcs	Ms. Wanda K. WILLIAMS
28	Chief Academic Diversity Officer	Dr. Ronald JOHNSON
25	Asst VP Sponsored Projects Admin	Ms. Jodi OGDEN
88	Assoc Dean for Practice Nursing	Dr. Thomas A. MACKEY
14	Director Data Center Operations	Mr. Kevin B. GRANHOLD
22	EEO Advisor	Ms. Kimberly FRAYNE
88	Assoc Dean Tech Svcs Dentistry	Dr. Peter T. TRIOLO
88	Director Educational Tech Nursing	Ms. Linda L. CRAYS
88	Director Biomedical Info Tech Med	Dr. Stephen J. FATH
07	Assoc Dean Admissions/Stdt Aff-Med	Dr. Margaret MCNEESE
29	Assoc Dean Student & Alumni-SOD	Dr. Hugh P. PIERPONT
07	Asst Director Admissions-GSBS	Ms. Karen WEINBERG
35	Dir of Student Affairs-SBMI	Ms. Jaime HARGRAVE
35	Director Student Affairs-SON	Ms. Laurie G. RUTHERFORD
35	Assoc Dean of Student Affairs-SPH	Dr. Mary A. SMITH

*University of Texas Health Science Center at San Antonio (A)

7703 Floyd Curl Drive, San Antonio TX 78229-3900
County: Bexar FICE Identification: 003659
Unit ID: 228644
Telephone: (210) 567-7000 Carnegie Class: Spec/Med
FAX Number: (210) 567-2025 Calendar System: Other
URL: www.uthscsa.edu
Established: 1959 Annual Undergrad Tuition & Fees (In-State): $7,338
Enrollment: 3,249 Coed
Affiliation or Control: State IRS Status: 501(c)3
Highest Offering: Doctorate
Program: Professional
Accreditation: SC, ARCPA, BBT, COARC, DENT, @DIETC, EMT, HT, IPSY, #MED, MT, NURSE, OT, PTA, RADDOS

02 President .... Dr. William L. HENRICH
03 Sr Exec Vice President & COO .... Mr. Michael E. BLACK
11 Exec VP for Facility Planning/Admin .... Mr. James D. KAZEN
10 Vice President & CFO .... Ms. Andrea M. MARKS
05 VP Acad/Fac & Student Affairs .... Dr. Michael GARGANO
13 Vice Pres & Chief Information Ofcr .... Mr. Yeman COLLIER
46 Vice President for Research .... Dr. David WEISS
86 VP for Governmental Relations .... Mr. Armando DIAZ
30 VP for Institutional Advancement .... Ms. Deborah H. MORRILL
15 Vice Pres of Human Resources .... Mr. J. Michael TESH
100 VP Communications & Chief of Staff .... Ms. Mary G. DELAY
21 Asst Vice Pres for Business Affairs .... Mr. Gerard E. LONG
46 Asst VP Research Administration .... Ms. Jane A. YOUNGERS
18 Asst VP for Strategic Initiatives .... Mr. Darrell MAATSCH
63 Dean School of Medicine .... Dr. Francisco GONZALEZ-SCARANO
52 Dean Dental School .... Dr. William W. DODGE
58 Dean Graduate Biomed Science .... Dr. David WEISS
76 Int Dean School Health Professions .... Dr. Michael GARGANO
66 Dean School of Nursing .... Dr. Eileen T. BRESLIN
32 Exec Dir for Student Services .... Vacant
06 Registrar .... Ms. Blanca GUERRA
08 Exec Director of Libraries .... Ms. Rajia C. TOBIA
19 Chief of Police .... Mr. Michael PARKS
88 Exec Dir Acad/Fac/Studnt Ombudspers .... Dr. Bonnie L. BLANKMEYER
37 Director of Financial Aid .... Ms. Ellen NYSTROM
38 Director of Counseling .... Dr. Kozue SHIBAZAKI
43 Asst VP/Chief Legal Officer .... Mr. Jack C. PARK
96 Sr Dir Supply Chain Mngmt/HUB Coord .... Ms. Vikki F. ROSS

*The University of Texas M.D. Anderson Cancer Center (B)

1515 Holcombe Boulevard, Houston TX 77030-4000
County: Harris FICE Identification: 025554
Unit ID: 416801
Telephone: (713) 792-6161 Carnegie Class: Spec/Health
FAX Number: N/A Calendar System: Semester
URL: www.mdanderson.org
Established: 1941 Annual Undergrad Tuition & Fees (In-District): N/A
Enrollment: 290 Coed
Affiliation or Control: State/Local IRS Status: 501(c)3
Highest Offering: Doctorate
Program: Professional
Accreditation: SC, CGTECH, CYTO, DENT, DMOLS, HT, MT, RAD, RADDOS, RTT

02 President .... Dr. Ronald DEPINHO
05 Provost/Executive Vice President .... Dr. Ethan DMITROVSKY

*The University of Texas Medical Branch (C)

301 University Boulevard, Galveston TX 77555-0100
County: Galveston FICE Identification: 004952
Unit ID: 228653
Telephone: (409) 772-1011 Carnegie Class: Spec/Med
FAX Number: N/A Calendar System: Semester
URL: www.utmb.edu
Established: 1891 Annual Undergrad Tuition & Fees (In-State): $6,598
Enrollment: 3,012 Coed
Affiliation or Control: State IRS Status: 170(c)1
Highest Offering: Doctorate
Program: Professional
Accreditation: SC, ARCPA, BBT, COARC, DENT, @DIETI, MED, MT, NURSE, OT, PH, PTA

02 President .... Dr. David L. CALLENDER
04 Exec Asst to the President .... Ms. Jandee ALARID
05 Exec VP Provost/Dean Sch of Med .... Dr. Danny O. JACOBS
17 Exec VP & CEO Health System .. Ms. Donna K. SOLLENBERGER
10 Exec VP & Chief Business/Fin Ofcr .... Mr. William R. ELGER
86 Sr VP Health Policy & Legis Affairs .... Dr. Ben G. RAIMER
88 VP & Chief Physician .... Dr. Rex M. MCCALLUM
17 Interim Chief Medical Officer .... Dr. Oscar W. BROWN
20 VP Education & Dean Sch of Nursing .... Dr. Pamela G. WATSON
76 VP & Dean Sch of Health Professions ... Dr. Elizabeth J. PROTAS
58 VP & Dean Grad Sch of Biomed Sci .... Dr. Cary W. COOPER
16 VP HR & Employee Services .... Dr. Ronald B. MCKINLEY
13 VP Information Services & CIO .... Mr. Ralph E. FARR
18 VP Business Oper & Facilities .... Mr. Michael B. SHRINER
21 VP Chief Oper Officer AE .... Mr. Cameron W. SLOCUM
21 VP Finance Clinical Enterprise ...... Mr. David M. CONNAUGHTON
45 VP for Strategic Mgmt .... Dr. Rebecca SAAVEDRA
43 Sr VP General Counsel .... Ms. Carolee KING
26 VP Marketing & Communications .... Mr. Stephen CAMPBELL
35 Sr Assoc Dean Grad Sch Biomed Sci .... Dr. Dorian H. COPPENHAVER
35 Assoc Dean Admissions Sch of Med .... Dr. Lauree THOMAS
07 Dir Student Affairs Admissions SON .... Ms. Dorothy PEARROW
35 Assoc Dean Health Professions .... Dr. Henry CAVAZOS
46 Interim Dir Institutional Research .... Dr. James L. MAHON
08 Int Assoc VP Academic Res/Library .... Ms. Patricia A. CIEJKA
09 Assoc VP Inst Effectiveness .... Dr. John C. MCKEE
26 Assoc VP Public Affairs .... Ms. Mary G. HAVARD
21 Assoc VP Fin Plng & Perf Mgmt .... Mr. Matthew FURLONG
21 Assoc VP Budget & Analysis .... Ms. Celia BAILEY-OCHOA
88 Assoc VP Audit Services .... Ms. Kimberly K. HAGARA
30 Assoc VP Chief Develop Officer .... Ms. Betsy B. CLARDY
32 Assoc VP for Univ Student Services .... Dr. James MARTIN
29 Asst VP Alumni Relations .... Ms. Dixie MULLINS
28 VP & Chief Compliance Officer .... Mr. Tobin R. BOENIG
84 Dir Enrollment Svcs/Univ Registrar .... Mr. Shawn DEVEAU
19 Chief of University Police .... Mr. Thomas ENGELLS
22 Dir of Diversity and Inclusion .... Ms. Adeola ODUWOLE
23 Director Student Wellness .... Ms. Cynthia A. DESANTO
96 Exe Dir Supply Chain Management .... Mr. Frank REIGHARD
39 Dir Aux Enterprises-Housing/Bkstore .... Mr. Bruno P. CRISTELLI
38 Director Student Counseling .... Ms. Cynthia DESANTOS

*University of Texas of the Permian Basin (D)

4901 E University Boulevard, Odessa TX 79762-8122
County: Ector FICE Identification: 009930
Unit ID: 229018
Telephone: (432) 552-2020 Carnegie Class: Master's M
FAX Number: (432) 552-2374 Calendar System: Semester
URL: www.utpb.edu
Established: 1969 Annual Undergrad Tuition & Fees (In-State): $6,457
Enrollment: 4,021 Coed
Affiliation or Control: State IRS Status: 501(c)3
Highest Offering: Master's
Program: Liberal Arts And General; Teacher Preparatory; Professional
Accreditation: SC, ART, BUS, ENG, SW, TED

02 President .... Dr. W. David WATTS
04 Assistant to the President .... Ms. Carla P. NELSON
05 Provost/Vice Pres Academic Affairs .... Dr. William R. FANNIN
10 Vice President Business Affairs .... Mr. Dale CASSIDY
32 Sr AVP Academic & Student Services .... Ms. Teresa SEWELL
58 AVP Research/Dean Graduate Studies .... Dr. Juli RATHEAL
13 Asst Vice Pres/Dir Info Resources .... Mr. J. Keith YARBROUGH
49 Dean College of Arts & Science .... Dr. Mylan REDFERN
50 Dean School of Business .... Mr. Jack LADD
53 Dean School of Education .... Dr. Frank HERNANDEZ
30 Director Institutional Advancement .... Ms. Lee Anna GOOD
07 Director Admissions .... Mr. Scott SMILEY
06 Interim Registrar .... Mr. Joe SANDERS
37 Director Financial Aid .... Mr. Joe SANDERS
08 Director of Library Services .... Ms. Michele KUCHEL
15 Director Human Resources .... Ms. Caron PERKINS
51 Director Continuing Education .... Mr. Rey LASCANO
26 Interim Public Information Officer .... Ms. Travis WOODWARD
41 Director Athletics .... Dr. Steve AICINENA
19 Chief of Police .... Chief Tom HAIN
18 Chief Facilities/Physical Plant .... Mr. Michael RULAND
36 Dir Student Placement/Counseling .... Mr. Tony LOVE
96 Interim Director of Purchasing .... Ms. Ynez ALDERSON
09 Director of Institutional Research .... Dr. Denise WATTS
29 Alumni Relations .... Mrs. Maribea MERRITT

*University of Texas Southwestern Medical Center (E)

5323 Harry Hines Boulevard, Dallas TX 75390-9002
County: Dallas FICE Identification: 010019
Unit ID: 228635
Telephone: (214) 648-3111 Carnegie Class: Spec/Med
FAX Number: N/A Calendar System: Other
URL: www.utsouthwestern.edu
Established: 1943 Annual Undergrad Tuition & Fees (In-State): $8,036
Enrollment: 2,454 Coed
Affiliation or Control: State IRS Status: 501(c)3
Highest Offering: Doctorate
Program: Professional
Accreditation: SC, ARCPA, CLPSY, CORE, DIETC, EMT, IPSY, MED, OPE, PTA, RTT

02 President .... Dr. Daniel K. PODOLSKY
100 Vice President & Chief of Staff .... Dr. Robin M. JACOBY
05 Exec VP Acad Aff/Provost/Dean SMS .... Dr. Gregory FITZ
03 Exec VP Health System Affairs .... Dr. Bruce A. MEYER
10 Exec Vice Pres Business Affairs .... Mr. Arnim DONTES
46 Vice Provost/Dean of Basic Research .... Dr. David W. RUSSELL
23 Vice President Clinical Operations ...... Dr. John D. RUTHERFORD
88 Vice President University Hospitals .... Dr. John WARNER
88 Chief Quality Officer .... Dr. Gary REED
10 Vice President Financial Affairs .... Mr. Michael SERBER
86 Vice Pres Govt Affairs & Policy .... Ms. Angelica MARIN-HILL
27 Vice Pres Comm Mktg & Public Affs .... Ms. Nimisha SAVANI
16 Vice President Human Resource .... Dr. William M. BEHRENDT
43 Vice President Legal Affairs .... Ms. Leah A. HURLEY
72 Vice Pres Technology Development .... Mr. Frank P. GRASSLER
30 Vice President Development .... Ms. Amanda BILLINGS
102 Vice Pres Community and Corp Rels ...... Mr. Ruben E. ESQUIVEL
13 Vice Pres Information Resources .... Mr. Kirk A. KIRKSEY
18 Vice President Facilities Mgmt .... Mr. Kirby L. VAHLE
29 Vice Pres Stdnt/Alumni Affs/Admiss .... Mr. J. W. NORRED
88 Vice President Research Admin .... Ms. Angela WISHON
88 Asst Vice Pres Ambulatory Care .... Dr. Stan TAYLOR
88 Assoc Vice Pres Chief Admin Ofcr .... Dr. Randall F. JONES
88 Chief Med Officer University Hosp .... Dr. Steven LEACH
88 Assoc Vice Pres Chief Nursing Ofcr ..... Ms. Donna RICHARDSON
96 Asst Vice Pres Materials Mgmt .... Mr. Paul D. BELEW
88 Asst Vice Pres Parkland HHS Affairs ...... Dr. Christopher MADDEN
88 Asst Vice Pres Marketing .... Ms. Dorothea BONDS
21 Asst Vice President Accounting .... Ms. Sharon LEARY
08 Asst Vice Pres Library Services .... Mrs. Laurie L. THOMPSON
20 Sr Assoc Dean Academic Admin .... Dr. Charles M. GINSBURG
45 Sr Assoc Dean Strategic Development .... Dr. Dwain L. THIELE
28 Assoc Dean Faculty Diversity & Dev .... Dr. Byron L. CRYER
88 Assoc Dean Global Health .... Dr. Fiemu E. NWARIAKU
51 Assoc Dean Grad Medical Education .... Dr. Bradley MARPLE
63 Assoc Dean Undergrad Medical Educ .... Dr. Steve CANNON
32 Assoc Dean Student Affairs .... Dr. Angela MIHALIC
32 Assoc Dean Student Affairs .... Dr. James M. WAGNER
93 Assoc Dean Minority Student Affairs .... Dr. Shawna NESBITT
88 Associate Dean .... Dr. Perrie M. ADAMS
58 Dean Grad School Biomedical Science ..... Dr. David W. RUSSELL
76 Dean School of Health Professions .... Dr. Raul CAETANO
06 Registrar/Financial Aid .... Mr. Charles L. KETTLEWELL
07 Assoc Director of Admissions .... Ms. Anne P. MCLANE
11 Assoc Vice Pres Chief Oper Officer .... Ms. Becky MCCULLEY
13 Assoc Vice Pres Health Sys Info Res .... Mr. Suresh GUNASEKARAN
88 Asst Vice Pres Administrative Sys .... Mr. Mark FLETCHER

Vernon College (F)

4400 College Drive, Vernon TX 76384-4092
County: Wilbarger FICE Identification: 010060
Unit ID: 229504
Telephone: (940) 552-6291 Carnegie Class: Assoc/Pub-R-M
FAX Number: (940) 553-3902 Calendar System: Semester
URL: www.vernoncollege.edu
Established: 1970 Annual Undergrad Tuition & Fees (In-District): $2,064
Enrollment: 3,124 Coed
Affiliation or Control: State/Local IRS Status: 501(c)3
Highest Offering: Associate Degree
Program: Occupational; 2-Year Principally Bachelor's Creditable
Accreditation: SC, CAHIIM, SURGT

01 President .... Dr. Dusty R. JOHNSTON
04 Admin Secretary to the President .... Ms. Mary KING
05 Dean of Instructional Services .... Dr. Gary Don HARKEY
11 Dean of Administrative Services .... Mr. Garry DAVID
32 Dean of Student Svs/Athletic Dir .... Mr. John B. HARDIN, III
07 Dean Admiss/Registr/Financial Aid .... Mr. Joe HITE
103 Assoc Dean of Workforce Ed & Trng .... Mrs. Shana MUNSON
21 Assoc Dean Administrative Svcs .... Vacant
30 Director of Inst Advancement .... Ms. Michelle ALEXANDER
09 Director of Institutional Research .... Mrs. Betsy HARKEY
37 Director Financial Aid .... Mrs. Melissa J. ELLIOTT
13 Director of Information Technology .... Mr. Jim BINION
08 Director of Library Services .... Ms. Marion GRONA
18 Director Physical Plant .... Mr. John MAHONEY
15 Director of Human Resources .... Mrs. Haven DAVID
39 Director of Housing .... Mr. Tony PEREZ
35 Assoc Dean of Student Services .... Mrs. Kristin HARRIS
06 Assistant Registrar .... Mrs. Sarah DAVENPORT
66 Dir Associate Degree in Nursing .... Ms. Cathy BOLTON
66 Dir Licensed Vocational Nursing .... Mr. Lynn KALSKI
88 Director of Student Relations .... Ms. Brandi BRANNON
35 Director of Student Activities .... Mr. Sjohonton FANNER
19 Director of Campus Police .... Mr. Chris BELL
51 Coordinator Continuing Education .... Mrs. Anne PATTERSON
88 Coordinator of Testing .... Mrs. Sharron SHELTON
56 Coordinator of Distance Learning .... Vacant
24 Media Specialist .... Mr. Gene FROMMELT

Vet Tech Institute of Houston (G)

4669 Southwest Freeway, Suite 100, Houston TX 77027
County: Harris FICE Identification: 021448
Unit ID: 223472
Telephone: (713) 629-8940 Carnegie Class: Assoc/PrivFP
FAX Number: (713) 629-0059 Calendar System: Semester
URL: www.vettechinstitute.edu/houston
Established: 2007 Annual Undergrad Tuition & Fees: $13,530
Enrollment: 256 Coed
Affiliation or Control: Proprietary IRS Status: Proprietary
Highest Offering: Associate Degree
Program: Occupational
Accreditation: ACICS

01 Director/Chief Academic Officer .... Mr. Elbert HAMILTON, JR.

Victoria College (H)

2200 E Red River, Victoria TX 77901-4494
County: Victoria FICE Identification: 003662
Unit ID: 229540
Telephone: (361) 573-3291 Carnegie Class: Assoc/Pub-R-M
FAX Number: (361) 572-3850 Calendar System: Semester
URL: www.victoriacollege.edu
Established: 1925 Annual Undergrad Tuition & Fees (In-District): $1,992
Enrollment: 4,460 Coed

Affiliation or Control: Local IRS Status: 501(c)3
Highest Offering: Associate Degree
Program: Occupational; 2-Year Principally Bachelor's Creditable
Accreditation: SC, ADNUR, COARC, MLTAD, PTAA

01 President Dr. Thomas E. BUTLER
05 Vice President of Instruction Dr. Patricia A. VANDERVOORT
10 VP Administrative Svcs Mr. Keith BLUNDELL
32 Vice President of Student Services Dr. Florinda CORREA
30 VP College Advance/External Affairs Ms. Jennifer L. YANCEY
45 Exec Director Special Projects Dr. Larry GARRETT
09 Dir Inst Effect/Research/Assess Ms. Patricia REHAK
08 Director of Libraries Dr. Joe F. DAHLSTROM
06 Registrar Admissions & Records Ms. Michelle KLIMITCHEK
18 Director Physical Plant Mr. Robert DUFFIE
37 Director Financial Aid Ms. Kim OBSTA
15 Director Human Resources Ms. Terri KURTZ
26 Dir Marketing & Communications Mr. Darin KAZMIR
38 Director Advising/Counseling Mr. Robert CUBRIEL, III
96 Director of Purchasing Ms. Lydia HUBER
21 Director of Finance Ms. Tracey BERGSTROM
35 Student Center/Activities Director Ms. Elaine EVERETT-HENSLEY
38 Director of Testing Center Ms. Donna RODRIGUEZ
13 Director Technology Services Mr. Andy FARRIOR
04 Admin Asst to President Ms. Debbie RAINS

Virginia College Austin (A)

6301 E Highway 290, Austin TX 78723-1027
Telephone: (512) 371-3500 Identification: 666074
Accreditation: ACICS, #COARC, DMS, MAAB, SURGT

† Main campus is Virginia College in Birmingham, AL.

Vista College (B)

3440 Bell Street, Suite 100, Amarillo TX 79109
Telephone: (806) 372-3700 Identification: 770548
Accreditation: COE

† Main campus is Vista College in El Paso, TX.

Vista College (C)

6101 Montana Avenue, El Paso TX 79925-2021
County: El Paso FICE Identification: 025720
Unit ID: 365204
Telephone: (915) 779-8031 Carnegie Class: Assoc/PrivFP
FAX Number: (915) 779-8097 Calendar System: Semester
URL: www.vistacollege.edu
Established: 1987 Annual Undergrad Tuition & Fees: $18,100
Enrollment: 2,220 Coed
Affiliation or Control: Proprietary IRS Status: Proprietary
Highest Offering: Associate Degree
Program: Occupational
Accreditation: COE, MAAB, MAC

01 Campus Director Mr. Antonio RICO
01 Campus Director Ms. Rebecca CANCHOLA
06 Registrar Ms. Valerie PARKS
07 Director of Admissions Ms. Andre ROYOS
36 Director Career Services Mr. Jesus ACOSTA
37 Director Student Financial Aid Mr. Brian JONES
63 Director Medical Ms. Juana CERVANTES

Vista College (D)

4620 50th Street, Lubbock TX 79414
Telephone: (806) 785-2100 Identification: 770549
Accreditation: COE

† Main campus is Vista College in El Paso, TX.

Wade College Infomart (E)

1950 Stemmons Fwy, Ste 4080, LB 562, Dallas TX 75207
County: Dallas FICE Identification: 010130
Unit ID: 226879
Telephone: (214) 637-3530 Carnegie Class: Assoc/PrivFP
FAX Number: (214) 637-0827 Calendar System: Trimester
URL: www.wadecollege.edu
Established: 1962 Annual Undergrad Tuition & Fees: $12,275
Enrollment: 235 Coed
Affiliation or Control: Proprietary IRS Status: Proprietary
Highest Offering: Baccalaureate
Program: Fine Arts Emphasis
Accreditation: SC

01 President Dr. Harry DAVROS
03 Vice President Mr. John CONTE
05 Director of Academic Affairs Ms. Elizabeth JOHNSTON
11 Director of Institutional Support Ms. Kim PARKER
08 Head Librarian Mrs. Bobbie BAUMGARTEN
36 Director of Career Services Mrs. Jennifer MAGEE
07 Director of Admissions Mrs. Julie ROBINSON
37 Director Student Financial Aid Ms. Lisa HOOVER

Wayland Baptist University (F)

1900 West Seventh, Plainview TX 79072-6998
County: Hale FICE Identification: 003663
Unit ID: 229780
Telephone: (806) 291-1000 Carnegie Class: Master's L
FAX Number: (806) 291-1960 Calendar System: Semester
URL: www.wbu.edu
Established: 1908 Annual Undergrad Tuition & Fees: $12,800
Enrollment: 6,837 Coed
Affiliation or Control: Southern Baptist IRS Status: 501(c)3
Highest Offering: Master's
Program: 2-Year Principally Bachelor's Creditable; Liberal Arts And General; Teacher Preparatory; Professional
Accreditation: SC, MUS, NUR

01 President Dr. Paul W. ARMES
05 Executive Vice President/Provost Dr. Bobby L. HALL
84 Vice Pres Enrollment Management Dr. D. Claude LUSK
20 Vice Pres of External Campuses Dr. Elane SEEBO
10 Interim Chief Financial Officer Ms. Lezlie HUKILL
20 Associate Academic Vice President Dr. Stan DEMERRITT
12 Exec Dir/Campus Dean Albuquerque Dr. Steve SMITH
12 Exec Dir/Campus Dean Altus Dr. Tom FISHER
12 Exec Dir/Campus Dean Amarillo Dr. J. B BOREN
12 Exec Dir/Campus Dean Anchorage Dr. Eric ASH
12 Exec Dir/Campus Dean Clovis Dr. Gary MITCHELL
12 Exec Dir/Campus Dean Fairbanks Dr. Nancy WAGNER
12 Exec Dir/Campus Dean Hawaii Dr. David HOWLE
12 Exec Dir/Campus Dean Lubbock Dr. David BISHOP
12 Exec Dir/Campus Dean Phoenix Dr. D. Glenn SIMMONS
12 Exec Dir/Campus Dean San Antonio Dr. James ANTENEN
12 Exec Dir/Campus Dean Sierra Vista Dr. Robert MORRIS, III
12 Exec Dir/Campus Dean Wichita Falls Dr. Dean DANIEL
83 Acad Dean School Behav & Soc Sci Dr. Estelle OWENS
50 Academic Dean School of Business Dr. Otto B. SCHACHT
53 Academic Dean School of Education Dr. Jimmie L. TODD
57 Academic Dean School of Fine Arts Dr. Marti R. RUNNELS
79 Academic Dean School of Lang & Lit Dr. Cindy M. MCCLENAGAN
81 Academic Dean School Math/Sciences Dr. Herbert GROVER
64 Academic Dean School of Music Dr. Ann B. STUTES
66 Academic Dean School of Nursing Dr. Diane FRAZOR
73 Academic Dean Religion & Philosophy Dr. Paul L. SADLER
06 Registrar Mrs. Julie BOWEN
32 Exec Dir Student Development Mr. Tom HALL
30 Executive Dir Univ Advancement Mr. Mike MELCHER
21 Controller Mrs. Lezlie HUKILL
41 Athletic Director Dr. Greg FERIS
07 Director Admissions Mrs. Debbie STENNETT
29 Director Alumni Development Mr. Danny ANDREWS
88 Director Church Services Mr. Micheal SUMMERS
44 Director Annual Fund Vacant
44 Director Donor Relations Ms. Hope ENGLISH
37 Director Financial Aid Mrs. Karen LAQUEY
58 Coordinator of Graduate Studies Mrs. Amanda STANTON
15 Director Human Resources Mr. Ron APPLING
13 Director Information Technology Mrs. Katrina SMITH
09 Dir Inst Research/Effectiveness Mrs. Crhistina SPRUILL
12 Director Kenya Campus Dr. Richard SHAW
08 Director Library Dr. Polly R. LACKEY
88 Director Property Management Mr. Danny W. MURPHREE
26 Director Public Relations Mr. Jonathan PETTY
88 Director Special Projects Mrs. Penny POOLE
39 Director Student Housing Mrs. Nancy KEITH
35 Dir Student Leadership & Activities Mrs. Teresa MOORE
42 Director Student Ministries Mr. Donnie BROWN
40 Director University Services Mr. Eddie C. TURNER
106 Director Virtual Campus Dr. Scott FRANKLIN
105 Director Web Services Mrs. Charlotte SCHUMACHER
88 Director External Records Mr. Daniel BROWN
38 Coord Stdnt Counseling/Career Plng Mr. Michael COX
19 Chief of Police/WBU Mr. Lonnie BURTON
18 Chief Facilities/Physical Plant Mr. David MURPHREE
04 Exec Admin Asst to President Mrs. Carolyn ANDREWS

Weatherford College (G)

225 College Park Drive, Weatherford TX 76086-5699
County: Parker FICE Identification: 003664
Unit ID: 229799
Telephone: (817) 594-5471 Carnegie Class: Assoc/Pub-S-SC
FAX Number: (817) 598-6210 Calendar System: Semester
URL: www.wc.edu
Established: 1869 Annual Undergrad Tuition & Fees (In-District): $1,824
Enrollment: 5,717 Coed
Affiliation or Control: Local IRS Status: 501(c)3
Highest Offering: Associate Degree
Program: Occupational; 2-Year Principally Bachelor's Creditable
Accreditation: SC, ADNUR, COARC, DMS, EMT, IFSAC, PHLEB, @PTAA, RAD

01 President Dr. Kevin EATON
04 Exec Asst to the President Mrs. Theresa R. HUTCHISON
32 VP of Inst & Stdnt Services Dr. Richard BOWERS
10 Vice Pres Financial/Admin Affairs Mrs. Andra R. CANTRELL
30 Vice Pres Institutional Advancement Mr. Brent BAKER
76 Dean of Health & Human Sciences Ms. Katherine BOSWELL
05 Executive Dean of Academics Mr. Michael ENDY
53 Dean Educational/Instructional Sppt Ms. Rhonda TORRES
35 Executive Dean of Student Services Ms. Kathy BASSHAM
103 Dean Workforce & Economic Devel Ms. Kay YOUNG
27 Dir Communications/Public Relations Mrs. Linda BAGWELL
56 Dean of Extended Campuses Mr. Duane DURRETT
88 Director Truck Driving Mr. Bubba SWEARINGIN
09 Dir Institutional Research Mr. Dewayne BERRY
35 Exec Director Student Development Mr. Doug JEFFERSON
36 Dir of Career and Transfer Center Ms. Teresa BROCK
88 Director Food Services Ms. Erin DAVIDSON
37 Director Student Financial Aid Mr. Donnie PURVIS
21 Controller Mrs. Ruth CAMPFIELD
15 Director Human Resources Mrs. Ralinda STONE
07 Director of Admissions/Veterans Mr. Ralph WILLINGHAM
13 Director Technology Services Mr. Steven SANDIDGE
08 Director of Library Services Ms. Valorie STARR
18 Director of Facilities Ms. Rhonda JOHNSON
96 Director of Purchasing Mrs. Jeanie HOBBS
45 Director of Resource Development Dr. Shirley CHENAULT
19 Chief of Campus Police Mr. Paul STONE
38 Student Counseling Ms. Phyllis TIFFIN
88 Director Upward Bound Mr. Jeff KHALDEN
29 Director Alumni Relations Mr. Brent BAKER
103 Director of Workforce Education Ms. Janetta KRUSE
53 Director of Teacher Education Dr. Joyce MELTON PAGES
06 Registrar Mrs. Vicki TRAWEEK
88 Exec Dir of Student Engagement Mr. Adam FINLEY
88 Director of Testing Ms. Lela MORRIS
88 Dir of Outreach/Student Success Ms. Kay LANDRUM
88 Director Special Populations Ms. Bernadean CONNELL

West Coast University (H)

8435 N Stemmons Freeway, Dallas TX 75247-3900
Telephone: (214) 453-4533 Identification: 770485
Accreditation: &WC

† Main campus is West Coast University in North Hollywood, CA.

Western Technical College (I)

9451 Diana Drive, El Paso TX 79924-6936
Telephone: (915) 566-9621 Identification: 666103
Accreditation: ACCSC

† Main campus is Western Technical College in El Paso, TX.

Western Technical College (J)

9624 Plaza Circle, El Paso TX 79927-2105
County: El Paso FICE Identification: 020983
Unit ID: 224679
Telephone: (915) 532-3737 Carnegie Class: Assoc/PrivFP
FAX Number: (915) 532-6946 Calendar System: Other
URL: www.westerntech.edu
Established: 1969 Annual Undergrad Tuition & Fees: $31,000
Enrollment: 806 Coed
Affiliation or Control: Proprietary IRS Status: Proprietary
Highest Offering: Associate Degree
Program: Occupational; Technical Emphasis
Accreditation: ACCSC, PTAA

01 President/Director Mr. Allan SHARPE
88 Assistant Director Mr. Randy KUYKENDALL
11 Chief Administrative Officer Mr. Bill TERRELL
03 Excecutive VP/School Director Ms. Mary CANO
05 Academic Dean Ms. Lynda CERVANTES
10 Accountant Ms. Celi AVILA
37 Director Student Financial Services Ms. Danielle PICCHI
36 Director Career Services Ms. Helen GARCIA
07 Director Admission Mr. Marco MARTINEZ
13 Director Information Technology Mr. Jose PEREZ

Western Texas College (K)

6200 College Avenue, Snyder TX 79549-6189
County: Scurry FICE Identification: 009549
Unit ID: 229832
Telephone: (325) 573-8511 Carnegie Class: Assoc/Pub-R-M
FAX Number: (325) 573-9321 Calendar System: Semester
URL: www.wtc.edu
Established: 1969 Annual Undergrad Tuition & Fees (In-District): $1,898
Enrollment: 2,424 Coed
Affiliation or Control: State/Local IRS Status: 501(c)3
Highest Offering: Associate Degree
Program: Occupational; 2-Year Principally Bachelor's Creditable
Accreditation: SC

01 President Dr. Barbara R. BEEBE
05 Int Vice President of Instruction Dr. Jim PALMER
04 Assistant to the President Ms. Melanie SCHWERTNER
10 Chief Financial Officer Ms. Patricia CLAXTON
11 Chief Operation Officer Mr. Mike THORTON
09 Dean Inst Research & Effectiveness Mr. Britt CANADA
32 Dean of Student Services Mr. Ralph RAMON
72 Dean of Technology Mr. Roy BARTELS
30 Dean Col Advancement/Exec Dir Dev Mr. Jeremiah BOATRIGHT
41 Athletic Director Ms. Tammy DAVIS
06 Registrar Ms. Ann GALYEAN
37 Director Financial Aid Mr. Greg TORRES
21 Controller Ms. Marjann MORROW
16 Director of Human Resources Ms. Kelly MCGINNIS
85 Dir International Student Services Ms. Melissa DOUCETTE
96 Director of Purchasing & Compliance Mr. Travis BAWCUM

Wharton County Junior College (L)

911 Boling Highway, Wharton TX 77488-3298
County: Wharton FICE Identification: 003668
Unit ID: 229841
Telephone: (979) 532-4560 Carnegie Class: Assoc/Pub-R-L
FAX Number: (979) 532-6545 Calendar System: Semester
URL: www.wcjc.edu
Established: 1946 Annual Undergrad Tuition & Fees (In-District): $2,880
Enrollment: 7,407 Coed

Affiliation or Control: Local IRS Status: 501(c)3
Highest Offering: Associate Degree
Program: Occupational; 2-Year Principally Bachelor's Creditable
Accreditation: SC, CAHIIM, DH, #EMT, PTAA, RAD, SURGT

01 President .... Ms. Betty A. MCCROHAN
05 Vice President of Instruction .... Ms. Leigh Ann COLLINS
10 Vice President Administrative Svcs .... Mr. Bryce KOCIAN
13 Vice President of Technology & IR ... Ms. Pamela YOUNGBLOOD
32 Vice President of Student Services .... Mr. David LEENHOUTS
21 Dean of Financial & Business Svcs .... Mr. Gus WESSELS
26 Director of Marketing & Comm .... Ms. Zina CARTER
07 Director Admissions & Registration .... Ms. Christy BERRY
37 Director of Financial Aid .... Mr. Richard D. HYDE
08 Director Library Info/Tech Services .... Ms. Kwei HSU
18 Director of Facilities Management .... Mr. Mike FEYEN
15 Director of Human Resources .... Ms. Judy JONES
09 Director of Inst Effectiveness .... Dr. Danson JONES
96 Director of Purchasing .... Mr. Philip WUTHRICH

Wiley College (A)

711 Wiley Avenue, Marshall TX 75670-5199
County: Harrison FICE Identification: 003669
Unit ID: 229887
Telephone: (903) 927-3300 Carnegie Class: Bac/Diverse
FAX Number: (903) 938-8100 Calendar System: Semester
URL: www.wileyc.edu
Established: 1873 Annual Undergrad Tuition & Fees: $11,382
Enrollment: 1,401 Coed
Affiliation or Control: United Methodist IRS Status: 501(c)3
Highest Offering: Baccalaureate
Program: Liberal Arts And General; Teacher Preparatory
Accreditation: SC, ACBSP

01 President and CEO .... Dr. Haywood L. STRICKLAND
03 Executive Vice President & Provost .... Dr. Glenda F. CARTER
10 Vice Pres for Business & Finance .... Mrs. Willie M. HUGHEY
05 Vice President Academic Affairs .... Dr. Ernest J. PLATA
32 Vice President Student Affairs .... Dr. Joseph L. MORALE
30 Vice Pres Institutional Advancement .... Vacant
13 Vice Pres Information Technology .... Mr. Nathaniel HEWITT
21 Assoc VP Business/Fiscal Affairs .... Ms. Pamela PRESSLEY
53 Dean of Education .... Vacant
42 College Chaplain .... Rev. Tori BUTLER
04 Assistant to the President .... Mrs. Karen HELTON
50 Dean of Business & Technology .... Dr. Abdalla F. HAGAN
49 Dean of Sciences .... Dr. Walter SHUMANTE
97 Dean General Studies .... Dr. Sonya BURNETT-ANDRUS
79 Dean Social Sciences & Humanities .... Dr. Sherlynn H. BYRD
26 Director of Public Relations .... Ms. Tammy TAYLOR
08 Director of Library Services .... Vacant
06 Registrar .... Dr. Lalita ROGERS
07 Director of Admissions .... Vacant
15 Director Personnel Services .... Mrs. Krystal MOODY
18 Chief Facilities/Physical Plant .... Mr. Percy MURRAY
20 Assistant VP Academic Affairs .... Dr. Sherlynn BYRD
37 Director of Financial Aid .... Mr. Alan D. JACKSON
29 Director of Alumni Relations .... Ms. Alvena JONES
09 Director of Institutional Research .... Dr. Warren H. HAWKINS
11 Director Administrative Svcs .... Mr. O. Ivan WHITE
23 College Nurse .... Ms. Shonte EPPERSON
36 Dir Student Placement/Counseling .... Ms. LaDonna GAUT
41 Director of Athletics .... Ms. Janet EATON
96 Director of Purchasing .... Mr. Darius Z. KIMBLE
35 Director of Student Development .... Vacant
84 Director Enrollment Management .... Vacant

UTAH

Argosy University, Salt Lake City (B)

121 Election Road Suite 300, Draper UT 84020-7724
Telephone: (801) 601-5000 Identification: 666655
Accreditation: &WC

† Main campus is Argosy University, Orange County in Orange, CA.

The Art Institute of Salt Lake City (C)

121 West Election Road, Draper UT 84020
Telephone: (801) 601-4700 Identification: 666694
Accreditation: ACICS

† Main campus is The Art Institute of Phoenix in Phoenix, AZ.

Brigham Young University (D)

Provo UT 84602-0002
County: Utah FICE Identification: 003670
Unit ID: 230038
Telephone: (801) 422-4000 Carnegie Class: RU/H
FAX Number: (801) 422-0684 Calendar System: Semester
URL: www.byu.edu
Established: 1875 Annual Undergrad Tuition & Fees: $4,850
Enrollment: 34,409 Coed
Affiliation or Control: Latter-day Saints IRS Status: 501(c)3
Highest Offering: Doctorate
Program: Liberal Arts And General; Teacher Preparatory; Professional
Accreditation: NW, ART, BUS, BUSA, CLPSY, CONST, COPSY, CS, DANCE, DIETD, DIETI, ENG, ENGT, IPSY, JOUR, LAW, MFCD, MT, MUS, NRPA, NURSE, PH, SP, SPAA, SW, TEAC, THEA

01 President .... Dr. Cecil O. SAMUELSON
05 Academic Vice President .... Dr. Brent W. WEBB
11 Administrative Vice President .... Mr. Brian K. EVANS
44 Advancement Vice President .... Dr. Kevin J. WORTHEN
13 Vice Pres Info Tech/Chief Info Ofcr .... Dr. J. Kelly FLANAGAN
88 International Vice President .... Dr. Sandra ROGERS
32 Student Life Vice President .... Dr. Janet S. SCHARMAN
43 Asst to President/General Counsel .... Mr. Michael R. ORME
45 Asst to Pres Planning/Assessment ..... Mr. James D. GORDON, III
27 Asst to Pres Univ Communications .... Mrs. Carri P. JENKINS
20 Assoc Acad Vice President Faculty .... Dr. Craig H. HART
20 Assoc Acad VP Undergraduate Stds .... Dr. Jeffrey D. KEITH
46 Assoc Acad VP Research/Grad Stds .... Dr. Alan R. HARKER
35 Assoc Student Life Vice Pres .... Dr. Ronald K. CHAPMAN
10 Chief Financial Officer .... Mr. Brian K. EVANS
18 Asst Admin VP Physical Facilities .... Mr. Ole M. SMITH
15 Asst Admin VP Human Resource Svcs .... Mr. Forrest FLAKE
35 Asst Admin VP/Stdnt Auxil Svc .... Mr. David A. HUNT
26 Assoc Advance VP External Relations .... Mr. John C. LEWIS
30 Exec Dir LDS Philanthropies @ BYU ... Dr. Tanise CHUNG-HOON
36 Exec Dir Stdnt Acad/Advisement Svcs .... Mr. Norm FINLINSON
35 Dean Student Life .... Mr. Vernon L. HEPERI
37 Director Financial Aid/Scholarships .... Mr. Stephen E. HILL
88 Dean Undergraduate Education .... Dr. John D. BELL
08 University Librarian .... Ms. Jennifer PAUSTENBAUGH
58 Dean Graduate Studies .... Dr. Wynn C. STIRLING
51 Dean Continuing Education .... Dr. Wayne J. LOTT
47 Dean Life Sciences .... Dr. Rodney J. BROWN
54 Dean Engineering & Technology .... Dr. Alan R. PARKINSON
83 Dean Family Home & Social Science .... Dr. Benjamin M. OGLES
57 Dean Fine Arts & Communications .... Dr. Stephen M. JONES
79 Dean Humanities .... Dr. John ROSENBERG
61 Dean Law School .... Dr. James R. RASBAND
50 Dean Marriott School Management .... Dr. Gary C. CORNIA
53 Dean McKay School of Education .... Dr. K. Richard YOUNG
81 Dean Physical & Math Science .... Dr. Scott D. SOMMERFELDT
66 Dean Nursing .... Dr. Patricia RAVERT
73 Dean Religious Education .... Dr. Terry BALL
38 Director Counseling & Career Ctr .... Dr. Steve A. SMITH
09 Dir Institutional Assess/Analysis .... Dr. Danny R. OLSEN
06 Registrar .... Mr. Barry ALLRED
07 Director of Admissions .... Mr. R. Kirk STRONG
29 Managing Director Alumni Relations .... Ms. Linda PALMER
96 Director of Purchasing .... Mr. W. Timothy HILL

Broadview Entertainment Arts University (E)

240 East Morris Avenue, Salt Lake City UT 84115
Telephone: (801) 300-4300 Identification: 770809
Accreditation: ACICS

† Main campus is Broadview University in West Jordan, UT.

Broadview University (F)

869 West Hill Field Road, Layton UT 84041
Telephone: (801) 660-6000 Identification: 770810
Accreditation: ACICS, MAAB

† Main campus is Broadview University in West Jordan, UT.

Broadview University (G)

898 North 1200 West, Orem UT 84057
Telephone: (801) 822-5800 Identification: 770811
Accreditation: ACICS, MAAB

† Main campus is Broadview University in West Jordan, UT.

Broadview University (H)

1902 W 7800 S, West Jordan UT 84088-4021
County: Salt Lake FICE Identification: 011166
Unit ID: 230056
Telephone: (801) 304-4224 Carnegie Class: Spec/Health
FAX Number: (801) 304-4229 Calendar System: Quarter
URL: www.broadviewuniversity.edu
Established: 1971 Annual Undergrad Tuition & Fees: $14,400
Enrollment: 343 Coed
Affiliation or Control: Proprietary IRS Status: Proprietary
Highest Offering: Master's
Program: Occupational; Technical Emphasis
Accreditation: ACICS, MAAB

01 President .... Mr. Terry MYHRE
05 Director .... Ms. Deeann KERR

Eagle Gate College (I)

915 North 400 West, Layton UT 84041
Telephone: (801) 546-7500 Identification: 770812
Accreditation: ACICS

† Main campus is Eagle Gate College in Murray, UT.

Eagle Gate College (J)

5588 S Green Street, Murray UT 84123-6965
County: Salt Lake FICE Identification: 021785
Unit ID: 230366
Telephone: (801) 333-8100 Carnegie Class: Assoc/PrivFP4
FAX Number: (801) 263-6520 Calendar System: Other
URL: www.eaglegatecollege.edu
Established: 1979 Annual Undergrad Tuition & Fees: $13,609
Enrollment: 285 Coed
Affiliation or Control: Proprietary IRS Status: Proprietary
Highest Offering: Baccalaureate
Program: 2-Year Principally Bachelor's Creditable; Technical Emphasis
Accreditation: ACICS

01 President .... Ms. Janet HEAD
03 Campus VP .... Ms. Jana COLYAR

Everest College (K)

3280 W 3500 South, West Valley City UT 84119
County: Salt Lake FICE Identification: 022985
Unit ID: 230472
Telephone: (801) 840-4800 Carnegie Class: Assoc/PrivFP4
FAX Number: (801) 969-0828 Calendar System: Quarter
URL: www.everest.edu
Established: 1982 Annual Undergrad Tuition & Fees: $12,852
Enrollment: 374 Coed
Affiliation or Control: Proprietary IRS Status: Proprietary
Highest Offering: Baccalaureate
Program: Occupational; 2-Year Principally Bachelor's Creditable; Business Emphasis
Accreditation: ACICS, MAC, SURGT

01 President .... Ms. Natalie WILLIAMS
05 Academic Dean .... Ms. Daisy HERNANDEZ
10 Business Manager .... Ms. Amanda DUNN
07 Director of Admissions .... Ms. Roshae GARNER
36 Director Career Services .... Mr. Robert PETERSON

Fortis College (L)

3949 South 700 East, Suite 150, Salt Lake City UT 84107
Telephone: (801) 713-0915 Identification: 666762
Accreditation: ACCSC, ADNUR, DH

† Main campus is Fortis College in Cuyahoga Falls, OH.

Independence University (M)

4021 South 700 East, Suite 400,
Salt Lake City UT 84107-2453
County: Salt Lake FICE Identification: 022061
Unit ID: 465812
Telephone: (800) 972-5149 Carnegie Class: Not Classified
FAX Number: (801) 263-0345 Calendar System: Other
URL: www.independence.edu
Established: 1978 Annual Undergrad Tuition & Fees: $12,696
Enrollment: 969 Coed
Affiliation or Control: Proprietary IRS Status: Proprietary
Highest Offering: Master's
Program: Professional
Accreditation: ACCSC, COARC

01 Executive Director .... Mr. Carl BARNEY

ITT Technical Institute (N)

920 West LeVoy Drive, Murray UT 84123-2500
Telephone: (801) 263-3313 FICE Identification: 023610
Accreditation: ACICS

† Main campus is ITT Technical Institute in Indianapolis, IN.

LDS Business College (O)

95 N 300 W, Salt Lake City UT 84101-3500
County: Salt Lake FICE Identification: 003672
Unit ID: 230418
Telephone: (801) 524-8100 Carnegie Class: Assoc/PrivNFP
FAX Number: (801) 524-1900 Calendar System: Semester
URL: www.ldsbc.edu
Established: 1886 Annual Undergrad Tuition & Fees: $3,060
Enrollment: 2,200 Coed
Affiliation or Control: Latter-day Saints IRS Status: 501(c)3
Highest Offering: Associate Degree
Program: Occupational; 2-Year Principally Bachelor's Creditable; Business Emphasis
Accreditation: NW, MAC

01 President .... Mr. Larry J. RICHARDS
04 Executive Admin Asst .... Ms. Cathy A. SMITH
05 Chief Academic Officer .... Mr. Ronald E. GUYMON
88 Director of Instructional Design .... Mr. Jared WRIGHT
27 Chief Information Officer .... Mr. R. Brent CHERRINGTON
10 Vice President Finance/Controller .... Mr. Bob H. WISER
88 Director of Business Solutions .... Mr. Glenn MCGETTIGAN
30 VP Advancement .... Mr. Craig V. NELSON
20 Dean of Instuctional Support .... Mr. Tyler S. MORGAN
09 Director of Marketing & Research .... Mr. Matthew D. TITTLE
15 Director of Human Resources .... Mr. Brady KIMBER
84 Director of Enrollment Management .... Ms. Renae L. RICHARDS
07 Asst Director of Admissions .... Ms. Dawn FELLOWS
06 Registrar .... Ms. Tamra TAYLOR
06 Associate Registrar .... Mrs. Cindy LAMPROPOULOS
08 Dir of Library/Inform Resources .... Ms. Sarah SORENSEN
88 Accounting Program Director .... Mr. Bruce SCHREINER
50 Business Skills Program Director .... Mr. Scott NEWMAN
88 Entrepreneurship Program Director .... Mr. Ralph LITTLE
88 Professional Sales Program Director .... Mr. Kenneth DEVALL
50 Director Business Applications .... Mr. Mitch PENDLETON

50 Bus Admin Support Program Director .... Mrs. Marjean LAKE
23 Health Professions Program Director .... Mr. Brett MERKLEY
107 Paralegal Program Director .... Ms. Kimberly GARNER
97 Integrated Studies Program Director .... Mr. Paul RICHARDS
88 Interior Design Program Director .... Mr. Miles HUNSAKER
72 Business Info Systems Program Dir .... Mr. Spencer DEGRAW
73 Institute of Religion Director .... Mr. Tracy WILLIAMS
21 Assistant Controller .... Mr. Chris REITZ
37 Director of Financial Aid .... Mr. J. Douglas HORNE
37 Manager Student Financial Services .... Ms. Melanie CONOVER
40 Bookstore Manager .... Ms. Rachel BINGHAM
35 Director of Student Support .... Mr. Adrian JUCHAU
26 Public Affairs Director .... Mrs. Louise BROWN
88 Director of Learning Assistance Lab .... Mrs. Kathy SKENE
103 Director of Employment & Career Svc .... Mr. Wyton DUNFORD

Midwives College of Utah (A)

1174 E Graystone Way Suite 2,
Salt Lake City UT 84106-2671

County: Utah — Identification: 666281
Telephone: (866) 680-2756 — Carnegie Class: Not Classified
FAX Number: (866) 207-2024 — Calendar System: Semester
URL: www.midwifery.edu
Established: 1980 — Annual Undergrad Tuition & Fees: $19,050
Enrollment: 265 — Coed
Affiliation or Control: Independent Non-Profit — IRS Status: 501(c)3
Highest Offering: Master's
Program: Occupational; 2-Year Principally Bachelor's Creditable
Accreditation: MEAC

01 President .... Ms. Kristi RIDD-YOUNG
05 Academic Dean .... Ms. Nicole CROFT
06 Registrar .... Ms. Cindy WINWARD
04 Administrative Assistant .... Ms. Cindy WINWARD

Neumont University (B)

143 South Main, Salt Lake City UT 84111

County: Salt Lake — FICE Identification: 010098
Unit ID: 445692
Telephone: (801) 302-2800 — Carnegie Class: Spec/Tech
FAX Number: (801) 302-2811 — Calendar System: Quarter
URL: www.neumont.edu
Established: 2003 — Annual Undergrad Tuition & Fees: $23,100
Enrollment: 368 — Coed
Affiliation or Control: Proprietary — IRS Status: Proprietary
Highest Offering: Master's
Program: Professional; Technical Emphasis
Accreditation: ACICS

01 President/Campus Dir Utah .... Ned LEVINE
05 Provost .... Sam PUICH
32 Dean of Students .... Erin MCCORMACK
06 Registrar/Dir Academic Programs .... Larry CRANDALL
07 Director of Admissions .... Karick HEATON

Nightingale College (C)

4155 Harrison Blvd, Ste 100, Ogden UT 84403

County: Weber — FICE Identification: 038383
Unit ID: 44787
Telephone: (801) 689-2160 — Carnegie Class: Not Classified
FAX Number: (801) 689-3114 — Calendar System: Semester
URL: www.nightingale.edu
Established: — Annual Undergrad Tuition & Fees: $35,000
Enrollment: 48 — Coed
Affiliation or Control: Proprietary — IRS Status: Proprietary
Highest Offering: Associate Degree
Program: Occupational
Accreditation: ABHES

01 President/CEO .... Mr. Mikhail SHNEYDER

Ogden-Weber Applied Technology College (D)

200 North Washington Boulevard, Ogden UT 84404-4089

County: Weber — FICE Identification: 023465
Unit ID: 230490
Telephone: (801) 627-8300 — Carnegie Class: Assoc/Pub-U-MC
FAX Number: (801) 395-3727 — Calendar System: Other
URL: www.owatc.edu
Established: 1971 — Annual Undergrad Tuition & Fees (In-District): $2,916
Enrollment: 2,803 — Coed
Affiliation or Control: State/Local — IRS Status: 501(c)3
Highest Offering: Associate Degree
Program: Occupational; Technical Emphasis
Accreditation: COE, DA, MAC, PNUR

01 President & Chief Executive Officer .... Collette MERCIER
05 VP for Instructional Services .... James R. TAGGART
32 VP for Student Services .... Rhonda LAURITZEN
10 VP for College Services/CFO .... Tyler CALL

† Campus of Utah College of Applied Technology, Salt Lake City, UT.

Provo College (E)

1262 South 820 East, American Fork UT 84003
Telephone: (801) 333-7164 — Identification: 770813
Accreditation: ACICS

† Main campus is Provo College in Provo, UT.

Provo College (F)

1450 W 820 N, Provo UT 84601-1305

County: Utah — FICE Identification: 023608
Unit ID: 380438
Telephone: (801) 818-8900 — Carnegie Class: Assoc/PrivFP
FAX Number: (801) 375-9728 — Calendar System: Other
URL: www.provocollege.edu
Established: 1984 — Annual Undergrad Tuition & Fees: $14,835
Enrollment: 331 — Coed
Affiliation or Control: Proprietary — IRS Status: Proprietary
Highest Offering: Associate Degree
Program: Occupational; Nursing Emphasis
Accreditation: ACICS, ADNUR, PTAA

01 Campus President .... Mr. Todd SMITH
05 Academic Dean .... Mrs. Kristy THOMPSON
10 Business Manager .... Mr. Mickel BLOMQUIST
07 Director of Admissions .... Mr. Stewart HAGBERG
37 Financial Services Assoc Director .... Mr. Nick JOHNSON
06 Registrar .... Mrs. Natalia AROCHI
32 Director of Student Services .... Ms. Traci CLARIDA
36 Director of Career Services .... Mr. Gary NORMAN

Rocky Mountain University of Health Professions (G)

561 East 1860 South, Provo UT 84606-7312

County: Utah — FICE Identification: 041932
Unit ID: 475495
Telephone: (801) 375-5125 — Carnegie Class: Not Classified
FAX Number: (801) 375-2125 — Calendar System: Trimester
URL: www.rmuohp.edu
Established: 1998 — Annual Graduate Tuition & Fees: $20,000
Enrollment: 500 — Coed
Affiliation or Control: Proprietary — IRS Status: Proprietary
Highest Offering: Doctorate; No Undergraduates
Program: Professional
Accreditation: NW, PTA

01 President .... Dr. Richard P. NIELSEN
03 Executive Vice President of Admin .... Dr. Les SMITH
10 Vice President Finance .... Mr. Jeff BATE
30 VP Inst Effect/Strategic Planning .... Dr. Michael SKURJA
05 Provost .... Dr. Sandra PENNINGTON
20 Vice Provost/Academic Dean .... Dr. Hani GHAZI-BIRRY
46 Director of Research .... Dr. Brent ALVAR
09 Dir of Institutional Effectiveness .... Ms. Jessica D. EGBERT

Stevens-Henager College (H)

755 South Main Street, Logan UT 84321
Telephone: (435) 792-6970 — Identification: 770603
Accreditation: ACCSC, MAC

† Main campus is Stevens-Henager College in Ogden, UT.

Stevens-Henager College (I)

PO Box 9428, Ogden UT 84409-0428

County: Weber — FICE Identification: 003674
Unit ID: 230621
Telephone: (801) 394-7791 — Carnegie Class: Bac/Assoc
FAX Number: (801) 621-0853 — Calendar System: Quarter
URL: www.stevenshenager.edu
Established: 1891 — Annual Undergrad Tuition & Fees: $16,554
Enrollment: 472 — Coed
Affiliation or Control: Independent Non-Profit — IRS Status: 501(c)3
Highest Offering: Baccalaureate
Program: Occupational; 2-Year Principally Bachelor's Creditable
Accreditation: ACCSC, ADNUR, MAC, SURGT

01 Pres of Ogden Campus/Regional Dir .... Ms. Vicky DEWSNUP
07 Director of Admissions .... Mr. Brandon KELSON
32 Director of Student Services .... Mr. Doug BURCH
05 Chief Academic Officer .... Ms. Dixie MATHIS
10 Chief Business Officer .... Mr. Ryan MUNSON
35 Director Student Affairs .... Mr. Doug BURCH
36 Director Student Placement .... Ms. Kelly STONE

Stevens-Henager College (J)

1476 S Sandhill Road, Orem UT 84058-7310
Telephone: (801) 418-1450 — FICE Identification: 030030
Accreditation: ACCSC, MAC

† Main campus is Stevens-Henager College in Ogden, UT.

Stevens-Henager College (K)

720 South River Road, Suite C-130, St. George UT 84790
Telephone: (435) 628-9903 — Identification: 770604
Accreditation: ACCSC

† Main campus is Stevens-Henager College in Ogden, UT.

Stevens-Henager College (L)

383 W Vine Street, Salt Lake City UT 84123
Telephone: (801) 281-7620 — Identification: 666038
Accreditation: ACCSC, COARC

† Main campus is Stevens-Henager College in Ogden, UT.

Uintah Basin Applied Technology College (M)

1100 East Lagoon Street, Roosevelt UT 84066

FICE Identification: 011165
Unit ID: 230676
Telephone: (435) 722-6900 — Carnegie Class: Assoc/Pub-R-S
FAX Number: (435) 722-6999 — Calendar System: Semester
URL: www.ubatc.edu
Established: 1968 — Annual Undergrad Tuition & Fees (In-State): $1,800
Enrollment: 1,300 — Coed
Affiliation or Control: State — IRS Status: 501(c)3
Highest Offering: Associate Degree
Program: Occupational; Technical Emphasis
Accreditation: COE, PNUR

01 Campus President .... David R. WOOLSTENHULME
30 Vice Pres Economic Development .... Jean MOLD
32 Vice Pres of Student Services .... Robert PETERSON
10 Vice Pres of Finance .... Keith SPROUSE
05 Vice Pres of Instruction .... John WAHL
04 Exec Assistant to the President .... Trenna BALLOU
06 Registrar .... Julene OLSEN
37 Financial Aid Coordinator .... Mark ANDERTON

† Campus of Utah College of Applied Technology, Salt Lake City, UT.

University of Phoenix Utah Campus (N)

5373 South Green Street, Salt Lake City UT 84123-4642
Telephone: (801) 263-1444 — Identification: 770232
Accreditation: &NH, ACBSP, CACREP

† Main campus is University of Phoenix in Tempe, AZ.

The Utah College of Dental Hygiene at Careers Unlimited (O)

1176 S 1480 W, Orem UT 84058-4905

County: Utah — FICE Identification: 034633
Unit ID: 448239
Telephone: (801) 426-8234 — Carnegie Class: Spec/Health
FAX Number: (801) 224-5437 — Calendar System: Other
URL: www.ucdh.edu
Established: 2006 — Annual Undergrad Tuition & Fees: $24,970
Enrollment: 120 — Coed
Affiliation or Control: Proprietary — IRS Status: Proprietary
Highest Offering: Baccalaureate
Program: Occupational; 2-Year Principally Bachelor's Creditable
Accreditation: ACCSC, DH

01 College President .... Mr. Brent MOLEN
05 Director of Education .... Mr. Kenneth MOLEN

*Utah System of Higher Education (P)

The Gateway, 60 S 400 W, Salt Lake City UT 84101-1284

County: Salt Lake — FICE Identification: 009339
Telephone: (801) 321-7101 — Carnegie Class: N/A
FAX Number: (801) 321-7199
URL: www.higheredutah.org

01 Exec Ofcr/Commissioner of Higher Ed .... Mr. David L. BUHLER
05 Assoc Commissioner Academic Affairs .... Dr. Elizabeth J. HITCH
10 Assoc Commissioner Finance/Facilit .... Dr. Gregory STAUFFER
37 Exec Director Student Financial Aid .... Mr. David A. FEITZ
88 UESP Executive Director .... Ms. Lynne WARD

*The University of Utah (Q)

201 South 1460 East, Salt Lake City UT 84112-1107

County: Salt Lake — FICE Identification: 003675
Unit ID: 230764
Telephone: (801) 581-7200 — Carnegie Class: RU/VH
FAX Number: (801) 581-3007 — Calendar System: Semester
URL: www.utah.edu
Established: 1850 — Annual Undergrad Tuition & Fees (In-State): $7,457
Enrollment: 32,388 — Coed
Affiliation or Control: State — IRS Status: 501(c)3
Highest Offering: Doctorate
Program: Liberal Arts And General; Teacher Preparatory; Professional
Accreditation: NW, ARCPA, AUD, BUS, BUSA, CEA, CLPSY, COPSY, CYTO, DANCE, DENT, DIETC, EMT, ENG, ENGR, HSA, IPSY, LAW, MED, MIDWF, MT, MUS, NMT, NRPA, NURSE, OT, PH, PHAR, PLNG, PTA, SCPSY, SP, SPAA, SW, TEAC

02 President .... Dr. David W. PERSHING
05 Sr Vice Pres Academic Affairs .... Dr. Ruth WATKINS
17 Sr VP Hlth Sci/CEO Univ Ut Hlth Ctr .... Dr. Vivian S. LEE
43 Vice President & General Counsel .... Mr. John K. MORRIS
11 Vice Pres Administrative Services .... Mr. Arnold B. COMBE
32 Vice President Student Affairs .... Dr. Barbara H. SNYDER
30 Vice Pres Institutional Advancement .... Mr. Fred C. ESPLIN

86 Vice President Government Relations .... Mr. Jason PERRY
16 Assoc Vice Pres for Human Resources .... Ms. Joan GINES
46 Vice President Research .... Dr. Thomas N. PARKS
04 Exec Asst to the President .... Ms. Elizabeth W. MCCOY
27 Chief Information Officer .... Dr. Eric DENNA
21 Chief Strategy Officer .... Ms. Patricia A. ROSS
88 Chief Global Officer .... Dr. Michael L. HARDMAN
15 Chief Human Resources Officer .... Mr. Jeff HERRING
26 Chief Mktg & Commun Officer .... Mr. William J. WARREN
20 Assoc VP AA & Dean Undergrad Stds .... Dr. Martha S. BRADLEY
84 Sr Assoc VP for Enrollment Mgmt .... Ms. Mary G. PARKER
45 Assoc VP Acad Affs/Budget/Planning .... Ms. Cathy ANDERSON
18 Assoc VP Admin Services/Facilities .... Mr. Michael G. PEREZ
10 Assoc VP Admin/Finance & Bus Svcs .... Mr. Jeffrey J. WEST
20 Assoc VP Acad Affs/Equity/Diversity .... Dr. Octavio VILLALPANDO
88 Associate Vice President Research .... Dr. Cynthia M. FURSE
15 Associate Vice Pres Human Resources .... Ms. Joan E. GINES
88 Assoc VP Acad Affs/Faculty .... Dr. Amy WILDERMUTH
35 Assoc VP Stdnt Affs/Bus/Auxil Svcs .... Dr. Jerry L. BASFORD
21 Asst Vice Pres Admin Svc/Aux Svc .... Mr. Gordon N. WILSON
58 Dean Graduate School .... Dr. David B. KIEDA
48 Dean Architecture & Planning .... Vacant
50 Dean David Eccles Sch of Business .... Dr. Taylor RANDALL
52 Dean School of Dentistry .... Dr. Rena N. D'SOUZA
53 Interim Dean College of Education .... Dr. John MCDONNELL
54 Dean College of Engineering .... Dr. Richard B. BROWN
57 Dean Col of Fine Arts/AVP the Arts .... Dr. Raymond TYMAS-JONES
68 Dean College of Health .... Vacant
92 Dean Honors College .... Dr. Sylvia TORTI
79 Dn Col Hum/AVP Acad Affs/Indply Std .... Dr. Robert D. NEWMAN
61 Int Dean S J Quinney College of Law .... Dr. Robert ADLER
65 Dean Coll of Mines & Earth Science .... Dr. Francis H. BROWN
63 Dean School of Medicine .... Dr. Vivian S. LEE
66 Dean College of Nursing .... Dr. Patricia MORTON
67 Dean College of Pharmacy .... Dr. Chris M. IRELAND
81 Dean College of Science .... Dr. Pierre V. SOKOLSKY
83 Int Dean Col Social/Behav Science .... Dr. Cynthia BERG
70 Dean College of Social Work .... Dr. Jannah H. MATHER
88 Dean of Students .... Ms. Annie NEBEKER-CHRISTENSEN
06 University Registrar .... Mr. Timothy J. EBNER
23 CEO University Hospitals & Clinics .... Mr. David E. ENTWISTLE
91 Exec Dir Proj/Apps/Univ Info Tech .... Mr. Joseph R. TAYLOR
88 Director Institutional Review Board .... Mr. John P. STILLMAN
96 Director Purchasing .... Mr. James T. PARKER
94 Director Gender Studies .... Dr. Susie PORTER
77 Department Chair Sch of Computing .... Dr. Martin BERZINS
52 Dir Dental Clinic/Gen Prac Resideny .... Dr. Craige J. OLSON
07 Director Admissions .... Mr. Matthew LOPEZ
29 Exec Director Alumni Association .... Mr. M. John ASHTON
44 Director Planned Giving .... Ms. Karin S. HARDY
37 Dir Financial Aid & Scholarships .... Mr. John CURL
08 Int Exec Director Marriott Library .... Mr. Rick ANDERSON
62 Dir Eccles Health Sciences Library .... Ms. Jean P. SHIPMAN
62 Dir S J Quinney Col of Law/Lib .... Ms. Melissa BERNSTEIN
36 Director of Career Services .... Mr. Stan D. INMAN
38 Director Counseling Center .... Dr. Lauren WEITZMAN
39 Director Housing & Res Education .... Ms. Barbara REMSBURG
39 Director Univ Student Apartments .... Mr. Richard L. JAMES
88 Dir Natural History Museum of Utah .... Dr. Sarah B. GEORGE
19 Chief of Police .... Mr. Scott D. FOLSOM
40 Director Campus Bookstore .... Mr. Earl L. CLEGG
85 Director International Center .... Dr. Sabine KLAHR
41 Director Athletics .... Dr. Chris HILL
25 Dir Office of Sponsored Projects .... Mr. Brent K. BROWN
31 Director Univ-Neighborhood Partners .... Dr. Rosemarie HUNTER
09 Director Institutional Analysis .... Dr. Paul A. GORE

*Southern Utah University (A)

351 W Center Blvd, Cedar City UT 84720-2470
County: Iron FICE Identification: 003678
Unit ID: 230603
Telephone: (435) 586-7700 Carnegie Class: Master's L
FAX Number: (435) 586-5475 Calendar System: Semester
URL: www.suu.edu
Established: 1897 Annual Undergrad Tuition & Fees (In-State): $5,942
Enrollment: 8,125 Coed
Affiliation or Control: State IRS Status: 501(c)3
Highest Offering: Master's
Program: Occupational; Liberal Arts And General; Teacher Preparatory
Accreditation: NW, ART, ACBSP, BUS, CS, DANCE, ENG, MUS, NURSE, TEAC

02 President .... Dr. Richard E. KENDELL
05 Provost .... Dr. Bradley COOK
10 Vice Pres of Finance & Govt Rels .... Mr. Dorian PAGE
32 Interim VP Student Services .... Dr. Stephen ALLEN
26 Vice Pres for University Relations .... Mr. Dean O'DRISCOLL
30 Vice Pres Advancement .... Mr. Stuart JONES
58 Assoc Provost/Dean of Graduate Stds .... Mr. William J. BYRNES
13 Chief Information Officer .... Mr. Thomas MCFARLAND
18 Executive Director of FM .... Mr. Tiger FUNK
08 Dean/Director Library/Univ Studies .... Mr. John EYE
51 Dean of Continuing/Profess Studies .... Mr. Mark ATKINSON
21 Director Budget .... Mr. Bryant FLAKE
75 Director CTE .... Mr. David A. WARD
06 Registrar .... Mr. John ALLRED
15 Director Human Resources .... Mr. David T. MCGUIRE
88 Dean of University College .... Dr. Patrick CLARKE
27 Director of Communications .... Mrs. Jennifer A. BURT
37 Director of Financial Aid .... Ms. Jan CAREY-MCDONALD
29 Exec Director of Alumni Relations .... Ms. Mindy BENSON
41 Athletic Director .... Mr. Ken BEAZER

43 Legal Counsel .... Mr. D. Michael CARTER
79 Dean Col Humanities/Soc Sci .... Dr. James MCDONALD
50 Dean School of Business .... Dr. Carl R. TEMPLIN
53 Dean College of Education .... Dr. Deborah HILL
81 Dean College of Sci and Engineering .... Dr. Robert EVES
57 Dean College Performing/Visual Arts .... Mrs. Shauna MENDINI
96 Director of Purchasing .... Mr. Peter J. HEILGEIST
09 Director of Institutional Research .... Mr. Christian REINER
38 Director Student Counseling .... Dr. Curtis HILL

*Utah State University (B)

Logan UT 84322-0001
County: Cache FICE Identification: 003677
Unit ID: 230728
Telephone: (435) 797-1000 Carnegie Class: RU/H
FAX Number: (435) 797-3880 Calendar System: Semester
URL: www.usu.edu
Established: 1888 Annual Undergrad Tuition & Fees (In-State): $6,185
Enrollment: 28,786 Coed
Affiliation or Control: State IRS Status: 501(c)3
Highest Offering: Doctorate
Program: Liberal Arts And General; Teacher Preparatory; Professional
Accreditation: NW, AUD, BUS, BUSA, CEA, CIDA, CORE, CS, DIETC, DIETD, DIETI, ENG, ENGR, FOR, IPSY, LSAR, MFCD, MUS, NRPA, PSPSY, SP, SW, TEAC

02 President .... Dr. Stan L. ALBRECHT
05 Provost .... Dr. Noelle E. COCKETT
43 General Counsel .... Mr. Craig J. SIMPER
10 Vice President Business & Finance .... Mr. Dave COWLEY
32 Vice President Student Services .... Mr. James MORALES
56 Vice Pres Extension & Agriculture .... Dr. Kenneth L. WHITE
46 VP Research/Dn Sch Graduate Stds .... Dr. Mark R. MCLELLAN
30 COO/University Advancement .... Ms. Annette HERMAN
13 CIO/Assoc VP Information Technology .... Dr. Eric HAWLEY
18 Associate VP for Facilities .... Mr. Darrell E. HART
44 Associate VP University Advancement .... Ms. Joan SCHEFFKE
07 Asst VP Recruitment/Enrollment Svcs .... Mr. John MORTENSEN
20 Vice Provost .... Dr. Laurens H. SMITH
51 Vice Prov Regional Camp/Dist Educ .... Dr. Ronda R. MENLOVE
08 Dean Libraries .... Mr. Richard CLEMENT
29 Exec Director Alumni Relations .... Mrs. Patty HALAUFIA
26 Exec Dir Public Relations/Marketing .... Mr. Tim VITALE
09 Dir Analysis Assess/Accreditation .... Mr. Michael TORRENS
22 Director Affirmative Action/EEO .... Ms. Stacy STURGEON
41 Athletic Director .... Mr. Scott BARNES
25 Director Sponsored Programs .... Mr. Jeff COLEMAN
86 Director Government Relations .... Mr. Neil N. ABERCROMBIE
15 Director of Human Resources .... Ms. BrandE FAUPELL
19 Director University Police Dept .... Mr. Steven J. MECHAM
06 Registrar .... Mr. Roland SQUIRE
36 Director Career Services/Coop Educ .... Ms. Donna E. CROW
37 Director of Financial Aid .... Ms. Patti KOHLER
38 Director Counseling Center .... Dr. David BUSH
40 Director of Bookstore .... Mr. David PARKINSON
92 Director of Honors .... Dr. Nicholas MORRISON
96 Director of Purchasing .... Mr. Paul BOWMAN
47 Dean of Agriculture .... Dr. Kenneth L. WHITE
57 Dean of Arts .... Dr. Craig JESSOP
50 Dean of Business .... Mr. Douglas D. ANDERSON
53 Dean of Education .... Dr. Beth FOLEY
54 Dean of Engineering .... Mr. H. Scott HINTON
79 Dean Humanities/Social Science .... Dr. John C. ALLEN
65 Interim Dean of Natural Resources .... Dr. Chris LUECKE
81 Dean of Science .... Dr. James MACMAHON

*Utah Valley University (C)

800 W University Parkway, Orem UT 84058-5999
County: Utah FICE Identification: 004027
Unit ID: 230737
Telephone: (801) 863-8000 Carnegie Class: Bac/Diverse
FAX Number: (801) 226-5207 Calendar System: Semester
URL: www.uvu.edu
Established: 1941 Annual Undergrad Tuition & Fees (In-State): $2,543
Enrollment: 31,562 Coed
Affiliation or Control: State IRS Status: 501(c)3
Highest Offering: Master's
Program: Occupational; 2-Year Principally Bachelor's Creditable; Liberal Arts And General; Teacher Preparatory; Professional
Accreditation: NW, ADNUR, BUS, CEA, CS, DH, EMT, IFSAC, NUR, @SW, TEAC

02 President .... Dr. Matthew S. HOLLAND
05 Senior Vice Pres Academic Affairs .... Dr. Ian WILSON
03 Vice Pres Finance & Administration .... Dr. Val L. PETERSON
32 Vice President Student Affairs .... Dr. Michelle O. TAYLOR
30 Vice Pres Deveopment/Alumni .... Mr. Marc ARCHAMBAULT
26 Vice Pres University Relations .... Dr. Cameron K. MARTIN
45 VP Planning/Budgets & HR .... Ms. Linda MAKIN
10 Assoc Vice Pres Finance .... Mr. Michael R. FRANCIS
20 Assoc Vice Pres Engaged Learning .... Dr. Brian BIRCH
18 Assoc Vice Pres Facilities Planning .... Mr. Jim MICHAELIS
20 Assoc VP Programs .... Dr. Maureen ANDRADE
84 Assc VP Recruitment & Outreach .... Mr. Kirk YOUNG
26 Assoc VP College Mktg/Communication .... Mr. Chris TAYLOR
44 Assoc Vice Pres Development .... Vacant
20 Assoc VP Academic Affairs/Admin .... Dr. Kathren BROWN
88 Asst VP Student Success & Retention .... Vacant
88 Asst VP AA Community College Pgm .... Dr. Craig KLEIN
21 Asst VP/Controller Business Svcs .... Mr. Kedric BLACK
88 Asst VP Scholarship & Faculty Dev .... Vacant

07 Sr Director Admissions/One Stop .... Ms. Liz CHILDS
32 Assoc VP Student Life/Dean Students .... Dr. Shad SORENSON
72 Dean Computing/Technology .... Mr. Ernie CAREY
57 Dean School of the Arts .... Dr. Newell DAYLEY
81 Dean Science & Health .... Dr. Samuel RUSHFORTH
50 Dean School of Business .... Dr. Norman WRIGHT
97 Dean University College .... Dr. K.D TAYLOR
53 Dean School of Education .... Dr. Briant J. FARNSWORTH
15 Assoc VP Human Res/Equity Officer .... Mr. Mark WIESENBERG
37 Director Financial Aid/Scholarship .... Ms. Trish HOWARD
19 Dir Public Safety/Chief of Police .... Mr. John BREWER
44 Director of Planned Giving .... Ms. Cristina PIANEZZOLA
09 Director Institutional Research .... Mr. Robert LOVERIDGE
41 Assoc VP Athletics .... Mr. Vince OTOUPAL
24 Director Studios & Engineering .... Mr. Will MCKINNON
40 Director Bookstore .... Ms. Louise BRIDGE
06 Registrar .... Ms. LuAnn SMITH
28 Director Multicultural Center .... Vacant
29 Director Alumni Relations .... Ms. Jeri L. ALLPHIN
38 Dir Career & Academic Counseling .... Mr. Adam BLACK
96 Director of Purchasing .... Mr. Ryan LINDSTROM

*Weber State University (D)

1001 University Circle, Ogden UT 84408-1001
County: Weber FICE Identification: 003680
Unit ID: 230782
Telephone: (801) 626-6000 Carnegie Class: Master's M
FAX Number: (801) 626-7922 Calendar System: Semester
URL: www.weber.edu
Established: 1889 Annual Undergrad Tuition & Fees (In-State): $4,786
Enrollment: 26,532 Coed
Affiliation or Control: State IRS Status: 501(c)3
Highest Offering: Master's
Program: Occupational; 2-Year Principally Bachelor's Creditable; Liberal Arts And General; Teacher Preparatory; Professional; Fine Arts Emphasis
Accreditation: NW, ADNUR, ART, BUS, BUSA, CAHIIM, CEA, CIDA, COARC, CONST, DH, EMT, ENGT, HSA, MLTAD, MT, MUS, NUR, SW, @TEAC, TED

02 President .... Dr. Charles A. WIGHT
05 Provost .... Dr. Michael B. VAUGHAN
10 Vice Pres Administrative Services .... Dr. Norm TARBOX
30 Vice Pres for Univ Advancement .... Dr. Brad MORTENSEN
32 Vice President Student Affairs .... Dr. Janet WINNIFORD
13 VP for Information Technology .... Dr. Bret R. ELLIS
88 Vice Provost Innovation & Econo Dev .... Mr. Alexander LAWRENCE
51 Vice Prov & Dean Continuing Educ .... Dr. Bruce DAVIS
35 Assoc VP for Student Affairs .... Dr. Brett PEROZZI
21 Asst VP for Financial Services .... Mr. Steven E. NABOR
15 Asst Vice Pres for Human Resources .... Ms. Cherrie NELSON
11 Asst VP for Administrative Services .... Mr. Jerry G. GRAYBEAL
18 Assoc VP for Facilities Management .... Mr. Kevin HANSEN
20 Associate Provost .... Dr. Bruce BOWEN
20 Associate Provost .... Dr. Ryan THOMAS
76 Dean Health Professions .... Dr. Yasmen SIMONIAN
50 Dean Business/Economics .... Dr. Jeffrey STEAGALL
53 Dean of Education .... Dr. Jack L. RASMUSSEN
83 Dean Social Behavioral Science .... Dr. Frank HARROLD
79 Dean of Arts & Humanities .... Dr. Madonne MINER
81 Dean of Science .... Dr. David MATTY
72 Dean of Applied Science & Tech .... Dr. David FERRO
35 Dean of Students .... Dr. Jeffrey J. HURST
06 Registrar .... Mr. Mark SIMPSON
19 Director Public Safety .... Vacant
29 Exec Director Alumni Association .... Ms. Nancy COLLINWOOD
38 Dir Counseling & Psycholog Services .... Dr. Dianna K. ABEL
36 Director of Career Services .... Dr. Winn STANGER
37 Director of Financial Aid .... Mr. Jed SPENCER
27 Director of Media Relations .... Mr. John L. KOWALEWSKI
07 Director of Admissions .... Mr. Scott TEICHERT
08 University Librarian .... Ms. Joan HUBBARD
22 Dir Equal Opportunity/Affirm Action .... Dr. Barry G. GOMBERG
41 Dir of Intercollegiate Athletics .... Mr. Jerry BOVEE
40 Bookstore Director .... Mr. Tim ECK
25 Director Sponsored Projects .... Mr. James TAYLOR
85 Director Services Intl Students .... Mr. Morteza EMAMI
23 Director Student Health Center .... Ms. Juliana P. LARSEN
26 Director Public Relations .... Ms. Allison B. HESS
91 Director Administrative Computing .... Vacant
43 University Counsel .... Dr. G. Richard HILL
39 Director Housing & Residence Life .... Mr. Daniel KILCREASE
96 Director of Purchasing .... Ms. Nancy E. EMENGER
28 Asst to President for Diversity .... Dr. Forrest C. CRAWFORD
92 Director of Honors Program .... Dr. Judy ELSLEY
88 Director Budget & Investments .... Mr. Brian L. SHUPPY
09 Director of Institutional Research .... Mr. Steve KERR
94 Coordinator of Women's Studies .... Dr. Parrilla DE KOKAL

*Dixie State College of Utah (E)

225 S 700 E, Saint George UT 84770-3876
County: Washington FICE Identification: 003671
Unit ID: 230171
Telephone: (435) 652-7500 Carnegie Class: Bac/Assoc
FAX Number: (435) 656-4001 Calendar System: Semester
URL: www.dixie.edu
Established: 1911 Annual Undergrad Tuition & Fees (In-State): $4,291
Enrollment: 9,086 Coed
Affiliation or Control: State IRS Status: 501(c)3
Highest Offering: Baccalaureate
Program: Occupational; 2-Year Principally Bachelor's Creditable; Liberal Arts And General; Teacher Preparatory; Professional

Accreditation: NW, ADNUR, COARC, DH, EMT, NUR, PTAA, RAD, SURGT, TEAC

02 President .... Dr. Stephen D. NADAULD
11 Vice Pres Administrative Services .... Mr. Paul MORRIS
05 Exec Vice Pres Academic Services .... Dr. Donna DILLINGHAM-EVANS
32 VP Student Services/Govt Relations .... Mr. Frank LOJKO
44 Vice Pres Development .... Mr. George WHITEHEAD
30 Vice President Advancement .... Ms. Christina SCHULTZ
49 Dean School Arts & Letters .... Dr. Don HINTON
66 Dean School Nursing/Allied Health .... Dr. Carole GRADY
50 Dean School Business .... Dr. William CHRISTENSEN
81 Dean Science & Technology .... Dr. Victor HASFURTHER
53 Dean Sch Education/Family Studies .... Dr. Brenda SABEY
51 Dean Continuing Education .... Mr. Steve BRINGHURST
35 Dean of Students .... Mr. Del BEATTY
13 Chief Information Officer .... Mr. Gary J. KOEVEN
10 Exec Director Business Services .... Mr. A. Scott TALBOT
15 Exec Director of Human Resources .... Ms. Pamela MONTRALLO
18 Executive Director Campus Services .... Ms. Sherry RUESCH
08 Director Library .... Ms. Daphne SELBERT
40 Executive Director Auxiliaries .... Mr. T. Randy JUDD
37 Director Student Financial Aid .... Mr. J. D ROBERTSON
84 Exec Dir Enrollment Services .... Mr. David ROOS
06 Registrar .... Ms. Julie STENDER
07 Director of Admissions .... Mr. Josh SINE
38 Director Student Counseling .... Mr. Rick PALMER
26 Director Public Relations .... Mr. Steve JOHNSON
18 Director Facilities Operation .... Mr. Doug WHITEHEAD
19 Director Security/Safety .... Mr. Don C. REID
41 Athletic Director .... Mr. Jason BOOTHE
39 Director Resident Life .... Mr. Seth GUBLER
09 Director of Institutional Research .... Ms. Andrea BROWN
04 Exec Assistant to the President .... Mrs. Marilyn LAMOREAUX
35 Director of Student Involvement .... Mr. Jordon SHARP
96 Director of Purchasing .... Ms. Jackie FREEMAN
29 Director of Alumni Relations .... Ms. Kalynn LARSON

*Snow College (A)

150 E College Avenue, Ephraim UT 84627-1299
County: Sanpete — FICE Identification: 003679
Unit ID: 230597
Telephone: (435) 283-7000 — Carnegie Class: Assoc/Pub-R-M
FAX Number: (435) 283-6879 — Calendar System: Semester
URL: www.snow.edu
Established: 1888 — Annual Undergrad Tuition & Fees (In-State): $3,220
Enrollment: 4,599 — Coed
Affiliation or Control: State — IRS Status: 501(c)3
Highest Offering: Associate Degree
Program: Occupational; 2-Year Principally Bachelor's Creditable
Accreditation: NW, ACBSP, MUS, PNUR, THEA

02 President .... Dr. Scott L. WYATT
05 Vice President for Academic Affairs .... Dr. Gary SMITH
10 VP Finance/Administrative Services .... Mr. Marvin DODGE
32 Vice President Student Success .... Mr. Craig MATHIE
35 Dean of Student Life .... Ms. Michelle BROWN
75 Dean Business & Applied Tech .... Mr. Mike MEDLEY
36 Director of Student Success .... Ms. Susan LARSEN
08 Director Library/Information Svcs .... Mr. Jon OSTLER
09 Director Institutional Research .... Ms. Beckie HERMANSEN
15 Director Human Resource Development .... Mr. David DYCHES
18 Director Physical Plant Operations .... Mr. Bob OLIVER
24 Director TTC .... Mr. Chase MITCHELL
39 Director Student Housing .... Ms. Jessica SIEGFRIED
41 Athletic Director .... Mr. Robert NIELSON
06 Registrar .... Ms. Margie ANDERSON
07 Director Admissions/Communications .... Mr. Greg DART
21 Associate Business Officer .... Mr. John RUELL
26 Chief Public Relations Officer .... Vacant
35 Director Student Affairs .... Ms. Lindsey FIELD
37 Director Student Financial Aid .... Mr. Jack DALENE
38 Director Student Counseling .... Mr. Allen RIGGS
96 Director of Purchasing .... Mr. Michael JORGENSEN
30 Chief Development .... Ms. Rosie CONNOR

† Granted candidacy at the Baccalaureate level.

*Salt Lake Community College (B)

4600 S Redwood Road, Salt Lake City UT 84123-3197
County: Salt Lake — FICE Identification: 005220
Unit ID: 230746
Telephone: (801) 957-4111 — Carnegie Class: Assoc/Pub-U-MC
FAX Number: (801) 957-4444 — Calendar System: Semester
URL: www.slcc.edu
Established: 1948 — Annual Undergrad Tuition & Fees (In-State): $3,342
Enrollment: 26,161 — Coed
Affiliation or Control: State — IRS Status: 501(c)3
Highest Offering: Associate Degree
Program: Occupational; 2-Year Principally Bachelor's Creditable
Accreditation: NW, ACBSP, ACFEI, ADNUR, DH, FUSER, MAC, OTA, PTAA, RAD, SURGT

02 President .... Dr. Cynthia A. BIOTEAU
05 Provost .... Dr. Chris PICARD
10 Business Services Vice Pres .... Mr. Dennis KLAUS
32 Student Services Vice President .... Dr. Deneece HUFTALIN
30 Vice Pres Institutional Advancement .... Ms. Alison MCFARLANE
86 Govt & Community Relations VP .... Mr. Tim SHEEHAN
20 Assoc Prov Educ/Cmty Partnerships .... Dr. Ryan CARSTENS
107 Asst VP/Dean Professnal & Econ Dev .... Ms. Karen GUNN
09 Asst Provost Inst Effectiveness .... Ms. Barbara GROVER
21 Asst Vice Pres of Budget Services .... Dr. Kimberly HENRIE
15 Asst Vice Pres of Human Resources .... Mr. Craig GARDNER
18 Assistant VP of Facilities .... Mr. Robert ASKERLUND
35 Dean of Students/Asst Vice Pres .... Dr. Marlin CLARK
45 Asst VP Student Planning & Support .... Dr. Nancy SINGER
84 Asst VP Student Enrollment Services .... Mr. Eric WEBER
26 AVP Inst Mktg/Communicatns .... Mr. Kent FROGLEY
49 Int Dean Arts/Commun/New Media .... Mr. Richard SCOTT
50 Dean School of Business .... Mr. Dennis BROMLEY
76 Int Dean Health Sciences .... Dr. Tim BEAGLEY
79 Dean Humanities & Social Sciences .... Dr. John MCCORMICK
81 Dean Science/Math & Engineering .... Dr. Clifton SANDERS
75 Dean Technical Specialties .... Mr. Rick BOUILLON
08 Director Learning Resources .... Vacant
41 Athletic Director .... Ms. Norma CARR
88 Director Student Ctr/Auxiliary Svc .... Mr. Jason BEAL
88 Executive Director Grand Theatre .... Mr. Richard SCOTT
38 Director Academic Advising .... Ms. Sonia PARKER
78 Director of Co-operative Education .... Mr. Jack HESLEPH
36 Dir Student Assessment/Placement .... Ms. Diana HARVEY
06 Registrar .... Ms. MaryEtta CHASE
37 Director Financial Aid .... Ms. Cristi MILLARD
19 Director Parking & Security .... Mr. Shane CRABTREE
27 Chief Information/Security Officer .... Mr. Bill ZOUMADAKIS
21 Controller/Business Manager .... Mr. Douglas HANSEN
22 EEO Director .... Ms. Mozelle ORTON
96 Director of Purchasing .... Ms. Lois WIESEMANN
25 Director of Grants & Contracts .... Ms. Susan SALEM
30 Exec Director of Development .... Vacant
09 Dir Institutional Research .... Mr. Joseph DIAZ
88 Int Coord EEO/Risk Management .... Ms. Natalie SEELEY
29 Alumni Coordinator .... Vacant

* *Utah State University Eastern* (C)

451 E 400 N, Price UT 84501-2699
Telephone: (435) 613-5000 — FICE Identification: 003676
Accreditation: &NW, ADNUR, PNUR

† Main campus is Utah State University in Logan, UT.

Vista College (D)

1785 E 1450 South, Suite 300, Clearfield UT 84015
County: Davis — FICE Identification: 025728
Unit ID: 377342
Telephone: (801) 774-9900 — Carnegie Class: Assoc/PrivFP
FAX Number: (801) 774-0111 — Calendar System: Other
URL: www.vistacollege.edu
Established: — Annual Undergrad Tuition & Fees: $18,600
Enrollment: 160 — Coed
Affiliation or Control: Proprietary — IRS Status: Proprietary
Highest Offering: Associate Degree
Program: Occupational
Accreditation: ACCSC

01 Director .... Mr. Scott TOMLIN

Western Governors University (E)

4001 S 700 E, Suite 700, Salt Lake City UT 84107-2533
County: Salt Lake — FICE Identification: 033394
Unit ID: 433387
Telephone: (801) 274-3280 — Carnegie Class: Master's L
FAX Number: (801) 274-3305 — Calendar System: Other
URL: www.wgu.edu
Established: 1996 — Annual Undergrad Tuition & Fees: $5,780
Enrollment: 39,000 — Coed
Affiliation or Control: Independent Non-Profit — IRS Status: 501(c)3
Highest Offering: Master's
Program: Teacher Preparatory; Professional
Accreditation: NW, CAHIIM, NURSE, TED

01 President .... Dr. Robert W. MENDENHALL
10 Vice Pres Finance/Administration .... David GROW
09 Vice Pres Quality/Inst Research .... Jason LEVIN
88 Vice Pres of Strategic Relations .... Ken SORBER
26 Vice President of Marketing .... Linda Jean WESTERN
15 Vice President of Human Resources .... Bonnie PATTEE
37 Vice Pres of Financial Aid .... Bob COLLINS
20 Associate Provost Student Mentoring .... Mitsu PHILLIPS
20 Assoc Provost Program Management .... Chris MALLETT
20 Associate Provost Academic Services .... Dr. Stacey LUDWIG-JOHNSON
20 Assoc Provost Teachers Col/Accred .... Dr. Phil SCHMIDT
76 Dean College of Health Professions .... Jan JONES-SCHENK
27 Chief Marketing Officer .... Patrick PARTRIDGE
88 Director of Assessment .... Mike RANDALL
26 Director of Public Relations .... Joan MITCHELL
84 Director of Enrollment .... Eddie RIOS

Westminster College (F)

1840 S 1300 E, Salt Lake City UT 84105-3697
County: Salt Lake — FICE Identification: 003681
Unit ID: 230807
Telephone: (801) 484-7651 — Carnegie Class: Master's M
FAX Number: (801) 466-6916 — Calendar System: Semester
URL: www.westminstercollege.edu
Established: 1875 — Annual Undergrad Tuition & Fees: $29,500
Enrollment: 3,301 — Coed
Affiliation or Control: Independent Non-Profit — IRS Status: 501(c)3
Highest Offering: Master's
Program: Liberal Arts And General; Teacher Preparatory; Professional
Accreditation: NW, AAB, ACBSP, ANEST, NURSE, PH, TEAC

01 President .... Dr. Brian L. LEVIN-STANKEVICH
05 Provost & VP Academic Affairs .... Dr. James E. SEIDELMAN
30 Vice Pres Institutional Advancement .... Mr. Stephen R. MORGAN
10 Vice Pres Finance & Administration .... Mr. Curtis W. RYAN
84 Vice President Enrollment Mgmt .... Vacant
44 Asst VP Institutional Advancement .... Ms. Lisa ACTOR
26 Exec Dir Intgrated Marketing Comm .... Ms. Sheila YORKIN
49 Dean School of Arts & Sciences .... Dr. Lisa GENTILE
66 Dean School of Nursing/Hlth Science .... Dr. Sheryl STEADMAN
50 Dean School of Business .... Dr. Jin WANG
53 Dean School of Education .... Dr. Robert A. SHAW
88 Assoc Provost Academic Support/ALO .... Dr. Paul PRESSON
35 Dean of Students .... Mr. Mark FERNE
29 Director Alumni Relations .... Ms. Michelle BARBER-LYHNAKIS
32 Assoc Provost Student Development .... Mr. Mark FERNE
09 Assoc Provost Inst Research/Assess .... Ms. Nichole GREENWOOD
88 Assoc Provost Integrative Learning .... Ms. Annalisa HOLCOMBE
28 Assoc Provost Diversity/Global Lrng .... Dr. Nohemy SOLORZANO-THOMPSON
13 Chief Information Officer .... Mr. Robert ALLRED
88 Director of New Ventures .... Mr. Rex FALKENRATH
43 General Counsel/Risk Management .... Vacant
21 Director of Accounting Services .... Ms. Jennifer MEDRANO
15 Director of Human Resources .... Mr. Darin JONES
06 Registrar .... Ms. Mindy WENNERGREN
37 Director of Financial Aid .... Ms. Jenny RYAN
07 Director of Admissions .... Ms. Elizabeth KEY
18 Director Plant/Facilities .... Mr. Richard A. BROCKMYER
36 Director of Career Resource Center .... Mr. Mike CALDWELL
08 Director of Library .... Ms. Diane VANDERPOL
96 Director of Purchasing .... Mr. Alfred W. JOHANSEN
35 Dir Student Involvement/Leadership .... Ms. Trisha TEIG
39 Asst Director of Residential Life .... Ms. Aimee FROST
88 Director Start Center .... Ms. Deborah VICKERY
88 Director of Conferences .... Mr. Jeff BROWN
19 Director of Campus Patrol/Safety .... Mr. Saeed REZAI
41 Director of Athletics .... Mr. Shay WYATT
42 Director of Spiritual Life .... Ms. Jan SAAED
38 Director of Campus Counseling .... Ms. Lisa JONES
92 Director of Honors Program .... Dr. Richard BADENHAUSEN
91 Database Administrator .... Mr. Kyle RIMA

VERMONT

Bennington College (G)

One College Drive, Bennington VT 05201-6003
County: Bennington — FICE Identification: 003682
Unit ID: 230816
Telephone: (802) 442-5401 — Carnegie Class: Bac/A&S
FAX Number: (802) 447-4269 — Calendar System: Semester
URL: www.bennington.edu
Established: 1932 — Annual Undergrad Tuition & Fees: $45,680
Enrollment: 826 — Coed
Affiliation or Control: Independent Non-Profit — IRS Status: 501(c)3
Highest Offering: Master's
Program: Liberal Arts And General
Accreditation: EH

01 President .... Dr. Mariko SILVER
05 Dean of the College .... Ms. Isabel ROCHE
10 VP and Chief Financial Officer .... Ms. Laura KRAUSE
45 Sr VP for Planning & Administration .... Mr. David G. REES
30 VP for External Relations .... Ms. Paige BARTELS
07 VP for Admissions and Communication .... Ms. Janet L. MARSDEN
20 Associate Dean of the College .... Mr. Duncan DOBBELMANN

Bread Loaf School of English in Vermont (H)

4265 Ripton 125, Middlebury VT 05753
Telephone: (802) 443-5418 — Identification: 770119
Accreditation: &EH

† Main campus is Middlebury College in Middlebury, VT.

Burlington College (I)

351 North Avenue, Burlington VT 05401-8477
County: Chittenden — FICE Identification: 012183
Unit ID: 230825
Telephone: (802) 862-9616 — Carnegie Class: Bac/A&S
FAX Number: (802) 660-4331 — Calendar System: Semester
URL: www.burlington.edu
Established: 1972 — Annual Undergrad Tuition & Fees: $22,860
Enrollment: 198 — Coed
Affiliation or Control: Independent Non-Profit — IRS Status: 501(c)3
Highest Offering: Master's
Program: Liberal Arts And General
Accreditation: EH

01 President .... Ms. Christine A. PLUNKETT
05 Vice Pres Academic/Student Affairs .... Dr. Stephen ST ONGE
10 Director of Administration/Finance .... Vacant
29 Dir Community & Alumni Relations .... Vacant
32 Director of Student Life .... Mr. Greg LITCHFIELD
18 Director of Physical Plant .... Mr. John HAWKINS
07 Director of Admissions .... Ms. Gillian HOMSTED
13 Director Information Technology .... Mr. Jordan M. YOUNG

06 Registrar ... Ms. Rachel MOYER
08 Dir Library/Information Services ... Ms. Jessica ALLARD
37 Director of Financial Aid ... Ms. Lindy WALSH

Champlain College (A)

163 S Willard Street, Burlington VT 05402-0670
County: Chittenden　FICE Identification: 003684
Unit ID: 230852
Telephone: (802) 860-2700　Carnegie Class: Bac/Diverse
FAX Number: (802) 860-2750　Calendar System: Semester
URL: www.champlain.edu
Established: 1956　Annual Undergrad Tuition & Fees: $31,250
Enrollment: 3,235　Coed
Affiliation or Control: Independent Non-Profit　IRS Status: 501(c)3
Highest Offering: Master's
Program: Liberal Arts And General; Teacher Preparatory; Professional
Accreditation: EH, RAD, SW

01 President ... Dr. David F. FINNEY
05 Provost ... Dr. Robin ABRAMSON
10 Vice President Finances ... David J. PROVOST
84 Vice President Enrollment ... Ian MORTIMER
30 Vice President Advancement ... Michele RICHARDSON
32 Vice President Student Life ... Dr. Leslie AVERILL
13 Asst Vice Pres Information Systems ... Theodore LASKARIS
36 Assistant Vice Pres Career Services ... Sarah POTTER
15 Assoc Vice Pres Human Resources ... Mary Margaret LEE
20 Senior Associate Provost ... Dr. Michelle MILLER
104 Associate Provost-Education Abroad ... Dr. James CROSS
101 VP & Secretary of Corporation ... Katie HAWLEY
53 Dean Education/Human Stds Div ... Dr. Laurel BONGIORNO
88 Dean Comm/Creative Media Div ... Dr. Paula WILLOQUET-MARICONDI
50 Dean Business Division ... Dr. David STRUBLER
77 Int Dean Information Tech/Science ... Dr. Thomas MANN
51 Exec Dir Continuing Education ... Vacant
09 Institutional Effectiveness Dir ... Susan POWERS
07 Director of Admissions ... Sarah ANDRIANO
06 Registrar ... Rebecca PETERSON
37 Director of Financial Aid ... Kristi JOVELL
38 Director of Counseling ... Carol MORAN-BROWN
18 Director of Physical Plant ... Thomas BONNETTE
19 Director of Security & Safety ... Richard LONG
23 Director Health Services ... Cissy MCCLELLAN
22 Director of Affirmative Action ... Mary Margaret LEE
39 Director of Residential Life ... Danelle BERUBE
85 Foreign Students Advisor ... Kathy LYNN
21 Treasurer ... Shelley NAVARI
27 Public Information & News Director ... Stephen MEASE
29 Director of Alumni Relations ... Erik OLIVER
08 Director Library ... Janet COTTRELL
28 Dir Student Diversity/Inclusion ... Ame LAMBERT
103 Director Workforce Development ... Melissa HERSH
102 Dir Foundation/Corporate Relations ... Susan PANKEY
04 Executive Assistant ... Diana AGUSTA
40 Bookstore Manager ... Susan BROWN

College of St. Joseph (B)

71 Clement Road, Rutland VT 05701-3899
County: Rutland　FICE Identification: 003685
Unit ID: 231077
Telephone: (802) 773-5900　Carnegie Class: Master's S
FAX Number: (802) 776-5258　Calendar System: Semester
URL: www.csj.edu
Established: 1956　Annual Undergrad Tuition & Fees: $21,200
Enrollment: 314　Coed
Affiliation or Control: Roman Catholic　IRS Status: 501(c)3
Highest Offering: Master's
Program: 2-Year Principally Bachelor's Creditable; Liberal Arts And General; Teacher Preparatory; Professional
Accreditation: EH

01 President ... Dr. Richard B. LLOYD
05 Interim Academic Dean ... Dr. David BALFOUR
07 Dean of Admissions ... Vacant
32 Dean of Student Services ... Mr. Robert P. LUKASKIEWICZ
37 Director of Financial Aid ... Mrs. Julie ROSMUS
30 Dir Development/Alumni Relations ... Mr. Bates CHILDRESS
41 Director of Athletics ... Mr. Phil BARTLETT
06 Registrar ... Mr. Greg CHAMBERLAND
14 CIS Administrator ... Mr. Raymond GIBBS
35 Director of Student Support Svcs ... Ms. Susan BOYCE
21 Controller ... Mrs. Karen REYNOLDS
18 Chief Facilities/Physical Plant ... Mr. Thomas BELAND
10 Business Manager ... Mrs. Kristie JOHNSON
49 Interim Chair Arts & Sciences ... Dr. Jonas PRIDA
50 Chair Business ... Dr. Robert GODDARD
53 Chair Education ... Dr. Maria BOVE
15 Chair Psychology/Human Services ... Dr. Michael KESLER
08 Librarian ... Ms. Doreen MCCULLOUGH

Goddard College (C)

123 Pitkin Road, Plainfield VT 05667-9432
County: Washington　FICE Identification: 003686
Unit ID: 230889
Telephone: (800) 468-4888　Carnegie Class: Master's M
FAX Number: (802) 454-1029　Calendar System: Semester
URL: www.goddard.edu
Established: 1863　Annual Undergrad Tuition & Fees: $14,218
Enrollment: 703　Coed
Affiliation or Control: Independent Non-Profit　IRS Status: 501(c)3
Highest Offering: Master's
Program: Liberal Arts And General; Teacher Preparatory
Accreditation: EH

01 President ... Dr. Barbara VACARR
05 Academic Dean ... Dr. Jacqueline HAYES
10 Chief Financial Officer ... Ms. Faith BROWN
100 Spec Asst to Pres/Chief of Staff ... Ms. Sarah JARVIS
30 Chief Advancement Officer ... Ms. Lauren MOYE
32 Associate Dean of Community Life ... Ms. Susan A. WILSON
06 Registrar ... Mr. Josh CASTLE
15 Director of Human Resources ... Ms. Jill MUHR
37 Director of Financial Aid ... Ms. Beverly JENE
88 Director of Campus Services ... Mr. Paul SHPER
08 Director of Information Access ... Ms. Clara BRUNS
18 Director of Facilities Operations ... Mr. Scott BLANCHARD
12 Director of Port Townsend Campus ... Ms. Erin FRISTAD
21 Director of Business Office ... Ms. Sherri MOLLEUR
88 Manager of WGDR/WGDH Radio ... Mr. Kris GRUEN

Green Mountain College (D)

1 Brennan Circle, Poultney VT 05764-1199
County: Rutland　FICE Identification: 003687
Unit ID: 230898
Telephone: (802) 287-8000　Carnegie Class: Bac/A&S
FAX Number: (802) 287-8099　Calendar System: Semester
URL: www.greenmtn.edu
Established: 1834　Annual Undergrad Tuition & Fees: $32,192
Enrollment: 733　Coed
Affiliation or Control: Independent Non-Profit　IRS Status: 501(c)3
Highest Offering: Master's
Program: Liberal Arts And General; Teacher Preparatory
Accreditation: EH

01 President ... Dr. Paul J. FONTEYN
05 Vice President Academic Affairs ... Dr. William M. THROOP
10 Vice Pres Finance/Operations ... Mr. Robert J. GOULD
32 Vice President Student Affairs ... Dr. Joseph E. PETRICK
84 Vice Pres Enrollment Management ... Mr. Robert J. GOULD
04 Executive Assistant to President ... Ms. Jeanne V. ROOT
20 Dean of Faculty ... Dr. Thomas J. MAUHS-PUGH
30 Director of Development ... Ms. Mary Lou WILLITS
06 Registrar ... Ms. Sharon L. HOFFMAN
18 Director of Facilities ... Mr. Glenn LAPLANTE
19 Director of Public Safety ... Mr. Steven BROWN
26 Director of Public Relations ... Mr. Kevin COBURN
41 Athletic Director ... Mr. Keith BOSLEY
08 Director Library & Information Svcs ... Mr. Paul MILLETTE
85 Director of International Pgms ... Mr. Joel SHAPIRO
13 Director Computing & Info Mgmt ... Mr. Jeffrey WRIGHT
42 Chaplain ... Ms. Shirley OSKAMP
29 Dir Alumni Relations/Annual Giving ... Vacant
36 Director of Career Counseling ... Ms. Maia HANRON-SANFORD
92 Director of College Honors Program ... Dr. Jennifer SELLERS
37 Director Student Financial Aid ... Ms. Wendy ELLIS
15 Director Human Resources ... Ms. Janie EVANS
38 Director Student Counseling ... Vacant
09 Director of Institutional Research ... Ms. Sharon L. HOFFMAN
40 Manager of Bookstore ... Ms. Heather LYNG

Landmark College (E)

River Road South, Putney VT 05346
County: Windham　FICE Identification: 025326
Unit ID: 247649
Telephone: (802) 387-4767　Carnegie Class: Assoc/PrivNFP
FAX Number: (802) 387-6868　Calendar System: Semester
URL: www.landmark.edu
Established: 1985　Annual Undergrad Tuition & Fees: $49,500
Enrollment: 473　Coed
Affiliation or Control: Independent Non-Profit　IRS Status: 501(c)3
Highest Offering: Baccalaureate
Program: 2-Year Principally Bachelor's Creditable
Accreditation: EH

01 President ... Dr. Peter A. EDEN
03 Senior Vice President ... Dr. Brent BETIT
05 Academic Dean ... Dr. Adrienne MAJOR
30 Vice Pres Institutional Advancement ... Ms. Chelsea GWYTHER
10 Vice Pres Administration/Finance ... Mr. Jon MACCLAREN
26 Director Marketing Communication ... Mr. Mark DIPIETRO
84 Vice Pres Enrollment Management ... Mr. Gregory MATTHEWS
04 Assistant to the President ... Vacant
88 Dean Short-Term Pgms/Transfer Svcs ... Dr. John NISSEN
35 Dean of Students ... Mr. Michael LUCIANI
18 Director of Physical Plant ... Mr. James LOVERING
08 Head Librarian ... Ms. Jennifer LANN
13 Chief Technology Officer ... Ms. Corinne BELL
06 Registrar ... Ms. Karen DAMIAN
41 Director Activities/Athletics ... Mr. James AUSTIN
37 Director Student Financial Aid ... Ms. Jennifer DESMARAIS
38 Director of Student Counseling ... Mrs. Julie OSHERSON
23 Director of Health Services ... Ms. Simone HOLTON
40 Bookstore Manager ... Ms. Kimberly JUDD

Marlboro College (F)

PO Box A, Marlboro VT 05344-9999
County: Windham　FICE Identification: 003690
Unit ID: 230940
Telephone: (802) 257-4333　Carnegie Class: Bac/A&S
FAX Number: (802) 257-4154　Calendar System: Semester
URL: www.marlboro.edu
Established: 1946　Annual Undergrad Tuition & Fees: $38,110
Enrollment: 291　Coed
Affiliation or Control: Independent Non-Profit　IRS Status: 501(c)3
Highest Offering: Master's
Program: Liberal Arts And General
Accreditation: EH

01 President ... Ms. Ellen M. LOVELL
10 Senior Financial Mgmt Officer ... Ms. Anne PRATT
05 Dean of Faculty/Graduate Educ ... Mr. Richard GLEJZER
07 Dean of Admissions ... Ms. Nicole CURVIN
32 Dean of Students ... Mr. Ken SCHNECK
58 Associate Dean Graduate School ... Mr. Sean CONLEY
84 Dir Enrollment Stdt Svc at Grad Ctr ... Mr. Joseph HESLIN
46 Chief Planning & Budget Officer ... Mr. Bryant MORGAN
08 Librarian ... Ms. Emily ALLING
06 Registrar ... Mr. Tobias GELSTON
30 Chief Advancement Officer ... Ms. Lisa M. CHRISTENSEN
44 Annual Giving Director ... Ms. Patricia CAVANAUGH
18 Director of Plant Operations ... Mr. Dan J. COTTER
82 World Studies Director ... Ms. Cathy OSMAN
40 Bookstore Manager ... Ms. Rebecca BARTLETT

Marlboro College Graduate School (G)

28 Vernon Street, Brattleboro VT 05301
Telephone: (802) 258-9200　Identification: 770120
Accreditation: &EH

† Main campus is Marlboro College in Marlboro, VT.

Middlebury College (H)

Old Chapel, Middlebury VT 05753-6200
County: Addison　FICE Identification: 003691
Unit ID: 230959
Telephone: (802) 443-5000　Carnegie Class: Bac/A&S
FAX Number: (802) 443-2071　Calendar System: 4/1/4
URL: www.middlebury.edu
Established: 1800　Annual Undergrad Tuition & Fees: $57,075
Enrollment: 2,516　Coed
Affiliation or Control: Independent Non-Profit　IRS Status: 501(c)3
Highest Offering: Doctorate
Program: Liberal Arts And General
Accreditation: EH

01 President ... Dr. Ronald D. LIEBOWITZ
05 Vice President for Academic Affairs ... Dr. Tim SPEARS
10 Vice Pres for Finance/Treasurer ... Mr. Patrick J. NORTON
88 Sr Vice Pres/Philanthropic Advisor ... Mr. Michael SCHOENFELD
58 VP Language Sch/Sch Abroad/Grad Pgm ... Dr. Michael GEISLER
30 Vice Pres College Advancement ... Mr. James R. KEYES
20 VP Plng/Assess/Dir Col Self Study ... Dr. Susan BALDRIDGE
26 Vice President Communications ... Mr. Bill BURGER
37 Assoc VP Student Financial Services ... Ms. Kim DOWNS
21 Assoc VP Budget/Financial Planning ... Ms. Kristen C. ANDERSON
15 Assoc VP for HR/Organiz Development ... Ms. Drew MACAN
29 Assoc VP for Alumni Relations ... Ms. Margaret STOREY GROVES
06 AVP Planning/Assess/Col Registrar ... Mr. LeRoy GRAHAM
20 Dean Faculty Dev & Rsch/Curriculum ... Dr. James RALPH
20 Dean of the Faculty ... Dr. Andrea LLOYD
28 Dean of College/Chf Diversity Ofcr ... Dr. Shirley COLLADO
08 Dean of Library & Information Svcs ... Mr. Michael D. ROY
07 Dean of Admissions ... Mr. Gregory B. BUCKLES
21 Asst Treasurer/Dir of Business Svcs ... Mr. Thomas CORBIN
32 Assoc Dn of the Col/Dir Pub Safety ... Ms. Elizabeth B. BURCHARD
38 Exec Dir Health & Counseling Svcs ... Dr. Augustus JORDAN
42 Chaplain ... Ms. Laurel JORDAN
41 Director of Athletics ... Mr. Erin QUINN
26 Director of Public Affairs ... Ms. Sarah RAY
88 President MIIS ... Dr. Sunder RAMASWAMY
40 Bookstore Manager ... Ms. Georgia BEST

† Tuition figure is a comprehensive fees figure.

New England Culinary Institute (I)

56 College Street, Montpelier VT 05602-9720
County: Washington　FICE Identification: 022540
Unit ID: 230977
Telephone: (802) 223-6324　Carnegie Class: Spec/Other
FAX Number: (802) 225-3280　Calendar System: Quarter
URL: www.neci.edu
Established: 1980　Annual Undergrad Tuition & Fees: $30,140
Enrollment: 517　Coed
Affiliation or Control: Proprietary　IRS Status: Proprietary
Highest Offering: Baccalaureate
Program: Occupational; Technical Emphasis
Accreditation: ACCSC

01 CEO/President ... Mr. Francis VOIGT
11 Chief Financial Officer ... Mr. Phillip HARKER
05 Program Director of Education ... Mr. Lyndon VIRKLER
88 Exec Chef & VP Culinary Operations ... Chef Jean-Louis GERIN
88 Chair Baking & Pastry Programs ... Chef Kathleen KESSLER
88 Chair HRM Program ... Ms. Michelle FORD
20 Director Academic Svcs ... Ms. Laureen GAUTHIER
106 Chair Online Programs ... Chef Peg CHECCI
06 Registrar ... Ms. Liz FITZGERALD
07 Director of Admissions ... Mr. Dwight CROSS
08 Head Librarian ... Ms. Rachel BORNSTEIN
15 Director Human Resources ... Ms. Jennifer ZETARSKI

18 Director of Facilities .... Mr. William COLGAN
36 Manager Career Services .... Mr. Garth WALKER
20 Sr Dir Operations & Education .... Chef David MILES

Norwich University (A)

158 Harmon Drive, Northfield VT 05663-1000
County: Washington FICE Identification: 003692
Unit ID: 230995
Telephone: (802) 485-2000 Carnegie Class: Master's L
FAX Number: (802) 485-2032 Calendar System: Semester
URL: www.norwich.edu
Established: 1819 Annual Undergrad Tuition & Fees: $31,550
Enrollment: 2,321 Coed
Affiliation or Control: Independent Non-Profit IRS Status: 501(c)3
Highest Offering: Master's
Program: Liberal Arts And General; Teacher Preparatory; Professional
Accreditation: EH, ACBSP, ENG, NURSE

01 President .... Dr. Richard W. SCHNEIDER
05 Senior VPAA & Dean of Faculty .... Dr. Guiyou HUANG
107 VP CGCS .... Dr. William CLEMENTS
32 VP Student Affs/Enrollment/Tech .... Dr. Frank VANECEK
30 Vice Pres Institutional Advancement .... Mr. David J. WHALEY
13 VP Strategic Partnership .... Mr. Phillip SUSMANN
107 Dean Col of Professional Schools .... Mr. Aron TEMKIN
83 Dean College of Liberal Arts .... Dr. Andrea TALENTINO
81 Dean College of Science/Mathematics .... Dr. Michael MCGINNIS
88 Dean School of National Services .... Col. Lawrence OLIVER
29 Asst VP for Alumni and Vol Progrms .... Mr. Paul BOVA
20 Associate VP Academic Affairs .... Dr. Joseph BYRNE
04 Assistant to President .... Ms. Laura AMELL
10 Chief Financial Officer .... Ms. Lauren WOBBY
11 Chief Administrative Officer .... Mr. David MAGIDA
88 Director Center for Student Success .... Ms. Shelby GILE
88 Coord Office of Communications .... Mr. Mark ALBURY
35 Dean of Students .... Ms. Martha MATHIS
09 Dir Inst Research/Effectiveness .... Ms. Ellalou ZIRBLIS
15 Director of Human Resources .... Mr. Jay WISNER
08 Head Librarian .... Mr. Ravil VELI
41 Athletic Director .... Mr. Anthony A. MARIANO
18 Director Facilities/Operations .... Mr. Bizhan YAHYAZADEH
37 Director Student Financial Aid .... Mr. Martin DANIELS
38 Director Student Counseling .... Dr. Melvin MILLER
07 Director of Admissions .... Ms. Sherri GILMORE

Saint Michael's College (B)

One Winooski Park, Colchester VT 05439-0001
County: Chittenden FICE Identification: 003694
Unit ID: 231059
Telephone: (802) 654-2000 Carnegie Class: Bac/A&S
FAX Number: (802) 654-2297 Calendar System: Semester
URL: www.smcvt.edu
Established: 1904 Annual Undergrad Tuition & Fees: $38,690
Enrollment: 2,410 Coed
Affiliation or Control: Roman Catholic IRS Status: 501(c)3
Highest Offering: Master's
Program: Liberal Arts And General; Teacher Preparatory
Accreditation: EH, CEA

01 President .... Dr. John J. NEUHAUSER
04 Assistant to the President .... Ms. Tara L. ARCURY
05 Vice Pres Academic Affairs .... Dr. Karen A. TALENTINO
10 Vice President for Finance .... Mr. Neal ROBINSON
32 Vice President for Student Affairs .... Ms. Dawn M. ELLINWOOD
84 Vice President for Enrollment .... Mr. Jerry E. FLANAGAN
16 Vice President for Human Resources .... Mr. Michael J. NEW
30 VP for Institutional Advancement .... Mr. Patrick J. GALLIVAN
20 Dean of the College .... Dr. Jeffrey A. TRUMBOWER
42 Director Edmundite Campus Ministry .... Rev. Brian J. CUMMINGS, SSE
07 Director of Admission .... Ms. Jacqueline MURPHY
37 Director Student Financial Services .... Mr. Daniel R. COUTURE
06 Registrar .... Mr. John D. SHEEHEY
09 Director of Institutional Research .... Mr. John P. KULHOWVICK
29 Director of Alumni/Parent Relations .... Ms. Angela ARMOUR
35 Director Student Activities .... Ms. Grace A. KELLY
93 Dir Multicultural Student Affairs .... Mr. Moise ST. LOUIS
39 Director of Residence Life .... Mr. Louis DIMASI
88 Associate Dean of the College .... Dr. Jonathan L. D'AMORE
104 Director of Study Abroad .... Ms. Peggy H. IMAI
92 Honors Program Faculty Coordinator .... Dr. Nicholas CLARY
94 Coord of Gender/Women's Studies .... Dr. Michael BOSIA
08 Dir Library & Information Services .... Mr. John K. PAYNE
13 Chief Information Officer .... Mr. William O. ANDERSON
14 Director of Information Tech .... Vacant
26 Dir of Marketing/Communications .... Dr. Buff L. LINDAU
86 Dir Government/Community Relations .... Ms. Marilyn E. CORMIER
19 Director of Public Safety .... Mr. Peter D. SOONS
18 Director of Facilities .... Mr. David A. CUTLER
38 Director of Personal Counseling .... Ms. Linda HOLLINGDALE
36 Director of Career Development .... Ms. Christine CLARY
23 Director of Health Services .... Ms. Mary MASSON
41 Director of Athletics .... Dr. Geraldine KNORTZ
44 Director of Advancement Services .... Ms. Linda V. DONAHUE
102 Director of Foundation Relations .... Ms. Angela IRVINE
88 Financial Accounting Manager .... Ms. Shirley J. GOODELL-LACKEY
21 Director of Finance .... Ms. Mary Jane RUSSELL
96 Director of Business Services .... Mr. Robert ROBINSON
40 Bookstore Manager .... Mr. Stephen MCMAHON
31 Community Service Coordinator .... Ms. Heidi ST. PETER
105 Dir of Web Site Development .... Mr. Brian MACDONALD
44 Director of Individual Giving .... Ms. Terri P. SELBY

SIT (C)

Kipling Road, Brattleboro VT 05302-0676
County: Windham FICE Identification: 008860
Unit ID: 231068
Telephone: (802) 257-7751 Carnegie Class: Master's L
FAX Number: (802) 258-3248 Calendar System: Other
URL: www.worldlearning.org
Established: 1964 Annual Undergrad Tuition & Fees: $20,200
Enrollment: 1,130 Coed
Affiliation or Control: Independent Non-Profit IRS Status: 501(c)3
Highest Offering: Master's
Program: Liberal Arts And General; Teacher Preparatory; Professional
Accreditation: EH

01 President .... Mr. Don STEINBERG
05 Senior VP of Academic Affairs/CAO .... Dr. John LUCAS
10 CFO .... Ms. Nancy R. BROCK
16 Senior VP of Global Human Resources .... Mr. Ross GIBSON
43 General Counsel .... Ms. Lisa RAE
58 Dean SIT Graduate Institute .... Mr. Daniel YALOWITZ
84 Dean External Rels/Strtgc Enrol Mgt .... Ms. Laurie BLACK
30 Director of Advancement .... Mr. Tom NAVIN
88 Director Language and Culture Dept .... Ms. Beatriz FANTINI
07 Director of Admissions .... Ms. Kim DEREGO
06 Registrar .... Ms. Ginny NELLIS
37 Assistant Director Financial Aid .... Ms. Erin CRAW
32 Director of Campus Life .... Mr. Stephen SWEET

Southern Vermont College (D)

982 Mansion Drive, Bennington VT 05201-6002
County: Bennington FICE Identification: 003693
Unit ID: 231086
Telephone: (802) 442-5427 Carnegie Class: Bac/Diverse
FAX Number: (802) 447-4695 Calendar System: Semester
URL: www.svc.edu
Established: 1926 Annual Undergrad Tuition & Fees: $21,725
Enrollment: 465 Coed
Affiliation or Control: Independent Non-Profit IRS Status: 501(c)3
Highest Offering: Baccalaureate
Program: Occupational; Liberal Arts And General
Accreditation: EH, RAD

01 President .... Ms. Karen GROSS
10 Chief Financial Officer/COO .... Ms. Claire WURMFELD
04 Executive Assistant .... Ms. Colleen LITTLE
41 Director of Athletics .... Mr. Michael MCDONOUGH
05 Provost .... Dr. Albert C. DECICCIO
20 Associate Academic Dean .... Vacant
50 Chair Business .... Dr. Stacey HILLS
66 Chair Nursing .... Vacant
79 Chair of Humanities .... Dr. Jennifer RICHARDSON
81 Chair of Science and Technology .... Dr. Barry FLANARY
83 Chair of Social Sciences .... Mr. Scott STEIN
08 Director Learning Resources .... Ms. Sarah SANFILIPPO
06 Registrar .... Mr. Eric PARSONS
36 Director of Career Services .... Ms. Denise SPENCER
18 Director of Facilities .... Mr. Mark J. KLAUDER
32 Dean of Students .... Ms. Anne M. HOPKINS GROSS
38 Director of Counseling .... Mr. Michael GOODWIN
39 Director of Residence Life .... Ms. Sara PATCH
19 Director of Security .... Mr. George MARSHALL
07 Director of Admissions .... Mr. Jeremy GIBBONS
37 Director of Financial Aid .... Ms. Joel PHELPS
30 Dean of Development .... Vacant
27 Director of Communications .... Vacant
29 Dir Alumni Relations/Annual Fund .... Vacant
16 Director of Human Resources .... Ms. Sue METZNER
88 Coord Learning Disabilities .... Mr. David A. LINDENBERG

Sterling College (E)

PO Box 72, Craftsbury Common VT 05827-0072
County: Orleans FICE Identification: 021435
Unit ID: 231095
Telephone: (802) 586-7711 Carnegie Class: Bac/A&S
FAX Number: (802) 586-2596 Calendar System: Semester
URL: www.sterlingcollege.edu
Established: 1958 Annual Undergrad Tuition & Fees: $29,744
Enrollment: 105 Coed
Affiliation or Control: Independent Non-Profit IRS Status: 501(c)3
Highest Offering: Baccalaureate
Program: Liberal Arts And General
Accreditation: EH

01 President .... Mr. Matthew DERR
05 Dean of the College and Faculty .... Dr. Pavel CENKL
36 Dean of Work .... Ms. Jennifer PAYNE
07 Director of Admissions & Fin Aid .... Mr. Tim PATTERSON
04 Administrative Asst to President .... Ms. Michele MARTIN
10 Director of Finance .... Ms. Deborah CLARK
08 Librarian .... Ms. Petra VOGEL
18 Director of Facilities .... Mr. Steve SMITH
32 Dean of Students .... Ms. Favor ELLIS
30 Director of Advancement .... Ms. Judy BEVANS
06 Registrar .... Ms. Laurie LAGGNER
26 Director of Communications .... Ms. Christian FEUERSTEIN

University of Vermont (F)

South Prospect Street, Burlington VT 05405-0160
County: Chittenden FICE Identification: 003696
Unit ID: 231174
Telephone: (802) 656-3131 Carnegie Class: RU/H
FAX Number: N/A Calendar System: Semester
URL: www.uvm.edu
Established: 1791 Annual Undergrad Tuition & Fees (In-State): $15,718
Enrollment: 13,097 Coed
Affiliation or Control: State IRS Status: 501(c)3
Highest Offering: Doctorate
Program: Liberal Arts And General; Teacher Preparatory; Professional
Accreditation: EH, BUS, CACREP, CLPSY, DIETC, DIETD, ENG, IPSY, MED, MT, NMT, NURSE, PTA, RTT, SP, SPAA, SW, TED

01 President .... Dr. E. Thomas SULLIVAN
05 Senior Vice President & Provost .... Dr. David V. ROSOWSKY
10 VP for Finance & Treasurer & CFO .... Mr. Richard H. CATE
86 VP University Relations & Admin .... Dr. Thomas J. GUSTAFSON
46 Interim VP Research .... Dr. John N. EVANS
30 CEO & President The UVM Foundation .... Mr. O. Richard BUNDY, III
43 VP Legal Affairs & General Counsel .... Ms. Francine T. BAZLUKE
84 Vice Pres Enrollment Management .... Mr. Christopher H. LUCIER
20 Assoc Prov Faculty & International .... Dr. Gayle R. NUNLEY
20 Assoc Provost Curricular Affairs .... Dr. Brian V. REED
32 Assoc Provost Student & Campus Life .... Dr. Annie STEVENS
28 VP for Human Resources & Diversity .... Dr. Wanda R. HEADING-GRANT
100 VP for Executive Operations .... Dr. Gary L. DERR
18 Assoc VP Admin & Facility Services .... Mr. William P. BALLARD
15 Assoc VP Human Resource Services .... Ms. Barbara L. JOHNSON
35 Dean of Students .... Dr. David A. NESTOR
29 Assoc VP for Alumni Relations .... Mr. Alan E. RYEA
63 Dean College of Medicine .... Dr. Frederick C. MORIN, III
66 Dean Nursing & Health Sciences .... Dr. Patricia A. PRELOCK
49 Dean Arts & Sciences .... Dr. Antonio CEPEDA-BENITO
47 Dean Agriculture & Life Sciences .... Dr. Thomas C. VOGELMANN
54 Dean Engineering & Math Sciences .... Dr. Luis A. GARCIA
53 Dean Education & Social Services .... Dr. Fayneese S. MILLER
50 Dean Business Administration .... Dr. Sanjay SHARMA
92 Dean Honors College .... Dr. S. Abu RIZVI
65 Int Dean Environment & Natural Res .... Dr. Jon D. ERICKSON
56 Dean Extension .... Dr. Douglas O. LANTAGNE
58 Interim Dean Graduate College .... Dr. Cynthia J. FOREHAND
51 Dean Continuing & Distance Educ .... Ms. Cynthia L. BELLIVEAU
08 Dean Libraries & Learning Res & CIO .... Ms. Mara R. SAULE
06 Registrar .... Mr. Keith P. WILLIAMS
09 Director Institutional Research .... Dr. John F. RYAN
27 Director University Communications .... Mr. Enrique CORREDERA
13 Int Asc Chief Information Officer .... Ms. Julia H. RUSSELL
25 Assoc VP Research Administration .... Ms. Ruth A. FARRELL
21 University Budget Director .... Mr. Alberto CITARELLA
19 Chief of Police Services .... Ms. Lianne M. TUOMEY
41 Director of Athletics .... Dr. Robert CORRAN
36 Director Career Services .... Ms. Pamela K. GARDNER
23 Director Ctr for Health & Wellbeing .... Dr. Jon K. PORTER
38 Counsel/Psych Services Program Dir .... Dr. Todd N. WEINMAN
39 Director Residential Life .... Ms. Stacey A. MILLER
40 Director University Bookstore .... Mr. Jay E. MENNINGER
85 Director Intl Education Services .... Ms. Kimberly A. HOWARD
102 COO & VP The UVM Foundation .... Mr. Shane M. JACOBSON
44 Director Planned Giving .... Ms. Becky P. ARNOLD
22 Director AA & EO .... Mr. Jes S. KRAUS
07 Director Graduate Admissions .... Mr. Ralph M. SWENSON, III
07 Director Undergraduate Admissions .... Dr. Elizabeth A. WISER
37 Director Student Financial Services .... Ms. Marie D. JOHNSON
96 Director Procurement Services .... Ms. Natalie L. GUILLETTE
94 Director Women's Center .... Ms. LuAnn K. ROLLEY
24 Access/Media Services Librarian .... Mr. Aaron F. NICHOLS
101 Board of Trustees Coordinator .... Ms. Corinne B. THOMPSON

Vermont College of Fine Arts (G)

36 College Street, Montpelier VT 05602-3145
County: Washington FICE Identification: 003697
Unit ID: 455992
Telephone: (802) 828-8600 Carnegie Class: Assoc/PrivNFP4
FAX Number: (802) 828-8649 Calendar System: Semester
URL: www.vcfa.edu
Established: 2008 Annual Graduate Tuition & Fees: $20,306
Enrollment: 334 Coed
Affiliation or Control: Independent Non-Profit IRS Status: 501(c)3
Highest Offering: Master's; No Undergraduates
Program: Liberal Arts And General; Fine Arts Emphasis
Accreditation: EH

01 President .... Mr. Thomas Christopher GREENE
05 Academic Dean .... Mr. Matthew MONK
10 Chief Financial Ofcr/VP for Admin .... Ms. Erica METZGER HARE
26 VP for External Affairs .... Ms. Lyn CHAMBERLIN

† Carnegie Graduate Instructional Program classification is Postbac-A&S

Vermont Law School (H)

164 Chelsea Street, PO Box 96,
South Royalton VT 05068-0096
County: Windsor FICE Identification: 011934
Unit ID: 231147
Telephone: (802) 831-1000 Carnegie Class: Spec/Law
FAX Number: (802) 831-1163 Calendar System: Semester
URL: www.vermontlaw.edu

Established: 1972 Annual Graduate Tuition & Fees: $46,110
Enrollment: 570 Coed
Affiliation or Control: Independent Non-Profit IRS Status: 501(c)3
Highest Offering: First Professional Degree; No Undergraduates
Program: Professional
Accreditation: EH, LAW

01 President & Dean ... Mr. Marc MIHALY
05 Vice Dean for Academic Affairs ... Mr. Mark LATHAM
36 VP Operations/Office Career Svcs ... Mr. Dennis STERN
10 Vice President for Finance & Admin ... Ms. Lorraine ATWOOD
88 Asoc Dn Env Law Pgm/Dir Env Law Ctr ... Ms. Melissa SCANLAN
32 Assoc Dean Student Affs & Diversity ... Ms. Shirley JEFFERSON
84 Assoc Dean for Enrollment Mgmt ... Ms. Cheryl HANNA
30 Exec Director Inst Advancement ... Mr. Matt RIZZO
101 Special Assistant to the President ... Ms. Kim EVANS
15 Director Human Resources ... Ms. Diane HAYES
08 Dir Cornell Library & Professor ... Mr. Carl A. YIRKA
21 Comptroller ... Mr. James OUELLETTE
06 Registrar ... Ms. Maureen MORIARTY
37 Director of Financial Aid ... Ms. Cathy MULLINS
18 Physical Plant Director ... Ms. Lori CAMPBELL
26 Dir of Marketing/Communications ... Mr. Peter GLENSHAW
13 Director of Information Technology ... Mr. Duncan SUTHERLAND
04 Exec Asst to the President/Dean ... Ms. Tori JONES
40 Manager Barrister's Bookstore ... Ms. Amy MCDOWELL

*Vermont State Colleges System Office (A)

PO Box 7, Montpelier VT 05601
County: Washington FICE Identification: 029162
Unit ID: 231156
Telephone: (802) 224-3000 Carnegie Class: N/A
FAX Number: (802) 224-3035
URL: www.vsc.edu

01 Chancellor ... Mr. Timothy J. DONOVAN
04 Exec Assistant to the Chancellor ... Ms. Elaine SOPCHAK
43 Vice President/General Counsel ... Mr. William REEDY
10 Vice Pres/Chief Financial Officer ... Mr. Thomas ROBBINS
86 Director Cmty Rels & Public Policy ... Mr. Daniel SMITH
27 Chief Information Officer ... Ms. Linda HILTON
18 Director of Facilities ... Mr. Richard ETHIER
91 Director Admin Information Systems ... Ms. Dianne POLLACK
13 Director of System Info Tech ... Mr. Rick BLOOD
15 Director of Human Resources ... Ms. Nancy SHAW
09 Director of Institutional Research ... Ms. Hope SWANSON
88 Director of Payroll/Benefits ... Ms. Tracy SWEET

*Castleton State College (B)

62 Alumni Drive, Castleton VT 05735-4454
County: Rutland FICE Identification: 003683
Unit ID: 230834
Telephone: (802) 468-5611 Carnegie Class: Bac/A&S
FAX Number: (802) 468-6470 Calendar System: Semester
URL: www.castleton.edu
Established: 1787 Annual Undergrad Tuition & Fees (In-State): $9,864
Enrollment: 2,156 Coed
Affiliation or Control: State IRS Status: 501(c)3
Highest Offering: Master's
Program: Liberal Arts And General; Teacher Preparatory
Accreditation: EH, ADNUR, SW

02 President ... Mr. David S. WOLK
04 Exec Assistant to the President ... Ms. Rita B. GENO
05 Academic Dean ... Dr. Tony PEFFER
11 Dean of Administration ... Mr. Scott DIKEMAN
10 Controller ... Ms. Heidi WHITNEY
32 Dean of Students ... Mr. Dennis PROULX
30 Dean of College Advancement ... Ms. Colleen KLATT
84 Dean of Enrollment ... Mr. Maurice OUIMET
26 Director of Communications ... Mr. Ennis DULING
15 Director of Human Resources ... Ms. Janet HAZELTON
35 Assistant Dean for Campus Life ... Ms. Victoria ANGIS
06 Registrar ... Ms. Lori PATTEN
08 Director Calvin Coolidge Library ... Ms. Sandra DULING
37 Director Student Financial Aid ... Ms. Kathy O'MEARA
53 Director of Student Teaching ... Mr. Tim CLEARY
18 Director of Physical Plant ... Mr. Chuck LAVOIE
27 Director of College Relations ... Mr. Jeff WELD
36 Dir of Career Planning/Placement ... Ms. Judith CARRUTHERS
23 Wellness Center Director ... Ms. Martha COULTER
38 Director Student Counseling ... Vacant

*Community College of Vermont (C)

PO Box 489, Montpelier VT 05601
County: Washington FICE Identification: 011167
Unit ID: 230861
Telephone: (802) 828-2800 Carnegie Class: Assoc/Pub-R-L
FAX Number: (802) 828-2805 Calendar System: Semester
URL: www.ccv.edu
Established: 1970 Annual Undergrad Tuition & Fees (In-State): $7,090
Enrollment: 6,928 Coed
Affiliation or Control: State IRS Status: 501(c)3
Highest Offering: Associate Degree
Program: Occupational; 2-Year Principally Bachelor's Creditable
Accreditation: EH

02 President ... Ms. Joyce M. JUDY
03 Executive Dean ... Ms. Susan P. HENRY
11 Dean of Administration ... Dr. Barbara MARTIN
05 Dean of Academic Services ... Ms. Linda GABRIELSON
32 Dean of Student Services ... Ms. Deborah STEWART
84 Assoc Dean Enrollment Services ... Ms. Pam CHISHOLM
20 Associate Academic Dean ... Ms. Darlene MURPHY
20 Associate Academic Dean ... Ms. Diane HERMANN-ARTIM
12 Exec Director of Academic Center ... Ms. Penne CIARALDI
12 Exec Director of Academic Center ... Mr. Elmer KIMBALL
12 Exec Director of Academic Center ... Ms. Dee STEFFAN
12 Exec Director of Academic Center ... Ms. Tapp BARNHILL
24 Dean of Learning Technologies ... Mr. Eric SAKAI
15 Director Personnel Services ... Mrs. Lisa YAEGER
06 Registrar ... Mr. Thomas ARNER
07 Director of Admissions ... Mr. Adam WARRINGTON
09 Dir Institutional Research/Planning ... Ms. Laura MASSELL
88 Director Student Support Services ... Ms. Heather WEINSTEIN
29 Director Alumni Relations/Develop ... Vacant
26 Chief Public Relations Officer ... Ms. Josh LARKIN
10 Chief Business Officer ... Vacant
88 Director of Secondary Initiatives ... Ms. Natalie SEARLE
36 Director of Career Training Program ... Vacant
26 Dir of Marketing/Communications ... Ms. Janette SHAFFER

*Johnson State College (D)

337 College Hill, Johnson VT 05656-9898
County: Lamoille FICE Identification: 003688
Unit ID: 230913
Telephone: (802) 635-2356 Carnegie Class: Master's S
FAX Number: (802) 635-1230 Calendar System: Semester
URL: www.jsc.edu
Established: 1828 Annual Undergrad Tuition & Fees (In-State): $10,543
Enrollment: 1,783 Coed
Affiliation or Control: State IRS Status: 501(c)3
Highest Offering: Master's
Program: 2-Year Principally Bachelor's Creditable; Liberal Arts And General; Teacher Preparatory; Professional
Accreditation: EH

02 President ... Ms. Barbara E. MURPHY
05 Academic Dean ... Dr. Dan REGAN
11 Dean Administration/Chief Tech Ofcr ... Ms. Sharron R. SCOTT
32 Dean of Students ... Dr. David BERGH
84 Dean of Enrollment Services ... Ms. Penny HOWRIGAN
35 Asst Dean of Students ... Ms. Michele WHITMORE
06 Registrar ... Mr. Douglas EASTMAN
51 Co-Director External Degree Program ... Mr. David CAVANAGH
51 Co-Director of External Degree Prgm ... Ms. Valerie EDWARDS
18 Director of Physical Plant ... Mr. Woody DIONNE
41 Director of Athletics & Recreation ... Mr. Jamey VENTURA
38 Director of Counseling Services ... Ms. Cynthia HENNARD
30 Director Development/Alumni Rels ... Ms. Lauren PHILIE
36 Director Advising/Career Svcs ... Ms. Sara KINERSON
89 Director of First-Year Experience ... Ms. Margo WARDEN
19 Director Safety & Security ... Mr. Michael PALAGONIA
26 Dir College Communications ... Ms. Deborah BOUTON
37 Director Student Financial Aid ... Ms. Lisa CUMMINGS
15 Director Human Resources ... Ms. Sharon SCOTT
08 Librarian ... Mr. Joseph FARARA
79 Chair Humanities ... Dr. Paul SILVER
53 Chair Education ... Dr. David MCGOUGH
65 Chair Environ/Health Sciences ... Dr. Elizabeth DOLCI
57 Co-Chair Fine & Performing Arts ... Ms. Bethany PLISSEY
57 Co-Chair Fine & Performing Arts ... Ms. Mary MARTIN
50 Chair Business/Economics ... Mr. Henrique CEZAR
60 Chair Writing/Literature ... Dr. Sharon TWIGG
81 Chair Mathematics ... Dr. Julie THEORET
83 Co-Chair Behavioral Sciences ... Dr. Susan GREEN
83 Co-Chair Behavioral Sciences ... Dr. Eleanor WEBBER

*Lyndon State College (E)

1001 College Road, PO Box 919,
Lyndonville VT 05851-0919
County: Caledonia FICE Identification: 003689
Unit ID: 230931
Telephone: (802) 626-6200 Carnegie Class: Bac/Diverse
FAX Number: (802) 626-9770 Calendar System: Semester
URL: www.lyndonstate.edu
Established: 1911 Annual Undergrad Tuition & Fees (In-State): $10,286
Enrollment: 1,497 Coed
Affiliation or Control: State IRS Status: 501(c)3
Highest Offering: Master's
Program: Liberal Arts And General; Teacher Preparatory; Professional
Accreditation: EH, EXSC

02 President ... Dr. Joseph A. BERTOLINO
05 Provost/Dean of Academic Affairs ... Dr. Kellie H. BEAN
10 Dean of Administration ... Mr. Wayne T. HAMILTON
20 Associate Provost/Dean of Faculty ... Dr. Alison S. LATHROP
11 Dean of Institutional Advancement ... Mr. Robert E. WHITTAKER
32 Dean of Student Affairs ... Mr. Jonathan M. DAVIS
07 Director of Admissions ... Mr. Vincent U. MALONEY
88 Associate Academic Dean Enrollment ... Dr. Heather A. BOUCHEY
18 Director of Physical Plant ... Mr. Thomas R. ARCHER
91 Chief Technology Officer ... Mr. Michael A. DENTE
29 Director of Development & Alumni ... Ms. Hannah J. MANLEY
21 Controller ... Ms. Sheilah M. LADD
08 Library Director ... Mr. Garet B. NELSON
06 Registrar ... Ms. Kathryn J. MAIELI

39 Director of Residential Life ... Ms. Erin S. ROSSETTI
41 Director of Athletics ... Mr. Christopher T. UMMER
37 Director of Financial Aid ... Ms. Tanya W. BRADLEY
36 Director of Career Services ... Vacant
19 Director Public Safety ... Mr. George B. HACKING
88 Director Student Academic Support ... Mr. Robert G. MCCABE
88 Director of Broadcast Operations ... Ms. Darlene R. BOLDUC
88 Dir of Student Academic Development ... Ms. Debra M. BAILIN
26 Director Communications & Marketing ... Mr. Keith B. CHAMBERLIN
88 Director of Advising Resources ... Ms. Kathleen E. GOLD
89 Director of First-Year Experience ... Ms. Donna J. KEELY
15 Director Human Resources ... Ms. Sandra L. FRANZ

*Vermont Technical College (F)

PO Box 500, Randolph Center VT 05061-0500
County: Orange FICE Identification: 003698
Unit ID: 231165
Telephone: (802) 728-1000 Carnegie Class: Bac/Assoc
FAX Number: (802) 728-1390 Calendar System: Semester
URL: www.vtc.edu
Established: 1866 Annual Undergrad Tuition & Fees (In-State): $12,344
Enrollment: 1,645 Coed
Affiliation or Control: State IRS Status: 501(c)3
Highest Offering: Baccalaureate
Program: Occupational; 2-Year Principally Bachelor's Creditable; Professional; Technical Emphasis
Accreditation: EH, ADNUR, COARC, DH, ENGT, PNUR

02 President ... Dr. Philip CONROY, JR.
05 Dean Academic Affairs ... Mr. Philip PETTY
11 Dean of Administration ... Mr. Geoffrey LINDEMER
32 Dean of Enrollment/Student Affairs ... Mr. John PATERSON
13 Int Chief Technology Officer ... Mr. James SMITH
88 Exec Dir Strategic Col Operations ... Mr. Jay PATERSON
30 Assoc Dean Inst Advancement ... Ms. Martha TROMBLEY OAKES
35 Assistant Dean Student Life ... Ms. Mary Kathryn JUSKIEWICZ
06 Registrar ... Ms. Sarah LEVIN
37 Director Financial Aid ... Ms. Catherine MCCULLOUGH
29 Director Alumni Relations ... Ms. Ingrid VAN STEAMBURG
19 Director Security/Safety ... Mr. Emile FREDETTE
18 Director Physical Plant ... Mr. Theodore MANAZIR
36 Career Counseling/Placement ... Ms. Karry BOOSKA
66 Director Nursing Education ... Ms. Anna GERAC
15 Director of Human Resources ... Ms. Pamela ANKUDA
26 Director of Marketing ... Ms. Leandre WALDO-JOHNSON
40 Manager Bookstore ... Mr. Joe HIRAK

VIRGINIA

Advanced Technology Institute (G)

5700 Southern Boulevard, Virginia Beach VA 23462-2409
County: City of Virginia Beach FICE Identification: 031275
Unit ID: 231411
Telephone: (757) 490-1241 Carnegie Class: Assoc/PrivFP
FAX Number: (757) 499-5929 Calendar System: Semester
URL: www.auto.edu
Established: 1993 Annual Undergrad Tuition & Fees: $23,150
Enrollment: 600 Coed
Affiliation or Control: Proprietary IRS Status: Proprietary
Highest Offering: Associate Degree
Program: Occupational; Technical Emphasis
Accreditation: ACCSC

01 Campus President ... Mr. Dick DAIGLE
05 Chief Academic Officer ... Mr. Chenek PICKA
07 Director of Admissions ... Mr. Mike CORCORAN
32 Director of Student Services ... Mr. Kirk CLAYTON
37 Director Student Financial Aid ... Mr. Chad MARTS

American National University (H)

1813 E Main Street, Salem VA 24153-4598
County: Independent City FICE Identification: 003726
Unit ID: 232797
Telephone: (540) 986-1800 Carnegie Class: Assoc/PrivFP4
FAX Number: (540) 986-1344 Calendar System: Quarter
URL: www.an.edu
Established: 1886 Annual Undergrad Tuition & Fees: $11,412
Enrollment: 576 Coed
Affiliation or Control: Proprietary IRS Status: Proprietary
Highest Offering: Master's
Program: Business Emphasis
Accreditation: ACICS, EMT, MAC

01 President ... Mr. Frank E. LONGAKER
03 Vice President VA & WV Division ... Ms. Lenora S. DOWNING
05 Campus Director ... Mr. Ron BRADBURY
07 Regional Director of Admissions ... Mr. Larry W. STEELE

Appalachian College of Pharmacy (I)

1060 Dragon Road, Oakwood VA 24631
County: Buchanan FICE Identification: 041806
Unit ID: 449922
Telephone: (276) 498-4190 Carnegie Class: Spec/Health
FAX Number: (276) 498-4193 Calendar System: Semester
URL: www.acpharm.org
Established: 2003 Annual Graduate Tuition & Fees: $35,800
Enrollment: 223 Coed

Affiliation or Control: Independent Non-Profit IRS Status: 501(c)3
Highest Offering: Doctorate; No Undergraduates
Program: Professional
Accreditation: SC, PHAR

01 President .... Mr. Michael G. MCGLOTHLIN
05 Dean .... Dr. Susan L. MAYHEW

Appalachian School of Law (A)

PO Box 2825, Grundy VA 24614-2825
County: Buchanan FICE Identification: 035593
Unit ID: 432348
Telephone: (800) 895-7411 Carnegie Class: Spec/Law
FAX Number: (276) 935-8261 Calendar System: Semester
URL: www.asl.edu
Established: 1995 Annual Undergrad Tuition & Fees: $31,525
Enrollment: 350 Coed
Affiliation or Control: Independent Non-Profit IRS Status: 501(c)3
Highest Offering: First Professional Degree
Program: Professional
Accreditation: LAW

01 Dean & President .... Ms. Lucy MCGOUGH
08 Director of Library .... Mr. Charlie CONDON
36 Director of Career Services .... Ms. Janie CASTLE
13 Director of Information Services .... Mr. Brian PRESLEY
31 Director of Community Services .... Ms. Jina M. SAULS
32 Dir Student Services/Admissions .... Ms. Mary RAGLAND
30 Director of Development .... Ms. Karen HARVEY

Argosy University, Washington DC (B)

1550 Wilson Boulevard, Suite 600,
Arlington VA 22209-2435
Telephone: (703) 526-5800 Identification: 666788
Accreditation: &WC, CACREP, CLPSY

† Main campus is Argosy University, Orange County in Orange, CA.

Atlantic University (C)

215 67th Street, Virginia Beach VA 23451-8101
County: Virginia Beach Identification: 666653
Unit ID: 231402
Telephone: (757) 631-8101 Carnegie Class: Not Classified
FAX Number: (757) 631-8096 Calendar System: Trimester
URL: www.atlanticuniv.edu
Established: 1930 Annual Graduate Tuition & Fees: $18,576
Enrollment: 13,000 Coed
Affiliation or Control: Independent Non-Profit IRS Status: 501(c)3
Highest Offering: Master's; No Undergraduates
Program: Professional
Accreditation: DETC

01 CEO .... Kevin TODESCHI
05 Dir Academic & Administrative Affs .... James VAN AUKEN
07 Dean Admissions/Academic Advisings .... Candis COLLINS
06 Registrar .... Lynne MICELI
88 Education Services Coordinator .... Rachel ALVIDREZ
84 Enrollment Clerk .... Megan STORY

Averett University (D)

420 W Main Street, Danville VA 24541-3692
County: Independent City FICE Identification: 003702
Unit ID: 231420
Telephone: (434) 791-5600 Carnegie Class: Bac/Diverse
FAX Number: (434) 791-5637 Calendar System: Semester
URL: www.averett.edu
Established: 1859 Annual Undergrad Tuition & Fees: $27,500
Enrollment: 2,307 Coed
Affiliation or Control: Independent Non-Profit IRS Status: 501(c)3
Highest Offering: Master's
Program: Liberal Arts And General; Teacher Preparatory
Accreditation: SC

01 President .... Dr. Tiffany M. FRANKS
32 Executive Vice President .... Mr. Charles S. HARRIS
05 Vice Pres for Academic Affairs .... Dr. Janet LAUGHLIN
10 Vice President Business & Finance .... Mr. Thomas DAVIS
30 Vice Pres Institutional Advancement .... Mr. Albert RAWLEY
15 Director of Human Resources .... Mrs. Kathie TUNE
84 Vice Pres Enrollment Management .... Vacant
37 Director Student Financial Services .... Mr. Carl BRADSHER
21 Controller .... Mr. Andy FITCH
08 Director of Library .... Ms. Elaine DAY
36 Director of Career Services .... Ms. Petrina CARTER
06 Registrar .... Mrs. Janet ROBERSON
26 Dir of Marketing/Communications .... Mr. Ed JONES
29 Director Alumni Relations .... Mr. Dan HAYES
09 Dir Institutional Research/Effect .... Dr. Metta ALSOBROOK
07 Director of Admissions .... Mr. Joel NESTER
18 Chief Facilities/Physical Plant .... Mr. Alonzo JONES
35 Director of Student Affairs .... Mr. Bill WOODWARD
38 Director of Student Counseling .... Mrs. Joan KAHWAJY-ANDERSON

Aviation Institute of Maintenance (E)

10640 Davidson Place, Manassas VA 20109
County: Prince William FICE Identification: 038834
Unit ID: 445762
Telephone: (703) 257-5515 Carnegie Class: Not Classified
FAX Number: (703) 257-5523 Calendar System: Semester
URL: www.aviationmaintenance.edu
Established: 2001 Annual Undergrad Tuition & Fees: $39,097
Enrollment: 100 Coed
Affiliation or Control: Proprietary IRS Status: Proprietary
Highest Offering: Associate Degree
Program: Occupational; Technical Emphasis
Accreditation: ACCSC

01 Campus Executive Director .... Keith ZOBEL
11 Director of Compliance and Admin .... Teresa GOBER
05 Director of Education .... Richard BAKER
10 Bursar .... Dominique DOUGLAS

Baptist Theological Seminary at Richmond (F)

8040 Villa Park Drive, Henrico VA 23228
County: Independent City FICE Identification: 031169
Unit ID: 366793
Telephone: (804) 355-8135 Carnegie Class: Spec/Faith
FAX Number: (804) 355-8182 Calendar System: Semester
URL: www.btsr.edu
Established: 1991 Annual Graduate Tuition & Fees: $13,970
Enrollment: 102 Coed
Affiliation or Control: Independent Non-Profit IRS Status: 501(c)3
Highest Offering: Doctorate; No Undergraduates
Program: Professional; Religious Emphasis
Accreditation: THEOL

01 President .... Dr. Ronald W. CRAWFORD
05 Dean .... Dr. Timothy GILBERT
30 VP Institutional Advancement .... Mr. Timothy Bruce HEILMAN
10 Dir Business Affairs & Facilities .... Dr. James F. PEAK, JR.
07 Director Admissions & Recruitment .... Ms. Tiffany KELLOGG PITTMAN
06 Registrar .... Ms. Erin SPENGEMAN

Bethel College (G)

1705 Todds Lane, Hampton VA 23666
County: Hampton City FICE Identification: 041538
Unit ID: 458113
Telephone: (757) 826-1883 Carnegie Class: Not Classified
FAX Number: (757) 826-5436 Calendar System: Semester
URL: www.bethel-college.com
Established: 2004 Annual Undergrad Tuition & Fees: $8,000
Enrollment: 71 Coed
Affiliation or Control: Assemblies Of God Church IRS Status: 501(c)3
Highest Offering: Baccalaureate
Program: Professional; Religious Emphasis
Accreditation: BI

01 President .... Mr. Glenn REYNOLDS
05 Academic Dean .... Dr. Ron DEBERRY
32 Dean of Students .... Dr. Jerry GOULD
06 Registrar .... Ms. Nanette BARTHOLOMEW
08 Library Director .... Ms. Janell SANFORD

Bluefield College (H)

3000 College Drive, Bluefield VA 24605-1799
County: Tazewell FICE Identification: 003703
Unit ID: 231554
Telephone: (276) 326-3682 Carnegie Class: Bac/Diverse
FAX Number: (276) 326-4288 Calendar System: Semester
URL: www.bluefield.edu
Established: 1922 Annual Undergrad Tuition & Fees: $22,390
Enrollment: 734 Coed
Affiliation or Control: Baptist IRS Status: 501(c)3
Highest Offering: Master's
Program: Liberal Arts And General; Teacher Preparatory; Professional
Accreditation: SC, TEAC

01 President .... Dr. David W. OLIVE
04 Assistant to the President .... Mrs. Diane T. SHOTT
05 VP for Academic Affairs .... Vacant
30 VP for Advancement .... Mrs. Ruth BLANKENSHIP
10 VP for Finance & Admin .... Ms. Laura WHITE
32 VP for Student Development .... Rev. David TAYLOR
84 VP for Enrollment Management .... Mr. Trent ARGO
07 Director of Adult Admissions .... Mrs. Cathy PAYNE
06 Registrar .... Mrs. Amanda JORDAN
08 Director of Library Services .... Ms. Barbara GILLESPIE
26 Director of Public Relations .... Mr. Chris SHOEMAKER
29 Director of Alumni Relations .... Mr. Mark HIPES
09 Director of Institutional Research .... Mrs. Amanda JORDAN
37 Director of Financial Aid .... Ms. Carly KESTNER
42 Campus Minister .... Rev. David TAYLOR
41 Athletic Director .... Mr. Peter DRYER
40 Bookstore Manager .... Mrs. Judy AKERS
18 Director of Maintenance .... Mr. Blair TAYLOR
19 Director of Campus Safety .... Dr. Kelly WALLS
15 Human Resources Director .... Ms. Judy PEDNEAU

Bon Secours Memorial College of Nursing (I)

8550 Magellan Pkwy, Ste 1100, Richmond VA 23227
County: Henrico FICE Identification: 010043
Unit ID: 233356
Telephone: (804) 627-5300 Carnegie Class: Not Classified
FAX Number: (804) 627-5330 Calendar System: Semester
URL: www.bsmcon.edu
Established: 1961 Annual Undergrad Tuition & Fees: $13,464
Enrollment: 290 Coed
Affiliation or Control: Independent Non-Profit IRS Status: 501(c)3
Highest Offering: Baccalaureate
Program: Liberal Arts And General; Nursing Emphasis
Accreditation: ACICS, NURSE

05 Vice Pres Academic Affairs/Provost .... Dr. Melanie H. GREEN
66 Dean of the College .... Dr. James MCCANN
20 Asst Dean of Curriculum/Instruction .... Vacant
11 Dean of Administration and Finance .... Dr. Regina WELCH

Bridgewater College (J)

402 E College Street, Bridgewater VA 22812-1599
County: Rockingham FICE Identification: 003704
Unit ID: 231581
Telephone: (540) 828-8000 Carnegie Class: Bac/A&S
FAX Number: (540) 828-5479 Calendar System: 4/1/4
URL: www.bridgewater.edu
Established: 1880 Annual Undergrad Tuition & Fees: $28,500
Enrollment: 1,756 Coed
Affiliation or Control: Church Of The Brethren IRS Status: 501(c)3
Highest Offering: Baccalaureate
Program: Liberal Arts And General; Teacher Preparatory
Accreditation: SC

01 President .... Dr. David W. BUSHMAN
03 Executive Vice President .... Mr. Roy W. FERGUSON, JR.
05 Vice Pres/Dean of Academic Affairs .... Dr. Carol A. SCHEPPARD
10 Vice Pres for Finance & Treasurer .... Ms. Anne B. KEELER
26 Dir of Marketing & Communications .... Ms. Abbie PARKHURST
84 Vice President for Enrollment Mgmt .... Mr. Reggie WEBB
30 Director Institutional Advancement .... Mr. Todd D. LILLEY
18 Director of Sustainability .... Mr. Teshome H. MOLALENGE
40 Bookstore Manager .... Ms. Brandi LIVESAY
20 Associate Dean of Academic Affairs .... Dr. Edward W. HUFFSTETLER
32 Dean of Students .... Dr. William D. MIRACLE
36 Director of Career Services .... Ms. Sherry TALBOTT
88 Director of Academic Support Svcs .... Dr. Raymond W. STUDWELL, II
42 Chaplain .... Rev. Robert R. MILLER
07 Director of Admissions .... Mr. Jarret L. SMITH
37 Director of Financial Aid .... Mr. Scott D. MORRISON
21 Director of Budget & Analysis .... Mr. Jeffrey FIKE
13 Director of Info Tech Center .... Ms. Kristy K. RHEA
41 Director of Athletics .... Mr. Curtis L. KENDALL
38 Director of Counseling Services .... Mr. Randall HOOK
29 Director of Alumni Relations .... Ms. Ellen B. MILLER
09 Director of Institutional Research .... Ms. Dawn S. DALBOW
15 Director of Human Resources .... Ms. Victoria L. INGRAM
08 Library Director .... Mr. Andrew L. PEARSON
06 Registrar .... Ms. Cynthia K. HOWDYSHELL
21 Controller .... Ms. Mary S. SCHWAB
27 Editor/Dir of Media Relations .... Mr. Charles R. CULBERTSON
18 Director of Facilities .... Mr. David R. VANDEVANDER
19 Campus Police Chief .... Mr. Nicholas P. PICERNO
28 Minority Mentor .... Mr. James E. RAEFORD
23 Director of Student Health Services .... Ms. Paige FRENCH
35 Associate Dean of Students .... Ms. Crystal LYNN
28 Director of Multicultural Services .... Ms. Stephanie WILSON
88 Director of Dining Services .... Ms. Mary SPEIR

Bryant & Stratton College (K)

8141 Hull Street Road, North Chesterfield VA 23235-6411
Telephone: (804) 745-2444 Identification: 666496
Accreditation: &M, MAC

† Main campus is Bryant & Stratton College in Buffalo, NY.

Bryant & Stratton College (L)

301 Centre Pointe Drive, Virginia Beach VA 23462-4417
Telephone: (757) 499-7900 FICE Identification: 010061
Accreditation: &M, MAC

† Main campus is Bryant & Stratton College in Buffalo, NY.

California University of Management and Sciences Virginia (M)

400 North Washington Street, Falls Church VA 22046
Telephone: (703) 663-8088 Identification: 666734
Accreditation: ACICS

† Main campus is California University of Management and Sciences in Anaheim, CA.

Career Training Solutions (N)

10304 Spotsylvania Avenue, Ste. 400,
Fredericksburg VA 22408-8605
County: Stafford FICE Identification: 036543
Unit ID: 441858
Telephone: (540) 373-2200 Carnegie Class: Assoc/PrivFP
FAX Number: (540) 373-4465 Calendar System: Other
URL: www.careertrainingsolutions.com
Established: 2000 Annual Undergrad Tuition & Fees: N/A
Enrollment: 175 Coed

Affiliation or Control: Proprietary IRS Status: Proprietary
Highest Offering: Associate Degree
Program: Occupational
Accreditation: COE

01 Chief Executive Officer/President ....Ms. A. Christine CARROLL

The Catholic Distance University (A)

120 E Colonial Highway, Hamilton VA 20158-9012
County: Loudoun FICE Identification: 041242
Unit ID: 377430
Telephone: (540) 338-2700 Carnegie Class: Not Classified
FAX Number: (540) 338-4788 Calendar System: Trimester
URL: www.cdu.edu
Established: 1983 Annual Undergrad Tuition & Fees: $3,500
Enrollment: 800 Coed
Affiliation or Control: Independent Non-Profit IRS Status: 501(c)3
Highest Offering: Master's
Program: Religious Emphasis
Accreditation: DETC

01 President ....Dr. Marianne E. MOUNT
58 Dean Graduate Programs ....Dr. Robert ROYAL
05 Undergraduate Dean ....Fr. Bevil BRAMWELL
88 Dean of Catechetical Programs ....Sr. Mary Margaret SCHLATHER
06 Graduate Registrar ....Ms. Theresa SNIDER
06 Undergraduate Registrar ....Mrs. Kathleen WOODDELL
08 Head Librarian ....Vacant
10 Director of Finance ....Mr. Don FONG
30 Director of Development ....Vacant
26 Director of Communications ....Mrs. Marcia REGNERY
35 Director Student Affairs ....Vacant
07 Director of Admissions ....Ms. Carol CIULLO
29 Director Alumni Relations ....Vacant
37 Director Student Financial Aid ....Vacant
13 Director Computing Information Mgmt ....Mrs. Carol DALEY

Centra College of Nursing (B)

907 Lakeside Dr, Ste A, Lynchburg VA 24501
FICE Identification: 021758
Unit ID: 232618
Telephone: (434) 200-3070 Carnegie Class: Not Classified
FAX Number: (434) 200-5239 Calendar System: Semester
URL: www.centrahealth.com
Established: Annual Undergrad Tuition & Fees: $7,414
Enrollment: 167 Coed
Affiliation or Control: Independent Non-Profit IRS Status: 501(c)3
Highest Offering: Associate Degree
Program: Nursing Emphasis
Accreditation: ABHES, DNUR, PNUR

01 Dean ....Ms. Kathy JOHNSON

Central Baptist Theological Seminary (C)

2221 Centerville Turnpike, Virginia Beach VA 23464-6847
County: Virginia Beach FICE Identification: 039663
Telephone: (757) 479-3706 Carnegie Class: Not Classified
FAX Number: (757) 479-4232 Calendar System: Semester
URL: www.baptistseminary.edu
Established: 1995 Annual Undergrad Tuition & Fees: $4,320
Enrollment: 85 Coed
Affiliation or Control: Baptist IRS Status: 501(c)3
Highest Offering: Master's
Program: Professional; Religious Emphasis
Accreditation: TRACS

01 President ....Mr. Daniel K. DAVEY
05 Chief Academic Officer ....Mr. Eric J. LEHNER
07 Director of Admissions ....Mr. Kyle C. DUNHAM
10 Financial Officer ....Dr. Thomas KEISER
06 Registrar ....Mr. Edward ESTES
09 Dir Institutional Effectiveness ....Dr. Robert TOMENENDAL

Centura College (D)

932 Ventura Way, Chesapeake VA 23320
Telephone: (757) 549-2121 Identification: 770608
Accreditation: ACCSC

† Main campus is Centura College in Virginia Beach, VA.

Centura College (E)

616 Denbigh Boulevard, Newport News VA 23608
Telephone: (757) 874-2121 Identification: 770606
Accreditation: ACCSC

† Main campus is Centura College in Virginia Beach, VA.

Centura College (F)

7020 N Military Highway, Norfolk VA 23518-4202
Telephone: (757) 853-2121 Identification: 770605
Accreditation: ACCSC, DA

† Main campus is Centura College in Virginia Beach, VA.

Centura College (G)

7914 Midlothian Turnpike, North Chesterfield VA 23235
County: Chesterfield FICE Identification: 031264
Unit ID: 427982
Telephone: (804) 330-0111 Carnegie Class: Assoc/PrivFP
FAX Number: (804) 330-3809 Calendar System: Semester
URL: www.centuracollege.edu
Established: 1992 Annual Undergrad Tuition & Fees: $31,722
Enrollment: 211 Coed
Affiliation or Control: Proprietary IRS Status: Proprietary
Highest Offering: Associate Degree
Program: 2-Year Principally Bachelor's Creditable; Business Emphasis
Accreditation: ACCSC

01 Campus Executive Director ....Zoe THOMPSON
11 Director of Compliance and Admin ....Grace BLEVINS
05 Director of Education ....Ann TRIBBEY
07 Director of Admissions ....Paul WILLIAMS
06 Registrar ....Autre METAL
37 Financial Aid ....Korey HUGHES
10 Bursar ....Leslie CROCKER
32 Student Services ....Helena COOPER
36 Career Services ....Steven TERRY

Centura College (H)

7001 West Broad Street, Richmond VA 23294
Telephone: (804) 672-2300 Identification: 770607
Accreditation: ACCSC

† Main campus is Centura College in North Chesterfield, VA.

Centura College (I)

2697 Dean Drive, Suite 100,
Virginia Beach VA 23452-7431
County: City of Virginia Beach FICE Identification: 023344
Unit ID: 232016
Telephone: (757) 340-2121 Carnegie Class: Assoc/PrivFP4
FAX Number: (757) 340-9704 Calendar System: Semester
URL: www.centura.edu
Established: 1969 Annual Undergrad Tuition & Fees: $16,912
Enrollment: 1,484 Coed
Affiliation or Control: Proprietary IRS Status: Proprietary
Highest Offering: Baccalaureate
Program: Occupational, Business Emphasis
Accreditation: ACCSC

01 Campus Executive Director ....Jeremiah SCARBROUGH
11 Dir of Compliance & Administration ....Ruth HALL
05 Director of Education ....Lamar LEWIS
07 Director of Admissions ....Cliff MESSINA
06 Registrar ....Dennis RYAN
10 Bursar ....Debbie KRAUSE
32 Student Services ....Mary MORGAN
36 Career Services ....Brenda HOUCK
37 Financial Aid ....Jennifer BROADWELL

Chamberlain College of Nursing (J)

2450 Crystal Drive, Suite 319, Arlington VA 22202
Telephone: (703) 416-7300 Identification: 770497
Accreditation: &NH, NURSE

† Main campus is Chamberlain College of Nursing - Addison in Addison, IL.

Chester Career College (K)

751 West Hundred Road, Chester VA 23836-2516
County: Chesterfield FICE Identification: 034095
Telephone: (804) 751-9191 Carnegie Class: Not Classified
FAX Number: (804) 751-2599 Calendar System: Semester
URL: www.chestercareercollege.edu
Established: 1997 Annual Undergrad Tuition & Fees: N/A
Enrollment: N/A Coed
Affiliation or Control: Proprietary IRS Status: Proprietary
Highest Offering: Associate Degree
Program: Occupational
Accreditation: COE

01 Campus Director ....Debbie HARRIS
05 Academic Dean ....Sandra KERRICK

Christendom College (L)

134 Christendom Drive, Front Royal VA 22630-6534
County: Warren FICE Identification: 036653
Unit ID: 231703
Telephone: (540) 636-2900 Carnegie Class: Not Classified
FAX Number: (540) 636-1655 Calendar System: Semester
URL: www.christendom.edu
Established: 1977 Annual Undergrad Tuition & Fees: $22,720
Enrollment: 407 Coed
Affiliation or Control: Roman Catholic IRS Status: 501(c)3
Highest Offering: Master's
Program: Liberal Arts And General
Accreditation: SC

01 President ....Dr. Timothy T. O'DONNELL
03 Executive Vice President ....Mr. Kenneth H. FERGUSON
10 Exec Vice President Finance & Admin ....Mr. Mark C. MCSHURLEY
05 Vice President Academic Affairs ....Dr. Steven C. SNYDER
30 Vice President for Advancement ....Mr. John F. CISKANIK
18 Vice Pres Operations/Facility Plng ....Mr. Michael S. FOECKLER
32 Dean of Student Life ....Mr. Jesse DORMAN
20 Academic Dean ....Dr. Patrick KEATS
07 Director of Admissions & Marketing ....Mr. Thomas MCFADDEN
06 Registrar ....Mr. Walter A. JANARO
08 Director of Christendom Library ....Mr. Andrew V. ARMSTRONG
37 Financial Aid Officer ....Mrs. Alisa L. POLK
29 Director Alumni & Career Devel ....Ms. Marie ANTUNES
13 Director of Computer Services ....Mr. Douglas S. BRIGGS
88 Registrar/Business Officer NDGS ....Miss Heidi KALIAN
41 Athletic Director ....Mr. Chris VANDERWOUDE
30 Director Development Operations ....Mr. Paul JALSEVAC
04 Assistant to the President ....Miss Melanie BAKER
58 Dean of the Graduate School ....Dr. Kristen BURNS

Christopher Newport University (M)

1 Avenue of the Arts, Newport News VA 23606-3072
County: Independent City FICE Identification: 003706
Unit ID: 231712
Telephone: (757) 594-7000 Carnegie Class: Master's S
FAX Number: (757) 594-7713 Calendar System: Semester
URL: www.cnu.edu
Established: 1960 Annual Undergrad Tuition & Fees (In-State): $11,092
Enrollment: 5,169 Coed
Affiliation or Control: State IRS Status: 501(c)3
Highest Offering: Master's
Program: Liberal Arts And General
Accreditation: SC, BUS, ENG, MUS, SW, THEA

01 President ....Sen. Paul S. TRIBLE, JR.
100 Chief of Staff ....Mrs. Cynthia R. PERRY
05 Provost ....Dr. Mark W. PADILLA
03 Executive Vice President ....Mr. William L. BRAUER
43 University Counsel ....Ms. Maureen R. MATSEN
30 Vice Pres for Univ Advancement ....Mrs. Adelia P. THOMPSON
15 Director of Human Resources ....Mrs. Lorraine M. WESTPHAL
41 Director of Athletics ....Mr. Todd BROOKS
04 Exec Assistant to the President ....Mrs. Beverley D. MUELLER
10 University Comptroller ....Mrs. Diane REED
35 Dean of Students ....Dr. Kevin M. HUGHES
49 Int Dean College Arts & Humanities ....Dr. Lori J. UNDERWOOD
83 Dean College of Social Sciences ....Dr. Robert E. COLVIN
88 Dean College Natural/Behav Sciences ....Dr. David C. DOUGHTY
07 Dean of Admission ....Mr. Robert LANGE
06 Dean Enrollment Services/ Registrar ....Dr. Lisa D. DUNCAN RAINES
37 Director of Financial Aid ....Ms. Clara E. JOHNSON
36 Director Center of Career Planning ....Ms. Elizabeth K. WESTLEY
39 Assistant Director of Housing ....Ms. Janine W. KENNELL
09 Director of Institutional Research ....Ms. Donna A. VARNER
13 Chief Information Officer ....Mr. Stephen S. CAMPBELL
08 University Librarian ....Ms. Mary K. SELLEN
19 Chief of University Police ....Mr. Jeffrey S. BROWN
21 Director of University Audit ....Ms. Faith D. BELOTE
18 Asst Director of Plant Operations ....Mr. Albert C. METZGAR
44 Sr Dir Advancement/Planned Giving ....Ms. Lucy L. LATCHUM
96 Director of Materiel Management ....Mr. Ryan A. FEREBEE
29 Dir Alumni Relations/Univ Events ....Ms. Amie E. GRAHAM
26 Director of Public Relations ....Ms. Lori A. JACOBS
28 Director of EO/Faculty Recruitment ....Ms. Michelle L. MOODY
38 Exec Dir Counseling & HE Services ....Mr. William V. RITCHEY
26 Director of Communications ....Mr. Bruce S. BRONSTEIN, JR.

College of William & Mary (N)

PO Box 8795, Williamsburg VA 23187-8795
County: Independent City FICE Identification: 003705
Unit ID: 231624
Telephone: (757) 221-4000 Carnegie Class: RU/H
FAX Number: (757) 221-1259 Calendar System: Semester
URL: www.wm.edu
Established: 1693 Annual Undergrad Tuition & Fees (In-State): $9,232
Enrollment: 8,258 Coed
Affiliation or Control: State IRS Status: 501(c)3
Highest Offering: Doctorate
Program: Liberal Arts And General; Teacher Preparatory; Professional
Accreditation: SC, BUS, BUSA, CACREP, IPSY, LAW, TED

01 President ....Mr. W. Taylor REVELEY, III
05 Provost ....Dr. Michael HALLERAN
11 Vice President for Administration ....Ms. Anna B. MARTIN
10 Vice President for Finance ....Mr. Samuel E. JONES
30 Vice President for Development ....Mr. Matthew T. LAMBERT
45 Vice Pres for Strategic Initiatives ....Dr. James R. GOLDEN
32 Vice President for Student Affairs ....Dr. Virginia M. AMBLER
41 Director of Athletics ....Mr. Edward (Terry) C. DRISCOLL
29 Exec Vice Pres Alumni Association ....Ms. Karen R. COTTRELL
49 Dean Faculty of Arts & Sciences ....Dr. Katharine CONLEY
50 Dean School of Business Admin ....Dr. Lawrence B. PULLEY
53 Dean School of Education ....Dr. Spencer NILES
61 Dean School of Law ....Mr. Davison M. DOUGLAS
88 Dean/Dir School of Marine Science ....Dr. John T. WELLS
08 Dean University Libraries ....Ms. Carrie COOPER
43 University Counsel ....Ms. Deborah A. LOVE
20 Vice Provost for Academic Affairs ....Dr. Kathleen F. SLEVIN
82 Vice Prov Intl Affairs/Reves Ctr ....Dr. Stephen E. HANSON

46 Vice Provost Rsch & Grad Prof Stds .... Dr. Dennis M. MANOS
13 Assoc Prov Information Technology .... Mr. Courtney M. CARPENTER
27 Chief Information Officer .... Mr. Courtney CARPENTER
108 Assoc Prov Inst Analysis/Effective .... Dr. Susan L. BOSWORTH
84 Associate Provost for Enrollment .... Mr. Henry R. BROADDUS
07 Dean of Admission .... Mr. Henry R. BROADDUS
06 University Registrar .... Ms. Sara L. MARCHELLO
88 Dean for Educational Policy .... Dr. Lu Ann HOMZA
58 Dean Graduate Studies & Research .... Dr. Virginia TORCZON
92 Dean Honors/Interdisciplinary Stds .... Dr. Joel D. SCHWARTZ
88 Dean of Undergraduate Studies .... Dr. John GRIFFIN
104 Director of Global Education .... Ms. Sylvia MITTERNDORFER
86 Assoc VP Government Relations .... Ms. Frances C. BRADFORD
26 Director of University Relations .... Mr. Brian WHITSON
88 Assoc VP Development/Operations .... Ms. Teresa L. MUNFORD
44 Assoc VP Development/Fundraising .... Mr. Earl T. GRANGER
102 Director Corporate & Found Rels .... Ms. Suzanne ARMSTRONG
18 Assoc Vice Pres Facilities Mgmt .... Mr. Dave SHEPARD
35 Dean of Students .... Ms. Marjorie THOMAS
25 Director of Sponsored Programs .... Ms. Jane LOPEZ
22 Director of Equal Opportunity .... Ms. Sharron GATLING
37 Director Student Financial Aid .... Mr. Edward P. IRISH
15 Assoc VP Human Resources .... Mr. Ron PRICE
38 Director Counseling Center .... Dr. Warrenetta C. MANN
36 Director Career Center .... Ms. Mary E. SCHILLING
19 Chief W&M Police Department .... Mr. Donald R. CHALLIS
21 Director Financial Operations .... Mr. Edmund (Bert) E. BRUMMER
23 Director Student Health Center .... Dr. Virginia D. WELLS
28 Dir of Ctr for Student Diversity .... Dr. Vernon HURTE
39 Asst VP Stdnt Affs/Dir of Res Life .... Ms. Deborah BOYKIN
96 Director of Procurement .... Mr. Gregory W. JOHNSON
40 Manager W&M Bookstore .... Ms. Cathy PACHECO
100 Asst to President/Chief of Staff .... Mr. Michael J. FOX
101 Secretary to the Board of Visitors .... Mr. Michael J. FOX
04 Executive Asst to President .... Ms. Cynthia A. BRAUER
88 Director of Creative Services .... Ms. Tina L. COLEMAN
88 Assoc VP for Health & Wellness .... Dr. Robert K. CRACE

Columbia College (A)

8300 Merrifield Avenue, Fairfax VA 22031
County: Fairfax FICE Identification: 041273
Unit ID: 455983
Telephone: (703) 206-0508 Carnegie Class: Assoc/PrivFP
FAX Number: (703) 206-0488 Calendar System: Quarter
URL: www.ccdc.edu
Established: 1999 Annual Undergrad Tuition & Fees: $6,720
Enrollment: 434 Coed
Affiliation or Control: Proprietary IRS Status: Proprietary
Highest Offering: Associate Degree
Program: Occupational; 2-Year Principally Bachelor's Creditable
Accreditation: COE

01 President .... Dr. Richard K. KIM

Court Reporting Institute of Arlington (B)

4300 Wilson Boulevard, Suite 140, Arlington VA 22203
Telephone: (703) 875-1200 Identification: 770814
Accreditation: ACICS

† Main campus is Court Reporting Institute of Dallas in Dallas, TX.

DeVry University - Arlington Campus (C)

2450 Crystal Drive, Arlington VA 22202-3843
Telephone: (703) 414-4000 Identification: 666220
Accreditation: &NH, ENGT

† Main campus is DeVry University - Chicago Campus in Chicago, IL.

Eastern Mennonite University (D)

1200 Park Road, Harrisonburg VA 22802-2462
County: Independent City FICE Identification: 003708
Unit ID: 232043
Telephone: (540) 432-4000 Carnegie Class: Bac/A&S
FAX Number: (540) 432-4444 Calendar System: Semester
URL: www.emu.edu
Established: 1917 Annual Undergrad Tuition & Fees: $29,350
Enrollment: 1,622 Coed
Affiliation or Control: Mennonite Church IRS Status: 501(c)3
Highest Offering: Master's
Program: Liberal Arts And General; Teacher Preparatory; Professional
Accreditation: SC, CACREP, NURSE, PAST, SW, TED, THEOL

01 President .... Dr. Loren E. SWARTZENDRUBER
05 Provost .... Dr. Fred L. KNISS
30 Vice President for Advancement .... Mr. Kirk L. SHISLER
10 Vice President for Finance .... Mr. Daryl W. BERT
84 Vice Pres Enrollment & Marketing .... Mr. Luke HARTMAN
32 Vice President for Student Life .... Dr. Kenneth L. NAFZIGER
20 Vice Pres & Undergrad Academic Dean .... Dr. Deirdre SMELTZER
73 Seminary Dean .... Dr. Michael A. KING
06 University Registrar .... Mr. David A. DETROW
26 Director of Marketing Services .... Ms. Andrea S. WENGER
07 Director Undergraduate Admissions ..... Ms. Stephanie C. SHAFER
08 Director of Libraries .... Dr. Beryl H. BRUBAKER
37 Director of Financial Assistance .... Ms. Michele R. HENSLEY
36 Director Career Services/Testing .... Ms. Jennifer L. LITWILLER
29 Director of Alumni/Parent Relations .... Mr. Douglas J. NYCE
09 Director Institutional Research .... Dr. BJ MILLER
04 Assistant to the President .... Ms. Twila K. YODER
41 Athletic Director .... Mr. David A. KING
42 Campus Pastor .... Mr. Brian M. BURKHOLDER
13 Director of Information Systems .... Mr. Jack H. RUTT
18 Director of Physical Plant .... Mr. Eldon KURTZ
15 Director Human Resources .... Ms. Marcia J. ENGLE
21 Controller .... Mr. Timothy STUTZMAN
27 Chief Public Information Officer .... Mr. Michael J. ZUCCONI
35 Director Student Affairs .... Ms. Rachel R. SAWATZKY
38 Director Student Counseling .... Ms. Pamela D. COMER

Eastern Virginia Medical School (E)

Box 1980, Norfolk VA 23501-1980
County: Independent City FICE Identification: 010338
Unit ID: 231970
Telephone: (757) 446-5600 Carnegie Class: Spec/Med
FAX Number: (757) 446-5135 Calendar System: Other
URL: www.evms.edu
Established: 1973 Annual Graduate Tuition & Fees: $31,489
Enrollment: 1,090 Coed
Affiliation or Control: Independent Non-Profit IRS Status: 501(c)3
Highest Offering: Doctorate; No Undergraduates
Program: Professional
Accreditation: SC, ARCPA, CLPSY, IPSY, MED, PH, SURGA

01 † President/Provost/Dean .... Dr. Richard V. HOMAN
100 Chief of Staff .... Mr. Brandt COX
03 Senior Vice President .... Ms. Claudia KEENAN
10 Vice Pres Administration/Finance ..... Mr. Mark R. BABASHANIAN
88 Vice Pres/Dean Sch of Health Prof .... Dr. Charles D. COMBS
20 Associate Dean Education .... Dr. Ronald W. FLENNER
88 Assoc Dean Clinical Affairs .... Dr. Alfred Z. ABUHAMAD
43 General Counsel .... Ms. Stacy R. PURCELL
58 Assoc Dean Grad Medical Education .... Dr. Linda R. ARCHER
88 Assoc Dean Hum Sub Protection/IRB .... Dr. Robert F. WILLIAMS
09 Assoc Dean for Research .... Dr. William J. WASILENKO
50 Assoc Dean Business/Admin Affairs .... Mr. David E. HUBAND
08 Assoc Dean Library/Lrng Resource .... Ms. Judith R. MERCER
28 Vice President for Diversity .... Mr. Mekbib L. GEMEDA
32 Assoc Dean for Student Affairs .... Dr. Ann E. CAMPBELL
84 Asst Dean Admissions and Enroll .... Dr. Donald C. MEYER
88 Assoc Dean for Health Professions .... Mr. Jeff A. JOHNSON
88 Associate Dean for Faculty Affairs .... Dr. Elza MYLONA
06 Registrar .... Mr. Michael J. DONLAN
07 Director of Admissions .... Ms. Susan L. CASTORA
15 Director Human Resources .... Mr. Matthew R. SCHENK
21 Director of Finance .... Ms. Helen S. HESELIUS
18 Chief Facilities/Physical Plant .... Mr. Jack D. BEASLEY
37 Director Student Financial Aid .... Ms. Margaret L. MURPHY
93 Director Minority Affairs .... Ms. Gail C. WILLIAMS
96 Director of Materials Management .... Mr. Steven LEE
21 Director for Business Management .... Ms. Tammy A. CHRISMAN
26 Director of Mktg & Communications .... Mr. Vincent A. RHODES
29 Director Alumni Relations .... Ms. Melissa W. LANG
30 Director of Development .... Ms. Connie L. MCKENZIE
51 Director for Continuing Med Educ .... Ms. Drucie A. PAPAFIL
88 Director of the Brock Institute .... Dr. Karen REMLEY

† Member of Virginia Consortium for Professional Psychology.

ECPI College of Technology (F)

5555 Greenwich Road, Virginia Beach VA 23462-6554
County: Independent City FICE Identification: 010198
Unit ID: 248934
Telephone: (757) 671-7171 Carnegie Class: Assoc/PrivFP4
FAX Number: (757) 671-8661 Calendar System: Semester
URL: www.ecpi.edu
Established: 1966 Annual Undergrad Tuition & Fees: $13,980
Enrollment: 9,840 Coed
Affiliation or Control: Proprietary IRS Status: Proprietary
Highest Offering: Master's
Program: Occupational
Accreditation: SC, ACFEI, MAAB, NUR

01 President .... Mr. Mark B. DREYFUS
12 Campus President .... Mr. Kevin PAVEGLIO
13 VP Info Systems/Financial Aid .... Mr. Jeff ARTHUR

Edward Via College of Osteopathic Medicine (G)

2265 Kraft Drive, Blacksburg VA 24060
County: Montgomery FICE Identification: 037093
Unit ID: 442806
Telephone: (540) 231-4000 Carnegie Class: Spec/Med
FAX Number: (540) 231-5252 Calendar System: Semester
URL: www.vcom.vt.edu
Established: 2002 Annual Graduate Tuition & Fees: $39,990
Enrollment: 1,144 Coed
Affiliation or Control: Independent Non-Profit IRS Status: 501(c)3
Highest Offering: Doctorate; No Undergraduates
Program: Professional
Accreditation: OSTEO

01 President .... Dr. James F. WOLFE
05 Executive Vice President & Dean .... Dr. Dixie TOOKE-RAWLINS
10 Associate Vice Pres Finance/CFO .... Mr. Mark HAMRIC
32 Assoc Vice Pres Student Services .... Mr. William KING
46 Assoc Vice Pres Research/Grad Stds .... Dr. Hara P. MISRA
11 Assoc Vice President Operations .... Mr. Bill PRICE
12 Vice Dean Carolinas Campus .... Dr. Timothy J. KOWALSKI
12 Vice Dean Virginia Campus .... Dr. Jan M. WILLCOX
58 Vice Dean Post-Bac/Pre-med Program ... Dr. Francine ANDERSON
63 Vice Dean Post Baccalaureate Pgm .... Dr. Brian W. HILL

Emory & Henry College (H)

PO Box 947, 30461 Garnand Drive,
Emory VA 24327-0947
County: Washington FICE Identification: 003709
Unit ID: 232025
Telephone: (276) 944-4121 Carnegie Class: Bac/A&S
FAX Number: (276) 944-6934 Calendar System: Semester
URL: www.ehc.edu
Established: 1836 Annual Undergrad Tuition & Fees: $28,966
Enrollment: 945 Coed
Affiliation or Control: United Methodist IRS Status: 501(c)3
Highest Offering: Doctorate
Program: Liberal Arts And General; Teacher Preparatory
Accreditation: SC, TEAC

01 President .... Mr. Jake B. SCHRUM
04 Executive Assistant to President .... Mr. Mark R. GRAHAM
05 VP Academic Affairs/Dean .... Dr. David P. HANEY
10 Vice Pres for Business and Finance .... Dr. Dirk E. WILMOTH
32 VP Student Life/Dean of Students .... Ms. Pamela L. GOURLEY
30 VP for Institutional Advancement .... Mr. Joseph P. TAYLOR
84 Vice Pres for Enrollment Management .... Mr. David S. HAWSEY
09 Dir Institutional Research/Effect .... Mr. Gregory G. STEINER
29 Director of Alumni Affairs .... Ms. Monica S. HOEL
37 Director of Financial Aid .... Ms. Lauren PIZZO
06 Registrar/Dir of CSA .... Ms. Lynn ELLIOTT
36 Director of Career Planning .... Ms. Amanda GARDNER
38 Director Student Counseling .... Ms. Jill M. SMELTZER
26 Director Public Relations .... Mr. Dirk S. MOORE
08 Chief Information Officer/Librarian ...... Ms. Lorraine N. ABRAHAM
18 Int Dir of Facilities Management .... Mr. Josh NOLAND
40 Bookstore Manager .... Mr. Terry RICHARDSON
42 Chaplain .... Rev. Mary K. BRIGGS
15 Human Resources Manager .... Ms. Angie S. EDMONDSON
20 Associate VP Academic Affairs .... Dr. Michael J. PUGLISI
35 Associate Dean of Students .... Mr. Todd CLARK
21 Associate VP Business/Finance .... Ms. Benita BARE
07 Director of Admissions .... Ms. Gretchen TUCKER
39 Director of Housing .... Mr. Jimmy WHITED
41 Director of Athletics .... Ms. Myra SIMS
19 Chief of Campus Police .... Mr. Scott POORE

Everest College (I)

825 Greenbrier Circle, Chesapeake VA 23320
Telephone: (757) 361-3900 Identification: 770791
Accreditation: ACICS

† Main campus is Everest College in Newport News, VA.

Everest College (J)

803 Diligence Drive, Newport News VA 23606
County: Independent City FICE Identification: 009267
Unit ID: 232502
Telephone: (757) 873-1111 Carnegie Class: Assoc/PrivFP
FAX Number: (757) 873-0728 Calendar System: Other
URL: www.everest.edu
Established: Annual Undergrad Tuition & Fees: N/A
Enrollment: 351 Coed
Affiliation or Control: Proprietary IRS Status: Proprietary
Highest Offering: Associate Degree
Program: Occupational
Accreditation: ACICS

01 President .... Ms. Niki GOOD
05 Director of Education .... Mr. Michael GODFREY

† Tuition varies by degree program.

Everest College (K)

8620 Westwood Center Drive, Vienna VA 22182
Telephone: (703) 288-3131 Identification: 770792
Accreditation: ACICS

† Main campus is Everest College in Colorado Springs, CO.

Ferrum College (L)

PO Box 1000, 215 Ferrum Mtn Road,
Ferrum VA 24088-9001
County: Franklin FICE Identification: 003711
Unit ID: 232089
Telephone: (540) 365-2121 Carnegie Class: Bac/Diverse
FAX Number: (540) 365-4269 Calendar System: Semester
URL: www.ferrum.edu
Established: 1913 Annual Undergrad Tuition & Fees: $28,675
Enrollment: 1,510 Coed
Affiliation or Control: United Methodist IRS Status: 501(c)3
Highest Offering: Baccalaureate
Program: Liberal Arts And General
Accreditation: SC, SW

01 President ... Dr. Jennifer L. BRAATEN
11 Vice Pres for Admininstration ... Dr. Douglas E. CLARK
05 Interim VP for Academic Affairs ... Dr. Gail SUMMER
10 VP for Business and Finance ... Mrs. Barb HATCHER
30 Vice Pres Institutional Advancement ... Mrs. Kimberly P. BLAIR
84 Vice Pres Enrollment Management ... Dr. Douglas E. CLARK
32 Vice President of Student Affairs ... Dr. Andrea P. ZUSCHIN
42 Dean of Chapel/Religious Life ... Vacant
20 Dean Academic Pgms/Faculty Devel ... Dr. Gail SUMMER
04 Special Assistant to the President ... Mrs. Theresa M. POTTER
06 Registrar ... Mrs. Yvonne S. WALKER
84 Assoc VP for Enrollment Mgmt ... Mrs. Gilda Q. WOODS
09 Dir of Assessment & Inst Research ... Dr. Jolene D. HAMM
08 Exec Dir Stanley Library ... Ms. Brandi PORTER
37 Director of Financial Aid ... Ms. Heather HOLLANDSWORTH
29 Director Alumni & Family Programs ... Mrs. Tracy S. HOLLEY
26 Director of Public Relations ... Vacant
41 Director of Athletics ... Mr. J. Abraham NAFF
44 Regional Gift Officer ... Mr. Gene BOURNE
18 Director of Physical Plant ... Mr. Sam E. MORAN
88 Dir Student Leadership & Engagement . Mr. David A. NEWCOMBE
13 Director of Computer Services ... Mr. Daniel K. HODGES
15 Dir of Human Resources ... Mrs. Mary Alice WHISENANT
40 Bookstore Manager ... Ms. Patty SIGMON
19 Director Ferrum College Police Dept ... Ms. Elizabeth LEGG
36 Dir Career Svcs/Student Employment ... Mr. Roland WALTERS
88 Disability Services Coordinator ... Ms. Nancy S. BEACH
91 Coord of Administrative Computing ... Mr. Tim BELCHER
28 Coordinator Multicultural Programs ... Mr. Justin MUSE
79 Dean School Arts & Humanities ... Dr. John W. BRUTON
81 Dean School Natural Science & Math ... Dr. Jason POWELL
83 Dean School Social Sciences ... Dr. Kevin REILLY

Fortis College (A)

6300 Center Drive, Building 22, Norfolk VA 23502
County: Independent City FICE Identification: 023427
Unit ID: 233329
Telephone: (757) 499-5447 Carnegie Class: Assoc/PrivFP
FAX Number: N/A Calendar System: Quarter
URL: www.fortis.edu/campuses
Established: Annual Undergrad Tuition & Fees: $24,085
Enrollment: 392 Coed
Affiliation or Control: Proprietary IRS Status: Proprietary
Highest Offering: Associate Degree
Program: Occupational
Accreditation: ACICS

01 President ... Dr. Walter MERCHANT

Fortis College (B)

2000 Westmoreland Street, Suite A, Richmond VA 23230
Telephone: (804) 323-1020 Identification: 770815
Accreditation: ACICS, DA, SURGT

† Main campus is Fortis College in Norfolk, VA.

George Mason University (C)

4400 University Drive, Fairfax VA 22030-4444
County: Fairfax FICE Identification: 003749
Unit ID: 232186
Telephone: (703) 993-1000 Carnegie Class: RU/H
FAX Number: (703) 993-1009 Calendar System: Semester
URL: www.gmu.edu
Established: 1957 Annual Undergrad Tuition & Fees (In-State): $9,908
Enrollment: 32,961 Coed
Affiliation or Control: State IRS Status: 501(c)3
Highest Offering: Doctorate
Program: Liberal Arts And General; Teacher Preparatory; Professional
Accreditation: SC, ART, BUS, BUSA, CEA, CLPSY, CS, ENG, HSA, IPSY, LAW, MUS, NRPA, NURSE, PH, SPAA, SW, TED

01 President ... Dr. Ángel CABRERA
100 Chief of Staff ... Mr. Frank NEVILLE
03 Vice Pres for Administration ... Vacant
05 Provost ... Dr. Peter N. STEARNS
10 Vice Pres Finance/Administration ... Ms. Jennifer (J.J.) DAVIS
07 Vice President Enrollment Services ... Mr. Wayne SIGLER
18 Vice President for Facilities ... Mr. Thomas G. CALHOUN
86 VP Government & Community Relations ... Mr. Paul LIBERTY
30 VP University Devel/Alumni Affairs ... Vacant
13 Interim VP Information Tech/CIO ... Ms. Jennifer (J.J.) DAVIS
32 Vice President for University Life ... Ms. Rose PASCARELL
46 VP Research/Economic Development ... Dr. Vikas CHANDHOKE
22 VP Compliance/Diversity & Ethics ... Mr. Corey D. JACKSON
16 Assoc Vice Pres for HR/Payroll ... Ms. Linda HARBER
43 University Counsel ... Mr. Thomas M. MONCURE
45 Chief Budget Officer ... Mr. Guilbert L. BROWN
20 Vice Provost Academic Affairs ... Dr. Michelle MARKS
20 Assoc Prov for Undergrad Education ... Dr. Janette MUIR
84 Assoc Prov for Enroll Plng & Admin ... Ms. Renate H. GUILFORD
58 Assoc Prov for Graduate Education ... Dr. Cody EDWARDS
35 Director Ofc of Student Involvement ... Ms. Lauren LONG
35 Assistant Vice Pres University Life ... Ms. Patricia J. CARRETTA
06 Interim Registrar ... Mr. Brian SELINSKY
37 Director Student Financial Aid ... Ms. Heidi GRANGER
36 Director University Career Services ... Ms. Christine Y. CRUZVERGARA
08 University Librarian ... Mr. John G. ZENELIS
23 Exec Director Student Health Svcs ... Dr. Wagida A. ABDALLA
29 Assoc VP Alumni Affairs ... Ms. Christine CLARK-TALLEY
41 Dir of Intercollegiate Athletics ... Mr. Thomas J. O'CONNOR
19 Dir & Chief of University Police ... Mr. Eric HEATH
49 Dean Col of Humanities/Social Sci ... Dr. Deborah BOEHM-DAVIS
61 Dean School of Law ... Dr. Daniel D. POLSBY
80 Acting Dean School of Public Policy ... Dr. Mark ROZELL
50 Acting Dean School of Management ... Dr. Sarah NUTTER
53 Dean College of Educ & Human Devel ... Dr. Mark R. GINSBERG
54 Dean Volgenau School of Engineering ... Dr. Kenneth BALL
66 Dean College of Health/Human Svcs ... Dr. Thomas R. PROHASKA
81 Acting Dean College of Science ... Dr. Peggy AGOURIS
88 Actg Dean Sch Conflict/Anal & Resol ... Dr. Solon SIMMONS
88 Dean Col of Visual/Performing Arts ... Mr. William F. REEDER
38 Acting Exec Dir Counseling Center ... Dr. Adrienne M. BARNA
09 Assoc Prov Institutional Research ... Ms. Kris M. SMITH
35 Associate Dean University Life ... Dr. Todd S. ROSE
96 Director of Purchasing and AP ... Mr. Cliff SHORE

Global Health College (D)

25 South Quaker Lane, 1st Floor, Alexandria VA 22314
County: Independent City FICE Identification: 041400
Unit ID: 455390
Telephone: (703) 212-7410 Carnegie Class: Assoc/PrivFP
FAX Number: (703) 212-7414 Calendar System: Other
URL: www.global.edu
Established: 2004 Annual Undergrad Tuition & Fees: $15,500
Enrollment: 265 Coed
Affiliation or Control: Proprietary IRS Status: Proprietary
Highest Offering: Associate Degree
Program: Nursing Emphasis
Accreditation: ACICS

01 President ... Mariatu KARGBO
10 Vice Pres Administration/Fiscal Svc ... Bernard FRISBY

Hampden-Sydney College (E)

College Road, PO Box 128,
Hampden-Sydney VA 23943-0667
County: Prince Edward FICE Identification: 003713
Unit ID: 232256
Telephone: (434) 223-6000 Carnegie Class: Bac/A&S
FAX Number: (434) 223-6350 Calendar System: Semester
URL: www.hsc.edu
Established: 1775 Annual Undergrad Tuition & Fees: $37,732
Enrollment: 1,080 Male
Affiliation or Control: Presbyterian Church (U.S.A.) IRS Status: 501(c)3
Highest Offering: Baccalaureate
Program: Liberal Arts And General
Accreditation: SC

01 President ... Dr. Christopher B. HOWARD
04 Special Asst to the President ... Mr. William P. O MOSS
05 Provost & Dean of the Faculty ... Dr. Dennis G. STEVENS
10 VP Business Affairs & Finance ... Mr. W. Glenn CULLEY, JR.
30 VP Institutional Advancement ... Dr. H. Lee KING, JR.
11 VP Strategy/Admin & Board Affairs ... Dr. V. Dale JONES
07 Dean of Admissions ... Ms. Anita H. GARLAND
20 Associate Dean of the Faculty ... Dr. J. Michael UTZINGER
32 Dean of Students ... Dr. David A. KLEIN
20 Associate Dean Academic Support ... Ms. Christa D. FYE
41 Director of Athletics ... Mr. Richard P. EPPERSON, II
08 Director of the Library & Computing ... Dr. Cyrus I. DILLON, III
42 College Church Pastor/H-SC Chaplain ... Rev Dr. David A. KECK
06 Registrar ... Ms. Dawn L. CONGLETON
37 Director of Financial Aid ... Ms. Zita M. BARREE
29 Director of Alumni Relations ... Mr. Mark G. MEITZ
18 Director of Physical Plant ... Mr. John C. PRENGAMAN
36 Assoc Dean Career Educ/Voc Reflect . LtCol. L. Rucker SNEAD, III
23 Director of Student Health Center ... Ms. Margaret P. GRAHAM
15 Director of Human Resources ... Ms. Barbara S. ARMENTROUT
19 Chief of Police ... Mr. Jeffrey S. GEE
40 Bookstore Manager ... Vacant
09 Director Inst Research/Assessment ... Dr. Christine C. ROSS
26 Director Communications & Marketing ... Mr. Thomas H. SHOMO
21 Controller ... Mr. Michael A. SMITH
35 Assistant Dean of Students ... Mr. John R C. RAMSAY
39 Assoc Dean Students ... Mr. Wesley S. LAWSON
25 Director Grants & Special Projects ... Mrs. Eunice W. CARWILE
104 Dir Global Education & Study Abroad ... Mrs. Mary K. COOPER

Hampton University (F)

Hampton VA 23668-0199
County: Independent City FICE Identification: 003714
Unit ID: 232265
Telephone: (757) 727-5000 Carnegie Class: Master's M
FAX Number: (757) 727-5085 Calendar System: Semester
URL: www.hamptonu.edu
Established: 1868 Annual Undergrad Tuition & Fees: $20,724
Enrollment: 4,768 Coed
Affiliation or Control: Independent Non-Profit IRS Status: 501(c)3
Highest Offering: Doctorate
Program: Liberal Arts And General; Teacher Preparatory; Professional
Accreditation: SC, CS, ENG, IACBE, JOUR, MUS, NURSE, PHAR, PTA, SP, TED

01 President ... Dr. William R. HARVEY
03 Executive Vice President ... Dr. JoAnn HAYSBERT
05 Provost ... Dr. Pamela V. HAMMOND
10 Vice Pres Business Affs/Treasurer ... Mrs. Doretha J. SPELLS
32 Vice Pres for Student Affairs ... Dr. Barbara L. INMAN
43 Vice President/General Counsel ... Atty. Faye HARDY-LUCAS
30 Vice President for Development ... Mr. Laron J. CLARK
04 Executive Assistant to President ... Dr. Charrita D. DANLEY
46 Special Asst to President/Research ... Dr. Elnora DANIEL
31 Assoc Vice Pres External Relations ... Mrs. Joy JEFFERSON
35 Assoc Vice Pres for Student Affairs ... Vacant
21 Asst VP Business Affs/Comptroller ... Ms. Nellie CRAWFORD
25 Asst Vice Pres Grants Management ... Mrs. Lillie F. GREEN
20 Asst Provost Academic Affairs ... Dr. Pollie MURPHY
72 Int Assistant Provost Technology ... Gen. Wallace ARNOLD
33 Dean of Men ... Mr. Woodson H. HOPEWELL, JR.
34 Dean of Women ... Miss Jewel B. LONG
07 Director of Admissions ... Mrs. Angela BOYD
06 Registrar ... Mrs. Jorsene COOPER
36 Dir Career Counsel/Planning Ctr ... Mrs. Vivian DAVID
38 Interim Director the Counseling Ctr ... Dr. Linda KIRKLAND-HARRIS
08 Administrator University Libraries ... Ms. Faye WATKINS
29 Director of Alumni Affairs ... Mrs. Sharon FITZGERALD
15 Director of Human Resources ... Ms. Rikki THOMAS
14 Director Computer Center ... Vacant
37 Financial Aid Officer ... Mr. Martin MILES
26 Director of University Relations ... Mrs. Yuri Rodgers MILLIGAN
09 Director Institutional Research ... Mrs. Michelle CLAWSON
23 Director Student Health Services ... Dr. Bert HOLMES
42 University Chaplain ... Rev. Debra L. HAGGINS
18 Director Buildings & Grounds ... Mr. Lowell MIDDLETON
87 Director of Summer Sessions ... Dr. Pollie MURPHY
19 Chief of Campus Police ... Mr. David GLOVER
86 Director Government Relations ... Mr. Wilbert L. THOMAS
96 Director of Purchasing ... Mr. Malcolm HAINES
40 University Bookstore Manager ... Ms. Michelle R. MILLER
53 Dean School of Liberal Arts ... Dr. Mamie E. LOCKE
66 Dean School of Nursing ... Dr. Deborah JONES
81 Assistant Dean School of Science ... Dr. Michelle CLAVILLE
51 Dean Sch Educ/Human Development ... Dr. Cassandra HERRING
50 Dean School of Business ... Dr. Sid H. CREDLE
54 Dean Sch of Engineering/Technology ... Dr. Eric J. SHEPPARD
67 Dean School of Pharmacy ... Dr. Wayne HARRIS
58 Dean the Graduate College ... Dr. Patrena N. BENTON
60 Dean Scripps Howard Sch Journ/Comm ... Mr. Brett PULLEY
88 Dean University College ... Dr. Donnovon OUTTEN

Hollins University (G)

PO Box 9688, Roanoke VA 24020-1688
County: Roanoke FICE Identification: 003715
Unit ID: 232308
Telephone: (540) 362-6000 Carnegie Class: Bac/A&S
FAX Number: (540) 362-6642 Calendar System: 4/1/4
URL: www.hollins.edu
Established: 1842 Annual Undergrad Tuition & Fees: $32,710
Enrollment: 794 Female
Affiliation or Control: Independent Non-Profit IRS Status: 501(c)3
Highest Offering: Master's
Program: Liberal Arts And General; Teacher Preparatory
Accreditation: SC, TEAC

01 President ... Ms. Nancy O. GRAY
10 Vice Pres Finance/Administration ... Ms. Kerry EDMONDS
30 Vice Pres for External Relations ... Mr. Mark W. JONES
84 Vice President of Enrollment ... Ms. Stefanie NILES
05 Chair of the Faculty ... Ms. Julie PFEIFFER
32 Dean of Students ... Ms. Patty O'TOOLE
07 Dean of Admissions ... Ms. Nikki JOHNSON WILLIAMS
20 Dean Academic Services ... Ms. Rebecca BEACH
28 Associate Dean Intercultural Pgms ... Ms. Jeri L. SUAREZ
04 Executive Assistant to President ... Ms. Brook E. DICKSON
88 Director Alumnae & Donor Relations ... Ms. Laura ANDERSON
06 Registrar ... Ms. Anna GOODWIN
08 Director of the Library ... Mr. Luke VILELLE
15 Director of Human Resources ... Ms. Alicia GODZWA
26 Director of Public Relations ... Mr. Jeff HODGES
29 Assoc Dir of Alumnae Relations ... Ms. Anna MONCURE
36 Director Career Development Center ... Ms. Ashley GLENN
37 Director Financial Aid ... Ms. Mary Jean CORRISS
41 Director of Athletics ... Mr. David ZINN
09 Director of Institutional Research ... Ms. Anna GOODWIN
18 Director Plant Operations/Services ... Ms. May THOMAS

iGlobal University (H)

7700 Little River Turnpike, #600, Annandale VA 22003
County: Fairfax Identification: 667105
Telephone: (703) 941-2020 Carnegie Class: Not Classified
FAX Number: (703) 941-2025 Calendar System: Quarter
URL: www.iglobaluniversity.org
Established: 2008 Annual Undergrad Tuition & Fees: N/A
Enrollment: N/A Coed
Affiliation or Control: Proprietary IRS Status: Proprietary
Highest Offering: Master's
Program: Business Emphasis
Accreditation: ACICS

01 President & CEO ... Dr. David Y. SOHN

Institute for the Psychological Sciences (I)

2001 Jefferson Davis Hwy, Ste 511,
Arlington VA 22202-3609
County: Arlington FICE Identification: 038724
Unit ID: 445869

Telephone: (703) 416-1441 Carnegie Class: Spec/Health
FAX Number: (703) 416-8588 Calendar System: Semester
URL: www.ipsciences.edu
Established: 1998 Annual Graduate Tuition & Fees: $29,460
Enrollment: 84 Coed
Affiliation or Control: Independent Non-Profit IRS Status: 501(c)3
Highest Offering: Doctorate; No Undergraduates
Program: Professional
Accreditation: SC

00 President Emeritus .... Rev. John HOPKINS, LC
01 President .... Rev. Charles SIKORSKY, LC
05 Academic Dean/Chair .... Dr. William NORDLING
32 Dean of Students .... Dr. Peter MANGO
03 VP for Institutional Effectiveness .... Dr. Mary Ann LA FLEUR
30 VP for Advancement .... Mr. James O'DAY
106 Director of Distance Education .... Dr. Stephen GRUNDMAN
07 Director of Admissions .... Vacant
06 Registrar .... Ms. Jennifer E. KARNS
08 Library Director .... Mr. Jeffrey ELLIOTT
37 Financial Aid Officer .... Dr. Peter MANGO
10 Chief Business Officer .... Ms. LaRon NORRIS
42 Chaplain .... Fr. Daniel WILSON

ITT Technical Institute (A)

14420 Albemarle Point Pl, Suite 100,
Chantilly VA 20151-1750
Telephone: (703) 263-2541 Identification: 666324
Accreditation: ACICS

† Main campus is ITT Technical Institute in Indianapolis, IN.

ITT Technical Institute (B)

5425 Robin Hood Road, Suite 100, Norfolk VA 23513
Telephone: (757) 466-1260 Identification: 666555
Accreditation: ACICS

† Main campus is ITT Technical Institute in Indianapolis, IN.

ITT Technical Institute (C)

300 Gateway Centre Parkway, Richmond VA 23235-5139
Telephone: (804) 330-4992 Identification: 666040
Accreditation: ACICS

† Main campus is ITT Technical Institute in Indianapolis, IN.

ITT Technical Institute (D)

2159 Apperson Drive, Salem VA 24153
Telephone: (540) 989-2500 Identification: 770664
Accreditation: ACICS

† Main campus is ITT Technical Institute in Indianapolis, IN.

ITT Technical Institute (E)

7300 Boston Boulevard, Springfield VA 22153-2804
Telephone: (703) 440-9535 Identification: 666321
Accreditation: ACICS

† Main campus is ITT Technical Institute in Indianapolis, IN.

James Madison University (F)

800 S Main Street, Harrisonburg VA 22807-0001
County: Independent City FICE Identification: 003721
Unit ID: 232423
Telephone: (540) 568-6211 Carnegie Class: Master's L
FAX Number: N/A Calendar System: Semester
URL: www.jmu.edu
Established: 1908 Annual Undergrad Tuition & Fees (In-State): $9,176
Enrollment: 19,927 Coed
Affiliation or Control: State IRS Status: 501(c)3
Highest Offering: Doctorate
Program: Liberal Arts And General; Teacher Preparatory; Professional
Accreditation: SC, ARCPA, ART, AUD, BUS, BUSA, CACREP, CIDA, CS, DANCE, DIETD, ENGR, IPSY, MUS, NURSE, OT, PSPSY, SP, SPAA, SW, TED, THEA

01 President .... Mr. Jonathan R. ALGER
05 Provost/Senior VP Academic Affairs .... Dr. Jerry BENSON
11 Sr Vice Pres Administration/Finance .... Mr. Charles W. KING
32 Sr VP Student Affairs/Univ Planning .... Dr. Mark J. WARNER
30 Vice Pres University Advancement .... Mr. Nick LANGRIDGE
84 VP Access and Enrollment Mgmt .... Ms. Donna L. HARPER
04 Exec Assistant to the President .Mrs. Maggie BURKHART-EVANS
81 Dean College Science/Math .... Dr. David F. BRAKKE
49 Dean College Arts/Letters .... Dr. David K. JEFFREY
76 Dean Col of Health & Behav Studies .... Dr. Sharon LOVELL
50 Dean College of Business .... Dr. Mary GOWAN
57 Dean College Visual Performing Arts .... Dr. George E. SPARKS
53 Dean College of Education .... Dr. Phillip M. WISHON
72 Dean College of Int Science & Engr .... Dr. Robert KOLVOORD
58 Dean Graduate School .... Dr. Reid J. LINN
97 Dean University Studies .... Dr. Linda C. HALPERN
08 Dean of Libraries/Educ Technologies .... Mr. Ralph A. ALBERICO
43 University Counsel .... Ms. Susan L. WHEELER
45 Asst Vice Pres Budget Management .... Ms. Diane L. STAMP
07 Director of Admissions .... Mr. Michael D. WALSH
37 Dir Financial Aid & Scholarships .... Ms. Lisa L. TUMER
15 Director Human Resources .... Ms. Diane YERIAN
09 Director Institutional Research .... Dr. Frank J. DOHERTY
41 Director of Athletics .... Mr. Jeffrey T. BOURNE
26 Dir Public Affairs & Univ Spokesman .... Mr. Donald K. EGLE
06 University Registrar .... Ms. Michele M. WHITE
19 Chief of Police .... Mr. Lee A. SHIFFLETT

Jefferson College of Health Sciences (G)

101 Elm Ave. S.E., Roanoke VA 24013
County: Independent City FICE Identification: 006622
Unit ID: 231837
Telephone: (540) 985-8483 Carnegie Class: Spec/Health
FAX Number: (540) 985-9773 Calendar System: Semester
URL: www.jchs.edu
Established: 1982 Annual Undergrad Tuition & Fees: $22,400
Enrollment: 1,048 Coed
Affiliation or Control: Independent Non-Profit IRS Status: 501(c)3
Highest Offering: Master's
Program: Professional; Nursing Emphasis
Accreditation: SC, ARCPA, COARC, EMT, MT, NURSE, OT, OTA, PTAA

01 President .... Dr. Nathaniel L. BISHOP
05 Dean Academic Affairs .... Dr. Lisa ALLISON-JONES
10 Dean Administrative Services .... Ms. Anna S. MILLIRONS
84 Director Enrollment Management .... Ms. Connie S. COOK
32 Dean Student Affairs .... Mr. Scott HILL
108 Assoc Dean for Inst Effectiveness .... Dr. Glen R. MAYHEW
17 Chair Community Health Sciences .... Dr. Sharon L. HATFIELD
88 Director Healthcare Management .... Dr. Janet E. PHILLIPS
63 Program Director Emergency Services .... Mr. John C. COOK
17 Dept Chair Arts & Sciences .... Dr. Francis C. DANE
83 Pgm Dir Humanities & Soc Sci .... Mr. Darrell K. SHOMAKER
81 Director Biomed/Sci/Math .... Dr. James L. MCDONEL
66 Dept Chair Nursing .... Dr. Ava G. PORTER
66 Program Director BSN .... Dr. Rebecca M. GREER
66 Program Director BSN .... Dr. Melody F. SHARP
88 Dept Chr Rehab/Wellness .... Dr. Susan M. POLICH
88 Director Occupation Therapy Masters .... Dr. David A. HAYNES
27 Coord Communications/Col Relations .... Mr. Mark A. LAMBERT
29 Development Resource Officer .... Ms. Catherine P. TURNER
25 Sponsored Projects Coordinator .... Ms. Amanda M. ELLINGER
07 Director of Admissions .... Ms. Judith O. MCKEON
37 Director of Financial Aid .... Ms. Debra J. JOHNSON
06 Registrar .... Ms. Linda C. WILLIAMS
08 Director Library .... Ms. Ramona H. THISS
35 Coordinator Student Affairs .... Ms. Elizabeth A. COSTA
40 Manager Bookstore .... Ms. Suzanne M. ANDERSON
21 Bursar .... Ms. Vicki R. BROWN
09 Institutional Research Manager .... Dr. Timothy R. MILLARD
18 Safety/Physical Plant Officer .... Ms. Susan L. BOOTH
38 Director Counseling and Wellness .... Dr. Jennifer J. SLUSHER
21 Director Business Services .... Mr. Glenn S. HENSLEY
04 Admin Secretary to President .... Ms. Dorothy J. HALL
88 Program Director Health and Exc Sci .... Dr. Allison H. BOWERSOCK
88 Director Occupational Therapy Asst .... Ms. Ave M. MITTA
88 Program Dir Physician Asst Program .... Ms. Patricia J. AIREY
88 Program Director PTA program .... Ms. Rebecca DUFF

The John Leland Center for Theological Studies (H)

1306 N Highland Street, Arlington VA 22201
County: Arlington Identification: 666340
Telephone: (703) 812-4757 Carnegie Class: Not Classified
FAX Number: (703) 812-4764 Calendar System: Other
URL: www.leland.edu
Established: 1998 Annual Graduate Tuition & Fees: $11,620
Enrollment: 75 Coed
Affiliation or Control: Baptist IRS Status: 501(c)3
Highest Offering: Master's; No Undergraduates
Program: Religious Emphasis
Accreditation: THEOL

01 President .... Dr. Mark J. OLSON
05 Academic Dean/Vice President .... Dr. Jeffrey G. WILLETTS
04 Exec Assistant to the President .... Ms. Jovan PETTY
08 Librarian .... Ms. Monica LEAK
06 Registrar .... Ms. Andrea BAKKE
07 Director Recruiting/Admissions .... Mr. Elijah HEYWARD
10 Chief Business Officer .... Mrs. Ellen TEAGUE
21 Associate Business Officer .... Mr. Jonathan RIDER
26 Chief Public Relations Officer .... Mr. Elijah HEYWARD

Liberty University (I)

1971 University Boulevard, Lynchburg VA 24502-2269
County: Independent City FICE Identification: 020530
Unit ID: 232557
Telephone: (434) 582-2000 Carnegie Class: Master's L
FAX Number: (434) 582-2304 Calendar System: Semester
URL: www.liberty.edu
Established: 1971 Annual Undergrad Tuition & Fees: $20,768
Enrollment: 74,372 Coed
Affiliation or Control: Other IRS Status: 501(c)3
Highest Offering: Doctorate
Program: Liberal Arts And General; Teacher Preparatory; Professional
Accreditation: SC, ENG, EXSC, LAW, NURSE, TED

01 Chancellor/President .... Mr. Jerry FALWELL, JR.
88 Vice Chancellor Spiritual Affairs .... Rev. Jonathan FALWELL
05 Vice Chancellor/Acting Provost .... Dr. Ronald S. GODWIN
10 Chief Financial Officer .... Mr. Don MOON
32 Vice President Student Affairs .... Dr. Mark L. HINE
11 Vice President Administration .... Mrs. Sharon HARTLESS
15 Vice President Human Resources .... Mrs. Laura J. WALLACE
26 Vice Pres Exec Projects/Media Rels .... Mr. Johnnie MOORE
20 Vice Prov Grad Sch/Online Programs .... Dr. Ronald E. HAWKINS
20 Vice Prov Academic Administration .... Dr. Garth E. RUNION
09 Vice Pres for Admin Info Management .... Mr. Larry SHACKLETON
45 AVP for Institutional Effectiveness .... Dr. H. William WHEELER
13 Chief Information Officer .... Mr. Matthew J. ZEALAND
06 Registrar .... Mr. Larry SHACKLETON
84 Vice Pres Enrollment Management .... Mr. Chris JOHNSON
07 Director of Admissions .... Mr. Terry ELAM
29 Director of Alumni Affairs .... Mr. Tyler FALWELL
08 Dean of Library Services .... Ms. Marcy PRIDE
33 Dir Student Care/Conduct Offices .... Mr. Keith ANDERSON
34 Senior Student Conduct Officer .... Ms. Andrea ADAMS
42 Vice Pres & Dean of the Seminary .... Dr. Elmer TOWNS
86 Dean Helms School of Government .... Mr. Shawn D. AKERS
37 Vice President of Financial Aid .... Dr. Robert L. RITZ
41 Director of Athletics .... Mr. Jeff BARBER
49 Dean College of Arts & Sciences .... Dr. Roger D. SCHULTZ
50 Dean School of Business .... Dr. Scott M. HICKS
60 Dean School of Communication .... Dr. Cecil KRAMER
97 Dean Ctr Acad Support/Adv Svcs .... Dr. Brian YATES
73 Dean School of Religion .... Dr. Elmer L. TOWNS
53 Dean School of Education .... Dr. Karen L. PARKER
35 Director of Campus Recreation .... Mr. Chris MISIANO
18 Vice Pres of Field Operations .... Mr. Scott STARNES
19 Chief of Police LUPD .... Col. Richard HINKLEY
72 Dean School of Engineering and CSCI .... Mr. David DONAHOO
28 Dir Ctr for Multicltrl Enrichment .... Ms. Melany PEARL
106 Exec Director Online Programs .... Mrs. Tamela CRICKENBERGER
58 Dean Academic Admin Graduate School .... Dr. Kevin D. CORSINI
61 Dean School of Law .... Mr. Mathew D. STAVER
88 Dean School of Aeronautics .... Mr. David L. YOUNG

Longwood University (J)

201 High Street, Farmville VA 23909-1801
County: Prince Edward FICE Identification: 003719
Unit ID: 232566
Telephone: (434) 395-2000 Carnegie Class: Master's M
FAX Number: (434) 395-2635 Calendar System: Semester
URL: www.longwood.edu
Established: 1839 Annual Undergrad Tuition & Fees (In-State): $10,890
Enrollment: 4,834 Coed
Affiliation or Control: State IRS Status: 501(c)3
Highest Offering: Master's
Program: Liberal Arts And General; Teacher Preparatory; Professional
Accreditation: SC, BUS, EXSC, MUS, NRPA, NURSE, SP, SW, TED, THEA

01 President .... Mr. W. Taylor REVELEY, IV
05 Provost/Vice Pres Academic Affairs .... Dr. Kenneth B. PERKINS
10 Vice Pres Administration & Finance .... Mr. Kenneth COPELAND
32 Vice President for Student Affairs .... Dr. Tim J. PIERSON
86 VP for Commonwealth Relations .... Ms. Brenda L. ATKINS
18 VP Facilities Mgmt/Real Property .... Mr. Richard W. BRATCHER
30 Chief Development Officer .... Dr. Bryan K. ROWLAND
13 Chief Information Officer .... Ms. Penny G. HOWARD
84 Assoc VP Enrollment Management .... Dr. Jennifer K. GREEN
26 Assoc VP Marketing/Communications .... Ms. Sabrina BROWN
07 Dean of Admissions .... Ms. Sallie D. MCMULLIN
09 Director Assessment & Inst Research .... Dr. Ling Y. WHITWORTH
06 Registrar .... Ms. Vikki LEVINE
08 Dean of Library .... Mrs. Suzy SZASZ-PALMER
29 Associate VP for Alumni Relations .... Mrs. Nancy B. SHELTON
28 Director for Diversity & Inclusion .... Vacant
38 Director Student Counseling .... Dr. Wayne R. O'BRIEN
36 Director of Acad & Career Adv Ctr .... Ms. Mary M. SAUNDERS
37 Director Student Financial Aid .... Mrs. Karen M. SCHINABECK
15 Chief Human Resources Officer .... Ms. Della H. WICKIZER
18 Director Physical Plant .... Mr. Alvin B. MYERS
96 Director of Materiel Management .... Mr. James E. SIMPSON

Lynchburg College (K)

1501 Lakeside Drive, Lynchburg VA 24501-3199
County: Independent City FICE Identification: 003720
Unit ID: 232609
Telephone: (434) 544-8100 Carnegie Class: Master's S
FAX Number: (434) 544-8499 Calendar System: Semester
URL: www.lynchburg.edu
Established: 1903 Annual Undergrad Tuition & Fees: $33,565
Enrollment: 2,211 Coed
Affiliation or Control: Christian Church (Disciples Of Christ)
IRS Status: 501(c)3
Highest Offering: Doctorate
Program: Liberal Arts And General; Teacher Preparatory; Professional
Accreditation: SC, ACBSP, CACREP, EXSC, NURSE, PTA

01 President .... Dr. Kenneth R. GARREN
05 Vice Pres & Dean for Academic Affs .... Dr. Julius A. SIGLER
10 Vice President Business & Finance .... Mr. Steve BRIGHT
30 Vice Pres Advancement .... Ms. Denise MCDONALD
84 Vice Pres Enrollment Management .... Mrs. Rita DETWILER
32 Vice Pres & Dean of Student Develop .... Mr. John G. ECCLES
09 Vice Pres Institutional Research .... Mrs. Debbie DRISCOLL
50 Dean School Business & Economics .... Dr. Joseph TUREK

53 Dean School Education/Human Devel ....Dr. Jan STENNETTE
60 Dean Sch Communications & The Arts ....Dr. Oeida HATCHER
79 Dean Sch Humanities/Social Science ....Dr. Kim MCCABE
81 Dean School of Sciences ....Dr. Barry LOBB
76 Dean Sch Health Science/Human Perf ....Dr. Linda ANDREWS
06 Registrar/Asst Dean Acad/Stndt Info ....Mr. Jay K. WEBB
08 Director of the Library .. Mr. Christopher A. MILLSON-MARTULA
37 Director of Financial Aid ....Ms. Michelle DAVIS

Mary Baldwin College (A)

318 Prospect Street, Staunton VA 24401

County: Augusta FICE Identification: 003723
Unit ID: 232672
Telephone: (540) 887-7000 Carnegie Class: Master's S
FAX Number: (540) 886-5561 Calendar System: Other
URL: www.mbc.edu
Established: 1842 Annual Undergrad Tuition & Fees: $28,720
Enrollment: 1,797 Female
Affiliation or Control: Presbyterian Church (U.S.A.) IRS Status: 501(c)3
Highest Offering: Doctorate
Program: Liberal Arts And General; Teacher Preparatory
Accreditation: SC, SW, TEAC

01 President ....Dr. Pamela FOX
05 VP Academic Affairs/Dean ....Dr. Catharine O'CONNELL
10 Sr Vice President Business/Finance ....Mr. David MOWEN
84 Sr VP Enrollment Mgmt/Dean Stdnts ....Vacant
30 Vice Pres Institutional Advancement ....Vacant
26 Vice President for Public Relations ....Ms. Crista CABE
88 Assoc VP for Inclusive
Excellence ....Rev. Andrea CORNELL-SCOTT
58 Dean Adult & Graduate Studies ....Ms. Lallon POND
09 Dean Inst Research/Registrar ....Dr. Lewis D. ASKEGAARD
27 Chief Information Officer ....Mr. Angus MCQUEEN
07 Executive Director Enrollment Mgmt ....Mr. Andrew MODLIN
08 Director of Library ....Ms. Carol CREAGER
58 Graduate Teacher Education ....Dr. Rachel POTTER
57 Director MLitt/MFA ....Dr. Paul MENZER
88 Director Program for Excep Gifted ....Dr. Stephanie FERGUSON
15 Director of Human Resources ....Ms. Shelly IRVINE
32 Exec Dir Stdnt Life/Asc Dean Stdnts ....Ms. Lisa WELLS
18 Chief Facilities/Physical Plant ....Mr. Brent DOUGLASS
21 Dir of Budgets/Business Operation .... Mr. Rick CZERWINSKI
29 Director of Alumni Relations ....Vacant
36 Director Career Development Svcs ....Ms. Julie CHAPPELL
37 Director of Financial Aid ....Ms. Robin DIETRICH

Marymount University (B)

2807 N Glebe Road, Arlington VA 22207-4299

County: Arlington FICE Identification: 003724
Unit ID: 232706
Telephone: (703) 522-5600 Carnegie Class: Master's L
FAX Number: (703) 284-1637 Calendar System: Semester
URL: www.marymount.edu
Established: 1950 Annual Undergrad Tuition & Fees: $26,100
Enrollment: 3,702 Coed
Affiliation or Control: Roman Catholic IRS Status: 501(c)3
Highest Offering: Doctorate
Program: Liberal Arts And General; Teacher Preparatory; Professional
Accreditation: SC, ACBSP, CACREP, CIDA, HSA, NURSE, PTA, TED

01 President ....Dr. Matthew D. SHANK
05 Provost and Vice Pres Acad Affairs ....Dr. Sherri L. HUGHES
10 Vice Pres for Financial Affairs ....Dr. Ralph KIDDER
84 Vice Pres Stdnt Devel & Enrollment ....Vacant
30 Vice President for Development ....Mr. Joseph FOSTER
26 Vice Pres Communications/Marketing ......Ms. Shelley A. DUTTON
20 Assoc Vice President Acad Affairs ....Vacant
20 Assoc Vice President Acad Affairs .... Dr. Liane SUMMERFIELD
49 Dean Arts & Sciences ....Dr. George CHEATHAM
50 Dean Business Administration ....Dr. James RYERSON
53 Dean Education & Human Services ....Dr. Lois STOVER
76 Dean Health Professions ....Dr. Tess CAPPELLO
08 Dean Library & Learning Services ....Dr. Zary MOSTASHARI
06 University Registrar ....Mr. Scott SPENCER
13 Exec Director IT Services ....Mr. Steve MUNSON
09 Exec Director Inst Effectiveness .... Mr. Michael SCHUCHERT
32 Assoc Vice President Student Dev ....Vacant
07 Director of Admissions Undergrad ....Vacant
07 Director of Graduate Admissions ....Ms. Francesca REED
37 Director Financial Aid ....Ms. Deborah RAINES
42 Director Campus Ministry ....Rev. Brian BASHISTA
41 Director Athletics ....Mrs. Debbie WARREN
19 Dir of Campus Safety/Transportation ....Mr. Eric HOLS
91 Dir of Admin Information Services ....Vacant
39 Director of Residence Life ....Mr. Paul LYNCH
35 Director of Student Activities ....Mr. Vincent STOVALL
23 Director of Student Health Service ....Ms. Diane WHITE
38 Director Student Counseling ....Ms. Natalie MITCHELL
21 Asst Vice Pres and Controller ....Mr. Ronald SOMERVELL
15 Exec Dir Human Resource Svcs ....Mr. James HOBSON
18 Int Director of Physical Plant ....Vacant
96 Coordinator of Purchasing ....Mrs. Amy PAPPAS
29 Exec Dir Development/Alumni Rels ....Vacant
26 Director of Public Relations ....Ms. Laurie F. CALLAHAN

Medical Careers Institute (C)

1001 Omni Boulevard Suite 200,
Newport News VA 23606-4388
Telephone: (757) 873-2423 FICE Identification: 022472
Accreditation: &SC, MAAB, PTAA, RAD

† Main campus is ECPI College of Technology in Virginia Beach, VA.

Medical Careers Institute (D)

2809 Emerywood Parkway, Suite 400,
Richmond VA 23294
Telephone: (804) 521-5999 Identification: 667038
Accreditation: &SC, MAAB, SURTEC

† Main campus is ECPI College of Technology in Virginia Beach, VA.

Medtech College (E)

6565 Arlington Blvd., Suite 100, Falls Church VA 22042

County: Fairfax FICE Identification: 025889
Unit ID: 131742
Telephone: (703) 237-6200 Carnegie Class: Assoc/PrivFP
FAX Number: (703) 533-3750 Calendar System: Semester
URL: www.medtec.edu
Established: 1939 Annual Undergrad Tuition & Fees: $15,500
Enrollment: 1,545 Coed
Affiliation or Control: Proprietary IRS Status: Proprietary
Highest Offering: Associate Degree
Program: Occupational
Accreditation: COE

01 Executive Director ....Janet BARONE

Miller-Motte Technical College (F)

1011 Creekside Lane, Lynchburg VA 24502-4353

County: Lynchburg FICE Identification: 004992
Unit ID: 233091
Telephone: (434) 239-5222 Carnegie Class: Assoc/PrivFP
FAX Number: (434) 239-1069 Calendar System: Quarter
URL: www.miller-motte.edu
Established: 1997 Annual Undergrad Tuition & Fees: $11,904
Enrollment: 480 Coed
Affiliation or Control: Proprietary IRS Status: Proprietary
Highest Offering: Associate Degree
Program: Occupational; Technical Emphasis
Accreditation: ACICS, MAC, SURGT

01 Director ....Ms. Susie ROWLAND

Miller-Motte Technical College (G)

4444-A Electric Road, Roanoke VA 24018
Telephone: (540) 597-1010 Identification: 770816
Accreditation: ACICS

† Main campus is Miller-Motte Technical College in Lynchburg, VA.

National College (H)

3926 Seminole Trail, Charlottesville VA 22911-8397
Telephone: (434) 295-0136 Identification: 666501
Accreditation: ACICS, MAC

† Main campus is American National University in Salem, VA.

National College (I)

336 Old Riverside Drive, Danville VA 24541-1819
Telephone: (434) 793-6822 Identification: 666502
Accreditation: ACICS, MAC, SURGT

† Main campus is American National University in Salem, VA.

National College (J)

1515 Country Club Road, Harrisonburg VA 22801-9709
Telephone: (540) 432-0943 Identification: 666503
Accreditation: ACICS, MAC, SURGT

† Main campus is American National University in Salem, VA.

National College (K)

104 Candlewood Court, Lynchburg VA 24502-2653
Telephone: (434) 239-3500 Identification: 666504
Accreditation: ACICS, MAC

† Main campus is American National University in Salem, VA.

National College (L)

905 N. Memorial Boulevard, Martinsville VA 24112-2420
Telephone: (276) 632-5621 Identification: 666505
Accreditation: ACICS, MAC

† Main campus is American National University in Salem, VA.

Norfolk State University (M)

700 Park Avenue, Norfolk VA 23504-8000

County: Independent City FICE Identification: 003765
Unit ID: 232937
Telephone: (757) 823-8600 Carnegie Class: Master's L
FAX Number: (757) 823-2067 Calendar System: Semester
URL: www.nsu.edu
Established: 1935 Annual Undergrad Tuition & Fees (In-State): $7,226
Enrollment: 7,100 Coed
Affiliation or Control: State IRS Status: 501(c)3
Highest Offering: Doctorate
Program: Liberal Arts And General; Teacher Preparatory; Professional
Accreditation: SC, ADNUR, BUS, CLPSY, CS, DIETD, ENG, JOUR, KIN, MT, MUS, NAIT, NUR, SW, TED

01 Interim President ....Dr. Sandra J. DELOATCH
100 Chief of Staff ....Dr. Deborah C. FONTAINE
05 Provost/Vice Pres Academic Affs ....Dr. Sandra J. DELOATCH
10 Int Vice Pres Finance and Admin ....Mr. Earlie P. HORSEY
30 Acting Vice Pres Univ Advancement ....Mrs. Cheryl A. BATES-LEE
32 Vice Pres Student Affairs ....Mr. Edward M. WILLIS
20 Vice Provost for Undergrad ....Dr. Mildred K. FULLER
20 Vice Provost ....Dr. Clarence D. COLEMAN
84 Asst Vice Pres Enrollment Mgmt ....Mrs. Terricita E. SASS
43 University Counsel ....Ms. Pamela F. BOSTON
07 Dir of Recruitment & Admissions ....Mrs. Lakeisha E. MAYES
19 Chief of Campus Police ....Mr. Anthony H. WALKER
38 Acting Director of Counseling ....Mrs. Vanessa C. JENKINS
06 Interim Registrar ....Mr. Michael CARPENTER
08 Dean of Library Services ....Dr. Tommy BOGGER
37 Director of Financial Aid ....Mr. Kevin J. BURNS
36 Director of Career Services .... Mr. Nash D. MONTOGMERY
15 Human Resources Director ....Mrs. Edie H. ROGAN
14 Director Enterprise Information Sys .Mrs. Alison D. DAVIS-TARIQ
29 Director of Alumni Relations ....Ms. Michelle D. HILL
49 Dean of Liberal Arts ....Dr. Belinda C. ANDERSON
50 Interim Dean of Business ....Dr. Bidhu D. MOHANTY
53 Dean of Education ....Vacant
76 Acting Dean of Science & Technology .... Dr. Larry MATTIX
70 Interim Dean of Social Work ....Dr. Rowena C. WILSON
58 Dean of Graduate Studies and Resear ....Vacant
86 Legislative and Community Liason ....Ms. Paula C. THOMPSON
26 Asst VP of Univ Relations ....Mrs. Cheryl A. BATES-LEE
09 Dir Institutional Research ....Dr. Alona SMOLOVA
39 Director of Residential Life ....Mrs. Faith M. FITZGERALD
40 Bookstore Manager ....Ms. Pamela WILLIAMSON
41 Athletic Director ....Mr. Marty L. MILLER
18 Director of Facilities Management ....Vacant
85 Dir of Intl Student & Scholar Svcs ....Mrs. Beverly HARRIS
96 Director of Procurement ....Mr. Eugene ANDERSON
21 Controller ....Mr. Barry O. HERRING

† Member of Virginia Consortium for Professional Psychology.

Old Dominion University (N)

5115 Hampton Boulevard, Norfolk VA 23529-0001

County: Independent City FICE Identification: 003728
Unit ID: 232982
Telephone: (757) 683-3000 Carnegie Class: RU/H
FAX Number: (757) 683-4505 Calendar System: Semester
URL: www.odu.edu
Established: 1930 Annual Undergrad Tuition & Fees (In-State): $8,820
Enrollment: 24,670 Coed
Affiliation or Control: State IRS Status: 501(c)3
Highest Offering: Doctorate
Program: Liberal Arts And General; Teacher Preparatory; Professional
Accreditation: SC, ANEST, ART, BUS, BUSA, CACREP, CLPSY, CYTO, DH, ENG, ENGT, EXSC, MT, MUS, NMT, NRPA, NURSE, PH, PTA, SP, SPAA, TED, THEA

01 President ....Mr. John R. BRODERICK
05 Provost/VP Academic Affairs ....Dr. Carol SIMPSON
10 Vice President Admin & Finance ....Mr. Robert L. FENNING
46 Interim Vice President for Research .... Dr. Rodger HARVEY
15 Vice Pres for Human Resources ... Ms. September C. SANDERLIN
30 Vice Pres University Advancement ....Mr. Alonzo C. BRANDON
32 VP Student Engagement & Enroll Svcs ......Dr. Ellen J. NEUFELDT
09 Vice Prov Plng & Inst Effectiveness ....Dr. Martha S. SHARPE
88 Vice Provost for Faculty/Pgm Devel ....Dr. Chandra R. DESILVA
88 Vice Prov Grad/Undergrad Acad Pgms .... Dr. Brian K. PAYNE
20 Assoc Vice Pres Academic Affairs .... Mr. James P. DUFFY
21 Asc VP Admn & Fin/Univ Budget
Ofcr ....Ms. Deborah L. SWIECINSKI
88 Asst VP Regional/Higher Educ Ctrs ....Ms. Renee OLANDER
56 Assoc VP Distance Learning ....Mr. Andrew R. CASIELLO
84 Assoc Vice Pres Enrollment Mgmt ....Ms. Jane H. DANE
44 Assoc Vice Pres for Advancement ....Mr. Daniel J. GENARD
88 Assoc VP Student Engagement ....Dr. Johnny YOUNG
88 Asst Vice Pres Auxiliary Services ....Mr. Todd JOHNSON
21 Asst VP Finance/Univ Controller ....Ms. Mary DENEEN
13 Asst VP Information Technology
Svcs ....Mr. James R. WATERFIELD
31 Asst Vice Pres Community Engagement ....Ms. Karen F. MEIER
35 Asst Vice Pres Student Engagement .Mr. Donald M. STANSBURY
20 Asst VP Undergraduate Studies ....Ms. Judith M. BOWMAN
30 Asst Vice Pres for Development ....Dr. Anita S. FRIEDMAN
29 Asst Vice Pres of Alumni Relations ....Ms. Dana G. ALLEN
26 Asst VP Marketing & Communications .... Ms. Jennifer MULLEN
22 Asst VP Inst Equity & Diversity ....Ms. ReNee S. DUNMAN
58 Associate VP for Graduate Studies ....Dr. Brenda N. LEWIS
49 Dean College Arts & Letters ....Dr. Charles E. WILSON, JR.
81 Dean College of Sciences .... Dr. Christopher PLATSOUCAS
76 Dean College Health Sciences ....Dr. Shelley C. MISHOE
50 Dean Col Business/Public Admin ....Dr. Gilbert R. YOCHUM
53 Dean College of Education ....Vacant
54 Dean Col Engineering & Tech ....Dr. Oktay BAYSAL
92 Dean Honors College ....Dr. David D. METZGER
20 Int Dean Academic Enhancement ....Dr. David D. METZGER
36 Asst Dean Career Management Center .... Mr. Tom WUNDERLICH
93 Asst Dean Multicultural Stdnt Svcs ....Ms. Lesa C. CLARK

43 General Counsel ....Mr. Richard E. NANCE
85 Exec Dir International Programs ....Mr. Marcelo E. SILES
88 Exec Dir Cmty Development Corp ....Ms. E. Ann GRANDY
08 University Librarian ....Ms. Virginia S. O'HERRON
11 Chief Operating Officer ....Mr. David F. HARNAGE
06 University Registrar ....Ms. Mary K. SWARTZ
07 Exec Director of Admissions ....Dr. J. Christopher FLEMING
41 Director of Athletics ....Dr. C. Wood SELIG
37 Int Director Student Financial Aid ....Ms. Vera E. RIDDICK
04 Asst to Pres Community Relations ....Ms. Cecelia T. TUCKER
88 Director Military Affairs ....Vacant
38 Sr Exec Director Counseling Svcs ....Dr. Lenora H. THOMPSON
23 Director Student Health Center ....Ms. Jennifer J. FOSS
85 Director Intl Students & Faculty ....Ms. Robbin S. FULMORE
91 Director Computing Information Svcs ....Mr. Michael S. LITTLE
39 Exec Director of Student Housing ....Vacant
18 Director Facilities Management ....Mr. R. Dillard GEORGE
19 Chief of Police ....Ms. Rhonda L. HARRIS
27 Director of Public Relations ....Mr. Stephen P. DANIEL
28 Dir Inst Equity/Diversity/EO/AA ....Ms. Lanay NEWSOM
96 Director of Materiel Management ....Mr. Rick BERRY
94 Director Women's Studies ....Dr. Jennifer N. FISH
16 Interim Director of Human Resources ....Ms. Kathleen WILLIAMSON
35 Dir Student Activities/Leadership ....Ms. Nicole C. KIGER
40 Manager Bookstore ....Mr. Darryl ATKINSON
04 Asst to the President/Asst to COO ....Ms. Velvet L. GRANT
86 Asst to Pres for Govt Relations ....Ms. Elizabeth A. KERSEY

† Member of Virginia Consortium for Professional Psychology.

Patrick Henry College (A)

Ten Patrick Henry Circle, Purcellville VA 20132
County: Loudoun FICE Identification: 039513
Telephone: (540) 338-1776 Carnegie Class: Bac/A&S
FAX Number: (540) 441-8709 Calendar System: Semester
URL: www.phc.edu
Established: 2000 Annual Undergrad Tuition & Fees: $25,570
Enrollment: 347 Coed
Affiliation or Control: Independent Non-Profit IRS Status: 501(c)3
Highest Offering: Baccalaureate
Program: Liberal Arts And General
Accreditation: TRACS

00 Chancellor ....Dr. Michael P. FARRIS
01 President ....Dr. Graham WALKER
05 Provost ....Dr. Gene E. VEITH
03 Exec Vice President & Treasurer ....Mr. Carl W. SCHREIBER
30 Vice President for Advancement ....Mr. Colin STEWART
20 Dean of Academic Affairs ....Dr. Frank GULIUZZA
32 Dean of Student Affairs ....Ms. Sandra K. CORBITT
11 VP for Campus Services ....Mr. Earl W. HALL
10 Chief Financial Officer ....Mr. Daryl WOLKING
09 Senior Dir of Inst Effectiveness ....Mr. Rodney J. SHOWALTER
13 Chief Information Officer ....Mr. Jeff R. BURTNER
84 Asst VP for Enrollment Management ....Mr. William K. KELLARIS
06 Registrar ....Ms. Tamara L. WOLFGANG
08 Director of the Library ....Ms. Sara E. PENSGARD
26 Director of Communications ....Mr. David W. HALBROOK

Protestant Episcopal Theological Seminary in Virginia (B)

3737 Seminary Road, Alexandria VA 22304-5201
County: Independent City FICE Identification: 003731
Unit ID: 233259
Telephone: (703) 370-6600 Carnegie Class: Not Classified
FAX Number: (703) 370-6234 Calendar System: Semester
URL: www.vts.edu
Established: 1823 Annual Graduate Tuition & Fees: $12,850
Enrollment: 191 Coed
Affiliation or Control: Protestant Episcopal IRS Status: 501(c)3
Highest Offering: Doctorate; No Undergraduates
Program: Professional; Religious Emphasis
Accreditation: THEOL

01 President/Dean ....Rev. Ian S. MARKHAM
05 Vice Pres/Assoc Dean Academic Affs ....Rev. Melody KNOWLES
10 VP for Administration/Finance ....Mrs. Heather ZDANCEWICZ
30 VP Inst Advancement ....Rev. J. Barney HAWKINS
16 VP HR and Inst Effectiveness ....Ms. Katie GLOVER
88 Assoc Dean of Special Projects ....Dr. Amy DYER
32 Assoc Dean of Students ....Rev. Justin LEWIS-ANTHONY
06 Registrar ....Mrs. Tamara A. SHEPHERD
08 Director of the Library ....Dr. Mitzi J. BUDDE

Radford University (C)

810 E Main Street, Radford VA 24142-0002
County: Independent City FICE Identification: 003732
Unit ID: 233277
Telephone: (540) 831-5000 Carnegie Class: Master's L
FAX Number: (540) 831-5142 Calendar System: Semester
URL: www.radford.edu
Established: 1910 Annual Undergrad Tuition & Fees (In-State): $8,976
Enrollment: 9,573 Coed
Affiliation or Control: State IRS Status: 501(c)3
Highest Offering: Doctorate
Program: Liberal Arts And General; Teacher Preparatory; Professional
Accreditation: SC, BUS, CACREP, CIDA, COPSY, CS, DIETD, MUS, NRPA, NURSE, OT, @PTA, SP, SW, TED, THEA

01 President ....Ms. Penelope W. KYLE
04 Special Assistant to the President ....Ms. Jo A. KIERNAN
05 Provost & VP Academic Affairs ....Dr. Sam H. MINNER
10 Vice President for Finance & Admin ....Mr. Richard S. ALVAREZ
32 Vice President for Student Affairs ....Dr. Mark G. SHANLEY
30 Vice President Univ Advancement ....Dr. Deborah ROBINSON
26 Vice President and Chief Comm Ofc ....Mr. Larry J. CARPENTER
21 Associate VP for Finance & Admin ....Ms. Lisa H. RIDPATH
84 Interim Vice Prov Enroll Plng/Mgmt ....Mr. James PENNIX
20 Vice Prov for Academic Affairs ....Dr. William R. KENNAN
108 Asst Vice Provost for Assessment ....Dr. Ebenezer F. KOLAJO
49 Dean Col Hum/Behav Sci ....Dr. Katherine HAWKINS
50 Interim Dean of Business & Econ ....Dr. Dennis O. GRADY
53 Dean Education & Human Development ....Dr. Patricia B. SHOEMAKER
76 Dean Health & Human Services ....Dr. Kenneth M. COX
57 Dean Visual/Performing Arts ....Dr. Joseph P. SCARTELLI
58 Int Dean Col of Grad & Prof Studie ....Dr. Nora REILLY
72 Dean Col of Sci & Technology ....Dr. J. Orion ROGERS
35 Associate Dean of Students ....Ms. Susan TRAGESER
13 Associate VP Info Technology ....Mr. Edward B. OAKES
07 Dean of Admissions ....Mr. James PENNIX
06 Registrar ....Mr. Matthew S. BRUNNER
37 Director of Financial Aid ....Mrs. Barbara A. PORTER
39 Director of Residential Life ....Ms. Amber MULLEN
18 Asst VP & Chief Fac Officer ....Mr. Chris WILLIS
29 Executive Dir of Alumni Affairs ....Ms. Laura TURK
41 Director Intercollegiate Athletics ....Mr. Robert LINEBURG
08 Dean of the Library ....Mr. Steven P. HELM
27 Vice President Info Technology/CIO ....Mr. Danny M. KEMP
15 Exec Dir & Chief HR Officer ....Ms. Christina BROGDON
19 Director of University Police ....Chief Colleen T. ROBERTS
88 Dir Acad Engage/Career Svc ....Ms. Ellen TAYLOR
23 Director Student Health Services ....Ms. Abby UGLUM
85 Interim Dir of International Ed Ctr ....Ms. Teresa KING
24 Director TV/Radio/Comm Svcs ....Ms. Ashlee B. CLAUD
25 Dir Sponsored Pgms/Grant Mgmt ....Mr. Thomas CRUISE
40 Manager University Bookstore ....Mr. Benjie SAUNDERS
96 Dir Procurement & Contracts ....Ms. Pamela P. SIMPKINS
09 Asst Vice Pres/Dir Inst Research ....Dr. Debra R. TEMPLETON
38 Director Student Counseling ....Ms. Erin SULLIVAN
102 Asst VP for University Advancement ....Ms. Robyn J. PORTERFIELD
88 University Controller ....Mr. William H. SHORTER
88 Director Planning & Construction ....Mr. Roy E. SAVILLE
86 Dir Govt/Non-Profit Assistance Ctr ....Dr. Bruce W. CHASE
35 Assoc VP Student Affairs/Activities ....Mr. Kenneth J. BONK
39 Director of Housing Operations ....Mr. Jeffrey P. ORZOLEK
51 Dir Ctr Innovative Teach/Learn ....Mr. Charlie COSMATO
28 Dir Ctr for Diversity & Inclusion ....Ms. Crasha PERKINS
45 Dir Budget and Financial Planning ....Mr. Chad REED

Randolph College (D)

2500 Rivermont Avenue, Lynchburg VA 24503-1555
County: Independent City FICE Identification: 003734
Unit ID: 233301
Telephone: (434) 947-8000 Carnegie Class: Bac/A&S
FAX Number: (434) 947-8139 Calendar System: Semester
URL: www.randolphcollege.edu
Established: 1891 Annual Undergrad Tuition & Fees: $32,240
Enrollment: 645 Coed
Affiliation or Control: United Methodist IRS Status: 501(c)3
Highest Offering: Master's
Program: Liberal Arts And General; Teacher Preparatory
Accreditation: SC, TEAC

01 President ....Dr. Bradley W. BATEMAN
05 VP Academic Affs & Dean of College ....Dr. Carl A. GIRELLI
30 Vice Pres Institutional Advancement ....Ms. Jan MERIWETHER
10 VP Finance/Administration/Treasurer ....Mr. Mitch WESOLOWSKI
32 VP Student Affs & Dean of Students ....Dr. Matha THORNTON
26 Vice Pres College Relations ....Vacant
84 VP Enrollment Management ....Mr. Michael J. QUINN
101 Exec Asst to Pres/Sec Board Trust ....Mr. Wesley FUGATE
20 Associate Dean of the College ....Ms. Paula J. WALLACE
29 Alumnae Director ....Ms. Heather A. GARNETT
09 Dir Institutional Res/Plng/Asses ....Dr. John F. KEENER
15 Director Human Resources ....Ms. Sharon SAUNDERS
18 Chief Facilities/Physical Plant ....Mr. Bobby BENNETT
21 Controller ....Mr. Jonathan TYREE
38 Director Student Counseling ....Dr. Anne HERSHBELL
08 Librarian ....Mr. Theodore J. HOSTETLER
06 Registrar ....Ms. Barbara S. THRASHER
37 Dir Student Financial Services ....Mr. Michael C. FARRIS
36 Director of Career Development ....Vacant
13 Director of Information Technology ....Mr. Victor GOSNELL

Randolph-Macon College (E)

204 Henry Street, PO Box 5005, Ashland VA 23005-5505
County: Hanover FICE Identification: 003733
Unit ID: 233295
Telephone: (804) 752-7200 Carnegie Class: Bac/A&S
FAX Number: (804) 752-7231 Calendar System: Other
URL: www.rmc.edu
Established: 1830 Annual Undergrad Tuition & Fees: $34,850
Enrollment: 1,312 Coed
Affiliation or Control: United Methodist IRS Status: 501(c)3
Highest Offering: Baccalaureate
Program: Liberal Arts And General; Teacher Preparatory
Accreditation: SC, TEAC

01 President ....Mr. Robert R. LINDGREN
05 Provost/VP for Academic Affairs ....Dr. William T. FRANZ
10 Vice Pres of Admin & Finance ....Mr. Paul DAVIES
30 Vice Pres for College Advancement ....Ms. Diane M. LOWDER
84 Vice President for Enrollment ....Dr. David L. LESESNE
32 Vice President for Student Affairs ....Dr. Grant L. AZDELL
29 Exec Dir Col Advancement for Alumni ....Mrs. Susan H. DONAVANT
08 Director of Library ....Dr. Virginia E. YOUNG
26 Dir of Marketing & Communications ....Mrs. Anne Marie LAURANZON
07 Director of Admissions ....Mr. Anthony F. AMBROGI
37 Director of Financial Aid ....Mrs. Mary Y. NEAL
14 CIO and ITS Director ....Mr. Kirk BAUMBACH
06 Registrar ....Mrs. Alana DAVIS
36 Dir Counseling/Career Services ....Dr. D. Craig ANDERSON
09 Director of Institutional Research ....Dr. Timothy W. MERRILL
18 Dir of Operations & Physical Plant ....Mr. Thomas P. DWYER
42 Chaplain ....Rev. Darrell L. HEADRICK
19 Director of Campus Safety ....Mr. Maurice J. KIELY
41 Athletic Director ....Mr. Jeffrey S. BURNS
15 Director Human Resources ....Mrs. Sharon S. JACKSON
21 Controller ....Mrs. Barbara A. DAUBERMAN
20 Associate Dean of the College ....Dr. Lauren C. BELL
36 Director of Career Services ....Ms. Catherine A. ROLLMAN
35 Asst Dean of Students ....Mr. James D. MCGHEE, JR.
40 Bookstore Manager ....Mrs. Barclay F. DUPRIEST
88 Exec Dir Ctr Personal/Career Dev ....Mrs. Linda P. CARNE
21 Director of Budget/Financial Analys ....Mrs. Caroline C. BUSCH

Reformed Theological Seminary (F)

1651 Old Meadow Road, Suite 300, McLean VA 22102
Telephone: (703) 448-3393 Identification: 666079
Accreditation: &SC, &THEOL

† Main campus is Reformed Theological Seminary in Jackson, MS.

Regent University (G)

1000 Regent University Drive, Virginia Beach VA 23464-9800
County: Independent City FICE Identification: 030913
Unit ID: 231651
Telephone: (757) 352-4127 Carnegie Class: DRU
FAX Number: (757) 352-4381 Calendar System: Semester
URL: www.regent.edu
Established: 1977 Annual Undergrad Tuition & Fees: $15,960
Enrollment: 5,925 Coed
Affiliation or Control: Independent Non-Profit IRS Status: 501(c)3
Highest Offering: Doctorate
Program: Professional
Accreditation: SC, ACBSP, CACREP, CLPSY, LAW, TEAC, THEOL

01 President ....Dr. Carlos CAMPO
05 Exec Vice Pres for Academic Affairs ....Dr. Paul BONICELLI
30 Vice President for Advancement ....Mrs. Ann LEBLANC
14 Vice President for Info Technology ....Mrs. Tracy R. STEWART
10 VP of Finance ....Mr. Dean A. WOOTEN
15 Vice President for Human Resources ....Mrs. Martha J. SMITH
26 VP for Marketing & Public Relations ....Ms. Sherri MILLER
106 Assistant VP of Online Learning ....Mrs. Ginger ZILLGES
60 Dean Communication & the Arts ....Dr. Mitch LAND
50 Dean School of Business/Leadership ....Dr. Bruce E. WINSTON
38 Dean Psychology & Counseling ....Dr. William HATHAWAY
73 Dean School of Divinity ....Dr. Michael D. PALMER
53 Interim Dean School of Education ....Dr. Gail DERRICK
80 Dean School of Government ....Dr. Eric PATTERSON
61 Dean School of Law ....Mr. Jeffrey A. BRAUCH
49 Dean College of Arts & Sciences ....Dr. Gerson MORENO-RIANO
08 Dean of Libraries ....Dr. Sara BARON
43 General Counsel ....Mr. Louis A. ISAKOFF
06 Registrar ....Ms. Althea KIMES
37 Director of Financial Aid ....Ms. Dotti DAVIDSON
09 Director of Institutional Research ....Dr. Amanda WYNN
84 Director of Enrollment Management ....Mr. Matthew CHADWICK
18 Dir of Facilities & Engineering ....Mr. Richard JEMIOLA
29 Director of Alumni Relations ....Ms. Melissa FUQUAY
35 Director of Student Life ....Mr. Roger CHEEKS
96 Manager of Purchasing ....Mrs. Pauline CARRAWAY
42 Director of Campus Ministries ....Dr. Richard KIDD
84 Exec Dir Enrollment Marketing ....Mr. David PROFFITT
108 Director of Assessment ....Mr. Ryan MURNANE
88 Director of Military Affairs ....Mr. Dave BOISSELLE

Richard Bland College (H)

11301 Johnson Road, Petersburg VA 23805-7100
County: Independent City FICE Identification: 003707
Unit ID: 233338
Telephone: (804) 862-6100 Carnegie Class: Assoc/Pub2in4
FAX Number: (804) 862-6207 Calendar System: Semester
URL: www.rbc.edu
Established: 1960 Annual Undergrad Tuition & Fees (In-State): $2,010
Enrollment: 1,532 Coed
Affiliation or Control: State IRS Status: 501(c)3
Highest Offering: Associate Degree
Program: 2-Year Principally Bachelor's Creditable
Accreditation: SC

01 President ....Dr. Debbie L. SYDOW
05 Provost & Dean of Faculty ....Vacant

10 Vice Pres Administration & Finance ... Mrs. Annette S. PARKER
19 Director Security/Safety ... Mr. Jesse B. WRAY
30 Director Institutional Advancement ... Dr. C. Scott DAVIS
09 Dir of Institutional Effectiveness ... Mr. James T. HART
06 Registrar ... Ms. Lois WRAY
08 Director of Library ... Mr. Daniel L. REAM
32 Director of Student Affairs ... Vacant
13 Director of Info Tech Services ... Vacant
37 Director of Financial Aid ... Mrs. Jeanne E. HOLMES
07 Assoc Dir of Enrollment Services ... Mrs. Whitney GERSHOWITZ
15 Director of Human Resources ... Mr. Jason BROWN
18 Facilities/Physical Plant Manager ... Mr. George JELLERSON
96 Director of Purchasing ... Ms. Nichole COLLINS
35 Assoc Dir of Student Services ... Ms. Evanda WATTS-MARTINEZ
39 Assoc Dir of Residence Life ... Vacant

Riverside School of Health Careers (A)

316 Main Street, Newport News VA 23601
FICE Identification: 021400
Unit ID: 233408
Telephone: (757) 240-2200 Carnegie Class: Not Classified
FAX Number: (757) 240-2225 Calendar System: Semester
URL: www.riverside.edu
Established: Annual Undergrad Tuition & Fees: $25,500
Enrollment: 326 Coed
Affiliation or Control: Independent Non-Profit IRS Status: 501(c)3
Highest Offering: Associate Degree
Program: Occupational
Accreditation: ABHES, DNUR, PNUR, RAD, SURGT

03 Vice President & Administrator ... Ms. Tracee B. CARMEAN

Roanoke College (B)

221 College Lane, Salem VA 24153-3747
County: Independent City FICE Identification: 003736
Unit ID: 233426
Telephone: (540) 375-2500 Carnegie Class: Bac/A&S
FAX Number: (540) 375-2205 Calendar System: Semester
URL: www.roanoke.edu
Established: 1842 Annual Undergrad Tuition & Fees: $36,472
Enrollment: 2,060 Coed
Affiliation or Control: Evangelical Lutheran Church In America
IRS Status: 501(c)3
Highest Offering: Baccalaureate
Program: Liberal Arts And General; Teacher Preparatory
Accreditation: SC, ACBSP, TEAC

01 President ... Mr. Michael C. MAXEY
05 Vice President/Dean of the College ... Dr. Richard A. SMITH
84 VP of Enrollment Services ... Dr. Brenda P. POGGENDORF
32 Vice President Student Affairs ... Dr. Eugene L. ZDZIARSKI, II
10 Vice President Business Affairs ... Mr. Mark P. NOFTSINGER
30 Vice President Resource Development ... Ms. Connie K. CARMACK
13 Chief Information Officer ... Ms. Rebecca SANDLIN
09 Exec Dir Institutional Research ... Dr. Jack K. STEEHLER
20 Assoc Dean Academic Affairs/Admin ... Dr. Jennifer K. BERENSON
06 Assoc Dean Acad Affairs/Registrar ... Ms. Leah R. RUSSELL
07 Director of Admissions ... Ms. Patricia N. LEDONNE
35 Associate Dean of Student Life ... Dr. Brian T. CHISOM
39 Director of Residence Life/Housing ... Ms. Teresa P. BLETHYN
88 Director of Colket Ctr/Student Act ... Mr. Mark T. PETERSEN
92 Director of Honors Programs ... Dr. Michael A. HAKKENBERG
08 Director of the Library ... Mr. Stanley F. UMBERGER
36 Director of Career Services ... Ms. Toni D. MCLAWHORN
24 Director Instructional Tech/Res Ctr ... Mr. David H. MULFORD
31 Director Cmty Pgms/Special Events ... Ms. Stephanie P. GARST
26 Director of Public Relations ... Ms. Teresa T. GEREAUX
44 Director of Gift Planning ... Mr. Richard J. POGGENDORF
29 Director of Development/Alumni ... Mr. Jonathan E. LEE
37 Director of Financial Aid ... Mr. Thomas S. BLAIR
21 Director of Finance & Budget ... Ms. Kathryn A. VANNESS
91 Dir Appllications Systems Inf Tech ... Ms. Mitzi B. STEELE
18 Manager Planning and Projects ... Mr. Larry S. WALKER
15 Director Human Resources ... Ms. Cathy S. DICKERSON
40 Bookstore Coordinator/Buyer ... Ms. Melissa B. RUTLEDGE
19 Director Campus Safety ... Mr. Thomas H. TURNER
23 Director Student Health Services ... Ms. Sandra W. MCGHEE
41 Athletic Director ... Mr. M. Scott ALLISON
42 Chaplain ... Rev. Christopher M. BOWEN
43 General Counsel ... Mr. G. Michael PACE, JR.
104 Director International Education ... Dr. Pamela SEROTA COTE
38 Director Counseling Center ... Dr. J. P. Hap COX
28 Director of Multicultural Affairs ... Ms. Juliet J. LOWERY
04 Executive Assistant to President ... Ms. Joyce A. SINK

Sanford-Brown College-Tysons Corner (C)

1761 Old Meadow Road, McLean VA 22102
County: Fairfax FICE Identification: 009420
Unit ID: 234216
Telephone: (703) 556-8888 Carnegie Class: Bac/Assoc
FAX Number: (703) 556-0953 Calendar System: Quarter
URL: www.wbscareer.com
Established: 1950 Annual Undergrad Tuition & Fees: $15,703
Enrollment: 733 Coed
Affiliation or Control: Proprietary IRS Status: Proprietary
Highest Offering: Baccalaureate
Program: Occupational; 2-Year Principally Bachelor's Creditable; Liberal Arts And General
Accreditation: ACICS

01 President ... Dr. Raul GARZA

Sentara College of Health Sciences (D)

1441 Crossways Blvd, Ste 105, Chesapeake VA 23320
County: Chesapeake City FICE Identification: 031065
Unit ID: 232885
Telephone: (757) 388-2900 Carnegie Class: Not Classified
FAX Number: (757) 388-2905 Calendar System: Semester
URL: www.sentara.edu
Established: 1892 Annual Undergrad Tuition & Fees: $12,500
Enrollment: 460 Coed
Affiliation or Control: Independent Non-Profit IRS Status: 501(c)3
Highest Offering: Baccalaureate
Program: Professional; Nursing Emphasis
Accreditation: ACICS, CVT, NURSE, SURGT

01 Dean Sentara Col of Health Sciences ... Ms. Shelly COHEN
66 Dean of Nursing ... Dr. Angela TAYLOR
45 Asst Dean Institutional Effective ... Ms. Monique BAUCHAM
76 Asst Dean Dept of Allied Health ... Ms. Nora LEONARD
88 Asst Dean Information Technology ... Mr. Christopher NELSON
32 Asst Dean Dept of Student Svcs ... Mrs. Sandy MOORE
08 Librarian ... Ms. Suzanne DUNCAN
37 Financial Aid Representative ... Ms. Mary Ann RIVERA
07 Admissions Recruiter ... Ms. Sue LAMB

Shenandoah University (E)

1460 University Drive, Winchester VA 22601-5195
County: Independent City FICE Identification: 003737
Unit ID: 233541
Telephone: (540) 665-4500 Carnegie Class: Master's L
FAX Number: N/A Calendar System: Semester
URL: www.su.edu
Established: 1875 Annual Undergrad Tuition & Fees: $29,704
Enrollment: 4,176 Coed
Affiliation or Control: United Methodist IRS Status: 501(c)3
Highest Offering: Doctorate
Program: Liberal Arts And General; Teacher Preparatory; Professional
Accreditation: SC, ARCPA, BUS, COARC, MIDWF, MUS, NURSE, OT, PHAR, PTA, TEAC

01 President ... Dr. Tracy FITZSIMMONS
05 VP for Academic Affairs ... Dr. Adrienne G. BLOSS
10 Vice Pres Administration/Finance ... Mr. Richard C. SHICKLE, SR.
32 Vice President for Student Life ... Dr. Rhonda VANDYKE COLBY
30 Vice Pres for Advancement ... Mr. Mitchell L. MOORE
84 VP for Enrol Mgmt & Student Success ... Dr. Clarresa MORTON
39 Dir Resident Life & Student Conduct ... Ms. Sue O'DRISCOLL
29 Assoc Vice Pres for Alumni Affairs ... Ms. Jane D. PITTMAN
44 Assoc Vice Pres for Advancement ... Ms. Vicky MEDLOCK
26 Director of Media Relations ... Ms. Emily BURNER
49 Dean of College of Arts & Sciences ... Dr. Calvin H. ALLEN, JR.
50 Dean of Byrd School of Business ... Dr. Miles DAVIS
64 Dean of Shenandoah Conservatory ... Dr. Michael J. STEPNIAK
67 Dean of Dunn School of Pharmacy ... Dr. Alan B. MCKAY
07 Exec of Recruitment & Admissions ... Mr. Andy WOODALL
35 Dir of Student Engagement ... Mr. Rick MCCLENDON
08 Director of Library Services ... Mr. Christopher A. BEAN
06 Registrar ... Vacant
21 Controller ... Ms. Courtney JARRETT
37 Director of Financial Aid ... Ms. Nancy S. BRAGG
36 Director of Career Services ... Ms. Jennifer A. SPATARO-WILSON
18 Director of Physical Plant ... Mr. Barry SCHNOOR
23 Director of Wellness Center ... Mr. Ronald G. STICKLEY
15 Director of Human Resources ... Ms. Marie C. LANDES
41 Athletic Director ... Mr. Doug ZIPP
91 Database & System Administrator ... Mr. David HOFFMAN
13 Director of Institutional Computing ... Mr. Quaiser ABSAR
66 Director Custer School of Nursing ... Dr. Kathryn M. GANSKE
88 Director Div of Athletic Training ... Dr. Rose A. SCHMIEG
88 Dir Div of Occupational Therapy ... Dr. Leslie DAVIDSON
88 Director Div of Physical Therapy ... Dr. Karen E. ABRAHAM
88 Sr Dir Advancement - Conservatory ... Mr. Bradley C. SNOWDEN
19 Interim Director of Public Safety ... Mr. Robin EBERSOLE
102 Director Foundation Relations ... Ms. Jennifer BOUSQUET
31 Director Auxiliary Services ... Mr. John V. STEVENS
88 Dir Div of Physician Asst Studies ... Dr. Rachel CARLSON
20 Dir Learning Resources & Services ... Dr. Audrey ROBINSON
42 Dean of Spiritual Life ... Rev Dr. Justin ALLEN
88 Dir Division of Respiratory Care ... Ms. Beverly WATSON
09 Director Institutional Research ... Vacant
40 Bookstore Manager ... Ms. Mary Ellen WELCH
96 Purchasing & Accts Pay Manager ... Ms. Ginny L. NORMAN
24 Coordinator Media Services ... Ms. Val GANGWER
38 Director Student Counseling ... Ms. Nancy SCHULTE

Skyline College (F)

5234 Airport Road, Roanoke VA 24012-1603
County: Roanoke FICE Identification: 030927
Unit ID: 261931
Telephone: (540) 563-8000 Carnegie Class: Bac/Assoc
FAX Number: (540) 362-5400 Calendar System: Semester
URL: www.skyline.edu
Established: 1966 Annual Undergrad Tuition & Fees: $13,900
Enrollment: 250 Coed
Affiliation or Control: Proprietary IRS Status: Proprietary
Highest Offering: Baccalaureate
Program: Occupational; 2-Year Principally Bachelor's Creditable; Technical Emphasis
Accreditation: ACCSC, MAAB

01 Campus President ... Mr. John GUISE

South Baylo University (G)

7535 Little River Tnpk Unit 325-A, Annandale VA 22003
Telephone: (703) 642-7518 Identification: 770912
Accreditation: @ACUP

† Main campus is South Baylo University in Anaheim, CA.

South University (H)

2151 Old Brick Road, Richmond VA 23060
Telephone: (804) 727-6800 Identification: 770919
Accreditation: &SC

† Main campus is South University in Savannah, GA.

South University (I)

301 Bendix Road, Suite 100, Virginia Beach VA 23452
Telephone: (757) 493-6900 Identification: 770920
Accreditation: &SC, NURSE

† Main campus is South University in Savannah, GA.

Southeast Culinary and Hospitality College (J)

100 Piedmont Avenue, Bristol VA 24201-5699
County: Bristol FICE Identification: 041338
Unit ID: 451608
Telephone: (276) 591-5699 Carnegie Class: Assoc/PrivFP
FAX Number: (276) 591-5677 Calendar System: Semester
URL: www.southeastculinary.edu
Established: 2004 Annual Undergrad Tuition & Fees: $20,090
Enrollment: 94 Coed
Affiliation or Control: Proprietary IRS Status: Proprietary
Highest Offering: Associate Degree
Program: Occupational
Accreditation: COE

01 Chief Executive Officer ... Richard K. ERSKINE
05 Dean ... Joshua WILLIAMSON

Southern Virginia University (K)

One University Hill Drive, Buena Vista VA 24416-3097
County: Rockbridge FICE Identification: 003738
Unit ID: 233611
Telephone: (540) 261-8400 Carnegie Class: Bac/A&S
FAX Number: (540) 261-8451 Calendar System: Semester
URL: www.svu.edu
Established: 1867 Annual Undergrad Tuition & Fees: $18,900
Enrollment: 721 Coed
Affiliation or Control: Independent Non-Profit IRS Status: 501(c)3
Highest Offering: Baccalaureate
Program: Liberal Arts And General
Accreditation: SC

01 President ... Mr. Paul K. SYBROWSKY
05 Provost ... Dr. Madison U. SOWELL
10 Vice President Finance ... Mr. Robert E. HUCH
30 VP Institutional Advancement ... Mr. Richard G. WHITEHEAD
26 VP Communications & Marketing ... Vacant
07 VP Enrollment and Marketing ... Mr. Brett GARCIA
13 VP Operations/Student Services ... Mr. Scott Y. DOXEY
20 Associate Provost ... Dr. Alan WHITEHURST
44 Director of Institutional Advance ... Mr. William BRADDY
32 Associate Dean of Students ... Mr. Joseph BOUCHELLE
10 Controller ... Mr. Jesse SEEGMILLER
08 Director of Library Services ... Dr. Christopher RICHARDSON
36 Director of Student Support ... Mr. Michael GIBBONS
41 Athletic Director ... Mr. Scott Y. DOXEY
06 Registrar ... Ms. Whitney LARSEN
37 Director of Financial Aid ... Mr. John BRANDT
29 Director of Alumni Relations ... Mr. John FEINAUER
09 Director of Institutional Research ... Dr. Alan WHITEHURST
15 Human Resources Assistant ... Mr. Tyson COOPER

Southside Regional Medical Center Professional Schools (L)

737 South Sycamore Street, Petersburg VA 23803-5133
County: Independent City FICE Identification: 012744
Unit ID: 233082
Telephone: (804) 765-5800 Carnegie Class: Not Classified
FAX Number: (804) 765-5937 Calendar System: Semester
URL: www.srmconline.com
Established: 1895 Annual Undergrad Tuition & Fees: $10,650
Enrollment: 130 Coed
Affiliation or Control: Proprietary IRS Status: Proprietary
Highest Offering: Associate Degree
Program: Occupational
Accreditation: ABHES, ADNUR, DMS, DNUR, RAD

03 Vice Pres for Professional Schools ... Ms. Cynthia PARSONS

Standard Healthcare Services College of Nursing (A)

1073 West Broad Street #201, Falls Church VA 22046
Identification: 667129
Telephone: (703) 891-1787 Carnegie Class: Not Classified
FAX Number: (703) 891-1789 Calendar System: Semester
URL: www.standardcollege.edu
Established: 2004 Annual Undergrad Tuition & Fees: N/A
Enrollment: N/A Coed
Affiliation or Control: Proprietary IRS Status: Proprietary
Highest Offering: Associate Degree
Program: Nursing Emphasis
Accreditation: **ABHES**

01 Executive Director .... Ms. Isibor Joy NOSEGBE

Stratford University (B)

7777 Leesburg Pike, Falls Church VA 22043
County: Fairfax FICE Identification: 025412
Unit ID: 438498
Telephone: (703) 821-8570 Carnegie Class: Master's L
FAX Number: N/A Calendar System: Quarter
URL: www.stratford.edu
Established: 1976 Annual Undergrad Tuition & Fees: $14,985
Enrollment: 1,823 Coed
Affiliation or Control: Proprietary IRS Status: Proprietary
Highest Offering: Master's
Program: Professional; Business Emphasis
Accreditation: **ACICS**, ACFEI, NURSE

00 President .... Dr. Richard SHURTZ
03 Executive Vice President .... Mary Ann SHURTZ
05 Chief Academic Officer .... Dr. James FLAGGERT
11 Chief Operations Officer .... Benoit COSSART
10 Chief Financial Officer .... John DOVI
85 Vice President Intl Development .... Feroze KHAN
12 Campus Director DC Metro .... Voytek PANAS
107 Campus Dean .... Dr. Abed ALMALA
06 Registrar .... Mark ORTIZ
07 Director of Admissions .... Ann CONNORS
36 Career Services Manager .... Stephanie DEBAHA
37 Student Financial Services Manager .... Ali MONDLOCK
36 Student Services Manager .... Aerin GILBERT
12 Campus Director Woodbridge .... Vacant
107 Campus Dean .... Dr. Richelle JOHNSON
37 Student Financial Services Manager .... Nancy KELLEWAY
06 Registrar .... Missy TAYLOR
36 Career Services Manager .... Peter BARTELL
35 Student Services Manager .... Anita GRAY
07 Director of Admissions .... James CAMERON
12 Campus Director Richmond .... Susan MERRITT
107 Campus Dean .... Dr. Mary Anne RAMIREZ
37 Student Financial Services Manager .... Noshuo RIVERS
06 Registrar .... Michele THOMPSON
36 Career Services Manager .... Jessica HARLOW
35 Student Services Manager .... Vacant
07 Director of Admissions .... David MAYLE
12 Campus Director Baltimore .... Darryl CAMPBELL
107 Campus Dean .... Eric FRAUWIRTH
37 Student Financial Services Manager .... Lesley OTTERBEIN
06 Registrar .... Kelly KU
36 Career Services Manager .... Dhavani GANATRA
35 Student Services Manager .... Deborah KAI KAI
07 Director of Admissions .... Nick GRASSO
12 Campus Director Newport News .... Aisha NEWSOME
107 Campus Dean .... Dr. Michelle BICEY
37 Student Financial Services Manager .... Ovette FINNELL
06 Registrar .... Sandra APPLETON
36 Career Services Manager .... Yoges NATHAN
35 Student Services Manager .... Jawuan WHEATON
07 Director of Admissions .... Shawn KOHLMAN
12 Campus Director Virginia Beach .... Aisha NEWSOME
107 Campus Dean .... Dr. Hermann BAYER
37 Student Financial Services Manager .... Helen GARLAND
07 Director of Admissions .... Vivian PENA

Stratford University (C)

11104 West Broad Street, Glen Allen VA 23060
Telephone: (804) 290-4231 Identification: 770819
Accreditation: **ACICS**

† Main campus is Stratford University in Falls Church, VA.

Stratford University (D)

836 J. Clyde Morris Boulevard,
Newport News VA 23601-1303
Telephone: (757) 873-4235 Identification: 770818
Accreditation: **ACICS**

† Main campus is Stratford University in Falls Church, VA.

Stratford University (E)

14349 Gideon Drive, Woodbridge VA 22192
Telephone: (703) 897-1982 Identification: 770817
Accreditation: **ACICS**

† Main campus is Stratford University in Falls Church, VA.

Sweet Briar College (F)

134 Chapel Road, Sweet Briar VA 24595-9998
County: Amherst FICE Identification: 003742
Unit ID: 233718
Telephone: (434) 381-6100 Carnegie Class: Bac/A&S
FAX Number: (434) 381-6173 Calendar System: 4/1/4
URL: www.sbc.edu
Established: 1901 Annual Undergrad Tuition & Fees: $33,130
Enrollment: 739 Female
Affiliation or Control: Independent Non-Profit IRS Status: 501(c)3
Highest Offering: Master's
Program: Liberal Arts And General
Accreditation: **SC**, ENG

01 President .... Dr. Jo Ellen PARKER
100 Vice President and Chief of Staff .... Mrs. Louise S. ZINGARO
04 Exec Asst Office of the President .... Mrs. Theresa P. MCNABB
09 Director Institutional Research .... Ms. Christy C. COLE
88 Director of the Tusculum Institute .... Dr. Lynn RAINVILLE
42 Chaplain .... Rev. Dori BAKER
05 Dean of the FacultyVP Acad Affs ... Dr. Amy JESSEN-MARSHALL
20 Assoc Dean Academic Affairs .... Dr. Jill GRANGER
08 Dir Integrated Information Systems .... Dr. John G. JAFFE
06 Registrar .... Ms. Deborah L. POWELL
25 Faculty Grants Officer .... Ms. Kathleen PLACIDI
85 Director International Studies .... Dr. Tiffany N. CUMMINGS
41 Director of Athletics .... Ms. Kelly S. MORRISON
104 Director Junior Year in Spain .... Ms. M. Celeste DELGADO-LIBRERO
104 Director Junior Year in France .... Dr. Margaret A. SCOUTEN
88 Director of Academic Advising .... Mrs. Kelly KRAFT-MEYER
84 Dean of Enrollment Mgmt .... Mr. Steven W. NAPE
10 Vice Pres Finance/Administration .... Mr. Scott SHANK
21 Assoc VP Finance/Administration .... Ms. Gail D. PAYNE
15 Director of Human Resources .... Ms. Caroyn BURTON
18 Director Physical Plant .... Mr. Steve BAILEY
19 Chief of Campus Police .... Mr. David GARDNER
37 Director Financial Aid .... Mrs. Bobbi CARPENTER
40 Book Shop Manager .... Ms. Lynn LEWIS
96 Director Purchasing .... Ms. Cynthia L. PONTON
88 Coordinator Benefits .... Mrs. Judy SPROUSE
31 Director of Auxiliary Services .... Vacant
30 Vice Pres for Alumnae/ Development .... Ms. Heidi HANSEN-MCCRORY
29 Director of Alum Rel/Annual Giving ..... Mrs. Melissa WITHEROW
44 Director of Donor Relations .... Mrs. Donna WHITEHOUSE
32 VP/Dean of Co-Curricular Life .... Ms. Cheryl L. STEELE
38 Mental Health Counselor/Health Svcs ... Ms. Elizabeth S. BLEVINS
36 Director Career Services .... Mr. Wayne F. STARK
39 Director Residence Life & Housing .... Ms. Annie JONES
23 Nurse Practioner/Dir Health Svcs .... Ms. Rose TAYLOR
27 Director of Media/Marketing & Comm .... Ms. Christy JACKSON

Union Presbyterian Seminary (G)

3401 Brook Road, Richmond VA 23227-4597
County: Independent City FICE Identification: 003743
Unit ID: 233842
Telephone: (804) 355-0671 Carnegie Class: Spec/Faith
FAX Number: (804) 355-3919 Calendar System: Semester
URL: www.upsem.edu
Established: 1812 Annual Graduate Tuition & Fees: $13,500
Enrollment: 211 Coed
Affiliation or Control: Presbyterian Church (U.S.A.) IRS Status: 501(c)3
Highest Offering: Doctorate; No Undergraduates
Program: Professional; Religious Emphasis
Accreditation: **SC**, THEOL

01 President .... Dr. Brian K. BLOUNT
11 Vice President for Administration .... Mr. Michael B. CASHWELL
30 Vice Pres Institutional Advancement .... Mr. Richard WONG
84 VP of Enrollment Management .... Ms. Michelle WALKER
05 Dn Union Presbyterian Sem(Richmond) ..... Dr. Stanley SKRESLET
12 Dean Union Presby Sem (Charlotte) .... Dr. Thomas W. CURRIE
20 Associate Dean Academic Programs .... Dr. E. Carson BRISSON
07 Director of Admissions .... Ms. Kate Fiedler BOSWELL
06 Registrar .... Mr. Stanley HARGRAVES
08 Librarian .... Dr. Milton J. COALTER
13 Director Technology Services .... Mr. John R. WILSON
36 Director Student Placement .... Dr. Susan E. FOX

University of Fairfax (H)

1980 Gallows Road, Suite 220, Vienna VA 22182
County: Fairfax Identification: 667094
Telephone: (703) 790-3203 Carnegie Class: Not Classified
FAX Number: (703) 790-3201 Calendar System: Other
URL: www.ufairfax.net
Established: 2002 Annual Graduate Tuition & Fees: N/A
Enrollment: N/A Coed
Affiliation or Control: Independent Non-Profit IRS Status: 501(c)3
Highest Offering: Doctorate; No Undergraduates
Program: Professional
Accreditation: **DETC**

01 President/CEO .... Dr. Christopher V. FEUDO

University of Management & Technology (I)

1901 Fort Myer Drive, Suite 700, Arlington VA 22209-1609
County: Arlington FICE Identification: 041103
Unit ID: 437097
Telephone: (703) 516-0035 Carnegie Class: Not Classified
FAX Number: (703) 516-0985 Calendar System: Semester
URL: www.umtweb.edu
Established: 1998 Annual Undergrad Tuition & Fees: $11,820
Enrollment: 1,061 Coed
Affiliation or Control: Proprietary IRS Status: Proprietary
Highest Offering: Doctorate
Program: Professional; Business Emphasis
Accreditation: **DETC**

01 President .... Dr. Yanping CHEN
05 Academic Dean .... Dr. J. Davidson FRAME

University of Mary Washington (J)

1301 College Avenue, Fredericksburg VA 22401-5300
County: Independent City FICE Identification: 003746
Unit ID: 232681
Telephone: (540) 654-1000 Carnegie Class: Master's L
FAX Number: (540) 654-1073 Calendar System: Semester
URL: www.umw.edu
Established: 1908 Annual Undergrad Tuition & Fees (In-State): $9,660
Enrollment: 5,093 Coed
Affiliation or Control: State IRS Status: 501(c)3
Highest Offering: Master's
Program: Liberal Arts And General; Teacher Preparatory
Accreditation: **SC**, MUS

01 President .... Mr. Richard V. HURLEY
05 Provost .... Dr. Jonathan LEVIN
100 Chief of Staff .... Dr. Martin A. WILDER
10 VP for Admin & Finance .... Mr. Richard R. PEARCE
32 Vice President Student Affairs .... Mr. Douglas N. SEARCY
30 Vice Pres for Advance & Univ Rels .... Mr. Salvatore M. MERINGOLO
102 CEO of UMW Foundation .... Mr. Jeffrey W. ROUNTREE
13 Actg CIO .... Mr. Hall CHESHIRE
88 VP Econ Dev & Regional Engagement .... Dr. Meta R. BRAYMER
15 Asst Vice Pres/Human Res/AAEEO .... Ms. Sabrina C. JOHNSON
105 Director of Digital Communication .... Ms. Shelley KEITH
21 Asst Vice Pres Business Svcs/CPO .... Ms. Erma A. BAKER
20 Assocate Provost .... Dr. John T. MORELLO
18 Assoc Vice Pres Facilities Services .... Mr. John P. WILTENMUTH, III
09 Asst Prov Inst Analy & Effect .... Mr. Taiwo A. ANDE
07 Assoc Prov Admissions & Fin Aid .... Ms. Carol DESCAK
53 Dean of College of Education .... Dr. Mary L. GENDERNALIK-COOPER
50 Dean College of Business .... Dr. Lynne D. RICHARDSON
20 Dean College of Arts & Sciences .... Dr. Richard FINKELSTEIN
35 Dean of Student Life .... Mr. Cedric B. RUCKER
37 Director of Financial Aid .... Ms. Debra J. HARBER
09 Director of Institutional Research ...... Mr. Mathew C. WILKERSON
21 Internal Audit Director .... Ms. Tera D. KOVANES
39 Director of Residence Life .... Ms. Christine M. PORTER
06 Registrar .... Ms. Rita DUNSTON
41 Director of Athletics .... Mr. Ken D. TYLER
08 University Librarian .... Ms. Rosemary ARNESON
88 Director of Publications .... Ms. Neva S. TRENIS
24 Director of Dodd Auditorium .... Mr. Doug NOBLE
88 Assoc Dean of Advising Services .... Ms. Sallie W. BRAXTON
19 Chief of University Police .... Mr. Eddie L. PERRY
29 Exec Director Alumni Relations .... Mr. Mark THADEN
38 Director of Counseling/Psych Svcs ...... Dr. Nicole A. SURETHING
88 Director of Disability Services .... Ms. Sally SCOTT
23 University Physician .... Dr. P. Thomas RILEY
88 Director of University Galleries .... Ms. Anne TIMPANO
27 Director Media & Public Relations .... Ms. Marty G. MORRISON
28 Spec Asst Diversity & Inclusion .... Dr. Leah COX
26 Associate VP University Rels .... Ms. Anna B. BILLINGSLEY
88 Director of Design Services .... Ms. AJ NEWELL
29 Director National Alumni Engagement .... Ms. Cindy L. SNYDER
44 Assoc VP Univ Advancemnt/Alumni Rel ...... Mr. Kenneth L. STEEN
26 Director of Marketing .... Mr. Malcolm HOLMES

University of Phoenix Richmond-Virginia Beach Campus (K)

9750 West Broad Street, Glen Allen VA 23060-4169
Telephone: (804) 281-3900 Identification: 770233
Accreditation: **&NH**, ACBSP

† Main campus is University of Phoenix in Tempe, AZ.

University of Richmond (L)

28 Westhampton Way, Richmond VA 23173-1903
County: Independent City FICE Identification: 003744
Unit ID: 233374
Telephone: (804) 289-8000 Carnegie Class: Bac/A&S
FAX Number: (804) 287-6540 Calendar System: Semester
URL: www.richmond.edu
Established: 1830 Annual Undergrad Tuition & Fees: $45,320
Enrollment: 4,361 Coordinate
Affiliation or Control: Independent Non-Profit IRS Status: 501(c)3
Highest Offering: Doctorate
Program: Liberal Arts And General; Professional

Accreditation: SC, BUS, BUSA, LAW, TEAC

01 President .... Dr. Edward L. AYERS
05 Provost .... Dr. Stephen ALLRED
10 Vice President Business & Finance .... Mr. David B. HALE
32 Vice President Student Affairs .... Dr. Stephen D. BISESE
30 Vice President Advancement .... Mr. Thomas C. GUTENBERGER
13 Vice Pres for Information Services .... Ms. Kathryn J. MONDAY
84 Vice Pres Enrollment Management .... Ms. Nanci TESSIER
100 Chief of Staff .... Dr. Lori G. SCHUYLER
101 Secretary Board of Trustees .... Ms. Ann Lloyd BREEDEN
04 Executive Assistant to President .... Mrs. Carolyn R. MARTIN
88 CEO Spider Mgmt Company .... Mr. Steve KNEELEY
16 Assoc Vice Pres Human Resources .... Mr. Carl K. SORENSEN
18 Assoc Vice Pres Facilities .... Mr. Andrew S. MCBRIDE
29 Asst VP Alumni & Career Services .... Ms. Kristin J. WOODS
102 Asst VP Foundation/Corp/Govt Rels ... Ms. Michelle E. WAMSLEY
42 University Chaplain .... Rev. Craig T. KOCHER
07 Asst VP and Dean of Admissions .... Mr. Gil VILLANUEVA
08 University Librarian .... Mr. Kevin BUTTERFIELD
09 Dir Institutional Effectiveness .... Dr. Patricia B. MURPHY
06 University Registrar .... Ms. Susan D. BREEDEN
37 Director of Financial Aid .... Ms. Cynthia B. DEFFENBAUGH
36 Director Career Development Center .. Ms. Leslie W. STEVENSON
38 Director of CAPS .... Dr. Peter O. LEVINESS
96 Director of Procurement .... Ms. Jean C. HINES
35 Assoc VP Student Development .... Dr. Tinina Q. CADE
41 Director of Athletics .... Mr. Keith GILL
104 Director Study Abroad .... Ms. Michele D. COX
105 Director Web Services .... Mr. Eric F. PALMER
33 Dean of Richmond College .... Dr. Joseph R. BOEHMAN
34 Dean Westhampton College .... Dr. Juliette L. LANDPHAIR
49 Dean School of Arts & Sciences .... Dr. Kahtleen R. SKERRETT
50 Dean School of Business .... Dr. Nancy A. BAGRANOFF
61 Dean TC Williams Law School .... Dr. Wendy C. PERDUE
51 Dean School Continuing Studies .... Dr. James L. NARDUZZI
88 Dean Jepson School Leader Stds .... Dr. Sandra J. PEART
19 Assoc VP Publc Sfty/Chief of Police .... Mr. David M. MCCOY
23 Director Health Center .... Dr. Lynne P. DEANE
26 Asst VP for Communications .... Ms. Lisa VAN RIPER
40 Manager University Bookstore .... Mr. Roger L. BROOKS

University of the Potomac (A)

2070 Chain Bridge Road Suite G100, Vienna VA 22182
Telephone: (888) 380-1192 Identification: 666178
Accreditation: &M

† Main campus is University of the Potomac in Washington, DC.

University of Virginia (B)

Charlottesville VA 22903
County: Independent City FICE Identification: 003745
Unit ID: 234076
Telephone: (434) 924-0311 Carnegie Class: RU/VH
FAX Number: (434) 924-0938 Calendar System: Semester
URL: www.virginia.edu
Established: 1819 Annual Undergrad Tuition & Fees (In-State): $12,668
Enrollment: 23,907 Coed
Affiliation or Control: State IRS Status: 501(c)3
Highest Offering: Doctorate
Program: Liberal Arts And General; Teacher Preparatory; Professional
Accreditation: SC, BUS, BUSA, CACREP, CLPSY, CS, DENT, DIETI, ENG, IPSY, LAW, LSAR, MED, NURSE, PCSAS, PH, PLNG, RTT, SP, TEAC

01 President .... Dr. Teresa A. SULLIVAN
03 Exec Vice Pres/Chief Operating Ofcr .... Mr. Patrick D. HOGAN
101 Secretary Board of Visitors .... Ms. Susan G. HARRIS
05 Exec Vice President & Provost .... Dr. John D. SIMON
30 Sr Vice Pres Devel/Public Affairs .... Mr. Robert D. SWEENEY
46 Vice President for Research .... Mr. Thomas C. SKALAK
10 Vice Pres/Chief Financial Officer .... Vacant
21 Vice President Management/Budget .... Ms. Colette SHEEHY
17 Vice President & CEO Medical Center .... Mr. R. Edward HOWELL
32 Vice Pres/Chief Student Affs Ofcr .... Ms. Patricia M. LAMPKIN
13 Vice Pres/Chief Info Officer .... Mr. James L. HILTON
63 VP & Dean School of Medicine .... Dr. Steven T. DEKOSKY
28 VP/Chief Officer Diversity/Equity .... Mr. Marcus L. MARTIN
100 Chief of Staff/Assoc VP for Admin .... Ms. Nancy A. RIVERS
44 Sr Asc VP Dev/Principal Relship Dev .... Mr. Charles B. FITZGERALD
105 Dir of Web Services & Interac Media .... Mr. Zach WHEAT
88 Senior Vice Provost .... Mr. J. Milton ADAMS
20 Vice Prov for Academic Affairs .... Ms. Maurie D. MCINNIS
88 Vice Prov Faculty Recruitmt/Retent .... Ms. Gertrude J. FRASER
88 Vice Provost for Global Affairs .... Mr. Jeffrey w. LEGRO
11 Vice Prov for Administration .... Ms. Anda L. WEBB
88 Vice Provost for the Arts .... Mr. Jody K. KIELBASA
88 Vice Prov for Faculty Development .... Dr. Sharon L. HOSTLER
88 Vice Prov for Academic Outreach .... Mr. Billy K. CANNADAY, JR.
20 Asc Prov Acad Spprt/Classroom Mgmt .... Ms. Martha Wynne STUART
88 Assoc VP Business Operations .... Mr. Richard A. KOVATCH
15 VP/Chief Human Resource Officer .... Ms. Susan CARKEEK
21 Asst Vice Pres Student Finan Svcs .... Mr. Stephen A. KIMATA
88 Asst VP Research Admin .... Mr. Gerald J. KANE
26 Interim Chief Communications Ofc .... Mr. Anthony P. DE BRUYN
88 Chief Investment Officer .... Mr. Lawrence E. KOCHARD
18 Chief Facilities Officer .... Mr. Donald E. SUNDGREN
06 Registrar .... Ms. Carol A J. STANLEY
07 Dean Undergraduate Admission .... Mr. Gregory W. ROBERTS
49 Dean School of Arts & Sciences .... Ms. Meredith J. WOO
61 Dean School of Law .... Mr. Paul G. MAHONEY
66 Dean School of Nursing .... Ms. Dorrie K. FONTAINE
54 Dean Schl Engr/Applied Science .... Mr. James H. AYLOR
48 Dean School of Architecture .... Ms. Kim TANZER
50 Dean Grad School Business Admin .... Mr. Robert F. BRUNER
50 Dean School of Commerce .... Mr. Carl P. ZEITHAML
53 Dean School of Education .... Mr. Robert C. PIANTA
80 Dean Sch Leadership/Public Policy .... Mr. Harry HARDING
51 Dean Cont & Prof Studies .... Mr. Billy K. CANNADAY
35 Associate VP/Dean of Students .... Mr. Allen W. GROVES
23 Exec Director Student Health .... Dr. James C. TURNER
41 Dir Intercollegiate Athletic Pgms .... Mr. Craig K. LITTLEPAGE
43 Gen Counsel & Corporate Secretary .... Mr. Paul J. FORCH
31 Director Community Relations .... Ms. Ida Lee WOOTTEN
22 Director Equal Opportunity Pgms ... Ms. Darlene SCOTT-SCURRY
08 University Librarian .... Ms. Karin WITTENBORG
09 Dir Institutional Assess & Studies .... Mr. George A. STOVALL
88 Exec Director The Jefferson Trust .... Mr. Wayne COZART
37 Director Student Financial Svcs .... Ms. Yvonne B. HUBBARD
36 Exec Dir Univ Career Services .... Mr. James L. MCBRIDE, JR.
87 Dir Summer & Special Academic Pgms .... Mr. Dudley J. DOANE
104 Dir International Studies Office .... Mr. Dudley J. DOANE
19 Chief of Police .... Mr. Michael A. GIBSON
39 Exec Dir Housing & Residence Life .... Ms. Gay PEREZ
29 Executive Director of UVa Bookstore .... Mr. Jonathan A. KATES
38 Director Counseling/Psych Services .... Mr. Russell FEDERMAN
93 Dean African-American Affairs .... Dr. Maurice APPREY
94 Dir Studies in Women & Gender .... Ms. Charlotte PATTERSON
96 Director of Procurement Services .... Mr. Eric N. DENBY

The University of Virginia's College at Wise (C)

One College Avenue, Wise VA 24293-4412
County: Wise FICE Identification: 003747
Unit ID: 233897
Telephone: (276) 328-0100 Carnegie Class: Bac/A&S
FAX Number: (276) 376-1012 Calendar System: Semester
URL: www.uvawise.edu
Established: 1954 Annual Undergrad Tuition & Fees (In-State): $8,509
Enrollment: 2,420 Coed
Affiliation or Control: State IRS Status: 501(c)3
Highest Offering: Baccalaureate
Program: Liberal Arts And General; Teacher Preparatory
Accreditation: SC, CS, ENG, NURSE, TEAC

01 Chancellor .... Dr. Donna P. HENRY
46 Ex Asst to Chanc/Dir Strategic Plng .... Ms. Marcia K. QUESENBERRY
05 Provost/Vice Chan for Acad Affairs .... Dr. Sanders HUGUENIN
30 Vice Chanc Devel/College Relations .... Ms. Tami ELY
10 Vice Chanc Finance/Administration .... Mr. Sim E. EWING
84 Vice Chancellor Enrollment Mgmt .... Mr. Russell D. NECESSARY
41 Ast Vice Chanc Athletic Development .... Mr. Carroll W. DALE
20 Academic Dean .... Dr. Amelia J. HARRIS
32 Dean of Students .... Mrs. Jewell B. WORLEY
21 Comptroller .... Mrs. Kristy KISER
06 Registrar .... Ms. Narda PORTER
08 Director of the Library .... Mr. Robin P. BENKE
15 Director of Human Resources .... Ms. Stephanie D. PERRY
88 Director of College Services .... Mr. Joseph B. KISER
26 Director of News & Media Relations .... Ms. Kathy STILL
44 Director of Development .... Ms. Valerie LAWSON
29 Director of Alumni Relations .... Ms. Pamela J. COLLIE
37 Director of Financial Aid .... Ms. Rebecca HUFFMAN
35 Asst Dir of Student Activities .... Mr. Joshua JUSTICE
36 Director of Career Development .... Vacant
38 Personal Counselor/Health Services .... Ms. Rachel ROSE
19 Campus Police Chief .... Mr. Stephen L. MCCOY
12 Site Director UVA-Wise Programs .... Ms. Courtney L. CONNER
18 Interim Dir Facility Planning/Mgmt .... Mr. David SHORT
09 Director of Institutional Research .... Dr. P. Scott BEVINS
24 Director of Media Services .... Vacant
40 Bookstore Manager .... Mr. Scott LAWSON
39 Director of Residence Life .... Mr. Josh JUSTICE
13 Interim Exec Dir of Info Technology .... Dr. P. Scott BEVINS

Virginia Baptist College (D)

4105 Plank Road, Fredericksburg VA 22407-4803
County: Spotsylvania FICE Identification: 038626
Telephone: (540) 785-5440 Carnegie Class: Not Classified
FAX Number: (540) 785-5441 Calendar System: Semester
URL: www.vbc.edu
Established: 1984 Annual Undergrad Tuition & Fees: $4,800
Enrollment: 100 Coed
Affiliation or Control: Baptist IRS Status: 501(c)3
Highest Offering: Master's
Program: Religious Emphasis
Accreditation: TRACS

01 President .... Dr. Don FORRESTER

Virginia College (E)

7200 Midlothian Turnpike, Richmond VA 23225
Telephone: (804) 977-5100 Identification: 770837
Accreditation: ACICS, MAAB

† Main campus is Virginia College in Birmingham, AL.

Virginia Commonwealth University (F)

901 W Franklin Street, Box 842527,
Richmond VA 23284-2527
County: Independent City FICE Identification: 003735
Unit ID: 234030
Telephone: (804) 828-0100 Carnegie Class: RU/VH
FAX Number: N/A Calendar System: Semester
URL: www.vcu.edu
Established: 1838 Annual Undergrad Tuition & Fees (In-State): $10,299
Enrollment: 9,885 Coed
Affiliation or Control: State IRS Status: 501(c)3
Highest Offering: Doctorate
Program: Liberal Arts And General; Teacher Preparatory; Professional
Accreditation: SC, ANEST, ART, BUS, BUSA, CACREP, CIDA, CLPSY, COPSY, CORE, CS, DANCE, DENT, DH, DIETI, EMT, ENG, FEPAC, HSA, IPSY, JOUR, MED, MT, MUS, NMT, NUR, OT, PH, PHAR, PLNG, PTA, RAD, RTT, SPAA, SW, TED, THEA

01 President VCU & VCU Health System .... Dr. Michael RAO
05 Provost & Sr VP Academic Affs .... Dr. Beverly J. WARREN
17 Sr Vice Pres Health Sciences .... Dr. Sheldon M. RETCHIN
10 Sr Vice Pres Finance & COO .... Dr. David W. HANSON
46 Vice President for Research .... Dr. Francis L. MACRINA
30 Vice Pres Development & Alumni Rel .... Ms. Marti HEIL
86 Executive Dir For Government Rels .... Mr. Mark E. RUBIN
32 Vice Prov Student Affairs .... Dr. Henry G. RHONE
88 Vice Provost for Life Sciences .... Dr. Thomas F. HUFF
09 Vice Prov Planning & Decision Supp .... Ms. Kathleen SHAW
84 Vice Prov for Strategic Enrollment .... Mr. Luke D. SCHULTHEIS
91 Chief Information Officer Tech Svcs .... Mr. Alexander L. HENSON
18 Assoc Vice Pres Facilities Mgmt .... Mr. Brian J. OHLINGER
88 Assoc Vice Pres Gift Development .... Ms. Anne D. JACOBSON
21 Assoc Vice Pres Finance & Admin .... Ms. Pamela A. CURREY
84 Assoc Vice Provost Enroll Svcs .... Ms. Delores T. TAYLOR
22 Asst VP for Inst Equity .... Ms. Velma J. WILLIAMS
16 Asst Vice Pres for Human Resource .... Ms. Cathleen C. BURKE
08 University Librarian .... Mr. John E. ULMSCHNEIDER
43 University Counsel .... Mr. David E. JOHNSON
41 Director of Athletics .... Mr. Edward K. MCLAUGHLIN
88 Director of Business Services .... Ms. Diane L. REYNOLDS
39 Exec Dir Resdential Life & Housing .... Mr. Curtis ERWIN
06 Univ Registrar & Dir Records/Regis .... Mr. Anjour B. HARRIS
07 Asst VP Student Records & Admission .. Ms. Sybil C. HALLORAN
37 Director of Financial Aid .... Ms. Brenda L. BURKE
38 Dir of Counseling Services .... Dr. Jihad N. AZIZ
36 Dir of University Career Center .... Mr. Joseph A. TESTANI
35 Assoc VProv/Dean Student Affs .... Dr. Reuban B. RODRIGUEZ
29 Assoc VP University Alum Relations .... Mr. Gordon A. MCDOUGALL
88 Exec Dir Global Eduation Office .... Dr. R. McKenna BROWN
88 Dir Ctr for Environmental Studies .... Dr. Gregory C. GARMAN
25 Asst VP Research Admin .... Ms. Susan E. ROBB
19 Chief of Police .... Mr. John A. VENUTI
31 VProv/Div Community Engagement .... Dr. Catherine W. HOWARD
94 Director Women's Studies .... Dr. Diana H. SCULLY
92 Dean Honors College .... Dr. Timothy L. HULSEY
67 Dean of Pharmacy .... Dr. Victor A. YANCHICK
66 Dean of School of Nursing .... Dr. Jean GIDDENS
63 Dean of School of Medicine .... Dr. Jerome F. STRAUSS
53 Dean School of Education .. Dr. Christine S. WALTHER-THOMAS
52 Dean of Dentistry .... Dr. David C. SARRETT
50 Dean School of Business .... Mr. Ed A. GRIER
49 Dean Humanities & Sciences .... Dr. James S. COLEMAN
57 Dean School of Arts .... Mr. Joseph H. SEIPEL
70 Dean School of Social Work .... Dr. James E. HINTERLONG
76 Dean Allied Health Professions .... Dr. Cecil B. DRAIN
58 Dean Graduate School .... Dr. F. Douglas BOUDINOT
54 Interim Dean School of Engineering .... Dr. Charles JENNETT
35 Asst Vice Prov Student Affairs .... Dr. Charles J. KLINK
88 Assoc Director of GEO .... Mr. Osama ALAMI
96 Director Procurement Payment Svcs .... Mr. C. Edward GIBBS
26 Exec Dir University Relations .... Ms. Pamela D. LEPLEY

*Virginia Community College System Office (G)

101 N 14th Street, Richmond VA 23219-3658
County: Independent City FICE Identification: 008904
Unit ID: 234146
Telephone: (804) 819-4901 Carnegie Class: N/A
FAX Number: (804) 819-4760
URL: www.vccs.edu

01 Chancellor .... Dr. Glenn DUBOIS
11 Vice Chanc Administrative Services .... Ms. Donna VANCLEAVE
05 Vice Chancellor Academic Services .... Dr. Susan WOOD
103 Vice Chanc Workforce Development .... Dr. Craig HERNDON
13 Vice Chancellor Information Tech .... Dr. Joy A. HATCH
30 Vice Chanc Institutional Advance .... Dr. Jennifer SAGER GENTRY
15 Assoc Vice Chanc Human Resource Svc .... Dr. Christopher LEE
18 Assoc Vice Chanc/Facility Mgmt .... Mr. Bert JONES
43 General Counsel .... Ms. Greer SAUNDERS
88 Director of Internal Audit .... Ms. Helen VANDERLAND
21 Controller .... Mr. Dave MAIR
04 Exec Assistant to the Chancellor .... Ms. Marlene MONDZIEL

*Blue Ridge Community College (H)

PO Box 80, Weyers Cave VA 24486-0080
County: Augusta FICE Identification: 006819
Unit ID: 231536
Telephone: (540) 234-9261 Carnegie Class: Assoc/Pub-R-M
FAX Number: (540) 234-8189 Calendar System: Semester

URL: www.brcc.edu
Established: 1965 Annual Undergrad Tuition & Fees (In-State): $4,584
Enrollment: 4,694 Coed
Affiliation or Control: State IRS Status: 501(c)3
Highest Offering: Associate Degree
Program: Occupational; 2-Year Principally Bachelor's Creditable
Accreditation: SC, ADNUR

02 President .... Dr. John A. DOWNEY
05 Vice Pres Instruction/Student Svcs .... Dr. Robert YOUNG
10 VP Finance/Administrative Svcs .... Dr. Robert BALDYGO
15 Director of Human Resources .... Mr. Tim NICELY
30 Executive Director Development .... Ms. Amy LASER KIGER
81 Dean Math/Physical Sciences/Tech .... Dr. Tara CARTER
79 Dean Humanities/SoclSci/Workforce .... Dr. Kevin RATLIFF
76 Dean Life Sciences/Human Services .... Dr. David URSO
20 Dean Academic Support Services .... Ms. Annette WILLIAMS
08 Dean Learning Resources .... Mr. Francis J. MORAN
26 Chief Public Relations Officer .... Ms. Bridget BAYLOR
21 Financial Services Manager .... Ms. Franki HAMPTON
19 Security & Compliance Coordinator .... Mr. Wayne MARTIN
09 Coordinator Institutional Research .... Dr. Susan E. CROSBY
37 Financial Aid Coordinator .... Mr. Robert CLEMMER
36 Coord Career Services/Recruitment .... Ms. Jenny HARVEY

*Central Virginia Community College (A)

3506 Wards Road, Lynchburg VA 24502-2498
County: Independent City FICE Identification: 004988
Unit ID: 231697
Telephone: (434) 832-7600 Carnegie Class: Assoc/Pub-R-M
FAX Number: (434) 386-4700 Calendar System: Semester
URL: www.cvcc.vccs.edu
Established: 1966 Annual Undergrad Tuition & Fees (In-State): $4,065
Enrollment: 4,905 Coed
Affiliation or Control: State IRS Status: 501(c)3
Highest Offering: Associate Degree
Program: Occupational; 2-Year Principally Bachelor's Creditable
Accreditation: SC, COARC, EMT, RAD

02 President .... Dr. John CAPPS
05 Int VP Academic Affs/Stdnt Svcs .... Mr. Will SANDIDGE
10 Vice President Finance & Admin Svcs .... Mr. John POOLE
103 VP Ctr Workforce Dev/Cont Educ .... Dr. Ruth HENDRICK
30 Vice Pres Institutional Advancement .... Mr. Michael BRADFORD
13 Vice Pres of Information Technology .... Mr. James D. LIGHTFOOT
45 Dean Instnl Effectiveness/Planning .... Dr. Joey FRONHEISER
21 Chief Business Officer .... Ms. Cathryn MOBLEY
29 Director Alumni/Public Relations .... Vacant
96 Director of Purchasing .... Dr. Kimely DAVIS
37 Financial Aid Officer .... Ms. Deborah A. MARSHALL
15 Human Resource Manager .... Ms. Leticia FORSTER
18 Capital Outlay Project Engineer .... Mr. Tom BUSHLEY
56 Distance Education Supervisor .... Ms. Susan S. BEASLEY
07 Coordinator of Admissions/Records .... Ms. Julie LOVING
08 Coordinator of Library Services .... Mr. Michael T. FEIN
78 Coord Apprenticeship/Coop Education .... Vacant
79 Dean Humanities/Social Science .... Dr. Muriel B. MICKLES
50 Dean of Business & Allied Health .... Dr. James LEMONS
81 Dean of Science/Math/Engineering .... Dr. Jeffrey W. LAUB

*Dabney S. Lancaster Community College (B)

PO Box 1000, Clifton Forge VA 24422-1000
County: Independent City FICE Identification: 004996
Unit ID: 231873
Telephone: (540) 863-2800 Carnegie Class: Assoc/Pub-R-S
FAX Number: (540) 863-2915 Calendar System: Semester
URL: www.dslcc.edu
Established: 1967 Annual Undergrad Tuition & Fees (In-State): $4,770
Enrollment: 1,463 Coed
Affiliation or Control: State IRS Status: 501(c)3
Highest Offering: Associate Degree
Program: Occupational; 2-Year Principally Bachelor's Creditable
Accreditation: SC, ACFEI, ADNUR

02 President .... Dr. John J. RAINONE
10 Vice President Finance/Admin Svcs .... Mrs. Angela GRAHAM
51 VP Continuing Educ/Workforce Svcs .... Mr. Gary S. KEENER
49 Dean Arts & Sciences .... Dr. Michael R. SCOTT
32 Director of Student Services .... Mr. Matthew MCGRAW
35 Acting Director of Student Services .... Dr. Michael SCOTT
08 Director of Learning Resources .... Ms. Nova WRIGHT
09 Assessment Officer .... Dr. Michael SCOTT
06 Registrar .... Ms. Lorrie FERGUSON
21 Business Officer .... Ms. Melanie RICKETT
18 Buildings & Grounds Supervisor .... Mr. Edward N. KENNY
13 Coord of Computer Info Systems .... Ms. Tamra LIPSCOMB
37 Coord of Student Financial Aid .... Mrs. Sandra J. HAVERLACK
45 Planning & Funding Specialist .... Ms. Lynda N. THOMPSON
15 Director of Personnel Services .... Ms. April TOLLEY

*Danville Community College (C)

1008 S Main Street, Danville VA 24541-4088
County: Independent City FICE Identification: 003758
Unit ID: 231882
Telephone: (434) 797-2222 Carnegie Class: Assoc/Pub-R-M
FAX Number: (434) 797-8514 Calendar System: Semester
URL: www.dcc.vccs.edu
Established: 1967 Annual Undergrad Tuition & Fees (In-State): $3,960
Enrollment: 4,420 Coed
Affiliation or Control: State IRS Status: 501(c)3
Highest Offering: Associate Degree
Program: Occupational; 2-Year Principally Bachelor's Creditable
Accreditation: SC

02 President .... Dr. Bruce R. SCISM
05 Vice Pres Academic/Student Services .... Dr. Christopher C. EZELL
10 Vice Pres Financial/Admin Services .... Mr. Scott BARNES
09 Dir of Plng/Effectiveness/Research .... Dr. Sherri H. HUFFMAN
30 Director of Development .... Mr. Shannon HAIR
26 Chief Public Relations Officer .... Ms. Andrea BURNEY

*Eastern Shore Community College (D)

29300 Lankford Highway, Melfa VA 23410-9755
County: Accomack FICE Identification: 003748
Unit ID: 232052
Telephone: (757) 789-1789 Carnegie Class: Assoc/Pub-R-S
FAX Number: (757) 789-1737 Calendar System: Semester
URL: www.es.vccs.edu
Established: 1971 Annual Undergrad Tuition & Fees (In-State): $3,795
Enrollment: 1,338 Coed
Affiliation or Control: State IRS Status: 501(c)3
Highest Offering: Associate Degree
Program: Occupational; 2-Year Principally Bachelor's Creditable
Accreditation: SC

02 President .... Dr. Linda THOMAS-GLOVER
05 Vice Pres Academic & Student Svcs .... Vacant
10 Vice Pres Finance & Administration .... Mrs. Annette EDWARDS
32 Dean of Student Services .... Mr. Bryan SMITH
08 Director Learning Resources .... Mrs. Janet JUSTIS
06 Registrar .... Mrs. Connie FENTRESS
09 Director of Institutional Research .... Ms. Judith M. GRIER
26 Chief Public Relations Officer .... Ms. Laurie SWAIN
37 Director of Student Financial Aid .... Mr. Bryan SMITH
15 Director Personnel Services .... Ms. Diane WHEATLEY
18 Chief Facilities/Physical Plant .... Mr. Bobby MEARS
29 Director Alumni Relations/Devel .... Ms. Eve BELOTE
20 Associate Academic Officer .... Mrs. Robin RICH-COATES

*Germanna Community College (E)

2130 Germanna Highway, Locust Grove VA 22508-2102
County: Orange FICE Identification: 008660
Unit ID: 232195
Telephone: (540) 423-9030 Carnegie Class: Assoc/Pub-R-M
FAX Number: (540) 727-3207 Calendar System: Semester
URL: www.germanna.edu
Established: 1970 Annual Undergrad Tuition & Fees (In-State): $3,336
Enrollment: 7,514 Coed
Affiliation or Control: State IRS Status: 501(c)3
Highest Offering: Associate Degree
Program: Occupational; 2-Year Principally Bachelor's Creditable
Accreditation: SC, ADNUR, DA

02 President .... Dr. David A. SAM
04 Exec Assistant to the President .... Ms. Pamela D. SHIFFLETT
05 VP Academic & Student Services .... Dr. Ann WOOLFORD
11 VP Finance & Administrative Svcs .... Mr. Richard BREHM
103 VP Workforce & Community Educ .... Dr. Jeanne WESLEY
30 VP Institutional Advancement .... Mr. Doug ELLIOTT
32 Dean of Student Services .... Ms. Pam FREDERICK
09 Exec Dir of Planning & Assessement .... Dr. Deborah BROCK
08 Head Librarian .... Mr. George OBERLE
72 Dean Professional & Technical Study .... Ms. Denise GUEST
55 Dean Distance Educ & Lrng Resources .... Dr. Yan Yan YONG
66 Dean of Nursing & Health Technology .... Vacant
15 Exec Director of Human Resources .... Mr. Reginald RYALS
18 Building & Ground Supervisor .... Mr. Garland FENWICK
07 Dean of Enrollment Services/Registr .... Ms. Ali HEIBER
13 Manager Technology Services .... Ms. Jacque LARSEN
26 Director of Marketing .... Ms. Barbara TAYLOR
49 Dean of Arts & Sciences .... Dr. Shashuna GRAY
103 Dean of Workforce Prof Development .... Ms. Martha O'KEEFE
19 Chief of Police .... Mr. Craig BRANCH

*J. Sargeant Reynolds Community College (F)

PO Box 85622, Richmond VA 23285-5622
County: Henrico FICE Identification: 003759
Unit ID: 232414
Telephone: (804) 371-3000 Carnegie Class: Assoc/Pub-U-MC
FAX Number: (804) 371-3650 Calendar System: Semester
URL: www.reynolds.edu
Established: 1972 Annual Undergrad Tuition & Fees (In-State): $4,248
Enrollment: 12,846 Coed
Affiliation or Control: State IRS Status: 501(c)3
Highest Offering: Associate Degree
Program: Occupational; 2-Year Principally Bachelor's Creditable
Accreditation: SC, ACFEI, ADNUR, COARC, DA, DT, EMT, MLTAD, OPD, POLYT

02 President .... Dr. Gary L. RHODES
03 Executive Vice President .... Dr. Genene D. LEROSEN
05 Vice President Academic Affairs .... Dr. David R. LOOPE
30 Vice President Advancement .... Mrs. Elizabeth S. LITTLEFIELD
103 VP Comm Col Workforce Alliance .... Mr. Louis L. MCGINTY
10 VP Finance and Administration .... Ms. Amelia M. BRADSHAW
32 Vice President Student Affairs .... Dr. Thomas N. HOLLINS, JR.
45 Assoc VP Policy/Inst Effectiveness .... Mrs. Diane F. BRASINGTON
13 Assoc Vice President Technology .... Mr. John N. AMBROSE
79 Dean School of Humanities/Soc Sci .... Dr. Barbara M. GLENN
50 Dean School of Business .... Mr. David J. BARRISH
76 Dean School of Nursing/Allied Hlth .... Dr. Susan S. HUNTER
81 Dean School of Math Sci Engineering .... Mr. Raymond A. BURTON
20 Dean Educational Support Services .... Mr. Ty CORBIN
09 Director Office Inst Effectiveness .... Dr. Jackie R. BOURQUE
15 Director of Human Resources .... Ms. Corliss B. WOODSON
37 Director of Financial Aid .... Mrs. Kiesha L. POPE
07 Director of Admissions & Records .... Mrs. Karen M. PETTIS-WALDEN
88 Assistant VP Workforce Development .... Vacant
88 Director Outreach and Recruitment .... Ms. Tracy S. GREEN
26 Dir Communications/Public Affairs .... Mr. Malcolm T. HOLMES
26 Director of Marketing .... Ms. Kelly A. SMITH
08 Director of Info/Library Services .... Mr. Hong WU
88 Director of Learning Communities .... Mr. Charles PETERSON, JR.
18 Director Facilities Mgmt/Planning .... Mr. Mark W. PROBST
21 Director of Financial Operations .... Ms. Shirley L. HOPKINS
30 Director of Development .... Ms. Marianne S. MCGHEE
88 Director of Middle College .... Ms. Mary Jo WASHKO
06 Registrar .... Ms. Denise S. TUNSTALL
96 Purchasing Manager .... Mr. Christopher L. COLE
19 Chief of Police & Security Services .... Mr. Paul L. RONCA

*John Tyler Community College (G)

13101 Jefferson Davis Highway, Chester VA 23831-5316
County: Chesterfield FICE Identification: 004004
Unit ID: 232450
Telephone: (804) 796-4000 Carnegie Class: Assoc/Pub-S-MC
FAX Number: (804) 796-4163 Calendar System: Semester
URL: www.jtcc.edu
Established: 1965 Annual Undergrad Tuition & Fees (In-State): $3,970
Enrollment: 10,145 Coed
Affiliation or Control: State IRS Status: 501(c)3
Highest Offering: Associate Degree
Program: Occupational; 2-Year Principally Bachelor's Creditable
Accreditation: SC, ADNUR, FUSER

02 President .... Dr. Ted RASPILLER
04 Executive Assistant to President .... Ms. Mara M. HILLIAR
05 VP Academic Affairs .... Dr. William FIEGE
32 VP for Student Affairs .... Dr. L. Ray DRINKWATER
10 VP for Finance & Admin Services .... Mr. William F. TAYLOR
103 Vice Pres for CC Workforce Alliance .... Mr. Mac L. MCGINTY
35 Dean of Students .... Ms. Sandra KIRKLAND
54 Dean Engr/Business/Public Svcs .... Dr. Melody L. MOORE
49 Dean Arts/Humanities/Soc Sciences .... Dr. Mikell BROWN
81 Dean Math/Natural & Behavorial Sci .... Dr. Johanna WEISS
102 Executive Director Foundation .... Ms. Beverley DEW
09 Dir Institutional Effectiveness .... Dr. Donna JOVANOVICH
08 Librarian Chester Campus .... Ms. Linda LUEBKE
15 Director Human Resources .... Ms. Susan GRINNAN
13 Director Information Services .... Mr. Larry RUBES
37 Director Financial Aid .... Mr. Tony JONES
07 Dir Admission/Records/Registration .... Mrs. Joy L. JAMES
21 Business Manager .... Mr. Leon R. BROWN
19 Security Manager .... Mr. Frank MEDAGLIA
35 Coordinator Student Activities .... Ms. Amanda CARPENTER
36 Director Counseling Chester Campus .... Ms. Michelle TINDALL
36 Dir Counseling Midlothian Campus .... Dr. Ruth VARNEY
18 Director Facilities Operations .... Mr. Greg A. DUNAWAY
26 Director College Relations .... Vacant
66 Dean of Health Sciences .... Dr. Deborah ULMER
08 Librarian Midlothian Campus .... Ms. Helen MCKANN
06 Registrar .... Ms. Joy L. JAMES
96 Director of Purchasing .... Ms. Nancy M. JIMISON

*Lord Fairfax Community College (H)

173 Skirmisher Lane, Middletown VA 22645-1745
County: Frederick FICE Identification: 008659
Unit ID: 232575
Telephone: (540) 868-7000 Carnegie Class: Assoc/Pub-R-L
FAX Number: (540) 868-7100 Calendar System: Semester
URL: www.lfcc.edu
Established: 1970 Annual Undergrad Tuition & Fees (In-State): $4,005
Enrollment: 7,288 Coed
Affiliation or Control: State IRS Status: 501(c)3
Highest Offering: Associate Degree
Program: Occupational; 2-Year Principally Bachelor's Creditable; Business Emphasis
Accreditation: SC

02 President .... Dr. Cheryl THOMPSON-STACY
05 VP of Academic and Student Affairs .... Dr. Chris COUTTS
10 VP of Financial & Admin Services .... Mr. Chris BOIES
32 Vice President of Student Success .... Vacant
103 Vice Pres Workforce Solutions .... Ms. Jeanian CLARK
20 Assoc VP of Instruction Middletown .... Ms. Kim BLOSSER
20 Assoc VP of Instruction Fauquier .... Dr. Judy BATSON
76 Assoc Dean Health Prof & Science .... Ms. Tammy WAGNER
88 Dean Bus/Tech/Dir HS Outreach .... Ms. Brenda K. BYARD
81 Dean Hum/Math/Social Sciences .... Dr. Richard L. ELAM
15 Human Resource Manager .... Ms. Karen N. FOREMAN
30 Director of Development .... Ms. Liv HEGGOY
12 Manager Luray-Page County Center .... Ms. Judith J. SUDDITH
08 Director Learning Resources Center .... Mr. David R. GRAY
09 Dir Planning/Inst Effectiveness .... Dr. John H. MILAM

13 Coordinator Network Security .... Mr. Douglas M. SHRIER
35 Dean of Students - Middletown .... Dr. Karen H. BUCHER
84 Dir of Enrollment Mgt & Reg Service ....Vacant
38 Dir Stdnt Learning Svcs/Counseling ....Ms. Amber FOLTZ
37 Coordinator Student Financial Aid ....Mr. Aaron WHITACRE
96 Procurement Officer ....Ms. Anastasia TRIPLETT
21 Budget and Finance Director ....Ms. Margaret J. BARNETT
19 Law Enforcement Manager ....Mr. Rob MARSHALL
26 Public Relations Marketing Manager ....Ms. Leslie G. KELLY
07 Coord Student Success ....Vacant
35 Coord Student Life & Info Services .... Ms. Brandy BOIES
36 Counselor Middle College ....Ms. Stacy DREW
08 Librarian .... Mr. Gregory MACDONALD
88 Coord of Dual Enrollment ....Ms. Heather BURTON
88 Coord Student Learning & TRIO SS .... Ms. Mia S. LEGGETT
88 Coord/Dir LF Small Bus Dev Center ....Mr. William A. SIRBAUGH
88 Coord Business & Industry Trng ....Mr. Bill PENCE
35 Dean of Students - Fauquier ....Ms. Heather BURTON
88 Director of Transition Programs ....Ms. Lyda KISER
27 Public Info/Grant & Sponsored Pgm ....Mr. Darryl D. CRAWFORD
06 Registrar ....Ms. Karen BUCHER
18 Chief Facilities/Physical Plant .... Mr. David L. BUSHMAN

*Mountain Empire Community College (A)

3441 Mountain Empire Road,
Big Stone Gap VA 24219-4634
County: Wise FICE Identification: 009629
Unit ID: 232788
Telephone: (276) 523-2400 Carnegie Class: Assoc/Pub-R-M
FAX Number: (276) 523-8297 Calendar System: Semester
URL: www.mecc.edu
Established: 1972 Annual Undergrad Tuition & Fees (In-State): $3,192
Enrollment: 3,089 Coed
Affiliation or Control: State IRS Status: 501(c)3
Highest Offering: Associate Degree
Program: Occupational; 2-Year Principally Bachelor's Creditable
Accreditation: SC, ADNUR, COARC

02 President ....Dr. Scott HAMILTON
05 Int VP Academic & Student Svcs ....Ms. Vickie RATLIFF
10 Vice Pres Finance & Admin Services ....Ms. Donna SHELTON
30 Vice Pres Institutional Advancement .... Ms. Donna G. STANLEY
32 Dean of Student Services ....Mr. Brandon DOTSON
07 Director of Enrollment Services ....Ms. Kristy HALL
08 Director of Library Services .... Mr. Michael GILLEY
51 Dir Continuing & Distance Education .... Ms. Sue Ella BOATRIGHT-WELLS
37 Director Financial Aid/Registrar ....Ms. Kristy HALL
13 Dir Ctr Computing & Info Technology .. Mr. Rickie N. CAMPBELL
15 Director Personnel Services ....Ms. Pam GILES
18 Chief Facilities/Physical Plant ....Mr. Jim VICARS
49 Dean Arts & Sciences ....Ms. Carolyn H. REYNOLDS
72 Dean of Industrial Tech/Health Sci .... Mr. Tommy CLEMENTS
50 Int Dean of Business & Info Tech .... Mr. Ricky BOLLING
26 Chief Public Relations Officer .... Ms. Amy GREEAR

*New River Community College (B)

PO Box 1127, Dublin VA 24084-1127
County: Pulaski FICE Identification: 005223
Unit ID: 232867
Telephone: (540) 674-3600 Carnegie Class: Assoc/Pub-R-M
FAX Number: (540) 674-3642 Calendar System: Semester
URL: www.nr.edu
Established: 1969 Annual Undergrad Tuition & Fees (In-State): $3,977
Enrollment: 5,083 Coed
Affiliation or Control: State IRS Status: 501(c)3
Highest Offering: Associate Degree
Program: Occupational; 2-Year Principally Bachelor's Creditable
Accreditation: SC

02 President ....Dr. Jack M. LEWIS
04 Assistant to the President .... Mrs. Amy J. HALL
05 VP for Instruction/Student Svcs .... Dr. Patricia B. HUBER
10 Vice Pres for Finance & Technology ...Mr. John L. VAN HEMERT
30 VP for WD and External Relations ....Dr. Mark C. ROWH
20 Assoc VP/Assessment Coordinator .... Mrs. Teri D. MOORE
49 Interim Dean of Arts & Sciences .... Dr. Janice SHELTON
72 Dean Business & Technologies .... Mr. Dan A. LOOKADOO
09 Dir Inst Effectiveness/Research ....Dr. Frederick M. STREFF
06 Registrar ....Ms. Margaret G. TAYLOR
15 Human Resources & Business Ofc Mgr ....Ms. Melissa P. ANDERSON
102 Executive Director of Foundation ....Ms. Angie E. COVEY
32 Counselor/Student Life Coordinator ....Dr. Benjamin KRAMER
35 Director of Student Affairs ....Ms. Margaret G. TAYLOR
37 Director of Student Financial Aid .... Mrs. Lori A. TIBBS
38 Director of Student Counseling ....Ms. Margaret G. TAYLOR
18 Chief Facilities/Physical Plant ....Mr. Anthony J. NICOLO
21 Associate Vice President of Finance ....Ms. Bridget M. SAYLES
96 Inventory and Purchasing Technician ......Ms. Monica W. CARDEN
56 Dir Dist Educ/Offsite Campus Svcs ....Mrs. Linda C. CLAUSSEN
51 Director Transitional Programs ....Mrs. Jenny L. BOLTE
08 Coordinator of Library Services .... Mrs. Sandra B. SMITH
07 Coord Admissions/Records/Stdnt Svcs ..Ms. Margaret G. TAYLOR
88 Coordinator of WorkKeys Center ....Mrs. Patricia RYAN
88 Coordinator Center Hearing Impaired ....Ms. Lucy J. HOWLETT
88 Coordinator of Learning Disabled ....Ms. Lucy J. HOWLETT
84 Enrollment Manager Coordinator .... Mrs. Deborah D. KENNEDY

*Northern Virginia Community College (C)

4001 Wakefield Chapel Road, Annandale VA 22003-3796
County: Fairfax FICE Identification: 003727
Unit ID: 232946
Telephone: (703) 323-3000 Carnegie Class: Assoc/Pub-S-MC
FAX Number: (703) 323-3767 Calendar System: Semester
URL: www.nvcc.edu
Established: 1965 Annual Undergrad Tuition & Fees (In-State): $3,678
Enrollment: 51,864 Coed
Affiliation or Control: State IRS Status: 501(c)3
Highest Offering: Associate Degree
Program: Occupational; 2-Year Principally Bachelor's Creditable
Accreditation: SC, ADNUR, CAHIIM, COARC, DA, DH, DMS, EMT, MLTAD, PTAA

02 President .... Dr. Robert G. TEMPLIN, JR.
05 Exec VP/Chief Academic Officer ....Dr. Mel D. SCHIAVELLI
10 Vice President Finance .... Ms. Dimitrina DIMKOVA
11 Vice Pres/Chief Administrative Ofcr ....Mr. Tony A. BANSAL
13 Vice Pres of Information Technology ....Dr. Steven G. SACHS
103 Vice Pres of Workforce Development ...Mr. William H. GARY, SR.
09 VP Inst Research/Planning/Assess ....Dr. George E. GABRIEL
20 Assoc VP Academic Services .... Dr. Sharon N. ROBERTSON
104 Assoc Vice Pres Global Studies ....Dr. Paul J. MCVEIGH
84 Assoc VP Stdnt Svcs & Enroll Mgmt .... Dr. Elizabeth HARPER
12 Acting Provost Alexandria Campus .... Dr. Ron BUCHANAN
12 Provost Annandale Campus .... Dr. Barbara L. SAPERSTONE
12 Provost Loudoun Campus ....Dr. Julie LEIDIG
12 Provost Manassas Campus .... Dr. Roger RAMSAMMY
12 Provost Medical Education Campus .... Mr. Brian P. FOLEY
12 Provost Woodbridge Campus .... Dr. Sam HILL
102 Exec Dir NVCC Education Foundation ....Mr. John J. RUFFINO
22 Dir Affirm Act/Minority/Legal Affs .... Mr. Everett V. EBERHARDT
29 Director Alumni Relations ....Ms. Bonnie L. IDLE
25 Director of Grants/Special Projects .... Ms. Deborah E. MOTTSMAN-ROSEN
15 Director of Human Resources .... Ms. Shelli W. JARVIS
96 Director of Purchasing ....Mr. Edward J. MELLON
37 Dir Stdnt Financial Aid/Support Svc ....Ms. Joan A. ZANDERS
21 Controller ....Ms. Jill FRISTOE
18 Dir Facilities Plng/Support Svcs .... Mr. William CHAMBERLIN
27 Public Information Officer ....Ms. Jessica M. BAXTER
19 Director Security/Safety .... Chief Daniel DUSSEAU
86 Director Government Affs/Cmty Rels .... Mr. Dana KAUFFMAN

*Patrick Henry Community College (D)

645 Patriot Avenue, Martinsville VA 24112
County: Henry FICE Identification: 003751
Unit ID: 233019
Telephone: (276) 638-8777 Carnegie Class: Assoc/Pub-R-M
FAX Number: (276) 656-0320 Calendar System: Semester
URL: www.ph.vccs.edu
Established: 1962 Annual Undergrad Tuition & Fees (In-State): $3,970
Enrollment: 2,327 Coed
Affiliation or Control: State IRS Status: 501(c)3
Highest Offering: Associate Degree
Program: Occupational; 2-Year Principally Bachelor's Creditable
Accreditation: SC, ADNUR

02 President ....Dr. Angeline D. GODWIN
05 VP Academic/Student Develop Svcs .... Dr. Kristin WESTOVER
10 Vice Pres Finance & Admin Services ....Mr. John HANBURY
30 Vice Pres Inst Advancement .... Mr. Christopher PARKER
103 Dean Workforce Devel/Continuing Ed ....Mrs. Rhonda HODGES
20 Dean Institutional Support Svcs ....Mr. Greg HODGES
72 Dean Prof Tech/Hlth Sci/Accel Lrng ....Mr. Jeff FIELDS
32 Dean of Student Development .... Mr. Jeff PORTER
37 Financial Aid/Veterans Admin ....Mrs. Cindy KELLER
06 Registrar ....Ms. Jessica CARTER
15 Director of Human Resources .... Ms. Lori MCCARTY
18 Chief Facilities/Physical Plant .... Mr. Wayne CARDWELL
26 Chief Public Relations/Dir Alumni ....Mrs. Kristin LANDRUM
22 Affirmative Action Coordinator .... Ms. Lori MCCARTY
96 Director of Purchasing ....Ms. Carline DEAL
09 Coord Inst Research/Plng/Evaluation ....Vacant
07 Coord of Admissions & Records ....Mr. Travis TISDALE

*Paul D. Camp Community College (E)

100 N College Drive, Franklin VA 23851-0737
County: Independent City FICE Identification: 009159
Unit ID: 233037
Telephone: (757) 569-6700 Carnegie Class: Assoc/Pub-R-S
FAX Number: (757) 569-6795 Calendar System: Semester
URL: www.pdc.edu
Established: 1970 Annual Undergrad Tuition & Fees (In-State): $3,965
Enrollment: 1,493 Coed
Affiliation or Control: State IRS Status: 501(c)3
Highest Offering: Associate Degree
Program: Occupational; 2-Year Principally Bachelor's Creditable
Accreditation: SC

02 President ....Dr. Paul W. CONCO
05 VP Academic/Student Development ....Dr. Tara ATKINS-BRADY
10 Vice President Finance/Admin Svcs ....Dr. Joe EDENFIELD
30 Vice Pres Institutional Advancement ....Ms. Felicia BLOW
20 Dean Occupational/Tech Programs ....Ms. Renee FELTS
32 Dean Student Services ....Ms. Trina JONES
20 Dean of Suffolk Academic Programs .....Dr. Harriette ARRINGTON
08 Director of Learning Resources ....Ms. Linza M. WEAVER
12 Academic Director-Smithfield ....Dr. Carl SWEAT
103 VP of Workforce Development ....Mr. Randy BETZ
09 Director of Institutional Research .... Dr. Jerry J. STANDAHL
18 Chief Facilities/Physical Plant .... Mr. James C. GORHAM
15 Human Resources Manager ....Ms. Jackie SPIKER
21 Business Office Manager ....Ms. Deanna DAVENPORT
88 Development Studies Program Head ......Dr. Tara ATKINS-BRADY
26 Public Relations Specialist ....Ms. Wendy HARRISON
96 Buyer Specialist ....Vacant
37 Financial Aid Coordinator .... Ms. Teresa HARRISON
04 Assistant to the President .... Ms. Cathy CUTCHINS

*Piedmont Virginia Community College (F)

501 College Drive, Charlottesville VA 22902-7589
County: Independent City FICE Identification: 009928
Unit ID: 233116
Telephone: (434) 977-3900 Carnegie Class: Assoc/Pub-R-M
FAX Number: (434) 971-8232 Calendar System: Semester
URL. www.pvcc.edu
Established: 1972 Annual Undergrad Tuition & Fees (In-State): $3,208
Enrollment: 5,693 Coed
Affiliation or Control: State IRS Status: 501(c)3
Highest Offering: Associate Degree
Program: Occupational; 2-Year Principally Bachelor's Creditable; Liberal Arts And General
Accreditation: SC, ADNUR, EMT, RAD, SURGT

02 President .... Dr. Frank FRIEDMAN
05 VP Instruction/Student Svcs ....Dr. John DONNELLY
10 Vice President Finance/Admin Svcs ....Mr. Stephen PARKER
30 Vice Pres Advancement/Development .... Dr. James ROSS
79 Dean Humanities/Fine Arts/Soc Sci ....Dr. Clifford W. HAURY
50 Dean Business/Math/Technologies .... Dr. Chuck BOHLEKE
17 Dean Health & Life Sciences ....Dr. Kathy HUDSON
103 Dean Workforce Services .... Ms. Valerie PALAMOUNTAIN
32 Director of Student Services ....Ms. Mary Lee WALSH
13 Dir Information Technology/CIO ....Mr. Shivajl SAMANTA
09 Dir Instl Research/Planning/Effect ....Vacant
06 Registrar .... Ms. Allyson REA
96 Director of Purchasing ....Ms. Marie C. MELTON
18 Facilities Manager .... Mr. Dennis WEIR
15 Human Resources Manager .... Ms. Jennifer ATKINS
26 Manager Marketing/Media Relations .... Ms. Anita SHOWERS
84 Outreach Manager ....Ms. Kathryn SNOW
08 Coordinator Library Services .... Ms. Linda CAHILL
37 Coordinator Financial Aid .... Ms. Carol LARSON
36 Coordinator Advising & Transfer .... Mr. Kemper STEELE

*Rappahannock Community College (G)

12745 College Drive, Glenns VA 23149-0287
County: Gloucester FICE Identification: 009160
Unit ID: 233310
Telephone: (804) 758-6700 Carnegie Class: Assoc/Pub-S-MC
FAX Number: (804) 758-3852 Calendar System: Semester
URL: www.rappahannock.edu
Established: 1970 Annual Undergrad Tuition & Fees (In-State): $4,064
Enrollment: 5,023 Coed
Affiliation or Control: State IRS Status: 501(c)3
Highest Offering: Associate Degree
Program: Occupational; 2-Year Principally Bachelor's Creditable
Accreditation: SC

02 President ....Dr. Elizabeth H. CROWTHER
10 Vice Pres Finance & Admin Services ....Mr. D. Kim MCMANUS
05 VP Instruction/Student Development .... Dr. A. Donna ALEXANDER
32 Dean Student Development ....Ms. Anne KORNEGAY
106 Dean of Distance Learning/Tech .... Ms. Leslie SMITH
08 Dean of Learning Resources .... Ms. Cherie CARL
30 Dean of College Advancement ....Mr. Victor W. CLOUGH, JR.
09 Dir Institutional Effectiveness ....Dr. Glenda D. HAYNIE
06 College Registrar ....Ms. Felicia B. PACKETT
37 Financial Aid/Veteran Affairs Ofcr ....Ms. Carolyn A. WARD
15 Human Resources Manager ....Mrs. Caroline W. STELTER
18 Facilities/Physical Plant Manager ....Mr. Mark P. BEAVER
21 Business Manager ....Ms. Susan S. BROADDUS

*Southside Virginia Community College (H)

109 Campus Drive, Alberta VA 23821-2930
County: Brunswick FICE Identification: 008661
Unit ID: 233639
Telephone: (434) 949-1000 Carnegie Class: Assoc/Pub-R-L
FAX Number: (434) 949-7863 Calendar System: Semester
URL: www.southside.edu
Established: 1970 Annual Undergrad Tuition & Fees (In-State): $3,810
Enrollment: 6,042 Coed
Affiliation or Control: State IRS Status: 501(c)3
Highest Offering: Associate Degree
Program: Occupational; 2-Year Principally Bachelor's Creditable
Accreditation: SC, EMT

02 President ....Dr. John J. CAVAN
12 Provost John H Daniel Campus .... Dr. Paula M. GASTENVELD
12 Provost Christanna Campus ....Dr. Al ROBERTS

10 Vice Pres Finance & Administration ... Mr. Peter G. HUNT
25 VP Adult Education & Grants ... Dr. Linda SHEFFIELD
13 Dean Information Services ... Mr. Jack ANCELL
84 Dean Enrollment Mgt & Assoc Prof ... Mrs. Shannon FEINMAN
20 Dean of Instruction Daniel Campus ... Ms. Elizabeth ELAM
20 Dean of Instruction Christanna ... Mr. Chad PATTON
09 Dean Planning & Inst Effectiveness ... Vacant
66 Dean of Nursing/Health Technology ... Ms. Michelle K. EDMONDS
102 Exec Director SVCC Foundation ... Mrs. Mary Jane ELKINS
08 College Librarian ... Ms. Rosa TOWNSEND
26 Public Relations & Mktg Specialist ... Ms. Christie C. HALES
37 Director of Financial Aid ... Ms. Sally THARRINGTON
15 Human Resources Manager ... Ms. Bethany W. HARRIS
18 Buildings/Grounds Supt Christanna ... Mr. Roger WRAY
38 Dir Student Counseling Christanna ... Ms. Judy SHEPHERD
38 Director Student Counseling Daniel ... Mrs. Dorethea SIZEMORE
21 Business Manager ... Mrs. Juanita Nita GRIZZARD
29 Alumni Relations SVCC ... Mrs. Mary Jane ELKINS

*Southwest Virginia Community College (A)

Box SVCC, Richlands VA 24641-1101

County: Tazewell FICE Identification: 007260
Unit ID: 233648

Telephone: (276) 964-2555 Carnegie Class: Assoc/Pub-R-M
FAX Number: (276) 964-9307 Calendar System: Semester
URL: www.sw.edu
Established: 1967 Annual Undergrad Tuition & Fees (In-State): $3,336
Enrollment: 2,766 Coed
Affiliation or Control: State IRS Status: 501(c)3
Highest Offering: Associate Degree
Program: Occupational; 2-Year Principally Bachelor's Creditable
Accreditation: SC, ADNUR, EMT, OTA, RAD

02 President ... Dr. J. Mark ESTEPP
05 VP Academics & Student Services ... Dr. Barbara J. FULLER
10 Vice Pres Finance & Admin Services ... Dr. Leonard V. KOGUT
30 Vice Pres Institutional Advancement ... Ms. Phyllis A. ROBERTS
11 General Admin Coordinator ... Ms. Rhonda L. VANDYKE
79 Dean Humanit/Sci/Math/Health Tech ... Ms. Cathy SMITH-COX
50 Dean Business/Engr & Indust Tech ... Mr. James DYE
103 Dean Cmty/Workforce & Econ Sol ... Ms. Sharon PEERY
32 Dean Student Success ... Ms. Mary A. RAGLAND
09 Institutional Research Officer ... Dr. Edmond C. SMITH
102 Exec Dir SWCC Educ Foundation ... Ms. Mary W. LAWSON
15 Human Resources Manager ... Ms. Martha L. RASNAKE
21 Business Manager ... Mr. Michael BALES
19 Campus Police Chief ... Mr. Ronnie KISER
18 Physical Plant Superintendent ... Mr. Tony MCGHEE
26 Public Relations Coordinator ... Ms. Patsy G. BUSSARD
08 Coordinator of Library Services ... Ms. Teresa A. YEAROUT
106 Director Distance Learning ... Ms. Dyan E. LESTER

*Thomas Nelson Community College (B)

99 Thomas Nelson Drive, Hampton VA 23666

County: Independent City FICE Identification: 006871
Unit ID: 233754

Telephone: (757) 825-2700 Carnegie Class: Assoc/Pub-S-SC
FAX Number: (757) 825-2763 Calendar System: Semester
URL: www.tncc.edu
Established: 1967 Annual Undergrad Tuition & Fees (In-State): $3,981
Enrollment: 9,242 Coed
Affiliation or Control: State IRS Status: 501(c)3
Highest Offering: Associate Degree
Program: Occupational; 2-Year Principally Bachelor's Creditable
Accreditation: SC, ADNUR, DH

02 President ... Dr. John T. DEVER
12 Provost Historic Triangle Campus ... Dr. William TRAVIS
05 Vice President for Academic Affairs ... Dr. Lonnie SCHAFFER
32 Vice President for Student Affairs ... Dr. Daniel LUFKIN
11 Vice President for Admin/Finance ... Mr. Charles A. NURNBERGER
103 Vice Pres for Workforce Development ... Dr. Deborah G. WRIGHT
44 Vice Pres Institutional Advancement ... Ms. Cynthia CALLAWAY
35 Assoc VP for Student Affairs ... Dr. Vicki RICHMOND
13 Director of Information Tech ... Mr. Wayne DAVIS
106 Dir Distance/Distributive Learning ... Ms. Ruth SMITH
84 Director of Enrollment Management ... Ms. Kris RARIG
10 Assoc VP for Financial Services ... Ms. Teresa BAILEY
103 Assoc VP for Workforce Training/CE ... Dr. Carmen BURROWS
60 Dean Communications/Social Sciences ... Mr. Patrick TOMKINS
81 Int Dean Science/Engr/Technology ... Dr. Michael REYNOLDS
50 Int Dean Bus/Public Ser/IT/Math ... Mr. Raymond MUZIA
76 Dean Health Professions ... Dr. William TRAVIS
38 Dean of Student Development ... Ms. Joyce JOHNSON
37 Dir Financial Aid/Veteran Affairs ... Ms. Kathryn ANDERSON
18 Physical Plant Manager ... Mr. Mark KRAMER
26 Director Public Relations/Marketing ... Ms. Cecilia RAMIREZ
30 Director of Development ... Ms. Lara OVERY
08 Director of Learning Resources ... Mr. Richard HODGES
09 Dir Inst Research and Effectiveness ... Mr. Steven FELKER
21 Business Office Manager ... Ms. Virginia HAIDERER
15 Director of Human Resources ... Ms. Joy COOKE

*Tidewater Community College (C)

121 College Place, Norfolk VA 23510

County: Independent City FICE Identification: 003712
Unit ID: 233772

Telephone: (757) 822-1122 Carnegie Class: Assoc/Pub-S-SC
FAX Number: (757) 822-1060 Calendar System: Semester
URL: www.tcc.edu
Established: 1968 Annual Undergrad Tuition & Fees (In-State): $3,788
Enrollment: 30,134 Coed
Affiliation or Control: State IRS Status: 501(c)3
Highest Offering: Associate Degree
Program: Occupational; 2-Year Principally Bachelor's Creditable
Accreditation: SC, ACFEI, ADNUR, CAHIIM, COARC, DMS, EMT, FUSER, OTA, PTAA, RAD

02 President ... Dr. Edna V. BAEHRE-KOLOVANI
11 Exec Vice President Administration ... Mr. Franklin T. DUNN
05 VP Academic Affairs/Chief Acad Ofcr ... Dr. Daniel DEMARTE
10 Vice President Finance ... Ms. Phyllis MILLOY
13 Vice President Info Systems ... Dr. Robin L P. YING
103 Vice Pres Workforce Development ... Dr. Theresa BRYANT
32 VP for Student Affairs ... Dr. Charles W. LEPPER
44 Vice Pres Institutional Advancement ... Mr. James P. TOSCANO
20 Int Assoc VP Academic Effectiveness ... Dr. Kellie SOREY
20 AVP Faculty Dev/Curriculum Innovat ... Dr. Diann HOLT
106 Interim Assoc Vice Pres eLearning ... Ms. Deborah EDSON
25 Assoc Vice Pres Grants/Spons Pgms ... Ms. Valerie CHEESEMAN
26 AVP Interactive Communications ... Ms. Marian ANDERFUREN
35 AVP for Student Services ... Dr. Kathy MAALOUF
20 Provost Chesapeake Campus ... Dr. Lisa B. RHINE
20 Provost Portsmouth Campus ... Dr. Michelle WOODHOUSE
20 Provost Virginia Beach Campus ... Dr. Michael SUMMERS
20 Provost Norfolk Campus ... Dr. Marvin L. BRIGHT
32 Int Dean of Student Svcs Chesapeake ... Mr. Kevin MCCARTHY
81 Dean Lang/Math/Science Chesapeake ... Dr. Cynthia CADIEUX
50 Dean Bus/Pub Svc/Tech Chesapeake ... Mr. James PERKINSON
32 Dean of Student Svcs Portsmouth ... Dr. Raphael TURNER
50 Dean Bus/Pub Svcs/Tech Portsmouth ... Ms. Ann AMBROSE
81 Dean Lang/Math/Science Portsmouth ... Ms. Jenefer SNYDER
32 Dean of Student Svcs Va Beach ... Dr. Marilyn HODGE
50 Dean IT & Business Va Beach ... Ms. Carolyn MCLELLAN
54 Dean Eng & Ind Tech Va Beach ... Mr. David EKKER
76 Dean Health Professions ... Mr. Thomas CALOGRIDES, JR.
79 Dean Humanities Va Beach ... Ms. Marcane ANDERSON
81 Int Dean Natural Sciences Va Beach ... Mr. Fred STEMPLE
83 Dean Social Sci/Pub Svcs Va Beach ... Dr. Joseph FAIRCHILD
32 Int Dean of Student Svcs Norfolk ... Ms. Mecca MARSH
50 Dean Bus/Pub Svcs/Tech Norfolk ... Dr. Caroline RIVERA
81 Int Dean Lang/Math/Science Norfolk ... Ms. Kerry RAGNO
66 Dean of Nursing ... Dr. Phyllis EATON
30 Interim Director of Development ... Ms. Ashley ALLMAN
06 Interim Registrar ... Ms. Christine DAMROSE-MAHLMANN
96 Director of Materiel Management ... Ms. Robin MOORE
09 Dir Institutional Effectiveness ... Mr. Curtis K. AASEN
57 Director Visual Arts Center ... Ms. Christina RUPSCH
18 Director Facilities Management ... Mr. David GUGLIELMO
15 Director Human Resources ... Ms. Gretna SMITH
37 Director Student Financial Aid ... Ms. Jennifer HARPHAM

*Virginia Highlands Community College (D)

PO Box 828, Abingdon VA 24212-0828

County: Washington FICE Identification: 007099
Unit ID: 233903

Telephone: (276) 739-2400 Carnegie Class: Assoc/Pub-R-M
FAX Number: (276) 739-2590 Calendar System: Semester
URL: www.vhcc.edu
Established: 1967 Annual Undergrad Tuition & Fees (In-State): $3,810
Enrollment: 2,570 Coed
Affiliation or Control: State IRS Status: 501(c)3
Highest Offering: Associate Degree
Program: Occupational; 2-Year Principally Bachelor's Creditable
Accreditation: SC, ADNUR, OTA

02 President ... Dr. Ron PROFFITT
05 VP Instruction & Student Services ... Dr. Hara CHARLIER
10 VP Financial/Administrative Svcs ... Ms. Christine FIELDS
30 Vice Pres Institutional Advancement ... Mr. David N. MATLOCK
49 Dean Business/Human/Soc Sci ... Ms. Alma Z. ROWLAND
72 Dean of Science & Engr Technologies ... Mr. Robert F. MAY
66 Dean of Nursing and Allied Health ... Ms. Kathy J. MITCHELL
103 Dean Workforce Training & Cont Educ ... Ms. Melinda T. LELAND
08 Director Library/Instructional Svcs ... Mr. Charles BOLING
37 Director of Financial Aid ... Ms. Karen T. CHEERS
07 Director Admission/Records ... Ms. Karen T. CHEERS
06 Registrar ... Ms. Charlene EASTRIDGE
15 Director Personnel Services ... Ms. Laura MCCLELLAN
32 Director Student Affs/Alumni Rels ... Vacant
88 Director of Talent Search ... Ms. Beth M. PAGE
88 Director Project EXCEL ... Ms. Jackie T. CRAFT
38 Director Student Counseling ... Vacant
21 Business Manager ... Mr. Roger W. SPENCER
96 Director of Purchasing ... Ms. Chelsa TAYLOR
88 Institutional Effectiveness ... Ms. Jennifer D. ADDISON
90 Coord Academic Computing/Technology ... Mr. Glen JOHNSON
26 Public Relations Officer ... Ms. Anne M. DUNHAM
09 Institutional Research Officer ... Mr. Jeff D. RUSSELL
18 Chief Facilities/Physical Plant ... Mr. Ernest L. NUNLEY
19 Director of Security/Safety ... Mr. David NECESSARY
36 Career Plng/Placement Spclst ... Mr. Tony FULLER

*Virginia Western Community College (E)

PO Box 14007, Roanoke VA 24038-4007

County: Independent City FICE Identification: 003760
Unit ID: 233949

Telephone: (540) 857-8922 Carnegie Class: Assoc/Pub-R-L
FAX Number: (540) 857-6526 Calendar System: Semester
URL: www.virginiawestern.edu
Established: 1966 Annual Undergrad Tuition & Fees (In-State): $4,278
Enrollment: 8,440 Coed
Affiliation or Control: State IRS Status: 501(c)3
Highest Offering: Associate Degree
Program: Occupational; 2-Year Principally Bachelor's Creditable
Accreditation: SC, ACBSP, DH, RAD, RTT

02 President ... Dr. Robert H. SANDEL
10 Vice Pres of Finance/Admin Services ... Ms. Cheryl MILLER
05 Int Vice Pres Academic/Student Affs ... Dr. Elizabeth WILMER
30 Vice Pres Institutional Advancement ... Dr. Angela M. FALCONETTI
103 Vice Pres Workforce Development Svc ... Mr. James POYTHRESS
45 Dean Institutional Effectiveness ... Ms. Rachelle KOUDELIK-JONES
49 Int Dean Lib Arts/Social Sciences ... Ms. Amy ANGUIANO
81 Dean Nat Sci/Math/Health Tech Div ... Ms. Carole GRAHAM
50 Int Dean Bus/Sciences/Engrng/WFD ... Ms. Deborah YANCEY
32 Dean of Student Services ... Ms. Lori BAKER
09 Director Institutional Research ... Ms. Carol ROWLETT
18 Director of Facilities Mgmt Svcs ... Mr. Kevin G. WITTER
26 Chief Public Relations Officer ... Mr. Josh MEYER
06 Registrar ... Ms. Lorraine CONKLIN
19 Campus Police Chief ... Mr. Craig HARRIS
37 Financial Aid Officer ... Mr. Chad SARTINI
103 Workforce Development Officer ... Ms. Leah COFFMAN
13 Information Technology Manager ... Vacant
15 Human Resources Manager ... Mr. Garry M. SHELTON
21 Business Manager ... Mrs. Fredona AARON
35 Coordinator Advising/Retention Svc ... Vacant
08 Coordinator of the Library ... Ms. Lynn HURT
36 Counselor Career Services ... Vacant
24 Coordinator Learning Tech Center ... Vacant
25 Coord Grants Dev & Special Projects ... Ms. Marilyn J. HERBERT-ASHTON
29 Alumni/Annual Giving Coord/Communic ... Mr. Erik W. WILLIAMS

*Wytheville Community College (F)

1000 E Main Street, Wytheville VA 24382-3308

County: Wythe FICE Identification: 003761
Unit ID: 234377

Telephone: (276) 223-4700 Carnegie Class: Assoc/Pub-R-M
FAX Number: (276) 223-4778 Calendar System: Semester
URL: www.wcc.vccs.edu
Established: 1963 Annual Undergrad Tuition & Fees (In-State): $3,990
Enrollment: 3,717 Coed
Affiliation or Control: State IRS Status: 501(c)3
Highest Offering: Associate Degree
Program: Occupational; 2-Year Principally Bachelor's Creditable
Accreditation: SC, ADNUR, DH, MLTAD, PTAA

02 President ... Dr. Charlie WHITE
05 Vice Pres Instruction/Student Devel ... Dr. William H. HIGHTOWER, JR.
10 Vice Pres Finance & Admin Services ... Ms. Crystal Y. CREGGER
09 Director of Institutional Research ... Dr. Kent E. GLINDEMANN
30 Vice Pres of College Development ... Dr. Rhonda K. CATRON-WOOD
75 Vice Pres Cont Ed & Tech/Occ Pgms ... Ms. Angela Y. LAWSON
50 Dean of Business & Humanities ... Ms. Donna FENDER
76 Dean of Health & Science ... Dr. Lorri M. HUFFARD
32 Dean of Student Services ... Mr. Michael L. MCHONE
13 Director Acad/Admin Computing ... Mr. Shawn MCREYNOLDS
06 Registrar ... Ms. Karen ALEXANDER
15 Human Resources Manager ... Ms. Linda R. NYE
26 Public Relations Coordinator ... Mr. William A. VESELIK
08 Coordinator of Library Services ... Mr. George E. MATTIS, JR.
96 Procurement Officer ... Ms. Vivian FANNING
106 Dir of Distance & Distrib Learning ... Mr. Kenneth E. FAIRBANKS
37 Coordinator Financial Aid ... Ms. Mary Beth GALLAGHER

Virginia Intermont College (G)

1013 Moore Street, Bristol VA 24201-4298

County: Independent City FICE Identification: 003752
Unit ID: 233912

Telephone: (276) 669-6101 Carnegie Class: Bac/A&S
FAX Number: (276) 669-5763 Calendar System: Semester
URL: www.vic.edu
Established: 1884 Annual Undergrad Tuition & Fees: $24,642
Enrollment: 496 Coed
Affiliation or Control: Baptist IRS Status: 501(c)3
Highest Offering: Baccalaureate
Program: Liberal Arts And General; Teacher Preparatory; Business Emphasis
Accreditation: #SC, SW

01 President ... Dr. E. Clorisa PHILLIPS
05 Sr Vice President/Provost ... Mr. Mark ROBERTS
10 Sr Vice President Administration ... Ms. Linda MORGAN
30 Vice Pres Institutional Advancement ... Ms. Ronda COLE GENTRY
10 Vice President Finance ... Mr. Terry HAVERTY
04 Executive Assistant to President ... Mr. Robert BAIRD
07 Dean of Admissions ... Mr. Richard CARROLL
37 Director of Financial Aid ... Vacant
08 Librarian ... Mr. Jonathan TALLMAN
36 Dir Placement & Career Planning ... Ms. Ronan KING
06 Registrar ... Ms. Pamela HAMMOND
09 Director of Institutional Research ... Ms. Charlotte INGRAM
21 Associate Business Officer ... Ms. Becky COVEY

29 Director of Alumni Relations ... Mr. Sean TRENT
38 Director of Student Counseling ... Ms. Deborah PATTERSON
92 Director of Honors Program ... Dr. Robert RAINWATER
15 Director Human Resources ... Vacant
26 Dir of Marketing/Communications ... Ms. Mary Anne HOLBROOK
18 Chief Facilities/Physical Plant ... Mr. Con SAULS

Virginia International University (A)

11200 Waples Mill Road, Suite 360, Fairfax VA 22030

County: Fairfax | FICE Identification: 041440
Telephone: (703) 591-7042 | Carnegie Class: Not Classified
FAX Number: (703) 591-7046 | Calendar System: Semester
URL: www.viu.edu
Established: 1998 | Annual Undergrad Tuition & Fees: $9,174
Enrollment: 337 | Coed
Affiliation or Control: Independent Non-Profit | IRS Status: 501(c)3
Highest Offering: Master's
Program: Professional; Business Emphasis
Accreditation: ACICS

01 President ... Dr. Isa SARAC
03 Vice President University Affairs ... Ms. Sue Ann MYERS

Virginia Military Institute (B)

319 Letcher Avenue, Lexington VA 24450-0304

County: Independent City | FICE Identification: 003753
Unit ID: 234085
Telephone: (540) 464-7230 | Carnegie Class: Bac/A&S
FAX Number: (540) 464-7583 | Calendar System: Semester
URL: www.vmi.edu
Established: 1839 | Annual Undergrad Tuition & Fees (In-State): $22,492
Enrollment: 1,664 | Coed
Affiliation or Control: State | IRS Status: 501(c)3
Highest Offering: Baccalaureate
Program: Liberal Arts And General
Accreditation: SC, BUS, CS, ENG

01 Superintendent ... Gen. J. H. Binford PEAY
05 Dean of the Faculty ... BGen. R. Wane SCHNEITER
10 Deputy Superintendent Finance/Admin ... BGen. Robert L. GREEN
32 Commandant of Cadets ... Col. Thomas H. TRUMPS
100 Chief of Staff ... Col. James P. INMAN
04 Assistant to the Superintendent ... Col. Jeffrey H. CURTIS
21 Assoc Business Exec/Treasurer ... Col. Gary R. KNICK
07 Director of Admissions ... Col. Vernon L. BEITZEL
88 Exec Director Museum Programs ... Col. Keith E. GIBSON
37 Director of Financial Aid ... Col. Timothy P. GOLDEN
35 Deputy Commandant ... Col. L. E. HURLBUT
36 Director of Career Services ... Col. R. Samuel RATCLIFFE
41 Director Intercollegiate Athletics ... Mr. Donald T. WHITE
26 Director Communications & Marketing ... Col. Stewart D. MACINNIS
29 Executive VP Alumni Association ... LTC. Adam C. VOLANT
30 Exec VP VMI Foundation/Fund Raising ... Mr. Brian S. CROCKETT
88 Exec VP Keydet Club/Athletic Fund . Mr. Gregory M. CAVALLARO
06 Registrar ... Col. Janet M. BATTAGLIA
15 Director Human Resources ... Col. Robert B. SPORE
18 Director Physical Plant ... LTC. James L. WILLIAMS, JR.
09 Director Institutional Research ... Col. Elizabeth S. SECHLER
88 Director Auxiliary Services ... Col. David K. HOUGH
40 Manager Bookstore ... Ms. Patricia T. RULEY
42 Institute Chaplain ... Col. James S. PARK
17 Institute Physician ... Dr. David L. COPELAND
88 Director of Sports Information ... Mr. Wade H. BRANNER
08 Head Librarian ... Col. Donald H. SAMDAHL, JR.
38 Director of Cadet Counseling ... LtCol. Sarah L. JONES
14 Director Information Technology ... Col. Thomas F. HOPKINS
96 Director of Purchasing ... Maj. Kathy H. TOMLIN

† Tuition includes required room and board and quartermaster charges.

Virginia Polytechnic Institute and State University (C)

Blacksburg VA 24061-0202

County: Montgomery | FICE Identification: 003754
Unit ID: 233921
Telephone: (540) 231-6000 | Carnegie Class: RU/VH
FAX Number: (540) 231-9263 | Calendar System: Semester
URL: www.vt.edu
Established: 1872 | Annual Undergrad Tuition & Fees (In-State): $11,455
Enrollment: 31,087 | Coed
Affiliation or Control: State | IRS Status: 501(c)3
Highest Offering: Doctorate
Program: Liberal Arts And General; Teacher Preparatory; Professional
Accreditation: SC, ART, BUS, BUSA, CACREP, CEA, CIDA, CLPSY, CONST, CS, DIETD, DIETI, ENG, FOR, IPSY, LSAR, MFCD, MUS, PH, PLNG, SPAA, TED, THEA, VET

01 President ... Charles W. STEGER
05 Senior Vice President & Provost ... Mark G. MCNAMEE
11 Vice President for Admin Services ... Sherwood G. WILSON
13 Vice Pres for Information Tech ... Scott F. MIDKIFF
32 Vice President Student Affairs ... Patricia A. PERILLO
30 Vice Pres Devel & University Rels ... Elizabeth A. FLANAGAN
29 Vice President Alumni Relations ... Thomas C. TILLAR, JR.
28 VP Diversity and Inclusion ... William T. LEWIS, SR.
46 Vice President for Research ... Robert WALTERS
20 Vice Prov for Undergrad Acad Affs ... Vacant
58 Vice President and Dean Grad Educ ... Karen P. DEPAUW
56 VP Outreach/International Affs ... Guru GHOSH
10 Vice President for Finance and CFO ... M. Dwight SHELTON
07 Director of Undergrad Admissions ... Mildred JOHNSON
35 Dean of Students ... Thomas BROWN
16 Assoc Vice Pres for Human Resources ... Hal IRVIN
09 Asst Provost Institutional Research ... Kristen BUSH
43 General Counsel ... Kay K. HEIDBREDER
84 Asst VP for Enroll & Degree Mgmt ... Wanda H. DEAN
45 Dir for Planning & Administration ... Jeb STEWART
37 Dir of Scholarships/Financial Aid ... Vacant
23 Director Schiffert Health Center ... Kanitta CHAROENSIRI
18 Assoc Vice President for Facilities ... Michael J. COLEMAN
39 Director of Dining Services ... Ted FAULKNER
39 Director of Housing and Res Life ... Eleanor FINGER
41 Athletic Director ... James WEAVER
26 Assoc Vice Pres Univ Relations ... Larry HINCKER
38 Director Student Counseling ... Chris FLYNN
40 Executive Director Bookstore ... Donald J. WILLIAMS
62 Dean of Libraries ... Tyler WALTERS
47 Dean of Agriculture/Life Sciences ... Alan GRANT
48 Dean of Architecture/Urban Studies ... Jack DAVIS
49 Dean College of Science ... Lay N. CHANG
50 Dean of Business ... Robert T. SUMICHRAST
54 Dean of Engineering ... Richard BENSON
79 Dean Liberal Arts & Human Sciences ... Sue OTT ROWLANDS
74 Dean of Veterinary Medicine ... Vacant
65 Dean of Natural Resources & Environ ... Paul M. WINISTORFER
96 Director of Purchasing ... W. Thomas KALOUPEK
90 Director Educational Technology ... John F. MOORE
91 Assoc Vice Pres for Enterprise Sys ... Deborah M. FULTON
12 Interim Exec Dir Natl Cap Region ... James BOHLAND
102 CEO Virginia Tech Foundation ... John E. DOOLEY

Virginia State University (D)

One Hayden Street,
Virginia State University VA 23806-0001

County: Chesterfield | FICE Identification: 003764
Unit ID: 234155
Telephone: (804) 524-5000 | Carnegie Class: Master's S
FAX Number: (804) 524-6506 | Calendar System: Semester
URL: www.vsu.edu
Established: 1882 | Annual Undergrad Tuition & Fees (In-State): $7,784
Enrollment: 6,208 | Coed
Affiliation or Control: State | IRS Status: 501(c)3
Highest Offering: Doctorate
Program: Liberal Arts And General; Teacher Preparatory
Accreditation: SC, ART, BUS, CS, DIETD, DIETI, ENG, ENGT, MUS, NAIT, @SW, TED

01 President ... Dr. Keith T. MILLER
100 Chief of Staff ... Mr. Cortez K. DIAL
10 Vice Pres Finance & Administration ... Mr. David J. MEADOWS
05 Provost/VP for Academic Affairs ... Dr. W. Weldon HILL
32 VP of Student Affairs & Enroll Mgmt ... Dr. Michael SHACKLEFORD
20 Vice Provost ... Dr. James E. HUNTER
15 Assoc VP for Human Resource ... Dr. Elliot WHEELAN
84 Asst VP/Student Enrollment Services ... Mr. Henry DEBOSE
30 Assoc VP for Institutional Advance ... Ms. Adrienne WHITAKER
21 Associate Business Officer ... Ms. Sheila MCNAIR
50 Dean Reginald F. Lewis Co Business ... Dr. Mirta M. MARTIN
54 Dean College of Engineering & Tech . Dr. Keith M. WILLIAMSON
79 Dean Col of Humananities & Soc Sci ... Dr. Andrew KANU
47 Dean College of Agriculture ... Dr. Jewel E. HAIRSTON
58 Dean Graduate Studies ... Dr. James E. HUNTER
62 Dean Library & Media Services ... Dr. Elsie S. WEATHERINGTON
76 Dean College of Natural Health Sci ... Dr. Larry BROWN
44 Director of Development ... Vacant
06 Registrar ... Ms. Debera BONNER
09 Director Inst Planning/Assessment ... Dr. Emmett L. RIDLEY
37 Director of Financial Aid ... Mrs. Myra PHILLIPS
19 Director Police/Public Safety ... Mr. Michael WALLACE
04 Special Assistant to the President ... Mr. Jesse VAUGHAN
18 Director of Facilities ... Mr. Gilbertt HANZLIK
07 Director Admissions & Recruitment ... Ms. Irene F. LOGAN
26 Director University Relations ... Mr. Thomas REED
22 Human Resources Manager ... Ms. Gayle ONEAL
14 Assoc VP & Chief Information ... Mr. Hubert B. HARRIS
39 Director Residence Facilities ... Dr. LaVerne BRIGGS
36 Director Career Plng & Placement ... Ms. Yolanda M. CREWS
40 Bookstore Manager ... Mr. Kevin POWELL
92 Director Honors Program ... Mr. Daniel M. ROBERTS
41 Athletic Director ... Mrs. Peggy DAVIS
42 Minister ... Rev. Delano DOUGLAS
29 Coordinator of Alumni Relations ... Ms. Andrea COLLINS
27 Deputy Chief Information Officer ... Ms. Stephanie A. HAYES
23 Director Student Health Services ... Mrs. Rebecca BRANCH-GRIFFIN
25 Contract Manager ... Ms. Linda SCOTT
87 Director Summer School Session ... Dr. Vykuntapathi THOTA
96 Director of Purchasing ... Mrs. Yolanda BUCK
38 Director Student Counseling ... Ms. LaKesha RONEY

Virginia Tech Carilion School of Medicine (E)

2 Riverside Circle, Suite M140, Roanoke VA 24016

County: Independent City | Identification: 667148
Telephone: (540) 526-2500 | Carnegie Class: Not Classified
FAX Number: (540) 581-0741 | Calendar System: Other
URL: www.vtc.vt.edu
Established: 2007 | Annual Graduate Tuition & Fees: $43,751
Enrollment: 128 | Coed
Affiliation or Control: State | IRS Status: 501(c)3
Highest Offering: Doctorate; No Undergraduates
Program: Professional
Accreditation: @SC, #MED

01 President & Dean ... Dr. Cynda Ann JOHNSON

Virginia Union University (F)

1500 N Lombardy Street, Richmond VA 23220-1784

County: Independent City | FICE Identification: 003766
Unit ID: 234164
Telephone: (804) 257-5600 | Carnegie Class: Bac/Diverse
FAX Number: (804) 257-5818 | Calendar System: Semester
URL: www.vuu.edu
Established: 1865 | Annual Undergrad Tuition & Fees: $14,930
Enrollment: 1,750 | Coed
Affiliation or Control: Baptist | IRS Status: 501(c)3
Highest Offering: Doctorate
Program: Liberal Arts And General; Teacher Preparatory; Professional
Accreditation: SC, ACBSP, SW, TED, THEOL

01 President ... Dr. Claude G. PERKINS
05 Vice President for Academic Affairs ... Dr. Julius E. SCIPIO
32 VP Enrollmnt Mgmt & Stdnt Affs ... Mr. Lee D. YOUNG
10 VP Financial Affairs ... Mr. Gregory LEWIS
30 Vice Pres Institutional Advancement ... Mr. Dennis C. WASHINGTON
09 VP Research/Planning & Spec Pgms ... Dr. Joy P. GOODRICH
26 Asst to Pres/Dir Public Relations ... Ms. Vanessa COOMBS
53 Dean Evelyn R Syphax Sch Ed/Psy ... Dr. David A. ADEWUYI
81 Dean Math/Science & Technology ... Dr. Latrelle A. GREEN
50 Dean Sydney Lewis Sch of Business ... Dr. Adelaja O. ODUTOLA
79 Dean School of Humanities & Soc Sci ... Dr. Linda G. SCHLICHTING
73 Dean School of Theology ... Dr. John W. KINNEY
25 Asst to President Title III Pgms ... Mr. Samuel T. RHOADES
15 Director Human Resources ... Ms. Hollace J. ENOCH
06 Registrar ... Ms. Marilyn A. BROOKS
38 Director Counseling ... Ms. Melody M. PANNELL
29 Director of Alumni Relations ... Ms. Charmica D. EPPS
08 Library Director ... Ms. Pamela FOREMAN
37 Director Financial Aid ... Mrs. Karen L. GEE
27 Director Information Technology ... Mr. Robert R. GRAY
88 Lan Administrator ... Vacant
36 Director Career Services ... Dr. Penni SWEETENBURG-LEE
84 Director of Enrollment Management ... Ms. Kristie L. WHITE
42 University Pastor ... Rev. Angelo V. CHATMON
41 Athletic Director ... Mr. Michael L. BAILEY
19 Chief University Police ... Col. Carlton G. EDWARDS
24 Audio Visual Coordinator ... Mr. JaPrince L. CARTER
21 Comptroller ... Ms. Stephanie M. WHITE
40 Bookstore Manager ... Ms. Terri WYATT
39 Int Director of Residence Life ... Mr. Ullin K. RIGBY
23 University Physician ... Dr. Walton M. BELLE
31 Dir of Community & Student Rels ... Ms. Claudia E. WALL
18 Director Facilities ... Mr. David E. GORDON
96 Director of Purchasing ... Mr. Michael T. ADKINS

Virginia University of Lynchburg (G)

2058 Garfield Avenue, Lynchburg VA 24501-6417

County: Independent City | FICE Identification: 003762
Unit ID: 234137
Telephone: (434) 528-5276 | Carnegie Class: Spec/Faith
FAX Number: (434) 528-4257 | Calendar System: Semester
URL: www.vul.edu
Established: 1886 | Annual Undergrad Tuition & Fees: $7,880
Enrollment: 588 | Coed
Affiliation or Control: Independent Non-Profit | IRS Status: 501(c)3
Highest Offering: Doctorate
Program: Liberal Arts And General; Business Emphasis
Accreditation: TRACS

01 President ... Dr. Ralph REAVIS
05 Provost/Executive Vice President ... Dr. Kathy C. FRANKLIN
10 Vice President of Finance ... Mr. Donald LESLIE
32 Vice Pres Div Student Affairs ... Dr. Terrie E. GRIFFIN
30 VP for Institutional Advancement ... Dr. Doris S. CRAWFORD
09 Registrar ... Mr. Layman FRANKLIN
38 Director Student Counseling ... Mr. Eugene HENRY
84 Director Enrollment Management ... Mrs. Bindiya SHAH

Virginia Wesleyan College (H)

1584 Wesleyan Drive, Norfolk VA 23502-5599

County: Independent City | FICE Identification: 003767
Unit ID: 234173
Telephone: (757) 455-3200 | Carnegie Class: Bac/A&S
FAX Number: (757) 461-4944 | Calendar System: 4/1/4
URL: www.vwc.edu
Established: 1961 | Annual Undergrad Tuition & Fees: $32,182
Enrollment: 1,431 | Coed
Affiliation or Control: United Methodist | IRS Status: 501(c)3
Highest Offering: Baccalaureate
Program: Liberal Arts And General; Teacher Preparatory
Accreditation: SC, NRPA, @SW

01 President ... Dr. William T. GREER, JR.
05 VP Academic Affs/Dean of College ... Dr. Timothy G. O'ROURKE

10 Vice President of Finance ... Mr. Cary A. SAWYER
32 VP Student Affs/Dean of Enrollment .. Mr. David E. BUCKINGHAM
30 VP for College Advancement ... Ms. Mita K. VAIL
11 Vice President of Operations ... Mr. Bruce F. VAUGHAN
45 Dir Strategic Plng/Spec Ast to Pres ... Ms. Laynee H. TIMLIN
45 Director Institutional Research ... Mr. Donald STAUFFER
09 Dir Instl Effective/Accreditation ... Dr. David DIRLAM
26 Director of College Communications ... Ms. Leona BAKER
35 Dean of Students ... Dr. Keith E. MOORE
88 Assoc VP for College Advancement ... Ms. Suzanne SAVAGE
07 Dean of Admissions ... Mr. Nelson DAVIS
20 Assoc Dean Special Acad Projects ... Ms. Debbie L. HICKS
20 Assoc Dean of the College ... Dr. Sally SHEDD
39 Assoc Dean Students for Res Life ... Ms. McCarren CAPUTA
13 Chief Technology Officer ... Mr. Jack L. DMOCH
41 Director of Athletics ... Ms. Joanne M. RENN
55 Director of Adult Studies Program ... Mr. Thomas R. FARLEY
08 Library Director ... Mrs. Susan ERICKSON
15 Director of Human Resources ... Ms. Karla R. RASMUSSEN
06 Registrar ... Ms. Regina BYNUM
37 Director of Financial Aid ... Ms. Teresa L. RHYNE
96 Director of Purchasing ... Ms. Midge ZIMMERMAN
31 Director of Community Service ... Ms. Diane E. HOTALING
36 Director of Career Services ... Ms. Lisa I. FENTRESS
19 Director of Security ... Mr. Jerry MANCE
29 Director of Alumni Relations ... Ms. Lina GREEN
91 Manager of Admin Computer Systems ... Mr. Greg BAPTISTE
18 Director of Physical Plant ... Mr. David R. HOPPER
42 Chaplain ... Rev. Greg WEST
38 Director of Counseling ... Mr. James W. BROWN
44 Director of Special Gifts ... Vacant
44 Director of Annual Giving ... Ms. Kristin WILLIAMS
44 Director Leadership Giving ... Ms. Lori L. MCCAREL
40 Bookstore Manager ... Ms. Kim S. BROWN
92 Director Honors and Scholars ... Dr. Joyce B. EASTER
28 Director of International Programs ... Ms. Lena H. JOHNSON
88 Director of Student Activities ... Ms. Jennifer E. MITCHELL
23 Director of Health Services ... Ms. Valerie L. COVINGTON

Washington and Lee University (A)

204 W Washington Street, Lexington VA 24450-2116
County: Independent City FICE Identification: 003768
Unit ID: 234207
Telephone: (540) 458-8400 Carnegie Class: Bac/A&S
FAX Number: (540) 458-8945 Calendar System: Other
URL: www.wlu.edu
Established: 1749 Annual Undergrad Tuition & Fees: $44,507
Enrollment: 2,302 Coed
Affiliation or Control: Independent Non-Profit IRS Status: 501(c)3
Highest Offering: Doctorate
Program: Liberal Arts And General; Professional
Accreditation: SC, BUS, JOUR, LAW, TEAC

01 President ... Dr. Kenneth P. RUSCIO
05 Provost ... Dr. Daniel WUBAH
20 Associate Provost ... Dr. Marc CONNER
10 Vice Pres for Finance and Admin ... Mr. Steven G. MCALLISTER
30 Vice Pres University Advancement ... Mr. Dennis W. CROSS
32 VP for Stdnt Affs & Dean of Stdnts ... Ms. Sidney S. EVANS
04 Senior Asst to the President ... Dr. Elizabeth KNAPP
101 Sr Asst to Pres/Sec of University ... Mr. James D. FARRAR
43 General Counsel ... Ms. Leanne M. SHANK
22 Assoc Gen Counsel Compliance Spprt ... Ms. Jennifer E. KIRKLAND
49 Interim Dean of the College ... Dr. Suzanne P. KEEN
50 Dean of Commerce/Economics/Politics ... Dr. Larry C. PEPPERS
61 Dean of Law School ... Ms. Nora V. DEMLEITNER
26 Exec Dir of Comm/Public Affairs ... Mr. Jeffery G. HANNA
35 Dean of Student Life ... Mr. David M. LEONARD
35 Assoc Dean of Students ... Ms. Tamara Y. FUTRELL
30 Exec Dir of University Development ... Mr. Tres MULLIS
41 Director of Athletics ... Ms. Janine M. HATHORN
35 Dir Univ Commons/Campus Activities .. Mr. Jason L. RODOCKER
07 Dean of Admissions/Financial Aid ... Mr. William M. HARTOG
09 Dir Institutional Effectiveness ... Mr. Bryan PRICE
06 Associate University Registrar ... Ms. Barbara L. ROWE
08 University Librarian ... Mr. John TOMBARGE
85 Director International Education ... Dr. Larry BOETSCH
29 Exec Director of Alumni Affairs ... Mr. Walter T. DUDLEY
15 Exec Director of Human Resources ... Ms. Amy BARNES
37 Director of Financial Aid ... Mr. James D. KASTER
18 Exec Dir Facilities/Capital Plng ... Mr. John HOOGAKKER
21 Associate Treasurer & Controller ... Mrs. Deborah Z. CAYLOR
13 Chief Technology Officer ... Mr. David SAACKE
24 Senior Academic Technologist ... Mr. Brandon R. BUCY
36 Director Undergrad Career Services ... Ms. Beverly T. LORIG
23 Director Student Health/Counseling ... Dr. Jane T. HORTON
96 Director of Auxiliary Services ... Mr. Paul F. RENZI
40 Director of Univ Bookstore ... Mr. K. C SCHAEFER

Washington Baptist University (B)

4300 Evergreen Lane, Annandale VA 22003
County: Fairfax Identification: 666234
Telephone: (703) 333-5904 Carnegie Class: Not Classified
FAX Number: (703) 333-5906 Calendar System: Semester
URL: www.wbcs.edu
Established: Annual Undergrad Tuition & Fees: $4,675
Enrollment: N/A Coed
Affiliation or Control: Baptist IRS Status: 501(c)3
Highest Offering: Doctorate
Program: Religious Emphasis
Accreditation: BI

01 President ... Dr. Peter M. CHANG
03 Executive Vice President ... Dr. Davis S. KIM
32 Dean of Students ... Mr. David Y. LEE

Westwood College-Annandale (C)

7619 Little River Turnpike 5th Fl, Annandale VA 22003
Telephone: (877) 305-0049 Identification: 666599
Accreditation: ACICS

† Main campus is Westwood College-South Bay in Torrance, CA.

Westwood College-Arlington Ballston (D)

4420 North Fairfax Drive, Arlington VA 22203
Telephone: (703) 243-3900 Identification: 666660
Accreditation: ACICS

† Main campus is Westwood College-South Bay in Torrance, CA.

World College (E)

5193 Lake Shore Drive, Suite 105,
Virginia Beach VA 23455-2500
County: Henrico FICE Identification: 041361
Unit ID: 419448
Telephone: (757) 464-4600 Carnegie Class: Not Classified
FAX Number: (757) 464-3687 Calendar System: Other
URL: www.cie-wc.edu
Established: 1992 Annual Undergrad Tuition & Fees: $4,150
Enrollment: 470 Coed
Affiliation or Control: Proprietary IRS Status: Proprietary
Highest Offering: Baccalaureate
Program: Technical Emphasis
Accreditation: DETC

01 President ... Mr. Randy DRINKO
05 Dean of Instruction ... Mr. Keith CONN
07 Admissions Counselor ... Mr. Scott KATZENMEYER

WASHINGTON

Antioch University Seattle (F)

2326 Sixth Avenue, Seattle WA 98121-1814
Telephone: (206) 441-5352 Identification: 666812
Accreditation: &NH, CACREP, MFCD

† Main campus is Antioch University in Yellow Springs, OH.

Argosy University, Seattle (G)

2601 A Elliott Avenue, Seattle WA 98121-1318
Telephone: (206) 283-4500 Identification: 666080
Accreditation: &WC

† Main campus is Argosy University, Orange County in Orange, CA.

The Art Institute of Seattle (H)

2323 Elliott Avenue, Seattle WA 98121-1622
County: King FICE Identification: 022913
Unit ID: 234492
Telephone: (206) 448-0900 Carnegie Class: Spec/Arts
FAX Number: (206) 448-2501 Calendar System: Quarter
URL: www.ais.edu
Established: 1946 Annual Undergrad Tuition & Fees: $23,088
Enrollment: 1,703 Coed
Affiliation or Control: Proprietary IRS Status: Proprietary
Highest Offering: Baccalaureate
Program: Occupational
Accreditation: NW, ACFEI, CIDA

01 President ... Elden R. MONDAY, JR.
05 Dean of Academic Affairs ... Dr. Scott CARNZ
15 Director of Human Resources ... Natasha J. OILAR
32 Dean of Student Affairs ... Megan KIJEWSKI
07 Senior Director of Admissions ... Liane SOOHOO
11 Dir Administrative/Financial Svcs ... Greg WOODARD
36 Director Career Services ... Jim MCGUIRE

Bainbridge Graduate Institute (I)

220 2nd Avenue South, Suite 400,
Seattle WA 98104-2617
FICE Identification: 041612
Unit ID: 458159
Telephone: (206) 855-9559 Carnegie Class: Not Classified
FAX Number: (206) 855-9045 Calendar System: Quarter
URL: www.bgi.edu
Established: 2002 Annual Undergrad Tuition & Fees: $27,720
Enrollment: 165 Coed
Affiliation or Control: Independent Non-Profit IRS Status: 501(c)3
Highest Offering: Master's
Program: Professional; Business Emphasis
Accreditation: ACICS

01 President ... Mr. Gifford PINCHOT, III
05 Provost/Dean of Academic Affairs ... Dr. John GARDNER
26 Vice President of External Relation ... Ms. Michele MORGAN
11 CFO/Vice President of Operations ... Mr. Jim MCRAE
06 Registrar ... Ms. Lynn BRAUN

Bakke Graduate University (J)

1013 8th Avenue, Suite 401, Seattle WA 98104-1222
County: King FICE Identification: 031108
Unit ID: 420705
Telephone: (206) 264-9100 Carnegie Class: Not Classified
FAX Number: (206) 264-8828 Calendar System: Semester
URL: www.bgu.edu
Established: 1990 Annual Graduate Tuition & Fees: N/A
Enrollment: 183 Coed
Affiliation or Control: Independent Non-Profit IRS Status: 501(c)3
Highest Offering: Doctorate; No Undergraduates
Program: Professional; Religious Emphasis
Accreditation: TRACS

00 Chancellor ... Dr. Ray BAKKE
01 President ... Dr. Brad SMITH
05 Academic Dean ... Dr. Gwen DEWEY
30 Vice President Advancement ... Mr. Robert STEINHAGEN
10 Chief Operations/Financial Ofcr ... Mr. Art ZYLSTRA
06 Registrar ... Dr. Judi MELTON
07 Dir Admiss Svcs/Personnel/Facil Dir ... Ms. Julie GUSTAVSON

Bastyr University (K)

14500 Juanita Drive NE, Kenmore WA 98028-4966
County: King FICE Identification: 022425
Unit ID: 235547
Telephone: (425) 602-3000 Carnegie Class: Spec/Health
FAX Number: (425) 823-6222 Calendar System: Quarter
URL: www.bastyr.edu
Established: 1978 Annual Undergrad Tuition & Fees: $22,695
Enrollment: 1,035 Coed
Affiliation or Control: Independent Non-Profit IRS Status: 501(c)3
Highest Offering: Doctorate
Program: Professional
Accreditation: NW, ACUP, DIETD, DIETI, MEAC, NATUR

01 President ... Dr. Daniel K. CHURCH
05 Senior Vice President/Provost ... Dr. Timothy C. CALLAHAN
10 Vice President for Finance & Admin ... Mr. Sheldon R. HABER
100 Chief of Staff ... Vacant
30 Chief Development Officer ... Ms. Sheryl STIEFEL
32 Vice President of Student Affairs ... Ms. Susan WEIDER
07 Asst Vice Pres Recruitment & Retent ... Ms. Christine MASTERSON
08 Director of Library Services ... Ms. Jane SAXTON
29 Dir Career and Alumni Svcs ... Ms. Susan FARLEY
23 Chf Medical Ofcr Ctr Natural Health ... Dr. Jamey WALLACE
15 Exec Dir of Human Resources/IT ... Mr. Keith WOODY
13 Director of Information Technology ... Ms. Marsha MCGOUGH
09 Director of Research Development ... Dr. Mark MARTZEN
26 Assoc Dir of Media/Public Rels ... Mr. Derek WING
46 Senior Research Scientist ... Dr. Leanna STANDISH
40 Bookstore Manager ... Mr. Marty PETERSEN
07 Director of Admissions ... Vacant
37 Director Financial Aid ... Ms. Danette CARTER
18 Director Facilities and Safety ... Mr. Daniel CLARK
21 Controller ... Mr. Joe PLOUF
38 Director Counseling ... Ms. Cherlyn STOVER

Bates Technical College (L)

1101 S Yakima Avenue, Tacoma WA 98405-4895
County: Pierce FICE Identification: 005306
Unit ID: 235671
Telephone: (253) 680-7000 Carnegie Class: Assoc/Pub-U-MC
FAX Number: (253) 680-7101 Calendar System: Quarter
URL: www.bates.ctc.edu
Established: 1940 Annual Undergrad Tuition & Fees (In-State): $6,864
Enrollment: 4,557 Coed
Affiliation or Control: State IRS Status: 501(c)3
Highest Offering: Associate Degree
Program: Occupational; 2-Year Principally Bachelor's Creditable; Technical Emphasis
Accreditation: NW, DA, DT, OTA

01 President ... Dr. Ron LANGRELL
04 Exec Asst to the President ... Vacant
05 Vice President of Instruction ... Ms. Cheri LOILAND
32 Vice President of Student Services ... Mr. Ivan GORNE
15 Director of Human Resources ... Mr. Geof KAUFMAN
12 Executive Dean Mohler Campus ... Mr. Ed ULMAN
12 Executive Dean South Campus ... Ms. Chen LOILAND
88 Dean of Educational Systems ... Ms. Gloria GARNER
09 Exec Dn Inst Rsrch/Plng/Assessment ... Ms. Summer KENESSON
20 Dean of Academic Programs ... Mr. Mike BRANDSTETTER
30 Director of Development ... Ms. Kimberly PLEGER
21 Executive Dean of Fiscal Services ... Mr. John GINTHER
18 Director Facilities & Operations ... Mr. Marty MATTES
06 Registrar ... Mr. Patrick BROWN
96 General Services Manager ... Mr. Alexander KENESSON
37 Financial Aid Officer ... Ms. Susan NEESE
35 Director of Student Services ... Mr. Dion TEAGUE
13 Director of Information Technology ... Mr. Tom GEORGE
28 College Diversity Coordinator ... Ms. Kathy FLORES

Bellevue College (A)

3000 Landerholm Circle, SE, Bellevue WA 98007-6484
County: King FICE Identification: 003769
Unit ID: 234669
Telephone: (425) 564-1000 Carnegie Class: Assoc/Pub4
FAX Number: (425) 564-4065 Calendar System: Quarter
URL: www.bellevuecollege.edu
Established: 1965 Annual Undergrad Tuition & Fees (In-State): $4,240
Enrollment: 14,156 Coed
Affiliation or Control: State IRS Status: 501(c)3
Highest Offering: Baccalaureate
Program: Occupational; 2-Year Principally Bachelor's Creditable; Professional
Accreditation: NW, ADNUR, CIDA, DMS, NDT, NMT, RADDOS, RTT

01 President ...... Dr. David RULE
04 Exec Asst to the President ...... Ms. Lisa CORCORAN
11 Vice Pres Administrative Services ...... Mr. Ray WHITE
05 Vice President of Instruction ...... Mr. Tom NIELSEN
15 Interim VP Human Resources ...... Ms. Yvonne MCGOOKIN
30 Vice Pres Institutional Advancement ...... Mr. Larry HERRON
32 Interim VP of Student Services ...... Dr. Ata KARIM
103 Vice Pres of Workforce Development ...... Dr. Paula BOYUM
28 Vice President of Diversity ...... Ms. Yoshiko HARDEN
13 Vice Pres of Information Resources ...... Mr. Russell BEARD
09 Assoc VP Effect & Strat Planning ...... Ms. Patricia JAMES
51 Dean Continuing Education ...... Ms. Janis MACHALA
79 Dean of Arts and Humanities ...... Ms. Margaret HARADA
76 Dean of HSEWI ...... Mr. Kevin MCCARTHY
83 Dean of Social Science ...... Ms. Virginia BRIDWELL
88 Associate Dean of Student Programs ...... Mr. Faisal JASWAL
35 Associate Dean of Student Services ...... Mr. Matt GROSHONG
85 Asst Dean Internatl Student Pgms ...... Mr. Cris SAMIA
10 Exec Dir of Finance & Auxiliary Svc ...... Ms. Jennifer STROTHER
08 Dean Library/Media ...... Ms. Myra VAN VACTOR
26 Director College & Community Rels ...... Mr. Bart BECKER
37 Director Financial Aid ...... Vacant
19 Director of Public Safety ...... Mr. Tommy VU
13 Director Computing Services ...... Mr. Jason AQUI
91 Director Networking Svcs & Security ...... Mr. Gary FARRIS
41 Director of Athletics ...... Mr. Bill O'CONNOR
38 Student Counseling ...... Mr. Harlan LEE
40 Director Bellevue College Bookstore ...... Ms. Kristen CONNELY
96 Exec Director Proc Mgmt & Fac Plng ...... Mr. Dexter JOHNSON

Bellingham Technical College (B)

3028 Lindebergh Avenue, Bellingham WA 98225-1599
County: Whatcom FICE Identification: 004999
Unit ID: 234696
Telephone: (360) 752-7000 Carnegie Class: Assoc/Pub-R-M
FAX Number: (360) 676-2798 Calendar System: Quarter
URL: www.btc.ctc.edu
Established: 1957 Annual Undergrad Tuition & Fees (In-District): $4,680
Enrollment: 3,255 Coed
Affiliation or Control: State/Local IRS Status: 501(c)3
Highest Offering: Associate Degree
Program: Occupational
Accreditation: NW, ACFEI, DA, DH, SURGT

01 President ...... Dr. Patricia MCKEOWN
04 Exec Assistant to the President ...... Ms. Ronda LAUGHLIN
05 Vice President of Instruction ...... Ms. Carol LAGER
32 Vice President of Student Services ...... Dr. Linda FOSSEN
11 VP of Administrative Services ...... Ms. Debra JONES
72 Dean of Professional Technical Educ ...... Vacant
30 Exec Director College Advancement ...... Mr. Dean FULTON
15 Director Human Resources ...... Vacant
37 Director Financial Aid ...... Mr. Mike FENTRESS
06 Director Registration/Enrollment ...... Ms. Joan KAMMERZELL
13 Dir Computer/Inform Support Svcs ...... Mr. Curtis PERERA
08 Director Library ...... Ms. Jane BLUME
18 Chief Facilities/Physical Plant ...... Mr. David JUNGKUNTZ
26 Director of Communications ...... Ms. Marni Saling MAYER

Big Bend Community College (C)

7662 Chanute Street NE, Moses Lake WA 98837-3299
County: Grant FICE Identification: 003770
Unit ID: 234711
Telephone: (509) 793-2222 Carnegie Class: Assoc/Pub-R-M
FAX Number: (509) 762-6329 Calendar System: Quarter
URL: www.bigbend.edu
Established: 1962 Annual Undergrad Tuition & Fees (In-State): $4,000
Enrollment: 2,310 Coed
Affiliation or Control: State IRS Status: 501(c)3
Highest Offering: Associate Degree
Program: Occupational; 2-Year Principally Bachelor's Creditable
Accreditation: NW, ADNUR

01 President ...... Dr. Terry LEAS
10 Vice Pres Administrative Services ...... Ms. Gail HAMBURG
05 Vice Pres Instruction/Student Svcs ...... Mr. Bob MOHRBACHER
15 VP of Human Resources & Labor ...... Mrs. Kim GARZA
75 Dean Prof Technical Education ...... Mr. Clyde RASMUSSEN
49 Dean of Arts & Sciences ...... Ms. Kara GARRETT
53 Dean Educ/Health/Language Skills ...... Vacant
32 Assoc VP of Student Services ...... Ms. Candis LACHER
35 Director of Student Programs ...... Ms. Kim JACKSON
37 Director of Financial Aid ...... Ms. Jille SHANKAR
08 Dean of Library Resources ...... Mr. Tim FUHRMAN
41 Director of Athletics ...... Mr. Preston WILKS
06 Registrar ...... Ms. Candis LACHER
102 Dir Inst Advancement/Exec Dir Found ...... Mrs. LeAnne PARTON
27 Publication & Information Director ...... Mr. Doug SLY
21 Director of Business Services ...... Ms. Charlene RIOS
40 Director of Bookstore ...... Mrs. Caren COURTRIGHT
18 Chief Facilities/Physical Plant ...... Ms. Gail HAMBURG
96 Director of Purchasing ...... Ms. Kathy ARITA
39 Residence Hall Coordinator ...... Mr. Hugh SCHOLTE
09 Dean of Institutional Research ...... Ms. Valerie KIRKWOOD

Carrington College - Spokane (D)

10102 E Knox Ave., Suite 200, Spokane WA 99206-4187
County: Spokane Identification: 666385
Unit ID: 439118
Telephone: (509) 532-8888 Carnegie Class: Not Classified
FAX Number: (509) 533-5983 Calendar System: Other
URL: www.carrington.edu
Established: 1998 Annual Undergrad Tuition & Fees: $14,212
Enrollment: 448 Coed
Affiliation or Control: Proprietary IRS Status: Proprietary
Highest Offering: Associate Degree
Program: Occupational; 2-Year Principally Bachelor's Creditable
Accreditation: ACICS, MAAB, RAD

01 Executive Campus Director ...... Mr. Peter TENNEY

Cascadia Community College (E)

18345 Campus Way, NE, Bothell WA 98011-8205
County: King FICE Identification: 034835
Unit ID: 439190
Telephone: (425) 352-8000 Carnegie Class: Assoc/Pub-S-SC
FAX Number: (425) 352-8313 Calendar System: Quarter
URL: www.cascadia.edu
Established: 2000 Annual Undergrad Tuition & Fees (In-District): $4,000
Enrollment: 3,159 Coed
Affiliation or Control: State/Local IRS Status: Exempt
Highest Offering: Associate Degree
Program: 2-Year Principally Bachelor's Creditable
Accreditation: NW

01 President ...... Dr. Eric MURRAY
05 Vice Pres Student Learning/Success ...... Vacant
20 Dean for Student Learning ...... Dr. Erik TINGELSTAD
06 Registrar ...... Ms. Bonnie ELLIS
09 Dir Institutional Research ...... Ms. Susan HAMILTON
10 Chief Business Officer ...... Mr. Terrence HSIAO
15 Director Personnel Services ...... Ms. Gina LORENZ
18 Chief Facilities/Physical Plant ...... Vacant
21 Associate Business Officer ...... Vacant
27 Chief Information Officer ...... Ms. Meagan WALKER
32 Chief Student Life Officer ...... Vacant
37 Director Student Financial Aid ...... Ms. Sybil SMITH
30 Chief Development ...... Ms. Rebecca HASTINGS
38 Director Student Counseling ...... Ms. Ana BLACKSTAD
84 Director Enrollment Management ...... Ms. Erin BLAKENEY

Central Washington University (F)

400 E University Way, Ellensburg WA 98926-7501
County: Kittitas FICE Identification: 003771
Unit ID: 234827
Telephone: (509) 963-1111 Carnegie Class: Master's M
FAX Number: (509) 963-3206 Calendar System: Quarter
URL: www.cwu.edu
Established: 1890 Annual Undergrad Tuition & Fees (In-State): $8,997
Enrollment: 10,737 Coed
Affiliation or Control: State IRS Status: 501(c)3
Highest Offering: Master's
Program: Liberal Arts And General; Teacher Preparatory; Professional
Accreditation: NW, BUS, CACREP, CONST, DIETD, DIETI, EMT, ENGT, IPSY, MUS

01 President ...... Dr. James L. GAUDINO
05 Provost/VP Academic & Student Life ...... Dr. Marilyn LEVINE
10 CFO/VP Business & Financial Affairs ...... Mr. George CLARK
100 Chief of Staff ...... Ms. Sherer HOLTER
20 Assoc Provost ...... Mr. Tracy PELLETT
21 Dir Organizational Effectiveness ...... Mr. Edward DAY
84 Assoc VP Enrollment Management ...... Mr. John SWINEY
32 Dean of Student Success ...... Dr. Sarah L. SWAGER
35 Assoc Dean Student Development ...... Mr. Keith M. CHAMPAGNE
88 Assoc Dean Student Achievement ...... Mr. Jesse NELSON
18 Dir Plant Operations and Maintenenc ...... Mr. Robert TOSCH
15 Dir Faculty and Labor Relations ...... Mr. James BUSALACCHI
14 Asst VP for Information Tech Svcs ...... Mr. Carmen RAHM
58 Dean Graduate Studies and Research ...... Dr. Holly CRAWFORD
49 Dean College of Arts/Humanities ...... Dr. Marji MORGAN
50 Dean College of Business ...... Dr. Kathryn MARTELL
53 Dean College of Educ/Prof Studies ...... Dr. Connie LAMBERT
83 Dean College of the Sciences ...... Dr. Kirk JOHNSON
08 Dean of Library Services ...... Dr. Patricia CUTRIGHT
30 Dir University Advancement ...... Mr. Scott WADE
85 Asst VP Intl Stds and Programs ...... Dr. Michael LAUNIUS
06 Registrar ...... Ms. Tracy TERRELL
22 Dir Employ/Student Svc/ Compliance ...... Ms. Staci SLEIGH-LAYMAN
41 Director Athletics ...... Mr. Jack BISHOP
51 Director Continuing Education ...... Mr. Richard N. BYHAM
12 Asst VP University Centers ...... Vacant
07 Director of Admissions ...... Ms. Kathy GAER-CARLTON
37 Director of Financial Aid ...... Ms. Agnes F. CANEDO
39 Assoc Dean Student Living ...... Mr. Richard DESHIELDS
19 Director Public Safety ...... Mr. Michael LUVERA
26 Director Public Affairs ...... Ms. Linda SCHACTLER
09 Dir Institutional Research ...... Vacant
28 Director of Diversity ...... Vacant
29 Exec Officer Office Alumni Relation ...... Ms. Grace GREENWICH
36 Director Student Placement ...... Vacant
38 Director Student Counseling ...... Vacant
96 Purchasing Manager ...... Mr. Stuart THOMPSON
21 Assoc VP Fin & Business Auxiliaries ...... Ms. Connie WILLIAMS
88 Assistant VP Information Security ...... Mr. Andreas BOHMAN

Centralia College (G)

600 Centralia College Boulevard, Centralia WA 98531-4035
County: Lewis FICE Identification: 003772
Unit ID: 234845
Telephone: (360) 736-9391 Carnegie Class: Assoc/Pub-R-M
FAX Number: (360) 330-7573 Calendar System: Quarter
URL: www.centralia.edu
Established: 1925 Annual Undergrad Tuition & Fees (In-State): $4,000
Enrollment: 2,167 Coed
Affiliation or Control: State IRS Status: 501(c)3
Highest Offering: Associate Degree
Program: Occupational; 2-Year Principally Bachelor's Creditable
Accreditation: NW

01 President ...... Dr. James M. WALTON
05 Vice President Instruction ...... Mr. John MARTENS
32 Vice President of Students ...... Ms. Lucretia FOLKS
10 Vice Pres Finance/Administration ...... Mr. Steve WARD
15 VP Human Resources/Legal Affairs ...... Ms. Julie LEDFORD
103 Dean Workforce Education ...... Ms. Durelle SULLIVAN
08 Dean of Library Services/E-Learning ...... Ms. Sue GALLAWAY
88 Dean of Academic Transfer Programs ...... T. R. GRATZ
09 Director of Institutional Research ...... Vacant
103 Dir WorkFirst & Worker Retraining ...... Ms. Beverley GESTRINE
84 Director of Enrollment Services ...... Ms. Qy-Ana MANNING
37 Director of Financial Aid ...... Ms. Tracy DAHL
13 Director Information Technology ...... Mr. Patrick ALLISON
41 Director of Sports Programs ...... Mr. Bob PETERS
29 Director Alumni Relations ...... Ms. Julie JOHNSON
96 Director of Purchasing ...... Ms. Bonnie MYER
26 Dir College Relations & Events Plng ...... Mr. Don FREY
40 Bookstore Manager ...... Ms. Tammy STRODEMIER
97 Program Coordinator ...... Ms. Joanie ROGERSON

† Granted candidacy at the Baccalaureate level.

Charter College (H)

410 W Bakerview Road, Suite 112, Bellingham WA 98226
Telephone: (360) 647-5000 Identification: 770820
Accreditation: ACICS

† Main campus is Charter College in Anchorage, AK.

Charter College (I)

5278 Outlet Drive, Pasco WA 99301
Telephone: (509) 543-3388 Identification: 770821
Accreditation: ACICS

† Main campus is Charter College in Anchorage, AK.

Charter College (J)

17200 SE Mill Plain Blvd, Suite 100, Vancouver WA 98683
Telephone: (775) 849-9900 Identification: 770822
Accreditation: ACICS

† Main campus is Charter College in Anchorage, AK.

Charter College-Fife (K)

3700 Pacific Highway E, Suite 150, Fife WA 98424
Telephone: (775) 525-2117 Identification: 770623
Accreditation: ACICS

† Main campus is Charter College in Anchorage, AK.

Charter College-Lynnwood (L)

19401 49th Avenue West, Lynnwood WA 98036
Telephone: (425) 275-4900 Identification: 770624
Accreditation: ACICS

† Main campus is Charter College in Anchorage, AK.

City University of Seattle (M)

521 Wall Street, Suite 100, Seattle WA 98121
County: King FICE Identification: 013022
Unit ID: 234915
Telephone: (206) 239-4500 Carnegie Class: Master's L
FAX Number: N/A Calendar System: Quarter
URL: www.cityu.edu
Established: 1973 Annual Undergrad Tuition & Fees: $15,615
Enrollment: 1,175 Coed
Affiliation or Control: Independent Non-Profit IRS Status: 501(c)3

Highest Offering: Master's
Program: 2-Year Principally Bachelor's Creditable; Liberal Arts And General; Teacher Preparatory; Professional; Business Emphasis
Accreditation: NW

01 President .... Mr. Richard CARTER
101 Exec Asst Office of the President .... Ms. Ruth NICHOLS
84 Vice President Enrollment/Registrar .... Dr. Melissa E. MECHAM
05 Provost .... Dr. Steven OLSWANG
10 CFO/VP Finance & Administration .... Mr. Bruce K. BRYANT
30 Vice President for Univ Advancement .... Mr. Christopher ROSS
88 Vice President European Operations .... Dr. Jan REBRO
50 Dean School of Management .... Dr. Kurt KIRSTEIN
53 Dean School of Education .... Dr. Craig SCHIEBER
20 Dean Academic Affs-Europe .... Mr. David GRIFFIN
108 Director of Inst Effectiveness .... Vacant
21 Director of Finance .... Ms. Maria KREY
15 Director of Human Resources .... Mr. Timothy SPRAKE
08 Director Library Services .... Ms. Mary MARA
37 Assoc Dir Student Financial Svcs .... Ms. Linda COOKE
29 Alumni Relations Manager .... Mr. Alex WEBSTER
90 Director of Information Technology .... Mr. Kevin H. BROWN
88 Veterans Affairs Officer .... Ms. Ry-Yon SAO
07 Director Admissions .... Ms. Alyssa BORELLI
85 Director Intl Student Office .... Ms. Sabine SAWAY
18 Facilities Manager .... Mr. Troy CRABREE

† Granted candidacy at the Doctorate level.

Clark College (A)

1933 Fort Vancouver Way, Vancouver WA 98663-3598
County: Clark FICE Identification: 003773
Unit ID: 234933
Telephone: (360) 992-2000 Carnegie Class: Assoc/Pub-U-SC
FAX Number: (360) 992-2871 Calendar System: Quarter
URL: www.clark.edu
Established: 1933 Annual Undergrad Tuition & Fees (In-State): $3,743
Enrollment: 10,000 Coed
Affiliation or Control: State IRS Status: 501(c)3
Highest Offering: Associate Degree
Program: Occupational; 2-Year Principally Bachelor's Creditable
Accreditation: NW, ADNUR, DH, MAC

01 President .... Mr. Robert KNIGHT
05 Vice President of Instruction .... Dr. Tim COOK
32 Vice President of Student Affairs .... Mr. William BELDON
11 Vice President of Admin Services .... Mr. Bob WILLIAMSON
16 Assoc Vice Pres of Human Resources .... Ms. Darcy ROURK
45 Assoc VP Planning/Instnl Effective .... Ms. Shanda DIEHL
51 Assoc VP Corp & Continuing Educ .... Mr. Kevin KUSSMAN
84 Dean of Enrollment Services .... Ms. Diane DREBIN
50 Dean Business/Technology .... Ms. Genevieve HOWARD
79 Dean English/Comm/Hum/Basic Educ .... Dr. Ray KORPI
76 Dean Life Sci/Health & Phys Ed .... Mr. Blake BOWERS
83 Dean Social Sciences/Fine Arts .... Mr. Miles JACKSON
66 Assoc Dean of Nursing .... Ms. Cynthia MYERS
52 Director of Dental Hygiene .... Ms. Brenda WALSTEAD
04 Exec Assistant to the President .... Ms. Leigh KENT
06 Registrar .... Ms. Kimberly MARSHEL
41 Director of Athletics .... Mr. Charles GUTHRIE
15 Associate Director Human Resources .... Ms. Sue WILLIAMS
08 Dir of Library Services .... Ms. Michelle BAGLEY
13 Director of Computing Services .... Mr. Phil SHEEHAN
18 Director of Plant Services .... Vacant
26 Exec Director of Communications .... Mr. Chato HAZELBAKER
36 Director Career/Employment Services .... Ms. Edie BLAKELY
37 Director of Financial Aid .... Ms. Karen DRISCOLL
07 Director of Admissions .... Vacant
10 Director of Business Services .... Ms. Karen WYNKOOP
35 Dir Stdnt Life/Multicult Stdnt Affs .... Ms. Sarah GRUHLER
38 Director Advising & Counseling .... Ms. Kelsey DUPRIE
25 Director of Grant Development .... Mr. Travis KIBOTA
28 Director of Equity & Diversity .... Ms. Sirius BONNER
19 Director of Security & Safety .... Mr. Ken PACHECO
85 International Recruitment Manager .... Ms. Jody SHULNAK
40 Bookstore Manager .... Ms. Monica KNOWLES
88 Mature Learning & Travel Stds Mgr .... Ms. Tracy REILLY-KELLY
96 Purchasing Manager .... Ms. Lisa NELSON

Clover Park Technical College (B)

4500 Steilacoom Boulevard, SW,
Lakewood WA 98499-4004
County: Pierce FICE Identification: 005752
Unit ID: 234951
Telephone: (253) 589-5800 Carnegie Class: Assoc/Pub-S-MC
FAX Number: (253) 589-5601 Calendar System: Quarter
URL: www.cptc.edu
Established: 1942 Annual Undergrad Tuition & Fees (In-State): $7,810
Enrollment: 4,366 Coed
Affiliation or Control: State IRS Status: 501(c)3
Highest Offering: Associate Degree
Program: Occupational; 2-Year Principally Bachelor's Creditable; Technical Emphasis
Accreditation: NW, DA, HT, MAC, MLTAD, SURGT

01 President .... Dr. John W. WALSTRUM
04 Executive Assistant .... Cherie STEELE
05 Vice President Instruction .... Joyce LOVEDAY
10 Vice President Administrative Svcs .... Linda SCHOONMAKER
32 Vice President Student Services .... June STACEY-CLEMONS
20 Associate Vice Pres Instruction .... Mabel EDMONDS
16 Chief Human Res/Legal Affairs Off .... James TUTTLE
103 Dean of Workforce Development .... Vacant
13 Dir Information Technology .... Michael TAYLOR
37 Director Financial Aid .... Wendy JOSEPH
19 Director Plant Services & Security .... Mike ANDERSON
12 Dir Northwest Career/Technical HS .... Loren DAVIS
56 Director Extended Learning .... Vacant
84 Director of Enrollment Services .... Cynthia MOWRY
21 Controller .... Larry CLARK
96 Purchasing Coord/Capital Projects .... Kate PURATICH
26 Marketing/Outreach Coordinator .... Janet HOLM
36 WorkFirst Special Projects Coord .... Christeen CROUCHET
09 Institutional Researcher .... Teresa GREENE
40 Bookstore Coordinator .... Donna KOEHLER
18 Custodial Maintenance Coordinator .... Morris MILLER
06 Registrar .... Cynthia MOWRY

Columbia Basin College (C)

2600 N 20th Avenue, Pasco WA 99301-3397
County: Franklin FICE Identification: 003774
Unit ID: 234979
Telephone: (509) 547-0511 Carnegie Class: Assoc/Pub-R-L
FAX Number: (509) 546-0401 Calendar System: Quarter
URL: www.columbiabasin.edu
Established: 1955 Annual Undergrad Tuition & Fees (In-State): $4,176
Enrollment: 6,294 Coed
Affiliation or Control: State IRS Status: 170(c)1
Highest Offering: Baccalaureate
Program: Occupational; 2-Year Principally Bachelor's Creditable
Accreditation: NW, ADNUR, DH, EMT, MAC, SURGT

01 President .... Dr. Richard CUMMINS
05 Vice President Instruction .... Mr. Curt FREED
11 Vice President of Administration .... Mr. William SARACENO
28 Vice Pres of Diversity/Outreach .... Mr. Martin VALADEZ
32 Vice President of Student Services .... Vacant
15 VP Human Resources/Legal Affairs .... Ms. Camilla GLATT
21 Assist VP Fiscal Operations .... Mr. Mike GRINNELL
09 Dean for Institutional Effectivenes .... Dr. Joe MONTGOMERY
49 Dean Arts & Humanities .... Mr. Bill MCKAY
62 Assoc Dean Library Services .... Ms. Melissa MCBURNEY
102 Executive Director Foundation .... Mr. Robert ROSSELLI
36 Exec Dean Career/Technical Ed .... Mr. Frank POWERS
84 Registrar/Assoc Dean Enroll Svcs .... Ms. Patricia CAMPBELL
13 Director of Technology Services .... Mr. Brian DEXTER
40 Bookstore Director .... Ms. Debra BRUCE
18 Director of Plant Operations .... Mr. Chuck SCHMIDT
41 Athletic Director .... Mr. Scott ROGERS
26 Director of Communications .... Mr. Frank MURRAY
35 Director of Student Programs .... Ms. Alice SCHLEGEL
37 Director Student Financial Aid .... Mr. Ben BEUS
96 Director of Purchasing .... Ms. Sarah BROOKS
06 Associate Registrar .... Ms. Donna KORSTAD

*Community Colleges of Spokane District 17 (D)

501 N Riverpoint Boulevard, Ste 126,
Spokane WA 99217-6000
County: Spokane FICE Identification: 010784
Telephone: (509) 434-5107 Carnegie Class: N/A
FAX Number: (509) 434-5120
URL: www.ccs.spokane.edu

01 Chancellor .... Dr. Christine JOHNSON
12 Pres Spokane Community College .... Mr. Scott MORGAN
12 Pres Spokane Falls Comm College .... Dr. Janet GULLICKSON
05 Provost/Chief Learning Officer .... Dr. Nancy FAIR-SZOFRAN
20 Vice President of Learning SCC .... Ms. Rebecca RHODES
20 Vice President of Learning SFCC .... Dr. Jim MINKLER
32 Vice Pres of Student Services SCC .... Dr. Amy MCCOY
32 VP of Student Services SFCC .... Mr. Darrin PITCHER
10 Chief Financial Officer .... Mr. Keith FOSTER
11 Chief Administration Officer .... Mr. Greg L. STEVENS
13 Chief Information Officer .... Vacant
26 Public Information Officer .... Ms. Anne M. TUCKER
41 Dist Director of Athletics PE/Rec .... Mr. Ken BURRUS
102 Executive Director CCS Foundation .... Mr. Tony D. HIGLEY
40 Director College Bookstores .... Ms. Catherine R. SCOTT
18 District Director of Facilities .... Mr. Dennis DUNHAM
103 Dist Dir Wkforce/Cont Ed/Corp Trng .... Ms. Sara SEXTON-JOHNSON
07 District Outreach Coordinator .... Vacant
96 Purchasing Manager .... Mr. Rod RAMER

*Spokane Community College (E)

North 1810 Greene Street, Spokane WA 99217-5499
County: Spokane FICE Identification: 003793
Unit ID: 236692
Telephone: (509) 533-7000 Carnegie Class: Assoc/Pub-R-L
FAX Number: (509) 533-8839 Calendar System: Quarter
URL: www.scc.spokane.edu
Established: 1963 Annual Undergrad Tuition & Fees (In-State): $4,389
Enrollment: 6,961 Coed
Affiliation or Control: State IRS Status: 501(c)3
Highest Offering: Associate Degree
Program: Occupational; 2-Year Principally Bachelor's Creditable; Technical Emphasis
Accreditation: NW, ACFEI, ADNUR, CAHIIM, COARC, CVT, DA, DMS, MAC, RAD, SURGT

00 District Chancellor .... Dr. Christine JOHNSON
02 President .... Mr. Scott MORGAN
05 Acting VP Instruction .... Dr. Rebecca RHODES
32 Acting VP Student Services .... Ms. Amy MCCOY
88 District Director Head Start .... Ms. Patty ALLEN
32 Dean of Student Support Services .... Mr. Michael LENKER
07 Director Admissions & Registration .... Ms. Roxanne BELOIT
35 Director Student Development .... Mr. Connan CAMPBELL
51 Dean Adult Basic Education .... Ms. Geri SWOPE
49 Interim Dean Arts & Sciences .... Ms. Vicki TRIER
50 Dean Business/Hospitality/Info Tech .... Mr. Jeff BROWN
88 Dean Corrections Education .... Mr. David MURLEY
56 Dean Extended Learning .... Ms. Jenni MARTIN
76 Dean Health & Environmental Science .... Dr. JL HENRIKSEN
66 Acting Dean of Nursing .... Ms. Heather STEPHEN-SELBY
75 Dean for Technical Education .... Mr. Dave COX
41 Director Athletics/PE/Recreation .... Mr. Ken BURRUS
09 Director of Planning & Research .... Mr. Ben WOLFE
51 Assistant Dean Adult Basic Ed .... Mr. Brian DUDAK
88 Assistant Dean PACE Services .... Ms. Linda DEFORD
75 Associate Dean Technical Education .... Mr. Rod TAYLOR
06 Registrar .... Ms. Roxanne BELOIT
88 Director Head Start Operations .... Ms. Debbie DOLAN
88 Director Head Start Program Svcs .... Mr. David COLBURN
88 Director Head Start Admin Services .... Ms. Karin CARTER
37 Director Financial Aid .... Ms. Tammy ZIBELL
28 Director Multicultural & Outreach .... Ms. Lori HUNT
10 Chief Financial Officer .... Mr. Keith FOSTER
40 Director of College Bookstores .... Ms. Cathy SCOTT
11 Chief Administration Officer .... Mr. Greg STEVENS
26 Chief Public Information Officer .... Ms. Anne TUCKER
30 District Development Officer .... Mr. Tony HIGLEY
20 District Provost .... Dr. Nancy FAIR-SZOFRAN
29 Director Alumni Relations .... Ms. Janice EATHERTON
38 Student Counseling Department Chair .... Ms. Cathy SHAFFER
96 Director of Purchasing .... Mr. Rodney RAMER
90 District Dir Information Technology .... Mr. Dick HOL

*Spokane Falls Community College (F)

3410 W Fort George Wright Drive,
Spokane WA 99224-5288
County: Spokane FICE Identification: 009544
Unit ID: 236708
Telephone: (509) 533-3500 Carnegie Class: Assoc/Pub-R-L
FAX Number: (509) 533-3237 Calendar System: Quarter
URL: www.spokanefalls.edu
Established: 1967 Annual Undergrad Tuition & Fees (In-State): $3,467
Enrollment: 8,527 Coed
Affiliation or Control: State IRS Status: 501(c)3
Highest Offering: Associate Degree
Program: Occupational; 2-Year Principally Bachelor's Creditable; Music Emphasis
Accreditation: NW, PTAA

02 President .... Dr. Janet GULLICKSON
04 Exec Asst to the President .... Ms. Ann KIENHOLZ JURCEVICH
05 Vice President of Learning .... Dr. James MINKLER
32 Vice President of Student Services .... Mr. Darren PITCHER
81 Dean Computing/Math & Science .... Mr. James BRADY
22 Dn Equity/Diversity/Spec Initiative .... Vacant
83 Dean Soc Science/Acct/Econ/Hum Svcs .... Mr. James BRADY
79 Dean Humanities/Acad Initiatives .... Dr. Glen COSBY
08 Dean Library/Instruct Support Svcs .... Dr. Mary Ann GOODWIN
103 Dean Bus/Prof Stds/Workforce .... Dr. Glen COSBY
85 Dean of International Programs .... Dr. Lisa AVERY
79 Dean Visual & Performing Arts .... Dr. Bonnie BRUNT
84 Assoc Dean Enrollment Services .... Mr. Steven BAYS
38 Chair of Student Counseling .... Mr. Loren PEMBERTON
19 Security & Safety Supervisor .... Mr. Kenneth DEMELLO
37 Assoc Director of Financial Aid .... Ms. Marjorie DAVIS
36 Assoc Dean of Student Development .... Ms. Chrissy DAVIS
07 Dir Recruit/New Stdnt Entry Center .... Ms. Chrissy JONES
30 Exec Director CCS Foundation .... Mr. Tony HIGLEY
41 Athletic Director .... Mr. Ken BURRUS
51 Director Marketing/Outreach .... Ms. Penny BUTTERS
15 Chief Human Resources Officer .... Mr. Greg STEVENS
18 Director of Facilities .... Mr. Dennis DUNHAM
26 Public Information Officer .... Ms. Anne TUCKER
96 Director of Purchasing .... Mr. Rod RAMER
09 Dir Inst Effectiveness/Research .... Ms. Sally JACKSON

Cornish College of the Arts (G)

1000 Lenora Street, Seattle WA 98121-2707
County: King FICE Identification: 012315
Unit ID: 235024
Telephone: (206) 726-5151 Carnegie Class: Spec/Arts
FAX Number: (206) 720-1011 Calendar System: Semester
URL: www.cornish.edu
Established: 1914 Annual Undergrad Tuition & Fees: $33,550
Enrollment: 788 Coed
Affiliation or Control: Independent Non-Profit IRS Status: 501(c)3
Highest Offering: Baccalaureate
Program: Liberal Arts And General; Fine Arts Emphasis
Accreditation: NW, ART

01 President .... Dr. Nancy J. USCHER
05 Provost .... Ms. Moira SCOTT PAYNE

30 VP Institutional Advancement ... Ms. Gwendolyn FREED
10 Chief Finance Officer ... Mr. Jeffrey R. RIDDELL
11 VP of Special Project ... Ms. Vicki CLAYTON
84 Interim VP of Enrollment Management ... Ms. Victoria DUTCHER
57 Art Department Chairperson ... Ms. Christy JOHNSON
57 Dance Department Chairperson ... Ms. Kathryn DANIELS
57 Interim Design Dept Chairperson ... Mr. Jeff BRICE
64 Music Department Chairperson ... Mr. Kent DEVEREAUX
57 Performance Production Dept Chair ... Mr. Dave TOSTI-LANE
57 Theater Department Chairperson ... Mr. Richard E T. WHITE
79 Humanities & Sciences Dept Chair ... Dr. Chris KELLETT
20 Dean of the College ... Dr. Jenifer WARD
32 Dean of Student Affairs ... Mr. Jerry HEKKEL
06 Dean of Academic Services/Registrar ... Ms. Adrienne M. BOLYARD
26 Director of Communications ... Ms. Karen L. BYSTROM
38 Director of Counseling Services ... Ms. Lori KOSHORK
15 Director of Human Resources ... Ms. Beverly PAGE
13 Director of Information Technology ... Mr. Mark LEDESMA
21 Controller ... Ms. Tina CHAMBERLAIN
08 Director of Library Services ... Ms. Hollis NEAR
30 Dir of Development/Alumni Relations ... Ms. Chris STOLLERY
07 Director of Admissions ... Ms. Sharron STARLING
18 Facilities Director ... Ms. Jenny FRAZIER
88 Business & Student Accounts Manager ... Mr. Jeff WYBORNY
19 Dir of Campus Safety & Security ... Mr. Brandon BIRD
37 Director of Financial Aid ... Ms. Monique THERIAULT

DeVry University - Federal Way Campus (A)

3600 S 344th Way, Federal Way WA 98001-9558
Telephone: (253) 943-2800 Identification: 666224
Accreditation: &NH, ENGT

† Main campus is DeVry University - Chicago Campus in Chicago, IL.

DigiPen Institute of Technology (B)

9931 Willows Road, NE, Redmond WA 98052
County: King FICE Identification: 037243
Unit ID: 443410
Telephone: (425) 558-0299 Carnegie Class: Bac/Diverse
FAX Number: (425) 558-0378 Calendar System: Semester
URL: www.digipen.edu
Established: 1988 Annual Undergrad Tuition & Fees: $26,400
Enrollment: 1,055 Coed
Affiliation or Control: Proprietary IRS Status: Proprietary
Highest Offering: Master's
Program: Professional; Technical Emphasis
Accreditation: ACCSC

01 President ... Mr. Claude COMAIR
03 Chief Operating Officer ... Mr. Jason Y. CHU
05 Dean of Faculty ... Mr. Xin LI
11 Sr Vice President of Administration ... Ms. Meighan SHOESMITH
10 Sr Vice President of Operations ... Mr. Raymond YAN
37 Director of Financial Aid ... Ms. Kimberly KING
32 Director of Student Services ... Mr. Gordon DUTRISAC
26 VP of External Affairs ... Ms. Angela KUGLER

Eastern Washington University (C)

526 5th Street, Cheney WA 99004-1619
County: Spokane FICE Identification: 003775
Unit ID: 235097
Telephone: (509) 359-6200 Carnegie Class: Master's L
FAX Number: (509) 359-6927 Calendar System: Quarter
URL: www.ewu.edu
Established: 1882 Annual Undergrad Tuition & Fees (In-State): $7,933
Enrollment: 12,537 Coed
Affiliation or Control: State IRS Status: 501(c)3
Highest Offering: Doctorate
Program: Liberal Arts And General; Teacher Preparatory; Professional
Accreditation: NW, BUS, CACREP, CEA, CS, DH, ENG, ENGT, MUS, NRPA, OT, PLNG, PTA, SP, SW

01 President ... Dr. Rodolfo AREVALO
05 Vice Pres/Prov Academic Affs ... Dr. Rex FULLER
10 Vice President for Business/Finance ... Ms. Mary VOVES
32 Vice President for Student Affairs ... Ms. Stacey MORGAN FOSTER
30 Vice President of Advancement ... Mr. Michael WESTFALL
20 Vice Prov Academic Res/Admin/Plng ... Dr. Linda KIEFFER
58 Vice Prov/Dean Grad/Undergrad Std ... Dr. Ronald DALLA
08 Dean of Libraries ... Dr. Suzanne MILTON
84 Int Assoc VP Enrollment Services ... Ms. Erin MORGAN
41 Director Intercollegiate Athletics ... Mr. William CHAVES
21 Assoc VP Finance/Chief Fin Officer ... Ms. Toni HABEGGER
18 Assoc Vice Pres for Facilities ... Mr. Shawn KING
04 Exec Assistant to the President/BOT ... Ms. Catherine MOSS
100 Assoc to the President ... Ms. Laurie CONNELLY
86 Director of Government Relations ... Mr. David BURI
36 Assoc Dir Career Services Center ... Ms. Virginia HINCH
92 Director of University Honors ... Dr. Dana ELDER
07 Director of Admissions ... Ms. Shannon CARR
37 Director of Fin Aid & Scholarships ... Mr. Bruce DEFRATES
40 Dir of Bookstore/Pence Union Bldg ... Mr. Robert ANDERSON
51 Dir of Continuing Education & RS ... Vacant
06 Director of Registration & Records ... Ms. Debra FOCKLER
20 Interim Vice Provost ... Dr. Colin ORMSBY
15 Director of Human Resources ... Ms. Jolynn ROGERS
29 Director of Alumni Advancement ... Ms. Lisa POPLAWSKI
96 Director Purchasing ... Ms. LeeAnn CASE
39 Director Housing/Residential Life ... Mr. Josh ASHCROFT
38 Director Counseling & Psych Svcs ... Dr. Robert QUACKENBUSH
19 Director Public Safety/Chief Police ... Chief Timothy L. WALTERS
44 Assoc Director of Annual Giving ... Ms. Pat SPANJER
27 Media Relations Specialist ... Mr. David MEANY
22 Dir Equal Opp/Affirm Action Coord ... Mrs. Gayla WRIGHT
50 Int Dean College of Business Admin ... Dr. Martine DUCHATELET
49 Dean College Arts/Letters/Education ... Dr. Lynn BRIGGS
83 Dean Col Social/Behav Sci/Soc Work ... Dr. Vickie SHIELDS
81 Dean Col Science Math & Technology ... Dr. Judd CASE
66 Dean Intercol Center Nursing Educ ... Dr. Patricia BUTTERFIELD
35 Dean of Student Life ... Dr. Amy JOHNSON
09 Director of Institutional Research ... Dr. Colin ORMSBY
26 Chief Public Relations Officer ... Ms. Teresa CONWAY
28 Director of Diversity ... Ms. Gayla WRIGHT

Edmonds Community College (D)

20000 68th Avenue W, Lynnwood WA 98036-5999
County: Snohomish FICE Identification: 005001
Unit ID: 235103
Telephone: (425) 640-1459 Carnegie Class: Assoc/Pub-S-MC
FAX Number: (425) 771-3366 Calendar System: Quarter
URL: www.edcc.edu
Established: 1967 Annual Undergrad Tuition & Fees (In-State): $4,409
Enrollment: 9,537 Coed
Affiliation or Control: State IRS Status: 501(c)3
Highest Offering: Associate Degree
Program: Occupational; 2-Year Principally Bachelor's Creditable
Accreditation: NW, CA, CONST

01 President ... Dr. Jean HERNANDEZ
05 Interim Vice President Instruction ... Ms. Gail GIULLI
10 Vice Pres/Chief Financial Ofcr ... Mr. Kevin MCKAY
30 Vice Pres Col Relations/Advancement ... Ms. Carol SUMMERS
16 Vice Pres Human Resources ... Mr. Mark CASSIDY
32 Vice President Student Services ... Mr. George SMITH
103 VP Workforce Devel/Training ... Ms. Susan LOREEN
85 Vice Pres International Education ... Mr. David J. CORDELL
08 Dean Learning Resources ... Ms. Lauri KRAM
84 Sr Asc Dean Stdnt Enroll/Fin Svcs ... Ms. Rae-Ellen REAS
35 Sr Assoc Dean Student Life/Devel ... Ms. Nicola SMITH
36 Dean Student Success/Reten ... Dr. Alicia LEWIS
88 Director Advising ... Ms. Stephanie BARON
04 Executive Asst to the President ... Ms. Patty MICHAJLA
102 Director College Foundation ... Ms. Pam WANSER
25 Exec Dir Grants Research/Effective ... Ms. Beth NICHOLS
26 Director Communications/Marketing ... Ms. Stephanie WIEGAND
13 Director Information Technology ... Ms. Eva SMITH
18 Chief Facilities/Physical Plant ... Mr. Paul DOHERTY
28 Equity & Inclusion ... Dr. Tonya DRAKE
96 Director of Purchasing ... Ms. Marian PAANANEN
27 Interim Public Information Officer ... Ms. Marisa PIERCE
19 Director Safety & Security ... Mr. Paul DOHERTY
41 Athletic Director ... Mr. Jorge DE LA TORRE
85 Dir International Student Services ... Ms. Lisa THOMPSON
09 Institutional Researcher ... Ms. Pat HUFFMAN

Everest College (E)

155 Washington Ave, Ste 200, Bremerton WA 98337
County: Kitsap FICE Identification: 023001
Unit ID: 234739
Telephone: (360) 473-1120 Carnegie Class: Not Classified
FAX Number: (360) 792-2404 Calendar System: Quarter
URL: www.everest.edu
Established: 1960 Annual Undergrad Tuition & Fees: $11,788
Enrollment: 332 Coed
Affiliation or Control: Proprietary IRS Status: Proprietary
Highest Offering: Associate Degree
Program: Occupational
Accreditation: ACICS, MAC

01 President ... Mr. Tim ALLEN

Everest College (F)

906 SE Everett Mall Parkway, 6th FL, Everett WA 98208
Telephone: (425) 789-7960 Identification: 770793
Accreditation: ACICS, MAC

† Main campus is Everest College in Bremerton, WA.

Everest College (G)

2156 Pacific Avenue, Tacoma WA 98402
Telephone: (253) 207-4000 Identification: 770794
Accreditation: ACICS

† Main campus is Everest College in Bremerton, WA.

Everest College (H)

120 NE 136th Avenue, Suite 130, Vancouver WA 98684
Telephone: (360) 254-3282 Identification: 666737
Accreditation: ACICS, MAC

† Main campus is Everest College in Portland, OR.

Everett Community College (I)

2000 Tower Street, Everett WA 98201-1390
County: Snohomish FICE Identification: 003776
Unit ID: 235149
Telephone: (425) 388-9100 Carnegie Class: Assoc/Pub-U-SC
FAX Number: (425) 388-9129 Calendar System: Quarter
URL: www.everettcc.edu
Established: 1941 Annual Undergrad Tuition & Fees (In-State): $3,609
Enrollment: 6,980 Coed
Affiliation or Control: State IRS Status: 501(c)3
Highest Offering: Associate Degree
Program: Occupational; 2-Year Principally Bachelor's Creditable
Accreditation: NW, ADNUR, MAC

01 President ... Dr. David BEYER
04 Executive Assistant to President ... Ms. Cheryl BLACKBURN
05 Vice Pres Instruction/Student Svcs ... Dr. Sandra FOWLER-HILL
30 Vice Pres of College Advancement ... Dr. John OLSON
11 Vice Pres of Administrative Svcs ... Ms. Jennifer L. HOWARD
26 Vice Pres of College Services ... Mr. Patrick SISNEROS
12 Exec Dir Univ Ctr North Puget Sound ... Vacant
60 Dean Communication/Social Sciences ... Mr. Eugene MCAVOY
81 Dean of Math & Science ... Mr. Al FRIEDMAN
62 Dean of Arts & Learning Resources ... Ms. Jeanne LEADER
76 Dean Health Sciences/Public Safety ... Mr. Jason SMITH
53 Dean of Basic & Adult Education ... Ms. Katie JENSEN
28 Dean Student Dev/Diversity Advocacy ... Ms. Christina CASTORENA
51 Director Continuing Education ... Ms. Karen LANDRY
84 Dean Enrollment/Student Finan Svcs ... Ms. Laurie FRANKLIN
19 Dir of Campus Safety & Security ... Vacant
12 Exec Director of Corporate Training ... Mr. John B. BONNER
09 Director Institutional Research ... Vacant
41 Director of Athletics ... Mr. Larry WALKER
40 Director of Bookstore ... Ms. Kerri KIRK
88 Dir Center for Disability Services ... Ms. Kathy COOK
88 Program Manager A ... Vacant

The Evergreen State College (J)

2700 Evergreen Parkway, NW, Olympia WA 98505-0005
County: Thurston FICE Identification: 008155
Unit ID: 235167
Telephone: (360) 867-6000 Carnegie Class: Master's S
FAX Number: (360) 867-6577 Calendar System: Quarter
URL: www.evergreen.edu
Established: 1967 Annual Undergrad Tuition & Fees (In-State): $7,486
Enrollment: 4,509 Coed
Affiliation or Control: State IRS Status: 501(c)3
Highest Offering: Master's
Program: Liberal Arts And General
Accreditation: NW

01 President ... Dr. Thomas L. PURCE
05 Vice President/Provost ... Dr. Michael ZIMMERMAN
32 Vice President Student Affairs ... Dr. Wendy ENDRESS
10 Vice President Finance/Admin ... Dr. John HURLEY
30 Vice President College Advancement ... Ms. D. Lee HOEMANN
84 Assoc Vice Pres for Enrollmt Mgmt ... Mr. Steve HUNTER
15 Assoc Vice Pres for Human Resources ... Ms. Laurel UZNANSKI
08 Interim Dean of Library Services ... Ms. Sarah PEDERSEN
35 Dean Student/Academic Support Svcs ... Dr. Phyllis LANE
04 Deputy to President/Secretary BOT ... Mr. John CARMICHAEL
45 Exec Dir Operational Plng/Budget ... Mr. Steve TROTTER
22 Spec Asst to Pres/Equal Opportunity ... Mr. Paul GALLEGOS
22 Civil Rights Officer ... Ms. Nicole ACK
86 Director of Government Relations ... Dr. Julie GARVER
14 Director Computing & Communications ... Mr. Aaron POWELL
26 Dir Marketing/Comm/College Rels ... Mr. Todd SPRAGUE
37 Director of Financial Aid ... Ms. Tracy HALL
06 Interim Registrar ... Ms. Elaine HAYASHI-PETERSEN
09 Director of Institutional Research ... Ms. Laura COGHLAN
18 Director of Facilities ... Ms. Jeanne RYNNE
21 Director of Business Services ... Mr. Collin ORR
29 Asst VP Develop/Alumni Relations ... Ms. Amanda WALKER
36 Director Career Development Center ... Mr. Steve LAING
38 Dir Counseling & Health Services ... Ms. Elizabeth MCHUGH
96 Purchasing and Contracts Manager ... Mr. Jay FIELD
07 Director of Admissions ... Mr. Bryan GOULD
88 Director of Sustainability ... Mr. Scott MORGAN

Faith Evangelical College & Seminary (K)

3504 N Pearl Street, Tacoma WA 98407-2607
County: Pierce FICE Identification: 036894
Unit ID: 443049
Telephone: (253) 752-2020 Carnegie Class: Spec/Faith
FAX Number: (253) 759-1790 Calendar System: Quarter
URL: www.faithseminary.edu
Established: 1969 Annual Undergrad Tuition & Fees: $8,280
Enrollment: 340 Coed
Affiliation or Control: Interdenominational IRS Status: 501(c)3
Highest Offering: Doctorate
Program: Professional; Religious Emphasis
Accreditation: TRACS

01 President ... Dr. Michael J. ADAMS
05 Executive Dean ... Dr. James D. GIBSON
09 Dir of Institutional Effectiveness ... Dr. Eric L. RICE
07 Admissions Officer ... Mrs. Lorrie WHATELY
08 Director Information/Library Svcs ... Dr. Timothy HYUN
88 Director of Korean Studies ... Dr. Kyu H. LEE
37 Financial Aid Officer ... Ms. Debi RICE
10 Chief Financial Officer ... Dr. Douglas COLLIER
06 Registrar ... Rev. Tyrone M. HARDY
35 Office Manager/Student Services ... Mrs. Alison B. HARDY

Gonzaga University (A)

502 E Boone Avenue, Spokane WA 99258-0001
County: Spokane FICE Identification: 003778
Unit ID: 235316
Telephone: (509) 313-4220 Carnegie Class: Master's L
FAX Number: (509) 313-5718 Calendar System: Semester
URL: www.gonzaga.edu
Established: 1887 Annual Undergrad Tuition & Fees: $34,570
Enrollment: 7,781 Coed
Affiliation or Control: Roman Catholic IRS Status: 501(c)3
Highest Offering: Doctorate
Program: Liberal Arts And General; Teacher Preparatory; Professional; Fine Arts Emphasis
Accreditation: NW, ANEST, BUS, BUSA, CACREP, CEA, ENG, LAW, MUS, NURSE, TED

01 President ....Dr. Thayne M. MCCULLOH
05 Academic Vice President ....Dr. Patricia OCONNELL KILLEN
03 Executive Vice President ....Mr. Earl F. MARTIN
10 Vice President for Finance ....Mr. Charles J. MURPHY
88 Vice President for Mission ....Rev. Frank E. CASE, SJ
32 VP for Student Development ....Dr. Judith BIGGS GARBUIO
26 Acting VP University Relations ....Mr. Joe POSS
30 Sr Vice President Principal Gifts ....Ms. Margot J. STANFIELD
20 Assoc AVP/Chief Diversity Officer ....Dr. Raymond REYES
06 Asst Academic Vice Pres/Registrar ....Ms. Jolanta A. WEBER
15 Asst Vice President Human Resources ....Mr. Kirk WOOD-GAINES
88 Assistant VP for Marketing/Comm ....Mr. Dave SONNTAG
07 Dean of Admission ....Ms. Julie A. MCCULLOH
35 Asst VP Dean of Students ....Ms. Kassi KAIN
08 Dean of Libraries ....Dr. Eileen K. BELL-GARRISON
37 Dean of Student Finance Services ....Mr. James WHITE
13 Chief Information Officer ....Mr. Chris G. GILL
26 Director Cmty/Public Relations ....Ms. Mary Joan HAHN
29 Director Alumni ....Mr. Bob D. FINN
36 Director Career Center ....Dr. Mary HEITKEMPER
38 Dir Counseling/Career Assessment ....Dr. Fernando ORITZ
49 Dean Arts & Sciences ....Dr. Elisabeth MERMANN-JOZWIAK
50 Dean School of Business ....Dr. Clarence D. BARNES
107 Dean School of Prof Studies ....Dr. Joe ALBERT
53 Dean of Education ....Dr. Vincent ALFONSO
54 Dean of Engineering & Applied Scien ....Dr. Steve SILLIMAN
61 Dean of Law ....Ms. Jane KORN
09 Director of Institutional Research ....Ms. Jolanta A. WEBER
41 Director of Athletics ....Mr. Michael L. ROTH
42 Acting Dir of University Ministry ....Mrs. Michelle M. WHEATLEY
43 Corporation Counsel ....Ms. Maureen MCGUIRE
18 Director Plant Services ....Mr. Kenneth R. SAMMONS
92 Director Honors Program ....Rev. Tim R. CLANCY, SJ
96 Manager of Purchasing ....Mr. Steve M. LUNDEN
104 Director Study Abroad ....Mr. Richard O. MENARD
25 Director Sponsored Research & Pgm ....Ms. Joann WAITE
108 Faculty Director of Assessment ....Dr. Patrick T. MCCORMICK
20 Assoc Academic Vice President ....Dr. Ron LARGE
66 Dean of Nursing & Human Physiology ....Dr. Brenda STEVENSON MARSHALL
20 Asst AVP for Global Engagement ....Dr. Joseph J. KINSELLA
35 Asst Dean of Students ....Ms. Sima THORPE
35 Asst Dean of Students ....Mr. Jeffery HART
106 Dean of Virtual Campus ....Dr. Michael CAREY
71 Dean of Florence ....Dr. Patrick BURKE
100 Chief of Staff ....Dr. Michael HERZOG
21 Assoc Vice President of Finance ....Mr. Joe SMITH
88 Controller ....Mr. Kevin MANN
88 Director of Publications ....Mr. Dale GOODWIN

Grays Harbor College (B)

1620 Edward P. Smith Drive, Aberdeen WA 98520-7500
County: Grays Harbor FICE Identification: 003779
Unit ID: 235334
Telephone: (360) 532-9020 Carnegie Class: Assoc/Pub-R-M
FAX Number: (360) 538-4299 Calendar System: Quarter
URL: www.ghc.edu
Established: 1930 Annual Undergrad Tuition & Fees (In-District): $4,000
Enrollment: 1,984 Coed
Affiliation or Control: State/Local IRS Status: 501(c)3
Highest Offering: Associate Degree
Program: Occupational; 2-Year Principally Bachelor's Creditable
Accreditation: NW, ADNUR

01 President ....Dr. Edward BREWSTER
05 Vice President for Instruction ....Ms. Laurie CLARY
10 Chief Financial Officer ....Ms. Barbara MCCULLOUGH
32 Vice President for Student Services ....Dr. Arlene TORGERSEN
75 Dean of Vocational Instruction ....Mr. Mike KELLY
35 Assoc Dean for Student Services ....Ms. Nancy DEVERSE
08 Assoc Dean Library/Media Services ....Mr. Stanley W. HORTON
07 Assoc Dean of Admissions ....Ms. Nancy DE VERSE
15 Chief Human Resources Officer ....Mr. David HALVERSTADT
37 Director Student Financial Aid ....Vacant
18 Dir Campus Operations/Sfty/Security ....Mr. Tony SIMONE
38 Director of Counseling ....Ms. Melissa BARNES
30 Chief Development Officer ....Ms. Jan JORGENSON
26 Director Public Relations ....Ms. Jane F. GOLDBERG
09 Chief Instnl Effect/Research/Plng ....Ms. Kristy ANDERSON
06 Registrar ....Ms. Nancy DEVERSE

Green River Community College (C)

12401 SE 320th Street, Auburn WA 98092-3699
County: King FICE Identification: 003780
Unit ID: 235343
Telephone: (253) 833-9111 Carnegie Class: Assoc/Pub-S-MC
FAX Number: (253) 288-3470 Calendar System: Quarter
URL: www.greenriver.edu
Established: 1965 Annual Undergrad Tuition & Fees (In-State): $3,961
Enrollment: 7,709 Coed
Affiliation or Control: State IRS Status: 501(c)3
Highest Offering: Associate Degree
Program: Occupational; 2-Year Principally Bachelor's Creditable
Accreditation: NW, OTA, PTAA

01 President ....Dr. Eileen E. ELY
05 Vice President of Instruction ....Mr. Derek BRANDES
13 Exec Dir of Information Technology ....Ms. Camella MORGAN
10 Vice President Business Affairs ....Mr. Rick BRUMFIELD
15 Vice President for Human Resources ....Ms. Lesley HOGAN
32 Vice President of Student Services ....Dr. Deborah CASEY
56 Vice Pres Extended Learning ....Ms. Edith BANNISTER
85 Assoc VP of International Programs ....Mr. Ross JENNINGS
75 Dn Prof/Tech Ed/Trades & Technology ....Mr. Josh CLEARMAN
49 Dean Instr/Math/Soc Sci/Fine Arts ....Ms. Christie GILLILAND
76 Dean of Instr/Health/Family Studies ....Ms. Krista FOX
88 Dean of Instr/Capital Project ....Mr. Sam BALL
88 Dean Inst Lang/Acad Skill/Wellnes ....Ms. Laura DIZAZZO
79 Assoc Dean Instr/English/Humanities ....Dr. Joyce HAMMER
81 Assoc Dean Instr/Science ....Ms. Cathy WELLS
84 Dean of Enrollment & Completion ....Ms. Jessica GILMORE
35 Dean of Student Success/Retention ....Ms. Joanne MARTIN
06 Registrar ....Ms. Denise BENNATTS
37 Director of Financial Aid ....Ms. Mary EDINGTON
30 Exec Director of Development/Found ....Mr. George FRASIER
21 Director of Business Services ....Ms. Debbie KNIPSCHIELD
21 Controller ....Ms. Teresa COLLINS
18 Director of Facilities ....Mr. Michael LAMONTAGNE
27 Exec Director of College Relations ....Vacant
51 Exec Dir Cont Educ/Off-Campus Sites ....Ms. Leslie MOORE
09 Exec Dir Institutional Effectivenes ....Mr. Christopher JOHNSON
28 Dir Multicultural & Diversity Svcs ....Mr. Michael TUNCAP
96 Purchasing Manager ....Ms. Patty SIKORA
31 Community Relations Coordinator ....Mr. Josh GERTSMAN
19 Director of Campus Safety ....Mr. Fred A. CREEK
41 Director Athletics ....Mr. Robert KICKNER

Heritage University (D)

3240 Fort Road, Toppenish WA 98948-9599
County: Yakima FICE Identification: 003777
Unit ID: 235422
Telephone: (509) 865-8500 Carnegie Class: Master's M
FAX Number: (509) 865-4469 Calendar System: Semester
URL: www.heritage.edu
Established: 1982 Annual Undergrad Tuition & Fees: $17,664
Enrollment: 1,170 Coed
Affiliation or Control: Independent Non-Profit IRS Status: 501(c)3
Highest Offering: Master's
Program: 2-Year Principally Bachelor's Creditable; Liberal Arts And General; Teacher Preparatory; Professional
Accreditation: NW, MT, SW

01 President ....Dr. John E. BASSETT
05 Vice President Academic Affairs ....Dr. Curtis GUAGLIANONE
32 Vice Pres Student Life ....Ms. Melissa FILOWSKI
100 Chief of Staff ....Ms. Crystal LAME BULL
30 Vice President Advancement ....Mr. Michael P. MOORE
21 Controller ....Ms. Siri J. STROM
06 Registrar ....Vacant
53 Dean of Education & Psychology ....Ms. Mea MOORE
18 Director Physical Plant ....Mr. Rob CARROLL
37 Director of Financial Aid ....Mr. Oscar VERDUZCO
08 Library Director ....Mr. Bill MCCAY
13 Director Information Services ....Mr. Jim BUSH
07 Dir of Admissions & Recruitment ....Mrs. Olivia GUTIERREZ
26 Communications Officer ....Ms. Bonnie HUGHES
04 Manager Executive Offices ....Ms. Betty J. SAMPSON
09 Director of Institutional Research ....Ms. Nina OMAN
10 Chief Business Officer ....Mr. Rick R. GAGNIER
15 Director Personnel Services ....Ms. Veronica NARANJO
49 Dean Arts & Sciences ....Dr. Kazuhiro SONODA
35 Dir Stdnt Affs/Plcmnt/Counseling ....Ms. Melissa HILL
29 Dir Alumni Rels/Annual Giving Ofcr ....Ms. Betsy NAGLE-MCNAUGHTON
36 Director Student Placement ....Ms. Irma DEPRIETO
84 Director Enrollment Management ....Mrs. Olivia GUTIERREZ
96 Director of Purchasing ....Ms. Geneva SAPP
38 Counselor for Student Life ....Ms. Erica MACIAS

Highline Community College (E)

PO Box 98000, 2400 S 240th Street,
Des Moines WA 98198-9800
County: King FICE Identification: 003781
Unit ID: 235431
Telephone: (206) 878-3710 Carnegie Class: Assoc/Pub-S-MC
FAX Number: (206) 870-3754 Calendar System: Quarter
URL: www.highline.edu
Established: 1961 Annual Undergrad Tuition & Fees (In-State): $4,000
Enrollment: 7,063 Coed
Affiliation or Control: State IRS Status: 501(c)3
Highest Offering: Associate Degree
Program: Occupational; 2-Year Principally Bachelor's Creditable
Accreditation: NW, ADNUR, COARC, MAC, POLYT

01 President ....Dr. Jack BERMINGHAM
11 Vice President for Administration ....Mr. Larry YOK
05 Vice Pres for Academic Affairs ....Mr. Jeff WAGNITZ
30 VP Inst Advancement/Cmty Rels ....Dr. Lisa SKARI
32 Vice Pres for Student Services ....Ms. Toni CASTRO
20 Dean of Instruction-Vocational ....Ms. Alice MADSEN
20 Dean of Instruction-Academics ....Dr. Rolita EZEONU
24 Dean Instructional Resources ....Ms. Monica LUCE
35 Assoc Dean Student Programs ....Mr. Jonathan BROWN
84 Assoc Dean for Enrollment Services ....Vacant
51 Exec Dir Community Education ....Ms. Judy PERRY
37 Director Financial Aid ....Ms. Lorraine ODOM
26 Director Communications & Marketing ....Mr. Jason PRENOVOST
15 Exec Director of Human Resources ....Ms. Sue WILLIAMSON
21 Director Financial Services ....Ms. Shirley BEAN
13 Exec Dir Administrative Technology ....Mr. Dennis COLGAN
18 Director Plant Operations ....Mr. Barry HOLLDORF
19 Director Security & Safety ....Mr. Rich NOYER
41 Director Athletics ....Mr. John DUNN
44 Director Resources & Development ....Mr. Rod STEPHENSON
09 Director Institutional Research ....Vacant
38 Assoc Dean Counseling/Judicial ....Dr. Allison LAU
40 Bookstore Manager ....Ms. Laura NOLE
96 Director of Purchasing ....Ms. Dianna THIELE
06 Interim Registrar ....Ms. Debbie FAISON
07 Director of Admissions ....Ms. L. Michelle KUWASAKI
22 Dir Multicultural Affairs/Leadershp ....Ms. Natasha BURROWES
29 Coordinator Alumni Relations ....Ms. Madison GRIDLEY

Interface College (F)

178 South Stevens Street, Spokane WA 99201
County: Spokane FICE Identification: 023265
Unit ID: 235495
Telephone: (509) 467-1727 Carnegie Class: Assoc/PrivFP
FAX Number: (509) 467-3804 Calendar System: Semester
URL: www.interface.edu
Established: 1982 Annual Undergrad Tuition & Fees: $14,710
Enrollment: 145 Coed
Affiliation or Control: Proprietary IRS Status: Proprietary
Highest Offering: Associate Degree
Program: Occupational
Accreditation: CNCE

01 President ....Walt LEATHERS
03 Director ....Dave WILSON
37 Director of Financial Aid ....Rick SINCLAIR
07 Asst Director of Admissions ....Kathy HAMMONDS

International Academy of Design and Technology (G)

645 Andover Park West, Seattle WA 98188-3319
Telephone: (206) 575-1865 Identification: 666265
Accreditation: ACICS

† Main campus is International Academy of Design and Technology in Tampa, FL.

ITT Technical Institute (H)

1615 75th Street SW, Everett WA 98203-6261
Telephone: (425) 583-0200 Identification: 666326
Accreditation: ACICS

† Main campus is ITT Technical Institute in Indianapolis, IN.

ITT Technical Institute (I)

12720 Gateway Drive, Suite 100, Seattle WA 98168-3334
Telephone: (206) 244-3300 FICE Identification: 008443
Accreditation: ACICS

† Main campus is ITT Technical Institute in Indianapolis, IN.

ITT Technical Institute (J)

13518 East Indiana Avenue,
Spokane Valley WA 99216-1589
County: Spokane FICE Identification: 030718
Unit ID: 235510
Telephone: (509) 926-2900 Carnegie Class: Spec/Tech
FAX Number: (509) 926-2908 Calendar System: Quarter
URL: www.itt-tech.edu
Established: 1985 Annual Undergrad Tuition & Fees: N/A
Enrollment: 317 Coed
Affiliation or Control: Proprietary IRS Status: Proprietary
Highest Offering: Baccalaureate
Program: Technical Emphasis
Accreditation: ACICS

Lake Washington Institute of Technology (K)

11605 132nd Avenue NE, Kirkland WA 98034-8506
County: King FICE Identification: 005373
Unit ID: 235699
Telephone: (425) 739-8100 Carnegie Class: Assoc/Pub-S-MC
FAX Number: (425) 739-8299 Calendar System: Quarter
URL: www.lwtech.edu
Established: 1949 Annual Undergrad Tuition & Fees (In-State): $3,211
Enrollment: 4,787 Coed
Affiliation or Control: State IRS Status: 170(c)1

Highest Offering: Baccalaureate
Program: Occupational; Technical Emphasis
Accreditation: NW, ACFEI, DA, DH, FUSER, MAC, OTA, PTAA

01 President .... Ms. Amy M. GOINGS
04 Executive Asst to President .... Ms. Debbie Z. ALMSTEDT
05 Interim VP of Instruction .... Dr. Brinton SPRAGUE
88 Special Assistant to the President .... Ms. Andrea I. OLSON
53 Dean Gen Educ/Hospitality & Svcs .... Mr. Douglas J. EMORY
76 Dean Instruction Allied Health .... Ms. Maria MACEDO
72 Dean Applied Design Programs .... Ms. Nancy DICK
08 Assoc Dean Library/E-Learning .... Vacant
76 Dir Phys Therapist Assistant Pgm .... Ms. Molly VERSCHUYL
76 Director Occupational Therapy .... Ms. Kay BRITTINGHAM
88 Director Funeral Services .... Ms. Erin WILCOX
66 Interim Director Nursing .... Mr. Paul BOWLUS-ROOT
27 Chief Information Officer .... Mr. Mike POTTER
18 Director Facilities & Operations .... Mr. Tim WHEELER
21 Controller .... Ms. Debbie DEBEAUCHAMP
88 Food Service Operations Manager .... Mr. Eric SAKAI
96 Purchasing Manager .... Ms. Betty CONWELL
106 Director of eLearning .... Ms. Jennifer DALBY
26 Director Marketing .... Ms. Regine ADAMS
102 Interim Exec Director Foundation .... Ms. Terry BYINGTON
32 Vice President Student Services .... Mr. Dennis LONG
89 Principal/Dean High School Programs .... Ms. Kim INFINGER
37 Director Financial Aid .... Mr. Bill CHANEY
35 Director of Student Services .... Dr. Ruby HAYDEN
103 Director Workforce Development .... Ms. Demetra BIROS
88 Director TRiO Student Support Svcs .... Dr. Patricia HUNTER
06 Registrar .... Dr. Ruby HAYDEN
88 Director Title III .... Ms. Christina HARTER
88 Manager Student Programs .... Ms. Sheila WALTON
40 Manager Bookstore .... Mr. Greg LEPAGE
85 Exec Dir Global Pgms & Partners .... Ms. Myung PARK
25 Director of Grant Development .... Ms. Mary WILLIAMS
30 Executive Dir College Advancement .... Ms. Terry BYINGTON
15 Executive Director Human Resources ... Mr. Gregory W. ROBERTS

Lower Columbia College (A)

PO Box 3010, Longview WA 98632-0310
County: Cowlitz FICE Identification: 003782
Unit ID: 235750
Telephone: (360) 442-2000 Carnegie Class: Assoc/Pub-R-M
FAX Number: (360) 442-2109 Calendar System: Quarter
URL: www.lowercolumbia.edu
Established: 1934 Annual Undergrad Tuition & Fees (In-State): $4,262
Enrollment: 3,595 Coed
Affiliation or Control: State IRS Status: 170(c)1
Highest Offering: Associate Degree
Program: Occupational; 2-Year Principally Bachelor's Creditable
Accreditation: NW, ADNUR, MAC

01 President .... Mr. Christopher C. BAILEY
05 Int Vice President of Instruction .... Mr. Brendan GLASER
11 Vice President Administrative Svcs .... Mr. Nolan WHEELER
32 Vice President for Student Success . Ms. Lisa MATYE EDWARDS
103 Dean Workforce/Continuing Educ .... Mr. Brendan GLASER
20 Dean Instructional Programs .... Ms. Maggie STUART
20 Dean Instructional Programs .... Mr. Kyle HAMMON
76 Associate Dean Allied Health/Nurse .... Ms. Karen JOINER
09 Director Institutional Research .... Ms. Wendy HALL
18 Director of Campus Services .... Mr. Richard HAMILTON
102 Director of Foundation .... Ms. Erin BROWN
41 Athletic Director .... Mr. Kirc J. ROLAND
21 Controller .... Mr. Joe QUIRK
26 Director of College Relations .... Ms. Sue GROTH
15 Director of Personnel Services .... Ms. Kendra SPRAGUE
37 Financial Aid Officer .... Ms. Marisa GREEAR
08 Director of Library Services .... Ms. Maggie STUART
13 Director of Information Technology .... Mr. Brandon RAY
40 Director of Bookstore .... Vacant
07 Director of Admissions/Registrar .... Ms. Lynn LAWRENCE
10 Chief Business Officer .... Mr. Nolan WHEELER
84 Director Enrollment Management ..... Ms. Lisa MATYE EDWARDS
96 Director of Purchasing .... Ms. Sherry GOHN
04 Executive Assistant .... Ms. Linda J. CLARK

Moody Bible Institute-Spokane (B)

611 E Indiana Avenue, Spokane WA 99207
Telephone: (509) 570-5900 Identification: 770082
Accreditation: &NH

† Main campus is Moody Bible Institute in Chicago, IL.

Northwest College of Art & Design (NCAD) (C)

16301 Creative Drive NE, Poulsbo WA 98370-8651
County: Kitsap FICE Identification: 026021
Unit ID: 377546
Telephone: (360) 779-9993 Carnegie Class: Spec/Arts
FAX Number: (360) 779-9933 Calendar System: Semester
URL: www.ncad.edu
Established: 1982 Annual Undergrad Tuition & Fees: $18,200
Enrollment: 80 Coed
Affiliation or Control: Proprietary IRS Status: Proprietary
Highest Offering: Baccalaureate
Program: Fine Arts Emphasis
Accreditation: ACCSC

01 President .... Craig FREEMAN
06 Registrar/Financial Aid .... Ryan MARTIN
05 Director of Education .... Julius FINLEY

Northwest Indian College (D)

2522 Kwina Road, Bellingham WA 98226-9278
County: Whatcom FICE Identification: 021800
Unit ID: 380377
Telephone: (360) 676-2772 Carnegie Class: Tribal
FAX Number: (360) 738-0136 Calendar System: Quarter
URL: www.nwic.edu
Established: 1978 Annual Undergrad Tuition & Fees: $4,960
Enrollment: 699 Coed
Affiliation or Control: Tribal Control IRS Status: 501(c)3
Highest Offering: Baccalaureate
Program: Occupational; 2-Year Principally Bachelor's Creditable
Accreditation: NW

01 President .... Dr. Justin GUILLORY
10 Vice President/Admin & Finance .... Ms. Karyl JEFFERSON
05 Vice Pres Instruction/Student Svcs .... Ms. Carole RAVE
11 Vice President Campus Development .... Mr. David OREIRO
45 VP for Research/Sponsored Programs .... Ms. Barbara ROBERTS
04 Exec Assistant to the President .... Ms. Corby DAVIS
106 Dean of Academic/Distant Learning ...... Ms. Bernice PORTERVINT
20 Assoc Dean for Instruction .... Mr. Don MCCLUSKEY
37 Asc Dn Students/Fin Aid Dir/Admiss .... Ms. Crystal BAGBY
13 IT Director .... Mr. Michael JAMES
08 Library Director .... Ms. Valerie MCBETH

Northwest Institute of Literary Arts (E)

P.O. Box 639, Freeland WA 98249
County: Island FICE Identification: 041889
Unit ID: 460941
Telephone: (360) 331-0307 Carnegie Class: Not Classified
FAX Number: N/A Calendar System: Semester
URL: www.nila.edu
Established: 2005 Annual Graduate Tuition & Fees: $12,650
Enrollment: 38 Coed
Affiliation or Control: Independent Non-Profit IRS Status: 501(c)3
Highest Offering: Master's; No Undergraduates
Program: Professional; Fine Arts Emphasis
Accreditation: DETC

01 Program Director .... Mr. Wayne UDE
06 Registrar .... Ms. Susan JANOW

Northwest School of Wooden Boatbuilding (F)

42 N Water Street, Port Hadlock WA 98339-8706
County: Jefferson FICE Identification: 041550
Unit ID: 236124
Telephone: (360) 385-4948 Carnegie Class: Not Classified
FAX Number: (360) 385-5089 Calendar System: Other
URL: www.nwboatschool.org
Established: 1981 Annual Undergrad Tuition & Fees: $13,050
Enrollment: 45 Coed
Affiliation or Control: Independent Non-Profit IRS Status: 501(c)3
Highest Offering: Associate Degree
Program: Occupational
Accreditation: ACCSC

01 Executive Director .... Mr. Peter LEENHOUTS
05 Director of Education .... Ms. Pamela ROBERTS

Northwest University (G)

PO Box 579, Kirkland WA 98083-0579
County: King FICE Identification: 003783
Unit ID: 236133
Telephone: (425) 822-8266 Carnegie Class: Bac/Diverse
FAX Number: (425) 889-5224 Calendar System: Semester
URL: www.northwestu.edu
Established: 1934 Annual Undergrad Tuition & Fees: $25,390
Enrollment: 1,355 Coed
Affiliation or Control: Assemblies Of God Church IRS Status: 501(c)3
Highest Offering: Master's
Program: Liberal Arts And General; Religious Emphasis
Accreditation: NW, ACBSP, NURSE

01 President .... Dr. Joseph CASTLEBERRY
05 Provost .... Dr. Jim HEUGEL
10 Chief Financial Officer .... Mr. John JORDAN
30 Senior VP of Advancement .... Mr. Jason MILES
42 Campus Pastor .... Rev. Phil RASMUSSEN
06 Registrar .... Mrs. Sandy HENDRICKSON
07 Director of Admissions .... Mrs. Anna PFLUG
37 Director of Financial Aid .... Mr. Roger WILSON
41 Athletic Director .... Mr. Gary MCINTOSH
08 College Librarian .... Mr. Adam EPP
38 Director of Counseling Services .... Ms. Teresa REGAN
29 Director of Alumni Services .... Mr. Dustin SHIRLEY
15 Director Human Resources .... Ms. Victoria CLARK
36 Director Student Success .... Mrs. Amy JONES

† Granted candidacy at the Doctorate level.

Olympic College (H)

1600 Chester Avenue, Bremerton WA 98337-1699
County: Kitsap FICE Identification: 003784
Unit ID: 236188
Telephone: (360) 792-6050 Carnegie Class: Assoc/Pub4
FAX Number: (360) 475-7151 Calendar System: Quarter
URL: www.olympic.edu
Established: 1946 Annual Undergrad Tuition & Fees (In-State): $3,999
Enrollment: 8,545 Coed
Affiliation or Control: State IRS Status: 501(c)3
Highest Offering: Baccalaureate
Program: Occupational; 2-Year Principally Bachelor's Creditable
Accreditation: NW, ACFEI, ADNUR, MAC, NURSE, PTAA

01 President .... Dr. David C. MITCHELL
05 Vice President of Instruction .... Ms. Mary GARGUILE
11 Vice President of Administration .... Mr. Bruce RIVELAND
32 Vice President of Student Services .... Dr. Damon BELL
26 Vice President College Relations .... Dr. Joan HANTEN
16 Exec Director Human Resource Svcs .... Ms. Lynnette DE SHAW
51 Admin Svcs Mgr Continuing Education ... Dr. Samantha POWERS
04 Exec Assistant to the President .... Ms. Allison SMITH
37 Director Financial Aid .... Ms. Heidi TOWNSEND
27 Int Director of Communications .... Ms. Amanda GEBHARDT-FUENTES
84 Dn Enroll Svcs/Registrar/Dir Admiss .... Ms. Dianna LARSEN
18 Chief Facilities/Physical Plant .... Mr. William WILKIE
21 Director of Business Services .... Ms. Janell WHITELEY
96 Procurement Officer .... Ms. Diana LAKE
40 Director of Auxiliary Services .... Vacant
36 Director Student Placement .... Ms. Teresa MCDERMOTT
09 Dir Research/Planning/ Assessment .... Dr. Michelle CHANDRASEKHAR
28 Multicultural Services Manager .... Vacant
103 Dean Workforce Development .... Ms. Amy HATFIELD
08 Dean Library-Media .... Ms. Ruth M. SAUCIER
35 Dean of Student Development .... Mr. James MOHR
50 Dean Business & Technology .... Dr. Norma WHITACRE
81 Dean Math/Engineer/Sci/Health .... Dr. Mark HARRISON
79 Dean Humanities/Social Science .... Dr. Gina HUSTON

Pacific Lutheran University (I)

Tacoma WA 98447-0003
County: Pierce FICE Identification: 003785
Unit ID: 236230
Telephone: (253) 531-6900 Carnegie Class: Master's M
FAX Number: (253) 535-8320 Calendar System: 4/1/4
URL: www.plu.edu
Established: 1890 Annual Undergrad Tuition & Fees: $34,440
Enrollment: 3,473 Coed
Affiliation or Control: Evangelical Lutheran Church In America
IRS Status: 501(c)3
Highest Offering: Master's
Program: Liberal Arts And General; Teacher Preparatory; Professional
Accreditation: NW, BUS, CS, ENG, MFCD, MUS, NURSE, SW, TED

01 President .... Dr. Thomas W. KRISE
05 Provost/Dean Graduate Studies .... Dr. Steven P. STARKOVICH
10 Vice President Finance & Operations .... Dr. Sheri J. TONN
30 Vice Pres Development/Univ Rels .... Dr. Steve J. OLSON
32 Vice Pres Stdnt Life/Dean of Stdnts .... Dr. Laura F. MAJOVSKI
07 Vice Pres Admission/Enrollment Svcs .... Mr. Karl A. STUMO
27 Vice Pres Marketing & Communication .... Vacant
20 Associate Provost for Curriculum .... Dr. Jan P. LEWIS
21 Assoc Vice Pres Finance/Controller .... Mr. Robert K. RILEY
08 Assoc Provost for Information Tech .... Dr. Frank X. MOORE
42 University Pastor .... Rev. Dennis G. SEPPER
42 University Pastor .... Rev. Nancy J. CONNOR
57 Dean School of Arts & Communication .... Dr. Cameron D. BENNETT
50 Dean of School of Business .... Dr. James L. BROCK
53 Dean School of Educ & Kinesiology .... Dr. Frank M. KLINE
66 Dean School of Nursing .... Dr. Terry W. MILLER
79 Dean of Humanities .... Dr. James M. ALBRECHT
88 Dean of Natural Sciences .... Dr. Matthew J. SMITH
83 Dean of Social Sciences .... Dr. David R. HUELSBECK
35 Dean Stdnt Dev/Dir of Stdnt Involve .... Dr. Eva R. JOHNSON
58 Assoc Dean Grad & Special Programs .... Dr. Laura J. POLCYN
88 Exec Dir Wang Ctr for Global Ed .... Dr. Tamara R. WILLIAMS
88 Director Academic Advising .... Mr. Hal DELAROSBY
41 Athletic Director .... Ms. Laurie L. TURNER
06 Registrar .... Ms. Kristin H. PLAEHN
39 Asst Dean of Stdnts/Dir of Res Life .... Mr. Tom A. HUELSBECK
18 Director Facilities Management .... Mr. David L. KOHLER
29 Exec Dir Constituent Relations .... Vacant
19 Director of Campus Safety & Info .... Mr. Greg V. PREMO
36 Exec Dir of Career Connections .... Vacant
23 Director of Health & Counseling Ctr .... Dr. Matt FREEMAN
15 Assoc Vice Pres Human Resources .... Ms. Teri P. PHILLIPS
90 Dir of Enterprise Systems & Comm .... Mr. David P. ALLEN
37 Director of Student Financial Aid .... Ms. Kay W. SOLTIS
40 Manager of Bookstore .... Ms. Amanda B. HAWKINS
09 Dir Assessment/Accreditation/Rsrch .... Dr. David A. VEAZEY

Pacific Northwest University of Health Sciences (J)

111 University Parkway, Suite 202, Yakima WA 98901
County: Yakima FICE Identification: 041305
Unit ID: 455406
Telephone: (509) 452-5100 Carnegie Class: Assoc/PrivNFP4

FAX Number: (509) 452-5101 Calendar System: Semester
URL: www.pnwu.edu
Established: 2005 Annual Graduate Tuition & Fees: $48,000
Enrollment: 300 Coed
Affiliation or Control: Independent Non-Profit IRS Status: 501(c)3
Highest Offering: Doctorate; No Undergraduates
Program: Professional
Accreditation: OSTEO

01 President ... Dr. Keith WATSON
05 Chief Academic Officer ... Dr. Robert E. SUTTON
10 Chief Financial Officer ... Ms. Ann O'BRIEN
11 Interim Chief Business Officer ... Vacant
30 Chief Advancement Officer ... Mr. Wendell SNODGRASS
63 Dean Col of Osteopathic Medicine ... Dr. Robyn PHILLIPS-MADSON

Peninsula College (A)

1502 East Lauridsen Boulevard,
Port Angeles WA 98362-6698
County: Clallam FICE Identification: 003786
Unit ID: 236258
Telephone: (360) 452-9277 Carnegie Class: Assoc/Pub4
FAX Number: (360) 457-8100 Calendar System: Quarter
URL: www.pc.ctc.edu
Established: 1961 Annual Undergrad Tuition & Fees (In-District): $4,192
Enrollment: 2,408 Coed
Affiliation or Control: State/Local IRS Status: 501(c)3
Highest Offering: Baccalaureate
Program: Occupational; 2-Year Principally Bachelor's Creditable
Accreditation: NW, ADNUR

01 President ... Dr. Luke ROBINS
05 Vice President Instruction ... Dr. Mary O'NEIL-GARRETT
11 Vice President Administrative Svcs ... Ms. Deborah FRAZIER
32 Vice President Student Services ... Mr. Jack HULS
45 VP Institutional Effectiveness ... Dr. Paula DOHERTY
50 Exec Dir Cmty/Business Education ... Mr. Bob LAWRENCE-MARKARIAN
55 Dean Adult Basic Education ... Dr. Evelyn SHORT
35 Dean of Student Services ... Ms. Maria PENA
13 Director Information Technology ... Mr. Steven BAXTER
37 Dir Finan Aid/Enrollment Services ... Ms. Krista FRANCIS
04 Executive Asst to the President ... Ms. Pattie FISCHER
27 Public Information Officer ... Ms. Phyllis L. VAN HOLLAND
15 Director Human Resources ... Ms. Bonnie H. CAUFFMAN
85 Director of International Programs ... Ms. Sophia ILIAKIS-DOHERTY
102 Exec Director of the Foundation ... Ms. Mary HUNCHBERGER
41 Director Athletics/Student Programs ... Mr. Rick ROSS
09 Director of Institutional Research ... Vacant
18 Physical Plant Director ... Mr. Rick CROOT
40 Bookstore Manager ... Mrs. Camilla RICO
06 Enrollment Services Manager ... Ms. Cindy LAUDERBACK

Perry Technical Institute (B)

2011 W. Washington Ave, Yakima WA 98903
County: Yakima FICE Identification: 009387
Unit ID: 236212
Telephone: (509) 453-0375 Carnegie Class: Not Classified
FAX Number: (509) 453-0473 Calendar System: Quarter
URL: www.perrytech.edu
Established: 1939 Annual Undergrad Tuition & Fees: $9
Enrollment: 748 Coed
Affiliation or Control: Independent Non-Profit IRS Status: 501(c)3
Highest Offering: Associate Degree
Program: Occupational
Accreditation: ACCSC

01 President ... Christine COTE

Pierce College District (C)

9401 Farwest Drive SW, Lakewood WA 98498-1999
County: Pierce FICE Identification: 005000
Unit ID: 235237
Telephone: (253) 964-6500 Carnegie Class: Assoc/Pub-S-MC
FAX Number: N/A Calendar System: Quarter
URL: www.pierce.ctc.edu
Established: 1967 Annual Undergrad Tuition & Fees (In-State): $3,826
Enrollment: 11,837 Coed
Affiliation or Control: State IRS Status: 501(c)3
Highest Offering: Associate Degree
Program: Occupational; 2-Year Principally Bachelor's Creditable
Accreditation: NW, ADNUR, DH

01 District Chancellor ... Dr. Michele JOHNSON
12 President Pierce College Puyallup ... Dr. Marty L. CAVALLUZZI
12 President Fort Steilacoom ... Ms. Denise YOCHUM
05 VP Learning/Student Success-PY ... Dr. Matthew CAMPBELL
05 Vice Pres Learning/Stdnt Success-FS ... Ms. Debra GILCHRIST
10 Vice Pres Administrative Services ... Mr. Choi HALLADAY
30 Vice President of Advancement ... Vacant
15 Vice President for Human Resources ... Ms. Holly GORSKI
13 Dean of Institutional Technology ... Mr. Mike STOCKE
06 Registrar/Dir Enrollment Svcs-Dist ... Ms. Anne WHITE
08 Dean Libraries & Learning Resources ... Ms. Christie FLYNN
26 Dir Marketing and Communications ... Mr. Brian BENEDETTI
36 Dir Student Development-District ... Ms. Agnes STEWARD
35 Dir Student Programs-Ft Steilacoom ... Mr. Cameron COX
41 Director of Athletics ... Mr. Duncan STEVENSON
18 Director of Facilities & Const Mgt ... Mr. Jim TAYLOR
32 Dir of Student Life-Puyallup ... Mr. Sean COOKE
85 Director of International Education ... Vacant
19 District Manager Campus Safety ... Mr. Chris MACKERSIE
21 Director of Budget and Finance ... Ms. Sylvia DERRICK
37 Interim Director Financial Aid ... Ms. Anne WHITE
84 Director Enrollment Services-Puy ... Ms. Els DEMING
09 Institutional Researcher ... Ms. Kris CUMMINGS
49 District Dean Arts & Humanities ... Dr. Holly SMITH
88 District Dean Transitional Ed ... Ms. Lori GRIFFIN
76 District Dean Tech/Allied Health ... Mr. Ronald MAY
88 District Dean Natural Sciences ... Mr. Thomas BROXSON
83 District Dean Social Sciences ... Mr. Greg BRAZELL
29 Alumni Relations Manager ... Ms. Paula HENSON-WILLIAMS
96 Procurement Officer ... Mr. Curtis LEE

Pima Medical Institute-Renton (D)

555 South Renton Village Place, Renton WA 98057
Telephone: (800) 477-7462 Identification: 770517
Accreditation: ABHES, COARC

† Main campus is Pima Medical Institute-Tucson in Tucson, AZ.

Pima Medical Institute-Seattle (E)

9709 3rd Avenue NE, Suite 400, Seattle WA 98115-2052
Telephone: (206) 322-6100 Identification: 666172
Accreditation: ABHES, DH, OTA, PTAA, RAD

† Main campus is Pima Medical Institute-Tucson in Tucson, AZ.

Renton Technical College (F)

3000 NE Fourth Street, Renton WA 98056-4123
County: King FICE Identification: 010434
Unit ID: 236382
Telephone: (425) 235-2352 Carnegie Class: Assoc/Pub-S-SC
FAX Number: (425) 235-7832 Calendar System: Quarter
URL: www.rtc.edu
Established: 1942 Annual Undergrad Tuition & Fees (In-State): $4,855
Enrollment: 5,445 Coed
Affiliation or Control: State IRS Status: 501(c)3
Highest Offering: Associate Degree
Program: Occupational; Technical Emphasis
Accreditation: NW, ACFEI, DA, MAC, SURGT

01 President ... Mr. Steven J. HANSON
10 VP Finance/Administration ... Ms. Melinda M. MERRELL
05 Vice President Instruction ... Vacant
32 Vice President Student Services ... Mr. Dave PELKEY
97 Dean Basic Studies ... Ms. Jodi NOVOTNY
76 Dean Allied Health ... Vacant
72 Dean Apprentice/Trade & Industry ... Ms. Gay KIESLING
50 Dean Bus/Educ/Hum Svcs/Gen Educ ... Ms. Peggy MOE
72 Dean Automotive/Tech/Distance Educ ... Mr. Dante J. LEON
102 Foundation Director ... Ms. Heather WINFREY
13 Director Technology ... Vacant
07 Director Enrollment Services ... Ms. Robin YOUNG
46 Director Institutional Planning ... Ms. Mary Kate RICHARDSON
08 Director Library ... Mr. Eric E. PALO
21 Director Financial Services ... Mr. Mark JOHNSON
15 Director Human Resources Develop ... Ms. Lesley HOGAN
37 Director Financial Aid ... Ms. Debbie SOLOMON
18 Director Plant Operations ... Mr. Barry A. BAKER
40 Bookstore Manager ... Mr. Jose A. PERDOMO
19 Safety & Security Manager ... Vacant
103 Director Workforce Development ... Ms. Maggi SUTTHOFF
88 Associate Dean Culinary Arts ... Mr. Doug MEDBURY
26 Director Communications & Marketing ... Ms. Kendra SMITH
38 Director Counseling & Advising ... Mr. Scott LATIOLAIS
35 Director Student Programs ... Ms. Jessica SUPINSKI
88 Custodial Manager ... Mr. Mark DANIELS
88 Outreach Manager ... Ms. Andrea LANCASTER

Saint Martin's University (G)

5000 Abbey Way, SE, Lacey WA 98503-7500
County: Thurston FICE Identification: 003794
Unit ID: 236452
Telephone: (360) 491-4700 Carnegie Class: Master's S
FAX Number: (360) 459-4124 Calendar System: Semester
URL: www.stmartin.edu
Established: 1895 Annual Undergrad Tuition & Fees: $39,950
Enrollment: 1,800 Coed
Affiliation or Control: Roman Catholic IRS Status: 501(c)3
Highest Offering: Master's
Program: Liberal Arts And General; Teacher Preparatory; Professional
Accreditation: NW, ENG, TEAC

00 Chancellor ... Abbot Neal G. ROTH, OSB
01 President ... Dr. Roy F. HEYNDERICKX
05 Provost & Vice President ... Dr. Molly E. SMITH
10 Vice President of Finance ... Ms. Susan D. HELTSLEY
30 Vice Pres Inst Advancement ... Ms. Rosanne NICHOLS
85 Vice Pres Intl Programs/Development ... Ms. Josephine YUNG
26 VP of Marketing/Communications ... Ms. Jennifer FELLINGER
32 Dean Student Services ... Ms. Melanie RICHARDSON
84 Dean Enrollment Management ... Vacant
07 Dean Admission/Stdnt Financial Svcs ... Mr. Scott SCHULZ
21 Treasurer ... Fr. Bede CLASSICK
37 Financial Aid Director ... Ms. Isabelle MORA
29 Director Alumni Relations ... Vacant
06 Registrar ... Mr. Alex ARCENEAUX
13 Associate Vice President/CIO ... Mr. Greg DAVIS
18 Director Facilities Management ... Mr. Alan TYLER
44 Dir of Development/Planned Giving ... Ms. Katie WOJKE
36 Director of Career Placement ... Ms. Ann ADAMS
41 Athletic Director ... Mr. Bob GRISHAM
49 Dean Col of Arts & Sciences ... Dr. Eric APFELSTADT
81 Dean of Science & Math ... Dr. Katherine PORTER
83 Dean of Social Sciences ... Dr. Rex CASILLAS
53 Dean of Education ... Dr. Joyce WESTGARD
50 Dean of Business ... Dr. Richard BEER
54 Dean of Engineering ... Dr. Zella KAHN-JETTER
56 Director Extension Programs ... Mr. Cruz ARROYO
08 Library Director ... Mr. Scot HARRISON
42 Director Campus Ministry ... Mr. Jon DWYER
39 Director of Housing/Residence Life ... Mr. Tim MCCLAIN
38 Director Counseling Center ... Ms. Jan BERNEY
09 Director Institutional Grants/Rsrch ... Vacant
15 Associate VP of Human Resources ... Ms. Cynthia JOHNSON
89 Director of Freshmen Studies ... Dr. Sharon TAYLOR
104 Dir International Programs/Dev ... Vacant
40 Manager Bookstore ... Mr. Mark MORRIS

*Seattle Community Colleges (H)

1500 Harvard Avenue, Seattle WA 98122-3803
County: King FICE Identification: 010106
Unit ID: 236498
Telephone: (206) 934-4100 Carnegie Class: N/A
FAX Number: (206) 934-3883
URL: www.seattlecolleges.edu

01 Chancellor ... Dr. Jill WAKEFIELD
03 Vice Chancellor ... Dr. Carin S. WEISS
10 Vice Chanc for Finance & Technology ... Dr. Kurt BUTTLEMAN
15 Chief Human Resources Officer ... Mr. Charles E. SIMS
26 Public Information Officer ... Ms. Patricia PAQUETTE
30 Interim Exec Dir for Advancement ... Ms. Evelyn YENSON
12 President South Seattle Cmty Col ... Mr. Gary OERTLI
12 President North Seattle Cmty Col ... Mr. Mark MITSUI
12 President Seattle Central Cmty Col ... Dr. Paul KILLPATRICK

*North Seattle Community College (I)

9600 College Way N, Seattle WA 98103-3599
County: King FICE Identification: 009704
Unit ID: 236072
Telephone: (206) 934-3600 Carnegie Class: Assoc/Pub-U-MC
FAX Number: (206) 934-3606 Calendar System: Quarter
URL: www.northseattle.edu
Established: 1970 Annual Undergrad Tuition & Fees (In-State): $3,862
Enrollment: 6,047 Coed
Affiliation or Control: State IRS Status: 170(c)1
Highest Offering: Associate Degree
Program: Occupational; 2-Year Principally Bachelor's Creditable
Accreditation: NW, ADNUR, MAC

02 Interim President ... Dr. Mary Ellen O'KEEFFE
05 Vice President for Instruction ... Dr. Mary Ellen O'KEEFFE
32 Int Vice Pres Student Development ... Ms. Marci MYER
11 Vice President of Administration ... Dr. Monty MONTERECY
36 Exec Dean Career/Workforce Educ ... Mr. Steve MILLER
79 Dean Art/Humanities/Social Sciences ... Dr. Alison STEVENS
81 Dean Math & Science ... Mr. Peter LORTZ
17 Dean Health & Human Services ... Dr. Robert FINEMAN
50 Dean Business/Eng Info Tech ... Ms. Terry COX
08 Dean Library & Media Services ... Ms. Sharon SIMES
35 Assoc Dean Student Develop Svcs ... Ms. Alice MELLING
88 Assoc Dean Basic/Transitional Stds ... Ms. Kim CHAPMAN
56 Assoc Dean e-Learning ... Dr. Tom BRAZIUNAS
30 Director of Development ... Ms. Anne ZACOVIC
26 Dir Marketing & Public Relations ... Ms. Judy KITZMAN
84 Dean Enrollment Svcs/Registrar ... Ms. Kathy RHODES
51 Director Continuing Education ... Ms. Heidi STUBER
37 Int Director Financial Aid Services ... Ms. Eileen ROBISON
35 Dir Student Ldrshp/Multi Cult Pgms ... Mr. Jeffrey VASQUEZ
103 Director Workforce Education ... Mr. John BOWERS
09 Dir Institutional Effectiveness ... Dr. Jack BAUTSCH
104 Director International Programs ... Ms. Mari ACOB-NASH
15 Director Personnel Services ... Mr. David BITTENBENDER
18 Dir Facilities & Plant Operations ... Mr. Bruce KIESER
38 Lead Counselor ... Dr. Lydia MINATOYA
45 Director Strategic Initiatives ... Mr. Gary GORLAND

† Granted candidacy at the Baccalaureate level.

*Seattle Central Community College (J)

1701 Broadway, Seattle WA 98122-2400
County: King FICE Identification: 003787
Unit ID: 236513
Telephone: (206) 587-3800 Carnegie Class: Assoc/Pub-U-MC
FAX Number: (206) 344-4390 Calendar System: Quarter
URL: seattlecentral.edu
Established: 1966 Annual Undergrad Tuition & Fees (In-State): $3,493
Enrollment: 16,680 Coed
Affiliation or Control: State IRS Status: 170(c)1
Highest Offering: Baccalaureate
Program: Occupational; 2-Year Principally Bachelor's Creditable
Accreditation: NW, ACFEI, ADNUR, COARC, DH, OPD, #SURGT

02 President .... Dr. Paul KILLPATRICK
05 Vice Pres of Instruction & Student .... Dr. Warren BROWN
11 Vice Pres Administrative Services .... Mr. Michael PHAM
103 Associate Vice President Workforce .... Mr. Al GRISWOLD
09 Exec Dir Strategic Initiatives & IR .... Dr. Cherisa YARKIN
35 Dean of Student Resources & Support .... Ms. Brigid MCDEVITT
37 Director of Financial Aid .... Ms. Noel MCBRIDE
102 Executive Director Foundation .... Mr. Adam NANCE
27 Interim Director of Communications .... Ms. Janet GRIMLEY
08 Exec Dean Instructional Resources .... Dr. Wai-Fong LEE
49 Dean Basic Studies .... Ms. Laura DIZAZZO
50 Dean Business IT & Creative Arts .... Ms. Jody LAFLEN
76 Dean of Allied Health .... Mr. David GOURD
81 Dean Science & Mathematics .... Dr. Wendy ROCKHILL
83 Interim Dean Humanities/Social Sci .... Dr. Bradley LANE
88 Exec Dean International Education .... Dr. Andrea INSLEY
35 Dean Student Life & Engagement .... Ms. Lexie EVANS
12 Assoc Dean Seattle Culinary Academy .... Ms. Linda CHAUNCEY
13 Assoc Dean Information Technology .... Ms. Harriet WASSERMAN
12 Asst Dean Seattle Maritime Academy .... Dr. Carl ELLIS
51 Director Cmty Educ/Evening Pgm .... Mr. Jeff WEST
06 Assoc Dean Enrollment/Registrar .... Ms. Diane COLEMAN
19 Director Security/Safety .... Mr. Elman MCCLAIN
18 Director Facilities .... Mr. Chuck DAVIS

*South Seattle Community College (A)

6000 16th Avenue, SW, Seattle WA 98106-1499
County: King
FICE Identification: 009706
Unit ID: 236504
Telephone: (206) 934-5300
Carnegie Class: Assoc/Pub4
FAX Number: (206) 934-5393
Calendar System: Quarter
URL: www.southseattle.edu
Established: 1969
Annual Undergrad Tuition & Fees (In-State): $4,267
Enrollment: 7,356
Coed
Affiliation or Control: State
IRS Status: 501(c)3
Highest Offering: Baccalaureate
Program: Occupational; 2-Year Principally Bachelor's Creditable
Accreditation: NW

02 President .... Mr. Gary L. OERTLI
05 Vice Pres Instruction .... Ms. Donna MILLER-PARKER
11 Vice Pres Administrative Services .... Dr. Frank ASHBY
32 Vice President Student Services .... Dr. Rosie RIMANDO-CHAREUNSAP
45 Dean Instructional Resources .... Ms. Mary Jo WHITE
75 Executive Dean Technical Education .... Dr. Malcom P. GROTHE
88 Exec Dn Apprenticeshp/Special Trng .... Ms. Holly MOORE
97 Dean Basic & Transitional Studies .... Mr. John BOWERS
20 Dean of Academic Programs .... Dr. Chad E. HICKOX
35 Dean Student Life .... Ms. Cessa HEARD-JOHNSON
103 Dean Workforce Educ/New Initiatives .... Ms. Wendy PRICE
88 Dean Hosp & Service Occupations .... Mr. Robert GLATT
88 Dean Multi-Trades/Infor Technology .... Mr. Duncan BURGESS
84 Associate Dean Enrollment Services .... Mr. Greg DEMPSEY
72 Dean of Technical Education .... Ms. Kim ALEXANDER
20 Assoc Dean Academic Programs .... Ms. Laura KINGSTON
51 Director Continuing Education .... Ms. Luisa MOTTEN
103 Dir Worksource Dev/Employment Svcs .... Ms. Kelly DEFORREST
37 Dir Student Financial Assistance .... Ms. Patricia L. BILLINGS
27 Director Communications .... Mr. Kevin MALONEY
15 Director Human Resources .... Ms. Kathryn A. VEDVICK
108 Dir of Planning/Research/Assessment .... Ms. Marsha D. BROWN
13 Director Computer Services .... Vacant
18 Dir Facilities & Plant Operations .... Mr. Steve MORGAN
30 Exec Dir Foundation/College Advance .... Ms. Elizabeth A. PLUHTA
28 Director of Diversity & Retention .... Mr. Ricardo LEYVA-PUEBLA
19 Manager Safety/Security .... Mr. James E. LEWIS
40 Manager Bookstore .... Ms. Jen ROHLFS

Seattle Institute of Oriental Medicine (B)

444 Ravenna Boulevard, Suite 101, Seattle WA 98115
County: King
FICE Identification: 032803
Unit ID: 439914
Telephone: (206) 517-4541
Carnegie Class: Spec/Health
FAX Number: N/A
Calendar System: Trimester
URL: www.siom.edu
Established: 1994
Annual Undergrad Tuition & Fees: $19,365
Enrollment: 40
Coed
Affiliation or Control: Proprietary
IRS Status: Proprietary
Highest Offering: Master's; No Lower Division
Program: Professional
Accreditation: ACUP

Seattle Pacific University (C)

3307 Third Avenue W, Seattle WA 98119-1997
County: King
FICE Identification: 003788
Unit ID: 236577
Telephone: (206) 281-2111
Carnegie Class: Master's L
FAX Number: (206) 281-2115
Calendar System: Quarter
URL: www.spu.edu
Established: 1891
Annual Undergrad Tuition & Fees: $33,444
Enrollment: 4,095
Coed
Affiliation or Control: Free Methodist
IRS Status: 501(c)3
Highest Offering: Doctorate
Program: Liberal Arts And General; Teacher Preparatory; Professional
Accreditation: NW, BUS, CLPSY, DIETD, ENG, MFCD, MUS, NURSE, TED

01 President .... Dr. Daniel J. MARTIN
05 Provost .... Dr. Jeffrey B. VAN DUZER
11 Sr VP for University Relations .... Mrs. Marjorie R. JOHNSON
10 Sr VP for Planning & Administration .... Mr. Donald W. MORTENSON
32 VP for Student Life .... Dr. Jeffrey C. JORDAN
10 VP for Business & Finance .... Mr. Craig G. KISPERT
20 Assoc VP Academic Affairs .... Dr. Cynthia J. PRICE
13 Assoc VP Information/Data Mgmt .... Ms. Janet L. WARD
18 Asst VP Facility Management .... Mr. David B. CHURCH
14 Asst VP Technology Services .... Mr. David W. TINDALL
102 President of Seattle Pacific Fdn .... Mr. Thomas W. BOX
50 Dean School of Business & Economics .... Dr. Joseph WILLIAMS
53 Dean School of Education .... Dr. Rick EIGENBROOD
66 Dean School of Health Sciences .... Dr. Lorie WILD
49 Dean College of Arts & Sciences .... Dr. Bruce D. CONGDON
88 Dean School of Psych/Fam & Cmty .... Dr. Micheal D. ROE
73 Dean School of Theology .... Dr. Douglas M. STRONG
42 Dean of Students for Community Life .... Mr. Joel PEREZ
36 Director Career Development Center .... Dr. Jacqui S. SMITH-BATES
08 University Librarian .... Mr. Michael PAULUS
38 Director Student Counseling Center .... Dr. Steven A. MAYBELL
07 Director Undergraduate Admissions .... Mr. Jobe S. KORB-NICE
07 Dir Graduate Admissions/Marketing .... Dr. John L. GLANCY
06 University Registrar .... Mrs. Ruth L. ADAMS
27 Director University Communications .... Mrs. Jennifer J. GILNETT
37 Director Student Financial Services .... Mr. Jordan L. GRANT
27 News & Media Relations Manager .... Mrs. Tracy C. NORLEN
45 Assoc Director Projects & Planning .... Mr. Wayne H. ELLING
31 Director of University Services .... Mr. Murray J. LAWSON
19 Director of Safety & Security .... Mr. Mark REID
44 Director of Annual Giving .... Mr. Dean O. CARRELL
29 Director of Alumni Relations .... Mr. Kenneth E. CORNELL
41 Director of Athletics .... Ms. Erin E. O'CONNELL
15 Director of Human Resources .... Mr. Gary E. WOMELSDUFF
28 Director of the John Perkins Center .... Mr. Tali HAIRSTON
39 Director of Residence Life .... Mr. Gabe JACOBSEN
35 Interim Director Student Programs .... Mrs. Susan OKAMOTO LANE
88 Director of Multi-Ethnic Programs .... Mrs. Susan OKAMOTO LANE

The Seattle School of Theology and Psychology (D)

2501 Elliot Avenue, Seattle WA 98121-1177
County: King
FICE Identification: 034664
Unit ID: 441131
Telephone: (206) 876-6100
Carnegie Class: Spec/Health
FAX Number: (206) 876-6195
Calendar System: Trimester
URL: www.theseattleschool.edu
Established: 2001
Annual Graduate Tuition & Fees: $14,576
Enrollment: 266
Coed
Affiliation or Control: Independent Non-Profit
IRS Status: 501(c)3
Highest Offering: Master's; No Undergraduates
Program: Religious Emphasis
Accreditation: @THEOL, TRACS

01 President .... Dr. Keith R. ANDERSON
04 Assistant to the President .... Vacant
05 Sr Vice Pres Academic Affs/CAO .... Dr. J. Derek MCNEIL
10 Chief Financial Officer .... Mr. Phil BISHOP
20 Assistant Academic Dean .... Dr. Stephanie NEIL
08 Dir Library Svcs/Inst Assessment .... Ms. Cheryl GOODWIN
06 Dir Academic Services/Registrar .... Ms. Kristen HOUSTON
07 Director of Recruitment .... Ms. Nicole GREENWALD
13 Director Computer & Info Services .... Mr. Jason BEST
15 Human Resources .... Ms. Kartha HEINZ
18 Facilities Manager .... Ms. Daniel TIDWELL

Seattle University (E)

901 12th Avenue, Seattle WA 98122-1090
County: King
FICE Identification: 003790
Unit ID: 236595
Telephone: (206) 296-6000
Carnegie Class: Master's L
FAX Number: N/A
Calendar System: Quarter
URL: www.seattleu.edu
Established: 1891
Annual Undergrad Tuition & Fees: $35,865
Enrollment: 7,484
Coed
Affiliation or Control: Roman Catholic
IRS Status: 501(c)3
Highest Offering: Doctorate
Program: Liberal Arts And General; Teacher Preparatory; Professional
Accreditation: NW, BUS, CACREP, DMS, ENG, LAW, MIDWF, NURSE, SPAA, SW, TED, THEOL

01 President .... Rev. Stephen V. SUNDBORG, SJ
05 Provost .... Dr. Isiaah CRAWFORD
03 Executive Vice President .... Dr. Tim LEARY
10 Chief Financial Officer .... Ms. Connie KANTER
43 Vice Pres and University Counsel .... Ms. Mary S. PETERSEN
30 Vice Pres University Advancement .... Ms. Mary Kay MCFADDEN
32 Interim VP Student Development .... Dr. Michele MURRAY
88 Vice President Mission & Ministry .... Rev. Peter ELY, SJ
45 Vice President University Planning .... Dr. Robert DULLEA
84 Vice President for Enrollment Svcs .... Ms. Marilyn CRONE
26 Vice President for Communications .... Mr. Scott MCCLELLAN
15 Vice President Human Resources .... Mr. Gerald HUFFMAN
49 Dean of Arts & Sciences .... Dr. David POWERS
50 Dean of Business & Economics .... Dr. Joseph M. PHILLIPS
53 Dean of Education .... Dr. Deanna SANDS
66 Interim Dean of Nursing .... Dr. Janiece DESOCIO
54 Dean of Science & Engineering .... Dr. Michael QUINN
79 Dean of Matteo Ricci College .... Dr. Jodi OLSEN KELLY
61 Dean of Law .... Ms. Annette C. CLARK
73 Dean of Theology & Ministry .... Dr. Mark MARKULY
08 University Librarian .... Mr. John P. POPKO
20 Assoc Provost Academic Achievement .... Dr. Charles LAWRENCE
20 Assoc Provost Global Engagement .... Dr. Victoria JONES
46 Assoc Provost Research & Grad Educ .... Dr. William EHMANN
27 Chief Information Officer/AVP .... Mr. Charles PORTER
21 Assoc VP of Finance .... Mr. Andrew O'BOYLE
18 Assoc VP Facilities Administration .... Mr. Robert SCHWARTZ
29 Asst VP Alumni Relations .... Ms. Susan VOSPER
13 Chief Technology Officer .... Mr. Dennis GENDRON
30 Assoc VP University Advancement .... Mr. Mark BURNETT
44 Sr Director of Planned Giving .... Ms. Sarah FINNEY
44 Director of Annual Giving .... Ms. Leigh Ann GILMER
102 Dir of Foundation & Corporate Rels .... Ms. Jane SPALDING
35 Assoc Vice Pres Student Development .... Dr. Alvin STURDIVANT
06 Registrar .... Ms. Joyce ALLEN
07 Dean of Admissions .... Ms. Melore NIELSEN
09 Director of Institutional Research .... Dr. Robert DUNIWAY
42 Director Campus Ministry .... Fr. Mike BAYARD, SJ
37 Interim Dir Student Financial Svcs .... Ms. Lindy HALL
41 Director of Athletics .... Mr. Bill HOGAN
19 Executive Director of Public Safety .... Mr. Timothy MARRON
33 Interim Dean of Students .... Mr. Darrell GOODWIN
85 Director International Student Ctr .... Mr. Ryan GREENE
104 Director Education Abroad .... Ms. Gina LOPARDO
36 Executive Director Career Services .... Ms. Bethany KREITL
38 Director Counseling Center .... Dr. Kimberly CALUZA
28 Dir Multicultural Student Affairs .... Dr. Monica NIXON
39 Dir Housing & Resid Life .... Ms. Kathleen BAKER
25 Director Research & Sponsored Proj .... Dr. Nalini IYER
96 Director of Purchasing .... Ms. Marie PETERSON
23 Director Student Health Center .... Ms. Maura O'CONNOR
40 Bookstore Manager .... Mr. Robert SPENCER

Shoreline Community College (F)

16101 Greenwood Avenue N, Shoreline WA 98133-5696
County: King
FICE Identification: 003791
Unit ID: 236610
Telephone: (206) 546-4101
Carnegie Class: Assoc/Pub-S-SC
FAX Number: (206) 546-4630
Calendar System: Quarter
URL: www.shoreline.edu
Established: 1964
Annual Undergrad Tuition & Fees (In-State): $4,410
Enrollment: 6,884
Coed
Affiliation or Control: State
IRS Status: 170(c)1
Highest Offering: Associate Degree
Program: Occupational; 2-Year Principally Bachelor's Creditable; Nursing Emphasis
Accreditation: NW, ADNUR, CAHIIM, DH, MLTAD

01 Interim President .... Mr. Daryl J. CAMPBELL
05 VP Academic & Student Affairs .... Mr. James JANSEN
11 Vice Pres Administrative Svcs .... Vacant
15 VP Human Resources/Legal Affairs .... Mr. Stephen SMITH
27 Spec Asst to Pres/Public Info/Mkt .... Mr. Jim HILLS
96 Special Asst to President Budget .... Ms. Holly M. WOODMANSEE
04 Exec Asst to the President .... Ms. Lori YONEMITSU
85 Exec Dir International Programs .... Ms. Diana SAMPSON
51 Director Cntr for Bus & Cont Educ .... Mr. Dave CUNNINGHAM
72 Director Technology Support Service .... Mr. Gary KALBFLEISCH
06 Registrar .... Ms. Chris MELTON
18 Director Facilities .... Mr. Bob ROEHL
19 Director Safety & Security .... Ms. Robin BLACKSMITH
66 Program Director Nursing .... Ms. Lynn VON SCHLIEDER
37 Director Financial Aid .... Mr. Ted HAASE
38 Dir Advis/Counsel/High School Pgm .... Dr. Yvonne L. TERRELL-POWELL
40 Director Auxiliary Services .... Ms. Mary E. KELEMEN
88 Director Essential Skills .... Mr. William SPERLING
09 Asst Director Inst Effectiveness .... Vacant
08 Acting Dean Library/Media/Tech .... Mr. Robert FRANCIS
35 Interim Co-Dean of Students .... Dr. Yvonne L. TERRELL-POWELL
35 Interim Co-Dean of Students .... Ms. Kim THOMPSON
103 Dean Workforce Education .... Mr. Dave CUNNINGHAM
31 Dean Capital Projects/Cmty Rels .... Ms. Gillian O. LEWIS
79 Acting Dean Humanities Division .... Ms. Kathy HUNT
104 Actg Dean Global Stds/Trans/Honors .... Mr. Robert FRANCIS
88 Dean Student Enroll/Environ Init .... Dr. Susan H. HOYNE

Skagit Valley College (G)

2405 College Way, Mount Vernon WA 98273-5899
County: Skagit
FICE Identification: 003792
Unit ID: 236638
Telephone: (360) 416-7600
Carnegie Class: Assoc/Pub-R-L
FAX Number: (360) 416-7890
Calendar System: Quarter
URL: www.skagit.edu
Established: 1926
Annual Undergrad Tuition & Fees (In-State): $4,208
Enrollment: 4,834
Coed
Affiliation or Control: State
IRS Status: 501(c)3
Highest Offering: Associate Degree
Program: Occupational; 2-Year Principally Bachelor's Creditable
Accreditation: NW, ACFEI, ADNUR, MAC

01 President .... Dr. Thomas KEEGAN
05 Vice President Educational Services .... Dr. Mick DONAHUE
10 Vice Pres Administrative Services .... Ms. Mary Alice GROBINS
12 Vice President of Whidbey Campus .... Dr. Mick DONAHUE
32 Dean of Student Services .... Dr. David PAUL
13 Dean Technology/eLearning/Library .... Mr. Tom BATES

103 Dean Workforce Education ....Ms. Laura CAILLOUX
20 Dean Academic Education ....Dr. Joan YOUNGQUIST
37 Financial Aid Officer ....Mr. Steve EPPERSON
15 Exec Director of Human Resources ....Ms. Sue WILLIAMSON
18 Director of Physical Plant ....Mr. Dave SCOTT
27 Director of Public Information ....Ms. Arden AINLEY
104 Director of International Programs ....Ms. Christa SCHULZ
40 Bookstore Manager ....Ms. Kim HALL
41 Director of Athletics ....Mr. Gary KNUTZEN
09 Director of Institutional Research ....Dr. Maureen PETTITT

South Puget Sound Community College (A)

2011 Mottman Road, SW, Olympia WA 98512-6292
County: Thurston FICE Identification: 005372
Unit ID: 236656
Telephone: (360) 754-7711 Carnegie Class: Assoc/Pub-R-L
FAX Number: (360) 664-0780 Calendar System: Quarter
URL: www.spscc.ctc.edu
Established: 1962 Annual Undergrad Tuition & Fees (In-State): $4,069
Enrollment: 6,308 Coed
Affiliation or Control: State IRS Status: 501(c)3
Highest Offering: Associate Degree
Program: Occupational; 2-Year Principally Bachelor's Creditable
Accreditation: NW, ACFEI, DA, IFSAC, MAC

01 President ....Dr. Timothy STOKES
04 Special Assistant to the President ....Ms. Diana TOLEDO
05 Int Vice President for Instruction ....Dr. Michelle ANDREAS
32 Vice President for Student Services ....Dr. Rhonda COATS
11 Vice Pres Administrative Services ....Ms. Nancy MCKINNEY
07 Dean of Enrollment Svcs/Registrar ....Mr. Jerad SORBER
18 Dean of Facilities Planning & Opers ....Ms. Penny KOAL
26 Dean of College Relations ....Ms. Kellie BRASETH
35 Dean of Student Life ....Dr. Dave RECTOR
37 Dean of Student Financial Services .... Ms. Carla IDOHL-CORWIN
16 Chief Human Resources Officer ....Ms. Sheila EMERY
30 Exec Director College Foundation ....Ms. Cecelia LOVELESS
28 Director of Diversity & Equity ....Ms. Eileen YOSHINA
09 Director of Institutional Research ....Ms. Jennifer TUIA
10 Chief Business Officer ....Ms. Nancy MCKINNEY
08 Dir of Library/Media & eLearning ....Dr. Elizabeth HILL
19 Director of Security ....Mr. Lonnie HATMAN
40 Director of Auxiliary Services ....Mr. Bryce WINKELMAN
27 Chief Information Officer ....Ms. Lori CASILE
72 Dean of Applied Technology ....Mr. Andrew BIRD
45 Dean of Instruc Planning & Develop ....Ms. Lorna PATTERSON
76 Dean of Natural & Applied Sciences ....Mr. Allen OLSON
79 Dean of Humanities/Communications ....Ms. Mary SOLTMAN
83 Dean of Social Sciences & Business ....Dr. Debbie TEED

Tacoma Bible College (B)

106 S. 28th Street, Tacoma WA 98402
County: Pierce Identification: 667139
Telephone: (253) 396-0467 Carnegie Class: Not Classified
FAX Number: (253) 396-0462 Calendar System: Semester
URL: www.tacomabiblecollege.org
Established: Annual Undergrad Tuition & Fees: N/A
Enrollment: 9,200 Coed
Affiliation or Control: Independent Non-Profit IRS Status: 501(c)3
Highest Offering: Baccalaureate
Program: Religious Emphasis
Accreditation: @TRACS

01 President ....Dr. Keith DIETRICH

Tacoma Community College (C)

6501 S 19th Street, Tacoma WA 98466-6100
County: Pierce FICE Identification: 003796
Unit ID: 236753
Telephone: (253) 566-5000 Carnegie Class: Assoc/Pub-U-MC
FAX Number: (253) 566-5169 Calendar System: Quarter
URL: www.tacomacc.edu
Established: 1965 Annual Undergrad Tuition & Fees (In-State): $3,717
Enrollment: 8,337 Coed
Affiliation or Control: State IRS Status: 501(c)3
Highest Offering: Associate Degree
Program: Occupational; 2-Year Principally Bachelor's Creditable
Accreditation: NW, ADNUR, CAHIIM, COARC, DMS, EMT, RAD

01 President ....Dr. Pamela TRANSUE
05 Vice Pres Academic/Student Affairs ....Dr. Tod TREAT
11 Vice Pres Administrative Services ....Ms. Silvia BARAJAS
32 Vice Pres Student Services ....Ms. Mary CHIKWINYA
20 Dean for Academic Services ....Mr. Charlie CRAWFORD
88 Director K-12 Ptnshps/Stdnt Conduct ....Ms. Dolores HAUGEN
07 Dean for Entry & Enrollment Svcs ....Mr. Steve ASHPOLE
88 Dean for Advising and Counseling ....Ms. Shema HANEBUTTE
108 Dir Inst Effective/Instr Assessment ....Mr. Scott MARSH
18 Director Facilities/CapitalProjects ....Mr. Clint STEELE
35 Director of Student Life ....Ms. Jen MANLEY
37 Director Student Financial Aid ....Ms. Kim MATISON

Trinity Lutheran College (D)

2802 Wetmore Avenue, Everett WA 98201
County: Snohomish FICE Identification: 021067
Unit ID: 235769
Telephone: (425) 249-4800 Carnegie Class: Bac/Diverse
FAX Number: (425) 249-4801 Calendar System: 4/1/4
URL: www.tlc.edu
Established: 1944 Annual Undergrad Tuition & Fees: $26,442
Enrollment: 194 Coed
Affiliation or Control: Independent Non-Profit IRS Status: 501(c)3
Highest Offering: Baccalaureate
Program: Liberal Arts And General; Religious Emphasis
Accreditation: NW

01 President ....Mr. John REED
05 Academic Dean ....Dr. Michael DELASHMUTT
10 Vice President Finance ....Mr. Tom RAMSEY
32 Dean of Students ....Ms. Andrea IDE
30 Associate Director of Development ....Mr. Lance GEORGESON
06 Registrar ....Sir Charles NELSON
08 Director of Educ Tech & Library ....Mr. Seong Heon LEE
37 Director of Financial Aid ....Ms. Shanna PYZER
29 Alumni Relations Coordinator ....Ms. Linda KENT
31 Campus Pastor ....Mr. Erik SAMUELSON
13 IT Administrator ....Mr. Seong Heon LEE
21 Accounting Manager ....Mrs. Miwa EASTON

University of Phoenix Western Washington Campus (E)

7100 Fort Dent Way, Suite 100, Tukwila WA 98188-8553
Telephone: (425) 572-1600 Identification: 770234
Accreditation: &NH, ACBSP

† Main campus is University of Phoenix in Tempe, AZ.

University of Puget Sound (F)

1500 N Warner St., Tacoma WA 98416-0002
County: Pierce FICE Identification: 003797
Unit ID: 236328
Telephone: (253) 879-3100 Carnegie Class: Bac/A&S
FAX Number: (253) 879-3500 Calendar System: Semester
URL: www.pugetsound.edu
Established: 1888 Annual Undergrad Tuition & Fees: $41,868
Enrollment: 2,857 Coed
Affiliation or Control: Independent Non-Profit IRS Status: 501(c)3
Highest Offering: Doctorate
Program: Liberal Arts And General; Teacher Preparatory; Professional
Accreditation: NW, MUS, OT, PTA

01 President ....Dr. Ronald R. THOMAS
101 Board Secy/Dir Ofc of President ....Ms. Mary Elizabeth COLLINS
05 Academic VP/Dean of University ....Dr. Kristine M. BARTANEN
10 Vice Pres Finance & Admin ....Ms. Sherry B. MONDOU
26 Vice President University Relations ....Mr. David BEERS
84 Vice President for Enrollment ....Dr. Jenny RICKARD
32 VP Student Affairs/Dean of Students ....Mr. Mike SEGAWA
21 Assoc VP Accounting/Budget Svcs ....Ms. Janet S. HALLMAN
15 Assoc Vice Pres Human Resources ....Ms. Cindy MATERN
21 Assoc Vice Pres Business Services ....Mr. John M. HICKEY
18 Assoc Vice Pres Facilities Services ....Mr. Bob KIEF
37 Assoc VP for Student Financial Svcs .....Ms. Maggie A. MITTUCH
26 Executive Dir of Communications ....Ms. Gayle MCINTOSH
13 Chief Information Officer ....Mr. William MORSE
28 Dean Diversity and Inclusion ....Mr. Michael BENITEZ
20 Associate Academic Dean ....Dr. Martin JACKSON
20 Associate Academic Dean ....Dr. Sunil KUKREJA
20 Associate Academic Dean ....Dr. Lisa L. FERRARI
09 Dir Inst Research & Retention ....Ms. C. Ellen PETERS
06 Registrar ....Mr. Brad TOMHAVE
08 Library Director ....Ms. Jane CARLIN
41 Director of Athletics ....Ms. Amy E. HACKETT
29 Director Alumni & Parent Relations ....Ms. Allison CANNADY-SMITH
85 Director International Programs ....Mr. Roy ROBINSON
53 Dean School of Education ....Dr. John WOODWARD
50 Dir School of Business/Leadership ....Dr. Alva BUTCHER
64 Director of School of Music ....Dr. Keith C. WARD
88 Director of Occupational Therapy ....Dr. George TOMLIN
88 Director of Physical Therapy ....Dr. Jennifer D. HASTINGS

University of Washington (G)

Seattle WA 98195-0001
County: King FICE Identification: 003798
Unit ID: 236948
Telephone: (206) 543-2100 Carnegie Class: RU/VH
FAX Number: (206) 543-9285 Calendar System: Quarter
URL: www.washington.edu
Established: 1861 Annual Undergrad Tuition & Fees (In-State): $11,305
Enrollment: 42,446 Coed
Affiliation or Control: State IRS Status: 501(c)3
Highest Offering: Doctorate
Program: Liberal Arts And General; Teacher Preparatory; Professional
Accreditation: NW, ARCPA, AUD, BUS, BUSA, CAHIIM, CEA, CLPSY, CONST, DENT, DIETC, EMT, ENG, FOR, HSA, IPSY, JOUR, LAW, LIB, LSAR, MED, MIDWF, MT, NURSE, OPE, OT, PDPSY, PH, PHAR, PLNG, PTA, SCPSY, SP, SPAA, SW

01 President ....Mr. Michael K. YOUNG
12 Chancellor Bothell Campus ....Dr. Kenyon S. CHAN
12 Chancellor Tacoma Campus ....Dr. Debra FRIEDMAN
05 Provost ....Dr. Ana Mari CAUCE
20 Vice Chanc Academic Affairs Tacoma ....Dr. James W. HARRINGTON
10 Sr Vice Pres Finance/Facilities ....Ms. V'Ella WARREN
28 VP Minority Affs/V Prov Diversity ..Dr. Sheila EDWARDS LANGE
17 Exec VP Med Affs/CEO UW Med/Dean ....Dr. Paul G. RAMSEY
30 Vice Pres for Univ Advancement ....Dr. Connie KRAVAS
15 Vice President Human Resources ....Ms. Mindy KORNBERG
13 VP & Vice Prov UW Info Tech ....Ms. Kelli TROSVIG
26 Vice President for External Affairs ....Mr. Randy HODGINS
46 Vice Provost Research ....Dr. Mary E. LIDSTROM
51 V Provost UW Prof & Cont Education ... Dr. David P. SZATMARY
45 Vice Prov Planning & Budgeting ....Mr. Paul JENNY
20 Executive V Provost Acad Affs ....Mr. Douglas J. WADDEN
20 Vice Prov/Dean Undergrad Acad Affs ....Dr. Ed TAYLOR
32 VP & Vice Provost Student Life ....Mr. Denzil SUITE
88 V Provost for Academic Personnel ....Dr. Cheryl A. CAMERON
88 V Prov/UW Ctr for Commercialization ....Ms. Linden RHOADS
86 Director Federal Relations ....Ms. Christy D. GULLION
43 Division Chief Attorney General ....Mr. Gary L. IKEDA
06 University Registrar ....Ms. Virjean EDWARDS
29 Exec Dir & Assoc VP Alum Assoc ....Mr. Paul RUCKER
17 Exec Dir UW Medical Ctr Admin ....Mr. Stephen P. ZIENIEWICZ
17 Exec Dir Harborview Med Ctr ....Ms. Eileen WHALEN
37 Asst Vice Pres Student Life/Dir Fin ....Ms. S. Kay LEWIS
86 Director State Relations ....Ms. Margaret A. SHEPHERD
07 Asst VP Enrollment/Admissions ....Dr. Philip BALLINGER
09 AVP Inst Research & Data Mgmt ....Mr. Todd B. MILDON
36 Director Career Center ....Ms. Susan TERRY
13 CFO UW Information Technology ....Mr. Bill FERRIS
18 Assoc Vice Pres Facilities Services ....Mr. Charles KENNEDY
92 Director Honors Program ....Dr. James J. CLAUSS
41 Director Athletics ....Mr. Scott WOODWARD
08 Dean Libraries ....Ms. Lizabeth A. WILSON
96 Assoc Director Purchasing Services ....Mr. Mark CONLEY
58 Vice Prov/Dean Graduate School ....Dr. Gerald J. BALDASTY
49 Dean Arts & Sciences ....Dr. Robert STACEY
47 Int Dean Col of Built Environments ....Dr. John SCHAUFELBERGER
50 Dean Business School ....Dr. Jim JIAMBALVO
54 Interim Dean Engineering ....Dr. Judith RAMEY
61 Dean Law School ....Dr. Kellye Y. TESTY
70 Dean Social Work ....Dr. Edwina UEHARA
52 Dean Dentistry ....Dr. Joel H. BERG
63 Dean Medicine ....Dr. Paul G. RAMSEY
66 Dean Nursing ....Dr. Azita EMAMI
67 Dean Pharmacy ....Dr. Thomas BAILLIE
69 Dean School of Public Health ....Dr. Howard FRUMKIN
53 Dean Education ....Dr. Tom STRITIKUS
80 Dean of Public Affairs ....Dr. Sandra O. ARCHIBALD
88 Dean Information School ....Dr. Harry BRUCE
88 Dean Col of the Environment ....Dr. Lisa GRAUMLICH

Walla Walla Community College (H)

500 Tausick Way, Walla Walla WA 99362-9267
County: Walla Walla FICE Identification: 005006
Unit ID: 236887
Telephone: (509) 522-2500 Carnegie Class: Assoc/Pub-R-L
FAX Number: (509) 527-4480 Calendar System: Quarter
URL: www.wwcc.edu
Established: 1967 Annual Undergrad Tuition & Fees (In-State): $4,375
Enrollment: 5,096 Coed
Affiliation or Control: State IRS Status: 170(c)1
Highest Offering: Associate Degree
Program: Occupational; 2-Year Principally Bachelor's Creditable; Technical Emphasis
Accreditation: NW, ADNUR, MAC

01 President ....Dr. Steven L. VANAUSDLE
11 VP of Administrative Services ....Mr. James R. PETERSON
05 Vice President of Academic Educ ....Dr. Marleen RAMSEY
32 Vice Pres of Student Services ....Mrs. Wendy SAMITORE
10 Vice Pres of Financial Services ....Mrs. Davina K. FOGG
76 Dean of Health Sciences Education ....Ms. Kathleen ADAMSKI
30 Director of Resource Development ....Mr. Doug BAYNE
07 Director of Admissions/Registrar ....Mr. Carlos E. DELGADILLO
38 Int Dir Student Development Center ....Ms. Kristi WELLINGTON-BAKER
37 Financial Aid Director ....Ms. Danielle HODGEN
35 Director of Student Activities ....Dr. David D. CHASE
08 Director of Library Services ....Mrs. Stacy PREST
12 Director of Clarkston Campus ....Dr. Janet V. DANLEY
41 Athletic Director ....Mr. Jeffrey E. REINLAND
15 Director of Human Resources ....Mrs. Sharon M. HARTFORD
18 Director of Plant Facilities ....Vacant
106 Director of eLearning ....Ms. Lisa CHAMBERLIN
88 Dean of Transitional Studies ....Ms. Darlene SNIDER
51 Dean of Correctional Education ....Dr. Joe A. SMALL
28 Director of Multicultural Svcs ....Vacant
40 Bookstore Manager ....Ms. Alecia ANGELL
31 Coordinator of Community Education ....Vacant
27 Dir Marketing & Communications ....Ms. Melissa HARRISON

Walla Walla University (I)

204 S College Avenue, College Place WA 99324-1198
County: Walla Walla FICE Identification: 003799
Unit ID: 236896
Telephone: (509) 527-2615 Carnegie Class: Master's M
FAX Number: (509) 527-2397 Calendar System: Quarter
URL: www.wallawalla.edu
Established: 1892 Annual Undergrad Tuition & Fees: $28,725
Enrollment: 1,940 Coed
Affiliation or Control: Seventh-day Adventist IRS Status: 501(c)3
Highest Offering: Master's
Program: Liberal Arts And General; Teacher Preparatory; Professional
Accreditation: NW, ACBSP, ACFEI, ENG, MUS, NUR, SW

01 President .... Dr. John MCVAY
05 Vice Pres Academic Administration .... Dr. Bob CUSHMAN
10 Vice Pres Financial Administration .... Mr. Steve ROSE
32 Vice Pres Student Life and Mission .... Dr. David RICHARDSON
84 VP University Relations and Advance .... Ms. Jodi WAGNER
28 Asst to President for Diversity .... Dr. Pedrito MAYNARD-REID
04 Executive Asst Office of President .... Ms. Deirdre BENWELL
20 Associate Vice Pres Academic Admin .... Dr. Scott LIGMAN
21 Associate Vice Pres Financial Admin .... Mr. Glenn CARTER
08 Director of Libraries .... Ms. Carolyn GASKELL
06 Registrar .... Ms. Carolyn DENNEY
42 Chaplain .... Mr. Paddy MCCOY
29 Director of Alumni Relations .... Mrs. Terri DICKINSON NEIL
14 Director Information Services .... Mr. Scott MCFADDEN
37 Director Student Financial Services .... Ms. Cassie RAGENOVICH
15 Director Human Resources .... Mr. Rafael SIGUENZA
18 Director of Plant Services .... Mr. George BENNETT
26 Dir Marketing/University Relations .... Ms. Holley BRYANT
33 Dean of Men .... Mr. Tom BLACKWELDER
34 Dean of Women .... Mr. Kristen TAYLOR
58 Dean of Graduate Programs .... Dr. Joseph GALUSHA
66 Dean of School of Nursing .... Ms. Lucille KRULL
73 Dean of School of Theology .... Dr. David THOMAS
54 Dean of School of Engineering .... Mr. Doug LOGAN
07 Director of Admissions .... Mr. Dallas WEIS
36 Director Career Center .... Vacant
38 Director Student Counseling .... Mr. Don WALLACE

Washington State University (A)

PO Box 645910, Pullman WA 99164-5910

County: Whitman FICE Identification: 003800
Unit ID: 236939
Telephone: (509) 335-3564 Carnegie Class: RU/VH
FAX Number: N/A Calendar System: Semester
URL: www.wsu.edu
Established: 1890 Annual Undergrad Tuition & Fees (In-District): $12,300
Enrollment: 27,679 Coed
Affiliation or Control: State/Local IRS Status: 501(c)3
Highest Offering: Doctorate
Program: Liberal Arts And General; Teacher Preparatory; Professional
Accreditation: NW, BUS, BUSA, CEA, CIDA, CLPSY, CONST, COPSY, CS, DIETC, ENG, HSA, IPSY, LSAR, MUS, NURSE, PHAR, SP, VET

01 President .... Dr. Elson S. FLOYD
05 Interim Provost/Exec Vice President .... Dr. Daniel BERNARDO
10 VP Business and Finance .... Mr. Roger D. PATTERSON
43 Div Chief State Attorney Gen Office .... Ms. Danielle HESS
20 Vice Provost for Faculty Affairs .... Dr. Frances MCSWEENEY
106 VP Global Campus .... Dr. David CILLAY
84 VP Student Affairs & Enrollment .... Mr. John FRAIRE
27 VP Information Systems & CIO .... Dr. Viji MURALI
46 VP Research/Dean Grad School .... Dr. Nancy MAGNUSON
12 Chancellor WSU Spokane .... Ms. Lisa BROWN
12 Chancellor WSU Tri-Cities .... Dr. Keith MOO-YOUNG
12 Chancellor WSU Vancouver .... Dr. Mel NETZHAMMER
47 Int Dean Agric/Human Natl Res Sci .... Dr. Ronald MITTELHAMMER
50 Dean Business & Economics .... Dr. Eric SPANGENBERG
53 Dean Education .... Dr. Michael TREVISAN
54 Dean Engineering & Architecture .... Dr. Candis CLAIBORN
66 Dean Nursing .... Dr. Patricia BUTTERFIELD
67 Dean Pharmacy .... Dr. Gary POLLACK
60 Dean Communication .... Dr. Lawrence E. PINTAK
49 Dean Arts & Sciences .... Dr. Daryll DEWALD
74 Dean Veterinary Medicine .... Dr. Bryan K. SLINKER
92 Dean Honors College .... Dr. M. Grant NORTON
45 Assoc VP & Chief Budget Office .... Ms. Joan KING
71 Dean University College .... Dr. Mary F. WACK
08 Dean Libraries .... Mr. Joseph STARRATT
06 Registrar .... Ms. Julia POMERENK
07 Director Admissions .... Ms. Wendy PETERSON
09 Assoc Dir Institutional Research .... Ms. Fran HERMANSTON
18 Assoc VP Facilities Services .... Ms. Olivia YANG
37 Director Financial Aid .... Ms. Chio FLORES
41 Director Intercollegiate Athletics .... Mr. William H. MOOS
86 Assoc VP Government Relations .... Ms. Colleen KERR
88 Director Internal Audit .... Ms. Heather LOPEZ
56 Director Extension .... Dr. Daniel BERNARDO

Wenatchee Valley College (B)

1300 Fifth Street, Wenatchee WA 98801-1799

County: Chelan FICE Identification: 003801
Unit ID: 236975
Telephone: (509) 682-6800 Carnegie Class: Assoc/Pub-R-M
FAX Number: (509) 682-6541 Calendar System: Quarter
URL: www.wvc.edu
Established: 1939 Annual Undergrad Tuition & Fees (In-State): $3,718
Enrollment: 3,668 Coed
Affiliation or Control: State IRS Status: 501(c)3
Highest Offering: Associate Degree
Program: Occupational; 2-Year Principally Bachelor's Creditable
Accreditation: NW, ADNUR, MAC, MLTAD

01 President .... Mr. James RICHARDSON
05 Vice President of Instruction .... Dr. Carli SCHIFFNER
11 VP of Administrative Services .... Ms. Suzie BENSON
38 Vice President Student Development .... Vacant
49 Dean Lib Arts/Sciences/Basic Skills .... Dr. Rick UNDERBAKKE
12 Dean Omak Campus .... Vacant
103 Dean Workforce Education .... Ms. Mary WATSON
23 Dean Allied Health/Nursing .... Ms. Jenny CAPELO
15 Director Human Resources .... Ms. Reagan BELLAMY
45 Director Institution Effectiveness .... Dr. Susan MURRAY
32 Director Student Programs/Outreach .... Vacant
37 Director Financial Aid .... Mr. Kevin BERG
18 Facilities & Operations Manager .... Mr. Greg RANDALL
06 Registrar .... Mr. Bruce MAXWELL
08 Dn Libraries/Learning Technologies .... Mr. Andrew HERSH-TUDOR
10 Director of Fiscal Services .... Ms. Janice FREDSON
27 Communications Manager .... Ms. Libby SIEBENS
20 Coordinator of Adult Basic Skills .... Mr. Aaron PARROTT

Western Washington University (C)

516 High Street, Bellingham WA 98225-5950

County: Whatcom FICE Identification: 003802
Unit ID: 237011
Telephone: (360) 650-3000 Carnegie Class: Master's L
FAX Number: (360) 650-3022 Calendar System: Quarter
URL: www.wwu.edu
Established: 1893 Annual Undergrad Tuition & Fees (In-State): $8,253
Enrollment: 14,833 Coed
Affiliation or Control: State IRS Status: 501(c)3
Highest Offering: Beyond Master's But Less Than Doctorate
Program: Liberal Arts And General; Teacher Preparatory; Professional
Accreditation: NW, ART, BUS, CACREP, CORE, CS, ENGT, MUS, NRPA, SP, TED

01 President .... Dr. Bruce SHEPARD
05 Vice Pres Academic Affairs/Provost .... Dr. Brent CARBAJAL
10 Vice Pres Business/Financial Affs .... Mr. Richard D. VAN DEN HUL
84 VP Enrollment/Student Services .... Dr. Eileen V. COUGHLIN
26 Vice Pres for University Relations .... Mr. Steve SWAN
30 Vice Pres University Advancement .... Ms. Stephanie BOWERS
32 Asst VP Enrollment/Student Services .... Dr. Kunle OJIKUTU
13 Vice Prov Info/Chief Info Officer .... Dr. John D. LAWSON
58 Act Vice Prov Rsch/Act Dn Grad Sch .... Dr. Kathleen KITTO
53 Vice Prov Undergraduate Education .... Dr. Steven L. VANDERSTAAY
22 Vice Prov Equal Oppty/Employmt Div .... Dr. Sue GUENTER-SCHLESINGER
51 Vice Provost Extended Education .... Dr. Earl F. GIBBONS
35 Dean of Students .... Mr. Theodore W. PRATT, JR.
15 Asst VP for Human Resources .... Ms. Chyerl WOLFE-LEE
06 Registrar .... Mr. David BRUNNEMER
07 Exec Dir Admissions/Financial Aid .... Ms. Clara CAPRON
36 Director Career Services Center .... Ms. Tina LOUDON
37 Director Financial Aid .... Ms. Clara CAPRON
29 Executive Director Alumni Relations .... Ms. Deborah DEWEES
27 Director University Communications .... Mr. Paul COCKE
44 Dir Plan Giving/Sr Advisor to Pres .... Vacant
08 Dean of Libraries .... Dr. Mark GREENBERG
39 Director University Residences .... Mr. Leonard JONES
04 Sr Executive Assistant to President .... Dr. Paul DUNN
09 Director of Institutional Research .... Dr. Ming ZHANG
18 Director of Facilities Management .... Mr. John A. FURMAN
19 Chief of Public Safety .... Mr. Randy STEGMEIER
41 Interim Athletic Director .... Mr. Steven CARD
92 Director of Honors Program .... Dr. George MARIZ
96 Purchasing Manager .... Ms. Sally MCKECHNIE
79 Dean College of Humanities/Soc Sci .... Vacant
72 Dean College of Science/Technology .... Dr. Jeff WRIGHT
50 Dean College Business & Economics .... Dr. Brian K. BURTON
65 Dean Huxley Col of the Environment .... Dr. Steven HOLLENHORST
57 Dean College Fine & Performing Arts .... Dr. Daniel G. GUYETTE
53 Dean Woodring College of Education .... Dr. Francisco RIOS
12 Dean Fairhaven College .... Dr. Jack HERRING

Whatcom Community College (D)

237 W Kellogg Road, Bellingham WA 98226-8003

County: Whatcom FICE Identification: 010364
Unit ID: 237039
Telephone: (360) 383-3000 Carnegie Class: Assoc/Pub-R-M
FAX Number: (360) 383-4000 Calendar System: Quarter
URL: www.whatcom.ctc.edu
Established: 1970 Annual Undergrad Tuition & Fees (In-State): $4,180
Enrollment: 3,998 Coed
Affiliation or Control: State IRS Status: 501(c)3
Highest Offering: Associate Degree
Program: Occupational; 2-Year Principally Bachelor's Creditable; Technical Emphasis
Accreditation: NW, ADNUR, MAC, PTAA

01 President .... Dr. Kathi HIYANE-BROWN
05 Vice President for Instruction .... Dr. Ronald LEATHERBARROW
11 Int VP for Administrative Services .... Mr. Nate LANGSTRAAT
20 Vice Pres for Educational Services .... Ms. Patricia ONION
97 Dean for Instruction .... Mr. Ed HARRI
08 Library Director .... Ms. Linda LAMBERT
10 Director for Business & Finance .... Mr. Ken BRONSTEIN
06 Registrar .... Mr. Michael SINGLETARY
07 Coordinator of Admissions Outreach .... Ms. Laine JOHNSTON
37 Director of Financial Aid .... Mr. Jack WOLLENS
32 Director Student/Athletic Pgms .... Mr. Kris BAIER
85 Director of International Programs .... Mr. Kelly KESTER
26 Exec Director for Comm/Marketing .... Ms. Mary VERMILLION
40 Bookstore Manager .... Mr. Jon SPORES
18 Facilities Director .... Mr. Brian KEELEY
04 Exec Assistant to the President .... Ms. Keri PARRIERA
15 Director Human Resources .... Ms. Becky RAWLINGS
09 Director for Institutional Research .... Dr. Anne Marie KARLBERG
30 Executive Director for Advancement .... Ms. Anne BOWEN
27 Chief Public Information Officer .... Ms. Mary VERMILLION

Whitman College (E)

345 Boyer Avenue, Walla Walla WA 99362-2083

County: Walla Walla FICE Identification: 003803
Unit ID: 237057
Telephone: (509) 527-5411 Carnegie Class: Bac/A&S
FAX Number: (509) 527-5859 Calendar System: Semester
URL: www.whitman.edu
Established: 1882 Annual Undergrad Tuition & Fees: $43,150
Enrollment: 1,520 Coed
Affiliation or Control: Independent Non-Profit IRS Status: 501(c)3
Highest Offering: Baccalaureate
Program: Liberal Arts And General
Accreditation: NW

01 President .... Dr. George S. BRIDGES
05 Provost/Dean of Faculty .... Dr. Timothy KAUFMAN-OSBORN
30 Vice President for Development .... Mr. John W. BOGLEY
10 Treasurer/Chief Financial Officer .... Mr. Peter W. HARVEY
32 Dean of Students .... Mr. Charles E. CLEVELAND
20 Associate Dean of Faculty .... Dr. Lisa R. PERFETTI
84 Dean of Admission/Financial Aid .... Mr. Tony A. CABASCO
13 Chief Technology Officer .... Mr. Dan M. TERRIO
18 Chief Facilities/Physical Plant .... Mr. Daniel L. PARK
08 Librarian .... Mrs. Dalia L. CORKRUM
91 Director of Enterprise Technology .... Mr. Michael W. QUINER
07 Director of Admissions .... Mr. Adam MILLER
09 Director of Institutional Research .... Dr. Neal J. CHRISTOPHERSON
20 Assistant Dean of Faculty .... Ms. Kendra J. GOLDEN
35 Associate Dean of Students .... Ms. Barbara A. MAXWELL
26 Director of Communications .... Ms. Ruth S. WARDWELL
38 Director Student Counseling .... Mr. F. "Thatcher" CARTER
39 Director Residence Life & Housing .... Ms. Nancy J. TAVELLI
29 Director Alumni Relations .... Ms. Nancy L. MITCHELL
104 Director of Off-Campus Studies .... Ms. Susan H. BRICK
15 Director Human Resources .... Mr. Dennis T. HOPWOOD
06 Registrar .... Ms. Stacey J. GIUSTI
19 Director of Security .... Mr. Terry E. THOMPSON
23 Director Health Services .... Ms. Claudia L. NESS
36 Director of Career Center .... Ms. Susan M. BUCHANAN
37 Director of Financial Aid Services .... Ms. Marilyn K. PONTI
41 Athletic Director .... Mr. Dean C. SNIDER
42 Coordinator of Spiritual Life .... Mr. Adam M. KIRTLEY
04 Executive Assistant to President .... Ms. Jennifer A. CASPER

Whitworth University (F)

300 W Hawthorne Road, Spokane WA 99251-0001

County: Spokane FICE Identification: 003804
Unit ID: 237066
Telephone: (509) 777-1000 Carnegie Class: Master's M
FAX Number: (509) 777-4763 Calendar System: 4/1/4
URL: www.whitworth.edu
Established: 1890 Annual Undergrad Tuition & Fees: $35,320
Enrollment: 2,875 Coed
Affiliation or Control: Presbyterian IRS Status: 501(c)3
Highest Offering: Master's
Program: Liberal Arts And General; Teacher Preparatory; Professional
Accreditation: NW, MUS, NURSE, TED

01 President .... Dr. Beck A. TAYLOR
03 Provost & Executive Vice President .... Dr. Caroline J. SIMON
10 VP Finance & Administration .... Dr. Brian L. BENZEL
30 VP Institutional Advancement .... Dr. Scott A. MCQUILKIN
32 VP for Student Life .... Dr. Richard G. MANDEVILLE
84 VP Admissions & Financial Aid .... Mr. Greg ORWIG
28 Asst VP Diversity/Intercultural .... Dr. Lawrence A. BURNLEY
15 Assoc VP Human Resources .... Ms. Dolores J. HUMISTON
42 Dean of Spiritual Life .... Dr. Terry P. MCGONIGAL
88 Assoc Provost Fac Devel/Schlrshp .... Dr. Kathleen H. STORM
06 Registrar .... Ms. Beverly S. KLEEMAN
35 Associate Dean of Students .... Dr. Jolyn DAHLVIG
20 Associate Provost of Instruction .... Dr. Randall B. MICHAELIS
91 Director of Information Systems .... Mr. Kenneth BROWN
62 Int Dean Library/Instrct Resources .... Mr. Kenneth D. PECKA
21 Assoc VP Finance & Administration .... Ms. Luz I. MERKEL
29 Dir Alumni/Parent Relations .... Mr. Aaron P. MCMURRAY
51 Dean of Continuing Studies .... Dr. Terry D. RATCLIFF
07 Director of Admissions .... Ms. Marianne W. HANSEN
58 AVP Grad & Cont Studies Enroll Mgt .... Ms. Cheryl D. VAWTER
18 Director of Facilities Services .... Mr. Christopher EICHORST
23 Director of Health Center .... Ms. Kristiana L. HOLMES
53 Interim Dean of School of Education .... Dr. Barbara SANDERS
41 Interim Director of Athletics .... Ms. Melinda LARSON
37 Director of Financial Aid .... Ms. Wendy Z. OLSON
35 Assoc Dean of Students/Dir HUB .... Ms. Dayna L. COLEMAN
39 Assoc Director of Student Housing .... Mr. Alan B. JACOB
40 Manager of Bookstore .... Ms. Nancy G. LOOMIS
26 Director of Communications .... Ms. Nancy G. HINES
38 Director of Counseling Services .... Ms. Janelle R. THAYER
09 Director of Institutional Research .... Mr. Gary D. WHISENAND
50 Dean Sch Global Commerce Mgmt .... Dr. Timothy J. WILKINSON

Yakima Valley Community College (G)

PO Box 22520, S 16th Ave & Nob Hill,
Yakima WA 98907-2520

County: Yakima FICE Identification: 003805
Unit ID: 237109
Telephone: (509) 574-4600 Carnegie Class: Assoc/Pub-R-M

FAX Number: (509) 574-6860 Calendar System: Quarter
URL: www.yvcc.edu
Established: 1928 Annual Undergrad Tuition & Fees (In-State): $4,000
Enrollment: 4,302 Coed
Affiliation or Control: State IRS Status: 170(c)1
Highest Offering: Associate Degree
Program: Occupational; 2-Year Principally Bachelor's Creditable
Accreditation: NW, ADNUR, DH, MAC, SURGT

01 President .... Dr. Linda KAMINSKI
05 Vice Pres Instruction/Student Svcs .... Mr. Tomas YBARRA
10 Vice Pres Administrative Services .... Ms. Teresa HOLLAND
12 Dean Basic Skills/Grandview Campus .... Dr. Bryce HUMPHREYS
13 Director Tech Services .... Mr. Scott TOWSLEY
32 Dean Student Services .... Ms. Leslie BLACKABY
49 Dean Arts & Sciences .... Ms. Kerrie ABB
75 Dean Workforce Education .... Ms. Paulette LOPEZ
08 Library Director .... Ms. Joan WEBER
37 Director Student Financial Aid .... Ms. Janet CANTELON
06 Registrar .... Mr. Luis GUTIERREZ
07 Director of Admissions .... Mr. Luis GUTIERREZ
09 Dir Institutional Effectiveness .... Ms. Sheila DELQUADRI
29 Director Alumni Relations .... Ms. Deborah WILSON
26 Community Relations Coordinator .... Ms. Nicole HOPKINS
15 Director Human Resources .... Mr. Mark ROGSTAD
18 Director Facilities/Physical Plant .... Mr. Jeff WOOD
96 Purchasing Manager .... Ms. Claudia HOFFBAUER
35 Student Life Coordinator .... Ms. Kelly ROBBINS

WEST VIRGINIA

Alderson Broaddus University (A)

101 College Hill Drive, Philippi WV 26416-4600
County: Barbour FICE Identification: 003806
Unit ID: 237118
Telephone: (304) 457-1700 Carnegie Class: Bac/Diverse
FAX Number: (304) 457-6239 Calendar System: Semester
URL: www.ab.edu
Established: 1871 Annual Undergrad Tuition & Fees: $22,740
Enrollment: 870 Coed
Affiliation or Control: American Baptist IRS Status: 501(c)3
Highest Offering: Master's
Program: 2-Year Principally Bachelor's Creditable; Liberal Arts And General; Teacher Preparatory; Professional
Accreditation: NH, #ARCPA, NUR, TEAC

01 President .... Dr. Richard A. CREEHAN
05 Provost/Exec VP for Academic Affs .... Dr. Joan L. PROPST
10 Vice Pres Administration & Finance . Mr. Bruce A. BLANKENSHIP
30 Vice Pres Institutional Advancement .... Mr. Jay NUSSEL
84 Vice Pres Enrollment Management .... Vacant
44 Asst VP Adv/Major Gifts/Donor Rels .... Dr. Carl W. GITTINGS
20 Asst VP Institutional Accreditation .... Mr. Eric M. SHOR
108 Asst VP Institutional Assessment .... Mr. Tom J. BERLIN
101 Exec Asst to Pres/Sec to the Board .... Ms. Juliet A. SPRUILL
32 Dean of Student Affairs .... Ms. Sarah E. WARD
53 College of Education and Music .... Dr. Mary K. DEVONO
79 Col of Humanities/Social Sciences .... Dr. Andrea J. BUCKLEW
81 College of Science/Technology/Math .... Dr. Ross A. BRITTAIN
50 College of Business and Management .... Vacant
76 College of Health Sciences .... Dr. Brenda A. MASON
88 Col of Physician Assistant Studies .... Ms. Ginger A. BOLES
13 Director of Information Technology .... Mr. Byron A. SAYRES
35 Dir of Student Engagement/Orient .... Ms. Koreen VILLERS
42 Chaplain .... Dr. James M. STINESPRING
08 Director of Library Services .... Mr. David E. HOXIE
41 Athletic Director .... Mr. Dennis W. CREEHAN
37 Director of Financial Aid .... Ms. Amy L. KING
26 Director of Mktg/Communications ... Ms. Ashley E. MITTELMEIER
29 Director of Alumni Relations .... Vacant
06 Registrar .... Ms. Saundra E. HOXIE
102 Major Gifts Officer .... Ms. J. Nikky LUNA
08 Dir Academic Ctr for Educ Success .... Ms. Amy MASON
18 Chief Facilities/Physical Plant .... Mr. Elton Lee DUNCAN
27 Dir of Information and Research .... Ms. Julia M. MORRIS
40 Director of Campus Services .... Mr. Ed BURDA
21 Director of Accounting Services .... Ms. Jill BAKER
07 Director of Admissions .... Mr. Zachary A. WARD
38 Director of Counseling Services .... Mr. Chad HOSTETLER
36 Director of Career Services .... Ms. Teresa D. VAN ALSBURG
44 Director of Annual Giving .... Ms. Dionne T. ANDREWS
88 Director of Development .... Ms. M. Annette FETTY
105 Web Content Editor .... Mr. Aaron P. KITTLE

American Public University System (B)

111 W Congress Street, Charles Town WV 25414-1621
County: Jefferson FICE Identification: 035393
Unit ID: 449339
Telephone: (304) 724-3700 Carnegie Class: Master's L
FAX Number: (304) 724-3780 Calendar System: Other
URL: www.apus.edu
Established: 1991 Annual Undergrad Tuition & Fees: $6,400
Enrollment: 50,838 Coed
Affiliation or Control: Proprietary IRS Status: Proprietary
Highest Offering: Master's
Program: 2-Year Principally Bachelor's Creditable; Liberal Arts And General; Professional
Accreditation: NH, ACBSP, NURSE

01 President/CEO .... Dr. Wallace E. BOSTON
05 Exec VP & Provost .... Dr. Karan H. POWELL
10 Exec VP & CFO .... Mr. Harry T. WILKINS
26 Exec VP Programs & Marketing .... Ms. Carol S. GILBERT
03 Exec VP/Chief Operations Officer .... Dr. Sharon VAN WYK
11 Senior VP/Chief Admin Officer .... Mr. Pete W. GIBBONS
13 Senior VP/Chief Information Officer .... Mr. W. Dale YOUNG
20 Senior VP/Academic Opers Officer .... Dr. Gwen HALL
06 VP/Registrar .... Ms. Lyn GEER
84 VP Enrollment Mgt & Student Support .... Ms. Terry GRANT
31 VP Cmty Col Relations & Outreach .... Dr. John HOUGH
46 VP Research & Development .... Dr. Phil ICE
86 VP Regulatory & Govt Relations .... Dr. Russell KITCHNER
88 VP Strategic Initiatives .... Mr. Phil MCNAIR
32 VP Student Services .... Ms. Caroline SIMPSON
09 VP Institutional Research & Assess .... Dr. Jennifer HELM
08 VP Library and Educ Materials .... Dr. Fred STIELOW
88 VP Military Relations .... Mr. Jim SWEIZER
15 VP Human Resources .... Ms. Amy PANZARELLA
37 VP Financial Aid Services .... Mr. Gary SPOALES
88 VP Institutional Accreditation .... Ms. Lynn C. WRIGHT

Appalachian Bible College (C)

161 College Drive, Mt. Hope WV 25880
County: Raleigh FICE Identification: 007544
Unit ID: 237136
Telephone: (304) 877-6428 Carnegie Class: Spec/Faith
FAX Number: (304) 877-5082 Calendar System: Semester
URL: www.abc.edu
Established: 1950 Annual Undergrad Tuition & Fees: $12,945
Enrollment: 302 Coed
Affiliation or Control: Independent Non-Profit IRS Status: 501(c)3
Highest Offering: Master's
Program: Liberal Arts And General; Teacher Preparatory; Religious Emphasis
Accreditation: NH, BI

01 President .... Dr. Daniel L. ANDERSON
05 Vice President for Academics .... Mr. Daniel S. HANSHEW
10 Vice President for Business .... Mr. Kenneth E. LILLY
30 Vice President for Development .... Rev. Jonathan A. RINKER
32 Vice President for Student Services .... Rev. David E. CHILDS
42 Vice Pres for Extension Ministries .... Mr. David J. HOLLOWAY
33 Dean of Men .... Mr. John M. SHARP
34 Dean of Women .... Mrs. Linda J. CHILDS
06 Registrar .... Dr. Charles N. BETHEL
07 Director of Admissions .... Mr. Scott T. ROSS
08 Librarian .... Mr. David W. DUNKERTON
37 Acting Director of Financial Aid .... Mrs. Deana B. STEINKE
04 Admin Assistant to the President .... Mrs. Elisabeth I. GOLDEN
26 Director of Public Relations .... Mr. Jarod K. BURRER

Bethany College (D)

Main Street, Bethany WV 26032-0417
County: Brooke FICE Identification: 003808
Unit ID: 237181
Telephone: (304) 829-7000 Carnegie Class: Bac/A&S
FAX Number: (304) 829-7700 Calendar System: 4/1/4
URL: www.bethanywv.edu
Established: 1840 Annual Undergrad Tuition & Fees: $25,736
Enrollment: 1,080 Coed
Affiliation or Control: Christian Church (Disciples Of Christ)
IRS Status: 501(c)3
Highest Offering: Master's
Program: Liberal Arts And General; Teacher Preparatory
Accreditation: NH, SW, TED

01 President of the College .... Dr. Scott D. MILLER
30 Senior Vice President .... Mr. Sven M. DE JONG
05 Interim Provost .... Dr. David R. BLACK
10 Vice President for Finance .... Mr. Thomas E. RHINE
04 Executive Asst to the President .... Ms. Deidra R. HALL-NUZUM
100 Executive Asst to the President .... Dr. Mort GAMBLE
20 Asst Vice President Academic Affs .... Dr. Katrina D'AQUIN
32 Dean of Students .... Mr. Gerald STEBBINS
37 Director of Financial Aid .... Mr. Jason MCCLAIN
41 Director of Athletics & Recreation .... Mr. Brian ROSE
09 Dir Institutional Research/Records .... Dr. Jason HARTZ
88 Director of McCann Learning Center .... Dr. Christina SAMPSON
88 Director of Student Support Service .... Ms. Hilary LOSO
89 Director of First Year Experience .... Dr. Katrina D'AQUIN
88 Director of International Programs .... Dr. Harald MENZ
36 Director of Student Placement .... Mr. John OSBORNE
23 Director of the Byrd Health Center .... Mrs. Carol TYLER
27 Director of Communications .... Ms. Rebecca ROSE
29 Director of Alumni/Parent Relations .... Ms. Ashley KANOTZ
88 Director of Advancement Services .... Ms. Shirley KEMP
88 Director of Sports Information .... Vacant
88 Director of Church Relations .... Dr. Larry GRIMES
18 Director of Physical Plant .... Mr. Theodore D. WILLIAMS
10 Director of Financial Affairs .... Mr. Daniel T. PAJAK
21 Director of Business Affairs .... Ms. Saralyn DAGUE
19 Director of Safety & Security .... Mr. Robert RIBAR
15 Director of Personnel Services .... Ms. Merlinda LEES
39 Director of Residence Life .... Mr. Andrew LEWIS
35 Director of Student Activiites .... Mr. Samuel GOODGE
42 Chaplain .... Rev. Scott THAYER
08 Director of the Libraries .... Mrs. Heather MAY-RICCIUTI
13 Dir Info Technology/Network Admin .... Mr. Ron SHAW
24 Dir Media Services/Classroom Tech .... Mr. Thomas V. FURBEE
88 Public Services Librarian .... Mr. Trevor ONEST
06 Registrar .... Ms. Lisa CUCARESE
84 Director of Enrollment .... Ms. Mollie CECERE
88 General Manager Conference Center .... Ms. Donna WHITE
88 Director of Dining Services .... Mrs. Necol M. DUNSON
40 Manager of the Bookstore .... Ms. Ann CRAFT
38 College Counselor .... Ms. Renee STOCK

Davis & Elkins College (E)

100 Campus Drive, Elkins WV 26241-3996
County: Randolph FICE Identification: 003811
Unit ID: 237358
Telephone: (304) 637-1900 Carnegie Class: Bac/Diverse
FAX Number: (304) 637-1413 Calendar System: 4/1/4
URL: www.dewv.edu
Established: 1904 Annual Undergrad Tuition & Fees: $24,500
Enrollment: 818 Coed
Affiliation or Control: Presbyterian Church (U.S.A.) IRS Status: 501(c)3
Highest Offering: Baccalaureate
Program: 2-Year Principally Bachelor's Creditable; Liberal Arts And General; Teacher Preparatory; Business Emphasis
Accreditation: NH, ADNUR, IACBE, TEAC, THEA

00 Chancellor and Provost .... Vacant
01 President .... Dr. Michael P. MIHALYO, JR.
84 Executive Vice President/COO .... Mr. Kevin H. WILSON
10 Chief Financial Officer .... Ms. Greta J. TROASTLE
05 Vice President for Academic Affairs .... Dr. Joseph M. ROIDT
30 Vice President College Advancement .... Vacant
32 Vice President for Student Affairs .... Mr. Scott D. GODDARD
26 Assoc VP for Commun & Marketing .... Ms. Carol M. SCHULER
15 Director Human Resources .... Ms. M. J. COREY
06 Registrar .... Dr. Stephanie C. HAYNES
18 Exec Director of Physical Plant .... Mr. Ronald J. SELDERS
37 Director Financial Planning .... Mr. Matthew A. SUMMERS
08 Assistant Director Booth Library .... Ms. Mary Jo DEJOICE
42 Chaplain .... Rev. Kevin M. STARCHER
41 Director of Athletics .... Mr. Ron PALMER
19 Director of Campus Safety/Security .... Mr. Michael R. JORDAN
44 Director of Advancement Operations .... Ms. Karen L. WILMOTH
04 Executive Asst to the President .... Ms. Robin PRICE
09 Director of Institutional Research .... Ms. Lindsey GRAHAM

Everest Institute (F)

5514 Big Tyler Road, Cross Lanes WV 25313-1399
County: Kanawha FICE Identification: 010356
Unit ID: 237604
Telephone: (304) 776-6290 Carnegie Class: Assoc/PrivFP
FAX Number: (304) 776-6262 Calendar System: Other
URL: www.everest-institute.com
Established: 1968 Annual Undergrad Tuition & Fees: $18,700
Enrollment: 292 Coed
Affiliation or Control: Proprietary IRS Status: Proprietary
Highest Offering: Associate Degree
Program: Occupational
Accreditation: ACCSC

01 President .... Ms. Aimee SWITZER
05 Director of Education .... Ms. Melesa HAYNES
07 Director of Admission .... Ms. Karen WILKINSON
10 Director of Finance .... Mr. Matt LANE
36 Director Career Services .... Vacant

Future Generations Graduate School (G)

400 Road Less Traveled, Franklin WV 26807-9201
County: Pendleton Identification: 666714
Telephone: (304) 358-2000 Carnegie Class: Not Classified
FAX Number: (304) 358-3008 Calendar System: Other
URL: www.future.edu
Established: 2003 Annual Graduate Tuition & Fees: $17,500
Enrollment: 38 Coed
Affiliation or Control: Independent Non-Profit IRS Status: 501(c)3
Highest Offering: Master's; No Undergraduates
Program: Liberal Arts And General
Accreditation: NH

01 President .... Dr. Chris CLUETT
05 Dean .... Dr. Mike RECHLIN

Huntington Junior College (H)

900 Fifth Avenue, Huntington WV 25701-2004
County: Cabell FICE Identification: 009047
Unit ID: 237437
Telephone: (304) 697-7550 Carnegie Class: Assoc/PrivFP
FAX Number: (304) 697-7554 Calendar System: Quarter
URL: www.huntingtonjuniorcollege.edu
Established: 1936 Annual Undergrad Tuition & Fees: $7,470
Enrollment: 802 Coed
Affiliation or Control: Proprietary IRS Status: Proprietary
Highest Offering: Associate Degree
Program: 2-Year Principally Bachelor's Creditable; Technical Emphasis
Accreditation: NH, MAC

01 President .... Carolyn A. SMITH
03 Director .... Dr. Catherine E. SNODDY
05 Academic Affairs Director .... Linda J. WEST

ITT Technical Institute (A)

5183 US Route 60, Bldg 1, Suite 40,
Huntington WV 25705
Telephone: (304) 733-8700 Identification: 666709
Accreditation: ACICS

† Main campus is ITT Technical Institute in Indianapolis, IN.

Martinsburg College (B)

341 Aikens Center, Martinsburg WV 25404
County: Berkeley Identification: 667035
Telephone: (304) 263-6262 Carnegie Class: Not Classified
FAX Number: (866) 703-6611 Calendar System: Other
URL: www.martinsburgcollege.edu
Established: 1980 Annual Undergrad Tuition & Fees: $3,000
Enrollment: 775 Coed
Affiliation or Control: Proprietary IRS Status: Proprietary
Highest Offering: Associate Degree
Program: Occupational; 2-Year Principally Bachelor's Creditable; Technical Emphasis
Accreditation: DETC

01 President .... Paul VIBOCH
05 Chief Academic Officer .... Stella GARLICK
07 Director of Admissions .... Laurie MAURO
06 Registrar .... Rita CLAYPOLE

Mountain State College (C)

1508 Spring Street, Parkersburg WV 26101
County: Wood FICE Identification: 005008
Unit ID: 237598
Telephone: (304) 485-5487 Carnegie Class: Assoc/PrivFP
FAX Number: (304) 485-3524 Calendar System: Quarter
URL: www.msc.edu
Established: 1888 Annual Undergrad Tuition & Fees: $8,100
Enrollment: 262 Coed
Affiliation or Control: Proprietary IRS Status: Proprietary
Highest Offering: Associate Degree
Program: Occupational; 2-Year Principally Bachelor's Creditable; Business Emphasis
Accreditation: ACICS

01 President .... Mrs. Judith SUTTON

National College (D)

110 Park Center Drive, Parkersburg WV 26101
Telephone: (304) 699-3005 Identification: 770787
Accreditation: ACICS

† Main campus is American National University in Salem, VA.

National College (E)

421 Hilltop Drive, Princeton WV 24740
Telephone: (304) 487-3845 Identification: 666499
Accreditation: ACICS, MAC

† Main campus is American National University in Salem, VA.

Ohio Valley University (F)

1 Campus View Drive, Vienna WV 26105-8000
County: Wood FICE Identification: 003819
Unit ID: 237640
Telephone: (304) 865-6000 Carnegie Class: Bac/Diverse
FAX Number: (304) 865-6001 Calendar System: Semester
URL: www.ovu.edu
Established: 1958 Annual Undergrad Tuition & Fees: $18,750
Enrollment: 459 Coed
Affiliation or Control: Churches Of Christ IRS Status: 501(c)3
Highest Offering: Master's
Program: Liberal Arts And General; Teacher Preparatory
Accreditation: #NH, IACBE, @TEAC

01 President .... Dr. Harold SHANK
10 Executive Vice President/CFO .... Mr. Jeffrey A. DIMICK
03 Chancellor .... Dr. Keith STOTTS
05 VP for Academic Affairs .... Dr. Jim BULLOCK
41 Sr VP/Athletic Director .... Mr. Dennis W. COX
30 VP University Outreach .... Mr. Jeremy JACOBY
04 Admn Asst to the President .... Mrs. Kimberly HAYNES
26 Director of Community Relations .... Mrs. Christine PARKER
43 General Counsel .... Dr. Becky D. MATHIS-STUMP
18 Director of Campus Operations .... Mr. David STEWART
36 Director of Career Services .... Mrs. Kathy MULLER
32 Dean of Student Life .... Mr. Jason DOUGHERTY
08 Library Director .... Mr. Rodney WOOTEN
06 Registrar .... Mrs. Sarah BARTON
07 Director of Admissions .... Mrs. Lisa WEST

Salem International University (G)

223 W Main Street, Box 500, Salem WV 26426-0500
County: Harrison FICE Identification: 003820
Unit ID: 237783
Telephone: (304) 326-1109 Carnegie Class: Master's M
FAX Number: (304) 326-1246 Calendar System: Semester
URL: www.salemu.edu
Established: 1888 Annual Undergrad Tuition & Fees: $17,700
Enrollment: 850 Coed
Affiliation or Control: Proprietary IRS Status: Proprietary
Highest Offering: Master's
Program: 2-Year Principally Bachelor's Creditable; Teacher Preparatory; Professional; Business Emphasis
Accreditation: NH

00 Chancellor/CEO .... Mr. James W. BROOKS
01 President .... Mr. John A. LUOTTO
03 Executive Vice President .... Dr. Cecil E. KIRKLAND
05 Interim Provost .... Dr. Cecil E. KIRKLAND
10 CFO .... Mr. Dan NELANT
37 VP Financial Aid & Compliance .... Mr. Marty MEHRINGER
106 Director Online Operations .... Mr. Timothy RAUSCHENBACH
27 CIO .... Mr. Pieter BRESLER
15 Director Human Resources .... Vacant
06 Registrar .... Ms. Rebecca HALL
06 Registrar Online .... Ms. Jennifer HALER
53 Dean School of Education .... Dr. Craig MCCLELLAN
66 Director Nursing Education .... Dr. Susie WILSON
107 Dean Online Operations .... Dr. Kimberly PADDOCK-O'REILLY
08 Dean Library Services .... Dr. Phyllis D. FREEDMAN
32 Director Student Life .... Ms. Sarah SHEETS
19 Director Campus Security .... Mr. Joseph SHAVER
18 Director Physical Plant & Maint .... Vacant
41 Athletic Director .... Mr. Keith BULLION

University of Charleston (H)

2300 Maccorkle Avenue, SE, Charleston WV 25304-1099
County: Kanawha FICE Identification: 003818
Unit ID: 237312
Telephone: (304) 357-4800 Carnegie Class: Bac/Diverse
FAX Number: (304) 357-4715 Calendar System: Semester
URL: www.ucwv.edu
Established: 1888 Annual Undergrad Tuition & Fees: $19,500
Enrollment: 1,455 Coed
Affiliation or Control: Independent Non-Profit IRS Status: 501(c)3
Highest Offering: Doctorate
Program: Liberal Arts And General; Teacher Preparatory; Professional; Fine Arts Emphasis
Accreditation: NH, ACFEI, #ARCPA, NUR, OTA, PHAR, RAD, SW, TEAC

01 President .... Dr. Edwin H. WELCH
05 Provost & Dean of Faculty .... Dr. Letha ZOOK
10 Vice Pres Administration & Finance .... Mrs. Cleta M. HARLESS
30 Vice Pres for Development .... Mr. Ben BEAKES
07 Vice President for Admissions .... Ms. Joan CLARK
32 Vice President Student Development .... Mrs. Jennie FERRETTI
26 Vice President for Marketing .... Ms. Susan BACKOFEN
12 Regional Pres Beckley/Martinsburg .... Dr. Jerry FORSTER
06 Registrar .... Ms. Carol SPRADLING
29 Alumni Director .... Ms. Bridgette BORST
21 Controller .... Mr. Steve DAVIS
27 Chief Information Officer .... Mr. Scott TERRY
08 Director of Library .... Ms. Judy ALTIS
85 Director International Student Pgms .... Mr. Dan MEADOWS
37 Associate Director Financial Aid .... Ms. Nina MORTON
35 Coordinator of Student Programs .... Ms. Meghan SPARROW
40 Bookstore Manager .... Mr. Glenn JOHNSON
18 Director Plant & Property .... Mr. Gary BOYD
41 Athletic Director .... Dr. Bren STEVENS
88 Director of Colleague Program .... Dr. Barbara WRIGHT
09 Director of Institutional Research .... Ms. Lisa DAWKINS
50 Dean Graduate School of Business .... Dr. Scott BELLAMY
67 Dean School of Pharmacy .... Dr. Michelle EASTON
49 Dean School of Arts & Sciences .... Dr. Barbara WRIGHT
76 Dean School of Health Sciences .... Dr. Josephine KAHLER

Valley College - Beckley Campus (I)

120 New River Town Center, Suite C, Beckley WV 25801
County: Raleigh FICE Identification: 030844
Unit ID: 377652
Telephone: (304) 252-9547 Carnegie Class: Assoc/PrivFP
FAX Number: (304) 252-1694 Calendar System: Other
URL: www.valley.edu
Established: 1983 Annual Undergrad Tuition & Fees: $9,800
Enrollment: 163 Coed
Affiliation or Control: Proprietary IRS Status: Proprietary
Highest Offering: Associate Degree
Program: Occupational; Business Emphasis
Accreditation: ACICS

01 Corp Ex Dir of Academics/Stdnt Affs .... Ms. Beth GARDNER

Valley College - Martinsburg Campus (J)

287 Aikens Center, Martinsburg WV 25404-6203
County: Berkeley FICE Identification: 026094
Unit ID: 377661
Telephone: (304) 263-0979 Carnegie Class: Assoc/PrivFP
FAX Number: (304) 263-2413 Calendar System: Other
URL: www.valley.edu
Established: 1983 Annual Undergrad Tuition & Fees: $11,300
Enrollment: 77 Coed
Affiliation or Control: Proprietary IRS Status: Proprietary
Highest Offering: Associate Degree
Program: Occupational; Business Emphasis
Accreditation: ACICS

01 Executive Director .... Mr. Matt JENKINS

West Virginia Business College (K)

116 Pennsylvania Avenue, Nutter Fort WV 26301-4516
Telephone: (304) 624-7695 Identification: 666507
Accreditation: ACICS

† Main campus is West Virginia Business College in Wheeling, WV.

West Virginia Business College (L)

1052 Main Street, Wheeling WV 26003-2702
County: Ohio FICE Identification: 010861
Unit ID: 237978
Telephone: (304) 232-0361 Carnegie Class: Assoc/PrivFP
FAX Number: (304) 232-0363 Calendar System: Quarter
URL: www.wvbc.edu
Established: 1881 Annual Undergrad Tuition & Fees: $9,150
Enrollment: 93 Coed
Affiliation or Control: Proprietary IRS Status: Proprietary
Highest Offering: Associate Degree
Program: Occupational
Accreditation: ACICS

01 Director .... Ms. Rebecca SUTER

*West Virginia Council for Community & Technical College Education (M)

1018 Kanawha Boulevard E, Suite 700,
Charleston WV 25301-2800
County: Kanawha Identification: 666993
Telephone: (304) 558-0265 Carnegie Class: N/A
FAX Number: (304) 558-1646
URL: www.wvctcs.org

01 Chancellor .... James L. SKIDMORE

*Blue Ridge Community and Technical College (N)

13650 Apple Harvest Drive, Martinsburg WV 25403
County: Berkeley FICE Identification: 039573
Unit ID: 446774
Telephone: (304) 260-4380 Carnegie Class: Assoc/Pub-R-M
FAX Number: (304) 260-4376 Calendar System: Semester
URL: www.blueridgectc.edu
Established: 1974 Annual Undergrad Tuition & Fees (In-State): $3,120
Enrollment: 4,360 Coed
Affiliation or Control: State IRS Status: 501(c)3
Highest Offering: Associate Degree
Program: Occupational; 2-Year Principally Bachelor's Creditable
Accreditation: NH, ADNUR, EMT, PTAA

02 President .... Dr. Peter G. CHECKOVICH
05 Vice President of Curriculum .... Dr. George PERRY
103 VP Economic and Workforce Devel .... Dr. Ann M. SHIPWAY
84 VP of Enrollment Management .... Ms. Leslie SEE
10 Chief Financial Officer .... Ms. Kimberly LINEBERG
50 Associate VP of Business and Tech .... Mr. Randall C. MILLER
06 Registrar .... Ms. Angie M. KINDER
07 Director of Access .... Ms. Brenda NEAL
15 Director Human Resources .... Dr. Justin RUBLE
13 Assoc Director of IT .... Mr. Michael BYERS
38 Director of Student Success .... Vacant
37 Director of Financial Aid .... Ms. Doris GLENN

*Bridgemont Community and Technical College (O)

619 2nd Avenue, Montgomery WV 25136
County: Fayette FICE Identification: 040473
Unit ID: 445674
Telephone: (304) 734-6600 Carnegie Class: Assoc/Pub-S-SC
FAX Number: (304) 734-6630 Calendar System: Semester
URL: www.bridgemont.edu
Established: 2004 Annual Undergrad Tuition & Fees (In-District): $3,560
Enrollment: 1,074 Coed
Affiliation or Control: State/Local IRS Status: 501(c)3
Highest Offering: Associate Degree
Program: Occupational; 2-Year Principally Bachelor's Creditable
Accreditation: NH, COARC, DH, ENGT

02 President .... Dr. Beverly Jo HARRIS
05 VP Academic & Student Affairs .... Dr. Kristin MALLORY
10 Chief Financial Officer .... Dr. Patricia HUNT
29 President of Alumni Association .... Ms. Alicia SYNER
06 Registrar .... Mr. Roy SIMMONS
37 Director of Financial Aid .... Ms. Mary BLIZZARD
35 Director of Student Services .... Ms. Jeanne SMITH
26 Director of Institutional Marketing .... Mr. Brian BOLYARD
13 Director of Computer Services .... Mr. Thomas MINNICH
09 Director of Institutional Research .... Mr. James F. FAUVER
08 Interim Director of Library .... Ms. Kathleen PHILLIPS
51 Dean of Extended Learning .... Ms. Connie FOX
18 Director of Physical Plant .... Mr. George HYPES
78 Director Career Svcs/Cooperative Ed .... Mr. James MCDOUGLE
22 Dir Affirm Action/Equal Opportunity .... Mr. Gene LOPEZ
07 Director of Admissions .... Ms. Joyce SURBAUGH

15 Chief Human Resources Officer .... Mr. Gene LOPEZ
21 Associate Business Officer .... Ms. Cathy AQUINO
28 Director of Diversity .... Mr. Gene LOPEZ
30 Chief Development .... Mr. Jack NUCKOLS
32 Chief Student Life Officer .... Ms. Jeanne SMITH
36 Director Student Placement .... Mr. James MCDOUGLE
96 Director of Purchasing .... Mr. John POWELL
84 Director Enrollment Management .... Ms. Joyce SURBAUGH
38 Director Student Counseling .... Ms. Tammy BIBBEE

*Eastern West Virginia Community and Technical College (A)

316 Eastern Drive, Moorefield WV 26836-1155
County: Hardy FICE Identification: 041190
Unit ID: 438708
Telephone: (304) 434-8000 Carnegie Class: Assoc/Pub-R-S
FAX Number: (304) 434-7001 Calendar System: Semester
URL: www.eastern.wvnet.edu
Established: 1999 Annual Undergrad Tuition & Fees (In-State): $2,688
Enrollment: 833 Coed
Affiliation or Control: State IRS Status: Exempt
Highest Offering: Associate Degree
Program: Occupational; 2-Year Principally Bachelor's Creditable; Technical Emphasis
Accreditation: NH

02 President .... Dr. Charles TERRELL
10 Exec Dean for Financial & Operation .... Ms. Penny REARDON
32 Dean for Academic & Student Service .... Mr. Robert EAGLE
32 Assoc Dean Academic & Student Svcs .... Ms. Sherry BECKER-GORBY
103 Director of Workforce Education .... Ms. Sherry WATTS
75 Dean of Career/Technical/Workforce .... Mr. Ward MALCOLM

*Kanawha Valley Community & Technical College (B)

PO Box 1000; Cole Complex 102, Institute WV 25112
County: Kanawha FICE Identification: 040386
Unit ID: 445018
Telephone: (304) 205-6600 Carnegie Class: Assoc/Pub-R-S
FAX Number: N/A Calendar System: Semester
URL: www.kvctc.edu
Established: 1953 Annual Undergrad Tuition & Fees (In-District): $3,560
Enrollment: 1,578 Coed
Affiliation or Control: State/Local IRS Status: Exempt
Highest Offering: Associate Degree
Program: Occupational; 2-Year Principally Bachelor's Creditable
Accreditation: NH, ADNUR, NMT

02 President .... Dr. Joseph L. BADGLEY
10 Vice President Finance .... Dr. Patricia HUNT
32 Vice President of Student Services .... Dr. Susan GARDNER
04 Special Assistant to President .... Vacant
05 Vice President Academic Affairs .... Dr. Cindy KELLEY
103 Vice Pres Workforce Economic Devel .... Mrs. Laura L. MCCULLOUGH
06 Registrar .... Mr. Roy SIMMONS
07 Director of Admissions .... Ms. Michelle D. WICKS
37 Associate Director of Financial Aid .... Ms. Carla BLANKENBEUHLER
26 PR Associate and Webmaster .... Mrs. Kristin LEDFORD
16 Human Resources Representative .... Ms. Michelle BISSELL
51 Director of Continuing Education .... Mrs. Kim SOVINE
21 Business Manager .... Mrs. Kristi WILLIAMS
96 Chief Purchasing Officer .... Mr. John POWELL

*Mountwest Community and Technical College (C)

1 Mountwest Way, Huntington WV 25701
County: Cabell FICE Identification: 040414
Unit ID: 444954
Telephone: (304) 710-3141 Carnegie Class: Assoc/Pub-R-M
FAX Number: (304) 710-3187 Calendar System: Semester
URL: www.mctc.edu
Established: 1975 Annual Undergrad Tuition & Fees (In-District): $2,952
Enrollment: 2,608 Coed
Affiliation or Control: State/Local IRS Status: 501(c)3
Highest Offering: Associate Degree
Program: Occupational; 2-Year Principally Bachelor's Creditable
Accreditation: NH, ACBSP, CAHIIM, MAC, PTAA

02 President .... Dr. Keith J. COTRONEO
05 Executive Dean .... Ms. Carol A. PERRY
32 Dean of Student Services .... Ms. Billie K. BROOKS
103 Dean Workforce Dev/Business/Tech .... Mr. Steven L. BROWN
15 Director Employee Development/HR .... Ms. Stephanie A. NEAL
27 Chief Information Officer/COO .... Mrs. Terri L. TOMBLIN-BYRD

*New River Community and Technical College (D)

221 George Street, Suite 2, Beckley WV 25801
County: Raleigh FICE Identification: 039603
Unit ID: 447582
Telephone: (304) 929-5472 Carnegie Class: Assoc/Pub-R-M
FAX Number: (304) 929-5478 Calendar System: Semester
URL: www.newriver.edu
Established: 2003 Annual Undergrad Tuition & Fees (In-State): $3,460
Enrollment: 3,066 Coed
Affiliation or Control: State IRS Status: 501(c)3
Highest Offering: Associate Degree
Program: Occupational; 2-Year Principally Bachelor's Creditable
Accreditation: NH, EMT

02 President .... Dr. L. Marshall WASHINGTON
04 Exec Secretary to the President .... Ms. Lori A. MIDKIFF
05 Interim Vice Pres and CAO .... Dr. Carry DEATLEY
10 Vice Pres Financial/Admin Affairs .... Mr. Stephen M. BENSON
30 VP Inst Advancement/Workforce Educ .... Mr. William J. LOOPE
32 Vice Pres Student Services .... Dr. Allen B. WITHERS
13 Vice Pres/Chief Technology Officer .... Dr. David J. AYERSMAN
16 Chief Human Resources Officer .... Ms. Leah A. TAYLOR
27 Chief Communications Officer .... Ms. Elizabeth M. BELCHER
20 Assoc VP of Academic Affairs .... Dr. Carry DEATLEY
12 Campus Dean Advanced Tech Ctr .... Ms. Lisa M. HATCHER
12 Campus Dean Beckley .... Dr. Carolyn G. SIZEMORE
12 Campus Dean Greenbrier Valley .... Mr. Roger D. GRIFFITH
12 Campus Dean Mercer County .... Mr. Steve WISE
12 Campus Dean Nicholas County .... Mr. Fred B. CULLER
45 Director of Inst Effectiveness .... Dr. Renae R. MCGINNIS
06 Registrar .... Ms. Donna M. LEWIS
08 Staff Librarian .... Mr. Robert H. COSTON
37 Director of Financial Aid .... Ms. Patricia HARMON
96 Director of Purchasing .... Ms. Twana JACKSON
21 Controller .... Ms. Heike I. SOEFFKER-CULICERTO
18 Director of Physical Plant .... Mr. Robert RUNION
26 Director of Public Relations .... Ms. Barbara A. ELLIOTT
07 Director of Enrollment Services .... Ms. Tracy L. EVANS
24 Dir Ctr for Teaching Excellence .... Mr. Ralph C. PAYNE

*Pierpont Community & Technical College (E)

1201 Locust Avenue, Fairmont WV 26554-2470
County: Marion FICE Identification: 040385
Unit ID: 443492
Telephone: (304) 367-4692 Carnegie Class: Assoc/Pub-R-M
FAX Number: (304) 367-4881 Calendar System: Semester
URL: www.pierpont.edu
Established: 1974 Annual Undergrad Tuition & Fees (In-State): $3,860
Enrollment: 2,925 Coed
Affiliation or Control: State IRS Status: 501(c)3
Highest Offering: Associate Degree
Program: Occupational; 2-Year Principally Bachelor's Creditable
Accreditation: NH, ACFEI, CAHIIM, #COARC, MLTAD, NAIT, PTAA

02 President .... Dr. Doreen M. LARSON
10 VP for Finance and Administration .... Mr. Dale R. BRADLEY
05 Provost/VP for Academic Affairs .... Ms. Leslie LOVETT
86 VP for Organization and Development .... Mr. Stephen E. LEACH
103 VP Workforce & Economic Development .... Mr. Paul SCHREFFLER
27 Chief Information Officer .... Mr. Rob LINGER
97 Dean School of Academic Studies .... Dr. Raymond MAINENTI
88 Dean Sch of Business/Aviation/Tech .... Dr. Gerald BACZA
76 Dean School of Health Careers .... Dr. Rosemarie ROMESBURG
88 Dean School of Human Services .... Dr. Brian FLOYD

*Southern West Virginia Community and Technical College (F)

P. O. Box 2900, Mount Gay WV 25637-2900
County: Logan FICE Identification: 003816
Unit ID: 237817
Telephone: (304) 792-7098 Carnegie Class: Assoc/Pub-R-M
FAX Number: (304) 792-7046 Calendar System: Trimester
URL: www.southernwv.edu
Established: 1971 Annual Undergrad Tuition & Fees (In-State): $2,904
Enrollment: 2,178 Coed
Affiliation or Control: State IRS Status: 501(c)3
Highest Offering: Associate Degree
Program: Occupational; 2-Year Principally Bachelor's Creditable; Technical Emphasis
Accreditation: NH, ADNUR, COARC, DH, MLTAD, RAD, SURGT

02 President .... Ms. Joanne J. TOMBLIN
10 VP for Finance & Administration .... Mr. Samuel LITTERAL
05 VP Academic Affairs & Student Svcs .... Vacant
103 VP Economic & Workforce Development .... Ms. Allyn S. BARKER
14 Chief Information Officer .... Mr. Gary HOLEMAN
30 Vice President for Development .... Mr. Ronald E. LEMON
15 Interim Human Resources Director .... Ms. Debbie C. DINGESS
04 Exec Asst to President & BOG .... Ms. Emma L. BAISDEN
20 Dean Career and Techncial Programs .... Ms. Pamela L. ALDERMAN
20 Dean University Transfer Programs .... Vacant
12 Director Wyoming Campus Operations .... Mr. David LORD
12 Director Wmson Campus Operations .... Ms. Rita G. ROBERSON
12 Director Logan Campus Operations .... Mr. Randy SKEENS
12 Director Boone Campus Operations .... Mr. William COOK
76 Chair Allied Health & Nursing Dept .... Ms. Alyce PATTERSON-DIAZ
50 Chair Business Department .... Dr. Gail HALL
72 Chair Technology & Engineering Dept .... Ms. Carol A. HOWERTON
81 Chair Science Department .... Mr. Guy LOWES, JR.
88 Chair Transitional Studies .... Mr. Steven LACEK
83 Chair Social Sciences Department .... Vacant
81 Chair Mathematics Department .... Ms. Melinda D. SAUNDERS
79 Chair Humanities Department .... Mr. George H. MORRISON
06 Interim Registrar .... Ms. Teri WELLS
37 Director Student Financial Asst .... Ms. Cindy POWERS
08 Director of Libraries .... Ms. Kimberly L. MAYNARD
88 Director of Media .... Mr. Marcus GIBBS
96 Director of Purchasing .... Ms. Melissa CREAKMAN
84 Dean Enrollment Mgmt & Student Dev .... Mr. Darrell TAYLOR
26 Public Relations Specialist .... Ms. Carol A. COLE

*West Virginia Northern Community College (G)

1704 Market Street, Wheeling WV 26003-3643
County: Ohio FICE Identification: 009054
Unit ID: 238014
Telephone: (304) 233-5900 Carnegie Class: Assoc/Pub-R-M
FAX Number: (304) 232-4651 Calendar System: Semester
URL: www.wvncc.edu
Established: 1972 Annual Undergrad Tuition & Fees (In-State): $2,890
Enrollment: 2,505 Coed
Affiliation or Control: State IRS Status: 501(c)3
Highest Offering: Associate Degree
Program: Occupational; 2-Year Principally Bachelor's Creditable
Accreditation: NH, ACFEI, ADNUR, CAHIIM, COARC, MAC, RAD, SURGT

02 President .... Dr. Martin OLSHINSKY
05 Vice President Academic Affairs .... Dr. Vicki RILEY
10 CFO & VP Administrative Services .... Mr. Stephen LIPPIELLO
103 Vice Pres Workforce Dev .... Mr. J. Michael KOON
32 Vice President Student Services .... Mrs. Janet FIKE
31 Dean Community Relations .... Mr. Robert DEFRANCIS
13 Director Information Technology .... Mr. David HANES
09 Dir Inst Research .... Mrs. Pamela WOODS
18 Director of Facilities .... Mr. Jim BALLER
06 Dir of Records/Registrar .... Ms. Nancy ALBERT
15 Chief Human Resource Officer .... Mrs. Peggy CARMICHAEL
36 Counselor I Career Plng/Placement .... Vacant
12 Campus Dean Weirton .... Mr. J. Michael KOON
12 Campus Dean Wheeling .... Vacant
12 Campus Dean New Martinsville .... Mr. Larry TACKETT
32 Director Student Union Activities .... Mrs. Shannon PAYTON
07 Associate Director Admissions .... Vacant

*New River Technical College Greenbrier Valley Campus (H)

101 Church Street, Lewisburg WV 24901-1303
Telephone: (304) 647-6560 Identification: 770468
Accreditation: &NH

† Main campus is New River Community and Technical College in Beckley, WV.

*New River Technical College Mercer County Campus (I)

1397 Stafford Drive, Princeton WV 24740-8230
Telephone: (304) 818-2009 Identification: 770469
Accreditation: &NH

† Main campus is New River Community and Technical College in Beckley, WV.

*New River Technical College Nicholas County Campus (J)

6101 Webster Road, Summersville WV 26651
Telephone: (304) 872-1236 Identification: 770470
Accreditation: &NH

† Main campus is New River Community and Technical College in Beckley, WV.

*Southern West Virginia Community and Technical College-Boone/Lincoln Campus (K)

3505 Daniel Boone Parkway, Suite A,
Foster WV 25608-8126
Telephone: (304) 369-2952 Identification: 770471
Accreditation: &NH

† Main campus is Southern West Virginia Community and Technical College in Mount Gay, WV.

*Southern West Virginia Community and Technical College-Williamson Campus (L)

1601 Armory Drive, Williamson WV 25661
Telephone: (304) 235-6046 Identification: 770473
Accreditation: &NH

† Main campus is Southern West Virginia Community and Technical College in Mount Gay, WV.

*Southern West Virginia Community and Technical College-Wyoming/McDowell Campus (M)

128 College Drive, Saulsville WV 25876
Telephone: (304) 294-8346 Identification: 770472
Accreditation: &NH

† Main campus is Southern West Virginia Community and Technical College in Mount Gay, WV.

* *West Virginia Northern Community College* (A)

141 Main Street, New Martinsville WV 26155
Telephone: (304) 455-4684 Identification: 770474
Accreditation: &NH

† Main campus is West Virginia Northern Community College in Wheeling, WV.

* *West Virginia Northern Community College* (B)

150 Park Avenue, Weirton WV 26062
Telephone: (304) 723-2210 Identification: 770475
Accreditation: &NH

† Main campus is West Virginia Northern Community College in Wheeling, WV.

*West Virginia Higher Education Policy Commission (C)

1018 Kanawha Boulevard E, Ste 700,
Charleston WV 25301-2887
County: Kanawha FICE Identification: 033440
Unit ID: 237941
Telephone: (304) 558-2101 Carnegie Class: N/A
FAX Number: (304) 558-5719
URL: www.hepc.wvnet.edu

01 Chancellor ... Dr. Paul L. HILL
05 Chancellor Comm/Tech College Educ ... Mr. James L. SKIDMORE
88 Interim Program Director ... Dr. Jan TAYLOR
100 Sr Director Board Public Relation ... Ms. Ashley L. SCHUMAKER
20 Vice Chancellor for Academic Affs ... Dr. Kathy BUTLER
10 Vice Chancellor for Finance ... Dr. Edward MAGEE
45 Vice Chancellor Policy and Planning ... Dr. Angela BELL
15 Vice Chancellor for Human Resources ... Mr. Mark TOOR
43 General Counsel ... Mr. Bruce R. WALKER
11 Exec Vice Chancellor Administration ... Mr. Robert E. ANDERSON
32 Dir Student/Educational Services ... Mr. Daniel E. CROCKETT
37 Senior Director of Financial Aid ... Mr. Brian WEINGART
88 Director Administrative Services ... Ms. Cindy L. ANDERSON

*Bluefield State College (D)

219 Rock Street, Bluefield WV 24701-2198
County: Mercer FICE Identification: 003809
Unit ID: 237215
Telephone: (304) 327-4000 Carnegie Class: Bac/Diverse
FAX Number: (304) 325-7747 Calendar System: Semester
URL: www.bluefieldstate.edu
Established: 1895 Annual Undergrad Tuition & Fees (In-State): $5,564
Enrollment: 1,935 Coed
Affiliation or Control: State IRS Status: 501(c)3
Highest Offering: Baccalaureate
Program: Liberal Arts And General; Teacher Preparatory
Accreditation: NH, ACBSP, ADNUR, ENGT, NURSE, RAD, TED

02 President ... Dr. Martha V. KROTSENG
05 Vice Pres Academic Affs/Provost ... Vacant
10 Vice Pres Financial/Admin Affairs ... Ms. Shelia JOHNSON
32 Vice President Student Affairs ... Vacant
04 Dir Inst/Media Rels/Asst to Pres ... Mr. James A. NELSON
88 Executive Director Title III ... Dr. Felica WILLIAMS
06 Registrar ... Vacant
08 Director Library Services ... Ms. Joanna THOMPSON
24 Interim Chief Technology Officer ... Mr. Tom G. COOK
14 Director of Computer Services ... Mr. Tom G. COOK
36 Director of Placement ... Mr. Thomas HARRISON
07 Director of Admissions ... Mr. Kenneth MANDEVILLE
37 Director of Financial Aid ... Mr. Thomas ILSE
15 Director of Human Resources ... Ms. Jonette AUGHENBAUGH
18 Admin Asst Senior of Physical Plant ... Ms. Diana GIBSON
19 Director Public Safety ... Mr. Richard AKERS
09 Director of Institutional Research ... Dr. Tracey ANDERSON
38 Director of Counseling ... Dr. Cravor JONES
29 Director Alumni Affairs ... Ms. Deirdre GUYTON
40 Manager Bookstore ... Ms. Virginia RICHARDSON
41 Athletic Director ... Mr. Terry BROWN
50 Dean School of Business ... Dr. Steve BOURNE
49 Dean School of Arts and Sciences ... Dr. Martha EBORALL
54 Dean School of Eng Tech/Comp Sci ... Dr. Shannon BOWLING
53 Interim Dean School of Education ... Dr. Betsy STEENKEN
66 Dean School Nursing/Allied Health ... Ms. Angela LAMBERT
66 ADN Program Director ... Ms. Sandra WYNN
66 BSN Program Director ... Ms. Beth PRITCHETT
88 Program Dir of Radiologic Tech ... Ms. Melissa HAYE
61 Program Dir Criminal Justice ... Vacant
28 Director of Multicultural Affs ... Vacant
96 Director of Purchasing ... Mr. Paul RUTHERFORD
30 Director of Advancement/Planning ... Ms. Betty CARROLL

*Concord University (E)

PO Box 1000, Athens WV 24712-1000
County: Mercer FICE Identification: 003810
Unit ID: 237330
Telephone: (304) 384-3115 Carnegie Class: Bac/Diverse
FAX Number: (304) 384-9044 Calendar System: Semester
URL: www.concord.edu
Established: 1872 Annual Undergrad Tuition & Fees (In-State): $6,002
Enrollment: 2,834 Coed
Affiliation or Control: State IRS Status: 501(c)3
Highest Offering: Master's
Program: Liberal Arts And General; Teacher Preparatory; Professional
Accreditation: NH, SW, TED

02 Interim President ... Dr. Kendra BOGGESS
05 Interim VP & Academic Dean ... Dr. Jane SMITH
30 VP for Advancement ... Vacant
20 Associate Dean ... Dr. Cheryl BARNES
32 VP Student Aff/Dir of Retention ... Dr. Marjie FLANIGAN
10 VP for Business & Finance ... Dr. Charles P. BECKER
07 VP for Admissions & Financial Aid ... Vacant
11 VP of Administration ... Mr. Rick DILLON
06 Registrar ... Mrs. Carolyn COX
08 Director of Libraries ... Mrs. Connie SHUMATE
37 Director of Student Financial Aid ... Mrs. Debra TURNER
84 Chief Enrollment Management Ofcr ... Mrs. Jacqueline NOTTINGHAM
29 Director of Alumni Relations ... Ms. Sarah TURNER
88 Director Bonner Scholars Program ... Mrs. Kathy BALL
13 Chief Technology Officer ... Mr. Charles ELLIOTT
15 Human Resources Director ... Mr. Marshall CAMPBELL
18 Director Physical Plant ... Mr. Gerry VONVILLE
19 Director of Public Safety ... Chief Mark STELLA
36 Director of Career Services ... Ms. Tammy MONK
38 Director of Counseling ... Ms. Sandy GRIM
40 Bookstore Manager ... Mr. Randy JONES
41 Athletic Director ... Mr. Kevin GARRETT
21 Financial Reporting Officer ... Ms. Elizabeth J. CAHILL
09 Director of Institutional Research ... Vacant
24 Ctr for Academic Technologies ... Mr. Steve MEADOWS
26 Public Relations/Mktg Specialist ... Mr. Lance MCDANIEL
25 Director of Grants and Contracts ... Mr. Scott INGHRAM
12 Director of the Beckley Center ... Dr. Susan WILLIAMS
96 Interim Purchasing Agent ... Mr. Gary HYLTON

*Fairmont State University (F)

1201 Locust Avenue, Fairmont WV 26554-2470
County: Marion FICE Identification: 003812
Unit ID: 237367
Telephone: (304) 367-4000 Carnegie Class: Master's S
FAX Number: (304) 367-4789 Calendar System: Semester
URL: www.fairmontstate.edu
Established: 1865 Annual Undergrad Tuition & Fees (In-State): $5,824
Enrollment: 4,451 Coed
Affiliation or Control: State IRS Status: 501(c)3
Highest Offering: Master's
Program: Liberal Arts And General; Teacher Preparatory; Business Emphasis
Accreditation: NH, ACBSP, ADNUR, ENGR, ENGT, NURSE, TED

02 President FSU ... Dr. Maria C. ROSE
05 Interim Provost/VP Academic Affairs . Dr. Christina M. LAVORATA
10 Vice Pres Admin & Fiscal Affairs ... Mr. Enrico A. PORTO
27 Interim VP/Chief Info Officer ... Mr. Andy RAISOVICH
32 VP Student Services ... Ms. Kaye WIDNEY
108 VP Inst Assessment & Effectiveness ... Vacant
04 Executive Asst to the President ... Ms. Judith E. BIAFORE
20 Assoc Provost for Academic Affs ... Dr. Jack R. KIRBY
26 AVP Univ Comm and Inst Advancement ... Ms. Ann B. BOOTH
18 Asst Vice Pres for Facilities ... Mr. Raymond T. TUCKER
16 AVP for Human Resources ... Mrs. Cynthia S. CURRY
06 Registrar ... Ms. Evie BRANTMAYER
49 Dean College of Liberal Arts ... Dr. Deanna J. SHIELDS
72 Dean College of Science and Tech ... Dr. Anthony F. GILBERTI
50 Dean School of Business ... Dr. Richard C. HARVEY
53 Dean School of Education ... Dr. Van O. DEMPSEY
57 Dean School of Fine Arts ... Mr. Peter LACH
66 Dean School of Nursing ... Dr. Sharon BONI
07 Director of Recruiting ... Ms. Amie M. FAZALARE
29 Director Alumni Relations ... Ms. Emily L. SWAIN
91 Dir of Applications Develop Svcs ... Mr. Andy RAISOVICH
41 Director of Athletics ... Mr. Timothy A. MCNEELY
19 Dir of Emerg Mgmt/Chief of Police ... Mr. Jack A. CLAYTON
38 Dir of Counseling and Disab Srvs ... Ms. Andrea M. PAMMER
37 Director Financial Aid/Scholarships ... Ms. Cynthia K. HUDOK
39 Interim Director of Housing ... Mr. Timothy S. RICE
08 Director of Library Services ... Ms. Thelma J. HUTCHINS
96 Director of Procurement ... Ms. Monica J. COCHRAN
26 Director of Public Relations ... Ms. Amy E. PELLEGRIN
36 Director of Student Development ... Ms. Sally V. FRY
90 Director of Solutions Center ... Ms. Joanie RAISOVICH
23 Director of Student Health Services ... Ms. Mary P. WATSON

*Glenville State College (G)

200 High Street, Glenville WV 26351-1292
County: Gilmer FICE Identification: 003813
Unit ID: 237385
Telephone: (304) 462-7361 Carnegie Class: Bac/Diverse
FAX Number: (304) 462-7610 Calendar System: Semester
URL: www.glenville.edu
Established: 1872 Annual Undergrad Tuition & Fees (In-State): $3,192
Enrollment: 1,898 Coed
Affiliation or Control: State IRS Status: 501(c)3
Highest Offering: Baccalaureate
Program: Liberal Arts And General; Teacher Preparatory
Accreditation: NH, TED

02 President ... Dr. Peter B. BARR
05 Provost & Senior Vice President ... Dr. John M. PEEK
10 Exec Vice Pres Business & Finance . Mr. Robert O. HARDMAN, II
26 Sr Vice Pres for External Relations ... Mr. James W. SPEARS
30 VP Advancement/Exec Dir GSC Found ... Mr. Dennis J. POUNDS
84 Vice Pres for Enrollment Management ... Mr. D. Duane CHAPMAN
04 Executive Assistant to President ... Ms. Teresa G. STERNS
53 Dean of Teacher Education ... Dr. Kevin G. CAIN
15 Chief Human Resources Officer ... Ms. Krystal D. SMITH
37 Director of Financial Aid ... Ms. Karen D. LAY
18 Exec Director of Physical Plant ... Mr. Thomas R. RATLIFF
39 Director of Residence Life ... Mr. Jerry L. BURKHAMMER
19 Director of Public Safety ... Mr. Daniel R. BELL
41 Director of Athletics ... Ms. Janet K. BAILEY
23 Director Campus Health Services ... Ms. Ronda L. WILLIAMS
08 Director of Library ... Ms. Gail L. WESTBROOK
27 Dir Public Relations & Marketing ... Ms. Annette D. BARNETTE
21 Controller ... Mr. Richard D. ACCORD
96 Director of Purchasing ... Ms. Joyce E. RIDDLE
29 Director of Alumni Affairs ... Ms. Debra A. NAGY
35 Director of Student Activities ... Ms. Jodi OCHELTREE
06 Associate Registrar ... Ms. Ann M. REED
14 Manager Of Database Admin D ... Mr. Neal L. BENSON
36 Career Services Counselor ... Ms. Joanna M. DISTEFANO
38 Professional Counselor ... Mr. Timothy J. UNDERWOOD
84 Supervisor for Enrollment ... Ms. Ashley M. WEIR

*Marshall University (H)

1 John Marshall Drive, Huntington WV 25755-0001
County: Cabell FICE Identification: 003815
Unit ID: 237525
Telephone: (304) 696-3170 Carnegie Class: Master's L
FAX Number: (304) 696-6565 Calendar System: Semester
URL: www.marshall.edu
Established: 1837 Annual Undergrad Tuition & Fees (In-State): $6,216
Enrollment: 13,715 Coed
Affiliation or Control: State IRS Status: 501(c)3
Highest Offering: Doctorate
Program: Occupational; 2-Year Principally Bachelor's Creditable; Liberal Arts And General; Teacher Preparatory; Professional
Accreditation: NH, ADNUR, ANEST, BUS, BUSA, CAHIIM, CLPSY, COARC, CYTO, DIETD, DIETI, ENG, ENGR, FEPAC, JOUR, #MED, MLTAD, MT, MUS, NUR, @PHAR, @PTA, SP, SW, TED

02 President ... Dr. Stephen J. KOPP
05 Provost/Sr VP Academic Affairs ... Dr. Gayle L. ORMISTON
43 Sr VP/Exec Affairs & Gen Counsel ... Mr. F. Layton COTTRILL
63 Dean of Medicine ... Dr. Joseph I. SHAPIRO
102 CEO MU Foundation Inc ... Dr. Ron AREA
11 Sr VP for Administration ... Ms. Karen KIRTLEY
46 VP Research ... Mr. John MAHER
86 VP Federal Programs/Dir CEO RCBI ... Ms. Charlotte WEBER
53 Dean College of Education ... Dr. Teresa EAGLE
26 Sr VP Communication/Chief of Staff ... Mr. Matt TURNER
29 Vice President Alumni Relations ... Mr. Matthew D. HAYES
13 VP Information Technology/CIO ... Dr. Jan I. FOX
44 Vice President Development ... Mr. Lance WEST
28 VP Multicultural Affairs ... Dr. Shari CLARKE
51 Assoc VP Outreach & Cont Studies ... Dr. David PITTENGER
14 Asst VP Information Technology ... Dr. Arnold R. MILLER
10 Chief Financial Officer ... Ms. Mary Ellen HEUTON
07 Dir Admission Undergrad/Grad Pgms ... Ms. Tammy JOHNSON
32 Dean Student Affairs ... Mr. Stephen W. HENSLEY
106 Asst VP for OnLine learning Lib/IT ... Ms. Monica BROOKS
58 Dean Graduate College ... Dr. Donna SPINDEL
49 Interim Dean College Liberal Arts ... Dr. Robert BOOKWALTER
50 Dean College of Business ... Dr. Haiyang CHENG
57 Dean College of Arts & Media ... Mr. Donald L. VAN HORN
67 Dean School of Pharmacy ... Dr. Kevin W. YINGLING
66 Dean College of Health Prof ... Dr. Michael PREWITT
54 Dean Col of Info Tech/Engr ... Dr. Wael ZATAR
81 Dean College of Science ... Dr. Charles SOMERVILLE
41 Director of Athletics ... Mr. Mike HAMRICK
06 Registrar ... Ms. Roberta FERGUSON
37 Director Student Financial Aid ... Ms. Kathy BIALK
36 Director Career Services ... Ms. Denise HOGSETT
15 Director Human Resource Services ... Ms. Michelle DOUGLAS
19 Director of Public Safety ... Mr. James E. TERRY
96 Director of Purchasing ... Ms. Stephanie SMITH
18 Director of Physical Plant ... Mr. Mark CUTLIP
39 Director Residence Services ... Mr. John YAUN
09 Asst to the Pres/Dir Inst Rsch/Plng ... Mr. Michael J. MCGUFFEY
85 Exec Dir Ctr for Intl Programs ... Dr. Clark EGNOR
40 Manager of Bookstore ... Mr. Mike CAMPBELL
22 Director Equity Programs ... Ms. Debra HART
88 Director Recruitment ... Ms. Elizabeth WOLFE

*Shepherd University (I)

PO Box 5000, Shepherdstown WV 25443-5000
County: Jefferson FICE Identification: 003822
Unit ID: 237792
Telephone: (304) 876-5000 Carnegie Class: Master's S
FAX Number: (304) 876-3101 Calendar System: Semester
URL: www.shepherd.edu
Established: 1871 Annual Undergrad Tuition & Fees (In-State): $6,256
Enrollment: 4,326 Coed
Affiliation or Control: State IRS Status: 501(c)3
Highest Offering: Master's
Program: Liberal Arts And General; Teacher Preparatory
Accreditation: NH, IACBE, MUS, NURSE, SW, TED

02 President ... Dr. Suzanne SHIPLEY
05 Vice President Academic Affairs ... Dr. Christopher AMES
10 Vice Pres Finance & Administration ... Ms. Deborah JUDD
32 Vice President Student Affairs ... Dr. Thomas SEGAR

Code	Title	Name
30	Acting Vice President Advancement	Mr. Aaron RYAN
84	Vice Pres Enrollment Management	Ms. Kimberly SCRANAGE
43	General Counsel	Mr. K. Alan PERDUE
100	Chief of Staff	Ms. Shelli DRONSFIELD
88	Assoc VP/Business Decision Support	Mr. James VIGIL
35	Asst VP Stdnt Aff/Student Success	Ms. Christana JOHNSON
81	Dean Sch of Natural Sciences/Math	Dr. Colleen NOLAN
79	Dean School of Arts & Humanities	Mr. Dow BENEDICT
50	Dean Sch of Bus/Social Sciences	Dr. Ann M. LEGREID
53	Dean Sch Educ/Profess Studies	Dr. Virginia HICKS
58	Dean Grad Studies/Cont Education	Dr. Scott BEARD
88	Dean Teaching & Learning	Dr. Laura RENNINGER
26	Exec Director Univ Communications	Ms. Valerie OWENS
09	Director Institutional Research	Ms. Sara MAENE
39	Director Residence Life	Ms. Elizabeth SECHLER
21	Comptroller	Ms. Rebecca STOTTLEMEYER
35	Asst VP Student Aff/Student Engage	Ms. Holly FRYE
15	Director Human Resources	Dr. Marie DEWALT
13	Director Info Technology Services	Mr. Joey DAGG
06	Registrar	Ms. Tracy SEFFERS
07	Director of Admissions	Mr. Matthew HUBER
37	Assoc VP Enroll/Dir FA	Ms. Sandra OERLY-BENNETT
19	Univ Police Chief	Mr. John MCAVOY
53	Director Teacher Education	Dr. Douglas KENNARD
18	Director Physical Plant	Mr. Dan YANNA
41	Athletics Director	Mr. B.J PUMROY
96	Director of Purchasing	Ms. Debra LANGFORD
38	Director Student Counseling	Ms. Barbara BYERS
29	Director Alumni Relations	Ms. Alexis REED
92	Director Honors Program	Dr. Sally BRASHER
44	Director Annual Giving	Ms. Julia KRALL

*West Liberty University (A)

208 University Drive, West Liberty WV 26074

County: Ohio — FICE Identification: 003823 — Unit ID: 237932

Telephone: (304) 336-5000 — Carnegie Class: Bac/Diverse

FAX Number: (304) 336-8403 — Calendar System: Semester

URL: www.westliberty.edu

Established: 1837 — Annual Undergrad Tuition & Fees (In-State): $6,226

Enrollment: 2,795 — Coed

Affiliation or Control: State — IRS Status: 501(c)3

Highest Offering: Master's

Program: Liberal Arts And General; Teacher Preparatory; Professional; Business Emphasis

Accreditation: NH, #ARCPA, DH, IACBE, MT, MUS, NURSE, @SW, TED

Code	Title	Name
02	President	Mr. Robin C. CAPEHART
05	Vice Provost	Vacant
43	Vice President & General Counsel	Mr. John L. DAVIS
32	Vice President of Student Affairs	Vacant
10	Executive VP & CFO	Mr. John E. WRIGHT
11	Provost	Dr. Brian CRAWFORD
88	VP for Community Engagement	Mr. Jeff KNIERIM
81	Dean College of Sciences	Dr. Robert KREISBERG
49	Dean College Liberal Arts	Dr. Robert KRUSE
57	Dean College Arts & Comm	Dr. William M. BARONAK
53	Dean College of Education	Dr. Keely O. CAMDEN
66	Dir of Nursing Programs	Dr. Rose KUTLENIOS
50	Dean College of Business	Dr. Loren A. WENZEL
35	Assoc Dean Student Services	Ms. Marcella SNYDER
06	Ex Dir Enr Svc/Regr/Dean Std	Ms. Stacy A. COOK
15	Vice President of Human Resources	Mr. James L. STULTZ
13	Chief Technology Officer	Mr. James T. CLARK
09	Dir of Inst Research & Assessment	Ms. Paula J. TOMASIK
41	Director of Athletics	Mr. James W. WATSON
07	Director of Admissions	Ms. Brenda M. KING
51	Director of Cont Educ/Special Pgm	Vacant
08	Director of Library	Ms. Cheryl R. HARSHMAN
26	Director of University Engagement	Mr. Jeff KNIERIM
29	Director of Alumni Association	Mr. Shane STACK
37	Director Student Financial Aid	Mrs. Katie COOPER
30	VP of Institutional Advancement	Mr. Jason W. KOEGLER
31	Director of Auxiliary Services	Mr. John L. DAVIS
18	Chief of Operations	Mr. Patrick J. HENRY
38	Director of Counseling	Ms. Bridgette DAWSON
92	Director of the Honors Program	Dr. Peter L. STAFFEL
93	Minority Student Coordinator	Ms. Amena ANDERSON-OLIVER
88	Director Dental Hygiene Programs	Ms. Margaret J. SIX
88	Dir Clinical Lab Science Program	Dr. William C. WAGENER
20	Associate Academic Officer	Vacant
21	Associate Business Officer	Ms. Cindy R. MCGEE
84	Assoc Dean Enrollment Services	Ms. Brenda M. KING
23	Director of Health Services	Ms. Cheryl BENNINGTON
88	Vice President of Broadcasting	Vacant
88	Director Physican Assistant Program	Dr. Allan M. BEDASHI
21	Controller	Ms. Stephanie L. HOOPER
04	Executive Asst to the President	Dr. John P. MCCULLOUGH
85	Coord International Student Rec	Ms. Mihaela A. SZABO
88	Marketing Director	Ms. Tammi SECRIST
44	Director of Major Gifts	Ms. Angela R. ZAMBITO

*West Virginia School of Osteopathic Medicine (B)

400 N Lee Street, Lewisburg WV 24901-1196

County: Greenbrier — FICE Identification: 011245 — Unit ID: 237880

Telephone: (304) 645-6270 — Carnegie Class: Spec/Med

FAX Number: (304) 645-4859 — Calendar System: Semester

URL: www.wvsom.edu

Established: 1972 — Annual Graduate Tuition & Fees: $21,150

Enrollment: 824 — Coed

Affiliation or Control: State — IRS Status: 501(c)3

Highest Offering: First Professional Degree; No Undergraduates

Program: Professional

Accreditation: @NH, OSTEO

Code	Title	Name
02	President	Dr. Michael D. ADELMAN
05	Vice Pres Academic Affairs & Dean	Dr. Lorence L. PENCE
10	Vice Pres Finance & Facilities	Mr. Larry WARE
11	Vice Pres for Administration	Dr. James W. NEMITZ
16	Associate VP of Human Resources	Ms. Leslie BICKSLER
100	Associate VP Administrative Affairs	Ms. Marilea BUTCHER
43	General Counsel	Mr. Jeffrey SHAWVER
20	Assoc Dean Osteopathic Medical Educ	Dr. Robert W. FOSTER
20	Assoc Dean Graduate Med Education	Dr. Victoria SHUMAN
20	Assoc Dean Preclinical Education	Dr. John SCHRIEFER
20	Assoc Dean Predoctoral Clin Educ	Dr. Craig BOISVERT
108	Assoc Dean Assessment/Educ Devel	Dr. Elaine SOPER
20	Assoc Dean Affiliated/Spons Pgms	Dr. Malcolm MODRZAKOWSKI
20	Asst Dean Graduate Med Educ	Dr. David LEECH
88	Exec Dir Clinical Evaluation Ctr	Ms. Stephanie SCHULER
88	Director National Boards Office	Dr. Robert FISK
13	Director Information Technology	Ms. Kimberly RANSOM
35	Director of Student Affairs	Dr. Rebecca MORROW
06	Registrar	Ms. Jennifer SEAMS
37	Director Financial Aid	Ms. Sharon L. HOWARD
30	Director Institutional Development	Ms. Heather ANTOLINI
29	Director Alumni Relations	Ms. Shannon WARREN
07	Director of Admissions	Ms. Patricia PERKINS
08	Director of Library	Ms. Mary ESSIG
26	Director of Marketing and PR	Ms. Denise GETSON
25	Director of Contracts	Ms. Pam OCHALA
24	Director of Media Services	Mr. Richard MCMAHAN
18	Director of Physical Plant II	Mr. William ALDER
40	Business Manager	Ms. Cindi KNIGHT
101	Executive Administrative Assistant	Ms. Cheryl BAKER

*West Virginia State University (C)

PO Box 1000, Institute WV 25112-1000

County: Kanawha — FICE Identification: 003826 — Unit ID: 237899

Telephone: (304) 766-3000 — Carnegie Class: Bac/A&S

FAX Number: (304) 768-9842 — Calendar System: Semester

URL: www.wvstateu.edu

Established: 1891 — Annual Undergrad Tuition & Fees (In-State): $5,932

Enrollment: 2,644 — Coed

Affiliation or Control: State — IRS Status: 501(c)3

Highest Offering: Master's

Program: Liberal Arts And General; Teacher Preparatory

Accreditation: NH, ACBSP, SW, TED

Code	Title	Name
02	President	Dr. Brian O. HEMPHILL
10	Vice President for Finance	Mr. Melvin JONES
05	Provost and VP for Academic Affairs	Dr. R. Charles BYERS
09	Coord Institutional Research	Dr. Danny R. CANTRELL
32	Vice President Student Affairs	Ms. Katherine MCCARTHY
30	VP for University Advancement	Ms. Patricia J. SCHUMANN
20	Asst Provost & Asst VP Acad Affs	Dr. T. Ramon STUART
20	Assoc Prov and Assoc VP Acad Aff	Dr. Kimberly WHITEHEAD
35	Asst Vice Pres Student Affairs	Mr. Joseph ODEN, JR.
26	Asst VP Univ and Legis Relations	Mr. Thomas BENNETT, II
86	VP for Research & Public Service	Dr. Orlando F. MCMEANS
100	Chief of Staff Spec Asst to Pres	Ms. Ashley SCHUMAKER
79	Dean College of Arts & Humanities	Dr. Barbara LADNER
81	Dean College of Natural Sci/Math	Dr. Katherine HARPER
107	Dean Col of Professional Studies	Dr. Robert L. HARRISON, JR.
50	Inter Dean Col of Bus Admin/Soc Sci	Dr. Lois LUCAS
53	Chrmn Department of Education	Dr. Sandra ORR
70	Chairman Department Sociology	Dr. Gail MOSBY
64	Chairman Music Department	Ms. Brenda VANDERFORD
68	Chrmn Health & Human Performance	Mrs. Debra ANDERSON-CONLIFFE
26	Director for Public Relations	Mr. Jack BAILEY
14	Director Computer Services	Mr. Robert H. HUSTON
09	Dir Inst Research & Effectiveness	Vacant
18	Director Physical Facilities	Mr. Philip H. JUDD
06	Director Records & Registration	Ms. Donna L. HUNTER
19	Director of Public Safety	Chief Joseph SAUNDERS
21	Asst Vice President for Business	Ms. Lori ELLIOTT
08	Interim Director Library Services	Ms. Mary HORN
37	Director Student Financial Aid	Ms. JoAnn L. ROSS
29	Director Alumni Relations	Ms. Belinda FULLER
15	Acting Director of Human Resources	Ms. Julie SALDIVAR
36	Dir Career Services & Coop Educ	Ms. Sandhya (Sandy) G. MAHARAJ
07	Interim Director of Admissions	Ms. Amanda ANDERSON
38	Director New Student Programs	Mrs. Sharon S. BANKS
96	Director of Purchasing	Mrs. Janis A. BENNETT
88	Associate Director of Admissions	Ms. Christina KAST

*West Virginia University (D)

1500 University Avenue, Morgantown WV 26506-0002

County: Monongalia — FICE Identification: 003827 — Unit ID: 238032

Telephone: (304) 293-0111 — Carnegie Class: RU/H

FAX Number: (304) 293-5883 — Calendar System: Semester

URL: www.wvu.edu

Established: 1867 — Annual Undergrad Tuition & Fees (In-State): $6,456

Enrollment: 29,707 — Coed

Affiliation or Control: State — IRS Status: 501(c)3

Highest Offering: Doctorate

Program: Liberal Arts And General; Teacher Preparatory; Professional

Accreditation: NH, ART, AUD, BUS, BUSA, CACREP, CLPSY, COPSY, CORE, CS, DENT, DH, DIETD, DIETI, DMS, ENG, ENGR, FEPAC, FOR, HT, IPSY, JOUR, LAW, LSAR, MED, MT, MUS, NMT, NURSE, OT, PA, PH, PHAR, PTA, RAD, RADMAG, RTT, SP, SPAA, SW, TED, THEA

Code	Title	Name
02	President	Dr. James P. CLEMENTS
05	Provost & VP Acad Affairs	Dr. Michele G. WHEATLY
10	Vice President for Admin & Finance	Mr. Narvel G. WEESE, JR.
26	Vice Pres for University Relations	Ms. Sharon L. MARTIN
17	Chancellor of Health Sciences	Dr. Christopher C. COLENDA
32	Vice President Student Affairs	Mr. Kenneth D. GRAY
46	VP Research & Econ Develop	Dr. Fred L. KING
15	Vice President for Human Resources	Ms. Margaret R. PHILLIPS
58	Vice Pres Health Sci Rsrch/Grad Ed	Dr. Glen DILLON
76	Interim Sr Assoc VP/Health Sciences	Mr. Fred R. BUTCHER
20	Sr Assoc Provost Academic Affairs	Dr. Russell K. DEAN
20	Assoc Provost Academic Personnel	Dr. Cecil B. WILSON
88	Director Research & Rural Health	Ms. Jodie JACKSON
100	Chief of Staff	Mr. John J. COLE
88	Exec Officer for Policy Development	Dr. Jennifer L. FISHER
43	VP Legal Affairs/General Counsel	Mr. William H. HUTCHENS, III
21	Assoc VP & Chief Financial Officer	Ms. Wendy L. KING
21	Sr Assoc Vice Pres for Finance	Mr. Daniel A. DURBIN
56	Interim Director of Extension Svcs	Dr. Steve BONANNO
102	President WVU Foundation	Mr. R. Wayne KING
20	Assoc Provost Academic Programs	Dr. Elizabeth A. DOOLEY
13	Assoc Provost IT/CIO	Dr. John P. CAMPBELL
18	Assoc VP Facilities & Svcs	Mr. Randy HUDAK
35	Assoc Vice Pres Student Affairs	Mr. Michael A. ELLINGTON
88	Asst VP Hlth Sci & Tech Academy	Ms. Ann M. CHESTER
88	Associate VP University Relations	Ms. Tricia L. PETTY
84	Associate VP Enroll Mgmt Svcs	Ms. Brenda S. THOMPSON
45	Assoc Vice Pres Planning & Treasury	Ms. Elizabeth P. REYNOLDS
25	Asst VP Office of Sponsored Pgms	Mr. Alan B. MARTIN
09	Director of Institutional Research	Vacant
39	Director Res Life/Dean of Students	Mr. G. Corey FARRIS
41	Director Intercollegiate Athletics	Mr. Oliver F. LUCK
23	Director of Health Services	Dr. Jan E. PALMER
24	Director of Radio & TV Services	Mr. John E. DUWALL
27	Asst VP News/Information Services	Ms. Rebecca B. LOFSTEAD
29	Exec Director Alumni Association	Mr. Stephen L. DOUGLAS
37	Interim Director Financial Aid	Ms. Tresa WEIMER
07	Exec Director Admissions	Dr. Stephen E. LEE
06	University Registrar	Dr. Steve E. ROBINSON
08	Interim Dean of Library Services	Ms. Myra LOWE
38	Asst VP Student Wellness	Dr. Catherine A. YURA
21	Director Financial Services	Ms. Lisa A. LIVELY
19	Chief of Police/Univ Police Dept	Capt. Bob E. ROBERTS
96	Dir Purchasing/Cont & Pay	Ms. Brenda K. MOWEN
88	Assoc VP Intl & Global Outreach	Dr. David C. STEWART
50	Dean Business and Economics	Dr. Jose V. SARTARELLI
49	Dean of Arts & Sciences	Dr. Robert H. JONES
57	Dean College Creative Arts	Dr. Paul K. KREIDER
53	Dean Educ & Human Resources	Dr. Lynn SCHRUM
61	Dean of Law	Dr. Joyce E. MCCONNELL
63	Dean of Medicine	Dr. Arthur J. ROSS
52	Dean of Dentistry	Dr. David A. FELTON
54	Dean of Engr/Mineral Resources	Dr. Eugene V. CILENTO
47	Dean of Agriculture & Forestry	Dr. Daniel J. ROBISON
67	Dean of Pharmacy	Dr. Patricia A. CHASE
60	Dean of Journalism	Dr. Maryanne REED
68	Dean Physical Education	Dr. Dana D. BROOKS
66	Interim Dean of Nursing	Ms. Elisabeth SHELTON
88	Assoc VP Academic Innovation	Dr. Susan D. DAY-PERROOTS
36	Director Career Services	Mr. David L. DURHAM
88	Assoc Provost Intl Acad Affairs	Dr. Michael LASTINGER
88	Assoc VP Acad Strategic Plng	Dr. Nigel N. CLARK
88	Int Assoc Provost Grad Acad Affairs	Dr. Katherine KARRAKER
35	Interim Dean Students & Dir Housing	Mr. G. Corey FARRIS
88	Director of Internal Audit	Mr. William R. QUIGLEY

*West Virginia University at Parkersburg (E)

300 Campus Drive, Parkersburg WV 26104-8647

County: Wood — FICE Identification: 003828 — Unit ID: 237686

Telephone: (304) 424-8000 — Carnegie Class: Bac/Assoc

FAX Number: (304) 424-8315 — Calendar System: Semester

URL: www.wvup.edu

Established: 1961 — Annual Undergrad Tuition & Fees (In-State): $2,712

Enrollment: 3,829 — Coed

Affiliation or Control: State — IRS Status: 501(c)3

Highest Offering: Baccalaureate

Program: Occupational; 2-Year Principally Bachelor's Creditable; Liberal Arts And General; Teacher Preparatory

Accreditation: NH, ACBSP, ADNUR, SURGT, TED

Code	Title	Name
02	President	Dr. Marie FOSTER GNAGE
04	Executive Asst to the President	Mr. Brady WHIPKEY
05	Sr Vice President Academic Affairs	Dr. Rhonda TRACY
32	Vice President for Student Services	Mr. Anthony UNDERWOOD
103	Vice Pres Workforce/Community Educ	Dr. Tabitha ANDERSON
10	Chief Financial Officer	Dr. Vincent MENSAH
26	Director Marketing/Communications	Mrs. Katie WOOTTON
13	Director Information Technology	Mr. Dan BONINE
22	Special Asst to President	Mrs. Debbie RICHARDS
12	Director Jackson County Center	Mr. John GORRELL
102	Director of Development	Mrs. Geni ASTORG
18	Director Facilities & Services	Mr. David WHITE
15	Director Human Resources	Mr. Scott POE
09	Dir Inst Rsrch/Outcomes Assessment	Mr. Jeremy STARKEY

06 Registrar .... Mrs. Leslie SIMS
07 Asst Dean of Enrollment .... Mrs. Christine POST
37 Director of Financial Aid .... Mrs. Heather SKIDMORE
96 Director of Purchasing .... Ms. Lynne WOOLLARD
35 Director Student Activities .... Mr. Tom YENCHA
08 Director of Library .... Mr. Stephen HUPP
50 Chair Business/Economics/Math Div .... Mr. Steven MORGAN
53 Chair Education/Humanities Division .... Dr. Cindy GISSY
76 Chair Health Sciences Division .... Mrs. Rose BEEBE
83 Chair Social Science/Languages Div .... Mrs. Denise MCCLUNG
72 Chair Science/Technology Division .... Mr. David THOMPSON

* *Marshall University-South Charleston Campus* (A)

100 Angus E Peyton Drive, South Charleston WV 25303
Telephone: (304) 746-2500 Identification: 770467
Accreditation: &NH

† Main campus is Marshall University in Huntington, WV.

* *Potomac State College of West Virginia University* (B)

Keyser WV 26726-2698
Telephone: (304) 788-6800 FICE Identification: 003829
Accreditation: &NH

† Main campus is West Virginia University in Morgantown, WV.

* *West Virginia University Institute of Technology* (C)

405 Fayette Pike, Montgomery WV 25136-2436
Telephone: (304) 442-1000 FICE Identification: 003825
Accreditation: &NH, ENG, ENGT

† Main campus is West Virginia University in Morgantown, WV.

West Virginia Junior College (D)

176 Thompson Drive, Bridgeport WV 26330
Telephone: (304) 842-4007 Identification: 770823
Accreditation: ACICS

† Main campus is West Virginia Junior College in Charleston, WV.

West Virginia Junior College (E)

1000 Virginia Street East, Charleston WV 25301-2817
County: Kanawha FICE Identification: 010573
Unit ID: 237987
Telephone: (304) 345-2820 Carnegie Class: Assoc/PrivFP
FAX Number: (304) 345-1425 Calendar System: Quarter
URL: www.wvjc.edu
Established: 1892 Annual Undergrad Tuition & Fees: $12,650
Enrollment: 163 Coed
Affiliation or Control: Proprietary IRS Status: Proprietary
Highest Offering: Associate Degree
Program: 2-Year Principally Bachelor's Creditable
Accreditation: ACICS

01 President .... Mr. Alexander R. HULT

West Virginia Junior College (F)

148 Willey Street, Morgantown WV 26505-5596
County: Monongalia FICE Identification: 005007
Unit ID: 237996
Telephone: (304) 296-8282 Carnegie Class: Assoc/PrivFP
FAX Number: (304) 581-6990 Calendar System: Quarter
URL: www.wvjcmorgantown.edu
Established: 1922 Annual Undergrad Tuition & Fees: $12,650
Enrollment: 260 Coed
Affiliation or Control: Proprietary IRS Status: Proprietary
Highest Offering: Associate Degree
Program: 2-Year Principally Bachelor's Creditable; Business Emphasis
Accreditation: ACICS

01 President & CEO .... Ms. Patricia A. CALLEN
05 Academic Director .... Ms. Leanne CARDOSA
36 Career Services .... Ms. Holly HILDRETH
37 Financial Aid Director .... Ms. Savannah MCCONNELL

West Virginia Wesleyan College (G)

59 College Avenue, Buckhannon WV 26201-2699
County: Upshur FICE Identification: 003830
Unit ID: 237969
Telephone: (304) 473-8000 Carnegie Class: Bac/Diverse
FAX Number: (304) 472-2571 Calendar System: Semester
URL: www.wvwc.edu
Established: 1890 Annual Undergrad Tuition & Fees: $26,794
Enrollment: 1,394 Coed
Affiliation or Control: United Methodist IRS Status: 501(c)3
Highest Offering: Master's
Program: Liberal Arts And General; Teacher Preparatory; Professional
Accreditation: NH, MUS, NUR, TED

01 President .... Dr. Pamela BALCH
05 VP Academic Affairs & Dean of Col .... Dr. Boyd CREASMAN
10 VP Administration & Finance .... Dr. Barry PRITTS
84 VP Enrollment Management .... Mr. Bernard VALENTO
32 VP Student Development .... Ms. Julia KEEHNER
30 VP Advancement .... Mr. Robert SKINNER
13 VP Information Technology .... Mr. R. Duwane SQUIRES
42 Dean of the Chapel .... Rev. Angela Gay KINKEAD
102 Director Foundation/Govt Relations .... Ms. Nicki BENTLEY-COLTHART
07 Director of Admission .... Mr. John WALTZ
11 Director of Administrative Services .... Mr. Keith NICHOLS
37 Director Financial Aid .... Ms. Susan GEORGE
29 Director of Alumni Affairs .... Ms. Kristi WILKERSON
08 Director of Library Services .... Ms. Paula MCGREW
06 Dir Acad & Career Svcs/Registrar .... Ms. Alice CREASMAN
39 Director Campus Life & Housing .... Ms. Alisa LIVELY
09 Director of Institutional Research .... Ms. Tammy CRITES
15 Director of Human Resources .... Ms. Vickie CROWDER
18 Director of the Physical Plant .... Mr. Kenneth ANDREW
30 Director Advancement Operations .... Ms. Rose Ellen LOUDIN
88 Director of Learning Center .... Dr. Shawn KUBA
41 Director of Athletics .... Mr. Randall TENNEY
21 Comptroller .... Mr. Randall CRITES
40 Director of Bookstore .... Ms. Jennifer DALTON
92 Director Honors Program .... Mr. Douglas VAN GUNDY
93 Director Intercultural Relations .... Ms. Courtney HAND
44 Planned Giving Coordinator .... Rev. David PETERS
38 Dir of Counseling & Wellness Center .... Mr. Michael KUBA
31 Dir of Leadership Development .... Ms. LeeAnn BROWN

Wheeling Jesuit University (H)

316 Washington Avenue, Wheeling WV 26003-6295
County: Ohio FICE Identification: 003831
Unit ID: 238078
Telephone: (304) 243-2000 Carnegie Class: Bac/Diverse
FAX Number: (304) 243-2243 Calendar System: Semester
URL: www.wju.edu
Established: 1954 Annual Undergrad Tuition & Fees: $27,830
Enrollment: 1,581 Coed
Affiliation or Control: Roman Catholic IRS Status: 501(c)3
Highest Offering: Doctorate
Program: Liberal Arts And General; Professional
Accreditation: NH, ACBSP, COARC, NMT, NURSE, PTA, TEAC

01 President .... Rev. James FLEMING, SJ
05 Chief Academic Officer .... Dr. Robert PHILLIPS
76 Dean for Health Sciences .... Dr. Helen FASO
10 Chief Financial Officer .... Mr. Kevin LUSK
88 VP for Mission & Ministy .... Rev. William RICKLE, SJ
30 VP for Institutional Advancement .... Vacant
84 VP for Enrollment Management .... Mr. Larry VALLAR
32 Dean for Student Development .... Ms. Christine OHL-GIGLIOTTI
90 Assoc VP for Info Tech Services .... Mr. Daniel T. FEELEY
11 Associate VP for Administration .... Mr. Donald KAMINSKI
37 Director Financial Aid .... Ms. Christie L. TOMCZYK
21 Controller .... Mr. Stephen CRINITI
21 Senior Accountant .... Mr. Donald YAQUINTA
06 Registrar .... Ms. Joy CRONIN
08 Librarian .... Ms. Kelly MUMMERT
91 Systems Administrator .... Mr. Richard M. KLEMPA
42 Director of Campus Ministry .... Mr. Jamey BROGAN
41 Athletic Director .... Mr. Danny SANCOMB
18 Director of Physical Plant .... Mr. Frank P. CONNELLY
85 International Student Coordinator .... Ms. Sunnie MCCABE

WISCONSIN

Alverno College (I)

3400 S 43rd Street, Box 343922,
Milwaukee WI 53234-3922
County: Milwaukee FICE Identification: 003832
Unit ID: 238193
Telephone: (414) 382-6000 Carnegie Class: Master's S
FAX Number: (414) 382-6066 Calendar System: Semester
URL: www.alverno.edu
Established: 1887 Annual Undergrad Tuition & Fees: $23,231
Enrollment: 2,522 Female
Affiliation or Control: Independent Non-Profit IRS Status: 501(c)3
Highest Offering: Master's
Program: Liberal Arts And General; Teacher Preparatory; Professional
Accreditation: NH, MUS, NURSE, TED

01 President .... Dr. Mary J. MEEHAN
10 Sr Vice Pres Finance & Mgmt Svcs .... Mr. James OPPERMANN
05 Sr Vice Pres Academic Affairs .... Dr. Kathleen O'BRIEN
30 Vice President College Advancement .... Ms. Julie QUINLAN BRAME
20 Exec Director Academic Services .... Sr. Marlene NEISES
84 VP for Enrollment Services .... Ms. Kate LUNDEEN
32 Assoc Vice Pres/Dean of Students .... Ms. Virginia WAGNER
07 Dir Communications for Admissions .... Ms. Cecelia CASPRAM
20 Associate Vice President Academic .... Dr. Kathy LAKE
20 Associate Vice President Academic .... Dr. Jeanna ABROMEIT
06 Registrar .... Ms. Patricia HARTMANN
08 Director Library .... Ms. Carol BRILL
36 Director Career Development .... Ms. Joanna PATTERSON
13 Exec Dir Information Technology .... Ms. Anita EIKENS
37 Assoc Dir Student Financial Plng .... Mr. Mary ROWE
29 Director Alumnae Relations .... Ms. Mary FRIESEKE
38 Director Advising .... Ms. Katherine BUNDALO
51 Dir Institute Educational Outreach .... Ms. Judith REISETTER-HART
15 Director Human Resources .... Ms. Sharon WILCOX
41 Director of Athletics .... Mr. Brad DUCKWORTH
42 Campus Minister .... Ms. Connie POPP
96 Purchasing Agent .... Ms. Anne MCCARRON
09 Director of Institutional Research .... Dr. Glen ROGERS
27 Chief Information Officer .... Mr. Jim HILBY
50 Dean School of Business .... Mr. Dan HORTON
66 Dean School of Nursing .... Ms. Patricia SCHROEDER
53 Dean of School of Education .... Dr. Nancy ATHANASIOU
49 Dean School of Arts & Sciences .... Dr. Sandra GRAHAM
50 Director Master of Business Admin .... Dr. Patricia JENSEN
79 Assoc Dean Humanities Division .... Dr. John SAVAGIAN
81 Asc Dean Natl Science/Math/Tech Div .... Dr. Angela FREY
83 Assoc Dean Behavioral Sciences Div .... Dr. Julie ULLMAN
72 Assoc Dean Comm & Tech Div .... Dr. Jennifer MIKULAY
60 Assoc Dean Arts Div .... Dr. Kat GILBERT
28 Sp Asst to VP Acad Affs/Multclt Iss .... Dr. Celia JACKSON
04 Assistant to the President .... Ms. Jill DESMOND
101 Executive Assistant .... Ms. Joan WALTER-SCHUMACHER

Anthem College-Milwaukee (J)

440 South Executive Drive, Ste 200,
Brookfield WI 53005-4283
Telephone: (262) 641-9944 Identification: 666613
Accreditation: ABHES, SURTEC

† Main campus is Anthem College in Maryland Heights, MO.

The Art Institute of Wisconsin (K)

320 East Buffalo Street, Suite 100, Milwaukee WI 53202
Telephone: (877) 285-4234 Identification: 770824
Accreditation: ACICS

† Main campus is The Art Institute of Phoenix in Phoenix, AZ.

Bellin College, Inc. (L)

3201 Eaton Road, Green Bay WI 54311
County: Brown FICE Identification: 006639
Unit ID: 238324
Telephone: (920) 433-6699 Carnegie Class: Spec/Health
FAX Number: (920) 433-1923 Calendar System: Semester
URL: www.bellincollege.edu
Established: 1909 Annual Undergrad Tuition & Fees: $21,943
Enrollment: 271 Coed
Affiliation or Control: Independent Non-Profit IRS Status: 501(c)3
Highest Offering: Master's
Program: Professional; Nursing Emphasis
Accreditation: NH, NURSE, RAD

01 President & CEO of the College .... Dr. Connie BOERST
10 Vice President Business & Finance .... Mr. Joseph E. KEEBAUGH
05 Dean of Academic Affairs .... Dr. Stephanie M. STEWART
32 Dean of Student Services .... Dr. Nancy M. BURRUSS
30 Vice President Development & PR .... Mr. Matt G. RENTMEESTER
13 Director of Technology .... Mr. Lucas KOENIG
06 Registrar .... Mr. Russell J. LEARY
37 Director Financial Aid .... Ms. Lena C. GOODMAN
07 Director of Admissions .... Ms. Katie KLAUS

Beloit College (M)

700 College Street, Beloit WI 53511-5595
County: Rock FICE Identification: 003835
Unit ID: 238333
Telephone: (608) 363-2000 Carnegie Class: Bac/A&S
FAX Number: (608) 363-2718 Calendar System: Semester
URL: www.beloit.edu
Established: 1846 Annual Undergrad Tuition & Fees: $41,250
Enrollment: 1,274 Coed
Affiliation or Control: Independent Non-Profit IRS Status: 501(c)3
Highest Offering: Baccalaureate
Program: Liberal Arts And General; Teacher Preparatory
Accreditation: NH

01 President .... Dr. Scott BIERMAN
05 Provost .... Dr. Ann DAVIES
11 Vice President Budget & Planning .... Ms. Laurie STICKELMAIER
84 Vice President Enrollment Services .... Ms. Nancy BENEDICT
30 VP Development & Alumni Relations .... Mr. Jeff PUCKETT
32 Dean of Students .... Dr. Christina KLAWITTER
06 Registrar .... Ms. Mary BOROS-KAZAI
07 Director of Admissions .... Mr. James S. ZIELINSKI
09 Director of Institutional Research .... Mr. Russell CANNON
08 Chief Information Officer .... Ms. Megan E. FITCH
15 VP Human Resources and Operations .... Ms. Lori RHEAD
29 Sr Dir Annual Supp & Alumni/Parent .... Mr. Mark C. WOLD
26 Director of Communications .... Mr. Jason HUGHES
39 Director Resident Life/Conferences .... Mr. John F. WINKELMANN
18 Director of Physical Plant .... Mr. Michael BRADY
36 Director of Career Development .... Ms. Jessica FOX-WILSON
38 College Counselor .... Vacant
40 Bookstore Director .... Mr. Peter FRONK
37 Dir of Student Financial Services .... Mr. Jonathan E. URISH
41 Athletic Director .... Ms. Peggy CARL
28 Dir Intercult Pgm/Asst Dean Stdnts .... Mr. Cecil YOUNGBLOOD

Bryant & Stratton College (A)

310 W Wisconsin Avenue, Suite 500 E,
Milwaukee WI 53203
Telephone: (414) 276-5200 FICE Identification: 005009
Accreditation: &M, ADNUR, MAC

† Main campus is Bryant & Stratton College in Buffalo, NY.

Cardinal Stritch University (B)

6801 N Yates Road, Milwaukee WI 53217-3985
County: Milwaukee FICE Identification: 003837
Unit ID: 238430
Telephone: (414) 410-4000 Carnegie Class: DRU
FAX Number: (414) 410-4239 Calendar System: Semester
URL: www.stritch.edu
Established: 1937 Annual Undergrad Tuition & Fees: $25,450
Enrollment: 4,595 Coed
Affiliation or Control: Roman Catholic IRS Status: 501(c)3
Highest Offering: Doctorate
Program: 2-Year Principally Bachelor's Creditable; Liberal Arts And General; Teacher Preparatory; Professional
Accreditation: NH, ACBSP, ADNUR, NUR, NURSE, TED

01 President .... Dr. James P. LOFTUS
00 Chancellor .... Sr. Camille KLIEBHAN
04 Assistant to the President .... Ms. Kathryn HOWELL
03 Executive Vice President/CFO .... Vacant
05 Executive VP Academic Affairs .... Dr. Anthea L. BOJAR
42 Vice President Mission & Identity .... Fr. James G. GANNON
84 Vice President Enrollment Services .... Mr. John P. MUELLER
10 Vice President Business & Finance .... Ms. Tammy M. HOWARD
13 Vice President Info Services/CIO .... Mr. Thomas J. RAINS
26 Sr Director of Univ Communications .... Mr. Scott H. RUDIE
30 Vice President for Univ Advancement .... Dr. Robert J. BUCKLA
30 Assoc VP for University Advancement . Ms. Judy M. HAUGSLAND
32 Vice Pres for Student Development .. Ms. Christine M. ROBINSON
21 Asst VP for Business & Finance .... Vacant
21 Dir Treasury & Risk Management .... Ms. Janet MCKNIGHT
15 Director of Human Resources/Payroll .... Ms. Melissa STAUBER
49 Dean College of Arts & Sciences .... Dr. Daniel J. SCHOLZ
50 Dean College of Business & Mgmt .... Dr. Peter J. HOLBROOK
53 Dean College of Education & Ldrship .... Dr. Freda R. RUSSELL
66 Dean College of Nursing .... Ms. Kelly J. DRIES
06 Registrar .... Vacant
21 Bursar .... Ms. Lisa M. LEWIN
20 Director of Academic Affairs .... Ms. Nancy A. DAWKINS
85 Director of International Programs .... Ms. Laine M. PHILIPPA
39 Director of Residence Life .... Mr. Joseph R. NISWONGER
41 Director of Athletics .... Mr. Patrick J. CLEMENS
07 Sr Dir of Student Recruitment .... Mr. Kirk D. MESSER
08 Director of University Library .. Mr. David W. WEINBERG-KINSEY
37 Director of Financial Aid .... Mr. Ben J. BAERBOCK
36 Director of Career Services .... Mr. Tom E. KIPP
09 Dir of Quality Data & Inst Research .... Ms. Lynsey A. SCHWABROW
18 Director of Facilities .... Mr. John B. GLYNN
91 Director of Enterprise Systems .... Ms. Susan L. INGLES
19 Director of Security .... Mr. Andrew DE RUBERTIS
44 Director Major Gifts/Planned Giving .... Mr. Chris J. LANGE
29 Dir Alumni Relations/Annual Giving .... Mr. Joel F. CENCIUS
38 Dir for Counseling/Mental Wellness .... Ms. Laura J. HEMPE

Carroll University (C)

100 N East Avenue, Waukesha WI 53186-5593
County: Waukesha FICE Identification: 003838
Unit ID: 238458
Telephone: (262) 547-1211 Carnegie Class: Master's S
FAX Number: (262) 524-7646 Calendar System: Semester
URL: www.carrollu.edu
Established: 1846 Annual Undergrad Tuition & Fees: $25,899
Enrollment: 3,571 Coed
Affiliation or Control: Presbyterian Church (U.S.A.) IRS Status: 501(c)3
Highest Offering: Doctorate
Program: Liberal Arts And General; Teacher Preparatory; Professional
Accreditation: NH, #ARCPA, NURSE, PTA

01 President .... Dr. Doug N. HASTAD
05 Provost .... Dr. Joanne PASSARO
10 Vice President for Finance .... Mr. Ron LOSTETTER
84 Vice President for Enrollment .... Mr. James V. WISEMAN
30 Vice President for Advancement .... Mr. Stephen KUHN
32 Vice President Student Affairs .... Dr. Theresa BARRY
13 Chief Information Officer .... Ms. Debra JENKINS
06 Registrar .... Ms. Ann HANDFORD
21 Controller .... Ms. Deidre ERWIN
44 Sr Advancement Ofcr for Development .... Ms. Cherie SWENSON
26 Director of Public Relations .... Ms. Claire M. BEGLINGER
15 Director of Human Resources .... Ms. Lorraine FORCINITO
08 Interim Library Director .... Ms. Amelia OSTERUD
37 Director of Student Financial Svcs .... Ms. Dawn M. SCOTT
41 Athletic Director .... Mr. Joe BAKER
88 Assoc Director of Part-Time Studies .... Ms. Jan SNYDER
28 Director of Cultural Diversity .... Mr. Carl ERVIN
29 Director Alumni Relations .... Ms. Dolores M. BROWN
96 Director of Purchasing .... Ms. Char RICHARDS
07 Director of Admissions .... Ms. Kelly J. HEIMAN
18 Chief Facilities/Physical Plant .... Mr. Alan PESCHL
38 Director Student Counseling .... Ms. Angie R. BRANNAN
04 Exec Assistant to the President .... Ms. Gina M. EHLER

Carthage College (D)

2001 Alford Park Drive, Kenosha WI 53140-1994
County: Kenosha FICE Identification: 003839
Unit ID: 238476
Telephone: (262) 551-8500 Carnegie Class: Bac/A&S
FAX Number: (262) 551-6208 Calendar System: 4/1/4
URL: www.carthage.edu
Established: 1847 Annual Undergrad Tuition & Fees: $34,850
Enrollment: 3,029 Coed
Affiliation or Control: Evangelical Lutheran Church In America
IRS Status: 501(c)3
Highest Offering: Master's
Program: Liberal Arts And General; Teacher Preparatory
Accreditation: NH, MUS, SW

01 President .... Dr. Gregory S. WOODWARD
100 Special Assistant to the President .... Mr. Paul R. HEGLAND
05 Provost .... Dr. Julio C. RIVERA
20 Associate Dean of the College .... Dr. David STEEGE
06 Registrar .... Ms. Abby HEINRICHS
51 Assoc VP Adult Education .... Mr. Michael WEST
58 Director of Graduate Program .... Dr. Paul ZAVADA
92 Director of Honors Program .... Dr. Paul ULRICH
36 Director Career Center .... Ms. Jean FREDERICK
108 Director Institutional Assessment .... Dr. Dana GARRIGAN
104 Study Abroad Director .... Dr. Erik KULKE
11 Sr VP Administration/Business .... Mr. William R. ABT
90 VP Academic Information Services .... Mr. Todd D. KELLEY
14 Director of Computer Center .... Mrs. Carol SABBAR
91 Director Administrative Computing .... Mr. Richard HUENINK
105 Dir Tech Integration & Infrastructr .... Mr. David ROBINSON
105 Director Online Communications .... Mrs. Elizabeth YOUNG
24 Director Media Services .... Mr. Mike LOVE
21 Associate VP for Business .... Mr. William D. HOARE
10 Assoc VP/Controller .... Mr. Scot ECKER
41 Director of Athletics .... Dr. Robert R. BONN
40 Bookstore Manager .... Mrs. Pam ROBERS
18 Physical Plant Superintendent .... Mr. Dave PERTTULA
19 Director of Campus Security .... Mr. John KLABECHEK, IV
30 Sr VP Institutional Advancement .... Dr. Bradley J. ANDREWS
26 Assoc VP Institutional Advancement .... Ms. Elaine L. WALTON
102 Director Corp & Foundatino Rels .... Mr. Greg HUSS
29 Asst Director Advancement Programs .... Mrs. Mardell FISHER
44 Asst Dir Alumni/Parent Programs .... Ms. Lauren HANSEN
27 Assoc VP for Communications .... Ms. Molly POLK
07 VP for Enrollment .... Mr. Dean CLARK
37 Director Student Financial Aid .... Mr. Vatistas VATISTAS
84 Dean of Admissions .... Mr. Nick MULVEY
32 Dean of Students .... Mr. Jason RAMIREZ
35 Assoc Dean of Students .... Mr. Nick WINKLER
35 Asst Dean of Students .... Ms. Nina FLEMING
35 Director of Student Success .... Mr. Gary WILLIAMS
35 Director Student Activities .... Ms. Becky WINDBERG
38 Director Student Counseling .... Ms. Deborah BETSWORTH
42 Dean of Siebert Chapel .... Vacant

College of Menominee Nation (E)

PO Box 1179, Keshena WI 54135-1179
County: Menominee FICE Identification: 031251
Unit ID: 413617
Telephone: (800) 567-2344 Carnegie Class: Tribal
FAX Number: (715) 799-1336 Calendar System: Semester
URL: www.menominee.edu
Established: 1992 Annual Undergrad Tuition & Fees: $7,670
Enrollment: 721 Coed
Affiliation or Control: Tribal Control IRS Status: 501(c)3
Highest Offering: Baccalaureate
Program: Occupational; 2-Year Principally Bachelor's Creditable; Teacher Preparatory; Business Emphasis
Accreditation: NH, ADNUR

01 President .... Dr. Verna M. FOWLER
05 Chief Academic Officer .... Dr. Diana MORRIS
10 Chief Financial Officer .... Ms. Laurie REITER
12 Vice Pres of CMN Green Bay Campus .... Mr. Chad WAUKECHON
26 Dean External Relations .... Dr. Holly YOUNGBEAR-TIBBETS
32 Dean of Student Services .... Mr. Gary BESAW
49 Dean of Letters & Science .... Dr. Diana MORRIS
66 Dean of Nursing .... Ms. Linda TAYLOR
75 Dean of Technical Education .... Mrs. Deanna BISLEY
51 Dean of Continuing Education .... Mr. Brian BOWALKOWSKI
04 Assistant to the President .... Ms. Melinda COOK
09 Director Institutional Research .... Mr. Ronald JURGENS
30 Advancement Director .... Ms. Irene KIEFER
25 Director of Sponsored Programs .... Mrs. Jill MARTIN
13 IT Director .... Ms. Renita WILBER
18 Director of Operations .... Mr. Richard WARRINGTON
21 Business Manager .... Mr. Victor ESCALANTE
15 Human Resources Director .... Ms. Rachel RICE
37 Director Financial Aid .... Ms. Nicole FISH
06 Registrar .... Mrs. Juanita WAUKAU-WILBER
07 Admissions Director .... Ms. Tessa JAMES
29 Director Alumni Relations .... Ms. Irene KIEFER
88 Voc Rehab Director .... Mr. Norman SHAWANOKASIC
08 Library Director .... Ms. Maria ESCALANTE
88 Campus Planner .... Mr. Joel KROENKE
40 Director of Bookstore .... Ms. Verna DELEON

College of Menominee Nation Oneida Campus (F)

2733 S Ridge Road, Green Bay WI 54304
Telephone: (920) 965-0070 Identification: 770424
Accreditation: &NH

† Main campus is College of Menominee Nation in Keshena, WI.

Columbia College of Nursing (G)

4425 N Port Washington Rd, Milwaukee WI 53212-1099
County: Milwaukee FICE Identification: 006640
Unit ID: 238573
Telephone: (414) 326-2330 Carnegie Class: Not Classified
FAX Number: (414) 236-2331 Calendar System: Semester
URL: www.ccon.edu
Established: 1901 Annual Undergrad Tuition & Fees: $25,698
Enrollment: 157 Coed
Affiliation or Control: Independent Non-Profit IRS Status: 501(c)3
Highest Offering: Baccalaureate
Program: Professional; Nursing Emphasis
Accreditation: NH, NURSE

01 President & Dean .... Dr. Jill M. WINTERS
10 Chief Financial/Business Officer .... Ms. Christina ITALIANO
05 Associate Dean of Academic Affairs .... Ms. Catherine KNUTESON
88 Associate Dean of Practice .... Ms. Heather VARTANIAN
04 Admin Assistant to the President .... Ms. Gail PETERSON
20 Associate Academic Officer .... Ms. Haley GEIGER
37 Director Student Financial Aid .... Ms. Wendy HILVO
06 Registrar .... Ms. Joua XIONG
24 Director Educational Media .... Mr. Keith JACKSON
07 Admissions Specialist .... Ms. Joanne ROBIS

Concordia University Wisconsin (H)

12800 N Lake Shore Drive, Mequon WI 53097-2402
County: Ozaukee FICE Identification: 003842
Unit ID: 238616
Telephone: (262) 243-5700 Carnegie Class: Master's L
FAX Number: (262) 243-4351 Calendar System: 4/1/4
URL: www.cuw.edu
Established: 1881 Annual Undergrad Tuition & Fees: $24,930
Enrollment: 7,751 Coed
Affiliation or Control: Lutheran Church - Missouri Synod
IRS Status: 501(c)3
Highest Offering: Doctorate
Program: Liberal Arts And General; Teacher Preparatory; Professional
Accreditation: NH, #ARCPA, IACBE, MAC, NURSE, OT, @PHAR, PTA, SW

01 President .... Rev Dr. Patrick T. FERRY
11 Executive VP & Chief Oper Ofcr .... Mr. Allen J. PROCHNOW
05 Senior Vice President of Academics .... Dr. William R. CARIO
32 Vice President of Student Life .... Dr. Andrew J. LUPTAK
07 Sr Vice Pres of Enrollment Services .... Mr. Kenneth K. GASCHK
13 Vice Pres of Information Technology .... Mr. Thomas G. PHILLIP
26 Vice President of Marketing .... Ms. Anita CLARK
10 VP Finance & CFO .... Ms. Joan M. SCHOLZ
20 Assistant Vice Pres of Academics .... Rev Dr. Randy L. FERGUSON
20 Assistant Vice Pres of Academics .... Dr. Bernard D. BULL
20 Assistant Vice Pres of Academics .... Dr. Leah M. DVORAK
30 Vice Pres of Advancement .... Rev Dr. Roy PETERSON
42 Campus Pastor .... Rev. Steven N. SMITH
36 Director Counseling .... Mr. David I. ENTERS
37 Financial Aid Officer .... Mr. Steve P. TAYLOR
06 Registrar .... Dr. Steven MONTREAL
50 Dean School of Business .... Dr. David BORST
88 Dean School Human Services .... Dr. Terri S. KAUL
49 Dean School Arts/Sciences .... Dr. Gaylund K. STONE
53 Dean School of Education .... Dr. Michael UDEN
35 Dean of Students .... Dr. Sarah E. HOLTAN
08 Library Director .... Mr. Christian HIMSEL
09 Institutional Research .... Dr. Tamara R. FERRY
29 Director of Alumni Relations .... Mr. Josh KRAEGEL
39 Director Student Housing .... Ms. Barbara A. WILSON
41 Athletic Director .... Dr. Rob M. BARNHILL
88 Chair Faculty Senate .... Dr. Brad CONDIE
36 Director Career Services .... Ms. Kim DUNISCH
40 Director Bookstore .... Ms. Kia LOR
19 Director Campus Safety .... Mr. Mario VALDES
18 Superintendent Buildings & Grounds .... Mr. Steve V. HIBBARD
15 Director Human Resources .... Ms. Kim MASENTHIN
24 Director Instructional Technology .... Mr. Sean B. YOUNG
26 Public Relations Officer .... Mr. Jeff J. BANDURSKI
28 Minority Student Group Advisor .... Mr. Adam WALKER
86 Asst to President for Govern & Plng .... Dr. Ross STUEBER

Edgewood College (I)

1000 Edgewood College Drive, Madison WI 53711-1997
County: Dane FICE Identification: 003848
Unit ID: 238661
Telephone: (608) 663-4861 Carnegie Class: DRU
FAX Number: (608) 663-3291 Calendar System: Semester
URL: www.edgewood.edu
Established: 1927 Annual Undergrad Tuition & Fees: $24,666
Enrollment: 3,064 Coed
Affiliation or Control: Roman Catholic IRS Status: 501(c)3
Highest Offering: Doctorate
Program: Liberal Arts And General; Teacher Preparatory; Professional
Accreditation: NH, ACBSP, MFCD, NURSE, TED

01 President .... Dr. Daniel J. CAREY
03 Executive Vice President .... Dr. Scott FLANAGAN
05 VP Academic Affs/Academic Dean .... Dr. Dean PRIBBENOW
32 VP Student Devel/Dean of Students .... Dr. Margaret R. BALISTRERI-CLARKE
10 Vice President Business & Finance .... Mr. Michael GUNS
30 Vice Pres Inst Advancement .... Ms. Marcia WHITTINGTON
13 Director of Information Technology .... Mr. Deron KLING
20 Associate Academic Dean .... Dr. Kelly GRORUD
58 Dean Grad Adult/Profess Studies .... Dr. Scott CAMPBELL
09 Director of Inst Assessment & Rsrch .... Dr. Edward J. KEELEY
06 Registrar .... Ms. Michelle KELLY
08 Library Director .... Dr. Sylvia CONTRERAS
36 Exec Director for Career Services .... Ms. Ellen BARTKOWIAK
29 Alumni Director .... Ms. Kathleen O'CONNOR
26 Director Public Relations .... Mr. Edward TAYLOR
15 Director of Human Resources .... Ms. Carrie MICKELSON
18 Director Facilities & Operations .... Ms. Susan SERRAULT
35 Director Student Activities .... Dr. Beth JOHN
38 Director Student Counseling .... Dr. Stephanie GRAHAM
07 Director of Admissions .... Ms. Christine BENEDICT
21 Controller .... Ms. Jane WILHELM
28 Director of Diversity & Inclusion .... Mr. Tony GARCIA
37 Director Student Financial Aid .... Ms. Kari GRIBBLE

George Williams College of Aurora University (A)

350 Constance Boulevard, Williams Bay WI 53191
Telephone: (262) 245-5531 Identification: 770066
Accreditation: &NH

† Main campus is Aurora University in Aurora, IL.

Globe University-Appleton (B)

5045 West Grande Market Drive, Grande Chute WI 54914
Telephone: (920) 364-1100 Identification: 770800
Accreditation: ACICS

† Main campus is Globe University in Woodbury, MN.

Globe University-Eau Claire (C)

4955 Bullis Farm Road, Eau Claire WI 54702
Telephone: (715) 855-6600 Identification: 770801
Accreditation: ACICS

† Main campus is Globe University in Woodbury, MN.

Globe University-Green Bay (D)

2620 Development Drive, Bellevue WI 54311
Telephone: (920) 264-1600 Identification: 770802
Accreditation: ACICS

† Main campus is Globe University in Woodbury, MN.

Globe University-La Crosse (E)

2651 Midwest Drive, Third FL, Onalaska WI 54650
Telephone: (608) 779-2600 Identification: 770803
Accreditation: ACICS

† Main campus is Globe University in Woodbury, MN.

Globe University-Madison East (F)

4901 Eastpark Boulevard, Madison WI 53718
Telephone: (608) 216-9400 Identification: 770804
Accreditation: ACICS

† Main campus is Globe University in Woodbury, MN.

Globe University-Middleton (G)

1345 Deming Way, Middleton WI 53562
Telephone: (608) 830-6900 Identification: 770805
Accreditation: ACICS

† Main campus is Globe University in Woodbury, MN.

Globe University-Wausau (H)

1480 County Road Xx, Rothschild WI 54474
Telephone: (715) 301-1300 Identification: 770806
Accreditation: ACICS

† Main campus is Globe University in Woodbury, MN.

Herzing University (I)

5218 E Terrace Drive, Madison WI 53718-8340
County: Dane FICE Identification: 009621
Unit ID: 240392
Telephone: (608) 249-6611 Carnegie Class: Bac/Assoc
FAX Number: (608) 249-8593 Calendar System: Semester
URL: www.herzing.edu
Established: 1948 Annual Undergrad Tuition & Fees: $17,670
Enrollment: 743 Coed
Affiliation or Control: Proprietary IRS Status: Proprietary
Highest Offering: Master's
Program: Technical Emphasis
Accreditation: NH, ADNUR, MAAB, NURSE

01 President .... Ms. Renee HERZING
12 Campus President .... Mrs. Chris MONTAGNINO
10 CFO & Vice President of Finance .... Mr. Ryan O'DESKY
05 Academic Dean .... Mr. Brian WILLISON
37 Educational Funding Manager .... Mr. Clayton GROTH
32 Director of Student Services/Regist .... Ms. Carolyn KENT
07 Director of Admissions .... Ms. Jodi MERGENER
36 Director of Career Development .... Mr. Jeff WESTRA

Herzing University Brookfield Campus (J)

555 South Executive Drive, Brookfield WI 53005
Telephone: (262) 649-1710 Identification: 770429
Accreditation: &NH

† Main campus is Herzing University in Madison, WI.

Herzing University Kenosha Campus (K)

4006 Washington Road, Kenosha WI 53144
Telephone: (262) 671-0675 Identification: 770430
Accreditation: &NH, MAAB

† Main campus is Herzing University in Madison, WI.

Herzing University Online Campus (L)

W140N8917 Lilly Road, Menomonee Falls WI 53051
Telephone: (866) 508-0748 Identification: 770431
Accreditation: &NH, CAHIIM

† Main campus is Herzing University in Madison, WI.

ITT Technical Institute (M)

W177 N9886 RiverCrest Dr, Suite 200, Germantown WI 53022
Telephone: (262) 257-7100 Identification: 770665
Accreditation: ACICS

† Main campus is ITT Technical Institute in Indianapolis, IN.

ITT Technical Institute (N)

470 Security Boulevard, Green Bay WI 54313-9705
Telephone: (920) 662-9000 Identification: 666317
Accreditation: ACICS

† Main campus is ITT Technical Institute in Indianapolis, IN.

ITT Technical Institute (O)

6300 West Layton Avenue, Greenfield WI 53220-4612
Telephone: (414) 282-9494 FICE Identification: 030875
Accreditation: ACICS

† Main campus is ITT Technical Institute in Indianapolis, IN.

ITT Technical Institute (P)

2450 Rimrock Road, Suite 100, Madison WI 53713
Telephone: (608) 288-6301 Identification: 770666
Accreditation: ACICS

† Main campus is ITT Technical Institute in Indianapolis, IN.

Lac Courte Oreilles Ojibwa Community College (Q)

13466 W Trepania Road, Hayward WI 54843-2181
County: Sawyer FICE Identification: 025322
Unit ID: 260372
Telephone: (715) 634-4790 Carnegie Class: Tribal
FAX Number: (715) 634-5049 Calendar System: Semester
URL: www.lco.edu
Established: 1982 Annual Undergrad Tuition & Fees: $3,870
Enrollment: 535 Coed
Affiliation or Control: Tribal Control IRS Status: 501(c)3
Highest Offering: Associate Degree
Program: 2-Year Principally Bachelor's Creditable
Accreditation: NH, MAC

01 President .... Mr. Raymond BURNS
05 Interim Academic Dean .... Dr. Beth PAAP
32 Dean of Students .... Ms. Sarah BUTLER
10 Business Office Manager .... Ms. Gwen WELTER
06 Registrar .... Mrs. Annette WIGGINS
37 Financial Aid Director .... Ms. Jill MATCHETT
46 Office of Sponsored Programs .... Mr. Dan GETZ
15 Human Resource Director .... Ms. Shanna BURNS

Lakeland College (R)

PO Box 359, Sheboygan WI 53082-0359
County: Sheboygan FICE Identification: 003854
Unit ID: 238980
Telephone: (920) 565-1000 Carnegie Class: Master's L
FAX Number: (920) 565-1206 Calendar System: Semester
URL: www.lakeland.edu
Established: 1862 Annual Undergrad Tuition & Fees: $22,950
Enrollment: 3,769 Coed
Affiliation or Control: United Church Of Christ IRS Status: 501(c)3
Highest Offering: Master's
Program: Liberal Arts And General
Accreditation: NH, TEAC

01 President .... Mr. Dan W. ECK
04 Assistant to the President .... Ms. Ann M. FLAD-JESION
05 Vice Pres Academic Affairs .... Dr. Margaret L. ALBRINCK
30 Vice President for Advancement .... Dr. Kenneth D. STRMISKA
32 Vice President Student Development .... Mr. Nathan D. DEHNE
56 Vice Pres Kellett Adult Education .... Mr. Zach r. VOELZ
06 Registrar .... Ms. Erin K. KOHL
09 Director of Institutional Research .... Ms. Deb L. HAGEN-FOLEY
08 Director of Library Services .... Ms. Ann K. PENKE
07 Director of Admissions .... Mr. Nick A. SPAETH
37 Director of Financial Aid .... Ms. Patty L. TAYLOR
27 Director of Communications .... Mr. David D. GALLIANETTI
41 Interim Athletic Director .... Dr. April ARVAN
21 Controller .... Ms. Sharon L. ROOB
29 Director of Alumni Relations .... Ms. Lisa B. VIHOS
36 Director of Career Development .... Ms. Lisa M. STEPHAN
15 Director of Personnel Services .... Mr. Peter G. PLATTEN
18 Chief Facilities/Physical Plant .... Mr. Rich N. HAEN
38 Director of Student Counselling .... Dr. Carey A. KNIER

Lawrence University (S)

711 E. Boldt Way, Appleton WI 54911
County: Outagamie FICE Identification: 003856
Unit ID: 239017
Telephone: (920) 832-7000 Carnegie Class: Bac/A&S
FAX Number: (920) 832-6606 Calendar System: Other
URL: www.lawrence.edu
Established: 1847 Annual Undergrad Tuition & Fees: $41,226
Enrollment: 1,518 Coed
Affiliation or Control: Independent Non-Profit IRS Status: 501(c)3
Highest Offering: Baccalaureate
Program: Liberal Arts And General
Accreditation: NH, MUS

01 President .... Dr. Mark BURSTEIN
04 Executive Asst to the President .... Ms. Laurie PETRICK
05 Provost and Dean of the Faculty .... Dr. David BURROWS
10 VP Business & Operations .... Mr. Brian RISTE
30 VP Development/Alumni Rels .... Mr. Calvin D. HUSMANN
32 VP Student Affairs & Dean .... Ms. Nancy D. TRUESDELL
29 VP Alumni/Constituency Engagement .... Mr. Mark D. BRESEMAN
27 Assoc Vice Pres Communications .... Mr. Craig L. GAGNON
44 Assoc VP Major & Planned Giving .... Ms. Barbara J. STACK
30 Assoc Vice Pres Development .... Ms. Stacy J. MARA
21 Director Financial Services .... Ms. Elizabeth MILLER
64 Dean Conservatory of Music .... Mr. Brian G. PERTL
36 Dean of Career Services .... Ms. Mary T. MEANY
35 Dean Student Academic Services .... Mr. Geoff GAJEWSKI
20 Associate Dean of the Faculty .... Ms. Ruth M. LUNT
28 Asst Dean Students Multicul Affs .... Ms. Pa Lee MOUA
09 Director of Research Administration .... Dr. William F. SKINNER
07 Director of Admissions .... Mr. Kenneth L. ANSELMENT
37 Director of Financial Aid .... Ms. Sara C. HOLMAN
06 Registrar .... Ms. Anne S. NORMAN
08 Librarian .... Mr. Peter J. GILBERT
41 Athletic Director .... Mr. Michael W. SZKODZINSKI
13 Director Information Tech Svcs .... Mr. Steven M. ARMSTRONG
15 Director of Human Resources .... Ms. Sandy ISSELMANN
18 Director of Facility Services .... Mr. Daniel R. MEYER
38 Director Counseling Services .... Ms. Kathleen F. FUCHS

Madison Media Institute-College of Media Arts (T)

2702 Agriculture Drive, Madison WI 53718-6787
County: Dane FICE Identification: 010913
Unit ID: 364168
Telephone: (608) 663-2000 Carnegie Class: Assoc/PrivFP
FAX Number: (608) 442-0141 Calendar System: Semester
URL: www.mediainstitute.edu
Established: 1969 Annual Undergrad Tuition & Fees: $17,300
Enrollment: 488 Coed
Affiliation or Control: Proprietary IRS Status: Proprietary
Highest Offering: Baccalaureate
Program: 2-Year Principally Bachelor's Creditable; Technical Emphasis
Accreditation: ACCSC

01 President .... Mr. Donald G. MADELUNG
10 Chief Financial/Business Officer .... Mr. Kent SHEPLER
07 Admissions Director .... Mr. Francisco TORRES
53 Dean of Education .... Mr. Rich DENHART
36 Director Student Placement .... Ms. Laura MAEL

Maranatha Baptist Bible College & Seminary (U)

745 W Main Street, Watertown WI 53094-7600
County: Jefferson FICE Identification: 023172
Unit ID: 239071
Telephone: (920) 261-9300 Carnegie Class: Bac/Diverse
FAX Number: (920) 261-9109 Calendar System: Semester
URL: www.mbbc.edu
Established: 1968 Annual Undergrad Tuition & Fees: $13,120
Enrollment: 995 Coed
Affiliation or Control: Independent Non-Profit IRS Status: 501(c)3
Highest Offering: Master's
Program: Liberal Arts And General; Teacher Preparatory; Professional; Religious Emphasis

Accreditation: NH, NURSE

01 President ... Dr. Martin MARRIOTT
03 Executive Vice President ... Dr. Matthew DAVIS
05 Vice President for Academic Affairs ... Dr. John R. BROCK
30 Vice President for Inst Advancement ... Dr. Jim H. HARRISON
10 Vice President for Business Affairs ... Mr. Mark W. STEVENS
32 Dean of Students ... Mr. John DAVIS
06 Registrar ... Dr. Steve CARLSON
07 Director of Admissions ... Dr. James H. HARRISON
30 Director of Development ... Mr. Steve BOARD
09 Director of Institutional Research ... Dr. Matthew DAVIS
15 Director Personnel Services ... Mr. Kevin MONTNEY
18 Chief Facilities/Physical Plant ... Dr. Werner LUMM
26 Chief Public Relations Officer ... Mr. Peter WRIGHT
41 Athletic Director ... Mr. Robert THOMPSON
08 Librarian ... Mr. Mark HANSON
35 Director Student Affairs ... Mr. Peter HUBER
29 Director Alumni Relations ... Mr. John DAVIS
37 Director Student Financial Aid ... Mr. Randy HIBBS

Marian University (A)

45 S National Avenue, Fond Du Lac WI 54935-4699
County: Fond Du Lac
FICE Identification: 003861
Unit ID: 239080
Telephone: (920) 923-7600
Carnegie Class: Master's L
FAX Number: (920) 923-7154
Calendar System: Semester
URL: www.marianuniversity.edu
Established: 1936
Annual Undergrad Tuition & Fees: $24,720
Enrollment: 2,306
Coed
Affiliation or Control: Roman Catholic
IRS Status: 501(c)3
Highest Offering: Doctorate
Program: Liberal Arts And General; Teacher Preparatory; Professional
Accreditation: NH, IACBE, NURSE, RAD, SW, TED

01 Interim President ... Mr. Robert A. FALE
05 Exec VP Academic Affairs ... Dr. Edward H. OGLE
84 VP Enrollment Management ... Ms. Stacey L. AKEY
32 VP for Mission & Student Engagement ... Ms. Kate CANDEE
30 Vice President for Advancement ... Vacant
10 Dir Business & Finance/Controller ... Ms. Mary K. KOSMER
04 Executive Assistant to President ... Ms. Carey C. GARDIN
53 Dean School of Education ... Dr. Sue A. STODDART
66 Dean Nursing/Health Professions .. Dr. Julie A. LUETSCHWAGER
49 Dean Arts/Sciences ... Dr. James VAN DYKE
50 Dean Business/Public Safety ... Dr. Jeffrey G. REED
35 Dean of Student Engagement ... Mr. Paul KRIKAU
08 Director of Libraries ... Ms. Mary Ellen GORMICAN
55 Exec Dir Adult/Graduate Studies ... Vacant
18 General Manager/Facilities ... Mr. Artie L. GOLD
06 Registrar ... Ms. Cheryl A. TEICHMILLER
09 Director of Institutional Research ... Dr. Sylvia K. REED
37 Director of Financial Aid ... Ms. Pamela WARREN
42 Director of Campus Ministry ... Sr. Marie SCOTT, CSA
26 Director University Relations ... Ms. Lisa L. KIDD
29 Director Alumni Relations ... Ms. Mary SCHWINER
07 Dean of Admission ... Ms. Shannon S. LALUZERNE
16 Director of Human Resources ... Ms. Cathy T. FLOOD
41 Director of Athletics ... Mr. Jason J. MURPHY
88 Dean Advising/Academic Services ... Ms. Cathy M. MATHWEG
23 Director of Health Services ... Ms. Connie DIENER
36 Director Career & Grad School Svcs ... Ms. Ashly G. GARNER
88 Director of Campus Dining Services ... Ms. Nikki A. KRAMER
13 Director of Information Technology ... Mr. Keith L. FALK
40 Director of Bookstore ... Ms. Mary MANGAN-FLOOD
30 Director of Counseling ... Ms. Ellen MERCER
92 Director Honors Program ... Dr. Abbey E. ROSEN
108 Director of Inst Assessment ... Mr. Gregory M. CANARD
39 Director of Student Services ... Ms. Dee HARMSEN
104 Coordinator of Study Abroad ... Vacant
25 Director Research & Sponsored Grnts ... Mr. Marc D. HEIMERL

Marquette University (B)

PO Box 1881, Milwaukee WI 53201-1881
County: Milwaukee
FICE Identification: 003863
Unit ID: 239105
Telephone: (414) 288-7700
Carnegie Class: DRU
FAX Number: (414) 288-3300
Calendar System: Semester
URL: www.mu.edu
Established: 1881
Annual Undergrad Tuition & Fees: $34,200
Enrollment: 11,746
Coed
Affiliation or Control: Roman Catholic
IRS Status: 501(c)3
Highest Offering: Doctorate
Program: Liberal Arts And General; Teacher Preparatory; Professional
Accreditation: NH, ARCPA, BUS, BUSA, CLPSY, COPSY, DENT, ENG, JOUR, LAW, MIDWF, MT, NURSE, PTA, SP, TED, THEA

01 President ... Rev. Scott R. PILARZ, SJ
03 Executive Vice President ... Dr. Mary DISTANISLAO
05 Interim Provost ... Dr. Margaret CALLAHAN
10 Vice President Finance ... Mr. John C. LAMB
11 Vice President Administration ... Mr. Arthur F. SCHEUBER
32 Vice President for Student Affairs ... Dr. L. Christopher MILLER
30 Interim VP University Advancement . Mr. Thomas S. MACKINNON
27 Vice President Public Affairs ... Ms. Rana H. ALTENBURG
43 Vice President/General Counsel ... Ms. Cynthia M. BAUER
26 Interim VP Marketing/Communication ... Mr. David MURPHY
35 Assoc Vice Pres Student Affairs ... Dr. Linda J. LEE
15 Asst Vice Pres/Dir Human Resources ... Mr. Octavio CASTRO
39 Asst Vice Pres/Dean Residence Life ... Dr. James P. MCMAHON
88 Sr Assoc VP Development ... Mr. Timothy RIPPINGER
20 Vice Prov Undergrad Pgms/Teaching ... Dr. Gary MEYER
58 V Prov Research/Dean Graduate Sch ... Dr. Jeanne HOSSENLOPP
90 Assoc Vice Prov Educational Tech ... Mr. G. Jon PRAY
88 Assoc Vice Prov Acad Support Pgm ... Ms. Anne D. DEAHL
28 Associate Prov Diversity/Inclusion ... Dr. William WELBURN
06 Registrar ... Ms. Georgia D. MCRAE
49 Dean of Arts & Sciences ... Dr. Richard HOLZ
50 Interim Dean of Business Admin ... Dr. Mark EPPLI
52 Dean of Dentistry ... Dr. William K. LOBB
54 Dean of Engineering ... Dr. Robert BISHOP
60 Dean of Communication ... Dr. Lori BERGEN
76 Dean of Health Sciences ... Dr. William CULLINAN
61 Dean of the Law School ... Mr. Joseph D. KEARNEY
66 Dean of Nursing ... Dr. Margaret CALLAHAN
53 Dean College of Education ... Dr. William A. HENK
107 Dean Col of Professional Studies ... Dr. Robert J. DEAHL
08 Dean of Libraries ... Ms. Janice WELBURN
07 Dean of Admissions ... Mr. Robert BLUST
35 Dean of Students ... Dr. Stephanie QUADE
25 Exec Director of Research Support ... Ms. Katherine DURBEN
104 Dir Office International Education ... Mr. Terence MILLER
37 Director of Financial Aid ... Ms. Susan M. TEERINK
36 Director Career Services Center ... Ms. Laura F. KESTNER
41 VP and Director of Athletics ... Mr. Lawrence WILLIAMS
23 Exec Dir Student Health Services ... Dr. Carolyn S. SMITH
38 Director of Counseling Center ... Dr. Michael J. ZEBROWSKI
42 Vice Pres of Univ Mission/Ministry ... Dr. Stephanie J. RUSSELL
13 Chief Information Officer ... Ms. Kathy J. LANG
18 Director Facilities Services ... Mr. Ronald L. RIPLEY
19 Director Public Safety ... Mr. Lawrence R. RICKARD
40 Director Marquette Spirit Shop ... Mr. James K. GRAEBERT
96 Director of Purchasing ... Ms. Jenny ALEXANDER
29 Exec Director of Alumni Association ... Mr. Timothy J. SIMMONS

Medical College of Wisconsin (C)

PO Box 26509, Milwaukee WI 53226-0509
County: Milwaukee
FICE Identification: 024535
Unit ID: 239169
Telephone: (414) 955-8296
Carnegie Class: Spec/Med
FAX Number: (414) 955-6560
Calendar System: Other
URL: www.mcw.edu
Established: 1893
Annual Graduate Tuition & Fees: $49,180
Enrollment: 1,209
Coed
Affiliation or Control: Independent Non-Profit
IRS Status: 501(c)3
Highest Offering: Doctorate; No Undergraduates
Program: Professional
Accreditation: NH, DENT, MED, PDPSY, PH

01 President & CEO ... Dr. John R. RAYMOND, SR.
05 Dean/Executive Vice President ... Dr. Joseph E. KERSCHNER
10 Sr Vice Pres Finance/Administration ... Mr. Glenn Allen BOLTON, JR.
88 Dean Grad Sch Biomedical Science ... Dr. Ravi P. MISRA
30 Vice Pres Institutional Advancement ... Mr. James W. HEALD
15 Vice President Human Resources ... Ms. Sherri DUCHARME-WHITE
86 Vice Pres Government/Community Affs ... Ms. Kathryn A. KUHN
28 VP Corporate Compliance Risk Mgmt ... Mr. Daniel WICKEHAM
100 Chief of Staff ... Ms. Mara LORD
44 Assoc Vice President Development ... Ms. Pamela J. GARVEY
26 Assoc Vice Pres Public Affairs ... Mr. Richard N. KATSCHKE
20 Int Sr Assoc Dean for Academic Affs ... Dr. Kenneth B. SIMONS
22 Sr Asc Dean Faculty Affs/Diversity ... Dr. Alonzo P. WALKER
32 Assoc Dean for Student Affairs ... Dr. Richard L. HOLLOWAY
63 Assoc Dean Graduate Med Educ ... Dr. Kenneth B. SIMONS
46 Senior Associate Dean Research ... Dr. David D. GUTTERMAN
20 Associate Dean Curriculum ... Dr. Philip N. REDLICH
45 Assoc Dean Educ Support/Evaluation ... Vacant
21 Director Budget Administration ... Ms. Deidre ERWIN
13 Director Application Development ... Ms. Rebecca L. MORRISON
08 Director Medical Libraries ... Ms. Mary B. BLACKWELDER
07 Director Admissions ... Ms. Jennifer L. HALUZAK
06 Registrar ... Ms. Lesley A. MACK
18 Dir Facil Engineering/Maintenance ... Mr. Jeffrey BORNEMANN
37 Director Student Financial Services ... Ms. Linda L. PASCHAL
25 Director Grants & Contracts ... Ms. April HAVERTY
29 Exec Director Alumni Relations ... Mr. William A. SCHULTZ
21 Director Business Services ... Ms. Paulette PECARD
88 Medical Dir Clinical Informatics ... Dr. Rick D. GILLIS
40 Manager of Bookstore ... Ms. Cathy GRANFIELD

Midwest College of Oriental Medicine (D)

6232 Bankers Road, Racine WI 53403-9747
County: Racine
FICE Identification: 030612
Unit ID: 383020
Telephone: (800) 593-2320
Carnegie Class: Spec/Health
FAX Number: (262) 554-7475
Calendar System: Quarter
URL: www.acupuncture.edu
Established: 1979
Annual Undergrad Tuition & Fees: $15,751
Enrollment: 218
Coed
Affiliation or Control: Proprietary
IRS Status: Proprietary
Highest Offering: Master's; No Lower Division
Program: Professional
Accreditation: ACUP

01 President ... Dr. William J. DUNBAR
05 Academic Director ... Dr. Robert CHELNICK
20 Academic Dean/Research Director ... Dr. Alan URETZ
88 Projects Director ... Dr. Kristine L. LA POINT
37 Director of Financial Aid ... Ms. Elizabeth M. HOJAN
07 Admissions Coord/Transfer Credit ... Mr. Lawrence PILOCZEWSKI
06 Records Officer/Registrar ... Ms. Amy L. BENISH
08 Dean of Students/Librarian ... Mr. John BALLARINI
32 Dean of Students ... Ms. Olga GAJDOSIK
09 Research Director ... Mr. Jin Hua XIE
63 Dean of Biomedicine Science ... Dr. Peter NIKAS
85 Dean of Foreign Students ... Dr. Duckin SUH
17 Internship Director ... Dr. Helen WU
09 Clinic Tracking/Inst Evaluation ... Ms. Deirdre M. DUNBAR
86 Compliance Officer ... Mr. Harry S. HEIFETZ
91 Information Systems ... Mr. William H. LEHMAN
26 Marketing/Student Affairs ... Mr. Chris A. KRAJNIAK
88 Office Manager ... Ms. Stephanie M. PITTMAN

Milwaukee Career College (E)

3077 North Maryfair Rd #300, Milwaukee WI 53222
County: Milwaukee
FICE Identification: 041174
Unit ID: 449861
Telephone: (414) 257-2939
Carnegie Class: Not Classified
FAX Number: (414) 727-9557
Calendar System: Other
URL: www.mkecc.edu
Established: 2002
Annual Undergrad Tuition & Fees: $129,600
Enrollment: 61
Coed
Affiliation or Control: Proprietary
IRS Status: Proprietary
Highest Offering: Associate Degree
Program: Occupational
Accreditation: ABHES

01 President ... Jack TAKAHASHI

Milwaukee Institute of Art & Design (F)

273 E Erie Street, Milwaukee WI 53202-6003
County: Milwaukee
FICE Identification: 020771
Unit ID: 239309
Telephone: (414) 847-3200
Carnegie Class: Spec/Arts
FAX Number: (414) 291-8077
Calendar System: Semester
URL: www.miad.edu
Established: 1974
Annual Undergrad Tuition & Fees: $30,704
Enrollment: 720
Coed
Affiliation or Control: Independent Non-Profit
IRS Status: 501(c)3
Highest Offering: Baccalaureate
Program: Liberal Arts And General; Fine Arts Emphasis
Accreditation: NH, ART

01 President ... Mr. Neil J. HOFFMAN
05 VP of Academic Affairs ... Mr. David MARTIN
84 VP for Enrollment Management ... Ms. Mary C. SCHOPP
04 Executive Assistant to President ... Ms. Dagmar L. CARNDUFF
09 Assoc VP Academic Plng/Assessment ... Ms. Cynthia LYNCH
10 Chief Financial Officer ... Ms. Brenda JONES
32 Dean of Students ... Mr. Tony J. NOWAK
37 Executive Director of Financial Aid ... Ms. Carol MASSE
07 Executive Director of Admissions ... Ms. Stacey STEINBERG
30 Director of Development ... Mr. Ryan DANIELS
26 Director of Communications ... Ms. Vivian M. ROTHSCHILD
08 Director of Library Services ... Ms. Cynthia D. LYNCH
36 Director of Career Services ... Mr. Duane P. SEIDENSTICKER
51 Dir Pre-College & Adult Learning ... Ms. Jill F. KUNSMANN
19 Director Security/Safety ... Mr. Keith A. KOTOWICZ
06 Director of Registration Services ... Ms. Jean WEIMER
38 Director of College Advising ... Ms. Rebecca BALISTRERI
29 Dir Cultural & Alumni Relations ... Ms. Melissa RICHARDS
15 Director of Human Resources ... Ms. Edie MCCLELLAN
20 Director of Academic Operations ... Ms. Marie KAMINSKI
18 Building Maintenance Manager ... Mr. Michael A. GOETZ

Milwaukee School of Engineering (G)

1025 N Broadway, Milwaukee WI 53202-3109
County: Milwaukee
FICE Identification: 003868
Unit ID: 239318
Telephone: (414) 277-7300
Carnegie Class: Master's S
FAX Number: (414) 277-7454
Calendar System: Quarter
URL: www.msoe.edu
Established: 1903
Annual Undergrad Tuition & Fees: $32,880
Enrollment: 2,564
Coed
Affiliation or Control: Independent Non-Profit
IRS Status: 501(c)3
Highest Offering: Master's
Program: Professional; Technical Emphasis
Accreditation: NH, CONST, ENG, ENGT, NURSE, PERF

01 President ... Dr. Hermann VIETS
05 Vice President Academics ... Dr. Fred BERRY
10 Vice President of Finance and CFO ... Ms. Dawn THIBEDEAU
30 Vice President of Development ... Mr. A. Frank HABIB
18 Director Of Operations ... Mr. Kevin MORIN
32 Vice President Student Life ... Mr. Patrick J. COFFEY
84 Vice Pres of Enrollment Management ... Mr. Timothy VALLEY
09 Dean of Institutional Research ... Mr. Leonard A. VANDEN BOOM
25 Dean Grants & Projects ... Mr. Thomas E. BRAY
48 Chair Architectural Engr Dept ... Dr. Deborah JACKMAN
50 Chair School of Business ... Mr. Steve BIALEK
54 Chair Electrical Engr/CPU Sci Dept ... Dr. Stephen WILLIAMS
97 Chair General Studies Department ... Dr. David KENT
81 Chair Mathematics Department ... Dr. Karl H. DAVID
54 Chair Mechanical Engineering Dept ... Dr. Matthew A. PANHANS
81 Chair Physics/Chemistry Dept ... Dr. Matey KALTCHEV

66 Chair Nursing Department .... Dr. Debra JENKS
21 Controller .... Ms. Janda VAVRICKA
06 Registrar .... Ms. Mary F. NIELSEN
26 Director Marketing Public Affairs .... Ms. Sandra L. EVERTS
27 Director Public & Media Relations .... Ms. JoEllen BURDUE
15 Director of Human Resources .... Mr. Kevin A. MORIN
37 Director of Financial Aid .... Mr. Steve MIDTHUN
21 Director of Student Accounts .... Ms. Debra A. DANNECKER
44 Director of Development .... Mr. Jonathan V. KOWALSKI, JR.
38 Director of Counseling .... Mr. Joseph P. MELOY
88 Director Learning Resource Center .... Mr. Brian E. BURKE
35 Director Student Activities .... Mr. Richard GAGLIANO
39 Director Residence Halls .... Dr. William E. BREESE
41 Director Athletics .... Mr. Dan I. HARRIS
08 Director of Library & Info Services .... Mr. Gary S. SHIMEK
105 Director of Services/Webmaster .... Mr. Kent A. PETERSON
19 Director of Public Safety .... Mr. William P. FADROWSKI
88 Director Fluid Power Institute .... Mr. Tom S. WANKE
29 Director Alumni Affairs .... Ms. Cathy VAREBROOK
13 Dir Computer/Communications Svcs .... Vacant
07 Director of Admissions .... Ms. Dana GRENNIER
36 Director Student Placement .... Ms. Mary SPENCER
88 Asst Director of Student Life .... Mr. Nick SEIDLER
40 Bookstore Manager .... Mr. David P. ABRAHAMSON

Mount Mary University (A)

2900 N Menomonee River Parkway,
Milwaukee WI 53222-4597

County: Milwaukee | FICE Identification: 003869 | Unit ID: 239390
Telephone: (414) 258-4810 | Carnegie Class: Master's S
FAX Number: (414) 256-1224 | Calendar System: Semester
URL: www.mtmary.edu
Established: 1913 | Annual Undergrad Tuition & Fees: $24,848
Enrollment: 1,640 | Female
Affiliation or Control: Roman Catholic | IRS Status: 501(c)3
Highest Offering: Doctorate
Program: Liberal Arts And General; Teacher Preparatory; Professional
Accreditation: NH, CIDA, DIETC, DIETI, OT, SW

01 President .... Dr. Eileen SCHWALBACH
05 Acting VP Academic/Student Affairs .... Dr. Karen FRIEDLEN
10 Vice Pres Finance & Administration .... Mr. Reyes GONZALEZ
84 Vice Pres Enrollment Services .... Mr. David WEGENER
26 VP Communications/Comm Engage .... Ms. Lynn SPRANGERS
30 Sr Director of Univ Advancement .... Ms. Angela MANCUSO
88 Vice President Mission/ Identity .... Sr. Joan PENZENSTADLER, SSND
20 Acting Dean Academic Affairs .... Dr. Wendy WEAVER
32 Acting Dean Student Affairs .... Ms. Nicole GAHAGAN
58 Dean ofGraduate Education .... Dr. Doug MICKELSON
66 Dean Nursing Program .... Dr. Jill WINTERS
88 Exec Dir Women's Leadership Inst .... Ms. Beth WNUK
21 Controller .... Ms. Mary REEVES
06 Registrar .... Dr. Mary KARR
44 Annual Giving Officer .... Ms. Courtney MEYER
27 Senior Dir of Mktg/Public Relations .... Ms. Susan SEILER
29 Senior Dir of Alumnae Engage .... Ms. Susan NIEBERLE
07 Director of Graduate Admission .... Ms. Judy BORAWSKI
07 Director of Undergraduate Admission .... Ms. Rachel SONNENTAG
09 Director of Inst Research .... Dr. Jill MEYER
08 Director of Library .... Mr. Eric ROBINSON
13 Director of Information Technology .... Mr. Praveen KRISHNAMURTI
37 Director Financial Aid .... Ms. Debra DUFF
35 Director of Student Engagement .... Ms. Amy DANIELSON
39 Director of Residence Life .... Ms. Beth SCHOENWETTER
36 Dir of Advising/Career Development .... Ms. Michelle SMALLEY
104 Director of International Studies .... Ms. Nan METZGER
15 Director of Human Resources .... Vacant
41 Athletic Director .... Vacant
42 Director of Campus Ministry .... Ms. Lea ROSENBERG
18 Director of Buildings & Grounds .... Mr. Barry BRANDENBURG
19 Director of Security .... Mr. Paul LESHOK
40 Mgr Barnes & Noble Bookstore .... Ms. Whitney BAUMGARTEN
105 Website and Photo Manager .... Ms. Eichelle THOMPSON
04 Executive Assistant to President .... Ms. Pamela SALOUN

Nashotah House (B)

2777 Mission Road, Nashotah WI 53058-9793

County: Waukesha | FICE Identification: 003874 | Unit ID: 239424
Telephone: (262) 646-6500 | Carnegie Class: Spec/Faith
FAX Number: (262) 646-6504 | Calendar System: Semester
URL: www.nashotah.edu
Established: 1842 | Annual Graduate Tuition & Fees: $11,850
Enrollment: 145 | Coed
Affiliation or Control: Protestant Episcopal | IRS Status: 501(c)3
Highest Offering: Doctorate; No Undergraduates
Program: Professional; Religious Emphasis
Accreditation: THEOL

01 President & Dean .... Rt Rev. Edward L. SALMON
04 Dean's Office Administrator .... Mrs. Sandy MILLS
11 Associate Dean of Administration .... Mr. Ryan R. DELANEY
05 Associate Dean for Academic Affairs .... Rev. Steven A. PEAY
32 Assoc Dean Student Affs/Dir Admiss .... Dr. Carol K. KLUKAS
08 Library Director .... Mr. David G. SHERWOOD
30 Dir Development & Alumni Relations .... Mr. Charleston D. WILSON
18 Chief Facilities/Physical Plant .... Mr. Rich BRAZELTON
40 Bookstore Director .... Vacant
07 Director of Student Recruitment .... Mrs. Sarah PROSSER
106 Director of Distance Learning .... Rev. Tony BLEYTHING
06 Registrar .... Mrs. Sarah POKORNY

National-Louis University Milwaukee/Beloit Campus (C)

12000 W Park Place, Suite 100,
Milwaukee WI 53224-3007

Telephone: (414) 577-2658 | Identification: 770088
Accreditation: &NH

† Main campus is National-Louis University in Chicago, IL.

Northland College (D)

1411 Ellis Avenue, Ashland WI 54806-3999

County: Ashland | FICE Identification: 003875 | Unit ID: 239512
Telephone: (715) 682-1699 | Carnegie Class: Bac/A&S
FAX Number: (715) 682-1308 | Calendar System: Other
URL: www.northland.edu
Established: 1892 | Annual Undergrad Tuition & Fees: $29,990
Enrollment: 575 | Coed
Affiliation or Control: United Church Of Christ | IRS Status: 501(c)3
Highest Offering: Baccalaureate
Program: Liberal Arts And General; Teacher Preparatory
Accreditation: NH

01 President .... Dr. Michael MILLER
05 Vice President of Academic Affairs .... Ms. Cheryl CONTANT
30 VP of Institutional Advancement .... Mr. Scott SHRODE
10 VP Finance & Administration .... Mr. Robert JACKSON
84 VP of Inst Marketing & Enroll Mgmt .... Mr. Rick SMITH
32 VP of Stdnt Affairs & Inst Sustain .... Ms. Michele MEYER
88 Exec Director Environmental Inst .... Mr. Mark PETERSON
88 Exec Director of Development .... Ms. Kristy LIPHART
20 Associate Academic Dean .... Mr. Alan BREW
07 Director of Admissions .... Mr. Teege METTILLE
06 Registrar .... Ms. Kathy TRAYNOR
08 Library Director .... Ms. Julia WAGGONER
29 Director of Alumni Relations .... Ms. Michelle CHASE
13 Information Service Manager .... Mr. Todd PYDO
41 Athletic Director .... Mr. William WILSON
15 Director Human Resources .... Mr. Paul SKORACZEWSKI
18 Director of Facilities .... Mr. Thomas HMIELEWSKI
37 Director of Student Financial Aid .... Ms. Heather SHELLY
21 Controller .... Ms. Lori BENNETTS
44 Director of Annual Giving .... Ms. Carrie SLATER-DUFFY
09 Institutional Research Specialist .... Ms. Petra HOFSTEDT
04 Exec Assistant to the President .... Ms. Lisa MCGINLEY
39 Director of Residential Life .... Mr. Jared FRIESEN
42 Campus Minister .... Mr. David SAETRE
25 Director of Grant Dev and Admin .... Ms. Lisa WILLIAMSON
26 Int Director of Inst Marketing .... Mr. Bob GROSS

Northland International University (E)

W10085 Pike Plains Road, Dunbar WI 54119-9285

County: Marinette | FICE Identification: 038725 | Unit ID: 239503
Telephone: (715) 324-6900 | Carnegie Class: Bac/Diverse
FAX Number: (715) 324-6214 | Calendar System: Semester
URL: www.ni.edu
Established: 1976 | Annual Undergrad Tuition & Fees: $13,380
Enrollment: 493 | Coed
Affiliation or Control: Baptist | IRS Status: 501(c)3
Highest Offering: Doctorate
Program: 2-Year Principally Bachelor's Creditable; Teacher Preparatory; Professional; Religious Emphasis
Accreditation: TRACS

01 President .... Vacant
05 Vice President Academic Affairs/CAO .... Dr. Antone GOYAK
10 Vice Pres Financial Affairs/CFO .... Vacant
11 Vice Pres Operational Affairs/COO .... Mr. Hugh MCCOY
32 Vice President Student Affairs .... Mr. Hugh MCCOY
06 Registrar .... Dr. Kevin PRIEST
07 Admissions Director .... Mr. Trevor GEARHART
09 Dir Institutional Effectiveness .... Vacant
37 Director Student Financial Aid .... Mrs. Mandy MCLAIN
08 Head Librarian .... Mr. Van CARPENTER
41 Athletic Director .... Mr. Michael MCCARTY

Ottawa University Wisconsin (F)

245 South Executive Drive, Brookfield WI 53005-4204

Telephone: (262) 879-0200 | Identification: 666084
Accreditation: &NH

† Main campus is Ottawa University in Ottawa, KS.

Rasmussen College - Appleton (G)

3500 E. Destination Drive, Appleton WI 54915

Telephone: (920) 750-5900 | Identification: 667059
Accreditation: &NH, MAAB

† Main campus is Rasmussen College - St. Cloud in Saint Cloud, MN.

Rasmussen College - Green Bay (H)

904 South Taylor Street, Suite 100, Green Bay WI 54303

Telephone: (920) 593-8400 | Identification: 667063
Accreditation: &NH, CAHIIM, MAC, MLTAD

† Main campus is Rasmussen College - St. Cloud in Saint Cloud, MN.

Rasmussen College - Wausau (I)

1101 Westwood Drive, Wausau WI 54401

Telephone: (715) 841-8000 | Identification: 667068
Accreditation: &NH, MAAB

† Main campus is Rasmussen College - St. Cloud in Saint Cloud, MN.

Ripon College (J)

300 West Seward Street, PO Box 248,
Ripon WI 54971-0248

County: Fond du Lac | FICE Identification: 003884 | Unit ID: 239628
Telephone: (920) 748-8115 | Carnegie Class: Bac/A&S
FAX Number: (920) 748-7243 | Calendar System: Semester
URL: www.ripon.edu
Established: 1851 | Annual Undergrad Tuition & Fees: $31,602
Enrollment: 904 | Coed
Affiliation or Control: Independent Non-Profit | IRS Status: 501(c)3
Highest Offering: Baccalaureate
Program: Liberal Arts And General; Teacher Preparatory
Accreditation: NH

01 President .... Zachariah P. MESSITTE
04 Admin Asst to President .... Danielle FICEK
05 Vice President & Dean of Faculty .... Gerald E. SEAMAN
30 Vice President for Advancement .... Wayne P. WEBSTER
10 Interim Vice President for Finance .... Lori A. SCHULZE
32 Vice President Dean of Students .... Christophor M. OGLE
84 Vice President for Enrollment .... Jennifer MACHACEK
06 Assoc Dean of Faculty/Registrar .... Michele A. WITTLER
36 Assoc Dean Students/Dir Career Dev .... Thomas M. VAUBEL
88 Exec Dir Ethical Leadership Program .... Lindsay A. BLUMER
07 Dean of Admissions .... Leigh D. MLODZIK
21 Controller .... Lori A. SCHULZE
08 User Services Librarian .... Andrew R. PRELLWITZ
35 Dir Student Activities/Orientation .... Melissa L. BEMUS
88 Director Student Support Svcs .... Daniel J. KRHIN
39 Director of Residence Life .... Jessica L. JOANIS
26 Dir Publication/Institutional Image .... Richard T. DAMM
26 Exec Dir Marketing & Communications .... Melissa K. ANDERSON
44 Director of Development-Major Gifts .... Larry P. MALCHOW
14 Dir Information Technology Services .... Ronald I. HAEFNER
88 General Manager Food Service .... Sarjit SINGH
18 Director Physical Plant .... Brian SKAMRA
41 Director of Athletics .... Julie H. JOHNSON
102 Dir Foundation & Gov Relations .... Terri L. HOLZMAN
44 Director Annual Fund .... Nancy L. HINTZ
29 Dir of Alumni & Parent Rels Pgms .... Amy L. GERRETSEN
15 Human Resource Administrator .... Jennifer FRANZ
38 Director of Counseling Services .... Cynthia S. VIERTEL
40 Bookstore Manager .... Rose OLKIEWICZ

Sacred Heart School of Theology (K)

7335 S Highway 100, Box 429,
Hales Corners WI 53130-0429

County: Milwaukee | FICE Identification: 020780 | Unit ID: 239637
Telephone: (414) 425-8300 | Carnegie Class: Spec/Faith
FAX Number: (414) 529-6999 | Calendar System: Semester
URL: www.shst.edu
Established: 1933 | Annual Graduate Tuition & Fees: $15,750
Enrollment: 147 | Coed
Affiliation or Control: Roman Catholic | IRS Status: 501(c)3
Highest Offering: Master's; No Undergraduates
Program: Professional; Religious Emphasis
Accreditation: NH, THEOL

01 President-Rector .... Msgr. Ross A. SHECTERLE
10 VP Finance .... Ms. Sally A. SMITS
03 Vice Rector .... Vacant
05 VP Intellectual Formation .... Dr. Patrick J. RUSSELL
42 VP Human Formation .... Rev. Stephen MALKIEWICZ, OFM
20 VP Pastoral Formation .... Rev. Donald LOSKOT, SDS
88 Vice Pres for Spiritual Formation .... Rev. Paul KELLY, SCJ
08 Director Acad Information Services .... Ms. Susanna PATHAK
07 Vice President of External Affairs .... Rev. Javier BUSTOS
06 Registrar .... Ms. Rose M. KOPENEC
26 Director Communications .... Mr. Jonathan DRAYNA
18 Director Plant Operations .... Mr. Michael J. ERATO
04 Executive Asst to President-Rector .... Ms. Josephine A. CALCAGNINO
13 Information Systems Coordinator .... Mr. Thomas WEIS

Saint Norbert College (L)

100 Grant Street, De Pere WI 54115-2099

County: Brown | FICE Identification: 003892 | Unit ID: 239716
Telephone: (920) 403-3181 | Carnegie Class: Bac/A&S
FAX Number: (920) 403-4008 | Calendar System: Semester
URL: www.snc.edu
Established: 1898 | Annual Undergrad Tuition & Fees: $31,866

Enrollment: 2,223 Coed
Affiliation or Control: Roman Catholic IRS Status: 501(c)3
Highest Offering: Master's
Program: Liberal Arts And General; Teacher Preparatory; Professional
Accreditation: NH

01 President .... Mr. Thomas KUNKEL
05 Vice Pres Acad Affs/Dean of Col .... Dr. Jeffrey FRICK
10 Vice President Business & Finance .... Ms. Eileen JAHNKE
30 Vice Pres Institutional Advancement .... Mr. Phil OSWALD
32 Vice Pres Mission & Student Affairs .... Rev. Jay J. FOSTNER
84 Vice Pres Enrollment Mgmt/Comm .... Mr. Edward LAMM
44 Assoc Vice Pres Inst Advancement .... Mr. Patrick WAGNER
09 Assoc VP Institutional Effective .... Dr. Ray ZURAWSKI
20 Associate Academic Dean .... Dr. Kevin QUINN
36 Director Career Services .... Ms. Mandy NYCZ
35 Associate Dean Student Life .... Vacant
38 Dir Counseling/Career Programs .... Mr. Bruce ROBERTSON
07 Exec Director of Admissions .... Vacant
29 Director Alumni & Parent Relations .... Mr. Todd DANEN
21 Director of Finance .... Mr. Curt KOWALESKI
37 Director of Financial Aid .... Mr. Jeffrey A. ZAHN
26 Director Communications/Marketing .... Mr. Drew VAN FOSSEN
08 Director of Library .... Dr. Kristin D. VOGEL
15 Director Human Resources .... Mr. Gary A. UMHOEFER
41 Director Physical Educ/Athletics .... Mr. Tim BALD
06 Registrar .... Mr. Richard L. GUILD
14 Dir Technology Support Services .... Ms. Raechelle CLEMMONS
104 Director of VIE & Study Abroad .... Vacant
28 Dir Multicultural Student Services .... Ms. Bridgit MARTIN
18 Director Facilities/Physical Plant .... Mr. John J. BARNES
40 Manager Bookstore Operations .... Ms. Monica WITTROCK

Silver Lake College of the Holy Family (A)

2406 S Alverno Road, Manitowoc WI 54220-9319
County: Manitowoc FICE Identification: 003850
Unit ID: 239743
Telephone: (920) 684-6691 Carnegie Class: Bac/Diverse
FAX Number: (920) 684-7082 Calendar System: Semester
URL: www.sl.edu
Established: 1935 Annual Undergrad Tuition & Fees: $22,950
Enrollment: 655 Coed
Affiliation or Control: Roman Catholic IRS Status: 501(c)3
Highest Offering: Master's
Program: Liberal Arts And General; Teacher Preparatory; Professional
Accreditation: NH, MUS, NURSE

01 President .... Dr. Chris E. DOMES
05 VP Academic Affs/Dean Faculty .... Ms. Vicki ANSORGE
10 VP of Finance & Business .... Ms. Debra WIGAND
32 VP Admissions/Stdnt Life/Dean Stdts .... Dr. Julie MAYROSE
30 VP Advancement/External Relations .... Mr. Jake CZARNIK-NEIMEYER
42 Director of Campus Ministry .... Mr. Tommy NELSON
06 Registrar .... Ms. Rachel FISCHER
08 Head Librarian .... Sr. Ritarose STAHL
37 Director Student Financial Aid .... Ms. Jodi POPP
29 Director Alumni/Parent Relations .... Mr. Dan CONNOLLY
18 Director of Facilities .... Mr. Dale FETTERER
13 Director Technology Services .... Mr. Joe PUTMAN
15 Director Human Resources .... Ms. Jan GRAUNKE
36 Dir Career Res/Experiential Lrng .... Ms. Jan L. ALGOZINE
21 Associate Business Officer .... Ms. Melissa DIENER
26 Director Marketing/Communications .... Ms. Carrie KOST
20 Associate Academic Officer .... Dr. Erik HOYER
09 Director of Institutional Research .... Ms. Kim BARRON
28 Director of Diversity .... Ms. Julie KAUTZER
19 Director of Campus Security .... Mr. Randy AMMERMAN
44 Director of Annual Fund/Major Gifts .... Ms. Roxanna STRAWN
07 Director of Admissions/Traditional .... Ms. Jamie GRANT
07 Director of Admissions/Adult Market .... Ms. Cynthia ST. JOHN
41 Athletic Director .... Mr. Mike FLENTJE
35 Director Student Affairs .... Ms. Jessica EHMLER

University of Phoenix Milwaukee Main Campus (B)

10850 West Park Place, Suite 150,
Milwaukee WI 53224-3606
Telephone: (414) 410-7900 Identification: 770235
Accreditation: &NH

† Main campus is University of Phoenix in Tempe, AZ.

*University of Wisconsin System (C)

1220 Linden Dr, 1720 Van Hise Hall,
Madison WI 53706-1559
County: Dane FICE Identification: 003894
Unit ID: 240435
Telephone: (608) 262-2321 Carnegie Class: N/A
FAX Number: (608) 262-3985
URL: www.wisconsin.edu

01 President .... Kevin P. REILLY
05 Sr Vice Pres Academic Affairs .... Mark NOOK
11 Sr VP Administration/Fiscal Affairs .... David MILLER
10 Vice President Finance .... Deborah A. DURCAN
16 Associate Vice Pres Human Resources .... Alan N. CRIST
09 Assoc VP Policy Analysis/Research .... Heather H. KIM
91 Int Assoc VP Learning/Inform Tech .... Lori DOCKEN
45 Assoc VP Budget & Planning .... Freda J. HARRIS
43 General Counsel .... Tomas L. STAFFORD

*University of Wisconsin-Madison (D)

500 Lincoln Drive, Madison WI 53706-1380
County: Dane FICE Identification: 003895
Unit ID: 240444
Telephone: (608) 262-1234 Carnegie Class: RU/VH
FAX Number: (608) 262-0123 Calendar System: Semester
URL: www.wisc.edu
Established: 1848 Annual Undergrad Tuition & Fees (In-State): $10,378
Enrollment: 42,820 Coed
Affiliation or Control: State IRS Status: 501(c)3
Highest Offering: Doctorate
Program: Liberal Arts And General; Teacher Preparatory; Professional
Accreditation: NH, ARCPA, ART, AUD, BUS, BUSA, CIDA, CLPSY, COPSY, CORE, CYTO, DIETD, DMS, ENG, FOR, IPSY, LAW, LIB, LSAR, MED, MUS, NURSE, OT, PH, PHAR, PLNG, PTA, RAD, SCPSY, SP, SW, THEA, VET

02 Chancellor .... Dr. Rebecca BLANK
05 Provost Academic Affairs .... Dr. Paul M. DELUCA
11 Vice Chancellor Administration .... Mr. Darrell BAZZELL
13 CIO/Vice Provost Info Technology .... Mr. Bruce MAAS
43 Director of Admin Legal Services .... Vacant
100 Chancellor's Chief of Staff .... Ms. Becci MENGHINI
58 VC Research/Dean Graduate School .... Dr. Martin T. CADWALLADER
30 Vice Chanc University Relations .... Mr. Vince SWEENEY
84 Interim Vice Prov Enrollment Mgmt .... Mr. Steven HAHN
49 Dean College Letters & Science .... Dr. John K. SCHOLZ
63 Dean Medicine and Public Health .... Dr. Robert N. GOLDEN
53 Dean School of Education .... Dr. Julie K. UNDERWOOD
50 Dean School of Business .... Dr. Francois ORTALO-MAGNE'
67 Dean School of Pharmacy .... Dr. Jeanette C. ROBERTS
54 Dean of College of Engineering .... Dr. Ian ROBERTSON
32 Dean of Students .... Ms. Lori BERQUAM
47 Dean of Agricultural/Life Sciences .... Dr. Kathryn VANDENBOSCH
66 Dean of School of Nursing .... Dr. Katharyn A. MAY
59 Dean of Human Ecology .... Dr. Soyeon SHIM
74 Dean of Veterinary Medicine .... Dr. Mark D. MARKEL
61 Dean of the Law School .... Dr. Margaret RAYMOND
18 Assoc Vice Chanc Facil Plng/Mgmt .... Mr. William ELVEY
82 Int Dean International Studies .... Dr. Guido PODESTÁ
88 Int Director Environmental Studies .... Dr. Paul ROBBINS
41 Director Intercollegiate Athletics .... Mr. Barry L. ALVAREZ
88 Director of Physical Plant .... Mr. John HARROD
88 Director of Arboretum .... Mr. Kevin D. MCSWEENEY
88 Director State Lab of Hygiene .... Dr. Charles BROKOPP
88 Director of Wisconsin Union .... Mr. Mark C. GUTHIER
07 Director of Admissions .... Ms. Adele BRUMFIELD
08 Director of Libraries .... Mr. Edward VANGEMERT
26 Director University Communications .... Ms. Amy TOBUREN
102 President UW Foundation .... Dr. Michael M. KNETTER
29 Director of Alumni Association .... Ms. Paula E. BONNER
37 Director Student Financial Services .... Ms. Susan FISCHER
38 Director of Counseling Services .... Dr. Danielle OAKLEY
16 Director Human Resources .... Mr. Robert LAVIGNA
39 Director of University Housing .... Mr. Paul N. EVANS
51 Dean Continuing Studies .... Dr. Jeffrey RUSSELL
19 Director of University Police .... Ms. Susan RISELING
88 Director of Archives .... Mr. David NULL
28 Vice Provost Diversity and Climate .... Vacant
20 Assoc Vice Chanc Faculty/Staff Pgms .... Dr. Steve STERN
23 Director University Health Service .... Dr. Sarah A. VAN ORMAN
88 Assoc Vice Chanc Teaching/Learning .... Dr. Chris W. OLSEN
88 Director of Space Management .... Mr. Douglas N. ROSE
17 President Hospital & Clinics .... Ms. Donna KATEN-BAHENSKY
21 Dir Auxiliary Operations Analysis .... Ms. Donna HALLERAN
10 Asst Vice Chanc Business Services .... Ms. Martha KERNER
88 Asst Vice Chanc Extended Pgms .... Mr. Peyton SMITH
25 Assoc Dean/Graduate/Research Svcs .... Mr. Petra SCHROEDER
06 Registrar .... Mr. Scott OWCZAREK
88 Secretary of the Faculty .... Ms. Andrea POEHLING
88 Secretary of Academic Staff .... Vacant
88 Director of Recreational Sports .... Mr. Dale CARRUTHERS
15 Director of Academic Personnel .... Mr. Stephen R. LUND
15 Director Classified Personnel .... Mr. Mark WALTERS
85 Director Intl Student Services .... Ms. Laurie COX
22 Dir Office of Equity & Diversity .... Mr. Luis A. PINERO
96 Director of Purchasing .... Mr. Michael R. HARDIMAN
09 Dir Instl Rsrch/Acad Plng/Analysis .... Dr. Jocelyn L. MILNER
88 Special Asst to Provost .... Dr. Eden INOWAY-RONNIE
86 Sr Special Asst to Chanc Fed Rels .... Ms. Rhonda D. NORSETTER

*University of Wisconsin-Eau Claire (E)

105 Garfield Avenue, PO Box 4004,
Eau Claire WI 54702-4004
County: Eau Claire FICE Identification: 003917
Unit ID: 240268
Telephone: (715) 836-2637 Carnegie Class: Master's M
FAX Number: (715) 836-2902 Calendar System: Semester
URL: www.uwec.edu
Established: 1916 Annual Undergrad Tuition & Fees (In-State): $8,786
Enrollment: 11,046 Coed
Affiliation or Control: State IRS Status: 501(c)3
Highest Offering: Doctorate
Program: Liberal Arts And General; Teacher Preparatory; Professional
Accreditation: NH, BUS, CS, JOUR, MUS, NURSE, SP, SW

02 Chancellor .... Dr. James C. SCHMIDT
05 Prov/Vice Chanc Academic Affairs .... Dr. Patricia A. KLEINE
10 Vice Chanc Administration/Finance .... Mr. David GESSNER
32 Vice Chanc Student Affairs .... Dr. Beth A. HELLWIG
46 Asst VC Research/Sponsored Pgm .... Dr. Karen G. HAVHOLM
18 Asst Chanc Facil/Univ Relations .... Mr. Michael J. RINDO
20 Assoc Vice Chanc Academic Affairs .... Dr. Michael R. WICK
97 Asc Vice Chanc Undergraduate Stds .... Dr. Robert KNIGHT
35 Associate Dean of Student Affairs .... Ms. Jodi THESING-RITTER
45 Dir Marketing/Comm/Strategic Plng .... Ms. Mary Jane BRUKARDT
22 Director of Affirmative Action .... Ms. Teresa O'HALLORAN
102 Pres UWEC Foundatn/Dir Univ Advanc .... Ms. Kimera WAY
32 Dean of Students .... Dr. Brian A. CARLISLE
07 Director of Admission .... Ms. Heather KRETZ
28 Director of Multicultural Affairs .... Mr. Jesse L. DIXON
08 Director of Libraries .... Mr. John H. POLLITZ
13 Dir Learning & Technology Services .... Mr. Craig A. MEY
27 Chief Information Officer .... Mr. Chip ECKARDT
15 Director of Human Resources .... Ms. Donna J. WEBER
37 Director of Financial Aid .... Ms. Kathleen A. SAHLHOFF
38 Director of Counseling .... Ms. Lynn WILSON
06 Registrar .... Ms. Tessa PERCHINSKY
36 Assoc Director Career Services .... Ms. Staci L. HEIDTKE
18 Director of Facilities Mgmt .... Mr. Terry L. CLASSEN
19 Director of University Police .... Mr. David W. SPRICK
23 Director of Student Health Services .... Ms. Laura G. CHELLMAN
39 Director of Housing/Residence Life .... Mr. Charles H. MAJOR
41 Director of Athletics .... Mr. J. Scott KILGALLON
51 Director Continuing Education .... Mr. Durwin LONG
85 Director International Education .... Dr. Karl F. MARKGRAF
29 Director Alumni Relations .... Mr. John BACHMEIER
92 Director of Honors Program .... Dr. Jefford B. VAHLBUSCH
21 Director of Business Services .... Mr. Mark REEVES
26 Chief Public Relations Officer .... Mr. Michael J. RINDO
30 Chief Development/Alumni Relations .... Ms. Kimera WAY
96 Director of Purchasing .... Mr. Steve SLIND
09 Institutional Planner .... Mr. Andrew J. NELSON
49 Int Dean College of Arts & Sciences .... Dr. David BAKER
66 Dean Col of Nursing/Health Sciences .... Dr. Linda K. YOUNG
53 Dean Col Education/Human Sciences .... Dr. Gail SCUKANEC
50 Dean College of Business .... Ms. Diane HOADLEY

*University of Wisconsin-Green Bay (F)

2420 Nicolet Drive, Green Bay WI 54311-7001
County: Brown FICE Identification: 003899
Unit ID: 240277
Telephone: (920) 465-2000 Carnegie Class: Master's S
FAX Number: (920) 465-2032 Calendar System: Semester
URL: www.uwgb.edu
Established: 1965 Annual Undergrad Tuition & Fees (In-State): $7,648
Enrollment: 7,000 Coed
Affiliation or Control: State IRS Status: 501(c)3
Highest Offering: Master's
Program: Liberal Arts And General; Teacher Preparatory; Professional
Accreditation: NH, DIETD, DIETI, MUS, NURSE, SW

02 Chancellor .... Dr. Thomas K. HARDEN
05 Provost/Vice Chancellor .... Dr. Julia E. WALLACE
10 Vice Chanc Business & Finance .... Mr. Kelly FRANZ
30 Asst Chanc University Advancement .... Vacant
32 Dean of Students .... Dr. Brenda AMENSON-HILL
14 Assoc Provost Information Services .... Dr. Rajeev BUKRALIA
20 Assoc Provost for Academic Affairs .... Dr. Andrew KERSTEN
31 Assoc Provost Outreach/Adult Access .... Dr. Steve VANDENAVOND
107 Dean Professional Studies .... Dr. Sue JOSEPH MATTISON
49 Dean Liberal Arts & Sciences .... Dr. Scott FURLONG
43 Legal Counsel .... Vacant
07 Director of Admissions .... Ms. Pam HARVEY-JACOBS
15 Director of Human Resources .... Ms. Sheryl VAN GRUENSVEN
18 Dir Facilities Management/Planning .... Mr. Paul PINKSTON
19 Director Public Safety .... Mr. Thomas KUJAWA
41 Director Athletics .... Mr. Ken BOTHOF
21 Controller .... Ms. SuAnn DETAMPEL
09 Director Institutional Research .... Dr. Deborah FURLONG
84 Dean Enrollment & Acad Svcs .... Mr. Michael STEARNEY
82 Director of International Education .... Mr. Brent BLAHNIK
46 Director of Institute for Research .... Ms. Lidia NONN
37 Director Financial Aid .... Mr. James P. ROHAN
39 Director of Residence Life .... Vacant
40 Manager Bookstore .... Mr. Patrick SORELLE
24 Director Media Svcs/Telecomm .... Mr. William HUBBARD
23 Director Health Services .... Ms. Amy HENNIGES
96 Director of Institutional Support .... Vacant
38 Director Counseling Services .... Mr. Gregory L. SMITH
100 Special Asst to Chancellor .... Mr. Dan SPIELMANN
27 Director University Communications .... Mr. Christopher SAMPSON
36 Director Career Services .... Ms. Linda G. PEACOCK-LANDRUM
29 Director Alumni Relations .... Ms. Kari MOODY
35 Director Student Life .... Ms. Lisa TETZLOFF
06 Registrar .... Ms. Amanda HRUSKA

*University of Wisconsin-La Crosse (G)

1725 State Street, La Crosse WI 54601-3788
County: La Crosse FICE Identification: 003919
Unit ID: 240329
Telephone: (608) 785-8000 Carnegie Class: Master's L
FAX Number: (608) 785-8492 Calendar System: Semester
URL: www.uwlax.edu
Established: 1909 Annual Undergrad Tuition & Fees (In-State): $8,725
Enrollment: 10,227 Coed
Affiliation or Control: State IRS Status: 501(c)3
Highest Offering: Doctorate

Program: Liberal Arts And General; Teacher Preparatory; Professional
Accreditation: NH, ANEST, ARCPA, BUS, MUS, NRPA, OT, PH, PTA, RADDOS, RTT

02 Chancellor ... Dr. Joe GOW
05 Provost/Vice Chanc Acad Affairs ... Ms. Heidi MACPHERSON
30 Asst Chancellor Advancement ... Mr. Greg REICHERT
10 Vice Chancellor Admin & Finance ... Dr. Bob HETZEL
50 Dean of Business Administration ... Dr. Bruce MAY
53 Director School of Education ... Dr. Marcie WYCOFF-HORN
79 Dean of Liberal Studies ... Dr. Ruthann E. BENSON
76 Dean Science Health ... Dr. Bruce RILEY
58 Assoc V Chan Acad/Dir Univ Grad Std ... Dr. Robert HOAR
32 Asst Chancellor & Dean of Students ... Dr. Paula M. KNUDSON
27 Chief Information Officer ... Dr. Mohamed ELHINDI
15 Director of Human Resources ... Ms. Madeline HOLZEM
51 Director Continuing Educ/Exten ... Ms. Penny TIEDT
08 Director of Library ... Ms. Catherine LAVALLÉE-WELCH
85 Director International Education ... Mr. Jay M. LOKKEN
07 Director ES/Admissions ... Mr. Corey SJOQUIST
06 Registrar ... Dr. Christine S. BAKKUM
37 Director ES/Financial Aid ... Ms. Louise L. JANKE
38 Exec Director Counseling/Testing ... Vacant
36 Director of Career Services ... Ms. Karla E. STANEK
41 Athletic Director ... Mr. Joshua WHITMAN
26 Director News and Marketing ... Mr. Brad R. QUARBERG
29 Director Alumni Relations ... Ms. Janie M. SPENCER
23 Director Student Health Center ... Dr. Brian K. ALLEN
09 Director Institutional Research ... Ms. Natalie SOLVERSON
19 Chief of University Police ... Mr. Scott W. ROHDE
18 Director Physical Plant ... Mr. Hank M. KLOS
28 Assoc Dean Campus Climate/Diversity ... Ms. Barbara E. STEWART
22 Director Affirmative Action ... Mr. Nizam ARAIN

*University of Wisconsin-Milwaukee (A)

PO Box 413, Milwaukee WI 53201-0413
County: Milwaukee   FICE Identification: 003896
Unit ID: 240453
Telephone: (414) 229-1122   Carnegie Class: RU/H
FAX Number: (414) 229-6329   Calendar System: Semester
URL: www.uwm.edu
Established: 1885   Annual Undergrad Tuition & Fees (In-State): $9,300
Enrollment: 29,145   Coed
Affiliation or Control: State   IRS Status: 501(c)3
Highest Offering: Doctorate
Program: Liberal Arts And General; Teacher Preparatory; Professional; Business Emphasis
Accreditation: NH, BUS, CEA, CLPSY, COPSY, CS, CYTO, DANCE, DMS, ENG, LIB, MT, MUS, NURSE, OT, PLNG, PTA, SCPSY, SP, SW

02 Chancellor ... Dr. Michael R. LOVELL
05 Provost/Vice Chanc Academic Affairs ... Dr. Johannes BRITZ
10 Vice Chanc Finance & Admin Affs ... Ms. Robin L. VAN HARPEN
26 Vice Chanc Univ Rels/Communications ... Mr. Thomas L. LULJAK
46 Vice Chanc Research/Dean Grad Sch ... Vacant
32 Vice Chancellor Student Affairs ... Dr. Michael R. LALIBERTE
30 Vice Chancellor Development ... Dr. Patricia A. BORGER
88 Vice Chanc Global Inclusion & Engag ... Dr. Joan M. PRINCE
20 Assoc Vice Chanc Academic Affairs ... Dr. Devarajan VENUGOPALAN
20 Actg Assoc Vice Chanc Academic Affs ... Dr. Phyllis KING
28 Act Assoc Vice Chancellor Diversity ... Dr. Cheryl S. AJIROTUTU
84 Assoc Vice Chanc Enrollment Mgmt ... Dr. Jeffrey S. MEECE
13 Interim Chief Information Officer ... Dr. Jacques DU PLESSIS
18 Assoc VC Facilities Planning/Mgmt ... Mr. Geoffrey HURTADO
04 Senior Advisor to the Chancellor ... Mr. David H. GILBERT
76 Dean College Health Sciences ... Dr. Chukuka S. ENWEMEKA
48 Dean Architecture & Urban Planning ... Dr. Robert C. GREENSTREET
50 Dean School Business Administration ... Dr. Timothy L. SMUNT
53 Dean School of Education ... Dr. Barbara J. DALEY
54 Dean Col Engr & Applied Science ... Dr. Brett PETERS
57 Int Dean Peck School of the Arts ... Dr. Scott EMMONS
88 Dean of Freshwater Science ... Dr. David GARMAN
69 Dean School of Public Health ... Dr. Magda PECK
58 Interim Dean Graduate School ... Dr. David YU
49 Dean College Letters & Science ... Dr. Rodney SWAIN
62 Int Dean School Information Studies ... Dr. Wooseob JEONG
66 Dean of College of Nursing ... Dr. Sally LUNDEEN
70 Dean Helen Bader Sch Social Welfare ... Dr. Stan STOJKOVIC
51 Int Dean School of Continuing Educ ... Dr. Sammis B. WHITE
35 Dean of Students ... Dr. Timothy GORDON
22 Dir Equity/Diversity Services ... Ms. Francene BOTTS, L.
08 Director of the Library ... Ms. Ewa BARCZYK
43 Interim Director Legal Affairs ... Ms. Joely B. URDAN
06 Interim Registrar ... Mr. Seth J. ZLOTOCHA
15 Director of Human Resources ... Ms. Suzanne WESLOW
19 Director University Police ... Mr. Michael J. MARZION
25 Director Office Sponsored Research ... Mr. Thomas MARCUSSEN
23 Director Health Center ... Dr. Julia BONNER
09 Dir Assessment/Institutional Rsrch ... Dr. Gesele DURHAM
85 Director Center for Intl Education ... Dr. Patrice S. PETRO
37 Director Student Financial Aid ... Ms. Jane HOJAN-CLARK
39 Director of Residence Life ... Mr. Scott S. PEAK
41 Athletic Director ... Ms. Amanda BRAUN
40 Director Bookstore ... Mr. Erik G C. HEMMING
36 Int Dir Career Development Center ... Ms. Cindy PETRITES
27 Dir Univ Communications & Media Rel ... Ms. Laura GLAWE
21 Int Dir Business & Financial Svcs ... Mr. Jerry TARRER
29 Interim Director Alumni Relations ... Ms. Amy L. TATE
96 Purchasing Manager ... Ms. Joan C. AGUADO-WARE

09 Coordinator Resource Analysis ... Mr. Donald A. WEILL
07 Director of Admissions & Recruiting ... Vacant

*University of Wisconsin-Oshkosh (B)

800 Algoma Boulevard, Oshkosh WI 54901-3551
County: Winnebago   FICE Identification: 003920
Unit ID: 240365
Telephone: (920) 424-1234   Carnegie Class: Master's L
FAX Number: (920) 424-7317   Calendar System: Semester
URL: www.uwosh.edu
Established: 1871   Annual Undergrad Tuition & Fees (In-State): $7,360
Enrollment: 13,519   Coed
Affiliation or Control: State   IRS Status: 501(c)3
Highest Offering: Doctorate
Program: Liberal Arts And General; Teacher Preparatory; Professional
Accreditation: NH, BUS, CACREP, CS, EXSC, JOUR, MUS, NURSE, SW

02 Chancellor ... Dr. Richard H. WELLS
05 Provost & Vice Chancellor ... Dr. Lane R. EARNS
20 Asst Vice Chanc Curricular Affairs ... Dr. Carleen VANDE ZANDE
20 Int Asst Vice Chanc Acad Support ... Ms. Irma BURGOS
51 Asst Vice Chanc Lifelong Learning ... Dr. Karen HEIKEL
32 Vice Chancellor Student Affairs ... Dr. Petra ROTER
10 Vice Chancellor Administrative Svcs ... Mr. Thomas G. SONNLEITNER
21 Associate Vice Chanc Admin Svcs ... Ms. Lori M. WORM
06 Registrar ... Ms. Lisa M. DANIELSON
22 Affirmative Action Officer ... Ms. Pamela LASSITER
09 Director of Institutional Research ... Mr. Michael W. WATSON
38 Director of Counseling Center ... Dr. Joseph J. ABHOLD
14 Int CIO Director Info Technology ... Mr. Nick DVORACEK
50 Dean Business ... Dr. William TALLON
66 Dean Nursing ... Dr. Rosemary SMITH
53 Dean Education & Human Services ... Dr. Frederick L. YEO
49 Dean Letters & Sciences ... Dr. John J. KOKER
102 Pres Univ of Wisc Oshkosh Foundatn ... Mr. Arthur H. RATHJEN
29 Director of Alumni Association ... Ms. Christine M. GANTNER
37 Director of Financial Aid ... Mr. Kim DONAT
26 Exec Director Integrated Marketing ... Ms. Jamie CEMAN
25 Director Grants/Faculty Development ... Mr. Robert W. ROBERTS
35 Dean of Students ... Dr. Sharon KIPETZ
58 Director Graduate Studies ... Mr. Gregory WYPISZYNSKI
07 Director of Admissions ... Ms. Jill M. ENDRIES
15 Director of Human Resources ... Mr. Timothy DANIELSON
18 Facilities/Physical Plant Director ... Mr. Steven A. ARNDT
36 Director of Career Services ... Ms. Jaime PAGE-STADLER
96 Purchasing/Printing Manager ... Mr. Brian KLINGER
92 Director University Honors Program ... Dr. Laurence CARLIN
08 Director Library ... Mr. Patrick J. WILKINSON

*University of Wisconsin-Parkside (C)

900 Wood Road, Box 2000, Kenosha WI 53141-2000
County: Kenosha   FICE Identification: 005015
Unit ID: 240374
Telephone: (262) 595-2345   Carnegie Class: Bac/A&S
FAX Number: (262) 595-2202   Calendar System: Semester
URL: www.uwp.edu
Established: 1968   Annual Undergrad Tuition & Fees (In-State): $7,293
Enrollment: 4,769   Coed
Affiliation or Control: State   IRS Status: 501(c)3
Highest Offering: Master's
Program: Liberal Arts And General; Teacher Preparatory; Professional
Accreditation: NH, BUS

02 Chancellor ... Deborah L. FORD
05 Interim Provost/Vice Chancellor ... Fred EBEID
10 Vice Chanc Admin/Fiscal Affairs ... Melvin KLINKNER
32 Dean of Students ... Tammy MCGUCKIN
84 Assoc Vice Chanc Enrollment Mgmt ... DeAnn L. POSSEHL
30 Asst Chanc Univ Rels/Advancement ... John JARACZEWSKI
20 Associate Provost ... Dennis ROME
88 Asst VC Ofc of Inst Effectiveness ... Kimberly KELLEY
28 Senior Diversity Officer ... Edward TWYMAN
50 Int Dean Col of Bus Econ & Comput ... Dirk BALDWIN
49 Dean College of Arts/Humanities ... Dean YOHNK
51 Dean College of Nat & Hlth Sciences ... Emmanual OTU
31 Exec Dir Ctr for Comty Partnerships ... Jane SCHAEFER
08 Director of the Library ... Jo CATES
13 Chief Information Officer ... Ilya YAKOVLEV
92 Director of Honors Program ... Gary M. WOOD
92 Director Minority Student Services ... Damian EVANS
21 Dir Business Services/Controller ... Scott MENKE
15 Director Human Resources ... Elaine TINCHER-JOHNSON
19 Dir Campus Police/Public Safety ... James HELLER
51 Manager Continuing Education ... Vacant
37 Director Financial Aid ... Randall MCCREADY
26 Director of Public Information ... Vacant
29 Interim Alumni Relations Manager ... Priscilla O'NEILL
06 Registrar ... Rhonda KIMMEL
36 Int Dir of Advising/Career Center ... Gwen JONES
18 Director Facilities Management ... Donald A. KOLBE
94 Director of Women's Studies ... Mary LENARD
96 Director of Purchasing ... Vacant
35 Interim Director of Student Life ... Steve WALLNER
38 Director Student Health/Counseling ... Sandra LEICHT
40 Manager Bookstore ... Daryl COHEN
07 Director of Admissions ... Vacant
09 Dir of Research Administration ... Vacant

*University of Wisconsin-Platteville (D)

1 University Plaza, Platteville WI 53818-3099
County: Grant   FICE Identification: 003921
Unit ID: 240462
Telephone: (608) 342-1491   Carnegie Class: Master's L
FAX Number: (608) 342-1232   Calendar System: Semester
URL: www.uwplatt.edu
Established: 1866   Annual Undergrad Tuition & Fees (In-State): $7,484
Enrollment: 8,624   Coed
Affiliation or Control: State   IRS Status: 501(c)3
Highest Offering: Master's
Program: Liberal Arts And General; Teacher Preparatory; Professional
Accreditation: NH, ENG, MUS, NAIT, TED

02 Chancellor ... Mr. Dennis J. SHIELDS
05 Provost & Vice Chancellor ... Dr. Mittie NIMOCKS DEN HERDER
103 Spec Asst to Chanc/Chief of Staff ... Ms. Rose M. SMYRSKI
11 Vice Chanc Administrative Services ... Mr. Robert G. CRAMER
32 Assoc Vice Chanc Student Affairs ... Dr. Laura BAYLESS
30 Asst Chanc Univ Advance/Foundation ... Mr. Dennis R. COOLEY
58 Director Graduate School ... Dr. Dominic BARRACLOUGH
06 Registrar ... Mr. David S. KIECKHAFER
07 Dir Admissions and Enrollment Svcs ... Ms. Angela M. UDELHOFEN
37 Director of Financial Aid ... Ms. Tracey K. MINGO
09 Director of Institutional Research ... Mr. Mark R. MAILLOUX
38 Director Student Counseling ... Ms. Deirdre L. DALSING
26 Dir Univ Info/Comm/Public Rels ... Mr. Paul J. ERICKSON
41 Director Intercollegiate Athletics ... Mr. Mark D. MOLESWORTH
39 Director of Student Housing ... Ms. Linda A. MULROY-BOWDEN
15 Director Personnel Services ... Ms. Elaine Jeanne DURR
19 Director Security/Safety ... Mr. Scott E. MARQUARDT
92 Director of Honors Program ... Dr. Nancy L. TURNER
93 Dir Multicultural Educ Resource Ctr ... Ms. Angela M. MILLER
96 Director of Purchasing ... Mr. Lewis BETTINGER
08 Director of Library ... Ms. Zora J. SAMPSON
18 Director of Physical Plant ... Mr. Pete D. DAVIS
36 Director of Placement Services ... Ms. Diana J. TRENDT
51 Director Continuing Education ... Ms. Marian G. MACIEJ-HINER
29 Coordinator Alumni Relations ... Ms. Kimberly G. SCHMELZ
49 Dean Col Liberal Arts/Education ... Dr. Elizabeth A. THROOP
54 Dean Col of Engr/Math/Science ... Dr. William B. HUDSON
47 Dean Business Life Sci/Agric ... Dr. Wayne C. WEBER

*University of Wisconsin-River Falls (E)

410 S Third Street, River Falls WI 54022-5013
County: Pierce   FICE Identification: 003923
Unit ID: 240471
Telephone: (715) 425-3911   Carnegie Class: Master's M
FAX Number: (715) 425-4487   Calendar System: Semester
URL: www.uwrf.edu
Established: 1874   Annual Undergrad Tuition & Fees (In-State): $8,084
Enrollment: 6,455   Coed
Affiliation or Control: State   IRS Status: 501(c)3
Highest Offering: Beyond Master's But Less Than Doctorate
Program: Liberal Arts And General; Teacher Preparatory; Professional
Accreditation: NH, BUS, MUS, SP, SW

02 Chancellor ... Dr. Dean A. VAN GALEN
05 Vice Chancellor & Provost ... Dr. Fernando P. DELGADO
10 Assistant Chancellor Bus/Finance ... Ms. Elizabeth FRUEH
20 Associate VC Academic Affairs ... Dr. Michael MILLER
32 Assoc Vice Chanc Student Affs ... Mr. Gregg HEINSELMAN
47 Dean Agricult/Food/Environ Sci ... Dr. Dale GALLENBERG
53 Dean Education/Profess Studies ... Dr. Larry SOLBERG
49 Dean of Arts & Sciences ... Dr. Bradley J. CASKEY
50 Dean Business & Economics ... Dr. Glenn T. POTTS
58 Director Graduate Studies ... Dr. Michael MILLER
04 Special Assistant to Chancellor ... Dr. Blake W. FRY
30 Exec Director for Advancement ... Mr. Chris MUELLER
07 Director of Admissions ... Mr. Mark R. MEYDAM
06 Registrar ... Mr. Dan VANDE YACHT
08 Director of Library ... Ms. Valerie I. MALZACHER
46 Director Grants & Research ... Ms. Molly VAN WAGNER
13 Chief Information Officer ... Mr. Stephen REED
22 Director Affirmative Action ... Ms. Andriel DEES
35 Director of Student Life ... Mr. Paul SHEPHERD
41 Athletic Director ... Mr. Roger TERNES
40 Manager Bookstore ... Ms. Sherry REHNELT
37 Director Financial Assistance ... Ms. Barbara J. STINSON
15 Director of Human Resources ... Ms. Donna ROBOLE
18 Exec Dir Facilities/Planning/Mgmt ... Mr. Michael J. STIFTER
45 Director Campus Planning ... Mr. Dale K. BRAUN
19 Director of Public Safety ... Mr. Richard TRENDE
21 Controller ... Mr. Joel HEUSCHELE
26 Chief Public Relations Officer ... Mr. Blake FRY
96 Director Purchasing Services ... Ms. Gail ANDERSON
88 Int Dir Academic Success Center ... Vacant
35 Dir Student Services & Programs ... Mr. Gregg M. HEINSELMAN
85 Director International Programs ... Vacant
29 Director Alumni Relations ... Mr. Daniel E. MCGINTY
09 Director of Institutional Research ... Ms. Jennifer PAWELKO
92 Interim Director Honors Program ... Mr. Michael MILLER
28 Director of Diversity ... Ms. Andriel DEES
38 Director Student Counseling ... Ms. Alice REILLY-MYKLEBUST
84 Assoc Vice Chan for Enroll/Success ... Dr. Kristina ANDERSON
56 Director Outreach Programs ... Ms. Katrina LARSEN
88 Director of McNair Scholars Program ... Dr. Louis PORTER, II

*University of Wisconsin-Stevens Point (A)

2100 Main Street, Stevens Point WI 54481-3871
County: Portage FICE Identification: 003924
Unit ID: 240480
Telephone: (715) 346-0123 Carnegie Class: Master's M
FAX Number: (715) 346-4841 Calendar System: Semester
URL: www.uwsp.edu
Established: 1894 Annual Undergrad Tuition & Fees (In-State): $7,578
Enrollment: 9,677 Coed
Affiliation or Control: State IRS Status: 501(c)3
Highest Offering: Doctorate
Program: Liberal Arts And General; Teacher Preparatory; Professional
Accreditation: NH, ART, AUD, CIDA, DANCE, DIETD, ENG, FOR, MT, MUS, SP, @SW, THEA

02 Chancellor ... Dr. Bernie PATTERSON
05 Provost & Vice Chancellor ... Dr. Greg SUMMERS
10 Vice Chancellor Business Affairs ... Mr. Gregory M. DIEMER
32 Vice Chancellor Student Affairs ... Dr. Al THOMPSON
20 Interim AVC for Tech/Lrng/Acad Pgms ... Dr. James SAGE
100 Chief of Staff ... Mr. Rob MANZKE
15 AVC Person/Bdgt/Grants/Summer Pgms ... Dr. Katie JORE
51 Exec Dir UWSP Continuing Ed ... Mr. Tom GOSPODARCZYK
07 Director Admissions ... Ms. Terri CRUMLEY
37 Interim Director of Financial Aid ... Mr. Paul WATSON
19 Director Safety & Loss Control ... Mr. Jeff KARCHER
30 Vice Chanc Univ Advancement ... Mr. Chris RICHARDS
29 Director of Alumni Affairs ... Ms. Laura GEHRMAN-ROTTIER
26 Director University Relations/Comm ... Ms. Kate WORSTER
16 Director of Personnel ... Mr. Robert TABOR
38 Director Counseling Center ... Dr. Stacey GERKEN
13 Dir of Information Technology ... Ms. Marsha HENFER
22 Director Equity & Affirm Act ... Ms. Mai VANG
08 Director University Library ... Dr. Kathy DAVIS
06 Registrar ... Mr. Dan KELLOGG
18 Chief Facilities/Physical Plant ... Mr. Paul HASLER
36 Director Student Placement ... Dr. Angie KELLOGG
96 Director of Purchasing ... Ms. Katie SCHROTH
57 Dean Col of Fine Arts & Communic ... Mr. Jeff MORIN
49 Dean College of Letters & Science ... Dr. Christopher CIRMO
65 Dean Coll of Natural Resources ... Dr. Christine L. THOMAS
107 Dean Col of Professional Studies ... Dr. Marty LOY
09 Director of Institutional Research ... Vacant
28 Director of Multicultural Affairs ... Mr. Ron STREGE
35 Director Student Affairs ... Dr. Al THOMPSON

*University of Wisconsin-Stout (B)

712 South Broadway, Menomonie WI 54751-2458
County: Dunn FICE Identification: 003915
Unit ID: 240417
Telephone: (715) 232-1122 Carnegie Class: Master's L
FAX Number: (715) 232-1416 Calendar System: 4/1/4
URL: www.uwstout.edu
Established: 1891 Annual Undergrad Tuition & Fees (In-State): $8,600
Enrollment: 9,247 Coed
Affiliation or Control: State IRS Status: 501(c)3
Highest Offering: Beyond Master's But Less Than Doctorate
Program: Liberal Arts And General; Teacher Preparatory; Professional
Accreditation: NH, ART, CACREP, CIDA, CONST, CORE, DIETD, DIETI, ENG, MFCD, TED

02 Chancellor ... Dr. Charles W. SORENSEN
05 Provost & Vice Chancellor ... Dr. Joseph BESSIE
11 Vice Chanc for Admin/Student Life ... Mr. Phil LYONS
20 Associate Vice Chancellor ... Dr. Jackie WEISSENBURGER
30 Vice Chanc Univ Advance/Mktg ... Mr. Mark PARSON
32 Asst VC Student Life Svcs ... Mr. Scott GRIESBACH
28 Asst Vice Chanc for Diversity ... Vacant
45 Asst Chanc Plng/Assess/Rsrch/Qual ... Dr. Meridith DRZAKOWSKI
50 Dean College of Management ... Dr. Abel ADEKOLA
49 Dean Col Arts/Humanities/Social Sci ... Dr. Maria ALM
53 Dean Col of Ed/Hlth/Hum Sci ... Dr. Mary HOPKINS-BEST
81 Dean Col of Science/Tech/Engr/Math ... Dr. Jeff ANDERSON
32 Dean of Students ... Ms. Joan THOMAS
06 Registrar ... Mr. Scott CORRELL
84 Director Enrollment Management ... Dr. Pamela HOLSINGER-FUCHS
36 Director Career Services ... Ms. Amy LANE
08 Director University Library ... Mr. Marlys BRUNSTING
04 Special Assistant to the Chancellor ... Ms. Kristi KRIMPELBEIN
37 Director Student Financial Aid ... Ms. Beth BOISEN
26 Director University Communications ... Mr. Doug MELL
21 Director Business/Financial Svcs ... Ms. Kim SCHULTE-SHOBERG
13 Chief Information Officer ... Mr. Doug J. WAHL
76 Exec Director Health & Safety ... Mr. James UHLIR
15 Director Human Resources ... Ms. Deb GEHRKE
38 Director Counseling Center ... Dr. John ACHTER
88 Director Online Services ... Mr. Doug STEVENS
23 Director Student Health Services ... Ms. Janice LAWRENCE-RAMAEKER
40 Director Bookstore ... Ms. Cathy CLOSE
44 Director of the Annual Fund ... Ms. Jennifer RUDIGER
85 Director International Education ... Mr. Hong ROST
18 Director Physical Plant ... Ms. Shirley KLEBESADEL
96 Director Procurement/Materials Mgmt ... Mr. Brent TILTON
39 Interim Dir University Housing ... Mr. Martin FRITZ
41 Director Athletics ... Mr. Duey NAATZ
29 Director Alumni Relations ... Ms. Juliet FOX
19 Dir of Safety & Risk Management ... Mr. Dean A. SANKEY
19 Coordinator University Police ... Ms. Lisa A. WALTER

*University of Wisconsin-Superior (C)

Belknap and Catlin, PO Box 2000,
Superior WI 54880-4500
County: Douglas FICE Identification: 003925
Unit ID: 240426
Telephone: (715) 394-8101 Carnegie Class: Master's S
FAX Number: (715) 394-8454 Calendar System: Semester
URL: www.uwsuper.edu
Established: 1893 Annual Undergrad Tuition & Fees (In-State): $7,542
Enrollment: 2,700 Coed
Affiliation or Control: State IRS Status: 501(c)3
Highest Offering: Beyond Master's But Less Than Doctorate
Program: Liberal Arts And General; Teacher Preparatory; Professional
Accreditation: NH, MUS, SW

02 Chancellor ... Dr. Renee WACHTER
05 Provost/Vice Chanc Academic Affairs ... Dr. Faith HENSRUD
11 Vice Chanc Administration & Finance ... Ms. Janet K. HANSON
30 Vice Chanc University Advancement ... Ms. Jeanne E. THOMPSON
32 Dean of Students ... Ms. Vicki HAJEWSKI
10 Controller ... Mr. Robert B. WAKSDAHL
15 Director Human Resources ... Ms. Peggy A. FECKER
18 Director Facilities Management ... Mr. Tom FENNESSEY
26 Director Marketing & Communications ... Ms. Lynne M. WILLIAMS
06 Registrar ... Dr. Diane J. DOUGLAS
08 Librarian ... Ms. Debra L. NORDGREN
07 Director of Admissions ... Ms. Tonya ROTH
41 Athletic Director ... Mr. Steve NELSON
37 Director Student Financial Aid ... Ms. Donna R. DAHLVANG
14 Director Administrative Info Svcs ... Vacant
51 Dir Center Cont Educ/Online Svcs ... Vacant
88 Dir Distance Learning & Cont Educ ... Dr. Peter D. NORDGREN
40 Director Bookstore ... Mr. Vaughn N. RUSSOM
29 Director Alumni Relations ... Mr. Thomas K. BERGH
38 Director Advisement ... Dr. Christopher CHERRY
28 Director of Diversity ... Mr. Alvin (Chip) BEAL
84 Director Enrollment Management ... Vacant

*University of Wisconsin-Whitewater (D)

800 W Main, Whitewater WI 53190-1790
County: Walworth FICE Identification: 003926
Unit ID: 240189
Telephone: (262) 472-1234 Carnegie Class: Master's L
FAX Number: (262) 472-1518 Calendar System: Semester
URL: www.uww.edu
Established: 1868 Annual Undergrad Tuition & Fees (In-State): $7,578
Enrollment: 12,031 Coed
Affiliation or Control: State IRS Status: 501(c)3
Highest Offering: Beyond Master's But Less Than Doctorate
Program: Liberal Arts And General; Teacher Preparatory; Professional
Accreditation: NH, ART, BUS, CACREP, MUS, SP, SW, TED, THEA

02 Chancellor ... Dr. Richard J. TELFER
05 Prov/Vice Chanc Academic Affs ... Dr. Beverly KOPPER
32 Vice Chancellor Student Affairs ... Dr. Thomas R. RIOS
30 VC Univ Advance/Foundation Pres ... Mr. Jonathan ENSLIN
11 Vice Chanc Administrative Affs ... Mr. Jeff (Dean) ARNOLD
20 Assoc Vice Chanc Academic Affairs ... Dr. Greg COOK
13 Asst Vice Chanc Tech/Info Resource ... Dr. Elena POKOT
84 Asst Vice Chanc Enroll/Retention ... Mr. Matt ASCHENBRENER
09 Director of Institutional Research ... Vacant
20 AVC Multicult Affs/Stdnt Success ... Dr. Richard MCGREGORY
37 Director of Financial Aid ... Ms. Carol A. MILLER
10 Chief Business Officer ... Mr. Jeff (Dean) ARNOLD
26 Chief Public Relations Officer ... Ms. Sara KUHL
21 Director of Budget ... Ms. Aimee C. ARNOLD
07 Director of Admissions ... Mr. Jeff BLAHNIK
06 Registrar ... Ms. Jodi M. HARE-PAYNTER
36 Director of Career Services ... Mr. Ron BUCHHOLZ
15 Director Human Resources/Diversity ... Ms. Judith M. TRAMPF
85 Dir Center for Global Education ... Ms. Candace A. CHENOWETH
44 Exec Dir University Development ... Ms. Kate LOFTUS
18 Director Facility Planning/Mgmt ... Mr. Greg SWANSON
38 Exec Dir Univ Health/Counseling Svc ... Dr. Richard L. JAZDZEWSKI
96 Director of Purchasing ... Mr. Michael T. HIRSCHFIELD
28 Director of Diversity ... Dr. Elizabeth OGUNSOLA
92 Director of Honors Program ... Dr. Rex HANGER
88 Int Dir Acad Advising/Explor Ctr ... Ms. Pamela TANNER
35 Dean Student Life ... Ms. Mary Beth MACKIN
57 Dean Arts/Communication ... Dr. Mark MCPHAIL
50 Dean of Business & Economics ... Dr. Christine CLEMENTS
53 Dean Education/Professional Studies ... Dr. Katharina E. HEYNING
49 Dean Letters & Sciences ... Dr. Mary PINKERTON
58 Dean Grad Stds/Continuing Educ ... Dr. John STONE

*University of Wisconsin Colleges (E)

780 Regent Street, Suite 130, Madison WI 53715-2635
County: Dane FICE Identification: 003897
Unit ID: 240055
Telephone: (608) 262-3786 Carnegie Class: Assoc/Pub2in4
FAX Number: (608) 262-7872 Calendar System: Semester
URL: www.uwc.edu
Established: 1964 Annual Undergrad Tuition & Fees (In-State): $4,882
Enrollment: 14,162 Coed
Affiliation or Control: State IRS Status: 501(c)3
Highest Offering: Baccalaureate
Program: 2-Year Principally Bachelor's Creditable
Accreditation: NH

02 Chancellor ... Dr. Raymond CROSS
05 Provost/Vice Chancellor ... Dr. Gregory P. LAMPE
10 Vice Chancellor Admin & Fin Svcs ... Mr. Steven C. WILDECK
32 Assoc VC Stdt Svcs & Enroll Mgmt ... Dr. Richard BARNHOUSE
12 Int Vice Chanc/Provost UW-Extension ... Dr. Greg HUTCHINS
20 Associate Vice Chancellor ... Dr. Lisa SEALE
13 Chief Information Officer ... Ms. Marsha HENFER
15 Director Human Resources ... Ms. Pam DOLLARD
06 Registrar ... Mr. Larry GRAVES
37 Director Student Financial Aid ... Mr. William TRIPPETT
26 Exec Director University Relations ... Ms. Teri H. VENKER
28 Director of Diversity ... Dr. Stephan GILCHRIST
51 Dir Continuing Ed/Extended Svcs ... Mr. Tim URBONYA
12 Dean UW Baraboo/Sauk County ... Dr. Tom PLEGER
12 Int Dean UW Barron Cty (Rice Lake) ... Dr. Tracy WHITE
12 Dean UW Fond Du Lac ... Dr. John SHORT
12 Dean UW Fox Valley (Menasha) ... Dr. Martin RUDD
12 Dean UW Manitowoc ... Dr. Charles E. CLARK
12 Dean UW Marathon County ... Dr. Keith MONTGOMERY
12 Dean UW Marinette ... Ms. Paula LANGTEAU
12 Dean UW Marshfield/Wood Co. ... Dr. Patricia L. STUHR
12 Dean UW Richland ... Dr. Patrick HAGEN
12 Dean UW Rock County ... Dr. Carmen WILSON
12 Dean UW Sheboygan ... Dr. Al HARDERSEN
12 Dean UW Washington County ... Dr. Alan Paul PRICE
12 Dean UW Waukesha ... Dr. Harry P. MUIR, JR.

*University of Wisconsin Baraboo/Sauk County (F)

1006 Connie Road, Baraboo WI 53913
Telephone: (608) 355-5200 Identification: 770450
Accreditation: &NH

† Main campus is University of Wisconsin Colleges in Madison, WI.

*University of Wisconsin Barron County (G)

1800 College Drive, Rice Lake WI 54868
Telephone: (715) 234-8176 Identification: 770457
Accreditation: &NH

† Main campus is University of Wisconsin Colleges in Madison, WI.

*University of Wisconsin Fond du Lac (H)

400 University Drive, Fond du Lac WI 54935
Telephone: (920) 929-1100 Identification: 770451
Accreditation: &NH

† Main campus is University of Wisconsin Colleges in Madison, WI.

*University of Wisconsin Fox Valley (I)

1478 Midway Road, Menasha WI 54952
Telephone: (920) 832-2600 Identification: 770456
Accreditation: &NH

† Main campus is University of Wisconsin Colleges in Madison, WI.

*University of Wisconsin Manitowoc (J)

705 Viebahn Street, Manitowoc WI 54220-6699
Telephone: (920) 683-4700 Identification: 770453
Accreditation: &NH

† Main campus is University of Wisconsin Colleges in Madison, WI.

*University of Wisconsin Marathon County (K)

518 South 7th Avenue, Wausau WI 54401
Telephone: (715) 261-6235 Identification: 770461
Accreditation: &NH

† Main campus is University of Wisconsin Colleges in Madison, WI.

*University of Wisconsin Marinette (L)

750 W Bay Shore Street, Marinette WI 54143-4253
Telephone: (715) 735-4300 Identification: 770454
Accreditation: &NH

† Main campus is University of Wisconsin Colleges in Madison, WI.

*University of Wisconsin Marshfield/Wood County (M)

2200 West 5th Street, Marshfield WI 54449
Telephone: (715) 389-6530 Identification: 770455
Accreditation: &NH

† Main campus is University of Wisconsin Colleges in Madison, WI.

*University of Wisconsin Richland (N)

1200 Highway 14 West, Richland Center WI 53581-1316
Telephone: (608) 647-6186 Identification: 770458
Accreditation: &NH

† Main campus is University of Wisconsin Colleges in Madison, WI.

* *University of Wisconsin Rock County* (A)
2909 Kellogg Avenue, Janesville WI 53546
Telephone: (608) 758-6565 Identification: 770452
Accreditation: &NH

† Main campus is University of Wisconsin Colleges in Madison, WI.

* *University of Wisconsin Sheboygan* (B)
One University Drive, Sheboygan WI 53081-4760
Telephone: (920) 459-6600 Identification: 770459
Accreditation: &NH

† Main campus is University of Wisconsin Colleges in Madison, WI.

* *University of Wisconsin Washington County* (C)
400 University Drive, West Bend WI 53095
Telephone: (262) 335-5200 Identification: 770462
Accreditation: &NH

† Main campus is University of Wisconsin Colleges in Madison, WI.

* *University of Wisconsin Waukesha* (D)
1500 N University Drive, Waukesha WI 53188-2799
Telephone: (262) 521-5200 Identification: 770460
Accreditation: &NH

† Main campus is University of Wisconsin Colleges in Madison, WI.

Viterbo University (E)
900 Viterbo Drive, La Crosse WI 54601-8802
County: La Crosse FICE Identification: 003911
Unit ID: 240107
Telephone: (608) 796-3000 Carnegie Class: Master's L
FAX Number: (608) 796-3050 Calendar System: Semester
URL: www.viterbo.edu
Established: 1890 Annual Undergrad Tuition & Fees: $22,670
Enrollment: 2,788 Coed
Affiliation or Control: Roman Catholic IRS Status: 501(c)3
Highest Offering: Doctorate
Program: Liberal Arts And General; Teacher Preparatory; Professional
Accreditation: NH, ACBSP, DIETC, DIETI, MUS, NURSE, SW, TED

01 President ... Dr. Richard B. ARTMAN
05 Vice President for Academic Affairs ... Dr. Barbara M. GAYLE
32 Vice President Student Development ... Dr. Diane L. BRIMMER
10 Vice Pres Administration/Finance ... Mr. Todd M. ERICSON
30 Vice Pres Institutional Advancement ... Mr. Gary L. KLEIN
26 Vice Pres Communications Marketing ... Mr. Patrick G. KERRIGAN
21 Assistant Vice President Finance ... Mr. Eugene R. ALBERTS
07 Dean of Admission ... Mr. Robert L. FORGET
42 Chaplain ... Fr. Conrad A. TARGONSKI
66 Dean School of Nursing ... Dr. Silvana F. RICHARDSON
53 Dean School of Education ... Dr. Sue S. BATELL
49 Dean School Letters & Sciences ... Dr. Glena G. TEMPLE
57 Dean School of Fine Arts ... Dr. Timothy B. SCHORR
50 Dean School of Business ... Dr. Thomas E. KNOTHE
58 Dean Graduate/Prof/Adult Education ... Vacant
88 Director of Ethics in Leadership ... Dr. Richard L. KYTE
06 Registrar ... Ms. Amy S. GLEASON
26 Director of Marketing ... Mr. Paul WILHELMSON
08 Director of Library ... Ms. Gretel L. STOCK KUPPERMAN
14 Director of Computer Services ... Mr. Tom L. HAUSMANN
41 Athletic Director ... Mr. Barry J. FRIED
37 Director of Financial Aid ... Ms. Terry W. NORMAN
29 Director Alumni/Parent Relations ... Ms. Kathleen A. DUERWACHTER
36 Director Career Planning/Placement . Ms. Beth D. DOLDER-ZIEKE
15 Director of Human Resources ... Ms. Sonya GANTHER
09 Director Institutional Research ... Ms. Naomi R. STENNES-SPIDAHL
18 Director Physical Plant ... Mr. Eugene M. MCCURDY
38 Dir Counseling/Student Development ... Ms. Lesley A. STUGELMAYER
39 Director of Residence Life ... Ms. Vickie L. UNFERTH
53 Director Grad Studies in Education ... Ms. Rhonda M. RABBITT
88 Dir Faculty Dev/Internship Coord ... Dr. Theresa MOORE
88 Director of Global Education ... Mr. Shaojie JIANG
19 Campus Safety & Security Director ... Mr. David J. PLEASANTS
07 Assoc Dir of Freshman Admissions ... Ms. Jessica K. MILLER
07 Associate Director of Admissions ... Mr. Eric R. SCHMIDT
04 Executive Admin Asst to President ... Ms. Sheila SEVERSON

Wisconsin Lutheran College (F)
8800 W Bluemound Road, Milwaukee WI 53226-4699
County: Milwaukee FICE Identification: 021366
Unit ID: 240338
Telephone: (414) 443-8800 Carnegie Class: Bac/A&S
FAX Number: (414) 443-8514 Calendar System: Semester
URL: www.wlc.edu
Established: 1973 Annual Undergrad Tuition & Fees: $23,620
Enrollment: 1,090 Coed
Affiliation or Control: Independent Non-Profit IRS Status: 501(c)3
Highest Offering: Master's
Program: Liberal Arts And General
Accreditation: NH, NURSE

01 President ... Dr. Daniel W. JOHNSON
05 Provost & VP of Academic Affairs ... Dr. John D. KOLANDER
32 Vice President Student Affairs ... Dr. Dennis L. MILLER
10 Vice Pres Finance & Administration ... Mr. Gary SCHMID
26 Exec Dir Marketing & Communication ... Mr. Jason VANACKER
30 Vice Pres Development ... Mr. Craig RUSSOW
15 VP of Human Resources ... Mr. Steven SCHROEDER
21 Asst VP Finance ... Mrs. Diane HOEHNKE
84 Exec Director of Enrollment ... Mr. Lucas FAUST
06 Registrar ... Mr. Brett VALERIO
08 Director of Library Services ... Mrs. Starla C. SIEGMANN
37 Director Student Financial Aid ... Mrs. Linda L. LOEFFEL
42 Campus Pastor ... Rev. Nathan STROBEL
53 Director Teacher Education ... Prof. James HOLMAN
39 Director Residential Life/Housing ... Mrs. Judy K. EGGERS
07 Executive Director of Admissions ... Mr. Jeff WEBER
41 Athletic Director ... Mr. Edward NOON
35 Dean of Student Success ... Mr. Joel P. MISCHKE
88 Director of Arts Programming ... Mr. Daniel SCHMAL
27 Director of Information Technology ... Mr. John MEYER
29 Director of Alumni Relations ... Mrs. Lisa LEFFEL
44 Exec Director of Planned Giving ... Mrs. Kris METZGER
09 Information Systems Analyst ... Mrs. Olya FINNEGAN
102 Director Corp/Foundation Relations ... Ms. Sharon PATTERSON
18 Chief Facilities/Physical Plant ... Mr. Gary SCHMID
24 Media Services Coordinator ... Mr. Tim SNYDER

Wisconsin School of Professional Psychology (G)
9120 W Hampton Avenue, Suite 212,
Milwaukee WI 53225-4960
County: Milwaukee FICE Identification: 022713
Unit ID: 240213
Telephone: (414) 464-9777 Carnegie Class: Spec/Health
FAX Number: (414) 358-5590 Calendar System: Semester
URL: www.wspp.edu
Established: 1979 Annual Graduate Tuition & Fees: $31,550
Enrollment: 91 Coed
Affiliation or Control: Independent Non-Profit IRS Status: 501(c)3
Highest Offering: Doctorate; No Undergraduates
Program: Professional
Accreditation: NH, CLPSY

01 President ... Dr. Kathleen M. RUSCH
05 Dean ... Dr. Dale A. BESPALEC
04 Assistant to the President ... Ms. Sheri LINDGREN
17 Director Clinical Training ... Dr. Susan DVORAK

* Wisconsin Technical College System (H)
PO Box 7874, Madison WI 53707-7874
County: Dane Identification: 666185
Telephone: (608) 266-1207 Carnegie Class: N/A
FAX Number: (608) 266-1285
URL: www.wtcsystem.edu

01 President ... Ms. Morna K. FOY
03 Executive Vice President ... Mr. James ZYLSTRA
05 Provost/Vice Pres Student Success ... Ms. Kathleen CULLEN
86 Dir Strategic Ptrnshp/External Rels ... Mr. Conor SMYTH

* Blackhawk Technical College (I)
PO Box 5009, Janesville WI 53547-5009
County: Rock FICE Identification: 005390
Unit ID: 238397
Telephone: (608) 758-6900 Carnegie Class: Assoc/Pub-R-M
FAX Number: (608) 757-7740 Calendar System: Semester
URL: www.blackhawk.edu
Established: 1912 Annual Undergrad Tuition & Fees (In-District): $3,969
Enrollment: 2,967 Coed
Affiliation or Control: State/Local IRS Status: 501(c)3
Highest Offering: Associate Degree
Program: Occupational; Technical Emphasis
Accreditation: NH, ACFEI, ADNUR, DA, DMS, MAC, MLTAD, PTAA, RAD

02 President ... Dr. Thomas C. ECKERT
05 Vice President Learning ... Dr. Diane NYHAMMER
11 Vice President Finance/College Oper ... Ms. Renea L. RANGUETTE
16 Vice President Human Resources ... Mr. Brian B. GOHLKE
32 Vice President Student Services ... Mr. Edward G. ROBINSON
09 Dir Institutional Effectiveness ... Mr. Michael J. GAGNER
04 Asst to President/Board Liaison ... Ms. Jacqueline J. PINS
14 Chief Information Officer ... Ms. Mary SCHOELER
26 Marketing & Communications Mgr ... Mr. Gary KOHN
97 Dean Gen Ed/Academic Support ... Dr. Gabrielle BANICK
88 Assoc Dean Gen Ed/Academic Supp ... Mr. Darian SNOW
76 Dean Health Sciences ... Ms. Nancy R. LIGHTFIELD
88 Dean Public Safety ... Mr. Mark I. BROWN
88 Emergency Preparedness Coordinator ... Vacant
88 EMS Fire Service & Paramedic Coord ... Mr. David F. PETERSON
66 Assoc Dean Nursing ... Vacant
72 Dean Advanced Mfg & Transportation ... Vacant
50 Dean Business and Econ Dev ... Dr. Gina MCCONOUGHEY
12 Director of Monroe Campus ... Vacant
21 Controller ... Mr. David MCDONALD
25 Manager Grants Administration ... Mr. Andrew S. MCGRATH
37 Director of Financial Aid ... Ms. Dorothy THOMAS
06 Director Student Development ... Ms. Kerry K. FROEHLICH-MUELLER
18 Facilities Director ... Vacant
96 Manager Purchasing/Fac Design ... Ms. Kelly J. DEMPSEY
51 Continuing Education Coord ... Mr. Mark V. TRILLER
08 Director of Learning Resources ... Dr. Elizabeth REZEL
102 Director of Foundation & Alumni ... Ms. Kelli CAMERON

* Chippewa Valley Technical College (J)
620 W Clairemont Avenue, Eau Claire WI 54701-6162
County: Eau Claire FICE Identification: 005304
Unit ID: 240116
Telephone: (715) 833-6200 Carnegie Class: Assoc/Pub-R-M
FAX Number: (715) 833-6470 Calendar System: Semester
URL: www.cvtc.edu
Established: 1912 Annual Undergrad Tuition & Fees (In-District): $3,524
Enrollment: 6,086 Coed
Affiliation or Control: Local IRS Status: 501(c)3
Highest Offering: Associate Degree
Program: Occupational; 2-Year Principally Bachelor's Creditable; Technical Emphasis
Accreditation: NH, ADNUR, CAHIIM, COARC, DH, DMS, MAC, MLTAD, PNUR, PTAA, RAD, SURGT

02 President ... Bruce A. BARKER
05 Vice President Education ... Roger J. STANFORD
11 Vice President Operations ... Tom G. HUFFCUTT
32 Vice President Student Services ... Margo A. KEYS
12 River Falls Campus Administrator ... Beth A. HEIN
12 Chippewa Falls Campus Manager ... Timothy M. SHEPARDSON
12 Menomonie Campus Manager ... Roxann S. VANDERWYST
12 Nanorite Innovation Center Manager ... Pam D. OWEN
46 Dir of Research/Special Projects ... Margaret A. DICKENS
47 Dean Industry/Agricul & Energy ... Aliesha R. CROWE
06 Registrar ... Jessica SCHWARTZ
07 Director of Enrollment Services ... Paige WEGNER
37 Financial Aid Officer ... Mary E. GORUD
26 Manager of College Marketing ... Pam HALLER
31 Director of Community Relations ... Doug A. OLSON
10 Director of Budget & Finance ... Kirk L. MOIST
88 Director of Prof Development ... Debra WALSH
13 Director of Info Technology ... Tom J. LANGE
88 Customer Service Center Spec/Mgr ... Karen L. CALLAWAY
35 Student Life Specialist ... Alisa S. SCHLEY
96 Purchasing Agent ... Doug D. DEKAN
21 Budget Manager ... Tracy M. DRIER
19 Safety/Security and Risk Manager ... Carrie L. HALLQUIST
28 Diversity/Equal Opportunity Spec ... Michael A. OJIBWAY
35 Student Services Grants/Operations ... Natalyn M. MARLAIRE
35 Dean Academic and Develop Services ... Kristen A. RANEY
102 Dir of CVTC Foundation/Alumni Assoc ... Heidi L. FISHER
25 Grants Specialist ... Shana SCHMIDT
108 Manager of Assessment ... Philip V. PALSER
97 Assoc Dean of Gen Edun & Curric ... Lynette LIVINGSTON
18 Facilities Manager ... Rod BAGLEY
15 Human Resources Director ... Tam BURGAU
21 Business Office Manager ... Sara J. NICK
76 Dean Health & Emergency Services ... Shelly Y. OLSON
97 Dean General Educ & Business ... Cherrie BERGANDI
88 Assoc Dean of Transportation ... Tim STANTON
88 Assoc Dean of Manufacturing ... Jeff SULLIVAN
88 Assoc Dean of Emergency Services ... Eric ANDERSON
50 Assoc Dean of Business ... Jeff PEPPER
76 Assoc Dean of Health ... Linda KRUEGER

* Fox Valley Technical College (K)
1825 N Bluemound Drive, Appleton WI 54914-1643
County: Outagamie FICE Identification: 009744
Unit ID: 238722
Telephone: (920) 735-5600 Carnegie Class: Assoc/Pub-R-L
FAX Number: (920) 735-2582 Calendar System: Semester
URL: www.fvtc.edu
Established: 1967 Annual Undergrad Tuition & Fees (In-District): $4,178
Enrollment: 10,580 Coed
Affiliation or Control: State/Local IRS Status: 501(c)3
Highest Offering: Associate Degree
Program: Occupational; 2-Year Principally Bachelor's Creditable
Accreditation: NH, ACFEI, ADNUR, DA, DH, MAC, OTA

02 President ... Dr. Susan A. MAY
05 VP Instructional Services ... Mr. Christopher MATHENY
11 VP Administrative Services ... Ms. Jill MCEWEN
32 VP Student/Community Development ... Ms. Patti JORGENSEN
04 Assistant to the President ... Ms. Vicky VAN HOUT
76 Exec Dean Business/Health/Service ... Ms. Donna ELLIOTT
72 Ex Dn Mnfctng/Transp/Info/Agri Tech ... Mr. Steve STRAUB
19 Executive Dean Public Safety ... Dr. Patricia ROBINSON
10 Chief Financial Officer ... Ms. Amy VAN STRATEN
13 Chief Information Officer ... Mr. Troy KOHL
97 Dean General Studies ... Ms. Carol MAY
102 Exec Dir FVTC Foundation/Cmty Rels ... Ms. Alyce DUMKE
12 Oshkosh Campus Director ... Ms. Melissa KOHN
37 Director Student Financial Svcs ... Ms. Stacy DORAN
35 Director Student Affairs ... Ms. Denise MARTINEZ
06 Registrar ... Mr. Brian BUSS
26 Director of College Marketing ... Ms. Barb DREGER
88 Director Compensation & Benefits ... Ms. Barb KIEFFER
88 Director Venture Center ... Ms. Amy PIETSCH
15 Director Employee Rels/Staff Dev ... Ms. Deb GORMAN
88 NCJTC Technology Director ... Ms. Karen ALESCH
88 Director Articulated Programs ... Ms. Marge RUBIN
46 Director College Effectiveness ... Dr. Patti FROHRIB

36 Specialist Student Employment Svcs ... Mr. Bruce WEILAND
35 Director Student Life ... Ms. Vicky BARKE

*Gateway Technical College (A)

3520 30th Avenue, Kenosha WI 53144-1690
County: Kenosha
FICE Identification: 005389
Unit ID: 238759
Telephone: (262) 564-2200
Carnegie Class: Assoc/Pub-R-L
FAX Number: (262) 564-2201
Calendar System: Semester
URL: www.gtc.edu
Established: 1912
Annual Undergrad Tuition & Fees (In-District): $3,507
Enrollment: 8,720
Coed
Affiliation or Control: State/Local
IRS Status: 501(c)3
Highest Offering: Associate Degree
Program: Occupational
Accreditation: NH, ADNUR, CAHIIM, DA, MAC, PTAA, SURGT

02 President ... Dr. Bryan D. ALBRECHT
05 Exec VP/Prov/Chief Academic Officer ... Ms. Zina HAYWOOD
12 Dean Racine Campus ... Mr. Ray KOUKARI
12 Dean Elkhorn Campus ... Mr. Michael O'DONNELL
12 Dean Kenosha Campus ... Mr. Dennis SHERWOOD
10 Vice President Finance ... Ms. Bane THOMEY
86 VP Government/Community Relations ... Ms. Stephanie SKLBA
103 VP Workforce/Economic Develop Div ... Ms. Debbie DAVIDSON
20 Asst Provost/VP IE/Student Success ... Dr. John THIBODEAU
84 Dean of Student Enrollment ... Ms. Stacy RILEY
32 Dean Student Development ... Mr. Steve WILKES
06 Registrar ... Ms. Chrystal MOEZ
09 Assoc VP Institutional Research ... Ms. Anne WHYNOTT
15 VP Human Resources and Facilities ... Mr. William WHYTE
26 Marketing Director ... Ms. Jayne HERRING
07 Director of Admissions ... Ms. Susan ROBERTS
18 Chief Facilities/Physical Plant ... Mr. William WHTYE
21 Associate Business Officer ... Ms. Beverly HANSEN
37 Director Student Financial Aid ... Ms. Janice RIUTTA
28 Director of Diversity ... Ms. Debbie MILLER
102 Foundation Executive Director ... Dr. Jennifer CHARPENTIER

*Lakeshore Technical College (B)

1290 North Avenue, Cleveland WI 53015-1414
County: Manitowoc
FICE Identification: 009194
Unit ID: 239008
Telephone: (920) 693-1000
Carnegie Class: Assoc/Pub-R-M
FAX Number: (920) 693-1363
Calendar System: Semester
URL: www.gotoltc.edu
Established: 1913
Annual Undergrad Tuition & Fees (In-District): $4,000
Enrollment: 2,252
Coed
Affiliation or Control: State/Local
IRS Status: 501(c)3
Highest Offering: Associate Degree
Program: Occupational; 2-Year Principally Bachelor's Creditable; Technical Emphasis
Accreditation: NH, ADNUR, EMT, RAD

02 President ... Dr. Michael LANSER
04 Executive Assistant ... Ms. Allison WEBER
05 Vice President of Instruction ... Vacant
32 Vice President of Student Services ... Dr. Douglas GOSSEN
103 Vice President Workforce Solutions ... Mr. Peter THILLMAN
15 Director Human Resources ... Ms. Kathy KOTAJARVI
10 Director Financial Services ... Ms. Cindy DROSS
09 Dir Institutional Effectiveness ... Ms. Nikki KISS
26 Dir Marketing & College Relations ... Ms. Julie MIRECKI
28 Diversity Coordinator ... Ms. Nicole YANG
88 Dean of Apprenticeship/Transportati ... Vacant
50 Dean Business & Technology ... Mr. Ed JANAIRO
97 Dean General Education/Basic Skills ... Ms. Lynn RETZAK
76 Exec Dean Health & Business ... Dr. Barbara DODGE
47 Exec Dean Mfg Trades/Agriculture ... Mr. Richard HOERTH
07 Student Services Manager ... Mr. Don GEIGER
37 Financial Aid Manager ... Ms. Corey GIVENS
32 Student Success Manager ... Ms. Foua HANG
18 Physical Plant Manager ... Mr. Bryan KOESER
08 Library Services Manager ... Ms. Karla ZAHN
22 Affirm Action Officer ... Ms. Kathy KOTAJARVI
40 Bookstore Manager ... Ms. Kelly WOLFERT
13 Dir Information Technology ... Mr. Chris LEWINSKI
30 Director of Advancement ... Ms. Katie WILLINGER
29 Director Alumni Relations ... Ms. Katie WILLINGER

*Madison Area Technical College (C)

1701 Wright Street, Madison WI 53704-2599
County: Dane
FICE Identification: 004007
Unit ID: 238263
Telephone: (608) 246-6100
Carnegie Class: Assoc/Pub-R-L
FAX Number: (608) 246-6880
Calendar System: Semester
URL: www.madisoncollege.org
Established: 1912
Annual Undergrad Tuition & Fees (In-District): $4,053
Enrollment: 18,046
Coed
Affiliation or Control: State/Local
IRS Status: 501(c)3
Highest Offering: Associate Degree
Program: Occupational; 2-Year Principally Bachelor's Creditable
Accreditation: NH, ACFEI, ADNUR, COARC, DH, MAC, MLTAD, OPTT, OTA, PTAA, RAD, SURGT

02 President ... Dr. Jack E. DANIELS, III
05 Provost ... Mr. Terrance S. WEBB
11 Vice Pres Administrative Svcs ... Mr. Aaron BURKES
32 Vice Pres Student Development ... Dr. Keith T. CORNILLE
84 Vice Pres Enrollment Management ... Ms. Diane K. WALLESER
15 Vice Pres Human Resources ... Mr. Charles E. MCDOWELL
45 Asst Vice Pres Budget/Public Affair ... Mr. Timothy L. CASPER
07 Asst Vice Pres Marketing/Enrollment ... Ms. Jennifer L. HOEGE
20 Assoc Vice Pres Learner Success ... Ms. Turina R. BAKKEN
88 Director Operations ... Ms. Lori A. SEBRANEK
18 Director Facilities Services ... Mr. Michael M. STARK
10 Chief Finance Officer/Controller ... Mr. Edwin R. NOEHRE
13 Chief Information Officer ... Mr. Mirwais QADER
21 Budget Director ... Mr. Peter MATERNOWSKI
25 Director Grants & Special Projects ... Ms. Emily J. SANDERS
41 Athletic Director ... Mr. Stephen C. HAUSER
09 Dir Inst Research & Effectiveness ... Mr. Ali R. ZARRINNAM
88 Dir International Education ... Dr. Geoffrey W. BRADSHAW
35 Director Student Life ... Ms. Renee M. ALFANO
108 Director Testing and Assessment ... Mr. James A. MERRITT
26 Manager Public Relations ... Mr. Cary R. HEYER
08 Director Library Services ... Ms. Julie C. GORES
40 Bookstore Manager ... Mr. Scott R. HEIMAN
37 Manager Financial Aid ... Mr. William PENA
22 Dir Employ/Diversity & Cmty Rels ... Ms. Malika S. EVANCO
19 Chief of Public Safety ... Mr. James A. BOTTONI
102 Chief Exec Officer Foundation ... Ms. Tammy THAYER
88 Dean Academic Advancement ... Mr. Christopher P. VANDALL
88 Assoc Dean Retention & Student Devt ... Ms. Carlotta V. CALMESE
38 Assoc Dean Couns & Stdnt Conduct ... Dr. Geraldo G. VILA CRUZ
106 Assoc Dean Online/Accelerated Lrng ... Dr. Shawna M. CARTER
88 Assoc Dean Academic Advancement ... Ms. Janice L. METTAUER
54 Dean Applied Science Engr & Tech ... Mr. Kenneth J. STARKMAN
50 Dean Business & Applied Arts ... Mr. Bryan M. WOODHOUSE
88 Dean Human & Protective Services ... Vacant
49 Dean Arts & Sciences ... Dr. Todd H. STEBBINS
76 Dean Health Education ... Dr. Mark C. LAUSCH
51 Dean Community & Corporate Learning ... Ms. Kathleen A. RADIONOFF
88 Dir Ctr Excellence Teaching/Learn ... Mr. Patrick BARLOW
12 Director Eastern Region ... Ms. Lynn M. FORSETH
12 Director Northern Region ... Mr. John W. ALT
12 Director Southwest Region ... Dr. Lorin K. TOEPPER
12 Downtown Campus Manager ... Dr. Kathleen A. PARIS
12 South Campus Manager ... Ms. Valentina AHEDO
26 Marketing Promotions Manager ... Mr. Christopher SCHELL
96 Purchasing Manager ... Ms. Kristin MURPHY

*Mid-State Technical College (D)

500 32nd Street N, Wisconsin Rapids WI 54494-5599
County: Wood
FICE Identification: 005380
Unit ID: 239220
Telephone: (715) 422-5300
Carnegie Class: Assoc/Pub-R-M
FAX Number: (715) 422-5345
Calendar System: Semester
URL: www.mstc.edu
Established: 1967
Annual Undergrad Tuition & Fees (In-District): $3,969
Enrollment: 3,622
Coed
Affiliation or Control: State/Local
IRS Status: 501(c)3
Highest Offering: Associate Degree
Program: 2-Year Principally Bachelor's Creditable; Technical Emphasis
Accreditation: NH, ADNUR, CAHIIM, COARC, MAC, PHLEB, SURGT

02 President ... Dr. Susan BUDJAC
05 Vice President Academic Affairs ... Dr. Ann Marie KRAUSE
32 VP Student Affairs/Information Tech ... Ms. Connie WILLFAHRT
10 Vice President Finance ... Mr. Nelson D. DAHL
15 Vice President Human Resources ... Mr. Richard O'SULLIVAN
50 Dean General Education & Business ... Dr. John HIGGS
75 Dean Technical/Industrial Division ... Mr. Alan JAVOROSKI
76 Dean Service & Health Careers ... Ms. Janet NEWMAN
12 Dean Stevens Point Campus ... Mr. Steven SMITH
12 Dean Marshfield Campus ... Ms. Brenda DILLENBURG
26 Director of Communications ... Mr. Karl EASTTORP
30 Director College Advancement ... Ms. Patty FAIRCHILD
102 Foundation and Alumni Director ... Ms. Chris MAGUIRE
18 Director of Facilities/Procurement ... Mr. Larry CIHLAR
84 Director of Enrollment Management ... Ms. Mandy LANG
35 Director Student Support ... Ms. Nancy SCHAPERKOTTER
96 Director of Purchasing ... Vacant
06 Student Records Manager ... Ms. Denise KINNEY
08 Library Services Manager ... Ms. Maria HERNANDEZ
37 Financial Aid Supervisor ... Mrs. Mary Jo GREEN

*Milwaukee Area Technical College (E)

700 W State Street, Milwaukee WI 53233-1443
County: Milwaukee
FICE Identification: 003866
Unit ID: 239248
Telephone: (414) 297-6600
Carnegie Class: Assoc/Pub-U-MC
FAX Number: (414) 297-7990
Calendar System: Semester
URL: www.matc.edu
Established: 1912
Annual Undergrad Tuition & Fees (In-District): $5,121
Enrollment: 27,942
Coed
Affiliation or Control: Local
IRS Status: 501(c)3
Highest Offering: Associate Degree
Program: Occupational; 2-Year Principally Bachelor's Creditable
Accreditation: NH, ACFEI, ADNUR, COARC, CVT, DH, DIETT, FUSER, MAC, MLTAD, OTA, PHLEB, PNUR, PTAA, RAD, SURGT

02 President ... Dr. Michael L. BURKE
05 Provost ... Dr. Vicki J. MARTIN
32 Vice Pres Student Services ... Dr. Trevor KUBATZKE
10 Vice President of Finance ... Dr. James WILLIAMS
43 Vice President & Legal Counsel ... Ms. Janice FALKENBERG
15 Assoc Vice Pres Human Resource ... Dr. Pablo CARDONA
13 Assoc VP Information Technology ... Mr. Michael WALSH
23 Dean Health Occupation ... Dr. Dessie LEVY
49 Int Dean Liberal Arts & Sciences ... Dr. Wilma BONAPARTE
50 Int Dean Business & Graphic Arts ... Dr. Mohammad DAKWAR
24 General Manager Public Television ... Mr. Ellis BROMBERG
11 Director Operations ... Mr. Richard DRIES
35 Director Student Life ... Mr. Archie GRAHAM
08 Director of Library ... Vacant
37 Interim Director Student Finances ... Ms. Camille NICOLAI
90 Director Technical Services ... Mr. Michael GAVIN
21 Controller ... Ms. Terri GAYHART
19 Director Public Safety ... Mr. Bradford HINES
06 Registrar ... Ms. Sarah ADAMS
09 Director Institutional Research ... Vacant
84 Director Recruitment ... Vacant
29 Director Alumni Relations ... Ms. Christine MCGEE
38 Int Director Student Counseling ... Dr. Daniel BURRELL
26 Chief Public Relations Officer ... Ms. Kathleen HOHL
96 Procurement Manager ... Mr. Edward BUSHMAN
41 Coordinator Athletics ... Mr. Randy CASEY

*Moraine Park Technical College (F)

235 N National Avenue, Fond Du Lac WI 54935-2884
County: Fond Du Lac
FICE Identification: 009256
Unit ID: 239372
Telephone: (920) 922-8611
Carnegie Class: Assoc/Pub-R-L
FAX Number: (920) 929-2471
Calendar System: Semester
URL: www.morainepark.edu
Established: 1967
Annual Undergrad Tuition & Fees (In-District): $3,986
Enrollment: 6,074
Coed
Affiliation or Control: State/Local
IRS Status: 501(c)3
Highest Offering: Associate Degree
Program: Occupational; 2-Year Principally Bachelor's Creditable; Technical Emphasis
Accreditation: NH, ADNUR, CAHIIM, COARC, MAC, MLTAD, RAD, SURGT

02 President ... Sheila RUHLAND
05 Vice Pres Academic Affairs ... James R. EDEN
10 Vice Pres Finance & Facilities ... Bonnie BAERWALD
15 Vice President Human Resources ... Kathleen M. BROSKE
30 VP Marketing/College Advancement ... Sharon N. HOLMES
32 Vice President Student Affairs ... Stanley CRAM
13 CIO/Vice Pres Inform Technology ... Jim BLAKESLEE
84 Vice Pres of Enrollment Management ... Bethany M. RAFFAELLI
30 Director of College Advancement ... Kelly NORTON
12 WB & Online Campus/Cmty Partner ... Peter J. RETTLER
12 Beaver Dam Campus/Cmty Prtnr ... Karen COLEY
20 Executive Dean of Instruction ... James V. EDEN
24 Exec Dean Instructional Support ... Gerald R. EDGREN, III
76 Exec Dean Hlth Sciences/Public Svcs ... Kathy S. VANEERDEN
88 Dean of Health Sciences/Public Svcs ... Kristin M. FINNEL
06 Registrar ... Amanda HRUSKA
26 Dir Marketing/Communications ... Melissa WORTHINGTON
07 Recruitment & Retention Associate ... Sally A. RUBACK
08 Learning Resource Center Associate ... Charlene M. PETTIT
40 Auxiliary Services Associate ... Jon A. SHAPIRO
18 Facilities Associate ... Timothy J. FLOOD
22 Employment/Affirmative Action Assoc ... Beth A. MENDOZA
96 Purchasing Associate ... Charles E. BIRRINGER
37 Student Financials Partner ... Karen A. ZUEHLKE

*Nicolet Area Technical College (G)

Box 518, Rhinelander WI 54501-0518
County: Oneida
FICE Identification: 005384
Unit ID: 239442
Telephone: (715) 365-4410
Carnegie Class: Assoc/Pub-R-S
FAX Number: (715) 365-4445
Calendar System: Semester
URL: www.nicoletcollege.edu
Established: 1967
Annual Undergrad Tuition & Fees (In-State): $3,666
Enrollment: 1,306
Coed
Affiliation or Control: State
IRS Status: 501(c)3
Highest Offering: Associate Degree
Program: Occupational; 2-Year Principally Bachelor's Creditable
Accreditation: NH, ADNUR, DH, MAC

02 President ... Ms. Elizabeth BURMASTER
10 Vice Pres Finance/Coll Operations ... Ms. Roxanne M. LUTGEN
05 VP Teaching/Learning/Stdnt Success ... Dr. Kenneth E. URBAN
88 Dean of Trade & Industry ... Ms. Brigitte PARSONS
49 Dean of Liberal Arts ... Ms. Rose PRUNTY
50 Dean Business/Institutional Effect ... Mr. Chuck KOMP
76 Dean of Health Occupations ... Ms. Lenore MANGLES
103 Exec Dean Wrkfce/Econ Dev/Security ... Mr. Ron SKALLERUD
102 Executive Director Foundation ... Ms. Heather SCHALLOCK
16 Director of Human Resources ... Dr. Dan GROLEAU
21 Dir of Accounting/Business Services ... Mr. John VAN DE LOO
18 Director of Facilities ... Mr. Pete VANNEY
26 Exec Dir Comm/Col Cmty Init ... Ms. Sandy KINNEY
37 Director Financial Aid ... Ms. Jill PRICE
28 Dir Ctr for Diversity/Inclusion ... Ms. Rachelle ASHLEY
88 Disability Support Case Manager ... Vacant
19 Director Protective Services ... Mr. Jason GOELDNER
06 Registrar/Dir Welcome Center ... Mr. Kyle GRUENING
08 Director Library Services ... Mr. Todd MOUNTJOY
13 Director Information Technology ... Mr. Greg MILJEVICH
103 Director Workforce Development ... Ms. Sandy BISHOP
88 Director Learner Success ... Vacant
09 Planning/Development/Evaluation Mgr ... Ms. Kelly HAVERKAMPF
07 PK-16/Admissions Coordinator ... Ms. Teri PHALIN

*Northcentral Technical College (A)

1000 W Campus Drive, Wausau WI 54401-1880

County: Marathon FICE Identification: 005387
Unit ID: 239460
Telephone: (715) 675-3331 Carnegie Class: Assoc/Pub-R-M
FAX Number: (715) 675-9776 Calendar System: Semester
URL: www.ntc.edu
Established: 1912 Annual Undergrad Tuition & Fees (In-District): $4,026
Enrollment: 4,764 Coed
Affiliation or Control: Local IRS Status: 501(c)3
Highest Offering: Associate Degree
Program: Occupational; 2-Year Principally Bachelor's Creditable
Accreditation: NH, ADNUR, DH, EMT, MAC, MLTAD, PHLEB, RAD, SURGT

02 President ....Dr. Lori A. WEYERS
05 Vice President for Learning ....Mrs. Shelly MONDEIK
15 Vice President of HR/College Advanc ...Mrs. Jeannie M. WORDEN
32 Vice President of Student Services ....Dr. Laurie BOROWICZ
10 Vice President of Finance & CFO ....Ms. Jane KITTEL
13 Chief Information Officer ....Mr. Chet A. STREBE
18 Director of Facilities ....Mr. Rob ELLIOTT
26 Dirctor of Marketing & PR ....Mrs. Katrina FELCH
19 Dean Public Safety ....Mr. Bryce KOLPACK
97 Dean General Studies & Learning Ctr ....Mrs. Rachelle PHAKITTHONG
47 Dean Agricultural Sciences ....Ms. Vicky PIETZ
50 Dean Business/Cmty Svc/Intntl Ed .... Mr. Christopher SEVERSON
103 Dean Business & Industry Solutions ....Mr. Mark BOROWICZ
12 Dean East & Southeast Campuses ....Mr. Larry KIND
12 Dean North/West/Southwest Campuses ....Ms. Bobbi DAMROW
76 Dean of Health Sciences ....Ms. Lorraine ZOROMSKI
22 Employment Coord/Affirm Action Ofcr ....Ms. Cindy THELEN
88 Director Quality/Continuous Improv ....Mrs. Beth ELLIE
35 Director of Student Relations ....Mr. Shawn P. SULLIVAN
19 Director of Security ....Mr. Dan JACOBSON
06 Registrar ....Mr. Nick BLANCHETTE
88 Dean K-12 Programs ....Mr. Dan NOWAK
84 Director of Enrollment ....Ms. Sarah DILLON
15 Director of Human Resources ....Ms. Karen BRZEZINSKI
106 Dean Educational Support Services ....Ms. Debra STENCIL
36 Director of Transfer & Placement ....Ms. Suzi MATHIAS
38 Dean of Student Success ....Mrs. Shannon LIVINGSTON
75 Dean of Technical & Trades ....Mr. Darren ACKLEY

*Northeast Wisconsin Technical College (B)

PO Box 19042, 2740 W Mason Street,
Green Bay WI 54307-9042

County: Brown FICE Identification: 005301
Unit ID: 239488
Telephone: (920) 498-5500 Carnegie Class: Assoc/Pub-R-L
FAX Number: (920) 498-6260 Calendar System: Semester
URL: www.nwtc.edu
Established: 1913 Annual Undergrad Tuition & Fees (In-District): $3,884
Enrollment: 9,944 Coed
Affiliation or Control: State/Local IRS Status: 501(c)3
Highest Offering: Associate Degree
Program: Occupational; 2-Year Principally Bachelor's Creditable; Technical Emphasis
Accreditation: NH, ADNUR, CAHIIM, COARC, DA, DH, DMS, EMT, ENGT, MAC, MLTAD, PTAA, RAD, SURGT

02 President ....Dr. H. Jeffrey RAFN
05 Vice President of Learning ....Ms. Lori SUDDICK
32 Vice President of Student Services ....Dr. Pamela PHILLIPS
30 Vice Pres of College Advancement ....Ms. Karen SMITS
15 Vice President of Human Resources ....Ms. Sandy RYCZKOWSKI
13 Chief Information Officer ....Ms. Linda HARTFORD
10 Chief Financial Officer ....Mr. Jim BLUMREICH
12 Dean Marinette Campus ....Mr. Patrick O'HARA
12 Dean Sturgeon Bay Campus ....Vacant
50 Dn Business/Information Technology ....Mr. Randy SMITH
76 Dean Health Science ....Ms. Kay TUPALA
72 Dean Trades & Engr Technologies ....Mr. Mark WEBER
97 Dean General Education ....Ms. Michele SCHMIT
31 Dean Community/Regional Lrning Svcs ....Mrs. Sally L. MARTIN
20 Dean Learning Solutions ....Ms. Anne KAMPS
103 Dean Corp Training & Economic Devel ....Mr. Dean STEWART
38 Dean of Student Success ....Ms. Vickie LOCK
28 Director of College Diversity ....Dr. Alem ASRES
06 Registrar & Dean Enrollment Svcs ....Mr. Mark FRANKS
84 Dir Assessment/Enrollment/Retention ....Ms. Sally LANGAN
37 Financial Aid Director ....Ms. Emily YSEBAERT
09 Director Planning and Development ....Ms. Karen J. SMITS
96 Director of Purchasing ....Mr. Mark CICHON
102 Director Educational Foundation ....Ms. Crystal HARRISON
40 Director Bookstore ....Ms. Bonita ZIMA
26 Chief Public Relations Officer ....Vacant
18 Director of Facilities ....Mr. Daniel J. SEIDL
24 Media & Telecom Services Manager ....Mr. John SIEMERING
08 Manager Library Services ....Ms. Kim LAPLANTE
104 Manager Center for Global Cultures ....Vacant
21 Director of Financial Operations ....Mr. Clark WAGNER

*Southwest Wisconsin Technical College (C)

1800 Bronson Boulevard, Fennimore WI 53809-9778

County: Grant FICE Identification: 007669
Unit ID: 239910
Telephone: (608) 822-3262 Carnegie Class: Assoc/Pub-R-M
FAX Number: (608) 822-6019 Calendar System: Semester
URL: www.swtc.edu
Established: 1967 Annual Undergrad Tuition & Fees (In-District): $4,010
Enrollment: 3,386 Coed
Affiliation or Control: State/Local IRS Status: 501(c)3
Highest Offering: Associate Degree
Program: Occupational; 2-Year Principally Bachelor's Creditable
Accreditation: NH, ADNUR, MAC, MLTAD, PTAA

02 President ....Dr. Duane M. FORD
10 VP for Administrative Services ....Mr. Caleb WHITE
05 VP for Student & Academic Services ....Dr. Phil THOMAS
50 Dean Business/Agric/General Educ ....Dr. Joyce CZAJKOWSKI
76 Dean Health Occupations ....Ms. Kathleen E. GARRITY
47 Dean of Industry/Trades/Agriculture ....Mr. Derek DACHELET
13 Director of Information Technology ....Vacant
15 Director of Human Resources ....Ms. Laura BODENBENDER
30 Director Institutional Advancement ....Ms. Barbara TUCKER
32 Director of Student Services ....Ms. Laura NYBERG-COMINS
37 Financial Aid Manager ....Ms. Joy A. KITE
18 Director of Facilities ....Mr. Doug PEARSON
39 Resident/Student Life Manager ....Ms. Heather FIFRICK
88 Human Resources Assistant ....Ms. Connie HABERKORN
88 Administrative Asst Admin Services ....Ms. Helen LAUFENBERG
88 Fire EMS & Early Childhood Coord ....Ms. Rita LUNA
88 Criminal Justice & Drivers Ed Coord ....Ms. Kris WUBBEN
04 Executive Asst to Board/President ....Ms. Karen M. CAMPBELL
21 Finance Accountant/Payroll Suprvsr ....Ms. Mary UREN
88 Curriculum/Staff Development ....Ms. Julie PLUEMER

*Waukesha County Technical College (D)

800 Main Street, Pewaukee WI 53072-4696

County: Waukesha FICE Identification: 005294
Unit ID: 240125
Telephone: (262) 691-5566 Carnegie Class: Assoc/Pub-S-MC
FAX Number: (262) 691-5593 Calendar System: Semester
URL: www.wctc.edu
Established: 1923 Annual Undergrad Tuition & Fees (In-District): $3,885
Enrollment: 10,286 Coed
Affiliation or Control: State/Local IRS Status: 501(c)3
Highest Offering: Associate Degree
Program: Occupational; 2-Year Principally Bachelor's Creditable; Technical Emphasis
Accreditation: NH, ACFEI, ADNUR, CAHIIM, DH, EMT, ENGT, MAC, SURGT

02 President ....Dr. Barbara A. PRINDIVILLE
03 Executive VP ....Ms. Kaylen BETZIG
45 VP Strategic Effectiveness & Advanc ....Ms. Kaylen BETZIG
05 VP Learning ....Ms. Denine ROOD
10 Chief Financial Officer ....Ms. Cary A. TESSMANN
32 VP Student Services ....Ms. Deborah WALLENDAL
75 Dean Industrial Occupations ....Mr. Michael SHIELS
76 Dean Service Occupations ....Mr. Greg WEST
76 Dean Health Occupations ....Ms. Sandra STEARNS
50 Dean Business Occupations ....Mr. Bradley PIAZZA
103 Dean Center/Business Performance ....Dr. Joseph WEITZER
97 Dean Academic Support ....Ms. Susan MINNICK
15 VP Human Resource Svcs ....Mr. David BROWN
06 Registrar ....Ms. Jacki VANDYKE
38 Director Counsel/Acad Sup/Spec Svcs ....Ms. Deborah JILBERT
14 Chief Information Officer ....Mr. Rodney NOBLES
40 Bookstore Manager ....Mr. Rick MILLER
18 Director Facilities Services ....Mr. Jeffrey LEVERENZ
35 Director Student Development ....Ms. Susanne FENSKE
90 Director Academic Technology ....Mr. Randall COOROUGH
08 Director of Library Services ....Ms. Terry KEMPER
88 Mgr Executive Operations Pres Ofc ....Mr. James F. REHAGEN
26 Marketing & Communications Mgr ....Ms. Susan STERN
07 Manager Admiss/Advis & Assessment ....Ms. Kathleen KAZDA
37 Manager Financial Aid ....Mr. Timothy K. JACOBSON
35 Student Life Coordinator ....Mr. Jonathan N. PEDRAZA
28 Recruitment Supervisor ....Ms. Trisha L. HORNBURG
25 Director of Grants & Contracts ....Ms. Linda J. MILLER
23 Enviro Health & Safety Supervisor ....Mr. Bruce NEUMANN
24 Media Services Coordinator ....Mr. Donald DUGAN
96 Purchasing Specialist ....Ms. Victoria NASH
36 Mgr Career Development Services ....Ms. Barbara SUYAMA
85 International Educ Coordinator ....Mr. K.Austin BAADE
28 Diversity Coordinator ....Mr. Rolando DELEON

*Western Technical College (E)

400 N Seventh Street, La Crosse WI 54601-3368

County: La Crosse FICE Identification: 003840
Unit ID: 240170
Telephone: (608) 785-9200 Carnegie Class: Assoc/Pub-R-M
FAX Number: (608) 785-9205 Calendar System: Trimester
URL: www.westerntc.edu
Established: 1912 Annual Undergrad Tuition & Fees (In-District): $3,989
Enrollment: 4,798 Coed
Affiliation or Control: State/Local IRS Status: 501(c)3
Highest Offering: Associate Degree
Program: Occupational; 2-Year Principally Bachelor's Creditable; Technical Emphasis
Accreditation: NH, ADNUR, CAHIIM, COARC, DA, MAC, MLTAD, OTA, PTAA, RAD, SURGT

02 President ....Dr. J. Lee RASCH
10 Vice President Finance/Operations ....Mr. Michael C. PIEPER
05 Vice President for Instruction ....Dr. Peg BOUDREAU
32 VP Student Services ....Dr. Denise T. VUJNOVICH
45 AVP Strategic Effectiveness & Engag ....Ms. Amy THORNTON
12 Director of Ops-Regional Locations ....Ms. Jennifer BRAVE
102 Executive Director Foundation ....Mr. Michael SWENSON
14 Director Computer/Telecomm Svcs ....Mr. Bruce E. MATHEW
37 Financial Aid Manager ....Ms. Jerolyn R. GRANDALL
21 Business Services Director ....Ms. Amy SCHMIDT
56 Director Economic Development ....Ms. Patti BALACEK
38 Director Counseling Enroll Svcs ....Ms. Ann BRANDAU-HYNEK
29 Director Alumni Relations ....Ms. Sally EMERSON
07 Manager Admissions/Registration ....Ms. Sandy PETERSON
35 Manager of Campus Activities ....Ms. Shelley MCNEELY
08 Manager Library Services ....Mr. Ron EDWARDS
24 Manager Instructional Media Center ....Ms. Joan PIERCE
40 Bookstore Manager ....Mr. David R. WIGNES
72 Dean Industrial Technologies ....Mr. William BRENDEL
76 Dean Health & Public Safety ....Ms. Diane NEEFE
97 Dean General Education ....Dr. Douglas STRAUSS
50 Dean Business Education ....Mr. Gary BROWN

*Wisconsin Indianhead Technical College (F)

505 Pine Ridge Drive, Shell Lake WI 54871-9300

County: Washburn FICE Identification: 011824
Unit ID: 240198
Telephone: (715) 468-2815 Carnegie Class: Assoc/Pub-R-M
FAX Number: (715) 468-2819 Calendar System: Semester
URL: www.witc.edu
Established: 1968 Annual Undergrad Tuition & Fees (In-State): $3,798
Enrollment: 3,596 Coed
Affiliation or Control: State IRS Status: Exempt
Highest Offering: Associate Degree
Program: Occupational; 2-Year Principally Bachelor's Creditable; Technical Emphasis
Accreditation: NH, ADNUR, MAC, OTA

02 President ....Dr. Robert M. MEYER
10 Vice Pres Finance/Bus Svcs/CFO ....Mr. Steven DECKER
05 Vice President Academic Affairs ....Dr. Bonny COPENHAVER
32 Vice President Student Affairs ....Mr. Steve BITZER
20 Vice President Instruct Technology ....Mr. Joe HUFTEL
51 Vice President Cont Educ/Foundation ....Mr. Craig FOWLER
09 VP Institutional Effectiveness ....Ms. Ellen RILEY HAUSER
15 VP Human Res/Employee Rels ....Ms. Cher VINK
13 Sr Director Information Technology ....Mr. James DAHLBERG
37 Director Financial Aid ....Mr. Terry KLEIN
06 Registrar ....Mr. Shane EVENSON
08 Director Learning Resources ....Mr. Scott VRIEZE
84 Director of Enrollment ....Ms. Laura SULLIVAN
26 Director Marketing & Recruitment ....Ms. Elizabeth LYDEN

*Chippewa Valley Technical College-Chippewa Falls Campus (G)

770 Scheidler Road, Chippewa Falls WI 54729

Telephone: (715) 738-3841 Identification: 770419
Accreditation: &NH

† Main campus is Chippewa Valley Technical College in Eau Claire, WI.

*Chippewa Valley Technical College-Gateway (H)

2320 Alpine Road, Eau Claire WI 54703

Telephone: (715) 874-4600 Identification: 770420
Accreditation: &NH

† Main campus is Chippewa Valley Technical College in Eau Claire, WI.

*Chippewa Valley Technical College Menomonie Campus (I)

403 Technology Drive East, Menomonie WI 54751

Telephone: (715) 232-2685 Identification: 770422
Accreditation: &NH

† Main campus is Chippewa Valley Technical College in Eau Claire, WI.

*Chippewa Valley Technical College River Falls Campus (J)

500 South Wasson Lane, River Falls WI 54022

Telephone: (715) 425-3301 Identification: 770423
Accreditation: &NH

† Main campus is Chippewa Valley Technical College in Eau Claire, WI.

*Chippewa Valley Technical College-West (K)

4000 Campus Road, Eau Claire WI 54703

Telephone: (715) 833-6221 Identification: 770421
Accreditation: &NH

† Main campus is Chippewa Valley Technical College in Eau Claire, WI.

*Fox Valley Technical College (L)

150 N Campbell Road, Oshkosh WI 54902

Telephone: (920) 233-9191 Identification: 770425
Accreditation: &NH

† Main campus is Fox Valley Technical College in Appleton, WI.

***Gateway Technical College Burlington Center** (A)*
496 McCanna Parkway, Burlington WI 53105
Telephone: (262) 767-5200 Identification: 770426
Accreditation: &NH

† Main campus is Gateway Technical College in Kenosha, WI.

***Gateway Technical College Elkhorn Campus** (B)*
400 County Road H, Elkhorn WI 53121
Telephone: (262) 741-8200 Identification: 770427
Accreditation: &NH

† Main campus is Gateway Technical College in Kenosha, WI.

***Gateway Technical College Racine Campus** (C)*
1001 S Main Street, Racine WI 53403
Telephone: (262) 619-6200 Identification: 770428
Accreditation: &NH

† Main campus is Gateway Technical College in Kenosha, WI.

***Madison Area Technical College Commercial Avenue Education Center** (D)*
2125 Commercial Avenue, Madison WI 53704
Telephone: (608) 246-6100 Identification: 770436
Accreditation: &NH

† Main campus is Madison Area Technical College in Madison, WI.

***Madison Area Technical College Downtown Education Center** (E)*
211 North Carroll Street, Madison WI 53703
Telephone: (608) 246-6100 Identification: 770437
Accreditation: &NH

† Main campus is Madison Area Technical College in Madison, WI.

***Madison Area Technical College Portage** (F)*
330 West Collins Street, Portage WI 53901
Telephone: (608) 745-3100 Identification: 770438
Accreditation: &NH

† Main campus is Madison Area Technical College in Madison, WI.

***Madison Area Technical College Fort Atkinson** (G)*
827 Banker Road, Fort Atkinson WI 53538
Telephone: (920) 568-7200 Identification: 770435
Accreditation: &NH

† Main campus is Madison Area Technical College in Madison, WI.

***Madison Area Technical College Reedsburg** (H)*
300 Alexander Avenue, Reedsburg WI 53959
Telephone: (608) 524-7800 Identification: 770439
Accreditation: &NH

† Main campus is Madison Area Technical College in Madison, WI.

***Madison Area Technical College Watertown** (I)*
1300 West Main Street, Watertown WI 53098
Telephone: (920) 206-8000 Identification: 770440
Accreditation: &NH

† Main campus is Madison Area Technical College in Madison, WI.

***Mid-State Technical College Marshfield Campus** (J)*
2600 West 5th Street, Marshfield WI 54449
Telephone: (715) 387-2538 Identification: 770441
Accreditation: &NH

† Main campus is Mid-State Technical College in Wisconsin Rapids, WI.

***Mid-State Technical College Stevens Point Campus** (K)*
933 Michigan Avenue, Stevens Point WI 54481
Telephone: (715) 344-3063 Identification: 770442
Accreditation: &NH

† Main campus is Mid-State Technical College in Wisconsin Rapids, WI.

***Milwaukee Area Technical College** (L)*
5555 West Highlands Road, Mequon WI 53092
Telephone: (262) 238-2200 Identification: 770443
Accreditation: &NH

† Main campus is Milwaukee Area Technical College in Milwaukee, WI.

***Milwaukee Area Technical College** (M)*
6665 South Howell Avenue, Oakcreek WI 53154-1107
Telephone: (414) 571-4500 Identification: 770444
Accreditation: &NH

† Main campus is Milwaukee Area Technical College in Milwaukee, WI.

***Milwaukee Area Technical College** (N)*
1200 South 71st Street, West Allis WI 53214-3110
Telephone: (414) 456-5500 Identification: 770445
Accreditation: &NH

† Main campus is Milwaukee Area Technical College in Milwaukee, WI.

***Moraine Park Technical College** (O)*
700 Gould Street, Beaver Dam WI 53916
Telephone: (920) 887-1428 Identification: 770446
Accreditation: &NH

† Main campus is Moraine Park Technical College in Fond Du Lac, WI.

***Moraine Park Technical College** (P)*
2151 North Main Street, West Bend WI 53090
Telephone: (262) 335-5713 Identification: 770447
Accreditation: &NH

† Main campus is Moraine Park Technical College in Fond Du Lac, WI.

***Northeast Wisconsin Technical College-Marinette Campus** (Q)*
1601 University Drive, Marinette WI 54143
Telephone: (715) 735-9361 Identification: 770448
Accreditation: &NH

† Main campus is Northeast Wisconsin Technical College in Green Bay, WI.

***Northeast Wisconsin Technical College-Sturgeon Bay Campus** (R)*
229 N 14th Avenue, Sturgeon Bay WI 54235
Telephone: (920) 746-4900 Identification: 770449
Accreditation: &NH

† Main campus is Northeast Wisconsin Technical College in Green Bay, WI.

***Wisconsin Indianhead Technical College-Ashland Campus** (S)*
2100 Beaser Avenue, Ashland WI 54806
Telephone: (715) 682-8040 Identification: 770463
Accreditation: &NH, MAC

† Main campus is Wisconsin Indianhead Technical College in Shell Lake, WI.

***Wisconsin Indianhead Technical College-New Richmond Campus** (T)*
1019 S Knowles Avenue, New Richmond WI 54017
Telephone: (715) 246-6561 Identification: 770464
Accreditation: &NH, MAC

† Main campus is Wisconsin Indianhead Technical College in Shell Lake, WI.

***Wisconsin Indianhead Technical College-Rice Lake Campus** (U)*
1900 College Drive, Rice Lake WI 54868
Telephone: (715) 234-7082 Identification: 770465
Accreditation: &NH, EMT, MAC

† Main campus is Wisconsin Indianhead Technical College in Shell Lake, WI.

***Wisconsin Indianhead Technical College-Superior Campus** (V)*
600 North 21st Street, Superior WI 54880
Telephone: (715) 394-6677 Identification: 770466
Accreditation: &NH

† Main campus is Wisconsin Indianhead Technical College in Shell Lake, WI.

WYOMING

***Carbon County Higher Education Center/ Rawlins** (W)*
705 Rodeo Street, Rawlins WY 82301
Telephone: (307) 328-9204 Identification: 770481
Accreditation: &NH

† Main campus is Western Wyoming Community College in Rock Springs, WY.

Casper College (X)
125 College Drive, Casper WY 82601-2458
County: Natrona FICE Identification: 003928
Unit ID: 240505
Telephone: (307) 268-2110 Carnegie Class: Assoc/Pub-R-M
FAX Number: (307) 268-2682 Calendar System: Semester
URL: www.caspercollege.edu
Established: 1945 Annual Undergrad Tuition & Fees (In-District): $2,448
Enrollment: 4,384 Coed
Affiliation or Control: Local IRS Status: 501(c)3
Highest Offering: Associate Degree
Program: Occupational; 2-Year Principally Bachelor's Creditable
Accreditation: NH, ACBSP, ADNUR, ART, COARC, EMT, MLTAD, MUS, OTA, RAD, THEA

01 President ....Dr. Walter H. NOLTE
05 Vice President Academic Affairs ....Dr. Tim WRIGHT
32 Int Vice President Student Services ....Ms. Kim BYRD
11 Vice Pres Administrative Services ....Ms. Lynnde COLLING
51 Dean of Continuing Education ....Dr. Laura DRISCOLL
15 Director Human Resources ....Mr. Chauncy JOHNSON
07 Director Admissions/Student Records ....Ms. Kyla FOLTZ
26 Director College Relations ....Mr. Rich FUJITA
18 Director Physical Plant ....Mr. Michael SAWYER
38 Director Student Counseling ....Ms. Teresa WALLACE
08 Director of the Library ....Mr. Brad MATTHIES
13 Director Information Technology ....Mr. Kent BROOKS
36 Director Placement ....Ms. Janet DEVRIES
39 Director of Housing ....Ms. Barb MERYHEW
41 Athletic Director ....Mr. William LANDEN
24 Director of Media Services ....Mr. Todd WYKERT
19 Director Campus Security ....Mr. Lance JONES
102 Exec Director Foundation ....Ms. Paulann T. DOANE
09 Institutional Researcher ....Ms. Lynn FLETCHER
37 Director of Student Financial Aid ....Mr. Darry VOIGT
21 Dir Financial Services/Controller ....Ms. Robyn LANDEN
96 Purchasing Coordinator ....Mr. Paul CHRISTMAN
06 Registrar ....Ms. Linda NICHOLS

Central Wyoming College (Y)
2660 Peck Avenue, Riverton WY 82501-1520
County: Fremont FICE Identification: 007289
Unit ID: 240514
Telephone: (307) 855-2000 Carnegie Class: Assoc/Pub-R-M
FAX Number: (307) 855-2095 Calendar System: Semester
URL: www.cwc.edu
Established: 1966 Annual Undergrad Tuition & Fees (In-District): $2,568
Enrollment: 2,228 Coed
Affiliation or Control: Local IRS Status: 501(c)3
Highest Offering: Associate Degree
Program: Occupational; 2-Year Principally Bachelor's Creditable
Accreditation: NH, ADNUR

01 President ....Dr. JoAnne Y. MCFARLAND
03 Exec Vice Pres Student/Acad Svcs ....Dr. Jason WOOD
10 Vice Pres Admin Svcs/CFO ....Mr. Ron GRANGER
13 Chief Information Officer ....Mr. John WOOD
18 Chief Facilities/Physical Plant ....Mr. Wayne ROBINSON
08 Director of Library Services ....Ms. Nicole POUGET
27 Director of Public Information ....Ms. Carolyn AANESTAD
15 Exec Dir for Human Resources ....Ms. Jennifer REY
21 Finance Officer ....Ms. Lindy PASKETT
19 Director of Campus Safety/Security ....Mr. Dan LADD
96 Director of Purchasing ....Ms. Suzie KOEHN
84 Asst Dean for Enrollment Services ....Ms. Jacquelyn BURNS
103 Dean for Workforce & Cmty Educ ....Ms. Lynne MCAULIFFE
41 Director of Athletics ....Mr. Serol STAUFFENBERG
06 Assistant Registrar ....Ms. Connie NYBERG
49 Dean for Arts/English/Math ....Dr. Mark NORDEEN
50 Dean for Commerce/Allied Health ....Ms. Charlotte DONELSON
32 Assoc VP Student Services ....Ms. Cory DALY
35 Asst Dean Student Services ....Mr. Steve BARLOW
05 Assoc VP Academic Services ....Ms. Martha DAVEY

***CollegeAmerica Cheyenne** (Z)*
6101 Yellowstone Road, Cheyenne WY 82009
Telephone: (307) 637-2044 Identification: 770609
Accreditation: ACCSC

† Main campus is CollegeAmerica Denver in Denver, CO.

Eastern Wyoming College (a)
3200 W C Street, Torrington WY 82240-1699
County: Goshen FICE Identification: 003929
Unit ID: 240596
Telephone: (307) 532-8200 Carnegie Class: Assoc/Pub-R-S
FAX Number: (307) 532-8229 Calendar System: Semester
URL: ewc.wy.edu/
Established: 1948 Annual Undergrad Tuition & Fees (In-District): $2,472
Enrollment: 1,934 Coed
Affiliation or Control: State/Local IRS Status: 501(c)3
Highest Offering: Associate Degree
Program: Occupational; 2-Year Principally Bachelor's Creditable
Accreditation: NH

01 President ....Dr. Thomas J. ARMSTRONG
04 Exec Asst to President/Board ....Ms. Holly L. BRANHAM

Code	Title	Name
05	Vice President for Learning	Dr. Dee LUDWIG
11	VP for Admin Services	Mr. Ron LAHER
32	VP for Student Services	Dr. Rex COGDILL
20	Assoc VP for Outreach & Learning	Mr. Mike DURFEE
30	Dir of Institutional Development	Mr. Oliver SUNDBY
08	Director of Library Services	Mrs. Casey DEBUS
41	Director of College Athletics	Mr. Verl E. PETSCH
26	Director of College Relations	Ms. Tami AFDAHL
09	Director of Institutional Research	Ms. Kimberly RUSSELL
18	Director of Physical Plant	Mr. Keith JARVIS
39	Director of Residence Life	Ms. Kellee GOODER
37	Director of Financial Aid	Ms. Susan STEPHENSON
38	Director Counseling & Testing	Mrs. Debbie OCHSNER
15	Director Human Resources	Mr. Stuart NELSON
21	Business Office Director	Ms. Karen PARRIOTT

Eastern Wyoming College-Douglas Campus (A)

203 N 6th Street, Douglas WY 82633

Telephone: (307) 358-5622 Identification: 770476

Accreditation: &NH

† Main campus is Eastern Wyoming College in Torrington, WY.

Gillette College (B)

300 West Sinclair, Gillette WY 82718

Telephone: (888) 544-5538 Identification: 770478

Accreditation: &NH

† Main campus is Northern Wyoming Community College District in Sheridan, WY.

Institute of Business and Medical Careers (C)

1854 Dell Range Boulevard, Cheyenne WY 82009

Telephone: (307) 433-8363 Identification: 666738

Accreditation: ACICS

† Main campus is Institute of Business and Medical Careers in Fort Collins, CO.

Laramie County Community College (D)

1400 E College Drive, Cheyenne WY 82007-3299

County: Laramie FICE Identification: 009259

Unit ID: 240620

Telephone: (307) 778-5222 Carnegie Class: Assoc/Pub-R-M

FAX Number: (307) 778-1399 Calendar System: Semester

URL: www.lccc.wy.edu

Established: 1968 Annual Undergrad Tuition & Fees (In-District): $2,736

Enrollment: 5,141 Coed

Affiliation or Control: State/Local IRS Status: 501(c)3

Highest Offering: Associate Degree

Program: Occupational; 2-Year Principally Bachelor's Creditable

Accreditation: NH, ADNUR, DH, DMS, EMT, PTAA, RAD, SURGT

Code	Title	Name
01	President	Dr. Joe SCHAFFER
05	Vice Pres of Academic Affairs	Dr. Jose FIERRO
10	Vice Pres of Administration/Finance	Ms. Carol HOGLUND
32	Vice President of Student Services	Ms. Judy HAY
13	Chief Technology Officer	Mr. Chad MARLEY
16	Executive Director Human Resources	Ms. Peggie KRESL-HOTZ
30	Assoc VP Inst Advancement	Ms. Lisa MURPHY
12	Assoc VP of Albany County Campus	Dr. Lynn STALNAKER
45	Assc VP Institutional Effectiveness	Vacant
08	Librarian	Ms. Karen LANGE
37	Director of Financial Aid	Ms. Julie WILSON
26	Int Director of Public Relations	Mr. Ty STOCKTON
18	Director of Physical Plant	Mr. Timothy MACNAMARA
21	Director of Accounting Services	Mr. Herry ANDREWS
29	Dir Alumni Affairs/Event Planning	Ms. Lisa TRIMBLE
44	Dir Scholarships & Annual Giving	Ms. Brenda LAIRD
09	Manager of Institutional Research	Ms. Ann MURRAY
96	Director of Contracting/Procurement	Mr. Jerry HARRIS
07	Director of Admissions	Ms. Holly BRUEGMAN
06	Registrar	Ms. Stacy MAESTAS
35	Dean of Campus Living & Learning	Ms. Jenny RIGG
36	Dir Advising & Career Services	Ms. Chrissy RENFRO
49	Dean School of Arts & Humanities	Ms. Kathleen URBAN
50	Dean Sch of Bus/Ag & Tech Studies	Mr. Melvin O. HAWKINS, JR.
69	Dean Sch of Health Sci & Wellness	Ms. Therese HARPER
81	Dean School of Math & Science	Vacant
103	Dean Sch of Outreach/Workforce Dev	Ms. Maryellen TAST
20	Dir Instructional Technologies	Mr. Les BALSIGER

Laramie County Community College Albany County Campus (E)

1125 Boulder Drive, Laramie WY 82070

Telephone: (307) 721-5138 Identification: 770477

Accreditation: &NH

† Main campus is Laramie County Community College in Cheyenne, WY.

Northern Wyoming Community College District (F)

PO Box 1500, 3059 Coffeen Avenue, Sheridan WY 82801-1500

County: Sheridan FICE Identification: 003930

Unit ID: 240666

Telephone: (307) 674-6446 Carnegie Class: Assoc/Pub-R-M

FAX Number: (307) 674-4293 Calendar System: Semester

URL: www.sheridan.edu

Established: 1948 Annual Undergrad Tuition & Fees (In-District): $2,782

Enrollment: 4,273 Coed

Affiliation or Control: Local IRS Status: 501(c)3

Highest Offering: Associate Degree

Program: Occupational; 2-Year Principally Bachelor's Creditable

Accreditation: NH, ADNUR, DH

Code	Title	Name
01	President	Dr. Paul R. YOUNG
05	VP Academic Affairs	Dr. Jon H. CONNOLLY
10	VP Admin & Finance/CFO	Ms. Cheryl A. HEATH
12	VP Gillette College	Dr. Mark G. ENGLERT
30	VP Development	Dr. Susan BIGELOW
20	Asst VP Academic Affairs	Vacant
06	Dean Enrollment Services	Ms. Sharon K. ELWOOD
32	Dean of Students	Ms. Carol GARCIA
49	Dean Arts/Humanities & Social Science	Dr. Mercedes AGUIRRE BATTY
76	Dean Health Sciences	Ms. Trudy R. MUNSICK
47	Dean Culinary/Ag & Natural Science	Dr. Ami N. ERICKSON
75	Dean Technical Education	Mr. Jed JENSEN
15	Director Human Resources	Ms. Jennifer MCARTHUR
26	Dir Marketing/College Information	Ms. Wendy M. SMITH
37	Director Financial Aid Services	Ms. Jennifer SMITH
13	Dir Information Technology Services	Mr. Brady R. FACKRELL
21	Controller	Ms. Karen B. BURTIS
39	Director Housing & Residential Ed	Ms. Larissa B. BONNET
07	Director of Admissions - SC	Mr. Zane S. GARSTAD
07	Director of Admissions - GC	Ms. Jeri L. RUSSELL
88	Director Veteran Services	Mr. Brett K. BURTIS
18	Director Facilities/Physical Plant	Mr. Kent A. ANDERSEN
18	Director Gillette Facilities	Mr. Mark N. ANDERSEN
106	Dir Distance & Distributive Learn	Mr. Stoney GADDY
103	Dir Workforce Development & CE	Ms. Karen ST. CLAIR
08	Librarian	Ms. Katrina M. BROWN

Northwest College (G)

231 W 6th Street, Powell WY 82435

County: Park FICE Identification: 003931

Unit ID: 240657

Telephone: (307) 754-6000 Carnegie Class: Assoc/Pub-R-S

FAX Number: (307) 754-6245 Calendar System: Semester

URL: www.northwestcollege.edu

Established: 1946 Annual Undergrad Tuition & Fees (In-District): $2,653

Enrollment: 2,136 Coed

Affiliation or Control: State/Local IRS Status: 501(c)3

Highest Offering: Associate Degree

Program: Occupational; 2-Year Principally Bachelor's Creditable

Accreditation: NH, ADNUR, MUS

Code	Title	Name
01	President	Dr. Stefani HICSWA
05	Vice Pres Academic Affairs	Dr. Gerald GIRAUD
32	Vice Pres Student Affairs	Dr. Sean FOX
11	Vice Pres Administrative Services	Mr. Kim MILLS
26	Vice Pres College Relations	Mr. Mark KITCHEN
102	Executive Director NWC Foundation	Ms. Shelby WETZEL
20	Dean Student Learning/Acad Support	Dr. Matthew EWERS
103	Dean Extended Campus/Workforce	Ms. Ronda PEER
08	Library Director	Dr. Susan RICHARDS
10	Finance Director	Mr. Sheldon FLOM
15	Human Resources Director	Ms. Jill ANDERSON
14	Computing Services Director	Mr. Casey DEARCORN
18	Facilities Director	Mr. David PLUTE
06	Registrar/Admissions Director	Mr. Brad HAMMOND
37	Financial Aid/Scholarships Director	Mr. Shaman QUINN
39	Residence/Campus Life Director	Mr. Dee HAVIG

Oyster Ridger Higher Education/Kemmerer (H)

20 Adaville Drive, Diamondville WY 83116

Telephone: (307) 877-6958 Identification: 770479

Accreditation: &NH

† Main campus is Western Wyoming Community College in Rock Springs, WY.

University of Wyoming (I)

Dept 3434, 1000 E University Avenue, Laramie WY 82071-3434

County: Albany FICE Identification: 003932

Unit ID: 240727

Telephone: (307) 766-1121 Carnegie Class: RU/H

FAX Number: (307) 766-2271 Calendar System: Semester

URL: www.uwyo.edu

Established: 1886 Annual Undergrad Tuition & Fees (In-State): $4,404

Enrollment: 13,929 Coed

Affiliation or Control: State IRS Status: 501(c)3

Highest Offering: Doctorate

Program: Liberal Arts And General; Teacher Preparatory; Professional

Accreditation: NH, BUS, CACREP, CLPSY, CS, DIETD, ENG, LAW, MUS, NURSE, PHAR, SP, SW, TED

Code	Title	Name
01	President	Dr. Robert STERNBERG
05	Interim Vice Pres Academic Affairs	Dr. Richard MCGINITY
10	Vice President Administration	Vacant
86	Vice Pres Govt & Community Affairs	Mr. Chris BOSWELL
46	Vice President Research & Econ Dev	Dr. William A. GERN
32	Vice President Student Affairs	Dr. Sara L. AXELSON
13	Vice President Information Tech	Mr. Robert R. AYLWARD
30	Vice Pres Institutional Advancement	Mr. W. Ben BLALOCK, III
43	Vice President & General Counsel	Mr. Richard H. MILLER
41	Director Intercollegiate Athletics	Mr. Tom BURMAN
20	Associate VP Academic Affairs	Dr. Nicole BALLENGER
20	Associate VP Academic Affairs	Dr. Carol FROST
20	Associate VP Academic Affairs	Dr. Andrew C. HANSEN
11	Assoc Vice Pres Operations	Mr. Mark A. COLLINS
21	Assoc VP Fiscal Administration	Ms. Janet S. LOWE
21	Asst Vice Pres Budget/Inst Analysis	Ms. Arley WILLIAMS
88	Assoc Vice President Research	Ms. Dorothy C. YATES
35	AVP Student Affairs/Dn of Students	Dr. David COZZENS
88	Assoc VP Institutional Advancement	Mr. John D. STARK
47	Dean of Agriculture	Dr. Frank D. GALEY
49	Dean of Arts & Sciences	Dr. Paula LUTZ
50	Interim Dean of Business	Dr. John MITTELSTAEDT
53	Dean of Education	Dr. Kay A. PERSICHITTE
54	Dean of Engineering	Dr. Robert ETTEMA
76	Dean of Health Sciences	Dr. Joseph F. STEINER
61	Dean of Law	Mr. Stephen D. EASTON
08	Dean of Libraries	Ms. Maggie FARRELL
56	Dean Outreach	Dr. Susan FRYE
12	Assoc Dean UW/Casper College Center	Dr. Brent PICKETT
88	Director School of Energy Resources	Dr. Mark NORTHAM
65	Director Haub Sch Env/Nat Resources	Dr. Ingrid BURKE
07	Director of Admissions	Ms. Shelley DODD
36	Director Advising/Career Services	Ms. Evelyn J. CHYTKA
28	Director Affirmative Action/EEO	Ms. Oneida BLAGG
29	Director Alumni Relations	Mr. Keener FRYE
88	Director American Heritage Center	Mr. Mark GREENE
88	Director Art Museum	Ms. Susan MOLDENHAUER
88	Director Auxiliary Services	Ms. Carolyn SMITH
88	Director Campus Recreation	Mr. Patrick MORAN
45	Director Facilities Planning	Vacant
92	Director Honors Program	Dr. Duncan HARRIS
15	Director Human Resources	Mr. Rick DELACASTRO
18	Director Physical Plant	Mr. James SCOTT
26	Director Inst Communications	Mr. Chad BALDWIN
22	Director Inst Marketing	Ms. Montica WILLMSCHEN
06	Registrar	Mr. David MICUS
39	Exec Dir Res Life/Dining/Stdnt Un	Mr. Patrick N. CALL
37	Director Student Financial Aid	Ms. Joanna CARTER
23	Director Student Health Services	Dr. Joanne E. STEANE
38	Director Univ Counseling Ctr	Dr. Keith EVASHEVSKI
19	Chief University Police Dept	Mr. Mike SAMP

Western Wyoming Community College (J)

PO Box 428, Rock Springs WY 82902-0428

County: Sweetwater FICE Identification: 003933

Unit ID: 240693

Telephone: (307) 382-1600 Carnegie Class: Assoc/Pub-R-M

FAX Number: (307) 382-1636 Calendar System: Semester

URL: www.wwcc.wy.edu

Established: 1959 Annual Undergrad Tuition & Fees (In-District): $1,141

Enrollment: 3,734 Coed

Affiliation or Control: State/Local IRS Status: 501(c)3

Highest Offering: Associate Degree

Program: Occupational; 2-Year Principally Bachelor's Creditable

Accreditation: NH

Code	Title	Name
01	President	Dr. Karla N. LEACH
05	VP of Student Learning	Mr. Lou FLAIM
32	VP of Student Success Services	Dr. Jackie FREEZE
11	VP for Administrative Services	Mr. Marty KELSEY
88	Assoc VP for Administrative Svcs	Ms. Carla BUDD
21	Controller	Ms. Debbie BAKER
07	Director of Admissions	Mr. Joseph MUELLER
06	Registrar	Ms. Kay LEUM
37	Director of Financial Aid	Mr. Javier FLORES
08	Director of Library Services	Ms. Janice GROVER-ROOSA
18	Director of Physical Resources	Mr. Paul ROSS
39	Director Housing/Student Activities	Mr. Dustin CONOVER
40	Bookstore Manager	Ms. Natalie LANE
35	Director Student Development Center	Ms. Kim DRANE
41	Athletic Director	Dr. Lu SWEET
92	Director of Honors Program	Mr. Richard KEMPA
09	Director of Institutional Research	Vacant
15	Director Personnel Services	Ms. Carla BUDD
26	Coord of Marketing/Public Info	Mr. Christopher SHEID
30	Director Community College Relation	Mr. David TATE
36	Director Student Placement	Mr. Mark REMBACZ
10	Chief Business Officer	Ms. Debbie BAKER
20	Associate VP of Student Learning	Vacant
88	Associate VP for Student Success	Ms. Laurie WATKINS
38	Director Student Counseling	Ms. Kim DRANE
96	Director of Purchasing	Ms. Tammy REGISTER

Western Wyoming Community College Outreach Afton/Star Valley (K)

247 N Washington, Box 1237, Afton WY 83110

Telephone: (307) 886-3834 Identification: 770483

Accreditation: &NH

† Main campus is Western Wyoming Community College in Rock Springs, WY.

Western Wyoming Community College Outreach Evanston (A)

1013 Cheyenne Drive, Evanston WY 82930
Telephone: (307) 789-3988 Identification: 770482
Accreditation: &NH

† Main campus is Western Wyoming Community College in Rock Springs, WY.

WyoTech (B)

4373 N 3rd Street, Laramie WY 82072-9519
County: Albany FICE Identification: 009157
Unit ID: 240718
Telephone: (307) 742-3776 Carnegie Class: Assoc/PrivFP
FAX Number: (307) 721-4854 Calendar System: Other
URL: www.wyotech.edu
Established: 1966 Annual Undergrad Tuition & Fees: $29,250
Enrollment: 1,650 Coed
Affiliation or Control: Proprietary IRS Status: Proprietary
Highest Offering: Associate Degree
Program: Occupational
Accreditation: ACCSC

01 President .... Mr. Wm. Guy WARPNESS
05 Director of Education .... Mr. Caleb PERRITON
07 Director of Admissions .... Mr. Glenn HALSEY
37 Director of Financial Aid .... Ms. Brenda COSSITT
32 Director of Student Services .... Mr. Kyle MORRIS
36 Director of Career Services .... Mr. Martin AXLUND
06 Registrar .... Ms. Revalee WEERHEIM
84 Admissions Manager .... Mr. Greg TAYLOR
39 Housing Manager .... Mr. Gabe LUCERO
04 Admin Assistant to the President .... Ms. Courtney SCHELL

US SERVICE SCHOOLS

Air Force Institute of Technology (C)

2950 Hobson Way, Wright Patterson AFB OH 45433-7765
County: Greene FICE Identification: 003009
Unit ID: 200697
Telephone: (937) 255-2321 Carnegie Class: DRU
FAX Number: (937) 656-7600 Calendar System: Quarter
URL: www.afit.edu
Established: 1919 Annual Graduate Tuition & Fees: $16,560
Enrollment: 806 Coed
Affiliation or Control: Federal IRS Status: Exempt
Highest Offering: Doctorate; No Undergraduates
Program: Professional; Technical Emphasis
Accreditation: NH, ENG

01 Chancellor .... Dr. Todd I. STEWART
05 Director of Academic Affairs .... Vacant
54 Dean Graduate School of Engr & Mgt .... Vacant
20 Associate Dean for Academic Affairs .... Dr. Paul J. WOLF
46 Dean for Research .... Dr. Heidi R. RIES
10 Chief Financial Officer .... Ms. Ann M. MARBURGER
09 Director Institutional Research .... Vacant
06 Director Admissions/Registrar .... Mr. Robert J. LAVERRIERE
32 Associate Dean of Students .... Col. Michael L. HASTRITER
13 Dir Communications & Information .... LtCol. Darin LADD
08 Director D'Azzo Research Library .... Dr. Laurene E. ZAPROROZHETZ
15 Director Personnel Services .... Ms. Leanne HEAGLE
18 Chief Facilities/Physical Plant .... Mr. Daniel W. ROHRBACH
29 Manager Alumni Affairs .... Ms. Kathleen E. SCOTT
35 Director Student Services .... Mr. Richard GAMMON
85 Director of Intl Student Affairs .... Ms. Annette D. ROBB
40 Bookstore Supervisor .... Mr. Joseph SCOTT

Air University (D)

55 LeMay Plaza South, Maxwell AFB AL 36112-6335
County: Montgomery FICE Identification: 001001
Telephone: (334) 953-5613 Carnegie Class: Not Classified
FAX Number: (334) 953-2749 Calendar System: Other
URL: www.au.af.mil
Established: 1946 Annual Undergrad Tuition & Fees: N/A
Enrollment: 54,754 Coed
Affiliation or Control: Federal IRS Status: Exempt
Highest Offering: Doctorate
Program: Professional
Accreditation: SC

01 Commander and President .... Lt Gen. David S. FADOK
03 Vice Commander .... MajGen. Waldo D. GIVHAN
05 Vice President for Academic Affairs .... Dr. Bruce T. MURPHY
06 Registrar .... Dr. Michael J. MASTERSON
88 Chief Advisory Boards .... Mrs. Diana BUNCH
20 Director Academic Affairs .... Dr. Chris CAIN

† Parent institution of Community College of the Air Force, School of Advanced Air and Space Studies, and the Air Force Institute of Technology

Community College of the Air Force (E)

100 South Turner Blvd,
Maxwell AFB, Gunter Annex AL 36114-3011
Telephone: (334) 649-5000 FICE Identification: 012308
Accreditation: &SC, PTAA

† Main campus is Air University in Maxwell AFB, AL.

Defense Language Institute (F)

Presido of Monterey CA 93944-3229
County: Monterey FICE Identification: 001195
Unit ID: 428222
Telephone: (831) 242-5828 Carnegie Class: Not Classified
FAX Number: (831) 242-6495 Calendar System: Other
URL: www.dliflc.edu
Established: 1941 Annual Undergrad Tuition & Fees: N/A
Enrollment: 3,800 Coed
Affiliation or Control: Federal IRS Status: Exempt
Highest Offering: Associate Degree
Program: Occupational; 2-Year Principally Bachelor's Creditable
Accreditation: WJ

01 Commandant .... Col. Danial PICK
05 Provost .... Dr. Betty Lou LEAVER
20 Associate Provost .... Dr. Jielu ZHAO
46 Dean Program Eval Research Testing .... Mr. Deniz BILGIN
06 Registrar .... Dr. Robert SAVUKINAS

† Associate Arts in Foreign Language authorized by US Congress in December 2001 and approved by ACCJC/WASC in June 2002.

59th Dental Training Squadron (G)

Bldg 3352, Lackland AFB TX 78236
Telephone: (210) 292-7251 Identification: 770122
Accreditation: &M

† Main campus is Uniformed Services University of the Health Sciences in Bethesda, MD.

Joint Forces Staff College (H)

7800 Hampton Boulevard, Norfolk VA 23511-1702
Telephone: (757) 443-6000 Identification: 770121
Accreditation: &M

† Main campus is National Defense University in Washington, DC.

The Judge Advocate General's Legal Center & School (I)

600 Massie Road, Charlottesville VA 22903-1781
County: Albermarle Identification: 666974
Telephone: (434) 971-3300 Carnegie Class: Not Classified
FAX Number: (434) 971-3338 Calendar System: Quarter
URL: www.jagcnet.army.mil/tjaglcs
Established: 1951 Annual Graduate Tuition & Fees: N/A
Enrollment: 115 Coed
Affiliation or Control: Federal IRS Status: Exempt
Highest Offering: Master's; No Undergraduates
Program: Professional
Accreditation: LAW

01 Acting Commander/Commandant .... Col. Sharon E. RILEY
05 Dean .... Col. James F. GARRETT
20 Associate Dean of Academics .... Mr. Maurice A. LESCAULT, JR.

Marine Corps University (J)

2076 South Street, Quantico VA 22134-5068
County: Prince William Identification: 666745
Unit ID: 438513
Telephone: (703) 784-2105 Carnegie Class: Not Classified
FAX Number: (703) 784-1271 Calendar System: Semester
URL: www.mcu.usmc.mil
Established: 1989 Annual Graduate Tuition & Fees: N/A
Enrollment: 535 Coed
Affiliation or Control: Federal IRS Status: Exempt
Highest Offering: Master's; No Undergraduates
Program: Professional; Technical Emphasis
Accreditation: SC

01 President .... Col. Tom WEIDLEY
05 Vice President for Academic Affairs .... Dr. Jerre W. WILSON
20 Director Academic Support Division .... Mr. Jay HATTON
09 Director Institutional Research .... Dr. Susan JOHNSTON

National Defense University (K)

Fort Lesley J. McNair, Washington DC 20319-5066
FICE Identification: 031893
Unit ID: 423494
Telephone: (202) 685-0080 Carnegie Class: Not Classified
FAX Number: (202) 685-3920 Calendar System: Semester
URL: www.ndu.edu
Established: 1976 Annual Graduate Tuition & Fees: N/A
Enrollment: 1,915 Coed
Affiliation or Control: Federal IRS Status: Exempt
Highest Offering: Master's; No Undergraduates
Program: Professional
Accreditation: M

01 President .... MG. Gregg F. MARTIN
03 Senior VP Intl Programs & Outreach .... Mr. Stephen R. PIETROPAOLI
05 Provost/Vice Pres Academic Affairs .... Dr. John W. YAEGER
20 Deputy Vice Pres Academic Affairs .... Dr. Brenda F. ROTH
09 Dir Inst Rsrch/Plng & Assessment .... Dr. R. Joel FARRELL, II
06 University Registrar .... Mr. Larry JOHNSON
08 Director of Libraries .... Ms. Helen (Meg) TULLOCH
23 Director Health Fitness .... Mr. Tony SPINOSA
26 Director Public Affairs .... Vacant
27 Chief Information Officer .... COL. Stewart LILES
10 Director Resource Management .... Mr. Jay HELMING
25 Director Contracting .... Ms. Jenifer CUOZZO
43 General Counsel .... Ms. Mollie MURPHY
15 Director Personnel .... Vacant
102 NDU Foundation .... Ms. Cathleen PEARL
85 Director International Fellows .... Mr. John CHARLTON
18 Chief Facilities/Physical Plant .... Mr. Charles FANSHAW
88 Events Director .... Mr. Jerry FABER
11 Chief of Staff & Administration .... Mr. Michael CANNON
88 Deputy Chief of Staff & Admin .... COL. Bradley W. BOOTH
28 Director of Diversity .... Vacant
86 Director University Outreach .... Vacant

National Intelligence University (L)

200 MacDill Boulevard, Washington DC 20340-5100
Identification: 666393
Unit ID: 131380
Telephone: (202) 231-3344 Carnegie Class: Not Classified
FAX Number: (202) 231-3294 Calendar System: Quarter
URL: www.ni-u.edu/
Established: 1962 Annual Undergrad Tuition & Fees: N/A
Enrollment: 715 Coed
Affiliation or Control: Federal IRS Status: Exempt
Highest Offering: Master's
Program: Professional
Accreditation: M

01 President .... Dr. David R. ELLISON
100 Chief of Staff .... Col. James C. LAUGHREY
04 Executive Assistant to President .... Ms. Jessica M. STEINRUCK
05 Provost .... Dr. Susan M. STUDDS
88 Dir Ctr for International Pgms .... Mr. Lorenzo S. HIPONIA
46 Dir Ctr for Strategic Intel Rsrch .... Dr. Cathryn Q. THURSTON
09 Dir Inst Effectiveness .... Dr. Felicia BRADSHAW
10 VP Finance & Administration .... Vacant
11 Director of Operations .... Mr. Stephen J. KERDA
18 Facilities .... Dr. Richard MESTAS
19 Security Officer .... Ms. Thelma FLAMER
06 Registrar .... Mr. Eric H. STUPAR
07 Director of Admissions .... Ms. Alteia L. ROBINSON
90 Director Eductional Technology .... Ms. Elvia E. CORTES
08 Director Library Services .... Ms. Denise CAMPBELL
58 Acting Dean College Strat Intel .... Col. Douglas W. KIELY
12 Director NSA Campus .... Mr. Dax NORMAN
12 Director NGA Campus .... Mr. Timothy J. CHRISTENSON
12 Director Reserve Monthly Prog .... Mr. Christopher BAILEY
12 Director European Academic Cntr .... Dr. Jimmie NEWTON
12 Director Southern Academic Cntr .... Mr. Kevin TALIAFERRO
58 Dean School of Science & Tech Intel .... Dr. Brian R. SHAW
88 Associate Dean School of S&T Intel .... Dr. Duncan MCGILL
29 Dir Outreach & Alumni Affairs .... Mr. Thomas VAN WAGNER

Naval Postgraduate School (M)

1 University Circle, Room M10, Monterey CA 93943-5100
County: Monterey FICE Identification: 001310
Unit ID: 119678
Telephone: (831) 656-2441 Carnegie Class: Master's L
FAX Number: (831) 656-2921 Calendar System: Quarter
URL: www.nps.edu
Established: 1909 Annual Undergrad Tuition & Fees: N/A
Enrollment: 3,090 Coed
Affiliation or Control: Federal IRS Status: Exempt
Highest Offering: Doctorate
Program: Professional
Accreditation: WC, BUS, ENG, SPAA

01 Interim President .... RAdm. Jan TIGHE
100 Acting Chief of Staff .... Capt. Deidre MCLAY
05 Provost .... Dr. Douglas A. HENSLER
13 Chief Information Officer .... Dr. Christine M. HASKA
20 Vice Provost for Academic Affairs .... Dr. Orrin Douglas MOSES
46 Dean of Research .... Dr. Jeffrey D. PADUAN
54 Dean Grad Sch Engr/Applied Sci .... Dr. Phillip A. DURKEE
58 Dean Sch of Intl Graduate Studies .... Dr. James J. WIRTZ
50 Dean Grad Sch Bus/Public Policy .... Dr. William R. GATES
72 Dean Grad Sch Oper & Info Sciences .... Dr. Gordon MCCORMICK
32 Dean of Students .... Capt. Tom MACRAE
10 Comptroller .... Mr. Kevin K. LITTLE
18 Director Facilities/Support Svcs .... Mr. Peter G. DAUSEN
08 University Librarian .... Ms. Eleanor S. UHLINGER
06 Registrar .... Mr. Mike ANDERSEN
15 Director Human Resources .... Ms. Julie CARPENTER
29 Director of Alumni Relations .... Mr. Kari L. MIGLAW
19 Sr Lecturer NPS/Chief Security Ofcr .... CAPT. Robert SIMERAL, RET.
88 Senior Intelligence Officer .... Capt. Jennith E. HOYT
09 Exec Dir Inst Plng/Communications .... Dr. Fran HORVATH
28 EEO Director .... Ms. Deborah A. BAITY
56 Dir Office of Continuous Learning .... Mr. Tom M. MASTRE
07 Director of Admissions .... Ms. Sue DOOLEY

88 Deputy Comptroller ... Mr. Jack L. SHISIDO
88 Director of Programs ... CDR. Mary J. SIMS

Naval War College (A)

686 Cushing Road, Newport RI 02841-1207
County: Newport
FICE Identification: 003413
Unit ID: 432320
Telephone: (401) 841-3089
Carnegie Class: Not Classified
FAX Number: (401) 841-1297
Calendar System: Trimester
URL: www.usnwc.edu
Established: 1884
Annual Graduate Tuition & Fees: N/A
Enrollment: N/A
Coed
Affiliation or Control: Federal
IRS Status: Exempt
Highest Offering: Master's; No Undergraduates
Program: Professional
Accreditation: EH

01 President ... RADM. Walter E. CARTER, JR.
04 Exec Assistant to the President ... LCDR. Jay BREWER
05 Provost ... Amb. MaryAnn PETERS, RET.
88 Chief of Staff to the Provost ... Mr. Richard R. MENARD
20 Associate Provost ... Prof. William R. SPAIN
100 Chief of Staff ... CAPT. George LANG
20 Dean of Academic Affairs ... Prof. John GAROFANO
09 Dean Center for Warfare Studies ... Prof. Robert J. RUBEL
32 Dean of Students ... CAPT. John GRIFFIN
08 Director Library Services ... Dr. Allen C. BENSON
56 Dir College of Distance Education ... Dr. Jay HICKEY
06 Registrar ... CAPT. John GRIFFIN
46 Chairman Strategy & Policy ... Dr. Michael PAVKOVIC
88 Chairman National Security Affairs ... Dr. David COOPER
88 Chairman Joint Military Operations ... CAPT. Alan ABRAMSON
10 Chief Business Officer ... Mr. Robert SAMPSON
15 Director Military Personnel Svcs ... CDR. Melanie HA'O
15 Civilian Human Resources Officer ... Ms. Charlene HANSON
18 Chief Facilities/Physical Plant ... Ms. Beth LEINBERRY
26 Chief Public Relations Officer ... CDR. Carla M. MCCARTHY
27 Chief Information Officer ... Mr. Joseph PANGBORN
19 Director of Security ... Mr. Paul GATELY
29 Director Alumni Affairs ... Prof. Julia A. GAGE
88 Director Writing Center ... Dr. Donna CONNOLLY
88 Director International Programs ... Prof. Thomas MANGOLD
88 Dean Col Operatnl/Strategic Ldrshp ... Prof. James KELLY

School of Advanced Air and Space Studies (B)

125 Chennault Circle, Maxwell AFB AL 36112-6424
Telephone: (334) 953-5155
Identification: 666746
Accreditation: &SC

† Main campus is Air University in Maxwell AFB, AL.

Uniformed Services University of the Health Sciences (C)

4301 Jones Bridge Road, Bethesda MD 20814-4799
County: Montgomery
FICE Identification: 021610
Unit ID: 164137
Telephone: (301) 295-3013
Carnegie Class: Not Classified
FAX Number: (301) 295-3431
Calendar System: Quarter
URL: www.usuhs.mil
Established: 1972
Annual Graduate Tuition & Fees: N/A
Enrollment: 1,019
Coed
Affiliation or Control: Federal
IRS Status: Exempt
Highest Offering: Doctorate; No Undergraduates
Program: Professional
Accreditation: M, ANEST, CLPSY, ENGR, MED, NURSE, PH

01 President ... Dr. Charles L. RICE
03 Senior Vice President ... Vacant
05 Sr Vice Pres University Programs ... Dr. Patrick SCULLEY
10 Vice Pres Finance & Administration ... Mr. Stephen C. RICE
26 Interim Vice Pres External Affairs ... Dr. Jeffrey LONGACRE
46 Acting Vice President for Research ... Dr. Richard LEVINE
88 VP Affiliation/International Affs ... Dr. Jeffrey LONGACRE
04 Exec Assistant to the President ... Ms. Mary L. SCHWARTZ
100 Chief of Staff ... Mr. Robert J. THOMPSON
63 Dean School of Medicine ... Dr. Arthur KELLERMANN
63 Vice Dean School of Medicine ... Dr. John MCMANIGLE
58 Assoc Dean Graduate Education ... Dr. Eleanor S. METCALF
07 Assoc Dean Admiss & Recruiting SOM ... LTC. Aaron SAGUIL
88 Assoc Dean Graduate Medical Educ ... Capt. Jerri CURTIS
32 Assoc Dean Student Affairs ... Col. Lisa MOORES
88 Assistant Dean Academic Support ... Dr. William WITTMAN
88 Assistant Dean Clinical Sciences ... Dr. Patricia MCKAY
66 Dean Graduate School of Nursing ... Dr. Ada Sue HINSHAW
20 Associate Dean Acad Affairs GSN ... Dr. Carol A. ROMANO
46 Director AFRRI ... Col. Lester HUFF
27 Chief Information Officer ... Mr. Timothy RAPP
43 Acting General Counsel ... Mr. Jason KARR
06 Registrar ... Ms. Gail HEWITT-CLARKE
15 Director Civilian Human Res ... Mr. Darryl BROWN
08 Acting University Librarian ... Ms. Linda SPITZER
18 Director of Facilities ... Ms. Cheryl KING
96 Director of Contracting ... Mr. Anthony REVENIS
21 Associate Business Officer ... Mr. Walter TINLING
29 Director Alumni Relations ... Ms. Sharon WILLIS
20 Assistant Dean for Curriculum ... Col. Arnyce POCK
88 Assoc Dean for Faculty ... Dr. Brian REAMY
88 Assoc Dean for Medical Education ... Dr. William GILLILAND
52 Dean Army Postgrad Dental School ... Col. Priscilla HAMILTON
52 Dean Naval Postgrad Dental School ... Capt. Glenn MUNRO
52 Dean Air Force Postgrad Dental Sch ... Col. Thomas SCHNEID

United States Air Force Academy (D)

2304 Cadet Drive, Suite 2400,
USAF Academy CO 80840-5025
County: El Paso
FICE Identification: 001369
Unit ID: 128328
Telephone: (719) 333-3070
Carnegie Class: Bac/A&S
FAX Number: (719) 333-3647
Calendar System: Semester
URL: www.academyadmissions.com
Established: 1954
Annual Undergrad Tuition & Fees: N/A
Enrollment: 4,120
Coed
Affiliation or Control: Federal
IRS Status: Exempt
Highest Offering: Baccalaureate
Program: Liberal Arts And General; Professional
Accreditation: NH, BUS, CS, DENT, ENG

United States Army Command and General Staff College (E)

1 Reynolds Avenue, Building 111,
Fort Leavenworth KS 66027-1352
County: Leavenworth
FICE Identification: 001947
Unit ID: 156055
Telephone: (913) 684-3097
Carnegie Class: Not Classified
FAX Number: (913) 684-2906
Calendar System: Trimester
URL: www.cgsc.army.mil
Established: 1881
Annual Graduate Tuition & Fees: N/A
Enrollment: 1,002
Coed
Affiliation or Control: Federal
IRS Status: Exempt
Highest Offering: Master's; No Undergraduates
Program: Professional
Accreditation: NH

01 Commandant ... LtGen. David G. PERKINS
03 Deputy Commandant ... BGen. Gordon DAVIS, JR.
04 Assistant Deputy Commandant ... Col. Michael J. JOHNSON
05 Dean of Academics ... Dr. Wendell C. KING
100 Chief of Staff ... Col. Jeff P. LAMOE
58 Director Graduate Degree Programs ... Dr. Robert BAUMANN
08 Director of Library ... Mr. Ed BURGESS
32 Director CGSS School ... Col. Drew MEYEROWICH
06 Registrar ... Mr. Kenneth A. NORRIS
26 Chief Public Relations Officer ... Mr. Harry SARLES

United States Army War College (F)

122 Forbes Avenue, Carlisle PA 17013-5050
County: Cumberland
Identification: 666235
Telephone: (717) 245-4711
Carnegie Class: Not Classified
FAX Number: (717) 245-4721
Calendar System: Other
URL: www.carlisle.army.mil
Established:
Annual Graduate Tuition & Fees: N/A
Enrollment: N/A
Coed
Affiliation or Control: Federal
IRS Status: Exempt
Highest Offering: Master's; No Undergraduates
Program: Professional
Accreditation: M

01 Commandant ... MajGen. Anthony CUCOLO
05 Provost ... Dr. Lance BETROLS

United States Coast Guard Academy (G)

15 Mohegan Avenue, New London CT 06320-8100
County: New London
FICE Identification: 001415
Unit ID: 130624
Telephone: (860) 444-8444
Carnegie Class: Bac/Diverse
FAX Number: (860) 444-8288
Calendar System: Semester
URL: www.cga.edu
Established: 1876
Annual Undergrad Tuition & Fees: N/A
Enrollment: 967
Coed
Affiliation or Control: Federal
IRS Status: Exempt
Highest Offering: Baccalaureate
Program: Occupational; Technical Emphasis
Accreditation: EH, BUS, ENG

01 Superintendent ... RADM. Sandra L. STOSZ
03 Assistant Superintendent ... CAPT. Eric C. JONES
45 Planning Officer ... CDR. Alan G. LAPENNA
05 Dean of Academics ... Dr. Kurt J. COLELLA
20 Associate Dean ... CDR. David C. CLIPPINGER
45 Assoc Dean Acad Support Services ... Vacant
07 Director of Admissions ... CAPT. Stephan FINTON
32 Commandant of Cadets ... CAPT. James L. MCCAULEY
06 Registrar ... Mr. Donald E. DYKES
08 Librarian ... Ms. Lucia MAZIAR
10 Comptroller ... CDR. Richard G. BOSTON
26 Public Affairs Officer ... LT. Megan MERVAR
09 Institutional Research ... Dr. Leonard M. GIAMBRA
46 Director of Research ... Vacant
13 Head of Information Services ... CDR. Robert R. OATMAN
15 Personnel Management Specialist ... Mrs. Sunnie ROBINSON
16 Chief Personnel/Administration ... CAPT. Sean P. GILL
18 Chief Facilities Engineer ... CDR. Michael A. CLYBURN
19 Security Chief ... CGPO. Timothy M. NUGENT
22 Civil Rights Officer ... Vacant
23 Chief Health Services ... CDR. Joseph L. PEREZ
29 President Alumni Association ... CDR. James SYLVESTER
38 Chief Cadet Counselor ... Dr. Robert MURRAY
40 Bookstore Manager ... Ms. Lauri KERP
41 Director of Athletics ... Mr. Timothy M. FITZPATRICK
42 Command Chaplain ... CAPT. Brian K. FINCH
43 Staff Legal Officer ... CDR. Stephen J. ADLER
85 International Cadet Advisor ... Dr. Alina M. ZAPALSKA
28 Director of Diversity ... Mr. Antonio FARIAS
88 Director Leadership Development Ctr ... CAPT. Andrea M. MARCILLE

† There is a one-time entrance fee of $3,000 to cover uniform, laptop, and supplies.

United States Merchant Marine Academy (H)

300 Steamboat Road, Kings Point NY 11024-1634
County: Nassau
FICE Identification: 002892
Unit ID: 197027
Telephone: (516) 773-5000
Carnegie Class: Bac/Diverse
FAX Number: (516) 773-5509
Calendar System: Trimester
URL: www.usmma.edu
Established: 1943
Annual Undergrad Tuition & Fees: $1,032
Enrollment: 1,012
Coed
Affiliation or Control: Federal
IRS Status: Exempt
Highest Offering: Master's
Program: Liberal Arts And General; Professional
Accreditation: M, ENG

01 Superintendent & Dean ... RADM. James HELIS
03 Deputy Superintendent ... RDML. Susan L. DUNLAP
05 Academic Dean/Asst Supt Acad Affs ... Dr. Shashi KUMAR
18 Asst Supt for Facilities ... Capt. Theodore DOGONNIUCK
20 Assistant Academic Dean ... Ms. Dianne TAHA
32 Commandant Midshipmen ... Capt. John KENNEDY
30 Director Office of External Affairs ... Capt. Marcie KATCHER
07 Director of Admissions ... Capt. Robert JOHNSON
06 Registrar ... Ms. Lisa JERRY
08 Chief Librarian ... Dr. George J. BILLY
13 Director Computer/Information Mgmt ... Mr. Kevin CLARKE
15 Director Human Resources ... Mr. Andrew GREEN
10 Chief Financial Officer ... Mr. Jose ESCOTO
29 Director Alumni Relations ... Mr. Peter RACKETT
35 Director Student Affairs ... Ms. Mary CUNNINGHAM
36 Dir of Prof Develop/Career Services ... Capt. Gene ALBERT
37 Director Student Financial Aid ... Vacant
96 Director of Purchasing ... Mr. Max DIAH

United States Military Academy (I)

West Point NY 10996-5000
County: Orange
FICE Identification: 002893
Unit ID: 197036
Telephone: (845) 938-4041
Carnegie Class: Bac/A&S
FAX Number: (845) 938-3021
Calendar System: Semester
URL: www.westpoint.edu
Established: 1802
Annual Undergrad Tuition & Fees: N/A
Enrollment: 4,592
Coed
Affiliation or Control: Federal
IRS Status: Exempt
Highest Offering: Baccalaureate
Program: Liberal Arts And General; Professional
Accreditation: M, CS, ENG

01 Superintendent/President ... LTG. David H. HUNTOON, JR.
05 Dean of Academic Board ... BG. Timothy TRAINOR
20 Vice Dean ... Dr. Jean BLAIR
32 Commandant of Cadets ... BG. Richard D. CLARKE
100 Chief of Staff ... COL. Charles A. STAFFORD
88 Garrison Commander ... COL. Dane RIDEOUT
07 Director of Admissions ... COL. Deborah MCDONALD
06 Assoc Dean Operations/Registrar ... Dr. James DALTON
45 Associate Dean for Research ... LTC. John GRAHAM
09 Institutional Research ... LTC. Holly WEST
13 Chief Information Officer ... COL. Ron DODGE
10 Director of Resource Management ... Mrs. Deborah A. POOL
26 Public Affairs Officer ... LTC. Webster WRIGHT
08 USMA Library ... Mr. Christopher BARTH
29 President Association of Graduates ... COLRet. Robert MCCLURE
38 Dir Center for Personal Development ... LTC. Brian CRANDALL
41 Director Intercollegiate Athletics ... Mr. Boo CORRIGAN
18 Chief Facilities/Physical Plant ... Mr. Matthew TALABER
15 Dir Center for Faculty Excellence ... Dr. Mark EVANS
35 Dir Ctr for Enchanced Performance ... COL. Carl J. OHLSON
88 Director of Cadet Activities ... LTC. Todd MESSITT

United States Naval Academy (J)

121 Blake Road, Annapolis MD 21402-5000
County: Anne Arundel
FICE Identification: 030430
Unit ID: 164155
Telephone: (410) 293-1000
Carnegie Class: Bac/A&S
FAX Number: (410) 293-3734
Calendar System: Semester
URL: www.usna.edu
Established: 1845
Annual Undergrad Tuition & Fees: N/A
Enrollment: 4,442
Coed
Affiliation or Control: Federal
IRS Status: Exempt
Highest Offering: Baccalaureate
Program: Liberal Arts And General; Professional; Technical Emphasis
Accreditation: M, CS, ENG

01 Superintendent VADM. Michael H. MILLER
32 Commandant of Midshipmen Capt. William D. BYRNE
05 Academic Dean & Provost Dr. Andrew T. PHILLIPS
20 Vice Academic Dean Dr. Boyd A. WAITE
07 Dean of Admissions Capt. Bruce J. LATTA
10 Associate Dean for Finances Capt. Peter A. NARDI
20 Assoc Dean for Academic Affairs Dr. Jennifer WATERS
08 Assoc Dean Information Svcs/Library Mr. James RETTIG
21 Deputy for Finance Mr. Joseph RUBINO
100 Chief of Staff Capt. Steven S. VAHSEN
11 CO Naval Support Activity Annapolis Capt. Thomas L. REESE
06 Registrar Dr. Christopher A. DAVIS
26 Public Affairs Officer CDR. John SCHOFIELD
29 Exec Director Alumni Association Mr. William OCONNER
21 Comptroller CDR. Todd W. HAUGE
14 Chief Information Officer CDR. Louis J. GIANNOTTI
88 Director Academic Center Dr. Bruce J. BUKOWSKI
09 Director Institutional Research Capt. Glenn F. GOTTSCHALK
18 Public Works Officer Capt. Scott BERNOTAS
41 Athletic Director Mr. Chet GLADCHUK
42 Command Chaplain Capt. Michael PARISI
30 Director Officer Development Capt. Mike MICHEL
15 Director Human Resources Mr. William COFFIN
28 Director of Diversity Capt. Roger ISOM

AMERICAN SAMOA

American Samoa Community College (A)

PO Box 2609, Pago Pago AS 96799-2609
County: American Samoa FICE Identification: 010010
Unit ID: 240736
Telephone: (684) 699-9155 Carnegie Class: Assoc/Pub-S-SC
FAX Number: (684) 699-6259 Calendar System: Semester
URL: www.amsamoa.edu
Established: 1970 Annual Undergrad Tuition & Fees (In-State): $3,600
Enrollment: 1,764 Coed
Affiliation or Control: State IRS Status: 501(c)3
Highest Offering: Baccalaureate
Program: Occupational; 2-Year Principally Bachelor's Creditable
Accreditation: WC, WJ

01 President Dr. Seth P. GALEA'I
05 Vice Pres Academic/Student Affairs Dr. Kathleen KOLHOFF
11 Vice Pres Administrative Services Dr. Rosevonne PATO
32 Dean of Student Services Dr. Emilia LE'I
51 Dir of Adult Educ/Lit Ext Learning Mr. Tauvela FALE
20 Dean of Academic Affairs Dr. Irene HELSHAM
08 Director of Library Services Mrs. Emma FUNG CHEN PENN
25 Dir Land Grant/Cmty & Natural Res Dr. Daniel F. AGA
45 Dir Institutional Effectiveness Vacant
37 Financial Aid Manager Mr. Peteru LAM YUEN
88 Dir Teacher Education Program Dr. Lina GALEA'I-SCANLAN
10 Chief Financial Officer Ms. Emey SILAFAU
88 Director of SAMPAC Mrs. Okenaisa FAUOLO-MANILA
88 Director of Upward Bound Program Vacant
102 Dir of ASCC Research Foundation Mrs. Matesina WILLIS
88 Director of Small Business Devel Mr. Herbert THWEATT
06 Dir of Admissions Records Finan Aid Mrs. Sifagatogo TUITASI
15 Director Human Resources Mrs. Komiti EMMSLEY
26 Press Officer Mr. James KNEUBUHL
72 Acting Dean Trades & Technology Mr. Michael LEAU
27 Chief Information Officer Ms. Grace TULAFONO
38 Director of Student Support Svcs Mrs. Repeka ALAIMOANA-NUUSA
18 Dir Physical Facilities-Maintenance Mr. Loligi SEUMANUTAFA

FEDERATED STATES OF MICRONESIA

College of Micronesia-FSM (B)

PO Box 159 Kolonia, Pohnpei FM 96941-0159
FICE Identification: 010343
Unit ID: 243638
Telephone: (691) 320-2480 Carnegie Class: Assoc/Pub-R-M
FAX Number: (691) 320-2479 Calendar System: Semester
URL: www.comfsm.fm
Established: 1963 Annual Undergrad Tuition & Fees (In-State): $4,940
Enrollment: 2,744 Coed
Affiliation or Control: State IRS Status: 501(c)3
Highest Offering: Associate Degree
Program: Occupational; 2-Year Principally Bachelor's Creditable
Accreditation: WJ

01 President Mr. Joseph DAISY
05 Vice Pres Instructional Affairs Mrs. Mariana BEN DEREAS
32 Vice Pres Support/Student Affairs Vacant
56 VP Coop Research/Ext (Land Grant) Mr. Walter James CURRIE
11 Vice Pres Dept of Admin Services Mr. Joseph HABUCHMAI
12 Dean Chuuk Campus Mr. Kind KANTO
12 Dean Pohnpei Campus Vacant
12 Dean Kosrae Campus Mr. Kalwin KEPHAS
12 Dean Yap Campus Ms. Lourdes ROBOMAN
10 Comptroller Mr. Danilo DUMANTAY
12 Director FSM-FMI Campus Mr. Matthias EWARMAI
45 Director Research & Planning Mr. Jimmy HICKS
15 Director Human Resources Ms. Rencelly NELSON
20 Director Academic Programs Mrs. Karen SIMION
08 Director Learning Resource Center Mrs. Jennifer HAINRICK
75 Dir Career & Technical Education Mr. Grilly JACK
18 Director Physical Plant/Maintenance Mr. Francisco MENDIOLA
06 Registrar Mr. Joey ODUCADO
21 Business Officer Manager Vacant
37 Director Student Financial Aid Mr. Eddie HALEYALIG
38 Counselor Ms. Penselyn ETSE
26 Director Devel/Public Relations Vacant
13 Director Information Technology Mr. Gordon SEGAL
35 Director Residential/Campus Life Vacant

GUAM

Guam Community College (C)

PO Box 23069, Barrigada GU 96921-3069
County: Guam FICE Identification: 015361
Unit ID: 240745
Telephone: (671) 735-5531 Carnegie Class: Assoc/Pub-R-S
FAX Number: (671) 734-5238 Calendar System: Semester
URL: www.guamcc.edu
Established: 1977 Annual Undergrad Tuition & Fees (In-District): $4,446
Enrollment: 2,577 Coed
Affiliation or Control: State/Local IRS Status: 501(c)3
Highest Offering: Associate Degree
Program: Occupational; 2-Year Principally Bachelor's Creditable; Technical Emphasis
Accreditation: WJ, MAC

01 President Dr. Mary Y. OKADA
05 Vice President Academic Affairs Dr. R. Ray D. SOMERA
10 Vice President Finance & Admin Ms. Carmen K. SANTOS
10 Controller Mr. Edwin E. LIMTUATCO
75 Dean Trades & Professional Services Dr. Juan P. FLORES
72 Dean Technology & Student Services Dr. Virginia C. TUDELA
26 Asst Dir Communications & Promo Ms. Jayne T. FLORES
04 Private Secretary Ms. Esther A. MUNA
101 Admin Secretary II BOT-Pres Ofc Ms. Bertha M. GUERRERO
06 Coordinator Admissions/Registration Mr. Patrick L. CLYMER
45 Asst Dir Planning & Development Ms. Doris U. PEREZ
103 Asst Dir Cont Ed & Workforce Dev Mr. Victor RODGERS
88 Assoc Dean Dr. Michael L. CHAN
88 Assoc Dean Dr. Karen M. SABLAN
32 Assoc Dean Ms. Joanne A. IGE
15 Administrator Human Resources Ms. Joann W. MUNA
18 Facilities Engineer Administrator Mr. Lawrence P. PEREZ
08 Librarian Ms. Christine B. MATSON
20 Admin Ofcr VP's Ofc-Academic Affs Ms. Ana Mari C. ATOIGUE
09 Asst Dir AIER Ms. Marlena O. MONTAGUE
88 Pgm Specialist Adult Basic Edu Ms. Priscilla C. JOHNS
88 Pgm Specialist CACGP Ms. Christine B. SISON
35 Pgm Spc Ctr Student Involvement Ms. Barbara B. LEON GUERRERO
23 School Health Counselor Ms. Emma R. BATACLAN
26 Program Specialist Mr. Wesley T. GIMA
37 Coordinator Student Financial Aid Ms. Esther A. RIOS
88 Pgm Specialist TRIO Programs Mr. Huan F. HOSEI
29 Pgm Specialist Alumni & Fundraising Ms. Bonnie Mae M. DATUIN
88 Pgm Specialist POST Mr. Dennis SANTOTOMAS
88 Pgm Specialist Alumni & Fundraising Mr. Danilo Philbert BILONG
96 Supply Management Administrator Ms. Joleen M. EVANGELISTA
14 Data Processing Administrator Mr. Francisco C. CAMACHO
51 Pgm Specialist Continuing Educ Ms. Terry L. BARNHART
51 Pgm Specialist Continuing Educ Ms. Rowena Ellen PEREZ
40 Bookstore Manager Mr. Daniel T. OKADA
55 Pgm Specialist Night Administrator Ms. Ava M. GARCIA
19 Safety Admin Envir Safety Ofc Mr. Gregorio T. MANGLONA
88 Adjunct Assoc Dean TSS Vacant
88 Pgm Specialist Accomodative Svcs Mr. John F. PAYNE

Pacific Islands University (D)

172 Kinney's Road, Mangilao GU 96913
County: Guam FICE Identification: 034383
Unit ID: 439862
Telephone: (671) 734-1812 Carnegie Class: Spec/Faith
FAX Number: (671) 734-1813 Calendar System: Semester
URL: www.piu.edu
Established: 1976 Annual Undergrad Tuition & Fees: $10,580
Enrollment: 81 Coed
Affiliation or Control: Independent Non-Profit IRS Status: 501(c)3
Highest Offering: Master's
Program: Liberal Arts And General; Religious Emphasis
Accreditation: TRACS

01 President/CEO Dr. David L. OWEN
03 Administrative Vice President Mr. Nino T. PATE
05 Academic Vice President Dr. Shirley A. MABINI
20 Seminary Dean Mr. Michael OWEN
20 Liberal Studies Chair Ms. Sarah BRUBAKER
20 Biblical Studies Chair Mr. Iotaka CHORAM
32 Student Life Director Mr. Robert WATT
06 Registrar Ms. Anne STINNETTE
21 Operations Director Ms. Celia ATOIGE
04 Exec Assistant to the President Ms. Samantha OWEN

University of Guam (E)

UOG Station, Mangilao GU 96923-1800
County: Guam FICE Identification: 003935
Unit ID: 240754
Telephone: (671) 735-2990 Carnegie Class: Master's S
FAX Number: (671) 734-2296 Calendar System: Semester
URL: www.uog.edu
Established: 1952 Annual Undergrad Tuition & Fees (In-State): $5,098
Enrollment: 3,411 Coed
Affiliation or Control: State IRS Status: 501(c)3
Highest Offering: Master's
Program: Occupational; Liberal Arts And General; Teacher Preparatory; Professional
Accreditation: WC, IACBE, NUR, SW, TED

01 President Dr. Robert A. UNDERWOOD
05 Actg Sr VP Academic & Student Aff Dr. Anita B. ENRIQUEZ
10 Vice Pres Administration & Finance Mr. David M. O'BRIEN
58 AVP Graduate Studies/Research & SP Dr. John A. PETERSON
43 University Legal Counsel Ms. Victorina M Y. RENACIA
88 Institutional Compliance Officer Ms. Elaine FACULO-GOGUE
04 Executive Assistant to President Ms. Louise M. TOVES
26 Director Integrated Mktg Comm Mr. Jonas D. MACAPINLAC
45 Chief Planning Officer Mr. David S. OKADA
29 Director Dev & Alumni Affairs Mr. Norman ANALISTA
102 Exec Director Endowment Foundation Mr. Mark B. MENDIOLA
108 Dir Academic Assess/Inst Research Ms. Deborah D. LEON GUERRERO
49 Dean Col of Lib Arts & Social Sci Dr. James D. SELLMANN
47 Dean Col of Natural & Applied Sci Dr. Lee S. YUDIN
50 Dean Sch Bus & Pub Admin Dr. Anita B. ENRIQUEZ
53 Dean School of Education Dr. Frankie S. LAANAN
66 Actg Dir Sch of Nursing & Hlth Sci Ms. Kathryn WOOD
84 Dean Enroll Mgmt & Student Services Ms. Remy B. CRISTOBAL
06 Registrar Ms. Remy B. CRISTOBAL
37 Director Financial Aid Mr. Mark A. DUARTE
32 Student Life Officer Ms. Sallie MCDONALD
88 Director Guam CEDDERS Dr. Heidi E. SAN NICOLAS
08 Director Learning Resources Ms. Christine K. SCOTT-SMITH
14 Dir Info Tech Resource/Computer Ctr Dr. Luan P. NGUYEN
88 Actg Dir Micronesia Area Res Center Ms. Monique C. STORIE
88 Director Marine Laboratory Dr. Laurie RAYMUNDO
88 Dir Watr Env Rsrch Inst Wstrn Pac Dr. Shahram KHOSROWPANAH
88 Dir Ctr for Island Sustainability Dr. John A. PETERSON
51 Director Prof/International Pgm Ms. Cathleen MOORE-LINN
88 Director TRIO Programs Mr. Yoichi K. RENGIIL
15 Chief Human Resources Officer Mr. Larry GAMBOA
18 Chief Plant Fac Ofcr Fac & Util Mr. Sonny P. PEREZ
41 Actg Field House/Athletics Director Ms. Ann S.A. LEON GUERRERO
19 Acting Chief of Safety Mr. Felix MANSAPIT
40 Director Bookstore & Auxillary Svcs Ms. Ann S.A. LEON GUERRERO
21 Comptroller Ms. Zeny ASUNCION-NACE

MARSHALL ISLANDS

College of the Marshall Islands (F)

PO Box 1258, Majuro MH 96960-1258
County: Marshalls FICE Identification: 030224
Unit ID: 376695
Telephone: (692) 625-3394 Carnegie Class: Assoc/Pub-R-S
FAX Number: (692) 625-7203 Calendar System: Semester
URL: www.cmi.edu
Established: 1989 Annual Undergrad Tuition & Fees (In-State): $4,415
Enrollment: 989 Coed
Affiliation or Control: State IRS Status: 501(c)3
Highest Offering: Associate Degree
Program: 2-Year Principally Bachelor's Creditable
Accreditation: WJ

01 Interim President Dr. Carl HACKER
05 VP Academic & Student Affairs Mr. Donald HESS
11 Vice Pres Administration Ms. Diane C. MYAZOE-DEBRUM
10 VP Finance//Chief Financial Officer Mr. Stevenson KOTTON
45 VP for Research & Planning Dr. Rafe Edward TRICKEY, JR.
20 Dean of Academic Affairs Ms. Ruth ABBOTT
32 Dean of Students Ms. Rachel SALOMON
46 Dean of Voc & Continuing Education Ms. Diane C. MYAZOE-DEBRUM
06 Registrar Ms. Monica GORDON
07 Director of Admissions & Records Ms. Rosita V. CAPELLE
08 Director of Library Services Vacant
15 Human Resources Director Mr. Robert W. WILLSON
51 Director Continuing/Adult Education Vacant
18 Director Physical Plant Mr. William REIHER
88 Dir Stdnt Support Svcs/Upward Bound Ms. Aluka RAKIN
13 Director Information & Technology Mr. Bonifacio SANCHEZ
88 Director Nuclear Institute Ms. Mary L. SILK
53 Chair Education/Marshallese Stds Mr. Max VOELZKE
37 Financial Aid Director Ms. Jacinta SAMUEL
49 Chair Liberal Arts Ms. Janet HESS
50 Chair Business & IT Vacant
66 Chair Nursing Ms. Florence L. PETER
81 Chair Mathematics/Science Mr. Donald HESS
04 Special Assistant to the President Vacant
19 Director Security/Safety Mr. David DEBRUM
38 Director of Student Counseling Dr. Donna SEPPY
09 Dean Rsrch/Planning/Effectiveness Vacant

NORTHERN MARIANAS

Northern Marianas College (A)

PO Box 501250, Saipan MP 96950-1250
FICE Identification: 030330
Unit ID: 240790
Telephone: (670) 234-5498 Carnegie Class: Bac/Assoc
FAX Number: (670) 234-0759 Calendar System: Semester
URL: www.nmcnet.edu
Established: 1976 Annual Undergrad Tuition & Fees (In-District): $3,820
Enrollment: 1,207 Coed
Affiliation or Control: State/Local IRS Status: 501(c)3
Highest Offering: Baccalaureate
Program: 2-Year Principally Bachelor's Creditable; Liberal Arts And General; Teacher Preparatory
Accreditation: WC, WJ

01 President .... Dr. Sharon Y. HART
05 Dean of Academic Programs & Svcs .. Ms. Barbara K. MERFALEN
32 Dean of Student Services .... Mr. Leo PANGELINAN
10 Chief Financial Officer .... Ms. Tracy GUERRERO
11 Dean of Administration .... Mr. David J. ATTAO
31 Dean-Director of CREES .... Mr. Ross MANGLONA
04 Executive Secretary to President .... Ms. Becky SABLAN
13 Director of Information Technology .... Mr. Jonathan LIWAG
09 Dir Institutional Effectiveness .... Ms. Jacqueline CHE
30 Director of External Relations .... Mr. Frankie M. ELIPTICO
08 Director Library Services .... Mr. Christopher TODD
53 Director School of Education .... Ms. Charlotte R. CEPEDA
51 Director of Adult Basic Education .... Ms. Lorraine T. CABRERA
07 Director Admissions & Records .... Mr. Manny CASTRO
38 Director of Counseling Services .... Dr. Timothy BAKER
37 Director of Financial Aid .... Ms. Daisy MANGLONA-PROPST
96 Procurement Manager .... Ms. Anita C. CAMACHO
15 Director of Human Resources .... Mr. Christopher TIMMONS
21 Chief Accountant .... Ms. Solita K. BARNES
36 Career Planning/Placement Coord .... Ms. Neda C. DELEON GUERRERA
18 Facilities Manager .... Mr. John GUERRERO
29 President NMC Alumni Association .... Mr. Jack O. KIYOSHI
106 Director of Distance Learning & ALO .... Ms. Amanda ALLEN

PALAU

Palau Community College (B)

PO Box 9, Koror PW 96940-0009
County: Koror FICE Identification: 011009
Unit ID: 243647
Telephone: (680) 488-2470 Carnegie Class: Assoc/Pub-R-S
FAX Number: (680) 488-2447 Calendar System: Semester
URL: www.palau.edu
Established: 1969 Annual Undergrad Tuition & Fees: $4,215
Enrollment: 680 Coed
Affiliation or Control: Federal IRS Status: Exempt
Highest Offering: Associate Degree
Program: Occupational; 2-Year Principally Bachelor's Creditable
Accreditation: WJ

01 President .... Dr. Patrick U. TELLEI
05 Vice President Education & Training .... Vacant
11 Vice Pres Administration & Finance .... Mr. Jay OLEGERIIL
46 Vice Pres Cooperative Rsrch/Exten .... Mr. Thomas TARO
04 Exec Assistant to the President .... Mr. Todd NGIRAMENGIOR
32 Dean of Students .... Mr. Sherman DANIEL
20 Dean of Academic Affairs .... Mr. Robert RAMARUI
51 Dean of Continuing Education .... Mr. William WALLY
30 Director of Development .... Mr. Tzuchie TADAO
07 Director Admissions & Financial Aid . Mrs. Dahlia M. KATOSANG
06 Registrar .... Ms. Lesley B. ADACHI
15 Director of Human Resources .... Mr. Omdasu T. UEKI
18 Director of Physical Plant .... Mr. Clement KAZUMA
13 Director of Computer Systems .... Mr. Bruce RIMIRCH
35 Director of Student Life .... Ms. Hilda NGIRALMAU
10 Director of Finance .... Ms. Uroi N. SALII
09 Institutional Researcher .... Ms. Ligaya SARA
38 Counselor .... Ms. Maurine ALEXANDER
38 Counselor .... Mr. Winfred RECHEIUNGEL
38 Counselor .... Ms. Glendalynn NGIRMERIIL
91 System Analyst .... Ms. Grace ALEXANDER
88 Accreditation Liaison Officer .... Ms. Deikola OLIKONG

PUERTO RICO

American University of Puerto Rico (C)

Box 2037, Bayamon PR 00960-2037
County: Bayamon FICE Identification: 011941
Unit ID: 241100
Telephone: (787) 620-2040 Carnegie Class: Bac/Diverse
FAX Number: (787) 785-7377 Calendar System: Other
URL: www.aupr.edu
Established: 1963 Annual Undergrad Tuition & Fees: $5,496
Enrollment: 2,460 Coed
Affiliation or Control: Independent Non-Profit IRS Status: 501(c)3
Highest Offering: Master's
Program: Liberal Arts And General; Teacher Preparatory; Business Emphasis
Accreditation: M

01 President .... Mr. Juan C. NAZARIO-TORRES
05 Vice President Acad Student Affairs .... Dr. Consuelo CASTRO-MELENDEZ
10 Vice Pres Finance & Admin Affairs .... Mrs. Magda A. CANCEL-PEREZ
32 Dean Student Affairs .... Prof. Tamara FELIX-RODRIGUEZ
06 Registrar .... Prof. Maria RODRIGUEZ-PAZ
07 Admissions Officer .... Ms. Keren LLANOS
08 Learning Resources Center Director .... Mrs. Wanda HERNANDEZ-SANCHEZ
35 Dir Student Affairs/Public Rels .... Mrs. Nereida CRISTOBAL
37 Director Financial Aid .... Mrs. Yahaira MELENDEZ
21 Director Accounting .... Mrs. Jeanette AVILES-FERRAN
38 Director Guidance Counseling .... Mrs. Luz S. HERNANDEZ
24 Director Educational Media .... Ms. Carol SANTIAGO
41 Athletic Director .... Mr. Manfredo VEGA
14 Director Computer Center .... Mr. Juan L. RIVERA
15 Director Personnel Services .... Mrs. Lillian BELEN-NAZARIO
12 Director Bayamon Campus .... Dr. Josephine RESTO-OLIVO
12 Director Manati Campus .... Prof. Rosa RODRIGUEZ
09 Dir Research/Institutional Planning .... Vacant
18 Chief Facilities/Physical Plant .... Mr. Efrain LUGO
36 Director of Student Placement .... Vacant
84 Director Enrollment Management .... Mrs. Mariela CRUZ
96 Director of Purchasing .... Mrs. Celeste TRAVERSO
92 Director of Honors Program .... Prof. Claribel RODRIGUEZ
30 Chief Development .... Mr. Jaime GONZALEZ
20 Associate Academic Officer .... Prof. Milagros RIVERA
14 Director Acad Computer Center .... Vacant
53 Dept Chair School of Education .... Dr. Jose RAMIREZ
50 Dept Chair Business Admin/Sec Sci .... Prof. Norma ORTIZ
49 Department Chair Arts & Sciences .... Prof. Carmen T. LANDRON

Atenas College (D)

Paseo de las Atenas #101, Manati PR 00674
FICE Identification: 035443
Unit ID: 440651
Telephone: (787) 884-3838 Carnegie Class: Assoc/PrivNFP4
FAX Number: (787) 884-6754 Calendar System: Semester
URL: www.atenascollege.edu
Established: 1996 Annual Undergrad Tuition & Fees: $6,945
Enrollment: 1,390 Coed
Affiliation or Control: Independent Non-Profit IRS Status: 501(c)3
Highest Offering: Baccalaureate
Program: Liberal Arts And General
Accreditation: ACCSC

01 President .... Prof. Maria L. HERNANDEZ NUNEZ

Atlantic University College (E)

PO Box 3918, Guaynabo PR 00970
County: Guaynabo FICE Identification: 025054
Unit ID: 241216
Telephone: (787) 720-1022 Carnegie Class: Bac/Diverse
FAX Number: (787) 720-1092 Calendar System: Quarter
URL: www.atlanticu.edu
Established: 1983 Annual Undergrad Tuition & Fees: $6,755
Enrollment: 1,416 Coed
Affiliation or Control: Independent Non-Profit IRS Status: 501(c)3
Highest Offering: Baccalaureate
Program: 2-Year Principally Bachelor's Creditable; Liberal Arts And General; Professional
Accreditation: ACICS

01 President .... Dr. Teresa DE DIOS UNANUE
05 Dean of Academics .... Prof. Ivette CARBONELL
11 Dean of Administration .... Prof. Heriberto MARTINEZ-ABREU
26 Exec VP/Dean Technology/ Marketing .... Prof. Heriberto MARTINEZ-DE DIOS
81 Dean of Science and Digital Arts .... Prof. Frances GRAU
06 Registrar .... Ms. Edna I. GUTIERREZ
38 Dir Student Counseling/ Placement .... Mrs. Maria C. LOPEZ-CEPERO
37 Director Financial Aid .... Mrs. Janice RIVERA
08 Head Librarian .... Mrs. Tania DÍAZ
07 Officer of Admissions .... Mrs. Margarita FIGUEROA
21 Bursar's Officer .... Mrs. María del C MONTESINO
15 Officer of Human Services .... Mrs. Urania GONZALEZ

Bayamon Central University (F)

PO Box 1725, Bayamon PR 00960-1725
County: Bayamon FICE Identification: 005022
Unit ID: 241225
Telephone: (787) 786-3030 Carnegie Class: Master's M
FAX Number: (787) 740-2200 Calendar System: Semester
URL: www.ucb.edu.pr
Established: 1961 Annual Undergrad Tuition & Fees: $5,900
Enrollment: 2,256 Coed
Affiliation or Control: Roman Catholic IRS Status: 501(c)3
Highest Offering: Master's
Program: Liberal Arts And General; Teacher Preparatory; Professional
Accreditation: M, CORE, @TEAC

01 President .... Dr. Lillian NEGRON
05 Academic Dean .... Dr. Pura ECHANDI
11 Administrative Dean .... Mrs. Rosimar FERRER
32 Dean of Students .... Mrs. Niza ZAYAS
49 Dir College Liberal Arts/Humanities .... Dr. Oscar CRUZ
53 Dir Col of Education and Behaviora .... Dr. Caroline GONZALEZ
50 Dir Business Development & Tech .... Prof. Nidia COLON
08 Director Learning Resources .... Mrs. Annette VALENTIN
15 Director of Human Resources .... Mrs. Virna RIVERA
30 Director Institutional Development .... Mr. Pedro BERMUDEZ
07 Director of Admissions .... Mrs. Christine HERNANDEZ
37 Director Student Financial Aid .... Mrs. Edna ORTIZ
38 Director Guidance Center .... Mrs. Milagros M. RIVERA
06 Registrar .... Mr. Victor COLON
35 Director Transition Services (STAE) .... Mrs. Myrna PEREZ
90 Dir Center for Faculty Development .... Mr. Jorge DIAZ
68 Director of Sports Facilities .... Mr. Edwin MORALES
13 Director of Information System .... Vacant
18 Director Physical Facilities .... Eng. Eliezer GARCIA
26 Public Relations Officer .... Mrs. Niza ZAYAS
96 Purchase Officer .... Mrs. Jessica OJEDA
09 Specialist Institutional Research .... Mrs. Luz M. PALACIOS
66 Nursing Program Coordinator .... Prof. Floridalia VIDAL
20 Associate Academic Dean .... Dr. Luz C. VALENTIN
29 Alumni Relations .... Prof. Josean FELICIANO
84 Director Enrollment Management .... Mrs. Christine HERNANDEZ
58 Graduate Studies Director .... Dr. Nitza MARQUEZ
88 Dir College Sciences/Health Profes .... Dr. Pedro ROBLES

Caribbean University (G)

Box 493, Bayamon PR 00960-0493
County: Bayamon FICE Identification: 012525
Unit ID: 241377
Telephone: (787) 780-0070 Carnegie Class: Master's M
FAX Number: (787) 785-0101 Calendar System: Semester
URL: www.caribbean.edu
Established: 1969 Annual Undergrad Tuition & Fees: $5,635
Enrollment: 1,615 Coed
Affiliation or Control: Independent Non-Profit IRS Status: 501(c)3
Highest Offering: Doctorate
Program: Liberal Arts And General; Teacher Preparatory
Accreditation: M, @TEAC

01 President/CEO .... Dr. Ana E. CUCURELLA-ADORNO
03 Executive Director .... Mr. Victor T. ADORNO
05 Vice President of Academic Affairs .... Dr. Luis J. DELGADO
45 Vice President of Planning and Info .... Mr. Jorge RIEFKOHL
11 Dean Administration Affairs .... Mr. Israel RODRIGUEZ
32 Dean of Student Affairs .... Mr. Luis J. DELGADO
13 IT Interim Director .... Mr. Luis N. PRATTS
15 Human Resources Director .... Vacant
37 Director Student Financial Aid .... Mr. Hector GRACIA
06 Registrar .... Mrs. Kendra ORTIZ
08 Librarian/Director Audio-Visual .... Mrs. Carmen L. APONTE
07 Director of Admissions .... Mrs. Rosalie MORALES
12 Director of Carolina Campus .... Dr. Jaime CRUZ
12 Director of Ponce Campus .... Dr. Ramon VAZQUEZ
12 Director Vega Baja Campus .... Dr. Angel MEJIAS
20 Provost .... Ms. Lillian MATOS
71 Director Special Service Program .... Mrs. Maryliz AUBRET
26 Public Relations Director .... Dr. Enrique ROSARIO
49 Director Department Arts/Science .... Prof. William PEREZ
50 Director Dept Business Admin/Sec Sc .... Mr. Jose M. CUETO
76 Health Services .... Ms. Mara MEDINA
54 Director Department of Engineering .... Dr. Hermes CALDERON
66 Director Department of Nursing .... Dr. Mildred FLORES
53 Director Department Education .... Dr. Edgardo REYES
77 Director of Computer Science .... Dr. Augusto CARVAJAL
18 Chief Facilities/Physical Plant .... Mr. Henry SEVILLA
43 Legal Advisor .... Mr. Rafael SANTIAGO
38 Director Student Counseling .... Dr. Ida Y. ALVARADO
41 Athletic Director .... Mr. Jaime VAZQUEZ
22 Director of Compliance .... Mrs. Elena GARCIA
84 Director Enrollment Management .... Vacant
09 Director of Institutional Research .... Dr. Luz D. SERRANO
96 Director of Purchasing .... Mrs. Carmen J. ROSA

Carlos Albizu University (H)

Box 9023711, San Juan PR 00902-3711
County: San Juan FICE Identification: 010724
Unit ID: 241331
Telephone: (787) 725-6500 Carnegie Class: Spec/Health
FAX Number: (787) 721-7187 Calendar System: Semester
URL: www.albizu.edu
Established: 1966 Annual Undergrad Tuition & Fees: $4,990
Enrollment: 930 Coed
Affiliation or Control: Independent Non-Profit IRS Status: 501(c)3
Highest Offering: Doctorate
Program: Professional
Accreditation: M, CLPSY, SP

00 Chair Board of Trustees .... Mr. Jaime L. ALBORS BIGAS
01 President .... Dr. Ileana RODRIGUEZ-GARCIA
12 Chancellor of San Juan Campus . Dr. Jose J. CABIYA-MORALES
12 Chancellor of Miami Campus .... Dr. Carmen ROCA
07 Vice Pres Admissions/Student Affs .... Mr. Ram LAMBA
11 Spec Asst to Chanc for Admin Affs .... Mr. Luis ECHEGARAY
05 Spec Asst to Chanc for Acad Affs .... Dr. Jaime VERAY
88 Special Assistant to Vice President .... Ms. Sylvia LOPEZ
10 Exec Director of Finance .... Mrs. Syvia LOPEZ
46 Director Research Training .... Dr. Lymaries PADILLA-COTTO
88 Director General Psychology Program .... Dr. Jaime VERAY
51 Director Continuing Education Ofc .... Vacant
88 Director Internship .... Dr. Aida GARCIA

37 Director Student Financial Aid .... Mrs. Doris QUERO-MENDEZ
08 Librarian ....Ms. Yolanda ROSARIO-ROSARIO
06 Registrar ....Mr. Victor BONILLA-RODRIGUEZ
88 Dir Industrial/Org Psych Program ... Dr. Miguel MARTINEZ-LUGO
13 Dir Information Technology Svcs .... Mr. Luis CAMACHO
88 Administrator Community Svcs Clinic .... Mr. Rafael ORTIZ
31 Director Community Services Clinic ....Dr. Jose RODRIGUEZ-QUINONES
88 Director PhD Clinical Psych Program ....Dr. Aida JIMENEZ-TORRES
88 Dir PsyD Clinical Psychology Pgm ..Dr. Nanet LOPEZ-CORDOVA
15 Director of Human Resources ....Mrs. Carmen ACEVEDO-RIOS
30 Director Development ....Ms. Angeles PEREZ-TORO
88 Director Clinical Training .... Dr. Noel QUINTERO-JIMENEZ
88 Director Bachelor's Program ....Dr. Jaime VERAY
38 President Student Counseling ....Mr. Ricardo DEL RIO-MORALES
11 Director Administration ....Mr. John FERNANDEZ
26 Public Relations Officer ....Rochely ESCALANTE
29 Director Alumni Relations ....Ms. Angeles PEREZ

Center for Advanced Studies On Puerto Rico and the Caribbean (A)

PO Box 902-3970, Old San Juan PR 00902-3970
County: San Juan FICE Identification: 021660
Unit ID: 241793
Telephone: (787) 723-4481 Carnegie Class: Spec/Other
FAX Number: (787) 723-1023 Calendar System: Semester
URL: www.ceaprc.edu
Established: 1976 Annual Graduate Tuition & Fees: $5,080
Enrollment: 573 Coed
Affiliation or Control: Independent Non-Profit IRS Status: 501(c)3
Highest Offering: Doctorate; No Undergraduates
Program: Professional; Fine Arts Emphasis
Accreditation: M

01 Chancellor .... Mr. Miguel A. RODRIGUEZ-LOPEZ
05 Academic Dean .... Dr. Jaime L. RODRIGUEZ-CANCEL
06 Registrar ....Mrs. Mayra I. RAMIREZ
08 Head Librarian ....Mr. Francis J. MOJICA
10 Administration Dean ....Mrs. Lizzette CARRILLO
04 Chancellor's Assistant .... Ms. Clarissa SANTIAGO-TORO
07 Marketing and Enrollment Director .....Mrs. Monica D. GONZALEZ
37 Financial Aid Officer ....Mrs. Lillian M. OLIVER

Centro de Estudios Multidisciplinarios (B)

Calle Degetau #25, Bayamon PR 00961
Telephone: (787) 780-8900 Identification: 770590
Accreditation: ACCSC

† Main campus is Centro de Estudios Multidisciplinarios in Rio Piedras, PR.

Centro de Estudios Multidisciplinarios (C)

Calle Dr. Vidal #8 y #53, Humacau PR 00791
Telephone: (787) 850-8333 Identification: 770589
Accreditation: ACCSC

† Main campus is Centro de Estudios Multidisciplinarios in Rio Piedras, PR.

Centro de Estudios Multidisciplinarios (D)

Calle Cristy #56, Mayaguez PR 00681
Telephone: (787) 986-7440 Identification: 770591
Accreditation: ACCSC

† Main campus is Centro de Estudios Multidisciplinarios in Rio Piedras, PR.

Centro de Estudios Multidisciplinarios (E)

Calle 13 #1206, Ext San Agustin, Rio Piedras PR 00926
County: San Juan FICE Identification: 021891
Unit ID: 241517
Telephone: (787) 765-4210 Carnegie Class: Assoc/PrivNFP
FAX Number: (787) 765-4277 Calendar System: Semester
URL: www.cempr.edu
Established: 1980 Annual Undergrad Tuition & Fees: $6,561
Enrollment: 1,243 Coed
Affiliation or Control: Independent Non-Profit IRS Status: 501(c)3
Highest Offering: Baccalaureate
Program: Occupational; 2-Year Principally Bachelor's Creditable; Nursing Emphasis
Accreditation: ACCSC

01 President .... Mr. Juan C. PAGANI-SOTO
05 Academic Dean .... Dr. Nereida NALES
07 Director of Admissions .... Mr. Juan RESTO TORRES
06 Registrar ....Mrs. Margarita RIVERA
10 Finance Director .... Mr. Carlos RODRIGUEZ
12 Branch Director ....Mrs. Laura M. DELGADO
15 Human Resources Director ...... Mrs. Lilliana M. LOPEZ-MEDERO

Colegio de Cinematografia, Artes y Television (F)

51 Dr. Veve St, Degetau St Corner, Bayamon PR 00960
County: Bayamon FICE Identification: 031576
Unit ID: 430935
Telephone: (787) 779-2500 Carnegie Class: Assoc/PrivFP
FAX Number: (787) 995-2525 Calendar System: Semester
URL: www.ccatpr.com/nosotros/
Established: 1993 Annual Undergrad Tuition & Fees: $6,550
Enrollment: 854 Coed
Affiliation or Control: Proprietary IRS Status: Proprietary
Highest Offering: Associate Degree
Program: Occupational
Accreditation: ACCSC

01 President ....Mr. Jorge GARCIA

Colegio Universitario de San Juan (G)

180 Jose R. Oliver Street, San Juan PR 00918
County: San Juan FICE Identification: 010567
Unit ID: 241720
Telephone: (787) 480-2400 Carnegie Class: Bac/Assoc
FAX Number: (787) 250-7395 Calendar System: Semester
URL: www.cunisanjuan.edu
Established: 1972 Annual Undergrad Tuition & Fees (In-District): $2,950
Enrollment: 2,950 Coed
Affiliation or Control: Local IRS Status: 501(c)3
Highest Offering: Baccalaureate
Program: Occupational; 2-Year Principally Bachelor's Creditable; Business Emphasis
Accreditation: M, ADNUR

01 Acting Chancellor ....Dr. Haydee M. ZAYAS-HERNÁNDEZ
45 Dir Planning/Inst Research/Ext Rels ....Dr. Haydee M. ZAYAS-HERNANDEZ
04 Special Asst to the Chancellor ....Dr. Melvin VEGA-GONZALEZ
11 Acting Dean Administrative Affairs .....Mr. Victor RIVERA-FLORES
05 Acting Dean Academic Affairs .... Dr. Phaedra GELPI-RODRÍGUEZ
51 Dir Continuing Educ/Extension Pgm .. Mrs. Mercy FALERO-SOTO
37 Manager Student Financial Aid ...... Ms. Gloria MIRABAL-RIVERA
08 Head Librarian .... Mrs. Sheila VERA-MORALES
06 Registrar ....Mrs. Evelyn GUZMAN-LOPEZ
38 Counselor ....Mrs. Mara MALAVE-LASSO
07 Retention Officer .... Mrs. Kennia I. SANTOS-PEREZ
36 Placement Officer .... Mrs. Margarita COLON-CALZADA
13 Administrator Info Systems/ Telecomm .... Mr. Zacarias POURIET-DE LA CRUZ
72 Director Science & Technology ....Prof. Marcus DROZ
76 Director Health Related Science .....Prof. Luz D. ORTEGA-RAMOS
50 Director Business Administration ....Prof. Mariamelia GONZALEZ-RODRIGUEZ
97 Manager General Education .... Prof. Carmen J. RODRIGUEZ

Columbia Centro Universitario (H)

PO Box 8517, Caguas PR 00726-8517
County: Caguas FICE Identification: 008902
Unit ID: 241304
Telephone: (787) 743-4041 Carnegie Class: Master's S
FAX Number: (787) 746-5616 Calendar System: Semester
URL: www.columbiaco.edu
Established: 1966 Annual Undergrad Tuition & Fees: $9,435
Enrollment: 6,290 Coed
Affiliation or Control: Proprietary IRS Status: Proprietary
Highest Offering: Master's
Program: Business Emphasis
Accreditation: M

01 President ....Mr. Alex R. DEJORGE
05 VP Academic Affairs ....Mrs. Carmen J. LOPEZ
03 Senior VP of Operations .... Mrs. Carmen M. RIVERA
10 VP Finance and Administration .... Mrs. Daritza MULERO
32 VP Student Affairs .... Mrs. Brendaliz ZAYAS
26 VP Marketing and Communication .... Mr. Angel QUIÑONES
12 Chancellor of Caguas Campus ....Dra. Gladys SERRANO
12 Chancellor of Yauco Branch .... Ms. Rosario PADILLA
35 Executive Director Student Affairs ....Mrs. Belmarie HUERTAS
20 Dean Academic Affairs .... Mr. Luis LOPEZ
08 Institutional Librarian ....Ms. Luz NEGRON
11 Administrative Support Director .... Ms. Carmen I. ROJAS
37 Financial Aid Director ....Mrs. Virginia GUANG
07 Coordinator of Admissions ....Mrs. Xiomara SANCHEZ
06 Registrar .... Ms. Wilmarie TORRES
38 Student Counselor ....Ms. Ingrid CARRION
15 Director Human Resources ....Ms. Elsie M. TORRES
36 Director Student Placement ....Ms. Iris TIZOL
18 Facilities & Development Director .... Mr. Jesus M. RIVERA

Columbia Centro Universitario (I)

Box 3062, Yauco PR 00698-3062
Telephone: (787) 856-0845 Identification: 666036
Accreditation: &M

† Main campus is Columbia Centro Universitario in Caguas, PR.

Conservatory of Music of Puerto Rico (J)

951 Ponce de Leon Ave. Miramar, Santurce PR 00907
County: San Juan FICE Identification: 010819
Unit ID: 241766
Telephone: (787) 751-0160 Carnegie Class: Spec/Arts
FAX Number: (787) 766-1216 Calendar System: Semester
URL: www.cmpr.edu
Established: 1959 Annual Undergrad Tuition & Fees (In-State): $4,420
Enrollment: 455 Coed
Affiliation or Control: State IRS Status: 501(c)3
Highest Offering: Master's
Program: Music Emphasis
Accreditation: M

01 Chancellor .... Prof. Lui HERNANDEZ-MERGAL
05 Dean of Academic Affairs .... Prof. Ariel GUZMAN
11 Dean of Administration ....Mr. Juan Carlos HERNANDEZ
32 Dean Student Affairs/Financial Aid ...... Mr. Michael RAJABALLEY
88 Dean of Preparatory School ....Prof. Magdalena NOGUERAS
07 Director of Admissions ....Mrs. Ilsamar HERNANDEZ
08 Librarian ....Mrs. Damaris CORDERO
20 Associate Dean of Studies ....Vacant
30 Development & Public Relations Dir ....Ms. Ciara MELENDEZ
15 Human Resources Director ....Ms. Alba DAVILA
38 Counselor ....Mrs. Pilar RUIBAL

Dominican Study Center of the Caribbean (K)

PO Box 1968, Bayamon PR 00960-1968
County: Bayamon Identification: 666337
Telephone: (787) 786-4508 Carnegie Class: Not Classified
FAX Number: (787) 798-2712 Calendar System: Semester
URL: www.cedoc.edu
Established: 1980 Annual Undergrad Tuition & Fees: $5,100
Enrollment: 70 Coed
Affiliation or Control: Independent Non-Profit IRS Status: 501(c)3
Highest Offering: Master's
Program: Religious Emphasis
Accreditation: THEOL

01 Dean ....Rev Dr. Yamil A. SAMALOT-RIVERA, OP
05 Associate Dean ....Dr. Oscar CRUZ-CUEVAS

EDIC College (L)

PO Box 9120, Caguas PR 00726-9120
County: Caguas FICE Identification: 030219
Unit ID: 376321
Telephone: (787) 744-8519 Carnegie Class: Assoc/PrivFP
FAX Number: (787) 743-0855 Calendar System: Semester
URL: www.ediccollege.com
Established: 1987 Annual Undergrad Tuition & Fees: $6,485
Enrollment: 916 Coed
Affiliation or Control: Proprietary IRS Status: Proprietary
Highest Offering: Associate Degree
Program: Occupational
Accreditation: ACICS

01 President/CEO ....Mr. Jose A. CORDOVA
11 Administrator .... Mrs. Milagros CARTAGENA
12 Director of Branch Campus .... Mr. Reinaldo GONZALEZ
05 Academic Dean ....Mrs. Loida R. RAMIREZ

EDP University of Puerto Rico (M)

PO Box 192303, San Juan PR 00919-2303
County: San Juan FICE Identification: 021651
Unit ID: 243832
Telephone: (787) 765-3560 Carnegie Class: Bac/Diverse
FAX Number: (787) 777-0025 Calendar System: Semester
URL: www.edpuniversity.edu
Established: 1968 Annual Undergrad Tuition & Fees: $5,940
Enrollment: 1,198 Coed
Affiliation or Control: Independent Non-Profit IRS Status: 501(c)3
Highest Offering: Master's
Program: Occupational; Business Emphasis
Accreditation: M

01 President ....Mrs. Gladys T. NIEVES
05 Academic Dean ....Mr. Sandra ARROYO
10 Vice President Finance .... Mr. Luis RIVERA
26 VP Institutional/International Rels .... Dr. Marilyn PASTRANA
108 VP Acreditation & Inst Assessment ....Dr. Alberto LOPEZ
13 VP Tcchnology/Distance Education .... Prof Mayra RIVERA
14 Inst Information Systems Dir .... Dr. Ramon MALLOL
06 Registrar ....Mrs. Glenda RODRÍGUEZ
08 Librarian ....Mrs. Igrí ENRIQUEZ
21 Finance Dean ....Mrs. Marie Luz PASTRANA
32 Student Services Dean ....Dr. Enid CARTAGENA
18 Director Facilities/Physical Plant ....Eng. Luis FUSTER
37 Director of Financial Aid .... Ms. Maria COLON
07 Director of Admissions ....Mrs. Dendy VILA

EDP University of Puerto Rico (N)

PO Box 1674, 49 Betances Street, San Sebastian PR 00685-1674
Telephone: (787) 896-2137 Identification: 666488
Accreditation: &M

† Main campus is EDP University of Puerto Rico in San Juan, PR.

Escuela de Artes Plasticas de Puerto Rico (O)

PO Box 9021112, San Juan PR 00902-1112
County: San Juan FICE Identification: 025694
Unit ID: 241951
Telephone: (787) 725-8120 Carnegie Class: Spec/Arts
FAX Number: (787) 725-8111 Calendar System: Semester

URL: www.eap.edu
Established: 1966 Annual Undergrad Tuition & Fees (In-State): $3,248
Enrollment: 489 Coed
Affiliation or Control: State IRS Status: 501(c)3
Highest Offering: Baccalaureate
Program: Liberal Arts And General; Teacher Preparatory; Fine Arts Emphasis
Accreditation: M, ART

01 Acting Chancellor .... Arch. Ivonne M. MARCIAL VEGA
11 Dean of Administration .... Mr. Ismael GARCIA ORTEGA
05 Acting Dean Acad/Student Affairs .... Prof. Teresa LOPEZ
06 Registrar .... Ms. Ileana MALDONADO
07 Officer of Admissions .... Ms. Nitza MELENDEZ
13 Director Information Technology .... Ms. Limaris SOTO
37 Director Student Financial Aid .... Mr. Alfred DIAZ
36 Counselor Stdnt Affairs/Placement .... Ms. Ivette MUNOZ
45 Director of Planning Office .... Mr. Carlos E. RIVERA
09 Assistant Institutional Research .... Dr. Shirley A. TAVARES
10 Chief Financial Officer .... Ms. Mayra E. DIAZ
18 Coord Facilities/Physical Plant .... Mr. Edwin ALICEA
56 Coordinator Extension Program .... Ms. Liliam NIEVES
38 Counselor Stdnt Life/Counseling .... Dr. Yadira ORTIZ COLON
88 Coordinator Cultural Activities ... Mr. Adrian O. RIVERA NEGRON
105 Director Web Services .... Mr. Celso E. PORTELA IRIGOYEN
96 Officer of Purchasing .... Vacant
20 Asst Dean Acad/Student Affairs .... Mr. Marcos VÉLEZ RIVERA
15 Director Personnel Services .... Ms. Carmen D. ROSARIO-MORALES
28 Director of Projects .... Dr. Shirley A. TAVARES
53 Director Education .... Prof. Noemi RIVERA
97 Director General Studies .... Dr. Maria VAZQUEZ
88 Director Fashion/Apparel Design .... Prof. Ana COLORADO
88 Director Industrial/Product Design .... Prof. Vladimir GARCIA
88 Dir Design/Visual Communications .... Prof. Mayela CARDENAS
88 Director Painting .... Prof. Jvelisse JIMENEZ
88 Director Sculpture .... Prof. Linda SÁNCHEZ PINTOR
88 Director Graphics .... Prof. Luis A. ORTIZ

Evangelical Seminary of Puerto Rico (A)

Ponce De Leon Avenue 776, San Juan PR 00925-2207
County: San Juan FICE Identification: 006823
Unit ID: 243498
Telephone: (787) 763-6700 Carnegie Class: Spec/Faith
FAX Number: (787) 751-0847 Calendar System: Semester
URL: www.se-pr.edu
Established: 1919 Annual Undergrad Tuition & Fees: $5,094
Enrollment: 241 Coed
Affiliation or Control: Interdenominational IRS Status: 501(c)3
Highest Offering: Doctorate
Program: Professional
Accreditation: M, THEOL

01 President .... Dr. Sergio OJEDA-CARCAMO
05 Academic Dean/Chaplain .... Dr. Francisco J. GOITIA PADILLA
10 Director Administration & Finances .. Ms. Myrna E. PEREZ-LOPEZ
06 Registrar .... Miss Mari Lillian RIVERA
08 Head Librarian .... Mrs. Sonia ARRILLAGA MONTALVO
30 Director of Development/Planning .... Ms. Ruth M. DIAZ
37 Student Financial Aid .... Ms. Lourdes JESUS CESAREO

Huertas Junior College (B)

PO Box 8429, Caguas PR 00726-8429
County: Caguas FICE Identification: 022608
Unit ID: 242112
Telephone: (787) 746-1400 Carnegie Class: Assoc/PrivFP
FAX Number: (787) 747-0170 Calendar System: Semester
URL: www.huertas.edu
Established: 1945 Annual Undergrad Tuition & Fees: $9,600
Enrollment: 1,450 Coed
Affiliation or Control: Proprietary IRS Status: Proprietary
Highest Offering: Associate Degree
Program: Occupational; 2-Year Principally Bachelor's Creditable; Technical Emphasis
Accreditation: M, CAHIIM, @PTAA

01 President .... Maria del Mar LOPEZ-AVILES
03 Exec Vice President and Compliance .... Raul HERNANDEZ
05 Vice Pres of Students & Academics .... Amarillys GARCIA
30 VP Planning and Development .... Barbara FLORES
15 VP of Human Resources .... Sarai GONZALEZ
32 Associate VP of Student Services .... Eva VEGA
06 Registrar .... Krishna MARQUEZ
08 Head Librarian .... Glenda PEREZ
38 Director Student Counseling .... Evelyn COTTO
21 Director of Finance & Federal Funds .... Celestino CRUZ
22 Compliance Officer .... Vacant
88 Counselor .... Vacant

Humacao Community College (C)

PO Box 9139, Humacao PR 00792-9139
County: Humacao FICE Identification: 023406
Unit ID: 242121
Telephone: (787) 852-1430 Carnegie Class: Assoc/PrivNFP
FAX Number: (787) 850-1577 Calendar System: Trimester
URL: www.hccpr.edu
Established: 1978 Annual Undergrad Tuition & Fees: $5,640
Enrollment: 763 Coed
Affiliation or Control: Independent Non-Profit IRS Status: 501(c)3
Highest Offering: Baccalaureate
Program: Occupational; 2-Year Principally Bachelor's Creditable; Business Emphasis
Accreditation: ACICS

01 President .... Lic. Jorge E. MOJICA
03 Executive Vice President .... Prof. Aida E. RODRIGUEZ
05 Exec Director/Chief Academic Ofcr .... Mrs. Gladys E. FLECHA
55 Director of Evening Session .... Prof. Ada BAEZ
37 Director Student Financial Aid .... Mrs. Cheryle PEREZ
36 Student Placement Officer .... Mr. Luis GARCIA
07 Director Admissions .... Vacant
06 Registrar .... Mrs. Nildalee MELENDEZ
08 Head Librarian .... Mrs. Lourdes ELIZA
10 Treasury Officer (Finance) .... Mrs. Diana RODRIGUEZ
38 Student Counselor .... Mr. Neftali DIAZ
11 Chief College Administrator .... Mrs. Marianne BERRIOS
04 Adm Asst to Pres/Dir Personnel .... Mrs. Nilda E. RODRIGUEZ

ICPR Junior College (D)

558 Munoz Rivera Avenue, Hato Rey PR 00919-0304
County: San Juan FICE Identification: 011940
Unit ID: 243841
Telephone: (787) 753-6000 Carnegie Class: Assoc/PrivFP
FAX Number: (787) 622-3416 Calendar System: Semester
URL: www.icprjc.edu
Established: 1946 Annual Undergrad Tuition & Fees: $6,330
Enrollment: 682 Coed
Affiliation or Control: Proprietary IRS Status: Proprietary
Highest Offering: Associate Degree
Program: Occupational; 2-Year Principally Bachelor's Creditable; Business Emphasis
Accreditation: M

01 President/Chief Executive Officer .... Dr. Olga RIVERA
12 Hato Rey Campus Director .... Mrs. Maria de los M. RIVERA
20 Academic Affairs Dean .... Mrs. Maribel BAYONA
07 Admissions Director Hato Rey .... Mr. Axel CALDERON
07 Admissions Director Mayaguez .... Mrs. Aracelis GASTON
07 Admissions Director Arecibo .... Ms. Meysaliz GARCIA
07 Admissions Director Manati .... Mrs. Viviana TORRES
10 Finance and Accounting Director .... Mr. Noel ORTIZ
37 Financial Aid Director .... Mr. Arroyo PALMIRA
12 Mayaguez Campus Director .... Dr. Luz M. ORTIZ
12 Arecibo Campus Director .... Mrs. Ivette CHARRIEZ
12 Manati Campus Director .... Mr. Fernando GONZALEZ
06 Registrar Hato Rey .... Mrs. María C. VELEZ
06 Registrar Mayaguez .... Mrs. Olga NEGRON
06 Registrar Arecibo .... Mrs. Glenda PADIN
06 Registrar Manati .... Mrs. Vanessa TRINIDAD
06 Registrar Bayamon Extension .... Mrs. Diana FREYTES
26 Institutional Admissions/Mrktng Dir .... Mr. Isander VELAZQUEZ
13 Information Systems Director .... Mr. Nelson MEJIAS
08 Learning Res Librarian Hato Rey .... Mrs. Sulynet TORRES
08 Lrng Resources Librarian Mayaguez .... Mrs. Jessica CARO
08 Lrng Resources Librarian Arecibo .... Mrs. Irma JIMENEZ
08 Learning Resources Librarian .... Mr. Martin ROSADO
38 Professional Counselor Mayaguez .... Mrs. Barbarita CUMPIANO
38 Professional Counselor Arecibo .... Mrs. Milagros AGUILAR
38 Professional Counselor Manati .... Mrs. Lourdes RIOS
38 Professional Counselor Hato Rey .... Mrs. Yarelis COLON
15 Human Resources Director .... Mrs. Daisy CASTRO
88 Institutional Compliance Director .... Mrs. Lizzette VARGAS
56 Bayamon Extension Director .... Mr. Manuel MELO
20 Academic Coordinator Mayaguez .... Dr. Mayra RUIZ
20 Academic Coordinator Arecibo .... Mrs. Edith RAMOS
20 Academic Coordinator Manati .... Mrs. Maribel TORRES
20 Academic Coordinator Hato Rey .... Mr. Josue CINTRON

ICPR Junior College-Arecibo Campus (E)

PO Box 146007, Arecibo PR 00614-0067
Telephone: (787) 878-6000 Identification: 770166
Accreditation: &M

† Main campus is ICPR Junior College in Hato Rey, PR.

ICPR Junior College-Manati Branch Campus (F)

PO Box 49, Manati PR 00674-0049
Telephone: (787) 884-6000 Identification: 770168
Accreditation: &M

† Main campus is ICPR Junior College in Hato Rey, PR.

ICPR Junior College-Mayaguez Campus (G)

PO Box 1108, Mayaguez PR 00681-9913
Telephone: (787) 832-6000 Identification: 770167
Accreditation: &M

† Main campus is ICPR Junior College in Hato Rey, PR.

Instituto de Banca y Comercio (H)

709 Ferrocarril Street, Ponce PR 00717
Telephone: (787) 840-6119 Identification: 770773
Accreditation: ACICS

† Main campus is Instituto de Banca y Comercio in San Juan, PR.

Instituto de Banca y Comercio (I)

61 Ponce de Leon Ave, San Juan PR 00917
Identification: 667107
Telephone: (787) 754-7120 Carnegie Class: Not Classified
FAX Number: (787) 754-7143 Calendar System: Other
URL: www.ibanca.net
Established: Annual Undergrad Tuition & Fees: N/A
Enrollment: N/A Coed
Affiliation or Control: Proprietary IRS Status: Proprietary
Highest Offering: Associate Degree
Program: Occupational
Accreditation: ACICS

01 President .... Sr. Guillermo NIGAGLIONI
05 Director .... Mr. Wilfredo HERNANDEZ

*Inter American University of Puerto Rico Central Office (J)

GPO Box 363255, San Juan PR 00936-3255
County: San Juan FICE Identification: 008242
Unit ID: 242671
Telephone: (787) 766-1912 Carnegie Class: N/A
FAX Number: (787) 751-3375
URL: www.inter.edu

01 President .... Mr. Manuel J. FERNOS
03 Exec Director President's Office .... Mr. Tomas M. JIMENEZ
05 Vice Pres Academic & Student Affrs .... Mr. Agustin ECHEVARRIA
10 VP Financial Affairs/Services .... Mr. Luis ESQUILIN
42 Vice President Religious Affairs .... Rev. Norberto DOMINGUEZ
20 Associate VP Academic Affairs .... Dr. Rafael CABRERA
21 Assoc VP Financial Affairs/Services .... Ms. Olga LUNA
32 Associate Vice Pres Student Affairs .... Dr. Elba ENCARNACION
04 Exec Assistant to the President .... Mr. Dominique GILORMINI
26 Exec Dir Public Rels & Marketing .... Ms. Rosa MELENDEZ
30 Executive Director Development .... Mr. Eduardo LAMADRID
09 Exec Director Inst Research .... Dr. Elizabeth SCALLEY
13 Dir Information/Telecommunications .... Mrs. Jossie SALGUERO
43 Director Legal Services .... Mrs. Lorraine JUARBE
43 Director Federal Legal Services .... Mr. Vladimir ROMAN
15 Exec Director Human Resources .... Ms. Maggie COLON

*Inter American University of Puerto Rico Aguadilla Campus (K)

Box 20000, Aguadilla PR 00605-9001
County: Aguadilla FICE Identification: 003939
Unit ID: 242626
Telephone: (787) 891-0925 Carnegie Class: Master's S
FAX Number: (787) 882-3020 Calendar System: Other
URL: www.aguadilla.inter.edu
Established: 1957 Annual Undergrad Tuition & Fees: $5,614
Enrollment: 4,631 Coed
Affiliation or Control: Independent Non-Profit IRS Status: 501(c)3
Highest Offering: Master's
Program: Occupational; Liberal Arts And General; Teacher Preparatory; Professional
Accreditation: M, NUR, @TEAC

02 Chancellor .... Dr. Elie AGESILAS
05 Dean of Studies .... Prof. Nilsa M. ROMAN
32 Dean of Student Affairs .... Mrs. Ana C. LAUSELL
13 Director Information and Technology .... Mr. Asdrubal JIMENEZ
90 Information Systems Administrator .... Mr. Jossue MORALES
11 Dean of Administrative Affairs .... Mr. Israel AYALA
20 Associate Dean of Studies .... Mrs. Lymari NEGRON
30 Development Director .... Miss Sacha M. RUIZ
08 Library Director .... Mrs. Monserrate YULFO
07 Admissions Director .... Mrs. Doris PEREZ
06 Registrar .... Mrs. Maria PEREZ
37 Financial Aid Director .... Mrs. Gloria CORTES
21 Bursar .... Mrs. Yanira GONZALEZ
16 Human Resources Director .... Mr. Jose R. AREIZAGA
96 Purchasing Officer .... Ms. Wanda VARGAS
35 Student Support Services Director .... Mrs. Ivonne ACEVEDO
81 Director of Science and Technology .... Prof. Rosa GONZALEZ
79 Director of Education & Hum Studies .... Mrs. Ramonita ROSA
50 Director Economic Science & Admin .... Prof. Elidine GONZALEZ
53 Dir of Social & Behavioral Sciences .... Prof. Ricardo BADILLO
42 Chaplain .... Mr. Francisco GONZALEZ
88 Director of Upward Bound Program .... Ms. Mayra ROZADA
88 Dir Campus Learning Center .... Ms. Yamilette PROSPER
18 Dir Building Maintenance/Univ Guard .... Mr. Jose CABAN
38 Director of Counseling Office .... Ms. Gladys ACEVEDO
41 Sports Director .... Ms. Yolanda PAGAN
84 Enrollment Manager .... Prof. Myriam MARCIAL

*Inter American University of Puerto Rico Arecibo Campus (L)

PO Box 4050, Arecibo PR 00614-4050
County: Arecibo FICE Identification: 005026
Unit ID: 242635
Telephone: (787) 878-5475 Carnegie Class: Master's S
FAX Number: (787) 880-1624 Calendar System: Semester
URL: www.arecibo.inter.edu
Established: 1957 Annual Undergrad Tuition & Fees: $4,660
Enrollment: 4,965 Coed
Affiliation or Control: Independent Non-Profit IRS Status: 501(c)3
Highest Offering: Master's

Program: Occupational; Liberal Arts And General; Teacher Preparatory
Accreditation: M, ANEST, NUR, SW, @TEAC

02 Chancellor ....Dr. Rafael RAMIREZ- RIVERA
05 Dean of Academic Affairs ....Dr. Annette VEGA
11 Dean of Administrative Affairs ....Ms. Wanda PEREZ
32 Dean of Student Affairs ....Prof. Ilvis AGUIRRE
20 Assoc Dean of Academic Affairs ....Prof. Wanda BALSEIRO
08 Educational Resources Center Dir ....Mrs. Sara ABREU
10 Bursar ....Mr. Victor MALDONADO
37 Student Financial Aid Director ....Mr. Ramon DE JESUS
06 Registrar ....Mrs. Carmen RODRIGUEZ
07 Director of Admissions ....Mrs. Provi MONTALVO
04 Executive Assistant to Chancellor ....Mrs. Enid ARBELO
56 Distance Learning Director ....Prof. Aida ALVAREZ
45 Planning Director ....Mrs. Enid ARBELO
42 Religious Life Director ....Mr. Amilcar SOTO
15 Personnel Director ....Mrs. Maritza SANTOS
41 Athletic Department ....Ms. Ileana MORALES
50 Director Econ & Adms Sciences Dept ....Prof. Elba TORO
51 Continuing Education Director ....Mrs. Mariel LLERANDI
53 Director of Education Department ....Prof. Magda VAZQUEZ
66 Director of Nursing Department ....Dr. Frances CORTES
79 Dir of Humanities Department ....Prof. Maria L. DELGADO
81 Director of Sciences & Tech Dept ....Prof. Hector PAGAN
83 Director of Social Sciences Dept ....Prof. Lourdes CARRION
30 Development Director ....Vacant
38 Director Student Counseling ....Ms. Nydia DELGADO
14 Director of Computing Center ....Mr. Jose SEGARRA
58 Director Graduate Program in Educ ....Dra. Ramonita DIAZ
18 Chief Facilities/Physical Plant ....Mr. Jose SANCHEZ
84 Director Enrollment Management ....Mrs. Carmen MONTALVO
88 Dir Graduate Program Anesthesia ....Prof. Josue RAMOS
96 Purchasing Officer ....Mrs. Sonia VILLAIZAN
92 Coordinator Honor Program ....Ms. Vilmaris VAZQUEZ

*Inter American University of Puerto Rico Barranquitas Campus (A)

PO Box 517, Barranquitas PR 00794-0517
County: Barranquitas FICE Identification: 005027
Unit ID: 242644
Telephone: (787) 857-3600 Carnegie Class: Bac/Diverse
FAX Number: (787) 857-2244 Calendar System: Semester
URL: www.br.inter.edu
Established: 1957 Annual Undergrad Tuition & Fees: $6,000
Enrollment: 2,491 Coed
Affiliation or Control: Independent Non-Profit IRS Status: 501(c)3
Highest Offering: Master's
Program: 2-Year Principally Bachelor's Creditable; Liberal Arts And General
Accreditation: M, TEAC

02 Chancellor ....Dr. Irene FERNANDEZ
05 Dean Academic Affairs ....Dr. Patricia ALVAREZ
09 Director of Institutional Research ....Dr. Maribel LÓPEZ
10 Bursar Director ....Mr. Antonio J. ROSARIO
06 Registrar ....Mrs. Sandra M. MORALES
32 Dean Student Affairs ....Mrs. Aramilda CARTAGENA
11 Dean Administrative Affairs ....Mr. Jose E. ORTIZ-ZAYAS
08 Librarian ....Mrs. Maria del C RIVERA
38 Director Upward Bound Program ....Mrs. Saraliz GONZALEZ
84 Director Recruitment/Promotion ....Mrs. Ana Isabel COLON
37 Financial Aid Director ....Mr. Eduardo FONTANEZ
84 Enrollment Manager ....Mrs. Lydia ARCE
07 Director of Admissions ....Mr. Edgardo CINTRON
53 Dir Education/Social Sci/Humanities ....Dr. Filonena CINTRON
81 Dir Natural Sciences/Technology ....Prof. José PÉREZ
88 Director Admin & Economics Sciences ....Vacant
51 Director Continuing Education ....Mrs. Aixa SERRANO
29 Director Alumni Relations ....Mr. Elvin J. ORTIZ
15 Director Human Resources ....Mr. Victor SANTIAGO
30 Chief Development ....Dr. Patricia ALVAREZ
18 Chief Facilities/Physical Plant ....Mr. Jose E. ORTIZ-ZAYAS

*Inter American University of Puerto Rico Bayamon Campus (B)

500 Road 830, Bayamon PR 00957
County: Bayamon FICE Identification: 005028
Unit ID: 242705
Telephone: (787) 279-1912 Carnegie Class: Bac/Diverse
FAX Number: (787) 279-2205 Calendar System: Semester
URL: bayamon.inter.edu
Established: 1912 Annual Undergrad Tuition & Fees: $5,120
Enrollment: 4,934 Coed
Affiliation or Control: Independent Non-Profit IRS Status: 501(c)3
Highest Offering: Master's
Program: Technical Emphasis
Accreditation: M, AAB, ENG, OPTR

02 Chancellor ....Prof. Juan F. MARTINEZ
04 Assistant to Chancellor ....Mr. Antonio L. PANTOJA
30 Chief Development ....Mr. Jaime COLON
05 Chief Academic Officer ....Dr. Carlos OLIVARES
20 Associate Academic Officer ....Dra. Irma ALVARADO
55 Assoc Dean Studies II-Evening Pgm ....Mr. Carlos N. ALICEA
88 Director Student Support Services ....Mrs. Zoraida CRUZ
08 Head Librarian ....Mrs. Sandra ROSA
36 Student Placement and Coop Educ ....Mrs. Maritza ZAMBRANA
88 Dean School of Aeronautics ....Prof. Jorge CALAF
54 Dean School of Engineering ....Dr. Javier QUINTANA
54 Director Electrical Engr Dept ....Prof. Ruben FLORES
54 Director Industrial Engr Dept ....Dr. Heriberto BARRIERA
54 Director Mechanical Engr Dept ....Prof. Amilcar RINCON
81 Director Mathematics/Sciences ....Dr. Omar CUETO
50 Dir Business Administration Dept ....Dr. Francisco MONTALVO
60 Director Communications Dept ....Prof. Ruth E. HERNANDEZ
77 Director Computer Sciences Dept ....Prof. Jose RODRIGUEZ
76 Director of Health Science ....Dra. Silvia ROSADO
79 Director Humanities/Language Dept ....Prof. Laura RIOS
75 Director Tech Institute ....Mrs. Liza FREYTES
32 Chief Students Life Officer ....Mrs. Gema C. TORRES
35 Student Affairs Assistant ....Mrs. Grace GOMEZ
38 Director Student Counseling ....Mrs. Magali PALMER
35 Student Activities Director ....Mrs. Cybel BETANCOURT
41 Athletic Director ....Mr. Reynaldo ROLON
23 Infirmary ....Mrs. Maria ROSADO
10 Chief Financial/Business Officer ....Mr. Luis M. CRUZ
96 Director of Purchasing ....Mrs. Gladys ARROYO
21 Associate Business Officer ....Mr. Serafin RIVERA
18 Chief Facilities/Physical Plant ....Eng. Jose A. FUENTES
15 Human Resources Director ....Mrs. Migdalia ORTIZ
46 Chief Research and Development ....Dr. Armando RODRIGUEZ
84 Director Enrollment Services ....Miss Ivette NIEVES
07 Director of Admissions ....Mr. Hector VARGAS
06 Registrar ....Mr. Eddie AYALA
13 Director Information Technology ....Mr. Edwin RIVERA
45 Planning Inst Research Officer ....Vacant
42 Director of Chaplaincy Office ....Rvda. Carmen I. PEREZ

*Inter American University of Puerto Rico Fajardo Campus (C)

Call Box 70003, Fajardo PR 00738-7003
County: Fajardo FICE Identification: 022828
Unit ID: 242680
Telephone: (787) 863-2390 Carnegie Class: Bac/Diverse
FAX Number: (787) 860-3470 Calendar System: Semester
URL: fajardo.inter.edu
Established: 1960 Annual Undergrad Tuition & Fees: $6,300
Enrollment: 2,211 Coed
Affiliation or Control: Independent Non-Profit IRS Status: 501(c)3
Highest Offering: Master's
Program: Liberal Arts And General; Fine Arts Emphasis
Accreditation: M, SW, TEAC

02 Chancellor ....Dr. Ismael SUAREZ-HERRERO
05 Dean Academic Affairs ....Dr. Paula SAGARDIA OLIVERAS
11 Dean Administrative Affairs ....Ms. Lydia E. SANTIAGO ROSADO
32 Dean for Student Affairs ....Prof. Javier MARTINEZ
06 Registrar ....Mrs. Arlene PARRILLA
07 Director of Admissions ....Mrs. Ada CARABALLO
37 Director Student Financial Aid ....Mrs. Marilyn MARTINEZ
08 Librarian ....Ms. Angie COLON
15 Director of Personnel Office ....Mrs. Maria A. RAMOS
09 Planning Director ....Ms. Hilda L. ORTIZ
41 Athletic Director ....Mr. Jose RUIZ
18 Physical Plant Supervisor ....Mrs. Milagros RONDÓN
42 Chaplain/Director Campus Ministry ....Rev. Rafael HIRALDO
50 Chairperson Business Department ....Prof. Wilfredo DEL VALLE
53 Chairperson Educ & Social Sci Dept ....Dr. Porfirio MONTES
79 Chairperson Humanities Dept ..Prof. Lourdes PEREZ DEL VALLE
81 Chairperson Math/Science Dept ....Prof. Irma MORALES
84 Director Enrollment Management ....Mrs. Glenda DIAZ

*Inter American University of Puerto Rico Guayama Campus (D)

Call Box 10004, Guayama PR 00785
County: Guayama FICE Identification: 022827
Unit ID: 242699
Telephone: (787) 864-2222 Carnegie Class: Bac/Diverse
FAX Number: (787) 866-5006 Calendar System: Semester
URL: www.guayama.inter.edu
Established: 1956 Annual Undergrad Tuition & Fees: $4,702
Enrollment: 2,249 Coed
Affiliation or Control: Independent Non-Profit IRS Status: 501(c)3
Highest Offering: Master's
Program: 2-Year Principally Bachelor's Creditable; Liberal Arts And General; Nursing Emphasis
Accreditation: M, TEAC

02 Chancellor ....Prof. Carlos E. COLON-RAMOS
06 Registrar ....Mr. Luis A. SOTO
08 Librarian ....Mrs. Edny SANTIAGO
10 Bursar ....Ms. Teresa MANAUTOU
05 Dean of Studies ....Dr. Angela DE JESUS
11 Dean of Administration ....Mr. Nestor A. LEBRON
32 Dean of Students ....Dr. Rosa J. MARTINEZ
07 Director Admissions ....Mrs. Laura FERRER
37 Director Financial Aid ....Mr. Jose A. VECHINI
29 Director Alumni Relations ....Dr. Rosa J. MARTINEZ
51 Director Continuing Education ....Mrs. Dianne RIVERA
15 Human Resources Officer ....Mrs. Maria MARES
18 Chief Facilities/Physical Plant ....Mr. Benjamin AYALA
45 Chief Plng Officer/Research & Devel ....Mrs. Nitza J. TORRES
30 Chief Devel/Dir Annual Plan Giv ....Vacant
42 Chaplain Director ....Rvdo. Arnaldo CINTRON
84 Director Enrollment Management ....Mrs. Eileen RIVERA
96 Director of Purchasing ....Mrs. Maria VAZQUEZ
31 Dir of Community & New Student Rels ....Mrs. Luz ORTIZ
23 Director Health Services ....Mrs. Arcilia RIVERA
66 Director Nursing Program ....Dr. Minerva MULERO
88 Dir Adult Higher Education Program ....Mrs. Carmen G. RIVERA
50 Dir Dept Business Admin/Econ Sci ....Dr. Rosalia MORALES
53 Dir Dept Education/Soc Sci/Hum Std ....Dr. Ray ROBLES
81 Dir Dept Natural & Applied Science ....Prof. Carmen TORRES

*Inter American University of Puerto Rico Metropolitan Campus (E)

PO Box 191293, San Juan PR 00919-1293
County: San Juan FICE Identification: 003940
Unit ID: 242653
Telephone: (787) 250-1912 Carnegie Class: DRU
FAX Number: (787) 250-0742 Calendar System: Trimester
URL: www.metro.inter.edu
Established: 1962 Annual Undergrad Tuition & Fees: $6,723
Enrollment: 10,703 Coed
Affiliation or Control: Independent Non-Profit IRS Status: 501(c)3
Highest Offering: Doctorate
Program: 2-Year Principally Bachelor's Creditable; Liberal Arts And General; Teacher Preparatory; Professional
Accreditation: M, ADNUR, MT, NUR, SW, TEAC

02 Chancellor ....Prof. Marilina L. WAYLAND
05 Dean of Studies ....Prof. Migdalia TEXIDOR
32 Dean of Students ....Dr. Carmen OQUENDO
10 Dean of Administration ....Mr. Jimmy CANCEL
11 Dean of Faculty Cs Economics & Adm ....Prof. Fredrick VEGA
53 Dean of Education & Behavioral Sci ....Dr. Carmen COLLAZO
83 Director School of Psychology ....Dr. Jaime SANTIAGO
79 Dean Faculty of Humanities ....Dr. Olga VILLAMIL
66 Director of Nursing ....Dr. Ivette CORA
72 Director of Medical Technology ....Dr. Ida A. MEJIAS
81 Dean Faculty of Science & Technolog ....Dr. Izander ROSADO
06 Registrar ....Ms. Lisette RIVERA
84 Enrollment Management ....Mr. Luis E. RUIZ
20 Associate Dean of Studies ....Ms. Blanca M. GONZALEZ
08 Actg Dir of Ctr for Access Infom ....Ms. Mirna ROSARIO
15 Human Resources Officer ....Mrs. Darlin TORRES
37 Director of Financial Aid ....Vacant
18 Dir Conservation & General Services ....Ing. Keyla O. MARRERO
38 Dir Student Placement/Guidanc/Couns ....Ms. Beatriz RIVERA
83 Director School of Social Work ....Dr. Elizabeth MIRANDA
58 Director School of Education ....Dr. Maria D. RUBERO
88 Director International Rel Office ....Prof. Ramon AYALA
73 Dir School of Theology ....Dr. Angel VELEZ
88 Dir School of Criminal Justice ....Prof. Luis ACEVEDO
26 Public Relations Officer ....Vacant
14 Director Informatic/Telecomm Center ....Mr. Eduardo ORTIZ
36 Director Student Placement ....Mrs. Adabel-Vanessa COLON
07 Director of Admissions ....Ms. Janies OLIVIERI
09 Dean Inst Research/External Rsrch ....Vacant
21 Associate Dean of Administration ....Vacant
30 Development & Fund Raising ....Mrs. Evelyn VEGA
96 Purchasing Officer ....Mrs. Patricia GONZALEZ
92 Coordinator of Honors Program ....Prof. Mariusz JACKO
88 Bursar ....Ms. Carmen RIVERA

*Inter American University of Puerto Rico Ponce Campus (F)

104 Turpo Industrial Park Road, #1,
Mercedita PR 00715-1602
County: Ponce FICE Identification: 005029
Unit ID: 242662
Telephone: (787) 284-1912 Carnegie Class: Bac/Diverse
FAX Number: (787) 841-0103 Calendar System: Semester
URL: ponce.inter.edu
Established: 1962 Annual Undergrad Tuition & Fees: $4,634
Enrollment: 5,983 Coed
Affiliation or Control: Independent Non-Profit IRS Status: 501(c)3
Highest Offering: Master's
Program: 2-Year Principally Bachelor's Creditable; Liberal Arts And General; Teacher Preparatory
Accreditation: M, OTA, @PTAA, RAD, TEAC

02 Chancellor ....Dr. Vilma E. COLON
05 Dean of Studies ....Dr. Jacqueline ALVAREZ
32 Dean of Students ....Mrs. Edda COSTAS
11 Dean of Administrative Affairs ....Eng. Victor A. FELIBERTY
08 Director Education Resource Center ....Mrs. Maria SILVESTRINI
35 Director Student Services ....Mrs. Miriam MARTINEZ
10 Bursar ....Mrs. Nilda RODRIGUEZ
06 Registrar ....Mrs. Maria del C PEREZ
84 Director Enrollment Management ....Mrs. Miriam MARTINEZ
30 Director of Development ....Mrs. Hilde V. STELLA
07 Director of Admissions ....Mr. Franco L. DIAZ
88 Ctr Academic Retention/Integration ....Vacant
15 Human Resource Officer ....Mrs. Ivonne COLLAZO
19 Supervisor of University Guard ....Mr. Reinaldo ROSADO
37 Director Student Financial Aid ....Mrs. Debra MARTINEZ
41 Athletic Director ....Mr. Raul HERNANDEZ
58 Director of Graduate Programs ....Dr. Lilliam LABOY
50 Director Business & Administration ....Vacant
51 Director Continuing Education ....Mrs. Maria MUNOZ
79 Act Dir Humanistics/Pedagogical Std ....Mrs. Santy CORREA
81 Director Mathematics/Sciences ....Prof. Lourdes DIAZ
83 Dir Social/Behavioral Science ....Vacant
76 Director Health Science ....Prof. Gerardo RIVERA
38 Dir Univ Integration Services Ofc ....Mr. Hector MARTINEZ
14 Director Computer Center ....Mr. Antonio RAMOS
26 Public Relations Officer ....Mr. Rolando J. MENDEZ

04 Chief Executive Assistant .... Mrs. Diana RIVERA
88 Dir Marketing & Student Promotion .... Mrs. Yinaira SANTIAGO
106 Director Distance Education Program ..... Dr. Omayra CARABALLO
88 Accreditation/Certification Officer .... Mrs. Evelyn CASTILLO
45 Director of Evaluation & Planning .... Mr. Anselmo ALVAREZ
18 Chief Facilities/Physical Plant .... Mr. Julio C. MUNOZ

*Inter American University of Puerto Rico San German Campus (A)

PO Box 5100, San German PR 00683-9801

County: San German FICE Identification: 003938
Unit ID: 242617
Telephone: (787) 264-1912 Carnegie Class: Master's M
FAX Number: (787) 892-6350 Calendar System: Semester
URL: www.sg.inter.edu
Established: 1912 Annual Undergrad Tuition & Fees: $5,680
Enrollment: 5,355 Coed
Affiliation or Control: Independent Non-Profit IRS Status: 501(c)3
Highest Offering: Doctorate
Program: Occupational; 2-Year Principally Bachelor's Creditable; Liberal Arts And General; Teacher Preparatory; Professional
Accreditation: M, MT, RAD, TEAC

02 Chancellor .... Prof. Agnes MOJICA
05 Dean of Studies .... Dr. Nyvia ALVARADO
11 Dean of Administration .... Mrs. Frances CARABALLO
32 Dean of Students .... Mr. Raúl MEDINA
20 Associate Dean of Studies .... Prof. Carmen TORRES
21 Auxiliary Dean of Administration .... Mrs. Marisol GONZALEZ
15 Director of Human Resources .... Mrs. Evelyn TORES
18 Chief Facilities/Physical Plant .... Mr. Jose A. RIVERA
37 Director Financial Aid .... Mrs. Maria Ines LUGO
06 Registrar .... Mrs. Arleen SANTANA
07 Director of Admissions .... Mrs. Mildred CAMACHO
08 Director of Library .... Mrs. Doris ASENCIO
38 Director Student Counseling .... Mrs. Daisy PEREZ
09 Dir Plng Evaluation/Inst Studies .... Miss Maria MORALES-MARTINEZ
19 Director of Security .... Mr. Victor BONILLA
14 Director of Computer Center .... Mr. Rogelio TORO-ZAPATA
41 Athletic Director .... Prof. Francisco ACEVEDO
39 Director of Men Student Housing .... Mrs. Erlinda VEGA
39 Director of Women Student Housing .... Mrs. Hilda CRUZ
40 Bookstore Manager .... Vacant
42 Dir Chaplaincy/Spiritual Well-being .... Rev. Pablo CARABALLO
04 Special Assistant of the Chancellor .... Mrs. Tary GARCIA
35 Manager of Student Services .... Mrs. Maria Gil MARTINEZ
51 Director of Continuing Education .... Vacant
58 Director Graduate Programs .... Dr. Elba T. IRIZARRY
88 Manager of Food Services .... Mr. Héctor CABASSA
17 Director of Medical Services .... Vacant
88 Auxiliary Dean of Students .... Mrs. Janet RIVERA
30 Chief Development Officer .... Miss Leticia MARTINEZ
96 Director of Purchasing .... Mr. Israel CRUZ
10 Director Bursar's Office .... Mr. Carlos SEGARRA
53 Director of Education .... Dr. Miriam PADILLA
83 Director of Social Scieces & Libera .... Dr. Maritza VÉLEZ
50 Director of Entreprenurial & Mgmt .... Dr. Milsa MORALES
88 Director of Biology & Environmental .... Dr. Angela GONZÁLEZ
72 Director of Technical Studies .... Prof. Mildred ORTIZ
57 Director of Fine Arts .... Prof. Samuel ROSADO
76 Director of Health Sciences .... Prof. Maritza ORTIZ
88 Director of Language & Literature .... Dr. Marta VIADA
81 Director of Math & Applied Sciences .... Dr. Pedro JAVIER
88 Director of TRIO Programs .... Mrs. Yolanda PÉREZ
92 Director of Honor Program .... Dr. Zulma QUIÑONES
26 Director of External Resources .... Prof. Mildred DE SANTIAGO

*Inter American University of Puerto Rico School of Law (B)

PO Box 70351, San Juan PR 00936-8351

County: San Juan Identification: 666813
Unit ID: 242723
Telephone: (787) 751-1912 Carnegie Class: Spec/Law
FAX Number: (787) 751-2975 Calendar System: Semester
URL: www.derecho.inter.edu
Established: 1961 Annual Graduate Tuition & Fees: $15,303
Enrollment: 797 Coed
Affiliation or Control: Independent Non-Profit IRS Status: 501(c)3
Highest Offering: First Professional Degree; No Undergraduates
Program: Professional
Accreditation: M, LAW

02 Dean .... Dr. Julio E. FONTANET-MALDONADO
05 Dean of Studies .... Dr. Yanira REYES-GIL
32 Dean of Students .... Dr. Iris M. CAMACHO-MELÉNDEZ
11 Dean of Administration .... Mr. Heriberto SOTO-LÓPEZ
06 Registrar .... Mrs. Maria de Lourdes RIVERA
08 Head Librarian .... Mr. Hector Ruben SANCHEZ
61 Director of Legal Aid Clinic .. Mr. Rafael E. RODRÍGUEZ-RIVERA
37 Director of Financial Aid .... Mr. Ricardo CRESPO
07 Director of Admissions .... Mrs. Angela TORRES
18 Chief Facilities/Physical Plant .... Mr. Jose A. RIVERA
96 Director of Purchasing .... Mrs. Yajahira VIDAL
88 Director of Bursar Office .... Mr. Samuel SANCHEZ

*Inter American University of Puerto Rico School of Optometry (C)

500 John Will Harris Road, Bayamon PR 00957-6257

County: San Juan Identification: 666601
Unit ID: 404222
Telephone: (787) 765-1915 Carnegie Class: Spec/Health
FAX Number: (787) 767-3920 Calendar System: Semester
URL: www.optonet.inter.edu
Established: 1981 Annual Graduate Tuition & Fees: $26,000
Enrollment: 224 Coed
Affiliation or Control: Independent Non-Profit IRS Status: 501(c)3
Highest Offering: First Professional Degree; No Undergraduates
Program: Professional
Accreditation: M, OPT

02 Dean .... Dr. Andres PAGAN
05 Dean for Academic Affairs .... Dr. Angel ROMERO
11 Dean of Administration .... Mr. Francisco RIVERA
32 Dean of Student Affair .... Dra. Iris CABELLO
42 Director Religious Life .... Dra. Ileana VARGAS
07 Director Admissions .... Vacant
30 Director Development .... Mrs. Maria J. AULET
88 Director Basic Sciences .... Dr. John MORDI
20 Director Academic Affairs .... Dr. José M. DE JESÚS
88 Dean of Clinical Affairs .... Dra. Damaris PAGAN
08 Library Director .... Mrs. Wilma MARRERO
90 Director of Computing .... Mr. Elias SANTIAGO
21 Bursar's Officer .... Mr. Eduardo SALICHS
15 Director Human Resources .... Ms. Milagros RODRIGUEZ
37 Financial Aid Officer .... Mrs. Lourdes M. NIEVES
04 Executive Assistant of the Dean .... Mrs. Arleen E. CORREA

John Dewey College (D)

PO Box 19538, San Juan PR 00910-1538

County: San Juan FICE Identification: 031121
Unit ID: 431309
Telephone: (787) 753-0039 Carnegie Class: Assoc/PrivNFP
FAX Number: (787) 764-6303 Calendar System: Other
URL: www.jdc.edu
Established: Annual Undergrad Tuition & Fees: $8,553
Enrollment: 332 Coed
Affiliation or Control: Independent Non-Profit IRS Status: 501(c)3
Highest Offering: Baccalaureate
Program: Occupational
Accreditation: ACICS

01 President/CEO .... Mr. Carlos A. QUINONES
10 Director of Finance .... Ms. Mirna BAEZ

John Dewey College-Bayamon (E)

Road 2 Corujo Industrial Park, Bayamon PR 00959
Telephone: (787) 778-1200 Identification: 770777
Accreditation: ACICS

† Main campus is John Dewey College in San Juan, PR.

John Dewey College-Carolina (F)

Road 3 Compound 11, Lot 7, Carolina PR 00986
Telephone: (787) 769-1515 Identification: 770776
Accreditation: ACICS

† Main campus is John Dewey College in San Juan, PR.

John Dewey College-Fajardo (G)

267 General Valero Street, Fajardo PR 00738
Telephone: (787) 860-1212 Identification: 770775
Accreditation: ACICS

† Main campus is John Dewey College in San Juan, PR.

John Dewey College-Juana Diaz (H)

Rd 149, KM 55.9 Lomas Industrial PK, Juana Diaz PR 00795
Telephone: (787) 260-1023 Identification: 770774
Accreditation: ACICS

† Main campus is John Dewey College in San Juan, PR.

John Dewey College-Manati (I)

Rd 604,KM 49.1,Tierra Nueva Salient, Manati PR 00674
Telephone: (789) 854-3800 Identification: 770807
Accreditation: ACICS

† Main campus is John Dewey College in San Juan, PR.

Mech-Tech College (J)

PO Box 6118, Caguas PR 00726

County: Caguas FICE Identification: 030255
Unit ID: 414461
Telephone: (787) 744-1060 Carnegie Class: Assoc/PrivFP
FAX Number: (787) 744-1035 Calendar System: Quarter
URL: www.mechtech.edu
Established: 1984 Annual Undergrad Tuition & Fees: $8,754
Enrollment: 4,014 Coed
Affiliation or Control: Proprietary IRS Status: Proprietary
Highest Offering: Associate Degree
Program: Occupational; 2-Year Principally Bachelor's Creditable; Technical Emphasis
Accreditation: CNCE

01 President .... Mr. Edwin J. COLON COSME
03 Chief Operating Officer .... Miss Yadexy SIERRA CONCEPCION
32 Vice President of Student Affairs .... Mrs. Lydia ROJAS
88 Lead Coordinator .... Mr. Carlos CRUZ GORRITZ
88 Occupational Comptroller .... Mr. Isaias ROJAS
05 Vice President for Academic Affairs .... Mr. Armando DEL VALLE
12 Academic Director .... Dr. César TORO
45 Vice President Planning & Develop .... Mr. Jose ALGORRI NAVARRO
11 Vice President for Administration .... Mrs. Aguilda GOMEZ
13 Vice President Information Tech .... Mr. Victor FIGUEROA
10 Comptroller .... Mr. Edwin RODRIGUEZ
88 Vice President for Compliance .... Mrs. Belen GONZALEZ
06 Registrar .... Mrs. Blanca RIVERA SANTIAGO
37 Financial Aid Director .... Mrs. Jessica CRUZ BONILLA
07 Admissions Director .... Miss Rocio ROSARIO
36 Placement Director .... Mrs. Maria RAMON
20 Dean of Academic Affairs .... Mrs. Carla FONTÁN
35 Dean of Student Affairs .... Mrs. Aurea ROQUE
08 Library Director .... Mrs. Carmen AVILES
12 Bayamon Branch Campus Coordinator ... Mr. Julio MONSERRATE
12 Ponce Branch Campus Coordinator .... Mr. Luis MORALES
12 Vega Baja Branch Campus Coordinator .... Mrs. Carla FONTAN
12 Mayaguez Branch Campus Coordinator .... Mr. Hector LEBRON
12 Orlando Branch Campus Director .... Mrs. Maribel RAMOS

National University College (K)

MSC 452, PO Box 144035, Arecibo PR 00614
Telephone: (787) 879-5044 Identification: 666489
Accreditation: ACICS

† Main campus is National University College in Bayamon, PR.

National University College (L)

State Road#2 Km.11.2 #1660, Bayamon PR 00960-2036

County: Bayamon FICE Identification: 022606
Unit ID: 242972
Telephone: (787) 780-5134 Carnegie Class: Bac/Assoc
FAX Number: (787) 779-4906 Calendar System: Trimester
URL: www.nuc.edu
Established: 1982 Annual Undergrad Tuition & Fees: $7,030
Enrollment: 2,400 Coed
Affiliation or Control: Proprietary IRS Status: Proprietary
Highest Offering: Master's
Program: 2-Year Principally Bachelor's Creditable; Nursing Emphasis
Accreditation: M, ACICS, @TEAC

01 President .... Dr. Gloria E. BAQUERO
88 VP of Compliance .... Mr. Desi LOPEZ
05 VP Academic Affairs .... Dr. Maria ESTRADA
32 VP of Student Affairs .... Ms. Ana M. LUCUMI
00 Chancellor .... Ms. Daliana RIVERA
46 Director Research & Development .... Mr. Angel AVILES
37 Institutional Dir Financial Aid .... Ms. Elizabeth CRUZ
07 Enrollment & Admissions Coord .... Ms. Blanca GONZALEZ
06 Registrar .... Ms. Glorimar RODRIGUEZ

National University College Ponce Campus (M)

Carretera PR 506, KM 1.0, Coto Laurel PR 00780
Telephone: (787) 840-4474 Identification: 770169
Accreditation: ACICS

† Main campus is National University College in Bayamon, PR.

National University College Rio Grande Campus (N)

Carr.#3 Km 22.01, Bo. Cienaga Baja, Rio Grande PR 00745
Telephone: (787) 809-5100 Identification: 770170
Accreditation: ACICS

† Main campus is National University College in Bayamon, PR.

Ponce Paramedical College (O)

1213 Acacia Street Villa Flores Urb, Ponce PR 00716-2901

County: Ponce FICE Identification: 025349
Unit ID: 243072
Telephone: (787) 848-1589 Carnegie Class: Assoc/PrivFP
FAX Number: (787) 259-0169 Calendar System: Other
URL: www.popac.edu
Established: 1983 Annual Undergrad Tuition & Fees: $13,985
Enrollment: 4,546 Coed
Affiliation or Control: Proprietary IRS Status: Proprietary
Highest Offering: Associate Degree
Program: Occupational; 2-Year Principally Bachelor's Creditable
Accreditation: ACCSC

01 President .... Mrs. Maria PAGAN
04 Executive Assistant .... Vacant
05 Academic Dean .... Mrs. Rosa E. CRUZ
06 Registrar .... Mrs. Ivette OLIVERAS
37 Director Student Financial Aid .... Mrs. Amarilis ROCHE

Ponce School of Medicine & Health Sciences (A)

PO Box 7004, Ponce PR 00732-7004
County: Ponce FICE Identification: 024824
Unit ID: 243081
Telephone: (787) 840-2575 Carnegie Class: Assoc/PrivNFP4
FAX Number: (787) 840-9756 Calendar System: Semester
URL: www.psm.edu
Established: 1977 Annual Graduate Tuition & Fees: $24,359
Enrollment: 664 Coed
Affiliation or Control: Independent Non-Profit IRS Status: 501(c)3
Highest Offering: Doctorate; No Undergraduates
Program: Professional; Business Emphasis
Accreditation: M, CLPSY, MED, PH

01 Interim President/Dean .... Dr. Olga RODRIGUEZ DE ARZOLA
05 Assoc Dean Faculty/Clinical Affairs .... Dr. Raul ARMSTRONG
58 Int Director of Graduate Studies .... Dra. Kenira THOMPSON
11 Asst Dean Administration & Finance ... Ms. Bethzaida CRUZ SOTO

The Pontifical Catholic University of Puerto Rico (B)

2250 Las Americas Avenue, Suite 564,
Ponce PR 00717-9997
County: Ponce FICE Identification: 003936
Unit ID: 241410
Telephone: (787) 841-2000 Carnegie Class: DRU
FAX Number: (787) 651-2034 Calendar System: Semester
URL: www.pucpr.edu
Established: 1948 Annual Undergrad Tuition & Fees: $5,560
Enrollment: 11,015 Coed
Affiliation or Control: Roman Catholic IRS Status: 501(c)3
Highest Offering: Doctorate
Program: Liberal Arts And General; Teacher Preparatory; Professional
Accreditation: M, CORE, LAW, MT, NUR, SW, @TEAC

00 Chancellor .... M.Rev. Felix LAZARO
01 President .... Dr. Jorge I. VELEZ AROCHO
04 Executive Assistant to President .... Lic. Liza RIESTRA
05 Vice President Academic Affairs .... Dr. Leandro COLON
10 Vice President of Finance .... Prof. Irma I. RODRIGUEZ
32 Vice President for Student Affairs .... Prof. Freddie MARTINEZ
20 Assoc Vice Pres Academic Affairs .... Dr. Herminio IRIZARY
35 Asst to Vice Pres Student Affairs .... Prof. Myriam D. LOPEZ
09 Vice President Inst Rsrch/Dev Plng .... Dr. Felix CORTES
12 Rector Arecibo Branch .... Dr. Edwin HERNANDEZ
12 Rector Mayaguez Branch .... Dr. Olga HERNÁNDEZ
06 Registrar .... Prof. Ivan E. DAVILA
07 Director of Admissions .... Dr. Ana O. BONILLA
08 Director of the Library .... Prof. Magda VARGAS
37 Director of Student Aid .... Mrs. Rosalia MARTINEZ
36 Director of Placement Services .... Mr. Enrique ARROYO
14 Director Computer Center .... Mr. Moises CABRERA
55 Director of Evening Studies .... Dra. Adalecia HASSELL
24 Director Educational Technology .... Dr. Edgar RODRIGUEZ
79 Dean of Arts & Humanities .... Prof. Alfonso SANTIAGO
81 Dean of Sciences .... Dra. Alma L. SANTIAGO
61 Dean of the School of Law .... Lic. Jose A. FRONTERA
50 Dean Business Administration .... Dr. Jaime L. SANTIAGO-CANET
53 Dean of Education .... Dr. Myriam ZAYAS
58 Dean Institute of Graduate Studies .... Dr. Hernan VERA
48 Organizing Dean School of Arquit .... Mr. Javier DEJESUS
51 Coord Continuing Education Inst .... Mrs. Karen G. MORALES
27 Communications .... Mrs. Jalibeth RODRIGUEZ
29 Alumni Relations Officer .... Mrs. Maria S. MASCARO
15 Director Human Resources .... Mr. Wilfredo CORNIER
40 Director Bookstore .... Mrs. Ashley VELEZ
41 Athletic Director .... Prof. Louis ARCHEVAL
42 Chaplain .... Rev. Juan C. RIVERA
31 Director Auxiliary Enterprises .... Mr. Julio FELIU
26 Director Public Relations .... Mrs. Irem POVENTUD
38 Director Student Counseling .... Prof. Carmen GONZALEZ
18 Physical Plant/Safety & Security .... Mr. Julio PALMER
21 Treasurer Bursar's Office .... Mr. Juan E. ROMAN
28 Director of Diversity .... Vacant
96 Director of Purchasing .... Mrs. Zoraida VELAZQUEZ
88 Exec Dir International Relations .... Dra. Enid MIRANDA
88 Director of Biotechnology .... Dra. Cariluz SANTIAGO
88 Acreditation Liaison Officer .... Dr. Carmen J. ACOSTA-FUMERO
30 Infrastructure Director .... Ing. Armando RODRIGUEZ
84 Coord Institutional Recruitment .... Mrs. Linnette MILETTI
108 Coordinator of Outcomes Assessment .... Prof. Maria MUÑIZ
89 Director of Freshmen .... Prof. Carmen Z. TORRES

Pontifical Catholic University of Puerto Rico-Arecibo Campus (C)

Box 144045, Arecibo PR 00614-4045
Telephone: (787) 881-1212 Identification: 666603
Accreditation: &M, @TEAC

† Main campus is The Pontifical Catholic University of Puerto Rico in Ponce, PR.

Pontifical Catholic University of Puerto Rico-Mayaguez Campus (D)

Box 1326, Mayaguez PR 00681-1326
Telephone: (787) 834-5151 Identification: 666605
Accreditation: &M, @TEAC

† Main campus is The Pontifical Catholic University of Puerto Rico in Ponce, PR.

San Juan Bautista School of Medicine (E)

PO Box 4968, Carretera 172, Caguas PR 00726-4968
County: San Juan FICE Identification: 031773
Unit ID: 430670
Telephone: (787) 743-3038 Carnegie Class: Spec/Med
FAX Number: (787) 743-3042 Calendar System: Semester
URL: www.sanjuanbautista.edu
Established: 1978 Annual Graduate Tuition & Fees: $23,500
Enrollment: 246 Coed
Affiliation or Control: Proprietary IRS Status: Proprietary
Highest Offering: First Professional Degree; No Undergraduates
Program: Professional
Accreditation: M, #MED

01 President/Dean .... Dr. Yocasta BRUGAL-MENA
11 Dean of Administration .... Mr. Carlos F. ABREU

Seminario Teologico de Puerto Rico (F)

Urb. Roosevelt, Calle Jose Canals, Hato Rey PR 00918
Telephone: (787) 274-1142 Identification: 770142
Accreditation: &M

† Main campus is Nyack College in Nyack, NY.

*Sistema Universitario Ana G. Mendez (G)

Apartado 21345, Rio Piedras PR 00928-1341
County: San Juan FICE Identification: 029078
Unit ID: 242060
Telephone: (787) 751-0178 Carnegie Class: N/A
FAX Number: (787) 766-1706
URL: www.suagm.edu

01 President .... Mr. Jose F. MENDEZ
03 Executive Vice President .... Mr. Jose F. MENDEZ, JR.
05 Vice President for Academic Affairs .... Mr. Jorge L. CRESPO
10 Vice Pres Financial Affairs .... Mr. Alfonso L. DAVILA
32 Int VP Student/Marketing Affairs .... Ms. Mayra CRUZ
45 Vice President Planning & Research .... Mr. Jorge CRESPO
11 Vice Pres Administrative Affairs .... Mr. Jesus A. DIAZ
15 Vice President Human Resources .... Dr. Victoria DE JESUS
13 Chief Information Officer .... Sr. Kenneth MALDONADO
26 Director Public Relations .... Ms. Maria MARTINEZ
04 Exec Assistant to President .... Ms. Lydia I. MASSARI

*Universidad del Este (H)

PO Box 2010, Carolina PR 00984-2010
County: San Juan FICE Identification: 003941
Unit ID: 243346
Telephone: (787) 257-7373 Carnegie Class: Master's L
FAX Number: (787) 776-1220 Calendar System: Semester
URL: www.suagm.edu/une
Established: 1949 Annual Undergrad Tuition & Fees: $5,216
Enrollment: 13,630 Coed
Affiliation or Control: Independent Non-Profit IRS Status: 501(c)3
Highest Offering: Master's
Program: Occupational; 2-Year Principally Bachelor's Creditable; Liberal Arts And General; Teacher Preparatory
Accreditation: M, ACBSP, ACFEI, @SW, @TEAC

02 Chancellor .... Mr. Alberto MALDONADO-RUIZ
05 Vice Chancellor Academic Affairs .... Dr. Mildred HUERTAS
11 Vice Chanc Admin Affs/Ofce of Chanc .... Mrs. Maria S. DIAZ
32 Vice Chancellor Student Affairs .... Dr. Nahomy CURET
24 Vice Chanc Information Resources .... Mrs. Carmen ORTEGA
46 Vice Chanc External Resources .... Mrs. Mayra M. FERRAN
20 Assoc VC Licensing/Accreditation .... Mrs. Nilda I. ROSADO
88 Assoc Vice Chanc Admin Affairs .... Mrs. Magalie ALVARADO
35 Assoc Vice Chanc Student Affairs .... Mrs. Karen RIVERA
84 Assoc VC Enrollment Management .... Mrs. Magda E. OSTOLAZA
38 Assoc VC for Multidisciplinary Svcs .... Vacant
23 AVC Stdnt Quality of Life/Wellness . Mrs. Carmen G. VELAZQUEZ
07 Asst Vice Chan Admiss/Financial Aid .... Mr. Ramon FUENTES
09 Asst Vice Chanc Academic Effective .... Dr. Claribette RODRIGUEZ
36 Exec Director Employment Placement .... Mrs. Diana M. COLON
30 Asst VC for University Advancement ... Mrs. Maria I. DE GUZMAN
15 Asst Vice Pres Human Resources .... Mr. Jorge RODRIGUEZ
10 Assistant Vice President of Budget .... Mr. Jorge A. TORRES
88 Dean Intl Sch Hosp/Culinary Arts .... Mr. Ivan O. PUIG
107 Assoc Dean Professional Studies .... Mrs. Johanna VIVONI
18 Physical Plant/Operations Manager .... Mr. Edgar D. RODRIGUEZ
06 Registrar .... Mrs. Elisa QUILES
37 Director of Financial Aid .... Mr. Norberto PAGAN
08 Director of Library .... Mrs. Elsa MARIANI
26 Director Public Relations .... Mrs. Ivonne D. ARROYO
29 Director Alumni & Fund Raising .... Ms. Gisela NEGRON
13 Information/Telecommunications Dir .... Mr. Nestor MAS
41 Athletic Director .... Mr. Julio FIGUEROA
19 Safety & Security Director .... Mr. Carlos E. BERROA

*Universidad Del Turabo (I)

Estacion Universidad, Box 3030, Gurabo PR 00778-3030
County: Gurabo FICE Identification: 011719
Unit ID: 243601
Telephone: (787) 743-7979 Carnegie Class: DRU
FAX Number: (787) 744-5394 Calendar System: Semester
URL: www.suagm.edu
Established: 1972 Annual Undergrad Tuition & Fees: $5,216
Enrollment: 17,040 Coed
Affiliation or Control: Independent Non-Profit IRS Status: 501(c)3
Highest Offering: Doctorate
Program: Liberal Arts And General; Teacher Preparatory; Professional
Accreditation: M, BUS, DIETC, ENG, NURSE, SP, @SW, TEAC

02 Chancellor .... Dr. Dennis ALICEA
11 Vice Chancellor of Admin Affairs .... Dr. Gladys BETANCOURT
05 Vice Chancellor Academic Affairs .... Dr. Roberto LORAN
32 Vice Chancellor of Student Affairs .... Dra. Brunilda APONTE
08 Vice Chancellor Information Res .... Dr. Sarai LASTRA
92 Vice Chancellor Honors Program .... Ms. Maricarmen SANTOS
88 Asst Vice Chanc Eval & Development .. Dra. Maria del C. SANTOS
21 Asst Vice Chanc Admin Affairs .... Mrs. Edna ORTA
53 Dean Education .... Mr. Israel RODRÍGUEZ
50 Dean Business Administration .... Dr. Marcelino RIVERA
54 Dean Engineering .... Dr. Jack T. ALLISON
72 Dean Science & Technology .... Dr. Teresa LIPSETT
83 Dean Social Sciences & Humanities .... Vacant
58 Dean of Graduate Studies .... Dr. Sharon CANTRELL
06 Registrar .... Mrs. Zoraida ORTIZ
27 Director of Marketing .... Ms. Melba G. SÁNCHEZ
37 Director Office of Financial Aid .... Mrs. Carmen J. RIVERA
26 Director Public Relations .... Ms. Iris SERRANO
18 Chief Facilities/Physical Plant .... Eng. Mayra RODRIGUEZ
29 Coordinator Alumni Relations .... Ms. René S. RONDA
30 Chief Development Officer .... Ms. Alba RIVERA
96 Director of Purchasing .... Mr. Jose BERRIOS
07 Director of Admissions .... Mrs. Virginia GONZALEZ
09 Director of Institutional Research .... Ms. Mari G. GONZALEZ
15 Director Personnel Services .... Mrs. Iris BERRIOS
36 Assoc Vice Chanc Student Placement .... Ms. Carmen PULLIZA
84 Director Enrollment Management .... Ms. Maria V. FIGUEROA
10 Chief Business Officer .... Ms. Jessica M. PERRY
38 Assoc Vice Chanc Student Counseling .... Ms. Samaris COLLAZO

*Universidad Metropolitana (J)

PO Box 21150, Rio Piedras PR 00928-1150
County: San Juan FICE Identification: 025875
Unit ID: 241739
Telephone: (787) 766-1717 Carnegie Class: Master's L
FAX Number: (787) 759-7663 Calendar System: Quarter
URL: www.suagm.edu/umet
Established: 1980 Annual Undergrad Tuition & Fees: $5,184
Enrollment: 13,616 Coed
Affiliation or Control: Independent Non-Profit IRS Status: 501(c)3
Highest Offering: Doctorate
Program: Liberal Arts And General; Teacher Preparatory; Professional; Business Emphasis
Accreditation: M, ADNUR, NUR, @TEAC

02 SUAGM President .... Dr. José F. MENDEZ
00 Chancellor .... Dr. Carlos M. PADIN
05 Vice Chancellor Academic Affairs .... Dra. Zaida VEGA
108 Int Vice Chanc Inst Assessment .... Dr. Carmen LUNA
29 Vice Chanc Alumni Relations .... Ms. Belissa AQUINO
32 Vice Chanc for Student Affairs .... Mrs. Carmen ROSADO
102 Vice Chanc of International Affairs .... Dr. Zaida VEGA
88 Vice Chanc External Resources .... Mrs. Gladys CORA
11 Assoc Vice Chanc Admin Affairs .... Mrs. Maria del Pilar CHARNECO
08 Head Librarian .... Mrs. Maria de los A. LUGO
88 Asst Vice Chanc for Eval/Devel .... Prof. Adanid PRIETO
11 Asst Vice Chanc for Admin Affairs .... Dr. Mildred ARBONA
15 Asst Vice Pres for Human Resources .... Mrs. Marisol MUNOZ
18 Int Chief Facilities/Physical Plant .... Mr. Egenero FRANCISCO-CABALLO
13 Vice Pres Information Resources .... Mr. Carlos M. DELGADO
20 Assoc Vice Chanc Eval and Develop .... Mr. Eric BARRIOS
32 Assoc Vice Chanc Dev/Retention .... Mrs. Awilda PEREZ
10 Asst Vice Pres Analysis & Budget .... Mrs. Aixa ALDARONDO
45 Asst Vice President of Planning .... Mrs. Mariela COLLAZO
49 Dean of Liberal Arts/Human & Commun .... Dr. Eloisa GORDON
50 Dean of Business Administration .... Dr. Juan OTERO
53 Dean of Education .... Dr. Judith GONZALEZ
76 Dean of Health Science .... Dr. Lourdes MALDONADO
81 Dean of Science & Technology .... Dr. Karen GONZALEZ
32 Asst Vice Chanc Retention/Develop .... Mr. Ariel MENDEZ
65 Dean of Environmental Affairs .... Dr. Carlos PADIN
83 Assoc Dean of Social Sciences .... Dr. Mariveliz CABAN
107 Assoc Dean of Professional Studies .... Ms. Melissa GUILLIANI
60 Assoc Dean of Communications .... Mr. Alfredo NIEVES
79 Assoc Dean of Humanities .... Dr. Martin CRUZ
75 Assoc Dean of Technical Studies .... Prof. Felipe ROSA
51 Assoc Dean of Continuing Education .... Ms. Lorna MARTINEZ
53 Assoc Dean of Education .... Dr. Daisy RODRIGUEZ
53 Assoc Dean of Education .... Dr. Angel CANALES
72 Director Educational Production .... Mr. Luis MARTINEZ
76 Director of Respiratory Therapy .... Mrs. Yolanda TORRES
66 Director of Nursing .... Mrs. Yolanda TORRES
26 Director Public Relations Officer .... Ms. Yvonne GUADALUPE
06 Registrar .... Mrs. Beatriz NIEVES
12 Additional Location Dir Bayamón .... Mrs. Ibis RODRÍGUEZ
12 Addtional Location Dir Aguadilla .... Mr. Luis A. RUIZ
12 Additional Location Dir Jayuya .... Mrs. Irma del Pilar CRUZ
12 Additional Location Dir Comerío .... Mr. José I. CARMONA
07 Director of Admissions .... Mr. Julio RODRIGUEZ
41 Athletic Director .... Mr. Ariel ORTIZ

Universal Technology College of Puerto Rico (A)

111 Comercio Street, Aguadilla PR 00603

County: Aguadilla FICE Identification: 030297
Unit ID: 376385
Telephone: (787) 882-2065 Carnegie Class: Assoc/PrivNFP
FAX Number: (787) 891-2370 Calendar System: Semester
URL: www.unitecpr.edu
Established: 1987 Annual Undergrad Tuition & Fees: $10,920
Enrollment: 1,217 Coed
Affiliation or Control: Independent Non-Profit IRS Status: 501(c)3
Highest Offering: Baccalaureate
Program: Occupational; 2-Year Principally Bachelor's Creditable; Technical Emphasis
Accreditation: ACCSC

01 Chief Executive Officer ....Mrs. Keila LOPEZ
11 Administrative Manager ....Mr. Ivan F. ROMAN
04 Executive Secretary ....Mrs. Marilyn GONZALEZ
05 Chief Academic Officer ....Vacant
06 Registrar ....Ms. Maria ALVAREZ
08 Director of Library ....Ms. Airlyn VAZQUEZ
10 Controller ....Mr. Alexis ROSADO
12 Director of Branch Campus ....Ms. Nelida CARDONA
14 Director Computer Center ....Mr. Zain CORDERO
15 Director Human Resources ....Ms. Jemilis GONZALEZ
18 Chief Facilities/Physical Plant ....Mr. Danily NIEVES
32 Director Student Affairs ....Vacant
36 Director Student Placement ....Mrs. Ada MORALES
45 Director Planning & Development ....Mrs. Evelyn TORRES
37 Director Student Financial Aid ....Mr. Samuel HERNANDEZ
38 Director Student Counsel ....Mrs. Dalia SANTIAGO
96 Purchasing Officer ....Mrs. Dolores MITJANS
23 Healthcare Services ....Mr. Silverio JIMENEZ
07 Coordinator of Admissions ....Mrs. Teresita RIVERA
50 Director of Business Administration ....Mrs. Sandra GONZALEZ
72 Director of Industrial Technology ....Mr. Eduardo FIGUEROA

Universidad Adventista de las Antillas (B)

Box 118, Mayaguez PR 00681-0118

County: Mayaguez FICE Identification: 005019
Unit ID: 241191
Telephone: (787) 834-9595 Carnegie Class: Bac/Diverse
FAX Number: (787) 834-9597 Calendar System: Semester
URL: www.uaa.edu
Established: 1961 Annual Undergrad Tuition & Fees: $11,320
Enrollment: 1,312 Coed
Affiliation or Control: Seventh-day Adventist IRS Status: 501(c)3
Highest Offering: Master's
Program: 2-Year Principally Bachelor's Creditable; Liberal Arts And General; Teacher Preparatory; Professional
Accreditation: M, NUR, @TEAC

01 President ....Dr. Obed JIMENEZ
05 Vice President for Academic Affairs ....Dr. Myrna COLÓN
10 Vice President Financial Affairs ....Mr. Misael JIMENEZ
32 Vice President for Students Affairs ....Dr. Javier DIAZ
30 VP Planning and Development ....Dr. José D. GÓMEZ
42 Religious Affairs Director ....Mr. Abiezer RODRIGUEZ
20 Associate for VP Academic Affairs ....Mrs. Yolanda PEREZ
21 Associate Financial Vice President ....Mrs. Madeline CRUZ
66 Dean of the School of Nursing ....Mrs. Alicia FRANCO
53 Dean of the School of Education ....Mrs. Maritza LAMBOY
50 Director of Business Administration ....Mr. Julio DE LA CRUZ
81 Director Mathematics/Sciences/Comp ....Mrs. Alicia MORADILLOS
73 Director Theology Department ....Dr. Efren PAGAN
06 Registrar ....Mrs. Ana D. TORRES
07 Director of Admissions ....Mrs. Yolanda FERRER
37 Director of Student Financial Aid ....Mrs. Awilda MATOS
26 Dir Public Relations & Promotion ....Miss Lorell VARELA
108 Director of Institutional Effectiv ....Mrs. Milca MADURO
13 Director Computing and Information ....Mr. Heber VAZQUEZ
08 Librarian ....Mrs. Aixa VEGA
38 Counselor ....Mrs. Ivelisse PEREZ
96 Director of Purchasing ....Mr. Obed RODRIGUEZ
18 Chief Facilities/Physical Plant ....Mr. Abel RODRIGUEZ
34 Dean of Women ....Mrs. Felicita CRUZ
33 Dean of Men ....Mr. Angel RODRIGUEZ
09 Institutional Research Officer ....Mrs. Esther N. LABOY

Universidad Central Del Caribe (C)

PO Box 60-327, Bayamon PR 00960-6032

County: Bayamon FICE Identification: 021633
Unit ID: 243568
Telephone: (787) 798-3001 Carnegie Class: Spec/Med
FAX Number: (787) 798-6836 Calendar System: Semester
URL: www.uccaribe.edu
Established: 1976 Annual Undergrad Tuition & Fees: $8,045
Enrollment: 498 Coed
Affiliation or Control: Independent Non-Profit IRS Status: 501(c)3
Highest Offering: Doctorate
Program: 2-Year Principally Bachelor's Creditable; Professional
Accreditation: M, MED, RAD

01 President ....Dr. Jose Ginel RODRIGUEZ
05 Dean for Academic Affairs ....Dr. Nereida DIAZ-RODRIGUEZ
11 Dean Administrative Affairs ....Ms. Emilia SOTO
32 Dean Student Affairs ....Dr. Omar PEREZ
17 Dean of Medicine ....Dr. Jose Ginel RODRIGUEZ
63 Associate Dean of Medicine ....Mrs. Zilka RIOS
53 Asst Dean Professional Services ....Ms. Emilia SOTO
06 Registrar ....Ms. Nilda MONTANEZ-LOPEZ
07 Director of Admissions ....Ms. Irma L. CORDERO
37 Director Student Financial Aid ....Ms. Lisandra VIERA
10 Director of Finances ....Mrs. Iris J. FONT
08 Librarian ....Ms. Mildred RIVERA
51 Director of Continuing Education ....Dr. Frances GARCIA
38 Counselor ....Ms. Yari M. MARRERO
46 Dean of Research and Graduate Pgms ....Dr. Luis A. CUBANO
20 Dean for Clinical & Faculty Affairs ....Dr. Harry MERCADO

Universidad Pentecostal Mizpa (D)

PO Box 20966, San Juan PR 00928-0966

County: San Juan FICE Identification: 031983
Unit ID: 441690
Telephone: (787) 720-4476 Carnegie Class: Spec/Faith
FAX Number: (787) 720-2012 Calendar System: Semester
URL: www.mizpa.edu
Established: 1937 Annual Undergrad Tuition & Fees: $3,640
Enrollment: 1,274 Coed
Affiliation or Control: Pentecostal Church of God IRS Status: 501(c)3
Highest Offering: Master's
Program: Religious Emphasis
Accreditation: BI

01 President ....Mr. Angel A. RIVERA
05 Dean of Academic Affairs ....Mr. Leonardo MELENDEZ
11 Dean Administration/Finance ....Mr. Elisamuel RODRIGUEZ
32 Dean of Student Affairs ....Mr. Jorge BURGOS
42 Director Christian Service ....Vacant
18 Director of Physical & Facilities ....Vacant
06 Registrar ....Ms. Sara MARTINEZ
08 Librarian ....Mr. Julio RAMOS
37 Student Financial Aid Officer ....Mrs. Myriam JUARBE
26 Chief Public Relations Officer ....Mr. Rafael LABOY

Universidad Politecnica De Puerto Rico (E)

Ponce de Leon 377, Box 192017, San Juan PR 00919

County: San Juan FICE Identification: 021000
Unit ID: 243577
Telephone: (787) 622-8000 Carnegie Class: Spec/Engg
FAX Number: (787) 754-8268 Calendar System: Trimester
URL: www.pupr.edu
Established: 1966 Annual Undergrad Tuition & Fees: $7,548
Enrollment: 4,743 Coed
Affiliation or Control: Independent Non-Profit IRS Status: 501(c)3
Highest Offering: Master's
Program: Liberal Arts And General
Accreditation: M, ENG, ENGR, IACBE, LSAR

01 President ....Prof. Ernesto VAZQUEZ-BARQUET
84 Vice Pres Enrollment Management ....Mr. Carlos PEREZ
05 Chief Academic Officer ....Dr. Miguel A. RIESTRA
06 Registrar ....Mrs. Mayra I. LOPEZ
07 Director Admissions ....Mrs. Teresa CARDONA
08 Head Librarian ....Mrs. Mirta COLON
37 Director Financial Aid ....Mr. Sergio VILLOLDO
09 Director of Institutional Research ....Dr. Miguel A. RIESTRA
10 Chief Business Officer ....Mr. Ernesto VÁZQUEZ-MARTÍNEZ
15 Director Personnel Services ....Ms. Ana CASTELLANO
18 Chief Facilities/Physical Plant ....Mr. Herminio ROMERO
29 Alumni Relations ....Ms. Lourdes ALCRUDO
35 Director Student Affairs ....Mr. Carlos PEREZ
36 Director Student Placement ....Mrs. Angie ESCALANTE
38 Director Student Counseling ....Ms. Claribel DÍAZ-DÍAZ
21 Associate Business Officer ....Ms. Olga CANCEL
96 Director of Purchasing ....Mr. Ramón RIVERA

Universidad Teologica Del Caribe (F)

PO Box 901, Saint Just PR 00978-0901

County: Trujillo Alto FICE Identification: 023355
Unit ID: 241614
Telephone: (787) 761-0640 Carnegie Class: Spec/Faith
FAX Number: (787) 748-9220 Calendar System: Semester
URL: www.utcpr.edu
Established: 1956 Annual Undergrad Tuition & Fees: $3,784
Enrollment: 172 Coed
Affiliation or Control: Church Of God IRS Status: 501(c)3
Highest Offering: Baccalaureate
Program: Religious Emphasis
Accreditation: BI

01 President ....Francisco ORTIZ
05 Academic Dean ....Carmen AYALA
06 Registrar ....Carolina FIGUEROA
10 Administration Dean ....Frankie NEGRON
32 Dean of Students ....Elizabeth GONZALEZ
37 Financial Aid Director ....Sandra BARRETO
08 Librarian ....Velma Leticia SOSA

*University of Puerto Rico-Central Administration (G)

1187 Flamboyan Street, San Juan PR 00926-1117

County: San Juan FICE Identification: 003942
Unit ID: 243160
Telephone: (787) 250-0000 Carnegie Class: N/A
FAX Number: (787) 759-6917
URL: www.upr.edu

01 President ....Dr. José A. LASALDE DOMINICCI
03 Executive Director ....Dra. Gladys ESCALONA
05 Vice President for Academic Affairs ....Dra. Celeste E. FREYTES
09 Vice President for Research ....Dr. José A. LASALDE-DOMINICCI
32 Vice Pres Student Affairs ....Vacant
12 Chancellor Rio Piedras Campus ....Dra. Ethel RÍOS ORLANDI
12 Acting Chancellor Mayaguez Campus ....Dr. Andrés CALDERÓN-COLÓN
12 Chanc Medical Sciences Campus ....Dr. José RODRÍGUEZ-CRESPO
12 Chanc University College at Cayey ....Dr. José N. CARABALLO
12 Chanc University Col Humacao ....Dra. Carmen A. MIRANDA RIVERA
12 Chanc Univ College at Bayamon ....Dr. Orlando GONZÁLEZ-GONZÁLEZ
12 Chanc Univ College at Ponce ....Dra. Margarita E. VILLAMIL-TORRES
12 Chanc Univ College at Carolina ....Dr. Luis D. TORRES-TORRES
12 Chanc Univ College at Utuado ....Prof. Raúl M. NUÑEZ-ACEVEDO
12 Chanc Univ College Aguadilla ....Dr. José M. PLANAS-RIVERA
12 Chanc Univ College at Arecibo ....Dr. José RODRÍGUEZ-VÁZQUEZ
30 Dir Devel & Alumni Affairs Office ....Vacant
18 Dir Ctrl Designer Construction Ofc ....Eng. René BEAUCHAMP-OCASIO
10 Director Finance Office ....Mr. Basilio RIVERA ARROYO
15 Director Human Resources Office ....Mrs. Edna M. SCHARRÓN
11 Director Administrative Service ....Ms. Miriam D. MARTÍNEZ
13 Director Information Systems Office ....Mr. Alfredo FIGUEROA-LLAVAT
37 Director Student Financial Aid ....Vacant
43 Director Legal Affairs Office ....Ms. Martha L. VÉLEZ
88 Administrator Botanical Garden ....Mr. Carlos R. DÍAZ-PÉREZ
27 University Press & Communications ....Vacant
101 Exec Secretary University Board ....Dra. Ana N. LÓPEZ-FUENTES
21 Director Budget Office ....Mr. Basilio RIVERA-ARROYO

*University of Puerto Rico-Aguadilla (H)

PO Box 6150, Aguadilla PR 00604-6150

County: Aguadilla FICE Identification: 012123
Unit ID: 243106
Telephone: (787) 890-2681 Carnegie Class: Bac/Diverse
FAX Number: (787) 891-3455 Calendar System: Semester
URL: www.uprag.edu
Established: 1972 Annual Undergrad Tuition & Fees (In-State): $2,014
Enrollment: 3,000 Coed
Affiliation or Control: State IRS Status: 501(c)3
Highest Offering: Baccalaureate
Program: Occupational; 2-Year Principally Bachelor's Creditable; Liberal Arts And General
Accreditation: M, ACBSP, TED

02 Acting Chancellor ....Dr. Jose M. PLANAS RIVERA
05 Acting Dean Academic Affairs ....Dr. Sandra I. PEREZ RODRIGUEZ
11 Acting Dean Administrative Affairs ....Prof. Edna E. HERNANDEZ BONILLA
32 Acting Dean Student Affairs ....Prof. Luis R. RIVERA LOPEZ
06 Registrar ....Mrs. Zaida SERRANO
07 Admissions Officer ....Mrs. Melba SERRANO
08 Head Librarian ....Prof. Sharon RIVERA
14 Director of Computer Center ....Mr. Carlos JIMENEZ
16 Acting Director of Personnel ....Mrs. Carmen A. RODRIGUEZ PEREZ
19 Director of Security/Safety ....Mr. Edwin VAZQUEZ MEDINA
37 Director Student Financial Aid ....Mr. Luis ALVAREZ
51 Director Continuing Education ....Prof. U. Birilo SANTIAGO VELAZQUEZ
38 Director Student Counseling ....Dr. Gilberto HERRERA
45 Dir Planning/Inst Research Office ....Mr. Gerardo JAVARIZ
18 Chief Facilities/Physical Plant ....Vacant
29 Director Alumni Relations ....Mrs. Jeannette AQUINO
96 Purchasing Supervisor ....Mrs. Widylia MEDINA

*University of Puerto Rico at Arecibo (I)

Call Box 4010, Arecibo PR 00614-4010

County: Arecibo FICE Identification: 007228
Unit ID: 243115
Telephone: (787) 815-0000 Carnegie Class: Bac/Diverse
FAX Number: (787) 880-2245 Calendar System: Semester
URL: www.upra.edu
Established: 1967 Annual Undergrad Tuition & Fees (In-State): $2,819
Enrollment: 3,693 Coed
Affiliation or Control: State IRS Status: 501(c)3
Highest Offering: Baccalaureate
Program: Occupational; Liberal Arts And General
Accreditation: M, ACBSP, ADNUR, CS, ENGT, JOUR, NUR, TED

02 Chancellor ....Dr. Jose J. RODRIGUEZ

05 Dean of Academic Affairs .... Dra. Maiella RAMOS FONTEN
11 Dean of Administrative Affairs .... Prof. Rafael GARCIA TOULET
32 Dean of Student Affairs ....Prof. Luis GONZALEZ
09 Dir Planning/Institutional Research .... Prof. Soriel SANTIAGO
06 Registrar ....Mrs. Widilia RODRIGUEZ
07 Director of Admissions ....Mrs. Magaly MENDEZ
08 Head Librarian ....Prof. Robert ROSADO
15 Director Human Resources ....Ms. Sandra DE JESUS
38 Director Student Counseling ....Prof. Jose RODRIGUEZ
04 Assistant to the Chancellor ....Prof. Fernendo MEDINA
51 Dir Continuing Education/Prof Stds ....Prof. Nayla BAEZ
37 Director Student Financial Aid ....Ms. Myrta ORTIZ
41 Athletic Director ....Prof. Jose COLON
13 Computing & Information Management ....Prof. Aixa RAMIREZ
20 Assoc Dean of Academic Affairs ....Prof. Ana GARCIA
29 Director Alumni Relations ....Mrs. Mercedes PEREZ
92 Director Honors Program ....Dra. Jane ALBERDESON
96 Director of Purchasing ....Mrs. Rosaura QUINTANA
18 Chief Facilities/Physical Plant ....Mr. Ruben SANTIAGO

*University of Puerto Rico at Bayamon (A)

Carr. 174 #170 Industrial Minillas,
Bayamon PR 00959-1911
County: Bayamon FICE Identification: 010975
Unit ID: 243133
Telephone: (787) 993-0000 Carnegie Class: Bac/Diverse
FAX Number: (787) 993-8900 Calendar System: Semester
URL: www.uprb.edu
Established: 1971 Annual Undergrad Tuition & Fees (In-State): $3,012
Enrollment: 5,062 Coed
Affiliation or Control: State IRS Status: 501(c)3
Highest Offering: Baccalaureate
Program: Liberal Arts And General
Accreditation: M, ACBSP, ENGT, TED

02 Chancellor ....Dr. Orlando GONZÁLEZ-GONZÁLEZ
05 Dean Academic Affairs .... Dr. Javier AVALOS-SÁNCHEZ
32 Dean Student Affairs ....Ms. Elsa FLORES-ORTIZ
06 Registrar ....Ms. Carmen CINTRON-OTERO
07 Director Admissions .... Mrs. Carmen MONTES-BURGOS
08 Director Learning Resources ....Prof. Maria de los Angeles ZAVALA-COLÓN
11 Dean Administrative Affairs ....Mr. Abdiel MARTÍNEZ-BARRIOS
15 Director Human Resources ....Mrs. Idalia MORELL-MARRERO
35 Director Student Activities ....Mrs. Maribelle PERGOLA-RIVERA
36 Director Student Placement ....Prof. Nelson VÁZQUEZ-ESPEJO
37 Director Student Financial Aid ...Mr. Héctor CUADRADO-GARCÍA
38 Director Student Counseling ....Mr. Angel RUCABADO
81 Director Biology ....Dr. Nilda APONTE-AVELLANET
50 Director Business Administration ...Prof. Lydia UBARRI-DE LEÓN
51 Director Continuing Education .... Ms. Verónica FUENTES-RUÍZ
09 Director Planning & Inst Research ....Mr. Javier ZAVALA-QUIÑONES
53 Director Education ....Prof. María A. GONZÁLEZ DE RESENDE
54 Director Engineering ....Prof. Jesús ORTIZ-CINTRÓN
68 Director Physical Education ....Prof. Carlos MARICHAL-LUGO
79 Director Humanities ....Dr. Luis H. PABÓN-BATLLE
83 Director Social Sciences ....Dr. Elizabeth CRESPO-KEBLER
77 Director Computer Science .... Prof. Antonio HUERTAS-BERMÚDEZ
75 Director Secretarial Sciences .... Prof. Nancy JIMÉNEZ-PÉREZ
72 Director Electronics ....Prof. Jesús ORTIZ-CINTRÓN
23 Director Health Services ....Dr. Jorge L. TORRES-SÁNCHEZ
96 Director Purchasing ....Mr. Agustin GRATEROLE-ROSARIO
88 Director Special Services ....Ms. Shelciy COLLAZO
81 Director Physics ....Dr. Alfredo TORRUELLA-LAWTON
88 Director English ....Dr. Luis PABÓN-BATLLE
88 Director Spanish ....Dr. Luis H. PABÓN-BATLE
81 Director Mathematics ....Prof. Angel MORERA-GONZÁLEZ
88 Director Chemistry ....Dr. Solange BENÍTEZ-RAMÍREZ
18 Coord Facilities/Physical Plant ...Mr. Samuel SÁEZ-HERNÁNDEZ
10 Director Finance ....Ms. María PÉREZ-SÁNCHEZ
21 Director Budget ....Mr. Wilfredo ORTIZ-RUÍZ
13 Director Information Systems ....Ms. Barbara LANDRAU

*University of Puerto Rico-Carolina (B)

PO Box 4800, Carolina PR 00984-4800
County: San Juan FICE Identification: 030160
Unit ID: 243142
Telephone: (787) 257-0000 Carnegie Class: Bac/Diverse
FAX Number: (787) 750-7940 Calendar System: Quarter
URL: www.uprc.edu
Established: 1974 Annual Undergrad Tuition & Fees (In-State): $3,821
Enrollment: 3,837 Coed
Affiliation or Control: State IRS Status: 501(c)3
Highest Offering: Baccalaureate
Program:
Accreditation: M, ACBSP

02 Chancellor ....Dr. Luis D. TORRES
05 Dean of Academic Affairs ....Dr. Juan BONILLA
11 Dean Administrative Affairs ....Ing. Jose MEZA
32 Dean Student Affairs ....Dr. Jaime M. CABRERA
06 Registrar ....Mr. Abelardo MARTINEZ
16 Human Resources Director ....Mrs. Sandra HERNANDEZ
09 Director of Planning/Inst Research ....Prof. Carmen L. CRUZ
08 Director Learning Resources Center ....Prof. Stanley PORTELA
51 Director Continuing Education ....Prof. Roberto VIZCARRONDO
07 Admissions Officer ....Mrs. Celia MENDEZ

14 Coord/Dir Computer Sys Center ....Prof. Miguel A. VELEZ
37 Financial Aid Director ....Mr. Rafael RUIZ
22 Affirmative Action Officer ....Mrs. Rosa QUINONES
88 Director Graphic Arts/Advertising ....Prof. Jose AYALA
50 Director Banking/Finance/Insurance ....Dr. Eldra HERANANDEZ
81 Director Natural Sciences ....Dr. Rafael MENDEZ
88 Director Secretarial Sciences ....Prof. Josefina RODRIGUEZ
83 Director Social Sciences ....Dr. Olga COLON
68 Director Physical Education ....Dr. Awilda NUÑEZ
88 Director Auto Tech/Mech Engineering ....Prof. Narcisa MEZA
79 Director Humanities ....Dra. Amalia ALSINA
88 Director Spanish ....Prof. Zulma PENCHI
88 Director English ....Prof. Wanda RODRIGUEZ
88 Dean Hotel Administration School ....Prof. Paul RIVERA
23 Director Health Care ....Dr. Ruben D'ACOSTA
18 Supt Operations & Maintenance ....Mr. Herman MUNIZ
41 Athletic Director ....Mr. Arcadio OCASIO
96 Director of Purchasing ....Mrs. Lourdes Z. ORTIZ
10 Chief Business Officer ....Mrs. Sarahi GUADALUPE

*University of Puerto Rico at Cayey (C)

205 Antonio R Barcelo Avenue, Cayey PR 00736
County: Cayey FICE Identification: 007206
Unit ID: 243151
Telephone: (787) 738-2161 Carnegie Class: Bac/Diverse
FAX Number: (787) 738-8039 Calendar System: Semester
URL: web1.oss.cayey.upr.edu/main/
Established: 1967 Annual Undergrad Tuition & Fees (In-State): $3,012
Enrollment: 3,696 Coed
Affiliation or Control: State IRS Status: 501(c)3
Highest Offering: Baccalaureate
Program: Liberal Arts And General; Teacher Preparatory; Professional; Business Emphasis
Accreditation: M, ACBSP, TED

02 Interim Chancellor ....Dr. Jose N. CARABALLO
05 Interim Dean of Academic Affairs ....Dr. Glorivee ACEVEDO
11 Dean of Administration Affairs ....Mr. Samuel GONZÁLEZ
32 Interim Dean of Student Affairs ....Dr. Sarah MALAVE
08 Director Library ....Prof. Sonia DAVILA
06 Registrar ....Mrs. Daisy RAMOS
15 Interim Director Human Resources ....Mr. Juan M. ORTIZ
56 Head Extension Division ....Mr. Luis R. SANTIAGO
37 Director Student Financial Aid ....Mrs. Sonia PLACERES
38 Director Student Counseling ....Dr. Lino HERNANDEZ
36 Interim Director Student Placement ....Mrs. Rosa ORTIZ
14 Director Computer Center ....Mr. Ramon MARTINEZ
45 Director Planning & Development ....Prof. Irmannette TORRES-LUGO
07 Director Admissions ....Mrs. Jesus MARTINEZ
18 Director Facilities/Physical Plant ....Mr. Luis LATORRE
23 Director Health Services ....Dr. Sandra LISBOA
19 Director Security/Safety ....Mr. Edgardo CASTRO
92 Director Honor Program ....Dr. Jannette GAVILLAN
88 Director External Resources ....Prof. Gladys RAMOS
20 Associate Academic Officer ....Dr. William RIOS
04 Assistant to the Chancellor ....Prof. Gladys RAMOS
41 Director Athletic Program ....Prof. Stacey LOPEZ
26 Chief Public Relations Officer ....Mr. Angel R. ROSA
29 Director Alumni Relations ....Mrs. Gema C. FIGUEROA
96 Director Purchasing ....Mrs. Candida COLON
43 Director Legal Services ....Mr. Francisco MORENO
88 Student Ombudsman ....Prof. Evelyn COLLAZO
53 Education ....Dr. William RIOS
79 Humanities ....Prof. Harry HERNANDEZ
83 Social Sciences ....Dr. Nelson MIRANDA
88 Hispanic Studies ....Prof. Jose PEREZ
88 English ....Prof. David LIZARDI
81 Chemistry ....Dr. Wilfredo RESTO
65 Natural Science ....Vacant
88 Biology ....Dr. Ricardo CHIESA
94 Women's Studies ....Dr. Sarah MALAVE
09 Director Assess & Inst Research ....Prof. Irmannette TORRES-LUGO
10 Chief Business Officer ....Mr. Jose COLON
88 Director Budgeting ....Mr. Gonzalo COLON
81 Mathematics-Physics ....Dr. Julia RODRIGUEZ
50 Business Administration ....Prof. Edfel RIVERA
72 Technology & Office Administration ....Prof. Awilda M. CARABALLO
68 Physical Education ....Dr. Edwin FLORES
88 RISE Program ....Dr. Robert ROSS
88 Commission on Prevention of Viol ....Dr. Jose VARGAS
88 Iterdisciplinary Research Institute ....Ms. Vionet MARTI
88 Museum ....Dr. Humberto FIGUEROA

*University of Puerto Rico-Humacao (D)

Call box 860, Humacao PR 00792
County: Humacao FICE Identification: 003943
Unit ID: 243179
Telephone: (787) 850-0000 Carnegie Class: Bac/Diverse
FAX Number: (787) 852-4638 Calendar System: Semester
URL: www.uprh.edu
Established: 1962 Annual Undergrad Tuition & Fees (In-State): $2,280
Enrollment: 3,603 Coed
Affiliation or Control: State IRS Status: 501(c)3
Highest Offering: Baccalaureate
Program: Occupational; 2-Year Principally Bachelor's Creditable; Liberal Arts And General; Teacher Preparatory
Accreditation: M, ACBSP, ADNUR, ENGT, NUR, PTAA, SW, TED

02 Acting Chancellor ....Dr. Carmen A. MIRANDA
05 Acting Dean of Academic Affairs ....Dr. Ivelisse RIVERA
11 Acting Dean Administrative Affairs ....Mrs. Mariolga ROTGER
04 Assistant to the Chancellor ....Prof. Milagros MARRERO
32 Acting Dean of Student Affairs ....Prof. Wanda L. RODRÍGUEZ
20 Assistant Dean of Academic Affairs ....Dr. Esther Z. VEGA
09 Dir Planning/IR and Accreditation ....Vacant
06 Registrar ....Mr. Jorge ACEVEDO
07 Director of Admissions ....Mrs. Elizabeth GERENA
08 Director of the Library ....Mr. Luis RODRÍGUEZ
13 Dir Computer/Commun & Info Mgmt ....Mr. Hiram ORTIZ
15 Acting Director Human Resources ....Mrs. Maria ROSA
10 Director of Finance ....Mrs. Ines SANCHEZ
37 Asst Financial Aid Officer ....Mrs. Brunilda LÓPEZ
88 Director Interdis/Intreg Dev Std ....Dr. Pedro VÁZQUEZ
51 Dir Continuing Education/Extension ....Prof. José LÓPEZ
23 Director Health Services ....Vacant
18 Chief Facilities/Physical Plant ....Vacant
19 Director Security/Safety ....Mr. Carlos O. FIGUEROA
96 Director of Purchasing ....Mr. Javier A. MUYET
88 Student Ombuds Person ....Dr. Cástula SANTIAGO
41 Athletic Coordinator ....Mrs. Miriam LASANTA
21 Director of Budget Office ....Mrs. Iris N. CARRASQUILLO
108 Office of Institutional Assessment ....Prof. Luis NEGRÓN
88 Director Svcs Population Disabil .... Prof. Carmen SEPÚLVEDA
88 Envir Health & Occupational Safety .... Mrs. Angélica TORRES
101 Sec of Academic Senate/Adm Board ...Prof. Amelia MALDONADO

*University of Puerto Rico-Mayaguez Campus (E)

PO Box 9000, Mayaguez PR 00681-9000
County: Mayaguez FICE Identification: 003944
Unit ID: 243197
Telephone: (787) 832-4040 Carnegie Class: DRU
FAX Number: (787) 834-3031 Calendar System: Semester
URL: www.uprm.edu
Established: 1911 Annual Undergrad Tuition & Fees (In-State): $2,819
Enrollment: 11,984 Coed
Affiliation or Control: State IRS Status: 501(c)3
Highest Offering: Doctorate
Program: Occupational; Liberal Arts And General; Teacher Preparatory; Professional
Accreditation: M, ENG, NUR, TED

02 Acting President ....Dr. Jorge RIVERA SANTOS
05 Dean of Academic Affairs ....Dr. Darnyd W. ORTIZ SEDA
11 Dean Administration ....Lcdo. Angel L. MATOS FLORES
32 Dean of Students ....Arq. Wilma SANTIAGO GABRIELINI
49 Dean of Arts & Sciences ....Dr. Juan LÓPEZ GARRIGA
54 Dean of Engineering ....Dr. Jaime SEGUEL
47 Dean of Agricultural Sciences .....Dr. Héctor SANTIAGO ANADON
50 Dean Business Administration ....Prof. Héctor BRAVO VICK
58 Director of Graduate Studies ....Dr. Anand D. SHARMA
14 Director of Computer Center ....Mr. José CUEVAS
06 Registrar ....Mrs. Briseida MELENDEZ
08 Acting Director of the Library ....Prof. Norma I. SOJO
07 Director of Admissions ....Ms. Norma TORRES
37 Director Student Financial Aid ....Mrs. Lynette FELICIANO RIOS
36 Director Student Placement ....Mrs. Nancy NIEVES
26 Press Office Director ....Mrs. Mariam L. ROSA VELEZ
45 Director Inst Research/Planning ....Dr. Noel ARTILES LEON
29 Director Alumni Association ....Miss Yomarachaliff LUCIANO-FIGUEROA
15 Director of Personnel Services ....Mrs. Cynthia THOMAS FRATICELLI
18 Director of Physical Resources ....Eng. Roberto AYALA
38 Director Student Counseling ....Mr. Edwin MORALES
21 Acting Director Financial Services ....Mr. José E. AVILES
51 Director Continuing Education ....Prof. Silvestre COLÓN
19 Director Security/Safety ....Mr. Roberto TORRES
23 Director Health Services ....Mrs. Rosie TORRES
41 Athletic Director ....Prof. Fernando GAZTAMBIDE
43 Director Legal Services ....Lcda. Lizbeth J. RIVERA MORALES

*University of Puerto Rico-Medical Sciences Campus (F)

PO Box 365067, San Juan PR 00936-5067
County: San Juan FICE Identification: 024600
Unit ID: 243203
Telephone: (787) 758-2525 Carnegie Class: Spec/Med
FAX Number: (787) 758-2556 Calendar System: Other
URL: www.rcm.upr.edu
Established: 1950 Annual Undergrad Tuition & Fees (In-State): $3,746
Enrollment: 2,802 Coed
Affiliation or Control: State IRS Status: 501(c)3
Highest Offering: Doctorate
Program: Professional
Accreditation: M, ANEST, AUD, CAHIIM, CYTO, DA, DENT, DIETI, HSA, MED, MIDWF, MT, NMT, NURSE, OT, PH, PHAR, PTA, RAD, SP

02 Interim Chancellor ....Dr. Jose RODRIGUEZ-ORENGO
05 Interim Dean Academic Affairs ....Dr. Ricardo C. GONZALEZ-MENDEZ
32 Interim Dean Students Affairs ....Dr. Nitza RIVERA
11 Interim Dean of Administration ....Prof. Carlos ORTIZ
63 Interim Dean School of Medicine .....Dr. Ines J. GARCIA-GARCIA
52 Interim Dean School Dental Medicine ....Dr. Noel AYMAT

69 Dean Grad School Public Health .... Dr. Jose CORDERO
67 Dean School of Pharmacy .... Dr. Wanda MALDONADO
76 Interim Dean School Health Prof .... Dr. Ruben GARCIA
66 Interim Dean School of Nursing .... Dr. Nancy DAVILA
100 Interim Chief of Staff .... Dr. Margarita IRIZARRY
20 Associate Academic Officer .... Dr. Juanita VILLAMIL
13 Director Information Technology .... Prof. Sandra SANTOS
43 Director Legal Services .... Mr. Raul BANDAS
27 Chief Information Officer .... Ms. Milady GOMEZ
06 Registrar .... Mr. Reinaldo POMALES
08 Library Director .... Dr. Irma QUINONES
09 Director Inst & Academic Research .... Dr. Wanda BARRETO
24 Director Educational Media .... Prof. Efrain FLORES
35 Director Student Affairs .... Mrs. Rosa VELEZ
07 Director of Admissions .... Mrs. Yolanda RIVERA
38 Director of Student Counseling .... Prof. Blanca AMOROS
37 Director of Student Financial Aid .... Mr. Rafael SOLIS
10 Interim Chief Financial Officer .... Mrs. Antonia REYES
15 Interim Director Personnel Services .... Mrs. Maria ZAYAS
18 Chief Facilities/Physical Plant .... Mr. Julio A. COLLAZO
96 Director of Purchasing .... Mr. Jose CARDONA
19 Director Security Office .... Mr. William FIGUEROA

*University of Puerto Rico at Ponce (A)

PO Box 7186, Ponce PR 00732-7186
County: Ponce FICE Identification: 009652
Unit ID: 243212
Telephone: (787) 844-8181 Carnegie Class: Bac/Diverse
FAX Number: (787) 844-8679 Calendar System: Semester
URL: www.uprp.edu
Established: 1970 Annual Undergrad Tuition & Fees (In-State): $14,510
Enrollment: 3,089 Coed
Affiliation or Control: State IRS Status: 501(c)3
Highest Offering: Baccalaureate
Program: Occupational; Liberal Arts And General
Accreditation: M, ACBSP, PTAA, TED

02 Chancellor .... Dr. Margarita E. VILLAMIL
04 Assistant to the Chancellor .... Mrs. Reina M. GONZALEZ
04 Assistant to the Chancellor .... Mr. Pedro I. MARTINEZ
05 Dean Academic Affairs .... Prof. Evelyn GONZALEZ
11 Dean Administrative Affairs .... Dr. Drianfel VAZQUEZ
32 Dean Student Affairs .... Mrs. Acmin VELAZQUEZ
20 Associate Academic Dean .... Prof. Hernando VALERO
45 Dir Inst Research/Planning Officer .... Dr. Jennifer ALICEA
08 Director Library .... Prof. Brett DIAZ
06 Registrar .... Mrs. Marya Z. SANTIAGO
38 Director of Student Counseling .... Dr. Efrain RIOS
07 Director of Admissions .... Mrs. Emily MATOS
37 Director of Financial Aid .... Mrs. Ada HERENCIA
15 Director of Personnel Services .... Mr. Juan C. LEON
88 Director of Cultural Activities .... Mr. Jose L. PONS
14 Director of Computer Center .... Prof. Juan VEGA
18 Chief Facilities/Physical Plant .... Mr. Alberto GARCIA
40 Director Bookstore .... Vacant
41 Athletic Director .... Mrs. Lesbia COLON
23 Director Health Services .... Dr. Claudio SANTOS
29 Director Alumni Relations .... Mrs. Acmin VELAZQUEZ
30 Chief Development .... Vacant
19 Director of Security/Traffic .... Mr. German PIMENTEL
88 Coordinator Security/Safety .... Mr. Francisco HERNANDEZ
22 Coordinator Affirmative Action .... Mrs. Ginny VELEZ

*University of Puerto Rico-Rio Piedras Campus (B)

PO Box 23300, Rio Piedras PR 00931-3300
County: San Juan FICE Identification: 007108
Unit ID: 243221
Telephone: (787) 763-3877 Carnegie Class: RU/H
FAX Number: (787) 764-8799 Calendar System: Semester
URL: www.uprrp.edu
Established: 1903 Annual Undergrad Tuition & Fees (In-State): $2,819
Enrollment: 15,259 Coed
Affiliation or Control: State IRS Status: 501(c)3
Highest Offering: Doctorate
Program: Liberal Arts And General; Teacher Preparatory; Professional
Accreditation: M, ACBSP, CORE, CS, DIETD, JOUR, LAW, LIB, PLNG, SPAA, SW, TED

02 Chancellor .... Dr. Ana R. GUADALUPE
05 Dean Academic Affairs .... Dr. Beatriz RIVERA
11 Dean of Administration .... Mr. Alberto FELICIANO
32 Dean of Students .... Dr. Mayra CHARRIEZ
20 Associate Dean Academic Affairs .... Dr. Tania GARCIA RAMOS
50 Dean Business Administration .... Dr. Paul LATORTUE
48 Dean of Architecture .... Prof. Francisco RODRIGUEZ
81 Dean of Natural Sciences .... Dr. Brad WEINER
83 Dean of Social Sciences .... Dr. Blanca ORTIZ
61 Dean of Law .... Ms. Vivian NEPTUNE
97 Dean of General Studies .... Dr. Luis FERRAO
79 Dean of Humanities .... Dr. Luis A. ORTIZ
58 Dean Graduate Studies/Research .... Dr. Haydee SEIJO
53 Dean of Education .... Dr. Juanita RODRIGUEZ
35 Asst Dean Student Affairs .... Ms. Michele COLON GARCIA
38 Director of Student Counseling .... Mrs. Maritza PEREZ
30 Int Dir Devel & Alumni Relations .... Mrs. Rosita A. RIVERA
06 Registrar .... Mr. Juan M. APONTE
08 Director of Library System .... Dr. Snejanka PENKOVA
15 Director of Human Resources .... Mrs. Aida ROSARIO
07 Director of Admissions .... Mrs. Cruz Belinda VALENTIN

14 Director of Computer Center .... Mr. Rafael LLANOS
62 Director Grad Sch Library/Info Sci .... Dr. Luisa VIGO
60 Director School of Communication .... Dr. Eliseo COLON
58 Dir Graduate Sch of Planning .... Dr. Elias R. GUTIERREZ
51 Dir Continuing Educ/Extension .... Mrs. Melba MARTINEZ
09 Director of Institutional Research .... Prof. Zulyn RODRIGUEZ
18 Chief Planning/Physical Devel Ofc .... Ing. Raul CINTRON
26 Chief Public Relations Officer .... Mrs. Lorna CASTRO
37 Director of Student Financial Aid .... Mrs. Ana HERNANDEZ
96 Director of Purchasing .... Mrs. Ivonne MATIENZO-CARRERO

*University of Puerto Rico at Utuado (C)

PO Box 2500, Utuado PR 00641-2500
County: Utuado FICE Identification: 029384
Unit ID: 243188
Telephone: (939) 292-8924 Carnegie Class: Bac/Diverse
FAX Number: (787) 894-1081 Calendar System: Semester
URL: www.uprutuado.edu/cormo.htm
Established: 1979 Annual Undergrad Tuition & Fees (In-State): $2,944
Enrollment: 1,476 Coed
Affiliation or Control: State IRS Status: 501(c)3
Highest Offering: Baccalaureate
Program: Occupational; 2-Year Principally Bachelor's Creditable; Liberal Arts And General; Business Emphasis
Accreditation: M, ACBSP, TED

02 Acting Chancellor .... Prof. Raúl M. NÚÑEZ
05 Chief Academic Officer .... Prof. Debra GONZALEZ
10 Chief Business Officer .... Mrs. Teresita MATTEI
32 Chief Student Life Officer .... Prof. Carolyn MERCADO
08 Head Librarian .... Dr. Miguel SANTIAGO
09 Director Institutional Research .... Dr. Javier LUGO
06 Registrar .... Mrs. Marilia SANTIAGO
07 Director of Admission .... Mrs. María V. ROBLES
15 Director Personnel Services .... Ms. Luz E. MARTÍNEZ
38 Director Student Counseling .... Mr. Amilcar GONZALEZ
37 Director Student Financial Aid .... Mrs. Edymariel CORTES
14 Director Computer Center .... Mr. Héctor L. LÓPEZ
18 Chief Facilities/Physical Plant .... Mr. Josue LUGO
19 Director Security/Safety .... Mr. Miguel TORRES
41 Director of Athletics .... Mr. Miguel RODRIGUEZ
47 Director of Agriculture .... Prof. Eladio GONZALEZ
50 Dir Office Systems/Business Admin .... Prof. Vivian VELEZ
96 Director of Purchasing .... Mrs. Luz MARTINEZ
51 Director Continuing Education .... Prof. Miralys PEREZ
53 Director Education .... Prof. Vilmaris CESTERO
88 Director Natural Sciences .... Dr. Vilmari LÓPEZ
79 Director Humanities/Spanish/English .... Prof. Adolfo J. GARCÍA

University of the Sacred Heart (D)

PO Box 12383, San Juan PR 00914-8505
County: San Juan FICE Identification: 003937
Unit ID: 243443
Telephone: (787) 728-1515 Carnegie Class: Master's M
FAX Number: (787) 728-1692 Calendar System: Semester
URL: www.sagrado.edu
Established: 1935 Annual Undergrad Tuition & Fees: $6,500
Enrollment: 6,335 Coed
Affiliation or Control: Roman Catholic IRS Status: 501(c)3
Highest Offering: Master's
Program: Occupational; Liberal Arts And General; Teacher Preparatory; Professional
Accreditation: M, NUR, SW

01 President .... Dr. Jose J. RIVERA
84 Dir Inst Plng/Assessmt/Enroll Mgmt .... Prof. Lilia PLANELL
05 Dean Academic/Student Affairs .... Dr. Lydia ESPINET
11 Dean of Administration .... Mr. Jose L. RICCI
30 Dean of Development .... Prof. Adlin RIOS
20 Associate Academic Dean .... Prof. Yezmin HERNANDEZ
32 Associate Students Dean .... Prof. Pedro FRAILE
09 Director of Inst Research Office .... Dr. Carmen PADIAL
07 Director of Admissions .... Prof. Lilia PLANELL
06 Registrar .... Ms. Mildred PINEIRO
26 Chief Public Relations Officer .... Mrs. Maria E. MADRID
21 Director of Budgeting .... Mrs. Lourdes BERTRAN
91 Director Admin Computer Center .... Ms. Carmen CINTRON
18 Chief Facilities/Physical Plant .... Mr. Jose L. RICCI
15 Director Personnel Services .... Ms. Sol A. GOMILA
29 Director Alumni Relations .... Mrs. Elizabeth VARGAS
08 Head Librarian .... Mrs. Sonia DIAZ
37 Director of Financial Aid .... Ms. June ANDRADE
39 Director Student Housing .... Ms. Livia D. PASTRANA
41 Athletic Director .... Mr. Jose L. BURGOS
42 Chaplain .... Vacant
10 Director Finance Office .... Vacant
50 Director Business Administration .... Prof. Marta ALMEYDA
53 Director Education Department .... Dr. Migdalia OQUENDO
60 Director Communication Department .... Prof. Modesto AGUAYO
81 Director Natural Sciences .... Prof. Zaida GRACIA
79 Dir Fac Intdspln Human/Social Stds .... Prof. Isabel YAMÍN
21 Internal Auditor .... Mr. Ricardo AGUIRRE
24 Dir Center for FAC/Rchmnt/Educ Tech .... Mrs. Sylvia ALVAREZ
51 Assoc Director Continuing Education .... Mrs. Elvia AGOSTO
19 Coordinator Security/Safety .... Mr. Jose LOZADA
21 Coord Inst Devel Center for CFRET .... Mr. Wally ALVARANZA
88 Coord Edu Tech CFRET/FAC/Rchmnt .... Ms. Sylvia ALVAREZ
24 Coord Multimedia Product of CFRET .... Mr. Benigno ROSA

VIRGIN ISLANDS

University of the Virgin Islands (E)

8266 John Brewers Bay, Saint Thomas VI 00802-6025
FICE Identification: 003946
Unit ID: 243665
Telephone: (340) 776-9200 Carnegie Class: Bac/Diverse
FAX Number: (340) 693-1005 Calendar System: Semester
URL: www.uvi.edu
Established: 1962 Annual Undergrad Tuition & Fees (In-State): $4,794
Enrollment: 2,423 Coed
Affiliation or Control: State IRS Status: 501(c)3
Highest Offering: Master's
Program: Liberal Arts And General; Teacher Preparatory; Professional
Accreditation: M, ADNUR, NUR

01 President .... Dr. David HALL
100 Interim Chief of Staff .... Ms. Pamela RICHARDS SAMUEL
88 Special Asst to the President .... Dr. Haldane DAVIES
05 Interim Provost .... Dr. Camille MCKAYLE-STOLZ
25 Asst Dir Spec Proj/Grants/Agreement .... Dr. Angela MCGHEE
53 Interim Dean School of Education .... Dr. Linda THOMAS
81 Interim Dean College of Sci & Math .... Dr. Sandra ROMANO
50 Interim Dean School of Business ..... Prof. Aubrey WASHINGTON
79 Int Dean College Lib Arts/Soc Sci .... Dr. Simon B. JONES-HENDRICKSON
66 Dean School of Nursing .... Dr. Cheryl P. FRANKLIN
46 Interim Vice Provost .... Dr. Frank MILLS
84 Vice Provost Access/Enroll Services .... Vacant
07 Dir Admissions/Recruitment .... Dr. Xuri M. ALLEN
06 Registrar .... Ms. Heather HOGARTH-SMITH
37 Director of Financial Aid .... Ms. Cheryl A. ROBERTS
41 Director of Athletics .... Mr. Peter SAUER
88 Dir Community/Personal Develop .... Ms. ILene HEYWARD
30 VP Institutional Advancement .... Ms. Dionne V. JACKSON
29 Director of Alumni Affairs .... Ms. Linda SMITH
44 Director of Major Gifts .... Mr. Mitchell NEAVES
26 Interim Director Public Relations .... Ms. Nanyamka FARRELLY
88 Director of Special Events .... Ms. Liza MARGOLIS
102 Dir Corporate/Foundation/Govt Rels .... Mr. Richard CLEAVER
96 Purchasing Supervisor .... Mr. Eric CHRISTIAN
10 VP Administration & Finance .... Ms. Shirley LAKE-KING
21 Controller .... Ms. Peggy SMITH
15 Acting Dir of HR/Org Development .... Ms. Valena V. RICHARDS
88 Assoc Dir HR/Org Development .... Ms. Yvonne D. LAWRENCE
88 Director of Capital Projects .... Mr. Gerard BUGGY
40 Bookstore Manager-STT Campus .... Mr. Mervin V. TAYLOR
40 Bookstore Manager-AAS Campus .... Ms. Laurel A. HECKER
19 Chief of Security .... Mr. Roderick C. PULLEN
18 Plant Maintenance Manager .... Mr. Charles MARTIN
27 Chief Information Officer .... Ms. Tina M. KOOPMANS
14 Mgr Enterprise Data/User Services .... Ms. Sharlene J. HARRIS
08 Manager of Library/Fac Tech Svcs .... Ms. Judith ROGERS
35 Dean of Students-STT Campus .... Dr. Doris BATTISTE
36 Counseling Supervisor-STT Campus .... Ms. Verna RIVERS
35 Dean of Students - AAS Campus .... Ms. Miriam OSBORNE-ELLIOTT
36 Counseling Supervisor-AAS Campus .... Ms. Patricia TOWAL

University of the Virgin Islands-St. Croix (F)

RR1 10,000, Kingshill VI 00850-9781
Telephone: (340) 778-1620 Identification: 770173
Accreditation: &M

† Main campus is University of the Virgin Islands in Saint Thomas, VI.

Index of Key Administrators

A

AABERGE, Nancy .... 406-874-6161. 286 E aabergen@milescc.edu
AADLAND, Susan, R ...... 605-394-6884. 452 A susan.aadland@sdsmt.edu
AAKER, Sherry .... 850-729-4901. 109 I aakers@nwfsc.edu
AAKHUS, Michael, K ...... 812-464-1855. 174 D MAakhus@usi.edu
AALBERS, Jeffrey, R .... 651-361-3320. 256 N jaalbers@mcnallysmith.edu
AALTO, David, W .... 508-767-7355. 222 C daalto@assumption.edu
AAMODT, Peter, W .... 859-344-3352. 199 H peter.aamodt@thomasmore.edu
AANES, Jacquelyn .... 641-269-3200. 178 H aanesjac@grinnell.edu
AANESTAD, Carolyn .... 307-855-2103. 542 Y carolyn@cwc.edu
AARON, Belinda .... 318-473-6515. 205 A baaron@lsua.edu
AARON, Fredona .... 540-857-6053. 514 E faaron@virginiawestern.edu
AARON, Judith .... 718-636-3677. 336 F jaaron@pratt.edu
AARON, Kenneth .... 518-327-6297. 336 B kaaron@paulsmiths.edu
AARSVOLD, Bruce, N ..... 507-933-7020. 255 I aarsvold@gustavus.edu
AASEN, Curtis, K .... 757-822-1070. 514 C caasen@tcc.edu
AASTED, Jon .... 661-362-5406... 40 E jon.aasted@canyons.edu
ABADIE, Bonnie .... 210-341-1366. 477 L babadie@ost.edu
ABADIE, Chuck .... 601-403-1312. 269 D cabadie@prcc.edu
ABADIE, Rene, G .... 985-549-2341. 208 C rabadie@selu.edu
ABALDO, Michelle .... 772-462-7265. 106 P mabaldo@irsc.edu
ABARAY, Christyn .... 712-749-2253. 176 D abarayc@bvu.edu
ABARE, JR., William, T . 904-819-6288. 103 E abare@flagler.edu
ABASA-NYARKO, Charles .... 541-383-7205. 402 D cabasanyarko@cocc.edu
ABATEMARCO, Vincent .. 313-993-1508. 250 K vabatemarco@udmercy.edu
ABB, Kerrie .... 509-574-4870. 525 G kabb@yvcc.edu
ABBA, Crystal .... 775-784-4901. 294 D crystal_abba@nshe.nevada.edu
ABBAS, Asma .... 413-528-7215. 222 E aabbas@simons-rock.edu
ABBASCHIAN, Reza .... 951-827-5190... 71 E reza.abbaschian@ucr.edu
ABBASI, Umair .... 620-341-5454. 186 D uabbasi@emporia.edu
ABBATE, Anthony .... 505-438-8884. 312 A abbate@acupuncturecollege.edu
ABBATE, Skya .... 505-438-8884. 312 A skya@acupuncturecollege.edu
ABBEY, Craig, W .... 716-645-2791. 341 F cwabbey@buffalo.edu
ABBOTT, Andy .... 541-885-1720. 405 J andy.abbott@oit.edu
ABBOTT, Cameron .... 916-660-7102... 66 B
ABBOTT, Charlene, R ...... 337-475-5977. 207 G cabbott@mcneese.edu
ABBOTT, Chuck .... 514-244-8448. 376 J chuck.abbott@ccuniversity.edu
ABBOTT, Douglas, M ..... 406-496-4127. 287 F dabbott@mtech.edu
ABBOTT, James, W .... 605-677-5641. 451 F james.abbott@usd.edu
ABBOTT, Jill .... 218-846-3796. 259 F jill.abbott@minnesota.edu
ABBOTT, Judy, A .... 936-468-2901. 482 A collegeofeducation@sfasu.edu
ABBOTT, Karen, D .... 603-645-9623. 297 I k.abbott@snhu.edu
ABBOTT, Larry .... 606-679-8501. 196 D larry.abbott@kctcs.edu
ABBOTT, Mark, R .... 541-737-3504. 406 A mark@coas.oregonstate.edu
ABBOTT, Mary .... 605-668-1464. 450 F mabbott@mtmc.edu
ABBOTT, Michael .... 518-320-1529. 341 C michael.abbott@suny.edu
ABBOTT, Mike .... 903-675-6393. 488 D abbott@tvcc.edu
ABBOTT, Patrick, W .... 512-223-7720. 466 I pabbott@austincc.edu
ABBOTT, Paula, J .... 308-254-7404. 293 E abbottp@wncc.edu
ABBOTT, Ruth .... 692-625-3394. 546 F
ABBOTT, Shawn, L .... 212-998-4584. 334 D shawn.abbott@nyu.edu
ABBOTT, Steve .... 507-786-3231. 264 B abbott@stolaf.edu
ABBOTT, Steven, W .... 207-581-1052. 212 B steven.abbott@maine.edu
ABBOTT, Thomas, E .... 207-621-3342. 212 C tabbott@maine.edu
ABBRUZZESE, John, A ... 570-422-3277. 428 D abbruzzese@po-box.esu.edu
ABBS, Guy .... 770-531-6305. 128 B gabbs@laniertech.edu
ABBUHL, James, M .... 330-569-5174. 380 I abbuhljm@hiram.edu
ABBY, Dean .... 617-332-3666. 233 D dean_abby@mspp.edu
ABDALLA, Wagida, A ..... 703-993-2826. 505 C wabdalla@gmu.edu
ABDALLAH, Blanche .... 651-690-6516. 263 O beabdallah@stkate.edu
ABDALLAH, Chaouki, T .. 505-277-2611. 312 F provost@unm.edu
ABDEL, Maria .... 305-474-6950. 112 F mabdel@stu.edu
ABDELAL, Ahmed .... 978-934-2635. 229 B Ahmed_Abdelal@uml.edu
ABDELKARIM, Shehadeh .... 216-687-6964. 377 F s.abdelkarim@csuohio.edu
ABDELLA, Stephen .... 716-338-1031. 327 J steveabdella@mail.sunyjcc.edu
ABDELRAHMAN, Mohamed .... 361-593-2809. 484 A mohamed.abdelrahman@tamuk.edu
ABDULLAH, Makala, M .. 386-481-2042... 99 C
ABEAR, Lichele .... 631-687-5158. 339 B labear@sjcny.edu
ABED, Donna, M .... 302-573-5430... 93 F dma@dtcc.edu
ABEGG, Robert, M .... 214-887-5321. 471 F babegg@dts.edu
ABEL, Dianna, K .... 801-626-6406. 497 D diannaabel@weber.edu
ABEL, Eileen .... 908-526-1200. 305 B eabel@raritanval.edu
ABEL, Jason, T .... 858-499-0202... 40 C jabel@coleman.edu
ABEL, Jeff .... 301-447-7437. 217 B abel@msmary.edu
ABEL, Kevin .... 561-803-2552. 110 B kevin_abel@pba.edu
ABEL, Richard, L .... 620-792-9333. 184 F abelr@bartonccc.edu
ABEL, Sean .... 408-298-2181... 63 P sean.abel@sjcc.edu
ABEL, Susan .... 513-745-3334. 393 H abel@xavier.edu
ABELA, Andrew, V .... 202-319-5290... 94 G abela@cua.edu
ABELA, Ella .... 918-663-9000. 398 L ellaa@plattcollege.org
ABELES, Robert .... 213-740-4611... 74 A rabeles@usc.edu
ABELES, Susan, K .... 310-794-8686... 71 C sabeles@finance.ucla.edu
ABELL, Carol .... 320-363-5511. 254 J cabell@csbsju.edu
ABELL, Carol .... 320-363-5511. 263 P abell@csbsju.edu
ABELL, Debbie .... 618-453-6727. 159 G kohley@siu.edu
ABELL, Donna .... 270-686-4575. 196 C donna.abell@kctcs.edu
ABELL, Mark .... 740-245-7370. 392 A mabell@rio.edu
ABELL, Martha .... 912-478-5111. 126 C martha@georgiasouthern.edu
ABELL, Russ .... 718-636-3684. 336 F rabell@pratt.edu
ABELL, Tracey .... 503-244-0726. 401 M traceyabell@achs.edu
ABELS, Eileen, G .... 617-521-2811. 236 G eileen.abels@simmons.edu
ABENT, Rita, E .... 724-738-2919. 429 F rita.abent@sru.edu
ABER, Suzanne .... 860-297-2525... 91 F suzanne.aber@trincoll.edu
ABERA, Hideki .... 949-480-4208... 66 F habera@soka.edu
ABERCROMBIE, Barbara, A .... 479-575-2159... 23 I barbaraa@uark.edu
ABERCROMBIE, Neil, N . 435-797-0258. 497 B neil.abercrombie@usu.edu
ABERNATHY, Cammy ..... 352-392-6000. 116 A caber@ufl.edu
ABERNATHY, Jeff .... 989-463-7146. 239 B abernathyj@alma.edu
ABERNATHY, Linda .... 636-481-3337. 275 I labernat@jeffco.edu
ABERNATHY, Sharon, A . 573-875-7360. 272 G saabernathy@ccis.edu
ABERNETHY, Michael ..... 813-974-3305. 116 C abernethy@usf.edu
ABERNETHY, William ..... 734-973-3488. 252 A bill@wccnet.edu
ABEYIE, Nana .... 212-650-6899. 317 D nana@ccny.cuny.edu
ABHOLD, Joseph, J .... 920-424-2061. 537 B abhold@uwosh.edu
ABIKO, Ken .... 415-575-6112... 31 D kabiko@ciis.edu
ABLES, Jim .... 740-587-6545. 379 D ables@denison.edu
ABLESER, Judith .... 248-370-2466. 248 J ableser@oakland.edu
ABNEY, Lisa .... 318-357-5361. 208 B abney@nsula.edu
ABNEY KORN, Karen ..... 937-294-0592. 388 M karenkorn@saa.edu
ABORN, Lucinda .... 562-860-2451... 37 I laborn@cerritos.edu
ABOUELENEIN, Baz .... 913-288-7668. 187 L baz@kckcc.edu
ABOUFADEL, Kathy .... 616-451-3511. 241 H kaboufadel@davenport.edu
ABOUSERHAL, Mike .... 216-987-4709. 378 D mike.abouserhal@tri-c.edu
ABOWITZ, Alexa .... 978-837-5150. 234 A abowitzc@merrimack.edu
ABPLANALP, Mike .... 570-484-2525. 429 B mabplanalp@lhup.edu
ABRAHAM, Doug .... 303-724-2000... 86 A doug.abraham@ucdenver.edu
ABRAHAM, Edward .... 336-716-1445. 370 D
ABRAHAM, Jennifer, S ... 215-576-0800. 431 E jabraham@rrc.edu
ABRAHAM, Jim .... 317-578-7353. 171 I
ABRAHAM, Karen, A ...... 505-277-5808. 312 F kabraham@unm.edu
ABRAHAM, Karen, E ...... 540-665-5520. 509 E kabraham@su.edu
ABRAHAM, Keshia, N .... 305-626-3157. 104 J Keshia.Abraham@fmuniv.edu
ABRAHAM, Lawrence, D 512-475-7000. 491 C l.abraham@austin.utexas.edu
ABRAHAM, Lorraine, N .. 276-944-6212. 504 H labraham@ehc.edu
ABRAHAM, Magdalene ... 662-246-6318. 268 B mabraham@msdelta.edu
ABRAHAM, Martin, A ..... 330-941-3009. 394 A martin.abraham@ysu.edu
ABRAHAM, Mercy .... 303-360-4788... 81 C mercy.abraham@ccaurora.edu
ABRAHAM, Nabeel .... 313-845-6460. 243 H nabraham@hfcc.edu
ABRAHAM, Paul .... 740-654-6711. 387 C abraham@ohio.edu
ABRAHAM, Philippe, J ... 518-437-4903. 341 D pabraham@albany.edu
ABRAHAM, Reed .... 662-246-6273. 268 B rabraham@msdelta.edu
ABRAHAM, Shondra, N .. 803-536-7013. 446 G sabraham@scsu.edu
ABRAHAM, Tekeste, B ... 570-662-4890. 429 C tabraham@mansfield.edu
ABRAHAM, Tracie .... 225-771-3590. 206 J tracie_abraham@subr.edu
ABRAHAMN, Keshia, N .. 305-626-3157. 104 J Keshia.Abraham@fmuniv.edu
ABRAHAMOWICZ, Dan .. 937-775-2808. 393 G dan.abrahamowicz@wright.edu
ABRAHAMS, Shayne, D . 317-466-2121. 167 B sdabrahams@indianatech.edu
ABRAHAMSON, David, P .... 414-277-7173. 534 G abrahams@msoe.edu
ABRAHAMSON, Duc ...... 248-689-8282. 251 I duc.abrahamson@walshcollege.edu
ABRAHAMSON, Kris ...... 707-521-7950... 65 B kabrahamson@santarosa.edu
ABRAHAMSON, Kyle ...... 208-459-5622. 138 A kabrahamson@collegeofidaho.edu
ABRAJANO, Barbara .... 312-939-0111. 144 D
ABRAM, Nadine .... 973-877-3275. 301 H shaw@essex.edu
ABRAMS, Albert, J .... 478-471-2722. 128 I albert.abrams@maconstate.edu
ABRAMS, Albert, J .... 478-471-2770. 128 I albert.abrams@maconstate.edu
ABRAMS, Andrew, L .... 843-377-2145. 441 G aabrams@charlestonlaw.edu
ABRAMS, Christopher, T 330-471-8273. 383 D cabrams@malone.edu
ABRAMS, Elizabeth .... 831-459-4188... 72 C esabrams@ucsc.edu
ABRAMS, Eve .... 315-568-3163. 333 C eabrams@nycc.edu
ABRAMS, Hal .... 503-768-7921. 403 K habrams@lclark.edu
ABRAMS, Nairobi .... 305-237-3240. 109 D nabrams@mdc.edu
ABRAMSON, Alan .... 401-841-3556. 545 A
ABRAMSON, Nancy .... 212-678-8036. 328 A naabramson@jtsa.edu
ABRAMSON, Robin .... 802-860-2729. 499 A abramson@champlain.edu
ABREU, Carlos, F .... 787-743-3038. 552 E cabreu@sanjuanbautista.edu
ABREU, Jonathan .... 212-752-1530. 328 G jonathan.abreu@limcollege.edu
ABREU, Sara .... 787-878-5475. 549 L sabreu@arecibo.inter.edu
ABREU-HORNBOSTEL, Esmilda, M .... 973-655-5114. 303 D abreue@mail.montclair.edu
ABRIOLA, Linda .... 617-627-3237. 237 C linda.abriola@tufts.edu
ABROMEIT, Jeanna .... 414-382-6084. 531 I jeanna.abromeit@alverno.edu
ABROMITIS, Barbara ...... 630-942-3020. 142 G abromitisb@cod.edu
ABRUSCATO, Tony .... 813-342-5601... 18 I tony.abruscato@phoenix.edu
ABSAR, Quaiser .... 540-665-4937. 509 E qabsar@su.edu
ABSHER, Keith .... 731-661-5361. 462 F kabsher@uu.edu
ABSHIRE, Paula .... 912-650-5687. 131 H pabshire@southuniversity.edu
ABSTON, Byron .... 205-391-2388..... 6 H babston@sheltonstate.edu
ABSTON, Kara .... 501-279-4442... 21 C kabston@harding.edu
ABT, Phyllis .... 970-204-8363... 81 N phyllis.abt@frontrange.edu
ABT, William, R .... 262-551-6200. 532 D wabt@carthage.edu
ABU-GHAZALEH, Nabil, S .... 310-287-4325... 52 F abughans@wlac.edu
ABUHAMAD, Alfred, Z ... 757-446-7979. 504 E abuhamaz@evms.edu
ABUKHALAF, Ronnie ...... 561-912-2166. 103 C rabukhalaf@evergladesuniversity.edu
ABUTIN, Albert .... 714-992-7076... 56 F aabutin@fullcoll.edu

ABUZNEID, Abdelshakour, A .... 203-576-4113... 91 G
abuzneid@bridgeport.edu
ACCAPADI, Mamta .... 407-646-2185. 111 Q
maccapadi@rollins.edu
ACCAPADI, Mamta .... 541-737-8748. 406 A
mamta.accapadi@oregonstate.edu
ACCARDI, Michael .... 978-837-5062. 234 A
accardim@merrimack.edu
ACCARDI, Theresa .... 516-323-3468. 331 J
taccardi@molloy.edu
ACCIARDO, Linda, A ...... 401-874-2116. 440 D
lindaa@advance.uri.edu
ACCOMANDO, Annette ... 504-278-6422. 203 F
aaccomando@nunez.edu
ACCORD, Richard, D ...... 304-462-4107. 529 G
richard.accord@glenville.edu
ACCORNERO, Chris .... 864-644-5294. 446 I
caccornero@swu.edu
ACEBO, Kayla .... 918-631-2565. 401 F
kayla-acebo@utulsa.edu
ACEVEDO, Beatriz .... 212-924-5900. 347 B
bursar@swedishinstitute.edu
ACEVEDO, Francisco ...... 787-264-1912. 551 A
facevedo@sg.inter.edu
ACEVEDO, Gladys .... 787-891-0925. 549 K
gacevedo@aguadilla.inter.edu
ACEVEDO, Glorivee .... 787-738-2161. 554 C
glorivee.rosario@upr.edu
ACEVEDO, Ivonne .... 787-891-0925. 549 K
iaecheva@ns.inter.edu
ACEVEDO, Jorge .... 787-850-9380. 554 D
jorge.acevedo4@upr.edu
ACEVEDO, Luis .... 787-250-1912. 550 E
laacevedo@metro.inter.edu
ACEVEDO-RIOS, Carmen 787-725-6500. 547 H
cacevedo@albizu.edu
ACEVES, William, C .... 619-239-0391... 36 D
waceves@cwsl.edu
ACHARYA, Suresh .... 269-749-7666. 249 A
sacharya@olivetcollege.edu
ACHEMIRE, Roy .... 918-293-4724. 398 B
roy.achemire@okstate.edu
ACHENBACH, USMS, Gerard .... 231-995-1203. 248 B
gachenbach@nmc.edu
ACHENBACH, Laurie .... 618-453-7984. 159 G
laurie@micro.siu.edu
ACHESON, Carol .... 503-253-3443. 405 E
cacheson@ocom.edu
ACHING, Gerard, L .... 607-255-4625. 322 A
gla23@cornell.edu
ACHS, Carol .... 480-461-7742... 15 A
carol.achs@mmesacc.edu
ACHTER, John .... 715-232-2468. 538 B
achterj@uwstout.edu
ACHTERBERG, Cheryl, L 614-292-2461. 386 E
achterberg.1@osu.edu
ACHTERMAN, Douglas ... 408-848-4809... 45 F
dachterman@gavilan.edu
ACIERNO, Lou .... 212-752-1530. 328 G
lou.acierno@limcollege.edu
ACK, Nicole .... 360-867-5371. 519 J
ackn@evergreen.edu
ACKER, Don .... 724-339-7542. 425 B
dacker@nbi.edu
ACKERKNECHT, Steven, M .... 518-255-5214. 344 E
ackerksm@cobleskill.edu
ACKERLEY, Roseanne ..... 513-487-3234. 325 G
rackerley@huc.edu
ACKERMAN, Debbie .... 217-732-3155. 151 C
dackerman@lincolncollege.edu
ACKERMAN, Deborah ..... 503-253-3443. 405 E
dackerman@ocom.edu
ACKERMAN, Denise .... 845-758-7625. 314 D
ackerman@bard.edu
ACKERMAN, Eric .... 954-262-2063. 109 K
esa@nova.edu
ACKERMAN, Judy .... 240-567-5010. 216 F
judy.ackerman@montgomerycollege.edu
ACKERMAN, Kate .... 617-217-9225. 222 G
kackerman@baystate.edu
ACKERMAN, Kathy .... 828-395-1522. 361 C
kackerman@isothermal.edu
ACKERMAN, Mary .... 320-762-4673. 257 O
marya@alextech.edu
ACKERMAN, Traci .... 954-492-5353. 100 A
ackerman@citycollege.edu
ACKERMANN, Arthur, J .. 314-935-5582. 284 L
ackermann@wustl.edu
ACKLAND, Terri .... 520-494-5227... 12 P
terri.ackland@centralaz.edu
ACKLEY, Brian .... 607-844-8222. 347 I
ackleyb@TC3.edu
ACKLEY, Darren .... 715-675-3331. 541 A
ackley@ntc.edu
ACKLEY, Lavon .... 229-430-0415. 120 A
lackley@albanytech.edu
ACOB-NASH, Mari .... 206-934-7804. 522 I
mari.acob-nash@seattlecolleges.edu
ACORACE, Joan .... 603-206-8012. 296 A
jacorace@ccsnh.edu
ACOSTA, Araceli .... 210-924-4338. 467 E
araceli.acosta@bua.edu
ACOSTA, Christy .... 312-226-6294. 151 A
ACOSTA, Esmeralda .... 623-845-3012... 14 M
esmeralda.acosta@gccaz.edu
ACOSTA, Jesse .... 903-566-7044. 492 D
jacosta@uttyler.edu
ACOSTA, Jesus .... 915-779-8031. 494 C
jacosta@computercareercenter.com
ACOSTA, Lydia, M .... 954-262-4640. 109 K
lacosta@nova.edu
ACOSTA, Pilar .... 407-708-2432. 113 E
acostap@seminolestate.edu
ACOSTA, R. Alexander .... 305-348-1118. 115 B
ACOSTA, Reynold .... 407-303-8016... 97 H
reynold.acosta@adu.edu
ACOSTA, Sylvia, Y .... 915-747-8533. 492 A
syacosta3@utep.edu
ACOSTA-FUMERO, Carmen, J .... 787-841-2000. 552 B
cacosta@pucpr.edu
ACQUAAH, George .... 301-860-3610. 220 A
gacquaah@bowiestae.edu
ACREE, Elizabeth, A .... 520-621-3432... 18 F
acree@email.arizona.edu
ACREE, Jenny .... 785-243-1435. 185 M
jacree@cloud.edu
ACREY, Autry .... 903-730-4890. 474 O
autry.acrey@jarvis.edu
ACTON, Anne .... 617-422-7282. 235 B
aacton@nesl.edu
ACTON, James .... 561-297-3057. 114 L
jacton2@fau.edu
ACTON, James .... 312-567-5000. 147 F
jacton@iit.edu
ACTOR, Lisa .... 801-832-2731. 498 F
lactor@westminstercollege.edu
ACUESTA, Sylvia .... 718-636-3750. 336 F
sacuesta@pratt.edu
ACUNA, Matt .... 714-556-3610... 74 D
foundersclerk@vanguard.edu
ADACHI, Lesley, B .... 680-488-2471. 547 B
lbadachi@gmail.com
ADACHI, Themy .... 510-430-3285... 54 F
themy@mills.edu
ADADE, Anthony .... 508-929-8714. 230 G
aadade@worcester.edu
ADADEVOH, Vidal .... 205-453-6300... 96 F
ADAIR, Adam .... 870-512-7801... 20 B
adam_adair@asun.edu
ADAIR, Russell, K .... 203-432-4469... 93 A
russell.adair@yale.edu
ADAIR, Wendy, H .... 713-313-7455. 485 F
adairw@tsu.edu
ADALIAN, Paul .... 541-552-6833. 406 C
adalianp@sou.edu
ADAM, Audrey .... 508-286-5839. 238 B
adam_audrey@wheatonma.edu
ADAM, Baba .... 530-895-2987... 30 F
adamba@butte.edu
ADAM, Charles, A .... 563-333-6151. 182 B
AdamCharlesA@sau.edu
ADAM, Don .... 512-313-3000. 469 L
don.adam@concordia.edu
ADAM, Johnna .... 309-794-7578. 139 L
johnnaadam@augustana.edu
ADAMES, Jose .... 845-431-8954. 323 C
Jose.adames@sunydutchess.edu
ADAMO, Clare .... 860-632-3009... 90 C
library@holyapostles.edu
ADAMO, Paul, J .... 607-436-2535. 343 E
adamopj@oneonta.edu
ADAMS, Adam .... 870-759-4142... 25 K
aadams@wbcoll.edu
ADAMS, Amy .... 614-236-6242. 375 H
adams@capital.edu
ADAMS, Andrea .... 434-582-2681. 506 I
ahepburn@liberty.edu
ADAMS, Ann .... 312-503-0054. 155 D
a-adams@northwestern.edu
ADAMS, Ann .... 541-917-4353. 404 B
adamsa@linnbenton.edu
ADAMS, Ann .... 360-438-4382. 522 G
aadams@stmartin.edu
ADAMS, Ann Clay .... 404-687-4524. 123 C
adamsa@ctsnet.edu
ADAMS, Anthony, T .... 334-229-5176..... 1 D
anthony-adams@alasu.edu
ADAMS, Barbara, B .... 847-866-3939. 145 E
barbara.adams@garrett.edu
ADAMS, Barresa .... 850-526-2761... 99 N
stantong@chipola.edu
ADAMS, Beth .... 218-855-8186. 258 B
badams@clcmn.edu
ADAMS, Betty .... 713-797-7000. 482 F
bnadams@pvamu.edu
ADAMS, Billy .... 254-647-3234. 478 H
badams@rangercollege.edu
ADAMS, Brett, C .... 443-352-4250. 218 E
bcadams@stevenson.edu
ADAMS, Bridgett .... 229-217-4148. 129 F
badams@moultrietech.edu
ADAMS, Brittany .... 909-599-5433... 50 J
badams@lifepacific.edu
ADAMS, Carey .... 912-344-2589. 120 G
carey.adams@armstrong.edu
ADAMS, Carol, J .... 314-968-6907. 284 N
caroladams05@webster.edu
ADAMS, Cathryn .... 972-860-8269. 470 H
cadams@dcccd.edu
ADAMS, Chadd .... 205-665-6155..... 9 B
cadams3@montevallo.edu
ADAMS, Chris .... 573-840-9428. 282 K
cadams@trcc.edu
ADAMS, Christopher, J .. 631-451-4118. 346 E
adamsc@sunysuffolk.edu
ADAMS, Cynthia .... 620-365-5116. 183 I
adams@allencc.edu
ADAMS, Dana .... 773-508-8077. 151 H
dadams2@luc.edu
ADAMS, David, R .... 626-584-5462... 45 E
dadams@fuller.edu
ADAMS, Dean .... 270-384-8036. 197 D
adamsd@lindsey.edu
ADAMS, DeAnna .... 901-843-3885. 458 E
registrar@rhodes.edu
ADAMS, Debbie .... 423-697-2493. 460 C
ADAMS, Denise .... 530-895-2329... 30 F
adamsde@butte.edu
ADAMS, Dennis, R .... 865-694-6448. 461 D
dadams@pstcc.edu
ADAMS, Don .... 210-485-0088. 464 I
dadams@alamo.edu
ADAMS, Elisa .... 617-578-7100. 236 E
eadams@sbboston.com
ADAMS, Elizabeth, T .... 818-677-2969... 34 C
elizabeth.t.adams@csun.edu
ADAMS, Ellen .... 718-631-6269. 319 D
eadams@qcc.cuny.edu
ADAMS, Gary .... 218-733-2005. 259 A
g.adams@lsc.edu
ADAMS, Gary .... 972-241-3371. 470 E
gadams@dallas.edu
ADAMS, Grantley .... 860-738-6333... 89 C
gadams@nwcc.commnet.edu
ADAMS, Guy .... 916-789-8600... 47 C
guy_adams@heald.edu
ADAMS, J. Milton .... 434-924-3728. 511 B
jma@virginia.edu
ADAMS, Jacob .... 909-607-3318... 39 C
jacob.adams@cgu.edu
ADAMS, Jamele .... 781-736-3600. 224 F
jadams@brandeis.edu
ADAMS, James, E .... 325-942-2071. 465 K
james.adams@angelo.edu
ADAMS, James, J .... 909-599-5433... 50 J
jjadams@lifepacific.edu
ADAMS, JR., James, P .. 859-257-6654. 200 C
j.p.adams@uky.edu
ADAMS, Jan .... 903-510-3287. 488 E
jada@tjc.edu
ADAMS, Jane, A .... 352-392-4574. 116 A
jane-adams@ufl.edu
ADAMS, Janieth .... 601-979-0928. 267 E
janieth.f.wilson_adams@jsums.edu
ADAMS, Jason .... 303-762-6936... 81 G
jason.adams@denverseminary.edu
ADAMS, Jeff .... 479-788-7221... 24 A
jeff.adams@uafs.edu
ADAMS, Jeffrey, M .... 336-841-4581. 355 C
jeadams@highpoint.edu
ADAMS, Jeffrey, R .... 717-872-3703. 429 D
jeffrey.adams@millersville.edu
ADAMS, Jennifer .... 925-439-2181... 42 A
jadams@losmedanos.edu
ADAMS, Jennifer .... 315-792-7810. 346 C
jennifer.adams@sunyit.edu
ADAMS, Jennifer .... 614-236-6170. 375 H
jadams@capital.edu
ADAMS, Jimmy .... 409-839-2014. 486 E
jimmy.adams@lit.edu
ADAMS, Joe .... 601-856-5400. 267 B
jadams@holmescc.edu
ADAMS, John .... 570-662-4000. 429 C
jadams@mansfield.edu
ADAMS, John .... 512-313-3000. 469 L
john.adams@concordia.edu
ADAMS, Josh .... 707-527-4492... 65 B
jadams@santarosa.edu
ADAMS, Julie .... 973-655-7067. 303 D
adamsju@mail.montclair.edu
ADAMS, Karen .... 785-242-5200. 189 I
karen.adams@ottawa.edu
ADAMS, Karen .... 918-495-7163. 398 H
kaadams@oru.edu
ADAMS, Karen, H .... 812-856-5596. 167 E
kadams@indiana.edu
ADAMS, Katherine .... 601-974-1124. 267 I
adamska@millsaps.edu
ADAMS, Keith .... 318-345-9266. 203 C
kadams@ladelta.edu
ADAMS, Kelly, L .... 315-792-3047. 349 F
kadams@utica.edu
ADAMS, Ken .... 814-453-6016. 434 G
ADAMS, Kent .... 620-672-5641. 190 A
kenta@prattcc.edu
ADAMS, Kevin .... 718-270-6050. 319 A
kadams@mec.cuny.edu
ADAMS, Kim .... 815-394-4376. 157 C
KAdams@rockford.edu
ADAMS, Kim .... 800-422-2418... 99 A
kadams@baymedical.org
ADAMS, Kimberly .... 325-942-2122. 465 K
kadams15@angelo.edu
ADAMS, LaVerne .... 731-668-7240. 464 F
laverne.adams@wtbc.edu
ADAMS, Lesley .... 315-781-3671. 326 C
ladams@hws.edu
ADAMS, Linda .... 706-379-3111. 134 L
leadams@yhc.edu
ADAMS, Linda .... 610-738-3892. 430 A
ladams@wcupa.edu
ADAMS, Lisa .... 678-839-6428. 133 I
ladams@westga.edu
ADAMS, Lisa .... 413-565-1000. 222 F
ladams@baypath.edu
ADAMS, Lita .... 413-748-3695. 236 I
ladams@springfieldcollege.edu
ADAMS, Lu .... 417-255-7976. 278 F
luadams@missouristate.edu
ADAMS, Mack .... 575-527-7550. 311 B
madams@nmsu.edu
ADAMS, Mark .... 936-294-1158. 487 A
ucs_mca@shsu.edu
ADAMS, Mary, A .... 303-991-1575... 78 D
mary.adams@americansentinel.edu
ADAMS, Melvin .... 207-255-1305. 212 F
melvin.adams@maine.edu
ADAMS, Merrill .... 505-566-3371. 311 I
adamsm@sanjuancollege.edu
ADAMS, Michael, J .... 888-777-7675. 519 K
mjadams@faithseminary.edu
ADAMS, Michelle .... 773-291-6359. 142 D
madams@ccc.edu
ADAMS, Molly-Dodd ...... 352-588-8291. 112 D
molly-dodd.adams@saintleo.edu
ADAMS, N. Scott .... 828-669-8012. 357 H
nadams@montreat.edu
ADAMS, Natasha, A .... 302-857-6009... 93 C
nadams@desu.edu
ADAMS, Neale, J .... 515-574-1284. 179 D
adams_n@iowacentral.edu
ADAMS, Patrick .... 516-876-3194. 343 D
adamsp@oldwestbury.edu
ADAMS, Paul, S .... 570-408-4114. 437 F
paul.adams@wilkes.edu
ADAMS, Perrie, M .... 214-648-2258. 493 E
perrie.adams@utsouthwestern.edu
ADAMS, Phillip, D .... 912-358-3059. 131 C
adamsp@savannahstate.edu
ADAMS, Randall .... 202-885-8664... 97 D
radams@wesleyseminary.edu
ADAMS, Regine .... 425-739-8389. 520 K
regine.adams@lwtech.edu
ADAMS, Richard, E .... 212-749-2802. 330 A
radams@msmnyc.edu
ADAMS, Ricky .... 334-244-3930..... 2 A
radams7@aum.edu
ADAMS, Rita, S .... 618-393-2982. 146 H
adamsr@iecc.edu
ADAMS, Robert .... 575-492-2597. 310 G
radams@nmjc.edu
ADAMS, Robert, H .... 501-569-3202... 24 B
rhadams@ualr.edu
ADAMS, Robert, J .... 386-226-6119. 102 B
robert.adams@erau.edu
ADAMS, Rodney .... 843-525-8219. 447 C
radams@tcl.edu
ADAMS, Ruth, L .... 206-281-2548. 523 C
radams@spu.edu
ADAMS, Sarah .... 618-252-5400. 159 E
sarah.adams@sic.edu
ADAMS, Sarah .... 414-297-6595. 540 E
adamss@matc.edu
ADAMS, Shawn .... 404-627-2681. 121 H
shawn.adams@beulah.org
ADAMS, Sheila, V .... 662-329-7299. 268 E
sadams@nsgslp.muw.edu
ADAMS, Shirley, M .... 860-515-3836... 87 I
sadams@charteroak.edu
ADAMS, Stephen .... 229-732-5943. 120 D
stephenadams@andrewcollege.edu
ADAMS, Stephen .... 413-572-5394. 230 F
sadams@westfield.ma.edu
ADAMS, Susan, B .... 817-257-7926. 484 I
s.adams@tcu.edu
ADAMS, Susanne, H .... 910-755-7302. 358 D
adamss@brunswickcc.edu
ADAMS, Tammy .... 254-647-3234. 478 H
tadams@rangercollege.edu

ADAMS, Tila .... 401-277-4909. 440 A
madams@risd.edu
ADAMS, Tracy, R .... 205-853-1200..... 5 B
tadams@jeffstateonline.com
ADAMS, Vic .... 606-242-0416. 196 F
vic.adams@kctcs.edu
ADAMS, Vickie .... 256-782-5006..... 4 K
vadams@jsu.edu
ADAMS, William, D .... 207-859-4604. 209 J
wadams@colby.edu
ADAMS COWES, Sheila . 810-762-9532. 244 Q
sadams@kettering.edu
ADAMS-DUNFORD,
Jane .... 828-227-7234. 369 E
jdunford@wcu.edu
ADAMS-GASTON,
Javaune .... 614-292-9334. 386 E
adams-gaston.1@osu.edu
ADAMSKI, Kathleen .... 509-527-4240. 524 H
kathleen.adamski@wwcc.edu
ADAMSKI, M. Patricia ..... 516-463-6800. 326 D
patricia.adamski@hofstra.edu
ADAMSON, Bonnie, J ..... 910-630-7192. 356 H
adamson@methodist.edu
ADAMSON, Liz .... 432-264-5608. 473 E
ladamson@howardcollege.edu
ADAMSON, Richard .... 320-363-3164. 263 P
radamson@csbsju.edu
ADAMSPERRY, Stacy ..... 610-796-8221. 409 E
stacy.adamsperry@alvernia.edu
ADAMUS, Anne M, G ..... 248-204-2208. 245 I
aadamus@ltu.edu
ADAMUS LIOTTA,
Sheila, M .... 401-865-2600. 439 E
sadamus@providence.edu
ADANU, Sesime .... 610-399-2053. 428 B
sadanu@cheyney.edu
ADARKWA, Joshua .... 510-261-8500... 58 G
joshua.adarkwa@patten.edu
ADAUTO, III, Ricardo .... 915-747-5555. 492 A
radauto@utep.edu
ADCOX, Gary .... 615-333-3344. 457 N
gadcox@national-college.edu
ADCOX, Kathy, S .... 252-451-8274. 362 D
kadcox@nashcc.edu
ADCOX, William .... 713-792-2275. 492 E
william.adcox@uth.tmc.edu
ADDERLEY, Cedric .... 614-236-6204. 375 H
cadderley@capital.edu
ADDINGTON, Eric, J ...... 218-299-3010. 255 A
eaddingt@cord.edu
ADDINGTON, Gary .... 719-384-6859... 83 M
gary.addington@ojc.edu
ADDISON, Jennifer, D .... 276-739-2458. 514 D
jaddison@vhcc.edu
ADDISON, Lynn .... 912-583-3285. 122 B
laddison@bpc.edu
ADDISON, Steve .... 501-450-3199... 25 H
saddison@uca.edu
ADDISON REID,
Barbara .... 617-349-8507. 228 B
baddison@lesley.edu
ADDLEMAN, John .... 717-766-2511. 423 L
jaddlema@messiah.edu
ADDY, Cathryn, L .... 860-255-3601... 89 G
caddy@txcc.commnet.edu
ADEBIYI, Songie .... 708-596-2000. 159 C
sadebiyi@ssc.edu
ADEGBOYE, David, S ..... 504-286-5327. 206 K
dadegboye@suno.edu
ADEGOKE, Nancy .... 718-429-6600. 349 H
nancy.adegoke@vaughn.edu
ADEKOLA, Abel .... 715-232-1325. 538 B
adekolaa@uwstout.edu
ADELAINE, Michael .... 605-688-4988. 452 B
michael.adelaine@sdstate.edu
ADELANI, Lateef .... 314-340-3319. 275 A
adelanil@hssu.edu
ADELBERG, Robert .... 718-261-5800. 315 F
radelberg@bramsonort.edu
ADELMAN, Michael, D ... 304-647-6200. 530 B
madelman@osteo.wvsom.edu
ADELSBERG, Lester .... 504-762-3224. 203 A
ladels@dcc.edu
ADELSPERGER, Donna ... 219-989-2436. 171 N
adelsper@purduecal.edu
ADEN-FOX, Nancy .... 402-472-4344. 292 I
naden1@unl.edu
ADER, Elaine .... 916-558-2062... 53 D
adere@scc.losrios.edu
ADERA, Rosette, B .... 570-941-6645. 436 A
rosette.adera@scranton.edu
ADERA, Tilahuan .... 575-646-2810. 310 I
tadera@nmsu.edu
ADERHOLD, Mary .... 770-537-5719. 134 H
mary.aderhold@westgatech.edu
ADERO, Chad .... 301-846-2531. 214 H
cadero@frederick.edu
ADESIDA, Ilesanmi .... 217-244-4545. 162 A
iadesida@illinois.edu
ADEWUMI, Michael, A ... 814-863-4030. 426 A
m2a@psu.edu
ADEWUYI, David, A .... 804-257-5742. 515 F
daadewuyi@vuu.edu
ADEY, Penelope, S .... 518-388-6109. 348 J
adeyp@union.edu
ADEYANJU, Matthew ...... 231-591-2324. 242 F
Matthew_Adeyanju@ferris.edu
ADKINS, Cathy, L .... 828-689-1395. 356 F
cadkins@mhc.edu
ADKINS, Deborah .... 417-269-8910. 273 D
daadkin@coxcollege.edu
ADKINS, Ernest .... 480-517-8202... 15 D
ernest.adkins@riosalado.edu
ADKINS, Kay .... 606-326-2043. 194 J
kay.adkins@kctcs.edu
ADKINS, Marc .... 440-826-2768. 374 F
madkins@bw.edu
ADKINS, Michael .... 602-275-7133... 17 L
michael.adkins@rsiaz.edu
ADKINS, Michael, T .... 804-257-5752. 515 F
mtadkins@vuu.edu
ADKINS, Robert .... 724-503-1001. 436 G
radkins@washjeff.edu
ADKINS, Sheldon .... 405-425-5250. 397 D
sheldon.adkins@oc.edu
ADKINSON, Stacy, J ...... 260-399-7700. 174 C
sadkinson@sf.edu
ADKISON, Linda .... 816-654-7313. 275 K
ladksion@kcumb.edu
ADKISON, Stephen .... 541-962-3511. 405 H
sadkison@eou.edu
ADLEMAN, Rick .... 970-248-1525... 79 F
radleman@coloradomesa.edu
ADLER, Brian .... 610-758-3375. 422 A
bla212@lehigh.edu
ADLER, Brian, D .... 580-774-3063. 400 B
brian.adler@swosu.edu
ADLER, Brian, U .... 229-928-1361. 126 D
brian.adler@gsw.edu
ADLER, Charles, M .... 240-895-4343. 218 A
cladler@smcm.edu
ADLER, Jackie .... 254-867-3620. 486 B
jackie.adler@tstc.edu
ADLER, Robert .... 801-581-3791. 496 Q
robert.adler@law.utah.edu
ADLER, Shmuel .... 773-463-7738. 160 H
sadler@telshe.edu
ADLER, Stephen, J .... 860-444-8255. 545 G
stephen.j.adler@uscg.mil
ADLER, Steven .... 858-534-1709... 71 F
sadler@ucsd.edu
ADLER, Wendy .... 508-541-1542. 225 F
wadler@dean.edu
ADLEY, Jerald .... 662-254-3636. 269 A
jerald.adley@mvsu.edu
ADLING, Jennifer .... 806-742-3844. 487 D
jennifer.adling@ttu.edu
ADORNO, Margaret .... 909-621-8147... 60 A
margaret.adorno@pomona.edu
ADORNO, Victor, T .... 787-780-0070. 547 G
vadorno@caribbean.edu
ADOVASIO, James, M ..... 814-824-2545. 423 J
jadovasio@mercyhurst.edu
ADRIAN, Janet .... 913-360-7117. 184 H
jadrian@benedictine.edu
ADRIAN, Loretta, P .... 714-241-6152... 39 I
ladrian@coastline.edu
ADRIANO, Jonalee .... 707-638-5259... 69 K
jonalee.adriano@tu.edu
ADUKAITIS, Megan .... 610-796-8225. 409 E
mega.adukaitis@alvernia.edu
ADWELL, Jack .... 217-875-7200. 156 J
jadwell@richland.edu
ADY, Tina .... 254-526-1903. 468 G
martina.ady@ctcd.edu
AEILTS, Larry .... 734-973-3480. 252 A
laeilts@wccnet.edu
AELION, C. Marjorie ...... 413-545-2526. 228 F
maelion@schoolph.umass.edu
AESCHLIMANN,
Rodney, L .... 775-784-1113. 294 J
rod@admin.edu
AFDAHL, Gordon .... 812-535-5125. 172 F
gafdahl@smwc.edu
AFDAHL, Tami .... 307-532-8206. 542 a
tami.afdahl@ewc.wy.edu
AFFENITO, Sandra .... 860-231-5769... 92 F
saffenito@usj.edu
AFFLECK, Mary Ann .... 860-906-5010... 88 D
maffleck@ccc.commnet.edu
AFFLECK-GRAVES,
John, F .... 574-631-4700. 174 A
affleck-graves.1@nd.edu
AFGHANI, Carmen .... 407-708-2044. 113 E
afghanic@seminolestate.edu
AFIELD, W. Edward .... 239-687-5303... 98 J
weafield@avemarialaw.edu
AFROOKHTEH, Afshin ..... 714-816-0366... 70 A
afshin.afrookhteh@trident.edu
AFSAHI, Armin .... 858-534-3902... 71 F
aafsahi@ucsd.edu
AFTON-BACKLUND,
Lee Ann, M .... 931-598-1238. 458 H
lafton@sewanee.edu
AGA, Daniel, F .... 684-699-1575. 546 A
d.aga@amsamoa.edu
AGAFONOV, Alexander ... 718-522-9073. 314 B
agafonov@asa.edu
AGAR, John, R .... 610-359-5082. 414 D
jagar@dccc.edu
AGARWAL, Anupam .... 205-996-6670..... 8 E
agarwal@uab.edu
AGARWAL, Vaibhav .... 574-631-0946. 174 A
vagarwal@nd.edu
AGARWAL, Vijendra .... 507-389-5998. 259 G
vijendra.agarwal@mnsu.edu
AGATHA, Rachelle .... 760-591-3012. 118 I
ragatha@usa.edu
AGAZZI, David .... 847-543-2631. 143 A
dagazzi@clcillinois.edu
AGBARAJI, Casmir .... 505-786-4113. 310 D
cagbaraji@navajotech.edu
AGBAYANI, Amefil .... 808-956-4567. 136 B
agbayani@hawaii.edu
AGBOOLA, Isaac .... 202-651-5224... 95 C
isaac.agboola@gallaudet.edu
AGEE, Doug, A .... 636-584-6714. 273 M
daagee@eastcentral.edu
AGEE, Patty, A .... 660-263-3900. 272 A
pagee@cccb.edu
AGEE, Steve .... 405-208-5276. 397 F
sagee@okcu.edu
AGER, Christina .... 215-572-2115. 409 H
ager@arcadia.edu
AGESILAS, Elie .... 787-891-0925. 549 K
eagesilas@aguadilla.inter.edu
AGGERS, Steve .... 310-287-4513... 52 F
aggerss@wlac.edu
AGGREH, Julia .... 215-951-2990. 430 E
aggrehj@philau.edu
AGHA-JAFFAR, Tamara .. 913-288-7689. 187 L
taghajaf@kckcc.edu
AGHO, Austin, O .... 317-274-4702. 168 D
aagho@iupui.edu
AGJMURATI, Nick .... 212-592-2000. 340 H
nagjmurati@sva.edu
AGNE, Anissa .... 904-620-2698. 116 B
anissa.agne@unf.edu
AGNELLO-VAZQUEZ,
Jacqueline .... 914-633-2548. 327 C
jagnellovazquwz@iona.edu
AGNESE, JR., Louis, J ... 210-829-3900. 490 A
agnese@uiwtx.edu
AGNETTA, Daniel .... 269-471-3302. 243 G
agnetta@andrews.edu
AGNETTA, Daniel, E .... 269-471-3302. 239 D
agnetta@andrews.edu
AGNEW, Alice .... 814-824-2362. 423 J
aagnew@mercyhurst.edu
AGNEW, Donna .... 847-578-8316. 157 F
donna.agnew@rosalindfranklin.edu
AGNEW, F. Raymond ...... 518-327-6317. 336 B
ragnew@paulsmiths.edu
AGNEW, Ina .... 918-293-4761. 398 B
ina.agnew@okstate.edu
AGNEW, Robyn, R .... 864-379-8701. 443 F
ragnew@erskine.edu
AGNEW, Scott .... 701-224-5597. 372 B
scott.agnew@bismarckstate.edu
AGNO, Malvin .... 415-955-2036... 26 L
AGNOSTAK, Harry, M .... 848-932-3929. 306 A
harry.agnostak@rutgers.edu
AGO, Emmanuel .... 718-862-7996. 329 M
emmanuel.ago@manhattan.edu
AGOSTA, Frank .... 212-592-2000. 340 H
fagosta@sva.edu
AGOSTA, William .... 814-472-3035. 432 D
wagosta@francis.edu
AGOSTO, Elvia .... 787-728-1515. 555 D
eagosto@sagrado.edu
AGOURIS, Peggy .... 703-993-1362. 505 C
pagouris@gmu.edu
AGRAS, James, R .... 412-359-1000. 434 H
jagras@triangle-tech.edu
AGRAS, James, R .... 412-359-1000. 434 G
AGRAS, James, R .... 412-359-1000. 434 I
jagras@triangle-tech.edu
AGRAS, Rudy, K .... 412-359-1000. 434 G
AGRAWAL, C. Mauli ...... 210-458-6859. 492 C
mauli.agrawal@utsa.edu
AGRAWAL, Gail, B .... 319-335-9034. 175 I
gail-agrawal@uiowa.edu
AGRAWAL, Jagdish .... 510-885-3291... 33 C
jagdish.agrawal@csueastbay.edu
AGRE-KIPPENHAN,
Susan .... 503-883-2409. 404 A
sagreki@linfield.edu
AGRELA, Ramona .... 949-824-5962... 71 B
ragrela@uci.edu
AGUADO-WARE,
Joan, C .... 414-229-4304. 537 A
aguadowa@uwm.edu
AGUAYO, Modesto .... 787-728-1515. 555 D
maguayo@sagrado.edu
AGUE, Paul, E .... 619-201-8701... 62 B
Paul.Ague@sdcc.edu
AGUIAR, Aracely .... 310-287-4238... 52 F
aguiara@wlac.edu
AGUIAR, Jenny .... 508-541-1519. 225 F
jaguiar@dean.edu
AGUILA, Nayda, G .... 617-964-1100. 222 A
naguila@ants.edu
AGUILAR, Alisha .... 909-748-8047... 73 H
alisha_aguilar@redlands.edu
AGUILAR, Carmen .... 508-678-2811. 231 B
carmen.aguilar@bristolcc.edu
AGUILAR, Cheryl, M ...... 909-607-1232... 39 D
cheryl.aguilar@cmc.edu
AGUILAR, Greg .... 309-794-8275. 139 L
gregaguilar@augustana.edu
AGUILAR, Hector .... 512-223-7663. 466 I
haguilar@austincc.edu
AGUILAR, Jose, A .... 951-827-3878... 71 E
jose.aguilar@ucr.edu
AGUILAR, Margie .... 915-842-0422. 474 B
AGUILAR, Milagros .... 787-878-6000. 549 D
maguilar@icprjc.edu
AGUILAR, Steven .... 956-721-5361. 475 F
steven.aguilar@laredo.edu
AGUILERA, Rafael .... 806-894-9611. 480 H
raguilera@southplainscollege.edu
AGUILLARD, Joe .... 318-487-7401. 202 F
joe.aguillard@lacollege.edu
AGUINALDO, Teresa ...... 847-543-2288. 143 A
com401@clcillinois.edu
AGUIRRE, Arturo .... 213-487-0110... 42 K
info@dula.edu
AGUIRRE, Carlos .... 210-486-4951. 464 J
caguirre57@alamo.edu
AGUIRRE, Ilvis .... 787-878-5475. 549 L
iaguirre@arecibo.inter.edu
AGUIRRE, Juan Carlos ... 956-872-6782. 480 I
jcaguirre@southtexascollege.edu
AGUIRRE, Ray .... 408-270-6468... 63 O
ray.aguirre@sjeccd.edu
AGUIRRE, Ricardo .... 787-728-1515. 555 D
raguirre@sagrado.edu
AGUIRRE, Richard .... 574-535-7571. 166 A
rraguirre@goshen.edu
AGUIRRE, Thomas .... 505-277-3361. 312 F
doso@unm.edu
AGUIRRE, Tina .... 760-355-6347... 48 A
tina.aguirre@imperial.edu
AGUIRRE-ACUNA, Maria 325-235-7349. 486 C
maria.aguirre@tstc.edu
AGUIRRE BATTY,
Mercedes .... 307-674-6446. 543 F
mbatty@sheridan.edu
AGUNDEZ, Adrian .... 661-763-7737... 69 D
aagundez@taftcollege.edu
AGUSTA, Diana .... 802-860-2733. 499 A
agusta@champlain.edu
AHEARN, Michael, J ...... 978-867-4004. 226 H
michael.ahearn@gordon.edu
AHEDO, Valentina .... 608-246-6461. 540 C
vahedo@madisoncollege.edu
AHERN, Carrie, A .... 605-256-5663. 451 H
carrie.ahern@dsu.edu
AHERN, Jack .... 413-545-2710. 228 F
jfa@ipo.umass.edu
AHERN, Joseph, F .... 845-758-7178. 314 D
ahern@bard.edu
AHERN, Martin .... 617-984-1635. 235 I
mahern@quincycollege.edu
AHERN, Michael .... 620-227-9359. 186 B
mfahern@dc3.edu
AHERN, Tim .... 319-208-5247. 182 G
tahern@scciowa.edu
AHERNE, John .... 845-341-4710. 335 H
john.aherne@sunyorange.edu
AHLBAUM, Mitch .... 212-772-4946. 318 C
mahlbaum@hunter.cuny.edu
AHLBURG, Dennis, A ..... 210-999-8401. 488 C
dennis.ahlburg@trinity.edu
AHLEMANN, Tina .... 843-574-6142. 447 E
tina.ahlemann@tridenttech.edu
AHLQUIST, Michelle .... 320-762-4918. 257 O
michellea@alextech.edu
AHMAD, Maria .... 765-455-9203. 168 A
activities@iuk.edu
AHMADI, Goodarz .... 315-268-6446. 320 A
ahmadi@clarkson.edu
AHMED, Andrea .... 520-383-8401... 18 B
aahmed@tocc.cc.az.us
AHMED, Haseeb .... 419-448-2284. 380 G
hahmed@heidelberg.edu
AHMED, Ismael .... 313-593-5030. 251 D
inahmed@umich.edu
AHMED, Juzar .... 812-465-7160. 174 D
juzar@usi.edu

AHMED, M. Monir ... 909-537-3139... 34 E
AHMED, Mirza, F ... 313-496-2674. 252 B fahmed1@wcccd.edu
AHMED, Mustaq ... 419-358-3237. 374 J ahmedm@bluffton.edu
AHMED, Shariq ... 909-748-8352... 73 H shariq_ahmed@redlands.edu
AHMED, Zahir ... 573-986-6863. 282 B zahmed@semo.edu
AHN, Hee Young ... 323-731-2383... 57 I president@psuca.edu
AHN, Karen ... 213-385-2322... 77 A karenahn@wmu.edu
AHN, Kelly ... 718-862-8000. 329 M kelly.ahn@manhattan.edu
AHN, Young Jin ... 714-533-1495... 66 H admission@southbaylo.edu
AHNER, Yolanda ... 915-831-7724. 472 B yahner@epcc.edu
AHO, Duane ... 906-487-7349. 242 G duane.aho@finlandia.edu
AHO, Lynn ... 906-353-4602. 245 A laho@kbocc.org
AHOLA, Scott ... 605-642-6359. 451 G scott.ahola@bhsu.edu
AHORRIO, Beatriz ... 212-694-1000. 315 E bahorrio@boricuacollege.edu
AHRENS, Jennifer ... 478-240-5143. 129 H jahrens@oftc.edu
AICINENA, Steve ... 432-552-2675. 493 D aicinena_s@utpb.edu
AIKEN, Deborah, J ... 401-825-2100. 439 A daiken@ccri.edu
AIKEN, George ... 415-433-9200... 65 C gaiken@saybrook.edu
AIKEN, Katherine ... 208-885-6448. 139 D provost@uidaho.edu
AIKEN, Katherine, G ... 208-885-6426. 139 D kaiken@uidaho.edu
AIKEN, Ryan ... 413-775-1309. 231 E aikenr@gcc.mass.edu
AILSTOCK, M. Stephen ... 410-777-2230. 213 D smailstock@aacc.edu
AIMONE, Chris ... 812-877-8498. 172 C aimone@rose-hulman.edu
AINLAY, Stephen, C ... 518-388-6101. 348 J ainlays@union.edu
AINLEY, Arden ... 360-416-7716. 523 G arden.ainley@skagit.edu
AINSLEIGH, Susan ... 413-565-1000. 222 F sainsleigh@baypath.edu
AINSLEY, Sharon ... 610-647-4400. 418 I sainsley@immaculata.edu
AINSLIE, Carolyn, N ... 609-258-1447. 304 E ainslie@princeton.edu
AINSWORTH, Emma, L .. 662-685-4771. 266 C eainsworth@bmc.edu
AINSWORTH, Jerald ... 423-425-4666. 463 D jerald-ainsworth@utc.edu
AINSWORTH, Jerald ... 423-425-4633. 463 D jerald-ainsworth@utc.edu
AINSWORTH, Jerry ... 618-634-3396. 158 M jerrya@shawneecc.edu
AINSWORTH, Patricia ... 978-542-6446. 230 E painsworth@salemstate.edu
AIREN, Osaro ... 936-468-1073. 482 A aireno@sfasu.edu
AIREY, Patricia, J ... 540-985-8376. 506 G pjairey@jchs.edu
AIROZO, Paul ... 508-830-5051. 230 D pairozo@maritime.edu
AITCHISON, Cecile ... 207-780-4708. 212 H caitchison@usm.maine.edu
AITSON-ROESSLER, Mechelle ... 405-733-7308. 399 F maitson-roessler@rose.edu
AIZENSTAT, Stephen ... 805-969-3626... 57 K saizenstat@pacifica.edu
AJE, John ... 609-984-1100. 308 A
AJI, Aron, R ... 563-333-6053. 182 B AjiAronR@sau.edu
AJIROTUTU, Cheryl, S ... 414-229-3038. 537 A yinka@uwm.edu
AKAJUOBI, Cajetan ... 334-229-4316..... 1 D cakajuobi@alasu.edu
AKAKPO, Koffi ... 419-755-4702. 385 D kakakpo@ncstatecollege.edu
AKANDE, Benjamin, O ... 314-968-5951. 284 N akandeb@webster.edu
AKBASHEVA, Bela ... 770-394-8300. 120 H spatilla@aii.edu
AKCHIN, Lisa, G ... 410-455-2889. 219 D akchin@umbc.edu
AKE, Barbara ... 505-566-3218. 311 I akeb@sancollege.edu
AKENS, Cathy ... 305-919-5943. 115 B akens@fiu.edu
AKENS, Jeff ... 916-388-2800... 36 G jakens@carrington.edu
AKERMAN, Kate ... 617-217-9006. 222 G kakerman@baystate.edu
AKERMAN, Patricia ... 320-308-5966. 261 C pakerman@sctcc.edu
AKERS, Judy ... 276-326-4260. 502 H
AKERS, Lex, A ... 309-677-2721. 140 I lakers@bradley.edu
AKERS, Mary Anne ... 443-885-3225. 217 A maryanne.akers@morgan.edu
AKERS, Richard ... 304-327-4181. 529 D rakers@bluefieldstate.edu
AKERS, Shawn, D ... 434-592-5451. 506 I sdakers@liberty.edu
AKERSON, Joni ... 320-308-6158. 261 C jakerson@sctcc.edu
AKEY, Stacey, L ... 920-923-7652. 534 A sakey@marianuniversity.edu
AKHAVI, Seyed ... 212-594-4000. 347 H sakhavi@tricollege.edu
AKHAVI, Seyed ... 315-792-5469. 331 I sakhavi@mvcc.edu
AKIE, Ronald, E ... 617-928-4790. 234 E reakie@mountida.edu
AKIN, Daniel, L ... 919-761-2222. 366 I dakin@sebts.edu
AKIN, Hudson ... 765-285-1633. 164 B hakin@bsu.edu
AKIN, Jamie ... 325-942-2116. 465 K jamie.akin@angelo.edu
AKIN, Joeleen ... 404-471-6133. 119 I jakin@agnesscott.edu
AKIN, Renea ... 270-534-3461. 196 G renea.akin@kctcs.edu
AKIN-SITKA, Becky ... 972-241-3371. 470 E rakin-sitka@dallas.edu
AKINKUOYE, Nicholas ... 415-239-3000... 38 L nakinkuoye@ccsf.edu
AKINLEYE, Johnson, O .. 910-962-3876. 369 C akinleyej@uncw.edu
AKINS, Erick ... 210-486-2778. 465 B eakins@alamo.edu
AKINS, Richie ... 912-478-5393. 126 C rakins@georgiasouthern.edu
AKKAWI, Kayed ... 312-935-6025. 156 K kakkawi@robertmorris.edu
AKL, Fred, A ... 610-499-4036. 437 E faakl@widener.edu
AKL, Hatem ... 732-255-0400. 304 A hakl@ocean.edu
AKMAN, Jeffrey, S ... 202-741-2880... 95 D akman@gwu.edu
AKOJIE, Patricia, A ... 270-686-4200. 192 G patricia.akojie@brescia.edu
AKRIDGE, Jay, T ... 765-494-8391. 171 M akridge@purdue.edu
AKST JONES, Ellen ... 641-472-7000. 180 N eajones@mum.edu
AKSU, Mert ... 313-994-6620. 250 K aksumn@udmercy.edu
AL-AMIN, John ... 925-229-6942... 41 J jalamin@4cd.edu
AL-ASSAF, Yousef ... 585-475-2411. 337 L ymacad@rit.edu
AL-HAZZAM DAWASARI, Elizabeth ... 480-860-2700... 13 Q edawsari@taliesin.edu
ALADE, Ayodele, J ... 410-651-6327. 219 E ajalade@umes.edu
ALAIMO, Joseph ... 570-408-4512. 437 F joseph.alaimo@wilkes.edu
ALAIMO, Kathleen ... 773-298-3090. 158 E alaimo@sxu.edu
ALAIMOANA-NUUSA, Repeka ... 684-699-9155. 546 A r.nuusa@amsamoa.edu
ALAM, Maria ... 901-678-2867. 460 B malam@memphis.edu
ALAM, Mohammad ... 212-220-1299. 317 A malam@bmcc.cuny.edu
ALAMI, Osama ... 804-827-7474. 511 F oalami@vcu.edu
ALAMPI, Janet ... 860-512-2813... 88 G jalampi@manchestercc.edu
ALANDER, Link ... 832-813-6842. 476 A link.s.alander@lonestar.edu
ALANGAR, Sadhana ... 734-929-9089. 241 A sadhana@cleary.edu
ALARCIO, Rebecca ... 805-922-6966... 26 K ralarcio@hancockcollege.edu
ALARID, Jandee ... 409-772-9868. 493 C jalarid@utmb.edu
ALASIO, Claire ... 732-571-3463. 303 C calasio@monmouth.edu
ALAWIYE, Osman ... 320-308-3023. 261 B oalawiye@stcloudstate.edu
ALBANESE, Karli ... 909-599-5433... 50 J kalbanese@lifepacific.edu
ALBANESE, Linda ... 516-323-4025. 331 J lalbanese@molloy.edu
ALBANESE, Marc ... 610-282-1100. 414 F marc.albanese@desales.edu
ALBANO, John ... 209-386-6777... 54 D albano.j@mccd.edu
ALBANO, Ralph ... 202-319-5218... 94 G albano@cua.edu
ALBANO, Stephen, D ... 609-984-1100. 308 A salbano@tesc.edu
ALBANO, Thomas ... 219-785-5307. 172 A talbano@pnc.edu
ALBARRAN, Agustin ... 619-644-7161... 46 E agustin.albarran@gcccd.edu
ALBARRAN, Charo ... 707-864-7122... 66 G charo.albarran@solano.edu
ALBAYYARI, J ... 260-481-6391. 168 C albayyaj@ipfw.edu
ALBEE, David ... 415-257-1308... 42 J david.albee@dominican.edu
ALBERDESON, Jane ... 787-815-0000. 553 I jane.alberdeson@upr.edu
ALBERICO, Ralph, A ... 540-568-3828. 506 F alberira@jmu.edu
ALBERS, Jhett ... 605-642-6885. 451 G jhett.albers@bhsu.edu
ALBERS, Mia ... 605-455-6016. 450 I malbers@olc.edu
ALBERT, Angelique ... 406-275-4820. 288 C angelique_albert@skc.edu
ALBERT, Barbara, J ... 570-326-3761. 427 B balbert@pct.edu
ALBERT, David ... 860-768-4482... 92 D dalbert@hartford.edu
ALBERT, Eric ... 847-566-6401. 162 G ealbert@usml.edu
ALBERT, Gene ... 516-773-5000. 545 H albertg@usmma.edu
ALBERT, George ... 412-291-6313. 410 B galbert@aii.edu
ALBERT, J, L ... 404-413-4519. 126 E jalbert@gsu.edu
ALBERT, Joe ... 509-313-3564. 520 A albert@gonzaga.edu
ALBERT, Juline ... 712-274-6400. 183 G juline.albert@witcc.edu
ALBERT, Karen ... 215-951-2847. 430 E albertk@philau.edu
ALBERT, Katrice ... 612-624-0594. 264 G ka225@umn.edu
ALBERT, Laurie ... 919-508-2025. 370 F lalbert@peace.edu
ALBERT, Louis ... 520-206-6752... 17 A lalbert@pima.edu
ALBERT, Marianne ... 724-222-5330. 425 K malbert@penncommercial.edu
ALBERT, Nancy ... 304-214-8852. 528 G nalbert@wvncc.edu
ALBERT, OP, Peg ... 517-264-7000. 250 B palbert@sienaheights.edu
ALBERT, Rachel, E ... 207-834-7510. 212 E realbert@maine.edu
ALBERT, Rita ... 561-237-7231. 108 X ralbert@lynn.edu
ALBERT, Robert ... 606-783-5158. 198 A r.albert@moreheadstate.edu
ALBERT-GREEN, DeEadra ... 512-313-3000. 469 L deeadra.green@concordia.edu
ALBERT-KNOPP, Heather ... 207-801-5640. 210 A halbert-Knopp@coa.edu
ALBERT LINK, Cindy ... 617-266-1400. 223 D
ALBERTA, Richard ... 415-282-7600... 27 L richardalberta@actcm.edu
ALBERTELLI, Denise ... 718-409-4946. 346 D dalbertelli@sunymaritime.edu
ALBERTO, Paul, A ... 404-413-8100. 126 E palberto@gsu.edu
ALBERTS, David ... 724-938-4324. 428 A alberts@calu.edu
ALBERTS, Eugene, R ... 608-796-3849. 539 E eralberts@viterbo.edu
ALBERTS, Kristin, R ... 904-256-7180. 107 Q kalbert@ju.edu
ALBERTS, Trev ... 402-554-2305. 293 A talberts@unomaha.edu
ALBERTSON, Eugene ... 336-887-3000. 355 N ealbertson@laureluniversity.edu
ALBERTSON, Kay, H ... 919-735-5151. 364 H kha@waynecc.edu
ALBERTSON, Ron ... 503-517-7421. 407 E ron.albertson@reed.edu
ALBIN, Martha ... 918-456-5511. 396 H albinml@nsuok.edu
ALBIN-HILL, Jill ... 708-524-6980. 144 C jalbin@dom.edu
ALBINA, Adam, R ... 603-641-7266. 297 G aalbina@anselm.edu
ALBINI, Marisa ... 401-333-7150. 439 A malbini@ccri.edu
ALBINSON, Erik ... 319-399-8843. 176 G ealbinson@coe.edu
ALBINSON, Erik ... 319-399-8741. 176 G ealbinso@coe.edu
ALBISTON, Steve, K ... 208-524-3000. 138 D steven.albiston@my.eitc.edu
ALBON, Darrell, J ... 740-368-3070. 387 J djalbon@owu.edu
ALBORS BIGAS, Jaime, L ... 787-725-6500. 547 H jalbors@pfizer.com
ALBRECHT, Bryan, D ... 262-564-3000. 540 A albrechtb@gtc.edu
ALBRECHT, Catherine ... 419-772-2130. 386 D c-albrecht@onu.edu
ALBRECHT, Christal, M .. 904-381-3410. 105 E christal.albrecht@fscj.edu
ALBRECHT, Daniel ... 408-278-4343... 76 J dalbrecht@jessup.edu
ALBRECHT, Don ... 361-825-2612. 483 F don.albrecht@tamucc.edu
ALBRECHT, James, M ... 253-535-7317. 521 I albrecjm@plu.edu
ALBRECHT, Jana ... 309-438-2231. 147 J jlalbre2@ilstu.edu
ALBRECHT, Jon ... 813-257-3375. 118 L jalbrecht@ut.edu
ALBRECHT, Shauna ... 406-265-3711. 287 D albrecht@msun.edu
ALBRECHT, Stan, L ... 435-797-7172. 497 B stan.albrecht@usu.edu
ALBRIGHT, Bev ... 815-455-8676. 152 F balbright@mchenry.edu
ALBRIGHT, Geri ... 205-929-6315..... 5 D galbright@lawsonstate.edu
ALBRIGHT, Ken ... 530-895-2298... 30 F albrightke@butte.edu
ALBRIGHT, Mike ... 845-341-4728. 335 H mike.albright@sunyorange.edu
ALBRIGHT, Thomas ... 601-979-2580. 267 E thomas.e.albright@jsums.edu
ALBRINCK, Jill ... 630-515-4526. 144 A jalbrinck@devry.edu
ALBRINCK, Margaret, L .. 920-565-1290. 533 R albrinckm@lakeland.edu
ALBRITTON, Rosie, L ... 936-261-1510. 482 F rlalbritton@pvamu.edu
ALBRITTON, Sheila ... 423-697-4710. 460 C
ALBURCHER, Ronald ... 650-723-2300... 68 E
ALBURY, Mark ... 802-485-2305. 500 A malbury@norwich.edu
ALBUS, Alana, M ... 484-664-3170. 424 H aalbus@muhlenberg.edu
ALCAINO, Ricardo ... 805-893-4504... 72 B ricardo.alcaino@oeo.ucsb.edu
ALCALA, Celena ... 310-287-4244... 52 F alcalac@wlac.edu
ALCALA, Juana, J ... 406-243-2049. 286 H juana.alcala@umontana.edu
ALCOCK, Sherry, B ... 563-387-1862. 180 M alcock@luther.edu
ALCORN, Charles ... 361-570-4354. 489 E alcornc@uhv.edu
ALCORN, Gena ... 309-341-5327. 141 A galcorn@sandburg.edu
ALCORTA, Joe, H ... 325-670-1594. 472 O jalcorta@hsutx.edu
ALCRUDO, Lourdes ... 787-622-8000. 553 E lalcrudo@pupr.edu
ALDAMA, Ben ... 479-986-6939... 22 C baldama@nwacc.edu
ALDARONDO, Aixa ... 787-766-1717. 552 J aialdarondo@suagm.edu
ALDAY, Katherine, E ... 770-423-6290. 127 N kalday@kennesaw.edu
ALDEN, Alison ... 617-253-6512. 233 B
ALDEN, Michael, F ... 573-882-2055. 283 C aldenm@missouri.edu
ALDEN, III, Raymond, W ... 815-753-0493. 154 I ralden@niu.edu
ALDENDERFER, Mark, S 209-228-7742... 71 D maldenderfer@UCMerced.edu
ALDER, William ... 304-647-6203. 530 B walder@osteo.wvsom.edu
ALDERMAN, Charles, W 334-844-6406..... 1 G aldercw@auburn.edu
ALDERMAN, Norman, M 863-667-5129. 113 P nmalderman@seu.edu
ALDERMAN, Pamela, L .. 304-896-7302. 528 F pamela.alderman@southernwv.edu
ALDERMAN, Richard ... 713-743-2100. 489 B alderman@uh.edu
ALDERMAN, Steve ... 713-646-1812. 480 J salderman@stcl.edu
ALDERSON, Diane ... 810-762-9770. 244 Q dalderso@kettering.edu
ALDERSON, Philip, O ... 314-977-9801. 281 I palderso@slu.edu
ALDERSON, Ynez ... 432-552-2795. 493 D alderson_y@utpb.edu
ALDERTON, Karen, S ... 814-371-6920. 415 C mainc@dbcollege.edu
ALDRETE, Christina ... 210-486-3733. 465 A caldrete@alamo.edu
ALDRICH, Adrian, M ... 630-637-5201. 154 F amaldrich@noctrl.edu

ALDRICH, Allison, S .... 315-268-6590. 320 A
aldricas@clarkson.edu
ALDRICH, B.J .... 907-474-7043... 10 I
bjaldrich@alaska.edu
ALDRICH, Kimberly, J .... 269-337-7302. 244 K
Kim.Aldrich@kzoo.edu
ALDRICH, Maria .... 704-894-2113. 353 J
maaldrich@davidson.edu
ALDRICH, Michael .... 808-675-3851. 135 C
michael.aldrich@byuh.edu
ALDRIDGE, Dale .... 229-225-5293. 132 D
daldridge@southwestgatech.edu
ALDRIDGE, Doug .... 417-626-1234. 279 J
aldridge.doug@occ.edu
ALDRIDGE, Gary .... 229-225-5293. 132 D
galdridge@southwestgatech.edu
ALDRIDGE, Jim .... 706-385-1050. 130 F
jim.aldridge@point.edu
ALDRIDGE, R. Mark ...... 817-202-6355. 481 E
aldridge@swau.edu
ALDRIDGE, Shelley .... 859-253-3637. 194 A
shelley.aldridge@frontier.edu
ALDRIDGE, Susan .... 501-760-4204... 22 A
saldridge@npcc.edu
ALDRIDGE, Terrance ...... 803-536-7757. 446 G
taldridge@scsu.edu
ALDRIDGE, William, D ... 202-885-8686... 97 D
caldridge@wesleyseminary.edu
ALEEM, Marsha .... 229-333-5954. 134 B
mlaleem@valdosta.edu
ALEJANDRO, Agustin, C 830-591-7215. 481 C
acalejandro@swtjc.edu
ALEJANDRO, Juan .... 254-710-3867. 467 G
juan_alejandro@baylor.edu
ALEMAN, Jorge .... 650-493-4430... 66 E
jorge.aleman@sofia.edu
ALEMU, Katiso .... 334-874-5700..... 3 A
kalemu@ccal.edu
ALESCH, Karen .... 920-831-4397. 539 K
alesch@fvtc.edu
ALESH, Tammy .... 719-632-7626... 82 J
talesh@intellitec.edu
ALESSANDRO, Lisa .... 216-221-8584. 392 G
lisaalessand@vmcad.edu
ALEWINE, Jerry .... 864-941-8536. 446 C
alewine.j@ptc.edu
ALEX-ASSENSOH, Yvette 541-346-3175. 406 D
yalex@uoregon.edu
ALEXANDER, A. Donna .. 804-758-6704. 513 G
dalexander@rappahannock.edu
ALEXANDER, Adrian, W . 918-631-2356. 401 F
adrian-alexander@utulsa.edu
ALEXANDER, SJ,
Andrew, F .... 402-280-2779. 289 D
alexa@creighton.edu
ALEXANDER, Anthony .... 660-359-3948. 279 H
aalexander@mail.ncmissouri.edu
ALEXANDER, Ashley ..... 718-390-3304. 350 B
ashley.alexander@wagner.edu
ALEXANDER, Bertha, P .. 813-974-2393. 116 C
bertha@admin.usf.edu
ALEXANDER, Beth, A ..... 317-940-6378. 164 J
balexand@butler.edu
ALEXANDER, Brenda ...... 325-649-8045. 473 F
balexander@hputx.edu
ALEXANDER, Bruce .... 315-786-2364. 327 L
balexander@sunyjefferson.edu
ALEXANDER, Bruce, D ... 203-432-8611... 93 A
bruce.alexander@yale.edu
ALEXANDER, Bryant, K .. 310-338-7430... 53 E
bryant.alexander@lmu.edu
ALEXANDER, Carol .... 701-349-5776. 373 A
carolalexander@trinitybiblecollege.edu
ALEXANDER, Charlene ... 765-285-5466. 164 B
calexander@bsu.edu
ALEXANDER, Charles .... 803-536-7017. 446 G
calexander@scsu.edu
ALEXANDER,
Christine, D .... 717-291-4168. 416 J
christine.alexander@fandm.edu
ALEXANDER, Chuck .... 510-841-9230... 77 B
calexander@wi.edu
ALEXANDER, Cindy .... 864-294-3324. 444 C
cindy.alexander@furman.edu
ALEXANDER, Colins .... 256-726-8471..... 6 B
calexander@oakwood.edu
ALEXANDER, Dana, C .... 805-565-6237... 76 D
dalexand@westmont.edu
ALEXANDER, David .... 208-282-3234. 138 E
alexdav2@isu.edu
ALEXANDER, David, C ... 208-467-8521. 139 A
president@nnu.edu
ALEXANDER, Debra .... 989-328-1276. 247 D
debraj@montcalm.edu
ALEXANDER, Dona .... 508-531-2622. 229 D
dona.alexander@bridgew.edu
ALEXANDER, Donna .... 330-494-6170. 389 F
dalexander@starkstate.edu
ALEXANDER, Donna, R .. 813-253-6272. 118 L
dalexander@ut.edu
ALEXANDER, Eugene ..... 516-561-0050. 316 B
ALEXANDER, Eva .... 501-786-7367... 19 J
eva.alexander@arkansasbaptist.edu
ALEXANDER, F. King ..... 225-578-2111. 204 N
ALEXANDER, Fred .... 601-977-7813. 270 A
falexander@tougaloo.edu
ALEXANDER, George ...... 239-590-7045. 115 A
galexand@fgcu.edu
ALEXANDER, Grace .... 680-488-2471. 547 B
gracea@palau.edu
ALEXANDER,
Gwendolyn .... 620-341-5203. 186 D
galexan1@emporia.edu
ALEXANDER, J Neil .... 931-598-1288. 458 H
jnalexan@sewanee.edu
ALEXANDER, Jacklan ..... 305-626-3718. 104 J
Jacklan.Alexander@fmuniv.edu
ALEXANDER, Janet .... 706-295-6321. 125 C
jalexand@highlands.edu
ALEXANDER, Jay .... 908-835-2329. 308 G
jayalex@warren.edu
ALEXANDER, Jennifer .... 361-593-2793. 484 A
jennifer.alexander@tamuk.edu
ALEXANDER, Jenny .... 414-288-7362. 534 B
jenny.alexander@marquette.edu
ALEXANDER, Jill .... 973-748-9000. 299 F
jill_alexander@bloomfield.edu
ALEXANDER, John .... 847-491-8100. 155 D
j-alexander8@md.northwestern.edu
ALEXANDER, Juan .... 502-597-6813. 197 A
juan.alexander@kysu.edu
ALEXANDER, Karen .... 252-335-0821. 359 F
karen_alexander@albemarle.edu
ALEXANDER, Karen .... 276-223-4702. 514 F
kalexander@wcc.vccs.edu
ALEXANDER, Karla, K ..... 260-399-7700. 174 C
kalexander@sf.edu
ALEXANDER, Kevin, L .... 714-449-7450... 67 D
kalexander@scco.edu
ALEXANDER, Kim .... 206-934-6660. 523 A
kim.alexander@seattlecolleges.edu
ALEXANDER, Kim .... 828-395-1759. 361 C
kalexander@isothermal.edu
ALEXANDER, Kimberly ... 570-484-2955. 429 B
kalexand@lhup.edu
ALEXANDER, King .... 225-578-2111. 204 O
alexander@lsu.edu
ALEXANDER, Laura .... 217-206-7148. 161 E
lalex5@u8is.edu
ALEXANDER, Laurie .... 409-933-8482. 469 E
lalexander@com.edu
ALEXANDER, Lex .... 336-272-7102. 354 E
lex.alexander@greensboro.edu
ALEXANDER, Lynn, M ..... 731-881-7490. 463 E
lalexand@utm.edu
ALEXANDER,
M. Christopher .... 704-894-2337. 353 J
chalexander@davidson.edu
ALEXANDER, Marijo .... 507-433-0606. 260 I
malexand@riverland.edu
ALEXANDER, Mary .... 615-514-2787. 457 P
admissions@nossi.edu
ALEXANDER, Maurine .... 680-488-3036. 547 B
maurinea@palau.edu
ALEXANDER, Michael, B 617-243-2221. 227 K
malexander@lasell.edu
ALEXANDER,
Michael, D .... 601-635-2111. 266 H
malexander@eccc.edu
ALEXANDER, Michelle ... 940-552-6291. 493 F
malexander@vernoncollege.edu
ALEXANDER, Otis .... 903-593-8311. 485 A
oalexander@texascollege.edu
ALEXANDER, P. Paul ...... 617-541-5386. 232 G
palexander@rcc.mass.edu
ALEXANDER, Pati .... 817-531-4214. 488 A
palexander@txwes.edu
ALEXANDER, Paul .... 701-349-5444. 373 A
paulalexander@trinitybiblecollege.edu
ALEXANDER, Paul, H ..... 714-879-3901... 47 K
palexander@hiu.edu
ALEXANDER, Pearl .... 404-894-0300. 125 D
pearl.alexander@ohr.gatech.edu
ALEXANDER, Peter .... 336-334-5789. 369 A
p_alexan@uncg.edu
ALEXANDER, Peter, C .... 260-422-5561. 167 B
pcalexander@indiantech.edu
ALEXANDER, Rachel .... 337-521-8913. 203 I
rachel.alexander@southlouisiana.edu
ALEXANDER, Renee, T ... 607-255-3693. 322 A
rta3@cornell.edu
ALEXANDER, Robert .... 601-974-1062. 267 I
robert.alexander@millsaps.edu
ALEXANDER, Ross .... 765-973-8318. 167 G
roscalex@iue.edu
ALEXANDER, Sanquita ... 334-291-4996..... 2 H
sanquita.alexander@cv.edu
ALEXANDER, Seth .... 617-253-4900. 233 B
ALEXANDER, Shawn .... 602-383-8228... 18 E
ALEXANDER,
Sheldon, H .... 919-761-2217. 366 I
salexander@sebts.edu
ALEXANDER, Sherry .... 918-343-7867. 399 C
salexander@rsu.edu
ALEXANDER, Sheryl .... 650-949-6149... 44 M
alexandersheryl@fhda.edu
ALEXANDER, State .... 704-216-6067. 356 D
salexan@livingstone.edu
ALEXANDER, State, W .... 704-216-6067. 356 D
salexan@livingstone.edu
ALEXANDER, Susan, L ... 651-962-6031. 265 C
slalexander@stthomas.edu
ALEXANDER,
Suzanne, T .... 410-334-2900. 221 D
salexander@worwic.edu
ALEXANDER, Terry .... 404-527-4536. 122 E
talexander@carver.edu
ALEXANDER, Theodore .. 314-977-8843. 281 I
talexander@slu.edu
ALEXANDER, Thomas, L 570-577-3216. 411 A
t.alexander@bucknell.edu
ALEXANDER, Tiffany ...... 252-985-5137. 365 D
talexander@ncwc.edu
ALEXANDER, Walter .... 256-372-4871..... 1 A
walter.alexander@aamu.edu
ALEXANDER, William ..... 205-226-4736..... 2 C
walexand@bsc.edu
ALEXANDER, William ..... 305-443-9170. 112 A
ALEXANDER, William, B 215-898-7021. 435 B
wba2@upenn.edu
ALEXANDER, Willie .... 954-201-7471... 99 D
walexand@broward.edu
ALEXANDER, Yvonne ...... 501-370-5271... 22 F
yalexander@philander.edu
ALEXANDER-HARVEY,
Annie .... 863-784-7104. 113 G
annie.alexander-harvey@southflorida.edu
ALEXANDER-LEWIS,
Sandi .... 812-866-6101. 166 C
alexanderlewis@hanover.edu
ALEXANDER-WALLACE,
Linda .... 718-518-4432. 318 B
lalexander@hostos.cuny.edu
ALEXANDERSON,
Sara, C .... 716-839-8200. 322 E
sara.alexanderson@daemen.edu
ALEXANDROU, Cyprian . 315-858-0450. 326 E
cyprian@hts.edu
ALEXIOU, Mildred .... 845-398-4310. 340 A
malexiou@stac.edu
ALEXIS, Eloise .... 404-270-5040. 132 E
ealexis@spelman.edu
ALEXIS, Marnelle .... 312-922-1884. 152 C
malexis@maccormac.edu
ALEXO, Kenneth .... 973-408-3067. 301 C
kalexojr@drew.edu
ALFANO, Michael, C ...... 212-998-4090. 334 D
michael.alfano@nyu.edu
ALFANO, Michael, P ...... 860-832-2102... 87 K
malfano@ccsu.edu
ALFANO, Renee, M .... 608-243-4539. 540 C
ralfano@madisoncollege.edu
ALFARO, Fela .... 214-860-2454. 470 J
falfaro@dcccd.edu
ALFARO, Jose .... 561-732-4424. 112 G
jalfaro@svdp.edu
ALFARO, Vanessa .... 305-222-2812. 103 L
valfaro@careercollege.edu
ALFERNESS, Rod .... 805-893-7789... 72 B
alferness@engineering.ucsb.edu
ALFIE, Rebeca .... 305-642-4104. 111 C
ALFIERI, Linda, L .... 315-255-1743. 316 D
alfieri@cayuga-cc.edu
ALFONSO, August .... 361-698-1300. 471 G
aalfonso@delmar.edu
ALFONSO, Jorge .... 305-821-3333. 105 A
jalfonso@fnu.edu
ALFONSO, Peter .... 401-874-4576. 440 D
peteralfonso@uri.edu
ALFONSO, Vincent .... 509-313-3444. 520 A
alfonso@gonzaga.edu
ALFORD, Bobby, R .... 713-798-5906. 467 F
balford@bcm.edu
ALFORD, Deborah .... 618-235-2700. 160 A
deborah.alford@swic.edu
ALFORD, Frederick .... 860-297-2157... 91 F
frederick.alford@trincoll.edu
ALFORD, Marie .... 562-985-8403... 33 F
malford@csulb.edu
ALFORD, Mike, J .... 972-860-8146. 470 H
mja3320@dcccd.edu
ALFORD, Randall, L .... 321-674-8080. 104 H
rlalford@fit.edu
ALFORD, Sara .... 972-899-8414. 477 I
salford@nctc.edu
ALFORD, Tarome .... 413-748-3508. 236 I
talford@springfieldcollege.edu
ALFRED, Tangelia .... 323-241-5333... 52 C
alfredtm@lasc.edu
ALFRED, Valarie .... 256-362-4489..... 7 F
valfred@talladega.edu
ALFULTIS, Michael .... 860-405-9010... 92 A
michael.alfultis@uconn.edu
ALGER, Jonathan, R .... 540-568-6868. 506 F
algerjr@jmu.edu
ALGIER, Anne-Marie .... 585-275-9390. 349 C
anne-marie.algier@rochester.edu
ALGORRI NAVARRO,
Jose .... 787-744-1060. 551 J
jalgorri@mechtech.edu
ALGOZINE, Jan, L .... 920-686-6192. 536 A
Jan.Algozine@sl.edu
ALI, Abe .... 661-336-5141... 49 M
abeali@kccd.edu
ALI, Aneesah .... 773-702-5671. 161 B
aali@uchicago.edu
ALI, Hesham .... 402-554-2380. 293 A
hali@unomaha.edu
ALI, Masoom .... 516-572-7113. 332 C
masoom.ali@ncc.edu
ALI, Mohammad .... 937-376-6235. 376 E
mail@centralstate.edu
ALI, Nicholas, D .... 412-531-4433. 414 C
info@deantech.edu
ALI, Noorjhan .... 847-679-3135. 149 G
nali@ksi.edu
ALI, Raagini .... 650-543-3722... 54 C
rali@menlo.edu
ALI, Richard, D .... 412-531-4433. 414 C
info@deantech.edu
ALI, Rita .... 309-694-5561. 146 E
rali@icc.edu
ALI, Yasmin .... 718-951-2407. 317 C
yali@brooklyn.cuny.edu
ALIBERTI, Fred .... 518-629-7210. 326 G
f.aliberti@hvcc.edu
ALIBRANDI, Cynthia, A .. 315-445-4462. 328 F
alibraca@lemoyne.edu
ALIC, Mersiha .... 260-203-2914. 173 E
alicm@trine.edu
ALICANDRO, Jean .... 860-832-1664... 87 K
alicandro@ccsu.edu
ALICEA, Carlos, N .... 787-279-1912. 550 B
calicea@bayamon.inter.edu
ALICEA, Dennis .... 787-743-7979. 552 I
ut_dalicea@suagm.edu
ALICEA, Edwin .... 787-725-8120. 548 O
ealicea@eap.edu
ALICEA, Jennifer .... 787-844-8181. 555 A
jennifer.alicea@upr.edu
ALICEA, Jose .... 617-541-5307. 232 G
jalicea@rcc.mass.edu
ALICEA, Joseph .... 718-518-4377. 318 B
jalicea@hostos.cuny.edu
ALICEA, Marisa .... 312-362-8772. 143 H
malicea@depaul.edu
ALICEA, Priscilla .... 401-232-6715. 438 K
palicea@bryant.edu
ALICEA, Victor, G .... 212-694-1000. 315 E
valicea@boricuacollege.edu
ALICEA-MALDONADO,
Rafael .... 585-345-6820. 325 C
ralicea-maldonado@genesee.edu
ALIG, Julie .... 978-934-2506. 229 B
Julie_Alig@uml.edu
ALISHIO, Kip, C .... 513-529-4634. 384 G
alishikc@miamioh.edu
ALIX, Jeff .... 419-289-5093. 374 C
jalix@ashland.edu
ALKIRE, Garry, R .... 308-635-6032. 293 E
galkire@wncc.edu
ALKIRE, Laurie, A .... 308-635-6036. 293 E
alkirel@wncc.edu
ALKIRE, Leonica .... 701-854-8005. 372 J
leonicaa@sbci.edu
ALLADA, Venkata .... 573-341-4573. 284 A
allada@mst.edu
ALLAN, Bill .... 316-295-5891. 186 H
ballan@friends.edu
ALLAN, Carol .... 413-265-2289. 225 C
allanc@elms.edu
ALLAN, Linda .... 412-809-5100. 430 H
allan.linda@pti.edu
ALLAN, Mark .... 215-951-1395. 420 B
allanm@lasalle.edu
ALLAN, Peter .... 760-245-4271... 75 B
peter.allan@vvc.edu
ALLAN-LINDBLOM,
Ronald .... 412-392-8101. 431 B
rlindblom@pointpark.edu
ALLARD, Don .... 919-761-2310. 366 I
dallard@sebts.edu
ALLARD, Ingrid, M .... 518-262-5919. 313 D
allardi@mail.amc.edu
ALLARD, Jessica .... 802-862-9616. 498 I
jallard@burlington.edu
ALLARD, Lee .... 518-782-6737. 340 J
lallard@siena.edu
ALLARD, Michael .... 518-828-4181. 321 C
allard@sunycgcc.edu
ALLARD, Nicholas, W ..... 718-780-7902. 315 H
nicholas.allard@brooklaw.edu
ALLBEE, Bob .... 563-288-6002. 178 B
ballbee@eicc.edu

ALLBRIGHT, A. Rodney .. 281-756-3598. 465 D
ara@alvincollege.edu
ALLBRIGHT, Jacque .... 512-245-2521. 487 C
ja14@txstate.edu
ALLBRITTEN, Jeffery .... 239-489-9211. 101 O
president@edison.edu
ALLCORN, Terry, A .... 417-268-6062. 271 I
tallcorn@gobbc.edu
ALLEE, Kelly .... 217-234-5215. 150 D
kallee@lakeland.cc.il.us
ALLEGRANTE, John, P ... 212-678-3991. 347 G
allegrante@tc.edu
ALLEMAN, Michael .... 337-550-1308. 205 B
ALLEMAN, Vickie .... 713-942-3466. 490 L
alleman@stthom.edu
ALLEN, Al .... 386-822-8808. 117 C
aallen@stetson.edu
ALLEN, Algia .... 972-563-9573. 488 D
aallen@tvcc.edu
ALLEN, Amanda .... 670-234-5498. 547 A
amandaal@nmcnet.edu
ALLEN, Andrea .... 305-899-3310... 98 O
aallen@barry.edu
ALLEN, Andrew, T .... 619-260-4553... 73 I
provost@sandiego.edu
ALLEN, Anita, L .... 215-898-4032. 435 B
aallen@law.upenn.edu
ALLEN, Ann .... 217-854-5506. 140 G
aalle@blackburn.edu
ALLEN, Ann, M .... 217-854-5506. 140 G
aalle@blackburn.edu
ALLEN, Anna, M .... 215-951-1374. 420 B
aallen@lasalle.edu
ALLEN, Anthony .... 718-933-6700. 331 K
aallen@monroecollege.edu
ALLEN, Anthony, W .... 573-629-3252. 274 J
anthony.allen@hlg.edu
ALLEN, B. Connie .... 919-516-4001. 366 C
bcallen@st-aug.edu
ALLEN, Bill .... 252-985-5111. 365 D
ballen@ncwc.edu
ALLEN, Bonita .... 251-405-7053..... 2 D
ballen@bishop.edu
ALLEN, Bonnie, J .... 615-898-2772. 459 D
bonnie.allen@mtsu.edu
ALLEN, Brenda .... 336-750-2200. 370 A
allenba@wssu.edu
ALLEN, Brian .... 815-939-5258. 155 H
ballen@olivet.edu
ALLEN, Brian, K .... 608-785-8558. 536 G
ballen@uwlax.edu
ALLEN, JR., Calvin, H .... 540-665-4587. 509 E
callen@su.edu
ALLEN, Carl .... 212-799-5000. 328 B
ALLEN, Carol, M .... 443-412-2144. 215 C
caallen@harford.edu
ALLEN, Carolyn, H .... 479-575-6702... 23 I
challen@uark.edu
ALLEN, Charles .... 650-949-6150... 44 L
allencharles@fhda.edu
ALLEN, SJ, Charles, H ... 203-254-4000... 89 I
executive@fairfield.edu
ALLEN, Chaunda .... 225-578-4339. 204 O
call18@lsu.edu
ALLEN, Cheryl .... 404-215-2618. 129 D
callen@morehouse.edu
ALLEN, Cindy .... 517-787-0800. 244 J
allencynthiaa@jccmi.edu
ALLEN, Craig .... 817-257-7865. 484 I
c.allen2@tcu.edu
ALLEN, Dale .... 508-854-4337. 232 F
dallen@qcc.mass.edu
ALLEN, Dana, G .... 757-683-3097. 507 N
dallen@odu.edu
ALLEN, Daniel, T .... 267-502-2636. 410 I
daniel.allen@brynathyn.edu
ALLEN, Darren .... 205-929-6361..... 5 D
dallen@lawsonstate.edu
ALLEN, David .... 508-678-2811. 231 B
david.allen@bristolcc.edu
ALLEN, David .... 817-923-1921. 481 G
dallen@swbts.edu
ALLEN, David, D .... 662-915-7265. 270 B
allen@olemiss.edu
ALLEN, David, N .... 520-626-4606... 18 F
davida@tla.arizona.edu
ALLEN, David, P .... 253-535-7524. 521 I
david.allen@plu.edu
ALLEN, David, W .... 916-339-1500... 55 D
dallen@mticollege.edu
ALLEN, Dee Dee .... 501-450-1228... 21 E
allendd@hendrix.edu
ALLEN, Diane, D .... 410-548-3374. 220 D
ddallen@salisbury.edu
ALLEN, Donna, Y .... 870-235-4012... 23 F
dyallen@saumag.edu
ALLEN, Douglas, W .... 320-222-5202. 260 H
douglas.allen@ridgewater.edu
ALLEN, Elizabeth .... 760-630-1555... 49 L
eallen@kaplan.edu
ALLEN, OP,
Elizabeth Anne .... 615-297-7545. 452 J
sreanne@aquinascollege.edu
ALLEN, Emily .... 212-226-5500. 314 A
eaallen@aii.edu
ALLEN, Eric .... 724-589-2186. 434 B
eallen@thiel.edu
ALLEN, Erin .... 704-991-0261. 364 C
eallen4640@stanly.edu
ALLEN, Forrest .... 432-685-4580. 476 G
fallen@midland.edu
ALLEN, Gary, K .... 573-882-9200. 283 C
allengk@missouri.edu
ALLEN, Gary, K .... 573-882-9200. 283 B
allengk@umsystem.edu
ALLEN, Greg .... 402-557-7581. 288 G
greg.allen@bellevue.edu
ALLEN, Gregg, N .... 207-780-5097. 212 H
gregg@usm.maine.edu
ALLEN, Helen .... 205-348-7949..... 8 D
helen.allen@ua.edu
ALLEN, Hengameh, G ..... 919-516-4488. 366 C
hgallen@st-aug.edu
ALLEN, Hilary .... 919-760-8548. 356 G
allenh@meredith.edu
ALLEN, Ivan .... 478-757-3501. 122 F
iallen@centralgatech.edu
ALLEN, Ivan, H .... 478-988-6800. 122 G
iallen@centralgatech.edu
ALLEN, JR., James .... 301-387-3059. 214 I
james.allen@garrettcollege.edu
ALLEN, JR., James .... 301-387-3006. 214 I
james.allen@garrettcollege.edu
ALLEN, James, S .... 618-453-7653. 159 G
jsallen@siu.edu
ALLEN, Janel, S .... 812-464-1756. 174 D
jallen@usi.edu
ALLEN, Janine .... 503-581-8166. 403 A
jallen@corban.edu
ALLEN, Jason, K .... 816-414-3700. 277 L
president@mbts.edu
ALLEN, Jay .... 601-928-6250. 268 C
jay.allen@mgccc.edu
ALLEN, Jeff .... 903-223-3049. 484 C
jeff.allen@tamut.edu
ALLEN, Jeffrey .... 814-536-5168. 412 C
jallen@crbc.net
ALLEN, Jen .... 706-419-1119. 123 F
jennifer.allen@covenant.edu
ALLEN, Jennie .... 909-447-2502... 39 E
jallen@cst.edu
ALLEN, Jerry .... 510-594-3641... 30 K
jallen@cca.edu
ALLEN, Jim .... 316-295-5513. 186 H
jim_allen@friends.edu
ALLEN, Jim .... 419-434-4207. 393 D
jallen@winebrenner.edu
ALLEN, Jo .... 919-760-8511. 356 G
jallen@meredith.edu
ALLEN, Joanne .... 559-438-4222... 46 K
joanne_allen@heald.edu
ALLEN, Jodi .... 270-789-6229. 193 D
jmallen@campbellsville.edu
ALLEN, Joel .... 704-991-0294. 364 C
jallen7581@stanly.edu
ALLEN, John .... 217-824-4004. 150 D
john.d.allen@doc.illinois.gov
ALLEN, John, A .... 614-885-5585. 388 C
jallen@pcj.edu
ALLEN, John, C .... 435-797-1195. 497 B
john.allen@usu.edu
ALLEN, John, M .... 718-270-2680. 342 D
jallen@downstate.edu
ALLEN, Johnny, L .... 662-720-7226. 269 B
jlallen@nemcc.edu
ALLEN, Joseph, L .... 864-242-5100. 441 D
ALLEN, Joyce .... 206-296-2000. 523 E
jallen@seattleu.edu
ALLEN, Judy .... 207-801-5680. 210 A
jallen@coa.edu
ALLEN, Julia .... 704-922-6511. 360 F
allen.julia@gaston.edu
ALLEN, Julian, O .... 404-413-4723. 126 E
joallen@gsu.edu
ALLEN, Justin .... 540-535-3561. 509 E
jallen3@su.edu
ALLEN, Kanya .... 270-707-3827. 195 E
kanya.allen@kctcs.edu
ALLEN, Karen, H .... 919-742-2715. 359 B
kallen@cccc.edu
ALLEN, Katherine .... 313-593-5300. 251 D
kmaallen@umich.edu
ALLEN, Kathy .... 828-694-1773. 358 C
allenkc@blueridge.edu
ALLEN, Kellie .... 606-326-2044. 194 J
kellie.allen@kctcs.edu
ALLEN, Kent .... 405-425-5194. 397 D
kent.allen@oc.edu
ALLEN, Kirsten .... 316-322-3192. 185 D
kallen@butlercc.edu
ALLEN, Kitty .... 605-995-2612. 450 A
kiallen1@dwu.edu
ALLEN, Kristi .... 212-229-8947. 332 E
allenk@newschool.edu
ALLEN, Lawrence, R .... 864-656-7640. 442 C
lalln@clemson.edu
ALLEN, Linda, A .... 319-296-4201. 178 J
linda.allen@hawkeyecollege.edu
ALLEN, Linda, D .... 617-373-2307. 235 F
ALLEN, Lonny .... 419-448-3359. 389 J
lallen@tiffin.edu
ALLEN, Lori .... 312-942-8708. 157 G
lori_j_allen@rush.edu
ALLEN, Lori .... 575-527-7727. 311 B
allen@nmsu.edu
ALLEN, Mark .... 719-384-6830... 83 M
mark.allen@ojc.edu
ALLEN, Mark .... 918-293-4830. 398 B
mark.allen@okstate.edu
ALLEN, Mark, R .... 570-408-4103. 437 F
mark.allen@wilkes.edu
ALLEN, Mary .... 410-225-4255. 216 C
mallen01@mica.edu
ALLEN, Mary Louise .... 610-896-1183. 418 F
mlallen@haverford.edu
ALLEN, Max .... 910-962-3030. 369 C
allenm@uncw.edu
ALLEN, Melissa .... 607-431-4130. 325 F
allenm2@hartwick.edu
ALLEN, Michael .... 406-496-4399. 287 F
mallen@mtech.edu
ALLEN, Michael .... 954-771-0376. 108 Q
mallen@knoxseminary.edu
ALLEN, Michael, D .... 615-898-2840. 459 D
michael.allen@mtsu.edu
ALLEN, Michael, K .... 818-364-7635... 52 A
allenm@lamission.edu
ALLEN, Michael, S .... 202-319-5286... 94 G
allen@cua.edu
ALLEN, Michele .... 816-604-4023. 277 H
michele.allen@mcckc.edu
ALLEN, Myrna, L .... 386-312-4249. 112 C
myrnaallen@sjrstate.edu
ALLEN, Nancy .... 919-684-2965. 354 A
nancy.allen@duke.edu
ALLEN, Nancy .... 325-942-2165. 465 K
nancy.allen@angelo.edu
ALLEN, Nancy, T .... 303-871-2007... 86 B
nallen@du.edu
ALLEN, Owen .... 336-887-3000. 355 N
oallen@laureluniversity.edu
ALLEN, Patricia .... 718-951-5074. 317 C
pallen@brooklyn.cuny.edu
ALLEN, Patricia .... 503-534-7022. 404 C
pallen@marylhurst.edu
ALLEN, Patrick .... 518-631-9875. 348 K
allenp@uniongraduatecollege.edu
ALLEN, Patrick .... 301-934-7539. 214 D
pallen@csmd.edu
ALLEN, Patty .... 509-533-4820. 518 E
patty.allen@scc.spokane.edu
ALLEN, Philip, D .... 229-333-5939. 134 B
pdallen@valdosta.edu
ALLEN, Preston, C .... 805-756-1226... 32 F
pallen@calpoly.edu
ALLEN, Ray .... 410-225-2289. 216 C
rallen@mica.edu
ALLEN, Regina .... 256-761-6285..... 7 F
rallen@talladega.edu
ALLEN, Remy, E .... 504-568-4802. 205 C
rall1@lsuhsc.edu
ALLEN, Rosemary .... 502-863-8146. 194 C
rosemary_allen@georgetowncollege.edu
ALLEN, Rusty .... 620-947-3121. 190 J
rustya@tabor.edu
ALLEN, Samira .... 845-848-7407. 322 G
samira.allen@dc.edu
ALLEN, JR., Samuel .... 603-641-7492. 297 G
sallen@anselm.edu
ALLEN, Scott, T .... 203-596-4590... 90 I
scallen@post.edu
ALLEN, Seth .... 909-621-8134... 60 A
seth.allen@pomona.edu
ALLEN, Sharon .... 928-428-8342... 13 J
sharon.allen@eac.edu
ALLEN, Sheila, W .... 706-542-3461. 133 C
sallen01@uga.edu
ALLEN, Shelli .... 816-604-3175. 277 G
shelli.allen@mcckc.edu
ALLEN, Stacey .... 505-566-3515. 311 I
allens@sancollege.edu
ALLEN, Stacey .... 505-566-3515. 311 I
allens@sanjuancollege.edu
ALLEN, Stanley, T .... 609-258-3737. 304 E
stallen@princeton.edu
ALLEN, Stephen .... 435-865-8499. 497 A
allen@suu.edu
ALLEN, Steve .... 606-539-4219. 200 B
steve.allen@ucumberlands.edu
ALLEN, Susan .... 478-445-5650. 125 A
susan.allen@gcsu.edu
ALLEN, Susan, K .... 603-862-3600. 298 C
suzy.allen@unh.edu
ALLEN, T. Muriel .... 267-502-2632. 410 I
muriel.allen@brynathyn.edu
ALLEN, Ted .... 503-554-2161. 403 C
tallen@georgefox.edu
ALLEN, Teresa .... 912-287-5809. 130 B
tallen@okefenokeetech.edu
ALLEN, Terry, D .... 859-257-8927. 200 C
tallen@uky.edu
ALLEN, Thomas .... 845-437-7267. 349 G
thallen@vassar.edu
ALLEN, Tim .... 360-473-1120. 519 E
ALLEN, Tom .... 443-334-2955. 218 E
tallen@stevenson.edu
ALLEN, Tom .... 864-977-7135. 445 H
tom.allen@ngu.edu
ALLEN, Tony .... 731-989-6055. 454 J
tallen@fhu.edu
ALLEN, W. Clayton .... 903-510-2507. 488 E
call2@tjc.edu
ALLEN, Wanda .... 610-543-2500... 96 F
ALLEN, William, R .... 530-898-5623... 33 A
ballen@csuchico.edu
ALLEN, Xuri, M .... 340-693-1224. 555 E
xallen@live.uvi.edu
ALLEN, Yvonne .... 216-373-5343. 385 G
yallen@ndc.edu
ALLEN, Zachery .... 701-224-2524. 372 B
zachery.allen@bismarckstate.edu
ALLEN-COVINO, Carol ... 973-278-5400. 299 D
cja@berkeleycollege.edu
ALLEN-DIAZ, Barbara, H 510-987-9359... 70 H
barbara.allen-diaz@ucop.edu
ALLEN-KELSEY, Janice ... 386-481-2459... 99 C
kelseyj@cookman.edu
ALLEN-MEARES, Paula ... 312-413-3350. 161 D
pameares@uic.edu
ALLEN-MEARES, Paula ... 312-413-3350. 161 C
pameares@uic.edu
ALLEN-PERRY, Lynette ... 215-572-2173. 409 H
collins@arcadia.edu
ALLEN-SHARPE,
Regina, C .... 302-356-6790... 94 E
regina.a.sharpe@wilmu.edu
ALLENBY, Daniel .... 617-353-1068. 224 D
dallenby@bu.edu
ALLER, Gary .... 202-448-6968... 95 C
gary.aller@gallaudet.edu
ALLES, Patrick .... 317-788-2063. 173 I
alles@uindy.edu
ALLETTO, Philip .... 912-525-5000. 131 B
palletto@scad.edu
ALLEVA, Joe .... 225-578-3600. 204 O
athletics@lsu.edu
ALLEY, Ashlee, E .... 620-229-6362. 190 G
ashlee.alley@sckans.edu
ALLEY, Brien .... 402-363-5624. 293 I
balley@york.edu
ALLEY, Carolyn .... 828-694-1730. 358 C
carolyna@blueridge.edu
ALLEY, Christy .... 620-672-5641. 190 A
christya@prattcc.edu
ALLEY, Jerome .... 303-867-1155... 87 E
Alley@TaftU.edu
ALLEY, Kathryn, E .... 605-394-6952. 452 A
kate.jansak@sdsmt.edu
ALLEY, Kristen .... 660-359-3948. 279 H
kalley@mail.ncmissouri.edu
ALLGOOD, John .... 225-214-6975. 206 D
john.allgood@ololcollege.edu
ALLGRETTI, Marguerite ... 312-752-2432. 149 E
marguerite.allgretti@kendall.edu
ALLIGOOD, Bennye, J ..... 352-395-5182. 113 C
bennye.alligood@sfcollege.edu
ALLIGOOD, Phillip, N ..... 252-334-2014. 357 A
phillip.alligood@macuniversity.edu
ALLINA, Babette .... 401-454-6317. 440 A
ballina@risd.edu
ALLING, David, C .... 860-628-4751... 90 D
dalling@lincolncollegene.edu
ALLING, Emily .... 802-258-9221. 499 F
ealling@marlboro.edu
ALLIS, Celeste, H .... 336-342-4261. 363 C
allisc@rockinghamcc.edu
ALLISON, Angela .... 559-934-2152... 75 G
angelaallison@whccd.edu
ALLISON, Dale .... 808-236-5811. 135 F
dallison@hpu.edu
ALLISON, Jack, T .... 787-743-7979. 552 I
jaallison@suagm.edu
ALLISON, JR.,
James, M .... 410-810-7490. 221 C
jallison2@washcoll.edu
ALLISON, Jennifer, R ...... 864-597-4030. 449 I
allisonjr@wofford.edu
ALLISON, Jim .... 502-863-7922. 194 C
jim_allison@georgetowncollege.edu
ALLISON, Lon, J .... 630-752-5918. 163 F
lon.allison@wheaton.edu

ALLISON, Lorri ... 336-506-4133. 357 M
lorri.allison@alamancecc.edu
ALLISON, M. Scott ... 540-375-2337. 509 B
allison@roanoke.edu
ALLISON, Maria, T ... 480-965-7279... 11 K
icmta@asu.edu
ALLISON, Patrick ... 360-736-9391. 517 G
pallison@centralia.edu
ALLISON, Robert ... 724-503-1001. 436 G
rallison@washjeff.edu
ALLISON, Robert ... 610-902-8275. 411 E
robert.allison@cabrini.edu
ALLISON, Rose Mariee ... 864-231-2099. 441 B
rallison@andersonuniversity.edu
ALLISON, Sherry ... 505-346-2348. 312 E
sherry.allison@bie.edu
ALLISON, Terry, L ... 574-520-4220. 168 E
tlalliso@iusb.edu
ALLISON, William ... 914-594-4226. 334 A
william_allison@nymc.edu
ALLISON-JONES, Lisa ... 540-224-6970. 506 G
LAllisonjones@jchs.edu
ALLMAKER, Peter ... 413-662-5592. 230 C
peter.allmaker@mcla.edu
ALLMAN, Ashley ... 757-822-1642. 514 C
aallman@tcc.edu
ALLMAN, Joyce, L ... 405-325-3221. 401 B
joyceallman@ou.edu
ALLMAN, Marion, K ... 513-751-1206. 374 A
aic@theartinstituteofcincinnati.com
ALLMAN, Martha, B ... 336-758-5201. 370 D
allanmb@wfu.edu
ALLMON, Suzanne ... 325-674-2412. 464 H
allmons@acu.edu
ALLOWAY, Laura ... 740-753-6171. 380 K
allowayl@hocking.edu
ALLPHIN, Jeri, L ... 801-863-8553. 497 C
jeri.allphin@uvu.edu
ALLRED, Barry ... 801-422-2631. 495 D
barry_allred@byu.edu
ALLRED, J. Michael ... 530-754-9868... 70 J
jmallred@ucdavis.edu
ALLRED, Jeremy, P ... 323-265-8802... 51 F
allredjp@elac.edu
ALLRED, John ... 435-586-7715. 497 A
johnallred1@suu.edu
ALLRED, Judy ... 970-675-3305... 80 B
judy.allred@cncc.edu
ALLRED, Robert ... 801-832-2013. 498 F
rallred@westminstercollege.edu
ALLRED, Stephen ... 804-289-8153. 510 L
sallred@richmond.edu
ALLSHOUSE, Kent ... 316-284-5279. 184 J
kellshouse@bethelks.edu
ALLSTON, Tim ... 256-726-8103..... 6 B
tallston@oakwood.edu
ALLWEISS, Stephanie ... 504-247-1746. 207 C
sallweis@tulane.edu
ALLY, H. David ... 504-280-5470. 205 G
hally@uno.edu
ALLY, Ron ... 847-925-6380. 145 H
rally@harpercollege.edu
ALM, Deborah ... 413-748-3215. 236 I
dalm@springfieldcollege.edu
ALM, Janet ... 269-488-4326. 244 L
jalm@kvcc.edu
ALM, Maria ... 715-232-2596. 538 B
almm@uwstout.edu
ALMAGUER, Michael ... 925-969-2347... 41 L
malmaguer@dvc.edu
ALMALA, Abed ... 703-821-8570. 510 B
aalmala@stratford.edu
ALMALA, Abed, H ... 703-329-9601... 96 F
aal@strayer.edu
ALMEIDA, Craig ... 508-565-1325. 237 A
calmeida@stonehill.edu
ALMEIDA, Enga ... 817-202-6494. 481 E
ealmeida@swau.edu
ALMEIDA, James ... 201-692-7200. 301 J
almeida@fdu.edu
ALMENDAREZ, Juan ... 210-829-3932. 490 A
jaalmend@uiwtx.edu
ALMENDARIZ, Moises ... 214-860-8711. 471 A
malmendariz@dcccd.edu
ALMER, Deb ... 507-537-6243. 261 F
Deb.Almer@smsu.edu
ALMEYDA, Marta ... 787-728-1515. 555 D
malmeyda@sagrado.edu
ALMOGELA, Lovellie ... 909-537-4155... 34 E
lalmogel@csusb.edu
ALMOND, B.J ... 713-348-6770. 479 A
balmond@rice.edu
ALMOND, James, S ... 765-494-9706. 171 M
jsalmond@purdue.edu
ALMOND, Paula ... 910-755-7422. 358 D
almondp@brunswickcc.edu
ALMONTE, Loreto ... 305-821-3333. 105 A
lalmonte@fnu.edu
ALMQUIST, Arne, J ... 859-572-5483. 198 I
almquista@nku.edu
ALMQUIST, Brian ... 843-574-6011. 447 E
brian.almquist@tridenttech.edu
ALMQUIST, Cathy ... 843-574-6750. 447 E
cathy.almquist@tridenttech.edu
ALMSTEDT, Debbie, Z ... 425-739-8200. 520 K
debbie.almstedt@lwtech.edu
ALNUTT, Mark ... 573-651-2227. 282 B
malnutt@semo.edu
ALO, Richard ... 601-979-2153. 267 E
richard.a.alo@jsums.edu
ALOIA, Gregory, F ... 912-279-5705. 123 B
president@ccga.edu
ALONSO, Carlos, J ... 212-854-6935. 321 D
ca2201@columbia.edu
ALONSO, Daniel ... 415-808-3000... 47 E
daniel_alonso@heald.edu
ALONSO, David ... 212-998-1077. 334 D
david.alonso@nyu.edu
ALONSO, John ... 860-628-4751... 90 D
jalonso@lincolncollegene.edu
ALONSO, Marcos ... 619-961-2174. 463 J
malonso@victory.edu
ALONSO, Tony, J ... 918-595-7840. 400 E
antonio.alonso@tulsacc.edu
ALONZO, Donette ... 913-621-8762. 186 C
dalonzo@donnelly.edu
ALONZO, Patricia ... 989-775-4123. 249 F
alonzo.patricia@sagchip.edu
ALOYO, JR., Victor ... 609-688-1940. 304 D
victor.aloyo@ptsem.edu
ALP, Funda, F ... 203-396-8241... 91 C
alpf@sacredheart.edu
ALPERIN, Diane ... 561-297-2011. 114 L
alperind@fau.edu
ALPERIN, Diane ... 561-297-3068. 114 L
alperind@fau.edu
ALPERIN, Samantha ... 901-321-3116. 453 H
salperin@cbu.edu
ALPERN, Robert, J ... 203-785-4672... 93 A
robert.alpern@yale.edu
ALPERT, Gregg ... 213-749-4244. 325 G
galpert@huc.edu
ALSAIDI, Yasin ... 603-428-2230. 297 D
yalsaidi@nec.edu
ALSDURF, Karalin ... 913-651-2111. 187 L
kalsdurf@kckcc.edu
ALSINA, Amalia ... 787-257-0000. 554 B
maria.perez25@upr.edu
ALSIP, Morgan ... 405-691-3800. 396 D
malsip@macu.edu
ALSOBROOK, Joe ... 636-949-4853. 276 D
jalsobrook@lindenwood.edu
ALSOBROOK, Metta ... 434-791-5618. 502 D
malsobrook@averett.edu
ALSOBROOKS, David, S 601-403-1241. 269 D
salsobrooks@prcc.edu
ALSOP, Robert ... 641-585-8130. 183 D
alsopb@waldorf.edu
ALSTER, Kristine ... 617-287-5638. 228 G
kristine.alster@umb.edu
ALSTON, Karen ... 315-443-2744. 347 C
kalston@syr.edu
ALSTON, Lakesha ... 252-328-6804. 367 B
alstonl@ecu.edu
ALSTON, Melissa, F ... 706-771-4171. 121 D
mfalston@augustatech.edu
ALSTON, Reginald ... 217-333-6394. 162 A
alston@illinois.edu
ALSTON, Sharon ... 202-885-6053... 94 F
salston@american.edu
ALSTON-BROWN,
Michelle ... 404-756-4442. 121 A
malston@atlm.edu
ALSTON-PINCKNEY,
Elizabeth ... 704-216-6100. 356 D
ealston-pinckney@livingstone.edu
ALSTOTT, Melissa ... 270-686-4567. 196 C
melissa.alstott@kctcs.edu
ALSTROM, Mike ... 231-777-0307. 247 G
mike.alstrom@muskegoncc.edu
ALSUP, Greer ... 931-393-1529. 461 A
galsup@mscc.edu
ALT, Greg, L ... 309-438-2143. 147 J
gaalt@ilstu.edu
ALT, John, W ... 608-524-7825. 540 C
jalt@madisoncollege.edu
ALTABEF, Nomi ... 480-212-1704... 17 N
ALTAMIRANO,
Rodolfo, R ... 215-573-6332. 435 B
rudiea@pobox.upenn.edu
ALTAYLI, Z. Benek ... 719-255-3257... 85 M
azltayli@uccs.edu
ALTEMOSE, Jane ... 610-758-4637. 422 A
jca209@lehigh.edu
ALTEMOSE, Rodney, E ... 215-258-7750. 411 B
altemose@bucks.edu
ALTEMOSE, Rodney, H ... 215-258-7750. 411 B
altemose@bucks.edu
ALTEMUS, Virginia ... 207-326-2241. 211 D
ginny.altemus@mma.edu
ALTENBURG,
Deborah, E ... 202-220-1320. 337 I
altend@rpi.edu
ALTENBURG, Rana, H ... 414-288-7430. 534 B
rana.altenburg@marquette.edu
ALTENKIRCH, Robert, A . 256-824-6340..... 8 F
robert.altenkirch@uah.edu
ALTER, Steven ... 215-572-2825. 409 H
alters@arcadia.edu
ALTIER, Jeffrey, P ... 386-822-8100. 117 C
jaltier@stetson.edu
ALTIERE, Ralph ... 303-724-2631... 86 A
ralph.altiere@ucdenver.edu
ALTIERI, Guy ... 240-500-2000. 215 B
galtieri@hagerstowncc.edu
ALTIERI, Jason, C ... 281-873-0262. 469 H
j.altieri@commonwealth.edu
ALTIERI, Paul ... 570-484-2278. 429 B
paltieri@lhup.edu
ALTIERO, Nicholas, J ... 504-865-5764. 207 C
altiero@tulane.edu
ALTIKULAC, John ... 770-426-2644. 128 D
jaltikulac@life.edu
ALTIS, Judy ... 304-929-1414. 527 H
judyaltis@ucwv.edu
ALTMAN, Arla, S ... 727-816-3404. 110 E
altmana@phcc.edu
ALTMAN, Carolyn ... 912-486-1149. 126 C
caltman@georgiasouthern.edu
ALTMAN, Don ... 660-626-2820. 271 A
daltman@atsu.edu
ALTMAN, J.J ... 912-871-1648. 129 J
jaltman@ogeecheetech.edu
ALTMAN, Joanne, D ... 336-841-9613. 355 C
jaltman0@highpoint.edu
ALTOMARE, Carl ... 610-341-1775. 415 G
caltomar@eastern.edu
ALTON, Beth ... 858-795-5138... 64 E
balton@sanfordburnham.org
ALTON, Stevan ... 586-445-7374. 246 A
altons@macomb.edu
ALTSCHULER, Glenn, C .. 607-255-4987. 322 A
gca1@cornell.edu
ALTSHULER, Gina ... 215-335-0800. 422 C
galtshuler@lincolntech.com
ALTUCHER, Kristine ... 607-844-8222. 347 I
altuchk@tc3.edu
ALTUSKY,
Shlomo Avidgor ... 718-868-2300. 314 I
ALTWINE, Chad ... 402-375-7274. 291 F
chaltwi1@wsc.edu
ALTY, James ... 504-862-8262. 207 C
jalty@tulane.edu
ALUTTO, Joseph, A ... 614-292-2424. 386 E
alutto.1@osu.edu
ALVA, Gerardo ... 956-326-2284. 483 B
gerardo.alva@tamiu.edu
ALVA, Sylvia, A ... 818-677-3001... 34 C
sylvia.alva@csun.edu
ALVAR, Brent ... 801-375-5125. 496 G
balvar@rmuohp.edu
ALVARADO, Cecilia ... 951-222-8000... 61 A
ALVARADO, Christian ... 949-582-4860... 67 C
calvarado@saddleback.edu
ALVARADO, Eddie, D ... 661-336-5143... 49 M
ealvarad@kccd.edu
ALVARADO, Ida, Y ... 787-780-0070. 547 G
ialvarado@caribbean.edu
ALVARADO, Irma ... 787-279-1912. 550 B
ialvarado@bayamon.inter.edu
ALVARADO,
Johnathan, E ... 404-627-2681. 121 H
johnathan.alvarado@beulah.org
ALVARADO, Magalie ... 787-257-7373. 552 H
ue_malvarado@suagm.edu
ALVARADO, Nick ... 325-235-7331. 486 C
nick.alvarado@sweetwater.tstc.edu
ALVARADO, Norman ... 718-779-1430. 336 D
nalvarado@plazacollege.edu
ALVARADO, Nyvia ... 787-892-4300. 551 A
nalvarad@sg.inter.edu
ALVARADO, Phil ... 530-938-5233... 41 A
alvarado@siskiyous.edu
ALVARANZA, Wally ... 787-728-1515. 555 D
walvaranza@sagrado.edu
ALVAREZ, Aida ... 787-878-5475. 549 L
aalvarez@arecibo.inter.edu
ALVAREZ, Anselmo ... 787-284-1912. 550 F
aalvarez@ponce.inter.edu
ALVAREZ, Antonia ... 361-593-3606. 484 A
antonia.alvarez@tamuk.edu
ALVAREZ, Aubree ... 502-456-6506. 199 G
aalvarez@sullivan.edu
ALVAREZ, Barry, L ... 608-262-4312. 536 D
bla@athletics.wisc.edu
ALVAREZ, Celso, J ... 305-474-6868. 112 F
cjalvarez@stu.edu
ALVAREZ, Ivonne ... 619-388-2689... 62 E
ialvarez@sdccd.edu
ALVAREZ, Jacqueline ... 787-284-1912. 550 F
jalvarez@ponce.inter.edu
ALVAREZ, Leticia ... 559-638-3641... 69 A
leticia.alvarez@reedleycollege.edu
ALVAREZ, Lourdes ... 203-932-7257... 92 E
lavarez@newhaven.edu
ALVAREZ, Luis ... 787-890-2681. 553 H
luis.alvarez8@upr.edu
ALVAREZ, Maria ... 787-882-2065. 553 A
registraduria@unitecpr.net
ALVAREZ, Maria, L ... 305-899-3085... 98 O
malvarez@barry.edu
ALVAREZ, Patricia ... 559-730-3988... 40 I
patriciaa@cos.edu
ALVAREZ, Patricia ... 787-857-3600. 550 A
palvarez@br.inter.edu
ALVAREZ, Raul ... 714-484-7128... 56 E
ralvarez@cypresscollege.edu
ALVAREZ, Richard, S ... 540-831-5411. 508 C
ralvarez@radford.edu
ALVAREZ, Sylvia ... 787-728-1515. 555 D
salvarez@sagrado.edu
ALVAREZ BROWN,
Carmen ... 216-687-2054. 377 F
c.a.brown38@csuohio.edu
ALVES, Jeffrey ... 570-408-4725. 437 F
jeffrey.alves@wilkes.edu
ALVES, Stephanie ... 925-969-2082... 41 L
salves@dvc.edu
ALVES-FERREIRA, Rosa .. 973-642-8187. 307 D
rosa.alves-ferreira@shu.edu
ALVESTED, Scott ... 660-543-8000. 283 A
alvested@ucmo.edu
ALVIDREZ, Rachel ... 757-457-8101. 502 C
rachel.alvidrez@atlanticuniv.edu
ALVIN, Stephen, R ... 815-224-0491. 148 A
steve_alvin@ivcc.edu
ALVINO, Kathleen, M ... 401-865-2430. 439 E
kalvino@providence.edu
ALVIS, Robert ... 812-357-6543. 173 A
ralvis@saintmeinrad.edu
ALY, Mai ... 773-481-8061. 142 F
maly@ccc.edu
ALY, Nael ... 707-654-1018... 31 I
naly@csum.edu
ALZAHABI, Basem ... 810-762-7893. 244 Q
balzahab@kettering.edu
AMACK, April ... 970-542-3187... 83 E
april.amack@morgancc.edu
AMADOR, Dora ... 210-999-7227. 488 C
damador@trinity.edu
AMAKER, Corey, R ... 803-705-4344. 441 C
amakerc@benedict.edu
AMAN, Rick ... 541-440-4600. 408 D
Rick.Aman@umpqua.edu
AMARAL, George ... 510-780-4500... 50 I
gamaral@lifewest.edu
AMASON, Amy ... 706-776-0104. 130 E
aamason@piedmont.edu
AMATO, Paula, A ... 603-428-2461. 297 D
pamato@nec.edu
AMAYA, Mercedes ... 305-237-2325. 109 D
mamaya@mdc.edu
AMBACH, Robert ... 513-556-2413. 390 G
robert.ambach@uc.edu
AMBAR, Carmen, T ... 610-606-4612. 412 I
president@cedarcrest.edu
AMBLER, Anthony, P ... 803-777-7356. 447 G
ambler@cec.sc.edu
AMBLER, Virginia, M ... 757-221-1236. 503 N
vmambl@wm.edu
AMBRA, Stephen ... 603-271-6484. 296 C
sambra@ccsnh.edu
AMBRIZ, Rick ... 915-351-8100. 465 I
AMBRIZ-GALAVIZ,
Norma ... 510-436-2501... 59 D
nambrizgalaviz@peralta.edu
AMBROGI, Anthony, F ... 804-752-7362. 508 E
aambrogi@rmc.edu
AMBRON, Sueann ... 303-315-8001... 86 A
sueann.ambron@ucdenver.edu
AMBROSE, Allison, S ... 563-333-6155. 182 B
AmbroseAllisonS@sau.edu
AMBROSE, Ann ... 757-822-2301. 514 C
aambrose@tcc.edu
AMBROSE, AnneMarie ... 315-866-0300. 326 A
ambroseac@herkimer.edu
AMBROSE, Charles, M ... 660-543-4112. 283 A
ambrose@ucmo.edu
AMBROSE, James ... 315-786-2490. 327 L
jambrose@sunyjefferson.edu
AMBROSE, John, N ... 804-523-5612. 512 F
jambrose@reynolds.edu
AMBROSE, Molly, B ... 617-228-2457. 231 C
mambrose@bhcc.mass.edu
AMBROSE, Pam ... 312-915-7602. 151 H
pambros@luc.edu
AMBROSE, Susan ... 617-373-2170. 235 F
AMBROSETTI, Ronald, J . 504-398-2214. 206 C
rambrosetti@olhcc.edu
AMBROSON, Gene ... 712-274-5293. 181 B
ambroson@morningside.edu

AMBRUSO, Diane 717-299-7754. 434 A
ambruso@stevenscollege.edu
AMBUR, Roberta, S 605-677-5661. 451 F
roberta.ambur@usd.edu
AMBURGEY, Jeff, S 859-985-3082. 192 F
jeff_amburgey@berea.edu
AMBUSKE, Joseph 614-236-6116. 375 H
jambuske@capital.edu
AMEER, Inge-Lise 603-643-3113. 296 G
inge-lise.ameer@dartmouth.edu
AMEIGH, Michael 315-312-3500. 344 A
michael.ameigh@oswego.edu
AMELANG, Mary Ann 281-425-6256. 475 I
mamelang@lee.edu
AMELING, Brian, F 864-488-8200. 444 L
bameling@limestone.edu
AMELL, Laura 802-485-2065. 500 A
lamell@norwich.edu
AMELSBERG, James 641-585-8164. 183 D
amelsbergj@waldorf.edu
AMEN, Barbara, A 503-777-7259. 407 E
barbara.amen@reed.edu
AMEND, John 402-554-2242. 293 A
jamend@unomaha.edu
AMENSON-HILL, Brenda 920-465-2159. 536 F
hillb@uwgb.edu
AMENT, Rebecca, R 740-588-1322. 394 C
bament@zanestate.edu
AMENTA, Paula 847-214-7273. 144 F
pamenta@elgin.edu
AMENTA, Peter, S 732-235-6300. 306 B
amenta@rutgers.edu
AMERIO, Barbara 661-763-7881... 69 D
bamerio@taftcollege.edu
AMERO, Carolina 678-466-4217. 123 A
carolinaamero@clayton.edu
AMERSHEK, Tom 620-235-4775. 189 L
tamershe@pittstate.edu
AMERSON, Philip, A 847-866-3901. 145 E
philip.amerson@garrett.edu
AMES, Christopher 304-876-5176. 529 I
cames@shepherd.edu
AMES, Lynda, J 518-564-3310. 344 B
ameslj@plattsburgh.edu
AMES, Marilyn 914-337-9300. 321 E
marilyn.ames@concordia-ny.edu
AMES, Mark 405-382-9950. 399 I
m.ames@sscok.edu
AMES, Orrin 334-983-6556..... 7 H
oames@troy.edu
AMES, Pam 714-997-6712... 38 A
ames@chapman.edu
AMES, Susan, E 315-445-4227. 328 F
amesse@lemoyne.edu
AMES, Trevor, R 612-624-6244. 264 G
amesx001@umn.edu
AMES, W. Edward 407-582-5528. 118 M
eames@valenciacollege.edu
AMEY, Carol, J 859-858-3511. 192 B
camey@asbury.edu
AMEY, Tracey 570-327-4503. 427 B
tamey@pct.edu
AMEZCUA, Victoria 626-396-2278... 28 P
victoria.amezcua@artcenter.edu
AMICK, Michael 218-855-8268. 258 B
mamick@clcmn.edu
AMICK, Patricia, A 816-604-1130. 277 C
patricia.amick@mcckc.edu
AMIDON, Howard 978-921-4242. 234 C
howard.amidon@montserrat.edu
AMIDON, Jacob, E 585-785-1418. 324 D
amidonje@flcc.edu
AMIDON, James, I 765-361-6364. 175 B
amidonj@wabash.edu
AMIE, Torrion 952-358-8505. 260 B
torrion.amie@normandale.edu
AMIN, Shamima 334-727-8011..... 8 A
samin@tuskegee.edu
AMIRIDIS, Michael 803-777-2808. 447 G
provost@sc.edu
AMIRTHARAJ, Merlin 704-991-0207. 364 C
mamirtharaj5283@stanly.edu
AMLANER, Charles, J 770-423-6738. 127 N
camlaner@kennesaw.edu
AMLER, Robert, W 914-594-4531. 334 A
robert_amler@nymc.edu
AMMAR, Salwa 718-862-7440. 329 M
salwa.ammar@manhattan.edu
AMMERMAN, Amy 281-459-7175. 479 G
amy.ammerman@sjcd.edu
AMMERMAN, Randy 920-686-6179. 536 A
randy.ammerman@sl.edu
AMMERMAN, Richard 973-655-5460. 303 D
ammermanr@mail.montclair.edu
AMMERMAN, Rocky 218-683-8540. 260 D
rocky.ammerman@northlandcollege.edu
AMMIDOWN, Darla 603-577-6533. 296 F
dammidown@dwc.edu
AMMIGAN, Ravi 302-831-2115... 94 B
rammigan@udel.edu
AMMIRATI, Theresa, P 860-439-2050... 89 H
tpamm@conncoll.edu
AMMON, Janice, S 609-497-7890. 304 D
chapel@ptsem.edu
AMMONS, Brian 828-298-3325. 370 E
bammons@warren-wilson.edu
AMMONS, Don 704-922-6240. 360 F
ammons.don@gaston.edu
AMMONS, Kevin 334-347-2623..... 3 G
kammons@escc.edu
AMODIO, Francis 845-569-3154. 332 B
francis.amodio@msmc.edu
AMODIO, Greg, J 412-396-5589. 415 F
amodiog@duq.edu
AMOKE, William 619-298-1829... 68 A
wamoke@ssu.edu
AMON, Julie 856-225-6108. 306 C
julie.amon@camden.rutgers.edu
AMOO, Judith, L 308-635-6702. 293 E
amooj@wncc.edu
AMORE, Elizabeth 305-284-6266. 118 F
eamore@miami.edu
AMOROS, Blanca 787-758-2525. 554 F
blanca.amoros@upr.edu
AMORY, Deborah 518-587-2100. 346 A
deb.amory@esc.edu
AMOS, Anthea 850-484-4436. 110 G
aamos@pensacolastate.edu
AMOS, Maureen, T 773-442-5000. 154 H
m-amos@neiu.edu
AMOS, Ralph 310-206-8962... 71 C
ralphamos@support.ucla.edu
AMOS, Ralph 301-405-2102. 219 B
ramos@umd.edu
AMOS PALMER,
Susan, M 651-793-1823. 259 C
sueamos.palmer@metrostate.edu
AMOTT, Teresa, L 309-341-7210. 150 A
tamott@knox.edu
AMOUZEGAR, Mahyar 909-869-2472... 32 G
mahyar@csupomona.edu
AMPARO, Frank 623-935-8872... 14 K
frank.amparo@estrellamountain.edu
AMPERSAND, Stephen 410-287-1003. 214 B
sampersand@cecil.edu
AMPUERO, Rosemary 212-774-0739. 330 E
rampuero@mmm.edu
AMREIN, Mark 865-288-6810... 18 I
mark.amrein@phoenix.edu
AMRHEIN, Rick 219-464-5777. 174 E
rick.amrhein@valpo.edu
AMRIKHAS, Violet 818-947-2533... 52 E
amrikhv@lavc.edu
AMSELMI, Michael, A 410-704-4008. 220 E
manselmi@towson.edu
AMSPAUGH, Melissa, A 440-525-7357. 382 M
mamspaugh@lakelandcc.edu
AMSTER, Yosef 516-295-5700. 351 N
AMSTUTZ, Margaret 706-542-0383. 133 C
mastutz@uga.edu
AMUNDSEN, Scott 714-816-0366... 70 A
scott.amundsen@trident.edu
AMUNDSON,
Elizabeth, A 202-994-4900... 95 D
amundson@gwu.edu
AMYOT, Maribeth 513-745-3445. 393 H
amyotm@xavier.edu
AMYX, Tim 615-230-3614. 461 G
tim.amyx@volstate.edu
AN, Nana 202-885-2729... 94 F
nanaan@american.edu
ANACKER, Gayne 951-343-4682... 30 H
ganaker@calbaptist.edu
ANAHITA, Sine 907-474-6515... 10 I
sine.anahita@alaska.edu
ANALISTA, Norman 671-735-2586. 546 E
nanalista@uguam.uog.edu
ANAND, Brij, B 718-990-6350. 339 A
anandb@stjohns.edu
ANANDALINGAM,
G. Anand 301-405-2308. 219 B
ganand@rhsmith.umd.edu
ANANOU, Simeon 410-543-6112. 220 D
CIO@salisbury.edu
ANASAGASTI, Rogelio 713-718-5001. 473 C
rogelio.anasagasti@hccs.edu
ANASTASIO, Rosemary 718-390-3422. 350 B
ranastas@wagner.edu
ANASTASIOU, Maria 803-641-3671. 448 A
maria@usca.edu
ANASTASSIOU,
Pamela, L 928-523-2109... 16 C
pamela.anastassiou@nau.edu
ANAWALT, Deborah 410-626-2504. 217 G
debbie.anawalt@sjca.edu
ANAYA, Angela 505-888-8898. 312 A
financialaid@acupuncturecollege.edu
ANAYA, Jose 310-660-6464... 43 B
janaya@elcamino.edu
ANAYA, Lorena 510-580-3508... 77 C
lanaya@cci.edu
ANAYA, Nena 505-424-2331. 309 J
nanaya@iaia.edu
ANAYA, Victor 201-447-7100. 299 C
vanaya@bergen.edu
ANCAAR, Kathy, T 504-816-4304. 201 K
kancar@dillard.edu
ANCELL, Jack 434-949-1066. 513 H
jack.ancell@southside.edu
ANCHOR, Rebecca, E 585-245-5100. 343 C
anchor@geneseo.edu
ANCI, Diane 413-538-2515. 234 D
danci@mtholyoke.edu
ANCTIL, Robin 641-844-5571. 179 H
robin.anctil@iavalley.edu
ANCTIL, Robin 641-844-5571. 179 J
robin.anctil@iavalley.edu
ANDALI, Sophia 928-350-1001... 17 K
sophia.andali@prescott.edu
ANDE, Taiwo, A 540-654-1282. 510 J
tande@umw.edu
ANDELMAN, Julia 212-678-8893. 328 A
juandelman@jtsa.edu
ANDERECK, Barbara, S 740-368-3773. 387 J
bsandere@owu.edu
ANDERFUREN, Marian 757-822-1940. 514 C
manderfuren@tcc.edu
ANDERLEY, Gerald, M 651-962-6061. 265 C
ANDERMAN, Lynea 610-892-1524. 427 E
landerman@pit.edu
ANDERS, Lee 620-862-5252. 184 E
andle@barclaycollege.edu
ANDERS, Peter, J 717-872-3433. 429 D
peter.anders@millersville.edu
ANDERS, Steven 641-784-5178. 178 F
anders@graceland.edu
ANDERSEN, Charles, N 208-496-1124. 137 H
andersenc@byui.edu
ANDERSEN, Jim 209-384-6396... 54 D
andersen.j@mccd.edu
ANDERSEN, Kathy 717-728-2503. 412 J
kathyandersens@centralpenn.edu
ANDERSEN, Kent 205-226-4679..... 2 C
kanderse@bsc.edu
ANDERSEN, Kent, A 307-674-6446. 543 F
kandersen@sheridan.edu
ANDERSEN, Laura, A 269-337-7248. 244 K
Laura.Andersen@kzoo.edu
ANDERSEN, Leslie 714-816-0366... 70 A
leslie.andersen@trident.edu
ANDERSEN, Margaret 302-831-7299... 94 B
mla@udel.edu
ANDERSEN, Mark, N 307-686-0254. 543 F
mandersen@sheridan.edu
ANDERSEN, Mary 719-775-8873... 83 E
mary.andersen@morgancc.edu
ANDERSEN, Mike 831-656-2845. 544 M
manderse@nps.edu
ANDERSEN, Patricia, M 605-394-1261. 452 A
patricia.andersen@sdsmt.edu
ANDERSEN, Robert 309-298-2446. 162 K
r-andersen@wiu.edu
ANDERSEN, Russ 402-557-7069. 288 G
russ.andersen@bellevue.edu
ANDERSEN, Sherry 508-362-2131. 231 D
sanderse@capecod.edu
ANDERSEN, Stephen 706-764-6936. 125 F
sandersen@gntc.edu
ANDERSEN,
Thomas Ove 828-884-8320. 352 I
ove.andersen@brevard.edu
ANDERSON, Aime 662-562-3305. 269 C
aanderson@northwestms.edu
ANDERSON, Al 406-275-4833. 288 C
al_anderson@skc.edu
ANDERSON, Alice 219-989-2335. 171 N
Andersag@purduecal.edu
ANDERSON, Amanda 304-204-4340. 530 C
aanderson13@wvstateu.edu
ANDERSON, Amy 813-253-7264. 106 M
aanderson@hccfl.edu
ANDERSON, Amy 269-782-1367. 250 C
aanderson@swmich.edu
ANDERSON, Amy, A 212-749-2802. 330 A
admission@msmnyc.edu
ANDERSON, Andrew 207-780-5585. 212 H
andrew@usm.maine.edu
ANDERSON, Angela 970-521-6659... 83 L
angela.anderson@njc.edu
ANDERSON, Angela, D 301-322-0699. 217 F
andersad@pgcc.edu
ANDERSON, Angela, R 252-328-6747. 367 B
andersona@ecu.edu
ANDERSON, Antje 402-461-7351. 289 I
aanderson@hastings.edu
ANDERSON, Barbara 660-248-6320. 272 B
banderso@centralmethodist.edu
ANDERSON, Barbara 206-708-4995. 194 A
barbara.anderson@frontier.edu
ANDERSON, Barry, L 901-334-5806. 457 A
banderson@memphisseminary.edu
ANDERSON, Belinda, C 757-823-8118. 507 M
bcanderson@nsu.edu
ANDERSON, Ben 859-572-5282. 198 I
andersonb5@nku.edu
ANDERSON,
Benjamin, J 828-298-3325. 370 E
benjand@warren-wilson.edu
ANDERSON, Beth 937-376-6588. 376 E
banderson@centralstate.edu
ANDERSON, Beth 423-461-8316. 457 H
banderson@milligan.edu
ANDERSON, Beth 218-322-2451. 258 I
beth.anderson@itascacc.edu
ANDERSON, Betty, H 337-475-5127. 207 G
anderson@mcneese.edu
ANDERSON, Betty, L 573-629-3055. 274 J
banderson@hlg.edu
ANDERSON, Bobby 209-386-6730... 54 D
robert.anderson@mccd.edu
ANDERSON, ESQ,
Bradford 805-756-5210... 32 F
bpanders@calpoly.edu
ANDERSON, Brett, B 970-491-7530... 80 I
brett.anderson@colostate.edu
ANDERSON, Bridges 334-222-6591..... 5 E
banderson@lbwcc.edu
ANDERSON, Bridgette 845-431-8655. 323 C
banderso@sunydutchess.edu
ANDERSON, Bruce, W 651-635-8051. 253 K
bw-anderson@bethel.edu
ANDERSON, C. Colt 718-817-4802. 324 G
coltanderson@fordham.edu
ANDERSON, Carl, A 202-526-3799... 96 D
ANDERSON, Cary, M 610-660-1045. 432 E
cander01@sju.edu
ANDERSON, Cathleen, R 315-445-4300. 328 F
anderscr@lemoyne.edu
ANDERSON, Cathy 302-736-2410... 94 C
andersca@wesley.edu
ANDERSON, Cathy 801-581-6940. 496 Q
cathy.anderson@hsc.utah.edu
ANDERSON, JR.,
Charles 606-436-5721. 195 C
chuck.anderson@kctcs.edu
ANDERSON, Charlise 731-410-6723. 455 J
canderson@lanecollege.edu
ANDERSON, Charlotte 785-227-3380. 184 I
andersonc@bethanylb.edu
ANDERSON, Cheryl 912-344-2586. 120 G
cheryl.anderson@armstrong.edu
ANDERSON, Cheryl 210-829-3837. 490 A
cheryla@uiwtx.edu
ANDERSON, Christi 806-894-9611. 480 H
canderson@southplainscollege.edu
ANDERSON, Christina 815-394-4388. 157 C
canderson@rockford.edu
ANDERSON, Cindy, L 304-558-4016. 529 C
canderson@hepc.wvnet.edu
ANDERSON, Claudette 601-979-0695. 267 E
claudette.d.anderson@jsums.edu
ANDERSON, Cody 828-835-4287. 364 E
canderson@tricountycc.edu
ANDERSON, Corey, R 541-684-7354. 405 C
canderson@nwcu.edu
ANDERSON, D. Craig 804-752-7270. 508 E
canderson@rmc.edu
ANDERSON, Dale, O 301-405-5648. 219 B
danderso@umd.edu
ANDERSON, Dan, J 515-574-2813. 179 D
anderson_dan@iowacentral.edu
ANDERSON, Daniel, J 336-278-7410. 354 B
andersd@elon.edu
ANDERSON, Daniel, L 304-877-6428. 526 C
president@abc.edu
ANDERSON, Danny 901-722-3204. 458 K
danderson@sco.edu
ANDERSON, Danny, J 785-864-3661. 190 L
djand@ku.edu
ANDERSON, Daryl 718-779-1430. 336 D
danderson1@mail.plazacollege.edu
ANDERSON, Dave 877-476-8674. 472 K
ANDERSON, David 949-582-4835... 67 C
danderson@saddleback.edu
ANDERSON, David 405-682-1611. 397 E
danderson@occc.edu
ANDERSON, David, R 507-786-3000. 264 B
anderson@stolaf.edu
ANDERSON, Dawn, L 619-260-7733... 73 I
dawn@sandiego.edu
ANDERSON, Deborah 906-786-5802. 240 K
andersod@baycollege.edu
ANDERSON, Dee Dee 423-425-4761. 463 D
deedee-anderson@utc.edu
ANDERSON, Delia, C 617-732-2910. 233 E
delia.anderson@mcphs.edu
ANDERSON, Della 808-455-0598. 137 A
dellaand@hawaii.edu
ANDERSON, Diane, K 269-387-2152. 252 I
diane.anderson@wmich.edu
ANDERSON, Dianna 704-886-6500... 96 F

ANDERSON, Dianne .... 505-277-1807. 312 F danderson@unm.edu
ANDERSON, Don, K .... 515-964-0601. 178 E andersond@faith.edu
ANDERSON, Donna .... 607-431-4827. 325 F andersond@hartwick.edu.
ANDERSON, Donna, M .. 941-359-6116. 111 O danderso@ringling.edu
ANDERSON, Douglas, A 814-863-1484. 426 A daa7@psu.edu
ANDERSON, Douglas, D 435-797-2376. 497 B douglas.anderson@usu.edu
ANDERSON, Douglas, P 651-523-2203. 256 A danderson@hamline.edu
ANDERSON, Duane, C ... 580-559-5204. 395 F dandersn@ecok.edu
ANDERSON, Elizabeth .... 717-264-4141. 437 H eanderson@wilson.edu
ANDERSON, Eric .... 712-707-7132. 181 H eric.anderson@nwciowa.edu
ANDERSON, Eric .... 715-855-7512. 539 J eanderson72@cvtc.edu
ANDERSON, Eric, D .... 817-202-6202. 481 E eanderson@swau.edu
ANDERSON, Eric, R .... 614-236-6606. 375 H eanderson@capital.edu
ANDERSON, Eugene .... 305-284-4643. 118 F genea@miami.edu
ANDERSON, Eugene .... 757-823-8053. 507 M
ANDERSON, Faith .... 912-443-5776. 131 D fanderson@savannahtech.edu
ANDERSON, Francine ..... 540-231-4000. 504 G
ANDERSON, G. Scott ..... 212-220-8051. 317 A sanderson@bmcc.cuny.edu
ANDERSON, G. Scott ..... 718-270-6113. 319 A gsanderson@mec.cuny.edu
ANDERSON, Gail .... 715-425-3232. 537 E gail.anderson@uwrf.edu
ANDERSON, George, W . 713-221-8449. 489 D andersong@uhd.edu
ANDERSON, Gloria .... 334-872-2533..... 6 G
ANDERSON, Gordon, K .. 423-439-5671. 459 C andersgk@etsu.edu
ANDERSON, Gordon, L .. 612-343-4741. 262 X president@northcentral.edu
ANDERSON, Greg .... 215-204-8017. 433 K greg.anderson@temple.edu
ANDERSON, Gregory ...... 650-306-3353... 64 B andersong@smccd.edu
ANDERSON, Heather ...... 207-801-5623. 210 A handerson@coa.edu
ANDERSON, Heidi .... 215-596-8863. 435 H h.anderson@usciences.edu
ANDERSON, Heidi .... 605-394-4034. 452 E heidi.anderson@wdt.edu
ANDERSON, Ian .... 207-775-3052. 210 H ianderson@meca.edu
ANDERSON, Jaclyn .... 913-288-7670. 187 L jaanderson@kckcc.edu
ANDERSON, Jade .... 870-307-7540... 21 H jade.anderson@lyon.edu
ANDERSON, James .... 208-426-2384. 137 G jamesanderson@boisestate.edu
ANDERSON, James .... 912-344-3128. 120 G James.Anderson@armstrong.edu
ANDERSON, James .... 570-208-5858. 419 P jamesanderson@kings.edu
ANDERSON, James, A .... 910-672-1141. 367 D janderson@uncfsu.edu
ANDERSON, James, T .... 973-655-7022. 303 D andersonja@mail.montclair.edu
ANDERSON, Janet .... 541-463-5803. 403 I andersonj@lanecc.edu
ANDERSON, Janice .... 254-526-1116. 468 G janice.anderson@ctcd.edu
ANDERSON, Jeanette ...... 626-571-8811... 74 B jeanettea@uwest.edu
ANDERSON, Jeanette ...... 626-873-2144... 55 C janderson@mtsierra.edu
ANDERSON, Jeff .... 715-232-4053. 538 B andersonjeff@uwstout.edu
ANDERSON, Jeffery .... 334-244-3502..... 2 A janderso@aum.edu
ANDERSON, Jeffrey .... 561-297-1165. 114 L janderson@fau.edu
ANDERSON, Jeffrey .... 352-588-8657. 112 D jeffrey.anderson@saintleo.edu
ANDERSON, Jeffrey .... 518-255-5413. 344 E andersjm@cobleskill.edu
ANDERSON, Jeffrey, R ... 260-481-6116. 168 C andersjr@ipfw.edu
ANDERSON, Jeffrey, W .. 423-439-6846. 459 C andersjw@etsu.edu
ANDERSON, Jeffrey, W .. 423-439-5381. 459 C andersjw@etsu.edu
ANDERSON, Jennifer ...... 614-287-5581. 378 B jander02@cscc.edu
ANDERSON, Jeremy .... 606-337-1533. 193 F janderson@ccbbc.edu
ANDERSON, Jill .... 307-754-6401. 543 G Jill.Anderson@northwestcollege.edu
ANDERSON, Jillian .... 508-929-8072. 230 G Jillian.Anderson@worcester.edu
ANDERSON, Jim .... 563-588-4948. 180 L jim.anderson@loras.edu
ANDERSON, JoAn .... 281-756-3517. 465 D janderson@alvincollege.edu
ANDERSON, Joan, E ...... 508-793-3644. 225 B janderso@holycross.edu
ANDERSON, Joanna .... 660-596-7223. 282 G janderson@sfccmo.edu
ANDERSON, Joel, E .... 501-569-3200... 24 B jeanderson@ualr.edu
ANDERSON, John, A ...... 770-499-3132. 127 N janders2@kennesaw.edu
ANDERSON, John, L ...... 312-567-5198. 147 F johna@iit.edu
ANDERSON, John, M ..... 717-872-3591. 429 D mupresident@millersville.edu
ANDERSON, Jon .... 678-839-6445. 133 I janderso@westga.edu
ANDERSON, Joyce .... 208-376-7731. 137 F joycea@boisebible.edu
ANDERSON, JP .... 585-594-6400. 337 K anderson_jp@roberts.edu
ANDERSON, Judith .... 507-538-0162. 254 F anderson.judith@mayo.edu
ANDERSON, Judy .... 620-341-5379. 186 D jander21@emporia.edu
ANDERSON, Karen .... 515-643-6791. 181 A kanderson8@mercydesmoines.org
ANDERSON, Karen, L ..... 860-685-2337... 92 H kanderson@wesleyan.edu
ANDERSON, Kathleen ..... 410-837-5249. 221 A kanderson@ubalt.edu
ANDERSON, Kathleen, M .... 610-989-1450. 436 D kanderson@vfmac.edu
ANDERSON, Kathryn ...... 757-825-2851. 514 B andersonk@tncc.edu
ANDERSON, Kathy .... 617-724-6356. 234 B kanderson@mghihp.edu
ANDERSON, Kay .... 478-445-6286. 125 A kay.anderson@gcsu.edu
ANDERSON, Keith .... 434-582-2320. 506 I kranderson@liberty.edu
ANDERSON, Keith, R ..... 206-876-6101. 523 D kanderson@theseattleschool.edu
ANDERSON, Kelly .... 419-772-2073. 386 D k-anderson@onu.edu
ANDERSON, Kenny .... 407-628-5870. 102 K kanderson@cci.edu
ANDERSON, Kevin .... 301-314-7075. 219 B athleticdir@umd.edu
ANDERSON, Kevin, L ..... 563-589-0211. 183 F kanderson@wartburgseminary.edu
ANDERSON, Kim .... 484-365-7565. 422 D kanderson@lincoln.edu
ANDERSON, Kristen, C .. 802-443-5092. 499 H kanderso@middlebury.edu
ANDERSON, Kristin, K ... 901-722-3216. 458 K kanderson@sco.edu
ANDERSON, Kristina .... 715-425-0699. 537 E Kristina.Anderson@uwrf.edu
ANDERSON, Kristy .... 530-938-5521... 41 A kanderson@siskiyous.edu
ANDERSON, Kristy .... 360-538-4101. 520 B kanderso@ghc.edu
ANDERSON, Larry .... 318-797-5371. 205 F larry.anderson@lsus.edu
ANDERSON, Larry .... 218-879-0842. 258 E larrya@fdltcc.edu
ANDERSON, Larry .... 218-879-0822. 258 E larrya@fdltcc.edu
ANDERSON, Larry .... 660-248-6251. 272 B landerso@centralmethodist.edu
ANDERSON, Laura .... 540-362-7439. 505 G ltanderson@hollins.edu
ANDERSON, Leah .... 864-503-5240. 448 H landerson@uscupstate.edu
ANDERSON, Leesa, P .... 706-778-3000. 130 E landerson@piedmont.edu
ANDERSON, Leif, B .... 612-330-1497. 253 H andersol@augsburg.edu
ANDERSON, Leslie .... 309-796-5933. 140 E andersonle@bhc.edu
ANDERSON, Leslie .... 870-733-6732... 21 I landerson@midsouthcc.edu
ANDERSON, Linda .... 503-297-5544. 405 D landerson@ocac.edu
ANDERSON, Linda, M ..... 412-268-1939. 412 H la18@andrew.cmu.edu
ANDERSON, Linda, S ..... 816-604-2380. 277 F linda.anderson@mcckc.edu
ANDERSON, Lisa .... 218-723-6738. 254 K landerso@css.edu
ANDERSON, Lisa .... 479-619-2227... 22 C landerson7@nwacc.edu
ANDERSON, Louise .... 269-488-4777. 244 L landerson@kvcc.edu
ANDERSON, LuAnne ...... 218-733-7680. 259 A l.anderson@lsc.edu
ANDERSON, Lydia .... 907-474-7037... 10 I lmanderson@alaska.edu
ANDERSON, Lynda .... 480-732-7019... 14 J lynda.anderson@cgc.edu
ANDERSON, Marcane ..... 757-822-7183. 514 C manderson@tcc.edu
ANDERSON, Margaret .... 413-565-1000. 222 F panderso@baypath.edu
ANDERSON, Margie .... 435-283-7145. 498 A margie.anderson@snow.edu
ANDERSON, Marie .... 909-469-5485... 76 B manderson@westernu.edu
ANDERSON, Mark .... 860-628-4751... 90 D manderson@lincolncollegene.edu
ANDERSON, Mark .... 650-949-7156... 44 N andersonmark@foothill.edu
ANDERSON, Mark, R ..... 770-423-6160. 127 N mande126@kennesaw.edu
ANDERSON, Marlene ..... 701-224-5578. 372 B marlene.anderson@bismarckstate.edu
ANDERSON, Martha .... 602-285-7553... 15 C martha.anderson@phoenixcollege.edu
ANDERSON, Mary .... 815-939-5243. 155 H manderso@olivet.edu
ANDERSON, Mary Ellen . 812-855-9845. 167 F manderso@indiana.edu
ANDERSON, Max .... 312-942-6832. 157 G max_anderson@rush.edu
ANDERSON, Melinda, F . 318-619-2916. 205 A manderson@lsua.edu
ANDERSON, Melissa, K . 920-748-8365. 535 J andersonmk@ripon.edu
ANDERSON, Melissa, L . 336-841-9220. 355 C manderson@highpoint.edu
ANDERSON, Melissa, P . 540-674-3635. 513 B manderson@nr.edu
ANDERSON, Michael ...... 312-369-8652. 143 D manderson@colum.edu
ANDERSON, Michael ...... 402-375-7208. 291 F miander1@wsc.edu
ANDERSON, Michael ...... 718-951-5280. 317 C manderson@brooklyn.cuny.edu
ANDERSON, Michelle ..... 707-476-4170... 40 H michelle-anderson@redwoods.edu
ANDERSON, Michelle ..... 724-503-1001. 436 G manderson@washjeff.edu
ANDERSON, Mike .... 253-589-5529. 518 B mike.anderson@cptc.edu
ANDERSON, Molllie .... 402-554-2321. 293 A mkanderson@unomaha.edu
ANDERSON, Monique, W .... 865-974-2101. 463 C manders@utk.edu
ANDERSON, Myron .... 303-556-3022... 83 D mande118@msudenver.edu
ANDERSON, N. Douglas 740-376-4536. 383 E doug.anderson@marietta.edu
ANDERSON, Nancy .... 978-867-4828. 226 H nancy.anderson@gordon.edu
ANDERSON, Nancy, K .... 325-649-8610. 473 F nanderson@hputx.edu
ANDERSON, Nina .... 732-571-7577. 303 C nanderso@monmouth.edu
ANDERSON, Norma, J .... 210-434-6711. 477 N njanderson@lake.ollusa.edu
ANDERSON, Patricia ...... 775-753-2115. 294 F pat.anderson@gbcnv.edu
ANDERSON, Patty .... 386-752-1822. 104 G patty.anderson@fgc.edu
ANDERSON, Per .... 218-299-3932. 255 A anderson@cord.edu
ANDERSON, Phyllis .... 510-559-2710... 57 F president@plts.edu
ANDERSON, Rachel .... 541-881-5590. 408 C randerson@tvcc.cc
ANDERSON, Rachel, L ... 302-453-3721... 93 F rachel.anderson@dtcc.edu
ANDERSON, Randy .... 323-953-4000... 51 G andersr@lacitycollege.edu
ANDERSON, Rayelle .... 208-769-5978. 138 I rayelle_anderson@nic.edu
ANDERSON, Rebecca ..... 704-337-2485. 365 G andersonr@queens.edu
ANDERSON, Rhonda, C . 989-837-4455. 248 C rca@northwood.edu
ANDERSON, Richard, L .. 512-863-1471. 481 I andersor@southwestern.edu
ANDERSON, Rick .... 252-940-6417. 358 A ricka@beaufortccc.edu
ANDERSON, Rick .... 701-777-3171. 371 C rick.anderson@und.edu
ANDERSON, Rick .... 801-585-9521. 496 Q rick.anderson@utah.edu
ANDERSON, Rick, L .... 785-670-1634. 191 D rick.anderson@washburn.edu
ANDERSON, Robert .... 941-359-4200. 117 A
ANDERSON, Robert .... 509-359-2531. 519 C randerson@ewu.edu
ANDERSON, Robert, E ... 304-558-4016. 529 C randerson@hepc.wvnet.edu
ANDERSON, Robin .... 503-943-7224. 408 F anderson@up.edu
ANDERSON, Roger .... 908-852-1400. 300 D andersonr@centenarycollege.edu
ANDERSON, Ron .... 651-779-3368. 258 C ron.anderson@century.edu
ANDERSON, Ronald, M . 859-858-3511. 192 B ron.anderson@asbury.edu
ANDERSON, Russell .... 601-266-4153. 270 E rusty.anderson@usm.edu
ANDERSON, Sandra, E ... 605-256-5143. 451 H sandy.anderson@dsu.edu
ANDERSON, Scott, R ..... 815-599-3604. 146 D scott.anderson@highland.edu
ANDERSON, Sharee .... 208-524-3000. 138 D sharee.anderson@my.eitc.edu
ANDERSON, Sharon, D .. 336-734-7735. 360 E sanderson@forsythtech.edu
ANDERSON, Shawn .... 218-299-6535. 259 F shawn.anderson@minnesota.edu
ANDERSON, Sherry .... 270-534-3145. 196 G sherry.anderson@kctcs.edu
ANDERSON, Stephanie ... 512-245-2803. 487 C sa35@txstate.edu
ANDERSON, Stephen, P . 830-372-8020. 485 C sanderson@tlu.edu
ANDERSON, Steve .... 816-415-7805. 285 C andersonst@william.jewell.edu
ANDERSON, Steven .... 620-365-5116. 183 I anderson@allencc.edu
ANDERSON, Steven .... 724-503-1001. 436 G sanderson@washjeff.edu
ANDERSON, Susan .... 216-373-6396. 385 G andersons@ndc.edu
ANDERSON, Susan, M ... 530-898-6472... 33 A sanderson@csuchico.edu
ANDERSON, Suzanne ..... 701-777-2711. 371 C suzanne.anderson@und.edu
ANDERSON, Suzanne, M .... 540-853-0691. 506 G srmcquire@carilionclinic.org
ANDERSON, Tabitha .... 304-424-8271. 530 E tabitha.anderson@wvup.edu
ANDERSON, Tamara .... 508-565-1661. 237 A tanderson@stonehill.edu
ANDERSON, Teri .... 620-278-4202. 190 I tanderson@sterling.edu
ANDERSON, Therese ...... 215-596-8813. 435 H registrar@uschiences.edu
ANDERSON, Timothy, J . 413-545-6388. 228 F tjanderson@ecs.umass.edu
ANDERSON, Tina, K .... 229-891-7000. 129 F tanderson@moultrietech.edu
ANDERSON, Tina, K .... 229-333-2119. 134 K tina.anderson@wiregrass.edu
ANDERSON, Toby .... 218-749-0319. 259 B t.anderson@mr.mnscu.edu
ANDERSON, Todd .... 910-521-6371. 369 B todd.anderson@uncp.edu
ANDERSON, Tracey .... 304-327-4331. 529 D tanderson@bluefieldstate.edu
ANDERSON, Trudy, J ..... 208-364-4002. 139 D tanderso@uidaho.edu
ANDERSON, Vanessa ..... 303-797-5930... 78 F vanessa.anderson@arapahoe.edu
ANDERSON, Wanda .... 302-736-2443... 94 C wanda.anderson@wesley.edu
ANDERSON, Warren .... 315-268-3785. 320 A wanderso@clarkson.edu
ANDERSON, Wayne, K ... 716-645-2823. 341 F wka@buffalo.edu
ANDERSON, William .... 845-431-8961. 323 C william.anderson@sunydutchess.edu
ANDERSON, William .... 901-435-1226. 455 M william_anderson@loc.edu
ANDERSON, William, J .. 603-646-2485. 296 G william.j.anderson@dartmouth.edu
ANDERSON, William, L .. 301-322-0622. 217 F wanderson@pgcc.edu
ANDERSON, William, O . 610-660-1276. 432 E banderso@sju.edu
ANDERSON, William, O . 802-654-2252. 500 B wanderson@smcvt.edu
ANDERSON-BINA, Cindy .... 218-235-2121. 261 G c.bina@vcc.edu
ANDERSON-CONLIFFE, Debra .... 304-766-3237. 530 C andersonde@wvstateu.edu
ANDERSON-OLIVER, Amena .... 304-336-8274. 530 A aanderson@westliberty.edu
ANDERSON-SAPATA, Barbara .... 847-233-7700. 155 B banderson-sapata@nc.edu
ANDERTON, Mark .... 435-722-6900. 496 M marka@ubatc.edu
ANDINO, Trinidad .... 610-917-1431. 436 C t_andino@vfcc.edu
ANDORS, Allison .... 516-686-7737. 333 H aandors@nyit.edu

ANDRADE, Alicia .... 559-453-2220... 45 D
alicia.andrade@fresno.edu

ANDRADE, Anne, M .... 401-254-3207. 440 B
amandrade@rwu.edu

ANDRADE, June .... 787-728-1515. 555 D
jandrade@sagrado.edu

ANDRADE, Kim .... 405-422-1267. 399 B
andradek@redlandscc.edu

ANDRADE, Maureen .... 801-863-6158. 497 C
maureen.andrade@uvu.edu

ANDRADE, Ruddys .... 201-200-3364. 303 F
randrade@njcu.edu

ANDRAWES, Janette .... 415-749-4515... 62 G
jandrawes@sfai.edu

ANDREA, Francine .... 201-559-6181. 302 A
andreaf@felician.edu

ANDREA, Robert .... 518-956-8206. 341 D
randrea@albany.edu

ANDREADIS, Clea .... 781-280-3911. 232 B
andreadisc@middlesex.mass.edu

ANDREAS, Michelle .... 360-596-5209. 524 A
mandreas@spscc.edu

ANDREASEN,
Michael, C .... 541-346-0869. 406 D
miandrea@uoregon.edu

ANDREASEN,
Niels-Erik, A .... 269-471-3100. 239 D
neaa@andrews.edu

ANDRECHAK, Mike .... 217-333-4493. 162 A
mandrech@illinois.edu

ANDREI, Michael, G .... 716-839-8472. 322 E
mandrei@daemen.edu

ANDREINI, Janelle, S ..... 402-465-2414. 291 G
jsa@nebrwesleyan.edu

ANDREJCZYK, Rose, L ... 413-205-3248. 221 F
rose.andrejczyk@aic.edu

ANDREOLA, Michael .... 412-536-1096. 420 A
michael.andreola@laroche.edu

ANDRESEN, Julie, A .... 573-629-4001. 274 J
jandresen@hlg.edu

ANDRESEN, Kirsten .... 310-338-1998... 53 E
kandresen@lmu.edu

ANDRESEN, Sharla .... 541-383-7208. 402 D
sandresen@cocc.edu

ANDRESS, Reinhard .... 773-508-3505. 151 H
randress@luc.edu

ANDRESS-MARTIN,
Holly .... 583-288-6421. 273 F
handress@culver.edu

ANDREU, Angel, E .... 585-292-3031. 332 A
aandreu@monroecc.edu

ANDREU, Frank .... 305-821-3333. 105 A
fandreu@fnu.edu

ANDREW, Aletha .... 919-735-5151. 364 H
raandrew@waynecc.edu

ANDREW, Damon .... 334-670-3712..... 7 H
dandrew@troy.edu

ANDREW, Damon, P .... 225-578-2043. 204 O
damonandrew@lsu.edu

ANDREW, Kenneth .... 304-473-8367. 531 G
andrew_k@wvwc.edu

ANDREW, Matt .... 314-968-6955. 284 N
matthewandrew91@webster.edu

ANDREWS, Aaron .... 870-759-4105... 25 K
aandrews@wbcoll.edu

ANDREWS, Adrienne .... 530-642-5644... 53 C

ANDREWS, Arthur, W ...... 919-866-5688. 364 G
awandrews@waketech.edu

ANDREWS, Beverly .... 269-467-9945. 242 H
bandrews@glenoaks.edu

ANDREWS, Bradley, J ..... 262-551-5850. 532 D
bandrews@carthage.edu

ANDREWS, Brett .... 918-335-6250. 398 F
bandrews@okwu.edu

ANDREWS, Carolyn .... 806-291-3400. 494 F
andrewsc@wbu.edu

ANDREWS, Chip, L .... 770-534-6759. 122 A
candrews@brenau.edu

ANDREWS, Cyndi .... 503-594-3025. 402 F
cyndia@clackamas.edu

ANDREWS, Danielle .... 614-825-6255. 373 G
dandrews@aiam.edu

ANDREWS, Danny .... 806-291-3600. 494 F
andrewsd@wbu.edu

ANDREWS, David, W .... 410-516-7820. 215 H
davidandrews@jhu.edu

ANDREWS, Dianna, L ..... 904-264-2172. 111 P
dianna.andrews@iws.edu

ANDREWS, Dionne, T .... 304-457-6324. 526 A
andrewsdt@ab.edu

ANDREWS, Donald, R .... 225-771-5640. 206 J
jazandrews@yahoo.com

ANDREWS, Douglas, M . 863-784-7177. 113 G
doug.andrews@southflorida.edu

ANDREWS, Evelyn .... 707-654-1794... 31 I
eandrews@csum.edu

ANDREWS, George .... 305-237-3316. 109 D
gandrews@mdc.edu

ANDREWS, Herry .... 307-778-1231. 543 D
handrews@lccc.wy.edu

ANDREWS, Jeannette ..... 803-777-3862. 447 G
jandrews@mailbox.sc.edu

ANDREWS, Jeff .... 601-318-6741. 270 I
jeff.andrews@wmcarey.edu

ANDREWS, Karen, B .... 770-423-6555. 127 N
kandrews@kennesaw.edu

ANDREWS, Karren .... 541-880-2203. 403 H
andrews@klamathcc.edu

ANDREWS, Larry .... 903-823-3349. 482 D
larry.andrews@texarkanacollege.edu

ANDREWS, Lenora .... 716-286-8708. 334 F
laa@niagara.edu

ANDREWS, Lewis .... 410-276-0306. 218 D
landrews@host.sdc.edu

ANDREWS, Linda .... 434-544-8324. 506 K
andrews@lynchburg.edu

ANDREWS, Linda .... 713-798-4606. 467 F
landrews@bcm.edu

ANDREWS, Loretta .... 406-447-4508. 285 G
landrews@carroll.edu

ANDREWS, Lynn .... 503-699-6309. 404 C
landrews@marylhurst.edu

ANDREWS, Margaret .... 810-762-3420. 251 E
mmandrew@umflint.edu

ANDREWS, Mark .... 770-228-7367. 132 B
mandrews@sctech.edu

ANDREWS, Michael, F ... 503-943-8628. 408 F
andrews@up.edu

ANDREWS, Mitch .... 903-510-2034. 488 E
mand@tjc.edu

ANDREWS, Nancy .... 919-684-2455. 354 A
nancy.andrews@mc.duke.edu

ANDREWS, Nikki .... 508-373-9701. 223 A
nikki.andrews@becker.edu

ANDREWS, Penelope ...... 518-445-2321. 313 C
pandr@albanylaw.edu

ANDREWS, Richard .... 916-691-7423... 53 B
andrewr@crc.losrios.edu

ANDREWS, Sabrina, L .... 330-972-6959. 390 E
sabrin7@uakron.edu

ANDREWS, Serena .... 979-230-3245. 468 A
serena.andrews@brazosport.edu

ANDREWS, Sona .... 503-725-5257. 406 B
sona.andrews@pdx.edu

ANDREWS, Stacie .... 814-254-0557. 413 C
standrews@pa.gov

ANDREWS, Susan .... 309-677-3296. 140 I
susancan@bradley.edu

ANDREWS, Terri .... 954-923-4440. 108 P
financial@keycollege.edu

ANDREWS, Tim .... 913-360-7367. 184 H
tandrews@benedictine.edu

ANDREWS, Todd, G .... 401-863-6331. 438 J
todd_andrews@brown.edu

ANDREWS, Todd, J .... 860-727-6937... 90 A
tandrews@goodwin.edu

ANDREWS, Trisha .... 847-543-2007. 143 A
tandrews@clcillinois.edu

ANDREWS, Wayne, D ..... 606-783-2022. 198 A
w.andrews@moreheadstate.edu

ANDRIANO, Sarah .... 802-865-5740. 499 A
sandriano@champlain.edu

ANDRIATCH, Michael ...... 585-395-5809. 342 F
mandriat@brockport.edu

ANDRIOTIS-BAITINGER,
Katerina .... 908-737-7030. 302 F
andriotk@kean.edu

ANDRITZ, Mary, H .... 317-940-9735. 164 J
mandritz@butler.edu

ANDROUIN, George .... 904-620-4222. 116 B
gandroui@unf.edu

ANDRZEJEWSKI,
Margaret .... 716-827-2564. 348 G
andrzejewskim@trocaire.edu

ANDRZJEWSKI,
Linda, M .... 302-356-6754... 94 E
linda.m.andrzjewski@wilmu.edu

ANDUJAR-WENDLAND,
Sandra .... 212-686-9040. 350 G
s.andujar@woodtobecoburn.edu

ANELAUSKAS, Jillian ...... 617-730-7105. 235 D
jill.anelauskas@newbury.edu

ANEMA, Laurie .... 708-974-5343. 153 F
anema@morainevalley.edu

ANGE, Crystal .... 252-940-6216. 358 A
crystala@beaufortccc.edu

ANGEL, Carmen .... 505-428-1000. 311 J
carmen.angel@sfcc.edu

ANGEL, Daniel, D .... 415-442-6570... 45 I
dangel@ggu.edu

ANGEL, David, P .... 508-793-7320. 225 A
dangel@clarku.edu

ANGELES, Rocio .... 805-893-6189... 72 B
rangeles@ltsc.ucsb.edu

ANGELIS, Peter .... 310-825-4941... 71 C
pangelis@ha.ucla.edu

ANGELL, Alecia .... 509-527-3683. 524 H
alecia.angell@wwcc.edu

ANGELL, Lance, R .... 270-707-3709. 195 E
lance.angell@kctcs.edu

ANGELL, Mary .... 505-473-6322. 311 K
mary.angell@santafeuniversity.edu

ANGELL, Townsend .... 503-777-7283. 407 E
townsend.angell@reed.edu

ANGELO, Caroline .... 706-355-5013. 120 J
cangelo@athenstech.edu

ANGELO, Larian .... 646-313-8000. 319 E

ANGELONE, Lenora .... 724-938-4439. 428 A
angelone@calu.edu

ANGELONI, Lisa .... 609-771-3080. 300 E
angeloni@tcnj.edu

ANGELOTTI, Linda .... 408-855-5123... 75 K
linda.angelotti@wvm.edu

ANGEMI, Karen .... 909-621-8384... 46 H
karen_angemi@hmc.edu

ANGER, Donna .... 907-474-6131... 10 I
dmanger@alaska.edu

ANGER, Paul .... 928-428-6260... 13 J
paul.anger@eac.edu

ANGEVINE, Roger, L .... 606-878-4801. 196 D
roger.angevine@kctcs.edu

ANGIOLLIO, Elise .... 561-297-0202. 114 L
elise@fau.edu

ANGIS, Victoria .... 802-468-1231. 501 B
victoria.angis@castleton.edu

ANGLE, J. Scott .... 706-542-3924. 133 C
caesdean@uga.edu

ANGLE, Nick .... 517-629-0305. 239 A
nangle@albion.edu

ANGLE, Ray .... 919-962-4481. 368 D
rayangle@email.unc.edu

ANGLE, Steven .... 423-425-4141. 463 D
steven-angle@utc.edu

ANGLEA, John .... 937-484-1395. 392 C
janglea@urbana.edu

ANGLIM, Sean .... 315-568-3092. 333 C
sanglim@nycc.edu

ANGLIN, Jennifer .... 866-251-3244... 97 I

ANGLIN, Marcus .... 213-763-7227... 52 D
anglimj@lattc.edu

ANGLIN, Mark .... 209-575-2000... 77 J
anglinm@mjc.edu

ANGLIN, Pamela, D .... 903-785-7661. 478 B
panglin@parisjc.edu

ANGRISANI, Vincent .... 718-997-5600. 319 C
vincent.angrisani@qc.cuny.edu

ANGST, JR., Arthur, H ... 516-876-3094. 343 D
angsta@oldwestbury.edu

ANGSTADT, Peter .... 541-956-7000. 407 F
pangstadt@roguecc.edu

ANGSTER, Sherrie .... 626-966-4576... 27 P
studentservices@agu.edu

ANGUIANO, Amy .... 540-857-7385. 514 E

ANGULO, Susan .... 305-628-6566. 112 F
cangulo@stu.edu

ANID, Nada .... 516-686-7931. 333 H
nanid@nyit.edu

ANKE, Sharla, M .... 724-287-8711. 411 C
sharla.anke@bc3.edu

ANKENBAUER, Marilyn .. 817-923-8459. 469 F
marilyn.ankenbauer@fishermore.edu

ANKENY, Mark .... 503-352-2924. 407 A
mankeny@pacificu.edu

ANKER, Laura, M .... 516-876-3460. 343 D
ankerl@oldwestbury.edu

ANKER, Perryne .... 310-824-1586... 26 B

ANKER, Steve .... 661-255-1050... 31 C
sanker@calarts.edu

ANKERSEN, Lynne .... 843-574-6137. 447 E
lynne.ankersen@tridenttech.edu

ANKROM, Jeff .... 937-327-6142. 393 E
jankrom@wittenberg.edu

ANKROM, Jeff, A .... 937-327-6231. 393 E
jankrom@wittenberg.edu

ANKUDA, Pamela .... 802-728-1530. 501 F
pankuda@vtc.edu

ANNA, Gary, M .... 309-677-3150. 140 I
gma@bradley.edu

ANNAN, Jack .... 970-521-6690... 83 L
jack.annan@njc.edu

ANNARELLI, James, J .... 727-864-8421. 101 N
annarejj@eckerd.edu

ANNETT, JR., Bruce, J ... 248-204-2200. 245 I
bannett@ltu.edu

ANNETTE, Harold .... 218-322-2353. 258 I
harold.annette@itascacc.edu

ANNING, Peter .... 408-855-5125... 75 K
peter.anning@wvm.edu

ANNINO, Louis .... 203-932-7153... 92 E
lannino@newhaven.edu

ANNIS, David, L .... 405-325-2300. 401 B
dannis@ou.edu

ANNIS, Dominique, A ..... 815-740-3398. 162 F
dannis@stfrancis.edu

ANNIS, Patricia, O .... 207-942-6781. 209 E
pannis@bts.edu

ANNIS, Robert, L .... 609-921-7100. 305 D
annis@rider.edu

ANNUNZIATO, Frank .... 215-204-7366. 433 K
frank.annunziato@temple.edu

ANSARI, Parviz .... 856-256-4850. 305 E
ansari@rowan.edu

ANSARI, Shahid .... 781-239-4277. 222 D
sansari@babson.edu

ANSBOURY, Pamela .... 210-485-0307. 464 I
pansboury@alamo.edu

ANSEL, Stuart .... 718-252-7800. 348 B
sansel@touro.edu

ANSELMENT, Kenneth, L 920-832-6992. 533 S
ken.anselment@lawrence.edu

ANSON, Dena .... 785-670-1154. 191 D
dena.anson@washburn.edu

ANSON, Regan .... 402-872-2429. 291 E
ranson@peru.edu

ANSORGE, Vicki .... 920-686-6203. 536 A
Vicki.Ansorge@sl.edu

ANSTROM, Deborah .... 828-298-3325. 370 E
purchasing@warren-wilson.edu

ANSTROM, Deborah .... 828-298-3325. 370 E
danstrom@warren-wilson.edu

ANTCZAK, Frederick .... 616-331-2495. 243 C
antczakf@gvsu.edu

ANTEL, Lisa .... 203-596-4585... 90 I
lantel@post.edu

ANTENEN, James .... 210-826-7595. 494 F
antenenj@wbu.edu

ANTENORCRUC, Connie . 714-953-6500... 43 I

ANTENUCCI, Lindsay ...... 818-785-2726... 37 F
lindsay.antenucci@casalomacollege.edu

ANTER, David .... 805-378-1415... 74 F
danter@vcccd.edu

ANTES, Joann, B .... 570-372-4049. 433 H
antes@susqu.edu

ANTHONY, Cynthia .... 205-929-3510..... 5 D
canthony@lawsonstate.edu

ANTHONY, Kathy .... 610-526-6045. 417 H
kanthony@harcum.edu

ANTHONY, Lewis .... 301-736-3631. 216 B
lewis.anthony@msbbcs.edu

ANTHONY, Linda .... 410-843-8217. 265 D
Linda.Anthony@laureate.net

ANTHONY, Lorraine .... 518-587-2100. 346 A
lorraine.anthony@esc.edu

ANTHONY, Michael .... 847-635-1745. 155 F
manthony@oakton.edu

ANTHONY, Miriam .... 708-596-2000. 159 C
manthony@ssc.edu

ANTHONY, Pamela .... 515-294-1022. 175 H
panthony@iastate.edu

ANTHONY, Patrick .... 404-385-7344. 125 D
patrick.anthony@dopp.gatech.edu

ANTHONY, Philadelphia . 336-750-3301. 370 A
philadelphiaw@wssu.edu

ANTHONY, Richard, M ... 202-408-2400... 96 F

ANTHONY, Sharon .... 215-572-2850. 409 H
anthony@arcadia.edu

ANTHWAL, Sunny .... 845-398-4061. 340 A
sunny@stac.edu

ANTILLA, Margaret .... 503-338-2428. 402 G
mantilla@clatsopcc.edu

ANTILLON, Susan .... 386-506-3656. 101 G
antills@DaytonaState.edu

ANTKOWIAK, Alex .... 410-337-6060. 215 A
alex.antkowiak@goucher.edu

ANTMAN, Karen, H .... 617-638-5300. 224 D
kha4@bu.edu

ANTOINE, Kevin .... 718-270-1738. 342 D
kevin.antoine@downstate.edu

ANTOINE, Linda, B .... 225-771-4580. 206 J
linda_antoine@subr.edu

ANTOKHIN, Kathleen ...... 510-649-2469... 38 J
kantokhin@gtu.edu

ANTOKHIN, Kathleen ...... 510-649-2463... 46 B
kantokhin@gtu.edu

ANTOLINI, Heather .... 304-647-6374. 530 B
hantolini@osteo.wvsom.edu

ANTON, Janis, K .... 312-777-8508. 147 D
janton@aii.edu

ANTONIA, Keith .... 706-867-2886. 133 D
keith.antonia@ung.edu

ANTONICH, Cheryl .... 708-456-0300. 161 A
cantonic@triton.edu

ANTONIO, Edward .... 303-765-3163... 82 E
eantonio@iliff.edu

ANTONS,
Christopher, M .... 210-431-6718. 479 D
cantons@stmarytx.edu

ANTONUCCI, Carl .... 860-832-2099... 87 K
antonucci@ccsu.edu

ANTONUCCI,
Dorothy, M .... 412-578-8770. 412 G
dmantonucci@carlow.edu

ANTONUCCI, Frank .... 716-896-0700. 350 A
antonucci@villa.edu

ANTONUCCI, Robert, V .. 978-665-3101. 229 E
rantonucci@fitchburgstate.edu

ANTONUCCI, Toni, C ...... 734-763-5846. 251 C
tca@umich.edu

ANTROBUS, Barbara .... 859-858-2285. 192 A

ANTUNES, Marie .... 540-636-2900. 503 L
alumni@christendom.edu

ANTURKAR, Anjali, N ..... 734-764-5132. 251 C anturkar@umich.edu
ANUZZI, Carmen .... 484-384-2976. 425 I canuzzi@eastern.edu
ANYANWU, FitzPatrick ... 337-421-6905. 204 E fitzpatrick.anyanwu@sowela.edu
ANYANWU, Fitzpatrick, U .... 337-421-6905. 204 E fitzpatrick.anyanwu@sowela.edu
ANZ, Susan .... 254-710-8641. 467 G susan_anz@baylor.edu
ANZALDVA, Ricardo .... 212-237-8316. 318 D
ANZALONE, Roseann ..... 518-743-2242. 345 E anzalonr@sunyacc.edu
ANZELONE, Paulette, A .. 716-839-8214. 322 E panzelon@daemen.edu
AOUN, Joseph, E .... 617-373-2101. 235 F
APANOVICH, Val .... 570-674-6749. 424 A vapanovi@misericordia.edu
APAW, David .... 410-225-2464. 216 C dapaw@mica.edu
APEL, Scott .... 562-985-4031... 33 F sapel@csulb.edu
APELIAN, Bill .... 864-242-5100. 441 D
APER, Jeffery, P .... 217-854-3231. 140 G japer@blackburn.edu
APFELSTADT, Eric .... 360-438-4564. 522 G eapfelstadt@stmartin.edu
APFELTHALER, Gerhard .. 805-493-3352... 31 H apfeltha@callutheran.edu
APLIN, Greg .... 334-222-6591..... 5 E jgaplin@lbwcc.edu
APODACA, Phillip, C ...... 719-389-6613... 79 D papodaca@coloradocollege.edu
APODACA, Rennette .... 575-646-2916. 310 I rennette@nmsu.edu
APOLD, Susan, M .... 914-337-9300. 321 E susan.apold@concordia-ny.edu
APOLINSKI, Lisa .... 619-684-8808... 56 C lapolinski@newschoolarch.edu
APOLLO, Richard, M ...... 516-463-5405. 326 D richard.apollo@hofstra.edu
APONTE, Brunilda .... 787-743-7979. 552 I baponte@suagm.edu
APONTE, Carmen, L .... 787-780-0070. 547 G caponte@caribbean.edu
APONTE, Edwin, D .... 317-931-2306. 165 B edaponte@cts.edu
APONTE, Juan, M .... 787-764-0000. 555 B juan.aponte6@upr.edu
APONTE, Julio .... 787-274-1142. 335 C japonte@stdpr.edu
APONTE-AVELLANET, Nilda .... 787-993-8861. 554 A nilda.aponte2@upr.edu
APPAVOO, Suresh .... 415-485-3598... 42 J sappavoo@dominican.edu
APPELGATE, Michele, R . 641-422-4435. 181 D appelmic@niacc.edu
APPELGET, Kristin .... 609-258-3018. 304 E appelget@princeton.edu
APPELL, Breck, H .... 515-964-0601. 178 E appellb@faith.edu
APPELQUIST, Donald, L . 863-784-7181. 113 G donald.appelquist@southflorida.edu
APPELT, Uschi .... 812-866-7221. 166 C appelt@hanover.edu
APPENZELLER, Allan ...... 515-961-1677. 182 E allan.appenzeller@simpson.edu
APPIAH-PADI, Stephen, K .... 570-577-3796. 411 A s.appiahpadi@bucknell.edu
APPIGNANI, Georgianna 212-217-5380. 324 C georgianna_appignani@fitnyc.edu
APPLE, Mark .... 317-955-6775. 170 V mapple@marian.edu
APPLE, MaryLou .... 931-393-1682. 461 A mapple@mscc.edu
APPLE, Thomas, M .... 808-956-7651. 136 B tapple@hawaii.edu
APPLE VANALSTINE, Judy .... 317-788-3271. 173 I japplevanal@uindy.edu
APPLEBEE, Elizabeth, M . 928-523-6347... 16 C beth.applebee@nau.edu
APPLEBURY, Gene .... 901-751-8453. 457 B gapplebury@mabts.edu
APPLEBY, Alice .... 803-822-3588. 445 C applebya@midlandstech.edu
APPLEBY, Charley .... 870-680-8717... 20 B charley_appleby@asun.edu
APPLEGATE, J. Phillip .... 918-631-2070. 401 F phil-applegate@utulsa.edu
APPLEGATE, John .... 812-855-9198. 167 E jsapple@iu.edu
APPLEGATE, John, S ...... 812-855-9198. 167 F jsapple@indiana.edu
APPLEGATE, Rachel .... 317-278-2376. 168 D rapplega@iupui.edu
APPLEGRAD, Yaakov ...... 718-853-8500. 348 A y2appleg@aol.com
APPLEMAN, Bramer .... 508-559-5208. 395 F bappleman@ecok.edu
APPLETON, Judith, A ..... 607-255-9970. 322 A jaa2@cornell.edu
APPLETON, Kevin .... 225-771-5550. 206 I kevin_appleton@sus.edu
APPLETON, Russ .... 205-226-4923..... 2 C rappleton@bsc.edu
APPLETON, Sandra .... 757-873-4235. 510 B sappleton@stratford.edu
APPLIN, Cynthia .... 937-328-6147. 377 A applinc@clarkstate.edu
APPLIN, Mary Beth .... 601-857-3253. 267 A mary.applin@hindscc.edu
APPLING, Ron .... 806-291-3451. 494 F applingr@wbu.edu
APPOLONIA, Terry .... 814-938-6711. 428 F Terry.Appolonia@iup.edu
APPREY, Maurice .... 434-243-6950. 511 B ma9h@virginia.edu
AQUI, Jason .... 425-564-4128. 517 A jason.aqui@bellevuecollege.edu
AQUILA, Dominic .... 866-323-0233... 60 E
AQUILA, Dominic .... 713-525-2164. 490 L aquilad@stthom.edu
AQUILA, Jennifer, K .... 610-799-1120. 421 I jaquila@lccc.edu
AQUILA, Scott, W .... 610-799-1550. 421 I saquila@lccc.edu
AQUINO, Belissa .... 787-766-1717. 552 J beaquino@suagm.edu
AQUINO, Carlos .... 815-740-3398. 162 F caquino@stfrancis.edu
AQUINO, Cathy .... 304-734-6611. 527 O caquino@bridgemont.edu
AQUINO, Eufemia .... 650-493-4430... 66 E eufemia.aquino@sofia.edu
AQUINO, Felix, J .... 405-682-7546. 397 E faquino@occc.edu
AQUINO, Jeannette .... 787-890-2681. 553 H jeanette.aquino@upr.edu
ARAB, Christine, C .... 904-632-3320. 105 E ccarab@fscj.edu
ARABIA, Caprice .... 716-926-8942. 326 B carabia@hilbert.edu
ARACENA, Beth .... 610-796-8365. 409 E beth.aracena@alvernia.edu
ARADHYA, Jennifer, M .. 781-280-3511. 232 B loucksb@middlesex.mass.edu
ARAGON, Ruben .... 505-454-3330. 310 E rubenaragon@nmhu.edu
ARAIMO, Angelo .... 718-390-3411. 350 B aaraimo@wagner.edu
ARAIN, Nizam .... 608-785-8541. 536 G narain@uwlax.edu
ARAIS, Mercy .... 860-465-4527... 87 L araism@easternct.edu
ARAIZA, Claudia .... 619-298-1829... 68 A caraiza@ssu.edu
ARAMMASH, Fouzi, H ..... 803-705-4311. 441 C arammashf@benedict.edu
ARANDA, Jennifer .... 605-256-5121. 451 H jennifer.aranda@dsu.edu
ARANDA, Romelia .... 830-758-4125. 481 C rdaranda@swtjc.edu
ARANEO, Mary Lou .... 631-451-4611. 346 E araneom@sunysuffolk.edu
ARANT, Mark .... 479-788-7611... 24 A mark.arant@uafs.edu
ARANT, TJ .... 316-295-5888. 186 H president@friends.edu
ARASIMOWICZ, George . 908-737-4376. 302 F garasimo@kean.edu
ARATA, Beverly .... 619-594-6336... 35 D arata@mail.sdsu.edu
ARAUJO, Lisa .... 516-877-3230. 313 A araujo@adelphi.edu
ARAUZ, Patricia, O .... 502-852-5511. 200 D poarau01@louisville.edu
ARAVAMUDAN, Srinivas 919-684-6811. 354 A srinivas@duke.edu
ARAVENA, Carmen .... 217-424-6202. 153 C caravena@millikin.edu
ARBELO, Enid .... 787-878-5475. 549 L earbelo@arecibo.inter.edu
ARBIDE, Donna, A .... 305-284-2873. 118 F darbide@miami.edu
ARBOGAST, Laura .... 212-217-3762. 324 C laura_arbogast@fitnyc.edu
ARBONA, Mildred .... 787-766-1717. 552 J um_marbona@suagm.edu
ARBUCKLE, Joanne .... 212-217-4680. 324 C joanne_arbuckle@fitnyc.edu
ARBUSTO, Joan .... 203-575-8091... 89 B jarbusto@nvcc.commnet.edu
ARBUTHNOT, Beth .... 706-864-1441. 133 D beth.arbuthnot@ung.edu
ARCARIO, Paul .... 718-482-5400. 318 F ARCARIOP@lagcc.cuny.edu
ARCE, Elsa, M .... 412-365-1282. 412 K arce@chatham.edu
ARCE, Francisco, M .... 310-660-3119... 43 B fmarce@elcamino.edu
ARCE, Frank .... 312-752-2478. 149 E frank.arce@kendall.edu
ARCE, Joshua .... 785-749-8482. 187 B jarce@haskell.edu
ARCE, Lydia .... 787-857-3600. 550 A larce@br.inter.edu
ARCE, Marisela .... 530-749-7994... 77 M marce@yccd.edu
ARCELUS, Victor .... 717-337-6901. 417 B varcelus@gettysburg.edu
ARCELUS, Victor, J .... 860-439-2834... 89 H victor.arcelus@conncoll.edu
ARCENEAUX, Alex .... 360-438-4356. 522 G aarceneaux@stmartin.edu
ARCHAMBAULT, Marc .... 801-863-8568. 497 C marc.archambault@uvu.edu
ARCHAMBEAU, Blair ...... 773-702-8813. 161 B b-archambeau@uchicago.edu
ARCHBOLD, David, J ..... 248-370-3358. 248 J archbold@oakland.edu
ARCHER, Daniel, R .... 580-774-3001. 400 B daniel.archer@swosu.edu
ARCHER, Deborah .... 212-431-2860. 333 I Deborah.Archer@nyls.edu
ARCHER, Gie .... 940-668-7731. 477 I marcher@nctc.edu
ARCHER, Keith .... 765-658-4165. 165 F keitharcher@depauw.edu
ARCHER, Len .... 407-303-5619... 97 H len.archer@adu.edu
ARCHER, Linda, R .... 757-446-6190. 504 E archerlr@evms.edu
ARCHER, Robert .... 740-774-6300. 378 J rarcher@daymarcollege.edu
ARCHER, Ron .... 714-879-3901... 47 K rarcher@hiu.edu
ARCHER, Ryan .... 316-295-5410. 186 H archerr@friends.edu
ARCHER, Santee .... 229-732-5977. 120 D santeearcher@andrewcollege.edu
ARCHER, Thomas, R .... 802-626-6454. 501 E thomas.archer@lyndonstate.edu
ARCHER-RIERSON, Abbey .... 620-242-0439. 188 G archera@mcpherson.edu
ARCHEVAL, Louis .... 787-841-2000. 552 B louis_archeval@pucpr.edu
ARCHEY, Larry .... 413-559-5767. 227 B
ARCHEY, Mary Frances .. 412-237-3126. 413 D marchey@ccac.edu
ARCHIBALD, Eileen .... 602-285-7870... 15 C eileen.archibald@phoenixcollege.edu
ARCHIBALD, Michael ..... 909-621-8152... 65 D michael.archibald@scrippscollege.edu
ARCHIBALD, Richard, L . 530-226-4739... 66 D rarchibald@simpsonu.edu
ARCHIBALD, Sandra, O .. 206-616-1648. 524 G sarch@uw.edu
ARCHINAL, Ginette .... 336-278-7230. 354 B garchinal@elon.edu
ARCHULETA, Irma .... 408-223-6749... 63 O irma.archuleta@evc.edu
ARCHULETA, Renee .... 303-914-6345... 84 I renee.archuleta@rrcc.edu
ARCILA, Luz .... 727-864-7748. 101 N arcilal@eckerd.edu
ARCOLEO, Joseph, J ...... 212-217-3750. 324 C joseph_arcoleo@fitnyc.edu
ARCUINO, Cathy, L .... 620-235-4680. 189 L carcuino@pittstate.edu
ARCURY, Tara, L .... 802-654-2212. 500 B tarcury@smcvt.edu
ARDAIOLO, Frank, P ...... 803-323-2251. 449 G ardaiolof@winthrop.edu
ARDALAN, Shah .... 281-290-2777. 476 A shah.ardalan@lonestar.edu
ARDEN, Warwick, A .... 919-515-2195. 368 B warwick_arden@ncsu.edu
ARDITO, Marilyn .... 315-268-6497. 320 A mardito@clarkson.edu
ARDIZZONE, Ronald, M 781-891-2148. 223 C rardizzone@bentley.edu
ARDOIN, Ken .... 337-482-0911. 208 D kenardoin@louisiana.edu
ARDREY, Melantha .... 843-953-3257. 443 A ardreym@cofc.edu
AREA, Ron .... 304-696-2826. 529 H area@marshall.edu
AREIZAGA, Jose, R .... 787-891-0925. 549 K jareizag@aguadilla.inter.edu
ARELLANES-MILLER, Toni .... 626-529-8094... 57 G tmiller@pacificoaks.edu
ARELLANO, Margarita .... 512-245-2124. 487 C ma33@txstate.edu
ARELLANO, Margarita, M .... 512-245-2124. 487 C ma33@txstate.edu
AREMU, Kola .... 256-761-6175..... 7 F karemu@talladega.edu
ARENA, Jeffrey .... 847-214-7810. 144 F jarena@elgin.edu
ARENA, John .... 706-771-5730. 121 D jarena@augustatech.edu
ARENA, Maryanne .... 585-345-6802. 325 C mcarena@genesee.edu
ARENAZ, Pablo .... 956-326-2240. 483 B pablo.arenaz@tamiu.edu
AREND, Lori .... 412-536-2506. 420 A lori.arend@laroche.edu
AREND, Matthew .... 517-629-0521. 239 A marend@albion.edu
AREND, Tait .... 336-278-7429. 354 B tarend@elon.edu
ARENDS, Stuart .... 734-432-5366. 246 B sarends@madonna.edu
ARENDT, Thomas, K .... 562-902-3355... 67 H tomarendt@scuhs.edu
ARENIVAS, Marisol .... 520-417-4115... 12 R arenivasm@cochise.edu
ARENS, Dave .... 712-279-1715. 176 B dave.arens@briarcliff.edu
ARENS, Timothy, E .... 312-329-4191. 153 E tarens@moody.edu
ARENS, William .... 631-632-7030. 342 C william.arens@stonybrook.edu
ARES, Doreen .... 978-665-3123. 229 E dares@fitchburgstate.edu
ARESON, Ann, H .... 814-332-6556. 409 D ann.areson@allegheny.edu
ARETS, Wiel .... 312-567-3263. 147 F wiel.arets@iit.edu
ARETZ, Anthony, J .... 513-244-4232. 377 G president@mail.msj.edu
AREVALO, Rodolfo .... 509-359-6362. 519 C president@ewu.edu
AREY, George, A .... 617-552-4725. 224 A george.arey@bc.edu
AREY, Sherrie .... 479-979-1211... 25 J sarey@ozarks.edu
ARFSTEN, Cheri .... 719-502-3054... 84 A cheri.arfsten@ppcc.edu
ARGENTIERI, Colleen ..... 607-587-3932. 345 D argentch@alfredstate.edu
ARGIRI, Elizabeth .... 586-445-7306. 246 A argiril@macomb.edu
ARGO, Mike, A .... 870-235-4083... 23 F maargo@saumag.edu
ARGO, Trent .... 276-326-4217. 502 H targo@bluefield.edu
ARGOSINGER, C. Chad . 508-999-8515. 229 A cargosinger@umassd.edu
ARGUELLES, Adrianna .... 718-939-5100. 329 B aarguelles@libi.edu
ARGUIJO, JR., Daniel .... 713-718-2335. 473 C dan.arguijo@hccs.edu
ARGYRIS, Steven, G .... 510-649-2430... 46 B sargyris@gtu.edu
ARHIN, Afua .... 910-672-1924. 367 D aarhin@uncfsu.edu
ARIANO, Pat .... 630-829-6003. 140 B pariano@ben.edu
ARIAS, Michael, R .... 949-824-5661... 71 B mrarias@uci.edu
ARIAS, Susan .... 805-493-3139... 31 H sarias@callutheran.edu
ARICK, Bruce, E .... 317-940-9481. 164 J barick@butler.edu
ARICO, Laura .... 812-866-7087. 166 C arico@hanover.edu
ARILSON, Barbara .... 440-375-7000. 382 L barilson@lec.edu
ARIOLA, Victor .... 310-527-7105... 43 K
ARIOSTO, Robert .... 609-894-9311. 299 I rariosto@bcc.edu
ARITA, Kathy .... 509-793-2016. 517 C kathyar@bigbend.edu
ARIZA, Cristina .... 210-829-3870. 490 A mariza@uiwtx.edu
ARIZA, Diana, M .... 203-582-8939... 91 A diane.ariza@quinnipiac.edu
ARIZA, Ricardo .... 402-280-2469. 289 D ariza@creighton.edu
ARJUNE, Ricky, B .... 904-620-2502. 116 B rarjune@unf.edu
ARLITSCH, Kenning .... 406-994-6978. 287 B kenning.arlitsch@montana.edu
ARMAGOST, Mark, S ...... 814-863-4308. 426 A msa17@psu.edu
ARMBRUSTER, Jane, A .. 716-878-4658. 343 A armbruja@buffalostate.edu
ARMBRUSTER, Shirley ... 559-278-2795... 33 D shirleya@csufresno.edu
ARMENDARIZ, John .... 617-373-2133. 235 F
ARMENDARIZ, Louis ...... 602-242-6265... 12 E
ARMENIA, Rita .... 212-217-3820. 324 C rita_armenia@fitnyc.edu
ARMENOIX, Leslie .... 808-933-3116. 136 A armenoix@hawaii.edu

ARMENTA, Richard, R ... 512-223-7795. 466 I
rarmenta@austincc.edu
ARMENTOR, Melissa ... 409-880-8853. 486 E
mfarmentor@lit.edu
ARMENTROUT, Barbara, S ... 434-223-6220. 505 E
barmentrout@hsc.edu
ARMENTROUT, Renae ... 319-385-6242. 179 K
rarmentrout@iwc.edu
ARMES, Paul, W ... 806-291-3400. 494 F
armesp@wbu.edu
ARMESTO, Laura ... 859-846-5726. 197 I
larmesto@midway.edu
ARMEY, Edith ... 701-662-1593. 372 D
edith.armey@lrsc.edu
ARMIJO, Lillian ... 575-835-5780. 310 F
larmijo@admin.nmt.edu
ARMINANA, Ruben ... 707-664-2156... 36 B
ruben.arminana@sonoma.edu
ARMINI, Michael, A ... 617-373-5718. 235 F
ARMINIAK, Anthony ... 734-374-3227. 252 B
aarmini1@wcccd.edu
ARMONT, Bob ... 417-862-9533. 274 F
barmont@globaluniversity.edu
ARMOO, A. Kobina ... 410-238-9000... 96 F
ARMOR, Thomas, W ... 317-738-8045. 165 I
tarmor@franklincollege.edu
ARMOUR, Angela ... 802-654-2527. 500 B
aarmour@smcvt.edu
ARMOUR, Catherine ... 202-639-1803... 95 B
carmour@corcoran.org
ARMOUR, Janet, Y ... 662-842-5192. 267 C
jyamour@iccms.edu
ARMOUR, Lisa ... 352-381-3642. 113 C
lisa.armour@sfcollege.edu
ARMOUR, Mary Alice ... 724-805-2209. 432 G
maryalice.armour@email.stvincent.edu
ARMOUR, Robert ... 606-546-1799. 200 A
rarmour@unionky.edu
ARMOUR, Robin ... 925-439-2181... 42 A
rarmour@losmedanos.edu
ARMOZA, Marcela ... 718-260-4999. 319 B
marmoza@citytech.cuny.edu
ARMSTRONG, Amy ... 830-792-7405. 480 F
anarmstrong@schreiner.edu
ARMSTRONG, Andrew, V ... 540-636-2900. 503 L
armstrong@christendom.edu
ARMSTRONG, Booker, S 816-604-6732. 277 D
booker.armstrong@mcckc.edu
ARMSTRONG, Chris ... 770-859-9779. 128 F
ARMSTRONG, Colleen ... 719-549-3005... 84 G
colleen.armstrong@pueblocc.edu
ARMSTRONG, Dave ... 719-389-6870... 79 D
david.armstrong@coloradocollege.edu
ARMSTRONG, David ... 706-865-2134. 133 B
darmstrong@truett.edu
ARMSTRONG, David, A .. 859-344-3348. 199 H
armstrd@thomasmore.edu
ARMSTRONG, David, M . 816-501-2423. 271 H
david.armstrong@avila.edu
ARMSTRONG, Donald ... 716-614-5950. 334 E
hr@niagaracc.suny.edu
ARMSTRONG, Donald ... 716-614-5950. 334 E
Armstrong@niagaracc.suny.edu
ARMSTRONG, Eleanor ... 925-969-3353... 49 B
earmstrong@jfku.edu
ARMSTRONG, Eric ... 541-684-4644. 407 B
earmstrong@pioneerpacific.edu
ARMSTRONG, Franca ... 315-792-5321. 331 I
farmstrong@mvcc.edu
ARMSTRONG, Gary ... 816-415-7651. 285 C
armstrongg@william.jewell.edu
ARMSTRONG, JR., J. David ... 954-201-7401... 99 D
darmstro@broward.edu
ARMSTRONG, Jane ... 973-328-5181. 300 G
jarmstrong@ccm.edu
ARMSTRONG, Jeffrey, D 805-756-1111... 32 F
presidentsoffice@calpoly.edu
ARMSTRONG, Kelli, J ... 617-552-0585. 224 A
kelli.armstrong@bc.edu
ARMSTRONG, Kim ... 309-796-5006. 140 E
armstrongk@bhc.edu
ARMSTRONG, Lee, F ... 334-844-5176..... 1 G
armstlf@auburn.edu
ARMSTRONG, Lori, B ... 410-704-3570. 220 E
larmstrong@towson.edu
ARMSTRONG, Mary Beth ... 205-665-6720.... 9 B
armstrom@montevallo.edu
ARMSTRONG, Molly ... 252-246-1236. 365 C
marmstrong@wilsoncc.edu
ARMSTRONG, Myeisha .. 760-757-2121... 54 G
marmstrong@miracosta.edu
ARMSTRONG, Nancy, A . 419-772-2251. 386 D
n-armstrong@onu.edu
ARMSTRONG, Neal, E ... 512-232-3305. 491 C
neal_armstrong@mail.utexas.edu
ARMSTRONG, Pamla ... 580-559-5239. 395 F
parmstro@ecok.edu
ARMSTRONG, Peter ... 402-465-2153. 291 G
parmstro@nebrwesleyan.edu
ARMSTRONG, Raul ... 787-840-2575. 552 A
ARMSTRONG, Scott ... 815-825-2086. 149 F
scott.armstrong@kishwaukeecollege.edu
ARMSTRONG, Shane ... 310-377-5501... 53 F
sarmstrong@marymountcalifornia.edu
ARMSTRONG, Shelly ... 231-591-3825. 242 F
armstros@ferris.edu
ARMSTRONG, Shirley ... 229-430-3511. 120 A
sarmstrong@albanytech.edu
ARMSTRONG, Steven, M ... 920-832-6769. 533 S
steven.m.armstrong@lawrence.edu
ARMSTRONG, Suzanne .. 757-221-7647. 503 N
smarmstrong@wm.edu
ARMSTRONG, Terri ... 541-880-2287. 403 H
armstrong@klamathcc.edu
ARMSTRONG, Thomas, J ... 307-532-8202. 542 a
tom.armstrong@ewc.wy.edu
ARMSTRONG, William, L ... 303-963-3350... 79 C
warmstrong@ccu.edu
ARMUSEWICZ, Allison ... 716-614-6238. 334 E
aarmusewicz@niagaracc.suny.edu
ARN, Diana ... 501-977-2001... 25 C
arn@uaccm.edu
ARNADE, Peter ... 808-956-6460. 136 B
parnade@hawaii.edu
ARNDT, Steven, A ... 920-424-0220. 537 B
arndt@uwosh.edu
ARNDT, Wayne, S ... 732-987-2237. 302 B
arndt@georgian.edu
ARNELL, Terri, J ... 941-359-7592. 111 O
tarnell@ringling.edu
ARNER, Lynette ... 330-263-2139. 377 H
larner@wooster.edu
ARNER, Thomas ... 802-828-2800. 501 C
arnert@ccv.edu
ARNESON, Rosemary ... 540-654-1000. 510 J
rarneso3@umw.edu
ARNETT, Brad, K ... 770-484-1204. 128 E
lru@lru.edu
ARNETT, David, J ... 978-478-3400. 235 G
darnett@northpoint.edu
ARNETT, Harold ... 785-442-6125. 187 E
harnett@highlandcc.edu
ARNETT, Katy ... 240-895-2000. 218 A
kearnett@smcm.edu
ARNETT, Ron, W ... 606-474-3151. 194 H
rarnett@kcu.edu
ARNN, III, Larry, P ... 517-607-2301. 243 I
president@hillsdale.edu
ARNO, Rachel ... 617-588-1354. 223 B
rarno@bfit.edu
ARNOLD, Aimee, C ... 262-472-5955. 538 D
mccanna@uww.edu
ARNOLD, Becky, P ... 802-656-9535. 500 F
becky.arnold@uvm.edu
ARNOLD, Carl ... 903-233-4320. 475 J
carlarnold@letu.edu
ARNOLD, Carolyn ... 510-723-6965... 37 K
carnold@chabotcollege.edu
ARNOLD, Christina ... 616-234-3532. 243 B
carnold@grcc.edu
ARNOLD, Clinton, E ... 562-903-4816... 29 L
clinton.arnold@biola.edu
ARNOLD, David ... 770-499-3013. 127 N
darnol22@kennesaw.edu
ARNOLD, David ... 575-492-2124. 312 M
darnold@usw.edu
ARNOLD, Donna, C ... 619-482-6371... 68 B
darnold@swccd.edu
ARNOLD, Harvey, E ... 772-462-6210. 106 P
harnold@irsc.edu
ARNOLD, J. David ... 309-467-6322. 145 C
arnold@eureka.edu
ARNOLD, Jane ... 412-536-1786. 420 A
jane.arnold@laroche.edu
ARNOLD, Jeanne, J ... 616-331-3296. 243 C
arnoljea@gvsu.edu
ARNOLD, Jeff (Dean) ... 262-472-1922. 538 D
arnoldd@uww.edu
ARNOLD, Jim ... 415-485-9506... 40 G
jim.arnold@marin.edu
ARNOLD, Joseph ... 657-278-3256... 33 E
jarnold@fullerton.edu
ARNOLD, Joshua ... 909-599-5433... 50 J
jarnold@lifepacific.edu
ARNOLD, Joshua ... 706-233-7233. 131 E
jarnold@shorter.edu
ARNOLD, Julie ... 419-448-2953. 380 G
jarnold3@heidelberg.edu
ARNOLD, Kelly ... 405-224-3140. 401 E
karnold@usao.edu
ARNOLD, Kenneth, L ... 707-256-3331... 55 F
karnold@napavalley.edu
ARNOLD, Lorene, R ... 260-399-7700. 174 C
larnold@sf.edu
ARNOLD, Lorin ... 856-256-4290. 305 E
arnold@rowan.edu
ARNOLD, Mary, M ... 651-641-8268. 255 B
arnold@csp.edu
ARNOLD, Melody ... 575-492-2102. 312 M
marnold@usw.edu
ARNOLD, Michael, A ... 302-831-1195... 94 B
marnold@udel.edu
ARNOLD, Nancy ... 615-297-7545. 452 J
arnoldn@aquinascollege.edu
ARNOLD, Philip, M ... 518-255-5228. 344 E
arnoldpm@cobleskill.edu
ARNOLD, Robert ... 765-983-1217. 165 G
boba@earlham.edu
ARNOLD, Robert ... 815-836-5488. 150 H
arnoldro@lewisu.edu
ARNOLD, Rodney ... 870-743-3000... 22 B
rarnold@northark.edu
ARNOLD, Ronald, M ... 312-935-6646. 156 K
rarnold@robertmorris.edu
ARNOLD, Sally ... 978-232-2029. 226 C
sarnold@endicott.edu
ARNOLD, Shirley, E ... 828-884-8329. 352 I
arnoldse@brevard.edu
ARNOLD, Stephen ... 409-984-6249. 486 H
stephen.arnold@lamarpa.edu
ARNOLD, Sue ... 281-487-1170. 484 H
sarnold@txchiro.edu
ARNOLD, Susan ... 610-606-4609. 412 I
swarnold@cedarcrest.edu
ARNOLD, Tai ... 518-587-2100. 346 A
tai.arnold@esc.edu
ARNOLD, Tisha ... 870-575-8946... 24 E
arnoldt@uapb.edu
ARNOLD, III, W. Ellis ... 501-450-1223... 21 E
arnold@hendrix.edu
ARNOLD, III, W. Ellis ... 501-450-1351... 21 E
arnold@hendrix.edu
ARNOLD, Wallace ... 757-727-6988. 505 F
wallace.arnold@hamptonu.edu
ARNONE, Harriet ... 516-686-7517. 333 H
harnone@nyit.edu
ARNOULD, Karen, A ... 810-762-3344. 251 E
karnould@umflint.edu
ARNST, Scott ... 810-762-3123. 251 E
sarnst@umflint.edu
ARNUM, Waynette ... 860-906-5125... 88 D
warnum@ccc.commnet.edu
ARNZEN, Diane ... 636-481-3282. 275 I
darnzen@jeffco.edu
AROCHI, Natalia ... 801-818-8900. 496 F
natalia.arochi@provocollege.edu
AROCHO, Fotini ... 617-984-1652. 235 I
farocho@quincycollege.edu
AROMANDO, Drew, C ... 609-896-5178. 305 D
aromando@rider.edu
ARONBERG, Susan ... 561-912-2166. 103 C
saronberg@evergladesuniversity.edu
ARONSON, Donna ... 507-457-6900. 264 A
daronson@smumn.edu
ARONSON, Ed ... 541-881-5875. 408 C
earonson@tvcc.cc
ARONSON, Linda ... 508-849-3458. 222 B
laronson@annamaria.edu
ARONSON, Roberta, C ... 412-396-1818. 415 F
aronson@duq.edu
ARORA SINGH, Alka ... 623-845-3968... 14 M
alka.arora.singh@gcmail.maricopa.edu
ARP, Alissa ... 541-552-8173. 406 C
arpa@sou.edu
ARP, Dan ... 541-737-2331. 406 A
dan.arp@oregonstate.edu
ARP, Mary ... 217-641-4200. 148 M
marp@jwcc.edu
ARP, William ... 225-771-3092. 206 J
william_arp@subr.edu
ARPEY, Sharon, A ... 518-580-5590. 341 A
sarpey@skidmore.edu
ARPINO, Donald ... 617-879-7899. 230 B
darpino@massart.edu
ARQUETTE, Mary ... 419-824-3969. 383 C
marquette@lourdes.edu
ARRA, Linda, N ... 610-330-5115. 420 D
arral@lafayette.edu
ARREDONDO, Arnold ... 423-493-4215. 462 B
arredondoa@tntemple.edu
ARREDONDO, Marisol ... 714-628-7339... 38 A
arredond@chapman.edu
ARREDONDO, Patricia ... 213-627-2580... 38 G
ARRIAZA, Cecilia ... 714-992-7087... 56 F
carriaza@fullcoll.edu
ARRILLAGA MONTALVO, Sonia ... 787-763-6700. 549 A
sarrillaga@se-pr.edu
ARRINGTON, Cedric ... 256-551-1711..... 4 I
cedric.arrington@drakestate.edu
ARRINGTON, Doris, B ... 860-906-5085... 88 D
darrington@ccc.commnet.edu
ARRINGTON, Harriette ... 757-925-6302. 513 E
harrington@pdc.edu
ARRINGTON, Jodey ... 806-742-4105. 487 D
jodey.arrington@ttu.edu
ARRINGTON, Michelle ... 601-266-6698. 270 E
michelle.arrington@usm.edu
ARRINGTON, Pam ... 330-966-5460. 389 F
parrington@starkstate.edu
ARRINGTON, Pamela ... 334-241-9592..... 7 H
parrington@troy.edu
ARRINGTON, Teresa, R .. 662-685-4771. 266 C
tarrington@bmc.edu
ARRINGTON, Tom ... 281-459-7613. 479 G
tom.arrington@sjcd.edu
ARRINGTON-JONES, Angela ... 773-291-6297. 142 D
ARRIOLA, Benjamin ... 915-778-4001. 481 D
ARROSSA, Monty, J ... 208-732-6267. 138 B
marrossa@csi.edu
ARROWOOD, Roarke ... 828-835-4305. 364 E
rarrowood@tricountycc.edu
ARROYO, Cruz ... 253-964-4688. 522 G
carroyo@stmartin.edu
ARROYO, Enrique ... 787-841-2000. 552 B
earroyo@pucpr.edu
ARROYO, Ethel ... 847-233-7700. 155 B
earroyo@nc.edu
ARROYO, Gladys ... 787-279-1912. 550 B
garroyo@bayamon.inter.edu
ARROYO, Hope ... 510-580-5521... 77 C
harroyo@cci.edu
ARROYO, Ivonne, D ... 787-257-7323. 552 H
iarroyo@suagm.edu
ARROYO, Sandra ... 787-765-3560. 548 M
sarroyo@edpuniversity.edu
ARRUDA, Yvonne, D ... 401-865-2480. 439 E
yarruda@providence.edu
ARSHADI, Nasser ... 314-516-5899. 283 E
arshadi@umsl.edu
ARSLANIAN, Susan ... 978-468-7111. 227 A
sarslanian@gcts.edu
ARTALE, Maureen, P ... 607-436-3216. 343 E
artalemp@oneonta.edu
ARTBAUER, Michael ... 216-687-3544. 377 F
m.artbauer@csuohio.edu
ARTEAGA, Eddie ... 310-377-5501... 53 F
EArteaga@marymountcalifornia.edu
ARTEAGA, Joseph ... 805-546-3205... 42 C
joseph_arteaga@cuesta.edu
ARTEAGA, Patricia ... 973-748-9000. 299 F
patricia_arteaga@bloomfield.edu
ARTECONA, Sarah, N ... 305-284-5490. 118 F
sartecona@miami.edu
ARTER, Neil ... 405-425-5906. 397 D
neil.arter@oc.edu
ARTERIAN, Hannah ... 315-443-9580. 347 C
arterian@syr.edu
ARTHO, Donna ... 936-294-3101. 487 A
artho@shsu.edu
ARTHUR, Christon ... 269-471-3405. 239 D
christon@andrews.edu
ARTHUR, Dave ... 512-476-2772. 466 J
finaid@austingrad.edu
ARTHUR, Gwendolynne .. 508-793-7384. 225 A
garthur@clarku.edu
ARTHUR, Jeff ... 757-671-7171. 504 F
ARTHUR, Mark ... 405-789-7661. 400 A
mark.arthur@swcu.edu
ARTHUR, Salinda ... 912-478-5253. 126 C
sarthur@georgiasouthern.edu
ARTHUR, Virginia ... 651-793-1920. 259 C
virginia.arthur@metrostate.edu
ARTIBISE, Alan ... 956-882-8266. 491 D
alan.artibise@utb.edu
ARTILES LEON, Noel ... 787-265-3877. 554 E
director.oiip@upr.edu
ARTIM, Amanda ... 814-536-5168. 412 C
amanda@crbc.net
ARTIM, Michael ... 814-536-5168. 412 C
martim@crbc.net
ARTIS, Christine ... 718-933-6700. 331 K
cartis@monroecollege.edu
ARTIS, Frederick, D ... 918-595-7898. 400 E
frederick.artis@tulsacc.edu
ARTIS, Lori ... 618-468-3200. 150 G
lartis@lc.edu
ARTMAN, Richard, B ... 608-796-3001. 539 E
rbartman@viterbo.edu
ARTMAN, Vicky ... 618-634-3219. 158 M
vickya@shawneecc.edu
ARUL, Jebapriya ... 863-667-5086. 113 P
jfarul@seu.edu
ARUNACHALAM, Vairam 573-882-3225. 283 C
arunachalam@missouri.edu
ARVAN, April ... 920-565-1222. 533 R
arvanaa@lakeland.edu
ARVELO, Wildolfo ... 603-427-7602. 295 K
warvelo@ccsnh.edu
ARVIN, Ann ... 650-498-6227... 68 E
aarvin@stanford.edu
ARVIZU, Mimi ... 408-848-4840... 45 F
marvizu@gavilan.edu

ARVIZU, Primavera 661-395-4863 49 N prarvizu@bakersfieldcollege.edu
ARZOLA, Fernando 646-378-6150 335 C fernando.arzola@nyack.edu
ARZROUNI-CHAHINIAN, Chaghig 510-987-9452 28 A
ASAMOAH, Yaw, A 724-357-2280 428 F osebo@iup.edu
ASARE, Esi, A 315-445-4693 328 F asareea@lemoyne.edu
ASARO, Diane, C 773-508-2543 151 H dasaro@luc.edu
ASATO, Susan 760-757-2121 54 G sasato@miracosta.edu
ASAWA, Archibald, E 949-480-4006 66 F asawa@soka.edu
ASBILL, Jonathan 918-456-5511 396 H asbill01@nsuok.edu
ASBURY, Denise 423-652-4895 455 I dasbury@king.edu
ASBURY, Jo-Ellen 410-334-2181 218 E jasbury@stevenson.edu
ASCARELLI, Daniela 215-895-6280 415 B ascareld@drexel.edu
ASCENCIO, Jorge 714-895-8107 39 J jascencio@gwc.cccd.edu
ASCENCIO, Margarita 617-670-4404 226 F mascencio@fisher.edu
ASCENCIO, Mario 202-478-1543 95 B mascencio@corcoran.org
ASCHE, Hylee 308-398-7407 288 I hasche@cccneb.edu
ASCHENBRENER, Matt 262-472-1570 538 D aschenbm@uww.edu
ASCHER, Erin, E 513-556-6381 390 G erin.ascher@uc.edu
ASCHIM, Joan 541-463-5591 403 I aschimj@lanecc.edu
ASCHIM, Sue 503-491-7247 404 E sue.aschim@mhcc.edu
ASCHLIMAN, David, A 260-422-5561 167 B daaschliman@indianatech.edu
ASCIONE, Frank, J 734-764-7144 251 C fascione@umich.edu
ASCIONE, Lou 619-388-7873 62 F lascione@sdccd.edu
ASDURIAN, Emil 718-261-5800 315 F easdurianmd@bramsonort.edu
ASENCIO, Doris 787-892-5115 551 A asencio@sg.inter.edu
ASENCIO-PINTO, Aida 708-209-3492 143 E aida.asencio-pinto@cuchicago.edu
ASGHAR, Farhad 212-961-3402 314 C fasghar@bankstreet.edu
ASH, Carol 402-280-1272 289 D carolash@creighton.edu
ASH, Christine, A 216-368-4350 375 J caa2@case.edu
ASH, Eric 907-375-4515 494 F ash@wbu.edu
ASH, Kenya, D 513-529-7157 384 G ashkd@miamioh.edu
ASH, Michael 319-208-5050 182 G mash@scciowa.edu
ASH, Portia 419-772-2047 386 D p-ash@onu.edu
ASH, Steven 352-854-2322 100 K ashs@cf.edu
ASHBAUGH, Jackie, E 330-684-8973 390 F jackie1@uakron.edu
ASHBEE, Emma, M 530-226-4166 66 D 1004mgr@fheg.follett.com
ASHBRIDGE, Susie 541-956-7239 407 F sashbridge@roguecc.edu
ASHBROOK, Richard, M 614-236-6108 375 H rashbrook@capital.edu
ASHBURN, Beth, D 336-725-8344 365 F piedmontu@pbc.edu
ASHBURN, Charlene 575-538-6328 312 N ashburnc@wnmu.edu
ASHBURN, Elyse 410-455-2065 219 D eashburn@umbc.edu
ASHBURN, Gwen 828-251-6505 368 C gashburn@unca.edu
ASHBURN, Maureen, A 617-333-2294 225 E mashburn1010@curry.edu
ASHBY, Brendan 651-846-1314 261 D brendan.ashby@saintpaul.edu
ASHBY, Frank 206-934-6417 523 A frank.ashby@seattlecolleges.edu
ASHBY, Jamie 903-823-3319 482 D jamie.ashby@texarkanacollege.edu
ASHBY, Kalie 301-387-3060 214 I kalie.ashby@garrettcollege.edu
ASHBY, Patti 405-912-9017 395 K pashby@hc.edu
ASHCRAFT, Kelley 864-578-8770 446 F kashcraft@sherman.edu
ASHCRAFT, Matthew 480-461-7215 15 A Matthew.Aschcraft@mesacc.edu
ASHCROFT, Josh 509-359-6916 519 C jashcroft@ewu.edu
ASHCROFT, Judy 813-974-8128 116 C jashcroft@usf.edu
ASHDOWN, Jane 516-877-4065 313 A jashdown@adelphi.edu
ASHE, Janet 216-373-5308 385 G jashe@ndc.edu
ASHE, Mardy 828-227-7134 369 E mashe@wcu.edu
ASHENMACHER, Robert, J 218-723-6075 254 K rashenma@css.edu
ASHER, Bernadette 404-627-2681 121 H bernadette.asher@beulah.org
ASHER, Curt 661-654-3042 32 H casher@csub.edu
ASHER, Herb 614-292-0803 386 E asher.1@osu.edu
ASHER, Pamela 816-268-5442 279 G pjasher@nts.edu
ASHFORD, Bruce, R 919-761-2435 366 I bashford@sebts.edu
ASHFORD, Rebecca, L 865-694-6552 461 D rlashford@pstcc.edu
ASHFORD-LIGON, Latonya 609-586-4800 302 G ashfordl@mccc.edu
ASHIDA, Gary 719-384-6951 83 M gary.ashida@ojc.edu
ASHIN, Annette 617-559-8775 227 D aashin@hebrewcollege.edu
ASHLEY, Bill 601-276-3707 269 H bashley@smcc.edu
ASHLEY, Bonnie 406-994-2603 287 B bashley@montana.edu
ASHLEY, Donna 646-717-9706 325 B ashley@gts.edu
ASHLEY, Garrett, P 562-951-4625 32 E gashley@calstate.edu
ASHLEY, George 256-726-8455 6 B gashley@oakwood.edu
ASHLEY, Gwen 803-641-3495 448 A gwena@usca.edu
ASHLEY, Kurt 724-589-2115 434 B kashley@thiel.edu
ASHLEY, Mark 909-621-8090 46 H mark_ashley@hmc.edu
ASHLEY, Mary Ellen 978-738-7401 232 E meashley@necc.mass.edu
ASHLEY, Mary Ellen 978-556-3627 232 E meashley@necc.mass.edu
ASHLEY, Rachelle 715-365-4517 540 G rashley@nicoletcollege.edu
ASHLEY, Traci, D 919-209-2563 361 E tdashley@johnstoncc.edu
ASHLEY, SR., Willard W.C 732-247-5241 303 E washley@nbts.edu
ASHLEY-PAULEY, Jonita 423-798-7830 462 E jpauley@tusculum.edu
ASHMAN, Theresa, L 305-284-5450 118 F tashman@miami.edu
ASHMORE, Don, P 325-670-1448 472 O dashmore@hsutx.edu
ASHOUR, Cheryl 780-744-1150 58 D cashour@palomar.edu
ASHPOLE, Steve 253-566-5326 524 C sashpole@tacomacc.edu
ASHTON, M. John 801-581-3055 496 Q john.ashton@alumni.utah.edu
ASHTON, Nadine 313-664-7673 241 C nashton@collegeforcreativestudies.edu
ASHTON, Sharon 904-620-2115 116 B sashton@unf.edu
ASHTON-PRITTING, Randi, L 860-768-4268 92 D pritting@hartford.edu
ASHWELL, Dru 417-626-1234 279 J dashwell@occ.edu
ASHWORTH, Dennis 706-355-5167 120 J dashworth@athenstech.edu
ASHWORTH, Edward, N 207-581-3202 212 B edward.ashworth@maine.edu
ASHWORTH, Linda, R 651-631-5109 263 A lrashworth@nwc.edu
ASIAMAH-ANDRADE, Akua 856-225-6322 306 C andradea@camlink.rutgers.edu
ASIDAO, Christine 773-442-4650 154 H
ASIM, Paul 714-432-5796 39 K pasim@occ.cccd.edu
ASKA, Aaron 201-200-3035 303 F aaska@njcu.edu
ASKEGAARD, Lewis, D 540-887-7071 507 A laskegaa@mbc.edu
ASKELAND, Lori, J 937-327-7061 393 E laskeland@wittenberg.edu
ASKELSON, Denise 218-935-0417 265 E denise.askelson@wetcc.edu
ASKELSON, Mary 503-788-6644 407 E askelsom@reed.edu
ASKELSON, Mindi 507-379-3361 260 I mindi.askelson@riverland.edu
ASKERLUND, Robert 801-957-4101 498 B robert.askerlund@slcc.edu
ASKEW, Christie 202-238-2546 95 G caskew@howard.edu
ASKEW, Joseph 731-989-6651 454 J jaskew@fhu.edu
ASKEW, Rebecca 601-403-1317 269 D raskew@prcc.edu
ASKEW, Susan, S 931-598-1710 458 H saskew@sewanee.edu
ASKEW, Tara 706-649-1901 123 E taskew@columbustech.edu
ASKEW-ROBINSON, Jipaum 270-534-3420 196 G jaskewgibson0001@kctcs.edu
ASKIN, Jacalyn, A 480-732-7298 14 J jacalyn.askin@cgc.edu
ASKREN, Mark 402-472-2311 292 I maskren1@unl.edu
ASMUS, Colleen, M 850-474-2642 117 B casmus@uwf.edu
ASMUTH, Shawn, C 334-844-7771 1 G asmutsc@auburn.edu
ASONEVICH, Walter, J 814-262-3820 427 C wasonevich@pennhighlands.edu
ASOODEH, Mike, M 985-549-2314 208 C asoodeh@selu.edu
ASPELUND, Jan 970-945-8691 79 G
ASPERGER, Joseph 810-762-9749 244 Q jasperge@kettering.edu
ASPINALL, David 910-221-2224 354 D
ASPINALL, Robin, J 909-621-8116 39 D robin.aspinall@cmc.edu
ASPINWALL, Neil 337-421-6900 204 E neil.aspinwall@sowela.edu
ASQUINO, Daniel, M 978-632-0001 232 C d_asquino@mwcc.mass.edu
ASRES, Alem 920-498-6826 541 B alem.asres@nwtc.edu
ASSAD, Arjang, A 716-645-3221 341 F aassad@buffalo.edu
ASSAD, Jean-Claude 601-979-2411 267 E jean-claude.assad@jsums.edu
ASSAEL, Leon 612-624-2424 264 G assael@umn.edu
ASSAF, Michael 413-775-1318 231 E assafm@gcc.mass.edu
ASSANIS, Dennis, N 631-632-4360 342 C dassanis@stonybrook.edu
ASSANTE, Javonda, T 979-313-6211 307 C javonda.assante@shu.edu
ASSELIN, Edward 518-255-5215 344 E asselie@cobleskill.edu
ASSELIN, Edward, E 518-255-5215 344 E asselie@cobleskill.edu
ASSELIN, Martha, J 518-381-1336 340 G asselimj@sunysccc.edu
ASSIGNON, Selmon 773-602-2028 142 B sassignon@ccc.edu
ASSING, Wayne 401-454-6639 440 A wassing@risd.edu
AST, Nicholas 405-878-5411 399 G frnicholas@stgregorys.edu
ASTI, Martha, S 704-233-8123 370 G asti@wingate.edu
ASTON, Mary Kay 570-941-5984 436 A marykay.aston@scranton.edu
ASTON, Rollah 575-624-7281 309 I rollah.aston@roswell.enmu.edu
ASTON, Sheree 909-706-3502 76 B saston@westernu.edu
ASTORG, Geni 304-424-8340 530 E geni.astorg@wvup.edu
ASTROM, Mark 505-473-6121 311 K mark.astrom@santafeuniversity.edu
ASUKILE, Imani, D 727-816-3192 110 E asukili@phcc.edu
ASUNCION-NACE, Zeny 671-735-2942 546 E znace@uguam.uog.edu
ASWEGAN, Kathie 319-226-2003 175 D Kathie.Aswegan@AllenCollege.edu
ATALLAH, Zahi 831-755-6960 46 G zatallah@hartnell.edu
ATCHESON, Marshall, L 864-644-5020 446 I matcheson@swu.edu
ATCHISON, Kathryn 310-794-0212 71 C katchison@resadmin.ucla.edu
ATENCIO, Elaine 619-260-4520 73 I atencio@sandiego.edu
ATENCIO, Wilma 719-846-5555 85 H wilma.atencio@trinidadstate.edu
ATES, Clarence 508-853-2300 232 F cates@qcc.mass.edu
ATEWOLOGUN, Adenuga 507-433-0607 260 I adenuga.atewologun@riverland.edu
ATHANASIOU, Nancy 414-382-6195 531 I nancy.athanasiou@alverno.edu
ATHANS, Stephan 919-718-7287 359 B sathans@cccc.edu
ATHERTON, Dennis 575-492-2763 310 G datherton@nmjc.edu
ATHEY, Rochelle 702-895-5541 294 I rochelle.athey@unlv.edu
ATHEY, Rochelle 515-294-5225 175 H rathey@iastate.edu
ATIEH, Lute 816-279-7000 271 B lutea@acot.edu
ATIEH, Sam 816-279-7000 271 B president@acot.edu
ATKIN, Michael, B 818-947-2600 52 E atkinmb@lavc.edu
ATKINS, Angie, S 662-329-7126 268 E aatkins@rm.muw.edu
ATKINS, Brenda, L 434-395-2027 506 J atkinsbl@longwood.edu
ATKINS, Bridget 912-280-4000 120 B batkins@altamahatech.edu
ATKINS, Christine 203-401-4071 87 G catkins@albertus.edu
ATKINS, Clark 501-812-2200 22 G catkins@pulaskitech.edu
ATKINS, Cynthia, A 270-707-3761 195 E cynthia.atkins@kctcs.edu
ATKINS, Darlenna, M 318-797-5237 205 F darlenna.atkins@lsus.edu
ATKINS, Douglas, G 603-526-3750 295 I datkins@colby-sawyer.edu
ATKINS, Elizabeth, A 856-225-6161 306 C atkins1@camden.rutgers.edu
ATKINS, Garry, L 205-726-2763 6 F glatkins@samford.edu
ATKINS, James, H 859-238-6223 193 E jh.atkins@centre.edu
ATKINS, Jennifer 434-961-5245 513 F jatkins@pvcc.edu
ATKINS, Kemal 302-857-6300 93 C katkins@desu.edu
ATKINS, Lisa 618-545-3110 149 D latkins@kaskaskia.edu
ATKINS, Norman 212-228-1888 337 H
ATKINS, Paula, B 318-795-5365 205 F paula.atkins@lsus.edu
ATKINS, Priscilla, D 616-395-7986 244 A atkinsp@hope.edu
ATKINS, Rachel 325-793-4709 476 E ratkins@mcm.edu
ATKINS, Rodney 903-730-4890 474 O RAtkins@jarvis.edu
ATKINS-BRADY, Tara 757-569-6713 513 E tatkins-brady@pdc.edu
ATKINSON, Darryl 757-683-3407 507 N datkinso@odu.edu
ATKINSON, Denese 606-886-3863 194 K denese.atkinson@kctcs.edu
ATKINSON, Eva, G 270-686-4282 192 G eva.atkinson@brescia.edu
ATKINSON, Frank 405-466-3370 395 N fatkinson@langston.edu
ATKINSON, J. Scott 585-395-2137 342 F satkinso@brockport.edu
ATKINSON, Jane, M 503-768-7200 403 K
ATKINSON, Jeffrey 704-233-8117 370 G atkinson@wingate.edu
ATKINSON, Joseph, C 202-526-3799 96 D
ATKINSON, Judith 856-415-2115 302 C jatkinson@gccnj.edu
ATKINSON, Linda 301-784-5000 213 B latkinson@allegany.edu
ATKINSON, Mark 435-586-1966 497 A markatkinson@suu.edu
ATKINSON, Rose 406-768-6317 286 C ratkinson@fpcc.edu
ATKINSON, Sander 601-484-8707 267 G satkinso@meridiancc.edu
ATKINSON, Stacy, R 843-857-4298 442 F satkinson@coker.edu
ATKINSON, Susan, J 714-449-7442 67 D satkinson@scco.edu
ATKINSON, Thomas 269-782-1262 250 C tatkinson@swmich.edu
ATKINSON, Tim 386-752-1822 104 G tim.atkinson@fgc.edu
ATKINSON, Vicki 847-925-6208 145 H vatkinso@harpercollege.edu
ATKINSON-ALSTON, Stephanie 310-233-4025 51 H
ATKINSON-ALSTON, Stephanie 818-364-7758 52 A atkinssa@lamission.edu
ATLAS, Gordan 607-871-2924 313 E atlas@alfred.edu
ATLAS, Jamie 615-794-4254 457 Q jatlas@omorecollege.edu
ATO, Gladys 408-273-2683 55 H gato@nhu.edu

ATO, Gladys ... 408-273-2204... 55 H gato@nhu.edu
ATOIGE, Celia ... 671-734-1812. 546 D catoige@piu.edu
ATOIGUE, Ana Mari, C .. 671-735-5527. 546 C anamari.atoigue@guamcc.edu
ATTALLA, Lory ... 603-513-5103. 298 D lory.attalla@law.unh.edu
ATTANASIO, Ann ... 410-617-7745. 216 A aattanasio@loyola.edu
ATTAO, David, J ... 670-234-5498. 547 A dattao@nmcnet.edu
ATTARDO, Salvatore ... 903-886-5166. 483 E salvatore.attardo@tamuc.edu
ATTEBERY, Philip ... 903-586-2501. 467 D attebery@bmats.edu
ATTENBOROUGH, Charlotte ... 973-877-3055. 301 H attenbor@essex.edu
ATTERBURY, G. Burnham "Burnie" ... 209-932-2967... 73 A batterbury@pacific.edu
ATTIA, Magdy ... 704-378-1140. 355 K mattia@jcsu.edu
ATTIG, Ann, M ... 719-884-5000... 83 K amattig@nbc.edu
ATTOH, Samuel, A ... 773-508-8948. 151 H sattoh@luc.edu
ATTOH, Samuel, A ... 773-508-2975. 151 H sattoh@luc.edu
ATTRIDGE, Daniel, F ... 202-319-5139... 94 G attridge@cua.edu
ATWATER, Brent ... 336-272-7102. 354 E brent.atwater@greensboro.edu
ATWATER, Ken ... 813-253-7050. 106 M katwater@hccfl.edu
ATWELL, Scott ... 850-644-2761. 115 C satwell@fsu.edu
ATWOOD, Beverlee ... 208-882-1566. 138 H batwood@nsa.edu
ATWOOD, Beverly, A ... 270-707-3721. 195 E beverly.atwood@kctcs.edu
ATWOOD, Julie ... 601-477-4055. 267 F julie.atwood@jcjc.edu
ATWOOD, Kim ... 502-456-6504. 199 G katwood@sullivan.edu
ATWOOD, Lorraine ... 802-831-1204. 500 H latwood@vermontlaw.edu
ATWOOD, Roy, A ... 208-882-1566. 138 H dratwood@nsa.edu
ATZERT, Andy ... 212-229-8947. 332 E atzerta@newschool.edu
AU, Peggy ... 510-628-8038... 51 A peggyau@lincolnuca.edu
AU, Sau Fong ... 718-951-5476. 317 C sau@brooklyn.cuny.edu
AUBIN, Mary Ann ... 314-792-6302. 275 L aubin@kenrick.edu
AUBRET, Maryliz ... 787-780-0070. 547 G maubret@caribbean.edu
AUBREY, Leonard ... 516-686-1100. 333 H laubrey@nyit.edu
AUBRY, Nadine ... 617-373-2154. 235 F
AUBUT, Irene ... 603-271-6484. 296 C iaubut@ccsnh.edu
AUCLAIR, Billye, W ... 508-849-3359. 222 B bauclair@annamaria.edu
AUCOIN, Judi, F ... 205-726-2728..... 6 F jfaucoin@samford.edu
AUDAS, Jean Paul ... 405-325-2395. 401 B jaudas@ou.edu
AUDET, Suzanne ... 508-999-8076. 229 A saudet@umassd.edu
AUDETTE, Bert ... 207-948-9277. 211 I baudette@unity.edu
AUDUS, Kenneth, L ... 785-864-3591. 190 L audus@ku.edu
AUDUSSEAU, Loic ... 718-289-5168. 317 B loic.audusseau@bcc.cuny.edu
AUDYATIS, Todd ... 508-531-2608. 229 D taudyatis@bridgew.edu
AUEN, Mike ... 402-844-7058. 291 I mike@northeast.edu
AUER, Margaret ... 313-993-1090. 250 K auerme@udmercy.edu
AUER, Matthew ... 812-855-3550. 167 F mauer@indiana.edu
AUER, Matthew, R ... 207-786-6066. 209 F mauer@bates.edu
AUERBACH, Michael ... 843-953-5991. 443 A auerbachmh@cofc.edu
AUFDERHEIDE, Keith ... 404-364-8405. 130 A kaufderheide@oglethorpe.edu
AUGENSEN, Harry ... 610-499-4014. 437 E hjaugensen@widener.edu
AUGENSPEIN, Amee ... 260-459-4567. 169 C aaugenspein@ibcfortwayne.edu
AUGENSTEIN, Amee ... 260-459-4545. 169 C aaugenstein@ibcfortwayne.edu
AUGHENBAUGH, Barbara ... 410-837-5719. 221 A baughenbaugh@ubalt.edu
AUGHENBAUGH, Jonette ... 304-327-4049. 529 D jaughenbaugh@bluefieldstate.edu
AUGHINBAUGH, Robert 207-768-9577. 212 G robert.aughinbaugh@umpi.edu
AUGMAN, JR., William, J ... 937-376-2946. 388 B
AUGOSTINI, Christopher, L ... 202-687-7330... 95 E cla4@georgetown.edu
AUGSBURGER, Arol, R .. 312-949-7700. 146 G aaugsburger@ico.edu
AUGSBURGER, Carrie, A ... 515-964-0601. 178 E augsburgerc@faith.edu
AUGSBURGER, Lance, A 515-964-0601. 178 E augsburgerl@faith.edu
AUGUISTE, Andrea ... 303-444-0202... 83 F aauguiste@naropa.edu
AUGUST, Bonne ... 718-260-5560. 319 B baugust@citytech.cuny.edu
AUGUST-SCHWARTZ, Suzanne ... 510-869-6511... 61 I saugustschwartz@samuelmerritt.edu
AUGUSTE, Wadner ... 212-749-2802. 330 A wauguste@msmnyc.edu
AUGUSTIN, Monica, L ... 408-554-6908... 64 M mlaugustin@scu.edu
AUGUSTINE, Lisa ... 440-365-5222. 383 B
AUGUSTINE, Robert, M .. 217-581-2220. 144 E rmaugustine@eiu.edu
AUGUSTINE-PLAISANCE, Lu-Ann ... 718-409-7302. 346 D laugustine@sunymaritime.edu
AUGUSTINE-PLAISANCE, LuAnn ... 718-409-7304. 346 D laugustine@sunymaritime.edu
AUGUSTUS, Edward ... 508-793-2011. 225 B eaugustu@holycross.edu
AULD, Sandra ... 908-709-7010. 308 B auld@ucc.edu
AULET, Maria, J ... 787-765-1915. 551 C mjaulet@inter.edu
AULIN, Kirsi ... 805-893-3285... 72 B kirsi.aulin@ombuds.ucsb.edu
AULL, JR., Zeke ... 251-460-6609..... 9 E zaull@southalabama.edu
AULT, Allen ... 859-622-3565. 193 P allen.ault@eku.edu
AULT, Brian ... 410-857-2262. 216 E bault@mcdaniel.edu
AULT, Jill, K ... 530-226-4103... 66 D jault@simpsonu.edu
AUM, Seok Joo ... 213-487-0110... 42 K provost@dula.edu
AUMAN, Timothy, L ... 336-758-5210. 370 D aumantl@wfu.edu
AUNE, Jeff ... 952-446-4152. 255 D aunej@crown.edu
AUNGST, Donald ... 914-455-2650. 330 J daungst@mercy.edu
AURAND, Nancy ... 503-222-3225. 403 B naurand@cci.edu
AURE, Aaron ... 605-688-6195. 452 B aaron.aure@sdstate.edu
AURIEMMA, Lisa ... 207-859-1233. 211 H libdir@thomas.edu
AURORA, Rosleen ... 818-785-2726... 37 F rosleen.aurora@casalomacollege.edu
AURYAN, Mosen ... 609-771-2143. 300 E
AUSBAND, Avrohom ... 718-601-3523. 351 L
AUSBORN, Dawn ... 910-630-7610. 356 H dausborn@methodist.edu
AUSBURY, Brad ... 417-862-9533. 274 F bausbury@globaluniversity.edu
AUSEL, Jill ... 412-365-1244. 412 K jausel@chatham.edu
AUSEN, Orrin, J ... 507-344-7350. 253 J oausen@blc.edu
AUSMUS, Ryan ... 620-225-0186. 186 B rausmus@dc3.edu
AUSTAD, Dianne, M ... 319-368-6464. 181 C daustad@mtmercy.edu
AUSTER, Julie ... 914-395-2365. 340 E jauster@sarahlawrence.edu
AUSTIN, Aaron, L ... 316-284-5324. 184 J aaustin@bethelks.edu
AUSTIN, Alvin ... 704-378-1110. 355 K aaustin@jcsu.edu
AUSTIN, Anne ... 870-612-2058... 25 A anne.austin@uaccb.edu
AUSTIN, April ... 404-270-5153. 132 E aprila@spelman.edu
AUSTIN, Brian ... 865-471-3273. 453 F baustin@cn.edu
AUSTIN, Charles ... 803-705-4967. 441 C austinc@benedict.edu
AUSTIN, Chris ... 270-247-8521. 197 H caustin@midcontinent.edu
AUSTIN, Dale, F ... 616-395-7950. 244 A austin@hope.edu
AUSTIN, Deborah ... 717-264-4141. 437 H daustin@wilson.edu
AUSTIN, Diane ... 617-243-2124. 227 K daustin@lasell.edu
AUSTIN, Faires ... 334-386-7180..... 3 H faustin@faulkner.edu
AUSTIN, James ... 802-387-6786. 499 E jaustin@landmark.edu
AUSTIN, Jane ... 570-288-8400. 416 H
AUSTIN, Joseph, M ... 207-780-5158. 212 H austin@usm.maine.edu
AUSTIN, L. Bruce ... 847-214-7366. 144 F baustin@elgin.edu
AUSTIN, Laurie ... 718-960-8706. 318 A laurie.austin@lehman.cuny.edu
AUSTIN, Marlisa ... 502-213-5073. 195 F marlisa.austin@kctcs.edu
AUSTIN, Michael ... 316-942-4291. 189 E austinm@newmanu.edu
AUSTIN, Robert, C ... 806-371-5024. 465 E rcaustin@actx.edu
AUSTIN, Suzanne, E ... 205-934-6290..... 8 E seaustin@uab.edu
AUSTIN, Tiffany ... 845-675-4581. 335 C tiffany.austin@nyack.edu
AUSTIN, Timothy, R ... 412-396-6054. 415 F austint@duq.edu
AUSTIN, Tracey, M ... 603-526-3886. 295 I taustin@colby-sawyer.edu
AUSTIN, William ... 908-689-7618. 308 G will@warren.edu
AUSTIN-BRUNS, Emily ... 978-665-3025. 229 E eaustinb@fitchburgstate.edu
AUTIO, Wesley ... 413-545-2963. 228 F autio@umass.edu
AUTREY, Denny ... 713-634-0011. 481 G dautrey@swbts.edu
AUTRY, Dean ... 270-686-4464. 196 C dean.autry@kctcs.edu
AUTRY, Shanna ... 850-201-8918. 117 D autrys@tcc.fl.edu
AUVENSHINE, Donnie ... 325-649-8408. 473 F dauvenshine@hputx.edu
AVALONE, Valarie, L ... 585-292-3021. 332 A vavalone@monroecc.edu
AVALOS, Juan ... 949-582-4566... 67 C javalos@saddleback.edu
AVALOS, Natalie ... 818-767-0888... 76 K Natalie.Avalos@woodbury.edu
AVALOS-SÁNCHEZ, Javier ... 787-993-8860. 554 A javier.avalos@upr.edu
AVANT, Jacqueline ... 678-260-3538. 131 E javant@shorter.edu
AVANT, Linda ... 918-293-4678. 398 B linda.avant@okstate.edu
AVANT, Toni, D ... 662-915-7174. 270 B tavant@olemiss.edu
AVEILLE, Candido ... 305-821-3333. 105 A caveille@fnu.edu
AVENDANO, John ... 815-802-8110. 149 C president@kcc.edu
AVENT, Sherri, M ... 336-334-7973. 367 E avent@ncat.edu
AVERETTE, Don ... 864-646-1341. 447 D daveret1@tctc.edu
AVERILL, Ken ... 270-444-9676. 193 N kaverill@daymarcollege.edu
AVERILL, Leslie ... 802-651-5907. 499 A averill@champlain.edu
AVERILL, Sue ... 330-672-2220. 382 B saveril2@kent.edu
AVERRE, Amy ... 207-941-7187. 210 B averrea@husson.edu
AVERSA, Ann ... 212-854-5561. 314 G aaversa@barnard.edu
AVERY, Alice, M ... 203-371-7927... 91 C averya@sacredheart.edu
AVERY, Annalea ... 406-657-1032. 288 B annalea.avery@rocky.edu
AVERY, Annette ... 417-873-7312. 273 H aavery@drury.edu
AVERY, Barbara ... 323-259-2500... 56 I bavery@oxy.edu
AVERY, Brigid ... 616-632-2494. 239 E brigid.avery@aquinas.edu
AVERY, Donald ... 478-289-2015. 124 C davery@ega.edu
AVERY, Earl, L ... 781-891-2907. 223 C eavery@bentley.edu
AVERY, Faith ... 513-721-7944. 380 D favery@gbs.edu
AVERY, James ... 731-661-5329. 462 F javery@uu.edu
AVERY, Joshua ... 513-721-7944. 380 D javery@gbs.edu
AVERY, Kathy ... 918-293-4988. 398 B kathy.avery@okstate.edu
AVERY, Kristine ... 207-893-7755. 211 G kavery@sjcme.edu
AVERY, Lisa ... 509-533-3844. 518 F lisa.avery@spokanefalls.edu
AVERY, Margery, L ... 585-567-9350. 326 F margery.avery@houghton.edu
AVERY, Martin, D ... 315-386-7222. 345 F averym@canton.edu
AVERY, Michael, R ... 513-721-7944. 380 D president@gbs.edu
AVERY, Paula ... 310-303-7213... 53 F pavery@marymountcalifornia.edu
AVERY, Robert, H ... 401-254-3236. 440 B ravery@rwu.edu
AVERY, Susan ... 508-289-2500. 238 E savery@whoi.edu
AVILA, Arcadio ... 562-860-2451... 37 I aavila@cerritos.edu
AVILA, Celi ... 915-532-3737. 494 J cavila@westerntech.edu
AVILA, Glenna ... 661-255-1050... 31 C glenna@calarts.edu
AVILA, Lauri ... 928-428-8915... 13 J lauri.avila@eac.edu
AVILA, Linda, C ... 310-794-0691... 71 C lcavila@saa.ucla.edu
AVILA, Mike ... 909-607-9224... 39 C mike.avila@cgu.edu
AVILA, Patricia ... 951-222-8000... 61 A
AVILA, Pedro ... 559-324-6474... 68 H
AVILA, Pedro ... 559-324-6474... 68 I pedro.avila@scccd.edu
AVILA, Susan ... 510-594-3661... 30 K savila@cca.edu
AVILES, Angel ... 787-780-5134. 551 L aaviles@nuc.edu
AVILES, Carmen ... 787-744-1060. 551 J cre_caguas@mechtech.edu
AVILES, Gladys, M ... 248-204-4123. 245 I gaviles@ltu.edu
AVILES, John ... 859-371-9393. 192 D javiles@beckfield.edu
AVILES, José ... 302-831-8123... 94 B javiles@udel.edu
AVILES, José, E ... 787-265-3767. 554 E finanzaz@uprm.edu
AVILES-FERRAN, Jeanette ... 787-620-2040. 547 C javiles@aupr.edu
AVISSAR, Roni ... 305-421-4000. 118 F avissar@miami.edu
AW, Fanta ... 202-885-3357... 94 F fanta@american.edu
AWBREY, Susan, M ... 248-370-4955. 248 J awbrey@oakland.edu
AWE, Jacqueline ... 912-358-3114. 131 C awej@savannahstate.edu
AWN, Peter ... 212-854-1932. 321 D pja3@columbia.edu
AWOLAJU, Tafa ... 508-678-2811. 231 B tafa.awolaju@bristolcc.edu
AWOLOLA, Oluyemi ... 727-725-2688. 102 I Yemi@cci.edu
AWONIYI, Beatrice ... 352-395-5513. 113 C bea.awoniyi@sfcollege.edu
AWUAH, Agatha ... 315-498-2500. 335 G awuaha@sunyocc.edu
AWUAH, Emmanuel ... 315-498-7270. 335 G awuahe@sunyocc.edu
AXELRAD, Albert, S ... 617-824-8036. 226 A albert_axelrad@emerson.edu
AXELROD, Larry ... 604-482-5510. 139 F laxelrod@adler.edu
AXELSON, Sara, L ... 307-766-5123. 543 I saxelson@uwyo.edu
AXLER, Sheldon ... 415-338-1571... 35 E axler@sfsu.edu
AXLUND, Martin ... 307-755-2169. 544 B maxlund@wyotechstaff.edu
AXTELL, Denise ... 530-242-7770... 65 G daxtell@shastacollege.edu
AXTELL, Richard, D ... 859-238-5342. 193 E rick.axtell@centre.edu
AXTELL, Thomas, B ... 309-341-7212. 150 A taxtell@knox.edu
AXTON, Faith, M ... 660-263-3900. 272 A fma@cccb.edu
AYALA, Benjamin ... 787-864-2222. 550 D benaya@inter.edu
AYALA, Carlos ... 707-664-2132... 36 B dean.education@sonoma.edu
AYALA, Carmen ... 787-761-0640. 553 F decanaasuntosacademicos@utcpr.edu
AYALA, Eddie ... 787-279-1912. 550 B eayala@bayamon.inter.edu
AYALA, Gladys, M ... 914-594-4498. 334 A gladys_ayala@nymc.edu
AYALA, Israel ... 787-891-0925. 549 K iayala@aguadilla.inter.edu

AYALA, Javier, I ... 585-292-3672. 332 A
jayala5@monroecc.edu
AYALA, Jose ... 787-257-0000. 554 B
jose.ayala5@upr.edu
AYALA, Mary ... 575-562-2421. 309 H
mary.ayala@enmu.edu
AYALA, Paul ... 210-805-5863. 490 A
peayala@uiwtx.edu
AYALA, Ramon ... 787-250-1912. 550 E
rayala@metro.inter.edu
AYALA, Roberto ... 787-265-5413. 554 E
roberto.ayala@uprm.edu
AYBAR, Jose, M ... 773-838-7511. 142 E
jaybar@ccc.edu
AYCOCK, Greg ... 951-739-7802... 60 L
greg.aycock@norcocollege.edu
AYCOCK, Larry, K ... 909-794-2161... 61 K
laycock@sbccd.edu
AYDELOTT, Carla ... 541-684-7241. 405 C
caydelott@nwcu.edu
AYDELOTTE, Elise ... 661-362-2267... 53 G
eaydelotte@masters.edu
AYER, Bernice ... 270-686-4518. 196 C
bernice.ayer@kctcs.edu
AYERS, Beth ... 707-654-1186... 31 I
BookStore@csum.edu
AYERS, David, J ... 724-458-2025. 417 E
djayers@gcc.edu
AYERS, Edward, L ... 804-289-8102. 510 L
eayers@richmond.edu
AYERS, Keith ... 251-460-6211... 9 E
kayers@southalabama.edu
AYERS, Kenya ... 847-925-6404. 145 H
kayers@harpercollege.edu
AYERS, Michael ... 718-758-8127. 317 C
mrayers@brooklyn.cuny.edu
AYERS, Michael ... 828-766-1272. 361 H
mayers@mayland.edu
AYERS, Michael, V ... 336-734-7478. 360 E
mayers@forsythtech.edu
AYERS, Nancy, A ... 208-467-8542. 139 A
naayers@nnu.edu
AYERS, Shari, L ... 614-235-4136. 390 A
sayers@TLSohio.edu
AYERS, Tom ... 810-762-9787. 244 Q
tayers@kettering.edu
AYERS, William, J ... 302-857-1814... 93 G
ayers@dtcc.edu
AYERSMAN, David, J ... 304-256-0281. 528 D
dayersman@newriver.edu
AYI, Richard, S ... 712-279-3149. 182 C
ayirs@stlukescollege.edu
AYLESBURY, Tom ... 626-568-8850... 50 E
AYLMER, Francoise ... 503-725-5037. 406 B
francoise@pdx.edu
AYLOR, James, H ... 434-924-3310. 511 B
jha@virginia.edu
AYLOR, Jerri ... 806-457-4200. 472 G
jaylor@fpctx.edu
AYLOR, Joshua ... 336-272-7102. 354 E
jaylor@greensboro.edu
AYLOR, Pete ... 864-587-4229. 447 B
aylorp@smcsc.edu
AYLWARD, Robert, R ... 307-766-4860. 543 I
raylward@uwyo.edu
AYMAT, Noel ... 787-758-2525. 554 F
noel.aymat@upr.edu
AYNES, Danny ... 541-917-4822. 404 B
aynesd@linnbenton.edu
AYON, Violet, R ... 714-808-4793... 56 D
vayon@nocccd.edu
AYOOB, Kenneth ... 707-826-4491... 35 C
kpa1@humboldt.edu
AYOUBI, Amjad ... 504-865-5107. 207 C
aamjad@tulane.edu
AYRAVAINEN, Eija ... 212-772-4878. 318 C
eija.ayravainen@hunter.cuny.edu
AYRE, Joyce ... 406-377-9447. 286 A
ayre@dawson.edu
AYRE, Joyce ... 406-377-9421. 286 A
ayre@dawson.edu
AYRE-BOGGS, Rebecca .. 810-766-4044. 239 H
rebecca.boggs@baker.edu
AYRES, Angel ... 617-989-4159. 237 G
ayresa@wit.edu
AYRES, Christina, M ... 573-458-0101. 273 M
cmayres@eastcentral.edu
AYRES, Dana ... 214-768-2841. 481 A
dwayres@smu.edu
AYRES, Gary ... 618-468-3000. 150 G
glayres@lc.edu
AYRES, Ted, D ... 316-978-6791. 191 F
ted.ayres@wichita.edu
AYTCH, Keith ... 408-270-6450... 63 O
keith.aytch@evc.edu
AYTES, Kregg ... 406-994-4423. 287 B
kregg.aytes@montana.edu
AZADIAN, Patrick ... 626-873-2113... 55 C
pazadian@mtsierra.edu
AZAIR, Cheryl ... 310-824-1586... 26 B
cheryl@cherylazair.com
AZAR, Dimitri ... 312-996-3500. 161 D
dazar@uic.edu
AZAR, Eve ... 908-835-2335. 308 G
azar@warren.edu
AZAR, James, A ... 401-254-3124. 440 B
jazar@rwu.edu
AZARI, Cynthia ... 951-222-8804... 61 A
AZARI, Cynthia, E ... 951-222-8800... 60 J
cynthia.azari@rccd.edu
AZBELL, Kristen ... 805-581-1233... 43 G
AZCUNAGA, Cecilia ... 401-949-2820. 439 C
cazcunaga@inteducators.org
AZCUY, Alex ... 305-629-2929. 112 H
AZDELL, Grant, L ... 804-752-7266. 508 E
gazdell@rmc.edu
AZEBEOKHAI, I. Charles 678-915-7485. 132 C
cazebeok@spsu.edu
AZEKE, Mercy ... 732-571-4409. 303 C
mazeke@monmouth.edu
AZEVEDO, Christinia ... 530-541-4660... 50 D
azevedo@ltcc.edu
AZHAND, Hamid, U ... 909-537-5136... 34 E
hazhand@csusb.edu
AZIZ, Jihad, N ... 804-828-6200. 511 F
jnaziz@vcu.edu
AZIZ, Kareem ... 410-276-0306. 218 D
kaziz@host.sdc.edu
AZIZ, Nadim ... 864-656-0542. 442 C
aziz@clemson.edu
AZIZAN-GARDNER,
Noor ... 573-882-6282. 283 C
azizan-gardnern@missouri.edu
AZKOUL, Emilie ... 616-222-1447. 241 F
emilie.azkoul@cornerstone.edu
AZLIN WRIGHT, Taisha . 714-816-0366... 70 A
taisha.wright@trident.edu
AZOTEA, Gary, A ... 216-475-7520. 388 G
gary.azotea@remingtoncollege.edu
AZURE, Jackie ... 406-768-3213. 286 C
jazure@fpcc.edu
AZURE, Melody ... 701-854-8020. 372 J
melodya@sbci.edu
AZURE, Tracy ... 701-477-7862. 373 B
tazure@tm.edu
AZZIZ, Ricardo ... 706-721-2301. 126 B
president@gru.edu

B

BAADE, K.Austin ... 262-691-5550. 541 D
kbaade@wctc.edu
BAAKKO, Lori ... 906-487-7360. 242 G
lori.baakko@finlandia.edu
BAAR, Rachael ... 270-831-9803. 195 D
rachael.baar@kctcs.edu
BAART, Aaron ... 712-722-6079. 177 J
aaron.baart@dordt.edu
BAAS, John ... 712-722-6020. 177 J
john.baas@dordt.edu
BAAS, Mark ... 507-332-5876. 261 E
mark.baas@southcentral.edu
BABA, Marietta ... 517-355-6675. 246 H
mbaba@msu.edu
BABALIS, Eva ... 718-779-1430. 336 D
ebabalis@mail.plazacollege.edu
BABASHANIAN,
Mark, R ... 757-446-6000. 504 E
babashmr@evms.edu
BABB, Brian ... 386-506-4457. 101 G
babbb@DaytonaState.edu
BABB, Brian, T ... 386-506-4457. 101 G
babbb@DaytonaState.edu
BABB, Mike ... 847-925-6825. 145 H
mbabb@harpercollege.edu
BABB, Phillip ... 619-702-9400... 31 G
phillip.babb@cibu.edu
BABB, Randy ... 719-389-6379... 79 D
randy.babb@coloradocollege.edu
BABBITT, Jeff ... 585-567-9211. 326 F
jeff.babbitt@houghton.edu
BABBITT, Steven ... 516-463-5019. 326 D
steven.babbitt@hofstra.edu
BABBITT, Terry ... 505-277-8392. 312 F
tbabbitt@unm.edu
BABCOCK, Bernie ... 541-881-5706. 408 C
bbabcock@tvcc.cc
BABCOCK, Whit ... 513-556-4603. 390 G
whit.babcock@uc.edu
BABEL, Rebecca ... 815-753-1395. 154 I
rbabel@niu.edu
BABEL, Thomas ... 630-515-3029. 144 A
tbabel@devry.edu
BABER, James ... 740-264-5591. 379 F
jbaber@egcc.edu
BABER, Karen ... 309-796-5362. 140 E
baberk@bhc.edu
BABESHOFF, Ruth ... 714-628-4775... 60 H
babeshoff_ruth@sccollege.edu
BABETZ, Jeffrey ... 843-863-7921. 441 H
jbabetz@csuniv.edu
BABICH-SPECK,
Kimberly ... 216-987-4000. 378 D
kimberly.babich-speck@tri-c.edu
BABICK-SAQUI,
Christine ... 219-866-6177. 172 E
cbs@saintjoe.edu
BABIN, Louis ... 225-752-4233. 202 C
lbabin@iticollege.edu
BABINGTON, Cynthia ... 765-658-4270. 165 F
cbabington@depauw.edu
BABINGTON, Lynn ... 203-254-4150... 89 I
lbabington@fairfield.edu
BABIZE, Mollie ... 413-369-4044. 225 D
babize@csld.edu
BABYAK, Joyce ... 440-775-8534. 385 H
joyce.babyak@oberlin.edu
BABYAK, Joyce ... 440-775-8410. 385 H
Joyce.Babyak@oberlin.edu
BACA, Amy ... 575-538-6145. 312 N
bacaamym@wnmu.edu
BACA, Brad ... 970-943-2114... 86 I
bbaca@western.edu
BACA, Max ... 505-454-3117. 310 E
mbaca@nmhu.edu
BACA, Randy ... 254-298-8582. 482 C
randy.baca@templejc.edu
BACA-DOSTER,
Carmen, E ... 303-765-3127... 82 E
cbaca@iliff.edu
BACARISSE, Charles ... 281-649-3428. 473 B
cbacarisse@hbu.edu
BACCHETTA, Aldo ... 816-802-3334. 275 J
abacchetta@kcai.edu
BACCI, Diana, S ... 610-341-5854. 415 G
dbacci@eastern.edu
BACCI, Nancy ... 973-748-9000. 299 F
nancy_bacci@bloomfield.edu
BACH, Alex ... 800-955-2527. 274 I
abach@grantham.edu
BACH, Bert, C ... 423-439-4219. 459 C
bachb@etsu.edu
BACH, Bruce ... 215-641-6519. 424 B
bbach@mc3.edu
BACH, Carol Anne ... 615-547-1200. 454 A
cbach@cumberland.edu
BACH, Larry, C ... 612-343-4703. 262 X
lcbach@northcentral.edu
BACH, Lee ... 248-476-1122. 246 G
lbach@mispp.edu
BACHAND, Donald, J ... 989-964-4296. 249 G
dbachand@svsu.edu
BACHARACH, Valerie, S . 724-439-4900. 421 F
vbacharach@laurel.edu
BACHAS, Leonidas, G ... 305-284-4117. 118 F
bachas@miami.edu
BACHELER, Linda ... 239-590-1212. 115 A
lbachele@fgcu.edu
BACHLE, Lori ... 402-552-3100. 288 L
BACHMAN, Desirae ... 712-325-3445. 179 L
dbachman@iwcc.edu
BACHMAN, Gary ... 517-586-3001. 241 A
gbachman@cleary.edu
BACHMAN, Rob ... 303-762-6970... 81 G
rob.bachman@denverseminary.edu
BACHMANN,
Christopher ... 618-468-3100. 150 G
cbachman@lc.edu
BACHMANN, Kirk, T ... 312-944-0882. 150 F
BACHMANN, Robin ... 714-895-8382... 39 J
rbachmann@gwc.cccd.edu
BACHMEIER, James ... 616-331-2188. 243 C
bachmeij@gvsu.edu
BACHMEIER, John ... 715-836-5189. 536 E
bachmejg@uwec.edu
BACHOO, Richard, R ... 860-832-1776... 87 K
bachoor@ccsu.edu
BACHOVCHIN, Jeffery, J 610-660-1676. 432 E
bachovch@sju.edu
BACHRACH, Beverly ... 305-623-2355. 112 F
bbachrach@stu.edu
BACHRATY, James, J ... 716-839-8461. 322 E
jbachrat@daemen.edu
BACIK, Johanna ... 216-987-2283. 378 D
johanna.bacik@tri-c.edu
BACK, Andy ... 610-526-6027. 417 H
aback@harcum.edu
BACK, Richard ... 315-312-2285. 344 A
richard.back@oswego.edu
BACKELS, Kelsey, K ... 717-872-3122. 429 D
kelsey.backels@millersville.edu
BACKER, Carol ... 800-782-2422... 32 B
cbacker@mail.cnuas.edu
BACKLIN, William, W ... 641-422-4326. 181 D
backwil@niacc.edu
BACKLUND, Mary, I ... 845-758-7472. 314 D
backlund@bard.edu
BACKMAN, Carey ... 585-389-2320. 332 D
cbackma2@naz.edu
BACKMAN, Kelli ... 402-481-8698. 288 H
kelli.backman@bryanhealthcollege.edu
BACKMAN, Stephen, M .. 251-343-8200... 6 E
stephen.backman@remingtoncollege.edu
BACKOFEN, Susan ... 304-357-4789. 527 H
susanbackofen@ucwv.edu
BACKSCHEIDER,
Nickolas, A ... 334-844-4512... 1 G
backsni@auburn.edu
BACKUS, Bruce, D ... 314-935-9882. 284 L
backusb@wustl.edu
BACKUS, Robert, H ... 607-746-4677. 345 G
backusrh@delhi.edu
BACON, Curt ... 541-552-6487. 406 C
bacon@sou.edu
BACON, Jack ... 610-892-1007. 427 E
jbacon@pit.edu
BACON, Karen ... 212-340-7700. 351 M
kbacon@yu.edu
BACON, Pamela ... 210-458-6551. 492 C
pamela.bacon@utsa.edu
BACOT, Hunter ... 501-569-8572... 24 B
ahbacot@ualr.edu
BACZA, Gerald ... 304-367-4632. 528 E
Gerald.Bacza@pierpont.edu
BACZEWSKI, Philip, C ... 940-565-3886. 490 C
baczewski@unt.edu
BADAL, Amy, A ... 570-577-1638. 411 A
amy.badal@bucknell.edu
BADAL, Ashour ... 209-664-6747... 35 B
abadal@csustan.edu
BADAL, Robert, S ... 701-252-3467. 373 D
badal@jc.edu
BADALYAN, Anna ... 213-763-7064... 52 D
badalya@lattc.edu
BADE, Michael ... 415-502-6460... 72 A
Michael.Bade@ucsf.edu
BADE, Robert, E ... 727-816-3767. 110 E
badeb@phcc.edu
BADE, William, D ... 217-786-2326. 151 F
bill.bade@llcc.edu
BADEAUX, Stephanie ... 985-543-4120. 203 D
BADENHAUSEN,
Richard ... 801-832-2460. 498 F
rbadenhausen@westminstercollege.edu
BADERMAN, Barbara ... 602-943-2311... 19 C
Barb.Baderman@west.edu
BADGER, Nancy ... 423-425-4438. 463 D
nancy-badger@utc.edu
BADGLEY, Joseph, L ... 304-205-6613. 528 B
jbadgley@kvctc.edu
BADILLO, Ricardo ... 787-891-0925. 549 K
rbadillo@aguadilla.inter.edu
BADILLO, Toni ... 915-831-2164. 472 B
mbadill4@epcc.edu
BADINELLI, Sigrid ... 415-433-9200... 65 C
sbadinelli@saybrook.edu
BADOLATO, Greg ... 617-266-1400. 223 D
BADOLATO, Michael ... 978-762-4000. 232 D
mbadolat@northshore.edu
BADOVINAC, Amanda ... 406-496-4828. 287 F
abadovinac@mtech.edu
BADOVINAC, John, C ... 406-496-4249. 287 F
jbadovinac@mtech.edu
BADWAL, Avi ... 619-260-2943... 73 I
abadwal@sandiego.edu
BAEHR, Marie ... 319-399-8616. 176 G
mbaehr@coe.edu
BAEHRE-KOLOVANI,
Edna, V ... 757-822-1050. 514 C
ekolovani@tcc.edu
BAENEN, Michael ... 617-627-3300. 237 C
michael.baenen@tufts.edu
BAENNINGER, MaryAnn 320-363-5505. 254 J
csbpres@csbsju.edu
BAER, Candace ... 401-454-6426. 440 A
cbaer@risd.edu
BAER, Catherine, E ... 845-437-5401. 349 G
cabaer@vassar.edu
BAER, Eugen ... 315-781-3300. 326 C
baer@hws.edu
BAER, Karim ... 415-575-6176... 31 D
kbaer@ciis.edu
BAER, Natasha ... 763-433-1707. 257 P
natasha.baer@anokaramsey.edu
BAER, Robert ... 203-857-7369... 89 D
rbaer@norwalk.edu
BAER, Ulrich, C ... 212-998-8695. 334 D
ulrich.baer@nyu.edu
BAERBOCK, Ben, J ... 414-410-4050. 532 B
bjbaerbock@stritch.edu
BAERWALD, Bonnie ... 920-929-2131. 540 F
bbaerwald@morainepark.edu
BAESLACK, III,
William, A ... 216-368-4346. 375 J
william.baeslack@case.edu
BAESSLER, Laura ... 937-382-6661. 393 B
laura_baessler@wilmington.edu
BAETHKE, Mark ... 515-965-7312. 177 B
mdbaethke@dmacc.edu
BAEZ, Ada ... 787-285-5457. 549 C
abaez4@hccpr.edu

BAEZ, Annecy .... 718-289-5868. 317 B
annecy.baez@bcc.cuny.edu
BAEZ, Mirna .... 787-753-0039. 551 D
BAEZ, Nayla .... 787-878-4146. 553 I
nayla.baez@upr.edu
BAEZ MILAN, Tony .... 724-653-2183. 415 A
tbaez@dec.edu
BAEZA-ORTEGO, Gilda ... 575-538-6350. 312 N
ortegog@wnmu.edu
BAFFA, Joe .... 714-556-3610... 74 D
joe.baffa@vanguard.edu
BAFFORD-BUBEL,
Karen, M .... 585-266-0430. 324 A
karen.baffordbubel@cci.edu
BAGBY, Crystal .... 360-676-2772. 521 D
cbagby@nwic.edu
BAGDAZIAN, Robert, A .. 805-525-4417... 69 H
rbagdazian@thomasaquinas.edu
BAGEL, George .... 770-534-6265. 122 A
gbagel@brenau.edu
BAGEL, Jeffrey .... 716-851-1991. 323 I
bagel@ecc.edu
BAGENTS, Bill .... 256-766-6610..... 4 B
bbagents@hcu.edu
BAGG, Eva .... 562-938-4736... 51 D
ebagg@lbcc.edu
BAGG, Mary Beth .... 317-788-3220. 173 I
bagg@uindy.edu
BAGGER, Jonathan, A .... 410-516-3355. 215 H
bagger@jhu.edu
BAGGETT, Cody .... 217-641-4360. 148 M
cbaggett@jwcc.edu
BAGGIO, Bobbe, G .... 215-951-1238. 420 B
baggio@lasalle.edu
BAGGOT, Joseph .... 507-222-4075. 254 D
jbaggot@carleton.edu
BAGGS, Adam .... 817-257-6814. 484 I
a.baggs@tcu.edu
BAGGS, David .... 843-863-7513. 441 H
dbaggs@csuniv.edu
BAGGSON, Gulizar .... 479-619-2203... 22 C
gbaggson@nwacc.edu
BAGILEO, Nick, J .... 202-526-3799... 96 D
BAGINSKI, Kristen .... 412-392-4750. 431 B
kbaginski@pointpark.edu
BAGLEY, Elizabeth .... 404-471-6339. 119 I
ebagley@agnesscott.edu
BAGLEY, Michelle .... 360-992-2472. 518 A
mbagley@clark.edu
BAGLEY, Rod .... 715-833-6480. 539 J
rbagley1@cvtc.edu
BAGLEY, Shawn .... 330-823-2280. 391 E
bagleysp@mountunion.edu
BAGLEY, Vera, L .... 301-322-0801. 217 F
vbagley@pgcc.edu
BAGNALL, James .... 928-428-8414... 13 J
jim.bagnall@eac.edu
BAGNELL, William .... 252-328-6858. 367 B
bagnellw@ecu.edu
BAGNO, Sherry .... 847-578-3262. 157 F
sherry.bagno@rosalindfranklin.edu
BAGNOLI, Joseph, P ...... 641-269-3600. 178 H
bagnolij@grinnell.edu
BAGRANOFF, Nancy, A .. 804-289-8550. 510 L
nbagrano@richmond.edu
BAGSTAD, Kristi .... 563-588-6314. 176 F
kristi.bagstad@clarke.edu
BAGWELL, Andrea .... 202-274-5400... 97 A
abagwell@udc.edu
BAGWELL, Elizabeth .... 828-251-6525. 368 C
bbagwell@unca.edu
BAGWELL, Jack .... 803-327-8021. 449 J
bagwell@yorktech.edu
BAGWELL, Linda .... 817-598-6274. 494 G
lbagwell@wc.edu
BAGWELL, Lydia .... 575-527-7560. 311 B
lbagwell@nmsu.edu
BAHAR, Sonya .... 314-516-7150. 283 E
bahars@umsl.edu
BAHARANYI, Ntam .... 334-727-8659..... 8 A
nbaharanyi@tuskegee.edu
BAHLS, Steven, C .... 309-794-7208. 139 L
stevenbahls@augustana.edu
BAHNEMAN, Molly .... 651-846-1514. 261 D
molly.bahneman@saintpaul.edu
BAHNEY, Steve .... 217-245-1488. 150 D
steve.bahney@doc.illinois.gov
BAHR, Christine, M .... 618-537-6810. 152 G
cmbahr@mckendree.edu
BAHR, Christopher .... 979-230-3119. 468 A
christopher.bahr@brazosport.edu
BAHR, Jonathon .... 734-995-7311. 241 E
barhj@cuaa.edu
BAI, Yifeng .... 973-748-9000. 299 F
yifeng_bai@bloomfield.edu
BAIA, Larissa .... 603-524-3207. 295 L
lbaia@ccsnh.edu
BAICK, Seung-ju .... 770-279-0507. 124 I
academic@gcuniv.edu
BAIER, Henry, D .... 734-764-3402. 251 C
hbaier@umich.edu
BAIER, Kris .... 360-383-3003. 525 D
kbaier@whatcom.ctc.edu
BAIER, Valerie, A .... 570-326-3761. 427 B
vbaier@pct.edu
BAIERL, Kenneth, W .... 574-520-4560. 168 E
kbaierl@iusb.edu
BAIGENT, Peter .... 631-632-6700. 342 C
peter.baigent@stonybrook.edu
BAIGENT, Peter, M .... 631-632-6700. 342 C
peter.baigent@stonybrook.edu
BAILARD, Rhiannon .... 310-506-4702... 58 H
Rhiannon.Bailard@pepperdine.edu
BAILES, Loretta .... 773-907-4418. 142 A
lcanett-bailes@ccc.edu
BAILEY, Aileen, M .... 240-895-4338. 218 A
ambailey@smcm.edu
BAILEY, Alison .... 309-438-2947. 147 J
baileya@ilstu.edu
BAILEY, Ann .... 662-325-3555. 268 D
housing@saffairs.msstate.edu
BAILEY, Anthony .... 213-740-2852... 74 A
arbailey@usc.edu
BAILEY, Barbara .... 773-252-5311. 156 I
barbara.bailey@resu.edu
BAILEY, Beth .... 706-419-1104. 123 F
beth.bailey@covenant.edu
BAILEY, Birdie, I .... 256-765-4311..... 9 C
bibailey@una.edu
BAILEY, Bliss .... 334-844-3500..... 1 G
bailebn@auburn.edu
BAILEY, Cassandra, L .... 310-258-8772... 53 E
cbailey8@lmu.edu
BAILEY, Cassy .... 785-594-8484. 184 C
cassy.bailey@bakeru.edu
BAILEY, Cheryl .... 701-355-8180. 373 E
cbailey@mail.cdln.lib.nd.us
BAILEY, Chris, C .... 570-372-4149. 433 H
baileycj@susqu.edu
BAILEY, Christopher .... 202-231-3866. 544 L
christopher.bailey@dodiis.mil
BAILEY, Christopher, C .. 360-442-2101. 521 A
cbailey@lowercolumbia.edu
BAILEY, Clint .... 252-328-2606. 367 B
baileyrc@ecu.edu
BAILEY, Darlene .... 816-415-5943. 285 C
baileyd@william.jewell.edu
BAILEY, David .... 912-280-4000. 120 B
dbailey@altamahatech.edu
BAILEY, David .... 303-361-7381... 81 C
david.bailey@ccaurora.edu
BAILEY, David, C .... 574-631-1097. 174 A
bailey.77@nd.edu
BAILEY, Dennis, A .... 850-644-8136. 115 C
dbailey@fsu.edu
BAILEY, Dexter .... 631-632-4490. 342 C
dexter.bailey@stonybrook.edu
BAILEY, Dixon .... 325-734-3651. 486 C
dixon.bailey@tstc.edu
BAILEY, Donald Russell . 401-865-1188. 439 E
drbailey@providence.edu
BAILEY, Donna .... 800-818-2261. 296 F
dbailey@dwc.edu
BAILEY,
Dudley (Skip), L .... 585-292-2833. 332 A
dbailey@monroecc.edu
BAILEY, Ed .... 231-995-1215. 248 B
ebailey@nmc.edu
BAILEY, Gary .... 616-538-2330. 243 A
gbailey@gbcol.edu
BAILEY, Helen .... 423-869-6387. 456 A
hbailey@lmunet.edu
BAILEY, Howard, E .... 270-745-2791. 200 G
howard.bailey@wku.edu
BAILEY, Jack .... 304-766-4109. 530 C
jbaile19@wvstateu.edu
BAILEY, Jana, K .... 606-539-4234. 200 B
jana.bailey@ucumberlands.edu
BAILEY, Janet, K .... 304-462-4102. 529 G
janet.bailey@glenville.edu
BAILEY, Janie .... 870-633-4480... 21 A
jbailey@eacc.edu
BAILEY, Jaye .... 203-392-5552... 88 A
baileyj10@southernct.edu
BAILEY, Jeff .... 870-972-3077... 19 N
jbailey@astate.edu
BAILEY, Jessica, H .... 601-984-6300. 270 C
jhbailey@umc.edu
BAILEY, Jessica, M .... 336-750-3277. 370 A
baileyjm@wssu.edu
BAILEY, John .... 808-675-3458. 135 C
baileyj@byuh.edu
BAILEY, Joseph, A .... 585-345-6900. 325 C
jabailey@genesee.edu
BAILEY, Julie .... 432-264-5030. 473 E
jbailey@howardcollege.edu
BAILEY, Karen .... 404-460-2482. 130 F
karen.bailey@point.edu
BAILEY, Kathy .... 864-977-7170. 445 H
kim.bailey@ngu.edu
BAILEY, Kelly .... 805-525-4417... 69 H
kbailey@thomasaquinas.edu
BAILEY, Kelly .... 724-738-4223. 429 F
kelly.bailey@sru.edu
BAILEY, Kevin .... 850-474-2214. 117 B
baileyk@uwf.edu
BAILEY, Kim .... 816-322-0110. 271 O
kim.bailey@calvary.edu
BAILEY, Kristi .... 281-487-1170. 484 H
kbailey@txchiro.edu
BAILEY, Lisa .... 909-652-6532... 37 M
lisa.bailey@chaffey.edu
BAILEY, Lora .... 219-980-6989. 168 B
lorbaile@iun.edu
BAILEY, Maggie .... 619-849-2535... 59 L
maggiebailey@pointloma.edu
BAILEY, Marcia .... 636-584-6551. 273 M
baileymc@eastcentral.edu
BAILEY, Margaret, A .... 803-934-3192. 445 F
mbailey@morris.edu
BAILEY, Mark .... 909-621-8219... 59 G
mark_bailey@pitzer.edu
BAILEY, Mark .... 205-853-1200..... 5 B
mbailey@jeffstateonline.com
BAILEY, Mark, L .... 214-887-5001. 471 F
mbailey@dts.edu
BAILEY, Mary, H .... 910-672-1390. 367 D
mhbailey@uncfsu.edu
BAILEY, Mary Kaye .... 702-651-4362. 294 E
mary.kaye.bailey@csn.edu
BAILEY, Michael .... 914-251-6915. 344 D
michael.bailey@purchase.edu
BAILEY, Michael, L .... 804-342-1497. 515 F
mbailey@vuu.edu
BAILEY, Michelle .... 563-441-4152. 178 C
BAILEY, Mike .... 620-417-1019. 190 F
mike.bailey@sccc.edu
BAILEY, Mitchell .... 937-512-3050. 388 O
mitchell.bailey@sinclair.edu
BAILEY, Neil .... 478-289-2162. 124 C
nabailey@ega.edu
BAILEY, Patrick, X .... 504-865-3434. 205 H
pbailey@loyno.edu
BAILEY, Paul .... 678-466-4377. 123 A
paulbailey@clayton.edu
BAILEY, Peter, A .... 302-295-1191... 94 E
peter.a.bailey@wilmu.edu
BAILEY, JR., Philip, S ... 805-756-2226... 32 F
pbailey@calpoly.edu
BAILEY, Richard .... 281-458-4050. 479 E
richard.bailey@sjcd.edu
BAILEY, Richard .... 281-458-4050. 479 G
richard.bailey@sjcd.edu
BAILEY, Richard, L .... 717-361-1181. 415 H
baileyrl@etown.edu
BAILEY, Robyn .... 847-635-1444. 155 F
rbailey@oakton.edu
BAILEY, S. Elizabeth .... 706-542-0006. 133 C
sebailey@uga.edu
BAILEY, Scott .... 706-272-4435. 123 G
sbailey@daltonstate.edu
BAILEY, Stephanie .... 615-963-7245. 459 E
sbaile11@tnstate.edu
BAILEY, Steve .... 434-381-6110. 510 F
sbailey@sbc.edu
BAILEY, Stuart, A .... 512-492-3033. 466 B
sbailey@aoma.edu
BAILEY, Teresa .... 757-825-2770. 514 B
baileyt@tncc.edu
BAILEY, Terry .... 706-272-2611. 123 G
tbailey@daltonstate.edu
BAILEY, William .... 252-493-7434. 362 G
wbailey@email.pittcc.edu
BAILEY, William, D .... 814-393-2306. 428 C
wbailey@clarion.edu
BAILEY-AYE, Regena ...... 785-654-2416. 183 I
rbailey@allencc.edu
BAILEY-CHEN, Robin ...... 661-255-1050... 31 C
rbaileychen@calarts.edu
BAILEY CLARK, Denise .. 301-934-7724. 214 D
dbclark@csmd.edu
BAILEY-FOUGNIER,
Dennis .... 831-479-6317... 30 G
debailey@cabrillo.edu
BAILEY-JONES, Rachel ... 585-389-5139. 332 D
rjones3@naz.edu
BAILEY-OCHOA, Celia .... 409-772-8909. 493 C
cebailey@utmb.edu
BAILIN, Debra, M .... 802-626-6210. 501 E
debra.bailin@lyndonstate.edu
BAILLARGEON, Betty .... 860-885-2605... 89 F
BAILLIE, Harold, W .... 570-941-7520. 436 A
harold.baillie@scranton.edu
BAILLIE, Joan, M .... 856-351-2601. 307 B
baillie@salemcc.edu
BAILLIE, Thomas .... 206-543-5050. 524 G
tbaillie@uw.edu
BAILO, Carole Anne .... 480-212-1704... 17 N
BAILON, Kathy .... 213-624-1200... 44 D
kbailon@fidm.edu
BAILY, Jessica .... 914-674-7611. 330 J
jbaily@mercy.edu
BAILY, Michael .... 906-487-7276. 242 G
michael.baily@finlandia.edu
BAILY, Scott .... 970-491-7655... 80 I
scott.baily@colostate.edu
BAIMA, Thomas, A .... 847-566-6401. 162 G
tbaima@usml.edu
BAIN, Andrew, C .... 410-951-4231. 220 B
acbain@coppin.edu
BAIN, Daniel .... 251-809-1551..... 5 A
daniel.bain@jdcc.edu
BAIN, Donald, E .... 585-385-8010. 338 H
dbain@sjfc.edu
BAIN, Jeff, N .... 931-363-9872. 456 C
jbain@martinmethodist.edu
BAIN, Michael, L .... 404-669-2097. 130 F
michael.bain@point.edu
BAIN-DOWELL, Astra ...... 718-270-1234. 342 D
astra.dowell@downstate.edu
BAINTER, Bradley .... 309-298-1808. 162 K
bl-bainter@wiu.edu
BAIR, Ava .... 719-336-1574... 82 R
ava.bair@lamarcc.edu
BAIR, Ginny, V .... 218-477-2581. 259 H
ginny.bair@mnstate.edu
BAIR, Peggy .... 928-350-1110... 17 K
pbair@prescott.edu
BAIR, Susanne, P .... 716-878-4324. 343 A
bairsp@buffalostate.edu
BAIRD, Bridget, R .... 423-439-8222. 459 C
bairdb@etsu.edu
BAIRD, David, L .... 714-895-8125... 39 J
dbaird@gwc.cccd.edu
BAIRD, Davis .... 508-793-7673. 225 A
dbaird@clarku.edu
BAIRD, Denise, M .... 317-738-8270. 165 I
dbaird@franklincollege.edu
BAIRD, Jeffrey .... 215-951-2620. 430 E
bairdj@philau.edu
BAIRD, Karen .... 312-322-1720. 160 D
kbaird@spertus.edu
BAIRD, Kathy .... 707-256-7168... 55 F
kbaird@napavalley.edu
BAIRD, Lynn, N .... 208-885-6534. 139 D
lbaird@uidaho.edu
BAIRD, Phil .... 701-255-3285. 373 C
pbaird@uttc.edu
BAIRD, Robert .... 276-466-7911. 514 G
robertbaird@vic.edu
BAIRD, Timothy, R .... 724-847-6490. 417 A
trbaird@geneva.edu
BAISDEN, Emma, L .... 304-896-7402. 528 F
emma.baisden@southernwv.edu
BAITMAN, Clay, L .... 618-235-2700. 160 A
clay.baitman@swic.edu
BAITY, Deborah, A .... 831-656-2480. 544 M
dbaity@nps.edu
BAJOIE, Diane, E .... 504-568-4810. 205 C
dbajoi@lsuhsc.edu
BAJOR, William .... 201-200-3409. 303 F
wbajor@njcu.edu
BAJUSZIK, Pattie, A .... 724-287-8711. 411 C
pattie.bajuszik@bc3.edu
BAK, Doug .... 719-846-5513... 85 H
doug.bak@trinidadstate.edu
BAKARI, Sentwali .... 515-271-2835. 177 K
sentwali.bakari@drake.edu
BAKAS, Joanna .... 617-850-1280. 227 E
jbakas@hchc.edu
BAKEMEIR, Emily, P .... 203-432-4440... 93 A
emily.bakemeir@yale.edu
BAKER, Adria .... 713-348-6095. 479 A
abaker@rice.edu
BAKER, Alvin .... 606-326-2422. 194 J
abaker00016@kctcs.edu
BAKER, Amy .... 573-288-6493. 273 F
abaker@culver.edu
BAKER, Barbara .... 970-521-6611... 83 L
barbara.baker@njc.edu
BAKER, Barry .... 407-823-2564. 115 E
barry.baker@ucf.edu
BAKER, Barry .... 989-686-9346. 242 C
bgbaker@delta.edu
BAKER, Barry, A .... 425-235-5839. 522 F
bbaker@rtc.edu
BAKER, Ben, J .... 256-765-4278..... 9 C
bjbaker@una.edu
BAKER, Bill .... 405-422-1282. 399 B
bakerb@redlandscc.edu
BAKER, Brent .... 817-598-6275. 494 G
bbaker@wc.edu
BAKER, Brent, A .... 765-641-4072. 163 L
babaker@anderson.edu
BAKER, Brian .... 812-749-1212. 171 K
bbaker@oak.edu
BAKER, Brian, K .... 240-567-1787. 216 F
brian.baker@montgomerycollege.edu
BAKER, Bruce .... 603-427-7604. 295 K
bbaker@ccsnh.edu
BAKER, Caroline .... 410-455-8171. 219 D
cbaker@umbc.edu

BAKER, Carrie, B .... 850-873-3565. 106 H
cbaker@gulfcoast.edu
BAKER, Chad .... 717-299-7702. 434 A
baker@stevenscollege.edu
BAKER, Cheryl .... 304-647-6201. 530 B
cbaker@osteo.wvsom.edu
BAKER, Connie .... 805-289-6400... 74 H
cbaker@vcccd.edu
BAKER, Crystal .... 812-237-2215. 167 A
crystal.baker@indstate.edu
BAKER, Danette .... 806-743-2786. 487 E
danette.baker@ttuhsc.edu
BAKER, David .... 715-836-2542. 536 E
bakerda@uwec.edu
BAKER, David, A .... 541-737-3871. 406 A
david.baker@oregonstate.edu
BAKER, David, E .... 312-567-3561. 147 F
bakerd@iit.edu
BAKER, Dawn .... 503-760-3131. 402 B
dawn@birthingway.edu
BAKER, Debbie .... 307-382-1611. 543 J
dbaker@wwcc.wy.edu
BAKER, Debra .... 662-246-6301. 268 B
dbaker@msdelta.edu
BAKER, Don .... 408-924-7820... 36 A
don.baker@sjsu.edu
BAKER, Donald, B .... 401-825-2134. 439 A
dbaker@ccri.edu
BAKER, Donna .... 816-584-6847. 280 C
donna.baker@park.edu
BAKER, Dori .... 434-381-6113. 510 F
dbaker@sbc.edu
BAKER, Douglas, D .... 815-753-9500. 154 I
ddbaker@niu.edu
BAKER, Dyann, J .... 860-701-5016... 90 G
baker_dy@mitchell.edu
BAKER, Eliott, G .... 724-738-2010. 429 F
eliott.baker@sru.edu
BAKER, Elisha (Bear) ...... 907-786-1050... 10 H
provost@uaa.alaska.edu
BAKER, Elizabeth .... 252-222-6216. 358 G
bakere@carteret.edu
BAKER, Erinnae .... 803-981-7075. 449 J
ebaker@yorktech.edu
BAKER, Erma, A .... 540-654-2043. 510 J
ebaker@umw.edu
BAKER, Fred .... 501-450-1362... 21 E
baker@hendrix.edu
BAKER, Gail .... 402-554-2232. 293 A
gbaker@unomaha.edu
BAKER, Gilbert .... 501-852-0871... 25 H
gilbertb@uca.edu
BAKER, Gordon .... 678-466-4334. 123 A
gordonbaker@clayton.edu
BAKER, Greg .... 808-981-2790. 135 E
gbaker@hicom.edu
BAKER, Hilary .... 818-677-7750... 34 C
hilary.baker@csun.edu
BAKER, Jackie .... 507-457-6695. 264 A
jbaker@smumn.edu
BAKER, James, P .... 417-836-8501. 278 E
jbaker@missouristate.edu
BAKER, Janet .... 610-740-3765. 412 I
jlbaker@cedarcrest.edu
BAKER, Jeff .... 619-644-7108... 46 E
jeff.baker@gcccd.edu
BAKER, Jeffrey, A .... 704-687-8457. 368 E
jbaker88@uncc.edu
BAKER, Jennifer .... 417-823-3469. 281 M
jbaker@forest.edu
BAKER, Jill .... 619-388-2320... 62 E
jbaker@sdccd.edu
BAKER, Jill .... 304-457-6337. 526 A
bakersj@ab.edu
BAKER, Jim .... 817-272-2261. 491 B
jimbaker@uta.edu
BAKER, Jo Nell .... 909-593-3511... 72 E
jbaker@laverne.edu
BAKER, Joe .... 262-524-7319. 532 C
jrbaker@carrollu.edu
BAKER, John, T .... 508-856-5538. 229 C
john.baker@umassmed.edu
BAKER, Johnny .... 256-835-5463..... 3 M
jbaker@gadsdenstate.edu
BAKER, Joseph, J .... 610-499-4151. 437 E
jjbaker@widener.edu
BAKER, Joyce .... 740-695-9500. 374 H
jbaker@belmontcollege.edu
BAKER, Judy .... 650-949-7388... 44 N
bakerjudy@foothill.edu
BAKER, Karen, M .... 817-257-5566. 484 I
k.baker@tcu.edu
BAKER, Kathleen .... 206-296-6305. 523 E
bakerkat@seattleu.edu
BAKER, Lee, D .... 919-684-3465. 354 A
ldbaker@duke.edu
BAKER, Leona .... 757-455-3366. 515 H
lbaker@vwc.edu
BAKER, Linda .... 906-487-3381. 247 A
lpbaker@mtu.edu
BAKER, Lori .... 540-857-6067. 514 E
lbaker@virginiawestern.edu
BAKER, LuAnn .... 870-307-7425... 21 H
luann.baker@lyon.edu
BAKER, Marilyn .... 816-271-4200. 279 A
mbaker3@missouriwestern.edu
BAKER, Matt .... 660-562-1219. 279 I
mcbaker@nwmissouri.edu
BAKER, Matt .... 215-951-2870. 430 E
bakerm@philau.edu
BAKER, Maureen .... 402-844-7258. 291 I
maureen@northeast.edu
BAKER, Melanie .... 540-636-2900. 503 L
melaniebaker@christendom.edu
BAKER, Michael .... 907-564-8259... 10 C
mbaker@alaskapacific.edu
BAKER, Michael, F .... 508-856-3040. 229 C
michael.baker@umassmed.edu
BAKER, Mike .... 859-442-1153. 195 B
mike.baker@kctcs.edu
BAKER, Molly .... 815-288-5511. 158 K
bakerm@svcc.edu
BAKER, Monica .... 928-226-4262... 13 B
monica.baker@coconino.edu
BAKER, Nancy .... 704-636-6882. 355 D
nbaker@hoodseminary.edu
BAKER, Natalie .... 404-880-6879. 122 J
nbaker@cau.edu
BAKER, Neal .... 765-983-1355. 165 G
bakerne@earlham.edu
BAKER, Nelson .... 404-894-8920. 125 D
nelson.baker@pe.gatech.edu
BAKER, Nick .... 989-275-5000. 245 B
nick.baker@kirtland.edu
BAKER, Pearl .... 606-539-4211. 200 B
pearl.baker@ucumberlands.edu
BAKER, Quincee .... 701-627-4638. 371 A
qbaker@fbcc.bia.edu
BAKER, Richard .... 601-643-8404. 266 F
richard.baker@colin.edu
BAKER, Richard .... 703-257-5515. 502 E
directoredamm@aviationmaintenance.edu
BAKER, Richard, A .... 713-743-8834. 489 B
rabaker4@central.uh.edu
BAKER, Robert .... 518-631-9862. 348 K
bakerr@uniongraduatecollege.edu
BAKER, Robert .... 617-984-1642. 235 I
bbaker@quincycollege.edu
BAKER, Robert .... 617-984-5959. 235 I
rbaker@quincycollege.edu
BAKER, Robert, D .... 972-238-6174. 471 C
rbaker1@dcccd.edu
BAKER, Robert, T .... 336-758-5224. 370 D
bakerrt@wfu.edu
BAKER, Robin, E .... 503-554-2101. 403 C
rbaker@georgefox.edu
BAKER, Russell, D .... 317-921-4313. 169 K
rbaker80@ivytech.edu
BAKER, Ruth, E .... 410-334-2815. 221 D
rbaker@worwic.edu
BAKER, Sallie .... 828-835-4202. 364 E
sbaker@tricountycc.edu
BAKER, Sally, A .... 207-859-4609. 209 J
sabaker@colby.edu
BAKER, Sandi, J .... 770-531-6408. 128 B
sbaker@laniertech.edu
BAKER, Sandy .... 951-222-8408... 61 A
sandy.baker@rccd.edu
BAKER, Sara .... 706-233-7323. 131 E
sbaker@shorter.edu
BAKER, Sarah .... 910-672-1185. 367 D
sbaker@uncfsu.edu
BAKER, Scott, R .... 740-427-5148. 382 J
bakersr@kenyon.edu
BAKER, Shane .... 919-761-2285. 366 I
sbaker@sebts.edu
BAKER, Shawn .... 402-461-7303. 289 I
sbaker@hastings.edu
BAKER, Sherry .... 731-286-3242. 460 F
baker@dscc.edu
BAKER, Stephen .... 212-353-4131. 321 F
baker@cooper.edu
BAKER, Stephen, N .... 401-874-4980. 440 D
majorbaker@uri.edu
BAKER, Steve .... 619-644-7155... 46 E
steve.baker@gcccd.edu
BAKER, Steven .... 561-803-2223. 110 B
steven_baker@pba.edu
BAKER, Susan, D .... 585-292-2124. 332 A
sbaker@monroecc.edu
BAKER, Thomas, N .... 315-267-2900. 344 C
bakertn@potsdam.edu
BAKER, Timothy .... 670-234-3690. 547 A
timothyb@nmcnet.edu
BAKER, Todd .... 716-896-0700. 350 A
bakert@villa.edu
BAKER, Twila .... 701-627-4738. 371 A
BAKER, Val .... 863-297-1000. 110 H
vbaker@polk.edu
BAKER, Wayne .... 432-335-6574. 477 M
wbaker@odessa.edu
BAKER, William, P .... 602-386-4137... 11 G
william.baker@arizonachristian.edu
BAKER, Winston .... 936-468-2601. 482 A
bakerwa@sfasu.edu
BAKER-TATE, Ixchel .... 910-962-1112. 369 C
tatei@uncw.edu
BAKER-WATSON, Stevie 765-658-6075. 165 F
steviebaker-watson@depauw.edu
BAKEWELL-SACHS,
Susan .... 503-494-7445. 405 I
sondeansoffice@ohsu.edu
BAKHIET, Raga .... 619-482-6381... 68 B
BAKHIT, Izzeldin .... 267-256-0210... 96 F
izzeldin.bakhit@strayer.edu
BAKHIT, Norm .... 574-535-7507. 166 A
nbakhit@goshen.edu
BAKK, Kelly .... 218-749-7765. 259 B
k.bakk@mr.mnscu.edu
BAKKE, Andrea .... 703-812-4757. 506 H
abakke@leland.edu
BAKKE, Lisa .... 702-651-4211. 294 E
lisa.bakke@csn.edu
BAKKE, Ray .... 360-927-5744. 516 J
rayb@bgu.edu
BAKKEN, Jeffrey .... 309-677-3997. 140 I
jbakken@bradley.edu
BAKKEN, Turina, R .... 608-246-6516. 540 C
bakken@madisoncollege.edu
BAKKER, Joseph .... 850-599-3211. 114 K
joseph.bakker@famu.edu
BAKKUM, Barclay .... 312-225-1700. 146 G
bbakkum@ico.edu
BAKKUM, Christine, S ... 608-785-8951. 536 G
cbakkum@uwlax.edu
BAKSH-JARRETT, Gail .... 718-482-5116. 318 F
gailbj@lagcc.cuny.edu
BAKST, M, S .... 248-968-3360. 253 A
BAKST, Y .... 248-968-3360. 253 A
BAKY, John, S .... 215-951-1286. 420 B
baky@lasalle.edu
BALA, Devi .... 480-517-8343... 15 D
devi.bala@riosalado.edu
BALABAN, Carey, D .... 412-624-5749. 435 C
cbalaban@pitt.edu
BALABAN, Michael .... 845-431-8044. 323 C
michael.balaban@sunydutchess.edu
BALACEK, Patti .... 608-785-9201. 541 E
balacekp@westerntc.edu
BALACHANDRAN, Betsy 847-851-5309. 139 I
BALAGOUR, Nina .... 215-612-6600. 419 J
n_balagour@chicareers.com
BALAKRISHNAN, Raju ... 313-593-5248. 251 D
rajub@umich.edu
BALANOFF, Janet .... 407-823-1336. 115 E
janet.balanoff@ucf.edu
BALAS, E. Andrew .... 706-721-2621. 126 B
andrew.balas@gru.edu
BALAS, Heather .... 724-589-2014. 434 B
hbalas@thiel.edu
BALASCO, Vincent .... 401-825-1179. 439 A
vbalasco@ccri.edu
BALASKI, Keith .... 612-659-6842. 259 D
keith.balaski@minneapolis.edu
BALASON, Severo .... 708-974-5346. 153 F
balasonjrs@morainevalley.edu
BALATBAT, Joseph .... 212-924-5900. 347 B
jbalatbat@swedishinstitute.edu
BALBACH, Donna, M ...... 812-357-6525. 173 A
dbalbach@saintmeinrad.edu
BALCH, Angela .... 432-685-4508. 476 G
abalch@midland.edu
BALCH, Glenna .... 512-404-4828. 467 A
gbalch@austinseminary.edu
BALCH, Maggie .... 781-736-3600. 224 F
balch@brandeis.edu
BALCH, Pamela .... 304-473-8181. 531 G
balch@wvwc.edu
BALD, Tim .... 920-403-3030. 535 L
tim.bald@snc.edu
BALDASTY, Gerald, J ..... 206-543-7468. 524 G
baldasty@uw.edu
BALDERAS, Maggie .... 805-966-3888... 30 A
mbalderas@brooks.edu
BALDERRAMA, Sylvia .... 845-437-5700. 349 G
sybalderrama@vassar.edu
BALDESCHWIELER,
Karen .... 415-738-8107... 56 A
kbaldeschwieler@new.edu
BALDIN, Antoinette .... 419-995-8222. 381 Q
baldin.a@rhodesstate.edu
BALDIN, Antoinette .... 419-995-8887. 381 Q
baldin.a@rhodesstate.edu
BALDINI, Fred .... 916-278-7256... 34 D
baldinif@csus.edu
BALDONADO, Hernando 713-718-5069. 473 C
nandy.baldonado@hccs.edu
BALDONEDO, Claudia .... 718-482-5236. 318 F
claudiab@lagcc.cuny.edu
BALDREE, Megan .... 325-793-4801. 476 E
baldree.megan@mcm.edu
BALDRIDGE, Amanda ...... 580-371-2371. 396 E
abaldridge@mscok.edu
BALDRIDGE, Patricia, M 215-951-2851. 430 E
baldridgep@philau.edu
BALDRIDGE, Susan .... 802-443-5518. 499 H
scbaldridge@middlebury.edu
BALDUCCI, Laureen .... 650-949-7823... 44 N
balduccilaureen@foothill.edu
BALDUS, Lisa .... 507-281-7771. 261 A
lisa.baldus@rctc.edu
BALDWIN, Alphonso ...... 847-543-2113. 143 A
abaldwin@clcillinois.edu
BALDWIN, Anne, E .... 585-245-5547. 343 C
baldwina@geneseo.edu
BALDWIN, Beatrice .... 225-342-6950. 207 D
Beatrice.Baldwin@la.gov
BALDWIN, Bryan .... 508-531-2609. 229 D
bbaldwin@bridgew.edu
BALDWIN, Chad .... 307-766-2929. 543 I
cbaldwin@uwyo.edu
BALDWIN, Charlene .... 714-532-7747... 38 A
baldwin@chapman.edu
BALDWIN, Christine, A .. 714-850-4800... 87 E
Baldwin@TaftU.edu
BALDWIN, Darin .... 334-745-6437..... 7 C
dbaldwin@suscc.edu
BALDWIN, David, N .... 508-626-4645. 230 A
dbaldwin@framingham.edu
BALDWIN, Deborah, J .... 501-569-3296... 24 B
djbaldwin@ualr.edu
BALDWIN, Dirk .... 262-595-2379. 537 C
baldwin@uwp.edu
BALDWIN, Dorsey .... 912-478-5409. 126 C
dbaldwin@georgiasouthern.edu
BALDWIN, Gail .... 601-643-8322. 266 F
gail.baldwin@colin.edu
BALDWIN, Jackie .... 856-227-7200. 300 B
jbaldwin@camdencc.edu
BALDWIN, Joelle .... 616-632-2076. 239 E
baldwjoe@aquinas.edu
BALDWIN, Karen .... 205-348-4767..... 8 D
kbaldwin@advance.ua.edu
BALDWIN, Laura .... 215-572-2970. 409 H
baldwinl@arcadia.edu
BALDWIN, Mary Sue ...... 205-726-4097..... 6 F
msbaldwi@samford.edu
BALDWIN, R. Chad .... 636-584-6609. 273 M
rcbaldwin@eastcentral.edu
BALDWIN, Sarah .... 503-554-2321. 403 C
sbaldwin@georgefox.edu
BALDWIN, Stan .... 601-925-3321. 268 A
sbaldwin@mc.edu
BALDWIN, Thomas .... 218-281-8340. 264 E
tbaldwin@umn.edu
BALDWIN, Tony .... 704-216-6272. 356 D
tbaldwin@livingstone.edu
BALDWIN, Veria .... 606-589-3018. 196 F
cookie.baldwin@kctcs.edu
BALDWIN, William, J ..... 212-678-3052. 347 G
wjb12@tc.columbia.edu
BALDWIN-DIMEO,
Caren .... 603-526-3714. 295 I
cbaldwin-dimeo@colby-sawyer.edu
BALDYGO, Robert .... 540-234-9261. 511 H
baldygor@brcc.edu
BALE, Shelly .... 775-445-3324. 295 A
shelly.bale@wnc.edu
BALENTINE, Kim .... 417-626-1234. 279 J
kbalentine@occ.edu
BALES, Jennifer .... 913-621-8733. 186 C
jennifer@donnelly.edu
BALES, John Anthony ..... 208-885-5953. 139 D
jbales@uidaho.edu
BALES, Kay .... 765-285-5344. 164 B
kbales@bsu.edu
BALES, Michael .... 276-964-7323. 514 A
michael.bales@sw.edu
BALES, Richard, C .... 419-772-2205. 386 D
r-bales@onu.edu
BALES, William, J .... 615-898-5818. 459 D
joe.bales@mtsu.edu
BALESTRERI, Teresa, A .. 314-516-5002. 283 E
tkb@umsl.edu
BALFOUR, David .... 802-773-5900. 499 B
david.balfour@csj.edu
BALGE, Daniel, N .... 507-354-8221. 256 M
balgedn@mlc-wels.edu
BALIK, Daniel, J .... 651-696-6265. 256 L
balik@macalester.edu
BALINT, Bill .... 724-357-7854. 428 F
wsbalint@iup.edu
BALISTRERI, Rebecca ..... 414-847-3262. 534 F
beckybalistreri@miad.edu
BALISTRERI-CLARKE,
Margaret, R .... 608-663-2212. 532 I
balistr@edgewood.edu
BALIT-MOUSSALLI,
Cinzia .... 334-833-4452..... 4 D
cinziam@huntingdon.edu
BALL, Angela .... 254-867-3938. 486 B
angela.ball@systems.tstc.edu

BALL, Charles ... 574-239-8318. 166 N cball@hcc-nd.edu
BALL, Christine ... 706-771-4150. 121 D cball@augustatech.edu
BALL, Daniel, W ... 864-388-8300. 444 K dball@lander.edu
BALL, Dave ... 319-296-4204. 178 J david.ball@hawkeyecollege.edu
BALL, Deborah, L ... 734-615-4415. 251 C dball@umich.edu
BALL, Diane ... 239-513-1122. 106 O dball@hodges.edu
BALL, Don ... 330-494-6170. 389 F dball@starkstate.edu
BALL, Donald ... 352-365-3532. 108 S balld@lssc.edu
BALL, Drexel, B ... 803-535-5263. 442 B dball@claflin.edu
BALL, Gerald, D ... 828-689-1242. 356 F gball@mhc.edu
BALL, James, D ... 410-386-8192. 214 A jball@carrollcc.edu
BALL, Jason ... 561-297-3440. 114 L jball@fau.edu
BALL, John ... 504-568-4500. 205 C jball@lsuhsc.edu
BALL, Justin ... 309-677-3850. 140 I Jball@bradley.edu
BALL, Karen ... 559-791-2420... 49 P kball@portervillecollege.edu
BALL, Karen ... 717-720-4050. 427 G kball@passhe.edu
BALL, Kathy ... 304-384-6009. 529 E bonner@concord.edu
BALL, Kenneth ... 703-993-1500. 505 C kball@gmu.edu
BALL, Kevin ... 330-941-1560. 394 A keball@ysu.edu
BALL, Kim ... 704-894-2521. 353 J kiball@davidson.edu
BALL, Kimberly ... 657-278-4968... 33 E kball@fullerton.edu
BALL, Larry, P ... 480-245-7969... 14 B larry.ball@ibcs.edu
BALL, Margaret, A ... 405-208-5060. 397 F mball@okcu.edu
BALL, Margaret, T ... 718-817-3010. 324 G mball@fordham.edu
BALL, Mary ... 402-552-6067. 288 L ballmary@clarksoncollege.edu
BALL, Michael ... 859-246-6512. 194 L michael.ball@kctcs.edu
BALL, Molly, A ... 309-457-2323. 153 D maball@monmouthcollege.edu
BALL, Sam ... 253-833-9111. 520 C sball@greenriver.edu
BALL, Scott ... 423-236-2881. 458 J sball@southern.edu
BALL, Shelley ... 865-471-3235. 453 F sball@cn.edu
BALL, Terri ... 913-367-6204. 187 E tball@highlandcc.edu
BALL, Terry ... 801-422-2736. 495 D terry_ball@byu.edu
BALL, Thomas, G ... 724-458-2163. 417 E tgball@gcc.edu
BALL, Travis ... 903-886-5060. 483 E travis.ball@tamuc.edu
BALL, William, S ... 513-558-0026. 390 G william.s.ball@uc.edu
BALL-DAVIS, Marsha ... 860-906-5127... 88 D mball-davis@ccc.commnet.edu
BALL-PARKER, Gayle ... 310-243-2801... 33 B gball@csudh.edu
BALL-WILLIAMSON, Carrie ... 662-862-8123. 267 C cbball@iccms.edu
BALLA, Ruth Ann ... 305-237-3702. 109 D rballa@mdc.edu
BALLABAN, David, C ... 610-921-7256. 409 A dballaban@alb.edu
BALLAGH DE TOVAR, Jane ... 913-621-8791. 186 C jane@donnelly.edu
BALLAM, Gary, O ... 816-654-7562. 275 K gballam@kcumb.edu
BALLANTINE, Clay ... 413-559-5590. 227 B
BALLANTYNE, Trina ... 201-216-8165. 307 E tballant@stevens.edu
BALLARD, Carol ... 863-680-6236. 105 D cballard@flsouthern.edu
BALLARD, Carol ... 334-670-3182..... 7 H csupri@troy.edu
BALLARD, Chris ... 217-362-6419. 153 C cballard@millikin.edu
BALLARD, Donna ... 662-476-5054. 266 I dballard@eastms.edu
BALLARD, Glenda ... 903-223-3073. 484 C glenda.ballard@tamut.edu
BALLARD, Jennifer ... 870-512-7861... 20 B jennifer_ballard@asun.edu
BALLARD, Jennifer ... 503-883-2509. 404 A jballard@linfield.edu
BALLARD, Katie ... 270-686-4529. 196 C katie.ballard@kctcs.edu
BALLARD, Lowell, W ... 630-752-5222. 163 F lowell.ballard@wheaton.edu
BALLARD, Margaret ... 617-745-3876. 225 G margaret.ballard@enc.edu
BALLARD, Phillip ... 870-862-8131... 23 D pballard@southark.edu
BALLARD, Robin ... 309-694-8511. 146 E rballard@icc.edu
BALLARD, Steve ... 870-543-5910... 23 E sballard@seark.edu
BALLARD, Steve ... 252-328-6212. 367 B chancellor@ecu.edu
BALLARD, Susan ... 513-244-4955. 377 G susan_ballard@mail.msjl.edu
BALLARD, Terri ... 412-536-1251. 420 A terri.ballard@laroche.edu
BALLARD, William, H ... 419-772-2020. 386 D b-ballard@onu.edu
BALLARD, William, P ... 802-656-2240. 500 F william.ballard@uvm.edu
BALLARD GORMAN, Shannon ... 518-244-3142. 338 C ballas@sage.edu
BALLARD-THROWER, Rhea ... 202-806-8047... 95 G rballard@law.howard.edu
BALLARINI, John ... 262-554-6110. 534 D jaballarini@yahoo.com
BALLARO, Mollie ... 716-888-3272. 316 C Mallarom@canisius.edu
BALLATE, Henry ... 954-322-4460. 107 V ballateh@jmvu.edu
BALLENGEE, Greg, A ... 740-351-3574. 388 N gballengee@shawnee.edu
BALLENGER, John, P ... 256-824-6565..... 8 F ballenj@uah.edu
BALLENGER, Nicole ... 307-766-4286. 543 I nicoleb@uwyo.edu
BALLENGER, Sherry ... 404-756-5727. 129 E sballenger@msm.edu
BALLENTINE, Angela ... 252-492-2061. 364 F ballentine@vgcc.edu
BALLENTINE, Howard ... 302-736-2529... 94 C ballentine@wesley.edu
BALLER, Jim ... 304-214-8960. 528 G jballer@wvncc.edu
BALLESTEROS, Victor ... 972-438-6932. 478 C vballesteros@parkercc.edu
BALLEW, Marcy ... 903-875-7335. 477 G marcy.ballew@navarrocollege.edu
BALLEW, Steve ... 601-266-4131. 270 E steve.ballew@usm.edu
BALLHEIM, John ... 563-242-4023. 175 F john.ballheim@ashford.edu
BALLING, John, D ... 503-370-6004. 408 J jballing@willamette.edu
BALLINGER, Andrea ... 309-438-8990. 147 J asballi@ilstu.edu
BALLINGER, Jamie ... 207-859-1102. 211 H ballingerj@thomas.edu
BALLINGER, Kevin ... 714-432-5531... 39 K sballinger@occ.cccd.edu
BALLINGER, Marcia, J ... 440-365-5222. 383 B
BALLINGER, Philip ... 206-221-2305. 524 G philipba@uw.edu
BALLINGER, Stacy ... 423-614-8630. 455 L sballinger@leeuniversity.edu
BALLMAN, Terry ... 909-537-5800... 34 E
BALLOM, Kenneth ... 217-333-2121. 162 A ballom@illinois.edu
BALLOU, Dawn ... 617-732-2077. 233 E dawn.ballou@mcphs.edu
BALLOU, Trenna ... 435-722-6900. 496 M trenna@ubatc.edu
BALLS, Jennifer ... 252-789-0219. 361 G jballs@martincc.edu
BALMER, Shannon ... 541-684-7222. 405 C sbalmer@nwcu.edu
BALMER, Stephanie ... 717-245-1287. 414 H balmers@dickinson.edu
BALMOS, Donald ... 254-299-8602. 476 D dbalmos@mclennan.edu
BALOG, Scott ... 850-201-8632. 117 D balogs@tcc.fl.edu
BALOGA, Monica ... 321-674-7397. 104 H mbaloga@fit.edu
BALOGH, Deborah Ware 317-788-3212. 173 I dbalogh@uindy.edu
BALOGUN, Lateef ... 252-536-6371. 361 A lbalogun916@halifaxcc.edu
BALOUBI, Desire' ... 919-546-8307. 366 E dbaloubi@shawu.edu
BALOUGH, Sandra, A ... 814-472-3151. 432 D sbalough@francis.edu
BALRAM, Arlette ... 212-686-9040. 350 G abalram@woodtobecoburn.edu
BALSAM, Carl, E ... 773-244-5610. 154 G cbalsam@northpark.edu
BALSAMO, Michael ... 586-445-7141. 246 A balsamom@macomb.edu
BALSANO, Gregory, R ... 562-903-4708... 29 L greg.balsano@biola.edu
BALSEIRO, Wanda ... 787-878-5475. 549 L wbalseiro@arecibo.inter.edu
BALSER, Deborah, B ... 314-516-5146. 283 E balserd@umsl.edu
BALSER, Jeffrey, R ... 615-936-3030. 463 G jeff.balser@vanderbilt.edu
BALSER, Teresa, C ... 352-392-1961. 116 A tcbalser@ufl.edu
BALSIGER, Les ... 307-778-4359. 543 D lbalsiger@lccc.wy.edu
BALSLEY, Richard ... 229-317-6930. 124 A rich.balsley@darton.edu
BALTER-REITZ, Susan ... 406-657-2214. 287 C sbalter-reitz@msubillings.edu
BALTES, Erin ... 207-859-1327. 211 H baltese@thomas.edu
BALTES, Tim ... 417-447-2631. 279 K baltest@otc.edu
BALTHAZAR, Judith ... 610-526-5374. 410 J jbalthaz@brynmawr.edu
BALTHAZARD, Pierre ... 716-375-2200. 338 E pbalthaz@sbu.edu
BALTIMORE, Lester ... 516-877-3142. 313 A baltimore@adelphi.edu
BALTRUS, Susan, C ... 207-795-2846. 209 I baltruss@cmhc.org
BALTZIS, Basil ... 973-596-5534. 303 G basil.c.baltzis@njit.edu
BALTZLEY, Dennis ... 602-978-7751... 18 A Dennis.Baltzley@Thunderbird.edu
BALZA, Stephen, J ... 507-354-8221. 256 M balzasj@mlc-wels.edu
BALZANO, Wanda ... 336-758-4455. 370 D balzanow@wfu.edu
BALZER, Brenda ... 443-334-2176. 218 E bbalzer@stevenson.edu
BALZER, Jackie ... 503-725-5249. 406 B jbalzer@pdx.edu
BALZER, William ... 419-372-0623. 374 K wbalzer@bgsu.edu
BAMBARA, Cynthia, S ... 301-784-5000. 213 B cbambara@allegany.edu
BAMBERGER, Gregory ... 610-683-4095. 429 A gbamberg@kutztown.edu
BAMBHROLIA, Savita ... 609-586-4800. 302 G bambhros@mccc.edu
BAMBINA, Antonia, D ... 812-461-5357. 174 D adbambina@usi.edu
BAMBURAK, Michele ... 412-263-6600. 410 B mbamburak@aii.edu
BAME, Kevin ... 618-453-2474. 159 G kbame@siu.edu
BAMFORD, Carol, M ... 515-263-6129. 178 G cbamford@grandview.edu
BAMFORD, Penny ... 510-869-6744... 61 I pbamford@samuelmerritt.edu
BAMMAN, Chris ... 660-543-4331. 283 A bamman@ucmo.edu
BAMONTE, Paul ... 718-409-7254. 346 D pbamonte@sunymaritime.edu
BANA, Mark ... 303-914-6220... 84 I Mark.Bana@rrcc.edu
BANACH, Michael ... 718-940-5584. 339 B mbanach@sjcny.edu
BANACH, Patricia, S ... 860-465-5000... 87 L banachp@easternct.edu
BANAHAN, Richard ... 314-644-9766. 281 E rbanahan@stlcc.edu
BANASZAK, Larry ... 614-823-1693. 387 K lbanaszak@otterbein.edu
BANAVAR, Jayanth, R ... 301-405-2316. 219 B banavar@umd.edu
BANCHOFF, Thomas ... 202-687-5117... 95 E banchoff@georgetown.edu
BANCROFT, Blake ... 615-361-7555. 454 D bbancroft@daymarinstitute.edu
BANCROFT-MORELY, Carol ... 302-573-5497... 93 F bancroft@dtcc.edu
BANDA, Magda ... 708-656-8000. 153 H magna.banda@morton.edu
BANDAS, Mark ... 615-322-6400. 463 G mark.bandas@vanderbilt.edu
BANDAS, Raul ... 787-758-2525. 554 F raul.bandas@upr.edu
BANDELIN, Janis, M ... 864-294-2191. 444 C janis.bandelin@furman.edu
BANDO, Chris ... 609-201-8767... 62 B cbando@sdcc.edu
BANDOIAN, Nancy ... 617-989-4476. 237 G bandoiann@wit.edu
BANDRE, Mark, A ... 785-827-5541. 188 C mark.bandre@kwu.edu
BANDS, Kathleen ... 301-696-3400. 215 D bands@hood.edu
BANDSTRA, Travis ... 708-239-4854. 160 K travis.bandstra@trnty.edu
BANDURSKI, Jeff, J ... 262-243-5700. 532 H jeffrey.bandurski@cuw.edu
BANDY, JR., John, M ... 404-413-4600. 126 E jbandy@gsu.edu
BANDY, Kanoe ... 661-763-7779... 69 D kbandy@taftcollege.edu
BANDY, Kenneth ... 704-463-1360. 365 E kenneth.bandy@fsmail.pfeiffer.edu
BANDY-NEAL, LaMel ... 615-327-6767. 456 E lbneal@mmc.edu
BANDYOPADHYAY, Santanu ... 714-484-7331... 56 E sbandyopadhyay@cypresscollege.edu
BANEGAR, Michael ... 575-528-7548. 311 B mbanegar@nmsu.edu
BANERJEE, Nantoo ... 269-471-6615. 243 G banerjee@andrews.edu
BANERJI, Debashish ... 323-663-2167... 73 B
BANESS KING, Deborah 708-456-0300. 161 A dbanessk@triton.edu
BANEY, Mary Ellen ... 412-396-6575. 415 F baney@duq.edu
BANEY, Todd ... 704-922-6485. 360 F baney.todd@gaston.edu
BANG, Barbara ... 701-671-2277. 372 E barbara.bang@ndscs.edu
BANG, Sam ... 626-584-5398... 45 E sbang@fuller.edu
BANGASSER, Karen ... 605-331-6684. 452 D karen.bangasser@usiouxfalls.edu
BANGASSER, Kathy ... 815-599-3448. 146 D kathy.bangasser@highland.edu
BANGASSER, Susan ... 909-384-8650... 62 A sbangasser@sbccd.cc.ca.us
BANGERT, Darci, M ... 515-574-1035. 179 D bangert@iowacentral.edu
BANGERT, Stephanie ... 510-869-1528... 61 I sbangert@samuelmerritt.edu
BANGERT-DROWNS, Robert ... 518-442-4988. 341 D rbangert@albany.edu
BANGOLAME, Yaw ... 706-396-7608. 130 C ybangolame@paine.edu
BANGS, Joann ... 651-690-6500. 263 O jmbangs@stkate.edu
BANICK, Gabrielle ... 608-757-6320. 539 I gbanick@blackhawk.edu
BANISTER, Mickey, D ... 405-425-5200. 397 D mickey.banister@oc.edu
BANISTER, Stephen ... 701-858-3855. 371 F stephen.banister@minotstateu.edu
BANKEN, Mary Jo ... 573-882-6211. 283 C bankenm@missouri.edu
BANKER, Bonnie ... 859-858-3511. 192 B bonnie.banker@asbury.edu
BANKEY, Michael ... 216-987-3237. 378 D michael.bankey@tri-c.edu
BANKIRER, Marcia ... 303-292-0015... 81 F m.bankirer@denverschoolofnursing.edu
BANKIRER, Marcia ... 303-248-2701... 28 M mbankirer@argosy.edu
BANKOLE-MEDINA, Katherine ... 410-951-3431. 220 B kbankole@coppin.edu
BANKS, Cara ... 309-779-7704. 160 L cara.banks@trinitycollegeqc.edu
BANKS, Cerri ... 413-538-2481. 234 D cbanks@mtholyoke.edu
BANKS, Christopher ... 213-613-2200... 67 E christopher_banks@sciarc.edu
BANKS, Dacia, L ... 315-684-6289. 345 A banksdl@morrisville.edu
BANKS, Darrell, L ... 859-233-8207. 199 I dbanks@transy.edu
BANKS, Heather, R ... 260-982-5306. 170 U hrbanks@manchester.edu
BANKS, Julie, M ... 937-229-3233. 391 C jbanks1@udayton.edu
BANKS, Kathryn, M ... 252-638-7367. 359 G banksk@cravencc.edu
BANKS, Kay ... 803-321-5146. 445 G kay.banks@newberry.edu
BANKS, Kevin ... 443-885-3527. 217 A kevin.banks@morgan.edu
BANKS, Lynne ... 814-472-3002. 432 D lbanks@francis.edu
BANKS, M. Katherine ... 979-845-7203. 483 C k-banks@tamu.edu
BANKS, Marcus ... 510-869-8692... 61 I mbanks@samuelmerritt.edu
BANKS, Mary ... 239-590-1172. 115 A mbanks@fgcu.edu
BANKS, McRae ... 336-334-5338. 369 A mcbanks@uncg.edu
BANKS, Melissa ... 912-443-3388. 131 D mbanks@savannahtech.edu
BANKS, Michael ... 816-604-6544. 277 D michael.banks@mcckc.edu

BANKS, Nicole, P .... 561-862-4310. 110 C
banksn@palmbeachstate.edu
BANKS, Ronald .... 502-597-5948. 197 A
ron.banks@kysu.edu
BANKS, Sharon, S .... 304-766-3078. 530 C
banksss@wvstateu.edu
BANKS, Wayne .... 870-574-4493... 23 G
wbanks@sautech.edu
BANKS, III, Wayne, S .... 205-397-6601.... 3 B
stan.banks@vc.edu
BANKS, Yvonne, R .... 651-631-5221. 263 A
yrbanks@nwc.edu
BANKS-DEAVER,
Yolanda, E .... 919-530-6204. 368 A
ybanks@nccu.edu
BANKSTON, Patrick .... 219-980-6562. 168 B
pbanks@iun.edu
BANKSTON, Tony .... 309-556-3031. 148 B
iwuadmit@iwu.edu
BANKY, Lori .... 281-899-1240. 478 J
BANNAN, Denise, A .... 810-766-4272. 239 G
denise.bannan@baker.edu
BANNER, Carolyn .... 803-584-3446. 448 D
cmbanner@mailbox.sc.edu
BANNER, Josephina, E ... 610-558-5548. 424 I
bannerj@neumann.edu
BANNER, Lilliam .... 908-737-0367. 302 F
lbanner@kean.edu
BANNISTER, Darlene .... 830-792-7357. 480 F
bannistr@schreiner.edu
BANNISTER, Edith .... 253-833-9111. 520 C
ebannister@greenriver.edu
BANNISTER, Geoff .... 808-544-0202. 135 F
gbannister@hpu.edu
BANNISTER, Mark .... 785-628-5339. 186 F
markbannister@fhsu.edu
BANNON, Douglas, F .... 319-398-5517. 180 J
doug.bannon@kirkwood.cc.ia.us
BANNON, Stephen .... 401-232-6001. 438 K
sbannon@bryant.edu
BANOCY-PAYNE, Marge 850-201-6070. 117 D
banocym@tcc.fl.edu
BANOS, Anne .... 504-865-5201. 207 C
apbanos@tulane.edu
BANREY, Vincent .... 718-270-6046. 319 A
vbanrey@mec.cuny.edu
BANSAL, Tony, A .... 703-323-5304. 513 C
tbansal@nvcc.edu
BANSAVICH, John .... 415-422-5529... 73 J
bansavich@usfca.edu
BANTA, Trudy, W .... 317-274-4111. 168 D
tbanta@iupui.edu
BANTO, Andrea .... 770-612-2170... 96 F
BANTON, Cris .... 503-554-2167. 403 C
cbanton@georgefox.edu
BANTZ, Charles .... 317-274-4417. 167 E
cbantz@iupui.edu
BANTZ, Charles .... 317-274-4417. 167 F
cbantz@iupui.edu
BANTZ, Charles, R .... 317-274-4417. 168 D
cbantz@iupui.edu
BANTZ, Don .... 907-564-8201... 10 C
dbantz@alaskapacific.edu
BANWARTH, Gregory .... 508-362-2131. 231 D
gbanwarth@capecod.edu
BANYCKY, Elizabeth .... 618-453-4918. 159 G
lbanyck@siu.edu
BANZ, Clint, J .... 215-368-7538. 412 A
cbanz@cbs.edu
BAPTISTE, Greg .... 757-455-3350. 515 H
gbaptiste@vwc.edu
BAPTISTE, Jo Rae .... 808-245-8323. 136 H
jorae@hawaii.edu
BAPTISTE, Michele .... 212-650-6310. 317 D
mbaptiste@ccny.cuny.edu
BAQUERO, Gloria, E .... 787-780-5134. 551 L
gbaquero@nuc.edu
BARABINO, Gilda .... 212-650-5435. 317 D
BARABINO, Joseph .... 305-348-2494. 115 B
joseph.barabino@fiu.edu
BARAGONA, Fred .... 318-342-5141. 208 E
baragona@ulm.edu
BARAJAS, Daniel .... 928-344-7769... 11 L
daniel.barajas@azwestern.edu
BARAJAS, Leticia .... 213-763-7071... 52 D
barajal@lattc.edu
BARAJAS, Silvia .... 253-566-5050. 524 C
sbarajas@tacomacc.edu
BARAKAT, Nabeel .... 310-233-4351... 51 H
barakanm@lahc.edu
BARAKAT, Nabeel, M .... 310-233-4351... 51 H
barakanm@lahc.edu
BARAKEH, Zeina .... 415-641-1241... 62 G
zbarakeh@sfai.edu
BARAKER, Eli .... 347-394-1036. 315 A
BARALLE, Ralph .... 636-227-2100. 276 F
ralph.baralle@logan.edu
BARANOWSKI, Donna .... 941-907-2262. 103 C
dbaranowski@evergladesuniversity.edu
BARANOWSKI, Thomas . 732-987-2219. 302 B
baranowskit@georgian.edu
BARATO, Ruben .... 914-606-6777. 350 F
Ruben.Barato@sunywcc.edu
BARAZZONE, Esther, L .. 412-365-1160. 412 K
barazzone@chatham.edu
BARBA, Robert .... 413-775-1606. 231 E
barba@gcc.mass.edu
BARBA, Steve .... 603-535-2722. 298 G
sbarba@plymouth.edu
BARBARAK, Thomas .... 314-256-8886. 271 F
barbarak@ai.edu
BARBAREE, Joel .... 870-850-4821... 23 E
jbarbaree@seark.edu
BARBARI, Mary Pat .... 312-235-3539. 159 A
m.barbari@shimer.edu
BARBARI, Timothy .... 617-353-2141. 224 D
barbari@bu.edu
BARBATIS, Peter .... 561-868-3142. 110 C
barbatip@palmbeachstate.edu
BARBEE, Brent .... 910-410-1809. 362 I
brentb@richmondcc.edu
BARBEE, Chris, W .... 616-331-3590. 243 C
barbeec@gvsu.edu
BARBER,
Bernadette (BJ) .... 626-584-5238... 45 E
bjbarber@fuller.edu
BARBER, Billy .... 252-789-0303. 361 G
bbarber@martincc.edu
BARBER, Catherine .... 985-858-5746. 203 B
catherine.barber@fletcher.edu
BARBER, Deborah, G .... 803-323-2191. 449 G
barberdg@winthrop.edu
BARBER, Elizabeth .... 812-749-1242. 171 K
bbarber@oak.edu
BARBER, Ella .... 972-273-3009. 471 B
ebarber@dcccd.edu
BARBER, Glynis .... 410-951-3078. 220 B
gbarber@coppin.edu
BARBER, Jacques .... 516-877-4800. 313 A
jbarber@adelphi.edu
BARBER, Jeff .... 434-582-2100. 506 I
jbarber2@liberty.edu
BARBER, Jennifer .... 916-278-6295... 34 D
jbarbar@csus.edu
BARBER, Jerald .... 870-777-5722... 25 B
jerald.barber@uacch.edu
BARBER, Kimberly .... 850-644-6127. 115 C
kabarber@admin.fsu.edu
BARBER, Liane .... 513-244-4711. 377 G
liane_barber@mail.msj.edu
BARBER, Luanne .... 870-612-2119... 25 A
luanne.barber@uaccb.edu
BARBER, Marcia, A .... 315-470-6611. 345 B
mabarber@esf.edu
BARBER, Michael .... 858-653-6740... 49 C
BARBER, SJ, Michael .... 314-977-2701. 281 I
barbermd@slu.edu
BARBER, Michael, J .... 406-247-5750. 287 C
mbarber@msubillings.edu
BARBER, Ray, G .... 812-749-1213. 171 K
ocuexec@oak.edu
BARBER, Sharon .... 563-441-3500. 180 E
sbarber@kucampus.edu
BARBER, Susan, C .... 405-208-5287. 397 F
sbarber@okcu.edu
BARBER, Tamara .... 701-224-5476. 372 B
tamara.barber@bismarckstate.edu
BARBER, Tim .... 513-244-8615. 376 J
tim.barber@ccuniversity.edu
BARBER, Tracy .... 719-255-7507... 85 M
tbarber@uccs.edu
BARBER-LYHNAKIS,
Michelle .... 801-832-2755. 498 F
mbarber@westminstercollege.edu
BARBERA, Anthony .... 516-876-3135. 343 D
barberaa@oldwestbury.edu
BARBERA, Anthony .... 516-876-3292. 343 D
barberaa@oldwestbury.edu
BARBERICH, Judith .... 610-282-1100. 414 F
judy.barberich@desales.edu
BARBICH, Michelle .... 814-732-1457. 428 E
mbarbich@edinboro.edu
BARBIERI, Dean .... 925-969-3559... 49 B
dbarbieri@jfku.edu
BARBIERI, Dean .... 925-969-3562... 49 B
dbarbieri@jfku.edu
BARBIERI, Lina .... 610-282-1100. 414 F
lina.barbieri@desales.edu
BARBONI, Edward .... 908-737-3350. 302 F
ebarboni@kean.edu
BARBOSA, Isaac .... 409-880-8195. 486 E
ibarbosa@lit.edu
BARBOSA, Miguel .... 570-422-3547. 428 D
mbarbosa@po-box.esu.edu
BARBOUR, Cheryl .... 303-546-3565... 83 F
cheryl@naropa.edu
BARBOUR, Darrell .... 641-585-8138. 183 D
darrell.barbour@waldorf.edu
BARBOUR, Heather .... 401-341-2225. 440 C
heather.barbour@salve.edu
BARBOUR, Kathryn, A .... 410-827-5806. 214 C
kbarbour@chesapeake.edu
BARBOUR, Monica .... 313-993-1951. 250 K
barbourm@udmercy.edu
BARBOUR, Sandy .... 510-642-5316... 70 I
athletic.director@berkeley.edu
BARCALOW, Douglas, A 260-399-7700. 174 C
dbarcalow@sf.edu
BARCELO,
Nancy (Rusty) .... 505-747-2140. 311 E
nbarcelo@nnmc.edu
BARCHI, Robert, L .... 848-932-7454. 306 A
president@rutgers.edu
BARCKHOLTZ, Beatriz .... 956-882-5141. 491 D
beatriz.becerra@utb.edu
BARCKHOLTZ, Benjamin 406-657-1714. 287 C
benjamin.barckholtz@msubillings.edu
BARCLAY, Angela .... 513-241-4338. 373 J
angela.barclay@antonellicollege.edu
BARCLAY, Donald, A .... 209-658-4444... 71 D
dbarclay@UCMerced.edu
BARCLAY, Kent .... 978-232-2282. 226 C
kbarclay@endicott.edu
BARCLAY, Raymond .... 386-822-7255. 117 C
rbarclay@stetson.edu
BARCLIFT, Mark .... 417-862-9533. 274 F
mbarclift@globaluniversity.edu
BARCUS, Susan, L .... 706-721-0275. 126 B
sbarcus@gru.edu
BARCUS, Tracy .... 301-387-3164. 214 I
tracy.barcus@garrettcollege.edu
BARCZYK, Ewa .... 414-229-4781. 537 A
ewa@uwm.edu
BARD, Sharon, K .... 704-463-3428. 365 E
sharon.bard@fsmail.pfeiffer.edu
BARDEN, John, H .... 512-404-4829. 467 A
jbarden@austinseminary.edu
BARDEN, Nancy .... 303-644-4034... 83 E
nancy.barden@morgancc.edu
BARDILL MOSCARITOLO,
Lisa .... 914-773-3860. 335 J
lbardillmoscaritolo@pace.edu
BARDO, John, W .... 316-978-3001. 191 F
john.bardo@wichita.edu
BARE, Benita .... 276-944-6800. 504 H
bbare@ehc.edu
BARE, James, S .... 516-739-1545. 333 F
admin_dean@nyctcm.edu
BAREFIELD, Frank .... 334-556-2235..... 3 N
fbarefield@wallace.edu
BAREFIELD, Kevin .... 662-685-4771. 266 C
kbarefield@bmc.edu
BAREFOOT, Clark .... 405-691-3800. 396 D
cbarefoot@macu.edu
BAREFOOT, Russell .... 908-526-1200. 305 B
rbarefoot@raritanval.edu
BARELMAN, Jason .... 402-375-7327. 291 F
jabarel1@wsc.edu
BARENDS, Bobbi, J .... 302-259-6030... 93 E
bobbi.barends@dtcc.edu
BARENDS, Frans .... 404-894-5000. 125 D
frans.barends@business.gatech.edu
BARES, Donna .... 440-375-7075. 382 L
dbares@lec.edu
BARFIELD, Craig .... 919-760-8516. 356 G
craigb@meredith.edu
BARFIELD, Virginia, C .... 803-461-3253. 445 A
ginger.barfield@lr.edu
BARFOOT, D. Scott .... 214-887-5151. 471 F
sbarfoot@dts.edu
BARGAR, Robin .... 312-369-8222. 143 D
rbargar@colum.edu
BARGAS, Peter .... 661-362-2836... 53 G
pbargas@masters.edu
BARGE, Gayle .... 937-376-6142. 376 E
gbarge@centralstate.edu
BARGE, Scott .... 574-535-7110. 166 A
scottcb@goshen.edu
BARGE-MILES, Linda .... 850-599-3225. 114 K
linda.barge-miles@famu.edu
BARGER, Brett .... 636-949-4366. 276 D
bbarger@lindenwood.edu
BARGER, David .... 203-582-8956... 91 A
david.barger@quinnipiac.edu
BARGER, Debbie .... 828-327-7000. 359 A
dbarger@cvcc.edu
BARGER, Debbie, M .... 515-263-6012. 178 G
dbarger@grandview.edu
BARGER, Debra, E .... 530-898-6105... 33 A
dbarger@csuchico.edu
BARGER, Eric .... 503-943-7337. 408 F
barger@up.edu
BARGER, Kyle .... 215-248-6325. 422 F
kbarger@ltsp.edu
BARGER, Robert, C .... 614-235-4136. 390 A
rbarger@TLSohio.edu
BARHAM, James .... 731-286-3206. 460 F
jbarham@dscc.edu
BARHORST, Michael .... 937-512-2152. 388 O
michael.barhorst@sinclair.edu
BARILAR, Stephen, J .... 570-577-3333. 411 A
steve.barilar@bucknell.edu
BARILLO, Madeline, K .... 203-857-7039... 89 D
mbarillo@norwalk.edu
BARIMANI, Adel .... 610-436-2828. 430 A
abarimani@wcupa.edu
BARINOWSKI, Sandra .... 256-824-2771..... 8 F
sandra.patterson@uah.edu
BARIOLA, Kristi .... 662-246-6376. 268 B
kbariola@msdelta.edu
BARISH, Robert, A .... 318-675-5240. 205 D
rbaris@lsuhsc.edu
BARKALOW, Susan, L .... 252-451-8258. 362 D
barkalow@nashcc.edu
BARKAN, Chester .... 516-572-7370. 332 C
chester.barkan@ncc.edu
BARKE, Brady, L .... 573-651-2322. 282 B
bbarke@semo.edu
BARKE, Vicky .... 920-735-2468. 539 K
barke@fvtc.edu
BARKELOO, Mary, E .... 308-635-6033. 293 E
barkeloo@wncc.edu
BARKER, Allyn, S .... 304-896-7404. 528 F
allyn.barker@southernwv.edu
BARKER, Allyson .... 256-782-5820..... 4 K
abarker@jsu.edu
BARKER, Allyson .... 256-782-5002..... 4 K
abarker@jsu.edu
BARKER, Anna, M .... 240-500-2000. 215 B
ambarker@hagerstowncc.edu
BARKER, Brent .... 334-386-7231..... 3 H
bbarker@faulkner.edu
BARKER, Brian .... 970-943-3038... 86 I
bbarker@western.edu
BARKER, Bruce, A .... 715-833-6221. 539 J
bbarker@cvtc.edu
BARKER, Catherine, A .... 816-235-1375. 283 D
barkerca@umkc.edu
BARKER, David, F .... 502-852-4676. 200 D
david.barker@louisville.edu
BARKER, Helen, G .... 301-369-2800. 213 G
hgbarker@capitol-college.edu
BARKER, James, F .... 864-656-3413. 442 C
jbarker@clemson.edu
BARKER, Jeffrey, H .... 864-596-9091. 443 D
jeff.barker@converse.edu
BARKER, Joe .... 830-591-7284. 481 C
jcbarker@swtjc.edu
BARKER, John .... 617-628-5000. 237 C
john.barker@tufts.edu
BARKER, John, D .... 864-294-2106. 444 C
john.barker@furman.edu
BARKER, John, F .... 716-286-8220. 334 F
jfb@niagara.edu
BARKER, Joshua .... 252-398-6319. 353 H
barkej@chowan.edu
BARKER, Lee .... 773-256-3000. 152 H
lbarker@meadville.edu
BARKER, Lisa .... 731-425-8835. 460 G
lbarker@jscc.edu
BARKER, Lorie .... 559-791-2370... 49 P
lbarker@portervillecollege.edu
BARKER, Michael .... 919-843-5684. 368 D
michael_barker@unc.edu
BARKER, Neva .... 909-621-8306... 65 D
neva.barker@scrippscollege.edu
BARKER, Randy .... 910-892-3178. 355 B
rbarker@heritagebiblecollege.edu
BARKER, Rhonda .... 850-872-3857. 106 H
rbarker@gulfcoast.edu
BARKER, Rod .... 503-491-7666. 404 E
rod.barker@mhcc.edu
BARKER, Stan .... 541-463-5608. 403 I
barkers@lanecc.edu
BARKER, Tom .... 503-223-2245. 403 J
tbarker@portland.chefs.edu
BARKER, Tom .... 937-433-3410. 379 J
tbarker@edaff.com
BARKETT, Pamela .... 864-294-2217. 444 C
pam.barkett@furman.edu
BARKIS, Marita .... 816-235-1219. 283 D
barkism@umkc.edu
BARKLEY, Alan .... 203-332-5967... 88 F
abarkley@hcc.commnet.edu
BARKLEY, Camille .... 334-844-9999..... 1 G
barklnc@auburn.edu
BARKLEY, Eric .... 573-288-6363. 273 F
ebarkley@culver.edu
BARKLEY, Heather, R .... 260-359-4129. 166 O
hbarkley@huntington.edu
BARKLEY, Robert, S .... 864-656-5463. 442 C
rbrtbkl@clemson.edu
BARKLEY, Susan, E .... 972-238-6943. 471 C
sbarkley@dcccd.edu
BARKLEY-GIFFIN,
Adrienne .... 618-985-3741. 148 J
adriennebarkley@jalc.edu
BARKMAN, Jeff .... 731-989-6051. 454 J
facilities@fhu.edu
BARKO, Valerie .... 618-985-3741. 148 J
valeriebarko@jalc.edu
BARKSCHAT, Kate .... 828-395-1163. 361 C
kbarkschat@isothermal.edu

BARKSDALE, Gary .... 859-622-5094. 193 P gary.barksdale@eku.edu
BARKSDALE, Tina, M ..... 302-356-6940... 94 E tina.m.barksdale@wilmu.edu
BARKWILL, Joseph .... 516-463-6623. 326 D joseph.barkwill@hofstra.edu
BARLAAM, Maria .... 718-289-5608. 317 B maria.barlaam@bcc.cuny.edu
BARLAND, Karen .... 410-951-3704. 220 B kbarland@coppin.edu
BARLETT, Alisa .... 605-856-5880. 451 B alisa.barlett@sintegleska.edu
BARLETT, Paul .... 913-234-0632. 185 L paul.barlett@cleveland.edu
BARLOK, Tracy .... 508-793-2011. 225 B tbarlok@holycross.edu
BARLOW, Charlene .... 859-344-3348. 199 H barlowc@thomasmore.edu
BARLOW, David .... 910-672-1659. 367 D dbarlow@uncfsu.edu
BARLOW, Gloria .... 570-408-4440. 437 F gloria.barlow@wilkes.edu
BARLOW, Jerry, N .... 504-282-4455. 206 A jbarlow@nobts.edu
BARLOW, Jill, M .... 978-468-7111. 227 A jbarlow@gcts.edu
BARLOW, John .... 207-326-2485. 211 D john.barlow@mma.edu
BARLOW, Justin .... 678-839-5000. 133 I jbarlow@westga.edu
BARLOW, Kevin .... 281-283-3065. 489 C barlowk@uhcl.edu
BARLOW, Marlene, T ..... 215-968-8000. 411 B barlowm@bucks.edu
BARLOW, Michael .... 270-706-8614. 195 A michael.barlow@kctcs.edu
BARLOW, Patrick .... 608-246-6910. 540 C wbarlowe@madisoncollege.edu
BARLOW, Steve .... 307-855-2143. 542 Y barlow@cwc.edu
BARLOW, Thomas, M .... 813-879-6000. 103 B tbarlow@cci.edu
BARLOW, William .... 440-775-8273. 385 H bill.barlow@oberlin.edu
BARLOW-KELLEY, Jill .... 207-801-5633. 210 A jbk@coa.edu
BARLOWE, Jamie .... 419-530-2413. 392 B jamie.barlowe@utoledo.edu
BARNA, Adrienne, M ...... 703-993-2380. 505 C abarna@gmu.edu
BARNA, Peter .... 718-636-3744. 336 F provost@pratt.edu
BARNABY, Mike .... 218-855-8039. 258 B mbarnaby@clcmn.edu
BARNARD, Cheryl, A ..... 860-231-5267... 92 F cbarnard@usj.edu
BARNARD, Melinda .... 707-664-3236... 36 B melinda.barnard@sonoma.edu
BARNARD, Monica .... 806-720-7232. 476 B monica.barnard@lcu.edu
BARNARD, Susan .... 201-447-7938. 299 C sbarnard@bergen.edu
BARNARD, Tom .... 217-351-2582. 155 J tbarnard@parkland.edu
BARNDS, W. Kent .... 309-794-7314. 139 L wkentbarnds@augustana.edu
BARNER, John, C .... 812-488-2362. 173 H jb295@evansville.edu
BARNES, Amy .... 540-458-8920. 516 A abarnes@wlu.edu
BARNES, Andre .... 415-239-3151... 38 L abarnes@ccsf.edu
BARNES, Andrew .... 718-636-3570. 336 F awbarnes@pratt.edu
BARNES, April .... 859-622-3855. 193 P april.barnes@eku.edu
BARNES, Ashley .... 620-278-4276. 190 I abarnes@sterling.edu
BARNES, Brian, M .... 907-474-7649... 10 I bmbarnes@alaska.edu
BARNES, Candice .... 252-399-6393. 352 F cdbarnes@barton.edu
BARNES, Carolyn .... 940-898-3456. 488 B cbarnes@twu.edu
BARNES, Cheryl .... 304-384-6303. 529 E
BARNES, Clarence, D ..... 509-313-3404. 520 A barnes@jepson.gonzaga.edu
BARNES, Dan .... 312-662-4041. 139 F barnes@adler.edu
BARNES, David, M .... 402-449-2809. 289 H gupres@graceu.edu
BARNES, Edwin, A .... 909-869-3020... 32 G eabarnes@csupomona.edu
BARNES, Elizabeth, A .... 248-689-8282. 251 I bbarnes@walshcollege.edu
BARNES, Emanuel .... 601-877-6147. 265 G ebarnes@alcorn.edu
BARNES, Fred .... 310-665-6968... 57 C fbarnes@otis.edu
BARNES, Gary, W .... 806-651-2095. 484 D gbarnes@mail.wtamu.edu
BARNES, Harold, B .... 815-224-0450. 148 A harold_barnes@ivcc.edu
BARNES, III, James, H .. 651-638-6230. 253 K j-barnes@bethel.edu
BARNES, Jeffrey .... 951-552-8639... 30 H jbarnes@calbaptist.edu
BARNES, John .... 831-459-2973... 72 C barnes@ucsc.edu
BARNES, John, J .... 920-403-3255. 535 L john.barnes@snc.edu
BARNES, Juiliana .... 619-388-2678... 62 E jbarnes@sdccd.edu
BARNES, Julie .... 870-460-1127... 24 D barnesj@uamont.edu
BARNES, Karen .... 601-925-3241. 268 A misscoll@bkstr.com
BARNES, Katharine, T ..... 401-863-1914. 438 J katharine_barnes@brown.edu
BARNES, Kathleen .... 978-232-2292. 226 C kbarnes@endicott.edu
BARNES, Kelly .... 706-295-6842. 125 F kbarnes@gntc.edu
BARNES, Kenneth, J .... 716-851-1157. 323 I barnesk@ecc.edu
BARNES, Kimberly .... 989-386-6622. 247 B kbarnes@midmich.edu
BARNES, M. Craig .... 609-497-7800. 304 D president@ptsem.edu
BARNES, Marc .... 504-816-4359. 201 K mbarnes@dillard.edu
BARNES, Melissa .... 360-538-4095. 520 B mbarnes@ghc.edu
BARNES, Michael, W ...... 918-631-2359. 401 F michael-barnes@utulsa.edu
BARNES, Pamela .... 618-634-3349. 158 M pamelab@shawneecc.edu
BARNES, Peter .... 404-727-0419. 124 E peter.barnes@emory.edu
BARNES, Randall .... 619-388-3523... 62 D rbarnes@sdccd.edu
BARNES, Ray .... 617-217-9000. 222 G rbarnes@baystate.edu
BARNES, Rita .... 931-372-3797. 460 A ritabarnes@tntech.edu
BARNES, Russell .... 713-348-4350. 479 A rcb@rice.edu
BARNES, Scott .... 434-797-8409. 512 C sbarnes@dcc.vccs.edu
BARNES, Scott .... 435-797-2060. 497 B scott.barnes@usu.edu
BARNES, Sharon, E .... 817-257-7095. 484 I s.barnes@tcu.edu
BARNES, Shelly .... 574-239-8362. 166 N sbarnes@hcc-nd.edu
BARNES, Solita, K .... 670-284-5698. 547 A solitab@nmcnet.edu
BARNES, Ted .... 254-295-4678. 490 B tbarnes@umhb.edu
BARNES, Wilson, C .... 678-915-5481. 132 C wbarnes@spsu.edu
BARNES PHARR, Cindy . 480-732-7093... 14 J cindy.barnes.pharr@cgc.edu
BARNES-TEAMER, Toya . 504-816-4916. 201 K tbteamer@dillard.edu
BARNES WHYTE, Susan 503-883-2517. 404 A swhyte@linfield.edu
BARNET, John .... 914-961-8313. 340 B jbarnet@svots.edu
BARNETT, Alan .... 660-359-3948. 279 H abarnett@mail.ncmissouri.edu
BARNETT, Alan .... 731-286-3259. 460 F barnett@dscc.edu
BARNETT, Amy .... 765-998-5565. 173 C ambarnett@tayloru.edu
BARNETT, Beth .... 201-684-7529. 305 A bbarnett@ramapo.edu
BARNETT, Charles .... 662-246-6304. 268 B cbarnett@msdelta.edu
BARNETT, Charlie .... 662-720-7375. 269 B cbarnett@nemcc.edu
BARNETT, Daniel .... 410-617-1466. 216 A djbarnett@loyola.edu
BARNETT, David, L .... 770-531-3172. 122 A dlbarnett@brenau.edu
BARNETT, Gina .... 415-565-4614... 71 A barnettg@uchastings.edu
BARNETT, Jacqualine ..... 717-720-4038. 428 B jbarnett@paisshe.edu
BARNETT, Jahnae, H ...... 573-592-4216. 285 D jbarnett@williamwoods.edu
BARNETT, James, R .... 850-474-2005. 117 B jbarnett@uwf.edu
BARNETT, Jay .... 606-337-1142. 193 F jbarnett@ccbbc.edu
BARNETT, Kimberly .... 719-502-2012... 84 A kimberly.barnett@ppcc.edu
BARNETT, Larry, E .... 619-260-7777... 73 I larryb@sandiego.edu
BARNETT, Lenice .... 954-486-7728. 118 E
BARNETT, Margaret, J .... 540-868-7123. 512 H mbarnett@lfcc.edu
BARNETT, Michael .... 803-754-4100. 443 C
BARNETT, Mike .... 785-328-4251. 186 F mbarnett@fhsu.edu
BARNETT, Nicole .... 256-551-3114..... 4 I nicole.barnett@drakestate.edu
BARNETT, Randal .... 251-368-7603..... 5 A randal.barnett@jdcc.edu
BARNETT, Robert .... 810-766-6878. 251 E rbarnett@umflint.edu
BARNETT, Theresa .... 903-463-8753. 472 M tbarnett@grayson.edu
BARNETT, Timothy, L ..... 217-206-6581. 161 E barnett.timothy@uis.edu
BARNETTE, Andrew .... 724-925-4047. 437 D barnettea@wccc.edu
BARNETTE, Annette, D ... 304-462-4115. 529 G annette.barnette@glenville.edu
BARNETTE, F. Gary .... 229-317-6728. 124 A gary.barnette@darton.edu
BARNETTE, Jennifer, C ... 334-683-2313..... 5 F jbarnette@marionmilitary.edu
BARNETTE, Vivian, D ..... 336-334-7727. 367 E vdbarnet@ncat.edu
BARNETTT, Karen, L .... 203-576-5264... 91 D Karen.Barnett@stvincentscollege.edu
BARNEY, Alfred .... 678-891-2362. 125 G alfred.barney@gpc.edu
BARNEY, Carl .... 800-972-5149. 495 M
BARNEY, James, N .... 317-916-7827. 169 L jbarney6@ivytech.edu
BARNEY, Patti .... 954-201-7520... 99 D pbarney@broward.edu
BARNEY, Rick .... 502-585-9911. 199 C rbarney@spalding.edu
BARNHARDT, Denise ..... 326-249-8186. 360 A dsbarnh@davidsonccc.edu
BARNHARDT, Wendy ..... 704-216-3700. 363 D wendy.barnhardt@rccc.edu
BARNHART, Amy .... 937-775-5721. 393 G amy.barnhart@wright.edu
BARNHART, Bruce .... 724-938-4407. 428 A barnhart@calu.edu
BARNHART, Mitch .... 859-257-8015. 200 C mbarn@uky.edu
BARNHART, Ross .... 719-549-3365... 84 G ross.barnhart@pueblocc.edu
BARNHART, Roy, R .... 724-852-3241. 437 A rbarnhar@waynesburg.edu
BARNHART, Terry, L ...... 671-735-5571. 546 C terry.barnhart@guamcc.edu
BARNHILL, Belinda .... 252-638-7341. 359 G barnhillb@cravencc.edu
BARNHILL, Carol .... 870-972-2028... 19 N cbarnhil@astate.edu
BARNHILL, John .... 850-644-1224. 115 C jbarnhill@admin.fsu.edu
BARNHILL, Kristopher, C .... 864-488-4606. 444 L kbarnhill@limestone.edu
BARNHILL, Rob, M .... 262-243-5700. 532 H rob.barnhill@cuw.edu
BARNHILL, Tapp .... 802-254-6370. 501 C barnhilt@ccv.edu
BARNHOUSE, Richard .... 608-262-3786. 538 E richard.barnhouse@uwc.edu
BARNUM, Martin .... 847-566-6401. 162 G mbarnum@usml.edu
BARNWELL, John .... 504-214-4098. 207 C jon@tulane.edu
BARNWELL, Larry .... 864-977-7161. 445 H larry.barnwell@ngu.edu
BARNWELL, Vollie .... 828-251-6700. 368 C vbarnwel@unca.edu
BARON, Bruce .... 909-382-4091... 61 J bbaron@sbccd.cc.ca.us
BARON, Joshua, D .... 845-575-3000. 330 D josh.baron@marist.edu
BARON, Kit .... 626-396-2322... 28 P
BARON, Melissa, M .... 724-946-7927. 437 B baronmm@westminster.edu
BARON, Sara .... 757-352-4182. 508 G sbaron@regent.edu
BARON, Stephanie .... 425-640-1049. 519 D stephanie.baron@edcc.edu
BARON, Stuart .... 302-622-8000... 93 B
BARONAK, William, M ... 304-336-8061. 530 A wbaronak@westliberty.edu
BARONE, OSF, Ann Carmen .... 419-824-3703. 383 C acarmen@lourdes.edu
BARONE, Janet .... 703-237-6200. 507 E
BARONE, Joseph .... 848-445-6814. 306 B jbarone@rci.rutgers.edu
BARONE, Michael .... 716-673-3323. 342 A michael.barone@fredonia.edu
BARONIO, Lisa .... 210-999-7328. 488 C lbaronio@trinity.edu
BAROODY, Daniel, A ..... 607-735-1870. 323 H dbaroody@elmira.edu
BAROUDI, George .... 516-299-3790. 329 C george.baroudi@liu.edu
BARQUINERO, James, M .... 203-365-4763... 91 C barquineroj@sacredheart.edu
BARQUINERO, Jim .... 203-365-4763... 91 C barquineroj@sacredheart.edu
BARR, Ann .... 503-352-7200. 407 A ann.barr@pacificu.edu
BARR, Carol, A .... 413-545-6330. 228 F cbarr@provost.umass.edu
BARR, Jared .... 813-988-5131. 104 A barrj@floridacollege.edu
BARR, K. Jill .... 410-455-1337. 219 D jbarr@umbc.edu
BARR, Karah .... 612-375-1900. 256 E kbarr@ipr.edu
BARR, Kevin .... 812-237-3600. 167 A kevin.barr@indstate.edu
BARR, Krispin, W .... 336-721-2627. 366 D krispin.barr@salem.edu
BARR, Mary, G .... 812-877-8258. 172 C mary.g.barr@rose-hulman.edu
BARR, Peter, B .... 304-462-4110. 529 G peter.barr@glenville.edu
BARR, Robin .... 386-506-4473. 101 G barrr@DaytonaState.edu
BARR, Sarah .... 402-465-2193. 291 G sbarr@nebrwesleyan.edu
BARR, Susan .... 631-656-2129. 324 F susan.barr@ftc.edu
BARR, Suzy .... 843-574-6181. 447 E suzy.barr@tridenttech.edu
BARR, Victor .... 865-974-2196. 463 C vbarr@utk.edu
BARRACLOUGH, Diana .. 610-499-4153. 437 E dbarraclough@widener.edu
BARRACLOUGH, Dominic .... 608-342-1262. 537 D barracld@uwplatt.edu
BARRACLOUGH, Jessica 785-670-1723. 191 D jessica.barraclough@washburn.edu
BARRAM, Dirk .... 503-554-2822. 403 C dbarram@georgefox.edu
BARRANTES, Jane .... 408-554-5416... 64 M jbarrantes@scu.edu
BARRANTES, Laura .... 301-431-5401. 217 C lbarrantes@nlc.edu
BARRAR, Elena .... 610-558-5516. 424 I barrare@neumann.edu
BARRAS, Janet .... 678-359-5022. 127 A janetb@gordonstate.edu
BARRATT, Marguerite ..... 202-994-6130... 95 D barratt@gwu.edu
BARREE, Zita, M .... 434-223-6265. 505 E zbarree@hsc.edu
BARREIRA, Paul, J .... 617-495-2010. 227 C pbarreira@huhs.harvard.edu
BARRENTINE, Debra, A .. 256-228-6001..... 5 H barrentined@nacc.edu
BARRENTINE, Jim .... 719-502-2344... 84 A jim.barrentine@ppcc.edu
BARRENTINE, Roger, A .. 636-481-3106. 275 I rbarrent@jeffco.edu
BARRERA, Adriana, D .... 213-891-2201... 51 F preid@email.laccd.edu
BARRERA, Merrynoll .... 408-934-4900... 47 A merrynoll_barrera@heald.edu
BARRERA, Rosa .... 316-284-5241. 184 J rbarrera@bethelks.edu
BARRERA, Steve, V .... 210-458-4249. 492 C steve.barrera@utsa.edu
BARRETO, Mary Jo .... 803-323-2233. 449 G mannm@winthrop.edu
BARRETO, Sandra .... 787-761-0640. 553 F asistenciaeconomica@cbp.edu
BARRETO, Wanda .... 787-758-2480. 554 F wanda.barreto@upr.edu
BARRETT, Adam .... 212-431-2888. 333 I Adam.Barrett@nyls.edu
BARRETT, Brian, D .... 817-515-6960. 482 B brian.barrett@tccd.edu
BARRETT, Carolyn .... 904-256-7090. 107 Q cbarret@ju.edu
BARRETT, Christina .... 413-236-2112. 231 A cbarrett@berkshirecc.edu
BARRETT, David .... 620-242-0412. 188 G barrettd@mcpherson.edu
BARRETT, Dawn .... 617-879-7100. 230 B dawn.barrett@massart.edu
BARRETT, Denise .... 662-846-1967. 194 A denise.barrett@frontier.edu
BARRETT, Dustin .... 912-650-6250. 131 H dbarrett@southuniversity.edu
BARRETT, Jeannie .... 706-754-7704. 129 G jbarrett@northgatech.edu
BARRETT, Joan .... 417-447-6914. 279 K barrettj@otc.edu
BARRETT, John .... 770-426-2616. 128 D jbarrett@life.edu
BARRETT, Juanita .... 773-244-4892. 154 G jbarrett@northpark.edu

BARRETT, Karinda 850-201-6209. 117 D barrettk@tcc.fl.edu
BARRETT, Kim, E 858-534-6655... 71 F graduatedean@ucsd.edu
BARRETT, Kimberly 937-775-5240. 393 G kimberly.barrett@wright.edu
BARRETT, Laura 919-344-2517. 120 G laura.barrett@armstrong.edu
BARRETT, Lawrence, M .. 207-974-4691. 210 K lbarrett@emcc.edu
BARRETT, Leah 585-395-2122. 342 F lbarrett@brockport.edu
BARRETT, Leah, A 585-395-2772. 342 F lbarrett@brockport.edu
BARRETT, Linda 620-242-0457. 188 G barrettl@mcpherson.edu
BARRETT, Linda 401-874-2509. 440 D lindab@uri.edu
BARRETT, Mark 978-837-5075. 234 A barrettm@merrimack.edu
BARRETT, Michael 850-644-1768. 115 C mgbarrett@admin.fsu.edu
BARRETT, Michael 616-977-0599. 249 B michael.barrett@puritanseminary.org
BARRETT, Pam, J 770-534-6176. 122 A pbarrett@brenau.edu
BARRETT, Robert, T 803-536-8980. 446 G rbarrett1@scsu.edu
BARRETT, Rosemary 845-341-4200. 335 H rosemary.barrett@sunyorange.edu
BARRETT, Stephen 817-735-2261. 490 E Stephen.Barrett@unthsc.edu
BARRETT, Valoree 785-227-3380. 184 I barrettv@bethanylb.edu
BARRETT, Zunilka 617-287-7005. 228 E zbarrett@umassp.edu
BARRIE, John 845-848-7500. 322 G john.barrie@dc.edu
BARRIENTOS, Joseph 808-544-0267. 135 F jbarrientos@hpu.edu
BARRIER, Jeremy 256-766-6610..... 4 B jbarrier@hcu.edu
BARRIERA, Heriberto 787-279-1912. 550 B hbarriera@bayamon.inter.edu
BARRILLEAUX, Allayne .. 985-448-4011. 208 A laynie.barrilleaux@nicholls.edu
BARRINGER, Judy 212-659-7215. 328 E jbarringer@tkc.edu
BARRINGTON, Ruth, A .. 401-825-2184. 439 A rbarrington@ccri.edu
BARRIOS, Eric 787-766-1717. 552 J ca_ebarrios@suagm.edu
BARRIOS, Eugenio 212-220-1266. 317 A ebarrios@bmcc.cuny.edu
BARRIOS, Francisco 573-651-2154. 282 B fbarrios@semo.edu
BARRIS, Julie 814-472-3012. 432 D jbarris@francis.edu
BARRISH, David, J 804-523-5934. 512 F dbarrish@reynolds.edu
BARRITT, Eric, D 248-364-6150. 248 J barritt@oakland.edu
BARRON, Alexandra, L ... 512-464-8878. 479 C alexb@stedwards.edu
BARRON, Brad, E 864-294-2033. 444 C brad.barron@furman.edu
BARRON, Caulyne 602-648-5750... 13 I cbarron@dunlap-stone.edu
BARRON, Dave 334-670-3657..... 7 H wdbarron@troy.edu
BARRON, David 918-343-7852. 399 C dbarron@rsu.edu
BARRON, Dianne 334-670-3189..... 7 H dlbarron@troy.edu
BARRON, Eric, J 850-644-1085. 115 C ebarron@fsu.edu
BARRON, Glenda, O 254-298-8600. 482 C glenda.barron@templejc.edu
BARRON, Katie 970-542-3108... 83 E katie.barron@morgancc.edu
BARRON, Kim 920-686-6275. 536 A Kim.Barron@sl.edu
BARRON, Maria, V 954-308-2180... 98 G mbarron@aii.edu
BARRON, Michael 319-335-1548. 175 I michael-barron@uiowa.edu
BARRON, Nicole 312-915-8903. 151 H nbarron@luc.edu
BARRON, Robert, E 847-970-4800. 162 G rector@usml.edu
BARROS, Michael 808-845-9135. 136 G mbarros@hawaii.edu
BARROTT, Jim 423-697-3211. 460 C
BARROW, Carla 229-225-5077. 132 D cbarrow@southwestgatech.edu
BARROW, Christine, E ... 301-322-0419. 217 F barowce@pgcc.edu
BARROW, Deborah, L .... 940-397-4212. 476 H debbie.barrow@mwsu.edu
BARROW, Jerry 706-369-5763. 120 J jbarrow@athenstech.edu
BARROW, Linda, M 770-531-6331. 128 B lbarrow@laniertech.edu
BARROWS, Barbara 641-585-8143. 183 D barbara.barrows@waldorf.edu
BARROWS, David 217-206-6730. 161 E barrows.david@uis.edu
BARROWS, Karen, A 585-475-2396. 337 L karen.barrows@rit.edu
BARROWS, Karen, A 585-475-2396. 337 L kab7050@rit.edu
BARROWS, Robert 617-228-2241. 231 C rbarrows@bhcc.mass.edu
BARRRIS, Brad 706-236-2272. 121 G bbarris@berry.edu
BARRY, Ann Marie 847-635-1699. 155 F annmarie@oakton.edu
BARRY, Catherine 603-882-6923. 296 B cbarry@ccsnh.edu
BARRY, Ceal, R 303-492-6591... 85 L ceal.barry@colorado.edu
BARRY, Christine 713-525-3156. 490 L cbarry@stthom.edu
BARRY, Donna, M 973-655-4361. 303 D barryd@mail.montclair.edu
BARRY, Ernie 214-768-2004. 481 A ebarry@smu.edu
BARRY, Jeannette 402-375-7466. 291 F jebarry1@wsc.edu
BARRY, Jessica 937-294-0592. 388 M jessica@saa.edu
BARRY, Joanne 607-753-2302. 343 B joanne.barry@cortland.edu
BARRY, John 254-710-1412. 467 G john_barry@baylor.edu
BARRY, Kevin, G 302-295-1170... 94 E kevin.g.barry@wilmu.edu
BARRY, Laura 201-559-3504. 302 A barryl@felician.edu
BARRY, Liz 858-566-1200... 42 G lbarry@disd.edu
BARRY, Richard 610-526-6532. 410 J rbarry@brynmawr.edu
BARRY, Theresa 262-524-7334. 532 C tbarry@carrollu.edu
BARRY, Thomas, E 214-768-4320. 481 A tbarry@smu.edu
BARTA, Barbara 614-234-1788. 384 J bbarta@mccn.edu
BARTA, Gary 319-335-9435. 175 I gary-barta@uiowa.edu
BARTA, James 218-755-2965. 258 A jbarta@bemidjistate.edu
BARTA, Lou 217-641-4215. 148 M lbarta@jwcc.edu
BARTA, Sharon 510-261-8500... 58 G sharon.barta@patten.edu
BARTANEN, Kristine, M . 253-879-3205. 524 F acadvp@pugetsound.edu
BARTEE, Robert, D 402-559-4203. 292 J bbartee@unmc.edu
BARTEL, Alexa 843-383-8126. 442 F abartel@coker.edu
BARTEL, Brad, N 615-898-2953. 459 D brad.bartel@mtsu.edu
BARTEL, Kyle, J 580-774-3705. 400 B kyle.bartel@swosu.edu
BARTEL, LeRoy 972-825-4827. 481 F lbartel@sagu.edu
BARTEL, Steven, J 605-256-5146. 451 H steve.bartel@dsu.edu
BARTEL, Tonia 660-831-4105. 278 I bartelt@moval.edu
BARTELL, Peter 703-897-1972. 510 B pbartell@stratford.edu
BARTELL, William 605-331-6703. 452 D bill.bartell@usiouxfalls.edu
BARTELMAY, Ryan 312-752-2454. 149 E ryan.bartelmay@kendall.edu
BARTELS, Dennis 614-416-6200. 375 B dbartels@bradfordschoolcolumbus.edu
BARTELS, Jean 912-478-5258. 126 C jbartels@georgiasouthern.edu
BARTELS, Marilyn 800-955-2527. 274 I mbartels@grantham.edu
BARTELS, Paige 802-440-4336. 498 G pbartels@bennington.edu
BARTELS, Roy 325-574-7629. 494 K rbartels@wtc.edu
BARTELS, Sharon, J 770-962-7580. 127 D sbartels@gwinnetttech.edu
BARTELS, Suzanne 336-316-2000. 355 A
BARTELSON, Gretchen, G 712-324-5061. 181 G gbartelson@nwicc.edu
BARTFIELD, Joel 518-262-7302. 313 D bartfi@mail.amc.edu
BARTGES, Ellyn 320-308-0125. 261 B elbartges@stcloudstate.edu
BARTH, Brad 701-671-2131. 372 E brad.barth@ndscs.edu
BARTH, Christopher 845-938-3833. 545 I Christopher.Barth@usma.edu
BARTH, Cynthia 410-225-4223. 216 C cbarth@mica.edu
BARTH, Doug 785-594-4526. 184 C doug.barth@bakeru.edu
BARTH, Michael 406-496-4233. 287 F mbarth@mtech.edu
BARTH, Richard, P 410-706-7794. 219 C rbarth@ssw.umaryland.edu
BARTH, Rick 205-665-6239..... 9 B rbarth@montevallo.edu
BARTHA, Jaimee 847-628-2514. 149 B jbartha@judsonu.edu
BARTHELEMY, Jennifer .. 618-544-8657. 147 A barthelemyj@iecc.edu
BARTHELL, John 405-974-3371. 400 K jbarthell@uco.edu
BARTHELMAS, Frederick 518-587-2100. 346 A rick.barthlemas@esc.edu
BARTHELMES, David 810-762-3324. 251 E dwbarth@umflint.edu
BARTHOLMEY, Theresa .. 660-263-3900. 272 A tbart@cccb.edu
BARTHOLOMEW, Lynda . 256-726-7210..... 6 B lbartholomew@oakwood.edu
BARTHOLOMEW, Nanette 757-826-1883. 502 G registrar@bethel-college.com
BARTHOLOMEW-FEIS, Dixee 712-749-2131. 176 D bartholomew@bvu.edu
BARTINE, Hunt 201-200-2016. 303 F hbartine@njcu.edu
BARTINI, Michael, D 207-725-3146. 209 H mbartini@bowdoin.edu
BARTKOVICH, Jeffrey, P 585-292-3018. 332 A jbartkovich@monroecc.edu
BARTKOWIAK, Ellen 608-663-2312. 532 I ebartkowiak@edgewood.edu
BARTL, Noelle 575-562-2412. 309 H noelle.bartl@enmu.edu
BARTLE, Gamin 973-408-3106. 301 C gbartle@drew.edu
BARTLE, John, R 402-554-3989. 293 A jbartle@unomaha.edu
BARTLEBAUGH, Brenda, P 318-797-5009. 205 F brenda.bartlebaugh@lsus.edu
BARTLETT, Anita 580-628-6233. 396 M anita.bartlett@noc.edu
BARTLETT, Anne 979-230-3202. 468 A anne.bartlett@brazosport.edu
BARTLETT, Annemarie, M 610-660-1299. 432 E abartlet@sju.edu
BARTLETT, Julia 913-234-0758. 185 L julia.bartlett@cleveland.edu
BARTLETT, Phil 802-773-5900. 499 B phil.bartlett@csj.edu
BARTLETT, Raymond 713-743-8780. 489 A rbartlett@uh.edu
BARTLETT, Rebecca 802-258-9226. 499 F rbartlet@marlboro.edu
BARTLETT, Stacy 706-385-1100. 130 F stacy.bartlett@point.edu
BARTLETT, Walter, C 336-322-2100. 362 F Walter.Bartlett@piedmontcc.edu
BARTLEY, Mary, E 515-961-1511. 182 E mimi.bartley@simpson.edu
BARTLEY, Patricia, A 773-256-0717. 152 B pbartley@lstc.edu
BARTLEY, Ron 843-921-6901. 446 A rbartley@netc.edu
BARTLING, Kaitlyn 641-648-4611. 179 I kaitlyn.bartling@iavalley.edu
BARTLING, Kelly, H 308-865-8455. 292 H bartlingkh@unk.edu
BARTNETT, Jane 718-409-7277. 346 D jbartnett@sunymaritime.edu
BARTO, Christopher, T ... 212-752-1530. 328 G christopher.barto@limcollege.edu
BARTOL, Michelle, M 814-641-3432. 419 H bartolm@juniata.edu
BARTOLD, Melissa 312-225-1700. 146 G mbartold@ico.edu
BARTOLINI, Brian, J 401-865-1554. 439 E bbartoli@providence.edu
BARTOLO, Tony 423-478-6208. 460 D tbartolo@clevelandstatecc.edu
BARTOLOTTA, Charles ... 631-451-4790. 346 F bartolc@sunysuffolk.edu
BARTON, Aimee 216-791-5000. 377 E aimee.barton@case.edu
BARTON, Bill 912-871-1690. 129 J bbarton@ogeecheetech.edu
BARTON, Carolina 949-214-3093... 41 I carolina.barton@cui.edu
BARTON, Catherine 404-237-7573. 121 F cbarton@bauder.edu
BARTON, Charles "Lennie" 919-760-8375. 356 G bartonl@meredith.edu
BARTON, Connie 530-242-7719... 65 G cbarton@shastacollege.edu
BARTON, David 660-284-4800. 275 B
BARTON, Delores 404-270-5376. 132 E dbarton@spelman.edu
BARTON, Gayle, R 413-542-2180. 221 G gbarton@amherst.edu
BARTON, J. Mark 479-394-7622... 23 B mbarton@rmcc.edu
BARTON, Jacqueline, K .. 626-395-3646... 31 E jkbarton@caltech.edu
BARTON, Jennifer, K 520-621-3512... 18 F barton@email.arizona.edu
BARTON, John, D 248-218-2026. 249 D jbarton@rc.edu
BARTON, Laurence 610-526-1301. 409 F larry.barton@theamericancollege.edu
BARTON, Mary 940-565-2085. 490 C mary.barton@unt.edu
BARTON, Michelle 760-744-1150... 58 D mbarton@palomar.edu
BARTON, Nancy 203-837-8588... 88 B bartonn@wcsu.edu
BARTON, Pat 678-466-4185. 123 A patbarton@clayton.edu
BARTON, Patricia 510-136-1220... 47 J barton@hnu.edu
BARTON, Sarah 304-865-6034. 527 F sarah.barton@ovu.edu
BARTON, Todd 727-726-1153. 100 E toddbarton@clearwater.edu
BARTOW, Margaret 440-525-7096. 382 M mbartow@lakelandcc.edu
BARTOW, Patricia 619-216-6694... 68 B pbartow@swccd.edu
BARTRAM, Lydia 561-297-0180. 114 L lbartram@fau.edu
BARTSCH, Jonathan 617-236-8800. 226 F jbartsch@fisher.edu
BARTSCHER, Patricia, B . 415-338-2998... 35 E pattyb@sfsu.edu
BARTUS, Thomas, J 609-258-7720. 304 E tbartus@princeton.edu
BARWICK, Daniel, W 620-331-4100. 187 G dbarwick@indycc.edu
BARZACCHINI, Mike 847-925-6510. 145 H mbarzacc@harpercollege.edu
BASCH, Hersch 718-438-1002. 331 A
BASCHSHI, Maria 760-630-1555... 49 L mbaschshi@kaplan.edu
BASEL, Barbara 605-773-3455. 451 E barbara.basel@sdbor.edu
BASER, Ric, N 918-595-7980. 400 E ricky.baser@tulsacc.edu
BASFORD, Jerry, L 801-581-7793. 496 Q jbasford@sa.utah.edu
BASH, Cassaundra 574-936-8898. 163 K cassaundra.bash@ancilla.edu
BASHAM, Bob 660-626-2307. 271 A bbasham@atsu.edu
BASHARA, Teri 318-678-6000. 202 I tbashara@bpcc.edu
BASHAW, Edward 479-968-0490... 20 E ebashaw@atu.edu
BASHAW, Pat 501-279-4315... 21 C pbashaw@harding.edu
BASHFORD, Mike 870-574-4480... 23 G mbashfor@sautech.edu
BASHISTA, Brian 703-284-1607. 507 B brian.bashista@marymount.edu
BASILE, Carole, G 314-516-5109. 283 E basilec@umsl.edu
BASILE, Elizabeth 718-368-4539. 318 E ebasile@kbcc.cuny.edu
BASINGER, Randall, G ... 717-796-5375. 423 L rbasinge@messiah.edu
BASINGER, Scott, F 713-798-4100. 467 F scottb@bcm.edu
BASINSKI, Judith, B 716-878-4011. 343 A basinsjb@buffalostate.edu
BASIRATMAND, Mehran 561-297-0230. 114 L mehran@fau.edu
BASKIN, Richard 678-359-5018. 127 A rbaskin@gordonstate.edu
BASKIN, William 914-251-6485. 344 D bill.baskin@purchase.edu
BASKO, Aaron, M 410-543-6161. 220 D ambasko@salisbury.edu
BASLER, Julie 303-369-5151... 84 E julie.basler@plattcolorado.edu
BASLER, Sandra, K 636-481-3298. 275 I sbasler@jeffco.edu
BASLER, Thomas, G 843-792-9211. 445 B basler@musc.edu
BASLEY, Carolyn 312-935-4556. 156 K cbasley@robertmorris.edu
BASMADJIAN, Kevin 203-582-3497... 91 A kevin.basmadjian@quinnipiac.edu

BASNIGHT, Beth .... 617-323-6662. 233 D
beth_basnight@mspp.edu
BASOM, Richard .... 717-361-4762. 415 H
basomr@etown.edu
BASRI, Gibor .... 510-642-7294... 70 I
vcei@berkeley.edu
BASS, Brenda .... 319-273-2221. 176 A
brenda.bass@uni.edu
BASS, Brittany .... 618-395-7777. 147 B
bassb@iecc.edu
BASS, Charles .... 619-260-4819... 73 I
charlesb@sandiego.edu
BASS, Chris .... 909-607-6999... 39 C
chris.bass@cuc.edu
BASS, Donna .... 334-222-6591..... 5 E
dbass@lbwcc.edu
BASS, Harry, S .... 252-335-3189. 367 C
hsbass@mail.ecsu.edu
BASS, Jan .... 850-474-3132. 117 B
jbass@uwf.edu
BASS, Jimmy .... 910-962-4292. 369 C
bassj@uncw.edu
BASS, Mary, T .... 252-823-5166. 360 C
bassm@edgecombe.edu
BASS, Randall .... 202-687-4535... 95 E
bassr@georgetown.edu
BASS, Scott, A .... 202-885-2127... 94 F
provost@american.edu
BASS, Wanda, S .... 334-493-3573..... 5 E
wsbass@lbwcc.edu
BASSETT, Baylor .... 678-839-6582. 133 I
bbassett@westga.edu
BASSETT, Cheryl .... 810-762-0553. 247 F
cheryl.bassett@edtech.mcc.edu
BASSETT, Claire, M .... 713-798-4712. 467 F
bassett@bcm.edu
BASSETT, Dorothy, E ...... 412-396-5839. 415 F
bassettd@duq.edu
BASSETT, Heidi, M .... 972-860-7255. 470 I
HBassett@dcccd.edu
BASSETT, Joanne .... 901-333-5020. 461 F
jbassett@southwest.tn.edu
BASSETT, John, E .... 509-865-8600. 520 D
bassett_j@heritage.edu
BASSETT, Mary .... 630-889-6527. 154 E
mbassett@nuhs.edu
BASSETT, Matthew, D ..... 315-445-4450. 328 F
bassetmd@lemoyne.edu
BASSETT, Robert .... 714-997-6715... 38 A
bassett@chapman.edu
BASSETT, Sally .... 607-274-3209. 327 E
sbassett@ithaca.edu
BASSETTE, Lorraine, P .... 301-322-0524. 217 F
lbasssette@pgcc.edu
BASSETTE, Lynda, D .... 607-436-2407. 343 E
bassetld@oneonta.edu
BASSETTI, Mimi .... 215-572-2941. 409 H
bassetti@arcadia.edu
BASSHAM, Donna .... 417-255-7243. 278 F
donnabassham@missouristate.edu
BASSHAM, Kathy .... 817-598-6427. 494 G
kbassham@wc.edu
BASSHAM, Mia, W .... 570-740-0420. 422 G
mbassham@luzerne.edu
BASSI, Susan, E .... 309-556-3151. 148 B
sbassi@iwu.edu
BASSI-COOK, Teresa ...... 724-838-4295. 433 E
bassi@setonhill.edu
BASSINGER, Donnie .... 828-726-2286. 358 E
dbassinger@cccti.edu
BASSO, Mary .... 732-987-2427. 302 B
basso@georgian.edu
BASSO, Sharon, K .... 610-758-4156. 422 A
sbr2@lehigh.edu
BASSO, Susan .... 814-863-6188. 426 A
smb43@psu.edu
BAST, Carrie .... 330-325-6718. 385 E
cbast@neomed.edu
BASTECKI-PEREZ,
Victoria .... 215-641-6482. 424 B
vbasteck@mc3.edu
BASTIAN, Joni .... 618-537-6555. 152 G
jjbastian@mckendree.edu
BASTIN, Judy .... 316-322-3235. 185 D
jbastin@butlercc.edu
BASTIONY, Peter .... 305-949-9500. 102 E
pbastiony@cci.edu
BASTON, Michael .... 718-482-5180. 318 F
mbaston@lagcc.cuny.edu
BASU, Andra, M .... 610-921-7634. 409 A
abasu@alb.edu
BASUALDO, Maria .... 607-778-5030. 315 I
basualdomi@sunybroome.edu
BATACLAN, Emma, R ...... 671-735-8889. 546 C
emma.bataclan@guamcc.edu
BATAILLON, Pamela .... 402-559-9567. 292 J
pdbataillon@unmc.edu
BATAYEH, Ed .... 248-349-5454. 251 I
ed.batayeh@walshcollege.edu
BATCHELDER, Kathy ...... 330-684-8944. 390 F
ksbatch@uakron.edu
BATCHELDER, Rick .... 518-562-4106. 320 B
rick.batchelder@clinton.edu
BATCHELLER, Tamara ..... 313-578-0346. 250 K
batchets@udmercy.edu
BATCHELOR, Gerald .... 731-425-2619. 460 G
gbatchelor@jscc.edu
BATCHELOR, Susan .... 618-545-3033. 149 D
sbatchelor@kaskaskia.edu
BATCHELOR, Susan .... 215-955-2867. 434 C
susan.mcfadden@jefferson.edu
BATCHELOR, William, D 334-844-3209..... 1 G
wdb0007@auburn.edu
BATE, Carol .... 315-229-5906. 339 F
cbate@stlawu.edu
BATE, Jeff .... 801-375-5125. 496 G
jbate@rmuohp.edu
BATE, Joel, C .... 208-732-6836. 138 B
jbate@csi.edu
BATELL, Sue, S .... 608-796-3380. 539 E
ssbatell@viterbo.edu
BATEMAN, Bradley, W ... 434-947-8140. 508 D
bbateman@randolphcollege.edu
BATEMAN, Joyce .... 417-447-6973. 279 K
BATEMAN, Linda .... 260-665-4124. 173 E
batemanl@trine.edu
BATEMAN, Mathew .... 814-866-8148. 420 E
mbateman@lecom.edu
BATEMAN, JR., Rick ...... 337-421-6965. 204 E
rick.bateman@sowela.edu
BATEMAN, William, K ..... 989-837-4448. 248 C
batemanw@northwood.edu
BATENHORST, Jim Ann . 806-894-9611. 480 H
jbatenho@southplainscollege.edu
BATENHORST, Mandy .... 580-349-1396. 397 G
mandyb@opsu.edu
BATES, Alan .... 256-840-4129..... 6 I
abates@snead.edu
BATES, Becky .... 612-332-3361. 253 G
bbates@aii.edu
BATES, Brad .... 617-552-4680. 224 A
brad.bates@bc.edu
BATES, Brent .... 660-596-7252. 282 G
bbates@sfccmo.edu
BATES, Brian .... 408-924-6518... 36 A
brian.bates@sjsu.edu
BATES, Carol .... 318-678-6000. 202 I
cbates@bpcc.edu
BATES, Carol .... 906-487-7258. 242 G
carol.bates@finlandia.edu
BATES, Cathy, J .... 828-262-6276. 367 A
batescj@appstate.edu
BATES, Damien .... 928-317-5892... 11 L
damien.bates@azwestern.edu
BATES, Doug .... 931-372-3408. 460 A
dbates@tntech.edu
BATES, Evola, C .... 225-771-4680. 206 I
evola_bates@sus.edu
BATES, Janice .... 610-647-4400. 418 I
jbates@immaculata.edu
BATES, Jennifer .... 315-279-5646. 328 D
jbates@mail.keuka.edu
BATES, Joan .... 423-478-6205. 460 D
jbates@clevelandstatecc.edu
BATES, Julie .... 501-660-1002... 19 L
jbates@asusystem.edu
BATES, Lynette .... 909-558-4561... 51 C
lbates@llu.edu
BATES, Mark, R .... 440-775-8477. 385 H
mark.bates@oberlin.edu
BATES, Mary Lou, W ...... 518-580-5588. 341 A
mbates@skidmore.edu
BATES, Michael .... 731-426-7560. 455 J
mbates@lanecollege.edu
BATES, Michael, D .... 816-235-6910. 283 D
batesmd@umkc.edu
BATES, Mike .... 503-375-7003. 403 A
mbates@corban.edu
BATES, Pamela .... 859-246-6335. 194 L
pamela.bates@kctcs.edu
BATES, Patrick, M .... 585-292-2820. 332 A
pbates@monroecc.edu
BATES, Ren .... 859-246-4605. 194 L
ren.bates@kctcs.edu
BATES, Starnell .... 803-822-3235. 445 C
batess@midlandstech.edu
BATES, Suzanne .... 330-263-2365. 377 H
sbates@wooster.edu
BATES, Tom .... 360-416-7745. 523 G
tom.bates@skagit.edu
BATES, Tom .... 281-756-3561. 465 D
tbates@alvincollege.edu
BATES, Winfrey .... 270-858-6501. 196 D
winfrey.bates@kctcs.edu
BATES-LEE, Cheryl, A ..... 757-823-8323. 507 M
cabates-lee@nsu.edu
BATH, Michael, J .... 906-227-2151. 248 A
mbath@nmu.edu
BATIC, Marjorie .... 317-955-6150. 170 V
mbatic@marian.edu
BATIE, Larry .... 205-929-1517..... 5 G
lbatie@miles.edu
BATISTA, Adrian .... 440-775-8472. 385 H
adrian.Batista@oberlin.edu
BATISTA, Angela, E .... 812-464-1862. 174 D
BATISTA, Jorge .... 347-964-8600. 315 E
jbatista@boricuacollege.edu
BATISTE, Sophia .... 859-282-8989. 127 F
sbatiste@ict-ils.edu
BATISTE, Sophia .... 678-450-0550. 127 F
sbatiste@ict-ils.edu
BATKER, Carol, J .... 415-422-4523... 73 J
cjbatker@usfca.edu
BATSON, Barbara .... 479-575-2806... 23 I
bbatson@uark.edu
BATSON, James .... 847-925-6340. 145 H
jbatson@harpercollege.edu
BATSON, Judy .... 540-351-1513. 512 H
jbatson@lfcc.edu
BATSON, Marie .... 251-442-2370..... 9 A
mbatson@umobile.edu
BATSON, Rebecca .... 302-857-7887... 93 C
rbatson@desu.edu
BATSON-BOREL, Dawn .. 305-626-3150. 104 J
dawn.batson@fmuniv.edu
BATT, Ellen .... 208-459-5814. 138 A
ebatt@collegeofidaho.edu
BATT, Marylou .... 617-349-8564. 228 B
mbatt@lesley.edu
BATTAGLIA, Janet, M ..... 540-464-7213. 515 B
battagliajm@vmi.edu
BATTAGLINO, Lisa .... 508-531-1347. 229 D
lbattaglino@bridgew.edu
BATTALORA, Elizabeth .... 318-473-6459. 205 A
ebattalora@lsua.edu
BATTEN, Melissa .... 843-349-5228. 444 F
melissa.batten@hgtc.edu
BATTEN-MICKENS,
Meloyde .... 202-651-5337... 95 C
meloyde.batten-mickens@gallaudet.edu
BATTERSBY, Gerard .... 313-883-8552. 249 E
battersby.gerard@shms.edu
BATTERSON, Brett .... 312-431-2391. 157 D
bbatterson@roosevelt.edu
BATTIATA, Russell .... 305-273-4499. 100 H
russell.battiata@cbt.edu
BATTISTA, Elizabeth ...... 718-855-3661. 327 B
ebattista@idc.edu
BATTISTA, Vincent, C ..... 718-855-3661. 327 B
vcbattista@idc.edu
BATTISTE, Doris .... 340-693-1121. 555 E
dbattis@live.uvi.edu
BATTISTE, Leilani .... 415-241-2294... 38 L
lbattist@ccsf.edu
BATTISTEL, George .... 503-768-7807. 403 K
georgeb@lclark.edu
BATTISTELLA, Diane .... 630-829-6415. 140 B
dbatistella@ben.edu
BATTISTI, Francis .... 607-778-5138. 315 I
battistifl@sunybroome.edu
BATTLE, Bill .... 205-348-3600..... 8 D
bbattle@ia.ua.edu
BATTLE, Bruce .... 661-362-3432... 40 E
bruce.battle@canyons.edu
BATTLES, Denise .... 910-962-3389. 369 C
battlesd@uncw.edu
BATTRAW, Danny .... 928-428-8605... 13 J
danny.battraw@eac.edu
BATTURS, Beth Anne ...... 410-777-7352. 213 D
babatturs@aacc.edu
BATTY, Philip .... 616-331-8648. 243 C
battyp@gvsu.edu
BATTY-HERBERT,
Kimberly .... 863-784-7329. 113 G
battyhek@southflorida.edu
BAUCHAM, Monique .... 757-388-2900. 509 D
msbaugh@sentara.com
BAUDER, Lee .... 405-912-9019. 395 K
books@hc.edu
BAUDER, Megan .... 610-841-3333. 427 F
mbauder@psb.edu
BAUDER, Sarah, J .... 301-314-8279. 219 B
sbauder@umd.edu
BAUDRY, Michel .... 909-706-8271... 76 B
mbaudry@westernu.edu
BAUER, C. Jon .... 636-584-6501. 273 M
bauerj@eastcentral.edu
BAUER, Cynthia, M .... 414-288-7343. 534 B
cindy.bauer@marquette.edu
BAUER, Daniel, C .... 314-367-8700. 281 C
daniel.bauer@stlcop.edu
BAUER, Daniel, L .... 502-272-8240. 192 E
dbauer@bellarmine.edu
BAUER, David .... 859-858-3581. 192 A
BAUER, Deb .... 401-949-2820. 439 C
BAUER, Don .... 620-365-5116. 183 I
bauer@allencc.edu
BAUER, Frank .... 724-938-5717. 428 A
bauer_f@calu.edu
BAUER, Jackie .... 320-308-5486. 261 C
jbauer@sctcc.edu
BAUER, James .... 313-664-7412. 241 C
jbauer@collegeforcreativestudies.edu
BAUER, James, M .... 305-284-2270. 118 F
jbauer@miami.edu
BAUER, James, R .... 503-370-6112. 408 J
jbauer@willamette.edu
BAUER, Jason, K .... 515-263-2887. 178 G
jbauer@grandview.edu
BAUER, Jeffery .... 740-351-3550. 388 N
jbauer@shawnee.edu
BAUER, Jody .... 215-751-8060. 413 I
jbauer@ccp.edu
BAUER, John .... 678-915-7334. 132 C
jbauer@spsu.edu
BAUER, Kelli .... 620-252-7360. 185 O
kellib@coffeyville.edu
BAUER, Kent .... 970-542-3111... 83 E
kent.bauer@morgancc.edu
BAUER, Kimberly, P .... 404-413-0728. 126 E
kimbauer@gsu.edu
BAUER, Mary Claire .... 518-629-7309. 326 G
m.bauer@hvcc.edu
BAUER, Michelle .... 217-732-3155. 151 C
mbauer@lincolncollege.edu
BAUER, Patrick .... 847-925-6827. 145 H
pbauer@harpercollege.edu
BAUER, Sarah .... 415-338-2174... 35 E
sbauer@sfsu.edu
BAUER, Susan .... 212-752-1530. 328 G
susan.bauer@limcollege.edu
BAUER, Thomas .... 928-523-6126... 16 C
thomas.bauer@nau.edu
BAUER, Thomas, G .... 805-565-6043... 76 D
tbauer@westmont.edu
BAUER, Tom .... 650-358-6782... 64 A
bauert@smccd.edu
BAUER, Warren, K .... 515-574-1120. 179 D
bauer@iowacentral.edu
BAUER-LEVESQUE,
Angela .... 617-682-1551. 226 D
abauer-levesque@eds.edu
BAUGH, Anita, G .... 320-308-5936. 261 C
abaugh@sctcc.edu
BAUGH, Frank .... 601-318-6772. 270 I
frank.baugh@wmcarey.edu
BAUGH, Robbie .... 940-668-7731. 477 I
rbaugh@nctc.edu
BAUGHER, Kathy .... 615-248-1320. 462 D
kbaugher@trevecca.edu
BAUGHMAN, Leslie .... 214-692-8080. 131 H
lbaughman@southuniversity.edu
BAUGHMAN, Matthew ... 618-453-2341. 159 G
baughman@siu.edu
BAUGHMAN, Patricia ..... 936-261-1944. 482 F
pabaughman@pvamu.edu
BAUGUS, John .... 626-815-4622... 29 H
jbaugus@apu.edu
BAUHS, Raymond .... 615-226-3990. 455 N
rbauhs@lincolntech.com
BAUHS, Timothy .... 312-369-7054. 143 D
tbauhs@colum.edu
BAUM, Christina .... 203-392-5760... 88 A
baumc1@southernct.edu
BAUM, Courtney .... 724-805-2253. 432 G
courtney.baum@email.stvincent.edu
BAUM, Cynthia, G .... 410-627-7859. 265 D
cynthia.baum@waldenu.edu
BAUM, Daniel, B .... 410-777-2011. 213 D
dbbaum@aacc.edu
BAUM, Robert .... 724-805-2590. 432 G
bob.baum@email.stvincent.edu
BAUM, Robin .... 914-594-4882. 334 A
robin_baum@nymc.edu
BAUMAL, Robert .... 978-656-3244. 232 B
baumalr@middlesex.mass.edu
BAUMAN, Curtis .... 570-945-8506. 419 N
curtis.bauman@keystone.edu
BAUMAN, Dallas .... 631-632-6974. 342 C
dallas.bauman@stonybrook.edu
BAUMAN, David .... 218-723-6179. 254 K
dbauman@css.edu
BAUMAN, Jerry .... 312-996-2497. 161 D
jbauman@uic.edu
BAUMAN, Jerry .... 312-413-5473. 161 D
jbauman@uic.edu
BAUMAN, Joel .... 386-822-7100. 117 C
jbauman@stetson.edu
BAUMANN, Anita, M .... 814-472-3902. 432 D
abaumann@francis.edu
BAUMANN, Benjamin ...... 508-678-2811. 231 B
ben.baumann@bristolcc.edu
BAUMANN, Erick .... 708-524-5054. 144 C
ebauman@dom.edu
BAUMANN, Joe .... 979-830-4075. 467 I
joe.baumann@blinn.edu
BAUMANN, Julianne, D . 607-735-1806. 323 H
jbaumann@elmira.edu
BAUMANN, Melissa, J ... 334-844-5860..... 1 G
mjb0041@auburn.edu
BAUMANN, Robert .... 913-684-2741. 545 E
robert.baumann@leavenworth.army.mil
BAUMANN, Terry .... 727-726-1153. 100 E
terrybaumann@clearwater.edu

BAUMBACH, Kirk ... 804-752-7263. 508 E kirkbaumbach@rmc.edu
BAUMER, Julie ... 541-956-7346. 407 F jbaumer@roguecc.edu
BAUMERT, Karen, D ... 208-732-6279. 138 B kbaumert@csi.edu
BAUMET, Robert, L ... 716-878-5304. 343 A baumetrl@buffalostate.edu
BAUMGAERTNER, Jill, P 630-752-5060. 163 F jill.baumgaertner@wheaton.edu
BAUMGARDNER, Brice, D ... 573-629-3279. 274 J bbaumgardner@hlg.edu
BAUMGARDNER, Deidra 317-738-8189. 165 I dbaumgardner@franklincollege.edu
BAUMGARDNER, Michael ... 518-244-2207. 338 C baumgm@sage.edu
BAUMGARDNER, Waylon ... 951-343-4876... 30 H wbaumgardner@calbaptist.edu
BAUMGART, Reilly ... 618-262-8641. 147 C baumgartr@iecc.edu
BAUMGARTEN, Bobbie .. 214-637-3530. 494 F bbaumgarten@wadecollege.edu
BAUMGARTEN, Whitney . 414-256-1272. 535 A MMC-Bookstore@mtmary.edu
BAUMGARTNER, Bruce .. 814-732-2776. 428 E bbaumgartner@edinboro.edu
BAUMGARTNER, Carolyn, G ... 419-530-5812. 392 B carolyn.baumgartner@utoledo.edu
BAUMGARTNER, David, A ... 319-335-1023. 175 I david-baumgartner@uiowa.edu
BAUMGARTNER, Eric, T 419-772-2372. 386 D e-baumgartner@onu.edu
BAUMGARTNER, Holly, J ... 419-824-3756. 383 C hbaumgartner@lourdes.edu
BAUMLER, Angela ... 410-532-3150. 217 E abaumler@ndm.edu
BAUMLER, Kim, M ... 563-556-5110. 181 E baumlerk@nicc.edu
BAUMLER, Scott ... 319-368-6460. 181 C sbaumler@mtmercy.edu
BAUN, Dan ... 507-537-6978. 261 F Dan.Baun@smsu.edu
BAUN, Jeffrey, S ... 610-359-5315. 414 D jbaun@dccc.edu
BAUR, John ... 309-438-7661. 147 J jebaur@ilstu.edu
BAURAIN, Thomas, S ... 816-322-0110. 271 O thomas.baurain@calvary.edu
BAUS, Amy ... 563-589-3132. 182 J abaus@dbq.edu
BAUSHKE, Ken ... 270-745-3056. 200 G ken.baushke@wku.edu
BAUSILI, Mark, T ... 716-878-4907. 343 A bausilmt@buffalostate.edu
BAUSINGER, Patricia, E . 570-321-4049. 422 H baus@lycoming.edu
BAUSLER, Katie ... 907-796-6530... 11 A katie.bausler@uas.alaska.edu
BAUSS, Celia, N ... 864-592-4754. 447 A baussc@sccsc.edu
BAUSTISTA PERTUZ, Sofia ... 718-817-0664. 324 G spertuz@fordham.edu
BAUTISTA MOLLER, Lydia, B ... 954-607-4344. 118 D
BAUTSCH, Jack ... 206-934-3655. 522 I jack.bautsch@seattlecolleges.edu
BAVA, Brian ... 208-459-5319. 138 A bbava@collegeofidaho.edu
BAVERO, Gary, S ... 973-642-8502. 307 D gary.bavero@shu.edu
BAWCOM, Amy ... 254-526-1264. 468 G amy.bawcom@ctcd.edu
BAWCOM, Jerry, G ... 254-295-4500. 490 B jbawcom@umhb.edu
BAWCUM, Travis ... 325-574-7612. 494 K tbawcum@wtc.edu
BAXTER, Agnes ... 919-546-8212. 366 E abaxter@shawu.edu
BAXTER, Aimee, F ... 318-257-2641. 207 F abaxter@latech.edu
BAXTER, Barbara, C ... 870-733-6722... 21 I bbaxter@midsouthcc.edu
BAXTER, Donna ... 910-755-7336. 358 D baxterd@brunswickcc.edu
BAXTER, Ginny ... 562-938-4634... 51 D gbaxter@lbcc.edu
BAXTER, Jan ... 541-440-4600. 408 D Jan.Baxter@umpqua.edu
BAXTER, Jessica, M ... 703-323-3288. 513 C jbaxter@nvcc.edu
BAXTER, Keith ... 580-745-2250. 399 J kbaxter@se.edu
BAXTER, Marty, A ... 859-246-6239. 194 L marty.baxter@kctcs.edu
BAXTER, Pat ... 212-229-8947. 332 E baxterp@newschool.edu
BAXTER, Richard, L ... 706-507-8043. 123 D baxter_richard@columbusstate.edu
BAXTER, Robert ... 402-878-2380. 290 D bbaxter@littlepriest.edu
BAXTER, Steven ... 360-452-9277. 522 A sbaxter@pencol.edu
BAYARD, SJ, Mike ... 206-296-6052. 523 E bayardm@seattleu.edu
BAYARD, Patrick ... 217-443-8776. 143 G pbayard@dacc.edu
BAYARDELLE, Eddy ... 718-289-5185. 317 B eddy.bayardelle@bcc.cuny.edu
BAYER, Hermann ... 757-493-6000... 96 F
BAYER, Hermann ... 757-497-4466. 510 B hbayer@stratford.edu
BAYER, Richard, L ... 865-974-2105. 463 C rbayer@utk.edu
BAYERL, Sue ... 320-308-2111. 261 B sjbayerl@stcloudstate.edu
BAYLES, Kenneth ... 402-559-4945. 292 J kbayles@unmc.edu
BAYLESS, Laura ... 608-342-1854. 537 D
BAYLESS, Rita ... 970-945-8691... 79 G
BAYLESS, Robert ... 816-802-3399. 275 J rbayless@kcai.edu
BAYLIS, Gordon ... 270-745-6733. 200 G gordon.baylis@wku.edu
BAYLOR, Bridget ... 540-234-9261. 511 H baylorb@brcc.edu
BAYLOR, Gail ... 828-298-3325. 370 E gbaylor@warren-wilson.edu
BAYLOR, Jeffrey, S ... 605-677-5759. 451 F jeffrey.baylor@usd.edu
BAYLOR, Martin ... 956-665-2121. 492 B baylormv@utpa.edu
BAYNARD, Donald ... 617-287-7799. 228 G donald.baynard@umb.edu
BAYNE, Deann ... 308-635-6018. 291 D dbayne@csc.edu
BAYNE, Doug ... 509-527-4253. 524 H doug.bayne@wwcc.edu
BAYNE, Suzanne ... 423-472-7141. 460 D sbayne@clevelandstatecc.edu
BAYNHAM, Donald ... 972-860-7119. 470 I Baynham@dcccd.edu
BAYNHAM, Patricia, J .... 512-233-1675. 479 C patricib@stedwards.edu
BAYNUM, Thomas, B ... 309-796-5001. 140 E baynumt@bhc.edu
BAYONA, Maribel ... 787-753-6335. 549 D mbayona@icprjc.edu
BAYOUMI, Magdy, A ... 337-482-6147. 208 D mab@louisiana.edu
BAYS, Sherri, A ... 575-538-6150. 312 N bayss@wnmu.edu
BAYS, Steven ... 509-533-3570. 518 F steve.bays@spokanefalls.edu
BAYSAL, Oktay ... 757-683-3787. 507 N obaysal@odu.edu
BAYTCH, Karen ... 617-349-8726. 228 B kbaytch@lesley.edu
BAYTO, Tammy ... 478-274-7852. 129 I tbayto@oftc.edu
BAYUSIK, Linda ... 203-332-5085... 88 F lbayusik@hcc.commnet.edu
BAZAN, Teresita ... 512-223-7950. 466 I tbazan@austincc.edu
BAZAN, Yamilet ... 951-785-2100... 50 B ybazan@lasierra.edu
BAZANT, Robert, S ... 724-222-5330. 425 K rbazant@penncommercial.edu
BAZAR, Leon ... 361-593-2258. 484 A kulgb000@tamuk.edu
BAZARNIC, Steve ... 301-784-5000. 213 B sbazarnic@allegany.edu
BAZEMORE, Dennis ... 910-893-1540. 352 K bazemored@campbell.edu
BAZEMORE, Haywood, M ... 803-705-4321. 441 C bazemoreh@benedict.edu
BAZHDARI, Lauren ... 212-752-1530. 328 G lauren.bazhdari@limcollege.edu
BAZIJIAN, Rosann, V ... 336-334-3418. 369 A rvbazirj@uncg.edu
BAZIL, Ted ... 914-961-8313. 340 B ted@svots.edu
BAZIL, Theodore ... 914-961-8313. 340 B tbazil@svots.edu
BAZLEY, Lisa ... 740-587-6526. 379 D bazleyl@denison.edu
BAZLUKE, Francine, T .... 802-656-8585. 500 F francine.bazluke@uvm.edu
BAZZELL, Darrell ... 608-263-2467. 536 D dbazzell@vc.wisc.edu
BEA, David ... 520-206-4519... 17 A dbea@pima.edu
BEACH, Aaron, T ... 231-995-1342. 248 B abeach@nmc.edu
BEACH, Gary ... 541-737-2815. 406 A gary.beach@oregonstate.edu
BEACH, Nancy, S ... 540-365-4262. 504 L nbeach@ferrum.edu
BEACH, Natalie ... 503-399-5105. 402 E natalie.beach@chemeketa.edu
BEACH, Rebecca ... 540-362-6414. 505 G rbeach@hollins.edu
BEACH, Vincent, W ... 575-234-9215. 311 A vbeach@nmsu.edu
BEACHAM, David, M ... 864-597-4206. 449 I beachamdm@wofford.edu
BEACHLER, Judith ... 916-691-7205... 53 B beachlj@crc.losrios.edu
BEACHNAU, Andrew, J .. 616-331-2120. 243 C beachnaa@gvsu.edu
BEACHY, Randy ... 574-807-7350. 164 D beachyr@bethelcollege.edu
BEACON, John ... 812-237-3560. 167 A john.beacon@indstate.edu
BEADENKOPF, Scott ... 610-361-5327. 424 I beadenks@neumann.edu
BEADLE, Paul ... 724-832-1050. 434 H pbeadle@triangle-tech.edu
BEAGHAN, John, W ... 248-370-2445. 248 J beaghan@oakland.edu
BEAGLE, Deborah ... 734-384-4202. 247 C dbeagle@monroeccc.edu
BEAGLE, Donald ... 704-461-6740. 352 G donaldbeagle@bac.edu
BEAGLE, Mike ... 541-552-6127. 406 C beaglem@sou.edu
BEAGLEY, Tim ... 801-957-4846. 498 B tim.beagley@slcc.edu
BEAHON, Mary Ann ... 573-592-1127. 285 D mbeahon@williamwoods.edu
BEAIL, Linda ... 619-849-2408... 59 L lindabeail@pointloma.edu
BEAKES, Ben ... 304-357-4849. 527 H benbeakes@ucwv.edu
BEAL, Alvin (Chip) ... 715-394-8297. 538 C abeal@uwsuper.edu
BEAL, Billy ... 601-484-8765. 267 G bbeal@meridiancc.edu
BEAL, Jason ... 801-957-4205. 498 B jason.beal@slcc.edu
BEAL, Judy ... 617-521-2139. 236 G judy.beal@simmons.edu
BEAL, Stephen ... 510-594-3630... 30 K sbeal@cca.edu
BEALE, Charles, L ... 302-831-8107... 94 B cbeale@udel.edu
BEALE, Connie, L ... 973-761-9401. 307 C concetta.beale@shu.edu
BEALES, Sharon ... 215-619-7472. 424 B sbeales@mc3.edu
BEALL, David ... 773-508-2391. 151 H dbeall@luc.edu
BEALL, Jim ... 912-583-3257. 122 B jbeall@bpc.edu
BEALS, Linda, M ... 937-327-6374. 393 E lbeals@wittenberg.edu
BEALS, Michael, J ... 714-556-3610... 74 D michael.beals@vanguard.edu
BEAM, Brian ... 309-438-8404. 147 J babeam@ilstu.edu
BEAM, Carla ... 907-786-1359... 10 G cjbeam@alaska.edu
BEAM, Donny ... 423-493-4100. 462 B security@tntemple.edu
BEAM, Jay ... 704-971-8500. 353 F
BEAM, John ... 510-464-3474... 59 C jbeam@peralta.edu
BEAM, Julie ... 574-807-7020. 164 D julie.beam@bethelcollege.edu
BEAM, Linda ... 310-660-3401... 43 B lbeam@elcamino.edu
BEAM, Marc ... 530-242-7670... 65 G mbeam@shastacollege.edu
BEAM, Ruthanne ... 865-573-4517. 455 G rubeam@johnsonU.edu
BEAM, Tony ... 864-977-2008. 445 H tony.beam@ngu.edu
BEAMAN, Patricia, L ... 716-839-8538. 322 E pbeaman@daemen.edu
BEAMAN, Riley ... 910-576-6222. 362 C beamanr@montgomery.edu
BEAMAN, Warren, J ... 503-517-1050. 408 H wbeaman@warnerpacific.edu
BEAMON, Cynthia ... 919-546-8476. 366 E cbeamon@shawu.edu
BEAMON, Stanley ... 312-850-7038. 142 C sbeamon3@ccc.edu
BEAMON, Vincent, L ... 252-335-3299. 367 C vlbeamon@mail.ecsu.edu
BEAN, Al ... 207-780-5588. 212 H albean@usm.maine.edu
BEAN, Athena ... 325-649-8810. 473 F abean@hputx.edu
BEAN, Carlena ... 207-941-7064. 210 B beanc@husson.edu
BEAN, Christopher, A ..... 540-665-4553. 509 E cbean@su.edu
BEAN, Debra ... 858-642-8106... 55 J dbean@nu.edu
BEAN, Ethelle, S ... 605-256-5205. 451 H ethelle.bean@dsu.edu
BEAN, Gary ... 315-792-7106. 346 C gary.bean@sunyit.edu
BEAN, Kellie, H ... 802-626-6406. 501 E kellie.bean@lyndonstate.edu
BEAN, Nancy ... 731-352-4000. 453 D beann@bethelu.edu
BEAN, Norma, P ... 713-313-4420. 485 F bean_np@tsu.edu
BEAN, Paul ... 785-242-5200. 189 I paul.bean@ottawa.edu
BEAN, Shirley ... 206-878-3710. 520 E sbean@highline.edu
BEAN, Steve ... 218-322-2351. 258 I steve.bean@itascacc.edu
BEAR, William ... 763-433-1132. 257 Q william.bear@anokaramsey.edu
BEARCE, Jacqueline, S ... 413-542-2354. 221 G jsbearce@amherst.edu
BEARCE, John ... 702-651-7454. 294 E john.bearce@csn.edu
BEARD, Aileen ... 218-723-6000. 254 K abeard@css.edu
BEARD, Casey ... 541-278-5838. 402 C cbeard@bluedd.edu
BEARD, David ... 706-880-8175. 128 A dbeard@lagrange.edu
BEARD, John, P ... 843-349-6441. 442 E johnb@coastal.edu
BEARD, Richard, L ... 717-867-6363. 421 H rbeard@lvc.edu
BEARD, Russell ... 425-564-4200. 517 A russ.beard@bellevuecollege.edu
BEARD, Scott ... 304-876-5370. 529 I sbeard@shepherd.edu
BEARD, Timothy, L ... 727-816-3413. 110 E beardt@phcc.edu
BEARDMORE, Kevin ... 270-686-4504. 196 C kevin.beardmore@kctcs.edu
BEARDMORE, Melissa, A ... 410-777-2532. 213 D mabeardmore@aacc.edu
BEARDSLEE, Bill ... 603-899-4188. 296 H beardsleeb@franklinpierce.edu
BEARDSLEY, Kathleen .... 215-572-2838. 409 H beardsley@arcadia.edu
BEARE, Paul ... 559-278-0210... 33 D pbeare@csufresno.edu
BEARMAN, Alan ... 785-670-1855. 191 D alan.bearman@washburn.edu
BEARROWS, Thomas, R . 217-333-0563. 161 C bearrows@uillinois.edu
BEARROWS, Thomas, R . 312-996-7762. 161 D bearrows@uillinois.edu
BEARSS, Carrie ... 810-989-5501. 249 H cbearss@sc4.edu
BEARY, Richard ... 407-823-5242. 115 E richard.beary@ucf.edu
BEASIMER, Linda, M ... 845-431-8979. 323 C beasimer@sunydutchess.edu
BEASLEY, Barbara ... 941-907-2262. 103 C bbeasley@evergladesuniversity.edu
BEASLEY, David ... 870-972-2088... 19 N dbeasley@astate.edu
BEASLEY, Jack, D ... 757-446-5035. 504 E beaslejd@evms.edu
BEASLEY, Linda ... 706-821-8316. 130 C lbeasley@paine.edu
BEASLEY, Lori ... 405-974-3371. 400 K lbeasley@uco.edu
BEASLEY, Marcia ... 330-263-2165. 377 H mbeasley@wooster.edu
BEASLEY, Sharon ... 203-576-6262... 91 D sharon.beasley@stvincentscollege.edu
BEASLEY, Susan, S ... 434-832-7742. 512 A beasleys@cvcc.vccs.edu
BEATA, Anthony ... 239-280-2577... 98 K tony.beata@avemaria.edu
BEATRICE, Jonelle ... 330-941-1450. 394 A jabeatrice@ysu.edu
BEATSON, Bonnie ... 808-235-7374. 137 C beatson@hawaii.edu
BEATTIE, George, A ... 218-723-6562. 254 K gbeattie@css.edu
BEATTIE, Linda ... 502-585-9911. 199 C lbeattie@spalding.edu
BEATTIE, Martha, J ... 603-646-2258. 296 G martha.j.beattie@dartmouth.edu
BEATTY, Anthony ... 859-257-8200. 200 C a.beatty@uky.edu
BEATTY, Brian ... 415-338-6833... 35 E bjbeatty@sfsu.edu
BEATTY, Del ... 435-652-7514. 497 E beatty@dixie.edu
BEATTY, Kimberly, A ... 817-515-5636. 482 B kimberly.beatty@tccd.edu

BEATTY, Lisa, L .... 563-588-8000. 178 D
lbeatty@emmaus.edu
BEATTY, Paul, V .... 406-496-4198. 287 F
pbeatty@mtech.edu
BEATTY, Robert .... 856-256-4025. 305 E
beatty@rowan.edu
BEATTY, Scott .... 207-741-5832. 211 A
sbeatty@smccme.edu
BEATTY, Susan .... 503-725-5061. 406 B
susan.beatty@pdx.edu
BEATTY, Tracy .... 269-965-3931. 244 O
beattyt@kellogg.edu
BEATY, Katherine, M ...... 309-677-3107. 140 I
kbeaty@bradley.edu
BEATY, Lori .... 254-968-1885. 483 A
lbeaty@tarleton.edu
BEATY, Michael .... 303-368-7462... 84 B
BEATY, Vivian .... 313-845-9698. 243 H
vbeaty@hfcc.edu
BEAUBIEN, Richard .... 678-891-3237. 125 G
richard.beaubien@gpc.edu
BEAUCHAMP, Becky, M . 405-878-5420. 399 G
bmbeauchamp@stgregorys.edu
BEAUCHAMP, Darrell ..... 575-492-2676. 310 G
dbeauchamp@nmjc.edu
BEAUCHAMP, Denise ...... 610-526-6665. 417 H
dbeauchamp@harcum.edu
BEAUCHAMP, CSC,
E. William .... 503-943-7101. 408 F
beaucham@up.edu
BEAUCHAMP, Eddie .... 678-407-5381. 125 B
ebeauchamp@ggc.edu
BEAUCHAMP, Lance ...... 904-256-7067. 107 Q
lbeauch@ju.edu
BEAUCHAMP, Mary Jo ... 812-749-1399. 171 K
mbeauchamp@oak.edu
BEAUCHAMP, Robin, L .. 401-254-3244. 440 B
rbeauchamp@rwu.edu
BEAUCHAMP-OCASIO,
René .... 787-250-0000. 553 G
rene.beauchamp@upr.edu
BEAUDIN, Giselda .... 407-646-2466. 111 Q
gbeaudin@rollins.edu
BEAUDOIN, Amy, L .... 606-679-8501. 196 D
amy.beaudoin@kctcs.edu
BEAUDOIN, Susan .... 518-381-1327. 340 G
beaudose@sunysccc.edu
BEAUGH, Richard .... 985-549-2000. 208 C
richard.beaugh@selu.edu
BEAUJON, Francis .... 530-257-6181... 50 F
fbeaujon@lassencollege.edu
BEAULIEU, Adrian, G ...... 401-865-2114. 439 E
abeaulie@providence.edu
BEAULIEU, Ellen .... 207-602-2334. 213 A
ebeaulieu@une.edu
BEAULIEU, Gary, R .... 317-940-9624. 164 J
gbeaulie@butler.edu
BEAULIEU, Sharen .... 207-602-2339. 213 A
sbeaulieu@une.edu
BEAUMONT, Karen .... 413-528-7293. 222 E
karen@simons-rock.edu
BEAUPRE, David, R .... 412-396-6063. 415 F
beaupred@duq.edu
BEAUPRE, Walter .... 302-736-2436... 94 C
security@wesley.edu
BEAUPRE', Eugene, L ..... 513-745-4271. 393 H
beaupre@xavier.edu
BEAUREGARD, Amy .... 410-644-6400. 218 G
BEAUREGARD, Debbie ... 603-228-1541. 298 D
dbeauregard@piercelaw.edu
BEAUREGARD, Jill .... 320-589-6036. 264 F
beaureja@morris.umn.edu
BEAUREGARD, Kathy ...... 269-387-3061. 252 I
kathy.beauregard@wmich.edu
BEAUREGARD, Michelle 401-232-6722. 438 K
mbeaureg@bryant.edu
BEAUREGARD, Stephen . 508-565-1375. 237 A
sbeauregard@stonehill.edu
BEAUVAIS, Laura .... 401-874-4341. 440 D
beauvais@uri.edu
BEAVER, Jeff, S .... 864-388-8208. 444 K
jbeaver@lander.edu
BEAVER, John .... 979-830-4000. 467 I
BEAVER, John .... 979-209-7300. 467 I
john.beaver@blinn.edu
BEAVER, Kevin .... 301-937-8448. 218 H
kbeaver@tesst.com
BEAVER, Mark, P .... 804-758-6764. 513 G
mbeaver@rappahannock.edu
BEAVER, Mindi .... 609-984-1114. 308 A
mbeaver@tesc.edu
BEAVER, Shirley .... 515-643-6615. 181 A
sbeaver@mercydesmoines.org
BEAVERS, Dennis .... 316-264-1580. 162 I
dennis.beavers@vatterott-college.edu
BEAVERS, Dennis .... 314-264-1580. 293 D
dennis.beavers@vatterott-college.edu
BEAVERS, Dennis .... 314-264-1500. 284 G
dennis.beavers@vatterott-college.edu
BEAVERS, Gerald .... 502-456-6509. 199 F
gbeavers@sctd.edu

BEAVERS, Judy .... 517-321-0242. 243 F
jbeavers@glcc.edu
BEAVERS, Philip, E .... 517-321-0242. 243 F
pbeavers@glcc.edu
BEAZER, Ken .... 435-865-8354. 497 A
beazer@suu.edu
BEBBER, Glenda, H .... 704-233-8242. 370 G
gbebber@wingate.edu
BEBENSEE, Mark, A .... 843-953-5156. 442 A
mark.bebensee@citadel.edu
BECENTI, Delores .... 505-786-4104. 310 D
dbecenti@navajotech.edu
BECERRA, Cynthia .... 209-478-0800... 47 M
cbecerra@humphreys.edu
BECERRA, Gilbert .... 361-698-2474. 471 G
gbecerra@delmar.edu
BECERRA-FERNANDEZ,
Irma .... 305-348-2000. 115 B
Irma.Fernandez@fiu.edu
BECHARD, Matthew .... 785-243-1435. 185 M
mbechard@cloud.edu
BECHER, Amy .... 724-589-2182. 434 B
abecher@thiel.edu
BECHER, Eric .... 606-218-5282. 200 F
ericbecher@upike.edu
BECHER, Gregory, J .... 805-525-4417... 69 H
gbecher@thomasaquinas.edu
BECHERER, Bob .... 618-468-3700. 150 G
rbecherer@lc.edu
BECHERER, Jack, J .... 815-921-4001. 157 A
j.becherer@rockvalleycollege.edu
BECHERER, Jeffery .... 212-431-2158. 333 I
jeffery.becherer@nyls.edu
BECHTEL, Brian .... 816-604-3036. 277 G
brian.bechtel@mcckc.edu
BECHTEL, Janice, L .... 419-783-2444. 379 C
jbechtel@defiance.edu
BECHTOLD, Brad .... 864-294-3166. 444 C
brad.bechtold@furman.edu
BECHTOLD, Julie .... 312-261-3270. 153 I
julie.bechtold@nl.edu
BECK, Alan .... 617-327-6777. 233 D
alan_beck@mspp.edu
BECK, Alissa .... 513-244-4892. 377 G
alissa_beck@mail.msj.edu
BECK, Anne, D .... 313-664-7473. 241 C
abeck@collegeforcreativestudies.edu
BECK, Barbara, E .... 518-580-5800. 341 A
bbeck@skidmore.edu
BECK, Carina .... 406-994-4353. 287 B
cbeck@montana.edu
BECK, Cherie .... 517-371-5140. 250 G
beckc@cooley.edu
BECK, Chris .... 512-313-3000. 469 L
chris.beck@concordia.edu
BECK, Deborah .... 803-777-3957. 447 G
dbeck@gwm.sc.edu
BECK, Deborah, C .... 803-777-3957. 447 G
dbeck@sc.edu
BECK, Erika .... 702-992-2500. 294 G
erika.beck@nsc.edu
BECK, Jeffrey .... 908-737-5900. 302 F
jbeck@kean.edu
BECK, Jen .... 512-245-2152. 487 C
jb32@txstate.edu
BECK, Jennifer .... 225-768-1779. 206 D
jbeck@ololcollege.edu
BECK, Joan .... 773-256-0756. 152 B
jbeck@lstc.edu
BECK, Jocelyn, M .... 610-799-1155. 421 I
jbeck@lccc.edu
BECK, John .... 517-750-1200. 250 E
jbeck@arbor.edu
BECK, Julie .... 417-268-6004. 271 I
jbeck@gobbc.edu
BECK, Kenneth, L .... 606-474-3135. 194 H
kbeck@kcu.edu
BECK, Leesa .... 805-893-4165... 72 B
leesa.beck@sa.ucsb.edu
BECK, Lynn .... 209-946-2680... 73 A
lbeck@pacific.edu
BECK, Margaret, Z .... 941-752-5597. 114 I
beckm@scf.edu
BECK, Marilyn, C .... 256-306-2555..... 2 F
mcb@calhoun.edu
BECK, Maryann, M .... 334-833-4522..... 4 D
mbeck@huntingdon.edu
BECK, Maureen, A .... 443-334-2231. 218 E
mbeck@stevenson.edu
BECK, Morgan .... 620-223-2700. 186 G
morganb@fortscott.edu
BECK, Pam .... 567-661-7334. 387 L
pamela_beck@owens.edu
BECK, Richard .... 918-343-7615. 399 C
rbeck@rsu.edu
BECK, Ronda .... 859-257-4759. 200 C
rsbeck0@uky.edu
BECK, Ronda .... 517-371-5140. 250 G
beckr@cooley.edu
BECK, Stacie .... 480-423-6536... 15 E
stacie.beck@scottsdalecc.edu

BECK-DUDLEY, Caryn .... 850-644-3090. 115 C
cbeckdudley@cob.fsu.edu
BECK-LITTLE, Rebecca .... 704-406-4358. 354 C
rbeck-little@gardner-webb.edu
BECKEMEYER, Wendy .... 412-365-1100. 412 K
wbeckemeyer@chatham.edu
BECKEMEYER,
Wendy, C .... 412-397-5255. 431 I
beckemeyer@rmu.edu
BECKENHAUER,
Charles, D .... 254-710-3821. 467 G
charles_beckenhauer@baylor.edu
BECKER, Barbara .... 817-272-3071. 491 B
bbecker@uta.edu
BECKER, Bart .... 425-564-3081. 517 A
bart.becker@bellevuecollege.edu
BECKER, Brian .... 815-753-8980. 154 I
bbecker@niu.edu
BECKER, Bryan .... 312-413-8202. 161 D
bryanb@uic.edu
BECKER, Carol .... 212-854-9847. 321 D
cbecker@columbia.edu
BECKER, Charles, P .... 304-384-5190. 529 E
beckerc@concord.edu
BECKER, Dennis, M .... 303-871-3897... 86 B
dbecker@du.edu
BECKER, Elizabeth, M ..... 708-209-3020. 143 E
elizabeth.becker@cuchicago.edu
BECKER, Frederick, W .... 570-326-3761. 427 B
fbecker@pct.edu
BECKER, J. Thomas .... 215-951-2945. 430 E
beckert@philau.edu
BECKER, Janine .... 570-408-8009. 437 F
janine.becker@wilkes.edu
BECKER, Jim .... 812-855-4884. 167 F
jambecke@indiana.edu
BECKER, Jonathan .... 845-758-7378. 314 D
jbecker@bard.edu
BECKER, Joyce, D .... 573-651-2189. 282 B
jbecker@semo.edu
BECKER, Joyce, K .... 443-352-4031. 218 E
jbecker@stevenson.edu
BECKER, Karen .... 815-802-8405. 149 C
kbecker@kcc.edu
BECKER, Karl, D .... 215-222-4200. 431 H
kbecker@walnuthillcollege.edu
BECKER, Kurt .... 718-260-3608. 336 E
kbecker@poly.edu
BECKER, Larry .... 951-785-2460... 50 B
lbecker@lasierra.edu
BECKER, Linda .... 402-486-2507. 292 E
libecker@ucollege.edu
BECKER, Lois, S .... 904-256-7030. 107 Q
lbecker1@ju.edu
BECKER, Mark, P .... 404-413-1300. 126 E
mbecker@gsu.edu
BECKER, Mary .... 507-457-1503. 264 A
mbecker@smumn.edu
BECKER, Mike .... 925-439-2181... 42 A
mbecker@losmedanos.edu
BECKER, Nancy .... 973-618-3314. 300 A
nbecker@caldwell.edu
BECKER, Pete, D .... 708-209-3092. 143 E
pete.becker@cuchicago.edu
BECKER, Raymond .... 215-567-7080. 410 A
rbecker@aii.edu
BECKER, Richard, A .... 561-868-3137. 110 C
beckerr@palmbeachstate.edu
BECKER, Ron .... 201-761-6415. 306 L
rbecker@saintpeters.edu
BECKER, S. Ann .... 321-674-7327. 104 H
abecker@fit.edu
BECKER, Scott .... 517-355-2070. 246 H
beckersc@msu.edu
BECKER, Sheila, R .... 563-556-5110. 181 C
beckers@nicc.edu
BECKER, Stefan .... 718-960-8764. 318 A
stefan.becker@lehman.cuny.edu
BECKER-CORNBLATT,
Robin, A .... 240-500-2000. 215 B
rabecker-cornblatt@hagerstowncc.edu
BECKER-GORBY, Sherry . 304-434-8000. 528 A
sherrybg@eastern.wvnet.edu
BECKER-RICHARDS,
Joicy .... 609-497-7900. 304 D
joicy.becker@ptsem.edu
BECKETT, Alice .... 415-503-6251... 62 H
abeckett@sfcm.edu
BECKETT, Keith .... 330-263-2500. 377 H
kbeckett@wooster.edu
BECKETT, Thomas, A ...... 203-432-1414... 93 A
thomas.beckett@yale.edu
BECKFORD, John, S .... 864-294-2007. 444 C
john.beckford@furman.edu
BECKHORN, Roy .... 916-568-3190... 52 K
beckhor@losrios.edu
BECKLER, Larry .... 843-525-8282. 447 C
lbeckler@tcl.edu
BECKLEY, Clark .... 913-234-0609. 185 L
clark.beckley@cleveland.edu

BECKLEY, David, L .... 662-252-2491. 269 F
dlbeckley@rustcollege.edu
BECKLEY, Gemma .... 662-252-8000. 269 F
gbeckley@rustcollege.edu
BECKMAN, Donald, C ..... 503-370-6315. 408 J
dbeckman@willamette.edu
BECKMAN, John, H .... 212-998-6848. 334 D
john.beckman@nyu.edu
BECKMANN, Terry, J ...... 207-786-8339. 209 F
tbeckman@bates.edu
BECKNER, Scott .... 478-445-5800. 125 A
scott.beckner@gcsu.edu
BECKS, Crystal .... 661-654-3012... 32 H
cbecks@csub.edu
BECKSTED, Scott, M ...... 315-470-4992. 345 B
smbeckst@esf.edu
BECKSTROM, Brian, A .... 319-352-8217. 183 E
brian.beckstrom@wartburg.edu
BECKSTROM, Robert, A .. 440-365-5222. 383 B
BECKSTROM, Ronald ...... 651-793-1889. 259 C
ronald.beckstrom@metrostate.edu
BECKUM, Randy .... 913-971-3461. 188 H
rbeckum@mnu.edu
BECKWITCH, Peter .... 517-437-7341. 243 I
peter.beckwitch@hillsdale.edu
BECKWITH, Cynthia, A ... 909-621-8512... 46 H
cynthia_beckwith@hmc.edu
BECKWITH, Ryan .... 661-395-4266... 49 N
ryan.beckwith@bakersfieldcollege.edu
BECKWITH, Steven V, W 510-987-9436... 70 H
steven.beckwith@ucop.edu
BECTON, Charles, L .... 252-335-3228. 367 C
clbecton@mail.ecsu.edu
BEDAR, Gerald, J .... 440-943-7600. 388 J
jerrybednar@juno.com
BEDARD, Martha .... 860-486-0497... 92 A
martha.bedard@uconn.edu
BEDARD, Martha .... 505-277-4241. 312 F
mbedard@unm.edu
BEDARD, Richard, F .... 413-205-3532. 221 F
richard.bedard@aic.edu
BEDASHI, Allan, M .... 304-336-5100. 530 A
abedashi@westliberty.edu
BEDDALL, Tina .... 559-278-2191... 33 D
tina_beddall@csufresno.edu
BEDDALL, Tina .... 559-278-6111... 33 D
tina_beddall@csufresno.edu
BEDDO, Leslie .... 785-242-2067. 189 D
lbeddo@neosho.edu
BEDDOW, Lucinda .... 256-306-2784..... 2 F
lmb@calhoun.edu
BEDELL, Frank .... 803-754-4100. 443 C
BEDENBAUGH, Diana, L 864-488-4589. 444 L
dbedenbaugh@limestone.edu
BEDFORD, Allen .... 267-502-2567. 410 I
allen.bedford@brynathyn.edu
BEDFORD, Chris .... 781-736-3432. 224 F
cbedford@brandeis.edu
BEDFORD, John .... 405-208-5322. 397 F
jbedford@okcu.edu
BEDFORD, Laura .... 315-792-3179. 349 F
lbedford@utica.edu
BEDFORD, Norm .... 702-774-8000. 294 I
norm.bedford@unlv.edu
BEDI, Param, S .... 570-577-1557. 411 A
param.bedi@bucknell.edu
BEDINI, Ken .... 860-465-5247... 87 L
bedini@easternct.edu
BEDITZ, Stephen .... 518-956-8120. 341 D
sbeditz@albany.edu
BEDNAR, Cynthia .... 610-436-2231. 430 A
cbednar@wcupa.edu
BEDNAR, Jean .... 847-628-2087. 149 B
jean.bednar@judsonu.edu
BEDNARZ, Bridgette .... 254-968-9271. 483 A
bednarz@tarleton.edu
BEDNEY, Elynda, A .... 269-471-6040. 239 D
bedney@andrews.edu
BEDOYA, Eduardo .... 231-777-0332. 247 G
eduardo.bedoya@muskegoncc.edu
BEDOYA, Theresa .... 410-225-2434. 216 C
tbedoya@mica.edu
BEDTKE, James .... 507-457-1458. 264 A
jbedtke@smumn.edu
BEDWELL, Pamela .... 478-757-2666. 128 I
pamela.bedwell@maconstate.edu
BEE, Allan, C .... 530-898-6322... 33 A
abee@csuchico.edu
BEE, Richard .... 562-903-4728... 29 L
richard.e.bee@biola.edu
BEE, Timothy, S .... 520-621-1737... 18 F
timbee@email.arizona.edu
BEEBE, Barbara, R .... 325-574-6501. 494 K
bbeebe@wtc.edu
BEEBE, Craig .... 504-865-3579. 205 H
cwbeebe@loyno.edu
BEEBE, Gayle, D .... 805-565-6024... 76 D
president@westmont.edu
BEEBE, Norman .... 413-775-1333. 231 E
beebe@gcc.mass.edu

BEEBE, Robert, D .... 909-593-3511... 72 E
rbeebe@laverne.edu
BEEBE, Rose .... 304-424-8286. 530 E
rose.beebe@wvup.edu
BEECH, Amanda .... 661-255-1050... 31 C
abeech@calarts.edu
BEECH, Bettina .... 601-984-1020. 270 C
bbeech@umc.edu
BEECH, JR., Derrick .... 404-756-5294. 129 E
dbeech@msm.edu
BEECH, Rachel, A .... 520-621-6123... 18 F
rabeech@email.arizona.edu
BEECHAM, Sarah .... 706-649-1800. 123 E
sbeecham@columbustech.edu
BEECHER, Brian .... 847-543-2464. 143 A
bbeecher@clcillinois.edu
BEECHING,
Angela Myles .... 617-585-1118. 234 I
angela.beeching@necmusic.edu
BEEHLER, John .... 412-397-5445. 431 I
beehler@rmu.edu
BEEKE, Joel, R .... 616-977-0599. 249 B
BEEKMAN, Emily .... 646-717-9761. 325 B
registrar@gts.edu
BEEKMAN, William, R .... 517-353-9818. 246 H
beekman@msu.edu
BEELEN, Joan .... 616-957-6027. 240 M
jrb44@calvinseminary.edu
BEELER, Jeremy .... 908-835-2301. 308 G
jbeeler@warren.edu
BEELER, Shannon .... 720-855-6014... 82 C
shannonb@heritage-education.com
BEELER, Sydney .... 816-604-1070. 277 C
sydney.beeler@mcckc.edu
BEEMAN, Greg .... 845-675-4417. 335 C
greg.beeman@nyack.edu
BEEMER, Elizabeth .... 937-376-6444. 376 E
ebeemer@centralstate.edu
BEEMER, Matthew .... 904-596-2473. 117 H
mbeemer@tbc.edu
BEEMER, Pamela .... 847-491-7505. 155 D
p-beemer@northwestern.edu
BEEN, Sharon, A .... 501-882-8836... 19 M
sabeen@asub.edu
BEENK, Rose .... 775-831-1314. 295 F
rbeenk@sierranevada.edu
BEER, Jenny .... 574-535-7474. 166 A
jlbeer@goshen.edu
BEER, Laura .... 503-699-3361. 404 C
lbeer@maryhurst.edu
BEER, Linda .... 507-389-7351. 261 E
linda.beer@southcentral.edu
BEER, Patrick .... 478-387-4720. 125 E
pbeer@gmc.cc.ga.us
BEER, Richard .... 360-486-8784. 522 G
jrbeer@stmartin.edu
BEERS, David .... 253-879-3902. 524 F
dbeers@pugetsound.edu
BEERS, George, S .... 650-949-7077... 44 N
beersgeorge@foothill.edu
BEERS, Josh .... 717-560-8240. 421 A
jbeers@lbc.edu
BEERS, Maggie .... 415-338-3613... 35 E
mbeers@sfsu.edu
BEERS, Peter .... 717-560-8267. 421 A
pbeers@lbc.edu
BEERS, Robert .... 406-657-1124. 288 B
robert.beers@rocky.edu
BEERS, Stephen, T .... 479-524-7252... 21 G
sbeers@jbu.edu
BEERY, Kevin, E .... 610-917-1401. 436 C
kebeery@vfcc.edu
BEERY, Wendy .... 610-917-1429. 436 C
wmbeery@vfcc.edu
BEESON, Duane, L .... 712-707-7116. 181 H
beeson@nwciowa.edu
BEESON, Patricia, E .... 412-624-4223. 435 C
beeson@pitt.edu
BEETS, A. Ray .... 319-296-4042. 178 J
aurel.beets@hawkeyecollege.edu
BEETS, Shannon .... 775-831-1314. 295 F
sbeets@sierranevada.edu
BEEZHOLD, Philip, D ..... 616-526-6481. 240 L
pdb2@calvin.edu
BEG, Christina .... 216-397-1998. 381 R
cbeg@jcu.edu
BEGANY, James .... 724-357-7544. 428 F
jbegany@iup.edu
BEGAY, Darryl, R .... 928-724-6698... 13 H
darbegay@dinecollege.edu
BEGAY, Janice .... 785-749-8419. 187 B
janice.begay@bie.edu
BEGAY, Karen, F .... 520-626-9809... 18 F
kfbegay@email.arizona.edu
BEGGETT, Kimberly .... 352-638-9727... 99 B
kbaggett@beaconcollege.edu
BEGIN, Gene .... 781-239-4512. 222 D
gbegin@babson.edu
BEGLEY, John, B .... 270-384-8505. 197 D
begleyj@lindsey.edu
BEGLEY, Mary Ann .... 415-338-2722... 35 E
begley@sfsu.edu
BEGLEY, Thomas .... 518-276-2525. 337 I
begley@rpi.edu
BEGLINGER, Claire, M ... 262-524-7242. 532 C
cbegling@carrollu.edu
BEHAN, C. Joseph .... 315-655-7284. 316 E
jbehan@cazenovia.edu
BEHAN KRAUS,
Carolyn, A .... 203-773-8521... 87 G
cbehan@albertus.edu
BEHAUNEK, Luke .... 515-961-1562. 182 E
luke.behaunek@simpson.edu
BEHBEHANI, Khosrow ... 817-272-2571. 491 B
kb@uta.edu
BEHE, Phil .... 252-399-6528. 352 F
pbehe@barton.edu
BEHEN, Joseph .... 312-499-4272. 158 L
jbehen@saic.edu
BEHLING, Laura, L .... 309-341-7216. 150 A
llbehling@knox.edu
BEHLING, Laura, L .... 317-940-9278. 164 J
lbehling@butler.edu
BEHM, Bonnie Lee .... 610-519-6456. 436 F
bonnie.behm@villanova.edu
BEHM, Rhonda, K .... 651-641-8894. 255 B
rbehm@csp.edu
BEHMER, Scott .... 440-610-2240. 131 H
sbehmer@southuniversity.edu
BEHN, Julie .... 408-944-6121. 182 A
julie.behn@palmer.edu
BEHR, Fred, C .... 507-786-3636. 264 B
behr@stolaf.edu
BEHR, John .... 914-961-8313. 340 B
jbehr@svots.edu
BEHR, Kate, E .... 914-337-9300. 321 E
kate.behr@concordia-ny.edu
BEHR, Michelle .... 970-351-2707... 86 C
michelle.behr@unco.edu
BEHR, Richard, A .... 239-590-7399. 115 A
rbehr@fgcu.edu
BEHRE, William .... 609-771-2797. 300 E
behre@tcnj.edu
BEHRENDT, William, M . 214-648-6342. 493 E
william.behrendt@utsouthwestern.edu
BEHRENS, Ann .... 217-228-5432. 156 C
behrens@quincy.edu
BEHRENS, James .... 516-572-7700. 332 C
james.behrens@ncc.edu
BEHRENS, Kim .... 559-791-2322... 49 P
kbehrens@portervillecollege.edu
BEHRENS, Susanne .... 713-623-2040. 466 G
sbehrens@aii.edu
BEHRENS, Troy, T .... 214-768-2288. 481 A
tbehrens@smu.edu
BEHRS, David .... 562-902-3345... 67 H
davebehrs@scuhs.edu
BEHRS, David .... 562-902-3345... 67 H
davidbehrs@scuhs.edu
BEHUL, Paula .... 561-297-3004. 114 L
pbehul@fau.edu
BEHUNEK, Sarah .... 303-458-3535... 84 M
sbehunek@regis.edu
BEI, Yongshun .... 516-739-1545. 333 F
clinicdirector@nyctcm.edu
BEIDLEMAN, David, C ... 717-361-1493. 415 H
beidlemand@etown.edu
BEIER, Nancy, A .... 410-777-2834. 213 D
nabeier@aacc.edu
BEIERSCHMITT, Bill .... 918-338-8030. 399 C
bbeierschmitt@rsu.edu
BEIKIRCH, Dale .... 432-685-5539. 476 G
dbeikirch@midland.edu
BEIL, Cheryl .... 202-994-6712... 95 D
cbeil@gwu.edu
BEIL, Don .... 202-651-5005... 95 C
don.beil@gallaudet.edu
BEILBY, Rod .... 530-741-6838... 77 M
rbeilby@yccd.edu
BEILBY, Rodney .... 530-741-6707... 77 M
rbeilby@yccd.edu
BEINHOFF, Lisa .... 575-835-5615. 310 F
lbeinhoff@admin.nmt.edu
BEIRNE, Chris .... 706-385-1120. 130 F
chris.beirne@point.edu
BEIRNE, Jay .... 617-578-7100. 236 E
jbeirne@sbboston.com
BEISECKER, Mark .... 805-893-4071... 72 B
mark.beisecker@bkstr.ucsb.edu
BEISWANGER,
Robert, C .... 716-839-8218. 322 E
rbeiswan@daemen.edu
BEITEL, Leland .... 443-334-2064. 218 E
lbeitel@stevenson.edu
BEITEY, George .... 619-388-7860... 62 F
gbeitey@sdccd.edu
BEITL, Thomas, R .... 330-972-8643. 390 E
tbeitl@uakron.edu
BEITNER, Veronica .... 616-632-2458. 239 E
beitnver@aquinas.edu
BEITTEL, Lisa, B .... 508-421-5913. 229 C
Lisa.Beittel@umassmed.edu
BEITZEL, Vernon, L .... 540-464-7211. 515 B
beitzelvl@vmi.edu
BEJAR, Elizabeth .... 305-348-2151. 115 B
elizabeth.bejar@fiu.edu
BEJNAROWICZ, Ewa ...... 312-553-3193. 141 N
ebejnarowicz@ccc.edu
BEKKEN, Joseph .... 208-769-3368. 138 I
jmbekken@nic.edu
BEKRITSKY, Brett .... 845-848-7405. 322 G
brett.bekritsky@dc.edu
BELAND, Thomas .... 802-773-5900. 499 B
tom.beland@csj.edu
BELANGER, OFM,
Brian, C .... 518-783-5047. 340 J
bbelanger@siena.edu
BELANGER, David, J ...... 413-585-2530. 236 H
dbelange@smith.edu
BELANGER, Elise .... 617-296-8300. 227 I
elise_belanger@laboure.edu
BELANGER, Lisa .... 860-768-4666... 92 D
belanger@hartford.edu
BELAUSKAS, August, J .. 847-566-6401. 162 G
gbelauskas@usml.edu
BELCHER, C. Gary .... 512-313-3000. 469 L
charles.belcher@concordia.edu
BELCHER, Carol .... 843-574-6230. 447 E
carol.belcher@tridenttech.edu
BELCHER, Chris .... 918-495-6529. 398 H
cbelcher@oru.edu
BELCHER, Chris, P .... 701-483-2984. 371 D
chris.belcher@dickinsonstate.edu
BELCHER, David, O .... 828-227-7100. 369 E
dbelcher@wcu.edu
BELCHER, Elizabeth, M .. 304-929-5464. 528 D
ebelcher@newriver.edu
BELCHER, Keith, E .... 912-279-5922. 123 B
kbelcher@ccga.edu
BELCHER, Michael .... 978-934-3929. 229 B
michael_belcher@uml.edu
BELCHER, Michael .... 209-946-2537... 73 A
mbelcher@pacific.edu
BELCHER, Nicholas .... 617-850-1297. 227 E
nbelcher@hchc.edu
BELCHER, Tim .... 540-365-4366. 504 L
tbelcher@ferrum.edu
BELCHER, Trevor .... 415-738-8042... 56 A
BELD, Jo, M .... 507-786-3910. 264 B
beld@stolaf.edu
BELDAN, Chris .... 717-290-8755. 421 D
cbeldan@lancasterseminary.edu
BELDEN, Eric .... 330-490-7337. 392 H
ebelden@walsh.edu
BELDON, William .... 360-992-2103. 518 A
wbeldon@clark.edu
BELEN-NAZARIO, Lillian 787-620-2040. 547 C
lbelen@aupr.edu
BELEW, Paul, D .... 214-648-6062. 493 E
paul.belew@utsouthwestern.edu
BELEW, Valerie, S .... 615-353-3342. 461 B
valerie.belew@nscc.edu
BELFIELD, Sherri .... 704-378-1032. 355 K
sbelfield@jcsu.edu
BELFIORE, Michael .... 718-289-5338. 317 B
michael.belfiore@bcc.cuny.edu
BELFIORE, Phil, J .... 814-824-2268. 423 J
pbelfiore@mercyhurst.edu
BELIN, Jackie .... 908-526-1200. 305 B
jbelin@raritanval.edu
BELIN, Joanne .... 205-970-9215..... 7 B
jbelin@sebc.edu
BELINSKI, Victor .... 909-274-4365... 55 A
vbelinski@mtsac.edu
BELISLE, William, R .... 504-284-5539. 206 K
wbelisle@suno.edu
BELK, Peter .... 913-469-8500. 187 J
pbelk@jccc.edu
BELK, Wesley, C .... 864-429-8728. 448 G
wcbelk@mailbox.sc.edu
BELKIN, Betsey .... 440-646-8184. 392 D
bbelkin@ursuline.edu
BELKNAP, Cindy .... 570-577-3654. 411 A
cindy.belknap@bucknell.edu
BELKNAP, Peggy .... 928-536-6231... 16 E
peggy.belknap@npc.edu
BELKO, Dawn .... 763-424-0715. 260 C
dbelko@nhcc.edu
BELL, Aimee .... 440-826-2071. 374 F
abell@bw.edu
BELL, Amy .... 870-743-3000... 22 B
abell@northark.edu
BELL, Angela .... 304-558-1112. 529 C
abell@hepc.wvnet.edu
BELL, Brett .... 619-388-7810... 62 F
bbell@sdccd.edu
BELL, Bryon .... 916-608-6500... 53 C
BELL, Chris .... 940-552-6291. 493 F
cbell@vernoncollege.edu
BELL, Christina .... 847-259-1840. 141 L
cbell@christianlifecollege.edu
BELL, Christopher A, R .. 207-768-9511. 212 G
chris.bell@umpi.edu
BELL, Corinne .... 802-387-6863. 499 E
corinnebell@landmark.edu
BELL, Cynthia, M .... 330-941-3101. 394 A
cmbell02@ysu.edu
BELL, Damon .... 360-475-7474. 521 H
dbell@olympic.edu
BELL, Daniel, R .... 304-462-4132. 529 G
dan.bell@glenville.edu
BELL, Danielle .... 803-321-5128. 445 G
danielle.bell@newberry.edu
BELL, David, D .... 614-823-1300. 387 K
dbell@otterbein.edu
BELL, Dean .... 312-322-1791. 160 D
dbell@spertus.edu
BELL, Denise .... 508-793-2397. 225 B
dbell@holycross.edu
BELL, Denise .... 850-973-9481. 109 H
belld@nfcc.edu
BELL, Geraldine .... 205-929-1715..... 5 G
gbell@mail.miles.edu
BELL, Glenn, R .... 251-380-3099..... 7 D
bell@shc.edu
BELL, Gregory, J .... 570-321-4395. 422 H
bell@lycoming.edu
BELL, Gretchen, M .... 336-322-2154. 362 F
Gretchen.Bell@piedmontcc.edu
BELL, Harold .... 404-270-5269. 132 E
hbell@spelman.edu
BELL, Hershey .... 814-866-6641. 420 E
hbell@lecom.edu
BELL, Jacquelin .... 619-388-3428... 62 D
jbell@sdccd.edu
BELL, Jeff, W .... 903-923-3221. 486 A
jeff.bell@tstc.edu
BELL, Jennifer .... 856-256-4410. 305 E
bellj@rowan.edu
BELL, Jenny .... 205-665-6565..... 9 B
jbell8@montevallo.edu
BELL, John, D .... 801-422-3037. 495 D
john_bell@byu.edu
BELL, Jorge .... 415-239-3000... 38 L
jbell@ccsf.edu
BELL, Julie .... 217-228-5432. 156 C
bellju@quincy.edu
BELL, Juliette, B .... 410-651-6101. 219 E
jbbell@umes.edu
BELL, Karen .... 617-266-1400. 223 D
BELL, Kathleen .... 317-931-2305. 165 B
kbell@cts.edu
BELL, Kathleen .... 651-779-3438. 258 C
kathy.bell@century.edu
BELL, Katrina .... 386-506-3635. 101 G
bellk@daytonastate.edu
BELL, Kelli .... 740-593-4797. 387 C
bellk@ohio.edu
BELL, Kelly, A .... 864-662-6064. 441 B
kbell@andersonuniversity.edu
BELL, Laura .... 215-871-6609. 430 D
laurab@pcom.edu
BELL, Lauren, C .... 804-752-7268. 508 E
lbell@rmc.edu
BELL, Leia .... 860-512-2903... 88 G
lbell@manchestercc.edu
BELL, Leia .... 860-727-6967... 90 A
lbell@goodwin.edu
BELL, Lillie, F .... 318-357-6171. 208 B
bell@nsula.edu
BELL, Linda .... 610-372-4721. 431 D
lbell@racc.edu
BELL, Linda .... 212-854-2708. 314 G
labell@barnard.edu
BELL, Lisa, G .... 859-246-6564. 194 L
lisag.bell@kctcs.edu
BELL, Lynn .... 334-556-2223..... 3 N
lbell@wallace.edu
BELL, Marcus, V .... 803-376-5700. 441 A
mbell@allenuniversity.edu
BELL, Margaret, G .... 410-857-2203. 216 E
mbell@mcdaniel.edu
BELL, Marjorie .... 617-964-1100. 222 A
mbell@ants.edu
BELL, Marty .... 217-228-5432. 156 C
bellma@quincy.edu
BELL, Melleta .... 432-837-8388. 487 B
mbell@sulross.edu
BELL, Michael .... 847-259-1840. 141 L
mbell@christianlifecollege.edu
BELL, Mike .... 907-796-6140... 11 A
mike.bell@uas.alaska.edu
BELL, Norma, G .... 205-853-1200..... 5 B
ngbell@jeffstateonline.com
BELL, Pam .... 314-264-1852. 162 I
pam.bell@vatterott-college.edu
BELL, Pam .... 314-264-1852. 183 C
pam.bell@vatterott-college.edu
BELL, Pam .... 334-833-4570..... 4 D
0377mgr@fheg.follett.com
BELL, Pam .... 904-620-2372. 116 B
pbell@unf.edu

BELL, Pam .... 314-264-1852. 293 D
pam.bell@vatterott-college.edu
BELL, Patty .... 903-983-8678. 475 E
pbell@kilgore.edu
BELL, Paul .... 405-325-4411. 401 B
pbell@ou.edu
BELL, Rebecca .... 432-685-4556. 476 G
rbell@midland.edu
BELL, Richard, S .... 803-938-3715. 448 F
richbell@uscsumter.edu
BELL, Robert, H .... 626-585-7205... 58 F
rhbell@pasadena.edu
BELL, Roberta .... 615-322-4359. 463 G
roberta.bell@vanderbilt.edu
BELL, Ruffin .... 610-399-2240. 428 B
rbell@cheyney.edu
BELL, Scott .... 907-474-6265... 10 I
svbell2@alaska.edu
BELL, Sharon, B .... 401-874-2378. 440 D
sbbell@mail.uri.edu
BELL, Sheree .... 636-481-3119. 275 I
sbell6@jeffco.edu
BELL, Stephen .... 847-543-2238. 143 A
sbell@clcillinois.edu
BELL, Stephen .... 610-558-5549. 424 I
bells@neumann.edu
BELL, Steven, K .... 724-847-6530. 417 A
skbell@geneva.edu
BELL, Stuart, R .... 225-578-1519. 204 O
sbell@lsu.edu
BELL, Tommy .... 260-481-5443. 168 C
belljt@ipfw.edu
BELL, Trudy .... 805-546-3206... 42 C
tbell@cuesta.edu
BELL ADAMS, Sandra .... 718-262-2363. 319 F
sadams@york.cuny.edu
BELL-GARRISON,
Eileen, K .... 509-313-6533. 520 A
bellgarrison@gonzaga.edu
BELLA, Carlos .... 956-326-2347. 483 B
cbella@tamiu.edu
BELLACK, Janis, P .... 617-726-8002. 234 B
jbellack@mghihp.edu
BELLAFIORE, April .... 508-678-2811. 231 B
april.bellafiore@bristolcc.edu
BELLAH, Eric .... 865-981-8225. 456 D
eric.bellah@maryvillecollege.edu
BELLAIRS, Bart .... 985-549-2253. 208 C
bart.bellairs@selu.edu
BELLALTA, Maria .... 617-262-5000. 223 F
Maria.Bellalta@the-bac.edu
BELLAMEY, Tim .... 618-634-3221. 158 M
timb@shawneecc.edu
BELLAMY, Antoinette, P . 910-630-7257. 356 H
abellamy@methodist.edu
BELLAMY, Reagan .... 509-682-6445. 525 B
rbellamy@wvc.edu
BELLAMY, Sandra .... 212-694-1000. 315 E
sbellamy@boricuacollege.edu
BELLAMY, Scott .... 304-357-6696. 527 H
scottbellamy@ucwv.edu
BELLAMY, Timothy, R .... 919-530-5326. 368 A
timothy.bellamy@nccu.edu
BELLANCA, Rose .... 734-973-3491. 252 A
rbellanca@wccnet.edu
BELLANI, Raj .... 765-658-4622. 165 F
rajbellani@depauw.edu
BELLARDINE, Louis .... 212-851-0623. 321 D
lbellardine@columbia.edu
BELLAS, Peter .... 661-362-3144... 40 E
peter.bellas@canyons.edu
BELLATTI, Tom .... 918-495-7018. 398 H
tbellatti@oru.edu
BELLAVANCE, Leslie .... 607-871-2412. 313 E
bellavance@alfred.edu
BELLAVIA, Rand .... 716-829-7616. 323 D
bellavia@dyc.edu
BELLE, Walton, M .... 804-257-5885. 515 F
BELLE-ISLE,
G. Christopher .... 585-292-2271. 332 A
cbelleisle@monroecc.edu
BELLEFEUILLE, Kate .... 315-498-2291. 335 G
BELLEFEUILLLE,
Barbara, K .... 574-807-7250. 164 D
barb.bellefeuille@bethelcollege.edu
BELLEMAN, Ben .... 740-420-5933. 385 L
bbelleman@ohiochristian.edu
BELLER, Wendy .... 217-228-5432. 156 C
bellewe@quincy.edu
BELLICINI, Pierre, A .... 814-866-8121. 420 E
pbellicini@lecom.edu
BELLINA, Amy .... 732-571-3586. 303 C
abellina@monmouth.edu
BELLING, Karen .... 630-752-5021. 163 F
karen.belling@wheaton.edu
BELLINGER, Eunice .... 716-614-6450. 334 E
ebellinger@niagaracc.suny.edu
BELLINGER, Jesse .... 803-705-4326. 441 C
bellingerj@benedict.edu
BELLIPANNI, Domino ..... 662-246-6471. 268 B
dbellipanni@msdelta.edu
BELLIVEAU, Cynthia, L ... 802-656-3890. 500 F
cynthia.belliveau@uvm.edu
BELLO, Chippi .... 503-594-3099. 402 F
chippi@clackamas.edu
BELLO, Diane .... 631-632-6175. 342 C
diane.bello@stonybrook.edu
BELLO-BRUNSON,
Jane, M .... 219-464-6769. 174 E
jane.bellobrunson@valpo.edu
BELLO-DECASTRO,
Leigh .... 973-877-3484. 301 H
bellodecastro@essex.edu
BELLO-OGUNU, John .... 843-953-5079. 443 A
belloogunuj@cofc.edu
BELLOLI, Ronald .... 928-724-6676... 13 H
rbelloli@dinecollege.edu
BELLONA, Steven, J .... 315-859-4502. 325 E
sbellona@hamilton.edu
BELLONI, Francis, L .... 914-594-4110. 334 A
francis_belloni@nymc.edu
BELLOWS, Charlene, M .. 508-831-5577. 238 F
cbellows@wpi.edu
BELLOWS, Kathryn, S ..... 202-687-5867... 95 E
bellowsk@georgetown.edu
BELLSOM, Lou .... 773-380-6880. 163 D
lbellsom@westwood.edu
BELLUCCI, Anthony .... 973-642-8818. 307 D
anthony.bellucci@shu.edu
BELLUCCI, Debbie .... 413-755-4334. 233 A
dbellucci@stcc.edu
BELLUCCI, Keith .... 617-732-2145. 233 E
keith.bellucci@mcphs.edu
BELLUM, Kim .... 605-882-5284. 450 D
bellumk@lakeareatech.edu
BELMAN, David .... 925-439-2181... 42 A
dbelman@losmedanos.edu
BELMAR, Ricardo .... 305-274-1021. 109 K
belmar@nova.edu
BELMODIS, Cassie .... 503-399-5159. 402 E
cassie.belmodis@chemeketa.edu
BELOBRAJDIC, Scott ...... 618-650-2298. 159 H
sbelobr@siue.edu
BELOIT, Roxanne .... 509-533-7067. 518 E
roxanne.beloit@scc.spokane.edu
BELOTE, David, J .... 731-881-7525. 463 E
dbelote@utm.edu
BELOTE, Eve .... 757-789-1767. 512 D
ebelote@es.vccs.edu
BELOTE, Faith, D .... 757-594-7618. 503 M
faith.belote@cnu.edu
BELOTE, Michael, R .... 478-301-2850. 128 H
michael.r.belote@mercer.edu
BELOW, Debbie .... 573-986-6888. 282 B
dbelow@semo.edu
BELROSE, Jacqueline ...... 978-632-6600. 232 C
j_belrose@mwcc.mass.edu
BELSKY, Jeff .... 412-809-5100. 430 H
belsky.jeff@pti.edu
BELSKY, Yisroel .... 718-941-8000. 331 C
BELSTRA, James, E .... 708-239-4720. 160 K
jim.belstra@trnty.edu
BELTON, Ada, A .... 803-705-4327. 441 C
beltona@benedict.edu
BELTON, Annie, R .... 803-536-8406. 446 G
zs_abelton@scsu.edu
BELTON, Ray, L .... 318-670-9312. 207 A
rbelton@susla.edu
BELTRAN, Cherie .... 254-647-1414. 478 H
cbeltran@rangercollege.edu
BELTRAN, Dulce .... 305-237-2222. 109 D
dbeltran@mdc.edu
BELTRAN, JD .... 415-351-3530... 62 G
jdbeltran@sfai.edu
BELTRAN, Philip .... 408-554-5082... 64 M
pjbeltran@scu.edu
BELTRONE, Gail .... 212-854-6031. 314 G
gbeltron@barnard.edu
BELWOOD, Marilyn .... 660-831-4085. 278 I
belwoodmf@moval.edu
BELYEA, Daniel .... 207-974-4664. 210 K
dbelyea@emcc.edu
BELYEA, Elizabeth .... 916-691-7367... 53 B
belyeae@crc.losrios.edu
BEMBRY, Walter .... 785-784-5225. 183 B
bembry@uiu.edu
BEMELEN, Jeff .... 303-871-3256... 86 B
jbemelen@du.edu
BEMIS, Carol .... 574-807-7370. 164 D
bemisc@bethelcollege.edu
BEMIS, Scot, R .... 781-736-4464. 224 F
bemis@brandeis.edu
BEMUS, Melissa, L .... 920-748-8112. 535 J
bemusm@ripon.edu
BEN-AVI, Simon, S .... 516-463-7107. 326 D
simon.ben-avi@hofstra.edu
BEN DEREAS, Mariana ... 691-320-2480. 546 B
mben@comfsm.fm
BENAICHA, Hedi .... 401-456-8053. 439 F
hbenaicha@ric.edu
BENALLY, Rebecca, M ... 928-724-6610... 13 H
benallym@dinecollege.edu
BENALLY, Steven .... 505-786-4110. 310 D
sbenally@navajotech.edu
BENARD, Jane .... 502-863-8437. 194 C
jane_benard@georgetowncollege.edu
BENARD, Mary .... 760-757-2121... 54 G
mbenard@miracosta.edu
BENATAN, Ethan .... 503-699-6325. 404 C
ebenatan@marylhurst.edu
BENAVENTE, Debra .... 562-902-3336... 67 H
debramitchell@scuhs.edu
BENAVIDES, Adolfo .... 903-886-5018. 483 E
adolfo.benavides@tamuc.edu
BENAVIDES, Elma, F ...... 512-863-1441. 481 I
benavide@southwestern.edu
BENAVIDES, Lewis .... 940-898-3555. 488 B
lbenavides@twu.edu
BENAVIDES-FRANKE,
Joanna .... 361-825-6052. 483 F
joanna.benavides-franke@tamucc.edu
BENAVIDEZ, Max .... 909-621-8099... 39 D
max.benavidez@cmc.edu
BENBOW, Camilla, P .... 615-322-8407. 463 G
camilla.benbow@vanderbilt.edu
BENCA, Melissa .... 212-774-4860. 330 E
mbenca@mmm.edu
BENCHIMOL, Daniel .... 212-875-4633. 314 C
dbenchimol@bankstreet.edu
BENCHOFF, Bryan .... 740-593-0061. 387 C
benchoff@ohio.edu
BENDAPUDI, Neeli .... 785-864-7573. 190 L
neeli@ku.edu
BENDECK, Yvette .... 281-283-3022. 489 C
bendeck@uhcl.edu
BENDELE, Jennifer .... 419-227-3141. 391 F
jennifer@unoh.edu
BENDER, David, L .... 989-837-4374. 248 C
bender@northwood.edu
BENDER, George .... 412-396-4895. 415 F
benderg@duq.edu
BENDER, James, E .... 651-631-5493. 263 A
jebender@nwc.edu
BENDER, Jennie, M .... 606-474-3226. 194 H
jbender@kcu.edu
BENDER, Joe .... 812-855-6017. 167 F
jbender@bncollege.com
BENDER, Judith, A .... 201-360-4279. 302 D
jbender@hccc.edu
BENDER, Judy .... 585-475-4315. 337 L
jebpsn@rit.edu
BENDER, Karla .... 713-718-8247. 473 C
karla.bender@hccs.edu
BENDER, Kathryn .... 843-953-5079. 443 A
benderkc@cofc.edu
BENDER, Laurie .... 732-224-2059. 299 G
lbender@brookdalecc.edu
BENDER, Michael .... 203-325-4351... 87 H
BENDER, Rick .... 432-685-4529. 476 G
rbender@midland.edu
BENDER, Starr, S .... 407-303-1631... 97 H
starr.bender@adu.edu
BENDER, Stephanie .... 410-337-6431. 215 A
stephanie.bender@goucher.edu
BENDER, Thomas, B ...... 504-866-7426. 206 B
librarian@nds.edu
BENDER, Tracy .... 803-786-3551. 443 B
tbender@columbiasc.edu
BENDER, Trudy .... 928-524-7324... 16 E
trudy.bender@npc.edu
BENDER, Virginia .... 201-761-6023. 306 L
vbender@saintpeters.edu
BENDER, Yaakov .... 718-868-2300. 314 I
BENDETTI, Debbie .... 707-546-4000... 43 E
dbendetti@empirecollege.com
BENDICKSON, Mary .... 813-253-7210. 106 M
mbendickson@hccfl.edu
BENDIKAS, Kristina .... 413-662-5526. 230 C
k.bendikas@mcla.edu
BENDOLPH, Arthur .... 904-470-8151. 102 A
a.bendolph@ewc.edu
BENDYNA, OP, Mary ..... 615-297-7545. 452 J
srmary@aquinascollege.edu
BENECKI, Anita .... 716-896-0700. 350 A
benecki@villa.edu
BENEDETTI, Brian .... 253-864-3235. 522 C
bbenedetti@pierce.ctc.edu
BENEDETTO, Mark .... 605-331-6684. 452 D
mark.benedetto@usiouxfalls.edu
BENEDETTO, Robert .... 510-649-2540... 46 B
rbenedetto@gtu.edu
BENEDETTO, Robert .... 510-559-2540... 57 F
rbenedetto@gtu.edu
BENEDETTO, Robert .... 510-649-2540... 57 H
rbenedetto@gtu.edu
BENEDETTO, William ...... 845-431-8096. 323 C
benedett@sunydutchess.edu
BENEDICT, Christine .... 608-663-2294. 532 I
cbenedict@edgewood.edu
BENEDICT, David .... 727-376-6911. 117 I
david.benedict@trinitycollege.edu
BENEDICT, Dow .... 304-876-5393. 529 I
dbenedic@shepherd.edu
BENEDICT, Dwight .... 202-651-5064... 95 C
dwight.benedict@gallaudet.edu
BENEDICT, Jody, C .... 585-385-8322. 338 H
jbenedict@sjfc.edu
BENEDICT, Mike, A .... 563-884-5753. 182 A
mike.benedict@palmer.edu
BENEDICT, Nancy .... 608-363-2380. 531 M
benedict@beloit.edu
BENEDICT, Russel, K ...... 208-496-1910. 137 H
benedictr@byui.edu
BENEDICT-AUGUSTINE,
Amy .... 607-436-2534. 343 E
amy.benedict-augstine@oneonta.edu
BENEDIK, Michael .... 979-845-4274. 483 C
benedik@tamu.edu
BENEKE, Ginny .... 858-642-8357... 55 J
gbeneke@nu.edu
BENEKE, Thomas, J .... 515-574-1050. 179 D
beneke@iowacentral.edu
BENEVEDES, Julie, K ...... 209-667-3440... 35 B
jbenevedes@csustan.edu
BENFANTI, William, J .... 716-878-5557. 343 A
benfanwj@buffalostate.edu
BENFATTI, Angela .... 719-384-6834... 83 M
angela.benfatti@ojc.edu
BENFER, Beverly, J .... 610-799-1591. 421 I
bbenfer@lccc.edu
BENFIELD, John, S .... 843-377-2147. 441 G
jbenfield@charlestonlaw.edu
BENFORD, Gladys .... 870-575-8405... 24 E
benfordg@uapb.edu
BENFORD, James, R .... 810-762-9899. 244 Q
jbenford@kettering.edu
BENFORD, Jeffrey .... 925-439-2181... 42 A
jbenford@losmedanos.edu
BENGE, Robert .... 423-236-2855. 458 J
rcbenge@southern.edu
BENGEL, Jo Ann .... 626-815-5003... 29 H
jbengel@apu.edu
BENGINIA, Francis, A .... 610-330-5090. 420 D
benginif@lafayette.edu
BENGSTON, Carl .... 562-860-2451... 37 I
cbengston@cerritos.edu
BENGTSON, John .... 559-244-5957... 68 H
john.bengtson@scccd.edu
BENHAM, Maenette .... 808-956-0980. 136 B
mbenham@hawaii.edu
BENISH, Allan .... 732-247-5241. 303 E
abenish@nbts.edu
BENISH, Amy, L .... 262-554-2010. 534 D
albenish@aol.com
BENITEZ, Hubert .... 516-918-3615. 315 G
hbenitez@bcl.edu
BENITEZ, Michael .... 253-879-3929. 524 F
mbenitez@pugetsound.edu
BENITZ-HODGE, Grissel 808-735-4852. 135 D
ghodge@chaminade.edu
BENJAMIN, Bill .... 727-873-4199. 116 D
benjamin@mail.usf.edu
BENJAMIN, Eric, V .... 931-598-1241. 458 H
ebenjami@sewanee.edu
BENJAMIN, Gregory .... 610-399-2419. 428 B
gbenjamin@cheyney.edu
BENJAMIN, Helen .... 925-229-6820... 41 J
hbenjamin@4cd.edu
BENJAMIN, Jodi .... 402-941-6102. 290 K
benjamin@midlandu.edu
BENJAMIN, Mary .... 620-227-9240. 186 B
mbenjamin@dc3.edu
BENJAMIN, Mary, E .... 870-575-8475... 24 E
benjaminm@uapb.edu
BENJAMIN, Robert .... 617-745-3595. 225 G
robert.j.benjamin@enc.edu
BENJAMIN, Robert .... 269-471-3310. 239 D
robertb@andrews.edu
BENJAMIN, William .... 805-546-3129... 42 C
william_benjamin@cuesta.edu
BENKE, Jack .... 573-592-5555. 285 B
jack.benke@westminster-mo.edu
BENKE, Robin, P .... 276-328-0151. 511 C
rpb@wise.edu
BENKOV, Edith .... 619-594-6111... 35 D
ebenkov@mail.sdsu.edu
BENLOLO, Henri .... 352-854-2322. 100 K
benloloh@cf.edu
BENMERGUI, Diana .... 212-960-5277. 351 M
benmergui@yu.edu
BENN, Sherri .... 512-245-2278. 487 C
sb17@txstate.edu
BENNATTS, Denise .... 253-833-9111. 520 C
dbennatts@greenriver.edu
BENNECKE, Margie .... 708-237-5050. 155 B
mbennecke@nc.edu
BENNER, Brent, W .... 813-253-6211. 118 L
bbenner@ut.edu
BENNETT, Albert, F .... 949-824-5315... 71 B
abennett@uci.edu
BENNETT, Amy .... 317-955-6768. 170 V
abennett@marian.edu
BENNETT, Barbara .... 956-364-4697. 485 H
barb.bennett@tstc.edu

BENNETT, Barbara, L ...... 401-598-2838. 439 B
bbennett@jwu.edu
BENNETT, Blaine .... 830-591-7275. 481 C
blaine.bennett@swtjc.edu
BENNETT, Bobby .... 434-947-8109. 508 D
bbennett@randolphcollege.edu
BENNETT, Cameron, D ... 253-535-7150. 521 I
bennetcd@plu.edu
BENNETT, Carolyn .... 516-876-3203. 343 D
bennettc@oldwestbury.edu
BENNETT, Cathy .... 740-695-9500. 374 H
cbennett@belmontcollege.edu
BENNETT, Chris .... 765-998-4574. 173 C
chbennett@taylor.edu
BENNETT, Christina, L ... 973-642-8818. 307 D
christina.bennett@shu.edu
BENNETT, Christopher .... 440-375-7000. 382 L
cbennett@lec.edu
BENNETT, Daniel, P .... 906-487-2216. 247 A
dpbennet@mtu.edu
BENNETT, Derwin .... 518-255-5836. 344 E
bennetdd@cobleskill.edu
BENNETT, Douglas .... 714-432-5126... 39 K
dbennett@occ.cccd.edu
BENNETT, Drew, A .... 417-255-7900. 278 E
drewbennett@missouristate.edu
BENNETT, Elbert .... 870-575-8504... 24 E
bennette@uapb.edu
BENNETT, Elizabeth, C .. 949-824-7982... 71 B
bennette@uci.edu
BENNETT, Eric .... 212-659-7290. 328 E
ebennett@tkc.edu
BENNETT, Gene .... 870-780-1201... 19 K
gbennett@smail.anc.edu
BENNETT, George .... 509-527-2930. 524 I
george.bennett@wallawalla.edu
BENNETT, Helen .... 270-686-4285. 192 G
helen.bennett@brescia.edu
BENNETT, Holly, L .... 561-993-1126. 110 C
bennetth@palmbeachstate.edu
BENNETT, James .... 913-288-7259. 187 L
jbennett@kckcc.edu
BENNETT, Jamie .... 213-613-2200... 67 E
jamie_bennett@sciarc.edu
BENNETT, Janis, A .... 304-766-3010. 530 C
bennetja@wvstateu.edu
BENNETT, Jeff .... 405-425-5903. 397 D
jeff.bennett@oc.edu
BENNETT, Jeffrey, L .... 570-321-4031. 422 H
bennett@lycoming.edu
BENNETT, Joan, W .... 732-932-9375. 306 A
profmycogirl@yahoo.com
BENNETT, JoAnn .... 937-327-6185. 393 E
jbennett@wittenberg.edu
BENNETT, Josh .... 406-447-6932. 287 A
josh.bennett@umhelelna.edu
BENNETT, Julia .... 208-377-8080. 137 K
jbennett@carrington.edu
BENNETT, Karen .... 520-515-5417... 12 R
bennettk@cochise.edu
BENNETT, Kari .... 518-438-3111. 330 C
bennettk@mariacollege.edu
BENNETT, Kerrie .... 401-874-5053. 440 D
kbennett@uri.edu
BENNETT, Kim .... 260-665-4438. 173 E
bennettk@trine.edu
BENNETT, Lea, S .... 662-685-4771. 266 C
lbennett@bmc.edu
BENNETT, Linda .... 870-612-2020... 25 A
linda.bennett@uaccb.edu
BENNETT, Linda, L .... 570-577-1149. 411 A
linda.bennett@bucknell.edu
BENNETT, Linda L, M .... 812-464-1756. 174 D
bennettl@usi.edu
BENNETT, Lori .... 805-378-1403... 74 F
lbennett@vcccd.edu
BENNETT, Maybelle, T ... 202-806-4771... 95 G
maybelle.bennett@howard.edu
BENNETT, Michael, J ..... 727-341-3012. 112 E
bennett.michael@spcollege.edu
BENNETT, Mitchell .... 214-333-5139. 470 D
mitch@dbu.edu
BENNETT, Patricia .... 850-729-4901. 109 I
bennettp@nwfsc.edu
BENNETT, Patrick .... 614-947-6836. 380 A
patrick.bennett@franklin.edu
BENNETT, Rashad .... 954-923-4440. 108 P
registrar@keycollege.edu
BENNETT, Rene .... 816-604-5412. 277 E
rene.bennett@mcckc.edu
BENNETT, Richard .... 678-915-7443. 132 C
rbennett@spsu.edu
BENNETT, Rick .... 408-855-5232... 75 K
rick.bennett@wvm.edu
BENNETT, Rodger .... 972-860-4802. 470 G
rpbfape@dcccd.edu
BENNETT, Rodney, D ..... 601-266-5001. 270 E
president@usm.edu
BENNETT, Sari, M .... 603-862-4285. 298 C
sari.bennett@unh.edu
BENNETT, Scott .... 904-620-2002. 116 B
sbennett@unf.edu
BENNETT, Sherri .... 870-838-2945... 19 K
sbennett@smail.anc.edu
BENNETT, Sonja .... 803-535-5668. 442 B
sbennett@claflin.edu
BENNETT, Sonja, A .... 803-536-7000. 446 G
BENNETT, Stephen, R .... 507-933-7526. 255 I
sbennett@gustavus.edu
BENNETT, Susan, A .... 240-895-4336. 218 A
sabennett@smcm.edu
BENNETT, Tanya Lynn .... 973-408-3718. 301 C
tbennett@drew.edu
BENNETT, II, Thomas .... 304-766-3032. 530 C
tbennett3@wvstateu.edu
BENNETT, Todd .... 404-364-8329. 130 A
tbennett1@oglethorpe.edu
BENNETT, Valesie .... 309-677-3961. 140 I
vbennett@bradley.edu
BENNETT-BEALER,
Nichole .... 609-894-9311. 299 I
nbennett-bealer@bcc.edu
BENNETT-CAMPBELL,
Bonnie, L .... 815-224-0481. 148 A
bonnie_campbell@ivcc.edu
BENNETT-WILLIAMS,
Emma .... 843-953-3989. 442 A
ebennett@citadel.edu
BENNETTS, Lori .... 715-682-1824. 535 D
lbennetts@northland.edu
BENNIE, Roanna .... 805-922-6966... 26 K
rbennie@hancockcollege.edu
BENNIE, Scott .... 949-794-9090... 68 D
sbennie@stanbridge.edu
BENNIGHOFF, James ..... 254-710-6500. 467 G
james_bennighoff@baylor.edu
BENNING, Tom .... 314-529-9304. 276 G
tbenning@maryville.edu
BENNINGER, Paul .... 336-917-5460. 366 D
paul.benninger@salem.edu
BENNINGTON, Cheryl .... 304-336-8049. 530 A
cbennington@westliberty.edu
BENNION, Paul .... 208-459-5841. 138 A
pbennion@collegeofidaho.edu
BENOIT, Andy .... 337-482-6474. 208 D
ajbenoit@louisiana.edu
BENOIT, Anthony .... 617-588-1324. 223 B
abenoit@bflt.edu
BENOIT, Barbara, Z .... 508-767-7387. 222 C
bz.benoit@assumption.edu
BENOIT, OSB, Charles ... 985-867-2225. 206 H
acdean@sjasc.edu
BENOIT, Debra .... 985-493-2563. 208 A
debi.benoit@nicholls.edu
BENOIT, Doug .... 714-432-5605... 39 K
dbenoit@occ.cccd.edu
BENOIT, Joseph, N .... 605-668-1514. 450 F
joseph.benoit@mtmc.edu
BENOIT, Kate .... 828-726-2375. 358 E
kbenoit@cccti.edu
BENOIT, Michele .... 541-888-7421. 407 H
mbenoit@socc.edu
BENOIT, Pam .... 740-593-2600. 387 C
benoit@ohio.edu
BENOIT, Thomas .... 325-793-3869. 476 E
tbenoit@mcm.edu
BENOIT, Tyra .... 707-524-1519... 65 B
tbenoit@santarosa.edu
BENOLIEL, Abraham .... 718-339-1090. 351 G
rabenoliel@mikdashmelech.org
BENOLIEL, Haim .... 718-339-1090. 351 G
roshyeshiva@mikdashmelech.org
BENOLKEN, Julie .... 651-450-3622. 258 H
jbenolk@inverhills.edu
BENRUD, Ann .... 612-874-3793. 257 B
abenrud@mcad.edu
BENSE, Judy, A .... 850-474-2200. 117 B
jbense@uwf.edu
BENSEL, Terry .... 814-332-3391. 409 D
tbensel@allegheny.edu
BENSEN, Steven, P .... 701-788-4761. 371 E
Steven.Bensen@mayvillestate.edu
BENSINK, Michael .... 508-678-2811. 231 B
michael.bensink@bristolcc.edu
BENSLEY, James, S .... 231-995-1034. 248 B
jbensley@nmc.edu
BENSON, Allen, C .... 401-841-3397. 545 A
BENSON, Bill .... 541-962-3241. 405 H
wbenson@eou.edu
BENSON, Brenda .... 310-434-4433... 65 A
benson_brenda@smc.edu
BENSON, Bruce, D .... 303-860-5600... 85 K
officeofthepresident@cu.edu
BENSON, Bryan, E .... 903-233-3809. 475 J
bryanbenson@letu.edu
BENSON, Carrie, R .... 412-578-8776. 412 G
crbenson@carlow.edu
BENSON, Daniel .... 507-389-6838. 259 G
daniel.benson@mnsu.edu
BENSON, Dawn .... 406-275-4985. 288 C
dawn_benson@skc.edu
BENSON, Duane .... 712-274-5133. 181 B
bensond@morningside.edu
BENSON, Ella .... 757-424-0333. 224 G
Ella.Benson@cambridgecollege.edu
BENSON, Erin, V .... 207-768-9453. 212 G
erin.benson@umpi.edu
BENSON, George .... 843-953-5500. 443 A
bensong@cofc.edu
BENSON, Gus .... 859-622-3636. 193 P
gus.benson@eku.edu
BENSON, Holly .... 334-244-3125..... 2 A
hbenson@aum.edu
BENSON, Jerry .... 540-568-3429. 506 F
bensonaj@jmu.edu
BENSON, Jocelyn .... 313-577-3933. 252 G
jbenson@wayne.edu
BENSON, Joe .... 205-348-4566..... 8 D
joe.benson@ua.edu
BENSON, Kristin .... 651-846-2882... 28 M
kbenson@argosy.edu
BENSON, Matt, A .... 423-775-7295. 453 E
matt.benson@bryan.edu
BENSON, Michael .... 859-622-2977. 193 P
michael.benson@eku.edu
BENSON, Mindy .... 435-586-7763. 497 A
benson@suu.edu
BENSON, Mitchel .... 916-568-3041... 52 K
bensonm@losrios.edu
BENSON, Neal, L .... 304-462-4117. 529 G
neal.benson@glenville.edu
BENSON, Patricia .... 610-626-6142. 417 H
pbenson@harcum.edu
BENSON, Paul, H .... 937-229-2601. 391 C
pbenson1@udayton.edu
BENSON, Peter .... 203-287-3017... 90 H
paier.admin@snet.net
BENSON, Richard .... 540-231-9752. 515 C
deaneng@vt.edu
BENSON, Robert, M .... 865-882-4553. 461 E
bensonrm@roanestate.edu
BENSON, Robin .... 918-647-1344. 394 I
rbenson@carlalbert.edu
BENSON, Ruthann, E ...... 608-785-8116. 536 G
rbenson@uwlax.edu
BENSON, Samantha .... 910-879-5567. 358 B
sbenson@bladencc.edu
BENSON, Stephanie, G ... 706-355-5112. 120 J
sbenson@athenstech.edu
BENSON, Stephen, M ..... 304-929-5486. 528 D
sbenson@newriver.edu
BENSON, Suzie .... 509-682-6505. 525 B
sbenson@wvc.edu
BENSON, Terra .... 520-206-4640... 17 A
tbenson@pima.edu
BENSON, Todd .... 503-251-5726. 408 G
tbenson@uws.edu
BENSON, Vaughn .... 402-375-7245. 291 F
vabenso1@wsc.edu
BENSON, Wade, M .... 706-379-3111. 134 L
wadeb@yhc.edu
BENSON-TYUS, Hasanna 202-462-2101... 96 A
benson@iwp.edu
BENSTON, Kimberly .... 610-896-1014. 418 F
kbenston@haverford.edu
BENT, Lauren .... 978-837-5250. 234 A
BENTE, James .... 630-942-2409. 142 G
bentej@cod.edu
BENTIVEGNA,
Saverio, S .... 914-594-3368. 334 A
saverio_bentivegna@nymc.edu
BENTLEY, Dean .... 404-727-6039. 124 E
dean.bentley@emory.edu
BENTLEY, Jane .... 708-974-5703. 153 F
jane.bentley@morainevalley.edu
BENTLEY, Kelvin .... 216-987-4577. 378 D
kelvin.bentley@tri-c.edu
BENTLEY, Pamela .... 270-706-8731. 195 A
pamela.bentley@kctcs.edu
BENTLEY, Sarah .... 512-492-3034. 466 B
sbentley@aoma.edu
BENTLEY, Tiffanie, L .... 207-741-5610. 211 A
tbentley@smccme.edu
BENTLEY, Tony .... 309-347-5448. 141 A
abentley@sandurg.edu
BENTLEY-COLTHART,
Nicki .... 304-472-8488. 531 G
bentley-colthart@wvwc.edu
BENTON, Andrew, K .... 310-506-4451... 58 H
andrew.benton@pepperdine.edu
BENTON, Debra, M .... 740-593-4260. 387 C
bentond@ohio.edu
BENTON, Gayle .... 928-226-4204... 13 B
Gayle.Benton@coconino.edu
BENTON, James .... 828-659-0444. 362 A
jimbenton@mcdowelltech.edu
BENTON, Katherine .... 405-382-9263. 399 I
k.benton@sscok.edu
BENTON, Patrena, N .... 757-727-5000. 505 F
patrena.benton@hamptonu.edu
BENTON, Ronald, W .... 303-963-3221... 79 C
rbenton@ccu.edu
BENTON, Sherry .... 352-392-1575. 116 A
benton@counsel.ufl.edu
BENTON, William .... 717-815-1232. 438 D
wbenton@ycp.edu
BENTON-MESTAS,
Andrea .... 719-587-8333... 78 B
andrea@adams.edu
BENTSON, Kenneth .... 505-454-3080. 310 E
kbentson@nmhu.edu
BENTZ, Mandy .... 865-539-7203. 461 D
mdbentz@pstcc.edu
BENULIS, Joan, R .... 585-385-8010. 338 H
jbenulis@sjfc.edu
BENVENGER,
Deborah, A .... 215-871-6711. 430 D
admissions@pcom.edu
BENVENISTE,
Lawrence, M .... 404-727-6377. 124 E
larry_benveniste@bus.emory.edu
BENVENUTTI, Mary Beth 510-748-2211... 59 B
mbenvenutti@peralta.edu
BENWAY, Elizabeth .... 508-830-5086. 230 D
ebenway@maritime.edu
BENWAY, Jennifer .... 617-349-8498. 228 B
jbenway@lesley.edu
BENWELL, Deirdre .... 509-527-2066. 524 I
deirdre.benwell@wallawalla.edu
BENZ, Deborah .... 507-457-5069. 262 A
dbenz@winona.edu
BENZ, Kathleen .... 661-362-3032... 40 E
kathleen.benz@canyons.edu
BENZEL, Brian, L .... 509-777-3208. 525 F
bbenzel@whitworth.edu
BENÍTEZ-RAMÍREZ,
Solange .... 787-993-8874. 554 A
solange.benitez@upr.edu
BEOKU-BETTS,
Josephine, A .... 561-297-2057. 114 L
beokubet@fau.edu
BEQUETTE, Angela, L ..... 919-866-5394. 364 G
albequette@waketech.edu
BEQUETTE, Barry .... 601-877-6137. 265 G
bequette@alcorn.edu
BEQUETTE, Lori .... 704-355-3920. 353 D
lori.bequette@carolinascollege.edu
BERALDI, JR.,
Thomas, F .... 603-645-9695. 297 I
t.beraldi@snhu.edu
BERAN, Connie .... 512-313-3000. 469 L
connie.beran@concordia.edu
BERAN, Paul, B .... 479-788-7007... 24 A
paul.beran@uafs.edu
BERAN, Wayne, B .... 361-570-4811. 489 E
beranw@uhv.edu
BERARDI, William .... 508-678-2811. 231 B
william.berardi@bristolcc.edu
BERARDI-DEMO, Linda .. 570-504-9612. 413 B
BERBERET, James, M ..... 815-599-3406. 146 D
jim.berberet@highland.edu
BERBRICK, Antonia .... 828-694-1716. 358 C
a_berbrick@blueridge.edu
BERDANIER, Bruce .... 203-254-4000... 89 I
bberdanier@fairfield.edu
BEREAUD, Francois .... 619-388-7503... 62 F
fbereaud@sdccd.edu
BERENBACK, Steven .... 401-454-6156. 440 A
sberenba@risd.edu
BERENBAUM, Devorah ... 718-645-0536. 331 G
mirrer@thejnet.com
BERENBAUM, Osher ...... 917-645-0536. 331 G
mirrer@thejnet.com
BERENBAUM, Rachel ..... 718-645-0536. 331 G
mirrer@thejnet.com
BERENDT, Sherri .... 312-427-2737. 148 L
6berendt@jmls.edu
BERENSON, Jennifer, K .. 540-375-2204. 509 B
berenson@roanoke.edu
BERENSON, Jerry, A ...... 610-526-5160. 410 J
jberenso@brynmawr.edu
BERESFORD, Jack .... 619-388-6914... 62 C
jberesford@sdccd.edu
BEREZNIAK, Ronald .... 941-756-0690. 420 E
rberezniak@lecom.edu
BERG, Alicia, M .... 312-369-7102. 143 D
aberg@colum.edu
BERG, Amy .... 607-753-5942. 343 B
amy.berg@cortland.edu
BERG, Beth .... 413-585-2108. 236 H
bberg@smith.edu
BERG, Cynthia .... 801-581-8620. 496 Q
cynthia.berg@csbs.utah.edu
BERG, Dale .... 520-326-1600... 17 J
BERG, Denise .... 570-662-4853. 429 C
dberg@mansfield.edu
BERG, Diana .... 952-888-4777. 263 B
dberg@nwhealth.edu
BERG, Eric .... 218-723-6630. 254 K
eberg@css.edu
BERG, Gary .... 805-437-8580... 32 I
gary.berg@csuci.edu

BERG, Hunter .... 701-255-3285. 373 C
hberg@uttc.edu
BERG, Jerry .... 815-394-5058. 157 C
jberg@rockford.edu
BERG, Joel, H .... 206-543-5980. 524 G
joelberg@uw.edu
BERG, John .... 215-972-2007. 426 Y
jberg@pafa.edu
BERG, John, A .... 314-935-7311. 284 L
jberg@wustl.edu
BERG, Kevin .... 509-682-6815. 525 B
kberg@wvc.edu
BERG, Linda, K .... 651-290-6321. 265 F
linda.berg@wmitchell.edu
BERG, Richard, R .... 717-290-8704. 421 D
rberg@lancasterseminary.edu
BERG, Roger .... 913-621-8744. 186 C
rberg@donnelly.edu
BERG, Scott, M .... 413-748-3859. 236 I
sberg@springfieldcollege.edu
BERG, Shelton, G .... 305-284-2241. 118 F
sberg@miami.edu
BERG, Stacey, L .... 832-824-4588. 467 F
sberg@bcm.edu
BERG, Tamara .... 507-457-5460. 262 A
tberg@winona.edu
BERG, Terry .... 806-371-5008. 465 E
tlberg@actx.edu
BERGAMO, Anne, M ...... 856-691-8600. 301 A
abergamo@cccnj.edu
BERGAN, Maureen .... 251-380-3498..... 7 D
mbergan@shc.edu
BERGANDI, Cherrie .... 715-833-6483. 539 J
cbergandi@cvtc.edu
BERGEN, Lori .... 414-288-7133. 534 B
lori.bergen@marquette.edu
BERGEN, Michael .... 718-951-5186. 317 C
mbergen@brooklyn.cuny.edu
BERGER, Amy, C .... 818-677-2932... 34 C
amy.berger@csun.edu
BERGER, Aron .... 845-426-3276. 350 I
ydm@thejnet.com
BERGER, Brandi .... 706-233-7205. 131 E
bberger@shorter.edu
BERGER, David .... 212-960-5253. 351 M
dberger@yu.edu
BERGER, Edward, E .... 620-665-3505. 187 F
bergere@hutchcc.edu
BERGER, Patrice .... 402-472-5425. 292 I
pberger1@unl.edu
BERGER, Pearl .... 212-960-5363. 351 M
berger@yu.edu
BERGER, Scott .... 320-762-4475. 257 O
scottb@alextech.edu
BERGER, Sheri, L .... 818-947-2316... 52 E
bergersl@lavc.edu
BERGER, Susan, A .... 315-655-7126. 316 E
sberger@cazenovia.edu
BERGER, Susan, A .... 315-655-7122. 316 E
sberger@cazenovia.edu
BERGER, Vance, J .... 423-775-7212. 453 E
bergerva@bryan.edu
BERGER, William .... 814-732-1107. 428 E
wberger@edinboro.edu
BERGER-SWEENEY,
Joanne, E .... 617-627-3864. 237 C
joanne.berger-sweeney@tufts.edu
BERGERON, Bette .... 618-650-3350. 159 H
bberger@siue.edu
BERGERON, Florence ..... 617-912-9146. 224 B
fbergeron@bostonconservatory.edu
BERGERON, Iva .... 214-860-8735. 471 A
ibergeron@dcccd.edu
BERGERON, Katherine .... 401-863-2573. 438 J
katherine_bergeron@brown.edu
BERGERON, Mindy .... 925-969-3385... 49 B
bergeron@jfku.edu
BERGERON,
Stephanie, W .... 248-689-8282. 251 I
sbergeron@walshcollege.edu
BERGES, Cherry, L .... 270-824-8677. 196 A
cherry.berges@kctcs.edu
BERGESON, Daniel .... 507-222-5992. 254 D
dbergeso@carleton.edu
BERGESON, Patricia ...... 312-369-7478. 143 D
pbergeson@colum.edu
BERGESON, Rachel .... 631-632-6740. 342 C
rachel.bergeson@stonybrook.edu
BERGFELD, Julie .... 314-529-9620. 276 G
jbergfeld@maryville.edu
BERGFELD, Steve .... 708-216-6648. 151 H
sbergfeld@luc.edu
BERGGREN, Jeffrey, C ... 260-359-4016. 166 O
jberggren@huntington.edu
BERGGREN, Kent, E ...... 208-524-3000. 138 D
kent.berggren@my.eitc.edu
BERGGREN, Marie, N ..... 510-287-3306... 70 H
marie.berggren@ucop.edu
BERGGREN, Stacey, L .... 208-467-8994. 139 A
BERGH, David .... 802-635-1200. 501 D
david.bergh@jsc.edu
BERGH, Thomas, K .... 715-394-8081. 538 C
tbergh@uwsuper.edu
BERGHOFF, Carolyn ...... 312-788-1151. 162 H
cberghoff@vandercook.edu
BERGHOLZ, John .... 312-261-3871. 153 I
john.bergholz@nl.edu
BERGHORN, George ...... 517-483-1319. 245 H
berghorg@lcc.edu
BERGIN, Bonita, M .... 707-545-3647... 29 J
BERGKAMP, Sheila .... 620-227-9404. 186 B
sbergkamp@dc3.edu
BERGLAND, Arne .... 805-493-3152... 31 H
bergland@clunet.edu
BERGLER, Michael .... 949-214-3187... 41 I
michael.bergler@cui.edu
BERGLUND, Bruce .... 616-526-6194. 240 L
brb6@calvin.edu
BERGMAN, Beverly .... 478-471-2721. 128 I
beverly.bergman@maconstate.edu
BERGMAN, Bruce .... 308-535-3676. 290 J
bergmanb@mpcc.edu
BERGMAN, Dave .... 606-539-4167. 200 B
dave.bergman@ucumberlands.edu
BERGMAN, Jessica .... 606-546-1639. 200 A
jbergman@unionky.edu
BERGMAN,
Maeve Katherine .... 510-981-5014... 59 A
mbergman@peralta.edu
BERGMAN, Matthew .... 217-228-5432. 156 C
bergmma@quincy.edu
BERGMAN, Stephanie ..... 616-988-1000. 241 D
BERGMAN, JR.,
William, T .... 215-204-6550. 433 K
William.Bergman@temple.edu
BERGMANN, Hans .... 203-582-8960... 91 A
hans.bergmann@quinnipiac.edu
BERGMANN, Michelle .... 541-440-4620. 408 D
Michelle.Bergmann@umpqua.edu
BERGMANN, Ronald .... 718-960-8421. 318 A
ron.bergmann@lehman.cuny.edu
BERGMANN, Tom .... 847-947-5516. 153 I
tbergmann@nl.edu
BERGMEIER, Tyler .... 603-752-1113. 296 E
tbergmeier@ccsnh.edu
BERGQUIST, Eric .... 502-597-7008. 197 A
eric.bergquist@kysu.edu
BERGQUIST, Viola .... 320-308-5177. 261 C
vbergquist@sctcc.edu
BERGREN, Rebecca, A ... 717-337-6866. 417 B
rbergren@gettysburg.edu
BERGRUD, Erik .... 816-584-6412. 280 C
erik.bergrud@park.edu
BERGSTROM, Andrew .... 843-953-5294. 443 A
bergstroma@cofc.edu
BERGSTROM, Chip .... 617-217-9070. 222 G
cbergstrom@baystate.edu
BERGSTROM, Paula .... 870-574-4488... 23 G
pbergstr@sautech.edu
BERGSTROM, Scott, J .... 208-496-1136. 137 H
bergstroms@byui.edu
BERGSTROM, Tracey ...... 361-582-2535. 493 H
tracey.bergstrom@victoriacollege.edu
BERGUM, Mike .... 765-983-1483. 165 G
bergumi@earlham.edu
BERGVALL, Dennis .... 503-370-6397. 408 J
dbergval@willamette.edu
BERHE, Annette .... 901-435-1351. 455 M
annette.berhe@loc.edu
BERISH, Michele .... 718-409-6079. 346 D
mberish@sunymaritime.edu
BERK, Anne-Marie .... 309-341-7793. 150 A
apberk@knox.edu
BERK, Bradford, C .... 585-275-3407. 349 C
bradford_berk@urmc.rochester.edu
BERK, Steven, L .... 806-743-3000. 487 E
steven.berk@ttuhsc.edu
BERKELAND, Rondell ..... 218-723-7033. 254 K
rberkela@css.edu
BERKELEY, Fred .... 706-385-1459. 130 F
fred.berkeley@point.edu
BERKHEIMER, Eric, J .... 410-677-6553. 220 D
ejberkheimer@salisbury.edu
BERKHEIMER, Karen ...... 410-334-2915. 221 D
kberkheimer@worwic.edu
BERKHOF, Robert, A ...... 616-526-6091. 240 L
berk@calvin.edu
BERKICH, Carla .... 361-825-2703. 483 F
carla.berkich@tamucc.edu
BERKLAS, Jennifer, L .... 909-621-8000... 65 D
jennifer.berklas@scrippscollege.edu
BERKLEY, Scott .... 505-566-3162. 311 I
berkleys@sancollege.edu
BERKMAN, Ronald, M .... 216-687-3544. 377 F
ronald.berkman@csuohio.edu
BERKNER, Paul, D .... 207-859-4460. 209 J
pberkner@colby.edu
BERKOW, Daniel .... 209-667-3381... 35 B
dberkow@csustan.edu
BERKOWITZ, Bobbie .... 212-305-3582. 321 D
bb2509@columbia.edu
BERKOWITZ, David .... 256-824-6952..... 8 F
david.berkowitz@uah.edu
BERKOWITZ, Justin .... 386-267-0565. 101 F
director@daytonacollege.edu
BERKSTEINER, Ethel .... 912-443-5894. 131 D
eberksteiner@savannahtech.edu
BERLAND, Eti .... 847-982-2500. 146 C
berland@htc.edu
BERLEY, Susan .... 820-652-0636. 362 A
susanberley@mcdowelltech.edu
BERLIN, Eileen .... 973-278-5400. 299 D
eml@berkeleycollege.edu
BERLIN, Ingrid .... 402-457-2717. 290 G
iberlin@mccneb.edu
BERLIN, Robert, Y .... 781-736-3720. 224 F
drb@brandeis.edu
BERLIN, Tom, J .... 304-457-6352. 526 A
berlintj@ab.edu
BERLINER, Donna .... 630-942-2475. 142 G
berliner@cod.edu
BERLINER, Herman, A .... 516-463-5402. 326 D
herman.a.berliner@hofstra.edu
BERLINER, Thomas .... 847-628-1520. 149 B
tberliner@judsonu.edu
BERLO, Josh .... 218-726-8168. 264 D
jpberlo@d.umn.edu
BERLYN, Mark, A .... 314-516-6515. 283 E
berlynm@umsl.edu
BERMAN, Audrey .... 510-869-6129... 61 I
aberman@samuelmerritt.edu
BERMAN, Harris .... 617-636-2177. 237 C
harris.berman@tufts.edu
BERMAN, Joel .... 954-262-2130. 109 K
jb@nova.edu
BERMAN, Larry, S .... 404-413-5570. 126 E
larryberman@gsu.edu
BERMAN, Lou Ann .... 903-566-7052. 492 D
lberman@uttyler.edu
BERMAN, Marc .... 619-961-4271... 69 I
mberman@tjsl.edu
BERMAN, Mark, A .... 518-782-6957. 340 J
mberman@siena.edu
BERMAN, Mark, R .... 413-205-3008. 221 F
mark.berman@aic.edu
BERMAN, Mary Jane ...... 513-529-1943. 384 G
bermanmj@miamioh.edu
BERMAN, Michael .... 805-437-2099... 32 I
michael.berman@csuci.edu
BERMAN, Morris, S ...... 714-449-7455... 67 D
mberman@scco.edu
BERMAN, Paula .... 617-277-3915. 224 C
BERMAN, Richard, T ...... 440-775-8140. 385 H
Richard.Berman@oberlin.edu
BERMAN-MARTIN,
Gail, L .... 508-999-8660. 229 A
gberman@umassd.edu
BERMANN, Todd .... 706-864-1451. 133 D
todd.berrman@ung.edu
BERMEA, Gilbert, S .... 830-758-4111. 481 C
gbermea@swtjc.edu
BERMINGHAM, Jack .... 206-878-3710. 520 E
jbermingham@highline.edu
BERMUDEZ, Jose Luis ... 979-845-5141. 483 C
jbermudez@tamu.edu
BERMUDEZ, Megan .... 610-921-7510. 409 A
mbermudez@alb.edu
BERMUDEZ, Pedro .... 787-786-3030. 547 F
pbermudez@ucb.edu.pr
BERMUDEZ, Shaila .... 910-221-2224. 354 D
sbermundez@gcd.edu
BERNA, Francis, J .... 215-951-1346. 420 B
berna@lasalle.edu
BERNABE, Arnaldo .... 718-518-6888. 318 B
abernabe@hostos.cuny.edu
BERNAD, Manuel, A .... 858-499-0202... 40 C
manuelb@coleman.edu
BERNADELLE, Guary ...... 815-967-7300. 157 B
bernadelle@rockfordcareercollege.edu
BERNAL, Deanna .... 818-785-2726... 37 F
deanna.bernal@casalomacollege.edu
BERNAL, Elena .... 781-283-1000. 237 F
ebernal@wellesley.edu
BERNAL-OLSON,
Patricia .... 937-229-4211. 391 C
pbernalolson1@udayton.edu
BERNARD, Bill .... 212-924-5900. 347 B
wbernard@swedishinstitute.edu
BERNARD, David, K .... 314-921-9290. 284 D
dbernard@ugst.edu
BERNARD, Dee .... 651-450-3522. 258 H
dbernar@inverhills.edu
BERNARD, Frances .... 518-438-3111. 330 C
franb@mariacollege.edu
BERNARD, Kacey .... 610-341-1481. 415 G
kbernard@eastern.edu
BERNARD, Kacey .... 610-341-1389. 425 I
kbernard@eastern.edu
BERNARD, Marcella, J .... 207-859-4342. 209 J
mbernard@colby.edu
BERNARD, Marjorie, P .... 412-578-8880. 412 G
mpbernard@carlow.edu
BERNARD, Nancy, M .... 334-844-4744..... 1 G
bernanm@auburn.edu
BERNARD, Nesta .... 202-238-2340... 95 G
nbernard@howard.edu
BERNARD, Pamela .... 919-684-3955. 354 A
pamela.bernard@duke.edu
BERNARD, Philip .... 617-989-4162. 237 G
bernardp@wit.edu
BERNARD, Renee .... 814-472-2766. 432 D
rbernard@francis.edu
BERNARD, Richard .... 405-974-3493. 400 K
rbernard1@uco.edu
BERNARD, Sue .... 207-768-2808. 210 M
BERNARD, Thomas .... 413-662-5205. 230 C
t.bernard@mcla.edu
BERNARD, Vicki .... 314-340-5112. 275 A
bernardv@hssu.edu
BERNARDI, Robert .... 985-448-4794. 208 A
rob.bernardi@nicholls.edu
BERNARDINO, Maria ..... 209-954-5065... 63 C
mbernardino@deltacollege.edu
BERNARDIS, Tim .... 406-638-3113. 286 D
tim@lbhc.edu
BERNARDO, Daniel .... 509-335-4561. 525 A
bernardo@wsu.edu
BERNARDO, Daniel .... 509-335-5581. 525 A
bernardo@wsu.edu
BERNARDO, Lisa, M ...... 209-667-3094... 35 B
lbernardo@csustan.edu
BERNARDO, Peter, R ..... 216-397-4217. 381 R
pbernardo@jcu.edu
BERNARDO-SOUSA,
Marie .... 401-598-1754. 439 B
mbernardo@jwu.edu
BERNAS, Judith, A .... 602-827-2017... 18 F
jbernas@email.arizona.edu
BERNAUER, Edmund ...... 808-521-2288. 135 I
dean@orientalmedicine.edu
BERNDT, Michael .... 952-358-8498. 260 B
michael.berndt@normandale.edu
BERNE, Robert .... 212-998-2283. 334 D
robert.berne@nyu.edu
BERNECKER, Kim .... 972-825-4634. 481 F
kbernecker@sagu.edu
BERNEL, Liz .... 219-785-5719. 172 A
ebernel@pnc.edu
BERNER, Albert, J .... 973-618-3660. 300 A
aberner@caldwell.edu
BERNER, JR.,
Howard, E .... 314-275-3514. 156 B
howard.berner@principia.edu
BERNER, Nancy .... 931-598-1172. 458 H
nberner@sewanee.edu
BERNET, Glenn, H .... 417-865-2815. 274 B
bernetg@evangel.edu
BERNEY, Jan .... 360-438-4513. 522 G
jberney@stmartin.edu
BERNHARD, Andrew ...... 503-654-8000. 407 B
abernhard@pioneerpacific.edu
BERNHARD, Mark, C ..... 812-464-1829. 174 D
mbernhard@usi.edu
BERNHARD, Robert, J .... 574-631-3902. 174 A
bernhard.9@nd.edu
BERNHARDSON, Bonnie 218-879-0828. 258 E
bonnie@fdltcc.edu
BERNHARDSON, Mark ... 218-879-0703. 258 E
mbernhar@fdltcc.edu
BERNHEISEL, Susan .... 419-251-1583. 383 G
susan.bernheisel@mercycollege.edu
BERNICK, Lee .... 702-895-1068. 294 I
lee.bernick@unlv.edu
BERNIER, Jessica .... 845-437-5320. 349 G
jebernier@vassar.edu
BERNIER, Jose .... 845-341-4689. 335 H
jose.bernier@sunyorange.edu
BERNIER, Joseph .... 401-454-6394. 440 A
jbernier01@risd.edu
BERNIER, Julie, N .... 603-535-2230. 298 G
jbernier@plymouth.edu
BERNOTAS, Scott .... 410-293-1010. 545 J
scott.bernotas@navy.mil
BERNOTSKY, Lorraine .... 610-425-7447. 430 A
lbernotsky@wcupa.edu
BERNSTEIN, Aimee .... 718-409-5979. 346 D
abernstein@sunymaritime.edu
BERNSTEIN, Alan .... 229-333-5870. 134 B
abernste@valdosta.edu
BERNSTEIN, David .... 845-406-4308. 351 A
BERNSTEIN, Jennifer .... 212-346-1095. 335 J
jbernstein@pace.edu
BERNSTEIN, Melissa ...... 801-581-3386. 496 Q
melissa.bernstein@law.utah.edu
BERNSTEIN, Melvin .... 617-373-4160. 235 F
BERNSTEIN, Michael ...... 504-865-5261. 207 C
mbernstein@tulane.edu
BERNSTEIN, Pamela .... 603-880-8308. 298 A
tmc@thomasmorecollege.edu
BERNSTEIN, Robin .... 402-557-7300. 288 G
robin.bernstein@bellevue.edu
BERNTSON, Joan, L .... 218-751-8670. 263 C
joanberntson@oakhills.edu

BERONA, David .... 603-535-2817. 298 G daberona@plymouth.edu
BEROTTE JOSEPH, Carole, M .... 718-289-5151. 317 B president@bcc.cuny.edu
BERQUAM, Lori .... 608-263-5700. 536 D lberquam@studentlife.wisc.edu
BERQUIST, Gina .... 503-255-0332. 404 F ginab@multnomah.edu
BERRAHOU, Catherine ... 248-689-8282. 251 I cberraho@walshcollege.edu
BERRIDGE, Bob .... 773-256-0783. 152 B bberridg@lstc.edu
BERRIER, David .... 773-702-9800. 161 B dberrier@uchicago.edu
BERRIOS, Iris .... 787-743-7979. 552 I
BERRIOS, Jose .... 787-751-0178. 552 I ac_jberrios@suagm.edu
BERRIOS, Marianne .... 787-852-1430. 549 C mberrios@hccpr.edu
BERRIOS, William .... 212-592-2000. 340 H wberrios@sva.edu
BERROA, Carlos, E .... 787-257-7373. 552 H ceberroa@suagm.edu
BERROL, Jerry, M .... 718-260-5800. 319 B jberrol@citytech.cuny.edu
BERRY, Amy .... 918-631-3288. 401 F amy-berry@utulsa.edu
BERRY, Brian .... 870-612-2014... 25 A brian.berry@uaccb.edu
BERRY, Chad .... 859-985-3490. 192 F chad_berry@berea.edu
BERRY, Christy .... 979-532-6381. 494 L berryc@wcjc.edu
BERRY, Clay .... 870-508-6124... 20 A cberry@asumh.edu
BERRY, Dewayne .... 817-598-6227. 494 G dberry@wc.edu
BERRY, Donald, K .... 251-442-2203..... 9 A dberry@umobile.edu
BERRY, Donna .... 559-638-3641... 69 A donna.berry@reedleycollege.edu
BERRY, Evan .... 207-893-7750. 211 G eberry@sjcme.edu
BERRY, Evan .... 772-462-7945. 106 P eberry@irsc.edu
BERRY, Fred .... 414-277-7324. 534 G berry@msoe.edu
BERRY, J. William .... 972-721-5226. 488 F berry@udallas.edu
BERRY, Joanne .... 603-427-7609. 295 K jberry@ccsnh.edu
BERRY, Joe .... 501-882-4407... 19 M jlberry@asub.edu
BERRY, John .... 740-366-9395. 376 A berry.19@osu.edu
BERRY, John, N .... 305-626-1443. 104 J john.berry@fmuniv.edu
BERRY, Joyce .... 970-491-6675... 80 I joyce.berry@colostate.edu
BERRY, Kathy .... 760-355-6215... 48 A kathy.berry@imperial.edu
BERRY, Larry .... 423-614-8086. 455 L lberry@leeuniversity.edu
BERRY, Laura .... 870-743-3000... 22 B lberry@northark.edu
BERRY, Laurie, M .... 812-468-2000. 174 D lberry@usi.edu
BERRY, Linda, C .... 708-209-3209. 143 E linda.berry@cuchicago.edu
BERRY, Malinda .... 800-287-8822. 164 C berryma@bethanyseminary.edu
BERRY, Mario .... 281-290-3960. 476 A mario.berry@lonestar.edu
BERRY, Mildred .... 305-626-1444. 104 J Mildred.Berry@fmuniv.edu
BERRY, Richard, A .... 936-468-2707. 482 A rberry@sfasu.edu
BERRY, Rick .... 757-683-3109. 507 N rberry@odu.edu
BERRY, Robert, L .... 904-620-2851. 116 B robert.berry@unf.edu
BERRY, Ronald .... 318-342-1100. 208 E rberry@ulm.edu
BERRY, Scott, A .... 260-359-4006. 166 O sberry@huntington.edu
BERRY, Scott, D .... 864-488-4525. 444 L sberry@limestone.edu
BERRY, Steve .... 775-831-1314. 295 F sberry@sierranevada.edu
BERRY, Trey .... 870-235-4004... 23 F tcberry@saumag.edu
BERRY, Yvonne .... 603-513-5215. 298 D yvonne.berry@law.unh.edu
BERRYHILL, Cathy .... 505-747-2194. 311 E cathyb@nnmc.edu
BERRYHILL, Jimmilea .... 706-842-0341. 458 A jberryhill@ogs.edu
BERRYMAN, Davis .... 405-491-6680. 399 K dberryma@snu.edu
BERRYMAN, Joanne .... 502-585-9911. 199 C jberryman@spalding.edu
BERRYMAN, Theresa .... 847-543-2890. 143 A tberryman@clcillinois.edu
BERRYMAN, Treva, G .... 615-366-4482. 459 A treva.berryman@tbr.edu
BERS, Trudy, H .... 847-635-1894. 155 F tbers@oakton.edu
BERSHAD, Carolyn .... 607-753-4728. 343 B carolyn.bershad@cortland.edu
BERSI, Janna .... 310-243-3161... 33 B jbersi@csudh.edu
BERSON, Gail .... 508-286-8251. 238 B gberson@wheatonma.edu
BERT, Daryl, W .... 540-432-4101. 504 D daryl.bert@emu.edu
BERTCH, Dennis .... 269-488-4205. 244 L dbertch@kvcc.edu
BERTEAUX, Susan .... 508-830-5035. 230 D sberteaux@maritime.edu
BERTHELOT, Yves .... 404-385-3383. 125 D yves.berthelot@provost.gatech.edu
BERTHELSEN, Mike .... 612-624-6837. 264 G berth004@umn.edu
BERTHELSEN, Rita .... 712-325-3356. 179 L rberthelsen@iwcc.edu
BERTHIAUME, Joe .... 940-898-3676. 488 B jberthiaume@twu.edu
BERTHIAUME, Peter, L ... 603-526-3675. 295 I pberthia@colby-sawyer.edu
BERTI, David, M .... 617-422-7215. 235 B dberti@nesl.edu
BERTINI, Kristine .... 207-780-5180. 212 H bertini@usm.maine.edu
BERTOCCHI, Bonnie, M . 775-445-4450. 295 A bonnie.bertocchi@wnc.edu
BERTOLI, Jim .... 812-877-8359. 172 C bertoli@rose-hulman.edu
BERTOLINE, Gary, R .... 765-494-2552. 171 M bertoline@purdue.edu
BERTOLINI, Leonard .... 815-836-5244. 150 H bertolle@lewisu.edu
BERTOLINO, Joseph, A .. 802-626-6404. 501 E joseph.bertolino@lyndonstate.edu
BERTOLUCCI, Linda .... 619-644-7799... 46 E linda.bertolucci@gcccd.edu
BERTONE, Genevieve ...... 310-434-3911... 65 A bertone_genevieve@smc.edu
BERTOZZI, Nicholas .... 603-577-6640. 296 F bertozzi@dwc.edu
BERTRAM, Bob .... 207-780-4546. 212 H rbertram@usm.maine.edu
BERTRAM, Brian .... 517-264-7676. 250 B bbertram@sienaheights.edu
BERTRAM, Robert, G ...... 585-292-2626. 332 A rbertram@monroecc.edu
BERTRAN, Lourdes .... 787-728-1515. 555 D lbertran@sagrado.edu
BERTRAND, Andre, E ..... 404-215-2717. 129 D abertran@morehouse.edu
BERTSCH, Lynda .... 701-858-3360. 371 F lynda.bertsch@minotstateu.edu
BERTSCH, Lynn .... 513-244-4975. 377 G lynn_bertsch@mail.msj.edu
BERTSCHINGER, Edmund .... 617-253-1000. 233 B
BERTSOS, Daniel .... 937-775-4172. 393 G dan.bertsos@wright.edu
BERUBE, Danelle .... 802-860-2702. 499 A dberube@champlain.edu
BERUBE, Eric .... 661-763-7720... 69 D eberube@taftcollege.edu
BERUBE, Patricia .... 413-572-5415. 230 F pberube@westfield.ma.edu
BERWICK, Robert .... 202-408-2400... 96 F
BERZAS, Elizabeth .... 225-768-1706. 206 D eberzas@ololcollege.edu
BERZINS, Martin .... 801-581-8224. 496 Q mb@cs.utah.edu
BESANA, GianMario .... 312-362-5554. 143 H gbesana@depaul.edu
BESAW, Gary .... 800-567-2344. 532 E gbesaw@menominee.edu
BESHARA, Alexa .... 201-360-4771. 302 D abeshara@hccc.edu
BESHARA, John .... 330-941-3527. 394 A jbeshara@ysu.edu
BESIKOF, Rudolph, J ..... 818-947-2625... 52 E besikorj@lavc.edu
BESKID, Novella .... 803-777-0958. 447 G novella@sc.edu
BESNARD, Pamela .... 909-621-8192... 60 A pamela.besnard@pomona.edu
BESPALEC, Dale, A .... 414-464-9777. 539 G dbespalec@wspp.edu
BESS, Janie .... 617-349-8542. 228 B jbess@lesley.edu
BESS, Vivian, E .... 301-736-3631. 216 B vbess@msbbcs.edu
BESSER, Pamela .... 502-213-2616. 195 F pam.besser@kctcs.edu
BESSESEN, Marit .... 619-594-6395... 35 D bessesen@mail.sdsu.edu
BESSETTE, Jamie .... 205-665-6230..... 9 B jbessette@montevallo.edu
BESSETTE, Roger .... 413-755-4390. 233 A rbessette@stcc.edu
BESSEY, Dean .... 207-948-9232. 211 I dbessey@unity.edu
BESSIE, Joseph .... 715-232-2421. 538 B bessiej@uwstout.edu
BESSLER, Joseph .... 918-610-8303. 398 I joe.bessler@ptstulsa.edu
BEST, JR., A. Reginald ... 313-317-1700. 243 H Arbest1@hfcc.edu
BEST, Ebony, S .... 512-505-3039. 473 G esbest@htu.edu
BEST, Georgia .... 802-443-2258. 499 H best@middlebury.edu
BEST, Jason .... 206-876-6100. 523 D jbest@theseattleschool.edu
BEST, Mark, W .... 252-638-7247. 359 G bestm@cravencc.edu
BEST, Mickey .... 972-860-8201. 470 H mbest@dcccd.edu
BEST, Neil, A .... 724-847-6643. 417 A nabest@geneva.edu
BEST, Robert .... 864-455-9812. 448 E rbest@greenvillemed.sc.edu
BEST, Roger, J .... 660-543-8597. 283 A best@ucmo.edu
BEST, Sandra, M .... 912-358-4194. 131 C bestsm@savannahstate.edu
BEST, Sara .... 701-349-3621. 373 A sarabest@trinitybiblecollege.edu
BEST, Sharon .... 386-752-1822. 104 G sharon.best@fgc.edu
BEST, Susan .... 252-985-5141. 365 D sbest@ncwc.edu
BEST, Trinda .... 760-252-2411... 29 I tbest@barstow.edu
BESTE, Jeff .... 937-766-7858. 375 K bestej@cedarville.edu
BESTOCK, Donna, J .... 650-738-4121... 64 D bestock@smccd.edu
BESTUL, Michael, J .... 216-397-4261. 381 R mbestul@jcu.edu
BETANCOURT, Cybel ...... 787-279-1912. 550 B cbetancourt@bayamon.inter.edu
BETANCOURT, Gladys .... 787-743-7979. 552 I ut-gbetancou@suagm.edu
BETANCOURT VELEZ, Ismael, J .... 563-425-5832. 183 B betancourti@uiu.edu
BETECK, Ellis, B .... 410-651-6621. 219 E ebbeteck@umes.edu
BETH, Amy .... 201-447-7999. 299 C abeth@berger.edu
BETHEA, Edward .... 843-661-8060. 443 G ed.bethea@fdtc.edu
BETHEL, Charles, N .... 304-877-6428. 526 C registrar@abc.edu
BETHKE, Earl .... 808-689-2411. 136 C bethke@hawaii.edu
BETHKE, Jeffrey .... 312-362-6986. 143 H jbethke@depaul.edu
BETHKE-GOMEZ, Jesse .. 651-793-1805. 259 C jesse.bethkegomez@metrostate.edu
BETHMAN, Brenda .... 816-235-1643. 283 D bethmanb@umkc.edu
BETHSCHEIDER, John .... 281-756-5601. 465 D jbethscheider@alvincollege.edu
BETHUNE, Andrew, J ..... 989-964-4071. 249 G ajbethune@svsu.edu
BETHUNE, Lawrence, E .. 617-266-1400. 223 D
BETIT, Brent .... 802-387-6797. 499 E bbetit@landmark.edu
BETKER, Pam .... 303-762-6898... 81 G pam.betker@denverseminary.edu
BETORI, John .... 567-661-7575. 387 L john_betori@owens.edu
BETROLS, Lance .... 717-245-4711. 545 F
BETSCHART, Joseph, V .. 503-845-3406. 404 D joseph.betschart@mtangel.edu
BETSWORTH, Deborah ... 262-551-5725. 532 D dbetsworth@carthage.edu
BETTELYOUN, Kim .... 605-455-6093. 450 I kbettelyoun@olc.edu
BETTENCOURT, Patrick ... 209-575-6362... 77 J bettencourtp@mjc.edu
BETTING, Laurie .... 701-777-6055. 371 C laurie.betting@und.edu
BETTINGER, Lewis .... 608-342-1221. 537 D bettingerl@uwplatt.edu
BETTISON-VARGA, Lori .. 909-621-8148... 65 D president@scrippscollege.edu
BETTS, Albert .... 856-256-4200. 305 E betts@rowan.edu
BETTS, Diane .... 870-574-4560... 23 G dbetts@sautech.edu
BETTS, Keith .... 203-837-8600... 88 B bettsk@wcsu.edu
BETTS, Keith .... 912-344-2514. 120 G keith.betts@armstrong.edu
BETTS, Russell .... 312-567-3800. 147 F betts@iit.edu
BETZ, Bridget, K .... 573-341-4282. 284 A berry@mst.edu
BETZ, Don .... 405-974-2311. 400 K betz@uco.edu
BETZ, Erica .... 610-398-5300. 422 B ebetz@lincolntech.com
BETZ, Jon .... 505-566-3505. 311 I betzj@sanjuancollege.edu
BETZ, Kimberly .... 507-222-4295. 254 D kbetz@carleton.edu
BETZ, Leslie .... 309-556-3161. 148 B iwureg@iwu.edu
BETZ, Norma .... 732-255-0400. 304 A nbetz@ocean.edu
BETZ, Randy .... 757-569-6064. 513 E rbetz@pdc.edu
BETZIG, Kaylen .... 262-691-5198. 541 D kbetzig@wctc.edu
BEU, Pat .... 605-394-1999. 452 A pat.beu@sdsmt.edu
BEUKELMAN, Doug, D ... 712-707-7121. 181 H dougb@nwciowa.edu
BEUS, Ben .... 509-542-4811. 518 C bbeus@columbiabasin.edu
BEUSSMAN, Victoria .... 507-786-3325. 264 B beussman@stolaf.edu
BEUTEL, Charles, M .... 815-740-5037. 162 F cbeutel@stfrancis.edu
BEUTLER, Randy, L .... 580-774-3766. 400 B randy.beutler@swosu.edu
BEVANS, Judy .... 802-586-7111. 500 E jbevans@sterlingcollege.edu
BEVANS, Patricia, A ...... 315-445-4185. 328 F bevanspa@lemoyne.edu
BEVERAGE, JR., Morris, W .... 440-525-7118. 382 M mbeverage@lakelandcc.edu
BEVERIDGE, Kim .... 800-869-7223. 131 B kveverid@scad.edu
BEVERIDGE, Thomas ...... 805-565-6017... 76 D tbeverid@westmont.edu
BEVERLY, Aleza, D .... 765-641-4004. 163 L adbeverly@anderson.edu
BEVERLY, Pearlie .... 254-710-6939. 467 G pearl_beverly@baylor.edu
BEVERLY, Roger, D .... 423-585-2620. 462 A roger.beverly@ws.edu
BEVERSLUIS, Claudia ..... 616-526-6102. 240 L cbeversl@calvin.edu
BEVILACQUA, Linda .... 305-899-3010... 98 O lbevilacqua@barry.edu
BEVILLE, Jill .... 336-334-4013. 369 A jmbevill@uncg.edu
BEVINS, P. Scott .... 276-376-0144. 511 C pb8q@uvawise.edu
BEVINS, P. Scott .... 276-376-1066. 511 C pb8q@uvawise.edu
BEWSEY, Jeff .... 828-227-7322. 369 E bewsey@wcu.edu
BEX, Darcee .... 337-262-5962. 203 J darcee.bex@solacc.edu
BEY, George, J .... 601-974-1385. 267 I beygj@millsaps.edu
BEY, Laura .... 617-521-2181. 236 G laura.bey@simmons.edu
BEYDLER, Julie .... 970-542-3126... 83 E julie.beydler@morgancc.edu
BEYER, Bryan .... 803-754-4100. 443 C
BEYER, David .... 425-388-9573. 519 I dbeyer@everettcc.edu
BEYER, Kirk, D .... 507-933-6075. 255 I kbeyer@gustavus.edu
BEYER, Paul, N .... 443-997-5600. 215 H pbeyer@jhu.edu
BEYER HOUPT, Julia ..... 740-587-6636. 379 D houpt@denison.edu
BEYL, Caula .... 865-974-7303. 463 C cbeyl@utk.edu
BEYROUTY, Craig .... 970-491-6274... 80 I craig.beyrouty@colostate.edu
BEZA, Mary .... 573-681-5561. 276 C bezam@lincolnu.edu
BEZETTE-FLORES, Noel .. 713-226-5570. 489 D bezetten@uhd.edu
BEZOTTE, Christine .... 607-735-1852. 323 H cbezotte@elmira.edu
BEZROUKOVA, Irina .... 218-726-8369. 264 D ibezrouk@umn.edu
BHADA, Farokh .... 401-232-6005. 438 K fbhada@bryant.edu
BHANDARI, Rupa .... 415-565-8909... 71 A bhandari@uchastings.edu
BHARGAVA, Vivek .... 601-877-6450. 265 G vivek@alcorn.edu
BHARUCHA, Jamshed .... 212-353-4240. 321 F president@cooper.edu

BHATI, Karni .... 864-294-3019. 444 C
karni.bhati@furman.edu
BHATTACHARYA,
Debasis .... 808-984-3619. 137 B
debasisb@hawaii.edu
BHATTACHARYA,
Somnath .... 561-297-3638. 114 L
sbhatt@fau.edu
BIA, Johnson .... 520-206-5001... 17 A
jbia@pima.edu
BIAFORA, Frank .... 727-873-4292. 116 D
fbiafora@mail.usf.edu
BIAFORE, Judith, E .... 304-367-4151. 529 F
Judy.Biafore@fairmontstate.edu
BIAGIOTTI, Eugene .... 610-647-4400. 418 I
ebiagiotti@immaculata.edu
BIALEK, Steve .... 414-277-7364. 534 G
bialek@msoe.edu
BIALK, Kathy .... 304-696-2281. 529 H
bialkk@marshall.edu
BIANCAMANO, John, J .. 740-593-2626. 387 C
biancama@ohio.edu
BIANCHI, Amy, M .... 617-333-2236. 225 E
abianchi@curry.edu
BIANCHI, Ashley .... 610-330-5055. 420 D
biancia@lafayette.edu
BIANCHI, Ashley .... 901-843-3810. 458 E
bianchia@rhodes.edu
BIANCHI, Julius .... 805-493-3483... 31 H
bianchi@clunet.edu
BIANCHI, Mark .... 732-987-2678. 302 B
bianchim@georgian.edu
BIANCO, Amy .... 845-848-4065. 322 G
amy.bianco@dc.edu
BIBB, Shawn .... 408-924-1500... 36 A
shawn.bibb@sjsu.edu
BIBBEE, Tammy .... 304-734-6618. 527 O
tbibbee@bridgemont.edu
BIBBENS, Matthew, G .... 909-607-8966... 39 D
matthew.bibbens@cmc.edu
BIBEAU, Shelley .... 651-846-1683. 261 D
shelley.bibeau@saintpaul.edu
BIBEAU, Susan .... 860-701-5000... 90 G
bibeau_s@mitchell.edu
BIBI, Khalid, W .... 716-888-8293. 316 C
bibi@canisius.edu
BIBLE, Doug .... 501-205-8453... 20 I
dbible@cbc.edu
BIBLE, Doug, S .... 318-797-5383. 205 F
doug.bible@lsus.edu
BIBLE, J. Brice .... 740-597-3246. 387 C
bibleb@ohio.edu
BIBLE, Robert .... 918-549-2800. 395 A
BICAK, Charles, J .... 308-865-8209. 292 H
bicakc@unk.edu
BICE, Cynthia .... 636-949-4618. 276 D
cbice@lindenwood.edu
BICE, Diane, K .... 810-762-7491. 244 Q
dbice@kettering.edu
BICE, JR., Gary, L .... 716-673-3341. 342 A
gary.bice@fredonia.edu
BICE, Patricia .... 914-251-6360. 344 D
patricia.bice@purchase.edu
BICEY, Michelle .... 757-873-4235. 510 B
mbicey@stratford.edu
BICHEL, Rebecca .... 817-272-1413. 491 B
rbichel@uta.edu
BICHELMEYER,
Barbara, A .... 812-941-2200. 168 F
bic@iu.edu
BICKEL, Kathy .... 541-737-2351. 406 A
kathy.bickel@oregonstate.edu
BICKEL, Linda, S .... 573-681-5489. 276 C
bickell@lincolnu.edu
BICKEL, Meghan .... 215-222-4200. 431 H
mbickel@walnuthillcollege.edu
BICKEL, Sarah .... 928-523-7608... 16 C
sarah.bickel@nau.edu
BICKEL, Teri .... 301-846-2446. 214 H
tbickel@frederick.edu
BICKELL, Kris .... 203-576-4851... 91 G
ubonline@bridgeport.edu
BICKERS, Eugene, N .... 213-740-1114... 74 A
bickers@usc.edu
BICKFORD, David .... 480-557-1946... 18 I
david.bickford@phoenix.edu
BICKFORD, Deborah, J .. 937-229-2245. 391 C
dbickford1@udayton.edu
BICKFORD, George .... 312-553-5896. 141 N
gbickford@ccc.edu
BICKFORD, Jeffrey .... 978-556-3745. 232 E
jbickford@necc.mass.edu
BICKFORD, Sonja .... 406-791-5389. 288 E
sbickford01@ugf.edu
BICKING, Michael, D ...... 610-436-3478. 430 A
mbicking@wcupa.edu
BICKLEY, Carol, A .... 803-321-5124. 445 G
carol.bickley@newberry.edu
BICKNELL, Brian .... 617-588-1365. 223 B
bbicknell@bfit.edu
BICKNELL-HOLMES,
Tracy .... 605-394-2511. 137 G
BICKSLER, Leslie .... 304-647-6279. 530 B
lbicksler@osteo.wvsom.edu
BIDDINGS-MURO,
Regina, D .... 219-989-2323. 171 N
reginab@purduecal.edu
BIDDISCOMBE, John, S . 860-685-2895... 92 H
jbiddiscombe@wesleyan.edu
BIDDLE, Chris .... 615-226-3990. 455 N
cbiddle@nadcedu.com
BIDDY, Scott .... 510-642-7374... 70 I
fsb@berkeley.edu
BIDWELL, Lorena, L .... 269-471-6124. 239 D
lorena@andrews.edu
BIEBER, Ann, D .... 610-799-1581. 421 I
abieber@lccc.edu
BIEBER, Deborah .... 773-256-3000. 152 H
dbieber@meadville.edu
BIEBER, Kori .... 541-956-7196. 407 F
kbieber@roguecc.edu
BIEBIGHAUSER,
Victor, K .... 334-395-8800. 131 H
vbiebighauser@southuniversity.edu
BIEBUYCK, Bill .... 563-588-6405. 176 F
bill.biebuyck@clarke.edu
BIEBUYCK, Brent .... 586-445-7119. 246 A
Biebuyckb@macomb.edu
BIEDSCHEID, Thomas ..... 970-491-6321... 80 I
tom.biedscheid@colostate.edu
BIEGEL, Peter, J .... 904-632-3131. 105 E
pbiegel@fscj.edu
BIEGEN, M. Sharon .... 314-516-5711. 283 E
sharon_biegen@umsl.edu
BIEGENZAHN, Nathan .... 919-497-3250. 356 E
nbiegenzahn@louisburg.edu
BIEHN, Christopher .... 607-274-3115. 327 E
cbiehn@ithaca.edu
BIEL, Alan .... 814-732-2856. 428 E
abiel@edinboro.edu
BIELEC, John .... 215-895-1434. 415 B
jbielec@drexel.edu
BIELEN, Paul .... 707-524-1608... 65 B
pbielen@santarosa.edu
BIELER, Glenn, M .... 410-516-8631. 215 H
gbieler1@jhu.edu
BIELMAN, Jess .... 503-517-1140. 408 H
jbielman@warnerpacific.edu
BIELSKI, Bradley, A .... 859-344-3305. 199 H
bradley.bielski@thomasmore.edu
BIENENFELD, Sheila .... 408-924-5300... 36 A
sheila.bienenfeld@sjsu.edu
BIENERT, Bonnie .... 847-628-2083. 149 B
bbienert@judsonu.edu
BIENFANG, Kim .... 763-433-1483. 257 P
kim.bienfang@anokaramsey.edu
BIENKOWSKI, Kathleen .. 404-727-0737. 124 E
kathleen.bienkowski@emory.edu
BIENVENUE, Scott .... 603-882-6923. 296 B
sbienvenue@ccsnh.edu
BIENZ, Richard, A .... 260-399-7700. 174 C
rbienz@sf.edu
BIER, Alice, G .... 718-951-5189. 317 C
abier@brooklyn.cuny.edu
BIER, Debbie .... 412-521-6200. 432 A
debbie.bier@rosedaletech.org
BIER, Jill .... 815-825-2086. 149 F
jill.bier@kishwaukeecollege.edu
BIERBAUER, Charles ...... 803-777-4105. 447 G
bierbauer@sc.edu
BIERLICH, Sue .... 714-432-5562... 39 K
sbierlich@occ.cccd.edu
BIERMAN, Derek .... 402-844-7060. 291 I
derek@northeast.edu
BIERMAN, Scott .... 402-557-7245. 280 G
scott.bierman@bellevue.edu
BIERMAN, Scott .... 608-363-2201. 531 M
biermans@beloit.edu
BIERMAN, Steve .... 417-447-8856. 279 K
biermans@otc.edu
BIERMANN, Mark, L .... 319-352-8284. 183 E
mark.biermann@wartburg.edu
BIERMANN, Theodore ..... 734-432-5515. 246 B
tbiermann@madonna.edu
BIERNACKI, Steve .... 505-566-3284. 311 I
biernackis@sanjuancollege.edu
BIERNBAUM, Dana .... 309-298-1800. 162 K
dm-biernbaum@wiu.edu
BIERNBAUM, John .... 309-298-3320. 162 K
j-biernbaum@wiu.edu
BIERYLA, John .... 570-389-4297. 427 H
jbieryla@bloomu.edu
BIES, James, B .... 605-274-4124. 449 K
jim.bies@augie.edu
BIES, Julia .... 315-279-5204. 328 D
jbies@mail.keuka.edu
BIESECKER, James .... 717-337-6700. 417 B
jbieseck@gettysburg.edu
BIETELCHIES, Wade .... 517-265-5161. 238 G
BIETZ, Gordon .... 423-236-2801. 458 J
bietz@southern.edu
BIGARD, Heather .... 217-854-3231. 140 G
heather.bigard@blackburn.edu
BIGBY, Angela, D .... 702-968-2046. 295 E
abigby@roseman.edu
BIGCRANE, Michael .... 406-275-4789. 288 C
michael_bigcrane@skc.edu
BIGELOW, Holly .... 507-280-3509. 261 A
holly.bigelow@rctc.edu
BIGELOW, Scott .... 910-521-6351. 369 B
scott.bigelow@uncp.edu
BIGELOW, Susan .... 307-674-6446. 543 F
sbigelow@sheridan.edu
BIGG, Dort .... 954-763-9840... 98 I
executivedirector@atom.edu
BIGGER, Kimberly .... 870-248-4000... 20 G
kim.bigger@blackrivertech.edu
BIGGER, Roberta, H .... 864-597-4040. 449 I
biggerrh@wofford.edu
BIGGERS, Carla, D .... 409-944-1200. 472 I
cbiggers@gc.edu
BIGGERS, Darlene .... 281-283-3000. 489 C
biggers@uhcl.edu
BIGGERS, Leisa .... 310-660-3593... 43 B
lbiggers@elcamino.edu
BIGGERS, Weslynn .... 706-385-1081. 130 F
weslynn.biggers@point.edu
BIGGERSTAFF, Patrick .... 704-233-8247. 370 G
dpbigg@wingate.edu
BIGGIO, Nancy .... 205-726-4267..... 6 F
ncbiggio@samford.edu
BIGGS, Becca .... 503-821-8892. 406 F
beca@pnca.edu
BIGGS, Kristen .... 231-843-5875. 252 H
BIGGS, Patsy .... 501-370-4002... 19 J
patsy.biggs@arkansasbaptist.edu
BIGGS, Shirley, A .... 803-535-5268. 442 B
sbiggs@claflin.edu
BIGGS, Sue, A .... 325-670-1314. 472 O
sbiggs@hsutx.edu
BIGGS GARBUIO,
Judith .... 509-313-4100. 520 A
biggsgarbuio@gonzaga.edu
BIGHAM, William, L .... 937-766-7810. 375 K
bbigham@cedarville.edu
BIGLER, Thomas .... 717-464-7050. 421 B
BIGLIENI, Lindy .... 417-269-3083. 273 D
admissions@coxcollege.edu
BIGNEY, Tracy .... 207-973-3234. 212 A
bigney@maine.edu
BIHL, Andy, J .... 330-569-5335. 380 I
bihlsj@hiram.edu
BIKLEN, Douglas, P .... 315-443-4751. 347 C
dpbiklen@syr.edu
BILACH, Matt .... 480-994-9244... 17 Q
mattb@swiha.edu
BILBRUCK, Tom .... 661-362-3235... 40 E
tom.bilbruck@canyons.edu
BILDER, Kevin .... 480-517-8464... 15 D
kevin.bilder@riosalado.edu
BILDERBACK, Rebecca ... 620-365-5116. 183 I
bilderback@allencc.edu
BILDERBACK, Ryan .... 620-365-5116. 183 I
rbilderback@allencc.edu
BILELLA, Jamieson, A .... 973-655-4352. 303 D
bilellaj@mail.montclair.edu
BILES, Deron .... 817-923-1921. 481 G
dbiles@swbts.edu
BILGER, Cindy, L .... 570-577-1631. 411 A
cbilger@bucknell.edu
BILGER, Jackie .... 570-321-4309. 422 H
bilger@lycoming.edu
BILGIN, Deniz .... 831-242-3744. 544 F
deniz.i.bilgin.civ@mail.mil
BILIONIS, Louis, D .... 513-556-0121. 390 G
louis.bilionis@uc.edu
BILLARD, Trisha .... 516-876-3053. 343 D
billardt@oldwestbury.edu
BILLEAUDEAU, Kim, A .... 337-262-5300. 208 D
kimberlyb@louisiana.edu
BILLEAUX, David .... 361-825-2393. 483 F
david.billeaux@tamucc.edu
BILLECI, Celesta .... 805-893-3437... 72 B
celesta.billeci@sa.ucsb.edu
BILLEN, Isabelle .... 405-733-7356. 399 F
ibillen@rose.edu
BILLER, Gary, M .... 309-298-1814. 162 K
gm-biller@wiu.edu
BILLEY, Terry, L .... 580-928-5533. 400 B
terry.billey@swosu.edu
BILLHARTZ, Scott, L ...... 618-537-6869. 152 G
slbillhartz@mckendree.edu
BILLI, John, E .... 734-936-5214. 251 C
jbilli@umich.edu
BILLIE, Marie, H .... 410-651-7502. 219 E
mhbillie@umes.edu
BILLIE, Natasha, M .... 405-466-3445. 395 N
nmbillie@langston.edu
BILLIG, Michael .... 717-291-4152. 416 J
michael.billig@fandm.edu
BILLINGER, Kristi, M ..... 785-864-7231. 190 L
kristib@ku.edu
BILLINGS, Amanda .... 214-648-2344. 493 E
amanda.billings@utsouthwestern.edu
BILLINGS, Chuck .... 415-485-3263... 42 J
cbillings@dominican.edu
BILLINGS, Debra .... 810-766-4278. 239 G
debra.billings@baker.edu
BILLINGS, Frank .... 516-572-7771. 332 C
frank.billings@ncc.edu
BILLINGS, Patricia, L ..... 206-934-6739. 523 A
patricia.billings@seattlecolleges.edu
BILLINGSLEA, Aldo .... 408-554-5578... 64 M
abillingslea@scu.edu
BILLINGSLEY, Anna, B ... 540-654-1055. 510 J
abilling@umw.edu
BILLINGSLEY, Dale, B .... 502-852-5209. 200 D
dbbill01@louisville.edu
BILLINGSLEY, Jodie .... 806-742-2020. 487 D
jodie.billingsley@ttu.edu
BILLINGSLEY, Linda .... 318-487-7630. 202 F
linda.billingsley@lacollege.edu
BILLINGSLEY, Tiffany ..... 870-633-4480... 21 A
tbillingsley@eacc.edu
BILLINGTON,
Suzanne K, L .... 208-885-5867. 139 D
suzib@uidaho.edu
BILLITTIER, Anthony .... 716-829-8124. 323 D
billitti@dyc.edu
BILLMAN, Kathleen .... 773-256-0770. 152 B
kbillman@lstc.edu
BILLMAN, Rhonda .... 330-287-1213. 386 F
billman.36@osu.edu
BILLS, Andy .... 336-841-4538. 355 C
abills@highpoint.edu
BILLS, Joyce .... 918-465-1777. 395 G
jbills@eosc.edu
BILLS, Linda, G .... 814-332-3362. 409 D
linda.bills@allegheny.edu
BILLS-WINDT, Caryn, A . 312-413-8145. 161 D
cabw@uic.edu
BILLUPS, Kurt .... 806-457-4200. 472 G
kbillups@fpctx.edu
BILLUPS, Vory .... 404-225-4474. 121 B
vbillups@atlantatech.edu
BILLY, Beth .... 251-809-1555..... 5 A
beth.billy@jdcc.edu
BILLY, George, J .... 516-726-5747. 545 H
billyg@usmma.edu
BILMONT, John .... 415-241-2230... 38 L
jbilmont@ccsf.edu
BILODEAU, Denise .... 978-232-2102. 226 C
bilodeau@endicott.edu
BILODEAU, Gene .... 970-824-1103... 80 B
gene.bilodeau@cncc.edu
BILONG, Danilo Philbert 671-735-5554. 546 C
danilophilbert.bilong@guamcc.edu
BILOTTA, Barbara, J .... 716-880-2265. 330 F
barbara.bilotta@medaille.edu
BILOTTA, Leone .... 610-917-1483. 436 C
l_bilotta@vfcc.edu
BILSKY, Edward .... 207-602-2707. 213 A
ebilsky@une.edu
BILSKY, Steven .... 215-898-6121. 435 B
athdir@pobox.upenn.edu
BIMONTE-YERGANIAN,
Maria .... 203-582-3446... 91 A
maria.bimonte@quinnipiac.edu
BIMROSE, Irene .... 309-692-4092. 152 J
ibimrose@midstate.edu
BINA, Shawn .... 218-235-2170. 261 G
s.bina@vcc.edu
BINA, III, William, F ...... 478-301-5570. 128 H
bina_wf@mercer.edu
BINARD, Kris .... 303-404-5103... 81 N
kris.binard@frontrange.edu
BINAU, Brad, A .... 614-235-4136. 390 A
bbinau@TLSohio.edu
BINDER, George .... 985-867-2229. 206 H
gbinderfinaid@sjasc.edu
BINDER, Jan .... 602-285-7869... 15 C
jan.binder@phoenixcollege.edu
BINDEWALD, Kurt .... 504-865-3226. 205 H
kjbindew@loyno.edu
BINEK, Gordy .... 701-224-5697. 372 B
gordon.binek@bismarckstate.edu
BINESH, Behzad .... 714-744-7099... 38 A
binesh@chapman.edu
BING, Richard, N .... 212-998-2391. 334 D
richard.bing@nyu.edu
BINGAMON, Cindy .... 314-837-6777. 280 K
cbingamon@slcconline.edu
BINGEL, Laurie, A .... 618-235-2700. 160 A
laurie.bingel@swic.edu
BINGER, Nancy .... 847-628-2510. 149 B
nbinger@judsonu.edu
BINGHAM, C. Sam .... 864-503-5073. 448 H
sbingham@uscupstate.edu
BINGHAM, Charlotte .... 806-742-3627. 487 D
charlotte.bingham@ttu.edu
BINGHAM, Charlotte .... 806-742-3627. 487 E
charlotte.bingham@ttu.edu

BINGHAM, Daniel .... 406-444-6800. 287 A
daniel.bingham@umhelena.edu
BINGHAM, Jeff .... 405-425-5152. 397 D
jeff.bingham@oc.edu
BINGHAM, Jeri .... 773-252-5131. 156 I
jeri.bingham@resu.edu
BINGHAM, OP,
Mary Rose .... 615-297-7545. 452 J
srmrose@aquinascollege.edu
BINGHAM, Michael .... 828-448-6025. 365 A
mbingham@wpcc.edu
BINGHAM, Millard .... 601-432-6234. 267 E
millard.j.bingham@jsums.edu
BINGHAM, Nelson .... 765-983-1205. 165 G
nelsonb@earlham.edu
BINGHAM, Nelson .... 765-983-1211. 165 G
nelsonb@earlham.edu
BINGHAM, Rachel .... 801-524-8129. 495 O
rbingham@ldsbc.edu
BINGHAM, Rosie, P .... 901-678-2114. 460 B
rbingham@memphis.edu
BINGHAM, Thomas, E ... 808-956-3469. 136 B
bingham@hawaii.edu
BINGHAM BLEVINS,
Granetta .... 502-863-8000. 194 C
BINION, Jim .... 940-552-6291. 493 F
jbinion@vernoncollege.edu
BINK, Cynthia .... 718-260-5030. 319 B
cbink@citytech.cuny.edu
BINKERD, James .... 707-638-5883... 69 K
jim.binkerd@tu.edu
BINKOWSKI, Marcella .... 215-637-7700. 418 G
smbinkowski@holyfamily.edu
BINNEY, Craig .... 508-565-1107. 237 A
cbinney@stonehill.edu
BINNICKER, Paul .... 816-833-0524. 178 F
binnicke@graceland.edu
BINNS, Andrew, N .... 215-898-7225. 435 B
abinns@sas.upenn.edu
BINSFELD, Douglas .... 218-855-8184. 258 B
dbinfeld@clcmn.edu
BINSTOCK, Neal, F .... 412-397-6290. 431 I
binstock@rmu.edu
BINTNER, Leslie .... 515-244-4221. 175 C
bintnerl@aib.edu
BIO, Cathy .... 808-984-3519. 137 B
cbio@hawaii.edu
BIOTEAU, Cynthia, A ...... 801-957-4226. 498 B
cbioteau@slcc.edu
BIR, Chad .... 317-955-6040. 170 V
cbir@marian.edu
BIRBERICK, Anne .... 815-753-0494. 154 I
annie@niu.edu
BIRCH, Andrea, C .... 770-718-5325. 122 A
abirch@brenau.edu
BIRCH, Barbara .... 212-960-5373. 351 M
birch@yu.edu
BIRCH, Brian .... 801-863-8361. 497 C
brian.birch@uvu.edu
BIRCH, Esther .... 301-736-3631. 216 B
esther.birch@msbbcs.edu
BIRCH, Laura, A .... 217-420-6661. 153 C
lbirch@millikin.edu
BIRCHAK, Chris .... 713-221-8007. 489 D
birchakc@uhd.edu
BIRCHARD, Michael .... 763-424-0850. 260 C
mbirchard@nhcc.edu
BIRCHWOOD, Rachel ..... 845-451-1459. 322 D
r_birchw@culinary.edu
BIRCKBICHLER, Carrie .... 724-738-2150. 429 F
carrie.birckbichler@sru.edu
BIRCKBICHLER,
Carrie, J .... 724-738-2150. 429 F
carrie.birckbichler@sru.edu
BIRD, Andrew .... 360-596-5219. 524 A
abird@spscc.edu
BIRD, Brandon .... 206-726-5024. 518 G
bbird@cornish.edu
BIRD, Lee, E .... 405-744-5328. 397 H
lee.bird@okstate.edu
BIRD, Lori .... 419-267-1266. 385 F
lbird@northweststate.edu
BIRD, Lyly .... 909-537-7096... 34 E
lbird@csusb.edu
BIRD, Sheila .... 620-278-4247. 190 I
sbird@sterling.edu
BIRD, Su Ann .... 229-931-2110. 131 G
sbird@southgatech.edu
BIRD, SuAnn .... 229-931-2110. 131 G
sbird@southgatech.edu
BIRD, Veronica .... 610-917-1422. 436 C
rabird@vfcc.edu
BIRDINE, Phil .... 580-477-7700. 401 J
phil.birdine@wosc.edu
BIRDSELL, David .... 646-660-6700. 316 J
David.Birdsell@baruch.cuny.edu
BIRDSONG, Jeff .... 918-540-6348. 396 G
jbirdsong@neo.edu
BIRDSONG, Ronnie .... 575-562-4490. 309 H
ronnie.birdsong@enmu.edu
BIRDWELL, Cindy, A ...... 517-264-7194. 250 B
cbirdwell@sienaheights.edu
BIRDWHISTELL, Terry, L 859-218-1871. 200 C
terry.bird@uky.edu
BIRELINE, David .... 949-214-3209... 41 I
david.bireline@cui.edu
BIRENBAUM, Elizabeth .. 714-432-6196... 39 K
ebirenbaum@occ.cccd.edu
BIRGE, James, F .... 603-899-4129. 296 H
birgej@franklinpierce.edu
BIRGE, Susan, N .... 203-254-4000... 89 I
sbirge@fairfield.edu
BIRGEN, Mariah, H .... 319-352-8565. 183 E
mariah.birgen@wartburg.edu
BIRGEN, Mike .... 606-626-2681. 451 I
Mike.Birgen@northern.edu
BIRINGER, Bobbi .... 312-261-3550. 153 I
bobbi.biringer@nl.edu
BIRK, Michelle, L .... 618-235-2700. 160 A
michelle.birk@swic.edu
BIRKE, Richard .... 503-370-6046. 408 J
rbirke@willamette.edu
BIRKEDAHL, Patrice .... 510-659-6208... 57 A
pbirkedahl@ohlone.edu
BIRKEDAHL, Walter .... 510-659-6216... 57 A
wbirkedahl@ohlone.edu
BIRKENHOLTZ,
Kenneth, I .... 515-961-1512. 182 E
ken.birkenholtz@simpson.edu
BIRKHEAD, Kathryn .... 479-986-4052... 22 C
kbirkhead@nwacc.edu
BIRKHEAD, Mary .... 610-282-1100. 414 F
mary.birkhead@desales.edu
BIRKHOLZ, Amberleigh .. 708-209-3629. 143 E
amberleigh.birkholz@cuchicago.edu
BIRKNER, Linda, M .... 501-977-2006... 25 C
birkner@uaccm.edu
BIRKY, Ian, T .... 610-758-3880. 422 A
itb0@lehigh.edu
BIRMINGHAM, John ...... 630-353-9010. 144 A
jbirmingham@devry.edu
BIRMINGHAM, Jolene ... 312-226-6294. 151 A
jbirmingham@lexingtoncollege.edu
BIRMINGHAM, Stacy, G 724-458-3841. 417 E
sgbirmingham@gcc.edu
BIRNBACH, David, J ...... 305-284-2002. 118 F
dbirnbach@miami.edu
BIRNBAUM, Ben .... 617-552-3353. 224 A
ben.birnbaum@bu.edu
BIRNBAUM, Roger .... 323-856-7600... 27 O
BIRO, Susan .... 410-386-8419. 214 A
sbiro@carrollcc.edu
BIRON, Jackie .... 510-780-4500... 50 I
jbiron00@lifewest.edu
BIRON, Louise .... 518-255-5623. 344 E
bironl@cobleskill.edu
BIRON, Ronald .... 603-448-2445. 297 A
rbiron@lebanoncollege.edu
BIROS, Demetra .... 425-739-8315. 520 K
demetra.biros@lwtech.edu
BIROS, Janice .... 215-895-2200. 415 B
jan.biros@drexel.edu
BIRREN, Susan, J .... 781-736-3451. 224 F
birren@brandeis.edu
BIRRINGER, Charles, E .. 920-924-3420. 540 F
cbirringer@morainepark.edu
BIRTWISTLE, Heidi .... 610-341-1738. 415 G
hbirtwis@eastern.edu
BISBEY, CDP, Michele ... 412-536-1255. 420 A
michele.bisbey@laroche.edu
BISCH, Debbie .... 620-227-9209. 186 B
debbieb@dc3.edu
BISCHOFF, Jeannette ...... 916-660-7000... 66 B
jbischoff@sierracollege.edu
BISCHOFF, Margaretha ... 956-872-8310. 480 I
etybuh@southtexascollege.edu
BISCHOFF, Richard, W ... 216-368-5445. 375 J
richard.bischoff@case.edu
BISCONTI, Ursula .... 941-694-1122. 299 D
uhn@berkeleycollege.edu
BISESE, Stephen, D .... 804-289-8615. 510 L
sbisese@richmond.edu
BISESI, Linda .... 415-565-4645... 71 A
bisesil@uchastings.edu
BISESI, Michael, S .... 614-292-8350. 386 E
bisesi.12@osu.edu
BISH, Courtney, D .... 315-386-7120. 345 F
bish@canton.edu
BISH, Douglas .... 415-239-3720... 38 L
dbish@ccsf.edu
BISH, Kevin .... 859-858-2272. 192 A
BISHARA, Heather .... 561-297-4159. 114 L
hbishara@fau.edu
BISHEL, Mary, A .... 219-785-5204. 172 A
mbishel@pnc.edu
BISHOP, Angalynn .... 361-698-1255. 471 G
abishop3@delmar.edu
BISHOP, Brandan .... 616-222-1954. 241 F
brandan.bishop@cornerstone.edu
BISHOP, Carol .... 518-255-5520. 344 E
bishopcm@cobleskill.edu
BISHOP, Carol, M .... 607-746-4582. 345 G
bishopcm@delhi.edu
BISHOP, Catherine .... 405-325-1543. 401 B
cbishop@ou.edu
BISHOP, Christopher ...... 888-384-0849... 27 E
cjbishop@allied.edu
BISHOP, Christopher ...... 970-675-3251... 80 B
christopher.bishop@cncc.edu
BISHOP, David .... 806-785-9285. 494 F
bishop@wbu.edu
BISHOP, Donald .... 574-631-7505. 174 A
dbishop1@nd.edu
BISHOP, Eric .... 909-652-7405... 37 M
eric.bishop@chaffey.edu
BISHOP, Eric .... 928-524-7400... 16 E
eric.bishop@npc.edu
BISHOP, George .... 850-872-3803. 106 H
gbishop@gulfcoast.edu
BISHOP, Ginger .... 828-328-7335. 356 B
ginger.bishop@lr.edu
BISHOP, Jack .... 509-963-1914. 517 F
bishopj@cwu.edu
BISHOP, Jeffrey .... 314-977-6663. 281 I
jbisho12@slu.edu
BISHOP, Kelley .... 301-314-7236. 219 B
kbishop@umd.edu
BISHOP, Kristy, A .... 816-604-1165. 277 C
kristy.bishop@mcckc.edu
BISHOP, Kyle, K .... 240-895-4289. 218 A
kkbishop@smcm.edu
BISHOP, Lisa, J .... 812-888-4274. 174 F
bishop@vinu.edu
BISHOP, Nancy .... 803-778-6638. 441 F
bishopnw@cctech.edu
BISHOP, Nathaniel, L ..... 540-985-8484. 506 G
nlbishop@jchs.edu
BISHOP, Pamela .... 614-287-2437. 378 B
pbishop2@cscc.edu
BISHOP, Patty .... 925-631-4793... 61 F
pbishop@stmarys-ca.edu
BISHOP, Paul .... 805-965-0581... 64 L
pwbishop@sbcc.edu
BISHOP, Phil .... 206-876-6100. 523 D
pbishop@theseattleschool.edu
BISHOP, Rex .... 770-975-4522. 122 I
BISHOP, Richard .... 860-832-2201... 87 K
bishopr@ccsu.edu
BISHOP, Robert .... 510-780-4500... 50 I
rbishop@lifewest.edu
BISHOP, Robert .... 414-288-6591. 534 B
robert.bishop@marquette.edu
BISHOP, Sandy .... 715-365-4564. 540 G
sbishop@nicoletcollege.edu
BISHOP, Selah .... 904-470-8220. 102 A
selah.bisho0911@ewc.edu
BISHOP, Shane .... 406-377-9421. 286 A
sbishop@dawson.edu
BISHOP, Steve .... 417-447-8152. 279 K
bishops@otc.edu
BISHOP, Steve .... 601-276-3701. 269 H
bishop@smcc.edu
BISHOP, Wesley, T .... 504-286-5325. 206 K
wbishop@suno.edu
BISHOP, William .... 504-861-5431. 205 H
wgbishop@loyno.edu
BISHOP, William .... 916-278-7469... 34 D
william.bishop@csus.edu
BISHOP, Wilsie, S .... 423-439-4811. 459 C
bishopws@etsu.edu
BISHOP-STUART, Aimee 419-251-1203. 383 G
aimee.bishopstuart@mercycollege.edu
BISHOP STUART, Aimee 419-251-1802. 383 G
aimee.bishopstuart@mercycollege.edu
BISIGNANO, Chris .... 914-251-6530. 344 D
chris.bisignanoi@purchase.edu
BISKING, Robert .... 210-343-2132. 477 N
rbisking@lake.ollusa.edu
BISKUP, Susan .... 570-408-4355. 437 F
susan.biskup@wilkes.edu
BISKUPIAK, Walter, H .... 406-447-5420. 285 G
bbiskupi@carroll.edu
BISLEY, Deanna .... 800-567-2344. 532 E
dbisley@menominee.edu
BISMARK, Jeanie .... 870-235-4078... 23 F
mjbismark@saumag.edu
BISSELL, Michelle .... 304-205-6640. 528 B
mbissell@kvctc.edu
BISSELL, Sandra .... 315-781-3312. 326 C
bissell@hws.edu
BISSELL PAULSON,
Lisa .... 707-965-7362... 57 J
lpaulson@puc.edu
BISSET, Matthew, S .... 727-864-8222. 101 N
bissetms@eckerd.edu
BISSET, William, J .... 718-862-7200. 329 M
william.bisset@manhattan.edu
BISSETTE, Callie .... 252-399-6336. 352 F
cbissette@barton.edu
BISSONETTE, David .... 218-855-8178. 258 B
dbissonette@clcmn.edu
BISSONETTE, Matt .... 507-379-3335. 260 I
matt.bissonette@riverland.edu
BISWAS, Harun .... 678-466-4240. 123 A
harunbiswas@clayton.edu
BITIKOFER, Scott .... 407-646-2121. 111 Q
sbitikofer@rollins.edu
BITNER, Hannah .... 816-322-0110. 271 O
hannah.bitner@calvary.edu
BITNER, Scott .... 410-706-3822. 219 C
sbitner@af.umaryland.edu
BITNER, Teddy .... 816-322-0110. 271 O
teddy.bitner@calvary.edu
BITOK, Abraham .... 928-724-6611... 13 H
akbitok@dinecollege.edu
BITTENBENDER, David ... 206-934-7792. 522 I
david.bittenbender@seattlecolleges.edu
BITTERBAUM, Erik, J ..... 607-753-2201. 343 B
erik.bitterbaum@cortland.edu
BITTERSFELD, Y .... 718-692-0208. 351 E
BITTINGER, Dale .... 410-455-2278. 219 D
bittinger@umbc.edu
BITTLE, Carolyn .... 910-410-1751. 362 I
carolynb@richmondcc.edu
BITTORF, David, C .... 240-500-2000. 215 B
dcbittorf@hagerstowncc.edu
BITZER, Michael .... 704-637-4466. 353 E
jmbitzer@catawba.edu
BITZER, Steve .... 715-682-4591. 541 F
Steve.Bitzer@witc.edu
BIVENS, Leon, J .... 410-651-6681. 219 E
ljbivens@umes.edu
BIXBY, David, E .... 626-815-5334... 29 H
dbixby@apu.edu
BIXBY, John, L .... 305-284-2211. 118 F
jbixby@miami.edu
BIXEL, Gil .... 850-484-1575. 110 G
gbixel@pensacolastate.edu
BIXLER, Cindy .... 386-226-7959. 102 B
cynthia.bixler@erau.edu
BIXLER, Kirk, J .... 317-738-8801. 165 I
kbixler@franklincollege.edu
BIZON, Walter, G .... 248-204-3020. 245 I
wbizon@ltu.edu
BJELLAND, David .... 320-762-4407. 257 O
davidb@alextech.edu
BJERKAAS, Douglas .... 303-937-4035... 79 E
dbjerkaas@chu.edu
BJERKLIE, Joseph, R ...... 207-834-8621. 212 E
joseph.bjerklie@maine.edu
BJOKNE, Daniel, H .... 515-964-0601. 178 E
bjokned@faith.edu
BJORK, Ross .... 662-915-7546. 270 B
rbjork@olemiss.edu
BJORKE, Joell .... 507-457-5014. 262 A
jbjorke@winona.edu
BJORKLUND, Robert, B . 651-638-6396. 253 K
robert-bjorklund@bethel.edu
BJORKMAN, David, J ..... 561-297-0113. 114 L
dbjorkm1@fau.edu
BJORKMAN, Karen .... 419-530-7842. 392 B
karen.bjorkman@utoledo.edu
BJORLAND, Kirk .... 641-784-5110. 178 F
kdbjorla@graceland.edu
BJORN, Thorr, D .... 401-874-5245. 440 D
tbjorn@uri.edu
BJUR, Jared .... 909-599-5433... 50 J
jbjur@lifepacific.edu
BLACK, Adam .... 801-863-6378. 497 C
blackad@uvu.edu
BLACK, Angel .... 303-837-0825... 78 H
ablack@aii.edu
BLACK, Bettye, R .... 405-466-3294. 395 N
brblack@langston.edu
BLACK, Britt .... 630-752-5072. 163 F
britt.black@wheaton.edu
BLACK, Christopher, B ... 260-422-5561. 167 B
cbblack@indianatech.edu
BLACK, Connie .... 208-562-3000. 138 C
BLACK, David, R .... 304-829-7313. 526 D
dblack@bethanywv.edu
BLACK, Dennis, R .... 716-645-2982. 341 F
dblack@buffalo.edu
BLACK, Diane .... 251-442-2209..... 9 A
dblack@umobile.edu
BLACK, Eliza, E .... 803-934-3264. 445 F
eblack@morris.edu
BLACK, Ellen .... 843-349-5211. 444 F
ellen.black@hgtc.edu
BLACK, Heather .... 412-365-1281. 412 K
hblack@chatham.edu
BLACK, Jane .... 740-695-9500. 374 H
jblack@belmontcollege.edu
BLACK, Jason .... 205-726-3673..... 6 F
jjblack@samford.edu
BLACK, Jeff .... 410-972-3303. 217 G
jeffrey.black@sjca.edu
BLACK, Jerry, D .... 937-775-2411. 393 G
jerry.black@wright.edu
BLACK, John .... 478-471-2712. 128 I
john.black@maconstate.edu

BLACK, John Paul .... 252-527-6223. 361 F
jpblack@lenoircc.edu
BLACK, John Paul .... 252-527-6223. 361 F
jblack@lenoircc.edu
BLACK, Joshua .... 423-614-8370. 455 L
jblack@leeuniversity.edu
BLACK, Joshua .... 864-941-8540. 446 C
black.j@ptc.edu
BLACK, Kedric .... 801-863-8536. 497 C
kedric.black@uvu.edu
BLACK, Laurie .... 802-258-3273. 500 C
laurie.black@worldlearning.org
BLACK, Lendley, C .... 218-726-7106. 264 D
chan@d.umn.edu
BLACK, Linda .... 970-351-1638... 86 C
linda.black@unco.edu
BLACK, Lynda, K .... 336-838-6148. 365 B
lynda.black@wilkescc.edu
BLACK, Mark .... 615-966-5709. 456 B
mark.black@lipscomb.edu
BLACK, Maryann .... 919-668-3792. 354 A
maryann.black@duke.edu
BLACK, Michael .... 404-894-2486. 125 D
mike.black@housing.gatech.edu
BLACK, Michael .... 805-922-6966... 26 K
mblack@pcpa.org
BLACK, Michael, E .... 210-567-7103. 493 A
blackm@uthscsa.edu
BLACK, Michael, M .... 229-333-7838. 134 B
mmblack@valdosta.edu
BLACK, Rochelle, A .... 248-370-3682. 248 J
black@oakland.edu
BLACK, Rose Ann .... 718-779-1430. 336 D
rblack@plazacollege.edu
BLACK, Sarah .... 318-427-4407. 205 A
sblack@lsua.edu
BLACK, Shaun, C .... 315-445-4569. 328 F
blacksc@lemoyne.edu
BLACK, Sherry .... 775-445-3000. 295 A
sherry.black@wnc.edu
BLACK, Sul .... 803-705-4334. 441 C
blacks@benedict.edu
BLACK, Tanja .... 864-429-8728. 448 G
trblack@mailbox.sc.edu
BLACK, Thomas .... 650-723-1550... 68 E
thomas.black@stanford.edu
BLACK, Wilhemena .... 305-284-3064. 118 F
wblack@miami.edu
BLACK, William, N .... 215-204-4760. 433 K
william.black@temple.edu
BLACK-ARIAS, Maxinee .. 404-237-7573. 121 F
mblackarias@bauder.edu
BLACK-GOLD, Tonia .... 704-637-4393. 353 E
tblackgo@catawba.edu
BLACKABY, Leslie .... 509-574-6806. 525 G
lblackaby@yvcc.edu
BLACKBOURN,
Richard, L .... 662-325-3717. 268 D
rlb277@msstate.edu
BLACKBURN, Alison, A .. 617-627-6272. 237 C
alison.blackburn@tufts.edu
BLACKBURN, Cheryl ...... 425-388-9572. 519 I
cblackburn@everettcc.edu
BLACKBURN, David .... 716-286-8405. 334 F
deb@niagara.edu
BLACKBURN, David .... 423-425-4495. 463 D
david-blackburn@utc.edu
BLACKBURN, J. Blair ..... 214-333-5122. 470 D
blair@dbu.edu
BLACKBURN, James ...... 315-279-5215. 328 D
jblackbu@mail.keuka.edu
BLACKBURN, John, D .... 217-732-3155. 151 C
jblackburn@lincolncollege.edu
BLACKBURN, Kristi, V ... 310-233-4044... 51 H
blackbkv@lahc.edu
BLACKBURN, Michael .... 713-500-6087. 492 E
Michael.R.Blackburn@uth.tmc.edu
BLACKBURN, Steven ..... 860-509-9560... 90 B
sblackburn@hartsem.edu
BLACKBURN, Terri .... 208-467-8673. 139 A
tblackburn@nnu.edu
BLACKBURN-SMITH,
Jefferson .... 614-823-1031. 387 K
jblackburnsmith@otterbein.edu
BLACKHURST, Anne, E ... 218-477-2415. 259 H
blackhurst@mnstate.edu
BLACKKETTER,
Donald, M .... 406-496-4129. 287 F
dblackketter@mtech.edu
BLACKLAW, Stuart .... 928-445-7300... 19 H
BLACKLEY, Scott .... 662-407-1501. 267 C
jsblackley@iccms.edu
BLACKMAN, Ronda .... 828-277-5521. 366 G
rblackman@southcollegenc.edu
BLACKMAN, Sharon, L ... 214-378-1748. 470 F
sblackman@dcccd.edu
BLACKMAN, Sherry .... 973-748-9000. 299 F
sherry_blackman@bloomfield.edu
BLACKMON, Bruce .... 910-410-1723. 362 I
bblackmon@richmondcc.edu
BLACKMON, Chianti .... 301-447-6932. 217 B
blackmon@msmary.edu
BLACKMON, Luke .... 843-863-8004. 441 H
lblackmon@csuniv.edu
BLACKMON, Terry, W .... 731-426-7601. 455 J
tblackmon@lanecollege.edu
BLACKMON, Velma, B ... 252-335-3294. 367 C
vbblackmon@mail.ecsu.edu
BLACKNEY, Kenneth .... 215-895-1505. 415 B
ksb@drexel.edu
BLACKSMITH, Lourdes ... 630-466-7900. 162 J
lblacksmith@waubonsee.edu
BLACKSMITH, Robin ...... 206-546-4503. 523 F
rblacksmith@shoreline.edu
BLACKSON, Valora, N .... 718-390-4439. 339 A
blacksov@stjohns.edu
BLACKSTAD, Ana .... 425-352-8359. 517 E
ablackstad@cascadia.edu
BLACKSTON, Barbara .... 931-221-6163. 459 B
blackstonb@apsu.edu
BLACKSTON, Michael ..... 559-438-4222... 46 K
michael_blackston@heald.edu
BLACKSTONE,
Tondelaya .... 410-951-4265. 220 B
tblackstone@coppin.edu
BLACKWELDER, Mary, B 414-955-8323. 534 C
blackwel@mcw.edu
BLACKWELDER, Murray . 816-235-2672. 283 D
blackwelderm@umkc.edu
BLACKWELDER, Tom ..... 509-527-2113. 524 I
tom.blackwelder@wallawalla.edu
BLACKWELL, Amy .... 864-294-3496. 444 C
amy.blackwell@furman.edu
BLACKWELL, Ann .... 601-266-4568. 270 E
ann.blackwell@usm.edu
BLACKWELL, Billie Jo .... 908-852-1400. 300 D
blackwellb@centenarycollege.edu
BLACKWELL, David .... 859-257-8939. 200 C
dblackwell@uky.edu
BLACKWELL, David .... 870-584-4471... 24 F
dblackwell@cccua.edu
BLACKWELL, Deborah ... 704-355-5970. 353 D
debbie.blackwell@carolinascollege.edu
BLACKWELL, Jeannine ... 859-257-1759. 200 C
blackwell@uky.edu
BLACKWELL, Joe .... 405-789-7661. 400 A
joe.blackwell@swcu.edu
BLACKWELL, Joyce .... 336-517-2154. 352 H
Jblackwell@bennett.edu
BLACKWELL, Mary, D .... 623-845-3305... 14 M
m.blackwell@gcmail.maricopa.edu
BLACKWELL, Mike .... 803-754-4100. 443 C
BLACKWELL, Samuel ...... 803-780-1239. 449 E
blackwell@voorhees.edu
BLACKWELL, Scott .... 601-266-4783. 270 E
edward.blackwell@usm.edu
BLACKWOOD, James ..... 706-880-8050. 128 A
jblackwood@lagrange.edu
BLACKWOOD,
Jothany, L .... 559-442-4600... 68 I
jothany.blackwood@fresnocitycollege.edu
BLACKWOOD, Kathy ...... 650-358-6790... 64 A
blackwoodk@smccd.edu
BLACKWOOD, Phyllis .... 254-299-8659. 476 D
pblackwood@mclennan.edu
BLACKWOOD,
Rodney, B .... 806-720-7402. 476 B
rod.blackwood@lcu.edu
BLADDICK, Jerry .... 636-949-2000. 276 D
BLADES, Dawn .... 845-257-3171. 342 B
bladesd@newpaltz.edu
BLAES, Ziuta .... 337-521-8896. 203 I
ziuta.blaes@southlouisiana.edu
BLAESING, Ron .... 334-244-3758...... 2 A
rblaesin@aum.edu
BLAGDAN, Donna .... 760-872-2000... 42 E
dblagdan@deepsprings.edu
BLAGG, Oneida .... 307-766-3459. 543 I
oblagg@uwyo.edu
BLAGG, Rosalyn .... 870-508-6128... 20 A
rblagg@asumh.edu
BLAGUSZEWSKI,
Edward, F .... 413-545-0444. 228 F
edblag@admin.umass.edu
BLAHNIK, Brent .... 920-465-2190. 536 F
blahnikb@uwgb.edu
BLAHNIK, Jeff .... 262-472-1440. 538 D
blahnikj@uww.edu
BLAHNIK, Sheryl .... 217-875-7200. 156 J
sblahnik@richland.edu
BLAICH, Charles, F .... 765-361-6311. 175 B
blaichc@wabash.edu
BLAIFEDER, Mark .... 212-217-4020. 324 C
mark_blaifeder@fitnyc.edu
BLAIN, Daniel .... 330-325-6261. 385 E
dblain@neomed.edu
BLAIN, Judy .... 931-221-7691. 459 B
blainj@apsu.edu
BLAINE, Louise .... 641-673-1038. 183 H
blainel@wmpenn.edu
BLAINE, Robert .... 601-979-2141. 267 E
robert.blaine@jsums.edu
BLAINE-WALLACE,
William .... 207-786-8272. 209 F
wblainew@bates.edu
BLAIR, Anothony, L .... 717-866-5775. 416 E
ablair@evangelical.edu
BLAIR, Brian .... 202-885-2842... 94 F
bblair@american.edu
BLAIR, Christine .... 903-693-2075. 478 A
cblair@panola.edu
BLAIR, Cinnamon .... 505-277-1806. 312 F
cblair@salud.unm.edu
BLAIR, David, A .... 512-428-1286. 479 C
davidab@stedwards.edu
BLAIR, Dena .... 734-973-3356. 252 A
dlblair@wccnet.edu
BLAIR, Eric .... 816-584-6858. 280 C
eric.blair@park.edu
BLAIR, Jean .... 845-938-3615. 545 I
Jean.Blair@usma.edu
BLAIR, Jeff .... 614-251-4735. 386 B
blairj@ohiodominican.edu
BLAIR, John, P .... 270-745-6520. 200 G
jp.blair@wku.edu
BLAIR, Kimberly, P .... 540-365-4211. 504 L
kblair@ferrum.edu
BLAIR, Larry .... 415-749-4560... 62 G
lblair@sfai.edu
BLAIR, Linda .... 502-447-1000. 199 E
lblair@spencerian.edu
BLAIR, Maureen .... 309-438-8611. 147 J
meblair@ilstu.edu
BLAIR, Michael, R .... 563-387-1040. 180 M
blairmic@luther.edu
BLAIR, Ray .... 413-755-4868. 233 A
rblair@stcc.edu
BLAIR, Rob, M .... 806-894-9611. 480 H
rblair@southplainscollege.edu
BLAIR, Sylvia .... 410-386-8411. 214 A
sblair@carrollcc.edu
BLAIR, Thomas .... 770-216-2960. 127 F
tblair@ict-ils.edu
BLAIR, Thomas, S .... 540-375-2235. 509 B
blair@roanoke.edu
BLAIR, Timothy, V .... 610-436-2739. 430 A
tblair@wcupa.edu
BLAIR, Wendell .... 312-553-5662. 141 N
wblair@ccc.edu
BLAIR, Wray .... 301-687-4201. 220 C
wnblair@frotburg.edu
BLAIS, Roger, N .... 918-631-2554. 401 F
roger-blais@utulsa.edu
BLAISING, Craig, A .... 817-923-1921. 481 G
cblaising@swbts.edu
BLAKE, Alan .... 603-271-6484. 296 C
ablake@ccsnh.edu
BLAKE, Aretha .... 704-971-8500. 353 F
BLAKE, Barb .... 309-438-2143. 147 J
bblake@ilstu.edu
BLAKE, Ben .... 860-465-5283... 87 L
blakeb@easternct.edu
BLAKE, Charles, E .... 901-322-0120. 452 F
BLAKE, Darcy .... 650-543-3901... 54 C
dblake@menlo.edu
BLAKE, David .... 912-525-5000. 131 B
dblake@scad.edu
BLAKE, David .... 541-737-0123. 406 A
david.blake@oregonstate.edu
BLAKE, Diane, T .... 518-388-6104. 348 J
blaked@union.edu
BLAKE, Erin .... 225-216-8000. 202 H
blakee@mybrcc.edu
BLAKE, Erin .... 337-421-6946. 204 E
erin.blake@sowela.edu
BLAKE, F. Phyllis .... 914-633-2462. 327 C
pblake@iona.edu
BLAKE, Ira .... 570-389-4308. 427 H
iblake@bloomu.edu
BLAKE, James, E .... 203-392-5457... 88 A
blakej2@southernct.edu
BLAKE, John .... 907-474-5188... 10 I
jeblake@alaska.edu
BLAKE, Joi Lin .... 650-738-4333... 64 D
blakej@smccd.edu
BLAKE, Karen .... 203-575-8269... 89 B
kblake@nvcc.commnet.edu
BLAKE, Katherine, H .... 781-891-2074. 223 C
kblake@bentley.edu
BLAKE, Larry .... 859-572-1907. 198 I
blakel1@nku.edu
BLAKE, Lisa .... 309-341-5282. 141 A
lblake@sandburg.edu
BLAKE, Lori .... 325-670-5896. 472 O
lblake@hsutx.edu
BLAKE, M. Brian .... 305-284-2211. 118 F
m.brian.blake@miami.edu
BLAKE, Paul .... 231-591-3030. 242 F
blakep@ferris.edu
BLAKE, Peg .... 707-826-3361... 35 C
plb91@humboldt.edu
BLAKE, Richard, D .... 214-887-5231. 471 F
rblake@dts.edu
BLAKE, Robert, C .... 202-994-6870... 95 D
rblake@gwu.edu
BLAKE, Scott .... 906-487-7242. 242 G
scott.blake@finlandia.edu
BLAKE, Shontell .... 225-216-8703. 202 H
blakes@mybrcc.edu
BLAKE, Susan, N .... 770-499-3576. 127 N
sblake@kennesaw.edu
BLAKE, William, J .... 330-941-2086. 394 A
wjblake@ysu.edu
BLAKEFIELD, Mary .... 765-973-8522. 167 G
mblakefi@iue.edu
BLAKELEY, Mary Ann ..... 440-525-7119. 382 M
mblakeley@lakelandcc.edu
BLAKELY, Craig, H .... 502-852-3297. 200 D
crag.blakely@louisville.edu
BLAKELY, Dee .... 618-634-3247. 158 M
deeb@shawneecc.edu
BLAKELY, Edie .... 360-992-2239. 518 A
eblakely@clark.edu
BLAKELY, Zeledith .... 252-638-1587. 359 G
blakelyz@cravencc.edu
BLAKEMAN, Donald, L .... 502-863-8091. 194 C
don_blakeman@georgetowncollege.edu
BLAKEMORE, Jerry, D .... 815-753-1000. 154 I
jblakemore@niu.edu
BLAKEMORE, Patricia ..... 401-739-5000. 439 D
pblakemore@neit.edu
BLAKENEY, Erin .... 425-352-8307. 517 E
eblakeney@cascadia.edu
BLAKENEY, Sara .... 704-337-2536. 365 G
blakeneys@queens.edu
BLAKESLEE, Jim .... 920-929-2114. 540 F
jblakeslee@morainepark.edu
BLAKEY, Linda, S .... 734-973-3536. 252 A
blakey@wccnet.edu
BLAKLEY, Jackie .... 864-646-1305. 447 D
jblakle1@tctc.edu
BLAKLEY, Ramon .... 361-593-2315. 484 A
ramon.blakley@tamuk.edu
BLAKNEY, Rob .... 972-825-4643. 481 F
rblakney@sagu.edu
BLALOCK, Reed .... 318-767-2603. 205 A
rblalock@lsua.edu
BLALOCK, Tim .... 270-247-8521. 197 H
tblalock@midcontinent.edu
BLALOCK, III, W. Ben ... 307-766-3948. 543 I
bblalock@uwyo.edu
BLANCHARD, Andrew .... 972-883-6706. 491 E
ablanch@utdallas.edu
BLANCHARD, Gina, A ... 740-392-6868. 384 K
gina.blanchard@mvnu.edu
BLANCHARD, Gordon .... 847-578-3232. 157 F
gordon.blanchard@rosalindfranklin.edu
BLANCHARD, John .... 907-796-6340... 11 A
john.blanchard@uas.alaska.edu
BLANCHARD, John .... 212-749-2802. 330 A
jblanchard@msmnyc.edu
BLANCHARD, Jon .... 207-893-6604. 211 G
jblanchard@sjcme.edu
BLANCHARD, Joyce .... 207-621-3403. 212 C
joyceb@maine.edu
BLANCHARD, Kendall, A 229-928-1360. 126 D
kendall.blanchard@gsw.edu
BLANCHARD, Loren .... 504-520-7525. 209 D
lblancha@xula.edu
BLANCHARD, Marsha, L 573-888-0513. 282 B
mblanchard@semo.edu
BLANCHARD, Myrtho ...... 202-274-5946... 97 A
mblanchard@udc.edu
BLANCHARD,
Nicholas, R .... 410-651-3777. 219 E
nrblanchard@umes.edu
BLANCHARD, Scott .... 802-322-1640. 499 C
scott.blanchard@goddard.edu
BLANCHARD, Teri, L ...... 740-427-5181. 382 J
blanchard@kenyon.edu
BLANCHET, Robert .... 518-255-5525. 344 E
blanchrc@cobleskill.edu
BLANCHETT, Russell ...... 972-882-7520. 483 E
russell.blanchett@tamuc.edu
BLANCHETT, Wanda, J .... 816-235-2231. 283 D
blanchettw@umkc.edu
BLANCHETTE, David, M . 401-456-8009. 439 F
dblanchette@ric.edu
BLANCHETTE, Diane, F .. 401-341-2135. 440 C
blanched@salve.edu
BLANCHETTE, Nick .... 715-675-3331. 541 A
blanchette@ntc.edu
BLANCO, Julio, R .... 831-582-4401... 34 B
jrblanco@csumb.edu
BLANCO, Mark, E .... 914-337-9300. 321 E
mark.blanco@concordia-ny.edu
BLAND, Byron .... 650-433-3814... 58 B
bbland@paloaltou.edu
BLAND, Constance .... 662-254-3421. 269 A
cgbland@mvsu.edu
BLAND, Dorothy .... 940-367-4927. 490 C
dorothy.bland@unt.edu

BLAND, Earl .... 913-971-3617. 188 H
ebland@mnu.edu
BLAND, Glenda .... 256-378-2004..... 2 G
gbland@cacc.edu
BLAND, James .... 937-393-3431. 389 B
jbland@sscc.edu
BLAND, John, D .... 704-687-5822. 368 E
jdbland@uncc.edu
BLAND, Marissa .... 816-415-5938. 285 C
blandm@william.jewell.edu
BLAND, Terry .... 662-562-3271. 269 C
tbland@northwestms.edu
BLANDA, Diane, M .... 401-874-2024. 440 D
dblanda@advance.uri.edu
BLANDFORD, David, K .. 989-463-7147. 239 B
blandford@alma.edu
BLANDING, Bruce .... 731-424-3520. 460 G
bblanding@jscc.edu
BLANDON, Darwin .... 423-493-4328. 462 B
helpdesk@tntemple.edu
BLANEY, Diana .... 219-464-7867. 174 E
diana.blaney@valpo.edu
BLANEY, Tari .... 614-287-5021. 378 B
tblaney@cscc.edu
BLANK, Bonnie .... 415-451-2819... 63 A
bblank@sfts.edu
BLANK, Dave, L .... 336-278-6705. 354 B
dblank@elon.edu
BLANK, James .... 330-672-3614. 382 B
jblank@kent.edu
BLANK, Michelle .... 419-783-2490. 379 C
mblank@defiance.edu
BLANK, Rebecca .... 608-262-9946. 536 D
chancellor@news.wisc.edu
BLANK DOUCETTE,
Margot .... 858-566-1200... 42 G
m.blank@disd.edu
BLANKE, Raymond .... 405-733-7306. 399 F
rblanke@rose.edu
BLANKENBAKER, Zarina 972-238-6025. 471 C
zblankenbaker@dcccd.edu
BLANKENBEUHLER,
Carla .... 304-205-6706. 528 B
cblankenbeuhler@kvctc.edu
BLANKENHORN, Stacie . 503-359-1082. 407 A
bookstore@pacificu.edu
BLANKENSHIP, Anne ..... 850-644-0170. 115 C
ablankenship@fsu.edu
BLANKENSHIP,
Bruce, A .... 304-457-6220. 526 A
blankenshipba@ab.edu
BLANKENSHIP,
Bryan, P .... 859-858-2228. 192 A
BLANKENSHIP, Candice 870-762-3137... 19 K
cblankenship@smail.anc.edu
BLANKENSHIP,
Daniel, J .... 219-866-6154. 172 E
djb@saintjoe.edu
BLANKENSHIP, Karen .... 281-476-1850. 479 F
karen.blankenship@sjcd.edu
BLANKENSHIP, Mark ...... 859-252-0361. 197 C
mblankenship@lextheo.edu
BLANKENSHIP, Mike ..... 601-856-5400. 267 B
mblankenship@holmescc.edu
BLANKENSHIP, Ruth ...... 276-326-4556. 502 H
rblankenship@bluefield.edu
BLANKENSHIP, Tim .... 404-471-5465. 119 I
tblankenship@agnesscott.edu
BLANKENSHIP, Vince .... 903-923-2002. 471 J
vblankenship@etbu.edu
BLANKINSHIP, Blair .... 410-837-5714. 221 A
bblankinship@ubalt.edu
BLANKMEYER,
Bonnie, L .... 210-567-2691. 493 A
blankmeyer@uthscsa.edu
BLANKS, Janet .... 561-297-2230. 114 L
blanks@ccs.fau.edu
BLANSETT, Dewey .... 662-329-7396. 268 E
dblansett@oe.muw.edu
BLANSETT, H. Wayne ..... 662-846-4150. 266 G
wblanset@deltastate.edu
BLANTON, Carmen .... 910-755-7332. 358 D
blantonc@brunswickcc.edu
BLANTON, Jason .... 606-783-9361. 198 A
j.blanton@moreheadstate.edu
BLANTON, Jay .... 859-257-3303. 200 C
jay.blanton@uky.edu
BLANTON, Ryan .... 918-463-2931. 395 D
ryan.blanton@connorsstate.edu
BLANTON, Shannon .... 901-678-5044. 460 B
sblanton@memphis.edu
BLANTON, Sharon .... 808-543-8000. 135 F
sblanton@hpu.edu
BLANTON, Wynn .... 614-882-2551. 379 M
BLAPPERT, Gerald .... 985-732-6640. 203 D
BLASDEL, Audra .... 317-955-6254. 170 V
ablasdel@marian.edu
BLASE, Kristen .... 603-428-2226. 297 D
kblase@nec.edu
BLASHAK, Theodore .... 248-675-0200. 131 H
tblashak@southuniversity.edu
BLASIC, Michael, D .... 607-735-1830. 323 H
mblasic@elmira.edu
BLASIG, Jerry, A .... 402-557-7075. 288 G
jerry.blasig@bellevue.edu
BLASINGAME, David, T . 314-935-5850. 284 L
david_blasingame@wustl.edu
BLASS, Tammy .... 323-226-6511... 52 G
tblass@dhs.lacounty.gov
BLASSINGAME, Susan ... 806-720-7602. 476 B
susan.blassingame@lcu.edu
BLASTING, Ralph .... 716-673-3111. 342 A
ralph.blasting@fredonia.edu
BLASZAK, Julie .... 616-632-2945. 239 E
jab008@aquinas.edu
BLATCHLEY, Richard, L .. 651-631-5321. 263 A
rlblatchley@nwc.edu
BLATTNER, Nancy .... 973-618-3217. 300 A
nblattner@caldwell.edu
BLAU, Diane .... 248-476-1122. 246 G
dblau@mispp.edu
BLAU, Kathy .... 620-276-9598. 187 A
kathy.blau@gcccks.edu
BLAU, Phil .... 740 351 3137. 388 N
pblau@shawnee.edu
BLAU, Thomas .... 614-251-4567. 386 B
blaut@ohiodominican.edu
BLAUSER, Lisa .... 910-672-1163. 367 D
lsblauser@uncfsu.edu
BLAUSTEIN, Marilyn, H .. 413-545-0941. 228 F
blaustein@oirp.umass.edu
BLAUWKAMP, Christi .... 760-366-3791... 42 B
cblauwkamp@cmccd.edu
BLAYLOCK, Benny .... 318-342-1600. 208 E
blaylock@ulm.edu
BLAYLOCK, John, V .... 402-844-7292. 291 I
johnb@northeast.edu
BLAYLOCK, Reginald ...... 619-594-3557... 35 D
blaylock@mail.sdsu.edu
BLAYLOCK, Stephen .... 813-988-5131. 104 A
blaylocks@floridacollege.edu
BLAYLOCK, Vicki .... 601-635-2111. 266 H
vblaylock@eccc.edu
BLAZE, Douglas .... 865-974-2521. 463 C
blaze@utk.edu
BLAZEJOWSKI, Carol, A 973-655-3031. 303 D
blazejowskic@mail.montclair.edu
BLAZIS, Enoch .... 507-786-3002. 264 B
blazis@stolaf.edu
BLEDSOE, Chad, A .... 828-448-6048. 365 A
cbledsoe@wpcc.edu
BLEDSOE, Christopher ... 212-998-2040. 334 D
christopher.bledsoe@nyu.edu
BLEDSOE, Kelly .... 478-757-5140. 134 G
kbledsoe@wesleyancollege.edu
BLEDSOE, Lisa .... 971-722-5852. 407 D
lbledsoe@pcc.edu
BLEDSOE, Mary, C .... 865-694-6415. 461 D
mcbledsoe@pstcc.edu
BLEDSOE, W. Craig .... 615-966-1789. 456 B
craig.bledsoe@lipscomb.edu
BLEEKER, Joshua, J .... 214-887-5041. 471 F
jbleeker@dts.edu
BLEEKER, Justin .... 866-323-0233... 60 E
BLEICH, Michael .... 314-362-0956. 274 G
mbleich@bjc.org
BLEICHER, Joe .... 860-253-3050... 88 C
jbleicher@asnuntuck.edu
BLEICKEN, Linda, M ...... 912-344-2535. 120 G
linda.bleicken@armstrong.edu
BLEIFIELD, Elaina .... 763-424-0868. 260 C
ebleifield@nhcc.edu
BLENIS, Brian, G .... 610-861-1344. 424 E
bblenis@moravian.edu
BLESSING, Gale .... 503-491-7219. 404 E
gale.blessing@mhcc.edu
BLETHYN, Teresa, P .... 540-375-2308. 509 B
blethyn@roanoke.edu
BLEVINS, Anita, F .... 423-478-7021. 458 B
ablevins@ptseminary.edu
BLEVINS, Bob .... 601-318-6155. 270 I
bblevins@wmcarey.edu
BLEVINS, Elizabeth .... 740-351-3112. 388 N
eblevins@shawnee.edu
BLEVINS, Elizabeth, S .... 434-381-6141. 510 F
bblevins@sbc.edu
BLEVINS, Grace .... 804-330-0111. 503 G
dcacrim@centura.edu
BLEVINS, Karen .... 606-326-2063. 194 J
karen.blevins@kctcs.edu
BLEVINS, Lori .... 336-249-8186. 360 A
lblevins@davidsonccc.edu
BLEVINS, Mark .... 913-621-8780. 186 C
mblevins@donnelly.edu
BLEVINS, Robert .... 601-318-6155. 270 I
robert.blevins@wmcarey.edu
BLEVINS, Ryan .... 219-464-5413. 174 E
ryan.blevins@valpo.edu
BLEW, Denise, M .... 610-758-3179. 422 A
dmb3@lehigh.edu
BLEWETT, Patrick, A .... 530-226-4033... 66 D
pblewett@simpsonu.edu
BLEY, Maya .... 973-290-4223. 300 F
mbley@cse.edu
BLEY-VROMAN, Robert .. 808-956-8516. 136 B
vroman@hawaii.edu
BLEYMAIER, Gene .... 408-924-1200... 36 A
gene.bleymaier@sjsu.edu
BLEYTHING, Tony .... 262-646-6510. 535 B
tbleything@nashotah.edu
BLEZIEN, Paul .... 952-446-4161. 255 D
blezienp@crown.edu
BLICHARZ, Marcia .... 609-771-2848. 300 E
blicharz@tcnj.edu
BLICKHAN, Lynn .... 217-641-4206. 148 M
lblickhan@jwcc.edu
BLIFFEN, John .... 901-375-4400. 457 C
johnbliffen@midsouthcc.org
BLILEY, Sean .... 814-732-1304. 428 E
sbliley@edinboro.edu
BLINKA, Sonja .... 409-933-8474. 469 E
sblinka@com.edu
BLISS, Chris .... 415-703-9545... 30 K
cbliss@cca.edu
BLISS, Frances .... 413-265-2314. 225 C
blissf@elms.edu
BLISS, Michael, B .... 808-675-3705. 135 C
blissm@byuh.edu
BLISS, Patricia, J .... 315-445-4141. 328 F
blisspj@lemoyne.edu
BLISS, Robert, M .... 314-516-6874. 283 E
rmbliss@umsl.edu
BLISS, Shannon .... 831-755-6875... 46 G
sbliss@hartnell.edu
BLISS, Steve .... 912-525-5000. 131 B
sbliss@scad.edu
BLISS-FURR, Carol .... 617-541-5394. 232 G
cbliss@rcc.mass.edu
BLISSERT, Julie, H .... 315-312-2265. 344 A
julie.blissert@oswego.edu
BLITT, William, J .... 972-377-1730. 469 G
bblitt@collin.edu
BLITZ, Phebe .... 480-461-7000... 15 A
phebe.blitz@mesacc.edu
BLITZ, Y .... 248-968-3360. 253 A
BLITZER, Donna, M .... 831-459-3983... 72 C
dblitzer@ucsc.edu
BLIVEN, Gail .... 651-690-6845. 263 O
gnbliven@stkate.edu
BLIZZARD, Mary .... 304-558-4614. 527 O
mblizzard@wvctcs.org
BLOCH, Darren .... 212-431-2845. 333 I
Darren.Bloch@nyls.edu
BLOCK, Derryl .... 815-753-6155. 154 I
dblock@niu.edu
BLOCK, Gene, D .... 310-825-2151... 71 C
chancellor@conet.ucla.edu
BLOCK, Greg .... 619-594-2176... 35 D
gblock@mail.sdsu.edu
BLOCK, Jayme, E .... 410-543-6156. 220 D
jeblock@salisbury.edu
BLOCK, Jeff .... 406-447-6958. 287 A
jeff.block@umhelena.edu
BLOCK, Ken, W .... 419-772-2036. 386 D
k-block@onu.edu
BLOCK, Murray .... 518-608-8336. 324 B
mblock@excelsior.edu
BLOCK, Peggy .... 270-534-3464. 196 G
peggy.block@kctcs.edu
BLOCK, Regina, M .... 815-740-5047. 162 F
rblock@stfrancis.edu
BLOCKER, Bill .... 832-252-4604. 468 L
bill.blocker@cbshouston.edu
BLOCKER, Peggy, J .... 303-765-3114... 82 E
pblocker@iliff.edu
BLOCKER, Robert, L .... 203-432-4160... 93 A
robert.blocker@yale.edu
BLOCKSIDGE, Charles .... 412-237-4476. 413 D
cblocksidge@ccac.edu
BLODGETT, Bruce, M ...... 315-255-1743. 316 D
blodgett@cayuga-cc.edu
BLODGETT, Martha Lee .. 850-474-2712. 117 B
mblodget@uwf.edu
BLODGETT, Patricia, A ... 603-358-2280. 298 F
pblodget@keene.edu
BLODGETT, Steve .... 507-786-3316. 264 B
blodgett@stolaf.edu
BLOECHLE, Michael .... 217-206-6653. 161 E
bloechle.michael@uis.edu
BLOEM, Russell, J .... 616-526-6651. 240 L
rjb42@calvin.edu
BLOEMENDAAL,
Mark, R .... 712-707-7127. 181 H
markb@nwciowa.edu
BLOEMENDAAL-GRUETT,
Joan .... 320-629-5116. 260 F
gruettj@pinetech.edu
BLOEMKE, Jody .... 507-389-7492. 261 E
jody.bloemke@southcentral.edu
BLOEMKER,
Geraldine, A .... 610-499-4107. 437 E
gabloemker@widener.edu
BLOHM, Jason .... 402-941-6435. 290 K
blohm@midlandu.edu
BLOHOWIAK, Shelly .... 847-578-8355. 157 F
shelly.blohowiak@rosalindfranklin.edu
BLOK, Tamara, L .... 818-767-0888... 76 K
tamara.blok@woodbury.edu
BLOMBERG, Thomas ...... 850-644-7380. 115 C
tblomber@fsu.edu
BLOMGREN, Rebecca ..... 336-272-7102. 354 E
blomgrenr@greensboro.edu
BLOMGREN, Richard ...... 828-298-3325. 370 E
rickb@warren-wilson.edu
BLOMQUIST, Mickel ...... 801-818-8900. 496 F
mikelb@provocollege.edu
BLOMQUIST, William, A 317-274-3976. 168 D
blomquis@iupui.edu
BLONDE, Mitchell, P ...... 517-264-7146. 250 B
mblonde@sienaheights.edu
BLONDIN, Jo, A .... 937-328-6001. 377 A
blondinj@clarkstate.edu
BLONDIN, Monica, M .... 508-831-5469. 238 F
mmlucey@wpi.edu
BLONIARZ, Peter .... 518-956-8240. 341 D
pbloniarz@albany.edu
BLOOD, Janet .... 207-974-4606. 210 K
jblood@emcc.edu
BLOOD, Rick .... 802-224-3000. 501 A
rick.blood@vsc.edu
BLOODGOOD, Jane .... 785-320-4503. 188 E
janebloodgood@matc.net
BLOODSAW, Marti .... 309-694-5593. 146 E
marti.bloodsaw@icc.edu
BLOOM, Joel .... 973-596-3102. 303 G
joel.s.bloom@njit.edu
BLOOM, John, S .... 214-887-5591. 471 F
jbloom@dts.edu
BLOOM, Ronald, L .... 516-463-5940. 326 D
ronald.bloom@hofstra.edu
BLOOM, Steven .... 617-243-2440. 227 K
sbloom@lasell.edu
BLOOM, Vicki .... 574-520-4448. 168 E
vdbloom@iusb.edu
BLOOMBERG, Sandra .... 201-200-3321. 303 F
sbloomberg@njcu.edu
BLOOMBERG, Steven ..... 405-682-7814. 397 E
smbloomberg@occc.edu
BLOOMER, Dennis, L ..... 864-488-4561. 444 L
dbloomer@limestone.edu
BLOOMFIELD, Stewart .... 212-938-5540. 345 C
sbloomfield@sunyopt.edu
BLOOMFIELD, Susan, R . 919-866-5452. 364 G
srbloomfield@waketech.edu
BLOOMINGDALE,
Mary, E .... 641-422-4351. 181 D
bloommar@niacc.edu
BLOSS, Adrienne, G .... 540-665-4525. 509 E
abloss@su.edu
BLOSS, Kim, K .... 870-235-4055... 23 F
kkbloss@saumag.edu
BLOSSER, Joseph, D ...... 336-841-9000. 355 C
jblosser@highpoint.edu
BLOSSER, Kim .... 540-868-7111. 512 H
kblosser@lfcc.edu
BLOSSOM, Michael .... 415-355-1601... 27 L
michaelblossom@actcm.edu
BLOUIN, Robert, A .... 919-966-1122. 368 D
bob_blouin@unc.edu
BLOUNT, Brian, K .... 804-355-0671. 510 G
bblount@upsem.edu
BLOUNT, Cameron .... 662-562-3354. 269 C
cblount@northwestms.edu
BLOUNT, Joanna .... 574-936-8898. 163 K
joanna.blount@ancilla.edu
BLOUNT, Nicole .... 404-880-8710. 122 J
nblount@cau.edu
BLOUNT, Sally, E .... 847-491-2840. 155 D
sallyblount@kellogg.northwestern.edu
BLOW, Felicia .... 757-569-6791. 513 E
fblow@pdc.edu
BLOW, Trevor .... 954-783-7339. 102 M
tblow@cci.edu
BLOW, William .... 256-549-8200..... 3 M
BLOWERS, Debbie .... 661-654-3381... 32 H
dblowers@csub.edu
BLOWERS, Jerimy .... 315-568-3123. 333 C
jblowers@nycc.edu
BLOWERS, Kelsy .... 218-683-8543. 260 D
kelsy.blowers@northlandcollege.edu
BLOXOM, Donald, R ...... 318-797-5267. 205 F
don.bloxom@lsus.edu
BLOYED, Carolyn .... 541-962-3519. 405 H
cbloyed@eou.edu
BLUE, Damon, A .... 323-563-4856... 38 B
damonblue@cdrewu.edu
BLUE, Debbie .... 405-585-4120. 397 C
debbie.blue@okbu.edu
BLUE, Deborah, G .... 559-244-5901... 68 H
deborah.blue@scccd.edu
BLUE, Lynn .... 616-331-2035. 243 C
bluel@gvsu.edu

BLUESTONE, Jeffrey, A ... 415-476-4451... 72 A jeff.bluestone@ucsf.edu
BLUESTONE, Leslie .... 215-641-6529. 424 B lbluesto@mc3.edu
BLUM, Blair .... 858-646-3170... 64 E bblum@sanfordburnham.org
BLUM, Robert .... 817-272-2771. 491 B rwblum@uta.edu
BLUM, Susan .... 631-444-8250. 342 C susan.blum@stonybrook.edu
BLUM, Thomas, L .... 914-395-2203. 340 E tblum@sarahlawrence.edu
BLUMBERG, Audrey, S .. 516-877-3159. 313 A blumberg@adelphi.edu
BLUMBERG, Bruce, K .... 803-938-3838. 448 F bruceb@uscsumter.edu
BLUMBERG, Elizabeth .... 781-239-2762. 231 G eblumberg@massbay.edu
BLUMBERG, James, J .... 309-556-3066. 148 B jblumber@iwu.edu
BLUMBERG, Paulette ...... 657-278-4717... 33 E pblumberg@fullerton.edu
BLUME, Jane .... 360-752-8472. 517 B jblume@btc.ctc.edu
BLUME, Steven, W .... 800-431-8488... 28 J sblume@aptc.edu
BLUME, Travis, A .... 260-422-5561. 167 B tablume@indianatech.edu
BLUMENSTEIN, Robert ... 610-282-1100. 414 F robert.blumenstein@desales.edu
BLUMENTHAL, Eric .... 503-251-5715. 408 G eblumenthal@uws.edu
BLUMENTHAL, George, R .... 831-459-2058... 72 C chancellor@ucsc.edu
BLUMENTHAL, Jon .... 651-604-4101. 257 A
BLUMER, Lindsay, A ...... 920-748-8316. 535 J blumerl@ripon.edu
BLUMHARDT, Jon .... 808-845-9126. 136 G blumhard@hawaii.edu
BLUMREICH, Jim .... 920-498-5701. 541 B jim.blumreich@nwtc.edu
BLUNDELL, Caitlin .... 978-837-5128. 234 A blundellc@merrimack.edu
BLUNDELL, Keith .... 361-582-2535. 493 H keith.blundell@victoriacollege.edu
BLUNT, Grace .... 508-767-7172. 222 C gblunt@assumption.edu
BLUNT, Lisa .... 406-874-6214. 286 E bluntl@milescc.edu
BLUNT, Shelly, B .... 812-465-7020. 174 D sblunt@usi.edu
BLUST, Robert .... 414-288-7004. 534 B robert.blust@marquette.edu
BLY, Marie .... 603-752-1113. 296 E mbly@ccsnh.edu
BLYTHE, Gretchen, S ...... 816-604-2251. 277 F gretchen.blythe@mcckc.edu
BLYTHE, Janett .... 270-534-3079. 196 G janett.blythe@kctcs.edu
BLYTHE-SMITH, Karen ... 256-549-8357..... 3 M ksmith@gadsdenstate.edu
BOAL, John, R .... 832-252-4603. 468 L john.boal@cbshouston.edu
BOALS-GILBERT, Beverly .... 870-972-3052... 19 N bboals@astate.edu
BOARD, A. Jill .... 760-384-6212... 49 O jboard@cerrocoso.edu
BOARD, Cristine .... 216-987-3467. 378 D cristine.board@tri-c.edu
BOARD, Steve .... 920-206-2371. 533 U steve.board@mbbc.edu
BOARDLEY, Thomaicc .... 301-860-3394. 220 A tboardley@bowiestate.edu
BOARDLEY SUBER, Dianne .... 919-516-4200. 366 C dbsuber@st-aug.edu
BOARDMAN, David .... 215-204-8421. 433 K david.boardman@temple.edu
BOARDMAN, Gregory, E 650-725-1808... 68 E gboardman@stanford.edu
BOAT, Thomas, F .... 513-558-7333. 390 G thomas.boat@uc.edu
BOATMUN, Tim .... 580-745-2370. 399 J tboatmun@se.edu
BOATRIGHT, Christine ... 386-752-1822. 104 G christine.boatright@fgc.edu
BOATRIGHT, Jeremiah ... 325-574-6572. 494 K jboatright@wtc.edu
BOATRIGHT-WELLS, Sue Ella .... 276-523-7489. 513 A sboatright@me.vccs.edu
BOATWRIGHT, Betty, R .. 803-536-8556. 446 G bboatwright@scsu.edu
BOATWRIGHT, Cassie .... 850-484-1778. 110 G cboatwright@pensacolastate.edu
BOATWRIGHT, Jennifer .. 281-649-3321. 473 B jboatwright@hbu.edu
BOATWRIGHT, Tamara ... 678-359-5259. 127 A tamarab@gordonstate.edu
BOATWRIGHT, Wally ..... 843-383-8088. 442 F wboatwright@coker.edu
BOAZ, Matthew, L .... 513-556-5508. 390 G boazmw@ucmail.uc.edu
BOB-PENNYPACKER, Beaulah .... 928-524-7326... 16 E beaulah.bob-pennypacker@npc.edu
BOBAK, Karen, A .... 315-568-3864. 333 C kbobak@nycc.edu
BOBART, David .... 410-837-4331. 221 A dbobart@ubalt.edu
BOBB, June .... 718-997-5780. 319 C june.bobb@qc.cuny.edu
BOBBETT, Tricia .... 417-667-8181. 273 A tbobbett@cottey.edu
BOBBIN, Michael, J .... 904-256-7055. 107 Q mbobbin@ju.edu
BOBBIN, Steffi .... 617-559-8640. 227 D sbobbin@hebrewcollege.edu
BOBBITT, Donald, R .... 501-686-2505... 23 H president@uasys.edu
BOBBY, Anna .... 330-941-3675. 394 A ambobby@ysu.edu
BOBICH, Marni .... 909-607-8533... 59 G marni_bobich@pitzer.edu
BOBINSKI, Michael .... 404-894-5411. 125 D mbobinski@athletics.gatech.edu
BOBO, David .... 205-853-1200..... 5 B dbobo@jeffstateonline.com
BOBO, Lori .... 601-925-3252. 268 A lbobo@mc.edu
BOBROWSKI, Paul .... 937-229-3349. 391 C pbobrowki1@udayton.edu
BOBZIEN, Randy .... 303-722-5724... 83 A rbobzien@lincolntech.com
BOCCHICCHIO, Rebecca . 916-660-8000... 66 B rbocchicchio@sierracollege.edu
BOCCHINFUSO-COHEN, Rita .... 559-278-2381... 33 D ritab@csufresno.edu
BOCCHINO, Bud .... 713-798-2195. 467 F bocchino@bcm.edu
BOCCIA, Lenore .... 215-222-4200. 431 H lboccia@walnuthillcollege.edu
BOCIAN, David, F .... 951-827-2304... 71 E vpap@ucr.edu
BOCIAN, Terry, M .... 616-632-2475. 239 E bociater@aquinas.edu
BOCK, Darrell, L .... 214-887-5251. 471 F dbock@dts.edu
BOCK, Jim .... 610-328-8529. 433 I jbock1@swarthmore.edu
BOCK, Lisa, L .... 336-862-7986. 362 H llbock@randolph.edu
BOCK, Mike .... 260-665-4878. 173 E bockm@trine.edu
BOCK, Wendy .... 309-796-5180. 140 E bockw@bhc.edu
BOCKMAN, Edward .... 847-543-2259. 143 A ebockman@clcillinois.edu
BOCZER, Amy .... 203-254-4000... 89 I aboczer@fairfield.edu
BODDIE-LAVAN, Jeanine .... 334-244-3610..... 2 A jblavan@aum.edu
BODDY, Michael .... 314-252-3132. 274 A mboddy@eden.edu
BODE, Brian .... 913-288-7667. 187 L bbode@kckcc.edu
BODE, Lori .... 636-949-4925. 276 D lbode@lindenwood.edu
BODEN, Alison .... 609-258-6244. 304 E aboden@princeton.edu
BODEN, Janet .... 773-256-0744. 152 B jboden@lstc.edu
BODEN, Michael .... 845-431-8952. 323 C michael.boden@sunydutchess.edu
BODENBENDER, Laura ... 608-822-2315. 541 C lbodenbender@swtc.edu
BODENSTEINER, Ivan .... 219-465-7852. 174 E ivan.bodensteiner@valpo.edu
BODERMAN, Don .... 503-838-8063. 406 E boderman@wou.edu
BODIE, Cindy, H .... 336-315-8660. 353 C cbodie@carolinagrad.edu
BODIE, Darryl, A .... 336-315-8660. 353 C dbodie@carolinagrad.edu
BODIFORD, Wayne .... 386-312-4041. 112 C waynebodiford@sjrstate.edu
BODIN, Susan .... 312-915-7454. 151 H sbodin@luc.edu
BODISON, Sacared, A ..... 301-314-8091. 219 B sbodison@umd.edu
BODMAN, Andrew, R .... 909-537-5024... 34 E abodman@csusb.edu
BODNAR, Molly .... 719-389-6351... 79 D molly.bodnar@coloradocollege.edu
BODNAR, Richard .... 718-997-5191. 319 C richard.bodnar@qc.edu
BODONI, June .... 978-867-4217. 226 H june.bodoni@gordon.edu
BODRATO, Kelli .... 718-405-3234. 320 G kelli.bodrato@mountsaintvincent.edu
BODRATTI, Robert .... 518-828-4181. 321 C bodratti@sunycgcc.edu
BODRI, Michael .... 706-864-1958. 133 D michael.bodri@ung.edu
BODUR, Niyazi .... 516-686-7724. 333 H nbodur@nyit.edu
BODVARSSON, Orn .... 320-308-2225. 261 B obbodvarsson@stcloudstate.edu
BOE, Eugene .... 218-739-3375. 256 K eboe@lbs.edu
BOECKERMANN, Gabriele .... 513-569-1550. 376 L gabriele.boeckermann@cincinnatistate.edu
BOEDEKER, Katrina, P ... 260-399-7700. 174 C kboedeker@sf.edu
BOEDER, John, C .... 507-354-8221. 256 M boederjc@mlc-wels.edu
BOEGEL, Tom .... 415-239-3360... 38 L tboegel@ccsf.edu
BOEH, Thomas .... 559-244-5641... 33 D tboeh@csufresno.edu
BOEHLKE, Cassandra ..... 219-785-5748. 172 A cboehlke@pnc.edu
BOEHM, Beth, A .... 502-852-3975. 200 D baboeh01@louisville.edu
BOEHM, Christopher ...... 205-552-1222..... 3 B chris.boehm@ecacolleges.com
BOEHM, Christopher, H . 610-921-7700. 409 A cboehm@alb.edu
BOEHM, J, J .... 989-964-4055. 249 G jjboehm@svsu.edu
BOEHM, J. J .... 989-964-4055. 249 G jjboehm@svsu.edu
BOEHM, Michael .... 574-284-4610. 172 G mboehm@saintmarys.edu
BOEHM, Michael, J .... 614-292-5881. 386 E boehm.1@osu.edu
BOEHM-DAVIS, Deborah 703-993-8720. 505 C dbdavis@gmu.edu
BOEHMAN, Joseph, R .... 804-289-8000. 510 L jboehman@richmond.edu
BOEHME, Michael, J .... 320-234-8509. 260 H mike.boehme@ridgewater.edu
BOEHMER, Brian .... 740-364-9535. 376 A bboehmer@newark.ohio-state.edu
BOEHMER, Robert, G ..... 478-289-2027. 124 C bboehmer@ega.edu
BOEHNE, Cheryl .... 618-545-3184. 149 D cboehne@kaskaskia.edu
BOEHNE, Rhonda .... 618-545-3022. 149 D rboehne@kaskaskia.edu
BOEHNER, Joel .... 574-807-7116. 164 D joel.boehner@bethelcollege.edu
BOEKER, Cathy .... 979-830-4455. 467 I cboeker@blinn.edu
BOELE, Erin .... 599-278-2345... 33 D eboele@csufresno.edu
BOENIG, Tobin, R .... 409-747-8702. 493 C trboenig@utmb.edu
BOENINGER, Candice .... 740-593-4100. 387 C boeningc@ohio.edu
BOENKER, Norma, J ...... 260-399-7700. 174 C nboenker@sf.edu
BOER, Larry .... 708-239-4608. 160 K larry.boer@trnty.edu
BOERBOOM, Chris .... 701-231-7867. 371 G chris.boerboom@ndsu.edu
BOERGERMANN, Gary ... 918-343-7625. 399 C gboergermann@rsu.edu
BOERIO, Bibiana .... 724-834-2200. 433 E
BOERNER, Anne .... 503-297-5544. 405 D aboerner@ocac.edu
BOERNER, William .... 716-673-3358. 342 A william.boerner@fredonia.edu
BOERSIG, Pam .... 612-332-3361. 253 G pboersig@aii.edu
BOERSMA, Paul, H .... 616-395-7145. 244 A boersma@hope.edu
BOERST, Connie .... 920-433-6622. 531 L connie.boerst@bellincollege.edu
BOESCH, Donald, F .... 410-221-2001. 219 A boesch@umces.edu
BOESDORFER, Nancy, A 217-443-8856. 143 G nboes@dacc.edu
BOESE, Donna .... 620-229-6208. 190 G
BOETSCH, Larry .... 540-458-8145. 516 A lboetsch@wlu.edu
BOETTCHER, Marlene, F . 719-384-6824... 83 M marlene.boettcher@ojc.edu
BOEVINGLOH, Linda .... 636-481-3488. 275 I lboeving@jeffco.edu
BOEZAART, Arn .... 616-331-6905. 243 C boezaara@gvsu.edu
BOGAGE, Alan .... 410-386-8339. 214 A abogage@carrollcc.edu
BOGAN, Gerri .... 706-821-8262. 130 C gbogan@paine.edu
BOGAN, Ivory .... 601-984-1400. 270 C bogan@umc.edu
BOGAN, Jeremy .... 518-454-5155. 321 A boganj@strose.edu
BOGAN, Kim .... 619-849-2481... 59 L kimbogan@pointloma.edu
BOGAN, Yolanda .... 850-599-3145. 114 K yolanda.bogan@famu.edu
BOGART, Denise .... 229-333-5709. 134 B dbogart@valdosta.edu
BOGART, Marti, S .... 630-637-5355. 154 F msbogart@noctrl.edu
BOGART, William, T .... 865-981-8101. 456 D tom.bogart@maryvillecollege.edu
BOGATSKI, Anatole .... 510-780-4500... 50 I abogatski@lifewest.edu
BOGDAN, Sharon .... 410-532-5332. 217 E sbogdan@ndm.edu
BOGEN, Janice, M .... 215-503-4335. 434 C janice.bogen@jefferson.edu
BOGER, John, C .... 919-962-4417. 368 D jcboger@email.unc.edu
BOGER-HAWKINS, Caitlin .... 860-738-6441... 89 C cboger-hawkins@nwcc.commnet.edu
BOGERT, Brian .... 570-408-4015. 437 F brian.bogert@wilkes.edu
BOGGAN, Jeff .... 678-717-2842. 133 D jeff.boggan@ung.edu
BOGGAN, Laura, K .... 423-652-4707. 455 I lkboggan@king.edu
BOGGER, Tommy .... 757-823-2004. 507 M tlbogger@nsu.edu
BOGGESS, Jonathan .... 601-974-1502. 267 I boggejc@millsaps.edu
BOGGESS, Kendra .... 304-384-5224. 529 E president@concord.edu
BOGGIE, Mark .... 520-515-5451... 12 R boggiem@cochise.edu
BOGGIO, Pamela, J .... 508-213-2483. 235 E pamela.boggio@nichols.edu
BOGGS, Allan .... 937-775-3224. 393 G allan.boggs@wright.edu
BOGGS, Beverly .... 931-221-6540. 459 B boggsb@apsu.edu
BOGGS, Bonnie, B .... 734-384-4268. 247 C bboggs@monroeccc.edu
BOGGS, Doyle, W .... 864-597-4182. 449 I boggsdw@wofford.edu
BOGGS, Gretchen, M ...... 410-250-1088. 219 E contedoc@ezy.net
BOGGS, John .... 281-998-6150. 479 H john.boggs@sjcd.edu
BOGGS, Larry .... 662-862-8252. 267 C laboggs@iccms.edu
BOGGS, Paul, R .... 903-233-3981. 475 J paulboggs@letu.edu
BOGGS, Rainie .... 859-253-3637. 194 A rainie.boggs@frontier.edu
BOGH, Wayne .... 909-389-3309... 61 K wbogh@craftonhills.edu
BOGHOSIAN, Bruce, M ... 510-987-9452... 28 A
BOGHOSSIAN, Fikru .... 443-885-3160. 217 A fikru.boghossian@morgan.edu
BOGLE, Barry, J .... 915-831-7116. 472 B bbogle@epcc.edu
BOGLE, Darcy .... 661-763-7889... 69 D dbogle@taftcollege.edu
BOGLE, Yvonne .... 413-782-1594. 238 A ybogle@wne.edu
BOGLEY, John, W .... 509-527-5979. 525 E bogleyj@whitman.edu
BOGNER, Drew .... 516-323-3200. 331 J dbogner@molloy.edu
BOGOMILSKY, Moshe .... 718-434-0784. 316 F
BOGOMOLNY, Robert, L 410-837-4866. 221 A rbogomolny@ubalt.edu
BOHACH, Gregory .... 662-325-3006. 268 D gbohach@dafvm.msstate.edu
BOHACZ, Candy .... 269-467-9945. 242 H cbohacz@glenoaks.edu
BOHAKER, Linda, A .... 618-374-5495. 156 B linda.bohaker@principia.edu
BOHAM, Kenneth, A .... 828-726-2211. 358 E kboham@cccti.edu
BOHAN, David .... 973-378-9801. 307 C david.bohan@shu.edu
BOHAN, Ken .... 562-907-4261... 76 I kbohan@whittier.edu
BOHANNON, Betsy .... 859-622-1500. 193 P betsy.bohannon@eku.edu
BOHANON, Janet .... 770-531-6315. 128 B jbohanon@laniertech.edu
BOHASKA, Chris .... 410-225-2490. 216 C cbohaska@mica.edu
BOHL, Kyle .... 616-538-2330. 243 A kbohl@gbcol.edu
BOHLAND, James .... 540-231-6000. 515 C jayjon@vt.edu
BOHLEKE, Briant .... 717-334-6286. 422 E bbohleke@ltsg.edu
BOHLEKE, Chuck .... 434-961-5348. 513 F cbohleke@pvcc.edu

BOHMAN, Andreas .... 509-963-2499. 517 F
BohmanA@cwu.edu
BOHMFALK, Rachel, C ... 956-721-5816. 475 F
rbohmfalk@laredo.edu
BOHN, Bill .... 541-506-6090. 402 H
bbohn@cgcc.cc.or.us
BOHN, Nicole .... 415-405-3583... 35 E
nbohn@sfsu.edu
BOHNENBLUST, Delyna . 620-421-6700. 188 D
delynab@labette.edu
BOHNET, Sandra .... 269-488-4409. 244 L
sbohnet@kvcc.edu
BOHNETT, Sally .... 419-251-8985. 383 G
sally.bohnett@mercycollege.edu
BOHNSACK, Jennifer ...... 602-331-7500... 12 A
jbohnsack@aii.edu
BOHNY, David .... 973-618-3440. 300 A
dbohny@caldwell.edu
BOHREN, Karen .... 231-591-2607. 242 F
bksferrisstate@bncollege.com
BOHRER, Robert, E .... 717-337-6823. 417 B
rbohrer@gettysburg.edu
BOICE, Daniel .... 563-876-3353. 177 I
dboice@dwci.edu
BOIES, Brandy .... 540-868-7161. 512 H
bboies@lfcc.edu
BOIES, Chris .... 540-868-7129. 512 H
cboies@lfcc.edu
BOIKE, Kristine .... 763-424-0964. 260 C
kboike@nhcc.edu
BOILINI, Laura, L .... 386-312-4199. 112 C
lauraboilini@sjrstate.edu
BOISE, Craig .... 216-687-2300. 377 F
c.boise@law.csuohio.edu
BOISEN, Beth .... 715-232-1695. 538 B
boisenb@uwstout.edu
BOISJOLY, Russell, P .... 716-673-4813. 342 A
russell.boisjoly@fredonia.edu
BOISSEAU, Tracey, J ...... 765-494-1494. 171 M
BOISSELLE, Dave .... 757-352-4757. 508 G
daviboi@regent.edu
BOISSELLE, Vincent .... 315-781-3549. 326 C
boisselle@hws.edu
BOISSONEAULT, Susan . 508-678-2811. 231 B
susan.boissoneault@bristolcc.edu
BOISVERT, Craig .... 304-647-6290. 530 B
cboisvert@osteo.wvsom.edu
BOISVERT, David .... 631-244-3009. 323 B
BOITNOTT, Tina .... 903-886-5110. 483 E
tina.boitnott@tamuc.edu
BOJAR, Anthea, L .... 414-410-4006. 532 B
albojar@stritch.edu
BOKOWSKI, Debrah .... 503-534-4038. 404 C
dbokowski@marylhurst.edu
BOKSAN, George .... 610-861-1421. 424 E
megjb01@moravian.edu
BOKTOR, Monir .... 949-794-9090... 68 D
mboktor@stanbridge.edu
BOLA, William .... 207-602-2365. 213 A
wbola@une.edu
BOLA, William .... 207-206-2365. 213 A
wbola@une.edu
BOLAND, Carolyn .... 513-244-4717. 377 G
carolyn_boland@mail.msj.edu
BOLAND, Catherine .... 928-350-4001... 17 K
cboland@prescott.edu
BOLAND, Kristine .... 419-783-2469. 379 C
kboland@defiance.edu
BOLAND, Mary, G .... 808-956-8522. 136 B
mgboland@hawaii.edu
BOLAND, Mary Kate .... 610-647-4400. 418 I
mboland@immaculata.edu
BOLAND, Patrick, O .... 203-857-7032... 89 D
pboland@norwalk.edu
BOLAND-CHASE, Ann .... 590-961-4728. 423 B
chase@marywood.edu
BOLDEN, Errol .... 410-951-3542. 220 B
ebolden@coppin.edu
BOLDEN, Gary .... 423-775-6596. 458 A
gbolden@ogs.edu
BOLDEN, John .... 313-496-2536. 252 B
jbolden1@wcccd.edu
BOLDMAN, Denise .... 937-484-1243. 392 C
dboldman@urbana.edu
BOLDREY, Penny .... 989-358-7297. 239 C
boldreyp@alpenacc.edu
BOLDT, Deborah .... 505-428-1704. 311 J
deborah.boldt@sfcc.edu
BOLDT, William .... 702-895-5895. 294 I
william.boldt@unlv.edu
BOLDUC, Darlene, R .... 802-626-6490. 501 E
darlene.bolduc@lyndonstate.edu
BOLDUC, Michael, C .... 561-237-7180. 108 X
mbolduc@lynn.edu
BOLEK, Catherine .... 410-651-6714. 219 E
csbolek@umes.edu
BOLEMAN, Roger, P .... 320-589-6150. 264 F
bolemarp@morris.umn.edu
BOLERATZ, Jonathan .... 814-332-5206. 409 D
jboleratz@allegheny.edu
BOLES, Ginger, A .... 304-457-6230. 526 A
bolesgr@ab.edu
BOLES, Jessica .... 580-559-5539. 395 F
jboles@ecok.edu
BOLES, Sonja .... 407-708-2148. 113 E
boless@seminolestate.edu
BOLEY, Stacie .... 318-798-6868. 201 D
BOLGER, Eric .... 417-690-2278. 272 E
bolger@cofo.edu
BOLICK-FLOSS, Annie .... 707-826-3341... 35 C
amb2@humboldt.edu
BOLIG, Kimberly, L .... 570-326-3761. 427 B
kbolig@pct.edu
BOLIN, Alexis .... 408-848-4742... 45 F
0282mgr@fheg.follett.com
BOLIN, Mark .... 256-352-8102..... 9 G
mark.bolin@wallacestate.edu
BOLIN-REECE, Mary .... 859-257-8701. 200 C
mcreec01@uky.edu
BOLING, Charles .... 276-739-2514. 514 D
cboling@vhcc.edu
BOLING, Cindy .... 405-974-2547. 400 K
cboling@uco.edu
BOLISH, Jennifer .... 651-905-3428. 254 B
jbolish@browncollege.edu
BOLL, Julie .... 217-228-5432. 156 C
bollju@quincy.edu
BOLLARD, Kathleen .... 303-860-5600... 85 K
Kathleen.Bollard@cu.edu
BOLLEN, Kathryn, A .... 585-785-1228. 324 D
bollenka@flcc.edu
BOLLIER, John, H .... 203-432-6754... 93 A
john.bollier@yale.edu
BOLLIG, Nicole .... 785-320-4554. 188 E
nicolefischer@matc.net
BOLLING, Phyllis .... 973-596-3420. 303 G
phyllis.bolling@njit.edu
BOLLING, Ricky .... 276-523-7462. 513 A
rbolling@me.vccs.edu
BOLLINGER, Bruce .... 701-231-6177. 371 G
bruce.bollinger@ndsu.edu
BOLLINGER, Lee, C .... 212-854-9970. 321 D
bollinger@columbia.edu
BOLLINGER, Mary .... 603-888-1311. 297 F
mbollinger@rivier.edu
BOLLINGER, Richard .... 903-223-3068. 484 C
rbolinger@tamut.edu
BOLLINGER, Robert, D ... 218-755-4147. 258 A
rbollinger@bemidjistate.edu
BOLLMAN, Lois .... 612-659-6305. 259 D
lois.bollman@minneapolis.edu
BOLLMAN-DALANSKY,
Terri, L .... 814-641-3424. 419 H
bollmat@juniata.edu
BOLLMANN, Janice, A ... 314-286-4805. 280 F
jabollmann@ranken.edu
BOLMAN, Dave .... 602-383-8228... 18 E
dbolman@uat.edu
BOLOWSKI, Mary .... 201-200-3041. 303 F
mbolowski@njcu.edu
BOLSTER, Jeff .... 619-849-2480... 59 L
jeffbolster@pointloma.edu
BOLT, Barb .... 814-868-9900. 416 C
barbb@erieit.edu
BOLT, Carolyn .... 212-517-0454. 330 E
cbolt@mmm.edu
BOLT, Dave .... 559-925-3222... 75 I
davebolt@whccd.edu
BOLT, Gary .... 630-844-6878. 140 A
gbolt@aurora.edu
BOLT, Gita .... 504-861-2657. 205 H
gbolt@loyno.edu
BOLT, Susan .... 574-284-4556. 172 G
sbolt@saintmarys.edu
BOLT, Tracy, L .... 443-334-2270. 218 E
tbolt@stevenson.edu
BOLT, Wendy .... 513-569-1640. 376 L
wendy.bolt@cincinnatistate.edu
BOLTE, Jenny, L .... 540-674-3645. 513 B
jbolte@nr.edu
BOLTE, Michael .... 831-459-2991... 72 C
bolte@ucolick.org
BOLTON, Cathy .... 940-552-6291. 493 F
cbolton@vernoncollege.edu
BOLTON, David .... 417-328-1538. 282 C
dbolton@sbuniv.edu
BOLTON, Denny, G .... 336-841-9202. 355 C
ebolton@highpoint.edu
BOLTON, JR.,
Glenn Allen .... 414-955-8704. 534 C
abolton@mcw.edu
BOLTON, Harry .... 707-654-1192... 31 I
hbolton@csum.edu
BOLTON, Janice .... 770-962-7580. 127 D
jbolton@gwinnetttech.edu
BOLTON, Lance .... 719-502-2200... 84 A
lance.bolton@ppcc.edu
BOLTON, Melanie .... 256-378-4900..... 2 G
mbolton@cacc.edu
BOLTON, Robert, D .... 517-750-1200. 250 E
rbolton@arbor.edu
BOLTON, Sarah, R .... 413-597-4171. 238 D
sarah.r.bolton@williams.edu
BOLTON, Stanley .... 803-822-3523. 445 C
boltons@midlandstech.edu
BOLTON, Tama .... 831-477-3548... 30 G
tabolton@cabrillo.edu
BOLTON, Tonya, D .... 870-759-4130... 25 K
tbolton@wbcoll.edu
BOLTZ, Fran .... 716-286-8751. 334 F
fboltz@niagara.edu
BOLYAI, Stephen .... 973-720-2233. 308 I
bolyais@wpunj.edu
BOLYARD, Adrienne, M . 206-726-5021. 518 G
abolyard@cornish.edu
BOLYARD, Brian .... 304-734-6600. 527 O
bbolyard@bridgemont.edu
BOLYARD, Melissa .... 404-727-0692. 124 E
mbolyar@emory.edu
BOMAN, Victoria .... 205-247-8837..... 7 E
vbowen@stillman.edu
BOMBA, Jody, L .... 909-593-3511... 72 E
jbomba@laverne.edu
BOMBARO, Christine ..... 570-372-4320. 433 H
bombaro@susqu.edu
BOMBERGER, Sherry ..... 717-757-1100. 438 H
sherry.bomberger@yti.edu
BOMERSBACH, Bob .... 212-280-1428. 349 A
bbomersbach@uts.columbia.edu
BOMOTTI, Gerry .... 702-895-3571. 294 I
gerry.bomotti@unlv.edu
BONA, Dennis .... 269-965-3931. 244 O
bonad@kellogg.edu
BONAGURO, John, A ..... 270-745-7003. 200 G
john.bonaguro@wku.edu
BONAHUE, Edward .... 352-381-3822. 113 C
ed.bohahue@sfcollege.edu
BONANDO, John, S .... 724-738-2728. 429 F
john.bonando@sru.edu
BONANNO, Barbara .... 726-926-8924. 326 B
bbonnano@hilbert.edu
BONANNO, Janice, M .... 617-228-2436. 231 C
jbonanno@bhcc.mass.edu
BONANNO, Joseph .... 812-855-4440. 167 F
jbonanno@indiana.edu
BONANNO, Steve .... 304-293-6967. 530 D
steve.bonanno@mail.wvu.edu
BONAPARTE, Donna .... 781-239-6434. 222 D
dbonaparte@babson.edu
BONAPARTE, Wallace, T 843-792-1568. 445 B
bonaparw@musc.edu
BONAPARTE, Wilma .... 414-297-7396. 540 E
bonaparw@matc.edu
BONATAKIS, Valerie .... 413-265-2227. 225 C
bonatakisv@elms.edu
BONATO, Frederick .... 973-655-4280. 303 D
bonatof@mail.montclair.edu
BONCUORE, Cheryl .... 312-752-2646. 149 E
cheryl.boncuore@kendall.edu
BOND, Alicia .... 570-408-6024. 437 F
alicia.bond@wilkes.edu
BOND, Bill, E .... 406-756-3818. 286 B
bbond@fvcc.edu
BOND, Bradley .... 815-753-9403. 154 I
bbond@niu.edu
BOND, Cheryl .... 601-947-4201. 268 C
cheryl.bond@mgccc.edu
BOND, Cindy, R .... 208-732-6454. 138 B
cbond@csi.edu
BOND, Emma .... 601-426-6346. 269 G
ebond@southeasternbaptist.edu
BOND, Erin .... 212-431-2199. 333 I
Erin.Bond@nyls.edu
BOND, Inge .... 408-741-2166... 75 L
inge.bond@westvalley.edu
BOND, Jan .... 419-289-5054. 374 C
jbond1@ashland.edu
BOND, Jay .... 657-278-4355... 33 E
jbond@fullerton.edu
BOND, Martha .... 315-781-3780. 326 C
mbond@hws.edu
BOND, Meredith, R .... 216-687-9321. 377 F
m.bond40@csuohio.edu
BOND, Michelle .... 334-386-7275..... 3 H
mbond@faulkner.edu
BOND, Nola .... 660-562-1127. 279 I
nbond@nwmissouri.edu
BOND, Peter .... 972-883-2301. 491 E
pbond@utdallas.edu
BOND, Roy, L .... 972-391-1087. 470 I
RoyBond@dcccd.edu
BOND, Susan, E .... 610-359-1222. 414 D
sbond@dccc.edu
BOND-HUIE,
Stephanie, A .... 512-499-4798. 491 A
shuie@utsystem.edu
BONDAVALLI, Bonnie .... 815-836-5242. 150 H
bondavbo@lewisu.edu
BONDAVALLI, Bruno ...... 773-878-3439. 158 B
bbondavalli@staugustine.edu
BONDI, Tony .... 626-229-1300... 50 H
BONDS, Dorothea .... 214-648-7500. 493 E
dorothea.bonds@utsouthwestern.edu
BONDS, Jess .... 209-478-0800... 47 M
jbonds@humphreys.edu
BONDS, Jonathon .... 770-960-1298. 127 F
jbonds@ict-ils.edu
BONDS, Nell .... 870-743-3000... 22 B
nbonds@northark.edu
BONDS, Thomas .... 662-862-8131. 267 C
tabonds@iccms.edu
BONDUM, Victoria .... 315-228-7481. 320 F
vbondum@colgate.edu
BONDURANT, Derrith ..... 903-566-7444. 492 D
dbondurant@uttyler.edu
BONDURANT, Glenda, P 252-246-1333. 365 C
gbondurant@wilsoncc.edu
BONDURANT, Jennifer ... 573-592-5313. 285 B
jenny.bondurant@westminster-mo.edu
BONDURANT,
William, S .... 606-474-3234. 194 H
bbondurant@kcu.edu
BONE, Andrew .... 503-399-6593. 402 E
andrew.bone@chemeketa.edu
BONE, Don .... 215-573-3444. 435 B
donbone@upenn.edu
BONE, Robyn .... 817-531-6552. 488 A
rbone@txwes.edu
BONEBRIGHT, Terri .... 765-658-4359. 165 F
tbone@depauw.edu
BONELLI, Vicky .... 618-544-8657. 147 A
bonelliv@iecc.edu
BONES, Rafael .... 413-572-8277. 230 F
rbones@westfield.ma.edu
BONEWALD, Karen, I ..... 603-526-3748. 295 I
kbonewald@colby-sawyer.edu
BONEWITZ, Stan .... 512-313-3000. 469 L
stan.bonewitz@concordia.edu
BONEZ, Allison .... 317-955-6080. 170 V
abonez@marian.edu
BONFANTI, Philip .... 662-325-8853. 268 D
pgb13@msstate.edu
BONFIGLIO, Robert, A ... 585-245-5618. 343 C
bonfig@geneseo.edu
BONGARD, Joseph, W ... 610-785-6271. 432 C
jbongard@scs.edu
BONGARTEN, Bruce, C .. 315-470-6510. 345 B
bcbongarten@esf.edu
BONGARTZ, Michael ...... 816-235-1515. 283 D
bongartzm@umkc.edu
BONGIORNO, Laurel ...... 802-651-5978. 499 A
bongiorno@champlain.edu
BONGO, Catherine, N .... 973-655-7137. 303 D
bongoc@mail.montclair.edu
BONI, Bethyn .... 315-568-3252. 333 C
bboni@nycc.edu
BONI, Sharon .... 304-367-0205. 529 F
sharon.boni@fairmontstate.edu
BONICELLI, Paul .... 757-352-4320. 508 G
pbonicelli@regent.edu
BONIFER, Duane .... 270-384-8043. 197 D
boniferd@lindsey.edu
BONIFORTI, Alfredo, H .. 561-237-7173. 108 X
aboniforti@lynn.edu
BONIFORTI, Chris, G ..... 561-237-7163. 108 X
cboniforti@lynn.edu
BONILLA, Ana, O .... 787-841-2000. 552 B
abonilla@pucpr.edu
BONILLA, Angelita .... 973-353-1494. 306 D
bonillan@andromeda.rutgers.edu
BONILLA, Anie .... 954-492-5353. 100 A
abonilla@citycollege.edu
BONILLA, Charles .... 312-369-8611. 143 D
cbonilla@colum.edu
BONILLA, Diana .... 818-364-7699... 52 A
bonilldi@lamission.edu
BONILLA, Juan .... 787-769-2043. 554 B
juan.bonilla3@upr.edu
BONILLA, Kathleen .... 559-489-2221... 68 I
kathy.bonilla@fresnocitycollege.edu
BONILLA, Mary Kay .... 406-771-5123. 287 E
mbonilla@gfcmsu.edu
BONILLA, Matthew, F ..... 212-346-1200. 335 J
mbonilla@pace.edu
BONILLA, Ray .... 979-458-6000. 482 E
rbonilla@tamus.edu
BONILLA, Victor .... 787-892-4675. 551 A
vicbonil@sg.inter.edu
BONILLA, Wendy .... 951-698-6389... 75 A
BONILLA-RODRIGUEZ,
Victor .... 787-725-6500. 547 H
vbonilla@albizu.edu
BONIN, Charles, G .... 207-768-9550. 212 G
charles.bonin@umpi.edu
BONINE, Dan .... 304-420-8639. 530 E
dan.bonine@wvup.edu
BONINI, Robin .... 906-487-7225. 242 G
robin.bonini@finlandia.edu
BONK, Kenneth, J .... 540-831-5332. 508 C
kjbonk@radford.edu
BONK, Sharon, B .... 617-588-1356. 223 B
sbonk@bfit.edu

BONN, Cynthia, L .... 401-874-7100. 440 D deanofadmission@uri.edu
BONN, Robert, R .... 262-551-5942. 532 D rbonn@carthage.edu
BONNE, Connie .... 563-441-2450. 180 E cbonne@kucampus.edu
BONNEAU, Elizabeth .... 508-849-3459. 222 B ebonneau@annamaria.edu
BONNER, A. Frank .... 704-406-4236. 354 C fbonner@gardner-webb.edu
BONNER, Beverly, J .... 865-882-4550. 461 E bonner@roanestate.edu
BONNER, Davita .... 386-481-2143... 99 C bonnerd@cookman.edu
BONNER, Debera .... 804-524-5276. 515 D dbonner@vsu.edu
BONNER, Gloria, L .... 615-898-2622. 459 D gloria.bonner@mtsu.edu
BONNER, Hugh, W .... 315-464-6560. 342 E bonnerh@upstate.edu
BONNER, James .... 215-572-2187. 409 H bonner@arcadia.edu
BONNER, Jo .... 205-348-6149..... 8 C jo.bonner@uasystem.ua.edu
BONNER, John, B .... 425-276-9520. 519 I jbonner@everettcc.edu
BONNER, Judd .... 951-343-4256... 30 H jbonner@calbaptist.edu
BONNER, Judy, L .... 205-348-5103..... 8 D judy.bonner@ua.edu
BONNER, Julia .... 414-229-4716. 537 A jbonner@uwm.edu
BONNER, Mason .... 205-247-8025..... 7 E mbonner@stillman.edu
BONNER, Paula, E .... 608-262-9630. 536 D pbonner@waastaff.com
BONNER, Sirius .... 360-992-2355. 518 A sbonner@clark.edu
BONNER, Thomas, P .... 651-696-6295. 256 L bonner@macalester.edu
BONNER, William, L .... 803-754-3950. 449 H
BONNET, Larissa, B .... 307-674-6446. 543 F lbonnet@sheridan.edu
BONNETTE, Clarence .... 803-793-5248. 443 E bonnettec@denmarktech.edu
BONNETTE, Margaree .... 803-793-5175. 443 E bonnettem@denmarktech.edu
BONNETTE, Thomas .... 802-860-2705. 499 A bonnette@champlain.edu
BONNIN, Linda .... 901-678-2843. 460 B lmichael@memphis.edu
BONNIN, Richard .... 713-743-0945. 489 A rjbonnin@uh.edu
BONNIN, Richard .... 713-743-8155. 489 B rjbonnin@central.uh.edu
BONNSTETTER, Bret .... 847-925-6224. 145 H bbonnste@harpercollege.edu
BONO, John .... 831-459-4747... 72 C jbono@ucsc.edu
BONOFIGLIO, Carrie .... 517-338-3314. 241 A cbono@cleary.edu
BONONES, Patrick .... 404-471-6396. 119 I pbonones@agnesscott.edu
BONSANG, Stacy .... 781-595-6768. 228 C sbonsang@mariancourt.edu
BONSIGNORE, Diana .... 770-650-3000... 96 F
BONTA, Anthony .... 305-899-3653... 98 O abonta@barry.edu
BONTATIBUS, Donna .... 860-343-5805... 89 A dbontatibus@mxcc.commnet.edu
BONTE, Troy .... 724-503-1001. 436 G tbonte@washjeff.edu
BONTINELLI, Stasi .... 303-751-8700... 78 J bontinelli@bel-rea.com
BONTRAGER, Cindy, A .. 785-532-6226. 188 A cab@ksu.edu
BONTRAGER, Cindy, A .. 785-532-6767. 188 A cab@ksu.edu
BONTRAGER, Katherine, A .... 859-572-6132. 198 I bontragerk1@nku.edu
BONTRAGER, Kimberlee . 423-869-6314. 456 A kimberlee.bontrager@lmunet.edu
BONUCHI, Molly, A .... 308-635-6112. 293 E bonuchim@wncc.edu
BONURA, Kimberlee .... 850-443-0126. 265 D kimberlee.bonura@waldenu.edu
BONURA, Nancy .... 432-264-3752. 473 E nbonura@howardcollege.edu
BONURA, Rocky .... 310-660-3670... 43 B abonura@elcamino.edu
BONVENUTO, Christopher, M .... 818-947-2336... 52 E bonvencm@lavc.edu
BONVILLIAN, Gary .... 229-226-1621. 132 F gbonvillian@thomasu.edu
BONVILLIAN, William, B 202-789-1828. 233 B
BOOCKER, David, J .... 402-554-2338. 293 A dboocker@unomaha.edu
BOOG, Melissa, M .... 410-543-6330. 220 D mmboog@salisbury.edu
BOOHER, Doug .... 812-855-9529. 167 F dbooher@indiana.edu
BOOHER, Mark .... 805-922-6966... 26 K mbooher@pcpa.org
BOOK, Cheryl, A .... 612-343-4163. 262 X cabook@northcentral.edu
BOOK, Connie .... 336-278-5661. 354 B cbook@elon.edu
BOOK, Wes .... 612-343-4143. 262 X wcbook@northcentral.edu
BOOKER, Alicia .... 412-788-7360. 413 D abooker@ccac.edu
BOOKER, Kathy, J .... 217-424-6348. 153 C kbooker@millikin.edu
BOOKER, Kevin .... 404-653-7893. 129 D kbooker@morehouse.edu
BOOKER, Latoya .... 616-632-2455. 239 E latoya.booker@aquinas.edu
BOOKER, Marc .... 602-557-4609... 18 I marc.booker@phoenix.edu
BOOKER, Mary .... 909-621-8205... 60 A mary.booker@pomona.edu
BOOKER, Michael .... 636-481-3312. 275 I mbooker@jeffco.edu
BOOKER, Sid .... 814-732-2810. 428 E sbooker@edinboro.edu
BOOKER, Steve .... 407-646-2395. 111 Q sbooker@rollins.edu
BOOKMAN, Douglas .... 800-672-3060. 366 F
BOOKMEYER, Paul, G .... 816-942-8400. 271 H paul.bookmeyer@avila.edu
BOOKOUT, James .... 334-670-3617..... 7 H jbookout@troy.edu
BOOKOUT, Jeff .... 870-358-8614... 20 B jeff_bookout@asun.edu
BOOKSTAVER, John .... 636-922-8722. 280 J jbookstaver@stchas.edu
BOOKWALTER, Robert ... 304-696-2350. 529 H bookwalt@marshall.edu
BOOM, Bill .... 320-363-3996. 263 P bboom@csbsju.edu
BOOM, Philip .... 563-588-8000. 178 D pboom@emmaus.edu
BOOMGAARDEN, Donald .... 504-865-3039. 205 H deancmfa@loyno.edu
BOOMS, Carole .... 734-432-5811. 246 B cbooms@madonna.edu
BOONE, Dan .... 615-248-1251. 462 D dboone@trevecca.edu
BOONE, Debbie .... 334-291-4927..... 2 H debbie.boone@cv.edu
BOONE, J. Allen .... 901-843-3760. 458 E boone@rhodes.edu
BOONE, John, B .... 919-866-5923. 364 G jbboone@waketech.edu
BOONE, Katherine, B .... 410-455-3768. 219 D kboone@umbc.edu
BOONE, Kathleen, C .... 716-839-8301. 322 E kboone@daemen.edu
BOONE, LaShanda, R .... 314-340-3301. 275 A boonel@hssu.edu
BOONE, Loren .... 320-308-3151. 261 B ljboone@stcloudstate.edu
BOONE, Phil .... 325-674-2659. 464 H phil.boone@acu.edu
BOONE, Rebecca .... 318-357-5621. 208 B booner@nsula.edu
BOONE, Susan .... 773-702-8815. 161 B sboone@uchicago.edu
BOONSTRA, Brenda .... 706-776-0103. 130 E bboonstra@piedmont.edu
BOOR, Kathryn, J .... 607-255-2241. 322 A kjb4@cornell.edu
BOORD, Peggy, L .... 904-632-3251. 105 E pboord@fscj.edu
BOOREN, Diane .... 303-457-2757... 81 L dbooren@cci.edu
BOOROS, Deborah .... 610-282-1100. 414 F deborah.booros@desales.edu
BOOS, Jean .... 843-355-4167. 449 F boosj@wiltech.edu
BOOSINGER, Timothy, R .... 334-844-5771..... 1 G provost@auburn.edu
BOOSKA, Karry .... 802-728-1320. 501 F kbooska@vtc.edu
BOOSTER, Richard .... 541-683-5141. 403 D dbooster@gutenberg.edu
BOOTH, Ann, B .... 304-367-4047. 529 F Ann.Booth@fairmontstate.edu
BOOTH, Austin .... 716-645-0983. 341 F abooth@buffalo.edu
BOOTH, Bradley, W .... 202-685-2387. 544 K bradley.booth@ndu.edu
BOOTH, Derrick .... 916-484-8361... 53 A boothd@arc.losrios.edu
BOOTH, Eric .... 512-313-3000. 469 L eric.booth@concordia.edu
BOOTH, George, E .... 302-259-6206... 93 E gbooth@dtcc.edu
BOOTH, James, M .... 713-525-6960. 490 L booth@stthom.edu
BOOTH, Jane, E .... 212-854-0286. 321 D jeb@gc.columbia.edu
BOOTH, Jennifer .... 803-754-4100. 443 C
BOOTH, Julie .... 530-541-4660... 50 D booth@ltcc.edu
BOOTH, LaQuita .... 334-229-4124..... 1 D lbooth@alasu.edu
BOOTH, Paige .... 512-448-8429. 479 C paigeb@stedwards.edu
BOOTH, Richard .... 618-374-5127. 156 B richard.booth@principia.edu
BOOTH, Ronnie, L .... 864-646-1773. 447 D rlbooth@tctc.edu
BOOTH, Scott .... 614-947-6592. 380 A scott.booth@franklin.edu
BOOTH, Susan, A .... 573-629-3002. 274 J sbooth@hlg.edu
BOOTH, Susan, L .... 540-224-4640. 506 G slbooth1@jchs.edu
BOOTH, Terry, L .... 803-778-6624. 441 F boothtl@cctech.edu
BOOTHBY, Mandy .... 712-749-2123. 176 D boothbym@bvu.edu
BOOTHBY, Rebecca .... 318-342-1982. 208 E ulm@campuscornerinc.com
BOOTHE, Alan .... 334-242-7710..... 7 H aboothe@troy.edu
BOOTHE, Diane .... 208-426-1611. 137 G dianeboothe@boisestate.edu
BOOTHE, Jason .... 435-652-7526. 497 E boothe@dixie.edu
BOOTHE, M. Shane .... 832-252-4646. 468 L shane.boothe@cbshouston.edu
BOOTMAN, J, L .... 520-626-1657... 18 F bootman@pharmacy.arizona.edu
BOOZER, Andrew .... 803-461-3296. 445 A andrew.boozer@lr.edu
BOPKO, Patricia .... 909-652-6152... 37 M patricia.bopko@chaffey.edu
BOPP, Ruthane, I .... 847-735-5025. 150 B bopp@lakeforest.edu
BOQUET, OSB, Gregory, M .... 985-867-2232. 206 H rector@sjasc.edu
BOQUETTE, Troy .... 810-762-0243. 247 F troy.boquette@mcc.edu
BORASI, Raffaella .... 585-275-3950. 349 C raffaella.borasi@rochester.edu
BORAWSKI, Judy .... 414-258-4810. 535 A borawskj@mtmary.edu
BORCHERS, Mitch .... 913-469-8500. 187 J mborchers@jccc.edu
BORCHERS, Timothy, A .. 218-477-2764. 259 H tim.borchers@mnstate.edu
BORCK, Pat .... 478-471-2865. 128 I pat.borck@maconstate.edu
BORDEAUX, Lionel .... 605-856-5880. 451 B lionel.bordeaux@sintegleska.edu
BORDEAUX, Lynette .... 605-856-5880. 451 B lynette.bordeaux@sintegleska.edu
BORDEAUX, Shirley .... 701-255-3285. 373 C sbordeaux@uttc.edu
BORDELON, Deborah .... 708-534-8045. 145 F dbordelon@govst.edu
BORDEN, David, S .... 512-223-7738. 466 I dborden@austincc.edu
BORDEN, John, S .... 212-875-4603. 314 C jborden@bankstreet.edu
BORDEN, M. Paige .... 407-823-4765. 115 E paige.borden@ucf.edu
BORDEN, Oliver .... 505-566-3490. 311 I bordeno@sanjuancollege.edu
BORDEN, Robert .... 216-421-7467. 377 C rborden@cia.edu
BORDEN, Susan .... 410-626-2506. 217 G susan.borden@sjca.edu
BORDEN, Vic .... 812-855-9893. 167 F vborden@indiana.edu
BORDER, Debra .... 402-481-3804. 288 H deb.border@bryanhealthcollege.edu
BORDERS, Julianna .... 419-559-2228. 389 I jborders01@terra.edu
BORDERS, Katrina .... 713-221-2740. 489 D bordersk@uhd.edu
BORDERS, Marianne .... 803-981-7320. 449 J borders@sctechsystem.edu
BORDIN, Cristina, L .... 512-464-8893. 479 C cristinb@stedwards.edu
BORDONARO, Vilma .... 914-594-4900. 334 A vilma_bordonaro@nymc.edu
BOREK, Jarrod .... 315-733-2300. 349 D jborek@uscny.edu
BORELLI, Alyssa .... 206-239-4500. 517 M aborelli@cityu.edu
BOREN, Carla .... 816-584-6317. 280 C carla.boren@park.edu
BOREN, David, L .... 405-325-3916. 401 B dboren@ou.edu
BOREN, J. B .... 806-352-5207. 494 F borenjb@wbu.edu
BOREN, Laura .... 918-456-5511. 396 H borenld@nsuok.edu
BORER, Jim .... 763-424-0736. 260 C jborer@nhcc.edu
BORER, Ralph (Sam), J .. 402-557-7355. 288 G sam.borer@bellevue.edu
BORES, Gerald .... 503-552-2007. 404 H gbores@ncnm.edu
BORGE, Keith .... 914-654-5552. 320 H kborge@cnr.edu
BORGER, Jennika .... 610-861-1411. 424 E
BORGER, Patricia, A .... 414-229-3013. 537 A pborger@uwm.edu
BORGES, Dan .... 831-477-5220... 30 G daborges@cabrillo.edu
BORGES, Eduardo .... 281-649-3299. 473 B eborges@hbu.edu
BORGES, Silvia .... 305-821-3333. 105 A sborges@fnu.edu
BORGLUM, Karen, M .... 407-582-3455. 118 M kborglum@valenciacollege.edu
BORGMAN, Cathleen, M 203-254-4081... 89 I cborgman@fairfield.edu
BORGMAN, Kenneth, L .. 989-463-7314. 239 B borgman@alma.edu
BORGMANN-INGWERSEN, Marian .... 402-465-2415. 291 G mborgman@nebrwesleyan.edu
BORGOGNONI, Mary, E 716-286-8352. 334 F meb@niagara.edu
BORGONAH, Darryl .... 512-245-2550. 487 C djb129@txstate.edu
BORGSMILLER, Stephen 573-472-3210. 282 B sjborgsmiller@semo.edu
BORGSTROM, Karen .... 603-513-5189. 298 D karen.borgstrom@law.unh.edu
BORGUS, Donna .... 585-389-2471. 332 D dborgus8@naz.edu
BORICH, Joe .... 419-448-3014. 389 J borichj@tiffin.edu
BORIS, Barbara, A .... 610-409-3605. 436 B bboris@ursinus.edu
BORIS, Patricia, A .... 716-673-3131. 342 A patricia.boris@fredonia.edu
BORJESSON, Peggy .... 503-399-2537. 402 E peggy.borjesson@chemeketa.edu
BORK, Ronald .... 402-643-7475. 289 B ron.bork@cune.edu
BORKOVICH, Bruce .... 231-591-5000. 242 F borkovb@ferris.edu
BORKOWSKI, Donald, V 207-725-3947. 209 H dborkows@bowdoin.edu
BORKOWSKI, Ellen, Y .... 518-388-6293. 348 J borkowse@union.edu
BORLAND, James .... 312-777-8661. 147 D jborland@aii.edu
BORLANDOE, Janice, M 718-270-6046. 319 A jborlandoe@mec.cuny.edu
BORN, Bill .... 574-535-7543. 166 A billjb@goshen.edu
BORN, Brad .... 316-284-5239. 184 J bborn@bethelks.edu
BORNE, Jade .... 817-515-4742. 482 B jade.borne@tccd.edu
BORNEMANN, Jeffrey .... 414-955-8793. 534 C jbornema@mcw.edu
BORNER, John .... 315-792-7530. 346 C john.borner@sunyit.edu
BORNHEIMER, Mary, E .. 618-537-6524. 152 G mebornheimer@mckendree.edu
BORNSTEIN, Eva .... 718-960-8232. 318 A eva.bornstein@lehman.cuny.edu
BORNSTEIN, Leah, L .... 928-226-4100... 13 B leah.bornstein@coconino.edu
BORNSTEIN, Rachel .... 802-225-3318. 499 I rachel.bornstein@neci.edu
BORNUS, Susan .... 651-523-2929. 256 A sbornus@hamline.edu
BOROFSKY, David, B .... 605-256-5112. 451 H david.borofsky@dsu.edu
BORONICO, Jess .... 516-686-7838. 333 H jboronic@nyit.edu
BORONICO, L. Christie .. 203-576-5238... 91 D linda.boronico@stvincentscollege.edu
BOROS, Barbara .... 480-654-7702... 15 A barbara.boros@mesacc.edu
BOROS, Barbara .... 480-461-7128... 15 A barbara.boros@mesacc.edu
BOROS-KAZAI, Mary .... 608-363-2640. 531 M boroskaz@beloit.edu
BOROUGHS, SJ, Philip, L .... 508-793-2525. 225 B pborough@holycross.edu
BOROWIAK, Mary Marcine .... 716-896-0700. 350 A marcine@villa.edu
BOROWICK, Matthew .... 973-378-9847. 307 C matthew.borowick@shu.edu

BOROWICZ, Laurie .... 715-675-3331. 541 A borowiczl@ntc.edu
BOROWICZ, Mark .... 715-675-3331. 541 A Borowicz@ntc.edu
BORREGO, Paul .... 210-486-2194. 465 B pborrego4@alamo.edu
BORREGO, Susan, E ...... 310-243-3784... 33 B sborrego@csudh.edu
BORREN, Tammy .... 931-540-2553. 460 E tborren@columbiastate.edu
BORRERO, Harold .... 707-638-5267... 69 K harold.borrero@tu.edu
BORROW, Susan .... 256-215-4301..... 2 G sborrow@cacc.edu
BORSIG, Jim .... 662-329-7100. 268 E jborsig@pres.muw.edu
BORSKI, Brian .... 972-860-4116. 470 G
BORST, Andrew .... 309-295-1414. 162 K AJ-Borst@wiu.edu
BORST, Bridgette .... 304-357-4925. 527 H bridgetteborst@ucwv.edu
BORST, Charlotte .... 562-907-4204... 76 I cborst@whittier.edu
BORST, David .... 262-243-5700. 532 H david.borst@cuw.edu
BORTHWICK, Kristen .... 512-492-3011. 466 B registrar@aoma.edu
BORTMAN, Lisa .... 310-506-4393... 58 H lisa.bortman@pepperdine.edu
BORTMAN, Walter, J ...... 818-364-7800... 52 A bortmawj@lamission.edu
BORTUNK, Ayelet .... 305-653-8770. 119 G abortunk@lecfl.com
BORTZ, Carolyn .... 610-861-5375. 425 D cbortz@northampton.edu
BORUFF-JONES, Polly ... 417-873-7282. 273 H pboruffjones@drury.edu
BORUM, Art .... 618-545-3401. 149 D aborum@kaskaskia.edu
BORUNDA, Mario, R ...... 805-898-2940... 44 I mborunda@fielding.edu
BORUS, David, M .... 845-437-7583. 349 G daborus@vassar.edu
BORUSZEWSKI, Richard 517-371-5140. 250 G boruszer@cooley.edu
BOS, James .... 712-722-6030. 177 J jim.bos@dordt.edu
BOS, Saskia .... 212-353-4203. 321 F sbos@cooper.edu
BOSACK-KOSEK, Carol, A .... 570-408-5963. 437 F carol.bosack@wilkes.edu
BOSCHINI, JR., Victor, J .... 817-257-7783. 484 I v.boschini@tcu.edu
BOSCHMANN, Erv .... 765-455-9275. 168 A eboschma@iupui.edu
BOSCHUNG, Milla .... 205-348-6250...... 8 D mboschun@ches.ua.edu
BOSCO, Mike .... 617-588-1364. 223 B mbosco@bfit.edu
BOSCO, Pat, J .... 785-532-6237. 188 A bosco@ksu.edu
BOSE, Mohua .... 518-608-8288. 324 B mbose@excelsior.edu
BOSE, Pradeep .... 859-622-1761. 193 P pradeep.bose@eku.edu
BOSIA, Michael .... 802-654-2980. 500 B mbosia@smcvt.edu
BOSIO, Amy .... 215-895-6382. 415 B aab97@drexel.edu
BOSIO, Katherine .... 810-762-9537. 244 Q kbosio@kettering.edu
BOSIO, Laurie, A .... 401-333-7150. 439 A lbosio@ccri.edu
BOSKIE, Shawn .... 602-386-4811.... 11 G shawn.boskie@arizonachristian.edu
BOSKO, Ronna .... 585-245-5596. 343 C bosko@geneseo.edu
BOSLAND, Judy .... 575-646-1720. 310 I jbosland@nmsu.edu
BOSLEY, Amy, N .... 407-582-8255. 118 M abosley@valenciacollege.edu
BOSLEY, Barry .... 717-358-4663. 416 J barry.bosley@fandm.edu
BOSLEY, Gabriele .... 502-272-8476. 192 E gbosley@bellarmine.edu
BOSLEY, Keith .... 802-287-8238. 499 D bosleyk@greenmtn.edu
BOSMA, Tim .... 707-524-1635... 65 B tbosma@santarosa.edu
BOSS, Diane .... 479-936-5172... 22 C dboss@nwacc.edu
BOSS, JR., Edward, A .... 516-299-4095. 329 D edward.boss@liu.edu
BOSS, Ken .... 708-239-4830. 160 K ken.boss@trnty.edu
BOSS, Shannon .... 215-780-1318. 433 A sbaoss@salus.edu
BOSSA, Susan, G .... 617-984-1656. 235 I sbossa@quincycollege.edu
BOSSE, Jeannine .... 207-859-1105. 211 H sfs@thomas.edu
BOSSE, Patricia, A .... 410-532-5177. 217 E pbosse@ndm.edu
BOSSERT, Rodney .... 770-423-6030. 127 N rbossert@kennesaw.edu
BOSSIO, Lora, J .... 530-752-6449... 70 J ljbossio@ucdavis.edu
BOSSLE, Francis, X .... 443-997-6394. 215 H fbossle@jhu.edu
BOSSO, Edward, H .... 202-651-5346... 95 C edward.bosso@gallaudet.edu
BOST, Preston, R .... 765-361-6288. 175 B bostp@wabash.edu
BOST, Tim .... 704-216-7230. 363 D tim.bost@rccc.edu
BOSTER, Drew .... 510-780-4500... 50 I dboster@lifewest.edu
BOSTIAN, Susan .... 605-626-2520. 451 I sbostian@northern.edu
BOSTIC, Ann .... 410-276-4101. 218 D abostic@host.sdc.edu
BOSTIC, Deborah .... 717-846-5000. 438 F
BOSTIC, Don .... 325-641-5726. 478 H dbostic@rangercollege.edu
BOSTIC, Heather .... 314-340-3567. 275 A bostich@hssu.edu
BOSTIC, Peter .... 530-541-4660... 50 D bostic@ltcc.edu
BOSTIC, Renee .... 718-270-6071. 319 A rbostic@mec.cuny.edu
BOSTICK, Sharon .... 312-567-3293. 147 F sbostick@iit.edu
BOSTICK, Sharon, L .... 816-235-1531. 283 D bosticks@umkc.edu
BOSTICK-ISSAC, Sharon . 386-481-2957... 99 C bosticks@cookman.edu
BOSTON, McKinley .... 575-646-7630. 310 I boston@nmsu.edu
BOSTON, Pamela, F .... 757-823-2293. 507 M pfboston@nsu.edu
BOSTON, Richard, G .... 860-701-6728. 545 G richard.g.boston@uscg.mil
BOSTON, Wallace, E .... 304-724-3700. 526 B wboston@apus.edu
BOSTROM, Jennifer .... 317-738-8758. 165 I jbostrom@franklincollege.edu
BOSWELL, Chris .... 307-766-2238. 543 I cboswel1@uwyo.edu
BOSWELL, Kate Fiedler .. 804-355-0671. 510 G kboswell@upsem.edu
BOSWELL, Katherine .... 817-598-6216. 494 G kboswell@wc.edu
BOSWELL, Robert .... 303-735-1332... 85 L robert.boswell@colorado.edu
BOSWORTH, Blair .... 216-987-4899. 378 D blair.bosworth@tri-c.edu
BOSWORTH, Susan, L ..... 757-221-3584. 503 N slbosw@wm.edu
BOSWORTH, Theresa .... 541-278-5757. 402 C tbosworth@bluecc.edu
BOTANA, Joseph .... 706-385-1017. 130 F joseph.botana@point.edu
BOTELER, Trina .... 770-975-4000. 122 I
BOTELHO, Marla .... 781-768-7340. 236 A marla.botelho@regiscollege.edu
BOTERO, Nancy .... 954-201-7414... 99 D nbotero@broward.edu
BOTHNER, Peter, G .... 585-389-2196. 332 D pbothne4@naz.edu
BOTHOF, Ken .... 859-572-5193. 198 I
BOTHOF, Ken .... 920-465-2145. 536 F bothofk@uwgb.edu
BOTHWELL, Jennifer .... 508-541-1596. 225 F jbothwell@dean.edu
BOTKIN, Sarah, L .... 319-363-8213. 181 C sbotkin@mtmercy.edu
BOTLEY, Robert, L .... 910-672-1151. 367 D rbotley@uncfsu.edu
BOTSTEIN, Leon .... 914-758-7423. 222 E president@bard.edu
BOTSTEIN, Leon .... 845-758-7423. 314 D president@bard.edu
BOTT, Jennifer .... 765-285-1581. 164 B jpbott@bsu.edu
BOTTARO, Jesus .... 718-270-6263. 319 A jbottaro@mec.cuny.edu
BOTTELBERGHE, John ..... 970-675-3275... 80 B john.bottelberghe@cncc.edu
BOTTEMILLER, Sandi ...... 503-768-7183. 403 K sjb@lclark.edu
BOTTENFIELD, Gigi .... 406-447-6927. 287 A gigi.bottenfield@umhelena.edu
BOTTERUD, Carl .... 323-259-1441... 56 I botterud@oxy.edu
BOTTICELLI, Jill .... 817-461-8741. 466 D jbotticelli@arlingtonbaptistcollege.edu
BOTTOMLY, Kim .... 781-283-2237. 237 F kbottomly@wellesley.edu
BOTTOMS, Bette, L .... 312-996-5753. 161 D bbottoms@uic.edu
BOTTOMS, Rebecca .... 336-725-8344. 365 F bottomsb@piedmontu.edu
BOTTONE, Frances, H ..... 605-652-4988. 305 C frances.bottone@stockton.edu
BOTTONI, James, A .... 608-243-4552. 540 C jbottoni@madisoncollege.edu
BOTTORFF, Allen .... 772-462-7360. 106 P ebottorff@irsc.edu
BOTTORFF, Margaret, B . 302-831-2101... 94 B bottorff@udel.edu
BOTTRELL, Cynthia .... 319-296-4470. 178 J cynthia.bottrell@hawkeyecollege.edu
BOTTRELL, Marilyn .... 308-398-7335. 288 I marilynbottrell@cccneb.edu
BOTTRILL, Michael .... 505-473-6101. 311 K michael.bottrill@santafeuniversity.edu
BOTTS, L., Francene .... 414-229-6242. 537 A francene@uwm.edu
BOTTUM, James, R .... 864-656-3466. 442 C jb@clemson.edu
BOTZ, Daniel, J .... 785-827-5541. 188 C dbotz@kwu.edu
BOTZMAN, Thomas, J ... 570-674-6215. 424 A tbotzman@misericordia.edu
BOUABIDI, Debra .... 845-574-4492. 338 B moppenhe@sunyrockland.edu
BOUBEL, Diana .... 936-468-2206. 482 A dboubel@sfasu.edu
BOUCHARD, Beth .... 702-434-6599. 295 F bbouchard@sierranevada.edu
BOUCHARD, Christine, A .... 518-956-8140. 341 D cbouchard@albany.edu
BOUCHELLE, Joseph .... 540-261-8428. 509 K joseph.bouchelle@svu.edu
BOUCHER, Ed .... 931-372-3237. 460 A edboucher@tntech.edu
BOUCHER, Erica .... 970-943-2885... 86 I eboucher@western.edu
BOUCHER, Joceline .... 207-326-2489. 211 D joceline.boucher@mma.edu
BOUCHER, Lynne .... 585-389-2305. 332 D lbouche9@naz.edu
BOUCHEY, Heather, A .... 802-626-6615. 501 E heather.bouchey@lyndonstate.edu
BOUCIAS, Jean .... 413-775-1147. 231 E boucias@gcc.mass.edu
BOUDET, Lucy .... 407-582-1016. 118 M lboudet@valenciacollege.edu
BOUDINOT, F. Douglas . 804-828-2233. 511 F fdboudinot@vcu.edu
BOUDJOUK, Philip .... 701-231-6542. 371 G philip.boudjouk@ndsu.edu
BOUDOURIS, Jeff .... 937-512-2512. 388 O jeff.boudouris@sinclair.edu
BOUDREAU, Charles .... 630-466-7900. 162 J cboudreau@waubonsee.edu
BOUDREAU, George .... 314-256-8801. 271 F boudreau@ai.edu
BOUDREAU, Nancy, D ... 203-365-7599... 91 C boudreaun@sacredheart.edu
BOUDREAU, Peg .... 608-785-9102. 541 E boudreaum@westerntc.edu
BOUDREAU, Steven .... 401-454-6544. 440 A sboudrea@risd.edu
BOUDREAUX, David, E .. 985-448-4134. 208 A david.boudreaux@nicholls.edu
BOUEY, Joy .... 808-739-4619. 135 D jbouey@chaminade.edu
BOUFFARD, Patricia, A .. 860-738-6319... 89 C pbouffard@nwcc.commnet.edu
BOUGHMAN, Joann .... 301-445-1992. 219 A jboughman@usmd.edu
BOUILLON, Rick .... 801-957-2077. 498 B rick.bouillon@slcc.edu
BOUKNIGHT, H. Randall 864-388-8239. 444 K rbouknig@lander.edu
BOUL, Sarah .... 314-719-3663. 274 E sboul@fontbonne.edu
BOULANGER, Jennifer .... 315-792-5308. 331 I jboulanger@mvcc.edu
BOULAS, Karen .... 607-962-9291. 322 B boulas@corning-cc.edu
BOULDER, James .... 814-732-1047. 428 E jboulder@edinboro.edu
BOULDIN, Randy .... 615-966-5711. 456 B randy.bouldin@lipscomb.edu
BOULDING, William .... 919-660-7822. 354 A bb1@duke.edu
BOULER, David, E .... 423-493-4117. 462 B debouler@aol.com
BOULET, Scott .... 617-349-8610. 228 B sboulet@lesley.edu
BOULGER, Lynn .... 207-801-5620. 210 A lboulger@coa.edu
BOULTON, Matthew, M .. 317-931-2303. 165 B mboulton@cts.edu
BOULUKOS, Tracy .... 561-297-2738. 114 L tbouluko@fau.edu
BOUMA, Glenn .... 712-722-6035. 177 J glenn.bouma@dordt.edu
BOUMA, Sarah .... 515-309-9000. 183 C sarah.bouma@vatterott-college.edu
BOUNDY, Janice, F .... 309-655-2230. 158 C jan.f.boundy@osfhealthcare.org
BOUNIAEV, Mikhail .... 956-882-6701. 491 D mikhail.bouniaev@utb.edu
BOURA, Ahmad .... 712-274-5222. 181 B bouraa@morningside.edu
BOURA, Ahmad .... 603-899-1132. 296 H ahmadb@franklinpierce.edu
BOURASSA, Eileen .... 503-883-2507. 404 A ebouras@linfield.edu
BOURASSA, Tabitha .... 810-762-9648. 244 Q tbourass@kettering.edu
BOURDETTE, Marcia .... 575-538-6318. 312 N bourdettem@wnmu.edu
BOURDON, Steve .... 956-872-5051. 480 I sbourdon@southtexascollege.edu
BOURG, Chuck .... 318-357-5581. 208 B bourgc@nsula.edu
BOURG, Tammy .... 985-549-2316. 208 C tbourg@selu.edu
BOURGEOIS, David, L ... 919-658-7747. 357 I dbourgeois@moc.edu
BOURGEOIS, Donna .... 504-865-3523. 205 H dhbourg@loyno.edu
BOURGEOIS, Gene .... 512-245-2205. 487 C eb04@txstate.edu
BOURGEOIS, Jack, R ...... 864-592-4618. 447 A bourgeois@sccsc.edu
BOURGEOIS, Sheryl .... 714-997-6955... 38 A sbourgeo@chapman.edu
BOURGEOIS, Thomas .... 662-325-3611. 268 D thomasb@saffairs.msstate.edu
BOURGOIN, Jim .... 207-453-5035. 210 L jbourgoin@kvcc.me.edu
BOURHILL, Jane .... 973-290-4081. 300 F
BOURLIER, Julie .... 310-660-3383... 43 B jbourlier@elcamino.edu
BOURNE, Don, E .... 208-524-3000. 138 D don.bourne@my.eitc.edu
BOURNE, Gene .... 540-365-4310. 504 L gbourne@ferrum.edu
BOURNE, Jeffrey, T .... 540-568-6164. 506 F bournejt@jmu.edu
BOURNE, John .... 303-991-1575... 78 D john.bourne@americansentinel.edu
BOURNE, Linda, D .... 606-679-8501. 196 D linda.bourne@kctcs.edu
BOURNE, Steve .... 304-327-4087. 529 D sbourne@bluefieldstate.edu
BOURQUE, Alicia .... 504-865-3835. 205 H aabourqu@loyno.edu
BOURQUE, Carrie .... 617-912-9275. 224 B cbourque@bostonconservatory.edu
BOURQUE, Daniel, F .... 617-552-6067. 224 A daniel.bourque@bc.edu
BOURQUE, Elizabeth, B . 518-580-5700. 341 A ebourque@skidmore.edu
BOURQUE, Jackie, R ...... 804-523-5286. 512 F jbourque@reynolds.edu
BOURQUE, Kathleen .... 413-565-1000. 222 F kbourque@baypath.edu
BOURQUE, Michael, J ... 617-552-0343. 224 A michael.bourque.2@bc.edu
BOUSE, Gary .... 662-846-4704. 266 G gbouse@deltastate.edu
BOUSQUET, David .... 508-373-9558. 223 A david.bousquet@becker.edu
BOUSQUET, David .... 928-523-8483... 16 C david.bousquet@nau.edu
BOUSQUET, Jennifer ...... 540-665-4618. 509 E jbousque@su.edu
BOUSQUET, Suzanne ..... 908-737-0430. 302 F sbousque@kean.edu
BOUSSON, Eduardo .... 402-465-2222. 291 G ebousson@nebrwesleyan.edu
BOUTELL, Heather .... 502-272-8124. 192 E hboutell@bellamine.edu
BOUTIN, Karyn .... 508-588-9100. 232 A
BOUTON, Deborah .... 802-635-1664. 501 D deborah.bouton@jsc.edu
BOUTON, Deborah .... 704-330-6446. 359 C debbie.bouton@cpcc.edu
BOUTTE, Gwen .... 504-671-5091. 203 A gboutt@dcc.edu
BOUTWELL, Ashli .... 334-556-2226..... 3 N aboutwell@wallace.edu
BOUTWELL, Wendy .... 251-380-3030..... 7 D wboutwell@shc.edu
BOUYETT, Kathy, A .... 770-720-5508. 130 G kab1@reinhardt.edu
BOUZARD, Ramona, S ... 319-352-8217. 183 E ramona.bouzard@wartburg.edu
BOUZEK, Jeff .... 515-643-3180. 181 A jbouzek@mercydesmoines.org
BOVA, Paul .... 802-485-2079. 500 A pbova@norwich.edu
BOVARD, Charles .... 217-238-8260. 150 D jbeck31925@lakeland.cc.il.us

BOVE, Elena, M 310-338-2885 53 E ebove@lmu.edu
BOVE, Laurence 330-490-7123 392 H lbove@walsh.edu
BOVE, Maria 802-773-5900 499 B maria.bove@csj.edu
BOVEE, Jerry 801-626-7738 497 D jerrybovee@weber.edu
BOVIA, Marilyn 419-473-2700 378 I mmbovia@daviscollege.edu
BOWAB, Lynn 978-681-0800 233 C bowab@mslaw.edu
BOWALKOWSKI, Brian 800-567-2344 532 E bkowalkowski@menominee.edu
BOWDEN, Anita 508-854-4206 232 F abowden@qcc.mass.edu
BOWDEN, Ron 903-434-8157 477 J rbowden@ntcc.edu
BOWDEN, Russ 707-527-4262 65 B rbowden@santarosa.edu
BOWDEN, Vicky 626-815-2034 29 H vbowden@apu.edu
BOWDIN, Sarah 903-566-7057 492 D sbowdin@uttyler.edu
BOWDLER, Michelle, D 617-627-3766 237 C michelle.bowdler@tufts.edu
BOWE, Adraenne 212-817-7020 317 F abowe1@gc.cuny.edu
BOWE, Debbie 352-854-2322 100 K bowed@cf.edu
BOWE, Erik, R 770-499-3360 127 N ebowe@kennesaw.edu
BOWE, Mona 574-284-4587 172 G mbowe@saintmarys.edu
BOWELL, Daniel 765-998-5241 173 C dnbowell@taylor.edu
BOWEN, Alyncia 614-234-5177 384 J abowen@mccn.edu
BOWEN, Anne 360-383-3323 525 D abowen@whatcom.ctc.edu
BOWEN, Blannie, E 814-863-7494 426 A bxb1@psu.edu
BOWEN, Brendan 678-839-6348 133 I bbowen@westga.edu
BOWEN, Brian 585-475-2411 337 L bhbcms@rit.edu
BOWEN, Bruce 801-626-6006 497 D babowen@weber.edu
BOWEN, Candice 303-492-6893 85 L candice.bowen@colorado.edu
BOWEN, Carmen 818-766-8151 41 F cbowen@concordecareercolleges.com
BOWEN, Christopher, M 540-375-2300 509 B bowen@roanoke.edu
BOWEN, Corey, J 410-651-8100 219 E cjbowen@umes.edu
BOWEN, James 405-789-7661 400 A james.bowen@swcu.edu
BOWEN, Janine 410-337-6460 215 A jbowen@goucher.edu
BOWEN, John 713-743-0209 489 B jbowen@uh.edu
BOWEN, John, J 401-598-1900 439 B jbowen@jwu.edu
BOWEN, Jose, A 214-768-2880 481 A jabowen@smu.edu
BOWEN, Julie 806-291-3470 494 F bowenj@wbu.edu
BOWEN, Kara 701-228-5432 372 C kara.bowen@dakotacollege.edu
BOWEN, Laura 678-359-5585 127 A laurab@gordonstate.edu
BOWEN, Laura 704-669-4106 359 D bowen@clevelandcc.edu
BOWEN, Lauren, L 216-397-4374 381 R bowen@jcu.edu
BOWEN, Lucy 713-221-8024 489 D bowenl@uhd.edu
BOWEN, Patricia, A 606-693-5000 196 H pbowen@kmbc.edu
BOWEN, Rachel 610-526-6157 417 H rbowen@harcum.edu
BOWEN, Randyll 585-292-2215 332 A rbowen3@monroecc.edu
BOWEN, Robin, E 978-665-3421 229 E rbowen@fitchburgstate.edu
BOWEN, Roxanne 423-585-6806 462 A roxanne.bowen@ws.edu
BOWEN, Sam 320-222-5206 260 H sam.bowen@ridgewater.edu
BOWEN, Sharon, G 931-540-2548 460 E sbowen@columbiastate.edu
BOWEN, Sherri, W 336-734-7200 360 E sbowen@forsythtech.edu
BOWEN, Stephen, H 404-784-8300 124 E sbowen@emory.edu
BOWEN, Susan 229-317-6747 124 A susan.bowen@darton.edu
BOWEN, Susan 609-586-4800 302 G bowens@mccc.edu
BOWEN, Terry 410-386-8494 214 A tbowen@carrollcc.edu
BOWEN, Tom 901-678-5395 460 B tmbowen1@memphis.edu
BOWEN, W. Ann 423-585-6892 462 A ann.bowen@ws.edu
BOWENS, Laura Lee 201-216-5208 307 E lbowens@stevens.edu
BOWENS, Ollie 662-252-8000 269 F obowens@rustcollege.edu
BOWENS, Pacey 870-762-3134 19 K pbowens@smail.anc.edu
BOWER, Beth, A 978-542-7757 230 E bbower@salemstate.edu
BOWER, David, A 812-464-1918 174 D bower@usi.edu
BOWER, Eric 216-791-5000 377 E eric.bower@case.edu
BOWER, Jami 678-839-6464 133 I jbower@westga.edu
BOWER, Mike 567-661-7200 387 L mike_bower@owens.edu
BOWER, Shirley 585-475-5034 337 L slbwml@rit.edu
BOWER, SCC, Theresa 973-543-6528 298 I acslibrary@acs350.org
BOWERS, Blake 360-992-2938 518 A bbowers@clark.edu
BOWERS, Bonnie 602-331-7500 12 A bbowers@aii.edu
BOWERS, David, A 212-938-5666 345 C dbowers@sunyopt.edu
BOWERS, David, G 734-929-9095 241 A dbowers@cleary.edu
BOWERS, Gayln, K 707-965-6231 57 J gbowers@puc.edu
BOWERS, J. Betsy 850-474-2637 117 B bbowers@uwf.edu
BOWERS, James 312-235-3505 159 A j.bowers@shimer.edu
BOWERS, Jane 212-237-8801 318 D jbowers@jjay.cuny.edu
BOWERS, John 270-745-4278 200 G john.bowers@wku.edu
BOWERS, John 206-934-6869 523 A john.bowers@seattlecolleges.edu
BOWERS, John 206-934-3727 522 I john.bowers@seattlecolleges.edu
BOWERS, Kathy 417-626-1234 279 J kbowers@occ.edu
BOWERS, Kevin 618-544-8657 147 A bowersk@iecc.edu
BOWERS, Lynn 773-380-6786 140 D lynn.bowers@seabury.edu
BOWERS, Marilyn, R 423-318-2776 462 A marilyn.bowers@ws.edu
BOWERS, Marilyn, R 423-585-2633 462 A marilyn.bowers@ws.edu
BOWERS, Michael 616-698-7111 241 H mbowers8@davenport.edu
BOWERS, Michael, E 864-587-4220 447 B bowersme@smcsc.edu
BOWERS, Paul, E 330-569-5453 380 I bowerspe@hiram.edu
BOWERS, Richard 817-598-6213 494 G rbowers@wc.edu
BOWERS, Rodney 321-674-8080 104 H rbowers@fit.edu
BOWERS, Stephanie 360-650-2055 525 C stephanie.bowers@wwu.edu
BOWERSOCK, Allison, H 540-985-9943 506 G ahbowersock@jchs.edu
BOWERSOCK, Gary 303-273-3330 80 E gbowerso@mines.edu
BOWICK, Lesley 770-207-4080 120 J lbowick@athenstech.edu
BOWIE, DeWayne 337-482-6287 208 D dkbowie@louisiana.edu
BOWIE, Jalonna 913-234-0681 185 L jalonna.bowie@cleveland.edu
BOWIE, John 207-755-5432 210 J jbowie@cmcc.edu
BOWIE, Linda 410-951-3915 220 B lbowie@coppin.edu
BOWIE, Lois 903-593-8311 485 A lbowie@texascollege.edu
BOWIE, Michelle 202-884-9611 96 G bowiem@trinitydc.edu
BOWIE, Staci, A 843-349-2227 442 E sbowie@coastal.edu
BOWKER, Janet, L 814-732-2544 428 E bowker@edinboro.edu
BOWLAN, Ronald, E 215-503-7268 434 C ron.bowlan@jefferson.edu
BOWLDS, Joy 270-852-8965 196 C joy.bowlds@kctcs.edu
BOWLES, Adam 618-842-3711 146 I bowlesa@iecc.edu
BOWLES, Anita, K 864-587-4221 447 B bowlesa@smcsc.edu
BOWLES, Crystal 918-293-5274 398 B crystal.bowles@okstate.edu
BOWLES, Diane 704-378-1202 355 K dbowles@jcsu.edu
BOWLES, James, H 270-824-8588 196 A james.bowles@kctcs.edu
BOWLES, Ronald 214-333-5316 470 D ronb@dbu.edu
BOWLES, Ulisa 910-672-1411 367 D ubowles@uncfsu.edu
BOWLIN, Stephanie 909-469-5383 76 B sbowlin@westernu.edu
BOWLING, Doug 513-569-1752 376 L doug.bowling@cincinnatistate.edu
BOWLING, John, C 815-939-5221 155 H jbowling@olivet.edu
BOWLING, Shannon 304-327-4131 529 D sbowling@bluefieldstate.edu
BOWLING, Thomas, L 301-687-4311 220 C tbowling@frostburg.edu
BOWLUS, Robin 419-358-3453 374 J bowlusr@bluffton.edu
BOWLUS-ROOT, Paul 425-739-8244 520 K paul.root@lwtech.edu
BOWMAN, Alan 518-631-9890 348 K bowmanr@uniongraduatecollege.edu
BOWMAN, Barbara 312-893-7100 145 B bbowman@erikson.edu
BOWMAN, Bruce 903-233-3610 475 J brucebowman@letu.edu
BOWMAN, Chris 405-425-5161 397 D chris.bowman@oc.edu
BOWMAN, Corey, L 660-543-4114 283 A bowman@ucmo.edu
BOWMAN, David, B 214-459-8490 480 B
BOWMAN, Denise 901-572-2452 453 B denise.bowman@bchs.edu
BOWMAN, Denvy, A 614-236-6908 375 H dbowman@capital.edu
BOWMAN, Donald, R 941-752-5301 114 I bowmand@scf.edu
BOWMAN, Gail 859-985-3774 192 F bowmang@berea.edu
BOWMAN, Gina 870-972-2250 19 N gbowman@astate.edu
BOWMAN, Helen, Y 215-895-2803 415 B helen.y.bowman@drexel.edu
BOWMAN, Jane 336-838-6142 365 B jane.bowman@wilkescc.edu
BOWMAN, John 301-687-4211 220 C jbowman@frostburg.edu
BOWMAN, Judith, M 757-683-3260 507 N jbowman@odu.edu
BOWMAN, Kevin 808-687-7032 135 F kbowman@hpu.edu
BOWMAN, Leslie 903-233-3270 475 J lesliebowman@letu.edu
BOWMAN, Marjorie 937-775-2933 393 G marjorie.bowman@wright.edu
BOWMAN, Michael 510-659-6064 57 A mbowman@ohlone.edu
BOWMAN, Nelson, E 936-261-1550 482 F nebowman@pvamu.edu
BOWMAN, Pam 662-685-4771 266 C pbowman@bmc.edu
BOWMAN, Pamela, L 309-298-1971 162 K pl-bowman@wiu.edu
BOWMAN, Paul 435-797-1042 497 B paul.bowman@usu.edu
BOWMAN, Richard 781-239-5298 222 D rbowman@babson.edu
BOWMAN, Robert 575-624-7158 309 I robert.bowman@roswell.enmu.edu
BOWMAN, Ruby 317-917-3259 171 A rbowman@martin.edu
BOWMAN, Ryan 765-455-9413 168 A rsbowman@iuk.edu
BOWMAN, Scott 612-874-3677 257 B scott_bowman@mcad.edu
BOWMAN, Shannon 714-992-7001 56 F sbowman@fullcoll.edu
BOWMAN, Teri, A 660-543-4900 283 A tbowman@ucmo.edu
BOWMAN, Ty 562-860-2451 37 I tbowman@cerritos.edu
BOWNE, Kristine 626-396-2474 28 P kristine.bowne@artcenter.edu
BOWNES, Michael, A 205-348-8341 8 C mbownes@uasystem.ua.edu
BOWRON, Steve 507-433-0695 260 I steve.bowron@riverland.edu
BOWSER, Chris 641-683-5155 179 A chris.bowser@indianhills.edu
BOWSER, Robert 724-357-3077 428 F robert.bowser@iup.edu
BOWSER, Steve 404-270-5326 132 E sbowser@spelman.edu
BOWYER, Donald 870-972-3053 19 N dbowyer@astate.edu
BOWYER, Karen, A 731-286-3300 460 F kbowyer@dscc.edu
BOWYER, Roger 937-529-2201 390 D rogerbowyer@united.edu
BOX, Jay 859-256-3100 194 I jay.box@kctcs.edu
BOX, Jean, A 205-726-2565 6 F jabox@samford.edu
BOX, Margaret 325-942-2335 465 K
BOX, Thomas, W 206-281-2108 523 C twb@spu.edu
BOYAR, Virginia 530-541-4660 50 D boyar@ltcc.edu
BOYCE, Eric 828-251-6710 368 C eboyce@unca.edu
BOYCE, Glenn, F 662-472-2312 267 B gboyce@holmescc.edu
BOYCE, Lynn 405-224-3140 401 E lboyce@usao.edu
BOYCE, Mary 323-563-5854 38 B maryboyce@cdrewu.edu
BOYCE, Richard, D 812-877-8443 172 C richard.boyce@rose-hulman.edu
BOYCE, Robert 301-687-4043 220 C rjboyce@frostburg.edu
BOYCE, Susan 802-773-5900 499 B susan.boyce@csj.edu
BOYD, Amanda, L 419-866-0261 389 H alboyd@stautzenberger.com
BOYD, Angela 757-727-5328 505 F angela.boyd@hamptonu.edu
BOYD, Betsy, A 541-346-0946 406 D eaboyd@uoregon.edu
BOYD, Bill 910-323-5614 353 B billboyd@ccbs.edu
BOYD, Brian 407-823-3016 115 E brian.boyd@ucf.edu
BOYD, Carla, L 218-726-8795 264 D clboyd@d.umn.edu
BOYD, Carla, M 217-443-8753 143 G cboyd@dacc.edu
BOYD, Catherine, C 843-953-1826 443 A boydc@cofc.edu
BOYD, Cheri, L 785-827-5541 188 C kcherib@kwu.edu
BOYD, Cheri, L 405-878-5416 399 G clboyd@stgregorys.edu
BOYD, Chrispher 336-770-3322 369 D boydc@uncsa.edu
BOYD, Clarence 918-495-7767 398 H cboyd@oru.edu
BOYD, Cristine 330-325-6673 385 E cboyd@neomed.edu
BOYD, Cynthia 770-426-2756 128 D cboyd@life.edu
BOYD, Cynthia, E 312-942-5496 157 G cynthia_e_boyd@rush.edu
BOYD, Danielle 618-634-3298 158 M danielleb@shawneecc.edu
BOYD, David, L 714-850-4800 69 E boyd@taftu.edu
BOYD, Deborah 615-966-6263 456 B deborah.boyd@lipscomb.edu
BOYD, Debra, C 803-323-2220 449 G boydd@winthrop.edu
BOYD, Dorene 970-339-6412 78 C dorene.boyd@aims.edu
BOYD, Ernest 731-426-7531 455 J eboyd@lanecollege.edu
BOYD, Franette 803-535-5237 442 B fboyd@claflin.edu
BOYD, Frank, A 309-556-3255 148 B fboyd@iwu.edu
BOYD, Gary 304-357-4704 527 H garyboyd@ucwv.edu
BOYD, Gerald, L 240-629-7840 214 H gboyd@frederick.edu
BOYD, Heather 303-273-3221 80 E heather.boyd@is.mines.edu
BOYD, JR., James, I 707-965-7203 57 J jboyd@puc.edu
BOYD, Jean Ellen 618-634-3240 158 M jeanb@shawneecc.edu
BOYD, Jeff 847-214-7900 144 F jboyd@elgin.edu
BOYD, Jody 207-974-4633 210 K jboyd@emcc.edu
BOYD, John 405-682-7501 397 E jboyd@occc.edu
BOYD, John, C 828-766-1270 361 H jboyd@mayland.edu
BOYD, Karen 309-796-5225 140 E boydk@bhc.edu
BOYD, Karen, O 314-576-5923 283 E boyd@umsl.edu
BOYD, Karly 229-317-6775 124 A karly.boyd@darton.edu
BOYD, Kathleen 401-341-2374 440 C boydk@salve.edu
BOYD, Keith 312-942-2694 157 G keith_boyd@rush.edu
BOYD, Ken 913-443-5858 131 D kboyd@savannahtech.edu

BOYD, Kim 918-495-7108. 398 H
kboyd@oru.edu
BOYD, Linda, D 617-732-2800. 233 E
linda.boyd@mcphs.edu
BOYD, Lonnie 620-229-6136. 190 G
lonnie.boyd@sckans.edu
BOYD, Margaret, M 207-859-4312. 209 J
mbboyd@colby.edu
BOYD, Mary, K 512-448-8741. 479 C
mboyd@stedwards.edu
BOYD, Michael 706-754-7807. 129 G
mboyd@northgatech.edu
BOYD, Michael 309-694-5361. 146 E
mboyd@icc.edu
BOYD, Michael, J 563-588-7024. 180 L
michael.boyd@loras.edu
BOYD, Nick 530-283-0202... 44 H
nboyd@frc.edu
BOYD, Robert 559-278-4480... 33 D
robert_boyd@csufresno.edu
BOYD, III, Samuel 314-264-1000. 284 G
Samuel.boyd@vatterott.edu
BOYD, Sharon, H 910-962-7769. 369 C
boyds@uncw.edu
BOYD, Stephanie 502-220-4444. 194 A
stephanie.boyd@frontier.edu
BOYD, Steve 970-945-8691... 79 G
BOYD, Steven 916-484-8633... 53 A
boyds@arc.losrios.edu
BOYD, Susan 586-445-7408. 246 A
boyds@macomb.edu
BOYD, Thomas 303-273-3247... 80 E
tboyd@mines.edu
BOYD, Todd, T 580-774-3782. 400 B
todd.boyd@swosu.edu
BOYD-PUGH,
Jennifer, N 305-899-4057... 98 O
jboydpugh@barry.edu
BOYD-SCOTLAND,
Joann 803-793-5100. 443 E
boydscotland@denmarktech.edu
BOYD-STEWART, Ann 412-365-1258. 412 K
aboydstewart@chatham.edu
BOYDEN, Kenneth 718-982-2224. 317 E
kenneth.boyden@csi.cuny.edu
BOYDSTUN, Morris 479-394-7622... 23 B
mboydstun@rmcc.edu
BOYE-BEAMAN, Joni 989-964-4062. 249 G
jbb@svsu.edu
BOYENS, Kathy, R 815-939-5211. 155 H
kboyens@olivet.edu
BOYER, Alan, B 617-850-1222. 227 E
aboyer@hchc.edu
BOYER, Bruce 508-565-1380. 237 A
bboyer@stonehill.edu
BOYER, Bruce, E 573-875-7251. 272 G
beboyer@ccis.edu
BOYER, Charles, D 559-278-2061... 33 D
cboyer@csufresno.edu
BOYER, Debra, A 617-228-2403. 231 C
dboyer@bhcc.mass.edu
BOYER, Gary 315-279-5296. 328 D
gboyer@mail.keuka.edu
BOYER, John, W 773-702-8576. 161 B
jwboyer@uchicago.edu
BOYER, Mary 215-702-4541. 411 F
mboyer@cairn.edu
BOYER, Mary Jo 610-450-6524. 414 D
mboyer@dccc.edu
BOYER, Paul, J 413-597-4181. 238 D
paul.j.boyer@williams.edu
BOYER, Raymond, E 701-231-6539. 371 G
ray.boyer@ndsu.edu
BOYER, Scott 717-560-8271. 421 A
sboyer@lbc.edu
BOYER, Suzanne, L 410-777-2045. 213 D
slboyer1@aacc.edu
BOYER-OWENS, Linda 210-485-0230. 464 I
lboyer-owens@alamo.edu
BOYES, Jerry, S 716-878-6533. 343 A
boyesjs@buffalostate.edu
BOYETT, Chad 912-287-5808. 130 B
cboyett@okefenokeetech.edu
BOYETT, James, C 501-362-1125... 19 M
jcboyett@hebersprings.asub.edu
BOYETTE, Alan, J 336-334-5494. 369 A
alan_boyette@uncg.edu
BOYETTE, Barbara, G 336-316-2825. 355 A
boyettebg@guilford.edu
BOYETTE, Don, L 252-246-1275. 365 C
dboyette@wilsoncc.edu
BOYETTE, Rick 903-823-3274. 482 D
ricky.boyette@texarkanacollege.edu
BOYETTE, Sandra, C 336-758-6082. 370 D
boyette@wfu.edu
BOYE', Stephanie 617-369-3618. 236 F
sboye@smfa.edu
BOYKIN, Coretta 251-578-1313..... 6 D
cboykin@rstc.edu
BOYKIN, Deborah 757-221-3178. 503 N
boykin@wm.edu
BOYKIN, III, George, H 919-516-4888. 366 C
ghboykin@st-aug.edu
BOYKIN, Karen 215-780-1420. 433 A
kboykin@salus.edu
BOYKIN, Melinda 216-368-3245. 375 J
melinda.boykin@case.edu
BOYKIN, Regena 601-635-2111. 266 H
rboykin@eccc.edu
BOYKIN, Ted 570-586-2400. 410 D
tboykin@bbc.edu
BOYLAN, Ellen 570-348-6203. 423 B
eboylan@marywood.edu
BOYLAN, Joyce 626-873-2111... 55 C
BOYLAN, Stanley, L 212-463-0400. 348 B
stanley.boylan@touro.edu
BOYLE, Ann, M 618-650-3779. 159 H
aboyle@siue.edu
BOYLE, Antonio 502-597-7001. 197 A
antonio.boyle@kysu.edu
BOYLE, Antonio 803-536-7186. 446 G
aboyle@scsu.edu
BOYLE, Brian 251-442-2287..... 9 A
bboyle@umobile.edu
BOYLE, Christine 215-968-8058. 411 B
boylec@bucks.edu
BOYLE, Ellen 518-438-3111. 330 C
eboyle@mariacollege.edu
BOYLE, Jeanne 848-932-7505. 306 D
jeboyle@rulmail.rutgers.edu
BOYLE, Jeff 828-395-1456. 361 C
jboyle@isothermal.edu
BOYLE, Jill 970-945-8691... 79 G
BOYLE, Kevin 973-618-3372. 300 A
kboyle@caldwell.edu
BOYLE, Lori 619-239-0391... 36 D
lboyle@cwsl.edu
BOYLE, Mary-Ellen 508-793-7671. 225 A
mboyle@clarku.edu
BOYLE, Mike, A 615-898-2177. 459 D
mike.boyle@mtsu.edu
BOYLE, Nuala 585-389-2670. 332 D
nboyle5@naz.edu
BOYLE, Patrick, M 773-508-7070. 151 H
pboyle@luc.edu
BOYLE, Rebecca 716-827-2559. 348 G
boyler@trocaire.edu
BOYLE, Richard 713-221-8065. 489 D
boyler@uhd.edu
BOYLE, Richard, A 636-949-4477. 276 D
rboyle@lindenwood.edu
BOYLE, Robert, J 904-620-4663. 116 B
rboyle@unf.edu
BOYLE, Sharon, A 215-926-2295. 433 K
sharon.boyle@temple.edu
BOYLE, Susan, A 330-569-5119. 380 I
boylesa@hiram.edu
BOYLE, Taggart 617-984-1771. 235 I
tboyle@quincycollege.edu
BOYLES, Bob 618-842-3711. 146 I
boylesr@iecc.edu
BOYLES, Dixon 252-940-6223. 358 A
dixonb@beaufortccc.edu
BOYLES, Elinda, C 740-351-3005. 388 N
eboyles@shawnee.edu
BOYLES, Joel 662-562-3240. 269 C
jboyles@northwestms.edu
BOYLES, Rhonda, J 210-434-6711. 477 N
rjboyles@lake.ollusa.edu
BOYLES, Robin 662-846-4804. 266 G
rboyles@deltastate.edu
BOYLES, Shery 919-760-8581. 356 G
boyless@meredith.edu
BOYMELGREEN, Shaya 718-434-0784. 316 F
BOYNTON, Andrew, C 617-552-4107. 224 A
andy.boynton@bc.edu
BOYNTON, Robert, A 973-596-3441. 303 G
robert.boynton@njit.edu
BOYNTON, Russell 603-668-6660. 297 C
BOYS, Kevin, S 937-393-3431. 389 B
kboys@sscc.edu
BOYS, Mary 212-280-1558. 349 A
mboys@uts.columbia.edu
BOYSUN, Virginia 406-377-9404. 286 A
vboysun@dawson.edu
BOYUM, Paula 425-564-2265. 517 A
paula.boyum@bellevuecollege.edu
BOZARTH, Diane 573-288-6473. 273 F
dbozarth@culver.edu
BOZARTH, Peggy, I 270-707-3844. 195 E
peggy.bozarth@kctcs.edu
BOZEMAN, Joseph, C 443-885-3017. 217 A
joseph.bozeman@morgan.edu
BOZINSKI, Glenn 570-674-6434. 424 A
gbozinsk@misericordia.edu
BOZYLINSKY, Garrett, A 401-874-4599. 440 D
garry@uri.edu
BOZZUTO, Victoria 203-285-2408... 88 E
vbozzuto@gwcc.commnet.edu
BRAATEN, Beth 719-590-6758... 81 B
bbraaten@coloradotech.edu
BRAATEN, Jennifer, L 540-365-4202. 504 L
jbraaten@ferrum.edu
BRAATEN, Pamela, K 701-788-4773. 371 E
Pamela.Braaten@mayvillestate.edu
BRAATZ, Jay 312-362-7561. 143 H
jbraatz@depaul.edu
BRABAZON, Jodi 215-574-9600. 418 H
jbrabazon@hussianart.edu
BRABHAM, Sherry, F 212-217-4020. 324 C
sherry_brabham@fitnyc.edu
BRABHAM, Susan, S 803-938-3795. 448 F
brabhams@uscsumter.edu
BRACCIANO, Susan 816-271-4214. 279 A
braccian@missouriwestern.edu
BRACE, Liz 828-298-3325. 370 E
gathering@warren-wilson.edu
BRACE, Simon 704-847-5600. 366 J
sbrace@ses.edu
BRACERO, Cindy 407-831-9816... 99 O
cbracero@citycollege.edu
BRACEY, Carol 951-343-4456... 30 H
cbracey@calbaptist.edu
BRACEY, Gerald 228-897-7101. 270 I
jerry.bracey@wmcarey.edu
BRACEY, W. Earl 309-298-1900. 162 K
we-bracey@wiu.edu
BRACK, Jonathan, M 215-572-3878. 437 C
jbrack@wts.edu
BRACKEN, Damien, S 617-266-1400. 223 D
BRACKEN, Gary 816-415-7871. 285 C
brackeng@william.jewell.edu
BRACKEN, James 330-672-2962. 382 B
jbracke1@kent.edu
BRACKEN, Larry 850-484-1705. 110 G
lbracken@pensacolastate.edu
BRACKEN, Lisa 803-778-6652. 441 F
brackenlm@cctech.edu
BRACKENS, Roland 903-593-8311. 485 A
rbrackens@texascollege.edu
BRACKER, Beverly 619-961-4235... 69 I
bbracker@tjsl.edu
BRACKETT, Andrew 973-618-3519. 300 A
ABrackett@caldwell.edu
BRACKETT, Edmund 816-584-6588. 280 C
edmund.brackett@park.edu
BRACKETT, Geoffrey, L 845-575-3000. 330 D
geoffrey.brackett@marist.edu
BRACKETT, Jan 207-725-3142. 209 H
jbracket@bowdoin.edu
BRACKETT, Robert 708-563-1577. 147 F
rbrackett@iit.edu
BRACKIN, Chad 225-578-4736. 204 N
cmb@lsu.edu
BRACKIN, Donna 901-320-9700. 463 J
dbrackin@victory.edu
BRACKLEY, Paul 312-329-4225. 153 E
paul.brackley@moody.edu
BRACKMAN, Sarah 512-863-1987. 481 I
brackmas@southwestern.edu
BRACKNELL, Ann 205-391-2958..... 6 H
abracknell@sheltonstate.edu
BRACY, Marion 504-520-7507. 209 D
mbracy@xula.edu
BRADAC, John, P 607-274-3365. 327 E
jbradac@ithaca.edu
BRADACH, Carmen 218-749-7743. 259 B
c.bradach@mr.mnscu.edu
BRADACH, Carmen 218-749-7743. 261 G
c.bradach@mr.mnscu.edu
BRADBERRY, J. Chris 402-280-2950. 289 D
jcbradberry@creighton.edu
BRADBERRY, LeAnn 816-604-5430. 277 E
leann.bradberry@mcckc.edu
BRADBERRY, Richard 443-885-3488. 217 A
richard.bradberry@morgan.edu
BRADBURY, Boyd, L 218-477-2095. 259 H
bradbury@mnstate.edu
BRADBURY, Guy 252-633-4464. 357 I
gbradbury@moc.edu
BRADBURY, Ron 540-986-1800. 501 H
rjbradbury@an.edu
BRADBURY JONES,
Mary 503-675-3963. 404 C
mjones@marylhurst.edu
BRADDER, Kelley, L 515-961-1621. 182 E
kelley.bradder@simpson.edu
BRADDIX, D'Andre 314-516-5205. 283 E
braddixd@umsl.edu
BRADDY, William 540-261-8450. 509 K
bill.braddy@svu.edu
BRADEN, Crystal 325-942-2259. 465 K
crystal.braden@angelo.edu
BRADEN, Jeffery, P 919-515-2468. 368 B
jeff_braden@ncsu.edu
BRADEN, SJ,
Michael, L 201-761-6014. 306 L
mbraden@saintpeters.edu
BRADEN, Sandra 313-664-7471. 241 C
sbraden@collegeforcreativestudies.edu
BRADFIELD, Anna 508-531-1201. 229 D
abradfield@bridgew.edu
BRADFIELD, Brett 605-331-6712. 452 D
brett.bradfield@usiouxfalls.edu
BRADFIELD, Carol 407-303-9585... 97 H
carol.bradfield@adu.edu
BRADFIELD, Glynis 269-471-3432. 243 G
glynisb@andrews.edu
BRADFIELD, Katrina 731-661-5346. 462 F
kbradfie@uu.edu
BRADFIELD, Terry 202-885-8631... 97 D
tbradfield@wesleyseminary.edu
BRADFORD, SR.,
Corey, S 936-261-2150. 482 F
csbradford@pvamu.edu
BRADFORD, Frances, C 757-221-7802. 503 N
fcbrad@wm.edu
BRADFORD, James 615-343-5705. 463 G
james.w.bradford@vanderbilt.edu
BRADFORD, Jerry 256-233-8278..... 1 F
jerry.bradford@athens.edu
BRADFORD, Lawrence 323-953-4000... 51 G
bradfoll@lacitycollege.edu
BRADFORD, Linda 205-247-8001..... 7 E
lbradford@stillman.edu
BRADFORD, Margaret 541-956-7088. 407 F
mbradford@roguecc.edu
BRADFORD, Michael 434-832-7293. 512 A
bradfordm@cvcc.vccs.edu
BRADFORD, Michele 256-439-6822..... 3 M
mbradford@gadsdenstate.edu
BRADFORD, Peggy 410-462-8001. 213 F
pbradford@bccc.edu
BRADFORD, Sarah, E 423-439-8304. 459 C
bradfors@etsu.edu
BRADFORD, Susan, E 713-942-3436. 490 L
bradfords@stthom.edu
BRADFORD-PERRY,
Emma 225-771-4990. 206 J
emma_perry@subr.edu
BRADFORD ROUSE,
Teri 805-565-7255... 76 D
tbradfordrouse@westmont.edu
BRADFUTE, Robert, W 512-223-4721. 466 I
rbradfut@austincc.edu
BRADIN, Bernice 617-349-8685. 228 B
bbradin@lesley.edu
BRADLEY, Alan 615-297-7545. 452 J
alanb@aquinascollege.edu
BRADLEY, Alice 704-290-5832. 363 G
abradley@spcc.edu
BRADLEY, Brenda 712-274-6400. 183 G
brenda.bradley@witcc.edu
BRADLEY, Charles 406-496-4301. 287 F
cbradley@mtech.edu
BRADLEY, Colleen 610-436-2128. 430 A
cbradley@wcupa.edu
BRADLEY, Dale, R 304-367-4692. 528 E
Dale.Bradley@pierpont.edu
BRADLEY, Daniel, J 812-237-4000. 167 A
president@indstate.edu
BRADLEY, David, M 713-221-8610. 489 D
bradleyd@uhd.edu
BRADLEY, Dennis, J 814-732-1030. 428 E
bradley@edinboro.edu
BRADLEY, George, C 706-821-8230. 130 C
gbradley@paine.edu
BRADLEY, Jacquline 707-468-3110... 54 B
jbradley@mendocino.edu
BRADLEY, Jane 319-296-4230. 178 J
jane.bradley@hawkeyecollege.edu
BRADLEY, Jennifer 319-398-4913. 180 J
jbradley@kirkwood.edu
BRADLEY, Jennifer 808-734-9890. 136 E
jbradley@hawaii.edu
BRADLEY, Jim 817-272-5602. 491 B
jim@uta.edu
BRADLEY, JoAnn 718-270-4418. 342 D
jbradley@downstate.edu
BRADLEY, Joseph 410-617-5780. 216 A
jbradley@loyola.edu
BRADLEY, Judy 606-218-5253. 200 F
judybradley@upike.edu
BRADLEY, Julie 972-758-3821. 469 G
jbradley@collin.edu
BRADLEY, Kathy 717-337-6960. 417 B
kbradley@gettysburg.edu
BRADLEY, Marcy, K 607-871-2350. 313 E
bradlemk@alfred.edu
BRADLEY, Mark 360-882-2200... 45 H
markbradley@ggbts.edu
BRADLEY, Martha, S 801-585-3582. 496 Q
martha.bradley@utah.edu
BRADLEY, Monica 318-274-6118. 207 E
bradleym@gram.edu
BRADLEY, Natalie 707-256-7372... 55 F
nbradley@napavalley.edu
BRADLEY, Nate 602-429-4912... 16 O
nbradley@ps.edu
BRADLEY, Nedra 601-484-8674. 267 G
nbradley@meridiancc.edu
BRADLEY, Patrick, J 660-543-4515. 283 A
pbradley@ucmo.edu

BRADLEY, Paul, A .... 651-631-5592. 263 A
pabradley@nwc.edu
BRADLEY, Roger .... 386-267-0565. 101 F
director@daytonacollege.edu
BRADLEY, Tanya, W .... 802-626-6218. 501 E
tanya.bradley@lyndonstate.edu
BRADLEY, Tess .... 610-341-5827. 415 G
tbradley@eastern.edu
BRADLEY, Torey .... 706-291-2121. 131 E
tbradley@shorter.edu
BRADLEY, Tracey .... 865-539-7158. 461 D
tcbradley@pstcc.edu
BRADLEY, Winifred .... 850-484-2014. 110 G
wbradley@pensacolastate.edu
BRADLEY-DOPPES, Peg . 303-871-3399... 86 B
pbd@du.edu
BRADLEY-HASTY,
Barbara .... 252-536-3386. 361 A
bhasty399@halifaxcc.edu
BRADSHAW, Amelia, M . 804-523-5867. 512 F
abradshaw@reynolds.edu
BRADSHAW, Boyd .... 636-227-2100. 276 F
boyd.bradshaw@logan.edu
BRADSHAW, Brent .... 972-279-6511. 465 F
bbradshaw@amberton.edu
BRADSHAW, Debra .... 816-268-5472. 279 G
dlbradshaw@nts.edu
BRADSHAW, Felicia .... 202-231-3354. 544 L
felicia.bradshaw@dodiis.mil
BRADSHAW, Gail .... 708-534-4124. 145 F
gbradshaw@govst.edu
BRADSHAW,
Geoffrey, W .... 608-246-6165. 540 C
gbradshaw@madisoncollege.edu
BRADSHAW, George ...... 909-274-4419... 55 A
gbradshaw@mtsac.edu
BRADSHAW, John, F ..... 919-572-1625. 352 C
jbradshaw@apexsot.edu
BRADSHAW, Ken .... 270-534-3169. 196 G
ken.bradshaw@kctcs.edu
BRADSHAW, Kim .... 704-355-5584. 353 D
kim.bradshaw@carolinascollege.edu
BRADSHAW, Marjorie ..... 913-234-0607. 185 L
marjorie.bradshaw@cleveland.edu
BRADSHAW, Michael ..... 601-477-4120. 267 F
michael.bradshaw@jcjc.edu
BRADSHAW, Sheryl .... 903-813-2444. 466 H
sbradshaw@austincollege.edu
BRADSHAW, Steve .... 706-295-6934. 125 F
sbradshaw@gntc.edu
BRADSHAW, Wilson, G . 239-590-1055. 115 A
president@fgcu.edu
BRADSHER, Carl .... 434-791-5646. 502 D
cbradshe@averett.edu
BRADSHER, Judy, S .... 336-322-2211. 362 F
Judy.Bradsher@piedmontcc.edu
BRADT, Jeremy .... 815-599-3486. 146 D
jeremy.bradt@highland.edu
BRADT, Kay .... 785-594-8414. 184 C
kay.bradt@bakeru.edu
BRADY, Bridget .... 805-898-4003... 44 I
blbrady@fielding.edu
BRADY, Carolyn, M .... 610-861-5342. 425 D
cbrady@northampton.edu
BRADY, Christian .... 814-865-2631. 426 A
cmb44@psu.edu
BRADY, Claire .... 352-435-6308. 108 S
bradyc@lssc.edu
BRADY, David, M .... 203-576-4589... 91 G
dbrady@bridgeport.edu
BRADY, Glen .... 951-222-8561... 61 A
glen.brady@rccd.edu
BRADY, Henry .... 510-642-5116... 70 I
hbrady@econ.berkeley.edu
BRADY, James .... 509-533-3680. 518 F
jim.brady@spokanefalls.edu
BRADY, James .... 509-533-3660. 518 F
jim.brady@spokanefalls.edu
BRADY, Jeanne .... 610-660-3094. 432 E
jebrady@sju.edu
BRADY, Kathleen .... 314-977-8173. 281 I
bradyk@slu.edu
BRADY, Kevin .... 985-549-2001. 208 C
kevin.brady@selu.edu
BRADY, Linda, P .... 336-334-5266. 369 A
lpbrady@uncg.edu
BRADY, Linda Beth .... 512-313-3000. 469 L
lindabeth.brady@concordia.edu
BRADY, Michael .... 608-363-2200. 531 M
bradym@beloit.edu
BRADY, Reginald .... 323-953-4287... 51 G
bradyr@lacitycollege.edu
BRADY, Steven .... 315-464-4510. 342 E
bradys@upstate.edu
BRADY, Tara .... 781-768-7238. 236 A
tara.brady@regiscollege.edu
BRADY, Thomas, F .... 219-785-5740. 172 A
tfbrady@pnc.edu
BRADY, Todd .... 731-661-6566. 462 F
tbrady@uu.edu
BRAENDEL, Carly .... 828-669-8012. 357 H
cbraendel@montreat.edu
BRAEUTIGAM,
Ronald, R .... 847-491-7040. 155 D
braeutigam@northwestern.edu
BRAGG, Mark, S .... 423-439-4137. 459 C
bragg@etsu.edu
BRAGG, Martin, E .... 805-756-2511... 32 F
mbragg@calpoly.edu
BRAGG, Melissa .... 254-295-4608. 490 B
mbragg@umhb.edu
BRAGG, Nancy, S .... 540-665-4538. 509 E
nbragg@su.edu
BRAGG, Sadie .... 212-220-8320. 317 A
sbragg@bmcc.cuny.edu
BRAHA, Habtu .... 410-951-3014. 220 B
hbraha@coppin.edu
BRAHA, Habtu .... 410-951-3447. 220 B
hbraha@coppin.edu
BRAHAMS, Teri, T .... 865-694-6476. 461 D
tbrahams@pstcc.edu
BRAHM, Gary .... 949-753-4774... 29 M
chancellor@brandman.edu
BRAIDER, Christopher ..... 303-492-3261... 85 L
christopher.braider@colorado.edu
BRAIDES, Cheryl .... 215-612-6600. 419 J
cbraides@chicareers.com
BRAILER, James .... 410-516-8070. 215 H
jbraile1@jhu.edu
BRAILOFSKY, Yosef .... 845-362-3053. 314 H
yosefb@bytsem.org
BRAILOW, David, G .... 317-738-8017. 165 I
dbrailow@franklincollege.edu
BRAIM, Barry .... 413-775-1311. 231 E
braim@gcc.mass.edu
BRAINARD, Nancy .... 918-495-7119. 398 H
nbrainard@oru.edu
BRAINERD, Marian, J ..... 937-775-5588. 393 G
marian.brainerd@wright.edu
BRAISHER, Lyndsey .... 405-912-9007. 395 K
lbraisher@hc.edu
BRAISHER, Mark, H .... 405-912-9013. 395 K
mbraisher@hc.edu
BRAKEFIELD, Jean Ann . 843-349-2846. 442 E
jeanann@coastal.edu
BRAKKE, David, F .... 540-568-3508. 506 F
brakkedf@jmu.edu
BRAKSICK, Ben .... 317-955-6319. 170 V
bbraksick@marian.edu
BRALY, JR., Cliff .... 336-272-7102. 354 E
bralyc@greensboro.edu
BRAMANTE, Paula .... 617-951-2350. 234 G
paula.bramante@necb.edu
BRAMBILA, Albert .... 760-921-5447... 58 C
abrambila@paloverde.edu
BRAMBLE, Karen .... 602-944-3335... 11 D
kbramble@aicag.edu
BRAMBLETT, Jeff .... 800-955-2527. 274 I
jbramblett@grantham.edu
BRAMBLETT, Sandra, J .. 404-894-8874. 125 D
sandi@gatech.edu
BRAME, Tracey .... 616-301-6800. 250 G
bramet@cooley.edu
BRAMLAGE, SC, Nancy .. 513-244-4844. 377 G
nancy_bramlage@mail.msj.edu
BRAMLETT, Rebecca .... 919-962-4388. 368 D
rebecca_bramlett@unc.edu
BRAMMELL, Keith .... 606-326-2426. 194 J
Keith.brammell@kctcs.edu
BRAMMER, Erika .... 423-652-6301. 455 I
ebrammer@king.edu
BRAMUCCI, Robert, S .... 949-582-4960... 67 A
rbramucci@socccd.edu
BRAMWELL, Bevil .... 540-338-2700. 503 A
frbramwell@cdu.edu
BRANCA, Matthew, P ..... 570-326-3761. 427 B
mbranca@pct.edu
BRANCA, Mickey .... 415-241-2255... 38 L
mbranca@ccsf.edu
BRANCATO, Marco .... 781-239-2571. 231 G
mbrancato@massbay.edu
BRANCH, Craig .... 540-891-3007. 512 E
cbranch@germanna.edu
BRANCH, Deborah, G ...... 252-335-3271. 367 C
dgbranch@mail.ecsu.edu
BRANCH, Gary .... 256-395-2211..... 7 C
gbranch@suscc.edu
BRANCH, Gary, L .... 251-580-2202..... 4 L
gbranch@faulknerstate.edu
BRANCH, Kevin .... 404-215-7902. 129 D
kbranch@morehouse.edu
BRANCH, Teresa, S .... 406-243-5225. 286 H
teresa.branch@umontana.edu
BRANCH-GRIFFIN,
Rebecca .... 804-524-5674. 515 D
rbgriffi@vsu.edu
BRANCHEAU, Carrie .... 303-753-6046... 85 B
cbrancheau@rmcad.edu
BRANCHINI, Ann, Z .... 860-383-5204... 89 F
abranchini@trcc.commnet.edu
BRANCOLINI, Kristine .... 310-338-4593... 53 E
kbrancol@lmu.edu
BRAND, Amy .... 601-553-3455. 267 G
abrand@meridiancc.edu
BRAND, David .... 910-678-8307. 360 D
brandd@faytechcc.edu
BRAND, Frederick .... 609-984-1588. 308 A
fbrand@tesc.edu
BRAND, Jonathan .... 319-895-4324. 177 A
jbrand@cornellcollege.edu
BRAND, Latricia .... 503-768-7743. 403 K
lbrand@lclark.edu
BRAND, Richard .... 865-981-8011. 456 D
richard.brand@maryvillecollege.edu
BRAND, Ronald .... 609-894-9311. 299 I
rbrand@bcc.edu
BRANDAU-HYNEK, Ann . 608-785-9585. 541 E
BrandauHynekA@westerntc.edu
BRANDEBERRY, Shari .... 419-434-4245. 393 D
registrar@winebrenner.edu
BRANDEBURG, Rosanne 352-365-3515. 108 S
brandebr@lssc.edu
BRANDEBURY, Amy .... 812-488-2155. 173 H
ab288@evansville.edu
BRANDEL, Rick, L .... 928-523-6696... 16 C
rick.brandel@nau.edu
BRANDENBURG, Aurelia 859-985-3173. 192 F
aurelia_brandenburg@berea.edu
BRANDENBURG, Barry .. 414-258-4810. 535 A
brandenb@mtmary.edu
BRANDENBURG,
Mark, C .... 843-953-5252. 442 A
mark.brandenburg@citadel.edu
BRANDENBURG, Tricia .. 410-704-2000. 220 E
tbrandenburg@towson.edu
BRANDER, Kenneth .... 212-960-5400. 351 M
BRANDES, Derek .... 253-833-9111. 520 C
dbrandes@greenriver.edu
BRANDES, Rand .... 828-328-7077. 356 B
rand.brandes@lr.edu
BRANDFORD-CALVO,
Dania .... 401-874-2018. 440 D
brandford@uri.edu
BRANDIMORE,
Merry Jo .... 989-964-4289. 249 G
mjbrand@svsu.edu
BRANDING, Celeste, E ... 630-844-7520. 140 A
cbrandin@aurora.edu
BRANDKAMP, Katelyn .... 660-263-4110. 279 B
KatelynBrandkamp@macc.edu
BRANDON, Alonzo, C .... 757-683-3421. 507 N
abrandon@odu.edu
BRANDON, Dave, E .... 217-424-6330. 153 C
dbrandon@millikin.edu
BRANDON, David, A ...... 734-764-9416. 251 C
dabran@umich.edu
BRANDON, Deborah, L .. 909-869-3427... 32 G
dlbrandon@csupomona.edu
BRANDON, Elvis .... 615-230-3375. 461 G
elvis.brandon@volstate.edu
BRANDON, Eric .... 828-328-7301. 356 B
eric.brandon@lr.edu
BRANDON, John, R .... 419-289-5034. 374 C
jbrandon@ashland.edu
BRANDON, Kevin .... 708-209-3127. 143 E
kevin.brandon@cuchicago.edu
BRANDON, Lisa, K .... 618-537-6865. 152 G
lkbrandon@mckendree.edu
BRANDON, Maureen ...... 970-247-7264... 81 M
brandon_m@fortlewis.edu
BRANDON, Michaele ...... 505-566-3693. 311 I
brandonm@sancollege.edu
BRANDON, Sonia .... 970-248-1884... 79 F
sbrandon@coloradomesa.edu
BRANDSEN, Cheryl .... 616-526-8538. 240 L
brac@calvin.edu
BRANDSTETTER, Mike .... 253-680-7229. 516 L
mbrandstetter@bates.ctc.edu
BRANDT, Barry, M .... 712-707-7284. 181 H
brandt@nwciowa.edu
BRANDT, Elaine .... 573-897-5000. 276 E
BRANDT, Jay, J .... 561-237-7947. 108 X
jbrandt@lynn.edu
BRANDT, John .... 314-744-7639. 278 B
brandtJ@mobap.edu
BRANDT, John .... 540-261-4478. 509 K
john.brandt@svu.edu
BRANDT, Martin .... 631-420-2333. 346 B
martin.brandt@farmingdale.edu
BRANDT, Mary, A .... 701-355-8377. 373 E
mabrandt@umary.edu
BRANDT, Scott .... 831-459-2425... 72 C
sbrandt@ucsc.edu
BRANDT, Thompson, A .. 815-599-3450. 146 D
thompson.brandt@highland.edu
BRANDT, Troy, A .... 515-574-1985. 179 D
brandt@iowacentral.edu
BRANDT, William .... 973-278-5400. 314 K
wab@berkeleycollege.edu
BRANDT, William .... 973-278-5400. 299 D
wab@Berkeleycollege.edu
BRANDT, William, A .... 724-946-6216. 437 B
brandtwa@westminster.edu
BRANDT-RAUF, Paul ...... 312-996-5939. 161 D
pwb1@uic.edu
BRANDT STOVER,
Cynthia .... 510-430-2380... 54 F
cbrandtstover@mills.edu
BRANGMAN, Alan .... 302-831-1110... 94 B
BRANHAM, Celeste .... 207-778-7087. 212 D
cbranham@maine.edu
BRANHAM, Holly, L .... 307-532-8303. 542 a
holly.branham@ewc.wy.edu
BRANHAM, Keith .... 309-672-5916. 152 I
kbranham@methodistcol.edu
BRANHAM, LaTonya .... 937-376-6611. 376 E
lbranham@centralstate.edu
BRANHAM, Lorraine .... 315-443-3627. 347 C
lbranham@syr.edu
BRANICKY, Michael .... 785-864-3881. 190 L
mbranicky@ku.edu
BRANIFF, Wendall .... 713-226-5552. 489 D
braniffw@uhd.edu
BRANIGAN, David .... 814-863-9150. 426 A
deb7@psu.edu
BRANKLE, Steve .... 479-524-7209... 21 G
SBrankle@jbu.edu
BRANNAN, Angie, R ...... 262-524-7335. 532 C
abrannan@carrollu.edu
BRANNAN, Colleen, E .... 607-436-2748. 343 E
brannace@oneonta.edu
BRANNAN, Thomas, I .... 205-935-7240..... 8 E
tbrannan@uab.edu
BRANNEN, Andy .... 912-287-5858. 130 B
abrannen@okefenokeetech.edu
BRANNER, Wade, H .... 540-464-7253. 515 B
brannerwh@vmi.edu
BRANNOCK, Kathleen .... 518-783-2919. 340 J
kbrannock@siena.edu
BRANNON, Brandi .... 940-552-6291. 493 F
bbrannon@vernoncollege.edu
BRANNON, Tony, L .... 270-809-3328. 198 B
tbrannon@murraystate.edu
BRANSCOME, Tara .... 256-331-5299..... 6 A
tbranscome@nwscc.edu
BRANSFIELD, Sean .... 610-785-6205. 432 C
sbransfield@scs.edu
BRANSFORD, Denise, A . 312-341-2040. 157 D
dbrandsford@roosevelt.edu
BRANSKY, David .... 805-289-6153... 74 H
dbransky@vcccd.edu
BRANSON, Cathy .... 606-487-3148. 195 C
Cathy.Branson@kctcs.edu
BRANSON, David .... 207-775-3052. 210 H
dbranson@meca.edu
BRANSON, Kevin .... 619-388-2799... 62 E
kbranson@sdccd.edu
BRANSON, Mark .... 312-662-4121. 139 F
mbranson@adler.edu
BRANSON, Mark .... 336-249-8186. 360 A
mbranson@davidsonccc.edu
BRANSON, Salinda Jo .... 309-649-6217. 160 E
jo.branson@src.edu
BRANSON, Walter, J .... 260-481-6804. 168 C
branson@ipfw.edu
BRANSTETTER,
Jeffrey, C .... 402-280-2709. 289 D
jbranstetter@creighton.edu
BRANSTETTER, Marie ..... 913-288-7211. 187 L
marie@kckcc.edu
BRANT, Christine .... 734-432-5620. 246 B
cbrant@madonna.edu
BRANT, Curtis .... 612-977-4149. 254 C
curtis.brant@capella.edu
BRANT, David .... 310-506-4730... 58 H
david.brant@pepperdine.edu
BRANT, Felicia .... 202-274-5000... 97 A
fbrant@udc.edu
BRANT, Keith, E .... 925-631-4219... 61 F
keb5@stmarys-ca.edu
BRANTLEY, Brenda .... 318-678-6000. 202 I
bbrantley@bpcc.edu
BRANTLEY, Clarence, E .. 248-341-2101. 248 D
cebrantl@oaklandcc.edu
BRANTLEY, Clinton .... 478-757-5138. 134 G
cbrantley@wesleyancollege.edu
BRANTLEY, Kristina .... 386-822-7141. 117 C
kbrantle@stetson.edu
BRANTLEY, Kyle .... 601-925-7634. 268 A
brantley@mc.edu
BRANTLEY, Linda .... 978-762-4000. 232 D
lbrantley@northshore.edu
BRANTLEY, Martha, S .... 818-779-8041... 50 A
mbrantley@kingsuniversity.edu
BRANTLEY, Michael .... 972-860-7640. 470 I
MBrantley@dcccd.edu
BRANTLEY, Stephanie .... 803-376-5802. 441 A
sbrantley@allenuniversity.edu
BRANTMAYER, Evie .... 304-367-4141. 529 F
evie.brantmayer@fairmontstate.edu

BRANTON-HOUSLEY, Mary .... 970-204-8121... 81 N mary.branton-housley@frontrange.edu
BRANUM, Reina .... 785-890-3641. 189 H reina.branum@nwktc.edu
BRAS, Duane .... 616-222-3000. 245 C dbras@kuyper.edu
BRAS, Rafael .... 404-385-5700. 125 D provost@gatech.edu
BRASE, Don .... 503-399-5184. 402 E don.brase@chemeketa.edu
BRASE, Heather .... 314-744-5342. 278 B Matlock@mobap.edu
BRASE, Ruby, F .... 217-420-6029. 153 C rbrase@millikin.edu
BRASE, Ruby, F .... 217-424-5071. 153 C rbrase@millikin.edu
BRASE, Wendell, C .... 949-824-5107... 71 B wcbrase@uci.edu
BRASEL, Steve .... 312-329-4194. 153 E steve.brasel@moody.edu
BRASETH, Kellie .... 360-596-5214. 524 A kbraseth@spscc.edu
BRASFIELD, Julie, A .... 919-515-8008. 368 B julie_brasfield@ncsu.edu
BRASHEARS, Randolph .. 978-934-2384. 229 B Randolph_Brashears@uml.edu
BRASHER, Christine .... 337-482-1394. 208 D cbrasher@louisiana.edu
BRASHER, Melinda .... 512-313-3000. 469 L melinda.brasher@concordia.edu
BRASHER, Sally .... 304-876-5244. 529 I sbrasher@shepherd.edu
BRASHIER, Jason .... 731-989-6571. 454 J jbrashier@fhu.edu
BRASIER, Terry .... 828-398-7146. 357 N terrygbrasier@abtech.edu
BRASINGTON, Diane, F . 804-523-5130. 512 F dbrasington@reynolds.edu
BRASINGTON, Dyan, L .. 410-704-3780. 220 E dbrasington@towson.edu
BRASLEY, Stephanie, L .. 323-242-5512... 52 C braslesl@lasc.edu
BRASSARD, Kevin, F .... 508-213-2213. 235 E kevin.brassard@nichols.edu
BRASSEUR, Gary .... 989-686-9000. 242 C gvbrasse@delta.edu
BRASSORD, James, D .... 413-542-2202. 221 G jdbrassord@amherst.edu
BRASTETER, Christina .... 856-256-5173. 305 E brasteter@rowan.edu
BRASWELL, Clara .... 478-825-6347. 124 H braswellc@fvsu.edu
BRASWELL, Don .... 718-518-4340. 318 B dbraswell@hostos.cuny.edu
BRASWELL, James .... 281-476-2771. 479 F james.braswell@sjcd.edu
BRASWELL, Lee .... 704-355-6937. 353 D lee.braswell@carolinas.org
BRATCHER, Richard, W .. 434-395-2630. 506 J bratcherrw@longwood.edu
BRATCHER, Winnie .... 502-863-8024. 194 C winnie_bratcher@georgetowncollege.edu
BRATER, D. Craig .... 317-274-8416. 167 F dbrater@iupui.edu
BRATHWAITE, Joy, E ..... 330-471-8238. 383 D jbrathwaite@malone.edu
BRATSCH, John .... 559-730-3776... 40 I johnbr@cos.edu
BRATSCH-PRINCE, Dawn .... 515-294-6410. 175 H deprince@iastate.edu
BRATT, Jonathan .... 585-594-6830. 337 K bratt_jonathan@roberts.edu
BRATTIN, Emily .... 816-802-3561. 275 J ebrattin@kcai.edu
BRATTON, Chris .... 617-267-6100. 236 F
BRATTON, Christina .... 419-559-2319. 389 I cbratton01@terra.edu
BRATTON, Kate .... 225-578-4807. 204 O dwgs@lsu.edu
BRATTON, Kevin .... 910-642-7141. 364 A Kevin.Bratton@sccnc.edu
BRATTON, Phyllis, K ...... 701-252-3467. 373 D pbratton@jc.edu
BRAUCH, Jeffrey, A ...... 757-352-4040. 508 G jeffbra@regent.edu
BRAUCHLE, Ken .... 812-237-2334. 167 A ken.brauchle@indstate.edu
BRAUCKMULLER, Lois ... 352-854-2322. 100 K brauckml@cf.edu
BRAUER, Cynthia, A ...... 757-221-1693. 503 N cabra1@wm.edu
BRAUER, David, F .... 270-831-9625. 195 D david.brauer@kctcs.edu
BRAUER, Douglas .... 217-875-7200. 156 J dbrauer@richland.edu
BRAUER, Jeanna .... 417-667-8181. 273 A jbrauer@cottey.edu
BRAUER, William, L ...... 757-594-7040. 503 M wbrauer@cnu.edu
BRAUGHTON, Michael, L .... 317-788-3214. 173 I mbraughton@uindy.edu
BRAUN, Abraham .... 845-425-1370. 335 F
BRAUN, Amanda .... 414-229-6599. 537 A abraun25@uwm.edu
BRAUN, Dale, K .... 715-425-3840. 537 E dale.k.braun@uwrf.edu
BRAUN, Dennis .... 508-767-7541. 222 C dbraun@assumption.edu
BRAUN, Elizabeth .... 718-818-6470. 339 H
BRAUN, Eric .... 740-351-3257. 388 N ebraun@shawnee.edu
BRAUN, H. Elizabeth ...... 610-328-8365. 433 I lbraun1@swarthmore.edu
BRAUN, John .... 270-707-3795. 195 E jbraun0008@kctcs.edu
BRAUN, Keith .... 518-327-6072. 336 B kbraun@paulsmiths.edu
BRAUN, Keith, V .... 727-816-3336. 110 E braunk@phcc.edu
BRAUN, Lynn .... 206-780-6221. 516 I lynn.braun@bgi.edu
BRAUN, Mark .... 319-335-3549. 175 I mark-braun@uiowa.edu
BRAUN, Mark, J .... 507-933-7541. 255 I mbraun@gustavus.edu
BRAUN, Neil, S .... 212-346-1962. 335 J nbraun@pace.edu
BRAUN, Raymond .... 419-372-3411. 374 K rwbraun@bgsu.edu
BRAUN, Ronald .... 620-947-3121. 190 J ronb@tabor.edu
BRAUN, Thomas, W ...... 412-648-1938. 435 C twb3@pitt.edu
BRAUN PASTERNACK, Carol .... 805-893-2706... 72 B c.pasternack@summersessions.ucsb.edu
BRAUNGARD, Elizabeth, A .... 717-361-1525. 415 H braungarde@etown.edu
BRAUNINGER, Mike ...... 504-280-6590. 205 G rbraunin@uno.edu
BRAVAIS-SLYMAN, Karine .... 312-777-8674. 147 D kbravais-slyman@aii.edu
BRAVE, Jennifer .... 608-789-6248. 541 E bravej@westerntc.edu
BRAVEMAN, Daan .... 585-389-2004. 332 D dbravem7@naz.edu
BRAVERMAN, David ...... 413-748-3100. 236 I dbraverman@springfieldcollege.edu
BRAVERMAN, Stanley, A 215-713-3906. 420 B bravermans@lasalle.edu
BRAVMAN, John, C .... 570-577-1511. 411 A john.bravman@bucknell.edu
BRAVO VICK, Héctor ...... 787-265-3800. 554 E hectora.bravo@upr.edu
BRAVOS, Angelo .... 847-628-2086. 149 B abravos@judsonu.edu
BRAWNER, Dan .... 615-383-4848. 464 D dbrawner@watkins.edu
BRAWNER, Jeff .... 901-751-8453. 457 B jbrawner@mabts.edu
BRAXTON, Elizabeth, G .. 864-833-8006. 446 D egbraxton@presby.edu
BRAXTON, Joanne, E ..... 631-451-4160. 346 E braxtoj@sunysuffolk.edu
BRAXTON, Phyllis .... 310-287-4333... 52 F braxtopd@wlac.edu
BRAXTON, Sallie, W ...... 540-286-8016. 510 J sbraxton@umw.edu
BRAY, Carmen .... 985-549-2222. 208 C Carmen.Bray@selu.edu
BRAY, D. John .... 716-829-7818. 323 D brayjd@dyc.edu
BRAY, Heather .... 614-222-6191. 378 A hbray@ccad.edu
BRAY, Tammy .... 541-737-3220. 406 A tammy.bray@oregonstate.edu
BRAY, Thomas, E .... 414-277-7416. 534 G bray@msoe.edu
BRAY, Tim .... 612-624-2095. 264 G brayx010@umn.edu
BRAYMER, Meta, R .... 540-286-8014. 510 J mbraymer@umw.edu
BRAYSHAW, Laurie .... 505-424-2305. 309 J llogan@iaia.edu
BRAYTON, Kelley .... 310-434-3465... 65 A brayton_kelley@smc.edu
BRAYTON, Spencer .... 217-854-3231. 140 G spencer.brayton@blackburn.edu
BRAZ, Meredith .... 603-646-2246. 296 G meredith.braz@dartmouth.edu
BRAZA, Peter .... 719-255-4550... 85 M pbraza@uccs.edu
BRAZDA, Sara .... 978-837-5257. 234 A brazdas@merrimack.edu
BRAZEAU, Gayle .... 207-221-4366. 213 A gbrazeau@une.edu
BRAZELL, Greg .... 253-964-6696. 522 C gbrazell@pierce.ctc.edu
BRAZELTON, Rich .... 262-646-6528. 535 B rbrazelton@nashotah.edu
BRAZIER, Elise .... 512-313-3000. 469 L elise.brazier@concordia.edu
BRAZILE, Orella .... 318-670-9315. 207 A obrazile@susla.edu
BRAZIUNAS, Tom .... 206-934-3619. 522 I tom.braziunas@seattlecolleges.edu
BRAZZEL, Thomas .... 979-830-4041. 467 I Thomas.Brazzel@blinn.edu
BRAZZIL, Nancy, A .... 512-471-1232. 491 C nancy@po.utexas.edu
BREAU, Walter, C .... 413-265-2222. 225 C breauw@elms.edu
BREAULT, Susan .... 860-412-7362... 89 E sbreault@qvcc.commnet.edu
BREAUX, Aminta, H ...... 717-872-3594. 429 D aminta.breaux@millersville.edu
BRECHBILL, Ryan .... 614-823-1520. 387 K rbrechbill@otterbein.edu
BRECKENRIDGE, Jim ..... 650-433-3826... 58 B jbreckenridge@paloaltou.edu
BRECKENRIDGE, Joyce .. 412-237-3110. 413 D jbreckenridge@ccac.edu
BREDFELDT, Gary .... 717-560-8297. 421 A gbredfeldt@lbc.edu
BREE, Gretchen .... 217-732-3155. 151 C gbree@lincolncollege.edu
BREEDEN, Amy .... 804-527-1000... 96 F
BREEDEN, Ann Lloyd ..... 804-289-8732. 510 L abreeden@richmond.edu
BREEDEN, Kathy .... 931-540-2555. 460 E mbreeden@columbiastate.edu
BREEDEN, Susan, D ...... 804-289-8400. 510 L sbreeden@richmond.edu
BREEDING, Lesa .... 325-674-2996. 464 H breedingm@acu.edu
BREEDLOVE, Debbie ...... 479-788-7052... 24 A debbie.breedlove@uafs.edu
BREEDLOVE, Paul .... 541-880-2239. 403 H breedlove@klamathcc.edu
BREEN, Anne, L .... 603-271-6484. 296 C abreen@ccsnh.edu
BREEN, Catherine .... 617-495-9047. 227 C catherine_breen@harvard.edu
BREEN, Greg .... 858-653-6740... 49 C
BREEN, Robert .... 610-282-1100. 414 F lmgr1269@fheg.follett.com
BREEN, Thomas .... 518-292-1926. 338 C breent@sage.edu
BREER, Mary .... 217-234-5401. 150 D mbreer@lakeland.cc.il.us
BREERWOOD, Adam ...... 601-403-1132. 269 D abreerwood@prcc.edu
BREES, Chris .... 641-844-5763. 179 J chris.brees@iavalley.edu
BREESE, Jeffrey .... 816-501-4617. 280 I jeffrey.breese@rockhurst.edu
BREESE, Steven .... 203-392-5468... 88 A breeses1@southernct.edu
BREESE, William, E .... 414-277-7401. 534 G breese@msoe.edu
BREHLER, Elizabeth .... 336-506-4138. 357 M elizabeth.brehler@alamancecc.edu
BREHM, James, J .... 765-361-6027. 175 B brehmj@wabash.edu
BREHM, Richard .... 540-423-9042. 512 E rbrehm@germanna.edu
BREIER, Barbara .... 512-245-2396. 487 C blb137@txstate.edu
BREILAND, Chris .... 918-335-6831. 398 F cbreiland@okwu.edu
BREINER, Fred .... 865-539-7144. 461 D fjbreiner@pstcc.edu
BREINER, Ozzie .... 610-758-3500. 422 A lb05@lehigh.edu
BREITBACH, Nicole .... 563-588-6501. 176 F nicole.breitbach@clarke.edu
BREITBACH, William ...... 530-242-7555... 65 G wbreitbach@shastacollege.edu
BREITBARTH, Jonathan, S .... 651-641-8796. 255 B breitbarth@csp.edu
BREITENBACH, Ed .... 231-777-0295. 247 G
BREITHOLZ, Brian .... 216-523-7221. 377 F
BREITMAN, Paul .... 609-258-2676. 304 E breitman@princeton.edu
BREITMEYER, Chris .... 636-922-8356. 280 J cbreitmeyer@stchas.edu
BREJA, Lisa .... 641-844-5576. 179 H lisa.breja@iavalley.edu
BREKKE, Alice .... 701-777-3511. 371 C alice.brekke@und.edu
BREKKE, Tom .... 218-723-6717. 254 K tbrekke@css.edu
BREKKEN, Kathryn, C .... 702-651-7535. 294 E kc.brekken@csn.edu
BRELAND, Byron .... 408-298-2181... 63 P byron.breland@sjcc.edu
BRELAND, Garry, M ...... 601-318-6101. 270 I garry.breland@wmcarey.edu
BRELAND, Jason .... 601-528-8424. 268 C jason.breland@mgccc.edu
BRELAND, Roger .... 251-442-2216..... 9 A rbreland@umobile.edu
BRELLIS, Matthew .... 631-687-4561. 339 B mbrellis@sjcny.edu
BRELSFORD, George ...... 301-387-3748. 214 I george.brelsford@garrettcollege.edu
BREMER, Cris, M .... 559-489-2220... 68 I crism.bremer@fresnocitycollege.edu
BREMER, Geoff .... 828-669-8012. 357 H gbremer@montreat.edu
BREMER, John, H .... 928-524-7381... 16 E john.bremer@npc.edu
BREMET, Robert .... 985-448-4646. 208 A robert.bremer@nicholls.edu
BREMS, Christiane .... 503-352-7330. 407 A cbrems@pacificu.edu
BRENAN, Lindsey .... 212-678-3004. 347 G brenan@exchange.tc.columbia.edu
BRENDEL, William .... 608-785-9175. 541 E brendelw@westerntc.edu
BRENKMAN, John .... 646-660-6500. 316 J John.Brenkman@baruch.cuny.edu
BRENN, James, E .... 803-535-5326. 442 B jbrenn@claflin.edu
BRENNAN, Adriana .... 908-737-2586. 302 F adicecil@kean.edu
BRENNAN, Blair .... 308-432-6044. 291 D bbrennan@csc.edu
BRENNAN, Christopher .. 732-246-5604. 303 E cbrennan@nbts.edu
BRENNAN, Christopher, P .... 727-864-8311. 101 N brennacp@eckerd.edu
BRENNAN, Colleen .... 716-829-7809. 323 D brennanc@dyc.edu
BRENNAN, Deb .... 308-398-7305. 288 I dbrennan@cccneb.edu
BRENNAN, Fran .... 781-595-6768. 228 C fbrennan@mariancourt.edu
BRENNAN, James, F ...... 202-319-5244... 94 G brennan@cua.edu
BRENNAN, Jonathan, R . 607-746-4670. 345 G brennajr@delhi.edu
BRENNAN, Joseph, A .... 716-645-6969. 341 F brennanj@buffalo.edu
BRENNAN, Kara .... 914-633-2410. 327 C kbrennan@iona.edu
BRENNAN, Kelly .... 212-217-3800. 324 C kelly_brennan@fitnyc.edu
BRENNAN, Kelly .... 914-654-5294. 320 H kbrennan@cnr.edu
BRENNAN, Kevin .... 215-717-6437. 435 A kbrennan@uarts.edu
BRENNAN, Leah .... 860-701-5061... 90 G brennan_l@mitchell.edu
BRENNAN, Lipa .... 718-438-2727. 351 O rlb@novominsk.com
BRENNAN, Mary Rosita . 201-559-6024. 302 A brennanr@felician.edu
BRENNAN, Nicole .... 617-912-9120. 224 B nbrennan@bostonconservatory.edu
BRENNAN, Rick .... 708-974-5388. 153 F brennan@morainevalley.edu
BRENNAN, Robert, J ...... 301-447-7432. 217 B brennan@msmary.edu
BRENNAN, Shannon ...... 570-622-7622. 423 G shannon.brennan@mccann.edu
BRENNAN, Stephen, J ... 718-982-3214. 317 E stephen.brennan@csi.cuny.edu
BRENNAN, Terrence ...... 972-881-5734. 469 G tbrennan@collin.edu
BRENNAN, Thomas .... 215-951-1516. 420 B brennan@lasalle.edu
BRENNAN, Thomas, H ... 401-341-3232. 440 C brennant@salve.edu
BRENNAN, William, J .... 207-326-2220. 211 D bill.brennan@mma.edu
BRENNEMAN, Darnell .... 740-857-1311. 388 I dbrenneman@rosedale.edu
BRENNEMAN, James, E . 574-535-7180. 166 A president@goshen.edu
BRENNEMANN, Kyle, R . 573-629-3008. 274 J kbrennemann@hlg.edu
BRENNEN, David .... 859-257-1678. 200 C david.brennen@uky.edu
BRENNER, David, A ...... 858-534-1501... 71 F dbrenner@ucsd.edu
BRENNER, Paul .... 212-237-8968. 318 D pbrenner@jjay.cuny.edu
BRENNER-BUDER, Barbara .... 415-451-2817... 63 A bbrenner@sfts.edu
BRENNER-SCOTTI, Laura .... 609-984-1141. 308 A lbrennerscotti@tesc.edu
BRENT, Daniel .... 617-323-6662. 233 D dan_brent@mspp.edu

BRENTLINGER, Dustin ... 419-448-2062. 380 G
dbrentli@heidelberg.edu
BRENTON, Robin, A ... 410-857-2297. 216 E
rbrenton@mcdaniel.edu
BRESCIANI, Dean ... 701-231-7211. 371 G
dean.bresciani@ndsu.edu
BRESEE, Mikel ... 313-664-1546. 241 C
mbresee@collegeforcreativestudies.edu
BRESEMAN, Mark, D ... 920-832-6519. 533 S
mark.d.breseman@lawrence.edu
BRESHEARS, Pearlene ... 417-328-1729. 282 C
pbreshears@sbuniv.edu
BRESKO, Lynn ... 336-256-1283. 369 A
lynn_bresko@uncg.edu
BRESLAUER, George, W ... 510-642-1961... 70 I
bresl@berkeley.edu
BRESLAUER, Kenneth, J ... 732-445-3956. 306 A
kjbdna@rci.rutgers.edu
BRESLER, Pieter ... 317-805-1785. 527 G
pbresler@salemu.edu
BRESLIN, Beau ... 518-580-5705. 341 A
bbreslin@skidmore.edu
BRESLIN, Eileen, T ... 210-567-5800. 493 A
breslin@uthscsa.edu
BRESLIN, Kathleen, A ... 610-359-5131. 414 D
kbreslin@dccc.edu
BRESLIN, Lisa ... 410-857-2225. 216 E
lbreslin@mcdaniel.edu
BRESNAHAN, Carol ... 407-646-2355. 111 Q
cbresnahan@rollins.edu
BRESSETTE, Andrew ... 706-236-2229. 121 G
abressette@berry.edu
BRESSINGTON, Cheryl ... 308-865-8655. 292 H
bressingtonc@unk.edu
BRESSINGTON, Cheryl ... 308-865-8388. 292 H
bressingtonc@unk.edu
BRESSLER, Coleen ... 402-844-7006. 291 I
coleen@northeast.edu
BRESSLER, Darlene ... 765-677-2147. 169 B
darlene.bressler@indwes.edu
BRESSLER, Gregory, W ... 973-655-5457. 303 D
bresslerg@mail.montclair.edu
BRESSO, Michele ... 661-336-5041... 49 M
mbresso@kccd.edu
BRETL, Jim ... 402-280-2722. 289 D
bretlj@creighton.edu
BRETON, Gary ... 706-236-1756. 121 G
gbreton@berry.edu
BRETT, Jennifer ... 203-576-4122... 91 G
acup@bridgeport.edu
BRETTI, Anthony ... 918-595-7831. 400 E
anthony.bretti@tulsacc.edu
BRETTSCHNEIDER,
Marla, B ... 603-862-4676. 298 C
marla.brettschneider@unh.edu
BRETZ, Brenda, K ... 717-245-1587. 414 H
bretz@dickinson.edu
BREUDER, Robert, L ... 630-942-2200. 142 G
breuder@cod.edu
BREVETT, Renford A, B ... 484-365-7213. 422 D
rbrevett@lincoln.edu
BREW, Alan ... 715-682-1329. 535 D
abrew@northland.edu
BREWER, Athos, K ... 718-289-5869. 317 B
athos.brewer@bcc.cuny.edu
BREWER, Brent ... 269-782-1411. 250 C
bbrewer01@swmich.edu
BREWER, Clay ... 618-985-3741. 148 J
claybrewer@jalc.edu
BREWER, Craig ... 650-508-3500... 56 H
cbrewer@ndnu.edu
BREWER, Dawn, M ... 812-888-4225. 174 F
dbrewer@vinu.edu
BREWER, Deborah ... 716-614-5911. 334 E
dbrewer@niagaracc.suny.edu
BREWER, Jane, T ... 843-549-6314. 448 D
jtbrewer@mailbox.sc.edu
BREWER, Janet ... 501-760-4313... 22 A
jbrewer@npcc.edu
BREWER, Janet, L ... 765-641-4272. 163 L
jlbrewer@anderson.edu
BREWER, Jay ... 401-841-7008. 545 A
BREWER, Jerry, T ... 803-777-4172. 447 G
jerry-brewer@sc.edu
BREWER, Jill ... 760-872-2000... 42 E
BREWER, Jim, L ... 870-460-1274... 24 D
brewer@uamont.edu
BREWER, John ... 801-863-8320. 497 C
brewerjc@uvu.edu
BREWER, JR., John, B ... 301-447-5280. 217 B
brewer@msmary.edu
BREWER, Judy ... 319-656-2447. 182 D
BREWER, Kristina ... 260-665-4161. 173 E
brewerk@trine.edu
BREWER, Michael, H ... 484-664-3400. 424 H
brewer@muhlenberg.edu
BREWER, Michelle ... 318-678-6017. 202 I
mbrewer@bpcc.edu
BREWER, Nathan ... 618-664-6752. 145 G
nathan.brewer@greenville.edu

BREWER, Reta ... 785-832-8622. 187 B
reta.brewer@bie.edu
BREWER, Rick ... 843-863-7505. 441 H
rbrewer@csuniv.edu
BREWER, Robert, W ... 336-272-7102. 354 E
rbrewer@greensboro.edu
BREWER, Ryan ... 205-329-7865... 3 B
ryan.brewer@ecacolleges.com
BREWER, Stacey ... 864-596-9050. 443 D
stacey.brewer@converse.edu
BREWER, Susan ... 870-460-1050... 24 D
brewers@uamont.edu
BREWER, Theresa ... 617-427-0060. 232 G
tbrewer@rcc.mass.edu
BREWER, Tim ... 704-878-3205. 362 B
tbrewer@mitchellcc.edu
BREWERTON, Katie ... 303-762-6948... 81 G
katie.brewerton@denverseminary.edu
BREWINGTON, Delsey ... 910-592-8084. 363 E
dbrewington@sampsoncc.edu
BREWINGTON,
Donald, E ... 512-505-3054. 473 G
debrewington@htu.edu
BREWINGTON, Mazie ... 661-722-6300... 28 F
mbrewington@avc.edu
BREWSTER, Carrie ... 925-631-4643... 61 F
cbrewste@stmarys-ca.edu
BREWSTER, Edward ... 360-538-4000. 520 B
brewster@ghc.edu
BREWSTER, Geoffrey ... 918-610-8303. 398 I
geoffrey.brewster@ptstulsa.edu
BREWSTER, LaRita ... 256-761-6119... 7 F
lmbrewster@talladega.edu
BREY, Amanda ... 805-690-7640... 30 A
Abrey@brooks.edu
BREY, Richard ... 208-282-2902. 138 E
breyrich@isu.edu
BREZEL, Allen ... 404-872-3593. 121 C
abrezel@johnmarshall.edu
BREZIL, Chris ... 212-229-5300. 332 E
brezilc@newschool.edu
BREZINA, Jennifer ... 661-362-5919... 40 E
jennifer.brezina@canyons.edu
BREZINA, Kate ... 401-456-8086. 439 F
kbrezina@ric.edu
BREZINSKI, Donald ... 603-645-9688. 297 I
d.brezinski@snhu.edu
BRIA, Jeff ... 301-431-5410. 217 C
jbria@nlc.edu
BRIAN, Thomas, J ... 918-631-2200. 401 F
thomas-brian@utulsa.edu
BRIANT, Clyde, L ... 401-863-7408. 438 J
clyde_briant@brown.edu
BRIAR-LAWSON,
Katharine ... 518-442-5324. 341 D
kbriarlawson@albany.edu
BRIARE, Bill ... 503-594-3110. 402 F
billb@clackamas.edu
BRICE, Albie ... 919-761-2100. 366 I
abrice@sebts.edu
BRICE, Diane ... 806-371-5028. 465 E
kdbrice@actx.edu
BRICE, Jeff ... 206-726-5043. 518 G
jbricey@cornish.edu
BRICE, Michelle ... 312-662-4113. 139 F
mbrice@adler.edu
BRICE, Ruth ... 610-399-2033. 428 B
rbrice@cheyney.edu
BRICELAND, Cynthia ... 724-503-1001. 436 G
cbriceland@washjeff.edu
BRICHER, Gary ... 860-297-2331... 91 F
gary.bricher@trincoll.edu
BRICHTA, William ... 215-780-1307. 433 A
BRICK, George ... 575-624-8023. 310 H
brick@nmmi.edu
BRICK, III,
Harold (Ben), B ... 402-449-2893. 289 H
gu-library@graceu.edu
BRICK, Susan, H ... 509-527-5790. 525 E
bricksh@whitman.edu
BRICKER, J. Douglas ... 412-396-6361. 415 F
bricker@duq.edu
BRICKER, Susan ... 805-289-6044... 74 H
sbricker@vcccd.edu
BRICKER-THOMPSON,
Jason, A ... 330-569-5234. 380 I
brickerja@hiram.edu
BRICKETTO, Matthew, M 610-436-3301. 430 A
mbricketto@wcupa.edu
BRICKHOUSE, Nancy ... 302-831-2101... 94 B
nbrick@udel.edu
BRICKHOUSE,
Wendy, W ... 252-335-0821. 359 F
wbrickhouse@albemarle.edu
BRICKLE, Colleen ... 952-358-8158. 260 B
colleen.brickle@normandale.edu
BRICKNER-WOOD,
Larry ... 603-862-1165. 298 C
larry.brickner-wood@unh.edu
BRIDGE, Claire ... 909-621-8148... 65 D
claire.bridge@scrippscollege.edu

BRIDGE, David ... 660-562-1181. 279 I
dbridge@nwmissouri.edu
BRIDGE, Louise ... 801-863-8689. 497 C
bridgelo@uvu.edu
BRIDGEFORTH, Valerie ... 601-318-6188. 270 I
vbridgeforth@wmcarey.edu
BRIDGEMAN, Curtis ... 503-370-6402. 408 J
BRIDGEMAN, Doris ... 601-977-7836. 270 A
dbridgeman@tougaloo.edu
BRIDGEMAN, Gregory ... 270-707-3904. 195 E
gbridgeman0001@kctcs.edu
BRIDGEMAN, Robert ... 352-638-9761... 99 B
bbridgeman@beaconcollege.edu
BRIDGEN, Erin, R ... 412-578-8725. 412 G
erbridgen@carlow.edu
BRIDGENS, Marc, E ... 570-326-3761. 427 B
mbridgen@pct.edu
BRIDGEO, Kim ... 978-837-5938. 234 A
kim.bridgeo@merrimack.edu
BRIDGER, Donald ... 303-458-4206... 84 M
dbridger@regis.edu
BRIDGERS, Amy ... 252-399-6397. 352 F
abbridgers@barton.edu
BRIDGES, Amanda ... 706-864-1546. 133 D
amanda.bridges@ung.edu
BRIDGES, Angela ... 662-846-4380. 266 G
abridges@deltastate.edu
BRIDGES, Avie ... 714-564-6910... 60 G
bridges_avie@sac.edu
BRIDGES, Bradley ... 816-604-1086. 277 C
bradley.bridges@mcckc.edu
BRIDGES, Carl ... 740-753-6087. 380 K
bridgesc@hocking.edu
BRIDGES, Ceil, L ... 870-235-4079... 23 F
clbridges@saumag.edu
BRIDGES, Christopher ... 570-662-4342. 429 C
cbridges@mansfield.edu
BRIDGES, Clarence, E ... 312-413-5946. 161 D
cbridges@uic.edu
BRIDGES, Craig ... 218-723-4822. 254 K
cbridges@css.edu
BRIDGES, Daniel ... 323-343-3080... 34 A
dbridges@cslanet.calstatela.edu
BRIDGES, Darryl ... 843-661-1295. 444 B
dbridges@fmarion.edu
BRIDGES, David ... 229-391-5050. 119 H
dbridges@abac.edu
BRIDGES, Deborah, K ... 504-280-6173. 205 G
dkbridge@uno.edu
BRIDGES, Dennis ... 309-556-3345. 148 B
dbridges@iwu.edu
BRIDGES, George, S ... 509-527-5132. 525 E
bridges@whitman.edu
BRIDGES, Joey ... 704-406-4647. 354 C
jbridges@gardner-webb.edu
BRIDGES, Kermit, S ... 972-825-4652. 481 F
president@sagu.edu
BRIDGES, LaDonna ... 508-626-4906. 230 A
lbridges@framingham.edu
BRIDGES, Martin ... 910-410-1818. 362 I
mwbridges@richmondcc.edu
BRIDGES, Ruth ... 254-298-8309. 482 C
ruth.bridges@templejc.edu
BRIDGES, Shelton ... 502-451-0815. 199 G
sbridges@sullivan.edu
BRIDGES, Shelton ... 502-451-0815. 199 F
sbridges@sullivan.edu
BRIDGES, Steven, J ... 812-465-7048. 174 D
sjbridge@usi.edu
BRIDGES, Tharsteen ... 334-874-5700... 3 A
tbridges@ccal.edu
BRIDGES, Vernon, D ... 818-947-2541... 52 E
bridgevd@lavc.edu
BRIDGMAN, Christa, L ... 828-298-3325. 370 E
cbridgma@warren-wilson.edu
BRIDGMON, Phillip ... 918-456-5511. 396 H
bridgmon@nsuok.edu
BRIDWELL, Virginia ... 425-564-2198. 517 A
virginia.bridwell@bellevuecollege.edu
BRIELL, Scott, A ... 770-538-4706. 122 A
sbriell@brenau.edu
BRIEN, Jane ... 845-758-4294. 314 D
brien@bard.edu
BRIER, Bonnie ... 212-998-4095. 334 D
bb91@nyu.edu
BRIER, Stephen, F ... 503-370-6022. 408 J
sbrier@willamette.edu
BRIERE, Donna ... 603-752-1113. 296 E
dbriere@ccsnh.edu
BRIGDON, Beth, P ... 706-721-9667. 126 B
bbrigdon@gru.edu
BRIGGANCE, Richard ... 615-963-5171. 459 E
rbriggance@tnstate.edu
BRIGGS, Baily ... 903-923-3217. 486 A
Baily.briggs@tstc.edu
BRIGGS, Catherine, R ... 609-894-9311. 299 I
cbriggs@bcc.edu
BRIGGS, Charlotte ... 413-565-1000. 222 F
cbriggs@baypath.edu
BRIGGS, Darcy ... 303-797-5623... 78 F
darcy.briggs@arapahoe.edu

BRIGGS, De Armond ... 641-472-1162. 180 N
dbriggs@mum.edu
BRIGGS, Douglas, S ... 540-636-2900. 503 L
dougb@christendom.edu
BRIGGS, Eddie ... 864-388-8222. 444 K
ebriggs@lander.edu
BRIGGS, Jackie ... 507-453-2743. 259 E
jbriggs@southeastmn.edu
BRIGGS, Jeff ... 785-628-4200. 186 F
jbriggs@fhsu.edu
BRIGGS, Jerryl ... 937-376-6387. 376 E
jbriggs@centralstate.edu
BRIGGS, Julie, A ... 585-245-5616. 343 C
briggsja@geneseo.edu
BRIGGS, Karen ... 662-476-5041. 266 I
kbriggs@eastms.edu
BRIGGS, Karen ... 619-260-2762... 73 I
karenbriggs@sandiego.edu
BRIGGS, Karen, M ... 215-670-9230. 425 J
kmbriggs@peirce.edu
BRIGGS, LaNae, R ... 803-786-3856. 443 B
lrbriggs@columbiasc.edu
BRIGGS, LaVerne ... 804-524-5011. 515 D
lbriggs@vsu.edu
BRIGGS, Lynn ... 509-359-2227. 519 C
lbriggs@ewu.edu
BRIGGS, Mary, K ... 276-944-6836. 504 H
mkbriggs@ehc.edu
BRIGGS, Michelle, A ... 570-321-4190. 422 H
briggs@lycoming.edu
BRIGGS, Patrick ... 231-591-2163. 242 F
briggsp@ferris.edu
BRIGGS, Pertrina ... 630-743-0695. 163 C
pbriggs@westwood.edu
BRIGGS, Peter, F ... 517-353-1720. 246 H
pbriggs@msu.edu
BRIGGS, Sarah, F ... 517-629-0244. 239 A
sbriggs@albion.edu
BRIGGS, Stephen, R ... 706-236-2281. 121 G
sbriggs@berry.edu
BRIGGS, Susan ... 406-683-7031. 286 I
s_briggs@umwestern.edu
BRIGGS, Thyra ... 909-607-4408... 46 H
thyra_briggs@hmc.edu
BRIGGS, William ... 657-278-3355... 33 E
wbriggs@fullerton.edu
BRIGGS KITTREDGE,
Cynthia ... 512-472-4133. 480 G
cynthia.kittredge@ssw.edu
BRIGHAM, Bettie Ann ... 610-341-5823. 415 G
bbrigham@eastern.edu
BRIGHAM, David, R ... 215-972-2056. 426 Y
skesskler@pafa.edu
BRIGHAM, Jeffrey ... 617-964-1100. 222 A
BRIGHT, Brett, O ... 903-923-3240. 486 A
brett.bright@tstc.edu
BRIGHT, Harry ... 641-472-1178. 180 N
hbright@mum.edu
BRIGHT, James (Phillip) 731-881-7845. 463 E
pbright@utm.edu
BRIGHT, Jessica ... 512-313-3000. 469 L
jessica.bright@concordia.edu
BRIGHT, Kristina ... 573-592-4257. 285 D
kbright@williamwoods.edu
BRIGHT, Marvin, L ... 757-822-1180. 514 C
mlbright@tcc.edu
BRIGHT, Sarah ... 636-481-3218. 275 I
sbright@jeffco.edu
BRIGHT, Steve ... 434-544-8208. 506 K
bright@lynchburg.edu
BRIGMAN, Leellen ... 212-217-3800. 324 C
leellen_brigman@fitnyc.edu
BRILEY, Brantley ... 252-527-6223. 361 F
bbriley@lenoircc.edu
BRILEY, Jana ... 912-478-1301. 126 C
janawms@georgiasouthern.edu
BRILL, Ann ... 309-341-7130. 150 A
abrill@knox.edu
BRILL, Ann, M ... 785-864-4755. 190 L
abrill@ku.edu
BRILL, Carol ... 414-382-6054. 531 I
carol.brill@alverno.edu
BRILLER, Vladimir ... 718-636-4245. 336 F
vbriller@pratt.edu
BRILLHART, David ... 740-366-9319. 376 A
brillhart.5@osu.edu
BRIMAGE, Yira ... 602-285-7229... 15 C
yira.brimage@phoenixcollege.edu
BRIMHALL, Carrie ... 218-736-1524. 259 F
carrie.brimhall@minnesota.edu
BRIMHALL, Joseph ... 503-251-5712. 408 G
jebrimhall@uws.edu
BRIMI, Barbara ... 865-251-1800. 458 I
bbrimi@southcollegetn.edu
BRIMMER, Diane, L ... 608-796-3801. 539 E
dlbrimmer@viterbo.edu
BRIMMER, Donald, L ... 607-735-1900. 323 H
dbrimmer@elmira.edu
BRINDLE, Denise ... 508-213-2372. 235 E
denise.brindle@nichols.edu

BRINDLEY, Roger 813-974-3460. 116 C brindley@usf.edu
BRINGAZE, Tammy 413-572-5491. 230 F tbringaze@westfield.ma.edu
BRINGER, Michael 573-288-6300. 273 F mbringer@culver.edu
BRINGHURST, Steve 435-652-7901. 497 E brings@dixie.edu
BRINGLE, Mary, L 828-884-8142. 352 I mbringle@brevard.edu
BRINGSJORD, Elizabeth 518-320-1251. 341 C elizabeth.bringsjord@suny.edu
BRINING, Patricia, N 856-691-8600. 301 A pbrining@cccnj.edu
BRINK, Benita 719-587-7426... 78 B babrink@adams.edu
BRINK, Laura 617-521-2127. 236 G laura.brink@simmons.edu
BRINK, Matthew 302-831-2392... 94 B mbrink@udel.edu
BRINKER, Cynthia, S 812-464-1774. 174 D cbrinker@usi.edu
BRINKMAN, Cathy 818-364-7723... 52 A brinkmanc@lamission.edu
BRINKOETTER, Darbe 217-875-7200. 156 J dbrinkoetter@richland.edu
BRINN, Tracy 423-461-8736. 457 H tnbrinne@milligan.edu
BRINNEMAN, Charlotte 859-525-6510. 198 E cbrinneman@national-college.edu
BRINSON, Anne 317-921-4831. 169 K aebrinson@ivytech.edu
BRINSON, Donna 770-781-6963. 128 B dbrinson@laniertech.edu
BRINSON, Leigh 312-935-4408. 156 K lbrinson@robertmorris.edu
BRINSON, Marla 732-906-2513. 303 B MBrinson@middlesexcc.edu
BRINSON, Reginald 404-880-8779. 122 J rbrinson@cau.edu
BRINSON, Willie, L 919-735-5151. 364 H wlbrinson@waynecc.edu
BRIONES, Eloisa, M 650-738-4227... 64 D briones@smccd.edu
BRISBANE, Frances, L 631-444-2139. 342 C frances.brisbane@stonybrook.edu
BRISCO, Thomas, V 325-670-1211. 472 O tbrisco@hsutx.edu
BRISCOE, Chad 574-372-5100. 166 B chad.briscoe@grace.edu
BRISCOE, Doris 573-288-6511. 273 F dbriscoe@culver.edu
BRISCOE, Stephen, A 641-269-4570. 178 H briscoe@grinnell.edu
BRISEBOIS, Robin 619-684-8793... 56 C rbrisebois@newschoolarch.edu
BRISENO, Nancy, M 361-698-1293. 471 G nbriseno3@delmar.edu
BRISKEY, Marvin 614-947-6002. 380 A marv.briskey@franklin.edu
BRISLAWN, Kimberly 319-273-2761. 176 A kimberly.brislawn@uni.edu
BRISSON, Caitrin 617-951-2350. 234 G caitrin.brisson@necb.edu
BRISSON, E. Carson 804-355-0671. 510 G cbrisson@upsem.edu
BRISSON, Jerry 314-529-9356. 276 G jbrisson@maryville.edu
BRISSON, Michelle 973-408-3454. 301 C mbrisson@drew.edu
BRISTLE, Shawn 928-758-3926... 15 L sbristle@mohave.edu
BRISTOL, Cecelia, M 815-226-4083. 157 C cbristol@rockford.edu
BRISTOL, Louis 860-738-6328... 89 C lbristol@nwcc.commnet.edu
BRISTOR, Valerie 561-297-3357. 114 L bristor@fau.edu
BRISTOW, Aimee 573-592-5364. 285 B aimee.bristow@westminster-mo.edu
BRISTOW, Jessica 248-218-2038. 249 D jbristow@rc.edu
BRISTOW, Vance 662-325-3707. 268 D vbristow@foundation.msstate.edu
BRITIGAN, Bradley, E 402-599-8878. 292 J bradley.britigan@unmc.edu
BRITO, Sandra 508-362-2131. 231 D sbrito@capecod.edu
BRITSCH, James 575-492-2873. 310 G jbritsch@nmjc.edu
BRITT, Ann, R 252-789-0222. 361 G abritt@martincc.edu
BRITT, Denise 404-752-1500. 129 E dbritt@msm.edu
BRITT, James 312-629-6869. 158 L jbrittjr1@saic.edu
BRITT, Jeanette 814-824-2247. 423 J jbritt@mercyhurst.edu
BRITT, Julianne 781-891-3456. 223 C jbritt@bentley.edu
BRITT, Maria 770-423-6021. 127 N mbritt6@kennesaw.edu
BRITT PIPE, Teri 602-496-2644... 11 K teri.pipe@asu.edu
BRITTAIN, Andrew 808-544-0216. 135 F abrittain@hpu.edu
BRITTAIN, Andrew 808-236-5288. 135 F abrittain@hpu.edu
BRITTAIN, Frederick, L 207-778-7303. 212 D brittain@maine.edu
BRITTAIN, Lee 936-468-3206. 482 A lbrittain@sfasu.edu
BRITTAIN, Linda, D 717-264-4141. 437 H lbrittain@wilson.edu
BRITTAIN, Ross, A 304-457-6428. 526 A brittainra@ab.edu
BRITTENHAM, Marti 505-224-4340. 309 E mbrittenham@cnm.edu
BRITTINGHAM, Kay 425-739-8178. 520 K kay.brittingham@lwtech.edu
BRITTO, Marwin 281-290-3718. 476 A Marwin@lonestar.edu
BRITTON, Brian, J 401-232-6051. 438 K bbritton@bryant.edu
BRITTON, Dana, J 717-766-2511. 423 L dbritton@messiah.edu
BRITTON, Keith, E 803-938-3882. 448 F kbritton@uscsumter.edu
BRITTON, Malcolm, E 719-884-5000... 83 K mebritton@nbc.edu
BRITTON, Mark 620-441-5595. 186 A britton@cowley.edu
BRITZ, Johannes 412-229-4501. 537 A britz@uwm.edu
BRKOVICH, LeAnna 814-536-5168. 412 C lbrkovich@crbc.net
BROADDUS, Henry, R 757-221-3980. 503 N hrbroa@wm.edu
BROADDUS, Susan, S 804-758-6724. 513 G sbroaddus@rappahannock.edu
BROADDUS, Virginia 202-884-9220... 96 G broaddusv@trinitydc.edu
BROADED, C. Montgomery 317-940-8312. 164 J mbroaded@butler.edu
BROADHEAD, Fenton, L 208-496-1123. 137 H broadheadf@byui.edu
BROADIE, II, Paul 845-341-4020. 335 H paul.broadie@sunyorange.edu
BROADUS, Alicia 330-684-8901. 390 F broadus@uakron.edu
BROADWATER, Bonnie 301-387-3050. 214 I bonnie.broadwater@garrettcollege.edu
BROADWATER, Larry 865-251-1800. 458 I lbroadw@southcollegetn.edu
BROADWAY, Michael, J 906-227-2700. 248 A mbroadwa@nmu.edu
BROADWELL, Jennifer 757-340-2121. 503 I finaidcvab@centura.edu
BROADWELL, Phyllis 912-279-5816. 123 B pbroadwell@ccga.edu
BROCATO, MaryAnne 662-332-8750. 268 B mbrocato@msdelta.edu
BROCK, Amber 229-226-1621. 132 F abrock@thomasu.edu
BROCK, Deborah 540-423-9179. 512 E dbrock@germanna.edu
BROCK, Donna 404-880-8337. 122 J dbrock@cau.edu
BROCK, Gary 419-251-1780. 383 G gary.brock@mercycollege.edu
BROCK, III, Harry, B 205-726-4071..... 6 F bbrock@samford.edu
BROCK, J, C 727-341-4495. 112 E brock.jc@spcollege.edu
BROCK, James, L 253-535-7445. 521 I brockjl@plu.edu
BROCK, Jeanette 239-513-1122. 106 O jbrock@hodges.edu
BROCK, John, R 920-206-2320. 533 U jbrock@mbbc.edu
BROCK, Kathy 218-736-1500. 259 F kathy.brock@minnesota.edu
BROCK, Kishia 480-517-8567... 15 D kishia.brock@riosalado.edu
BROCK, Lynn, A 937-766-7846. 375 K brockl@cedarville.edu
BROCK, Marcius 507-389-1180. 259 G marcius.brock@mnsu.edu
BROCK, Marilyn 562-938-4127... 51 D mbrock@lbcc.edu
BROCK, Michael 610-989-1246. 436 D mbrock@vfmac.edu
BROCK, Michelle 704-272-5357. 363 G mbrock@spcc.edu
BROCK, Nancy, R 802-258-3357. 500 C Nancy.brock@worldlearning.org
BROCK, Nikki 336-917-5473. 366 D nikki.brock@salem.edu
BROCK, Regan 419-251-8968. 383 G regan.brock@mercycollege.edu
BROCK, Sabra 212-742-8770. 348 B sabra.brock@touro.edu
BROCK, Summer 252-399-6383. 352 F sebrock@barton.edu
BROCK, Teresa 817-598-6348. 494 G tbrock@wc.edu
BROCK, Todd 270-686-9551. 192 G todd.brock@brescia.edu
BROCKEL, Sarah 406-247-5780. 287 C sbrockel@msubillings.edu
BROCKENBROUGH, Karl, B 301-860-3470. 220 A kbrockenbrough@bowiestate.edu
BROCKER, Rachel 773-256-0726. 152 B rbrocker@lstc.edu
BROCKETT, Lori 760-750-4405... 35 A brockett@csusm.edu
BROCKGREITENS, Kathy 636-922-8229. 280 J kbrockgreitens@stchas.edu
BROCKHOFF, Jennifer 502-585-9911. 199 C jbrockhoff@spalding.edu
BROCKIE, Clarena 406-353-2607. 285 E cbrockie@ancollege.edu
BROCKIE, Dixie 406-353-2607. 285 E dbrockie@ancollege.edu
BROCKIE, Kimberly 406-353-2607. 285 E kbrockie@ancollege.edu
BROCKINGTON, Joseph, L 269-337-7133. 244 K Joe.Brockington@kzoo.edu
BROCKINTON, W. Joseph 864-644-5142. 446 I jbrockinton@swu.edu
BROCKMAN, Diane 660-596-7205. 282 G dbrockman@sfccmo.edu
BROCKMYER, Richard, A 801-832-2516. 498 F rbrockmyer@westminstercollege.edu
BROCKWAY, David, J 601-318-6199. 270 I david.brockway@wmcarey.edu
BROCKWELL, Gerri, S 423-323-0226. 461 C gsbrockwell@northeaststate.edu
BROD, Catherine 630-942-2448. 142 G brodc@cod.edu
BRODA, Joanna 212-346-1652. 335 J jbroda@pace.edu
BRODERHAUSEN, Cathryn 843-863-7523. 441 H cbroderhausen@csuniv.edu
BRODERICK, Christopher 503-725-3773. 406 B christopher.broderick@pdx.edu
BRODERICK, Deborah 212-998-6825. 334 D deborah.broderick@nyu.edu
BRODERICK, Jo 978-921-4242. 234 C jo.broderick@montserrat.edu
BRODERICK, John, R 757-683-3159. 507 N jbroderi@odu.edu
BRODERICK, JR., John, T 603-513-5101. 298 D john.broderick@law.unh.edu
BRODERICK, Katherine, S 202-274-7332... 97 A sbroderick@udc.edu
BRODERICK, Mark, C 410-617-2713. 216 A mbroder@loyola.edu
BRODERICK, Marybeth 845-848-7824. 322 G marybeth.broderick@dc.edu
BRODERICK, Michael 860-515-3885... 87 I mbroderick@charteroak.edu
BRODERICK, Victor, K 217-786-2414. 151 F victor.broderick@llcc.edu
BRODERSEN, Lyn, A 641-422-4002. 181 D brodelyn@niacc.edu
BRODERSON, Maureen, A 818-779-8040... 50 A mbroderson@kingsuniversity.edu
BRODEUR, Thomas 860-832-2531... 87 K brodeur@ccsu.edu
BRODHEAD, Richard, H 919-684-2424. 354 A president@duke.edu
BRODIE, Carol 209-946-2261... 73 A cbrodie@pacific.edu
BRODIE, Lyman 407-823-1113. 115 E Lyman.Brodie@ucf.edu
BRODIE, Marilyn 408-298-2181... 63 P marilyn.brodie@sjcc.edu
BRODIGAN, Becky 207-721-5235. 209 H rbrodiga@bowdoin.edu
BRODL, Mark 210-999-8201. 488 C mbrodl@trinity.edu
BRODMERKEL, Darcy 570-674-6466. 424 A dbrodmer@misericordia.edu
BRODRICK, Tracy 970-248-1422... 79 F tbrodrick@coloradomesa.edu
BRODSKY, Mikhail 510-208-2803... 51 A rector@lincolnuca.edu
BRODSKY, Stephen 212-346-1274. 335 J sbrodksy@pace.edu
BRODY, Charmain 610-398-5300. 422 B cbrody@lincolntech.com
BRODY, Gerald, D 512-863-1582. 481 I brodyj@southwestern.edu
BRODY, Michael 503-777-7521. 407 E brodym@reed.edu
BRODZINSKI, Deborah 312-935-6659. 156 K dbrody@robertmorris.edu
BRODZINSKI, James 219-464-6758. 174 E jim.brodzinski@valpo.edu
BROEKER, Christine 407-708-2396. 113 E broekerc@seminolestate.edu
BROERING, Naomi 619-574-6909... 57 E nbroering@pacificcollege.edu
BROGAN, Frank, T 850-245-0466. 114 J chancellor@flbog.edu
BROGAN, Jamey 304-243-2385. 531 H jbrogan@wju.edu
BROGAN, Michael, S 716-839-8227. 322 E mbrogan@daemen.edu
BROGDEN, Jeff, D 919-658-7171. 357 I jbrogden@moc.edu
BROGDON, Bethanie, B 229-333-5666. 134 B bbbass@valdosta.edu
BROGDON, Christina 540-831-5421. 508 C cbrogdon@radford.edu
BROGE, Jason 989-275-5000. 245 B jason.broge@kirtland.edu
BROGHAMMER, Sean, M 970-351-2806... 86 C ean.broghammer@unco.edu
BROIDA, Judith 410-888-9048. 216 D jbroida@muih.edu
BROKAW, Melinda, S 319-399-8617. 176 G mbrokaw@coe.edu
BROKENSHIRE, Catherine 312-777-8619. 147 D cbrokenshire@aii.edu
BROKKE, Dan 952-944-2121. 253 I
BROKKEN, Patty 319-385-6391. 179 K pbrokken@iwc.edu
BROKOPP, Charles 608-890-1569. 536 D cdb@mail.slh.wisc.edu
BROLLEY, Francis, R 815-224-0466. 148 A fran_brolley@ivcc.edu
BROM, Donald 215-637-7700. 418 G dbrom@holyfamily.edu
BROMAN, Erica 413-552-2747. 231 F ebroman@hcc.edu
BROMANDER, Lowell 651-523-2225. 256 A lbromander@hamline.edu
BROMBERG, Ellis 414-297-6600. 540 E brombere@matc.edu
BROMFIELD, Robert, L 415-422-2786... 73 J rlbromfield@usfca.edu
BROMFIELD, Wayne, A 570-577-1149. 411 A wayne.bromfield@bucknell.edu
BROMLEY, Dennis 801-957-4357. 498 B dennis.bromley@slcc.edu
BROMLEY, Michael, D 203-576-4641... 91 G mbromley@bridgeport.edu
BROMSTAD, Peter, J 770-720-5521. 130 G pjb@reinhardt.edu
BROND, David 706-721-9556. 126 B dbrond@gru.edu
BRONDER, James, S 419-227-3141. 391 F jsbronde@unoh.edu
BRONET, Frances 541-346-3631. 406 D fbronet@uoregon.edu
BRONFMAN, Jane 860-906-5103... 88 D jbronfman@ccc.commnet.edu
BRONFORT, Gert 952-888-4777. 263 B gbronfort@nwhealth.edu
BRONISZ, John 505-224-3730. 309 E jbronisz@cnm.edu
BRONK, Leslie 612-977-4222. 254 C leslie.bronk@capella.edu
BRONNER, Gwethalyn 847-543-2685. 143 A gbronner@clcillinois.edu
BRONNER, Jennifer 740-826-8131. 384 L jbronner@muskingum.edu
BRONSDON, Chris 619-594-7985... 35 D cbronsdo@mail.sdsu.edu
BRONSKI, Suzanne 973-655-4334. 303 D bronskis@mail.montclair.edu
BRONSON, Jennifer 412-365-1862. 412 K jbronson@chatham.edu
BRONSTEIN, JR., Bruce, S 757-594-7699. 503 M bruce.bronstein@cnu.edu
BRONSTEIN, Ken 360-383-3359. 525 D kbronstein@whatcom.ctc.edu
BRONSTEIN, Laura 607-777-5572. 341 E lbronst@binghamton.edu
BRONSTEIN, Susan 716-338-1035. 327 J susanbronstein@mail.sunyjcc.edu
BROOK, Kathleen 575-646-4083. 310 I kbrook@nmsu.edu
BROOK, Raymond 540-986-1800. 198 E rbrook@national-college.edu
BROOKBANK, Julie 605-995-3026. 450 E julie.brookbank@mitchelltech.edu

BROOKE, Judith .... 321-674-8053. 104 H
jbrooke@fit.edu
BROOKE, Patrick, T .... 630-752-5126. 163 F
patrick.brooke@wheaton.edu
BROOKER, Paulita .... 704-463-7302. 365 E
paulita.brooker@fsmail.pfeiffer.edu
BROOKER, Sarah .... 717-564-4112. 419 I
sbrooker@kaplan.edu
BROOKET, Jenn .... 517-264-7159. 250 B
jbrooket@sienaheights.edu
BROOKEY, Lauren, F ...... 918-595-7977. 400 E
lauren.brookey@tulsacc.edu
BROOKNER, Laurie .... 415-565-8813... 71 A
brookner@uchastings.edu
BROOKS, Anthony, M .... 919-530-6298. 368 A
abrooks@nccu.edu
BROOKS, Barbara .... 315-228-7417. 320 F
bbrooks@colgate.edu
BROOKS, Beth, A .... 773-252-5311. 156 I
beth.brooks@resu.edu
BROOKS, Bill .... 727-736-5082. 113 D
bbrooks@schiller.edu
BROOKS, Billie, K .... 304-710-3141. 528 C
hendersb@mctc.edu
BROOKS, Bryan .... 972-825-4821. 481 F
BBrooks@sagu.edu
BROOKS, Carlton .... 719-502-2003... 84 A
carlton.brooks@ppcc.edu
BROOKS, Carolyn .... 323-856-7742... 27 O
cbrooks@afi.com
BROOKS, Carrie Allison . 901-272-5160. 456 F
cbrooks@mca.edu
BROOKS, Chris .... 800-422-2418... 99 A
cbrooks@baymedical.org
BROOKS, Cindy, L .... 610-799-1121. 421 I
cbrooks@lccc.edu
BROOKS, Craig .... 719-336-1674... 82 R
craig.brooks@lamarcc.edu
BROOKS, Cynthia .... 615-963-7410. 459 E
cbrooks@tnstate.edu
BROOKS, Dana, D .... 304-293-8026. 530 D
dbrooks@mail.wvu.edu
BROOKS, Danny, K .... 205-226-4699..... 2 C
dbrooks@bsc.edu
BROOKS, Darlene, D ...... 901-843-3901. 458 E
brooksd@rhodes.edu
BROOKS, DeeAnna .... 803-323-2225. 449 G
brooksd@winthrop.edu
BROOKS, Delores, J .... 708-974-5376. 153 F
brooks@morainevalley.edu
BROOKS, II, Earl, D ...... 260-665-4101. 173 E
brookse@trine.edu
BROOKS, Fred .... 252-451-8233. 362 D
fbrooks@nashcc.edu
BROOKS, Gail .... 562-951-4455... 32 E
gbrooks@calstate.edu
BROOKS, Gene .... 605-575-2030. 452 D
gene.brooks@usiouxfalls.edu
BROOKS, Glee, R .... 530-226-4188... 66 D
gbrooks@simpsonu.edu
BROOKS, II, H. Gordon . 337-482-6224. 208 D
gbrooks@louisiana.edu
BROOKS, Henry, M .... 410-651-6206. 219 E
hmbrooks@umes.edu
BROOKS, Ian .... 510-883-2056... 42 I
ibrooks@dspt.edu
BROOKS, James, J .... 541-346-6121. 406 D
brooksja@uoregon.edu
BROOKS, James, W .... 317-805-1730. 527 G
jwb@salemu.edu
BROOKS, Jane .... 219-785-5657. 172 A
jbrooks@pnc.edu
BROOKS, Jason .... 620-341-5481. 186 D
jbrooks5@emporia.edu
BROOKS, John .... 337-482-2976. 208 D
jmb5961@louisiana.edu
BROOKS, John, I .... 910-672-1060. 367 D
jibrooks@uncfsu.edu
BROOKS, Joseph .... 303-963-3463... 79 C
jbrooks@ccu.edu
BROOKS, Julia .... 503-223-2245. 403 J
jbrooks@portland.chefs.edu
BROOKS, Juliette .... 201-692-7050. 301 J
juliette_brooks@fdu.edu
BROOKS, Justin, P .... 619-239-0391... 36 D
jbrooks@cwsl.edu
BROOKS, Katrina .... 904-724-2229. 118 J
BROOKS, Keith .... 410-706-7131. 219 C
kbrooks@umaryland.edu
BROOKS, Kent .... 307-268-2703. 542 X
kbrooks@caspercollege.edu
BROOKS, Krista .... 217-732-3168. 151 B
kjbrooks@lincolnchristian.edu
BROOKS, L. Rayburn ...... 864-941-8301. 446 C
brooks.r@ptc.edu
BROOKS, Larry .... 701-228-5457. 372 C
larry.brooks@dakotacollege.edu
BROOKS, Lois .... 541-737-0739. 406 A
lois.brooks@oregonstate.edu
BROOKS, Lyvette .... 215-751-8046. 413 I
lbrooks@ccp.edu
BROOKS, Madelene .... 252-222-6224. 358 G
brooksm@carteret.edu
BROOKS, Marilyn, A ...... 804-257-5846. 515 F
mabrooks2@vuu.edu
BROOKS, Mark .... 229-931-2246. 131 G
mbrooks@southgatech.edu
BROOKS, Mark, D .... 270-901-1117. 196 E
mark.brooks@kctcs.edu
BROOKS, Michael .... 912-650-5640. 131 H
jmbrooks@southuniversity.edu
BROOKS, Monica .... 304-696-6474. 529 H
brooks@marshall.edu
BROOKS, Nancy, S .... 515-294-8757. 175 H
nsbrook@iastate.edu
BROOKS, Patricia .... 662-621-4168. 266 D
pbrooks@coahomacc.edu
BROOKS, Paul .... 972-825-4616. 481 F
pbrooks@sagu.edu
BROOKS, Randy, M .... 217-424-6205. 153 C
rbrooks@millikin.edu
BROOKS, Robert .... 617-928-4602. 234 E
rbrooks@mountida.edu
BROOKS, Roger, L .... 860-439-2030... 89 H
roger.brooks@conncoll.edu
BROOKS, Roger, L .... 804-289-8491. 510 L
rbrooks@richmond.edu
BROOKS, Ronnie .... 615-963-5671. 459 E
rbrooks6@tnstate.edu
BROOKS, Sandra, L .... 606-474-3247. 194 H
bookstore@kcu.edu
BROOKS, Sarah .... 509-542-4837. 518 C
sbrooks@columbiabasin.edu
BROOKS, Sean .... 410-951-3455. 220 B
sbrooks@coppin.edu
BROOKS, Sherry .... 906-635-2216. 245 G
sbrooks@lssu.edu
BROOKS, Sherry, L .... 906-635-2216. 245 G
sbrooks1@lssu.edu
BROOKS, Susan, H .... 704-687-5770. 368 E
sbrooks@uncc.edu
BROOKS, Telaekah .... 202-884-9519... 96 G
brookst@trinitydc.edu
BROOKS, Tim .... 303-871-3030... 86 B
tim.brooks@du.edu
BROOKS, Tim .... 617-627-3986. 237 C
tim.brooks@tufts.edu
BROOKS, Todd .... 757-594-7217. 503 M
todd.brooks@cnu.edu
BROOKS, Tom .... 828-339-4202. 364 B
tbrooks@southwesterncc.edu
BROOKS, Tyrone, W .... 208-885-5255. 139 D
tyroneb@uidaho.edu
BROOKS, Vera .... 410-462-8500. 213 F
vbrooks@bccc.edu
BROOKS, Walter .... 609-586-4800. 302 G
brooksw@mccc.edu
BROOKS, Walter, T .... 508-362-2131. 231 D
wbrooks@capecod.edu
BROOKS, Wendy .... 989-358-7299. 239 C
brooksw@alpenacc.edu
BROOKS, Wesley, H .... 319-352-8260. 183 E
wes.brooks@wartburg.edu
BROOKS BLAIR,
Sarah, D .... 937-529-2201. 390 D
sblair@united.edu
BROOKSHIRE, Kathy .... 601-484-8612. 267 G
kbrooksh@meridiancc.edu
BROOM, Cheryl .... 760-795-2121... 54 G
cbroom@miracosta.edu
BROOM, Mahailier, L ...... 318-670-9345. 207 A
mbroom@susla.edu
BROOMALL, James, K ... 302-831-2795... 94 B
jbroom@udel.edu
BROOME, JR., David, E . 704-687-5732. 368 E
debroome@uncc.edu
BROOME, Marion, E .... 317-274-1486. 168 D
mbroome@iupui.edu
BROOME, Melba .... 202-274-6118... 97 A
mbroome@udc.edu
BROOMHEAD, Keiko .... 617-989-4034. 237 G
broomheadk@wit.edu
BROPHY, Ann .... 314-968-6922. 284 N
annbrophy26@webster.edu
BROPHY, George .... 860-768-4608... 92 D
brophy@hartford.edu
BROPHY, Michael, S .... 310-377-5501... 53 F
mbrophy@marymountcalifornia.edu
BROPHY, JR.,
William, E .... 256-824-6144..... 8 F
william.brophy@uah.edu
BRORSON, Susan .... 218-281-8186. 264 E
sbrorson@umn.edu
BROSCHART, Jim .... 607-431-4026. 325 F
broschartj@hartwick.edu
BROSCHEIT, James .... 303-556-2866... 86 A
james.broscheit@ucdenver.edu
BROSIUS, Jo .... 859-622-2474. 193 P
jo.brosius@eku.edu
BROSKE, Kathleen, M .... 920-924-2139. 540 F
kbroske@morainepark.edu
BROSKI, Annette .... 315-792-5411. 331 I
abroski@mvcc.edu
BROSKY, Lisa .... 502-213-2400. 195 F
lisa.brosky@kctcs.edu
BROSNAN, Joseph, S .... 215-489-2203. 414 E
Joseph.Brosnan@delval.edu
BROSSETTE, Alicia .... 214-768-2030. 481 A
abrosset@smu.edu
BROSSMANN,
William, D .... 517-321-0242. 243 F
wbrossmann@glcc.edu
BROSTROM, Nathan, E ... 510-987-9029... 70 H
nathan.brostrom@ucop.edu
BROTHERS, Gregory, A .. 713-646-1888. 480 J
gbrothers@stcl.edu
BROTHERS, James, F ..... 937-229-2829. 391 C
JBrothers1@udayton.edu
BROTHERS, Wes .... 740-477-7757. 385 L
wbrothers@ohiochristian.edu
BROTHERTON, Jeffrey .... 614-222-4014. 378 A
jbrotherton@ccad.edu
BROTHERTON,
Thomas, S .... 712-852-5224. 179 E
tbrotherton@iowalakes.edu
BROUCEK, Willard .... 605-626-2401. 451 I
broucekw@northern.edu
BROUDE, Nancy .... 617-587-5585. 234 H
brouden@neco.edu
BROUGH, Amy, F .... 860-297-5315... 91 F
amy.brough@trincoll.edu
BROUGHTON, Nancy ...... 218-879-0837. 258 E
sam@fdltcc.edu
BROUGHTON, Sandy, S . 732-255-0400. 304 A
sbroughton@ocean.edu
BROUILLETTE,
Domenick, R .... 816-604-1370. 277 C
domenick.brouillette@mcckc.edu
BROUK, Susan .... 660-263-4110. 279 B
susanbr@macc.edu
BROUNK, Thomas, M .... 314-935-5955. 284 L
tom_brounk@wustl.edu
BROUSSARD, Camille .... 212-431-2354. 333 I
cbroussard@nyls.edu
BROUSSARD, Michael .... 337-550-1292. 205 B
BROUSSARD, William .... 225-771-3170. 206 J
will_broussard@subr.edu
BROUWER, Peter, S .... 315-267-2515. 344 C
brouweps@potsdam.edu
BROUWERS, Mariette ..... 541-737-2131. 406 A
mariette.brouwers@oregonstate.edu
BROWDER, Steven, K .... 317-738-8301. 165 I
sbrowder@franklincollege.edu
BROWER, Bob .... 619-849-2216... 59 L
bobbrower@pointloma.edu
BROWER, Laura .... 805-289-6460... 74 H
lbrower@vcccd.edu
BROWER, Paul, O .... 508-213-2271. 235 E
paul.brower@nichols.edu
BROWER, Pearl, K .... 907-852-3333... 10 F
pearl.brower@ilisagvik.edu
BROWER, Roderick .... 910-678-8232. 360 D
browerr@faytechcc.edu
BROWER, William .... 585-245-5626. 343 C
brower@geneseo.edu
BROWN, A. Ramona .... 718-982-2335. 317 E
aramona.brown@csi.cuny.edu
BROWN, Aaron .... 951-222-8789... 60 J
aaron.brown@rccd.edu
BROWN, Adrienne .... 912-358-4166. 131 C
brownad@savannahstate.edu
BROWN, Albert, F .... 740-588-1210. 394 C
abrown@zanestate.edu
BROWN, Alfreda .... 330-672-2442. 382 B
abbrown@kent.edu
BROWN, Alistair .... 630-620-2101. 155 A
abrown@seminary.edu
BROWN, Amy .... 704-463-3046. 365 E
amy.brown@fsmail.pfeiffer.edu
BROWN, Amy, L .... 607-746-4584. 345 G
brownal@delhi.edu
BROWN, Andrea .... 435-652-7595. 497 E
abrown@dixie.edu
BROWN, Angela, C .... 254-968-9128. 483 A
abrown@tarleton.edu
BROWN, Angela, P .... 731-425-2347. 460 G
abrown@jscc.edu
BROWN, Anne .... 617-228-3267. 231 C
abrown@bhcc.mass.edu
BROWN, Ansel, E .... 919-530-7477. 368 A
browna@nccu.edu
BROWN, Anthony .... 252-335-3277. 367 C
abrown@mail.ecsu.edu
BROWN, Anthony .... 225-247-8019. 202 H
browna@mybrcc.edu
BROWN, Arlene .... 256-840-4171...... 6 I
abrown@snead.edu
BROWN, Arthur .... 870-862-8131... 23 D
abrown@southark.edu
BROWN, Arthur, E .... 212-217-3650. 324 C
arthur_brown@fitnyc.edu
BROWN, B, T .... 252-536-7245. 361 A
btbrown920@halifaxcc.edu
BROWN, Barry .... 617-928-4502. 234 E
barrybrown@mountida.edu
BROWN, Bernetta, H ...... 252-335-3596. 367 C
bhbrown@mail.ecsu.edu
BROWN, Bill .... 919-760-2367. 356 G
brownw@meredith.edu
BROWN, Bill .... 913-469-8500. 187 J
bbrown@jccc.edu
BROWN, Bill .... 863-638-7228. 119 C
bill.brown@warner.edu
BROWN, Bill .... 417-328-1601. 282 C
bbrown@sbuniv.edu
BROWN, Bob .... 903-886-5024. 483 E
bob.brown@tamuc.edu
BROWN, Bobbie .... 806-742-3661. 487 D
bobbie.brown@ttu.edu
BROWN, Bonita, J .... 336-334-4244. 369 A
bjbrown3@uncg.edu
BROWN, Braden .... 405-382-9277. 399 I
b.brown@sscok.edu
BROWN, Brandon .... 706-821-8233. 130 C
bbrown@paine.edu
BROWN, Breighan .... 269-782-1294. 250 C
bbrown02@swmich.edu
BROWN, Brenda .... 309-796-4815. 140 E
brownb@bhc.edu
BROWN, Brenda, L .... 478-988-6851. 122 G
bbrown@centralgatech.edu
BROWN, Brent, K .... 801-581-3003. 496 Q
brent.brown@osp.utah.edu
BROWN, Brian .... 315-364-3207. 350 E
bbrown@wells.edu
BROWN, JR., Buck, F .... 864-379-8805. 443 F
brown@erskine.edu
BROWN, Calvin .... 205-348-5966..... 8 D
cbrown@alumni.ua.edu
BROWN, Canter .... 478-825-6156. 124 H
brownc@fvsu.edu
BROWN, JR., Canter ...... 478-825-6156. 124 H
brownc@fvsu.edu
BROWN, Carl .... 614-947-6080. 380 A
carl.brown@franklin.edu
BROWN, Carlton, E .... 404-880-8566. 122 J
cbrown@cau.edu
BROWN, Carly .... 412-747-7800... 96 F
BROWN, Carmen .... 803-584-3446. 448 D
cdbrown@mailbox.sc.edu
BROWN, Carol .... 559-791-2316... 49 P
cbrown@portervillecollege.edu
BROWN, Carol .... 901-333-4462. 461 F
cbrown@southwest.tn.edu
BROWN, Carol, J .... 309-341-7980. 150 A
cbrown@knox.edu
BROWN, Carolanne .... 561-803-2050. 110 B
carolanne_brown@pba.edu
BROWN, Carrie .... 936-468-3971. 482 A
brownch@sfasu.edu
BROWN, Cassandra .... 205-226-4643..... 2 C
clbrown@bsc.edu
BROWN, Chad .... 740-588-1260. 394 C
cbrown@zanestate.edu
BROWN, Charity .... 559-453-2236... 45 D
charityb@fresno.edu
BROWN, Charles .... 502-456-6773. 199 G
cbrown@sullivan.edu
BROWN, Charles, L .... 561-297-3988. 114 L
clbrown@fau.edu
BROWN, Cheryl-Ann ...... 321-674-7581. 104 H
cbrown@fit.edu
BROWN, Chris .... 408-924-1950... 36 A
chris.brown@sjsu.edu
BROWN, Christopher ...... 949-376-6000... 50 C
cbrown@lagunacollege.edu
BROWN, Christopher ...... 919-962-1000. 366 K
csbrown@northcarolina.edu
BROWN, Christopher, D . 570-577-3164. 411 A
chris.brown@bucknell.edu
BROWN, Christopher, M 517-355-6509. 246 H
brownc28@msu.edu
BROWN, Cindy .... 417-455-5540. 273 E
CindyBrown@crowder.edu
BROWN, Clarence .... 909-274-4121... 55 A
cbrown@mtsac.edu
BROWN, Constance .... 212-854-2011. 314 G
cbrown@barnard.edu
BROWN, Constance .... 516-561-0050. 316 B
BROWN, Cynthia .... 706-754-7714. 129 G
cbrown@northgatech.edu
BROWN, Cynthia, F .... 413-662-5242. 230 C
c.brown@mcla.edu
BROWN, Cynthia, L .... 508-213-2215. 235 E
cindy.brown@nichols.edu
BROWN, Dale .... 308-535-8112. 290 J
brownd@mpcc.edu
BROWN, Dan .... 502-863-7035. 194 C
dan_brown@georgetowncollege.edu
BROWN, Dana .... 601-979-5848. 267 E
dana.a.brown@jsums.edu

BROWN, Danene .... 619-388-2803... 62 E
dmbrown@sdccd.edu
BROWN, Daniel .... 512-245-3579. 487 C
sp15@txstate.edu
BROWN, Daniel .... 806-291-3575. 494 F
brownd@wbu.edu
BROWN, Daniel, W .... 203-582-8927... 91 A
daniel.brown@quinnipiac.edu
BROWN, Danielle .... 407-275-9696... 99 K
BROWN, Danita .... 203-857-7004... 89 D
dbrown@norwalk.edu
BROWN, Danita .... 612-624-3560. 264 G
dbyoung@umn.edu
BROWN, Darlene .... 215-248-7158. 413 A
brown@chc.edu
BROWN, Darrell .... 254-968-9083. 483 A
dwbrown@tarleton.edu
BROWN, Darryl .... 301-295-3412. 545 C
darryl.brown@usuhs.edu
BROWN, David .... 352-638-9721... 99 B
dbrown@beaconcollege.edu
BROWN, David .... 314-434-4044. 273 C
david.brown@covenantseminary.edu
BROWN, David .... 910-668-7731. 477 I
dbrown@nctc.edu
BROWN, David .... 617-369-3870. 236 F
dbrown@smfa.edu
BROWN, David .... 262-691-5346. 541 D
dbrown@wctc.edu
BROWN, David, H .... 845-437-5315. 349 G
brown@vassar.edu
BROWN, Deanie .... 217-206-6222. 161 E
brown.deanie@uis.edu
BROWN, Debbi .... 808-984-3204. 137 B
debbi@hawaii.edu
BROWN, Deborah .... 512-863-1944. 481 I
brownd@southwestern.edu
BROWN, Delbert, W .... 585-245-5566. 343 C
brown@geneseo.edu
BROWN, Dennis .... 281-425-6300. 475 I
dbrown@lee.edu
BROWN, DeShanna .... 404-270-5128. 132 E
dbrown56@spelman.edu
BROWN, Diane, M .... 484-365-8055. 422 D
dbrown@lincoln.edu
BROWN, Dina .... 978-556-3701. 232 E
dbrown@necc.mass.edu
BROWN, Dolores, M .... 262-524-7133. 532 C
docampo@carrollu.edu
BROWN, Donna .... 479-248-7236... 21 B
registrar@ecollege.edu
BROWN, Donna .... 660-626-2790. 271 A
dbrown@atsu.edu
BROWN, Donna, L .... 218-477-2721. 259 H
donna.brown@mnstate.edu
BROWN, Donnie .... 806-291-3596. 494 F
brownd@wbu.edu
BROWN, Dorothy .... 404-712-8218. 124 E
daborw7@emory.edu
BROWN, Doug, E .... 515-964-0601. 178 E
brownd@faith.edu
BROWN, Doug, M .... 505-277-6148. 312 F
browndm@mgt.unm.edu
BROWN, Douglas .... 508-588-9100. 232 A
BROWN, Eleanor, J .... 718-855-3661. 327 B
ebrown@idc.edu
BROWN, Elizabeth, A ..... 312-329-4141. 153 E
elizabeth.brown@moody.edu
BROWN, Eric, A .... 843-355-4170. 449 F
browne@wiltech.edu
BROWN, Erica .... 217-854-3231. 140 G
erica.brown@blackburn.edu
BROWN, Erica .... 205-226-4733..... 2 C
ebrown@bsc.edu
BROWN, Erin .... 360-442-2131. 521 A
mbrown@lowercolumbia.edu
BROWN, JR., Ermen ...... 701-766-1342. 370 H
ermen.brown@littlehoop.edu
BROWN, Ethel .... 678-891-2526. 125 G
ebrown@gpc.edu
BROWN, Ethel, M .... 404-413-1300. 126 E
ebrown@gsu.edu
BROWN, Evelyn .... 731-426-7532. 455 J
ebrown@lanecollege.edu
BROWN, Faith .... 802-322-1616. 499 C
faith.brown@goddard.edu
BROWN, Felicia .... 252-335-3642. 367 C
fdbrown@mail.ecsu.edu
BROWN, Fran .... 248-476-1122. 246 G
fbrown@mispp.edu
BROWN, Francis, H .... 801-581-8767. 496 Q
fbrown@mines.utah.edu
BROWN, Frankie, M .... 316-978-3065. 191 F
frankie.brown@wichita.edu
BROWN, Fred .... 850-872-3843. 106 H
fbrown@gulfcoast.edu
BROWN, Fred .... 970-339-6640... 78 C
fred.brown@aims.edu
BROWN, Gary .... 608-785-9167. 541 E
browng@westerntc.edu
BROWN, Gary .... 814-824-2036. 423 J
gbrown@mercyhurst.edu
BROWN, Gary, L .... 919-530-7466. 368 A
gbrown@nccu.edu
BROWN, Geoffrey .... 315-268-7633. 320 A
gbrown@clarkson.edu
BROWN, George .... 773-291-6613. 142 D
gbrown34@ccc.edu
BROWN, Giles .... 903-463-8620. 472 M
browng@grayson.edu
BROWN, Gladys .... 951-827-5604... 71 E
gladys.brown@ucr.edu
BROWN, Greg .... 760-366-5290... 42 B
gbrown@cmccd.edu
BROWN, Gregory, N .... 212-854-2003. 314 G
gbrown@barnard.edu
BROWN, Guilbert, L .... 703-993-8743. 505 C
gbrowne@gmu.edu
BROWN, H. David .... 816-271-4327. 279 A
browndav@missouriwestern.edu
BROWN, Heather .... 213-477-2966... 54 J
hbrown@msmc.la.edu
BROWN, Hilrie .... 615-383-4848. 464 D
hbrown@watkins.edu
BROWN, Isiah, D .... 713-313-1318. 485 F
brownid@tsu.edu
BROWN, J. Kevin .... 863-784-7424. 113 G
kevin.brown@southflorida.edu
BROWN, J.J .... 828-262-2060. 367 A
brownjj1@appstate.edu
BROWN, Jacqueline, L .... 301-322-0918. 217 F
jbrown@pgcc.edu
BROWN, James .... 508-854-4324. 232 F
jbrown@qcc.mass.edu
BROWN, James .... 570-389-4410. 427 H
jbrown@bloomu.edu
BROWN, James, C .... 315-792-3001. 349 F
jbrown@utica.edu
BROWN, James, W .... 319-895-4485. 177 A
jbrown@cornellcollege.edu
BROWN, James, W .... 757-455-5730. 515 H
bbrown@vwc.edu
BROWN, Jamie, L .... 989-774-3945. 240 N
brown3jl@cmich.edu
BROWN, Jane, B .... 617-373-4810. 235 F
BROWN, Janet, M .... 219-464-5289. 174 E
janet.brown@valpo.edu
BROWN, Janice .... 301-846-2484. 214 H
jbrown@frederick.edu
BROWN, Jared .... 610-436-3305. 430 A
jbrown@wcupa.edu
BROWN, Jasmin, K .... 910-630-7034. 356 H
jabrown@methodist.edu
BROWN, Jason .... 804-862-6214. 508 H
jbrown@rbc.edu
BROWN, Jeff .... 801-832-2900. 498 F
jbrown@westminstercollege.edu
BROWN, Jeff .... 509-533-7373. 518 E
jeff.brown@scc.spokane.edu
BROWN, Jeff .... 828-250-2350. 368 C
jbrown@unca.edu
BROWN, Jeffrey, D .... 573-629-3015. 274 J
jbrown@hlg.edu
BROWN, Jeffrey, S .... 757-594-7053. 503 M
jsbrown@cnu.edu
BROWN, Jennifer .... 785-738-9085. 189 F
jbrown@ncktc.edu
BROWN, Jennifer .... 203-582-3246... 91 A
jennifer.brown@quinnipiac.edu
BROWN, Jennifer, A .... 617-287-5420. 228 G
jennifer.brown@umb.edu
BROWN, Jeremy .... 970-248-1962... 79 F
jbrown@coloradomesa.edu
BROWN, Jeremy .... 971-722-4365. 407 D
president@pcc.edu
BROWN, Jerri .... 928-350-2113... 17 K
jbrown@prescott.edu
BROWN, Jesse, M .... 260-359-4028. 166 O
jbrown@huntington.edu
BROWN, Jim .... 770-229-3455. 132 B
jbrown@sctech.edu
BROWN, Jim .... 731-989-6449. 454 J
jbrown@fhu.edu
BROWN, JoAnn .... 318-670-6651. 207 A
jwarren@susla.edu
BROWN, Joann .... 318-274-6153. 207 E
brownj@gram.edu
BROWN, Joanna .... 413-552-2253. 231 F
jbrown@hcc.edu
BROWN, Joanne .... 409-832-2956. 486 E
jcbrown@lit.edu
BROWN, Johanna .... 810-762-0409. 247 F
johanna.brown@mcc.edu
BROWN, John .... 404-962-3206. 134 A
john.brown@usg.edu
BROWN, John .... 619-482-6573... 68 B
jbrown@swccd.edu
BROWN, Jonathan .... 206-878-3710. 520 E
jbrown@highline.edu
BROWN, Joseph .... 910-246-4957. 363 F
brownj@sandhills.edu
BROWN, Joseph, D .... 903-923-2277. 471 J
jbrown@etbu.edu
BROWN, Joyce .... 443-885-3015. 217 A
joyce.brown@morgan.edu
BROWN, Joyce, F .... 212-217-4000. 324 C
joyce_brown@fitnyc.edu
BROWN, JT .... 563-588-7810. 180 L
jt.brown@loras.edu
BROWN, Julia .... 662-472-9011. 267 B
jubrown@holmescc.edu
BROWN, June, E .... 918-631-2584. 401 F
june-brown@utulsa.edu
BROWN, Kali .... 252-492-2061. 364 F
brownk@vgcc.edu
BROWN, Karen .... 607-962-9221. 322 B
kbrown7@corning-cc.edu
BROWN, Karen .... 432-839-8697. 487 B
kbrown2@sulross.edu
BROWN, Karen, A .... 607-436-2524. 343 E
brownka@oneonta.edu
BROWN, Kate .... 603-899-1090. 296 H
0212mgr@fhet.follett.com
BROWN, Katherine .... 662-241-6101. 268 E
kbrown@edhs.muw.edu
BROWN, Kathleen .... 502-776-1443. 199 A
BROWN, Kathleen, M ...... 574-284-4557. 172 G
kbrown@saintmarys.edu
BROWN, Kathren .... 801-863-8517. 497 C
kbrown@uvu.edu
BROWN, Kathryn, F .... 612-624-3533. 264 G
brown059@umn.edu
BROWN, Katrina, M .... 307-674-6446. 543 F
kbrown@sheridan.edu
BROWN, Keith .... 440-365-5222. 383 B
BROWN, Keith, A .... 318-342-5422. 208 E
kbrown@ulm.edu
BROWN, Keith, A .... 205-853-1200..... 5 B
kbrown@jeffstateonline.com
BROWN, Kelli .... 478-445-4715. 125 A
kelli.brown@gcsu.edu
BROWN, Kelly .... 405-224-3140. 401 E
kbrown@usao.edu
BROWN, Ken .... 563-588-8193. 176 F
ken.brown@clarke.edu
BROWN, Kendal, N .... 712-290-8737. 421 D
kbrown@lancasterseminary.edu
BROWN, Kenneth .... 509-777-4486. 525 F
kbrown@whitworth.edu
BROWN, Kent .... 573-635-4971. 276 C
kentbrown@molawcenter.com
BROWN, Kevin .... 215-572-2854. 409 H
brownka@arcadia.edu
BROWN, Kevin .... 541-784-5149. 178 F
brown@graceland.edu
BROWN, Kevin .... 423-236-2874. 458 J
kbrown@southern.edu
BROWN, Kevin .... 843-349-5398. 444 F
kevin.brown@hgtc.edu
BROWN, Kevin, A .... 919-866-5475. 364 G
kabrown@waketech.edu
BROWN, Kevin, H .... 206-239-4500. 517 M
khbrown@cityu.edu
BROWN, Kim, S .... 757-455-3275. 515 H
kbrown@vwc.edu
BROWN, Kimberly, A ..... 630-515-6044. 153 B
kbrown@midwestern.edu
BROWN, Kimberly, S ..... 850-474-2200. 117 B
kimbrown@uwf.edu
BROWN, Kristen .... 626-395-8395... 31 E
kbrown@caltech.edu
BROWN, Kristen, C .... 336-272-7102. 354 E
kristen.brown@greensboro.edu
BROWN, Kyle .... 315-386-7164. 345 F
brownk@canton.edu
BROWN, Larry .... 804-524-1162. 515 D
lbrown@vsu.edu
BROWN, Laura, J .... 815-455-3700. 152 F
lbrown@mchenry.edu
BROWN, Laura, S .... 607-255-3062. 322 A
lsb7@cornell.edu
BROWN, LeAnn .... 763-576-4784. 257 Q
lbrown@anokatech.edu
BROWN, LeeAnn .... 304-473-8160. 531 G
brown_l@wvwc.edu
BROWN, Lenice .... 936-261-1068. 482 F
ldbrown@pvamu.edu
BROWN, Leon, R .... 804-706-5020. 512 G
lbrown@jtcc.edu
BROWN, JR.,
Leonard, E .... 717-245-1736. 414 H
brownl@dickinson.edu
BROWN, Levy .... 910-755-7304. 358 D
brownl@brunswickcc.edu
BROWN, Lewis .... 605-688-4161. 452 B
lewis.brown@sdstate.edu
BROWN, Linda .... 660-359-3948. 279 H
lbrown@mail.ncmissouri.edu
BROWN, Linda, J .... 218-299-4206. 255 A
linbrown@cord.edu
BROWN, Lisa .... 509-358-7551. 525 A
lisaj.brown@wsu.edu
BROWN, Lisa .... 563-441-4016. 178 C
lbrown@eicc.edu
BROWN, Lisa, M .... 202-687-0325... 95 E
lbrown@georgetown.edu
BROWN, Lisa, M .... 216-397-4184. 381 R
lmbrown@jcu.edu
BROWN, Llatetra, D .... 443-518-4766. 215 E
llatetrabrown@howardcc.edu
BROWN, Lori, A .... 973-313-6132. 307 C
lori.brown@shu.edu
BROWN, Lougene .... 706-507-8902. 123 D
brown_lougene@columbusstate.edu
BROWN, Louise .... 801-524-8174. 495 O
LBrown@ldsbc.edu
BROWN, Lucille .... 203-285-2114... 88 E
lbrown@gwcc.commnet.edu
BROWN, Luther .... 662-846-4312. 266 G
lbrown@deltastate.edu
BROWN, Lynne .... 212-998-2350. 334 D
lynne.brown@nyu.edu
BROWN, II,
M.Christopher .... 601-877-6100. 265 G
president@alcorn.edu
BROWN, Mae, W .... 858-534-3156... 71 F
mbrown@ucsd.edu
BROWN, Marcus .... 217-875-7200. 156 J
mbrown@richland.edu
BROWN, Margo .... 904-819-6474. 103 E
mbrown@flagler.edu
BROWN, Marinell .... 859-442-1120. 195 B
marinell.brown@kctcs.edu
BROWN, Mark .... 712-324-5061. 181 G
mbrown@nwicc.edu
BROWN, Mark, C .... 703-247-2500... 96 F
mbrown@strayer.edu
BROWN, Mark, I .... 608-743-4526. 539 I
mbrown55@blackhawk.edu
BROWN, Marsha, D .... 206-934-5136. 523 A
marsha.brown@seattlecolleges.edu
BROWN, Mary .... 504-988-7800. 207 C
mwbrown@tulane.edu
BROWN, Mary .... 217-544-6464. 158 D
BROWN, Mary, L .... 864-596-9094. 443 D
mary.brown@converse.edu
BROWN, Mary Lee .... 215-898-7260. 435 B
marylb@upenn.edu
BROWN, Matthew, S ...... 405-744-9164. 397 H
brownms@okstate.edu
BROWN, Melanie, A .... 386-312-4202. 112 C
melaniebrown@sjrstate.edu
BROWN, Melissa .... 412-809-5100. 430 H
brown.melissa@pti.edu
BROWN, Melvin, L .... 973-353-5872. 306 D
melbrown@rci.rutgers.edu
BROWN, Merri .... 215-248-6323. 422 F
mbrown@ltsp.edu
BROWN, Merv, R .... 208-496-2010. 137 H
brownme@byui.edu
BROWN, Michael, B .... 252-985-5136. 365 D
mbrown@ncwc.edu
BROWN, Michael, E .... 202-994-6241... 95 D
brownm@gwu.edu
BROWN, Michael, R .... 724-589-2167. 434 B
mbrown@thiel.edu
BROWN, Michael, T .... 805-893-2944... 72 B
michael.brown@els.ucsb.edu
BROWN, Michaela .... 910-672-1287. 367 D
mbrown38@uncfsu.edu
BROWN, Michele .... 847-635-1724. 155 F
mbrown@oakton.edu
BROWN, Michelle .... 678-717-3877. 133 D
michelle.brown@ung.edu
BROWN, Michelle .... 435-283-7127. 498 A
michelle.brown@snow.edu
BROWN, Mike .... 574-936-8898. 163 K
mike.brown@ancilla.edu
BROWN, Mike .... 903-463-8772. 472 M
mbrown@grayson.edu
BROWN, Mikell .... 804-594-1509. 512 G
mbrown@jtcc.edu
BROWN, Monte .... 919-684-0317. 354 A
monte.brown@duke.edu
BROWN, Naima .... 352-395-5648. 113 C
naima.brown@sfcollege.edu
BROWN, Nancy, B .... 423-318-2709. 462 A
nancy.brown@ws.edu
BROWN, Nicci, C .... 704-233-8126. 370 G
brown@wingate.edu
BROWN, Nicole .... 708-802-7750. 145 D
nbrown@foxcolleg.edu
BROWN, Nicole, R .... 417-625-3137. 278 D
brown-n@mssu.edu
BROWN, O. Ted .... 270-809-6937. 198 B
obrown@murraystate.edu
BROWN, Oscar, W .... 409-772-3303. 493 C
owbrown@utmb.edu
BROWN, Pamela .... 718-260-5008. 319 B
pbrown@citytech.cuny.edu
BROWN, Pamela .... 843-574-6246. 447 E
pamela.brown@tridenttech.edu

BROWN, Pamela, S .... 217-228-5520. 140 H
pbrown@brcn.edu
BROWN, Patricia, R .... 716-839-8484. 322 E
pbrown@daemen.edu
BROWN, Patrick .... 253-680-7014. 516 L
pbrown@bates.ctc.edu
BROWN, Patty .... 423-697-2437. 460 C
BROWN, Paul .... 254-659-7860. 473 A
pbrown@hillcollege.edu
BROWN, Paul, M .... 404-880-8790. 122 J
pbrown@cau.edu
BROWN, Paul, P .... 856-225-6005. 306 C
peyton@camden.rutgers.edu
BROWN, Paul, R .... 732-571-3402. 303 C
president@monmouth.edu
BROWN, Paul, R .... 740-588-1200. 394 C
pbrown@zanestate.edu
BROWN, Paula .... 972-438-6932. 478 C
pbrown@parkercc.edu
BROWN, Perry .... 406-243-4689. 286 H
perry.brown@umontana.edu
BROWN, Peter, M .... 914-594-4560. 334 A
peter_brown@nymc.edu
BROWN, Philip, R .... 207-768-2708. 210 M
pbrown@nmcc.edu
BROWN, Phillip .... 219-989-2240. 171 N
brown@purduecal.edu
BROWN, Phillip, M .... 618-650-3415. 159 H
phbrown@siue.edu
BROWN, Quincy, D .... 706-880-8297. 128 A
qbrown@lagrange.edu
BROWN, R. McKenna ..... 804-828-8471. 511 F
mbrown@vcu.edu
BROWN, Rachel .... 215-204-7981. 433 K
rachel.brown@temple.edu
BROWN, Rachel, M .... 615-868-6503. 457 D
rachel.brown@mtsa.edu
BROWN, Rae Linda .... 310-338-5217... 53 E
raelinda.brown@lmu.edu
BROWN, Randy .... 408-848-4852... 45 F
rbrown@gavilan.edu
BROWN, Ray .... 573-592-5238. 285 B
ray.brown@westminster-mo.edu
BROWN, Raymond, A ..... 610-527-0200. 432 B
bbrown@rosemont.edu
BROWN, Raymond, A ..... 817-257-7490. 484 I
r.brown@tcu.edu
BROWN, Rebecca .... 707-826-4142... 35 C
rebecca.brown@humboldt.edu
BROWN, Rebecca .... 214-333-5426. 470 D
rebeccab@dbu.edu
BROWN, Rebekkah, L ..... 484-664-3247. 424 H
rbrown@muhlenberg.edu
BROWN, Renee, D .... 419-559-2367. 389 I
rbrown@terra.edu
BROWN, Reynolda .... 386-481-2602... 99 C
brownr@cookman.edu
BROWN, Rhodella .... 386-506-3969. 101 G
brownr@DaytonaState.edu
BROWN, Rhonda .... 708-534-4044. 145 F
rbrown11@govst.edu
BROWN, Rhonda, L .... 215-204-7303. 433 K
rhonda.brown@temple.edu
BROWN, Ricardo .... 601-979-8836. 267 E
ricardo.a.brown@jsums.edu
BROWN, Richard .... 856-415-2205. 302 C
rbrown@gccnj.edu
BROWN, Richard .... 423-425-4393. 463 D
richard-brown@utc.edu
BROWN, Richard, B .... 801-581-6912. 496 Q
brown@coe.utah.edu
BROWN, Richard, W ...... 530-226-4728... 66 D
rbrown@simpsonu.edu
BROWN, Ricky .... 252-493-7259. 362 G
rbrown@email.pittcc.edu
BROWN, Robert .... 410-386-8224. 214 A
rbrown@carrollcc.edu
BROWN, Robert .... 312-553-6029. 141 N
rbrown@ccc.edu
BROWN, Robert .... 478-289-2068. 124 C
bbrown@ega.edu
BROWN, Robert, A .... 617-353-2200. 224 D
rabrown@bu.edu
BROWN, Robert, C .... 479-968-0237... 20 E
rcbrown@atu.edu
BROWN, Robert, C .... 216-368-4306. 375 J
robert.c.brown@case.edu
BROWN, Robert, K .... 918-781-7218. 394 D
brownr@bacone.edu
BROWN, Robert, L .... 803-981-7375. 449 J
rbrown@yorktech.edu
BROWN, Robert, M .... 251-460-6151..... 9 E
rbrown@southalabama.edu
BROWN, Robin .... 219-785-5508. 172 A
rbrown@pnc.edu
BROWN, Robin, C .... 970-491-2682... 80 I
robin.brown@colostate.edu
BROWN, Rodney, J .... 801-422-3963. 495 D
rod_brown@byu.edu
BROWN, Roger .... 901-435-1535. 455 M
roger_brown@loc.edu
BROWN, Roger, H .... 617-266-1400. 223 D
BROWN, Ron .... 254-295-4517. 490 B
rbrown@umhb.edu
BROWN, Ronald .... 334-229-7680..... 1 D
rbrown@alasu.edu
BROWN, Ronald, C .... 512-245-2205. 487 C
rb04@txstate.edu
BROWN, Ronald, H .... 919-516-4859. 366 C
rhbrown@st-aug.edu
BROWN, Rosann .... 814-641-3133. 419 H
brownr@juniata.edu
BROWN, Russ .... 772-462-6004. 106 P
rbrown@irsc.edu
BROWN, Ryan .... 541-880-2225. 403 H
brownr@klamathcc.edu
BROWN, Sabrina .... 434-395-2021. 506 J
browncs2@longwood.edu
BROWN, Sandra .... 858-534-3526... 71 F
BROWN, Sandra .... 605-668-1555. 450 F
sbrown@mtmc.edu
BROWN, Shanita .... 615-327-6223. 456 E
sbrown@mmc.edu
BROWN, Shannon .... 828-726-2288. 358 E
sbrown@cccti.edu
BROWN, Sharon, A .... 610-625-7847. 424 E
mesab01@moravian.edu
BROWN, Shelley .... 330-490-7134. 392 H
sbrown@walsh.edu
BROWN, Shirley, F .... 828-652-0676. 362 A
shirleyb@mcdowelltech.edu
BROWN, Shondae .... 256-395-2211..... 7 C
sbrown@suscc.edu
BROWN, Simon .... 215-751-8039. 413 I
sbrown@ccp.edu
BROWN, Sloane .... 918-540-6393. 396 G
scbrown@neo.edu
BROWN, Stacy .... 305-534-7050. 117 E
stacyb@talmudicu.edu
BROWN, Stan .... 229-317-6721. 124 A
stan.brown@darton.edu
BROWN, Stephan .... 352-588-8331. 112 D
stephan.brown@saintleo.edu
BROWN, Stephanie .... 954-262-7456. 109 K
browstep@nova.edu
BROWN, Stephanie .... 252-451-8257. 362 D
sbrown@nashcc.edu
BROWN, Stephanie .... 417-447-2653. 279 K
browns@otc.edu
BROWN, Stephen, E .... 248-204-2300. 245 I
sbrown@ltu.edu
BROWN, Stephen, G ...... 530-221-4275... 65 F
sbrown@shasta.edu
BROWN, Steve .... 570-586-2400. 410 D
sbrown@bbc.edu
BROWN, Steve .... 724-805-2534. 432 G
steve.brown@email.stvincent.edu
BROWN, Steve, D .... 423-439-4841. 459 C
browsd02@etsu.edu
BROWN, Steven .... 802-287-8912. 499 D
browns@greenmtn.edu
BROWN, Steven, F .... 601-484-0221. 268 D
sb1812@meridian.msstate.edu
BROWN, Steven, L .... 304-710-3141. 528 C
brown175@mctc.edu
BROWN, Sue, C .... 309-655-2206. 158 C
sue.c.brown@osfhealthcare.org
BROWN, Susan .... 802-860-2754. 499 A
brown@champlain.edu
BROWN, Susan, M .... 859-233-8225. 199 I
subrown@transy.edu
BROWN, Susie, A .... 918-595-7884. 400 E
susie.brown@tulsacc.edu
BROWN, Sylvia .... 252-744-6422. 367 B
brownsy@ccu.edu
BROWN, T. Rhett .... 704-233-8022. 370 G
rhbrown@wingate.edu
BROWN, Tamara, L .... 936-261-5205. 482 F
tlbrown@pvamu.edu
BROWN, Tammy .... 334-386-7264..... 3 H
tcbrown@faulkner.edu
BROWN, Tanasha .... 225-216-8103. 202 H
brownt@mybrcc.edu
BROWN, Tavonda .... 870-743-3000... 22 B
tbrown@northark.edu
BROWN, Ted .... 516-299-2229. 329 D
ted.brown@liu.edu
BROWN, Ted, R .... 931-363-9802. 456 C
tbrown@martinmethodist.edu
BROWN, Teresa .... 404-225-4700. 121 B
tbrown@atlantatech.edu
BROWN, Teresa .... 615-230-3377. 461 G
teresa.brown@volstate.edu
BROWN, Teresa, L .... 401-456-8240. 439 F
tlbrown@ric.edu
BROWN, Terrence .... 901-751-8453. 457 B
tbrown@mabts.edu
BROWN, Terry .... 716-673-3335. 342 A
terry.brown@fredonia.edu
BROWN, Terry .... 304-327-4191. 529 D
tbrown@bluefieldstate.edu
BROWN, Therese .... 303-404-5535... 81 N
therese.brown@frontrange.edu
BROWN, Thomas .... 702-651-7543. 294 E
thomas.brown@csn.edu
BROWN, Thomas .... 540-231-3787. 515 C
tbrown@vt.edu
BROWN, Thomas, W .... 507-933-7005. 255 I
brownie@gustavus.edu
BROWN, Tim .... 843-574-6424. 447 E
tim.brown@tridenttech.edu
BROWN, Timothy .... 616-392-8555. 252 J
tim.brown@westernsem.edu
BROWN, SJ, Timothy ..... 410-617-5524. 216 A
tbrown@loyola.edu
BROWN, Trachanda .... 215-242-7989. 413 A
brownt@chc.edu
BROWN, Venessa .... 618-650-5867. 159 H
vbrown@siue.edu
BROWN, Vicki, R .... 540-985-9784. 506 G
vrbrown@jchs.edu
BROWN, Victor .... 478-825-6211. 124 H
BROWN, Victor .... 937-395-5604. 382 K
victor.brown@kc.edu
BROWN, Walter, E .... 412-648-3185. 435 C
walter.brown@ia.pitt.edu
BROWN, Warren .... 206-934-5481. 522 J
warren.brown@seattlecolleges.edu
BROWN, Wes, S .... 912-260-4430. 131 F
wes.brown@sgsc.edu
BROWN, Wilfred .... 918-687-3299. 394 D
brownw@bacone.edu
BROWN, Wilfred, E .... 805-893-4155... 72 B
wbrown@housing.ucsb.edu
BROWN, William .... 571-334-2600... 28 M
wbrown@argosy.edu
BROWN, William .... 520-494-5340... 12 P
william.brown@centralaz.edu
BROWN, William, E .... 937-766-7900. 375 K
bbrown@cedarville.edu
BROWN, William, H .... 704-894-2143. 353 J
wibrown@davidson.edu
BROWN, William, J .... 717-867-6180. 421 H
wbrown@lvc.edu
BROWN, William (Bill) ... 859-846-5358. 197 I
bbrown@midway.edu
BROWN, Winston, D .... 504-520-7577. 209 D
wbrown@xula.edu
BROWN, Yvette .... 305-899-3600... 98 O
ybrown@barry.edu
BROWN, Zachary .... 607-431-4547. 325 F
brownz@hartwick.edu
BROWN, Zachary, M .... 309-692-4092. 152 J
zbrown@midstate.edu
BROWN, Zaundra .... 404-297-9522. 126 A
brownz@gptc.edu
BROWN-BULLOCH,
Lynn .... 843-661-8141. 443 G
lynn.brown-bulloch@fdtc.edu
BROWN-CAYRUTH,
Desmona .... 704-216-6010. 356 D
dbrown-cayruth@livingstone.edu
BROWN-CORNELIUS,
Denise .... 502-272-8270. 192 E
dbrowncornelius@bellarmine.edu
BROWN GORDAN,
Loria .... 601-979-2107. 267 E
loria.c.brown@jsums.edu
BROWN-GUILLORY,
Elizabeth .... 713-313-1180. 485 F
brown_guillorye@tsu.edu
BROWN-HART, Denise ... 910-672-1856. 367 D
dbrownhart@uncfsu.edu
BROWN MARSDEN,
Margaret .... 972-721-5245. 488 F
mebrown@udallas.edu
BROWN MORRIS, Kelly . 404-756-8951. 129 E
kbrownmorris@msm.edu
BROWN-NEVERS,
Michelle, H .... 215-898-7233. 435 B
mbnevers@upenn.edu
BROWN-SOW, Lynette ... 215-751-8859. 413 I
lbrown@ccp.edu
BROWN-WADE, Glenda . 205-929-1404..... 5 G
plac@mail.miles.edu
BROWN-WELTY, Sharon 559-278-2448... 33 D
sharonb@csufresno.edu
BROWN WRIGHT,
Lynda .... 404-413-2574. 126 E
lwright39@gsu.edu
BROWNE, Brian .... 718-990-2762. 339 A
browneb@stjohns.edu
BROWNE, Doug .... 620-417-1201. 190 F
doug.browne@sccc.edu
BROWNE, Joan, M .... 202-806-7513... 95 G
jmbrowne@howard.edu
BROWNE, Kevin .... 312-413-3471. 161 D
kbrowne@uic.edu
BROWNE, Kevin, M .... 209-228-4567... 71 D
KBrowne@UCMerced.edu
BROWNE, Nancy, E .... 305-595-9500... 97 G
nancy@amcollege.edu
BROWNE, Pamela .... 386-481-2858... 99 C
brownep@cookman.edu
BROWNE, Patrick .... 503-256-3180. 408 G
pbrowne@uws.edu
BROWNE, Richard, M ...... 305-595-9500... 97 G
richard@amcollege.edu
BROWNE, Timm .... 562-907-4211... 76 I
tbrowne@whittier.edu
BROWNELL, Claire .... 303-871-4876... 86 B
cbrownel@du.edu
BROWNELL, Jennifer ...... 336-506-4140. 357 M
jennifer.brownell@alamancecc.edu
BROWNELL, Winifred, E . 401-874-4101. 440 D
winnie@uri.edu
BROWNER, Stephanie ..... 212-229-5100. 332 E
browners@newschool.edu
BROWNIE, Ronald .... 605-626-2568. 451 I
ronald.brownie@northern.edu
BROWNING, David, A ...... 214-860-2015. 470 J
dbrowning@dcccd.edu
BROWNING, Debbie .... 740-245-7209. 392 A
browning@rio.edu
BROWNING, Douglas, D 301-846-2442. 214 H
dbrowning@frederick.edu
BROWNING, Eric .... 740-392-6868. 384 K
eric.browning@mvnu.edu
BROWNING, Gari .... 510-659-6200... 57 A
gbrowning@ohlone.edu
BROWNING, Julie .... 713-348-2575. 479 A
jmb@rice.edu
BROWNING, Katherine ... 301-387-3097. 214 I
katherine.browning@garrettcollege.edu
BROWNING, Kimbra .... 412-291-6220. 410 B
kbrowning@aii.edu
BROWNING, Marguerite . 909-621-8125... 46 H
maggie_browning@hmc.edu
BROWNING, Marian .... 877-314-2380... 57 G
mbrowning@pacificoaks.edu
BROWNING, Mark .... 208-769-3316. 138 I
mark_browning@nic.edu
BROWNING, Midge .... 618-374-5776. 156 B
midge.browning@principia.edu
BROWNING, Roger .... 618-393-2982. 146 H
browningr@iecc.edu
BROWNING, Skye .... 620-229-6223. 190 G
skye.browning@sckans.edu
BROWNING, Steve .... 870-235-4102... 23 F
dsbrowning@saumag.edu
BROWNLEE, David, W ..... 610-558-5628. 424 I
dbrownle@neumann.edu
BROWNLEE, L. Lang .... 317-788-3382. 173 I
lbrownlee@uindy.edu
BROWNLEE, Mordecai ..... 979-830-4282. 467 I
mordecai.brownlee@blinn.edu
BROWNLEE, Reb .... 814-262-3842. 427 C
rbrownlee@pennhighlands.edu
BROWNLEE, Sibyl .... 508-929-8077. 230 G
sbrownlee@worcester.edu
BROWNSBERGER,
William .... 660-944-2914. 272 H
wbrownsberger@conception.edu
BROXSON, Thomas .... 253-840-8338. 522 C
tbroxson@pierce.ctc.edu
BROYLES, Bill .... 662-325-7532. 268 D
bill.broyles@msstate.edu
BROYLES, Jennifer .... 732-445-6127. 306 A
jbroyles@echo.rutgers.edu
BROYLES, Jennifer .... 848-932-0142. 306 B
jbroyles@echo.rutgers.edu
BROYLES, Ken .... 423-461-8734. 457 H
kbroyles@milligan.edu
BROYLES, Stephen .... 940-668-7731. 477 I
sbroyles@nctc.edu
BROZ, Roger .... 612-659-6805. 259 D
roger.broz@minneapolis.edu
BROZA, Dave .... 651-638-6459. 253 K
d-broza@bethel.edu
BRUBACHER, Don .... 517-607-3130. 243 I
don.brubacher@hillsdale.edu
BRUBAKER, Andy .... 229-732-5935. 120 D
andybrubaker@andrewcollege.edu
BRUBAKER, Beryl, H ...... 540-432-4170. 504 D
brubakeb@emu.edu
BRUBAKER, Clifford, E ... 412-383-6560. 435 C
cliffb@pitt.edu
BRUBAKER, David .... 585-567-9484. 326 F
david.brubaker@houghton.edu
BRUBAKER, Donald, C ... 818-779-8069... 50 A
dbrubaker@kingsuniversity.edu
BRUBAKER, Glenn, R ..... 607-587-4750. 345 D
brubakgr@alfredstate.edu
BRUBAKER, Jackie .... 870-733-6741... 21 I
jbrubaker@midsouthcc.edu
BRUBAKER, Joel, A .... 724-847-6503. 417 A
jabrubak@geneva.edu
BRUBAKER, Karl .... 620-327-8216. 187 D
karlb@hesston.edu
BRUBAKER, Kevin .... 503-375-7030. 403 A
kbrubaker@corban.edu
BRUBAKER, Linda .... 708-216-3960. 151 H
lbrubaker@lumc.edu

BRUBAKER, Sarah .... 671-734-1812. 546 D
sbrubaker@piu.edu
BRUCE, Aaron, I .... 619-594-5201... 35 D
abruce@mail.sdsu.edu
BRUCE, Alex, M .... 931-598-1919. 458 H
ambruce@sewanee.edu
BRUCE, Ben .... 334-386-7257..... 3 H
bbruce@faulkner.edu
BRUCE, Charles, W .... 405-744-7440. 397 H
charles.bruce@okstate.edu
BRUCE, Debra .... 509-542-4604. 518 C
dbruce@columbiabasin.edu
BRUCE, Gheric .... 870-733-6722... 21 I
gebruce@midsouthcc.edu
BRUCE, Gonzalo .... 620-341-5374. 186 D
gbruce@emporia.edu
BRUCE, Harry .... 206-616-0985. 524 G
harryb@uw.edu
BRUCE, J. Michael .... 812-866-7039. 166 C
bruce@hanover.edu
BRUCE, Jerry .... 936-294-1101. 487 A
psy_ajb@shsu.edu
BRUCE, Jimmie .... 210-486-4905. 464 J
jbruce10@alamo.edu
BRUCE, Kathy .... 217-351-2280. 155 J
kbruce@parkland.edu
BRUCE, Lisa .... 619-961-4209... 69 I
lbruce@tjsl.edu
BRUCE, Lori .... 662-325-7400. 268 D
lmb102@msstate.edu
BRUCE, Motice .... 601-977-4470. 270 A
mbruce@tougaloo.edu
BRUCE, Patricia, S .... 601-974-1127. 267 I
brucesp@millsaps.edu
BRUCE, Philip .... 912-478-5197. 126 C
pbruce@georgiasouthern.edu
BRUCE, Rob .... 919-962-2646. 368 D
rob_bruce@unc.edu
BRUCE, Stanyell .... 410-455-2632. 219 D
bruce@umbc.edu
BRUCE, Stephen .... 575-624-7127. 309 I
stephen.watters@roswell.enmu.edu
BRUCE, Terry .... 619-393-2982. 146 H
brucet@iecc.edu
BRUCE, Thomas, W .... 607-255-9929. 322 A
twb22@cornell.edu
BRUCE, Tom, S .... 765-641-4232. 163 L
tsbruce@anderson.edu
BRUCE, Will .... 805-922-6966... 26 K
wbruce@hancockcollege.edu
BRUCE, William, P .... 615-327-3927. 455 F
pbruce@guptoncollege.edu
BRUCE-SANFORD, Gail .. 303-556-6433... 83 D
brucesan@msudenver.edu
BRUCKER, Denise .... 518-743-2329. 345 E
bruckerd@sunyacc.edu
BRUCKI, Mark, J .... 248-204-2310. 245 I
mbrucki@ltu.edu
BRUCKNER, Michael, S . 484-664-3230. 424 H
bruckner@muhlenberg.edu
BRUDER, Edward, C .... 717-815-1314. 438 D
ebruder@ycp.edu
BRUDNOK, Celine, R ..... 724-805-2720. 432 G
celine.brudnok@email.stvincent.edu
BRUDVIG, James .... 845-758-7429. 314 D
brudvig@bard.edu
BRUECK, Joshua .... 217-641-4320. 148 M
jbrueck@jwcc.edu
BRUECKEN, John .... 515-271-1471. 177 H
john.bruecken@dmu.edu
BRUEGGEMANN, Chuck 618-537-6873. 152 G
cebrueggemann@mckendree.edu
BRUEGGEMEIER,
Robert, W .... 614-292-5711. 386 E
brueggemeier.1@osu.edu
BRUEGMAN, Holly .... 307-778-1117. 543 D
hbruegma@lccc.wy.edu
BRUEHL, Allen, A .... 508-767-7311. 222 C
abruehl@assumption.edu
BRUEN, Christina, M ...... 508-910-6633. 229 A
cbruen@umassd.edu
BRUENGINSEN, Gail .... 585-266-0430. 324 A
gbrueningsen@cci.edu
BRUESS, Brian .... 651-690-6778. 263 O
bjbruess@stkate.edu
BRUGAL-MENA, Yocasta 787-743-3038. 552 E
ybrugal@sanjuanbautista.edu
BRUGGEMAN, Bob .... 903-223-3153. 484 C
bob.bruggeman@tamut.edu
BRUGGEMAN, John, H .. 513-487-3269. 325 G
jbruggeman@huc.edu
BRUGGER, Janet .... 877-442-0505... 86 F
janet.brugger@rockies.edu
BRUGH, Larry .... 814-262-3849. 427 C
lbrugh@pennhighlands.edu
BRUGH, Suzanne .... 814-262-6463. 427 C
sbrugh@pennhighlands.edu
BRUGMAN, Donna, M ... 617-984-1776. 235 I
dbrugman@quincycollege.edu
BRUHN, Tobias .... 215-968-8223. 411 B
bruhnt@bucks.edu
BRUKARDT, Mary Jane .. 715-836-2320. 536 E
brukarmj@uwec.edu
BRULE, Lise, M .... 203-392-5722... 88 A
brulel1@southernct.edu
BRUM, Joseph, P .... 401-865-2416. 439 E
joebrum@providence.edu
BRUMAGIN, Ruth .... 570-288-8400. 416 H
ruthb@marcogrp.com
BRUMBACH, Alicia .... 717-815-1309. 438 D
brumbach@ycp.edu
BRUMELOW, Harvey .... 404-627-2681. 121 H
harvey.brumelow@beulah.org
BRUMFIEL, Byron .... 618-395-3011. 146 H
brumfielb@iecc.edu
BRUMFIELD, Adele .... 608-262-0464. 536 D
abrumfield@admissions.wisc.edu
BRUMFIELD, Rick .... 253-833-9111. 520 C
rbrumfield@greenriver.edu
BRUMFIELD,
Wendell, W .... 318-342-5215. 208 E
wbrumfie@ulm.edu
BRUMITT, Jane .... 312-629-6184. 158 L
jbrumitt@saic.edu
BRUMLEY, Larry, D .... 478-301-5700. 128 H
brumley_ld@mercer.edu
BRUMMEL, Ann .... 218-935-0417. 265 E
ann.brummel@wetcc.edu
BRUMMEL, Joe .... 641-628-5232. 176 E
brummelj@central.edu
BRUMMELS, Lin .... 402-375-7321. 291 F
librumm1@wsc.edu
BRUMMER,
Edmund (Bert), E .... 757-221-1218. 503 N
eabrum@wm.edu
BRUMMER, James, M .... 651-962-6595. 265 C
jbrummer@stthomas.edu
BRUMMETT, Ronald, L ... 303-273-3377... 80 E
rbrummet@mines.edu
BRUMMETT, Ronald, L ... 303-273-3297... 80 E
rbrummet@mines.edu
BRUMMETT, Ross .... 865-471-3235. 453 F
rbrummett@cn.edu
BRUN, James .... 859-371-9393. 192 D
jbrun@beckfield.edu
BRUNDAGE, Isaac .... 575-538-6339. 312 N
brundagei@wnmu.edu
BRUNDAGE, Ken .... 814-871-7551. 416 K
brundage001@gannon.edu
BRUNDAGE, Tracy, L ..... 570-326-3761. 427 B
tbrundag@pct.edu
BRUNDO-SHARRAR,
Tricia, A .... 402-280-3058. 289 D
sharrar@creighton.edu
BRUNDY, Curtis .... 319-352-8500. 183 E
curtis.brundy@wartburg.edu
BRUNE, Carolyn .... 847-574-5154. 150 C
cbrune@lfgsm.edu
BRUNEAU, Patrice .... 803-323-2266. 449 G
bruneaup@winthrop.edu
BRUNELLI, Leslie, G ...... 803-777-7478. 447 G
lesliebrunelli@sc.edu
BRUNEN, Meredith .... 479-619-4176... 22 C
mbrunen@nwacc.edu
BRUNER, Darl, L .... 208-467-8843. 139 A
dlbruner@nnu.edu
BRUNER, Greg .... 815-939-5249. 155 H
gbruner@olivet.edu
BRUNER, Jeremy .... 501-450-3183... 25 H
BRUNER, Joe, W .... 859-858-3511. 192 B
joe.bruner@asbury.edu
BRUNER, Michael .... 651-779-3288. 258 C
mike.bruner@century.edu
BRUNER, Robert, F .... 434-924-7481. 511 B
rfb9k@virginia.edu
BRUNET EAGAN,
Kathleen .... 973-328-5052. 300 G
keagan@ccm.edu
BRUNET-KOCH,
Cameron .... 231-348-6601. 247 H
ckoch@ncmich.edu
BRUNGARDT, Cherie ..... 970-521-6787... 83 L
cherie.brungardt@njc.edu
BRUNGARDT, Heather .... 970-521-6623... 83 L
heather.brungardt@njc.edu
BRUNING, Merribeth ...... 870-245-5154... 22 D
bruningm@obu.edu
BRUNING, Monica .... 218-726-7171. 264 D
mbruning@d.umn.edu
BRUNING, Steve .... 614-236-6528. 375 H
sbruning@capital.edu
BRUNKOW, Alan .... 402-761-8259. 292 C
abrunkow@southeast.edu
BRUNNEMER, David ...... 360-650-7732. 525 C
david.brunnemer@wwu.edu
BRUNNER, JR., Dan ...... 419-473-2700. 378 I
djbrunner@daviscollege.edu
BRUNNER, David .... 513-244-8485. 376 J
David.Brunner@ccuniversity.edu
BRUNNER, Diane .... 419-473-2700. 378 I
dbrunner@daviscollege.edu
BRUNNER, Jon, L .... 239-590-7950. 115 A
jbrunner@fgcu.edu
BRUNNER, Karen, L .... 865-882-4606. 461 E
brunnerkl@roanestate.edu
BRUNNER, Ludwig .... 716-375-7666. 338 E
lbrunner@sbu.edu
BRUNNER, Mark .... 573-876-2381. 282 H
mbrunner@stephens.edu
BRUNNER, Mary, K .... 810-989-5512. 249 H
mbrunner@sc4.edu
BRUNNER, Matthew, S ... 540-851-5271. 508 C
msbrunner@radford.edu
BRUNNER, Penelope, W 843-953-4994. 443 A
brunnerpw@cofc.edu
BRUNNER, Thomas .... 908-852-1400. 300 D
brunnert@centenarycollege.edu
BRUNNER, Tim .... 419-473-2700. 378 I
tbrunner@daviscollege.edu
BRUNO, Bonnie .... 336-278-6603. 354 B
bbruno2@elon.edu
BRUNO, Gene .... 800-290-4226. 454 M
gbruno@hchs.edu
BRUNO, Joanne, Z .... 201-200-3003. 303 F
jbruno@njcu.edu
BRUNO, Joseph, W .... 740-376-4701. 383 E
joseph.bruno@marietta.edu
BRUNO, Kimberly .... 504-568-4820. 205 C
kbruno@lsuhsc.edu
BRUNO, Laura .... 718-281-5212. 319 D
lbruno@qcc.cuny.edu
BRUNO, Mary .... 386-506-3618. 101 G
brunom@DaytonaState.edu
BRUNO, Michael, S .... 201-216-5338. 307 E
mbruno@stevens.edu
BRUNO, Nick, J .... 318-342-1000. 208 E
bruno@ulm.edu
BRUNO, Tania .... 212-280-1404. 349 A
tbruno@uts.columbia.edu
BRUNOLD, Timothy .... 213-740-6753... 74 A
admdean@usc.edu
BRUNS, Clara .... 802-322-1603. 499 C
clara.bruns@goddard.edu
BRUNS, Dale .... 570-408-4600. 437 F
dale.bruns@wilkes.edu
BRUNS, Lisa .... 631-420-2245. 346 B
lisa.bruns@farmingdale.edu
BRUNS, Sandy .... 712-324-5061. 181 G
sandy@nwicc.edu
BRUNSON, Claude .... 601-984-1012. 270 C
cbrunson@umc.edu
BRUNSON, Mary Nelle ... 936-468-2707. 482 A
mbrunson@sfasu.edu
BRUNSON, Mary Nelle ... 936-468-2807. 482 A
mbrunson@sfasu.edu
BRUNSON, Teesa .... 803-780-1194. 449 E
tbrunson@voorhees.edu
BRUNSTING, Marlys .... 715-232-1184. 538 B
brunstingm@uwstout.edu
BRUNT, Bonnie .... 509-533-3339. 518 F
bonnie.brunt@spokanefalls.edu
BRUNTMYER, Eric .... 214-333-5160. 470 D
eric@dbu.edu
BRUNTON, Elizabeth ...... 215-248-6301. 422 F
ebrunton@ltsp.edu
BRUNTON, Mark .... 702-579-3528. 294 B
mbrunton@kaplan.edu
BRUNTZ, Crystal .... 816-501-3600. 271 H
crystal.bruntz@avila.edu
BRUSATI, Gerianne .... 845-341-4060. 335 H
gerianne.brusati@sunyorange.edu
BRUSH, Diana .... 814-393-2323. 428 C
dbrush@clarion.edu
BRUSH, Richard, L .... 401-598-4621. 439 B
dbrush@jwu.edu
BRUSH, Thomas .... 410-617-2280. 216 A
tdbrush@loyola.edu
BRUSH, Tressa .... 912-201-8000. 131 H
tbrush@southuniversity.edu
BRUSHETT, Corey .... 203-773-8558... 87 G
cbrushett@albertus.edu
BRUSKI, Kathleen .... 989-358-7335. 239 C
bruskik@alpenacc.edu
BRUSS, Carl .... 908-709-7485. 308 B
bruss@ucc.edu
BRUSS, Dan, R .... 507-344-7315. 253 J
danbruss@blc.edu
BRUSSELL, Carlotta .... 859-336-5082. 198 J
cbrussell@sccky.edu
BRUSTEIN, William, I ..... 614-292-5881. 386 E
brustein.1@osu.edu
BRUSTKERN, Kari .... 406-447-5422. 285 G
kbrustkern@carroll.edu
BRUSZEWSKI, Roger .... 717-872-3043. 429 D
roger.bruszewski@millersville.edu
BRUTON, John, W .... 540-365-4332. 504 L
jbruton@ferrum.edu
BRUUN-HORRIGAN,
Christina .... 937-484-1320. 392 C
cbruunhorrigan@urbana.edu
BRUXVOORT, Debra .... 641-628-7671. 176 E
bruxvoortb@central.edu
BRUYN, Kimberly, A ...... 616-732-1165. 241 H
kbruyn@davenport.edu
BRUZGO, Serena .... 303-273-3296... 80 E
sbruzgo@mines.edu
BRVENIK, Andrea .... 843-746-5100... 96 F
BRY, Jay .... 978-665-3131. 229 E
jbry@fitchburgstate.edu
BRYAN, Alexander .... 937-395-8618. 382 K
alex.bryan@kc.edu
BRYAN, Angela .... 228-497-7870. 268 C
angela.bryan@mgccc.edu
BRYAN, Barbara, J .... 954-201-7931... 99 D
bbryan@broward.edu
BRYAN, Derek .... 336-917-5472. 366 D
derek.bryan@salem.edu
BRYAN, Doug .... 704-406-4398. 354 C
dbryan@gardner-webb.edu
BRYAN, G. William .... 214-887-5362. 471 F
bbryan@dts.edu
BRYAN, Jessica .... 603-271-6484. 296 C
jbryan@ccsnh.edu
BRYAN, John .... 413-545-2554. 228 F
johnbrayn@provost.umass.edu
BRYAN, John, S .... 678-466-4351. 123 A
johnbryan@clayton.edu
BRYAN, Joseph .... 561-803-2127. 110 B
joseph_bryan@pba.edu
BRYAN, Laura .... 410-837-6134. 221 A
lbryan@ubalt.edu
BRYAN, JR., Norman, B 864-833-8757. 446 D
nbbryan@presby.edu
BRYAN, Paul .... 215-893-5252. 414 B
paul.bryan@curtis.edu
BRYAN, Penelope .... 714-444-4141... 76 I
pbryan@law.whittier.edu
BRYAN, Robert .... 216-987-4684. 378 D
robert.bryan@tri-c.edu
BRYAN, Robert, G .... 865-539-7198. 461 D
jbryan@pstcc.edu
BRYAN, Sandy .... 520-417-4098... 12 R
bryans@cochise.edu
BRYAN, Sibley .... 706-453-0378. 120 J
sbryan@athenstech.edu
BRYAN, Susan .... 417-865-2815. 274 B
bryans@evangel.edu
BRYAN, Terry .... 832-252-4676. 468 L
terry.bryan@cbshouston.edu
BRYAN, Timothy, B .... 330-569-5288. 380 I
bryanta@hiram.edu
BRYAN, Traci .... 229-391-4985. 119 H
tbryan@abac.edu
BRYAN, W. Ross .... 504-247-1524. 207 C
wbryan2@tulane.edu
BRYAN, Wes .... 714-895-8101... 39 J
wbryan@gwc.cccd.edu
BRYAN, William .... 315-498-2989. 335 G
w.v.bryan@sunyocc.edu
BRYANT, America .... 650-433-3804... 58 B
a.bryant@paloaltou.edu
BRYANT, Angela .... 336-734-7618. 360 E
abryant@forsythtech.edu
BRYANT, Angela, V .... 229-928-1378. 126 D
angela.bryant@gsw.edu
BRYANT, Bruce, K .... 206-239-4500. 517 M
brucebryant@cityu.edu
BRYANT, Carlton, G .... 800-782-2422... 32 B
cbryant@mail.cnuas.edu
BRYANT, Cherie .... 207-741-5726. 211 A
cbryant@smccme.edu
BRYANT, Clint .... 706-737-1626. 126 B
cbryant1@gru.edu
BRYANT, Daniel, C .... 740-376-4718. 383 E
dan.bryant@marietta.edu
BRYANT, David, A .... 580-349-1302. 397 G
dbryant@opsu.edu
BRYANT, David, A .... 407-303-9305... 97 H
david.bryant@adu.edu
BRYANT, Felicia .... 856-227-7200. 300 B
fbryant@camdencc.edu
BRYANT, Fred .... 361-593-3922. 484 A
kffcb00@tamuk.edu
BRYANT, Gerald .... 417-447-7553. 279 K
bryantg@otc.edu
BRYANT, Holley .... 509-527-2772. 524 I
holley.bryant@wallawalla.edu
BRYANT, Jack .... 405-422-1256. 399 B
bryantj@redlandscc.edu
BRYANT, III, James, S .. 803-535-1330. 446 B
bryantj@octech.edu
BRYANT, Jay .... 602-978-7294... 18 A
jay.bryant@thunderbird.edu
BRYANT, Jocelyn .... 410-951-3922. 220 B
jbryant@coppin.edu
BRYANT, John .... 309-556-3449. 148 B
jbryant@iwu.edu
BRYANT, Joy, L .... 864-644-5385. 446 I
jbryant@swu.edu
BRYANT, Karen .... 618-842-3711. 146 I
bryantk@iecc.edu
BRYANT, Kimberly .... 215-895-1121. 435 H
k.bryant@usciences.edu

BRYANT, Kinney .... 405-425-5155. 397 D
kinney.bryant@oc.edu
BRYANT, Mark .... 661-722-6300... 28 F
mbryant6@avc.edu
BRYANT, Matthew .... 706-419-1651. 123 F
bryant@covenant.edu
BRYANT, Micki .... 714-564-6079... 60 G
bryant_micki@sac.edu
BRYANT, Morgan .... 601-925-3354. 268 A
mbryant@mc.edu
BRYANT, Pam .... 325-649-8401. 473 F
pbryant@hputx.edu
BRYANT, Paul .... 309-467-6377. 145 C
pbryant@eureka.edu
BRYANT, Paul .... 205-366-8987..... 7 E
pbryant@stillman.edu
BRYANT, Penny, J .... 314-367-8700. 281 C
penny.bryant@stlcop.edu
BRYANT, Randal, E .... 412-268-8821. 412 H
randy.bryant@cs.cmu.edu
BRYANT, Rhonda .... 229-903-3609. 119 J
rhonda.bryant@asurams.edu
BRYANT, Scott .... 903-923-2173. 471 J
sbryant@etbu.edu
BRYANT, Sharon .... 312-850-7136. 142 C
sbryant@ccc.edu
BRYANT, Sheila, M .... 931-221-7178. 459 B
bryantsm@apsu.edu
BRYANT, Stephanie .... 417-836-4408. 278 E
stephaniebryant@missouristate.edu
BRYANT, Stephanie .... 803-754-4100. 443 C
BRYANT, Theresa .... 757-822-1184. 514 C
tbryant@tcc.edu
BRYANT, Tim .... 513-244-4504. 377 G
tim_bryant@mail.msj.edu
BRYANT, Toni .... 830-792-7229. 480 F
tlbyrant@schreiner.edu
BRYANT, Vickie .... 817-461-8741. 466 D
vbryant@arlingtonbaptistcollege.edu
BRYANT, Wayne, H .... 318-670-9351. 207 A
wbryant@ssla.edu
BRYANT, William, C .... 208-524-3000. 138 D
bill.bryant@my.eitc.edu
BRYANT DAWSON,
David .... 401-341-2454. 440 C
david.bryant@salve.edu
BRYCE, Jeanne .... 928-428-8261... 13 J
jeanne.bryce@eac.edu
BRYCE, Mark .... 928-428-8231... 13 J
mark.bryce@eac.edu
BRYD, John .... 803-323-3374. 449 G
brydj@winthrop.edu
BRYDE, Beverly .... 610-902-8311. 411 E
beverly.reilly.bryde@cabrini.edu
BRYDEN, David, L .... 336-841-9101. 355 C
dbryden@highpoint.edu
BRYDGES, Bruce .... 315-267-2484. 344 C
brydgebc@potsdam.edu
BRYDON, Lucinda, C ...... 607-746-4603. 345 G
brydonlm@delhi.edu
BRYENTON, John .... 270-686-4615. 196 C
john.bryenton@kctcs.edu
BRYLINSKY, Jody .... 269-387-2314. 252 I
jody.brylinsky@wmich.edu
BRYNE, Kathryn .... 617-243-2176. 227 K
kbryne@lasell.edu
BRYNTESON, Susan .... 302-831-2231... 94 B
susanb@udel.edu
BRYS-WILSON, Jessica .. 252-985-5186. 365 D
jbrys-wilson@ncwc.edu
BRYSON, Allison .... 541-880-2288. 403 H
bryson@klamathcc.edu
BRYSON, Barbara .... 713-348-5151. 479 A
bwbryson@rice.edu
BRYSON, Ben .... 912-427-1928. 120 B
bbryson@altamahatech.edu
BRYSON, Cynthia .... 713-771-5336. 127 F
cbryson@ict-ils.edu
BRYSON, J. Richard .... 740-389-4636. 383 F
brysonr@mtc.edu
BRYSON, Lance .... 717-477-1451. 429 E
jlbrys@ship.edu
BRYSON, Suzanne .... 828-251-6128. 368 C
sbryson@unca.edu
BRYSON, Terri .... 256-890-4703..... 2 F
tbb@calhoun.edu
BRZEZINSKI, Karen .... 715-675-3331. 541 A
brzezinski@ntc.edu
BRZEZINSKI, Michael, A 765-494-9399. 171 M
mbrzezinski@purdue.edu
BRZORAD, John .... 828-328-7606. 356 B
john.brzorad@lr.edu
BRZOZOWSKI,
Samantha .... 615-383-4848. 464 D
sbrzozowski@watkins.edu
BUBAN, Jill .... 203-591-5601... 90 I
jbuban@post.edu
BUBB, Kevin .... 517-483-9764. 245 H
bubbk@lcc.edu
BUBLITZ, Josh .... 507-453-2735. 259 E
jbublitz@southeastmn.edu
BUBNOVA, Elena .... 775-673-8239. 294 H
ebubnova@tmcc.edu
BUCARO, S. Ted .... 937-229-4122. 391 C
sbucaro1@udayton.edu
BUCCILLI, Michael .... 203-285-2144... 88 E
mbuccilli@gwcc.commnet.edu
BUCELL, Michael .... 814-732-2252. 428 E
bucell@edinboro.edu
BUCHA, Edward, R .... 724-738-2183. 429 F
edward.bucha@sru.edu
BUCHANAN, Barbara ...... 903-785-7661. 478 B
bbuchanan@parisjc.edu
BUCHANAN, Deborah, B 731-426-7552. 455 J
dbuchanan@lanecollege.edu
BUCHANAN, Debra .... 601-979-2245. 267 E
debra.a.buchanan@jsums.edu
BUCHANAN, Harvey .... 850-644-2825. 115 C
buchanan@fsu.edu
BUCHANAN, Herbert .... 202-865-6660... 95 G
hbuchanan@huhosp.org
BUCHANAN, Janelle, M . 806-720-7476. 476 B
janelle.buchanan@lcu.edu
BUCHANAN, Kelly .... 619-201-8702... 62 B
kelly.buchanan@sdcc.edu
BUCHANAN, Kyrel, L ...... 256-765-4328..... 9 C
kbuchanan@una.edu
BUCHANAN, Linda, R .... 319-385-6284. 179 K
linda.buchanan@iwc.edu
BUCHANAN, Pam .... 251-442-2372..... 9 A
pbuchanan@umobile.edu
BUCHANAN, Pamela ...... 828-227-7640. 369 E
pbuchanan@wcu.edu
BUCHANAN, Rollie, O .... 516-876-4873. 343 D
buchananr@oldwestbury.edu
BUCHANAN, Ron .... 703-845-6222. 513 C
rbuchanan@nvcc.edu
BUCHANAN, Susan, M .. 509-527-5183. 525 E
buchansm@whitman.edu
BUCHANAN, Tenielle ..... 615-966-5264. 456 B
tenielle.buchanan@lipscomb.edu
BUCHANAN,
Timothy, M .... 724-938-5887. 428 A
buchanan@calu.edu
BUCHANAN, Tony .... 407-301-4928. 464 G
tony.buchanan@earthlink.net
BUCHANAN, Trey .... 512-313-3000. 469 L
trey.buchanan@concordia.edu
BUCHE, Nathan .... 620-665-3569. 187 F
buchen@hutchcc.edu
BUCHELI, Hernan .... 650-508-3512... 56 H
hbucheli@ndnu.edu
BUCHER, John, E .... 440-775-6727. 385 H
john.bucher@oberlin.edu
BUCHER, Karen .... 540-868-7132. 512 H
kbucher@lfcc.edu
BUCHER, Karen, H .... 540-868-7132. 512 H
kbucher@lfcc.edu
BUCHER, Oskar .... 541-684-7273. 405 C
oskar@nwcu.edu
BUCHHOLTZ, Gina .... 701-224-5702. 372 B
gina.buchholtz@bismarckstate.edu
BUCHHOLZ, Richard .... 405-422-6204. 399 B
richard.buchholz@redlandscc.edu
BUCHHOLZ, Robert .... 336-278-5500. 354 B
rbuchholz@elon.edu
BUCHHOLZ, Ron .... 262-472-1498. 538 D
buchholr@uww.edu
BUCHHOLZ, Stephen ...... 605-394-4034. 452 E
stephen.buchholz@wdt.edu
BUCHMAN, Ashley .... 870-358-8636... 20 B
ashley_buchman@asun.edu
BUCHMAN, Irene .... 212-217-4590. 324 C
irene_buchman@fitnyc.edu
BUCHMAN, Lorne, M ...... 626-396-2301... 28 P
lorne.buchman@artcenter.edu
BUCHOLC, Stanley .... 978-665-3215. 229 E
sbucholc@fitchburgstate.edu
BUCHWALD, Adam .... 503-768-7227. 403 K
buchwald@lclark.edu
BUCHWALD, Rosalinda .. 626-914-8897... 38 K
rbuchwald@citruscollege.edu
BUCHWALDER, Mary, P . 937-229-3131. 391 C
mbuchwalder1@udayton.edu
BUCK, A. Scott .... 252-328-6910. 367 B
bucka@ecu.edu
BUCK, Charles .... 208-292-1737. 139 D
buck@uidaho.edu
BUCK, James, E .... 937-393-3431. 389 B
jbuck@sscc.edu
BUCK, John .... 407-447-7300. 105 I
jbuck@ftccollege.edu
BUCK, John .... 314-968-7030. 284 N
buckjh@webster.edu
BUCK, Katherine .... 973-290-4204. 300 F
kbuck@cse.edu
BUCK, Kavin .... 503-821-8942. 406 F
kbuck@pnca.edu
BUCK, Kevan, C .... 918-631-3245. 401 F
kevan-buck@utulsa.edu
BUCK, Marilyn, M .... 765-285-3716. 164 B
mbuck@bsu.edu
BUCK, Mark .... 630-889-7570. 144 A
mbuck@devry.edu
BUCK, Ryan .... 718-951-5000. 317 C
ryanbuck@brooklyn.cuny.edu
BUCK, Sylvia, T .... 812-488-2724. 173 H
sb79@evansville.edu
BUCK, Yolanda .... 804-524-5297. 515 D
ybuck@vsu.edu
BUCK ELK, Tara .... 701-483-2370. 371 D
Tara.Buckelk@dickinsonstate.edu
BUCKALEW, Leslie .... 209-588-5115... 77 I
buckalewl@yosemite.edu
BUCKALEW, Thomas, D . 205-652-3581..... 9 F
db@uwa.edu
BUCKHAULTS, Tex .... 806-874-3571. 468 J
tex.buckhaults@clarendoncollege.edu
BUCKHAULTS, Tresea, L 318-342-5240. 208 E
buckhaults@ulm.edu
BUCKI, SJ, John, P .... 315-445-4110. 328 F
buckijp@lemoyne.edu
BUCKINGHAM, David, E 757-455-3273. 515 H
debuckingham@vwc.edu
BUCKINGHAM, John .... 319-656-2447. 182 D
BUCKINGHAM, Stacy ..... 618-985-3741. 148 J
stacybuckingham@jalc.edu
BUCKIUS, Richard, O .... 765-494-6209. 171 M
rbuckius@purdue.edu
BUCKLA, Robert, J .... 414-410-4201. 532 B
rbuckla@stritch.edu
BUCKLAND, Stephen ...... 513-721-7944. 380 D
sbuckland@gbs.edu
BUCKLE, Eileen .... 732-255-0400. 304 A
ebuckle@ocean.edu
BUCKLES, Beverly, J ...... 909-558-4528... 51 C
bbuckles@llu.edu
BUCKLES, Dale .... 270-706-8431. 195 A
dale.buckles@kctcs.edu
BUCKLES, Gregory, B ..... 802-443-5415. 499 H
deanofadmissions@middlebury.edu
BUCKLEW, Andrea, J ...... 304-457-6438. 526 A
bucklewaj@ab.edu
BUCKLEW, Kathy .... 863-297-1016. 110 H
kbucklew@polk.edu
BUCKLEY, Alison .... 302-259-6086... 93 E
abuckley@dtcc.edu
BUCKLEY, Alison .... 443-518-4133. 215 E
abuckley@howardcc.edu
BUCKLEY, Chris .... 910-893-1208. 352 K
buckley@campbell.edu
BUCKLEY, Cindy .... 719-502-3100... 84 A
cindy.buckley@ppcc.edu
BUCKLEY, Cynthia, S ..... 405-466-3201. 395 N
csbuckley@langston.edu
BUCKLEY, Debi .... 479-619-4217... 22 C
dbuckley@nwacc.edu
BUCKLEY, Emily .... 913-621-8731. 186 C
ebuckley@donnelly.edu
BUCKLEY, Gerard .... 585-475-6317. 337 L
gbuckley@ntid.rit.edu
BUCKLEY, Gregory, A ..... 717-867-6213. 421 H
buckley@lvc.edu
BUCKLEY, Irene .... 914-674-7308. 330 J
ibuckley@mercy.edu
BUCKLEY, Jeanne .... 215-572-4019. 409 H
buckleyj@arcadia.edu
BUCKLEY, Jennifer .... 630-844-6155. 140 A
jbuckley@aurora.edu
BUCKLEY, Jerry .... 619-388-7350... 62 F
jbuckley@sdccd.edu
BUCKLEY, John, M .... 302-857-1200... 93 G
jbuckley@dtcc.edu
BUCKLEY, John, W .... 718-817-4000. 324 G
buckley@fordham.edu
BUCKLEY, Lawrence .... 650-306-3238... 64 B
buckleyl@smccd.edu
BUCKLEY, Linda .... 415-338-3376... 35 E
lbuckley@sfsu.edu
BUCKLEY, Marcus .... 518-454-5216. 321 A
buckleym@strose.edu
BUCKLEY, Mary .... 314-966-3000. 276 I
maryb@metrobusinesscollege.edu
BUCKLEY, Neil .... 617-731-7109. 235 H
nbuckley@pmc.edu
BUCKLEY, Noah .... 541-737-4411. 406 A
osuadmit@oregonstate.edu
BUCKLEY, Patricia .... 518-458-5444. 321 A
buckleyp@strose.edu
BUCKLEY, Peter, F .... 706-721-2231. 126 B
pbuckley@gru.edu
BUCKLEY, Roseanne .... 609-894-9311. 299 I
rbuckley@bcc.edu
BUCKLEY, Sally, A .... 617-333-2374. 225 E
sbuckley@curry.edu
BUCKLEY, Stephanie .... 310-506-4893... 58 H
stephanie.buckley@pepperdine.edu
BUCKLEY, Susan, C .... 319-335-3558. 175 I
susan-buckley@uiowa.edu
BUCKLIN, Carolyn .... 515-643-6744. 181 A
cbucklin@mercydesmoines.org
BUCKMAN, Cathy, M ...... 574-520-4451. 168 E
cmbuckma@iusb.edu
BUCKMAN, Kenneth .... 956-665-3461. 492 B
buckman@utpa.edu
BUCKMAN, Ty .... 937-327-6134. 393 E
tbuckman@wittenberg.edu
BUCKMASTER, Claudia .. 405-733-7380. 399 F
cbuckmaster@rose.edu
BUCKNER, Barbara .... 706-507-8505. 123 D
buckner_barbara@columbusstate.edu
BUCKNER, Carole .... 213-252-5100... 26 A
BUCKNER, JR.,
Frank, W .... 334-833-4541..... 4 D
fbuckner@huntingdon.edu
BUCKNER, R. Ty .... 336-316-2248. 355 A
rbuckner@guilford.edu
BUCKNER, Ramona .... 918-647-1320. 394 I
rbuckner@carlalbert.edu
BUCKNER, Tina .... 417-667-8181. 273 A
tbuckner@cottey.edu
BUCKNER JACKSON,
Patrice .... 912-478-3326. 126 C
pbuckner@georgiasouthern.edu
BUCKNOR, Wayne .... 256-726-7282..... 6 B
wbucknor@oakwood.edu
BUCKOVICH, John .... 912-525-5000. 131 B
jbuckovi@scad.edu
BUCKRIDGE, Brett .... 215-637-7700. 418 G
bbuckridge@holyfamily.edu
BUCKSER, Andrew .... 518-564-3150. 344 B
abuck005@plattsburgh.edu
BUCKWALTER, John, B .. 785-532-5500. 188 A
jbb3@ksu.edu
BUCKWALTER, Kim .... 215-204-7357. 433 K
kim.buckwalter@temple.edu
BUCY, Brandon, R .... 540-458-8651. 516 A
bucyb@wlu.edu
BUDD, Carla .... 307-382-1832. 543 J
cbudd@wwcc.wy.edu
BUDD, Deborah .... 510-981-2850... 59 A
dbudd@peralta.edu
BUDD, Frank, C .... 843-953-5640. 443 A
buddf@cofc.edu
BUDD, Jordan .... 603-513-5122. 298 D
jordan.budd@law.unh.edu
BUDD, Steven .... 508-854-4375. 232 F
sbudd@qcc.mass.edu
BUDD KEPLER, Patricia . 617-627-3427. 237 C
patricia.kepler@tufts.edu
BUDDE, Bruce .... 309-694-5477. 146 E
bbudde@icc.edu
BUDDE, Jill .... 641-683-5165. 179 A
jill.budde@indianhills.edu
BUDDE, Mitzi, J .... 703-370-6600. 508 B
BUDDELMEYER,
Gregory .... 419-434-5733. 391 D
buddelmeyerg@findlay.edu
BUDDEN, Chris .... 303-352-6911... 81 D
chris.budden@ccd.edu
BUDERUS, Julie .... 970-339-6583... 78 C
julie.buderus@aims.edu
BUDESCU, Gila .... 212-327-8054. 338 A
gbudescu@rockefeller.edu
BUDESKI, Brittany .... 406-771-4309. 287 E
brittany.budeski@gfcmsu.edu
BUDINE, Julie .... 217-228-5432. 156 C
hendrju@quincy.edu
BUDJAC, Susan .... 715-422-5319. 540 D
sue.budjac@mstc.edu
BUDKOWSKI, Dennis .... 740-389-4636. 383 F
budkowskid@mtc.edu
BUDWIG, Nancy .... 508-793-7779. 225 A
nbudwig@clarku.edu
BUDZILOWICZ, Mary ..... 610-902-8352. 411 E
mary.m.budzilowicz@cabrini.edu
BUDZYNSKI, John .... 312-949-7020. 146 G
jbudzynski@ico.edu
BUECHELE, Angela, K .... 937-229-2941. 391 C
abuechele1@udayton.edu
BUECHELE, Thomas .... 312-899-7420. 158 L
tbuechele@saic.edu
BUECHNER, Marybeth .... 916-558-2512... 53 D
buechnm@scc.losrios.edu
BUEHLER, Julie, L .... 413-545-9339. 228 F
julie.buehler@umass.edu
BUEHLER, Kati .... 805-565-6883... 76 D
kbuehler@westmont.edu
BUEHLER, Lesley .... 510-742-3126... 57 A
lbuehler@ohlone.edu
BUEHRER, Danielle .... 912-260-4419. 131 F
danielle.buehrer@sgsc.edu
BUEKENS, Pierre .... 504-988-5397. 207 C
sphaward@tulane.edu
BUEL, Kevin, A .... 845-675-4597. 335 C
kevin.buel@nyack.edu
BUELL, Katie .... 630-829-6128. 140 B
kbuell@ben.edu
BUENAVENTURA, Lisa ..... 617-287-5800. 228 G
lisa.buenaventura@umb.edu
BUENTELLO, Michael ..... 713-525-3589. 490 L
buentem@stthom.edu
BUENTELLO, Rachel, L ... 361-593-4068. 484 A
rachel.buentello@tamuk.edu

BUERSTER, Tara 618-393-2982. 146 H buerstert@iecc.edu
BUETTNER, David 641-422-4000. 181 D buettdav@niacc.edu
BUETTNER, Kathryn, A 815-753-9504. 154 I kbuettner@niu.edu
BUFANO, Suzanne 843-953-6799. 442 A suzanne.bufano@citadel.edu
BUFF, Stacy 828-652-0663. 362 A stacybuff@mcdowelltech.edu
BUFFINGTON, Brenda 615-230-3494. 461 G brenda.buffington@volstate.edu
BUFFINGTON, James 714-437-9697... 39 G
BUFFINGTON, Sean, T 215-717-6380. 435 A president@uarts.edu
BUFFINTON, Keith, W 570-577-3711. 411 A keith.buffinton@bucknell.edu
BUFFONE, Nancy 413-545-2554. 228 F buffone@admin.umass.edu
BUFFUM, Don 662-325-2861. 268 D dbuffum@procurement.msstate.edu
BUFORD, N. Lynn 662-846-4155. 266 G lbuford@deltastate.edu
BUFORD, Shannon 573-334-9181. 276 I shannon@metrobusinesscollege.edu
BUGAIGHIS, Elizabeth 610-332-6272. 425 D ebugaighis@northampton.edu
BUGAJSKI, Tricia, J 260-399-7700. 174 C tbugajski@sf.edu
BUGAY, David, P 949-582-4699... 67 A dbugay@socccd.edu
BUGBEE, David 707-826-3626... 35 C drb7001@humboldt.edu
BUGBEE, Susan, H 619-260-2888... 73 I bugbee@sandiego.edu
BUGG, Elmer 510-436-2411... 59 D ebugg@peralta.edu
BUGG, Gary, D 859-238-5535. 193 E gary.bugg@centre.edu
BUGGLIN, Tracy 740-826-8142. 384 L tbugglin@muskingum.edu
BUGGS, Richard 415-575-6116... 31 D rbuggs@ciis.edu
BUGGY, Gerard 340-693-1568. 555 E gbuggy@live.uvi.edu
BUGGY, James 864-455-8203. 448 E jbuggy@greenvillemed.sc.edu
BUGOS, Michelle, L 309-649-6209. 160 E michelle.bugos@src.edu
BUHKS, Ephraim 718-261-5800. 315 F ebuhks@bramsonort.edu
BUHL, David, V 989-463-7143. 239 B buhldv@alma.edu
BUHL, Pat 651-450-3536. 258 H pbuhl@inverhills.edu
BUHL, Patti 918-456-5511. 396 H buhl@nsuok.edu
BUHLER, David, L 801-321-7103. 496 P commissioner@ushe.edu
BUHLER, Doug 517-884-3867. 246 H buhler@anr.msu.edu
BUHLER, Mary Ann 785-539-3571. 188 F mabuhler@mccks.edu
BUHR, Connie 319-296-4281. 178 J connie.buhr@hawkeyecollege.edu
BUHR, Rachel 217-641-4314. 148 M rbuhr@jwcc.edu
BUHRMAN, Robert, A 607-255-3732. 322 A rab8@cornell.edu
BUHROW, William, C 503-554-2340. 403 C bbuhrow@georgefox.edu
BUI, Vincent 650-325-5621... 61 G vincent.bui@stpatricksseminary.org
BUISMAN, Kevin 507-389-6111. 259 G kevin.buisman@mnsu.edu
BUITER, Mike 864-242-5100. 441 D
BUIZZARD, Nicholas 410-296-5350. 218 I
BUJAK, Jeanette, K 704-233-8149. 370 G jbujak@wingate.edu
BUJOLD, James 218-285-2253. 260 G james.bujold@rainyriver.edu
BUKER, Jennifer 807-859-1319. 211 H pr@thomas.edu
BUKOWIECKI, Richard 562-860-2451... 37 I rbukowiecki@cerritos.edu
BUKOWSKI, Bruce, J 410-293-2934. 545 J bukowski@usna.edu
BUKOWSKI, Joseph, E 740-695-9500. 374 H bukowski@belmontcollege.edu
BUKOWSKI, Tamzin 320-762-4415. 257 O tamzinb@alextech.edu
BUKRALIA, Rajeev 920-465-2383. 536 F bukralir@uwgb.edu
BULETTE, Nancy 415-458-3708... 42 J nancy.bulette@dominican.edu
BULEY, Paula Marie 603-897-8202. 297 F pbuley@rivier.edu
BULGER, Stephanie 313-496-2878. 252 B sbulger1@wcccd.edu
BULIK, Lou Anne 610-499-4458. 437 E labulik@widener.edu
BULL, Bernard, D 262-243-5700. 532 H bernard.bull@cuw.edu
BULL, Inger 719-227-8280... 79 D inger.bull@ColoradoCollege.edu
BULL, Kam 530-895-2376... 30 F bullka@butte.edu
BULL, Kimberly 501-208-5310... 25 C bull@uaccm.edu
BULL, Sharon, I 208-467-8609. 139 A sibull@nnu.edu
BULL, Vivian 973-408-3100. 301 C president@drew.edu
BULLARD, Cora 910-521-6219. 369 B cora.bullard@uncp.edu
BULLARD, Robert, D 713-313-6849. 485 F bullardrd@tsu.edu
BULLARD, II, Roland, N 919-516-4232. 366 C rnbullard@st-aug.edu
BULLARD, Sam, F 337-482-6841. 208 D sfb@louisiana.edu
BULLARD, Scott, W 334-683-5104..... 5 C sbullard@judson.edu
BULLARD, Steven 936-468-3304. 482 A bullardsh@sfasu.edu
BULLARD-DILLARD, Rebecca 910-521-6271. 369 B william.gash@uncp.edu
BULLEN, James 305-821-3333. 105 A jbullen@fnu.edu
BULLER, Jeff 561-799-8579. 114 L jbuller@fau.edu
BULLINGER, Cheryl 605-721-5213. 450 G cbullinger@national.edu
BULLINGHAM, Bree 212-517-0532. 330 E bbullingham@mmm.edu
BULLINGTON, Tena 256-233-8243..... 1 F tena.bullington@athens.edu
BULLINS, Nancy 336-633-0256. 362 H ndbullins@randolph.edu
BULLION, Keith 304-326-1262. 527 G kbullion@salemu.edu
BULLIS, Michael, D 541-346-3405. 406 D bullism@uoregon.edu
BULLOCK, Barbara, A 219-981-4235. 168 B babulloc@iun.edu
BULLOCK, Barbara, J 937-775-3759. 393 G barbara.bullock@wright.edu
BULLOCK, Brian 610-519-4070. 436 F brian.bullock@villanova.edu
BULLOCK, Charles 408-924-2900... 36 A charles.bullock@sjsu.edu
BULLOCK, Doris 919-516-4919. 366 C djbullock@st-aug.edu
BULLOCK, Galen 213-763-7210... 52 D bullockgw@lattc.edu
BULLOCK, James 704-337-2316. 365 G bullockj@queens.edu
BULLOCK, Jeffrey, F 563-589-3223. 182 J jbullock@dbq.edu
BULLOCK, Jim 304-865-6116. 527 F jim.bullock@ovu.edu
BULLOCK, John, D 858-499-0202... 40 C jbullock@coleman.edu
BULLOCK, Josh 217-234-5222. 150 D jbullock@lakeland.cc.il.us
BULLOCK, Linda, C 281-283-2574. 489 C bullock@uhcl.edu
BULLOCK, Michael 413-236-1602. 231 A mbullock@berkshirecc.edu
BULLOCK, Quintin, B 518-381-1304. 340 G bullocqb@sunysccc.edu
BULLOCK, Steven 402-941-6200. 290 K bullock@midlandu.edu
BULLS, Derald 903-785-7661. 478 B dbulls@parisjc.edu
BULLS, W. Kenneth 336-750-2921. 370 A bullswk@wssu.edu
BULLUCK, Bruce 256-551-5210..... 4 I bruce.bulluck@drakestate.edu
BULNISKI, Meredith 559-438-4222... 46 K meredith_bulniski@heald.edu
BULONE, Phil 813-889-3484. 107 C pbulone@academy.edu
BULOW, Daniel 708-524-6780. 144 C dbulow@dom.edu
BULT, Tracy 219-757-6132. 172 D
BULZONI, Donna, R 570-422-3485. 428 D dbulzoni@po-box.esu.edu
BUMANN, Susan 218-879-0808. 258 E sbumann@fdltcc.edu
BUMBACO, Dominick 914-923-2866. 335 J dbumbaco@pace.edu
BUMGARDNER, Lydia, R 212-870-1233. 334 C registrarlb@nyts.edu
BUMILLER, Taylor, J 636-327-4645. 277 K tjb@midwest.edu
BUMPERS, Claude 251-442-2587..... 9 A cbumpers@umobile.edu
BUMPERS, Richard 404-460-2098. 130 F richard.bumpers@point.edu
BUMPUS, Julie, A 706-236-2207. 121 G jbumpus@berry.edu
BUNCE, Larry 816-235-1045. 283 D buncel@umkc.edu
BUNCH, Diana 334-953-1303. 544 D lucy.bunch@us.af.mil
BUNCH, Joan 419-251-1722. 383 G joan.bunch@mercycollege.edu
BUNCH, Kirsten, H 828-694-1810. 358 C kristenb@blueridge.edu
BUNCH, Martha, M 336-272-7102. 354 E bunchm@greensboro.edu
BUNCH, Meredith, N 309-692-4092. 152 J mbunch@midstate.edu
BUNCH, Thomas, G 817-202-6207. 481 E buncht@swau.edu
BUNCH, Wes 828-327-7000. 359 A wbunch@cvcc.edu
BUNCH, Wilma, C 417-269-3051. 273 D wbunch@coxcollege.edu
BUNDALO, Katherine 414-382-6398. 531 I kathy.bundalo@alverno.edu
BUNDERS, Lisa 603-899-4237. 296 H
BUNDY, Barbara 213-624-1200... 44 D bbundy@fidm.edu
BUNDY, James, A 203-432-1505... 93 A james.bundy@yale.edu
BUNDY, O. Keith 605-256-5146. 451 H keith.bundy@dsu.edu
BUNDY, III, O. Richard 802-656-2010. 500 F rich.bundy@uvm.edu
BUNDY, Penny 269-387-2000. 252 I penny.bundy@wmich.edu
BUNGE, Sacha 415-338-2204... 35 E sbunge@sfsu.edu
BUNIS, David, A 781-736-3993. 224 F dbunis@brandeis.edu
BUNKER, Laurel 651-638-6372. 253 K l-bunker@bethel.edu
BUNKOWSKE, Heidi 619-388-3911... 62 D hbunkows@sdccd.edu
BUNN, Dumont, C 478-988-6800. 122 G dbunn@centralgatech.edu
BUNN, Sandra, J 912-279-5965. 123 B sbunn@ccga.edu
BUNNELL, Brian 951-343-4350... 30 H bbunnell@calbaptist.edu
BUNNELL, Robert, D 610-361-5291. 424 I bunnellr@neumann.edu
BUNNELL, Robin 541-888-7339. 407 H rbunnell@socc.edu
BUNNELL-RHYNE, Melinda, A 301-369-2800. 213 G melindabunnell@capitol-college.edu
BUNNING, Galen 785-227-3380. 184 I bunningb@bethanylb.edu
BUNTEN, Tricia 218-726-6995. 264 D tbunten@d.umn.edu
BUNTON, Tim, M 217-443-8780. 143 G tbunton@dacc.edu
BUNYI, Beth 760-630-1555... 49 L bbunyi@kaplan.edu
BUOL, Deborah, L 563-589-3223. 182 J dbuol@dbq.edu
BUONO, Lisa 805-493-3663... 31 H llbuono@callutheran.edu
BUOSCIO, Amy 708-237-5050. 155 B abuoscio@nc.edu
BURAK, Deborah 610-861-4137. 425 D dburak@northampton.edu
BURAK, Marshall, J 510-628-8016... 51 A mburak@lincolnuca.edu
BURBA, Dave 530-541-4660... 50 D burba@ltcc.edu
BURBA, Randy 714-997-6763... 38 A burba@chapman.edu
BURBAGE, Priscilla, D 843-953-5578. 443 A burbagep@cofc.edu
BURBANK, Lynn 218-726-8833. 264 D lburbank@d.umn.edu
BURBANTE, Gilberto 985-448-4208. 208 A gilberto.burbante@nicholls.edu
BURCH, Beth 503-253-3443. 405 E bburch@ocom.edu
BURCH, C. Vicki 731-668-7240. 464 F vicki.burch@wtbc.edu
BURCH, Carl 501-450-1377... 21 E burch@hendrix.edu
BURCH, Chuck, S 704-406-4342. 354 C cburch@gardner-webb.edu
BURCH, Doug 801-622-1573. 496 I doug.burch@stevenshenager.edu
BURCH, Doug 801-622-1573. 496 I doug.burch@stevenhenager.edu
BURCH, Franki 704-406-4724. 354 C fburch@gardner-webb.edu
BURCH, John 270-789-5015. 193 D jrburch@campbellsville.edu
BURCH, Rhonda 812-866-7014. 166 C burch@hanover.edu
BURCH, Susan 406-756-3839. 286 B sburch@fvcc.edu
BURCH, Terese, A 815-395-5088. 158 A terriburch@sacn.edu
BURCH-SIMS, G. Pamela 615-963-7437. 459 E psims@tnstate.edu
BURCHAM, David, W 310-258-5404... 53 E david.burcham@lmu.edu
BURCHAM, Timothy 870-972-2085... 19 N tburcham@astate.edu
BURCHAM, CFRE, Timothy, R 859-256-3100. 194 I tim.burcham@kctcs.edu
BURCHARD, Bob, P 573-875-7410. 272 G rpburchard@ccis.edu
BURCHARD, Elizabeth, B 802-443-5201. 499 H eboudah@middlebury.edu
BURCHARD, Eric 740-593-1804. 387 C burchard@ohio.edu
BURCHARD, Faye, C 573-875-7400. 272 G fcburchard@ccis.edu
BURCHETT, Amy 432-264-5063. 473 E aburchett@howardcollege.edu
BURCHETT, Bonnie, L 423-439-4446. 459 C bonnie@etsu.edu
BURCHETT, Lance, E 501-686-5987... 24 C leburchett@uams.edu
BURCHFIELD, Bill 814-868-9900. 416 C burchfield@erieit.edu
BURCHFIELD, James 406-243-5521. 286 H james.burchfield@umontana.edu
BURCHFIELD, Nettie, L 985-549-2068. 208 C nburchfield@selu.edu
BURCHILL, John, K 785-827-5541. 188 C john@kwu.edu
BURCKHARDT, Judy 303-991-1575... 78 D judy.burckhardt@americansentinel.edu
BURD, Barbara 843-349-2401. 442 E bburd@coastal.edu
BURD, Gail, D 520-626-4099... 18 F gburd@email.arizona.edu
BURDA, Bradley 541-885-1180. 405 J bradley.burda@oit.edu
BURDA, Ed 304-457-6238. 526 A burdaep@ab.edu
BURDEN, Kathlyn 770-229-3328. 132 B kburden@sctech.edu
BURDEN, Matthew 630-637-5433. 154 F mburden@noctrl.edu
BURDEN, Regina 931-393-1691. 461 A rburden@mscc.edu
BURDEN, Velma 912-478-5421. 126 C vburden@georgiasouthern.edu
BURDETTE, David, A 989-774-3334. 240 N burde1da@cmich.edu
BURDETTE, Ilona 859-336-5082. 198 J iburdette@sccky.edu
BURDETTE, Vinson 803-508-7244. 440 G BurdetteV@atc.edu
BURDGE, Amber 620-431-2820. 189 D aburdge@neosho.edu
BURDICK, Evelyn, P 708-209-3259. 143 E evelyn.burdick@cuchicago.edu
BURDICK, Jonathan 585-275-6805. 349 C jonathan.burdick@rochester.edu
BURDICK, Julie 330-972-8365. 390 E burdick@uakron.edu
BURDICK, Phil 847-925-6183. 145 H pburdick@harpercollege.edu
BURDICK, Rebekah 863-667-5026. 113 P rburdick@seu.edu
BURDINE, James, N 979-862-4445. 484 B jnburdine@srph.tamhsc.edu
BURDOWSKI, Allen 718-489-5324. 338 G aburdowski@sfc.edu
BURDSAL, Carol, A 570-577-3855. 411 A carol.burdsal@bucknell.edu
BURDSALL, Dawn, M 610-660-1333. 432 E dburdsal@sju.edu
BURDUE, JoEllen 414-277-7117. 534 G burdue@msoe.edu
BURDZINSKI, Donna, R 352-797-5001. 110 E burdzid@phcc.edu
BURDZINSKI, Kenneth, R 727-816-3412. 110 E burdzink@phcc.edu
BURFORD, Kristina 501-450-1362... 21 E burford@hendrix.edu
BURG, James 260-481-4146. 168 C burgj@ipfw.edu
BURG, Karen 864-656-6462. 442 C kburg@clemson.edu
BURG, Mary, G 785-864-3131. 190 L mburg@ku.edu
BURGARD, Bambi 816-802-3455. 275 J bburgard@kcai.edu
BURGARD, Jim, E 504-280-6698. 205 G jburgard@uno.edu

BURGAU, Tam ... 715-858-1377. 539 J tburgau@cvtc.edu
BURGAY, Stephen, P ... 617-353-1168. 224 D burgay@bu.edu
BURGE, Legand, L ... 334-727-8976... 8 A lburge@tuskegee.edu
BURGENER, Kelly, T ... 208-496-1135. 137 H burgenerk@byui.edu
BURGER, Arnold ... 615-329-8516. 454 F aburger@fisk.edu
BURGER, Avraham ... 516-295-5700. 351 N
BURGER, Bill ... 802-443-5707. 499 H bburger@middlebury.edu
BURGER, Cindy, L ... 717-766-2511. 423 L cburger@messiah.edu
BURGER, Edward, B ... 512-863-1454. 481 I burger@southwestern.edu
BURGER, Lisa ... 701-777-4463. 371 C lisa.burger@und.edu
BURGER, Michael ... 334-244-3380... 2 A mburger1@aum.edu
BURGER, Rosemary ... 570-340-6054. 423 B burger@marywood.edu
BURGER, Shmuel ... 516-295-5700. 351 N
BURGES, Jena ... 707-826-4192... 35 C jb139@humboldt.edu
BURGESON, John ... 320-308-3081. 261 B jcburgeson@stcloudstate.edu
BURGESON, Sharron ... 760-921-5444... 58 C sharron.burgeson@paloverde.edu
BURGESS, Aaron ... 513-244-8112. 376 J aaron.burgess@ccuniversity.edu
BURGESS, Brenda, K ... 580-774-3015. 400 B brenda.burgess@swosu.edu
BURGESS, Charlotte, G .. 909-748-8281... 73 H char_burgess@redlands.edu
BURGESS, Craig, E ... 803-533-3928. 446 G
BURGESS, Dawn ... 619-388-7681... 62 F dburgess@sdccd.edu
BURGESS, Debbie ... 910-521-6279. 369 B debbie.burgess@uncp.edu
BURGESS, Douglas ... 513-556-9900. 390 G douglas.burgess@uc.edu
BURGESS, Duncan ... 206-934-6882. 523 A duncan.burgess@seattlecolleges.edu
BURGESS, Ed ... 913-758-3033. 545 E burgesse@leavenworth.army.mil
BURGESS, Jay ... 603-428-2254. 297 D jburgess@nec.edu
BURGESS, Kimberly ... 229-430-3976. 119 J kimberly.burgess@asurams.edu
BURGESS, Marcus ... 803-780-1199. 449 E mburgess@voorhees.edu
BURGESS, Marrlee ... 585-389-2884. 332 D mburges4@naz.edu
BURGESS, Nancy, E ... 301-583-7011. 217 F burgesne@pgcc.edu
BURGESS, Norma ... 615-966-6146. 456 B norma.burgess@lipscomb.edu
BURGESS, Shane, C ... 520-621-7621... 18 F sburgess@cals.arizona.edu
BURGESS, Sylvia ... 580-581-2621. 394 G sylviab@cameron.edu
BURGESS, Valerie ... 603-880-8308. 298 A vburgess@thomasmorecollege.edu
BURGETT, Paul, J ... 585-274-3326. 349 C pburgett@admin.rochester.edu
BURGGRAF, JR., Thomas, F ... 970-641-2237... 86 I tburggraf@western.edu
BURGGRAFF, Dennis ... 727-726-1153. 100 E dennisburggraff@clearwater.edu
BURGGRAFF, Lucy ... 800-672-3060. 366 F
BURGGREN, Warren, W . 940-565-2550. 490 C warren.burggren@unt.edu
BURGHART, Michael ... 707-826-3512... 35 C msb39@humboldt.edu
BURGHER, Karl ... 812-237-8449. 167 A karl.burgher@indstate.edu
BURGHER, Louis, W ... 402-552-2586. 288 L burgherlouis@clarksoncollege.edu
BURGIE-BRYANT, Willette ... 484-384-2942. 415 G wburgie@eastern.edu
BURGIE-BRYANT, Willette, A ... 484-384-2942. 425 I wburgie@eastern.edu
BURGIN, Jeffery ... 256-372-5233... 1 A jeffery.burgin@aamu.edu
BURGIN, Vicki ... 251-442-2269... 9 A vburgin@umobile.edu
BURGMAYER, Sharon ... 610-526-5106. 410 J sburmay@brynmawr.edu
BURGMEIER, Julie ... 563-588-6374. 176 F julie.bergmeier@clarke.edu
BURGNER, Ryan, C ... 308-635-6798. 293 E burgnerr@wncc.edu
BURGOS, Henry ... 860-906-5007... 88 D hburgos@ccc.commnet.edu
BURGOS, Irma ... 920-424-3080. 537 B burgos@uwosh.edu
BURGOS, Jorge ... 787-720-4476. 553 D decanatoestudiantes@mizpa.edu
BURGOS, Jose, L ... 787-728-1515. 555 D jburgos@sagrado.edu
BURGOS, Maida ... 305-821-3333. 105 A mburgos@fnu.edu
BURGOS, Michael ... 858-642-8207... 55 J mburgos@nu.edu
BURHENN, Herbert ... 423-425-4635. 463 D herbert-burhenn@utc.edu
BURI, David ... 360-359-4958. 519 C dburi@ewu.edu
BURIK, Larry ... 909-607-2226... 59 G larry_burik@pitzer.edu
BURISH, Thomas, G ... 574-631-6631. 174 A burish.2@nd.edu
BURK, Ann, M ... 308-432-6311. 291 D aburk@csc.edu
BURK, Brandon ... 479-394-7622... 23 B bburk@rmcc.edu
BURK, Jan ... 972-721-5221. 488 F jburk@udallas.edu
BURK, Jill ... 254-968-9089. 483 A burk@tarleton.edu
BURK, Kelly ... 765-983-1501. 165 G burkke@earlham.edu
BURK, Thomas ... 973-328-5037. 300 G tburk@ccm.edu
BURKARD, Donald, C ... 843-953-1432. 443 A burkardd@cofc.edu
BURKE, Andrew, J ... 575-527-7650. 311 B aburke@nmsu.edu
BURKE, Andrew, J ... 575-527-7510. 311 B aburke@nmsu.edu
BURKE, Barbara ... 718-260-5173. 319 B bburke@citytech.cuny.edu
BURKE, Barbara, A ... 217-581-2319. 144 E baburke2@eiu.edu
BURKE, Brenda, L ... 804-828-7372. 511 F blburke@vcu.edu
BURKE, Brian, E ... 414-277-7266. 534 G burke@msoe.edu
BURKE, Brian, W ... 413-545-2204. 228 F bwburke@external.umass.edu
BURKE, Bridgit ... 518-445-3233. 313 C bburk@albanylaw.edu
BURKE, Carson ... 330-923-9959. 379 K cburke@fortiscollege.edu
BURKE, Cathleen, C ... 804-828-0179. 511 F ccburke@vcu.edu
BURKE, Christine ... 617-850-1216. 227 E cburke@hchc.edu
BURKE, Christy ... 740-376-4708. 383 E christy.burke@marietta.edu
BURKE, Clarence ... 919-572-1625. 352 C cburke@apexsot.edu
BURKE, Colleen ... 215-572-2785. 409 H burkec@arcadia.edu
BURKE, Connie ... 617-739-1700. 235 A conburke@aii.edu
BURKE, Dale ... 808-544-9394. 135 F dburke@hpu.edu
BURKE, Daniel ... 978-542-6096. 230 E daniel.burke@salemstate.edu
BURKE, David ... 626-812-3016... 29 H dburke@apu.edu
BURKE, Derek, A ... 252-398-6369. 353 H burked@chowan.edu
BURKE, Diane, M ... 315-279-5688. 328 D dburke@mail.keuka.edu
BURKE, Donald, S ... 412-624-3001. 435 C donburke@pitt.edu
BURKE, Elizabeth ... 507-457-5330. 262 A eburke@winona.edu
BURKE, Ellen ... 607-735-1774. 323 H eburke@elmira.edu
BURKE, Genevieve ... 312-752-2174. 149 E genevieve.burke@kendall.edu
BURKE, Greg ... 318-357-5251. 208 B burkeg@nsula.edu
BURKE, Ingrid ... 307-766-5080. 543 I burke@uwyo.edu
BURKE, Janice, P ... 215-503-9606. 434 C janice.burke@jefferson.edu
BURKE, Jeanmarie, R ... 315-568-3869. 333 C jburke@nycc.edu
BURKE, Joe ... 620-421-6700. 188 D joeburke@labette.edu
BURKE, John ... 845-848-4079. 322 G john.burke@dc.edu
BURKE, John ... 724-852-3307. 437 A jburke@waynesburg.edu
BURKE, Jonathan ... 949-376-6000... 50 C jburke@lagunacollege.edu
BURKE, Jonathan, L ... 816-604-6620. 277 D jon.burke@mcckc.edu
BURKE, Joseph, D ... 256-228-6001... 5 H burkej@nacc.edu
BURKE, Joy ... 570-662-4877. 429 C jburke@mansfield.edu
BURKE, Judith, A ... 765-285-1847. 164 B jmoore@bsu.edu
BURKE, Kelly ... 808-974-7400. 136 A kellyb@hawaii.edu
BURKE, Keri ... 503-883-2269. 404 A kburke@linfield.edu
BURKE, Kevin, L ... 704-337-2542. 365 G burkek@queens.edu
BURKE, Kimberly, G ... 601-974-1250. 267 I burkekg@millsaps.edu
BURKE, Kristin ... 617-824-8608. 226 A kristin_burke@emerson.edu
BURKE, JR., Lewis ... 270-901-1033. 196 E lewis.burke@kctcs.edu
BURKE, Mary ... 508-747-0400. 235 I mburke@quincycollege.edu
BURKE, Matthew ... 617-928-4500. 234 E mburke@mountida.edu
BURKE, Melinda, W ... 520-621-3557... 18 F melinda.burke@al.arizona.edu
BURKE, Michael, L ... 414-297-6320. 540 E burkem@matc.edu
BURKE, Michael, P ... 617-495-1546. 227 C mikeburke@fas.harvard.edu
BURKE, Molly ... 708-524-6826. 144 C burkemq@dom.edu
BURKE, Morgan, J ... 765-494-3189. 171 M mjb@purdue.edu
BURKE, Patrick ... 509-313-4220. 520 A burkep@gonzaga.edu
BURKE, Peggy ... 773-325-4605. 143 H pburke@depaul.edu
BURKE, Peggy, Y ... 716-375-2394. 338 E pyburke@sbu.edu
BURKE, Peggy, Y ... 716-375-2370. 338 E pyburke@sbu.edu
BURKE, Scott, M ... 404-413-2088. 126 E sburke@gsu.edu
BURKE, Susan ... 781-762-1211. 226 E sburke@fine-ne.com
BURKE, Ted ... 508-541-1774. 225 F tburke@dean.edu
BURKE, Tom, J ... 661-336-5117... 49 M tburke@kccd.edu
BURKE, Tracie, L ... 901-321-3357. 453 H tburke@cbu.edu
BURKE, Valerie ... 561-912-2166. 103 C vburke@evergladesuniversity.edu
BURKE, Vic ... 912-443-5799. 131 D vburke@savannahtech.edu
BURKE, William, R ... 570-941-7887. 436 A william.burke@scranton.edu
BURKE-KELLY, Kathleen . 818-719-6408... 52 B kbk@piercecollege.edu
BURKEE, James ... 914-337-9300. 321 E james.burkee@concordia-ny.edu
BURKERT, Amy, L ... 412-268-8494. 412 H ak11@andrew.cmu.edu
BURKES, Aaron ... 608-243-4045. 540 C aburkes@madisoncollege.edu
BURKES, Kate ... 479-619-4299... 22 C kburkes@nwacc.edu
BURKETT, Amy ... 704-330-5940. 359 C amy.burkett@cpcc.edu
BURKETT, Holly, L ... 865-981-5302. 461 D hlburkett@pstcc.edu
BURKETT, Nancy ... 610-328-8651. 433 I nburket1@swarthmore.edu
BURKETT, Norvel ... 865-974-3181. 463 C nburkett@utk.edu
BURKETT, Timothy ... 704-847-5600. 366 J itadmin@ses.edu
BURKEY, Daniel, E ... 402-280-2131. 289 D dburkey@creighton.edu
BURKHALTER, James ... 806-742-1452. 487 D j.burkhalter@ttu.edu
BURKHALTER, Shelia ... 410-837-4271. 221 A sburkhalter@ubalt.edu
BURKHAMMER, Jerry, L 304-462-4114. 529 G jerry.burkhammer@glenville.edu
BURKHARDT, Janet ... 303-871-4757... 86 B janet.burkhardt@du.edu
BURKHARDT, Lou Ann .. 312-461-0600. 139 H lburkhardt@aaart.edu
BURKHARDT, Paul ... 928-350-3210... 17 K pburkhardt@prescott.edu
BURKHARDT, Robert ... 256-216-6660... 1 F robert.burkhardt@athens.edu
BURKHARDT, Thomas, E ... 937-229-4333. 391 C tburkhardt1@udayton.edu
BURKHART, Dan ... 406-657-1104. 288 B burkhard@rocky.edu
BURKHART, Jenny ... 859-858-2318. 192 A
BURKHART, Patricia ... 954-492-5353. 100 A pburkhart@citycollege.edu
BURKHART, Patrick ... 480-654-7700... 15 A patrick.burkhart@mesacc.edu
BURKHART-EVANS, Maggie ... 540-568-5646. 506 F evansmb@jmu.edu
BURKHEAD, Ann, E ... 724-847-6737. 417 A aeburkhe@geneva.edu
BURKHOLDER, Brian, M 540-432-4132. 504 D brian.burkholder@emu.edu
BURKHOLDER, Gary ... 408-254-6900... 55 H gburkholder@nhu.edu
BURKHOLDER, Mary, E . 419-783-2360. 379 C mburkholder@defiance.edu
BURKHOLDER, Robert, C ... 215-503-6249. 434 C robert.burkholder@jefferson.edu
BURKINK, Timothy, J ... 308-865-8342. 292 H burkinktj@unk.edu
BURKMAN, Roger ... 502-585-9911. 199 C rburkman@spalding.edu
BURKMAN, Tom, A ... 612-343-4748. 262 X taburkma@northcentral.edu
BURKOS, Rivka ... 718-261-5800. 315 F rburkos@bramsonort.edu
BURKS, Barry, L ... 336-334-7995. 367 E blburks@ncat.edu
BURKS, Brent ... 254-295-4514. 490 B bburks@umhb.edu
BURKS, Bryan ... 501-279-4240... 21 C bburks@harding.edu
BURKS, Eric ... 785-738-9057. 189 F eburks@ncktc.edu
BURKS, Laura ... 334-580-2144... 4 L lburks@faulknerstate.edu
BURKS, Scott, A ... 502-852-4661. 200 D scott.burks@louisville.edu
BURKS, Suzanne, M ... 405-744-5458. 397 H suzanne.burks@okstate.edu
BURKS, Valerie, C ... 407-582-1373. 118 M vburks1@valenciacollege.edu
BURKUM, Karen, J ... 315-268-6576. 320 A kburkum@clarkson.edu
BURLAUD, Patricia ... 516-686-7443. 333 H pburlaud@nyit.edu
BURLESON, Burt ... 254-710-3517. 467 G burt_burleson@baylor.edu
BURLESON, Susan ... 336-249-8186. 360 A sdburl@davidsonccc.edu
BURLEW, Elizabeth ... 315-655-7375. 316 E eburlew@cazenovia.edu
BURLEW, Jon ... 606-679-8501. 196 D jon.burlew@kctcs.edu
BURLEW, Lynette ... 318-473-6401. 205 A lburlew@lsua.edu
BURLINGAME, Kathy ... 502-410-6200. 194 B kburlingame@galencollege.edu
BURLINGAME, Sherry ... 708-456-0300. 161 A sburling@triton.edu
BURLINGHAM, Kay, A ... 847-866-3988. 145 E kay.burlingham@garrett.edu
BURMA, William, H ... 515-263-2975. 178 G bburma@grandview.edu
BURMAN, Tom ... 307-766-2292. 543 I tburman@uwyo.edu
BURMASTER, Elizabeth .. 715-365-4415. 540 G eburmaster@nicoletcollege.edu
BURN, Killara ... 413-549-4600. 227 B
BURNAM, Paul ... 740-362-3435. 383 H pburnam@mtso.edu
BURNAM, Scott, M ... 937-778-7849. 379 G sburnam@edisonohio.edu
BURNE, Mary ... 617-739-1700. 235 A mburne@aii.edu
BURNER, Emily ... 540-545-7334. 509 E eburner@su.edu
BURNES, Michael ... 706-236-2245. 121 G mburnes@berry.edu
BURNETT, Alex ... 718-960-4992. 318 A alex.burnett@lehman.cuny.edu
BURNETT, Brian ... 719-255-3210... 85 M bburnett@uccs.edu
BURNETT, Catherine, G .. 713-646-1831. 480 J cburnett@stcl.edu
BURNETT, Daniel, C ... 606-679-8501. 196 D danielc.burnett@kctcs.edu
BURNETT, Donald, L ... 208-885-6365. 139 D president@uidaho.edu
BURNETT, Eric ... 208-882-1566. 138 H eburnett@nsa.edu
BURNETT, Eric ... 208-882-1566. 138 H eburnett@moscow.com
BURNETT, Gloria ... 907-852-3333... 10 F gloria.burnett@ilisagvik.edu
BURNETT, Jim, W ... 828-448-3100. 365 A jburnett@wpcc.edu
BURNETT, Linda, G ... 409-882-3998. 486 G linda.burnett@lsco.edu
BURNETT, Lori, W ... 229-430-6443. 119 J lori.burnett@asurams.edu
BURNETT, Marc ... 931-372-3411. 460 A mburnett@tntech.edu
BURNETT, Mark ... 206-296-6110. 523 E markb@seattleu.edu
BURNETT, Michael, F ... 225-578-5748. 204 O vocbur@lsu.edu

BURNETT, Myra ... 404-270-5027. 132 E
mburnett@spelman.edu
BURNETT, Sharron, T ... 731-426-7645. 455 J
sburnett@lanecollege.edu
BURNETT, Tod, A ... 949-582-4722... 67 C
tburnett@saddleback.edu
BURNETT-ANDRUS,
Sonya ... 903-927-3351. 495 A
SBurnett-Andrus@wileyc.edu
BURNETTE, Cindy ... 270-745-2755. 200 G
cindy.burnette@wku.edu
BURNETTE, Daarel ... 937-376-6201. 376 E
dburnette@centralstate.edu
BURNETTE, George ... 336-770-1480. 369 D
burnetteg@uncsa.edu
BURNETTE, JR.,
Glen, G ... 910-521-6201. 369 B
glen.burnette@uncp.edu
BURNETTE, Janet, K ... 828-339-4242. 364 B
janet@southwesterncc.edu
BURNETTE, Janet, K ... 828-339-4250. 364 B
janet@southwesterncc.edu
BURNETTE, Kendra ... 864-587-4298. 447 B
burnettek@smcsc.edu
BURNETTE, Kurt ... 412-321-7550. 411 D
BURNETTE, Richard ... 850-644-1532. 115 C
rburnette@admin.fsu.edu
BURNETTE, Sheryl, L ... 423-439-4230. 459 C
burnetts@etsu.edu
BURNETTE, Stephanie ... 321-433-7271. 101 M
burnettes@brevardcc.edu
BURNEY, Andrea ... 434-797-8458. 512 C
aburney@dcc.vccs.edu
BURNEY, Brenda, D ... 931-540-2582. 460 E
bburney1@columbiastate.edu
BURNEY, John ... 402-826-8221. 289 E
john.burney@doane.edu
BURNEY, Linda ... 910-879-5519. 358 B
lburney@bladencc.edu
BURNEY, Louise ... 601-974-1101. 267 I
burnesl@millsaps.edu
BURNEY, Ralonda ... 336-517-2225. 352 H
BURNEY, Rolanda, C ... 410-651-7800. 219 E
rcburney@umes.edu
BURNHAM, Don ... 601-856-5400. 267 B
dburnham@holmescc.edu
BURNHAM, Mark, A ... 517-353-9000. 246 H
mburnham@msu.edu
BURNHAM, Willette, S ... 843-792-2146. 445 B
burnham@musc.edu
BURNIM, Mickey, L ... 301-860-3555. 220 A
mlburnim@bowiestate.edu
BURNLEY, Lawrence, A .. 509-777-4215. 525 F
lburnley@whitworth.edu
BURNLEY, Linda ... 646-888-6639. 329 J
burnleyl@sloankettering.edu
BURNNETT, Susan ... 415-451-2864... 63 A
sburnnett@sfts.edu
BURNS, Andrew ... 970-247-7180... 81 M
burns_a@fortlewis.edu
BURNS, Anita ... 518-464-8545. 324 B
aburns@excelsior.edu
BURNS, Barb ... 314-392-2362. 278 B
burnsba@mobap.edu
BURNS, Beth ... 419-755-4324. 385 D
burns.152@osu.edu
BURNS, Betty ... 812-749-1237. 171 K
bburns@oak.edu
BURNS, Bob ... 617-627-3783. 237 C
bob.burns@tufts.edu
BURNS, Candace ... 973-720-2138. 308 I
burnsc@wpunj.edu
BURNS, Carl, F ... 573-341-4292. 284 A
carlb@mst.edu
BURNS, Carla ... 973-408-3560. 301 C
cburns@drew.edu
BURNS, Cathy ... 918-343-7538. 399 C
cburns@rsu.edu
BURNS, Connie ... 610-799-1740. 421 I
cburns1@lccc.edu
BURNS, Donna ... 909-274-4220... 55 A
dburns@mtsac.edu
BURNS, Elizabeth ... 315-312-4100. 344 A
elizabeth.burns@oswego.edu
BURNS, Gary ... 816-501-4854. 280 I
gary.burns@rockhurst.edu
BURNS, Gordon, G ... 336-838-6112. 365 B
gordon.burns@wilkescc.edu
BURNS, J. Joseph ... 617-552-3273. 224 A
john.burns@bc.edu
BURNS, Jacquelyn ... 307-855-2150. 542 Y
jburns@cwc.edu
BURNS, James, R ... 617-552-1603. 224 A
james.burns.3@bc.edu
BURNS, James, T ... 215-670-9235. 425 J
jtburns@peirce.edu
BURNS, Janie ... 731-352-4000. 453 D
burnsj@bethelu.edu
BURNS, Jeffrey, S ... 804-752-7367. 508 E
jburns@rmc.edu
BURNS, Jennifer, A ... 412-365-1849. 412 K
jburns@chatham.edu
BURNS, Joseph, A ... 607-255-4843. 322 A
deanoffaculty-mailbox@cornell.edu
BURNS, Karen, S ... 713-525-2124. 490 L
burns@stthom.edu
BURNS, Kathleen ... 508-678-2811. 231 B
kathleen.burns@bristolcc.edu
BURNS, Kelli ... 314-539-5371. 281 D
kburns@stlcc.edu
BURNS, Kevin, J ... 757-823-8381. 507 M
kburns@nsu.edu
BURNS, Kimberly ... 215-567-7080. 410 A
kburns@aii.edu
BURNS, Kristen ... 703-658-4304. 503 L
krisburns@christendom.edu
BURNS, Larry ... 909-537-5250... 34 E
lburns@csusb.edu
BURNS, Lawrence, J ... 419-530-1228. 392 B
lawrence.burns2@utoledo.edu
BURNS, Lita ... 208-769-3302. 138 I
lita_burns@nic.edu
BURNS, Marie-Elaine ... 408-288-3191... 63 P
marie-elaine.burns@sjcc.edu
BURNS, Marvin ... 405-466-6150. 395 N
mburns@langston.edu
BURNS, Matthew ... 585-275-4085. 349 C
matthew.burns@rochester.edu
BURNS, Max ... 678-359-5015. 127 A
mburns@gordonstate.edu
BURNS, Nancy ... 408-260-0208... 44 J
sjadmissions@fivebranches.edu
BURNS, Patrick ... 928-776-2055... 19 H
patrick.burns@yc.edu
BURNS, Patrick ... 970-491-1833... 80 I
patrick.burns@colostate.edu
BURNS, Pauletta ... 256-306-2598..... 2 F
pburns@calhoun.edu
BURNS, Paulette ... 817-257-7650. 484 I
p.burns@tcu.edu
BURNS, Peter, S ... 716-926-8895. 326 B
pburns@hilbert.edu
BURNS, Rachel ... 301-369-2800. 213 G
reburns@capitol-college.edu
BURNS, Randy ... 270-384-8170. 197 D
burnsr@lindsey.edu
BURNS, Raymond ... 715-634-4790. 533 Q
rburns@lco.edu
BURNS, Roger, E ... 252-334-2043. 357 A
roger.burns@macuniversity.edu
BURNS, Sarah, H ... 704-233-8128. 370 G
shburns@wingate.edu
BURNS, Shanna ... 715-634-4790. 533 Q
sburns@lco.edu
BURNS, Shawn, G ... 806-651-2300. 484 D
sburns@mail.wtamu.edu
BURNS, Sonya, L ... 270-824-1823. 196 A
sonyal.burns@kctcs.edu
BURNS, Susan ... 712-274-5388. 181 B
burns@morningside.edu
BURNS, Thomas ... 716-286-8580. 334 F
tburns@niagara.edu
BURNS, Thomas, D ... 615-460-6400. 453 C
thomas.burns@belmont.edu
BURNS, Todd ... 309-268-8046. 146 B
todd.burns@heartland.edu
BURNS, Wendy ... 651-523-2235. 256 A
wburns@hamline.edu
BURNS, William ... 701-231-7671. 371 G
william.burns@ndsu.edu
BURNS, Yvonne ... 210-829-3900. 490 A
yburns@uiwtx.edu
BURNSIDE, Alphonso ... 305-626-3668. 104 J
Alphonso.Burnside@fmuniv.edu
BURNSIDE, Michael ... 404-225-4448. 121 B
mburnside@atlantatech.edu
BURR, Donna ... 805-966-3888... 30 A
dburr@brooks.edu
BURR, Jason, H ... 864-597-4381. 449 I
burrjh@wofford.edu
BURR, O.D ... 916-568-3048... 52 K
burro@losrios.edu
BURR, Stephen ... 313-883-8623. 249 E
burr.stephen@shms.edu
BURRAGE, Marie ... 212-817-7209. 317 F
mburrage@gc.cuny.edu
BURRELL, Becky ... 419-995-8331. 381 Q
burrell.b@rhodesstate.edu
BURRELL, Daniel ... 414-297-7043. 540 E
burrelld@matc.edu
BURRELL, James ... 704-378-1081. 355 K
jburrell@jcsu.edu
BURRELL, Ray ... 919-735-5151. 364 H
rayb@waynecc.edu
BURRELL, Robyn ... 619-477-6310... 70 D
rburrell@asuniversity.edu
BURRELL, Steve ... 912-478-1294. 126 C
sburrell@georgiasouthern.edu
BURRELL, Tamara ... 704-337-2498. 365 G
burrellt@queens.edu
BURRELL, Todd, C ... 618-650-3705. 159 H
tburrel@siue.edu
BURRER, Dennis, J ... 903-923-3252. 486 A
dennis.burrer@tstc.edu
BURRER, Jarod, K ... 304-877-6428. 526 C
jarod.burrer@abc.edu
BURRIGHT, John ... 913-288-7240. 187 L
jburright@kckcc.edu
BURRILL, Jennifer, R ... 269-471-6601. 239 D
burrillj@andrews.edu
BURRIS, David ... 530-283-0202... 44 H
dburris@frc.edu
BURRIS, Deborah, J ... 314-516-5695. 283 E
dburris@umsl.edu
BURRIS, Janssen ... 225-214-1947. 206 D
janssen.burris@ololcollege.edu
BURRIS, Kendra ... 806-743-2786. 487 E
kendra.burris@ttuhsc.edu
BURRIS, Rolanda ... 847-628-1069. 149 B
rburris@judsonu.edu
BURRIS, Sandra ... 503-725-2845. 406 B
sandra.burris@pdx.edu
BURROUGHS, Cynthia ... 501-370-5337... 22 F
cburroughs@philander.edu
BURROUGHS, Dave ... 620-441-5246. 186 A
burroughsdav@cowley.edu
BURROUGHS, Lisa ... 229-248-2522. 121 E
lisa.burroughs@bainbridge.edu
BURROUGHS,
W. Jeffrey ... 808-675-3923. 135 C
burrougj@byuh.edu
BURROUGHS-DAVIS,
Robin ... 603-526-3752. 295 I
rdavis@colby-sawyer.edu
BURROW, Jeanavon ... 706-865-2134. 133 B
jburrow@truett.edu
BURROWES, Natasha ... 206-878-3710. 520 E
nburrowes@highline.edu
BURROWS, Angie ... 570-372-4120. 433 H
burrowsa@susqu.edu
BURROWS, Carmen ... 757-825-2939. 514 B
burrowsc@tncc.edu
BURROWS, David ... 920-832-6528. 533 S
david.burrows@lawrence.edu
BURROWS, SC,
Joanne, M ... 563-588-6385. 176 F
joanne.burrows@clarke.edu
BURROWS-SCHUMACHER,
Molly, A ... 563-588-4981. 180 L
molly.burrowsschumacher@loras.edu
BURRUS, Ken ... 509-533-7220. 518 D
kburrus@ccs.spokane.edu
BURRUS, Ken ... 509-533-7220. 518 E
ken.burrus@ccs.spokane.edu
BURRUS, Ken ... 509-533-3630. 518 F
ken.burrus@ccs.spokane.edu
BURRUS, Scott ... 928-541-7777... 16 B
sburrus@ncu.edu
BURRUSS, John, W ... 713-798-6265. 467 F
jburruss@bcm.edu
BURRUSS, Nancy, M ... 920-433-6632. 531 L
nancy.burruss@bellincollege.edu
BURRUTO, James ... 315-781-3319. 326 C
burruto@hws.edu
BURSAVICH, Gregory, F . 336-316-2841. 355 A
bursavichgf@guilford.edu
BURSON, Max ... 316-295-5521. 186 H
mburson@friends.edu
BURSTEIN, Mark ... 920-832-6525. 533 S
mark.burstein@lawrence.edu
BURSTYN, Yaakov ... 305-534-7050. 117 E
BURSZTYN, Jacob ... 732-367-1060. 299 E
jbursztyn@bmg.edu
BURT, Bruce, E ... 937-229-2131. 391 C
bburt1@udayton.edu
BURT, Cecil ... 601-554-5506. 269 D
jcburt@prcc.edu
BURT, Charles ... 617-745-3725. 225 G
charles.burt@enc.edu
BURT, Jennifer, A ... 435-586-1997. 497 A
burt@suu.edu
BURT, Mickey, G ... 563-884-5451. 182 A
mickey.burt@palmer.edu
BURT, Theresa, E ... 215-926-2010. 433 K
theresa.burt@temple.edu
BURT, Walter ... 269-387-1821. 252 I
walter.burt@wmich.edu
BURT, Yolanda ... 216-687-2246. 377 F
y.burt@csuohio.edu
BURT-GRACIK, Mélissa .. 619-849-2253... 59 L
melissaburtgracik@pointloma.edu
BURTIS, Brett, K ... 307-674-6446. 543 F
bburtis@sheridan.edu
BURTIS, Karen, B ... 307-674-6446. 543 F
kburtis@sheridan.edu
BURTLEY, Harold ... 219-980-6778. 168 B
hburtley@iun.edu
BURTNER, Jeff, R ... 540-338-1776. 508 A
BURTON, Adam ... 951-343-4286... 30 H
aburton@calbaptist.edu
BURTON, Alan ... 580-745-2731. 399 J
aburton@se.edu
BURTON, Andre ... 330-325-6733. 385 E
aburton@neomed.edu
BURTON, Becky ... 770-962-7580. 127 D
bburton@gwinnetttech.edu
BURTON, Ben ... 317-921-4712. 169 K
bburton@ivytech.edu
BURTON, Brian, K ... 360-650-3896. 525 C
brian.burton@wwu.edu
BURTON, Caroyn ... 434-381-6510. 510 F
cburton@sbc.edu
BURTON, Courtney ... 212-799-5000. 328 B
BURTON,
Crompton (Hub), B ... 740-376-4402. 383 E
hub.burton@marietta.edu
BURTON, Dan ... 513-244-8167. 376 J
dan.burton@ccuniversity.edu
BURTON, Donald, N ... 602-648-5750... 13 I
dburton@dunlap-stone.edu
BURTON, Elizabeth ... 610-399-2427. 428 B
eburton@cheyney.edu
BURTON, Gene ... 765-285-1832. 164 D
gburton@bsu.edu
BURTON, Gregory, A ... 973-761-9362. 307 C
gregory.burton@shu.edu
BURTON, Harold ... 606-886-3863. 194 K
harold.burton@kctcs.edu
BURTON, Heather ... 540-868-7201. 512 H
hburton@lfcc.edu
BURTON, Hyacinth ... 256-726-7070..... 6 B
hburton@oakwood.edu
BURTON, Jennus, L ... 928-523-2708... 16 C
jennus.burton@nau.edu
BURTON, Jeremy ... 918-495-6647. 398 H
jburton@oru.edu
BURTON, Lisa, E ... 256-765-4317..... 9 C
leburton@una.edu
BURTON, Liz ... 541-962-3359. 405 H
eburton@eou.edu
BURTON, Lonnie ... 806-291-3635. 494 F
burtonl@wbu.edu
BURTON, Marjorie ... 440-775-5782. 385 H
marjorie.burton@oberlin.edu
BURTON, Michele ... 503-842-8222. 408 B
burton@tillamookbay.cc
BURTON, Patrice ... 708-596-2000. 159 C
pburton@ssc.edu
BURTON, Raymond, A ... 804-523-5374. 512 F
rburton@reynolds.edu
BURTON, Rebecca ... 972-854-5611. 469 L
rebecca.burton@concordia.edu
BURTON, Robert ... 808-984-3245. 137 B
reburton@hawaii.edu
BURTON, Stacy ... 775-784-1740. 294 J
sburton@unr.edu
BURTON, Terrance ... 508-999-8664. 229 A
tburton@umassd.edu
BURTON, Timothy, P ... 516-877-3385. 313 A
burton@adelphi.edu
BURTON, JR.,
Velmer, S ... 662-915-5526. 270 B
vsburton@olemiss.edu
BURTON, William ... 312-996-5546. 161 D
burton@uic.edu
BURTON-GOSS, Sadie ... 781-239-6334. 222 D
sburtongoss@babson.edu
BURTON-GRAHAM,
Laura ... 410-337-6439. 215 A
lburtong@goucher.edu
BURTT, Edward, H ... 740-368-3886. 387 J
ehburtt@owu.edu
BURWELL, Elissia ... 903-730-4890. 474 O
elissia_burwell@jarvis.edu
BURWELL, Michelle ... 610-399-2302. 428 B
mburwell@cheyney.edu
BURWELL, Tim, H ... 828-262-2070. 367 A
burwellth@appstate.edu
BURY, Sandra ... 309-677-2808. 140 I
sandy@bradley.edu
BURZACHECHI,
Nancilee ... 412-237-8182. 413 D
nancilee@ccac.edu
BURZICHELLI, Dominick 856-415-2292. 302 C
dburzichelli@gccnj.edu
BURZINSKI, Jody ... 620-421-6700. 188 D
jodyb@labette.edu
BUSALACCHI, James ... 509-963-1202. 517 F
busalacchij@cwu.edu
BUSAM, Leah ... 513-745-4879. 393 H
busaml@xavier.edu
BUSBEE, Walter ... 803-508-7254. 440 G
busbeew@atc.edu
BUSBOOM, Margo ... 402-461-7494. 289 I
mbusboom@hastings.edu
BUSBY, Bruce ... 260-481-6140. 168 C
busbyb@ipfw.edu
BUSBY, Michael ... 615-963-7631. 459 E
mbusby@tnstate.edu
BUSBY, Teresa ... 601-446-1211. 266 F
teresa.busby@colin.edu

BUSCH, Brian .... 252-789-0293. 361 G
bbusch@martincc.edu
BUSCH, C. Lawrence ...... 419-772-2362. 386 D
c-busch@onu.edu
BUSCH, Caroline, C .... 804-752-3267. 508 E
cbusch@rmc.edu
BUSCH, Gregory .... 419-755-4570. 385 D
gbusch@ncstatecollege.edu
BUSCH, Mary, E .... 317-788-3302. 173 I
busch@uindy.edu
BUSCH, Marybeth .... 419-755-4549. 385 D
mbusch@ncstatecollege.edu
BUSCH, Nancy .... 402-472-2526. 292 I
nbusch2@unl.edu
BUSCH, Nancy .... 718-817-4400. 324 G
busch@fordham.edu
BUSCHART, W. David .... 303-762-6907... 81 G
david.buschart@denverseminary.edu
BUSCHER, Frank .... 901-321-3230. 453 H
fbuscher@cbu.edu
BUSCHMAN, John, E ..... 973-761-9005. 307 C
john.buschman@shu.edu
BUSCHUR, Carol .... 513-475-3600. 194 B
cbuschur@galencollege.edu
BUSE, Beth, H .... 651-201-1799. 257 N
beth.buse@so.mnscu.edu
BUSE, Jon .... 319-398-5584. 180 J
jbuse@kirkwood.edu
BUSE, Kathleen .... 973-618-3411. 300 A
kbuse@caldwell.edu
BUSE, William .... 212-799-5000. 328 B
BUSEL, Yaakov .... 732-985-6533. 304 F
BUSER, Boyd, R .... 606-218-5411. 200 F
boydbuser@upike.edu
BUSH, Abra .... 617-912-9124. 224 B
abush@bostonconservatory.edu
BUSH, Cathy .... 440-525-7112. 382 M
cbush@lakelandcc.edu
BUSH, David .... 435-797-1012. 497 B
david.bush@usu.edu
BUSH, David .... 972-825-4888. 481 F
dbush@sagu.edu
BUSH, Edward .... 951-222-8837... 61 A
edward.bush@rcc.edu
BUSH, Gary, W .... 678-915-5501. 132 C
gbush@spsu.edu
BUSH, Jean .... 940-565-2055. 490 C
jean.bush@unt.edu
BUSH, Jeffrey, A .... 504-862-8385. 207 C
jbush@tulane.edu
BUSH, Jim .... 509-865-8570. 520 D
bush_j@heritage.edu
BUSH, Katherine .... 845-437-5900. 349 G
kabush@vassar.edu
BUSH, Keith .... 218-751-8670. 263 C
it@oakhills.edu
BUSH, Kristen .... 540-231-6994. 515 C
khbush@vt.edu
BUSH, Lisa, F .... 828-398-7202. 357 N
lbush@abtech.edu
BUSH, Lonica .... 409-933-8413. 469 E
lbush@com.edu
BUSH, Michael .... 805-986-5813... 74 G
mbush@vcccd.edu
BUSH, Rachel .... 229-732-5962. 120 D
rachelbush@andrewcollege.edu
BUSH, Robert .... 318-473-6414. 205 A
rbush@lsua.edu
BUSH, TaJuan .... 215-335-0800. 422 C
tbush@lincolntech.com
BUSHER, Edward, J .... 937-429-8922. 377 A
bushere@clarkstate.edu
BUSHER, Edward, J .... 937-328-6095. 377 A
bushere@clarkstate.edu
BUSHEY, Jane .... 480-245-7930... 14 B
jane.bushey@ibcs.edu
BUSHEY, Stephanie .... 516-463-6853. 326 D
stephanie.bushey@hofstra.edu
BUSHLEY, Tom .... 434-832-7725. 512 A
bushleyt@cvcc.vccs.edu
BUSHMAN, David, L ...... 540-868-7143. 512 H
dbushman@lfcc.edu
BUSHMAN, David, W ..... 540-828-5605. 502 J
dbushman@bridgewater.edu
BUSHMAN, Edward .... 414-297-6641. 540 E
bushmane@matc.edu
BUSHNELL, Elizabeth, J . 260-982-5242. 170 U
ejbushnell@manchester.edu
BUSHNELL, Lynn, M ...... 203-582-8651... 91 A
lynn.bushnell@quinnipiac.edu
BUSHNELL, Rebecca, W . 215-898-7320. 435 B
bushnell@sas.upenn.edu
BUSHNELL, Ryan .... 517-321-0242. 243 F
rbushnell@glcc.edu
BUSHONG, Sara .... 419-372-2856. 374 K
sbushon@bgsu.edu
BUSHWAY, Deborah .... 612-977-4149. 254 C
deborah.bushway@capella.edu
BUSIC, David .... 816-268-5402. 279 G
lkneely@nts.edu

BUSKEY, Cynthia .... 404-880-8550. 122 J
cbuskey@cau.edu
BUSROE, Andrew .... 606-368-6113. 191 J
andrewbusroe@alc.edu
BUSS, Brian .... 920-735-5792. 539 K
buss@fvtc.edu
BUSS, James .... 410-543-6000. 220 D
BUSS, Marney .... 734-487-1300. 242 D
mbuss@emich.edu
BUSSARD, Patsy, G .... 276-964-7332. 514 A
pat.bussard@sw.edu
BUSSE, Dan .... 850-484-1158. 110 G
dbusse@pensacolastate.edu
BUSSELL, Helena .... 817-531-4405. 488 A
hbussell@txwes.edu
BUSSELL, Paige .... 903-468-3209. 483 E
paige.bussell@tamuc.edu
BUSSELL, Rachelle .... 909-558-4544... 51 C
rbussell@llu.edu
BUSSEY, Brenda .... 508-929-8455. 230 G
bbussey@worcester.edu
BUSSEY, Tosha .... 404-527-4520. 122 E
tbussey@carver.edu
BUSTA, Joseph, F .... 251-460-7616..... 9 E
jbusta@southalabama.edu
BUSTAMANTE, Camilla .. 505-747-5454. 311 E
cbustamante@nnmc.edu
BUSTAMANTE, Chris ...... 480-517-8118... 15 D
chris.bustamente@riosalado.edu
BUSTAMANTE, Mary .... 610-519-4300. 436 F
mary.bustamante@villanova.edu
BUSTARD, James .... 217-351-2211. 155 J
jbustard@parkland.edu
BUSTER-WILLIAMS,
Kimberley .... 815-753-5600. 154 I
kbusterwilliams@niu.edu
BUSTILLO, Pamela .... 408-273-2696... 55 H
pbustillo@nhu.edu
BUSTOS, Javier .... 414-425-8300. 535 K
jbustos@shst.edu
BUSTOS, Phillip .... 505-224-4741. 309 E
pbustos@cnm.edu
BUSTROM, Carla .... 612-977-5302. 254 C
carla.bustrom@capella.edu
BUTALA, Dick .... 612-977-5770. 254 C
richard.butala@capella.edu
BUTCHER, Alva .... 253-879-3394. 524 F
abutcher@pugetsound.edu
BUTCHER, Claudette .... 918-293-5256. 398 B
claudette.butcher@okstate.edu
BUTCHER, Fred, R .... 304-293-1536. 530 D
fbutcher@hsc.wvu.edu
BUTCHER, Marilea .... 304-647-6367. 530 B
mbutcher@osteo.wvsom.edu
BUTCHER, Michael .... 912-279-5815. 123 B
mbutcher@ccga.edu
BUTCHER, Phil .... 713-942-3409. 490 L
butchep@stthom.edu
BUTCHER, Sean .... 706-233-7491. 131 E
sbutcher@shorter.edu
BUTCHER, Thomas, A .... 616-331-2067. 243 C
butchert@gvsu.edu
BUTCHER, Tina .... 706-507-8265. 123 D
butcher_tina@columbusstate.edu
BUTCHKO, Thomas .... 570-208-5928. 419 P
thomasbutchko@kings.edu
BUTDORFF, Carla .... 419-747-5401. 385 D
196mgr@fheg.follett.com
BUTERA, Rae-Anne .... 781-292-2321. 226 G
rae-anne.butera@olin.edu
BUTIN, Dan .... 978-837-5338. 234 A
dan.butin@merrimack.edu
BUTKOVICH, Michelle .... 248-204-2111. 245 I
mbutkovic@ltu.edu
BUTLER, Allen, P .... 815-455-8999. 152 F
abutler@mchenry.edu
BUTLER, Andra .... 606-546-1224. 200 A
abutler@unionky.edu
BUTLER, Ann .... 910-592-8081. 363 E
abutler@sampsoncc.edu
BUTLER, Beatrice .... 210-486-2300. 465 B
bbutler@alamo.edu
BUTLER, Becky .... 214-333-5106. 470 D
beckyb@dbu.edu
BUTLER, Bruce, D .... 713-500-3369. 492 E
bruce.d.butler@uth.tmc.edu
BUTLER, Bryant .... 601-968-5930. 266 A
bbutler@belhaven.edu
BUTLER, Connie .... 402-643-7332. 289 B
connie.butler@cune.edu
BUTLER, D. Martin .... 816-268-5421. 279 G
dbutler@nts.edu
BUTLER, Dionne, K .... 714-879-3901... 47 K
dkbutler@hiu.edu
BUTLER, Doze .... 225-771-5390. 206 J
doze_butler@subr.edu
BUTLER, Greg .... 601-477-4113. 267 F
greg.butler@jcjc.edu
BUTLER, Harry, P .... 248-204-3925. 245 I
hbutler@ltu.edu

BUTLER, Heidi .... 610-861-5453. 425 D
hbutler@northampton.edu
BUTLER, Jack .... 931-372-3227. 460 A
jbutler@tntech.edu
BUTLER, Janice, R .... 570-577-3973. 411 A
janice.butler@bucknell.edu
BUTLER, Jay .... 718-405-3417. 320 G
jay.butler@mountsaintvincent.edu
BUTLER, Jennifer .... 708-656-8000. 153 H
jennifer.butler@morton.edu
BUTLER, Jessica .... 260-481-6807. 168 C
butljm01@ipfw.edu
BUTLER, Joan .... 972-825-4650. 481 F
jbutler@sagu.edu
BUTLER, Joe .... 972-599-3121. 469 G
jrbutler@collin.edu
BUTLER, SJ, John, T ...... 617-552-2257. 224 A
john.butler@bc.edu
BUTLER, Johnnella, E ..... 404-270-5022. 132 E
jebutler@spelman.edu
BUTLER, Kathleen .... 860-231-5322... 92 F
kbutler@usj.edu
BUTLER, Kathleen, P ...... 325-235-7311. 486 C
kathleen.butler@tstc.edu
BUTLER, Kathy .... 304-558-0261. 529 C
butler@hepc.wvnet.edu
BUTLER, Ken .... 484-664-3126. 424 H
butler@muhlenberg.edu
BUTLER, Kevin .... 702-992-2312. 294 G
kevin.butler@nsc.edu
BUTLER, Kevin .... 704-337-2253. 365 G
butlerk@queens.edu
BUTLER, Kim, I .... 515-263-2841. 178 G
maintenance@grandview.edu
BUTLER, LeRoy .... 419-824-3938. 383 C
lbutler@lourdes.edu
BUTLER, Markisha .... 912-427-1969. 120 B
mbutler@altamahatech.edu
BUTLER, Mary Edith .... 630-466-7900. 162 J
mbutler@waubonsee.edu
BUTLER, Michael .... 909-469-5534... 76 B
mbutler@westernu.edu
BUTLER, Patrick, B .... 319-335-3565. 175 I
patrick-butler@uiowa.edu
BUTLER, Paul, C .... 856-225-6637. 306 C
pbutler@camden.rutgers.edu
BUTLER, Peter, W .... 312-942-8801. 157 G
peter_butler@rush.edu
BUTLER, Rebecca, A .... 419-434-5797. 391 D
butlerr@findlay.edu
BUTLER, Renee .... 718-482-5292. 318 F
rbutler@lagcc.cuny.edu
BUTLER, Robert .... 707-256-7625... 55 F
rbutler@napavalley.edu
BUTLER, Roxanna .... 405-682-1611. 397 E
rbutler@occc.edu
BUTLER, Sarah .... 715-634-4790. 533 Q
sbutler@lco.edu
BUTLER, Shai .... 518-337-2306. 321 A
butlers@strose.edu
BUTLER, Sharon .... 517-884-0101. 246 H
sbutler@msu.edu
BUTLER, Shirley .... 843-349-5218. 444 F
shirley.butler@hgtc.edu
BUTLER, Stephen, L .... 251-626-3303..... 8 B
sbutler@ussa.edu
BUTLER, Thomas, E .... 361-582-2560. 493 H
tom.butler@victoriacollege.edu
BUTLER, Timothy .... 636-627-2935. 276 D
tbutler@lindenwood.edu
BUTLER, Timothy, J .... 215-951-2744. 430 E
butlert@philau.edu
BUTLER, Tori .... 903-923-2455. 495 A
tbutler@wileyc.edu
BUTLER, Vanessa .... 310-434-4792... 65 A
butler_vanessa@smc.edu
BUTLER, Walter .... 731-352-4000. 453 D
butlerw@bethelu.edu
BUTLER, Wendy .... 303-837-0825... 78 H
wlbutler@aii.edu
BUTLER, William, E .... 214-860-2057. 470 J
wbutler@dcccd.edu
BUTLER-LUDWIG,
John, L .... 773-442-4670. 154 H
j-butler-ludwig@neiu.edu
BUTLER-PURRY,
Karen, L .... 979-845-3628. 483 C
klbutler@tamu.edu
BUTNER, Dustie .... 405-382-9525. 399 I
d.butner@sscok.edu
BUTRUM, Michael .... 660-263-3900. 272 A
michaelb@cccb.edu
BUTT, Allen .... 505-473-6065. 311 K
allen.butt@santafeuniversity.edu
BUTT, Debi, S .... 336-841-4524. 355 C
debib@highpoint.edu
BUTTAFARRO, JR.,
Thomas .... 716-375-2155. 338 E
tbuttafa@sbu.edu

BUTTENSCHON,
Marianne .... 315-792-5631. 331 I
mbuttenschon@mvcc.edu
BUTTER, Karen .... 415-476-8293... 72 A
Karen.Butter@ucsf.edu
BUTTERBAUGH,
Randy, R .... 318-797-5116. 205 F
randy.butterbaugh@lsus.edu
BUTTERFIELD, Kevin ...... 804-289-8942. 510 L
kbutterf@richmond.edu
BUTTERFIELD, Patricia ... 509-324-7332. 519 C
pbutter@wsu.edu
BUTTERFIELD, Patricia ... 509-324-7332. 525 A
pbutter@wsu.edu
BUTTERMORE, Jim .... 724-964-8811. 425 A
jbuttermore@ncstrades.edu
BUTTERS, Penny .... 509-533-3527. 518 F
penny.butters@spokanefalls.edu
BUTTERWORTH, Sandra . 248-476-1122. 246 G
sbutterworth@mispp.edu
BUTTLEMAN, Kurt .... 206-934-4111. 522 H
kurt.buttleman@seattlecolleges.edu
BUTTON, Kyle, C .... 323-343-3060... 34 A
kbutton@cslanet.calstatela.edu
BUTTON, Sharon .... 815-455-7796. 152 F
sbutton@mchenry.edu
BUTTRY, Tonya .... 573-334-6825. 282 A
tbuttry@sehosp.org
BUTTS, III, Calvin, O ..... 516-876-3160. 343 D
buttsc@oldwestbury.edu
BUTTS, Carl .... 407-673-7406. 108 W
cbutts@lincolntech.com
BUTTS, Dawn .... 803-508-7332. 440 G
buttsd@atc.edu
BUTTS, Elvin .... 910-892-3178. 355 B
ebutts@heritagebiblecollege.edu
BUTTS, Jeffrey .... 212-237-8486. 318 D
jbutts@jjay.cuny.edu
BUTTS, Rachelle .... 913-385-7700. 191 H
rbutts@wrightcc.edu
BUTTS, Sue .... 251-981-3771..... 2 I
sue.butts@columbiasouthern.edu
BUTTS WILLIAMS,
Barbara .... 612-977-5335. 254 C
barbara.buttswilliams@capella.edu
BUTVILAS, George .... 906-487-2303. 247 A
gjbutvil@mtu.edu
BUTWELL, Justin .... 845-575-3000. 330 D
justin.butwell@marist.edu
BUTZINE, Craig, S .... 724-938-1675. 428 A
BUUCK, Thomas .... 260-399-7700. 174 C
tbuuck@sf.edu
BUXBAUM, Hannah .... 812-855-8886. 167 F
hbuxbaum@indiana.edu
BUXBAUM, Howard .... 973-748-9000. 299 F
howard_buxbaum@bloomfield.edu
BUXTON, Barry, M .... 828-898-8785. 356 A
buxtonb@lmc.edu
BUXTON, Bonnie .... 678-225-7465. 430 D
BUXTON, Carolyn .... 330-263-2631. 377 H
cbuxton@wooster.edu
BUXTON, Jasmine .... 256-372-5615..... 1 A
jasmine.buxton@aamu.edu
BUXTON, Ralph, W .... 212-220-1432. 317 A
rbuxton@bmcc.cuny.edu
BUXTON, Robert, E .... 423-478-7703. 458 B
rbuxton@ptseminary.edu
BUXTON, Sheldon .... 918-335-6291. 398 F
sbuxton@okwu.edu
BUYEA, James .... 518-327-6099. 336 B
jbuyea@paulsmiths.edu
BUYOK, Albert .... 970-339-6683... 78 C
albert.buyok@aims.edu
BUZANSKI, Catherine ..... 716-880-2179. 330 F
catherine.buzanski@medaille.edu
BUZHARDT, Landee .... 803-321-5106. 445 G
landee.buzhardt@newberry.edu
BUZZARD, Janet .... 575-562-2343. 309 H
janet.buzzard@enmu.edu
BUZZELL, Sidney, S .... 303-963-3421... 79 C
sbuzzell@ccu.edu
BUZZELLI, OSB,
Aaron, N .... 724-532-7961. 432 H
aaron.buzzelli@email.stvincent.edu
BUZZELLI, Andrew .... 210-883-1190. 490 A
optometry@uiwtx.edu
BYARD, Brenda, K .... 540-868-7208. 512 H
bbyard@lfcc.edu
BYARS, Don .... 936-261-1057. 482 F
dobyars@pvamu.edu
BYARS, Lauretta, F .... 936-261-2120. 482 F
lfbyars@pvamu.edu
BYARS, Roger, D .... 713-313-1814. 485 F
byarsrd@tsu.edu
BYARS, Susan .... 239-590-7980. 115 A
sbyars@fgcu.edu
BYARS, Tracy .... 650-493-4430... 66 E
tracy.byars@sofia.edu
BYAS, Renee .... 713-718-5059. 473 C
renee.byas@hccs.edu

BYELICH, David, S .... 517-355-9271. 246 H
byelich@msu.edu
BYERLY, Alison, R .... 610-330-5200. 420 D
byerlya@lafayette.edu
BYERLY, Gary, R .... 225-578-3885. 204 O
graddeanoffice@lsu.edu
BYERLY, James .... 208-376-7731. 137 F
jbyerly@boisebible.edu
BYERS, Arthur .... 617-262-5000. 223 F
art.byers@the-bac.edu
BYERS, Barbara .... 304-876-5276. 529 I
bbyers@shepherd.edu
BYERS, Beth .... 478-471-2732. 128 I
beth.byers@maconstate.edu
BYERS, Deborah .... 316-978-3430. 191 F
deb.byers@wichita.edu
BYERS, Merrie .... 970-675-3204... 80 B
merrie.byers@cnc.edu
BYERS, Michael .... 304-260-4380. 527 N
mbyers@blueridgectc.edu
BYERS, Michael .... 212-817-7730. 317 F
facilities@gc.cuny.edu
BYERS, Michael, T .... 336-334-5768. 369 A
mike_byers@uncg.edu
BYERS, Michelle, C .... 319-273-2423. 176 A
michelle.byers@uni.edu
BYERS, R. Charles .... 304-766-3148. 530 C
rcbyers@wvstateu.edu
BYERS, Richard .... 503-491-7131. 404 E
richard.byers@mhcc.edu
BYFORD, Tina .... 575-646-1613. 310 I
tbyford@nmsu.edu
BYHAM, Richard, N .... 509-963-1504. 517 F
byhamr@cwu.edu
BYINGTON, J. Ralph ...... 843-349-2086. 442 E
byington@coastal.edu
BYINGTON, Kathleen, M 410-706-2802. 219 C
kbyington@af.umaryland.edu
BYINGTON, Terry .... 425-739-8219. 520 K
terry.byington@lwtech.edu
BYL, Beverly .... 707-654-1037... 31 I
bbyl@csum.edu
BYLAND, Tamara, C .... 816-235-1208. 283 D
Bylandt@umkc.edu
BYLANDER, Joyce, A ..... 717-245-1411. 414 H
bylander@dickinson.edu
BYLSMA, Thomas, W ..... 616-395-7781. 244 A
bylsma@hope.edu
BYMAN, Gregory, P .... 260-422-5561. 167 B
gpbyman@indianatech.edu
BYNOG, Elizabeth .... 318-487-5443. 202 M
elizabethbynog@cltc.edu
BYNUM, DeWayne .... 912-583-3280. 122 B
dbynum@bpc.edu
BYNUM, James .... 919-735-5151. 364 H
jbynum@waynecc.edu
BYNUM, Jennifer .... 979-209-7640. 467 I
jennifer.bynum@blinn.edu
BYNUM, Leroy .... 229-430-4832. 119 J
leroy.bynum@asurams.edu
BYNUM, Lou Anne .... 562-938-5015... 51 D
lbynum@lbcc.edu
BYNUM, Lynn, M .... 502-272-8236. 192 E
lbynum@bellarmine.edu
BYNUM, Regina .... 757-455-3352. 515 H
rbynum@vwc.edu
BYNUM, Robin .... 334-983-6556..... 7 H
rbynum@troy.edu
BYNUM, Staci .... 618-985-3741. 148 J
stacibynum@jalc.edu
BYNUM, Torrance .... 415-550-4348... 38 L
tbynum@ccsf.edu
BYRD, Alan .... 314-516-6471. 283 E
byrdak@umsl.edu
BYRD, Amanda, P .... 336-633-0217. 362 H
apbyrd@randolph.edu
BYRD, Bonita, E .... 410-651-6088. 219 E
bebyrd@umes.edu
BYRD, Brandon .... 803-765-6023. 441 A
bbyrd@allenuniversity.edu
BYRD, Cal .... 847-608-5457. 144 F
cbyrd@elgin.edu
BYRD, Carl .... 334-387-3877..... 1 E
carlbyrd@amridgeuniversity.edu
BYRD, Christopher, D .... 803-777-3824. 447 G
cbyrd@sc.edu
BYRD, Damon, D .... 404-527-4522. 122 E
dbyrd@carver.edu
BYRD, David .... 401-874-5484. 440 D
dbyrd@uri.edu
BYRD, Devin .... 912-650-5642. 131 H
dbyrd@southuniversity.edu
BYRD, Donna .... 404-880-8411. 122 J
dbyrd@cau.edu
BYRD, Gina .... 770-229-3050. 132 B
gbyrd@sctech.edu
BYRD, Goldie, S .... 336-334-7806. 367 E
gsbyrd@ncat.edu
BYRD, Holly .... 404-471-6077. 119 I
hbyrd@agnesscott.edu
BYRD, James .... 918-293-4940. 398 B
james.w.byrd@okstate.edu
BYRD, Joseph, K .... 504-520-7357. 209 D
jbyrd@xula.edu
BYRD, Kim .... 307-268-2210. 542 X
kbyrd@caspercollege.edu
BYRD, LeAnne .... 325-481-9300. 473 E
lbyrd@howardcollege.edu
BYRD, Marcia .... 937-529-2201. 390 D
mbyrd@united.edu
BYRD, Margie, L .... 518-438-3111. 330 C
mbyrd@mariacollege.edu
BYRD, Michelle .... 704-922-6263. 360 F
byrd.michelle@gaston.edu
BYRD, Nita .... 919-516-4241. 366 C
nbyrd@st-aug.edu
BYRD, Sherilyn .... 940-898-3748. 488 B
sbyrd@twu.edu
BYRD, Sherlynn .... 903-927-3300. 495 A
sbyrd@wileyc.edu
BYRD, Sherlynn, H .... 903-927-3300. 495 A
sbyrd@wileyc.edu
BYRD, Sherry .... 910-410-1772. 362 I
sherryb@richmondcc.edu
BYRD, Sherryl .... 931-221-7341. 459 B
byrds@apsu.edu
BYRD, Sylvia .... 803-508-7494. 440 G
byrds@atc.edu
BYRD, Theresa .... 619-260-7522... 73 I
tsbyrd@sandiego.edu
BYRD, Traevena .... 607-274-3909. 327 E
tbyrd@ithaca.edu
BYRD-LEWIS, Renee .... 678-407-5685. 125 B
rbyrdlewis@ggc.edu
BYRDSONG-WOODS,
Tashaye .... 615-329-8894. 454 F
tbyrdsong@fisk.edu
BYRN, Mary Pat .... 651-290-6478. 265 F
marypat.byrn@wmitchell.edu
BYRNE, Brian, J .... 212-636-6265. 324 G
bbyrne@fordham.edu
BYRNE, Gregory, K .... 520-621-4622... 18 F
uofaad@arizona.edu
BYRNE, Jamie, M .... 501-569-3244... 24 B
jmbyrne@ualr.edu
BYRNE, Joseph .... 802-485-2312. 500 A
byrne@norwich.edu
BYRNE, Larry .... 309-341-5215. 141 A
lbyrne@sandburg.edu
BYRNE, William, D .... 410-293-7005. 545 J
wdbyrne@usna.edu
BYRNES, David .... 516-671-8355. 350 C
dbyrnes@webb.edu
BYRNES, Don .... 402-323-3408. 292 C
dbyrnes@southeast.edu
BYRNES, John, D .... 815-740-5038. 162 F
jbyrnes@stfrancis.edu
BYRNES, Julie .... 775-753-2271. 294 F
julie.byrnes@gbcnv.edu
BYRNES, Kathleen, J ...... 610-519-4550. 436 F
kathleen.byrnes@villanova.edu
BYRNES, Mark, E .... 615-898-2534. 459 D
mark.byrnes@mtsu.edu
BYRNES, Patrick .... 305-821-3333. 105 A
pbyrnes@fnu.edu
BYRNES, Robert, J .... 718-862-7230. 329 M
robert.byrnes@manhattan.edu
BYRNES, William, J .... 435-586-7703. 497 A
byrnes@suu.edu
BYRON, Shelley .... 607-729-1581. 322 F
sbyron@davisny.edu
BYRON, Tammy .... 860-701-5488... 90 G
byron_t@mitchell.edu
BYSTROM, Karen, L .... 206-726-5169. 518 G
kbystrom@cornish.edu
BYSTRY, Richard, L .... 217-245-3030. 146 F
rlbystry@ic.edu
BZBELL, Wally, B .... 518-783-2342. 340 J
wbzbell@siena.edu

C

CABALLERO, Cesar .... 909-537-5099... 34 E
ccaballe@csusb.edu
CABALLERO, Maria, C .... 323-226-4911... 52 G
mccaballero@dhs.lacounty.gov
CABALLERO, Sharon .... 505-454-3198. 310 E
sscaballero@nmhu.edu
CABALLERO DE CORDERO,
Angela .... 408-864-8945... 44 M
caballerodecorderoangela@deanza.edu
CABALUNA, Dawnette ...... 801-990-1656. 104 F
dawnette@ucmt.com
CABAN, Jose .... 352-588-8362. 112 D
jose.caban@saintleo.edu
CABAN, Jose .... 787-891-0925. 549 K
jcaban@aguadilla.inter.edu
CABAN, Mariveliz .... 787-766-1717. 552 J
marcaban@suagm.edu
CABASA-HESS, Virginia .. 708-456-0300. 161 A
vcabasah@triton.edu
CABASCO, Tony, A .... 509-527-5882. 525 E
cabascja@whitman.edu
CABASSA, Héctor .... 787-892-1365. 551 A
hector.cabassaramos@sodexo.com
CABE, Crista .... 540-887-7380. 507 A
ccabe@mbc.edu
CABELLO, Iris .... 787-765-1915. 551 C
icabello@inter.edu
CABINTE, Ryan .... 415-561-6555... 60 C
CABIYA-MORALES,
Jose, J .... 787-725-6500. 547 H
jcabiya@sju.albizu.edu
CABLE, Amy .... 870-733-6740... 21 I
adcable@midouthcc.edu
CABLE, Christine .... 314-837-6777. 280 K
ccable@slcconline.edu
CABONI, Timothy .... 785-864-7100. 190 L
caboni@ku.edu
CABOT, Jeri, O .... 843-953-5522. 443 A
cabotj@cofc.edu
CABRAL, Jennifer, G .... 740-427-5171. 382 J
cabral@kenyon.edu
CABRAL, Kathleen .... 808-455-0524. 137 A
CABRAL, Manuel, J .... 808-455-0665. 137 A
mcabral@hawaii.edu
CABRAL, Valerie .... 718-260-3982. 336 E
vcabral@poly.edu
CABRAL-MALY,
Margarita, A .... 904-646-2324. 105 E
mcabralm@fscj.edu
CABRALES, Joe .... 909-389-3368... 61 K
jcabrale@craftonhills.edu
CABRALES, Joe .... 909-384-4400... 62 A
jcabrale@sbccd.cc.ca.us
CABRALES-MEDINA,
Araceli .... 773-602-5365. 142 B
CABRERA, Ángel .... 703-993-8700. 505 C
president@gmu.edu
CABRERA, Jaime, M .... 787-768-2934. 554 B
jaime.cabrera1@upr.edu
CABRERA, Lorraine, T .... 670-234-3690. 547 A
lorrainec@nmcnet.edu
CABRERA, Mario .... 212-217-4995. 324 C
mario_cabrera@fitnyc.edu
CABRERA, Moises .... 787-841-2000. 552 B
mcabrera@pucpr.edu
CABRERA, Rafael .... 787-766-1912. 549 J
rcabrera@inter.edu
CABRERA, Yisel .... 305-628-6562. 112 F
ycabrera2@stu.edu
CABUCO, Tracy .... 818-299-5500... 75 E
tcabuco@westcoastuniversity.edu
CABUNGCAL, Christi .... 614-947-6542. 380 A
cabungcc@franklin.edu
CABUNGCAL, Christi, L .. 614-947-6542. 380 A
christi.cabungcal@franklin.edu
CACACE, Marie .... 301-447-5360. 217 B
cacace@msmary.edu
CACCIA, Stephen, P .... 603-271-6484. 296 C
scaccia@ccsnh.edu
CACCIATORE, Lawrence .. 212-353-4250. 321 F
caciatl@cooper.edu
CACKOWSKI, Sandra ...... 713-525-2162. 490 L
sandy2@stthom.edu
CADA, Elizabeth .... 708-534-4389. 145 F
ecada@govst.edu
CADDELL, Jenev .... 212-650-8236. 317 D
jcaddell@ccny.cuny.edu
CADDY, Kurt .... 417-328-1900. 282 C
kcaddy@sbuniv.edu
CADE, Alfred .... 417-659-4426. 278 D
cade-a@mssu.edu
CADE, Eulanda .... 402-872-2230. 291 E
ecade@peru.edu
CADE, John .... 615-963-5107. 459 E
jcade@tnstate.edu
CADE, Michelle, A .... 313-927-1485. 246 D
mcade4052@marygrove.edu
CADE, Tinina, Q .... 804-289-8032. 510 L
tcade@richmond.edu
CADEAU, Danise .... 906-353-4628. 245 A
dcadeau@kbocc.org
CADENA, Rosa .... 978-232-2064. 226 C
rcadena@endicott.edu
CADENHEAD, Robert, K . 662-325-2431. 268 D
rwc77@msstate.edu
CADIEUX, Cynthia .... 757-822-5185. 514 C
ccadieux@tcc.edu
CADLE, David .... 314-286-4480. 280 F
dacadle@ranken.edu
CADLE, Julie .... 229-732-5927. 120 D
juliecadle@andrewcollege.edu
CADLE, Shirley, A .... 719-884-5000... 83 K
sacadle@nbc.edu
CADLE, Wendi .... 479-619-3149... 22 C
wcadle@nwacc.edu
CADMAN, Lesley, A .... 212-517-3929. 341 B
CADWALLADER,
Martin, T .... 608-262-1044. 536 D
cadwallader@grad.wisc.edu
CADWALLADER,
Meghan .... 617-912-9211. 224 B
mcadwallader@bostonconservatory.edu
CADWALLADER, Sarah ... 620-431-2820. 189 D
scadwallader@neosho.edu
CADY, Paul, S .... 208-282-3475. 138 E
cady@pharmacy.isu.edu
CADY MELZER,
Deborah, M .... 315-445-4527. 328 F
cadymedm@lemoyne.edu
CAETANO, Raul .... 214-648-1500. 493 E
raul.caetano@utsouthwestern.edu
CAFARO, Thomas, R .... 508-213-2294. 235 E
tom.cafaro@nichols.edu
CAFASSO, Frank .... 718-420-4220. 350 B
frank.cafasso@wagner.edu
CAFFARELLI, Joseph ...... 973-720-2714. 308 I
caffarellij@wpunj.edu
CAFFERKEY, Elizabeth .... 914-323-6800. 340 E
ecafferkey@sarahlawrence.edu
CAFFERTY, Jack .... 208-459-5168. 138 A
jcafferty@collegeofidaho.edu
CAFFEY, III, Walter .... 617-573-8646. 237 B
wcaffey@suffolk.edu
CAFFIE, Janique .... 973-328-5149. 300 G
jcaffie@ccm.edu
CAFFO, David, C .... 302-356-2474... 94 E
david.c.caffo@wilmu.edu
CAFONCELLI, Kathy, L .... 610-921-7600. 409 A
kcafoncelli@alb.edu
CAFONE, James, M .... 973-761-9139. 307 C
james.cafone@shu.edu
CAGE, Beverly .... 361-698-1279. 471 G
bacage@delmar.edu
CAGE, Patrick .... 773-995-3524. 141 J
pcage@csu.edu
CAGE, Stephanie .... 615-329-8586. 454 F
scage@fisk.edu
CAGGIANO, Marion .... 973-655-3417. 303 D
caggianom@mail.montclair.edu
CAGIGAS, Marcia .... 323-415-5383... 51 F
cagigamp@elac.edu
CAGLE, Andy .... 910-410-1811. 362 I
dacagle@richmondcc.edu
CAGLE, David .... 815-802-8128. 149 C
dcagle@kcc.edu
CAGLE, Randy, L .... 218-477-2477. 259 H
caglera@mnstate.edu
CAGLE, Sheri .... 815-802-8822. 149 C
scagle@kcc.edu
CAGLE, Susie .... 918-781-7280. 394 D
cagles@bacone.edu
CAGNET, Danny .... 248-218-2190. 249 D
dcagnet@rc.edu
CAHALAN, Jodi .... 515-271-1369. 177 H
jodi.cahalan@dmu.edu
CAHALAN, SJ,
Patrick, J .... 310-338-5921... 53 E
pcahalan@lmu.edu
CAHALL, Perry, J .... 614-885-5585. 388 C
pcahall@pcj.edu
CAHEN, Robert .... 440-525-7097. 382 M
bcahen@lakelandcc.edu
CAHILL, Bridget .... 847-925-6889. 145 H
bcahill@harpercollege.edu
CAHILL, Elizabeth, A ...... 603-526-3729. 295 I
ecahill@colby-sawyer.edu
CAHILL, Elizabeth, J .... 304-384-6003. 529 E
lcahill@concord.edu
CAHILL, Heather .... 413-205-3972. 221 F
heather.cahill@aic.edu
CAHILL, Holly .... 701-477-7862. 373 B
hcahill@tm.edu
CAHILL, Linda .... 434-961-5304. 513 F
lcahill@pvcc.edu
CAHILL, Margaret, D .... 651-962-6131. 265 C
mdcahill@stthomas.edu
CAHILL, Michael, T .... 718-780-7943. 315 H
michael.cahill@brooklaw.edu
CAHILL, Regina .... 212-594-4000. 347 H
rcahill@tcicollege.edu
CAHILL, Richard .... 859-985-3451. 192 F
richard_cahill@berea.edu
CAHILL, Stanley, P .... 978-542-6400. 230 E
scahill@salemstate.edu
CAHN, Peter .... 617-724-6138. 234 B
pcahn@mghihp.edu
CAHOE, William, B .... 765-285-1486. 164 B
wcahoe@bsu.edu
CAHOON, Amm .... 907-852-3333... 10 F
amm.cahoon@ilisagvik.edu
CAHOON, Faye .... 252-451-8221. 362 D
fcahoon@nashcc.edu
CAHOON, Kirsten .... 507-786-3268. 264 B
cahoon@stolaf.edu
CAHOY, William .... 320-363-3182. 263 P
bcahoy@csbsju.edu
CAI, Maoyi .... 512-444-8082. 485 B
cai@thsu.edu
CAILLET, Barb .... 330-684-8935. 390 F
naumoff@uakron.edu

CAILLOUX, Laura .... 360-416-7729. 523 G
laura.cailloux@skagit.edu
CAIN, Candace .... 248-218-2040. 249 D
ccain@rc.edu
CAIN, Chad .... 626-584-5352... 45 E
adm-fpo2@dept.fuller.edu
CAIN, Cheryl .... 361-593-2138. 484 A
cheryl.cain@tamuk.edu
CAIN, Chris .... 334-953-5159. 544 D
anthony.cain@us.af.mil
CAIN, Darrell .... 317-917-5702. 169 L
dcain@ivytech.edu
CAIN, John .... 405-733-7458. 399 F
jcain@rose.edu
CAIN, Kevin, G .... 304-462-4119. 529 G
kevin.cain@glenville.edu
CAIN, Michael .... 716-829-2100. 341 F
vphs@buffalo.edu
CAIN, Michael, E .... 716-829-3955. 341 F
mcain@buffalo.edu
CAIN, Sandra .... 508-541-1658. 225 F
scain@dean.edu
CAIN, Sara Beth .... 619-388-2721... 62 E
scain@sdccd.edu
CAIN, Shelly .... 309-796-5052. 140 E
cains@bhc.edu
CAIN, Stephen, D .... 240-567-1796. 216 F
stephen.cain@montgomerycollege.edu
CAIN, Steven, R .... 805-525-4417... 69 H
scain@thomasaquinas.edu
CAIN, Wingate .... 820-652-0632. 362 A
wingatecain@mcdowelltech.edu
CAIOLA, Gregory .... 609-771-2765. 300 E
caiola@tcnj.edu
CAIRE, Cynthia, D .... 504-865-3388. 205 H
caire@loyno.edu
CAIRES, Matthew .... 406-994-2826. 287 B
mcaires@montana.edu
CAIRNS, Janet .... 918-631-3101. 401 F
janet-cairns@utulsa.edu
CAIRNS, Jill .... 207-834-7602. 212 E
jillb@maine.edu
CAIRNS, Linda .... 303-373-2008... 85 C
lcairns@rvu.edu
CAIRNS, Melissa .... 602-274-4300... 12 K
mcairns@brymanschool.edu
CAIRNS, Michael .... 415-433-9200... 65 C
mcairns@saybrook.edu
CAIRO, Jim, R .... 504-568-4246. 205 C
jcairo@lsuhsu.edu
CAIROL, Miguel .... 718-260-5600. 319 B
mcairol@citytech.cuny.edu
CAIRY, Timothy, J .... 610-499-1193. 437 E
tjcairy@widener.edu
CAISON, Anthony .... 919-866-6101. 364 G
amcaison@waketech.edu
CAJAYON, Felicito .... 213-891-2056... 51 E
cajayof@email.laccd.edu
CAL, John .... 305-348-4001. 115 B
john.cal@fiu.edu
CALA, Catherine .... 330-941-3119. 394 A
cacala@ysu.edu
CALABRESE, Nancy .... 410-626-2553. 217 G
nancy.calabrese@sjca.edu
CALABRESE, Walter .... 252-444-0739. 359 G
calabresew@cravencc.edu
CALABRIA, Patrick .... 631-420-2400. 346 B
patrick.calabria@farmingdale.edu
CALAF, Jorge .... 787-279-1912. 550 B
jcalaf@bayamon.inter.edu
CALAIS, Debra .... 337-482-6199. 208 D
dcalais@louisiana.edu
CALAMAI, Anthony, G .... 828-262-3078. 367 A
calamaiag@appstate.edu
CALAMAIO, Caprice .... 913-234-0733. 185 L
caprice.calamaio@cleveland.edu
CALAMARE, Susan, S ..... 617-422-7387. 235 B
scalamare@nesl.edu
CALAME, Catherine .... 516-299-2719. 329 D
catherine.calame@liu.edu
CALAME, Wanda .... 334-683-2304..... 5 F
wcalame@marionmilitary.edu
CALAMETTI, Jeffrey, D .... 251-442-2242..... 9 A
jcalametti@umobile.edu
CALAMIA, John, J .... 504-865-3946. 205 H
calamia@loyno.edu
CALANDRELLA, Drew ..... 530-898-6131... 33 A
dcalandrella@csuchico.edu
CALARESO, Jack, P .... 508-849-3333. 222 B
jcalareso@annamaria.edu
CALARESO, Joe .... 305-595-9500... 97 G
admissions@amcollege.edu
CALCADO, Antonio .... 848-445-2474. 306 A
acalcado@facilities.rutgers.edu
CALCAGNINO,
Josephine, A .... 414-425-8300. 535 K
jcalcagnino@shst.edu
CALDARELLO, Beth .... 660-359-3948. 279 H
bcaldarello@mail.ncmissouri.edu
CALDAS, Vicente .... 516-364-0808. 333 D
itsupport@nycollege.edu
CALDERÓN-COLÓN,
Andrés .... 787-832-4040. 553 G
rector.uprm@upr.edu
CALDER, Susan .... 215-951-0981. 430 E
calders@philau.edu
CALDERON, Ann Marie .. 615-230-3401. 461 G
annmarie.calderon@volstate.edu
CALDERON, Axel .... 787-753-6000. 549 D
acalderon@icprjc.edu
CALDERON, Hermes .... 787-780-0070. 547 G
hcalderon@caribbean.edu
CALDERON, Janet .... 407-303-6108... 97 H
janet.calderon@adu.edu
CALDERON, Kimberly ..... 619-594-1040... 35 D
kcalderon@mail.sdsu.edu
CALDERON, Nancy, T ..... 408-554-4400... 64 M
ntcalderon@scu.edu
CALDERON, Raoul .... 641-472-7000. 180 N
rcalderon@mum.edu
CALDERON, Sara .... 215-248-7384. 422 F
scalderon@ltsp.edu
CALDERON, Sonny .... 818-733-2600... 56 B
CALDERON, Victor .... 305-342-5272. 103 L
vcalderon@careercollege.edu
CALDERSON, Carl .... 619-201-8780... 62 B
Carl.Calderson@sdcc.edu
CALDON, Heather .... 760-252-2411... 29 I
hcaldon@barstow.edu
CALDWELL, Adonna .... 901-572-2592. 453 B
adonna.caldwell@bchs.edu
CALDWELL, Agnes .... 517-265-5161. 238 G
acaldwell@adrian.edu
CALDWELL, Angela .... 870-248-4000... 20 G
angelac@blackrivertech.edu
CALDWELL, Brinda, W .... 828-398-7134. 357 N
bcaldwell@abtech.edu
CALDWELL, Cary .... 704-406-3939. 354 C
ccaldwell@gardner-webb.edu
CALDWELL, Cheryl .... 417-255-7960. 278 F
cherylcaldwell@missouristate.edu
CALDWELL, Daniel .... 601-318-6115. 270 I
daniel.caldwell@wmcarey.edu
CALDWELL, David .... 508-286-3403. 238 B
dcaldwel@wheatoncollege.edu
CALDWELL, David .... 615-248-1311. 462 D
dcaldwell@trevecca.edu
CALDWELL, Diana .... 574-936-8898. 163 K
diana.caldwell@ancilla.edu
CALDWELL, Gail .... 256-726-7024..... 6 B
gcaldwell@oakwood.edu
CALDWELL, Getchel .... 910-672-1661. 367 D
gcaldwel@uncfsu.edu
CALDWELL, Helen .... 704-378-1014. 355 K
hcaldwell@jcsu.edu
CALDWELL, Hollie .... 303-369-5151... 84 E
hollie.caldwell@plattcolorado.edu
CALDWELL,
Jacqueline, H .... 918-631-2691. 401 F
jacqueline-caldwell@utulsa.edu
CALDWELL, James .... 215-780-1306. 433 A
jcaldwell@salus.edu
CALDWELL, Janet .... 615-327-6851. 456 E
jcaldwell@mmc.edu
CALDWELL, Jeff .... 405-733-7395. 399 F
jcaldwell@rose.edu
CALDWELL, Jodi, K .... 912-478-5541. 126 C
jodic@georgiasouthern.edu
CALDWELL, Katrina .... 815-753-1554. 154 I
kcaldwell1@niu.edu
CALDWELL, Leah .... 256-726-7000..... 6 B
lcaldwell@oakwood.edu
CALDWELL, Lin, D .... 310-434-4200... 65 A
caldwell_lin@smc.edu
CALDWELL, Linda .... 251-580-2247...... 4 L
lcaldwell@faulknerstate.edu
CALDWELL, Michael .... 559-278-3027... 33 D
mcaldwell@csufresno.edu
CALDWELL, Mike .... 801-832-2592. 498 F
mcaldwell@westminstercollege.edu
CALDWELL, Nina .... 314-529-9485. 276 G
ncaldwell@maryville.edu
CALDWELL, Patrice .... 575-562-2315. 309 H
patrice.caldwell@enmu.edu
CALDWELL, Sandra .... 559-638-3641... 69 A
sandra.caldwell@reedleycollege.edu
CALDWELL, Susan .... 606-589-0310. 196 F
susan.caldwell@kctcs.edu
CALDWELL, Tim .... 215-780-1313. 433 A
tcaldwell@salus.edu
CALDWELL, Vicki .... 704-878-3206. 362 B
vcaldwell@mitchellcc.edu
CALDWELL, Ward .... 336-770-3283. 369 D
caldwellw@uncsa.edu
CALDWELL, IV,
William, B .... 478-387-4776. 125 E
wcaldwell@gmc.cc.ga.us
CALE, Lynn .... 252-446-0436. 360 C
calel@edgecombe.edu
CALE, JR., William, G .... 256-765-4211..... 9 C
wgcale@una.edu
CALEB, Peter .... 212-749-2802. 330 A
library@msmnyc.edu
CALENDA, Marianne .... 717-361-1196. 415 H
calendam@etown.edu
CALERO, Teofilo .... 773-878-2998. 158 B
tcalero@staugustine.edu
CALFAS, Karen, J .... 858-822-7552... 71 F
kcalfas@ucsd.edu
CALFEE, Laura .... 512-499-8787. 489 A
lcalfee@uh.edu
CALHOUN, Barbara, S .... 770-423-6258. 127 N
bcalhoun@kennesaw.edu
CALHOUN, Deborah, C .. 803-934-3216. 445 F
dcalhoun@morris.edu
CALHOUN, Larry .... 478-289-2250. 132 A
lcalhoun@southeasterntech.edu
CALHOUN, Larry, D .... 423-439-2068. 459 C
calhoun@etsu.edu
CALHOUN, Layne .... 334-683-5110..... 5 C
lcalhoun@judson.edu
CALHOUN, Linda .... 270-686-4473. 196 C
linda.calhoun@kctcs.edu
CALHOUN, M.Grace .... 773-508-2560. 151 H
gcalhoun@luc.edu
CALHOUN, Matthew .... 602-222-9300... 11 H
mcalhoun@arizonacollege.edu
CALHOUN, Matthew .... 601-276-3718. 269 H
mattc@smcc.edu
CALHOUN, Paul .... 518-580-5590. 341 A
pcalhoun@skidmore.edu
CALHOUN, Ralph .... 901-435-1276. 455 M
ralph_calhoun@loc.edu
CALHOUN, Thomas .... 601-979-2244. 267 E
thomas.c.calhoun@jsums.edu
CALHOUN, JR.,
Thomas, C .... 256-765-4709..... 9 C
tcalhoun@una.edu
CALHOUN, Thomas, G ... 703-993-2541. 505 C
tcalhou2@gmu.edu
CALHOUN, Tony .... 731-426-7658. 455 J
tcalhoun@lanecollege.edu
CALHOUN, Valerie, A .... 717-290-8713. 421 D
vcalhoun@lancasterseminary.edu
CALHOUN, W. Rochelle . 518-580-5760. 341 A
rcalhoun@skidmore.edu
CALHOUN-BROWN,
Allison .... 404-413-2067. 126 E
acalhounbrown@gsu.edu
CALHOUN-FRENCH,
Diane .... 502-213-2120. 195 F
diane.calhoun-french@kctcs.edu
CALICO, Marla .... 770-274-5023. 125 G
marla.calico@gpc.edu
CALIENDO, Amy, A .... 215-670-9114. 425 J
aacaliendo@peirce.edu
CALIENDO, Evelyn .... 847-467-3622. 155 D
evelyn-caliendo@northwestern.edu
CALIFF, Robert, M .... 919-668-8820. 354 A
calif001@mc.duke.edu
CALILAN, Kimo .... 707-864-7104... 66 G
james.calilan@solano.edu
CALINGO, Luis .... 818-767-0888... 76 K
Luis.calingo@woodbury.edu
CALISTO, George, W ...... 312-553-3419. 141 N
gcalisto@ccc.edu
CALIXTO, Jeanette .... 510-436-1134... 47 J
calixto@hnu.edu
CALIZ, Jason .... 312-332-0707. 160 J
jason.caliz@tfa.edu
CALIZO, Lee .... 410-455-1754. 219 D
calizo@umbc.edu
CALKINS, Gregory .... 513-529-3020. 384 G
calkingp@miamioh.edu
CALL, Alyson .... 620-417-1103. 190 F
aly.call@sccc.edu
CALL, Christopher, D ...... 805-565-6023... 76 D
ccall@westmont.edu
CALL, Diane .... 718-631-6222. 319 D
dcall@qcc.cuny.edu
CALL, Gregory, S .... 413-542-2334. 221 G
gscall@amherst.edu
CALL, Patrick, N .... 307-766-3179. 543 I
pcall@uwyo.edu
CALL, Sandra .... 314-340-3502. 275 A
calls@hssu.edu
CALL, Tyler .... 801-627-8451. 496 D
callt@owatc.edu
CALL, Vickie, G .... 336-838-6146. 365 B
vickie.call@wilkescc.edu
CALLAGHAN,
Aloysius, R .... 651-962-5777. 265 C
arcallaghan@stthomas.edu
CALLAGHAN, James .... 740-826-8121. 384 L
jamesc@muskingum.edu
CALLAGHAN, Karen, A ... 305-899-3401... 98 O
kcallaghan@barry.edu
CALLAGHAN, Keith .... 941-637-5604. 101 O
kcallaghan@edison.edu
CALLAGHAN, MaryEllen . 914-633-2512. 327 C
mcallaghan@iona.edu
CALLAHAN, Audra .... 508-999-8643. 229 A
acallahan@umassd.edu
CALLAHAN, Brianne, S ... 508-213-2218. 235 E
brianne.callahan@nichols.edu
CALLAHAN, Candice .... 718-779-1430. 336 D
info@plazacollege.edu
CALLAHAN, IV, Charles . 718-779-1430. 336 D
ccc4@plazacollege.edu
CALLAHAN, III,
Charles, E .... 718-779-1430. 336 D
cec3@plazacollege.edu
CALLAHAN, SR.,
Charles, E .... 718-779-1430. 336 D
cec@plazacollege.edu
CALLAHAN, Cheryl, M .... 336-334-5099. 369 A
cmcallah@uncg.edu
CALLAHAN, Christopher . 602-496-5012... 11 K
christopher.callahan@asu.edu
CALLAHAN, Clara, A ...... 215-955-6983. 434 C
clara.callahan@jefferson.edu
CALLAHAN, Colleen .... 843-208-8258. 448 B
ccallaha@uscb.edu
CALLAHAN, Edward .... 781-736-4240. 224 F
ecallaha@brandeis.edu
CALLAHAN, Elizabeth, K . 718-779-1430. 336 D
ekc@plazacollege.edu
CALLAHAN, Emile .... 661-654-2497... 32 H
ecallahan@csub.edu
CALLAHAN, Josh .... 707-826-3815... 35 C
josh.callahan@humboldt.edu
CALLAHAN, Joy, T .... 919-209-2027. 361 E
jtcallahan@johnstoncc.edu
CALLAHAN, Julie .... 603-645-9611. 297 I
j.callahan@snhu.edu
CALLAHAN, Laurie, F ..... 703-284-1648. 507 B
laurie.callahan@marymount.edu
CALLAHAN, Margaret ...... 414-288-7511. 534 B
margaret.callahan@marquette.edu
CALLAHAN, Margaret ..... 414-288-3812. 534 B
margaret.callahan@marquette.edu
CALLAHAN, Mary .... 617-258-6432. 233 B
CALLAHAN, Michael .... 805-289-6344... 74 H
mcallahan@vcccd.edu
CALLAHAN, Michael .... 419-227-3141. 391 F
macallah@unoh.edu
CALLAHAN, North .... 914-337-9300. 321 E
north.callahan@concordia-ny.edu
CALLAHAN, Patricia .... 978-762-4000. 232 D
tcallaha@northshore.edu
CALLAHAN, Patrick, F ..... 914-251-6435. 344 D
patrick.callahan@purchase.edu
CALLAHAN, Paul, J .... 330-972-6166. 390 E
pcallah@uakron.edu
CALLAHAN, Phyllis .... 513-529-4432. 384 G
callahp@miamioh.edu
CALLAHAN, Robert .... 319-368-6462. 181 C
rcallahan@mtmercy.edu
CALLAHAN, Timothy, C .. 425-602-3110. 516 K
tcallaha@bastyr.edu
CALLAN, Mike .... 314-246-7559. 284 N
mikecallan@webster.edu
CALLAN, Terrance, D ..... 513-231-2223. 374 D
tcallan@athenaeum.edu
CALLAND, Dana .... 606-759-7141. 196 B
dana.calland@kctcs.edu
CALLAWAY, Cynthia .... 757-825-2725. 514 B
callawayc@tncc.edu
CALLAWAY, Karen, L ...... 715-852-1365. 539 J
kcallaway@cvtc.edu
CALLAWAY,
MaryKatherine .... 225-578-6144. 204 O
mkc@lsu.edu
CALLEN, Bruce .... 417-873-7546. 273 H
bcallen@drury.edu
CALLEN, Edward .... 803-641-3218. 448 A
edc@usca.edu
CALLEN, Patricia, A .... 304-296-8282. 531 F
pcallen@wvjc.com
CALLENDER, David, L .... 409-772-1902. 493 C
dcallender@utmb.edu
CALLIER, Theodore .... 504-816-4018. 201 K
tcallier@dillard.edu
CALLIHAM, Marty .... 512-444-8082. 485 B
mcalliham@thsu.edu
CALLIS, Keith .... 843-863-7133. 441 H
kcallis@csuniv.edu
CALLOWAY, Dwight .... 707-864-7176... 66 G
dwight.calloway@solano.edu
CALLOWAY, Terence .... 850-599-3256. 114 K
terence.calloway@famu.edu
CALLUZZO, Vincent .... 914-633-2256. 327 C
vcalluzzo@iona.edu
CALLWOOD, Angie .... 845-752-3000. 348 I
a.callwood@uts.edu
CALLWOOD-BRATHWAITE,
Denise .... 305-623-1415. 104 J
denise.callwood-brathwaite@fmuniv.edu
CALME, Paul, H .... 513-745-3142. 393 H
calme@xavier.edu
CALMES, Daphne .... 323-563-4816... 38 B
daphnecalmes@cdrewu.edu

CALMESE, Carlotta, V ..... 608-243-4270. 540 C
ccalmese@madisoncollege.edu
CALNAN, Kerry .... 508-213-2207. 235 E
kerry.calnan@nichols.edu
CALO, Andrew .... 617-296-8300. 227 I
andrew_calo@laboure.edu
CALO, Balbina .... 212-472-1500. 334 B
bcalo@nysid.edu
CALOGRIDES, JR.,
Thomas .... 757-822-7335. 514 C
tcalogrides@tcc.edu
CALOVINI, Susan .... 336-721-2617. 366 D
susan.calovini@salem.edu
CALPIN, Fran .... 570-945-8170. 419 N
fran.calpin@keystone.edu
CALTABIANO, Ronald ..... 317-940-8652. 164 J
rcalt@butler.edu
CALUS-MCLAIN, Martha . 503-352-2764. 407 A
martha@pacificu.edu
CALUZA, Kimberly .... 206-296-6090. 523 E
caluzak@seattleu.edu
CALVERT, Carolyn, A ..... 325-793-3808. 476 E
ccalvert@mcm.edu
CALVERT, Deb .... 651 290-6310. 265 F
deb.calvert@wmitchell.edu
CALVERT, Maxine .... 405-422-1466. 399 B
calvertm@redlandscc.edu
CALVERT, Mike .... 308-398-7400. 288 I
michaelcalvert@cccneb.edu
CALVERT, Ned .... 903-923-2120. 471 J
ncalvert@etbu.edu
CALVERT, Raymond, J .... 727-816-3418. 110 E
calverr@phcc.edu
CALVIN, Allen .... 650-433-3802... 58 B
acalvin@paloaltou.edu
CALVIN, Brent .... 559-730-3755... 40 I
brentc@cos.edu
CALVIN, Dennis, D .... 814-865-4028. 426 A
ifa@psu.edu
CALVIN, Larry .... 504-520-7537. 209 D
lcalvin@xula.edu
CALVO, Dean .... 909-607-3183... 39 C
dean.calvo@cgu.edu
CALZADA, Maria .... 504-865-3244. 205 H
calzada@loyno.edu
CALZONETTI, Frank, J .... 419-530-4749. 392 B
frank.calzonetti@utoledo.edu
CAMACHO, Anita, C .... 670-234-5498. 547 A
anitac@nmcnet.edu
CAMACHO, David, E .... 928-523-9204... 16 C
david.camacho@nau.edu
CAMACHO, Francisco, C 671-734-0540. 546 C
mis@guamcc.edu
CAMACHO, Irma, G .... 915-831-2848. 472 B
icamach7@epcc.edu
CAMACHO, Luis .... 787-725-6500. 547 H
lcamacho@sju.albizu.edu
CAMACHO, Mildred .... 787-892-3090. 551 A
milcama@sg.inter.edu
CAMACHO-MARON,
Wanda .... 617-236-8859. 226 F
wcamacho-maron@fisher.edu
CAMACHO-MELÉNDEZ,
Iris, M .... 787-751-1912. 551 B
icamacho@juris.inter.edu
CAMAK, Shelagh .... 951-222-8671... 61 A
shelagh.camak@rcc.edu
CAMARA, Nivia .... 718-933-6700. 331 K
ncamara@monroecollege.edu
CAMARENA, Phame, M .. 989-774-3902. 240 N
camar1pm@cmich.edu
CAMARERO, Patricia ...... 401-949-2820. 439 C
pcamarero@inteducators.org
CAMARILLO, Jane .... 925-631-4235... 61 F
jcl1@stmarys-ca.edu
CAMBRIA, Russell .... 610-917-1423. 436 C
rlcambria@vfcc.edu
CAMDEN, Keely, O .... 304-336-8047. 530 A
kcamden@westliberty.edu
CAMELO, Kathleen, M .... 518-564-2187. 344 B
camelokm@plattsburgh.edu
CAMERON, JR., A. Neill 864-656-2123. 442 C
cameron@clemson.edu
CAMERON, Ann .... 714-997-6611... 38 A
cameron@chapman.edu
CAMERON, Cheryl, A ..... 206-543-6616. 524 G
ccameron@uw.edu
CAMERON, Dwayne .... 860-628-4751... 90 D
dcameron@lincolncollegene.edu
CAMERON, Eleanor, W ... 504-821-5881. 201 E
eleanor.cameron@cameroncollege.com
CAMERON, Helene .... 910-672-1095. 367 D
hcamero4@uncfsu.edu
CAMERON, James .... 703-897-1972. 510 B
jcameron@stratford.edu
CAMERON, Karen, E .... 313-927-1446. 246 D
kcameron@marygrove.edu
CAMERON, Kelli .... 608-757-7704. 539 I
kcameron@blackhawk.edu
CAMERON, Mark .... 801-565-5112. 144 A
mcameron@devry.edu
CAMERON, Matthew, R .. 305-899-3875... 98 O
mcameron@barry.edu
CAMERON, Richard, L .... 478-301-5500. 128 H
cameron_rl@mercer.edu
CAMERON, Sally, C .... 508-678-2811. 231 B
sally.cameron@bristolcc.edu
CAMERON, Samantha ..... 906-248-8429. 240 J
scameron@bmcc.edu
CAMERON, Suzette .... 386-506-7301. 101 G
cameros@DaytonaState.edu
CAMERON, Thomas .... 630-942-2291. 142 G
cameron@cod.edu
CAMERON, William, D ... 412-392-3490. 431 B
bcameron@pointpark.edu
CAMEY, John .... 580-581-2267. 394 G
jcamey@cameron.edu
CAMFIELD, Paul .... 830-792-7206. 480 F
phcamfield@schreiner.edu
CAMFIELD, Peter .... 580-349-1514. 397 G
pcamfield@opsu.edu
CAMILLE, Marc .... 410-617-2323. 216 A
mcamille@loyola.edu
CAMILLE, Michael .... 318-342-1750. 208 E
camille@ulm.edu
CAMILLERI, Michael .... 507-284-9328. 254 F
camilleri.michael@mayo.edu
CAMMACK, Nancy .... 409-984-6390. 486 H
cammacknl@lamarpa.edu
CAMMARATA, Debbie ..... 716-827-2522. 348 G
cammaratad@trocaire.edu
CAMMARATA, Maria, R .. 973-290-4498. 300 F
mcammarata@cse.edu
CAMMARATA, Miki .... 201-684-7457. 305 A
mcammara@ramapo.edu
CAMMISH, Peter .... 707-864-7278... 66 G
peter.cammish@solano.edu
CAMOU, Fernando .... 623-845-3677... 14 M
f.camou@gcmail.maricopa.edu
CAMP, Aarika .... 954-262-7084. 109 K
aarika@nova.edu
CAMP, Andy .... 518-580-5745. 341 A
acamp@skidmore.edu
CAMP, Ann .... 657-278-8678... 33 E
acamp@fullerton.edu
CAMP, Billy .... 334-386-7255..... 3 H
bcamp@faulkner.edu
CAMP, Carol .... 251-442-2213..... 9 A
ccamp@umobile.edu
CAMP, James, C .... 213-738-5731... 68 C
jcamp@swlaw.edu
CAMP, Margaret .... 864-503-5199. 448 H
mcamp@uscupstate.edu
CAMP, Robert, C .... 724-357-7889. 428 F
bobcamp@iup.edu
CAMP, Stephen .... 336-249-8186. 360 A
spcamp@davidsonccc.edu
CAMP, Sue, C .... 704-406-4378. 354 C
scamp@gardner-webb.edu
CAMP, Susan .... 405-319-8571. 394 G
susanc@cameron.edu
CAMPA, Jeff .... 816-322-0110. 271 O
jeff.campa@calvary.edu
CAMPAGNA, Michele ..... 973-655-5369. 303 D
campagnam@mail.montclair.edu
CAMPANA, MaryJo .... 570-321-4237. 422 H
campanam@lycoming.edu
CAMPANELLA,
Barbara, A .... 413-782-1630. 238 A
bcampane@wne.edu
CAMPANELLA, Carl .... 248-204-3030. 245 I
bookstore@ltu.edu
CAMPANELLA,
Cynthia, B .... 302-831-2343... 94 B
ccampa@udel.edu
CAMPANINI, Bino .... 321-674-8434. 104 H
bcampanini@fit.edu
CAMPBELL, Alan .... 563-336-3308. 177 L
acampbell@eicc.edu
CAMPBELL, Alton .... 208-885-7702. 139 D
altonc@uidaho.edu
CAMPBELL, Amy .... 517-264-3910. 238 G
CAMPBELL, Ann, E .... 757-446-5255. 504 E
campbeae@evms.edu
CAMPBELL, Anthony .... 609-896-5101. 305 D
acampbel@rider.edu
CAMPBELL, Barbara .... 606-759-7141. 196 B
barbara.campbell@kctcs.edu
CAMPBELL, Bill .... 412-365-1140. 412 K
bcampbell@chatham.edu
CAMPBELL, Blake .... 515-271-3077. 177 K
blake.campbell@drake.edu
CAMPBELL, Bonnie .... 641-683-5108. 179 A
bonnie.campbell@indianhills.edu
CAMPBELL, Brenda .... 334-670-3178..... 7 H
bcamp@troy.edu
CAMPBELL, Brett, S .... 918-595-7723. 400 E
brett.campbell@tulsacc.edu
CAMPBELL, Brooke .... 309-467-6420. 145 C
bcampbell@eureka.edu
CAMPBELL, Catherine, C 252-638-7271. 359 G
campbelc@cravencc.edu
CAMPBELL, Celia, K .... 617-627-3313. 237 C
celia.campbell@tufts.edu
CAMPBELL, Christie .... 512-233-1635. 479 C
christie@stedwards.edu
CAMPBELL, Clark, D .... 562-903-4867... 29 L
clark.campbell@biola.edu
CAMPBELL, Connan .... 509-533-7081. 518 E
connan.campbell@scc.spokane.edu
CAMPBELL, Conway .... 508-767-7506. 222 C
ccampbel@assumption.edu
CAMPBELL, Dan .... 413-552-2567. 231 F
dcampbell@hcc.edu
CAMPBELL, Danny .... 432-264-3752. 473 E
dcampbell@howardcollege.edu
CAMPBELL, Darryl .... 410-752-4710. 510 B
dcampbell@stratford.edu
CAMPBELL, Daryl, J .... 206-546-4551. 523 F
dcampbell@shoreline.edu
CAMPBELL, David .... 270-831-9632. 195 D
david.campbell@kctcs.edu
CAMPBELL, David .... 601-643-8332. 266 F
david.campbell@colin.edu
CAMPBELL, Deanna .... 760-872-5301... 49 O
dcampbel@cerrocoso.edu
CAMPBELL, Debbie .... 231-843-5819. 252 H
djcampbell@westshore.edu
CAMPBELL, Denise .... 202-231-3797. 544 L
denise.campbell@dodiis.mil
CAMPBELL, Diane .... 609-586-4800. 302 G
campbeld@mccc.edu
CAMPBELL, Diane .... 706-355-5048. 120 J
dcampbell@athenstech.edu
CAMPBELL, Donald .... 610-896-1100. 418 F
dcampbel@haverford.edu
CAMPBELL, Elizabeth ...... 503-821-8881. 406 F
presidentsoffice@pnca.edu
CAMPBELL, Elizabeth, P . 847-866-3971. 145 E
elizabeth.campbell@garrett.edu
CAMPBELL, Elreo .... 617-730-7102. 235 D
elreo.campbell@newbury.edu
CAMPBELL, Evelyn, S ..... 309-794-7533. 139 L
evelyncampbell@augustana.edu
CAMPBELL, Frances .... 937-766-7653. 375 K
campf@cedarville.edu
CAMPBELL, Garikai .... 404-215-2647. 129 D
kai@morehouse.edu
CAMPBELL, J. David ...... 256-228-6001..... 5 H
campbelld@nacc.edu
CAMPBELL, Jack, M .... 937-327-6131. 393 E
jcampbell@wittenberg.edu
CAMPBELL, Jada, D .... 610-796-8298. 409 E
jada.campbell@alvernia.edu
CAMPBELL, Jana .... 903-233-4186. 475 J
janacampbell@letu.edu
CAMPBELL, Jane, S .... 712-362-7947. 179 E
jcampbell@iowalakes.edu
CAMPBELL, Jennifer, D .. 561-868-3280. 110 C
campbejd@palmbeachstate.edu
CAMPBELL, Jeremy .... 704-216-3577. 363 D
jermey.campbell@rccc.edu
CAMPBELL, Joann, N ..... 904-620-2002. 116 B
jcampbel@unf.edu
CAMPBELL, Joanne .... 479-248-7236... 21 B
jcampbell@ecollege.edu
CAMPBELL, Joeseph .... 870-680-8725... 20 B
joe_campbell@asun.edu
CAMPBELL, John, P .... 304-293-4874. 530 D
jpcampbe@mail.wvu.edu
CAMPBELL, John, T .... 843-953-7144. 443 A
campbelljt@cofc.edu
CAMPBELL, Jonathan ..... 870-230-5098... 21 D
campbej@hsu.edu
CAMPBELL, Joseph, A .... 215-895-2807. 415 B
jac47@drexel.edu
CAMPBELL, K. Celeste ... 405-744-6876. 397 H
celeste.campbell@okstate.edu
CAMPBELL, Karen, M ..... 608-822-2300. 541 C
kcampbell@swtc.edu
CAMPBELL, Kate .... 310-233-4655... 51 H
campbekl@lahc.edu
CAMPBELL, Kathy .... 503-399-5018. 402 E
kathy.campbell@chemeketa.edu
CAMPBELL, Kathy .... 269-488-4722. 244 L
kcampbell@kvcc.edu
CAMPBELL, Keith, E .... 404-413-4465. 126 E
kcampbell@gsu.edu
CAMPBELL, Kelly .... 330-490-7296. 392 H
kcampbell@walsh.edu
CAMPBELL, Kelly, D .... 404-687-4547. 123 C
campbellk@ctsnet.edu
CAMPBELL, Ken, B .... 208-732-6243. 138 B
kcampbell@csi.edu
CAMPBELL, Keni .... 907-796-6569... 11 A
keni.campbell@uas.alaska.edu
CAMPBELL, Kevin .... 325-674-2765. 464 H
kevin.campbell@acu.edu
CAMPBELL, Kim .... 614-234-5144. 384 J
kcampbell@mccn.edu
CAMPBELL, Kimberly ...... 913-971-3584. 188 H
kjcampbell@mnu.edu
CAMPBELL, Kimberly ...... 405-491-6335. 399 K
kcampbel@snu.edu
CAMPBELL, Kirby, D ...... 318-342-5147. 208 E
kcampbell@ulm.edu
CAMPBELL, Lauren .... 215-637-7700. 418 G
lcampbell@holyfamily.edu
CAMPBELL, Lea .... 713-221-5548. 489 D
campbellc@uhd.edu
CAMPBELL, Lisa .... 714-992-7085... 56 F
lcampbell@fullcoll.edu
CAMPBELL, Lisa .... 775-623-4824. 294 F
lisa.campbell@gbcnv.edu
CAMPBELL, Lisa, M .... 724-287-8711. 411 C
lisa.campbell@bc3.edu
CAMPBELL, Lori .... 423-585-6933. 462 A
lori.campbell@ws.edu
CAMPBELL, Lori .... 802-831-1233. 500 H
lcampbell@vermontlaw.edu
CAMPBELL, Lucy .... 619-684-8783... 56 C
lcampbell@newschoolarch.edu
CAMPBELL, Margareta .... 707-546-4000... 43 E
mcampbell@empirecollege.com
CAMPBELL, Mark .... 617-266-1400. 223 D
CAMPBELL, Marshall ...... 304-384-5276. 529 E
mcampbell@concord.edu
CAMPBELL, Martin .... 870-230-5150... 21 D
campbem@hsu.edu
CAMPBELL, Mary, B .... 314-935-3617. 284 L
marycampbell@wustl.edu
CAMPBELL, Mary, B .... 864-488-8280. 444 L
mcampbell@limestone.edu
CAMPBELL, Mary, K .... 213-740-9464... 74 A
mcampbell@caps.usc.edu
CAMPBELL, Mason .... 870-508-6168... 20 A
mcampbell@asumh.edu
CAMPBELL, Matthew ...... 253-840-8419. 522 C
mcampbell@pierce.ctc.edu
CAMPBELL, Megan .... 301-369-2800. 213 G
megan@capitol-college.edu
CAMPBELL, Michael. .... 760-384-6159... 49 O
michael.campbell@cerrocoso.edu
CAMPBELL, Michael, A ... 423-585-2682. 462 A
mike.campbell@ws.edu
CAMPBELL, Michele .... 580-745-2512. 399 J
mcampbell@se.edu
CAMPBELL, Mike .... 304-696-2456. 529 H
marshallbkstr@fheg.follett.com
CAMPBELL, Milt .... 641-673-1074. 183 H
campbellm@wmpenn.edu
CAMPBELL, Mitchell, L .. 916-558-2426... 53 D
campbem@scc.losrios.edu
CAMPBELL, Nicole, J ..... 405-325-2072. 401 B
njudice@ou.edu
CAMPBELL, Nina .... 412-392-3990. 431 B
ncampbell@pointpark.edu
CAMPBELL, Patricia .... 617-627-3331. 237 C
patricia.campbell@tufts.edu
CAMPBELL, Patricia .... 509-542-4761. 518 C
pcambell@columbiabasin.edu
CAMPBELL, Phyllis .... 731-352-4046. 453 D
campbellp@bethelu.edu
CAMPBELL, Ralph .... 623-935-8051... 14 K
ralph.campbell@estrellamountain.edu
CAMPBELL, Randy .... 607-778-5196. 315 I
campbellrj@sunybroome.edu
CAMPBELL, Renee .... 479-636-9222... 22 C
rcampbell@nwacc.edu
CAMPBELL, Ric .... 845-758-7154. 314 D
campbell@bard.edu
CAMPBELL, Richard .... 207-780-4484. 212 H
dcamp@usm.maine.edu
CAMPBELL, Richard .... 832-252-4616. 468 L
richard.campbell@cbshouston.edu
CAMPBELL, Rickie, N ..... 276-523-2400. 513 A
rcampbell@me.vccs.edu
CAMPBELL, Rina .... 949-214-3561... 41 I
rina.campbell@cui.edu
CAMPBELL, Rina .... 559-453-2289... 45 D
rina.campbell@fresno.edu
CAMPBELL, Rixon .... 704-378-1039. 355 K
rocampbell@jcsu.edu
CAMPBELL, Robert .... 410-704-2364. 220 E
rcampbell@towson.edu
CAMPBELL, Robert .... 631-244-5050. 323 B
campbelr@dowling.edu
CAMPBELL, Robert, D .... 212-817-7300. 317 F
rcampbell@gc.cuny.edu
CAMPBELL, Robin .... 336-517-2229. 352 H
rcampbell@bennett.edu
CAMPBELL, Rosana .... 570-484-2723. 429 B
rcampbel@lhup.edu
CAMPBELL, Rupert .... 718-940-5844. 339 B
rcampbell@sjcny.edu
CAMPBELL, Samerah ...... 559-244-5989... 68 H
CAMPBELL, Sandra .... 870-460-1080... 24 D
campbell@uamont.edu
CAMPBELL, Sara .... 803-641-3268. 448 A
sarac@usca.edu
CAMPBELL, Sarah .... 415-451-2830... 63 A
scampbell@sfts.edu

CAMPBELL, Scott ... 773-834-3390. 161 B
scottcampbell@uchicago.edu
CAMPBELL, Scott ... 608-663-3297. 532 I
SCampbell@edgewood.edu
CAMPBELL, Sharon ... 919-760-8011. 356 G
sharonca@meredith.edu
CAMPBELL,
Shoshanna, M ... 718-780-7501. 315 H
shoshanna.campbell@brooklaw.edu
CAMPBELL, Stanley, R ... 859-238-5271. 193 E
stan.campbell@centre.edu
CAMPBELL, Stephanie ... 318-357-5351. 208 B
campbells@nsula.edu
CAMPBELL, Stephen ... 409-772-9751. 493 C
stepcamp@utmb.edu
CAMPBELL, Stephen ... 216-368-5555. 375 J
stephen.campbell@case.edu
CAMPBELL, Stephen, S .. 757-594-7663. 503 M
stephen.campbell@cnu.edu
CAMPBELL, Steven ... 423-323-0205. 461 C
srcampbell@northeaststate.edu
CAMPBELL, Susan ... 207-780-4547. 212 H
scamp@usm.maine.edu
CAMPBELL, Susan, G ... 817-257-4690. 484 I
s.g.campbell@tcu.edu
CAMPBELL, Suzanne, P .. 814-886-6385. 424 G
suzanne.campbell@mtaloy.edu
CAMPBELL, Thomas, F ... 214-905-3001. 491 E
thomas.f.campbell@utdallas.edu
CAMPBELL, Thomas, L ... 610-282-1100. 414 F
thomas.campbell@desales.edu
CAMPBELL, Timothy, M . 443-334-2838. 218 E
tmcampbell@stevenson.edu
CAMPBELL, Tom ... 714-628-2516... 38 A
tcampbell@chapman.edu
CAMPBELL, Vincent ... 615-256-1463. 452 G
vcampbell@abcnash.edu
CAMPBELL, Yanka ... 410-238-9000... 96 F
CAMPBELL-HOOPS,
Toma ... 406-353-2607. 285 E
thoops@ancollege.edu
CAMPBELL JACKSON,
Candace ... 330-972-7075. 390 E
candac7@uakron.edu
CAMPBELL-PARCO,
Wendy ... 925-969-3485... 49 B
wparco@jfku.edu
CAMPER, Anne ... 406-994-2891. 287 B
research@montana.edu
CAMPER, Diane ... 731-286-3338. 460 F
camper@dscc.edu
CAMPER, Yolanda ... 318-342-3306. 208 E
camper@ulm.edu
CAMPERI, Marcelo, F ... 415-422-5939... 73 J
camperi@usfca.edu
CAMPFIELD, Ruth ... 817-598-6388. 494 G
rcampfield@wc.edu
CAMPION, James, R ... 518-828-4181. 321 C
campion@sunycgcc.edu
CAMPION, William, J ... 254-647-3234. 478 H
bcampion@rangercollege.edu
CAMPIRANO, Marisa ... 956-882-4322. 491 D
marisa.campirano@utb.edu
CAMPLESE, Cole ... 631-632-9085. 342 C
cole.camplese@stonybrook.edu
CAMPO, Carlos ... 757-352-4015. 508 G
ccampo@regent.edu
CAMPO, Juan, E ... 805-893-3945... 72 B
jcampo@religion.ucsb.edu
CAMPO, Kathy ... 516-299-2503. 329 C
kathy.campo@liu.edu
CAMPO, Regina, Z ... 717-337-6207. 417 B
rcampo@gettysburg.edu
CAMPOS, Becky ... 714-997-6943... 38 A
bcampos@chapman.edu
CAMPOS, Cesar ... 312-939-0111. 144 D
CAMPOS, Connie ... 408-848-4802... 45 F
ccampos@gavilan.edu
CAMPOS, Darcie, R ... 708-534-5000. 145 F
dcampos@govst.edu
CAMPOS, Diana ... 575-234-9227. 311 A
dcampos@nmsu.edu
CAMPOS, Jesus ... 956-872-8330. 480 I
jhcampos@southtexascollege.edu
CAMPOS, Lisa ... 928-523-5677... 16 C
lisa.campos@nau.edu
CAMPOS, Luis ... 505-224-4565. 309 E
lcampos@cnm.edu
CAMPOS, Pete ... 505-454-2555. 309 L
pcampos@luna.edu
CAMPOS, Tammie ... 575-646-3616. 310 I
tcampos@nmsu.edu
CAMPOS, Tom ... 210-486-0606. 465 C
tcampos1@alamo.edu
CAMUTI, Alice ... 931-372-3232. 460 A
acamuti@tntech.edu
CANACARIS, Diana ... 865-981-8198. 456 D
diana.canacaris@maryvillecollege.edu
CANADA, Allison, M ... 410-334-2918. 221 D
acanada@worwic.edu
CANADA, Britt ... 325-574-7671. 494 K
bcanada@wtc.edu
CANADA, Greg ... 415-565-4885... 71 A
canadag@uchastings.edu
CANADA, Lisa ... 910-775-4201. 369 B
lisa.canada@uncp.edu
CANADA, Mark ... 910-521-6431. 369 B
mark.canada@uncp.edu
CANADAY, John ... 719-384-6819... 83 M
john.canaday@ojc.edu
CANADAY, Joseph ... 215-596-7524. 435 H
j.canaday@usciences.edu
CANALES, Angel ... 787-766-1717. 552 J
acanales7@suagm.edu
CANALES, Carmen, I ... 336-758-3256. 370 D
ccanales@wfu.edu
CANALES, Jason, G ... 413-662-5413. 230 C
jason.canales@mcla.edu
CANALES, Jo Ann ... 361-825-3884. 483 F
joann.canales@tamucc.edu
CANALES, Luis ... 270-809-4152. 198 B
lcanales@murraystate.edu
CANALS, Alex ... 718-933-6700. 331 K
acanals@monroecollege.edu
CANAN, Michelle ... 918-293-5494. 398 B
michelle.canan@okstate.edu
CANARD, Gregory, M ... 920-923-8583. 534 A
gmcanard78@marianuniversity.edu
CANAS, Carlos ... 305-626-3698. 104 J
carlos.canas@fmuniv.edu
CANAVAN, Jessie ... 330-823-2674. 391 E
canavajl@mountunion.edu
CANAVAN, Linda, T ... 781-292-2341. 226 G
linda.canavan@olin.edu
CANAVAN, Terry ... 631-499-7100. 329 B
tcanavan@libi.edu
CANCEL, Jimmy ... 787-250-1912. 550 E
jcancel@metro.inter.edu
CANCEL, Olga ... 787-754-8000. 553 E
ocancel@pupr.edu
CANCEL-PEREZ,
Magda, A ... 787-620-2040. 547 C
mcancel@aupr.edu
CANCHOLA, Rebecca ... 915-779-8031. 494 C
rcanchola@computercareercenter.com
CANCILLA, Mike ... 256-549-8311... 3 M
mcancilla@gadsdenstate.edu
CANDEE, Kate ... 920-923-8727. 534 A
kcandee@marianuniversity.edu
CANDELA, Natalie ... 810-762-9832. 244 Q
ncandela@kettering.edu
CANDELARIA, J. Randel . 336-734-7216. 360 E
jcandelaria@forsythtech.edu
CANDELARIA, Rene ... 210-733-0777. 475 B
CANDELAS, Saul, C ... 915-831-2354. 472 B
scandel8@epcc.edu
CANDIA, Patricia ... 361-664-2981. 468 K
candia@coastalbend.edu
CANDIDO, Jacqueline, P 215-898-4970. 435 B
candido@sas.upenn.edu
CANDIELLO, Mario ... 410-532-5389. 217 E
mcandiello@ndm.edu
CANDIOTTI, Alan ... 973-408-3495. 301 C
acandiot@drew.edu
CANDLER, George, B ... 212-327-7801. 338 A
candler@rockefeller.edu
CANDREVA, Anne, M ... 412-578-6043. 412 G
candrevaam@carlow.edu
CANEDO, Agnes, F ... 509-963-3049. 517 F
canedoa@cwu.edu
CANEIRO-LIVINGSTON,
Graciela ... 563-588-6406. 176 F
graciela.caneiro-livingston@clarke.edu
CANEPA, Janet, A ... 203-254-4280... 89 I
jcanepa@fairfield.edu
CANEPA, Thomas ... 513-556-2495. 390 G
tom.canepa@uc.edu
CANEPI, Karen ... 702-968-2033. 295 E
kcanepi@roseman.edu
CANER, Emir ... 706-865-2134. 133 B
ecaner@truett.edu
CANER, Ergun ... 817-461-8741. 466 D
ecaner@arlingtonbaptistcollege.edu
CANFIELD, Anne ... 816-802-3426. 275 J
acanfield@kcai.edu
CANFIELD, Cheri ... 847-233-7700. 155 B
ccanfield@nc.edu
CANFIELD, Kathleen ... 847-925-6283. 145 H
kcanfiel@harpercollege.edu
CANFIELD, Merle ... 607-753-5565. 343 B
merle.canfield@cortland.edu
CANGELLARIS,
Andreas, C ... 217-333-2150. 162 A
cangella@illinois.edu
CANHAM, Drew ... 254-299-8692. 476 D
dcanham@mclennan.edu
CANHAM, Raymond, P ... 972-238-6248. 471 C
canham@dcccd.edu
CANIA, Lisa, M ... 315-229-5585. 339 F
lcania@stlawu.edu
CANICK, Simon ... 651-290-6301. 265 F
simon.canick@wmitchell.edu
CANIDA, II, Robert, L ... 910-522-5790. 369 B
canida@uncp.edu
CANIGLIA, Alan ... 717-291-4168. 416 J
alan.caniglia@fandm.edu
CANIGLIA, Alan, S ... 717-291-3985. 416 J
alan.caniglia@fandm.edu
CANIZARES, Claude, R ... 617-253-0879. 233 B
CANNADA, JR.,
Robert, C ... 601-923-1600. 269 E
rcannada@rts.edu
CANNADAY, Billy, K ... 434-982-5207. 511 B
bkc2p@Virginia.EDU
CANNADAY, JR.,
Billy, K ... 434-982-2507. 511 B
bkc2p@virginia.edu
CANNADAY SAULNY,
Helen ... 202-994-6710... 95 D
saulnyh@gwu.edu
CANNADY, Sonya, Y ... 919-516-4482. 366 C
sycannady@st-aug.edu
CANNADY-SMITH,
Allison ... 253-879-3450. 524 F
acannadysmith@pugetsound.edu
CANNAN, Erin ... 845-758-7454. 314 D
cannan@bard.edu
CANNELL, Stephen ... 269-488-4241. 244 L
scannell@kvcc.edu
CANNEY, Catherine, E ... 978-665-3653. 229 E
ccanney@fitchburgstate.edu
CANNEY, Jane, W ... 651-962-6120. 265 C
jwcanney@stthomas.edu
CANNICI, James, P ... 972-883-2575. 491 E
cannici@utdallas.edu
CANNIFF, James, F ... 617-228-2435. 231 C
jfcanniff@bhcc.mass.edu
CANNING, Fran ... 603-513-5171. 298 D
fran.canning@law.unh.edu
CANNING, Ian ... 401-598-4405. 439 B
icanning@jwu.edu
CANNING, John, B ... 401-232-6020. 438 K
jcanning@bryant.edu
CANNING, Mary ... 415-442-7885... 45 I
mcanning@ggu.edu
CANNING, Patricia ... 215-248-7144. 413 A
canningp@chc.edu
CANNON, Blake ... 870-612-2057... 25 A
blake.cannon@uaccb.edu
CANNON, Brenda ... 931-393-1546. 461 A
bcannon@mscc.edu
CANNON, Bunnie ... 225-578-0302. 204 O
bcannon@lsu.edu
CANNON, Chris ... 251-460-6933... 9 E
ccannon@southalabama.edu
CANNON, Danita ... 912-287-5806. 130 B
dcannon@okefenokeetech.edu
CANNON, Donald, G ... 334-291-4981... 2 H
glen.cannon@cv.edu
CANNON, Gordon ... 601-266-5116. 270 E
gordon.cannon@usm.edu
CANNON, Gregory ... 845-575-3000. 330 D
greg.cannon@marist.edu
CANNON, Jason ... 256-840-4150... 6 I
jcannon@snead.edu
CANNON, Katherine ... 508-793-7499. 225 A
kcannon@clarku.edu
CANNON, Kathleen ... 503-847-2557. 408 G
kcannon@uws.edu
CANNON, Leslie ... 254-659-7505. 473 A
lcannon@hillcollege.edu
CANNON, Marsha ... 205-652-3517... 9 F
mac@uwa.edu
CANNON, Mary ... 740-392-6868. 384 K
mary.cannon@mvnu.edu
CANNON, Michael ... 202-685-3927. 544 K
michael.cannon@ndu.edu
CANNON, Michael, R ... 314-935-5152. 284 L
michael_cannon@wustl.edu
CANNON, Rebecca ... 225-768-0810. 206 D
rebecca.cannon@ololcollege.edu
CANNON, Richard, J ... 603-862-2232. 298 C
dick.cannon@unh.edu
CANNON, Russell ... 608-363-2014. 531 M
cannonr@beloit.edu
CANNON, Sharon ... 432-335-5150. 487 E
sharon.cannon@ttuhsc.edu
CANNON, Sharon ... 610-399-2057. 428 B
scannon@cheyney.edu
CANNON, Sondra ... 732-224-2695. 299 G
scannon@brookdalecc.edu
CANNON, Steve ... 214-648-6709. 493 E
steve.cannon@ustouthwestern.edu
CANNON, Thomas ... 727-726-1153. 100 E
tomcannon@clearwater.edu
CANNON, Tonya ... 404-460-2460. 130 F
tonya.cannon@point.edu
CANNON, Tyrone, H ... 415-422-6167... 73 J
cannont@usfca.edu
CANNON SMITH,
Elizabeth ... 413-542-2031. 221 G
alumni@amherst.edu
CANNY, Eric ... 386-822-8166. 117 C
ecanny@stetson.edu
CANO, Mary ... 915-566-9621. 494 J
mcano@westerntech.edu
CANO, Mary ... 956-380-8128. 479 B
mcano@riogrande.edu
CANO-MONREAL, Gina .. 956-364-4361. 485 H
CANON, Susan ... 507-786-3647. 264 B
canon@stolaf.edu
CANON, Sybil ... 662-560-1103. 269 C
srcanon@northwestms.edu
CANONICA, James ... 856-227-7200. 300 B
jcanonica@camdencc.edu
CANOUGH, Corrine, M .. 585-785-1469. 324 D
canougcm@flcc.edu
CANOY, Eugenio ... 408-274-7900... 63 O
eugenio.canoy@evc.edu
CANOY, Robert, W ... 704-406-4395. 354 C
rcanoy@gardner-webb.edu
CANT, David ... 714-241-6224... 39 I
dcant@coastline.edu
CANT, Karen ... 714-484-7313... 56 E
kcant@cypresscollege.edu
CANTALUPA, Kathy ... 617-951-2350. 234 G
kathy.cantalupa@necb.edu
CANTANIO, Teri, T ... 215-702-4422. 411 F
tcatanio@cairn.edu
CANTARELLA,
Theresa, C ... 718-390-4350. 339 A
cantaret@stjohns.edu
CANTARERO, Maritza ... 408-741-2429... 75 L
maritza.cantarero@westvalley.edu
CANTELON, Janet ... 509-574-4937. 525 G
jcantelon@yvcc.edu
CANTER, Bridget ... 270-534-3088. 196 G
bridget.canter@kctcs.edu
CANTERBURY, Jay ... 419-434-4076. 391 D
canterbury@findlay.edu
CANTERBURY,
Mary Ann ... 601-643-8414. 266 F
maryann.canterbury@colin.edu
CANTERINO, Patricia ... 610-647-4400. 418 I
pcanterino@immaculata.edu
CANTLEY, Shelby, D ... 765-641-4292. 163 L
sdcantley@anderson.edu
CANTO-WILLIAMS,
Loretta ... 925-439-2181... 42 A
lcantowilliams@losmedanos.edu
CANTON, David, B ... 209-667-3396... 35 B
dcanton1@csustan.edu
CANTOR, Nancy ... 315-443-2235. 347 C
ncantor@syr.edu
CANTOR, Ronald, G ... 207-741-5501. 211 A
rcantor@smccme.edu
CANTRELL, Andra, R ... 817-598-6260. 494 G
acantrell@wc.edu
CANTRELL, Betty ... 678-717-3941. 133 D
betsy.cantrell@ung.edu
CANTRELL, Carol ... 212-229-5671. 332 E
cantrelc@newschool.edu
CANTRELL, Chuck ... 423-425-4363. 463 D
chuck-cantrell@utc.edu
CANTRELL, Danny, R ... 304-766-4183. 530 C
dcantrel@wvstateu.edu
CANTRELL, Hampton ... 310-338-2893... 53 E
hampton.cantrell@lmu.edu
CANTRELL, Jill ... 770-531-6303. 128 B
cantrell@laniertech.edu
CANTRELL, Peggy ... 501-205-8834... 20 I
pcantrell@cbc.edu
CANTRELL, JR.,
Pierce, E ... 979-845-2072. 483 C
p-cantrell@tamu.edu
CANTRELL, Rhonda ... 316-942-4291. 189 E
cantrellr@newmanu.edu
CANTRELL, Sharon ... 787-743-7979. 552 I
scantrel@suagm.edu
CANTRELL, Steve ... 215-489-2356. 414 E
Steve.Cantrell@delval.edu
CANTU, Benjamin ... 903-923-3375. 486 A
benjamin.cantu@tstc.edu
CANTU, Charles ... 210-436-3320. 479 D
ccantu@stmarytx.edu
CANTU, Larry, J ... 830-792-7223. 480 F
ljcantu@schreiner.edu
CANTU, Martha ... 956-665-2147. 492 B
cantum@utpa.edu
CANTU, Tony ... 559-489-2212... 68 I
tony.cantu@fresnocitycollege.edu
CANTU, Valeriano ... 870-862-8131... 23 D
vcantu@southark.edu
CANTU, Veronica ... 713-646-1796. 480 J
vcantu@stcl.edu
CANTWELL, Chris ... 618-393-2982. 146 H
cantwellc@iecc.edu
CANTWELL, Linda ... 405-491-6324. 399 K
lcantwel@snu.edu
CANTWELL, Linda ... 405-491-6324. 399 K

CANTY, Joan ... 817-531-4404. 488 A
jcanty@txwes.edu
CANUETTE, JR., William (Bill) ... 910-296-2449. 361 D
wcanuette@jamessprunt.edu
CANUP, Karen ... 864-578-8770. 446 F
kcanup@sherman.edu
CAO, Christina ... 516-739-1545. 333 F
admissions@nyctcm.edu
CAO, Hai Tao ... 512-444-8082. 485 B
tcao@thsu.edu
CAO, Jian ... 847-467-1032. 155 D
jcao@northwestern.edu
CAO, Nina ... 773-907-4473. 142 A
ncao@ccc.edu
CAPACCIO, John ... 707-826-3451... 35 C
capaccio@humboldt.edu
CAPALBO, Tony ... 815-455-8569. 152 F
tcapalbo@mchenry.edu
CAPANI, Peter ... 817-923-8459. 469 F
peter.capani@fishermore.edu
CAPASSO, Susan ... 203-576-5481... 91 D
scapasso@stvincentscollege.edu
CAPDEVILLE, Michelle ... 413-755-4454. 233 A
capdeville@stcc.edu
CAPE, Jane, A ... 937-328-6038. 377 A
capej@clarkstate.edu
CAPE, Robert, E ... 843-953-6402. 443 A
caper@cofc.edu
CAPECI, Jonathan ... 610-917-1409. 436 C
jcapeci@vfcc.edu
CAPEHART, Robin, C ... 304-336-8000. 530 A
wlpres@westliberty.edu
CAPELA, Michael ... 661-763-7768... 69 D
mcapela@taftcollege.edu
CAPELL, Carey, M ... 843-953-6847. 442 A
carey.capell@citadel.edu
CAPELLE, Rosita, V ... 692-625-3291. 546 F
taklib@yahoo.com
CAPELLI, Joe ... 928-776-2184... 19 H
joe.capelli@yc.edu
CAPELLI, Stephen, L ... 410-334-2813. 221 D
scapelli@worwic.edu
CAPELO, Jenny ... 509-682-6662. 525 B
jcapelo@wvc.edu
CAPENER, Don ... 904-256-7431. 107 Q
dcapene@ju.edu
CAPERS, Meggin ... 610-341-5902. 415 G
mcapers@eastern.edu
CAPILOUTO, Eli ... 859-257-1701. 200 C
elic@uky.edu
CAPISCIOLTO, Ken ... 616-222-3000. 245 C
kcapisciolto@kuyper.edu
CAPISTRANO, Marites ... 216-781-9400. 377 D
mcapis@cie-wc.edu
CAPO, Leslie, L ... 504-568-4806. 205 C
lcapo@lsuhsc.edu
CAPOBIANCO, Patrick ... 617-327-6777. 233 D
patrick_capobianco@mspp.edu
CAPOCCI, John ... 914-606-6931. 350 F
John.Capocci@sunywcc.edu
CAPOLUPO, Catherine ... 617-521-2057. 236 G
catherine.capolupo@simmons.edu
CAPOLUPO, Catherine ... 401-254-3540. 440 B
CAPOMACCHIO, Jacqueline ... 508-793-7397. 225 A
jcapomacchio@clarku.edu
CAPONE, Lucien ... 828-250-3835. 368 C
scapone@unca.edu
CAPONI, Kimberly ... 630-466-7900. 162 J
kcaponi@waubonsee.edu
CAPORUSCIO, Josie ... 718-636-3649. 336 F
jcaporus@pratt.edu
CAPOTOSTA, Amelia ... 610-372-4721. 431 D
acapotosta@racc.edu
CAPP, Maureen ... 561-868-3131. 110 C
cappm@palmbeachstate.edu
CAPPELLA, Michael ... 719-638-6580... 81 K
mcappella@cci.edu
CAPPELLERI, Mary Anne 508-565-1067. 237 A
mcappelleri@stonehill.edu
CAPPELLI, Michael ... 612-343-4440. 262 X
macappel@northcentral.edu
CAPPELLO, Gina ... 617-287-5335. 228 G
gina.cappello@umb.edu
CAPPELLO, Tess ... 703-284-1580. 507 B
tess.cappello@marymount.edu
CAPPETO, Michael ... 718-409-7353. 346 D
mcappeto@sunymaritime.edu
CAPPETO, Michael ... 718-409-7260. 346 D
mcappeto@sunymaritime.edu
CAPPS, Casey ... 931-363-9809. 456 C
ccapps@martinmethodist.edu
CAPPS, John ... 434-832-7601. 512 A
cappsj@cvcc.vccs.edu
CAPPS, Larry ... 907-277-1000... 10 D
larry.capps@chartercollege.edu
CAPPS, Matthew ... 940-397-4138. 476 H
matthew.capps@mwsu.edu
CAPPS, Steve ... 936-633-5281. 465 J
scapps@angelina.edu

CAPPS, Tammy ... 618-634-3280. 158 M
tammyc@shawneecc.edu
CAPPUZZO, Gianpaolo ... 757-873-3100... 96 F
CAPRIO, Anthony, S ... 413-782-1243. 238 A
acaprio@wne.edu
CAPRON, Clara ... 360-650-2422. 525 C
clara.capron@wwu.edu
CAPRON, Clara ... 360-650-3470. 525 C
clara.capron@wwu.edu
CAPRON, Rhonda ... 916-577-2200... 76 J
rcapron@jessup.edu
CAPSOURAS, Barbara ... 973-328-5059. 300 G
bcapsour@ccm.edu
CAPTAIN, Rosanne ... 413-748-3118. 236 I
rcaptain@springfieldcollege.edu
CAPUANO, Christopher .. 201-692-7094. 301 J
capuano@fdu.edu
CAPUTA, McCarren ... 757-455-3295. 515 H
mcaputa@vwc.edu
CAPUTO, Andrea, L ... 330-569-5441. 380 I
caputoal@hiram.edu
CARA, Robert ... 704-366-5066. 269 E
rcara@rts.edu
CARABALLO, Ada ... 787-863-2390. 550 C
ada.caraballo@fajardo.inter.edu
CARABALLO, Awilda, M . 787-738-2161. 554 C
awilda.caraballo@upr.edu
CARABALLO, Darryl ... 702-651-2677. 294 E
darryl.caraballo@csn.edu
CARABALLO, Frances ... 787-892-2315. 551 A
fcpadouani@sg.inter.edu
CARABALLO, José, N ... 787-738-2161. 553 G
josenoel.caraballo@upr.edu
CARABALLO, Jose, N ... 787-738-4660. 554 C
jose.caraballo5@upr.edu
CARABALLO, Luis ... 530-898-6222... 33 A
lcaraballo@csuchico.edu
CARABALLO, Omayra ... 787-284-1912. 550 F
ocarabal@ponce.inter.edu
CARABALLO, Pablo ... 787-264-1912. 551 A
pablo_caraballo_rodriguez@intersg.edu
CARABALLO, Sherri ... 817-531-7511. 488 A
scaraballo@txwes.edu
CARABINE, Veatrice ... 508-541-1629. 225 F
vcarabine@dean.edu
CARABUJAL, Kayleigh ... 530-741-6793... 77 K
kcarabuj@yccd.edu
CARACHILO, Dominick, A ... 570-702-8904. 419 G
dcarachilo@johnson.edu
CARACO, Candace ... 410-532-5109. 217 E
ccaraco@ndm.edu
CARALIS, George ... 718-270-4293. 342 D
george.caralis@downstate.edu
CARAMELLO, Charles, A 301-405-0358. 219 B
ccaramel@umd.edu
CARAWAY, Chris ... 800-354-1254... 16 K
ccaraway@brightoncollege.edu
CARAWAY, Deborah ... 937-769-1036. 373 I
dcaraway@antioch.edu
CARBAJAL, Brent ... 360-650-3480. 525 C
brent.carbajal@wwu.edu
CARBAUGH, Terri ... 562-985-8707... 33 F
CARBERRY, Gail, E ... 508-854-4203. 232 F
gcarberry@qcc.mass.edu
CARBERRY, Paul, K ... 781-891-2009. 223 C
pcarberry@bentley.edu
CARBIS, Kathryn ... 406-791-5274. 288 E
kcarbis01@ugf.edu
CARBONE, Frank ... 718-940-5833. 339 B
fcarbone@sjcny.edu
CARBONE, Judy ... 301-387-3046. 214 I
judy.carbone@garrettcollege.edu
CARBONE, Michele ... 808-564-5975. 136 B
mcarbone@hawaii.edu
CARBONELL, Ivette ... 787-720-1022. 547 E
icarbonell@atlanticcollege.edu
CARBONELL, John ... 731-661-5081. 462 F
jcarbone@uu.edu
CARBONI, Michelle, L ... 815-224-0417. 148 A
michelle_carboni@ivcc.edu
CARBUTO, Michael ... 562-985-4771... 33 F
mcarbuto@csulb.edu
CARCANAGUES, Amy ... 210-829-3912. 490 A
amyc@uiwtx.edu
CARD, Curtis ... 605-642-6093. 451 G
curtis.card@bhsu.edu
CARD, Michael ... 605-677-6926. 451 F
michael.card@usd.edu
CARD, Steven ... 360-650-3109. 525 C
steven.card@wwu.edu
CARDA, Sarah ... 605-668-1541. 450 F
scarda@mtmc.edu
CARDANI, John ... 928-526-7606... 13 B
john.cardani@coconino.edu
CARDARELLI, William ... 860-231-5246... 92 F
bcardarelli@usj.edu
CARDELLE, Alberto ... 570-422-3425. 428 D
acardelle@esu.edu
CARDEN, Monica, W ... 540-674-3600. 513 B
mcarden@nr.edu

CARDEN, Sandy ... 270-686-4536. 196 C
sandy.carden@kctcs.edu
CARDENA, Sonia ... 860-297-4193... 91 F
sonia.cardena@trincoll.edu
CARDENAS, Eric, D ... 813-253-6232. 118 L
ecardenas@ut.edu
CARDENAS, Jose, A ... 480-965-6479... 11 K
jcardenas@asu.edu
CARDENAS, Kerstin ... 507-222-4068. 254 D
kcardena@carleton.edu
CARDENAS, Mayela ... 787-725-8120. 548 O
mcardenas@eap.edu
CARDENAS, Michael ... 617-739-1700. 235 A
mcardenas@aii.edu
CARDENAS, Monique ... 248-689-8282. 251 I
mcardena@walshcollege.edu
CARDENAS, Raul ... 303-315-2109... 86 A
raul.cardenas@ucdenver.edu
CARDENAS, Rudolph ... 910-672-1433. 367 D
rcardena@uncfsu.edu
CARDENAS, Veronica ... 956-721-5138. 475 F
veronica.cardenas@laredo.edu
CARDENAS-ADAME, Patricia ... 623-845-3567... 14 M
patricia.cardenas-adame@gccaz.edu
CARDENAS-CLAGUE, Adeline ... 909-593-3511... 72 E
acardenas-clague@laverne.edu
CARDER, Rick ... 765-677-2110. 169 B
rick.carder@indwes.edu
CARDER, Sally ... 501-760-4200... 22 A
scarder@npcc.edu
CARDILLO, Rosaleen ... 845-437-5844. 349 G
roecardillo@vassar.edu
CARDIN, Matt ... 585-385-8143. 338 H
mcardin@sjfc.edu
CARDINAL, Donald ... 714-997-6920... 38 A
cardinal@chapman.edu
CARDINAL, Jason ... 651-779-3469. 258 C
jason.cardinal@century.edu
CARDINALLI, Marc ... 478-445-2037. 125 A
marc.cardinalli@gcsu.edu
CARDINE, Darla, S ... 630-466-7900. 162 J
dcardine@waubonsee.edu
CARDONA, Jose ... 856-256-4236. 305 E
cardona@rowan.edu
CARDONA, Jose ... 787-758-2525. 554 F
jose.cardona8@upr.edu
CARDONA, Nelida ... 787-262-5786. 553 A
CARDONA, Pablo ... 414-297-6867. 540 E
cardonap@matc.edu
CARDONA, Teresa ... 787-754-8000. 553 E
tcardona@pupr.edu
CARDONE, Stephen ... 609-497-7730. 304 D
housing@ptsem.edu
CARDOSA, Leanne ... 304-296-8282. 531 F
lcardosa@wvjcmorgantown.edu
CARDOZA, Carla ... 915-831-2638. 472 B
ccardoza@epcc.edu
CARDOZA, Lisa ... 956-665-2100. 492 B
president@utpa.edu
CARDUCCI, Vince ... 313-664-1488. 241 C
vcarducci@collegeforcreativestudies.edu
CARDWELL, Cathi, A ... 740-368-3246. 387 J
cacardwe@owu.edu
CARDWELL, Kenneth ... 760-572-2000... 42 E
cardwell@deepsprings.edu
CARDWELL, Thomas ... 402-228-3468. 292 C
tcardwel@southeast.edu
CARDWELL, Wayne ... 276-656-0215. 513 D
wcardwell@patrickhenry.edu
CAREAGA, Andrew, P ... 573-341-4183. 284 A
acareaga@mst.edu
CARELLA, Terry ... 517-371-5140. 250 G
carellat@cooley.edu
CAREN, William, L ... 585-245-5619. 343 C
caren@geneseo.edu
CARET, Robert, L ... 617-287-7050. 228 E
rcaret@umassp.edu
CAREW, William ... 863-680-4305. 105 D
wcarew@flsouthern.edu
CAREY, Amy, B ... 651-631-5220. 263 A
abcarey@nwc.edu
CAREY, Barbara ... 914-367-8262. 339 E
bcarey@corriganlibrary.org
CAREY, Chris ... 423-236-2828. 458 J
carey@southern.edu
CAREY, Chris, J ... 858-499-0202... 40 C
webmaster@coleman.edu
CAREY, Daniel, J ... 608-663-2262. 532 I
dcarey@edgewood.edu
CAREY, Ernie ... 801-863-8237. 497 C
ecarey@uvu.edu
CAREY, Francis, J ... 716-839-8478. 322 E
fcarey@daemen.edu
CAREY, Jay ... 503-838-8481. 406 E
careywj@wou.edu
CAREY, Karen ... 805-437-8986... 32 I
karen.carey@csuci.edu
CAREY, Kate ... 614-823-3209. 387 K
kcarey@otterbein.edu

CAREY, Kim ... 503-594-0760. 402 F
kimc@clackamas.edu
CAREY, Marita ... 404-876-1227. 122 C
maritacarey@bccr.edu
CAREY, Mary Beth ... 914-633-2120. 327 C
mcarey@iona.edu
CAREY, Michael ... 718-862-8000. 329 M
michael.carey@manhattan.edu
CAREY, Michael ... 509-313-3550. 520 A
carey@gonzaga.edu
CAREY, Patricia, M ... 860-439-2508... 89 H
pmcar@conncoll.edu
CAREY, Paula ... 508-854-7518. 232 F
pcarey@qcc.mass.edu
CAREY, Peter, M ... 716-878-6332. 343 A
careypm@buffalostate.edu
CAREY, Russell, C ... 401-863-9846. 438 J
russell_carey@brown.edu
CAREY, Sandra ... 859-246-6203. 194 L
sandra.carey@kctcs.edu
CAREY, Seamus ... 203-371-7730... 91 C
careys@sacredheart.edu
CAREY, Susan ... 530-895-2378... 30 F
careysu@butte.edu
CAREY, Thomas, P ... 207-786-6254. 209 F
tcarey@bates.edu
CAREY, Timothy ... 973-655-5210. 303 D
careyt@mail.montclair.edu
CAREY-FLETCHER, Kathi . 240-567-7674. 216 F
kc.carey-fletcher@montgomerycollege.edu
CAREY-MCDONALD, Jan 435-586-7735. 497 A
careymcdonald@suu.edu
CARFAGNA, Angelo ... 201-692-7025. 301 J
angelo@fdu.edu
CARFAGNA, John ... 216-397-4321. 381 R
jcarfagna@jcu.edu
CARGER, Mimi ... 202-639-1867... 95 B
mcarter@corcoran.org
CARGILE, Kenneth, R ... 731-989-6000. 454 J
kcargile@fhu.edu
CARGILL, Jennifer, S ... 225-578-2217. 204 O
cargill@lsu.edu
CARHIDE, Brian, M ... 386-226-6056. 102 B
brian.carhide@erau.edu
CARIAGA-LO, Liza ... 401-863-2216. 438 J
liza_cariaga-lo@brown.edu
CARICO, Nathan ... 901-381-3939. 464 C
nathan@visible.edu
CARIDEO, James, J ... 717-736-4160. 417 I
jjcaride@hacc.edu
CARIDI, James, A ... 614-251-4595. 386 B
caridij@ohiodominican.edu
CARIGNAN, Steven ... 413-528-7207. 222 E
scarignan@simons-rock.edu
CARIKER, Heath ... 903-675-6235. 488 D
hcariker@tvcc.edu
CARILLI, Vincent ... 570-941-7680. 436 A
vincent.carilli@scranton.edu
CARINO, Annie ... 718-260-3020. 336 E
acarino@poly.edu
CARIO, William, R ... 262-243-5700. 532 H
william.cario@cuw.edu
CARISSIMI, Laura, K ... 440-365-5222. 383 B
CARITO, Phyllis ... 518-828-4181. 321 C
carito@sunycgcc.edu
CARKEEK, Susan ... 434-924-4475. 511 B
sc9ym@virginia.edu
CARKUM, Duane ... 504-520-7490. 209 D
dcarkum@xula.edu
CARL, Ashley ... 813-253-7158. 106 M
acarl@hccfl.edu
CARL, Cathy ... 845-431-8635. 323 C
CARL, Cherie ... 804-333-6716. 513 G
ccarl@rappahannock.edu
CARL, David ... 505-984-6082. 311 H
gi@sjcsf.edu
CARL, Harold, F ... 903-233-4400. 475 J
haroldcarl@letu.edu
CARL, Heidi, A ... 765-361-6375. 175 B
carlh@wabash.edu
CARL, James, C ... 203-396-8454... 91 C
carlj@sacredheart.edu
CARL, Peggy ... 608-363-2296. 531 M
carlp@beloit.edu
CARL, III, William, J ... 412-924-1366. 431 A
wcarl@pts.edu
CARLBLOM, Shelia ... 765-677-2191. 169 B
sheila.carlblom@indwes.edu
CARLEO, A. Susan ... 818-947-2321... 52 E
carleoas@lavc.edu
CARLETON, Dia, M ... 570-662-4052. 429 C
dcarleto@mansfield.edu
CARLETON, Mary Ruth ... 619-594-4562... 35 D
maryruth.carleton@sdsu.edu
CARLETTA, Charles, F ... 518-276-6212. 337 I
carlec@rpi.edu
CARLEY, Michael ... 559-791-2275... 49 P
mcarley@portervillecollege.edu
CARLI, Gale ... 510-742-3102... 57 A
gcarli@ohlone.edu

CARLIN, Erin .... 717-620-0103. 438 H
erin.carlin@yti.edu
CARLIN, Hiedi .... 417-625-9329. 278 D
carlin-h@mssu.edu
CARLIN, Jane .... 253-879-3118. 524 F
jcarlin@pugetsound.edu
CARLIN, Laurence .... 920-424-7364. 537 B
carlin@uwosh.edu
CARLIN, Melanie .... 217-357-9117. 156 K
mcarlin@robertmorris.edu
CARLIN, Michael .... 704-687-5500. 368 E
Mike.Carlin@uncc.edu
CARLIN, Virginia, A .... 630-560-6311. 148 K
vcarlin@hancocku.edu
CARLISLE, Annessa .... 734-973-3624. 252 A
acarlisle@wccnet.edu
CARLISLE, Beth .... 602-943-2311... 19 C
Beth.Carlisle@west.edu
CARLISLE, Brian .... 909-621-8241... 59 G
brian_carlisle@pitzer.edu
CARLISLE, Brian, A .... 715-836-5626. 536 E
carlisba@uwec.edu
CARLISLE, David, M .... 323-563-4987... 38 B
davidcarlisle@cdrewu.edu
CARLISLE, Elizabeth .... 812-749-1241. 171 K
lcarlisle@oak.edu
CARLISLE, James .... 478-445-8137. 125 A
james.carlisle@gcsu.edu
CARLISLE, Jerry, H .... 501-882-8835... 19 M
jhcarlisle@asub.edu
CARLISLE, Siri .... 518-828-4181. 321 C
carlisle@sunycgcc.edu
CARLISLE, Susan .... 502-213-5200. 195 F
susan.carlisle@kctcs.edu
CARLISLE, Willie .... 334-229-4562..... 1 D
carlisle@alasu.edu
CARLO, Jaclyn .... 631-244-3138. 323 B
carloj@dowling.edu
CARLO, Jennifer .... 412-578-6087. 412 G
CARLO, Luis .... 646-378-6171. 335 C
luis.carlo@nyack.edu
CARLOCK, Jennifer .... 309-655-7100. 158 C
jennifer.carlock@osfhealthcare.org
CARLOCK, Myra .... 731-352-4000. 453 D
carlockm@bethelu.edu
CARLOCK, Ruth .... 402-363-5704. 293 I
rmcarlock@york.edu
CARLSEN, Guy, F .... 718-489-5468. 338 G
gcarlsen@sfc.edu
CARLSON, Andrew .... 402-935-9400. 290 N
acarlson@nechristian.edu
CARLSON, Annie .... 828-669-8012. 357 H
acarlson@montreat.edu
CARLSON, C. Robert ...... 630-682-6002. 147 F
carlson@iit.edu
CARLSON, Cathy .... 507-222-4075. 254 D
ccarlson@carleton.edu
CARLSON, Charles .... 914-637-2757. 327 C
ccarlson@iona.edu
CARLSON, Chris .... 951-222-8000... 60 J
chris.carlson@rcc.edu
CARLSON, David, H .... 979-845-8160. 483 C
CARLSON, David, S .... 979-862-3389. 484 B
dscarlson@tamhsc.edu
CARLSON, Deborah .... 402-354-7023. 291 B
deb.carlson@methodistcollege.edu
CARLSON, Denise, M .... 402-354-7256. 291 B
denise.carlson@methodistcollege.edu
CARLSON, Don .... 650-738-4362... 64 D
carlsond@smccd.edu
CARLSON, Douglas .... 415-476-4527... 72 A
doug.carlson@ucsf.edu
CARLSON, Douglas, W ... 712-707-7055. 181 H
carlson@nwciowa.edu
CARLSON, Dylana .... 309-341-5230. 141 A
dcarlson@sandburg.edu
CARLSON, Gerald, P .... 337-482-6678. 208 D
gcarlson@louisiana.edu
CARLSON, Gregory .... 701-845-7480. 372 A
gregory.carlson@vcsu.edu
CARLSON, Herbert, F ...... 724-738-2545. 429 F
herbert.carlson@sru.edu
CARLSON, Jean .... 914-831-0416. 321 B
jcarlson@cw.edu
CARLSON, Jeffrey .... 708-524-6814. 144 C
jcarlson@dom.edu
CARLSON, Jim .... 406-586-3585. 286 F
jim.carlson@montanabiblecollege.edu
CARLSON, Julie .... 402-844-7142. 291 I
juliec@northeast.edu
CARLSON, Kathleen .... 773-298-3305. 158 E
carlson@sxu.edu
CARLSON, Kenna Lee ...... 402-486-2503. 292 E
kecarlso@ucollege.edu
CARLSON, Kerri .... 612-659-6204. 259 D
kerri.carlson@minneapolis.edu
CARLSON, Kurt .... 919-497-3325. 356 E
kcarlson@louisburg.edu
CARLSON, Libby, L .... 662-846-4268. 266 G
lcarlson@deltastate.edu
CARLSON, Malinda, L .... 217-245-3011. 146 F
mcarlson@ic.edu
CARLSON, Mark .... 651-201-1827. 257 N
mark.carlson@so.mnscu.edu
CARLSON, Mary .... 616-222-3000. 245 C
mcarlson@kuyper.edu
CARLSON, Nancy .... 303-914-6389... 84 I
nancy.carlson@rrcc.edu
CARLSON, Neil .... 616-526-6420. 240 L
nec4@calvin.edu
CARLSON, Nels .... 816-414-3700. 277 L
ncarlson@mbts.edu
CARLSON, Paul .... 815-802-8652. 149 C
pcarlson@kcc.edu
CARLSON, Paul .... 323-953-4000... 51 G
carlsopr@lacitycollege.edu
CARLSON, Paula, J .... 507-786-3632. 264 B
carlsonp@stolaf.edu
CARLSON, Rachel .... 540-545-7382. 509 E
rcarlso2@su.edu
CARLSON, Ria, M .... 949-824-7911... 71 B
ria.carlson@uci.edu
CARLSON, Rich .... 402-486-2508. 292 E
ricarlso@ucollege.edu
CARLSON, Rosa, F .... 559-791-2316... 49 P
rcarlson@portervillecollege.edu
CARLSON, Stanley, E ...... 563-884-5684. 182 A
stan.carlson@palmer.edu
CARLSON, Steve .... 920-206-2342. 533 U
steve.carlson@mbbc.edu
CARLSON, Steven, T .... 574-372-5100. 166 B
carlsost@grace.edu
CARLSON, Tammy .... 309-438-8846. 147 J
tscarls@ilstu.edu
CARLSON, Tracey .... 423-614-6000. 455 L
tcarlson@leeuniversity.edu
CARLSON, Wayne, E .... 614-292-2872. 386 E
carlson.8@osu.edu
CARLSON HURST,
Marjorie, F .... 330-471-8244. 383 D
mcarlson@malone.edu
CARLSON ZINK,
DeAnna .... 701-777-2611. 371 C
deannac@undfoundation.org
CARLSTROM, Lester, H .. 773-244-5597. 154 G
lcarlstrom@northpark.edu
CARLTON, Keitha .... 903-785-7661. 478 B
kcarlton@parisjc.edu
CARLTON, LeAnn, K .... 816-654-7213. 275 K
lcarlton@kcumb.edu
CARLTON, William .... 912-279-5892. 123 B
wcarlton@ccga.edu
CARLUCCI, Carl .... 832-842-5504. 489 B
ccarlucci@uh.edu
CARLUCCI, Carl, P .... 832-842-5504. 489 A
ccarlucci@uh.edu
CARMACK, Connie, K ..... 540-375-2230. 509 B
carmack@roanoke.edu
CARMAN, Beth Anne ...... 614-236-6211. 375 H
bcarman@capital.edu
CARMAN, Kevin .... 775-784-1740. 294 J
kcarman@unr.edu
CARMAN, Philip .... 505-224-4000. 309 E
pcarman@cnm.edu
CARMEAN, Tracee, B ...... 757-240-2200. 509 A
CARMEL, Julie .... 508-929-8754. 230 G
jcarmel@worcester.edu
CARMEN, Kim .... 318-675-5000. 205 D
kcarme@lsuhsc.edu
CARMENA, Craig .... 530-242-7912... 65 G
ccarmena@shastacollege.edu
CARMER, Gregory, W ..... 978-867-4012. 226 H
greg.carmer@gordon.edu
CARMICAL, Beth .... 910-272-3343. 363 B
bcarmical@robeson.edu
CARMICHAEL, Ann, C .... 803-584-3446. 448 D
anncar@mailbox.sc.edu
CARMICHAEL,
Beverly, C .... 904-819-6290. 103 E
bcarmichael@flagler.edu
CARMICHAEL, Brenda .... 620-343-4600. 186 E
bcarmichael@fhtc.edu
CARMICHAEL, John .... 360-867-6100. 519 J
carmichj@evergreen.edu
CARMICHAEL, Matt .... 530-752-5350... 70 J
mecarmichael@ucdavis.edu
CARMICHAEL, Paul .... 860-343-5787... 89 A
pcarmichael@mxcc.commnet.edu
CARMICHAEL, Peggy ...... 304-214-8901. 528 G
pcarmichael@wvncc.edu
CARMICHAEL, Stacy .... 228-896-2503. 268 C
stacy.carmichael@mgccc.edu
CARMINE, Kevin .... 718-319-7965. 318 B
kcarmine@hostos.cuny.edu
CARMODY, Patricia .... 507-537-6206. 261 F
Patricia.Carmody@smsu.edu
CARMODY, Richard .... 805-922-6966... 26 K
rcarmody@hancockcollege.edu
CARMONA, José, I .... 787-875-4150. 552 J
jocarmona@suagm.edu
CARNAGHI, Jan .... 317-955-6154. 170 V
jcarnaghi@marian.edu
CARNAGHI, Jill, E .... 314-935-5022. 284 L
jill.carnaghi@wustl.edu
CARNAHAN, Jon .... 503-842-8222. 408 B
carnahan@tillamookbay.cc
CARNAHAN, Scott .... 503-883-2229. 404 A
scarnah@linfield.edu
CARNAROLI, Craig .... 215-898-6693. 435 B
carnarol@upenn.edu
CARNDUFF, Dagmar, L .. 414-847-3211. 534 F
dagmarcarnduff@miad.edu
CARNE, Kim .... 906-786-5802. 240 K
carnek@baycollege.edu
CARNE, Linda, P .... 804-752-3103. 508 E
lindacarne@rmc.edu
CARNEGIE, Kay .... 503-399-5058. 402 E
kay.carnegie@chemeketa.edu
CARNES, Allen .... 336-770-3320. 369 D
carnesa@uncsa.edu
CARNES, Gregory, A .... 256-765-4245..... 9 C
gacarnes@una.edu
CARNES, Kathy, M .... 252-493-7220. 362 G
kcarnes@email.pittcc.edu
CARNES, Peter .... 508-565-1206. 237 A
pcarnes@stonehill.edu
CARNEVALE, David .... 562-907-4284... 76 I
dcarneva@whittier.edu
CARNEY, Angela .... 727-736-5082. 113 D
acarney@schiller.edu
CARNEY, Conferlete .... 727-712-5742. 112 E
carney.conferlete@spcollege.edu
CARNEY, Diane, E .... 412-291-6250. 410 B
dcarney@aii.edu
CARNEY, Edward .... 856-227-7200. 300 B
ecarney@camdencc.edu
CARNEY, Gary .... 610-861-1300. 424 E
carneyg@moravian.edu
CARNEY, Kathleen .... 508-793-3371. 225 B
kcarney@holycross.edu
CARNEY, Kay .... 415-451-2835... 63 A
kcarney@sfts.edu
CARNEY, Leslie .... 407-646-2266. 111 Q
lcarney@rollins.edu
CARNEY, OSF, Margaret 716-375-2222. 338 E
mcarney@sbu.edu
CARNEY, Martin .... 216-421-7424. 377 C
mcarney@cia.edu
CARNEY, Paul .... 314-968-7086. 284 N
paulcarney89@webster.edu
CARNEY, Sheila, A .... 412-578-6424. 412 G
carneysa@carlow.edu
CARNEY, Tim .... 513-244-4426. 377 G
tim_carney@mail.msj.edu
CARNEY, Timothy .... 202-319-5619... 94 G
carneyt@cua.edu
CARNEY-DEBORD, Nan .. 740-587-6428. 379 D
carneydebord@denison.edu
CARNEY-HALL, Karla ...... 309-556-3111. 148 B
dstudent@iwu.edu
CARNIE, Andrew, H .... 520-621-2802... 18 F
carnie@email.arizona.edu
CARNLEY, Raymond .... 706-802-5457. 125 C
rcarnley@highlands.edu
CARNWATH, Thomas ..... 215-717-6640. 435 A
tcarnwath@uarts.edu
CARNZ, Scott .... 206-239-2320. 516 H
scarnz@aii.edu
CARO, Jessica .... 787-832-6000. 549 D
jcaro@icprjc.edu
CARO, M.J .... 386-226-6340. 102 B
carom1@erau.edu
CARO, Mary Ellen .... 609-984-1130. 308 A
mcaro@tesc.edu
CAROL, Steve .... 732-987-2414. 302 B
CAROLAN, Tammy .... 563-425-5337. 183 B
carolant@uiu.edu
CAROLINA, Kimberly ...... 203-575-8056... 89 B
kcarolina@nvcc.commnet.edu
CAROLLO, Chris .... 203-332-5078... 88 F
ccarollo@hcc.commnet.edu
CARON, Bob .... 818-779-8040... 50 A
bcaron@kingsuniversity.edu
CARON, Christina .... 207-992-1939. 210 B
caroncb@husson.edu
CARON, David, G .... 314-256-8860. 271 F
caron@ai.edu
CARONE, Joseph .... 567-661-7190. 387 L
joseph_carone@owens.edu
CAROTHERS, Amy .... 775-784-6620. 294 J
acarothers@unr.edu
CAROTHERS, Harry, G .... 303-963-3228... 79 C
hcarothers@ccu.edu
CAROTHERS, John .... 775-784-1394. 294 J
jcarothers@adv.unr.edu
CARP, Richard, M .... 925-631-4443... 61 F
rmcarp@gmail.com
CARPENTER, Amanda ..... 804-706-5189. 512 G
acarpenter@jtcc.edu
CARPENTER, Amber, L ... 419-772-2012. 386 D
a-carpenter@onu.edu
CARPENTER, Andrew ...... 630-560-6313. 148 K
acarpenter@hancocku.edu
CARPENTER, Barbara ...... 225-771-2613. 206 J
carp.subr@aol.com
CARPENTER, Bobbi .... 434-381-6156. 510 F
bcarpenter@sbc.edu
CARPENTER, Carol .... 616-977-5520. 241 F
carol.carpenter@cornerstone.edu
CARPENTER, Carolyn, A . 573-629-3116. 274 J
Carolyn.Carpenter@hlg.edu
CARPENTER, Courtney .... 757-221-4000. 503 N
cmcarp@wm.edu
CARPENTER,
Courtney, M .... 757-221-2001. 503 N
cmcarp@wm.edu
CARPENTER, Dale .... 828-227-7311. 369 E
carpenter@wcu.edu
CARPENTER, Dale, E ...... 260-982-5393. 170 U
decarpenter@manchester.edu
CARPENTER, Dana .... 225-771-2394. 206 J
dana_carpenter@subr.edu
CARPENTER, David .... 478-929-6700. 128 I
david.carpenter@maconstate.edu
CARPENTER, Debra .... 281-283-2150. 489 C
carpenter@uhcl.edu
CARPENTER, Denise .... 320-222-6073. 260 H
denise.carpenter@ridgewater.edu
CARPENTER, Dianna, M . 816-604-2230. 277 F
dianna.carpenter@mcckc.edu
CARPENTER, Earl .... 310-506-4700... 58 H
earl.carpenter@pepperdine.edu
CARPENTER, Ginny .... 708-239-4703. 160 K
ginny.carpenter@trnty.edu
CARPENTER, Heather ...... 617-236-8800. 226 F
hcarpenter@fisher.edu
CARPENTER, Julia .... 405-691-3800. 396 D
jcarpenter@macu.edu
CARPENTER, Julie .... 831-656-3054. 544 M
jcarpenter@nps.edu
CARPENTER, Kae .... 931-372-3269. 460 A
kcarpenter@tntech.edu
CARPENTER, Kathryn, H . 312-996-8974. 161 D
khc@uic.edu
CARPENTER, Katie .... 406-238-7390. 288 B
katie.carpenter@rocky.edu
CARPENTER, Kenneth ..... 225-578-5863. 204 O
kenc@lsu.edu
CARPENTER, Kimberly .... 323-241-5321... 52 C
carpenkc@lasc.edu
CARPENTER, Larry .... 423-614-8440. 455 L
lcarpenter@leeuniversity.edu
CARPENTER, Larry, J ...... 540-831-5182. 508 C
ljcarpenter@radford.edu
CARPENTER, Linda, M ... 814-641-3111. 419 H
carpenl@juniata.edu
CARPENTER, Lisa .... 808-566-2411. 135 F
lcarpenter@hpu.edu
CARPENTER, Marla .... 336-770-3337. 369 D
carpem@uncsa.edu
CARPENTER, Mary, V ..... 731-881-7070. 463 E
maryc@utm.edu
CARPENTER, Michael ..... 757-823-8104. 507 M
mcarpenter@nsu.edu
CARPENTER, Mike .... 618-262-8641. 147 C
carpenterm@iecc.edu
CARPENTER, Mike .... 402-826-6781. 289 E
mike.carpenter@doane.edu
CARPENTER, Molly .... 870-368-2045... 22 E
mcarpenter@ozarka.edu
CARPENTER, Monica, S . 828-682-7315. 361 H
mscarpenter@mayland.edu
CARPENTER, Patricia, A . 207-778-7091. 212 D
patc@maine.edu
CARPENTER, Paula .... 217-234-5217. 150 D
pcarpent@lakeland.cc.il.us
CARPENTER, Richard ...... 832-813-6515. 476 A
richard.carpenter@lonestar.edu
CARPENTER, Robert .... 423-323-0259. 461 C
rccarpenter@northeaststate.edu
CARPENTER, Rosalie ...... 386-822-7348. 117 C
rcarpent@stetson.edu
CARPENTER, Scott .... 541-881-5773. 408 C
scarpent@tvcc.cc
CARPENTER, Shirley .... 404-215-2656. 129 D
scarpenter@morehouse.edu
CARPENTER, Stan .... 402-471-2505. 291 C
scarpenter@nscs.edu
CARPENTER, Stan .... 512-245-2150. 487 C
sc33@txstate.edu
CARPENTER, Van .... 715-324-6900. 535 E
van.carpenter@ni.edu
CARPENTER, Wayne, D .. 413-782-1565. 238 A
wcarpent@wne.edu
CARPENTER, Wendi, B ... 718-409-7271. 346 D
wcarpenter@sunymaritime.edu
CARPENTER-DAVIS,
Cheryl .... 816-604-4003. 277 H
cheryl.carpenter@mcckc.edu
CARPENTER-HUBIN,
Julie .... 614-292-5915. 386 E
carpenter-hubin.16@osu.edu

CARPENTER-WILLIAMS, Oshunda ... 815-802-8513. 149 C
owilliams@kcc.edu
CARPER, Kellie ... 815-455-8670. 152 F
kcarper@mchenry.edu
CARPI, Anthony ... 212-237-8944. 318 D
acarpi@jjay.cuny.edu
CARPIO, Eric ... 719-587-7802... 78 B
ecarpio@adams.edu
CARPIO, Joseph ... 505-346-2361. 312 E
joseph.carpio@bie.edu
CARPIO, Joseph ... 505-346-2324. 312 E
joseph.carpio@bie.edu
CARR, Bonnie ... 813-253-7006. 106 M
bcarr@hccfl.edu
CARR, Charles ... 940-397-4748. 476 H
charles.carr@mwsu.edu
CARR, Dennis ... 541-463-5583. 403 I
carrd@lanecc.edu
CARR, Diane ... 803-738-7754. 445 C
carrd@midlandstech.edu
CARR, Frances ... 229-317-6744. 124 A
frances.carr@darton.edu
CARR, James, W ... 501-279-4406... 21 C
carr@harding.edu
CARR, Jeffrey ... 619-849-2415... 59 L
jeffreycarr@pointloma.edu
CARR, Jeffrey ... 215-972-7623. 426 Y
jcarr@pafa.edu
CARR, Jessica ... 505-348-3700. 450 G
jcarr@national.edu
CARR, Jill ... 419-372-2843. 374 K
jcarr2@bgsu.edu
CARR, John ... 404-364-8439. 130 A
jcarr1@oglethorpe.edu
CARR, Karen, A ... 315-786-2404. 327 L
kcarr@sunyjefferson.edu
CARR, Larry ... 617-989-4256. 237 G
carrl@wit.edu
CARR, Leslie ... 661-362-3100... 40 E
leslie.carr@canyons.edu
CARR, Meagan ... 603-752-1113. 296 E
mcarr@ccsnh.edu
CARR, Nancy ... 315-498-2834. 335 G
CARR, Nicole, T ... 251-460-6475... 9 E
ntcarr@southalabama.edu
CARR, Norma ... 801-957-4083. 498 B
norma.carr@slcc.edu
CARR, Pattie ... 701-483-2089. 371 D
pattie.carr@dickinsonstate.edu
CARR, Penelope ... 407-277-0311. 103 C
pcarr@evergladesuniversity.edu
CARR, Ricki ... 208-376-7731. 137 F
rcarr@boisebible.edu
CARR, Robert ... 601-877-6141. 265 G
rcarr@alcorn.edu
CARR, Rodger ... 281-283-2900. 489 C
carr@uhcl.edu
CARR, Rodney ... 229-243-6496. 121 E
rodney.carr@bainbridge.edu
CARR, Rosalie ... 336-315-8660. 353 C
rcarr@carolinagrad.edu
CARR, Shannon ... 509-359-6582. 519 C
scarr@ewu.edu
CARR, Sherrean ... 408-848-4757... 45 F
scarr@gavilan.edu
CARR, Steve ... 513-244-8473. 376 J
steve.carr@ccuniversity.edu
CARR, Thomas, F ... 607-962-9223. 322 B
carr_tom@corning-cc.edu
CARR, Tunya ... 816-600-3900. 450 G
tcarr@national.edu
CARR ROBINETT, Angie . 816-501-4541. 280 I
angie.carr@rockhurst.edu
CARRADINE, Tania ... 504-671-5155. 203 A
tcarra@dcc.edu
CARRAFIELLO, Susan ... 937-775-2660. 393 G
susan.carrafiello@wright.edu
CARRANCO, Emilio ... 512-245-2161. 487 C
ec05@txstate.edu
CARRANO, Jean, B ... 803-938-3708. 448 F
jeabrown@uscsumter.edu
CARRANZA, Mike ... 956-872-3420. 480 I
mcarranz@southtexascollege.edu
CARRARO, Francine ... 940-397-8948. 476 H
francine.carraro@mwsu.edu
CARRASCO, Hector ... 719-549-2696... 80 K
hector.carrasco@colostate-pueblo.edu
CARRASQUILLO, Iris, N . 787-850-9363. 554 D
iris.carrasquillo@upr.edu
CARRAWAY, Carl ... 803-738-7624. 445 C
carrawayc@midlandstech.edu
CARRAWAY, Jay ... 252-527-6223. 361 F
jcarraway@lenoircc.edu
CARRAWAY, Kevin ... 252-328-6434. 367 B
carrawayc@ecu.edu
CARRAWAY, Pauline ... 757-352-4007. 508 G
paulcar@regent.edu
CARREIRA, Robert ... 520-515-5370... 12 R
carreirar@cochise.edu
CARREIRO, Manuel, C ... 203-582-8721... 91 A
manuel.carreiro@quinnipiac.edu
CARRELL, Dean, O ... 206-281-2083. 523 C
carrell@spu.edu
CARRERA, Cheryl ... 714-564-6606... 60 G
carrera_cheryl@sac.edu
CARRERA, Magali ... 508-999-8024. 229 A
mcarrera@umassd.edu
CARRERE, Carol, G ... 919-658-7771. 357 I
ccarrere@moc.edu
CARRESCIA, John ... 718-420-4264. 350 B
jcarresc@wagner.edu
CARRETTA, Patricia, J ... 703-993-2367. 505 C
pcarrett@gmu.edu
CARRICK, Stacy ... 660-562-1124. 279 I
carrick@nwmissouri.edu
CARRICO, Angela ... 269-782-1323. 250 C
acarrico@swmich.edu
CARRICO, John ... 270-534-3089. 196 G
john.carrico@kctcs.edu
CARRICO, Sarah ... 651-846-1424. 261 D
sarah.carrico@saintpaul.edu
CARRIER, Steve, G ... 785-827-5541. 188 C
yotee@kwu.edu
CARRIG, Virginia ... 845-431-8686. 323 C
virginia.carrig@sunydutchess.edu
CARRIGAN, Joyce ... 714-484-7142... 56 E
jcarrigan@cypresscollege.edu
CARRIGAN, Sarah, D ... 336-256-0397. 369 A
sarah_carrigan@uncg.edu
CARRIGAN, Tena ... 501-812-2217... 22 G
tcarrigan@pulaskitech.edu
CARRILLO, Carmen ... 310-233-4250... 51 H
carrilc@lahc.edu
CARRILLO, Jessica ... 806-742-2121. 487 D
jessica.carrillo@ttu.edu
CARRILLO, Lee ... 505-224-3093. 309 E
lcarrillo@cnm.edu
CARRILLO, Lizzette ... 787-723-4481. 548 A
lcarrillo@ceaprc.edu
CARRILLO, Robin ... 210-486-4134. 464 J
rcarrillo71@alamo.edu
CARRINGTON, Margie ... 650-306-3174... 64 B
carringtonm@smccd.edu
CARRINGTON-IRWIN, Melissa ... 651-385-6309. 259 E
mcarrington@southeastmn.edu
CARRION, Estela ... 727-816-3261. 110 E
carrioe@phcc.edu
CARRION, Ingrid ... 787-743-4041. 548 H
icarrion@columbiaco.edu
CARRION, Lourdes ... 787-878-5475. 549 L
lcarrion@arecibo.inter.edu
CARRION-SILVA, Ana, M ... 718-518-4407. 318 B
amcarrion@hostos.cuny.edu
CARRISALEZ, Albert, A ... 210-458-5138. 492 C
albert.carrisalez@utsa.edu
CARRIUOLO, Nancy ... 401-456-8101. 439 F
ncarriuolo@ric.edu
CARRIZOSA, Stan, A ... 559-730-3731... 40 I
stanc@cos.edu
CARROCCI, Noreen ... 316-942-4291. 189 E
carroccin@newmanu.edu
CARROLL, A. Christine ... 540-373-2200. 502 N
christine.carroll@careertrainingsolutions.com
CARROLL, Andrew, G ... 419-334-8400. 389 I
acarroll@terra.edu
CARROLL, Anne ... 423-697-2603. 460 C
CARROLL, Barbara, L ... 919-515-3443. 368 B
barbara_carroll@ncsu.edu
CARROLL, Betty ... 304-327-4031. 529 D
bcarroll@bluefieldstate.edu
CARROLL, Brian ... 706-368-6944. 121 G
bc@berry.edu
CARROLL, Brian, C ... 863-667-5020. 113 P
bccaroll@seu.edu
CARROLL, Carrie ... 651-523-1641. 256 J
ekennedy001@luthersem.edu
CARROLL, Charley ... 575-492-2660. 310 G
ccarroll@nmjc.edu
CARROLL, Constance, M 619-388-6957... 62 C
ccarroll@sdccd.edu
CARROLL, David, J ... 409-880-8118. 486 F
david.carroll@lamar.edu
CARROLL, Denise ... 910-521-6337. 369 B
denise.carroll@uncp.edu
CARROLL, Dennis, G ... 336-841-9229. 355 C
dcarroll@highpoint.edu
CARROLL, Donna, M ... 708-524-6817. 144 C
dompres@dom.edu
CARROLL, Doris, W ... 410-581-1802. 218 D
dcarroll@host.sdc.edu
CARROLL, Elizabeth ... 717-815-6470. 438 D
bcarroll@ycp.edu
CARROLL, Erik, P ... 623-572-3326. 153 B
ecarro@midwestern.edu
CARROLL, Frances ... 513-241-4338. 373 J
frances.carroll@antonellicollege.edu
CARROLL, Fredda ... 870-575-8057... 24 E
carrollf@uapb.edu
CARROLL, Gracie ... 325-670-1480. 472 O
gcarroll@hsutx.edu
CARROLL, Gregory ... 386-822-7452. 117 C
gcarroll@stetson.edu
CARROLL, III, James, J . 734-487-3200. 242 D
jcarroll@emich.edu
CARROLL, Jerry ... 864-503-5168. 448 H
jcarroll@uscupstate.edu
CARROLL, Jodi ... 606-546-1278. 200 A
jcarroll@unionky.edu
CARROLL, John ... 718-817-4075. 324 G
jcarroll@fordham.edu
CARROLL, John, L ... 205-726-2704... 6 F
jlcarrol@samford.edu
CARROLL, Jonathan ... 617-989-4316. 237 G
carrollj3@wit.edu
CARROLL, Justin, X ... 314-935-5050. 284 L
carroll@wustl.edu
CARROLL, Karen ... 410-225-2297. 216 C
kcarroll@mica.edu
CARROLL, Kathleen, A ... 603-526-3888. 295 I
kcarroll@colby-sawyer.edu
CARROLL, Kathy ... 402-872-2224. 291 E
kcarroll@peru.edu
CARROLL, Kathy ... 202-462-2101... 96 A
carroll@iwp.edu
CARROLL, Kevin ... 303-871-2599... 86 B
kevin.carroll@du.edu
CARROLL, Lawrence, B ... 630-617-3114. 145 A
larryc@elmhurst.edu
CARROLL, Margaret, R ... 248-341-2028. 248 D
mrcarrol@oaklandcc.edu
CARROLL, Mary, E ... 563-588-7107. 180 L
maryellen.carroll@loras.edu
CARROLL, Matt ... 925-631-4378... 61 F
mcarroll@stmarys-ca.edu
CARROLL, Pamela ... 405-744-3373. 397 H
pamela.carroll@okstate.edu
CARROLL, Pauline ... 978-934-2407. 229 B
Pauline_Carroll@uml.edu
CARROLL, Perry ... 513-585-0365. 376 I
perry.carroll@thechristcollege.edu
CARROLL, Rebecca ... 912-344-3223. 120 G
rebecca.carroll@armstrong.edu
CARROLL, Richard ... 276-466-7873. 514 G
richardcarroll@vic.edu
CARROLL, Rob ... 509-865-8619. 520 D
carroll_r@heritage.edu
CARROLL, Sean, M ... 724-287-8711. 411 C
sean.carroll@bc3.edu
CARROLL, Shannon ... 806-457-4200. 472 G
scarroll@fpctx.edu
CARROLL, Timothy ... 847-578-8481. 157 F
timothy.carroll@rosalindfranklin.edu
CARROLL, Timothy, D ... 865-882-4560. 461 E
carrolltd@roanestate.edu
CARROLL, Trent ... 281-649-3804. 473 B
tcarroll@hbu.edu
CARROLL, William ... 617-217-9240. 222 G
wcarroll@baystate.edu
CARROLL, William, J ... 630-829-6005. 140 B
wcarroll@ben.edu
CARROLL KEELEY, Louise ... 508-767-7312. 222 C
lkeeley@assumption.edu
CARRON, Jennifer ... 254-710-3435. 467 G
jennifer_carron@baylor.edu
CARROW, Erwin ... 229-430-1730. 119 J
erwin.carros@asurams.edu
CARRUTH, Ann ... 985-549-3772. 208 C
acarruth@selu.edu
CARRUTHERS, Anthony ... 508-856-6074. 229 C
anthony.carruthers@umassmed.edu
CARRUTHERS, Becky ... 575-769-4913. 309 F
becky.carruthers@clovis.edu
CARRUTHERS, Brian, A .. 864-242-5100. 441 D
CARRUTHERS, Dale ... 608-262-8256. 536 D
dcarruthers@recsports.wisc.edu
CARRUTHERS, Garrey, E 575-646-2035. 310 I
president@nmsu.edu
CARRUTHERS, Judith ... 802-468-1339. 501 B
judith.carruthers@castleton.edu
CARSCALLEN, Carey ... 269-471-6003. 239 D
ccarey@andrews.edu
CARSON, Barrett, H ... 404-894-1868. 125 D
barrett.carson@dev.gatech.edu
CARSON, Beth ... 516-299-2589. 329 D
beth.carson@liu.edu
CARSON, Brenda, B ... 601-635-2111. 266 H
bcarson@eccc.edu
CARSON, Carol ... 706-754-7703. 129 G
ccarson@northgatech.edu
CARSON, Carolyn, N ... 865-694-6554. 461 D
ccarson@pstcc.edu
CARSON, Connie, L ... 864-294-2202. 444 C
connie.carson@furman.edu
CARSON, Daniel ... 713-348-3350. 479 A
dcarson@rice.edu
CARSON, David ... 912-344-2506. 120 G
david.carson@armstrong.edu
CARSON, Denise, K ... 785-227-3380. 184 I
carsond@bethanylb.edu
CARSON, Elizabeth, M ... 815-395-5102. 158 A
bethcarson@sacn.edu
CARSON, Geoffrey ... 912-478-7481. 126 C
gvcarson@georgiasouthern.edu
CARSON, Jay, T ... 412-397-6404. 431 I
carsonj@rmu.edu
CARSON, John, J ... 860-768-4273... 92 D
jcarson@hartford.edu
CARSON, Kenneth, P ... 724-847-6605. 417 A
kpcarson@geneva.edu
CARSON, Pat ... 740-351-3460. 388 N
pcarson@shawnee.edu
CARSON, Paula ... 337-482-5754. 208 D
plp6475@louisiana.edu
CARSON, Paula, P ... 337-482-5754. 208 D
plp6475@louisiana.edu
CARSON, Rebecca ... 310-506-4558... 58 H
rebecca.carson@pepperdine.edu
CARSON, Sylvia ... 678-915-7222. 132 C
sylvia@spsu.edu
CARSON, Virginia, M ... 912-260-4394. 131 F
virginia.carson@sgsc.edu
CARSON, William ... 443-885-3110. 217 A
william.carson@morgan.edu
CARSTARPHEN, Minnie .. 334-876-9345... 4 A
mcarstarphen@wccs.edu
CARSTENS, Jeffrey ... 402-375-7213. 291 F
jecarst1@wsc.edu
CARSTENS, Joel, B ... 215-898-1404. 435 B
carstens@sfs.upenn.edu
CARSTENS, Lisa ... 503-352-2141. 407 A
carstens@pacificu.edu
CARSTENS, Ryan ... 801-957-5057. 498 B
ryan.carstens@slcc.edu
CARSTENSEN, Lundie ... 619-201-8705... 62 B
Lundie.Carstensen@sdcc.edu
CARSWELL, Linda ... 828-438-6000. 365 A
lcarswell@wpcc.edu
CARSWELL, Pamela ... 386-752-1822. 104 G
pamela.carswell@fgc.edu
CART, Robert ... 973-655-7028. 303 D
cartr@mail.montclair.edu
CARTABUKE, Jacqueline 516-877-6004. 313 A
jcartabuke@adelphi.edu
CARTAGENA, Aramilda ... 787-857-3600. 550 A
acartagena@br.inter.edu
CARTAGENA, Carlos ... 520-417-5485... 12 R
cartagec@cochise.edu
CARTAGENA, Enid ... 787-765-3560. 548 M
ecartagena@edpuniversity.edu
CARTAGENA, Milagros ... 787-704-1020. 548 L
mcartagena@ediccollege.edu
CARTEE, Dawn, H ... 912-871-1638. 129 J
dcartee@ogeecheetech.edu
CARTER, Alfonza ... 919-546-5893. 366 E
acarter@shawu.edu
CARTER, Allison, A ... 906-487-2335. 247 A
allison@mtu.edu
CARTER, Andrew, V ... 580-327-8632. 396 N
avcarter@nwosu.edu
CARTER, Angela, M ... 336-334-4822. 360 G
amcarter@gtcc.edu
CARTER, Bernadette ... 610-399-2271. 428 B
bcarter@cheyney.edu
CARTER, Bessie ... 405-945-3211. 398 C
CARTER, Beth ... 352-588-8480. 112 D
beth.carter@saintleo.edu
CARTER, Brenda, C ... 214-491-6271. 469 G
bcarter@collin.edu
CARTER, Brett ... 607-778-5003. 315 I
carterbd@sunybroome.edu
CARTER, Charles, K ... 252-335-0821. 359 F
ckcarter@albemarle.edu
CARTER, Charlotte ... 205-366-8948... 7 E
ccarter@stillman.edu
CARTER, Cheryl ... 419-755-9020. 385 D
ccarter@ncstatecollege.edu
CARTER, Chris ... 925-631-4200... 61 F
ccarter@stmarys-ca.edu
CARTER, Cindy ... 641-585-8130. 183 D
carterc@waldorf.edu
CARTER, Clark ... 843-863-8008. 441 H
ccarter@csuniv.edu
CARTER, Clay ... 252-940-6357. 358 A
clayc@beaufortccc.edu
CARTER, Coletta ... 678-891-2455. 125 G
coletta.carter@gpc.edu
CARTER, Cynthia ... 229-931-2057. 131 G
ccarter@southgatech.edu
CARTER, Cynthia ... 254-968-9877. 483 A
carter@tarleton.edu
CARTER, Cynthia, A ... 906-786-5802. 240 K
carterc@baycollege.edu
CARTER, D. Michael ... 435-586-7738. 497 A
carter_m@suu.edu
CARTER, Danette ... 425-602-3083. 516 K
dcarter@bastyr.edu

CARTER, Danielle, J .... 216-397-4185. 381 R
dcarter@jcu.edu
CARTER, David .... 512-471-4441. 491 C
CARTER, Deborah .... 517-264-7100. 250 B
dcarter2@sienaheights.edu
CARTER, Debra .... 973-300-2306. 307 F
dcarter@sussex.edu
CARTER, Dorothy .... 252-789-0247. 361 G
dlcarter@martincc.edu
CARTER, Drake .... 701-224-5545. 372 B
fred.carter@bismarckstate.edu
CARTER, Ed .... 256-331-5277..... 6 A
cartere@nwscc.edu
CARTER, Eloise .... 334-727-8953..... 8 A
ecarter@mytu.tuskegee.edu
CARTER, Evonne .... 252-335-0821. 359 F
evonne_carter@albemarle.edu
CARTER, F. "Thatcher" .... 509-527-5195. 525 E
carterft@whitman.edu
CARTER, F. Perna .... 919-516-4420. 366 C
fpcarter@st-aug.edu
CARTER, Gary, L .... 731-661-5204. 462 F
gcarter@uu.edu
CARTER, Glenda, F .... 903-927-3336. 495 A
gcarter@wileyc.edu
CARTER, Glenn .... 509-527-2202. 524 I
glenn.carter@wallawalla.edu
CARTER, H. Steve .... 252-638-7400. 359 G
carters@cravencc.edu
CARTER, Hasani .... 973-275-2385. 307 C
hasani.carter@shu.edu
CARTER, Helene .... 706-821-8323. 130 C
hcarter@paine.edu
CARTER, Holly, R .... 512-428-1051. 479 C
hollyc@stedwards.edu
CARTER, Jacque .... 402-826-8253. 209 E
jacque.carter@doane.edu
CARTER, Jamail .... 714-992-7064... 56 F
jcarter@fullcoll.edu
CARTER, James, F .... 270-809-4894. 198 B
jcarter@murraystate.edu
CARTER, Jane .... 828 669-8012. 357 H
jcarter@montreat.edu
CARTER, JaPrince, L .... 804-342-3895. 515 F
jlcarter@vuu.edu
CARTER, Jeffrey, W .... 800-287-8822. 164 C
president@bethanyseminary.edu
CARTER, Jennifer, L .... 724-847-6603. 417 A
jlcarter@geneva.edu
CARTER, Jessica .... 276-656-0312. 513 D
jcarter@patrickhenry.edu
CARTER, Jo .... 610-647-4400. 418 I
jcarter@immaculata.edu
CARTER, Joanna .... 307-766-2118. 543 I
jcarte22@uwyo.edu
CARTER, Joe .... 254-442-5106. 468 I
joe.carter@cisco.edu
CARTER, Joelle .... 270-745-6169. 200 G
joelle.carter@wku.edu
CARTER, John .... 847-866-3995. 145 E
john.carter@garrett.edu
CARTER, John, B .... 413-542-2771. 221 G
jbcarter@amherst.edu
CARTER, John, M .... 601-477-4161. 267 F
john.carter@jcjc.edu
CARTER, Joyce, M .... 937-229-2554. 391 C
jcarter1@udayton.edu
CARTER, Justin .... 864-644-5144. 446 I
jccarter@swu.edu
CARTER, Karin .... 509-533-4835. 518 E
karin.carter@scc.spokane.edu
CARTER, Kathryn .... 978-934-2741. 229 B
kathryn_carter@uml.edu
CARTER, Kermit .... 256-306-2613..... 2 F
klc@calhoun.edu
CARTER, Kyle, R .... 910-521-6201. 369 B
chancellor@uncp.edu
CARTER, Lana .... 719-549-3253... 84 G
lana.carter@pueblocc.edu
CARTER, Lawrence, E ...... 404-215-2608. 129 D
lcarter@morehouse.edu
CARTER, Lawrence, L ..... 517-321-0242. 243 F
lcarter@glcc.edu
CARTER, Leah .... 661-395-4672... 49 N
CARTER, Lennie .... 202-687-2499... 95 E
carterl@georgetown.edu
CARTER, Leon .... 810-766-2190. 239 H
leon.carter@baker.edu
CARTER, Linda .... 816-604-3081. 277 G
linda.carter@mcckc.edu
CARTER, Linda .... 314-516-4165. 283 E
CARTER, Linda .... 606-539-4230. 200 B
linda.carter@ucumberlands.edu
CARTER, Linnie, S .... 717-780-2321. 417 I
lscarter@hacc.edu
CARTER, Lisa .... 617-427-0060. 232 G
ljenkins@rcc.mass.edu
CARTER, Luther, F .... 843-661-1210. 444 B
lcarter@fmarion.edu
CARTER, Malika .... 701-777-4259. 371 C
malika.carter@und.edu
CARTER, Mark .... 660-596-7221. 282 G
mcarter@sfccmo.edu
CARTER, Martin .... 404-527-4520. 122 E
mcarter@carver.edu
CARTER, Matt .... 505-277-3003. 312 F
mdcarter@unm.edu
CARTER, Max, L .... 336-316-2445. 355 A
mcarter@guilford.edu
CARTER, Melody .... 478-825-6959. 124 H
carterm0@fvsu.edu
CARTER, Melody .... 478-825-6397. 124 H
carterm0@fvsu.edu
CARTER, Michael .... 270-789-5001. 193 D
mvcarter@campbellsville.edu
CARTER, Michael .... 661-255-1050... 31 C
mcarter@calarts.edu
CARTER, Michael .... 937-512-3883. 388 O
michael.carter@sinclair.edu
CARTER, Michele .... 254-526-1668. 468 G
michele.carter@ctcd.edu
CARTER, Mike .... 714-879-3901... 47 K
mcarter@hiu.edu
CARTER, Mike .... 918-495-7150. 398 H
mcarter@oru.edu
CARTER, Niaomi .... 703-878-2800... 96 F
CARTER, Nick .... 617-964-1100. 222 A
ncarter@ants.edu
CARTER, Ninette .... 580-581-5577. 394 G
ncarter@cameron.edu
CARTER, Patricia .... 305-626-3190. 104 J
pcarter@fmuniv.edu
CARTER, Petrina .... 434-791-5629. 502 D
pcarter@averett.edu
CARTER, Phillip .... 615-547-1307. 454 A
pcarter@cumberland.edu
CARTER, R. Daphne .... 843-661-1188. 444 B
rcarter@fmarion.edu
CARTER, Richard .... 651-641-8271. 255 B
carter@csp.edu
CARTER, Richard .... 309-298-2501. 162 K
r-carter@wiu.edu
CARTER, Richard .... 309-298-1929. 162 K
r-carter@wiu.edu
CARTER, Richard .... 206-239-4500. 517 M
richardcarter@cityu.edu
CARTER, Ronald, L .... 909-558-4542... 51 C
rcarter@llu.edu
CARTER, Ronald, L .... 704-378-1006. 355 K
rcarter@jcsu.edu
CARTER, Rosalyn, Y .... 954-762-5640. 114 L
rcarter@fau.edu
CARTER, Sadie .... 919-516-4168. 366 C
sjcarter@st-aug.edu
CARTER, Saundra .... 202-274-6430... 97 A
scarter@udc.edu
CARTER, Saundra, M ...... 202-274-5531... 97 A
scarter@udc.edu
CARTER, Sharon, L .... 714-879-3901... 47 K
slcarter@hiu.edu
CARTER, Shawna, M .... 608-246-6249. 540 C
smcarter@madisoncollege.edu
CARTER, Sheila .... 312-369-7994. 143 D
scarter@colum.edu
CARTER, Shirley .... 336-887-3000. 355 N
scarter@laureluniversity.edu
CARTER, Shirley, P .... 336-315-8660. 353 C
scarter@carolinagrad.edu
CARTER, Shree .... 714-556-3610... 74 D
scarter@vanguard.edu
CARTER, Shree .... 714-556-3610... 74 D
VUTrustees@vanguard.edu
CARTER, Spencer, D .... 269-471-3395. 239 D
scarter@andrews.edu
CARTER, Steven .... 215-935-3879. 437 C
scarter@wts.edu
CARTER, Susan .... 503-699-3338. 404 C
scarter@marylhurst.edu
CARTER, Tara .... 540-453-2260. 511 H
cartert@brcc.edu
CARTER, Taysha .... 479-619-4396... 22 C
tcarter@nwacc.edu
CARTER, Tiffany .... 773-291-6315. 142 D
tcarter63@ccc.edu
CARTER, Tom .... 256-331-5263..... 6 A
tom.carter@nwscc.edu
CARTER, Virginia, M .... 610-359-5394. 414 D
gcarter@dccc.edu
CARTER, JR., Walter, E .. 401-841-2266. 545 A
CARTER, William, E .... 713-718-8708. 473 C
william.carter@hccs.edu
CARTER, William, M .... 412-648-1401. 435 C
wmc4@pitt.edu
CARTER, Yolanda .... 502-863-7967. 194 C
yolanda_carter@georgetowncollege.edu
CARTER, Zina .... 979-532-6417. 494 L
zinac@wcjc.edu
CARTER-CHAPMAN,
Renee, M .... 907-786-6486... 10 H
rmcarterchapman@uaa.alaska.edu
CARTER-COLEY, Stacey .. 919-718-7213. 359 B
scarter@cccc.edu
CARTER-COLEY, Stacey .. 252-492-2061. 364 F
cartercoley@vgcc.edu
CARTER-STEVENS,
Marilyn .... 718-862-7958. 329 M
marilyn.carter@manhattan.edu
CARTER-TELLISON,
Katrina .... 561-237-7210. 108 X
kcarter-tellison@lynn.edu
CARTHELL, Sidney, G ..... 270-809-6836. 198 B
scarthell@murraystate.edu
CARTIER, Jolie, L .... 619-239-0391... 36 D
jcartier@cwsl.edu
CARTIER, Missy, M .... 559-323-2100... 63 B
mcartier@sjcl.edu
CARTIER, Mose .... 410-951-3636. 220 B
mcartier@coppin.edu
CARTLEDGE, Ernest .... 240-567-7991. 216 F
ernest.cartledge@montgomerycollege.edu
CARTLEDGE, Maureen ...... 210-486-7173. 465 B
mcartledge@alamo.edu
CARTLEDGE, Vince, E ..... 740-284-5191. 379 N
vcartledge@franciscan.edu
CARTMELL, Brandy, D .... 731-881-7050. 463 E
bcartmel@utm.edu
CARTMILL, Mark .... 859-985-3922. 192 F
cartmillm@berea.edu
CARTNAL, Ryan .... 805-546-3946... 42 C
rcartnal@cuesta.edu
CARTNEY, Michael .... 605-882-5284. 450 D
cartneym@lakeareatech.edu
CARTOLANO, Joseph ..... 718-631-6231. 319 D
jcartolano@qcc.cuny.edu
CARTON, Shirley .... 702-651-7341. 294 E
shirley.carton@csn.edu
CARTWRIGHT,
Alexander .... 716-645-3321. 341 F
vpr@buffalo.edu
CARTWRIGHT,
Michael, G .... 317-788-3368. 173 I
mcartwright@uindy.edu
CARTWRIGHT, Peggy ..... 909-652-6115... 37 M
peggy.cartwright@chaffey.edu
CARTWRIGHT,
Rhonda, D .... 512-448-8403. 479 C
rhondac@stedwards.edu
CARTWRIGHT, Rick, E .... 260-399-7700. 174 C
rcartwright@sf.edu
CARTY, Karenann .... 718-933-6700. 331 K
kcarty@monroecollege.edu
CARTY, Raymond, W ...... 573-629-3265. 274 J
rcarty@hlg.edu
CARULLO, Susan, H .... 843-792-2071. 445 B
carullos@musc.edu
CARUSO, Anne-Marie ..... 617-989-4174. 237 G
carusoa@wit.edu
CARUSO, Elizabeth, S ..... 585-395-2414. 342 F
lcaruso@brockport.edu
CARUSO, Janet .... 516-572-7599. 332 C
janet.caruso@ncc.edu
CARUSO, Matt .... 908-737-0580. 302 F
mcaruso@kean.edu
CARUSO, Michael .... 903-510-2420. 488 E
mcar@tjc.edu
CARUSO, Michele, E ...... 985-448-4081. 208 A
michele.caruso@nicholls.edu
CARUTHERS, Janet .... 573-875-7372. 272 G
jaocaruthers@ccis.edu
CARVAJAL, Augusto .... 787-780-0070. 547 G
acarvajal@caribbean.edu
CARVAJAL, Richard .... 229-248-2510. 121 E
richard.carvajal@bainbridge.edu
CARVALHO, Susan .... 859-257-4611. 200 C
carvalho@uky.edu
CARVER, Barbara .... 516-364-0808. 333 D
bcarver@nycollege.edu
CARVER, Curt .... 404-962-3300. 134 A
curt.carver@usg.edu
CARVER, David, S .... 402-559-7276. 292 J
dcarver@unmc.edu
CARVER, Deborah, A .... 541-346-1892. 406 D
dcarver@uoregon.edu
CARVER, Doris, W .... 336-322-2111. 362 F
Doris.Carver@piedmontcc.edu
CARVER, Greg .... 912-279-5980. 123 B
gcarver@ccga.edu
CARVER, Helen .... 561-842-8324. 108 V
hcarver@lincolntech.com
CARVER, Jerelene .... 919-546-8525. 366 E
jcarver@shawu.edu
CARVER, Keith .... 865-974-0782. 463 B
carverk@tennessee.edu
CARVER, Matthew .... 785-227-3380. 184 I
carverm@bethanylb.edu
CARVER, Matthew, J .... 716-880-2288. 330 F
matthew.j.carver@medaille.edu
CARVER, Nancy, G .... 973-655-7410. 303 D
carvern@mail.montclair.edu
CARVER, Peta .... 208-459-5180. 138 A
pcarver@collegeofidaho.edu
CARVER, Petra .... 208-459-5180. 138 A
pcarver@collegeofidaho.edu
CARVER, II, William, S .. 252-451-8328. 362 D
bcarver@nashcc.edu
CARWEIN, Vicky, L .... 260-481-6103. 168 C
chancellor@ipfw.edu
CARWILE, Eunice, W ...... 434-223-6144. 505 E
ecarwile@hsc.edu
CARY, Wendy, M .... 315-697-8200. 349 D
wcary@uscny.edu
CASADA, Tracy, L .... 606-679-8501. 196 D
tracy.casada@kctcs.edu
CASADONTE, Dominick .. 806-742-1832. 487 D
dominick.casadonte@ttu.edu
CASALE, Amanda .... 301-447-5271. 217 B
casale@msmary.edu
CASALE, Franklyn, M ...... 305-628-6663. 112 F
fcasale@stu.edu
CASALEGNO, Gina .... 412-268-2075. 412 H
ginac@andrew.cmu.edu
CASAMENTO, Charlene .. 860-832-0033... 87 K
casamentoc@ccsu.edu
CASAMENTO, Laura .... 315-792-3219. 349 F
lcasamento@utica.edu
CASANOVA, Matthew ...... 718-997-4433. 319 C
matthew.casanova@qc.cuny.edu
CASANOVER, Scott .... 314-264-1740. 293 D
scott.casanover@vatterott-college.edu
CASANOVER, Scott .... 316-264-1740. 162 I
scott.casanover@vatterott-college.edu
CASAREZ, Melissa .... 269-749-7163. 249 A
mcasarez@olivetcollege.edu
CASARIEGO, Orlando ..... 904-724-2229. 118 J
CASAS, Alexander .... 305-348-1657. 115 B
alexander.casas@fiu.edu
CASAZZA, Jacqualyn ...... 847-491-4302. 155 D
jcasazza@northwestern.edu
CASCAMO, John .... 805-546-3973... 42 C
john_cascamo@cuesta.edu
CASCARANO, Andrea ...... 973-642-8818. 307 D
andrea.cascarano@shu.edu
CASCARDI, Anthony .... 510-642-5396... 70 I
ajcascardi@berkeley.edu
CASCIO, Joe .... 310-434-4840... 65 A
cascio_joe@smc.edu
CASCONE, Jason .... 516-299-2259. 329 D
jason.cascone@liu.edu
CASE, Allan .... 906-635-2693. 245 G
acase@lssu.edu
CASE, Daniel .... 601-643-8385. 266 F
daniel.case@colin.edu
CASE, Deborah .... 775-445-3270. 295 A
deborah.case@wnc.edu
CASE, SJ, Frank, E .... 509-313-6191. 520 A
casef@gonzaga.edu
CASE, Harold .... 405-682-1611. 397 E
hcase@occc.edu
CASE, Jackie, L .... 919-866-5649. 364 G
jlcase@waketech.edu
CASE, Jim .... 657-278-3121... 33 E
jcase@fullerton.edu
CASE, Jimmy .... 432-837-8368. 487 B
jcase@sulross.edu
CASE, Josh .... 913-758-6331. 191 B
Josh.Case@stmary.edu
CASE, Judd .... 509-359-2532. 519 C
jcase@ewu.edu
CASE, Kim .... 765-998-4557. 173 C
CASE, Laura, M .... 865-981-8102. 456 D
laura.case@maryvillecollege.edu
CASE, LeeAnn .... 509-359-6618. 519 C
lcase@ewu.edu
CASE, Mark, R .... 203-837-8657... 88 B
casem@wcsu.edu
CASE, Mary .... 312-996-2716. 161 D
marycase@uic.edu
CASE, Michael .... 260-982-5431. 170 U
mcase@manchester.edu
CASE, Michael, A .... 607-587-3535. 345 D
casema@alfredstate.edu
CASE, Ron .... 856-415-2257. 302 C
rcase@gccnj.edu
CASE, Tom .... 907-786-1800... 10 H
chancellor@uaa.alaska.edu
CASE, Verna, M .... 704-894-2327. 353 J
vecase@davidson.edu
CASE-KING, Barbara .... 970-248-1266... 79 F
bking@coloradomesa.edu
CASEBEER, Clarice .... 417-967-5466. 282 J
CASEBEER, James .... 928-523-6080... 16 C
james.casebeer@nau.edu
CASEBOLT, Paul .... 813-988-5131. 104 A
admissions@floridacollege.edu
CASEL, Michael .... 610-896-1000. 418 F
mcasel@haverford.edu
CASEY, Barbara, A .... 413-597-4979. 238 D
barbara.a.casey@williams.edu
CASEY, Becky .... 334-876-9271..... 4 A
bcasey@wccs.edu
CASEY, Bonnie-Jeanne ... 617-521-2489. 236 G
bonniejeanne.casey@simmons.edu
CASEY, Brian, W .... 765-658-4220. 165 F
president@depauw.edu

CASEY, Carol, E .... 901-843-3815. 458 E casey@rhodes.edu
CASEY, Catherine, M ...... 212-998-1245. 334 D catherine.casey@nyu.edu
CASEY, Deborah .... 253-833-9111. 520 C dcasey@greenriver.edu
CASEY, Donald, E .... 773-325-7256. 143 H dcasey@depaul.edu
CASEY, Gary, S .... 248-341-2034. 248 D gscaey@oaklandcc.edu
CASEY, George, C .... 510-780-4500... 50 I gcasey@lifewest.edu
CASEY, Janet .... 518-580-8111. 341 A jcasey@skidmore.edu
CASEY, Jason, P .... 202-687-7717... 95 E jpc240@georgetown.edu
CASEY, Jenn .... 803-461-3297. 445 A jennifer.casey@lr.edu
CASEY, Joanne .... 518-472-5875. 313 C jcase@albanylaw.edu
CASEY, Ken .... 270-707-3884. 195 E ken.casey@kctcs.edu
CASEY, Kevin .... 207-941-7123. 210 B caseyk@husson.edu
CASEY, Lawrence, J .... 607-871-2123. 313 E casey@alfred.edu
CASEY, Lucas, J .... 515-263-6195. 178 G lcasey@grandview.edu
CASEY, Mary, M .... 508-286-3464. 238 B mcasey@wheatonma.edu
CASEY, Michael, T .... 518-580-5660. 341 A mcasey@skidmore.edu
CASEY, Paul .... 831-755-6860... 46 G pcasey@hartnell.edu
CASEY, Paula, J .... 501-569-8661... 24 B pjcasey@ualr.edu
CASEY, Randy .... 414-297-7872. 540 E caseyr@matc.edu
CASEY, Richard .... 610-989-1491. 436 D rcasey@vfmac.edu
CASEY, Roger, N .... 410-857-2222. 216 E presoffice@mcdaniel.edu
CASEY, Terry .... 256-782-5492..... 4 K tcasey@jsu.edu
CASEY, Timothy .... 800-962-7682. 285 A tcasey@wma.edu
CASEY, Warren .... 501-279-4056... 21 C casey@harding.edu
CASEY-WHITEMAN, Trish, A .... 410-777-2776. 213 D pacaseywhiteman@aacc.edu
CASH, Arlene .... 336-370-8624. 352 H
CASH, Derek, J .... 662-685-4771. 266 C dcash@bmc.edu
CASH, Erin .... 859-280-1249. 197 C ecash@lextheo.edu
CASH, James, D .... 847-866-3926. 145 E james.cash@garrett.edu
CASH, Teresa, Y .... 501-977-2009... 25 C cash@uaccm.edu
CASHBURLESS, Martha, D .... 330-823-2838. 391 E cashbumd@mountunion.edu
CASHEL, Malorie .... 417-625-9669. 278 D cashel-m@mssu.edu
CASHMAN, Jesse .... 612-330-1644. 253 H cashman@augsburg.edu
CASHMAN, Laurie .... 312-341-3518. 157 D lcashman@roosevelt.edu
CASHMAN, Richard .... 914-606-8501. 350 F richard.cashman@sunywcc.edu
CASHWELL, Candace ...... 252-985-5232. 365 D ccashwell@ncwc.edu
CASHWELL, Debbie .... 910-410-1803. 362 I debbiec@richmondcc.edu
CASHWELL, Michael, B .. 804-355-0671. 510 G mcashwell@upsem.edu
CASHWELL, Suzie .... 850-973-9432. 109 H cashwells@nfcc.edu
CASIELLO, Andrew, R ..... 757-683-5314. 507 N acasiell@odu.edu
CASILE, Lori .... 360-596-5353. 524 A lcasile@spscc.edu
CASILLAS, Rex .... 360-438-4347. 522 G rcasillas@stmartin.edu
CASINI, Michelle .... 312-935-4436. 156 K mcasini@robertmorris.edu
CASKEY, Bradley, J .... 715-425-3366. 537 E bradley.j.caskey@uwrf.edu
CASKEY, James, K .... 574-535-7564. 166 A jimkc@goshen.edu
CASKEY, Katherine .... 312-226-6294. 151 A dev@lexingtoncolleg.edu
CASKEY, Timothy .... 218-726-7161. 264 D tjcaskey@d.umn.edu
CASLER, Tess, C .... 315-268-7970. 320 A tcasler@clarkson.edu
CASLIN, Miriam .... 770-228-7372. 132 B mcaslin@sctech.edu
CASO, Ann .... 508-626-4043. 230 A acaso@framingham.edu
CASON, Carolyn .... 817-272-1021. 491 B clcason@uta.edu
CASON, Craig .... 719-549-2211... 80 K craig.cason@colostate-pueblo.edu
CASON, Donna .... 620-365-5116. 183 I cason@allencc.edu
CASPER, George .... 208-282-3398. 138 E caspgeor@isu.edu
CASPER, Jennifer, A .... 509-527-5132. 525 E casper@whitman.edu
CASPER, Scott .... 410-455-2386. 219 D secasper@umbc.edu
CASPER, Timothy, L .... 608-246-6033. 540 C tcasper@madisoncollege.edu
CASPERSON, April .... 740-362-3372. 383 H acasperson@mtso.edu
CASPRAM, Cecelia .... 414-382-6031. 531 I cecelia.caspram@alverno.edu
CASS, Jeffrey .... 361-570-4321. 489 E cassj@uhv.edu
CASS, Lori .... 570-662-4202. 429 C lcass@mansfield.edu
CASS, Rose .... 508-830-5080. 230 D rcass@maritime.edu
CASSADY, Sandra, L ...... 563-333-6409. 182 B CassadySandraL@sau.edu
CASSAR, Josephine, R .... 810-989-5530. 249 H jcassar@sc4.edu
CASSARD, Courtney .... 985-448-4405. 208 A courtney.cassard@nicholls.edu
CASSARD, Steve .... 410-837-5069. 221 A scassard@ubalt.edu
CASSEL, Kimberly, R ...... 570-326-3761. 427 B kcassel@pct.edu
CASSEL, Stephen .... 215-702-4243. 411 F scassel@cairn.edu
CASSELL, Shelle, R .... 903-463-8628. 472 M cassells@grayson.edu
CASSENS, Cynthia, A ...... 803-323-2223. 449 G cassensc@winthrop.edu
CASSENS, David .... 314-977-3102. 281 I dcassens@slu.edu
CASSERLY, Mary, F .... 518-442-3568. 341 D mcasserly@albany.edu
CASSEUS, Claire .... 516-364-0808. 333 D ccasseus@nycollege.edu
CASSIDY, Annamarie ...... 610-892-1520. 427 E acassidy@pit.edu
CASSIDY, Dale .... 432-552-2700. 493 D cassidy_d@utpb.edu
CASSIDY, Derrah .... 803-738-7582. 445 C cassidyd@midlandstech.edu
CASSIDY, Jane .... 225-578-5513. 204 O jcassid@lsu.edu
CASSIDY, Jennie, M .... 843-349-2573. 442 E jcassidy@coastal.edu
CASSIDY, Joseph .... 610-660-1331. 432 E jcassi02@sju.edu
CASSIDY, Joseph .... 207-454-1000. 211 B
CASSIDY, Joseph .... 630-942-2316. 142 G cassidyj1180@cod.edu
CASSIDY, Kim, E .... 610-526-5156. 410 J president@brynmawr.edu
CASSIDY, Mark .... 425-640-1647. 519 D mark.cassidy@edcc.edu
CASSIDY, Susan .... 516-323-3601. 331 J scassidy@molloy.edu
CASSIRER, Christopher ... 312-261-3073. 153 I christopher.cassirer@nl.edu
CASSITY, Justin .... 323-343-4907... 34 A jcassit@exchange.calstatela.edu
CASTAGNERA, James, O 609-896-5035. 305 D castagne@rider.edu
CASTAGNO, Karen .... 401-456-8822. 439 F kcastagno@ric.edu
CASTALDO, Annalisa ...... 610-499-1112. 437 E acastaldo@widener.edu
CASTALDO, John .... 609-771-2230. 300 E castaldo@tcnj.edu
CASTANEDA, Rejino .... 408-541-0100... 40 A rcastaneda@cogswell.edu
CASTANEDA-CALLEROS, Russell .... 562-463-7234... 60 I rcastanedacalleros@riohondo.edu
CASTANHO, Bradley, J ... 314-747-0927. 284 L bjcastanho@wustl.edu
CASTANO, C. Gabriel ..... 516-918-3705. 315 G gcastano@bcl.edu
CASTEEL, Matt .... 918-631-2960. 401 F matthew-casteel@utulsa.edu
CASTELLANI, Patrick, E .. 570-348-6283. 423 B pcastellani@marywood.edu
CASTELLANO, Ana .... 787-622-8000. 553 E acastellano@pupr.edu
CASTELLANO, Deborah ... 215-871-6707. 430 D registrar@pcom.edu
CASTELLANO, Gene .... 610-902-8254. 411 E gene.castellano@cabrini.edu
CASTELLANOS, Danny .... 305-595-9500... 97 G finaid@amcollege.edu
CASTELLINI, Mike .... 907-474-7210... 10 I macastellini@alaska.edu
CASTELLINO, Lisa .... 910-962-3520. 369 C castellinol@uncw.edu
CASTELLO-BUTLER, Joy . 860-727-6712... 90 A jbutler@goodwin.edu
CASTELLOE, Stephen ...... 336-334-4822. 360 G srcastelloe@gtcc.edu
CASTER-BRAITHWAITE, Donene .... 402-486-2535. 292 E docaster@ucollege.edu
CASTERTON, Deanna .... 563-387-1038. 180 M castde01@luther.edu
CASTETE, Ralynn, F .... 337-475-5612. 207 G rcastete@mcneese.edu
CASTIGLIA, Beth .... 201-559-6140. 302 A castigliab@felician.edu
CASTIGLIONE, Joe .... 405-325-8208. 401 B jcastiglione@ou.edu
CASTIGLIONI, Randy ...... 713-348-5241. 479 A castigr@rice.edu
CASTILLE, Philip, D .... 361-570-4848. 489 E castillep@uhv.edu
CASTILLO, Angelina .... 815-455-8738. 152 F acastillo@mchenry.edu
CASTILLO, Candace .... 972-273-3013. 471 B ccastillo@dcccd.edu
CASTILLO, JR., Carmelino .... 956-721-5135. 475 F carmelino.castillo@laredo.edu
CASTILLO, David .... 559-934-2166... 75 H davidcastillo2@whccd.edu
CASTILLO, David .... 831-443-1700... 47 D david_castillo@heald.edu
CASTILLO, Dennis, A ...... 716-652-8900. 316 G dcastillo@cks.edu
CASTILLO, Diana .... 254-526-1348. 468 G diana.castillo@ctcd.edu
CASTILLO, Elisa .... 978-542-6410. 230 E elisa.castillo@salemstate.edu
CASTILLO, Evelyn .... 787-284-1912. 550 F ecastillo@ponce.inter.edu
CASTILLO, JR., Juan, J .. 956-326-2380. 483 B jjcastillo@tamiu.edu
CASTILLO, Keith .... 951-552-8720... 30 H kcastillo@calbaptist.edu
CASTILLO, Maggie .... 623-935-8839... 14 K maggie.castillo@estrellamountain.edu
CASTILLO, Nicole .... 209-946-2496... 73 A ncastillo@pacific.edu
CASTILLO, Nubia .... 773-777-4220. 155 B ncastillo@nc.edu
CASTILLO, Raul, V .... 818-947-2618... 52 E castilrv@lavc.edu
CASTILLO, Salvador .... 541-737-8083. 406 A salvador.castillo@oregonstate.edu
CASTILLO, Saundra .... 575-527-7599. 311 B scastillo@nmsu.edu
CASTILLO, Victor .... 773-838-7795. 142 E vcastillo@ccc.edu
CASTILLO-ALANIZ, Jo Elda .... 361-593-3991. 484 A jo.alaniz@tamuk.edu
CASTILLO-FRICK, Iliana .. 305-237-0294. 109 D ifrick@mdc.edu
CASTILOW, Nancy .... 402-554-3509. 293 A ncastilow@unomaha.edu
CASTLE, Clinton .... 218-683-8600. 260 D clinton.castle@northlandcollege.edu
CASTLE, Janie .... 276-935-4349. 502 A jcastle@asl.edu
CASTLE, Josh .... 802-322-1672. 499 C josh.castle@goddard.edu
CASTLE, Lyle, W .... 208-282-7852. 138 E castlyle@isu.edu
CASTLE, Ruthie .... 662-562-3213. 269 C rcastle@northwestms.edu
CASTLEBERRY, Gina .... 931-553-0071. 457 F gina.castleberry@miller-motte.com
CASTLEBERRY, Jeff .... 405-208-5384. 397 F jcastleberry@okcu.edu
CASTLEBERRY, Joseph ... 425-889-4202. 521 G joseph.castleberry@northwestu.edu
CASTLEBERRY, Robert .... 580-559-5377. 395 F rcastleberry@ecok.edu
CASTLEBURY, Lisa .... 812-357-6515. 173 A lcastlebury@saintmeinrad.edu
CASTLEMAN, Janet, L ..... 401-865-2816. 439 E jcastlem@providence.edu
CASTON, Gay Lynn .... 601-857-3396. 267 A GLCaston@hindscc.edu
CASTONGUAY, Suzette ... 937-769-1375. 373 H scastonguay@antioch.edu
CASTONGUAY, Suzette ... 937-769-1375. 373 I scastonguay@antioch.edu
CASTOR, Peter .... 717-560-8219. 421 A pcastor@lbc.edu
CASTOR, Tammy .... 661-362-3516... 40 E tammy.castor@canyons.edu
CASTORA, Susan, L .... 757-446-5812. 504 E castorsl@evms.edu
CASTORENA, Christina ... 425-388-9282. 519 I ccastore@everettcc.edu
CASTRIOTA, Nadia .... 518-445-2361. 313 C ncast@albanylaw.edu
CASTRO, Adam .... 973-748-9000. 299 F adam_castro@bloomfield.edu
CASTRO, Daisy .... 787-753-6335. 549 D dcastro@icprjc.edu
CASTRO, Donna .... 505-426-2240. 310 E dcastro@nmhu.edu
CASTRO, Edgardo .... 787-738-2161. 554 C edgardo.castro@upr.edu
CASTRO, Francia, L .... 212-694-1000. 315 E fcastro@boricuacollege.edu
CASTRO, Ida, L .... 570-504-9647. 413 B
CASTRO, Joseph, I .... 559-278-2324... 33 D josephcastro@csufresno.edu
CASTRO, Kaye, A .... 239-687-5336... 98 J kcastro@avemarialaw.edu
CASTRO, Lorna .... 787-764-0000. 555 B lorna.castro@upr.edu
CASTRO, Louise, P .... 915-747-8820. 492 A lpcastro@utep.edu
CASTRO, Manny .... 670-234-5498. 547 A mannyc@nmcnet.edu
CASTRO, Octavio .... 414-288-5629. 534 B octavio.castro@marquette.edu
CASTRO, Patricia .... 702-651-5684. 294 E patricia.castro@csn.edu
CASTRO, Rene .... 310-243-3766... 33 B rcastro@csudh.edu
CASTRO, Rosie .... 210-486-3100. 465 A mcastro66@alamo.edu
CASTRO, Toni .... 206-878-3710. 520 E tcastro@highline.edu
CASTRO-MELENDEZ, Consuelo .... 787-620-2040. 547 C castromelendez@aupr.edu
CASTRONOVO, Neil, R ... 508-767-7274. 222 C ncastron@assumption.edu
CASTRUITA, Javier .... 408-741-2042... 75 J javier_castruita@wvm.edu
CASWELL, Robert, S .... 207-780-4200. 212 H caswell@usm.maine.edu
CASWELL, Roger .... 620-341-5372. 186 D rcaswekk@emporia.edu
CATA, Virginia .... 505-747-2119. 311 E virginia_c@nnmc.edu
CATALANA, Paul .... 864-455-7992. 448 E
CATALANA, Paul, V .... 864-294-2180. 444 C paul.catalana@furman.edu
CATALANO, George .... 607-777-3583. 341 E catalano@binghamton.edu
CATALANO, Rita .... 724-805-2274. 432 G rita.catalano@email.stvincent.edu
CATALANO, Steven .... 718-489-5309. 338 G scatalano@sfc.edu
CATALDI, Jennifer .... 317-738-8256. 165 I jcataldi@franklincollege.edu
CATALDO, Linda .... 617-627-6272. 237 C linda.cataldo@tufts.edu
CATALFAMO, Kevin .... 856-351-2701. 307 B kcatalfamo@salemcc.edu
CATALLOZZI, Lori, A .... 617-228-2048. 231 C lacatallozzi@bhcc.mass.edu
CATALON, Linda, H .... 225-771-2520. 206 I linda_catalon@sus.edu
CATANESE, Anthony, J ... 321-674-7232. 104 H catanese@fit.edu
CATANIA, Guy .... 412-392-3952. 431 B gcatania@pointpark.edu
CATANIA, Raymond, P ... 773-298-3031. 158 E catania@sxu.edu
CATANZARO, James, L .. 423-697-4455. 460 C
CATANZARO, Sam .... 309-438-7018. 147 J catanzar@ilstu.edu
CATE, Caroline .... 704-290-5209. 363 G ccate@spcc.edu
CATE, Richard, H .... 802-656-0219. 500 F richard.cate@uvm.edu
CATELLA, Rosanne .... 440-934-3101. 385 K rcatella@ohiobusinesscollege.edu
CATENZARO, Ana .... 215-637-7700. 418 G acatanzaro@holyfamily.edu
CATER, Gloria, H .... 617-541-5144. 232 G gcater@rcc.mass.edu
CATES, Chris .... 865-471-3245. 453 F ccates@cn.edu
CATES, Janet .... 615-966-1788. 456 B janet.cates@lipscomb.edu
CATES, Jo .... 262-595-2167. 537 C cates@uwp.edu
CATES, Matthew .... 903-875-7338. 477 G matt.cates@navarrocollege.edu
CATES, Truett .... 903-813-2309. 466 H tcates@austincollege.edu
CATH, Tom .... 219-464-5005. 174 E tom.cath@valpo.edu
CATHCART, Scott .... 760-744-1150... 58 D scathcart@palomar.edu

CATHELINE, Jim ... 724-964-8811. 425 A
jcatheline@ncstrades.edu
CATHER, Michael ... 410-704-4679. 220 E
mcather@towson.edu
CATHERMAN, David ... 504-398-2279. 206 C
dcatherman@olhcc.edu
CATHEY, Ron ... 318-257-4336. 207 F
rcathey@latech.edu
CATHIE, Julie ... 530-541-4660... 50 D
cathie@ltcc.edu
CATIGGAY, James ... 415-422-6216... 73 J
catiggay@usfca.edu
CATLETT, Deborrah, L ... 859-246-6810. 194 L
deborrah.catlett@kctcs.edu
CATLETT, Jennifer ... 865-471-3530. 453 F
jcatlett@cn.edu
CATLETT, Lowell ... 575-646-3748. 310 I
agdean@nmsu.edu
CATLIN, Diane ... 602-386-4105... 11 G
diane.catlin@arizonachristian.edu
CATO, Amie ... 903-785-7661. 478 B
acato@parisjc.edu
CATON, Claire ... 713-226-5223. 489 D
catonc@uhd.edu
CATONE, John ... 814-393-1823. 428 C
jcatone@cuf-inc.org
CATRON, Jonathan ... 864-644-5662. 446 I
jcatron@swu.edu
CATRON, LaKeysha ... 937-376-6657. 376 E
lcatron@centralstate.edu
CATRON, Sue ... 918-456-5511. 396 H
catrons@nsuok.edu
CATRON-WOOD,
Rhonda, K ... 276-223-4772. 514 F
rcatronwood@wcc.vccs.edu
CATT, Helen ... 229-430-3506. 120 A
hcatt@albanytech.edu
CATT, Helen ... 229-248-2500. 121 E
helen.catt@bainbridge.edu
CATT, Stephen, R ... 724-287-8711. 411 C
stephen.catt@bc3.edu
CATTANACH, John, R ... 315-516-4100. 283 E
cattanachj@umsl.edu
CATTOOR, Chad, A ... 314-505-7304. 272 J
cattoorc@csl.edu
CAUBERE, Monique ... 914-674-7510. 330 J
mcaubere@mercy.edu
CAUCE, Ana Mari ... 206-543-2100. 524 G
provost@uw.edu
CAUDA, Lisa ... 585-475-7721. 337 L
lisa.cauda@rit.edu
CAUDILL, Alicia ... 678-839-6423. 133 I
acaudill@westga.edu
CAUDILL, Dave ... 678-915-3168. 132 C
dcaudill@spsu.edu
CAUDILL, Helene, L ... 512-448-8648. 479 C
helenec@stedwards.edu
CAUDLE, Patricia, M ... 909-748-8171... 73 H
pat_caudle@redlands.edu
CAUFFMAN, Bonnie, H ... 360-417-6212. 522 A
bcauffman@pencol.edu
CAUFIELD, Brian ... 503-725-5739. 405 G
brian_caufield@ous.edu
CAUGHEY, Martha ... 850-484-1604. 110 G
mcaughey@pensacolastate.edu
CAUGHMAN, Gretchen ... 706-721-4014. 126 B
gcaughma@gru.edu
CAUGHMAN, S. Wright .. 404-778-3774. 124 E
scaughm@emory.edu
CAULEY, Phil ... 828-227-2923. 369 E
cauley@wcu.edu
CAULFIELD, Jack ... 508-213-2398. 235 E
jack.caulfield@nichols.edu
CAULFIELD, Richard ... 907-796-6256... 11 A
provost@uas.alaska.edu
CAULFIELD, Thomas, M . 217-351-2477. 155 J
tcaulfield@parkland.edu
CAUPP, Jeffrey, G ... 480-245-7944... 14 B
jeff.caupp@ibcs.edu
CAUSEY, Bruce ... 256-306-2569... 2 F
bcausey@calhoun.edu
CAUSEY, Joy ... 229-317-6886. 124 A
joy.causey@darton.edu
CAUSEY, Katherine ... 901-435-1259. 455 M
katherine_causey@loc.edu
CAUSEY, Mary Frances .. 928-350-1112... 17 K
mcausey@prescott.edu
CAUWELS, Beth ... 805-565-6101... 76 D
bcauwels@westmont.edu
CAVACO, Frank ... 617-964-1100. 222 A
fcavaco@ants.edu
CAVAGE, Christina ... 912-443-5827. 131 D
ccavage@savannahtech.edu
CAVALIER, Donald, R ... 218-281-8585. 264 E
cavalier@umn.edu
CAVALIER, Philip Acree .. 309-467-6301. 145 C
pcavalier@eureka.edu
CAVALIERI, Correne ... 718-779-1430. 336 D
ccavalieri@plazacollege.edu
CAVALIERI, Cristina, G ... 215-503-9496. 434 C
cristina.cavalieri@jefferson.edu
CAVALLARO, Claire ... 657-278-4021... 33 E
ccavallaro@fullerton.edu
CAVALLARO,
Gregory, M ... 540-464-7328. 515 B
gcav@vmiaa.org
CAVALLARO, Vito ... 212-938-5500. 345 C
vito@sunyopt.edu
CAVALLI, Mario ... 914-606-6844. 350 F
mario.cavalli@sunywcc.edu
CAVALLO, Susana ... 773-508-2760. 151 H
scavall@luc.edu
CAVALLUZZI, Marty, L ... 253-840-8421. 522 C
mcavalluzzi@pierce.ctc.edu
CAVALOVITCH, Renee ... 412-397-5262. 431 I
cavalovitch@rmu.edu
CAVALUZZI, Joseph ... 201-447-7639. 299 C
jcavaluzzi@bergen.edu
CAVAN, John, J ... 434-949-1003. 513 H
john.cavan@southside.edu
CAVANAGH, David ... 802-635-1289. 501 D
david.cavanagh@jsc.edu
CAVANAGH, Stephen ... 413-545-5093. 228 F
dean@nursing.umass.edu
CAVANAUGH, Amy ... 503-943-7201. 408 F
cavanaug@up.edu
CAVANAUGH, Brian ... 716-829-7878. 323 D
cavanaub@dyc.edu
CAVANAUGH, Erica ... 701-766-1305. 370 H
erica.cavanaugh@littleloop.edu
CAVANAUGH, Kyle ... 919-684-2826. 354 A
kyle.cavanaugh@duke.edu
CAVANAUGH,
Mary Anne ... 803-641-3563. 448 A
maryanc@usca.edu
CAVANAUGH, Patricia ... 802-451-7588. 499 F
pcavanaugh@marlboro.edu
CAVANAUGH, Patrick, D 209-946-2345... 73 A
pcavanaugh@pacific.edu
CAVAZOS, Cyndi ... 210-434-6711. 477 N
cacavazos@lake.ollusa.edu
CAVAZOS, Henry ... 409-772-3004. 493 C
hcavazos@utmb.edu
CAVAZOS, Lisa ... 956-364-4050. 485 H
lisa.cavazos@tstc.edu
CAVAZOS, Rebecca ... 956-664-4680. 480 I
beckyc@southtexascollege.edu
CAVENAUGH, Andy ... 910-296-2480. 361 D
acavenaugh@jamessprunt.edu
CAVENY, Deanna, M ... 843-953-5527. 443 A
cavenyd@cofc.edu
CAVERLEY, Darla ... 320-629-5118. 260 F
calverleyd@pinetech.edu
CAVICCHI, Daniel ... 401-454-6580. 440 A
dcavicch@risd.edu
CAVIN, JR., Elmo, M ... 806-743-3080. 487 E
elmo.cavin@ttuhsc.edu
CAVINESS, Debbie, J ... 315-470-6632. 345 B
dcavines@esf.edu
CAVINS-TULL, Kathryn ... 817-257-7820. 484 I
k.cavins@tcu.edu
CAVIS, Mark ... 906-487-7315. 242 G
mark.cavis@finlandia.edu
CAVITT, Deborah ... 817-531-4298. 488 A
dcavitt@txwes.edu
CAWLEY, Steve ... 305-284-3515. 118 F
s.cawley@miami.edu
CAWLFIELD, Jeffrey ... 573-341-4557. 284 A
jdc@mst.edu
CAWOOD, J. Scott ... 215-702-4216. 411 F
scawood@cairn.edu
CAWOOD, Patti ... 423-614-8316. 455 L
pcawood@leeuniversity.edu
CAWTHON, Donald, L ... 254-968-9227. 483 A
cawthon@tarleton.edu
CAWTHON, Jim ... 574-936-8898. 163 K
jim.cawthon@ancilla.edu
CAWYER, Carol ... 406-466-6012. 395 N
CAYEA, Cynthia ... 516-364-0808. 333 D
library@nycollege.edu
CAYER, Cynthia, B ... 860-832-1741... 87 K
cayerc@ccsu.edu
CAYLOR, Deborah, Z ... 540-458-8730. 516 A
dcaylor@wlu.edu
CAYWOOD, Carter ... 907-564-8360... 10 C
ccaywood@alaskapacific.edu
CAYWOOD, Janet ... 620-278-4280. 190 I
jcaywood@sterling.edu
CAZARES, Rebecca ... 559-934-2159... 75 G
beckycazares@whccd.edu
CAZAUBON, Steve ... 504-762-3050. 203 A
scazau@dcc.edu
CAZZETTA, Vinnie ... 845-341-4726. 335 H
vinnie.cazzetta@sunyorange.edu
CEARLEY, Anna ... 619-684-8791... 56 C
acearley@newschoolarch.edu
CEASAR, Ted ... 760-355-6312... 48 A
ted.ceasar@imperial.edu
CEBELAK, Jane, P ... 772-462-7544. 106 P
jcebelak@irsc.edu
CEBRICK, Daniel, T ... 570-208-5870. 419 P
dtcebric@kings.edu
CEBRZYNSKI, Gerard, J . 847-735-5104. 150 B
cebrzynski@lakeforest.edu
CEBUKLO, Danielle ... 570-702-8990. 419 G
dcebulko@johnson.edu
CECALA, Dianna ... 843-349-5207. 444 F
dianna.cecala@hgtc.edu
CECCANECCHIO,
Domenic ... 215-895-1554. 415 B
dc444@drexel.edu
CECCHINI, Bernard ... 315-568-3127. 333 C
bcecchini@nycc.edu
CECCHINI, Dan ... 541-383-7700. 402 D
dcecchini@cocc.edu
CECERE, Janice ... 973-748-9000. 299 F
janice_cecere@bloomfield.edu
CECERE, Mollie ... 304-829-7591. 526 D
mcecere@bethanywv.edu
CECERO, Diane, M ... 585-292-2108. 332 A
dcecero@monroecc.edu
CECH, John ... 406-444-0314. 286 G
jcech@montana.edu
CECIL, Dale ... 270-686-4239. 192 G
dale.cecil@brescia.edu
CECIL, David, J ... 859-233-8239. 199 I
financialaid@transy.edu
CECIL, Jamie, N ... 717-867-6228. 421 H
cecil@lvc.edu
CECIL, Kristine ... 303-871-2412... 86 B
kristine.cecil@du.edu
CECIL, Patrick, A ... 502-895-3411. 197 F
pcecil@lpts.edu
CEDAR, Leslie ... 512-471-3800. 491 C
cedar@alumni.utexas.edu
CEDEL, Thomas ... 512-313-3000. 469 L
thomas.cedel@concordia.edu
CEDENO, Derena ... 717-394-6211. 413 J
dcedeno@csb.edu
CEDERGREN, Cindy ... 218-683-8611. 260 D
cindy.cedergren@northlandcollege.edu
CEDERHOLM, Annette ... 256-840-4142... 6 I
acederholm@snead.edu
CEDILLO, Arnulfo ... 415-485-9375... 40 G
arnulfo.cedillo@marin.edu
CEDRONE, David, C ... 617-994-6904. 228 D
dmcedrone@bhe.mass.edu
CEGLES, Victor ... 562-985-8527... 33 F
vcegles@csulb.edu
CEJA, Jared ... 909-652-6561... 37 M
jared.ceja@chaffey.edu
CELENTANA, Marc ... 609-771-2247. 300 E
mcelent@tcnj.edu
CELHAY, Lilia ... 510-464-3215... 59 C
lcelhay@peralta.edu
CELHAY, Lilia ... 510-981-2881... 59 A
lcelhay@peralta.edu
CELL, Paul, M ... 973-655-5123. 303 D
cellp@mail.montclair.edu
CELLA, Barbara ... 925-439-2181... 42 A
bcella@losmedanos.edu
CELLEMME, Patricia ... 518-292-1710. 338 C
cellep@sage.edu
CELLI, David, S ... 570-389-4882. 427 H
dcelli@bloomu.edu
CELLI, Lorraine ... 516-299-3134. 329 C
Lorraine.Celli@liu.edu
CELLINI, Roger ... 909-748-8020... 73 H
roger_cellini@redlands.edu
CELLINI, Todd ... 912-201-8007. 131 H
tcellini@southuniversity.edu
CELTEK, Serkan ... 956-872-5577. 480 I
sbceltek@southtexascollege.edu
CEMAN, Jamie ... 920-424-2442. 537 B
cemanj@uwosh.edu
CEN, Luozhu ... 530-879-4050... 30 F
cenlu@butte.edu
CENCIUS, Joel, F ... 414-410-4203. 532 B
jfcencius@stritch.edu
CENKL, Pavel ... 802-586-7711. 500 E
pcenkl@sterlingcollege.edu
CENSOR, Yerachmiel ... 845-356-7064. 351 D
CENTENO, Barbara ... 210-458-4037. 492 C
barbara.centeno@utsa.edu
CENTER, Mark, R ... 210-434-6711. 477 N
mrcenter@lake.ollusa.edu
CENTKO, John ... 218-333-6613. 260 E
johnb.centko@ntcmn.edu
CENTOPANTI,
Anthony (Tony) ... 203-857-7131... 89 D
acentopant@norwalk.edu
CENTOR, Josh ... 412-268-8555. 412 H
jcentor@andrew.cmu.edu
CEO, Nicolette ... 516-323-3282. 331 J
nceo@molloy.edu
CEPEDA, Charlotte, R ... 670-234-5498. 547 A
charlottec@nmcnet.edu
CEPEDA, Rita ... 408-270-6402... 63 N
chancellor.office@sjeccd.org
CEPEDA-BENITO,
Antonio ... 802-656-3166. 500 F
antonio.cepeda-benito@uvm.edu
CEPPI, Matthew ... 760-750-4040... 35 A
mceppi@csusm.edu
CEPPOS, Jerry ... 225-578-9294. 204 O
jceppos@lsu.edu
CEPRIANO, Lucia ... 631-420-2003. 346 B
lucia.cepriano@farmingdale.edu
CEPULL, Jeff ... 215-951-2516. 430 E
cepullj@philau.edu
CERCONE, Charles ... 517-371-5140. 250 G
cerconec@cooley.edu
CERDA, Manuel ... 210-486-4111. 464 J
mcerda9@alamo.edu
CERES, Joanne, T ... 252-493-7208. 362 G
jceres@email.pittcc.edu
CERES, Sharon ... 252-493-7561. 362 G
sceres@email.pittcc.edu
CEREZO, Juan, E ... 718-862-7328. 329 M
juan.cerezo@manhattan.edu
CEREZO, Sabrina ... 718-951-5622. 317 C
scerezo@brooklyn.cuny.edu
CERILLI, Annette ... 401-232-6323. 438 K
acerilli@bryant.edu
CERINO, Michael, H ... 864-488-4564. 444 L
mcerino@limestone.edu
CERNECH, John, C ... 402-280-2775. 289 D
jcer@creighton.edu
CERNOCH, Jeff ... 281-756-3539. 465 D
jcernoch@alvincollege.edu
CERNY, Glenn ... 734-462-4400. 250 A
gcerny@schoolcraft.edu
CERNY, Kirk, R ... 765-494-0764. 171 M
kcerny@purdue.edu
CERTA, Len ... 914-923-2847. 335 J
lcerta@pace.edu
CERULLO, Ralph ... 631-244-3101. 323 B
CERVANTES, Augustin ... 408-273-2751... 55 H
acervantes@nhu.edu
CERVANTES,
Cecillia Y, M ... 763-488-2414. 258 F
cecillia.cervantes@hennepintech.edu
CERVANTES, George ... 202-495-3828... 96 C
advance@dhs.edu
CERVANTES, Juana ... 915-779-8031. 494 C
jcervantes@computercareercenter.com
CERVANTES, Lynda ... 915-532-3737. 494 J
lcervantes@westerntech.edu
CERVANTES, Margaret ... 432-264-5009. 473 E
mcervantes@howardcollege.edu
CERVANTES, Mike ... 361-592-9335. 484 A
mike.cervantes@tamuk.edu
CERVANTES, Philip ... 972-438-6932. 478 C
pcervantes@parkercc.edu
CERVANTES, Richard ... 575-835-5675. 310 F
rcervantes@admin.nmt.edu
CERVASIO, Nancy ... 480-557-2100... 18 I
nancy.cervasio@phoenix.edu
CERVELLI, Janice, A ... 520-621-6751... 18 F
jcervell@email.arizona.edu
CERVENKA, Mark ... 713-221-8043. 489 D
cervenkam@uhd.edu
CERVENY, Alan ... 402-472-9531. 292 I
acerveny2@unl.edu
CERVENY, Mike, J ... 319-895-4357. 177 A
mcerveny@cornellcollege.edu
CERVENY, Terri ... 518-262-8043. 313 D
cervent@mail.amc.edu
CERVINI, John ... 517-607-2670. 243 I
john.cervini@hillsdale.edu
CERVONKA, Daniel ... 203-576-2400... 91 G
cervonka@bridgeport.edu
CERZA, Donna ... 570-208-5868. 419 P
donnacerza@kings.edu
CESARANO, Betty ... 505-473-6117. 311 K
betty.cesarano@santafeuniversity.edu
CESAREO, Francesco, C . 508-767-7321. 222 C
fcesareo@assumption.edu
CESARIO, David, R ... 617-287-6200. 228 G
david.cesario@umb.edu
CESCA, Michele ... 657-278-4869... 33 E
mcesca@fullerton.edu
CESELSKI, Teresa ... 660-831-4139. 278 I
ceselskit@moval.edu
CESMEBASI, Erol ... 201-216-5576. 307 E
ecesmeba@stevens.edu
CESSNA, Tammy ... 859-858-2306. 192 A
CESTERO, Nicolle, M ... 413-205-3800. 221 F
nicolle.cestero@aic.edu
CESTERO, Vilmaris ... 787-600-4427. 555 C
vilmaris.cestero@upr.edu
CESTONE, Amy ... 302-292-6100... 96 F
CEVALLOS, F. Javier ... 610-683-4102. 429 A
cevallos@kutztown.edu
CEZAR, Henrique ... 802-635-1297. 501 D
henrique.cezar@jsc.edu
CHA, Jason ... 805-565-6132... 76 D
jacha@westmont.edu
CHAAPEL, Barbara, A ... 609-497-7760. 304 D
comm-pub@ptsem.edu
CHABOT, Lisabeth ... 607-274-3182. 327 E
lchabot@ithaca.edu

CHABOT-WIEFERICH, Rebecca 617-262-5000. 223 F Joshua.White@the-bac.edu
CHABOTAR, Kent, J 336-316-2146. 355 A chabotar@guilford.edu
CHACKO, Abraham 408-541-0100... 40 A achacko@cogswell.edu
CHACONA, Julie, A 814-732-1779. 428 E jchacona@edinboro.edu
CHACONIS, Alexis 718-260-5250. 319 B achaconis@citytech.cuny.edu
CHADEN, Caryn 312-362-8885. 143 H cchaden@depaul.edu
CHADWELL, Faye 541-737-3411. 406 A faye.chadwell@oregonstate.edu
CHADWICK, Becky, J 313-317-1534. 243 H bchadwick@hfcc.edu
CHADWICK, Gregory 252-737-7030. 367 B chadwickg@ecu.edu
CHADWICK, Jennifer 706-867-2886. 133 D jennifer.chadwick@ung.edu
CHADWICK, Matthew 757-352-4826. 508 G mchadwick@regent.edu
CHADWICK, Scott 513-745-3838. 393 H chadwicks@xavier.edu
CHAFEE, Julie 508-929-8770. 230 G jchaffee1@worcester.edu
CHAFFEE, Alecia 417-626-1234. 279 J chaffee.alecia@occ.edu
CHAFFEE, Cynthia 312-567-3084. 147 F cchaffee@iit.edu
CHAFFEE, Reta 603-513-1350. 298 E reta.chaffee@granite.edu
CHAFFIN, Debbie 256-765-4297..... 9 C dkchaffin@una.edu
CHAFIN, Kristal, L 260-359-4290. 166 O kchafin@huntington.edu
CHAFIN-EVANS, Karen, S 606-218-5606. 200 F karenevans@upike.edu
CHAGNON-BURKE, Veronique 212-355-1501. 316 H vchagnon-burke@christies.edu
CHAH, Namyoung 323-731-2383... 57 I nchah@psuca.edu
CHAHIN, T. Jaime 512-245-3333. 487 C tc03@txstate.edu
CHAI, Lin 407-888-8689. 104 B lchai@fcim.edu
CHAIREZ, Gladys 575-527-7664. 311 B gchairez@nmsu.edu
CHAIRSELL, Christine 971-722-4005. 407 D christine.chairsell@pcc.edu
CHAISSON, Breck 985-858-5805. 203 B breck.chaisson@fletcher.edu
CHAITOVSKY, Myron, B 718-780-7906. 315 H myron.chaitovsky@brooklaw.edu
CHAKRABORTY, Dave 805-437-8496... 32 I dave.chakraborty@csuci.edu
CHAKRIN, Lewis 201-684-7377. 305 A lchakrin@ramapo.edu
CHALEUNPHONH, Seuth 812-941-2319. 168 F schaleun@ius.edu
CHALFONTE, Barb 413-755-4465. 233 A blchalfonte@stcc.edu
CHALK, Gregg 508-541-1668. 225 F gchalk@dean.edu
CHALK, Rebecca 410-276-0306. 218 D rchalk@host.sdc.edu
CHALKER, Peggy 937-695-0751. 389 B pchalker@sscc.edu
CHALLENGER, Susan 781-283-2335. 237 F schallen@wellesley.edu
CHALLIS, Don 201-291-1111. 314 K edc@berkeleycollege.edu
CHALLIS, Don 201-291-1111. 299 D edc@berkeleycollege.edu
CHALLIS, Donald, R 757-221-1143. 503 N drchal@wm.edu
CHALLY, Pam 904-620-2810. 116 B pchally@unf.edu
CHALMERS, John 516-463-5791. 326 D john.chalmers@hofstra.edu
CHALMERS, Scott 773-256-0727. 152 B schalmer@lstc.edu
CHALMIERS, Harry 651-361-3441. 256 N harry.chalmiers@mcnallysmith.edu
CHALOUX, Matthew, P 561-237-7699. 108 X mchaloux@lynn.edu
CHALUPA, Leo, M 202-994-7315... 95 D lmchalupa@gwu.edu
CHALYKOFF, John 203-396-8084... 91 C chalykoffj@sacredheart.edu
CHAMANDY, Susan 617-730-7157. 235 D susan.chamandy@newbury.edu
CHAMBERAS, Peter 617-850-1237. 227 E frpac@metrocast.net
CHAMBERLAIN, Dennis, R 678-359-5056. 127 A dennisc@gordonstate.edu
CHAMBERLAIN, Enrique 972-273-3405. 471 B echamberlain@dcccd.edu
CHAMBERLAIN, Harvey 314-264-1000. 284 G harvey.chamberlain@vatterott.edu
CHAMBERLAIN, LaShanda 228-497-7630. 268 C lashanda.chamberlain@mgccc.edu
CHAMBERLAIN, Mary Ellen, M 518-327-6220. 336 B mchamberlain@paulsmiths.edu
CHAMBERLAIN, Monica, L 260-422-5561. 167 B mlchamberlain@indianatech.edu
CHAMBERLAIN, Nancy 815-921-4517. 157 A n.chamberlain@rockvalleycollege.edu
CHAMBERLAIN, Tina 206-726-5197. 518 G tchamberlain@cornish.edu
CHAMBERLAND, CSC, Gary, S 503-943-8011. 408 F chamberg@up.edu
CHAMBERLAND, Greg 802-773-5900. 499 B gregory.chamberland@csj.edu
CHAMBERLIN, Christopher 212-353-4099. 321 F c.m.chamberlin@gmail.com
CHAMBERLIN, Heather 816-483-9600. 190 D heatherc@spst.edu
CHAMBERLIN, Jonathan 704-216-3765. 363 D Jonathan.Chamberlain@rccc.edu
CHAMBERLIN, Keith, B 802-626-6459. 501 E keith.chamberlin@lyndonstate.edu
CHAMBERLIN, Lisa 509-527-5145. 524 H lisa.chamberlin@wwcc.edu
CHAMBERLIN, Lyn 802-828-8599. 500 G lyn.chamberlin@vcfa.edu
CHAMBERLIN, Mona 918-631-2656. 401 F mona-chamberlin@utulsa.edu
CHAMBERLIN, Paul, D 603-862-2650. 298 C paul.chamberlin@unh.edu
CHAMBERLIN, William 703-323-2120. 513 C wchamberlin@nvcc.edu
CHAMBERS, Andy 314-392-2211. 278 B chambers@mobap.edu
CHAMBERS, Anthony 407-277-0311. 103 C achambers@evergladesuniversity.edu
CHAMBERS, Candace 314-529-9454. 276 G ccchambers@maryville.edu
CHAMBERS, Carolyn 562-860-2451... 37 I cchambers@cerritos.edu
CHAMBERS, Daniel, P 607-436-2491. 343 E daniel.cambers@oneonta.edu
CHAMBERS, Diane, M 330-471-8183. 383 D dchambers@malone.edu
CHAMBERS, Donna 405-382-9950. 399 I d.chambers@sscok.edu
CHAMBERS, Eric 734-995-7419. 241 E chambe@cuaa.edu
CHAMBERS, Franklin, D 410-951-3933. 220 B fchambers@coppin.edu
CHAMBERS, Jason 828-835-4297. 364 E jchambers@tricountycc.edu
CHAMBERS, Jessica, A 240-500-2000. 215 B jachambers@hagerstowncc.edu
CHAMBERS, Joy 951-222-8649... 61 A joy.chambers@rcc.edu
CHAMBERS, Kemba 256-551-1712..... 4 I kemba.chambers@drakestate.edu
CHAMBERS, Larry 518-276-6000. 337 I chamb@rpi.edu
CHAMBERS, Martha 865-471-4351. 453 F mchambers@cn.edu
CHAMBERS, Melody 660-785-4114. 282 L mchamber@truman.edu
CHAMBERS, Michael 314-837-6777. 280 K mchambers@slcconline.edu
CHAMBERS, Phyllis, P 336-272-7102. 354 E phyllis.chambers@greensboro.edu
CHAMBERS, Robert 617-879-7751. 230 B rchambers@massart.edu
CHAMBERS, Steve 575-624-7410. 309 I steve.chambers@roswell.enmu.edu
CHAMBERS, Terri 937-708-5785. 393 A tchambers@wilberforce.edu
CHAMBERS, Thomas, A 716-286-8352. 334 F chambers@niagara.edu
CHAMBERS STROHM, Leslie 919-962-7246. 368 D strohm@email.unc.edu
CHAMBLEE, David 706-396-8160. 130 C dchamblee@paine.edu
CHAMBLEE, Tim 662-325-3920. 268 D t.chamblee@msstate.edu
CHAMBLIN, Cheryl, L 217-424-6293. 153 C cchamblin@millikin.edu
CHAMBLISS, Mary 615-329-8585. 454 F mchambliss@fisk.edu
CHAMEIDES, William, L 919-613-8004. 354 A bill.chameides@duke.edu
CHAMLEE-WRIGHT, Emily 410-778-7202. 221 C echamleewright2@washcoll.edu
CHAMP, Vonice 214-860-8716. 471 A vchamp@dcccd.edu
CHAMPAGNE, Keith, M 509-963-1515. 517 F champagn@cwu.edu
CHAMPAGNE, Ronald, O 607-735-1790. 323 H rchampagne@elmira.edu
CHAMPAGNE, Roy 281-425-6594. 475 I rchampag@lee.edu
CHAMPEAUX, Alison 218-723-7016. 254 K achampea@css.edu
CHAMPION, John 704-337-2523. 365 G championj@queens.edu
CHAMPION, Laura 616-526-6678. 240 L ldc4@calvin.edu
CHAMPION, Thomas 415-749-4528... 62 G tchampion@sfai.edu
CHAMPION, Victoria 305-899-4063... 98 O vchampion@barry.edu
CHAMPION, Willie 903-593-8311. 485 A wchampion@texascollege.edu
CHAMPION-TINTORER, Susan 973-353-1919. 306 D susan.tintorer@rutgers.edu
CHAMRA, Louay, M 248-370-2217. 248 J chamra@oakland.edu
CHAN, Andy 336-758-4662. 370 D
CHAN, Bill 614-947-6054. 380 A bill.chan@franklin.edu
CHAN, Caleb, K 517-750-1200. 250 E cchan@arbor.edu
CHAN, Claudia 718-482-5005. 318 F ClChan@lagcc.cuny.edu
CHAN, Eva 718-270-6487. 319 A echan@mec.cuny.edu
CHAN, Gilen 718-260-4981. 319 B gchan@citytech.cuny.edu
CHAN, Gregory, S 305-628-6522. 112 F gchan@stu.edu
CHAN, Kenyon, S 425-352-5221. 524 G kschan@uwb.edu
CHAN, Mark 405-425-5960. 397 D mark.chan@oc.edu
CHAN, Michael, L 671-735-5606. 546 C michael.chan@guamcc.edu
CHAN, Paul, H 303-871-4646... 86 B phchan@du.edu
CHAN, Regina 212-517-0501. 330 E rchan@mmm.edu
CHAN, Yau-Gene 888-488-4968... 48 K
CHANAY, Marcus, A 601-979-2241. 267 E marcus.a.chanay@jsums.edu
CHANCE, Carla 513-569-4755. 376 L carla.chance@cincinnatistate.edu
CHANCE, Cindi 706-737-1499. 126 B lhchance@gru.edu
CHANCE, Connie 325-235-7393. 486 C connie.chance@tstc.edu
CHANCE, Katie 256-551-5214..... 4 I katie.chance@drakestate.edu
CHANCE, Steve, L 806-371-5161. 465 E slchance@actx.edu
CHANCE, William 207-221-4372. 213 A wchance@une.edu
CHANCEY, Christine 828-398-2556. 366 G cchancey@southcollegenc.edu
CHANCEY, Janna, L 903-510-2298. 488 E jcha@tjc.edu
CHANCEY, Kari 918-293-5195. 398 B kari.chancey@okstate.edu
CHANDA, Jacqueline 816-802-3422. 275 J jchanda@kcai.edu
CHANDHOKE, Vikas 703-993-2268. 505 C vchandho@gmu.edu
CHANDLER, Brandon 856-225-6473. 306 C brandonc@camden.rutgers.edu
CHANDLER, Christopher 610-896-1250. 418 F cchandle@haverford.edu
CHANDLER, Clark, T 402-465-2114. 291 G cchandle@nebrwesleyan.edu
CHANDLER, Clint 803-738-7807. 445 C chandlerc@midlandstech.edu
CHANDLER, Derrall 619-388-3537... 62 D dchandler@sdccd.edu
CHANDLER, Dianne, S 765-973-8232. 167 G dschandl@iue.edu
CHANDLER, G. Thomas 803-777-5032. 447 G tchandler@sc.edu
CHANDLER, John, M 319-399-8622. 176 G jchandle@coe.edu
CHANDLER, Kathy 205-652-3421..... 9 F kchandler@uwa.edu
CHANDLER, Kenneth 919-530-7856. 368 A kenneth.chandler@nccu.edu
CHANDLER, Kim 651-696-6366. 256 L kchandle@macalester.edu
CHANDLER, Luanne 701-349-5793. 373 A lchandler@trinitybiblecollege.edu
CHANDLER, Maria 803-641-3317. 448 A mariac@usca.edu
CHANDLER, Mary 315-470-6654. 345 B mchand01@esf.edu
CHANDLER, Nancy, W 334-347-2623..... 3 G nchandler@escc.edu
CHANDLER, Norma 602-787-7073... 15 B norma.chandler@paradisevalley.edu
CHANDLER, Rebecca 310-338-5118... 53 E rchandler@lmu.edu
CHANDLER, Rick 212-650-3258. 318 C rick.chandler@hunter.cuny.edu
CHANDLER, Roger 251-575-8224..... 1 C rchandler@ascc.edu
CHANDLER, Roger 303-963-3341... 79 C rchandler@ccu.edu
CHANDLER, Sabrina, J 914-606-6880. 350 F sabrina.johnson.chandler@sunywcc.edu
CHANDLER, Shelly 352-638-9710... 99 B schandler@beaconcollege.edu
CHANDLER, Stephen 701-349-5959. 373 A schandler@trinitybiblecollege.edu
CHANDLER, Sue 404-297-9522. 126 A chandles@gptc.edu
CHANDLER, Timothy 410-704-2125. 220 E provost@towson.edu
CHANDO, Kristen 610-499-4142. 437 E kmchando@widener.edu
CHANDRASEKHAR, Michelle 360-475-7108. 521 H mchandrasekhar@olympic.edu
CHANEY, Bill 425-739-8119. 520 K bill.chaney@lwtech.edu
CHANEY, C. Steven 916-348-4689... 43 F stevec@chaneyassociates.com
CHANEY, Carmela 818-401-1031... 41 B cchaney@columbiacollege.edu
CHANEY, Jayn 641-269-3200. 178 H chaneyj@grinnell.edu
CHANEY, Matthew 231-591-2617. 242 F chaneym@ferris.edu
CHANEY, Rob 850-201-6085. 117 D chaneyr@tcc.fl.edu
CHANG, Caroline 408-554-5360... 64 M cschang@scu.edu
CHANG, Chaw-ye 610-436-3043. 430 A cchang@wcupa.edu
CHANG, Christopher 845-687-5096. 348 H changc@sunyulster.edu
CHANG, Cindy 818-719-6425... 52 B changck@piercecollege.edu
CHANG, George 908-737-3600. 302 F gchang@kean.edu
CHANG, Gilbert 239-513-1135. 119 E gchang@wolford.edu
CHANG, Hubert 562-902-3317... 67 H hurbertchang@scuhs.edu
CHANG, Jerry 808-974-7567. 136 A jerry7@hawaii.edu
CHANG, Jong Sik 770-279-0507. 124 I changjongsik@hotmail.com
CHANG, Ken 212-226-7300. 336 G kchang@pbcny.edu
CHANG, Lay, N 540-231-5422. 515 C laynam@vt.edu
CHANG, Lillian 808-373-2849. 137 E dr.chang@wmi.edu
CHANG, Ling Ling 516-739-1545. 333 F library@nyctcm.edu
CHANG, Mari 808-934-2526. 136 F changm@hawaii.edu
CHANG, Maria Raquel 619-477-6310... 70 D mchang@usuniversity.edu
CHANG, Marty 603-513-1375. 298 E marty.chang@granite.edu
CHANG, Nancy, H 817-515-5222. 482 B nancy.chang@tccd.edu
CHANG, Otto, H 260-481-0219. 168 C chango@ipfw.edu
CHANG, Patrick 201-684-7456. 305 A pchang@ramapo.edu
CHANG, Peter, M 703-333-5904. 516 B
CHANG, Shi-Kuo 847-679-3135. 149 G changsk@ksi.edu
CHANG, Tim 323-259-2531... 56 I tchang@oxy.edu
CHANGNON, Susan, J 724-287-8711. 411 C susan.changnon@bc3.edu
CHANLATTE, Ruben, D 817-257-5022. 484 I r.chanlatte@tcu.edu
CHANLER, Annette 318-371-3035. 203 E achanler@ltc.edu
CHAO, Gloria 212-220-8304. 317 A gchao@bmcc.cuny.edu
CHAO, Xia 406-657-1705. 287 C xia.chao@msubillings.edu
CHAO, Yvonne 212-228-1888. 337 H
CHAPA, Paul 210-999-8328. 488 C Paul.Chapa@trinity.edu
CHAPA, Yolanda, M 512-223-9154. 466 I ymc@austincc.edu
CHAPARRO, Luis 915-831-2132. 472 B lchapa13@epcc.edu

CHAPDELAINE, Andrea, E .... 610-921-7643. 409 A
achapdelaine@alb.edu
CHAPDELAINE, Karen ..... 772-462-7465. 106 P
kchapdel@irsc.edu
CHAPEL, Edward, V .... 973-655-4040. 303 D
chapele@mail.montclair.edu
CHAPELLE, Tynara .... 610-353-7630. 419 L
CHAPIN, William .... 518-891-2915. 335 A
wchapin@nccc.edu
CHAPKIS, Wendy .... 207-780-4966. 212 H
chapkis@maine.edu
CHAPLIN, Patricia, M ..... 313-927-1249. 246 D
pchaplin@marygrove.edu
CHAPLIN, Paulette .... 603-623-0313. 297 E
pchaplin@nhia.edu
CHAPMAN, Ana .... 201-360-4244. 302 D
achapman@hccc.edu
CHAPMAN, April .... 707-836-2904... 65 B
achapman@santarosa.edu
CHAPMAN, Bethany .... 254-295-4167. 490 B
bchapman@umhb.edu
CHAPMAN, Brenda, J ..... 404-413-3505. 126 E
bchapman@gsu.edu
CHAPMAN, Brian Keith .. 678-891-3337. 125 G
brian.chapman@gpc.edu
CHAPMAN, Bryce .... 314-744-7631. 278 B
chapmanb@mobap.edu
CHAPMAN, Clint .... 816-415-7872. 285 C
chapmanc@william.jewell.edu
CHAPMAN, D. Duane ..... 304-462-4128. 529 G
donald.chapman@glenville.edu
CHAPMAN, Dale, T .... 618-468-2001. 150 G
dchapman@lc.edu
CHAPMAN, Dana, L .... 904-256-7682. 107 Q
dchapma@ju.edu
CHAPMAN, David, W ...... 205-726-2771..... 6 F
dwchapma@samford.edu
CHAPMAN, Elaine .... 626-585-7608... 58 F
efchapman@pasadena.edu
CHAPMAN, Elaine, F .... 626-585-7065... 58 F
efchapman@pasadena.edu
CHAPMAN, Emily .... 312-499-4184. 158 L
echapman@saic.edu
CHAPMAN, Grant .... 314-246-8755. 284 N
chapman@webster.edu
CHAPMAN, Jeffrey, D ..... 785-827-5541. 188 C
jeff.chapman@kwu.edu
CHAPMAN, John .... 919-572-1625. 352 C
jchapman@apexsot.edu
CHAPMAN, Katrina .... 651-638-6043. 253 K
k-chapman@bethel.edu
CHAPMAN, Kendall, P ..... 601-643-8364. 266 F
ken.chapman@colin.edu
CHAPMAN, Kim .... 206-934-4521. 522 I
kim.chapman@seattlecolleges.edu
CHAPMAN, Lenora .... 210-458-6914. 492 C
lenora.chapman@utsa.edu
CHAPMAN, Leslie, T .... 847-735-5030. 150 B
chapman@lakeforest.edu
CHAPMAN, Linda .... 618-468-4000. 150 G
lchapman@lc.edu
CHAPMAN, Lisa, M .... 919-718-7295. 359 B
lchapman@cccc.edu
CHAPMAN, Michelle .... 404-756-4054. 121 A
mchapman@atlm.edu
CHAPMAN, Richard, L ..... 615-898-2988. 459 D
richard.chapman@mtsu.edu
CHAPMAN, Richard, N ... 843-661-1281. 444 B
rchapman@fmarion.edu
CHAPMAN, Robbin .... 781-283-3511. 237 F
rchapman@wellesley.edu
CHAPMAN, Robyn, F ...... 828-327-7000. 359 A
rchapman@cvcc.edu
CHAPMAN, Ronald, K ..... 801-422-8157. 495 D
ron_chapman@byu.edu
CHAPMAN, Sharon, H ..... 803-938-3810. 448 F
hamptons@uscsumter.edu
CHAPMAN, Tasha .... 314-434-4044. 273 C
tasha.chapman@covenantseminary.edu
CHAPMAN, Tim .... 503-253-3443. 405 E
tchapman@ocom.edu
CHAPMAN, Warren .... 312-369-7390. 143 D
wchapman@colum.edu
CHAPMAN, Wayne .... 270-247-8521. 197 H
wchapman@midcontinent.edu
CHAPP, Belena .... 215-568-4010. 424 D
bchapp@moore.edu
CHAPPELL, Cindy .... 619-849-2531... 59 L
cindychappell@pointloma.edu
CHAPPELL, Dorothy, F ... 630-752-5627. 163 F
dorothy.chappell@wheaton.edu
CHAPPELL, Jean .... 513-569-1596. 376 L
jean.chappell@cincinnatistate.edu
CHAPPELL, Julie .... 540-887-7225. 507 A
jchappel@mbc.edu
CHAPPELL-WILLIAMS, Lynette .... 607-255-3976. 322 A
lc75@cornell.edu
CHAPPLE, Bernadette ...... 334-229-4286..... 1 D
cbernadette@alasu.edu
CHAPUT, JR., Maury, L . 410-777-2324. 213 D
mlchaput@aacc.edu
CHARD, David, J .... 214-768-5465. 481 A
dchard@smu.edu
CHARETTE, Reno .... 406-657-2144. 287 C
rcharette@msubillings.edu
CHARGIN, Jan .... 408-848-4724... 45 F
jbchargin@gavilan.edu
CHARLES, Curtis .... 910-672-2247. 367 D
ccharles@uncfsu.edu
CHARLES, Cynthia .... 504-816-4263. 201 K
ccharles@dillard.edu
CHARLES, Harvey .... 928-523-1308... 16 C
harvey.charles@nau.edu
CHARLES, Jeffrey, R .... 408-554-4607... 64 M
jcharles@scu.edu
CHARLES, Jim .... 864-503-5563. 448 H
jcharles@uscupstate.edu
CHARLES, Joanne .... 740-351-3560. 388 N
jcharles@shawnee.edu
CHARLES, John .... 217-545-8080. 159 F
jcharles@siu.edu
CHARLES, Kevin, E .... 603-862-1098. 298 C
kevin.charles@unh.edu
CHARLES, Kristin .... 415-239-3677... 38 L
kcharles@ccsf.edu
CHARLES, Madonna .... 718-951-5133. 317 C
mcharles@brooklyn.cuny.edu
CHARLES, Olivier .... 334-244-3615..... 2 A
ocharles@aum.edu
CHARLES, Roosevelt .... 413-755-4088. 233 A
rccharles@stcc.edu
CHARLESTON, Kathleen .. 217-353-2024. 155 J
kcharleston@parkland.edu
CHARLEY, Daphne .... 334-876-9234..... 4 A
daphne.charley@wccs.edu
CHARLEY, Susan .... 731-286-3226. 460 F
charley@dscc.edu
CHARLIER, Hara .... 276-739-2429. 514 D
hcharlier@vhcc.edu
CHARLTON, John .... 202-685-4242. 544 K
charltonj@ndu.edu
CHARLTON, Patricia, A ... 702-651-5667. 294 E
patty.charlton@csn.edu
CHARNECO, Maria del Pilar .... 787-766-1717. 552 J
um_mcharneco@suagm.edu
CHARNEY, Dennis, S ..... 212-241-5674. 327 A
CHARNEY, Len .... 617-262-5000. 223 F
len.charney@the-bac.edu
CHARNOW, Rebecca ...... 212-749-2802. 330 A
rcharnow@msmnyc.edu
CHAROENSIRI, Kanitta ... 540-231-5313. 515 C
charkx@vt.edu
CHARON, Joseph .... 413-662-5284. 230 C
joseph.charon@mcla.edu
CHARPENTIER, Heather .. 518-743-2342. 345 E
charpentierh@sunyacc.edu
CHARPENTIER, Jennifer . 262-564-2866. 540 A
charpentierj@gtc.edu
CHARPENTIER, Paul .... 207-741-5503. 211 A
pcharpentier@smccme.edu
CHARRIER, Elizabeth, H . 512-448-8538. 479 C
elizc@stedwards.edu
CHARRIEZ, Ivette .... 787-878-6000. 549 D
icharriez@icprjc.edu
CHARRIEZ, Mayra .... 787-764-0000. 555 B
mayra.charriez@upr.edu
CHARRON, Michael .... 507-457-1606. 264 A
mcharron@smumn.edu
CHARTON, Jacques .... 415-485-3227... 42 J
charton@dominican.edu
CHASAN, Bob .... 520-795-0787... 11 J
admissions@asaom.edu
CHASE, Anne .... 859-985-3266. 192 F
anne_chase@berea.edu
CHASE, Bruce, W .... 540-831-5278. 508 C
bchase@radford.edu
CHASE, Cheryl .... 641-269-3450. 178 H
chaseche@grinnell.edu
CHASE, David .... 203-857-7058... 89 D
dchase@norwalk.edu
CHASE, David, D .... 509-527-4261. 524 H
david.chase@wwcc.edu
CHASE, David, T .... 973-267-9404. 304 G
CHASE, Diane .... 407-823-6197. 115 E
diane.chase@ucf.edu
CHASE, Dina .... 626-585-7878... 58 F
dmchase@pasadena.edu
CHASE, Geoffrey, W .... 619-594-4167... 35 D
gchase@mail.sdsu.edu
CHASE, Gregory, M .... 336-734-7246. 360 E
gchase@forsythtech.edu
CHASE, Horace, W .... 731-425-2610. 460 G
hchase@jscc.edu
CHASE, John .... 323-663-2167... 73 B
CHASE, Julie .... 207-741-5874. 211 A
jchase@smccme.edu
CHASE, Marilyn, O .... 317-788-2192. 173 I
chase@uindy.edu
CHASE, Mary, E .... 402-280-2162. 289 D
marychase@creighton.edu
CHASE, MaryEtta .... 801-957-4799. 498 B
maryetta.chase@slcc.edu
CHASE, Michael, K .... 423-775-7327. 453 E
mchase5606@bryan.edu
CHASE, Michelle .... 715-682-1811. 535 D
mchase@northland.edu
CHASE, Patricia, A .... 304-293-5101. 530 D
pachase@hsc.wvu.edu
CHASE, Ryan .... 480-517-8314... 15 D
ryan.chase@riosalado.edu
CHASE, William .... 617-236-8880. 226 F
wchase@fisher.edu
CHASE PADULA, Allison 401-254-3793. 440 B
achasepadula@rwu.edu
CHASON, Foster .... 423-585-2681. 462 A
foster.chason@ws.edu
CHASON, Myra .... 310-289-5123... 75 C
CHASSAPIS, Constantin .. 201-216-5564. 307 E
cchassap@stevens.edu
CHASTAIN, Allen .... 478-471-2714. 128 I
achastain@mgc.edu
CHASTAIN, Andrea, J ..... 913-288-7270. 187 L
chastain@kckcc.edu
CHASTAIN, Clint .... 678-359-5733. 127 A
clintc@gordonstate.edu
CHASTAIN, Lesa, M .... 417-268-6091. 271 I
ir@gobbc.edu
CHASTAIN, Lisa .... 478-757-2647. 128 I
lisa.chastain@maconstate.edu
CHASTAIN, Wes .... 828-835-4253. 364 E
wchastain@tricountycc.edu
CHASTANT, Jane .... 713-623-2040. 466 G
jchastant@aii.edu
CHASZAR, Mark .... 432-837-8189. 487 B
mchaszar@sulross.edu
CHATAS, Geoffrey .... 614-292-9232. 386 E
chatas.1@osu.edu
CHATEAU, Dale .... 814-838-7673. 416 G
CHATFIELD, Brenda, L ... 785-890-3641. 189 H
bchatfield@nwktc.edu
CHATHAM, David, W ...... 864-833-7028. 446 D
dchatham@presby.edu
CHATMAN, Cheryl, T ...... 651-603-6151. 255 B
chatman@csp.edu
CHATMAN, Jesse .... 901-435-1470. 455 M
jesse_chatman@loc.edu
CHATMAN, Robert .... 803-536-7200. 446 G
zs_rchatman@scsu.edu
CHATMON, Angelo, V ..... 804-257-5856. 515 F
achatmon@vuu.edu
CHATMON, Catherine ..... 336-725-8344. 365 F
chatmonc@piedmontu.edu
CHATTERJEE, Achala ...... 909-384-8904... 62 A
achatterjee@sbccd.cc.ca.us
CHATTERJEE-SUTTON, Eva .... 724-503-1001. 436 G
echatterjeesutton@washjeff.edu
CHATTERTON, Jim .... 603-623-0313. 297 E
jimchatterton@nhia.edu
CHATTERTON, Stephen, A .... 208-282-2515. 138 E
chatstep@isu.edu
CHATTIN, Duane, H .... 812-888-4164. 174 F
dchattin@vinu.edu
CHATY, Karen .... 707-468-3065... 54 B
kchaty@mendocino.edu
CHAU, Kai Ton .... 616-222-3000. 245 C
kchau@kuyper.edu
CHAUDRY, Aliya .... 405-466-3565. 395 N
achaudry@langston.edu
CHAUHDRI, Aamer .... 502-456-6509. 199 F
achauhdri@sctd.edu
CHAULK, Elizabeth .... 859-572-1985. 198 I
chaulke1@nku.edu
CHAUNCEY, Linda .... 206-934-4386. 522 J
linda.chauncey@seattlecolleges.edu
CHAURET, Christian .... 765-455-9371. 168 A
cchauret@iuk.edu
CHAUVIN, Marc .... 985-732-6640. 203 D
CHAVES, William .... 509-359-2347. 519 C
wchaves@ewu.edu
CHAVEZ, April .... 575-769-4061. 309 F
april.chavez@clovis.edu
CHAVEZ, Consuelo, E ..... 575-461-4413. 309 M
conniec@mesalands.edu
CHAVEZ, Dennis, J .... 607-777-2428. 341 E
dchavez@binghamton.edu
CHAVEZ, Gloriann .... 909-384-8665... 62 A
gchavez@sbccd.cc.ca.us
CHAVEZ, Gloriann .... 909-389-3248... 61 K
gchavez@sbccd.cc.ca.us
CHAVEZ, Guadalupe .... 956-872-3499. 480 I
gchavez@southtexascollege.edu
CHAVEZ, Israel .... 563-588-8000. 178 D
ichavez@emmaus.edu
CHAVEZ, Katrina .... 417-823-3409. 281 M
kchavez@forest.edu
CHAVEZ, Kym .... 423-265-7784. 266 A
Kchavez@belhaven.edu
CHAVEZ, Lisa, M .... 323-343-3500... 34 A
lchavez@cslanet.calstatela.edu
CHAVEZ, Mario, J .... 308-635-6186. 293 E
chavezm@wncc.edu
CHAVEZ, Mary .... 719-549-3280... 84 G
mary.chavez@pueblocc.edu
CHAVEZ, Michael .... 661-654-3181... 32 H
mchavez14@csub.edu
CHAVEZ, Michael .... 432-685-4507. 476 G
mchavez@midland.edu
CHAVEZ, Miguel .... 330-490-7341. 392 H
mchavez@walsh.edu
CHAVEZ, Olga .... 915-831-3322. 472 B
ochave30@epcc.edu
CHAVEZ, Orquedia .... 916-649-2400... 30 C
CHAVEZ-SILVA, Monica . 641-269-3900. 178 H
chavezsm@grinnell.edu
CHAVIRA, Jessica .... 325-235-7342. 486 C
jessica.chavira@tstc.edu
CHAVIRA, Rejoice .... 909-389-3456... 61 K
rchavira@craftonhills.edu
CHAVIS, Donna .... 843-921-6907. 446 A
dchavis@netc.edu
CHAVIS, Gordon .... 407-823-3004. 115 E
gordon.chavis@ucf.edu
CHAVIS, Kimberly .... 773-602-5501. 142 B
kboyd@ccc.edu
CHAVIS, Kimberly .... 847-925-6000. 145 H
kchavis@harpercollege.edu
CHAVIS, Tim .... 248-204-3700. 245 I
tchavis@ltu.edu
CHAVOUS, Warren .... 803-584-3446. 448 D
chavousg@mailbox.sc.edu
CHAWKIN, Ken .... 641-472-4037. 180 N
kchawkin@mum.edu
CHAYA, Ramon, C .... 585-345-6999. 325 C
rcchaya@genesee.edu
CHAYKIN, Rachelle .... 610-892-1528. 427 E
rchaykin@pit.edu
CHE, Jacqueline .... 670-234-5498. 547 A
jacquelinec@nmcnet.edu
CHEAGLE, Dorothy, S ..... 803-934-3227. 445 F
dcheagle@morris.edu
CHEATEM, Michelle .... 410-617-5171. 216 A
micheatem@loyola.edu
CHEATHAM, Frank .... 270-789-5231. 193 D
fdcheatham@campbellsville.edu
CHEATHAM, George .... 703-284-1560. 507 B
george.cheatham@marymount.edu
CHEATHAM, Kathy .... 205-329-7853..... 3 B
kathy.cheatham@ecacolleges.com
CHEBATOR, Paul, J .... 617-552-3470. 224 A
paul.chebator@bc.edu
CHECCI, Peg .... 802-793-0728. 499 I
peg.checci@neci.edu
CHECCIO, Albert, R .... 213-740-2211... 74 A
checcio@usc.edu
CHECHOWICH, Faye .... 765-998-4571. 173 C
fychechow@taylor.edu
CHECK, Andrea, G .... 260-422-5561. 167 B
agcheck@indianatech.edu
CHECKETTS, Max, L .... 808-675-3455. 135 C
checkettsm@byuh.edu
CHECKOVICH, Irene, C .... 508-531-1231. 229 D
icheckovich@bridgew.edu
CHECKOVICH, Peter, G .. 304-260-4380. 527 N
pcheckov@blueridgectc.edu
CHECOV, Elissa .... 770-962-7580. 127 D
echecov@gwinnetttech.edu
CHEE, Kathleen .... 808-544-0292. 135 F
kchee@hpu.edu
CHEEK, Annesa .... 937-512-4115. 388 O
annesa.cheek@sinclair.edu
CHEEK, Claude .... 516-299-3780. 329 C
claude.cheek@liu.edu
CHEEK, Debbie, Q .... 843-921-6945. 446 A
dcheek@netc.edu
CHEEK, Jimmy, G .... 865-974-3265. 463 C
chancellor@utk.edu
CHEEK, Lee .... 478-289-2048. 124 C
lcheek@ega.edu
CHEEK, Sherrie .... 662-472-2312. 267 B
scheek@holmescc.edu
CHEEKS, Roger .... 757-352-4486. 508 G
rogeche@regent.edu
CHEERS, Karen, T .... 276-739-2490. 514 D
kcheers@vhcc.edu
CHEESEBRO, Deb .... 336-770-3321. 369 D
cheesebrod@uncsa.edu
CHEESEMAN, Valerie ...... 757-822-1994. 514 C
vcheeseman@tcc.edu
CHEETHAM, William, C ... 315-445-4400. 328 F
cheethwc@lemoyne.edu
CHEEVER, Rex .... 620-665-3382. 187 F
cheeverr@hutchcc.edu
CHEKWA, Emmanuel .... 205-929-1459..... 5 G
echekwa@miles.edu
CHELBERG, Gene .... 415-405-3728... 35 E
chelberg@sfsu.edu
CHELETTE, Newton .... 661-722-6300... 28 F
nchelette@avc.edu

CHELINE, OSB, Paschal . 503-845-3269. 404 D
paschal.cheline@mtangel.edu
CHELL, Travis, L .... 423-652-6368. 455 I
tlchell@king.edu
CHELLMAN, Laura, G ..... 715-836-5954. 536 E
chellmlg@uwec.edu
CHELNICK, Robert .... 773-975-1295. 534 D
krisbob1@cs.com
CHELSEN, Paul, O .... 630-752-5026. 163 F
Paul.Chelsen@wheaton.edu
CHEMA, Thomas, V .... 330-569-5120. 380 I
chematv@hiram.edu
CHEMERINSKY, Erwin .... 949-824-7722... 71 B
echemerinsky@law.uci.edu
CHEN, Bill .... 626-571-8811... 74 B
billchen@uwest.edu
CHEN, Chau-Kuang .... 615-327-6848. 456 E
ckchen@mmc.edu
CHEN, Daxing (Michael) . 210-431-5009. 479 D
mchen@stmarytx.edu
CHEN, Desiree .... 630-617-3033. 145 A
chend@elmhurst.edu
CHEN, Diane .... 484-384-2941. 425 I
semdean@eastern.edu
CHEN, Diane .... 610-896-5000. 415 G
dchen@eastern.edu
CHEN, Ekron .... 626-571-5110... 51 B
ekron@les.edu
CHEN, Hui-Ling .... 603-222-4203. 297 G
hchen@anselm.edu
CHEN, Jack .... 516-877-3334. 313 A
jchen@adelphi.edu
CHEN, Jane .... 212-452-4178. 334 B
jchen@nysid.edu
CHEN, Jie .... 208-885-6244. 139 D
jiechen@uidaho.edu
CHEN, Julie .... 978-934-2226. 229 B
Julie_Chen@uml.edu
CHEN, Karen .... 323-731-2383... 57 I
esl@psuca.edu
CHEN, Liana .... 408-260-0208... 44 J
accounting@fivebranches.edu
CHEN, Linda .... 574-520-4338. 168 E
lchen@iusb.edu
CHEN, Mary M, Y .... 302-454-3968... 93 F
mchen@dtcc.edu
CHEN, May .... 510-981-2820... 59 A
mchen@peralta.edu
CHEN, May, K .... 510-981-2820... 59 A
mchen@peralta.edu
CHEN, Meghan .... 909-274-5658... 55 A
mchen@mtsac.edu
CHEN, Nellie .... 212-349-4330. 325 D
nchen@globe.edu
CHEN, JR., Ronald, K .... 973-353-5561. 306 D
ronald.chen@rutgers.edu
CHEN, Steve .... 518-629-7311. 326 G
s.chen@hvcc.edu
CHEN, Tsuey-Hwa .... 612-977-5732. 254 C
tsuey-hwa.chen@capella.edu
CHEN, Wen-Hsin .... 617-989-4029. 237 G
chenw@wit.edu
CHEN, Xiangming .... 860-297-5170... 91 F
xiangming.chen@trincoll.edu
CHEN, Xueying .... 334-291-4979..... 2 H
xueying.chen@cv.edu
CHEN, Yanping .... 703-516-0035. 510 I
yanping.chen@umtweb.edu
CHEN, Yemeng .... 516-739-1545. 333 F
president@nyctcm.edu
CHEN-ORTEGA, Cathy .... 303-546-3517... 83 F
cchenortega@naropa.edu
CHENAULT, Shirley .... 817-598-6337. 494 G
chenault@wc.edu
CHENAULT, Venida .... 785-830-2770. 187 B
venida.chenault@bie.edu
CHENCO, William .... 610-917-1430. 436 C
bachenco@vfcc.edu
CHENETTE, Jonathan ...... 845-437-5300. 349 G
jochenette@vassar.edu
CHENEVERT, Peter, S ..... 207-859-5530. 209 J
pschenev@colby.edu
CHENEY, Christine .... 775-784-4345. 294 J
cheney@unr.edu
CHENEY, John .... 413-542-2331. 221 G
jycheney@amherst.edu
CHENEY, Victor .... 904-819-6213. 103 E
vcheney@flagler.edu
CHENG, Alex .... 662-915-7407. 270 B
acheng@olemiss.edu
CHENG, Haiyang .... 304-696-2682. 529 H
CHENG, Rita .... 618-453-2341. 159 G
rcheng@siu.edu
CHENG, Stephen Z, D .... 330-972-7500. 390 E
cheng@uakron.edu
CHENG, Terence .... 718-951-5771. 317 C
tcheng@brooklyn.cuny.edu
CHENG, Wayne .... 714-533-1495... 66 H
waynecheng@southbaylo.edu
CHENG, Yan .... 954-763-9840... 98 I
dean@atom.edu
CHENOWETH,
Candace, A .... 262-472-1592. 538 D
chenowec@uww.edu
CHENOWETH, Gregg, A . 574-807-7210. 164 D
gregg.chenoweth@bethelcollege.edu
CHERAGHI, S. Hossein .. 413-782-1272. 238 A
cheraghi@wne.edu
CHERENEGAR, Barbara .... 605-331-6671. 452 D
jessica.cherenegar@usiouxfalls.edu
CHEREWICK, Daniel, P ... 248-341-2011. 248 D
dpchere@oaklandcc.edu
CHERI, OFM, Ferd .... 217-228-5432. 156 C
cherife@quincy.edu
CHERLAND, Ryan, M ...... 949-824-4521... 71 B
ryan.cherland@uci.edu
CHERMAK, Jerry .... 954-262-4419. 109 K
chermack@nova.edu
CHERMONTE, Debra, J .... 440-775-8411. 385 H
debra.chermonte@oberlin.edu
CHERN, James .... 973-746-2323. 303 D
chernj@mail.montclair.edu
CHERNOW, Barbara .... 631-632-6340. 342 C
barbara.chernow@stonybrook.edu
CHERREY, Cynthia .... 609-258-3000. 304 E
CHERRIN, Bruce, E .... 505-277-1740. 312 F
cherrin@unm.edu
CHERRINGTON,
R. Brent .... 801-524-8190. 495 O
Brent@ldsbc.edu
CHERRY, Brian .... 906-227-1823. 248 A
bcherry@nmu.edu
CHERRY, Charles, D .... 252-335-3593. 367 C
cdcherry@mail.ecsu.edu
CHERRY, Christal, M ...... 404-527-7718. 127 I
ccherry@itc.edu
CHERRY, Christopher ..... 715-394-8580. 538 C
rcherry@uwsuper.edu
CHERRY, Evonne .... 254-647-3234. 478 H
echerry@rangercollege.edu
CHERRY, Jewel, B .... 336-734-7297. 360 E
jcherry@forsythtech.edu
CHERRY, Mark .... 321-433-7031. 101 M
cherrym@easternflorida.edu
CHERRY, Michelle .... 305-809-3237. 104 I
michelle.cherry@fkcc.edu
CHERRY, Stephanie .... 319-296-2320. 178 J
stephanie.cherry@hawkeyecollege.edu
CHERUBIN, Daniel .... 212-772-4161. 318 C
dcherubi@hunter.cuny.edu
CHERUBINI, Angela .... 914-395-2567. 340 E
acherubini@sarahlawrence.edu
CHERUBINO, Thomas ..... 908-709-7546. 308 B
cherubino@ucc.edu
CHESBRO, Steven, B ...... 334-229-5053..... 1 D
schesbro@alasu.edu
CHESBROUGH, Ronald .. 636-922-8380. 280 J
rchesbrough@stchas.edu
CHESHIRE, Hall .... 540-654-1379. 510 J
hcheshir@umw.edu
CHESLEY, Laurie .... 616-234-4230. 243 B
lchesley@grcc.edu
CHESNEY, Alan, P .... 410-778-7706. 221 C
achesney2@washcoll.edu
CHESNEY, Linda, H .... 718-262-5119. 319 F
chesney@york.cuny.edu
CHESNEY, Mark .... 202-291-9020... 96 E
mchesney@radianscollege.edu
CHESNEY, Scott .... 603-862-1870. 298 C
scott.chesney@unh.edu
CHESNEY, Thom, D .... 972-860-4809. 470 G
CHESNUT, Robert, W ...... 217-581-2125. 144 E
rwchesnut@eiu.edu
CHESSER, Ron .... 501-760-4230... 22 A
rchesser@npcc.edu
CHESSON, JR.,
Andrew, L .... 318-675-5000. 205 D
achess@lsuhsc.edu
CHESTER, Ann, M .... 304-293-1651. 530 D
achester@hsc.wvu.edu
CHESTER, Brandi .... 870-248-4000... 20 G
brandic@blackrivertech.edu
CHESTER, Cathie .... 914-251-5976. 344 D
cathie.chester@purchase.edu
CHESTER, Claudia .... 925-969-3108... 49 B
cchester@jfku.edu
CHESTER, Steven .... 860-343-5864... 89 A
schester@mxcc.commnet.edu
CHESTER, Timothy, M .... 706-542-3145. 133 C
tchester@uga.edu
CHESTERFIELD,
Alverne, W .... 410-651-6253. 219 E
awchesterfield@umes.edu
CHESTNUT, Jacki, L .... 612-874-3729. 257 B
jacki_chestnut@mcad.edu
CHEU, Susan .... 408-848-4739... 45 F
scheu@gavilan.edu
CHEUNG, Alvin .... 916-631-8108... 32 C
CHEUNG, Enos .... 718-939-5100. 329 B
echeung@libi.edu
CHEUNG, Lillian .... 651-631-0204. 253 D
lcheung@aaaom.edu
CHEVALIER,
Jim Langstraat .... 971-722-2913. 407 D
jim.langstraat@pcc.edu
CHEVALIER, JR.,
Joseph .... 404-756-5773. 129 E
jchevalier@msm.edu
CHEVES, Brad, E .... 214-768-2667. 481 A
bcheves@smu.edu
CHEW, Catherine .... 252-638-7200. 359 G
chewc@cravencc.edu
CHEW, Elaine .... 254-968-9611. 483 A
chew@tarleton.edu
CHEW, Kenneth .... 812-237-3939. 167 A
kenneth.chew@indstate.edu
CHEW, Roy .... 937-395-8688. 382 K
roy.chew@khnetwork.org
CHEZUM, Kelly, O .... 315-268-4483. 320 A
chezumk@clarkson.edu
CHI, Selina .... 323-265-8154... 51 F
chiss@elac.edu
CHIA, Samuel .... 214-887-5121. 471 F
schia@dts.edu
CHIACCHIERINI, Chris ... 503-253-3443. 405 E
cc@ocom.edu
CHIAL, Sally .... 612-977-5299. 254 C
sally.chial@capella.edu
CHIANG, Amber .... 661-395-4251... 49 N
amchiang@bakersfieldcollege.edu
CHIAPPETTA, Anthony .... 202-319-5623... 94 G
chiappetta@cua.edu
CHIAPPINI, Thomas, A .. 330-494-6170. 389 F
tchiappini@starkstate.edu
CHIARA, Mary Jo, B ...... 718-940-5574. 339 B
mchiara@sjcny.edu
CHIASSON, Shannon ...... 504-398-2250. 206 C
schiasson@olhcc.edu
CHICHESTER, Susan, E .. 585-245-5577. 343 C
sue@geneseo.edu
CHICKERING, F. William 609-896-5111. 305 D
wchickering@rider.edu
CHICOINE, David, L .... 605-688-4111. 452 B
david.chicoine@sdstate.edu
CHIDDICK, Troy .... 610-527-0200. 432 B
tchiddick@rosemont.edu
CHIELLI, Jack, A .... 570-408-4770. 437 F
jack.chielli@wilkes.edu
CHIESA, Ricardo .... 787-738-2161. 554 C
ricardo.chiesa@upr.edu
CHIEVES, Kevin .... 912-443-5491. 131 D
kchieves@savannahtech.edu
CHIGAWA, Steven .... 808-235-7457. 137 C
chigawa@hawaii.edu
CHIGOGIDZE, Alex .... 718-982-2430. 317 E
alex.chigogidze@csi.cuny.edu
CHIGOS, Lisa .... 619-961-4326... 69 I
lchigos@tjsl.edu
CHIH, Lo-Li .... 808-974-7595. 136 A
loli@hawaii.edu
CHIKUNI, Ticha .... 859-336-5082. 198 J
tichachikuni@sccky.edu
CHIKWEM, John, O .... 484-365-8253. 422 D
jchikwem@lincoln.edu
CHIKWINYA, Mary .... 253-566-5127. 524 C
mchikwinya@tacomacc.edu
CHILCOTE, Paul .... 419-289-5771. 374 C
pchilcot@ashland.edu
CHILDERS, Amber .... 501-337-5000... 20 J
amber@coto.edu
CHILDERS, Camille .... 316-978-3620. 191 F
camille.childers@wichita.edu
CHILDERS, Joseph .... 951-827-4302... 71 E
joseph.childers@ucr.edu
CHILDERS, Karen .... 909-389-3260... 61 K
CHILDERS, Karen .... 909-389-3392... 61 K
kchilder@craftonhills.edu
CHILDRESS, Bates .... 802-773-5900. 499 B
bates.childress@csj.edu
CHILDRESS, Jamie .... 919-718-7239. 359 B
jchildress@cccc.edu
CHILDRESS, John .... 615-322-3977. 463 G
john.childress@vanderbilt.edu
CHILDRESS, Layton .... 417-447-8102. 279 K
childrel@otc.edu
CHILDREY, Cynthia, A .... 928-523-5021... 16 C
cynthia.childrey@nau.edu
CHILDREY, Lauren, T ...... 336-272-7102. 354 E
lauren.childrey@greensboro.edu
CHILDS, Cindy, D .... 301-322-0014. 217 F
childscd@pgcc.edu
CHILDS, David, E .... 304-877-6428. 526 C
david.childs@abc.edu
CHILDS, Debbie .... 325-649-8054. 473 F
dchilds@hputx.edu
CHILDS, Dee .... 256-824-2555..... 8 F
dee.childs@uah.edu
CHILDS, Dena .... 870-543-5959... 23 E
dchilds@seark.edu
CHILDS, Kimberly, M ..... 936-468-2805. 482 A
kchilds@sfasu.edu
CHILDS, Linda, J .... 304-877-6428. 526 C
linda.childs@abc.edu
CHILDS, Liz .... 801-863-8460. 497 C
childsli@uvu.edu
CHILDS, Paige .... 864-941-8688. 446 C
childs.p@ptc.edu
CHILDS, Paige, K .... 864-941-8688. 446 C
childs.p@ptc.edu
CHILDS, Randal, V .... 919-530-5264. 368 A
rchilds@nccu.edu
CHILDS, Richard, G .... 410-864-4274. 218 B
rchilds@stmarys.edu
CHILDS, Sidney .... 419-372-2677. 374 K
sidneyc@bgsu.edu
CHILDS, William, P .... 301-687-4211. 220 C
wchilds@frostburg.edu
CHILES, Rebecca .... 318-795-2392. 205 F
rebecca.chiles@lsus.edu
CHILICKI, Stacy .... 207-216-4312. 211 C
schilicki@yccc.edu
CHILLAS, Jonathon .... 858-642-8014... 55 J
jchillas@nu.edu
CHILLO, Joseph .... 617-730-7019. 235 D
joseph.chillo@newbury.edu
CHILTON, Bette .... 815-825-2086. 149 F
bette.chilton@kishwaukeecollege.edu
CHILTON, Bruce, D .... 845-758-7335. 314 D
chilton@bard.edu
CHIMENTI, Vito, R .... 215-670-9297. 425 J
vrchimenti@peirce.edu
CHIMERA, Anthony .... 312-662-4031. 139 F
achimera@adler.edu
CHIN, Calvin .... 646-557-4552. 318 D
chin@jjay.cuny.edu
CHIN, Deborah .... 203-932-7020... 92 E
dchin@newhaven.edu
CHIN, Elaine .... 408-924-3601... 36 A
elaine.chin@sjsu.edu
CHIN, Jean, E .... 706-542-8715. 133 C
jchin@uhs.uga.edu
CHIN, Jim .... 559-674-4812... 69 A
jim.chin@reedleycollege.edu
CHIN, Julie .... 818-299-5500... 75 E
jChin@westcoastuniversity.edu
CHIN, Li-Chen .... 919-684-5480. 354 A
li-chen.chin@duke.edu
CHIN, Penny, J .... 516-876-3137. 343 D
chinp@oldwestbury.edu
CHIN, Sonia .... 619-849-2958... 59 L
soniachin@pointloma.edu
CHIN KEE FATT,
Camille .... 718-780-7963. 315 H
camille.chinkeefatt@brooklaw.edu
CHINARIS, Tim .... 334-386-7214..... 3 H
tchinaris@faulkner.edu
CHINCHILLA, Gladys ...... 312-939-4975. 146 A
gchinchilla@harrington.edu
CHINETTI, Peter .... 617-964-1100. 222 A
pchinetti@ants.edu
CHING, David, M .... 310-233-4091... 51 H
chingdm@lahc.edu
CHING-BUSH, Elizabeth . 863-680-3949. 105 D
echingbush@flsouthern.edu
CHING-RAPPA, Myrtle ... 808-956-4399. 136 B
chingrapp@hawaii.edu
CHINN-JOINTER, June ... 901-435-1500. 455 M
june_chinn-jointer@loc.edu
CHINNASWAMY,
Sainath .... 508-929-8511. 230 G
schinnaswamy@worcester.edu
CHINNAVASO, Michael .. 510-883-7159... 42 I
mchinnavaso@dspt.edu
CHINNIAH, Nim .... 773-702-8118. 161 B
nim.chinniah@uchicago.edu
CHINNICI, OFM, Joseph 510-848-5232... 45 A
jchinnici@fst.edu
CHINWAH, Lovette .... 937-376-6473. 376 E
lchinwah@centralstate.edu
CHIOU, Sophia .... 740-245-7226. 392 A
schiou@rio.edu
CHIPMAN, Nelson .... 412-392-4306. 431 B
nchipman@pointpark.edu
CHIPMAN, Stephanie ...... 217-245-3030. 146 F
stephanie.chipman@ic.edu
CHIPMAN, Sue .... 478-471-2732. 128 I
sue.chipman@maconstate.edu
CHIPPS, Michael, R .... 402-844-7054. 291 I
michaelc@northeast.edu
CHIPREAN, Kristina, B ... 724-738-2052. 429 F
kristina.chiprean@sru.edu
CHIQUITO, Yug Fon .... 626-529-8246... 57 G
ychiquito@pacificoaks.edu
CHIRICO, Donna .... 718-262-2804. 319 F
dchirico@york.cuny.edu
CHISEM, Lori .... 205-929-3409..... 5 D
lchisem@lawsonstate.edu
CHISHOLM, Arnett .... 734-973-3540. 252 A
achisholm@wccnet.edu
CHISHOLM, Barbara .... 334-727-8535..... 8 A
chisholm@mytu.tuskegee.edu
CHISHOLM, Brendan, H . 508-856-4031. 229 C
brendan.chisholm@umassmed.edu

CHISHOLM, Bruce .... 336-322-2146. 362 F
Bruce.Chisholm@piedmontcc.edu
CHISHOLM, Douglas, W 937-766-7992. 375 K
chisd@cedarville.edu
CHISHOLM, Michael, T .. 503-725-2500. 406 B
chisholm@pdx.edu
CHISHOLM, Pam .... 802-828-2800. 501 C
chisholp@ccv.edu
CHISHOLM, Rex .... 312-503-3209. 155 D
r-chisholm@northwestern.edu
CHISLER, Christi, R .... 909-869-3805... 32 G
crchisler@csupomona.edu
CHISMAR, William, G ..... 808-956-8866. 136 B
chismar@hawaii.edu
CHISOLM, Roxanne .... 662-472-2312. 267 B
rchisolm@holmescc.edu
CHISOM, Brian, T .... 540-375-2259. 509 B
chisom@roanoke.edu
CHISUM, Virginia, E .... 432-335-6415. 477 M
vchisum@odessa.edu
CHITRE, Manoj .... 909-607-9828... 39 C
manoj.chitre@cgu.edu
CHITTIM, Del .... 863-667-5008. 113 P
dchittim@seu.edu
CHITWOOD, Ashley .... 504-671-6607. 203 A
achitw@dcc.edu
CHITWOOD, Charles ...... 405-491-6455. 399 K
cchitwood@snu.edu
CHITWOOD, James .... 847-969-4915... 28 M
jchitwood@argosy.edu
CHITWOOD, Linda .... 662-915-7621. 270 B
lchitwoo@olemiss.edu
CHIU, Edward .... 978-934-4814. 229 B
Edward_Chiu@uml.edu
CHIU, Yuwen .... 415-282-7600... 27 L
yuwenchiu@actcm.edu
CHLAD, Lori .... 315-228-7411. 320 F
lchlad@colgate.edu
CHLARSON, Cathleen ..... 480-732-7030... 14 J
cathy.chlarson@cgc.edu
CHLEBICKI, Ann .... 310-243-3510... 33 B
achlebicki@csudh.edu
CHLIWNIAK, Luba .... 520-206-7100... 17 A
lchliwniak@pima.edu
CHMURA, Michael .... 781-239-4549. 222 D
mchmura@babson.edu
CHMURA, Thomas .... 617-287-4087. 228 E
tchmura@umassp.edu
CHO, Hyun Sung .... 770-279-0507. 124 I
revdrcho@gcuniv.edu
CHO, Karen .... 808-235-7404. 137 C
kcho@hawaii.edu
CHO, Katherine H, S .... 213-413-9500... 67 I
dean@scusoma.edu
CHO, Ruth .... 562-926-1023... 60 B
ruthsangacho@gmail.com
CHOATE, Edward .... 417-836-6616. 278 E
edchoate@missouristate.edu
CHOATE, Jim .... 319-398-7612. 180 J
jchoate@kirkwood.edu
CHOATE, Michael, J .... 972-883-2943. 491 E
mchoate@utdallas.edu
CHOATE, Regina .... 575-492-2774. 310 G
rchoate@nmjc.edu
CHOBOT, Karen, M .... 701-671-2385. 372 E
karen.chobot@ndscs.edu
CHODOSH, Hiram, E ...... 909-621-8111... 39 D
hiram.chodosh@cmc.edu
CHOI, Andrew .... 714-822-0006... 36 C
tkd@calums.edu
CHOI, Anthony .... 714-822-8541... 36 C
anthonychoi@calumn.edu
CHOI, Bo Yoon .... 213-487-0110... 42 K
officemanager@dula.edu
CHOI, David .... 910-221-2224. 354 D
dchoi@gcd.edu
CHOI, Hee-Sook .... 605-677-5612. 451 F
heesook.choi@usd.edu
CHOI, Henry .... 714-533-1495... 66 H
advising@southbaylo.edu
CHOI, Kyunam .... 714-525-0088... 46 A
qchoi3@yahoo.com
CHOI, Mun .... 860-486-4037... 92 A
mun.choi@uconn.edu
CHOI, Rebecca .... 888-488-4968... 48 K
CHOI, Stephen .... 209-478-0800... 47 M
schoi@humphreys.edu
CHOI, Sun Hee .... 718-639-3975. 124 I
eastersun@hanmail.net
CHOI, Susan .... 856-227-7200. 300 B
schoi@camdencc.edu
CHOICE, Thomas, L .... 815-825-2086. 149 F
tom.choice@kishwaukeecollege.edu
CHOJNICKI, Linda, M .... 413-782-1315. 238 A
lchojnic@wne.edu
CHOLETTE, Beth, K .... 585-245-5716. 343 C
cholette@geneseo.edu
CHOLICK, Fred, A .... 785-532-6266. 188 A
fcholick@ksu.edu
CHOMA, Michael .... 724-339-7542. 425 B
thedean@teacher.com
CHOMIAK,
Renee DeLong .... 562-860-2451... 37 I
rdlchomiak@cerritos.edu
CHONCEK, Christopher .. 412-392-3905. 431 B
cchoncek@pointpark.edu
CHONG, Bruce .... 912-650-6206. 131 H
bchong@southuniversity.edu
CHONG, Dawn .... 419-372-2723. 374 K
dchong@bgsu.edu
CHONG, Frank .... 707-527-4431... 65 B
fchong@santarosa.edu
CHONG, Jocelyn .... 310-434-4547... 65 A
chong_jocelyn@smc.edu
CHONG, Philip .... 800-782-2422... 32 B
pchong@prodigy.net
CHONKO, Arthur, J .... 740-587-6456. 379 D
chonko@denison.edu
CHOO, Jeff .... 617-327-6777. 233 D
jeff_choo@mspp.edu
CHOONOO, John .... 646-312-2196. 316 J
John.Choonoo@baruch.cuny.edu
CHOPIN, Connie .... 337-373-0011. 203 J
connie.chopin@solacc.edu
CHOPIN, Connie .... 337-373-0011. 204 D
connie.chopin@solacc.edu
CHOPKA, John, A .... 717-796-4780. 423 L
jchopka@messiah.edu
CHOPP, Rebecca, S .... 610-328-8314. 433 I
rchopp1@swarthmore.edu
CHORAM, Iotaka .... 671-734-1812. 546 D
ichoram@piu.edu
CHORBAJIAN, Gil .... 518-694-7394. 313 B
gil.chorbajian@acphs.edu
CHORNEY, Doris .... 215-965-4051. 424 D
dchorney@moore.edu
CHOROSZY, Melisa, N .... 775-784-6181. 294 J
choroszy@admin.unr.edu
CHOTTINER, Gregg .... 212-217-3400. 324 C
gregg_chottiner@fitnyc.edu
CHOU, David .... 601-984-1040. 270 C
dchou@umc.edu
CHOU, Lexer .... 808-455-0248. 137 A
achou@hawaii.edu
CHOW, Fred .... 408-741-2635... 75 L
fred.chow@westvalley.edu
CHOW, Raymond .... 650-358-6742... 64 A
chow@smccd.edu
CHOW, Timothy .... 812-877-8910. 172 C
timothy.chow@rose-hulman.edu
CHOWDHURY, Faruque . 908-737-3300. 302 F
fchowdhu@kean.edu
CHOWEN, Jodi .... 808-675-3260. 135 C
jodi.chowen@byuh.edu
CHOWN, Deborah .... 413-775-1832. 231 E
chown@gcc.mass.edu
CHOWNING, John, E ..... 270-789-5520. 193 D
jechowning@campbellsville.edu
CHOY, Jonathan .... 562-903-4742... 29 L
jonathan.choy@biola.edu
CHREST, Erin .... 410-225-2493. 216 C
echrest@mica.edu
CHRESTAY, Joan, F .... 610-660-1226. 432 E
joan.chrestay@sju.edu
CHRISLER, Jennifer, S .... 413-585-2040. 236 H
jchrisler@smith.edu
CHRISMAN, Dana .... 319-208-5017. 182 G
dchrisman@scciowa.edu
CHRISMAN, Rick .... 518-580-8340. 341 A
rchrisma@skidmore.edu
CHRISMAN, Tammy, A ... 757-446-8447. 504 E
chrismta@evms.edu
CHRISNER, Carl .... 417-862-9533. 274 F
cchrisner@globaluniversity.edu
CHRISOPE, Linda .... 314-392-2231. 278 B
chrislc@mobap.edu
CHRISPENS, Pamela .... 951-785-2002... 50 B
pchrispe@lasierra.edu
CHRIST, Andrew .... 201-200-3191. 303 F
achrist@njcu.edu
CHRIST, Barbara, J .... 814-865-2541. 426 A
ebf@psu.edu
CHRIST, Brad .... 541-552-6451. 406 C
christb@sou.edu
CHRIST, Suzanne .... 618-545-3069. 149 D
schrist@kaskaskia.edu
CHRISTAL, Melodie, E .... 785-670-1876. 191 D
melodie.christal@washburn.edu
CHRISTALDI, Antoinette . 610-526-1382. 409 F
antoinette.christaldi@theamericancollege.edu
CHRISTEL, Mark, A .... 330-263-2483. 377 H
mchristel@wooster.edu
CHRISTENBERRY, Reid .. 931-372-3387. 460 A
rchristenberry@tntech.edu
CHRISTENBURY,
Elizabeth, S .... 704-894-2700. 353 J
bechristenbury@davidson.edu
CHRISTENSEN, Angela ... 612-659-6229. 259 D
angela.christensen@minneapolis.edu
CHRISTENSEN, April .... 660-263-3900. 272 A
aprilc@cccb.edu
CHRISTENSEN,
Barbara, W .... 650-574-6560... 64 A
christensen@smccd.edu
CHRISTENSEN, Bill .... 641-472-1156. 180 N
bchristensen@mum.edu
CHRISTENSEN, Charles .. 419-448-3268. 389 J
christensenc@tiffin.edu
CHRISTENSEN, David ..... 207-799-5979. 211 E
CHRISTENSEN, Edward ... 732-263-5500. 303 C
echriste@monmouth.edu
CHRISTENSEN, Edward ... 732-571-3450. 303 C
echriste@monmouth.edu
CHRISTENSEN, Holly ...... 912-510-3303. 123 B
hchristensen@ccga.edu
CHRISTENSEN,
Jeffrey, T .... 217-333-1216. 162 A
jchriste@illinois.edu
CHRISTENSEN, John, E .. 402-554-2311. 293 A
johnchristensen@unomaha.edu
CHRISTENSEN,
Jolene, D .... 507-933-7538. 255 I
jolene@gustavus.edu
CHRISTENSEN,
Kathleen, E .... 512-223-7053. 466 I
kchriste@austincc.edu
CHRISTENSEN, Keith, J .. 563-387-1506. 180 M
chriskei@luther.edu
CHRISTENSEN, Laure ..... 816-584-6810. 280 C
laure.christensen@park.edu
CHRISTENSEN, Lisa, M .. 802-258-9259. 499 F
lmchrist@marlboro.edu
CHRISTENSEN, Marc ...... 214-768-3051. 481 A
dean@engr.smu.edu
CHRISTENSEN, Matt ...... 707-256-3343... 55 F
mchristensen@napavalley.edu
CHRISTENSEN, Michael .. 808-675-3935. 135 C
christem@byuh.edu
CHRISTENSEN,
Nicolette, D .... 215-572-2901. 409 H
christen@arcadia.edu
CHRISTENSEN, Rocky ..... 660-263-3900. 272 A
rockyc@cccb.edu
CHRISTENSEN, Scott ...... 972-438-6932. 478 C
schstnsn@parkercc.edu
CHRISTENSEN, Stephen . 949-214-3198... 41 I
stephen.christensen@cui.edu
CHRISTENSEN, Tracie ..... 310-794-2308... 71 C
traciec@support.ucla.edu
CHRISTENSEN, William .. 435-652-7887. 497 E
christenb@dixie.edu
CHRISTENSON, Larry ..... 478-445-5160. 125 A
larry.christenson@gcsu.edu
CHRISTENSON, Mike ...... 612-659-6499. 259 D
mike.christenson@minneapolis.edu
CHRISTENSON,
Timothy, J .... 571-557-4594. 544 L
timothy.christenson2@dodiis.mil
CHRISTENSON-JONES,
Marybeth .... 218-755-3966. 258 A
mchristensonjones@bemidjistate.edu
CHRISTIAN, Beth .... 570-389-4102. 427 H
bchristi@bloomu.edu
CHRISTIAN, Clayton, T ... 406-444-0374. 286 G
cchristian@montana.edu
CHRISTIAN, Donal .... 718-270-6081. 319 A
dchristian@mec.cuny.edu
CHRISTIAN, Donald .... 512-313-3000. 469 L
donald.christian@concordia.edu
CHRISTIAN, Donald, P .... 845-257-3288. 342 B
president@newpaltz.edu
CHRISTIAN, Eric .... 340-693-1491. 555 E
echrist@live.uvi.edu
CHRISTIAN, Jamie .... 601-984-1738. 270 C
jnchristian@umc.edu
CHRISTIAN, Jim .... 303-753-6046... 85 B
jchristian@rmcad.edu
CHRISTIAN, Kristeen, R .. 407-582-2909. 118 M
kchristian6@valenciacollege.edu
CHRISTIAN, Linda .... 800-962-7682. 285 A
lchristian@wma.edu
CHRISTIAN, Sonya .... 661-395-4211... 49 N
sonya.christian@bakersfieldcollege.edu
CHRISTIAN, Susan, C .... 609-895-5768. 305 D
christian@rider.edu
CHRISTIAN, Tim .... 518-355-4000. 457 B
tchristian@mabts.edu
CHRISTIAN DARK,
Okianer .... 202-806-8000... 95 G
okianer.c.dark@howard.edu
CHRISTIANO, Patricia ..... 914-674-7622. 330 J
pchristiano@mercy.edu
CHRISTIANSEN, Claudia 620-431-2820. 189 D
cchristiansen@neosho.edu
CHRISTIANSEN,
Douglas .... 615-322-2111. 463 G
douglas.christiansen@vanderbilt.edu
CHRISTIANSEN, Heath ... 402-872-2221. 291 E
hchristiansen@peru.edu
CHRISTIANSEN,
Jeanne, M .... 208-885-7941. 139 D
jeannec@uidaho.edu
CHRISTIANSEN, Kari ...... 218-855-8060. 258 B
kchristi@clcmn.edu
CHRISTIE, Marla .... 828-726-2203. 358 E
mchristie@cccti.edu
CHRISTIE, N. Bradley ..... 864-379-8872. 443 F
nbc@erskine.edu
CHRISTIE, Pamela, L ...... 989-837-4212. 248 C
christie@northwood.edu
CHRISTIE, Ray, L .... 989-774-7062. 240 N
chris2r@cmich.edu
CHRISTIE, Tori .... 712-325-3276. 179 L
tchristie@iwcc.edu
CHRISTIENSEN, Jared .... 847-317-8159. 160 M
jchristen@tiu.edu
CHRISTISON, Dominic ... 610-799-1560. 421 I
dchristison@lccc.edu
CHRISTMAN,
Harold (Bud), G .... 828-689-1102. 356 F
bchristman@mhc.edu
CHRISTMAN, Pamela ...... 401-456-8803. 439 F
pchristman@ric.edu
CHRISTMAN, Paul .... 307-268-2633. 542 X
pchristman@caspercollege.edu
CHRISTMAN, Rick .... 740-474-7217. 385 L
rchristman@ohiochristian.edu
CHRISTMAN, Vanessa ..... 610-526-6594. 410 J
vchristma@brynmawr.edu
CHRISTMAS, Erica, G ..... 803-938-3851. 448 F
mcleodeg@uscsumter.edu
CHRISTMON,
Kenneth, C .... 260-481-6605. 168 C
christmk@ipfw.edu
CHRISTOFFERS,
Pamela, M .... 515-263-6023. 178 G
pchristoffers@grandview.edu
CHRISTOFFERSON,
Kimberlee, K .... 724-946-7247. 437 B
christkk@westminster.edu
CHRISTOFFERSON,
Martin, G .... 607-844-8222. 347 I
christm@tc3.edu
CHRISTOPHER, Aaron .... 925-969-3581... 49 B
achristopher@jfku.edu
CHRISTOPHER, Curtis .... 740-420-2847. 385 L
cchristopher@ohiochristian.edu
CHRISTOPHER, Dan .... 518-631-9843. 348 K
christopherd@uniongraduatecollege.edu
CHRISTOPHER, Greg ...... 513-745-3414. 393 H
CHRISTOPHER, Greg, T .. 417-268-6009. 271 I
gchristopher@gobbc.edu
CHRISTOPHER, Jennifer . 201-360-4061. 302 D
jchristopher@hccc.edu
CHRISTOPHER, Kenneth . 816-584-6846. 280 C
kenneth.christopher@park.edu
CHRISTOPHER, Mario .... 312-332-0707. 160 J
CHRISTOPHER, Mary ...... 707-654-1050... 31 I
mchristopher@csum.edu
CHRISTOPHER, Renny .... 805-437-8094... 32 I
renny.christopher@csuci.edu
CHRISTOPHER, Robert .... 563-333-6260. 182 B
ChristopherRobert@sau.edu
CHRISTOPHER,
Ronald, J .... 716-880-2485. 330 F
ronald.j.christopher@medaille.edu
CHRISTOPHER-HICKS,
Joann .... 410-951-3933. 220 B
jchristopher-hicks@coppin.edu
CHRISTOPHERSON,
Carolyn .... 831-459-4886... 72 C
carolync@ucsc.edu
CHRISTOPHERSON,
Karen .... 707-468-3091... 54 B
kchristo@mendocino.edu
CHRISTOPHERSON,
Michelle .... 218-281-8679. 264 E
mchristo@umn.edu
CHRISTOPHERSON,
Neal, J .... 509-527-5056. 525 E
christnj@whitman.edu
CHRISTY, Benjamin, C ... 716-878-6326. 343 A
christy@buffalostate.edu
CHRISTY, Dick .... 910-521-6560. 369 B
dick.christy@uncp.edu
CHRISTY, Gregory, E ...... 712-707-7100. 181 H
president@nwciowa.edu
CHRISTY, John, R .... 256-961-7763..... 8 F
John.Christy@uah.edu
CHRISTY, Jon, A .... 563-387-1016. 180 M
chrijo01@luther.edu
CHRISTY, Kathleen .... 716-829-7801. 323 D
christyk@dyc.edu
CHRISTY, Kathy .... 417-447-6963. 279 K
christyk@otc.edu
CHRISTY, Michelle, D ..... 617-324-9022. 233 B
CHRISTY, Stephanie .... 704-991-0358. 364 C
CHRITE, E. LaBrent .... 973-655-4304. 303 D
chritee@mail.montclair.edu
CHRONISTER, Lynne ...... 251-460-6333..... 9 E
lchronister@southalabama.edu

CHRUSZCZYK, Cynthia, A .... 305-899-3125... 98 O
cchruszczyk@barry.edu
CHRYSANTHOU, Juanita 832-813-6504. 476 A
juanita.chrysanthou@lonestar.edu
CHRZASTEK, OP, Brian .. 202-495-3842... 96 C
bchrzastek@dhs.edu
CHU, Don .... 858-642-8339... 55 J
dchu@nu.edu
CHU, Dragon .... 512-444-8082. 485 B
ychu@thsu.edu
CHU, Jason, Y .... 425-558-0299. 519 B
jchu@digipen.edu
CHU, Rose .... 651-999-5959. 259 C
rose.chu@metrostate.edu
CHUA, Nate .... 641-844-5473. 179 J
nate.chua@iavalley.edu
CHUCHIAK, John, F .... 417-836-5425. 278 E
johnchuchiak@missouristate.edu
CHUDNOFSKY, Robert ... 707-778-3628... 65 B
rchudnofsky@santarosa.edu
CHUDNOVSKY, Marina .. 847-324-5588. 163 H
CHUDY-SZCZUR, Beverly .... 716-926-8940. 326 B
bchudy@hilbert.edu
CHUK, Bonnie .... 617-236-8800. 226 F
bchuk@fisher.edu
CHUKS, Samuel .... 251-405-7021..... 2 D
schuks@bishop.edu
CHULVICK, Charles, E .... 908-526-1200. 305 B
cchulvic@raritanval.edu
CHUMAN, Jerilyn .... 949-582-4573... 67 C
jchuman@saddleback.edu
CHUN, Edna .... 336-334-5167. 369 A
e_chun@uncg.edu
CHUN, Leanne .... 808-455-0676. 137 A
leannech@hawaii.edu
CHUN, Mi Sun .... 770-279-0507. 124 I
misun.chun@gcuniv.edu
CHUN, Patrick .... 561-297-3199. 114 L
pchun@fau.edu
CHUN, Victoria .... 315-228-7611. 320 F
vchun@colgate.edu
CHUNG, Bernie .... 610-896-1106. 418 F
bchung@haverford.edu
CHUNG, Chih-Ming (Ryan) .... 815-226-4186. 157 C
CChung@rockford.edu
CHUNG, Christina .... 661-362-3127... 40 E
christina.chung@canyons.edu
CHUNG, Jae Young .... 323-731-2383... 57 I
jychung@psuca.edu
CHUNG, Jaeyeon, L .... 847-866-3877. 145 E
jaeyeon.chung@garrett.edu
CHUNG, Jin .... 213-252-5100... 26 A
CHUNG, Lucy .... 847-866-3877. 140 D
lucy.chung@seabury.edu
CHUNG, Peggy .... 718-779-1430. 336 D
pchung@plazacollege.edu
CHUNG, Russell .... 614-688-1698. 386 E
chung.592@osu.edu
CHUNG, Sean .... 240-684-2542. 219 F
enroll@umuc.edu
CHUNG, Silvan .... 808-845-9404. 136 G
silvan@hawaii.edu
CHUNG, Wing-Kit .... 971-722-4250. 407 D
wchung@pcc.edu
CHUNG-HOON, Tanise ... 801-422-4403. 495 D
tanise@byu.edu
CHUNN, Robert .... 813-253-7260. 106 M
rchunn@hccfl.edu
CHUPP, Tim .... 616-222-3000. 245 C
tchupp@kuyper.edu
CHURCH, Cathy .... 928-350-4100... 17 K
cchurch@prescott.edu
CHURCH, Daniel, K .... 425-602-3003. 516 K
dchurch@bastyr.edu
CHURCH, David, B .... 206-281-2602. 523 C
dchurch@spu.edu
CHURCH, Jennifer, H ..... 517-264-7143. 250 B
jhchurch@sienaheights.edu
CHURCH, Lori .... 843-349-2751. 442 E
lchurch@coastal.edu
CHURCH, Marjorie, R ..... 336-841-4692. 355 C
mchurch@highpoint.edu
CHURCH, Melinda .... 614-247-4573. 386 E
church.104@osu.edu
CHURCH, Roy, A .... 440-365-5222. 383 B
CHURCH, Vicki .... 503-682-1862. 407 B
vchurch@pioneerpacific.edu
CHURCH-GONZALES, Hunter .... 559-730-3805... 40 I
hunterc@cos.edu
CHURCHILL, Carol, A ..... 989-386-6602. 247 B
cchurchill@midmich.edu
CHURCHILL, Clifford, W . 772-546-5534. 106 N
cliffchurchill@hsbc.edu
CHURCHILL, Mark .... 617-585-1130. 234 I
mark.churchill@necmusic.edu
CHURCHILL, Mary .... 978-542-4097. 230 E
mary.churchill@salemstate.edu
CHURCHILL, Monte .... 956-447-6631. 480 I
mchurch@southtexascollege.edu
CHURCHILL, Robert .... 573-884-9080. 283 C
churchillr@missouri.edu
CHURCHILL, Sally, J ...... 734-763-5553. 251 C
sjc@umich.edu
CHURCHILL, Steve .... 510-559-5264... 57 F
schurchill@plts.edu
CHUSID, Eileen .... 212-410-8127. 333 E
echusid@nycpm.edu
CHUTE, Katherine .... 951-343-5067... 30 H
kchute@calbaptist.edu
CHUTE, Mary .... 609-292-6201. 308 A
mchute@njstatelib.org
CHUTE, Patricia .... 516-686-3939. 333 H
pchute@nyit.edu
CHYCINSKI, Jodi .... 616-331-2025. 243 C
chycinsj@gvsu.edu
CHYKA, Robert, D .... 716-880-2343. 330 F
robert.d.chyka@medaille.edu
CHYR, Fred, A .... 909-593-3511... 72 E
fchyr@laverne.edu
CHYTKA, Evelyn, J .... 307-766-2398. 543 I
jchytka@uwyo.edu
CIABOCCHI, Elizabeth .... 516-299-3990. 329 C
liz.ciabocchi@liu.edu
CIACCIO, Dolores .... 631-420-2411. 346 B
dolores.ciaccio@farmingdale.edu
CIACCIO, Jen .... 718-390-3801. 350 B
jen.ciaccio@wagner.edu
CIACIUCH, Denis .... 419-267-1407. 385 F
dciaciuch@northweststate.edu
CIANCHETTA, Susan, A .. 410-827-5811. 214 C
scianchetta@chesapeake.edu
CIANCI, Karen .... 559-453-2273... 45 D
karen.cianci@fresno.edu
CIARALDI, Penne .... 802-828-4060. 501 C
ciaraldp@ccv.edu
CIARAVINO, Asia .... 210-434-6711. 477 N
ahciaravino@lake.ollusa.edu
CIBIRKA, Roman, M .... 706-721-3096. 126 B
rcibirka@gru.edu
CIBUZAR, Jean .... 202-651-5282... 95 C
jean.cibuzar@gallaudet.edu
CICALA, RSM, Joseph, J 610-796-8211. 409 E
joe.cicala@alvernia.edu
CICCARELLI, Denise .... 843-953-5018. 443 A
ciccarellimd@cofc.edu
CICCARELLI, Mark .... 740-264-5591. 379 F
mciccarelli@egcc.edu
CICCAZZO, Michele .... 305-348-5344. 115 B
Michele.Ciccazzo@fiu.edu
CICCOMOSCOLO, Lori .... 401-874-5454. 440 D
lecicco@uri.edu
CICERO, John .... 858-309-3411... 55 J
jcicero@nu.edu
CICHOCKI, Eileen .... 707-468-3067... 54 B
ecichock@mendocino.edu
CICHOMSKA, Grace, J .... 708-524-6288. 144 C
gcichomska@dom.edu
CICHON, Mark .... 920-498-5759. 541 B
mark.cichon@nwtc.edu
CICIRELLI, Anna .... 201-761-6036. 306 L
acicirelli@saintpeters.edu
CICIRELLO, Pam .... 501-812-2774... 22 G
pcicirello@pulaskitech.edu
CID, Carmen, R .... 860-465-5295... 87 L
cid@easternct.edu
CIEJKA, Patricia, A .... 409-772-8745. 493 C
pciejka@utmb.edu
CIEPLY, Kevin .... 404-872-3593. 121 C
kcieply@johnmarshall.edu
CIFONE, Rocky .... 949-582-4777... 67 C
rcifone@saddleback.edu
CIFRA, Jason .... 808-934-2510. 136 F
cifra@hawaii.edu
CIFUENTES, Luis .... 361-825-2577. 483 F
luis.cifuentes@tamucc.edu
CIGANOVIC, Denny, D .... 843-953-5692. 443 A
ciganovicd@cofc.edu
CIGARROA, Francisco, G .... 512-499-4201. 491 A
chancellor@utsystem.edu
CIGELMAN, M. Susan .... 515-244-4221. 175 C
cigelmans@aib.edu
CIHA, Lisa .... 319-399-8669. 176 G
lciha@coe.edu
CIHLAR, Larry .... 715-422-5308. 540 D
larry.cihlar@mstc.edu
CILENTO, Eugene, V .... 304-293-4157. 530 D
gene.cilento@mail.wvu.edu
CILIBERTI, Anne .... 973-720-3179. 308 I
cilibertia@wpunj.edu
CILIBERTI, Scott .... 415-575-6143... 31 D
sciliberti@ciis.edu
CILIBERTI, Scott .... 415-369-5365... 45 I
sciliberti@ggu.edu
CILLAY, David .... 509-335-5454. 525 A
dcillay@wsu.edu
CILLO, Robert .... 303-546-3506... 83 F
bcillo@naropa.edu
CIMALORE, Ann .... 205-853-1200..... 5 B
acimalore@jeffstateonline.com
CIMBOLIC, Peter .... 614-251-4690. 386 B
cimbolicp@ohiodominican.edu
CIMINELLI, Mary .... 972-273-3130. 471 B
marygciminelli@dcccd.edu
CIMINELLI, Thomas, E ... 716-888-2250. 316 C
ciminel1@canisius.edu
CIMINO, Chris .... 865-974-9880. 463 C
cimino@utk.edu
CIMITILE, Maria .... 616-331-2400. 243 C
cimitilm@gvsu.edu
CIMORELLI, Nick .... 843-863-7581. 441 H
ncimorel@csuniv.edu
CIMPERMAN, Jennifer .... 216-368-7577. 375 J
jennifer.cimperman@case.edu
CIMPL, Linda .... 605-995-2896. 450 A
licimpl@dwu.edu
CINAR, Ali .... 312-567-3637. 147 F
cinar@iit.edu
CINI, Marie .... 301-985-7174. 219 F
marie.cini@umuc.edu
CINNAMON, Gary .... 760-750-4675... 35 A
cinnamon@csusm.edu
CINTORINO, Salvatore ... 860-832-1889... 87 K
cintorino@ccsu.edu
CINTRON, Arnaldo .... 787-864-2222. 550 D
acintron@inter.edu
CINTRON, Carmen .... 787-728-1515. 555 D
crcintron@sagrado.edu
CINTRON, Edgardo .... 787-857-3600. 550 A
ecintron@br.inter.edu
CINTRON, Filonena .... 787-857-3600. 550 A
scintron@br.inter.edu
CINTRON, Josue .... 787-753-6000. 549 D
jcintron@icprjc.edu
CINTRON, Nancy, A .... 718-960-8366. 318 A
nancy.cintron@lehman.cuny.edu
CINTRON, Raul .... 787-764-0000. 555 B
raul.cintron4@upr.edu
CINTRON, Rene .... 504-671-6138. 203 A
rcintr@dcc.edu
CINTRON-OTERO, Carmen .... 787-993-8922. 554 A
carmen.cintron2@upr.edu
CIOCE, Michael .... 609-894-9311. 299 I
mcioce@bcc.edu
CIOPPA, Lee .... 212-799-5000. 328 B
CIOSEK, Edward .... 413-748-3108. 236 I
eciosek@springfieldcollege.edu
CIOTOLI, Carlo .... 212-443-1297. 334 D
carlo.ciotoli@nyu.edu
CIPFL, Joseph, J .... 618-537-6462. 152 G
jjcipfl@mckendree.edu
CIPOLLA, Anthony .... 845-848-7814. 322 G
anthony.cipolla@dc.edu
CIPRES, Elizabeth .... 949-451-5410... 67 B
ecipres@ivc.edu
CIPRIANI, Colleen .... 614-234-5828. 384 J
cciprian@mccn.edu
CIPRIANO, Eli .... 713-743-8901. 489 A
ecipriano@uh.edu
CIPRIANO, Eli, D .... 713-743-8901. 489 B
ecipriano@central.uh.edu
CIPRIANO, Matt, J .... 215-968-8255. 411 B
cipriano@bucks.edu
CIPRO, Cheryl .... 914-395-2535. 340 E
ccipro@sarahlawrence.edu
CIPULLO, Donald, D ...... 973-655-5105. 303 D
cipullod@mail.montclair.edu
CIRAULO, Paul .... 212-517-0531. 330 E
pciraulo@mmm.edu
CIRCE, Scott .... 305-223-4561. 112 B
scirce@sjvcs.edu
CIRI, Michael .... 907-796-6452... 11 A
michael.ciri@uas.alaska.edu
CIRI, Michael .... 907-796-6534... 11 A
maciri@uas.alaska.edu
CIRILLO, Laureen .... 413-565-1006. 222 F
lcirillo@baypath.edu
CIRILLO, Robert .... 914-606-6981. 350 F
Robert.Cirillo@sunywcc.edu
CIRILLO, Susan, E .... 978-542-6232. 230 E
scirillo@salemstate.edu
CIRMO, Christopher .... 715-346-4224. 538 A
ccirmo@uwsp.edu
CISAR, Mary .... 507-786-3015. 264 B
cisar@stolaf.edu
CISCO, OSB, Bede .... 812-357-6611. 173 A
bcisco@saintmeinrad.edu
CISKANIK, John, F .... 540-636-2900. 503 L
ciskanik@christendom.edu
CISNA, Jennifer .... 714-338-1702... 18 I
jennifer.cisna@phoenix.edu
CISNA, Shawn .... 309-796-5915. 140 E
cisnas@bhc.edu
CISNEROS, Maria .... 504-671-5603. 203 A
mcisne@dcc.edu
CISNEROS, Teo .... 210-924-4338. 467 E
teo.cisneros@bua.edu
CISSELL, Jason, A .... 502-272-8329. 192 E
jcissell@bellarmine.edu
CISSNA, Tamara .... 765-983-1295. 165 G
cissnta@earlham.edu
CITARELLA, Alberto .... 802-656-3244. 500 F
alberto.citarella@uvm.edu
CITRON, Chaim .... 323-937-3763... 77 F
ccitron@yoec.edu
CIUFFO, Patricia .... 212-463-0400. 348 B
patricia.ciuffo@touro.edu
CIULLO, Carol .... 888-254-4238. 503 A
cciullo@cdu.edu
CIVELLO, Dianna .... 716-888-8220. 316 C
civillod@canisius.edu
CLABBY, William, J .... 512-448-8704. 479 C
bclabby@stedwards.edu
CLACK, Olivia .... 870-574-4481... 23 G
oclack@sautech.edu
CLAFFEY, JR., George, F .... 860-515-3777... 87 I
gclaffey@charteroak.edu
CLAFFEY, Marian, A .... 773-508-7473. 151 H
mclaffe@luc.edu
CLAGETT, Craig, A .... 410-386-8163. 214 A
cclagett@carrollcc.edu
CLAGGETT, Mindy .... 937-298-3399. 382 K
mindy.claggett@kc.edu
CLAGHORN, Patricia ...... 856-468-5000. 302 C
pclaghorn@gccnj.edu
CLAGUE, Roger .... 707-864-7264... 66 G
roger.clague@solano.edu
CLAIBORN, Candis .... 509-335-5593. 525 A
claiborn@wsu.edu
CLAIRE, Michael .... 650-574-6222... 64 C
clairem@smccd.edu
CLAMURRO, William, H . 620-341-5899. 186 D
wclamurr@emporia.edu
CLANCY, Amanda .... 303-678-3736... 81 N
amanda.clancy@frontrange.edu
CLANCY, Pauline .... 617-296-8300. 227 I
pauline_clancy@laboure.edu
CLANCY, SJ, Tim, R .... 509-313-6701. 520 A
clancy@gonzaga.edu
CLANG, Heather .... 617-349-8769. 228 B
hclang@lesley.edu
CLANTON, Ann .... 251-575-8204..... 1 C
aclanton@ascc.edu
CLANTON, Janet .... 573-897-5000. 276 E
CLANTON, Karen .... 256-824-6013..... 8 F
karen.clanton@uah.edu
CLAPP, Jason .... 319-363-8213. 181 C
jclapp@mtmercy.edu
CLAPP, Kenneth, W .... 704-637-4446. 353 E
kclapp@catawba.edu
CLAPPER, Cara .... 260-459-4501. 169 C
cclapper@ibcfortwayne.edu
CLAPPER, Mark, A .... 717-361-1499. 415 H
clapperm@etown.edu
CLAPPER-DEWELL, Theophylact .... 315-858-3914. 326 E
frtheophylact@jordanville.org
CLARDY, Betsy, B .... 409-772-1991. 493 C
bbclardy@utmb.edu
CLARE, Judith .... 401-232-6090. 438 K
jclare@bryant.edu
CLARIDA, Traci .... 801-818-8900. 496 F
traci.clarida@provocollege.edu
CLARIDAY, Sandra .... 423-746-5249. 462 C
sclariday@twcnet.edu
CLARK, Alfred .... 909-593-3511... 72 E
aclark@laverne.edu
CLARK, Alfred, P .... 909-593-3511... 72 E
aclark@laverne.edu
CLARK, Alice, M .... 662-915-7482. 270 B
vcrsp@olemiss.edu
CLARK, Allen .... 940-565-2550. 490 C
allen.clark@unt.edu
CLARK, Andy, T .... 229-245-6815. 134 B
atclark@valdosta.edu
CLARK, Anita .... 262-243-5700. 532 H
anita.clark@cuw.edu
CLARK, Ann, B .... 860-727-6761... 90 A
aclark@goodwin.edu
CLARK, Annette, C .... 206-398-4000. 523 E
annclark@seattleu.edu
CLARK, Becky .... 480-858-9100... 17 P
b.clark@scnm.edu
CLARK, Benita, I .... 919-866-7894. 364 G
biclark@waketech.edu
CLARK, Bettye .... 404-880-8667. 122 J
bclark@cau.edu
CLARK, Beverly .... 228-896-2512. 268 C
beverly.clark@mgccc.edu
CLARK, Beverly, E .... 254-867-3128. 485 G
beverly.clark@systems.tstc.edu
CLARK, Billy, L .... 225-928-7770. 201 I
CLARK, Bob .... 310-506-6190... 58 H
bob.clark@pepperdine.edu
CLARK, Bonnie, M .... 352-340-4801. 110 E
clarkb@phcc.edu

CLARK, Bradd 337-482-6454. 208 D
deanclark@louisiana.edu
CLARK, Bradd 337-482-6986. 208 D
deanclark@louisiana.edu
CLARK, Brenda 803-705-4385. 441 C
clarkb@benedict.edu
CLARK, Bret 805-546-3125... 42 C
bclark@cuesta.edu
CLARK, Brian 401-427-6920. 440 A
bclark@risd.edu
CLARK, Brock 228-497-7634. 268 C
brock.clark@mgccc.edu
CLARK, Brooks 530-226-4763... 66 D
bclark@simpsonu.edu
CLARK, Bryon 580-745-2064. 399 J
bclark@se.edu
CLARK, Carol 931-221-7570. 459 B
clarkc@apsu.edu
CLARK, Carol, D 931-221-7570. 459 B
clarkc@apsu.edu
CLARK, Cate 303-464-2306... 84 K
ctclark@redstone.edu
CLARK, Catherine 315-268-2209. 320 A
cclark@clarkson.edu
CLARK, Charles 228-896-3809. 268 C
charles.clark@mgccc.edu
CLARK, Charles 706-737-1738. 126 B
cwclark@gru.edu
CLARK, Charles, E 920-683-4710. 538 E
charles.clark@uwc.edu
CLARK, Charles, L 309-341-7399. 150 A
clclark@knox.edu
CLARK, Cherry 919-466-4400... 96 F
CLARK, Chip 903-566-7431. 492 D
cclark@uttyler.edu
CLARK, Chris 618-634-3233. 158 M
chrisc@shawneecc.edu
CLARK, Craig, R 607-587-3913. 345 D
CLARK, Cynthia, A 860-628-4751... 90 D
cclark@lincolncollegene.edu
CLARK, Dan 503-838-8483. 406 E
clarkd@wou.edu
CLARK, Dana 570-740-0422. 422 G
dclark@luzerne.edu
CLARK, Daniel 630-752-5593. 163 F
daniel.clark@wheaton.edu
CLARK, Daniel 616-234-4354. 243 B
dbclark@grcc.edu
CLARK, Daniel 425-602-3064. 516 K
dclark@bastyr.edu
CLARK, David 559-638-3641... 69 A
david.clark@reedleycollege.edu
CLARK, David 212-346-1590. 335 J
dclark@pace.edu
CLARK, David 651-638-6553. 253 K
d-clark@bethel.edu
CLARK, David 701-224-5434. 372 B
david.clark@bismarckstate.edu
CLARK, David, W 714-556-3610... 74 D
officeofthepresident@vanguard.edu
CLARK, Dawn 610-789-6700. 431 C
dclark@prismcareerinstitute.edu
CLARK, Dean 262-551-6000. 532 D
dean@carthage.edu
CLARK, Debbie 309-457-2125. 153 D
dclark@monmouthcollege.edu
CLARK, Deborah 404-225-4714. 121 B
dclark@atlantatech.edu
CLARK, Deborah 802-586-7711. 500 E
dclark@sterlingcollege.edu
CLARK, Deborah, E 607-871-2170. 313 E
clarkd@alfred.edu
CLARK, Debra 970-943-7005... 86 I
dclark@western.edu
CLARK, Denise 301-405-6266. 219 B
djclark@umd.edu
CLARK, Dennis 815-802-8606. 149 C
dclark@kcc.edu
CLARK, Diane 318-371-3035. 203 E
dclark@ltc.edu
CLARK, Donald 207-602-2274. 213 A
dclark@une.edu
CLARK, Donald, A 417-836-5509. 278 E
donclark@missouristate.edu
CLARK, Douglas, E 540-365-4551. 504 L
dclark@ferrum.edu
CLARK, Douglas, P 260-422-5561. 167 B
dpclark@indianatech.edu
CLARK, Douglas, R 951-785-2244... 50 B
dclark@lasierra.edu
CLARK, Ed 507-389-6651. 259 G
edmund.clark@mnsu.edu
CLARK, Elizabeth 660-785-7200. 282 L
eclark@truman.edu
CLARK, Elizabeth 617-541-5332. 232 G
eclark@rcc.mass.edu
CLARK, Eric 937-258-8251. 381 F
eric.clark@icb.edu
CLARK, Frank, C 843-792-2211. 445 B
clarkf@musc.edu
CLARK, Fred 508-531-6189. 229 D
fred.clark@bridgew.edu
CLARK, G. Reynolds 412-624-7721. 435 C
clark@pitt.edu
CLARK, Gail 765-987-1439. 165 G
clarkga@earlham.edu
CLARK, Gary, A 785-532-5590. 188 A
gac@ksu.edu
CLARK, Gary, C 405-744-6384. 397 H
gary.clark@okstate.edu
CLARK, Gary, E 864-294-3460. 444 C
gary.clark@furman.edu
CLARK, Gaye 910-410-1804. 362 I
agclark@richmondcc.edu
CLARK, Geno 706-396-8118. 130 C
gclark@paine.edu
CLARK, George 509-963-2323. 517 F
clarkg@cwu.edu
CLARK, Ginger 813-253-7022. 106 M
gclark@hccfl.edu
CLARK, Greg 502-895-3411. 197 F
gclark@lpts.edu
CLARK, Harold, E 504-286-5119. 206 K
hclark@suno.edu
CLARK, Irvin 404-297-9522. 126 A
clarki@gptc.edu
CLARK, J. Milton 909-537-5032... 34 E
mclark@csusb.edu
CLARK, Jack 205-329-7900..... 3 B
jack.clark@vc.edu
CLARK, Jacqueline 256-549-8695..... 3 M
jclark@gadsdenstate.edu
CLARK, Jacqueline 718-262-5213. 319 F
jclark@york.cuny.edu
CLARK, James 763-576-4797. 257 Q
jclark@anokatech.edu
CLARK, James 513-556-4615. 390 G
clark2j9@ucmail.uc.edu
CLARK, James, A 334-844-4765..... 1 G
clarkj3@auburn.edu
CLARK, James, L 816-322-0110. 271 O
president@calvary.edu
CLARK, James, T 304-336-8043. 530 A
clarkj@westliberty.edu
CLARK, Jamie, K 740-588-1222. 394 C
jclark@zanestate.edu
CLARK, Jane, E 301-405-2437. 219 B
jeclark@umd.edu
CLARK, Janet 812-535-5182. 172 F
jclark@smwc.edu
CLARK, Jeanian 540-868-7122. 512 H
jclark@lfcc.edu
CLARK, Jeffrey, A 518-580-5929. 341 A
jclark@skidmore.edu
CLARK, Jennifer 724-589-2858. 434 B
jclark@thiel.edu
CLARK, Jennifer, R 312-915-7819. 151 H
jclark7@luc.edu
CLARK, Jerry 601-984-5012. 270 C
jclark@umc.edu
CLARK, Jill 712-325-3285. 179 L
jclark@iwcc.edu
CLARK, Jimmy 479-979-1481... 25 J
jclark@ozarks.edu
CLARK, Joan 914-633-2046. 327 C
jclark@iona.edu
CLARK, Joan 304-357-4750. 527 H
joanclark@ucwv.edu
CLARK, Joanne 405-466-3489. 395 N
jclark@langston.edu
CLARK, John, D 404-413-5057. 126 E
johnclark@gsu.edu
CLARK, John, P 603-535-2750. 298 G
jpclark@plymouth.edu
CLARK, John, S 865-694-6601. 461 D
jclark@pstcc.edu
CLARK, Joy 334-244-3600..... 2 A
jclark@aum.edu
CLARK, Karen 765-973-8257. 167 G
krclark@iue.edu
CLARK, Karen 254-299-8689. 476 D
kclark@mclennan.edu
CLARK, Kathleen 808-543-8022. 135 F
kclark@hpu.edu
CLARK, Kellie, E 708-709-3725. 156 A
kclark@prairiestate.edu
CLARK, Kevin 215-204-7759. 433 K
keviclar@temple.edu
CLARK, Kim, B 208-496-1111. 137 H
clarkk@byui.edu
CLARK, Kimbrely, S 678-359-5108. 127 A
kimbrelyc@gordonstate.edu
CLARK, Kristin 714-432-5765... 39 K
kclark@occ.cccd.edu
CLARK, Kyle 806-742-4250. 487 D
kyle.clark@ttu.edu
CLARK, Kym 432-264-5124. 473 E
kclark@howardcollege.edu
CLARK, L. Nathan, N 775-856-2266. 293 K
nclark@ccnn4u.com
CLARK, Lanette 406-758-6328. 286 C
lclark@fpcc.edu
CLARK, Laron, J 757-727-5356. 505 F
laron.clark@hamptonu.edu
CLARK, Larry 253-589-5602. 518 B
larry.clark@cptc.edu
CLARK, Lawrence, S 910-962-7301. 369 C
clarkl@uncw.edu
CLARK, Leanna 303-315-7734... 86 A
leanna.clark@ucdenver.edu
CLARK, Lela, C 910-522-5800. 369 B
lela.clark@uncp.edu
CLARK, Lesa, C 757-683-4406. 507 N
lclark@odu.edu
CLARK, Linda, J 360-442-2100. 521 A
lclark@lowercolumbia.edu
CLARK, Lloyd 502-863-7074. 194 C
lloyd_clark@georgetowncollege.edu
CLARK, Lynne 718-262-2698. 319 F
lclark@york.cuny.edu
CLARK, Margie 517-483-1461. 245 H
clarkm@lcc.edu
CLARK, Marlin 801-957-4004. 498 B
marlin.clark@slcc.edu
CLARK, Martin 937-395-8607. 382 K
martin.clark@khnetwork.org
CLARK, Mary 501-977-2011... 25 C
clark@uaccm.edu
CLARK, Mary, C 252-633-3879. 359 G
clarkm@cravencc.edu
CLARK, MaryAnn 516-299-2486. 329 D
maryann.clark@liu.edu
CLARK, OSB, Matthew ... 985-867-2245. 206 H
mrclark@sjasc.edu
CLARK, Michael 910-521-6815. 369 B
michael.clark@uncp.edu
CLARK, Michael 570-321-4249. 422 H
clark@lycoming.edu
CLARK, Michael, P 949-824-4501... 71 B
mpclark@uci.edu
CLARK, Murray, B 859-323-5220. 200 C
mbclar2@pop.uky.edu
CLARK, Nancy, L 225-578-2735. 204 O
nclark@lsu.edu
CLARK, Naoma 940-397-4544. 476 H
naoma.clark@mwsu.edu
CLARK, Nathaniel 323-357-3674... 38 B
nathanielclark@cdrewu.edu
CLARK, Nick 662-476-5075. 266 I
nclark@eastms.edu
CLARK, Nigel, N 304-293-6457. 530 D
nigel.clark@mail.wvu.edu
CLARK, Pam 989-686-9225. 242 C
pamelaclark@delta.edu
CLARK, Paul, E 610-921-7708. 409 A
pclark@alb.edu
CLARK, Phillip 727-736-5082. 113 D
pclark@schiller.edu
CLARK, R. Yvette 617-873-0171. 224 G
Yvette.Clark@cambridgecollege.edu
CLARK, Richard 404-894-1940. 125 D
rick.clark@admiss.gatech.edu
CLARK, Richard 702-895-1469. 294 I
richard.clark@unlv.edu
CLARK, Rob 585-275-4151. 349 C
rclark@rochester.edu
CLARK, Robert 404-880-6623. 122 J
rclark@cau.edu
CLARK, Robert, A 207-941-7138. 210 B
clarkr@husson.edu
CLARK, Robert, E 940-397-4179. 476 H
robert.clark@mwsu.edu
CLARK, Rodney 508-678-2811. 231 B
rodney.clark@bristolcc.edu
CLARK, Ron 309-649-6303. 160 E
ronald.clark@src.edu
CLARK, Ron, M 972-238-6277. 471 C
rclark@dcccd.edu
CLARK, S. Kay 615-366-4482. 459 A
kay.clark@tbr.edu
CLARK, III, Samuel, J 910-630-7020. 356 H
sclark@methodist.edu
CLARK, Sara, M 417-836-6105. 278 E
saraclark@missouristate.edu
CLARK, Scott 415-482-1816... 42 J
scott.clark@dominican.edu
CLARK, Scott 415-451-2833... 63 A
sclark@sfts.edu
CLARK, Shani 229-317-6926. 124 A
shani.clark@darton.edu
CLARK, Shaun 870-777-5722... 25 B
shaun.clark@uacch.edu
CLARK, Stant 317-788-3998. 173 I
sclark@uindy.edu
CLARK, Steve 541-737-4875. 406 A
steve.clark@oregonstate.edu
CLARK, Steven, P 773-244-5773. 154 G
sclark@northpark.edu
CLARK, Sunny 415-452-5384... 38 L
sclark@ccsf.edu
CLARK, Susan 517-629-0798. 239 A
sclark@albion.edu
CLARK, Susan, B 601-984-1290. 270 C
sbclark2@umc.edu
CLARK, Susan, G 330-972-7780. 390 E
sclark1@uakron.edu
CLARK, Tabitha 773-947-6309. 152 E
tclark@mccormick.edu
CLARK, Teresa 615-966-5859. 456 B
teresa.clark@lipscomb.edu
CLARK, Todd 317-632-5553. 170 T
tclark@lincolntech.com
CLARK, Todd 909-469-5473... 76 B
tclark@westernu.edu
CLARK, Todd 276-944-6529. 504 H
tclark@ehc.edu
CLARK, Tony 402-935-9400. 290 N
tclark@nechristian.edu
CLARK, Victoria 425-822-8266. 521 G
victoria.clark@northwestu.edu
CLARK, Vincent, W 718-960-8539. 318 A
vincent.clark@lehman.cuny.edu
CLARK, Wanda 336-887-3000. 355 N
wclark@laureluniversity.edu
CLARK, Wayne 501-450-1263... 21 E
clark@hendrix.edu
CLARK, Wayne, N 208-496-2510. 137 H
clarkw@byui.edu
CLARK, Wendell 706-880-8060. 128 A
wclark@lagrange.edu
CLARK, William 856-351-2602. 307 B
clark@salemcc.edu
CLARK, William 330-684-8772. 390 F
bclark3@uakron.edu
CLARK ARTIS, Roslyn .... 305-626-3600. 104 J
roslyn.artis@fmuniv.edu
CLARK-BETANCOURT,
Tammy, L 217-443-8778. 143 G
tbetancourt@dacc.edu
CLARK-EVANS, Barbara .. 913-288-7504. 187 L
bclark@kckcc.edu
CLARK-HOLLAND,
Veronica 205-247-8018..... 7 E
vclark@stillman.edu
CLARK JOHNSON,
Virginia, L 701-231-8211. 371 G
virginia.clark@ndsu.edu
CLARK-KAISER, Mary ..... 616-632-2489. 239 E
clarkmar@aquinas.edu
CLARK-TALLEY,
Christine 703-993-8757. 505 C
cclarkta@gmu.edu
CLARK-WHITE, Patricia .. 949-753-4774... 29 M
CLARKBERG, Marin, E ... 607-255-9101. 322 A
mec30@cornell.edu
CLARKE, Ann 315-443-5889. 347 C
anclarke@syr.edu
CLARKE, Ann 617-670-4421. 226 F
aclarke@fisher.edu
CLARKE, Anthony 910-410-1855. 362 I
ajclarke@richmondcc.edu
CLARKE, Arlene 770-962-7580. 127 D
aclarke@gwinnetttech.edu
CLARKE, Cara 606-759-7141. 196 B
cara.clarke@kctcs.edu
CLARKE, Claudia 607-778-5220. 315 I
clarkeck@sunybroome.edu
CLARKE, David 518-694-7252. 313 B
david.clarke@acphs.edu
CLARKE, Ed 570-372-4114. 433 H
clarkeed@susqu.edu
CLARKE, Germel 610-606-4666. 412 I
goclarke@cedarcrest.edu
CLARKE, Jennifer 315-268-3826. 320 A
Jclarke@clarkson.edu
CLARKE, Josh 731-661-5139. 462 F
jclarke@uu.edu
CLARKE, Karen, B 215-204-2606. 433 K
karen.clarke@temple.edu
CLARKE, Kathleen 914-633-2067. 327 C
kclarke@iona.edu
CLARKE, Kathy 916-348-4689... 43 F
kclarke@epic.edu
CLARKE, Kenneth, I 607-255-6002. 322 A
kic2@cornell.edu
CLARKE, Kevin 516-773-5000. 545 H
clarkek@usmma.edu
CLARKE, Malanie 212-621-4101. 318 D
maclarke@jjay.cuny.edu
CLARKE, Marcus 919-546-8314. 366 E
mclarke@shawu.edu
CLARKE, Maryellen 910-272-3324. 363 B
mclarke@robeson.edu
CLARKE, Patrick 435-586-5479. 497 A
clarke@suu.edu
CLARKE, Richard, D 845-938-3103. 545 I
8uscc@usma.edu
CLARKE, III, Robert, S ... 864-379-8775. 443 F
clarke@erskine.edu
CLARKE, Ryan 601-635-2111. 266 H
rclarke@eccc.edu

CLARKE, Shari .... 304-696-4676. 529 H
clarkes@marshall.edu
CLARKE, Sonia .... 985-858-5861. 203 B
sonia.clarke@fletcher.edu
CLARKE-TURNER, Kay .... 973-596-3082. 303 G
kay.turner@njit.edu
CLARKIN, Donna .... 615-361-7555. 454 D
dclarkin@daymarinstitute.edu
CLARKSON, Bobbie .... 423-636-7300. 462 E
bclarkson@tusculum.edu
CLARKSON, Kris, R .... 814-641-3152. 419 H
clarksk@juniata.edu
CLARKSON, Nancy, E ..... 585-785-1344. 324 D
clarksne@flcc.edu
CLARKSON, Sallie .... 843-349-2448. 442 E
sallie@coastal.edu
CLARKSON, Sarah, M .... 814-641-3161. 419 H
clarkss@juniata.edu
CLARKSON, William .... 610-917-1477. 436 C
wmclarkson@vfcc.edu
CLARY, Christine .... 802-654-2548. 500 B
cclary@smcvt.edu
CLARY, Dean .... 309-649-6316. 160 E
dean.clary@src.edu
CLARY, Donnie, O .... 252-398-6250. 353 H
claryd@chowan.edu
CLARY, Gail .... 229-931-2318. 131 G
gclary@southgatech.edu
CLARY, Jason .... 503-228-6528. 402 A
jclary@aii.edu
CLARY, Laurie .... 360-538-4009. 520 B
lclary@ghc.edu
CLARY, Michael, T .... 901-843-3940. 458 E
clary@rhodes.edu
CLARY, Nicholas .... 802-654-2390. 500 B
nclary@smcvt.edu
CLARY, Tia .... 806-720-7313. 476 B
tia.clary@lcu.edu
CLASON, Nate .... 616-222-1439. 241 F
nate.clason@cornerstone.edu
CLASS, Richard, T .... 212-472-1500. 334 B
rclass@nysid.edu
CLASSEN, Terry, L .... 715-836-5278. 536 E
classetl@uwec.edu
CLASSICK, Bede .... 360-438-4392. 522 G
fr_bede@stmartin.edu
CLATTERBUCK, Glen .... 217-479-7015. 152 D
glen.clatterbuck@mac.edu
CLAUD, Ashlee, B .... 540-831-5017. 508 C
aclaud@radford.edu
CLAUNCH, Jacqueline .... 210-486-4908. 464 I
jclaunch@alamo.edu
CLAUNCH, Jacqueline .... 210-486-4900. 464 J
jclaunch@alamo.edu
CLAUSEN, Dave .... 530-251-8826... 50 F
dclausen@lassencollege.edu
CLAUSEN, Doris .... 201-216-5189. 307 E
doris.clausen@stevens.edu
CLAUSEN, Greg .... 712-325-3228. 179 L
gclausen@iwcc.edu
CLAUSEN, Heather .... 402-844-7334. 291 I
heatherc@northeast.edu
CLAUSEN, Janice .... 661-654-3360... 32 H
jclausen@csub.edu
CLAUSER, Lisa .... 573-518-2129. 278 A
lisac@mineralarea.edu
CLAUSON, Kathleen, M .. 641-784-5064. 178 F
clauson@graceland.edu
CLAUSS, James, J .... 206-543-7444. 524 G
uwhonors@uw.edu
CLAUSS, Karl .... 610-690-5707. 433 I
kclauss1@swarthmore.edu
CLAUSSEN, Ann, E .... 610-861-1492. 424 E
meaec01@moravian.edu
CLAUSSEN, Linda, C .... 540-674-3614. 513 B
lclaussen@nr.edu
CLAUSSEN, Nicole .... 701-662-1568. 372 D
nicole.claussen@lrsc.edu
CLAVERIE, Mark .... 518-587-2100. 346 A
mark.claverie@esc.edu
CLAVIJO, Manuel .... 508-849-3205. 222 B
mclavijo@annamaria.edu
CLAVILLE, Michelle .... 757-727-5239. 505 F
michelle.claville@hamptonu.edu
CLAVIR, Kenneth, R .... 949-214-3080... 41 I
ken.clavir@cui.edu
CLAVIR, Pamela .... 949-214-3133... 41 I
pam.clavir@cui.edu
CLAWSON, Michelle .... 757-727-5474. 505 F
michelle.clawson@hamptonu.edu
CLAXTON, Brenda .... 432-264-5612. 473 E
bclaxton@howardcollege.edu
CLAXTON, Patricia .... 325-574-7607. 494 K
pclaxton@wtc.edu
CLAY, Aileen .... 603-206-8175. 296 A
aclay@ccsnh.edu
CLAY, Antoinette, M .... 732-255-0400. 304 A
aclay@ocean.edu
CLAY, Daniel .... 573-882-8524. 283 C
clayda@missouri.edu
CLAY, David, S .... 641-269-3500. 178 H
clayd@grinnell.edu
CLAY, Doreen .... 818-710-2510... 52 B
claydj@piercecollege.edu
CLAY, George, W .... 864-656-0723. 442 C
gclay@clemson.edu
CLAY, Gladys .... 904-470-8087. 102 A
gladys.clay@ewc.edu
CLAY, John, L .... 256-539-0834..... 4 E
president@hbc1.edu
CLAY, Karen .... 541-962-3792. 405 H
karen.clay@eou.edu
CLAY, Lauren .... 662-476-5060. 266 I
lclay@eastms.edu
CLAY, Makeba .... 301-934-2251. 214 D
CLAY, Martyn .... 813-757-2110. 106 M
mclay6@hccfl.edu
CLAY, Melanie, N .... 678-839-0627. 133 I
melaniec@westga.edu
CLAY, Mercedes .... 419-783-2362. 379 C
mclay@defiance.edu
CLAY, Patrick, G .... 816-654-7650. 275 K
pclay@kcumb.edu
CLAY, Philip, N .... 508-831-5201. 238 F
pclay@wpi.edu
CLAY, Rex, J .... 704-922-6243. 360 F
clay.rex@gaston.edu
CLAY, Sharon .... 913-758-6108. 191 B
sharon.clay@stmary.edu
CLAY, Terry, M .... 410-777-2305. 213 D
tmclay@aacc.edu
CLAYBORNE, Hannah ..... 502-272-8070. 192 E
hclayborne@bellarmine.edu
CLAYBORNE, Staci, G .... 618-235-2700. 160 A
staci.clayborne@swic.edu
CLAYBORNE SCOTT,
Monica .... 731-426-7523. 455 J
mclayborne@lanecollege.edu
CLAYBROOK,
Jennifer, D .... 706-880-8032. 128 A
jclaybrook@lagrange.edu
CLAYCOMB, Cindy .... 316-978-3200. 191 F
cindy.claycomb@wichita.edu
CLAYCOMB, Donald, M .. 573-897-5000. 276 E
CLAYDEN, Jon .... 323-860-1188... 55 E
jonc@mi.edu
CLAYMAN, Ralph, V .... 949-824-5926... 71 B
rclayman@uci.edu
CLAYPOLE, Rita .... 304-263-6262. 527 B
rclaypole@martinsburginstitute.edu
CLAYPOOL, Joe .... 859-323-5445. 200 C
joseph.claypool@uky.edu
CLAYPOOLE, Jack .... 803-777-4111. 447 G
jclapoole@mycarolina.org
CLAYTON, Carolyn .... 859-858-2210. 192 A
CLAYTON, Carrie .... 903-566-7184. 492 D
cclayton@uttyler.edu
CLAYTON, Dana .... 812-488-2500. 173 H
dc26@evansville.edu
CLAYTON, Donald, E ...... 314-286-0106. 284 L
claytond@wustl.edu
CLAYTON, Gene, T .... 910-630-7011. 356 H
gclayton@methodist.edu
CLAYTON, Jack, A .... 304-842-8269. 529 F
jclayton@fairmontstate.edu
CLAYTON, Jan, L .... 918-595-7902. 400 E
jan.clayton@tulsacc.edu
CLAYTON, Janet, S .... 803-934-3246. 445 F
jclayton@morris.edu
CLAYTON, Jason .... 859-858-3511. 192 B
jason.clayton@asbury.edu
CLAYTON, Jay, B .... 724-653-2202. 415 A
jclayton@dec.edu
CLAYTON, Jeffrey, A .... 954-492-5353. 100 A
jclayton@citycollege.edu
CLAYTON, John .... 316-942-4291. 189 E
claytonj@newmanu.edu
CLAYTON, John .... 417-447-2667. 279 K
claytonj@otc.edu
CLAYTON, Kirk .... 757-490-1241. 501 G
kclayton@auto.edu
CLAYTON, Lisa .... 413-528-7239. 222 E
lclayton@simons-rock.edu
CLAYTON, Rita .... 717-815-1615. 438 D
rclayton@ycp.edu
CLAYTON, Taffye, B .... 919-962-0202. 368 D
Taffye@unc.edu
CLAYTON, Tiffany .... 610-921-7795. 409 A
tclayton@alb.edu
CLAYTON, Tonya, M .... 989-386-6601. 247 B
tmclayton@midmich.edu
CLAYTON, Vicki .... 206-726-5006. 518 G
vclayton@cornish.edu
CLAYTON, Yvette .... 256-372-5690..... 1 A
yvette.clayton@aamu.edu
CLEAR, Todd .... 973-353-3311. 306 A
tclear@rutgers.edu
CLEAR, Todd, R .... 973-353-3311. 306 D
tclear@rutgers.edu
CLEARFIELD, Michael ..... 707-638-5982... 69 K
michael.clearfield@tu.edu
CLEARMAN, Josh .... 253-833-9111. 520 C
jclearman@greenriver.edu
CLEARY, Brian .... 860-512-2613... 88 G
bcleary@manchestercc.edu
CLEARY, Charles .... 860-255-3403... 89 G
ccleary@txcc.commnet.edu
CLEARY, CSC, Hugh .... 508-565-1487. 237 A
hcleary@stonehill.edu
CLEARY, Kathleen .... 937-512-3044. 388 O
kathleen.cleary@sinclair.edu
CLEARY, Kelly .... 610-896-1181. 418 F
kcleary@haverford.edu
CLEARY, Lynn .... 315-464-5387. 342 E
clearyl@upstate.edu
CLEARY, Michael, J .... 575-234-9220. 311 A
mcleary@nmsu.edu
CLEARY, Paul, C .... 203-785-2867... 93 A
paul.cleary@yale.edu
CLEARY, Thomas .... 210-485-0500. 464 I
tcleary1@alamo.edu
CLEARY, Thomas, R .... 619-260-4659... 73 I
tcleary@sandiego.edu
CLEARY, Tim .... 802-468-1458. 501 B
tim.cleary@castleton.edu
CLEAVER, Richard .... 340-693-1042. 555 E
richard.cleaver@live.uvi.edu
CLEAVES, Laura .... 800-818-2261. 296 F
lcleaves@dwc.edu
CLEBSCH, Bill .... 650-725-0056... 68 E
clebsch@stanford.edu
CLECKLER, Steven .... 205-970-9239..... 7 B
scleckler@sebc.edu
CLEEK, Linda, L .... 812-464-1863. 174 D
lcleek@usi.edu
CLEEK, Stu .... 805-565-6029... 76 D
scleek@westmont.edu
CLEERE, Ashley .... 706-778-8500. 130 E
acleere@piedmont.edu
CLEGG, Earl, L .... 801-581-7028. 496 Q
eclegg@bookstore.utah.edu
CLEGG, Melody .... 208-524-3000. 138 D
melody.clegg@my.eitc.edu
CLELAND, Jerry .... 773-325-7706. 143 H
jcleland@depaul.edu
CLELAND, William .... 601-815-4700. 270 C
wcleland@umc.edu
CLEM, Randy .... 916-558-2424... 53 D
clemrj@scc.losrios.edu
CLEM, Tyler .... 513-772-9888. 386 C
tyler.clem@omw.edu
CLEMENS, Bonnie .... 909-607-3679... 39 B
bonnie_clemens@cuc.claremont.edu
CLEMENS, John .... 229-391-4870. 119 H
jclemens@abac.edu
CLEMENS, Michael .... 818-779-8047... 50 A
mclemens@kingsuniversity.edu
CLEMENS, Patrick, J .... 414-410-4839. 532 B
pjclemens@stritch.edu
CLEMENS, Tom .... 612-977-5269. 254 C
tom.clemens@capella.edu
CLEMENT, Fred .... 512-472-4133. 480 G
fred.clement@ssw.edu
CLEMENT, Gregory .... 978-632-6600. 232 C
g_clement@mwcc.mass.edu
CLEMENT, James, A .... 205-726-2395..... 6 F
jaclemen@samford.edu
CLEMENT, Linda, M .... 301-314-8430. 219 B
lclement@umd.edu
CLEMENT, Mercedes .... 386-506-3440. 101 G
clemenm@DaytonaState.edu
CLEMENT, Richard .... 435-797-2631. 497 B
richard.clement@usu.edu
CLEMENTS, Christine ...... 262-472-1343. 538 D
clementc@uww.edu
CLEMENTS, Dede .... 541-888-7351. 407 H
dclements@socc.edu
CLEMENTS, Erica .... 605-256-5712. 451 H
erica.clements@dsu.edu
CLEMENTS, Gary .... 252-527-6223. 361 F
gclements@lenoircc.edu
CLEMENTS, Geri .... 478-553-2066. 129 H
gclememts@oftc.edu
CLEMENTS, James, P ..... 304-293-5531. 530 D
Jim.Clements@mail.wvu.edu
CLEMENTS, Lee Ann, J ... 904-256-7300. 107 Q
lclemen@ju.edu
CLEMENTS, Stephen, K .. 859-858-3511. 192 B
steve.clements@asbury.edu
CLEMENTS, Tommy .... 276-523-7431. 513 A
tclements@me.vccs.edu
CLEMENTS, William .... 802-485-2368. 500 A
bclements@norwich.edu
CLEMETSEN, Bruce .... 541-917-4806. 404 B
clemetb@linnbenton.edu
CLEMMER, Greg .... 704-233-8000. 370 G
clemmer@wingate.edu
CLEMMER, Robert .... 540-234-9261. 511 H
clemmerr@brcc.edu
CLEMMONS, Brian .... 828-398-7161. 357 N
brianoclemmons@abtech.edu
CLEMMONS, Raechelle ... 920-403-3866. 535 L
raechelle.clemmons@snc.edu
CLEMMONS, Sarah .... 850-718-2213... 99 N
clemmonss@chipola.edu
CLEMO, Lorrie, A .... 315-312-2290. 344 A
lorrie.clemo@oswego.edu
CLEMONS, Brian .... 816-415-7802. 285 C
clemonsb@william.jewell.edu
CLEMONS, Cheryl .... 270-686-4250. 192 G
cheryl.clemons@brescia.edu
CLEMONS, Chuck .... 352-395-5202. 113 C
chuck.clemons@sfcollege.edu
CLEMONS, Lai-L .... 620-229-6168. 190 G
lai-l.clemons@sckans.edu
CLEMONS, Rita .... 909-635-0250. 224 G
Rita.Clemons@cambridgecollege.edu
CLENDENEN, Mike .... 252-493-7645. 362 G
mclendenen@email.pittcc.edu
CLENDENEN, Paula .... 270-247-8521. 197 H
pclendenen@midcontinent.edu
CLENDENIN, Larry .... 505-984-6060. 311 H
admissions@sjcsf.edu
CLERE, Ray .... 502-863-8122. 194 C
ray_clere@georgetowncollege.edu
CLERKIN, Elizabeth .... 440-775-8450. 385 H
liz.clerkin@oberlin.edu
CLERKIN, Kris .... 603-314-7874. 297 I
k.clerkin@snhu.edu
CLEROU, Diane .... 559-244-5970... 68 H
diane.clerou@scccd.edu
CLESCERI, Michael .... 815-479-7833. 152 F
mclesceri@mchenry.edu
CLEVELAND, SR.,
Alvin, A .... 334-872-2533..... 6 G
aclevesr@aol.com
CLEVELAND, Andrew ...... 651-846-1733. 261 D
andrew.cleveland@saintpaul.edu
CLEVELAND, Angela .... 269-965-3931. 244 O
clevelanda@kellogg.edu
CLEVELAND, Arthur .... 951-343-4215... 30 H
acleveland@calbaptist.edu
CLEVELAND, Ashley .... 913-234-0648. 185 L
ashley.cleveland@cleveland.edu
CLEVELAND, III, Carl, S 913-234-0600. 185 L
carl.clevelandiii@cleveland.edu
CLEVELAND, Charles, E . 509-527-5158. 525 E
clevelan@whitman.edu
CLEVELAND, Iesha, M ..... 919-536-7202. 360 B
clevelai@durhamtech.edu
CLEVELAND, Reginald .... 731-426-7595. 455 J
rcleveland@lanecollege.edu
CLEVENGER, Brian .... 217-206-6174. 161 E
clevenger.brian@uis.edu
CLEVENGER, Julie .... 217-786-2365. 151 F
julie.clevenger@llcc.edu
CLEVENGER, Timothy, R 541-346-2104. 406 D
trc@uoregon.edu
CLEVENTURE, Sarah .... 423-652-4715. 455 I
scleventure@king.edu
CLEVERING, Peter .... 708-239-4770. 160 K
peter.clevering@trnty.edu
CLIATT, Cass .... 717-291-3981. 416 J
cass.cliatt@fandm.edu
CLICK, Ben, A .... 240-895-4253. 218 A
baclick@smcm.edu
CLICK, Sally, E .... 317-940-9854. 164 J
sclick@butler.edu
CLICK, Stanley .... 606-759-7141. 196 B
stanley.click@kctcs.edu
CLICK, Stanley, W .... 606-783-1538. 196 B
stanley.click@kctcs.edu
CLICKNER, David .... 518-629-8068. 326 G
d.clickner@hvcc.edu
CLIFFORD, Christopher .. 205-934-8229..... 8 E
cbcliff@uab.edu
CLIFFORD, Joan .... 518-244-2410. 338 C
cliffj3@sage.edu
CLIFFORD, Paul .... 252-328-6072. 367 B
cliffordp@ecu.edu
CLIFT, Carla .... 256-551-3120..... 4 I
carla.clift@drakestate.edu
CLIFT, Edward .... 818-767-0888... 76 K
edward.clift@woodbury.edu
CLIFTON, Betsy .... 706-385-1460. 130 F
betsy.clifton@point.edu
CLIFTON, Gaye, B .... 336-342-4261. 363 C
cliftong@rockinghamcc.edu
CLIFTON, Jamie .... 951-571-6293... 60 K
jamie.clifton@mvc.edu
CLIFTON, Lonzy .... 334-876-9251..... 4 A
lonzy.clifton@wccs.edu
CLIFTON, Maurice .... 570-504-7000. 413 B
CLINARD, Rhonda .... 931-363-9820. 456 C
rclinard@martinmethodist.edu
CLINE, Cathie .... 870-633-4480... 21 A
ccline@eacc.edu
CLINE, Elizabeth .... 330-325-6498. 385 E
ecline@neomed.edu
CLINE, Gina .... 321-433-7000. 101 M
clineg@easternflorida.edu

CLINE, Glen, E ... 607-587-3917. 345 D clinege@alfredstate.edu
CLINE, J. Robert ... 864-231-2077. 441 B bcline@andersonuniversity.edu
CLINE, Jack ... 240-477-9505. 190 L jackcline@ku.edu
CLINE, Joseph ... 775-784-1740. 294 J cline@unr.edu
CLINE, Kimberly, R ... 516-299-2501. 329 D president@liu.edu
CLINE, Kimberly, R ... 516-299-2501. 329 C president@liu.edu
CLINE, Laurel ... 610-796-8317. 409 E laurel.cline@alvernia.edu
CLINE, Michael, B ... 765-494-8000. 171 M mbcline@purdue.edu
CLINE, Patricia ... 931-553-0071. 457 F patricia.cline@miller-motte.com
CLINE, Robert, J ... 814-871-5615. 416 K cline001@gannon.edu
CLINE, Scott ... 415-703-9316... 30 K scline@cca.edu
CLINE, Scott ... 415-239-3546... 38 L
CLINE, Tamara ... 530-283-0202... 44 H tcline@frc.edu
CLINE, Thomas, G ... 847-491-5608. 155 D t-cline@northwestern.edu
CLINE, Tricia ... 785-628-4091. 186 F tcline@fhsu.edu
CLINGINGSMITH, Aaron 406-657-2243. 287 C aaron.clingingsmith@msubillings.edu
CLINGMAN, A. Michele .. 575-492-2545. 310 G mclingman@nmjc.edu
CLINK, Wendy ... 954-201-7533... 99 D wclink@broward.edu
CLINTON, Antwan, D ... 202-238-2661... 95 G aclinton@howard.edu
CLINTON, Christine, M .. 814-886-6380. 424 G cclinton@mtaloy.edu
CLINTON, Don ... 903-693-2055. 478 A dclinton@panola.edu
CLINTON, Francene ... 413-755-6306. 233 A clinton@stcc.edu
CLINTON, John ... 717-477-1377. 429 E jeclin@sufoundation.org
CLINTON, Joseph ... 845-848-7700. 322 G joseph.clinton@dc.edu
CLINTON, Linda, T ... 903-886-5139. 483 E linda.clinton@tamuc.edu
CLINTON, Ron ... 903-434-8186. 477 J rclinton@ntcc.edu
CLINTON-JONES, Karen, A ... 716-878-6210. 343 A joneska@buffalostate.edu
CLIPPINGER, Cathie ... 740-366-9226. 376 A cclip@cotc.edu
CLIPPINGER, David, C ... 860-444-8393. 545 G david.c.clippinger@uscga.edu
CLISH, Colleen ... 651-523-2468. 256 A cclish01@hamline.edu
CLITES, Mona ... 301-784-5000. 213 B mclites@allegany.edu
CLOAN, Deborah ... 951-222-8000... 61 A
CLOCK, Joyce ... 218-733-5930. 259 A j.clock@lsc.edu
CLODFELTER, Elaine ... 704-272-5302. 363 G eclodfelter@spcc.edu
CLODFELTER, JR., Roger, D ... 336-841-9156. 355 C rclodfel@highpoint.edu
CLOETE, Marion, E ... 619-239-0391... 36 D mcloete@cwsl.edu
CLOKEY, Michael ... 505-428-1214. 311 J michael.clokey@sfccc.edu
CLONINGER, Mindy, E ... 620-235-4241. 189 L mcloning@pittstate.edu
CLOOS, Kevin, P ... 716-673-3452. 342 A kevin.cloos@fredonia.edu
CLOPTON, John, D ... 319-296-4004. 178 J john.clopton@hawkeyecollege.edu
CLOSE, Cathy ... 715-232-1235. 538 B closec@uwstout.edu
CLOSE, Stacey ... 860-465-5000... 87 L closes@easternct.edu
CLOSE, Steve ... 443-334-2690. 218 E sclose@stevenson.edu
CLOSE CONOLEY, Jane .. 951-827-5201... 71 E jane.conoley@ucr.edu
CLOSSER, James, B ... 615-868-6503. 457 D jclosser@mtsa.edu
CLOSTERMAN, Jane, E ... 573-882-2411. 283 B clostermanj@umsystem.edu
CLOTFELTER, James, H .. 336-334-5426. 369 A james_clotfelter@uncg.edu
CLOTT, Christopher ... 815-740-3395. 162 F cclott@stfrancis.edu
CLOUD, Andy ... 432-837-8179. 487 B wacloud@sulross.edu
CLOUD, Gary ... 480-219-6013. 271 A gcloud@atsu.edu
CLOUD, Rodney ... 334-387-3877... 1 E rodneycloud@amridgeuniversity.edu
CLOUD, Sybil ... 850-718-2223... 99 N clouds@chipola.edu
CLOUD, Yvonne ... 870-245-5299... 22 D cloudy@obu.edu
CLOUGH, Kenneth, J ... 315-312-2212. 344 A kenneth.clough@oswego.edu
CLOUGH, Michael ... 478-218-3301. 122 F mclough@centralgatech.edu
CLOUGH, Susan ... 970-542-3127... 83 E susan.clough@morgancc.edu
CLOUGH, JR., Victor, W 804-333-6705. 513 G vclough@rappahannock.edu
CLOUGHERTY, Helen ... 832-813-6514. 476 A helen.clougherty@lonestar.edu
CLOUGHERTY, Robert ... 518-587-2100. 346 A robert.clougherty@esc.edu
CLOUNCH, Teresa ... 785-594-8473. 184 C teresa.clounch@bakeru.edu
CLOUSE, Andrew, D ... 814-886-6480. 424 G AClouse@mtaloy.edu
CLOUSE, Cindy, D ... 606-679-8501. 196 D cindy.clouse@kctcs.edu
CLOUSE, Dave ... 731-989-6019. 454 J dclouse@fhu.edu
CLOUSE, Jim, W ... 432-837-8777. 487 B jclouse@sulross.edu
CLOUSE, Ron ... 602-944-3335... 11 D rclouse@aicag.edu
CLOUSTON, Heather, O .. 336-633-0286. 362 H hoclouston@randolph.edu
CLOW, Todd ... 517-437-7341. 243 I todd.clow@hillsdale.edu
CLOW, William, T ... 309-298-1552. 162 K wt-clow@wiu.edu
CLOWERS, Laurie, C ... 919-866-5929. 364 G lcclowers@waketech.edu
CLUBB, Patricia, L ... 512-232-7742. 491 C pat.clubb@austin.utexas.edu
CLUBB, Sandy Hatfield ... 515-271-2889. 177 K sandra.clubb@drake.edu
CLUETT, Chris ... 304-358-2000. 526 G chris@future.edu
CLUFF, Richard ... 480-461-7095... 15 A richard.cluff@mesacc.edu
CLUNE-KNEUER, Elizabeth, A ... 240-895-4274. 218 A eaclune@smcm.edu
CLUNIS, Tamara, T ... 806-371-5429. 465 E ttclunis@actx.edu
CLUTTER, Archie ... 402-472-7084. 292 I aclutter2@unl.edu
CLUTTER, Michael, L ... 706-542-4741. 133 C mclutter@warnell.uga.edu
CLUTTER, Sam ... 724-357-2141. 428 F Samuel.Clutter@iup.edu
CLYBURN, Michael ... 423-869-6223. 456 A michael.clyburn@lmunet.edu
CLYBURN, Michael, A ... 860-701-6727. 545 G michael.a.clyburn@uscg.mil
CLYDE, Maria ... 724-983-0700. 421 G clydem@laurel.edu
CLYDE, William ... 718-862-7303. 329 M william.clyde@manhattan.edu
CLYDE, JR., William ... 516-299-2241. 329 D william.clyde@liu.edu
CLYMAR, Linda ... 717-394-6211. 413 J lclymar@csb.edu
CLYMER, Patrick, L ... 671-735-5561. 546 C gcc.registrar@guamcc.edu
CLYMER, Ron ... 203-575-8044... 89 B rclymer@nvcc.commnet.edu
COACHMAN, Kenneth ... 205-929-1457... 5 G kcoachman@mail.miles.edu
COAKLEY, Jim ... 615-226-3990. 455 N jcoakley@nadcedu.com
COAKLEY, Toni ... 580-477-7751. 401 J toni.coakley@wosc.edu
COALTER, Milton, J ... 804-355-0671. 510 G jcoalter@upsem.edu
COAN, John ... 413-265-2275. 225 C coanj@elms.edu
COASH, Julia ... 203-773-8973... 87 G jcoash@albertus.edu
COATE, Letitia ... 707-664-2836... 36 B letitia.coate@sonoma.edu
COATES, James ... 708-596-2000. 159 C jcoates@ssc.edu
COATES, Jo Ann ... 724-480-3401. 413 H joann.coates@ccbc.edu
COATES, Robin ... 910-576-6222. 362 C coatesr@montgomery.edu
COATES, Thomas, E ... 716-878-6114. 343 A coateste@buffalostate.edu
COATES, Tom ... 906-635-6670. 245 G tcoates@lssu.edu
COATNEY, Margie ... 573-592-1194. 285 D margie.coatney@williamwoods.edu
COATS, Carol ... 580-745-2134. 399 J ccoats@se.edu
COATS, Daryle ... 601-426-6346. 269 G dcoats@southeasternbaptist.edu
COATS, Jeffrey ... 334-347-2623... 3 G jcoats@escc.edu
COATS, Rhonda ... 360-596-5231. 524 A rcoats@spscc.edu
COATSWORTH, John ... 212-854-2404. 321 D jhc2125@columbia.edu
COAUETTE, Chad ... 320-762-4403. 257 O chadc@alextech.edu
COAXUM, Thomas ... 256-372-8876... 1 A thomas.coaxum@aamu.edu
COBALLES-VEGA, Carmen ... 718-518-6611. 318 B ccvega@hostos.cuny.edu
COBANE, Craig ... 270-745-4258. 200 G craig.cobane@wku.edu
COBANOGLU, Cihan ... 941-359-4200. 117 A
COBARRUBIAS, Maria ... 201-200-2349. 303 F mcobarrubias@njcu.edu
COBB, Beverly ... 937-395-5604. 382 K beverly.cobb@kc.edu
COBB, Charles ... 270-706-8566. 195 A charles.cobb@kctcs.edu
COBB, Charles, G ... 828-262-7825. 367 A cobbcg@appstate.edu
COBB, Christopher ... 562-907-4241... 76 I ccobb@whittier.edu
COBB, Cindy ... 303-861-1151... 81 E ccobb@concorde.edu
COBB, Edythe ... 901-435-1731. 455 M edythe_cobb@loc.edu
COBB, James ... 931-372-3234. 460 A jimcobb@tntech.edu
COBB, Katharine ... 646-660-6660. 316 J Katharine.Cobb@baruch.cuny.edu
COBB, Kathy ... 321-433-7100. 101 M cobbk@easternflorida.edu
COBB, Keith ... 714-484-7116... 56 E kcobb@cypresscollege.edu
COBB, Kim, S ... 256-549-8236... 3 M kcobb@gadsdenstate.edu
COBB, Kristi ... 903-823-3358. 482 D kristi.cobb@texarkanacollege.edu
COBB, Lisa ... 615-353-3369. 461 B lisa.cobb@nscc.edu
COBB, Malynda ... 580-371-2371. 396 E mcobb@mscok.edu
COBB, Myreon, K ... 419-434-4544. 391 D mcobb@findlay.edu
COBB, P. Denise ... 618-650-5609. 159 H pcobb@siue.edu
COBB, Stephen, H ... 270-809-3391. 198 B scobb@murraystate.edu
COBIAN, Oscar ... 323-241-5328... 52 C cobianom@lasc.edu
COBLE, Bridgette ... 303-556-3664... 83 D bcoble@msudenver.edu
COBLE, Dan ... 813-393-3675. 131 H dcoble@southuniversity.edu
COBLE, Tammi ... 252-222-6081. 358 G coblet@carteret.edu
COBLENTZ, Pablo ... 208-426-1616. 137 G pablocoblentz@boisestate.edu
COBLER, Paula ... 361-570-4350. 489 E coblerp@uhv.edu
COBOS, Terry ... 805-652-5558... 74 E tcobos@vcccd.edu
COBURN, Danielle ... 205-853-1200... 5 B dcoburn@jeffstateonline.com
COBURN, David, K ... 850-644-3035. 115 C dcoburn@fsu.edu
COBURN, Kari, C ... 702-895-3771. 294 I kari@nevada.edu
COBURN, Kevin ... 802-287-8926. 499 D commsgmc@greenmtn.edu
COBURN, Mary, B ... 850-644-5590. 115 C mcoburn@fsu.edu
COBURN, Oakley, H ... 864-597-4300. 449 I coburnoh@wofford.edu
COCCHIARELLA, Frank, L ... 603-535-2260. 298 G frankc@plymouth.edu
COCCO-MITTEN, Melissa 415-503-6231... 62 H mcocco@sfcm.edu
COCHRAN, B.Barnett ... 740-392-6868. 384 K barney.cochran@mvnu.edu
COCHRAN, Barry, A ... 260-359-4035. 166 O bcochran@huntington.edu
COCHRAN, Bob ... 503-594-6790. 402 F bobc@clackamas.edu
COCHRAN, Caleb ... 617-989-4076. 237 G cochranc@wit.edu
COCHRAN, Connie, L ... 713-313-7606. 485 F cochrancl@tsu.edu
COCHRAN, Daniel, J ... 574-239-8409. 166 N dcochran@hcc-nd.edu
COCHRAN, Douglas ... 541-737-4085. 406 A career.services@oregonstate.edu
COCHRAN, Edward, E ... 724-503-1001. 436 G ecochran@washjeff.edu
COCHRAN, Gerardine ... 727-816-3190. 110 E cochran@phcc.edu
COCHRAN, Glenn ... 508-626-4636. 230 A gcochran@framingham.edu
COCHRAN, Jeanne ... 619-849-2513... 59 L jeannecochran@pointloma.edu
COCHRAN, Jerome ... 412-624-4247. 435 C cochran@pitt.edu
COCHRAN, Kevin ... 860-231-5238... 92 F kcochran@usj.edu
COCHRAN, Linda ... 601-923-1661. 269 E lcochran@rts.edu
COCHRAN, Mark, J ... 501-686-2540... 23 H mjcochran@uasys.edu
COCHRAN, Maryjo ... 334-670-3869... 7 H macochran@troy.edu
COCHRAN, Monica, J ... 304-367-4711. 529 F monica.cochran@fairmontstate.edu
COCHRAN, Nancy ... 303-871-6986... 86 B Nancy.Cochran@du.edu
COCHRAN, Philip, L ... 317-274-2481. 168 D plcochra@iupui.edu
COCHRAN, Raylene ... 850-478-8496. 110 F
COCHRAN, Rodney ... 423-869-7101. 456 A rodney.cochran@lmunet.edu
COCHRAN, III, Sam, V .. 319-335-7294. 175 I sam-cochran@uiowa.edu
COCHRAN, Scott ... 864-597-4261. 449 I cochranws@wofford.edu
COCHRAN, Stuart ... 646-313-8000. 319 E
COCHRAN, Susan, E ... 207-778-7200. 212 D cochran@maine.edu
COCHRAN, Teri ... 918-456-5511. 396 H cochrant@nsuok.edu
COCHRAN, Theodore, J .. 770-423-6212. 127 N tcochran@kennesaw.edu
COCHRAN, Thomas ... 901-321-3381. 453 H tcochran@cbu.edu
COCHRANE, Ashley ... 859-985-3605. 192 F cochranea@berea.edu
COCHRANE, John, T ... 319-895-4230. 177 A jcochrane@cornellcollege.edu
COCHRANE, Kerry ... 312-662-4237. 139 F kcochrane@adler.edu
COCHRANE, Michelle ... 203-773-8535... 87 G mcochrane@albertus.edu
COCKE, Paul ... 360-650-3350. 525 C paul.cocke@wwu.edu
COCKER, James, B ... 845-368-7208. 340 C
COCKERILL, Ryan ... 815-836-5250. 150 H cockerry@lewisu.edu
COCKETT, Noelle, E ... 435-797-1167. 497 B noelle.cockett@usu.edu
COCKLEY, Anne ... 859-846-5408. 197 I acockley@midway.edu
COCKLIN, Joel ... 419-434-4250. 393 D jcocklin@winebrenner.edu
COCKRELL, David ... 719-384-6884... 83 M david.cockrell@ojc.edu
COCKRELL, Phillip ... 601-979-2329. 267 E phillip.a.cockrell@jsums.edu
COCKRIEL, Torie ... 270-745-5394. 200 G torie.cockriel@wku.edu
COCKRUM, Larry, L ... 606-539-4214. 200 B larry.cockrum@ucumberlands.edu
COCO, Karen ... 318-670-9324. 207 A kcoco@susla.edu
COCOZZOLI, Gary, R ... 248-204-3000. 245 I gcocozzol@ltu.edu
CODD, John ... 201-692-7071. 301 J johncodd@fdu.edu
CODDING, Amparo ... 201-447-7133. 299 C acodding@bergen.edu
CODDINGTON, Andrew .. 315-228-6921. 320 F acoddington@colgate.edu
CODJOE, Henry, M ... 706-272-4406. 123 G hcodjoe@daltonstate.edu
CODNER, Jackie ... 580-745-2810. 399 J jcodner@se.edu
CODNER, Renee ... 760-630-1555... 49 L rcodner@kaplan.edu
CODY, Denise ... 515-244-4221. 175 C codyd@aib.edu
CODY, Doni, S ... 910-576-6222. 362 C codyd@montgomery.edu
CODY, Martha ... 805-756-6770... 32 F mcody@calpoly.edu
CODY, Mary Ellen ... 203-285-2296... 88 E mcody@gwcc.commnet.edu
CODY, Robert ... 508-362-2131. 231 D rcody@capecod.edu
CODY, Susan ... 770-274-5402. 125 G susan.cody@gpc.edu
COE, Bonnie, L ... 740-364-9509. 376 A bcoe@cotc.edu
COE, Cheri ... 978-921-4242. 234 C cheri.coe@montserrat.edu
COE, Douglas, A ... 406-496-4207. 287 F dcoe@mtech.edu
COE, Lea ... 229-931-2352. 131 G lcoe@southgatech.edu

COE-SMITH, Jane 208-282-2794. 138 E coesjane@isu.edu
COEHOORN, Joel 402-363-5603. 293 I jcoehoorn@york.edu
COFER, Mildred 973-877-3468. 301 H cofer@essex.edu
COFER, Stacy 316-323-6729. 185 D scofer@butlercc.edu
COFFEE, Laura, F 336-342-4261. 363 C coffeel@rockinghamcc.edu
COFFEY, Amanda, A 717-796-5300. 423 L acoffey@messiah.edu
COFFEY, Laura 512-492-3021. 466 B lcoffey@aoma.edu
COFFEY, Patrick, J 414-277-7226. 534 G coffey@msoe.edu
COFFEY, Paul 312-899-5176. 158 L pcoffey@saic.edu
COFFEY, Ron, L 260-359-4029. 166 O rcoffey@huntington.edu
COFFEY, Suzanne, R 413-542-2274. 221 G scoffey@amherst.edu
COFFIN, Deborah, J 303-492-8447... 85 L deb.coffin@colorado.edu
COFFIN, John 847-214-7950. 144 F jcoffin@elgin.edu
COFFIN, Jonathan 765-658-4088. 165 F jonathancoffin@depauw.edu
COFFIN, Lee, A 617-627-5275. 237 C lee.coffin@tufts.edu
COFFIN, Sheila 312-341-3530. 157 D scoffin@roosevelt.edu
COFFIN, William 410-293-2809. 545 J coffin@usna.edu
COFFMAN, Leah 540-966-3984. 514 E lcoffman@virginiawestern.edu
COFFMAN, Marie, E 724-852-3399. 437 A mcoffman@waynesburg.edu
COFFMAN, Renee 702-968-2020. 295 E rcoffman@roseman.edu
COFFMAN, Robert, L 765-641-4063. 163 L rlcoffman@anderson.edu
COFIELD, Cindy 601-318-6167. 270 I cindy.cofield@wmcarey.edu
COFRESI, Norma 718-960-8761. 318 A norma.cofresi@lehman.cuny.edu
COGAN, Edward, P 716-829-8365. 323 D cogane@dyc.edu
COGAN, Michael, F 651-962-6657. 265 C mfcogan@stthomas.edu
COGBURN, Wendy, L 205-348-0537..... 8 D wcogburn@ctl.ua.edu
COGDELL, Edith 210-829-6037. 490 A cogdell@uiwtx.edu
COGDILL, Rex 307-532-8257. 542 a rex.cogdill@ewc.wy.edu
COGER, Robin, N 336-334-7589. 367 E rncoger@ncat.edu
COGGIN, Rod 662-720-7306. 269 B rcoggin@nemcc.edu
COGGIN, Steven, J 704-637-4110. 353 E scoggin@catawba.edu
COGHLAN, Cathan 817-257-7793. 484 I c.coghlan@tcu.edu
COGHLAN, Laura 360-867-6676. 519 J coghlanl@evergreen.edu
COGSWELL, Bob 910-893-1217. 352 K cogswell@campbell.edu
COGSWELL, James, A 573-882-4701. 283 C cogswellja@missouri.edu
COGSWELL, Katherine 315-445-6124. 328 F cogswek@lemoyne.edu
COHALL, Kirkpatrick, G 212-870-1208. 334 C kcohall@nyts.edu
COHEN, Alise 845-848-4036. 322 G alise.cohen@dc.edu
COHEN, Bernadette 404-270-5091. 132 E bcohen@spelman.edu
COHEN, Brian 212-541-0365. 316 I brian.cohen@cuny.edu
COHEN, Dale, S 916-558-2275... 53 D cohend@scc.losrios.edu
COHEN, Daryl 262-595-2301. 537 C bookstore@uwp.edu
COHEN, David 800-371-6105... 16 A david@nationalparalegal.edu
COHEN, David 718-268-4700. 337 F
COHEN, David, J 843-953-5530. 443 A cohenD@cofc.edu
COHEN, David, J 843-953-5530. 443 A cohend@cofc.edu
COHEN, Howard 716-878-4101. 343 A cohenh@buffalostate.edu
COHEN, Ilene 732-255-0400. 304 A icohen@ocean.edu
COHEN, Jason 413-755-4438. 233 A jlcohen@stcc.edu
COHEN, Jerry, L 631-656-2121. 324 F jerry.cohen@ftc.edu
COHEN, Joel, J 646-660-6060. 316 J
COHEN, Jonah 203-285-2094... 88 E jcohen@gwcc.commnet.edu
COHEN, Kathleen, L 607-735-1728. 323 H kcohen@elmira.edu
COHEN, Kristin 973-720-2903. 308 I cohenk4@wpunj.edu
COHEN, Laurie 480-423-6511... 15 E laurie.cohen@scottsdalecc.edu
COHEN, Leslie 732-255-0400. 304 A lcohen@ocean.edu
COHEN, Lisa 215-576-0800. 431 E lcohen@rrc.edu
COHEN, Lizabeth 617-495-8602. 227 C lizabeth_cohen@radcliffe.harvard.edu
COHEN, Margaret, W 314-516-4508. 283 E peggy_cohen@umsl.edu
COHEN, Mark, J 202-687-7491... 95 E cohenm@georgetown.edu
COHEN, Martin, L 631-656-2175. 324 F martin.cohen@ftc.edu
COHEN, Marvin 312-369-7226. 143 D mcohen@colum.edu
COHEN, Michael, E 772-466-4822... 98 L m.cohen@aviator.edu
COHEN, Morris 513-862-2743. 380 E
COHEN, Neal 212-396-7729. 318 C ncoh@hunter.cuny.edu
COHEN, Peter 718-368-5563. 318 E pcohen@kbcc.cuny.edu
COHEN, Peter, F 412-268-4395. 412 H pfcohen@andrew.cmu.edu
COHEN, Pinchas 213-740-1354... 74 A hassy@usc.edu
COHEN, Richard 215-985-2500. 423 M rjc@phmc.org
COHEN, Richard, L 847-735-5555. 150 B cohen@lakeforest.edu
COHEN, Ronald, A 570-372-4103. 433 H cohen@susqu.edu
COHEN, Shaya 516-295-5700. 351 N
COHEN, Shelly 757-388-2900. 509 D sgvinson@sentara.com
COHEN, Stanley, G 631-656-2157. 324 F mara.maltz@ftc.edu
COHEN, Steve 707-524-1731... 65 B scohen@santorosa.edu
COHEN, Steven 510-464-3213... 59 C scohen@peralta.edu
COHEN, Steven 215-567-7080. 410 A scohen@aii.edu
COHEN, Susan, J 215-574-9600. 418 H scohen@hussianart.edu
COHEN, Tamara 352-392-1261. 116 A tamararc@dso.ufl.edu
COHEN, Vicki 201-692-2525. 301 J cohen@fdu.edu
COHEN, Zoe 978-837-5121. 234 A cohenz@merrimack.edu
COHN, Josephine 973-748-9000. 299 F josephine_cohn@bloomfield.edu
COHN, Stephen, A 919-687-3606. 354 A stevec@acpub.duke.edu
COHRS, Daniel 303-963-3352... 79 C dcohrs@ccu.edu
COHUNE, Ellen 805-756-2527... 32 F ecohune@calpoly.edu
COICAUD, Jean-Marc 973-353-3285. 306 D jeanmarc.coicaud@rutgers.edu
COKER, Bryan, F 410-337-6150. 215 A bryan.coker@goucher.edu
COKER, Dawn 706-880-8267. 128 A dcoker@lagrange.edu
COKER, Jeffrey, W 904-620-2787. 116 B j.coker@unf.edu
COKER, Kim 870-574-4533... 23 G kcoker@sautech.edu
COKER, Melissa, A 843-355-4117. 449 F cokerm@wiltech.edu
COKER, Scott, A 309-298-1834. 162 K sa-coker@wiu.edu
COKER, Sherry 417-447-8884. 279 K cokers@otc.edu
COKER, T. Kent 843-355-4144. 449 F cokert@wiltech.edu
COKKINOS, Michael 212-217-4476. 324 C michael_cokkinos@fitnyc.edu
COLÓN, Myrna 787-834-9595. 553 B mcolon@uaa.edu
COLÓN, Silvestre 787-832-4040. 554 E decep@uprm.edu
COLÓN, Victor 515-289-9200. 179 C vcolon@inste.edu
COLA, Anita 570-504-0498. 420 C colaa@lackawanna.edu
COLABRARO, Anthony 973-290-4470. 300 F acolabraro@cse.edu
COLADARCI, Richard 718-489-5256. 338 G rcoladarci@sfc.edu
COLADARCI, Ted, T 207-581-1415. 212 B theo@maine.edu
COLAGROSS, Glenda 256-331-5275..... 6 A colg@nwscc.edu
COLANER, Kevin, T 909-869-3365... 32 G KTcolaner@csupomona.edu
COLANGELO, Carmon 314-935-9300. 284 L colangelo@wustl.edu
COLAPIETRO, Cathy 816-584-6728. 280 C cathy.colapietro@park.edu
COLARERI, Michael, L 978-468-7111. 227 A mcolareri@gcts.edu
COLARIC, Susan 352-588-7375. 112 D susan.colaric@saintleo.edu
COLAROSS, Glenda 256-395-2211..... 7 C gcolaross@suscc.edu
COLARULLI, Guy, C 860-768-4749... 92 D colarulli@hartford.edu
COLASURDO, Giuseppe, N 713-500-3000. 492 E giuseppe.n.colasurdo@uth.tmc.edu
COLASURDO, Giuseppe, N 713-500-5700. 492 E giuseppe.n.colasurdo@uth.tmc.edu
COLATCH, John, P 570-577-1592. 411 A john.colatch@bucknell.edu
COLAW, Lee, M 806-371-5151. 465 E lmcolaw@actx.edu
COLBECK, Ellen 217-875-7200. 156 J ecolbeck@richland.edu
COLBERT, Brandi 928-757-0853... 15 L bcolbert@mohave.edu
COLBERT, Claudia 718-270-6172. 319 A ccolbert@mec.cuny.edu
COLBERT, Jeff 415-380-1428... 45 H jeffcolbert@ggbts.edu
COLBERT, Mary, J 410-857-2214. 216 E mcolbert@mcdaniel.edu
COLBERT RILEY, Cynthia 713-525-3119. 490 L colbert@stthom.edu
COLBURN, David 509-533-4841. 518 E david.colburn@scc.spokane.edu
COLBURN-ALSOP, Sara . 317-738-8257. 165 I scolburnalsop@franklincollege.edu
COLBY, Adam 727-864-7732. 101 N colbyac@eckerd.edu
COLBY, Chuck 570-662-4952. 429 C ccolby@mansfield.edu
COLBY, Ira 713-743-8086. 489 B icolby@uh.edu
COLBY CLEMENTS, Paula 978-681-0800. 233 C pcolby@mslaw.edu
COLCOLOUGH, Sharon .. 864-646-1790. 447 D scolcolo@tctc.edu
COLDREN, Mark 607-274-3853. 327 E mcoldren@ithaca.edu
COLE, JR., Allan 512-404-4822. 467 A acole@austinseminary.edu
COLE, Amber 405-945-3310. 398 C
COLE, Bruce 704-922-6413. 360 F cole.bruce@gaston.edu
COLE, Carol, A 304-896-7429. 528 F carol.cole@southernwv.edu
COLE, Christopher, L 804-523-5843. 512 F ccole@reynolds.edu
COLE, Christy, C 434-381-6530. 510 F ccole@sbc.edu
COLE, Dan 402-363-5609. 293 I dcole@york.edu
COLE, Dayton, T 828-262-2751. 367 A coledt@appstate.edu
COLE, Donald, R 662-915-7474. 270 B dcole@olemiss.edu
COLE, Elyne 217-333-6677. 162 A egcole@illinois.edu
COLE, Frances, E 252-398-6452. 353 H colefr@chowan.edu
COLE, Frank 505-566-3511. 311 I colef@sancollege.edu
COLE, Holly 603-428-2440. 297 D hcole@nec.edu
COLE, Jack, T 717-766-2511. 423 L jcole@messiah.edu
COLE, Jim 478-301-2994. 128 H cole_jm@mercer.edu
COLE, Joey 501-812-2243... 22 G jcole@pulaskitech.edu
COLE, John, J 304-293-8470. 530 D jay.cole@mail.wvu.edu
COLE, Joshua 617-850-1217. 227 E jcole@hchc.edu
COLE, Judith 813-879-6000. 103 B jcole@cci.edu
COLE, Judith, M 617-253-8231. 233 B
COLE, Katharine, H 813-253-6130. 118 L kcole@ut.edu
COLE, Kathryn, B 601-857-3502. 267 A Kathryn.Cole@hindscc.edu
COLE, Kathy 251-981-3771..... 2 I kathy.cole@columbiasouthern.edu
COLE, Kristie, C 864-231-2067. 441 B kcole@andersonuniversity.edu
COLE, Lauren 334-670-3216..... 7 H lscole@troy.edu
COLE, Lauren 910-642-7141. 364 A Lauren.Cole@sccnc.edu
COLE, Lisa 318-257-4325. 207 F lcole@latech.edu
COLE, Maenecia 252-335-0821. 359 F mlewis@albemarle.edu
COLE, Mark 315-312-3672. 344 A rmark.cole@oswego.edu
COLE, Michael 216-421-7413. 377 C mcole@cia.edu
COLE, Milton, T 610-519-4220. 436 F milton.cole@villanova.edu
COLE, Nadara, L 662-720-7277. 269 B ncole@nemcc.edu
COLE, Nathan 828-395-1633. 361 C ncole@isothermal.edu
COLE, Patricia 205-226-4907..... 2 C pcole@bsc.edu
COLE, Rebecca, S 937-775-2350. 393 G rebecca.cole@wright.edu
COLE, Rebecca, S 512-223-1015. 466 I rcole@austincc.edu
COLE, Richard 732-906-4153. 303 B RCole@middlesexcc.edu
COLE, JR., Richard 914-633-2311. 327 C rcole@iona.edu
COLE, Robert 610-647-4400. 418 I rcole@immaculata.edu
COLE, Robert, A 401-254-3149. 440 B rcole@rwu.edu
COLE, Sarah 251-626-3303..... 8 B registrar@ussa.edu
COLE, Stephanie, A 716-286-8319. 334 F scole@niagara.edu
COLE, Stephen, W 845-575-3000. 330 D stephen.cole@marist.edu
COLE, Steve 870-584-4471... 24 F scole@cccua.edu
COLE, Susan, A 973-655-4212. 303 D coles@mail.montclair.edu
COLE, Timothy, P 619-477-6310... 70 D tcole@usuniversity.edu
COLE, W. Scott 407-823-2482. 115 E scott.cole@ucf.edu
COLE, Wayne 563-441-4011. 178 C wcole@eicc.edu
COLE, Wendy, P 484-664-3433. 424 H cole@muhlenberg.edu
COLE, Xavier 410-617-5171. 216 A xcole@loyola.edu
COLE GENTRY, Ronda 276-466-7915. 514 G rondacole@vic.edu
COLEAL, Sharlene 661-362-3405... 40 E sharlene.coleal@canyons.edu
COLEBROOK, Cynthia 415-749-4522... 62 G ccolebrook@sfai.edu
COLECCHIA, Carlo 201-355-1124. 302 A colecchiac@felician.edu
COLEGROVE, Michael 606-539-4230. 200 B michael.colegrove@ucumberlands.edu
COLELLA, Carlo 301-405-6400. 219 B ccolella@umd.edu
COLELLA, Kurt, J 860-444-8275. 545 G kurt.j.colella@uscg.mil
COLELLA, Laurie 508-831-4922. 238 F lcolella@wpi.edu
COLELLI, Joy 718-637-5917. 336 E jcolelli@poly.edu
COLELLI, Leonard, A 724-938-4169. 428 A colelli@calu.edu
COLEMAN, Alvin 870-633-4480... 21 A acoleman@eacc.edu
COLEMAN, Anne Marie .. 401-874-5270. 440 D amc@uri.edu
COLEMAN, Barbara 212-875-4472. 314 C bcoleman@bankstreet.edu
COLEMAN, Berniesha 718-997-5760. 319 C berniesha.coleman@qc.cuny.edu
COLEMAN, Carole, T 928-344-7521... 11 L carole.coleman@azwestern.edu
COLEMAN, Carrie 864-596-9055. 443 D carrie.coleman@converse.edu
COLEMAN, Catherine, T . 870-633-4480... 21 A ccoleman@eacc.edu
COLEMAN, Chad 928-317-6470... 11 L chad.coleman@azwestern.edu
COLEMAN, Chad 574-535-7292. 166 A chadc@goshen.edu
COLEMAN, Cheryl, C 913-288-7471. 187 L ccoleman@kckcc.edu
COLEMAN, Clarence, D .. 757-823-8408. 507 M cdcoleman@nsu.edu
COLEMAN, Clinton, R 443-885-3022. 217 A clinton.coleman@morgan.edu
COLEMAN, Craig, S 412-397-4912. 431 I colemanc@rmu.edu

COLEMAN, David ... 859-622-1403. 193 P david.coleman@eku.edu
COLEMAN, David ... 508-270-4004. 231 G dcoleman@massbay.edu
COLEMAN, Dayna, L ... 509-777-4565. 525 F dcoleman@whitworth.edu
COLEMAN, Deborah ... 903-923-3320. 486 A deborah.coleman@tstc.edu
COLEMAN, Dennis ... 214-379-5514. 478 D dcoleman@pqc.edu
COLEMAN, Diane ... 206-934-3842. 522 J diane.coleman@seattlecolleges.edu
COLEMAN, Don ... 423-354-2533. 461 C dscoleman@northeaststate.edu
COLEMAN, Doug ... 903-923-3357. 486 A doug.coleman@tstc.edu
COLEMAN, Ellen ... 302-736-2508... 94 C colemael@wesley.edu
COLEMAN, F. Paul ... 607-431-4449. 325 F colemanf@hartwick.edu
COLEMAN, Frances, N ... 662-325-7661. 268 D fcoleman@library.msstate.edu
COLEMAN, Gerald ... 504-816-4050. 201 K gcoleman@dillard.edu
COLEMAN, Hardin, L ... 617-353-3213. 224 D hardin@bu.edu
COLEMAN, James, S ... 804-828-1674. 511 F jscoleman@vcu.edu
COLEMAN, Jamie ... 208-467-8768. 139 A jcoleman@nnu.edu
COLEMAN, Jay, T ... 319-352-8264. 183 E todd.coleman@wartburg.edu
COLEMAN, Jeff ... 435-797-1223. 497 B jeff.coleman@usu.edu
COLEMAN, Joe ... 904-256-7550. 107 Q jcolema@ju.edu
COLEMAN, Joseph, L ... 386-481-2626... 99 C colemanj@cookman.edu
COLEMAN, Joyce ... 815-280-2568. 149 A jcoleman@jjc.edu
COLEMAN, Jules, L ... 212-998-2414. 334 D jules.coleman@nyu.edu
COLEMAN, June ... 620-341-5407. 186 D jcoleman@emporia.edu
COLEMAN, Karen, W ... 773-702-7770. 161 B Kwcoleman@uchicago.edu
COLEMAN, Lamar ... 860-465-0147... 87 L colemanl@easternct.edu
COLEMAN, Larry ... 305-626-3713. 104 J Larry.Coleman@fmuniv.edu
COLEMAN, Laura, L ... 906-786-5802. 240 K colemanl@baycollege.edu
COLEMAN, Linda ... 610-519-4074. 436 F linda.coleman@villanova.edu
COLEMAN, Lisa, M ... 617-495-1540. 227 C lisa_coleman@harvard.edu
COLEMAN, Lynn, C ... 443-518-4918. 215 E lcoleman@howardcc.edu
COLEMAN, Marcus ... 225-771-3920. 206 J marcus_coleman@subr.edu
COLEMAN, Marion, A ... 717-358-7194. 416 J marion.coleman@fandm.edu
COLEMAN, Mark ... 270-384-8040. 197 D colemanm@lindsey.edu
COLEMAN, Mary ... 617-349-8458. 228 B mcolema5@lesley.edu
COLEMAN, Mary, E ... 718-289-5128. 317 B mary.coleman@bcc.cuny.edu
COLEMAN, Mary Sue ... 734-764-6270. 251 C marysuec@umich.edu
COLEMAN, Michael ... 313-664-7676. 241 C mcoleman@collegeforcreativestudies.edu
COLEMAN, Michael, J ... 540-231-5530. 515 C colemanm@vt.edu
COLEMAN, Mick ... 612-659-6107. 259 D mick.coleman@minneapolis.edu
COLEMAN, Mike ... 850-201-8427. 117 D colemanm@tcc.fl.edu
COLEMAN, Ray ... 561-686-6600. 114 L colemanr@fau.edu
COLEMAN, Reggie ... 405-491-6366. 399 K rcoleman@snu.edu
COLEMAN, Richard, A ... 812-888-4280. 174 F rcoleman@vinu.edu
COLEMAN, Rob ... 562-907-4271... 76 I rcoleman@whittier.edu
COLEMAN, Roshell ... 870-733-6722... 21 I rfcoleman@midsouthcc.edu
COLEMAN, S. Michelle .. 415-575-6160... 31 D mcoleman@ciis.edu
COLEMAN, Sean ... 412-365-1164. 412 K scoleman1@chatham.edu
COLEMAN, Stefanie ... 312-935-4558. 156 K scaldwell@robertmorris.edu
COLEMAN, Stephen, F ... 607-735-1804. 323 H scoleman@elmira.edu
COLEMAN, Steve ... 727-784-0003... 99 J scoleman@cfi.edu
COLEMAN, Steve, B ... 864-941-8373. 446 C coleman.s@ptc.edu
COLEMAN, Susannah ... 609-497-7782. 304 D susannah.coleman@ptsem.edu
COLEMAN, Tammy ... 870-584-4471... 24 F tcoleman@cccua.edu
COLEMAN, Teresa ... 912-538-3103. 132 A tcoleman@southeasterntech.edu
COLEMAN, Tina, L ... 757-221-1791. 503 N tina.coleman@wm.edu
COLEMAN, Tonya, R ... 678-359-5435. 127 A tonya_c@gordonstate.edu
COLEMAN, Vicki ... 336-334-7782. 367 E vcoleman@ncat.edu
COLEMAN-KAISER, Theresa ... 906-487-2281. 247 A tacolema@mtu.edu
COLEMAN-WHITE, Lawanda ... 678-915-7352. 132 C lcoleman@spsu.edu
COLEMER, Dena ... 507-389-7272. 261 E dena.colemer@southcentral.edu
COLENDA, Christopher, C ... 304-293-4511. 530 D ccolenda@hsc.wvu.edu
COLES, Jeff ... 618-468-4200. 150 G jcoles@lc.edu
COLES, Julius ... 404-215-6040. 129 D jcoles@morehouse.edu
COLES, Patricia ... 847-317-7033. 160 M pcoles@tiu.edu
COLES, Roger, L ... 989-774-6099. 240 N coles1rl@cmich.edu
COLES, Uva, C ... 215-670-9206. 425 J uccoles@peirce.edu
COLEY, Karen ... 920-887-4426. 540 F kcoley@morainepark.edu
COLEY, Kathryn, S ... 631-420-2400. 346 B kathy.coley@farmingdale.edu
COLEY, Ron, T ... 510-643-1430... 70 I rcoley@berkeley.edu
COLEY, Soraya ... 661-654-2154... 32 H scoley@csub.edu
COLGAN, Dennis ... 206-878-3710. 520 E dcolgan@highline.edu
COLGAN, OSB, Tobias ... 812-357-6981. 173 A tcolgan@saintmeinrad.edu
COLGAN, William ... 802-225-3342. 499 I will.colgan@neci.edu
COLGATE, Beverly ... 805-893-2218... 72 B beverly.colgate@ia.ucsb.edu
COLGROVE, Marianne ... 503-777-7792. 407 E mcolgrov@reed.edu
COLIP, Mark ... 312-949-7405. 146 G mcolip@ico.edu
COLL, James, P ... 601-266-4491. 270 E james.coll@usm.edu
COLLADO, Diosa ... 312-777-8584. 147 D dcollado@aii.edu
COLLADO, Shirley ... 802-443-5382. 499 H scollado@middlebury.edu
COLLAR, Doug ... 419-448-2157. 380 G dcollar@heidelberg.edu
COLLARD, Bruce ... 603-668-2211. 297 I b.collard@snhu.edu
COLLAZO, Carmen ... 787-250-1912. 550 E ccollazo@metro.inter.edu
COLLAZO, Evelyn ... 787-738-2161. 554 C evlyn.collazo@upr.edu
COLLAZO, Ivonne ... 787-284-1912. 550 F icollazo@ponce.inter.edu
COLLAZO, Julio, A ... 787-758-2525. 554 F julio.collazo@upr.edu
COLLAZO, Mariela ... 787-766-1717. 552 J mcollazo@suagm.edu
COLLAZO, Samaris ... 787-743-7979. 552 I s_collazo@suagm.edu
COLLAZO, Shelciy ... 787-993-8876. 554 A shelciy.collazo@upr.edu
COLLEN, Dan ... 707-826-3666... 35 C dgc7001@humboldt.edu
COLLEN, Jodi ... 612-330-1107. 253 H collen@augsburg.edu
COLLER, Barry, S ... 212-327-7490. 338 A collerb@rockefeller.edu
COLLERAN, Jeanne ... 216-397-4460. 381 R jcolleran@jcu.edu
COLLETTE, Mark ... 508-849-3462. 222 B mcollette@annamaria.edu
COLLEY, Debra, A ... 716-286-8560. 334 F dcolley@niagara.edu
COLLEY, Karen ... 312-413-2175. 161 D karenc@uic.edu
COLLEY, Scott ... 860-434-5232... 90 F scolley@lymeacademy.edu
COLLIE, Cynthia ... 336-506-4410. 357 M cynthia.collie@alamancecc.edu
COLLIE, Pamela, J ... 276-328-0128. 511 C pjc9w@uvawise.edu
COLLIE, Susan, A ... 501-882-8967... 19 M sacollie@asub.edu
COLLIER, Adrienne ... 585-395-2109. 342 F acollier@brockport.edu
COLLIER, Barbara ... 323-226-4911... 52 G bcollier@dhs.lacounty.gov
COLLIER, Barry, S ... 317-940-8421. 164 J bcollier@butler.edu
COLLIER, Billie ... 850-644-1281. 115 C bcollier@fsu.edu
COLLIER, Bridget ... 312-341-2005. 157 D bcollier@roosevelt.edu
COLLIER, Cindy ... 661-395-4281... 49 N ccollier@bakersfieldcollege.edu
COLLIER, Diondrae ... 408-273-2688... 55 H dcollier@nhu.edu
COLLIER, Douglas ... 253-752-2020. 519 K accounting@faithseminary.edu
COLLIER, Jackie ... 859-622-1260. 193 P jackie.collier@eku.edu
COLLIER, Jay ... 402-375-7325. 291 F jacolli1@wsc.edu
COLLIER, Kristen, L ... 937-327-7523. 393 E kcollier@wittenberg.edu
COLLIER, Lisa ... 618-545-3081. 149 D lcollier@kaskaskia.edu
COLLIER, Lisa ... 217-786-2446. 151 F lisa.collier@llcc.edu
COLLIER, Roger ... 918-449-6521. 396 H collier@nsuok.edu
COLLIER, Sharon ... 870-633-4480... 21 A scollier@eacc.edu
COLLIER, Stephanie ... 559-730-3700... 40 I stephanieco@cos.edu
COLLIER, Willyerd, R ... 765-361-6384. 175 B collierw@wabash.edu
COLLIER, Yeman ... 210-567-7052. 493 A colliery@uthscsa.edu
COLLIER-WHITE, Nelva, G ... 410-651-7700. 219 E ngcollier@umes.edu
COLLIFLOWER, Natalie ... 406-638-3148. 286 D stewartn@lbhc.edu
COLLIN, Lor ... 530-541-4660... 50 D collin@ltcc.edu
COLLING, Lynnde ... 307-268-2247. 542 X lcolling@caspercollege.edu
COLLINGWOD, Tracy ... 716-673-3327. 342 A tracy.collingwood@fredonia.edu
COLLINS, Aaron ... 251-981-3771... 2 I aaron.collins@columbiasouthern.edu
COLLINS, Amber ... 606-218-5251. 200 F ambercollins@upike.edu
COLLINS, Andrea ... 804-524-5973. 515 D acollins@vsu.edu
COLLINS, Anthony, G ... 315-268-6444. 320 A president@clarkson.edu
COLLINS, Bob ... 801-274-3280. 498 E robert.collins@wgu.edu
COLLINS, Bryan ... 516-299-2847. 329 D bryan.collins@liu.edu
COLLINS, Buddy ... 662-862-8271. 267 C bacollins@iccms.edu
COLLINS, Candis ... 757-457-8101. 502 C candis.collins@atlanticuniv.edu
COLLINS, Carrie ... 215-596-8948. 435 H c.collins@usciences.edu
COLLINS, Celeste ... 212-472-1500. 334 B ccollins@nysid.edu
COLLINS, Chinneta ... 301-423-3600... 96 F
COLLINS, Christine ... 337-421-6969. 204 E christine.collins@sowela.edu
COLLINS, Dana ... 580-349-1574. 397 G danac@opsu.edu
COLLINS, Darron ... 207-801-5601. 210 A dcollins@coa.edu
COLLINS, Dave ... 937-512-2522. 388 O dave.collins@sinclair.edu
COLLINS, David ... 501-279-4291... 21 C dcollins@harding.edu
COLLINS, David, A ... 724-532-5089. 432 G david.collins@email.stvincent.edu
COLLINS, David, D ... 423-439-5884. 459 C collinsd@etsu.edu
COLLINS, Dean, C ... 706-385-1094. 130 F dean.collins@point.edu
COLLINS, Deborah ... 870-230-5000... 21 D collind@hsu.edu
COLLINS, Debra ... 717-262-2010. 437 H dcollins@wilson.edu
COLLINS, Debra ... 214-333-5213. 470 D debra@dbu.edu
COLLINS, Derrick, K ... 773-995-3505. 141 J dcollins@csu.edu
COLLINS, Diana ... 215-596-8815. 435 H d.collins@usciences.edu
COLLINS, Dwight ... 415-561-6555... 60 C
COLLINS, Elaine ... 616-331-6821. 243 C collinel@gvsu.edu
COLLINS, Elizabeth ... 303-860-5600... 85 K elizabeth.collins@cu.edu
COLLINS, Ellen ... 617-323-6662. 233 D ellen_collins@mspp.edu
COLLINS, Ellen ... 402-552-6140. 288 L collins@clarksoncollege.edu
COLLINS, Elsa, G ... 610-683-4101. 429 A collins@kutztown.edu
COLLINS, Fuji ... 209-228-4331... 71 D FCollins@UCMerced.edu
COLLINS, Gary ... 478-301-2970. 128 H collins_g@mercer.edu
COLLINS, Gary ... 951-343-4304... 30 H gcollins@calbaptist.edu
COLLINS, Jacqueline, F .. 207-795-2844. 209 I collinja@cmhc.org
COLLINS, Jacqueline, M . 410-651-6407. 219 E jmcollins@umes.edu
COLLINS, James ... 916-558-2279... 53 D collins@scc.losrios.edu
COLLINS, James, E ... 508-793-7443. 225 A jcollins@clarku.edu
COLLINS, James, E ... 563-588-7103. 180 L jim.collins@loras.edu
COLLINS, Jennifer ... 336-758-4900. 370 D collinjm@wfu.edu
COLLINS, Jim ... 256-766-6610... 4 B jcollins@hcu.edu
COLLINS, John ... 812-866-6837. 166 C collins@hanover.edu
COLLINS, John ... 609-771-2167. 300 E jcollins@tcnj.edu
COLLINS, John, D ... 727-816-3310. 110 E collinj@phcc.edu
COLLINS, Joseph ... 630-942-2690. 142 G collinsj@cod.edu
COLLINS, Justin ... 580-349-1522. 397 G jkcollins@opsu.edu
COLLINS, Kamari ... 413-755-4558. 233 A kacollins@stcc.edu
COLLINS, Kathy ... 713-348-5147. 479 A kcollins@rice.edu
COLLINS, Kimberley ... 585-292-2105. 332 A kcollins@monroecc.edu
COLLINS, Kristine ... 208-426-2484. 137 G kcollin@boisestate.edu
COLLINS, L. Kay ... 812-279-8126. 171 K dcollins@ocub.oak.edu
COLLINS, L. Victor ... 410-704-5059. 220 E vcollins@towson.edu
COLLINS, Lance, R ... 607-255-9679. 322 A lc246@cornell.edu
COLLINS, Laverne ... 412-536-1059. 420 A laverne.collins@laroche.edu
COLLINS, Leigh Ann ... 979-532-6520. 494 L lacollins@wcjc.edu
COLLINS, Lori, G ... 904-632-5112. 105 E lcollins@fscj.edu
COLLINS, M. Sue ... 218-471-0015. 258 G scollins@nhed.edu
COLLINS, Marianne ... 845-687-5093. 348 H collinsm@sunyulster.edu
COLLINS, Marie ... 239-489-9214. 101 O mcollins11@edison.edu
COLLINS, Mark ... 781-736-4380. 224 F collins@brandeis.edu
COLLINS, Mark, A ... 307-766-4196. 543 I mcollin7@uwyo.edu
COLLINS, Mary ... 724-805-2564. 432 G mary.collins@email.stvincent.edu
COLLINS, Mary, K ... 315-445-4791. 328 F collinsm@lemoyne.edu
COLLINS, Mary Elizabeth 253-879-3237. 524 F lcollins@pugetsound.edu
COLLINS, Matthew ... 502-895-3411. 197 F mcollins@lpts.edu
COLLINS, Megan ... 619-594-6709... 35 D mcollins@mail.sdsu.edu
COLLINS, Michael ... 641-673-1393. 183 H collinsm@wmpenn.edu
COLLINS, Michael ... 805-525-4417... 69 H mcollins@thomasaquinas.edu
COLLINS, Michael ... 714-564-6981... 60 G collins_michaelT@sac.edu
COLLINS, Michael ... 269-488-4255. 244 L mcollins@kvcc.edu
COLLINS, Michael, F ... 508-856-8100. 229 C michael.collins@umassmed.edu
COLLINS, Mildred, D ... 615-327-6413. 456 E mcollins@mmc.edu
COLLINS, Nichole ... 804-862-6268. 508 H dcollins@rbc.edu
COLLINS, Nicole ... 207-948-9213. 211 I ncollins@unity.edu
COLLINS, Patti-Ann ... 617-228-2027. 231 C pcollins@bhcc.mass.edu
COLLINS, Paul ... 312-662-4448. 139 F pcollins@adler.edu
COLLINS, Peggy, P ... 864-596-9019. 443 D peggy.collins@converse.edu
COLLINS, Phil ... 706-864-1545. 133 D phil.collins@ung.edu
COLLINS, Richard ... 661-654-2221... 32 H rcollins6@csub.edu
COLLINS, Robert ... 504-816-4092. 201 K rcollins@dillard.edu

COLLINS, Roger 904-680-7717. 103 Q
rcollins@fcsl.edu
COLLINS, SR.,
Ronnie, L 410-951-3392. 220 B
rcollins@coppin.edu
COLLINS, Sandra 312-235-3535. 159 A
s.collins@shimer.edu
COLLINS, Sean 617-521-2296. 236 G
sean.collins@simmons.edu
COLLINS, Steve 870-612-2026... 25 A
steve.collins@uaccb.edu
COLLINS, Steve 209-575-6149... 77 J
collinss@mjc.edu
COLLINS, Sue 708-456-0300. 161 A
scollins@triton.edu
COLLINS, Sue 218-254-7985. 259 B
scollins@nhed.edu
COLLINS, Susan, M 734-763-2258. 251 C
smcol@umich.edu
COLLINS, Sylvia 931-393-1679. 461 A
scollins@mscc.edu
COLLINS, Teresa 253-833-9111. 520 C
tcollins@greenriver.edu
COLLINS, Tina 205-934-8152..... 8 E
collinst@uab.edu
COLLINS, Trudy 406-657-1680. 287 C
tcollins@msubillings.edu
COLLINS, Valerie 516-323-3008. 331 J
office-of-academic-affairs@molloy.edu
COLLINS, Walter 707-965-7500... 57 J
wcollins@puc.edu
COLLINS, Wanda 202-885-3500... 94 F
wcollin@american.edu
COLLINS, Yadigar 740-587-6530. 379 D
collinsy@denison.edu
COLLINWOOD, Nancy 801-626-6569. 497 D
ncollinwood@weber.edu
COLLIS, Jennifer 440-375-7175. 382 L
jcollis@lec.edu
COLLMIER, Robert 973-748-9000. 299 F
robert_collmier@bloomfield.edu
COLLOPY, David 413-528-7773. 222 E
dcollopy@simons-rock.edu
COLLUM, Anne 310-825-2827... 71 C
acollum@asucla.ucla.edu
COLLUM, Tammy 770-975-4000. 122 I
COLLUM, Tracy, L 336-767-7107. 355 C
tcollum@highpoint.edu
COLMAN, Dan 410-462-8432. 213 F
dcolman@bccc.edu
COLMAN, Glenn 870-743-3000... 22 B
gcoleman@northark.edu
COLMONE, Val 602-393-5900... 12 M
vcolmone@carrington.edu
COLOCHO, Elizabeth 310-233-4033... 51 H
coloche@lahc.edu
COLOM, Albert, N 419-372-1528. 374 K
acolom@bgsu.edu
COLOMBAT, Andre 410-617-2910. 216 A
acp@loyola.edu
COLOMBO, Chris 617-253-8566. 233 B
COLOMBO, Diana 201-216-5213. 307 E
dcolombo@stevens.edu
COLOMBO, Samuel 607-753-2305. 343 B
samuel.colombo@cortland.edu
COLON, Adabel-Vanessa 787-250-1912. 550 E
avcolon@metro.inter.edu
COLON, Ana Isabel 787-857-3600. 550 A
acolon@br.inter.edu
COLON, Angie 787-863-2390. 550 C
angie.colon@fajardo.inter.edu
COLON, Candida 787-738-2161. 554 C
candida.colon@upr.edu
COLON, Diana, M 787-257-7373. 552 H
dmcolon@suagm.edu
COLON, Eliseo 787-764-0000. 555 B
eliseo.colon@upr.edu
COLON, George 800-955-2527. 274 I
gcolon@grantham.edu
COLON, Gonzalo 787-738-2161. 554 C
gonzalo.colon@upr.edu
COLON, Jaime 787-279-1912. 550 B
jcolon@bayamon.inter.edu
COLON, Jose 787-879-5270. 553 I
jose.colon14@upr.edu
COLON, Jose 787-738-2161. 554 C
jose.colon@upr.edu
COLON, Leandro 787-841-2000. 552 B
leandro_colon@pucpr.edu
COLON, Lesbia 787-844-8181. 555 A
lesbia.colon@upr.edu
COLON, Lynn 407-404-6060. 113 E
colonl@seminolestate.edu
COLON, Maggie 787-763-1912. 549 J
mcolon@inter.edu
COLON, Maria 787-765-3560. 548 M
mscolon@edpuniversity.edu
COLON, Mirta 787-754-8000. 553 E
mcolon@pupr.edu
COLON, Nidia 787-786-3030. 547 F
ncolon@ucb.edu.pr
COLON, Olga 787-257-0000. 554 B
olga.colon1@upr.edu
COLON, Victor 787-786-3030. 547 F
vcolon@ucb.edu.pr
COLON, Vilma, E 787-284-1912. 550 F
vcolon@ponce.inter.edu
COLON, Yarelis 787-753-6000. 549 D
ycolon@icprjc.edu
COLON-CALZADA,
Margarita 787-480-2401. 548 G
macolon@sanjuancapital.com
COLON COSME,
Edwin, J 787-744-1060. 551 J
edwincolon@mechtech.edu
COLON GARCIA,
Michele 787-764-0000. 555 B
mcolon@upr.edu
COLON-RAMOS,
Carlos, E 787-864-2222. 550 D
ccolon@inter.edu
COLORADO, Ana 787-725-8120. 548 O
acolorado0013@eap.edu
COLSON, Darrel, D 319-352-8450. 183 E
president@wartburg.edu
COLSON, John 714-241-6257... 39 I
dcolson@coastline.edu
COLSON, Matthew 631-632-4932. 342 C
matthew.colson@stonybrook.edu
COLTER-BRABHAM,
Constance 803-780-1189. 449 E
cbrabham@voorhees.edu
COLTHARP, Duane 210-999-8201. 488 C
dcolthar@trinity.edu
COLTHARP, Glenn 417-455-5740. 273 E
GlennColtharp@crowder.edu
COLTMAN, Heather 561-297-3803. 114 L
coltman@fau.edu
COLTRANE, Scott, L 541-346-3186. 406 D
provost@uoregon.edu
COLUCCI, Rita 508-626-4993. 230 A
rcolucci@framingham.edu
COLUMBUS, Kristi 319-895-4153. 177 A
kcolumbus@cornellcollege.edu
COLUSSY-ESTES, Kate 404-471-6437. 119 I
kcolussyestes@agnesscott.edu
COLVENBACH, Mark, W 813-258-7210. 118 L
mcolvenbach@ut.edu
COLVEY, Kirsten, S 909-389-3327... 61 K
kcolvey@craftonhills.educa.us
COLVILLE, John 903-988-3747. 475 E
jcolville@kilgore.edu
COLVIN, Dora 956-364-4119. 485 H
dora.olivares@tstc.edu
COLVIN, Larry 269-749-7159. 249 A
lcolvin@olivetcollege.edu
COLVIN, Robert, E 757-594-7972. 503 M
rcolvin@cnu.edu
COLVIN, Vicki, L 713-348-0000. 479 A
colvin@rice.edu
COLVSON, W. Mark 845-257-3719. 342 B
colvsonm@newpaltz.edu
COLWELL, Brad 419-372-7403. 374 K
bcolwell@bgsu.edu
COLWELL, Judy 580-628-6210. 396 M
judy.colwell@noc.edu
COLWELL, Kim, H 217-443-8769. 143 G
kcolwell@dacc.edu
COLWELL, Melodie 870-460-1522... 24 D
colwell@uamont.edu
COLYAR, Jana 801-333-8100. 495 J
COMAGE, Rebecca 978-542-6401. 230 E
rebecca.comage@salemstate.edu
COMAIR, Claude 425-558-0299. 519 B
ccomair@digipen.edu
COMANDA, Peter 815-280-6606. 149 A
pcomanda@jjc.edu
COMAS, Waldemar, A 914-594-4567. 334 A
waldemar@nymc.edu
COMBE, Arnold, B 801-581-6404. 496 Q
arnie.combe@admin.utah.edu
COMBINE, Mark, S 724-738-2251. 429 F
mark.combine@sru.edu
COMBS, Charles, D 757-446-6090. 504 E
combscd@evms.edu
COMBS, Delcie 606-487-3100. 195 C
Delcie.Combs@kctcs.edu
COMBS, Joseph, L 423-585-2675. 462 A
joseph.combs@ws.edu
COMBS, Kristina, A 415-485-9504... 40 G
kristina.combs@marin.edu
COMBS, Steven 808-544-0228. 135 F
scombs@hpu.edu
COMBS, Steven 814-732-2400. 428 E
COMBS, Tiffany 606-368-6055. 191 J
tiffanycombs@alc.edu
COMBS, Vickie 606-487-3110. 195 C
vickie.combs@kctcs.edu
COMEAU, Elise 617-585-1230. 234 I
elise.comeau@necmusic.edu
COMEAUX, David, P 337-482-0922. 208 D
dcomeaux@louisiana.edu
COMEAUX, Linda 303-797-5997... 78 F
linda.comeaux@arapahoe.edu
COMEAUX, Mark 714-879-3901... 47 K
mcomeaux@hiu.edu
COMEDY, Alan, V 508-531-1241. 229 D
acomedy@bridgew.edu
COMEDY, Edna 651-793-1278. 259 C
edna.comedy@metrostate.edu
COMEDY-HOLMES,
Jennifer 210-486-4857. 464 J
jcomedy-holmes@alamo.edu
COMER, Alberta 812-237-3700. 167 A
alberta.comer@indstate.edu
COMER, Christopher 406-243-2632. 286 H
chris.comer@umontana.edu
COMER, Crystal 612-330-1034. 253 H
comerc@augsburg.edu
COMER, Kimberly 229-928-1373. 126 D
kim.comer@gsw.edu
COMER, Pamela, D 540-432-4314. 504 D
pam.comer@emu.edu
COMERFORD, John 217-854-3231. 140 G
john.comerford@blackburn.edu
COMEY, William 301-934-7509. 214 D
billc@csmd.edu
COMFORT, Randy, C 517-750-1200. 250 E
rcomfort@arbor.edu
COMINGORE, Terry 979-230-3318. 468 A
terry.comingore@brazosport.edu
COMMISSO, Louis 516-918-3609. 315 G
lcommisso@bcl.edu
COMMON, Easter 601-977-7879. 270 A
ecommon@tougaloo.edu
COMMONS, Mary 803-508-7413. 440 G
commonsm@atc.edu
COMPAAN, Korey 916-577-2200... 76 J
kcompaan@jessup.edu
COMPARY, Kristin 361-593-3606. 484 A
kristin.compary@tamuk.edu
COMPHER, Jeff 252-737-4501. 367 B
compherj@ecu.edu
COMPLIMENT, Brad 562-985-4001... 33 F
brad.compliment@csulb.edu
COMPTON, Betsy 205-652-3892..... 9 F
bcompton@uwa.edu
COMPTON, D. Chad 808-675-3790. 135 C
chad.compton@byuh.edu
COMPTON, Jennifer 517-264-3175. 238 G
COMPTON, Kerry 510-981-2933... 59 A
kcompton@peralta.edu
COMRIE, Andrew, C 520-621-1856... 18 F
comrie@email.arizona.edu
COMSTOCK, Alysha 708-524-6296. 144 C
acomstock@dom.edu
COMSTOCK, Jane Marie . 803-323-2225. 449 G
president@winthrop.edu
COMVALIUS-GODDARD,
Sharon 617-552-8259. 224 A
sharon.comvalius-goddard@bc.edu
CONARD, T. Hunt 518-580-5940. 341 A
hconard@skidmore.edu
CONATSER, Diane 708-709-3579. 156 A
dconatser@prairiestate.edu
CONAWAY, Kathleen, M . 814-332-4799. 409 D
kathleen.conaway@allegheny.edu
CONBOY, Sheila "Katie" . 617-521-2077. 236 G
katie.conboy@simmons.edu
CONCEPCION, Beth 912-525-5000. 131 B
bconcepc@scad.edu
CONCHA, Lee 847-578-8848. 157 F
lee.concha@rosalindfranklin.edu
CONCILIO, Michael 215-335-0800. 422 C
mconcilio@lincolntech.com
CONCO, Paul, W 757-569-6712. 513 E
pconco@pdc.edu
CONDE, Jean 650-508-3513... 56 H
jconde@ndnu.edu
CONDE-FRAZIER,
Elizabeth 215-324-0746. 415 G
econdefr@eastern.edu
CONDIC, Elizabeth, S 701-355-8083. 373 E
escondic@umary.edu
CONDIE, Brad 262-243-5700. 532 H
brad.condie@cuw.edu
CONDINO, Francis 724-357-2782. 428 F
fcondino@iup.edu
CONDON, Charlie 276-935-4349. 502 A
ccondon@asl.edu
CONDON, Debra, A 610-799-1938. 421 I
dcondon@lccc.edu
CONDON, Jacquelyn, S .. 309-457-2113. 153 D
jackiec@monmouthcollege.edu
CONDON, Jennifer 813-974-6061. 116 C
jcondon@admin.usf.edu
CONDON, Jennifer, M 515-574-1190. 179 D
condon@iowacentral.edu
CONDON, Katherine 850-474-2236. 117 B
kcondon@uwf.edu
CONDON, Michael, A 214-768-2802. 481 A
mikec@smu.edu
CONDON, Patricia 508-678-2811. 231 B
patricia.condon@bristolcc.edu
CONDON, Sara, A 515-574-1005. 179 D
condon_s@iowacentral.edu
CONDON, Tami 269-471-3591. 239 D
alumni@andrews.edu
CONDON, Terry 617-287-7800. 228 G
terry.condon@umb.edu
CONDRA, Shawn, M 785-539-3571. 188 F
scondra@mccks.edu
CONDRON, Dan 707-664-2732... 36 B
condrond@sonoma.edu
CONE, Allen, J 323-265-8913... 51 F
coneaj@elac.edu
CONE, Diana 912-478-5258. 126 C
dcone@georgiasouthern.edu
CONE, Janet, R 828-251-6922. 368 C
jcone@unca.edu
CONELLI, Maria, A 718-951-3180. 317 C
MConelli@brooklyn.cuny.edu
CONEWAY, Raydor 478-553-2065. 129 H
rconeway@oftc.edu
CONEY, Lennetta 810-762-0269. 247 F
lennetta.coney@mcc.edu
CONGDON, Bruce, D 206-281-2899. 523 C
bcongdon@spu.edu
CONGER, Heather 609-894-9311. 299 I
hconger@bcc.edu
CONGER, Lora 918-270-6402. 398 I
lora.conger@ptstulsa.edu
CONGLETON, Dawn, L 434-223-6203. 505 E
dcongleton@hsc.edu
CONGLETON, O. Mort 919-866-5926. 364 G
omcongleton@waketech.edu
CONGRESSI, Karyn 386-752-1822. 104 G
karyn.congressi@fgc.edu
CONIGLIO, Michael 706-880-8184. 128 A
mconiglio@lagrange.edu
CONINE, Chris 423-614-8102. 455 L
cconine@leeuniversity.edu
CONINE, Frances 318-357-6703. 208 B
coninef@nsula.edu
CONISON, Jay 704-971-8500. 353 F
CONJAR, Catarin 610-647-4400. 418 I
cconjar@immaculata.edu
CONKLIN, Barbara 252-399-6570. 352 F
baconklin@barton.edu
CONKLIN, D. David 845-431-8980. 323 C
conklin@sunydutchess.edu
CONKLIN, David 716-488-3026. 327 I
david.conklin@jamestownbusinesscollege.edu
CONKLIN, Deborah, M 260-481-6118. 168 C
conklin@ipfw.edu
CONKLIN, Denise 405-912-9005. 395 K
dconklin@hc.edu
CONKLIN, Eileen 915-831-4432. 472 B
econklin@epcc.edu
CONKLIN, Elizabeth 860-486-2943... 92 A
elizabeth.conklin@uconn.edu
CONKLIN, Kathleen 517-371-5140. 250 G
conklink@cooley.edu
CONKLIN, Lara, L 217-443-8798. 143 G
lconklin@dacc.edu
CONKLIN, Lorraine 540-857-6500. 514 E
lconklin@virginiawestern.edu
CONKLIN, Margaret 212-355-1501. 316 H
mconklin@christies.edu
CONKLIN, Peter 603-513-1382. 298 E
peter.conklin@granite.edu
CONKLIN, Robin 845-574-4484. 338 B
CONKLIN, Sandra 607-729-1581. 322 F
sconklin@davisny.edu
CONLEY, Aaron 972-883-6402. 491 E
aconley@utdallas.edu
CONLEY, Bill 402-554-2358. 293 A
bconley@unomaha.edu
CONLEY, Cary 270-831-9610. 195 D
cary.conley@kctcs.edu
CONLEY, Colleen 218-733-7626. 259 A
c.conley@lsc.edu
CONLEY, Davis, B 607-431-4173. 325 F
conleyd@hartwick.edu
CONLEY, Dennis 618-395-7777. 147 B
conleyd@iecc.edu
CONLEY, Heather 319-398-5504. 180 J
heather.conley@kirkwood.edu
CONLEY, Jeremy, D 515-574-1086. 179 D
conley@iowacentral.edu
CONLEY, Jerome 513-529-2800. 384 G
conleyj@miamioh.edu
CONLEY, John 518-562-4219. 320 B
john.conley@clinton.edu
CONLEY, Katharine 757-221-2470. 503 N
kconley@wm.edu
CONLEY, Keith, A 828-448-3151. 365 A
kconley@wpcc.edu
CONLEY, Kimberley, S 270-831-9752. 195 D
kim.conley@kctcs.edu
CONLEY, Laura, H 330-972-5793. 390 E
lhc1@uakron.edu

CONLEY, Mark .... 206-543-4139. 524 G
mconley@uw.edu
CONLEY, Marsha, A .... 717-866-5775. 416 E
mconley@evangelical.edu
CONLEY, MeShawn .... 405-974-5944. 400 K
mconley@uco.edu
CONLEY, Michael Anne .. 415-442-7281... 45 I
maconley@ggu.edu
CONLEY, Sean .... 802-258-9203. 499 F
sconley@marlboro.edu
CONLEY, Sonja .... 620-331-4100. 187 G
sconley@indycc.edu
CONLEY, Susanne, H ..... 508-626-4926. 230 A
sconley@framingham.edu
CONLEY, Terry .... 580-581-2308. 394 G
tconley@cameron.edu
CONLEY, William, J .... 508-793-3423. 225 B
wjconley@holycross.edu
CONLEY, William, T .... 570-577-1618. 411 A
bill.conley@bucknell.edu
CONLIFFE, Marcia .... 863-297-1004. 110 H
mconliffe@polk.edu
CONLIN, Pam .... 214-768-3738. 481 A
pconlin@smu.edu
CONLOGUE, Jon .... 413-572-5572. 230 F
jconlogue@westfield.ma.edu
CONLON, Cindy, H .... 256-765-4206..... 9 C
chconlon@una.edu
CONLON, Joanne .... 610-436-3506. 430 A
jconlon@wcupa.edu
CONLON, Kevin, J .... 614-222-6171. 378 A
kconlon@ccad.edu
CONN, Brian .... 423-614-8621. 455 L
bconn@leeuniversity.edu
CONN, C. Paul .... 423-614-8600. 455 L
pconn@leeuniversity.edu
CONN, Keith .... 757-464-4600. 516 E
deankconn@cie-wc.edu
CONN, Melinda .... 314-434-4044. 273 C
melinda.conn@covenantseminary.edu
CONN, Richard .... 202-639-1764... 95 B
rconn@corcoran.org
CONN, Sam .... 678-915-3440. 132 C
sconn@spsu.edu
CONNAGHAN, Stephen .. 202-319-5055... 94 G
connaghan@cua.edu
CONNALLY, Sam .... 502-852-3698. 200 D
s0conn02@louisville.edu
CONNAUGHTON,
David, M .... 409-772-3446. 493 C
dmconnau@utmb.edu
CONNELL, Bernadean ..... 817-598-6350. 494 G
bconnell@wc.edu
CONNELL, Dan, J .... 606-783-2612. 198 A
d.connell@moreheadstate.edu
CONNELL, Mary Kay .... 401-341-2262. 440 C
connellm@salve.edu
CONNELL, Matthew, J .... 570-688-2466. 425 D
mconnell@northampton.edu
CONNELL, Patrick .... 518-454-2833. 321 A
connellp@strose.edu
CONNELL, Rich .... 218-281-8490. 264 E
rconnell@umn.edu
CONNELL, S. Jack .... 585-594-6200. 337 K
connell_jack@roberts.edu
CONNELL, Timothy .... 562-908-3413... 60 I
tconnell@riohondo.edu
CONNELLY, Carol .... 219-785-5267. 172 A
cconnelly@pnc.edu
CONNELLY, Edward, D .... 860-628-4751... 90 D
econnelly@lincolncollegene.edu
CONNELLY, Frank, P ...... 304-243-2241. 531 H
fconnelly@wju.edu
CONNELLY, Krysti, H ..... 618-537-6861. 152 G
khconnelly@mckendree.edu
CONNELLY, Laurie .... 509-359-2372. 519 C
lconnelly@ewu.edu
CONNELLY, Philip .... 908-737-7000. 302 F
pconnell@kean.edu
CONNELLY-WEIDA,
Cecelia, A .... 610-799-1630. 421 I
cconnellyweida@lccc.edu
CONNELY, Anne .... 610-398-5300. 422 B
aconnely@lincolntech.com
CONNELY, Kristen .... 425-564-2388. 517 A
kristen.connely@bellevuecollege.edu
CONNER, Andrea .... 641-269-3708. 178 H
conneran@grinnell.edu
CONNER, Arabie .... 785-242-5200. 189 I
arabie.conner@ottawa.edu
CONNER, B. Renee .... 301-784-5000. 213 B
rconner@allegany.edu
CONNER, Courtney, L ..... 276-619-4317. 511 C
cconner@swcenter.edu
CONNER, David .... 806-894-9611. 480 H
dconner@southplainscollege.edu
CONNER, Deborah .... 843-349-2300. 442 E
dconner@coastal.edu
CONNER, Jamelle .... 727-341-3358. 112 E
conner.jamelle@spcollege.edu
CONNER, Louis, M .... 931-540-2632. 460 E
lconner@columbiastate.edu
CONNER, Marc .... 540-458-8418. 516 A
connerc@wlu.edu
CONNER, Meg .... 828-565-4095. 361 B
mbconner@haywood.edu
CONNER, Phyllis .... 402-375-7510. 291 F
phconne1@wsc.edu
CONNER, Rita, D .... 828-694-1825. 358 C
ritac@blueridge.edu
CONNER, Shelly .... 559-324-6476... 68 H
shelly.conner@scccd.edu
CONNER, Susan .... 517-629-0221. 239 A
sconner@albion.edu
CONNERAT, Carolyn, K .. 512-475-9223. 491 C
cconnerat@austin.utexas.edu
CONNERS, John, R .... 607-844-8222. 347 I
connerj@tc3.edu
CONNERS, Mary Ann ..... 732-906-4681. 303 B
mconners@middlesexcc.edu
CONNERTY, Denise, A .... 215-204-0720. 433 K
denise.connerty@temple.edu
CONNERY, Elizabeth, A .. 570-348-6200. 423 B
connery@marywood.edu
CONNETT, David .... 909-469-5264... 76 B
dconnett@westernu.edu
CONNIFF, Brian, P .... 570-941-7560. 436 A
brian.conniff@scranton.edu
CONNIRY, JR.,
Charles, J .... 503-554-6152. 403 C
cconniry@georgefox.edu
CONNOLE, Kim .... 701-627-4738. 371 A
kconno@fbcc.bia.edu
CONNOLLY, Adam .... 843-383-8050. 442 F
aconnolly@coker.edu
CONNOLLY, Ann Marie .. 313-883-8500. 249 E
connolly.annmarie@shms.edu
CONNOLLY, Becky .... 505-473-6318. 311 K
becky.connolly@santafeuniversity.edu
CONNOLLY, Dan .... 920-686-6163. 536 A
dan.connolly@sl.edu
CONNOLLY, Derry .... 858-653-6740... 49 C
CONNOLLY, Donna .... 401-841-6499. 545 A
CONNOLLY, Elizabeth, A 315-386-7325. 345 F
connolly@canton.edu
CONNOLLY, Jim .... 203-332-5088... 88 F
jconnolly@hcc.commnet.edu
CONNOLLY, John .... 718-409-5979. 346 D
jconnolly@sunymaritime.edu
CONNOLLY, Jon, H .... 307-674-6446. 543 F
jconnolly@sheridan.edu
CONNOLLY, Lidy .... 858-653-6740... 49 C
CONNOLLY, Lynn .... 720-279-8990... 82 D
lconnolly@csl.org
CONNOLLY, Meg .... 314-977-7121. 281 I
burnsmm@slu.edu
CONNOLLY, Melissa, A .. 516-463-4160. 326 D
melissa.a.connolly@hofstra.edu
CONNOLLY, Michael .... 320-363-3512. 263 P
mconnolly@csbsju.edu
CONNOLLY, Monika .... 949-582-4602... 67 C
mconnolly@saddleback.edu
CONNOLLY, Patricia, A .. 412-536-1243. 420 A
patricia.connolly@laroche.edu
CONNOLLY, Robert .... 617-287-7073. 228 E
rconnolly@umassp.edu
CONNOLLY, Shawn .... 973-655-4643. 303 D
connollys@mail.montclari.edu
CONNOLLY, Tara .... 515-964-6447. 177 B
tkconnolly@dmacc.edu
CONNON, Ryan .... 207-453-5141. 210 L
rconnon@kvcc.me.edu
CONNOR, Caroline .... 415-869-2900. 227 F
caroline.connor@hult.edu
CONNOR, Catherine, H .. 610-519-4036. 436 F
catherine.connor@villanova.edu
CONNOR, Edward, J .... 508-831-5286. 238 F
econnor@wpi.edu
CONNOR, Francis, P ...... 260-399-7700. 174 C
fconnor@sf.edu
CONNOR, Joanne .... 856-256-4102. 305 E
connorj@rowan.edu
CONNOR, Nancy, J .... 253-535-7465. 521 I
connornj@plu.edu
CONNOR, Pat .... 812-855-1764. 167 F
connorp@indiana.edu
CONNOR, Roger .... 203-837-9301... 88 B
connorr@wcsu.edu
CONNOR, Rosie .... 435-283-7160. 498 A
rosie.connor@snow.edu
CONNOR, Syd .... 601-266-4119. 270 E
connie.wyldmon@usm.edu
CONNOR, Terrence .... 214-768-4909. 481 A
connor@smu.edu
CONNOR, Terry, D .... 859-344-3308. 199 H
terry.connor@thomasmore.edu
CONNORS, Ann .... 703-821-8570. 510 B
aconnorts@stratford.edu
CONNORS, Anne .... 207-453-5126. 210 L
aconnors@kvcc.me.edu
CONNORS, Chalese .... 940-898-2373. 488 B
cconnors@twu.edu
CONNORS, Cheryl, C ..... 401-739-5000. 439 D
cconnors@neit.edu
CONNORS, Chris .... 727-864-8404. 101 N
connorce@eckerd.edu
CONNORS, Christine, M 617-266-1400. 223 D
CONNORS, John .... 215-596-8973. 435 H
j.connors@usciences.edu
CONNORS, Michael, W .. 773-371-5484. 141 D
mconnors@ctu.edu
CONNORS, Nancy, J ...... 718-940-5580. 339 B
nconnors@sjcny.edu
CONNORS, Natalie .... 219-785-5498. 172 A
nconnors@pnc.edu
CONOLLY, Charlene .... 410-287-6060. 214 B
cconolly@cecil.edu
CONOVER, Dustin .... 307-382-1644. 543 J
dconover@wwcc.wy.edu
CONOVER, Melanie .... 801-524-1927. 495 O
ConoverM@ldsbc.edu
CONOVER, Randall .... 937-328-6180. 377 A
conoverr@clarkstate.edu
CONOVER, Wheeler .... 606-589-3038. 196 F
wheeler.conover@kctcs.edu
CONRAD, Jacqueline ...... 617-873-0621. 224 G
Jacqueline.Conrad@cambridgecollege.edu
CONRAD, Jeffrey .... 617-236-8800. 226 F
jconrad@fisher.edu
CONRAD, Jerry .... 202-319-5515... 94 G
conradj@cua.edu
CONRAD, Jon, B .... 610-861-1526. 424 E
jconrad@moravian.edu
CONRAD, Kari, M .... 570-577-1217. 411 A
kari.conrad@bucknell.edu
CONRAD, Karol, A .... 270-824-1741. 196 A
karol.conrad@kctcs.edu
CONRAD, Katie, A .... 859-846-5807. 197 I
kconrad@midway.edu
CONRAD, Rebecca .... 207-775-3052. 210 H
bconrad@meca.edu
CONRAD, Rhonda .... 641-683-5115. 179 A
rhonda.conrad@indianhills.edu
CONRAD, Scott .... 707-524-1553... 65 B
sconrad@santarosa.edu
CONRAD, Valarie .... 312-949-7304. 146 G
vconrad@ico.edu
CONRADSEN, Susan ...... 706-236-5494. 121 G
sconradsen@berry.edu
CONROE, Nicole .... 716-829-7645. 323 D
conroen@dyc.edu
CONROY, Michele .... 610-902-8526. 411 E
michele.r.conroy@cabrini.edu
CONROY, Nina .... 212-237-8606. 318 D
nconroy@jjay.cuny.edu
CONROY, JR., Philip ..... 802-728-1251. 501 F
pconroy@vtc.edu
CONROY, Sarah .... 207-948-9169. 211 I
sconroy@unity.edu
CONROY, Shelley, F .... 214-820-3361. 467 G
shelley_conroy@baylor.edu
CONROY, Timothy .... 207-974-4682. 210 K
tconroy@emcc.edu
CONSIVINE-FONTES,
Lisa, M .... 410-825-2444. 439 A
lfontes@ccri.edu
CONSOLVO, Camille .... 406-771-5133. 287 E
camille.consolvo@gfcmsu.edu
CONSOLVO, Camille .... 541-962-3635. 405 H
cconsolv@eou.edu
CONSTABLE, Catherine ... 858-534-2827... 71 F
CONSTABLE, Jean .... 830-372-8090. 485 C
jconstable@tlu.edu
CONSTANCE, Eric, F ...... 315-786-2252. 327 L
econstance@sunyjefferson.edu
CONSTANT, Alan .... 256-824-3142..... 8 F
alan.constant@uah.edu
CONSTANTIN, Michael ... 225-216-8615. 202 H
constantinm@mybrcc.edu
CONSTANTINE, Carol ..... 508-678-2811. 231 B
carol.constantine@bristolcc.edu
CONSTANTINE, OSB,
Cyprian, G .... 724-805-2332. 432 H
cyprian.constantine@email.stvincent.edu
CONSTANTINE, Doris, F . 512-448-8525. 479 C
dorisc@stedwards.edu
CONSTANTINE, Ruth, H . 413-585-2200. 236 H
rconstan@smith.edu
CONSTANTINO, John ...... 808-245-8245. 136 H
johncons@hawaii.edu
CONSTANTINO, Lisa ...... 303-447-3846... 83 F
lconstantino@naropa.edu
CONSTANTINOU,
Constantia .... 718-409-7236. 346 D
cconstantinou@sunymaritime.edu
CONSTON, Marcia .... 704-330-6647. 359 C
marcia.conston@cpcc.edu
CONTANT, Cheryl .... 715-682-1675. 535 D
ccontant@northland.edu
CONTARINO, Sue .... 847-925-6200. 145 H
scontari@harpercollege.edu
CONTE, Jeffrey, A .... 914-606-6795. 350 F
jeffrey.conte@sunywcc.edu
CONTE, John .... 214-637-3530. 494 E
jconte@wadecollege.edu
CONTE, Millie .... 718-631-6222. 319 D
mconte@qcc.cuny.edu
CONTI, Erik .... 336-506-4201. 357 M
erik.conti@alamancecc.edu
CONTOMANOLIS,
Emanuel .... 585-475-5464. 337 L
emcoce@rit.edu
CONTOMANOLIS, Laurel 585-275-3166. 349 C
laurel.contomanolis@rochester.edu
CONTOS, Tanya .... 617-850-1231. 227 E
tcontos@hchc.edu
CONTRELLA, R. Thomas . 412-373-6400. 433 B
tcontrella@western-school.com
CONTRERAS, Adriana .... 210-485-0020. 464 I
acontreras81@alamo.edu
CONTRERAS, Beatriz ...... 219-989-2510. 171 N
beatriz.contreras@purduecal.edu
CONTRERAS, James .... 202-274-6053... 97 A
jcontreras@udc.edu
CONTRERAS, Lisa .... 312-935-6620. 156 K
lcontreras@robertmorris.edu
CONTRERAS, Raquel, J .. 864-656-2451. 442 C
rcontre@clemson.edu
CONTRERAS, JR.,
Sebastian .... 847-635-1756. 155 F
scontrer@oakton.edu
CONTRERAS, Sylvia .... 608-663-3278. 532 I
scontreras@edgewood.edu
CONVER, M. Kathleen .... 309-677-2242. 140 I
mkc@bradley.edu
CONVERSE, Kenneth, L .. 712-749-2101. 176 D
conversek@bvu.edu
CONVERSE, Sharon, K .... 248-341-2154. 248 D
skconver@oaklandcc.edu
CONVERTINO, Gary .... 508-541-1681. 225 F
gconvertino@dean.edu
CONWAY, Cathy .... 847-317-8135. 160 M
cconway@tiu.edu
CONWAY, Cathy .... 580-745-2152. 399 J
cconway@se.edu
CONWAY, Charles .... 718-270-3049. 342 D
charles.conway@downstate.edu
CONWAY, Charlotte .... 269-471-6616. 243 G
charlott@andrews.edu
CONWAY, Christine, G ... 717-291-4083. 416 J
christine.conway@fandm.edu
CONWAY, Dan .... 317-955-6280. 170 V
dconway@marian.edu
CONWAY, David .... 607-431-4943. 325 F
conwayd@hartwick.edu
CONWAY, Dennis, S .... 518-580-5566. 341 A
dconway@skidmore.edu
CONWAY, Elizabeth .... 781-768-7249. 236 A
elizabeth.conway@regiscollege.edu
CONWAY, Guy .... 813-974-5400. 116 C
gconway@usf.edu
CONWAY, Jayne .... 760-744-1150... 58 D
jconway@palomar.edu
CONWAY, Jean, L .... 972-860-7001. 470 I
JConway@dcccd.edu
CONWAY, Karen .... 901-321-3536. 453 H
kconway@cbu.edu
CONWAY, Sandra .... 727-873-4775. 116 D
sconway@mail.usf.edu
CONWAY, Sharon .... 301-891-4005. 221 B
sconway@wau.edu
CONWAY, Teresa .... 509-359-6489. 519 C
tconway@ewu.edu
CONWAY, Thomas .... 910-672-2501. 367 D
tconway@uncfsu.edu
CONWAY-TURNER,
Katherine .... 301-696-3023. 215 D
conwayturner@hood.edu
CONWAY-WELCH,
Colleen .... 615-343-8876. 463 G
colleen.conway-welch@vanderbilt.edu
CONWELL, Betty .... 425-739-8215. 520 K
betty.conwell@lwtech.edu
CONWELL, James, C ...... 812-877-8000. 172 C
conwell@rose-hulman.edu
CONYERS, Rhyan, M ...... 859-233-8898. 199 I
rconyers@transy.edu
CONZA, Lisa .... 516-299-3810. 329 C
lisa.conza@liu.edu
CONZATTI, Maria, P .... 516-572-7600. 332 C
maria.conzatti@ncc.edu
COOGAN, Janet .... 563-441-4201. 178 C
jcoogan@eicc.edu
COOGAN, Jay .... 612-874-3737. 257 B
president@mcad.edu
COOK, Aaron .... 231-995-2914. 248 B
acook@nmc.edu
COOK, Aaron .... 303-546-5284... 83 F
acook@naropa.edu
COOK, Adrienne .... 978-867-4238. 226 H
adrienne.cook@gordon.edu

COOK, Allen, P ... 203-576-4206 ... 91 G
acook@bridgeport.edu
COOK, Amber ... 814-871-7421. 416 K
cook0692@gannon.edu
COOK, Andrea, P ... 503-517-1212. 408 H
acook@warnerpacific.edu
COOK, Angela ... 207-780-5737. 212 H
adcook@usm.maine.edu
COOK, Anthony ... 314-505-7774. 272 J
cooka@csl.edu
COOK, Arlene ... 229-248-2579. 121 E
acook@bainbridge.edu
COOK, Barbara ... 973-300-2263. 307 F
bcook@sussex.edu
COOK, Barbara Jo ... 770-467-6038. 132 B
bcook@sctech.edu
COOK, Blake ... 229-317-6726. 124 A
russell.cook@darton.edu
COOK, Bradley ... 435-586-7704. 497 A
bradcook@suu.edu
COOK, Brenda, A ... 334-683-2353 ... 5 F
bcook@marionmilitary.edu
COOK, Brian ... 440-525-7720. 382 M
bcook@lakelandcc.edu
COOK, Bruce ... 386-506-4417. 101 G
cookb@DaytonaState.edu
COOK, Carey, W ... 208-467-8661. 139 A
cwcook@nnu.edu
COOK, Carson, C ... 901-678-2713. 460 B
carson.cook@memphis.edu
COOK, Charles, M ... 713-718-5042. 473 C
charles.cook@hccs.edu
COOK, Chris ... 806-742-2136. 487 D
chris.cook@ttu.edu
COOK, Connie, S ... 540-985-8344. 506 G
cscook@jchs.edu
COOK, Constance, E ... 734-763-0159. 251 C
cecook@umich.edu
COOK, Darrell ... 202-885-3541 ... 94 F
dcook@american.edu
COOK, David ... 913-897-8400. 190 L
davidcook@ku.edu
COOK, David ... 309-268-8181. 146 B
david.cook@heartland.edu
COOK, David ... 415-485-9405 ... 40 G
david.cook@marin.edu
COOK, David, E ... 218-722-4000. 255 E
davidc@dbumn.edu
COOK, Dawn ... 678-664-0515. 134 H
dawn.cook@westgatech.edu
COOK, Debra ... 918-335-6264. 398 F
dcook@okwu.edu
COOK, Donelda ... 410-617-5171. 216 A
dcook@loyola.edu
COOK, Donna, L ... 575-439-3699. 310 J
donnac@nmsu.edu
COOK, Donna, M ... 401-341-2435. 440 C
donna.cook@salve.edu
COOK, Earl ... 334-291-4966 ... 2 H
earl.cook@cv.edu
COOK, Edith ... 724-830-1014. 433 E
ecook@setonhill.edu
COOK, Ellen, D ... 337-482-6306. 208 D
edcook@louisiana.edu
COOK, Elsie ... 510-567-6174 ... 69 C
drcook@sum.edu
COOK, Gary ... 580-371-2371. 396 E
gcook@mscok.edu
COOK, Gary, R ... 214-333-5130. 470 D
mitch@dbu.edu
COOK, Gary, W ... 770-484-1204. 128 E
lru@lru.edu
COOK, Greg ... 262-472-1077. 538 D
cookg@uww.edu
COOK, Howard, M ... 803-786-3343. 443 B
hcook@columbiasc.edu
COOK, James ... 336-734-7311. 360 E
jcook@forsythtech.edu
COOK, Jeffrey ... 657-278-4475 ... 33 E
jcook@exchange.fullerton.edu
COOK, Jenene ... 617-427-0060. 232 G
jcook@rcc.mass.edu
COOK, Jerry ... 918-456-5511. 396 H
COOK, Jessica ... 302-736-2435 ... 94 C
jessica.cook@wesley.edu
COOK, Jim ... 573-651-2206. 282 B
jcook@semo.edu
COOK, John ... 603-206-8009. 296 A
jcook@ccsnh.edu
COOK, John, C ... 540-985-8317. 506 G
jccook@jchs.edu
COOK, Jolane ... 870-777-5722 ... 25 B
jolane.cook@uacch.edu
COOK, Karen ... 650-723-2300 ... 68 E
kcook@stanford.edu
COOK, Kathy ... 425-388-9273. 519 I
kcook@everettcc.edu
COOK, Kevin ... 601-984-4100. 270 C
kcook@umc.edu
COOK, Larry ... 909-389-3384 ... 61 K
lcook@craftonhills.edu
COOK, Lenora ... 620-276-9521. 187 A
lenora.cook@gcccks.edu
COOK, Les, P ... 906-487-2465. 247 A
lpcook@mtu.edu
COOK, Mark ... 616-395-7833. 244 A
cook@hope.edu
COOK, Mary ... 713-222-5340. 489 D
cookm@uhd.edu
COOK, Melinda ... 617-670-4462. 226 F
mcook1@fisher.edu
COOK, Melinda ... 800-567-2344. 532 E
melcook@menominee.edu
COOK, Melissa ... 207-801-5610. 210 A
mcook@coa.edu
COOK, Michelle ... 405-208-5000. 397 F
michelle.cook@okcu.edu
COOK, Michelle ... 336-750-2184. 370 A
cookm@wssu.edu
COOK, Michelle, G ... 706-583-8195. 133 C
mgcook@uga.edu
COOK, Phil ... 423-614-8500. 455 L
pcook@leeuniversity.edu
COOK, Richard, D ... 585-785-1410. 324 D
cookrd@flcc.edu
COOK, Rosalie ... 650-493-4430 ... 66 E
rosalie.cook@sofia.edu
COOK, Royrickers ... 334-844-5700 ... 1 G
cookroy@auburn.edu
COOK, Sandra ... 619-594-4756 ... 35 D
scook@mail.sdsu.edu
COOK, Sandra ... 303-986-2320 ... 80 D
careers@csha.net
COOK, Scott, A ... 304-336-8137. 530 A
cookscot@westliberty.edu
COOK, Sharon, L ... 972-860-7629. 470 I
SCook@dcccd.edu
COOK, Stacy, A ... 408-864-8330 ... 44 M
cookstacy@deanza.edu
COOK, Steve ... 502-895-3411. 197 F
scook@lpts.edu
COOK, Tena ... 308-432-6213. 291 D
tcook@csc.edu
COOK, Terry ... 410-455-2939. 219 D
tcook@umbc.edu
COOK, Thomas ... 239-513-1135. 119 E
COOK, Tim ... 360-992-2217. 518 A
tcook@clark.edu
COOK, Tom, G ... 304-327-4111. 529 D
tcook@bluefieldstate.edu
COOK, Toni ... 510-748-2135 ... 59 B
tcook@peralta.edu
COOK, Tony ... 504-671-5478. 203 A
tcook@dcc.edu
COOK, Vicki ... 231-995-1144. 248 B
vcook@nmc.edu
COOK, Vickie ... 618-664-7081. 145 G
vickie.cook@greenville.edu
COOK, William ... 304-307-0716. 528 F
william.cook@southernwv.edu
COOK-FRANCIS, Lynette 212-237-8100. 318 D
lcook-francis@jjay.cuny.edu
COOK-HUFFMAN,
Daniel, J ... 814-641-3151. 419 H
cookhud@juniata.edu
COOK-NOBLES, Robin ... 784-283-2839. 237 F
rcooknob@wellesley.edu
COOKE, Connie, F ... 716-878-4902. 343 A
cookecf@buffalostate.edu
COOKE, Harry ... 704-922-6355. 360 F
cooke.harry@gaston.edu
COOKE, Joy ... 757-825-2728. 514 B
cookej@tncc.edu
COOKE, Linda ... 206-239-4500. 517 M
lcooke@cityu.edu
COOKE, Matthew ... 616-957-6076. 240 M
mkc071@calvinseminary.edu
COOKE, Peggy, S ... 248-370-2190. 248 J
cooke@oakland.edu
COOKE, Sean ... 253-840-8472. 522 C
scooke@pierce.ctc.edu
COOKE, Sunita ... 619-644-7100 ... 46 E
sunita.cooke@gcccd.edu
COOKER, Dianne ... 704-991-0282. 364 C
dcooker8019@stanly.edu
COOKMAN, John ... 972-825-4659. 481 F
jcookman@sagu.edu
COOKS, Owen, J ... 336-750-2855. 370 A
cooksoj@wssu.edu
COOKSEY, Beth ... 615-230-3560. 461 G
beth.cooksey@volstate.edu
COOKSEY, Gaye, M ... 972-881-5807. 469 G
gcooksey@collin.edu
COOKSEY, Lynita ... 870-972-2030 ... 19 N
lcooksey@astate.edu
COOKSEY, Marilyn ... 504-286-3275. 270 I
marilyn.cooksey@wmcarey.edu
COOKSON, Nancy, B ... 402-465-2117. 291 G
nbc@nebrwesleyan.edu
COOL, Sharon ... 605-331-6760. 452 D
sharon.cool@usiouxfalls.edu
COOLE, Gloria, G ... 218-722-4000. 255 E
finaid@dbumn.edu
COOLEY, Alvin, L ... 973-353-5882. 306 D
alvin.cooley@rutgers.edu
COOLEY, Dennis, R ... 608-342-1182. 537 D
cooleyde@uwplatt.edu
COOLEY, Francis ... 203-287-3029 ... 90 H
paier.dean@snet.net
COOLEY, John ... 614-287-2501. 378 B
jcooley@cscc.edu
COOLEY, Marianne, B ... 784-283-3344. 237 F
mcooley@wellesley.edu
COOLEY, Meghan, M ... 309-794-7314. 139 L
meghancooley@augustana.edu
COOLEY, Mike ... 972-860-7871. 471 B
mcooley@dcccd.edu
COOLEY, Tom ... 816-604-6538. 277 D
thomas.cooley@mcckc.edu
COOLING, Mike ... 619-688-0800 ... 41 H
mcooling@concorde.edu
COOMAR, Parmeshwar ... 734-384-4209. 247 C
pcoomar@monroeccc.edu
COOMBE, Robert, D ... 303-871-2111 ... 86 B
chancellor@du.edu
COOMBS, Gary, F ... 619-201-8989 ... 67 G
gcoombs@shadowmountain.org
COOMBS, Matt ... 831-755-6725 ... 46 G
mcoombs@hartnell.edu
COOMBS, Robert ... 207-741-5569. 211 A
rcoombs@smccme.edu
COOMBS, Vanessa ... 804-257-5856. 515 F
vcoombs@vuu.edu
COOMER, Sue, B ... 270-384-8024. 197 D
coomers@lindsey.edu
COOMES, Judy ... 270-686-4532. 196 C
judy.coomes@kctcs.edu
COOMES, Kerrie ... 620-431-2820. 189 D
kcoomes@neosho.edu
COON, David, W ... 415-485-9502 ... 40 G
davidwain.coon@marin.edu
COON, Omayra ... 910-221-2224. 354 D
COON, Thomas, G ... 517-355-2308. 246 H
coontg@msu.edu
COONAN, Daniel ... 408-554-5344 ... 64 M
dcoonan@scu.edu
COONAN, Patrick, R ... 516-877-4511. 313 A
coonan@adelphi.edu
COONEN, Ned ... 847-214-7557. 144 F
ncoonen@elgin.edu
COONEY, Marcia, J ... 570-577-1631. 411 A
marcia.cooney@bucknell.edu
COONEY, Terry ... 410-704-2128. 220 E
tcooney@towson.edu
COONEY MINER,
Dianne, C ... 585-385-8472. 338 H
dcooney-miner@sjfc.edu
COONING, Peggy, J ... 615-248-1355. 462 D
pcooning@trevecca.edu
COONROD, Curtis, C ... 314-516-5211. 283 E
curt_coonrod@umsl.edu
COONROD, Julie ... 505-277-2711. 312 F
jcoonrod@unm.edu
COONS, Christopher ... 814-824-3125. 423 J
ccoons@mercyhurst.edu
COONS, Maria ... 847-925-6143. 145 H
mcoons@harpercollege.edu
COONS, Patrick ... 502-272-8056. 192 E
pcoons@bellarmine.edu
COONS, Robert, A ... 812-877-8007. 172 C
robert.a.coons@rose-hulman.edu
COOPEE, Scott, J ... 413-782-1246. 238 A
sjcoopee@wne.edu
COOPER, Alan ... 212-678-8065. 328 A
alcooper@jtsa.edu
COOPER, Amy, M ... 270-384-8053. 197 D
coopera@lindsey.edu
COOPER, Aneita ... 870-759-4184 ... 25 K
acooper@wbcoll.edu
COOPER, Ann, A ... 803-778-6636. 441 F
cooperaa@cctech.edu
COOPER, Anne, M ... 727-341-3323. 112 E
cooper.anne@spcollege.edu
COOPER, Barbara, I ... 252-222-6225. 358 G
cooperb@carteret.edu
COOPER, Brett ... 870-759-4107 ... 25 K
bcooper@wbcoll.edu
COOPER, Candace ... 704-878-3256. 362 B
ccooper@mitchellcc.edu
COOPER, Carrie ... 601-984-1117. 270 C
cecooper@umc.edu
COOPER, Carrie ... 757-221-3055. 503 N
clcooper@wm.edu
COOPER, Cary, W ... 409-772-2665. 493 C
ccooper@utmb.edu
COOPER, Colleen, M ... 386-822-7481. 117 C
cmcooper@stetson.edu
COOPER, Cynthia, L ... 585-292-3015. 332 A
ccooper@monroecc.edu
COOPER, David ... 773-777-4220. 155 B
dcooper@nc.edu
COOPER, David ... 401-841-3540. 545 A
COOPER, Derek ... 215-368-5000. 410 F
dcooper@biblical.edu
COOPER, Donna ... 518-464-8632. 324 B
dcooper@excelsior.edu
COOPER, Doug ... 404-653-7882. 129 D
dacooper@morehouse.edu
COOPER, Ed ... 229-430-3577. 120 A
ecooper@albanytech.edu
COOPER, Frank ... 609-771-2357. 300 E
cooper@tcnj.edu
COOPER, Franklin ... 406-638-3161. 286 D
cooperf@lbhc.edu
COOPER, Fred ... 815-802-8752. 149 C
fcooper@kcc.edu
COOPER, Gail, S ... 626-585-7282 ... 58 F
gscooper@pasadena.edu
COOPER, Gayle ... 870-612-2004 ... 25 A
gayle.cooper@uaccb.edu
COOPER, Helena ... 804-330-0111. 503 G
stuadvcrim@centura.edu
COOPER, Hortense ... 310-660-3492 ... 43 B
hcooper@elcamino.edu
COOPER, James ... 773-291-6536. 142 D
jcooper53@ccc.edu
COOPER, James ... 610-409-3698. 436 B
jcooper@ursinus.edu
COOPER, James, E ... 334-727-8011 ... 8 A
cooper@tuskegee.edu
COOPER, James, M ... 619-239-0391 ... 36 D
jcooper@cwsl.edu
COOPER, James, W ... 678-915-4986. 132 C
jcooper@spsu.edu
COOPER, Jeffrey ... 215-898-1388. 435 B
jeffcoop@upenn.edu
COOPER, Jennifer ... 404-233-3949. 458 F
jcooper@richmont.edu
COOPER, Jeremy ... 405-945-7799. 398 L
jeremyc@plattcollege.org
COOPER, Joel ... 610-328-7679. 433 I
jcooper2@swarthmore.edu
COOPER, John, D ... 563-333-6480. 182 B
CooperJohnD@sau.edu
COOPER, Jorsene ... 757-727-5323. 505 F
jorsene.cooper@hamptonu.edu
COOPER, Karen ... 603-897-8508. 297 F
kcooper@rivier.edu
COOPER, Karen, S ... 650-723-0198 ... 68 E
karen.cooper@stanford.edu
COOPER, Karl, S ... 205-802-1200 ... 3 C
karl.cooper@vc.edu
COOPER, Karla ... 402-826-8111. 289 E
karla.cooper@doane.edu
COOPER, Katie ... 304-336-8131. 530 A
katie.mills@westliberty.edu
COOPER, Kelly ... 815-921-4092. 157 A
k.cooper@rockvalleycollege.edu
COOPER, Kenneth ... 845-758-7461. 314 D
cooper@bard.edu
COOPER, Kerrie, L ... 315-386-7616. 345 F
cooper@canton.edu
COOPER, Lisa, A ... 229-931-2921. 126 D
lcooper@gsw.edu
COOPER, Lisa, J ... 215-951-2940. 430 E
cooperl@philau.edu
COOPER, Margaret ... 815-802-8962. 149 C
mcooper@kcc.edu
COOPER, Marina ... 410-704-2356. 220 E
mcooper@towson.edu
COOPER, Mark ... 614-251-4576. 386 B
cooperm2@ohiodominican.edu
COOPER, Mark, E ... 740-368-3108. 387 J
mecooper@owu.edu
COOPER, Mary, K ... 434-223-6311. 505 E
mcooper@hsc.edu
COOPER, Mary-Beth ... 413-748-3241. 236 I
mcooper@springfieldcollege.edu
COOPER, MaryKay ... 210-999-7011. 488 C
marykay.cooper@trinity.edu
COOPER, Matthew ... 609-984-1140. 308 A
mcooper@tesc.edu
COOPER, Michael ... 908-737-4120. 302 F
mrcooper@kean.edu
COOPER, N. John ... 412-624-1164. 435 C
cooper@pitt.edu
COOPER, Nani Lou, S ... 864-488-4617. 444 L
mreger@limestone.edu
COOPER, Natalie ... 215-871-6560. 430 D
nataliecoo@pcom.edu
COOPER, Patricia, A ... 808-956-7541. 136 B
pcooper@hawaii.edu
COOPER, R. Scott ... 267-502-2681. 410 I
rscott.cooper@brynathyn.edu
COOPER, Reginald ... 870-574-4504 ... 23 G
rcooper@sautech.edu
COOPER, Rick ... 251-981-3771 ... 2 I
rick.cooper@columbiasouthern.edu
COOPER, Robert, A ... 213-740-2101 ... 74 A
racooper@usc.edu
COOPER, Ruth ... 512-313-3000. 469 L
ruth.cooper@concordia.edu

COOPER, Scott ... 718-933-6700. 331 K
scooper@monroecollege.edu
COOPER, Stephanie ... 973-300-2161. 307 F
scooper@sussex.edu
COOPER, Stewart, E ... 219-464-5002. 174 E
stewart.cooper@valpo.edu
COOPER, Susan ... 949-936-1605... 33 E
scooper@fullerton.edu
COOPER, Tami, L ... 580-327-8530. 396 N
tlcooper@nwosu.edu
COOPER, Tammi ... 254-295-4507. 490 B
tcooper@umhb.edu
COOPER, Tana ... 620-792-9241. 184 F
coopert@bartonccc.edu
COOPER, Tara, L ... 606-546-1241. 200 A
tcooper@unionky.edu
COOPER, Toya ... 805-565-6832... 76 D
tcooper@westmont.edu
COOPER, Tracey, L ... 440-525-7230. 382 M
tcooper@lakelandcc.edu
COOPER, Tyson ... 540-261-2716. 509 K
tyson.cooper@svu.edu
COOPER, Yolanda ... 305-284-3551. 118 F
ycooper@miami.edu
COOPER-WHITE,
Michael, L ... 717-334-6286. 422 E
mcooper@ltsg.edu
COOPWOOD, SR.,
Kenneth ... 417-836-3736. 278 E
kcoopwood@missouristate.edu
COOROUGH, Randall ... 262-691-5168. 541 D
rcoorough@wctc.edu
COOTER, Raelynn ... 215-503-6595. 434 C
raelynn.cooter@jefferson.edu
COOTER, Robert, B ... 502-272-7992. 192 E
rcooter@bellarmine.edu
COOTS, Kevin ... 606-326-2064. 194 J
kevin.coots@kctcs.edu
COPANS, Ruth, S ... 518-580-5506. 341 A
rcopans@skidmore.edu
COPAS, Lisa ... 937-393-3431. 389 B
lcopas@sscc.edu
COPE, Glen, H ... 314-516-5373. 283 E
copeg@umsl.edu
COPE, Henry ... 843-574-6606. 447 E
henry.cope@tridenttech.edu
COPE, Marla ... 913-234-0687. 185 L
marla.cope@cleveland.edu
COPE, Matthew ... 251-626-3303..... 8 B
mcope@ussa.edu
COPE, Melody ... 631-244-3023. 323 B
copem@dowling.edu
COPELAND, Alice ... 903-730-4890. 474 O
ACopeland@jarvis.edu
COPELAND, Brian ... 616-331-2831. 243 C
copelabr@gvsu.edu
COPELAND, David, L ... 540-464-7218. 515 B
copelanddl@vmi.edu
COPELAND, Dawn ... 931-393-1698. 461 A
dcopeland@mscc.edu
COPELAND,
Deborah Gayle ... 530-226-4133... 66 D
COPELAND, Elaine, J ... 803-327-7402. 442 D
ecopeland@clintonjuniorcollege.edu
COPELAND, Judson ... 405-425-5129. 397 D
judson.copeland@oc.edu
COPELAND, Kenneth ... 434-395-2016. 506 J
copelandpk@longwood.edu
COPELAND, Leigh ... 843-525-8231. 447 C
lcopeland@tcl.edu
COPELAND, Louise ... 651-290-6439. 265 F
louise.copeland@wmitchell.edu
COPELAND, Maura ... 912-478-7481. 126 C
mconley@georgiasouthern.edu
COPELAND, Paul ... 706-880-8051. 128 A
pcopeland@lagrange.edu
COPELAND, Robert ... 803-327-7402. 442 D
rcopeland@clintonjuniorcollege.edu
COPELAND, JR.,
Robert, M ... 803-327-7402. 442 D
rcopeland@clintonjuniorcollege.edu
COPELAND, Sandra ... 252-862-1225. 363 A
sandrac@roanokechowan.edu
COPELAND, Sarah ... 423-473-2368. 460 D
SCopeland01@clevelandstatecc.edu
COPELAND, Wanda ... 610-796-8437. 409 E
wanda.copeland@alvernia.edu
COPELAND-MORGAN,
Youlonda ... 310-825-2665... 71 C
ycopeland-morgan@saonet.ucla.edu
COPELY, Pat ... 937-376-2946. 388 B
pcopely@payne.edu
COPENAGLE, Lily ... 503-517-7916. 407 E
copenagl@reed.edu
COPENHAVER, Bonny ... 715-394-6677. 541 F
bonny.copenhaver@witc.edu
COPENHAVER, Michael .. 619-644-7000... 46 E
michael.coppenhaver@gcccd.edu
COPES, Marcella ... 410-951-3990. 220 B
mcopes@coppin.edu
COPLIN, Kimberly, A ... 740-587-6243. 379 D
coplin@denison.edu
COPLIN, Louis ... 518-629-7348. 326 G
l.coplin@hvcc.edu
COPONITI, Mike ... 405-224-3140. 401 E
mcoponiti@usao.edu
COPONITI, Mike, D ... 405-224-3140. 401 E
mcoponiti@usao.edu
COPP, Destini ... 404-432-3475. 131 H
acopp@southuniversity.edu
COPP, Joan ... 717-394-6211. 413 J
COPPEDGE, Robin ... 580-371-2371. 396 E
rcoppedge@mscok.edu
COPPENHAVER,
Dorian, H ... 409-772-2665. 493 C
dcoppenh@utmb.edu
COPPER-GLENZ, Becky .. 507-389-1333. 259 G
becky.coper-glenz@mnsu.edu
COPPERSMITH,
Clifford, P ... 570-326-3761. 427 B
ccoppers@pct.edu
COPPI, Carla, E ... 618-453-7661. 159 G
ccoppi@siu.edu
COPPINGER, Debbie ... 615-460-6474. 453 C
debbie.coppinger@belmont.edu
COPPLE, Chad ... 618-437-5321. 156 H
copplec@rlc.edu
COPPLE, James "Dean" .. 865-694-6536. 461 D
jdcopple@pstcc.edu
COPPOLA, David, L ... 570-945-8500. 419 N
david.coppola@keystone.edu
COPPOLA, Kristin ... 503-725-8799. 406 B
coppola@pdx.edu
COPPOLA, Sandra ... 973-278-5400. 299 D
sec@berkeleycollege.edu
COPPOLA, Stephen, A ... 704-687-5965. 368 E
scoppola@uncc.edu
COPPOLA, William ... 817-515-3001. 482 B
william.coppola@tccd.edu
COPPRUE, Lisa ... 313-845-9610. 243 H
lcopprue@hfcc.edu
COQUEREL, Phoebe ... 404-225-4529. 121 B
pcoquerel@atlantatech.edu
CORA, Gladys ... 787-766-1717. 552 J
um_gcora@suagm.edu
CORA, Ivette ... 787-250-1912. 550 E
icora@intermetro.com
CORAZZA, Anthony ... 718-368-5124. 318 E
acorazza@kbcc.cuny.edu
CORBA, David ... 586-286-2058. 246 A
corbad@macomb.edu
CORBAT, Carol ... 318-473-6431. 205 A
ccorbat@lsua.edu
CORBETT, Andy ... 303-352-3032... 81 D
andy.corbett@cccs.edu
CORBETT, Ann ... 207-621-3145. 212 C
annie@maine.edu
CORBETT, Carrie ... 901-272-5111. 456 F
ccorbett@mca.edu
CORBETT, Heather ... 860-768-2409... 92 D
hcorbett@hartford.edu
CORBETT, Idna, M ... 610-436-3416. 430 A
icorbett@wcupa.edu
CORBETT, Keith ... 605-688-4153. 452 B
keith.corbett@sdstate.edu
CORBETT, Kevin, J ... 785-864-4760. 190 L
kcorbett@ku.edu
CORBETT, Martin ... 315-781-3656. 326 C
corbett@hws.edu
CORBETT, Michele ... 619-849-2510... 59 L
michelecorbett@pointloma.edu
CORBETT, Mickey ... 432-837-8059. 487 B
mcorbett@sulross.edu
CORBIN, Amanda ... 912-583-3249. 122 B
acorbin@bpc.edu
CORBIN, Edith ... 609-894-9311. 299 I
ecorbin@bcc.edu
CORBIN, Rebecca, A ... 609-894-9311. 299 I
rcorbin@bcc.edu
CORBIN, Thomas ... 802-443-5504. 499 H
corbin@middlebury.edu
CORBIN, Ty ... 804-523-5726. 512 F
tcorbin@reynolds.edu
CORBINE, Theresa, C ... 315-386-7448. 345 F
corbine@canton.edu
CORBITT, Sandra, K ... 540-338-1776. 508 A
slife@phc.edu
CORBITT, Timothy ... 315-229-5392. 339 F
CORBITT, Timothy, J ... 315-268-2327. 320 A
tcorbitt@clarkson.edu
CORBITT, Zach ... 864-596-9215. 443 D
zach.corbitt@converse.edu
CORBLY, James, E ... 785-827-5541. 188 C
james.corbly@kwu.edu
CORBOY, Lynne ... 215-780-1392. 433 A
lcorboy@salus.edu
CORCORAN, Janenne ... 410-386-8444. 214 A
jcorcoran@carrollcc.edu
CORCORAN, Jerry, M ... 815-224-0404. 148 A
jerry_corcoran@ivcc.edu
CORCORAN, Kevin, J ... 248-370-2140. 248 J
corcoran@oakland.edu
CORCORAN, Lisa ... 425-564-2302. 517 A
lisa.corcoran@bellevuecollege.edu
CORCORAN, Mary, C ... 617-552-8647. 224 A
mary.corcoran@bc.edu
CORCORAN, Mike ... 757-490-1241. 501 G
mcorcoran@auto.edu
CORCORAN, Thomas, B . 212-678-3126. 347 G
CORCORAN, Tim ... 619-644-7649... 46 C
tim.corcoran@gcccd.edu
CORCORAN, William ... 201-612-5234. 299 C
wcorcoran@bergen.edu
CORCORAN, William, M . 570-208-5846. 419 P
wmcorcor@kings.edu
CORDANO, Mark ... 978-837-5000. 234 A
cordanom@merrimack.edu
CORDEIRO, Paula, A ... 619-260-4540... 73 I
cordeiro@sandiego.edu
CORDEIRO, Wayne ... 541-485-1780. 405 B
waynecordeiro@newhope.edu
CORDEIRO, William ... 805-437-8860... 32 I
william.corderio@csuci.edu
CORDELL, Barbara ... 903-694-4003. 478 A
bcordell@panola.edu
CORDELL, David, J ... 425-640-1412. 519 D
dcordell@edcc.edu
CORDELL, Janice, K ... 563-387-1018. 180 M
cordellj@luther.edu
CORDELL, Joyce ... 915-831-6530. 472 B
jyamasak@cpcc.edu
CORDELL, Michelle ... 479-619-4361... 22 C
mcordell@nwacc.edu
CORDELL, Peggy ... 706-295-6959. 125 F
pcordell@gntc.edu
CORDELL, Penny ... 706-272-4498. 123 G
pcordell@daltonstate.edu
CORDER, Colleen ... 503-552-1702. 404 H
ccorder@ncnm.edu
CORDERO, Bill ... 510-436-2478... 59 D
bcordero@peralta.edu
CORDERO, Damaris ... 787-751-0160. 548 J
dcordero@cmpr.gov.pr
CORDERO, Dona ... 847-491-3355. 155 D
d-cordero@northwestern.edu
CORDERO, Edwin ... 864-578-8770. 446 F
ecordero@sherman.edu
CORDERO, Heather ... 847-317-7071. 160 M
hcordero@tiu.edu
CORDERO, Irma, L ... 787-740-1611. 553 C
irma.cordero@uccaribe.edu
CORDERO, Jose ... 787-758-2525. 554 F
jose.cordero6@upr.edu
CORDERO, Maggie ... 562-860-2451... 37 I
mcordero@cerritos.edu
CORDERO, Zain ... 787-882-2065. 553 A
mis@unitecpr.net
CORDERY, Simon ... 706-864-1819. 133 D
simon.cordery@ung.edu
CORDES, Molly ... 319-226-2091. 175 D
Molly.Cordes@AllenCollege.edu
CORDIA, Judith ... 775-445-3295. 295 A
judith.cordia@wnc.edu
CORDISCO, Shelli ... 607-778-5222. 315 I
cordiscosl@sunybroome.edu
CORDLE, David ... 620-341-5171. 186 D
dcordle@emporia.edu
CORDLE, Robbie, L ... 301-687-4403. 220 C
rcordle@frostburg.edu
CORDOVA, Damion ... 970-339-6656... 78 C
damion.cordova@aims.edu
CORDOVA, Denise ... 775-682-6708. 294 J
dcordova@unr.edu
CORDOVA, Jose, A ... 787-704-1020. 548 L
jcordova@ediccollege.edu
CORDOVA, Mitchell ... 239-590-7074. 115 A
mcordova@fgcu.edu
CORDOVA, Ryan ... 505-747-2288. 311 E
rcordova@nnmc.edu
CORDOVA, Tracy, H ... 417-667-8181. 273 A
tcordova@cottey.edu
CORDRAY, John ... 843-953-8259. 443 A
cordrayj@cofc.edu
CORDULACK, John ... 217-875-7200. 156 J
jcordula@richland.edu
CORDULACK, Tricia ... 217-875-7200. 156 J
tcordulack@richland.edu
CORE, Gordon ... 724-938-5985. 428 A
core@calu.edu
CORE, Jaqueline ... 724-852-3295. 437 A
jcore@waynesburg.edu
CORE, Justin ... 541-881-5781. 408 C
jcore@tvcc.cc
COREN, Richard, H ... 401-825-2028. 439 A
rhcoren@ccri.edu
CORESSEL, James ... 419-783-2503. 379 C
jcoressel@defiance.edu
COREY, Barry, H ... 562-903-4701... 29 L
president@biola.edu
COREY, Frederick, C ... 602-496-0624... 11 K
frederick.corey@asu.edu
COREY, George, A ... 413-577-5211. 228 F
gcorey@uhs.umass.edu
COREY, M, J ... 304-637-1344. 526 E
coreym@dewv.edu
COREY, Steven, M ... 269-749-7642. 249 A
scorey@olivetcollege.edu
CORIA, Elizabeth ... 562-908-3411... 60 I
elizabeth.coria@riohondo.edu
CORIEL, Paul, D ... 318-743-6444. 205 A
pcoreil@lsua.edu
CORIELL, Bruce ... 719-389-6638... 79 D
bcoriell@coloradocollege.edu
CORINO, Mark, A ... 973-618-3412. 300 A
mcorino@caldwell.edu
CORJAY, Marcy ... 704-216-7217. 363 D
marcy.corjay@rccc.edu
CORKERY, John, E ... 312-987-1426. 148 L
7corkery@jmls.edu
CORKILL, Jim, R ... 805-893-5882... 72 B
jim.corkill@accounting.ucsb.edu
CORKRAN, Kenneth, F ... 508-541-1700. 225 F
kcorkran@dean.edu
CORKRUM, Dalia, L ... 509-527-5193. 525 E
corkrum@whitman.edu
CORKUM, David ... 617-552-4500. 224 A
david.corkum@bc.edu
CORLE, Trish ... 814-262-3841. 427 C
tcorle@pennhighlands.edu
CORLEY, Bruce ... 817-274-4284. 467 H
CORLEY, David ... 530-257-6181... 50 F
dcorley@lassencollege.edu
CORLEY, Diane ... 512-463-9976. 486 D
diane.corley@tsus.edu
CORLEY, John, C ... 870-230-5179... 21 D
corleyj@hsu.edu
CORLEY, Teresa ... 615-794-4254. 457 Q
tcorley@omorecollege.edu
CORLEY, Thomas ... 785-242-5200. 189 I
thomas.corley@ottawa.edu
CORLISS, Bruce ... 401-874-6222. 440 D
bruce.corliss@gso.uri.edu
CORLL, Thomas ... 432-685-5540. 476 G
tcorll@midland.edu
CORMACK, Barbara ... 530-283-0202... 44 H
bcormack@frc.edu
CORMAN, RJ ... 828-398-7286. 357 N
richardjcorman@abtech.edu
CORMIER, Marilyn, E ... 802-654-2215. 500 B
mcormier@smcvt.edu
CORMIER, Matthew ... 508-362-2131. 231 D
mcormier@capecod.edu
CORN, Melanie ... 510-594-3649... 30 K
mcorn@cca.edu
CORNACCHIA,
Eugene, J ... 201-761-6010. 306 L
ecornacchia@saintpeters.edu
CORNEJO-DARCY, Silvia 619-216-6755... 68 B
scornejo@swccd.edu
CORNELIA, Jim ... 712-274-5234. 181 B
cornelia@morningside.edu
CORNELIUS, Alice ... 602-286-8330... 14 L
Alice.cornelius@gwmail.maricopa.edu
CORNELIUS, Jerod, L ... 651-631-5320. 263 A
jlcornelius@nwc.edu
CORNELIUS, Michael ... 480-423-6573... 15 E
michael.cornelius@scottsdalecc.edu
CORNELIUS, Tim ... 479-619-3117... 22 C
tcornelius@nwacc.edu
CORNELIUS TAYLOR,
Carmen ... 406-353-2607. 285 E
ctaylor@ancollege.edu
CORNELL, Brian ... 718-409-7200. 346 D
bcornell@sunymaritime.edu
CORNELL, Craig ... 740-597-3280. 387 C
cornellc@ohio.edu
CORNELL, Dennis ... 213-740-2111... 74 A
dcornell@president.usc.edu
CORNELL, Dona, G ... 832-842-0949. 489 A
dhcornell@uh.edu
CORNELL, Dona, G ... 713-743-0949. 489 B
dhcornell@uh.edu
CORNELL, John ... 912-279-5703. 123 B
jcornell@ccga.edu
CORNELL, Kenneth, E ... 206-281-2405. 523 C
kcornell@spu.edu
CORNELL-SCOTT,
Andrea ... 540-887-7270. 507 A
ascott@mbc.edu
CORNER, William, T ... 616-526-6451. 240 L
wtc2@calvin.edu
CORNERO, Robert ... 732-571-3424. 303 C
rcornero@monmouth.edu
CORNETT, Jeff ... 317-921-4282. 169 L
jcornett29@ivytech.edu
CORNETT, Scott ... 606-368-6120. 191 J
scottcornett@alc.edu
CORNETT, Sherry, N ... 770-720-5543. 130 G
snc@reinhardt.edu
CORNFORD, Ernest, A ... 314-516-5092. 283 E
cornford@umsl.edu

CORNIA, Gary, C ... 801-422-4122. 495 D
gary_cornia@byu.edu
CORNIER, Wilfredo ... 787-841-2000. 552 B
wcornier@pucpr.edu
CORNILLE, Keith, T ... 608-246-6464. 540 C
kcornille@madisoncollege.edu
CORNISH, Irene, K ... 315-859-4999. 325 E
icornish@hamilton.edu
CORNISH, Letitia ... 336-750-2132. 370 A
cornishl@wssu.edu
CORNMAN, Thomas, H ... 937-766-7770. 375 K
tcornman@cedarville.edu
CORNNER, Ryan ... 323-265-8967... 51 F
cornnerm@elac.edu
CORNOG, Evan, W ... 516-463-5213. 326 D
evan.cornog@hofstra.edu
CORNUE, Amy, L ... 315-684-6041. 345 A
cornueal@morrisville.edu
CORNWELL, Grant, H ... 330-263-2311. 377 H
gcornwell@wooster.edu
CORNWELL, Nancy ... 406-994-6654. 287 B
nancy.cornwell@montana.edu
CORNWELL, Phillip, J ... 812-877-8232. 172 C
cornwell@rose-hulman.edu
CORNWELL, Shirley, A ... 937-393-3431. 389 B
scornwell@sscc.edu
COROMINAS, Mike ... 954-262-8840. 109 K
coromina@nova.edu
CORONA, Nayeli ... 610-574-6909... 57 E
ncorona@pacificcollege.edu
CORONA, Paul ... 847-491-8570. 155 D
p-corona@northwestern.edu
CORONA, Stacie ... 530-898-5931... 33 A
scorona@csuchico.edu
CORONADO, Ricardo ... 817-515-5234. 482 B
ricardo.coronado@tccd.edu
CORPUS, Ben ... 646-312-4570. 316 J
Ben.Corpus@baruch.cuny.edu
CORR, Daniel, P ... 480-423-6317... 15 E
daniel.corr@scottsdalecc.edu
CORR, John ... 215-571-4478. 415 B
john.m.corr@drexel.edu
CORR, Marianne ... 574-631-6411. 174 A
mcorr1@nd.edu
CORRADETTI, Arthur ... 718-631-6344. 319 D
acorradetti@qcc.cuny.edu
CORRADO, Rebecca ... 212-217-4202. 324 C
rebecca_corrado@fitnyc.edu
CORRAL, Nohel ... 650-738-4124... 64 D
corraln@smccd.edu
CORRAL-NAVA, Nita ... 915-831-2302. 472 B
ncorraln@epcc.edu
CORRAN, Robert ... 802-656-3075. 500 F
robert.corran@uvm.edu
CORREA, Arleen, E ... 787-765-1915. 551 C
acorrea@opto.inter.edu
CORREA, Florinda ... 361-582-2516. 493 H
florinda.correa@victoriacollege.edu
CORREA, Leslie, H ... 808-544-0235. 135 F
lcorrea@hpu.edu
CORREA, Omar ... 563-588-7823. 180 L
omar.correa@loras.edu
CORREA, Peter ... 814-838-7673. 416 G
pcorrea@fortisinstitute.edu
CORREA, Santy ... 787-284-1912. 550 F
scorrea@ponce.inter.edu
CORREA, Sylvia ... 256-233-8116..... 1 F
sylvia.correa@athens.edu
CORREDERA, Enrique ... 802-656-2005. 500 F
enrique.corredera@uvm.edu
CORREIA, Jorge ... 781-595-6768. 228 C
jcorreia@mariancourt.edu
CORREIA, Mark, E ... 724-357-2555. 428 F
mark.correia@iup.edu
CORRELL, Dennis, L ... 570-327-4761. 427 B
dcorrell@pct.edu
CORRELL, Jen ... 717-728-2362. 412 J
jencorrell@centralpenn.edu
CORRELL, Scott ... 715-232-2121. 538 B
corrells@uwstout.edu
CORRENTI, Bill ... 718-368-5066. 318 E
bcorrenti@kbcc.cuny.edu
CORRIE, Rosie ... 575-769-4021. 309 F
rosie.corrie@clovis.edu
CORRIGAN, Boo ... 845-938-3701. 545 I
Boo.Corrigan@usma.edu
CORRIGAN, Deborah ... 518-438-3111. 330 C
debc@mariacollege.edu
CORRIGAN, Kevin ... 404-727-6460. 124 E
kcorrig@emory.edu
CORRIGAN, JR.,
Robert, F ... 713-798-6392. 467 F
corrigan@bcm.edu
CORRIGAN, Tom ... 617-217-9205. 222 G
tcorrigan@baystate.edu
CORRISS, Mary Jean ... 540-362-6332. 505 G
corrissmj@hollins.edu
CORRY, Mac ... 706-542-2277. 133 C
mcorry@uga.edu
CORSELLO, Christine, L ... 704-403-4336. 352 J
christine.corsello@carolinashealthcare.org
CORSENTINO, Leanne ... 719-549-3206... 84 G
leanne.corsentino@pueblocc.edu
CORSINI, Kevin, D ... 434-592-4691. 506 I
kdcorsini@liberty.edu
CORSO, Michael ... 973-720-2202. 308 I
corsom1@wpunj.edu
CORSO, Teri ... 973-290-4266. 300 F
tcorso@cse.edu
CORSON-RIKERT,
Janet, L ... 607-255-3564. 322 A
jlc18@cornell.edu
CORTES, Chris ... 559-638-3641... 69 A
chris.cortes@reedleycollege.edu
CORTES, Dario, A ... 973-278-5400. 299 D
dario@berkeleycollege.edu
CORTES, Dario, A ... 212-986-4343. 314 K
dario@berkeleycollege.edu
CORTES, Edymariel ... 939-292-8918. 555 C
edymariel.cortes@upr.edu
CORTES, Elvia, E ... 202-231-5605. 544 L
elvia.cortes@dodiis.mil
CORTES, Felix ... 787-841-2000. 552 B
fcortes@pucpr.edu
CORTES, Frances ... 787-878-5475. 549 L
fcortes@arecibo.inter.edu
CORTES, Gloria ... 787-891-0925. 549 K
gcortes@aguadilla.inter.edu
CORTES, Graciela ... 503-845-3555. 404 D
graciela.cortes@mtangel.edu
CORTES, Reinaldo ... 352-323-3691. 108 S
cortesr@lssc.edu
CORTES, Tammy ... 831-813-6820. 476 A
tammy.a.cortes@lonestar.edu
CORTESE, Joseph ... 570-504-9620. 413 B
CORTEZ, Herbert ... 831-443-1700... 47 D
herbert_cortez@heald.edu
CORTEZ, Jack ... 973-748-9000. 299 F
jack_cortez@bloomfield.edu
CORTEZ, Lori ... 989-386-6622. 247 B
lcortez@midmich.edu
CORTEZ, Ray ... 956-721-5303. 475 F
rcortez@laredo.edu
CORTEZ, Ronald, S ... 415-338-2521... 35 E
rscortez@sfsu.edu
CORTEZ, Sandra, L ... 956-721-5374. 475 F
sandra.cortez@laredo.edu
CORTEZ-FARAH, Terre ... 619-684-8763... 56 C
tcortez@newschoolarch.edu
CORTHELL, Ronald ... 219-989-2401. 171 N
ronald.corthell@purduecal.edu
CORTI, Tom ... 631-420-2264. 346 B
tom.corti@farmingdale.edu
CORTINAS, Debra ... 361-825-5743. 483 F
debra.cortinas@tamucc.edu
CORVEY, Rebecca, J ... 478-471-2734. 128 I
rebecca.corvey@maconstate.edu
CORVIN, Clay, L ... 504-282-4455. 206 A
claycor@wbsn.com
CORY, Christopher ... 212-346-1117. 335 J
ccory@pace.edu
CORY, Jeff ... 845-675-4425. 335 C
jeff.cory@nyack.edu
CORYAT, Catherine, A ... 973-655-4199. 303 D
coryatc@mail.montclair.edu
COSBY, Glen ... 509-533-3576. 518 F
glen.cosby@spokanefalls.edu
COSBY, Glen ... 509-533-3681. 518 F
glen.cosby@spokanefalls.edu
COSBY, Kevin, W ... 502-776-1443. 199 A
COSBY, Laura ... 268-488-4440. 244 L
lcosby@kvcc.edu
COSCIA, Paul ... 336-316-2395. 355 A
pcoscia@guilford.edu
COSDEN, Julie ... 239-280-2558... 98 K
julie.cosden@avemaria.edu
COSENTINO, Lauren ... 310-506-4397... 58 H
lauren.cosentino@pepperdine.edu
COSENTINO, Richard, E ... 910-521-6209. 369 B
cosentino@uncp.edu
COSEY, Arnel ... 504-671-5055. 203 A
acosey@dcc.edu
COSGROVE, John ... 570-662-4586. 429 C
jcosgrov@mansfield.edu
COSGROVE, Maryellen ... 706-867-3230. 133 D
maryellen.cosgrove@ung.edu
COSIMO, Julie ... 630-829-6037. 140 B
jcosimo@ben.edu
COSKY, Alicia, C ... 630-844-5116. 140 A
acosky@aurora.edu
COSMATO, Charlie ... 540-831-6597. 508 C
ccosmato@radford.edu
COSO, Xuchitl ... 863-680-4390. 105 D
xcoso@flsouthern.edu
COSPER, Tracy ... 229-317-6838. 124 A
tracy.cosper@darton.edu
COSSART, Benoit ... 703-539-6890. 510 B
bcossart@stratford.edu
COSSICH, Marc ... 936-468-2608. 482 A
mcossich@sfasu.edu
COSSICH, Monique ... 936-468-2504. 482 A
cossichm@sfasu.edu
COSSITT, Brenda ... 307-755-2244. 544 B
bcossitt@wyotech.edu
COST, Timothy, P ... 904-256-7016. 107 Q
tcost@ju.edu
COSTA, Elizabeth, A ... 540-985-9701. 506 G
eacosta@jchs.edu
COSTA, Kathleen ... 925-551-1822... 41 L
Kcosta@dvc.edu
COSTA, Linda, J ... 732-932-7743. 306 B
linda.costa@rutgers.edu
COSTA, Maria, D ... 423-439-7737. 459 C
costa@etsu.edu
COSTA, JR., Richard, F ... 859-371-9393. 192 D
rcosta@beckfield.edu
COSTA, Xavier ... 617-373-3682. 235 F
COSTANTINO, Andrea ... 716-645-2171. 341 F
costanti@buffalo.edu
COSTANZA, Laina ... 334-387-3877..... 1 E
lainacostanza@amridgeuniversity.edu
COSTANZA, Laina, T ... 334-387-3878..... 1 E
lainacostanza@amridgeuniversity.edu
COSTANZO, Brian ... 570-961-7841. 420 C
costanzob@lackawanna.edu
COSTAS, Edda ... 787-284-1912. 550 F
ecostas@ponce.inter.edu
COSTAS, Pam ... 312-915-6239. 151 H
pcostas@luc.edu
COSTELLO, Bernard ... 914-674-7569. 330 J
bcostello@mercy.edu
COSTELLO, Dana ... 410-225-2338. 216 C
dcostello@mica.edu
COSTELLO, Dennis ... 586-445-7318. 246 A
costellod@macomb.edu
COSTELLO, Eileen ... 978-632-6600. 232 C
e_costello@mwcc.mass.edu
COSTELLO, Georgia ... 618-235-2700. 160 A
georgia.costello@swic.edu
COSTELLO, Gregory, W ... 507-344-7305. 253 J
costello@blc.edu
COSTELLO, Jamie ... 617-879-7703. 230 B
jcostello@massart.edu
COSTELLO, Janice ... 860-727-6919... 90 A
jcostello@goodwin.edu
COSTELLO, SJ, John ... 312-915-6186. 151 H
jcoste2@luc.edu
COSTELLO, Kathryn ... 270-745-6208. 200 G
kathryn.costello@wku.edu
COSTELLO, Kevin ... 617-327-6777. 233 D
kevin_costello@mspp.edu
COSTELLO,
Mary Elizabeth ... 973-761-9175. 307 C
maryelizabeth.costello@shu.edu
COSTELLO, Richard, J ... 219-989-2540. 171 N
richard.costello@purduecal.edu
COSTELLO, Rose, M ... 260-481-6677. 168 C
costellr@ipfw.edu
COSTELLO STANIEC,
Andria ... 315-443-1057. 347 C
costello@syr.edu
COSTIGAN, Harry ... 215-567-7080. 410 A
hcostigan@edmc.edu
COSTNER, Alan ... 937-376-2946. 388 B
acostner@payne.edu
COSTNER, Carl ... 828-652-0614. 362 A
carlc@mcdowelltech.edu
COSTON, Charlotte, M ... 716-851-1180. 323 I
coston@ecc.edu
COSTON, D.C ... 701-483-2326. 371 D
dc.coston@dickinsonstate.edu
COSTON, Linda ... 229-430-2751. 120 A
lcoston@albanytech.edu
COSTON, Robert, H ... 304-647-6574. 528 D
rcoston@newriver.edu
COSTON, Todd ... 661-395-4601... 49 N
tcoston@bakersfieldcollege.edu
COSTON-MCHUGH,
Rose ... 856-227-7200. 300 B
rcoston-mchugh@camdencc.edu
COTA, Amalia ... 925-288-5800... 46 J
amalia_cota@heald.edu
COTA, Marco ... 909-384-8952... 62 A
mcota@sbccd.cc.ca.us
COTE, Christine ... 509-453-0375. 522 B
COTE, Deborah ... 413-236-1022. 231 A
dcote@berkshirecc.edu
COTE, John, C ... 810-766-4191. 239 H
john.cote@baker.edu
COTE-BONANNO,
Joanne, F ... 973-655-6234. 303 D
bonannoj@mail.montclair.edu
COTGREAVE, Bruce ... 806-345-5565. 465 E
blcotgreave@actx.edu
COTHAM, Brian ... 559-278-2111... 33 D
bcotham@csufresno.edu
COTHERN, John, W ... 615-898-2852. 459 D
john.cothern@mtsu.edu
COTHERN, Richard ... 912-427-5824. 120 B
rcothern@altamahatech.edu
COTHERN, Susan, L ... 828-884-8373. 352 I
strombsl@brevard.edu
COTHRAN, Rick ... 864-646-1701. 447 D
rcothran@tctc.edu
COTLEUR,
Mary Elizabeth ... 216-373-5316. 385 G
mcotleur@ndc.edu
COTNOIR, Kathleen ... 413-565-1209. 222 F
kcotnoir@baypath.edu
COTNOIR, Paul ... 508-373-9731. 223 A
paul.cotnoir@becker.edu
COTREL, Jack, R ... 423-439-6900. 459 C
cotrel@etsu.edu
COTRONEO, Keith, J ... 304-710-3141. 528 C
cotroneo@mctc.edu
COTSONES, Rena ... 815-753-0834. 154 I
rcotsones@niu.edu
COTSONIS, Joachim ... 617-850-1243. 227 E
jcotsonis@hchc.edu
COTTEN, Melinda ... 713-348-6200. 479 A
cotten@rice.edu
COTTER, Anita ... 310-825-1443... 71 C
acotter@registrar.ucla.edu
COTTER, Dan, J ... 802-258-9297. 499 F
dcotter@marlboro.edu
COTTER, Geri, E ... 402-465-2159. 291 G
gec@nebrwesleyan.edu
COTTER, James, W ... 517-355-6532. 246 H
cotterj@msu.edu
COTTER, Jeff ... 805-922-6966... 26 K
jcotter@hancockcollege.edu
COTTER, Mary, L ... 315-445-5441. 328 F
cottemal@lemoyne.edu
COTTER, Michael ... 914-594-3675. 334 A
michael_cotter@nymc.edu
COTTERMAN, Susan ... 740-389-4636. 383 F
cottermans@mtc.edu
COTTIER, Mary ... 210-486-2597. 465 B
mcottier@alamo.edu
COTTINGHAM, Carolyn ... 914-674-7459. 330 J
ccottingham@mercy.edu
COTTINGHAM, Ryan, T ... 517-750-1200. 250 E
ryanc@arbor.edu
COTTO, Evelyn ... 787-746-1400. 549 B
ecotto@huertas.edu
COTTO, Marguerite, C ... 231-995-1775. 248 B
mcotto@nmc.edu
COTTON, Beverly ... 603-668-2211. 297 I
b.cotton@snhu.edu
COTTON, Beverly ... 817-257-5710. 468 B
beverly.cotton@tcu.edu
COTTON, Dwight ... 859-336-5082. 198 J
dwightcotton@sccky.edu
COTTON, Fran ... 806-894-9611. 480 H
fcotton@southplainscollege.edu
COTTON, Joel ... 847-628-1581. 149 B
jcotton@judsonu.edu
COTTON, Patricia ... 334-229-4324..... 1 D
pcotton@alasu.edu
COTTON, Sabrina ... 256-726-7408..... 6 B
cotton@oakwood.edu
COTTON, Trae ... 336-750-3200. 370 A
cottontt@wssu.edu
COTTON KELLY,
Montique, R ... 419-372-7673. 374 K
mcotton@bgsu.edu
COTTONE, John ... 607-753-2701. 343 B
john.cottone@cortland.edu
COTTONHAM, Patricia ... 337-482-6266. 208 D
patcottonham@louisiaiana.edu
COTTRAUX, Suzanne ... 817-515-1541. 482 B
suzanne.cottraux@tccd.edu
COTTRELL, Angela ... 816-235-1407. 283 D
cottrella@umkc.edu
COTTRELL, Debbie ... 830-372-8002. 485 C
dcottrell@tlu.edu
COTTRELL, Debbie ... 254-295-5059. 490 B
dcottrell@umhb.edu
COTTRELL, Janet ... 802-865-6492. 499 A
cottrell@champlain.edu
COTTRELL, Karen, R ... 757-221-1166. 503 N
krcott@wm.edu
COTTRELL, Leslie ... 378-839-6452. 133 I
lcottrel@westga.edu
COTTRELL, Rick ... 800-962-7682. 285 A
rcottrell@wma.edu
COTTRELL, Terrance, L ... 815-740-5041. 162 F
tcottrell@stfrancis.edu
COTTRILL, Chad ... 503-883-2506. 404 A
ccottril@linfield.edu
COTTRILL, F. Layton ... 304-696-6295. 529 H
cottrill@marshall.edu
COTY, Blake ... 229-732-5934. 120 D
blakecoty@andrewcollege.edu
COTY, Mark ... 941-782-5980. 420 E
mcoty@lecom.edu
COUCH, Alisha, M ... 740-368-3099. 387 J
amcouch@owu.edu
COUCH, Carl ... 480-423-6161... 15 E
carl.couch@scottsdalecc.edu
COUCH, Charlie ... 970-351-2231... 86 C
charlie.couch@unco.edu

COUCH, Daryl, D .... 864-644-5328. 446 I
dcouch@swu.edu
COUCH, JR., Gene, C .... 336-506-4154. 357 M
gene.couch@alamancecc.edu
COUCH, Lisa .... 760-384-6288... 49 O
lcouch@cerrocoso.edu
COUCH, Michael .... 513-745-1000. 393 H
couch@xavier.edu
COUCH, Valerie .... 405-208-5440. 397 F
vcouch@okcu.edu
COUCHEY, Evangeline .... 845-675-4733. 335 C
evangeline.couchey@nyack.edu
COUDRIET, Colleen, W .. 814-677-1322. 415 C
occ@dbcollege.edu
COUGHENOUR, Brenda .. 814-262-6434. 427 C
bcoughen@pennhighlands.edu
COUGHLIN, Cass, M ...... 773-508-3300. 151 H
ccough2@luc.edu
COUGHLIN, Devan .... 904-256-7054. 107 Q
dcoughl1@ju.edu
COUGHLIN, Eileen, V ..... 360-650-3839. 525 C
eileen.coughlin@wwu.edu
COUGHLIN, OFM,
F. Edward .... 716-375-2032. 338 E
coughlin@sbu.edu
COUGHLIN, John .... 248-370-4618. 248 J
jcoughli@oakland.edu
COUGHLIN, Kathleen ..... 210-829-6012. 490 A
coughlin@uiwtx.edu
COUGHLIN, Kevin .... 239-489-9040. 101 O
kcoughlin@edison.edu
COUGHLIN, Mary Ann .... 413-748-3959. 236 I
mcoughlin@springfieldcollege.edu
COUGHLIN, Rene .... 712-325-3306. 179 L
rcoughlin@iwcc.edu
COUGHLIN, Richard .... 660-785-4038. 282 L
coughlin@truman.edu
COULOMBE, Jennifer, B . 336-734-7723. 360 E
jcoulombe@forsythtech.edu
COULON, Richard .... 949-824-6510... 71 B
rcoulon@uci.edu
COULSTON, Susan .... 269-782-1396. 250 C
scoulston@swmich.edu
COULTER, Ann .... 641-782-1340. 182 I
coulter@swcciowa.edu
COULTER, Chris .... 719-389-6568... 79 D
chris.coulter@coloradocollege.edu
COULTER, Christy, M ..... 724-847-5566. 417 A
cmcoulte@geneva.edu
COULTER, Cindy .... 828-327-7000. 359 A
ccoulter@cvcc.edu
COULTER, Cynthia .... 201-360-4722. 302 D
ccoulter@hccc.edu
COULTER, Kristin .... 512-313-3000. 469 L
kristin.coulter@concordia.edu
COULTER, Laurie .... 903-813-2900. 466 H
lcoulter@austincollege.edu
COULTER, Martha .... 802-468-1314. 501 B
martha.coulter@castleton.edu
COUNCE, Bamby .... 901-572-2853. 453 B
bamby.counce@bchs.edu
COUNCIL, Juanette .... 910-672-1208. 367 D
jcouncil@uncfsu.edu
COUNCIL, William .... 910-410-1823. 362 I
bcouncil@richmondcc.edu
COUNIHAN, Patricia, B .. 207-581-1359. 212 B
counihan@maine.edu
COUNTEE, Jerome .... 916-484-8202... 53 A
countej@arc.losrios.edu
COUNTS, LaNeta .... 404-471-6483. 119 I
lcounts@agnesscott.edu
COURCHAINE, Jeff .... 714-892-7711... 39 J
jcourchaine@gwc.cccd.edu
COURET, Esther .... 845-431-8673. 323 C
Esther.couret@sunydutchess.edu
COUREY, Scott .... 616-394-4287. 241 F
scott.courey@cornerstone.edu
COURTEMANCHE, Brian . 978-927-2278. 226 C
bcourtem@endicott.edu
COURTEY, Susan .... 818-240-1000... 45 G
scourtey@glendale.edu
COURTLEY-TODD,
Laura, J .... 305-628-6677. 112 F
lcourtle@stu.edu
COURTNEY, Andolyn, M 716-888-2780. 316 C
courtnea@canisius.edu
COURTNEY, David, H ..... 716-888-2778. 316 C
courtned@canisius.edu
COURTNEY, Hugh .... 617-373-3232. 235 F
COURTNEY, Jim .... 773-947-6285. 152 E
jcourtney@mccormick.edu
COURTNEY, Justin .... 419-772-2145. 386 D
j-courtney@onu.edu
COURTNEY, Sharon, P .... 504-988-3390. 207 C
sharonc@tulane.edu
COURTRIGHT, Caren .... 509-793-2038. 517 C
carenc@bigbend.edu
COURTRIGHT,
Mary Beth .... 508-588-9100. 232 A
COURTWAY, Tom .... 501-450-5286... 25 H
tcourtway@uca.edu
COUSIN, Dennis .... 504-520-7330. 209 D
dcousin@xula.edu
COUSSONS-READ, Mary 303-315-5821... 86 A
mary.coussons-read@ucdenver.edu
COUSSONS-READ, Mary 719-255-3121... 85 M
mcousson@uccs.edu
COUTILISH,
Theodore, G .... 734-487-2483. 242 D
ted.coutilish@emich.edu
COUTTS, Chris .... 540-868-7083. 512 H
ccoutts@lfcc.edu
COUTTS, Kimberly .... 760-797-2121... 54 G
kcoutts@miracosta.edu
COUTURE, Daniel, R .... 802-654-3243. 500 B
dcouture@smcvt.edu
COUTURE, Donna, L .... 978-232-2026. 226 C
dcouture@endicott.edu
COUTURE, Richard .... 607-274-3225. 327 E
rcouture@ithaca.edu
COVAL, Scott .... 610-282-1100. 414 F
scott.coval@desales.edu
COVAR, Tom .... 864-388-8305. 444 K
tcovar@lander.edu
COVAULT, Pamela .... 785-242-2067. 189 D
pcovault@neosho.edu
COVE, Lorraine, D .... 617-573-8160. 237 B
lcove@acad.suffolk.edu
COVELLE, Fred .... 617-422-7205. 235 B
fcovelle@nesl.edu
COVELLI-KOVACH,
Andrea .... 215-572-4014. 409 H
covelli@arcadia.edu
COVER, Michael, S .... 570-577-3348. 411 A
mike.cover@bucknell.edu
COVERDALE, Pat .... 423-236-2276. 458 J
plcoverdale@southern.edu
COVERS, Beth, A .... 810-762-9925. 244 Q
bcovers@kettering.edu
COVERT, Sheree, S .... 319-352-8272. 183 E
sheree.covert@wartburg.edu
COVEY, Angie, E .... 540-674-3655. 513 B
acovey@nr.edu
COVEY, Becky .... 276-466-7192. 514 G
beckycovey@vic.edu
COVEY, Bruce .... 404-727-6223. 124 E
bcovey@emory.edu
COVEY, Douglass, F .... 404-413-1500. 126 E
dcovey@gsu.edu
COVILLE, Joanne .... 909-621-8211... 65 D
joanne.coville@scrippscollege.edu
COVINGTON, Amber .... 440-449-4433. 392 D
amber.covington@ursuline.edu
COVINGTON, Bill, C .... 512-245-2314. 487 C
bc18@txstate.edu
COVINGTON, Dan .... 606-546-1285. 200 A
dcovin@unionky.edu
COVINGTON, Dave, R .... 208-467-8060. 139 A
dcovington@nnu.edu
COVINGTON, Dean .... 870-307-7206... 21 H
dean.covington@lyon.edu
COVINGTON, Janet .... 713-348-6312. 479 A
jcov@rice.edu
COVINGTON, Kate .... 620-276-9642. 187 A
kate.covington@gcccks.edu
COVINGTON, Latrice .... 202-806-2763... 95 G
latrice.byam@howard.edu
COVINGTON, Mary .... 919-966-9176. 368 D
mary_covington@unc.edu
COVINGTON, Sim .... 315-792-7165. 346 C
sim.covington@sunyit.edu
COVINGTON, Sirena .... 312-788-1146. 162 H
scovington@vandercook.edu
COVINGTON, Valerie, L .. 757-455-3108. 515 H
vcovington@vwc.edu
COVINGTON-GRAHAM,
Adrianne .... 405-945-3383. 398 C
COVINO, Nicholas .... 617-327-6777. 233 D
nicholas_covino@mspp.edu
COVINO, William, A .... 323-343-3030... 34 A
bill.covino@cslanet.calstatela.edu
COVITZ, Bobby .... 513-487-3259. 325 G
rcovitz@huc.edu
COWAN, Carole, A .... 978-656-3101. 232 B
cowanc@middlesex.mass.edu
COWAN, Cindy .... 864-977-2058. 445 H
cindy.cowan@ngu.edu
COWAN, David .... 507-389-2267. 259 G
david.cowan@mnsu.edu
COWAN, David, G .... 713-646-1729. 480 J
dcowan@stcl.edu
COWAN, Judith .... 803-327-7402. 442 D
jcowan@clintonjuniorcollege.edu
COWAN, Kenneth, H .... 402-559-4238. 292 J
kcowan@unmc.edu
COWAN, Marianne .... 207-786-6128. 209 F
mcowan@bates.edu
COWAN, Vickie, M .... 718-862-7398. 329 M
vickie.cowan@manhattan.edu
COWARD, William .... 814-536-5168. 412 C
bcoward@crbc.net
COWART, Julian .... 406-470-2036. 400 A
julian.cowart@swcu.edu
COWART, Lisa .... 803-323-2273. 449 G
cowartl@winthrop.edu
COWART, Lisa .... 832-813-6780. 476 A
lisa.a.cowart@lonestar.edu
COWDREY, Scott .... 507-457-7800. 264 A
rcowdrey@smumn.edu
COWDREY, Terry, E .... 207-859-4802. 209 J
Terry.Cowdrey@colby.edu
COWELL, Aaron .... 419-473-2700. 378 I
aacowell@daviscollege.edu
COWELL, JR., James, W 626-395-4464... 31 E
jcowell@caltech.edu
COWELL, Karen .... 661-722-6300... 28 F
kcowell@avc.edu
COWEN, Scott, S .... 504-865-5201. 207 C
scowen@tulane.edu
COWEN, Sonia .... 417-667-8181. 273 A
scowen@cottey.edu
COWGER, John .... 701-594-8192. 372 D
john.cowger@lrsc.edu
COWGER, Tiffany .... 618-395-7777. 146 H
cowgert@iecc.edu
COWHEY, Peter, F .... 858-822-7523... 71 F
pcowhey@uscd.edu
COWHIG, Aja .... 603-880-8308. 298 A
tmc@thomasmorecollege.edu
COWIE, Anne .... 617-369-3659. 236 F
acowie@mfa.org
COWIE, Lettie .... 714-556-3610... 74 D
OfficeVPBF@vanguard.edu
COWLES, John .... 616-234-3673. 243 B
jcowles@grcc.edu
COWLES, Malinda .... 724-357-1358. 428 F
malinda@iup.edu
COWLEY, Dave .... 435-797-1146. 497 B
dave.cowley@usu.edu
COWLEY, Julie, A .... 512-863-1720. 481 I
cowleyj@southwestern.edu
COWLING,
William Richard .... 314-991-6200. 141 G
rcowling@chamberlain.edu
COWLING,
William Richard .... 877-751-5783. 141 F
COWMAN, Mary .... 718-260-3054. 336 E
mcowman@poly.edu
COWMAN, Shaun .... 561-912-1211. 103 C
scowman@evergladesuniversity.edu
COWSER, Erin, K .... 985-549-5861. 208 C
erin.moore@selu.edu
COWSER YANCY,
Dorothy .... 919-546-8300. 366 E
dyancy@shawu.edu
COX, Alan .... 336-725-8344. 365 F
coxa@piedmontu.edu
COX, Aleshia .... 731-410-6714. 455 J
acox@lanecollege.edu
COX, Barbara .... 850-599-3796. 114 K
barbara.cox@famu.edu
COX, Ben .... 254-867-3063. 486 B
ben.cox@tstc.edu
COX, Betty, B .... 713-313-4218. 485 F
cox_bb@tsu.edu
COX, Bob .... 970-339-6509... 78 C
bob.cox@aims.edu
COX, Bobbie .... 704-406-4627. 354 C
bcox@gardner-webb.edu
COX, Brandt .... 757-446-5200. 504 E
COX, Cameron .... 253-964-6598. 522 C
CMCox@pierce.ctc.edu
COX, Carolyn .... 304-384-5323. 529 E
ccox@concord.edu
COX, Carolyn, S .... 240-500-2000. 215 B
cscox@hagerstowncc.edu
COX, Cathy .... 706-379-3111. 134 L
ccox@yhc.edu
COX, Charlene .... 219-464-5093. 174 E
charlene.cox@valpo.edu
COX, Cheryl .... 864-592-4613. 447 A
coxc@sccsc.edu
COX, Christopher .... 319-273-2737. 176 A
chris.cox@uni.edu
COX, Christopher, P .... 419-372-8932. 374 K
cpcox@bgsu.edu
COX, Chuck .... 417-865-2815. 274 B
coxc@evangel.edu
COX, Cleve, H .... 252-249-1851. 362 E
ccox@pamlicocc.edu
COX, Craig, A .... 805-482-2755... 61 E
rector@stjohnsem.edu
COX, Darryl .... 949-451-5435... 67 B
dcox@ivc.edu
COX, Dave .... 217-234-5376. 150 D
dcox5612@lakeland.cc.il.us
COX, Dave .... 509-533-7179. 518 E
dave.cox@scc.spokane.edu
COX, David, N .... 901-678-5344. 460 B
davidcox@memphis.edu
COX, Deborah, M .... 270-824-8609. 196 A
deborah.cox@kctcs.edu
COX, Dennis .... 949-214-3182... 41 I
dennis.cox@cui.edu
COX, Dennis, W .... 304-865-6081. 527 F
dennis.cox@ovu.edu
COX, Dianne .... 423-425-4677. 463 D
dianne-cox@utc.edu
COX, Donna .... 870-543-5968... 23 E
dcox@seark.edu
COX, Ed .... 845-431-8071. 323 C
COX, Fran .... 662-472-2312. 267 B
fcox@holmescc.edu
COX, Frank .... 501-329-6811... 21 E
COX, Geoffrey .... 858-635-4000... 26 M
gcox@alliant.edu
COX, Geoffrey .... 415-955-2001... 26 L
gcox@alliant.edu
COX, Gloria .... 940-565-3305. 490 C
gcox@unt.edu
COX, Gregg .... 561-237-7210. 108 X
gcox@lynn.edu
COX, Gregg, C .... 561-237-7210. 108 X
gcox@lynn.edu
COX, Helen .... 808-245-8210. 136 H
helencox@hawaii.edu
COX, J. P. Hap .... 540-375-2302. 509 B
cox@roanoke.com
COX, James .... 714-620-3700... 28 M
jcox@argosy.edu
COX, Jamie, S .... 256-766-6610..... 4 B
jcox@hcu.edu
COX, Janet .... 513-244-4466. 377 G
janet_cox@mail.msj.edu
COX, Janet, L .... 513-529-6724. 384 G
coxjl@miamioh.edu
COX, Jason .... 270-686-2111. 192 G
jason.cox@brescia.edu
COX, Jeffrey, W .... 585-475-7433. 337 L
jwccst@rit.edu
COX, Jennifer .... 503-228-6528. 402 A
jcox@aii.edu
COX, Jesse .... 313-927-1404. 246 D
jcox@marygrove.edu
COX, John, L .... 508-362-2131. 231 D
jcox@capecod.edu
COX, Karen .... 508-854-4479. 232 F
kcox@qcc.mass.edu
COX, Kelly .... 803-786-3723. 443 B
kcox@columbiasc.edu
COX, Kenneth, M .... 540-831-7600. 508 C
kcox3@radford.edu
COX, Lane .... 205-348-8697..... 8 D
lcox@fa.ua.edu
COX, Laurie .... 608-262-7890. 536 D
cox@studentlife.wisc.edu
COX, Leah .... 540-654-1263. 510 J
lcox@umw.edu
COX, Leana .... 970-675-3334... 80 B
leana.cox@cncc.edu
COX, Lisa .... 423-869-6722. 456 A
lisa.cox@lmunet.edu
COX, Lori .... 618-252-5400. 159 E
lori.cox@sic.edu
COX, Lynne .... 541-917-4848. 404 B
coxly@linnbenton.edu
COX, Mary .... 724-830-1027. 433 E
cox@setonhill.edu
COX, Matthew .... 719-255-3375... 85 M
mcox4@uccs.edu
COX, Michael .... 806-291-3765. 494 F
coxm@wbu.edu
COX, Michele, D .... 804-289-8838. 510 L
mcox@richmond.edu
COX, Paul .... 305-428-5700. 109 E
pcox@aii.edu
COX, Randall .... 903-785-7661. 478 B
rcox@parisjc.edu
COX, Richard, A .... 831-443-1700... 47 D
richard_cox@heald.edu
COX, Robert .... 503-491-7374. 404 E
robert.cox@mhcc.edu
COX, Robert .... 212-220-8041. 317 A
rcox@bmcc.cuny.edu
COX, Ryan .... 916-568-3101... 52 K
coxr@losrios.edu
COX, Sandra .... 936-633-5211. 465 J
scox@angelina.edu
COX, Sandra, K .... 217-581-3413. 144 E
skcox@eiu.edu
COX, Steve .... 740-245-7438. 392 A
scox@rio.edu
COX, Susan, S .... 610-606-4609. 412 I
sue@cedarcrest.edu
COX, Terry .... 206-934-7798. 522 I
terry.cox@seattlecolleges.edu
COX, Tiffa .... 615-963-7494. 459 E
tcox9@tnstate.edu
COX, Traci, R .... 419-995-8040. 381 Q
cox.t@rhodesstate.edu
COX, Virgil .... 704-922-6295. 360 F
cox.virgil@gaston.edu

COX, William 931-221-1400. 459 B coxw@apsu.edu
COX-LANYON, Vickie 508-793-7258. 225 A vcoxlanyon@clarku.edu
COY, Katherine, C 417-836-5274. 278 E kathycoy@missouristate.edu
COY, Marisue, S 270-852-3300. 197 B marisuec@kwc.edu
COY-OGAN, Lynne 207-973-1077. 210 B coyoganl@husson.edu
COYKENDALL, John 785-227-3380. 184 I coykendallj@bethanylb.edu
COYLE, Catherine 215-204-1950. 433 K catherine.coyle@temple.edu
COYLE, James 714-997-7074... 38 A coyle@chapman.edu
COYLE, John 814-886-6465. 424 G jcoyle@mtaloy.edu
COYLE, Mark 208-426-1826. 137 G markcoyle@boisestate.edu
COYLE, Philip 903-233-3200. 475 J philipcoyle@letu.edu
COYLE, Philip, A 423-266-4574. 458 F pcoyle@richmont.edu
COYNE, Anthony, M 803-938-3749. 448 F acoyne@uscsumter.edu
COYNE, John, B 330-569-5284. 380 I CoyneJB@hiram.edu
COYNE, John, M 724-264-1328. 417 E jmcoyne@gcc.edu
COYNE, Michael 928-681-0800. 233 C coyne@mslaw.edu
COYNE, Michael 570-372-4128. 433 H coyne@susqu.edu
COZART, Melissa 859-858-3511. 192 B melissa.cozart@asbury.edu
COZART, Wayne 434-243-9041. 511 B wdc9q@virginia.edu
COZZA, Mary Ann 713-226-5504. 489 D cozzam@uhd.edu
COZZENS, David 307-766-3296. 543 I dcozzens@uwyo.edu
COZZENS, Susan 404-894-5054. 125 D susan.cozzens@iac.gatech.edu
COZZOCREA, Rebecca 518-736-3622. 325 A rswart@fmcc.suny.edu
CRABB, Charlie 805-756-2204... 32 F ccrabb@calpoly.edu
CRABB, Jenna, S 505-277-2531. 312 F jennas@unm.edu
CRABB, Robert, J 612-625-6510. 264 G rcrabb@umn.edu
CRABILL, Casey 315-498-2211. 335 G president@sunyocc.edu
CRABREE, Troy 206-239-4500. 517 M troy.crabtree@cityu.edu
CRABTREE, Candace 617-928-4633. 234 E ccrabtree@mountida.edu
CRABTREE, David 541-683-5141. 403 D dcrabtree@gutenberg.edu
CRABTREE, Gina, D 316-978-3672. 191 F gina.crabtree@wichita.edu
CRABTREE, JR., John, A 317-789-8288. 165 E jcrabtree@crossroads.edu
CRABTREE, Kacy 828-898-8739. 356 A crabtreek@lmc.edu
CRABTREE, Peter 510-464-3218... 59 C pcrabtree@peralta.edu
CRABTREE, Robbin, D 203-254-4000... 89 I rcrabtree@fairfield.edu
CRABTREE, Shane 801-957-4571. 498 B shane.crabtree@slcc.edu
CRACCO, Elizabeth 860-486-4705... 92 A elizabeth.cracco@uconn.edu
CRACE, Kelly 919-660-1000. 354 A kelly.crace@duke.edu
CRACE, Robert, K 757-221-1236. 503 N rkcrac@wm.edu
CRACKENBERG, Peter 503-554-2138. 403 C pcrackenberg@georgefox.edu
CRADDOCK, Alden 314-529-6687. 276 G acraddock@maryville.edu
CRADDOCK, Chris 903-983-8181. 475 E ccraddock@kilgore.edu
CRADDOCK, Jackie 510-594-3612... 30 K jcraddock@cca.edu
CRADIT, James, D 618-453-7960. 159 G dcradit@business.siu.edu
CRADY, Thomas, M 507-933-7676. 255 I tcrady@gustavus.edu
CRAFA, Robert 718-409-7460. 346 D rcrafa@sunymaritime.edu
CRAFT, Ann 304-829-7255. 526 D acraft@bethanywv.edu
CRAFT, Edwin 662-846-4840. 266 G ecraft@deltastate.edu
CRAFT, Jackie, T 276-739-2561. 514 D jcraft@vhcc.edu
CRAFT, Stephen 205-665-6540..... 9 B scraft@montevallo.edu
CRAFT, Tonya 601-974-1200. 267 I craftte@millsaps.edu
CRAFT, William, J 218-299-3000. 255 A president@cord.edu
CRAFTON, Michael 678-466-4100. 123 A michaelcrafton@clayton.edu
CRAFTON, Teresa 478-274-7833. 129 I tcrafton@oftc.edu
CRAGAR, Beth 931-598-1312. 458 H bcragar@sewanee.edu
CRAGER, Cindy 609-626-3658. 305 C cindy.crager@stockton.edu
CRAGG, Kristina 858-513-9240. 175 F Kristina.Cragg@ashford.edu
CRAGLE, Rachael, C 865-539-7219. 461 D rccragle@pstcc.edu
CRAGO, David, C 419-772-2034. 386 D d-crago@onu.edu
CRAHEN, Sherri, A 216-397-3010. 381 R scrahen@jcu.edu
CRAIG, Barbara 269-695-2995. 245 D craig@lakemichigancollege.edu
CRAIG, Chris 559-791-2365... 49 P ccraig@portervillecollege.edu
CRAIG, Chris, J 740-376-4857. 383 E chris.craig@marietta.edu
CRAIG, Christopher, J 417-836-5215. 278 E chriscraig@missouristate.edu
CRAIG, Clarissa 913-469-8500. 187 J ccraig@jccc.edu
CRAIG, David 406-657-2209. 287 C david.craig2@msubillings.edu
CRAIG, David 406-657-2908. 287 C david.craig2@msubillings.edu
CRAIG, Dennis 914-251-6300. 344 D dennis.craig@purchase.edu
CRAIG, Florence 617-541-3501. 232 G fcraig@rcc.mass.edu
CRAIG, Harold 404-225-4488. 121 B hcraig@atlantatech.edu
CRAIG, James 916-361-1660... 36 H jcraig@carrington.edu
CRAIG, Jayne 575-769-4031. 309 F jayne.craig@clovis.edu
CRAIG, Jennifer 617-964-1100. 222 A jcraig@ants.edu
CRAIG, Jo-Ann 910-362-7057. 358 F jcraig@cfcc.edu
CRAIG, Johnny 219-844-0100. 170 Q jcraig@kaplan.edu
CRAIG, Kathryn, M 330-569-5131. 380 I craigkm@hiram.edu
CRAIG, La Saundra 513-569-1532. 376 L lasaundra.craig@cincinnatistate.edu
CRAIG, Martha, P 865-981-8167. 456 D mardi.craig@maryvillecollege.edu
CRAIG, Marva 212-220-8131. 317 A mcraig@bmcc.cuny.edu
CRAIG, Michael 816-501-4065. 280 I michael.craig@rockhurst.edu
CRAIG, Paige 708-209-3509. 143 E paige.craig@cuchicago.edu
CRAIG, Randy 323-241-5238... 52 C craigrs@lasc.edu
CRAIG, Sandy 618-262-8641. 147 C craigs@iecc.edu
CRAIG, Stephanie, A 814-371-2090. 434 F scraig@triangle-tech.edu
CRAIG, Wendy 619-660-4240... 46 D wendy.craig@gcccd.edu
CRAIG, William, G 732-571-3427. 303 C craig@monmouth.edu
CRAIG KUNG, Pang-Jen 919-878-9900... 96 F
CRAIG-TAYLOR, Phyliss, V 919-530-6112. 368 A pcraigtaylor@nccu.edu
CRAIGIE, Ted, W 603-526-3717. 295 I tcraigie@colby-sawyer.edu
CRAIN, B, J 979-862-7777. 483 C bjcrain@tamu.edu
CRAIN, John, L 985-549-2280. 208 C jcrain@selu.edu
CRAIN, Laura, J 607-871-2101. 313 E crain@alfred.edu
CRAIN, Ronald, D 618-453-6214. 159 G dcrain@siu.edu
CRAIN, Steve 620-242-0400. 188 G
CRAIN, Terry 618-985-3741. 148 J terrycrain@jalc.edu
CRALL, Leslie, D 580-774-3282. 400 B les.crall@swosu.edu
CRAM, Stanley 920-924-6431. 540 F scram@morainepark.edu
CRAM-RAHLF, Shelly 563-288-6011. 178 B scramrahlf@eicc.edu
CRAMB, Alan, W 312-567-3163. 147 F cramb@iit.edu
CRAMER, Alicia 713-646-1808. 480 J acramer@stcl.edu
CRAMER, Ann 951-343-4210... 30 H acramer@calbaptist.edu
CRAMER, Gregory, D 630-889-6536. 154 E gcramer@nuhs.edu
CRAMER, Janet 303-546-3588... 83 F jcramer@naropa.edu
CRAMER, Joel 317-738-8197. 165 I jcramer@franklincollege.edu
CRAMER, Judy 978-542-6139. 230 E judy.cramer@salemstate.edu
CRAMER, Patricia 614-236-6714. 375 H pcramer@capital.edu
CRAMER, Paul 717-361-1400. 415 H cramerp@etown.edu
CRAMER, Rick 607-729-1581. 322 F rcramer@davisny.edu
CRAMER, Robert, G 608-342-1226. 537 D cramerr@uwplatt.edu
CRAMER, Walter 203-837-8547... 88 B cramerw@wcsu.edu
CRAMPTON, Anne-Marie 719-336-1520... 82 R anne-marie.crampton@lamarcc.edu
CRAMPTON, Tom 810-762-0506. 247 F thomas.crampto@mcc.edu
CRAMPTON, Troy, D 515-574-1114. 179 D crampton@iowacentral.edu
CRAMSEY, Rachel 217-228-5520. 140 H
CRANCE, Gina-Lyn 610-921-7611. 409 A gcrance@alb.edu
CRANDALL, Brian 845-938-3327. 545 I 8uscc@usma.edu
CRANDALL, Donald, W 479-524-7150... 21 G dcrandal@jbu.edu
CRANDALL, James 530-242-7989... 65 G jcrandall@shastacollege.edu
CRANDALL, Larry 801-302-2800. 496 B larry.crandall@neumont.edu
CRANDALL, Laura 315-470-4865. 345 B ldcranda@esf.edu
CRANDALL, Paige 914-395-2575. 340 E pcrandall@sarahlawrence.edu
CRANDALL, Stephen, S 607-871-2184. 313 E fcrandall@alfred.edu
CRANDELL, Gale, M 989-386-6664. 247 B gcrandell@midmich.edu
CRANE, Carol 480-732-7114... 14 J carol.crane@cgc.edu
CRANE, Crystal, D 714-895-8970... 39 J ccrane@gwc.cccd.edu
CRANE, Jeff 270-384-8150. 197 D cranej@lindsey.edu
CRANE, Malachi, D 517-750-1200. 250 E mcrane@arbor.edu
CRANE, Peter 203-432-5109... 93 A peter.crane@yale.edu
CRANE, Ramona 719-219-9636... 79 B rcrane@cavt.edu
CRANE, Rob, M 913-288-7283. 187 L rcrane@kckcc.edu
CRANE, Robert 956-380-8100. 479 B rcrane@riogrande.edu
CRANE, Ron 972-825-4818. 481 F rcrane@sagu.edu
CRANE, Stephen, J 417-268-6600. 271 I scrane@gobbc.edu
CRANE, Susan 914-337-9300. 321 E susan.crane@concordia-ny.edu
CRANE, Susan, L 989-964-4350. 249 G scrane@svsu.edu
CRANFORD, Bill 601-925-3283. 268 A cranford@mc.edu
CRANFORD, Carolyn 903-813-2281. 466 H ccranford@austincollege.edu
CRANFORD, Shannon 580-628-6229. 396 M shannon.cranford@noc.edu
CRANFORD, Sondra 727-784-0003... 99 J scranford@cfi.edu
CRANFORD, Timothy 510-869-6610... 61 I tcranford@samuelmerritt.edu
CRANFORD, Timothy 912-358-4154. 131 C cranfordt@savannahstate.edu
CRANHAM, John, B 919-508-2336. 370 F jbcranham@peace.edu
CRANK, Robert 816-322-0110. 271 O bob.crank@calvary.edu
CRANMER, Wendy 315-792-7191. 346 C wendy.cranmer@sunyit.edu
CRANMORE, Jill, A 217-443-8756. 143 G jcranmore@dacc.edu
CRANSTON, Carey 708-444-4500. 145 D
CRANSTON, Carolyn 412-924-1375. 431 A ccranston@pts.edu
CRANSTON, Pam 410-516-8993. 215 H pcranston@jhu.edu
CRANWELL, Mary, E 732-987-2285. 302 B cranwell@georgian.edu
CRAPANZANO, Vincent 845-398-4019. 340 A vcrapanz@stac.edu
CRARY, Kami 617-726-2947. 234 B
CRARY-STACHOWIAK, Sage 413-205-3521. 221 F sage.stachowiak@aic.edu
CRATER, Lucas 618-536-3331. 159 F lcrater@siumed.edu
CRATTY, Frederic 203-837-8665... 88 B crattyf@wcsu.edu
CRAVEN, Bryan, C 850-718-2375... 99 N cravenb@chipola.edu
CRAVEN, Heather 973-328-5281. 300 G hcraven@ccm.edu
CRAVEN, Randy 423-236-2732. 458 J rlcraven@southern.edu
CRAVEN, Tracy 303-333-4224... 78 I tracy.craven@aspen.edu
CRAVENS, Michael 419-824-3620. 383 C mcravens@sistersosf.org
CRAVER, Robert 303-369-5151... 84 E robert.craver@plattcolorado.edu
CRAVER, William 678-225-7509. 430 D williamcr@pcom.edu
CRAVEY, Irene 512-759-5614. 486 B irene.cravey@tstc.edu
CRAVO, Ana, M 201-761-6104. 306 L acravo@saintpeters.edu
CRAW, Erin 802-258-3261. 500 C erin.craw@sit.edu
CRAWFORD, Allison 615-794-4254. 457 Q acrawford@omorecollege.edu
CRAWFORD, Brian 304-336-8004. 530 A brian.crawford@westliberty.edu
CRAWFORD, Bruce 205-929-6312..... 5 D bcrawford@lawsonstate.edu
CRAWFORD, Bryan 719-562-7002... 84 G bryan.crawford@pueblocc.edu
CRAWFORD, Cardon, B 843-953-6966. 442 A cardon.crawford@citadel.edu
CRAWFORD, Carol 215-728-4415. 425 G carol.crawford@jevs.org
CRAWFORD, Catherine 903-923-2069. 471 J ccrawford@etbu.edu
CRAWFORD, Cathy, L 260-399-7700. 174 C ccrawford@sf.edu
CRAWFORD, Charlie 253-566-6005. 524 C ccrawford@tacomacc.edu
CRAWFORD, Chris 785-628-4531. 186 F ccrawfor@fhsu.edu
CRAWFORD, Clinton 718-270-5140. 319 A crawford@mec.cuny.edu
CRAWFORD, Darryl, D 540-869-0623. 512 H dcrawford@lfcc.edu
CRAWFORD, David 303-797-5762... 78 F david.crawford@arapahoe.edu
CRAWFORD, David 773-947-6250. 152 E dcrawford@mccormick.edu
CRAWFORD, David, S 202-526-3799... 96 D
CRAWFORD, Debbie 970-945-8691... 79 G
CRAWFORD, Deborah 215-895-6203. 415 B deborah.l.crawford@drexel.edu
CRAWFORD, Deena 601-266-4829. 270 E deena.crawford@usm.edu
CRAWFORD, Diane 919-546-8309. 366 E dcrawford@shawu.edu
CRAWFORD, Doris, S 434-528-5276. 515 G dorisscott@vul.edu
CRAWFORD, Forrest, C 801-626-7420. 497 D fcrawford@weber.edu
CRAWFORD, Galen 513-562-6273. 373 K gcrawford@artacademy.edu
CRAWFORD, Gregory, P 574-631-6456. 174 A gregory_crawford@nd.edu
CRAWFORD, Holly 509-963-3101. 517 F crawfordh@cwu.edu
CRAWFORD, Holly 585-273-4734. 349 C hcrawford@admin.rochester.edu
CRAWFORD, Isiaah 206-296-6963. 523 E crawford@seattleu.edu
CRAWFORD, J. Patrick 850-474-2426. 117 B pat@uwf.edu
CRAWFORD, John 330-672-2760. 382 B jcrawfor1@kent.edu
CRAWFORD, John, D 229-333-5339. 134 B jdcrawford@valdosta.edu
CRAWFORD, John, P 716-880-2879. 330 F jpc334@medaille.edu
CRAWFORD, Jonas 805-986-5870... 74 G jcrawford@vcccd.edu
CRAWFORD, Kevin 706-245-7226. 124 D kcrawford@lifespring.net
CRAWFORD, Lelia 404-727-3300. 124 E lcrawfo@emory.edu
CRAWFORD, Malinda 406-756-3828. 286 B mcrawfor@fvcc.edu
CRAWFORD, Matt 952-358-8454. 260 B matt.crawford@normandale.edu
CRAWFORD, Missie 478-289-2172. 124 C mcrawford@ega.edu
CRAWFORD, Nellie 757-727-5221. 505 F nellie.crawford@hamptonu.edu
CRAWFORD, Patricia 765-973-8625. 167 G pajames@iue.edu
CRAWFORD, R. Scott 765-361-6355. 175 B crawforr@wabash.edu

CRAWFORD, Ray Scott ... 318-678-6000. 202 I
rcrawford@bpcc.edu
CRAWFORD, Rhia .... 828-766-1280. 361 H
rcrawford@mayland.edu
CRAWFORD, Ronald, W . 804-204-1201. 502 F
rcrawford@btsr.edu
CRAWFORD, Steve .... 661-362-2203... 53 G
scrawford@masters.edu
CRAWFORD, Steven, R ... 740-587-5717. 379 D
crawfords@denison.edu
CRAWFORD, Teresa .... 863-784-7061. 113 G
teresa.crawford@southflorida.edu
CRAWFORD, Teri .... 281-998-6151. 479 E
teri.crawford@sjcd.edu
CRAWFORD, Tim .... 254-295-4180. 490 B
tcrawford@umhb.edu
CRAWFORD, Valerie .... 309-268-8145. 146 B
val.crawford@heartland.edu
CRAWFORD, Valerie, S .. 334-244-3667..... 2 A
vsamuel@aum.edu
CRAWFORD, Virginia .... 601-266-5390. 270 E
virginia.crawford@usm.edu
CRAWFORD, III,
William, H .... 480-732-7309... 14 J
bill.crawford.iii@cgc.edu
CRAWLEY, Cathy .... 478-445-5149. 125 A
cathy.crawley@gcsu.edu
CRAWLEY, Deborah .... 610-558-5519. 424 I
cawleyd@neumann.edu
CRAWMER, Martha .... 937-328-6031. 377 A
crawmerm@clarkstate.edu
CRAYS, Courtney .... 620-223-2700. 186 G
courtneyc@fortscott.edu
CRAYS, Linda, L .... 713-500-2080. 492 E
linda.l.crays@uth.tmc.edu
CREA, Catharine .... 914-594-4480. 334 A
catharine_crea@nymc.edu
CREAGER, Carol .... 540-887-7310. 507 A
ccreager@mbc.edu
CREAGH, Curtis .... 573-681-5079. 276 C
creaghc@lincolnu.edu
CREAHAN, Patricia, H .... 716-888-2616. 316 C
creahan@canisius.edu
CREAKMAN, Melissa .... 304-896-7411. 528 F
melissa.creakman@southernwv.edu
CREAMER, Barry .... 214-818-1326. 470 A
bcreamer@criswell.edu
CREAMER, David .... 513-529-4225. 384 G
creamerd@miamioh.edu
CREAMER, Stephen .... 978-762-4000. 232 D
Screamer@northshore.edu
CREAMER, William .... 302-292-6100... 96 F
CREASIA, Joan, L .... 865-974-7584. 463 C
jcreasia@utk.edu
CREASMAN, Alice .... 304-473-8440. 531 G
creasman_aj@wvwc.edu
CREASMAN, Boyd .... 304-473-8042. 531 G
creasman@wvwc.edu
CREASON, Paul .... 562-938-4171... 51 D
pcreason@lbcc.edu
CREASON, Rita, A .... 270-789-5233. 193 D
racreason@campbellsville.edu
CREASY, Rick .... 423-472-7141. 460 D
RCreasy@clevelandstatecc.edu
CRECELIUS, Carolyn .... 573-518-2100. 278 A
kayc@mineralarea.edu
CRECELIUS, Kathryn, J .... 443-997-2370. 215 H
kcrecelius@jhu.edu
CREDILLE, John .... 417-328-1606. 282 C
jcredille@sbuniv.edu
CREDLE, Sid, H .... 757-727-5361. 505 F
sid.credle@hamptonu.edu
CREECH, Bill .... 918-595-7888. 400 E
bill.creech@tulsacc.edu
CREECH, Pat .... 918-540-6294. 396 G
pcreech@neo.edu
CREED, J. Bradley .... 205-726-2718..... 6 F
jbcreed@samford.edu
CREED-DIKEOGU, Gloria 785-242-5200. 189 I
creeddikeogu@ottawa.edu
CREEDON, James .... 215-204-1991. 433 K
james.creedon@temple.edu
CREEGER, Joan .... 704-216-3602. 363 D
joan.creeger@rccc.edu
CREEHAN, Dennis, W ..... 304-457-6404. 526 A
creehandw@ab.edu
CREEHAN, Richard, A ..... 304-457-1700. 526 A
creehanra@ab.edu
CREEK, Fred, A .... 253-833-9111. 520 C
fcreek@greenriver.edu
CREEKMORE, Crystal ...... 575-562-2175. 309 H
crystal.creekmore@enmu.edu
CREEL, Angie .... 928-344-7776... 11 L
angela.creel-erb@azwestern.edu
CREEL, Ronnie .... 334-670-3496..... 7 H
rcreel@troy.edu
CREEL, Shane .... 361-593-2237. 484 A
randolph.creel@tamuk.edu
CREELY, Hilliary .... 724-357-7730. 428 F
Hilliary.Creely@iup.edu

CREER, John .... 636-949-4777. 276 D
jcreer@lindenwood.edu
CREFT, Dawn, H .... 407-303-7894... 97 H
dawn.creft@adu.edu
CREGGER, Crystal, Y ...... 276-233-4762. 514 F
ccregger@wcc.vccs.edu
CREIGHTON, Clarinda .... 816-584-6833. 280 C
clarinda.creighton@park.edu
CREIGHTON, Grace .... 914-674-7369. 330 J
gcreighton@mercy.edu
CREIGHTON, Karen .... 417-447-2601. 279 K
creightk@otc.edu
CREMER, Douglas .... 818-767-0888... 76 K
douglas.cremer@woodbury.edu
CREMER, Phyllis, A .... 818-767-0888... 76 K
phyllis.cremer@woodbury.edu
CRENSHAW, Chris .... 601-266-4414. 270 E
christopher.crenshaw@usm.edu
CRENSHAW, Christine .... 405-744-5358. 397 H
christine.crenshaw@okstate.edu
CRENSHAW, Jan .... 281-998-6150. 479 G
jan.crenshaw@sjcd.edu
CRENSHAW, Karen .... 724-503-1001. 436 G
kcrenshaw@washjeff.edu
CRESCENZO, Mario .... 212-650-5250. 317 D
mcrescenzo@ccny.cuny.edu
CRESPINO, Curt, J .... 816-235-1105. 283 D
crespinocj@umkc.edu
CRESPO, Jorge .... 787-751-0178. 552 G
ac_jcrespo@suagm.edu
CRESPO, Jorge, L .... 787-751-0178. 552 G
ac_jcrespo@suagm.edu
CRESPO, Lynn .... 864-455-7992. 448 E
CRESPO, Ricardo .... 787-751-1912. 551 B
rcnevarez@juris.inter.edu
CRESPO-KEBLER,
Elizabeth .... 787-993-8864. 554 A
elizabeth.crespo1@upr.edu
CRESPO-LOPEZ, Sylvia .. 212-237-8897. 318 D
sylopez@jjay.cuny.edu
CRESPY, Charles, T .... 989-774-2481. 240 N
cresp1ct@cmich.edu
CREW, Dwayne .... 478-825-6200. 124 H
crewd@fvsu.edu
CREW, Rudolph, F .... 718-270-5000. 319 A
rcrew@mec.cuny.edu
CREWE, Sandra .... 202-806-7300... 95 G
screwe@howard.edu
CREWELL, Don .... 626-395-6280... 31 E
dcrewell@caltech.edu
CREWS, Amy .... 256-765-4437..... 9 C
aecrews@una.edu
CREWS, Bradford, W ...... 561-297-2190. 114 L
bcrews2@fau.edu
CREWS, Denise .... 217-875-7200. 156 J
dcrews@richland.edu
CREWS, Kimberly .... 202-274-5857... 97 A
kcrews@udc.edu
CREWS, Micah, R .... 423-652-4773. 455 I
mrcrews@king.edu
CREWS, Michele .... 617-879-2114. 238 C
mcrews@wheelock.edu
CREWS, Sharon .... 205-929-6307..... 5 D
sharon.crews@lawsonstate.edu
CREWS, William, O .... 415-380-1326... 45 H
billcrews@ggbts.edu
CREWS, Yolanda, M .... 804-524-5189. 515 D
ycrews@vsu.edu
CRIBBY, William .... 617-928-4021. 234 E
wcribby@mountida.edu
CRICK, James .... 502-451-0815. 199 F
jcrick@sullivan.edu
CRICK, James .... 502-451-0815. 199 G
jcrick@sullivan.edu
CRICKENBERGER, Leslie 706-583-2818. 120 J
lcrickenberger@athenstech.edu
CRICKENBERGER,
Tamela .... 434-592-3508. 506 I
tlcrickenberger@liberty.edu
CRIDER, Charles, G .... 717-736-4121. 417 I
cgcrider@hacc.edu
CRIDER, Wayne .... 706-245-7226. 124 D
wcrider@ec.edu
CRILLEY, Bonnie .... 814-866-8144. 420 E
bcrilley@lecom.edu
CRILLY, Sam .... 405-912-9064. 395 K
scrilly@hc.edu
CRIM, Kim .... 717-846-5000. 438 E
CRIMMIN, Nancy, P .... 774-354-0460. 223 A
nancy.crimmin@becker.edu
CRIMMINS, Cindy .... 717-815-1216. 438 D
ccrimmins@ycp.edu
CRIMMINS, Kate .... 410-837-6135. 221 A
kcrimmins@ubalt.edu
CRIMMINS LECHOWICZ,
Catherine .... 860-685-2841... 92 H
ccrimmins@wesleyan.edu
CRING, Christine, A .... 315-684-6079. 345 A
cringca@morrisville.edu
CRINITI, Stephen .... 304-243-2424. 531 H
scriniti@wju.edu

CRIPPS, Kimberly .... 205-726-4180..... 6 F
kcripps@samford.edu
CRISCI, David, A .... 570-340-6077. 423 B
dacrisci@marywood.edu
CRISLER, Pat .... 402-457-2759. 290 G
pcrisler@mccneb.edu
CRISMAN, Steve .... 901-321-3278. 453 H
scrisman@cbu.edu
CRISMON, M. Lynn .... 512-471-3718. 491 C
lynn.crismon@austin.utexas.edu
CRISP, JR., Delmas, S .... 910-630-7031. 356 H
dcrisp@methodist.edu
CRISP, Kathryn .... 615-904-8167. 459 D
kathy.crisp@mtsu.edu
CRISP, Whitney .... 229-931-2299. 131 G
wcrisp@southgatech.edu
CRISP, Winston, B .... 919-966-4045. 368 D
wbcrisp@email.unc.edu
CRISPELL, Brian .... 813-988-5131. 104 A
deanofstudents@floridacollege.edu
CRISPIN, Jon .... 251-981-3771..... 2 I
jon.crispin@columbiasouthern.edu
CRISS, Arthur .... 732-255-0400. 304 A
acriss@ocean.edu
CRISS, Paul .... 901-888-3343. 266 A
pcriss@belhaven.edu
CRISSINGER, Amy, S ..... 605-256-5139. 451 H
amy.crissinger@dsu.edu
CRIST, Alan, N .... 608-263-4384. 536 C
acrist@uwsa.edu
CRIST, Diane, G .... 651-962-6765. 265 C
dgcrist@stthomas.edu
CRIST, William, J .... 337-482-2001. 208 D
wjc4092@louisiana.edu
CRISTANTELLO, David .... 716-286-8679. 334 F
dcristan@niagara.edu
CRISTELLI, Bruno, P .... 409-772-1939. 493 C
bcristel@utmb.edu
CRISTELLO, Justin .... 859-442-1687. 195 B
justin.cristello@kctcs.edu
CRISTIANO KELLY,
Patricia .... 215-955-1755. 434 C
patricia.kelly@jefferson.edu
CRISTOBAL, Nereida .... 787-620-2040. 547 C
ncristobal@aupr.edu
CRISTOBAL, Remy, B ...... 671-735-2290. 546 E
remybc@uguam.uog.edu
CRISTOBAL, Remy, B ..... 671-735-2218. 546 E
remybc@uguam.uog.edu
CRISTOFARO,
Theresa, R .... 856-225-6053. 306 C
terri.cristofaro@rutgers.edu
CRISWELL, John .... 972-860-7786. 470 F
jcriswell@dcccd.edu
CRISWELL-BLOOM,
Robyn .... 941-355-9080. 101 L
rcriswellbloom@ewcollege.org
CRITE, Ken .... 815-802-8222. 149 C
kcrite@kcc.edu
CRITEL-RATHJE, Dina ...... 402-643-7396. 289 B
Dina.critel-rathje@cune.edu
CRITES, Randall .... 304-473-8030. 531 G
crites@wvwc.edu
CRITES, Tammy .... 304-473-8186. 531 G
crites_t@wvwc.edu
CRITTENDEN, Barbara, J 641-782-1425. 182 I
crittenden@swcciowa.edu
CRITTENDEN, Steve .... 218-683-8565. 260 D
steve.crittenden@northlandcollege.edu
CROAT, Lisa .... 515-643-6720. 181 A
lcroat@mercydesmoines.org
CROCE, Edward .... 210-434-6711. 477 N
ecroce@lake.ollusa.edu
CROCHET, Monique .... 985-448-4110. 208 A
monique.crochet@nicholls.edu
CROCK, Veronica .... 334-347-2623..... 3 G
vcrock@escc.edu
CROCKER, Daniel .... 207-974-4623. 210 K
dcrocker@emcc.edu
CROCKER, Dennis .... 815-939-5213. 155 H
djcrocker@olivet.edu
CROCKER, Jack .... 575-538-6318. 312 N
jcrocker@wnmu.edu
CROCKER, Jane, S .... 856-415-2250. 302 C
jcrocker@gccnj.edu
CROCKER, Leslie .... 804-330-0111. 503 G
bursarcrim@centura.edu
CROCKER, Marjorie .... 706-419-1544. 123 F
crocker@covenant.edu
CROCKER, Rhonda .... 575-624-7382. 309 I
rhonda.crocker@roswell.enmu.edu
CROCKER, Robert, A .... 516-796-4800. 333 C
rcrocker@nycc.edu
CROCKER, Ryan, C .... 979-862-8007. 483 C
rcrocker@tamu.edu
CROCKER, Teresa .... 404-894-2500. 125 D
teresa.crocker@police.gatech.edu
CROCKER, Tillman .... 575-624-7486. 309 I
tillman.crocker@roswell.enmu.edu
CROCKETT, Bennie, R ..... 601-318-6116. 270 I
crockett@wmcarey.edu

CROCKETT, Betty, P .... 410-543-6050. 220 D
bpcrockett@salisbury.edu
CROCKETT, Brian, S .... 540-464-7287. 515 B
briancrockett@vmiaa.org
CROCKETT, Charles, E .... 936-261-2653. 482 F
cecrockett@pvamu.edu
CROCKETT, Daniel, E .... 304-558-4618. 529 C
crockett@hepc.wvnet.edu
CROCKETT, Dave .... 217-581-6250. 144 E
dmcrockett@eiu.edu
CROCKETT, Deborah .... 207-947-4591. 209 G
dcrockett@bealcollege.edu
CROCKETT, Hannah .... 912-525-5000. 131 B
hcrocket@scad.edu
CROCKETT, Julie, A .... 303-458-3524... 84 M
jcrocket@regis.edu
CROCKETT, Michael .... 928-428-8215... 13 J
mike.crockett@eac.edu
CROCKETT, William, P .... 410-706-3902. 219 C
bcrocket@umaryland.edu
CROCKETT-BELL, Sharon 210-486-2886. 465 B
scrockett-bell@alamo.edu
CROCKETT-BELL, Sharon 210-486-2887. 465 B
scrockett-bell@alamo.edu
CROCKROM, SR.,
Charles .... 205-929-1447..... 5 G
ccrockrom@miles.edu
CROCQUET, Marc .... 954-262-8842. 109 K
crocquet@nova.edu
CROFOOT-MORLEY,
Deborah .... 713-525-3109. 490 L
crofoot@stthom.edu
CROFT, Candace .... 319-296-4432. 178 J
candace.croft@hawkeyecollege.edu
CROFT, Lucy, S .... 904-620-2525. 116 B
lcroft@unf.edu
CROFT, Nicole .... 866-680-2756. 496 A
academicdean@midwifery.edu
CROGHAN, David .... 301-846-2491. 214 H
dcroghan@frederick.edu
CROGHAN, John .... 315-859-4129. 325 E
jcroghan@hamilton.edu
CROLEY, Linda .... 386-752-1822. 104 G
linda.croley@fgc.edu
CROMARTIE, Anthony .... 973-877-1873. 301 H
cromartie@essex.edu
CROMARTY, Geoffrey ..... 215-951-2970. 430 E
cromartyg@philau.edu
CROMBIE, Richard .... 651-635-8041. 253 K
r-crombie@bethel.edu
CROMEENS, Julie .... 325-738-3318. 486 C
julie.cromeens@abilene.tstc.edu
CROMER, Steve .... 706-646-6234. 132 B
scromer@sctech.edu
CROMLEY, Brenda .... 570-389-4674. 427 H
bcromley@bloomu.edu
CROMWELL, Dennis .... 812-855-4717. 167 F
dcromwel@indiana.edu
CROMWELL, James .... 808-689-2909. 136 C
cromwell@hawaii.edu
CROMWELL, Randy .... 731-352-4046. 453 D
cromwellr@bethelu.edu
CROMWELL, Ronald .... 256-233-8214..... 1 F
ronald.cromwell@athens.edu
CRON, Sarah .... 970-248-1029... 79 F
scron@coloradomesa.edu
CRONAN, Andrew .... 212-217-3400. 324 C
andrew_cronan@fitnyc.edu
CRONAN, David .... 708-709-3585. 156 A
dcronan@prairiestate.edu
CRONAUER, OSB,
Patrick, T .... 724-805-2324. 432 H
patrick.cronauer@email.stvincent.edu
CRONC, Sue .... 770-531-6332. 128 B
scronc@laniertech.edu
CRONE, Kimberly, M ...... 203-392-9999... 88 A
cronek1@southernct.edu
CRONE, Marilyn .... 206-296-5841. 523 E
cronem@seattleu.edu
CRONIN, Alice .... 508-565-1021. 237 A
acronin@stonehill.edu
CRONIN, Charles .... 610-526-1458. 409 F
tip.cronin@theamericancollege.edu
CRONIN, Deborah .... 207-948-9227. 211 I
dcronin@unity.edu
CRONIN, Debra .... 312-850-7154. 142 C
dcronin1@ccc.edu
CRONIN, Joy .... 304-243-2238. 531 H
jcronin@wju.edu
CRONIN, Kelly .... 806-742-1780. 487 D
kelly.overley@ttu.edu
CRONIN, Mary, A .... 713-348-4070. 479 A
cronin@rice.edu
CRONIN, Patrick .... 508-531-1004. 229 D
pcronin@bridgew.edu
CRONIN, Shawn .... 978-762-4000. 232 D
scronin@northshore.edu
CRONK, Nancy, L .... 765-285-1722. 164 B
ncronk@bsu.edu
CRONRATH, David .... 301-405-6287. 219 B
cronrath@umd.edu

CROOK, Evonne ... 423-236-2830. 458 J ercrook@southern.edu
CROOK, Jon ... 325-793-4700. 476 E crook.jon@mcm.edu
CROOK, Linda ... 303-914-6256... 84 I linda.crook@rrcc.edu
CROOK, Patricia ... 615-963-5280. 459 E pcrook@tnstate.edu
CROOK, Phylis ... 614-234-5681. 384 J pcrook@mccn.edu
CROOKENDALE, Humphrey ... 212-343-1234. 331 D hcrookendale@mcny.edu
CROOKER, Benjamin ... 718-817-3048. 324 G crooker@fordham.edu
CROOKER, Ron ... 563-425-5666. 183 B crookerr@uiu.edu
CROOKS, John, R ... 440-365-5222. 383 B
CROOKSHANK, Gail ... 217-420-6778. 153 C gcrookshank@millikin.edu
CROOP, Patricia ... 518-464-8642. 324 B pcroop@excelsior.edu
CROOT, Rick ... 360-417-6553. 522 A rcroot@pencol.edu
CROOT, Robert, A ... 315-655-7158. 316 E rcroot@cazenovia.edu
CROPPER, USMS, Thomas, A ... 707-654-1010... 31 I tacropper@csum.edu
CROPSEY, Jeffrey ... 800-955-2527. 274 I jcropsey@grantham.edu
CROSBY, Anita, L ... 334-387-3877... 1 E anitacrosby@amridgeuniversity.edu
CROSBY, Cheryl ... 352-854-2322. 100 K crosbyc@cf.edu
CROSBY, Craig ... 858-541-7780... 55 J ccrosby@nu.edu
CROSBY, Donnie, E ... 334-387-3877... 1 E donniecrosby@amridgeuniversity.edu
CROSBY, Faye ... 831-459-3568... 72 C fjcrosby@ucsc.edu
CROSBY, James, P ... 216-347-4282. 381 R jcrosby@jcu.edu
CROSBY, Jesse ... 207-947-4591. 209 G jcrosby@bealcollege.edu
CROSBY, Kim ... 870-307-7275... 21 H kim.crosby@lyon.edu
CROSBY, Larry ... 909-607-7008... 39 C larrycrosby@cgu.edu
CROSBY, Mark ... 207-859-5500. 209 J mcrosby@colby.edu
CROSBY, Mark ... 417-864-7220. 274 D mcrosby@cci.edu
CROSBY, Pamela ... 863-667-5041. 113 P pscrosby@seu.edu
CROSBY, Susan, E ... 540-453-2363. 511 H crosbys@brcc.edu
CROSIER, Sandy ... 806-742-2974. 487 D sandra.crosier@ttu.edu
CROSIER, Sonia ... 847-543-2224. 143 A scrosier@clcillinois.edu
CROSKERY, Patrick, T ... 419-772-2197. 386 D p-croskery@onu.edu
CROSLEY, Leslie, V ... 315-684-6046. 345 A croslelv@morrisville.edu
CROSLIN, Joey ... 405-208-5075. 397 F jcroslin@okcu.edu
CROSMAN, Karen ... 740-368-3104. 387 J klcrosma@owu.edu
CROSON, Rachel ... 817-272-2881. 491 B croson@uta.edu
CROSS, Berri, V ... 336-334-4822. 360 G bvcross@gtcc.edu
CROSS, Charles, E ... 415-422-6522... 73 J cross@usfca.edu
CROSS, Colette ... 281-649-3475. 473 B ccross@hbu.edu
CROSS, David ... 713-718-8636. 473 C david.cross@hccs.edu
CROSS, David ... 603-862-2090. 298 C counseling.center@unh.edu
CROSS, Dennis, W ... 540-458-8232. 516 A dcross@wlu.edu
CROSS, Douglas, D ... 423-585-6901. 462 A doug.cross@ws.edu
CROSS, Dwight ... 802-225-6324. 499 I dwight.cross@neci.edu
CROSS, Hal, G ... 570-586-2400. 410 D hcross@bbc.edu
CROSS, James ... 802-383-6633. 499 A jcross@champlain.edu
CROSS, Jeff ... 619-203-3681... 28 M jefcross@argosy.edu
CROSS, Jeffrey ... 248-476-1122. 246 G jcross@mispp.edu
CROSS, Jeffrey, F ... 217-581-2121. 144 E jfcross@eiu.edu
CROSS, Jesse ... 336-334-4822. 360 G jlcross@gtcc.edu
CROSS, Justin ... 406-377-9403. 286 A justin_c@dawson.edu
CROSS, Kris ... 937-393-3431. 389 B kcross@sscc.edu
CROSS, Kristen ... 870-612-2011... 25 A kristen.cross@uaccb.edu
CROSS, Mary, M ... 615-353-3301. 461 B mary.cross@nscc.edu
CROSS, Michael ... 309-677-2670. 140 I mcross@bradley.edu
CROSS, Michael ... 919-209-2051. 361 E mtcross@johnstoncc.edu
CROSS, Monique ... 225-216-8361. 202 H crossm@mybrcc.edu
CROSS, Myrna, J ... 580-477-7712. 401 J myrna.cross@wosc.edu
CROSS, Penny ... 828-652-0645. 362 A penncyc@mcdowelltech.edu
CROSS, Raymond ... 608-262-3786. 538 E ray.cross@uwex.uwc.edu
CROSS, Roberta ... 724-503-1001. 436 G rcross@washjeff.edu
CROSS, Stan ... 828-298-3325. 370 E scross@warren-wilson.edu
CROSS, Stephen ... 404-894-8885. 125 D cross@gatech.edu
CROSS, Teresa ... 660-359-3948. 279 H tcross@mail.ncmissouri.edu
CROSS, Terry ... 423-614-8140. 455 L tcross@leeuniversity.edu
CROSS, Tim, L ... 865-974-7114. 463 C tlcross@utk.edu
CROSS BAKER, Tracey ... 518-564-2071. 344 B cros1626@plattsburgh.edu
CROSSLAND, Martin ... 913-971-3514. 188 H mcrossland@mnu.edu
CROSSLAND, Rick ... 785-442-6110. 187 E rcrossland@highlandcc.edu
CROSSLEY, Angela ... 602-275-7133... 17 L angela.crossley@rsaiz.edu
CROSSLEY, John ... 315-733-2300. 349 D
CROSSLEY, John, L ... 315-733-2300. 349 D jcrossley@uscny.edu
CROSSMAN, Cynthia ... 508-362-2131. 231 D ccrossma@capecod.edu
CROSSMAN, Herb ... 518-580-5819. 341 A hcrossma@skidmore.edu
CROSSMAN, Linda ... 727-873-4143. 116 D crossman@mail.usf.edu
CROSSMAN, Raymond, E ... 312-662-4001. 139 F rec@adler.edu
CROSSON, Elaine ... 631-632-6265. 342 C
CROSWELL, Katrina ... 510-549-4719... 68 G kcroswell@sksm.edu
CROTHERS, Scott ... 618-545-3176. 149 D scrothers@kaskaskia.edu
CROTTS, Glenda, S ... 704-406-4236. 354 C gcrotts@gardner-webb.edu
CROTTS, Neal ... 803-778-6602. 441 F crottsna@cctech.edu
CROTZ, Steve ... 334-244-3541... 2 A scrotz@aum.edu
CROUCH, Bruce ... 714-556-3610... 74 D bcrouch@vanguard.edu
CROUCH, David ... 501-279-4316... 21 C dcrouch@harding.edu
CROUCH, Frank ... 610-861-1516. 424 E fcrouch@moravian.edu
CROUCH, Julia ... 918-335-6212. 398 F jcrouch@okwu.edu
CROUCH, Peter, E ... 808-956-7727. 136 B pcrouch@hawaii.edu
CROUCH, Steven ... 612-624-2006. 264 G crouch@umn.edu
CROUCH, Tony ... 620-441-5207. 186 A crouch@cowley.edu
CROUCHET, Christeen ... 253-589-5895. 518 B christeen.crouchet@cptc.edu
CROUERE, Vanessa ... 985-867-2242. 206 H vcrouere@sjasc.edu
CROUSE, Eileen ... 269-782-1369. 250 C ecrouse@swmich.edu
CROUSE, JR., Francis, C ... 814-886-6383. 424 G fcrouse@mtaloy.edu
CROUSE, Harry ... 513-721-7944. 380 D hcrouse@gbs.edu
CROUSE, Margaret ... 308-432-6330. 291 D mcrouse@csc.edu
CROUSE, Robert ... 573-592-5019. 285 B rob.crouse@westminster-mo.edu
CROUSE, Steve ... 864-977-7016. 445 H steve.crouse@ngu.edu
CROUTER, Ann, C ... 814-865-1420. 426 A ac1@psu.edu
CROW, C. Robert ... 616-526-6165. 240 L rcrow@calvin.edu
CROW, Donna, E ... 435-797-3588. 497 B donna.crow@usu.edu
CROW, Michael, G ... 912-358-4172. 131 C crowm@savannahstate.edu
CROW, Michael, M ... 480-965-8972... 11 K michael.crow@asu.edu
CROW, Scott ... 916-484-8647... 53 A crows@arc.losrios.edu
CROW, Sharon ... 386-506-3016. 101 G crows@DaytonaState.edu
CROW, Steven ... 619-482-6310... 68 B scrow@swccd.edu
CROW, Tony, L ... 303-458-4161... 84 M tcrow@regis.edu
CROWDER, Annette ... 573-681-5102. 276 C crowdera@lincolnu.edu
CROWDER, Darren ... 417-328-1817. 282 C dcrowder@sbuniv.edu
CROWDER, John ... 317-789-8267. 165 E jcrowder@crossroads.edu
CROWDER, Mike ... 806-743-7865. 487 E mike.crowder@ttuhsc.edu
CROWDER, Rick ... 423-869-6306. 456 A rcrowder@lmunet.edu
CROWDER, Vickie ... 304-473-8032. 531 G crowder_v@wvwc.edu
CROWE, Aliesha, R ... 715-852-1394. 539 J acrowe3@cvtc.edu
CROWE, Carl ... 410-778-7235. 221 C ccrowe2@washcoll.edu
CROWE, Chuck ... 303-404-5238... 81 N chuck.crowe@frontrange.edu
CROWE, Ellen ... 773-380-6860. 163 D ecrowe@westwood.edu
CROWE, Jason ... 314-454-7770. 274 G jcrowe@bjc.org
CROWE, Lisa ... 859-622-2696. 193 P lisa.crowe@eku.edu
CROWE, Mary, L ... 863-680-4181. 105 D mcrowe@flsouthern.edu
CROWE, Peggy, A ... 270-745-3159. 200 G peggy.crowe@wku.edu
CROWE, Richard ... 818-345-8414... 41 B rcrowe@columbiacollege.edu
CROWE, Sara ... 912-583-3240. 122 B scrowe@bpc.edu
CROWE, Thomas ... 847-543-2473. 143 A tcrowe@clcillinois.edu
CROWE, William, R ... 706-542-3451. 133 C william.crowe@georgiacenter.uga.edu
CROWELL, Anthony ... 212-431-2840. 333 I Anthony.Crowell@nyls.edu
CROWELL, Heidi ... 603-577-6523. 296 F crowell@dwc.edu
CROWELL, Perry ... 850-644-4780. 115 C pcrowell@admin.fsu.edu
CROWELL, Rebecca, C ... 972-516-5011. 469 G rcrowell@collin.edu
CROWELL, Scott ... 507-537-6844. 261 F Scott.Crowell@smsu.edu
CROWETIPTON, Vaughn ... 864-294-2138. 444 C vaughn.crowetipton@furman.edu
CROWFOOT, Rebecca ... 770-394-8300. 120 H rcrowfoot@aii.edu
CROWL, Rebecca, R ... 330-363-6164. 374 E rcrowl@aultman.com
CROWL, Ronald ... 330-829-2756. 391 E crowlrl@mountunion.edu
CROWLEY, Janelle ... 847-214-7415. 144 F jcrowley@elgin.edu
CROWLEY, Kim ... 504-314-1852. 207 C kcrowley@tulane.edu
CROWLEY, Kimberly, A ... 806-354-6087. 465 E kacrowley@actx.edu
CROWLEY, Rachel ... 605-331-6661. 452 D rachel.crowley@usiouxfalls.edu
CROWLEY, Suzanne ... 561-912-2166. 103 C scrowley@evergladesuniversity.edu
CROWLEY, Tim ... 785-628-4236. 186 F tcrowley@fhsu.edu
CROWLEY, Timothy, D ... 207-768-2811. 210 M tcrowley@nmcc.edu
CROWLEY, Tom ... 716-286-8601. 334 F tcrowley@niagara.edu
CROWLEY, Treacy ... 216-987-3245. 378 D treacy.crowley@tri-c.edu
CROWNE, Deborah ... 808-544-0283. 135 F dcrowne@hpu.edu
CROWSON, Allan ... 615-844-5221. 464 E acrowson@welch.edu
CROWSON, Dennis ... 979-830-4456. 467 I dennis.crowson@blinn.edu
CROWTHER, Edward ... 719-587-7811... 78 B ercrowth@adams.edu
CROWTHER, Elizabeth, H ... 804-758-6701. 513 G ecrowther@rappahannock.edu
CROWTHER, Jason ... 910-221-2224. 354 D jcrowther@gcd.edu
CROWTHER, Lori, D ... 620-792-9216. 184 F crowtherl@bartonccc.edu
CROWTHER, Steven ... 910-221-2224. 354 D scrowther@gcd.edu
CROWTHER, Susan ... 661-362-3098... 40 E susan.crowther@canyons.edu
CROY, Jason ... 706-245-7226. 124 D jcroy@ec.edu
CROY, Melanie ... 405-382-9210. 399 I m.croy@sscok.edu
CROYLE, Kristin ... 956-665-7919. 492 B kcroyle@utpa.edu
CROYLE, Mary ... 806-743-2143. 487 E mary.croyle@ttuhsc.edu
CRUDELE, Dennis ... 561-297-3450. 114 L president@fau.edu
CRUEY, Pam ... 717-901-5112. 418 E pcruey@HarrisburgU.net
CRUICKSHANK, Laura ... 860-486-2086... 92 A laura.cruickshank@uconn.edu
CRUIKSHANK, Nancy, L 724-738-4831. 429 F nancy.cruikshank@sru.edu
CRUISE, Deborah, J ... 443-412-2233. 215 C dcruise@harford.edu
CRUISE, Thomas ... 540-831-5479. 508 C tcruise@radford.edu
CRUISE-HARPER, Christie ... 314-529-9684. 276 G ccruiseharper@maryville.edu
CRUM, Claude ... 606-368-6061. 191 J claudecrum@alc.edu
CRUM, Tom ... 423-697-2417. 460 C
CRUMBLIN, Leon ... 870-575-8360... 24 E crumblinl@uapb.edu
CRUME, Gene ... 847-628-2002. 149 B gene.crume@judsonu.edu
CRUMEDY, Ron, C ... 409-944-1237. 472 I rcrumedy@gc.edu
CRUMLEY, Christopher ... 281-476-1810. 479 F christopher.crumley@sjcd.edu
CRUMLEY, Kristie ... 410-386-8408. 214 A kcrumley@carrollcc.edu
CRUMLEY, Terri ... 715-346-2441. 538 A Terri.Crumley@uwsp.edu
CRUMMIE, Carla, M ... 404-527-4525. 122 E ccrummie@carver.edu
CRUMMIE, Robert, W ... 404-527-4520. 122 E rcrummie@carver.edu
CRUMP, D'adra ... 718-940-5869. 339 B dcrump@sjcny.edu
CRUMP, Linda ... 402-472-3417. 292 I lcrump1@unl.edu
CRUMP, Tammy ... 704-991-0267. 364 C tcrump5648@stanly.edu
CRUMP, Virginia, S ... 731-410-6709. 455 J vcrump@lanecollege.edu
CRUMPTON, Beth ... 478-274-7850. 129 I bcrumpton@oftc.edu
CRUSCIEL, Robert ... 814-472-3021. 432 D rcrusciel@francis.edu
CRUSE, David ... 517-265-5161. 238 G
CRUSE, Susan ... 404-727-6061. 124 E scruse2@emory.edu
CRUSE, Terry ... 903-233-4310. 475 J TerryCruse@letu.edu
CRUSE, Tom ... 513-936-1538. 391 A thomas.cruse@uc.edu
CRUSTO-WAY, Kathy ... 817-515-5206. 482 B kathy.crustoway@tccd.edu
CRUTCHER, Ben ... 859-218-3378. 200 C bencrutcher@uky.edu
CRUTCHER, Caicey, L ... 620-792-9386. 184 F crutcherc@bartonccc.edu
CRUTCHER, Cheryl ... 602-243-8398... 15 F cheryl.crutcher@southmountaincc.edu
CRUTCHER, Gary ... 816-414-3700. 277 L gcrutcher@mbts.edu
CRUTCHER, Ronald, A ... 508-286-8244. 238 B crutcher_ronald@wheatoncollege.edu
CRUTCHER, Terri ... 615-452-8600. 461 G terri.crutcher@volstate.edu
CRUTCHFIELD, Carla ... 501-337-5000... 20 J ccrutchfield@coto.edu
CRUTHIS, Crystal, E ... 336-841-9131. 355 C ccruthis@highpoint.edu
CRUTSINGER, Christy ... 940-565-2550. 490 C christy.crutsinger@unt.edu
CRUZ, Abraham ... 347-964-8600. 315 E acruz@boricuacollege.edu
CRUZ, Anthony ... 937-512-2974. 388 O anthony.cruz@sinclair.edu
CRUZ, Beatriz ... 718-429-6600. 349 H beatriz.cruz@vaughn.edu
CRUZ, Carmen, L ... 787-257-0000. 554 B carmen.cruz3@upr.edu
CRUZ, Celestino ... 787-746-1400. 549 B ccruz@huertas.edu
CRUZ, Cynthia, A ... 815-740-2270. 162 F ccruz@stfrancis.edu
CRUZ, Elizabeth ... 787-780-5134. 551 L ecruz@nuc.edu
CRUZ, Erin ... 559-791-2222... 49 P ecruz@portervillecollege.edu
CRUZ, Erin ... 559-791-2332... 49 P ecruz@portervillecollege.edu
CRUZ, Esteban ... 217-786-2200. 151 F esteban.cruz@llcc.edu

CRUZ, Felicita 787-834-9595. 553 B
fcruz@uaa.edu
CRUZ, Heather, A 716-851-1858. 323 I
cruzh@ecc.edu
CRUZ, Hilda 787-164-1912. 551 A
hmcruz@sg.inte.edu
CRUZ, Irma del Pilar 787-828-1319. 552 J
um_idelpilar@suagm.edu
CRUZ, Israel 787-264-1912. 551 A
icruz@sg.inter.edu
CRUZ, Jackie 831-755-6810... 46 G
jcruz@hartnell.edu
CRUZ, Jaime 787-769-0007. 547 G
jacruz@carolina.caribbean.edu
CRUZ, Jose 657-278-2011... 33 E
jcruz@fullerton.edu
CRUZ, Jose 956-872-3554. 480 I
jcruz@southtexascollege.edu
CRUZ, Lambert 602-386-4160... 11 G
lambert.cruz@arizonachristian.edu
CRUZ, Lourdes 203-837-9202... 88 B
cruzl@wcsu.edu
CRUZ, Luis, M 787-279-2250. 550 B
lcruz@bayamon.inter.edu
CRUZ, Madeline 787-834-9595. 553 B
mcruz@uaa.edu
CRUZ, Mariela 787-620-2040. 547 C
marielacruz@aupr.edu
CRUZ, Martin 787-766-1717. 552 J
um_mcruzsa@suagm.edu
CRUZ, Mayra 787-751-0178. 552 G
mcruz@suagm.edu
CRUZ, Monica 361-354-2258. 468 K
mcruz@coastalbend.edu
CRUZ, Nathaniel 718-518-4253. 318 B
ncruz@hostos.cuny.edu
CRUZ, Octavio 408-270-6423... 63 O
octavio.cruz@evc.edu
CRUZ, Oscar 787-786-3030. 547 F
oscruz@ucb.edu.pr
CRUZ, Robert 201-360-4051. 302 D
rcruz@hccc.edu
CRUZ, Rosa, E 787-848-1589. 551 O
rcruz@popac.edu
CRUZ, Rosalia 212-694-1000. 315 E
rcruz@boricuacollege.edu
CRUZ, Tony 760-744-1150... 58 D
tcruz@palomar.edu
CRUZ, Villan 718-933-6700. 331 K
Vcrux@monroecollege.edu
CRUZ, Zoraida 787-279-1912. 550 B
zcruz@bayamon.inter.edu
CRUZ BONILLA, Jessica 787-744-1060. 551 J
jecbo@mechtech.edu
CRUZ-CUEVAS, Oscar 787-786-4508. 548 K
ocruz@cedoc.edu
CRUZ GORRITZ, Carlos . 787-744-1060. 551 J
ccruz@mechtech.edu
CRUZ-RICHMAN, Daisy .. 718-270-7631. 342 D
dcruzrichman@downstate.edu
CRUZ SOTO, Bethzaida .. 787-840-2575. 552 A
CRUZ-URIBE, Kathyrn 765-973-8201. 167 G
kathcruz@iue.edu
CRUZADO, Waded 406-994-2341. 287 B
president@montana.edu
CRUZVERGARA,
Christine, Y 703-993-2370. 505 C
ccruzver@gmu.edu
CRYDER, Dennis 660-543-4313. 283 A
cryder@ucmo.edu
CRYER, Byron, L 214-648-2590. 493 E
byron.cryer@utsouthwestern.edu
CRYLEN, Thomas 847-925-6169. 145 H
tcrylen@harpercollege.edu
CUADRA, Darla 510-261-8500... 58 G
darla.cuadra@patten.edu
CUADRADO-GARCÍA,
Héctor 787-993-8953. 554 A
hector.cuadrado@upr.edu
CUARON, Berta 760-744-1150... 58 D
bcuaron@palomar.edu
CUBANO, Luis, A 787-798-3001. 553 C
luis.cubano@uccaribe.edu
CUBBA, Stephanie 213-477-2766... 54 J
scubba@msmc.la.edu
CUBBAGE, Alan, K 847-491-4886. 155 D
a-cubbage@northwestern.edu
CUBBERLEY, Frances, M 610-359-5141. 414 D
fcubberl@dccc.edu
CUBBINS, Elaine 520-383-8401... 18 B
ecubbins@tocc.cc.az.us
CUBE, Joan 925-631-8317... 61 F
jic2@stmarys-ca.edu
CUBELIC, Chuck 412-809-5100. 430 H
cubelic.chuck@pti.edu
CUBIT, James, R 847-735-5054. 150 B
cubit@lakeforest.edu
CUBRIEL, III, Robert 361-572-6406. 493 H
robert.cubriel@victoriacollege.edu
CUCARESE, Lisa 304-829-7831. 526 D
lcucarese@bethanywv.edu

CUCCIA, Christopher 718-390-4094. 339 A
cucciac@stjohns.edu
CUCOLO, Anthony 717-245-4400. 545 F
CUCURELLA-ADORNO,
Ana, E 787-780-0070. 547 G
president@caribbean.edu
CUDE, Ruth 361-354-2767. 468 K
rcude@coastalbend.edu
CUDHEA, Renee, M 518-489-7436. 330 C
srcudhea@mariacollege.edu
CUELLAR, Leana 847-635-1655. 155 F
lcuellar@oakton.edu
CUELLAR, Toni 254-298-8333. 482 C
toni.cuellar@templejc.edu
CUENIN, Walter 781-736-3574. 224 F
cuenin@brandeis.edu
CUETO, Jose, M 787-780-0070. 547 G
jcueto@caribbean.edu
CUETO, Omar 787-279-1912. 550 B
ocueto@bayamon.inter.edu
CUEVAS, José 787-834-3718. 554 E
support@uprm.edu
CUFF, Michael 508-830-5037. 230 D
mcuff@maritime.edu
CUFFARI, Gina 216-447-8807... 18 I
gina.cuffari@phoenix.edu
CUFFARI, Stefania 516-364-0808. 333 D
scuffari@nycollege.edu
CUIMAN, Leonzo 718-270-1972. 342 D
lcuiman@downstate.edu
CUKANNA, Paul-James .. 412-396-5002. 415 F
cukanna@duq.edu
CUKROWSKI, Ken, R 325-674-3700. 464 H
cukrowskik@acu.edu
CULATTA, Victor 408-795-5600... 36 A
victor.culatta@sjsu.edu
CULBERSON, Roy 940-498-6282. 477 I
rculberson@nctc.edu
CULBERT, John 773-325-7954. 143 H
jculbert@depaul.edu
CULBERTSON,
Charles, R 540-828-5720. 502 J
cculbert@bridgewater.edu
CULBREATH, Jahan 937-376-6289. 376 E
jculbreath@centralstate.edu
CULBRETH, Paul 717-391-1375. 434 A
culbreth@stevenscollege.edu
CULHAM, Mark 405-789-7661. 400 A
mark.culham@swcu.edu
CULHAN, Timothy, P 859-238-5360. 193 E
tim.culhan@centre.edu
CULHANE, Marianne, B .. 402-280-3154. 289 D
mculhane@creighton.edu
CULL, Cecelia 617-682-1525. 226 D
ccull@eds.edu
CULLANDER, Chris 415-476-6881... 72 A
chris.cullander@ucsf.edu
CULLARS, Kyle 478-445-1976. 125 A
kyle.cullars@gcsu.edu
CULLEN, Andrew 505-277-6465. 312 F
acullen@unm.edu
CULLEN, Daryl 415-282-7600... 27 L
darylcullen@actcm.edu
CULLEN, Jim 570-961-7864. 420 C
cullenj@lakcawanna.edu
CULLEN, Kathleen 608-266-9399. 539 H
kathleen.cullen@wtcsystem.edu
CULLEN, Keith 334-244-3345..... 2 A
kcullen1@aum.edu
CULLEN, Kevin 302-736-2442... 94 C
cullenke@wesley.edu
CULLEN, Matt 323-357-3438... 38 B
mattcullen@cdrewu.edu
CULLEN, Richard, T 845-451-1300. 322 D
r_cullen@culinary.edu
CULLENBERG, Steven 951-827-2762... 71 E
steven.cullenberg@ucr.edu
CULLENEN, Rachel 607-274-3306. 327 E
rcullenen@ithaca.edu
CULLENS, Linda 831-477-3222... 30 G
licullen@cabrillo.edu
CULLER, Angela 336-758-4010. 370 D
culleraa@wfu.edu
CULLER, Fred, B 304-883-2424. 528 D
fculler@newriver.edu
CULLER, Kevin, J 313-845-9755. 243 H
kjculler@hfcc.edu
CULLER, Lori, L 260-359-4213. 166 O
lculler@huntington.edu
CULLER, Valerie 734-384-4139. 247 C
vculler@monroeccc.edu
CULLERTON, Laura 303-369-5151... 84 E
laura.cullerton@plattcolorado.edu
CULLEY, Christopher, M . 614-292-0611. 386 E
culley.8@osu.edu
CULLEY, JR., W. Glenn .. 434-223-6216. 505 E
gculley@hsc.edu
CULLIGAN, Rob 320-363-3388. 263 P
rculligan@csbsju.edu
CULLINAN, Carol 716-880-2211. 330 F
carol.cullinan@medaille.edu

CULLINAN, Mary 541-552-6111. 406 C
cullinanm@sou.edu
CULLINAN, William 414-288-5053. 534 B
william.cullinan@marquette.edu
CULLISON, Janet, L 443-518-4904. 215 E
jcullison@howardcc.edu
CULLITON, Pamela 314-529-9520. 276 G
pculliton@maryville.edu
CULLITON, Richard 860-685-2627... 92 H
rculliton@wesleyan.edu
CULLNANE, Chris 601-968-8505. 266 A
ccullnane@belhaven.edu
CULLUM, Carol, J 910-362-7040. 358 F
ccullum@cfcc.edu
CULLUM, Charles 508-929-8038. 230 G
ccullum@worcester.edu
CULLUM, Douglas 585-594-6331. 335 B
cullumd@nes.edu
CULOTTA, Cheryl, C 518-327-6340. 336 B
cculotta@paulsmiths.edu
CULOTTA, Sheryl 860-685-2008... 92 H
sculotta@wesleyan.edu
CULP, Kristin, J 937-328-6087. 377 A
culpk@clarkstate.edu
CULP, Mark, K 610-861-5301. 425 D
mculp@northampton.edu
CULPEPPER, Grady 404-756-4033. 121 A
gculpepper@atlm.edu
CULPEPPER, R. Alan 678-547-6471. 128 H
culpepper_ra@mercer.edu
CULPEPPER, Sammy 205-652-3414..... 9 F
sculpepper@uwa.edu
CULPEPPER, Suzann 229-430-3510. 120 A
sculpepper@albanytech.edu
CULSHAW, John, P 319-335-5867. 175 I
CULUM, Samra 208-732-6223. 138 B
sculum@csi.edu
CULVER, Dale 913-758-4372. 191 B
culverd@stmary.edu
CULVER, Jay 863-638-2947. 119 D
culverjr@webber.edu
CULVER, Richard, W 410-543-6017. 220 D
rwculver@salisbury.edu
CULVER, Sandi 907-786-1464... 10 H
smculver@uaa.alaska.edu
CULVER, Terry 212-217-4109. 324 C
terry_culver@fitnyc.edu
CULVERHOUSE, Renee ... 256-393-2999..... 4 D
rculverhouse@huntingdon.edu
CUMBERLAND, Denise 502-585-9911. 199 C
dcumberland@spalding.edu
CUMBERLAND, Lyndsay 662-329-7295. 268 E
lcumberland@alumni.muw.edu
CUMBIE, Donna, L 252-222-6161. 358 G
cumbied@carteret.edu
CUMENS, Chris 270-901-1113. 196 E
chris.cumens@kctcs.edu
CUMINGS, Victoria 503-517-1012. 408 H
vcumings@warnerpacific.edu
CUMMING, Carrie 269-387-4300. 252 I
carrie.cumming@wmich.edu
CUMMING, Tammie 718-260-5007. 319 B
tcumming@citytech.cuny.edu
CUMMINGS, Alison 404-270-5353. 132 E
acummin3@spelman.edu
CUMMINGS, SSE,
Brian, J 802-654-2386. 500 B
bcummings@smcvt.edu
CUMMINGS, Carmen 850-599-3707. 114 K
carmen.cummings@famu.edu
CUMMINGS, Carmen, M 386-312-4152. 112 C
carmencummings@sjrstate.edu
CUMMINGS, Corlis 678-466-4270. 123 A
corliscummings@clayton.edu
CUMMINGS, Cynthia 508-910-6402. 229 A
ccummings2@umassd.edu
CUMMINGS, Dee Dee 765-983-1513. 165 G
cummide@earlham.edu
CUMMINGS,
Edmond, M 504-286-5258. 206 K
ecumming@suno.edu
CUMMINGS, Eric 615-547-1323. 454 A
ecummings@cumberland.edu
CUMMINGS, Helen 973-642-8380. 307 D
helen.cummings@shu.edu
CUMMINGS, Jeff 707-476-4100... 40 H
jeff-cummings@redwoods.edu
CUMMINGS, Jim 270-745-2035. 200 G
jim.cummings@wku.edu
CUMMINGS, Joseph 718-489-5346. 338 G
jcummings@sfc.edu
CUMMINGS, Joyce 954-308-2177... 98 G
jcummings@aii.edu
CUMMINGS, Kevin, R 914-594-4536. 334 A
webmaster@nymc.edu
CUMMINGS, Kris 253-964-6529. 522 C
kycummings@pierce.ctc.edu
CUMMINGS, Leslie 205-387-0511..... 2 B
lcummings@bscc.edu
CUMMINGS, Lisa 802-635-1382. 501 D
lisa.cummings@jsc.edu

CUMMINGS, Marge 606-337-1407. 193 F
mcummings@ccbbc.edu
CUMMINGS, Mary 724-852-3271. 437 A
mcumming@waynesburg.edu
CUMMINGS, Owen 503-845-3547. 404 D
owen.cummings@mtangel.edu
CUMMINGS, Sara 617-824-8446. 226 A
sara_cummings@emerson.edu
CUMMINGS,
Terrence, M 803-533-3721. 446 G
tcummings@scsu.edu
CUMMINGS, Tiffany, N .. 434-381-6362. 510 F
tcummings@sbc.edu
CUMMINGS, Victor 707-527-4615... 65 B
vcummings@santarosa.edu
CUMMINGS,
Wm. Theodore 281-283-3100. 489 C
cummings@uhcl.edu
CUMMINGS-DANSON,
Gail, L 518-580-5370. 341 A
gcumming@skidmore.edu
CUMMINS, Cheryl 662-846-4405. 266 G
ccummins@deltastate.edu
CUMMINS, David, J 330-972-8396. 390 E
dcummins@uakron.edu
CUMMINS, F. James 810-766-4250. 239 G
jim.cummins@baker.edu
CUMMINS, Jim 417-455-5533. 273 E
JimCummins@crowder.edu
CUMMINS, Richard 509-542-4869. 518 C
rcummins@columbiabasin.edu
CUMMINS, Stephen 630-942-3007. 142 G
cummins@cod.edu
CUMMISKEY,
Raymond, V 636-481-3100. 275 I
rcummisk@jeffco.edu
CUMPIANO, Barbarita .... 787-832-6000. 549 D
bcumpiano@icprjc.edu
CUNDALL, JR., Michael . 336-285-2030. 367 E
mcundall@ncat.edu
CUNDARI, Alan 909-469-5670... 76 B
acundari@westernu.edu
CUNDIFF, H. Lynn 928-757-0801... 15 L
lcundiff@mohave.edu
CUNDIFF, Sarah 316-942-4291. 189 E
cundiffs@newmanu.edu
CUNDIFF, Wendy 330-684-8907. 390 F
wcundif@uakron.edu
CUNEAZ, Jodi 810-766-4015. 239 H
jodi.cuneaz@baker.edu
CUNHA, Sonia 973-642-8743. 307 D
sonia.cunha@shu.edu
CUNION, William 330-823-2450. 391 E
cunionwe@mountunion.edu
CUNNING, Charles, J 864-488-4540. 444 L
cunning@limestone.edu
CUNNINGHAM, Al 912-427-5847. 120 B
acunningham@altamahatech.edu
CUNNINGHAM,
Austin, J 972-883-2234. 491 E
cunning@utdallas.edu
CUNNINGHAM,
Bruce, W 919-684-9007. 354 A
bruce.cunningham@duke.edu
CUNNINGHAM, Carl, G . 251-460-6895..... 9 E
ccunningham@southalabama.edu
CUNNINGHAM, Cecelia . 616-632-2816. 239 E
cunnicec@aquinas.edu
CUNNINGHAM,
Chester, M 270-824-8699. 196 A
chet.cunningham@kctcs.edu
CUNNINGHAM, Dave 206-546-4595. 523 F
dcunningham@shoreline.edu
CUNNINGHAM, David .... 313-845-4106. 243 H
dccumingham@hfcc.edu
CUNNINGHAM, Diana, J 914-594-4200. 334 A
diana_cunningham@nymc.edu
CUNNINGHAM, Diane .... 270-707-3921. 195 E
diane.cunningham@kctcs.edu
CUNNINGHAM, Eddie .... 302-454-3922... 93 F
ecunning@dtcc.edu
CUNNINGHAM, Eric 573-875-7649. 272 G
ercunningham@ccis.edu
CUNNINGHAM, Jack, L . 302-356-6921... 94 E
john.l.cunningham@wilmu.edu
CUNNINGHAM, James ... 630-617-3012. 145 A
james.cunningham@elmhurst.edu
CUNNINGHAM,
James, E 570-326-3761. 427 B
jcunning@pct.edu
CUNNINGHAM, Janet, L 580-327-8400. 396 N
jlcunningham@nwosu.edu
CUNNINGHAM, Joan 973-328-5340. 300 G
jcunningham@ccm.edu
CUNNINGHAM, John 404-270-5074. 132 E
jcunning@spelman.edu
CUNNINGHAM, John 774-455-7601. 228 E
jcunningham@umassonline.net
CUNNINGHAM, Joi, M .. 248-370-3496. 248 J
cunning3@oakland.edu

CUNNINGHAM, Julie ..... 716-375-2301. 338 E
jcunning@sbu.edu
CUNNINGHAM, Karla, K 317-940-9570. 164 J
kcunning@butler.edu
CUNNINGHAM,
Kathleen .... 610-606-4635. 412 I
ksglass@cedarcrest.edu
CUNNINGHAM, Kay .... 901-321-3430. 453 H
kay.cunningham@cbu.edu
CUNNINGHAM,
Kevin, A .... 563-884-5898. 182 A
kevin.cunningham@palmer.edu
CUNNINGHAM,
Lawrence (Bubba), R ..... 919-962-8200. 368 D
BubbaC@email.unc.edu
CUNNINGHAM, Luana ... 318-487-7301. 202 F
luana.cunningham@lacollege.edu
CUNNINGHAM, Marina .. 973-655-7566. 303 D
cunninghamm@mail.montclair.edu
CUNNINGHAM, Mark ..... 404-756-4654. 121 A
mcunningham@atlm.edu
CUNNINGHAM, Mary ..... 516-726-5651. 545 H
cunninghamm@usmma.edu
CUNNINGHAM, Michael 504-862-3308. 207 C
mcunnin1@tulane.edu
CUNNINGHAM, II,
Michael, J .... 401-333-7121. 439 A
mjcunningham@ccri.edu
CUNNINGHAM,
Michael, M .... 570-326-3761. 427 B
mcunning@pct.edu
CUNNINGHAM,
Michael, R .... 858-642-8801... 55 J
mcunningham@nu.edu
CUNNINGHAM, Nancy ... 772-462-7275. 106 P
CUNNINGHAM, Pat .... 719-389-6707... 79 D
pat.cunningham@coloradocollege.edu
CUNNINGHAM,
Patrick, J .... 412-578-8842. 412 G
pjcunningham@carlow.edu
CUNNINGHAM,
Paul R, G .... 252-744-2201. 367 B
cunninghamp@ecu.edu
CUNNINGHAM,
R. Michael .... 217-443-8831. 143 G
mcunningham@dacc.edu
CUNNINGHAM, Rose ..... 201-360-4158. 302 D
rcunningham@hccc.edu
CUNNINGHAM, Sean ..... 512-463-4930. 486 D
sean.cunningham@tsus.edu
CUNNINGHAM,
Shannon .... 918-540-6272. 396 G
scunningham@neo.edu
CUNNINGHAM,
Shannon .... 918-540-6295. 396 G
scunningham@neo.edu
CUNNINGHAM, Sheila ... 803-780-1266. 449 E
scunningham@voorhees.edu
CUNNINGHAM, Steven .. 815-753-6009. 154 I
cunningham@niu.edu
CUNNINGHAM,
Steven, D .... 815-753-6021. 154 I
cunningham@niu.edu
CUNNINGHAM, Todd ..... 724-357-7872. 428 F
todd.cunningham@iup.edu
CUNNINGHAM, Tom ...... 513-861-6400. 390 C
tom.cunningham@myunion.edu
CUNNINGHAM,
William, J .... 215-596-8535. 435 H
w.cunningham@usciences.edu
CUNZ, Leonard .... 908-852-1400. 300 D
cunzl@centenarycollege.edu
CUOMO, Michele .... 718-631-6344. 319 D
mcuomo@qcc.cuny.edu
CUOZZO, Frank .... 201-200-3173. 303 F
fcuozzo@njcu.edu
CUOZZO, Jenifer .... 202-685-3785. 544 K
cuozzoj@ndu.edu
CUP, Jo Beth .... 312-662-4101. 139 F
jcup@adler.edu
CUPP, Dondi, L .... 734-647-6079. 251 C
dcupp@umich.edu
CUPPER, Barbara .... 415-433-6691... 44 D
bcupper@fidm.edu
CUPPS, Lowell .... 803-786-3686. 443 B
lcupps@columbiasc.edu
CUPRAK, Greg .... 610-436-3200. 430 A
gcuprak@wcupa.edu
CURAVO, Pam .... 419-824-3731. 383 C
pcuravo@lourdes.edu
CURBO, Billy, D .... 254-659-7701. 473 A
bdcurbo@hillcollege.edu
CURD, David .... 877-248-6724... 14 A
CURD, Michael .... 877-248-6724... 14 A
m.curd@hmu.edu
CURE, Nancy .... 972-860-8261. 470 H
ncure@dcccd.edu
CURET, Nahomy .... 787-257-7373. 552 H
ue_ncuret@suagm.edu
CURETON, Alan, S .... 651-631-5250. 263 A
ascureton@nwc.edu
CURETON, Archie, L .... 585-245-5731. 343 C
cureton@geneseo.edu
CURETON, Michael .... 513-556-4951. 390 G
michael.cureton@uc.edu
CURIN, Donna, B .... 312-915-6404. 151 H
dcurin@luc.edu
CURL, John .... 801-581-8788. 496 Q
jcurl@sa.utah.edu
CURLEE, Michelle .... 406-477-6215. 285 H
mcurlee@cdkc.edu
CURLESS, Chris .... 805-893-4638... 72 B
chris.curless@purc.ucsb.edu
CURLEY, Greg, M .... 814-641-3521. 419 H
curleyg@juniata.edu
CURLEY, Lauren .... 781-239-2572. 231 G
lcurley@massbay.edu
CURLEY, Meredith .... 480-557-1217... 18 I
meredith.curley@phoenix.edu
CURLEY, Michael, J .... 508-831-6919. 238 F
mjcurley@wpi.edu
CURLEY, Russell, L .... 270-745-2304. 200 G
russell.curley@wku.edu
CURLEY, Thomas .... 413-236-2103. 231 A
tcurley@berkshirecc.edu
CURLEY, William .... 814-768-3401. 429 B
wgc114@lhup.edu
CURLL, Steve .... 814-371-2090. 434 F
scurll@triangle-tech.edu
CURME, Michael, A .... 513-529-1877. 384 G
curmema@miamioh.edu
CURNUTT, Cindy .... 432-335-6601. 477 M
ccurnutt@odessa.edu
CURNUTT, Marlin, R .... 423-585-2690. 462 A
marlin.curnutt@ws.edu
CURPHY, Kathleen .... 402-457-2716. 290 G
kcurpy@mccneb.edu
CURRALL, Steven, C .... 530-752-4600... 70 J
scc@ucdavis.edu
CURRAN, Daniel, J .... 937-229-4122. 391 C
president@udayton.edu
CURRAN, Diana, T .... 810-762-3150. 251 E
dtcurran@umflint.edu
CURRAN, Jack .... 718-862-7934. 329 M
jack.curran@manhattan.edu
CURRAN, James, W .... 404-727-8720. 124 E
jcurran@sph.emory.edu
CURRAN, Joanne .... 518-292-1704. 338 C
SCADean@sage.edu
CURRAN, Linda .... 303-678-3620... 81 N
linda.curran@frontrange.edu
CURRAN, Susan .... 401-232-6020. 438 K
scurran3@bryant.edu
CURRAN, Terrence, M ..... 910-962-3876. 369 C
currant@uncw.edu
CURRAN, Thomas, B .... 816-501-4250. 280 I
thomas.curran@rockhurst.edu
CURREN, Robert, A .... 407-303-9372... 97 H
robert.curren@adu.edu
CURRENT, Amy, L .... 563-589-0274. 183 F
acurrent@wartburgseminary.edu
CURRERI, Joseph .... 323-343-3700... 34 A
joseph.curreri@calstatela.edu
CURRERI, Michelle, S ..... 401-874-4462. 440 D
michelle@uri.edu
CURREY, David .... 714-997-6789... 38 A
dcurrey@chapman.edu
CURREY, Pamela, A .... 804-828-2092. 511 F
pacurrey@vcu.edu
CURRIE, Catherine .... 401-232-6369. 438 K
ccurrie@bryant.edu
CURRIE, Dave .... 978-468-7111. 227 A
dcurrie@gcts.edu
CURRIE, Dean, W .... 626-395-6275... 31 E
dean.currie@caltech.edu
CURRIE, Eric .... 585-567-9561. 326 F
eric.Currie@houghton.edu
CURRIE, Eunice, M .... 817-272-5554. 491 B
currie@uta.edu
CURRIE, Jacqueline .... 205-366-8894..... 7 E
jcurrie@stillman.edu
CURRIE, John .... 785-532-6912. 188 A
ksuad@ksu.edu
CURRIE, John .... 215-572-3811. 437 C
jcurrie@wts.edu
CURRIE, Kevin, D .... 724-738-2082. 429 F
kevin.currie@sru.edu
CURRIE, Stephanie .... 716-286-8205. 334 F
sbc@niagara.edu
CURRIE, Thomas, W .... 704-337-2450. 510 G
tcurrie@upsem.edu
CURRIE, Walter James ..... 691-320-2480. 546 B
jimc@comfsm.fm
CURRIER, Chuck .... 630-942-2790. 142 G
currier@cod.edu
CURRIER, Michelle, L ...... 315-386-7228. 345 F
currierm@canton.edu
CURRIN, Alicia .... 903-886-5034. 483 E
alicia.currin@tamuc.edu
CURRIN, Bruce, A .... 402-472-3105. 292 I
bcurrin1@unl.edu
CURRIN, Catherine .... 252-789-0297. 361 G
ccurrin@martincc.edu
CURRIN, Thomas .... 678-915-7482. 132 C
tcurrin@spsu.edu
CURRISTINE, Eileen .... 609-343-6810. 299 A
ecurrist@atlantic.edu
CURRO, Margaret (Peg) . 508-678-2811. 231 B
peg.curro@bristolcc.edu
CURRY, Anne .... 205-226-4904..... 2 C
acurry@bsc.edu
CURRY, Bonita, P .... 517-353-3243. 246 H
curryb@msu.edu
CURRY, Carolyn .... 302-857-6060... 93 C
ccurry@desu.edu
CURRY, Cynthia .... 305-626-3619. 104 J
Cynthia.Curry@fmuniv.edu
CURRY, Cynthia, S .... 304-367-4386. 529 F
Cindy.Curry@fairmontstate.edu
CURRY, David .... 813-988-5131. 104 A
development@floridacollege.edu
CURRY, Dean, C .... 717-766-2511. 423 L
dcurry@messiah.edu
CURRY, Elizabeth .... 352-854-2322. 100 K
currye@cf.edu
CURRY, Evan .... 215-702-4863. 411 F
ecurry@cairn.edu
CURRY, JR., H. Pete ...... 717-337-6311. 417 B
pcurry@gettysburg.edu
CURRY, James .... 402-844-7063. 291 I
jamesc@northeast.edu
CURRY, James .... 252-249-1851. 362 E
pbanks@pamlicocc.edu
CURRY, JR., James, L ... 770-720-5577. 130 G
JLC1@reinhardt.edu
CURRY, Janel .... 978-867-4063. 226 H
janel.curry@gordon.edu
CURRY, Jason .... 615-329-8582. 454 F
jcurry@fisk.edu
CURRY, Michael .... 252-789-0268. 361 G
mcurry@martincc.edu
CURRY, Michael, D .... 989-837-4758. 248 C
currym@northwood.edu
CURRY, Rachel .... 845-752-3000. 348 I
r.curry@uts.edu
CURRY, Ralph, W .... 906-786-5802. 240 K
curryr@baycollege.edu
CURRY, Robert .... 662-252-8000. 269 F
rcurry@rustcollege.edu
CURRY, Susan .... 319-384-5452. 175 I
sue-curry@uiowa.edu
CURRY, Terri, A .... 712-274-5257. 181 B
curryte@morningside.edu
CURRY, II, Theodore, H . 517-353-5300. 246 H
thcurry@msu.edu
CURRY, Tim .... 606-546-1682. 200 A
tcurry@unionky.edu
CURRY, Tina .... 252-536-7263. 361 A
tcurry215@halifaxcc.edu
CURRY, Vicki .... 620-365-5116. 183 I
curry@allencc.edu
CURRY, William, N .... 601-318-6103. 270 I
bill.curry@wmcarey.edu
CURRY DAMATO,
Ellen, R .... 914-654-5854. 320 H
ecurry@cnr.edu
CURTIN, Brian .... 207-893-6670. 211 G
bcurtin@sjcme.edu
CURTIN, Kathleen, M ...... 410-857-2259. 216 E
kcurtin@mcdaniel.edu
CURTIN, Maria .... 508-565-1311. 237 A
mcurtin@stonehill.edu
CURTIN, Michael, J .... 502-852-6166. 200 D
mjcurt01@louisville.edu
CURTIN, Valerie .... 406-447-6913. 287 A
valerie.curtin@umhelena.edu
CURTIN, William .... 773-508-8851. 151 H
wcurtin@luc.edu
CURTIS, Alicia .... 803-938-3742. 448 F
curtisam@uscsumter.edu
CURTIS, Allison .... 805-965-0581... 64 L
curtis@sbcc.edu
CURTIS, Alyce .... 617-928-4556. 234 E
acurtis@mountida.edu
CURTIS, Amy .... 207-879-8757. 210 C
acurtis@idsva.org
CURTIS, Benjamin, J .... 607-735-1821. 323 H
bcurtis@elmira.edu
CURTIS, Carolyn, G .... 518-629-7204. 326 G
c.curtis@hvcc.edu
CURTIS, Christine, W ..... 803-777-9516. 447 G
curtisch@sc.edu
CURTIS, Cynthia, A .... 615-460-6408. 453 C
cynthia.curtis@belmont.edu
CURTIS, Deborah, J .... 660-543-4116. 283 A
curtis@ucmo.edu
CURTIS, Deloris, Y .... 203-332-5102... 88 F
dcurtis@hcc.commnet.edu
CURTIS, Elaine .... 931-540-2534. 460 E
bcurtis@columbiastate.edu
CURTIS, Jason .... 219-785-5586. 172 A
jcurtis@pnc.edu
CURTIS, Jeanne, F .... 215-898-6300. 435 B
curtis@isc.upenn.edu
CURTIS, Jeffrey, H .... 540-464-7102. 515 B
curtisjh@vmi.edu
CURTIS, Jerri .... 301-295-3638. 545 C
jerri.curtis@usuhs.edu
CURTIS, Judy .... 910-521-6238. 369 B
jcurtis@uncp.edu
CURTIS, K. Tyler .... 620-341-5440. 186 D
kcurtis2@emporia.edu
CURTIS, Kathleen, A .... 915-747-7201. 492 A
kacurtis@utep.edu
CURTIS, Kelly .... 310-377-5501... 53 F
kcurtis@marymountcalifornia.edu
CURTIS, Kelly, T .... 864-488-4601. 444 L
kcurtis@limestone.edu
CURTIS, Mark .... 775-753-2265. 294 F
mark.curtis@gbcnv.edu
CURTIS, Marvin .... 574-520-4170. 168 E
mcurtis@iusb.edu
CURTIS, Matt .... 914-831-0313. 321 B
mcurtis@cw.edu
CURTIS, Monty, L .... 318-869-5042. 201 H
mcurtis@centenary.edu
CURTIS, Pamela .... 209-473-5217... 47 F
pamela_curtis@heald.edu
CURTIS, Regina .... 413-775-1426. 231 E
curtis@gcc.mass.edu
CURTIS, Rick .... 406-243-2122. 286 H
rcurtis@mso.umt.edu
CURTIS, Robert .... 614-947-6127. 380 A
robert.curtis@franklin.edu
CURTIS, Santhia .... 404-752-1895. 129 E
scurtis@msm.edu
CURTIS, Seletha, R .... 314-286-4803. 280 F
srcurtis@ranken.edu
CURTIS, Susan .... 336-517-2289. 352 H
scurtis@bennett.edu
CURTIS, Ted .... 330-972-6107. 390 E
curtis4@uakron.edu
CURTIS, Timothy .... 928-428-8220... 13 J
tim.curtis@eac.edu
CURTIS, Tina .... 606-759-7141. 196 B
tina.curtis@kctcs.edu
CURTIS, Tommy .... 706-233-7358. 131 E
tcurtis@shorter.edu
CURTIS HANE, Audrey ... 316-942-4291. 189 E
hanea@newmanu.edu
CURTIS POWELL,
Melissa .... 614-235-4136. 390 A
mcpowell@TLSohio.edu
CURTO, Stephen, A .... 732-224-2593. 299 G
scurto@brookdalecc.edu
CURVIN, Nicole .... 802-258-9261. 499 F
ncurvin@marlboro.edu
CUSACK, Kristen .... 303-360-4701... 81 C
kristen.cusack@ccaurora.edu
CUSACK, Mary .... 810-762-0474. 247 F
CUSEO, Vincent .... 323-259-2700... 56 I
admission@oxy.edu
CUSHMAN, Bob .... 509-527-2603. 524 I
bob.cushman@wallawalla.edu
CUSHMAN, Jenifer, S ...... 814-641-3181. 419 H
cushmaj@juniata.edu
CUSHMAN, Ron .... 417-873-7323. 273 H
rcushman@drury.edu
CUSICK, Dianna .... 612-659-6319. 259 D
dianna.cusick@minneapolis.edu
CUSICK, Sherry .... 563-589-3721. 182 J
scusick@dbq.edu
CUSMANO, Jo Ann, M ... 313-927-1469. 246 D
jcusmano@marygrove.edu
CUSPARD, Lisa-Marie ..... 510-580-6740... 77 C
lcuspard@cci.edu
CUSSEN, Susan .... 845-451-1471. 322 D
s_cussen@culinary.edu
CUSSON, Regina .... 860-486-5126... 92 A
regina.cusson@uconn.edu
CUSTER, Cristeen .... 507-457-2569. 262 A
ccuster@winona.edu
CUSTER, Laura .... 859-344-3314. 199 H
laura.custer@thomasmore.edu
CUSTER, Rodney .... 605-642-6262. 451 G
rod.custer@bhsu.edu
CUTAIA, Diana .... 617-879-2238. 238 C
dcutaia@wheelock.edu
CUTCHIN, Claudine .... 812-749-1443. 171 K
ccutchin@oak.edu
CUTCHIN, Jeff .... 618-395-7777. 147 B
cutchinj@iecc.edu
CUTCHINS, Cathy .... 757-569-6712. 513 E
ccutchins@pdc.edu
CUTHBERT, James, E ...... 585-594-6860. 337 K
cuthbertj@roberts.edu
CUTIETTA, Robert, A ...... 213-740-5389... 74 A
musicdean@thornton.usc.edu
CUTLER, David, A .... 802-654-2653. 500 B
dcutler@smcvt.edu
CUTLER, Jared .... 937-512-2789. 388 O
jared.cutler@sinclair.edu

CUTLER, Nancy .... 408-554-4915... 64 M
ncutler@scu.edu
CUTLER, Sally, M .... 317-940-9742. 164 J
scutler@butler.edu
CUTLIP, Mark .... 304-696-3253. 529 H
cutlipm@marshall.edu
CUTOLO, Chuck .... 516-572-7811. 332 C
chuck.cutolo@ncc.edu
CUTONE, Joan .... 412-536-1079. 420 A
joan.cutone@laroche.edu
CUTRELL, Kathy .... 336-887-3000. 355 N
kcutrell@laureluniversity.edu
CUTRELL, Lori .... 615-230-4834. 461 G
lori.cutrell@volstate.edu
CUTRI, David .... 419-530-6294. 392 B
david.cutri@utoledo.edu
CUTRIGHT, John, D .... 814-641-3520. 419 H
cutrigj@juniata.edu
CUTRIGHT, Patricia .... 509-963-1902. 517 F
cutright@cwu.edu
CUTSHAW, Kathleen, D .. 808-956-9190. 136 B
cutshaw@hawaii.edu
CUTSINGER, Ginger .... 269-965-3931. 244 O
cutsingerg@kellogg.edu
CUTSPEC, John .... 828-251-6868. 368 C
jcutspec@unca.edu
CUTTING, Alicia .... 603-206-8006. 296 A
acutting@ccsnh.edu
CUTTING, Judy .... 903-875-7573. 477 G
judy.cutting@navarrocollege.edu
CUTTINO, Robert, E .... 770-538-4749. 122 A
rcuttino@brenau.edu
CUTTONE, Carl .... 219-473-4295. 164 K
ccuttone@ccsj.edu
CUYKENDALL, Lora, L ... 503-494-8252. 405 I
news@ohsu.edu
CUZZOLINO, Robert, G .. 215-871-6770. 430 D
bob@pcom.edu
CVITKOVIC, Kimberly, F . 269-660-8021. 249 C
cvitkovick@millercollege.edu
CVITKOVIC, Vicky .... 847-543-6504. 143 A
vcvitkovic@clcillinois.edu
CWALINA, Marianne .... 781-736-8318. 224 F
mcwalina@brandeis.edu
CWALINA, Marianne, F .. 781-891-2129. 223 C
mcwalina@bentley.edu
CYBORON, Robert .... 808-544-0215. 135 F
rcyboron@hpu.edu
CYGAN, Brian .... 570-326-3761. 427 B
brian.cygan@pct.edu
CYLKE, Catherine .... 703-579-3572. 294 B
CYNAR, Deana .... 908-852-1400. 300 D
cynar@centenarycollege.edu
CYPHERS,
Christopher, J .... 212-752-1530. 328 G
christopher.cyphers@limcollege.edu
CYPHERS BENSON,
Laura .... 530-242-7649... 65 G
lbenson@shastacollege.edu
CYPRESS, Sharen .... 731-989-6986. 454 J
scypress@fhu.edu
CYPRIAN, Alecia .... 504-816-4398. 201 K
acyprian@dillard.edu
CYREE, Kendall, B .... 662-915-5820. 270 B
kbcyree@olemiss.edu
CYRUS, Cynthia, J .... 615-322-4474. 463 G
cynthia.j.cyrus@vanderbilt.edu
CYTERSKI-ACOSTA,
Andrea .... 210-805-5864. 490 A
cyterski@uiwtx.edu
CZAJA, James .... 909-274-4225... 55 A
jczaja@mtsac.edu
CZAJKIEWICZ, Zbigniew 281-283-3703. 489 C
czajkiewiez@uhcl.edu
CZAJKOWSKI, Joyce ...... 608-822-2419. 541 C
jczajkowski@swtc.edu
CZARAPATA, Paul .... 859-256-3100. 194 I
paul.czarapata@kctcs.edu
CZARDA, Lawrence, D .... 336-272-7221. 354 E
lczarda@greensboro.edu
CZARNIK-NEIMEYER,
Jake .... 920-686-6176. 536 A
Jake.Czarnik-Neimeyer@sl.edu
CZEKAJ, Sandra .... 219-785-5696. 172 A
czekajs@pnc.edu
CZEKAJ, Walter, P .... 724-938-5244. 428 A
czekaj@calu.edu
CZERNIAK, Walter, L ...... 815-753-0783. 154 I
wczerniak@niu.edu
CZERWINSKI, Rick .... 540-887-7336. 507 A
rczerwin@mbc.edu
CZERWINSKI-ALJETS,
Sue .... 618-468-4800. 150 G
sczerwin@lc.edu
CZOHARA, Cami .... 603-623-0313. 297 E
cczohara@nhia.edu
CZUBERNAT, Crystal ...... 626-529-8064... 57 G
cczubernat@pacificoaks.edu
CZYZ, Vito .... 716-375-2525. 338 E
vczyc@sbu.edu

D

DA GRACA, John .... 956-968-2132. 484 A
j-dagraca@tamuk.edu
DAAKE, Mary .... 308-865-8501. 292 H
daakem@unk.edu
DAAR, Karen .... 818-947-2378... 52 E
daarkl@lavc.edu
DABBS, Melinda .... 615-794-4254. 457 Q
meldabbs@omorecollege.edu
DABIRIAN, Amir .... 657-278-5000... 33 E
adabirian@fullerton.edu
DABNEY, David, O .... 419-530-8776. 392 B
david.dabney@utoledo.edu
DABNEY, Jerome .... 773-602-5252. 142 B
jdabney@ccc.edu
DABOUB, Joel .... 817-735-2204. 490 E
Joel.Daboub@unthsc.edu
DABOVAL, Jeanne, M .... 337-475-5508. 207 G
jdaboval@mcneese.edu
DABROWSKI, Jan .... 503-699-6275. 404 C
jdabrowski@marylhurst.edu
DACAL, Anita, S .... 412-578-6343. 412 G
dacalas@carlow.edu
DACHELET, Derek .... 608-822-2417. 541 C
ddachelet@swtc.edu
DACHILLE, Nancy .... 215-248-7048. 413 A
ndachill@chc.edu
DACOSTA, Tracy, M .... 401-254-3541. 440 B
tdacosta@rwu.edu
DACUMOS, Carlo .... 406-265-4100. 287 D
carlo.dacumos@msun.edu
DACUS, Kent .... 951-343-4687... 30 H
kdacus@calbaptist.edu
DADABHOY, Khushnur .. 303-556-3519... 86 A
khushnur.dadabhoy@ucdenver.edu
DADABHOY, Zavareh ..... 661-395-4204... 49 N
DADDONA, Mark .... 678-466-4070. 123 A
markdaddona@clayton.edu
DADDONA, Sharon, N .... 860-727-6903... 90 A
sdaddona@goodwin.edu
DADEZ, Edward .... 352-588-8206. 112 D
ed.dadez@saintleo.edu
DADEZ, Teresa .... 352-588-8347. 112 D
teresa.dadez@saintleo.edu
DAFFER, Steve .... 405-733-7424. 399 F
sdaffer@rose.edu
DAFFRON, Eric .... 201-684-7532. 305 A
edaffron@ramapo.edu
DAFFRON, Jeanne .... 816-271-4234. 279 A
daffron@missouriwestern.edu
DAFFRON, SJ, Justin ..... 773-508-3770. 151 H
jdaffro@luc.edu
DAFLER, James, E .... 724-946-7317. 437 B
daflerje@westminster.edu
DAGANAAR, Mark .... 913-469-8500. 187 J
mdaganaar@jccc.edu
DAGAVARIAN, Debra ...... 609-652-4514. 305 C
dagavarian@stockton.edu
DAGES, John, R .... 202-994-5300... 95 D
dages@gwu.edu
DAGG, Joey .... 304-876-5395. 529 I
jdagg@shepherd.edu
DAGGETT, Natalie .... 575-769-4956. 309 F
natalie.daggett@clovis.edu
DAGGETT, Paula .... 210-486-0224. 465 C
pdaggett@alamo.edu
DAGHER, Lisa, M .... 773-947-6282. 152 E
DAGOSTIN, Jean .... 334-983-3521..... 3 N
jdagostin@wallace.edu
DAGUE, Saralyn .... 304-829-7835. 526 D
sdague@bethanywv.edu
DAHILL, Patricia .... 617-587-5632. 234 H
dahillp@neco.edu
DAHL, Carolyn, C .... 205-348-6331..... 8 D
cdahl@ccs.ua.edu
DAHL, Margaret, W .... 706-583-8209. 133 C
mwd@uga.edu
DAHL, Mark .... 503-768-7339. 403 K
dahl@lclark.edu
DAHL, Nelson, D .... 715-422-5327. 540 D
nelson.dahl@mstc.edu
DAHL, Noel .... 415-703-9537... 30 K
ndahl@cca.edu
DAHL, Tracy .... 360-736-9391. 517 G
tdahl@centralia.edu
DAHLBERG, Albert, A ..... 401-863-1885. 438 J
albert_a_dahlberg@brown.edu
DAHLBERG, James .... 715-468-2815. 541 F
jim.dahlberg@witc.edu
DAHLBERG, Margaret ..... 701-845-7200. 372 A
margaret.dahlberg@vcsu.edu
DAHLBERG, Steve .... 218-935-0417. 265 E
sdahlberg@wetcc.edu
DAHLE, Tammi .... 205-665-6262..... 9 B
dahlet@montevallo.edu
DAHLEN, Anne .... 651-385-6323. 259 E
adahlen@southeastmn.edu
DAHLEN, David, L .... 507-284-2749. 254 F
dahlen.david@mayo.edu

DAHLEN, David, L .... 507-284-4839. 254 G
dahlen.david@mayo.edu
DAHLGREN, Jerod, T ..... 716-878-5569. 343 A
dahlgrjt@buffalostate.edu
DAHLIN, Jim .... 828-669-0012. 357 H
jdahlin@montreat.edu
DAHLMAN, Chuck .... 303-964-3678... 84 M
cdahlman@regis.edu
DAHLQUIST, Kent, R ...... 610-683-4027. 429 A
dahlquis@kutztown.edu
DAHLQUIST, Sally .... 651-450-3567. 258 H
sdahlqu@inverhills.edu
DAHLSTRAND, John ...... 785-670-1972. 191 D
john.dahlstrand@washburn.edu
DAHLSTROM, Duane ...... 320-308-5572. 261 C
ddahlstrom@sctcc.edu
DAHLSTROM, Joe, F ...... 361-570-4150. 489 E
dahlstromj@uhv.edu
DAHLSTROM, Joe, F ...... 361-572-6421. 493 H
joe.dahlstrom@victoriacollege.edu
DAHLSTROM, Thomas ... 610-341-5898. 425 I
tdahlstro@eastern.edu
DAHLSTROM,
Thomas, A .... 610-341-5898. 415 G
tdahlstr@eastern.edu
DAHLVANG, Donna, R ... 715-394-8393. 538 C
ddahlva1@uwsuper.edu
DAHLVIG, Jolyn .... 509-777-3208. 525 F
jdahlvig@whitworth.edu
DAHM, Lisa .... 713-646-1873. 480 J
ldahm@stcl.edu
DAHMES, Victoria .... 504-398-2237. 206 C
vdahmes@olhcc.edu
DAHSE, Winston .... 713-718-7564. 473 C
winston.dahse@hccs.edu
DAHULICH, Michael .... 570-561-1818. 432 F
mdahulich@stots.edu
DAI, Hai-Lung .... 215-204-4775. 433 K
provost@temple.edu
DAI, Hai-Lung .... 215-204-3177. 433 K
hai-lung.dai@temple.edu
DAIDONE, Angela .... 201-355-1309. 302 A
daidonea@felician.edu
DAIEK, Deborah .... 734-462-4400. 250 A
ddaiek@schoolcraft.edu
DAIGLE, Anna .... 337-421-6954. 204 E
anna.daigle@sowela.edu
DAIGLE, Claire .... 415-641-1241... 62 G
cdaigle@sfai.edu
DAIGLE, Darryl .... 985-380-2483. 203 H
darryldaigle@scl.edu
DAIGLE, David .... 207-216-4410. 211 C
ddaigle@yccc.edu
DAIGLE, Dick .... 757-490-1241. 501 G
ddaigle@auto.edu
DAIGLE, Thomas .... 508-999-8708. 229 A
tdaigle@umassd.edu
DAILEY, Bracken, J .... 951-827-3427... 71 E
bracken.dailey@ucr.edu
DAILEY, Brian .... 910-962-3711. 369 C
daileyb@uncw.edu
DAILEY, Brooke .... 615-460-6364. 453 C
brooke.dailey@belmont.edu
DAILEY, David .... 218-749-7772. 259 B
d.dailey@mr.mnscu.edu
DAILEY, Deborah .... 215-489-2915. 414 E
Deborah.Dailey@delval.edu
DAILEY, John, T .... 318-675-5000. 205 D
jdaile@lsuhsc.edu
DAILEY, Ronald .... 909-558-4683... 51 C
rdailey@llu.edu
DAILEY, Tim .... 541-888-7439. 407 H
tdailey@socc.edu
DAILY, Daniel, R .... 605-677-5371. 451 F
danlel.daily@usd.edu
DAILY, Hall, P .... 626-395-6256... 31 E
hdaily@caltech.edu
DAILY, Paula .... 239-489-9111. 101 O
pdaily@edison.edu
DAIN, Benny .... 580-349-1564. 397 G
bdain@opsu.edu
DAIN, Claudette .... 714-992-7018... 56 F
cdain@fullcoll.edu
DAIS, Olga .... 718-262-2140. 319 F
odais@york.cuny.edu
DAISEY, Mary Beth, B .... 856-225-2825. 306 C
daisey@camden.rutgers.edu
DAISY, Joseph .... 691-320-2480. 546 B
jdaisy@comfsm.fm
DAKE, Jean .... 423-425-4184. 463 D
jean-dake@utc.edu
DAKWAR, Mohammad ..... 414-297-8087. 540 E
dakwarmm@matc.edu
DALAVARIS, Christin ...... 618-545-3000. 149 D
cdalavaris@kaskaskia.edu
DALBEY, Mark .... 314-434-4044. 273 C
mark.dalbey@covenantseminary.edu
DALBOW, Dawn, S .... 540-828-5310. 502 J
ddalbow@bridgewater.edu
DALBY, Evelyn .... 760-795-6610... 54 G
edalby@miracosta.edu

DALBY, Jennifer .... 425-739-8312. 520 K
jennifer.dalby@lwtech.edu
DALE, Carroll, W .... 276-376-1081. 511 C
cwd7q@wise.edu
DALE, Cheryl .... 601-318-6199. 270 I
cheryl.dale@wmcarey.edu
DALE, Dianna .... 718-405-3227. 320 G
dianna.dale@mountsaintvincent.edu
DALE, Elizabeth .... 215-895-2436. 415 B
ead52@drexel.edu
DALE, Jean .... 402-375-7220. 291 F
jedale1@wsc.edu
DALE, Kim .... 970-204-8146... 81 N
kim.dale@frontrange.edu
DALE, Kimberly .... 954-776-4476. 108 C
kdale@keiseruniversity.edu
DALE, Louis .... 205-934-8762..... 8 E
ldale@uab.edu
DALE, Lynn, F .... 864-592-4833. 447 A
dalel@sccsc.edu
DALE, Lynn, F .... 864-592-4808. 447 A
dalel@sccsc.edu
DALE, Marc .... 630-466-7900. 162 J
mdale@waubonsee.edu
DALE, Melissa .... 732-263-5755. 303 C
mdale@monmouth.edu
DALE, Paul .... 602-787-6610... 15 B
paul.dale@paradisevalley.edu
DALE, Terri .... 620-431-2800. 189 D
tdale@neosho.edu
DALEN, Dean .... 218-683-8560. 260 D
dean.dalen@northlandcollege.edu
DALENE, Jack .... 435-283-7130. 498 A
jack.dalene@snow.edu
DALES, Sandra .... 910-695-3789. 363 F
daless@sandhills.edu
DALEY, Barbara, J .... 414-229-4721. 537 A
bdaley@uwm.edu
DALEY, Ben .... 619-398-4902... 47 I
DALEY, Carol .... 540-338-2700. 503 A
cdaley@cdu.edu
DALEY, Deborah .... 405-280-1786. 289 D
deborahdaley@creighton.edu
DALEY, Elizabeth, M .... 213-740-2804... 74 A
edaley@cinema.usc.edu
DALEY, Karen .... 616-698-7111. 241 H
rdaley@davenport.edu
DALEY, Michael, D .... 716-673-3434. 342 A
michael.daley@fredonia.edu
DALEY, Miesha, V .... 773-995-3555. 141 J
mdaley@csu.edu
DALGLISH, Jim .... 254-659-7771. 473 A
jdalglish@hillcollege.edu
DALGLISH, Lucy .... 301-405-2383. 219 B
dalglish@umd.edu
DALLA, Ronald .... 509-359-6566. 519 C
rdalla@ewu.edu
DALLAM, Colleen, C ...... 410-334-2864. 221 D
cdallam@worwic.edu
DALLAS, Sean, A .... 610-799-1584. 421 I
sdallas@lccc.edu
DALLEY, Annique .... 510-628-8023... 51 A
studentservices@lincolnuca.edu
DALLINGER, Deborah ..... 925-788-9131... 58 G
deborah.dallinger@patten.edu
DALLMAN, Bruce, D .... 620-235-4365. 189 L
bdallman@pittstate.edu
DALLMAN, Sara, E .... 303-963-3147... 79 C
sdallman@ccu.edu
DALO, Dave .... 301-934-7728. 214 D
ddalo@csmd.edu
DALONZO, Beth .... 740-826-8137. 384 L
bdalonzo@muskingum.edu
DALPE, J. Kyle .... 775-673-7166. 294 H
kdalpe@tmcc.edu
DALRYMPLE, Jim .... 417-626-1234. 279 J
dalrymple.jim@occ.edu
DALRYMPLE, Ruth .... 210-486-2174. 465 B
rdalrymple2@alamo.edu
DALRYMPLE, Scott .... 518-464-8684. 324 B
sdalrymple@excelsior.edu
DALSING, Deirdre, L ...... 608-342-1865. 537 D
dalsingd@uwplatt.edu
DALSKE, James .... 707-654-1070... 31 I
jdalske@csum.edu
DALTO, Diane .... 518-743-2337. 345 E
daltod@sunyacc.edu
DALTO, Joseph .... 251-344-1203..... 3 I
jdalto@fortiscollege.edu
DALTON, Ben .... 740-753-6516. 380 K
daltonb@hocking.edu
DALTON, Brenda .... 404-270-5245. 132 E
bdalton@spelman.edu
DALTON, Brenda .... 972-860-4677. 470 G
bdalton@dcccd.edu
DALTON, Brett, A .... 864-656-2444. 442 C
dbrett@clemson.edu
DALTON, Brian, F .... 814-332-2102. 409 D
bdalton@allegheny.edu
DALTON, Dana, L .... 336-734-7369. 360 E
ddalton@forsythtech.edu

DALTON, Deborah 508-626-4698. 230 A
ddalton@framingham.edu
DALTON, James 845-938-2050. 545 I
8ord@usma.edu
DALTON, Jennifer 304-473-8017. 531 G
daltont_j@wvwc.edu
DALTON, John 765-973-8450. 167 G
jodalton@iue.edu
DALTON, Judith 215-572-4088. 409 H
daltonj@arcadia.edu
DALTON, Karen 909-447-2534... 39 E
kdalton@cst.edu
DALTON, Linda 510-885-4120... 33 C
linda.dalton@csueastbay.edu
DALTON, Liz 706-355-5025. 120 J
edalton@athenstech.edu
DALTON, Thomas 518-464-8632. 324 B
tdalton@excelsior.edu
DALTON, Walter, H 828-395-1300. 361 C
wdalton@isothermal.edu
DALTON, William 225-216-8601. 202 H
daltonw@mybrcc.edu
DALTON-RANN, RaVonda 336-750-2046. 370 A
daltonrannr@wssu.edu
DALTON-RUSSELL, Belinda 270-534-3081. 196 G
belinda.dalton-russell@kctcs.edu
DALY, Adrian 216-791-5000. 377 E
adrian.daly@case.edu
DALY, Ashley 214-376-1000. 478 D
DALY, Carson 704-461-6728. 352 G
carsondaly@bac.edu
DALY, Christina 617-585-1103. 234 I
chris.daly@necmusic.edu
DALY, Cory 307-855-2186. 542 Y
cdaly@cwc.edu
DALY, Debra 402-280-2424. 289 D
dldaly@creighton.edu
DALY, Jennifer 504-762-3260. 203 A
jdaly@dcc.edu
DALY, Jonathan, P 805-525-4417... 69 H
jdaly@thomasaquinas.edu
DALY, Kathleen, M 850-644-4453. 115 C
kdaly@fsu.edu
DALY, Lois, K 518-783-2306. 340 J
daly@siena.edu
DALY, Michael 718-429-6600. 349 H
michael.daly@vaughn.edu
DALY, Patrick 972-721-5145. 488 F
mpdaly@udallas.edu
DALY, Robert, F 951-827-3296... 71 E
bob.daly@ucr.edu
DALY, Ross 914-251-6550. 344 D
ross.daly@purchase.edu
DALY, Shawn, p 716-286-8050. 334 F
sdaly@niagara.edu
DALY-EIMER, Anne, M 856-691-8600. 301 A
adaly@cccnj.edu
DALY-WESTON, Marilyn 212-650-3995. 318 C
marilyn.daley-weston@hunter.cuny.edu
DALZELL, Beth 603-513-1332. 298 E
beth.dalzell@granite.edu
DALZELL, Douglas 410-951-3826. 220 B
ddalzell@coppin.edu
DAMAR, Andrea 212-343-1234. 331 D
adamar@mcny.edu
DAMARI, David 231-591-3703. 242 F
damarid@ferris.edu
DAMAZO, Dennis, E 724-847-5678. 417 A
dedamazo@geneva.edu
DAMBROSIA, Pamela 718-261-5800. 315 F
pdambrosia@bramsonort.edu
DAME, Robert 630-889-6515. 154 E
rdame@nuhs.edu
DAMERON, Paul 270-789-5059. 193 D
padameron@campbellsville.edu
DAMES, Christopher 314-516-6473. 283 E
cdames@umsl.edu
DAMES, Jeanine 203-432-0800... 93 A
jeanine.dames@yale.edu
DAMEWOOD, Tony, M 402-552-6109. 288 L
damewood@clarksoncollege.edu
DAMHOFF, Russ 815-288-5511. 158 K
damhofr@svcc.edu
DAMIAN, Karen 802-387-6711. 499 E
kdamian@landmark.edu
DAMIANI, Glenn 505-224-3223. 309 E
GDamiani@cnm.edu
DAMIANI, Susan, M 718-990-7562. 339 A
damianis@stjohns.edu
DAMIANO, Ann, E 717-867-6077. 421 H
damiano@lvc.edu
DAMIANO, Fred 315-781-3955. 326 C
damiano@hws.edu
DAMICO, Debra, L 718-862-7213. 329 M
debra.damico@manhattan.edu
DAMM, Richard, T 920-748-8322. 535 J
dammr@ripon.edu
DAMMER, Bob 310-434-4397... 65 A
dammer_bob@smc.edu
DAMMINGER, Joanne, K 302-739-4052... 93 D
joanned@dtcc.edu
DAMMON, Robert 412-268-3696. 412 H
rd19@andrew.cmu.edu
DAMON, Brad 858-642-8318... 55 J
bdamon@nu.edu
DAMON, Jud 904-819-6252. 103 E
jdamon@flagler.edu
DAMON, Paula 712-279-5405. 176 B
paula.damon@briarcliff.edu
DAMONE, Bob 619-574-6909... 57 E
bdamone@pacificcollege.edu
DAMORE, Gary, P 602-386-4156... 11 G
gary.damore@arizonachristian.edu
DAMPEER, Susan, C 574-284-4601. 172 G
sdampeer@saintmarys.edu
DAMPIER, Pat 843-383-8062. 442 F
pdampier@coker.edu
DAMPIER, Paula 770-297-5896. 122 A
pland@brenau.edu
DAMRON, James 401-232-6261. 438 K
jdamron@bryant.edu
DAMRON, Kathy 785-864-7100. 190 L
mkdtopeka@aol.com
DAMRON, Nancy 913-971-3521. 188 H
nldamron@mnu.edu
DAMRON, Ron 606-218-5224. 200 F
ronalddamron@upike.edu
DAMROSE-MAHLMANN, Christine 757-822-1919. 514 C
cmahlmann@tcc.edu
DAMROW, Bobbi 715-675-3331. 541 A
damrow@ntc.edu
DAMSCHRODER, Matthew 309-556-3113. 148 B
orl@iwu.edu
DAMSKY, Sarah 212-650-5913. 317 D
sdamsky@ccny.cuny.edu
DAN, Chong 704-216-6035. 356 D
cdan@livingstone.edu
DANA, Robert, Q 207-581-1406. 212 B
rdana@maine.edu
DANAJOVITS, Joseph 860-738-6368... 89 C
jdanajovits@nwcc.commnet.edu
DANCE, Andrea 252-335-0821. 359 F
andrea_dance@albemarle.edu
DANCER, Erin 770-426-2974. 128 D
erin.dancer@life.edu
DANCHISE, Roger, A 781-891-2274. 223 C
rdanchise@bentley.edu
DANCIK, Deborah, B 503-370-6561. 408 J
ddancik@willamette.edu
DANCY, Regina, M 704-636-6818. 355 D
rdancy@hoodseminary.edu
DANDAPANI, Ramaswami 719-255-3551... 85 M
rdan@eas.uccs.edu
DANDELAKE, George 904-470-8150. 102 A
g.dandelake@ewc.edu
DANDRIDGE, Horace 313-927-1555. 246 D
hdandridge@marygrove.edu
DANE, Francis, C 540-224-4515. 506 G
fcdane@jchs.edu
DANE, Jane, H 757-683-6702. 507 N
jhdane@odu.edu
DANE, Kathy 904-743-1122. 107 T
kdane@jones.edu
DANE, Phil, W 731-881-7660. 463 E
pdane@utm.edu
DANEN, Todd 920-403-3943. 535 L
todd.danen@snc.edu
DANFORD, Richard, K 740-376-4899. 383 E
richard.danford@marietta.edu
DANFORD, Robert, E 610-499-4087. 437 E
redanford@widener.edu
DANFORD, Tom 615-366-4451. 459 A
tom.danford@tbr.edu
DANFORTH, Meridith 972-860-4823. 470 G
mdanforth@dcccd.edu
DANG, Connie 616-331-2177. 243 C
dangc@gvsu.edu
DANG-WILLIAMS, Thao 314-246-8757. 284 N
thaodangwilliams@webster.edu
DANGELO, Linda 617-732-2224. 233 E
linda.dangelo@mcphs.edu
DANGLER, Steven 607-753-2111. 343 B
steven.dangler@cortland.edu
DANHEISER, Priscilla, R 478-301-2089. 128 H
danheiser_p@mercer.edu
DANIEL, Andrea 706-355-5124. 120 J
adaniel@athenstech.edu
DANIEL, Brett 903-675-6239. 488 D
daniel@tvcc.edu
DANIEL, David, E 972-883-2201. 491 E
dedaniel@utdallas.edu
DANIEL, Dean 940-855-4322. 494 F
danield@wbu.edu
DANIEL, Elnora 757-727-5000. 505 F
elenora.daniel@hamptonu.edu
DANIEL, Floyd 501-279-4312... 21 C
rcoker@harding.edu
DANIEL, Kevin, S 719-587-7741... 78 B
ksdaniel@adams.edu
DANIEL, Larry 904-620-2520. 116 B
ldaniel@unf.edu
DANIEL, Linda 903-675-6350. 488 D
ldaniel@tvcc.edu
DANIEL, Lori 256-395-2211..... 7 C
ldaniel@suscc.edu
DANIEL, Margaret 615-297-7545. 452 J
daniel@aquinascollege.edu
DANIEL, Mary 254-867-3363. 486 B
mary.daniel@tstc.edu
DANIEL, Michael 251-981-3771..... 2 I
michael.daniel@columbiasouthern.edu
DANIEL, Nancy, C 617-348-6513. 237 E
nancy.daniel@urbancollege.edu
DANIEL, Richard 915-747-8600. 492 A
rjdaniel@utep.edu
DANIEL, Robin, L 336-272-7102. 354 E
rdaniel@greensboro.edu
DANIEL, Sandra, D 229-931-2275. 126 D
sandra.daniel@gsw.edu
DANIEL, Sharlene 423-775-6596. 458 A
sdaniel@ogs.edu
DANIEL, Sherman 680-488-2471. 547 B
shermand1961@yahoo.com
DANIEL, Stephen, P 757-683-3093. 507 N
sdaniel@odu.edu
DANIEL, Steve 706-646-6168. 132 B
sdaniel@sctech.edu
DANIEL, Thomas, E 404-656-2211. 134 A
tom.daniel@usg.edu
DANIEL, Tim 701-483-2100. 371 D
tim.daniel@dickinsonstate.edu
DANIEL, W. John 205-934-3474..... 8 E
wdaniel@uab.edu
DANIEL-ROBINSON, Kim 973-720-3766. 308 I
danielrobinsonk@wpunj.edu
DANIELL, Steven 817-531-4900. 488 A
sdaniell@txwes.edu
DANIELS, Brooke 617-369-3605. 236 F
bdaniels@smfa.edu
DANIELS, Calvin 913-234-0710. 185 L
calvin.daniels@cleveland.edu
DANIELS, Clayton 912-279-5775. 123 B
cdaniels@ccga.edu
DANIELS, Debra, S 815-280-2207. 149 A
ddaniels@jjc.edu
DANIELS, Dennis, E 936-261-3085. 482 F
dedaniels@pvamu.edu
DANIELS, Ellen, E 765-641-4254. 163 L
eedaniels@anderson.edu
DANIELS, Gerri, L 906-227-2650. 248 A
gdaniels@nmu.edu
DANIELS, Glynis, A 610-799-1936. 421 I
gdaniels@lccc.edu
DANIELS, III, Jack, E 608-246-6676. 540 C
DANIELS, James 760-252-2411... 29 I
jdaniels@barstow.edu
DANIELS, Jennifer 949-376-6000... 50 C
jdaniels@lagunacollege.edu
DANIELS, Jonathan 636-229-3200. 450 G
jdaniels@national.edu
DANIELS, Judy 337-550-1218. 205 B
DANIELS, Kathryn 206-726-5080. 518 G
kdaniels@cornish.edu
DANIELS, Kyle 585-266-0430. 324 A
kdaniels@cci.edu
DANIELS, LaMetrius 615-329-8773. 454 F
ldaniels@fisk.edu
DANIELS, Lisa 518-608-8398. 324 B
ldaniels@excelsior.edu
DANIELS, Lisa 518-464-8500. 324 B
ldaniels@excelsior.edu
DANIELS, Mark 425-235-2352. 522 F
mdaniels@rtc.edu
DANIELS, Martin 802-485-2969. 500 A
mdaniel2@norwich.edu
DANIELS, Matt 641-844-5708. 179 J
matt.daniels@iavalley.edu
DANIELS, Maurice, C 706-542-5424. 133 C
sswdean@uga.edu
DANIELS, Michael 828-448-3564. 365 A
mdaniels@wpcc.edu
DANIELS, Mildred, L 803-536-7171. 446 G
mdanie8@scsu.edu
DANIELS, JR., Mitchell, E 765-494-4600. 171 M
DANIELS, Nettie 318-274-6142. 207 E
danielsn@gram.edu
DANIELS, Orangel, J 910-362-7129. 358 F
odaniels@cfcc.edu
DANIELS, Pat, E 252-451-8329. 362 D
pdaniels@nashcc.edu
DANIELS, Patti, J 618-537-6936. 152 G
pjdaniels@mckendree.edu
DANIELS, Phil 573-592-5225. 285 B
phil.daniels@westminster-mo.edu
DANIELS, Randell, W 734-384-4224. 247 C
rdaniels@monroeccc.edu
DANIELS, Rebecca 315-229-5731. 339 F
rdaniels@stlawu.edu
DANIELS, Rochelle 803-822-3208. 445 C
danielsr@midlandstech.edu
DANIELS, Ronald, J 410-516-4170. 215 H
president@jhu.edu
DANIELS, Ronnie 606-573-3274. 196 F
ronnie.daniels@kctcs.edu
DANIELS, Ryan 414-847-3237. 534 F
ryandaniels@miad.edu
DANIELS, Scott 626-815-5441... 29 H
sdaniels@apu.edu
DANIELS, Shelia 386-822-7472. 117 C
sdaniels@stetson.edu
DANIELS, Terri 407-708-2126. 113 E
danielst@seminolestate.edu
DANIELS, Ursula 201-612-5355. 299 C
udaniels@bergen.edu
DANIELS, Wanda 251-405-7003..... 2 D
wdaniels@bishop.edu
DANIELS HERRON, Sally 612-330-1525. 253 H
herron@augsburg.edu
DANIELSEN, Randy 480-219-6009. 271 A
rdanielsen@atsu.edu
DANIELSON, Amy 414-443-3637. 535 A
danielsa@mtmary.edu
DANIELSON, Chad 269-660-8021. 249 C
danielsonc@millercollege.edu
DANIELSON, David 530-879-4078... 30 F
danielsonda@butte.edu
DANIELSON, David, D 651-631-5329. 263 A
dddanielson@nwc.edu
DANIELSON, Lisa, M 920-424-3007. 537 B
danielsn@uwosh.edu
DANIELSON, Mary Ann 402-280-2535. 289 D
maryanndanielson@creighton.edu
DANIELSON, Ronald, L 408-554-6813... 64 M
rdanielson@scu.edu
DANIELSON, Timothy 920-424-1037. 537 B
danielso@uwosh.edu
DANIK, Stephen, R 724-480-3356. 413 H
steve.danik@ccbc.edu
DANILOWICZ, Bret 405-744-5663. 397 H
bret.danilowicz@okstate.edu
DANKEL, Richard 401-232-6117. 438 K
rdankel@bryant.edu
DANKO, James, M 317-940-9900. 164 J
jdanko@butler.edu
DANLEY, Charrita, D 757-727-5231. 505 F
charrita.danley@hamptonu.edu
DANLEY, Janet, V 509-758-1703. 524 H
janet.danley@wwcc.edu
DANNA, Debra 504-864-7550. 205 H
danna@loyno.edu
DANNA, Stephen 518-792-5425. 344 B
dann1253@plattsburgh.edu
DANNECKER, Debra, A 414-277-7131. 534 G
schreite@msoe.edu
DANNECKER, Ronald 716-829-7600. 323 D
dannecrh@dyc.edu
DANNELLEY, Jenny 909-652-6231... 37 M
jenny.dannelley@chaffey.edu
DANNEN, Troy, A 319-273-2470. 176 A
troy.dannen@uni.edu
DANNENBAUM, Martha, C 979-458-8300. 483 C
mdannenbaum@tamu.edu
DANOS, Paul 603-646-2460. 296 G
paul.danos@dartmouth.edu
DANSBERRY, Elizabeth 859-344-3418. 199 H
dansbe@thomasmore.edu
DANSER, Dolores, A 717-245-1589. 414 H
danserd@dickinson.edu
DANT, Mary 618-545-3105. 149 D
mdant@kaskaskia.edu
DANTLEY, Michael 312-915-6992. 151 H
mdantley@luc.edu
DANTLEY, Scott, J 410-951-3828. 220 B
sdantley@coppin.edu
DANTSIN, Catherine 610-861-1509. 424 E
kdantsin@moravian.edu
DANUFF, Allan 352-854-2322. 100 K
danuffa@cf.edu
DANZELL, Linda 508-678-2811. 231 B
linda.danzell@bristolcc.edu
DANZEY, Ida 310-434-4792... 65 A
danzey_ida@smc.edu
DANZI, SJ, Rocco 201-761-7390. 306 L
rdanzi@saintpeters.edu
DANZY, Jamia 860-701-7708... 90 G
danzy_j@mitchell.edu
DAO, Chau 909-274-4450... 55 A
cdao@mtsac.edu
DAOUST, Carolyn 989-358-7211. 239 C
daoust@alpenacc.edu
DAPICE-WONG, Stephanie 631-665-1600. 348 B
stephanie.wong@touro.edu

DAPP, Scot .... 610-861-1534. 424 E
DAPRA, Joe .... 816-322-0110. 271 O
joe.dapra@calvary.edu
DARABI, Rachelle .... 417-836-8346. 278 E
rachelledarabi@missouristate.edu
DARANDARI, H. Sam ..... 314-516-6423. 283 E
darandarih@umsl.edu
DARBONE, Davidson .... 337-421-6940. 204 E
david.darbone@sowela.edu
DARBUT, Jeff .... 480-461-7382... 15 A
jeffrey.darbut@mesacc.edu
DARBY, Barbara, A .... 904-766-6551. 105 E
bdarby@fscj.edu
DARBY, Cindy .... 318-678-6000. 202 I
cdarby@bpcc.edu
DARBY, Mary, A .... 225-771-5923. 206 J
magdarby@yahoo.com
DARCANGELO, Robin ..... 707-864-7889... 66 G
robin.darcangelo@solano.edu
DARCY, Diane .... 718-482-5080. 318 F
ddarcy@lagcc.cuny.edu
DARCY, Kip .... 810-762-7331. 244 Q
kdarcy@kettering.edu
DARCY, Marsanda .... 212-349-4330. 325 D
mdarcy@globe.edu
DARDEN, Beth .... 618-634-3224. 158 M
bethda@shawneecc.edu
DARDEN, James .... 618-634-3325. 158 M
jamesda@shawneecc.edu
DARDEN, Mary .... 210-253-3264. 469 L
mary.darden@concordia.edu
DARDIS, Greg .... 503-675-3969. 404 C
gdardis@marylhurst.edu
DARE, Adebimpe .... 617-928-4763. 234 E
adare@mountida.edu
DARE, Donna .... 314-539-5288. 281 D
ddare@stlcc.edu
DARGA, Richard .... 773-995-2378. 141 J
rdarga@csu.edu
DARIN, Jessica .... 562-951-4700... 32 E
jdarin@calstate.edu
DARIN, Mary, K .... 972-238-6230. 471 C
mkdarin@dcccd.edu
DARING, William .... 508-854-4415. 232 F
wdaring@qcc.mass.edu
DARLAGE, Larry, J .... 817-515-6200. 482 B
larry.darlage@tccd.edu
DARLING, Douglas, D .... 701-662-1506. 372 D
doug.darling@lrsc.edu
DARLING, Joshua, J .... 864-488-8219. 444 L
jdarling@limestone.edu
DARLINGTON, Carol ...... 989-386-6625. 247 B
cdarlington@midmich.edu
DARNALL, Steve .... 707-826-6009... 35 C
wsd1@humboldt.edu
DARNALL BURKE,
Randi .... 707-826-3361... 35 C
darnall@humboldt.edu
DARNELL, Darrell, L .... 202-994-1000... 95 D
ddarnell@gwu.edu
DARNELL, Meg .... 212-924-5900. 347 B
ce@swedishinstitute.edu
DARNELL, Meg .... 212-924-5900. 347 B
placement@swedishinstitute.edu
DAROCA, Laura .... 310-665-6895... 57 C
otisalum@otis.edu
DAROSKY, Renee .... 312-939-4975. 146 A
rdarosky@harrington.edu
DARR, Eric, D .... 717-901-5111. 418 E
edarr@HarrisburgU.edu
DARR, Steven .... 863-638-7230. 119 C
steven.darr@warner.edu
DARRAH, SSJ, Mary ...... 215-248-7031. 413 A
darrahm@chc.edu
DARRIGRAND,
Denise, M .... 508-793-7423. 225 A
ddarrigrand@clarku.edu
DARRINGTON,
Jessyca, M .... 334-229-4894..... 1 D
jdarrington@alasu.edu
DARROW, David, W .... 937-229-4615. 391 C
DDarrow1@udayton.edu
DARROW, Karen .... 406-756-3900. 286 B
kdarrow@fvcc.edu
DARST, Valerie .... 660-263-4110. 279 B
valeried@macc.edu
DART, Greg .... 740-588-1220. 394 C
gdart@zanestate.edu
DART, Greg .... 435-283-7154. 498 A
greg.dart@snow.edu
DARTON, Ruth .... 909-777-3300... 43 N
DARVILLE, Dennis .... 919-761-2100. 366 I
ddarville@sebts.edu
DARVILLE, Robert, H ...... 706-233-7335. 131 E
rdarville@shorter.edu
DARWIN, Mike .... 205-726-4241..... 6 F
mdarwin@samford.edu
DAS, Dilip .... 410-951-6102. 220 B
ddas@coppin.edu
DAS, Pradeep, K .... 404-627-2681. 121 H
pradeep.das@beulah.org
DAS, Purna .... 219-785-5254. 172 A
pdas@pnc.edu
DASBURG, Deanne .... 828-884-8129. 352 I
dasburg@brevard.edu
DASENBROCK, Reed, W . 808-956-8447. 136 B
rdasenbr@hawaii.edu
DASEY-MORALES,
Maureen .... 316-978-3440. 191 F
maureen.dasey-morales@witchita.edu
DASGUPTA, Nandini ...... 510-869-8711... 61 I
ndasgupta@samuelmerritt.edu
DASHER, Glenn .... 256-824-6200..... 8 F
dasherg@uah.edu
DASHER, Josh .... 912-287-5819. 130 B
jdasher@okefenokeetech.edu
DASHIELD, Richeleen ..... 908-526-1200. 305 B
rdashield@raritanval.edu
DASILVA, Joseph .... 413-755-4889. 233 A
jdasilva@stcc.edu
DASINGER, Hank .... 334-285-5177..... 4 J
hank.dasinger@istc.edu
DASSANCE, Charles .... 970-945-8691... 79 G
DASTMOZD, Rassoul ..... 651-846-1335. 261 D
rassoul.dastmozd@saintpaul.edu
DATHER, Julie .... 605-668-1525. 450 F
jdather@mtmc.edu
DATSKO, Robert, G .... 814-472-3006. 432 D
rdatsko@francis.edu
DATTA, Asoke .... 808-544-1106. 135 F
adatta@hpu.edu
DATTA, Sumana .... 979-845-6774. 483 C
sumad@tamu.edu
DATTAGUPTA, Satyajit ... 410-778-7700. 221 C
sdattagupta2@washcoll.edu
DATUIN,
Bonnie Mae, M .... 671-735-5616. 546 C
bonniemae.datuin@guamcc.edu
DAUBERMAN,
Barbara, A .... 804-752-7300. 508 E
bdauberman@rmc.edu
DAUDISTEL, Howard ...... 915-747-8533. 492 A
hdaudistel@utep.edu
DAUER, Eve .... 443-537-1578. 265 D
eve.dauer@waldenu.edu
DAUGHADAY, David .... 410-617-2349. 216 A
daughaday@loyola.edu
DAUGHERTY, Carolyn .... 719-549-2830... 80 K
carolyn.daugherty@colostate-pueblo.edu
DAUGHERTY, Craig, A ... 740-427-5430. 382 J
daugherty@kenyon.edu
DAUGHERTY, Donna ...... 706-295-6306. 125 C
ddaugher@highlands.edu
DAUGHERTY, Eleanor ..... 773-702-5243. 161 B
ebd1@uchicago.edu
DAUGHERTY, Lorna .... 712-279-1705. 176 B
lorna.daugherty@briarcliff.edu
DAUGHERTY, Penny, J .. 541-346-2971. 406 D
penny@uoregon.edu
DAUGHERTY, Robyn ...... 479-524-7301... 21 G
rdaugherty@jbu.edu
DAUGHERTY, Tim .... 618-985-4872. 148 J
timdaugherty@jalc.edu
DAUGHERTY, Vernon, D 828-398-7220. 357 N
vdaugherty@abtech.edu
DAUGHETY, Kathy .... 252-399-6529. 352 F
kdaughety@barton.edu
DAUGHT, Gary .... 423-461-8799. 457 H
gfdaught@milligan.edu
DAUGHTREY, III,
Thomas, W .... 910-630-7316. 356 H
tdaughtrey@methodist.edu
DAUGHTRY, Dee Dee, D 919-209-2066. 361 E
dddaughtry@johnstoncc.edu
DAULTON, Jonathan, G .. 864-242-5100. 441 D
DAUM, Sarah .... 909-274-4750... 55 A
sdaum@mtsac.edu
DAUN, Eugene .... 847-578-3252. 157 F
eugene.daun@rosalindfranklin.edu
DAUPHINAIS, Michael ... 239-280-2505... 98 K
michael.dauphinais@avemaria.edu
DAURER, Jeffrey .... 815-753-2755. 154 I
jdaurer@niu.edu
DAUSEN, Peter, G .... 831-656-3037. 544 M
pgdausen@nps.edu
DAUTERIVE, Jerry .... 401-254-3444. 440 B
jdauterive@rwu.edu
DAUTREMONT-SMITH,
Julian .... 607-587-4011. 345 D
dautrej@alfredstate.edu
DAUWALDER, David, P .. 818-767-0888... 76 K
david.dauwalder@woodbury.edu
DAVALT, Greg .... 405-789-7661. 400 A
greg.davalt@swcu.edu
DAVAR, David .... 212-678-6161. 328 A
dadavar@jtsa.edu
DAVAULT, Joey .... 405-733-7392. 399 F
jdavault@rose.edu
DAVE-LAKHANI, Roopa .. 661-654-3370... 32 H
rdave@csub.edu
DAVENPORT, A. Wade ... 610-607-6271. 431 D
wdavenport@racc.edu
DAVENPORT, Daniel, D .. 208-885-6312. 139 D
dand@uidaho.edu
DAVENPORT, Darrien ..... 717-815-6663. 438 D
ddavenp2@ycp.edu
DAVENPORT, Deanna ..... 757-569-6704. 513 E
ddavenport@pdc.edu
DAVENPORT, Elizabeth ... 773-702-8282. 161 B
ejld@uchicago.edu
DAVENPORT, Fiona, E ... 215-887-5511. 437 C
fdavenport@wts.edu
DAVENPORT, Floyd .... 785-670-2066. 191 D
floyd.davenport@washburn.edu
DAVENPORT, Karen .... 914-964-4282. 320 C
DAVENPORT, Lechelle .... 901-333-4195. 461 F
ldavenport@southwest.tn.edu
DAVENPORT, Mary .... 507-433-0530. 260 I
mary.davenport@riverland.edu
DAVENPORT, Mike .... 270-824-8661. 196 A
mike.davenport@kctcs.edu
DAVENPORT, Mona .... 217-581-6690. 144 E
mydavenport@eiu.edu
DAVENPORT, Nancy .... 202-885-3200... 94 F
davenpor@american.edu
DAVENPORT, Richard ...... 507-389-1111. 259 G
richard.davenport@mnsu.edu
DAVENPORT, Robert .... 405-585-5301. 397 C
robert.davenport@okbu.edu
DAVENPORT, Robin .... 973-618-3905. 300 A
rdavenport@caldwell.edu
DAVENPORT, Robin .... 910-630-7609. 356 H
rdavenport@methodist.edu
DAVENPORT, Sarah .... 940-552-6291. 493 F
sdavenport@vernoncollege.edu
DAVENPORT, Shirley ...... 636-481-3333. 275 I
sdavenp1@jeffco.edu
DAVENPORT, Tamika ..... 312-850-7075. 142 C
Tatdavenport13@ccc.edu
DAVENPORT, Thomas .... 270-706-8699. 195 A
tom.davenport@kctcs.edu
DAVENPORT,
Zebulun, R .... 317-274-8990. 168 D
zrdavenp@iupui.edu
DAVENPORT-RAMIREZ,
Keisha .... 212-229-8996. 332 E
davenpok@newschool.edu
DAVENPORT SYPHER,
Beverly .... 513-556-2588. 390 G
provost@uc.edu
DAVEY, Andrew .... 816-414-3700. 277 L
adavey@mbts.edu
DAVEY, Cathleen .... 201-684-7612. 305 A
cdavey@ramapo.edu
DAVEY, Daniel, K .... 757-479-3706. 503 C
DAVEY, Martha .... 307-855-2235. 542 Y
mdavey@cwc.edu
DAVEY, Stephen .... 800-672-3060. 366 F
DAVID, Garry .... 940-552-6291. 493 F
gdavid@vernoncollege.edu
DAVID, Haven .... 940-552-6291. 493 F
hdavid@vernoncollege.edu
DAVID, Hope .... 412-760-9967. 131 H
hdavid@southuniversity.edu
DAVID, Jacob .... 212-563-6647. 348 I
jacobdavid835@yahoo.com
DAVID, Karl, H .... 414-277-7372. 534 G
david@msoe.edu
DAVID, Kenneth .... 212-463-0400. 348 B
kenneth.david@touro.edu
DAVID, Kevin .... 918-595-7925. 400 E
kevin.david@tulsacc.edu
DAVID, Kimberly, C .... 713-798-4975. 467 F
kcotner@bcm.edu
DAVID, Kyle .... 774-455-7560. 228 E
kdavid@umassp.edu
DAVID, Miriam .... 859-985-3212. 192 F
miriam_david@berea.edu
DAVID, Paula .... 508-793-7681. 225 A
pdavid@clarku.edu
DAVID, Richard .... 607-778-5199. 315 I
davidrc@sunybroome.edu
DAVID, Vivian .... 757-727-5331. 505 F
vivian.david@hamptonu.edu
DAVIDANN, Jon .... 808-544-0811. 135 F
jdavidann@hpu.edu
DAVIDHIZAR, Larry, J ... 312-329-4005. 153 E
larry.davidhizar@moody.edu
DAVIDOWITZ,
Menachem .... 585-473-2810. 347 D
DAVIDS, Cheryl .... 828-339-7018. 364 B
c_davids@southwesterncc.edu
DAVIDSEN, Susanna .... 612-312-2500. 265 D
Susanna.Davidsen@waldenu.edu
DAVIDSON, Andrew, R ... 212-854-6313. 321 D
ard2@columbia.edu
DAVIDSON, Anthony ...... 914-323-5315. 330 B
anthony.davidson@mville.edu
DAVIDSON, Conrad .... 701-858-3159. 371 F
conrad.davidson@minotstateu.edu
DAVIDSON, Debbie .... 262-564-3422. 540 A
davidsond@gtc.edu
DAVIDSON, Dennis, W .. 704-637-4474. 353 E
ddavidso@catawba.edu
DAVIDSON, Donald .... 603-641-7287. 297 G
ddavidson@anselm.edu
DAVIDSON, Dotti .... 757-352-4108. 508 G
dorobur@regent.edu
DAVIDSON, Elsa Jean .... 212-749-2802. 330 A
studentlife@msmnyc.edu
DAVIDSON, Erin .... 817-598-6285. 494 G
edavidson@wc.edu
DAVIDSON, Georglyn, L 215-968-8251. 411 B
davidson@bucks.edu
DAVIDSON, JaCenda ...... 615-329-8712. 454 F
jdavidson@fisk.edu
DAVIDSON, James, A .... 410-827-5846. 214 C
jdavidson@chesapeake.edu
DAVIDSON, Jamie .... 702-895-3627. 294 I
jamie.davidson@unlv.edu
DAVIDSON, Janet .... 724-480-3395. 413 H
janet.davidson@ccbc.edu
DAVIDSON, John .... 870-508-6122... 20 A
jdavidson@asumh.edu
DAVIDSON, Jon .... 810-762-3300. 251 E
jdavidso@umflint.edu
DAVIDSON, Katrena, J ... 330-941-1712. 394 A
katrena.davidson@ysu.edu
DAVIDSON, Keith, S ...... 410-651-6496. 219 E
kdavidson@umes.edu
DAVIDSON, Laura .... 919-760-8531. 356 G
davidsonl@meredith.edu
DAVIDSON, Laura-Lee ... 317-917-3628. 171 A
ldavidson@martin.edu
DAVIDSON, Leslie .... 413-528-7245. 222 E
leslied@simons-rock.edu
DAVIDSON, Leslie .... 540-665-5561. 509 E
ldavids2@su.edu
DAVIDSON, Lynda, J ...... 412-397-6801. 431 I
davidson@rmu.edu
DAVIDSON, Michael .... 317-921-4538. 169 L
mdavidson40@ivytech.edu
DAVIDSON, Michelle ...... 916-789-8600... 47 C
michelle_davidson@heald.edu
DAVIDSON, Mitch .... 207-741-5506. 211 A
mdavidson@smccme.edu
DAVIDSON, Nancy .... 605-274-5516. 449 K
nancy.davidson@augie.edu
DAVIDSON, Patricia .... 410-955-7544. 215 H
sondeansoffice@jhu.edu
DAVIDSON, Shane .... 812-488-2829. 173 H
sd10@evansville.edu
DAVIDSON, Sharon .... 718-262-2155. 319 F
sdavid@york.cuny.edu
DAVIDSON, Steve .... 270-444-9676. 193 N
sdavidson@daymarcollege.edu
DAVIDSON, Steve .... 615-966-6280. 456 B
steve.davidson@lipscomb.edu
DAVIDSON, Suellen .... 870-368-2059... 22 E
sdavidson@ozarka.edu
DAVIDSON, Valerie, J .... 317-940-9281. 164 J
vdavidso@butler.edu
DAVIDSON, Vicky, L ...... 937-775-2587. 393 G
vicky.davidson@wright.edu
DAVIDSON, Wayne, A .... 215-368-5000. 410 F
wdavidson@biblical.edu
DAVIE, Fred .... 212-280-1408. 349 A
fdavie@uts.columbia.edu
DAVIE, Karen .... 845-675-4608. 335 C
karen.davie@nyack.edu
DAVIE, Keith, A .... 845-675-4770. 335 C
keith.davie@nyack.edu
DAVIES, Ann .... 608-363-2667. 531 M
daviesa@beloit.edu
DAVIES, Anna .... 818-710-2281... 52 B
daviesa@piercecollege.edu
DAVIES, Becky .... 972-721-5206. 488 F
bdavies@udallas.edu
DAVIES, Bobby .... 201-327-8877. 301 G
bdavies@eastwick.edu
DAVIES, Dana .... 352-588-8283. 112 D
dana.davies@saintleo.edu
DAVIES, David .... 601-266-4533. 270 E
david.davies@usm.edu
DAVIES, Diana, K .... 609-258-2560. 304 E
ddavies@princeton.edu
DAVIES, Glyn .... 310-206-8041... 71 C
gdavies@ponet.ucla.edu
DAVIES, H. Dele, O .... 402-559-5131. 292 J
dele.davies@unmc.edu
DAVIES, Haldane .... 340-693-1004. 555 E
hdavies@live.uvi.edu
DAVIES, Helen .... 603-645-9631. 297 I
h.davies@snhu.edu
DAVIES, Mandy .... 916-660-7302... 66 B
mdavies@sierracollege.edu
DAVIES, Marilyn, S .... 909-593-3511... 72 E
mdavies@laverne.edu
DAVIES, Mark .... 405-208-5284. 397 F
mdavies@okcu.edu
DAVIES, Mark, D .... 570-577-1019. 411 A
mark.davies@bucknell.edu

DAVIES, Mark, Y ... 405-208-5284. 397 F mdavies@okcu.edu
DAVIES, Pamela, L ... 704-337-2216. 365 G daviesp@queens.edu
DAVIES, Paul ... 804-752-7399. 508 E pauldavies@rmc.edu
DAVIES, Peter ... 603-513-5255. 298 D peter.davies@law.unh.edu
DAVIES, Robert ... 541-962-3512. 405 H bob.davies@eou.edu
DAVIES, Susan ... 810-762-9927. 244 Q sdavies@kettering.edu
DAVIES, Susan ... 828-262-7244. 367 A daviess@appstate.edu
DAVIES, William, E ... 301-447-5234. 217 B davies@msmary.edu
DAVILA, Alba ... 787-751-0160. 548 J adavila@cmpr.pr.gov
DAVILA, Alfonso, L ... 787-751-0178. 552 G adavila@suagm.edu
DAVILA, David ... 361-825-2616. 483 F david.davila@tamucc.edu
DAVILA, Grace ... 713-221-8633. 489 D davilag@uhd.edu
DAVILA, Ivan, E ... 787-841-2000. 552 B idavila@pucpr.edu
DAVILA, Nancy ... 787-758-2525. 554 F nancy.davila@upr.edu
DAVILA, Sonia ... 787-738-2161. 554 C sonia.davila@upr.edu
DAVIN, Donna ... 706-290-2163. 121 G ddavin@berry.edu
DAVINO, Richard ... 508-541-1565. 225 F rdavino@dean.edu
DAVIS, A. Alex ... 323-953-4000... 51 G alexanal@lacitycollege.edu
DAVIS, Addie ... 773-291-6497. 142 D addavis@ccc.edu
DAVIS, Adrienne, D ... 314-935-8583. 284 L adriennedavis@wustl.edu
DAVIS, Alan ... 870-235-5059... 23 F dadavis@saumag.edu
DAVIS, Alan, B ... 205-853-1200..... 5 B adavis@jeffstateonline.com
DAVIS, Alana ... 804-752-7227. 508 E adavis@rmc.edu
DAVIS, Albert ... 985-448-4090. 208 A albert.davis@nicholls.edu
DAVIS, Amanda ... 916-558-2441... 53 D davisa@scc.losrios.edu
DAVIS, Andrew, B ... 706-778-8500. 130 E ddavis@piedmont.edu
DAVIS, Angella ... 859-246-6696. 194 L angie.davis@kctcs.edu
DAVIS, Anita, A ... 901-843-3889. 458 E adavis@rhodes.edu
DAVIS, Barbara ... 614-222-4035. 378 A bdavis@ccad.edu
DAVIS, Barbara ... 419-251-1704. 383 G barbara.davis@mercycollege.edu
DAVIS, Becky ... 904-743-1122. 107 T bdavis@jones.edu
DAVIS, Benjamin, A ... 765-641-4101. 163 L badavis@anderson.edu
DAVIS, Bob ... 417-823-3451. 281 M bdavis@forest.edu
DAVIS, Bonnie ... 207-221-4476. 213 A bdavis@une.edu
DAVIS, Bonnie, H ... 336-322-2104. 362 F Bonnie.Davis@piedmontcc.edu
DAVIS, Brad ... 405-789-7661. 400 A brad.davis@swcu.edu
DAVIS, Bradley ... 408-741-2668... 75 L bradley.davis@wvm.edu
DAVIS, Bradley, W ... 941-752-5388. 114 I davisb@scf.edu
DAVIS, Brenda ... 601-928-6381. 268 C brenda.davis2@mgccc.edu
DAVIS, Brent ... 559-730-3912... 40 I brentd@cos.edu
DAVIS, Brian, E ... 330-972-5302. 390 E bdavis@uakron.edu
DAVIS, Britt ... 910-893-1200. 352 K davisb@campbell.edu
DAVIS, Bruce ... 801-626-6789. 497 D brucedavis@weber.edu
DAVIS, Bryan ... 951-343-4721... 30 H bdavis@calbaptist.edu
DAVIS, C. Grant ... 334-844-4866..... 1 G daviscg@auburn.edu
DAVIS, C. Scott ... 804-862-6172. 508 H cdavis@rbc.edu
DAVIS, Carenado ... 252-527-6223. 361 F cdavis@lenoircc.edu
DAVIS, Carol ... 309-647-6395. 160 E carol.davis@src.edu
DAVIS, Carole ... 269-965-3931. 244 O davisc@kellogg.edu
DAVIS, Caroline ... 615-383-4848. 464 D cdavis@watkins.edu
DAVIS, Cassandra, E ... 973-761-7161. 307 C cassandra.davis@shu.edu
DAVIS, Catherine, C ... 609-497-7882. 304 D student.relations@ptsem.edu
DAVIS, Cathleen, M ... 937-775-5700. 393 G cathleen.davis@wright.edu
DAVIS, Cathy ... 773-995-2304. 141 J cdavis58@csu.edu
DAVIS, Charles, N ... 706-542-1704. 133 C cndavis@uga.edu
DAVIS, Cherie ... 209-384-6000... 54 D cherie.davis@mccd.edu
DAVIS, Chrissy ... 509-533-3743. 518 F chrissy.davis@spokanefalls.edu
DAVIS, Christine ... 239-433-6950. 101 O cdavis10@edison.edu
DAVIS, Christopher ... 865-573-4517. 455 G cdavis@johnsonU.edu
DAVIS, Christopher, A ... 410-293-6381. 545 J cdavis@usna.edu
DAVIS, Chuck ... 206-934-4340. 522 J chuck.davis@seattlecolleges.edu
DAVIS, Cliff ... 417-447-2652. 279 K davisc@otc.edu
DAVIS, Connie ... 985-549-2094. 208 C cdavis@selu.edu
DAVIS, Corby ... 360-676-2772. 521 D cdavis@nwic.edu
DAVIS, Curtis ... 404-215-2664. 129 D cdavis@morehouse.edu
DAVIS, Cynthia ... 240-684-2800. 219 F cynthia.davis@umuc.edu
DAVIS, D. Scott ... 478-301-2110. 128 H davis_ds@mercer.edu
DAVIS, Daisy ... 404-297-9522. 126 A davisd@gptc.edu
DAVIS, Dale, P ... 605-256-5238. 451 H dale.davis@dsu.edu
DAVIS, Dan ... 701-228-5621. 372 C danny.davis@dakotacollege.edu
DAVIS, Dana ... 478-757-3506. 122 F ddavis@centralgatech.edu
DAVIS, Daniel, P ... 417-624-7070. 476 F danield@pcg.org
DAVIS, Danny ... 413-748-3532. 236 I ddavis@springfieldcollege.edu
DAVIS, David ... 601-974-1432. 267 I davisdc@millsaps.edu
DAVIS, David, B ... 845-368-7200. 340 C david.davis@use.salvationarmy.org
DAVIS, David, H ... 828-694-1845. 358 C daviddav@blueridge.edu
DAVIS, Debbie ... 828-627-4521. 361 B ddavis@haywood.edu
DAVIS, Debbie ... 859-257-8311. 200 C deborah.davis@email.uky.edu
DAVIS, Deborah ... 212-650-3162. 318 C deborah.davis@hunter.cuny.edu
DAVIS, Debra ... 419-530-8355. 392 B debra.davis@utoledo.edu
DAVIS, Debra, C ... 251-434-3410..... 9 E ddavis@southalabama.edu
DAVIS, Deidra ... 207-326-2138. 211 D deidra.davis@mma.edu
DAVIS, Derek ... 816-268-5424. 279 G dldavis@nts.edu
DAVIS, Diana ... 513-244-4478. 377 G diana_davis@mail.msj.edu
DAVIS, Dianne, L ... 828-398-7841. 357 N ddavis@abtech.edu
DAVIS, Dirk ... 951-343-3905... 30 H ddavis@calbaptist.edu
DAVIS, Don ... 626-815-3828... 29 H ddavis@apu.edu
DAVIS, Donald, L ... 972-883-6176. 491 E don.davis@utdallas.edu
DAVIS, Donna ... 760-757-2121... 54 G ddavis@miracosta.edu
DAVIS, Donna ... 636-922-8300. 280 J ddavis@stchas.edu
DAVIS, Donna, J ... 415-422-6822... 73 J davisdj@usfca.edu
DAVIS, Dorothy, G ... 601-877-6460. 265 G djdavis@alcorn.edu
DAVIS, Ed ... 530-741-6853... 77 M edavis@yccd.edu
DAVIS, Eddie ... 972-825-4686. 481 F edavis@sagu.edu
DAVIS, Eddie, J ... 979-847-8700. 483 C edavis@tamu.edu
DAVIS, Elizabeth ... 203-932-7083... 92 E ebdavis@newhaven.edu
DAVIS, Elizabeth ... 254-710-3601. 467 G elizabeth_davis@baylor.edu
DAVIS, Ellen ... 512-863-1571. 481 I davise@southwestern.edu
DAVIS, Ernie ... 903-693-1112. 478 A edavis@panola.edu
DAVIS, Evelyn ... 423-624-0077. 453 G evelynd@chattanoogacollege.edu
DAVIS, Evett ... 706-771-4027. 121 D edavis@augustatech.edu
DAVIS, Faye ... 918-685-0724. 394 D davisf@bacone.edu
DAVIS, Fontaine ... 386-481-2005... 99 C davisf@cookman.edu
DAVIS, Gary ... 218-726-7572. 264 D gdavis@d.umn.edu
DAVIS, Gayle, R ... 616-331-2400. 243 C davisgr@gvsu.edu
DAVIS, Gene ... 870-307-7233... 21 H wesley.davis@lyon.edu
DAVIS, George ... 717-866-5775. 416 E george.davis@evangelical.edu
DAVIS, Gilda ... 504-286-5176. 206 K gdavis@suno.edu
DAVIS, Glenda ... 214-379-5526. 478 D gdavis@pqc.edu
DAVIS, Glenn ... 212-463-0400. 348 B glenn.davis@touro.edu
DAVIS, Glenn ... 330-672-3131. 382 B gdavis3@kent.edu
DAVIS, JR., Gordon ... 913-684-3443. 545 E gordon.davis@leavenworth.army.mil
DAVIS, Grant ... 610-647-4400. 418 I gdavis@immaculata.edu
DAVIS, Greg ... 360-438-8772. 522 G GDavis@stmartin.edu
DAVIS, Gregory ... 630-515-4554. 144 A gdavis@devry.edu
DAVIS, Gwenda, R ... 973-642-8803. 307 D gwenda.davis@shu.edu
DAVIS, Hazel ... 480-517-8273... 15 D hazel.davis@riosalado.edu
DAVIS, Heather ... 336-750-3350. 370 A davish@wssu.edu
DAVIS, Helane ... 518-445-2336. 313 C hdavi@albanylaw.edu
DAVIS, Henry ... 718-270-4985. 319 A hdavis@mec.cuny.edu
DAVIS, Henry, C ... 334-229-4401..... 1 D hdavis@alasu.edu
DAVIS, Herbert, R ... 919-572-1625. 352 C hdavis@apexsot.edu
DAVIS, Houston ... 404-962-3060. 134 A houston.davis@usg.edu
DAVIS, Howard ... 805-378-1457... 74 F hdavis@vcccd.edu
DAVIS, Howard ... 248-204-2316. 245 I hdavis@ltu.edu
DAVIS, Jack ... 540-231-6416. 515 C davisa@vt.edu
DAVIS, James ... 310-206-0011... 71 C jdavis@conet.ucla.edu
DAVIS, James ... 619-216-6759... 68 B jdavis@swccd.edu
DAVIS, James ... 410-225-4208. 216 C jdavis02@mica.edu
DAVIS, James ... 972-825-4803. 481 F jdavis@sagu.edu
DAVIS, James, A ... 515-294-0323. 175 H davis@iastate.edu
DAVIS, Janice ... 229-931-2381. 131 G jdavis@southgatech.edu
DAVIS, Jef, C ... 330-941-2336. 394 A jcdavis05@ysu.edu
DAVIS, Jeff ... 936-468-3407. 482 A jhdavis@sfasu.edu
DAVIS, Jeff ... 912-871-1640. 129 J jdavis@ogeecheetech.edu
DAVIS, Jeff ... 785-539-3571. 188 F mccweb@mccks.edu
DAVIS, Jeff ... 706-802-5105. 125 C jdavis@highlands.edu
DAVIS, Jeff ... 423-493-4230. 462 B davisj@tntemple.edu
DAVIS, Jeff ... 541-757-8944. 404 B jeff.davis@linnbenton.edu
DAVIS, Jeffrey, W ... 260-481-0739. 168 C davisj@ipfw.edu
DAVIS, Jenna ... 719-336-1589... 82 R jenna.davis@lamarcc.edu
DAVIS, Jennifer ... 252-246-1228. 365 C jdavis@wilsoncc.edu
DAVIS, Jennifer, L ... 740-374-8716. 392 I jdavis@wscc.edu
DAVIS, Jennifer (J.J.) ... 703-993-8750. 505 C jjdavis@gmu.edu
DAVIS, Jermyn ... 719-389-6748... 79 D jermyn.davis@coloradocollege.edu
DAVIS, Jerold ... 212-592-2000. 340 H jdavis@sva.edu
DAVIS, Jerome ... 212-854-5017. 321 D jd2145@columbia.edu
DAVIS, Jerome ... 205-226-4848..... 2 C jdavis@bsc.edu
DAVIS, Jerry, C ... 417-690-2470. 272 E pres@cofo.edu
DAVIS, Jim, L ... 701-477-7862. 373 B jdavis@tm.edu
DAVIS, Jimmy ... 615-460-5630. 453 C jimmy.davis@belmont.edu
DAVIS, Jimmy, H ... 731-661-5461. 462 F jdavis@uu.edu
DAVIS, Joan ... 214-333-6855. 470 D joan@dbu.edu
DAVIS, Joan, Y ... 205-391-5880..... 6 H jydavis@sheltonstate.edu
DAVIS, Joanne ... 561-297-3015. 114 L joannedavis@fau.edu
DAVIS, Joe, M ... 765-641-4084. 163 L jmdavis@anderson.edu
DAVIS, Joel ... 973-803-5000. 304 C jdavis@pillar.edu
DAVIS, John ... 605-677-5341. 451 F john.davis@usd.edu
DAVIS, John ... 626-873-2144... 55 C
DAVIS, John ... 920-206-2332. 533 U john.davis@mbbc.edu
DAVIS, John ... 920-206-2371. 533 U jdavis@mbbc.edu
DAVIS, John, L ... 304-336-8337. 530 A jdavis@westliberty.edu
DAVIS, John, L ... 304-336-8024. 530 A jdavis@westliberty.edu
DAVIS, John, R ... 740-376-4390. 383 E john.davis@marietta.edu
DAVIS, Jon ... 843-863-7218. 441 H jdavis@csuniv.edu
DAVIS, Jonathan, M ... 802-626-6419. 501 E jonathan.davis@lyndonstate.edu
DAVIS, Jud ... 731-989-6023. 454 J jdavis@fhu.edu
DAVIS, Julia, T ... 478-301-2644. 128 H davis_jt@mercer.edu
DAVIS, Julie ... 630-752-5079. 163 F Julie.Davis@wheaton.edu
DAVIS, Julie ... 315-268-6713. 320 A davisju@clarkson.edu
DAVIS, Julie, A ... 207-778-7142. 212 D jadavis@maine.edu
DAVIS, June ... 910-296-2424. 361 D jdavis@jamessprunt.edu
DAVIS, Karan, P ... 850-718-2205... 99 N davisk@chipola.edu
DAVIS, Karen ... 805-493-3164... 31 H kdavis@clunet.edu
DAVIS, Karen ... 401-863-3377. 438 J karen_davis@brown.edu
DAVIS, Karen, S ... 937-393-3431. 389 B ksdavis@sscc.edu
DAVIS, Kathleen ... 207-893-7741. 211 G kdavis@sjcme.edu
DAVIS, Kathy ... 352-854-2322. 100 K kathy.davis@cf.edu
DAVIS, Kathy ... 715-346-4193. 538 A kdavis@uwsp.edu
DAVIS, Kathy, K ... 207-768-9581. 212 G kathy.k.davis@umpi.edu
DAVIS, Katie ... 478-274-7775. 129 I kdavis@oftc.edu
DAVIS, Kelly ... 479-968-0242... 20 E kdavis@atu.edu
DAVIS, Kelly ... 817-272-2194. 491 B kdavis@uta.edu
DAVIS, Ken, R ... 423-478-7898. 458 B kdavis@ptseminary.edu
DAVIS, Kenneth, L ... 212-659-9003. 327 A
DAVIS, JR., Kenneth, M 919-658-2502. 357 I kdavis@moc.edu
DAVIS, Kerry ... 904-819-6200. 103 E KDavis@flagler.edu
DAVIS, Kim, D ... 806-371-2912. 465 E kddavis@actx.edu
DAVIS, Kimely ... 434-832-7627. 512 A davisk@cvcc.vccs.edu
DAVIS, LaDonna ... 301-937-8448. 218 H ldavis@tesst.com
DAVIS, Larry ... 903-223-3106. 484 C larry.davis@tamut.edu
DAVIS, Larry, D ... 501-977-2013... 25 C davis@uaccm.edu
DAVIS, Larry, E ... 412-624-6337. 435 C ledavis@pitt.edu
DAVIS, Larry, J ... 314-516-5606. 283 E ldavis@umsl.edu
DAVIS, Latacha ... 662-254-3579. 269 A latacha.davis@mvsu.edu
DAVIS, Laura ... 859-280-1236. 197 C ldavis@lextheo.edu
DAVIS, Lee ... 912-344-2535. 120 G lee.davis@armstrong.edu
DAVIS, LeeAnn ... 386-506-3404. 101 G davisl@DaytonaState.edu
DAVIS, Len, L ... 516-876-3191. 343 D davisl@oldwestbury.edu
DAVIS, Lily ... 619-849-2524... 59 L lilydavis@pointloma.edu
DAVIS, Linda ... 617-879-2341. 238 C ldavis@wheelock.edu

DAVIS, Linda .... 810-989-5765. 249 H
ldavis@sc4.edu
DAVIS, Linda .... 254-562-3848. 477 G
linda.davis@navarrocollege.edu
DAVIS, Linda, P .... 386-822-7710. 117 C
ldavis@stetson.edu
DAVIS, Lisa .... 202-687-3887... 95 E
davis1@georgetown.edu
DAVIS, Lois .... 503-725-2320. 406 B
loisd@pdx.edu
DAVIS, Loren .... 253-589-5771. 518 B
loren.davis@cptc.edu
DAVIS, Lori, A .... 502-597-6414. 197 A
lori.davis@kysu.edu
DAVIS, LuAnn .... 402-486-2503. 292 E
ludavis@ucollege.edu
DAVIS, Lynne .... 508-270-4021. 231 G
ldavis@massbay.edu
DAVIS, Maggie .... 513-244-4630. 377 G
maggie_davis@mail.msj.edu
DAVIS, Malcolm .... 832-842-4719. 489 B
mdavis@uh.edu
DAVIS, Margaret .... 845-368-7200. 340 C
margaret.davis@use.salvationarmy.org
DAVIS, Maria .... 269-749-7643. 249 A
mdavis@olivetcollege.edu
DAVIS, Marie .... 229-391-4988. 119 H
mdavis@abac.edu
DAVIS, Marilyn, S .... 217-424-6379. 153 C
mdavis@millikin.edu
DAVIS, Marjorie .... 509-533-4152. 518 F
marjorie.davis@spokanefalls.edu
DAVIS, Mark .... 310-506-4472... 58 H
mark.davis@pepperdine.edu
DAVIS, Marsha .... 845-758-7433. 314 D
davis@bard.edu
DAVIS, Martin .... 229-248-2516. 121 E
martin.davis@bainbridge.edu
DAVIS, Mary .... 212-217-4300. 324 C
mary_davis@fitnyc.edu
DAVIS, Mary .... 828-298-3325. 370 E
mdavis@warren-wilson.edu
DAVIS, Mary Ann .... 336-721-2774. 366 D
mary.davis@salem.edu
DAVIS, Matthew .... 402-557-7232. 288 G
matthew.davis@bellevue.edu
DAVIS, Matthew .... 920-206-2310. 533 U
matthew.davis@mbbc.edu
DAVIS, Matthew .... 920-261-9300. 533 U
mdavis@mbbc.edu
DAVIS, Matthew, D .... 812-877-8421. 172 C
matthew.davis@rose-hulman.edu
DAVIS, Meagon .... 478-757-3803. 134 G
mdavis@wesleyancollege.edu
DAVIS, Megan, W .... 603-862-2450. 298 C
megan.davis@unh.edu
DAVIS, Melvin .... 601-979-1400. 267 E
melvin.davis@jsums.edu
DAVIS, Michael .... 773-481-8182. 142 F
mdavis@ccc.edu
DAVIS, Michael .... 770-381-7200. 127 C
DAVIS, Michael, G .... 985-448-4030. 208 A
mike.davis@nicholls.edu
DAVIS, Michelle .... 781-292-2251. 226 G
michelle.davis@olin.edu
DAVIS, Michelle .... 434-544-8228. 506 K
davis@lynchburg.edu
DAVIS, Mike .... 386-752-1822. 104 G
mike.davis@fgc.edu
DAVIS, Miles .... 540-545-7253. 509 E
mdavis3@su.edu
DAVIS, Mitch .... 251-442-2334..... 9 A
mdavis@umobile.edu
DAVIS, Mitch .... 970-247-7010... 81 M
davis_m@fortlewis.edu
DAVIS, Mitchel, W .... 207-725-3930. 209 H
mwdavis@bowdoin.edu
DAVIS, Myriah .... 740-753-7020. 380 K
davism@hocking.edu
DAVIS, NaKesha .... 973-877-3306. 301 H
ngreen@essex.edu
DAVIS, Nan, M .... 903-813-3000. 466 H
ndavis@austincollege.edu
DAVIS, Nancy .... 413-265-2272. 225 C
davisn@elms.edu
DAVIS, Nancy .... 619-644-7000... 46 E
nancy.davis@gcccd.edu
DAVIS, Natalie .... 601-643-8354. 266 F
natalie.davis@colin.edu
DAVIS, Negar .... 619-594-4808... 35 D
ndavis@mail.sdsu.edu
DAVIS, Nelson .... 757-455-3201. 515 H
ndavis@vwc.edu
DAVIS, Nicolette .... 561-912-2166. 103 C
ndavis@evergladesuniversity.edu
DAVIS, Ora .... 334-387-3877..... 1 E
oradavis@amridgeuniversity.edu
DAVIS, Pamela .... 919-760-8360. 356 G
davisp@meredith.edu
DAVIS, Pamela, B .... 216-368-2825. 375 J
pamela.davis@case.edu
DAVIS, Patricia .... 207-780-5911. 212 H
patdavis@usm.maine.edu
DAVIS, Patricia .... 972-860-8180. 470 H
pdavis@dcccd.edu
DAVIS, Patricia, A .... 251-380-3063..... 7 D
pdavis@shc.edu
DAVIS, Patti .... 410-386-8066. 214 A
pdavis@carrollcc.edu
DAVIS, Paul .... 641-784-5422. 178 F
pjdavis@graceland.edu
DAVIS, Paul .... 936-468-1111. 482 A
pdavis@sfasu.edu
DAVIS, Paula .... 719-846-5680... 85 H
paula.davis@trinidadstate.edu
DAVIS, Paula .... 609-343-5091. 299 A
pdavis@atlantic.edu
DAVIS, Peggy .... 804-524-5030. 515 D
pdavis@vsu.edu
DAVIS, Pete, D .... 608-342-1147. 537 D
davisp@uwplatt.edu
DAVIS, Phillip .... 805-756-5301... 32 F
pdavis@calpoly.edu
DAVIS, Phillip, L .... 612-659-6300. 259 D
phil.davis@minneapolis.edu
DAVIS, Rachelle .... 301-387-3044. 214 I
rachelle.davis@garrettcollege.edu
DAVIS, Raeanne .... 212-237-8604. 318 D
radavis@jjay.cuny.edu
DAVIS, Ralph .... 770-426-2713. 128 D
ralph.davis@life.edu
DAVIS, Ralph, U .... 843-661-1110. 444 B
rdavis@fmarion.edu
DAVIS, Rance .... 315-229-5551. 339 F
rdavis@stlawu.edu
DAVIS, Randy .... 502-213-2122. 195 F
randall.davis@kctcs.edu
DAVIS, Ray, J .... 410-651-6083. 219 E
rjdavis@umes.edu
DAVIS, Rebecca .... 361-593-3344. 484 A
koosr00@tamuk.edu
DAVIS, Rebecca, F .... 512-448-8400. 479 C
DAVIS, Renee .... 334-386-7230..... 3 H
rdavis@faulkner.edu
DAVIS, Rhonda .... 417-624-7070. 476 F
rdavis@messengercollege.edu
DAVIS, Richard .... 317-931-2391. 165 B
ddavis@cts.edu
DAVIS, Richard, E .... 954-262-1203. 109 K
redavis@nova.edu
DAVIS, Rick .... 850-973-9492. 109 H
davisr@nfcc.edu
DAVIS, Rick .... 662-246-6441. 268 B
rdavis@msdelta.edu
DAVIS, Robert, H .... 303-492-7006... 85 L
robert.davis@colorado.edu
DAVIS, JR., Robert, W ... 570-941-7500. 436 A
robert.davis@scranton.edu
DAVIS, Roger .... 615-966-7161. 456 B
roger.davis@lipscomb.edu
DAVIS, Ron .... 901-383-6712... 96 F
rnd@strayer.edu
DAVIS, Ron .... 217-641-4500. 148 M
rmdavis@jwcc.edu
DAVIS, Ruth .... 718-855-3661. 327 B
rdavis@idc.edu
DAVIS, Sandie .... 706-295-6339. 125 C
sdavis@highlands.edu
DAVIS, Sandra .... 803-536-7067. 446 G
sdavis@scsu.edu
DAVIS, Sandra, L .... 909-869-2289... 32 G
sldavis@csupomona.edu
DAVIS, Sandra, S .... 803-535-1218. 446 B
davisss@octech.edu
DAVIS, Shane .... 318-487-7181. 202 F
shane.davis@lacollege.edu
DAVIS, Shara .... 440-365-5222. 383 B
DAVIS, Sharon .... 254-526-1346. 468 G
sharon.davis@ctcd.edu
DAVIS, Sharon .... 214-860-8705. 471 A
sdavis@dcccd.edu
DAVIS, Sharon .... 513-569-1475. 376 L
sharon.davis@cincinnatistate.edu
DAVIS, Shelly .... 207-893-7726. 211 G
sdavis@sjcme.edu
DAVIS, Sherri .... 606-672-2312. 194 A
sherri.davis@frontier.edu
DAVIS, Sherri .... 205-929-6357..... 5 D
sdavis@lawsonstate.edu
DAVIS, Sherry .... 254-659-7602. 473 A
sdavis@hillcollege.edu
DAVIS, Stan .... 205-726-2366..... 6 F
csdavis@samford.edu
DAVIS, Stefan, S .... 317-274-8828. 168 D
ssdavis@iupui.edu
DAVIS, Stephen .... 410-225-2355. 216 C
sdavis@mica.edu
DAVIS, Steve .... 304-357-4980. 527 H
stevedavis@ucwv.edu
DAVIS, Steven .... 707-638-5270... 69 K
steven.davis@tu.edu
DAVIS, Steven, J .... 208-496-3305. 137 H
daviss@byui.edu
DAVIS, Stewart .... 256-549-8603..... 3 M
sdavis@gadsdenstate.edu
DAVIS, Stuart .... 650-723-9406... 68 E
spdavis@stanford.edu
DAVIS, Sue .... 225-768-1802. 206 D
sue.davis@ololcollege.edu
DAVIS, Sue, E .... 330-941-2000. 394 A
sedavis@ysu.edu
DAVIS, Susan .... 803-935-4327. 131 H
sdavis@southuniversity.edu
DAVIS, Susan .... 314-529-9340. 276 G
sdavis5@maryville.edu
DAVIS, Susan, Y .... 573-875-7210. 272 G
sydavis@ccis.edu
DAVIS, Suzanne, E .... 315-268-6451. 320 A
daviss@clarkson.edu
DAVIS, Tamaria .... 404-270-5002. 132 E
tkdavis@spelman.edu
DAVIS, Tammy .... 325-574-7695. 494 K
tdavis@wtc.edu
DAVIS, Terry .... 619-482-6551... 68 B
tdavis@swccd.edu
DAVIS, Thomas .... 517-353-0722. 246 H
tdd@msu.edu
DAVIS, Thomas .... 434-791-5651. 502 D
thom.davis@averett.edu
DAVIS, Thomas .... 803-705-4687. 441 C
davist@benedict.edu
DAVIS, Tiffany .... 810-766-4277. 239 G
tiffany.davis@baker.edu
DAVIS, Tina .... 859-622-3876. 193 P
tina.davis@eku.edu
DAVIS, Todd .... 678-359-5061. 127 A
toddd@gordonstate.edu
DAVIS, Tom .... 954-545-4500. 113 F
registrar@sfbc.edu
DAVIS, Tom .... 334-670-3196..... 7 H
tomdavis@troy.edu
DAVIS, Tom .... 505-786-4113. 310 D
tdavis@navajotech.edu
DAVIS, Tom .... 440-375-7170. 382 L
tdavis@lec.edu
DAVIS, Tommye Lou .... 254-710-3750. 467 G
tommye_lou_davis@baylor.edu
DAVIS, Tracy .... 415-371-0002... 57 B
DAVIS, Tracy .... 641-782-1434. 182 I
davis@swcciowa.edu
DAVIS, Tyler .... 843-574-5505. 441 H
tdavis@csuniv.edu
DAVIS, Wayne .... 865-974-5321. 463 C
wtdavis@utk.edu
DAVIS, Wayne .... 757-825-3513. 514 B
davisw@tncc.edu
DAVIS, Wendell, M .... 919-530-6204. 368 A
wendell.davis@nccu.edu
DAVIS, Wendy .... 520-515-3623... 12 R
davisw@cochise.edu
DAVIS, Wendy .... 501-812-2273... 22 G
wdavis@pulaskitech.edu
DAVIS, Wesley .... 701-477-7862. 373 B
wdavis1@tm.edu
DAVIS, William .... 708-534-4105. 145 F
wdavis3@govst.edu
DAVIS, William .... 610-359-6500. 414 D
wdavis@dccc.edu
DAVIS AUSTIN, Patricia . 215-895-5844. 415 B
pda@drexel.edu
DAVIS-BLAKE, Alison .... 734-764-1363. 251 C
alisondb@umich.edu
DAVIS-DUKES, Janet .... 973-720-3096. 308 I
davisdukesj@wpunj.edu
DAVIS-FREEMAN,
Juana, L .... 803-934-3422. 445 F
jdavis@morris.edu
DAVIS FREEMAN,
Louisa, M .... 413-755-4333. 233 A
ldavisfreeman@stcc.edu
DAVIS-JOHNSON, Max .. 208-426-3033. 137 G
maxdavisjohnson@boisestate.edu
DAVIS OCHI, Megan .... 773-896-2400. 141 K
mdavis-ochi@ctschicago.edu
DAVIS-SAMUELS,
Ivanetta .... 615-327-6141. 456 E
DAVIS-TARIQ, Alison, D 757-823-2908. 507 M
adtariq@nsu.edu
DAVIS-VAN ATTA,
David .... 845-437-5276. 349 G
ddavisa@vassar.edu
DAVIS-WARNER,
Vanessa .... 785-825-5422. 185 B
vdavis-warner@brownmackie.edu
DAVISON, Brent .... 254-295-8642. 490 B
bdavison@umhb.edu
DAVISON, Dale .... 602-978-7873... 18 A
dale.davison@thunderbird.edu
DAVISON, Dale .... 602-978-7739... 18 A
dale.davison@thunderbird.edu
DAVISON, Don .... 513-721-7944. 380 D
ddavison@gbs.edu
DAVISON, Frieda, M .... 864-503-5610. 448 H
fdavison@uscupstate.edu
DAVISON, Ian, R .... 989-774-1870. 240 N
davis1ir@cmich.edu
DAVISON, James .... 412-924-1346. 431 A
jdavison@pts.edu
DAVISON, Kim, K .... 972-985-3781. 469 G
kdavison@collin.edu
DAVISON, Rodney .... 940-565-2592. 490 C
davison@union.admin.unt.edu
DAVISON, Ruth, L .... 850-474-2217. 117 B
rdavison@uwf.edu
DAVISON, Vickie .... 406-657-1005. 288 B
vicki.davison@rocky.edu
DAVISON-WILSON,
Sandra .... 616-451-2787. 242 F
davisons@ferris.edu
DAVISSON, Thomas, F ... 502-451-0815. 199 F
tdavisson@sullivan.edu
DAVISSON, Thomas, F ... 502-451-0815. 199 G
tdavisson@sullivan.edu
DAVITT, Alison .... 410-225-4219. 216 C
adavitt@mica.edu
DAVITT, Jeffrey .... 904-819-6489. 103 E
JDavitt@flagler.edu
DAVOLT, David .... 208-376-7731. 137 F
ddavolt@boisebible.edu
DAVOUD, Mohammad .... 912-478-7412. 126 C
mdavoud@georgiasouthern.edu
DAVROS, Harry .... 214-637-3530. 494 E
hdavros@wadecollege.edu
DAVY, Catherine, A .... 313-593-5030. 251 D
kdavy@umich.edu
DAW, Meredith .... 773-702-7040. 161 B
daw@uchicago.edu
DAW, Michael .... 415-442-6682... 45 I
mdaw@ggu.edu
DAWE, Lloyd, A .... 803-641-3338. 448 A
lloydd@usca.edu
DAWE, Richard, L .... 870-368-7371... 22 E
rdawe@ozarka.edu
DAWES, Charles .... 207-893-6621. 211 G
cdawes@sjcme.edu
DAWES, Daniel .... 404-752-1833. 129 E
ddawes@msm.edu
DAWES, Doug .... 701-845-7234. 372 A
doug.dawes@vcsu.edu
DAWES, Stephen .... 864-294-3031. 444 C
steve.dawes@furman.edu
DAWKINS, E. Janyce .... 706-542-7912. 133 C
edawkins@uga.edu
DAWKINS, Kelly, T .... 803-327-8047. 449 J
kdawkins@yorktech.edu
DAWKINS, Kemel, W .... 973-353-5541. 306 A
kemeld@andromeda.rutgers.edu
DAWKINS, Kemel, W .... 973-353-5541. 306 D
kemeld@andromeda.rutgers.edu
DAWKINS, Lisa .... 304-357-4374. 527 H
lisadawkins@ucwv.edu
DAWKINS, Nancy, A .... 414-410-4007. 532 B
nadawkins@stritch.edu
DAWKINS, Norman .... 212-431-2142. 333 I
ndawkins@nyls.edu
DAWKINS, Rita .... 704-330-6862. 359 C
rita.dawkins@cpcc.edu
DAWKINS, Thomas .... 213-763-7361... 52 D
dawkintl@lattc.edu
DAWLEY, Anna Marie .... 315-268-6475. 320 A
adawley@clarkson.edu
DAWLEY, Michael .... 508-793-7578. 225 A
mdawley@clarku.edu
DAWSON, Alan .... 941-487-4695. 115 D
adawson@ncf.edu
DAWSON, B. James .... 423-869-6391. 456 A
james.dawson@lmunet.edu
DAWSON, Brandon .... 978-232-2180. 226 C
bdawson@endicott.edu
DAWSON, Brian .... 310-506-7013... 58 H
brian.dawson@pepperdine.edu
DAWSON, Bridgette .... 304-336-8215. 530 A
bdawson@westliberty.edu
DAWSON, Cole .... 503-517-1221. 408 H
cdawson@warnerpacific.edu
DAWSON, Dave .... 479-575-5451... 23 I
daved@uark.edu
DAWSON, David .... 954-262-2119. 109 K
ddawson@nova.edu
DAWSON, Eric .... 662-329-7411. 268 E
edawson@oe.muw.edu
DAWSON, Imara, V .... 765-285-5422. 164 B
ivdawson@bsu.edu
DAWSON, Janice .... 808-983-4154. 135 G
jdawson@tokai.edu
DAWSON, Jennifer .... 616-632-2828. 239 F
dawsojen@aquinas.edu
DAWSON, Jim, T .... 615-353-3275. 461 B
jim.dawson@nscc.edu
DAWSON, John David .... 765-983-1211. 165 G
prexy@earlham.edu
DAWSON, L. Wayde .... 864-488-4522. 444 L
ldawson@limestone.edu

DAWSON, Rich ... 310-506-4246... 58 H
rich.dawson@pepperdine.edu
DAWSON, Royal ... 312-369-7514. 143 D
rdawson@colum.edu
DAWSON, Scott ... 503-725-3757. 406 B
dawsons@pdx.edu
DAWSON, Shela, B ... 903-233-4445. 475 J
sheladawson@letu.edu
DAWSON, Susan, P ... 512-223-7240. 466 I
sdawson@austincc.edu
DAWSON, Theresa, R ... 308-432-6053. 291 D
tdawson@csc.edu
DAWSON, JR.,
Thomas, E ... 410-951-3792. 220 B
thdawson@coppin.edu
DAWSON, Timothy ... 717-901-5158. 418 E
TDawson@HarrisburgU.edu
DAWSON, Tony ... 630-752-5203. 163 F
Tony.Dawson@wheaton.edu
DAWSON, Yolanda ... 818-401-1041... 41 B
ydawson@columbiacollege.edu
DAWTON, Dennis ... 215-965-4073. 424 D
academic@moore.edu
DAY, Barton ... 903-923-3302. 486 A
bart.day@tstc.edu
DAY, Dani ... 972-758-3804. 469 G
dday@collin.edu
DAY, Daniel ... 609-258-6108. 304 E
dday@princeton.edu
DAY, David ... 412-536-1070. 420 A
david.day@laroche.edu
DAY, Dennis ... 913-469-8500. 187 J
dday@jccc.edu
DAY, Dionne ... 773-371-5408. 141 D
dday@ctu.edu
DAY, Don ... 817-274-4284. 467 H
DAY, Donald ... 218-335-4285. 256 I
donald.day@lltc.edu
DAY, Edward ... 509-963-1856. 517 F
daye@cwu.edu
DAY, Elaine ... 434-791-5696. 502 D
eday@averett.edu
DAY, Heather ... 815-939-5011. 155 H
hday@olivet.edu
DAY, Ian ... 508-999-8722. 229 A
iday@umassd.edu
DAY, Janet ... 513-861-6400. 390 C
janet.day@myunion.edu
DAY, John, R ... 404-413-2564. 126 E
jday@gsu.edu
DAY, John, T ... 216-397-4207. 381 R
jday@jcu.edu
DAY, Leo ... 817-923-1921. 481 G
lday@swbts.edu
DAY, Mellani, J ... 303-963-3434... 79 C
mday@ccu.edu
DAY, Michelle ... 910-893-1232. 352 K
daym@campbell.edu
DAY, Patricia ... 518-828-4181. 321 C
day@sunycgcc.edu
DAY, Patricia, A ... 570-941-7767. 436 A
patricia.day@scranton.edu
DAY, Patrick ... 209-946-2365... 73 A
pday@pacific.edu
DAY, Rebeckah, J ... 210-436-3727. 479 D
rday@stmarytx.edu
DAY, Rondall, H ... 770-423-6074. 127 N
rday9@kennesaw.edu
DAY, Terri, L ... 817-515-5306. 482 B
terri.day@tccd.edu
DAY, Thelma ... 323-953-4000... 51 G
dayt@lacitycollege.edu
DAY, Thomas, C ... 410-706-7481. 219 C
tday@umaryland.edu
DAY-PERROOTS,
Susan, D ... 304-293-2834. 530 D
sue.day-perroots@mail.wvu.edu
DAYHOFF, Brenda ... 301-846-2481. 214 H
bdayhoff@frederick.edu
DAYLEY, Newell ... 801-863-7359. 497 C
newell.dayley@uvu.edu
DAYTON, Kay ... 615-230-3675. 461 G
kay.dayton@volstate.edu
DAYTON, Lynne ... 334-222-6591..... 5 E
ldayton@lbwcc.edu
DE ALMEIDA, Terry ... 973-642-8732. 307 D
terry.dealmeida@shu.edu
DE ANGELIS, John ... 212-678-3012. 347 G
deangelis@tc.edu
DE ANGULO, Bonnie ... 305-223-4561. 112 B
deangulo@sjvcs.edu
DE ARMOND, Rio ... 239-489-9015. 101 O
rndearmon@edison.edu
DE BEER, Fredrick, C ... 859-323-5079. 200 C
fcdebe1@uky.edu
DE BOER, David ... 616-451-3511. 241 H
ddeboer@davenport.edu
DE BONO, Chad ... 719-336-1517... 82 R
chad.debono@lamarcc.edu
DE BOTTON, Leonard ... 973-278-5400. 314 K
len@berkeleycollege.edu
DE BRUYN, Anthony, P . 512-499-4363. 491 A
adebruyn@utsystem.edu
DE BRUYN, Anthony, P . 434-924-1400. 511 B
apd5b@virginia.edu
DE CAROLIS, Robert, J .. 541-737-2547. 406 A
bob.decarolis@oregonstate.edu
DE CHANT, Richard ... 216-987-3125. 378 D
richard.dechant@tri-c.edu
DE DENUS, Christine ... 315-781-3304. 326 C
dedenus@hws.edu
DE DIOS UNANUE,
Teresa ... 787-720-0596. 547 E
tdedios@atlanticcollege.edu
DE FATIMA LIMA,
Maria ... 615-327-6533. 456 E
mflima@mmc.edu
DE FAZIO, Alice ... 201-200-3317. 303 F
adefazio@njcu.edu
DE FILIPPIS,
Daisy Cocco ... 203-575-8044... 89 B
ddefilippis@nvcc.commnet.edu
DE FINA, Allan ... 201-200-2101. 303 F
adefina@njcu.edu
DE GRAFFENREID,
Ellen ... 781-736-4213. 224 F
edegraff@brandeis.edu
DE GROAT, Arthur, S ... 785-532-0369. 188 A
degroata@ksu.edu
DE GUEVARA,
Maria Elena ... 408-554-5345... 64 M
mdeguevara@scu.edu
DE GUZMAN, Maria, I ... 787-257-7373. 552 H
ac_mguzman@suagm.edu
DE HAHN, Henri ... 619-684-8811... 56 C
hdehahn@newschoolarch.edu
DE HARO, Oscar ... 707-256-7365... 55 F
odeharo@napavalley.edu
DE JESUS, Angela ... 787-864-2222. 550 D
adejesus@inter.edu
DE JESUS, Ramon ... 787-878-5475. 549 L
rdjesus@arecibo.inter.edu
DE JESUS, Sandra ... 787-815-0000. 553 I
sandra.dejesus1@upr.edu
DE JESUS, Victoria ... 787-751-0178. 552 G
ac_vdejesus@suagm.edu
DE JESÚS, José, M ... 787-765-1915. 551 C
jmdejesus@inter.edu
DE JONG, Jinny ... 616-957-6046. 240 M
jinnydejong@calvinseminary.edu
DE JONG, Pamala, S ... 712-722-6488. 177 J
pam.dejong@dordt.edu
DE JONG, Sven, M ... 304-829-7281. 526 D
sdejong@bethanywv.edu
DE KALB, Jenifer ... 503-821-8901. 406 F
jenifer@pnca.edu
DE KLUYVER,
Cornelis, A ... 541-346-3843. 406 D
kees@uoregon.edu
DE KOKAL, Parrilla ... 801-626-8049. 497 D
mdekokal@weber.edu
DE LA CAMARA, Maria . 630-829-6539. 140 B
mdelacamera@ben.edu
DE LA CRUZ, Julio ... 787-834-9595. 553 B
jdelacruz@uaa.edu
DE LA CRUZ-REYES,
Pilar ... 619-477-6310... 70 D
pdelaacruzreyes@usuniversity.edu
DE LA GARZA, Marco ... 818-719-6448... 52 B
delagamj@piercecollege.edu
DE LA GUARDIA,
Teresa, S ... 305-284-2928. 118 F
tdelaguardia@miami.edu
DE LA MOTTE, Dean ... 401-341-2222. 440 C
dean.delamotte@salve.edu
DE LA PENA, Carolyn ... 530-752-6068... 70 J
ctdelapena@ucdavis.edu
DE LA RIVA, Yolanda ... 956-882-8804. 491 D
yolanda.delariva@utb.edu
DE LA ROSA, J. Manuel 915-215-4300. 487 E
jmanuel.delarosa@ttuhsc.edu
DE LA ROSSA, Arnie ... 860-383-5232... 89 F
adelarossa@trcc.commnet.edu
DE LA TORRE, Jorge ... 425-640-1233. 519 D
jorge.delatorre@edcc.edu
DE LA TORRE, Susana .. 510-436-2598... 59 D
sdelatorre@peralta.edu
DE LA TORRE-BURMEISTER,
Rosa ... 575-528-7009. 311 B
rosadela@nmsu.edu
DE LACEY, Lora ... 630-844-5510. 140 A
ldelacey@aurora.edu
DE LAROCHE,
Marilyn, A ... 404-413-1800. 126 E
madelaroche@gsu.edu
DE LATORRE, Adela, I ... 530-752-6866... 70 J
vcstudentaffairs@ucdavis.edu
DE LEEUW, Patricia ... 617-552-3263. 224 A
pat.deleeuw@bc.edu
DE LEO, Joyce ... 617-735-9958. 226 B
deleoj@emmanuel.edu
DE LEON, Dahlia ... 512-892-2640. 481 B
DE LEON, Daniel ... 956-872-5558. 480 I
ddeleon@southtexascollege.edu
DE LEON, Dreidre ... 859-622-2977. 193 P
dreidre.deleon@eku.edu
DE LEON, Jane ... 916-484-8307... 53 A
deleonj@arc.losrios.edu
DE LEON, Josephine ... 505-277-2611. 312 F
jdeleon@unm.edu
DE LEONARDIS,
David, J ... 614-885-5585. 388 C
ddeleon@pcj.edu
DE LISI, Richard ... 848-932-7496. 306 B
richard.delisi@gse.rutgers.edu
DE LOS REYES, Jose ... 415-749-4519... 62 G
jdelosreyes@sfai.edu
DE LUCA, Anne ... 510-642-2261... 70 I
adeluca@berkeley.edu
DE LUCA, James, P ... 843-953-6861. 442 A
jdeluca@citadel.edu
DE MARCO, Thomas ... 610-519-4155. 436 F
thomas.demarco@villanova.edu
DE MILIA, Frank ... 712-324-5061. 181 G
fdemilia@nwicc.edu
DE NOBLE, Timothy ... 785-532-5950. 188 A
tdenoble@ksu.edu
DE OCAMPO, Erlinda ... 323-415-4163... 51 F
deocamen@elac.edu
DE OLIVEIRA, Japhet ... 269-471-3211. 239 D
japhet@andrews.edu
DE PAULA, Anna ... 201-761-7450. 306 L
adepaula@saintpeters.edu
DE PIANO, Frank ... 954-262-5796. 109 K
depiano@nova.edu
DE ROSE, John ... 203-287-3034... 90 H
paier.fad@snet.net
DE ROSE, Robert, C ... 815-836-5201. 150 H
derosero@lewisu.edu
DE ROUEN, Stephani ... 615-547-1236. 454 A
sderouen@cumberland.edu
DE RUBERTIS, Andrew ... 414-410-4221. 532 B
aderubertis@stritch.edu
DE SANTIAGO, Mildred . 787-892-5131. 551 A
mdsantiago@sg.inter.edu
DE SHAW, Lynnette ... 360-475-7300. 521 H
ldeshaw@olympic.edu
DE SOUZA, Priscila ... 650-543-3786... 54 C
priscila.desouza@menlo.edu
DE SPAIN, Donna ... 630-844-3840. 140 A
ddespain@aurora.edu
DE VERSE, Nancy ... 360-538-4030. 520 B
ndeverse@ghc.edu
DE VINNE, Christine ... 410-532-5321. 217 E
cdevinne@ndm.edu
DE YAMPERT, Fredi ... 906-487-7306. 242 G
fredi.deyampert@finlandia.edu
DE YOUNG, Gene ... 541-684-7219. 405 C
gdeyoung@nwcu.edu
DEACON, Charles, A ... 202-687-3600... 95 E
deacon@georgetown.edu
DEACY, Deborah, S ... 909-593-3511... 72 E
ddeacy@laverne.edu
DEADWYLER, JR.,
Derrick ... 302-831-2113... 94 B
rdeadwy@udel.edu
DEAHL, Anne, D ... 414-288-6786. 534 B
anne.deahl@marquette.edu
DEAHL, Kathy, S ... 208-732-6201. 138 B
kdeahl@csi.edu
DEAHL, Robert, J ... 414-288-3154. 534 B
robert.deahl@marquette.edu
DEAKIN, Spencer, F ... 301-687-4234. 220 C
sdeakin@frostburg.edu
DEAL, Carline ... 276-656-0216. 513 D
cdeal@patrickhenry.edu
DEAL, Charley, T ... 731-881-7610. 463 E
cdeal@utm.edu
DEAL, Gregory, A ... 443-412-2391. 215 C
gdeal@harford.edu
DEAL, Josh ... 231-439-6349. 247 H
jdeal@ncmich.edu
DEAL, Kelley ... 252-443-4011. 362 D
kdeal@nashcc.edu
DEAL, Lisa ... 352-392-1331. 116 A
lsd@ufl.edu
DEAL, Pamela ... 912-478-8748. 126 C
pdeal@georgiasouthern.edu
DEAL, Shannon ... 731-881-7750. 463 E
sdeal@utm.edu
DEAL, Tammy ... 606-589-3086. 196 F
tdeal0002@kctcs.edu
DEAL, Todd ... 912-478-1435. 126 C
stdeal@georgiasouthern.edu
DEAN, Adam, S ... 417-667-8181. 273 A
adean@cottey.edu
DEAN, Amy ... 508-373-9534. 223 A
amy.dean@becker.edu
DEAN, Barbara ... 502-942-8503. 199 G
bsdean@sullivan.edu
DEAN, Becky ... 413-545-2211. 228 F
becky.dean@chancellor.umass.edu
DEAN, Bill ... 806-742-3641. 487 D
bill.dean@ttu.edu
DEAN, Christa ... 410-888-9048. 216 D
cdean@muih.edu
DEAN, Delores ... 850-599-3700. 114 K
delores.dean@famu.edu
DEAN, Denis, J ... 972-883-6852. 491 E
denis.dean@utdallas.edu
DEAN, Don ... 914-323-5219. 330 B
donald.dean@mville.edu
DEAN, Gayle ... 505-566-3204. 311 I
deang@sanjuancollege.edu
DEAN, James, H ... 941-359-7524. 111 O
jdean@ringling.edu
DEAN, James, S ... 412-531-4433. 414 C
info@deantech.edu
DEAN, JR., James, W ... 919-962-2198. 368 D
deanjr@email.unc.edu
DEAN, Jeffrey ... 502-272-8014. 192 E
jdean@bellarmine.edu
DEAN, Jeffrey, A ... 317-274-4417. 168 D
jadean1@iu.edu
DEAN, Jeffrey, L ... 856-225-2747. 306 C
jldean@camden.rutgers.edu
DEAN, Jerome ... 617-928-4500. 234 E
jdean@mountida.edu
DEAN, JR., Joe ... 205-226-4936..... 2 C
jdean@bsc.edu
DEAN, John, E ... 904-620-2800. 116 B
jdean@unf.edu
DEAN, Johnie, E ... 859-846-5779. 197 I
jdean@midway.edu
DEAN, Karol ... 412-365-2991. 412 K
kdean@chatham.edu
DEAN, Kathleen, L ... 216-397-1972. 381 R
kdean@jcu.edu
DEAN, Kathy, L ... 251-442-2215..... 9 A
kdean@umobile.edu
DEAN, Kenneth, D ... 573-882-6597. 283 C
deank@missouri.edu
DEAN, Kevin ... 610-436-2996. 430 A
kdean@wcupa.edu
DEAN, Kim ... 270-831-9707. 195 D
kim.dean@kctcs.edu
DEAN, Krystin ... 706-379-5237. 134 L
kndean@yhc.edu
DEAN, Laurie ... 575-492-2108. 312 M
ldean@usw.edu
DEAN, LeAnn ... 320-589-6173. 264 F
deanl@morris.umn.edu
DEAN, Lynne ... 210-486-4135. 464 J
ldean12@alamo.edu
DEAN, Mark, E ... 620-792-9235. 184 F
deanm@bartonccc.edu
DEAN, Marvin ... 810-766-4041. 239 H
marvin.dean@baker.edu
DEAN, Mary Anne ... 781-280-3580. 232 B
deanm@middlesex.mass.edu
DEAN, Paul, M ... 603-862-1427. 298 C
paul.dean@unh.edu
DEAN, Russell, K ... 304-293-7119. 530 D
rkdean@mail.wvu.edu
DEAN, Samuel, J ... 614-885-5585. 388 C
sdean@pcj.edu
DEAN, Sheryl, L ... 810-766-4062. 239 G
sheryl.dean@baker.edu
DEAN, Takem ... 973-684-5571. 304 B
tdean@pccc.edu
DEAN, Tanya ... 972-524-3341. 481 H
DEAN, Thomas, K ... 319-335-1995. 175 I
thomas-k-dean@uiowa.edu
DEAN, Troy ... 541-684-7293. 405 C
tdean@nwcu.edu
DEAN, Wanda, H ... 540-231-7951. 515 C
wdean@vt.edu
DEAN, Willow ... 316-677-9400. 191 E
wdean@watc.edu
DEAN-BAAR, Susan ... 314-516-6066. 283 E
deanbaar@umsl.edu
DEAN-KELLY, Louise ... 315-792-7296. 346 C
louise.deankelly@sunyit.edu
DEANE, Lynne, P ... 804-289-8064. 510 L
ldeane@richmond.edu
DEANE, Robert ... 270-745-2548. 200 G
robert.deane@wku.edu
DEANER, Kathy, F ... 954-308-2601... 98 G
kdeaner@aii.edu
DEANGELIS, Bill, J ... 770-720-9102. 130 G
wjd@reinhardt.edu
DEANGELIS, Brian ... 580-559-5604. 395 F
bdeangls@ecok.edu
DEANGELIS, Toni ... 719-846-5520... 85 H
toni.deangelis@trinidadstate.edu
DEANGELO, OFM CONV,
Jude ... 202-319-5575... 94 G
deangelo@cua.edu
DEANGELO, Mary ... 413-748-3757. 236 I
mdeangelo@springfieldcollege.edu
DEANNA, Linda ... 312-996-4857. 161 D
ldeanna@uic.edu

DEANS, Beverly .... 919-735-5151. 364 H bdeans@waynecc.edu
DEAR, Carley .... 601-857-3357. 267 A carley.dear@hindscc.edu
DEARBORN, Philip, E .... 717-560-8233. 421 A pdearborn@lbc.edu
DEARCORN, Casey .... 307-754-6084. 543 G Casey.Dearcorn@northwestcollege.edu
DEARING, Barbara .... 503-838-8094. 406 E dearingb@wou.edu
DEARSMAN, Matt .... 630-353-7049. 144 A mdearsman@devry.edu
DEARSTYNE, Kenneth ..... 610-607-6265. 431 D kdearstyne@racc.edu
DEARTH, John, C .... 716-673-3251. 342 A john.dearth@fredonia.edu
DEAS, Edwin .... 760-773-2511... 40 F edeas@collegeofthedesert.edu
DEASE, Dennis, J .... 651-962-6500. 265 C djdease@stthomas.edu
DEASE, Mary Ann .... 203-837-8248... 88 B deasem@wcsu.edu
DEASON, Michael .... 972-860-4670. 470 G mdeason@dcccd.edu
DEATER, Kate .... 814-262-6483. 427 C kdeater@pennhighlands.edu
DEATHERAGE, Eric .... 417-455-5610. 273 E EricDeatherage@crowder.edu
DEATHERAGE, Janet .... 312-915-6512. 151 H jdeathe@luc.edu
DEATLEY, Carry .... 304-929-5010. 528 D cdeatley@newriver.edu
DEATLEY, Janeen, S .... 937-393-3431. 389 B jdeatley@sscc.edu
DEATON, Amy .... 931-221-6131. 459 B deatona@apsu.edu
DEATON, Andrea, D .... 405-325-1646. 401 B adeaton@ou.edu
DEATON, Brady, J .... 573-882-3387. 283 C deatonb@missouri.edu
DEATON, Bruce .... 313-487-7017. 202 F bruce.deaton@lacollege.edu
DEATON, Judy .... 949-675-4451... 48 G interior_designer@msn.com
DEATON, Sharon .... 949-675-4451... 48 G interior_designer@msn.com
DEATS, Jacqueline .... 714-997-6851... 38 A deats@chapman.edu
DEATS, John .... 432-685-4726. 476 G jdeats@midland.edu
DEAVER, Christy .... 828-339-4406. 364 B christyd@southwesterncc.edu
DEAVER, David .... 254-647-3375. 478 H ddeaver@rangercollege.edu
DEAVER, Robin .... 910-678-8484. 360 D deaverr@faytechcc.edu
DEBAHA, Stephanie .... 703-821-8570. 510 B sdebaha@stratford.edu
DEBARROS, Angelia .... 210-485-0374. 464 I adebarros1@alamo.edu
DEBASIO, Nancy .... 816-995-2810. 280 I nancy.debasio@researchcollege.edu
DEBASIO, Nancy, O .... 816-995-2815. 280 G nancy.debasio@researchcollege.edu
DEBAUN, Amy .... 860-297-2305... 91 F amy.debaun@trincoll.edu
DEBEAUCHAMP, Debbie 425-739-8232. 520 K deborah.debeauchamp@lwtech.edu
DEBEER, Dean .... 718-779-1430. 336 D ddb@plazacollege.edu
DEBELA, Kenesa .... 773-256-0716. 152 B kdebela@lstc.edu
DEBELLIS, Ronald, A ...... 518-694-7319. 313 B ronalda.debellis@acphs.edu
DEBENEDETTI, Pablo ...... 609-258-5480. 304 E pdebene@princeton.edu
DEBENEDICTS, Elissa ...... 217-757-1190. 313 H edebenedicts@funeraleducation.org
DEBENEDITTIS, Lisa .... 212-229-8947. 332 E debenedl@newschool.edu
DEBERNARDI, Maureen . 617-779-4369. 236 B admissionsandrecords@sjs.edu
DEBERRY, Marilyn .... 803-376-5737. 441 A myoung@allenuniversity.edu
DEBERRY, Marilyn, C ..... 803-376-5827. 441 A myoung@allenuniversity.edu
DEBERRY, Ron .... 757-826-1883. 502 G execvp@bcva.edu
DEBIAK, Lauren .... 816-501-4232. 280 I lauren.debiak@rockhurst.edu
DEBIAS, Patti .... 773-256-0728. 152 B pdebias@lstc.edu
DEBLASIO, Denise, M .... 973-655-4340. 303 D deblasiod@mail.montclair.edu
DEBLOIS, Benjamin, A .... 910-755-7403. 358 D debloisb@brunswickcc.edu
DEBOARD, John .... 580-581-2237. 394 G jdeboard@cameron.edu
DEBOCK, Devin .... 918-293-4944. 398 B devin.debock@okstate.edu
DEBOER, Keith .... 616-222-1247. 241 F keith.deboer@cornerstone.edu
DEBOER-MORAN, Jason 651-641-8766. 255 B moran@csp.edu
DEBONO, Chad .... 719-336-6660... 82 R chad.debono@lamarcc.edu
DEBORD, Bonnie, H .... 770-720-5502. 130 G bhd@reinhardt.edu
DEBOSE, Angela, W .... 813-974-4018. 116 C awdebose@usf.edu
DEBOSE, Henry .... 804-524-5992. 515 D hdebose@vsu.edu
DEBOSKEY, Brian .... 303-876-7100. 450 G bdeboskey@national.edu
DEBOW, Arthur .... 503-297-5544. 405 D adebow@ocac.edu
DEBOWER, Lore .... 508-362-2131. 231 D ldebower@capecod.edu
DEBRAGA, Angie .... 775-775-2231. 294 F angie.debraga@gbcnv.edu
DEBRAGGIO, Michael, J 315-859-4654. 325 E mdebragg@hamilton.edu
DEBRITO, Joannie, L ...... 303-963-3378... 79 C jdebrito@ccu.edu
DEBRIZZI, JR., Thomas, A .... 203-576-4690... 91 G tdebriz@bridgeport.edu
DEBROCK, Larry .... 217-333-2747. 162 A ldebrock@business.uiuc.edu
DEBRUM, David .... 692-625-6416. 546 F ddebrum@cmi.edu
DEBS, Daisy .... 305-717-7000. 105 M
DEBUHR, Larry .... 812-866-6846. 166 C debuhr@hanover.edu
DEBURE, Olivier .... 727-864-8421. 101 N debureoc@eckerd.edu
DEBURRO, Jennifer .... 207-602-2132. 213 A jdeburro@une.edu
DEBUS, Casey .... 307-532-8311. 542 a casey.debus@ewc.wy.edu
DEBUSK, Frankie .... 423-636-7300. 462 E fdebusk@tusculum.edu
DEC, Ted .... 631-687-5155. 339 B tdec@sjcny.edu
DECAIRE, Maryann .... 847-578-8810. 157 F maryann.decaire@rosalindfranklin.edu
DECAIRE, Maryann .... 847-578-3217. 157 F maryann.decaire@rosalindfranklin.edu
DECALO, Ruth .... 212-678-8915. 328 A rudecalo@jtsa.edu
DECAMILLIS, Susan .... 231-995-1014. 248 B sdecamillis@nmc.edu
DECAPUA, Lynn .... 732-987-2729. 302 B decapual@georgian.edu
DECARBO, Diane, M ...... 724-658-1938. 411 C diane.decarbo@bc3.edu
DECARIE, Linette .... 617-353-2256. 224 D decarie@bu.edu
DECARLI, Kristen .... 203-773-8578... 87 G kdecarli@albertus.edu
DECARLO, Robert, L .... 516-877-3184. 313 A decarlo@adelphi.edu
DECAROLIS, Donna .... 215-895-1795. 415 B donna.marie.decarolis@drexel.edu
DECARVALHO, Fatima .... 973-655-7818. 303 D decarvalhf@mail.montclair.edu
DECASTRO-SALLIS, Kishma .... 412-397-6238. 431 I sallis@rmu.edu
DECATUR, Jane .... 508-626-4585. 230 A jdecatur@framingham.edu
DECATUR, Sean .... 740-427-5111. 382 J decatur@kenyon.edu
DECATUR, William .... 401-454-6474. 440 A wdecatur@risd.edu
DECELLE, Jerry, L .... 518-564-2082. 344 B decellejl@plattsburgh.edu
DECENA, Peter .... 408-924-2222... 36 A peter.decena@sjsu.edu
DECENZO, David, A .... 843-349-2001. 442 E ddecenzo@coastal.edu
DECHANT, Bill .... 828-565-4027. 361 B wmdechant@haywood.edu
DECHANT, Margaret .... 361-825-5951. 483 F margaret.dechant@tamucc.edu
DECHARINTE, Janeen ..... 815-838-0500. 150 H decharja@lewisu.edu
DECHIARO, Thomas .... 203-837-9800... 88 B dechiarot@wcsu.edu
DECHILLO, Neal .... 978-542-6630. 230 E ndechillo@salemstate.edu
DECICCIO, Albert, C .... 802-447-6333. 500 D adeciccio@svc.edu
DECICCO, Darlene .... 631-656-2134. 324 F darlene.decicco@ftc.edu
DECK, Joseph, G .... 210-434-6711. 477 N jgdeck@lake.ollusa.edu
DECKER, Amber .... 859-442-1147. 195 B amber.decker@kctcs.edu
DECKER, Ann .... 772-462-7240. 106 P adecker@irsc.edu
DECKER, Barbara, Q .... 515-643-6601. 181 A bdecker@mercydesmoines.org
DECKER, Blake .... 405-585-4102. 397 C blake.decker@okbu.edu
DECKER, Christy .... 518-828-4181. 321 C christy.decker@sunycgcc.edu
DECKER, David, R .... 614-947-6017. 380 A david.decker@franklin.edu
DECKER, Douglas .... 724-983-0700. 421 G ddecker@laurel.edu
DECKER, Douglas, S ...... 724-439-4900. 421 F ddecker@laurel.edu
DECKER, Kim .... 334-244-3636..... 2 A kdecker@aum.edu
DECKER, Nancy .... 724-983-0700. 421 G ndecker@laurel.edu
DECKER, Nancy, M .... 724-439-4900. 421 F ndecker@laurel.edu
DECKER, Pat .... 913-469-8500. 187 J pdecker5@jccc.edu
DECKER, Paul, W .... 818-767-0888... 76 K paul.decker@woodbury.edu
DECKER, Stephanie .... 973-684-6868. 304 B sdecker@pccc.edu
DECKER, Steven .... 715-468-2815. 541 F steven.decker@witc.edu
DECKER, Susan .... 812-535-5138. 172 F sdecker@smwc.edu
DECKER, Timothy .... 845-298-0755. 323 C tdecker@sunydutchess.edu
DECKLER, Dan .... 330-684-8940. 390 F dcd@uakron.edu
DECKLER, Daniel, B .... 330-684-8761. 390 E dcd@uakron.edu
DECLEENE, Catherine ..... 317-738-8090. 165 I cdecleene@franklincollege.edu
DECLUE, Gary .... 217-641-4999. 148 M declueg@jwcc.edu
DECLUE, Stephanie .... 816-415-7606. 285 C declues@william.jewell.edu
DECMAN, Mike .... 815-740-3427. 162 F mdecman@stfrancis.edu
DECOCK, Murray .... 315-228-7489. 320 F mdecock@colgate.edu
DECOLFMACKER, Robert, J .... 207-985-7976. 210 G robertdecolfmacker@landingschool.edu
DECONCILIS, Patricia, A . 724-653-2213. 415 A pdeconcilis@dec.edu
DECONINCK, Lori .... 603-668-2211. 297 I l.deconinck@snhu.edu
DECONNO, David .... 518-580-5719. 341 A ddecanno@skidmore.edu
DECONTI, Merlin, A .... 401-598-4700. 439 B mdeconti@jwu.edu
DECORDOVA, Endia .... 860-512-2903... 88 G edecordova@manchestercc.edu
DECOSTA, Jean .... 805-756-5198... 32 F jdecosta@calpoly.edu
DECOSTA, Melvin .... 808-735-4792. 135 D security@chaminade.edu
DECOSTER, Patrice .... 518-587-2100. 346 A pat.decoster@esc.edu
DECOTEAU, Steve .... 701-477-7862. 373 B sdecoteau@tm.edu
DECOUDREAUX, Alecia, A .... 510-430-2094... 54 F adecoudreaux@mills.edu
DECOURCY, Alan .... 513-244-4487. 377 G alan_decourcy@mail.msj.edu
DECOURSEY, Paul, A ..... 515-574-1055. 179 D decoursey@iowacentral.edu
DECOY, Dirk .... 740-695-9500. 374 H ddecoy@belmontcollege.edu
DECRISTO, James .... 336-734-2862. 369 D decristoj@uncsa.edu
DECROSTA, Tony .... 970-491-6947... 80 I tony.decrosta@colostate.edu
DEDE, Brenda, S .... 814-393-2337. 428 C bdede@clarion.edu
DEDEO, Patrick .... 973-720-2224. 308 I dedeop@wpunj.edu
DEDIEMAR, Jeanette .... 850-644-2466. 115 C jdediemar@fsu.edu
DEDIOS, Paul .... 714-484-7335... 56 E pdedios@cypresscollege.edu
DEDMAN, Tony .... 615-547-7610. 454 A tdedman@cumberland.edu
DEDOMINICIS, H. Ken ... 225-768-1754. 206 D ken@ololcollege.edu
DEE, Edward .... 718-779-1430. 336 D edee@plazacollege.edu
DEE, Kay, C .... 812-877-8502. 172 C dee@rose-hulman.edu
DEE, Shawn, G .... 336-334-4822. 360 G sgdee@gtcc.edu
DEE, Tina .... 231-777-0660. 247 G tina.dee@muskegoncc.edu
DEEB, Bassam, M .... 716-826-1200. 348 G deebb@trocaire.edu
DEEDRICK, Gary, A .... 864-242-5100. 441 D
DEEDS, Cher .... 330-684-8952. 390 F cher@uakron.edu
DEEDS, Sarene .... 417-873-7869. 273 H sdeeds@drury.edu
DEEDS, William, C .... 712-274-5103. 181 B deeds@morningside.edu
DEEG, Matthew .... 812-866-7081. 166 C deeg@hanover.edu
DEEGAN, Robert, P .... 760-744-1150... 58 D rdeegan@palomar.edu
DEEGAN, Rosemary, L ... 610-921-7202. 409 A rdeegan@alb.edu
DEEGEN, Lynn .... 601-928-6212. 268 C lynn.deegen@mgccc.edu
DEEHAN, Theresa, L .... 973-761-9746. 307 C theresa.deehan@shu.edu
DEEK, Fadi, P .... 973-596-3220. 303 G fadi.deek@njit.edu
DEEL, Connie .... 785-594-8362. 184 C connie.deel@bakeru.edu
DEEL, Susan, M .... 989-463-7348. 239 B deel@alma.edu
DEEM, Marie .... 412-536-1128. 420 A marie.deem@laroche.edu
DEEN, Candace .... 717-872-3771. 429 D candace.deen@millersville.edu
DEEN, Mary Stella .... 845-257-3520. 342 B deenm@newpaltz.edu
DEEN, Michael .... 903-813-2306. 466 H mdeen@austincollege.edu
DEER, Joe, W .... 308-635-6145. 293 E deerj234@wncc.edu
DEER, Susan .... 845-574-4000. 338 B
DEES, Andriel .... 715-425-3833. 537 E andriel.dees@uwrf.edu
DEES, Andriel .... 715-425-3711. 537 E andriel.dees@uwrf.edu
DEES, Charles .... 973-596-8293. 303 G charles.dees@njit.edu
DEESE, Nicole .... 318-869-5147. 201 H ndeese@centenary.edu
DEESE, Phyllis .... 903-823-3451. 482 D phyllis.deese@texarkanacollege.edu
DEESE, Todd .... 704-403-3218. 352 J todd.deese@carolinashealthcare.org
DEESS, Eugene, P .... 973-596-3110. 303 G deess@njit.edu
DEETER, Daniel, P .... 574-284-4543. 172 G ddeeter@saintmarys.edu
DEETZ, Kristi, R .... 812-888-4358. 174 F kdeetz@vinu.edu
DEFA, Dennis .... 406-994-3651. 287 B dennis.defa@montana.edu
DEFALCO, Ron, E .... 713-718-7586. 473 C ron.defalco@hccs.edu
DEFALUSSY, George .... 607-735-1978. 323 H gdefalussy@elmira.edu
DEFARIA, Lisa .... 619-477-6310... 70 D ldefaria@usuniversity.edu
DEFATTA, Jerry .... 601-266-5013. 270 E jerry.defatta@usm.edu
DEFEIS, Evelyn .... 973-684-5900. 304 B cdefeis@pccc.edu
DEFELICE, Robert, A .... 781-891-2256. 223 C rdefelice@bentley.edu
DEFEO, Gregory .... 412-809-5100. 430 H defeo.greg@pti.edu
DEFEO, Joseph .... 203-254-4025... 89 I jdefeo@fairfield.edu
DEFFENBAUGH, Cynthia, B .... 804-289-8438. 510 L cdeffenb@richmond.edu
DEFOE, Richard .... 504-278-6230. 203 F rdefoe@nunez.edu
DEFOOR, Keith .... 706-379-5156. 134 L kdefoor@yhc.edu
DEFORD, J. Kevin .... 423-652-4859. 455 I jkdeford@king.edu
DEFORD, Linda .... 509-279-6258. 518 E linda.deford@scc.spokane.edu
DEFORE, Matt .... 205-726-4021..... 6 F mdefore@samford.edu
DEFOREST, Kristin, A ...... 607-746-4590. 345 G deforeka@delhi.edu
DEFORREST, Kelly .... 206-934-7962. 523 A kelly.deforrest@seattlecolleges.edu
DEFRANCIS, Robert .... 304-214-8820. 528 G rdefrancis@wvncc.edu
DEFRANCO, Jeff .... 530-541-4660... 50 D defranco@ltcc.edu
DEFRANCO, Thomas .... 860-486-3813... 92 A thomas.defranco@uconn.edu
DEFRATES, Bruce .... 509-359-6329. 519 C bdefrates@ewu.edu
DEFREECE, Michele, T .... 607-746-4652. 345 G defreemt@delhi.edu
DEFREECE, Perri, D .... 607-746-4700. 345 G defreepd@delhi.edu
DEFREITAS, Jack .... 660-263-3900. 272 A
DEFRIES, Brandi .... 507-457-1750. 264 A bdefries@smumn.edu

DEGAIN, Sabrina .... 336-506-4161. 357 M
sabrina.degain@alamancecc.edu
DEGAISH, Ann .... 361-825-2612. 483 F
ann.degaish@tamucc.edu
DEGAZON, Karen .... 212-938-5654. 345 C
kdegazon@sunyopt.edu
DEGEN, Bruno .... 718-270-6110. 319 A
bdegen@mec.cuny.edu
DEGEN, Charlotte .... 413-662-5231. 230 C
charlotte.degen@mcla.edu
DEGENHART,
Mary Louise .... 314-367-8700. 281 C
mary.degenhart@stlcop.edu
DEGEORGE, Christine, C 941-359-7645. 111 O
ccarnegi@ringling.edu
DEGER, Beth .... 937-328-6023. 377 A
degerb@clarkstate.edu
DEGERMAN, Roger, E .... 218-299-3645. 255 A
degerman@cord.edu
DEGEUS, Marilyn, J .... 816-654-7262. 275 K
mdegeus@kcumb.edu
DEGIOIA, John (Jack), J 202-687-4134... 95 E
president@georgetown.edu
DEGIOVANNI, Kim .... 301-387-3040. 214 I
kim.degiovanni@garrettcollege.edu
DEGIOVINE, Christopher 518-454-5293. 321 A
frchris@strose.edu
DEGN, Jason .... 402-399-2431. 289 A
jdegn@csm.edu
DEGNAN, James, W .... 215-204-4643. 433 K
james.degnan@temple.edu
DEGNAN, Steven .... 734-995-7502. 241 E
security@cuaa.edu
DEGNAN, Susan .... 218-262-6710. 258 G
susandegnan@hibbing.edu
DEGRAFF, April .... 660-831-4172. 278 I
degraffa@moval.edu
DEGRAFFENREID,
Pamela .... 828-227-7346. 369 E
degraffen@wcu.edu
DEGRANGE, Karen, A ..... 812-877-8285. 172 C
karen.degrange@rose-hulman.edu
DEGRAW, Julie .... 419-358-3248. 374 J
degrawj@bluffton.edu
DEGRAW, Spencer .... 801-524-1947. 495 O
sdegraw2@ldsbc.edu
DEGROAT, Kevin .... 718-405-3400. 320 G
kevin.degroat@mountsaintvincent.edu
DEGROFT, Michael .... 717-391-3510. 434 A
degroft@stevenscollege.edu
DEGROOTE, David, K ..... 320-308-2192. 261 B
dkdegroote@stcloudstate.edu
DEHAAN, Laurens .... 415-433-9200... 65 C
ldehaan@saybrook.edu
DEHAEMERS, Jennifer .... 816-235-1143. 283 D
dehaemersj@umkc.edu
DEHART, Dan, J .... 818-779-8557... 50 A
ddehart@kingsuniversity.edu
DEHART, Joe .... 515-964-6279. 177 B
jcdehart@dmacc.edu
DEHART, Robert .... 402-363-5686. 293 I
bdehart@york.edu
DEHAVEN, Barbara .... 201-216-8762. 307 E
bdehaven@stevens.edu
DEHAVEN, Jane .... 515-244-4221. 175 C
dehavenj@aib.edu
DEHAY, Galen .... 864-646-2037. 447 D
gdehay@tctc.edu
DEHAYES, Donald, H ..... 401-874-4410. 440 D
ddehayes@uri.edu
DEHGHANI, Mo .... 201-216-8911. 307 E
mo.dehghani@stevens.edu
DEHN, Paula .... 270-852-3117. 197 B
pdehn@kwc.edu
DEHNE, Nathan, D .... 920-565-1588. 533 R
dehneND@lakeland.edu
DEHOYOS, Diane, N .... 915-747-5601. 492 A
dndehoyos@utep.edu
DEI ROSSI, Gary .... 209-468-9155... 69 F
DEI TOS, Nina Cecelia ... 570-504-9619. 413 B
DEIBERT, Glenn .... 912-287-5827. 130 B
gdeibert@okefenokeetech.edu
DEICHEN, Michael, G ..... 407-823-3702. 115 E
michael.deichen@ucf.edu
DEICHMANN, Wendy, J . 937-529-2201. 390 D
wjdedwards@united.edu
DEIERLING, Tara .... 573-592-4248. 285 D
tdeierli@williamwoods.edu
DEIGHTON, Joe .... 251-380-3023..... 7 D
jdeighton@shc.edu
DEIGNAN, Kathleen .... 609-258-5431. 304 E
kdeignan@princeton.edu
DEIKE, Randall .... 212-998-4553. 334 D
randall.deike@nyu.edu
DEIKE, Terri .... 903-233-3769. 475 J
terrideike@letu.edu
DEINES, Tye, A .... 603-526-3741. 295 I
tye.deines@colby-sawyer.edu
DEINNOCENTIIS, Maria .. 212-517-0482. 330 E
mdeinnocentiis@mmm.edu
DEIS, Michael .... 678-466-4500. 123 A
michaeldeis@clayton.edu
DEITCHMAN, Jay .... 518-629-7567. 326 G
j.deitchman@hvcc.edu
DEITEMEYER, Kandi, W . 252-335-0821. 359 F
kdeitemeyer@albemarle.edu
DEITRICK, Becky .... 570-372-4015. 433 H
deitrick@susqu.edu
DEITS, Will .... 805-986-5821... 74 G
wdeits@vcccd.edu
DEJESUS, Javier .... 787-841-2000. 552 B
javier_dejesus@pucpr.edu
DEJESUS, Lisa .... 229-430-3504. 120 A
ldejesus@albanytech.edu
DEJESUS-RUEFF,
Richard .... 585-385-8229. 338 H
rdejesus@sjfc.edu
DEJOICE, Mary Jo .... 304-637-1359. 526 E
dejoicem@dewv.edu
DEJONG, Carol .... 616-395-7760. 244 A
cdejong@hope.edu
DEJONG, David, N .... 412-624-4228. 435 C
dejong@pitt.edu
DEJORGE, Alex, R .... 787-258-1501. 548 H
aRdejorge@columbiaco.edu
DEJOY, Jennifer .... 207-326-2256. 211 D
jennifer.dejoy@mma.edu
DEJTHAI, Eddie .... 239-280-2507... 98 K
eddie.dejthai@avemaria.edu
DEJULIO, Rosemary, A .. 718-817-3009. 324 G
dejulio@fordham.edu
DEJULIO, Thomas, E ...... 718-817-3111. 324 G
tdejulio@fordham.edu
DEKAN, Doug, D .... 715-833-6238. 539 J
ddekan@cvtc.edu
DEKAY, Amy .... 716-880-2177. 330 F
adekay@medaille.edu
DEKAY, Amy, M .... 716-880-2224. 330 F
amy.marie.dekay@medaille.edu
DEKAY, Todd .... 717-358-6021. 416 J
todd.dekay@fandm.edu
DEKEYSER, Georgia .... 907-786-4048... 10 H
DEKKER, Jan .... 559-638-3641... 69 A
jan.dekker@reedleycollege.edu
DEKKER NETTLEMAN,
Mary .... 605-357-1309. 451 F
med@usd.edu
DEKLOTZ, Steve .... 503-493-6286. 402 J
sdeklotz@cu-portland.edu
DEKOSKY, Steven, T ...... 434-924-0311. 511 B
sd3zc@virginia.edu
DEKREY, Susan .... 845-437-7400. 349 G
sudekrey@vassar.edu
DEKRUIF, Kimberly .... 909-469-5342... 76 B
kdekruif@westernu.edu
DEKSHENIEKS, Craig ..... 770-426-2833. 128 D
craig.dekshenieks@life.edu
DEL BALZO, Mary Beth . 914-831-0463. 321 B
mdelbalzo@cw.edu
DEL BELLO, Wendy .... 281-756-3600. 465 D
wdelbello@alvincollege.edu
DEL BELLO, Wendy .... 281-756-3500. 465 D
wdebello@alvincollege.edu
DEL BELLO, Wendy .... 281-756-3686. 465 D
wdelbello@alvincollege.edu
DEL CERRO, Gerardo ..... 212-353-4321. 321 F
cerro@cooper.edu
DEL CONTE,
Christopher .... 817-257-7710. 484 I
c.delconte@tcu.edu
DEL GIUDICE,
Tristan, S .... 814-641-3390. 419 H
delgiut@juniata.edu
DEL PINO, Jennifer .... 515-961-1530. 182 E
jennifer.delpino@simpson.edu
DEL RIO, Esteban .... 619-260-7455... 73 I
edelrio@sandiego.edu
DEL RIO-MORALES,
Ricardo .... 787-725-6500. 547 H
consejoactivo@gmail.com
DEL ROSARIO, Dativa .... 510-436-2407... 59 D
ddelrosario@peralta.edu
DEL ROSARIO, Diana ..... 216-987-5027. 378 D
diana.del-rosario@tri-c.edu
DEL TONDO, Bruce .... 719-587-7227... 78 B
bdeltond@adams.edu
DEL TORO, Debra .... 210-829-6001. 490 A
ddeltoro@uiwtx.edu
DEL VALLE, Armando ..... 787-744-1060. 551 J
adelvalle@mechtech.edu
DEL VALLE, Deb .... 513-745-3877. 393 H
delvalle@xavier.edu
DEL VALLE, Wilfredo ...... 787-863-2390. 550 C
wilfredo.delvalle@fajardo.inter.edu
DEL VECCHIO, Ron .... 218-281-8109. 264 E
dsvedars@umn.edu
DELA CRUZ, Janis .... 808-847-9873. 136 G
janisdc@hawaii.edu
DELA ROSA,
Christopher .... 443-412-2000. 215 C
DELA ROSA,
Christopher .... 505-428-1000. 311 J
christopher.delarosa@sfcc.edu
DELA TEJA, Magdalena .. 817-515-6203. 482 B
magdalena.delateja@tccd.edu
DELABY, Lisa .... 530-895-2937... 30 F
delabyli@butte.edu
DELACASTRO, Rick .... 307-766-2215. 543 I
rdelacas@uwyo.edu
DELACH, Ruth .... 412-809-5100. 430 H
delach.ruth@pti.edu
DELAET, Lee .... 314-889-4539. 274 E
ldelaet@fontbonne.edu
DELAGUERRA, Christy ... 201-327-8877. 301 G
DELAHAYA, Richard .... 615-963-5331. 459 E
rdelahay@tnstate.edu
DELAHOUSSAYE,
Yasmin .... 323-241-5273... 52 C
delahoyj@lasc.edu
DELAHOUSSAYE,
Yasmin .... 213-891-2279... 51 E
delahoyj@email.laccd.edu
DELAHOYDE, Theresa .... 402-481-8843. 288 H
theresa.delahoyde@bryanhealthcollege.edu
DELAHUNT, Tom .... 515-271-2092. 177 K
tom.delahunt@drake.edu
DELAHUNTY, Jennifer .... 740-427-5778. 382 J
delahuntyj@kenyon.edu
DELAIN, Cindy .... 559-730-6265... 40 I
cindyd@cos.edu
DELALUE-KING,
Shontay .... 401-232-6448. 438 K
sdelalue@bryant.edu
DELAND, Jane, S .... 202-885-8602... 97 D
jdeland@wesleyseminary.edu
DELAND, Robert .... 312-788-1142. 162 H
rdeland@vandercook.edu
DELANEY, Anne Marie ... 781-239-6481. 222 D
delaneya@babson.edu
DELANEY, Christopher ... 717-337-6235. 417 B
cdelaney@gettysburg.edu
DELANEY, Connie, J ...... 612-624-1410. 264 G
delan108@umn.edu
DELANEY, John .... 423-425-4534. 463 D
john-delaney@utc.edu
DELANEY, John, A .... 904-620-2500. 116 B
jdelaney@unf.edu
DELANEY, John, T .... 412-648-1556. 435 C
jtd@pitt.edu
DELANEY, Kevin, J .... 310-338-5756... 53 E
kevin.delaney@lmu.edu
DELANEY, Melissa .... 510-841-9230... 77 B
mdelaney@wi.edu
DELANEY, Peggy .... 831-459-4375... 72 C
pdelaney@ucsc.edu
DELANEY, Ryan, R .... 262-646-6518. 535 B
rdelaney@nashotah.edu
DELANEY, Thomas .... 212-992-8851. 334 D
tom.delaney@nyu.edu
DELANEY, Timothy, J ..... 740-284-5210. 379 N
tdelaney@franciscan.edu
DELANEY, Timothy, R .... 412-624-4216. 435 C
tdelaney@pitt.edu
DELANEY, Ute .... 845-752-3000. 348 I
registrar@uts.edu
DELANOY, Debra .... 845-687-5088. 348 H
delanoyd@sunyulster.edu
DELANSKY, Barbara .... 541-463-5337. 403 I
delanskyb@lanecc.edu
DELANY, Mary, E .... 530-752-1605... 70 J
medelaney@ucdavis.edu
DELAP, Joe .... 256-782-5004..... 4 K
jdelap@jsu.edu
DELAP, Joe .... 256-782-5328..... 4 K
jdelap@jsu.edu
DELAP, Ronald .... 903-233-3900. 475 J
ronalddelap@letu.edu
DELAROSA, Sam .... 312-939-4975. 146 A
sdelarosa@harrington.edu
DELAROSBY, Hal .... 253-535-8259. 521 I
delarosby@plu.edu
DELASHMIT, Margaret .... 662-252-8000. 269 F
mdelashmit@rustcollege.edu
DELASHMUTT, Michael .. 425-249-4766. 524 D
michael.delashmutt@tlc.edu
DELAUTER, Leslie, J ...... 215-898-5551. 435 B
delauter@upenn.edu
DELAWALLA, Nooral .... 562-860-2451... 37 I
ndelawalla@cerritos.edu
DELAY, Mary, G .... 210-567-2010. 493 A
delay@uthscsa.edu
DELBELSO, Debra .... 518-783-2339. 340 J
ddelbelso@siena.edu
DELBRIDGE, Kristina ...... 518-587-2100. 346 A
kristina.delbridge@esc.edu
DELBUONO, Mary Gray . 412-536-1300. 420 A
mary.delbuono@laroche.edu
DELCAMBRE, Ken .... 409-944-1314. 472 I
kdelcamb@gc.edu
DELCAMP, Tom .... 215-222-4200. 431 H
tdelcamp@walnuthillcollege.edu
DELCID, Angela .... 516-299-4009. 329 D
angela.delcid@liu.edu
DELCOURE, Natalya .... 361-593-3801. 484 A
natalya.delcoure@tamuk.edu
DELCOURT, Veronica ...... 914-606-6963. 350 F
Veronica.Delcourt@sunywcc.edu
DELEGENCIA, Jess .... 925-969-3572... 49 B
jdelegencia@jfku.edu
DELEMEESTER,
Gregory, J .... 740-376-4630. 383 E
greg.delemeester@marietta.edu
DELENER, N.J .... 215-572-4691. 409 H
delenern@arcadia.edu
DELEON, Hilda .... 713-798-4612. 467 F
hildad@bcm.edu
DELEON, Javier .... 956-364-4562. 485 H
javier.deleon@tstc.edu
DELEON, Jerry .... 541-463-5870. 403 I
deleonj@lanecc.edu
DELEON, John .... 214-860-3673. 471 A
jdeleon@dcccd.edu
DELEON, Rocio .... 310-954-4025... 54 J
rdeleon@msmc.la.edu
DELEON, Rolando .... 262-691-5175. 541 D
rdeleon5@wctc.edu
DELEON, Verna .... 800-567-2344. 532 E
vdeleon@menominee.edu
DELEON, Zelma .... 940-565-3901. 490 C
zelma.deleon@unt.edu
DELEON GUERRERA,
Neda, C .... 670-234-5498. 547 A
nedac@nmcnet.edu
DELERME, Leslie, J .... 740-368-3152. 387 J
ljdelerm@owu.edu
DELEWSKY, Richard .... 561-912-2166. 103 C
rdelewsky@evergladesuniversity.edu
DELFORTE, Joseph, L ..... 585-785-1227. 324 D
delforjl@flcc.edu
DELGADILLO, Carlos, E . 509-527-4282. 524 H
carlos.delgadillo@wwcc.edu
DELGADO, Carlos, M ..... 787-766-1717. 552 J
DELGADO, Fernando, P . 715-425-3700. 537 E
fernando.delgado@uwrf.edu
DELGADO, Gilbert .... 954-732-6183. 103 L
gdelgado@careercollege.edu
DELGADO, Irene, R .... 718-409-5879. 346 D
idelgado@sunymaritime.edu
DELGADO, Jane Lee .... 212-220-1407. 317 A
jdelgado@bmcc.cuny.edu
DELGADO, Junior .... 413-572-5546. 230 F
jdelgado@westfield.ma.edu
DELGADO, Laura, M ...... 787-765-4210. 548 E
ldelgado@cempr.edu
DELGADO, Luis, J .... 787-780-0070. 547 G
ldelgado@caribbean.edu
DELGADO, Luis, J .... 787-780-0070. 547 G
jdelgado@caribbean.edu
DELGADO, Maria, L .... 787-878-5475. 549 L
mdelgado@arecibo.inter.edu
DELGADO, Nydia .... 787-878-5475. 549 L
ndelgado@arecibo.inter.edu
DELGADO, Ricardo .... 636-949-4735. 276 D
rdelgado@lindenwood.edu
DELGADO-LIBRERO,
M. Celeste .... 434-381-6334. 510 F
jys@sbc.edu
DELGAUDIO, Rose .... 562-938-4397... 51 D
rdelgaudio@lbcc.edu
DELGIORNO,
Christopher, M .... 845-575-3000. 330 D
christopher.delgiorno@marist.edu
DELGIUDICE, Candice .... 619-201-8741... 62 B
Candice.DelGiudice@sdcc.edu
DELGIZZO, Kimberley .... 617-353-3590. 224 D
delgizzo@bu.edu
DELGRECO, Michael .... 978-837-5292. 234 A
delgrecom@merrimack.edu
DELHOUSAYE, Darryl, L . 602-429-4932... 16 O
ddelhousaye@ps.edu
DELICH, John, T .... 651-631-5585. 263 A
jtdelich@nwc.edu
DELIETO, Mark .... 203-932-7014... 92 E
mdelieto@newhaven.edu
DELILE, John .... 207-453-5123. 210 L
jdelile@kvcc.me.edu
DELIN, Theresa, M .... 847-491-3293. 155 D
t-delin@northwestern.edu
DELINAR, Jon .... 216-987-4354. 378 D
jon.delinar@tri-c.edu
DELIO, Vincent .... 518-956-8010. 341 D
vdelio@albany.edu
DELISA, Kenneth, J .... 860-465-5269... 87 L
delisak@easternct.edu
DELISIO, Christopher, J . 740-368-3324. 387 J
cjdelisi@owu.edu
DELISLE, David, W .... 315-268-6666. 320 A
delisle@clarkson.edu
DELIZIO, Carissa .... 603-899-4142. 296 H
delizioc@franklinpierce.edu
DELK, Kim .... 405-733-7979. 399 F
kdelk@rose.edu

DELL, Erin, B ... 336-316-2196. 355 A
edell@guilford.edu
DELL, Jennifer ... 770-534-6164. 122 A
jdell@brenau.edu
DELL, Troy ... 301-687-4471. 220 C
tadell@frostburg.edu
DELLA POSTA,
Joseph, B ... 315-445-4564. 328 F
dellapjb@lemoyne.edu
DELLA TORRE, Thomas . 845-574-4465. 338 B
tdellato@sunyrockland.edu
DELLAPINA, Mario ... 718-960-8350. 318 A
mario.dellapina@lehman.cuny.edu
DELLAR, Dan ... 231-843-5985. 252 H
ddellar@westshore.edu
DELLAVECCHIA,
Nancy, J ... 330-672-2444. 382 B
ndellave@kent.edu
DELLER, Jean ... 260-665-4100. 173 E
dellerj@trine.edu
DELLHIME, Roberta, G ... 909-748-8040... 73 H
roberta_dellhime@redlands.edu
DELLI CARPINI,
Michael, X ... 215-898-4407. 435 B
dean@asc.upenn.edu
DELLICARPINI, Dominic . 717-815-1231. 438 D
dcarpini@ycp.edu
DELLINGER, Dewey ... 704-922-6236. 360 F
dewey.dellinger@gaston.edu
DELLINGER, Janice ... 864-503-5771. 448 H
dellinger@uscupstate.edu
DELLINGER, Tim ... 731-424-2603. 460 G
tdellinger1@jscc.edu
DELLIVENERI, Richard ... 303-964-3656... 84 M
rdellive@regis.edu
DELLUTRI, Alexandra ... 708-237-5030. 155 B
adellutri@nc.edu
DELLWO, Sarah ... 406-447-6908. 287 A
sarah.dellwo@umhelena.edu
DELL'AQUILO, Bobbie ... 516-686-7851. 333 H
rdellaqu@nyit.edu
DELL'OMO, Gregory, G .. 412-397-6400. 431 I
dellomo@rmu.edu
DELL'OSA, Lydia, J ... 610-359-7322. 414 D
ldellosa@dccc.edu
DELMAR, Cindy ... 585-345-6813. 325 C
cmdelmar@genesee.edu
DELMAR, James ... 845-687-5278. 348 H
delmarj@sunyulster.edu
DELNICK, Matt ... 219-464-6084. 174 E
matt.delnick@valpo.edu
DELOATCH, Eugene ... 443-885-3231. 217 A
eugene.deloatch@eng.morgan.edu
DELOATCH, Sandra, J ... 757-823-8670. 507 M
president@nsu.edu
DELOATCH, Sandra, J ... 757-823-8408. 507 M
provost@nsu.edu
DELOE, Mary ... 419-473-2700. 378 I
mdeloe@daviscollege.edu
DELONG, Allen, W ... 207-725-3536. 209 H
adelong2@bowdoin.edu
DELONG, Brian, C ... 610-799-1179. 421 I
bdelong2@lccc.edu
DELONG, Cliff ... 605-455-6079. 450 I
cdelong@olc.edu
DELONG, Jondavid, S ... 315-386-7328. 345 F
delongj@canton.edu
DELONG, Michael ... 501-812-2373... 22 G
mdelong@pulaskitech.edu
DELONG, Richard ... 810-766-4018. 239 G
richard.delong@baker.edu
DELONG, Shirley ... 610-799-1743. 421 I
sdelong3@lccc.edu
DELONGORIA, Maria ... 631-451-4174. 346 E
delongm@sunysuffolk.edu
DELORENZO, Donna ... 904-819-6255. 103 E
dDeLorenzo@flagler.edu
DELORENZO, Michael ... 217-333-1300. 162 A
michaeld@illinois.edu
DELORENZO, Patricia ... 410-888-9048. 216 D
pdelorenzo@muih.edu
DELORENZO,
Stephen, F ... 518-438-3111. 330 C
steved@mariacollege.edu
DELOREY, Mark, J ... 269-387-6005. 252 I
mark.delorey@wmich.edu
DELOZIER, Matt ... 423-323-0231. 461 C
jmdelozier@northeaststate.edu
DELP, Kevin ... 864-242-5100. 441 D
DELPHENICH, Pamela ... 617-253-1727. 233 B
DELPRETE, Angela ... 440-646-8371. 392 D
adelprete@ursuline.edu
DELQUADRI, Sheila ... 509-574-4655. 525 G
sdelquadri@yvcc.edu
DELROSSI, David ... 850-201-8255. 117 D
delrossd@tcc.fl.edu
DELUCA, Eileen ... 239-985-2498. 101 O
ecduluca@edison.edu
DELUCA, Mary ... 443-840-5215. 214 E
mdeluca@ccbcmd.edu
DELUCA, Paul, M ... 608-262-1304. 536 D
pmdeluca@wisc.edu
DELUCA, Peter, L ... 805-525-4417... 69 H
pdeluca@thomasaquinas.edu
DELUCA, Tony ... 610-359-5110. 414 D
tdeluca@dccc.edu
DELUCA, Vincent, J ... 212-817-7500. 317 F
vdeluca@gc.cuny.edu
DELUCCHI, Jennifer ... 916-568-3039... 52 K
deluccj@losrios.edu
DELUGACH, Harry, S ... 256-824-6614... 8 F
Harry.Delugach@uah.edu
DELUNAS, Linda ... 219-980-6643. 168 B
ldelunas@iun.edu
DELVECCHIO, Edie ... 201-200-3159. 303 F
edelvecchio@njcu.edu
DELVENTHAL, Bruce, W . 518-564-3140. 344 B
delvenbw@plattsburgh.edu
DELVISCIO, Gregory ... 607-777-2175. 341 E
gregdelv@binghamton.edu
DELYSER, Susan ... 315-279-5247. 328 D
sdelyser@mail.keuka.edu
DELZEIT, Greg ... 785-442-6039. 187 E
gdelzeit@highlandcc.edu
DEMA, Anne, C ... 816-415-5912. 285 C
demaa@william.jewell.edu
DEMAIO, Dennis ... 657-278-2900... 33 E
ddemaio@fullerton.edu
DEMARCO, Deborah ... 508-856-2903. 229 C
deborah.demarco@umassmed.edu
DEMARCO, Mary ... 401-874-2775. 440 D
mdemarco@uri.edu
DEMARESKI, Roger ... 609-258-8022. 304 E
rogerd@princeton.edu
DEMAREST, David, F ... 650-724-8887... 68 E
demarest@stanford.edu
DEMAREST, Geralynn ... 518-828-4181. 321 C
demarest@sunycgcc.edu
DEMARK, Paul ... 707-476-4358... 40 H
paul-demark@redwoods.edu
DEMARKEY, Nina ... 714-484-7188... 56 E
ndemarkey@cypresscollege.edu
DEMART-KRAUS, Gina ... 440-646-8334. 392 D
gdemart@ursuline.edu
DEMARTE, Daniel ... 757-822-1061. 514 C
ddemarte@tcc.edu
DEMASTERS, Janice ... 314-991-6200. 141 G
jdemasters@chamberlain.edu
DEMATTEO, Jeanne ... 925-631-4123... 61 F
jdematte@stmarys-ca.edu
DEMAYO, Andrea ... 518-244-2427. 338 C
demaya@sage.edu
DEMBECK, Brian, B ... 443-997-3728. 215 H
bdembeck@jhu.edu
DEMBOSKY,
Cassandra, C ... 607-255-3203. 322 A
ccd3@cornell.edu
DEMBOSKY, Deborah ... 910-630-7522. 356 H
driley@methodist.edu
DEMBY, Harod, C ... 919-516-4593. 366 C
hcdemby@st-aug.edu
DEMCIE, Christine ... 716-829-7688. 323 D
demciec@dyc.edu
DEMCZUK, Bernard ... 202-994-1000... 95 D
bdemczuk@gwu.edu
DEMEDEIROS, Joe ... 512-233-1443. 479 C
joed@stedwards.edu
DEMEIS, Debra ... 781-283-2322. 237 F
ddemeis@wellesley.edu
DEMELLO, Kenneth ... 509-533-3555. 518 F
DEMENT, Jennifer ... 503-491-7385. 404 E
jennifer.dement@mhcc.edu
DEMENT, Marilyn ... 773-907-4755. 142 A
mdement@ccc.edu
DEMENT, Mary ... 870-762-3113... 19 K
mdement@smail.anc.edu
DEMENT, Paul ... 732-263-5679. 303 C
pdement@monmouth.edu
DEMERCHANT, Doug, B . 630-752-5321. 163 F
doug.demerchant@wheaton.edu
DEMERITT, Linda, C ... 814-332-3393. 409 D
linda.demeritt@allegheny.edu
DEMERRITT, Stan ... 806-291-3415. 494 F
demerritt@wbu.edu
DEMERS, David ... 413-565-1315. 222 F
ddemers@baypath.edu
DEMERS, Mary ... 207-941-7131. 210 B
demersm@husson.edu
DEMERS, Paul ... 603-897-8537. 297 F
pdemers@rivier.edu
DEMERS, Susan, S ... 727-791-2501. 112 E
demers.susan@spcollege.edu
DEMERS, Suzanne ... 863-784-7041. 113 G
suzanne.demers@southflorida.edu
DEMES, Dennis ... 561-732-4424. 112 G
ddemes@svdp.edu
DEMETRIOU, Sophia ... 212-925-6625. 317 D
sdemetriou@ccny.cuny.edu
DEMIANCZYK, Jacquie ... 412-291-6286. 410 B
jdemianczyk@aii.edu
DEMICHAEL, Mark ... 765-677-2317. 169 B
mark.demichael@indwes.edu
DEMING, Elizabeth ... 229-430-3693. 120 A
edeming@albanytech.edu
DEMING, Els ... 253-840-8401. 522 C
edeming@pierce.ctc.edu
DEMITH, Lindsey ... 727-725-2688. 102 I
LDeMith@cci.edu
DEMITSAS, Yiani ... 260-422-5561. 167 B
jdemitsas@indianatech.edu
DEMLEITNER, Nora, V ... 540-458-8502. 516 A
demleitnern@wlu.edu
DEMMINGS, Elizabeth ... 765-658-4220. 165 F
betsydemmings@depauw.edu
DEMO, Tina ... 860-509-9549... 90 B
tdemo@hartsem.edu
DEMOSS, Brian ... 209-588-5222... 77 I
demossb@yosemite.edu
DEMOSS, Gerald, L ... 606-783-2623. 198 A
g.demoss@moreheadstate.edu
DEMOTT, Robin ... 309-341-5221. 141 A
rdemott@sandburg.edu
DEMPSEY, Connie ... 570-961-4692... 16 L
connie.dempsey@pennfoster.edu
DEMPSEY, Ellen, E ... 330-569-5340. 380 I
dempseyee@hiram.edu
DEMPSEY, George ... 404-233-3949. 458 F
gdempsey@richmont.edu
DEMPSEY, Grace ... 909-537-5005... 34 E
gdempsey@csusb.edu
DEMPSEY, Greg ... 206-934-5378. 523 A
greg.dempsey@seattlecolleges.edu
DEMPSEY, John, R ... 910-695-3700. 363 F
dempseyj@sandhills.edu
DEMPSEY, Kelly, J ... 608-757-6328. 539 I
kdempsey@blackhawk.edu
DEMPSEY, Marianne ... 301-447-5330. 217 B
dempsey@msmary.edu
DEMPSEY, Michael ... 845-848-4058. 322 G
michael.dempsey@dc.edu
DEMPSEY, Patricia ... 410-972-4511. 217 G
patricia.dempsey@sjca.edu
DEMPSEY, Richard ... 972-883-2141. 491 E
rmdempsey@utdallas.edu
DEMPSEY, Robert ... 718-289-5705. 317 B
robert.dempsey@bcc.cuny.edu
DEMPSEY, Ron ... 816-415-5034. 285 C
dempseyr@william.jewell.edu
DEMPSEY, Ron, D ... 678-915-7347. 132 C
dempsey@spsu.edu
DEMPSEY, Sarah ... 269-927-6188. 245 D
sdempsey@lakemichigancollege.edu
DEMPSEY, Van, O ... 304-367-4241. 529 F
van.dempsey@fairmontstate.edu
DEMPSEY, William ... 610-683-4575. 429 A
dempsey@kutztown.edu
DEMPSTER, Douglas, J .. 512-471-9601. 491 C
ddempster@austin.utexas.edu
DEMROVSKY, Amy ... 303-797-5753... 78 F
amy.demrovsky@arapahoe.edu
DEMSKI, Gary ... 574-520-4457. 168 E
gdemski@iusb.edu
DEMUTH, Paul ... 651-423-8370. 258 D
paul.demuth@dctc.edu
DEMYER, Craig ... 219-980-6937. 168 B
cdemyer@iusb.edu
DEN HARTOG, SR.,
Douglas, M ... 510-783-2100... 46 L
ddenhartog@heald.edu
DENARD, Carolyn, C ... 860-439-2035... 89 H
carolyn.denard@conncoll.edu
DENARD, Jeffrey, D ... 630-637-5142. 154 F
jddenard@noctrl.edu
DENARD, Letitia ... 404-270-5143. 132 E
ldenard@spelman.edu
DENARDO, Melissa, D ... 724-480-3439. 413 H
melissa.denardo@ccbc.edu
DENBOER, Marten ... 909-869-3443... 32 G
mdenboer@csupomona.edu
DENBY, Eric, N ... 434-924-4019. 511 B
end@virginia.edu
DENBY, Karlene ... 281-487-1170. 484 H
kdenby@txchiro.edu
DENDY, David ... 563-589-3618. 182 J
ddendy@dbq.edu
DENEEN, Linda ... 218-726-7588. 264 D
ldeneen@d.umn.edu
DENEEN, Mary ... 757-683-3030. 507 N
mdeneen@odu.edu
DENENBERG, Keely ... 773-697-2025. 144 B
kdenenberg@devry.edu
DENG, Yi ... 704-687-8450. 368 E
Yi.Deng@uncc.edu
DENHAM, Cynthia ... 256-840-4133... 6 I
cdenham@snead.edu
DENHAM, Kerriann ... 217-757-1190. 313 H
kdenham@funeraleducation.org
DENHAM, Mark ... 313-993-3250. 250 K
denhamma@udmercy.edu
DENHAM, Rena ... 541-956-7279. 407 F
rdenham@roguecc.edu
DENHART, Rich ... 608-663-2000. 533 T
rdenhart@mediainstitute.edu
DENHEETEN, Kathryn ... 989-775-4123. 249 F
denheeten.katy@sagchip.edu
DENHOLM, Jack ... 701-845-7160. 372 A
jack.denholm@vcsu.edu
DENIO, John ... 518-694-7337. 313 B
john.denio@acphs.edu
DENIO, John ... 401-232-6140. 438 K
jdenio@bryant.edu
DENISON, Bronda ... 334-670-5843... 7 H
bdenison@troy.edu
DENKER, Audria ... 502-410-6200. 194 B
adenker@galencollege.edu
DENKER, Lee ... 402-554-2444. 293 A
ldenker@unomaha.edu
DENLEY, Tristan ... 615-366-4482. 459 A
tristan.denley@tbr.edu
DENLINGER, Tammy ... 574-372-5100. 166 B
denlintl@grace.edu
DENLY, David ... 620-229-6104. 190 G
david.denly@sckans.edu
DENMAN, Bob, G ... 501-569-3194... 24 B
bgdenman@ualr.edu
DENNA, Eric ... 801-581-3100. 496 Q
eric.denna@utah.edu
DENNE, Cynthia, K ... 909-593-3511... 72 E
cdenne@laverne.edu
DENNEE, Mary Jo, R ... 716-851-1999. 323 I
dennee@ecc.edu
DENNEHY, Michael ... 972-860-4607. 470 G
mdennehy@dcccd.edu
DENNEY, Carolyn ... 509-527-2811. 524 I
carolyn.denney@wallawalla.edu
DENNEY, James ... 662-329-7462. 268 E
jdenney@vpaa.muw.edu
DENNEY, Karen ... 828-627-4546. 361 B
kdenney@haywood.edu
DENNEY, Martha ... 610-896-1232. 418 F
mdenney@haverford.edu
DENNING, CSC, John, F 508-565-1301. 237 A
jdenning@stonehill.edu
DENNING, Rusty ... 864-941-8417. 446 C
denning.r@ptc.edu
DENNIS, Anne ... 515-643-6640. 181 A
adennis@mercydesmoines.org
DENNIS, Carly ... 513-745-5671. 391 A
carly.dennis@uc.edu
DENNIS, Carolyn ... 318-487-7222. 202 F
carolyn.dennis@lacollege.edu
DENNIS, Dave, D ... 319-363-8213. 181 C
ddennis@mtmercy.edu
DENNIS, Denise ... 973-748-9000. 299 F
denise_bane@bloomfield.edu
DENNIS, Diana ... 815-753-2111. 154 I
ddennis@niu.edu
DENNIS, Dixie ... 931-221-7414. 459 B
dennisdi@apsu.edu
DENNIS, James, M ... 618-537-6936. 152 G
jdennis@mckendree.edu
DENNIS, Jeff ... 864-644-5521. 446 I
jdennis@swu.edu
DENNIS, Larry ... 850-644-5804. 115 C
ldennis@cci.fsu.edu
DENNIS, Peggy ... 419-372-8495. 374 K
fayed@bgsu.edu
DENNIS, Raymond, A ... 310-338-5994... 53 E
rdennis@lmu.edu
DENNIS, Roger, J ... 215-571-4755. 415 B
rjd45@drexel.edu
DENNIS, Sheryl ... 903-566-7222. 492 D
sdennis@uttyler.edu
DENNIS, Suzanne ... 718-780-7912. 315 H
suzanne.dennis@brooklaw.edu
DENNIS, Terry ... 863-680-3937. 105 D
vdennis@flsouthern.edu
DENNIS-PHILLIPS, Ruth 336-517-2207. 352 H
rdphillips@bennett.edu
DENNISON, Angela ... 419-227-3141. 391 F
ardennison@unoh.edu
DENNISON, Anne ... 207-775-3052. 210 H
adennison@meca.edu
DENNISON, Marla, K ... 651-631-5395. 263 A
mkdennison@nwc.edu
DENNISON, T. Wayne ... 770-499-3151. 127 N
wdenniso@kennesaw.edu
DENNISTON, Mark ... 937-382-6661. 393 B
mark_denniston@wilmington.edu
DENNISTON, Marsha ... 605-331-6633. 452 D
marsha.denniston@usiouxfalls.edu
DENNISTON, Terry ... 423-425-4203. 463 D
terry-denniston@utc.edu
DENNY, D ... 301-628-4253. 217 C
ddenny@nlc.edu
DENNY, David ... 503-699-6313. 404 C
ddenny@marylhurst.edu
DENON, Gregory ... 617-989-4112. 237 G
denong@wit.edu
DENSBERGER, Derek ... 714-556-3610... 74 D
ddensberger@vanguard.edu

DENSBERGER, Janelle .... 314-719-8057. 274 E
jdensberger@fontbonne.edu
DENSLOW, Kathy .... 325-793-4903. 476 E
kdenslow@mcm.edu
DENSON, John .... 205-665-6235..... 9 B
jdenson1@montevallo.edu
DENSON, Rob .... 515-964-6638. 177 B
rjdenson@dmacc.edu
DENT, Deborah, F .... 601-979-4299. 267 E
deborah.f.dent@jsums.edu
DENT, Gary, K .... 717-720-4158. 427 G
gkdent@passhe.edu
DENT, Patricia .... 508-678-2811. 231 B
patricia.dent@bristolcc.edu
DENT, Valeda .... 516-299-2307. 329 C
Valeda.Dent@liu.edu
DENTE, Michael, A .... 802-626-6375. 501 E
michael.dente@lyndonstate.edu
DENTE, Ron .... 239-489-9495. 101 O
rdente@edison.edu
DENTINO, Daniel .... 785-227-3380. 184 I
dentinod@bethanylb.edu
DENTLER, Amanda .... 313-993-1205. 250 K
dentleat@udmercy.edu
DENTON, Andy .... 417-865-2815. 274 B
dentona@evangel.edu
DENTON, David .... 931-221-6380. 459 B
dentond@apsu.edu
DENTON, Edward .... 510-643-7384... 70 I
edenton@cp.berkeley.edu
DENTON, Melissa .... 913-234-0750. 185 L
melissa.denton@cleveland.edu
DENUM, Michael .... 309-649-6268. 160 E
michael.denum@src.edu
DENVER, Genae .... 785-539-3571. 188 F
gdenver@mccks.edu
DENVIR, Cornelia .... 845-687-5034. 348 H
denvirc@sunyulster.edu
DENYS, Mark .... 215-204-7500. 433 K
mark.denys@temple.edu
DEO, Veena .... 651-523-2307. 256 A
vdeo@hamline.edu
DEOCAMPO, Erlinda, N .. 323-415-4163... 51 F
deocamen@elac.edu
DEOLALIKAR, Anil .... 951-827-1575... 71 E
anil.deolalikar@ucr.edu
DEOLIVEIRA,
Shushawana .... 718-270-2446. 342 D
shushawana.deoliveria@downstate.edu
DEORIO, Frank, A .... 718-817-4910. 324 G
deorio@fordham.edu
DEPACE, Paul .... 401-874-2725. 440 D
pauld@uri.edu
DEPALMA, Timothy .... 305-628-6788. 112 F
tdepalma@stu.edu
DEPAOLA, Natacha .... 312-567-3009. 147 F
depaola@iit.edu
DEPAOLIS, Cheryl .... 412-924-1384. 431 A
cdepaolis@pts.edu
DEPAUW, Karen, P .... 540-231-7581. 515 C
kpdepauw@vt.edu
DEPEDER, Suzanne .... 312-362-8648. 143 H
sdepeder@depaul.edu
DEPEDRO, Tracy .... 215-951-2738. 430 E
depedrot@philau.edu
DEPEDRO, Tracy .... 215-489-2312. 414 E
Tracy.DePedro@delval.edu
DEPERRO, Dennis, R ...... 315-445-4685. 328 F
deperrdr@lemoyne.edu
DEPEW, Chris .... 845-434-5750. 347 A
cdepew@sullivan.suny.edu
DEPEW, Dixie, A .... 937-328-6006. 377 A
depewd@clarkstate.edu
DEPEW, Elizabeth .... 219-785-5238. 172 A
ldepew@pnc.edu
DEPEW, Sally .... 231-591-3823. 242 F
depews@ferris.edu
DEPIANO, Michael .... 860-701-5194... 90 G
depiano_m@mitchell.edu
DEPINHO, Ronald .... 713-792-6161. 493 B
DEPLASCO, Patricia, A ... 302-739-4066... 93 D
pdeplasc@dtcc.edu
DEPOE, Robert .... 406-275-4974. 288 C
robert_depoe@skc.edu
DEPOMPEI, Roberta, A ... 330-972-6519. 390 E
rdepom1@uakron.edu
DEPONTIER, Woodrow ..... 316-978-3444. 191 F
woodrow.depontier@wichita.edu
DEPOO, Tilokie .... 212-343-1234. 331 D
tdepoo@mcny.edu
DEPORTER, Nick .... 480-860-2700... 13 Q
ndeporter@taliesin.edu
DEPOUTOT, Al .... 727-376-6911. 117 I
adepoutot@trinitycollege.edu
DEPOY, Byran .... 330-941-3625. 394 A
bwdepoy@ysu.edu
DEPPONG, Greg .... 517-355-5020. 246 H
deppong@msu.edu
DEPREY, Linda .... 207-834-7500. 212 E
lindad@maine.edu
DEPRIEST, Jon .... 619-201-8754... 62 B
Jon.DePriest@sdcc.edu
DEPRIEST, Tomika .... 404-270-5060. 132 E
tdepriest@spelman.edu
DEPRIETO, Irma .... 509-865-8537. 520 D
deprieto_i@heritage.edu
DEPUTY, Meghan .... 386-312-4169. 112 C
meghandeputy@sjrstate.edu
DER-KARABETIAN,
Aghop .... 909-593-3511... 72 E
ader-karabetian@laverne.edu
DERAMUS, Danny .... 501-279-4339... 21 C
dderamus@harding.edu
DERAVI, Fariba, S .... 334-244-3249..... 2 A
fderavi@aum.edu
DERBY, Dustin, C .... 563-884-5682. 182 A
dustin.derby@palmer.edu
DERCK, Amy .... 252-444-6012. 359 G
dercka@cravencc.edu
DEREGO, Kim .... 802-258-3324. 500 C
kim.derego@sit.edu
DERICKSON,
Christopher .... 919-962-8289. 368 D
cderickson@unc.edu
DERICO, Jeffrey .... 513-244-8110. 376 J
jeffrey.derico@ccuniversity.edu
DERIGGI, Nancy, M .... 914-606-6589. 350 F
nancy.deriggi@sunywcc.edu
DERITIS, Mark .... 315-268-6642. 320 A
mderitis@clarkson.edu
DERMODY, Sean .... 518-562-4122. 320 B
sean.dermody@clinton.edu
DEROCHI, Jack .... 803-323-2204. 449 G
derochij@winthrop.edu
DEROSA, Mary Lou .... 203-396-8321... 91 C
derosam@sacredheart.edu
DEROSA, Michael .... 510-869-6511... 61 I
mderosa@samuelmerritt.edu
DEROSE, Angela .... 203-287-3033... 90 H
paier.admin@snet.net
DEROSE, Maureen .... 203-287-3032... 90 H
paier.admin@snet.net
DEROSE, Michelle .... 616-632-2826. 239 E
derosmic@aquinas.edu
DEROSE, Paul .... 602-285-7417... 15 C
paul.derose@phoenixcollege.edu
DEROSE, Rae .... 312-777-8646. 147 D
rderose@aii.edu
DEROSIER, Stephen .... 603-752-1113. 296 E
sderosier@ccsnh.edu
DEROSIER DOUGLASS,
Diane .... 651-793-1919. 259 C
diane.derosierdouglass@metrostate.edu
DEROUIN, Karen .... 413-552-2248. 231 F
kderouin@hcc.edu
DERR, Debra .... 503-491-7211. 404 E
debra.derr@mhcc.edu
DERR, Ed .... 417-873-7418. 273 H
ederr@drury.edu
DERR, Gary, L .... 802-656-2212. 500 F
gary.derr@uvm.edu
DERR, Matthew .... 802-586-7711. 500 E
mderr@sterlingcollege.edu
DERRER, Meg .... 616-632-2843. 239 E
meg.derrer@aquinas.edu
DERRICK, Damon .... 936-468-4305. 482 A
derrickdc@sfasu.edu
DERRICK, Denise .... 618-545-3070. 149 D
dderrick@kaskaskia.edu
DERRICK, Gail .... 757-352-4859. 508 G
gailder@regent.edu
DERRICK, Scott .... 864-294-2267. 444 C
scott.derrick@furman.edu
DERRICK, Sylvia .... 253-964-6715. 522 C
DERRICO, Cindy .... 805-437-3340... 32 I
cindy.derrico@csuci.edu
DERRITT, Cindy .... 785-864-5170. 190 L
cderritt@ku.edu
DERRITT, Shawn .... 913-288-7437. 187 L
sderritt@kckcc.edu
DERRIVAN, Kevin .... 617-850-1222. 227 E
kderrivan@hchc.edu
DERRY, John, L .... 714-879-3901... 47 K
jderry@hiu.edu
DERRY, Patricia .... 734-432-5574. 246 B
pderry@madonna.edu
DERRY, Sebastian .... 718-405-3329. 320 G
sebastian.derry@mountsaintvincent.edu
DERSCH, Denise .... 856-351-2682. 307 B
ddersch@salemcc.edu
DERSH, Rhoda, E .... 610-375-1212. 425 H
redpaceset@aol.com
DERSTINE, Andria .... 440-775-8665. 385 H
Andria.Derstine@oberlin.edu
DERUBBO, Jeff .... 724-938-4415. 428 A
derubbo@calu.edu
DERVIN, Alice .... 618-374-5106. 156 B
alice.dervin@principia.edu
DERVISEVIC, Ajisa .... 516-686-7441. 333 H
ajisad@nyit.edu
DERYCZ-KESSLER,
Diana .... 323-464-5200... 52 H
DESALLES, Albert .... 310-434-4831... 65 A
desalles_albert@smc.edu
DESALVO, Dianne, S .... 989-774-4308. 240 N
desal1ds@cmich.edu
DESALVO, Patricia, D ..... 407-708-2136. 113 E
desalvop@seminolestate.edu
DESANCTIS, Joyce .... 617-726-8015. 234 B
jrdesanctis@mghihp.edu
DESANTIS, Charles, E ..... 202-687-1787... 95 E
ced33@georgetown.edu
DESANTIS, Linda .... 609-343-5093. 299 A
desantis@atlantic.edu
DESANTIS, Victor .... 717-872-3099. 429 D
victor.desantis@millersville.edu
DESANTIS, Victoria .... 845-368-7200. 340 C
victoria.desantis@use.salvationarmy.org
DESANTLO, William .... 610-917-1438. 436 C
wfdesanto@vfcc.edu
DESANTO, Cynthia, A ..... 409-747-9323. 493 C
cydesant@utmb.edu
DESANTO, Jerome, P ...... 570-941-6185. 436 A
jerome.desanto@scranton.edu
DESANTOS, Cynthia .... 409-747-9323. 493 C
cydesant@utmb.edu
DESAUTELS-POLIQUIN,
Lisa .... 207-859-1243. 211 H
desautelsl@thomas.edu
DESCAK, Carol .... 540-654-1618. 510 J
cdescak@umw.edu
DESCISCIO, Joseph, A .... 201-761-6366. 306 L
jdesciscio@saintpeters.edu
DESCUTNER, David .... 740-593-2431. 387 C
descutne@ohio.edu
DESCUTNER, David, N .... 740-593-1935. 387 C
descutne@ohio.edu
DESHAW, Carla, M .... 315-255-1743. 316 D
carla.deshaw@cayuga-cc.edu
DESHAZOR, Nicholas ...... 931-553-0071. 457 F
nicholas.deshazor@miller-motte.com
DESHIELDS, Richard ...... 509-963-2735. 517 F
deshielr@cwu.edu
DESHLER, Kirsten .... 805-893-4588... 72 B
kirsten.deshler@ia.ucsb.edu
DESHON, Eeva .... 415-808-1492... 46 I
eeva_deshon@heald.edu
DESHPANDE, Shekhar ..... 215-527-2918. 409 H
deshpande@arcadia.edu
DESILVA, Chandra, R ..... 757-683-4423. 507 N
cdesilva@odu.edu
DESIMONE, Albert, J ...... 269-337-7292. 244 K
Al.DeSimone@kzoo.edu
DESIMONE, Danette, J .... 315-470-6641. 345 B
djdesimo@esf.edu
DESJARDINS, Joseph ..... 320-363-5401. 254 J
jdesjardins@csbsju.edu
DESJARDINS, Joseph ..... 320-363-3147. 263 P
jdesjardins@csbsju.edu
DESJARDINS, Linda .... 413-775-1105. 231 E
desjardins@gcc.mass.edu
DESJARLAIS, Jennifer ..... 781-283-2273. 237 F
jdesjarl@wellesley.edu
DESLAURIERS, Faith ...... 386-226-6350. 102 B
faith.deslauriers@erau.edu
DESMARAIS, Charles ..... 415-749-4549... 62 G
cdesmarais@sfai.edu
DESMARAIS, Ethel, M .... 610-526-5245. 410 J
edesmara@brynmawr.edu
DESMARAIS, Gerald .... 413-662-5220. 230 C
g.desmarais@mcla.edu
DESMARAIS, Jennifer ..... 802-387-7179. 499 E
jenniferdesmarais@landmark.edu
DESMARAIS, Mark .... 603-752-1113. 296 E
mdesmarais@ccsnh.edu
DESMARAIS, Rachel, M . 336-734-7175. 360 E
rdesmarais@forsythtech.edu
DESMITH, Kristin .... 907-786-1263... 10 H
kadesmith@uaa.alaska.edu
DESMOND, Bill .... 309-796-5437. 140 E
desmondw@bhc.edu
DESMOND, Jill .... 414-382-6065. 531 I
jill.desmond@alverno.edu
DESMOND-HELLMANN,
Susan .... 415-476-2401... 72 A
sue.hellmann@ucsf.edu
DESOCIO, Janiece .... 206-296-2237. 523 E
desocioj@seattleu.edu
DESOL, Louis, P .... 717-872-3017. 429 D
louis.desol@millersville.edu
DESONIA, Amy .... 860-412-7260... 89 E
adesonia@qvcc.commnet.edu
DESOUZA,
Wellington, O .... 336-841-9196. 355 C
wdesouza@highpoint.edu
DESPAIN, Ira, L .... 785-594-8553. 184 C
ira.despain@bakeru.edu
DESPATHY, Carol .... 603-206-8136. 296 A
cdespathy@ccsnh.edu
DESPLAS, Ed .... 972-860-7752. 470 F
edesplas@dcccd.edu
DESPO, Pamela, M .... 724-589-2195. 434 B
pdespo@thiel.edu
DESROCHERS, Rebecca .. 603-623-0313. 297 E
rdesrochers@nhia.edu
DESROSIERS, Alicia .... 610-917-1414. 436 C
ardesrosiers@vfcc.edu
DESROSIERS, Jacque ..... 734-677-5306. 252 A
jdesrosiers@wccnet.edu
DESSELLE, Shane .... 916-631-8108... 32 C
DESSOYE, Jane, F .... 570-674-6168. 424 A
jdessoye@misericordia.edu
DESTEFANO, Joanne, M . 607-255-4242. 322 A
jmd11@cornell.edu
DESTEFANO, Joe .... 252-335-0821. 359 F
joseph_destefano@albemarle.edu
DESTEIGUER, John .... 405-425-5100. 397 D
john.desteiguer@oc.edu
DESTER, Lisa .... 518-743-2232. 345 E
desterl@sunyacc.edu
DESTITO, Connie .... 626-529-8202... 57 G
cdestito@pacificoaks.edu
DESTLER, William, W ..... 585-475-2394. 337 L
bill.destler@rit.edu
DESVIGNE, LaVora .... 718-482-5114. 318 F
ldesvigne@lagcc.cuny.edu
DESWERT, Lisa .... 541-506-6058. 402 H
ldeswert@cgcc.cc.or.us
DETAMORE, Ed .... 317-931-2318. 165 B
edetamore@cts.edu
DETAMPEL, SuAnn .... 920-465-2302. 536 F
detampes@uwgb.edu
DETAR, Eric .... 315-279-5378. 328 D
edetar@mail.keuka.edu
DETEMPLE, Jon Jay .... 610-526-6119. 417 H
jdetemple@harcum.edu
DETER, Richard, S .... 940-565-3000. 490 C
deter@unt.edu
DETGEN, Jim .... 580-327-8645. 396 N
ejdetgen@nwosu.edu
DETHERAGE, Larry .... 502-852-8185. 200 D
jldeth01@louisville.edu
DETISCH, John, C .... 724-925-4093. 437 D
detischj@wccc.edu
DETROW, David, A .... 540-432-4109. 504 D
detrowd@emu.edu
DETTBARN, Lana, J .... 563-336-3336. 177 L
ldettbarn@eicc.edu
DETTLAFF, Christine .... 405-422-1255. 399 B
dettlaffc@redlandscc.edu
DETTMAN, Kathleen .... 650-725-1327... 68 E
kathleen.dettman@stanford.edu
DETTORRE, Noell .... 740-374-8716. 392 I
ndettoree@wscc.edu
DETURK, Sabrina .... 610-660-1289. 432 E
sdeturk@sju.edu
DETURRIS, John .... 610-892-1543. 427 E
jdeturris@pit.edu
DETWEILER, Bob .... 805-756-2126... 32 F
rdetweil@calpoly.edu
DETWEILER, Sally .... 660-785-4031. 282 L
sallydet@truman.edu
DETWILER, Andrew, G .... 605-394-1995. 452 A
andrew.detwiler@sdsmt.edu
DETWILER, Nancy .... 617-745-3638. 225 G
nancy.l.detwiler@enc.edu
DETWILER, Rita .... 434-544-8300. 506 K
detwiler@lynchburg.edu
DETWILER, Robert .... 419-824-3880. 383 C
rdetwiler@lourdes.edu
DETWILER, Tim .... 616-949-5300. 241 F
tim.detwiler@cornerstone.edu
DETWILER, William .... 214-768-3237. 481 A
bdetwile@smu.edu
DEUSSING, Karin .... 215-935-3847. 437 C
kdeussing@wts.edu
DEUTER, Clayton .... 605-995-7132. 450 E
clayton.deuter@mitchelltech.edu
DEUTSCH, Gail, S .... 714-449-7459... 67 D
gdeutsch@scco.edu
DEUTSCH, Thomas, A .... 312-942-5567. 157 G
thomas_deutsch@rush.edu
DEUTSCH, Yeruchem .... 718-963-9770. 349 B
ed@utsb.org
DEUTSCHMAN, Kelly .... 507-786-3995. 264 B
deutschm@stolaf.edu
DEVALL, Kenneth .... 801-524-1965. 495 O
KDuvall@ldsbc.edu
DEVALL, Wendy .... 225-216-8503. 202 H
devallw@mybrcc.edu
DEVANE, Larry, F .... 405-422-1260. 399 B
devanel@redlandscc.edu
DEVANEY, Barbara, J ...... 207-768-9750. 212 G
barbara.devaney@umpi.edu
DEVAUGHN, Gerald .... 803-780-1265. 449 E
gdevaughn@voorhees.edu
DEVAULT, Sylvia, Y .... 812-488-2239. 173 H
sy5@evansville.edu
DEVAUX, April, A .... 585-785-1634. 324 D
devauxaa@flcc.edu
DEVEAU, Laura .... 617-928-4042. 234 E
ldeveau@mountida.edu

DEVEAU, Shawn .... 409-772-9803. 493 C
sjdeveau@utmb.edu
DEVELIN COLEY, Joan ... 410-435-0100. 217 E
DEVENNY, Marianne ...... 815-455-8716. 152 F
mdevenny@mchenry.edu
DEVENS, Philip .... 401-232-6119. 438 K
revdev@bryant.edu
DEVER, Carolyn .... 615-322-2851. 463 G
carolyn.dever@vanderbilt.edu
DEVER, David .... 310-434-4384... 65 A
dever_david@smc.edu
DEVER, John, T .... 757-825-2711. 514 B
deverj@tncc.edu
DEVER, Michael, K .... 517-750-1200. 250 E
miked@arbor.edu
DEVEREAUX, Kent .... 206-726-5029. 518 G
kdevereaux@cornish.edu
DEVEREAUX, Martin, C .. 561-237-7151. 108 X
mdevereaux@lynn.edu
DEVERES, Georgette .... 909-621-8088... 39 D
georgette.deveres@cmc.edu
DEVERS, James .... 570-941-6267. 436 A
james.devers@sranton.edu
DEVERS, Monica .... 320-308-4894. 261 B
mcdevers@stcloudstate.edu
DEVERS-JONES, Caitlin .. 727-784-0003... 99 J
cdeversjones@cfi.edu
DEVERSE, Nancy .... 360-538-4030. 520 B
ndeverse@ghc.edu
DEVERTEUIL, Johanna .... 863-638-2914. 119 D
deverteuilj@webber.edu
DEVERY, Dennis .... 609-777-5693. 308 A
ddevery@tesc.edu
DEVESTERN, Diane .... 610-436-3511. 430 A
ddevestern@wcupa.edu
DEVIER, David, H .... 937-328-6026. 377 A
devierd@clarkstate.edu
DEVILBISS, Mark, B .... 937-327-7808. 393 E
mdevilbiss@wittenberg.edu
DEVILLE, Lauren .... 706-396-8150. 130 C
ldeville@paine.edu
DEVINCENTIS, Mark .... 585-340-9501. 320 E
mdevincentis@crcds.edu
DEVINE, Christopher, F .. 412-397-6872. 431 I
devinec@rmu.edu
DEVINE, Dennis .... 406-771-5140. 287 E
dennis.devine@gfcmsu.edu
DEVINE, Donald .... 973-278-5400. 299 D
ded@berkeleycollege.edu
DEVINE, Donald, E .... 973-278-5400. 314 K
ded@berkeleycollege.edu
DEVINE, Flora, B .... 770-499-3562. 127 N
fdevine@kennesaw.edu
DEVINE, Jane .... 718-482-5421. 318 F
jane@lagcc.cuny.edu
DEVINE, Kathy .... 912-665-4472. 131 H
kdevine@southuniversity.edu
DEVINE, Linda, W .... 813-253-6203. 118 L
ldevine@ut.edu
DEVINE, Mary .... 218-846-3711. 259 F
mary.devine@minnesota.edu
DEVINE, Michelle .... 989-275-5000. 245 B
michelle.devine@kirtland.edu
DEVINE, Scott, W .... 240-895-4295. 218 A
swdevine@smcm.edu
DEVINE, Susan .... 510-780-4500... 50 I
sdevine@lifewest.edu
DEVINO, SJ,
Terrence, P .... 617-552-3636. 224 A
terrence.devino.1@bc.edu
DEVISSER, Kimberly .... 361-825-2763. 483 F
kimberly.devisser@tamucc.edu
DEVITO, Paul, L .... 773-298-3191. 158 E
devito@sxu.edu
DEVITO, Rose, M .... 617-984-1620. 235 I
rdevito@quincycollege.edu
DEVITO, William, J .... 215-951-1326. 420 B
devito@lasalle.edu
DEVITTO, John .... 704-290-5333. 363 G
jdevitto@spcc.edu
DEVIVO, Sharon, B .... 718-429-6600. 349 H
sharon.devivo@vaughn.edu
DEVLIN, Allison .... 661-362-3648... 40 E
allison.devlin@canyons.edu
DEVLIN, Diane, M .... 617-627-5878. 237 C
diane.devlin@tufts.edu
DEVLIN, George, A .... 803-705-4417. 441 C
devling@benedict.edu
DEVLIN, Jeff, P .... 412-578-8741. 412 G
jpdevlin@carlow.edu
DEVLIN, Thomas, C .... 510-642-3461... 70 I
tcd@berkeley.edu
DEVOE HEIDMAN,
Sheila .... 520-515-5362... 12 R
heidmans@cochise.edu
DEVONO, Mary, K .... 304-457-6484. 526 A
devonomk@ab.edu
DEVORE, Cynthia .... 651-793-1466. 259 C
cynthia.devore@metrostate.edu
DEVORE, Victor .... 619-660-4323... 46 D
victor.devore@gcccd.edu

DEVOS, Edward .... 617-327-6777. 233 D
edward_devos@mspp.edu
DEVOSS, David, V .... 270-809-2222. 198 B
public.safety@murraystate.edu
DEVRIES, Janet .... 307-268-2662. 542 X
jdevries@caspercollege.edu
DEVRIES, Lora .... 712-722-6422. 177 J
lora.devries@dordt.edu
DEVRIES, Warren, R .... 410-455-3270. 219 D
wdevries@umbc.edu
DEW, Beverley .... 804-594-1479. 512 G
bdew@jtcc.edu
DEW, John, R .... 334-670-5991..... 7 H
jrdew@troy.edu
DEWAARD, Chad .... 573-277-6694. 273 F
cdewaard@culver.edu
DEWALD, Barb .... 712-707-7192. 181 H
bdewald@nwciowa.edu
DEWALD, Daryll .... 509-335-5548. 525 A
daryll.dewald@wsu.edu
DEWALD, Howard .... 740-593-2600. 387 C
dewald@ohio.edu
DEWALT, Carol .... 603-668-6660. 297 C
DEWALT, Marie .... 304-876-5299. 529 I
mdewalt@shepherd.edu
DEWALT, Michael .... 410-323-6211. 214 F
admissions@faiththeological.org
DEWAN, Sue .... 518-464-8673. 324 B
sdewan@excelsior.edu
DEWBERRY, Angela, B ... 704-894-2227. 353 J
andewberry@davidson.edu
DEWBERRY, Thomas ...... 541-683-5141. 403 D
cdewberry@gutenberg.edu
DEWBRE, Dane .... 806-894-9611. 480 H
ddewbre@southplainscollege.edu
DEWBRE, Jeri Ann .... 806-894-9611. 480 H
jdewbre@southplainscollege.edu
DEWEERTH, Jennifer ...... 315-731-5818. 331 I
jdeweerth@mvcc.edu
DEWEES, Bridget .... 803-535-5793. 442 B
bdewees@claflin.edu
DEWEES, Deborah .... 360-560-3353. 525 C
deborah.dewees@wwu.edu
DEWEES, Julie .... 309-298-1800. 162 K
jk-dewees@wiu.edu
DEWEESE, Kass .... 580-477-7769. 401 J
kass.deweese@wosc.edu
DEWESE, Jerima .... 718-429-6600. 349 H
jerima.dewese@vaughn.edu
DEWEY, Amy .... 610-526-1000. 409 F
amy.dewey@theamericancollege.edu
DEWEY, Barbara, I .... 814-865-0401. 426 A
bid1@psu.edu
DEWEY, Gregory .... 909-593-3511... 72 E
gdewey@laverne.edu
DEWEY, Gwen .... 206-264-9100. 516 J
gwend@bgu.edu
DEWEY, Katie .... 918-540-6211. 396 G
katiebs@neo.edu
DEWEY, Marvin .... 620-278-4290. 190 I
mdewey@sterling.edu
DEWEY, Phyllis, K .... 716-926-8930. 326 B
pdewey@hilbert.edu
DEWEY, Susan .... 607-844-8222. 347 I
deweys@tc3.edu
DEWEY, Susan .... 501-977-2084... 25 C
dewey@uaccm.edu
DEWINE, Sue .... 812-866-7056. 166 C
dewine@hanover.edu
DEWINTER, Naomi .... 231-348-6618. 247 H
ndewinter@ncmich.edu
DEWIS, Rob .... 408-855-5327... 75 K
rob.dewis@wvm.edu
DEWITT, Bob .... 937-769-1852. 373 H
bdewitt@antioch.edu
DEWITT, Brenda, E .... 740-368-3329. 387 J
bedewitt@owu.edu
DEWITT, Charles, B .... 615-353-3346. 461 B
charles.dewitt@nscc.edu
DEWITT, Dan .... 502-897-4555. 199 B
ddewitt@sbts.edu
DEWITT, David .... 301-784-5000. 213 B
ddewitt@allegany.edu
DEWITT, Deborah, S .... 937-327-7001. 393 E
ddewitt@wittenberg.edu
DEWITT, Matt .... 314-837-6777. 280 K
mdewitt@slcconline.edu
DEWITT, Megan .... 660-359-3948. 279 H
mdewitt@mail.ncmissouri.edu
DEWITT, Siobhan, K .... 412-578-6651. 412 G
skdewitt@carlow.edu
DEWITT, Thomas, E .... 315-364-3266. 350 E
DEWOLF, Dawn .... 541-463-3000. 403 I
dewolfd@lanecc.edu
DEWOLF, William .... 617-824-8655. 226 A
william_dewolf@emerson.edu
DEWOODY, Susan .... 479-524-7371... 21 G
sdewoody@jbu.edu
DEWSNUP, Vicky .... 801-622-1569. 496 I
vicky.dewsnup@stevenshenager.edu

DEXTER, Ann .... 781-891-2640. 223 C
adexter@bentley.edu
DEXTER, Brian .... 509-542-4727. 518 C
bdexter@columbiabasin.edu
DEXTER, Kathleen, A ...... 207-621-3153. 212 C
dexter@maine.edu
DEXTER, Lena .... 251-580-2106..... 4 L
lena.dexter@faulknerstate.edu
DEXTER-HARRIS, Roz .... 904-632-3375. 105 E
rdexter@fscj.edu
DEXTER-WILSON,
Elizabeth .... 251-380-3470..... 7 D
edexterwilson@shc.edu
DEY, Farouk .... 650-723-1983... 68 E
fdey@stanford.edu
DEY, Farouk .... 412-268-2064. 412 H
fdey@andrew.cmu.edu
DEY, Kate .... 415-703-9575... 30 K
kdey@cca.edu
DEYOUNG, Michael .... 702-968-2006. 295 E
mdeyoung@roseman.edu
DEYOUNG, Paul .... 503-777-7290. 407 E
paul.deyoung@reed.edu
DEYOUNG, Renee .... 231-439-6347. 247 H
rdeyoung@ncmich.edu
DEZEMBER, Mary .... 575-835-5172. 310 F
dezember@nmt.edu
DEZIEL-EVANS, Lisa .... 954-262-1387. 109 K
lisad@nova.edu
DHANAK, Manhar .... 954-924-7242. 114 L
dhanak@fau.edu
DHILLON, Upinder, S ..... 607-777-2314. 341 E
dhillon@binghamton.edu
DHILLON, Vineeta .... 707-654-1086... 31 I
vdhillon@csum.edu
DHIR, Vijay, K .... 310-825-8507... 71 C
vdhir@seas.ucla.edu
DI DIO, Stephen .... 718-631-6044. 319 D
sdidio@qcc.cuny.edu
DI DONATO, Ana .... 352-588-8992. 112 D
ana.didonato@saintleo.edu
DI FAVA, John .... 617-252-1703. 233 B
DI GIACOMO, Michael .. 610-917-3949. 436 C
m_digiacomo@vfcc.edu
DI GUILIO, Raymond ..... 916-484-8484... 53 A
diguilr@arc.losrios.edu
DI LELLO, Joseph .... 914-968-6200. 339 E
Joseph.DiLello@archny.org
DI LULLO, Trish .... 256-233-8184..... 1 F
trish.dilullo@athens.edu
DI MARE, Lesley .... 719-549-2951... 80 K
presidentsoffice@colostate-pueblo.edu
DI NALLO, Benjamin ...... 201-559-3507. 302 A
dinallob@felician.edu
DI NARDI, Jason .... 914-594-4668. 334 A
jason_dinardi@nymc.edu
DI NUCCI, Jo Ellen .... 208-426-1200. 137 G
jedinucc@boisestate.edu
DI PASQUALE, Ray .... 401-825-2188. 439 A
rmdipasquale@ccri.edu
DI RADDO, Colleen .... 302-736-2420... 94 C
diraddo@wesley.edu
DI SANTO, Dusty .... 630-752-5490. 163 F
Dusty.DiSanto@wheaton.edu
DIAB, Dorey .... 419-755-4811. 385 D
ddiab@ncstatecollege.edu
DIACON, Todd .... 330-672-8529. 382 B
tdiacon@kent.edu
DIAH, Max .... 516-773-5000. 545 H
diahm@usmma.edu
DIAL, Bill .... 303-914-6298... 84 I
bill.dial@rrcc.edu
DIAL, Cortez, K .... 804-524-5070. 515 D
cdial@vsu.edu
DIAL, Eugene, A .... 985-448-4021. 208 A
eugene.dial@nicholls.edu
DIAMOND, Alice .... 617-349-8550. 228 B
adiamond@lesley.edu
DIAMOND, Beverly, E .... 843-953-5528. 443 A
diamondb@cofc.edu
DIAMOND,
Christopher, R .... 860-832-1934... 87 K
diamondchr@ccsu.edu
DIAMOND, Fred .... 626-914-8691... 38 K
fdiamond@citruscollege.edu
DIAMOND, Holly .... 313-845-9887. 243 H
hadiamond@hfcc.edu
DIAMOND, John, N .... 479-575-2000... 23 I
diamond@uark.edu
DIAMOND, Raymond, T . 225-578-8846. 205 E
DIAMOND BURROWAY,
Sarah .... 606-326-2106. 194 J
sdiamondburrowa0001@kctc.edu
DIANA, Kate .... 952-888-4777. 263 B
kdiana@nwhealth.edu
DIANGELO, JR.,
Joseph, A .... 610-660-1645. 432 E
jodiange@sju.edu
DIAS, James .... 518-956-8170. 341 D
jdias@albany.edu

DIAS, Margaret, S .... 508-999-8791. 229 A
mdias@umassd.edu
DIAS, Robert .... 408-270-6400... 63 N
robert.dias@sjeccd.org
DIAWARA, Patricia .... 719-549-3058... 84 G
Patricia.Diawara@pueblocc.edu
DIAZ, Alfred .... 787-725-8120. 548 O
adiaz@eap.edu
DIAZ, Alphonso, V .... 765-494-9705. 171 M
avdiaz@purdue.edu
DIAZ, Amy .... 815-921-4283. 157 A
a.diaz@rockvalleycollege.edu
DIAZ, Andrea .... 401-254-3317. 440 B
adiaz@rwu.edu
DIAZ, Armando .... 210-567-0372. 493 A
diaza@uthscsa.edu
DIAZ, Brett .... 787-844-8181. 555 A
brett.diaz@upr.edu
DIAZ, Emiliano .... 916-278-3901... 34 D
diaz@csus.edu
DIAZ, Fernando .... 773-995-2259. 141 J
fdiaz@csu.edu
DIAZ, Francisco .... 973-720-3244. 308 I
diazf@wpunj.edu
DIAZ, Franco, L .... 787-284-1912. 550 F
fldiaz@ponce.inter.edu
DIAZ, Glenda .... 787-863-2390. 550 C
glenda.diaz@fajardo.inter.edu
DIAZ, Jackie .... 254-710-3805. 467 G
jackie_diaz@baylor.edu
DIAZ, Janet .... 313-883-8696. 249 E
diaz.janet@shms.edu
DIAZ, Javier .... 787-834-9595. 553 B
jdiaz@uaa.edu
DIAZ, Jesus, A .... 787-751-0178. 552 G
ac_jdiaz@suagm.edu
DIAZ, Joel .... 805-986-5810... 74 G
jdiaz@vcccd.edu
DIAZ, Jorge .... 787-786-3030. 547 F
jdiaz@ucb.edu.pr
DIAZ, Joseph .... 801-957-4043. 498 B
joseph.diaz@slcc.edu
DIAZ, Leticia, M .... 321-206-5602... 98 O
ldiaz@barry.edu
DIAZ, Linda .... 201-529-7461. 305 A
ldiaz@ramapo.edu
DIAZ, Lourdes .... 787-284-1912. 550 F
ldiaz@ponce.inter.edu
DIAZ, Maria, S .... 787-257-7373. 552 H
ue_mdiaz@suagm.edu
DIAZ, Mario .... 312-850-7492. 142 C
mdiaz103@ccc.edu
DIAZ, Mark .... 305-284-2862. 118 F
markdiaz@miami.edu
DIAZ, Mayra, E .... 787-725-8120. 548 O
mediaz@eap.edu
DIAZ, Miguel, H .... 937-229-2105. 391 C
mdiaz3@udayton.edu
DIAZ, Mischelle, R .... 512-448-8404. 479 C
mischeld@stedwards.edu
DIAZ, Neftali .... 787-852-1430. 549 C
n.diz.r@hccpr.edu
DIAZ, Paula .... 312-935-3033. 156 K
pdiaz@robertmorris.edu
DIAZ, Ramonita .... 787-878-5475. 549 L
rdiaz@arecibo.inter.edu
DIAZ, Robert .... 212-220-8305. 317 A
rdiaz@bmcc.cuny.edu
DIAZ, Roberto .... 215-717-3107. 414 B
roberto.diaz@curtis.edu
DIAZ, Russell .... 845-848-4048. 322 G
russell.diaz@dc.edu
DIAZ, Ruth, M .... 787-763-6700. 549 A
rmdiaz@se-pr.edu
DIAZ, Sam .... 570-504-9069. 413 B
DIAZ, Sharon, C .... 510-869-6512... 61 I
sdiaz@samuelmerritt.edu
DIAZ, Sonia .... 787-728-1515. 555 D
sdiaz@sagrado.edu
DIAZ, Walter .... 860-465-5000... 87 L
diazw@easternct.edu
DIAZ, Walter .... 956-665-3551. 492 B
diazwr@utpa.edu
DIAZ, Yesenia .... 305-821-3333. 105 A
ydiaz@fnu.edu
DIAZ-ALONSO, Hernan .. 213-613-2200... 67 E
hernan@sciarc.edu
DIAZ-BONACQUISTI,
Judi .... 303-556-4498... 83 D
jbonacqu@msudenver.edu
DIAZ-HERRERA,
Jorge, L .... 315-279-5201. 328 D
jdiazh@mail.keuka.edu
DIAZ-RODRIGUEZ,
Nereida .... 787-798-6732. 553 C
nereida.diaz@uccaribe.edu
DIAZ-TORRES, Marie ...... 973-353-5372. 306 D
mdtorres@newark.rutgers.edu
DIBB, Andrew M, T .... 267-502-2582. 410 I
andrew.dibb@brynathyn.edu

DIBBERT, Douglas, S ... 919-962-7050. 368 D doug_dibbert@unc.edu
DIBBLE, Emily ... 617-228-2412. 231 C dibble@bhcc.mass.edu
DIBBLE, Rita ... 484-365-7429. 422 D rdibble@lincoln.edu
DIBELLO, Nan, M ... 716-686-7800. 346 A nan.dibello@esc.edu
DIBENEDETTO, Eileen, M ... 212-854-7732. 314 G edibened@barnard.edu
DIBENEDETTO, Steve ... 312-261-3461. 153 I steve.dibenedetto@nl.edu
DIBENEDETTO, Steve ... 847-947-5409. 153 I steve.dibenedetto@nl.edu
DIBIASIO, Daniel, A ... 419-772-2030. 386 D d-dibiasio@onu.edu
DIBLEY, Paula ... 704-216-3467. 363 D paula.dibley@rccc.edu
DIBONIFAZIO, Susan ... 570-408-4000. 437 F susan.dibonifazio@wilkes.edu
DIBRIGIDA, Vladimir ... 303-329-6355... 80 G director@cstcm.edu
DIBRITO, Kyle, J ... 717-736-4117. 417 I kjdibrit@hacc.edu
DICAMILLO, Thomas ... 520-494-5204... 12 P tom.dicamillo@centralaz.edu
DICAPRIO, Deborah, A ... 845-575-3000. 330 D deborah.dicaprio@marist.edu
DICARLO, Joseph ... 508-929-8090. 230 G jdicarlo1@worcester.edu
DICARO, David ... 585-385-8025. 338 H ddicaro@sjfc.edu
DICARO, Kim ... 313-496-2625. 252 B kdicaro1@wcccd.edu
DICE, Douglas ... 989-463-7162. 239 B dice@alma.edu
DICE, Frances ... 412-237-3064. 413 D fdice@ccac.edu
DICESARE, Deborah, A ... 818-778-5522... 52 E dicesad@lavc.edu
DICHRISTINA, Joseph, J ... 814-332-4356. 409 D joseph.dichristina@allegheny.edu
DICK, Beth ... 231-777-0314. 247 G
DICK, Larry ... 956-380-8179. 479 B personnel@riogrande.edu
DICK, Larry ... 956-380-8179. 479 B ldick@riogrande.edu
DICK, Nancy ... 425-739-8228. 520 K nancy.dick@lwtech.edu
DICKASON, John ... 909-447-2512... 39 E jdickason@cst.edu
DICKENS, Brian, K ... 713-313-1379. 485 F dickensbk@tsu.edu
DICKENS, Margaret, A ... 715-833-6419. 539 J mdickens@cvtc.edu
DICKENS, Martha ... 828-398-7302. 357 N mdickens@abtech.edu
DICKENS, Reginald ... 704-216-6025. 356 D rdickens@livingstone.edu
DICKENS, Reginald ... 903-730-4890. 474 O rdickens@jarvis.edu
DICKENS, Robert, E ... 775-784-1417. 294 J robertd@unr.edu
DICKENS, Susan ... 651-779-3298. 258 C susan.dickens@century.edu
DICKENS, Tony ... 419-720-6670. 388 E tdickens@proskills.edu
DICKENSON, J. Barry ... 267-341-3373. 418 G bdickinson@holyfamily.edu
DICKER, James, W ... 610-330-5021. 420 D dickerj@lafayette.edu
DICKERMAN, Christopher, M ... 610-359-5302. 414 D cdickerman@dccc.edu
DICKERMAN, Robert ... 413-755-4606. 233 A dickerman@stcc.edu
DICKERSON, Cathy, S ... 540-375-2262. 509 B cdickerson@roanoke.edu
DICKERSON, Darby ... 806-742-3990. 487 D
DICKERSON, Dee Ann ... 918-647-1300. 394 I ddickerson@carlalbert.edu
DICKERSON, John, R ... 662-325-2663. 268 D jdickerson@registrar.msstate.edu
DICKERSON, Larry ... 816-802-3363. 275 J ldickerson@kcai.edu
DICKERSON, Mark ... 626-387-5763... 29 H mdickerson@apu.edu
DICKERSON, Mary Ann ... 913-469-8500. 187 J mdkerson@jccc.edu
DICKERSON, Shirley ... 936-468-4109. 482 A sdickerson@sfasu.edu
DICKERSON, Valerie ... 208-377-8080. 137 K vdickerson@carrington.edu
DICKERT, Gerry ... 409-984-6342. 486 H dickertgl@lamarpa.edu
DICKEY, Daryl ... 678-839-6534. 133 I ddickey@westga.edu
DICKEY, Elizabeth, D ... 212-875-4595. 314 C edickey@bankstreet.edu
DICKEY, Jennifer ... 313-664-7428. 241 C jdickey@collegeforcreativestudies.edu
DICKEY, M. Thaxter ... 813-988-5131. 104 A dickeyt@floridacollege.edu
DICKEY, Marilyn ... 850-201-6652. 117 D dickeym@tcc.fl.edu
DICKEY, Matt ... 417-626-1234. 279 J dickey.matt@occ.edu
DICKEY, Serita ... 281-998-6150. 479 G serita.dickey@sjcd.edu
DICKEY, Todd, R ... 213-740-8184... 74 A svpadmin@usc.edu
DICKEY, Wanda ... 813-988-5131. 104 A library@floridacollege.edu
DICKEY, Wyman ... 904-269-7086. 105 N wdickey@fortiscollege.edu
DICKHERBER, David ... 636-949-4907. 276 D ddickherber@lindenwood.edu
DICKIE, Christopher ... 870-612-2139... 25 A christopher.dickie@uaccb.edu
DICKINSON, Marjorie, M ... 530-752-2619... 70 J mmdickinson@ucdavis.edu
DICKINSON, Mark, D ... 651-696-6278. 256 L dickinsonm@macalester.edu
DICKINSON, Michael, B ... 607-255-9300. 322 A mbd3@cornell.edu
DICKINSON, Rosie, A ... 956-326-2202. 483 B rosie@tamiu.edu
DICKINSON, Susan ... 308-635-6785. 293 E dickinso@wncc.edu
DICKINSON NEIL, Terri ... 509-527-2632. 524 I rosa.jimenez@wallawalla.edu
DICKMEYER, Nathan ... 718-482-6119. 318 F ndickmeyer@lagcc.cuny.edu
DICKS, Gary ... 979-230-3305. 468 A gary.dicks@brazosport.edu
DICKSON, Ann ... 859-257-7619. 200 C hdsawd@uky.edu
DICKSON, Brook, E ... 540-362-6287. 505 G bdickson@hollins.edu
DICKSON, Chris, M ... 260-422-5561. 167 B cmdickson@indianatech.edu
DICKSON, Jo Carole ... 502-213-2411. 195 F jocarole.dickson@kctcs.edu
DICKSON, John ... 202-639-1843... 95 B jdickerson@corcoran.org
DICKSON, John ... 727-873-4350. 116 D jdickson@mail.usf.edu
DICKSON, Nancy, A ... 724-480-3553. 413 H nancy.dickson@ccbc.edu
DICKSON, Richard, P ... 504-865-5500. 207 C rpd@tulane.edu
DICKSON, Stacy ... 352-854-2322. 100 K dicksons@cf.edu
DICOLA, Rose Ann ... 412-237-6517. 413 D rdicola@ccac.edu
DIDIER, Kim ... 515-965-7064. 177 B kmdidier@dmacc.edu
DIDION, John ... 714-480-7489... 60 F didion_john@rsccd.edu
DIDION, Judy ... 419-517-8905. 383 C jdidion@lourdes.edu
DIEBOLD, Ann ... 610-519-4560. 436 F ann.diebold@villanova.edu
DIECKMAN, Stacy ... 402-844-7288. 291 I stacyd@northeast.edu
DIECKMANN, Mike, F ... 850-474-2555. 117 B michaeldieckmann@uwf.edu
DIECKMEYER, Diane ... 951-372-7199... 60 L diane.dieckmeyer@norcocollege.edu
DIEDERICH, Nicole ... 419-434-4445. 391 D diederich@findlay.edu
DIEDRCHS, Carol, P ... 614-292-6151. 386 E diedrichs.1@0osu.edu
DIEDRICH, Guy ... 979-458-6000. 482 E gdiedrich@tamus.edu
DIEDRICK, James, K ... 404-471-6102. 119 I jdiedrick@agnesscott.edu
DIEDRIECH, Dan, C ... 314-516-4734. 283 E diedriechd@umsl.edu
DIEFENDORF, Wendy ... 518-244-2443. 338 C diefew@sage.edu
DIEHL, Bert ... 440-525-7140. 382 M rdiehl@lakelandcc.edu
DIEHL, Dave ... 301-696-3800. 215 D diehld@hood.edu
DIEHL, Hope, L ... 610-359-5333. 414 D hdiehl@dccc.edu
DIEHL, Joan ... 570-348-6248. 423 B 1226mgr@pheg.follett.com
DIEHL, Melissa, M ... 570-577-3776. 411 A melissa.diehl@bucknell.edu
DIEHL, Michele ... 215-646-7300. 417 F diehl.m@gmc.edu
DIEHL, Randy, L ... 512-471-4141. 491 C diehl@austin.utexas.edu
DIEHL, Roberta, L ... 570-577-3310. 411 A roberta.diehl@bucknell.edu
DIEHL, Shanda ... 360-992-2421. 518 A sdiehl@clark.edu
DIEHL, Timothy ... 207-725-3716. 209 H tdiehl@bowdoin.edu
DIEHM, Perry ... 913-971-3722. 188 H pdiehm@mnu.edu
DIEKER, R. Joseph ... 319-895-4210. 177 A jdieker@cornellcollege.edu
DIEKMANN, Beth ... 507-285-7259. 261 A beth.diekmann@rctc.edu
DIEM, Richard, A ... 210-458-6463. 492 C richard.diem@utsa.edu
DIEMER, Gregory, M ... 715-346-2641. 538 A gdiemer@uwsp.edu
DIEMER, Rene ... 215-248-6305. 422 F registrar@ltsp.edu
DIEMER, Robert ... 352-588-8974. 112 D robert.diemer@saintleo.edu
DIENER, Connie ... 920-923-7615. 534 A cdiener@marianuniversity.edu
DIENER, Melissa ... 920-686-6146. 536 A Melissa.Diener@sl.edu
DIENST, Tom ... 907-796-6497... 11 A tom.dienst@uas.alaska.edu
DIEPENBROCK, Amy ... 210-436-3102. 479 D adiepenbrock@stmarytx.edu
DIERCKX, Heidi ... 607-735-1954. 323 H hdierckx@elmira.edu
DIERENFIELD, Bruce, J ... 716-888-2683. 316 C derenfb@canisius.edu
DIERICKX, George ... 269-782-1207. 250 C gdierickx@swmich.edu
DIERINGER, Deanna, L ... 907-474-6629... 10 I dldieringer@alaska.edu
DIERINGER, Dennis, D ... 770-484-1204. 128 E lru@lru.edu
DIERINGER, Jerome, T ... 410-704-2516. 220 E jdieringer@towson.edu
DIERKS, David, R ... 319-335-3305. 175 I david-dierks@uiowa.edu
DIERLAM, Lois ... 914-337-9300. 321 E lois.dierlam@concordia-ny.edu
DIERS, Jane ... 217-544-6464. 158 D
DIESNER, Michael, R ... 717-867-6231. 421 H diesner@lvc.edu
DIETERLE, Sheila ... 719-336-1621... 82 R sheila.dieterle@lamarcc.edu
DIETRICH, Darryl ... 218-723-6165. 254 K ddietric@css.edu
DIETRICH, David ... 330-287-1203. 386 F dietrich.114@osu.edu
DIETRICH, John, F ... 321-433-7090. 101 M dietrichj@easternflorida.edu
DIETRICH, Keith ... 253-396-0467. 524 B
DIETRICH, Robert, C ... 570-326-3761. 427 B rdietric@pct.edu
DIETRICH, Robin ... 540-887-7025. 507 A rdietrich@mbc.edu
DIETRICH, Sandra ... 919-866-5674. 364 G sldietrich@waketech.edu
DIETZ, Carol, P ... 216-397-4314. 381 R cdietz@jcu.edu
DIETZ, Fred, K ... 270-809-2684. 198 B fdietz@murraystate.edu
DIETZ, Kenneth ... 502-852-6176. 200 D kenneth.dietz@louisville.edu
DIETZ, Larry ... 309-438-5451. 147 J ldietz@ilstu.edu
DIETZ, Sally ... 607-274-3385. 327 E sdietz@ithaca.edu
DIETZ, Sidney ... 602-286-8290... 14 L dietz@gatewaycc.edu
DIETZEL, Kristin, A ... 563-556-5110. 181 E dietzelk@nicc.edu
DIETZLER, Deborah, H ... 706-542-2251. 133 C dietzler@uga.edu
DIETZMAN, Steve ... 520-325-0123... 17 R sdietzman@suva.edu
DIEUDONNE', Jose' ... 706-385-1015. 130 F jose.dieudonne@point.edu
DIEZ, Mickey ... 985-448-7914. 203 B mickey.diez@fletcher.edu
DIEZ, Nicole ... 305-899-3593... 98 O ndiez@barry.edu
DIFELICIANTONIO, Richard, G ... 610-409-3200. 436 B rdifeliciantonio@ursinus.edu
DIFFEY, Steve ... 662-472-2312. 267 B sdiffey@holmescc.edu
DIFFIE, Rita Nell ... 432-685-4503. 476 G rndiffie@midland.edu
DIFFILY, Michael, E ... 603-577-6000. 296 F diffily@dwc.edu
DIFILIPO, Steve ... 410-287-1021. 214 B sdifilipo@cecil.edu
DIFOLCO PARKER, Jane 334-844-4000..... 1 G jdp0035@auburn.edu
DIFRANCO, Heidi ... 803-641-3397. 448 A heidid@usca.edu
DIFRONZO-HEITZER, Nicola ... 610-647-4400. 418 I ndifronzoheitzer@immaculata.edu
DIGATE, Russell, J ... 718-990-6411. 339 A digater@stjohns.edu
DIGBY, Annette ... 573-876-7213. 282 H adigby@stephens.edu
DIGBY, Joan ... 516-299-2840. 329 D joan.digby@liu.edu
DIGENNARO, John ... 440-826-2228. 374 F jdigenna@bw.edu
DIGERLANDO, Rose ... 847-214-7635. 144 F rdigerlando@elgin.edu
DIGGS, Charles ... 617-541-5310. 232 G cdiggs@rcc.mass.edu
DIGGS, Jeff ... 410-276-0306. 218 D jdiggs@host.sdc.edu
DIGGS, Mawine ... 313-922-3311. 252 B
DIGGS, Michael ... 217-875-7200. 156 J mdiggs@richland.edu
DIGIACOMO, Robert ... 631-656-2154. 324 F robert.digiacomo@ftc.edu
DIGIANFILIPPO, Denise . 602-787-6693... 15 B denise.digianfilippo@paradisevalley.edu
DIGIRONIMO, Joseph ... 215-468-8800. 419 F director@culinaryarts.edu
DIGMAN, Jo-Ann ... 314-539-5358. 281 D jdigman1@stlcc.edu
DIGRAZIA, Lauren ... 860-486-3903... 92 A lauren.digrazia@uconn.edu
DIGREGORIO, Christian . 570-348-6234. 423 B digregorio@marywood.edu
DIGREGORIO, Theresa ... 716-614-6430. 334 E digregor@niagaracc.suny.edu
DIGREORIO, Jeffrey ... 510-849-8283... 46 B jdigreorio@gtu.edu
DIGUISEPPE, Steven, A ... 717-872-3352. 429 D steve.diguiseppe@millersville.edu
DIINA-DEMPSEY, Stephanie, C ... 512-223-7736. 466 I diina@austincc.edu
DIJULIA, Dominick, J ... 610-660-1707. 432 E ddijulia@sju.edu
DIKEMAN, Scott ... 802-468-1214. 501 B scott.dikeman@castleton.edu
DILALLA, David ... 618-536-5535. 159 G ddilalla@siu.edu
DILANDO, Armand ... 617-254-2610. 236 B
DILAURO, Nanette ... 212-854-2154. 314 G ndilauro@barnard.edu
DILBECK, Jack ... 270-706-8892. 195 A jdilbeck0001@kctcs.edu
DILENO, Susan ... 440-826-2222. 374 F sdileno@bw.edu
DILEO, Jeffrey ... 361-570-4201. 489 E dileoj@uhv.edu
DILES, David ... 216-368-2866. 375 J dxd87@case.edu
DILGER, Patrick ... 203-392-6586... 88 A dilgerp1@southernct.edu
DILIBERTO, James, G ... 631-691-8733. 327 D dilibertoj@idti.edu
DILIBERTO, John, G ... 631-691-8733. 327 D johng@idti.edu
DILISIO, James ... 410-704-2131. 220 E jdilisio@towson.edu
DILL, Anna Maria ... 541-962-3774. 405 H adill@eou.edu
DILL, April ... 580-477-7710. 401 J april.dill@wosc.edu
DILL, Bonnie, T ... 301-405-2095. 219 B btdill@umd.edu
DILL, Gary, A ... 575-492-2123. 312 M gdill@usw.edu
DILL, Herb ... 440-375-7555. 382 L hdill@lec.edu
DILL, Jane, P ... 864-644-5404. 446 I jdill@swu.edu
DILL, Jeremy ... 207-741-5821. 211 A jdill@smccme.edu
DILL, Ken ... 864-644-5431. 446 I kdill@swu.edu
DILL, Marian ... 423-614-8304. 455 L mdill@leeuniversity.edu
DILL, Randy, G ... 208-732-6600. 138 B rdill@csi.edu
DILL, Rosemary ... 662-621-4201. 266 D rdill@coahomacc.edu
DILL, Tracy ... 218-755-4022. 258 A tdill@bemidjistate.edu
DILLABOUGH, Daniel, J 619-260-2247... 73 I dillaboughd@sandiego.edu
DILLALOGUE, Eric ... 305-809-3542. 104 I eric.dillalogue@fkcc.edu
DILLANE, Robert, J ... 717-867-6060. 421 H dillane@lvc.edu
DILLARD, III, Ben, P ... 843-661-8000. 443 G ben.dillard@fdtc.edu
DILLARD, Glenn ... 501-279-4407... 21 C gdillard@harding.edu
DILLARD, Maria, P ... 954-262-8051. 109 K mdillard@nova.edu
DILLAWAY, Colleen ... 661-654-2456... 32 H cdillaway@csub.edu

DILLBECK, Michael .... 641-472-1187. 180 N
sdillbeck@mum.edu
DILLBECK, Susan .... 641-472-1187. 180 N
sdillbeck@mum.edu
DILLE, Wayne .... 641-628-5268. 176 E
dille@central.edu
DILLEMUTH, Jim .... 612-659-6600. 259 D
jim.dillemuth@minneapolis.edu
DILLENBERG, Jack .... 480-219-6081. 271 A
jdillenberg@atsu.edu
DILLENBURG, Brenda .... 715-389-7011. 540 D
brenda.dillenburg@mstc.edu
DILLER, Donna .... 505-224-4000. 309 E
ddiller@cnm.edu
DILLER, Lisa, C .... 423-236-2417. 458 J
ldiller@southern.edu
DILLINGHAM, Martin ..... 615-383-4848. 464 D
mdillingham@watkins.edu
DILLINGHAM, Sabine .... 240-895-4192. 218 A
sldillingham@smcm.edu
DILLINGHAM, Tom .... 931-393-1756. 461 A
tdillingham@mscc.edu
DILLINGHAM-EVANS,
Donna .... 435-652-7506. 497 E
dillingh@dixie.edu
DILLION, Diana .... 605-856-2355. 451 B
diana.dillion@sintegleska.edu
DILLMAN, David .... 903-813-3000. 466 H
ddillman@austincollege.edu
DILLMAN, Joanna .... 985-732-6640. 203 D
DILLMAN, Rob .... 916-649-8168... 49 I
rdillman@kaplan.edu
DILLON, Anastacia .... 503-768-7095. 403 K
adillon@lclark.edu
DILLON, Andrew, P .... 512-471-3821. 491 C
adillon@ischool.utexas.edu
DILLON, Charles, T .... 231-843-5540. 252 H
ctdillon@westshore.edu
DILLON, Clotilde .... 212-594-4000. 347 H
cdillon@tcicollege.edu
DILLON, III, Cyrus, I ..... 434-223-6197. 505 E
cdillon@hsc.edu
DILLON, Ellen, M .... 308-635-6787. 293 E
dillone@wncc.edu
DILLON, Francis, X .... 508-565-1344. 237 A
fdillon@stonehill.edu
DILLON, Glen .... 304-293-7206. 530 D
ghdillon@hsc.wvu.edu
DILLON, Greg .... 765-658-4500. 165 F
gdillon@depauw.edu
DILLON, Howard .... 212-217-4040. 324 C
howard_dillon@fitnyc.edu
DILLON, James, S .... 717-720-4100. 427 G
jdillon@passhe.edu
DILLON, John .... 610-683-4002. 429 A
dillon@kutztown.edu
DILLON, Kendall .... 515-271-1661. 177 H
kendall.dillon@dmu.edu
DILLON, Mary Jane .... 904-819-6314. 103 E
dillonmj@flagler.edu
DILLON, Michael .... 410-455-2111. 219 D
mdillon@umbc.edu
DILLON, Mike .... 573-592-4209. 285 D
mike.dillon@williamwoods.edu
DILLON, Patricia .... 215-951-1430. 420 B
dillonp@lasalle.edu
DILLON, Paul .... 201-360-4631. 302 D
pdillon@hccc.edu
DILLON, R. Mark .... 630-752-5016. 163 F
mark.dillon@wheaton.edu
DILLON, Rick .... 304-384-5231. 529 E
rdillon@concord.edu
DILLON, Sarah .... 715-675-3331. 541 A
Dillon@ntc.edu
DILLON, T. Kevin .... 713-500-3535. 492 E
kevin.dillon@uth.tmc.edu
DILLON, Thomas .... 419-434-5777. 391 D
dillon@findlay.edu
DILLON HOGAN, Kate ... 716-375-2128. 338 E
khogan@sbu.edu
DILLOW, Al .... 217-245-3162. 146 F
al.dillow@ic.edu
DILLOW, Rhonda .... 618-634-3251. 158 M
rhondad@shawneecc.edu
DILLOW, Sarah, L .... 423-652-4739. 455 I
sldillow@king.edu
DILLSWORTH, Gary .... 716-926-8920. 326 B
gdillsworth@hilbert.edu
DILMORE, Donald, H ..... 814-732-2779. 428 E
ddilmore@edinboro.edu
DILORENZO, Peter .... 856-227-7200. 300 B
pdilorenzo@camdencc.edu
DILORENZO, Thomas .... 701-777-2167. 371 C
thomas.dilorenzo@und.edu
DILORENZO, Vicki .... 518-694-7331. 313 B
vicki.dilorenzo@acphs.edu
DILS, Keith .... 724-738-2292. 429 F
keith.dils@sru.edu
DILTS, Christine .... 845-848-7602. 322 G
DILUSTRO, John .... 252-398-6220. 353 H
dilusj@chowan.edu

DIMAGGIO,
Jacqueline, R .... 864-250-8179. 444 E
jacqui.dimaggio@gvltec.edu
DIMAIO, Amy .... 408-453-9900... 47 H
adimaio@henley-putnam.edu
DIMAIO, Judith .... 516-686-7594. 333 H
jdimaio@nyit.edu
DIMARCO, Casey .... 518-694-7278. 313 B
casey.dimarco@acphs.edu
DIMARCO, Erin .... 302-356-6924... 94 E
erin.j.dimarco@wilmu.edu
DIMARCO, Scott, R .... 570-662-4689. 429 C
sdimarco@mansfield.edu
DIMARIO, Joseph, X ...... 847-578-8633. 157 F
joseph.dimario@rosalindfranklin.edu
DIMARZO, Dean .... 845-569-3219. 332 B
dean.dimarzo@msmc.edu
DIMASI, Louis .... 802-654-2566. 500 B
ldimasi@smcvt.edu
DIMATTIA, Andrea .... 570-504-9634. 413 B
DIMAURO, JR., Alfred ... 508-831-6678. 238 F
fred@wpi.edu
DIMAURO, Giorgio, G .... 848-932-7787. 306 B
giorgio.dimauro@rutgers.edu
DIMENNA, Grey .... 732-571-3598. 303 C
gdimenna@monmouth.edu
DIMENT, Gregory, S .... 269-337-7149. 244 K
Greg.Diment@kzoo.edu
DIMICK, Jeffrey, A .... 304-865-6131. 527 F
jeffrey.dimick@ovu.edu
DIMINO, John, L .... 215-204-7276. 433 K
john.dimino@temple.edu
DIMINO, Laura .... 717-901-5139. 418 E
ldimino@harrisburgu.edu
DIMINO, Solweig .... 973-300-2215. 307 F
sdimino@sussex.edu
DIMITROV, Danielle, E ... 718-982-2250. 317 E
danielle.dimitrov@csi.cuny.edu
DIMITROVA, Diana .... 604-274-3306. 327 E
ddimitrova@ithaca.edu
DIMKOVA, Dimitrina ...... 703-323-3122. 513 C
ddimkova@nvcc.edu
DIMOLA, Anne .... 631-244-3020. 323 B
dimolaa@dowling.edu
DIMOLITSAS, Spiros ...... 202-687-3730... 95 E
seniorvp@georgetown.edu
DIMON, Denise .... 619-260-6824... 73 I
dimon@sandiego.edu
DIMOND, David .... 914-632-5400. 331 K
ddimond@monroecollege.edu
DIMOND, Marita .... 530-257-6181... 50 F
mdimond@lassencollege.edu
DINAN, Susan .... 973-720-3657. 308 I
dinans@wpunj.edu
DINARDO, N. John .... 215-895-2510. 415 B
dinardo@drexel.edu
DINDIAL-THOMPSON,
Heidi .... 727-725-2688. 102 I
HDindialthompson@cci.edu
DINDOFFER, Tamara, L . 517-750-1200. 250 E
tammyd@arbor.edu
DINEGAR, Leonard .... 303-860-5600... 85 K
leonard.dinegar@cu.edu
DINELLO, William, V ...... 718-262-2350. 319 F
wdinello@york.cuny.edu
DINGER, Tim .... 479-524-7234... 21 G
tdinger@jbu.edu
DINGESS, Debbie, C ...... 304-896-7416. 528 F
debbie.dingess@southernwv.edu
DINGLE, Terry .... 843-661-8321. 443 G
terry.dingle@fdtc.edu
DINGLEY, Clare .... 320-589-6030. 264 F
strandcd@morris.umn.edu
DINGMAN, Brandie .... 518-381-1280. 340 G
dingmabm@sunysccc.edu
DINGMANN, Melissa ..... 218-281-8576. 264 E
dingmann@umn.edu
DINICE, Elizabeth, M ...... 609-894-9311. 299 I
edinice@bcc.edu
DINIELLI, Michael .... 909-652-6904... 37 M
michael.dinielli@chaffey.edu
DINKEL, Georgianne ...... 530-226-4727... 66 D
jdinkel@simpsonu.edu
DINKEL, M.L. (Mel) .... 909-621-8026... 39 B
mel_dinkel@cuc.claremont.edu
DINKEL, Shirley .... 785-670-1470. 191 D
shirley.dinkel@washburn.edu
DINKINS, Marva .... 910-879-5570. 358 B
mdinkins@bladencc.edu
DINKINS, Sandy, E .... 904-264-2172. 111 P
sdinkins@iws.edu
DINNAN, Matthew, A ..... 203-254-4000... 89 I
madinnan@fairfield.edu
DINNDORF, Elizabeth, A 803-786-3178. 443 B
bdinndorf@columbiasc.edu
DINNO, Christopher .... 707-664-2870... 36 B
christopher.dinno@sonoma.edu
DINSE, Jayne .... 507-389-7269. 261 E
jayne.dinse@southcentral.edu
DINTINO, Dennis .... 718-260-3026. 336 E
ddintino@poly.edu

DINWIDDIE, Mollie, D ... 660-543-4140. 283 A
dinwiddie@ucmo.edu
DION, Kent .... 406-377-9416. 286 A
kent_d@dawson.edu
DIONNE, David .... 256-824-6820..... 8 F
david.dionne@uah.edu
DIONNE, Woody .... 802-635-1280. 501 D
woody.dionne@jsc.edu
DIORIO, Annette .... 610-330-5082. 420 D
diorioa@lafayette.edu
DIORIO, Mary Ann .... 860-255-3474... 89 G
mdiorio@txcc.commnet.edu
DIORIO, Nicole .... 508-767-7078. 222 C
nm.diorio@assumption.edu
DIPADOVA, Audra .... 949-582-4616... 67 C
adipadova@saddleback.edu
DIPADOVA-STOCKS,
Laurie .... 816-559-5617. 280 C
laurie.dipadovastocks@park.edu
DIPALMA, Allen, A .... 412-624-7415. 435 C
dipalma@pitt.edu
DIPAOLA, Robert, S .... 732-235-2465. 306 A
dipaolrs@cinj.rutgers.edu
DIPAOLO, Stephen, J ..... 848-445-5012. 306 A
sdip@uco.rutgers.edu
DIPETRO, David .... 412-396-5140. 415 F
dipetro@duq.edu
DIPIERRO, John .... 269-965-3931. 244 O
dipierroj@kellogg.edu
DIPIETRO, Joe .... 865-974-2241. 463 B
utpresident@tennessee.edu
DIPIETRO, Mark .... 802-387-1632. 499 E
markdepietro@landmark.edu
DIPIETRO, Stephen .... 215-895-4264. 415 B
stephen.l.dipietro@drexel.edu
DIPIETRO-STEWART,
Suze .... 609-652-4607. 305 C
suze.dipietro@stockton.edu
DIPIRO, Joseph, T .... 843-792-8450. 445 B
dipiroj@musc.edu
DIPIRO, Joseph, T .... 803-777-4151. 447 G
joseph.dipiro@sc.edu
DIPLOCK, Peter .... 860-486-2915... 92 A
peter.diplock@uconn.edu
DIPPMAN, Terry .... 419-473-2700. 378 I
tdippman@daviscollege.edu
DIPUCCIO, Denise .... 910-962-7933. 369 C
dipucciod@uncw.edu
DIRADDO, Colleen .... 484-384-2943. 425 I
cdiraddo@eastern.edu
DIRAIMO, Michael, J ...... 814-865-6563. 426 A
mjd256@psu.edu
DIRE, James .... 808-245-8229. 136 H
dire@hawaii.edu
DIRECTOR, Stephen, W .. 617-373-2170. 235 F
DIRIKER, Veronique, L ... 410-651-8142. 219 E
vdiriker@umes.edu
DIRK, Brian .... 440-375-7220. 382 L
bdirk@lec.edu
DIRKS, Nicholas, B .... 510-642-7464... 70 I
chancellor@berkeley.edu
DIRKSCHNEIDER, Carla . 402-552-6295. 288 L
dirkschneider@clarksoncollege.edu
DIRKSE, John .... 661-654-6181... 32 H
jdirkse@csub.edu
DIRKSEN, Dawn .... 866-323-0233... 60 E
DIRLAM, David .... 757-233-8893. 515 H
DIRST, Eric .... 630-515-4510. 144 A
edirst@devry.edu
DISABATINO, Gail .... 864-656-2161. 442 C
gaild@clemson.edu
DISABATO, Sharyn .... 352-588-7438. 112 D
sharyn.disabato@saintleo.edu
DISAIA, Kenneth, F .... 401-598-2346. 439 B
kdisaia@jwu.edu
DISALVIO, Philip .... 617-287-7925. 228 G
philip.disalvio@umb.edu
DISALVO, Stephen .... 314-529-9521. 276 G
sdisalvo@maryville.edu
DISALVO, Steven, R .... 603-641-7010. 297 G
sdisalvo@anselm.edu
DISANTI, Francis, J .... 610-660-1506. 432 E
disanti@sju.edu
DISATE, Nancy .... 303-861-1151... 81 E
ndisate@concorde.edu
DISCENZA, Tobias .... 239-489-9329. 101 O
tjdiscenza@edison.edu
DISCHINO, Maureen ...... 617-989-4009. 237 G
dischinom@wit.edu
DISHMAN, Leslie, B .... 985-448-4415. 208 A
leslie.dishman@nicholls.edu
DISHMAN, Marcie .... 919-718-7491. 359 B
mdishman@cccc.edu
DISHNER, Annette, H ..... 252-451-8236. 362 D
adishner@nashcc.edu
DISKIN, Becca, L .... 417-659-5422. 278 D
diskin-b@mssu.edu
DISLA, Jessica .... 973-748-9000. 299 F
jessica_disla@bloomfield.edu

DISMUKES, JR.,
Tommy, G .... 334-833-4402..... 4 D
tdismukes@huntingdon.edu
DISNEW, Carolyn .... 212-752-1530. 328 G
carolyn.disnew@limcollege.edu
DISORBO, Brenda .... 423-478-6215. 460 D
bdisorbo@clevelandstatecc.edu
DISPIGNO, OFM,
Francis, J .... 716-375-2142. 338 E
DISQUE, Carol .... 336-506-4138. 357 M
carol.disque@alamancecc.edu
DISS, Amy .... 941-907-2262. 103 C
adiss@evergladesuniversity.edu
DISS, Christina .... 503-883-2282. 404 A
cdiss@linfield.edu
DISTANISLAO, Mary ...... 414-288-7040. 534 B
mary.distanislao@marquette.edu
DISTASI, Vincent, F .... 724-458-2116. 417 E
vfdistasi@gcc.edu
DISTEFANO, Ann, L .... 570-577-3616. 411 A
ann.distefano@bucknell.edu
DISTEFANO, Anthony, F . 215-780-1420. 433 A
tdistefano@salus.edu
DISTEFANO, Dawn .... 516-572-7943. 332 C
dawn.distefano@ncc.edu
DISTEFANO,
Jacqueline, S .... 585-385-8013. 338 H
jdistefano@sjfc.edu
DISTEFANO, Jennifer ...... 603-668-2211. 297 I
j.distefano@snhu.edu
DISTEFANO, Joanna, M . 304-462-4118. 529 G
joanna.distefano@glenville.edu
DISTEFANO, Phillip, P ... 303-492-8908... 85 L
phil.distefano@colorado.edu
DISTISO, Christopher ..... 860-628-4751... 90 D
cdistiso@lincolncollegene.edu
DITCHFIELD, Dora .... 706-864-1951. 133 D
dora.ditchfield@ung.edu
DITCHIK, Jill .... 718-270-2075. 342 D
jditchik@downstate.edu
DITHOMAS, Deborah .... 760-252-2411... 29 I
ddithomas@barstow.edu
DITMAN, Mark .... 713-348-5441. 479 A
mditman@rice.edu
DITTEMORE, Nancy .... 951-785-2300... 50 B
ndittemo@lasierra.edu
DITTMAN, Jeff, L .... 605-256-5229. 451 H
jeff.dittman@dsu.edu
DITTMAN, Judith, L .... 605-256-5112. 451 H
judy.dittman@dsu.edu
DITTMANN, Mariam .... 404-297-9522. 126 A
dittmannm@gptc.edu
DITTMER, Amy .... 573-592-4313. 285 D
amy.dittmer@williamwoods.edu
DITTMER,
Harold "Hal", E .... 916-447-5171. 289 I
hdittmer@wellhead.com
DITTO, William, L .... 808-956-6451. 136 B
wditto@hawaii.edu
DITULIO, James, E .... 309-298-2453. 162 K
je-ditulio@wiu.edu
DITULLIO, Anthony .... 315-267-2135. 344 C
ditulija@potsdam.edu
DITULLIO, Daniel, F .... 508-767-7321. 222 C
df.ditullio@assumption.edu
DITZLER, Mauri, A .... 309-457-2127. 153 D
mditzler@monmouthcollege.edu
DIVELY, Mary Jo .... 412-268-9519. 412 H
mjdively@andrew.cmu.edu
DIVEN-BROWN, Laura ... 662-915-7175. 270 B
ldivenbr@olemiss.edu
DIVENS, Gary .... 856-338-1817. 300 B
gdivens@camdencc.edu
DIVERSI, Sarah .... 603-206-8004. 296 A
sdiversi@ccsnh.edu
DIVINE, Darren, D .... 702-651-5602. 294 E
darren.divine@csn.edu
DIVINE, David .... 409-933-8309. 469 E
ddivine@com.edu
DIVINO, Claudio .... 507-288-4563. 255 C
academic@crossroadscollege.edu
DIVITA, Brian .... 616-632-2929. 239 E
bjd002@aquinas.edu
DIVITA KOPACZ, Anne .. 312-893-7161. 145 B
adivitakopacz@erikson.edu
DIVITO, Catherine .... 501-812-2206... 22 G
cdivito@pulaskitech.edu
DIVJAK, Robert .... 203-575-8235... 89 B
rdivjak@nvcc.commnet.edu
DIWARA, Patrica .... 719-502-2037... 84 A
patricia.diawar@ppcc.edu
DIX, Rachel, T .... 252-985-5175. 365 D
rdix@ncwc.edu
DIXON, Ann .... 501-279-4349... 21 C
adixon@harding.edu
DIXON, Bradley .... 785-442-6028. 187 E
bdixon@highlandcc.edu
DIXON, Brenda .... 575-769-2811. 309 F
brenda.dixon@clovis.edu
DIXON, Bruce, W .... 606-474-3215. 194 H
bdixon@kcu.edu

DIXON, Carol, M 614-235-4136. 390 A cdixon@TLSohio.edu
DIXON, Cathy 410-626-2548. 217 G cathy.dixon@sjca.edu
DIXON, Chester, L 512-223-1222. 466 I cdixon@austincc.edu
DIXON, Diane 315-568-3065. 333 C ddixon@nycc.edu
DIXON, Gentry 567-661-7617. 387 L gentry_dixon@owens.edu
DIXON, Isaac 503-768-6239. 403 K idixon@lclark.edu
DIXON, Janet 701-224-5739. 372 B janet.dixon@bismarckstate.edu
DIXON, Jennifer 773-244-5530. 154 G jadixon@northpark.edu
DIXON, Jenny 928-681-5656. 15 L jdixon@mohave.edu
DIXON, Jeri, L 630-801-7900. 162 J jdixon@waubonsee.edu
DIXON, Jesse, L 715-836-3367. 536 E dixonjl@uwec.edu
DIXON, John 843-661-1335. 444 B jdixon@fmarion.edu
DIXON, Kris 609-894-9311. 299 I kdixon@bcc.edu
DIXON, Lloyd 937-708-5724. 393 A ldixon@wilberforce.edu
DIXON, Michael, G 260-982-5000. 170 U mgdixon@manchester.edu
DIXON, Patrick 870-972-2042. 19 N pdixon@astate.edu
DIXON, Paula 706-245-7226. 124 D pdixon@ec.edu
DIXON, JR., Ralph, W 704-406-4253. 354 C rdixon@gardner-webb.edu
DIXON, Richard 405-946-7799. 398 L richardd@plattcollege.org
DIXON, Rick, L 660-543-4255. 283 A dixon@ucmo.edu
DIXON, Robert 312-413-1878. 161 D robd@uic.edu
DIXON, Robert 405-744-6512. 397 H robert.dixon@okstate.edu
DIXON, Roger 478-471-2720. 128 I roger.dixon@maconstate.edu
DIXON, Samuel 678-466-4200. 123 A samdixon@clayton.edu
DIXON, Serafina Marie 734-432-5338. 246 B sserafina@madonna.edu
DIXON, Sherri, L 407-582-3306. 118 M sdixon@valenciacollege.edu
DIXON, Siri 503-222-3225. 403 B sdixon@cci.edu
DIXON, Sylvia 704-922-6475. 360 F dixon.sylvia@gaston.edu
DIXON, Terrance 404-954-6520. 129 D tdixon@morehouse.edu
DIXON, Terry 251-981-3771. 2 I terry.dixon@columbiasouthern.edu
DIXON, William 270-831-9650. 195 D bill.dixon@kctcs.edu
DIXSON, Mary 210-486-4937. 464 J mdixson1@alamo.edu
DIZAZZO, Laura 253-833-9111. 520 C lgriep@geenriver.edu
DIZAZZO, Laura 206-934-5492. 522 J laura.dizazzo@seattlecolleges.edu
DIZINNO, Janet, B 210-436-3737. 479 D jdizinno@stmarytx.edu
DJALALI, Chaden 319-335-2610. 175 I chaden-djalali@uiowa.edu
DJIN, Yana 212-247-3434. 329 L ydjin@mandl.edu
DLUGOS, James, S 207-893-7711. 211 G jdlugos@sjcme.edu
DLUGOS, OSA, Raymond 978-837-5130. 234 A raymond.dlugos@merrimack.edu
DMITROVSKY, Ethan 713-792-6161. 493 B
DMOCH, Jack, L 757-455-3114. 515 H jdmoch@vwc.edu
DMOHOWSKI, Emily 303-753-6046. 85 B edmohowski@rmcad.edu
DOAK, Bryan 928-344-7617. 11 L bryan.doak@azwestern.edu
DOAK, Greg 207-768-9571. 212 G greg.doak@umpi.edu
DOAK, James, W 254-710-2222. 467 G jim_doak@baylor.edu
DOAK, Josh 417-659-4460. 278 D doak-j@mssu.edu
DOAK, Rebecca 330-823-2889. 391 E doakaw@mountunion.edu
DOAK, Robert 773-380-6783. 140 D bob.doak@seabury.edu
DOAN, Cathy 706-886-6831. 133 A cdoan@tfc.edu
DOAN, Kathleen 207-741-5805. 211 A kdoan@smccme.edu
DOAN, Viet 701-231-5143. 371 G viet.doan@ndsu.edu
DOANE, Christopher 502-852-6907. 200 D doane@louisville.edu
DOANE, Dudley, J 434-924-6166. 511 B djd4j@virginia.edu
DOANE, Dudley, J 434-982-3013. 511 B djd4j@virginia.edu
DOANE, Paulann, T 307-268-2256. 542 X pdoane@caspercollege.edu
DOBBELAAR, Henry 201-216-5340. 307 E hdobbela@stevens.edu
DOBBELAERE, Arthur, G 630-515-7305. 153 B adobbe@midwestern.edu
DOBBELMANN, Duncan 802-440-4400. 498 G duncand@bennington.edu
DOBBERSTEIN, Trina 440-826-2111. 374 F tdobbers@bw.edu
DOBBINS, Eric 816-802-3468. 275 J edobbins@kcai.edu
DOBBINS, Kathleen 256-726-7266. 6 B dobbins@oakwood.edu
DOBBINS, Kenneth, W 573-651-2222. 282 B president@semo.edu
DOBBINS, Tamika 419-530-5923. 392 B Tamika.Dobbins@utoledo.edu
DOBBS, Gwen 479-636-9222. 22 C gdobbs@nwacc.edu
DOBBS, Paul 617-879-7105. 230 B pauldobbs@massart.edu
DOBBS, Ricky 903-886-5878. 483 E ricky.dobbs@tamuc.edu
DOBELLE, Evan, S 413-572-5201. 230 F edobelle@westfield.ma.edu
DOBI, Hanko, H 203-932-7191. 92 E hdobi@newhaven.edu
DOBISE, Michael 413-748-3880. 236 I mdobise@springfieldcollegel.edu
DOBISH, Rodney, W 412-396-4781. 415 F dobish@duq.edu
DOBKIN, Bethami 925-631-4408. 61 F bethami.dobkin4@stmarys-ca.edu
DOBKIN, David, P 609-258-3020. 304 E ddobkin@princeton.edu
DOBLIN, Stephen, A 409-880-8398. 486 F steve.doblin@lamar.edu
DOBMEYER, Ann 413-565-1000. 222 F dobmeyer@baypath.edu
DOBRANSKY, Mary 402-557-7160. 288 G mary.dobransky@bellevue.edu
DOBRICH, Carl 312-808-6300. 147 F
DOBRIN, Allan, H 646-664-2888. 316 I allan.dobrin@cuny.edu
DOBRINSKY, Herbert, C 212-960-0850. 351 M dobrinsk@yu.edu
DOBROTA, Joe 202-319-6369. 94 G dobrota@cua.edu
DOBROWSKI, Pauline 508-565-1363. 237 A pdobrowski@stonehill.edu
DOBROWSKI, Pauline 508-565-1290. 237 A pdobrowski@stonehill.edu
DOBRY, Diane 518-255-5443. 344 E dobrydf@cobleskill.edu
DOBSON, Alyssa 814-732-1965. 428 E adobson@edinboro.edu
DOBSON, Cheryl 417-625-9389. 278 D dobson-c@mssu.edu
DOBSON, Cheryl 914-323-5177. 330 B cheryl.dobson@mville.edu
DOBSON, Henry (Van), V 610-758-3774. 422 A hvd211@lehigh.edu
DOBSON, Jennie, P 256-549-8263. 3 M jdobson@gadsdenstate.edu
DOBSON, Lark, T 301-322-0616. 217 F ldobson@pgcc.edu
DOBSON, Lisa 910-592-8081. 363 E ldobson@sampsoncc.edu
DOBSON, Timothy 575-646-2101. 310 I tdobson@nmsu.edu
DOBSON-HOPKINS, Nina 443-885-3130. 217 A nina.hopkins@morgan.edu
DOCKEN, Lori 608-263-2571. 536 C ldocken@uwsa.edu
DOCKENDORF, Amy, L 605-256-5130. 451 H amy.dockendorf@dsu.edu
DOCKERY, Benjamin 502-897-4629. 199 B bdockery@sbts.edu
DOCKERY, David, S 731-661-5180. 462 F ddockery@uu.edu
DOCKERY, Sheila 910-879-5505. 358 B sdockery@bladencc.edu
DOCKETY, Maribeth, B 302-259-6155. 93 E mdockety@dtcc.edu
DOCKING, Jeffrey, R 517-265-5161. 238 G jdocking@adrian.edu
DOCKINS, Natalie, C 559-442-4600. 68 I natalie.culver-dockins@fresnocitycollege.edu
DOCKINS, Waynna 870-612-2009. 25 A waynna.dockins@uaccb.edu
DOCKMAN, David 410-290-7100. 215 J
DOCTOR, OFM, John 217-228-5432. 156 C docotjo@quincy.edu
DODD, Carley 325-674-2223. 464 H doddc@acu.edu
DODD, David 201-216-5491. 307 E ddodd@stevens.edu
DODD, Linda, M 724-287-8711. 411 C linda.dodd@bc3.edu
DODD, Paul 530-754-7806. 70 J pdodd@ucdavis.edu
DODD, Shelley 307-766-4273. 543 I shelley@uwyo.edu
DODD, William, M 956-882-3822. 491 D william.dodd@utb.edu
DODDS, DeLoss 512-471-5757. 491 C ddodds@mail.utexas.edu
DODDS, Gloria 706-649-1016. 123 E gdodds@columbustech.edu
DODDS, Jerrilynn, D 914-395-2303. 340 E jdodds@sarahlawrence.edu
DODDS, S. Curtis 530-226-4148. 66 D cdodds@simpsonu.edu
DODDS, Thomas, E 607-255-7445. 322 A ted56@cornell.edu
DODENHOFF, Michelle 803-777-2070. 447 G mdodenho@mailbox.sc.edu
DODGE, Barbara 920-693-1386. 540 B barbara.dodge@gotoltc.edu
DODGE, Billie, S 410-778-7760. 221 C bdodge2@washcoll.edu
DODGE, Brian, R 607-871-2154. 313 E dodgeb@alfred.edu
DODGE, Cabot, W 978-468-7111. 227 A
DODGE, Carole, E 561-237-7915. 108 X cdodge@lynn.edu
DODGE, Cynthia 636-573-9300. 278 G cdodge@motech.edu
DODGE, Darla 775-445-4224. 295 A darla.dodge@wnc.edu
DODGE, Georgina 319-335-3565. 175 I georgina-dodge@uiowa.edu
DODGE, Kevin 301-387-3328. 214 I kevin.dodge@garrettcollege.edu
DODGE, Marvin 435-283-7200. 498 A marvin.dodge@snow.edu
DODGE, Michelle 503-251-5710. 408 G mdodge@uws.edu
DODGE, Norma Jean 620-417-1171. 190 F normajean.dodge@sccc.edu
DODGE, Richard 954-262-3651. 109 K dodge@nova.edu
DODGE, Ron 845-938-3999. 545 I Ron.Dodge@usma.edu
DODGE, William, W 210-567-3160. 493 A dodge@uthscsa.edu
DODGE-REYOME, Nancy, M 315-267-2131. 344 C dodgenm@potsdam.edu
DODIER, Elizabeth 956-326-2412. 483 B edodier@tamiu.edu
DODSON, Al 662-562-3308. 269 C adodson@northwestms.edu
DODSON, Don, C 408-554-4055. 64 M ddodson@scu.edu
DODSON, JR., Howard 202-806-7234. 95 G howard.dodson@howard.edu
DODSON, Jennifer 269-467-9945. 242 H jdodson@glenoaks.edu
DODSON, Jerry 254-442-5152. 468 I jerry.dodson@cisco.edu
DODSON, Lloyd, R 312-329-4231. 153 E ldodson@moody.edu
DODSON, Lorraine 301-846-2486. 214 H ldodson@frederick.edu
DODSON, Shelley 765-973-8332. 167 G midodson@iue.edu
DODSON, Victor, H 443-412-2416. 215 C vdodson@harford.edu
DODSON, Wendy, B 910-695-3701. 363 F dodsonw@sandhills.edu
DODSWORTH, Melissa 419-473-2700. 378 I mdodsworth@daviscollege.edu
DOEBBERT, Jan 320-762-4504. 257 O jand@alextech.edu
DOEBLE, Gina 239-489-9029. 101 O gdoeble@edison.edu
DOELL, Elaine 603-535-2618. 298 G edoell@plymouth.edu
DOELL, Margaret 719-587-8383. 78 B mjdoell@adams.edu
DOELLER, Kathleen 480-990-3773. 14 H
DOEPKER, Joel 417-447-2655. 279 K doepkerj@otc.edu
DOERFER, Carol 518-828-4181. 321 C doerfer@sunycgcc.edu
DOERING, Dionne 612-330-1602. 253 H doering@augsburg.edu
DOERING, Douglas 207-775-3052. 210 H doug@meca.edu
DOERING, Laura 515-294-1840. 175 H ljdoeri@iastate.edu
DOERKSEN, Randall, C 316-295-5893. 186 H doerksen@friends.edu
DOERNER, Kinchel 605-688-4181. 452 B kinchel.doerner@sdstate.edu
DOERPINGHAUS, Helen, I 803-777-2808. 447 G doerp@sc.edu
DOERR, Bill 478-445-5768. 125 A bill.doerr@gcsu.edu
DOERR, Gail 410-888-9048. 216 D gdoerr@muih.edu
DOFFONEY, Ned 714-808-4797. 56 D ndoffoney@nocccd.edu
DOGAN, Can 832-230-5470. 477 H dogan@northamerican.edu
DOGBEVIA, Moses 402-461-7466. 289 I mdogbevia@hastings.edu
DOGGETT, Jeffrey 978-837-5207. 234 A doggettj@merrimack.edu
DOGONNIUCK, Theodore 516-773-5000. 545 H dogonniuck@usmma.edu
DOHERTY, Alison 310-577-3000. 77 G matcm@yosan.edu
DOHERTY, Art 541-962-3516. 405 H adoherty@eou.edu
DOHERTY, Brian 941-487-4300. 115 D bdoherty@ncf.edu
DOHERTY, Brian, E 413-265-2372. 225 C dohertyb@elms.edu
DOHERTY, Dan 970-339-6336. 78 C dan.doherty@aims.edu
DOHERTY, Eileen 773-298-5060. 158 E edoherty@sxu.edu
DOHERTY, Frank, J 540-568-6830. 506 F dohertfj@jmu.edu
DOHERTY, Kathryn 410-532-5316. 217 E kdoherty@ndm.edu
DOHERTY, Kenneth 313-577-3756. 252 G ac0578@wayne.edu
DOHERTY, Kevin 620-421-6700. 188 D kevind@labette.edu
DOHERTY, Kevin 312-369-7162. 143 D kdoherty@colum.edu
DOHERTY, Kristal 864-646-1795. 447 D kdoherty@tctc.edu
DOHERTY, Mary Jane 781-768-7015. 236 A mj.doherty@regiscollege.edu
DOHERTY, Paul 425-640-1713. 519 D paul.doherty@edcc.edu
DOHERTY, Paula 360-417-6275. 522 A pdoherty@pencol.edu
DOHERTY, Sharon 651-690-6783. 263 O sldoherty@stkate.edu
DOHERTY, Steve 269-488-4442. 244 L sdoherty@kvcc.edu
DOHM, Faith-Anne 203-254-4250. 89 I fdohm@fairfield.edu
DOHMAN, Gloria 701-671-2619. 372 E gloria.dohman@ndscs.edu
DOHNALIK, Judith 254-298-8600. 482 C j.dohnalik@templejc.edu
DOISY, Kathy 573-876-7157. 282 H kdoisy@stephens.edu
DOKEY, Denise 225-768-0818. 206 D denise.dokey@ololcollege.edu
DOKTOR, Caryn, G 212-799-5000. 328 B
DOLAK, James 970-491-4752. 80 I jim.dolak@colostate.edu
DOLAMORE, Joan 617-243-2485. 227 K jdolamore@lasell.edu
DOLAN, Abby 888-384-0849. 27 E adolan@allied.edu
DOLAN, Andrew, B 231-995-1019. 248 B adolan@nmc.edu
DOLAN, Barbara 605-394-2649. 452 A barbara.dolan@sdsmt.edu
DOLAN, Carol 912-358-4014. 131 C dolanc@savannahstate.edu
DOLAN, Daniel 212-237-8900. 318 D ddolan@jjay.cuny.edu
DOLAN, Debbie 509-533-4867. 518 E debbie.dolan@scc.spokane.edu
DOLAN, Donna, M 617-521-2111. 236 G donna.dolan@simmons.edu
DOLAN, Gayle 617-277-3915. 224 C
DOLAN, James, E 317-381-6028. 174 F jdolan@vinu.edu
DOLAN, John, F 315-445-4707. 328 F dolanjof@lemoyne.edu
DOLAN, Julie, L 508-793-7443. 225 A jdolan@clarku.edu
DOLAN, Linda 320-762-4439. 257 O lindad@alextech.edu
DOLAN, Mary, K 315-267-4816. 344 C dolanmk@potsdam.edu

DOLAN, Mary, K .... 315-386-7325. 345 F
dolanmk@potsdam.edu
DOLAN, Stacey, L .... 312-788-1147. 162 H
sdolan@vandercook.edu
DOLAN, Tim .... 303-762-6919... 81 G
tim.dolan@denverseminary.edu
DOLAN, Tina, M .... 781-283-3501. 237 F
cdolan@wellesley.edu
DOLANSKY, Brian, P ...... 914-606-6284. 350 F
brian.dolansky@sunywcc.edu
DOLBERRY, Carol .... 870-460-1034... 24 D
dolberryc@uamont.edu
DOLCI, Elizabeth .... 802-635-1482. 501 D
elizabeth.dolci@jsc.edu
DOLDER-ZIEKE, Beth, D 608-796-3828. 539 E
bdzieke@viterbo.edu
DOLDO, Frank .... 315-786-2250. 327 L
fdoldo@sunyjefferson.edu
DOLHEIMER, Mary, E .... 717-815-1274. 438 D
mdolheim@ycp.edu
DOLINSKY, Diane .... 570-702-8907. 419 G
ddolinsky@johnson.edu
DOLIVE, Mark .... 817-515-2113. 482 B
mark.dolive@tccd.edu
DOLIVE, Mark .... 817-515-3083. 482 B
mark.dolive@tccd.edu
DOLL, Caroline .... 805-437-3232... 32 I
caroline.doll@csuci.edu
DOLL, Cheryl, A .... 610-799-1087. 421 I
cdoll@lccc.edu
DOLL, Tammy .... 620-417-1131. 190 F
tammy.doll@sccc.edu
DOLLA, Marie .... 718-779-1430. 336 D
mdolla@plazacollege.edu
DOLLAR, Marek .... 513-529-4036. 384 G
dollarm@miamioh.edu
DOLLARD, Heidi .... 413-545-6133. 228 F
hdollard@oit.umass.edu
DOLLARD, Pam .... 608-890-1066. 538 E
pam.dollard@uwc.edu
DOLLASE, Beth .... 816-654-7282. 275 K
bdollase@kcumb.edu
DOLLENMAYER, Lisa ...... 727-726-1153. 100 E
lisadollenmayer@clearwater.edu
DOLLHOPF, Mark, R ...... 203-432-1941... 93 A
mark.dollhopf@yale.edu
DOLLING, David .... 202-994-6080... 95 D
dolling@gwu.edu
DOLLING, Lisa .... 201-216-5405. 307 E
ldolling@stevens.edu
DOLLOFF, Jane .... 617-348-6357. 237 E
jane.dolloff@urbancollege.edu
DOLLYHITE, Ronald .... 336-838-6281. 365 B
ronald.dollyhite@wilkescc.edu
DOLS, Kenn .... 218-855-8132. 258 B
kdols@clcmn.edu
DOLSEN, David, H .... 620-229-6298. 190 G
david.dolsen@sckans.edu
DOMANN, Jessica .... 713-942-5036. 490 L
domannj@sthom.edu
DOMAS, Matthew, S .... 662-562-3235. 269 C
gmdomas@northwestms.edu
DOMBCHEWSKYJ, Dan .. 704-290-5828. 363 G
bdombchewskyj@spcc.edu
DOMBROWSKI, Michael 716-614-5980. 334 E
mdombrowski@niagaracc.suny.edu
DOMBROWSKI,
Teresa, A .... 630-515-6479. 153 B
tdombr@midwestern.edu
DOMENECH, Tony .... 432-335-5360. 487 E
manuel.domenech@ttuhsc.edu
DOMENITZ, Linda .... 860-906-5153... 88 D
ldomenitz@ccc.commnet.edu
DOMERACKI, Kristin ...... 713-942-9505. 473 D
kdomeracki@hgst.edu
DOMES, Chris, E .... 920-686-6138. 536 A
Chris.Domes@sl.edu
DOMHOLDT, Elizabeth ... 218-723-6012. 254 K
bdomhold@css.edu
DOMIANO, Sam .... 985-549-2282. 208 C
sdomiano@selu.edu
DOMINE, Karen .... 541-888-7212. 407 H
khelland@socc.edu
DOMINELLI, Angela .... 518-694-7333. 313 B
angela.dominelli@acphs.edu
DOMINGO, Jannette .... 212-237-8757. 318 D
jdomingo@jjay.cuny.edu
DOMINGUEZ, Carmen ... 305-237-3374. 109 D
cdoming3@mdc.edu
DOMINGUEZ, Carmen ... 661-362-3116... 40 E
carmen.dominguez@canyons.edu
DOMINGUEZ, Edwin ...... 717-801-3264. 417 I
edomingu@hacc.edu
DOMINGUEZ, Joe .... 956-364-4341. 485 H
armando.dominguez@tstc.edu
DOMINGUEZ, Leo .... 432-837-8596. 487 B
leodo@sulross.edu
DOMINGUEZ, Leo, G ..... 432-837-8033. 487 B
leodo@sulross.edu
DOMINGUEZ, Maria .... 575-538-6611. 312 N
dominguezm@wnmu.edu
DOMINGUEZ, Mary .... 831-755-6714... 46 G
mdomingu@hartnell.edu
DOMINGUEZ, Norberto .. 787-296-0453. 549 J
dominguez@inter.edu
DOMINICK, Jay .... 609-258-5601. 304 E
jdominick@princeton.edu
DOMINY, Michele .... 845-758-7420. 314 D
dominy@bard.edu
DOMINY, Robert .... 478-757-3579. 122 F
rdominy@centralgatech.edu
DOMKE-DAMONTE,
Darla, J .... 843-349-2129. 442 E
ddamonte@coastal.edu
DOMMER, OSB, Ian .... 320-363-2791. 263 P
idommer@csbsju.edu
DOMNICK, Krista, R .... 919-515-2866. 368 B
krdomnic@ncsu.edu
DOMPE, Rudy .... 818-719-6440... 52 B
domperf@piercecollege.edu
DOMPIERRE, Michael, B 636-922-8355. 280 J
mdompierre@stchas.edu
DOMZALSKI, James .... 570-740-0342. 422 G
jdomzalski@luzerne.edu
DOMZALSKI, Jim .... 570-740-0342. 422 G
jdomzalski@luzerne.edu
DONA, David .... 541-383-7222. 402 D
ddona@cocc.edu
DONAHOE, Patrick .... 406-994-4531. 287 B
uccpd@montana.edu
DONAHOO, David .... 434-592-3084. 506 I
ddonahoo@liberty.edu
DONAHUE, Amy .... 860-486-0636... 92 A
amy.donahue@uconn.edu
DONAHUE, Annie .... 603-862-1540. 298 C
annie.donahue@unh.edu
DONAHUE, Bob .... 614-947-6010. 380 A
robert.donahue@franklin.edu
DONAHUE, Colin .... 818-677-2333... 34 C
colin.donahue@csun.edu
DONAHUE, David .... 510-430-3393... 54 F
ddonahue@mills.edu
DONAHUE, Eileen, B ...... 203-432-5850... 93 A
eileen.donahue@yale.edu
DONAHUE, Gabriel, M ... 973-290-4055. 300 F
gdonahue@cse.edu
DONAHUE, James, A ..... 925-631-4203... 61 F
president@stmarys-ca.edu
DONAHUE, James, P ..... 423-652-6002. 455 I
jpd@king.edu
DONAHUE, Janice, M .... 423-585-6921. 462 A
janice.donahue@ws.edu
DONAHUE, Jocelyn .... 904-680-7734. 103 Q
jdonahue@fcsl.edu
DONAHUE, Linda, V ...... 802-654-2563. 500 B
ldonahue@smcvt.edu
DONAHUE, Lorraine .... 814-262-3822. 427 C
ldonahue@pennhighlands.edu
DONAHUE, Mick .... 360-416-7732. 523 G
mick.donahue@skagit.edu
DONAHUE, Mick .... 360-679-5333. 523 G
mick.donahue@skagit.edu
DONAHUE, Nancy .... 865-694-6541. 461 D
ndonahue@pstcc.edu
DONAHUE, Patrick .... 812-855-3207. 167 F
donahued@indiana.edu
DONAHUE, Robert .... 617-353-9515. 224 D
rdonahue@bu.edu
DONAHUE, Sally, C .... 617-495-1580. 227 C
sdonahue@fas.harvard.edu
DONAHUE, Sandy .... 207-948-9229. 211 I
sdonahue@unity.edu
DONALD, Christopher ..... 601-974-1205. 267 I
chris.donald@millsaps.edu
DONALDSON, Adam ...... 334-386-7254..... 3 H
adonaldson@faulkner.edu
DONALDSON, Anthony .. 951-343-4841... 30 H
adonaldson@calbaptist.edu
DONALDSON, Colleen .... 585-395-5118. 342 F
cdonalds@brockport.edu
DONALDSON, Glen .... 618-546-5659. 150 D
glen.donaldson@doc.illinois.gov
DONALDSON, Janice, W 904-620-2476. 116 B
jdonalds@unf.edu
DONALDSON, Jody .... 319-398-7186. 180 J
jdonald@kirkwood.edu
DONALDSON, John, A ... 406-265-3520. 287 D
jdonaldson@msun.edu
DONALDSON, Lisa .... 970-204-8113... 81 N
lisa.donaldson@frontrange.edu
DONALDSON, Monde ..... 251-414-2291..... 7 D
mdonaldson@shc.edu
DONALDSON, Penny ...... 785-442-6054. 187 E
pdonaldson@highlandcc.edu
DONALDSON, Scott .... 510-780-4500... 50 I
sdonalds@lifewest.edu
DONALDSON, Stewart .... 909-607-9013... 39 C
stewart.donaldson@cgu.edu
DONALDSON, Tracey ..... 215-968-8091. 411 B
donaldso@bucks.edu
DONAT, Kim .... 920-424-3377. 537 B
donatk@uwosh.edu
DONAT, Patricia .... 706-864-1602. 133 D
patricia.donat@ung.edu
DONATH, Ben .... 712-749-2181. 176 D
donath@bvu.edu
DONATO, CSC, John, J .. 503-943-8532. 408 F
donato@up.edu
DONATO, Matt .... 909-621-8519... 59 G
matthew_donato@pitzer.edu
DONATUCCI, Nancy .... 724-339-7542. 425 B
gradeservices@nbi.edu
DONAUDY, Tom .... 561-297-2663. 114 L
tdonaudy@fau.edu
DONAVANT, Lori, A .... 731-881-7815. 463 E
ldonavant@utm.edu
DONAVANT, Susan, H ... 804-752-7222. 508 E
sdonavan@rmc.edu
DONCEVIC, John, G .... 724-847-6692. 417 A
jgdoncev@geneva.edu
DONCITS, Diane .... 651-641-3472. 256 J
ddoncits@luthersem.edu
DONCSECZ, Joseph, J .... 814-865-1355. 426 A
jjd7@psu.edu
DONDERO, Eileen .... 239-590-7967. 115 A
edondero@fgcu.edu
DONEGAN, Helen .... 407-317-7725. 115 E
helen.donegan@ucf.edu
DONEGAN, James .... 203-837-9600... 88 B
doneganj@wcsu.edu
DONEGAN, John, P .... 734-487-3591. 242 D
jdonega1@emich.edu
DONELSON, Charlotte .... 307-855-2154. 542 Y
donelson@cwc.edu
DONELSON, Rollin .... 336-334-5963. 369 A
rollin_donelson@uncg.edu
DONELSON, Tery .... 573-875-7490. 272 G
tldonelson@ccis.edu
DONER, Scott .... 229-333-7816. 134 B
sdoner@valdosta.edu
DONG, Suhua .... 717-337-6487. 417 B
sdong@gettysburg.edu
DONGES, James .... 812-855-3684. 167 F
jdonges@indiana.edu
DONHAM, Marilyn .... 734-973-3630. 252 A
mdonham@wccnet.edu
DONHARDT, Gary, L ...... 901-678-2231. 460 B
donhardt@memphis.edu
DONIN, Robert, B .... 603-646-0101. 296 G
robert.b.donin@dartmouth.edu
DONINI, Joseph .... 845-398-4040. 340 A
jdonini@stac.edu
DONKERSLOOT,
Norman .... 616-392-8555. 252 J
norman@westernsem.edu
DONLAN, Michael, J ...... 757-446-5890. 504 E
donlanmj@evms.edu
DONLEY, Bob .... 515-281-3934. 175 G
bdonley@iastate.edu
DONLIN, Linda .... 701-328-2962. 371 B
linda.donlin@ndus.edu
DONN, Denise, C .... 209-954-5114... 63 C
dcdonn@deltacollege.edu
DONNA, Jerry, A .... 217-581-3714. 144 E
jdonna@eiu.edu
DONNAY, Brent .... 320-308-3039. 261 B
btdonnay@stcloudstate.edu
DONNELL, Dorothy .... 662-252-8400. 269 F
ddonnell@rustcollege.edu
DONNELL, Kathy, S .... 951-487-3002... 55 B
kdonnell@msjc.edu
DONNELL, Richard, H .... 731-424-5883. 455 J
rdonnell@lanecollege.edu
DONNELL, Shauna, H .... 479-968-0343... 20 E
sdonnell@atu.edu
DONNELLA, II,
Joseph, A .... 717-337-6280. 417 B
donnella@gettysburg.edu
DONNELLAN, Barbara .... 617-369-3832. 236 F
bdonnellan@mfa.org
DONNELLI-SALLEE,
Emily .... 816-584-6779. 280 C
emily.donnelli@park.edu
DONNELLY, Daniel .... 615-297-7545. 452 J
donnelly@aquinascollege.edu
DONNELLY, Daniel .... 615-297-7545. 452 J
donnellyd@aquinascollege.edu
DONNELLY, Eileen, G .... 302-356-6812... 94 E
eileen.g.donnelly@wilmu.edu
DONNELLY, Gloria .... 215-762-4943. 415 B
gd27@drexel.edu
DONNELLY, John .... 434-961-5205. 513 F
jdonnelly@pvcc.edu
DONNELLY, JR.,
Joseph .... 617-373-2520. 235 F
DONNELLY, Liz .... 405-208-7910. 397 F
ldonnelly@okcu.edu
DONNELLY, Patrick, G ... 937-229-3334. 391 C
pdonnelly1@udayton.edu
DONNELLY, Sharon .... 215-489-2317. 414 E
Sharon.Donnelly@delval.edu
DONNELLY, Sherri .... 518-445-2396. 313 C
sdonn@albanylaw.edu
DONNELLY, Shirley, A ... 714-895-8121... 39 J
sdonnelly@gwc.cccd.edu
DONNELLY, William, H .. 740-376-4701. 383 E
whdonnelly@sbcglobal.net
DONOFF, R. Bruce .... 617-432-1401. 227 C
bruce_donoff@hms.harvard.edu
DONOFRIO, A. Steven ... 212-998-2362. 334 D
steven.donofrio@nyu.edu
DONOGHUE, Daniel, J ... 858-822-5155... 71 F
ddonoghue@ucsd.edu
DONOGHUE, Karen, A ... 203-254-4000... 89 I
kdonoghue@fairfield.edu
DONOHOE, Kerry .... 978-934-2542. 229 B
kerry_donohoe@uml.edu
DONOHOE, Nancy .... 312-935-6715. 156 K
ndonohoe@robertmorris.edu
DONOHOE, Neil .... 617-912-9143. 224 B
ndonohoe@bostonconservatory.edu
DONOHUE, Beth .... 315-568-3115. 333 C
bdonohue@nycc.edu
DONOHUE, Darrell .... 207-326-4311. 211 D
darrell.donohue@mma.edu
DONOHUE, James .... 717-544-7743. 421 C
jdonohue2@lancastergeneralcollege.edu
DONOHUE, John .... 609-771-2393. 300 E
jdonohue@tcnj.edu
DONOHUE, Mary .... 518-736-3622. 325 A
mdonohue@fmcc.suny.edu
DONOHUE, Michael .... 212-752-1530. 328 G
michael.donohue@limcollege.edu
DONOHUE, Patricia, C ... 609-586-4800. 302 G
donohuep@mccc.edu
DONOHUE, OSA,
Peter, M .... 610-519-8881. 436 F
peter.donohue@villanova.edu
DONOHUE, Timothy .... 215-568-9215. 423 M
tdonohue@phmc.org
DONOHUE, William .... 612-624-4100. 264 G
donohue@umn.edu
DONOHUE-MENDOZA,
Michelle .... 408-741-2185... 75 L
michelle.donohue@westvalley.edu
DONOHUE-SMITH,
Maureen .... 607-735-1957. 323 H
mdonohuesmith@elmira.edu
DONOTO, Chris .... 847-317-8113. 160 M
cdonoto@tiu.edu
DONOVAN, Amy .... 888-227-3552. 254 C
amy.donovan@capella.edu
DONOVAN, Amy, E .... 978-468-7111. 227 A
adonovan@gcts.edu
DONOVAN, Brooke .... 570-422-3659. 428 D
bdonovan@esufoundation.org
DONOVAN, Celeste .... 620-417-1016. 190 F
celeste.donovan@sccc.edu
DONOVAN, Donald, T .... 713-798-3380. 467 F
ddonovan@bcm.edu
DONOVAN, Gary, L .... 320-589-6065. 264 F
donovang@morris.umn.edu
DONOVAN, Jaclyn .... 229-931-2222. 126 D
jaclyn.donovan@gsw.edu
DONOVAN, James .... 657-278-3058... 33 E
jdonovan@fullerton.edu
DONOVAN, Joan .... 607-844-8222. 347 I
donovaj@TC3.edu
DONOVAN, Joseph .... 978-542-6119. 230 E
jdonovan@salemstate.edu
DONOVAN, Kara .... 515-643-6604. 181 A
kdonovan@mercydesmoines.org
DONOVAN, Kevin .... 716-896-0700. 350 A
kdonovan@villa.edu
DONOVAN, Mark .... 312-413-1401. 161 D
mdonovan@uic.edu
DONOVAN, RSM,
Nancy, E .... 814-886-6476. 424 G
ndonovan@mtaloy.edu
DONOVAN, R. Nowell .... 817-257-7101. 484 I
r.donovan@tcu.edu
DONOVAN, Stephen, J ... 603-862-2040. 298 C
steve.donovan@unh.edu
DONOVAN, Susan .... 410-617-2842. 216 A
sdonovan@loyola.edu
DONOVAN, Thomas, R .. 810-989-5755. 249 H
tdonovan@sc4.edu
DONOVAN, Timothy, J ... 802-224-3000. 501 A
tim.donovan@vsc.edu
DONOVAN, Veronica .... 913-758-4372. 191 B
veronica.donovan@stmary.edu
DONSBACH, Dave .... 217-351-2393. 155 J
ddonsbach@parkland.edu
DONTES, Arnim .... 214-648-3572. 493 E
arnim.dontes@utsouthwestern.edu
DOOCY, Christine .... 402-557-7002. 288 G
christine.doocy@bellevue.edu
DOODY, Josh .... 650-508-3685... 56 H
jdoody@ndnu.edu
DOODY, Mary .... 302-453-3760... 93 F
mary.doody@dtcc.edu
DOODY, Tom .... 651-846-1428. 261 D
thomas.doody@saintpaul.edu

DOOLEN, Toni ... 541-737-6400. 406 A
toni.doolen@oregonstate.edu

DOOLEY, Allen ... 715-564-6775... 60 G
dooley_allen@sac.edu

DOOLEY, Chris ... 803-535-1249. 446 B
dooleyc@octech.edu

DOOLEY, Dan ... 765-973-8348. 167 G
dadooley@iue.edu

DOOLEY, Daniel, M ... 510-987-0060... 70 H
dan.dooley@ucop.edu

DOOLEY, David, M ... 401-874-2444. 440 D
joyalewis@ds.uri.edu

DOOLEY, Deborah ... 585-389-2641. 332 D
ddooley5@naz.edu

DOOLEY, Donna ... 603-271-6484. 296 C
ddooley@ccsnh.edu

DOOLEY, Elizabeth, A ... 304-293-2661. 530 D
elizabeth.dooley@mail.wvu.edu

DOOLEY, John ... 718-270-2431. 342 D
john.dooley@downstate.edu

DOOLEY, John, E ... 540-231-2265. 515 C
jdooley@vt.edu

DOOLEY, Joseph, M ... 203-392-5375... 88 A
dooleyj1@southernct.edu

DOOLEY, Kathleen A, M 630-515-6078. 153 B
kdoole@midwestern.edu

DOOLEY, Kevin ... 732-263-5308. 303 C
kdooley@monmouth.edu

DOOLEY, Larry ... 864-656-3200. 442 C
dooley@clemson.edu

DOOLEY, Robert ... 423-425-4313. 463 D
robert-dooley@utc.edu

DOOLEY, Ronald ... 954-923-4440. 108 P
rdooley@keycollege.edu

DOOLEY, Sue ... 831-656-3023. 544 M
sgdooley@nps.edu

DOOLIN, Bobbie ... 606-546-1263. 200 A
bdoolin@unionky.edu

DOOLITTLE, Everett ... 763-657-3750. 259 C
everett.doolittle@metrostate.edu

DOOLITTLE, Martha ... 850-644-9719. 115 C
mdoolittle@fsu.edu

DOOLITTLE, Phillip, L ... 909-748-8180... 73 H
phillip_doolittle@redlands.edu

DOOLOS, Robert, K ... 225-578-1686. 204 O
rdoolos@lsu.edu

DOORES, Elizabeth, J ... 217-424-6335. 153 C
edoores@millikin.edu

DOORIS, Michael, J ... 814-863-8721. 426 A
mjd1@psu.edu

DOOROS, Daniel, J ... 949-824-7475... 71 B
djdooros@uci.edu

DOPSON, Brian ... 386-752-1822. 104 G
brian.dopson@fgc.edu

DORADO, Luis ... 213-763-7030... 52 D
doradol@lattc.edu

DORAME, Francisco ... 805-922-6966... 26 K
francisc.dorame@hancockcollege.edu

DORAN, Andrea ... 775-445-4265. 295 A
andrea.doran@wnc.edu

DORAN, Brenda ... 401-232-6106. 438 K
bdoran@bryant.edu

DORAN, Donald ... 732-255-0400. 304 A
ddoran@ocean.edu

DORAN, John ... 516-299-3579. 329 C
john.doran@liu.edu

DORAN, K. Brewer ... 978-542-6633. 230 E
kdoran@salemstate.edu

DORAN, Robert ... 505-277-9290. 312 F
rdoran@unm.edu

DORAN, Stacy ... 920-735-5698. 539 K
doran@fvtc.edu

DORAN COLLINS,
Marianne ... 401-598-2036. 439 B
marianne.dorancollins@jwu.edu

DORANTES, Andrew, R ... 909-621-8126... 46 H
andrew_dorantes@hmc.edu

DORCHEUS, Greg ... 503-338-2489. 402 G
gdorcheus@clatsopcc.edu

DORDICK, Jonathan, S .. 518-276-6000. 337 I
dordij@rpi.edu

DOREMUS, Brenda, K ... 517-264-7123. 250 B
bdoremus@sienaheights.edu

DORER, Thomas ... 860-768-4275... 92 D
dorer@hartford.edu

DORF, Laurie ... 718-997-3920. 319 C
laurie.dorf@qc.cuny.edu

DORFF, Robert ... 770-423-6124. 127 N
rdorff@kennesaw.edu

DORGAN, Sheila ... 508-910-6527. 229 A
sdorgan@umassd.edu

DORHOUT, Peter, K ... 785-532-6900. 188 A
dorhout@ksu.edu

DORIAN, James, C ... 401-456-9754. 439 F
jdorian@ric.edu

DORIS, Eugene, P ... 203-254-4000... 89 I
edoris@fairfield.edu

DORITY, Nancy ... 657-278-2350... 33 E
ndority@fullerton.edu

DORLAND, William ... 301-405-6771. 219 B
bdorland@umd.edu

DORMAN, Jay, A ... 334-833-4406..... 4 D
jdorman@huntingdon.edu

DORMAN, Jeremy ... 903-693-2009. 478 A
jdorman@panola.edu

DORMAN, Jesse ... 540-636-2900. 503 L
jdorman@christendom.edu

DORMAN, Laura ... 217-206-6005. 161 E
dorman.laura@uis.edu

DORMAN, Richard, H ... 724-946-7130. 437 B
dormanrh@westminster.edu

DORMAN, Steve, M ... 478-445-4444. 125 A
steve.dorman@gcsu.edu

DORN, Cheryl ... 406-791-5262. 288 E
cdorn01@ugf.edu

DORN, Ronald ... 208-769-3340. 138 I

DORNBERGER, Rich ... 765-983-1200. 165 G
dornbri@earlham.edu

DORNE, Clifford ... 989-964-7072. 249 G
cdorne@svsu.edu

DORNER, Kate ... 269-783-2110. 250 C
kdorner@swmich.edu

DORNER, Michael, H ... 651-641-8811. 255 B
dorner@csp.edu

DORNES, Delfina ... 618-468-5200. 150 G
dmlee@lc.edu

DORPH, Martin ... 212-992-8282. 334 D
martin.dorph@nyu.edu

DORR, Aimee ... 510-987-9020... 70 H
aimee.dorr@ucop.edu

DORR, Jodi, L ... 810-762-7996. 244 Q
jdorr@kettering.edu

DORR, Mary, I ... 913-288-7145. 187 L
mdorr@kckcc.edu

DORRELL, Martha ... 803-321-5373. 445 G
martha.dorrell@newberry.edu

DORRELL, Natalie ... 760-384-6260... 49 O
ndorrell@cerrocoso.edu

DORRILL, Lauri ... 334-670-3276..... 7 H
ldorrill@troy.edu

DORRIS, Pamela, L ... 248-232-4613. 248 D
pldorris@oaklandcc.edu

DORROH, Cynthia ... 661-362-3366... 40 E
cynthia.dorroh@canyons.edu

DORSA, Charles ... 701-483-2014. 371 D
Charles.Dorsa@sodexo.com

DORSA, Daniel ... 503-494-1084. 405 I
research@ohsu.edu

DORSEY, Al ... 501-370-5310... 22 F
adorsey@philander.edu

DORSEY, Alan, T ... 706-542-1561. 133 C
atdorsey@uga.edu

DORSEY, Andrew, R ... 303-404-5481... 81 N
andy.dorsey@frontrange.edu

DORSEY, Brynnmarie ... 484-664-3198. 424 H
dorsey@muhlenberg.edu

DORSEY, Ellen ... 212-353-4125. 321 F
dorsey2@cooper.edu

DORSEY, John, K ... 217-545-3625. 159 G
kdorsey@siumed.edu

DORSEY, Kerry ... 315-312-5558. 344 A
kerry.dorsey@oswego.edu

DORSEY, Lisa ... 314-977-8501. 281 I
ldorsey2@slu.edu

DORSEY, Lynn ... 203-576-4743... 91 G
ldorsey@bridgeport.edu

DORSEY, Michael ... 252-328-1283. 367 B
dorseym@ecu.edu

DORSEY, Michael, W ... 508-831-5609. 238 F
mwdorsey@wpi.edu

DORSEY, Myrtle E, B ... 314-539-5150. 281 D
mebdorsey@stlcc.edu

DORSEY, Patrick ... 312-915-7265. 151 H
pdorsey@luc.edu

DORSEY, Stuart, B ... 830-372-8000. 485 C
sdorsey@tlu.edu

DORSEY-ROBINSON,
Sylvia ... 559-925-3331... 75 I
sylviadorseyrobinson@whccd.edu

DORTA, Alvin ... 718-940-5982. 339 B
adorta@sjcny.edu

DORTON, Kevin ... 254-867-4802. 486 B
kevin.dorton@tstc.edu

DORY, Ondrea ... 641-784-5447. 178 F
dory@graceland.edu

DOSAL, Paul, J ... 813-974-5118. 116 C
pdosal@usf.edu

DOSCHER, Jeffrey ... 413-236-2816. 231 A
jdoscher@berkshirecc.edu

DOSKAL-SCAFFIDO,
Darese ... 607-844-8222. 347 I
doskald@TC3.edu

DOSS, Brad ... 507-433-0523. 260 I
brad.doss@riverland.edu

DOSSETT, Michael, S ... 336-322-2106. 362 F
Michael.Dossett@piedmontcc.edu

DOSTER, Betty ... 704-687-5769. 368 E
betty.doster@uncc.edu

DOSTIE, Diane ... 207-755-5281. 210 J
ddostie@cmcc.edu

DOSU, Tabzeera ... 916-278-5679... 34 D
dosut@csus.edu

DOTI, James, L ... 714-997-6611... 38 A
doti@chapman.edu

DOTSON, Barry ... 912-538-3141. 132 A
bdotson@southeasterntech.edu

DOTSON, Brandon ... 276-523-2400. 513 A
bdotson@me.vccs.edu

DOTSON, Ebbin ... 312-850-7856. 142 C
edotson4@ccc.edu

DOTSON, Michael, P ... 734-699-7008. 252 B
mdotson1@wcccd.edu

DOTSON, Robert ... 903-886-5523. 483 E
robert.dotson@tamuc.edu

DOTTAVIO, F. Dominic .. 254-968-9100. 483 A
president@tarleton.edu

DOTTER, Michelle ... 281-283-2100. 489 C
dotter@uhcl.edu

DOTTERER, Cathy ... 315-498-7251. 335 G
dotterec@sunyocc.edu

DOTTO, Ellen ... 908-709-7501. 308 B
dotto@ucc.edu

DOTTOREY, Mike ... 662-562-3319. 269 C
mldottorey@northwestms.edu

DOTY, Angela ... 541-684-7289. 405 C
adoty@nwcu.edu

DOTY, Dale ... 843-661-8101. 443 G
dale.doty@fdtc.edu

DOTY, Darla ... 254-968-9078. 483 A
ddoty@tarleton.edu

DOTY, Gregory, S ... 630-752-5384. 163 F
gregory.doty@wheaton.edu

DOTY, Harold ... 903-566-7346. 492 D
hdoty@uttyler.edu

DOTY, Jerry ... 925-288-5800... 46 J
jerry_doty@heald.edu

DOTY, Laura ... 916-660-7653... 66 B
ldoty@sierracollege.edu

DOTY, Laura ... 740-695-9500. 374 H
ldoty@belmontcollege.edu

DOTY, Marlene ... 973-278-5400. 314 K
md@berkeleycollege.edu

DOTY, Marlene ... 973-278-5400. 299 D
md@berkeleycollege.edu

DOTZLER, Ray ... 402-898-1000. 289 C
ray_d@creativecenter.edu

DOUCE, Louise, A ... 614-292-5766. 386 E
douce.1@osu.edu

DOUCET, Gayle ... 318-678-6000. 202 I
gdoucet@bpcc.edu

DOUCET, John ... 985-448-4385. 208 A
john.doucet@nicholls.edu

DOUCETT, Sandra ... 413-585-2686. 236 H
sdoucett@smith.edu

DOUCETTE, Diana, G ... 928-344-7526... 11 L
diana.doucette@azwestern.edu

DOUCETTE, Donald, S ... 563-336-3304. 177 L

DOUCETTE, Melissa ... 325-574-7650. 494 K
mdoucette@wtc.edu

DOUCETTE, Ronald ... 504-671-5475. 203 A
rdouce@dcc.edu

DOUGAN, Thomas, R ... 401-874-2427. 440 D
tdougan@uri.edu

DOUGAY, Kathleen, S ... 337-475-5509. 207 G
kdougay@mcneese.edu

DOUGHARTY,
W. Houston ... 641-269-3709. 178 H
doughart@grinnell.edu

DOUGHER, Kirk, M ... 561-297-3540. 114 L
mdough10@fau.edu

DOUGHER, Michael, J ... 505-277-2611. 312 F
dougher@unm.edu

DOUGHER, Michael, J ... 505-277-6128. 312 F
dougher@unm.edu

DOUGHERTY,
B. Christopher ... 610-527-0200. 432 B
cdougherty@rosemont.edu

DOUGHERTY, Charles, J 412-396-6060. 415 F
president@duq.edu

DOUGHERTY, Clint ... 760-384-6259... 49 O
cdougher@cerrocoso.edu

DOUGHERTY,
Cynthia, R ... 580-774-3767. 400 B
cindy.dougherty@swosu.edu

DOUGHERTY, Dennis, R 610-527-0200. 432 B
ddougherty@rosemont.edu

DOUGHERTY, Erin ... 972-883-2586. 491 E
erin.dougherty@utdallas.edu

DOUGHERTY, Gail ... 717-764-9550. 413 J
gdougherty@csb.edu

DOUGHERTY, Gail, E ... 717-764-9550. 414 A
gdougherty@csb.edu

DOUGHERTY, Jason ... 304-865-6084. 527 F
jason.dougherty@ovu.edu

DOUGHERTY, John ... 816-654-7303. 275 K
jdougherty@kcumb.edu

DOUGHERTY, John, M .. 607-871-2108. 313 E
dougherty@alfred.edu

DOUGHERTY, Lynne ... 516-463-6740. 326 D
lynne.dougherty@hofstra.edu

DOUGHERTY, Michael ... 303-273-3554... 80 E
mike.dougherty@is.mines.edu

DOUGHERTY, Michael, I 651-201-1801. 257 N
michael.dougherty@so.mnscu.edu

DOUGHERTY, Ryan ... 503-554-2246. 403 C
rdougherty@georgefox.edu

DOUGHERTY, Shanin, L 570-326-3761. 427 B
sdougher@pct.edu

DOUGHERTY, Tracy, D .. 806-371-5106. 465 E
tsdougherty@actx.edu

DOUGHERTY, Troy, J ... 208-496-9225. 137 H
doughertyt@byui.edu

DOUGHTY, Bruce ... 303-457-2757... 81 L
bdoughty@cci.edu

DOUGHTY, JR., Clyde ... 516-686-1133. 333 H
cdoughty@nyit.edu

DOUGHTY, Corinne ... 714-628-4883... 60 H
doughty_corine@sccollege.edu

DOUGHTY, David, C ... 757-594-7365. 503 M
doughty@cnu.edu

DOUGHTY, Delbert, D ... 260-359-4008. 166 O
ddoughty@huntington.edu

DOUGHTY, Karen ... 432-335-6404. 477 M
kdoughty@odessa.edu

DOUGLAS, Adrian, H ... 972-860-7603. 470 I
AdrianD@dcccd.edu

DOUGLAS, Alicia, R ... 816-501-4306. 280 I
alicia.douglas@rockhurst.edu

DOUGLAS, Andrew ... 410-516-4050. 215 H
douglas@jhu.edu

DOUGLAS, Ashley ... 785-243-1435. 185 M
adouglas@cloud.edu

DOUGLAS, Brian ... 508-286-8208. 238 B
douglas_brian@wheatonma.edu

DOUGLAS, Brianna ... 843-383-8060. 442 F
bbuncedouglas@coker.edu

DOUGLAS, Carmen ... 334-229-4667..... 1 D
cdouglas@alasu.edu

DOUGLAS, Davison, M .. 757-221-3790. 503 N
dmdoug@wm.edu

DOUGLAS, Deborah ... 773-995-3896. 141 J
ddougl22@csu.edu

DOUGLAS, Delano ... 804-524-5214. 515 D
ddouglas@vsu.edu

DOUGLAS, Derek ... 773-702-3627. 161 B
drbdouglas@uchicago.edu

DOUGLAS, Diane, J ... 715-394-8218. 538 C
ddougla2@uwsuper.edu

DOUGLAS, Dominique ... 703-257-5515. 502 E
bursaramm@aviationmaintenance.edu

DOUGLAS, Ian ... 518-694-7237. 313 B
ian.douglas@acphs.edu

DOUGLAS, Jeffrey, A ... 309-341-7491. 150 A
jdouglas@knox.edu

DOUGLAS, Jim ... 508-213-2333. 235 E
jim.douglas@nichols.edu

DOUGLAS, Katherine, P . 607-962-9232. 322 B
kdouglas@corning-cc.edu

DOUGLAS, Kelly, C ... 619-260-7974... 73 I
kdouglas@sandiego.edu

DOUGLAS, Kimberly ... 626-395-6416... 31 E
kdouglas@its.caltech.edu

DOUGLAS, Kristen ... 678-664-0529. 134 H
kristen.douglas@westgatech.edu

DOUGLAS, Laura ... 515-248-7206. 177 B
lldouglas@dmacc.edu

DOUGLAS, Linda ... 919-843-9393. 368 D
Linda_Douglas@unc.edu

DOUGLAS, Lisa ... 303-315-2769... 86 A
lisa.douglas@ucdenver.edu

DOUGLAS, Malcolm, C .. 847-574-5166. 150 C
mdouglas@lfgsm.edu

DOUGLAS, Michelle ... 304-696-2597. 529 H
douglasm@marshall.edu

DOUGLAS, Minnie, L ... 562-408-6969... 26 G

DOUGLAS, Renee ... 231-591-2614. 242 F
douglar3@ferris.edu

DOUGLAS, Renee ... 231-591-5968. 242 F
douglar3@ferris.edu

DOUGLAS, Scott, C ... 828-398-7147. 357 N
sdouglas@abtech.edu

DOUGLAS, Shawn ... 478-471-0779. 128 I
shawn.douglas@maconstate.edu

DOUGLAS, Sherry, L ... 308-432-6230. 291 D
sdouglas@csc.edu

DOUGLAS, Stephen, L ... 304-293-4731. 530 D
stephen.douglas@mail.wvu.edu

DOUGLAS, Tanya ... 317-543-4895. 171 A
tdouglas@martin.edu

DOUGLASS, Andraea ... 614-292-4164. 386 E
douglass.101@osu.edu

DOUGLASS, Barbara ... 860-738-6406... 89 C
bdouglass@nwcc.commnet.edu

DOUGLASS, Brent ... 540-887-7201. 507 A
bdouglass@mbc.edu

DOUGLASS, Carolinda ... 815-753-0492. 154 I
cdoug@niu.edu

DOUGLASS, Claudia, B .. 989-774-3632. 240 N
dougl1cb@cmich.edu

DOUGLASS, David, A ... 503-370-6447. 408 J
ddouglas@willamette.edu

DOUGLASS, Debbie ... 559-730-3736... 40 I
debbied@cos.edu

DOUGLASS, Georgia ... 630-752-5515. 163 F
georgia.douglass@wheaton.edu
DOUGLASS, James ... 507-433-0611. 260 I
jdouglas@riverland.edu
DOUGLASS, Jill ... 505-428-1351. 311 J
jill.douglass@sfcc.edu
DOUGLASS, Scott, R ... 302-831-2200... 94 B
douglass@udel.edu
DOUGLIS, Evan ... 518-276-6460. 337 I
douglis@rpi.edu
DOUILLARD, Paul ... 718-405-3258. 320 G
paul.douillard@mountsaintvincent.edu
DOUKAS, Peter, H ... 215-707-4990. 433 K
peter.doukas@temple.edu
DOULIS, Peter ... 215-871-6900. 430 D
peterd@pcom.edu
DOUMA, Debbie ... 850-484-1193. 110 G
ddouma@pensacolastate.edu
DOURLEIN, Peter ... 520-621-9414... 18 F
dourlein@u.arizona.edu
DOUTHIT, Tricia ... 303-273-3383... 80 E
tdouthit@mines.edu
DOVE, Bill ... 719-389-6384... 79 D
william.dove@coloradocollege.edu
DOVE, Cathy, S ... 212-255-8595. 322 A
csd3@cornell.edu
DOVE, Danyele ... 610-526-6047. 417 H
ddove@harcum.edu
DOVE, John ... 606-886-3863. 194 K
john.dove@kctcs.edu
DOVE, Krystal ... 423-461-8735. 457 H
DOVE, Robert, B ... 901-843-3800. 458 E
dove@rhodes.edu
DOVER, Gordon ... 901-272-5173. 456 F
gdover@mca.edu
DOVEY, Nicole ... 678-717-3839. 133 D
nicola.dovey@ung.edu
DOVI, John ... 703-539-6890. 510 B
jdovi@stratford.edu
DOVI, Sharon ... 607-844-8222. 347 I
dovis@TC3.edu
DOW, Brenda ... 845-257-3231. 342 B
dowb@newpaltz.edu
DOW, Evelyn ... 505-224-5217. 309 E
evdow@cnm.edu
DOW, Larry ... 860-297-2157... 91 F
larry.dow@trincoll.edu
DOW, Mary Ellen ... 202-884-9000... 96 G
dowm@trinitydc.edu
DOW, Sarah ... 617-585-1296. 234 I
sarah.dow@necmusic.edu
DOW, Steven, R ... 402-465-2255. 291 G
sdow@nebrwesleyan.edu
DOW-MCDONALD,
Jennifer ... 810-762-0533. 247 F
jennifer.dow@mcc.edu
DOW-ROYER, Cathy, A .. 413-205-3262. 221 F
cathy.dow-royer@aic.edu
DOWD, Bonnie Ann ... 619-388-6975... 62 C
bdowd@sdccd.edu
DOWD, Deirdre, M ... 516-876-3191. 343 D
dowdd@oldwestbury.edu
DOWD, Denny ... 214-333-5338. 470 D
denny@dbu.edu
DOWD, Jay ... 843-953-1411. 442 A
jdowd1@citadel.edu
DOWD, Julia, A ... 415-422-2531... 73 J
dowd@usfca.edu
DOWD, Sarah ... 864-646-1583. 447 D
sdowd@tctc.edu
DOWDEN, Luke ... 337-482-6022. 208 D
luke.downden@lousiana.edu
DOWDEY, Don ... 432-837-8124. 487 B
ddowdey@sulross.edu
DOWDLE, Deedie Kay ... 513-529-3637. 384 G
dowdledk@miamioh.edu
DOWDLE, Rita ... 662-562-3206. 269 C
rbdowdle@northwestms.edu
DOWDY, Kathleen, B ... 806-371-5389. 465 E
kbdowdy@actx.edu
DOWDY, Lawrence, A ... 610-436-6974. 430 A
ldowdy@wcupa.edu
DOWDY, Michael, B ... 410-706-3386. 219 C
mdowdy@umaryland.edu
DOWDY, Ronald ... 386-481-2031... 99 C
dowdyr@cookman.edu
DOWE, Peter ... 585-395-2531. 342 F
pdowe@brockport.edu
DOWELL, Chanda ... 309-854-1721. 140 E
dowellc@bhc.edu
DOWELL, David ... 562-985-4128... 33 F
david.dowell@csulb.edu
DOWELL, Elise ... 212-678-8950. 328 A
eldowell@jtsa.edu
DOWELL, Marcia, A ... 317-940-9257. 164 J
mdowell@butler.edu
DOWEN, Chris ... 303-556-4331... 86 A
chris.dowen@ucdenver.edu
DOWER, Debra ... 413-755-4468. 233 A
dfdower@stcc.edu
DOWER, Julia ... 603-542-7744. 296 D
jdower@ccsnh.edu
DOWER, Karyn ... 209-381-6585... 54 D
karyn.dower@mccd.edu
DOWLAND, Pam ... 812-357-6515. 173 A
pdowland@saintmeinrad.edu
DOWLESS, Donald, V ... 706-233-7201. 131 E
chimes@shorter.edu
DOWLING, Amy, S ... 570-321-4134. 422 H
dowling@lycoming.edu
DOWLING, Denise ... 406-243-4001. 286 H
denise.dowling@umontana.edu
DOWLING, Earl ... 630-942-3416. 142 G
dowlinge@cod.edu
DOWLING, Joseph, B ... 714-895-8158... 39 J
jdowling@gwc.cccd.edu
DOWLING, Victoria, A ... 618-537-2154. 152 G
vadowling@mckendree.edu
DOWNES, John ... 770-426-2646. 128 D
jdownes@life.edu
DOWNES, Kelly ... 618-437-5321. 156 H
downes@rlc.edu
DOWNES, Timothy ... 404-727-6532. 124 E
timothy.downes@emory.edu
DOWNEY, Catherine ... 503-552-1761. 404 H
cdowney@ncnm.edu
DOWNEY, James ... 412-924-1450. 431 A
jdowney@pts.edu
DOWNEY, John ... 704-337-2227. 365 G
downeyj@queens.edu
DOWNEY, John, A ... 540-234-9261. 511 H
downeyj@brcc.edu
DOWNEY, Nancy ... 207-859-4503. 209 J
ndowney@colby.edu
DOWNEY, Nora ... 610-785-6582. 432 C
ndowney@scs.edu
DOWNEY, Robert, F ... 724-938-4299. 428 A
downey_r@calu.edu
DOWNING, Amy ... 617-730-7174. 235 D
amy.downing@newbury.edu
DOWNING, Arthur ... 646-312-1020. 316 J
Arthur.Downing@baruch.cuny.edu
DOWNING, Charlotte, M 585-292-2000. 332 A
cdowning@monroecc.edu
DOWNING, Irvine ... 956-882-4238. 491 D
irv.downing@utb.edu
DOWNING, Kenneshia ... 510-783-2100... 46 L
kenneshia_downing@heald.edu
DOWNING, Kimberly ... 513-556-5028. 390 G
kimberly.downing@uc.edu
DOWNING, Lenora, S ... 540-986-1800. 501 H
ldowning@national-college.edu
DOWNING, Michael ... 508-336-8700. 439 B
mdowning@jwu.edu
DOWNING, Rossann ... 816-604-4071. 277 H
rossann.downing@mcckc.edu
DOWNING, Sherry ... 513-862-2743. 380 E
DOWNING, Steve ... 317-955-6351. 170 V
sdowning@marian.edu
DOWNING, Teresa ... 603-899-4105. 296 H
downingt@franklinpierce.edu
DOWNS, Colleen ... 518-891-2915. 335 A
cdowns@nccc.edu
DOWNS, Kim ... 802-443-5208. 499 H
kdowns@middlebury.edu
DOWNS, Lisa ... 913-971-3380. 188 H
ldowns@mnu.edu
DOWNS, Timothy, M ... 716-286-8342. 334 F
downs@niagara.edu
DOWNS, Wil ... 812-237-4114. 167 A
wil.downs@indstate.edu
DOWSE, Bruce ... 308-535-3605. 290 J
dowseb@mpcc.edu
DOXEY, Scott, Y ... 540-261-8577. 509 K
scott.doxey@svu.edu
DOXIE-DIXON, Eloise ... 504-520-7515. 209 D
edixon@xula.edu
DOYLE, Amanda ... 337-482-6730. 208 D
amandad@louisiana.edu
DOYLE, Catherine ... 585-389-2123. 332 D
cdoyle0@naz.edu
DOYLE, Cathleen, H ... 410-777-2902. 213 D
chdoyle@aacc.edu
DOYLE, Christine, M ... 610-355-7151. 414 D
cdoyle@dccc.edu
DOYLE, Christy ... 208-769-3481. 138 I
cadoyle@nic.edu
DOYLE, Clare ... 215-248-7071. 413 A
doylec@chc.edu
DOYLE, Creig ... 610-902-8245. 411 E
creig.w.doyle@cabrini.edu
DOYLE, Creig ... 603-535-2331. 298 G
cwdoyle@plymouth.edu
DOYLE, David ... 518-320-1311. 341 C
david.doyle@suny.edu
DOYLE, Denise ... 210-283-6827. 490 A
ddoyle@uiwtx.edu
DOYLE, Diana ... 303-797-5701... 78 F
diana.doyle@arapahoe.edu
DOYLE, Eileen ... 914-633-2483. 327 C
edoyle@iona.edu
DOYLE, Gerald ... 312-567-5203. 147 F
doyle@iit.edu
DOYLE, J. Griffin ... 706-542-8096. 133 C
gdoyle@uga.edu
DOYLE, Janice, B ... 301-445-1901. 219 A
jdoyle@usmd.edu
DOYLE, Jeff ... 254-710-1011. 467 G
jeff_doyle@baylor.edu
DOYLE, Joy, E ... 724-847-6636. 417 A
jedoyle@geneva.edu
DOYLE, Leslie ... 314-889-4503. 274 E
ldoyle@fontbonne.edu
DOYLE, Lori ... 215-895-2100. 415 B
lori.n.doyle@drexel.edu
DOYLE, Mary ... 831-459-4906... 72 C
mdoyle1@ucsc.edu
DOYLE, Michael, J ... 563-588-7823. 180 L
michael.doyle@loras.edu
DOYLE, Patrick ... 970-248-1847... 79 F
pdoyle@coloradomesa.edu
DOYLE, Sheila ... 607-777-3844. 341 E
sdoyle@binghamton.edu
DOYLE, Timothy ... 901-321-3548. 453 H
tdoyle1@cbu.edu
DOYNE, Diane ... 312-369-7524. 143 D
ddoyne@colum.edu
DOZIER, Cheryl ... 912-358-4000. 131 C
ssupresident@savannahstate.edu
DOZIER, Felecia ... 863-784-7231. 113 G
dozierf@southflorida.edu
DOZIER, Jack ... 417-447-7570. 279 K
dozierj@otc.edu
DOZIER, Kristine, L ... 317-788-3219. 173 I
dozierk@uindy.edu
DOZIER, Luann, D ... 504-865-5794. 207 C
ldozier@tulane.edu
DOZIER, Ronda ... 903-823-3422. 482 D
ronda.dozier@texarkanacollege.edu
DRABEK, Walter, J ... 716-888-8359. 316 C
drabek@canisius.edu
DRABIER, Renee ... 817-735-2146. 490 E
Renee.Drabier@unthsc.edu
DRABIK, Mary, A ... 954-545-4500. 113 F
mdrabik@sfbc.edu
DRABIK, Thomas ... 954-545-4500. 113 F
academics@sfbc.edu
DRAEGER, Darren ... 415-388-1133... 45 H
darren.draeger@lifeway.com
DRAGAN, Kimberly ... 860-738-6418... 89 C
kdragan@nwcc.commnet.edu
DRAGHI, Mary Kathleen . 814-871-7430. 416 K
draghi002@gannon.edu
DRAGO, Linda, S ... 412-396-5181. 415 F
drago@duq.edu
DRAGOO, Lloyd ... 432-837-8614. 487 B
ldragoo@sulross.edu
DRAIN, Cecil, B ... 804-828-7247. 511 F
cbdrain@vcu.edu
DRAIN, Timothy, S ... 903-510-2458. 488 E
tdra@tjc.edu
DRAKE, Autumn ... 405-912-9096. 395 K
adrake@hc.edu
DRAKE, Brent, M ... 765-494-6136. 171 M
bmdrake@purdue.edu
DRAKE, Carlene ... 909-558-4581... 51 C
cdrake@llu.edu
DRAKE, Carolyn, C ... 559-244-2604... 68 I
carolyn.drake@fresnocitycollege.edu
DRAKE, Charles, E ... 405-744-6494. 397 H
cedrake@okstate.edu
DRAKE, Chris ... 972-273-3301. 471 B
cdrake@dcccd.edu
DRAKE, Janet, M ... 701-845-7302. 372 A
jan.drake@vcsu.edu
DRAKE, Jennifer, A ... 317-791-5704. 173 I
jdrake@uindy.edu
DRAKE, Kay, L ... 859-238-5467. 193 E
kay.drake@centre.edu
DRAKE, Marianne ... 413-662-5224. 230 C
m.drake@mcla.edu
DRAKE, Michael, V ... 949-824-5111... 71 B
chancellor@uci.edu
DRAKE, Peter ... 212-966-0300. 333 A
info@nyaa.edu
DRAKE, Ricky ... 334-229-5104..... 1 D
rdrake@alasu.edu
DRAKE, Roger, D ... 660-248-6221. 272 B
rdrake@centralmethodist.edu
DRAKE, Steve ... 618-283-4170. 150 D
DRAKE, Susan, K ... 217-243-9071. 146 F
sdrake@ic.edu
DRAKE, Tom ... 575-769-4994. 309 F
tom.drake@clovis.edu
DRAKE, Tonya ... 425-640-1562. 519 D
tonya.drake@edcc.edu
DRAKE-DEESE, Kent ... 603-358-2346. 298 F
kdrakedeese@keene.edu
DRAKSLER, Vicki ... 309-692-4092. 152 J
vdraksler@midstate.edu
DRALE, Christina, S ... 501-569-3204... 24 B
csdrale@ualr.edu
DRANE, Kim ... 307-382-1645. 543 J
kdrane-n@wwcc.wy.edu
DRANGMEISTER, Cheryl 505-428-1162. 311 J
cheryl.drangmeister@sfcc.edu
DRAPEAU, Guy ... 860-297-4210... 91 F
guy.drapeau@trincoll.edu
DRAPER, David ... 310-377-5501... 53 F
ddraper@marymountcalifornia.edu
DRAPER, David, E ... 419-434-4202. 393 D
president@winebrenner.edu
DRAPER, Dennis ... 310-338-7504... 53 E
ddraper@lmu.edu
DRAPER, Frances ... 303-492-7531... 85 L
frances.draper@colorado.edu
DRAPER, James ... 603-358-2492. 298 F
jdraper@keene.edu
DRAPER, Jeri ... 215-751-8199. 413 I
jdraper@ccp.edu
DRAPER, Mary ... 727-726-1153. 100 E
marydraper@clearwater.edu
DRAPER, Mary, C ... 727-726-1153. 100 E
marydraper@clearwater.edu
DRAPER, Nancy, J ... 405-912-9024. 395 K
ndraper@hc.edu
DRAPER, Randall, W ... 303-492-2695... 85 L
randall.draper@colorado.edu
DRASGOW, Fritz ... 217-333-1480. 162 A
fdrasgow@illinois.edu
DRASS, Mike ... 302-736-2545... 94 C
drassmi@wesley.edu
DRAUDE, Barbara, J ... 615-904-8189. 459 D
barbara.draude@mtsu.edu
DRAUDT, Wayne, J ... 815-836-5235. 150 H
draudtwa@lewisu.edu
DRAUGHON, Bill ... 305-348-3961. 115 B
draughon@fiu.edu
DRAUGHON,
Katherine, A ... 812-465-7107. 174 D
kdraughon@usi.edu
DRAVES, Patricia, H ... 330-823-2690. 391 E
dravesph@mountunion.edu
DRAWDY, Lester, W ... 770-720-5927. 130 G
lwd@reinhardt.edu
DRAYER, Kevin, S ... 315-255-1743. 316 D
drayer@cayuga-cc.edu
DRAYFAHL, Perry, M ... 610-499-1291. 437 E
pmdrayfahl@widener.edu
DRAYNA, Jonathan ... 414-425-8300. 535 K
jdrayna@shst.edu
DRAYTON, Ronald ... 803-738-7606. 445 C
draytonr@midlandstech.edu
DREBIN, Diane ... 360-992-2080. 518 A
ddrebin@clark.edu
DREBLOW, Lewis, M ... 740-826-8050. 384 L
dreblow@muskingum.edu
DREES, Betty, M ... 816-235-1808. 283 D
dreesb@umkc.edu
DREES, Lynn ... 941-752-5428. 114 I
dreesl@scf.edu
DREESSEN, Angela ... 309-694-5353. 146 E
angela.dreessen@icc.edu
DREFFS, Daryl, A ... 603-668-2211. 297 I
d.dreffs@snhu.edu
DREGER, Barb ... 920-735-4776. 539 K
dreger@fvtc.edu
DREGIER, Denise, M ... 443-412-2428. 215 C
ddregier@harford.edu
DREHER, John ... 404-627-2681. 121 H
john.dreher@beulah.org
DREHER, Karolina ... 610-796-8218. 409 E
karolina.dreher@alvernia.edu
DREHER, Melanie ... 312-942-7117. 157 G
melanie_dreher@rush.edu
DREIBELBIS,
Elizabeth, M ... 717-846-5000. 438 E
DREIBELBIS, John, A ... 717-846-5000. 438 E
DREILING, Karolyn ... 913-758-6293. 191 B
Karolyn.Dreiling@stmary.edu
DREISBACH, Joseph, H .. 570-941-4760. 436 A
joseph.dreisbach@scranton.edu
DREITH, Michael ... 618-985-2637. 148 J
mikedreith@jalc.edu
DRENKOW, Daniel, D ... 605-274-5251. 449 K
dan.drenkow@augie.edu
DRESCHER, Greg ... 845-451-2401. 322 D
g_dresch@culinary.edu
DRESCHER, Kurt, W ... 978-468-7111. 227 A
kdrescher@gcts.edu
DRESSEN, Dan ... 507-786-3420. 264 B
dressen@stolaf.edu
DRESSER, Charles, E ... 312-329-4267. 153 E
cdresser@moody.edu
DRESSER-RECKTENWALD,
Wendy ... 607-587-4025. 345 D
dressews@alfredstate.edu
DREVON, CSC,
Charles, D ... 574-239-8392. 166 N
cdrevon@hcc-nd.edu
DREW, Dan ... 317-278-5323. 168 D
drew@iupui.edu

DREW, Daniel, J .... 716-888-2569. 316 C drewd@canisius.edu
DREW, Don .... 405-425-5577. 397 D don.drew@oc.edu
DREW, John .... 617-827-6047. 228 G john.drew@umb.edu
DREW, Rus .... 706-568-2022. 123 D drew_rus@columbusstate.edu
DREW, Stacy .... 540-868-7272. 512 H sdrew@lfcc.edu
DREW, Todd .... 402-872-2222. 291 E tdrew@peru.edu
DREWELOW, Lonna .... 319-368-6468. 181 C drewelow@mtmercy.edu
DREWENSKI, Shirley ...... 708-596-2000. 159 C sdrewenski@ssc.edu
DREWETT, Jerry, S .... 318-257-2769. 207 F uajsd@latech.edu
DREWS, David .... 517-265-5161. 238 G ddrews@adrian.edu
DREXLER, Brad .... 610-796-8216. 409 E bradley.drexler@alvernia.edu
DREXLER, Jim .... 706-419-1408. 123 F drexler@covenant.edu
DREXLER-HINES, Elizabeth .... 508-767-7343. 222 C ea.drexlerhines@assumption.edu
DREYER, Allen, R .... 570-586-2400. 410 D adreyer@bbc.edu
DREYER, Brenda .... 605-626-2552. 451 I brenda.dreyer@northern.edu
DREYER, CSC, Chris, J .. 574-239-8383. 166 N cdreyer@hcc-nd.edu
DREYER, John, M .... 260-452-3139. 165 D john.dreyer@ctsfw.edu
DREYER, Thomas .... 978-934-4801. 229 B Thomas_Dreyer@uml.edu
DREYFUS, Mark, B .... 757-671-7171. 504 F president@ecpi.edu
DREYFUSS, Simeon .... 503-699-3961. 404 C sdreyfuss@marylhurst.edu
DREYFUSS, Teresa .... 562-908-3404... 60 I tdreyfuss@riohondo.edu
DREYFUSS, Teresa .... 562-908-3403... 60 I tdreyfuss@riohondo.edu
DRICKEY, Nancy .... 503-883-2201. 404 A ndricke@linfield.edu
DRIER, Tracy, M .... 715-833-6498. 539 J tdrier@cvtc.edu
DRIES, Kelly, J .... 414-410-4390. 532 B kjdries@stritch.edu
DRIES, Richard .... 414-297-6572. 540 E driesr@matc.edu
DRIESSNER, Johnnie ...... 503-493-6549. 402 J jdriessner@cu-portland.edu
DRIFKA, Amy .... 612-977-5368. 254 C amy.drifka@capella.edu
DRIGGERS, Randy .... 504-282-4455. 206 A rdriggers@nobts.edu
DRILLING, Peter .... 716-652-8900. 316 G pdrilling@cks.edu
DRINAN, Helen, G .... 617-521-2070. 236 G helen.drinan@simmons.edu
DRINKARD, Gretchen ..... 314-454-7055. 274 G gdrinkard@bjc.org
DRINKO, J. Randall .... 216-781-9400. 377 D instruct@cie-wc.edu
DRINKO, Randy .... 757-464-4600. 516 E instruct@cie-wc.edu
DRINKWATER, L. Ray ..... 804-706-5064. 512 G ldrinkwater@jtcc.edu
DRISCOLL, Daniel, R ...... 630-889-6542. 154 E ddriscoll@nuhs.edu
DRISCOLL, Debbie .... 434-544-8125. 506 K driscoll@lynchburg.edu
DRISCOLL, Edward (Terry), C .... 757-221-3332. 503 N ecdris@wm.edu
DRISCOLL, Frederick ...... 617-989-4135. 237 G driscollf@wit.edu
DRISCOLL, Karen .... 360-992-2260. 518 A kdriscoll@clark.edu
DRISCOLL, Laura .... 307-268-2733. 542 X ldriscoll@caspercollege.edu
DRISCOLL, Lisa .... 508-849-3398. 222 B ldriscoll@annamaria.edu
DRISCOLL, Lori .... 850-769-1551. 106 H ldriscoll@gulfcoast.edu
DRISCOLL, Marcy, P .... 850-644-6885. 115 C mdriscoll@fsu.edu
DRISCOLL, Marsha .... 218-755-3984. 258 A mdriscoll@bemidjistate.edu
DRISCOLL, Mary, C .... 716-375-7673. 338 E mdriscol@sbu.edu
DRISCOLL, Mary Erina .... 212-650-5302. 317 D mdriscoll@ccny.cuny.edu
DRISCOLL, Michael .... 410-837-4865. 221 A mdriscoll@ubalt.edu
DRISCOLL, Michael .... 724-357-2200. 428 F Michael.Driscoll@iup.edu
DRISCOLL, Micheline ...... 718-368-5436. 318 E mdriscoll@kbcc.cuny.edu
DRISCOLL, JR., Robert, G .... 401-865-2090. 439 E rdriscol@providence.edu
DRISKELL, Lavon .... 662-685-4771. 266 C ldriskell@bmc.edu
DRIVER, C. Berry .... 817-923-1921. 481 G bdriver@swbts.edu
DRIVER, Doug .... 970-943-7010... 86 I ddriver@western.edu
DRIVER, Louise .... 501-882-8845... 19 M oldriver@asub.edu
DRIVER-LINN, Erin .... 617-384-9033. 227 C erin_driver-linn@harvard.edu
DRNEK, James .... 216-687-3977. 377 F j.drnek@csuohio.edu
DRODDY, Jason .... 225-578-5745. 204 O jdroddy@lsu.edu
DROEGEMEIER, Kelvin ... 405-325-3806. 401 B kkd@ou.edu
DROEL, Bill .... 708-974-5221. 153 F droel@morainevalley.edu
DROGE, Michael .... 816-584-6202. 280 C michael.droge@park.edu
DROKER, Stephanie .... 559-934-2221... 75 H stephaniedroker@whccd.edu
DROLL, Charlotte .... 570-389-4921. 427 H cdroll@bloomu.edu
DROMPP, Michael, R ...... 901-843-3795. 458 E drompp@rhodes.edu
DRONE-SILVERS, Scott .. 217-234-5338. 150 D dsilvers@lakeland.cc.il.us
DRONEY, Michael .... 330-494-6170. 389 F mdroney@starkstate.edu
DRONGOWSKI, OP, Stanley .... 616-632-8900. 239 E
DRONSFIELD, Shelli .... 304-876-5107. 529 I sdronsfi@shepherd.edu
DROOG, Sue .... 712-722-6017. 177 J sue.droog@dordt.edu
DROPKIN, Keith .... 617-588-1363. 223 B kdropkin@bfit.edu
DROPKIN, Shelley .... 617-588-1302. 223 B sdropkin@bfit.edu
DROSS, Cindy .... 920-693-1385. 540 B cindy.dross@gotoltc.edu
DROST, Donald .... 732-906-2568. 303 B ddrost@middlesexcc.edu
DROST, Jack .... 256-824-7407..... 8 F jack.drost@uah.edu
DROST, Jim .... 641-673-1104. 183 H drostj@wmpenn.edu
DROSTE, Pamela .... 843-574-6363. 447 E pamela.droste@tridenttech.edu
DROUGHT, Joe .... 815-921-4353. 157 A i.drought@rockvalleycollege.edu
DROUIN, Amy .... 816-501-4628. 280 I amy.drouin@rockhurst.edu
DROUIN, Jeff .... 510-723-6933... 37 K jdrouin@chabotcollege.edu
DROUIN, Nancy .... 207-216-4434. 211 C ndrouin@yccc.edu
DROZ, Marcus .... 787-480-2421. 548 G rrdroz@sanjuancapital.com
DRUCKER, David .... 508-541-1508. 225 F ddrucker@dean.edu
DRUCKER, Jesse .... 216-523-7440. 377 F jesse.s.drucker@csuohio.edu
DRUCKER, Monique, R ... 203-582-8723... 91 A monique.drucker@quinnipiac.edu
DRUCKER, Sheldon .... 201-692-7100. 301 J drucker@fdu.edu
DRUCKREY, Melissa .... 601-979-2123. 267 E melissa.l.druckrey@jsums.edu
DRUDING, Marlene .... 856-225-6768. 306 C mdruding@camden.rutgers.edu
DRUEKE, Tim .... 803-323-2228. 449 G drueket@winthrop.edu
DRUESEDOW, Gregory ... 615-361-7555. 454 D gdruesedow@daymarinstitute.edu
DRUGOVICH, Margaret, L .... 607-431-4990. 325 F president@hartwick.edu
DRUIN, Cathy .... 502-456-6509. 199 F cdruin@sctd.edu
DRUMLUK, Sandy .... 607-844-8222. 347 I drumlus@tc3.edu
DRUMM, C. Scott .... 504-282-4455. 206 A sdrumm@nobts.edu
DRUMM, Kathy .... 704-330-6717. 359 C kathy.drumm@cpcc.edu
DRUMM, Kevin .... 607-778-5100. 315 I drummke@sunybroome.edu
DRUMM, Rene' .... 423-236-2766. 458 J rdrumm@southern.edu
DRUMMER, Carlee .... 847-635-1671. 155 F cdrummer@oakton.edu
DRUMMER, Carol, J .... 516-463-4876. 326 D carol.j.drummer@hofstra.edu
DRUMMER FRANCIS, Raydora, S .... 315-470-4815. 345 B rsdrumme@esf.edu
DRUMMOND, Carl, N .... 260-481-5750. 168 C drummond@ipfw.edu
DRUMMOND, Gordon ...... 480-212-1704... 17 N
DRUMMOND, Jason, S .. 660-543-4157. 283 A drummond@ucmo.edu
DRUMMOND, Jerri .... 401-454-6655. 440 A jdrummon@risd.edu
DRUMMOND, Lew .... 205-391-2347..... 6 H ldrummondr@sheltonstate.edu
DRUMMOND, Peter .... 847-574-5234. 150 C pdrummond@lfgsm.edu
DRUMMOND, Sarah, B .. 617-964-1100. 222 A sdrummond@ants.edu
DRUMMY, Michael .... 714-997-6919... 38 A mdrummy@chapman.edu
DRURY, Joel .... 405-422-1257. 399 B druryj@redlandscc.edu
DRURY, Timothy .... 718-405-3239. 320 G timothy.drury@mountsaintvincent.edu
DRYDEN, Barbara .... 386-226-6300. 102 B dbfinaid@erau.edu
DRYDEN, Jonathan, N .... 440-365-5222. 383 B
DRYE, Theresea .... 813-974-5705. 116 C tdrye@usf.edu
DRYER, Christy .... 410-287-6060. 214 B cdryer@cecil.edu
DRYER, Peter .... 276-326-4281. 502 H pdryer@bluefield.edu
DRYGAS, Emily .... 907-474-6631... 10 I emily.drygas@alaska.edu
DRZAKOWSKI, Meridith . 715-232-5312. 538 B drzakowskim@uwstout.edu
DRZEWIECKI, Teresa ...... 443-537-1719. 265 D teresa.drzewiecki@laureate.net
DU, Fang .... 330-829-8175. 391 E dufang@mountunion.edu
DU PLESSIS, Jacques .. 414-229-3644. 537 A jacques@uwm.edu
DUARTE, Ivette .... 305-348-2423. 115 B duartei@fiu.edu
DUARTE, John .... 541-880-2282. 403 H duarte@klamathcc.edu
DUARTE, Lamar .... 210-486-3600. 465 A pacsfa8@alamo.edu
DUARTE, Mark, A .... 671-735-2266. 546 E mduarte@uguam.uog.edu
DUBACH, John, F .... 413-545-2211. 228 F dubach@chancellor.umass.edu
DUBAK, Izabela .... 630-889-6576. 154 E idubak@nuhs.edu
DUBE, CarolAnne .... 207-974-4817. 210 K cadube@emcc.edu
DUBEAU, Peter .... 410-225-2371. 216 C pdubeau@mica.edu
DUBEY, Steve .... 775-784-1331. 294 J sdubey@unr.edu
DUBIEL, Mandy .... 517-629-0600. 239 A adubiel@albion.edu
DUBIN, Bruce .... 303-373-2008... 85 C bdubin@rvu.edu
DUBINSKY, Zalman .... 973-267-8005. 304 G zalmandubinsky@gmail.com
DUBLE, Troy .... 706-419-1122. 123 F duble@covenant.edu
DUBLON, Felice .... 312-629-6800. 158 L fdublon@saic.edu
DUBOIS, Glenn .... 804-819-4903. 511 G gdubois@vccs.edu
DUBOIS, Keith .... 207-780-5250. 212 H dubois@usm.maine.edu
DUBOIS, Melinda, C .... 585-245-5736. 343 C dubois@geneseo.edu
DUBOIS, Philip, L .... 704-687-5729. 368 E pdubois@uncc.edu
DUBOIS, Russ .... 207-947-4591. 209 G rdubois@bealcollege.edu
DUBOIS, Shelly .... 602-749-7311. 144 A sdubois@devry.edu
DUBOIS, Toni .... 714-992-7074... 56 F tdubois@fullcoll.edu
DUBOSE, Cheryl .... 843-355-4162. 449 F dubosec@wiltech.edu
DUBOSE, Lisa .... 567-661-7263. 387 L lisa_dubose@owens.edu
DUBOSE, Richard, A .... 270-745-5405. 200 G rick.dubose@wku.edu
DUBRAY, Kirsten .... 916-484-8175... 53 A dubrayk@arc.losrios.edu
DUBRAY, Robert, R .... 412-365-1641. 412 K rdubray@chatham.edu
DUBROY, Tashni .... 919-546-8274. 366 E tdubroy@shawu.edu
DUBUC-PEDERSEN, Danielle .... 402-354-7259. 291 B danielle.dubuc-pedersen@ methodistcollege.edu
DUBUIS, Dina .... 734-432-5309. 246 B ddubuis@madonna.edu
DUBUQUE, Erick .... 502-585-9911. 199 C edubuque@spalding.edu
DUBUQUE, Jennifer .... 814-886-6319. 424 G jdubuque@mtaloy.edu
DUCHARME, Gaylene ..... 406-338-5421. 285 F gatk@bfcc.edu
DUCHARME-WHITE, Sherri .... 414-955-4145. 534 C sducharm@mail.mcw.edu
DUCHATELET, Martine .... 509-828-1223. 519 C mduchatelet@ewu.edu
DUCHON, Maire, I .... 718-862-7166. 329 M maire.duchon@manhattan.edu
DUCHSCHERER, Eric, D . 315-267-2350. 344 C duchsced@potsdam.edu
DUCIOAME, Lynn .... 940-397-4676. 476 H lynn.ducioame@mwsu.edu
DUCKETT, Dwaine, B ...... 510-987-0301... 70 H dwaine.duckett@ucop.edu
DUCKETT, Randy .... 803-648-6851. 448 A randyd@usca.edu
DUCKETT, Randy, R .... 803-641-3487. 448 A randyd@usca.edu
DUCKWORTH, Brad .... 414-382-6323. 531 I brad.duckworth@alverno.edu
DUCKWORTH, Cory, L ... 716-338-1060. 327 J coryduckworth@mail.sunyjcc.edu
DUCKWORTH, Latoya ..... 573-681-5970. 276 C duckworthl@lincolnu.edu
DUCKWORTH, Tony .... 918-444-3926. 396 H duckwo01@nsuok.edu
DUCLOS, Mark .... 478-445-4467. 125 A mark.duclos@gcsu.edu
DUCLOS-BARRETT, Victoria .... 401-341-2345. 440 C duclosv@salve.edu
DUCOFFE, Robert .... 574-520-4133. 168 E ducoffe@iusb.edu
DUCOTE, Melissa .... 318-345-9109. 203 C mducote@ladelta.edu
DUCRAY, Sarah .... 202-651-5000... 95 C sarah.ducray@gallaudet.edu
DUCUENNOIS, Sara .... 954-262-2103. 109 K ducuenno@nova.edu
DUDA, Laura .... 570-504-1588. 420 C dudal@lackawanna.edu
DUDA, Mark .... 570-961-7852. 420 C dudam@lackawanna.edu
DUDA, Stephen .... 570-504-1734. 420 C dudas@lackawanna.edu
DUDA, Teri .... 201-967-9667. 299 D td@berkeleycollege.edu
DUDA, Teri .... 201-967-9667. 314 K td@berkeleycollege.edu
DUDAK, Brian .... 509-279-6066. 518 E brian.dudak@scc.spokane.edu
DUDAK, Nancy, J .... 610-519-7300. 436 F nancy.dudak@villanova.edu
DUDAS, Bertalan .... 814-866-8142. 420 E bdudas@lecom.edu
DUDAS, Maryann .... 724-838-4275. 433 E dudas@setonhill.edu
DUDAS, Philip .... 651-905-3542. 254 B pdudas@browncollege.edu
DUDGEON, David .... 305-899-3727... 98 O ddudgeon@barry.edu
DUDLEY, Brad, D .... 310-506-6825... 58 H brad.dudley@pepperdine.edu
DUDLEY, Brandon .... 707-664-2986... 36 B brandon.dudley@sonoma.edu
DUDLEY, Charlotte .... 404-627-2681. 121 H charlotte.dudley@beulah.org
DUDLEY, Christopher, H 336-841-4530. 355 C cdudley@highpoint.edu
DUDLEY, Deborah, L ...... 315-267-2113. 344 C dudleydl@potsdam.edu
DUDLEY, Erlene .... 573-592-4291. 285 D edudley@williamwoods.edu
DUDLEY, Jacklyn, K .... 270-809-3774. 198 B jdudley@murraystate.edu
DUDLEY, Jacklyn, K .... 270-809-4126. 198 B jdudley@murraystate.edu
DUDLEY, Jacklyn, K .... 270-809-3774. 198 B kdudley@murraystate.edu
DUDLEY, Jason .... 239-489-9307. 101 O jdudley1@edison.edu
DUDLEY, Jennifer .... 201-360-4646. 302 D jdudley@hccc.edu
DUDLEY, Lavoyd, R .... 318-274-6227. 207 E dudleyr@gram.edu
DUDLEY, Manuel .... 336-334-4822. 360 G mcdudley@gtcc.edu
DUDLEY, Melissa .... 207-780-4110. 212 H mdudley@usm.maine.edu
DUDLEY, Sharese .... 219-980-6791. 168 B shaadudl@iun.edu
DUDLEY, Valerie .... 610-660-1015. 432 E vdudley@sju.edu
DUDLEY, Waller, T .... 540-458-8470. 516 A wdudley@wlu.edu

DUDLEY, William 713-222-5368. 489 D
dudleyw@uhd.edu
DUDLEY, William, C 413-597-4352. 238 D
william.c.dudley@williams.edu
DUDLEY-ESHBACH, Janet, E 410-543-6011. 220 D
jdudleyeshbach@salisbury.edu
DUDT, Susan 770-426-2700. 128 D
sdudt@life.edu
DUEKER, Tina, R 308-630-6571. 293 E
duekert@wncc.edu
DUENAS, Felicia 323-241-5376... 52 C
duenasmv@lasc.edu
DUENAS, Hector 305-273-4499. 100 H
hector@cbt.edu
DUERK, Jeffrey 216-368-3227. 375 J
duerk@case.edu
DUERKSEN, Deanne 620-947-3121. 190 J
deanned@tabor.edu
DUERWACHTER, Kathleen, A 608-796-3072. 539 E
kaduerwachter@viterbo.edu
DUESING, Jason, G 817-923-1921. 481 G
jduesing@swbts.edu
DUESTERHAUS, Molly 864-596-9614. 443 D
molly.duesterhaus@converse.edu
DUETT, Belinda, G 334-833-4519..... 4 D
bduett@huntingdon.edu
DUEWEKE, Anne, T 269-337-7418. 244 K
Anne.Dueweke@kzoo.edu
DUFAULT-HUNTER, David 626-815-2022... 29 H
ddhunter@apu.edu
DUFENDACH, Sarah 301-985-7252. 219 F
sarah.dufendach@umuc.edu
DUFF, Cathy 239-590-7043. 115 A
cduff@fgcu.edu
DUFF, Debra 414-256-1258. 535 A
duffd@mtmary.edu
DUFF, John, A 727-864-8318. 101 N
duffja@eckerd.edu
DUFF, Rebecca 540-985-8246. 506 G
rduff@jchs.edu
DUFF-ANDERSON, Rachel 419-824-3759. 383 C
DUFFEL-JONES, Mona 504-816-4024. 201 K
mduffeljones@dillard.edu
DUFFETT, Rick 320-308-2286. 261 B
rduffett@stcloudstate.edu
DUFFETT, Robert 610-341-5890. 415 G
rduffett@eastern.edu
DUFFETT, Robert, G 610-341-5890. 425 I
rduffett@eastern.edu
DUFFEY, Patrick 903-813-2361. 466 H
pduffey@austincollege.edu
DUFFIE, James, E 561-868-3077. 110 C
duffiej@palmbeachstate.edu
DUFFIE, Robert 361-582-2469. 493 H
robert.duffie@victoriacollege.edu
DUFFOURC, Danielle 504-520-7563. 209 D
dduffour@xula.edu
DUFFY, Arwen 626-396-2311... 28 P
arwen.duffy@artcenter.edu
DUFFY, Brad 225-768-1719. 206 D
brad.duffy@ololcollege.edu
DUFFY, Brian 901-320-9768. 463 J
bduffy@victory.edu
DUFFY, Brian 215-972-2030. 426 Y
bduffy@pafa.edu
DUFFY, Cami 270-809-3155. 198 B
cduffy@murraystate.edu
DUFFY, Dolly 574-631-2788. 174 A
eduffy@nd.edu
DUFFY, James, P 717-337-6240. 417 B
jpduffy@gettysburg.edu
DUFFY, James, P 757-683-5421. 507 N
jduffy@odu.edu
DUFFY, John 847-214-7374. 144 F
jduffyecc@aol.com
DUFFY, Julia, A 203-254-4000... 89 I
jduffy@fairfield.edu
DUFFY, Kristine 518-743-2237. 345 E
duffyk@sunyacc.edu
DUFFY, Larry, K 580-477-7705. 401 J
larry.duffy@wosc.edu
DUFFY, Michael 517-265-5161. 238 G
mduffy@adrian.edu
DUFFY, Michael 610-282-1100. 414 F
michael.duffy@desales.edu
DUFFY, Pamela, A 619-239-0391... 36 D
pduffy@cwsl.edu
DUFFY, Peter 508-999-9216. 229 A
pduffy@umassd.cdu
DUFFY, Rachelle, M 517-265-5161. 238 G
rduffy@adrian.edu
DUFFY, Susan 781-239-6425. 222 D
sduffy@babson.edu
DUFFY, II, William, R 563-425-5221. 183 B
duffyw@uiu.edu
DUFNER, Jessie 406-874-6226. 286 E
Dufnerj@milescc.edu
DUFORE, Timothy, R 330-972-7238. 390 E
tdufore@uakron.edu
DUFOUR, Graciela 815-836-5270. 150 H
dufourgr@lewisu.edu
DUFRENE, Uric 812-941-2208. 168 F
udufrene@ius.edu
DUFRESNE-REYES, Alice 408-848-4791... 45 F
adufresnereyes@gavilan.edu
DUGAN, Brendan, J 718-489-5416. 338 G
bdugan@sfc.edu
DUGAN, Christine, M 717-245-1180. 414 H
duganc@dickinson.edu
DUGAN, Donald 262-691-5309. 541 D
ddugan@wctc.edu
DUGAN, Jim 602-749-7311. 144 A
jdugan@devry.edu
DUGAN, Melinda, E 215-887-5511. 437 C
mdugan@wts.edu
DUGAN, Michael 410-827-5834. 214 C
mdugan@chesapeake.edu
DUGAN, Robert 850-474-3135. 117 B
rdugan@uwf.edu
DUGAN, Robert, E 617-573-8536. 237 B
rdugan@suffolk.edu
DUGAN, Sharon 818-785-2726... 37 F
sharon.dugan@casalomacollege.edu
DUGAN, Thomas, F 718-270-2626. 342 D
tdugan@downstate.edu
DUGAS, Ross, B 952-888-4777. 263 B
rdugas@nwhealth.edu
DUGATKIN, David 845-257-3802. 342 B
dugatkind@newpaltz.edu
DUGDALE, Kathy 218-733-5990. 259 A
k.dugdale@lsc.edu
DUGGAN, Adam 508-849-3424. 222 B
aduggan@annamaria.edu
DUGGAN, Christina 781-768-7228. 236 A
christina.duggan@regiscollege.edu
DUGGAN, David, B 315-464-9720. 342 E
duggand@upstate.edu
DUGGAN, Jamie 908-527-7213. 308 B
jconroy@ucc.edu
DUGGAN, Michael, B 617-573-8468. 237 B
mduggan@suffolk.edu
DUGGAN, Roberta 707-826-5833... 35 C
duggan@humboldt.edu
DUGGAN, Sean 806-742-2661. 487 D
s.duggan@ttu.edu
DUGGAN, Theresa 516-299-2783. 329 D
theresa.duggan@liu.edu
DUGGAN-GOLD, Lori 516-877-3262. 313 A
duggangold@adelphi.edu
DUGGER, Jim 901-435-1680. 455 M
jim_dugger@loc.edu
DUGGER, Karen 410-704-5456. 220 E
kdugger@towson.edu
DUGGER, Neil 214-333-5202. 470 D
neil@dbu.edu
DUGUID, Stephanie 601-643-8341. 266 F
stephanie.duguid@colin.edu
DUHON, Gail 616-222-1431. 241 F
gail.duhon@cornerstone.edu
DUHON, Stacey 318-274-6120. 207 E
duhons@gram.edu
DUIGNAN, Kevin 845-398-4017. 340 A
kduignan@stac.edu
DUIN, Diane 406-896-5841. 287 C
dduin@msubillings.edu
DUJARDIAN, Tamara 407-628-5870. 102 K
tdujardian@cci.edu
DUKE, Charles, R 828-262-2234. 367 A
dukecr@appstate.edu
DUKE, Del, G 870-235-4171... 23 F
dgduke@saumag.edu
DUKE, Jimmy 256-306-2846..... 2 F
jfd@calhoun.edu
DUKE, Kenneth 828-884-8144. 352 I
dukekm@brevard.edu
DUKE, Lori 919-760-2291. 356 G
dukel@meredith.edu
DUKE, Lynda 309-556-3760. 148 B
lduke@iwu.edu
DUKE, Phyllis 908-737-5000. 302 F
pduke@kean.edu
DUKE, Russell 626-650-2306... 45 K
DUKE, Shalamon 310-287-4423... 52 F
dukesa@wlac.edu
DUKE, Steven 336-758-5938. 370 D
dukest@wfu.edu
DUKE, Todd 765-973-8611. 167 G
mtduke@iue.edu
DUKERT, Tracey 610-436-2813. 430 A
tdukert@wcupa.edu
DUKES, Charlene, M 301-322-0400. 217 F
cdukes@pgcc.edu
DUKES, Gary 503-838-8221. 406 E
dukesg@wou.edu
DUKES, Kenya 919-878-9900... 96 F
DUKES, Melinda 423-636-7305. 462 E
mdukes@tusculum.edu
DUKES, Michael 601-965-5980. 266 A
mdukes@belhaven.edu
DUKES, Mona, B 843-355-4121. 449 F
dukesm@wiltech.edu
DUKES, Rebecca 408-924-1120... 36 A
rebecca.dukes@sjsu.edu
DUKETT, William 724-503-1001. 436 G
wdukett@washjeff.edu
DULABAUM, Mary 847-628-2089. 149 B
mdulabaum@judsonu.edu
DULAN, Garland 256-726-7005..... 6 B
gdulan@oakwood.edu
DULANY, Ann 740-284-5254. 379 N
adulany@franciscan.edu
DULAY, Rachel 415-351-3515... 62 G
rdulay@sfai.edu
DULAY, Sarah 708-237-5050. 155 B
sdulay@nc.edu
DULEPSKI, Deborah, L 203-576-2388... 91 G
ddulepsk@bridgeport.edu
DULEY, Victoria 518-562-4184. 320 B
victoria.duley@clinton.edu
DULGAR, Laura 623-935-8808... 14 K
laura.dulgar@estrellamountain.edu
DULIN, Bill 828-327-7000. 359 A
bdulin@cvcc.edu
DULIN, Scott 617-236-8800. 226 F
sdulin@fisher.edu
DULING, Ennis 802-468-1239. 501 B
ennis.duling@castleton.edu
DULING, Sandra 802-468-1396. 501 B
sandy.duling@castleton.edu
DULL, Lindsay, N 607-733-7177. 323 F
Ldull@ebi-college.com
DULLEA, Robert 206-296-2590. 523 E
dullea@seattleu.edu
DUMANCELA, Fanny 718-518-4434. 318 B
fdumancela@hostos.cuny.edu
DUMANTAY, Danilo 691-320-2480. 546 B
comptroller@comfsm.fm
DUMAS, Brandon 225-771-3922. 206 J
brandon_dumas@subr.edu
DUMAS, Carrie, M 404-752-1733. 129 E
cdumas@msm.edu
DUMAS, Dan 502-897-4131. 199 B
ddumas@sbts.edu
DUMAS, Maureen 401-598-2350. 439 B
mdumas@jwu.edu
DUMAS, Roxanne 617-879-2208. 238 C
rdumas@wheelock.edu
DUMAUAL, Roberto 718-522-9073. 314 B
rdumaual@asa.edu
DUMAY, Harry, E 603-641-7100. 297 G
hdumay@anselm.edu
DUMKE, Alyce 920-735-5695. 539 K
dumke@fvtc.edu
DUMM, Pamela 502-213-2109. 195 F
pamela.dumm@kctcs.edu
DUMMER, Robin, K 530-226-4130... 66 D
rdummer@simpsonu.edu
DUMONT, Cathy 207-859-1167. 211 H
alumni@thomas.edu
DUMONT, Ronald 201-692-2811. 301 J
ronald_dumont@fdu.edu
DUMONT, Sara, E 202-885-1321... 94 F
dumont@american.edu
DUMONTELLE, Janine 714-997-6553... 38 A
jpdumont@chapman.edu
DUMPSON, Kimberly, C 410-651-7686. 219 E
kdumpson@umes.edu
DUNAVANT, James, R 405-466-3394. 395 N
jrdunavant@langston.edu
DUNAVANT, James, R 405-466-3579. 395 N
jrdunavant@langston.edu
DUNAWAY, Greg 662-325-2646. 268 D
dunaway@soc.msstate.edu
DUNAWAY, Greg, A 804-594-1430. 512 G
llclair@jtcc.edu
DUNAWAY, Mark 650-493-4430... 66 E
mark.dunaway@sofia.edu
DUNBAR, Brenda 714-816-0366... 70 A
brenda.dunbar@trident.edu
DUNBAR, Deirdre, M 262-554-2010. 534 D
midwestcollege@aol.com
DUNBAR, Diana 805-289-6159... 74 H
ddunbar@vcccd.edu
DUNBAR, Joan 313-577-5542. 252 G
jcdunbar@wayne.edu
DUNBAR, Kristin 906-635-2625. 245 G
kdunbar@lssu.edu
DUNBAR, Nathan 503-517-1206. 408 H
ndunbar@warnerpacific.edu
DUNBAR, Shelley 308-432-6224. 291 D
sdunbar@csc.edu
DUNBAR, William, J 262-554-2010. 534 D
dunbarphd@aol.com
DUNBAR-JACOB, Jaqueline 412-624-2400. 435 C
dunbar@pitt.edu
DUNCAN, Christopher, M 937-327-7915. 393 E
cduncan@wittenberg.edu
DUNCAN, Darrell 615-966-6166. 456 B
darrell.duncan@lipscomb.edu
DUNCAN, David 417-626-1234. 279 J
duncan.david@occ.edu
DUNCAN, Douglas, S 727-341-3246. 112 E
duncan.doug@spcollege.edu
DUNCAN, Elton Lee 304-457-6247. 526 A
elton.duncan@sodexo.com
DUNCAN, Frances 850-484-2230. 110 G
fduncan@pensacolastate.edu
DUNCAN, JR., Gene 717-299-7782. 434 A
duncan@stevenscollege.edu
DUNCAN, Geri 704-290-5221. 363 G
gduncan@spcc.edu
DUNCAN, Ian 727-726-1153. 100 E
ianduncan@clearwater.edu
DUNCAN, Jane 954-262-5382. 109 K
janedunc@nova.edu
DUNCAN, Jennifer 610-917-1489. 436 C
jlduncan@vfcc.edu
DUNCAN, Jennifer 573-882-7560. 283 C
duncanjenn@missouri.edu
DUNCAN, Jenny 918-293-5488. 398 B
jenny.duncan@okstate.edu
DUNCAN, Jerelyn, L 501-244-5130... 19 J
jerelyn.duncan@arkansasbaptist.edu
DUNCAN, Jim 901-843-3850. 458 E
duncanjb@rhodes.edu
DUNCAN, John, B 843-863-7955. 441 H
jduncan@csuniv.edu
DUNCAN, Laura, H 334-833-4069..... 4 D
lduncan@huntingdon.edu
DUNCAN, Lewis 407-646-2120. 111 Q
lduncan@rollins.edu
DUNCAN, Linda 773-244-5697. 154 G
lduncan@northpark.edu
DUNCAN, Matthew 408-554-4583... 64 M
mduncan@scu.edu
DUNCAN, Michael, C 413-782-1240. 238 A
mduncan@wne.edu
DUNCAN, Mike 803-508-7283. 440 G
duncanm@atc.edu
DUNCAN, Nancy 503-399-2530. 402 E
nancy.duncan@chemeketa.edu
DUNCAN, Pamela 914-323-5158. 330 B
pamela.duncan@mville.edu
DUNCAN, Pete 740-351-3319. 388 N
pduncan@shawnee.edu
DUNCAN, Randy 704-687-7323. 368 E
rduncan@uncc.edu
DUNCAN, Renae, D 270-809-3027. 198 B
rduncan@murraystate.edu
DUNCAN, Robert 573-882-9582. 283 C
duncanrv@missouri.edu
DUNCAN, JR., Robert, J 918-781-6284. 394 D
duncanr@bacone.edu
DUNCAN, Steve 252-328-6105. 367 B
duncans@ecu.edu
DUNCAN, Steve 252-328-9094. 367 B
duncans@ecu.edu
DUNCAN, Susan 502-852-6373. 200 D
shdunc01@louisville.edu
DUNCAN, Susan, H 845-575-3000. 330 D
susan.duncan@marist.edu
DUNCAN, Suzanne 757-388-3693. 509 D
sxduncan@sentara.com
DUNCAN, Teresa, S 865-882-4648. 461 E
duncants@roanestate.edu
DUNCAN, Terry 270-707-3771. 195 E
terry.duncan@kctcs.edu
DUNCAN, Timothy 706-945-1358. 130 C
tduncan@paine.edu
DUNCAN, Todd 513-556-6445. 390 G
todd.duncan@uc.edu
DUNCAN, Tom, L 561-478-5555. 248 C
duncan@northwood.edu
DUNCAN, Tracey 931-372-6091. 460 A
tduncan@tntech.edu
DUNCAN, Wendy 515-271-1814. 177 K
wendy.duncan@drake.edu
DUNCAN, William, H 916-660-7000... 66 B
DUNCAN, William, R 423-439-6000. 459 C
duncanw@etsu.edu
DUNCAN JOSEPH, Cynthia 614-236-6621. 375 H
cduncan@capital.edu
DUNCAN-POITIER, Johanna 518-320-1276. 341 C
johanna.duncan-poitier@suny.edu
DUNCAN RAINES, Lisa, D 757-594-7846. 503 M
duncanl@cnu.edu
DUNCKLEE, Mary 508-565-3360. 237 A
stonehillbkstr@fheg.follett.com
DUNFEE, Lindsey, M 248-218-2018. 249 D
DUNFORD, Wyton 801-524-1922. 495 O
WDunford@ldsbc.edu

DUNG, Peter .... 213-613-2200... 67 E
peter_dung@sciarc.edu
DUNGEY, Deborah, J ..... 936-361-1000. 482 F
djdungey@pvamu.edu
DUNHAM, Andrew .... 517-629-0477. 239 A
adunham@albion.edu
DUNHAM, Andrew .... 517-629-0216. 239 A
adunham@albion.edu
DUNHAM, Anne, M .... 276-739-2456. 514 D
adunham@vhcc.edu
DUNHAM, David .... 209-228-4264... 71 D
DDunham@UCMerced.edu
DUNHAM, Dennis .... 509-533-8630. 518 D
ddunham@ccs.spokane.edu
DUNHAM, Dennis .... 509-533-8630. 518 F
dennis.dunham@ccs.spokane.edu
DUNHAM, Dennis .... 405-974-2374. 400 K
ddunham1@uco.edu
DUNHAM, Doug .... 660-562-1122. 279 I
dunham@nwmissouri.edu
DUNHAM, Kyle, C .... 757-479-3706. 503 C
kyle.dunham@baptistseminary.edu
DUNHAM, Mark, E .... 660-263-3900. 272 A
mdunham@cccb.edu
DUNHAM, Rhonda, J ..... 660-263-3900. 272 A
rdunham@cccb.edu
DUNHAM, Stephen, S .... 814-867-4088. 426 A
ssd13@psu.edu
DUNHAM, Thomas .... 773-907-4477. 142 A
tdunham@ccc.edu
DUNHAM, Wesley .... 508-849-3342. 222 B
wdunham@annamaria.edu
DUNHAM HOWIE,
Jules .... 937-376-2946. 388 B
jhowie@payne.edu
DUNHAM STRAND,
Amy .... 616-632-8900. 239 E
stranamy@aquinas.edu
DUNISCH, Kim .... 262-243-5700. 532 H
kimberly.dunisch@cuw.edu
DUNIWAY, Robert .... 206-296-2145. 523 E
rduniway@seattleu.edu
DUNKEL, Aaron .... 805-525-4417... 69 H
adunkel@thomasaquinas.edu
DUNKEL, Norbert, W ...... 352-392-2171. 116 A
norbd@housing.ufl.edu
DUNKELMAN, James ...... 562-907-4205... 76 I
jdunkelman@whittier.edu
DUNKERTON, David, W . 304-877-6428. 526 C
david.dunkerton@abc.edu
DUNKLE, John, H .... 847-491-2151. 155 D
j-dunkle@northwestern.edu
DUNKLE, Kurt .... 646-717-9740. 325 B
dunkle@gts.edu
DUNKLEBERGER,
Dennis, L .... 570-327-4772. 427 B
ddunkle@pct.edu
DUNKLEBERGER, Kay, E 570-326-3761. 427 B
kdunkleb@pct.edu
DUNKLEY, Eugene .... 618-664-6543. 145 G
eugene.dunkley@greenville.edu
DUNLAP, Doug .... 620-365-5116. 183 I
ddunlap@allencc.edu
DUNLAP, James, H .... 517-355-2223. 246 H
dunlap@msu.edu
DUNLAP, Joe, H .... 208-769-3303. 138 I
jhdunlap@nic.edu
DUNLAP, Lonnie, J .... 847-491-3707. 155 D
l-dunlap@northwestern.edu
DUNLAP, Lori .... 317-921-4949. 169 K
loridunlap@ivytech.edu
DUNLAP, Marilyn .... 808-956-8838. 136 B
mdunlap@hawaii.edu
DUNLAP, Nancy .... 615-248-1350. 462 D
ndunlap@trevecca.edu
DUNLAP, Scott .... 973-720-3232. 308 I
dunlaps@wpunj.edu
DUNLAP, Susan, L .... 516-726-5816. 545 H
dunlaps@usmma.edu
DUNLAY, Robert .... 402-280-2600. 289 D
robertdunlay@creighton.edu
DUNLEAVY, James, F ...... 610-861-5463. 425 D
jdunleavy@northampton.edu
DUNLEAVY, Patricia, E ... 570-348-6220. 423 B
dunleavy@marywood.edu
DUNMAN, ReNee, S .... 757-683-3141. 507 N
rdunman@odu.edu
DUNN, Amanda .... 801-840-4800. 495 K
adunn@cci.edu
DUNN, Andrew .... 714-438-4611... 39 H
adunn@mail.cccd.edu
DUNN, Andy .... 503-554-2162. 403 C
adunn@georgefox.edu
DUNN, Ashley .... 818-778-5518... 52 E
dunnAE@lavc.edu
DUNN, Barbara .... 870-543-5957... 23 E
bdunn@seark.edu
DUNN, Barry .... 605-688-4148. 452 B
barry.dunn@sdstate.edu
DUNN, Barry .... 605-688-4792. 452 B
barry.dunn@sdstate.edu
DUNN, Billie .... 440-375-7506. 382 L
bdunn@lec.edu
DUNN, Casey .... 440-449-6508. 392 D
0621mgr@follett.com
DUNN, Chris .... 419-372-8243. 374 K
dunncs@bgsu.edu
DUNN, Christopher .... 617-482-3103. 228 F
cdunn@admin.umass.edu
DUNN, Claire, B .... 315-470-6650. 345 B
cbdunn@esf.edu
DUNN, Daniel .... 312-329-4451. 153 E
daniel.dunn@moody.edu
DUNN, David .... 502-852-5184. 200 D
dldunn01@louisville.edu
DUNN, Denise, A .... 319-296-4267. 178 J
denise.dunn@hawkeyecollege.edu
DUNN, Douglas .... 210-690-9000. 472 N
ddunn@hallmarkcollege.edu
DUNN, Duane, M .... 620-417-1010. 190 F
duane.dunn@sccc.edu
DUNN, Elizabeth, E .... 574-520-4322. 168 E
elizdunn@iusb.edu
DUNN, Erin .... 727-873-4547. 116 D
edunn1@mail.usf.edu
DUNN, Franklin, T .... 757-822-1780. 514 C
fdunn@tcc.edu
DUNN, Galen .... 618-842-3711. 146 I
dunng@iecc.edu
DUNN, Hank .... 828-398-7112. 357 N
hdunn@abtech.edu
DUNN, Jaime .... 410-626-2500. 217 G
jaime.dunn@sjca.edu
DUNN, James, J .... 336-758-4240. 370 D
dunnjj@wfu.edu
DUNN, Jeanette, R .... 864-587-4271. 447 B
dunnj@smcsc.edu
DUNN, Joel .... 336-334-5834. 369 A
j_dunn@uncg.edu
DUNN, John .... 206-878-3710. 520 E
jdunn@highline.edu
DUNN, John, B .... 617-552-3350. 224 A
jack.dunn@bc.edu
DUNN, John, M .... 269-387-2351. 252 I
john.dunn@wmich.edu
DUNN, Judi, B .... 402-552-6123. 288 L
dunn@clarksoncollege.edu
DUNN, Julie, A .... 563-588-7136. 180 L
julie.dunn@loras.edu
DUNN, Keith .... 601-974-1010. 267 I
keith.dunn@millsaps.edu
DUNN, Leah .... 828-251-6545. 368 C
DUNN, Marilynn, C .... 419-434-4202. 393 D
mdunn@winebrenner.edu
DUNN, Mary, E .... 617-333-2193. 225 E
mdunn@curry.edu
DUNN, Meg .... 212-757-1190. 313 H
mdunn@funeraleducation.org
DUNN, Michael .... 513-745-3223. 393 H
dunn@xavier.edu
DUNN, Michele .... 201-684-7701. 305 A
mdunn@ramapo.edu
DUNN, Michelle .... 201-328-5196. 300 G
mdunn@ccm.edu
DUNN, Michelle .... 260-665-4421. 173 E
dunnm@trine.edu
DUNN, Paul .... 360-650-3472. 525 C
paul.dunn@wwu.edu
DUNN, Randy .... 706-379-5218. 134 L
rjdunn@yhc.edu
DUNN, Randy, J .... 330-941-3101. 394 A
randy.dunn@ysu.edu
DUNN, Robin .... 410-626-2540. 217 G
robin.dunn@sjca.edu
DUNN, Samuel .... 781-235-1200. 222 D
sdunn@babson.edu
DUNN, Samuel .... 781-239-6404. 222 D
sdunn@babson.edu
DUNN, Scott .... 229-248-2927. 121 E
sdunn@bainbridge.edu
DUNN, Susan .... 949-794-9090... 68 D
sdunn@stanbridge.edu
DUNN, T. Michael .... 334-833-4495..... 4 D
mdunn@huntingdon.edu
DUNN, Thomas, A .... 574-572-5100. 166 B
dunnta@grace.edu
DUNN, Tracy, H .... 803-705-4427. 441 C
dunnt@benedict.edu
DUNN, W. Brent .... 417-836-6666. 278 E
brentdunn@missouristate.edu
DUNN, Wendy, L .... 319-399-8710. 176 G
wdunn@coe.edu
DUNN-STEINKE, Molly .. 217-228-5432. 156 C
steinmo@quincy.edu
DUNNAGAN, Tim .... 208-426-4116. 137 G
timdunnagan@boisestate.edu
DUNNAM, Rob, W .... 770-720-9130. 130 G
rwd1@reinhardt.edu
DUNNAM, Vicki .... 325-793-4987. 476 E
dunnam.vicki@mcm.edu
DUNNE, Martha, L .... 212-998-2115. 334 D
marti.dunne@nyu.edu
DUNNE, Michele, A .... 515-263-2853. 178 G
mdunne@grandview.edu
DUNNE, Nicole .... 831-646-3007... 54 I
ndunn@mpc.edu
DUNNE, Thomas, A .... 718-817-0180. 324 G
tdunne@fordham.edu
DUNNE, Tim .... 207-216-4335. 211 C
tdunne@yccc.edu
DUNNE, Will .... 386-506-4486. 101 G
dunnew@DaytonaState.edu
DUNNE-CASCIO,
Colleen .... 541-962-3476. 405 H
ccascio@eou.edu
DUNNEGAN, Dawn .... 319-385-6238. 179 K
dawn.dunnegan@iwc.edu
DUNNETT, Stephen, C .... 716-645-2368. 341 F
dunnett@buffalo.edu
DUNNING, John .... 402-375-7286. 291 F
jodunni1@wsc.edu
DUNNING, Sue .... 863-638-2937. 119 D
dunnings@webber.edu
DUNNINGS, Lance .... 404-880-8051. 122 J
ldunning@cau.edu
DUNNINGTON,
Sandra, F .... 301-322-0406. 217 F
sdunnington@pgcc.edu
DUNNUCK, John .... 954-201-7405... 99 D
jdunnuck@broward.edu
DUNOVANT, Kevin .... 336-887-3000. 355 N
kdunovant@laureluniversity.edu
DUNOVICH, Marlayne ..... 610-902-8366. 411 E
marlayne.n.dundovich@cabrini.edu
DUNPHE, Beth .... 212-343-1234. 331 D
bdunphe@mcny.edu
DUNSEATH, Jennifer ...... 401-454-6386. 440 A
jdunseat@risd.edu
DUNSHEE, David, M ...... 248-232-4807. 248 D
dmdunshe@oaklandcc.edu
DUNSON, Kenneth .... 972-238-6171. 471 C
kdunson@dcccd.edu
DUNSON, Necol, M .... 304-829-7394. 526 D
ndunson@bethanywv.edu
DUNSTON, Karen .... 503-352-2218. 407 A
dunstonk@pacificu.edu
DUNSTON, Rita .... 540-654-1063. 510 J
rdunston@umw.edu
DUNSWORTH,
Richard, L .... 479-979-1242... 25 J
rdunsworth@ozarks.edu
DUNTLEY, Mark .... 503-768-7082. 403 K
duntley@lclark.edu
DUNWOODY, Joshua ..... 952-446-4170. 255 D
dunwoodyj@crown.edu
DUPAUL, Stephanie .... 214-768-2110. 481 A
sdupaul@smu.edu
DUPEE, Daniel .... 315-786-2401. 327 L
ddupee@sunyjefferson.edu
DUPEE, Ryan .... 727-726-1153. 100 E
ryandupee@clearwater.edu
DUPELL, Linda .... 978-665-4342. 229 E
ldupell@fitchburgstate.edu
DUPES, Steven .... 717-720-4100. 427 G
sdupes@passhe.edu
DUPIER, Charles .... 606-539-4316. 200 B
chuck.dupier@ucumberlands.edu
DUPIER, Jo .... 606-539-4208. 200 B
jo.dupier@ucumberlands.edu
DUPKE, Vicki .... 567-661-7172. 387 L
vicki_dupke@owens.edu
DUPLECHIN, Denise, M . 318-342-5336. 208 E
duplechin@ulm.edu
DUPONT, Joseph .... 781-736-3613. 224 F
dupont@brandeis.edu
DUPRA, JoAnn .... 870-543-5993... 23 E
jdupra@seark.edu
DUPRE, Carolyn .... 601-877-4701. 265 G
chinton@alcorn.edu
DUPRE, Terry, G .... 985-448-4031. 208 A
terry.dupre@nicholls.edu
DUPREE, Carol .... 325-794-4401. 468 I
carol.dupree@cisco.edu
DUPREE, Cathy, P .... 252-823-5166. 360 C
dupreec@edgecombe.edu
DUPREE, Jason, M .... 580-774-7081. 400 B
jason.dupree@swosu.edu
DUPREE, Jimmy .... 614-837-4088. 392 E
dupreej@valorcollege.com
DUPREE, Kathy .... 281-212-1610. 489 C
dupree@uhcl.edu
DUPREE, Paul, J .... 859-858-3511. 192 B
pdupree@asbury.edu
DUPREE, Robert, S .... 972-721-5311. 488 F
scott@udallas.edu
DUPREE, Stan .... 760-674-3777... 40 F
sdupree@collegeofthedesert.edu
DUPREY, Wayne, A .... 518-564-2033. 344 B
dupreywa@plattsburgh.edu
DUPRIE, Kelsey .... 360-992-2505. 518 A
sduprie@clark.edu
DUPRIEST, Barclay, F ..... 804-752-7371. 508 E
bdupries@rmc.edu
DURAJ, Jonathan .... 937-327-7814. 393 E
jduraj@wittenberg.edu
DURAL, Dalton .... 337-269-0620. 201 B
daltond@bluecliffcollege.com
DURAN, Alexandra .... 650-949-6973... 44 N
duranalexandra@fhda.edu
DURAN, Dorothy .... 712-325-3202. 179 L
dduran@iwcc.edu
DURAN, Kelly .... 716-839-8348. 322 E
kduran@daemen.edu
DURAN, Margret .... 806-743-2300. 487 E
margret.duran@ttuhsc.edu
DURAN, Michelle .... 361-593-5501. 484 A
michelle.duran@tamuk.edu
DURAN, Richard .... 805-986-5808... 74 G
rduran@vcccd.edu
DURAN, Veronica .... 520-494-5260... 12 P
veronica.duran@centralaz.edu
DURAN, William .... 505-224-4000. 309 E
wduran2@cnm.edu
DURAND, Bonita, R .... 716-878-4102. 343 A
durandbr@buffalostate.edu
DURANDETTA,
Donald, W .... 302-356-6780... 94 E
donald.w.durandetta@wilmu.edu
DURANT, Benjamin .... 252-335-8792. 367 C
bdurant@mail.ecsu.edu
DURANT, Brian .... 518-743-2236. 345 E
durantb@sunyacc.edu
DURANT, Joseph .... 843-661-8086. 443 G
joe.durant@fdtc.edu
DURANT, Joyce, M .... 843-661-1300. 444 B
jdurant@fmarion.edu
DURANT, Leroy, A .... 803-535-5341. 442 B
ldurant@claflin.edu
DURANT, Linda, S .... 610-499-4123. 437 E
lsdurant@widener.edu
DURANT, Natalie .... 860-512-3223... 88 G
ndurant@manchestercc.edu
DURANT, Nickeshia .... 718-357-0500. 339 G
ndurant@edaff.com
DURANT, Zoe, W .... 580-581-2288. 394 G
zoed@cameron.edu
DURANTI, Alessandro .... 310-825-4017... 71 C
aduranti@college.ucla.edu
DURBAK, Andres .... 773-907-4708. 142 A
adurbak@ccc.edu
DURBEN, Katherine .... 414-288-5470. 534 B
katherine.durben@marquette.edu
DURBIN, Bryce .... 706-236-2282. 121 G
bdurbin@berry.edu
DURBIN, Daniel, A .... 304-293-4008. 530 D
dan.durbin@mail.wvu.edu
DURBIN, Rachel .... 503-494-7800. 405 I
finaid@ohsu.edu
DURCAN, Deborah, A ..... 608-262-1311. 536 C
ddurcan@uwsa.edu
DURDELLA, Caroline ...... 949-582-4565... 67 C
cdurdella@saddleback.edu
DURDEN, Drew .... 478-289-2090. 124 C
ddurden@ega.edu
DURDEN, Lori .... 912-486-7607. 129 J
ldurden@ogeecheetech.edu
DURDEN, Tracey .... 734-432-5673. 246 B
tdurden@madonna.edu
DUREE, Christopher .... 641-844-5720. 179 H
christopher.duree@iavalley.edu
DUREE, Christopher, A ... 641-844-5720. 179 J
christopher.duree@iavalley.edu
DUREN, Andrew, M .... 708-974-5203. 153 F
duren@morainevalley.edu
DUREN, Deborah .... 573-876-7212. 282 H
debd@stephens.edu
DURETTE, Kristi .... 603-645-9780. 297 I
k.durette@snhu.edu
DURFEE, Carissa .... 617-989-4086. 237 G
durfeec@wit.edu
DURFEE, Mike .... 307-532-8346. 542 a
mike.durfee@ewc.wy.edu
DURFIELD, Jonathan ...... 832-813-6615. 476 A
jonathan.durfield@lonestar.edu
DURGIN, William .... 315-792-7200. 346 C
william.durgin@sunyit.edu
DURHAM, David, L .... 304-293-8220. 530 D
david.durham@mail.wvu.edu
DURHAM, Dawn, W .... 864-833-8477. 446 D
dwdurham@presby.edu
DURHAM, Ed .... 410-287-1010. 214 B
edurham@cecil.edu
DURHAM, Gesele .... 414-229-3305. 537 A
gerdurham@uwm.edu
DURHAM, Jerry .... 319-226-2015. 175 D
Jerry.Durham@AllenCollege.edu
DURHAM, John, R .... 610-519-7164. 436 F
john.durham@villanova.edu
DURHAM, Kim .... 954-262-8601. 109 K
durham@nsu.nova.edu
DURHAM, Lisa .... 704-378-1135. 355 K
ldurham@jcsu.edu
DURHAM, Lynn .... 404-894-8261. 125 D
lynn.durham@carnegie.gatech.edu

DURHAM, Rhonda ... 501-882-4442... 19 M
rsdurham@asub.edu
DURHAM, Tammara ... 785-864-4060. 190 L
tdurham@ku.edu
DURHAM, Timothy ... 740-587-6647. 379 D
durhamt@denison.edu
DURHAM, Wes, T ... 812-465-7016. 174 D
wdurham@usi.edu
DURHAM, William, H ... 704-233-8218. 370 G
durham@wingate.edu
DURIN, Lynne ... 815-825-2086. 149 F
lynne.durin@kishwaukeecollege.edu
DURISH, Aubrey, L ... 815-740-5047. 162 F
adurish@stfrancis.edu
DURKEE, Gene ... 603-428-2358. 297 D
edurkee@nec.edu
DURKEE, Phillip, A ... 831-656-2517. 544 M
padurkee@nps.edu
DURKEE, Robert, K ... 609-258-6428. 304 E
durkee@princeton.edu
DURKIN, Karen ... 856-415-2284. 302 C
kdurkin@gccnj.edu
DURKIN, Rebecca ... 847-578-8351. 157 F
rebecca.durkin@rosalindfranklin.edu
DURKLE, Robert, F ... 937-229-4411. 391 C
rdurkle1@udayton.edu
DURNEY, L. John ... 845-398-4116. 340 A
ldurney@stac.edu
DURNFORD, Ronald, R .. 504-520-5031. 209 D
rdurnfor@xula.edu
DURNIN, Ellen ... 203-392-5356... 88 A
durnine1@southernct.edu
DUROCHER, Becky, L ... 985-448-4510. 208 A
becky.leblanc-durocher@nicholls.edu
DUROSS, Frank ... 315-792-5526. 331 I
fduross@mvcc.edu
DUROUCHIC, Jennifer ... 281-931-7717. 127 F
jdurouchic@ict-ils.edu
DURR, Elaine ... 336-278-5229. 354 B
edurr@elon.edu
DURR, Elaine Jeanne ... 608-342-1176. 537 D
durrj@uwplatt.edu
DURR, Kimberly, H ... 618-650-2477. 159 H
kdurr@siue.edu
DURRETT, Duane ... 940-627-2690. 494 G
ddurrett@wc.edu
DURSI, Joseph, F ... 914-594-4487. 334 A
joseph_dursi@nymc.edu
DURSI, Joseph, F ... 914-594-4234. 334 A
joseph_dursi@nymc.edu
DURSKY, Jill ... 641-673-1046. 183 H
durskyje@wmpenn.edu
DURSKY, Jill ... 641-673-1046. 183 H
durskyj@wmpenn.edu
DURSO, Thomas, W ... 610-921-7526. 409 A
tdurso@alb.edu
DURST, Devoiry ... 732-414-2834. 308 K
DURST, Lisa ... 440-525-7721. 382 M
ldurst@lakelandcc.edu
DURST, Maribeth ... 352-588-8244. 112 D
maribeth.durst@saintleo.edu
DURST, Steve ... 231-591-2254. 242 F
dursts@ferris.edu
DURTSCHI, Lynn ... 208-524-3000. 138 D
lynn.durtschi@my.eitc.edu
DUSENBURY, Renata ... 919-546-8395. 366 E
rdusenbury@shawu.edu
DUSENBURY, Renata ... 919-546-8252. 366 E
rdusenbury@shawu.edu
DUSING, Roger ... 816-584-6386. 280 C
roger.dusing@park.edu
DUSSEAU, Daniel ... 703-323-3111. 513 C
ddusseau@nvcc.edu
DUSSOURD, Ellen, A ... 716-645-2258. 341 F
dussourd@buffalo.edu
DUTCHER, Dave ... 315-733-2300. 349 D
ddutcher@uscny.edu
DUTCHER, Debra ... 518-327-6082. 336 B
ddutcher@paulsmiths.edu
DUTCHER, Donald ... 315-866-0300. 326 A
dutcherdm@herkimer.edu
DUTCHER, James ... 518-255-5337. 344 E
dutchejm@cobleskill.edu
DUTCHER, Victoria ... 206-315-5825. 518 G
vdutcher@cornish.edu
DUTCHIK, Lisa ... 319-398-5431. 180 J
lisa.dutchik@kirkwood.edu
DUTLER, Sue ... 312-935-2210. 156 K
sdutler@robertmorris.edu
DUTREMBLE, Kathy ... 850-484-1630. 110 G
kdutremble@pensacolastate.edu
DUTREMBLE, Kathy ... 850-484-2076. 110 G
kdutremble@pensacolastate.edu
DUTRISAC, Gordon ... 425-558-0299. 519 B
gordon@digipen.edu
DUTSCHKE, Dennis ... 215-527-2901. 409 H
dutschkd@arcadia.edu
DUTTA, Debasish ... 217-333-6715. 162 A
ddutta@illinois.edu
DUTTA, Mitra ... 312-996-9450. 161 D
dutta@uic.edu
DUTTA, Soumitra ... 607-255-6418. 322 A
sd599@cornell.edu
DUTTO, Larry ... 559-730-3808... 40 I
larryd@cos.edu
DUTTON, Colleen ... 972-883-2221. 491 E
colleen.dutton@utdallas.edu
DUTTON, Shelley, A ... 703-284-1549. 507 B
shelley.dutton@marymount.edu
DUTTON COX, Deborah . 603-862-1627. 298 C
debbie.dutton@unh.edu
DUVAL, Derethia ... 415-338-2208... 35 E
derethia@sfsu.edu
DUVALL, Shannon ... 941-487-4801. 115 D
sduvall@ncf.edu
DUVALL, Staci ... 501-977-2087... 25 C
duvall@uaccm.edu
DUVENTRE, Amber ... 615-327-6813. 456 E
DUWALL, John, E ... 304-293-7171. 530 D
john.duwall@mail.wvu.edu
DUZIK, David, B ... 402-465-2144. 291 G
dduzik@nebrwesleyan.edu
DUZIK, Don ... 712-274-6400. 183 G
don.duzik@witcc.edu
DUZINSKI,
Jennifer Anne ... 317-738-8018. 165 I
jduzinski@franklincollege.edu
DVORACEK, Nick ... 920-424-7363. 537 B
dvoracek@uwosh.edu
DVORACSEK, Joe ... 727-341-6108. 112 E
dvoracsek.joe@spcollege.edu
DVORAK, Jerome ... 570-389-4216. 427 H
jdvorak@bloomufdn.org
DVORAK, Leah, M ... 262-243-5700. 532 H
leah.dvorak@cuw.edu
DVORAK, Robert ... 415-380-1358... 45 H
robertdvorak@ggbts.edu
DVORAK, Susan ... 414-466-9777. 539 G
sdvorak@wspp.edu
DVORSKE, Tom ... 337-475-5510. 207 G
tdvorske@mcneese.edu
DWIGHT, Beverly, J ... 413-782-2210. 238 A
bdwight@wne.edu
DWIGHT SMITH, Denise 704-687-2231. 368 E
ddsmith@uncc.edu
DWIRE, Steven, W ... 518-454-5464. 321 A
dwires@strose.edu
DWORACZYK, Bill ... 214-768-3140. 481 A
billd@smu.edu
DWORAK, Joseph, V ... 651-638-6400. 253 K
j-dworak@bethel.edu
DWORKIN, James, B ... 219-785-5331. 172 A
jdworkin@pnc.edu
DWORSHAK, Lydia ... 701-483-2091. 371 D
lydia.dworshak@dickinsonstate.edu
DWYER, Claire ... 203-576-5756... 91 D
Claire.Dwyer@stvincentscollege.edu
DWYER, Debra ... 585-292-2902. 332 A
ddwyer@monroecc.edu
DWYER, James, P ... 989-964-4209. 249 G
jdwyer@svsu.edu
DWYER, Jon ... 360-412-6152. 522 G
JDwyer@stmartin.edu
DWYER, Katelyn ... 617-296-8300. 227 I
katelyn_dwyer@laboure.edu
DWYER, Ken ... 508-854-4579. 232 F
krd@qcc.mass.edu
DWYER, Patricia ... 302-736-2352... 94 C
pdwyer@wesley.edu
DWYER, Sharon ... 805-289-8976... 74 H
sdwyer@vcccd.edu
DWYER, Thomas ... 502-410-6200. 194 B
tdwyer@galencollege.edu
DWYER, JR., Thomas, L 401-598-1410. 439 B
tdwyer@jwu.edu
DWYER, Thomas, P ... 804-752-7244. 508 E
tdwyer@rmc.edu
DYAL, Donald ... 806-742-2261. 487 D
donald.dyal@ttu.edu
DYBDAHL, Tammy ... 303-753-6046... 85 B
tdybdahl@rmcad.edu
DYBEN, Andrea ... 561-803-2062. 110 B
andrea_dyben@pba.edu
DYBICK, Thomas ... 413-205-3972. 221 F
thomas.dybick@aic.edu
DYBWAD, Peter ... 510-841-9230... 77 B
pdybwad@wi.edu
DYCHES, David ... 435-283-7058. 498 A
david.dyches@snow.edu
DYCKMAN, Lise ... 415-575-6181... 31 D
ldyckman@ciis.edu
DYE, Danny, L ... 502-231-5221. 197 E
ddye@myLBC.us
DYE, James ... 276-964-7284. 514 A
james.dye@sw.edu
DYE, Joanna ... 309-796-5442. 140 E
dyej@bhc.edu
DYE, John ... 330-337-6403. 373 F
college@awc.edu
DYE, Larry ... 580-628-6217. 396 M
larry.dye@noc.edu
DYE, Melissa ... 815-288-5511. 158 K
melissa.m.dye@svcc.edu
DYE, Michael ... 480-994-9244... 17 Q
michaeld@swiha.edu
DYE, Ryan, D ... 563-333-6389. 182 B
DyeRyanD@sau.edu
DYE, Teresa ... 651-730-5100. 255 H
tdye@globeuniversity.edu
DYER, Amy ... 703-370-6600. 508 B
DYER, Cynthia, M ... 515-961-1519. 182 E
cyd.dyer@simpson.edu
DYER, Edgar, L ... 843-349-2628. 442 E
dyer@coastal.edu
DYER, Esther, L ... 865-971-5216. 461 D
eldyer@pstcc.edu
DYER, Gail, A ... 401-865-2463. 439 E
gdyer@providence.edu
DYER, Jennifer ... 213-821-5002... 74 A
jennifer.dyer@stevens.usc.edu
DYER, John, C ... 214-887-5141. 471 F
jdyer@dts.edu
DYER, Karen ... 812-535-5101. 172 F
kdyer@smwc.edu
DYER, Kent ... 484-664-3140. 424 H
dyer@muhlenberg.edu
DYER, Kristyn, M ... 508-793-2418. 225 B
kdyer@holycross.edu
DYER, Mary ... 773-291-6225. 142 D
mdyer7@ccc.edu
DYER, Peggy, D ... 918-595-8100. 400 E
peggy.dyer@tulsacc.edu
DYER, Robin ... 704-669-4128. 359 D
dyer@clevelandcc.edu
DYER, Ruth ... 785-532-6224. 188 A
rdyer@ksu.edu
DYER, Stacey ... 843-470-8393. 447 C
sdyer@tcl.edu
DYER, Steve ... 818-767-0888... 76 K
steve.dyer@woodbury.edu
DYER, Tom ... 206-283-4500... 28 M
tdyer@argosy.edu
DYER, Tricia ... 207-621-3390. 212 C
triciad@maine.edu
DYER, Wayne ... 973-803-5000. 304 C
wdyer@pillar.edu
DYERLY, Kevin ... 909-748-8739... 73 H
kevin_dyerly@redlands.edu
DYESS, Hubert ... 601-426-6346. 269 G
hdyess@southeasternbaptist.edu
DYJAK, Mary Lou ... 413-748-3271. 236 I
mdyjak@springfieldcollege.edu
DYKE, Gary ... 281-649-3335. 473 B
gdyke@hbu.edu
DYKEMA, Mark ... 717-545-4747. 419 O
DYKES, Allison ... 404-727-8878. 124 E
allison.dykes@emory.edu
DYKES, Bill, G ... 513-772-9888. 386 C
bill.dykes@omw.edu
DYKES, Danny ... 601-643-8403. 266 F
danny.dykes@colin.edu
DYKES, Donald, E ... 860-444-8213. 545 G
donald.e.dykes@uscga.edu
DYKSHOORN, Sharon ... 712-274-6400. 183 G
sharon.dykshoorn@witcc.edu
DYKSTRA, Arlen, R ... 314-392-2201. 278 B
adykstra@mobap.edu
DYKSTRA, Doug ... 808-235-7402. 137 C
dykstra@hawaii.edu
DYKSTRA, Frank ... 520-515-5311... 12 R
poncho@cochise.edu
DYKSTRA, Joel ... 575-624-8203. 310 H
dykstra@nmmi.edu
DYKZEUL, Carin ... 503-682-3903. 407 B
cdykzeul@pioneerpacific.edu
DYLAK, Sandy ... 914-251-6953. 344 D
sandy.dylak@purchase.edu
DYMEK, Cheryle ... 270-707-3707. 195 E
cheryle.dymek@kctcs.edu
DYMENT, Christine ... 508-588-9100. 232 A
DYMOWSKI, Tom ... 210-829-3131. 490 A
dymowski@uiwtx.edu
DYMSKI, M, L ... 617-349-8208. 228 B
mld@lesley.edu
DYNAN-DOBBERTIEN,
Lisa ... 904-620-2900. 116 B
n00914995@unf.edu
DYRUD, Lars ... 218-683-8616. 260 D
lars.dyrud@northlandcollege.edu
DYSARD, Nancy, J ... 443-412-2408. 215 C
ndysard@harford.edu
DYSSON, Melissa, J ... 217-245-3080. 146 F
mdyson@ic.edu
DZADOVSKY, Indira ... 321-433-5687. 101 M
dzadovskyi@easternflorida.edu
DZAPOP, Kyle ... 309-677-2596. 140 I
kdzapo@bradley.edu
DZAU, Victor ... 919-684-2255. 354 A
victor.dzau@duke.edu
DZIAK, Mary Ann ... 570-961-7810. 420 C
dziakm@lackawanna.edu
DZIAK, SJ, Ted ... 504-865-2304. 205 H
dziak@loyno.edu
DZIEDZIAK, Michael ... 610-341-1376. 415 G
mdziedzi@eastern.edu
DZIEKAN, Rebecca ... 585-343-0055. 325 C
rldziekan@genesee.edu
DZIESINSKI, Lori ... 989-356-9021. 239 C
dziesinl@alpenacc.edu
DZIEWATKOSKI,
Julius, J ... 740-264-5591. 379 F
jdziewatkoski@egcc.edu
DZIJA, Alan ... 718-270-3176. 342 D
alan.dzija@downstate.edu
DZIK, John, L ... 706-778-8500. 130 E
jdzik@piedmont.edu
DZIK, Marianne ... 815-224-0433. 148 A
marianne_dzik@ivcc.edu
DZINANKA, John, S ... 631-420-2017. 346 B
john.dzinanka@farmingdale.edu
DZOMBAK, David ... 412-268-1180. 412 H
dzombak@cmu.edu
DZUBAY, Tim ... 816-412-5502. 450 G
tdzubay@national.edu
DZUREC, Laura ... 330-672-8794. 382 B
ldzurec@kent.edu
DZWONKOWSKI,
David, R ... 315-470-6641. 345 B
drdzwonk@esf.edu
DÍAZ, Tania ... 787-720-1022. 547 E
recursos@atlanticcollege.edu
DÍAZ-DÍAZ, Claribel ... 787-622-8000. 553 E
dadiaz@pupr.edu
DÍAZ-PÉREZ, Carlos, R .. 787-250-0000. 553 G
carlos.diaz14@upr.edu
D'ACIERNO, Michael ... 718-951-5150. 317 C
brooklyn@bkstore.com
D'ACOSTA, Ruben ... 787-257-0000. 554 B
ruben.dacosta@upr.edu
D'ADAMO, Caterina ... 310-377-5501... 53 F
CDAdamo@marymountcalifornia.edu
D'AGOSTINO, Jo Beth ... 773-508-7063. 151 H
jdagost@luc.edu
D'AGOSTINO, Julie ... 847-925-6523. 145 H
jdagosti@harpercollege.edu
D'AGOSTINO, Thomas ... 315-781-3307. 326 C
tdagostino@hws.edu
D'AGOSTO, Danielle ... 914-251-6507. 344 D
danielle.dagosto@purchase.edu
D'AIELLO, Christina ... 212-875-4645. 314 C
cdaiello@bankstreet.edu
D'ALESSANDRO,
Colleen ... 404-364-8319. 130 A
cdalessandro@oglethorpe.edu
D'ALLEGRO, Mary Lou .. 518-783-2307. 340 J
mdallegro@siena.edu
D'AMARO, Gina ... 516-918-3726. 315 G
gdamaro@bcl.edu
D'AMATO, Anthony ... 312-567-8821. 147 F
damato@iit.edu
D'AMBRA, Diane ... 401-598-1854. 439 B
ddambra@jwu.edu
D'AMBRA, Lauri ... 516-671-2213. 350 C
ldambra@webb.edu
D'AMBROSE, Martin ... 312-987-2396. 148 L
6dambrose@jmls.edu
D'AMBROSIO, Arnold ... 989-837-4205. 248 C
dambrosio@northwood.edu
D'AMBROSIO, Rose ... 201-692-2706. 301 J
rose_dambrosio@fdu.edu
D'AMICO, Catherine ... 702-968-1639. 295 E
cdamico@roseman.edu
D'AMICO, Janna ... 517-265-5161. 238 G
D'AMICO, Mary Lou ... 585-385-8280. 338 H
mdamico@sjfc.edu
D'AMORE, Jonathan, I .. 802-654-2347. 500 B
jdamore@smcvt.edu
D'AMOUR, Angela, L ... 805-565-6125... 76 D
adamour@westmont.edu
D'AMOUR, Gene ... 504-520-5444. 209 D
gdamour@xula.edu
D'ANGELO, Frank ... 928-771-4885... 19 H
frank.dangelo@yc.edu
D'ANGELO, Greg ... 617-369-3633. 236 F
gdangelo@smfa.edu
D'ANGELO, Kathryn, P ... 215-204-6545. 433 K
kathryn.dangelo@temple.edu
D'ANGELO, Louann ... 415-572-5622. 230 F
ldangelo@westfield.ma.edu
D'ANIERI, Paul, J ... 352-392-0780. 116 A
danieri@clas.ufl.edu
D'ANJOU, Sara ... 617-730-7059. 235 D
sara.danjou@newbury.edu
D'ANNA, Debora ... 828-884-8391. 352 I
debora.danna@brevard.edu
D'ANTONIO, Louis, S ... 203-285-2021... 88 E
ldantonio@gwcc.commnet.edu
D'APOLITO, Kristine ... 609-771-2504. 300 E
dapolito@tcnj.edu
D'APRIX, Kathleen ... 718-779-1430. 336 D
kdaprix@mail.plazacollege.edu

D'AQUIN, Katrina .... 304-829-7437. 526 D
kd'aquin@bethanywv.edu
D'ARCANGELIS, Linda ... 518-271-3285. 340 D
D'ARCANGELIS, Linda ... 518-271-3348. 330 I
darcangelisl@gmail.com
D'ARCY, Karen .... 708-534-8396. 145 F
kdarcy@govst.edu
D'ARGENIO, John .... 518-783-2450. 340 J
dargenio@siena.edu
D'ARRIGO, Diane .... 617-287-5052. 228 G
diane.darrigo@umb.edu
D'ATTILIO, Michael .... 518-454-5115. 321 A
dattilm@strose.edu
D'AVERSA, Robert .... 570-422-3324. 428 D
robert.daversa@po-box.esu.edu
D'EATH, Kelly .... 256-549-8266..... 3 M
kdeath@gadsdenstate.edu
D'ELIA, Christopher .... 225-578-7188. 204 O
cdelia@lsu.edu
D'IMPERIO, Pat .... 914-606-6846. 350 F
pat.d'imperio@sunywcc.edu
D'LENA, Brandye .... 949-582-4680... 67 C
bdlena@socccd.org
D'MONTE, Loreto .... 909-593-3511... 72 E
ldmonte@laverne.edu
D'ORAZIO, Peter .... 610-565-1095. 437 G
pdorazio@williamson.edu
D'OYLEY, Alicia .... 508-531-1214. 229 D
alicia.doyley@bridgew.edu
D'SOUZA, Rena, N .... 801-581-8951. 496 Q
rena.dsouza@hsc.utah.edu
D'URSO, Mary, D .... 610-785-6201. 432 C
mdurso@scs.edu

E

EADDY, Mary .... 843-349-5341. 444 F
mary.eaddy@hgtc.edu
EADES, Annmarie .... 404-752-8458. 129 E
aeades@msm.edu
EADES, Tim .... 740-477-7456. 385 L
teades@ohiochristian.edu
EADS, Jessica, L .... 516-463-6318. 326 D
jessica.l.eads@hofstra.edu
EADS, Linda, S .... 214-768-3754. 481 A
leads@smu.edu
EADS, Sonja .... 606-759-7141. 196 B
sonja.eads@kctcs.edu
EADY, Amy .... 989-328-1240. 247 D
amye@montcalm.edu
EADY, Niya .... 404-225-4452. 121 B
neady@atlantatech.edu
EAGAN, III, Aristide, C .. 504-762-3005. 203 A
aeagan@dcc.edu
EAGAN, Dennis, K .... 513-231-2223. 374 D
deagan@athenaeum.edu
EAGAN, Robert .... 215-248-7381. 422 F
reagan@ltsp.edu
EAGEN, Nancy .... 617-266-1400. 223 D
EAGLE, Elyse .... 941-355-9080. 101 L
admissions@ewcollge.org
EAGLE, Robert .... 304-434-8000. 528 A
reagle@eastern.wvnet.edu
EAGLE, Teresa .... 304-746-8924. 529 H
thardman@marshall.edu
EAGLEN, Robert .... 330-325-6121. 385 E
reaglen@neomed.edu
EAGLIN, Ron .... 386-506-4176. 101 G
eaglinr@DaytonaState.edu
EAKER, C, W .... 972-721-5384. 488 F
eaker@udallas.edu
EAKIN, J. Thomas .... 401-232-6046. 438 K
teakin@bryant.edu
EAKINS, Bill .... 308-535-3607. 290 J
eakinsw@mpcc.edu
EAKINS, Lewis .... 256-726-7374..... 6 B
leakins@oakwood.edu
EAKINS, Stanley, G .... 252-328-6966. 367 B
eakinss@ecu.edu
EALY, Edna .... 850-973-9474. 109 H
ealye@nfcc.edu
EAMOE, Deborah .... 513-861-6400. 390 C
deborah.eamoe@myunion.edu
EANES, Berenecea, J ...... 657-278-3221... 33 E
bjeanes@fullerton.edu
EANNACE, Maryrose .... 315-792-5301. 331 I
meannace@mvcc.edu
EAPEN, Jacob .... 609-586-4800. 302 G
eapenj@mccc.edu
EARDLEY, Larry .... 775-784-4901. 294 D
larry_eardley@nshe.nevada.edu
EARHART, Doug .... 202-722-8100... 96 F
EARHART, Peg .... 740-588-1315. 394 C
pearhart@zanestate.edu
EARHEART-BROWN,
Daniel, J .... 901-334-5809. 457 A
jebrown@memphisseminary.edu
EARL, Michael .... 252-536-5469. 361 A
mearl006@halifaxcc.edu
EARL, Renarde, D .... 336-734-7382. 360 E
rearl@forsythtech.edu
EARL, Robert .... 212-854-7758. 314 G
rearl@barnard.edu
EARLE, David .... 864-379-8772. 443 F
earle@erskine.edu
EARLE, James, P .... 603-899-4162. 296 H
earlejp@franklinpierce.edu
EARLE, James, V .... 412-648-1102. 435 C
earle@pitt.edu
EARLE, Shannon .... 282-250-3829. 368 C
searle@unca.edu
EARLE, Steven, R .... 562-903-4740... 29 L
steve.earle@biola.edu
EARLE, Susan .... 626-650-2306... 45 K
EARLES, Bobbi, L .... 563-588-7120. 180 L
bobbi.earles@loras.edu
EARLEY, P. Christopher .. 765-494-4366. 171 M
pcearley@purdue.edu
EARLEY, Rita .... 828-766-1290. 361 H
rearley@mayland.edu
EARLEY, Samantha .... 812-941-2342. 168 F
searley@ius.edu
EARLS, C. Anthony .... 308-865-8519. 292 H
earlsca@unk.edu
EARLY, Ida, H .... 314-935-5105. 284 L
Ida_Early@wustl.edu
EARLY, Johnnie .... 419-530-1931. 392 B
johnnie.early@utoledo.edu
EARLY, Lisa .... 410-951-3666. 220 B
learly@coppin.edu
EARLY, Loretta .... 405-325-9222. 401 B
learly@ou.edu
EARLY, Margaret .... 510-869-1524... 61 I
mearly@samuelmerritt.edu
EARLY, Matthew .... 404-727-7499. 124 E
matthew.early@emory.edu
EARLY, Patrick, M .... 217-581-7650. 144 E
pmearly@eiu.edu
EARLY, Peter .... 409-933-8404. 469 E
pearly@com.edu
EARLY, Robert .... 615-343-4601. 463 G
robert.early@vanderbilt.edu
EARNEST, Sarah .... 978-232-2458. 226 C
searnest@endicott.edu
EARNS, Lane, R .... 920-424-2220. 537 B
earns@uwosh.edu
EARP, Christy .... 336-838-6117. 365 B
christy.earp@wilkescc.edu
EARSHEN, Susan, J .... 716-878-3042. 343 A
earshesj@buffalostate.edu
EARST, Sherrye .... 850-599-3611. 114 K
sherrye.earst@famu.edu
EARVIN, Larry, L .... 512-505-3001. 473 G
llearvin@htu.edu
EARWICKER, David .... 916-278-3668... 34 D
earwicke@saclink.csus.edu
EASLEY, Jennifer .... 662-325-7404. 268 D
jbe2@spa.msstate.edu
EASLEY, Mike .... 704-233-8999. 370 G
m.easley@wingate.edu
EASON, Charles .... 707-864-3382... 66 G
charles.eason@solano.edu
EASON, Cynthia, G .... 864-250-8601. 444 E
cynthia.eason@gvltec.edu
EASON, Rod .... 641-472-7000. 180 N
reason@mum.edu
EASON, Wayne .... 601-635-2111. 266 H
weason@eccc.edu
EASSA, Emad .... 847-214-7885. 144 F
eeassa@elgin.edu
EASSON, Donald, D .... 508-831-4993. 238 F
deasson@wpi.edu
EAST, Jody, L .... 641-422-4218. 181 D
eastjody@niacc.edu
EAST, Patricia, A .... 319-296-4214. 178 J
patricia.east@hawkeyecollege.edu
EASTBURN, Meredith .... 615-383-4848. 464 D
meastburn@watkins.edu
EASTER, Benna .... 641-784-5372. 178 F
easter@graceland.edu
EASTER, Joyce, B .... 757-455-2126. 515 H
jeaster@vwc.edu
EASTER, Julian .... 480-677-7701... 12 P
julian.easter@centralaz.edu
EASTER, Kelvin .... 773-697-2155. 144 B
keaster@devry.edu
EASTER, Lisa .... 785-227-3380. 184 I
easterl@bethanylb.edu
EASTER, Michael .... 573-518-2188. 278 A
mreaster@mineralarea.edu
EASTER, Robert, A .... 217-333-3070. 161 C
reaster@uillinois.edu
EASTERLING, Cal .... 918-495-6538. 398 H
ceasterling@oru.edu
EASTERLING, Cynthia ..... 601-266-6579. 270 E
cynthia.easterling@usm.edu
EASTERLING, Doug .... 847-925-6955. 145 H
deasterl@harpercollege.edu
EASTERLING, Karen .... 810-767-4000. 239 H
karen.easterling@baker.edu
EASTERLING, Karen .... 989-872-6000. 239 G
karen.easterling@baker.edu
EASTERLING, Mayson .... 864-977-7055. 445 H
mayson.easterling@ngu.edu
EASTERLING, Vonda .... 919-516-4012. 366 C
vmeasterling@st-aug.edu
EASTERLING, III,
William, E .... 814-865-6546. 426 A
wee2@psu.edu
EASTERWOOD, Allyson .. 601-266-6986. 270 E
allyson.easterwood@usm.edu
EASTHAM, Yvette .... 270-707-3731. 195 E
yvette.eastham@kctcs.edu
EASTIN, Nichole .... 719-336-1572... 82 R
nichole.eastin@lamarcc.edu
EASTMAN, Callie .... 907-277-1000... 10 D
contact@chartercollege.edu
EASTMAN, III,
Donald, R .... 727-864-8211. 101 N
deastman@eckerd.edu
EASTMAN, Douglas .... 802-635-1677. 501 D
doug.eastman@jsc.edu
EASTMAN, Garrett .... 508-373-9709. 223 A
garrett.eastman@becker.edu
EASTMAN, Lori .... 518-580-5640. 341 A
leastman@skidmore.edu
EASTMAN, Michael .... 859-622-1583. 193 P
michael.eastman@eku.edu
EASTMAN, Michael .... 260-982-5412. 170 U
emeastman@manchester.edu
EASTMAN, Mindy, R ...... 641-422-4363. 181 D
eastmmin@niacc.edu
EASTON, Mark .... 928-226-4284... 13 B
mark.easton@coconino.edu
EASTON, Michelle .... 304-357-4879. 527 H
michelleeaston@ucwv.edu
EASTON, Miwa .... 425-249-4751. 524 D
miwa.easton@tlc.edu
EASTON, Shannon .... 518-608-8234. 324 B
seaston@excelsior.edu
EASTON, Stephen, D ...... 307-766-6416. 543 I
seaston3@uwyo.edu
EASTRIDGE, Charlene ..... 276-739-2461. 514 D
ceastridge@vhcc.edu
EASTTORP, Karl .... 715-422-5326. 540 D
karl.easttorp@mstc.edu
EASTTY, Michelle .... 907-822-3201... 10 A
meastty@akbible.edu
EASTUS, Victoria .... 212-431-2870. 333 I
veastus@nyls.edu
EASTWICK, Thomas .... 201-488-9400. 301 F
EASTWOOD, Candy .... 618-634-3231. 158 M
candye@shawneecc.edu
EATHERTON, Janice .... 509-434-5063. 518 E
janice.eatherton@ccs.spokane.edu
EATON, Arlinda .... 770-423-6117. 127 N
aeaton4@kennesaw.edu
EATON, Carol .... 386-506-3200. 101 G
Carol.Eaton@DaytonaState.edu
EATON, Curtis, H .... 208-732-6242. 138 B
ceaton@csi.edu
EATON, Eric, R .... 803-533-3782. 446 G
eeaton1@scsu.edu
EATON, Frank .... 603-668-2211. 297 I
f.eaton@snhu.edu
EATON, Harvill, C .... 615-547-1234. 454 A
eaton@cumberland.edu
EATON, James, M .... 708-709-3570. 156 A
jeaton@prairiestate.edu
EATON, Janet .... 903-927-3293. 495 A
jeaton@wileyc.edu
EATON, Joyce, A .... 336-316-2146. 355 A
jeaton@guilford.edu
EATON, Kent .... 620-242-0506. 188 G
eatonk@mcpherson.edu
EATON, Kevin .... 817-598-6270. 494 G
keaton@wc.edu
EATON, L. David .... 845-257-3210. 342 B
eatond@newpaltz.edu
EATON, Mark, A .... 636-584-6733. 273 M
maeaton@eastcentral.edu
EATON, Michael, B .... 662-862-8001. 267 C
mbeaton@iccms.edu
EATON, Phyllis .... 757-822-2308. 514 C
peaton@tcc.edu
EATON, Randy .... 828-227-7338. 369 E
jreaton@wcu.edu
EATON, Stephanie .... 314-516-5765. 283 E
stephanie@umsl.edu
EATON, Stephen, B .... 760-252-2411... 29 I
seaton@barstow.edu
EATON, Timothy, W .... 405-912-9456. 395 K
teaton@hc.edu
EATON-CRAWFORD,
Margaret .... 617-732-2132. 233 E
margaret.eaton-crawford@mcphs.edu
EATON-NEEB, Rosalyn ... 507-786-3615. 264 B
eatonnee@stolaf.edu
EATON-STULL,
Yvonne, M .... 814-332-4368. 409 D
yvonne.eatonstull@allegheny.edu
EAVES, Ken .... 760-252-2411... 29 I
keaves@barstow.edu
EAVES, Robert .... 803-934-3229. 445 F
reaves@morris.edu
EAVES, Stephen .... 316-295-5849. 186 H
stephen_eaves@friends.edu
EAVES FINN, Patricia ..... 505-428-1000. 311 J
patricia.eaves@sfcc.edu
EAVES-MCLENNAN,
Kristi .... 919-760-8455. 356 G
eavesk@meredith.edu
EBBELING, Jason .... 860-701-5197... 90 G
ebbeling_j@mitchell.edu
EBBERS, Susan .... 651-255-6143. 264 C
sebbers@unitedseminary.edu
EBBERT, Deborah .... 215-248-7069. 413 A
ebbertd@chc.edu
EBBS, George .... 570-389-4745. 427 H
gebbs@bloomu.edu
EBEID, Fred .... 262-595-2261. 537 C
ebeid@uwp.edu
EBEL, Jeffrey .... 618-545-3234. 149 D
jebel@kaskaskia.edu
EBELING, Phil .... 314-505-7591. 272 J
ebelingp@csl.edu
EBELTOFT, Gail .... 701-438-2530. 371 D
gail.ebeltoft@dickinsonstate.edu
EBEN, Brian .... 712-279-5239. 176 B
brian.eben@briarcliff.edu
EBER, John .... 773-298-3944. 158 E
eber@sxu.edu
EBERHARDT, David .... 205-226-4731..... 2 C
deberhar@bsc.edu
EBERHARDT, Everett, V .. 703-323-3266. 513 C
eeberhardt@nvcc.edu
EBERHARDT, Ronald, E .. 724-925-4071. 437 D
eberhardtr@wccc.edu
EBERHART, Becky, J ...... 847-866-3938. 145 E
becky.eberhart@garrett.edu
EBERHART, Cathy .... 563-884-5114. 182 A
cathy.eberhart@palmer.edu
EBERLE, Jeanette .... 863-638-2978. 119 D
eberleja@webber.edu
EBERLE, Matt .... 480-245-7969... 14 B
matt.eberle@tricityministries.org
EBERLE, OSB, Peter .... 503-845-3304. 404 D
peter.eberle@mtangel.edu
EBERLE, Sarah .... 512-313-3000. 469 L
sarah.eberle@concordia.edu
EBERLY, John, M .... 717-780-2648. 417 I
jmeberly@hacc.edu
EBERLY, Marian .... 607-962-9231. 322 B
meberly@corning-cc.edu
EBERSOLD, E. Douglas .. 573-592-4339. 285 D
doug.ebersold@williamwoods.edu
EBERSOLD, Julie, A .... 417-836-5654. 278 E
julieebersold@missouristate.edu
EBERSOLE, Bradley, J .... 740-374-8716. 392 I
bebersole@wscc.edu
EBERSOLE, Erin, R .... 610-647-4400. 418 I
eebersole@immaculata.edu
EBERSOLE, John, F .... 518-464-8524. 324 B
jebersole@excelsior.edu
EBERSOLE, Kenney .... 352-371-2833. 101 K
academicdean@dragonrises.edu
EBERSOLE, Mark .... 704-216-3601. 363 D
mark.ebersole@rccc.edu
EBERSOLE, Robin .... 540-545-7338. 509 E
rebersol@su.edu
EBERSOLE, Tim .... 717-477-1218. 429 E
tmeber@ship.edu
EBERT, Derry .... 303-963-3338... 79 C
debert@ccu.edu
EBERT, Sharon .... 570-961-7860. 420 C
eberts@lackawanna.edu
EBERTZ, Susan J, S .... 563-589-0265. 183 F
library@wartburgseminary.edu
EBERWEIN, Howard .... 413-662-5543. 230 C
h.eberwein@mcla.edu
EBNER, Timothy, J .... 801-581-5808. 496 Q
tebner@sa.utah.edu
EBNER-SMITH, Maria, E .. 248-370-4423. 248 J
ebnersmi@oakland.edu
EBONG, Imeh, D .... 904-620-2700. 116 B
i.ebong@unf.edu
EBORALL, Martha .... 304-327-4152. 529 D
meborall@bluefieldstate.edu
EBRAHIMPOUR, Maling . 727-873-4786. 116 D
mebrahimpour@umsl.edu
EBSTEIN, Gemma, F .... 860-685-2535... 92 H
gebstein@wesleyan.edu
EBY, Larry .... 302-225-6289... 93 H
ebylw@gbc.edu
EBY, Tim, J .... 314-516-6765. 283 E
ebyt@umsl.edu
ECCLES, John, G .... 434-544-8226. 506 K
eccles@lynchburg.edu
ECCLES, Tom .... 845-758-7598. 314 D
ccs@bard.edu
ECCLESTON, David .... 617-262-5000. 223 F
David.Eccleston@the-bac.edu
ECHANDI, Pura .... 787-786-3030. 547 F
pechandi@ucb.edu.pr

ECHARD, B. J ... 580-559-5769. 395 F brajec@ecok.edu

ECHEGARAY, Luis ... 787-725-6500. 547 H lechegaray@sju.albizu.edu

ECHEVARRI, Richard ... 215-780-1410. 433 A rech@salus.edu

ECHEVARRIA, Agustin ... 787-763-5845. 549 J aecheva@inter.edu

ECHEVARRIA, Fabian ... 209-478-0800... 47 M

ECHOLS, Carolyn, J ... 410-276-0306. 218 D cechols@host.sdc.edu

ECHOLS, Connie, C ... 530-226-4178... 66 D cechols@simpsonu.edu

ECHOLS, Jacqueline ... 404-297-9522. 126 A echolsj@gptc.edu

ECHOLS, Kimberly ... 410-276-0306. 218 D kechols@host.sdc.edu

ECHOLS, Mike ... 402-557-7851. 288 G mike.echols@bellevue.edu

ECHOLS, Steve ... 423-493-4100. 462 B

ECHOLS TOBE, Dorothy . 201-684-7008. 305 A dechols@ramapo.edu

ECK, Dan, W ... 920-565-1204. 533 R eckdw@lakeland.edu

ECK, Don ... 503-654-8000. 407 B deck@pioneerpacific.edu

ECK, James, C ... 919-497-3201. 356 E jeck@louisburg.edu

ECK, Stephen ... 405-425-5118. 397 D stephen.eck@oc.edu

ECK, Tim ... 801-626-6352. 497 D teck@weber.edu

ECKARDT, Chip ... 715-836-2381. 536 E eckardpp@uwec.edu

ECKARDT, Michael, J ... 207-581-3465. 212 B michael.eckardt@maine.edu

ECKARDT, Paula, J ... 212-924-5900. 347 B peckardt@swedishinstitute.edu

ECKEL, Mark ... 317-789-8282. 165 E meckel@crossroads.edu

ECKEL, Terri ... 928-776-2129... 19 H terri.eckel@yc.edu

ECKEL, Todd ... 909-593-3511... 72 E teckel@laverne.edu

ECKELS, Robert, T ... 417-836-6865. 278 E bobeckels@missouristate.edu

ECKEN, Lou ... 989-463-7245. 239 B ecken@alma.edu

ECKER, Brian ... 717-264-4141. 437 H brian.ecker@wilson.edu

ECKER, Scot ... 262-551-6200. 532 D secker@carthage.edu

ECKERT, Amber ... 858-513-9240. 175 F Amber.Eckert@ashford.edu

ECKERT, Gerald, C ... 717-872-3775. 429 D jerry.eckert@millersville.edu

ECKERT, Jason, C ... 937-229-2045. 391 C Jeckert1@udayton.edu

ECKERT, Phyllis ... 702-579-3539. 294 B peckert@kaplan.edu

ECKERT, Steve ... 928-317-6000... 11 L steve.eckert@azwestern.edu

ECKERT, Thomas, C ... 608-757-7772. 539 I tom.eckert@blackhawk.edu

ECKLES, Robert ... 212-410-8007. 333 E reckles@nycpm.edu

ECKLES, Robert ... 212-410-8480. 333 E reckles@nycpm.edu

ECKLEY, Lloydean, M ... 512-245-2158. 487 C le11@txstate.edu

ECKLIN, Laura ... 707-256-7105... 55 F lecklin@napavalley.edu

ECKLUND, Timothy, R ... 716-878-3506. 343 A eckluntr@buffalostate.edu

ECKMAN, Steven ... 386-506-3180. 101 G eckmans@DaytonaState.edu

ECKMAN, Steven, W ... 402-363-5621. 293 I seckman@york.edu

ECKRICH, Steve, E ... 541-737-4323. 406 A stevee@osubookstore.com

ECKSTEIN, Mark ... 716-829-8349. 323 D eckstein@dyc.edu

ECKSTEIN, Rebecca, R ... 740-368-3028. 387 J rreckste@owu.edu

ECONOMOU, James, S .. 310-825-7943... 71 C jeconomou@conet.ucla.edu

ECSEDY, Brenda ... 617-879-2225. 238 C becsedy@wheelock.edu

ECUNG, Antonia ... 559-791-2308... 49 P aecung@portervillecollege.edu

EDBURG, Lisa ... 573-518-2294. 278 A lisae@mineralarea.edu

EDDIE, Torrence ... 901-383-6501... 96 F

EDDINGER, Pam, Y ... 617-228-2400. 231 C peddinger@bhcc.mass.edu

EDDINGER, Terry, W ... 336-315-8660. 353 C teddinger@carolinagrad.edu

EDDINGTON, Natalie, D . 410-706-2176. 219 C neddingt@rx.umaryland.edu

EDDINS, Trevell ... 847-214-7391. 144 F teddins@elgin.edu

EDDINS-FOLENSBEE, Florence, F ... 713-798-4768. 467 F florence@bcm.edu

EDDLEMAN, Bill ... 573-651-2192. 282 B weddleman@semo.edu

EDDLEMAN, Bill ... 573-651-2062. 282 B weddleman@semo.edu

EDDS-ELLIS, Stacy ... 270-686-4573. 196 C stacy.edds@kctcs.edu

EDDY, Alex ... 513-244-8145. 376 J alex.eddy@ccuniversity.edu

EDDY, James, M ... 336-315-7317. 369 A jmeddy@uncg.edu

EDDY, Jean ... 401-454-6419. 440 A jeddy@risd.edu

EDDY, Laura, M ... 620-341-5465. 186 D leddy@emporia.edu

EDDY, Libby ... 907-474-7500... 10 I ofeddy@alaska.edu

EDDY, Rick ... 309-341-5234. 141 A reddy@sandburg.edu

EDDY, Shayna ... 508-626-4506. 230 A seddy@framingham.edu

EDDY, Tiffany ... 603-513-1373. 298 E tiffany.eddy@granite.edu

EDDY, Walter, D ... 973-655-7894. 303 D eddyw@mail.montclair.edu

EDELBROCK, Robert ... 877-442-0505... 86 F robert.edelbrock@rockies.edu

EDELEN, Charles ... 812-941-2400. 168 F cedelen@ius.edu

EDELMAN, David ... 805-898-2926... 44 I davidedelman@fielding.edu

EDELSON, Jeffrey ... 510-642-5039... 70 I swdean@berkeley.edu

EDELSON, Paul ... 631-632-7052. 342 C paul.edelson@stonybrook.edu

EDELSTEIN, Ronald, A ... 323-563-4980... 38 B ronaldedelstein@cdrewu.edu

EDEN, Bradford, L ... 219-464-5099. 174 E brad.eden@valpo.edu

EDEN, Gene, F ... 610-799-1146. 421 I geden@lccc.edu

EDEN, James, R ... 920-924-3317. 540 F jeden@morainepark.edu

EDEN, James, V ... 262-335-5705. 540 F jeden@morainepark.edu

EDEN, Peter, A ... 802-387-6730. 499 E petereden@landmark.edu

EDENFIELD, Carla ... 706-776-0112. 130 E cedenfield@piedmont.edu

EDENFIELD, Joe ... 757-569-6744. 513 E jedenfield@pdc.edu

EDENS, Gary ... 915-747-7471. 492 A gedens@utep.edu

EDENS, Michael, H ... 504-282-4455. 206 A medens@nobts.edu

EDENS, Mike ... 903-693-2021. 478 A medens@panola.edu

EDENS, Ruth ... 617-964-1100. 222 A redens@ants.edu

EDENS, Whitney ... 903-693-2067. 478 A wedens@panola.edu

EDGAR, Kimberly, S ... 615-898-2622. 459 D kimberly.edgar@mtsu.edu

EDGAR, Paula ... 973-642-8746. 307 D paula.edgar@shu.edu

EDGE, Johnnie ... 478-553-2124. 129 H jedge@oftc.edu

EDGECOMBE, Nydia ... 718-518-4180. 318 B nedgecombe@hostos.cuny.edu

EDGENS, Jeff ... 706-729-2127. 124 C jedgens@ega.edu

EDGERTON, Gary ... 317-940-9825. 164 J gedgerto@butler.edu

EDGERTON, Teresa ... 402-486-2540. 292 E teedgert@ucollege.edu

EDGETTE, Bill ... 903-813-2088. 466 H bedgette@austincollege.edu

EDGEWORTH, Lori ... 419-251-1614. 383 G lori.edgeworth@mercycollege.edu

EDGHILL-WALDEN, Vernese ... 312-553-2500. 141 M vedghill-walden@ccc.edu

EDGINGTON, Rick ... 580-628-6220. 396 M rick.edgington@noc.edu

EDGINGTON, Steve ... 714-879-3901... 47 K sedgington@hiu.edu

EDGINGTON, Thomas, J 574-372-5100. 166 B edging@grace.edu

EDGREN, III, Gerald, R .. 920-924-3184. 540 F gedgren@morainepark.edu

EDICK, Nancy ... 402-554-2719. 293 A nedick@unomaha.edu

EDIE, Shawn ... 781-768-7452. 236 A shawn.edie@regiscollege.edu

EDINBURGH, Mary ... 518-587-2100. 346 A mary.edinburgh@esc.edu

EDINGER, Joan, B ... 318-257-3036. 207 F jedinger@latech.edu

EDINGTON, Mary ... 253-833-9111. 520 C medington@greenriver.edu

EDINGTON, Maurice ... 850-412-5978. 114 K maurice.edington@famu.edu

EDINGTON, Pamela ... 203-857-7309... 89 D pedington@norwalk.edu

EDISON, Monica ... 616-632-2881. 239 E edisomon@aquinas.edu

EDLEMAN, Dan ... 903-886-5126. 483 E daniel.edelman@tamuc.edu

EDLER, Thomas ... 314-454-8515. 274 G tedler@bjc.org

EDLESTON, Robert, J ... 785-320-4500. 188 E robertedleston@matc.net

EDLEY, JR., Christopher 510-642-6483... 70 I edley@berkeley.edu

EDLUND, Kristy ... 303-762-6886... 81 G kristy.edlund@denverseminary.edu

EDLUND, Matthew ... 651-361-3450. 256 N medlund@mcnallysmith.edu

EDMAN, Neal, A ... 724-946-7110. 437 B nedman@westminster.edu

EDMAN, Patricia ... 612-374-5800. 255 F pedman@dunwoody.edu

EDMAN, Sally ... 712-707-7321. 181 H sedman@nwciowa.edu

EDMINSTER, Warren ... 270-809-3166. 198 B wedminster@murraystate.edu

EDMINSTON, David ... 337-482-0900. 208 D davidedminston@louisiana.edu

EDMISTON, Susan ... 314-644-9745. 281 E sedmiston@stlcc.edu

EDMOND, Georgia ... 478-289-2112. 124 C gedmond@ega.edu

EDMOND, Steven ... 512-505-3130. 473 G ssedmond@htu.edu

EDMONDS, Charles, W .. 570-321-4347. 422 H edmonds@lycoming.edu

EDMONDS, Kerry ... 540-362-6630. 505 G kedmonds@hollins.edu

EDMONDS, Lawson, C ... 205-652-3545..... 9 F ledmonds@uwa.edu

EDMONDS, Mabel ... 253-589-4333. 518 B mabel.edmonds@cptc.edu

EDMONDS, Melody ... 931-668-7010. 461 A medmonds@mscc.edu

EDMONDS, Michelle, K .. 434-949-1006. 513 H michelle.edmonds@southside.edu

EDMONDS, Mike ... 719-389-6684... 79 D medmonds@coloradocollege.edu

EDMONDS, William, A ... 724-938-4404. 428 A edmonds@calu.edu

EDMONDSON, Angie, S . 276-944-6108. 504 H aedmonds@ehc.edu

EDMONDSON, Charles, M ... 607-871-2101. 313 E edmondson@alfred.edu

EDMONDSON, Charles (Ricks) ... 817-515-7726. 482 B charles.edmondson@tccd.edu

EDMONDSON, Melanie, M ... 443-334-2272. 218 E medmondson@stevenson.edu

EDMONDSON, William .. 814-871-7298. 416 K edmondso002@gannon.edu

EDMONSON, Michele ... 661-362-3435... 40 E michele.edmonson@canyons.edu

EDMUNDS, Anne ... 314-246-8295. 284 N anneedmunds@webster.edu

EDMUNDSON, John ... 928-314-9500... 11 L john.edmundson@azwestern.edu

EDNEY, Kristyn ... 972-761-6884. 471 C kkedney@dcccd.edu

EDNEY, Norris ... 601-304-4300. 265 G nedney@alcorn.edu

EDOUARD, Randall ... 607-777-2791. 341 E redouard@binghamton.edu

EDRICH, Terri ... 972-860-4825. 470 G tedrich@dcccd.edu

EDSALL, Denese ... 954-201-7502... 99 D dedsall@broward.edu

EDSALL, Paul ... 724-838-4236. 433 E edsall@setonhill.edu

EDSCORN, Steven ... 918-456-5511. 396 H

EDSON, Deborah ... 757-822-7433. 514 C dedson@tcc.edu

EDSON, Rob ... 315-498-2097. 335 G edsonr@sunyocc.edu

EDSTROM, Julie ... 406-791-5271. 288 E jedstrom01@ugf.edu

EDUARDO, Marcelo ... 601-925-3214. 268 A eduardo@mc.edu

EDWALDS-GILBERT, Gretchen ... 909-607-2822... 65 D gretchen.edwalds-gilbert@scrippscollege.edu

EDWARDS, Amy ... 217-333-3551. 162 A aledward@illinois.edu

EDWARDS, Ana ... 770-423-6200. 127 N aedwar50@kennesaw.edu

EDWARDS, Angie ... 704-337-2531. 365 G edwardsa@queens.edu

EDWARDS, Annette ... 757-789-1768. 512 D aedwards@es.vccs.edu

EDWARDS, Bahola ... 432-685-4520. 476 G bahola@midland.edu

EDWARDS, Bambi ... 252-638-7317. 359 G edwardsb@cravencc.edu

EDWARDS, Barbara ... 314-286-4870. 280 F bedwards@ranken.edu

EDWARDS, Betty ... 334-420-4321..... 7 G bedwards@trenholmstate.edu

EDWARDS, Bradford, W . 904-256-7401. 107 Q bedward5@ju.edu

EDWARDS, Bruce ... 305-899-3050... 98 O bedwards@barry.edu

EDWARDS, Bud ... 765-658-4268. 165 F budedwards@depauw.edu

EDWARDS, Candace ... 410-386-8505. 214 A cedwards@carrollcc.edu

EDWARDS, Carlton, G ... 804-257-5851. 515 F cgedwards@vuu.edu

EDWARDS, Carmen ... 432-685-4589. 476 G cedwards@midland.edu

EDWARDS, Carol ... 806-742-0700. 487 D carol.edwards@ttu.edu

EDWARDS, Cathy ... 214-860-8685. 471 A cedwards@dcccd.edu

EDWARDS, JR., Charles 515-271-3194. 177 K charles.edwards@drake.edu

EDWARDS, JR., Charles 515-271-2871. 177 K charles.edwards@drake.edu

EDWARDS, Cody ... 703-993-5287. 505 C cedward7@gmu.edu

EDWARDS, Cynthia ... 404-297-9522. 126 A edwardsc@gptc.edu

EDWARDS, Daniel ... 631-656-3117. 324 F daniel.edwards@ftc.edu

EDWARDS, Danielle ... 515-244-4221. 175 C edwardsd@aib.edu

EDWARDS, David ... 732-906-2533. 303 B dedwards@middlesexcc.edu

EDWARDS, David ... 903-875-7348. 477 G david.edwards@navarrocollege.edu

EDWARDS, Donald ... 828-689-1246. 356 F dedwards@mhc.edu

EDWARDS, Doreen ... 607-871-2422. 313 E dedwards@alfred.edu

EDWARDS, Elizabeth ... 662-862-8265. 267 C eedwards@iccms.edu

EDWARDS, Ellen ... 207-947-4591. 209 G eedwards@bealcollege.edu

EDWARDS, Frank ... 404-880-8672. 122 J fedwards@cau.edu

EDWARDS, Gary ... 661-362-2291... 53 G gedwards@masters.edu

EDWARDS, George ... 606-886-3863. 194 K george.edwards@kctcs.edu

EDWARDS, Harry ... 562-903-4883... 29 L harry.edwards@biola.edu

EDWARDS, Holly ... 252-493-7252. 362 G hedwards@email.pittcc.edu

EDWARDS, Ian, C ... 412-396-6204. 415 F edwards181@duq.edu

EDWARDS, Ishmell, H ... 662-252-8000. 269 F iedwards@rustcollege.edu

EDWARDS, Jakki ... 651-291-0177. 256 N

EDWARDS, James, L ... 765-641-4011. 163 L jedwards@anderson.edu

EDWARDS, Jan ... 719-227-8285... 79 D jan.edwards@coloradocollege.edu

EDWARDS, Jane ... 203-432-8680... 93 A jane.edwards@yale.edu

EDWARDS, Jason ... 252-985-5102. 365 D jedwards@ncwc.edu

EDWARDS, Jeff ... 337-439-5765. 201 J jeff@deltatech.edu

EDWARDS, Jeff, E ... 517-750-1200. 250 E jedwards@arbor.edu

EDWARDS, Jennifer ... 215-717-6366. 435 A jedwards@uarts.edu

EDWARDS, Jennifer, T ... 254-968-9480. 483 A jtedwards@tarleton.edu

EDWARDS, Jessica ... 423-746-5331. 462 C jedwards@twcnet.edu

EDWARDS, Jodie ... 513-244-8430. 376 J jodie.edwards@ccuniversity.edu

EDWARDS, John ... 949-451-5255... 67 B jedwards@ivc.edu

EDWARDS, Jon ... 508-270-4102. 231 G jedwards@massbay.edu

EDWARDS, Joyce, P ... 336-334-7755. 367 E edwardsj@ncat.edu

EDWARDS, Judson ... 334-670-3989..... 7 H jcedwards@troy.edu

EDWARDS, Julie ... 417-447-8188. 279 K edwardsj@otc.edu

EDWARDS, Karen ... 251-460-7092..... 9 E cedwards@southalabama.edu

EDWARDS, Karen, K ... 641-269-3703. 178 H edwardsk@grinnell.edu

EDWARDS, Karin .... 860-885-5203... 89 F
kedwards@trcc.commnet.edu
EDWARDS, Kelly .... 406-657-1143. 288 B
kelly.edwards@rocky.edu
EDWARDS, Kevin, M ...... 413-265-2448. 225 C
edwardskevin@elms.edu
EDWARDS, Laurie, L ...... 712-324-5061. 181 G
ledwards@nwicc.edu
EDWARDS, Leeann .... 314-264-1000. 284 G
leeann.edwards@vatterott.edu
EDWARDS, Lisa, K .... 718-270-6238. 319 A
ledwards@mec.cuny.edu
EDWARDS, Louis, W ...... 713-313-6747. 485 F
edwards_lw@tsu.edu
EDWARDS, Mari "Beth" .. 512-471-1232. 491 C
beth@po.utexas.edu
EDWARDS, Mark .... 580-628-6240. 396 M
mark.edwards@noc.edu
EDWARDS, Mark, H .... 315-655-7334. 316 E
medwards@cazenovia.edu
EDWARDS, Marsha .... 503-594-3300. 402 F
marsha@clackamas.edu
EDWARDS, Mary Ruth ... 910-642-7141. 364 A
MaryRuth.Edwards@sccnc.edu
EDWARDS, Melinda .... 256-352-8172..... 9 G
melinda.edwards@wallacestate.edu
EDWARDS, Michael .... 641-673-2120. 183 H
edwardsm@wmpenn.edu
EDWARDS, Michael .... 713-718-7101. 473 C
michael.edwards@hccs.edu
EDWARDS, Michael .... 215-895-2311. 415 B
mte28@drexel.edu
EDWARDS, Michael, C .... 773-995-9544. 141 J
medwards@csu.edu
EDWARDS, Nigel .... 404-880-8151. 122 J
nedwards@cau.edu
EDWARDS, Randy, K ...... 828-262-2058. 367 A
edwardsrk@appstate.edu
EDWARDS, Richard .... 848-932-7821. 306 B
redwards@oldqueens.rutgers.edu
EDWARDS, Richard .... 848-932-7821. 306 A
redwards@oldqueens.rutgers.edu
EDWARDS, Rick .... 828-395-1676. 361 C
redwards@isothermal.edu
EDWARDS, Robert .... 828-227-7321. 369 E
edwardsr@wcu.edu
EDWARDS, Ron .... 608-785-9552. 541 E
edwardsr@westerntc.edu
EDWARDS, Rosie .... 334-285-5177..... 4 J
rosie.edwards@istc.edu
EDWARDS, Sandra, B .... 978-762-4000. 232 D
sedwards@northshore.edu
EDWARDS, Susie .... 316-322-3121. 185 D
sedwards@butlercc.edu
EDWARDS, Tami .... 404-876-1227. 122 C
tamiedwards@bccr.edu
EDWARDS, TerCraig, D .. 336-734-7953. 360 E
tedwards@forsythtech.edu
EDWARDS, Thomas .... 207-859-1362. 211 H
edwardst@thomas.edu
EDWARDS, Tim .... 205-652-3457..... 9 F
tedwards@uwa.edu
EDWARDS, Tobi .... 337-893-4984. 204 B
tedwards@solacc.edu
EDWARDS, Valerie .... 802-635-1290. 501 D
valerie.edwards@jsc.edu
EDWARDS, Virjean .... 206-543-2100. 524 G
vedwards@uw.edu
EDWARDS, Zenobia .... 704-378-1300. 355 K
zedwards@jcsu.edu
EDWARDS- EVANS,
Nicole .... 601-979-2244. 267 E
nicole.e.evans@jsums.edu
EDWARDS-ALEXANDER,
Shoshanna .... 610-660-1140. 432 E
sedwards@sju.edu
EDWARDS LANGE,
Sheila .... 206-543-2441. 524 G
sredward@uw.edu
EDWARDS SAUNDERS,
Abby .... 843-377-2413. 441 G
asaunders@charlestonlaw.edu
EFF, Ryan .... 517-265-5161. 238 G
reff@adrian.edu
EFFORD, Lelia, A .... 305-626-3180. 104 J
laefford@fmuniv.edu
EFFRAT, Andrew .... 617-521-2094. 236 G
andrew.effrat@simmons.edu
EFTHYMIOU,
Lampeto (Betty) .... 718-631-6611. 319 D
lefthymiou@qcc.cuny.edu
EFTINK, Maria .... 314-889-4533. 274 E
meftink@fontbonne.edu
EFTINK, Maurice, R .... 662-915-5974. 270 B
eftink@olemiss.edu
EGAN, Brian .... 973-684-5999. 304 B
began@pccc.edu
EGAN, Carolyn .... 850-644-4440. 115 C
cegan@admin.fsu.edu
EGAN, James .... 734-973-3390. 252 A
Jegan@wccnet.edu
EGAN, Jonathon .... 315-568-3311. 333 C
jegan@nycc.edu
EGAN, Maryan .... 239-590-1234. 115 A
megan@fgcu.edu
EGAN, Maureen, V .... 219-866-6123. 172 E
mo@saintjoe.edu
EGAN, Russi .... 760-921-5524... 58 C
regan@paloverde.edu
EGBE, Daniel .... 501-370-5259... 22 F
degbe@philander.edu
EGBE, Emmanuel .... 718-270-5170. 319 A
egbe@mec.cuny.edu
EGBELU, Pius, J .... 973-596-3314. 303 G
pius.j.egbelu@njit.edu
EGBERT, Jeb .... 949-783-4800... 75 E
jegbert@westcoastuniversity.edu
EGBERT, Jessica, D .... 801-375-5125. 496 G
jegbert@rmuohp.edu
EGBERT, Jessie, W .... 205-652-3535..... 9 F
jwe@uwa.edu
EGDORF, Randall .... 217-641-4973. 148 M
regdorf@jwcc.edu
EGE, Sybil .... 847-214-7034. 144 F
sege@elgin.edu
EGELAND, Hillary .... 845-434-5750. 347 A
hegeland@sullivan.suny.edu
EGELER, William, G .... 207-768-2792. 210 M
wegeler@nmcc.edu
EGENESS, Cynthia .... 651-690-6864. 263 O
cnegeness@stkate.edu
EGENREIDER, Michael ... 740-420-5926. 385 L
megenreider@ohiochristian.edu
EGERER, Sarah .... 706-233-4065. 121 G
segerer@berry.edu
EGGEBRAATEN, Allan ..... 641-585-8174. 183 D
eggebraaa@waldorf.edu
EGGENSPERGER, Martin 870-508-6102... 20 A
eggensperger@asumh.edu
EGGERS, John, M .... 320-308-0121. 261 B
jmeggers@stcloudstate.edu
EGGERS, Judy, K .... 414-443-8857. 539 F
judy.eggers@wlc.edu
EGGERS, Marilyn .... 909-558-7658... 51 C
meggers@llu.edu
EGGLESTON,
Anne-Marie .... 815-825-2086. 149 F
egglestn@kishwaukeecollege.edu
EGGLESTON, Joseph ...... 562-947-8755... 67 H
josepheggleston@scuhs.edu
EGGLESTON, Kathryn, K . 972-238-6364. 471 C
keggleston@dcccd.edu
EGGLESTON, Tami .... 618-537-6926. 152 G
teggleston@mckendree.edu
EGGLESTON, Theo .... 813-879-6000. 103 B
tegglest@cci.edu
EGGLESTON, Theresa ..... 562-902-3314... 67 H
theresaeggleston@scuhs.edu
EGGLETON, Freida, K ..... 270-745-5432. 200 G
freida.eggleton@wku.edu
EGITTO, Victor, T .... 323-259-2686... 56 I
egitto@oxy.edu
EGLE, Donald, K .... 540-568-5322. 506 F
egledk@jmu.edu
EGLSAER, Richard .... 936-294-1006. 487 A
eglsaer@shsu.edu
EGNOR, Clark .... 304-696-6265. 529 H
egnor3@marshall.edu
EGSEGIAN, Randall, J .... 919-536-7230. 360 B
egsegianr@durhamtech.edu
EHARDT, Thomas .... 713-743-8750. 489 A
tehardt@uh.edu
EHARDT, Tom .... 713-743-5325. 489 B
tehardt@uh.edu
EHASZ, Maribeth .... 407-823-4372. 115 E
maribeth.ehasz@ucf.edu
EHEREDGE, Katherine, C 850-474-2766. 117 B
ketheredge@uwf.edu
EHLER, Gina, M .... 262-524-7247. 532 C
gehler@carrollu.edu
EHLERS, Chris .... 918-781-7233. 394 D
ehlersc@bacone.edu
EHLERS, Nancy, M .... 716-652-8900. 316 G
nehlers@cks.edu
EHLERS, Pam .... 405-744-5253. 397 H
pam.ehlers@okstate.edu
EHLERS, Susan .... 651-773-1705. 258 C
susan.ehlers@century.edu
EHLERT, Alycia .... 615-230-3214. 461 G
alycia.ehlert@volstate.edu
EHMANN, Daniel, R .... 302-454-3935... 93 F
ehmann@dtcc.edu
EHMANN, William .... 206-220-8214. 523 E
ehmannw@seattleu.edu
EHMEN, Stacy, L .... 217-443-8746. 143 G
stacy@dacc.edu
EHMLER, Jessica .... 920-686-6278. 536 A
Jessica.Ehmler@sl.edu
EHNES, Gary .... 406-791-5926. 288 E
gehnes01@ugf.edu
EHREN, Judith, A .... 914-594-4495. 334 A
judith_ehren@nymc.edu
EHRENFELD, A .... 718-236-1171. 337 B
EHRENFELD, S, B .... 718-236-1171. 337 B
EHRENKRANTZ, Dan ...... 215-576-0800. 431 E
dehrenkrantz@rrc.edu
EHRHARDT, Tom .... 312-261-3200. 153 I
tom.ehrhardt@nl.edu
EHRLICH, Anne, R .... 818-767-0888... 76 K
anne.ehrlich@woodbury.edu
EHRLICH, Brian .... 321-674-8202. 104 H
behrlich@fit.edu
EHRLICH, Jonathan, D ... 828-298-3325. 370 E
jehrlich@warren-wilson.edu
EHRLICH, Margaret .... 770-274-5125. 125 G
margaret.ehrlich@gpc.edu
EHRLICH, Robert .... 660-626-2297. 271 A
rehrlich@atsu.edu
EHRMAN, Stephen, C ..... 202-994-4026... 95 D
sehrmann@gwu.edu
EHRMANTRAUT,
Dominic .... 901-321-3286. 453 H
dehrmant@cbu.edu
EHRMANTRAUT, Jan ...... 859-280-1232. 197 C
jehrmantraut@lextheo.edu
EIBECK, Pamela, A .... 209-946-2223... 73 A
president@pacific.edu
EICH, Melissa .... 413-775-1201. 231 E
eichm@gcc.mass.edu
EICHAS, Linda .... 321-433-7766. 101 M
eichasl@easternflorida.edu
EICHELBERGER, John ..... 907-474-7229... 10 I
jceichelberger@alaska.edu
EICHELBERGER, Lisa ...... 678-466-4900. 123 A
lisaeichelberger@clayton.edu
EICHELROTH, Kathleen ... 508-929-8098. 230 G
keichelroth@worcester.edu
EICHENLAUB, Mark, P ... 618-235-2700. 160 A
mark.eichenlaub@swic.edu
EICHENSTEIN, Joseph .... 732-985-6533. 304 F
EICHER, Michael .... 614-292-9858. 386 E
eicher@osu.edu
EICHFIELD, Tara .... 912-287-5809. 130 B
teichfield@okefenokeetech.edu
EICHHORN, Edward .... 201-216-5214. 307 E
eeichhor@stevens.edu
EICHHORN, Gregory, E .. 610-921-7260. 409 A
geichhorn@alb.edu
EICHLER, Barry .... 212-960-5214. 351 M
eichler@yu.edu
EICHLER, Richard .... 212-854-2878. 321 D
re1@columbia.edu
EICHMANN, Lauren .... 505-473-6440. 311 K
lauren.eichmann@santafeuniversity.edu
EICHNER, Kevin .... 785-242-5200. 189 I
kevin.eichner@ottawa.edu
EICHOLTZ, Kristin .... 610-282-1100. 414 F
kristin.eicholtz@desales.edu
EICHORST, Christopher .. 509-777-4780. 525 F
ceichorst@whitworth.edu
EICHORST, Shawn .... 402-472-3011. 292 I
seichorst@huskers.com
EICK, Caroline .... 301-447-5632. 217 B
eick@msmary.edu
EICKHOLT, Marcia .... 419-227-3141. 391 F
marcia@unoh.edu
EICKMEIER, Valerie ...... 317-920-2403. 168 D
veickmei@iupui.edu
EIDE, Greg .... 503-375-7021. 403 A
geide@corban.edu
EIDENBERG, Julia .... 503-517-1816. 408 I
jeidenberg@westernseminary.edu
EIDGAHY, Saeid .... 619-388-2795... 62 E
seidgahy@sdccd.edu
EIDSON, Kristi .... 270-686-4216. 192 G
kristi.eidson@brescia.edu
EIDSON, Marshall .... 210-829-3866. 490 A
meidson@uiwtx.edu
EIDSON, Paul .... 714-841-6252... 28 I
dreidson@apollosuniversity.edu
EIDSON, Rebecca, W ...... 864-646-1507. 447 D
reidson@tctc.edu
EIGENBROOD, Rick .... 206-281-2710. 523 C
eigend@spu.edu
EIGHMY, Taylor .... 865-974-8701. 463 C
vcresearch@utk.edu
EIKE, Claire .... 312-629-9379. 158 L
ceike@saic.edu
EIKENS, Anita .... 414-382-6343. 531 I
anita.eikens@alverno.edu
EILERING, Susan .... 217-479-7106. 152 D
susan.eilering@mac.edu
EILOLA, William .... 906-635-2757. 245 G
weilola@lssu.edu
EIMER, Greg, A .... 217-732-3155. 151 C
geimer@lincolncollege.edu
EIMERS, Mardy, T .... 573-882-3412. 283 C
eimersm@missouri.edu
EINHELLIG, Frank, E ...... 417-836-5119. 278 E
frankeinhellig@missouristate.edu
EINOLF, Karl, W .... 301-447-5396. 217 B
einolf@msmary.edu
EINSPAHR, Kent .... 402-643-7315. 289 B
kent.einspahr@cune.edu
EINSTEIN, Heath .... 817-257-7490. 484 I
h.einstein@tcu.edu
EIS, Linda .... 417-625-3797. 278 D
eis-l@mssu.edu
EISELE, Chad .... 309-341-7280. 150 A
ceisele@knox.edu
EISEN, Arnold, M .... 212-678-8072. 328 A
areisen@jtsa.edu
EISEN, George .... 585-389-2370. 332 D
geisen1@naz.edu
EISEN, Jeffrey, M .... 919-658-7759. 357 I
jeisen@moc.edu
EISENBACH, Regina .... 760-750-4253... 35 A
regina@csusm.edu
EISENBACH, Theresa ...... 203-332-5013... 88 F
teisenbach@hcc.commnet.edu
EISENBARTH, Jeffrey ...... 407-646-2117. 111 Q
jeisenbarth@rollins.edu
EISENBARTH, Kathryn, L 503-352-2705. 407 A
eisenbak@pacificu.edu
EISENBEISER,
Colleen, K .... 410-777-1963. 213 D
ckeisenbeiser@aacc.edu
EISENBERG, Eric .... 813-974-2804. 116 C
eisenberg@usf.edu
EISENBERG, Larry, A ...... 314-516-6469. 283 E
eisenbergl@umsl.edu
EISENBERG, Martin, J .... 740-368-3112. 387 J
mjeisenb@owu.edu
EISENBERGER, Israel ...... 845-362-3053. 314 H
EISENBERGER, Shlomo .. 440-943-5300. 388 F
seisenberger@telshehsihdmi.net
EISENHAUER, Joseph .... 313-993-1204. 250 K
eisenhjg@udmercy.edu
EISENHAUER, Walt .... 570-484-2168. 429 B
weisenha@lhup.edu
EISENHUTH, Wayne .... 507-222-4427. 254 D
weisenhu@carleton.edu
EISENMAN, Ann .... 563-244-7040. 178 A
aeisenman@eicc.edu
EISENMAN, Elaine .... 781-239-4355. 222 D
eeisenman@babson.edu
EISENMANN, Linda .... 508-286-8212. 238 B
eisenmann_linda@wheatonma.edu
EISENMENGER, Paul ...... 847-317-7087. 160 M
peisenme@tiu.edu
EISENSTADT, Robert, C .. 318-342-1151. 208 E
eisenstadt@ulm.edu
EISENSTEIN, Laya .... 718-268-4700. 337 F
EISENSTEIN, Paul .... 614-823-1609. 387 K
peisenstein@otterbein.edu
EISENTRAGER, Pete .... 816-235-2665. 283 D
eisentragerp@umkc.edu
EISGRUBER,
Cristopher, L .... 609-258-3026. 304 E
eisgrube@princeton.edu
EISINGER, David, W .... 563-588-4992. 180 L
david.eisinger@loras.edu
EISINGER, Robert .... 401-254-3043. 440 B
reisinger@rwu.edu
EISLER, David, L .... 231-591-2500. 242 F
eislerd@ferris.edu
EISNAUGLE, Eva .... 704-463-3424. 365 E
eva.eisnaugle@fsmail.pfeiffer.edu
EISNER, SND, Janet .... 617-735-9825. 226 B
president@emmanuel.edu
EITEL, Keith .... 817-923-1921. 481 G
keitel@swbts.edu
EITEL, Norine .... 660-626-2391. 271 A
neitel@atsu.edu
EITH, Gary, L .... 440-525-7084. 382 M
geith@lakelandcc.edu
EJIAGA, Romanus .... 504-286-5384. 206 K
rejiaga@suno.edu
EJIGU, Gebeyehu .... 708-534-8044. 145 F
gejigu@govst.edu
EJIGU, Gebeyehu .... 708-534-4120. 145 F
gejigu@govst.edu
EKBOLM, Kathleen .... 508-541-1530. 225 F
deanbkstr@fheg.follett.com
EKE, Kenoye, K .... 484-365-7436. 422 D
keke@lincoln.edu
EKKER, David .... 757-822-7287. 514 C
dekker@tcc.edu
EKKERS, Julie .... 651-290-6476. 265 F
julie.ekkers@wmitchell.edu
EKSTROM, Rodney .... 603-535-2217. 298 G
raekstrom@plymouth.edu
EL-AASSER,
Mohamed, S .... 610-758-2981. 422 A
mse0@lehigh.edu
EL-BERMAWY,
Mohamed .... 573-288-6344. 273 F
melbermawy@culver.edu
EL FATTAL, David .... 562-860-2451... 37 I
delfattal@cerritos.edu
EL-GAYAR, Omar, F .... 605-256-5799. 451 H
omar.el-gayar@dsu.edu

EL-HAGGAN, Ahmed 410-951-3850. 220 B elhaggan@coppin.edu
EL-HAQQ, Mahdi 410-276-0306. 218 D emahdi@host.sdc.edu
EL MOHANDES, Ayman 402-559-4950. 292 J aelmohandes@unmc.edu
EL-REWINI, Hesham 701-777-3412. 371 C rewini@engr.und.edu
EL-SAYED, Jacqueline, A 810-762-7992. 244 Q jelsayed@kettering.edu
EL-SHAMAA, Mariam, N 740-427-5820. 382 J elshamaam@kenyon.edu
EL SHAYEB, Tarek 270-745-4857. 200 G tarek.elshayeb@wku.edu
ELACHI, Charles 818-354-5673. 31 E charles.elachi@jpl.nasa.gov
ELAM, Becky 951-487-3011. 55 B belam@msjc.edu
ELAM, Demar 334-387-3877. 1 E demarelam@amridgeuniversity.edu
ELAM, Elizabeth 434-736-2085. 513 H elizabeth.elam@southside.edu
ELAM, Harry, J 650-723-2300. 68 E helam@stanford.edu
ELAM, Michael, A 252-862-1308. 363 A elamm@roanokechowan.edu
ELAM, Richard, L 540-868-7042. 512 H relam@lfcc.edu
ELAM, Terry 434-592-3966. 506 I tlelam@liberty.edu
ELAM, Terry, D 706-771-4005. 121 D telam@augustatech.edu
ELAND, Tom 612-659-6286. 259 D thomas.eland@minneapolis.edu
ELBE, Joyce 845-848-7900. 322 G joyce.elbe@dc.edu
ELBE, Michael 217-641-4300. 148 M melbe@jwcc.edu
ELBEL, Jacqueline 972-438-6932. 478 C jelbel@parkercc.edu
ELBERT, Dennis, J 701-777-2135. 371 C delbert@business.und.edu
ELBOUSHI, Toni, C 323-563-5827. 38 B tonielboushi@cdrewu.edu
ELBOW, Gary 806-742-2184. 487 D gary.elbow@ttu.edu
ELCHANANI, Matanya 203-576-4322. 91 G matanya@btidgeport.edu
ELDAYRIE, Elias, G 352-273-1788. 116 A eldayrie@ufl.edu
ELDE, Robert, P 612-624-2244. 264 G elde@umn.edu
ELDER, Dana 509-359-6305. 519 C delder@ewu.edu
ELDER, Darla 814-732-2743. 428 E delder@edinboro.edu
ELDER, Jill 605-394-4034. 452 E jill.elder@wdt.edu
ELDER, Laura 770-531-6318. 128 B lelder@laniertech.edu
ELDER, Reba 303-477-7240. 82 C relder@heritage-education.com
ELDER, Thomas 903-510-2405. 488 E teld@tjc.edu
ELDERT, John 617-266-1400. 223 D
ELDERTON, R. Brian 215-951-1540. 420 B elderton@lasalle.edu
ELDREDGE, Brad 406-756-3619. 286 B beldredge@fvcc.edu
ELDRIDGE, Daryl 866-931-4300. 280 H
ELDRIDGE, Jonathan 415-485-9619. 40 G jonathan.eldridge@marin.edu
ELDRIDGE, Joseph, T 202-885-3336. 94 F eldridg@american.edu
ELDRIDGE, Karen 865-981-8207. 456 D karen.eldridge@maryvillecollege.edu
ELDRIDGE, Kim 479-524-7424. 21 G keldridge@adm.jbu.edu
ELDRIDGE, Linda, P 859-846-5340. 197 I leldridge@midway.edu
ELDRIDGE, Marie 931-598-1111. 458 H police@sewanee.edu
ELDRIDGE, Maurice, G 610-328-8312. 433 I meldrid1@swarthmore.edu
ELDRIDGE, Paul 303-963-3093. 79 C peldridge@ccu.edu
ELDRIDGE, Randy 610-527-0200. 432 B reldridge@rosemont.edu
ELENICH, Richard 906-487-2763. 247 A rjelenic@mtu.edu
ELEY, Greg 765-998-5224. 173 C greley@taylor.edu
ELFRINK, Stephanie 314-529-9370. 276 G selfrink@maryville.edu
ELGARICO, Michael 805-493-3049. 31 H elgarico@callutheran.edu
ELGER, William, R 409-266-2006. 493 C welger@utmb.edu
ELGINBEHI, Iman 845-434-5750. 347 A ielginbehi@sullivan.suny.edu

ELGIRUS, Marie Lourdes 781-239-3140. 231 G melgirus@massbay.edu
ELHINDI, Mohamed 608-785-8309. 536 G Melhindi@uwlax.edu
ELIADI, Carol 617-373-5680. 233 E carol.eliadi@mcphs.edu
ELIAS, Charles 718-482-5052. 318 F celias@lagcc.cuny.edu
ELIAS, Helen 619-388-3709. 62 D helias@sdccd.edu
ELIAS, Michael 610-957-6149. 433 I
ELIAS, Sara 605-642-6397. 451 G sara.elias@bhsu.edu
ELIAS, Stephanny, J 617-333-2010. 225 E selias0104@curry.edu
ELIASON, Eric 218-299-3001. 255 A eliason@cord.edu
ELIASSEN, John 503-223-2245. 403 J jeliassen@portland.chefs.edu
ELIAV, Eli 585-275-2121. 349 C Eli_Eliav@URMC.Rochester.edu
ELICK, Cynthia, M 260-481-6204. 168 C elick@ipfw.edu
ELICKER, Beth 207-775-3052. 210 H belicker@meca.edu
ELICKER, Kreig 716-338-1040. 327 J kreigelicker@mail.sunyjcc.edu
ELIJAH, Rhonda 219-866-6134. 172 E rhondae@saintjoe.edu
ELIPTICO, Frankie, M 670-284-5498. 547 A frankiee@nmcnet.edu
ELIQUE, Jose 702-895-3668. 294 I chiefofpolice@unlv.edu
ELIZA, Lourdes 787-852-1430. 549 C leliza@hccpr.edu
ELIZALDE, Velma 361-354-2707. 468 K velmae@coastalbend.edu
ELIZALDE, Velma 361-354-2304. 468 K velmae@coastalbend.edu
ELIZANDRO, John 516-686-7605. 333 H jelizand@nyit.edu
ELIZONDO, Laura, M 956-326-2213. 483 B laura@tamiu.edu
ELIZONDO, Maria 956-664-4600. 480 I marye@southtexascollege.edu
ELIZONDO, Maria, G 956-872-3558. 480 I melizondo@southtexascollege.edu
ELKESHK, Abed 718-405-3300. 320 G abed.elkeshk@mountsaintvincent.edu
ELKINS, Becki, S 319-895-4595. 177 A belkins@cornellcollege.edu
ELKINS, Brian 620-672-5641. 190 A briane@prattcc.edu
ELKINS, Donna 502-213-7112. 195 F donna.elkins@kctcs.edu
ELKINS, Leah 513-241-4338. 373 J leah.elkins@antonellicollege.edu
ELKINS, Mark 904-596-2445. 117 H melkins@tbc.edu
ELKINS, Mary Jane 434-949-1063. 513 H maryjane.elkins@southside.edu
ELKINS, Mary Jane 434-949-1051. 513 H maryjane.elkins@southside.edu
ELKINS, Paula, S 706-886-6831. 133 A pelkins@tfc.edu
ELKINS, Penny, L 678-547-6556. 128 H elkins_pl@mercer.edu
ELKS, Martha 404-752-1881. 129 E melks@msm.edu
ELLARD, Mark 205-387-0511. 2 B mellard@bscc.edu
ELLARD, Peter, C 518-783-2307. 340 J pellard@siena.edu
ELLEFSON-KUEHN, Julie 847-925-6732. 145 H jellefso@harpercollege.edu
ELLENBERG, George, B 850-474-2077. 117 B GEllenberg@uwf.edu
ELLENBERGER, Sheila, J 740-826-8260. 384 L sheilaj@muskingum.edu
ELLENBOGEN, Jeffrey 518-587-2100. 346 A jeffrey.ellenbogen@esc.edu
ELLENS, S. Dean 630-617-3059. 145 A ellenss@elmhurst.edu
ELLENS, Timothy, L 616-526-6475. 240 L tje6@calvin.edu
ELLENSON, David 212-824-2201. 325 G dellenson@huc.edu
ELLENSTEIN, Peter 620-331-4100. 187 G pellenstein@ingefestival.org
ELLER, Enten 800-287-8822. 164 C enten@bethanyseminary.edu
ELLER, Greg 850-729-5332. 109 I eller@nwfsc.edu
ELLER, Greg 901-321-3307. 453 H elgo@cbu.edu
ELLERTSON, Christopher, J 210-999-7207. 488 C cellerts@trinity.edu
ELLERTSON, Shari 208-426-1614. 137 G shariellerston@boisestate.edu

ELLIBEE, Margaret 501-812-2216. 22 G mellibee@pulaskitech.edu
ELLIE, Beth 715-675-3331. 541 A ellie@ntc.edu
ELLIEHAUSEN-SLOBOZIEN, Kathryn 717-291-4215. 416 J kathy.elliehausenslobozien@fandm.edu
ELLIG, Tracy 406-994-5607. 287 B tellig@montana.edu
ELLIMAN, Don 303-315-7682. 86 A chancellor@ucdenver.edu
ELLING, Wayne, H 206-281-2599. 523 C elling@spu.edu
ELLINGER, Amanda, M 540-985-8206. 506 G amellinger@jchs.edu
ELLINGER, John, M 419-372-2006. 374 K johne@bgsu.edu
ELLINGHUYSEN, Scott 507-457-5696. 262 A sellinghuysen@winona.edu
ELLINGHUYSEN, Scott 507-457-5050. 262 A sellinghuysen@winona.edu
ELLINGSON, Mike 701-231-7307. 371 G michael.ellingson@ndsu.edu
ELLINGSON, Scott, D 218-299-3004. 255 A sellings@cord.edu
ELLINGSTON, Laura, L 408-551-7056. 64 M lellingson@scu.edu
ELLINGTON, Jim 208-732-6605. 138 B jellington@csi.edu
ELLINGTON, John 828-669-8012. 357 H jellington@montreat.edu
ELLINGTON, Keri 317-738-8086. 165 I kellington@franklincollege.edu
ELLINGTON, Michael, A 304-293-2702. 530 D michael.ellington@mail.wvu.edu
ELLINGTON, Ross 850-645-6900. 115 C wellington@fsu.edu
ELLINOR, Ben 941-359-4200. 117 A
ELLINWOOD, Dawn, M 802-654-2566. 500 B dellinwood@smcvt.edu
ELLIOT, Autumn 406-265-3770. 287 D autumn.elliot@msun.edu
ELLIOT, John 860-486-1361. 92 A john.elliot@uconn.edu
ELLIOT BROWN, Karin, A 323-343-3820. 34 A kbrown5@calstatela.edu
ELLIOTT, Angela, P 563-333-6339. 182 B ElliottAngelaP@sau.edu
ELLIOTT, Barbara 717-396-7833. 427 A belliott@pcad.edu
ELLIOTT, Barbara, A 304-929-6727. 528 D belliott@newriver.edu
ELLIOTT, Brian 503-588-9207. 403 A belliott@corban.edu
ELLIOTT, Charles 304-384-5334. 529 E celliott@concord.edu
ELLIOTT, Clara 413-552-2219. 231 F celliott@hcc.edu
ELLIOTT, Clifton, R 843-355-4138. 449 F elliottr@wiltech.edu
ELLIOTT, Craig 510-869-6627. 61 I celliott@samuelmerritt.edu
ELLIOTT, David, R 570-340-6075. 423 B delliott@marywood.edu
ELLIOTT, Diane 717-361-1198. 415 H elliottd@etown.edu
ELLIOTT, Donna 920-735-5638. 539 K elliott@fvtc.edu
ELLIOTT, Doug 540-423-9073. 512 E delliott@germanna.edu
ELLIOTT, Emily 603-752-1113. 296 E eelliott@ccsnh.edu
ELLIOTT, Gregg 719-587-7011. 78 B greggelliott@adams.edu
ELLIOTT, Holly 205-391-2211. 6 H helliott@sheltonstate.edu
ELLIOTT, Jacquelyn 870-743-3000. 22 B jelliott@northark.edu
ELLIOTT, James 312-329-4166. 153 E jim.elliott@moody.edu
ELLIOTT, Jeffrey 402-885-8228. 292 J jeffrey.elliott@unmc.edu
ELLIOTT, Jeffrey 703-416-1441. 505 I jelliott@ipsciences.edu
ELLIOTT, John, P 412-624-6127. 435 C jelliott@cfo.pitt.edu
ELLIOTT, Kathy 405-744-4188. 397 H kathy.elliott@okstate.edu
ELLIOTT, Ken 601-709-0966. 266 A kelliott@belhaven.edu
ELLIOTT, Ken 828-327-7000. 359 A kelliott@cvcc.edu
ELLIOTT, Kiersten 310-434-4173. 65 A elliott_kiersten@smc.edu
ELLIOTT, Lori 304-766-3026. 530 C lelliott1@wvstateu.edu
ELLIOTT, Lynn 276-944-6117. 504 H lelliott@ehc.edu
ELLIOTT, Marilyn 859-858-2033. 192 A

ELLIOTT, Mark 615-248-1271. 462 D melliott@trevecca.edu
ELLIOTT, Marvin, L 606-474-3253. 194 H melliott@kcu.edu
ELLIOTT, Melissa, J 940-552-6291. 493 F mjelliott@vernoncollege.edu
ELLIOTT, Michael, S 870-297-4261. 91 F michael.elliott@trincoll.edu
ELLIOTT, Michael, T 314-516-6109. 283 E melliott@umsl.edu
ELLIOTT, Patrick 607-777-2043. 341 E pelliott@binghamton.edu
ELLIOTT, Peter, A 863-297-1081. 110 H pelliott@polk.edu
ELLIOTT, Rennae 256-726-7533. 6 B elliott@oakwood.edu
ELLIOTT, Rita 815-226-3374. 157 C relliott@rockford.edu
ELLIOTT, Rob 715-675-3331. 541 A elliottr@ntc.edu
ELLIOTT, Scott, D 601-484-8619. 267 G selliott@meridiancc.edu
ELLIOTT, Stanley, J 919-658-2502. 357 I selliott@moc.edu
ELLIOTT, Steven 402-375-7394. 291 F stellio1@wsc.edu
ELLIOTT, Tracy 941-752-5399. 114 I elliott@scf.edu
ELLIOTT, Tracy, E 856-225-6324. 306 C telliott@camden.rutgers.edu
ELLIOTT, Trish 602-387-7000. 18 I trish.elliott@phoenix.edu
ELLIOTT, Wyley 479-936-5174. 22 C welliott@nwacc.edu
ELLIOTT CAIN, Pam 515-294-6218. 175 H pelliott@iastate.edu
ELLIOTT-NELSON, Linda 928-344-7516. 11 L linda.elliott-nelson@azwestern.edu
ELLIS, AJ 620-241-0723. 185 K
ELLIS, Annette, M 903-923-3313. 486 A annette.ellis@tstc.edu
ELLIS, Barbara, J 336-256-7856. 367 E ellis@ncat.edu
ELLIS, Bonnie 425-352-8125. 517 E bellis@cascadia.edu
ELLIS, Bonny, R 717-780-2583. 417 I brellis@hacc.edu
ELLIS, Brent 517-750-1200. 250 E bellis@arbor.edu
ELLIS, Bret, R 801-626-7660. 497 D bretellis@weber.edu
ELLIS, Brian 405-325-6211. 401 B be@ou.edu
ELLIS, Bridget 252-399-6371. 352 F bbellis@barton.edu
ELLIS, Carl 206-934-2647. 522 J carl.ellis@seattlecolleges.edu
ELLIS, Craig, D 717-764-9550. 414 A cellis@csb.edu
ELLIS, Craig, D 717-764-9550. 413 J cellis@csb.edu
ELLIS, David 503-768-7691. 403 K dgellis@lclark.edu
ELLIS, David, A 508-373-9464. 223 A david.ellis@becker.edu
ELLIS, David, A 513-529-3638. 384 G ellisda2@miamioh.edu
ELLIS, Dechelle 704-463-3411. 365 E dechelle.ellis@sodexo.com
ELLIS, Denise 402-826-8251. 289 E denise.ellis@doane.edu
ELLIS, Diane 870-307-7284. 21 H diane.ellis@lyon.edu
ELLIS, Donna 570 674 6266. 424 A dellis@misericordia.edu
ELLIS, Evelynn 603-646-3146. 296 G evelynn.ellis@dartmouth.Edu
ELLIS, Evelynn 603-646-3197. 296 G evelynn.ellis@dartmouth.edu
ELLIS, Favor 802-586-7711. 500 E fellis@sterlingcollege.edu
ELLIS, Gail 617-573-8144. 237 B gellis@acad.suffolk.edu
ELLIS, Genny 864-225-7653. 444 A gennyellis@forrestcollege.edu
ELLIS, George, W 813-974-5454. 116 C gellis@usf.edu
ELLIS, Graham 502-272-8218. 192 E gellis@bellarmine.edu
ELLIS, Heidi, B 903-813-2235. 466 H hellis@austincollege.edu
ELLIS, James, G 213-740-6422. 74 A dean@marshall.usc.edu
ELLIS, John 518-454-5166. 321 A ellisj@strose.edu
ELLIS, John 972-780-3600. 490 D
ELLIS, OSA, Kail, C 610-519-4521. 436 F kail.ellis@villanova.edu
ELLIS, Kenneth 443-885-3177. 217 A kenneth.ellis@morgan.edu

ELLIS, Kimberly ... 409-944-1234. 472 I kellis@gc.edu
ELLIS, Larry ... 607-729-1581. 322 F lellis@davisny.edu
ELLIS, Laura ... 315-229-5503. 339 F lellis@stlawu.edu
ELLIS, Leann ... 817-515-7701. 482 B leann.ellis@tccd.edu
ELLIS, Lee ... 618-374-5030. 156 B lee.ellis@principia.edu
ELLIS, Machelle ... 580-371-2371. 396 E mellis@mscok.edu
ELLIS, Marjorie, N ... 254-710-8669. 467 G Marjorie_Ellis@baylor.edu
ELLIS, Marjorie, N ... 828-262-2180. 367 A ellismr@appstate.edu
ELLIS, Michelle ... 330-972-5860. 390 E mellis@uakron.edu
ELLIS, Nicholle ... 317-955-6240. 170 V nellis@marian.edu
ELLIS, Pat ... 315-229-5392. 339 F pellis@stlawu.edu
ELLIS, Rodney ... 318-487-5443. 202 M rodneyellis@cltc.edu
ELLIS, Roger ... 636-949-4839. 276 D
ELLIS, Ronald, L ... 951-343-4210... 30 H rellis@calbaptist.edu
ELLIS, Rose, R ... 203-857-7202... 89 D rellis@norwalk.edu
ELLIS, Sabrina ... 202-994-9610... 95 D sellis@gwu.edu
ELLIS, Samuel ... 207-216-4436. 211 C sellis@yccc.edu
ELLIS, Shannon ... 775-784-6196. 294 J elliss@admin.unr.edu
ELLIS, Sharon ... 678-359-5158. 127 A sharone@gordonstate.edu
ELLIS, Stephanie ... 501-215-4898... 25 C ellis@uaccm.edu
ELLIS, Tom, M ... 423-425-4687. 463 D tom-ellis@utc.edu
ELLIS, Wade ... 951-487-3040... 55 B wellis@msjc.edu
ELLIS, Wade ... 760-773-2513... 40 F wellis@collegeofthedesert.edu
ELLIS, Wendy ... 802-287-8210. 499 D ellisw@greenmtn.edu
ELLIS, William, N ... 325-649-8000. 473 F hpupresident@hputx.edu
ELLIS DUKE, Rhea, V ... 570-945-8311. 419 N rhea.ellis@keystone.edu
ELLISON, Barbara ... 614-416-6230. 375 B bellison@bradfordschoolcolumbus.edu
ELLISON, David, R ... 202-231-3344. 544 L david.ellison@dodiis.mil
ELLISON, Diane ... 585-475-7284. 337 L dmeges@rit.edu
ELLISON, Jimmy ... 325-674-2305. 464 H jimmy.ellison@acu.edu
ELLISON, Kate ... 352-371-2833. 101 K faa@dragonrises.edu
ELLISON, Kimberly ... 513-732-5221. 391 B kimberly.ellison@uc.edu
ELLISON, Lori ... 239-513-1135. 119 E lellison@wolford.edu
ELLISON, Maderia ... 928-532-6743... 16 E maderia.ellison@npc.edu
ELLISON, Marjorie ... 573-288-6541. 273 F mellison@culver.edu
ELLISON, Mark, A ... 704-403-1616. 352 J mark.ellison@carolinashealthcare.org
ELLISON, Michael ... 817-531-7565. 488 A mellison@txwes.edu
ELLISON, Pamela ... 216-987-4459. 378 D pamela.ellison@tri-c.edu
ELLISON, Richard ... 530-898-3590... 33 A reellison@csuchico.edu
ELLISOR, Kimberly, M ... 843-661-1190. 444 B kellisor@fmarion.edu
ELLMORE, Philip, T ... 609-626-3546. 305 C philip.ellmore@stockton.edu
ELLRICH, Phillip ... 618-545-3149. 149 D pellrich@kaskaskia.edu
ELLWANGER, Carolyn ... 712-274-6400. 183 G carolyn.ellwanger@witcc.edu
ELLWOOD, David ... 617-495-1122. 227 C david_ellwood@harvard.edu
ELLZEY, Janet, L ... 512-471-7020. 491 C jellzey@mail.utexas.edu
ELLZY, James ... 615-963-7139. 459 E jellzy@tnstate.edu
ELMAN, Erin ... 215-717-6372. 435 A eelman@uarts.edu
ELMAN, Jeffrey ... 858-534-6073... 71 F deansocsci@ucsd.edu
ELMOGAHZY, Yehia ... 732-255-0400. 304 A yelmogahzy@ocean.edu
ELMOORE, Robert ... 937-294-6155. 382 A relmoore@kaplan.edu
ELMORE, Amy ... 270-534-3118. 196 G amy.elmore@kctcs.edu
ELMORE, Cecilia ... 573-341-6798. 284 A elmorec@mst.edu
ELMORE, Chris ... 336-272-7102. 354 E chris.elmore@greensboro.edu
ELMORE, Dana ... 601-925-3371. 268 A elmore@mc.edu
ELMORE, Donna ... 803-535-1374. 446 B elmored@octech.edu
ELMORE, Floyd ... 704-847-5600. 366 J felmore@ses.edu
ELMORE, Kenneth ... 617-353-4126. 224 D kennmore@bu.edu
ELMORE, Rheena ... 251-580-2145... 4 L relmore@faulknerstate.edu
ELMORE, Ricky ... 317-917-3626. 171 A relmore@martin.edu
ELMORE, Ronald ... 336-841-9128. 355 C relmore@highpoint.edu
ELMORE, Troy, A ... 270-384-8144. 197 D elmoret@lindsey.edu
ELNESS, Jodi, M ... 320-308-5087. 261 C jelness@sctcc.edu
ELNICK, William ... 215-572-2172. 409 H elnickb@arcadia.edu
ELOFIR, Stacey ... 410-704-4414. 220 E selofir@towson.edu
ELROD, David ... 706-272-4473. 123 G delrod@daltonstate.edu
ELROD, Eileen, R ... 408-554-4136... 64 M eelrod@scu.edu
ELROD, Roger ... 408-924-6112... 36 A rogere@sbcglobal.net
ELROD, Susan ... 559-278-3936... 33 D selrod@csufresno.edu
ELSASS, Susan ... 603-577-6581. 296 F elsass@dwc.edu
ELSBECK, George, J ... 607-431-4320. 325 F elsbeckg@hartwick.edu
ELSBERRY, Erin ... 302-736-2439... 94 C erin.elsberry@wesley.edu
ELSE, Iwalani ... 218-723-6583. 254 K ielse@css.edu
ELSE, Robert ... 805-965-0581... 64 L else@sbcc.edu
ELSEA, Kathy ... 660-785-4130. 282 L kelsea@truman.edu
ELSENBAUMER, Ronald, L ... 817-272-2103. 491 B elsenbaumer@uta.edu
ELSENER, Daniel, J ... 317-955-6100. 170 V delsener@marian.edu
ELSEROAD, Arleen ... 949-451-5416... 67 B alseroad@ivc.edu
ELSEROAD, Arleen ... 949-451-5416... 67 B aelseroad@ivc.edu
ELSLEY, Judy ... 801-626-6186. 497 D jelsley@weber.edu
ELSTAD, Pamela ... 218-723-2380. 259 A p.elstad@lsc.edu
ELSTER, Janette ... 315-568-3053. 333 C jelster@nycc.edu
ELSTON, Joseph, P ... 570-340-6024. 423 B
ELSTON, Randy, L ... 931-540-2521. 460 E relston@columbiastate.edu
ELSTON, Timothy, G ... 803-321-5197. 445 G timothy.elston@newberry.edu
ELSWICK, Clark ... 575-562-4352. 309 H clark.elswick@enmu.edu
ELTON, Nathan, J ... 704-894-2492. 353 J naelton@davidson.edu
ELVEY, William ... 608-262-3488. 536 D belvey@fpm.wisc.edu
ELWELL, Frank ... 918-343-7683. 399 C felwell@rsu.edu
ELWELL, Jan ... 518-255-5423. 344 E elwellja@cobleskill.edu
ELWELL, Katie ... 208-769-7806. 138 I katie_elwell@nic.edu
ELWOOD, Sharon, K ... 307-674-6446. 543 F elwood@sheridan.edu
ELWORTH, Edyce ... 336-734-7296. 360 E eelworth@forsythtech.edu
ELY, Aiden ... 916-608-6500... 53 C
ELY, Eileen, E ... 253-833-9111. 520 C eely@greenriver.edu
ELY, Janice ... 310-660-3109... 43 B jely@elcamino.edu
ELY, SJ, Peter ... 206-296-6158. 523 E ely@seattleu.edu
ELY, Tami ... 276-376-1057. 511 C tsd5p@uvawise.edu
ELZARKA, Sammy ... 909-593-3511... 72 E selzarka@laverne.edu
ELZEY, Thomas, J ... 803-536-7013. 446 G president@scsu.edu
EMADI, Matt ... 502-897-4720. 199 B memadi@sbts.edu
EMAMI, Azita ... 206-221-2472. 524 G emamia@uw.edu
EMAMI, Morteza ... 801-626-6853. 497 D memami@weber.edu
EMANUEL, Catherine, B . 770-720-9232. 130 G cbe@reinhardt.edu
EMANUEL, Tom ... 217-244-8671. 162 A emanuel@illinois.edu
EMBERTON, Sherilyn, R . 260-359-4050. 166 O semberton@huntington.edu
EMBLETON, Kathleen ... 215-717-6972. 435 A kembleton@uarts.edu
EMBREE, Adrienne ... 512-863-1226. 481 I embreea@southwestern.edu
EMBREE, Angela ... 515-271-1843. 177 K angela.embree@drake.edu
EMBRY, Greg ... 205-665-6030... 9 B embryg@montevallo.edu
EMBRY, Kathleen ... 312-980-9252. 148 D kembry@iadtchicago.edu
EMCH, Laura ... 419-372-2945. 374 K lemch@bgsu.edu
EMDY, Jim ... 831-476-9424... 44 K librarian@fivebranches.edu
EMENGER, Nancy, E ... 801-626-6017. 497 D nemenger@weber.edu
EMERICK, Sandra ... 330-325-6759. 385 E semerick@neomed.edu
EMERSON, Colleen ... 401-341-2331. 440 C emersonc@salve.edu
EMERSON, Nate ... 507-453-2711. 259 E nemerson@southeastmn.edu
EMERSON, Sally ... 608-789-6083. 541 E emersons@westerntc.edu
EMERSON, Steve ... 951-343-4415... 30 H semerson@calbaptist.edu
EMERSON, Wendy, R ... 336-734-7540. 360 E wemerson@forsythtech.edu
EMERSON, Yolanda ... 562-908-3405... 60 I yemerson@riohondo.edu
EMERY, John ... 661-654-2157... 32 H jemery@csub.edu
EMERY, Kathy, S ... 615-353-3259. 461 B kathy.emery@nscc.edu
EMERY, Monica ... 716-375-2400. 338 E memery@sbu.edu
EMERY, Rebecca, A ... 410-543-6075. 220 D raemery@salisbury.edu
EMERY, Sheila ... 360-596-5360. 524 A semery@spscc.edu
EMERZIAN, Janice ... 559-442-8237... 68 I janice.emerzian@fresnocitycollege.edu
EMERZIAN, Janice ... 559-638-3641... 69 A janice.emerzian@scccd.com
EMILIO, Linda ... 909-469-8421... 76 B lemilio@westernu.edu
EMIRU, Tadael ... 651-793-1508. 259 C tadael.emiru@metrostate.edu
EMIRU, Tadael ... 651-450-3572. 258 H temiru@inverhills.edu
EMLET, Jerry, D ... 860-727-6906... 90 A jemlet@goodwin.edu
EMM, William, T ... 585-345-6811. 325 C wtemm@genesee.edu
EMMANUEL, Narbeth, R . 618-650-2020. 159 H nemmanu@siue.edu
EMMANUEL-FRENEL, Rouseline ... 215-646-7300. 417 F Emmanuel.R@gmc.edu
EMMERICH, Linda ... 443-518-3825. 215 E lemmerich@howardcc.edu
EMMERLING, Andrew ... 717-757-1100. 438 H drew.emmerling@yti.edu
EMMERSON, Richard, K . 718-862-7345. 329 M richard.emmerson@manhattan.edu
EMMICK, Joseph, R ... 630-617-6422. 145 A joseph.r.emmick@elmhurst.edu
EMMIL, Bruce ... 701-224-5758. 372 B bruce.emmil@bismarckstate.edu
EMMONS, Carol-Ann ... 312-567-3827. 147 F emmons@iit.edu
EMMONS, Don ... 315-781-3559. 326 C emmons@hws.edu
EMMONS, Ken ... 619-644-7653... 46 E ken.emmons@gcccd.edu
EMMONS, Luli ... 650-433-3845... 58 B lemmons@paloaltou.edu
EMMONS, Sarah ... 859-233-8120. 199 I semmons@transy.edu
EMMONS, Scott ... 414-229-4762. 537 A semm@uwm.edu
EMMONS, Todd, C ... 603-526-3076. 295 I todd.emmons@colby-sawyer.edu
EMMSLEY, Komiti ... 684-699-9155. 546 A k.emmsley@amsamoa.edu
EMOND, Gean Ann ... 850-484-1728. 110 G gemond@pensacolastate.edu
EMONS, Margaret, L ... 402-465-2405. 291 G memons@nebrwesleyan.edu
EMORY, Cynthia ... 301-696-3566. 215 D emory@hood.edu
EMORY, Douglas, J ... 425-739-8311. 520 K doug.emory@lwtech.edu
EMORY, Fran ... 252-222-6144. 358 G emoryf@carteret.edu
EMORY, Julie, W ... 252-398-6252. 353 H emoryj@chowan.edu
EMSLIE, A. Gordon ... 270-745-2297. 200 G gordon.emslie@wku.edu
EMSWELLER, David, W .. 419-434-4570. 391 D emsweller@findlay.edu
EMSWELLER, David, W .. 419-434-4578. 391 D emsweller@findlay.edu
EMSWILER, Sue ... 717-299-7730. 434 A emswiler@stevenscollege.edu
ENCARNACION, Elba ... 787-766-1912. 549 J eencarnacion@inter.edu
ENCINA, Rosalinda ... 210-486-4609. 464 J rencina@alamo.edu
ENDER, Barbara, A ... 724-738-2004. 429 F barbara.ender@sru.edu
ENDER, Kenneth, L ... 847-925-6390. 145 H kender@harpercollege.edu
ENDER, Steven, C ... 616-234-3901. 243 B sender@grcc.edu
ENDERS, Naulayne, R ... 606-474-3276. 194 H nenders@kcu.edu
ENDERS, Thomas ... 562-985-5462... 33 F tenders@csulb.edu
ENDICOTT, Daniel, D ... 904-620-2019. 116 B dendicot@unf.edu
ENDICOTT, Jon ... 559-453-3484... 45 D jon.endicott@fresno.edu
ENDICOTT, Patricia ... 812-749-1435. 171 K pendicott@oak.edu
ENDICOTT, Wanda ... 620-235-4776. 189 L wendicot@pittstate.edu
ENDLICH, Norman, A ... 443-352-4140. 218 E nendlich@stevenson.edu
ENDRASKE, Mark ... 281-649-3148. 473 B mendraske@hbu.edu
ENDRESS, Wendy ... 360-867-6296. 519 J endressw@evergreen.edu
ENDRIES, Jill, M ... 920-424-0228. 537 B endries@uwosh.edu
ENDRIJONAS, Erika ... 805-986-5814... 74 G eendrijonas@vcccd.edu
ENDSLEY, Douglas ... 210-829-6004. 490 A douge@uiwtx.edu
ENDY, Michael ... 817-598-6211. 494 G mendy@wc.edu
ENEBO, Jeanette, E ... 701-231-7537. 371 G j.enebo@ndsu.edu
ENEGUESS, Katharine ... 603-752-1113. 296 E keneguess@ccsnh.edu
ENG, Carla ... 605-668-1514. 450 F ceng@mtmc.edu
ENG, Dave ... 845-398-4084. 340 A deng@stac.edu
ENG, Edwin ... 559-244-5910... 68 H ed.eng@scccd.edu
ENGBROCK, M. Jeff ... 409-944-1215. 472 I mengbroc@gc.edu
ENGEBRETSON, Pam ... 651-779-3994. 258 C pam.engebretson@century.edu
ENGEL, Cristi, L ... 402-461-5177. 290 E
ENGEL, Deidre ... 712-279-5448. 176 B deidre.engel@briarcliff.edu
ENGEL, Heather ... 585-475-2627. 337 L ncedar@rit.edu
ENGEL, Richard, R ... 530-752-9960... 70 J rrengel@ucdavis.edu
ENGEL, Shawna ... 901-272-5115. 456 F sengel@mca.edu
ENGELBACH, Karl, M ... 530-754-7237... 70 J kmengelbach@ucdavis.edu
ENGELBRECHT, Laci ... 217-479-7043. 152 D laci.engelbrecht@mac.edu
ENGELBRECHT, Sharon .. 417-626-1234. 279 J engelbrecht.sharon@occ.edu
ENGELBRIDE, Edward ... 518-320-1286. 341 C edward.engelbride@suny.edu
ENGELHARDT, Jon ... 254-710-3111. 467 G jon_engelhardt@baylor.edu
ENGELHARDT, Kelli ... 406-791-5237. 288 E kengelhardt01@ugf.edu
ENGELHART, Rene ... 916-646-2774... 61 I rengelhart@samuelmerritt.edu
ENGELLANT, Roxanne ... 406-683-7305. 286 I r_engellant@umwestern.edu
ENGELLS, Thomas ... 409-772-1503. 493 C tengells@utmb.edu
ENGELMAN, Denisa, A ... 580-774-3212. 400 B denisa.engelman@swosu.edu
ENGELMAN, Mark, D ... 580-774-3269. 400 B mark.engelman@swosu.edu
ENGELMAN, Tim ... 618-650-2662. 159 H tengelm@siue.edu
ENGELMEYER, Renee ... 507-285-7183. 261 A renee.engelmeyer@rctc.edu
ENGELSCHALL, Emily, D 951-827-3986... 71 E emily.engelschall@ucr.edu
ENGELSEN, Karen ... 805-986-5847... 74 G kengelsen@vcccd.edu
ENGEN, Stuart ... 701-671-2446. 372 E stuart.engen@ndscs.edu

ENGER, Lee .... 217-228-5432. 156 C
engerle@quincy.edu
ENGERT, Lara .... 312-752-2130. 149 E
lara.engert@kendall.edu
ENGFER, Tom .... 323-860-4349... 55 E
tengfer@mi.edu
ENGH, SJ, Michael, E .... 408-554-4100... 64 M
mengh@scu.edu
ENGH, Peter, M .... 508-213-2390. 235 E
peter.engh@nichols.edu
ENGLAND, A, W .... 313-593-5290. 251 D
england@umich.edu
ENGLAND, David .... 225-768-1711. 206 D
david.england@ololcollege.edu
ENGLAND, David .... 615-966-6210. 456 B
david.england@lipscomb.edu
ENGLAND, David, C .... 860-255-3500... 89 G
dengland@txcc.commnet.edu
ENGLAND, Richard .... 217-581-2017. 144 E
rengland@eiu.edu
ENGLAND, Sid .... 530-752-2432... 70 J
asengland@ucdavis.edu
ENGLAND, Tresa .... 970-675-3285... 80 B
tresa.england@cncc.edu
ENGLE, Chris .... 810-762-0242. 247 F
chris.engle@mcc.edu
ENGLE, Kevin, E .... 330-684-8948. 390 F
kengle@uakron.edu
ENGLE, Marcia, J .... 540-432-4148. 504 D
marcy.engle@emu.edu
ENGLEBERT, Mary, F ..... 828-262-6519. 367 A
englebertmf@appstate.edu
ENGLEHARDT, Richard ... 606-693-5000. 196 H
registrar@kmbc.edu
ENGLERT, Anne .... 210-458-7228. 492 C
anne.englert@utsa.edu
ENGLERT, Bradley, G ...... 512-232-1744. 491 C
b.englert@austin.utexas.edu
ENGLERT, Mark, G .... 307-686-0254. 543 F
menglert@sheridan.edu
ENGLERT, William, C ..... 310-233-4301... 51 H
englerbc@lahc.edu
ENGLESTATTER, Pauline . 301-447-5600. 217 B
englesta@msmary.edu
ENGLIN, Peter, D .... 515-294-5636. 175 H
penglin@iastate.edu
ENGLISH, Alison .... 714-556-3610... 74 D
aenglish@vanguard.edu
ENGLISH, Andrew .... 412-291-6423. 410 B
aenglish@aii.edu
ENGLISH, Chris .... 828-694-1728. 358 C
chrise@blueridge.edu
ENGLISH, Claude .... 816-584-6492. 280 C
claude.english@park.edu
ENGLISH, David .... 309-794-7203. 139 L
davidenglish@augustana.edu
ENGLISH, David .... 336-770-1546. 369 D
englishd@uncsa.edu
ENGLISH, Denise, K .... 352-365-3541. 108 S
englishd@lssc.edu
ENGLISH, Eva .... 406-353-2607. 285 E
eenglish@ancollege.edu
ENGLISH, Evon .... 361-825-3890. 483 F
evon.english@tamucc.edu
ENGLISH, Hope .... 806-291-3430. 494 F
hope@wbu.edu
ENGLISH, J. T .... 502-897-4121. 199 B
jenglish@sbts.edu
ENGLISH, La'Shea .... 619-684-8866... 56 C
lenglish@newschoolarch.edu
ENGLISH, Linda .... 970-945-8691... 79 G
ENGLISH, Lindsay .... 216-987-3610. 378 D
lindsay.english@tri-c.edu
ENGLISH, Matthew .... 503-280-8516. 402 J
menglish@cu-portland.edu
ENGLISH, Patricia .... 805-965-0581... 64 L
englishp@sbcc.edu
ENGLISH, Raymond, A ... 440-775-5666. 385 H
ray.english@oberlin.edu
ENGLISH, Susan .... 616-632-2045. 239 E
susan.english@aquinas.edu
ENGLISH, Suzanne .... 724-805-2660. 432 G
suzanne.english@email.stvincent.edu
ENGLISH, Zach .... 561-912-1211. 103 C
zenglish@evergladesuniversity.edu
ENGLUND, Melissa, M .. 215-895-6395. 415 B
englunmm@drexel.edu
ENGQUIST, John .... 507-389-7444. 261 E
john.engquist@southcentral.edu
ENGQUIST, John .... 218-751-8670. 263 C
johnengquist@oakhills.edu
ENGSTROM, Dan, M ...... 724-938-1523. 428 A
engstrom@calu.edu
ENGSTROM, Janet .... 708-732-7427. 194 A
janet.engstrom@frontier.edu
ENGSTROM, Royce, C .... 406-243-2311. 286 H
royce.engstrom@umontana.edu
ENICKS, Charles .... 706-721-9660. 126 B
cenicks@gru.edu
ENKE, Kathryn .... 320-363-5070. 254 J
kenke@csbsju.edu
ENLOE, Donald .... 303-871-2463... 86 B
denloe@du.edu
ENLOW, Todd .... 918-456-5511. 396 H
enlowm@nsuok.edu
ENNASSEF, Abdelilan ..... 973-328-5155. 300 G
aennassef@ccm.edu
ENNEKING, Thomas .... 317-955-6010. 170 V
tenneking@marian.edu
ENNEN, Rita .... 701-483-2883. 371 D
rita.ennen@dickinsonstate.edu
ENNIS, Daniel .... 843-349-2746. 442 E
dennis@coastal.edu
ENNIS, Daniel, G .... 410-516-2373. 215 H
danielgennis@jhu.edu
ENNIS, Jackie .... 252-399-6593. 352 F
jennis@barton.edu
ENNIS, Jackie .... 252-399-6571. 352 F
jennis@barton.edu
ENNIS, Kim .... 205-387-0511..... 2 B
kennis@bscc.edu
ENNIS, Matt .... 941-752-5574. 114 I
ennism@scf.edu
ENNIST, Phyllis .... 937-529-2201. 390 D
pjennist@united.edu
ENNS-REMPEL, Kevin ..... 559-453-2300... 45 D
kevin.enns.rempel@fresno.edu
ENOCH, Hollace, J .... 804-257-5841. 515 F
hjenoch@vuu.edu
ENOS, Elizabeth .... 781-239-2751. 231 G
eenos@massbay.edu
ENOS, Jonathan, C .... 717-291-3982. 416 J
jon.enos@fandm.edu
ENOS, Stacey .... 828-298-3325. 370 E
senos@warren-wilson.edu
ENRIGHT, Jacquelyn, K .. 301-369-2800. 213 G
jke@capitol-college.edu
ENRIGHT, John .... 213-613-2200... 67 E
john_enright@sciarc.edu
ENRIGHT, Judy .... 507-433-0636. 260 I
jenright@riverland.edu
ENRIGHT, Patrick .... 973-328-5700. 300 G
penright@ccm.edu
ENRIQUEZ, Anita, B .... 671-735-2994. 546 E
abe@uguam.uog.edu
ENRIQUEZ, Anita, B .... 671-735-2553. 546 E
abe@uguam.uog.edu
ENRIQUEZ, Igri .... 787-765-3560. 548 M
enriquez@edpuniversity.edu
ENSENBERGER,
Matthew .... 847-925-6586. 145 H
mensenbe@harpercollege.edu
ENSER, Jason .... 518-743-2277. 345 E
enserj@sunyacc.edu
ENSING, Kim .... 805-922-6966... 26 K
kensing@hancockcollege.edu
ENSLEY, Carol .... 916-278-7737... 34 D
censley@csus.edu
ENSLEY, Dana .... 706-379-5336. 134 L
ddensley@yhc.edu
ENSLEY, Kevin .... 817-923-1921. 481 G
kensley@swbts.edu
ENSLIN, Jonathan .... 262-472-1482. 538 D
enslinj@uww.edu
ENSMAN, JR.,
Richard, G .... 585-345-6809. 325 C
rgensman@genesee.edu
ENSMINGER, Todd .... 410-677-3160. 220 D
wtensminger@salisbury.edu
ENSOR, Pat .... 713-221-8011. 489 D
ensorp@uhd.edu
ENTERLINE, Keri .... 954-783-7339. 102 M
kenterline@cci.edu
ENTERS, David, T .... 262-243-5700. 532 H
dave.enters@cuw.edu
ENTESSARI, Abbass .... 305-623-1441. 104 J
Abbass.Entessari@fmuniv.edu
ENTREKIN, Cindy .... 256-215-4251..... 2 G
centrekin@cacc.edu
ENTRIKIN, Nicholas .... 574-631-5204. 174 A
Entrikin.1@nd.edu
ENTRINGER, Chris, E ..... 563-556-5110. 181 E
entringc@nicc.edu
ENTWISLE, Barbara .... 919-962-1319. 368 D
entwisle@unc.edu
ENTWISTLE, David, E ..... 801-581-7480. 496 Q
david.entwistle@hsc.utah.edu
ENTZ, Mary .... 515-791-1721. 177 B
mjentz@dmacc.edu
ENTZMINGER, Robert, L 501-450-1273... 21 E
entzminger@hendrix.edu
ENWEMEKA,
Chukuka, S .... 414-229-4712. 537 A
enwemeka@uwm.edu
ENYARD, Richard, K .... 217-581-3514. 144 E
renyard@eiu.edu
ENYEDI, Alexander .... 269-387-4350. 252 I
alex.enyedi@wmich.edu
ENZ FINKEN, Kathleen .. 805-756-2186... 32 F
kensfink@calpoly.edu
ENZOR, Sharon, B .... 662-685-4771. 266 C
senzor@bmc.edu
EOFF, Shirley .... 325-942-2722. 465 K
shirley.eoff@angleo.edu
EPEMA, Michael .... 712-722-6080. 177 J
michael.epema@dordt.edu
EPLEY, David .... 520-795-0787... 11 J
president@asaom.edu
EPLING, Linda .... 859-246-6584. 194 L
linda.epling@kctcs.edu
EPLING, Rob .... 513-569-1557. 376 L
rob.epling@cincinnatistate.edu
EPP, Adam .... 425-889-5263. 521 G
adam.epp@northwestu.edu
EPPEHIMER, Trevor .... 704-636-6534. 355 D
teppehimer@hoodseminary.edu
EPPEHIMER, Trevor .... 704-636-6743. 355 D
teppehimer@hoodseminary.edu
EPPERHART, David, H .... 870-230-5146... 21 D
epperd@hsu.edu
EPPERSON, Annissa .... 913-758-6172. 191 B
eppersona@stmary.edu
EPPERSON, Douglas ...... 805-756-2706... 32 F
dleppers@calpoly.edu
EPPERSON, II,
Richard, P .... 434-223-6153. 505 E
repperson@hsc.edu
EPPERSON, Shonte .... 903-927-3260. 495 A
sepperson@wileyc.edu
EPPERSON, Steve .... 360-416-7771. 523 G
steve.epperson@skagit.edu
EPPES, Thomas, E .... 662-915-5315. 270 B
teppes@olemiss.edu
EPPICH, David .... 505-566-3318. 311 I
eppichd@sanjuancollege.edu
EPPINETTE, Chance, W .. 318-342-5021. 208 E
eppinette@ulm.edu
EPPINGER, Beth .... 479-788-7334... 24 A
beth.eppinger@uafs.edu
EPPLER, Michelle .... 402-557-7010. 288 G
michelle.eppler@bellevue.edu
EPPLEY, Doug .... 814-472-3017. 432 D
deppley@francis.edu
EPPLI, Mark .... 414-288-5724. 534 B
mark.eppli@marquette.edu
EPPLING, Chris .... 706-865-2134. 133 B
ceppling@truett.edu
EPPLING, Marcie, T .... 256-824-6443..... 8 F
Marcie.Eppling@uah.edu
EPPS, Anna Cherrie .... 615-327-6904. 456 E
acepps@mmc.edu
EPPS, Bruce .... 614-236-6461. 375 H
bepps@capital.edu
EPPS, Carol .... 864-596-9595. 443 D
carol.epps@converse.edu
EPPS, Charmica, D .... 804-342-3938. 515 F
cdepps@vuu.edu
EPPS, Joanne, A .... 215-204-8993. 433 K
joanne.epps@temple.edu
EPPS, Ronald .... 254-299-8647. 476 D
repps@mclennan.edu
EPPS, Valerie .... 202-274-5210... 97 A
vepps@udc.edu
EPSTEIN, Adam .... 314-965-8363. 277 I
EPSTEIN, Chaim, L .... 718-438-1002. 331 A
EPSTEIN, Joanne .... 352-335-2332... 97 E
EPSTEIN, Meryl .... 602-331-7500... 12 A
mepstein@aii.edu
EPSTEIN, Scott .... 616-554-5691. 241 H
sepstein1@davenport.edu
EPTING, Bert .... 706-291-5338. 131 E
bepting@shorter.edu
EPTING, James, B .... 864-977-7018. 445 H
jimmy.epting@ngu.edu
EQUINOA, Kim .... 805-893-2920... 72 B
kim.parent@sa.ucsb.edu
ERARDI, Lauren .... 203-582-3606... 91 A
lauren.erardi@quinnipiac.edu
ERARDI, Scott, M .... 860-832-2032... 87 K
erardis@ccsu.edu
ERARIO, Vince .... 678-264-8808. 128 D
vince.erario@life.edu
ERATO, Michael, J .... 414-425-8300. 535 K
merato@shst.edu
ERB, Brian, I .... 706-236-2234. 121 G
berb@berry.edu
ERB, Daniel, E .... 336-841-4595. 355 C
derb@highpoint.edu
ERB, Jennifer .... 610-799-1034. 421 I
0617mgr@sheg.follett.com
ERB, Scott, D .... 207-778-7486. 212 D
scotterb@maine.edu
ERBERT, Daniel .... 970-339-6602... 78 C
daniel.erbert@aims.edu
ERBES, Fred, S .... 712-274-5168. 181 B
erbes@morningside.edu
ERCK, Lisa .... 916-631-8108... 32 C
ERCKERT, Joseph .... 215-489-2397. 414 E
Joseph.Erckert@delval.edu
ERDICE, Stephanie .... 717-477-7447. 429 E
smerdice@ship.edu
ERDMAN, Al .... 254-526-1331. 468 G
al.erdman@ctcd.edu
ERDMAN, Anne, C .... 269-927-8127. 245 D
erdman@lakemichigancollege.edu
ERDMAN, Howard .... 208-792-2456. 138 G
herdman@lcsc.edu
ERDMAN, Peg .... 928-532-6111... 16 E
peg.erdman@npc.edu
ERDMANN, David .... 407-646-2317. 111 Q
derdmann@rollins.edu
ERDMANN, James .... 215-503-6595. 434 C
james.erdmann@jefferson.edu
ERDMANN, Joel .... 251-460-7121..... 9 E
jerdmann@southalabama.edu
EREKSON, Charles, F ..... 408-554-4533... 64 M
cerekson@scu.edu
EREKSON, David .... 703-526-5842... 28 M
derekson@argosy.edu
EREKSON, Homer .... 817-257-7527. 484 I
h.erekson@tcu.edu
EREKSON, Thomas, L ..... 309-298-2442. 162 K
tl-erekson@wiu.edu
EREVELLES, Winston ...... 210-436-3996. 479 D
werevelles@stmarytx.edu
ERFAN, Shahir .... 718-482-5501. 318 F
serfan@lagcc.cuny.edu
ERFFMEYER, Kenneth ..... 616-526-6097. 240 L
kde2@calvin.edu
ERFORD, Dane .... 419-434-4524. 391 D
erford@findlay.edu
ERHAN, Ali .... 616-632-2819. 239 E
erhanali@aquinas.edu
ERICKSEN, Donald, O ..... 651-631-5249. 263 A
doericksen@nwc.edu
ERICKSEN, Robert, B ...... 310-825-1681... 71 C
bericksen@saonet.ucla.edu
ERICKSON, Ami, N .... 307-674-6446. 543 F
aerickson@sheridan.edu
ERICKSON, Christine .... 831-582-4091... 34 B
cherickson@csumb.edu
ERICKSON, Craig .... 763-488-2518. 258 F
craig.erickson@hennepintech.edu
ERICKSON, Fritz, J .... 231-591-3797. 242 F
ericksf@ferris.edu
ERICKSON, Janet .... 303-546-5295... 83 F
jerickson@naropa.edu
ERICKSON, Jon .... 218-723-6725. 254 K
jericksо@css.edu
ERICKSON, Jon, D .... 802-656-4280. 500 F
jon.erickson@uvm.edu
ERICKSON, Judith .... 904-256-7280. 107 Q
jericks2@ju.edu
ERICKSON, Karen .... 603-668-2211. 297 I
k.erickson@snhu.edu
ERICKSON, Karen .... 701-224-5424. 372 B
karen.erickson@bismarckstate.edu
ERICKSON, Kenneth, M .. 315-386-7401. 345 F
erickson@canton.edu
ERICKSON, Kenneth, W .. 208-524-3000. 138 D
kenneth.erickson@my.eitc.edu
ERICKSON, Kim .... 909-652-6021... 37 M
kim.erickson@chaffey.edu
ERICKSON, Kyle .... 218-335-4286. 256 I
kyle.erickson@lltc.edu
ERICKSON, Leslye, A ..... 502-852-4740. 200 D
leslye.erickson@louisville.edu
ERICKSON, Mark .... 845-451-1295. 322 D
m_ericks@culinary.edu
ERICKSON, Mark, H .... 610-861-5458. 425 D
merickson@northampton.edu
ERICKSON, Mary .... 952-851-0066. 253 B
merickson@academycollege.edu
ERICKSON, Maureen, N . 315-255-1743. 316 D
maureen.erickson@cayuga-cc.edu
ERICKSON, Michael .... 620-341-5298. 186 D
mericks2@emporia.edu
ERICKSON, Michelle, H .. 617-735-9825. 226 B
erickson@emmanuel.edu
ERICKSON, Micki .... 239-513-1122. 106 O
merickson@hodges.edu
ERICKSON, Pam .... 406-657-1015. 288 B
erisksop@rocky.edu
ERICKSON, Paul, J .... 608-342-1194. 537 D
ericksop@uwplatt.edu
ERICKSON, Regina .... 530-226-4718... 66 D
rerickson@simpsonu.edu
ERICKSON, Rodney, A .... 814-865-7611. 426 A
president@psu.edu
ERICKSON, Ron .... 740-753-7004. 380 K
ericksonr@hocking.edu
ERICKSON, Russell, E .... 651-286-7573. 263 A
reerickson@nwc.edu
ERICKSON, Scott .... 612-659-6831. 259 D
scott.erickson@minneapolis.edu
ERICKSON, Siri, C .... 507-933-7446. 255 I
ERICKSON, Susan .... 757-455-3220. 515 H
serickson@vwc.edu
ERICKSON, Suzanne .... 651-604-4119. 257 A
ERICKSON, Teri .... 719-384-6831... 83 M
teri.erickson@ojc.edu
ERICKSON, Tina, M .... 847-578-8589. 157 F
tina.erickson@rosalindfranklin.edu

ERICKSON, Todd 916-577-2200 76 J
terickson@jessup.edu
ERICKSON, Tony, W 651-962-4340 265 C
twerickson@stthomas.edu
ERICKSON, Wayne 402-844-7243 291 I
wayne@northeast.edu
ERICSON, III, Ed 479-238-8669 21 G
eericson@jbu.edu
ERICSON, MaryAnn 603-641-7402 297 G
mericson@anselm.edu
ERICSON, Todd, M 608-796-3856 539 E
tmericson@viterbo.edu
ERIK-SOUSSI, Catherine 860-629-6043 90 G
erik-soussi_c@mitchell.edu
ERIKSEN, Jennifer, A 207-778-7048 212 D
jennifer.eriksen@maine.edu
ERIKSEN, John 714-438-4680 39 H
jeriksen@mail.cccd.edu
ERIKSEN, John 401-232-6107 438 K
jeriksen@bryant.edu
ERIKSEN, Michael, P 404-413-1130 126 E
meriksen@gsu.edu
ERIKSMOEN, Lisa 701-858-3374 371 F
lisa.eriksmoen@minotstateu.edu
ERION, Cathy 402-557-7677 288 G
cathy.erion@bellevue.edu
ERJAVEC, Patricia 719-549-3213 84 G
patty.erjavec@pueblocc.edu
ERKKILA, Rachel 515-964-6210 177 B
rrerkkila@dmacc.edu
ERLANGER, Esrael 718-645-0536 331 G
ERLE, Sharon 850-973-1603 109 H
erles@nfcc.edu
ERMATINGER, James 217-206-6512 161 E
ermatinger.james@uis.edu
ERMER, Scott 319-398-4944 180 J
sermer@kirkwood.edu
ERMETI, Sara 574-520-4398 168 E
sermeti@iusb.edu
ERMIAS, Martha 323-265-8610 51 F
ermiasmy@elac.edu
ERMLER, Kathy 620-341-5403 186 D
kermler@emporia.edu
ERMOLI, Victor 912-525-5000 131 B
vermoli@scad.edu
ERNEST, Mark 386-822-7294 117 C
mernest@stetson.edu
ERNEY, Sherry 717-564-4112 419 I
serney@kaplan.edu
ERNST, Chris 502-456-6509 199 F
cernst@sctd.edu
ERNST, Dale, E 785-242-2067 189 D
dernst@neosho.edu
ERNST, John, P 606-783-2022 198 A
j.ernst@moreheadstate.edu
ERNST, Michelle 651-905-3445 254 B
mernst@browncollege.edu
ERNST, Nathan 630-515-6342 153 B
nernst@midwestern.edu
ERNST, Patricia 717-396-7833 427 A
pernst@pcad.edu
ERNST, Steve 518-608-8379 324 B
sernst@excelsior.edu
ERNST-LEONARD,
Amber 305-809-3531 104 I
amber.ernstleonard@fkcc.edu
ERPENBACH, Steve 605-697-7475 452 B
steve.erpenbach@sdsufoundation.org
ERPESTAD, Hanna 218-733-7667 259 A
h.erpestad@lsc.edu
ERPS, SJ, James, D 310-338-2720 53 E
james.erps@lmu.edu
ERRECA, Lori 619-388-3207 62 D
lerreca@sdccd.edu
ERRECA, Sarah 205-226-4905 2 C
serreca@bsc.edu
ERRICKSON, David, C 717-872-3015 429 D
david.errickson@millersville.edu
ERRICKSON, Niel 909-607-1272 65 D
nerricks@scrippscollege.edu
ERRICO, Joseph 570-504-8113 420 C
erricoj@lackawanna.edu
ERRIGO, Fred 803-321-5238 445 G
fred.errigo@newberry.edu
ERSKINE, George 254-526-1168 468 G
george.erskine@ctcd.edu
ERSKINE, Richard, K 276-591-5699 509 J
chefrke2@aol.com
ERSKINE, Robb 415-808-3000 47 E
robb_erskine@heald.edu
ERSKINE, Tina 207-454-1002 211 B
terskine@wccc.me.edu
ERSLAN, Bryan 423-869-6465 456 A
bryan.erslan@lmunet.edu
ERSLAND, Carolyn 402-826-8572 289 E
carolyn.ersland@doane.edu
ERSTE, Mark, A 740-284-5234 379 N
merste@franciscan.edu
ERTEL, Stefanie 910-221-2224 354 D
sertel@gcd.edu
ERTELT, Celeste 701-662-1533 372 D
celeste.m.ertelt@lrsc.edu
ERTELT, Victoria 503-845-3102 404 D
victoria.ertelt@mtangel.edu
ERTING, Carol 202-651-5400 95 C
carol.erting@gallaudet.edu
ERTLE, Anita 970-542-3140 83 E
anita.ertle@morgancc.edu
ERVIN, Archie 404-385-3686 125 D
archie.ervin@vpid.gatech.edu
ERVIN, Bob, J 910-678-8442 360 D
ervinb@faytechcc.edu
ERVIN, Carl 262-524-7378 532 C
cervin@carrollu.edu
ERVIN, Elonda 812-237-2877 167 A
elonda.ervin@indstate.edu
ERVIN, Elsie, L 662-846-4138 266 G
elervin@deltastate.edu
ERVIN, Erin 863-680-3905 105 D
eervin@flsouthern.edu
ERVIN, Kenneth 603-899-4178 296 H
ervink@franklinpierce.edu
ERVIN, Korrie 910-576-6222 362 C
ervink@montgomery.edu
ERVIN, Larry 865-981-8222 456 D
larry.ervin@maryvillecollege.edu
ERVIN, Leisa 662-325-7353 268 D
lbryant@audit.msstate.edu
ERVIN-BLANKENHEIM,
Elisabeth 215-491-5876 414 E
Elisabeth.Ervin@delval.edu
ERWIN, Clarissa 702-651-5863 294 E
clarissa.erwin@csn.edu
ERWIN, Connie, I 724-847-6666 417 A
cierwin@geneva.edu
ERWIN, Craig 512-863-1442 481 I
erwinc@southwestern.edu
ERWIN, Curtis 804-828-7666 511 F
cgerwin@vcu.edu
ERWIN, Deidre 262-524-7201 532 C
derwin@carrollu.edu
ERWIN, Deidre 414-955-8390 534 C
derwin@mcw.edu
ERWIN, Don, F 716-878-3424 343 A
erwindf@buffalostate.edu
ERWIN, Gary 313-317-6800 243 H
gjerwin@hfcc.edu
ERWIN, John, O 616-885-5585 388 C
jerwin@pcj.edu
ERWIN, John, S 309-694-5520 146 E
jerwin@icc.edu
ERWIN, Lisa 218-726-8501 264 D
laerwin@d.umn.edu
ERWIN, Pamela 651-638-6805 253 K
perwin@bethel.edu
ERWIN, Ryan 214-333-5436 470 D
rerwin@dbu.edu
ERWIN, Shari 918-293-4966 398 B
shari.erwin@okstate.edu
ERWIN, Steve 620-235-4231 189 L
serwin@pittstate.edu
ERWIN, W. Scott 512-245-2102 487 C
we10@txstate.edu
ERWIN-PLOOG, Patricia 603-513-1132 298 E
patricia.erwin-ploog@granite.edu
ERZ, Brad 312-629-6700 158 L
berz@saic.edu
ESCALANTE, Angie 787-765-5974 553 E
aescalan@pupr.edu
ESCALANTE, Eddie 626-571-8811 74 B
eddiee@uwest.edu
ESCALANTE, Maria 800-567-2344 532 E
mescalante@menominee.edu
ESCALANTE, Rochely 787-725-6500 547 H
rescalante@albizu.edu
ESCALANTE, Victor 800-567-2344 532 E
vescalante@menominee.edu
ESCALONA, Gladys 787-250-0000 553 G
gladys.escalona@upr.edu
ESCAMILLA, Cindy 210-829-3136 490 A
cyescami@uiwtx.edu
ESCAMILLA, Mark 361-698-1203 471 G
mescamilla@delmar.edu
ESCAMILLA, Sara 972-825-4837 481 F
Sescamilla@sagu.edu
ESCH, Terri 312-662-4151 139 F
tesch@adler.edu
ESCHEN, Thomas 314-529-9343 276 G
teschen@maryville.edu
ESCHENBRENNER,
Nancy 860-255-3398 89 G
neschenbrenner@txcc.commnet.edu
ESCHENBURG, Cynthia 313-845-9820 243 H
cmeschenburg@hfcc.edu
ESCHHOLZ, Ingrid 303-315-2600 86 A
ingrid.eschholz@ucdenver.edu
ESCOBAR, Estrella 915-747-5555 492 A
estrella@utep.edu
ESCOBAR, Jorge 408-273-2764 55 H
jorge.escobar@nhu.edu
ESCOBEDO, Duwayne 251-626-3303 8 B
descobedo@ussa.edu
ESCOLAS, Roger 614-222-3264 378 A
rescolas@ccad.edu
ESCOTET, Miguel 956-882-7220 491 D
miguel.escotet@utb.edu
ESCOTO, Ernesto, R 305-284-5511 118 F
e.escoto@miami.edu
ESCOTO, Jose 516-773-5000 545 H
escotoj@usmma.edu
ESCOTO, Sesario 831-479-6525 30 G
seescoto@cabrillo.edu
ESCRIBANO, Dorothy, A 914-654-5535 320 H
describano@cnr.edu
ESDALE, Joseph 248-689-8282 251 I
jesdale@walshcollege.edu
ESHAM, Sherry, L 520-626-6309 18 F
sesham@email.arizona.edu
ESHELMAN, Christopher 316-978-7007 191 F
christopher.eshelman@wichita.edu
ESHENBERG, Ardis 808-235-7370 137 C
ardise@hawaii.edu
ESHLEMAN, Nancy 717-291-3995 416 J
nancy.eshleman@fandm.edu
ESKANDARIAN, Ali 202-994-8192 95 D
ea1102@gwu.edu
ESKER, Brian 312-899-5177 158 L
besker@saic.edu
ESKES, Todd 909-599-5433 50 J
teskes@lifepacific.edu
ESKEW, Ron 716-926-8846 326 B
reskew@hilbert.edu
ESKIN, Jim 210-485-0047 464 I
jeskin@alamo.edu
ESLAHI, Farokh 217-206-7352 161 E
eslahi.farokh@uis.edu
ESLER, Beth 717-867-6210 421 H
esler@lvc.edu
ESLER, Tika 516-572-7210 332 C
tika.esler@ncc.edu
ESLINGER, Elise 507-222-5597 254 D
eeslinge@carleton.edu
ESLINGER, Michelle, D 701-777-4500 371 C
michelle.eslinger@und.edu
ESMAEILI, Ali 956-872-7270 480 I
esmaeili@southtexascollege.edu
ESNER, Ben 718-260-3511 336 E
besner@poly.edu
ESNES, Michael 908-709-7046 308 B
michael.esnes@ucc.edu
ESNES-JOHNSON,
Theresa 631-420-2104 346 B
theresa.esnes@farmingdale.edu
ESPARZA, Connie 312-935-4541 156 K
cesparza@robertmorris.edu
ESPARZA, Lou 214-333-5289 470 D
lou@dbu.edu
ESPER, Linda 508-373-9501 223 A
linda.esper@becker.edu
ESPESET, Rick 260-982-5390 170 U
rbespeset@manchester.edu
ESPEY, John 615-230-3300 461 G
john.espey@volstate.edu
ESPEY, Shellye 601-481-1309 267 G
sespey@meridiancc.edu
ESPINALES, Ricardo 914-251-5982 344 D
ricardo.espinales@purchase.edu
ESPINET, Lydia 787-727-7880 555 D
lespinet@sagrado.edu
ESPINO, Humberto 708-456-0300 161 A
hespino@triton.edu
ESPINOSA, Charles 361-593-3057 484 A
charles.espinosa@tamuk.edu
ESPINOSA, Rene 210-341-1366 477 L
respinosa@ost.edu
ESPINOSA, Rosa 210-434-6711 477 N
raespinosar@lake.ollusa.edu
ESPINOSA, Sarah 240-567-5382 216 F
sarah.espinosa@montgomerycollege.edu
ESPINOSA PIEB,
Christina 408-864-8995 44 M
espinosapiebchristina@deanza.edu
ESPINOSA-PIEB,
Christina 408-864-8958 44 M
espinosapiebchristina@deanza.edu
ESPINOZA, Beatriz, T 361-354-2200 468 K
bte@coastalbend.edu
ESPINOZA, Danielle 210-486-3366 465 A
despinoza@alamo.edu
ESPINOZA, Dora 847-578-8524 157 F
dora.espinoza@rosalindfranklin.edu
ESPINOZA, Gilda 505-428-1210 311 J
gilda.espinoza@sfcc.edu
ESPINOZA, Leticia 949-753-4774 29 M
lespinoz@brandman.edu
ESPINOZA, Lily 707-864-7000 66 G
lily.espinoza@solano.edu
ESPINOZA, Susan, B 210-486-0748 465 C
sespinoza@alamo.edu
ESPINOZA, Suzanne, M 209-667-3177 35 B
sespinoza1@csustan.edu
ESPINOZA, Yolanda 970-204-8366 81 N
yolanda.espinoza@frontrange.edu
ESPIRITU, Kira, A 619-260-8835 73 I
kespiritu@sandiego.edu
ESPLIN, Fred, C 801-581-4088 496 Q
fred.esplin@utah.edu
ESPOSITO, James 212-678-8095 328 A
jaesposito@jtsa.edu
ESPOSITO, Richard, C 412-396-6607 415 F
esposito@duq.edu
ESPOSITO-NOY, Celia 916-691-7487 53 B
esposic@crc.losrios.edu
ESPRIO, John 323-319-9500 70 C
ESPY, Kathlynne, D 614-234-5276 384 J
kespy@mccn.edu
ESPY, Kimberly, A 541-346-2090 406 D
kaespy@uoregon.edu
ESPY, Tracy, Y 704-463-3440 365 E
tracy.espy@fsmail.pfeiffer.edu
ESQUILIN, Luis 787-758-6260 549 J
esquilin@inter.edu
ESQUITH, Stephen, L 517-355-0210 246 H
esquith@msu.edu
ESQUIVEL, Ruben, E 214-648-0448 493 E
ruben.esquivel@utsouthwestern.edu
ESQUIVEL-SWINSON,
Adela 510-466-7394 59 A
aesquivelswinson@peralta.edu
ESQUIVEL-SWINSON,
Adela 510-466-7365 59 D
aesquivelswinson@peralta.edu
ESRY, Kip 800-955-2527 274 I
kesry@grantham.edu
ESSARY, Reba, J 205-348-7917 8 D
ressary@fa.ua.edu
ESSAYYAD, Musa, M 337-475-5010 207 G
messayyad@mcneese.edu
ESSENBURG, Curt 616-222-3000 245 C
cessenburg@kuyper.edu
ESSEX, Nathan, L 901-333-4200 461 F
nessex@southwest.tn.edu
ESSIG, Lori 605-995-2614 450 A
loessig@dwu.edu
ESSIG, Mary 304-647-6213 530 B
messig@osteo.wvsom.edu
ESTA, Daniel 847-578-3257 157 F
daniel.esta@rosalindfranklin.edu
ESTABROOK,
Madeleine, A 617-373-2772 235 F
ESTAPHAN, Charles, F 508-793-2514 225 B
cestapha@holycross.edu
ESTEBAN, A. Gabriel 973-761-9691 307 C
gabriel.esteban@shu.edu
ESTELL, Frank, E 208-467-8434 139 A
festell@nnu.edu
ESTEN, Dora, E 818-947-2761 52 E
estende@lavc.edu
ESTEP, Charles, R 864-379-8869 443 F
estep@erskine.edu
ESTEP, Gary 806-720-7627 476 B
gary.estep@lcu.edu
ESTEP, Kimberly, K 615-353-3326 461 B
kimberly.estep@nscc.edu
ESTEP, Leon, F 334-387-3877 1 E
leonestep@amridgeuniversity.edu
ESTEP, Tim 704-337-2460 365 G
estept@queens.edu
ESTEPP, J. Mark 276-964-7315 514 A
mark.estepp@sw.edu
ESTER, Joyce, C 773-602-5000 142 B
ESTERBERG, Kristin, G 978-542-6246 230 E
kesterberg@salemstate.edu
ESTERHUIZEN, Amy, H 563-556-5110 181 E
esterhuizena@portal.nicc.edu
ESTERS, Lorenzo 502-597-6822 197 A
lorenzo.esters@kysu.edu
ESTES, Bill 678-839-6447 133 I
bestes@westga.edu
ESTES, Edward 757-479-3706 503 C
eestes@baptistseminary.edu
ESTES, Eric 440-775-8462 385 H
eric.estes@oberlin.edu
ESTES, James 202-885-8696 97 D
jestes@wesleyseminary.edu
ESTES, Lane 205-226-4640 2 C
lestes@bsc.edu
ESTES, Michael 601-984-1130 270 C
mestes@umc.edu
ESTES, Susan 650-574-6404 64 C
estes@smccd.edu
ESTES, William 423-614-8175 455 L
bestes@leeuniversity.edu
ESTESS, Larry, M 318-342-5205 208 E
estess@ulm.edu
ESTEVEZ MARTINEZ,
Jacqueline 212-938-5500 345 C
jmartinez@sunyopt.edu
ESTILL, Donna 256-306-2756 2 F
dre@calhoun.edu
ESTILL, Sandi, L 606-759-7141 196 B
sandi.estill@kctcs.edu

ESTLACK, Scarlet ... 806-874-3571. 468 J scarlet.estlack@clarendoncollege.edu
ESTOCK, Steven ... 575-562-2632. 309 H steven.estock@enmu.edu
ESTRADA, Donna ... 985-448-7954. 203 B donna.estrada@fletcher.edu
ESTRADA, Ella Mae ... 212-431-2827. 333 I EllaMae.Estrada@nyls.edu
ESTRADA, George ... 530-242-7930... 65 G gestrada@shastacollege.edu
ESTRADA, George ... 203-576-4330... 91 G gestrada@bridgeport.edu
ESTRADA, James ... 860-832-2553... 87 K james.estrada@ccsu.edu
ESTRADA, Maria ... 787-780-5134. 551 L mestrada@nuc.edu
ESTRADA-HAMBY, Lisa . 940-397-4076. 476 H lisa.hamby@mwsu.edu
ESTRELLA, Fred ... 928-523-9998... 16 C fred.estrella@nau.edu
ESTRIDGE, Gwen ... 303-300-8740... 78 M gwen.estridge@collegeamerica.com
ESTRIN, Elena ... 212-349-4330. 325 D eestrin@globe.edu
ESTRY, Douglas ... 517-353-5380. 246 H estry@msu.edu
ETCHEMENDY, John, W . 650-724-4074... 68 E etch@stanford.edu
ETE, Sonia ... 310-360-8888... 26 E
ETESAMNIA, Hamid ... 909-748-8303... 73 H hamid_etesamnia@redlands.edu
ETHIER, Richard ... 802-224-3000. 501 A richard.ethier@vsc.edu
ETHINGTON, Robert ... 707-527-4573... 65 B rethington@santarosa.edu
ETINGE, Elias ... 706-821-8302. 130 C eetinge@paine.edu
ETSCHMAIER, Gale ... 619-594-1643... 35 D gale.etschmaier@sdsu.edu
ETSE, Penselyn ... 691-320-2480. 546 B petse@comfsm.fm
ETTARO, Barbara ... 814-863-1030. 426 A bxm7@psu.edu
ETTEMA, Robert ... 307-766-4253. 543 I rettema@uwyo.edu
ETTINGER, Sherri ... 617-521-2451. 236 G sherri.ettinger@simmons.edu
ETTLE, Violeta ... 202-885-2720... 94 F vi@american.edu
ETTLING, John ... 518-564-2010. 344 B president_office@plattsburgh.edu
ETTORE, JD ... 620-223-2700. 186 G jde@fortscott.edu
EUBANK, Charlotte ... 573-840-9662. 282 K ceubank@trcc.edu
EUBANK, Gary ... 937-529-2201. 390 D geubank@united.edu
EUBANK, Jeff ... 215-702-4202. 411 F jeubank@cairn.edu
EUBANKS, Audrey, C ... 251-442-2218... 9 A aeubanks@umobile.edu
EUBANKS, Cynthia ... 803-376-4746. 441 A ceubanks@allenuniversity.edu
EUBANKS, David, A ... 727-864-7888. 101 N eubankda@eckerd.edu
EUBANKS, David, L ... 865-573-4517. 455 G deubanks@johnsonU.edu
EUBANKS, Gail ... 912-443-5443. 131 D geubanks@savannahtech.edu
EUBANKS, Jamie ... 252-399-6368. 352 F jceubanks@barton.edu
EUBANKS, Karla, C ... 912-427-5899. 120 B keubanks@altamahatech.edu
EUBANKS, Kathleen, L ... 508-999-8086. 229 A keubanks@umassd.edu
EUBANKS, Philip, A ... 865-573-4517. 455 G peubanks@johnsonU.edu
EUBANKS, Taylor ... 662-329-7127. 268 E tleubanks@sa.muw.edu
EUDY, Kim ... 619-260-7967... 73 I keudy@sandiego.edu
EUDY, Kristina ... 704-991-0235. 364 C keudy5611@stanly.edu
EUNICE, E, E ... 850-201-7000. 117 D eunicee@tcc.fl.edu
EURE, Darius ... 252-335-3307. 367 C deure@mail.ecsu.edu
EURICH, Judy ... 252-638-7350. 359 G eurichj@cravencc.edu
EUSEBIO, Zenda Gay, P . 626-448-0023... 48 L
EUSTROM, Jim ... 503-399-5076. 402 E jim.eustrom@chemeketa.edu
EVAN, Joseph ... 570-208-5895. 419 P josephevan@kings.edu
EVANCHIK, Michele ... 609-292-2108. 308 A mevanchik@tesc.edu
EVANCO, Malika, S ... 608-243-4449. 540 C mevanco@madisoncollege.edu
EVANGELISTA, Joleen, M ... 671-735-5540. 546 C materialsmanagement@guamcc.edu
EVANGELISTA, Nancy ... 607-871-2649. 313 E fevangel@alfred.edu
EVANOSKY, Sonya ... 877-751-5783. 141 F
EVANOVICH, Dolan ... 614-292-8835. 386 E evanovich.1@osu.edu
EVANS, Alana ... 906-487-7358. 242 G alana.evans@finlandia.edu
EVANS, Aleia ... 216-201-9025. 383 A
EVANS, Amy, M ... 972-599-3144. 469 G aevans@collin.edu
EVANS, Angela, J ... 770-423-6300. 127 N aevans@kennesaw.edu
EVANS, Angie ... 912-260-4407. 131 F angie.evans@sgsc.edu
EVANS, Annette ... 706-542-7066. 133 C amevans@uga.edu
EVANS, April ... 765-998-4625. 173 C apevans@taylor.edu
EVANS, Atlas, D ... 617-726-5164. 234 B aevans3@mghihp.edu
EVANS, Beth ... 718-990-6999. 339 A evansb@stjohns.edu
EVANS, Beverly, A ... 717-815-1228. 438 D behinger@ycp.edu
EVANS, Brett ... 706-507-8434. 123 D evans_brett@columbusstate.edu
EVANS, Brian ... 502-863-8040. 194 C brian_evans@georgetowncollege.edu
EVANS, Brian ... 502-863-8223. 194 C brian_evans@georgetowncollege.edu
EVANS, Brian, K ... 801-422-3760. 495 D brian_evans@byu.edu
EVANS, Carol, A ... 231-995-1705. 248 B cevans@nmc.edu
EVANS, Carolyn, L ... 601-977-7764. 270 A cevans@tougaloo.edu
EVANS, Cheryl ... 580-628-6201. 396 M cheryl.evans@noc.edu
EVANS, Cheryl, O ... 585-385-8015. 338 H cevans@sjfc.edu
EVANS, Cynthia ... 970-351-3192... 86 C cynthia.evans@unco.edu
EVANS, Damian ... 262-595-2540. 537 C damian.evans@uwp.edu
EVANS, Dan ... 740-533-4610. 387 C evansd1@ohio.edu
EVANS, Dave ... 619-388-2737... 62 E devans@sdccd.edu
EVANS, Dave ... 916-278-6231... 34 D dave_evans@csus.edu
EVANS, David ... 229-391-2647. 129 F devans@moultrietech.edu
EVANS, David ... 972-273-3561. 471 B devans@dcccd.edu
EVANS, David, R ... 712-749-2243. 176 D evansd@bvu.edu
EVANS, Deborah, L ... 610-861-1340. 424 E debevans@moravian.edu
EVANS, Debra, C ... 740-376-4835. 383 E debbie.evans@marietta.edu
EVANS, Diane, T ... 936-261-2202. 482 F dtevans@pvamu.edu
EVANS, Doree ... 252-222-6282. 358 G evansd@carteret.edu
EVANS, Eric, D ... 781-981-7000. 233 B
EVANS, Erik ... 570-389-4047. 427 H eevans@bloomu.edu
EVANS, Frederick, M ... 803-516-4930. 446 G fevans6@scsu.edu
EVANS, Frederick M, G .. 803-536-7133. 446 G fevans3@scsu.edu
EVANS, Gary ... 507-457-5020. 262 A gevans@winona.edu
EVANS, George ... 618-545-3030. 149 D gevans@kaskaskia.edu
EVANS, JR., Gilbert, L ... 386-312-4127. 112 C gilbertevans@sjrstate.edu
EVANS, Gregory ... 815-455-8564. 152 F gevans@mchenry.edu
EVANS, Gwenn ... 706-357-5281. 120 J gevans@athenstech.edu
EVANS, Howard ... 909-941-3509... 32 G heevans@csupomona.edu
EVANS, J. David ... 770-423-6194. 127 N devans@kennesaw.edu
EVANS, Jack ... 813-253-7604. 106 M jevans@hccfl.edu
EVANS, JR., Jack ... 972-524-3341. 481 H
EVANS, SR., Jack ... 972-524-3341. 481 H
EVANS, James, D ... 636-949-4900. 276 D jevans@lindenwood.edu
EVANS, Jane ... 740-695-9500. 374 H jevans@belmontcollege.edu
EVANS, Janet, D ... 412-392-3824. 431 B jevans@pointpark.edu
EVANS, Janie ... 802-287-8203. 499 D evansj@greenmtn.edu
EVANS, Jaylene ... 970-542-3168... 83 E jaylene.evans@morgancc.edu
EVANS, Jeannette, H ... 315-684-6067. 345 A evansjh@morrisville.edu
EVANS, Jeffrey, L ... 313-593-5110. 251 D jlevan@umich.edu
EVANS, Jennifer, M ... 717-867-6271. 421 H jevans@lvc.edu
EVANS, Joe, W ... 405-224-3140. 401 E jwevans@usao.edu
EVANS, John, N ... 802-656-3117. 500 F john.evans@uvm.edu
EVANS, Joseph ... 410-706-8501. 219 C jevans@af.umaryland.edu
EVANS, Julia ... 909-607-3689... 39 C julia.evans@cgu.edu
EVANS, Julie ... 701-777-6345. 371 C jae@und.edu
EVANS, Julie ... 701-777-4171. 371 C und.affirmativeactionoffice@und.edu
EVANS, Kamira ... 610-892-1566. 427 E kevans@pit.edu
EVANS, Karen, V ... 610-921-7630. 409 A kevans@alb.edu
EVANS, Karyn ... 937-393-3431. 389 B kevans@sscc.edu
EVANS, Katherine ... 973-761-9500. 307 C katherine.evans@shu.edu
EVANS, Kenneth ... 973-300-2350. 307 F kevans@sussex.edu
EVANS, Kenneth, R ... 409-880-8405. 486 F kenneth.evans@lamar.edu
EVANS, Kevin ... 937-327-7520. 393 E kevans@wittenberg.edu
EVANS, Kim ... 802-831-1225. 500 H kevans@vermontlaw.edu
EVANS, Lana ... 419-267-1225. 385 F levans@northweststate.edu
EVANS, Laurie ... 313-664-1501. 241 C levans@collegeforcreativestudies.edu
EVANS, Leigh ... 478-553-2054. 129 H levans@oftc.edu
EVANS, Lexie ... 206-934-3890. 522 J lexie.evans@seattlecolleges.edu
EVANS, Linda ... 803-641-3342. 448 A lindae@usca.edu
EVANS, Lisa ... 513-569-1564. 376 L Lisa.evans@cincinnatistate.edu
EVANS, Lisa ... 828-398-7390. 357 N levans@abtech.edu
EVANS, Liz ... 412-392-5945. 431 B eevans@pointpark.edu
EVANS, III, Louis, D ... 713-221-2766. 489 D evansl@uhd.edu
EVANS, Marisa, L ... 814-886-6336. 424 G mevans@mtaloy.edu
EVANS, Mark ... 330-672-2972. 382 B mevans@kent.edu
EVANS, Mark ... 845-938-5502. 545 I Mark.Evans@usma.edu
EVANS, Mary ... 315-859-4668. 325 E mevans@hamilton.edu
EVANS, Mercedes ... 617-879-7060. 230 B msevans@massart.edu
EVANS, Michael ... 812-855-9249. 167 F mirevans@indiana.edu
EVANS, Michael ... 207-948-9151. 211 I mevans@unity.edu
EVANS, Michael ... 334-420-4302... 7 G mevans@trenholmstate.edu
EVANS, Michael ... 817-461-8741. 466 D mevans@arlingtonbaptistcollege.edu
EVANS, Michael, L ... 806-743-2738. 487 E michael.evans@ttuhsc.edu
EVANS, Nicole ... 614-251-4603. 386 B evansn@ohiodominican.edu
EVANS, Oliver ... 563-425-5284. 183 B evanso@uiu.edu
EVANS, Pamela ... 251-343-8200... 6 E pamela.evans@remingtoncollege.edu
EVANS, Paul ... 317-955-6290. 170 V pevans@marian.edu
EVANS, Paul, N ... 608-262-6982. 536 D paul.evans@housing.wisc.edu
EVANS, R. Gregory ... 912-478-2676. 126 C rgevans@georgiasouthern.edu
EVANS, JR., R. Lee ... 334-844-8348... 1 G evansrl@auburn.edu
EVANS, R. Scott ... 330-941-1585. 394 A sevans@ysu.edu
EVANS, Renee ... 201-761-7806. 306 L revans@saintpeters.edu
EVANS, Richard, W ... 585-785-1300. 324 D evansrw@flcc.edu
EVANS, Rick ... 818-677-2906... 34 C rick.evans@csun.edu
EVANS, Robert ... 501-660-1001... 19 L revans@asusystem.edu
EVANS, Robert ... 773-907-4817. 142 A REvans@ccc.edu
EVANS, Roberta ... 406-243-4911. 286 H roberta.evans@umontana.edu
EVANS, Sam ... 270-745-4664. 200 G sam.evans@wku.edu
EVANS, Sarah ... 317-931-2377. 165 B sevans@cts.edu
EVANS, Sharlotte ... 706-821-3965. 224 G Sharlotte.Evans@cambridgecollege.edu
EVANS, Shirley ... 410-276-0306. 218 D sevans@host.sdc.edu
EVANS, Sidney, S ... 540-458-8754. 516 A sevans@wlu.edu
EVANS, Steve ... 281-425-6887. 475 I sevans@lee.edu
EVANS, Susan ... 239-590-1057. 115 A sevans@fgcu.edu
EVANS, Tabitha ... 409-882-3319. 486 G tabitha.evans@lsco.edu
EVANS, Thomas ... 406-447-4401. 285 G tevans@carroll.edu
EVANS, Thomas, A ... 515-281-6527. 175 G taevans@iastate.edu
EVANS, Tiffany ... 704-290-5831. 363 G tiffanyevans@spcc.edu
EVANS, Tracy, L ... 304-929-5480. 528 D tevans@newriver.edu
EVANS, Valarie, J ... 919-536-7217. 360 B evansv@durhamtech.edu
EVANS, W. Franklin ... 803-536-7180. 446 G wevans1@scsu.edu
EVANS, Warren ... 808-791-5200... 28 M waevans@argosy.edu
EVANS, Wendy ... 570-955-1456. 420 C evansw@lackawanna.edu
EVANS, William, G ... 816-501-4659. 280 I bill.evans@rockhurst.edu
EVANS, Zina ... 352-392-1365. 116 A zevans@ufl.edu
EVANS-DAME, Kimberly . 315-792-5637. 331 I kevans-dame@mvcc.edu
EVANS JONES, Cheryl ... 706-821-8324. 130 C cevansjones@paine.edu
EVANS-PLANTS, Penny .. 706-232-5374. 121 G peplants@berry.edu
EVARIAN, Jane ... 661-654-3035... 32 H jevarian@csub.edu
EVASHEVSKI, Keith ... 307-766-2187. 543 I keski@uwyo.edu
EVE, Debra ... 406-353-2607. 285 E deve@ancollege.edu
EVE, Stacey ... 406-791-5306. 288 E
EVELAND, Larry ... 651-290-6356. 265 F larry.eveland@wmitchell.edu
EVELAND, Susan, M ... 541-346-3195. 406 D seveland@uoregon.edu
EVELER, Janet ... 915-831-5202. 472 B jeveler3@epcc.edu
EVELOFF, Vivian ... 314-516-6622. 283 E eveloffv@umsl.edu
EVELYN, Alan ... 646-312-2205. 316 J Alan.Evelyn@baruch.cuny.edu
EVEN, Susan, E ... 573-884-9388. 283 C EvenS@health.missouri.edu
EVENBECK, Scott ... 646-313-8000. 319 E
EVENSON, Eric ... 815-483-0062... 28 M eevenson@argosy.edu
EVENSON, Shane ... 715-468-2815. 541 F Shane.Evenson@witc.edu
EVENSON, Thomas, L ... 940-565-2239. 490 C evenson@unt.edu
EVENSVOLD, Marty ... 620-251-7700. 185 O martye@coffeyville.edu
EVERETT, Anna ... 805-893-5114... 72 B anna.everett@evc.ucsb.edu
EVERETT, Daniel, L ... 781-891-2113. 223 C deverett@bentley.edu
EVERETT, David, D ... 330-569-5353. 380 I everettdd@hiram.edu
EVERETT, Dennis, F ... 850-718-2216... 99 N everettd@chipola.edu
EVERETT, Gary, M ... 716-888-2330. 316 C everett@canisius.edu
EVERETT, Gwendolyn, H . 202-806-7040... 95 G geverett@howard.edu
EVERETT, Heidi ... 320-308-5937. 261 C heverett@sctcc.edu
EVERETT, Jamila ... 909-621-8129... 59 G jamila_everett@pitzer.edu
EVERETT, Joe ... 816-322-0110. 271 O joe.everett@calvary.edu
EVERETT, Kathy ... 704-669-4092. 359 D everett@clevelandcc.edu
EVERETT, Kelly ... 641-784-5144. 178 F keverett@graceland.edu
EVERETT, Lisa ... 925-424-1182... 37 L leverett@laspositascollege.edu
EVERETT, Marcia, K ... 330-471-8335. 383 D meverett@malone.edu
EVERETT, Margaret ... 503-725-5258. 406 B everettm@pdx.edu
EVERETT, Robert ... 480-732-7280... 14 J robert.everett@cgc.edu
EVERETT, Sarah (Sally) ... 813-253-7560. 106 M severett8@hccfl.edu

EVERETT, Steve .... 312-996-5611. 161 D
steve3@uic.edu
EVERETT, Tammy .... 641-784-5226. 178 F
teverett@graceland.edu
EVERETT, Todd .... 513-745-2993. 393 H
everett@xavier.edu
EVERETT-HENSLEY,
Elaine .... 361-572-6440. 493 H
elaine.hensley@victoriacollege.edu
EVERHART, Deborah .... 203-932-7330... 92 E
deverhart@newhaven.edu
EVERINGHAM, David ..... 727-873-4995. 116 D
devering@usfsp.edu
EVERS, Cynthia .... 404-756-4585. 121 A
cevers@atlm.edu
EVERS-MANLY, Shirley .. 323-568-3328... 38 B
shirleyeversmanly@cdrewu.edu
EVERT, Amanda .... 405-422-1445. 399 B
amanda.evert@redlandscc.edu
EVERTS, Sandra, L .... 414-277-7135. 534 G
everts@msoe.edu
EVERTS, Sheri, N .... 309-438-7018. 147 J
severts@ilstu.edu
EVES, Robert .... 435-586-1934. 497 A
eves@suu.edu
EVETOVICH, Tammy .... 402-375-7030. 291 F
taeveto1@wsc.edu
EVINGER, Donna, J .... 812-464-1770. 174 D
devinger@usi.edu
EVITT, Regula, M .... 719-389-6706... 79 D
regula.evitt@coloradocollege.edu
EVITTS, Beth, A .... 717-339-3527. 417 I
baevitts@hacc.edu
EVJEN, Art .... 831-582-3394... 34 B
aevjen@csumb.edu
EVON, Daniel, T .... 517-355-4727. 246 H
evon@cga.msu.edu
EWALD, Beth .... 810-762-9645. 244 Q
bewald@kettering.edu
EWALD, Edward .... 312-413-2992. 161 D
ewald@uic.edu
EWALD, Paul .... 650-508-3494... 56 H
pewald@ndnu.edu
EWALD, Paul, D .... 303-458-4040... 84 M
pewald@regis.edu
EWAN, Brian .... 856-691-8600. 301 A
bewan@cccnj.edu
EWARMAI, Matthias .... 691-350-5244. 546 B
mewarmai@comfsm.fm
EWART, Daniel .... 208-885-2271. 139 D
dewart@uidaho.edu
EWELL, Clint .... 928-776-2166... 19 H
clint.ewell@yc.edu
EWELL, Nicholas .... 626-300-5444... 59 H
EWELL, Robbi .... 619-388-3870... 62 D
rewell@sdccd.edu
EWEN, Bernadette .... 812-877-8697. 172 C
ewen@rose-hulman.edu
EWEN, Gary .... 303-963-3166... 79 C
gewen@ccu.edu
EWEN, Kurt, E .... 407-582-3413. 118 M
kewen@valenciacollege.edu
EWERS, Frank, W .... 909-869-4132... 32 G
fwewers@csupomona.edu
EWERS, Matthew .... 307-754-6125. 543 G
Matthew.Ewers@northwestcollege.edu
EWERS, Terri, L .... 641-422-4106. 181 D
ewerster@niacc.edu
EWICK, Sarah .... 415-749-4594... 62 G
sewick@sfai.edu
EWING, April .... 706-821-8307. 130 C
aewing@paine.edu
EWING, Carol .... 847-543-2937. 143 A
cewing@clcillinois.edu
EWING, David, W .... 716-888-2150. 316 C
ewingd@canisius.edu
EWING, Douglas .... 212-817-7490. 317 F
dewing@gc.cuny.edu
EWING, James .... 954-262-8981. 109 K
jewing@nova.edu
EWING, Jennifer .... 619-201-8682... 67 G
jewing@socalsem.edu
EWING, Kamesia .... 910-672-1325. 367 D
kewing@uncfsu.edu
EWING, Keith .... 320-308-2022. 261 B
EWING, Lori, K .... 573-875-7200. 272 G
lewing@ccis.edu
EWING, Mike, J .... 320-363-5605. 254 J
mjewing@csbsju.edu
EWING, II, Rick, M .... 419-289-5491. 374 C
pewing@ashland.edu
EWING, Sim, E .... 276-328-0133. 511 C
see4r@uvawise.edu
EWING, Sunnie .... 901-722-3231. 458 K
sewing@sco.edu
EWING-MORGAN, Dawn 718-960-8111. 318 A
dawn.ewing-morgan@lehman.cuny.edu
EWINS, Patricia .... 805-378-1408... 74 F
pewins@vcccd.edu
EXLER, Michael, J .... 215-895-6488. 415 B
mexler@drexel.edu
EXLEY, Robert .... 256-840-4100..... 6 I
rexley@snead.edu
EXLINE, Teresa, D .... 812-237-7783. 167 A
teresa.exline@indstate.edu
EXNER, Allen .... 301-369-2800. 213 G
ahexner@capitol-college.edu
EXNER, Charlotte, E .... 410-704-2132. 220 E
cexner@towson.edu
EXSTROM, Bruce .... 620-276-0473. 187 A
bruce.exstrom@gcccks.edu
EXTEJT, Marian .... 508-531-6151. 229 D
marian.extejt@bridgew.edu
EXUM, Melissa, E .... 765-494-5776. 171 M
exum@purdue.edu
EYE, John .... 435-865-8392. 497 A
eye@suu.edu
EYER, Paul .... 717-290-8705. 421 D
peyer@lancasterseminary.edu
EYERMANN, Therese .... 805-437-8410... 32 I
therese.eyermann@csuci.edu
EYLERS, Hinrich .... 602-557-7428... 18 I
hinrich.eylers@phoenix.edu
EYNON, Bret .... 718-482-5478. 318 F
beynon@lagcc.cuny.edu
EYNON, Matthew .... 717-291-3973. 416 J
matthew.eynon@fandm.edu
EYRING, Henry, J .... 208-496-1119. 137 H
eyringh@byui.edu
EYSTER, Michael, E .... 541-346-8393. 406 D
meyster@uoregon.edu
EYTCHESON, Greg .... 620-331-4100. 187 G
eytcheson@indycc.edu
EZAZ, Aron .... 334-874-5700..... 3 A
aezaz@ccal.edu
EZEIGBO, Anayo .... 704-330-1408. 355 K
aezeigbo@jcsu.edu
EZELL, Christopher, C .... 434-797-8410. 512 C
cezell@dcc.vccs.edu
EZELL, Cyn, D .... 813-257-3028. 118 L
cezell@ut.edu
EZELL, Glenda .... 479-979-1331... 25 J
gezell2@ozarks.edu
EZELL, Samantha .... 602-285-7569... 15 C
samantha.ezell@phoenixcollege.edu
EZEONU, Rolita .... 206-878-3710. 520 E
rezeonu@highline.edu
EZZEDDINE, Ahmad .... 313-577-8968. 252 G
a.m.ezzeddine@wayne.edu
EZZELL, Kevin .... 610-921-7248. 409 A
kezzell@alb.edu
EZZELL, Russell .... 325-649-8040. 473 F
rezzell@hputx.edu

F

FABATZ, Anna .... 636-481-3295. 275 I
afabatz@jeffco.edu
FABAZ, Jason .... 817-923-8459. 469 F
jason.fabaz@fishermore.edu
FABAZ, Jason .... 239-280-2480... 98 K
jason.fabax@avemaria.edu
FABBRUCCI, Stephen, W 978-556-3923. 232 E
sfabbrucci@necc.mass.edu
FABE, Barbara, A .... 718-862-7392. 329 M
barbara.fabe@manhattan.edu
FABER, Andrea .... 419-448-3375. 389 J
faberad@tiffin.edu
FABER, Charles .... 208-376-7731. 137 F
cfaber@boisebible.edu
FABER, Jerry .... 202-685-2372. 544 K
FaberG@ndu.edu
FABER, Paul, W .... 785-628-4234. 186 F
pfaber@fhsu.edu
FABIAN, Brenda .... 570-372-4325. 433 H
fabian@susqu.edu
FABIAN, James .... 631-632-6010. 342 C
james.fabian@stonybrook.edu
FABIAN, Kim .... 708-239-4855. 160 K
kim.fabian@trnty.edu
FABISH, David .... 562-860-2451... 37 I
fabish@cerritos.edu
FABOS, Kristin .... 831-479-6158... 30 G
krfabos@cabrillo.edu
FABREY, James .... 610-436-3228. 430 A
jfabrey@wcupa.edu
FABRITIUS, Stephanie, L 859-238-5226. 193 E
stephanie.fabritius@centre.edu
FABRIZIO, Dona, M .... 610-892-1514. 427 E
dfabrizio@pit.edu
FABRIZIO, Linda .... 212-614-6113. 336 C
lfabrizi@chpnet.org
FABRIZIO, Paul .... 325-793-3806. 476 E
fabrizip@mcm.edu
FABRY, Dee .... 858-642-8109... 55 J
dfabry@nu.edu
FACEY, Owen .... 954-486-7728. 118 E
FACKLER, Pete .... 814-393-2240. 428 C
pfackler@clarion.edu
FACKRELL, Brady, R .... 307-674-6446. 543 F
bfackrell@sheridan.edu
FACULO-GOGUE, Elaine . 671-735-2244. 546 E
efgogue@uguam.uog.edu
FADARIO, Adesina .... 718-270-6131. 319 A
sfadairo@mec.cuny.edu
FADDEN, R. Patricia .... 610-647-4400. 418 I
pfadden@immaculata.edu
FADENRECHT, Kirby .... 620-947-3121. 190 J
kirbyf@tabor.edu
FADOK, David, S .... 334-953-2044. 544 D
FADROWSKI, William, P 414-277-7210. 534 G
fadrowski@msoe.edu
FAEHNER, David, A .... 269-471-3122. 239 D
dfaehner@andrews.edu
FAEHNER, Frances, M .... 269-471-6686. 239 D
frances@andrews.edu
FAERMAN, Larry .... 561-297-3730. 114 L
lfaerman@fau.edu
FAERMAN, Sue, S .... 518-442-3950. 341 D
sfaerman@albany.edu
FAFFLER, Ken, K .... 651-631-5209. 263 A
kkfaffler@nwc.edu
FAGA, Kelly .... 641-648-4611. 179 I
kelly.faga@iavalley.edu
FAGAN, Charling .... 914-395-2471. 340 E
sha@slc.edu
FAGAN, Janice .... 401-232-6348. 438 K
jfagan@bryant.edu
FAGAN, Sue .... 352-365-3545. 108 S
fagans@lssc.edu
FAGAN, Thomas, W .... 580-774-3037. 400 B
tom.fagan@swosu.edu
FAGBEYIRO, Gabriel .... 318-670-9490. 207 A
gfagbeyiro@susla.edu
FAGELLA-D'ALOSIO,
Marguerite .... 631-420-2480. 346 B
marguerite.fagella@farmingdale.edu
FAGEN, Jeffrey, W .... 718-990-6068. 339 A
fagenj@stjohns.edu
FAGEN, Rich, E .... 626-395-2908... 31 E
rich@caltech.edu
FAGENSTROM, Linda ..... 406-791-5223. 288 E
lfagenstrom01@ugf.edu
FAGER, Karl, E .... 507-344-7451. 253 J
karlfager@blc.edu
FAGILLO, Jessica .... 559-730-3700... 40 I
jessicaf@cos.edu
FAGIN, Abbey .... 202-885-3411... 94 F
aes@american.edu
FAGLER, Mitchell .... 478-289-2272. 132 A
mfagler@southeasterntech.edu
FAHEY, Jack .... 330-941-1939. 394 A
jpfahey@ysu.edu
FAHEY, Scott .... 212-678-4194. 347 G
fahey@tc.edu
FAHEY, Sean .... 410-516-4107. 215 H
sfahey2@jhu.edu
FAHEY, William, E .... 603-880-8308. 298 A
tmc@thomasmorecollege.edu
FAHNESTOCK, Bethene .. 918-540-6202. 396 G
bfahnestock@neo.edu
FAHNESTOCK, Brian .... 805-652-5536... 74 E
bfahnestock@vcccd.edu
FAHNESTOCK, Carol .... 570-674-6216. 424 A
cfahnest@misericordia.edu
FAHRENWALD, Jeffrey ... 815-394-5026. 157 C
jfahrenwald@rockford.edu
FAHY, Greg .... 207-621-3255. 212 C
gregory.fahy@maine.edu
FAILING, Fred .... 800-962-7682. 285 A
ffailing@wma.edu
FAIN, James .... 508-999-8586. 229 A
jfain@umassd.edu
FAIN, Juanita .... 702-895-4387. 294 I
juanita.fain@unlv.edu
FAIN, Starr .... 334-387-3877..... 1 E
starrfain@amridgeuniversity.edu
FAIR, George, W .... 972-883-2350. 491 E
gwfair@utdallas.edu
FAIR, Kathy .... 903-983-8236. 475 E
kfair@kilgore.edu
FAIR, Kevin .... 312-996-7084. 161 D
kevinf@uillinois.edu
FAIR, Steve .... 205-391-2384..... 6 H
sfair@sheltonstate.edu
FAIR-SZOFRAN, Nancy .. 509-434-5060. 518 D
nancy.fair-szofran@ccs.spokane.edu
FAIR-SZOFRAN, Nancy .. 509-434-5060. 518 E
nancy.szofran@ccs.spokane.edu
FAIRBAIRN, Tina .... 650-543-3937... 54 C
tfairbairn@menlo.edu
FAIRBANKS, Anthony ...... 937-376-6373. 376 E
afairbanks@centralstate.edu
FAIRBANKS, Kenneth, E . 276-223-4868. 514 F
kfairbanks@wcc.vccs.edu
FAIRBANKS, Warren .... 508-626-4590. 230 A
wfairbanks@framingham.edu
FAIRCHILD, Diana .... 208-426-1664. 137 G
dfairchild@boisestate.edu
FAIRCHILD, Joseph .... 757-822-7207. 514 C
jfairchild@tcc.edu
FAIRCHILD, Patty .... 715-422-5535. 540 D
patty.fairchild@mstc.edu
FAIRCHILD, Thomas .... 817-735-5497. 490 E
Thomas.Fairchild@unthsc.edu
FAIRCHILDS, Angela, R .. 530-661-5711... 77 L
afairchi@yccd.edu
FAIRCLOTH, David .... 912-344-2685. 120 G
david.faircloth@armstrong.edu
FAIRFAX, Kathleen .... 605-688-4156. 452 B
kathleen.fairfax@sdstate.edu
FAIRFIELD-SONN,
James, W .... 860-768-4243... 92 D
fairfield@hartford.edu
FAIRLESS, Michael, J ..... 330-471-8100. 383 D
mfairless@malone.edu
FAIRLEY, Charlestine ...... 410-897-1244. 218 D
cfairley@host.sdc.edu
FAIRMAN, Jerilyn .... 315-786-2379. 327 L
jfairman@sunyjefferson.edu
FAIROW, Greg .... 503-493-6587. 402 J
gfairow@cu-portland.edu
FAISON, Brian .... 701-777-2234. 371 C
brian.faison@und.edu
FAISON, Debbie .... 206-878-3710. 520 E
dfaison@highline.edu
FAISON, Frederick .... 484-365-8075. 422 D
ffaison@lincoln.edu
FAITH, Helen .... 541-463-5266. 403 I
faithh@lanecc.edu
FAITHFUL, Mark .... 252-335-0821. 359 F
mark_faithful@albemarle.edu
FAIX, Peter, K .... 412-397-6271. 431 I
faix@rmu.edu
FAJACK, Deidra .... 859-572-5489. 198 I
fajackd@nku.edu
FAJACK, Matthew .... 352-392-2402. 116 A
mfajack@ufl.edu
FAJARDO, Arlene .... 650-574-6576... 64 C
fajardoa@smccd.edu
FAKHRI RAVARI, Saeed 949-480-4230... 66 F
sfakhriravari@soka.edu
FALA, Gregory .... 215-951-1907. 420 B
fala@lasalle.edu
FALARDEAU, George .... 626-396-2201... 28 P
george.falardeau@artcenter.edu
FALASTER, Marilyn .... 618-985-3741. 148 J
marilynfalaster@jalc.edu
FALBO, Mary Anna .... 716-896-0700. 350 A
falbo@villa.edu
FALCK-YI, Suzanne .... 641-585-8225. 183 D
falckyis@waldorf.edu
FALCO, James .... 815-479-7728. 152 F
jfalco@mchenry.edu
FALCO, Kathleen, P .... 207-778-7280. 212 D
kathleen.falco@maine.edu
FALCON, Kim .... 918-495-6928. 398 H
kfalcon@oru.edu
FALCON, Luis .... 978-934-4000. 229 B
Luis_Falcon@uml.edu
FALCON-CHANDLER,
Carole .... 406-353-2607. 285 E
cfalconchan@hotmail.com
FALCONE, Alice, A .... 978-867-4208. 226 H
alice.falcone@gordon.edu
FALCONETTI, Angela, M . 540-857-6020. 514 E
afalconetti@virginiawestern.edu
FALCONI, Stefano .... 617-521-2877. 236 G
stefano.falconi@simmons.edu
FALDER, Mike .... 765-998-5538. 173 C
mcfalder@taylor.edu
FALDUTO, Ellen .... 330-263-2230. 377 H
efalduto@wooster.edu
FALE, Robert, A .... 920-923-7617. 534 A
rfale@marianuniversity.edu
FALE, Tauvela .... 684-699-9155. 546 A
t.fale@amsamoa.edu
FALER, Kurt .... 630-889-6463. 154 E
kfaler@nuhs.edu
FALERO-SOTO, Mercy ..... 787-480-2480. 548 G
mfalero@sanjuancapital.com
FALES, Michael, F .... 269-749-7624. 249 A
mfales@olivetcollege.edu
FALESE, Joseph, T .... 815-836-5275. 150 H
falesejo@lewisu.edu
FALGOUT, Katherine .... 985-380-2483. 203 H
katherinefalgout@scl.edu
FALK, Adam, F .... 413-597-4233. 238 D
adam.f.falk@williams.edu
FALK, Dan .... 620-229-6267. 190 G
dan.falk@sckans.edu
FALK, Israel .... 845-356-7065. 351 D
FALK, Joyce .... 619-849-2534... 59 L
joycefalk@pointloma.edu
FALK, Keith, L .... 920-923-8594. 534 A
kfalk@marianuniversity.edu
FALK, Randy .... 541-917-4999. 404 B
falkr@linnbenton.edu
FALK, Richard, S .... 848-932-7896. 306 B
sasexecdean@sas.rutgers.edu
FALK, Stephanie, A .... 717-867-6696. 421 H
falk@lvc.edu

FALKE, Steve, J .... 814-863-0205. 426 A
sfalke@bncollege.com
FALKENBERG, Janice ..... 414-297-8718. 540 E
falkenjm@matc.edu
FALKENRATH, Rex .... 801-832-2588. 498 F
rfalkenrath@westminstercollege.edu
FALKENSTIEN, Sarah, N . 909-748-8044... 73 H
sarah_falkenstien@redlands.edu
FALKIEWICZ, Linda, K ... 313-577-3550. 252 G
lfalkiewicz@wayne.edu
FALKNER, Jeff .... 641-784-5341. 178 F
falkner@graceland.edu
FALKS, Delisa, F .... 979-458-5311. 483 C
delisa@tamu.edu
FALL, Diane .... 309-796-4840. 140 E
falld@bhc.edu
FALL, Stephany .... 850-599-3203. 114 K
stephany.fall@famu.edu
FALLACARO, Anthony ..... 603-645-9604. 297 I
a.fallacaro@snhu.edu
FALLERT, Danelle .... 323-265-8797... 51 F
fallerdj@elac.edu
FALLIN, Terri .... 417-667-8181. 273 A
tfallin@cottey.edu
FALLING, Cary .... 405-425-5290. 397 D
cary.falling@oc.edu
FALLING, Sali, K .... 765-285-5162. 164 B
sfalling@bsu.edu
FALLIS, Sue .... 925-631-4856... 61 F
sfallis@stmarys-ca.edu
FALLO, Thomas, M .... 310-660-3111... 43 B
tfallo@elcamino.edu
FALLON, Greg .... 973-684-5895. 304 B
gfallon@pccc.edu
FALLON, III, John, A ..... 765-289-1241. 164 B
jafallon@bsu.edu
FALLON, Melissa, A .... 607-436-3368. 343 E
fallonma@oneonta.edu
FALLON, Patricia, C .... 617-521-2018. 236 G
patricia.fallon@simmons.edu
FALLON, Thomas .... 978-556-3866. 232 E
tfallon@necc.mass.edu
FALLONE, Deborah, A .... 914-323-5224. 330 B
deborah.fallone@mville.edu
FALLOWS, John .... 215-335-0800. 422 C
jfallows@lincolntech.com
FALLS, Meda .... 731-925-5722. 460 G
mfalls@jscc.edu
FALLS, Mike .... 704-669-4147. 359 D
fallsm@clevelandcc.edu
FALLS, Sarah .... 212-472-1500. 334 B
sfalls@nysid.edu
FALOTICO, Michael .... 312-777-7735... 28 M
mfalotico@argosy.edu
FALSO, Frank .... 570-422-3333. 428 D
ffalso@esufoundation.org
FALTER, Ben .... 386-822-7201. 117 C
bfalter@stetson.edu
FALTYN, Timothy, W ...... 918-463-2931. 395 D
FALWELL, JR., Jerry ...... 434-582-2957. 506 I
jlfjr@liberty.edu
FALWELL, Jonathan .... 434-582-2000. 506 I
jonfalwell@liberty.edu
FALWELL, Tyler .... 434-592-3095. 506 I
twfalwell2@liberty.edu
FALZERANO,
Christine, E .... 203-576-4566... 91 G
cfalzera@bridgeport.edu
FALZONE, Kris .... 219-989-2217. 171 N
Kris.falzone@purduecal.edu
FAMA, Melissa .... 978-632-6600. 232 C
m_fama@mwcc.mass.edu
FAMBLE, JR., Freddie .... 325-793-4906. 476 E
ffamble@mcm.edu
FAMULA, Michelle, S ..... 530-752-2333... 70 J
msfamula@ucdavis.edu
FAMULARE,
Dominick, F .... 518-388-6532. 348 J
famularn@union.edu
FAMULARE, Marybeth .... 717-264-4141. 437 H
marybeth.famulare@wilson.edu
FAN, C. Cindy .... 310-825-4921... 71 C
cfan@international.ucla.edu
FAN, Lori .... 309-677-2245. 140 I
llw@bradley.edu
FANCHER, Karen, J .... 503-255-0332. 404 F
kfancher@multnomah.edu
FANDOZZI, Melissa .... 518-828-4181. 321 C
melissa.fandozzi@sunycgcc.edu
FANEK, Sami .... 727-725-2688. 102 I
sfanek@cci.edu
FANELLI, Sean, A .... 516-463-5740. 326 D
sean.fanelli@hofstra.edu
FANEUFF, Ken .... 706-379-5202. 134 L
kfaneuff@yhc.edu
FANFANX, Lerick .... 617-745-3869. 225 G
lerick.fanfanx@enc.edu
FANG, John .... 310-453-8300... 43 D
john@emperors.edu
FANGMEYER, Len, J ...... 308-865-8555. 292 H
fangmeyerlj@unk.edu

FANNAN, Lisa, L .... 816-604-2314. 277 F
lisa.fannan@mcckc.edu
FANNER, Sjohonton .... 940-552-6291. 493 F
sfanner@vernoncollege.edu
FANNIN, Larry .... 801-878-1053. 295 E
lfannin@roseman.edu
FANNIN, William, R .... 432-552-2110. 493 D
fannin_w@utpb.edu
FANNING, Vivian .... 276-223-4777. 514 F
vfanning@wcc.vccs.edu
FANSHAW, Charles .... 202-685-3929. 544 K
fanshawc@ndu.edu
FANSLAU, Michelle .... 239-489-9478. 101 O
mfanslau@edison.edu
FANSLER, A. Gigi .... 217-732-3155. 151 C
gfansler@lincolncollege.edu
FANT, Charlotte .... 662-915-5059. 270 B
cfant@olemiss.edu
FANT, Gene .... 731-661-5520. 462 F
gfant@uu.edu
FANT, Greg .... 575-646-2127. 310 I
gfant@nmsu.edu
FANT, Gregory .... 575-646-1727. 310 I
provost@nmsu.edu
FANTE, Cheryl .... 352-854-2322. 100 K
fantec@cf.edu
FANTER, Jeff .... 317-921-4502. 169 K
jfanter@ivytech.edu
FANTINI, Beatriz .... 802-258-3343. 500 C
beatriz.fantini@worldlearning.org
FANTOZZI, Joseph .... 212-650-7865. 317 D
jfantozzi@ccny.cuny.edu
FANUTTI, Carol .... 716-827-2662. 348 G
fanuttic@trocaire.edu
FAOUR, Sheila .... 318-675-5000. 205 D
sfaour@lsuhsc.edu
FAOUR, William, G .... 423-624-0077. 453 G
billf@chattanoogacollege.edu
FARACH-CARSON,
Cindy .... 713-348-5052. 479 A
farachca@rice.edu
FARAHANI, Gohar .... 301-846-2451. 214 H
gfarahani@frederick.edu
FARAHI, Dawood .... 908-737-7000. 302 F
dfarahi@kean.edu
FARAKISH, Negar .... 908-412-3590. 308 B
negar.farakish@ucc.edu
FARAN, Ellen, W .... 617-253-4078. 233 B
FARANDA, John, P .... 909-621-8153... 39 D
john.faranda@cmc.edu
FARARA, Joseph .... 802-635-1272. 501 D
joe.farara@jsc.edu
FARBANIEC, David .... 845-257-3196. 342 B
farbanid@newpaltz.edu
FARE, Bridget, M .... 412-396-6052. 415 F
fareb@duq.edu
FARES, Ted .... 575-562-2511. 309 H
ted.fares@enmu.edu
FARFAN, Erika, M .... 740-427-5571. 382 J
farfane@kenyon.edu
FARHA, Darron, C .... 219-464-6702. 174 E
darron.farha@valpo.edu
FARHANG, Ahad .... 718-951-5669. 317 C
afarhang@brooklyn.cuny.edu
FARIA, Cindy .... 850-474-2116. 117 B
cfaria@uwf.edu
FARIA, Geraldine .... 718-951-5214. 317 C
gfaria@brooklyn.cuny.edu
FARIA, Pamela .... 617-243-2221. 227 K
pfaria@lasell.edu
FARIAS, Antonio .... 860-701-6702. 545 G
antonio.farias@uscg.edu
FARIAS, Frank .... 520-621-6688... 18 F
ffarias@email.arizona.edu
FARIAS, Jaime, D .... 915-831-2394. 472 B
jfarias@epcc.edu
FARIAS, Richard .... 210-486-0130. 465 C
rfarias14@alamo.edu
FARIDIAN, Fred .... 909-884-8891... 41 G
ffaridian@concorde.edu
FARINELLA, Nicole .... 312-935-6689. 156 K
nfarinella@robertmorris.edu
FARINHOLT, Phil .... 910-362-7014. 358 F
pfarinholt@cfcc.edu
FARINOS, Jose, L .... 772-462-7611. 106 P
jfarinos@irsc.edu
FARISH, Donald, J .... 401-254-3201. 440 B
dfarish@rwu.edu
FARISH, Guy, E .... 440-826-2478. 374 F
gfarish@bw.edu
FARKAS, Abraham .... 707-524-1508... 65 B
afarkas@santarosa.edu
FARKAS, Scott, M .... 937-382-6661. 393 B
scott_farkas@wilmington.edu
FARLAND, William, H .... 970-491-7194... 80 I
william.farland@colostate.edu
FARLESS, John, A .... 812-228-5157. 174 D
jafarless@usi.edu
FARLEY, Barbara, A .... 217-245-3001. 146 F
barbara.farley@ic.edu

FARLEY, Christy .... 928-523-0185... 16 C
christy.farley@nau.edu
FARLEY, Erik, S .... 745-587-6605. 379 D
farleye@denison.edu
FARLEY, Jean .... 617-296-8300. 227 I
jean_farley@laboure.edu
FARLEY, Jeff, A .... 724-480-3366. 413 H
jeff.farley@ccbc.edu
FARLEY, Jerry, B .... 785-670-1556. 191 D
jerry.farley@washburn.edu
FARLEY, John .... 301-405-3205. 219 B
jfarley@umd.edu
FARLEY, Karen .... 563-336-3323. 177 L
kfarley@eicc.edu
FARLEY, Katherine .... 863-680-4735. 105 D
kfarley@flsouthern.edu
FARLEY, Kay .... 785-670-1049. 191 D
kay.farley@washburn.edu
FARLEY, Kenneth .... 626-395-6005... 31 E
farley@gps.caltech.edu
FARLEY, Kevin .... 800-962-7682. 285 A
kfarley@wma.edu
FARLEY, Lee .... 559-442-8231... 68 I
lee.farley@fresnocitycollege.edu
FARLEY, Michael .... 704-971-8500. 353 F
FARLEY, Patrick .... 301-891-4551. 221 B
pfarley@wau.edu
FARLEY, Penelope, L ...... 410-778-7224. 221 C
pfarley2@washcoll.edu
FARLEY, Susan .... 425-602-3354. 516 K
sfarley@bastyr.edu
FARLEY, Thomas, R .... 757-455-3263. 515 H
tfarley@vwc.edu
FARLEY, Tim .... 925-631-4830... 61 F
tif5@stmarys-ca.edu
FARLEY, Troy .... 616-331-3311. 243 C
farleytr@gvsu.edu
FARMER, Anne .... 708-209-3237. 143 E
anne.farmer@cuchicago.edu
FARMER, Bradley .... 614-287-2787. 378 B
bfarmer@cscc.edu
FARMER, Carla .... 417-667-8181. 273 A
cfarmer@cottey.edu
FARMER, David .... 910-695-3911. 363 F
farmerdj@sandhills.edu
FARMER, Jeff .... 423-493-4288. 462 B
farmerj@tntemple.edu
FARMER, Jennifer .... 713-646-1804. 480 J
jfarmer@stcl.edu
FARMER, John, J .... 848-932-7697. 306 A
jfarmer@oldqueens.rutgers.edu
FARMER, Joyce .... 610-282-1100. 414 F
joyce.farmer@desales.edu
FARMER, Karla .... 620-223-2700. 186 G
karlaf@fortscott.edu
FARMER, Larry, G .... 704-637-4227. 353 E
lfarmer@catawba.edu
FARMER, Linda .... 541-684-4644. 407 B
lfarmer@pioneerpacific.edu
FARMER, Lindsey .... 910-695-3726. 363 F
farmerl@sandhills.edu
FARMER, Lorna .... 908-852-1400. 300 D
farmer@centenarycollege.edu
FARMER, Megan Daly .... 202-319-6927... 94 G
farmer@cua.edu
FARMER, Pam .... 864-977-7009. 445 H
pam.farmer@ngu.edu
FARMER, Patricia .... 603-358-2370. 298 F
pfarmer@keene.edu
FARMER, Patricia J, B .... 315-229-5265. 339 F
pfarmer@stlawu.edu
FARMER, Richard .... 617-578-7100. 236 E
rfarmer@sbboston.com
FARMER, Scott .... 337-482-5393. 208 D
sfarmer@louisiana.edu
FARMER, Shakila, M ...... 713-221-8977. 489 D
farmers@uhd.edu
FARMER, Stephen, M ..... 919-966-3992. 368 D
smfarmer@email.unc.edu
FARMER, Steve .... 601-968-5929. 266 A
sfarmer@belhaven.edu
FARMER, Steve .... 419-227-3141. 391 F
wfarmer@unoh.edu
FARMER, Vickie, L .... 319-895-4243. 177 A
vfarmer@cornellcollege.edu
FARMER-DIXON,
Cherae .... 615-327-6207. 456 E
cdixon@mmc.edu
FARMER-KAISER, Mary .. 337-482-6965. 208 D
FARMER-NEAL,
Rochonda .... 254-710-1453. 467 G
rochonda_farmer-neal@baylor.edu
FARMER NOONAN, Erin 617-735-9991. 226 B
farmer@emmanuel.edu
FARNESKI, Anna .... 201-684-6844. 305 A
afarnesk@ramapo.edu
FARNHAM, Bruce .... 619-660-4347... 46 D
bruce.farnham@gcccd.edu
FARNHAM, Margaret, L .. 614-235-4136. 390 A
mfarnham@TLSohio.edu

FARNSWORTH, Briant, J 801-863-8006. 497 C
briant.farnsworth@uvu.edu
FARNSWORTH, Kent, A .. 417-455-5534. 273 E
KentFarnsworth@crowder.edu
FARNSWORTH, Scott ..... 928-776-2234... 19 H
scott.farnsworth@yc.edu
FARNSWORTH, Ward ..... 512-232-1322. 491 C
deansoffice@law.utexas.edu
FARO, Michael, E .... 585-594-6130. 337 K
farom@roberts.edu
FAROL, Dorothy .... 714-997-6611... 38 A
farol@chapman.edu
FARQUHARSON,
Janice, E .... 309-624-8980. 158 C
janice.farquharson@osfhealthcare.org
FARR, Betty .... 603-428-2480. 297 D
bfarr@nec.edu
FARR, C. Stephen .... 478-757-3700. 134 G
sfarr@wesleyancollege.edu
FARR, Lamar .... 215-953-5999... 96 F
lamar.farr@strayer.edu
FARR, Matthew .... 609-894-9311. 299 I
mfarr@bcc.edu
FARR, Pamela .... 912-287-5842. 130 B
pfarr@okefenokeetech.edu
FARR, Ralph, E .... 409-747-3810. 493 C
rfarr@utmb.edu
FARR, Sharon .... 573-288-6633. 273 F
sfarr@culver.edu
FARRA, Taline .... 617-587-5624. 234 H
farrat@neco.edu
FARRAND, Michael .... 423-775-6596. 458 A
mfarrand@ogs.edu
FARRAR, Carol .... 951-372-7017... 60 L
carol.farrar@norcocollege.edu
FARRAR, Gina, R .... 805-437-8400... 32 I
FARRAR, James, D .... 540-458-8465. 516 A
jdfarrar@wlu.edu
FARRAR, Jazaer .... 708-596-2000. 159 C
jfouad-farrar@ssc.edu
FARRAR, Margaret, E ..... 309-794-7313. 139 L
margaretfarrar@augustana.edu
FARRELL, Amy, E .... 717-245-1869. 414 H
farrell@dickinson.edu
FARRELL, Christina .... 610-558-5638. 424 I
farrellc@neumann.edu
FARRELL, Cynthia, H ...... 724-589-2178. 434 B
cfarrell@thiel.edu
FARRELL, Erin .... 859-985-3050. 192 F
farrelle@berea.edu
FARRELL, Gina .... 210-436-3517. 479 D
gfarrell@stmarytx.edu
FARRELL, Howard, M ..... 940-397-4782. 476 H
howard.farrell@mwsu.edu
FARRELL, Jack .... 315-279-5434. 328 D
jferrell@mail.keuka.edu
FARRELL, Jack .... 315-279-5405. 328 D
jfarrell@mail.keuka.edu
FARRELL, James .... 313-577-2017. 252 G
JimFarrell@wayne.edu
FARRELL, OSA,
Joseph, L .... 610-519-3546. 436 F
joseph.l.farrell@villanova.edu
FARRELL, Kathleen .... 914-251-6090. 344 D
kathleen.farrell@purchase.edu
FARRELL, Lauren, M ...... 724-925-4079. 437 D
farrelll@wccc.edu
FARRELL, Lisa, M .... 636-584-6558. 273 M
lmfarrell@eastcentral.edu
FARRELL, Maggie .... 307-766-3224. 543 I
farrell@uwyo.edu
FARRELL, Mark .... 412-392-3879. 431 B
mfarrell@pointpark.edu
FARRELL, Martin, F .... 610-660-1225. 432 E
mfarrell@sju.edu
FARRELL, Mary Ellen ...... 973 275-2293. 307 C
maryellen.farrell@shu.edu
FARRELL, Michael .... 716-851-1685. 323 I
farrell@ecc.edu
FARRELL, Nancy .... 413-265-2389. 225 C
farrelln@elms.edu
FARRELL, Pat .... 410-225-2367. 216 C
pfarrell@mica.edu
FARRELL, Patrick, V .... 610-758-3605. 422 A
pvf209@lehigh.edu
FARRELL, II, R. Joel ...... 202-685-2906. 544 K
robert.farrellll@ndu.edu
FARRELL, Robert, B .... 570-941-6213. 436 A
robert.farrell@scranton.edu
FARRELL, Ruth, A .... 802-656-3360. 500 F
ruth.farrell@uvm.edu
FARRELL, Terry .... 412-809-5100. 430 H
farrell.terry@pti.edu
FARRELL, Thomas .... 402-472-5242. 292 G
tfarrell@nebraska.edu
FARRELL, Thomas, J ...... 217-333-6293. 161 C
farrellt@uif.uillinois.edu
FARRELLY, Nanyamka .... 340-693-1058. 555 E
nfarrel@live.uvi.edu
FARRETTA, Annmarie ...... 617-928-4681. 234 E
afarretta@mountida.edu

FARRIN, Suzanne 914-251-6707. 344 D suzanne.farrin@purchase.edu
FARRINGTON, Anita 718-260-3773. 336 E afarring@poly.edu
FARRINGTON, David 541-440-4600. 408 D david.farrington@umpqua.edu
FARRINGTON, Edward 203-837-9013... 88 B farringtone@wcsu.edu
FARRIOR, Andy 361-582-2547. 493 H andy.farrior@victoriacollege.edu
FARRIOR, Carolyn, P 321-674-7118. 104 H cfarrior@fit.edu
FARRIS, Barry, N 501-882-8842... 19 M bnfarris@asub.edu
FARRIS, Edward, E 919-735-5151. 364 H edfarris@waynecc.edu
FARRIS, G. Corey 304-293-4491. 530 D corey.farris@mail.wvu.edu
FARRIS, Gary 425-564-3999. 517 A gary.farris@bellevuecollege.edu
FARRIS, Jeffery 662-846-4660. 266 G jfarris@deltastate.edu
FARRIS, Joe, R 662-325-3221. 268 D joe.farris@pres.msstate.edu
FARRIS, Lynn, L 406-756-2882. 286 B lfarris@fvcc.edu
FARRIS, Michael, C 434-947-8128. 508 D mfarris@randolphcollege.edu
FARRIS, Michael, P 540-338-1776. 508 A chancellor@phc.edu
FARRIS, Michael, W 512-245-2319. 487 C mf03@txstate.edu
FARRIS, Rachel 251-981-3771..... 2 I rachel.farris@columbiasouthern.edu
FARRIS, Robert 207-255-1315. 212 F robert.farris@maine.edu
FARRIS, Thomas, N 848-445-2214. 306 B tfarris@rutgers.edu
FARRIS, Tim 440-449-4471. 392 D tfarris@ursuline.edu
FARRON, Christie 510-780-4500... 50 I cfarron@lifewest.edu
FARROW, Al 314-367-8700. 281 C alvin.farrow@stlcop.edu
FARSACI, Daniel, P 585-785-1286. 324 D farsacdp@flcc.edu
FARVARDIN, Nariman 201-216-5213. 307 E president@stevens.edu
FARVER, Bill 503-491-7279. 404 E bill.farver@mhcc.edu
FARYNIAK, Karen, N 717-245-1323. 414 H faryniak@dickinson.edu
FARYNK, Linda, J 989-964-4236. 249 G lfarynk@svsu.edu
FASBINDER, Lori 714-628-5971... 60 H fasbinder_lori@sccollege.edu
FASHINPAUR, Diane, J 330-972-6577. 390 E djfl@uakron.edu
FASHOUER, Martha 518-489-7436. 330 C mfashouer@mariacollege.edu
FASO, Helen 304-243-2321. 531 H hmfaso@wju.edu
FASS, Richard, A 909-621-8507... 60 A richard.fass@pomona.edu
FASSERO, Matt 913-360-7420. 184 H mfassero@benedictine.edu
FASSETT, Linda 410-276-1844. 218 D lfassett@host.sdc.edu
FASSINGER, JoAnne, M 315-386-7951. 345 F fassingerj@canton.edu
FASSINGER, Polly, A 218-299-3549. 255 A fassinge@cord.edu
FASSINGER, Ruth 925-969-3300... 49 B rfassinger@jfku.edu
FAST, Joanne, R 402-449-2809. 289 H jofast@graceu.edu
FAST, Linda 479-575-6513... 23 I lfast@uark.edu
FAST, Marlene 620-947-3121. 190 J marlenef@tabor.edu
FASTNOW, Chris 406-994-2870. 287 B cfastnow@montana.edu
FATATO, Joel, R 518-629-4525. 326 G j.fatato@hvcc.edu
FATCHERIC, Michelle 774-354-0462. 223 A michelle.fatcheric@becker.edu
FATH, Stephen, J 713-500-5202. 492 E stephen.j.fath@uth.tmc.edu
FATICA, John 419-559-2353. 389 I jfatica@terra.edu
FATIMA, Nasrin 607-777-2365. 341 E nfatima@binghamton.edu
FATTIG, Teri, L 208-732-6501. 138 B tfattig@csi.edu
FATTOR, Stefany 718-817-4356. 324 G fattor@fordham.edu
FATTOUH, Said 713-221-8059. 489 D FattouhS@uhd.edu
FAUBERT, Bob 928-757-0840... 15 L bfaubert@mohave.edu
FAUCETT, Linford, P 302-259-6205... 93 E lfaucett@dtcc.edu
FAUCHER, Ola 785-864-4946. 190 L ofaucher@ku.edu
FAUCHET, Philippe, M 615-322-0720. 463 G philippe.m.fauchet@vanderbilt.edu
FAUCHEUX, Brenda 985-448-7909. 203 B brenda.faucheux@fletcher.edu
FAUGHANAN, Timothy 607-777-2275. 341 E tfaughn@binghamton.edu
FAUGHT, Daniel 406-496-4377. 287 F dfaught@mtech.edu
FAUL, Heidi 651-523-2204. 256 A hfaul01@hamline.edu
FAULCON, Gaddis 919-546-8373. 366 E gfaulcon@shawu.edu
FAULDS, Regina 203-596-4528... 90 I rfaulds@post.edu
FAULHABER, Gregory, M 716-652-8900. 316 G gfaulhaber@cks.edu
FAULK, Daniel 724-503-1001. 436 G dfaulk@washjeff.edu
FAULK, Jessica 617-521-1101. 236 G jessica.faulk@simmons.edu
FAULK, Ron, H 405-878-5407. 399 G rhfaulk@stgregorys.edu
FAULK, Sancy 501-205-8799... 20 I sfaulk@cbc.edu
FAULKENBERRY, Ron 843-661-1468. 444 B jfaulkenberry@fmarion.edu
FAULKNER, Audrey 315-279-5339. 328 D afaulkne@mail.keuka.edu
FAULKNER, Belinda 919-497-3207. 356 E bfaulkner@louisburg.edu
FAULKNER, Doug 618-664-6620. 145 G doug.faulkner@greenville.edu
FAULKNER, J. Todd 765-641-4204. 163 L jtfaulkner@anderson.edu
FAULKNER, Jerry 615-230-3501. 461 G jerry.faulkner@volstate.edu
FAULKNER, Jessica 501-205-8800... 20 I jfaulkner@cbc.edu
FAULKNER, Melissa 201-559-3620. 302 A faulknerm@felician.edu
FAULKNER, Ted 540-231-5618. 515 C thfaulkn@vt.edu
FAULKNER, Tony 813-879-6000. 103 B tfaulkner@cci.edu
FAULKNER, William 718-631-6244. 319 D wfaulkner@qcc.cuny.edu
FAUNA, Amari 503-760-3131. 402 B amari@birthingway.edu
FAUOLO-MANILA, Okenaisa 684-699-9155. 546 A o.fauolo@amsamoa.edu
FAUPELL, BrandE 435-797-1810. 497 B brande.faupell@usu.edu
FAUROT-CROWLEY, Sara 609-652-4469. 305 C sara.faurot@stockton.edu
FAUST, Anthony 402-844-7282. 291 I anthonyf@northeast.edu
FAUST, David, M 513-244-8492. 376 J president@ccuniversity.edu
FAUST, Deborah 906-635-2678. 245 G dfaust@lssu.edu
FAUST, Drew, G 617-495-1502. 227 C drew_faust@harvard.edu
FAUST, Jeffrey 251-809-1581..... 5 A jeffrey.faust@jdcc.edu
FAUST, Jennifer 657-278-4088... 33 E jfaust@fullerton.edu
FAUST, Kimberly, A 803-323-2225. 449 G faustk@winthrop.edu
FAUST, Lucas 414-443-8720. 539 F
FAUST, Margaret 704-637-4394. 353 E mfaust@catawba.edu
FAUST, Scott 218-755-2041. 258 A sfaust@bemidjistate.edu
FAUST, William Bryant 504-568-4829. 205 C wfaust@lsuhsc.edu
FAUSTINO, Tessie 808-675-3717. 135 C faustint@byuh.edu
FAUVER, James, F 304-734-6614. 527 O jfauver@bridgemont.edu
FAUX, Maureen 410-617-5817. 216 A mfaux@loyola.edu
FAVARA, JR., Leonard 620-241-0723. 185 K lenny.favara@centralchristian.edu
FAVATA, Joanne 845-398-4284. 340 A jfavata@stac.edu
FAVAZZA, Joseph 508-565-1311. 237 A jfavazza@stonehill.edu
FAVAZZA, Joseph 508-565-1650. 237 A jfavazza@stonehill.edu
FAVELA, Andres 760-750-4105... 35 A afavela@csusm.edu
FAVELA, Elena 218-285-2202. 260 G elena.favela@rainyriver.edu
FAVOLISE, Jeff, E 336-316-2845. 355 A favolisej@guilford.edu
FAVORITO, Barbara 951-785-2499... 50 B bfavorit@lasiera.edu
FAVORS, Toney 903-223-3061. 484 C toney.favors@tamut.edu
FAVRE, Beverly, C 504-286-5376. 206 K bfavre@suno.edu
FAVRE, Cynthia, L 507-933-7524. 255 I cfavre@gustavus.edu
FAVRE, Martha 978-665-3216. 229 E mfavre@fitchburgstate.edu
FAVRE, Sherry 618-235-2700. 160 A sherry.favre@swic.edu
FAW, Kim, E 336-838-6293. 365 B kim.faw@wilkescc.edu
FAWBUSH, Jennifer, M 260-399-7700. 174 C jfawbush@sf.edu
FAWBUSH, Shanon, L 260-982-5029. 170 U fawbush@manchester.edu
FAWCETT, Jeffrey, K 574-372-5100. 166 B fawcettj@grace.edu
FAWCETT, Patrick 812-941-2454. 168 F patfawce@ius.edu
FAWCETT, Tonya, L 574-372-5100. 166 B fawcettl@grace.edu
FAWTHROP, Lynn 617-732-1621. 226 B fawthropl@emmanuel.edu
FAXON, David 603-668-6660. 297 C
FAXON, Kristine 912-525-5000. 131 B kfaxon@scad.edu
FAY, III, Cornelius, R 301-696-3565. 215 D fay@hood.edu
FAY, Derek, R 208-496-1450. 137 H fayd@byui.edu
FAY, Ron 970-339-6359... 78 C ron.fay@aims.edu
FAY, Ron 619-849-2613... 59 L ronfay@pointloma.edu
FAY-REILLY, Tara 914-674-7762. 330 J tfreilly@mercy.edu
FAYAD, Barbara, H 864-938-3722. 446 D bfayad@presby.edu
FAYAD, Rosalie 718-368-5833. 318 E rfayad@kbcc.cuny.edu
FAYE, Janice, N 203-576-6355... 91 D jfaye@stvincentscollege.edu
FAYLOR, David, L 256-539-0834..... 4 E deaninst@hbc1.edu
FAYNE, Harriet 718-960-8401. 318 A harriet.fayne@lehman.cuny.edu
FAYOYIN, MaryJo 912-358-4329. 131 C fayoyinm@savannahstate.edu
FAYTAK, Shelley 814-838-7673. 416 G sfaytak@fortisinstitute.edu
FAZALARE, Amie, M 304-367-4867. 529 F Amie.Fazalare@fairmontstate.edu
FAZEKAS, Evelyn 315-792-3002. 349 F efazekas@utica.ucsu.edu
FAZIO, James, I 619-201-8978... 67 G jfazio@socalsem.edu
FAZIO, Linda 781-239-2522. 231 G lfazio@massbay.edu
FAZIO, Michael, A 201-761-6102. 306 L mfazio@saintpeters.edu
FAZIO, Patricia 860-486-5634... 92 A patricia.fazio@uconn.edu
FAZIOLI, Mark 860-727-6788... 90 A mfazioli@goodwin.edu
FAZZANO, Adriana 954-201-7518... 99 D afazzano@broward.edu
FAZZOLARE, Lorraine 707-524-1635... 65 B lfazzolare@santarosa.edu
FEAGIN, Susan, K 212-851-7999. 321 D skf17@columbia.edu
FEAN, Judith 574-284-5391. 172 G jfean@saintmarys.edu
FEAR, Kevin, G 724-653-2222. 415 A kfear@dec.edu
FEARN, Odell 865-882-4679. 461 E fearnao@roanestate.edu
FEARS, Lisa 317-738-8026. 165 I lfears@franklincollege.edu
FEASEL, Edward, M 949-480-4133... 66 F feasel@soka.edu
FEATHERSON, Vincent 314-644-9311. 281 E vfeatherson@stlcc.edu
FEATHERSTON, Guy 972-937-7612. 477 G guy.featherston@navarrocollege.edu
FEATHERSTONE, John 415-476-1323... 72 A jdbf@ucsf.edu
FEATHERSTONE, William 850-599-2978. 114 K william.featherstone@famu.edu
FEATHERSTONE-HANES, Robin 919-530-7934. 368 A rhanes@nccu.edu
FEATNER, Marlana 740-264-5591. 379 F mfeatner@egcc.edu
FEAVER, John, H 405-224-3140. 401 E jfeaver@usao.edu
FECKER, Peggy, A 715-394-8365. 538 C pfecker@uwsuper.edu
FEDDEMA, Lana, L 320-308-1595. 261 C lfeddema@sctcc.edu
FEDELE, Jennifer 412-392-3876. 431 B jfedele@pointpark.edu
FEDER, Mary 631-451-4256. 346 E federm@sunysuffolk.edu
FEDER-KANE, Abigail 212-854-1894. 314 G afederka@barnard.edu
FEDERER, Gina 972-273-3006. 471 B gfederer@dcccd.edu
FEDERLINE, Pamela 910-755-7397. 358 D federlinep@brunswickcc.edu
FEDERMAN, Robin 310-824-1586... 26 B robinfederman@hotmail.com
FEDERMAN, Russell 434-924-5150. 511 B rf5u@virginia.edu
FEDEROFF, Howard, J 202-687-4600... 95 E hjf8@georgetown.edu
FEDEROWICZ, Jane 610-527-0200. 432 B jfederowicz@rosemont.edu
FEDJE, Jay, T 651-638-6242. 253 K j-fedje@bethel.edu
FEDLER, Kyle 863-680-4124. 105 D kfedler@flsouthern.edu
FEDOCK, Laura 612-659-6765. 259 D laura.fedock@minneapolis.edu
FEDORCHAK, David 410-704-3974. 220 E dfedorchak@towson.edu
FEDORCHAK, Lynn 607-778-5319. 315 I fedorchaklm@sunybroome.edu
FEDORKO, Kathleen, C 215-968-8220. 411 B fedorkok@bucks.edu
FEDUCCIA, Mary, D 225-578-2162. 204 O mfeducc@lsu.edu
FEE, Glenn 503-253-3443. 405 E gfee@ocom.edu
FEE, Richard 714-484-7152... 56 E rfee@cypresscollege.edu
FEE, T. Joshua 859-858-3511. 192 B josh.fee@asbury.edu
FEEHERY, Peggy, C 770-720-5548. 130 G prc@reinhardt.edu
FEELER, William 432-685-4626. 476 G bfeeler@midland.edu
FEELEY, Daniel, T 304-243-2383. 531 H feeley@wju.edu
FEELEY, John 970-204-8131... 81 N john.feeley@frontrange.edu
FEENEY, David, F 508-678-2811. 231 B david.feeney@bristolcc.edu
FEENSTRA, Ronald, J 616-957-7193. 240 M feenro@calvinseminary.edu
FEERER, Pam 620-252-7357. 185 O pamf@coffeyville.edu
FEEZOR, Karen 828-328-7392. 356 B karen.feezor@lr.edu
FEGAN, Kevin, G 972-293-5449. 248 C fegan@northwood.edu
FEGELY, Neal, R 610-526-1501. 409 F neal.fegely@theamericancollege.edu
FEHE, Randy 563-425-5286. 183 B fehrr@uiu.edu
FEHLAU, Fred 626-396-2290... 28 P fred.fehlau@artcenter.edu
FEHLBERG, Mark 773-702-3321. 161 B mafehl@uchicago.edu
FEHLER, Tim, G 864-294-3347. 444 C tim.fehler@furman.edu
FEHLMAN, John, C 330-471-8236. 383 D jfehlman@malone.edu
FEHN, Bruce, C 848-932-5661. 306 A fehn@oldqueens.rutgers.edu
FEHN, Heather 609-771-2101. 300 E hfehn@tcnj.edu
FEHNRICH, Jennifer 567-661-7101. 387 L jennifer_fehnrich@owens.edu
FEHOKO, Lisa 808-675-3701. 135 C lisa.fehoko@byuh.edu
FEHRENBACH, Leslie, A 848-932-1352. 306 A fehrenbach@oldqueens.rutgers.edu
FEIBEL, Ann 718-482-5642. 318 F afeibel@lagcc.cuny.edu
FEICHTER, Kathryn 330-966-5452. 389 F kfeichter@starkstate.edu
FEICK, Andrew 610-409-3598. 436 B afeick@ursinus.edu
FEIER, Julie 970-943-2061... 86 I jfeier@western.edu
FEIERSTEIN, Barry 301-502-8639... 18 I barry.feierstein@phoenix.edu
FEIERTAG, Jason 484-664-3140. 424 H feiertag@muhlenberg.edu
FEIGELSTOCK, Yitzchok 516-225-4700. 337 C rcli@mlb.edu
FEIGENBAUM, Maurice 973-684-6036. 304 B mfeigenbaum@pccc.edu
FEIGERT, Kendra, M 717-867-6126. 421 H feigert@lvc.edu

FEIKES, David 219-785-5564. 172 A
dfeikes@pnc.edu
FEIL, Hallie, L 308-635-6126. 293 E
feilh@wncc.edu
FEIL, Kevin, D 717-815-6818. 438 D
kfeil@ycp.edu
FEILDS, Richard, A 404-527-4520. 122 E
rfeilds@carver.edu
FEIN, Cheri 212-217-4700. 324 C
cheri_fein@fitnyc.edu
FEIN, Gene 718-817-3900. 324 G
fein@fordham.edu
FEIN, Jason 973-408-3648. 301 C
jfein@drew.edu
FEIN, Michael, T 434-832-7751. 512 A
feinm@cvcc.vccs.edu
FEINAUER, John 540-261-4091. 509 K
john.feinauer@svu.edu
FEINBERG, David, T 310-267-9315... 71 C
dfeinberg@mednet.ucla.edu
FEINBERG, Debbie 202-639-1860... 95 B
finance@corcoran.org
FEINBERG, Diane 405-974-2661. 400 K
FEINER, Barbara, A 314-935-9842. 284 L
barbara.a.feiner@wustl.edu
FEINERMAN, Frances 413-236-2102. 231 A
ffeinerm@berkshirecc.edu
FEINGOLD, Marilyn 856-374-4932. 300 B
mfeingold@camdencc.edu
FEINMAN, Shannon 434-949-1012. 513 H
shannon.feinman@southside.edu
FEINSTEIN, Andy 408-924-2400... 36 A
andy.feinstein@sjsu.edu
FEINSTEIN, Bruce 818-767-0888... 76 K
bruce.feinstein@woodbury.edu
FEINSTEIN, David 212-964-2830. 331 B
FEINSTEIN, Jerald, L 301-548-5500... 96 F
FEISTHAMEL, Kevin, P 330-569-5952. 380 I
FEITELBERG, Daniel 209-228-4400... 71 D
dfeitelberg@UCMerced.edu
FEITZ, David, A 801-321-7211. 496 P
dfeitz@ushe.edu
FEKARIS, Cynthia 212-594-4000. 347 H
cfekaris@tcicollege.edu
FEKE, Donald, L 216-368-4389. 375 J
dlf4@case.edu
FEKETE, Michael 815-836-5549. 150 H
feketemi@lewisu.edu
FELCH, Katrina 715-675-3331. 541 A
felch@ntc.edu
FELDBLUM, Miriam 909-621-8017... 60 A
miriam.feldblum@pomona.edu
FELDER, Luther 706-821-8295. 130 C
lfelder@paine.edu
FELDER, Nigel 937-376-6566. 376 E
nfelder@centralstate.edu
FELDER-DEAS, Altoya, A 803-934-3167. 445 F
afdeas@morris.edu
FELDHAUS, Joseph, H 513-745-3908. 393 H
feldhausjl@xavier.edu
FELDHUES, Nicole 412-396-5675. 415 F
feldhuesn@duq.edu
FELDHUS, Karima 949-451-5232... 67 B
kfeldhus@ivc.edu
FELDMAN, Aharon 410-484-7200. 217 D
FELDMAN, Andrew 541-917-4741. 404 B
feldmana@linnbenton.edu
FELDMAN, Barbara 201-200-3001. 303 F
bfeldman@njcu.edu
FELDMAN, Dan 781-736-8405. 224 F
feldman@brandeis.edu
FELDMAN, Harriet, R 212-346-1200. 335 J
hfeldman@pace.edu
FELDMAN, Leonard, C 848-445-4524. 306 A
l.c.feldman@rutgers.edu
FELDMAN, Lori 219-989-2388. 171 N
feldman@purduecal.edu
FELDMAN, Mary Jane 716-614-5926. 334 E
feldman@niagaracc.suny.edu
FELDMAN, Rachelle 510-642-7117... 70 I
FELDMAN, Robert, S 413-545-4173. 228 F
feldman@sbs.umass.edu
FELDMAN, Stuart 212-851-1192. 348 B
sfeldman@touro.edu
FELDMANN, Deborah 510-594-3606... 30 K
dfeldmann@cca.edu
FELDMANN, Jacob 718-645-0536. 331 G
FELDMANN,
Raymond, C 410-704-4672. 220 E
rfeldmann@towson.edu
FELDMEIER, Theresa 614-236-6813. 375 H
tfeldmei@capital.edu
FELDNER, Lisa 701-328-2960. 371 B
lisa.feldner@ndus.edu
FELDSCHER, Donald 215-489-4978. 414 E
Donald.Feldscher@delval.edu
FELDSTEIN, Michael 704-216-3910. 363 D
michael.feldstein@rccc.edu
FELDT, Tina 318-869-5424. 201 H
tfeldt@centenary.edu

FELIBERTY, Victor, A 787-284-1912. 550 F
vfeliber@ponce.inter.edu
FELICE, Susan 708-656-8000. 153 H
susan.felice@morton.edu
FELICIANA, Jerrye, B 301-736-3631. 216 B
jerrye.feliciana@msbbcs.edu
FELICIANO, Alberto 787-764-0000. 555 B
alberto.feliciano@upr.edu
FELICIANO, Idali 517-265-5161. 238 G
ifeliciano@adrian.edu
FELICIANO, Javier 602-557-8049... 18 I
Javier.Feliciano@phoenix.edu
FELICIANO, Josean 787-786-3030. 547 F
jfeliciano@ucb.edu.pr
FELICIANO, Orlando 847-317-8072. 160 M
feliciano@tiu.edu
FELICIANO, Patsy 813-974-3827. 116 C
pfelicia@admin.usf.edu
FELICIANO RIOS,
Lynette 787-265-3863. 554 E
aeconomica@uprm.edu
FELIO, John, R 518-783-2471. 340 J
jfelio@siena.edu
FELIU, Julio 787-841-2000. 552 B
jfeliu@pucpr.edu
FELIX, Catherine 559-278-6715... 33 D
cdfelix@csufresno.edu
FELIX-MATA, Bertha 559-934-2217... 75 H
berthafelixmata@whccd.edu
FELIX-RODRIGUEZ,
Tamara 787-620-2040. 547 C
tdrodriguez@aupr.edu
FELKER, Sharon 618-634-3270. 158 M
sharonf@shawneecc.edu
FELKER, Sharon, M 303-963-3369... 79 C
sfelker@ccu.edu
FELKER, Steven 757-825-2716. 514 B
felkers@tncc.edu
FELKNOR, Bruce 312-629-6128. 158 L
bfelknor@saic.edu
FELL, Janet 732-923-4645. 303 C
jfell@monmouth.edu
FELL, Katherine, R 419-434-4510. 391 D
fell@findlay.edu
FELL, Stephanie 918-631-2241. 401 F
stephanie-fell@utulsa.edu
FELLEGY, Anna 218-879-0878. 258 E
afellegy@fdltcc.edu
FELLENBERG, William 201-200-3598. 303 F
wfellenberg@njcu.edu
FELLINGER, Jennifer 360-491-4700. 522 G
jfellinger@stmartin.edu
FELLMAN, Dorrea 207-621-3501. 212 C
dorrea.fellman@maine.edu
FELLMER, Jennine 641-472-1190. 180 N
alumni@mum.edu
FELLOWS, Dawn 801-524-8156. 495 O
DFellows@ldsbc.edu
FELLOWS, Gail 610-436-3333. 430 A
gfellows@wcupa.edu
FELLOWS, Maureen, O 315-470-6621. 345 B
mfellows@esf.edu
FELSER, Francis, J 716-250-7500. 315 J
fjfelser@bryantstratton.edu
FELSKE, Julie, L 989-837-4436. 248 C
felske@northwood.edu
FELSOVALYI, Erzsebet 973-748-9000. 299 F
elizabeth_felsovalyi@bloomfield.edu
FELT, K.C 208-282-3755. 138 E
feltkc@isu.edu
FELT, Suzanne 208-524-3000. 138 D
suzanne.felt@my.eitc.edu
FELTES, Carol 212-327-8909. 338 A
cfeltes@rockvax.rockefeller.edu
FELTMAN, Richard 718-951-5693. 317 C
rfeltman@brooklyn.cuny.edu
FELTMANN, Charles 636-227-2100. 276 F
charles.feltmann@logan.edu
FELTON, David, A 304-293-2521. 530 D
david.felton@hsc.wvu.edu
FELTON, Herman 704-216-6044. 356 D
hfelton@livingstone.edu
FELTON, James 828-227-2276. 369 E
jafelton@wcu.edu
FELTON, Jennifer 712-749-2120. 176 D
feltonj@bvu.edu
FELTON, Judith 860-343-5816... 89 A
jfelton@mxcc.commnet.edu
FELTON, Karen, S 202-994-6040... 95 D
kfelton@gwu.edu
FELTON, Pamela 312-322-1734. 160 D
pfelton@spertus.edu
FELTON, Rob 503-554-2129. 403 C
rfelton@georgefox.edu
FELTON, Shawn 607-255-2000. 322 A
FELTON, Terence 630-466-7900. 162 J
tfelton@waubonsee.edu
FELTS, Bennie, L 919-941-2920. 365 E
bennie.felts@fsmail.pfeiffer.edu
FELTS, Renee 757-569-6760. 513 E
rfelts@pdc.edu

FELTS, Ronald 661-726-1911... 70 G
ron.felts@uav.edu
FELTY, Donna, H 423-652-4752. 455 I
dhfelty@king.edu
FELTZ, Jason 325-793-6550. 476 E
feltz.jason@mcm.edu
FEMINO, Donald 978-232-5201. 226 C
dfemino@endicott.edu
FENCSIK, Alissa 510-204-0727... 38 J
afencsik@cdsp.edu
FENDER, Dan 402-872-2369. 291 E
dfender@peru.edu
FENDER, Donna 276-223-4729. 514 F
dfender@wcc.vccs.edu
FENDERS, Nancy 207-941-7153. 210 B
fendersn@husson.edu
FENDRICH, Chris 719-549-2149... 80 K
chris.fendrich@colostate-pueblo.edu
FENG, Janet 281-649-3748. 473 B
jfeng@hbu.edu
FENG, Tong 617-348-6511. 237 E
tongfeng@urbancollege.edu
FENLASON, Laurie 413-585-2170. 236 H
lfenlaso@smith.edu
FENN, Patricia 732-255-0400. 304 A
pfenn@ocean.edu
FENNELL, Angelia 903-593-8311. 485 A
afennell@texascollege.edu
FENNELL, Barbara 432-686-4250. 476 G
bfennell@midland.edu
FENNELL, Catherine 610-896-1221. 418 F
cfennell@haverford.edu
FENNELL, Catherine 610-527-0200. 432 B
fennell@roesmont.edu
FENNELL, Craig 215-204-1492. 433 K
craig.fennell@temple.edu
FENNELL, Dwight 903-593-8311. 485 A
dfennell@texascollege.edu
FENNELL, Sabrina 716-839-8228. 322 E
sfennell@daemen.edu
FENNELL, Shirley 919-546-8227. 366 E
sfennell@shawu.edu
FENNELL-MCGAY,
Carolyn 803-793-5108. 443 E
mcgayc@denmarktech.edu
FENNERN, Nicole 507-457-1781. 264 A
nfennern@smumn.edu
FENNESSEY, Tom 715-394-8122. 538 C
tfenness@uwsuper.edu
FENNING, Robert, L 757-683-3464. 507 N
rfenning@odu.edu
FENSKE, David, E 215-895-2479. 415 B
def23@drexel.edu
FENSKE, Sue 719-502-2017... 84 A
sue.fenske@ppcc.edu
FENSKE, Susanne 262-691-5295. 541 D
sfenske@wctc.edu
FENSTAD, Terry 413-572-5276. 230 F
tfenstad@westfield.ma.edu
FENTER, Glen, F 870-733-6722... 21 I
gfenter@midsouthcc.edu
FENTON, James, W 419-772-2070. 386 D
j-fenton@onu.edu
FENTON, Karlene 210-486-2000. 465 B
kfenton@alamo.edu
FENTON, Mimi 828-227-7398. 369 E
mfenton@wcu.edu
FENTON, Patrick 408-741-2056... 75 L
pat.fenton@westvalley.edu
FENTON, William, E 502-272-8059. 192 E
wfenton@bellarmine.edu
FENTON-MACE,
Christina 570-945-8162. 419 N
christina.mace@keystone.edu
FENTRESS, Connie 757-789-1728. 512 D
cfentress@es.vccs.edu
FENTRESS, Craig, M 240-500-2000. 215 B
cmfentress@hagerstowncc.edu
FENTRESS, Lisa, I 757-455-3337. 515 H
lfentress@vwc.edu
FENTRESS, Mike 360-752-8320. 517 B
mfentress@btc.ctc.edu
FENTRESS, Viki, P 318-797-5234. 205 F
viki.fentress@lsus.edu
FENVES, Gregory, L 512-471-1166. 491 C
fenves@utexas.edu
FENWICK, Garland 540-423-9046. 512 E
gfenwick@germanna.edu
FENWICK, Jim 818-947-2508... 52 E
fenwicjl@lavc.edu
FENWICK, Leslie, T 202-806-7340... 95 G
lfenwick@howard.edu
FERALDI, Corey 803-641-3280. 448 A
coreyf@usca.edu
FERALDI, Patricia, A 716-673-3553. 342 A
patricia.feraldi@fredonia.edu
FERBER, Maragaret, C 585-389-2020. 332 D
mferber6@naz.edu
FERBER, Moshe 718-601-3523. 351 L
mosheferber1@gmail.com

FERBRACHE, Jeanne 402-559-3937. 292 J
jferbrache@unmc.edu
FERCH, John 907-822-3201... 10 A
jferch@akbible.edu
FERCHLAND-PARELLA,
Joanne 619-594-7299... 35 D
jparella@mail.sdsu.edu
FERDINAND, Amy 973-655-4367. 303 D
ferdinanda@mail.montclair.edu
FERDMAN, Glenn 816-584-6707. 280 C
glenn.ferdman@park.edu
FERDOLAGE, Traci 707-826-4111... 35 C
traci.ferdolage@humboldt.edu
FEREBEE, Ryan, A 757-594-7033. 503 M
ryan.ferebee@cnu.edu
FEREIRA, James, A 864-231-2075. 441 B
jfereira@andersonuniversity.edu
FERGERSON, James 507-222-4292. 254 D
jfergers@carleton.edu
FERGERSON, Nicole 775-831-1314. 295 F
nfergerson@sierranevada.edu
FERGUSON, Angela 205-726-4841..... 6 F
adfergus@samford.edu
FERGUSON, Annette 806-874-3571. 468 J
annette.ferguson@clarendoncollege.edu
FERGUSON, Bennett 678-359-5023. 127 A
benf@gordonstate.edu
FERGUSON, Charity, F 270-384-8100. 197 D
fergusonc@lindsey.edu
FERGUSON, Chris 212-229-5900. 332 E
fergusoc@newschool.edu
FERGUSON, Christy 716-286-8345. 334 F
clf@niagara.edu
FERGUSON, Cristie 903-693-2005. 478 A
cferguson@panola.edu
FERGUSON, Darla 321-433-7080. 101 M
fergusond@easternflorida.edu
FERGUSON, Devin 972-825-4700. 481 F
dferguson@sagu.edu
FERGUSON, Douglas, J 610-359-7399. 414 D
dferguson@dccc.edu
FERGUSON, F. Joel 831-459-2412... 72 C
fjf@ucsc.edu
FERGUSON, Gail 940-397-4273. 476 H
gail.ferguson@mwsu.edu
FERGUSON, Jessame, E 410-857-2741. 216 E
jferguson@mcdaniel.edu
FERGUSON, Joseph, S 361-570-4390. 489 E
fergusonj@uhv.edu
FERGUSON, Judy 281-649-3450. 473 B
jferguson@hbu.edu
FERGUSON, Keith, D 615-353-3604. 461 B
keith.ferguson@nscc.edu
FERGUSON, Kenneth, H 540-636-2900. 503 L
kferguson@christendom.edu
FERGUSON, Kimberly 404-270-5132. 132 E
kfergu15@spelman.edu
FERGUSON, Larry 606-326-2232. 194 J
larry.ferguson@kctcs.edu
FERGUSON, Larry, W 803-323-2216. 449 G
fergusonl@winthrop.edu
FERGUSON, Lee 214-333-5363. 470 D
lee@dbu.edu
FERGUSON, Leonard 605-455-6000. 450 I
lferguson@olc.edu
FERGUSON, Lisa, M 740-283-6450. 379 N
lferguson@franciscan.edu
FERGUSON, Lori 580-349-1566. 397 G
lorif@opsu.edu
FERGUSON, Lorrie 540-863-2823. 512 B
lferguson@dslcc.edu
FERGUSON, Nicole 775-831-1314. 295 F
nferguson@sierranevada.edu
FERGUSON, Noreen 248-204-3106. 245 I
nferguson@ltu.edu
FERGUSON, Pamela 973-720-2615. 308 I
fergusonp4@wpunj.edu
FERGUSON, Paul 912-478-7288. 126 C
pferguson@georgiasouthern.edu
FERGUSON, Paul, W 207-581-1512. 212 B
president@umaine.edu
FERGUSON, Randy, L 262-243-5700. 532 H
randall.ferguson@cuw.edu
FERGUSON, Rebecca, C 419-372-8421. 374 K
fergusb@bgsu.edu
FERGUSON, Richard, T 937-229-5400. 391 C
dferguson1@udayton.edu
FERGUSON, Roberta 304-696-6632. 529 H
fergusor@marshall.edu
FERGUSON, Rose, A 815-599-3402. 146 D
rose.ferguson@highland.edu
FERGUSON, JR.,
Roy, W 540-828-5307. 502 J
rferguso@bridgewater.edu
FERGUSON, Sarah 972-860-4854. 470 G
sferguson@dcccd.edu
FERGUSON, Stephanie 540-887-7039. 507 A
sferguson@mbc.edu
FERGUSON, Stephanie 417-455-5566. 273 E
sferguso@crowder.edu

FERGUSON, Teresa, D ... 864-587-4003. 447 B
fergusont@smcsc.edu
FERGUSON, Theressa ..... 573-681-5128. 276 C
fergusont@lincolnu.edu
FERGUSON, Thomas ...... 614-231-3095. 374 I
thomas.ferguson@bexley.edu
FERGUSON, Tim .... 270-926-4040. 193 M
tferguson@daymarcollege.edu
FERGUSON, Timothy ...... 859-572-7770. 198 I
fergusont2@nku.edu
FERGUSON, Valerie .... 214-333-5113. 470 D
valerie@dbu.edu
FERGUSON, Vicki .... 510-235-7800... 41 K
vferguson@contracosta.edu
FERGUSON, Vicki .... 405-224-3140. 401 E
facfergusonv@usao.edu
FERGUSON, Vincent .... 215-248-4665. 422 F
vferguson@ltsp.edu
FERGUSON, William .... 315-228-7333. 320 F
wferguson@colgate.edu
FERGUSON, William, L .. 864-379-8881. 443 F
ferguson@erskine.edu
FERIS, Greg .... 806-291-3801. 494 F
gferis@wbu.edu
FERKETISH, B. Jean .... 412-624-6623. 435 C
ferkjean+@pitt.edu
FERKINGSTAD, Suzanne 612-375-1900. 256 E
sferkingstad@ipr.edu
FERLAAK MOTES,
Kimberly .... 320-363-5011. 254 J
kmotes@csbsju.edu
FERLAND, William, R ..... 401-825-1210. 439 A
wferland@ccri.edu
FERLEGER, Naomi, A ...... 845-575-3000. 330 D
Naomi.Ferleger@marist.edu
FERLISI, Nicholas .... 631-370-3300. 340 F
nferlisi@sbmelville.edu
FERLO, Roger .... 614-231-3095. 374 I
roger.ferlo@bexleyseabury.edu
FERLO, Roger, A .... 773-380-6782. 140 D
roger.ferlo@bexleyseabury.edu
FERN, Kathleen .... 602-557-1716... 18 I
kathleen.fern@phoenix.edu
FERN, Kathy, T .... 314-286-4895. 280 F
ktfern@ranken.edu
FERNALD, Julian, L .... 831-459-4341... 72 C
jfernald@ucsc.edu
FERNANDES, Brian .... 845-848-7807. 322 G
brian.fernandes@dc.edu
FERNANDES, Earl, K ...... 513-231-2223. 374 D
efernandes@athenaeum.edu
FERNANDES, Jamie .... 678-891-2379. 125 G
jamie.fernandes@gpc.edu
FERNANDES, Jane, K ..... 828-251-6470. 368 C
jfernand@unca.edu
FERNANDES, Jill .... 724-938-4415. 428 A
fernandes@calu.edu
FERNANDEZ, Diana .... 413-549-4600. 227 B
FERNANDEZ, Henry, B .... 954-486-7728. 118 E
FERNANDEZ, Irene .... 787-857-3600. 550 A
ifernandez@br.inter.edu
FERNANDEZ, J. Anthony 208-792-2216. 138 G
tfernandez@lcsc.edu
FERNANDEZ, Jack .... 203-371-7996... 91 C
fernandezj@sacredheart.edu
FERNANDEZ, Jeffrey .... 508-289-2325. 238 E
jfernandez@whoi.edu
FERNANDEZ, Jim .... 225-578-6916. 204 O
jfernan@lsu.edu
FERNANDEZ, John .... 787-725-6500. 547 H
jfernandez@albizu.edu
FERNANDEZ, Jose .... 609-586-4800. 302 G
fernandj@mccc.edu
FERNANDEZ, Jose, B ..... 407-823-2573. 115 E
jose.fernandez@ucf.edu
FERNANDEZ, Kennedy ... 305-273-4499. 100 H
kennedy@cbt.edu
FERNANDEZ, Luis .... 830-591-7276. 481 C
lmfernandez@swtjc.edu
FERNANDEZ, Raul .... 617-353-3635. 224 D
raul@bu.edu
FERNANDEZ, Ricardo, R 718-960-8111. 318 A
president.office@lehman.cuny.edu
FERNANDEZ, Rodolfo, J 305-284-4085. 118 F
rudyfernandez@miami.edu
FERNANDEZ,
Rudolph, J .... 305-284-4330. 118 F
rudyfernandez@miami.edu
FERNANDEZ, Victor, M .. 305-220-4120. 111 E
ultdir@ptcmatt.com
FERNANDEZ, Vivian .... 848-932-3020. 306 A
vfernandez@hr.rutgers.edu
FERNANDEZ, Wayne ...... 808-236-3597. 135 F
wfernandez@hpu.edu
FERNANDEZ, Yaniris ...... 413-559-5781. 227 B
FERNANDO, Gihan .... 202-885-1804... 94 F
gihan@american.edu
FERNE, Mark .... 801-832-2233. 498 F
mferne@westminstercollege.edu
FERNER, Ronald .... 215-702-4260. 411 F
rferner@cairn.edu
FERNETTE, Eric .... 713-500-3110. 492 E
eric.fernette@uth.tmc.edu
FERNHALL, Bo .... 312-996-7000. 161 D
fernhall@uic.edu
FERNIANY, Will .... 205-975-5362..... 8 E
ferniany@uab.edu
FERNOS, Manuel, J .... 787-763-4203. 549 J
mfernos@inter.edu
FERRAN, Mayra, M .... 787-257-7373. 552 H
mferran@suagm.edu
FERRAN, Peggy .... 315-781-3311. 326 C
ferran@hws.edu
FERRANTE, Jessica .... 212-924-5900. 347 B
jferrante@swedishinstitute.edu
FERRANTE, John .... 516-918-2787. 350 C
jferrante@webb.edu
FERRANTE, Regina .... 860-512-3633... 88 G
rferrant@manchestercc.edu
FERRANTI, Jeffrey .... 919-668-2166. 354 A
ferra007@mc.duke.edu
FERRAO, Luis .... 787-777-0677. 555 B
decanofeg@gmail.com
FERRARA, Brandi .... 315-781-3517. 326 C
bferrara@hws.edu
FERRARA, Hania .... 201-692-2381. 301 J
ferrara@fdu.edu
FERRARA, Joseph .... 202-687-4134... 95 E
jaf@georgetown.edu
FERRARA, Maria .... 201-447-7236. 299 C
mferrara@bergen.edu
FERRARA, Michael .... 603-862-1177. 298 C
mike.ferrara@unh.edu
FERRARA, Victoria .... 914-674-3094. 330 J
vferrara@mercy.edu
FERRARI, Bernard .... 410-234-9410. 215 H
bferrari@jhu.edu
FERRARI, Lisa, L .... 253-879-3207. 524 F
lferrari@pugetsound.edu
FERRARIO, Joyce, A .... 607-777-2311. 341 E
jferrari@binghamton.edu
FERRARO, Roger .... 860-906-5259... 88 D
rferraro@ccc.commnet.edu
FERRAUILO-DAVIS,
Mary-Jo .... 518-736-3622. 325 A
mary-jo.ferrauilo-davis@fmcc.suny.edu
FERRE, Loren .... 785-670-1794. 191 D
loren.ferre@washburn.edu
FERREIRA, Debora, D ..... 413-545-3464. 228 F
ferreira@admin.umass.edu
FERREIRA, Ken .... 603-899-4180. 296 H
finaid@franklinpierce.edu
FERREIRA, Lisa .... 619-961-4202... 69 I
lisaf@tjsl.edu
FERREIRA, Paul .... 207-326-2418. 211 D
paul.ferreira@mma.edu
FERREIRA, Robert .... 401-865-2407. 439 E
rferreir@providence.edu
FERRELL, Amber .... 910-296-2400. 361 D
aferrell@jamessprunt.edu
FERRELL, Ben, B .... 512-223-1099. 466 I
bferrell@austincc.edu
FERRELL, Donald .... 847-628-5051. 149 B
dferrell@judsonu.edu
FERRELL, Gregory, K ...... 330-287-0111. 386 F
ferrell.3@osu.edu
FERRELL, Michael, T .... 318-797-5278. 205 F
michael.ferrell@lsus.edu
FERRENTINO, Robert, C . 989-328-1221. 247 D
bobf@montcalm.edu
FERRER, Armando .... 305-237-4341. 109 D
aferrer@mdc.edu
FERRER, Laura .... 787-864-2222. 550 D
lferrer@inter.edu
FERRER, Rosimar .... 787-786-3030. 547 F
rferrer@ucb.edu.pr
FERRER, Shannon .... 480-990-3773... 14 H
FERRER, T.J .... 520-494-5577... 12 P
tj.ferrer@centralaz.edu
FERRER, Yolanda .... 787-834-9595. 553 B
yferrer@uaa.edu
FERRER-MUNIZ, Karen .. 518-629-7234. 326 G
k.ferrermuniz@hvcc.edu
FERRERO, JR., Ray .... 954-262-7585. 109 K
chancellor@nova.edu
FERRES, Steven .... 845-574-4770. 338 B
sferres@sunyrockland.edu
FERRETTI, Anthony, J ..... 941-756-0690. 420 E
aferretti@lecom.edu
FERRETTI, Bruce, S .... 610-330-5375. 420 D
ferrettb@lafayette.edu
FERRETTI, Jennie .... 304-357-4957. 527 H
jennieferretti@ucwv.edu
FERRETTI, John, M .... 814-866-6641. 420 E
hmckenzie@lecom.edu
FERRETTI, Kenneth, M .... 215-965-4007. 424 D
kferretti@moore.edu
FERRETTI, Silvia, M .... 814-866-6641. 420 E
ckonnerth@lecom.edu
FERREY, Patricia, A .... 814-332-2312. 409 D
patricia.ferrey@allegheny.edu
FERREYRA, Guillermo ..... 225-578-8859. 204 O
ferreyra@lsu.edu
FERRE', John, P .... 502-852-6976. 200 D
ferre@louisville.edu
FERRIBY, Peter, G .... 203-396-8283... 91 C
ferribyp@sacredheart.edu
FERRIER, Douglas, M ..... 956-326-2400. 483 B
douglas.ferrier@tamiu.edu
FERRIER, Lawrence .... 201-684-7494. 305 A
lferrier@ramapo.edu
FERRILL, Mary .... 561-803-2702. 110 B
mary_ferrill@pba.edu
FERRILLO, Patrick .... 415-929-6425... 73 A
pferrillo@pacific.edu
FERRIN, Susanne, E .... 215-895-1192. 435 H
s.ferrin@usciences.edu
FERRIS, Bill .... 206-543-9004. 524 G
bferris@uw.edu
FERRIS, Christian .... 361-593-2132. 484 A
christian.farris@tamuk.edu
FERRIS, Dan, J .... 815-939-5171. 155 H
djferris@olivet.edu
FERRIS, Diane, L .... 727-864-8381. 101 N
ferrisdl@eckerd.edu
FERRIS, Howard .... 781-239-3031. 231 G
hferris@massbay.edu
FERRIS, Jo .... 760-757-2121... 54 G
jferris@miracosta.edu
FERRIS, John .... 619-594-4967... 35 D
jferris@mail.sdsu.edu
FERRIS, Liz .... 765-973-8583. 167 G
liferris@iue.edu
FERRIS, Mary .... 805-893-2251... 72 B
mary.ferris@sa.ucsb.edu
FERRITOR, Daniel, E ...... 501-686-2531... 23 H
def@uark.edu
FERRO, David .... 801-626-6303. 497 D
dferro@weber.edu
FERRO, Deanna .... 315-731-5797. 331 I
dferro@mvcc.edu
FERRO, Jennifer .... 310-450-4613... 65 A
ferro_jennifer@smc.edu
FERRO, Jose .... 323-860-1135... 55 E
ferroj@mi.edu
FERRO, Lynn, P .... 717-815-1558. 438 D
lferro@ycp.edu
FERRO, Robert .... 617-989-4557. 237 G
ferrob@wit.edu
FERRUCCI, Rosemary ..... 516-686-1081. 333 H
rferrucc@nyit.edu
FERRUOLO, Stephen, C . 619-260-4527... 73 I
lawdean@sandiego.edu
FERRY, Catherine, T .... 717-291-3962. 416 J
cathie.ferry@fandm.edu
FERRY, MaryLou, J .... 909-607-9665... 65 D
marylou.ferry@scrippscollege.edu
FERRY, Michael .... 212-752-1530. 328 G
michael.ferry@limcollege.edu
FERRY, Patrick .... 734-995-7300. 241 E
patrick.ferry@cuw.edu
FERRY, Patrick, T .... 262-243-5700. 532 H
patrick.ferry@cuw.edu
FERRY, Richard, E .... 610-921-7825. 409 A
rferry@alb.edu
FERRY, Tamara, R .... 262-243-5700. 532 H
tamara.ferry@cuw.edu
FERST, Stephen .... 908-737-7140. 302 F
sferst@kean.edu
FERSZT, Edmund, J .... 413-545-6330. 228 F
edmund@provost.umass.edu
FERZELY, Eliza .... 402-941-6141. 290 K
ferzely@midlandu.edu
FESCOE, Michael .... 201-559-6004. 302 A
fescoem@felician.edu
FESER, Edward .... 217-333-1660. 162 A
feser@illinois.edu
FESER, Neil .... 504-468-2900. 207 B
neil@southwest.edu
FESKO, John .... 760-480-8474... 76 C
jvfesko@wscal.edu
FESSENBECKER, Denise . 310-377-5501... 53 F
dfessenbecker@marymountcalifornia.edu
FESSENDEN, June, S ..... 623-845-3406... 14 M
june.fessenden@gcmail.maricopa.edu
FESSLER, Brent .... 210-690-9000. 472 N
bfessler@hallmarkcollege.edu
FESSLER, Cale .... 816-271-4226. 279 A
cfessler@missouriwestern.edu
FESSLER, Deanne, K .... 660-263-4110. 279 B
deannef@macc.edu
FESSLER, Karen, P .... 570-326-3761. 427 B
kfessler@pct.edu
FESSLER, Robert .... 573-592-1181. 285 D
bfessler@williamwoods.edu
FESSLER, Robert .... 412-392-3479. 431 B
rfessler@pointpark.edu
FESSLER, Valerie, L .... 570-326-3761. 427 B
vlf1@pct.edu
FESTER, Rachel .... 718-405-3709. 320 G
rachel.fester@mountsaintvincent.edu
FETCHKO, Mary Beth ...... 412-536-1047. 420 A
marybeth.fetchko@laroche.edu
FETICK, Fay .... 314-529-9673. 276 G
ffetick@maryville.edu
FETROW, Aaron, L .... 336-316-2133. 355 A
afetrow@guilford.edu
FETROW, Jacquelyn .... 336-758-5311. 370 D
fetrowjs@wfu.edu
FETSCH, Cindy .... 701-777-3840. 371 C
cindy.fetsch@und.edu
FETTER, Wayne, R .... 337-475-5432. 207 G
wfetter@mcneese.edu
FETTERER, Dale .... 920-686-6158. 536 A
Dale.Fetterer@sl.edu
FETTERMAN, Ashley .... 570-961-7895. 420 C
fettermana@lackawanna.edu
FETTY, Gina .... 740-753-6445. 380 K
fettyg@hocking.edu
FETTY, M. Annette .... 304-457-6322. 526 A
fettyma@ab.edu
FEUCHT-HAVIAR,
Joyce, A .... 818-677-4711... 34 C
joyce.feucht-haviar@csun.edu
FEUDO, Christopher, V .. 703-790-3203. 510 H
FEUDO, John, A .... 617-552-4700. 224 A
feudo@bc.edu
FEUER, Avraham .... 732-367-1060. 299 E
AFeuer@bmg.edu
FEUER, Michael, J .... 202-994-6160... 95 D
mjfeuer@gwu.edu
FEUERBORN, Eric .... 405-224-3140. 401 E
efeuerborn@usao.edu
FEUERSTEIN, Christian ... 802-586-7711. 500 E
cfeuerstein@sterlingcollege.edu
FEULING, Michael .... 503-838-8449. 406 E
feulingm@wou.edu
FEUSTLE, Judith .... 443-352-4292. 218 E
jfeustle@stevenson.edu
FEVIG, David .... 219-464-5011. 174 E
david.fevig@valpo.edu
FEVOLA, Christopher, N . 516-299-3149. 329 C
christopher.fevola@liu.edu
FEWOX, Keli .... 706-355-5081. 120 J
kfewox@athenstech.edu
FEY, Jo .... 660-263-4110. 279 B
jof@macc.edu
FEY-YENSAN, Nancy ...... 704-687-8374. 368 E
nfeyyens@uncc.edu
FEYEN, Mike .... 979-532-6358. 494 L
mikef@wcjc.edu
FEYERHERM, Dianne, E . 254-299-8843. 476 D
dfeyerherm@mclennan.edu
FEYERHERM, Sarah, R ... 410-778-7228. 221 C
sfeyerherm2@washcoll.edu
FEYTEN, Carine .... 513-529-6317. 384 G
cfeyten@miamioh.edu
FIACCO, Marela .... 315-386-7608. 345 F
fiaccom@canton.edu
FIACCO, Phil .... 518-327-6300. 336 B
pfiacco@paulsmiths.edu
FIALA, Bill .... 626-815-2109... 29 H
bfiala@apu.edu
FIANO, Jason .... 541-956-7097. 407 F
jfiano@roguecc.edu
FICEK, Danielle .... 920-748-8118. 535 J
ficekd@ripon.edu
FICK, Kenneth, T .... 914-337-9300. 321 E
kenneth.fick@concordia-ny.edu
FICK, Paul .... 315-228-7130. 320 F
pfick@colgate.edu
FICK, Verlyn .... 520-515-5414... 12 R
fickv@cochise.edu
FICKE, Joan, C .... 973-655-4368. 303 D
fickej@mail.montclair.edu
FICKENSCHER, II,
Carl, C .... 260-452-2131. 165 D
carl.fickenscher@ctsfw.edu
FICKLER, Debra .... 610-519-7857. 436 F
debra.fickler@villanova.edu
FICTUM, Daniel .... 718-260-5931. 319 B
dfictum@citytech.cuny.edu
FIDLER, Jane, P .... 617-333-2355. 225 E
jfidler0803@curry.edu
FIEBELKORN, Donna ...... 906-635-2728. 245 G
dfiebelkorn@lssu.edu
FIEDLER, Daniel .... 903-233-3561. 475 J
danielfiedler@letu.edu
FIEDLER, Peter .... 617-353-6500. 224 D
pfiedler@bu.edu
FIEDLER, Thomas .... 617-353-3488. 224 D
tfiedler@bu.edu
FIEGE, William .... 804-594-1406. 512 G
bfiege@jtcc.edu
FIELD, Darryl .... 215-591-5880. 144 A
dfield@devry.edu
FIELD, Heather, M .... 415-565-4682... 71 A
fieldh@uchastings.edu
FIELD, Hilary .... 617-585-1701. 234 I
hilary.field@necmusic.edu
FIELD, Jay .... 562-938-4280... 51 D
jfield@lbcc.edu

- **FIELD**, Jay ... 360-867-6000. 519 J fieldj@evergreen.edu
- **FIELD**, Lindsey ... 435-283-7164. 498 A lindsey.field@snow.edu
- **FIELD**, Sherry ... 479-968-0350... 20 E sfield@atu.edu
- **FIELD**, Stephen, G ... 585-594-6150. 337 K fields@roberts.edu
- **FIELDER**, Marsha ... 517-265-5161. 238 G mfielder@adrian.edu
- **FIELDING**, Ahn ... 707-476-4140... 40 H ahn-fielding@redwoods.edu
- **FIELDING**, Chad ... 870-230-5420... 21 D fieldic@hsu.edu
- **FIELDING**, William ... 256-782-5773..... 4 K fielding@jsu.edu
- **FIELDS**, Ann ... 641-673-1076. 183 H fieldsa@wmpenn.edu
- **FIELDS**, Ann, Z ... 901-722-3230. 458 K annfields@sco.edu
- **FIELDS**, Beverly ... 806-457-4200. 472 G bfields@fpctx.edu
- **FIELDS**, Christine ... 276-739-2426. 514 D cfields@vhcc.edu
- **FIELDS**, Christopher ... 614-947-6803. 380 A christopher.fields@franklin.edu
- **FIELDS**, Darin ... 419-434-4553. 391 D fieldsd2@findlay.edu
- **FIELDS**, Dennis ... 717-545-4747. 419 O
- **FIELDS**, Gene ... 337-482-9246. 208 D gene.fields@louisiana.edu
- **FIELDS**, Jay ... 803-793-5286. 443 E fieldsj@denmarktech.edu
- **FIELDS**, Jeff ... 276-656-0222. 513 D jfields@patrickhenry.edu
- **FIELDS**, Joe ... 864-488-8347. 444 L jfields@limestone.edu
- **FIELDS**, John ... 229-430-4711. 119 J john.fields@asurams.edu
- **FIELDS**, Kimberly ... 229-430-1718. 119 J kimberly.fields@asurams.edu
- **FIELDS**, Lee, M ... 252-334-2080. 357 A lee.fields@macuniversity.edu
- **FIELDS**, Leonard, B ... 563-562-3263. 181 E fieldsl@nicc.edu
- **FIELDS**, M. Evelyn ... 803-536-4974. 446 G efields@scsu.edu
- **FIELDS**, Melea ... 562-902-3344... 67 H meleafields@scuhs.edu
- **FIELDS**, Michael ... 707-668-5663... 42 F
- **FIELDS**, Michael ... 713-221-8179. 489 D fieldsm@uhd.edu
- **FIELDS**, Mitch ... 315-312-6600. 344 A mitch.fields@oswego.edu
- **FIELDS**, Peter ... 406-994-4221. 287 B pfields@msubobcats.com
- **FIELDS**, Petra ... 704-991-0231. 364 C pfields7679@stanly.edu
- **FIELDS**, Richard ... 973-720-2397. 308 I fieldsr2j@wpunj.edu
- **FIELDS**, Russell ... 775-784-6987. 294 J rfields@unr.edu
- **FIELDS**, Todd, E ... 972-881-5174. 469 G tfields@collin.edu
- **FIELDS**, W. Bradley ... 859-238-5485. 193 E brad.fields@centre.edu
- **FIENE**, Jay ... 909-537-5600... 34 E jfiene@csusb.edu
- **FIENE**, John, L ... 402-554-3670. 293 A jfiene@unomaha.edu
- **FIENSY**, David, A ... 606-474-3263. 194 H dfiensy@kcu.edu
- **FIERBAUGH**, Lee ... 423-461-8719. 457 H lflerbaugh@milligan.edu
- **FIERKE**, Kimberly ... 607-431-4000. 325 F fierkek@hartwick.edu
- **FIERO**, Diane ... 661-362-3424... 40 E diane.fiero@canyons.edu
- **FIERO**, Tom, D ... 517-750-1200. 250 E tfiero@arbor.edu
- **FIERRO**, Jose ... 307-778-1104. 543 D jfierro@lccc.wy.edu
- **FIFE**, Jerry ... 615-343-6658. 463 G jerry.fife@vanderbilt.edu
- **FIFE**, Kaaren ... 913-288-7281. 187 L kfife@kckcc.edu
- **FIFE**, Linda, L ... 443-412-2377. 215 C lfife@harford.edu
- **FIFER**, Tom ... 660-831-4219. 278 I fifert@moval.edu
- **FIFRICK**, Heather ... 608-822-2366. 541 C hfifrick@swtc.edu
- **FIGA**, Jan ... 217-245-3020. 146 F jan.figa@ic.edu
- **FIGARI**, Charles, A ... 713-500-8400. 492 E charles.a.figari@uth.tmc.edu
- **FIGGS**, Joel ... 785-243-1435. 185 M jfiggs@cloud.edu
- **FIGHERA**, Joe ... 619-482-6446... 68 B jfighera@swccd.edu
- **FIGORA**, Luke ... 773-702-2265. 161 B lfigora@uchicago.edu
- **FIGUEIREDO**, Marianne . 617-521-2270. 236 G marianne.figueiredo@simmons.edu
- **FIGUEREDO**, Danilo, H .. 973-748-9000. 299 F danilo_figueredo@bloomfield.edu
- **FIGUEROA**, Ana, M ... 973-290-4434. 300 F afigueroa@cse.edu
- **FIGUEROA**, Carlos, O ... 787-850-9367. 554 D carlos.figueroa7@upr.edu
- **FIGUEROA**, Carolina ... 787-761-0640. 553 F oficialderegistroacademico@utcpr.edu
- **FIGUEROA**, Eduardo ... 787-882-2065. 553 A technoloa_industrial@unitecpr.net
- **FIGUEROA**, Fernando ... 361-698-1205. 471 G ffigueroa@delmar.edu
- **FIGUEROA**, Gema, C ... 787-738-2161. 554 C gema.figueroa@upr.edu
- **FIGUEROA**, Humberto ... 787-738-2161. 554 C humberto.figueroa@upr.edu
- **FIGUEROA**, Jennifer, E ... 570-577-1028. 411 A j.figueroa@bucknell.edu
- **FIGUEROA**, Julio ... 787-257-7373. 552 H ue_jfigueroa@suagm.edu
- **FIGUEROA**, Margarita ... 787-720-1022. 547 E admisiones@atlanticcollege.edu
- **FIGUEROA**, Maria, V ... 787-743-7979. 552 I ut_mfigueroa@suagm.edu
- **FIGUEROA**, Mark ... 503-768-7676. 403 K figueroa@lclark.edu
- **FIGUEROA**, Roberto ... 518-464-8800. 324 B rfigueroa@excelsior.edu
- **FIGUEROA**, Victor ... 787-744-1060. 551 J vfigueroa@mechtech.edu
- **FIGUEROA**, Vitaliano ... 701-845-7300. 372 A vitaliano.figueroa@vcsu.edu
- **FIGUEROA**, William ... 787-758-2525. 554 F william.figueroa2@upr.edu
- **FIGUEROA-LLAVAT**, Alfredo ... 787-250-0000. 553 G alfredo.figueroa@upr.edu
- **FIGURELLI**, Nicholas ... 973-761-9194. 307 C nicholas.figurelli1@shu.edu
- **FIJAL**, Amanda ... 773-702-7659. 161 B afijal@uchicago.edu
- **FIKE**, David, J ... 313-927-1208. 246 D dfike@marygrove.edu
- **FIKE**, Esther ... 954-492-5353. 100 A efike@citycollege.edu
- **FIKE**, Esther ... 407-831-9816... 99 O efike@citycollege.edu
- **FIKE**, Janet ... 304-214-8837. 528 G jfike@wvncc.edu
- **FIKE**, Jeffrey ... 540-828-5395. 502 J jfike@bridgewater.edu
- **FIKE**, Linda, K ... 301-387-3049. 214 I linda.fike@garrettcollege.edu
- **FIKSE**, Peggy ... 209-575-7707... 77 J
- **FILAN**, Sonia ... 480-461-7446... 15 A sonia.filan@mesacc.edu
- **FILARDI**, Salvatore ... 203-582-8800... 91 A salvatore.filardi@quinnipiac.edu
- **FILBRY**, Sandra ... 516-463-4335. 326 D sandra.filbry@hofstra.edu
- **FILBY**, Ivan ... 618-664-7000. 145 G presidentfilby@greenville.edu
- **FILBY**, Robert, G ... 740-284-5472. 379 N rfilby@franciscan.edu
- **FILE**, Carter ... 620-665-3509. 187 F
- **FILE**, David, C ... 319-385-6245. 179 K dfile@iwc.edu
- **FILEMYR**, Ann ... 505-424-2354. 309 J afilemyr@iaia.edu
- **FILIP**, Janet ... 517-586-3009. 241 A jfilip@cleary.edu
- **FILIPIAK**, Joseph, M ... 312-915-7671. 151 H jfilipi@luc.edu
- **FILIPP**, Robert, B ... 773-442-5300. 154 H r-filipp@neiu.edu
- **FILIPPELLI**, Karen, S ... 520-621-4789... 18 F filippek@email.arizona.edu
- **FILIPPIDIS**, Barbara ... 512-448-8558. 479 C barbaraf@stedwards.edu
- **FILIPPONE**, Anne ... 610-902-8407. 411 E anne.filippone@cabrini.edu
- **FILIPPONE**, Gregg, S ... 716-851-1073. 323 I filipponeg@ecc.edu
- **FILLINGER**, Barbara ... 734-973-3560. 252 A bfilling@wccnet.edu
- **FILLIPPI**, Carolyn ... 315-229-5267. 339 F cfillippi@stlawu.edu
- **FILLMORE**, Dre ... 706-233-7236. 131 E 1150mgr@fheg.follett.com
- **FILLNER**, Russ ... 406-447-6917. 287 A russ.fillner@umhelena.edu
- **FILLPOT**, Jim ... 909-652-6460... 37 M jim.fillpot@chaffey.edu
- **FILORAMO**, Dorothy ... 845-848-7400. 322 G dorothy.filoramo@dc.edu
- **FILOSA**, Bruce ... 718-951-5366. 317 C bfilosa@brooklyn.cuny.edu
- **FILOWSKI**, Melissa ... 509-865-8544. 520 D filowski_m@heritage.edu
- **FILSON**, Cori ... 518-580-5355. 341 A cfilson@skidmore.edu
- **FINALY**, Roy ... 619-477-6310... 70 D rfinaly@usuniversity.edu
- **FINCANNON**, Angie ... 765-998-5311. 173 C anfincann@taylor.edu
- **FINCH**, Amy ... 731-286-3347. 460 F finch@dscc.edu
- **FINCH**, Brian, K ... 860-444-8480. 545 G Bryan.K.Finch@uscg.mil
- **FINCH**, Christopher ... 201-559-6084. 302 A finchc@felician.edu
- **FINCH**, Daniel ... 419-720-6670. 388 E dfinch@proskills.edu
- **FINCH**, Irene ... 207-741-5715. 211 A ifinch@smccme.edu
- **FINCH**, J. Howard ... 205-726-2364..... 6 F hfinch@samford.edu
- **FINCH**, Jack, R ... 740-377-2520. 389 K jfinch1@zoominternet.net
- **FINCH**, Judy ... 503-768-7328. 403 K finchj@lclark.edu
- **FINCH**, Mary Ellen ... 314-529-9400. 276 G mfinch@maryville.edu
- **FINCH**, Thomas ... 315-786-2235. 327 L tfinch@sunyjefferson.edu
- **FINCH**, Tony ... 662-720-7304. 269 B tfinch@nemcc.edu
- **FINCH**, Tracy ... 870-972-2031... 19 N tfinch@astate.edu
- **FINCHER**, David, B ... 660-263-3900. 272 A academics@cccb.edu
- **FINCHER**, Wade ... 501-882-8866... 19 M wade@asub.edu
- **FINCK**, Konrad ... 312-329-4066. 153 E konrad.finck@moody.edu
- **FINDLEY**, Brenda ... 706-867-2705. 133 D brenda.findley@ung.edu
- **FINDLEY**, Donna ... 478-387-4846. 125 E dfindley@gmc.cc.ga.us
- **FINDLEY**, Lynette ... 734-487-6694. 242 D lfindley@emich.edu
- **FINDLEY**, Pamela, L ... 256-782-5151..... 4 K pfindley@jsu.edu
- **FINDT**, William ... 910-879-5502. 358 B wfindt@bladencc.edu
- **FINE**, Ricka, K ... 410-777-1868. 213 D rkfine@aacc.edu
- **FINEGAN, SC**, Carol, M . 718-405-3349. 320 G carol.finegan@mountsaintvincent.edu
- **FINEGAN**, James, M ... 814-871-7681. 416 K finegan001@gannon.edu
- **FINEGAN**, Kathleen ... 816-501-3621. 271 H kathleen.finegan@avila.edu
- **FINEMAN**, Robert ... 206-934-3791. 522 I robert.fineman@seattlecolleges.edu
- **FINEO**, Richard ... 860-632-3007... 90 C rfineo@holyapostles.edu
- **FINEOUT-OVERHOLT**, Ellen ... 903-923-2210. 471 J efineoutoverholt@etbu.edu
- **FINESILVER**, Jennifer ... 317-632-5553. 170 T jfinesilver@lincolntech.com
- **FINFROCK**, Randal, M ... 724-925-4060. 437 D finfrockr@wccc.edu
- **FINGER**, Eleanor ... 540-231-8893. 515 C efinger@vt.edu
- **FINGER**, Mary ... 312-362-8666. 143 H mfinger@depaul.edu
- **FINGLETON**, Samantha ... 212-472-1500. 334 B sfingleton@nysid.edu
- **FINK**, Brenda ... 626-914-8830... 38 K bfink@citruscollege.edu
- **FINK**, Ernest ... 718-409-7341. 346 D efink@sunymaritime.edu
- **FINK**, Gayle, M ... 301-860-3403. 220 A gfink@bowiestate.edu
- **FINK**, Jonathan ... 503-725-9944. 406 B jon.fink@pdx.edu
- **FINK**, Joseph, W ... 412-624-9510. 435 C fink@pitt.edu
- **FINK**, Michael ... 909-652-6453... 37 M michael.fink@chaffey.edu
- **FINK**, Michael ... 912-525-5000. 131 B mfink@scad.edu
- **FINKE**, Barbara ... 816-802-3434. 275 J bfinke@kcai.edu
- **FINKE**, John ... 317-955-6202. 170 V jfinke@marian.edu
- **FINKEL**, Lee ... 602-557-1595... 18 I lee.finkel@phoenix.edu
- **FINKELSTEIN**, Barbara, E ... 508-588-9100. 232 A
- **FINKELSTEIN**, Eric, M ... 718-990-2417. 339 A finkelse@stjohns.edu
- **FINKELSTEIN**, Jerry ... 212-229-1671. 332 E finkelsj@newschool.edu
- **FINKELSTEIN**, Larry, A ... 617-373-2462. 235 F
- **FINKELSTEIN**, Monte ... 850-201-8488. 117 D finkelsm@tcc.fl.edu
- **FINKELSTEIN**, Richard ... 540-654-1052. 510 J rfinkels@umw.edu
- **FINKS**, Frederick, J ... 419-289-5050. 374 C ffinks@ashland.edu
- **FINLAY**, Cheryl, S ... 412-624-4362. 435 C cfinlay@pitt.edu
- **FINLAYSON**, Al ... 218-733-7613. 259 A a.finlayson@lsc.edu
- **FINLAYSON**, Alexander (Sandy) ... 215-572-3823. 437 C sfinlayson@wts.edu
- **FINLAYSON**, Deborah ... 806-742-0502. 487 D deborah.finlayson@ttu.edu
- **FINLAYSON**, Jeanne ... 508-565-1337. 237 A jfinlayson@stonehill.edu
- **FINLEY**, Adam ... 817-598-8831. 494 G afinley@wc.edu
- **FINLEY**, David ... 906-635-2426. 245 G dfinley@lssu.edu
- **FINLEY**, Jane ... 251-442-2219..... 9 A jfinley@umobile.edu
- **FINLEY**, Jenna ... 970-351-2721... 86 C jenna.finley@unco.edu
- **FINLEY**, Jennifer ... 828-277-5521. 366 G jfinley@southcollegenc.edu
- **FINLEY**, Julius ... 360-779-9993. 521 C jfinley@ncad.edu
- **FINLEY**, Lucinda, M ... 716-645-3594. 341 F finleylu@buffalo.edu
- **FINLEY**, Matt ... 803-321-5166. 445 G matthew.finley@newberry.edu
- **FINLEY**, Meghan ... 203-777-8573... 87 G mfinley@albertus.edu
- **FINLEY**, Rebecca ... 215-503-9000. 434 C rebecca.finley@jefferson.edu
- **FINLEY**, Tony ... 501-279-4242... 21 C tfinley@harding.edu
- **FINLINSON**, Norm ... 801-422-4640. 495 D norm_finlinson@byu.edu
- **FINN**, Alan ... 503-725-3649. 406 B alan.finn@pdx.edu
- **FINN**, Alicia, A ... 603-641-7600. 297 G afinn@anselm.edu
- **FINN**, Bob, D ... 509-313-6100. 520 A finn@gonzaga.edu
- **FINN**, Edward, J ... 563-333-6289. 182 B FinnEdwardJ@sau.edu
- **FINN**, Erin ... 215-895-6712. 415 B emf332@drexel.edu
- **FINN**, Eugene, J ... 330-672-6000. 382 B gfinn@kent.edu
- **FINN**, John ... 330-263-2373. 377 H jfinn@wooster.edu
- **FINN**, Kevin ... 248-204-4100. 245 I kfinn@ltu.edu
- **FINN**, Louise ... 410-617-5252. 216 A lafinn@loyola.edu
- **FINN**, William ... 708-974-5727. 153 F finn@morainevalley.edu
- **FINN KENNEY**, Rebecca 415-458-3720... 42 J rebecca.finnkenney@dominican.edu
- **FINN-SHERMAN**, Miriam ... 781-768-7222. 236 A miriam.sherman@regiscollege.edu
- **FINN-WELCH**, Aliza ... 860-297-4054... 91 F aliza.finnwelch@trincoll.edu
- **FINNAN**, Diane, P ... 908-852-1400. 300 D finnand@centenarycollege.edu
- **FINNEGAN**, Barry ... 636-949-4455. 276 D bfinnegan@lindenwood.edu
- **FINNEGAN**, Faye, A ... 563-588-7155. 180 L faye.finnegan@loras.edu
- **FINNEGAN**, John ... 612-625-1179. 264 G finne001@umn.edu
- **FINNEGAN**, Michael, S .. 256-824-6480..... 8 F michael.finnegan@uah.edu
- **FINNEGAN**, Olya ... 414-443-8867. 539 F olya.finnegan@wlc.edu
- **FINNEL**, Kristin, M ... 920-922-8611. 540 F kfinnel@morainepark.edu
- **FINNELL**, Ovette ... 757-873-4235. 510 B ofinnell@stratford.edu
- **FINNELL**, Todd ... 760-355-6377... 48 A todd.finnell@imperial.edu
- **FINNELLY**, Ryan, L ... 847-317-8145. 160 M rfinnell@tiu.edu
- **FINNEN**, Mary ... 646-660-6549. 316 J Mary.Finnen@baruch.cuny.edu
- **FINNERTY**, Mary Beth ... 518-782-6818. 340 J mfinnerty@siena.edu
- **FINNERTY**, Pat ... 419-227-3141. 391 F pfinnert@unoh.edu
- **FINNERTY**, Robert ... 585-475-4733. 337 L bob.finnerty@rit.edu
- **FINNEY**, Andy ... 208-769-3266. 138 I andy_finney@nic.edu
- **FINNEY**, David, F ... 802-860-2734. 499 A finney@champlain.edu

FINNEY, Howard, H 214-860-2202. 470 J hfinney@dcccd.edu
FINNEY, Janice 850-644-1328. 115 C jfinney@admin.fsu.edu
FINNEY, Lesley, M 717-361-1445. 415 H finneylm@etown.edu
FINNEY, Marc 252-536-7237. 361 A mfinney295@halifaxcc.edu
FINNEY, Sarah 206-296-6390. 523 E sfinney@seattleu.edu
FINNEY, Terry 870-972-2398... 19 N tfinney@astate.edu
FINNIGAN, Kristia, H 803-777-6727. 447 G finnigan@sc.edu
FINNIN, Meredith 212-752-1530. 328 G meredith.finnin@limcollege.edu
FINNING, Shannon 781-239-4309. 222 D sfinning@babson.edu
FINTON, Stephan 860-444-8503. 545 G Stephan.P.Finton@uscga.edu
FINUCANE, Margaret, O . 216-397-1780. 381 R mfinucane@jcu.edu
FINZEL, Bart 320-589-6015. 264 F finzelbd@morris.umn.edu
FIORAVANTI, Emil 508-999-8106. 229 A efioravanti@umassd.edu
FIORE, Francesca 718-482-5332. 318 F ffiore@lagcc.cuny.edu
FIORE, James 631-632-7205. 342 C james.fiore@stonybrook.edu
FIORE CONTE, Johann ... 607-777-2221. 341 E jmfconte@binghamton.edu
FIORELLA, Cynthia 270-686-4445. 196 C cindy.fiorella@kctcs.edu
FIORENTINO, Christopher, M 610-436-2930. 430 A cfiorentino@wcupa.edu
FIORENTINO, Deanna .... 203-365-7626... 91 C fiorentinod@sacredheart.edu
FIORENTINO, JR., Michael 570-484-2000. 429 B mfiorentino@lhup.edu
FIORENZA, Anthony 305-237-2867. 109 D afiorenz@mdc.edu
FIORI, Christopher 781-280-3292. 232 B fioric@middlesex.mass.edu
FIORITO, Frank 312-567-7994. 147 F ffiorito@iit.edu
FIRESTONE, Bernard, J .. 516-463-5411. 326 D bernard.j.firestone@hofstra.edu
FIRESTONE, Elizabeth, E 865-694-6457. 461 D eefirestone@pstcc.edu
FIRESTONE, Luanne, C .. 716-888-2422. 316 C firestol@canisius.edu
FIRKUS, Greg 217-875-7200. 156 J gfirkus@richland.edu
FIRMAN, JR., William, H 412-536-1765. 420 A william.firman@laroche.edu
FIRMIN, Sally, E 254-710-3476. 467 G sally_firmin@baylor.edu
FIRTH, Ann, M 574-631-9164. 174 A firth.2@nd.edu
FIRZER, John 559-638-3641... 69 A john.fitzer@reedleycollege.edu
FISCH, Barry 617-587-5587. 234 H fischb@neco.edu
FISCHER, Alexander 718-384-5460. 351 H
FISCHER, Craig 914-606-6715. 350 F craig.fischer@sunywcc.edu
FISCHER, Donna 973-684-6333. 304 B dfischer@pccc.edu
FISCHER, Heidi 336-841-9636. 355 C hfischer@highpoint.edu
FISCHER, OSU, Helena .. 270-686-4248. 192 G helena.fischer@brescia.edu
FISCHER, Howard 602-749-5120. 189 I howard.fischer@ottawa.edu
FISCHER, Ita 630-752-5483. 163 F ita.fischer@wheaton.edu
FISCHER, Jacqueline 660-263-4110. 279 B JackieFischer@macc.edu
FISCHER, Jan 620-331-4100. 187 G janfischer@indycc.edu
FISCHER, Lynn 412-304-0712. 416 F lfischer@cci.edu
FISCHER, Mark 805-482-2755... 61 E fischer@stjohnsem.edu
FISCHER, Marvin 631-420-2702. 346 B marvin.fischer@farmingdale.edu
FISCHER, Michael, J 716-375-2121. 338 E mfischer@sbu.edu
FISCHER, Michael, R 210-999-8201. 488 C mfischer@trinity.edu
FISCHER, Noah, M 701-788-4647. 371 E noah.fischer@mayvillestate.edu
FISCHER, Patricia, L 918-595-7856. 400 E pat.fischer@tulsacc.edu
FISCHER, Pattie 360-417-6201. 522 A pfischer@pencol.edu
FISCHER, Patty 573-875-7260. 272 G pafischer@ccis.edu
FISCHER, Rachel 920-686-6231. 536 A Rachel.Fischer@sl.edu
FISCHER, JR., Robert, U 615-898-2613. 459 D bud.fischer@mtsu.edu
FISCHER, Sean 606-343-4910. 299 A sfischer@atlantic.edu
FISCHER, Susan 608-262-2087. 536 D susan.fischer@finaid.wisc.edu
FISCHER, William, M 937-229-3311. 391 C WFischer1@udayton.edu
FISCHER-FREE, Todd 815-226-3385. 157 C tfree@rockford.edu
FISCHLER, Abraham 954-262-3827. 109 K fischler@nova.edu
FISCHLER, Michael, L 603-535-2461. 298 G mfischle@plymouth.edu
FISCUS, Ronald 702-968-5570. 295 E rfiscus@roseman.edu
FISER, Dawn, M 734-929-9086. 241 A dfiser@cleary.edu
FISH, Alan 410-516-8767. 215 H afish6@jhu.edu
FISH, Alicia 607-431-4021. 325 F fisha@hartwick.edu
FISH, Chaya 847-982-2500. 146 C fish@htc.edu
FISH, David 417-626-1234. 279 J dfish@occ.edu
FISH, Jacqueline 843-863-7504. 441 H jfish@csuniv.edu
FISH, James, D 315-268-3859. 320 A fishj@carkson.edu
FISH, Jennifer, N 757-683-3823. 507 N jfish@odu.edu
FISH, Nicole 800-567-2344. 532 E nfish@menominee.edu
FISH, Thomas, E 606-539-4214. 200 B tom.fish@ucumberlands.edu
FISHBACK, Bill 325-649-8012. 473 F bfishback@hputx.edu
FISHBAUGH, Mary Susan 406-657-2285. 287 C mfishbaugh@msubillings.edu
FISHBECK, Donna 701-224-5638. 372 B donna.fishbeck@bismarckstate.edu
FISHBEIN, Michael 860-701-5028... 90 G fishbein_m@mitchell.edu
FISHBONE, Alexis 978-556-3615. 232 E afishbone@necc.mass.edu
FISHER, Alec 617-746-1209. 227 F alec.fisher@hult.edu
FISHER, Amy 617-521-2337. 236 G amy.fisher2@simmons.edu
FISHER, Ann 313-993-1582. 250 K fisheram@udmercy.edu
FISHER, Anne, E 941-487-4254. 115 D fisher@ncf.edu
FISHER, Anthony 912-525-5000. 131 B afisher@scad.edu
FISHER, Barrett 651-638-6083. 253 K fisbar@bethel.edu
FISHER, Brian 239-590-1786. 115 A bfisher@fgcu.edu
FISHER, Carol, M 585-292-2500. 332 A cfisher@monroecc.edu
FISHER, Christine 312-935-6696. 156 K cfisher@robertmorris.edu
FISHER, Courtney 870-762-3191... 19 K cfisher@smail.anc.edu
FISHER, Craig 325-674-2622. 464 H craig.fisher@acu.edu
FISHER, David 918-540-6233. 396 G dfisher@neo.edu
FISHER, David, A 864-242-5100. 441 D
FISHER, Dean 405-736-0223. 399 F dfisher@rose.edu
FISHER, Deborah, M 215-746-7981. 435 B debmarsh@sas.upenn.edu
FISHER, Dianna, L 657-278-4733... 33 E difisher@fullerton.edu
FISHER, Donna, M 620-417-1111. 190 F donna.fisher@sccc.edu
FISHER, Elizabeth 940-565-2085. 490 C elizabeth.fisher@unt.edu
FISHER, Ellen 212-452-4170. 334 B efisher@nysid.edu
FISHER, Gail 805-966-3888... 30 A gfisher@brooks.edu
FISHER, Gary, T 710-231-7672. 371 G gary.fisher@ndsu.edu
FISHER, Glenn, R 570-577-1921. 411 A glenn.fisher@bucknell.edu
FISHER, Gloria, M 909-384-4470... 62 A gfisher@sbccd.cc.ca.us
FISHER, Guy 574-807-7212. 164 D fisherg@bethelcollege.edu
FISHER, Heidi, L 715-833-6277. 539 J hfisher@cvtc.edu
FISHER, Hilry 212-817-7523. 317 F hfisher@gc.cuny.edu
FISHER, James, R 585-785-1208. 324 D fisherjr@flcc.edu
FISHER, Jane, E 716-888-2112. 316 C fisher@canisius.edu
FISHER, Jay 931-598-1142. 458 H jafisher@sewanee.edu
FISHER, Jeffrey, A 614-222-3277. 378 A jfisher@ccad.edu
FISHER, Jennifer, L 304-293-8531. 530 D jennifer.fisher@mail.wvu.edu
FISHER, John 229-219-1238. 134 K john.fisher@wiregrass.edu
FISHER, John, S 989-774-7472. 240 N john.s.fisher@cmich.edu
FISHER, Jon 334-244-3229..... 2 A jfisher@aum.edu
FISHER, Joseph 513-562-8754. 373 K jfisher@artacademy.edu
FISHER, Joseph, B 210-690-9000. 472 N jfisher@hallmarkcollege.edu
FISHER, Judith 269-471-3470. 239 D jfisher@andrews.edu
FISHER, Karla 316-322-3110. 185 D karla.fisher@butlercc.edu
FISHER, Katie 828-328-7247. 356 B katie.fisher@lr.edu
FISHER, Kelly 978-232-2328. 226 C kfisher@endicott.edu
FISHER, Kristi, D 512-232-1825. 491 C kfisher@austin.utexas.edu
FISHER, Kristie 319-398-4977. 180 J kfisher@kirkwood.edu
FISHER, Kyle 412-397-5290. 431 I fisherk@rmu.edu
FISHER, Linda 716-829-8400. 323 D fisherl@dyc.edu
FISHER, Lisa 405-682-1611. 397 E lisa.m.fisher@occc.edu
FISHER, Marc 805-893-3132... 72 B marc.fisher@vcadmin.ucsb.edu
FISHER, Mardell 262-551-5705. 532 D mfisher@carthage.edu
FISHER, Michael 401-232-6000. 438 K
FISHER, Michael 845-434-5750. 347 A mfisher@sullivan.suny.edu
FISHER, Michael 541-383-7238. 402 D mfisher@cocc.edu
FISHER, Patti 574-807-7625. 164 D patti.fisher@bethelcollege.edu
FISHER, Priscilla 662-252-8000. 269 F pfisher@rustcollege.edu
FISHER, Robert, C 615-460-6793. 453 C bob.fisher@belmont.edu
FISHER, Stephanie, B 252-451-8240. 362 D sfisher@nashcc.edu
FISHER, Terrell, F 504-861-5881. 205 H tfisher@loyno.edu
FISHER, Thomas, R 612-624-1013. 264 G fishe033@umn.edu
FISHER, Timothy 860-570-5127... 92 A timothy.fisher@uconn.edu
FISHER, Tom 580-481-5243. 494 F twfisher@wbu.edu
FISHER, William 508-793-7676. 225 A wfisher@clarku.edu
FISHER, William, J 843-792-4275. 445 B fisherj@musc.edu
FISHER, Witney 864-596-9016. 443 D witney.fisher@converse.edu
FISHER-OGDEN, Daryl 213-252-5100... 26 A
FISHERMAN, Bernadine . 505-346-2339. 312 E bernadine.fisherman@bie.edu
FISHEROWITZ, Shlomo .. 303-629-8200... 87 F
FISHMAN, Ariel 212-960-5400. 351 M afishma2@yu.edu
FISHMAN, David 845-406-4308. 351 A
FISHMAN, Joan, R 212-431-2850. 333 I jfishman@nyls.edu
FISHMAN, Yisroel 718-645-0536. 331 G
FISHSTEIN, Janet 617-521-2284. 236 G janet.fishstein@simmons.edu
FISK, Cheryl 952-446-4172. 255 D fiskc@crown.edu
FISK, Francine, J 918-631-2495. 401 F francine-fisk@utulsa.edu
FISK, Robert 304-647-6361. 530 B rfisk@osteo.wvsom.edu
FISKAA, Evelyn 845-848-4032. 322 G evelyn.fiskaa@dc.edu
FISKE, Joshua, A 315-268-6718. 320 A jfiske@clarkson.edu
FISKEAUX, Charlie, D .... 859-858-3511. 192 B charlie.fiskeaux@asbury.edu
FISSINGER, Matthew, X . 310-338-2750... 53 E mfissing@lmu.edu
FITCH, Andy 434-791-5679. 502 D afitch@averett.edu
FITCH, Brent 469-287-1345... 18 I brent.fitch@phoenix.edu
FITCH, Gene 972-883-6391. 491 E gene.fitch@utdallas.edu
FITCH, Jerome, H 803-535-5549. 442 B jfitch@claflin.edu
FITCH, Megan, E 608-363-2481. 531 M fitchm@beloit.edu
FITCH, Peggy 641-628-5148. 176 E fitchp@central.edu
FITE, David 909-748-8306... 73 H david_fite@redlands.edu
FITE, J, D 404-471-6000. 119 I jfite@agnesscott.edu
FITES, Catherine 510-235-7800... 41 K cfites@contracosta.edu
FITHIAN, David 773-702-2305. 161 B fithian@uchicago.edu
FITSIMMONS, Gary, N ... 423-775-7196. 453 E gary.fitsimmons@bryan.edu
FITTERER, Alex 512-313-3000. 469 L alex.fitterer@concordia.edu
FITTS, Alex 907-474-7980... 10 I affitts@alaska.edu
FITTS, Bev 503-517-1031. 408 H bfitts@warnerpacific.edu
FITTS, Michael, A 215-898-7061. 435 B mfitts@law.upenn.edu
FITZ, Gregory 214-648-8712. 493 E greg.fitz@utsouthwestern.edu
FITZ, SM, James, F 937-229-2899. 391 C jfitz1@udayton.edu
FITZ-GERALD, Jim 251-580-2205..... 4 L jim.fitz-gerald@faulknerstate.edu
FITZ-GERALD, Jim 251-580-2205..... 4 L jfitzgerald@faulknerstate.edu
FITZENBERGER, Jennifer, M 520-621-1877... 18 F jfitzen@email.arizona.edu
FITZGERALD, Ann 574-936-8898. 163 K ann.fitzgerald@ancilla.edu
FITZGERALD, Carol 541-881-4863. 408 C Carol.L.Fitzgerald@doc.state.or.us
FITZGERALD, Charles, B 434-924-3245. 511 B cbf2w@virginia.edu
FITZGERALD, Darren 800-962-7682. 285 A dfitzgerald@wma.edu
FITZGERALD, David 602-557-2387... 18 I david.fitzgerald@phoenix.edu
FITZGERALD, Deann 773-380-6820. 163 D dfitzgerald@westwood.edu
FITZGERALD, Deborah, K 617-253-3450. 233 B
FITZGERALD, Ed 618-252-5400. 159 E eddie.fitzgerald@sic.edu
FITZGERALD, Ed 765-973-8222. 167 G efitzger@iue.edu
FITZGERALD, Erin 860-493-0013... 87 J fitzgeralde@ct.edu
FITZGERALD, Erin 401-341-3108. 440 C erin.fitzgerald@salve.edu
FITZGERALD, Faith, M ... 757-823-8407. 507 M fmfitzgerald@nsu.edu
FITZGERALD, Francis, X 718-951-5504. 317 C fxfitzgerald@brooklyn.cuny.edu
FITZGERALD, Greg 503-594-3132. 402 F gregf@clackamas.edu
FITZGERALD, Hiram, E ... 517-353-8977. 246 H fitzger9@msu.edu
FITZGERALD, Ione 312-461-0600. 139 H ifitzgerald@aaart.edu
FITZGERALD, Joanne 518-631-9842. 348 K fitzerj@uniongraduatecollege.edu
FITZGERALD, Kathy 740-826-8468. 384 L kfitzgerald@muskingum.edu
FITZGERALD, Kevin 919-962-1591. 366 K kmfitzgerald@northcarolina.edu
FITZGERALD, Laura 716-896-0700. 350 A fitzgeraldl@villa.edu
FITZGERALD, Liz 802-225-3261. 499 I liz.fitzgerald@neci.edu
FITZGERALD, Maureen, F 818-677-5674... 34 C maureen.fitzgerald@csun.edu
FITZGERALD, Mike 618-833-3399. 158 M mikef@shawneecc.edu
FITZGERALD, Paul 312-662-4214. 139 F pfitzgerald@adler.edu
FITZGERALD, Paul 814-868-9900. 416 C paulf@erieit.edu
FITZGERALD, SJ, Paul, J 203-254-4000... 89 I pfitzgerald@fairfield.edu
FITZGERALD, Robert, F .. 401-863-2500. 438 J robert_fitzgerald@brown.edu
FITZGERALD, Sean, P .... 419-372-0464. 374 K sfitzge@bgsu.edu
FITZGERALD, Sharon 757-727-5425. 505 F alumni@hamptonu.edu
FITZGERALD, Susan 860-768-4011... 92 D fitzgeral@hartford.edu
FITZGERALD, Thomas .... 617-850-1212. 227 E tfitzgerald@hchc.edu

FITZGERALD MILLER, Judith .... 573-882-0278. 283 C
millerjud@missouri.edu
FITZGIBBON, Cecelia ..... 215-568-4515. 424 D
cfitzgibbon@moore.edu
FITZGIBBON, Heather, M .... 330-263-2576. 377 H
hfitzgibbon@wooster.edu
FITZGIBBON, John .... 831-582-4749... 34 B
jfitzgibbon@csumb.edu
FITZGIBBON, John .... 831-582-3000... 34 B
jfitzgibbon@csumb.edu
FITZGIBBON, III, William, E .... 713-743-3465. 489 B
fitz@uh.edu
FITZGIBBONS, Dorothy .. 516-323-3220. 331 J
dfitzgibbons@molloy.edu
FITZGIBBONS, James .... 510-231-5000... 49 D
FITZGIBBONS, John .... 303-458-4190... 84 M
president@regis.edu
FITZMAURICE, Patricia ... 212-752-1530. 328 G
patricia.fitzmaurice@limcollege.edu
FITZPATRICK, Beata .... 510-642-7464... 70 I
bfitzpatrick@berkeley.edu
FITZPATRICK, Holly .... 413-775-1813. 231 E
fitzpatrickh@gcc.mass.edu
FITZPATRICK, James .... 201-559-3565. 302 A
fitzpatrickj@felician.edu
FITZPATRICK, James, D . 203-254-4000... 89 I
jfitzpatrick@fairfield.edu
FITZPATRICK, Jane .... 606-783-2053. 198 A
j.fitzpatrick@moreheadstate.edu
FITZPATRICK, John, C .... 718-429-6600. 349 H
john.fitzpatrick@vaughn.edu
FITZPATRICK, Joseph ..... 312-235-3511. 159 A
j.fitzpatrick@shimer.edu
FITZPATRICK, M. Louise 610-519-4909. 436 F
louise.fitzpatrick@villanova.edu
FITZPATRICK, SC, Margaret, M .... 845-398-4013. 340 A
mfitzpat@stac.edu
FITZPATRICK, Mark .... 212-229-5300. 332 E
fitzpame@newschool.edu
FITZPATRICK, Mary Anne .... 803-777-7798. 447 G
fitzpatm@gwm.sc.edu
FITZPATRICK, Pat .... 718-390-3131. 350 B
pfitzpat@wagner.edu
FITZPATRICK, Robert ...... 207-948-9143. 211 I
rfitzpatrick@unity.edu
FITZPATRICK, Sharon ..... 405-945-3292. 398 C
FITZPATRICK, Susan ...... 906-635-2831. 245 G
sfitzpatrick@lssu.edu
FITZPATRICK, Timothy, J .... 352-392-2061. 116 A
timf@ufl.edu
FITZPATRICK, Timothy, M .... 860-444-8603. 545 G
timothy.m.fitzpatrick@uscga.edu
FITZSIMMONS, Joanne .. 518-445-2324. 313 C
jfitz@albanylaw.edu
FITZSIMMONS, John .... 207-629-4000. 210 I
jfitzsimmons@mccs.me.edu
FITZSIMMONS, Peter ..... 408-270-6130... 63 N
peter.fitzsimmons@sjeccd.org
FITZSIMMONS, Stephanie .... 732-224-2369. 299 G
sfitzsimmons@brookdalecc.edu
FITZSIMMONS, Tracy ..... 540-665-4505. 509 E
tfitzsim@su.edu
FITZSIMMONS, Verna, M .... 785-826-2601. 188 A
vfitzsimmons@ksu.edu
FITZSIMMONS, William, R .... 617-495-1557. 227 C
wrf@fas.harvard.edu
FITZSIMONS, Connie ...... 310-660-3715... 43 B
cfitzsimons@elcamino.edu
FITZSIMONS, Debra .... 949-582-4665... 67 A
dfitzsimons@socccd.edu
FITZWATER, Valerie ...... 972-825-5469. 481 F
VFitzwater@sagu.edu
FIVECOAT, Frederick .... 610-892-1519. 427 E
ffivecoat@pit.edu
FIX, John .... 256-824-6605..... 8 F
john.fix@uah.edu
FIXEN, Randall .... 701-662-1518. 372 D
randy.fixen@lrsc.edu
FJORTOFT, Nancy, F ...... 630-515-6072. 153 B
nfjort@midwestern.edu
FLACHMANN, Michael .... 661-654-2121... 32 H
mflachmann@csub.edu
FLACK, Anna .... 631-451-4008. 346 E
flacka@sunysuffolk.edu
FLACK, Bobby, L .... 301-447-5220. 217 B
flack@msmary.edu
FLACK, Felecia, J .... 906-227-1272. 248 A
fflack@nmu.edu
FLACK, Lisa .... 217-228-5432. 156 C
flackli@quincy.edu
FLACK, Wayne, R .... 218-299-3362. 255 A
flack@cord.edu
FLAD, Kiera .... 212-431-2164. 333 I
Kiera.Flad@nyls.edu
FLAD-JESION, Ann, M ... 920-565-1204. 533 R
flad-jesionad@lakeland.edu
FLADELAND, Diane .... 701-355-8140. 373 E
dflade@umary.edu
FLAGEL, Andrew .... 781-736-2005. 224 F
aflagel@brandeis.edu
FLAGG, Aaron .... 860-768-5236... 92 D
aflagg@hartford.edu
FLAGG, Chuck, S .... 248-232-4811. 248 D
csflagg@oaklandcc.edu
FLAGG, Mary .... 610-372-4721. 431 D
mflagg@racc.edu
FLAGGERT, James .... 703-539-6890. 510 B
jflaggert@stratford.edu
FLAGSTAD, Lois .... 605-642-6599. 451 G
lois.flagstad@bhsu.edu
FLAHARTY, Sue .... 910-938-6251. 359 E
flahartys@coastalcarolina.edu
FLAHAVEN, Jillian .... 563-441-2467. 180 E
jflahaven@kucampus.edu
FLAHERTY, Jane .... 979-845-8588. 483 C
jflaherty@tamu.edu
FLAHERTY, John .... 212-817-7769. 317 F
jflaherty@gc.cuny.edu
FLAHERTY, Michael .... 315-312-2106. 344 A
michael.flaherty@oswego.edu
FLAHERTY, Pamela, B .... 781-280-3631. 232 B
flahertyp@middlesex.mass.edu
FLAHERTY, Richard, A .... 617-746-5412. 236 B
FLAHIVE, Roger .... 973-328-5011. 300 G
rflahive@ccm.edu
FLAIM, Lou .... 307-382-1616. 543 J
lflaim@wwcc.wy.edu
FLAKE, Bryant .... 435-586-7725. 497 A
flake@suu.edu
FLAKE, Forrest .... 801-422-3861. 495 D
forrest_flake@byu.edu
FLAKE, Susan, R .... 704-272-5331. 363 G
sflake@spcc.edu
FLAMER, Thelma .... 202-231-2768. 544 L
thelma.flamer@dodiis.mil
FLAMM, Adele .... 302-736-2566... 94 C
adele.flamm@wesley.edu
FLAMM, Drew .... 260-982-5968. 170 U
arflamm@manchester.edu
FLAMM, Mara .... 215-717-6621. 435 A
mflamm@uarts.edu
FLAMMER, Rachel .... 716-888-2965. 316 C
flammer@canisius.edu
FLANAGAN, Alyce .... 256-352-8295..... 9 G
alyce.malcolm@wallacestate.edu
FLANAGAN, Elizabeth, A 540-231-7676. 515 C
betsyf@vt.edu
FLANAGAN, J. Kelly .... 801-422-3142. 495 D
kelly_flanagan@byu.edu
FLANAGAN, James .... 212-247-3434. 329 L
jflanagan@mandl.edu
FLANAGAN, James, L ..... 770-484-1204. 128 E
lru@lru.edu
FLANAGAN, James, P .... 603-641-6025. 297 G
jflanagan@anselm.edu
FLANAGAN, Jeanne .... 518-485-3902. 321 A
flanagaj@strose.edu
FLANAGAN, Jerry, E .... 802-654-3000. 500 B
jflanagan@smcvt.edu
FLANAGAN, John .... 973-642-8404. 307 D
john.flanagan@shu.edu
FLANAGAN, Justin .... 419-227-3141. 391 F
jdglanag@unoh.edu
FLANAGAN, Kathleen ..... 310-338-4482... 53 E
flanagan@lmu.edu
FLANAGAN, Lori .... 314-516-5661. 283 E
flanagamlo@umsl.edu
FLANAGAN, Mary Jane .. 989-774-3131. 240 N
flana1mj@cmich.edu
FLANAGAN, Maureen, P 215-574-9600. 418 H
mflanagan@hussianart.edu
FLANAGAN, Michael .... 610-399-2360. 428 B
mflanagan@cheyney.edu
FLANAGAN, Scott .... 608-663-2294. 532 I
sflanagan@edgewood.edu
FLANAGAN, Timothy ...... 309-438-5677. 147 J
FLANARY, Barry .... 802-447-4312. 500 D
bflanary@svc.edu
FLANDERS, Bruce .... 913-971-3568. 188 H
blflanders@mnu.edu
FLANDERS, Lorene .... 678-839-6369. 133 I
lflanders@westga.edu
FLANIGAN, Marjie .... 304-384-6035. 529 E
Mflanigan@concord.edu
FLANIGAN, Patricia .... 949-582-4365... 67 C
pflanigan@saddleback.edu
FLANIGAN, JR., Robert, D .... 404-270-5072. 132 E
rflaniga@spelman.edu
FLANIK, Greg, G .... 440-826-2700. 374 F
gflanik@bw.edu
FLANNAGAN, Dorothy, A .... 210-458-6878. 492 C
dorothy.flannagan@utsa.edu
FLANNAGAN, Larnell ..... 318-274-3235. 207 E
flannaganl@gram.edu
FLANNELY, SC, Jean ...... 718-405-3230. 320 G
jean.flannely@mountsaintvincent.edu
FLANNERY, Brenda .... 507-389-9423. 259 G
brenda.flannery@mnsu.edu
FLANNERY, Chad .... 618-252-5400. 159 E
chad.flannery@sic.edu
FLANNERY, Katherine ..... 215-951-2965. 430 E
flanneryk@philau.edu
FLANNERY, Kathleen ...... 620-231-7000. 189 L
kflannery@pittstate.edu
FLANNERY, Mary .... 510-780-4500... 50 I
mflannery@lifewest.edu
FLANNERY, Maura, C ..... 718-990-1860. 339 A
flannerm@stjohns.edu
FLANNERY, Patrick .... 517-607-2239. 243 I
patrick.flannery@hillsdale.edu
FLANNERY, Teresa (Terry) .... 202-885-2163... 94 F
flannery@american.edu
FLANZRAICH, Gerri .... 516-686-1158. 333 H
gflanzra@nyit.edu
FLATEAU, John .... 718-270-5067. 319 A
jflat@mec.cuny.edu
FLATT, Bonnie .... 503-251-5712. 408 G
bflatt@uws.edu
FLATT, Stephen .... 770-351-1407... 18 I
stephen.flatt@phoenix.edu
FLATTERY, Patrick .... 218-723-6042. 254 K
pflatter@css.edu
FLAVIN, Stephen, P .... 508-831-5095. 238 F
sflavin@wpi.edu
FLAX, Christine .... 443-394-9308. 218 E
cflax@stevenson.edu
FLAX, Gale .... 252-335-0821. 359 F
gale_flax@albemarle.edu
FLAX-HYMAN, Cheryl, L 850-747-3215. 106 H
cflax-hyman@gulfcoast.edu
FLEAGLE, Steven, R ...... 319-384-0595. 175 I
steve-fleagle@uiowa.edu
FLECHA, Gladys, E .... 787-852-1430. 549 C
gflecha@hccpr.edu
FLEENER, Harry .... 850-718-2310... 99 N
fleenerh@chipola.edu
FLEENER, Jayne .... 919-515-5900. 368 B
fleener@ncsu.edu
FLEENOR, Rick .... 606-539-4154. 200 B
rick.fleenor@ucumberlands.edu
FLEET, Frances .... 419-448-3326. 389 J
ffleet@tiffin.edu
FLEETWOOD, Janet .... 215-895-2141. 415 B
janet.fleetwood@drexel.edu
FLEGE, Kelly, A .... 319-273-5885. 176 A
kelly.flege@uni.edu
FLEISCHER, Stephen .... 323-343-4800... 34 A
sfleischer@cslanet.calstatela.edu
FLEISCHMAN, Jean .... 978-542-7765. 230 E
jfleischman@salemstate.edu
FLEISCHMAN, Linda .... 704-337-2543. 365 G
fleischmanl@queens.edu
FLEISCHMAN, Robert ...... 570-422-3589. 428 D
rfleischman@esu.edu
FLEISCHMANN, Kenneth 314-977-3948. 281 I
fleiske@slu.edu
FLEISHMAN, Joseph ...... 337-421-6960. 204 E
joseph.fleishman@sowela.edu
FLEIT, Jody .... 617-587-5511. 234 H
fleitj@neco.edu
FLEITAS, Dionisio .... 214-333-5303. 470 D
dion@dbu.edu
FLEMING, Allyson .... 615-327-6235. 456 E
afleming@mmc.edu
FLEMING, Carol .... 828-398-7307. 357 N
.cfleming@abtech.edu
FLEMING, David .... 269-782-1201. 250 C
dfleming@swmich.edu
FLEMING, Elizabeth .... 413-565-1000. 222 F
lfleming@baypath.edu
FLEMING, Elizabeth, A ... 864-596-9050. 443 D
betsy.fleming@converse.edu
FLEMING, Erika .... 305-428-5700. 109 E
efleming@aii.edu
FLEMING, Graham, R ..... 510-642-7540... 70 I
vcrfleming@berkeley.edu
FLEMING, J. Christopher .... 757-683-3685. 507 N
jcfleming@odu.edu
FLEMING, James .... 605-642-6270. 451 G
james.fleming@bhsu.edu
FLEMING, James .... 503-352-1510. 407 A
jfleming@pacificu.edu
FLEMING, SJ, James ..... 304-243-2233. 531 H
president@wju.edu
FLEMING, Jami .... 877-442-0505... 86 F
jami.fleming@rockies.edu
FLEMING, Jennifer .... 479-498-6020... 20 E
jfleming@atu.edu
FLEMING, Julie, C .... 770-720-5527. 130 G
jcf@reinhardt.edu
FLEMING, Justin .... 507-786-3615. 264 B
flemingj@stolaf.edu
FLEMING, Kay .... 618-985-3741. 148 J
kayfleming@jalc.edu
FLEMING, Kevin .... 951-739-7880... 60 L
kevin.fleming@norcocollege.edu
FLEMING, Kimberly .... 252-399-6540. 352 F
kmfleming@barton.edu
FLEMING, Kirsten .... 909-537-5300... 34 E
kfleming@csusb.edu
FLEMING, Linda .... 814-871-7549. 416 K
fleming006@gannon.edu
FLEMING, Lorraine .... 202-806-6565... 95 G
lfleming@howard.edu
FLEMING, Mark, J .... 610-861-1472. 424 E
memjf01@moravian.edu
FLEMING, Michael .... 404-222-2588. 129 D
mfleming@morehouse.edu
FLEMING, Mike, R .... 618-235-2700. 160 A
mike.fleming@swic.edu
FLEMING, Nina .... 262-551-5800. 532 D
nfleming@carthage.edu
FLEMING, Patricia, A ...... 574-284-4575. 172 G
pfleming@saintmarys.edu
FLEMING, Paul, C .... 504-864-7490. 205 H
pcflemin@loyno.edu
FLEMING, Richard .... 443-550-6021. 214 D
rfleming@csmd.edu
FLEMING, Rita .... 501-686-2920... 23 H
rfleming@uasys.edu
FLEMING, Robert .... 617-824-8670. 226 A
robert_fleming@emerson.edu
FLEMING, Saundra .... 773-878-4699. 158 B
sfleming@staugustine.edu
FLEMING, Scott, S .... 202-687-3455... 95 E
ssf2@georgetown.edu
FLEMING, Sherie .... 256-378-2021..... 2 G
sfleming@cacc.edu
FLEMING, Stephen .... 404-894-5217. 125 D
fleming@gatech.edu
FLEMING, Todd .... 815-394-5112. 157 C
tfleming@rockford.edu
FLEMING, Tom, O .... 310-338-2714... 53 E
tfleming@lmu.edu
FLEMING, Trish .... 215-836-2222. 409 G
tfleming@antonelli.edu
FLEMING, Vickie .... 919-497-3203. 356 E
vfleming@louisburg.edu
FLEMING, William .... 919-962-4651. 366 K
wafleming@northcarolina.edu
FLEMING, William, B ...... 561-803-2001. 110 B
william_fleming@pba.edu
FLEMING-WILLIS, Linda 614-825-6255. 373 G
lfleminlg-willis@aiam.edu
FLEMION, Meg .... 419-434-4510. 391 D
flemion@findlay.edu
FLEMMING, Joshua .... 518-736-3622. 325 A
joshua.flemming@fmcc.suny.edu
FLEMMING, Sondra, G ... 214-860-2146. 470 J
sflemming@dcccd.edu
FLENIKEN, Tracey .... 940-668-7731. 477 I
tfleniken@nctc.edu
FLENNER, Ronald, W ..... 757-446-5829. 504 E
Flennerw@evms.edu
FLENTJE, Mike .... 920-686-6137. 536 A
Mike.Flentje@sl.edu
FLESHER, Van .... 615-383-4848. 464 D
vflesher@watkins.edu
FLESHLER, David .... 216-368-2399. 375 J
david.fleshler@case.edu
FLETCHER, Anthony, S ... 972-860-7645. 470 I
AnthonyFletcher@dcccd.edu
FLETCHER, Bill .... 615-898-2500. 459 D
bill.fletcher@mtsu.edu
FLETCHER, Bridget .... 314-977-7778. 281 I
fletchb@slu.edu
FLETCHER, Carol .... 575-562-2611. 309 H
carol.fletcher@enmu.edu
FLETCHER, Christopher ... 305-809-3147. 104 I
chrisopher.fletcher@fkcc.edu
FLETCHER, Courtney ...... 402-559-4333. 292 J
cfletcher@unmc.edu
FLETCHER, Daryl .... 770-484-1204. 128 E
library@lru.edu
FLETCHER, Heidi, L .... 410-532-5105. 217 E
hfletcher@ndm.edu
FLETCHER, James, A ...... 208-282-3540. 138 E
fletjame@isu.edu
FLETCHER, Janice .... 617-243-2145. 227 K
jfletcher@lasell.edu
FLETCHER, Jeff .... 573-897-5000. 276 E
FLETCHER, John .... 252-328-5817. 367 B
fletcherjo@ecu.edu
FLETCHER, Kathy .... 432-685-4526. 476 G
kfletcher@midland.edu
FLETCHER, Lance .... 617-262-5000. 223 F
Lance.Fletcher@the-bac.edu
FLETCHER, Lynn .... 307-268-2211. 542 X
lfletcher@caspercollege.edu

FLETCHER, Maria ... 208-282-5304. 138 E fletmari@isu.edu
FLETCHER, Mark ... 214-648-8117. 493 E mark.fletcher@utsouthwestern.edu
FLETCHER, Randy ... 217-351-2236. 155 J rfletcher@parkland.edu
FLETCHER, Richard, L ... 440-826-2323. 374 F rfletche@bw.edu
FLETCHER, Scott ... 503-768-6001. 403 K graddean@lclark.edu
FLETCHER, Stephen ... 408-864-8642... 44 M fletcherstephen@deanza.edu
FLETCHER, Thomas ... 570-389-5161. 427 H tfletche@bloomu.edu
FLETCHER, Wesla ... 843-525-8293. 447 C wfletcher@tcl.edu
FLETCHER, William, A ... 843-953-5114. 442 A bill.fletcher@citadel.edu
FLEURY, Jane ... 518-631-9851. 348 K fleuryj@uniongraduatecollege.edu
FLEURY, Traci ... 704-971-8500. 353 F
FLEWELLING, Colleen ... 570-372-4183. 433 H flewelling@susq.edu
FLEWELLING, Colleen ... 570-372-4567. 433 H flewelling@susqu.edu
FLICK, Kenneth ... 843-525-8238. 447 C kflick@tcl.edu
FLICK, Larry ... 541-737-0123. 406 A larry.flick@oregonstate.edu
FLICK, Matt ... 937-294-0592. 388 M flick@saa.edu
FLICKINGER, Catherine .. 516-686-7792. 333 H cflickin@nyit.edu
FLICKINGER, Craig ... 734-432-5725. 246 B cflickinger@madonna.edu
FLICKINGER, Don ... 231-591-3578. 242 F flickind@ferris.edu
FLIEGE, Cheryl ... 309-694-5599. 146 E cfliege@icc.edu
FLIER, Jeffrey, S ... 617-432-1501. 227 C jeffrey_flier@hms.harvard.edu
FLIKEID, Ben ... 651-730-5100. 255 H bflikeid@globeuniversity.edu
FLING, Corey ... 619-849-2583... 59 L coreyfling@pointloma.edu
FLINN, Amy ... 254-298-8364. 482 C alflinn@templejc.edu
FLINN, Deborah ... 860-515-3873... 87 I
FLINN, Gordon, B ... 530-226-4735... 66 D gflinn@simpsonu.edu
FLINN, Nancy ... 510-436-1054... 47 J flinn@hnu.edu
FLINN, Randal ... 219-866-6165. 172 E rflinn@saintjoe.edu
FLINN, Ronald, T ... 517-355-3366. 246 H flinn@msu.edu
FLINT, Aaron ... 603-645-9678. 297 I a.flint@snhu.edu
FLINT, Juanita ... 972-860-4694. 470 G juanitazf@dcccd.edu
FLINT, Laury ... 812-855-7621. 167 F lbarthol@indiana.edu
FLINT, Tora ... 310-577-3000... 77 G registrar@yosan.edu
FLINTOFT, Rebecca ... 303-273-3050... 80 E rebecca.flintoft@is.mines.edu
FLINTON, JoElla ... 405-945-9106. 398 C
FLIPPO, Angela, D ... 870-759-4117... 25 K aflippo@wbcoll.edu
FLIS, Denise ... 405-208-5848. 397 F dflis@okcu.edu
FLOCCHINI, Randy ... 775-674-7688. 294 H rflocchini@tmcc.edu
FLOCKEN, Lise ... 760-757-2121... 54 G lflocken@miracosta.edu
FLOHR, Robin ... 740-264-5591. 379 F rflohr@egcc.edu
FLOM, Sheldon ... 307-754-6284. 543 G Sheldon.Flom@northwestcollege.edu
FLOMENHAFT, Marion ... 516-323-4702. 331 J mflomenhaft@molloy.edu
FLOOD, Carolyn ... 731-352-4020. 453 D floodc@bethelu.edu
FLOOD, Cathy, T ... 920-923-8082. 534 A cflood@marianuniversity.edu
FLOOD, David ... 215-762-3699. 415 B david.flood@drexel.edu
FLOOD, Flora ... 256-726-7287..... 6 B fflood@oakwood.edu
FLOOD, Malia ... 619-216-6682... 68 B mflood@swccd.edu
FLOOD, Pierre ... 323-563-4824... 38 B pierreflood@cdrewu.edu
FLOOD, Thomas ... 718-489-5443. 338 G thomasflood@sfc.edu
FLOOD, Tim ... 619-644-7141... 46 E tim.flood@gcccd.edu
FLOOD, Timothy, J ... 920-929-2136. 540 F tflood@morainepark.edu
FLOOR, Gregory ... 617-850-1285. 227 E gfloor@hchc.edu
FLORCZAK, Joan, E ... 203-576-4665... 91 G joan@bridgeport.edu
FLORENCE, Bob, K ... 816-604-6546. 277 D bob.florence@mcckc.edu
FLORENCE, Christopher . 314-434-4044. 273 C chris.florence@covenantseminary.edu
FLORENDO, Chava ... 541-552-6128. 406 C florendch@sou.edu
FLORENTINE, Dennis ... 908-835-2326. 308 G dflorentine@warren.edu
FLORES, Anna ... 480-517-8171... 15 D anna.flores@riosalado.edu
FLORES, Anthony ... 510-464-3592... 59 C aflores@peralta.edu
FLORES, Barbara ... 787-746-1400. 549 B bflores@huertas.edu
FLORES, Ben ... 915-747-5491. 492 A bflores@utep.edu
FLORES, Chio ... 509-335-9711. 525 A cflores@wsu.edu
FLORES, Deanna, L ... 407-303-1851... 97 H deanna.flores@adu.edu
FLORES, Edwin ... 787-738-2161. 554 C edwin.flores@upr.edu
FLORES, Efrain ... 787-758-2525. 554 F efrain.flores@upr.edu
FLORES, Elizabeth ... 915-747-7872. 492 A lizaf@utep.edu
FLORES, Fatima ... 561-912-2166. 103 C fflores@evergladesuniversity.edu
FLORES, Fernando ... 915-831-6391. 472 B fernief@epcc.edu
FLORES, Gustavo ... 707-664-4388... 36 B gustavo.flores@sonoma.edu
FLORES, Hector ... 585-475-4476. 337 L hefgrad@rit.edu
FLORES, Jacob, C ... 956-721-5148. 475 F jacob.flores@laredo.edu
FLORES, Javier ... 325-942-2047. 465 K javier.flores@angelo.edu
FLORES, Javier ... 307-382-1642. 543 J jflores@wwcc.wy.edu
FLORES, Jayne, T ... 671-735-5638. 546 C pio@guamcc.edu
FLORES, Juan, P ... 671-735-5530. 546 C juan.flores@guamcc.edu
FLORES, Kathy ... 253-680-7178. 516 L kflores@bates.ctc.edu
FLORES, Laureano ... 323-265-8640... 51 F floresl@elac.edu
FLORES, Marilyn ... 925-424-1382... 37 L mflores@laspositascollege.edu
FLORES, Marilyn ... 714-628-5030... 60 H marilyn_flores@sccollege.edu
FLORES, Mary ... 208-792-2325. 138 G mflores@lcsc.edu
FLORES, Matt ... 512-245-2922. 487 C mgf20@txstate.edu
FLORES, Michael ... 210-486-3963. 464 I mflores@alamo.edu
FLORES, Michael ... 210-486-3960. 465 A rflores@alamo.edu
FLORES, Mildred ... 787-780-0070. 547 G mflores@caribbean.edu
FLORES, Roberto ... 863-453-6661. 113 G robert.flores@southflorida.edu
FLORES, Ruben ... 787-279-1912. 550 B rflores@bayamon.inter.edu
FLORES, Rudy ... 530-895-2429... 30 F floresru@butte.edu
FLORES, Susan ... 956-364-4443. 485 H susan.flores@tstc.edu
FLORES, William, V ... 713-221-8001. 489 D president@uhd.edu
FLORES-CHURCH, Adriana ... 562-860-2451... 37 I achurch@cerritos.edu
FLORES-MEDINA, Donna ... 505-454-5328. 309 L dflores@luna.edu
FLORES-ORTIZ, Elsa ... 787-993-8899. 554 A elsa.flores@upr.edu
FLOREY, Nancy, E ... 717-361-1406. 415 H floreyne@etown.edu
FLOREZ, Viola ... 505-277-7267. 312 F vlforez@unm.edu
FLORIAN, Greg, E ... 217-875-7200. 156 J gflorian@richland.edu
FLORIAN, James, S ... 520-621-3680... 18 F florianj@email.arizona.edu
FLORIO, SJ, Philip, J ... 718-817-4503. 324 G pflorio2@fordham.edu
FLOROS, John ... 785-532-6147. 188 A floros@ksu.edu
FLORY, Lowell ... 800-287-8822. 164 C florylo@bethanyseminary.edu
FLOT, Rob ... 847-735-5200. 150 B flot@lakeforest.edu
FLOTTE, Terence, R ... 508-856-8000. 229 C terry.flotte@umassmed.edu
FLOUHOUSE, Steve ... 606-326-2055. 194 J steve.flouhouse@kctcs.edu
FLOURNOY, Bonita ... 404-756-4443. 121 A bflournoy@atlm.edu
FLOURNOY, Jacob, W ... 501-686-2901... 23 H jwflournoy@uasys.edu
FLOWER KIM, Laura ... 626-395-6330... 31 E laura.flowerkim@caltech.edu
FLOWERS, Damon ... 734-677-5322. 252 A dflowers@wccnet.edu
FLOWERS, Donald ... 415-485-9451... 40 G don.flowers@marin.edu
FLOWERS, George ... 334-844-4700..... 1 G flowegt@auburn.edu
FLOWERS, Kathleen ... 315-781-3825. 326 C kflowers@hws.edu
FLOWERS, Laura ... 615-771-7821. 464 G laura@williamsoncc.edu
FLOWERS, Lisa ... 406-771-4412. 287 E lflowers@montana.edu
FLOWERS, Marshall ... 828-669-8012. 357 H mflowers@montreat.edu
FLOWERS, Patricia, J ... 850-644-0415. 115 C pjflowers@fsu.edu
FLOWERS, Robert ... 315-781-3827. 326 C flowers@hws.edu
FLOWERS, Robert ... 817-531-4461. 488 A rflowers@txwes.edu
FLOYD, Andrew ... 229-430-3983. 119 J andrew.floyd@asurams.edu
FLOYD, Arlene ... 330-941-2333. 394 A afloyd@ysu.edu
FLOYD, Brenda, L ... 940-898-3505. 488 B bfloyd@twu.edu
FLOYD, Brian ... 304-367-4298. 528 E brian.floyd@pierpont.edu
FLOYD, Carey ... 580-371-2371. 396 E cfloyd@mscok.edu
FLOYD, Charlsie ... 636-949-4909. 276 D cfloyd@lindenwood.edu
FLOYD, Cindy ... 619-574-6909... 57 E cmfloyd@pacificcollege.edu
FLOYD, Cynthia ... 334-291-4905..... 2 H cynthia.floyd@cv.edu
FLOYD, David J, W ... 225-765-2437. 204 O rulife1@lsu.edu
FLOYD, Donna ... 510-235-7800... 41 K dfloyd@contracosta.edu
FLOYD, Elizabeth ... 864-225-7653. 444 A lizfloyd@forrestcollege.edu
FLOYD, Elson, S ... 509-335-4200. 525 A presidentsoffice@wsu.edu
FLOYD, Gerri ... 541-881-5838. 408 C gfloyd@tvcc.cc
FLOYD, Gregg, S ... 330-672-2422. 382 B gfloyd@kent.edu
FLOYD, James, J ... 909-621-8351... 39 D james.floyd@cmc.edu
FLOYD, Jennifer ... 606-539-4479. 200 B jennifer.floyd@ucumberlands.edu
FLOYD, Joseph ... 337-482-2148. 208 D jnf4727@louisiana.edu
FLOYD, Mark ... 541-737-4611. 406 A mark.floyd@oregonstate.edu
FLOYD, Polly, K ... 850-263-3261... 98 N pkfloyd@baptistcollege.edu
FLOYD, Steven ... 405-585-5132. 397 C steven.floyd@okbu.edu
FLOYD, Tony ... 843-383-8175. 442 F tfloyd@coker.edu
FLUEGEMAN, Tere ... 949-582-4920... 67 A tfluegeman@socccd.edu
FLUET, Gregoire, J ... 860-632-3010... 90 C rector@holyapostles.edu
FLUGUM, Deborah ... 818-677-2301... 34 C deborah.flugum@csun.edu
FLUHARTY, Steven, J ... 215-898-7236. 435 B vpr@pobox.upenn.edu
FLUKE, Donald, W ... 574-372-5100. 166 B dwfluke@grace.edu
FLUKE, Lauri, A ... 405-585-5131. 397 C lauri.fluke@okbu.edu
FLUKER, Zillah ... 334-229-5679..... 1 D zfluker@alasu.edu
FLUNDER, Urisonya ... 806-894-9611. 480 H uflunder@southplaincollege.edu
FLUNKER, Thomas, G ... 507-344-7577. 253 J tom.flunker@blc.edu
FLUOCCO, Edward ... 610-989-1200. 436 D efluocco@vfmac.edu
FLY, Jim ... 316-677-9400. 191 E jfly@watc.edu
FLY, Pam ... 918-444-2060. 396 H fly@nsuok.edu
FLY, Piper ... 615-269-8300. 455 H pfly@kaplan.edu
FLYER, Robert ... 440-365-5222. 383 B
FLYNN, Charles, L ... 718-405-3232. 320 G charles.flynn@mountsaintvincent.edu
FLYNN, Chris ... 540-231-6557. 515 C flynnc@vt.edu
FLYNN, Christie ... 253-964-6553. 522 C cflynn@pierce.ctc.edu
FLYNN, Erin ... 503-725-8490. 406 B erin.flynn@pdx.edu
FLYNN, Jackie ... 412-391-7021. 436 E admissions@vettechinstitute.edu
FLYNN, Joan ... 410-617-5161. 216 A jflynn@loyola.edu
FLYNN, John ... 205-726-2732..... 6 F jflynn@samford.edu
FLYNN, John, J ... 212-769-5055. 337 J
FLYNN, Karen ... 203-932-7317... 92 E kflynn@newhaven.edu
FLYNN, Kathy, A ... 319-296-4218. 178 J kathleen.flynn@hawkeyecollege.edu
FLYNN, Kevin ... 781-239-2549. 231 G kflynn@massbay.edu
FLYNN, Linda ... 979-830-4251. 467 I lflynn@blinn.edu
FLYNN, Mari ... 570-945-8335. 419 N mari.flynn@keystone.edu
FLYNN, Maria ... 270-534-3140. 196 G maria.flynn@kctcs.edu
FLYNN, Marilyn, L ... 213-740-8311... 74 A mflynn@usc.edu
FLYNN, Mark ... 706-568-2080. 123 D flynn_mark@columbusstate.edu
FLYNN, Maura ... 716-926-8822. 326 B mflynn@hilbert.edu
FLYNN, Michael ... 716-685-9631. 333 C mflynn@nycc.edu
FLYNN, Monty ... 315-498-2538. 335 G flynnm@sunyocc.edu
FLYNN, Ruth ... 903-510-3197. 488 E rfly@tjc.edu
FLYNN, Stuart, D ... 602-827-2066... 18 F flynns@email.arizona.edu
FLYNN, Thomas, F ... 610-796-8203. 409 E tom.flynn@alvernia.edu
FLYNN, Thomas, V ... 505-565-1413. 237 A tflynn@stonehill.edu
FLYNT, Samuel ... 334-244-3270..... 2 A sflynt@aum.edu
FOCARETO, Nicole ... 704-461-6665. 352 G NicoleFocareto@bac.edu
FOCHT, Jeffrey, W ... 610-861-5434. 425 D jfocht@northampton.edu
FOCKLER, Debra ... 509-359-6348. 519 C dfockler@ewu.edu
FODNESS, Kacie, M ... 605-256-5136. 451 H kacie.fodness@dsu.edu
FOECKLER, Michael, S ... 540-636-2900. 503 L foeckler@christendom.edu
FOEHL, Brooks, L ... 413-597-4408. 238 D Brooks.L.Foehl@williams.edu
FOERST, Cara Herrick ... 973-642-8726. 307 D cara.foerst@shu.edu
FOERSTER, Amy, C ... 570-577-1954. 411 A amy.foerster@bucknell.edu
FOERTSCH, James ... 701-774-4243. 372 F james.foertsch@willistonstate.edu
FOETSCH, Holly ... 860-512-3613... 88 G hfoetsch@manchestercc.edu
FOGARINO, Shirley ... 510-981-2852... 59 A sfogarino@peralta.edu
FOGARTY, John ... 850-644-1346. 115 C jfogarty@fsu.edu
FOGARTY, Raymond ... 401-232-6407. 438 K rfogarty@bryant.edu
FOGARTY, Timothy, P ... 814-393-2235. 428 C tfogarty@clarion.edu
FOGARTY, William ... 413-552-2221. 231 F bfogarty@hcc.edu
FOGEL, Henry ... 312-341-3782. 157 D hfogel@roosevelt.edu
FOGELGREN, John, A ... 302-454-3922... 93 F fogelgre@dtcc.edu
FOGERSON, Linda ... 760-757-2121... 54 G lfogerson@miracosta.edu
FOGERTY, Rebecca, R ... 302-831-8065... 94 B bfogerty@udel.edu
FOGG, Davina, K ... 509-527-4201. 524 H davina.fogg@wwcc.edu
FOGG, Neal ... 978-542-2495. 230 E nfogg@salemstate.edu
FOGG, Richard ... 785-320-4557. 188 E richardfogg@matc.net
FOGGS, Ranodore, M ... 618-537-6911. 152 G rmfoggs@mckendree.edu
FOGLEMAN, David ... 318-670-9590. 207 A dfogleman@susla.edu
FOHRMAN, Jonathan ... 760-757-2121... 54 G jfohrman@miracosta.edu
FOISY, Brian ... 701-858-3331. 371 F brian.foisy@minotstateu.edu
FOLBERG, Robert ... 248-370-3634. 248 J rfolberg@oakland.edu
FOLDA, Joe ... 719-549-2730... 80 K joe.folda@colostate-pueblo.edu
FOLDA, John, T ... 402-643-4052. 292 A sggs@stgregoryseminary.edu

FOLDEN, Tracey, Y .... 270-707-3825. 195 E
tracey.folden@kctcs.edu
FOLENSBEE, Michael ...... 215-635-7300. 417 C
mfolensbee@gratz.edu
FOLEY, Anne .... 312-369-7477. 143 D
afoley@colum.edu
FOLEY, Beth .... 435-797-1437. 497 B
beth.foley@usu.edu
FOLEY, Brian, P .... 703-822-6697. 513 C
bfoley@nvcc.edu
FOLEY, C. Brad .... 541-346-5661. 406 D
bfoley@uoregon.edu
FOLEY, Chris, J .... 317-274-0402. 168 D
cfoley@iupui.edu
FOLEY, Cindy .... 310-544-6405... 61 H
cindy.foley@usw.salvationarmy.org
FOLEY, Don .... 907-474-7317... 10 I
djfoley@alaska.edu
FOLEY, Erin .... 410-532-3586. 217 E
efoley@ndm.edu
FOLEY, Erin .... 541-885-1013. 405 J
erin.foley@oit.edu
FOLEY, Fred, J .... 215-951-1543. 420 B
foley@lasalle.edu
FOLEY, Gary, A .... 803-535-1264. 446 B
foleyg@octech.edu
FOLEY, Henry, C .... 573-882-6726. 283 B
foleyh@umsystem.edu
FOLEY, Jeff .... 706-721-6249. 126 B
jfoley@gru.edu
FOLEY, Jeremy, N .... 352-375-4683. 116 A
jeremy@gators.uaa.ufl.edu
FOLEY, John .... 508-793-7444. 225 A
jfoley@clarku.edu
FOLEY, John .... 716-851-1114. 323 I
foleyj@ecc.edu
FOLEY, Linda .... 402-354-7050. 291 B
linda.foley@methodistcollege.edu
FOLEY, Lisa .... 530-541-4660... 50 D
foley@ltcc.edu
FOLEY, Mark, R .... 251-442-2201..... 9 A
markfoley@umobile.edu
FOLEY, Mary .... 620-792-9278. 184 F
foleym@bartonccc.edu
FOLEY, Neil .... 845-341-4180. 335 H
neil.foley@sunyorange.edu
FOLEY, Phyllis .... 615-230-4828. 461 G
phyllis.foley@volstate.edu
FOLEY, Richard .... 212-992-8688. 334 D
dick.foley@nyu.edu
FOLEY, Robert, A .... 978-665-3194. 229 E
rfoley@fitchburgstate.edu
FOLEY, Ryan .... 912-688-6061. 129 J
rfoley@ogeecheetech.edu
FOLEY, Thomas, P .... 814-886-6411. 424 G
tfoley@mtaloy.edu
FOLEY, Tim .... 310-544-6461... 61 H
tim.foley@usw.salvationarmy.org
FOLEY, Timothy .... 251-626-3303..... 8 B
tfoley@ussa.edu
FOLGER, Pamela, M .... 217-424-6294. 153 C
pmfolger@millikin.edu
FOLKERT, Eva Dean .... 616-395-7956. 244 A
folkert@hope.edu
FOLKS, Liesl .... 716-645-2771. 341 F
seasdean@eng.buffalo.edu
FOLKS, Lonnie .... 609-652-4877. 305 C
lonnie.folks@stockton.edu
FOLKS, Lucretia .... 360-736-9391. 517 G
lfolks@centralia.edu
FOLLICK, David .... 718-990-5579. 339 A
follickd@stjohns.edu
FOLLICK, Edwin .... 714-533-1495... 66 H
edfollick@southbaylo.edu
FOLLICK, Edwin .... 714-533-3946... 36 C
efollick@calums.edu
FOLLINS, Craig .... 773-291-6313. 142 D
cfollins@ccc.edu
FOLLOSCO, David .... 818-710-2944... 52 B
follosd@piercecollege.edu
FOLSE, Victoria .... 309-556-3051. 148 B
vfolse@iwu.edu
FOLSOM, B. Kevin .... 214-887-5171. 471 F
kfolsom@dts.edu
FOLSOM, Scott, D .... 801-585-1158. 496 Q
scott.folsom@dps.utah.edu
FOLT, Carol, L .... 919-962-1365. 368 D
Carol.Folt@unc.edu
FOLTIN, Craig .... 216-987-4705. 378 D
craig.foltin@tri-c.edu
FOLTZ, Adele .... 302-736-2493... 94 C
adele.foltz@wesley.edu
FOLTZ, Amber .... 540-869-0799. 512 H
afoltz@lfcc.edu
FOLTZ, John .... 208-885-6681. 139 D
jfoltz@uidaho.edu
FOLTZ, Kyla .... 307-268-2111. 542 X
kfoltz@caspercollege.edu
FOLZ, James .... 518-828-4181. 321 C
folz@sunycgcc.edu
FOMBELLE, Douglas, W . 215-641-4801. 253 K
d-fombelle@bethel.edu
FONDETTO, Gina .... 973-642-8587. 307 D
gina.fondetto@shu.edu
FONDILLER, Jennifer ...... 212-854-2817. 314 G
jfondill@barnard.edu
FONG, Bobby .... 610-409-3587. 436 B
bfong@ursinus.edu
FONG, Bruce, W .... 713-917-3908. 471 F
bfong@dts.edu
FONG, Don .... 540-338-2700. 503 A
dfong@cdu.edu
FONG, Harry, M .... 408-554-4398... 64 M
hfong@scu.edu
FONG, Jennifer, C .... 818-947-2433... 52 E
fongjc@lavc.edu
FONG, Lindy .... 323-780-6738... 51 F
fonglw@elac.edu
FONG, Norman .... 916-631-8108... 32 C
FONG, Wyman .... 952-485-5261... 37 J
wfong@clpccd.org
FONG, Wyman .... 925-485-5261... 37 K
wfong@clpccd.org
FONG, Yaa-Yin .... 808-956-8259. 135 L
yaayin@hawaii.edu
FONGER, Ron .... 503-493-6510. 402 J
rfonger@cu-portland.edu
FONKEN, David .... 512-223-4606. 466 I
fonken@austincc.edu
FONS, August .... 575-492-2721. 310 G
afons@nmjc.edu
FONSECA, Anthony .... 413-265-2280. 225 C
fonsecaa@elms.edu
FONSECA, Mimi .... 503-517-1100. 408 H
mfonseca@warnerpacific.edu
FONTÁN, Carla .... 787-744-1060. 551 J
cfontan@mechtech.edu
FONT, Iris, J .... 787-740-4282. 553 C
iris.font@uccaribe.edu
FONTAINE,
Christopher, W .... 903-233-4071. 475 J
chrisfontaine@letu.edu
FONTAINE, David .... 315-792-3050. 349 F
dsfontaine@utica.edu
FONTAINE, Deborah, C .. 757-823-8670. 507 M
dcfontaine@nsu.edu
FONTAINE, Dorrie, K ...... 434-924-0141. 511 B
dkf2u@virginia.edu
FONTAINE, Kenneth .... 203-254-4000... 89 I
kfontaine@fairfield.edu
FONTAINE, Sheryl .... 657-278-2024... 33 E
sfontaine@fullerton.edu
FONTAINE, Yvette, M ..... 619-260-7691... 73 I
yvettef@sandiego.edu
FONTAN, Carla .... 787-744-1060. 551 J
cfontan@mechtech.edu
FONTANET-MALDONADO,
Julio, E .... 787-751-1912. 551 B
jfontane@juris.inter.edu
FONTANEZ, Eduardo .... 787-857-3600. 550 A
efontanez@br.inter.edu
FONTANILLA, Linda .... 949-451-5214... 67 B
lfontanilla@ivc.edu
FONTANO, Dominick ...... 718-390-3164. 350 B
dfontano@wagner.edu
FONTENETTE, Edward, J 870-575-8410... 24 E
fontenettee@uapb.edu
FONTENOT, Janet, S ...... 618-235-2700. 160 A
janet.fontenot@swic.edu
FONTENOT, Karen .... 985-549-2101. 208 C
kfontenot@selu.edu
FONTENOT, Laurie .... 337-363-2197. 204 A
lfontenot@acadiana.edu
FONTENOT, Laurie .... 337-948-0384. 204 C
laurie.fontenot@solacc.edu
FONTENOT, Patrick .... 210-486-4431. 464 J
pfontenot@alamo.edu
FONTENOT, Roxane .... 337-475-5883. 207 G
rfontenot@mcneese.edu
FONTES, Mary .... 218-793-2460. 260 D
mary.fontes@northlandcollege.edu
FONTEYN, Paul, J .... 802-287-8201. 499 D
fonteynp@greenmtn.edu
FONTHAM, Elizabeth ...... 504-559-1388. 205 C
efonth@lsuhsc.edu
FONTOURA, Ana .... 914-654-5456. 320 H
afontoura@cnr.edu
FONTS, Raul, A .... 401-865-2754. 439 E
rfonts@providence.edu
FONVILLE, John, A .... 252-638-7220. 359 G
fonvillj@cravencc.edu
FONZO, Crescenzo .... 201-761-6402. 306 L
cfonzo@saintpeters.edu
FOOSE, David .... 913-234-0650. 185 L
david.foose@cleveland.edu
FOOTE, Clarinda, L .... 870-307-7327... 21 H
clarinda.foote@lyon.edu
FOOTE, Jeffrey, C .... 518-255-5300. 344 E
footjc@cobleskill.edu
FOOTE, Joe, S .... 405-325-2721. 401 B
jfoote@ou.edu
FOOTE, Monica, W .... 718-939-5100. 329 B
mfoote@libi.edu
FOOTE, Rebecca, L .... 315-443-3765. 347 C
rlfoote@syr.edu
FOOTE, Teresa .... 912-650-6200. 131 H
tfoote@southuniversity.edu
FOOTE, Tom, J .... 708-209-3142. 143 E
tom.foote@cuchicago.edu
FOOTER, Nancy .... 940-565-2717. 490 C
nfooter@unt.edu
FORAKER, Wayne .... 480-557-3285... 18 I
wayne.foraker@phoenix.edu
FORBES, Cassie .... 828-766-1240. 361 H
cforbes@mayland.edu
FORBES, David, S .... 406-243-4621. 286 H
david.forbes@umontana.edu
FORBES, Don, L .... 320-363-2490. 254 J
dforbes@csbsju.edu
FORBES, Donald .... 320-363-2490. 263 P
dforbes@csbsju.edu
FORBES, Gerald .... 580-559-5208. 395 F
gforbes@ecok.edu
FORBES, J. Thomas .... 812-855-5394. 167 E
jtforbes@indiana.edu
FORBES, J.T .... 812-855-5700. 167 F
forbesjt@indiana.edu
FORBES, Karen, J .... 610-330-5005. 420 D
forbesk@lafayette.edu
FORBES, Kathryn, P .... 603-862-1505. 298 C
kathie.forbes@unh.edu
FORBES, Lindi, D .... 620-421-6700. 188 D
lindif@labette.edu
FORBES, Maribeth .... 781-595-6768. 228 C
mforbes@mariancourt.edu
FORBES, Michele .... 225-578-8491. 205 E
FORBES, Robert, P .... 678-915-3291. 132 C
rforbes@spsu.edu
FORBES, Scott .... 713-500-3289. 492 E
Scott.Forbes@uth.tmc.edu
FORBES, Sharon .... 708-237-5050. 155 B
sforbes@nc.edu
FORBES, Shawna .... 313-496-2587. 252 B
sforbes1@wcccd.edu
FORBES, Suzetta, R .... 906-932-4231. 242 I
suef@gogebic.edu
FORBES, Tonya .... 919-866-5595. 364 G
tpforbes@waketech.edu
FORBES ISAIS,
Geraldine .... 505-277-2879. 312 F
gforbes@unm.edu
FORBESS, Timothy .... 937-529-2201. 390 D
tforbess@united.edu
FORBIS, Brenda .... 912-344-2904. 120 G
brenda.forbis@armstrong.edu
FORBUSH, Dan .... 518-580-5746. 341 A
dforbush@skidmore.edu
FORCE, Bruce .... 918-293-5456. 398 B
bruce.force@okstate.edu
FORCE, Darcy .... 817-202-6629. 481 E
dforce@swau.edu
FORCH, Paul, J .... 434-924-3586. 511 B
pjf8t@virginia.edu
FORCINITO, Lorraine ...... 262-524-7124. 532 C
lforcini@carrollu.edu
FORD, Amy .... 580-559-5725. 395 F
aford@ecok.edu
FORD, Beth .... 216-373-5351. 385 G
bford@ndc.edu
FORD, Carol .... 601-643-8626. 266 F
carol.ford@colin.edu
FORD, Charles, W .... 270-247-8521. 197 H
cford@midcontinent.edu
FORD, Charlotte .... 205-226-4740..... 2 C
cford@bsc.edu
FORD, Chris .... 270-686-4291. 192 G
chris.ford@brescia.edu
FORD, Courtney .... 541-383-7700. 402 D
cford@cocc.edu
FORD, Daryl .... 617-349-8541. 228 B
dford@lesley.edu
FORD, Deborah, L .... 262-595-2211. 537 C
deborah.ford@uwp.edu
FORD, Dow .... 601-403-1214. 269 D
dford@prcc.edu
FORD, Duane, M .... 608-822-2300. 541 C
dford@swtc.edu
FORD, Gillian, F .... 814-332-2155. 409 D
gford@allegheny.edu
FORD, Glenn .... 541-737-2447. 406 A
glen.ford@oregonstate.edu
FORD, Glenn .... 870-633-4480... 21 A
gford@eacc.edu
FORD, III, Harrison .... 843-661-8231. 443 G
harrison.ford@fdtc.edu
FORD, James .... 503-682-3903. 407 B
jford@pioneerpacific.edu
FORD, Jean .... 734-384-4274. 247 C
jford@monroeccc.edu
FORD, Jeff .... 417-447-6930. 279 K
fordj@otc.edu
FORD, Jimmy .... 502-852-7155. 200 D
jimmy.ford@louisville.edu
FORD, John .... 415-476-4998... 72 A
jford@support.ucsf.edu
FORD, Josanne .... 215-569-9215. 423 M
jford@phmc.org
FORD, Kari .... 940-668-7731. 477 I
kford@nctc.edu
FORD, Kathy .... 909-469-5542... 76 B
kford@westernu.edu
FORD, Keenan .... 270-247-8521. 197 H
kford@midcontinent.edu
FORD, Kelli .... 317-917-5731. 169 L
kford50@ivytech.edu
FORD, Kim, R .... 202-274-7181... 97 A
kford@udc.edu
FORD, Kimberly .... 330-337-6403. 373 F
college@awc.edu
FORD, Lacy, K .... 803-777-2808. 447 G
ford@mailbox.sc.edu
FORD, Laura, C .... 309-794-7452. 139 L
lauraford@augustana.edu
FORD, Lynne, E .... 843-953-5527. 443 A
fordl@cofc.edu
FORD, Madeline .... 718-518-4211. 318 B
mford@hostos.cuny.edu
FORD, Marie .... 901-320-9700. 463 J
mford@victory.edu
FORD, Mark, C .... 913-971-3614. 188 H
mford@mnu.edu
FORD, Mary, E .... 573-629-3046. 274 J
mford@hlg.edu
FORD, Mary, J .... 603-822-5432. 298 E
mary.ford@granite.edu
FORD, Michael .... 312-341-2098. 157 D
mford@roosevelt.edu
FORD, Michael, B .... 503-768-7000. 403 K
mford@lclark.edu
FORD, Michelle .... 802-764-2139. 499 I
michelle.ford@neci.edu
FORD, Nadine, Y .... 919-516-4128. 366 C
nford@st-aug.edu
FORD, Nancy .... 620-365-5116. 183 I
ford@allencc.edu
FORD, Pamela, R .... 318-257-3031. 207 F
prford@latech.edu
FORD, Patrick .... 704-461-6545. 352 G
PatrickFord@bac.edu
FORD, Ralph .... 908-709-7142. 308 B
ford@ucc.edu
FORD, Regina .... 714-484-7344... 56 E
rford@cypresscollege.edu
FORD, Ricky .... 662-720-7302. 269 B
rgford@nemcc.edu
FORD, Ricky, G .... 662-720-7730. 269 B
rgford@nemcc.edu
FORD, Shelly .... 601-928-6222. 268 C
shelly.ford@mgccc.edu
FORD, Susan, M .... 618-453-4527. 159 G
sford@siu.edu
FORD, Sylverna, V .... 901-678-2201. 460 B
sford@memphis.edu
FORD, Tim .... 207-221-4523. 213 A
tford@une.edu
FORD, W. Glenn .... 503-883-2458. 404 A
gford@linfield.edu
FORD, William .... 215-968-8285. 411 B
fordw@bucks.edu
FORD FISHER, Margaret 713-718-8010. 473 C
margaret.fordfisher@hccs.edu
FORD-KEE, Dianthia .... 484-365-7391. 422 D
dfkee@lincoln.edu
FORDE, Althea .... 718-960-8066. 318 A
althea.forde@lehman.cuny.edu
FORDE, Dermot, M .... 419-372-9475. 374 K
dforde@bgsu.edu
FORDIS, JR.,
C. Michael .... 713-798-3395. 467 F
fordis@bcm.edu
FORDOSKI, Dori .... 814-371-2090. 434 F
dfordoski@triangle-tech.edu
FORDYCE, Richard, A ..... 660-263-3900. 272 A
rfordyce@cccb.edu
FORE, Janet, S .... 574-284-5281. 172 G
jfore@saintmarys.edu
FORE, Marilyn .... 843-349-5208. 444 F
marilyn.fore@hgtc.edu
FOREHAND, Cynthia, J .. 802-656-8060. 500 F
cynthia.forehand@uvm.edu
FORELL, K. Leigh .... 919-536-7200. 360 B
forellk@durhamtech.edu
FOREMAN, Artie .... 601-635-2111. 266 H
aforeman@eccc.edu
FOREMAN, David, M .... 570-577-3510. 411 A
david.foreman@bucknell.edu
FOREMAN, Dorine, M ..... 845-368-7202. 340 C
FOREMAN, Hank, T .... 828-262-7525. 367 A
foremanht@appstate.edu
FOREMAN, Karen, N .... 540-868-7109. 512 H
kforeman@lfcc.edu

FOREMAN, Kathy .... 904-470-8216. 102 A
kathy.foreman@ewc.edu
FOREMAN, Pamela .... 804-257-5821. 515 F
pforeman@vuu.edu
FOREMAN, Ronald, R ..... 845-368-7210. 340 C
FOREMAN, Todd, D .... 607-436-2081. 343 E
forematd@oneonta.edu
FOREST, Laura Ann .... 334-844-6444..... 1 G
laf0009@auburn.edu
FOREST, Rebecca .... 978-632-6600. 232 C
r_forest@mwcc.mass.edu
FOREST, Rebecca .... 978-630-9597. 232 C
r_forest@mwcc.mass.edu
FOREST, Robert .... 610-647-4400. 418 I
rforest@immaculata.edu
FORESTER, Lyn .... 402-826-8631. 289 E
lyn.forester@doane.edu
FORESTER, Sherri, L .... 270-901-1115. 196 E
sherri.forester@kctcs.edu
FORESYTH, Jan .... 432-264-5051. 473 E
jforesyth@howardcollege.edu
FORGER, James .... 517-355-4583. 246 H
forger@msu.edu
FORGET, Robert, L .... 608-796-3012. 539 E
rlforget@viterbo.edu
FORGETTE, Adrienne, M . 712-707-7077. 181 H
aforgett@nwciowa.edu
FORGEY, Glendon, S ...... 903-675-6211. 488 D
gforgey@tvcc.edu
FORGEY, Laura .... 612-359-6491. 253 H
forgey@augsburg.edu
FORINA, Olga .... 718-818-6470. 339 H
FORK, Patricia, A .... 614-235-4136. 390 A
pfork@TLSohio.edu
FORKUM, James .... 707-524-1849... 65 B
jforkum@santarosa.edu
FORLINES, Jon .... 615-844-5258. 464 E
jforlines@welch.edu
FORLINES, Susan .... 615-844-5259. 464 E
susan@welch.edu
FORMAN, Daniel, T .... 212-960-0863. 351 M
forman@yu.edu
FORMAN, Fran .... 417-690-3223. 272 E
fforman@cofo.edu
FORMAN, Gary .... 415-476-5544... 72 A
gary.forman@ucsf.edu
FORMAN, Peter .... 201-692-9612. 301 J
forman@fdu.edu
FORMAN, Robert, J .... 718-990-7552. 339 A
honors@stjohns.edu
FORMAN, Robin .... 404-727-6062. 124 E
robin.forman@emory.edu
FORMAN,
Scheherazade, W .... 301-322-0886. 217 F
formansw@pgcc.edu
FORNERIS, Glenda .... 815-802-8835. 149 C
gforneris@kcc.edu
FORNEY, Heather .... 605-773-3455. 451 E
heather.forney@sdbor.edu
FORNEY, Judith .... 940-565-2436. 490 C
judith.forney@unt.edu
FORNEY, Phyllis .... 314-687-2900. 281 K
pforney@sbc-hazelwood.com
FOROUDASTAN,
Hooshang .... 919-546-8323. 366 E
hooshang@shawu.edu
FORREST, Barbara .... 205-665-6055..... 9 B
forrestb@montevallo.edu
FORREST, Christy .... 336-249-8186. 360 A
clforrest@davidsonccc.edu
FORREST, Cynthia .... 207-602-2372. 213 A
cforrest@une.edu
FORREST, Haegan .... 617-243-2165. 227 K
hforrest@lasell.edu
FORREST, Seth .... 410-951-6183. 220 B
sforrest@coppin.edu
FORREST, Stephen, R ..... 734-764-1185. 251 C
stevefor@umich.edu
FORRESTER, Cynthia ...... 913-758-6114. 191 B
Cynthia.Forrester@stmary.edu
FORRESTER, Don .... 540-785-5440. 511 D
donforrester@vbc.edu
FORRESTER, Jill, M .... 717-245-1669. 414 H
forrestj@dickinson.edu
FORRESTER, Joe, D .... 724-480-3400. 413 H
joe.forrester@ccbc.edu
FORRESTER, Julia, P ...... 214-768-2574. 481 A
jforrest@smu.edu
FORRESTER, Michael, P . 864-592-4805. 447 A
forresterm@sccsc.edu
FORRESTER, Nancy .... 423-354-2521. 461 C
nfforrester@northeaststate.edu
FORRESTER, Risa .... 405-425-5954. 397 D
risa.forrester@oc.edu
FORRIDER, Holly .... 330-337-6403. 373 F
college@awc.edu
FORRIDER, Timothy .... 330-337-6403. 373 F
college@awc.edu
FORRISTER, Ann .... 517-264-3999. 238 G
FORRY, Jennifer .... 617-713-5901. 235 D
jennifer.forry@newbury.edu
FORSBERG, Peggy .... 785-442-6013. 187 E
pforsberg@highlandcc.edu
FORSETH, Eric, A .... 712-722-6004. 177 J
eric.forseth@dordt.edu
FORSETH, Lynn, M .... 920-568-7224. 540 C
forseth@madisoncollege.edu
FORSHEE, Scott .... 406-657-2298. 287 C
sforshee@msubillings.edu
FORSMAN, Carl .... 336-770-3235. 369 D
forsmanc@uncsa.edu
FORSMAN, Nadine .... 218-235-2154. 261 G
n.forsman@vcc.edu
FORSSTROM, Janice, M . 978-762-4000. 232 D
jforsstr@northshore.edu
FORST, Katherine .... 510-666-8248... 26 F
kforst@aimc.edu
FORSTEN, Michele .... 718-260-5109. 319 B
mforsten@citytech.cuny.edu
FORSTER, Daniel .... 617-521-2031. 236 G
daniel.forster@simmons.edu
FORSTER, David .... 573-592-4381. 285 D
dforster@williamwoods.edu
FORSTER, Jerry .... 304-929-1478. 527 H
jerryforster@ucwv.edu
FORSTER, Leticia .... 434-832-7617. 512 A
forsterl@cvcc.vccs.edu
FORSTER, Marjorie .... 410-706-6631. 219 C
mforster@umaryland.edu
FORSTER, Michael .... 601-266-5253. 270 E
michael.forster@usm.edu
FORSTER, Patrick .... 503-821-8912. 406 F
patrick@pnca.edu
FORSTER, Sarah .... 507-222-4206. 254 D
sforster@carleton.edu
FORSTER, Stefanie .... 207-216-4321. 211 C
sforster@yccc.edu
FORSTROM, Katharine .... 308-432-6246. 291 D
kforstrom@csc.edu
FORSYTH, Anne, S .... 805-525-4417... 69 H
aforsyth@thomasaquinas.edu
FORSYTH, Ashley .... 215-545-1347. 410 A
aforsyth@aii.edu
FORSYTH, Melissa .... 606-886-3863. 194 K
melissa.forsyth@kctcs.edu
FORSYTH, Nate .... 641-648-4611. 179 I
FORSYTH, Ryan .... 978-360-9290. 232 C
r_forsyth@mwcc.mass.edu
FORSYTHE, George, B .... 573-592-5315. 285 B
barney.forsythe@westminster-mo.edu
FORSYTHE, Mary, E .... 910-962-3154. 369 C
forsythem@uncw.edu
FORSYTHE, Micah .... 406-586-3585. 286 F
micah.forsythe@montanabiblecollege.edu
FORT, Gregg .... 716-926-8790. 326 B
gfort@hilbert.edu
FORT, Rebecca, L .... 330-471-8313. 383 D
rfort@malone.edu
FORTE, Gregory .... 216-987-4294. 378 D
gregory.forte@tri-c.edu
FORTE, Joseph .... 316-942-4291. 189 E
fortej@newmanu.edu
FORTE, Paul, D .... 401-456-8224. 439 F
pforte@ric.edu
FORTE, Teresa (Terrie) ... 413-747-0204. 224 G
teresa.forte@cambridgecollege.edu
FORTE, Tyrone .... 718-262-2228. 319 F
tforte@york.cuny.edu
FORTE-PARNELL,
Charlotte .... 661-722-6300... 28 F
cforteparnell@avc.edu
FORTENBERRY, Kim .... 813-424-4619. 107 C
kfortenberry@academy.edu
FORTHOFER, Scott .... 406-496-4500. 287 F
sforthofer@mtech.edu
FORTIN, Barbara .... 530-898-5945... 33 A
bfortin@csuchico.edu
FORTIN, Denis .... 269-471-3648. 239 D
fortind@andrews.edu
FORTIN, Jay .... 570-504-7000. 413 B
FORTIN, Maurice, G .... 325-942-2222. 465 K
maurice.fortin@angelo.edu
FORTIN, Shelley .... 843-661-8110. 443 G
shelley.fortin@fdtc.edu
FORTIN-WAVRA, Marion 402-554-4800. 293 A
mfortin-wavra@unomaha.edu
FORTINI, Mary-Ellen ...... 408-554-4806... 64 M
mfortini@scu.edu
FORTINO SHURTIFF,
Julie .... 989-386-6622. 247 B
jfortio@midmich.edu
FORTMAN, Susan .... 516-323-4311. 331 J
sfortman@molloy.edu
FORTMILLER, Dan .... 503-725-4446. 406 B
daniel.fortmiller@pdx.edu
FORTNER, James .... 404-894-7894. 125 D
james.fortner@business.gatech.edu
FORTNER, Martin .... 318-670-9322. 207 A
mfortner@susla.edu
FORTNER, Melissa .... 706-865-2134. 133 B
mfortner@truett.edu
FORTNER, Tom .... 601-984-1100. 270 C
tfortner@umc.edu
FORTON, Joseph .... 305-821-3333. 105 A
jforton@fnu.edu
FORTOSIS, Robert .... 727-864-8252. 101 N
fortoscr@eckerd.edu
FORTSCH, Peggy .... 319-226-2031. 175 D
Peggy.Fortsch@AllenCollege.edu
FORTUNE, Beth .... 615-322-4234. 463 G
beth.fortune@vanderbilt.edu
FORTUNE, Diana .... 518-891-2915. 335 A
dfortune@nccc.edu
FOS, Peter, J .... 504-280-5536. 205 G
president@uno.edu
FOSDYCK, Rick .... 641-683-5117. 179 A
rick.fosdyck@indianhills.edu
FOSGARD, Steven .... 989-386-6622. 247 B
sforgard@midmich.edu
FOSHEE, Brian, E .... 901-843-3870. 458 E
foshee@rhodes.edu
FOSKEY, Becky .... 478-289-2104. 124 C
bfoskey@ega.edu
FOSS, Anna .... 413-236-2107. 231 A
afoss@berkshirecc.edu
FOSS, Jennifer, J .... 757-683-3132. 507 N
jfoss@odu.edu
FOSS, Lisa .... 320-308-4028. 261 B
lhfoss@stcloudstate.edu
FOSS, Marcia, J .... 701-845-7534. 372 A
marcia.foss@vcsu.edu
FOSS, Michael, C .... 413-755-4510. 233 A
mfoss@stcc.edu
FOSS, Pedar, W .... 765-658-4359. 165 F
pfoss@depauw.edu
FOSS, Rick .... 651-641-3211. 256 J
rfoss001@luthersem.edu
FOSSEN, Linda .... 360-752-8440. 517 B
lfossen@btc.ctc.edu
FOSSUM, Dallas .... 701-671-2314. 372 E
dallas.fossum@ndscs.edu
FOSSUM, Scott .... 605-995-3025. 450 E
scott.fossum@mitchelltech.edu
FOSSUM, Theresa .... 979-458-6000. 482 E
tfossum@tamu.edu
FOSSUM, Tracy .... 507-786-3885. 264 B
fossum@stolaf.edu
FOSTER, Adrienne .... 310-287-4589... 52 F
fosteraa@wlac.edu
FOSTER, Alan .... 918-781-7285. 394 D
fostera@bacone.edu
FOSTER, Andrew .... 203-773-8542... 87 G
afoster@albertus.edu
FOSTER, Anita .... 859-336-5082. 198 J
afoster@sccky.edu
FOSTER, Anne .... 513-569-1898. 376 L
anne.foster@cincinnatistate.edu
FOSTER, Ben .... 972-524-3341. 481 H
FOSTER, Blair, W .... 716-888-2990. 316 C
foster@canisius.edu
FOSTER, Brandi .... 406-444-0332. 286 G
bfoster@montana.edu
FOSTER, Brian, L .... 573-882-6596. 283 C
fosterbl@missouri.edu
FOSTER, Cherie, A .... 248-341-2117. 248 D
cafoster@oaklandcc.edu
FOSTER, Clark, M .... 518-564-2130. 344 B
fostercm@plattsburgh.edu
FOSTER, Claybourne .... 901-435-1307. 455 M
claybourne_foster@loc.edu
FOSTER, Collins .... 678-891-2320. 125 G
collins.foster@gpc.edu
FOSTER, Connie .... 270-745-2904. 200 G
connie.foster@wku.edu
FOSTER, Delbert, T .... 803-536-8191. 446 G
dfoster@scsu.edu
FOSTER, Donald, W .... 614-823-1350. 387 K
dfoster@otterbein.edu
FOSTER, Donna .... 864-941-8430. 446 C
foster.d@ptc.edu
FOSTER, Eddie, D .... 252-638-3919. 359 G
fostere@cravencc.edu
FOSTER, Ellen .... 251-380-3460..... 7 D
efoster@shc.edu
FOSTER, Felecia .... 901-435-1740. 455 M
felecia_foster@loc.edu
FOSTER, Gaines .... 225-578-8619. 204 O
dnfost@lsu.edu
FOSTER, Gretchen, K .... 308-635-6183. 293 E
fosterg2@wncc.edu
FOSTER, Isaac .... 646-378-6125. 335 C
isaac.foster@nyack.edu
FOSTER, Ivan, V .... 336-750-2830. 370 A
fosteriv@wssu.edu
FOSTER, Jacqueline .... 910-362-7019. 358 F
jfoster@cfcc.edu
FOSTER, James, A .... 814-393-2225. 428 C
jafoster@clarion.edu
FOSTER, James, E .... 503-554-2144. 403 C
jfoster@georgefox.edu
FOSTER, Janet .... 562-985-5459... 33 F
jfoster4@csulb.edu
FOSTER, Jeanie .... 858-653-3000... 32 A
FOSTER, Joan, L .... 303-556-3215... 83 D
fosterjl@msudenver.edu
FOSTER, Joseph .... 703-284-1646. 507 B
joseph.foster@marymount.edu
FOSTER, Julie .... 775-831-1314. 295 F
jfoster@sierranevada.edu
FOSTER, Karen .... 318-342-5220. 208 E
kfoster@ulm.edu
FOSTER, Kathryn, A .... 207-778-7256. 212 D
kfoster@maine.edu
FOSTER, Kathy .... 512-232-3316. 491 C
k.foster@mail.utexas.edu
FOSTER, Kay, S .... 256-549-8224..... 3 M
kaysmith@gadsdenstate.edu
FOSTER, Keith .... 509-434-5275. 518 E
keith.foster@ccs.spokane.edu
FOSTER, Keith .... 509-434-5275. 518 D
kfoster@ccs.spokane.edu
FOSTER, LaTonya .... 630-617-6466. 145 A
latonya.foster@elmhurst.edu
FOSTER, Linda .... 904-470-8012. 102 A
lefoster@ewc.edu
FOSTER, Marie, C .... 219-785-5698. 172 A
mfoster@pnc.edu
FOSTER, Mary Jane .... 203-576-4696... 91 G
mjfoster@bridgeport.edu
FOSTER, Mary Louise ...... 402-844-7129. 291 I
marylouise@northeast.edu
FOSTER, Meezie .... 302-225-6235... 93 H
fosterm@gbc.edu
FOSTER, Meichele .... 573-876-7110. 282 H
mfoster@stephens.edu
FOSTER, Melanie .... 512-637-5677. 479 C
seubookstore@texasbook.com
FOSTER, Michelle .... 319-208-5063. 182 G
mfoster@scciowa.edu
FOSTER, Nicola .... 212-346-1949. 335 J
nfoster@pace.edu
FOSTER, Pamela .... 925-969-3449... 49 B
pfoster@jfku.edu
FOSTER, Paul .... 406-657-1705. 287 C
paul.foster4@msubillings.edu
FOSTER, Rita, F .... 334-242-5645..... 9 C
rffoster@una.edu
FOSTER, Robert, W .... 304-647-6285. 530 B
rfoster@osteo.wvsom.edu
FOSTER, Sandy .... 503-517-1851. 408 I
sfoster@westernseminary.edu
FOSTER, Scot .... 510-869-6744... 61 I
sfoster@samuelmerritt.edu
FOSTER, Shannon .... 907-834-1632... 11 B
sfoster@pwscc.edu
FOSTER, Sharon .... 858-635-4858... 26 M
sfoster@alliant.edu
FOSTER, JR., Sidney, C . 330-972-6102. 390 E
sfoster@uakron.edu
FOSTER, Stephen, P .... 937-775-2380. 393 G
stephen.foster@wright.edu
FOSTER, Steve .... 281-487-1170. 484 H
sfoster@txchiro.edu
FOSTER, Tim .... 970-248-1498... 79 F
tfoster@coloradomesa.edu
FOSTER, Tim .... 559-730-3902... 40 I
timf@cos.edu
FOSTER, Tim .... 309-268-4908. 151 C
tfoster@lincolncollege.edu
FOSTER, Timothy .... 717-757-1100. 438 H
tim.foster@yti.edu
FOSTER, Timothy, W .... 207-725-3228. 209 H
tfoster@bowdoin.edu
FOSTER, Yvonne .... 717-867-6161. 421 H
foster@lvc.edu
FOSTER BOYD, Marsha . 313-831-5200. 242 E
mboyd@etseminary.edu
FOSTER CURTIS, Ellen ... 708-534-8046. 145 F
efostercurtis@govst.edu
FOSTER-DAY, Emily .... 617-879-7016. 230 B
efoster-day@massart.edu
FOSTER GNAGE, Marie .. 304-424-8200. 530 E
marie.gnage@wvup.edu
FOSTER-JOHNSON,
Lynn .... 603-646-1187. 296 G
lynn.foster-johnson@dartmouth.edu
FOSTER ZSIGA, Erin .... 207-786-6215. 209 F
efoster@bates.edu
FOSTNER, Jay, J .... 920-403-3169. 535 L
jay.fostner@snc.edu
FOTH, Rodney .... 252-492-2061. 364 F
fothr@vgcc.edu
FOTOUHI, Farshad .... 313-577-3776. 252 G
fotouhi@wayne.edu
FOUBERG, Erin .... 605-626-3456. 451 I
ehfouberg@northern.edu
FOUCART, Steve .... 417-836-5632. 278 E
stevefoucart@missouristate.edu
FOUGERE, John .... 573-882-0601. 283 B
fougerej@umsystem.edu
FOUGERES, Michel .... 727-873-4040. 116 D
mfougeres@usfsp.edu

FOULSHAM, Linda, M .... 828-262-2144. 367 A
foulshamlm@appstate.edu
FOUNTAIN, Barbara .... 707-864-7000... 66 G
barbara.fountain@solano.edu
FOUNTAIN, Barbara .... 707-864-4000... 66 G
barbara.fountain@solano.edu
FOUNTAIN, Cheryl, A .... 904-620-2496. 116 B
fountain@unf.edu
FOUNTAIN, Jeffrey .... 702-579-3527. 294 B
jfountain@kaplan.edu
FOUNTAIN, Jennifer .... 541-552-6234. 406 C
fountainj@sou.edu
FOUNTAIN, Shanna .... 515-964-6441. 177 B
slfountain@dmacc.edu
FOUNTAINE, Cynthia ...... 618-453-8761. 159 G
fountaine@siu.edu
FOURMAN, Elizabeth ...... 574-284-4584. 172 G
efourman@saintmarys.edu
FOURMY CUTRER,
Emily .... 903-223-3001. 484 C
emily.cutrer@tamut.edu
FOURNIER, Jody .... 614-236-6445. 375 H
jfournie@capital.edu
FOURNIER, Marc .... 617-243-2291. 227 K
mfournier@lasell.edu
FOURNIER, Robert .... 313-577-4280. 252 G
ai5611@wayne.edu
FOUST, Cynthia, R .... 580-774-7172. 400 B
cindy.foust@swosu.edu
FOUST, Dane, R .... 410-543-6080. 220 D
drfoust@salisbury.edu
FOUST, Jasper .... 706-646-6302. 132 B
jfoust@sctech.edu
FOUST, Karen, R .... 501-450-1362... 21 E
foust@hendrix.edu
FOUST, Pam .... 217-641-4956. 148 M
pfoust@jwcc.edu
FOUT, Leslie, G .... 865-694-6529. 461 D
lgfout@pstcc.edu
FOUTCH, Tim .... 918-456-5511. 396 H
foutch@nsuok.edu
FOUTS, Paul .... 415-442-7026... 45 I
pfouts@ggu.edu
FOUTY, Dennis .... 832-842-4603. 489 A
dfouty@uh.edu
FOUTY, Dennis .... 832-842-4603. 489 B
dfouty@uh.edu
FOWLE, Marilyn .... 940-397-4117. 476 H
marilyn.fowle@mwsu.edu
FOWLER, Carlton .... 816-604-4101. 277 H
carlton.fowler@mcckc.edu
FOWLER, Craig .... 828-227-7282. 369 E
cfowler@wcu.edu
FOWLER, Craig .... 715-234-7082. 541 F
Craig.Fowler@witc.edu
FOWLER, David, G .... 601-815-1149. 270 C
dfowler@umc.edu
FOWLER, Derphelia .... 928-724-6950... 13 H
FOWLER, Dwight .... 610-341-1388. 415 G
dfowler@eastern.edu
FOWLER, Gregory .... 603-668-2211. 297 I
g.fowler@snhu.edu
FOWLER, Gregory, T ...... 928-523-1186... 16 C
gt.fowler@nau.edu
FOWLER, James .... 508-541-1547. 225 F
jfowler@dean.edu
FOWLER, Jeffrey .... 314-977-2849. 281 I
fowlerjl@slu.edu
FOWLER, Julie, H .... 903-983-8281. 475 E
jfowler@kilgore.edu
FOWLER, Liesl, A .... 309-794-7211. 139 L
lieslfowler@augustana.edu
FOWLER, Lindi .... 864-977-7200. 445 H
lindi.fowler@ngu.edu
FOWLER, Lisa .... 303-914-6302... 84 I
lisa.fowler@rrcc.edu
FOWLER, Lisa Therese ... 212-962-0002. 333 B
lfowler@nyci.edu
FOWLER, Marc .... 616-222-1443. 241 F
marc.fowler@cornerstone.edu
FOWLER, Matt .... 618-262-8641. 147 C
fowlerm@iecc.edu
FOWLER, Mike .... 502-451-0815. 199 G
mfowler@sullivan.edu
FOWLER, Pamela, W ...... 734-763-4119. 251 C
pfowler@umich.edu
FOWLER, Paul .... 404-727-0512. 124 E
pgfowle@emory.edu
FOWLER, Peter .... 617-989-4082. 237 G
fowlerp@wit.edu
FOWLER, S. Kevin .... 903-510-2419. 488 E
kfow@tjc.edu
FOWLER, Sandra .... 229-931-2237. 126 D
sandra.fowler@gsw.edu
FOWLER, Sandy .... 530-674-9199... 36 E
sfowler@cambridge.edu
FOWLER, Shaanette .... 330-490-7320. 392 H
sfowler@walsh.edu
FOWLER, Tammy, L .... 870-972-2617... 19 N
tlfowler@astate.edu
FOWLER, Verna, M .... 800-567-2344. 532 E
vfowler@menominee.edu
FOWLER, Vivia, L .... 478-757-5229. 134 G
vfowler@wesleyancollege.edu
FOWLER, Walter, B .... 412-365-1105. 412 K
wfowler@chatham.edu
FOWLER-HILL, Sandra ... 425-388-9216. 519 I
sfowler-hill@everettcc.edu
FOWLER-YOUNG,
Angela .... 410-706-7830. 219 C
ayoung@af.umaryland.edu
FOWLES, Erin .... 847-543-2375. 143 A
efowles@clcillinois.edu
FOWLES, Gareth .... 561-237-7601. 108 X
gfowles@lynn.edu
FOWLES, Michelle, R ..... 818-947-2437... 52 E
fowlesmr@lavc.edu
FOWLKES, Bruce, M .... 309-467-6423. 145 C
bfowlkes@eureka.edu
FOWLKES, Carolyn, J ..... 312-939-0111. 144 D
caroline@eastwest.edu
FOWLKES, Dane .... 903-923-2068. 471 J
dfowlkes@etbu.edu
FOWLKES, J. Brian .... 734-764-7516. 251 C
fowlkes@umich.edu
FOWLKES, J. Keith .... 859-238-5575. 193 E
keith.fowlkes@centre.edu
FOX, Amanda, T .... 205-665-6038..... 9 B
foxat@montevallo.edu
FOX, Andrea, D .... 404-752-1510. 129 E
afox@msm.edu
FOX, Anthony .... 989-386-6622. 247 B
aefox@midmich.edu
FOX, Brenda .... 903-463-8631. 472 M
foxb@grayson.edu
FOX, Carl, A .... 270-745-8794. 200 G
carl.fox@wku.edu
FOX, Carole, M .... 512-463-1808. 486 D
carole.fox@tsus.edu
FOX, Charles .... 508-929-8257. 230 G
cfox@worcester.edu
FOX, Chris .... 412-338-4770. 419 M
cfox@kaplan.edu
FOX, Christopher .... 617-369-3894. 236 F
cfox@mfa.org
FOX, Connie .... 304-734-6635. 527 O
cfox@bridgemont.edu
FOX, D. Jeff .... 208-732-6220. 138 B
jfox@csi.edu
FOX, Dan .... 303-273-3231... 80 E
dfox@mines.edu
FOX, David .... 937-708-5253. 393 A
dfox@wilberforce.edu
FOX, Debbie .... 225-768-1727. 206 D
Deborah.Fox@ololcollege.edu
FOX, Delcy .... 518-783-8300. 340 J
fox@siena.edu
FOX, Donnie, S .... 606-337-1530. 193 F
dfox@ccbbc.edu
FOX, Douglas .... 325-942-2333. 465 K
doug.fox@angelo.edu
FOX, Jan, I .... 304-696-6671. 529 H
fox@marshall.edu
FOX, Jeanne .... 574-807-7243. 164 D
foxj@bethelcollege.edu
FOX, John .... 229-931-6884. 126 D
john.fox@gsw.edu
FOX, John, T .... 404-778-4432. 124 E
john_fox@emory.org
FOX, Juliet .... 715-232-1151. 538 B
foxj@uwstout.edu
FOX, Karen, L .... 717-560-8254. 421 A
kfox@lbc.edu
FOX, Karmen .... 989-775-4123. 249 F
fox.karmen@sagchip.edu
FOX, Kelly, L .... 303-492-3224... 85 L
kelly.fox@colorado.edu
FOX, Krista .... 253-833-9111. 520 C
kfox@greenriver.edu
FOX, Linda, K .... 706-542-4879. 133 C
lkfox@uga.edu
FOX, Lori, E .... 212-678-3438. 347 G
lfox@exchange.tc.columbia.edu
FOX, Lynn .... 209-946-2421... 73 A
lfox@pacific.edu
FOX, Mark .... 423-461-8760. 457 H
mpfox@milligan.edu
FOX, Mark .... 704-669-4175. 359 D
foxm@clevelandcc.edu
FOX, Mary David .... 864-503-5040. 448 H
mdfox@uscupstate.edu
FOX, Michael, F .... 734-487-4190. 242 D
mfox13@emich.edu
FOX, Michael, J .... 757-221-1693. 503 N
mjfox1@wm.edu
FOX, P. Michael .... 585-395-2504. 342 F
mfox@brockport.edu
FOX, Pamela .... 540-887-7026. 507 A
pfox@mbc.edu
FOX, Pat .... 843-574-6307. 447 E
pat.fox@tridenttech.edu
FOX, Phyllis .... 423-461-8708. 457 H
pfox@milligan.edu
FOX, Richard .... 718-368-4799. 318 E
rfox@kbcc.cuny.edu
FOX, Robert .... 502-852-6745. 200 D
bob.fox@louisville.edu
FOX, Robert .... 215-468-8800. 419 F
admissions@culinaryarts.edu
FOX, BSG, Ronald, A ..... 773-380-7041. 140 D
ron.fox@seabury.edu
FOX, Rusty .... 817-515-3015. 482 B
rusty.fox@tccd.edu
FOX, Sean .... 307-754-6102. 543 G
Sean.Fox@northwestcollege.edu
FOX, Shari .... 615-794-4254. 457 Q
sfox@omorecollege.edu
FOX, Susan, E .... 804-355-0671. 510 G
sfox@upsem.edu
FOX, Thomas .... 909-706-3548... 76 B
tfox@westernu.edu
FOX, Timothy .... 410-617-2863. 216 A
tfox@loyola.edu
FOX, Todd .... 954-783-7339. 102 M
tfox@cci.edu
FOX, William .... 315-229-5892. 339 F
wfox@stlawu.edu
FOX, William, A .... 740-587-6271. 379 D
foxw@denison.edu
FOX-FORRESTER, Susan 432-837-8178. 487 B
sforrester@sulross.edu
FOX-WILSON, Jessica .... 608-363-2647. 531 M
foxjs@beloit.edu
FOXMAN, Philip, R .... 814-332-5383. 409 D
phil.foxman@allegheny.edu
FOXWORTH, Jessica, L .. 601-877-6479. 265 G
jfoxworth@alcorn.edu
FOY, Joycelyn .... 336-750-2264. 370 A
foyj@wssu.edu
FOY, Morna, K .... 608-267-9066. 539 H
president@wtcsystem.edu
FOYLE, Kevin, J .... 713-500-4472. 492 E
Kevin.J.Foyle@uth.tmc.edu
FOZARD, John, D .... 405-691-3800. 396 D
ecox@macu.edu
FOZARD, Jonathan .... 405-945-3284. 398 C
FRABONI, David, J .... 404-413-3405. 126 E
dfraboni@gsu.edu
FRACASSO, Jack .... 860-297-2361... 91 F
jack.fracasso@trincoll.edu
FRADEN, Rena .... 209-946-2023... 73 A
rfraden@pacific.edu
FRADKIN, Bernard .... 951-222-8038... 61 A
bernie.fradkin@rcc.edu
FRAGALE, Stephen .... 581-381-1339. 340 G
fragalsa@sunysccc.edu
FRAGE, Gary .... 229-430-3593. 120 A
gfrage@albanytech.edu
FRAGNOLI, Kristen, M ... 585-292-3369. 332 A
kfragnoli@monroecc.edu
FRAGOSO, Marcos .... 210-805-3014. 490 A
fragoso@uiwtx.edu
FRAIER, Whitney .... 618-537-6813. 152 G
wlfraier@mckendree.edu
FRAILE, Pedro .... 787-727-3583. 555 D
pfraile@sagrado.edu
FRAILING, Mallory .... 517-265-5161. 238 G
FRAINIER, Janine, L .... 317-940-9228. 164 J
jfrainie@butler.edu
FRAIRE, John .... 509-335-5900. 525 A
jfraire@wsu.edu
FRAIRE, Virginia, M .... 512-223-6019. 466 I
vfraire@austincc.edu
FRALEY, Doug .... 606-487-3086. 195 C
doug.fraley@kctcs.edu
FRALEY, F. Allen .... 330-471-8237. 383 D
afraley@malone.edu
FRALIC, Bradley, W .... 216-368-2126. 375 J
bradley.fralic@case.edu
FRALICKER, Tamara .... 618-395-7777. 147 B
fralickert@iecc.edu
FRAME, Adrienne .... 850-644-7999. 115 C
aframe@admin.fsu.edu
FRAME, J. Davidson .... 703-516-0035. 510 I
davidson.frame@umtweb.edu
FRAME, Randall, L .... 484-384-2980. 425 I
rframe@eastern.edu
FRAME, William, V .... 651-523-1660. 256 J
wframe001@luthersem.edu
FRAMPTON, John .... 845-687-5288. 348 H
framptoj@sunyulster.edu
FRANCE, Kathleen .... 419-473-2700. 378 I
kfrance@daviscollege.edu
FRANCE, Lucy .... 406-243-4742. 286 H
lucy.france@umontana.edu
FRANCE, Melissa, H .... 918-631-2516. 401 F
melissa-france@utulsa.edu
FRANCE, Nancy .... 503-838-8327. 406 E
francen@wou.edu
FRANCIES, Karen .... 281-649-3450. 473 B
kfrancies@hbu.edu
FRANCIOSI, Adrienne ..... 617-243-2214. 227 K
afranciosi@lasell.edu
FRANCIS, Amy .... 419-783-2376. 379 C
afrancis@defiance.edu
FRANCIS, Billy .... 501-337-5000... 20 J
bfrancis@coto.edu
FRANCIS, Charles .... 559-442-4600... 68 I
charles.francis@fresnocitycollege.edu
FRANCIS, JR.,
D. Morgan .... 336-838-6102. 365 B
morgan.francis@wilkescc.edu
FRANCIS, Diana .... 219-473-4211. 164 K
dfrancis@ccsj.edu
FRANCIS, Donald .... 301-846-2435. 214 H
dfrancis@frederick.edu
FRANCIS, Gerald, L .... 336-278-7900. 354 B
francis@elon.edu
FRANCIS, Heather .... 972-825-4627. 481 F
hfrancis@sagu.edu
FRANCIS, James, M .... 630-617-3041. 145 A
jimf@elmhurst.edu
FRANCIS, Jason .... 601-403-1041. 269 D
jfrancis@prcc.edu
FRANCIS, Jeff .... 972-825-4731. 481 F
JFrancis@sagu.edu
FRANCIS, Jeffrey .... 918-631-2084. 401 F
jeffrey-francis@utulsa.edu
FRANCIS, Karen .... 603-623-0313. 297 E
kfrancis@nhia.edu
FRANCIS, Krista .... 360-417-6393. 522 A
kfrancis@pencol.edu
FRANCIS, Lance .... 706-385-1062. 130 F
lance.francis@point.edu
FRANCIS, Laurie .... 201-447-7117. 299 C
lfrancis@bergen.edu
FRANCIS, Leon .... 610-558-5584. 424 I
francisl@neumann.edu
FRANCIS, Lesa-Gaye ...... 954-492-5353. 100 A
lgayefrancis@citycollege.edu
FRANCIS, CSV, Mark, R . 773-371-5420. 141 D
president@ctu.edu
FRANCIS, Michael, R ...... 801-863-8818. 497 C
francimi@uvu.edu
FRANCIS, Monty, E .... 214-860-2178. 470 J
mefrancis@dcccd.edu
FRANCIS, Norman, C ..... 504-520-7541. 209 D
nfrancis@xula.edu
FRANCIS, Paige .... 479-619-4337... 22 C
pfrancis@nwacc.edu
FRANCIS, Paige .... 203-254-4059... 89 I
pfrancis@fairfield.edu
FRANCIS, Patricia, L ...... 607-436-2846. 343 E
francipl@oneonta.edu
FRANCIS, Perry .... 734-487-0074. 242 D
emu_ombuds@emich.edu
FRANCIS, Robert .... 215-895-6966. 415 B
raf47@drexel.edu
FRANCIS, Robert .... 206-546-4797. 523 F
bfrancis@shoreline.edu
FRANCISCHETTI, Jessica 406-657-1041. 288 B
francisj@rocky.edu
FRANCISCO, Eva Lynn ... 904-819-6460. 103 E
efrancisco@flagler.edu
FRANCISCO-CABALLO,
Egenero .... 787-766-1717. 552 J
FRANCKA, Shelly .... 405-585-4602. 397 C
shelly.franka@okbu.edu
FRANCKO, David, A .... 205-348-8280..... 8 D
dfrancko@ua.edu
FRANCO, Alicia .... 787-834-9595. 553 B
afranco@uaa.edu
FRANCO, Barry .... 843-574-6796. 447 E
barry.franco@tridenttech.edu
FRANCO, Darlery .... 201-360-4191. 302 D
dfranco@hccc.edu
FRANCO, Juan .... 402-472-3755. 292 I
jfranco2@unl.edu
FRANCO, Maria .... 386-226-6225. 102 B
francom@erau.edu
FRANCO, Michael, R .... 410-225-2594. 216 C
mfranco@mica.edu
FRANCO, Onorina .... 575-538-6174. 312 N
francoo@wnmu.edu
FRANCO, Rita .... 209-478-0800... 47 M
rfranco@humphreys.edu
FRANCO, Robert .... 808-734-9514. 136 E
bfranco@hawaii.edu
FRANCOIS, K. Michael ... 936-261-1009. 482 F
kmfrancois@pvamu.edu
FRANCOIS-SEENY,
Denise .... 610-861-5066. 425 D
dfrancois@northampton.edu
FRANCOS, Richard .... 516-463-6613. 326 D
richard.francos@hofstra.edu
FRANDSEN, Michael, L .. 517-629-0210. 239 A
mfrandsen@albion.edu
FRANK, Anthony, A .... 970-491-6211... 80 I
presofc@colostate.edu
FRANK, Brian .... 727-341-4143. 112 E
frank.brian@spcollege.edu

FRANK, Brian .... 513-569-1579. 376 L brian.frank@cincinnatistate.edu
FRANK, Christine, D .... 312-942-8735. 157 G christine_frank@rush.edu
FRANK, David .... 541-346-4198. 406 D dfrank@uoregon.edu
FRANK, Dawn .... 605-455-6035. 450 I dfrank@olc.edu
FRANK, Isabel .... 718-817-4602. 324 G frank@fordham.edu
FRANK, Jonathan .... 312-793-7150. 145 B jfrank@erikson.edu
FRANK, Katherine .... 765-973-8521. 167 G kpfrank@iue.edu
FRANK, Kristin .... 602-331-7500... 12 A kfrank@aii.edu
FRANK, Larry .... 213-763-7052... 52 D franklb@lattc.edu
FRANK, Linda .... 518-587-2100. 346 A linda.frank@esc.edu
FRANK, Marie .... 225-578-2307. 204 O mfrank@lsu.edu
FRANK, Meghan .... 707-668-5663... 42 F
FRANK, Penny, M .... 814-332-4311. 409 D pfrank@allegheny.edu
FRANK, Richard .... 732-224-2753. 299 G rfrank@brookdalecc.edu
FRANK, Robert .... 740-593-2850. 387 C frank@ohio.edu
FRANK, Robert, G .... 505-277-2626. 312 F unmpres@unm.edu
FRANK, Sandy, K .... 812-464-1762. 174 D sfrank@usi.edu
FRANK, Shawn .... 828-328-7298. 356 B shawn.frank@lr.edu
FRANK, Thomas, E .... 401-865-2723. 439 E tfrank@providence.edu
FRANK, Vincent, P .... 717-901-5115. 418 E VFrank@HarrisburgU.edu
FRANK MAYS, Karen .... 978-665-3712. 229 E kfrankmays@fitchburgstate.edu
FRANKE, Mark, A .... 260-481-6258. 168 C franke@ipfw.edu
FRANKEL, Bonnie .... 312-362-6760. 143 H bfranke2@depaul.edu
FRANKEN, Kathy .... 319-232-6980. 183 B frankenk@uiu.edu
FRANKEN, Lynn .... 724-589-2200. 434 B lfranken@thiel.edu
FRANKENBURG, Doug .... 704-355-1549. 353 D doug.frankenburg@carolinascollege.edu
FRANKIEL, Tamar .... 310-824-1586... 26 B tamar.frankiel@ajrca.org
FRANKL, Molly, E .... 605-394-2414. 452 A molly.frankl@sdsmt.edu
FRANKLAND, Phil .... 603-882-6923. 296 B pfrankland@ccsnh.edu
FRANKLIN, Audrey .... 336-517-2247. 352 H afranklin@bennett.edu
FRANKLIN, Carol .... 216-987-5504. 378 D carol.franklin@tri-c.edu
FRANKLIN, Cheryl, P ..... 340-692-4117. 555 E cfrankl@live.uvi.edu
FRANKLIN, David .... 202-274-6168... 97 A david.franklin@udc.edu
FRANKLIN, Geralyn .... 936-468-3101. 482 A franklingm@sfasu.edu
FRANKLIN, Horace .... 256-551-3130..... 4 I horace.franklin@drakestate.edu
FRANKLIN, Janice .... 334-229-4106..... 1 D franklin@alasu.edu
FRANKLIN, Joseph .... 575-835-5700. 310 F jfranklin@admin.nmt.edu
FRANKLIN, K. Mike .... 406-447-5559. 285 G mfranklin@carroll.edu
FRANKLIN, Karen .... 575-624-7138. 309 I karen.franklin@roswell.enmu.edu
FRANKLIN, Kathy, C ...... 434-528-5276. 515 G kfranklin@vul.edu
FRANKLIN, Laura .... 831-646-4816... 54 I lfranklin@mpc.edu
FRANKLIN, Laura .... 828-884-8112. 352 I phillil@brevard.edu
FRANKLIN, Laura, L .... 828-883-8112. 352 I phillil@brevard.edu
FRANKLIN, Laurie .... 425-388-9035. 519 I lfranklin@everettcc.edu
FRANKLIN, Layman .... 434-528-5276. 515 G lfranklin@vul.edu
FRANKLIN, Marshall, E .. 864-242-5100. 441 D
FRANKLIN, Reginald ...... 575-624-8263. 310 H franklin@nmmi.edu
FRANKLIN, Roschoune .. 323-856-7621... 27 O rfranklin@afi.com
FRANKLIN, Scott .... 806-291-3745. 494 F franklins@wbu.edu
FRANKLIN, Susan .... 402-461-7411. 289 I sfranklin@hastings.edu
FRANKLIN, Teresa .... 918-587-6789. 400 J tfranklin@twsweld.com
FRANKLIN, Truitt .... 706-886-6831. 133 A tfranklin@tfc.edu
FRANKLIN, William .... 310-243-2828... 33 B wfranklin@csudh.edu
FRANKLIN, William .... 859-246-6771. 194 L william.franklin@kctcs.edu
FRANKMAN, Tom .... 573-592-4368. 285 D tfrankma@williamwoods.edu
FRANKS, Billie .... 606-589-3029. 196 F billie.franks@kctcs.edu
FRANKS, Brian .... 817-531-4452. 488 A bfranks@txwes.edu
FRANKS, Debra, J .... 864-388-8749. 444 K jfranks@lander.edu
FRANKS, Dennis .... 336-278-5555. 354 B dfranks3@elon.edu
FRANKS, Mark .... 920-498-6269. 541 B mark.franks@nwtc.edu
FRANKS, Peter .... 215-895-0226. 415 B pjf28@drexel.edu
FRANKS, Rita .... 318-257-2577. 207 F
FRANKS, Ronald .... 251-460-7189..... 9 E rfranks@southalabama.edu
FRANKS, Tammy .... 228-497-7800. 268 C tammy.franks@mgccc.edu
FRANKS, Tiffany, M .... 434-791-5670. 502 D tfranks@averett.edu
FRANSISCO, John .... 701-349-5788. 373 A johnfransisco@trinitybiblecollege.edu
FRANSISCO, Kerri .... 701-349-5415. 373 A kerrifransisco@trinitybiblecollege.edu
FRANSON, Terry .... 626-812-3061... 29 H tfranson@apu.edu
FRANTEL, Tracy, L .... 503-777-7505. 407 E tracy.frantel@reed.edu
FRANTZ, Betsy, C .... 713-500-3202. 492 E elizabeth.c.frantz@uth.tmc.edu
FRANTZ, David .... 765-973-8337. 167 G dfrantz@iue.edu
FRANTZ, Michael .... 712-749-2140. 176 D frantzm@bvu.edu
FRANTZ, Rita, A .... 319-335-7009. 175 I rita-frantz@uiowa.edu
FRANZ, Brad .... 719-384-6885... 83 M brad.franz@ojc.edu
FRANZ, Chris .... 303-953-3415... 79 C cfranz@ccu.edu
FRANZ, Jennifer .... 920-748-8108. 535 J franzj@ripon.edu
FRANZ, Jonathan, R .... 585-224-3200. 346 A jonathan.franz@esc.edu
FRANZ, Kelly .... 920-465-2210. 536 F franzk@uwgb.edu
FRANZ, Maggie .... 816-331-5700. 280 D mfranz@pcitraining.edu
FRANZ, Mark .... 314-889-1488. 274 E mfranz@fontbonne.edu
FRANZ, Matt .... 937-328-6045. 377 A franzm@clarkstate.edu
FRANZ, Sandra, L .... 802-626-4865. 501 E sandra.franz@lyndonstate.edu
FRANZ, Scott .... 620-947-3121. 190 J scottf@tabor.edu
FRANZ, William, T .... 804-752-7268. 508 E wfranz@rmc.edu
FRANZA, Thomas .... 631-244-3230. 323 B franzat@dowling.edu
FRANZBLAU, Alfred .... 734-763-1282. 251 C afranz@umich.edu
FRANZEN, Dale .... 310-434-3430... 65 A franzen_dale@smc.edu
FRANZEN, Kirsten .... 701-328-4156. 371 B kirsten.franzen@ndus.edu
FRANZEN, Kirsten .... 701-328-4156. 371 B kristen.franzen@ndus.edu
FRANZEN, Kristine .... 563-387-1330. 180 M frankr03@luther.edu
FRANZEN, Liisa, E .... 240-895-3220. 218 A lefranzen@smcm.edu
FRANZEO, Linda .... 903-813-2468. 466 H lfranzeo@austincollege.edu
FRANZINO, John .... 845-758-7862. 314 D jfranzin@bard.edu
FRANZMAN, Thomas ..... 847-566-6401. 162 G tfranzman@usml.edu
FRAONE, Kimberly .... 908-737-4600. 302 F kfraone@kean.edu
FRASER, Dori .... 919-735-5151. 364 H dori@waynecc.edu
FRASER, Gertrude, J .... 434-924-4095. 511 B gjf2u@virginia.edu
FRASER, Greg .... 313-664-7660. 241 C gfraser@collegeforcreativestudies.edu
FRASER, Jeanmarie .... 508-362-2131. 231 D jfraser@capecod.edu
FRASER, Julie .... 636-481-3200. 275 I jpierce@jeffco.edu
FRASER, Lynne .... 401-865-1534. 439 E lfrase1@providence.edu
FRASER, Oswald, E .... 718-270-6970. 319 A ofraser@mec.cuny.edu
FRASER, Robin .... 845-368-7200. 340 C robin.fraser@use.salvationarmy.org
FRASER, Sheri .... 207-621-3136. 212 C fraser@maine.edu
FRASER, Sherry, J .... 914-337-9300. 321 E sherry.fraser@concordia-ny.edu
FRASER, Tammy .... 937-382-6661. 393 B tammy_fraser@wilmington.edu
FRASER, Travis .... 212-431-2169. 333 I Travis.Fraser@nyls.edu
FRASHER, Kristy .... 765-973-8275. 167 G sm628@bncollege.com
FRASIER, Darryl .... 386-481-2165... 99 C frazierd@cookman.edu
FRASIER, George .... 253-833-9111. 520 C gfrasier@geenriver.edu
FRASSINELLI, David, W . 203-254-4254... 89 I dfrassinelli@fairfield.edu
FRAUWIRTH, Eric .... 410-752-4710. 510 B efrauwirth@stratford.edu
FRAWLEY, Becky .... 828-669-8012. 357 H bfrawley@montreat.edu
FRAWLEY, Maria, H .... 202-242-6817... 95 D mfrawley@gwu.edu
FRAYNE, Kimberly .... 713-500-3079. 492 E Kimberly.C.Frayne@uth.tmc.edu
FRAZEE, David .... 216-987-5339. 378 D david.frazee@tri-c.edu
FRAZER, Elmo .... 408-934-4900... 47 A elmo_frazer@heald.edu
FRAZER, Gael .... 850-484-1757. 110 G gfrazer@pensacolastate.edu
FRAZER, Gregory, H .... 412-396-5303. 415 F frazer@duq.edu
FRAZER, Thomas, K .... 352-392-9230. 116 A frazer@ufl.edu
FRAZIER, III, Arthur, E .. 404-270-5436. 132 E aefrazier@spelman.edu
FRAZIER, Deborah .... 360-417-6202. 522 A dfrazier@pencol.edu
FRAZIER, Deborah, J ...... 870-612-2001... 25 A debbie.frazier@uaccb.edu
FRAZIER, Desi .... 229-732-5959. 120 D desifrazier@andrewcollege.edu
FRAZIER, Diana .... 215-572-8520. 409 H frazierd@arcadia.edu
FRAZIER, Doug .... 912-344-2818. 120 G doug.frazier@armstrong.edu
FRAZIER, JR., Ernest, T . 504-278-6421. 203 F cfrazier@nunez.edu
FRAZIER, Herb .... 620-862-5252. 184 E herb.frazier@barclaycollege.edu
FRAZIER, Jami .... 816-531-5223. 272 I jfrazier@concorde.edu
FRAZIER, Jenny .... 206-726-5085. 518 G jfrazier@cornish.edu
FRAZIER, John .... 330-823-2243. 391 E fraziejl@mountunion.edu
FRAZIER, Kevan .... 828-251-6525. 368 C kfrazier@unca.edu
FRAZIER, Kevin, B .... 706-721-0955. 126 B kfrazier@gru.edu
FRAZIER, Larry .... 903-233-3951. 475 J larryfrazier@letu.edu
FRAZIER, Lorraine .... 501-686-8493... 24 C frazierlorraine@uams.edu
FRAZIER, Margaret .... 870-245-5220... 22 D frazierm@obu.edu
FRAZIER, Mike .... 254-295-4526. 490 B mfrazier@umhb.edu
FRAZIER, Renae .... 864-646-1550. 447 D rfrazier@tctc.edu
FRAZIER, Royce .... 620-862-5252. 184 E president@barclaycollege.edu
FRAZIER, Sandra .... 910-892-3178. 355 B sfrazier@heritagebiblecollege.edu
FRAZIER, Sean .... 815-753-1000. 154 I
FRAZIER, Sheryl .... 731-881-7040. 463 E sfraizer@utm.edu
FRAZIER, Steven, R .... 860-738-6409... 89 C sfrazier@nwcc.commnet.edu
FRAZIER, Sue .... 865-774-5800. 462 A sue.frazier@ws.edu
FRAZIER, Tina .... 918-444-4200. 396 H fraziert@nsuok.edu
FRAZIER-HELD, Jamie ... 912-650-5672. 131 H jfrazier-held@southuniversity.edu
FRAZOR, Diane .... 210-826-7595. 494 F frazord@wbu.edu
FRAZZA, Christian .... 406-447-4344. 285 G cfrazza@carroll.edu
FREAD, Susan, J .... 610-799-1072. 421 I sfread@lccc.edu
FRECHETTE, Michael ...... 312-942-6256. 157 G michael_frechette@rush.edu
FRED, Leota .... 406-586-3585. 286 F leota.fred@montanabiblecollege.edu
FREDA, Kristin .... 212-875-4450. 314 C kfreda@bankstreet.edu
FREDEEN, DonnaJean, A 609-896-5010. 305 D dfredeen@rider.edu
FREDERICK, Anita .... 701-477-7862. 373 B afrederick@tm.edu
FREDERICK, Athena, D ... 814-641-3171. 419 H fredera@juniata.edu
FREDERICK, Beth, E .... 215-717-6393. 435 A bfrederick@uarts.edu
FREDERICK, Brian .... 337-482-6480. 208 D jdh7220@louisiana.edu
FREDERICK, David .... 513-721-7944. 380 D dfrederick@gbs.edu
FREDERICK, Debra .... 605-274-5514. 449 K deb.frederick@augie.edu
FREDERICK, Edward, W . 609-586-4800. 302 G frederie@mccc.edu
FREDERICK, Jean .... 262-551-5959. 532 D jfrederick@carthage.edu
FREDERICK, John .... 210-458-4110. 492 C john.frederick@utsa.edu
FREDERICK, Julia .... 337-482-6700. 208 D jcg0624@louisiana.edu
FREDERICK, Lawrence, W .... 314-516-7170. 283 E frederickl@umsl.edu
FREDERICK, Lesley, J .... 217-786-2597. 151 F lesley.frederick@llcc.edu
FREDERICK, Linda, D ..... 504-286-5106. 206 K lfrederick@suno.edu
FREDERICK, Marcille ...... 708-239-4797. 160 K marci.frederick@trnty.edu
FREDERICK, Mary .... 480-857-5210... 14 J mary.frederick@cgc.edu
FREDERICK, Pam .... 540-423-9125. 512 E pfrederick@germanna.edu
FREDERICK, Richard .... 662-252-8000. 269 F rfrederick@rustcollege.edu
FREDERICK, Robert .... 518-381-1368. 340 G frederrg@sunysccc.edu
FREDERICK, Robert .... 256-824-7200..... 8 F robert.frederick@uah.edu
FREDERICK, Robert, J .... 319-273-6857. 176 A robert.frederick@uni.edu
FREDERICK, Steven, G ... 518-562-4195. 320 B steven.frederick@clinton.edu
FREDERICK, Thyssene .... 843-349-5246. 444 F thyssene.frederick@hgtc.edu
FREDERICK, Wayne, H ... 202-806-2550... 95 G wfrederick@howard.edu
FREDERICKS, Dan .... 601-968-5977. 266 A dfredericks@belhaven.edu
FREDERICKS, Kathleen ... 701-627-4738. 371 A
FREDERICKSON, Joel ..... 651-638-6317. 253 K frejoe@bethel.edu
FREDETTE, Emile .... 802-728-1292. 501 F efredett@vtc.edu
FREDRICH, Dolores .... 516-463-1800. 326 D dolores.fredrich@hofstra.edu
FREDRICK, Ashley .... 734-432-5421. 246 B afredrick@madonna.edu
FREDRICK, Erin .... 212-854-2005. 314 G efredrick@barnard.edu
FREDRICK, Kay .... 605-626-2518. 451 I kay.fredrick@northern.edu
FREDRICKSEN, Donovan 214-333-5337. 470 D donovan@dbu.edu
FREDRICKSON, Kurt ...... 626-584-5654... 45 E kurtf@fuller.edu
FREDS, Anthony .... 989-317-4602. 247 B afreds@midmich.edu
FREDSON, Janice .... 509-682-6505. 525 B jfredson@wvc.edu
FREDSTROM, Tim .... 309-438-5386. 147 J tcfreds@ilstu.edu
FREE, Carolyn, G .... 803-536-8402. 446 G zs_cfree@scsu.edu
FREE, Gordon .... 334-556-2447..... 3 N hgfree@wallace.edu
FREE, Jimmy, H .... 662-246-6330. 268 B jfree@msdelta.edu
FREE, Rhona, C .... 860-465-5246... 87 L free@easternct.edu
FREE, Rikky, L .... 501-882-4445... 19 M rlfree@asub.edu
FREEBAIRN, Paul, H .... 808-675-3599. 135 C freebaip@byuh.edu
FREEBOURN, Randal .... 219-989-2670. 171 N randal.freebourn@purduecal.edu
FREED, Carol .... 507-389-7211. 261 E carol.freed@southcentral.edu
FREED, Curt .... 509-542-4806. 518 C cfreed@columbiabasin.edu
FREED, Gwendolyn .... 206-726-5052. 518 G gfreed@cornish.edu
FREED, James .... 316-978-3030. 191 F james.freed@wichita.edu
FREED, Kate .... 412-365-1837. 412 K kfreed@chatham.edu
FREED, Linda .... 817-257-7516. 484 I linda.freed@tcu.edu
FREED, Michael .... 904-366-1500. 102 A
FREED, Mitchell .... 610-683-4175. 429 A freed@kutztown.edu

FREED, Richard, C .... 610-758-5991. 422 A
rcf2@lehigh.edu
FREED, Suzanne, K .... 518-442-3961. 341 D
sfreed@albany.edu
FREEDMAN, Daniel .... 845-257-3728. 342 B
freedmad@newpaltz.edu
FREEDMAN, Eric .... 704-337-2384. 365 G
freedmane@queens.edu
FREEDMAN, Michael ...... 301-985-7000. 219 F
FREEDMAN, Phyllis, D ... 304-326-1390. 527 G
pfreedman@salemu.edu
FREEDMAN, Stephen ...... 718-817-3040. 324 G
sfreedman@fordham.edu
FREEDMAN, Victoria ...... 212-430-3179. 351 M
vfreedman@aecom.yu.edu
FREEDMAN DOHERTY,
Elizabeth .... 617-287-5339. 228 G
elizabeth.doherty@umb.edu
FREEH, Mary Beth .... 610-606-4605. 412 I
mafreeh@cedarcrest.edu
FREEL, Lisa .... 301-846-2468. 214 H
lfreel@frederick.edu
FREELAND, Kay .... 770-426-2944. 128 D
freeland@life.edu
FREELAND, Richard, M .. 617-994-6901. 228 D
freeland@bhe.mass.edu
FREELANDER, Chichi ..... 405-491-6396. 399 K
cfreelan@snu.edu
FREELS, Ean .... 319-208-5015. 182 G
efreels@scciowa.edu
FREEMAN, Alston .... 803-934-3179. 445 F
afreeman@morris.edu
FREEMAN, Angela .... 952-888-4777. 263 B
afreeman@nwhealth.edu
FREEMAN, Carol Ann ..... 845-675-4794. 335 C
carol_ann.freeman@nyack.edu
FREEMAN, Charles .... 559-925-3145... 75 G
charlesfreeman@whccd.edu
FREEMAN, Chris .... 803-786-3886. 443 B
bookstore@columbiasc.edu
FREEMAN, Craig .... 360-779-9993. 521 C
cfreeman@ncad.edu
FREEMAN, Dave .... 530-242-2220... 65 G
dfreeman@shastacollege.edu
FREEMAN, Dennis .... 617-253-6056. 233 B
FREEMAN, Eddie .... 817-272-2106. 491 B
efreeman@uta.edu
FREEMAN, Elijah, T .... 252-789-0276. 361 G
efreeman@martincc.edu
FREEMAN, Everette, J ..... 229-430-2799. 119 J
everette.freeman@asurams.edu
FREEMAN, Gary .... 402-461-7752. 289 I
gfreeman@hastings.edu
FREEMAN, Ginger, C ...... 615-898-2922. 459 D
ginger.freeman@mtsu.edu
FREEMAN, Irving .... 724-552-2880. 420 E
ifreeman@lecom.edu
FREEMAN, Iva, M .... 312-752-2530. 149 E
iva.freeman@kendall.edu
FREEMAN, Jackie .... 435-652-7612. 497 E
freeman@dixie.edu
FREEMAN, Jennifer .... 662-254-3577. 269 A
jennifer.freeman@mvsu.edu
FREEMAN, John .... 707-864-7000... 66 G
john.freeman@solano.edu
FREEMAN, Karen, J .... 315-786-2234. 327 L
kfreeman@sunyjefferson.edu
FREEMAN, Kassie .... 601-877-6157. 265 G
kfreeman@alcorn.edu
FREEMAN, Kenneth .... 314-968-5990. 284 N
kennethfreeman@webster.edu
FREEMAN, Kenneth, W ... 617-353-6170. 224 D
kfreeman@bu.edu
FREEMAN, Larry .... 910-521-6601. 369 B
larry.freeman@uncp.edu
FREEMAN, Lisa .... 413-572-5204. 230 F
lfreeman@westfield.ma.edu
FREEMAN, Lisa, C .... 815-753-1000. 154 I
lfreeman1@niu.edu
FREEMAN, Makiko .... 215-893-5257. 414 B
makiko_freeman@curtis.edu
FREEMAN, Mark .... 215-571-3608. 415 B
maf375@drexel.edu
FREEMAN, Martha .... 207-228-8304. 212 H
mfreeman@maine.edu
FREEMAN, Matt .... 253-535-7337. 521 I
freeman@plu.edu
FREEMAN, Melanie, H .... 662-329-7222. 268 E
mfreeman@hr.muw.edu
FREEMAN, Michael, A .... 813-974-6677. 116 C
mafreeman@usf.edu
FREEMAN, Natalya .... 910-521-6262. 369 B
natalya.freeman@uncp.edu
FREEMAN, Roger .... 763-433-1378. 257 P
roger.freeman@anokaramsey.edu
FREEMAN, Russell, T ..... 773-577-8100. 143 F
FREEMAN, Sharon .... 662-254-3811. 269 A
sharonf@mvsu.edu
FREEMAN, Sheila, D ...... 662-685-4771. 266 C
sfreeman@bmc.edu
FREEMAN, Stella .... 937-395-8006. 382 K
stella.freeman@kc.edu
FREEMAN, Steve .... 270-534-3363. 196 G
steve.freeman@kctcs.edu
FREEMAN, Yancy .... 423-425-4662. 463 D
yancy-freeman@utc.edu
FREEMAN-GALLANT,
Corey .... 518-580-5720. 341 A
cfreeman@skidmore.edu
FREEMON, Yolanda .... 708-656-8000. 153 H
yolanda.freemon@morton.edu
FREER, Dana .... 513-244-4524. 377 G
dana_freer@mail.msj.edu
FREER, Douglas, R .... 909-869-3310... 32 G
drfreer@csupomona.edu
FREER, Michael .... 763-424-0955. 260 C
mfreer@nhcc.edu
FREER, Steven .... 845-687-5200. 348 H
freers@sunyulster.edu
FREER, Wayne .... 845-687-5053. 348 H
freerw@sunyulster.edu
FREEZE, Jackie .... 307-382-1639. 543 J
jfreeze@wwcc.wy.edu
FREGIA, Bertha .... 409-880-8355. 486 E
bertha.fregia@lit.edu
FREGIA, Bertha .... 409-880-8375. 486 F
bertha.fregia@lamar.edu
FREGIA, Olin .... 903-730-4890. 474 O
olin_fregia@jarvis.edu
FREHSE, Sandra .... 518-454-5244. 321 A
frehses@strose.edu
FREIBERGER, Amy, M .... 918-631-3727. 401 F
amy-freiberger@utulsa.edu
FREIBURGER, Chevy ...... 641-628-7637. 176 E
freiburger@central.edu
FREIBURGER, Lisa .... 616-234-4025. 243 B
lfreiburger@grcc.edu
FREIJE, Margaret .... 508-793-2541. 225 B
FREILER, Dan .... 717-396-7833. 427 A
dfreiler@pcad.edu
FREITAG, Paul, A .... 612-343-4455. 262 X
pafreita@northcentral.edu
FREITAG, Thomas .... 215-641-6538. 424 B
tfreitag@mc3.edu
FREITAS, Rockne, C .... 808-689-2770. 136 C
rfreitas@hawaii.edu
FREJOSKY, Joe .... 423-493-4225. 462 B
frejosj@tntemple.edu
FREJOSKY, Pam .... 423-493-4224. 462 B
frejosky@tntemple.edu
FREJOSKY, Pam .... 423-493-4100. 462 B
frejosky@tntemple.edu
FREMONT, Ronald .... 909-537-5004... 34 E
rfremont@csusb.edu
FRENCH, Barbara .... 415-476-6296... 72 A
bfrench@ucsf.edu
FRENCH, Christopher .... 860-297-5204... 91 F
christopher.french@trincoll.edu
FRENCH, Daphne .... 912-260-4232. 131 F
daphne.french@sgsc.edu
FRENCH, JR., George, T 205-929-1428..... 5 G
gtfrench@aol.com
FRENCH, Jeremiah .... 918-540-6113. 396 G
jerempf@neo.edu
FRENCH, Jessica .... 740-826-8171. 384 L
jfrench@muskingum.edu
FRENCH, Joy .... 303-724-2516... 86 A
joy.french@ucdenver.edu
FRENCH, Kelly .... 859-344-3619. 199 H
kelly.french@thomasmore.edu
FRENCH, Marjie, M .... 210-458-4228. 492 C
marjie.french@utsa.edu
FRENCH, Mark .... 614-287-2810. 378 B
mfrench1@cscc.edu
FRENCH, Paige .... 540-515-3749. 502 J
pfrench@bridgewater.edu
FRENCH, CSSP,
Raymond .... 412-396-5286. 415 F
french@duq.edu
FRENCH, Richard, G .... 781-283-3583. 237 F
rfrench@wellesley.edu
FRENCH, Robert, C .... 315-470-6511. 345 B
rcfrench@esf.edu
FRENCH, Stephanie .... 502-410-6200. 194 B
sfrench@galencollege.edu
FRENCH, Steve .... 404-894-3380. 125 D
steve.french@coa.gatech.edu
FRENCH, William, R .... 609-497-7789. 304 D
bill.french@ptsem.edu
FRENCH, William, R .... 609-497-7837. 304 D
FRENDEWEY, JR.,
James .... 906-487-2259. 247 A
jimf@mtu.edu
FRENDIAN, Michel .... 312-893-7145. 145 B
mfrendian@erikson.edu
FRENK, Julio .... 617-495-2936. 227 C
jfrenk@hsph.harvard.edu
FRENZEL, Michelle .... 218-755-2020. 258 A
mfrenzel@bemidjistate.edu
FRERE, Leslie .... 219-866-6116. 172 E
lfrere@saintjoe.edu
FRERICHS, Chris .... 515-961-1711. 182 E
chris.frerichs@simpson.edu
FRERIDGE, Jenifer .... 601-928-6288. 268 C
jenifer.freridge@mgccc.edu
FRESA-DILLON, Kerin .... 215-871-6864. 430 D
kerinf@pcom.edu
FRESCH, Cathy .... 814-871-5842. 416 K
fresch001@gannon.edu
FRESCHETTE, Brigitte ...... 701-662-1546. 372 D
brigitte.freschette@lrsc.edu
FRESE, Phil .... 814-393-2600. 428 C
pfrese@clarion.edu
FRESH, Frederick .... 404-270-5227. 132 E
ffresh@spelman.edu
FRESHOUR, Brett .... 330-490-7171. 392 H
bfreshour@walsh.edu
FRESHWATER, Laurie, A 252-222-6281. 358 G
freshwaterl@carteret.edu
FRESHWATER,
Thomas, A .... 910-962-7673. 369 C
freshwatert@uncw.edu
FRESQUEZ, Julie .... 951-343-4302... 30 H
jfresque@calbaptist.edu
FREUND, Deborah, A ..... 909-621-8025... 39 C
debbie.freund@cgu.edu
FREW, Erin .... 719-549-2207... 80 K
erin.frew@colostate-pueblo.edu
FREY, Angela .... 414-382-6206. 531 I
angela.frey@alverno.edu
FREY, Don .... 360-736-9391. 517 G
dfrey@centralia.edu
FREY, Donald .... 402-280-2300. 289 D
donaldfrey@creighton.edu
FREY, Isabel, D .... 516-463-4779. 326 D
isabel.d.frey@hofstra.edu
FREY, Joan, L .... 502-410-6200. 194 B
jfrey@galencollege.edu
FREY, Len, T .... 870-972-3303... 19 N
lfrey@astate.edu
FREY, Lori .... 717-264-4141. 437 H
lfrey@wilson.edu
FREY, Melissa .... 503-589-7652. 402 E
melissa.frey@chemeketa.edu
FREY, Sandy .... 636-481-3348. 275 I
sfrey@jeffco.edu
FREYBURGER, James ..... 912-650-6251. 131 H
jfreyburger@southuniversity.edu
FREYTAG, Peter .... 303-373-2008... 85 C
pfreytag@rvu.edu
FREYTES, Celeste, E .... 787-250-0000. 553 G
celeste.freytes@upr.edu
FREYTES, Diana .... 787-523-6000. 549 D
dfreytes@icprjc.edu
FREYTES, Elvin, R .... 212-966-0300. 333 A
elvin@nyaa.edu
FREYTES, Liza .... 787-279-1912. 550 B
lfreytes@bayamon.inter.edu
FRIANT, Jakim .... 910-362-7073. 358 F
jfriant@cfcc.edu
FRIAS, Frank .... 626-529-8064... 57 G
ffrias@pacificoaks.edu
FRIAS, Mary Lou .... 508-531-1252. 229 D
marylou.frias@bridgew.edu
FRICK, Caroline .... 706-754-7722. 129 G
cfrick@northgatech.edu
FRICK, Hedwig (Hedy) .... 937-484-1353. 392 C
hfrick@urbana.edu
FRICK, Jeffrey .... 920-403-3001. 535 L
jeffrey.frick@snc.edu
FRICK, Lillian, K .... 989-386-6605. 247 B
lfrick@midmich.edu
FRICKE, Bob .... 419-227-3141. 391 F
rlfricke@unoh.edu
FRICKE, David .... 732-906-2519. 303 B
dfricke@middlesexcc.edu
FRICKS, Brad .... 256-228-6001..... 5 H
fricksb@nacc.edu
FRICKX, Gretchen .... 312-939-4975. 146 A
gfrickx@harrington.edu
FRIDAY, Brenda .... 570-422-3534. 428 D
bfriday@po-box.esu.edu
FRIDAY-STROUD,
Shawnta .... 850-599-3565. 114 K
shawnta.friday-stroud@famu.edu
FRIDDELL, Melinda .... 229-226-1621. 132 F
mfriddell@thomasu.edu
FRIDGE, Rob .... 417-873-7527. 273 H
rfridge@drury.edu
FRIE, Vinetta .... 225-216-8504. 202 H
friev@mybrcc.edu
FRIEBEL, Thomas .... 718-368-6646. 318 E
tfriebel@kbcc.cuny.edu
FRIED, Barry, J .... 608-796-3811. 539 E
bjfried@viterbo.edu
FRIED, David .... 814-866-6641. 420 E
dfried@lecom.edu
FRIED, Linda, P .... 212-305-9300. 321 D
lpfried@columbia.edu
FRIED, Ray .... 325-235-7302. 486 C
ray.fried@tstc.edu
FRIED-GOODNIGHT,
Maud .... 856-691-8600. 301 A
mgoodnight@cccnj.edu
FRIEDBERG, Connie .... 412-809-5100. 430 H
friedberg.connie@pti.edu
FRIEDEL, Kristin, M .... 315-859-4637. 325 E
kfriedel@hamilton.edu
FRIEDENBERG,
Samantha .... 610-799-1754. 421 I
sfriedenberg@lccc.edu
FRIEDERICHS, Marla, J .. 651-962-6151. 265 C
mjfriederich@stthomas.edu
FRIEDHOFF, Scott .... 330-263-2118. 377 H
sfriedhoff@wooster.edu
FRIEDLANDER, Jack .... 805-965-0581... 64 L
friedlan@sbcc.edu
FRIEDLEN, Karen .... 414-256-1203. 535 A
friedlek@mtmary.edu
FRIEDLINE, Patrick .... 312-329-4414. 153 E
patrick.friedline@moody.edu
FRIEDLY, Allison .... 651-846-1305. 261 D
allison.friedly@saintpaul.edu
FRIEDMAN, Aaron .... 612-626-3700. 264 G
alfried@umn.edu
FRIEDMAN, Aaron .... 612-626-4949. 264 G
alfried@umn.edu
FRIEDMAN, Al .... 425-388-9399. 519 I
afriedman@everettcc.edu
FRIEDMAN, Anita, S .... 757-683-5789. 507 N
asfriedm@odu.edu
FRIEDMAN, Avraham ..... 847-982-2500. 146 C
friedman@htc.edu
FRIEDMAN, Beth .... 402-354-7236. 291 B
beth.friedman@methodistcollege.edu
FRIEDMAN, David .... 410-484-7200. 217 D
FRIEDMAN, Debra .... 253-692-5644. 524 G
debraf@u.washington.edu
FRIEDMAN, Elizabeth ..... 718-518-4314. 318 B
efriedman@hostos.cuny.edu
FRIEDMAN, Eric .... 201-360-4011. 302 D
efriedman@hccc.edu
FRIEDMAN, Frank .... 434-977-1620. 513 F
ffriedman@pvcc.edu
FRIEDMAN, Jay, R .... 716-645-3313. 341 F
jf5@buffalo.edu
FRIEDMAN, Jill, D .... 314-935-5261. 284 L
jill.friedman@wustl.edu
FRIEDMAN, Joel .... 401-825-2003. 439 A
jafriedman@ccri.edu
FRIEDMAN, Larry, S ...... 610-558-5522. 424 I
lfriedma@neumann.edu
FRIEDMAN, Lauren .... 203-575-8139... 89 B
lfriedman@nvcc.commnet.edu
FRIEDMAN, Mark .... 573-681-5316. 276 C
friedmanm@lincolnu.edu
FRIEDMAN, Melissa .... 212-280-6001. 328 A
mefriedman@jtsa.edu
FRIEDMAN, Mitchell ...... 415-561-6555... 60 C
FRIEDMAN, Natalie .... 212-854-2024. 314 G
nfriedma@barnard.edu
FRIEDMAN, Robert .... 212-960-5269. 351 M
rfriedm2@yu.edu
FRIEDMAN, Scott .... 847-925-6266. 145 H
sfriedma@harpercollege.edu
FRIEDMAN, Stephen, J .. 212-346-1097. 335 J
president@pace.edu
FRIEDMAN, William .... 312-369-7623. 143 D
bfriedman@colum.edu
FRIEDMAN, Yaakov .... 847-982-2500. 146 C
yfriedman@htc.edu
FRIEDMAN-LOMBARDO,
Jaclyn .... 973-655-7599. 303 D
friedmanlj@mail.montclair.edu
FRIEDMANN, Mina .... 212-217-3560. 324 C
mina_friedmann@fitnyc.edu
FRIEDRICH, Brian, L .... 402-643-7364. 289 B
brian.friedrich@cune.edu
FRIEDRICH, Dan .... 605-256-5555. 451 H
dan.friedrich@dsu.edu
FRIEDRICHSEN,
Steven, W .... 909-706-3911... 76 B
sfriedrichsen@westernu.edu
FRIEL, Kathern, R .... 302-292-3838... 93 F
friel@dtcc.edu
FRIEL, Lydia .... 215-780-1251. 433 A
lfriel@salus.edu
FRIEL, Terri, L .... 312-281-3320. 157 D
tfriel@roosevelt.edu
FRIEL, Wm. Jake .... 724-287-8711. 411 C
jake.friel@bc3.edu
FRIELER, Callie .... 570-340-6016. 423 B
frieler@marywood.edu
FRIEND, Dane .... 713-798-4300. 467 F
dfriend@bcm.edu
FRIEND, Dane, K .... 713-798-1544. 467 F
dfriend@bcm.edu
FRIEND, David .... 402-457-2770. 290 G
djfriend@mccneb.edu
FRIEND, Gwyn .... 312-362-6961. 143 H
gfriend@depaul.edu

FRIEND, Joanie 314-539-5157. 281 D jfriend4@stlcc.edu

FRIEND, Margaret 918-335-6238. 398 F mfriend@okwu.edu

FRIEND, Vivian, M 727-816-3427. 110 E friendv@phcc.edu

FRIERSON, Henry, T 352-392-6622. 116 A hfrierson@ufl.edu

FRIERSON, Muriel 856-256-4367. 305 E frierson@rowan.edu

FRIERY, Gary 281-998-6150. 479 G gary.friery@sjcd.edu

FRIES, James 505-454-3269. 310 E president_office@nmhu.edu

FRIES, Jane 970-542-3106. 83 E jane.fries@morgancc.edu

FRIESEKE, Mary 414-382-6098. 531 I mary.frieseke@alverno.edu

FRIESEN, Gary 765-998-4965. 173 C grfriesen@taylor.edu

FRIESEN, Jared 715-682-1290. 535 D jfriesen@northland.edu

FRIESEN, Wilbert 847-628-1001. 149 B will.friesen@judsonu.edu

FRIESZ, Mary 701-224-5748. 372 B mary.b.friesz@bismarckstate.edu

FRIGO, Sandy 213-613-2200. 67 E sandy_frigo@sciarc.edu

FRIGO, Terence 312-567-8973. 147 F frigo@iit.edu

FRIGOT, Pamela, J 724-738-2057. 429 F pamela.frigot@sru.edu

FRINDELL TEUSCHER, Karen 707-527-4377. 65 B kfrindell@santarosa.edu

FRIPPS, Kristina 610-892-1536. 427 E kfripps@pit.edu

FRISBEE, Holly 212-966-0300. 333 A hfrisbee@nyaa.edu

FRISBEE, Stephen 315-792-5399. 331 I sfrisbee@mvcc.edu

FRISBIE, Kathy 970-542-3240. 83 E kathy.frisbie@morgancc.edu

FRISBIE, Lorene, E 269-660-8021. 249 C frisbiel@millercollege.edu

FRISBIE-FULTON, Thomas 401-874-9463. 440 D tfrisbie@uri.edu

FRISBY, Anthony 215-503-4990. 434 C anthony.frisby@jefferson.edu

FRISBY, Bernard 703-212-7410. 505 D

FRISCH, Edward, G 520-621-7766. 18 F frisch@arizona.edu

FRISCH, Kim 303-458-4909. 84 M kfrisch@regis.edu

FRISCH, Randy, C 858-642-8110. 55 J rfrisch@nu.edu

FRISCH, Ronald, W 412-624-8030. 435 C paurf5@pitt.edu

FRISINA, Warren 516-463-4783. 326 D warren.frisina@hofstra.edu

FRISKICS, Scott 406-353-2607. 285 E friskics@hotmail.com

FRISKNEY, Paul 513-244-8128. 376 J paul.friskney@ccuniversity.edu

FRISKO, Peter 215-895-1389. 415 B peter.j.frisko@drexel.edu

FRISQUE, Megan 512-863-1584. 481 I frisquem@southwestern.edu

FRISTAD, Erin 360-344-4100. 499 C erin.fristad@goddard.edu

FRISTOE, Jill 703-323-3125. 513 C jfristoe@nvcc.edu

FRITCH, Jacque 800-962-7682. 285 A jfritch@wma.edu

FRITCH, Margie 619-388-2789. 62 E mfritch@sdccd.edu

FRITCH, Todd, G 413-205-3449. 221 F todd.fritch@aic.edu

FRITSCH, Robert 619-388-7515. 62 F rfritsch@sdccd.edu

FRITSCHE, Teresa 570-422-3422. 428 D tfritsche@po-box.esu.edu

FRITTS, Jack 630-829-6060. 140 B jfritts@ben.edu

FRITZ, Dave 702-567-1920. 293 N dafritz@cci.edu

FRITZ, Greg 402-399-2407. 289 A gfritz@csm.edu

FRITZ, Gretchen 570-348-6210. 423 B gfritz@marywood.edu

FRITZ, John 410-455-6596. 219 D fritz@umbc.edu

FRITZ, Lawrence, M 323-343-3820. 34 A lfritz@calstatela.edu

FRITZ, Martin 715-232-2131. 538 B fritzm@uwstout.edu

FRITZ, Stephen 806-742-1828. 487 D steve.fritz@ttu.edu

FRITZ, Stephen, J 651-962-5901. 265 C sjfritz@stthomas.edu

FRITZ, Susan, M 402-472-5242. 292 G smfritz@nebraska.edu

FRITZ, Thomas, R 814-472-3006. 432 D tfritz@francis.edu

FRITZ, William, J 718-982-2400. 317 E william.fritz@csi.cuny.edu

FRITZE, Barbara, B 717-337-6582. 417 B bfritze@gettysburg.edu

FRITZE, Ronald 256-216-5524. 1 F ron.fritze@athens.edu

FRIZADO, Joseph 419-372-7202. 374 K frizado@bgsu.edu

FRIZZELL, Christine 508-999-8648. 229 A cfrizzell@umassd.edu

FRIZZELL, Douglas, K 513-244-4239. 377 G doug_frizzell@mail.msj.edu

FRIZZELL, Robert 479-788-7205. 24 A robert.frizzell@uafs.edu

FROCHETTE, Carri 207-775-3052. 210 H cfrochette@meca.edu

FROCK, Gemma 803-508-7277. 440 G frockg@atc.edu

FRODYMA, Tina 773-298-3912. 158 E frodyma@sxu.edu

FROEHLE, Paula, M 312-332-0707. 160 J

FROEHLE, Ryan 312-939-4975. 146 A rfroehle@harrington.edu

FROEHLICH-MUELLER, Kerry, K 608-757-7654. 539 I kfroehlich-mueller@blackhawk.edu

FROGLEY, Kent 801-975-5094. 498 B kent.frogley@slcc.edu

FROHOFF, Katherine 816-501-4151. 280 I katherine.frohoff@rockhurst.edu

FROHRIB, Patti 920-735-5611. 539 K frohrib@fvtc.edu

FROLE, Angelo 740-203-8001. 378 B afrole@cscc.edu

FROMAN, John 352-323-3697. 108 S fromanj@lssc.edu

FROMBGEN, Liz 402-461-7321. 289 I lfrombgen@hastings.edu

FROMING, William 650-433-3830. 58 B bfroming@paloaltou.edu

FROMMELT, Gene 940-552-6291. 493 F gfrommelt@vernoncollege.edu

FROMMELT, Steve 816-604-1087. 277 C steve.frommelt@mcckc.edu

FRONCZEK, Andrew, F 216-397-4275. 381 R afronczek@jcu.edu

FRONCZEK, Walter 708-994-5372. 153 F fronczek@morainevalley.edu

FRONHEISER, Joey 434-832-7016. 512 A fronheiserj@cvcc.vccs.edu

FRONK, Michael, R 386-822-7523. 117 C mfronk@stetson.edu

FRONK, Peter 608-363-2375. 531 M fronkp@beloit.edu

FRONK, Suzette 828-898-8809. 356 A fronks@lmc.edu

FRONTERA, Jose, A 787-841-2000. 552 B jose_frontera@pucpr.edu

FRONTIERA, Charlene 650-574-6312. 64 C frontierac@smccd.edu

FRONZAGLIA, Shawn, G 412-268-4309. 412 H sgfronza@andrew.cmu.edu

FRONZONI, Susan 570-674-6249. 424 A sfronzon@misericordia.edu

FROSLID JONES, Karen, L 202-885-6155. 94 F kfroslid@american.edu

FROSS, Sharon 617-951-2350. 234 G sharon.fross@necb.edu

FROST, Aimee 807-832-5303. 498 F afrost@westminstercollege.edu

FROST, Amber 316-448-3150. 450 G afrost@national.edu

FROST, Carol 307-766-4121. 543 I frost@uwyo.edu

FROST, Dana, L 864-644-5004. 446 I dfrost@swu.edu

FROST, Eric 315-464-4393. 342 E froste@upstate.edu

FROST, Grif 808-981-2790. 135 E

FROST, Jacque, L 765-494-7126. 171 M frostj@purdue.edu

FROST, Judith 207-755-5265. 210 J jfrost@cmcc.edu

FROST, Julia, H 479-979-1401. 25 J jfrost@ozarks.edu

FROST, Lorraine 909-537-5100. 34 E lfrost@csusb.edu

FROST, Mark 518-276-8246. 337 I frostm@rpi.edu

FROST, Mark 518-783-4100. 340 J mfrost@siena.edu

FROST, Mike 406-243-4711. 286 H michael.frost@umontana.edu

FROST, Richard, A 616-395-7800. 244 A frost@hope.edu

FROST, Robert, A 530-938-5200. 41 A rfrost@siskiyous.edu

FROST, Scott 727-784-0003. 99 J sfrost@cfi.edu

FROST, Vivian 620-252-7199. 185 O vivianf@coffeyville.edu

FROSTMAN, Valerie 817-257-7513. 468 B v.forstman@tcu.edu

FROUDE, Bill 859-572-5112. 198 I froudew1@nku.edu

FRUCHTHANDLER, Abraham, H 718-377-0777. 336 I

FRUEH, Elizabeth 715-425-3737. 537 E elizabeth.frueh@uwrf.edu

FRUITTICHER, Lee 678-359-5009. 127 A leef@gordonstate.edu

FRUM, Jennifer, L 706-542-6126. 133 C jfrum@uga.edu

FRUMKIN, Howard 206-543-2100. 524 G frumkin@uw.edu

FRUMKIN, Jeffery, R 734-763-4551. 251 C jfrumkin@umich.edu

FRUMKIN, Michael 407-823-6424. 115 E michael.frumkin@ucf.edu

FRUMKIN, Steven 212-217-4330. 324 C steven_frumkin@fitnyc.edu

FRUSH, Karen 919-668-3749. 354 A frush002@mc.duke.edu

FRUTCHEY, Shelby 512-516-8703. 131 H sfrutchey@southuniversity.edu

FRUZZETTI, Armida 775-674-7550. 294 H afruzzetti@tmcc.edu

FRY, Angela 870-574-4523. 23 G afry@sautech.edu

FRY, Blake 715-425-3711. 537 E blake.fry@uwrf.edu

FRY, Blake, W 715-425-3711. 537 E blake.fry@uwrf.edu

FRY, Bobbye, G 210-829-6006. 490 A fry@uiwtx.edu

FRY, Eldon, E 717-766-2511. 423 L efry@messiah.edu

FRY, Jacy 605-256-5267. 451 H jacy.fry@dsu.edu

FRY, John, A 215-895-2100. 415 B jaf@drexel.edu

FRY, Matt 979-845-2217. 483 C mattfry@tamu.edu

FRY, Pamela 405-744-5627. 397 H provost@okstate.edu

FRY, Renae 763-493-0546. 260 C rfry@nhcc.edu

FRY, Sally, V 304-367-4214. 529 F sally.fry@fairmontstate.edu

FRY, Scott 918-825-4678. 398 B scott.fry@okstate.edu

FRYATT, Rayann 603-577-6511. 296 F rfryatt@dwc.edu

FRYE, Brandon 850-474-2384. 117 B bfrye@uwf.edu

FRYE, Curt 402-375-7200. 291 F cufrye1@wsc.edu

FRYE, Holly 304-876-5402. 529 I hfrye@shepherd.edu

FRYE, Jeffrey 419-434-4501. 391 D frye@findlay.edu

FRYE, Joseph 502-272-3333. 192 E jfrye@bellarmine.edu

FRYE, Karen 910-576-6222. 362 C fryek@montgomery.edu

FRYE, Keener 307-766-4166. 543 I hfry1@uwyo.edu

FRYE, Lela 352-395-5420. 113 C lela.frye@sfcollege.edu

FRYE, Susan 307-766-3152. 543 I frye@uwyo.edu

FRYER, Christopher 860-628-4751. 90 D cfryer@lincolncollegene.edu

FRYMAN, Thomas 937-778-7961. 379 G tfryman@edisonohio.edu

FUCHKO, III, John, M 404-962-3025. 134 A john.fuchko@usg.edu

FUCHS, Catherine 615-327-7264. 463 G catherine.fuchs@vanderbilt.edu

FUCHS, Kathleen, F 920-832-6574. 533 S kathleen.f.fuchs@lawrence.edu

FUCHS, Monique 617-989-4513. 237 G fuchsm@wit.edu

FUCHS, Tina, M 503-838-8220. 406 E fuchst@wou.edu

FUCHS, W. Kent 607-255-2364. 322 A provost@cornell.edu

FUCIARELLI, Sue, E 229-333-5800. 134 B semitchell@valdosta.edu

FUDA, Gary 254-526-1397. 468 G gary.fuda@ctcd.edu

FUDGE, Denise, G 270-384-8203. 197 D fudged@lindsey.edu

FUDGE, Sara 513-244-8445. 376 J sara.fudge@ccuniversity.edu

FUENTES, Angeles 831-582-4136. 34 B afuentes@csumb.edu

FUENTES, Jose, A 787-279-1912. 550 B jfuentes@bayamon.inter.edu

FUENTES, Juanita 719-549-3255. 84 G Juanita.Fuentes@pueblocc.edu

FUENTES, Pablo 915-351-8100. 465 I

FUENTES, Ramon 787-257-7373. 552 H ue_rfuentes@suagm.edu

FUENTES, Stephanie 303-753-6046. 85 B sfuentes@rmcad.edu

FUENTES-AFFLICK, Elena 415-476-1977. 72 A efuentes@sfghpeds.ucsf.edu

FUENTES-MARTIN, Mari 956-665-2260. 492 B fuentesmartinmm@utpa.edu

FUENTES-RUÍZ, Verónica 787-993-8916. 554 A veronica.fuentes@upr.edu

FUENTEZ, Tammy 620-421-6700. 188 D tammyf@labette.edu

FUERST, Nathan 860-486-3137. 92 A nathan.fuerst@uconn.edu

FUERY, Patrick 714-997-6947. 38 A fuery@chapman.edu

FUEYO, Vivian 727-873-4260. 116 D vfueyo@usfsp.edu

FUGALE, Stephen 610-519-4400. 436 F stephen.fugale@villanova.edu

FUGARD, Anne, S 904-620-1920. 116 B anne.fugard@unf.edu

FUGATE, Amy 810-762-0237. 247 F amy.fugate@mcc.edu

FUGATE, Mark 865-981-8145. 456 D mark.fugate@maryvillecollege.edu

FUGATE, Megan, A 620-421-6700. 188 D meganf@labette.edu

FUGATE, Wendy 814-838-7673. 416 G wfugate@fortisinstitute.edu

FUGATE, Wesley 434-947-8000. 508 D wfugate@randolphcollege.edu

FUGATE-ROBERTS, Kimberly 352-395-5510. 113 C kimberly.fugate-roberts@sfcollege.edu

FUGETT, Charlotte, A 520-206-7619. 17 A cfugett@pima.edu

FUGETT, Lana 870-307-7253. 21 H lana.fugett@lyon.edu

FUGITT, Gilbert 949-214-3057. 41 I gilbert.fugitt@cui.edu

FUHR, Thomas, W 315-267-2166. 344 C fuhrtw@potsdam.edu

FUHRMAN, JR., L. Clifton 864-938-3907. 446 D lcfuhrman@presby.edu

FUHRMAN, Susan, H 212-678-3131. 347 G susanf@tc.columbia.edu

FUHRMAN, Tim 509-793-2351. 517 C timf@bigbend.edu

FUHRMANN, Dave 805-652-5577. 74 E dfuhrmann@vcccd.edu

FUJI, Stephanie 480-423-6300. 15 E stephanie.fuji@scottsdalecc.edu

FUJIMOTO, Andrew 808-983-4115. 135 G andrewf@tokai.edu

FUJITA, Rich 307-268-3088. 542 X rfujita@caspercollege.edu

FUJIYOSHI, Lois, M 808-933-1944. 136 A lfujiyos@hawaii.edu

FUKS, Matt 605-697-5198. 452 B matt.fuks@statealum.com

FULCHER, D. Keith 662-846-4708. 266 G kfulcher@deltastate.edu

FULCHER, Kerry 619-849-2651. 59 L kerryfulcher@pointloma.edu

FULCOMER, Eric 815-226-3372. 157 C efulcomer@rockford.edu

FULD, Kenneth 603-862-2062. 298 C ken.fuld@unh.edu

FULDA, Henry 320-589-6060. 264 F fuldah@morris.umn.edu

FULFORD, Lynda 805-493-3839. 31 H fulford@clunet.edu

FULFORD, Sherri 334-242-2688. 1 G fulfosg@auburn.edu

FULFORD, William, J 251-460-7277. 9 E hfulford@southalabama.edu

FULIGNI, Paul 618-650-2560. 159 H pfulign@siue.edu

FULK, Scott 219-980-6792. 168 B sfulk@iun.edu

FULK, Sheryl, E 812-877-8344. 172 C sheryl.fulk@rose-hulman.edu

FULKERSON, Cathy 775-445-3219. 295 A cathy.fulkerson@wnc.edu

FULKERSON, Christopher, D 336-278-5055. 354 B fulkers@elon.edu

FULKERSON, Tahita, M 817-515-1002. 482 B tahita.fulkerson@tccd.edu

FULKERSON, JR., William, J ..... 919-684-8076. 354 A
fulke003@mc.duke.edu
FULL, Karen, A ..... 810-762-7496. 244 Q
kfull@kettering.edu
FULLEM, Wendy ..... 973-300-2120. 307 F
wfullem@sussex.edu
FULLEMAN, Robert ..... 973-720-2200. 308 I
fullemanr@wpunj.edu
FULLER, Barbara, J ..... 276-964-7200. 514 A
barbara.fuller@sw.edu
FULLER, Belinda ..... 304-766-3387. 530 C
bfuller@wvstateu.edu
FULLER, Brad ..... 800-962-7682. 285 A
bfuller@wma.edu
FULLER, Cindy ..... 217-424-3944. 153 C
cfuller@millikin.edu
FULLER, Dale ..... 229-243-6436. 121 E
dale.fuller@bainbridge.edu
FULLER, David ..... 701-858-3300. 371 F
president@minotstateu.edu
FULLER, Edwin, W ..... 607-274-3036. 327 E
efuller@ithaca.edu
FULLER, Elizabeth ..... 508-774-0657. 223 A
betsy.fuller@becker.edu
FULLER, JR., Henry, M .. 843-953-5185. 442 A
hank.fuller@citadel.edu
FULLER, Janet ..... 336-278-7729. 354 B
jfuller3@elon.edu
FULLER, Jennifer ..... 510-430-3131... 54 F
jfuller@mills.edu
FULLER, Jerry, A ..... 512-471-2866. 491 C
jfuller@austin.utexas.edu
FULLER, Jim ..... 765-677-2090. 169 B
jim.fuller@indwes.edu
FULLER, John, P ..... 405-744-9153. 397 H
eeo@okstate.edu
FULLER, Lana ..... 217-234-5222. 150 D
lfuller@lakeland.cc.il.us
FULLER, Laurinda ..... 562-985-4296... 33 F
lfuller@csulb.edu
FULLER, Lori ..... 661-654-2273... 32 H
1250mgr@fheg.follett.com
FULLER, Mark ..... 205-726-2711..... 6 F
dmfuller@samford.edu
FULLER, Mark, A ..... 413-545-5583. 228 F
dean@isenberg.umass.edu
FULLER, Mary ..... 508-531-6141. 229 D
mfuller@bridgew.edu
FULLER, Michael ..... 541-684-7248. 405 C
mfuller@nwcu.edu
FULLER, Mickey ..... 405-945-8645. 398 C
FULLER, Mildred, K ..... 757-823-2366. 507 M
mkfuller@nsu.edu
FULLER, Norine ..... 213-624-1200... 44 D
nfuller@fidm.edu
FULLER, Rex ..... 509-359-7900. 519 C
rfuller@ewu.edu
FULLER, Roger, D ..... 817-257-6122. 484 I
r.fuller@tcu.edu
FULLER, Sherry ..... 515-961-1543. 182 E
sherry.fuller@simpson.edu
FULLER, Tony ..... 276-739-2575. 514 D
mmcbride@vhcc.edu
FULLER, Vivian, L ..... 601-979-2360. 267 E
vivian.l.fuller@jsums.edu
FULLERTON, Darren, S .. 417-625-3135. 278 D
fullerton-d@mssu.edu
FULLERTON, Ernie ..... 412-200-3070... 18 I
ernie.fullerton@phoenix.edu
FULLERTON, Fred, C ..... 208-467-8530. 139 A
ffullerton@nnu.edu
FULLMAN, Joshua ..... 402-363-5719. 293 I
jfullman@york.edu
FULLMER, Paul ..... 717-867-6135. 421 H
fullmer@lvc.edu
FULMER, David ..... 918-495-7480. 398 H
dfulmer@oru.edu
FULMER, Deryl ..... 252-536-7289. 361 A
ddavis-fulmer985@halifaxcc.edu
FULMER, Gregory, L ..... 717-291-3993. 416 J
greg.fulmer@fandm.edu
FULMER, Hal ..... 334-670-3112..... 7 H
hfulmer@troy.edu
FULMER, Judy ..... 334-670-3102..... 7 H
jfulmer@troy.edu
FULMER, Terry ..... 617-373-2000. 235 F
FULMORE, Robbin, S ..... 757-683-3701. 507 N
rfulmore@odu.edu
FULOP, Timothy ..... 814-886-6302. 424 G
tfulop@mtaloy.edu
FULP, Andrew ..... 912-525-5000. 131 B
afulp@scad.edu
FULTON, Andrew ..... 914-323-5154. 330 B
andrew.fulton@mville.edu
FULTON, Dean ..... 360-752-8378. 517 B
dfulton@btc.ctc.edu
FULTON, Deborah, M ..... 540-231-0735. 515 C
dfulton@vt.edu
FULTON, DoVeanna ..... 713-221-8009. 489 D
fultond@uhd.edu

FULTON, Erica ..... 870-575-8491... 24 E
fultone@uapb.edu
FULTON, Jodie ..... 541-956-7200. 407 F
jfulton@roguecc.edu
FULTON, Kathy ..... 254-298-8426. 482 C
kath.library@templejc.edu
FULTON, Tara, L ..... 734-487-2573. 242 D
tfulton1@emich.edu
FULTZ, Angela ..... 606-759-7141. 196 B
angela.fultz@kctcs.edu
FULTZ, Larenda ..... 731-286-3234. 460 F
fultz@dscc.edu
FUNDERBURK, Dale ..... 903-886-5189. 483 E
dale.funderburk@tamuc.edu
FUNDERBURK, Dana ..... 618-664-7096. 145 G
dana.funderburk@greenville.edu
FUNDERBURK, Jerome .. 704-216-6248. 356 D
jfunderburk@livingstone.edu
FUNG, Hsin-Ming ..... 213-613-2200... 67 E
ming@sciarc.edu
FUNG CHEN PENN, Emma ..... 684-699-9155. 546 A
e.fungchenpenn@amsamoa.edu
FUNIGIELLO, Tony ..... 716-827-2481. 348 G
funigielloa@trocaire.edu
FUNK, Carla ..... 321-674-8921. 104 H
cfunk@fit.edu
FUNK, Chad ..... 916-484-8401... 53 A
funkc@arc.losrios.edu
FUNK, Cynthia ..... 615-322-3969. 463 G
cindy.funk@vanderbilt.edu
FUNK, David ..... 503-255-0332. 404 F
dfunk@multnomah.edu
FUNK, Nancy ..... 530-242-7689... 65 G
nfunk@shastacollege.edu
FUNK, Ruth ..... 620-947-3121. 190 J
ruthf@tabor.edu
FUNK, Tiger ..... 435-586-7888. 497 A
funk@suu.edu
FUNK, Tracy ..... 317-921-4371. 169 L
tfunk@ivytech.edu
FUNK-BAXTER, Kathryn . 361-825-2321. 483 F
kathryn.funk-baxter@tamucc.edu
FUNKE, Renata ..... 831-386-7100... 46 G
rfunke@hartnell.edu
FUQUA, Douglas ..... 808-983-4138. 135 G
dfuqua@tokai.edu
FUQUA, Heather ..... 502-447-1000. 199 E
hfuqua@spencerian.edu
FUQUAY, Melissa ..... 757-352-4270. 508 G
mfuquay@regent.edu
FURBEE, Thomas, V ..... 304-829-7749. 526 D
tfurbee@bethanywv.edu
FURDA, Eric, J ..... 215-898-2886. 435 B
furda@admissions.upenn.edu
FURE-SLOCUM, Carolyn . 507-222-4003. 254 D
cfureslo@carleton.edu
FURGAL, Charles, A ..... 508-286-8213. 238 B
cfurgal@wheatoncollege.edu
FURLANI, Thomas ..... 716-645-7979. 341 F
furlani@ccr.buffalo.edu
FURLONG, Deborah ..... 920-465-2374. 536 F
furlongd@uwgb.edu
FURLONG, Matthew ..... 409-772-5113. 493 C
mfurlong@utmb.edu
FURLONG, Scott ..... 920-465-2336. 536 F
furlongs@uwgb.edu
FURMAN, John, A ..... 360-650-3496. 525 C
john.furman@wwu.edu
FURNER, Jennifer ..... 315-279-5264. 328 D
jfurner@mail.keuka.edu
FURNISH, Shearle ..... 330-941-3409. 394 A
sfurnish@ysu.edu
FURNSTAHL, Doug ..... 218-235-2119. 261 G
d.furnstahl@vcc.edu
FURQUERON, Cherry ..... 432-264-5603. 473 E
cfurqueron@howardcollege.edu
FURR, James ..... 713-942-9505. 473 D
jfurr@hgst.edu
FURR, Kelia ..... 205-726-4230..... 6 F
kfurr@samford.edu
FURR, Sara ..... 405-945-8618. 398 C
FURR, Timothy, L ..... 320-222-5735. 260 H
tim.furr@ridgewater.edu
FURROW, Louise ..... 626-815-5328... 29 H
lfurrow@apu.edu
FURSE, Cynthia, M ..... 801-581-7236. 496 Q
cfurse@ece.utah.edu
FURST, Michele ..... 617-879-7366. 230 B
mfurst@massart.edu
FURST-BOWE, Julie ..... 618-650-2481. 159 H
jfurstb@siue.edu
FURTADO, Maria ..... 727-864-8331. 101 N
furtadm@eckerd.edu
FURTEK, Diane, H ..... 413-205-3212. 221 F
diane.furtek@aic.edu
FURTICK, Corrine ..... 317-917-3329. 171 A
cfurtick@martin.edu
FURTON, Kenneth ..... 305-348-2866. 115 B
kenneth.furton@fiu.edu

FURUI, Sadaoki ..... 773-834-2493. 160 I
furui@ttic.edu
FURUKAWA, Karen ..... 707-527-4302... 65 B
kfurukawa-schlereth@santarosa.edu
FURUKAWA, Tom ..... 323-265-8669... 51 F
furukat@elac.edu
FURUKAWA-SCHLERETH, Laurence ..... 707-664-2310... 36 B
laurence.furukawa-schlereth@sonoma.edu
FURULI, Andrea ..... 808-933-3112. 136 A
andrea.furuli@uhfoundation.org
FURUSA, Munashe ..... 310-243-3389... 33 B
mfurusa@csudh.edu
FURUSETH, Owen, J ..... 704-687-1302. 368 E
ojfuruse@uncc.edu
FURUTO, Brian ..... 808-845-9123. 136 G
bfuruto@hawaii.edu
FURUTO, Sandra ..... 808-956-7487. 135 L
yano@hawaii.edu
FURUYAMA, Ron ..... 310-434-4370... 65 A
furuyama_ron@smc.edu
FUSCHETTI, Deborah, M 863-784-7139. 113 G
deborah.fuschetti@southflorida.edu
FUSCO, David, J ..... 814-641-3684. 419 H
fusco@juniata.edu
FUSCO, Valerie ..... 315-792-7111. 346 C
valerie.fusco@sunyit.edu
FUSCO, William, J ..... 707-664-2639... 36 B
bill.fusco@sonoma.edu
FUSE-HALL, Rosalind ..... 336-517-2225. 352 H
rosalind.fuse-hall@bennett.edu
FUSILIER, LaDonna ..... 870-574-4519... 23 G
lfusilier@sautech.edu
FUSS, Kevin, J ..... 815-825-2086. 149 F
kevin.fuss@kishwaukeecollege.edu
FUSSELL, Carl ..... 408-554-4024... 64 M
cfussell@scu.edu
FUSSELL, Paula, V ..... 352-392-1075. 116 A
pvarnes@ufl.edu
FUSTER, Luis ..... 787-765-3560. 548 M
lfuster@edpuniversity.edu
FUTCH, Lynn ..... 912-871-1606. 129 J
lfutch@ogeecheetech.edu
FUTHEY, Carol ..... 970-248-1881... 79 F
cfuthey@coloradomesa.edu
FUTHEY, Tracy ..... 919-684-8111. 354 A
futhey@duke.edu
FUTRELL, Tamara, Y ..... 540-458-8766. 516 A
tfutrell@wlu.edu
FUTRELL, Terry ..... 937-708-5416. 393 A
tfutrell@wilberforce.edu
FUZY, Bob ..... 864-587-4295. 447 B
fuzyb@smcsc.edu
FYE, Christa, D ..... 434-223-6324. 505 E
cfye@hsc.edu
FYFE, Brenda, S ..... 314-968-6913. 284 N
fyfebr@webster.edu
FYFE, Dorothy, R ..... 718-270-2258. 342 D
dfyfe@downstate.edu
FYFE, John ..... 415-442-6540... 45 I
jfyfe@ggu.edu
FYFFE, Richard ..... 641-269-3351. 178 H
fyffe@grinnell.edu
FYFFE, Robert ..... 937-775-3336. 393 G
robert.fyffe@wright.edu
FYLES, Susan ..... 415-485-3283... 42 J
sfyles@dominican.edu
FYOCK, Debra, R ..... 412-648-1458. 435 C
dfyock@bc.pitt.edu

G

GÓMEZ, José, D ..... 787-834-9595. 553 B
jgomez@uaa.edu
GAALSWYK, Terry, B ..... 308-635-6103. 293 E
gaalswy2@wncc.edu
GAARDER, David, K ..... 972-883-6374. 491 E
dkg053000@utdallas.edu
GABA, Barbara ..... 908-965-6091. 308 B
gaba@ucc.edu
GABBARD, Billie, J ..... 727-816-3116. 110 E
gabbarb@phcc.edu
GABBARD, Clinton ..... 269-927-8120. 245 D
cgabbard@lakemichigancollege.edu
GABBARD, Elizabeth ..... 479-979-1307... 25 J
egabbard@ozarks.edu
GABBARD, Kurt, A ..... 512-404-4816. 467 A
kgabbard@austinseminary.edu
GABBARD, Ruth ..... 859-371-9393. 192 D
rgabbard@beckfield.edu
GABBARD, Veronica ..... 281-649-3747. 473 B
vgabbard@hbu.edu
GABBE, Steve, G ..... 614-292-1200. 386 E
gabbe.1@osu.edu
GABBERT, Jeri Pat ..... 219-981-4232. 168 B
jgabbert@iun.edu
GABBERT, Jill ..... 312-942-6302. 157 G
jill_gabbert@rush.edu
GABBERT, Paula, S ..... 864-294-2064. 444 C
paula.gabbert@furman.edu

GABEHART, Alan, D ..... 318-798-4117. 205 F
alan.gabehart@lsus.edu
GABEL, Ann-Marie ..... 562-938-4540... 51 D
agabel@lbcc.edu
GABEL, Barb ..... 419-448-2183. 380 G
bgabel@heidelberg.edu
GABEL, Joan ..... 573-882-6688. 283 C
gabelj@missouri.edu
GABEL, Stephen, H ..... 773-702-0790. 161 B
sgabel@uchicago.edu
GABER, Sharon ..... 479-575-2151... 23 I
sgaber@uark.edu
GABERT, Glen, E ..... 201-360-4003. 302 D
ggabert@hccc.edu
GABERT, Susan, S ..... 603-641-7231. 297 G
sgabert@anselm.edu
GABIANELLI, Barbara, A 203-576-4134... 91 G
bag@bridgeport.edu
GABIS, Mark, A ..... 270-926-1188. 193 N
mgabis@daymargroup.com
GABIS, Mark, A ..... 270-926-1188. 454 D
mgabis@daymargroup.com
GABLE, Carol ..... 315-229-5563. 339 F
cgable@stlawu.edu
GABLE, Marsha ..... 619-660-4302... 46 D
marsha.gable@gcccd.edu
GABOURY, Mario ..... 203-932-7253... 92 E
mgaboury@newhaven.edu
GABOVITCH, Rhonda ..... 508-678-2811. 231 B
rhonda.gabovitch@bristolcc.edu
GABRIEL, George, E ..... 703-323-3129. 513 C
ggabriel@nvcc.edu
GABRIEL, Lisa ..... 281-283-3032. 489 C
gabriel@uhcl.edu
GABRIEL, Rochelle ..... 973-748-9000. 299 F
rochelle_gabriel@bloomfield.edu
GABRIEL, Rochelle ..... 201-761-7130. 306 L
rgabriel@saintpeters.edu
GABRIEL, Sherine ..... 507-284-3268. 254 G
sherine.gabriel@mayo.edu
GABRIELE, Carol ..... 508-849-3380. 222 B
cgabriele@annamaria.edu
GABRIELE, Gary, A ..... 610-519-5860. 436 F
gary.gabriele@villanova.edu
GABRIELSE, Ken ..... 405-585-4300. 397 C
ken.gabrielse@okbu.edu
GABRIELSON, Kerry ..... 719-846-5643... 85 H
kerry.gabrielson@trinidadstate.edu
GABRIELSON, Linda ..... 802-828-2800. 501 C
linda.gabrielson@ccv.edu
GABY, Dennis ..... 714-449-7459... 67 D
dgaby@scco.edu
GACH, Sharon ..... 925-424-1001... 37 L
sgach@laspositascollege.edu
GACHETTE, Yves, M ..... 716-878-4521. 343 A
gachetym@buffalostate.edu
GACIOCH, Dennis, M ..... 860-768-4007... 92 D
gacioch@hartford.edu
GACKENHEIMER, Lois, M ..... 561-683-1400... 97 F
GACKLE, Joel ..... 714-556-3610... 74 D
joel.gackle@vanguard.edu
GADBERRY, Brad ..... 770-531-6319. 128 B
bgadberry@laniertech.edu
GADD, Dale ..... 574-807-7322. 164 D
gaddd@bethelcollege.edu
GADD, Elisabeth ..... 864-646-1812. 447 D
egadd@tctc.edu
GADDE, Sandee, A ..... 989-463-7146. 239 B
gadde@alma.edu
GADDIE, Faith ..... 717-396-7833. 427 A
fgaddie@pcad.edu
GADDIS, Glendi ..... 210-999-7011. 488 C
ggaddis@trinity.edu
GADDY, Stoney ..... 307-674-6446. 543 F
sgaddy@sheridan.edu
GADDY, Tina ..... 312-341-3558. 157 D
tgaddy@roosevelt.edu
GADIKIAN, Randolph Lee ..... 716-673-3181. 342 A
randolph.gadikian@fredonia.edu
GADSBY, Peter ..... 845-758-7457. 314 D
gadsby@bard.edu
GADSON, Mark, P ..... 610-409-3164. 436 B
mgadson@ursinus.edu
GADZINSKI, James, G ... 906-227-2971. 248 A
jgadzins@nmu.edu
GAEKLE, Robert ..... 219-785-5220. 172 A
rgaekle@pnc.edu
GAER-CARLTON, Kathy .. 509-963-1211. 517 F
gaerk@cwu.edu
GAERTE, Phyllis, E ..... 585-567-9620. 326 F
phyllis.gaerte@houghton.edu
GAERTNER, Gregory ..... 312-329-4125. 153 E
greg.gaertner@moody.edu
GAETA, Alexa ..... 404-471-6423. 119 I
agaeta@agnesscott.edu
GAETA, James ..... 512-863-1259. 481 I
gaetaj@southwestern.edu
GAETA, Michael ..... 503-253-3443. 405 E
president@ocom.edu

GAETJENS, Stuart .... 931-393-1663. 461 A
ssgaetjens@mscc.edu
GAETZ, Ivan .... 719-389-6070... 79 D
ivan.gaetz@coloradocollege.edu
GAFFNER, Lori .... 618-664-7120. 145 G
lori.gaffner@greenville.edu
GAFFNEY, Eva .... 508-531-1337. 229 D
egaffney@bridgew.edu
GAFFNEY, FSC, James ... 815-836-5230. 150 H
brjgaff@lewisu.edu
GAFFNEY, Kevin .... 610-921-7520. 409 A
kgaffney@alb.edu
GAFFNEY, Michelle .... 330-823-2496. 391 E
gaffnemi@mountunion.edu
GAFFNEY, Michelle .... 330-823-7288. 391 E
gaffnemi@mountunion.edu
GAFFNEY, Paul, J .... 512-863-1379. 481 I
gaffneyp@southwestern.edu
GAFFNEY, Phillip .... 706-204-2201. 125 C
pgaffney@highlands.edu
GAFFNEY, Tiffany, D ...... 401-865-2191. 439 E
tgaffne1@providence.edu
GAGAN, Kelly .... 585-389-2411. 332 D
kgagan8@naz.edu
GAGE, Adrian .... 508-929-8563. 230 G
agage@worcester.edu
GAGE, Amy .... 651-690-6829. 263 O
agage@stkate.edu
GAGE, Brent .... 205-934-4073..... 8 E
bgage@uab.edu
GAGE, Chris .... 812-866-7028. 166 C
gage@hanover.edu
GAGE, Chris .... 972-883-2055. 491 E
ccg034000@utdallas.edu
GAGE, Colin, C .... 816-235-1430. 283 D
gagec@umkc.edu
GAGE, David .... 315-781-3734. 326 C
gage@hws.edu
GAGE, J. Scott .... 978-837-5468. 234 A
j.scott.gage@merrimack.edu
GAGE, Jeannie .... 361-825-2332. 483 F
jeannie.gage@tamucc.edu
GAGE, Julia, A .... 401-841-6535. 545 A
GAGLIA, Anne .... 575-492-2114. 312 M
agaglia@usw.edu
GAGLIANO, Richard .... 414-277-7228. 534 G
gagliano@msoe.edu
GAGLIARDI, William ...... 989-837-4237. 248 C
gagliardi@northwood.edu
GAGNE PENDLETON,
Lori .... 860-515-3858... 87 I
lpendleton@charteroak.edu
GAGNER, Michael, J ...... 608-757-7754. 539 I
mgagner@blackhawk.edu
GAGNIER, Rick, R .... 509-865-8663. 520 D
gagnier_r@heritage.edu
GAGNON, Ann, M .... 603-358-2000. 298 F
agagnon@keene.edu
GAGNON, Craig, L .... 920-832-6587. 533 S
craig.l.gagnon@lawrence.edu
GAGNON, Joseph .... 570-342-7701... 16 L
joseph.gagnon@pennfoster.edu
GAGNON, Karen .... 712-274-5159. 181 B
gagnon@morningside.edu
GAGNON, Paula .... 207-216-4318. 211 C
pgagnon@yccc.edu
GAGNON, Roberta .... 269-965-3931. 244 O
gagnonr@kellogg.edu
GAHAGAN, Nicole .... 414-256-1211. 535 A
gahagann@mtmary.edu
GAHAGANS, Steve .... 479-575-6626... 23 I
steveg@uark.edu
GAHAN, Mick .... 402-457-2402. 290 G
mgahan@mccneb.edu
GAHL, Leslie, L .... 260-982-5256. 170 U
llgahl@manchester.edu
GAHM, Jamie, L .... 815-224-0428. 148 A
jamie_gahm@ivcc.edu
GAHMAN, Debora .... 215-699-5700. 421 E
dgahman@LSB.edu
GAIER, Mary .... 937-512-2163. 388 O
mary.gaier@sinclair.edu
GAIKO, Sylvia .... 270-745-8985. 200 G
sylvia.gaiko@wku.edu
GAILEY, Kim .... 970-943-3140... 86 I
kgailey@western.edu
GAILEY, Susan Coia .... 617-266-1400. 223 D
GAILLAT, Ana .... 269-467-9945. 242 H
agaillat@glenoaks.edu
GAILLIARD, Gary .... 817-735-2210. 490 E
Gary.Gailliard@unthsc.edu
GAILOR, Kathleen .... 845-451-1302. 322 D
k_gailor@culinary.edu
GAINES, Chad .... 660-248-6228. 272 B
cgaines@centralmethodist.edu
GAINES, David, J .... 512-863-1494. 481 I
gainesd@southwestern.edu
GAINES, Deborah .... 973-655-3123. 303 D
gainesd@mail.montclair.edu
GAINES, James, R .... 808-956-7490. 135 L
gaines@hawaii.edu
GAINES, John .... 615-936-2811. 463 G
john.gaines@vanderbilt.edu
GAINES, JR., Larry, R .... 856-225-6174. 306 A
gaines@camden.rutgers.edu
GAINES, JR., Larry, R .... 856-225-6174. 306 C
gaines@camden.rutgers.edu
GAINES, JR., Leonard .... 518-381-1283. 340 G
gaineslg@sunysccc.edu
GAINES, Michael .... 937-512-3829. 388 O
michael.gaines5421@sinclair.edu
GAINES, Randy .... 208-282-2872. 138 E
gainrand@isu.edu
GAINES, Shivaun, P .... 973-655-7648. 303 D
gainess@mail.montclair.edu
GAINES, Steven, D .... 805-893-4339... 72 B
gaines@bren.ucsb.edu
GAINEY, Karen, W .... 864-488-4504. 444 L
kgainey@limestone.edu
GAINSBOROUGH, Juliet 781-891-2868. 223 C
jgainsborough@bentley.edu
GAISBAUER,
Mary Catherine .... 765-494-7536. 171 M
mcgaisbauer@purdue.edu
GAITAN, Deborah .... 210-486-4454. 464 J
dgaitan@alamo.edu
GAITAN, Maria .... 707-527-4431... 65 B
mgaitan@santarosa.edu
GAITHER, Kimberly .... 573-288-6340. 273 F
kgaither@culver.edu
GAJDOSIK, Olga .... 262-554-2010. 534 D
GAJEWSKI, Geoff .... 920-832-6530. 533 S
geoffrey.c.gajewski@lawrence.edu
GAJEWSKI, Jennifer .... 410-704-2356. 220 E
jgajewski@towson.edu
GAJEWSKI, Linda .... 219-473-4217. 164 K
lgajewski@ccsj.edu
GAJOLI, Rita .... 619-594-6668... 35 D
rgajoli@mail.sdsu.edu
GAJRIA, Meenakshi .... 845-398-4154. 340 A
mgajria@stac.edu
GALA, Thomas .... 914-606-6856. 350 F
thomas.gala@sunywcc.edu
GALANES, Gloria .... 417-836-5247. 278 E
gloriagalanes@missouristate.edu
GALANSKI, Kay, A .... 724-946-7218. 437 B
galanska@westminster.edu
GALANTE, Dominic, J ..... 215-951-1020. 420 B
galante@lasalle.edu
GALARDI, Karen .... 215-504-2000. 418 G
kgalardi@holyfamily.edu
GALARRAGA, Francesca . 866-621-0124... 86 F
francesca.galarraga@rockies.edu
GALASKA, Vickie .... 419-448-3595. 389 J
galaskavm@tiffin.edu
GALATOLO, Ron, D .... 650-574-6550... 64 A
galatolo@smccd.edu
GALBALLY, James .... 517-629-0315. 239 A
jgalbally@albion.edu
GALBAVY, Tiffany .... 406-395-4313. 288 D
tgalbavy@stonechild.edu
GALBIATI, Jacqueline ..... 856-691-8600. 301 A
jgalbiati@cccnj.edu
GALBIERZ, Todd .... 636-922-8359. 280 J
tgalbierz@stchas.edu
GALBRAITH, Cynthia ...... 320-659-5143. 260 F
galbraithc@pinetech.edu
GALBRAITH, Mark .... 619-849-2489... 59 L
markgalbraith@pointloma.edu
GALBRAITH, OP,
Mary Sarah .... 615-297-7545. 452 J
srmsarah@quinascollege.edu
GALBRAITH, OP,
Mary Sarah .... 615-297-7545. 452 J
srmsarah@aquinascollege.edu
GALBREATH, Dodd .... 615-966-1771. 456 B
dodd.galbreath@lipscomb.edu
GALBREATH, Leslie .... 660-562-1590. 279 I
leslies@nwmissouri.edu
GALBREATH, Susan, C .. 615-966-5952. 456 B
susan.galbreath@lipscomb.edu
GALDIERI, Virginia .... 908-852-1440. 300 D
galdieriv@centenarycollege.edu
GALE, Andrea .... 909-607-1236... 39 D
andrea.gale@cmc.edu
GALE, Danon .... 417-626-1234. 279 J
gale.danon@occ.edu
GALE, Jennifer, D .... 610-917-1488. 436 C
jdgale@vfcc.edu
GALE, Lewis .... 209-946-2466... 73 A
lgale@pacific.edu
GALE, Mary, E .... 651-290-6438. 265 F
mary.gale@wmitchell.edu
GALE, Nicole, L .... 410-651-6458. 219 E
nlgale@umes.edu
GALEA'I, Seth, P .... 684-699-9155. 546 A
s.galeai@amsamoa.edu
GALEA'I-SCANLAN, Lina 684-699-9155. 546 A
l.scanlan@amsamoa.edu
GALECKE, Robert, M ...... 972-721-5203. 488 F
galecke@udallas.edu
GALENTINE, Karen, E ..... 412-578-6135. 412 G
galentineke@carlow.edu
GALEY, Frank, D .... 307-766-4133. 543 I
fgaley@uwyo.edu
GALICK, Robert .... 815-825-2086. 149 F
rob.galick@kishwaukeecollege.edu
GALIK, Barbara .... 309-677-2850. 140 I
barbara@bradley.edu
GALIL, Zvi .... 404-894-8357. 125 D
galil@gatech.edu
GALINDO, Elizabeth, A ... 858-499-0202... 40 C
egalindo@coleman.edu
GALINDO, Emily .... 530-752-0339... 70 J
ecgalindo@ucdavis.edu
GALINDO, Vickie .... 575-527-7526. 311 B
vigalind@nmsu.edu
GALINDO-BAIRD, Yibeli 256-551-3136..... 4 I
yibeli.baird@drakestate.edu
GALINSKI, Bonnie .... 978-542-2532. 230 E
bgalinski@salemstate.edu
GALITZ, Todd .... 718-636-3448. 336 F
tgalitz@pratt.edu
GALIZIO, Larry .... 503-338-2425. 402 G
lgalizio@clatsopcc.edu
GALL, Jen .... 510-849-8241... 57 H
jgall@psr.edu
GALL, John .... 724-480-3543. 413 H
john.gall@ccbc.edu
GALL RITCHIE, Amy, S .. 800-287-8822. 164 C
ritcham@bethanyseminary.edu
GALLAGAN, Marilynn ..... 978-656-3300. 232 B
gallaganm@middlesex.mass.edu
GALLAGHER, Abisola ..... 201-200-3165. 303 F
agallagher@njcu.edu
GALLAGHER, Beth, E ..... 805-756-2236... 32 F
begallag@calpoly.edu
GALLAGHER, AA,
Dennis, M .... 508-767-7419. 222 C
dgallagh@assumption.edu
GALLAGHER, Ed .... 256-766-6610..... 4 B
egallagher@hcu.edu
GALLAGHER, Elizabeth ... 925-631-4223... 61 F
egallagh@stmarys-ca.edu
GALLAGHER,
Geraldine M, P .... 407-582-3155. 118 M
ggallagher@valenciacollege.edu
GALLAGHER, Helen .... 404-965-6565. 315 G
hgallagher@careered.edu
GALLAGHER, Jody .... 814-732-1269. 428 E
jgallagher@edinboro.edu
GALLAGHER, Karen .... 607-753-4717. 343 B
karen.gallagher@cortland.edu
GALLAGHER, Karen, S ... 213-740-5756... 74 A
rsoedean@usc.edu
GALLAGHER, Leslie, D ... 281-425-6301. 475 I
lgallagher@lee.edu
GALLAGHER, Linda, A ... 724-480-3492. 413 H
linda.gallagher@ccbc.edu
GALLAGHER, Lori .... 713-525-3592. 490 L
irishstudies@stthom.edu
GALLAGHER, Mandy ...... 336-278-5797. 354 B
agallagher3@elon.edu
GALLAGHER, Mary .... 213-763-7040... 52 D
mgallagh@lattc.edu
GALLAGHER, Mary Beth 314-719-3554. 274 E
mbgallagher@fontbonne.edu
GALLAGHER, Mary Beth 276-223-4765. 514 F
mgallagher@wcc.vccs.edu
GALLAGHER, Maureen ... 914-395-2385. 340 E
mgallagher@sarahlawrence.edu
GALLAGHER, Patrick, G . 978-478-3400. 235 G
pgallagher@northpoint.edu
GALLAGHER, Richard ..... 914-968-6200. 339 E
richard.gallagher@archny.org
GALLAGHER, Scott .... 573-592-4337. 285 D
sgallagher@williamwoods.edu
GALLAGHER, Tanya, M .. 217-333-2131. 162 A
tmgallag@illinois.edu
GALLAHER, James .... 734-487-3430. 242 D
jgallahe@emich.edu
GALLANT, Danny, R .... 936-468-2203. 482 A
dgallant@sfasu.edu
GALLARDO, Gloria .... 361-825-2427. 483 F
gloria.gallardo@tamucc.edu
GALLARDO, Ignacio .... 805-893-4412... 72 B
ignacio.gallardo@sa.ucsb.edu
GALLARDO, Mark .... 573-341-4981. 284 A
gallardom@mst.edu
GALLARDO, Ruben, C .... 915-831-6306. 472 B
rgalla16@epcc.edu
GALLART, Stephen .... 845-687-5187. 348 H
gallarts@sunyulster.edu
GALLATIN, Cynthia .... 203-582-8521... 91 A
cynthia.gallatin@quinnipiac.edu
GALLAWAY, Sue .... 360-736-9391. 517 G
sgallaway@centralia.edu
GALLEGOS, Darlena .... 270-824-1758. 196 A
darlena.gallegos@kctcs.edu
GALLEGOS, Dora .... 208-459-5688. 138 A
dgallegos@collegeofidaho.edu
GALLEGOS, Joel, A .... 704-687-7755. 368 E
jagalleg@uncc.edu
GALLEGOS, John .... 916-348-4689... 43 F
jgallegos@epic.edu
GALLEGOS, Jose .... 303-937-4200... 79 E
jgallegos@chu.edu
GALLEGOS, Paul .... 360-867-6368. 519 J
gallegos@evergreen.edu
GALLEGOS, Sergio .... 415-272-5140. 397 E
sgallegos@occc.edu
GALLEGOS, Tommy .... 972-860-4799. 470 G
tgallegos@dcccd.edu
GALLEGOS, Tony .... 505-747-2161. 311 E
GALLEN, Michael, A .... 904-819-6206. 103 E
gallenm@flagler.edu
GALLEN, Peter, C .... 864-592-4680. 447 A
gallenp@sccsc.edu
GALLENBERG, Dale .... 715-425-3841. 537 E
dale.gallenberg@uwrf.edu
GALLENTINE, Jerry, L .... 605-721-5225. 450 G
jgallentine@national.edu
GALLEY, Cherryl .... 256-726-7047..... 6 B
cgalley@oakwood.edu
GALLIANETTI, David, D .. 920-565-1219. 533 R
gallianettidd@lakeland.edu
GALLIGAN, Chris .... 860-832-1764... 87 K
galliganc@ccsu.edu
GALLIGAN, Thomas, C .. 603-526-3451. 295 I
tgalligan@colby-sawyer.edu
GALLIMORE, Anna .... 336-721-2852. 366 D
anna.gallimore@ssalem.edu
GALLIMORE, Cindy, A ... 336-386-3277. 364 D
gallimorec@surry.edu
GALLINGER, Dawn .... 406-447-5179. 285 G
dgallinger@carroll.edu
GALLION, Melanie .... 843-525-8224. 447 C
mgallion@tcl.edu
GALLIVAN, Evan .... 617-262-5000. 223 F
Evan.Gallivan@the-bac.edu
GALLIVAN, Patrick, J ..... 802-654-2557. 500 B
pgallivan@smcvt.edu
GALLMAN, Kathleen .... 252-638-7233. 359 G
gallmank@cravencc.edu
GALLO, Kelly .... 562-902-3316... 67 H
kellygallo@scuhs.edu
GALLO, Liz .... 973-408-3097. 301 C
lgallo@drew.edu
GALLO, Maria .... 808-956-8234. 136 B
gallom@hawaii.edu
GALLO, Stephanie, L ...... 630-512-8859. 141 G
sgallo@chamberlain.edu
GALLON, Dennis, P .... 561-868-3500. 110 C
gallond@palmbeachstate.edu
GALLONIO, Anthony ...... 401-454-6636. 440 A
agalloni@risd.edu
GALLOS, Joan .... 617-879-2448. 238 C
jgallos@wheelock.edu
GALLOT, JR.,
Freddie, C .... 334-229-4223..... 1 D
fgallot@alasu.edu
GALLOWAY, Alison .... 831-459-3885... 72 C
cpevc@ucsc.edu
GALLOWAY, Curt .... 651-690-6980. 263 O
wcgalloway@stkate.edu
GALLOWAY, Heather ...... 512-245-2266. 487 C
hg02@txstate.edu
GALLOWAY, Merrill .... 606-589-3079. 196 F
merrill.galloway@kctcs.edu
GALLOWAY, Peter .... 610-436-3307. 430 A
pgalloway@wcupa.edu
GALLOWAY, Tami .... 740-389-4636. 383 F
GALLOWAY-PERRY,
Rulisa .... 212-237-8601. 318 D
rgalloway@jjay.cuny.edu
GALLUCCI, Nikki .... 518-631-9836. 348 K
galluccn@uniongraduatecollege.edu
GALLUP, Gary .... 816-501-3634. 271 H
gary.gallup@avila.edu
GALM, Molly, D .... 712-324-5061. 181 G
mgalm@nwicc.edu
GALOYAN, Nazy .... 650-949-7772... 44 N
galoyannazy@fhda.edu
GALUSHA, Joseph .... 509-527-2421. 524 I
joe.galusha@wallawalla.edu
GALVAN, Dennis .... 541-346-2851. 406 D
dgalvan@uoregon.edu
GALVAN, Efren .... 714-432-5774... 39 K
egalvan@occ.cccd.edu
GALVAN, Joan .... 805-965-0581... 64 L
jcgalvan@sbcc.edu
GALVAN, Jose, L .... 415-817-4260... 35 E
galvan1@sfsu.edu
GALVAN, Michael .... 575-492-2149. 312 M
mgalvan@usw.edu
GALVAN-GONZALEZ,
Sylvia .... 512-223-2106. 466 I
sgalvang@austincc.edu
GALVEZ, Kathleen .... 718-982-2355. 317 E
kathleen.galvez@csi.cuny.edu
GALVIN, Jeanne .... 718-631-6226. 319 D
jgalvin@qcc.cuny.edu

GALVIN, Nancy ... 617-349-8585. 228 B
ngalvin@lesley.edu
GALVINHILL, Paul ... 508-793-3363. 225 B
pgalvin@holycross.edu
GALYEAN, Ann ... 325-574-7914. 494 K
agalyean@wtc.edu
GALYEAN, Michael ... 806-742-2808. 487 D
michael.galyean@ttu.edu
GALYON, Kim ... 800-290-4226. 454 M
kgalyon@hchs.edu
GAMBA, Raymond ... 415-239-3174... 38 L
rgamba@ccsf.edu
GAMBACINI, Michelle ... 203-591-5615... 90 I
mgambacini@post.edu
GAMBAIANA, Mark ... 660-785-4133. 282 L
markg@truman.edu
GAMBILL, Todd ... 765-455-9360. 168 A
GAMBINO, Ellen ... 845-431-8966. 323 C
gambino@sunydutchess.edu
GAMBINO, Stephen ... 610-436-2133. 430 A
sgambino@wcupa.edu
GAMBLE, Barbara ... 256-830-2626... 3 H
bgamble@faulkner.edu
GAMBLE, Brad ... 417-328-1823. 282 C
bgamble@sbuniv.edu
GAMBLE, Carol ... 704-637-4411. 353 E
cgamble@catawba.edu
GAMBLE, Gregory ... 856-225-3999. 306 C
gambleg@camden.rutgers.edu
GAMBLE, Joan ... 419-559-2252. 389 I
jgamble@terra.edu
GAMBLE, John, E ... 361-825-6045. 483 F
john.gamble@tamucc.edu
GAMBLE, Kay ... 334-556-2397... 3 N
kgamble@wallace.edu
GAMBLE, Mort ... 304-829-7111. 526 D
mgamble@bethanywv.edu
GAMBLE, Patrick, K ... 907-450-8000... 10 G
ua.president@alaska.edu
GAMBLE, Sarah ... 615-966-6061. 456 B
sarah.gamble@lipscomb.edu
GAMBLE, Steven ... 575-562-2121. 309 H
steven.gamble@enmu.edu
GAMBLE, Thomas, J ... 814-824-2311. 423 J
tgamble@mercyhurst.edu
GAMBOA, David ... 310-243-3819... 33 B
dgamboa@csudh.edu
GAMBOA, Larry ... 671-735-2359. 546 E
lgamboa@uguam.uog.edu
GAMBOA, Noel ... 718-262-2372. 319 F
ngamboa@york.cuny.edu
GAMBRELL, Richard ... 423-425-5316. 463 D
richard-gambrell@utc.edu
GAMBRILL, Kaitlin ... 212-364-5789. 341 C
kaitlin.gambrill@suny.edu
GAMBRO, John, S ... 815-740-3829. 162 F
jgambro@stfrancis.edu
GAMELLI, Richard ... 708-216-9222. 151 H
rgamell@lumc.edu
GAMMON, Louise ... 209-468-9155... 69 F
GAMMON, Marcia ... 480-245-7918... 14 B
marcia.gammon@ibcs.edu
GAMMON, Richard ... 937-255-6800. 544 C
richard.gammon@afit.edu
GAMMON, Steven ... 541-962-3555. 405 H
sgammon@eou.edu
GAMPERT, Richard ... 718-518-6692. 318 B
rgampert@hostos.cuny.edu
GAN, Sonny ... 626-571-5110... 51 B
sonnygan@les.edu
GANA, Karen ... 315-568-3184. 333 C
kgana@nycc.edu
GANATRA, Dhavani ... 410-752-4710. 510 B
dganatra@stratford.edu
GANCZ, Aharon ... 973-960-6670. 304 G
rgancz@aol.com
GANDIA, Melodee ... 516-299-4090. 329 C
melodee.gandia@liu.edu
GANDOLFI, Franco ... 951-343-4968... 30 H
fgandolfi@calbaptist.edu
GANDRE, James ... 212-749-2802. 330 A
jgandre@msmnyc.edu
GANDU, Bobby ... 316-978-3162. 191 F
bobby.gandu@wichita.edu
GANDY, Ashley ... 404-364-8364. 130 A
agandy@oglethorpe.edu
GANDY, Beverly ... 310-506-4451... 58 H
berverly.gandy@pepperdine.edu
GANDY, Rex, F ... 361-593-3108. 484 A
rex.gandy@tamuk.edu
GANES, Andy ... 510-261-8500... 58 G
andy.ganes@patten.edu
GANESAN, Arasu ... 910-672-1477. 367 D
nganesan@uncfsu.edu
GANESH, Jaishankar ... 856-225-6217. 306 C
jganesh@camden.rutgers.edu
GANG, Martin ... 209-575-7979... 77 H
gangm@yosemite.edu
GANGENESS, Jeanine ... 218-755-3870. 258 A
jgangeness@bemidjistate.edu
GANGES, Tendaji, W ... 810-762-3365. 251 E
tganges@umflint.edu
GANGONE, Lynn ... 303-871-6801... 86 B
lynn.gangone@du.edu
GANGSTEAD, Sandra ... 478-445-4092. 125 A
sandra.gangstead@gcsu.edu
GANGWER, Val ... 540-665-4637. 509 E
vgangwer@su.edu
GANIO, John ... 845-687-5092. 348 H
ganioj@sunyulster.edu
GANIO, Mary ... 619-482-6301... 68 B
mganio@swccd.edu
GANN, Alexander ... 516-367-6890. 320 D
ganna@cshl.edu
GANN, John ... 903-223-3114. 484 C
john.gann@tamut.edu
GANN, Johnny ... 254-647-3234. 478 H
jgann@rangercollege.edu
GANN, Michael ... 662-846-4675. 266 G
mgann@deltastate.edu
GANN, Robert ... 310-660-3015... 43 B
bgann@elcamino.edu
GANNAWAY, Anne, A ... 563-333-6283. 182 B
GannawayAnneM@sau.edu
GANNAWAY, Dale ... 575-492-4712. 310 G
dgannaway@nmjc.edu
GANNAWAY, Paula ... 806-720-7327. 476 B
paula.gannaway@lcu.edu
GANNETT-MALICK,
Lynn ... 205-970-9218... 7 B
lynngm@sebc.edu
GANNON, Debbie, K ... 515-263-6020. 178 G
dgannon@grandview.edu
GANNON, James, G ... 414-410-4151. 532 B
jggannon@stritch.edu
GANNON, Kim ... 512-245-2371. 487 C
kg33@txstate.edu
GANNON, Marcy ... 301-934-7560. 214 D
marcyg@csmd.edu
GANNON, Susan ... 908-737-3461. 302 F
sgannon@kean.edu
GANNON, Violet ... 860-297-4033... 91 F
j.gannon@trincoll.edu
GANSBERG, Alan, L ... 818-401-1032... 41 B
agansberg@columbiacollege.edu
GANSCHOW, Darby ... 605-677-6623. 451 F
darby.ganschow@usd.edu
GANSKE, Kathryn, M ... 540-678-4381. 509 E
kganske@su.edu
GANSZ, David ... 937-778-7951. 379 G
dgansz@edisonohio.edu
GANT, Jocelind, E ... 814-393-2109. 428 C
jgant@clarion.edu
GANT, Patricia ... 415-485-9414... 40 G
patricia.gant@marin.edu
GANTENBEIN, Tony ... 320-629-5159. 260 F
gantenbeint@pinetech.edu
GANTHER, Sonya ... 608-796-3930. 539 E
sganther@viterbo.edu
GANTMAN, Amy ... 310-665-6851... 57 C
agantman@otis.edu
GANTNER, Christine, M ... 920-424-3414. 537 B
gantner@uwosh.edu
GANTNER, Myrna ... 678-839-6445. 133 I
mgantner@westga.edu
GANTT, Aubra, J ... 817-515-7778. 482 B
aubra.gantt@tccd.edu
GANTT, Bernard ... 718-289-5887. 317 B
bernard.gantt@bcc.cuny.edu
GANTT, Kevin ... 913-758-6230. 191 B
ganttk@stmary.edu
GANTT, Rachel ... 505-473-6622. 311 K
rachel.gantt@santafeuniversity.edu
GANTZ, Jennifer ... 316-942-4291. 189 E
gantzj@newmanu.edu
GANTZ, Katie, L ... 240-895-4491. 218 A
klgantz@smcm.edu
GANZEL, Toni ... 502-852-5192. 200 D
toni.ganzel@louisville.edu
GAO, Jing ... 215-646-7300. 417 F
gao.j@gmc.edu
GAONA, Selin ... 816-604-4190. 277 H
selin.gaona@mcckc.edu
GARAFOLA, David ... 972-438-6932. 478 C
dgarafola@parkercc.edu
GARAND, Bob ... 843-661-8326. 443 G
bob.garand@fdtc.edu
GARANZINI, SJ,
Michael, J ... 312-915-6400. 151 H
mgaranz@luc.edu
GARAT, Heather ... 916-649-2400... 30 C
GARAVASO, Pieranno ... 320-589-6250. 264 F
garavapf@morris.umn.edu
GARAWITZ, Amy ... 212-229-5662. 332 E
garawita@newschool.edu
GARAY, Stephanie ... 910-962-3188. 369 C
garays@uncw.edu
GARAYUA, Michelle ... 910-221-2224. 354 D
mgarayua@gcd.edu
GARBADE, Henry ... 843-208-8087. 448 B
hgarbade@uscb.edu
GARBARINO, James ... 816-444-0669. 280 I
bookstore@rockhurst.edu
GARBART, Hadley ... 410-225-2231. 216 C
hgarbart@mica.edu
GARBE, John ... 585-389-2038. 332 D
jgarbe6@naz.edu
GARBE, Theresa ... 423-461-8718. 457 H
tmgarbe@milligan.edu
GARBER, Alan, M ... 617-496-5100. 227 C
alan_garber@harvard.edu
GARBER, Barbara ... 415-351-3538... 62 G
bgarber@sfai.edu
GARBER,
Christopher, W ... 260-982-5027. 170 U
cwgarber@manchester.edu
GARBER, Darrell ... 610-683-4253. 429 A
garber@kutztown.edu
GARBER, Gail ... 860-486-5519... 92 A
gail.garber@uconn.edu
GARBER, Gena ... 641-628-5156. 176 E
garberg@central.edu
GARBER, Kevin, S ... 913-971-3275. 188 H
ksgarber@mnu.edu
GARBER, Philip ... 847-214-7285. 144 F
pgarber@elgin.edu
GARBER, Robert ... 619-388-2990... 62 E
rgarber@sdccd.edu
GARBER, Sandy ... 928-776-2117... 19 H
sandy.garber@yc.edu
GARBER BAX, Sharlene . 660-543-4114. 283 A
bax@ucmo.edu
GARBINI, Dennis, J ... 973-761-9011. 307 C
dennis.garbini@shu.edu
GARBIOGLU, Ibrahim ... 412-323-2323. 413 D
igarbioglu@ccac.edu
GARCEAU, Linda, R ... 423-439-4289. 459 C
garceaul@etsu.edu
GARCIA, Abigail ... 602-331-7500... 12 A
GARCIA, Adam ... 775-784-4689. 294 J
adam_garcia@police.unr.edu
GARCIA, Aida ... 787-725-6500. 547 H
agarcia@sju.albizu.edu
GARCIA, Al ... 212-349-4330. 325 D
agarcia@globe.edu
GARCIA, Albert ... 916-558-2337... 53 D
garciaaj@scc.losrios.edu
GARCIA, Alberto ... 787-848-0810. 555 A
alberto.garcia3@upr.edu
GARCIA, Alexandra ... 210-434-6711. 477 N
amgarcia08@lake.ollusa.edu
GARCIA, Alfredo ... 505-260-6180. 310 E
a_garcia@nmhu.edu
GARCIA, Amarillys ... 787-746-1400. 549 B
agarcia@huertas.edu
GARCIA, Ana ... 787-815-0000. 553 I
ana.garcia6@upr.edu
GARCIA, Andrea ... 707-638-5272... 69 K
andrea.garcia@tu.edu
GARCIA, Anita ... 409-933-8150. 469 E
agarcia@com.edu
GARCIA, Ava, M ... 671-735-5558. 546 C
ava.garcia@guamcc.edu
GARCIA, Bob ... 323-953-4000... 51 G
garciabj@lacitycollege.edu
GARCIA, Bob ... 989-463-7299. 239 B
garciab@alma.edu
GARCIA, Brenda, W ... 575-439-3697. 310 J
brgarcia@nmsu.edu
GARCIA, Brett ... 540-261-4503. 509 K
brett.garcia@svu.edu
GARCIA, Carlos ... 210-829-2717. 490 A
cagarci9@uiwtx.edu
GARCIA, Carol ... 718-779-1430. 336 D
cgarcia@plazacollege.edu
GARCIA, Carol ... 307-674-6446. 543 F
cgarcia@sheridan.edu
GARCIA, Caroline, M ... 520-621-3900... 18 F
cmgarcia@email.arizona.edu
GARCIA, Cathy ... 619-594-4723... 35 D
cgarcia@mail.sdsu.edu
GARCIA, Christian ... 305-284-5451. 118 F
christian@miami.edu
GARCIA, Christina ... 626-914-8825... 38 K
cmgarcia@citruscollege.edu
GARCIA, Daisy ... 940-668-7731. 477 I
dgarcia@nctc.edu
GARCIA, Dan, D ... 806-651-2031. 484 D
ddgarcia@mail.wtamu.edu
GARCIA, Daniel ... 810-762-9752. 244 Q
dgarcia@kettering.edu
GARCIA, David ... 604-274-1252. 327 E
dgarcia@ithaca.edu
GARCIA, David ... 330-672-1001. 382 B
tgarcia5@kent.edu
GARCIA, Delia ... 305-348-3598. 115 B
garciade@fiu.edu
GARCIA, Della ... 602-243-8124... 15 F
della.garcia@smcmail.maricopa.edu
GARCIA, Diana ... 630-743-0680. 163 C
dgarcia@westwood.edu
GARCIA, Elena ... 787-780-0070. 547 G
egarcia@caribbean.edu
GARCIA, Eliezer ... 787-786-3030. 547 F
egarcia@ucb.edu.pr
GARCIA, Elizabeth ... 860-439-2624... 89 H
elizabeth.garcia@conncoll.edu
GARCIA, Elizabeth ... 610-282-1100. 414 F
elizabeth.garcia@desales.edu
GARCIA, Florence ... 406-768-6300. 286 C
fgarcia@fpcc.edu
GARCIA, Frances ... 787-786-2412. 553 C
frances.garcia@uccaribe.edu
GARCIA, JR., Gilberto ... 202-994-9633... 95 D
ggarciajr@gwu.edu
GARCIA, Gilda ... 940-565-2711. 490 C
ggarcia@unt.edu
GARCIA, Gladys ... 661-654-3485... 32 H
ggarcia32@csub.edu
GARCIA, Heather ... 501-882-4434... 19 M
hngarcia@asub.edu
GARCIA, Helen ... 915-566-9621. 494 J
hgarcia@westerntech.edu
GARCIA, Irma ... 718-489-5490. 338 G
igarcia@sfc.edu
GARCIA, Janet, K ... 605-221-3234. 450 C
jgarcia@kilian.edu
GARCIA, Joann ... 760-252-2411... 29 I
jgarcia@barstow.edu
GARCIA, Joe ... 312-996-9450. 161 C
jggarcia@uic.edu
GARCIA, Jorge ... 787-779-2500. 548 F
ccat@coqui.edu
GARCIA, Joyce ... 323-265-8732... 51 F
garciajb@elac.edu
GARCIA, Juan ... 956-364-4604. 485 H
juan.garcia@tstc.edu
GARCIA, Juan, B ... 575-439-3717. 310 J
jbgarcia@nmsu.edu
GARCIA, JR., Juan, G ... 956-326-2267. 483 B
jgarcia@tamiu.edu
GARCIA, Juliet, V ... 956-882-8201. 491 D
president@utb.edu
GARCIA, Julio ... 408-273-2690... 55 H
jgarcia@nhu.edu
GARCIA, Kellie ... 661-654-3206... 32 H
kgarcia@csub.edu
GARCIA, Kim, L ... 408-274-6700... 63 N
kim.garcia@sjeccd.org
GARCIA, Leslie ... 503-494-5657. 405 I
cedma@ohsu.edu
GARCIA, Luis ... 787-285-5457. 549 C
lgarcia@hccpr.edu
GARCIA, Luis, A ... 802-656-3390. 500 F
luis.garcia@uvm.edu
GARCIA, Maria ... 305-595-9500... 97 G
registrar@amcollege.edu
GARCIA, Maria ... 210-341-1366. 477 L
mgarcia@ost.edu
GARCIA, Melissa ... 956-721-5189. 475 F
melissagarcia@laredo.edu
GARCIA, Meysaliz ... 787-878-6000. 549 D
mgarcia@icprjc.edu
GARCIA, Mildred ... 657-278-3456... 33 E
presidentgarcia@fullerton.edu
GARCIA, Myra ... 909-593-3511... 72 E
mgarcia2@laverne.edu
GARCIA, Orlando ... 305-348-3357. 115 B
orlando.garcia@fiu.edu
GARCIA, Oscar, S ... 830-591-7330. 481 C
osgarcia@swtjc.edu
GARCIA, Pete ... 305-348-0504. 115 B
pete.garcia@fiu.edu
GARCIA, Peter ... 925-969-2001... 41 L
pgarcia@dvc.edu
GARCIA, Phil ... 916-278-8758... 34 D
garciap@csus.edu
GARCIA, Racquel ... 212-247-3434. 329 L
GARCIA, Raul ... 847-635-1637. 155 F
rgarcia@oakton.edu
GARCIA, Rene ... 305-237-3519. 109 D
rgarcia@mdc.edu
GARCIA, Rick ... 310-338-6047... 53 E
rgarcia@lmu.edu
GARCIA, Rick ... 817-515-5292. 482 B
rick.garcia@tccd.edu
GARCIA, Roberto ... 719-389-6348... 79 D
rgarcia@coloradocollege.edu
GARCIA, Romeo ... 510-587-7890... 59 A
rgarcia@peralta.edu
GARCIA, Ron ... 505-454-3251. 310 E
garcia_rs@nmhu.edu
GARCIA, Rosemarie, M ... 505-428-1201. 311 J
rosemarie.garcia@sfcc.edu
GARCIA, Ruben ... 787-758-2525. 554 F
ruben.garcia3@upr.edu
GARCIA, Rudy ... 505-224-4342. 309 E
rudyg@cnm.edu
GARCIA, Sandra ... 713-221-8091. 489 D
garcias@uhd.edu
GARCIA, Sarah ... 208-769-3341. 138 I
sarah_garcia@nic.edu

GARCIA, Sergio ... 330-325-6259. 385 E
sgarcia@neomed.edu
GARCIA, Stella ... 956-364-4050. 485 H
stella.garcia@tstc.edu
GARCIA, Stephan ... 657-278-2115... 33 E
sgarcia@fullerton.edu
GARCIA, Steve ... 760-245-4271... 75 B
Steve.Garcia@vvc.edu
GARCIA, Steven, N ... 909-621-8030... 39 C
steve.garcia@cgu.edu
GARCIA, Sunshine ... 805-437-3776... 32 I
sunshine.garcia@csuci.edu
GARCIA, Susan, P ... 740-587-6592. 379 D
garcia@denison.edu
GARCIA, Tania ... 805-437-8452... 32 I
tania.garcia@csuci.edu
GARCIA, Tara ... 657-278-7295... 33 E
tgarcia@fullerton.edu
GARCIA, Tary ... 787-264-1912. 551 A
tdgarcia@sg.inter.edu
GARCIA, Teresa ... 319-208-1920. 182 G
tgarcia@scciowa.edu
GARCIA, Tony ... 608-663-2256. 532 I
tgarcia@edgewood.edu
GARCIA, Val ... 559-791-2459... 49 P
val.garcia@portervillecollege.edu
GARCIA, Valeria ... 813-974-9768. 116 C
vgarcia@usf.edu
GARCIA, Veronica ... 858-642-8265... 55 J
vgarcia@nu.edu
GARCIA, Veronica ... 971-722-7800. 407 D
veronica.garcia6@pcc.edu
GARCIA, Vladimir ... 787-725-8120. 548 O
vgarcia0068@eap.edu
GARCIA, Vonda ... 760-750-4852... 35 A
vgarcia@csusm.edu
GARCIA, William ... 973-596-5320. 303 G
william.garcia@njit.edu
GARCIA, Yessika ... 212-686-9040. 350 G
ygarcia@woodtobecoburn.edu
GARCIA-ANOYO,
Lemuel ... 512-404-4809. 467 A
lgarcia@austinseminary.edu
GARCIA-GARCIA, Ines, J 787-758-2525. 554 F
ines.garcia@upr.edu
GARCIA-HILLS,
Rosemarie ... 708-209-3257. 143 E
rosemarie.garcia@cuchicago.edu
GARCIA-MARENKO,
Emilio ... 269-471-3375. 239 D
egm@andrews.edu
GARCIA-MARENKO,
Emilio ... 269-471-3375. 243 G
egm@andrews.edu
GARCIA-MARENKO,
Emilio ... 269-471-3375. 239 D
egm@andrews.edu
GARCIA-MILLER, Maria .. 209-478-0800... 47 M
mgarcia@humphreys.edu
GARCIA ORTEGA,
Ismael ... 787-945-7013. 548 O
decanoadministracion@eap.edu
GARCIA RAMOS, Tania .. 787-764-0000. 555 B
tgarcia@upr.edu
GARCIA-REYES, Ana, I ... 718-518-4313. 318 B
agreyes@hostos.cuny.edu
GARCIA TOULET, Rafael 787-880-6577. 553 I
rafael.gaqrcia4@upr.edu
GARCIA VAN DE GRIEK,
Jessica ... 615-966-5210. 456 B
jessica.vandegriek@lipscomb.edu
GARCON, Reginald ... 410-888-9048. 216 D
rgarcon@muih.edu
GARCÍA, Adolfo, J ... 787-894-2828. 555 C
adolfo.garcia@upr.edu
GARD, Evelyn ... 203-285-2065... 88 E
egard@gwcc.commnet.edu
GARD, Krista, L ... 718-990-6749. 339 A
mcgowank@stjohns.edu
GARDEA, Oscar, M ... 415-338-2897... 35 E
omgardea@sfsu.edu
GARDELLA, Patrick ... 859-858-2130. 192 A
GARDI, Kerri ... 610-683-4647. 429 A
gardi@kutztown.edu
GARDIAL, Sarah ... 319-335-0866. 175 I
sarah-gardial@uiowa.edu
GARDIER PATERSON,
Mary, T ... 570-340-6018. 423 B
paterson@marywood.edu
GARDIN, Carey, C ... 920-923-7617. 534 A
cgardin@marianuniversity.edu
GARDIN, Kendra ... 219-785-5519. 172 A
kgardin@pnc.edu
GARDIN, T. Hershel ... 248-414-6900. 246 F
thgardin@mji.edu
GARDINER, Arthur, Z ... 603-448-2445. 297 A
GARDINER, Duane ... 361-593-2170. 484 A
duane.gardiner@tamuk.edu
GARDINER, Jane, W ... 910-630-7158. 356 H
jgardiner@methodist.edu
GARDNER, Amanda ... 276-944-6922. 504 H
agardner@ehc.edu
GARDNER, Andy ... 704-669-4041. 359 D
gardnera@clevelandcc.edu
GARDNER, Beth ... 304-252-9547. 527 I
GARDNER, Betina ... 859-622-1778. 193 P
betina.gardner@eku.edu
GARDNER, Brian ... 314-529-9387. 276 G
bgardner@maryville.edu
GARDNER, Brian ... 503-554-2112. 403 C
gardnerb@georgefox.edu
GARDNER, Butch ... 501-279-4454... 21 C
bgardner@harding.edu
GARDNER, Clinton ... 202-686-0876... 97 C
GARDNER, Clinton, D ... 928-541-7777... 16 B
president@ncu.edu
GARDNER, Craig ... 801-957-4601. 498 B
craig.gardner@slcc.edu
GARDNER, David ... 315-364-3229. 350 E
dgardner@wells.edu
GARDNER, David ... 434-381-6144. 510 F
dgardner@sbc.edu
GARDNER, David, M ... 785-864-0229. 190 L
gardner@ku.edu
GARDNER, Denise ... 865-974-4373. 463 C
d.gardner@utk.edu
GARDNER, Dinelia ... 201-559-6154. 302 A
gardnerd@felician.edu
GARDNER, Gail, A ... 518-458-5336. 321 A
gardnerg@strose.edu
GARDNER, Greg ... 405-682-7534. 397 E
ggardner@occc.edu
GARDNER, Guy, S ... 610-565-0999. 437 G
ggardner@williamson.edu
GARDNER,
Gwendolyn, S ... 704-894-2597. 353 J
gwgardner@davidson.edu
GARDNER, Helena ... 313-927-1650. 246 D
hgardner7910@marygrove.edu
GARDNER, James ... 660-359-3948. 279 H
jgardner@mail.ncmissouri.edu
GARDNER, Jeanne, W ... 719-549-3308... 84 G
jeanne.gardner@pueblocc.edu
GARDNER, Jeff ... 812-535-5299. 172 F
jgardner@smwc.edu
GARDNER, Jeff ... 231-348-6624. 247 H
jgardner@ncmich.edu
GARDNER, Jessica ... 847-574-5266. 150 C
jgardner@lfgsm.edu
GARDNER, John ... 206-780-6213. 516 I
john.gardner@bgi.edu
GARDNER, Judith ... 419-448-3420. 389 J
jgardner@tiffin.edu
GARDNER, Katherine, B . 919-658-7746. 357 I
kgardner@moc.edu
GARDNER, Kathy ... 704-991-0278. 364 C
kgardner5070@stanly.edu
GARDNER, Kelly, E ... 315-684-6363. 345 A
gardneke@morrisville.edu
GARDNER, Laurie, A ... 207-778-7272. 212 D
lgardner@main.edu
GARDNER, Marie ... 785-242-2067. 189 D
mgardner@neosho.edu
GARDNER, Mary ... 610-341-5961. 415 G
mgardner@eastern.edu
GARDNER, Mary ... 484-341-5961. 425 I
mgardner@eastern.edu
GARDNER, Melissa ... 330-823-6092. 391 E
gardnemf@mountunion.edu
GARDNER, Monique, G .. 504-861-5752. 205 H
mgardner@loyno.edu
GARDNER, Pamela, K ... 802-656-3450. 500 F
pamela.k.gardner@uvm.edu
GARDNER, Robert ... 909-537-5130... 34 E
rgardner@csusb.edu
GARDNER, Robert ... 817-202-6205. 481 E
gardnerr@swau.edu
GARDNER, Ronald, E ... 504-568-4810. 205 C
rgardner@lsuhsc.edu
GARDNER, Stephanie, F . 501-686-5558... 24 C
gardnerstephanief@uams.edu
GARDNER, Susan ... 304-205-6701. 528 B
sgardnerr@kvctc.edu
GARDNER, Suzanne ... 727-341-3364. 112 E
gardner.suzanne@spcollege.edu
GARDNER, Tammi ... 575-562-2991. 309 H
tammi.gardner@enmu.edu
GARDNER, Tracy ... 937-294-0592. 388 M
tracy@saa.edu
GAREWSKI, Jeffrey, A ... 860-465-4521... 87 L
garewskij@easternct.edu
GAREY, Ann ... 309-672-4766. 152 I
agarey@methodistcol.edu
GAREY, Cheri ... 704-534-4128. 145 F
cgarey@govst.edu
GAREY, Kelly ... 503-552-1603. 404 H
kgarey@ncnm.edu
GARFIELD, Gabriela ... 313-577-3049. 252 G
gabriela.garfield@wayne.edu
GARFINKEL, Stephen ... 212-678-8050. 328 A
stgarfinkel@jtsa.edu
GARFINKLE-WEITZ, Jill . 215-751-8368. 413 I
jweitz@ccp.edu
GARFOOT, John, R ... 716-338-1023. 327 J
johngarfoot@mail.sunyjcc.edu
GARGANO, Michael ... 210-567-4838. 493 A
gargano@uthscsa.edu
GARGANO, Michael ... 210-567-2004. 493 A
gargano@uthscsa.edu
GARGIULO, Joe ... 214-768-3474. 481 A
gargiulo@smu.edu
GARGIULO, Leslie ... 770-729-8400. 120 I
GARGUILE, Mary ... 360-475-7400. 521 H
mgarguile@olympic.edu
GARIBALDI, Antoine, M . 313-993-1455. 250 K
garibaldi@udmercy.edu
GARIC, John ... 406-496-3711. 287 F
jgaric@mtech.edu
GARIEPY, David ... 574-284-5000. 172 G
dgariepy@saintmarys.edu
GARIFI, Nelson, J ... 716-338-1045. 327 J
nelsongarifi@mail.sunyjcc.edu
GARIMELLA, Suresh ... 765-494-9095. 171 M
sureshg@purdue.edu
GARIPPA, Robert, J ... 214-887-5361. 471 F
rgarippa@dts.edu
GARIS, Jeffrey, W ... 814-865-2377. 426 A
jwg1@psu.edu
GARLAND, Anita, H ... 434-223-6120. 505 E
agarland@hsc.edu
GARLAND, Colleen, C ... 740-368-3015. 387 J
ccgarland@owu.edu
GARLAND, Daniel ... 412-291-6240. 410 B
dgarland@aii.edu
GARLAND, David ... 254-710-3755. 467 G
david_garland@baylor.edu
GARLAND, Doug ... 864-242-5100. 441 D
GARLAND, Helen ... 757-497-4466. 510 B
hgarland@stratford.edu
GARLAND, Jeffrey, W ... 302-831-2113... 94 B
jgarland@udel.edu
GARLAND, Peter, H ... 717-720-4010. 427 G
pgarland@passhe.edu
GARLAND, Philip ... 619-260-4724... 73 I
pgarland@sandiego.edu
GARLAND, Robert, R ... 330-823-3844. 391 E
garlanrr@mountunion.edu
GARLAND, Tina, M ... 937-382-6661. 393 B
tina_garland@wilmington.edu
GARLETT, Fred ... 626-815-5301... 29 H
fgarlett@apu.edu
GARLICH, Michael ... 407-708-2442. 113 E
garlichm@seminolestate.edu
GARLICK, Rebecca ... 979-743-5222. 467 I
bgarlick@blinn.edu
GARLICK, Stella ... 304-263-6262. 527 B
sgarlick@martinsburginstitute.edu
GARLIE, Gary ... 218-723-6104. 254 K
ggarlie@css.edu
GARMAN, David ... 414-382-1700. 537 A
garmand@uwm.edu
GARMAN, Deanna ... 423-585-6897. 462 A
deanna.garman@ws.edu
GARMAN, Gregory, C ... 804-828-1574. 511 F
ggarman@vcu.edu
GARMAN, Karen, M ... 937-382-6661. 393 B
karen_garman@wilmington.edu
GARMROTH, Nancy, T ... 864-592-4823. 447 A
garmrothn@sccsc.edu
GARN, Gregg ... 405-325-1081. 401 B
garn@ou.edu
GARNER, April ... 843-349-7870. 444 F
april.garner@hgtc.edu
GARNER, Ashly, G ... 920-923-7161. 534 A
aggarner54@marianuniversity.edu
GARNER, Billy ... 931-393-1576. 461 A
bgarner@mscc.edu
GARNER, Cheryl ... 361-698-1277. 471 G
cgarner6@delmar.edu
GARNER, Cindy ... 901-722-3223. 458 K
cgarner@sco.edu
GARNER, David ... 215-572-3839. 437 C
dgarner@wts.edu
GARNER, Doris ... 252-536-7255. 361 A
agarner939@halifaxcc.edu
GARNER, Gloria ... 253-680-7203. 516 L
ggarner@bates.ctc.edu
GARNER, Graham ... 319-352-8232. 183 E
graham.garner@wartburg.edu
GARNER, James ... 870-575-7035... 24 E
garnerj@uapb.edu
GARNER, Kimberly ... 801-524-8135. 495 O
KGarner9@ldsbc.edu
GARNER, Mark ... 610-398-5300. 422 B
mgarner@lincolntech.com
GARNER, Melissa ... 405-945-3315. 398 C
GARNER, Porter ... 979-845-7514. 483 C
porter-garner@tamu.edu
GARNER, Ray ... 256-824-6397... 8 F
ray.garner@uah.edu
GARNER, Regina ... 214-860-8553. 471 A
rgarner@dcccd.edu
GARNER, Richard ... 516-877-3800. 313 A
garner@adelphi.edu
GARNER, Roshae ... 801-840-4800. 495 K
rgarner@cci.edu
GARNER, Tim ... 256-782-8220... 4 K
tgarner@jsu.edu
GARNER, Timothy, L ... 317-738-8093. 165 I
tgarner@franklincollege.edu
GARNETT, Heather, A ... 434-947-8102. 508 D
hgarnett@randolphcollege.edu
GARNETT, Sherman, W .. 517-353-6753. 246 H
garnetts@msu.edu
GARNI, Kenneth, F ... 617-573-8226. 237 B
kgarni@suffolk.edu
GARNIC, Gary, G ... 814-871-7404. 416 K
garnic001@gannon.edu
GARNIGAN, Tina ... 404-527-7724. 127 I
tgarnigan@itc.edu
GAROFALO, Marise ... 570-504-7000. 413 B
GAROFALOW, Matthew .. 718-409-2866. 346 D
mgarofalow@sunymaritime.edu
GAROFANO, John ... 401-841-1812. 545 A
GARONE, Eugene ... 610-992-1700... 96 F
GARR, David, R ... 843-792-4431. 445 B
garrdr@musc.edu
GARR, Michael ... 209-954-5074... 63 C
mgarr@deltacollege.edu
GARR-BARNES, Andrea .. 270-745-5066. 200 G
andrea.garr-barnes@wku.edu
GARRABRANTS, Nancy .. 413-545-4764. 228 F
n.garrabrants@cns.umass.edu
GARRELL, Robin, L ... 310-825-4383... 71 C
rgarrell@gdnet.ucla.edu
GARREN, Kenneth, R ... 434-544-8200. 506 K
president@lynchburg.edu
GARREN, Mary Ann ... 870-762-3168... 19 K
mgarren@smail.anc.edu
GARREN, Steve ... 217-234-5459. 150 D
sgarren@lakeland.cc.il.us
GARRETSON, Janet ... 618-545-3333. 149 D
jgarretson@kaskaskia.edu
GARRETT, Bonnie, J ... 410-777-2503. 213 D
bjgarrett@aacc.edu
GARRETT, Dan, T ... 325-674-2508. 464 H
garrettd@acu.edu
GARRETT, David ... 315-792-7805. 346 C
david.garrett@sunyit.edu
GARRETT, Deborah, A ... 501-882-8986... 19 M
dagarrett@asub.edu
GARRETT, Don ... 325-674-2687. 464 H
don.garrett@acu.edu
GARRETT, Elizabeth ... 213-740-2101... 74 A
uscprovost@usc.edu
GARRETT, Gina ... 870-307-7557... 21 H
gina.garrett@lyon.edu
GARRETT, Glenda ... 214-860-8666. 471 A
ghall@dcccd.edu
GARRETT, Greg ... 281-443-8900. 485 D
GARRETT, Helen ... 541-463-5725. 403 I
garretth@lanecc.edu
GARRETT, J. Craig ... 504-282-4455. 206 A
cgarrett@nobts.edu
GARRETT, James ... 606-546-1244. 200 A
jgarrett@unionky.edu
GARRETT, James ... 412-268-5090. 412 H
garrett@cmu.edu
GARRETT, James, F ... 434-971-3303. 544 I
james.f.garrett.mil@mail.mil
GARRETT, Kara ... 509-793-2050. 517 C
karag@bigbend.edu
GARRETT, Kevin ... 304-384-5340. 529 E
garrettad@concord.edu
GARRETT, Larry ... 361-485-6803. 493 H
larry.garrett@victoriacollege.edu
GARRETT, Leonard ... 214-860-3697. 471 A
lgarrett@dcccd.edu
GARRETT, Louise, M ... 248-204-2000. 245 I
lgarrett@ltu.edu
GARRETT, Mark ... 270-901-1065. 196 E
mark.garrett@kctcs.edu
GARRETT, Mike ... 405-466-3262. 395 N
mgarrett@langston.edu
GARRETT, Natasha ... 412-536-1296. 420 A
natasha.garrett@laroche.edu
GARRETT, P, B ... 202-994-0108... 95 D
pgarrett@gwu.edu
GARRETT, Patricia ... 706-507-8898. 123 D
garrett_patricia@columbusstate.edu
GARRETT, Paul ... 864-977-7035. 445 H
paul.garrett@ngu.edu
GARRETT, Paula, K ... 828-298-3325. 370 E
academic@warren-wilson.edu
GARRETT, Rob, J ... 208-496-1450. 137 H
garrettr@byui.edu
GARRETT, Stacey, A ... 615-453-6301. 454 A
sgarrett@cumberland.edu
GARRETT, Susan, R ... 502-895-3411. 197 F
sgarrett@lpts.edu
GARRETT-MILLER, Holly 501-760-4364... 22 A
hgarrett@npcc.edu

GARRICK, Debbie ... 803-323-2145. 449 G garrickd@winthrop.edu
GARRICK DUHANEY, Laurel ... 845-257-3561. 342 B duhaneyl@newpaltz.edu
GARRIGAN, Dana ... 262-551-2373. 532 D dgarrigan@carthage.edu
GARRIOCH, Shaynan ... 845-451-4365. 322 D s_garrio@culinary.edu
GARRIS, Daffie, H ... 336-633-0290. 362 H dhgarris@randolph.edu
GARRIS, Eric, L ... 843-661-1160. 444 B egarris@fmarion.edu
GARRIS, Rick ... 303-963-3290... 79 C rgarris@ccu.edu
GARRISON, Bruce ... 918-343-7663. 399 C bgarrison@rsu.edu
GARRISON, David ... 706-880-8235. 128 A dgarrison@lagrange.edu
GARRISON, Deborah, R . 610-499-4214. 437 E drgarrison@widener.edu
GARRISON, Estella ... 949-582-4646... 67 C egarrison@saddleback.edu
GARRISON, Helene ... 949-376-6000... 50 C hgarrison@lagunacollege.edu
GARRISON, James, R ... 913-971-3296. 188 H jgarriso@mnu.edu
GARRISON, Mark ... 443-885-3185. 217 A mark.garrison@morgan.edu
GARRISON, Michael ... 651-962-5187. 265 C mgarrison@stthomas.edu
GARRISON, Peg ... 563-326-5319. 178 C pgarrison@eicc.edu
GARRISON, Scott ... 231-591-3729. 242 F garriss@ferris.edu
GARRISON, Walter ... 610-892-1504. 427 E wgarrison@pit.edu
GARRISON, Webb ... 505-467-6823. 312 D acadean@swc.edu
GARRISON, William ... 813-974-1642. 116 C wgarrison@usf.edu
GARRITY, Christopher ... 413-205-3366. 221 F christopher.garrity@aic.edu
GARRITY, Collette ... 612-374-5800. 255 F cgarrity@dunwoody.edu
GARRITY, Kathleen, E ... 608-822-2471. 541 C kgarrity@swtc.edu
GARRITY, Michael ... 708-456-0300. 161 A mgarrity@triton.edu
GARRITY, Patricia ... 608-897-8514. 297 F pgarrity@rivier.edu
GARRITY, Robert ... 239-280-2581... 98 K robert.garrity@avemaria.edu
GARROTT, Marci ... 214-860-8680. 471 A mgarrott@dcccd.edu
GARRY, Kirby ... 831-582-3534... 34 B kgarry@csumb.edu
GARST, Stephanie, P ... 540-375-2323. 509 B garst@roanoke.edu
GARSTAD, Zane, S ... 307-674-6446. 543 F zgarstad@sheridan.edu
GARSTECKI, Marcus ... 308-535-3610. 290 J garsteckim@mpcc.edu
GARTEN, Ann ... 310-660-3406... 43 B agarten@elcamino.edu
GARTEN, Ann, M ... 310-660-3670... 43 B agarten@elcamino.edu
GARTEN-SHUMAN, John ... 510-869-6727... 61 I jgartens@samuelmerritt.edu
GARTENMAYER, Charles 913-360-7583. 184 H cgartenmayer@benedictine.edu
GARTH, Bryant, G ... 213-738-6806... 68 C bgarth@swlaw.edu
GARTHOFF, Jerry ... 207-621-3067. 212 C garthoff@maine.edu
GARTIN, Stanton ... 970-521-6650... 83 L stanton.gartin@njc.edu
GARTNER, Lia ... 212-229-5192. 332 E gartnerl@newschool.edu
GARTNER, Maggie ... 979-845-4427. 483 C molona@tamu.edu
GARTON, Jilda ... 404-894-4819. 125 D jilda.garton@gtrc.gatech.edu
GARTRELL, William ... 626-396-2316... 28 P bill.gartrell@artcenter.edu
GARUS, Marcella Marie .. 716-896-0700. 350 A smgarus@villa.edu
GARVER, Julie ... 360-867-6453. 519 J garverj@evergreen.edu
GARVER, Robert, A ... 419-866-0261. 389 H ragarver@stautzenberger.com
GARVEY, Ann, L ... 612-330-1168. 253 H garvey@augsburg.edu
GARVEY, Carol ... 712-274-5178. 181 B garvey@morningside.edu
GARVEY, Diane ... 985-492-2009. 208 A diane.garvey@nicholls.edu
GARVEY, Hugh ... 217-786-2304. 151 F hugh.garvey@llcc.edu
GARVEY, James ... 618-453-4550. 159 G jgarvey@siu.edu
GARVEY, John, H ... 202-319-5100... 94 G cua-president@cua.edu
GARVEY, JR., Joseph, X 570-348-6222. 423 B jxgarvey@marywood.edu
GARVEY, Judy ... 714-241-6230... 39 I jgarvey@coastline.edu
GARVEY, Kathleen, M ... 508-373-9455. 223 A kathleen.garvey@becker.edu
GARVEY, Maxine ... 256-726-7000..... 6 B mgarvey@oakwood.edu
GARVEY, Meg ... 607-844-8222. 347 I garveym@TC3.edu
GARVEY, Pamela, J ... 414-955-4700. 534 C pgarvey@mcw.edu
GARVIN, Maureen ... 912-525-5000. 131 B mgarvin@scad.edu
GARY, Cynthia ... 405-682-1611. 397 E cynthia.d.gary@occc.edu
GARY, Kevin ... 574-535-7839. 166 A kgary@goshen.edu
GARY, Marc ... 212-678-8080. 328 A magary@jtsa.edu
GARY, SR., William, H .. 703-323-2399. 513 C wgary@nvcc.edu
GARZA, Felipe ... 361-593-2611. 484 A felipe.garza@tamuk.edu
GARZA, Fena ... 713-718-7748. 473 C fena.garza@hccs.edu
GARZA, Kim ... 509-793-2010. 517 C kimg@bigbend.edu
GARZA, Lanette ... 210-486-3731. 465 A lgarza@alamo.edu
GARZA, Lisa ... 972-883-4349. 491 E lisa.garza@utdallas.edu
GARZA, Noemi ... 956-872-2681. 480 I ngarza24@southtexascollege.edu
GARZA, Nora, R ... 956-721-5868. 475 F nrgarza@laredo.edu
GARZA, Rachel ... 814-332-2707. 409 D
GARZA, Raul ... 703-556-8888. 509 C
GARZA, Rebecca, J ... 214-860-2618. 470 J rgarza@dcccd.edu
GARZA, Robert ... 210-486-3930. 465 A rgarza@alamo.edu
GARZA, Roberto ... 305-223-4561. 112 B rgarza@sjvcs.edu
GARZA, JR., Victor ... 408-274-7900... 63 O victor.garza@evc.edu
GARZA, Wanda ... 956-872-2770. 480 I wgarza@southtexascollege.edu
GARZA-MITCHELL, Regina ... 956-364-4601. 485 H
GARZA-RODERICK, Jessie ... 209-833-7900... 63 C jgarza-roderick@deltacollege.edu
GASAWAY, Debbie ... 870-460-1622... 24 D gasaway@uamont.edu
GASCHK, Kenneth, K ... 262-243-5700. 532 H ken.gaschk@cuw.edu
GASCHO, Ron ... 303-762-6941... 81 G ron.gascho@denverseminary.edu
GASE, Chris ... 740-389-4636. 383 F gasec@mtc.edu
GASIOR, Donna ... 773-298-3165. 158 E gasior@sxu.edu
GASKELL, Carolyn ... 509-527-2133. 524 I carolyn.gaskell@wallawalla.edu
GASKILL, Gayle ... 651-690-6857. 263 O ggaskill@stkate.edu
GASKIN, Elizabeth ... 772-462-5604. 106 P egaskin@irsc.edu
GASKIN, Evelyn ... 480-927-0000... 18 I evelyn.gaskin@phoenix.edu
GASKIN, Lori ... 805-730-4011... 64 L lgaskin@sbcc.edu
GASKIN-FITCHUE, Leah . 937-376-2946. 388 B lfitchue@payne.edu
GASKINS, Frances ... 252-527-6223. 361 F fgaskins@lenoircc.edu
GASKINS, Laverne, L ... 229-333-5351. 134 B llgaskin@valdosta.edu
GASKINS, Leebrian, E ... 956-326-2310. 483 B lgaskins@tamiu.edu
GASOSKE, Betsy ... 314-434-4044. 273 C registrar@covenantseminary.edu
GASPAR, Leigh ... 781-891-2874. 223 C lgaspar@bentley.edu
GASPAR, Timothy ... 419-383-5858. 392 B timothy.gaspar@utoledo.edu
GASPAR JARVIS, Donna 207-602-2461. 213 A dgaspar@une.edu
GASPARD, Harold ... 504-671-6247. 203 A hgaspa@dcc.edu
GASPARIAN, Albert ... 714-895-8334... 39 J agasparian@gwc.cccd.edu
GASPARRO, Paul ... 216-987-2004. 378 D paul.gasparro@tri-c.edu
GASPER, Joseph ... 570-740-0372. 422 G jgasper@luzerne.edu
GASPER, William ... 213-763-7043... 52 D gasperw@lattc.edu
GASQUE, Jeanne, F ... 727-816-3213. 110 E gasquej@phcc.edu
GASS, C. Michael ... 240-895-3115. 218 A cmgass@smcm.edu
GASS, Melanie ... 704-403-1613. 352 J melanie.gass@carolinashealthcare.org
GASSAWAY, Kathy ... 530-938-5200... 41 A gassaway@siskiyous.edu
GASSEAU, Michelle ... 617-243-2150. 227 K mgaseau@lasell.edu
GASSER, Ray ... 208-885-6571. 139 D rgasser@uidaho.edu
GASSER, Stephanie ... 520-325-0123... 17 R registrar@suva.edu
GASSNER, Sheila ... 573-681-5084. 276 C gassners@lincolnu.edu
GASSNER, Taryn, E ... 302-857-1829... 93 D tgassner@dtcc.edu
GASSON, Grant ... 602-429-4949... 16 O ggasson@ps.edu
GAST, Alice, P ... 610-758-3156. 422 A apg206@lehigh.edu
GAST, Steve ... 712-279-1707. 176 B steve.gast@briarcliff.edu
GASTENVELD, Paula, M . 434-736-2085. 513 H paula.gastenveld@southside.edu
GASTEVICH, Donna ... 626-395-6651... 31 E dgastevi@caltech.edu
GASTON, Aracelis ... 787-832-6000. 549 D agaston@icprjc.edu
GASTON, Carmen ... 503-943-8506. 408 F kwong@up.edu
GASTON, David ... 785-864-3624. 190 L adgaston@ku.edu
GASTON, Della, J ... 336-342-4261. 363 C gastond@rockinghamcc.edu
GASTON, Kenneth ... 410-651-7550. 219 E klgaston@umes.edu
GASTON, Lori ... 704-894-2208. 353 J logaston@davidson.edu
GASTON, Neely ... 704-527-9909. 227 A ngaston@gcts.edu
GASTON-MARSH, Latonia, D ... 716-878-4618. 343 A marshld@buffalostate.edu
GATCH, Denise, D ... 941-752-5325. 114 I gatchd@scf.edu
GATCHELL, Michael, D ... 864-294-2475. 444 C mike.gatchell@furman.edu
GATELY, Kevin ... 781-280-3225. 232 B gatelyk@middlesex.mass.edu
GATELY, Kevin ... 603-897-8232. 297 F kgately@rivier.edu
GATELY, Paul ... 401-841-7531. 545 A
GATES, Alexander, E ... 973-353-5304. 306 D agates@andromeda.rutgers.edu
GATES, Amanda ... 617-585-1100. 234 I amanda.gates@necmusic.edu
GATES, Anne ... 216-421-7463. 377 C agates@cia.edu
GATES, Cynthia, K ... 405-585-5255. 397 C cynthia.gates@okbu.edu
GATES, Kathryn, F ... 662-915-7206. 270 B kfg@olemiss.edu
GATES, Leigh ... 312-939-4975. 146 A lgates@harrington.edu
GATES, Lori ... 503-842-8222. 408 B gates@tillamookbay.cc
GATES, Pamela, S ... 989-774-3342. 240 N gates1ps@cmich.edu
GATES, Reginald ... 817-515-5001. 482 B reginald.gates@tccd.edu
GATES, Robert ... 570-389-4015. 427 H rgates@bloomu.edu
GATES, Steve ... 479-936-5168... 22 C sgates@nwacc.edu
GATES, William, R ... 831-656-2754. 544 M bgates@nps.edu
GATES BLACK, Joy ... 817-515-5006. 482 B joy.gatesblack@tccd.edu
GATES-MILINER, Elaine . 619-574-6909... 57 E egates@pacificcollege.edu
GATEWOOD, Catherine .. 906-786-5802. 240 K cathi.gatewood@baycollege.edu
GATEWOOD, David ... 949-451-5650... 67 B dgatewood@ivc.edu
GATHERS, Avis ... 803-793-5241. 443 E gathersa@denmarktech.edu
GATHINGS, Kimberly ... 662-329-7138. 268 E kgathings@acadsupp.muw.edu
GATHJE, Pete ... 901-334-5832. 457 A pgathje@memphisseminary.edu
GATHMAN, Allen ... 573-651-2682. 282 B agathman@semo.edu
GATLIN, Greg ... 617-573-8428. 237 B ggatlin@suffolk.edu
GATLIN, Lavonne ... 256-765-4787..... 9 C lgatlin@una.edu
GATLING, Sharron ... 757-221-2617. 503 N sggatl@wm.edu
GATO, Stacy ... 207-221-4208. 213 A sgato@une.edu
GATOBU, Anne ... 859-858-3581. 192 A
GATRELL, Jay ... 812-237-3087. 167 A jay.gatrell@indstate.edu
GATTA, John, J ... 931-598-1248. 458 H jogatta@sewanee.edu
GATTAS, Joyce, M ... 619-594-1343... 35 D gattas@mail.sdsu.edu
GATTEN, Jeffrey ... 661-255-1050... 31 C jgatten@calarts.edu
GATTERDAM, Hans ... 817-272-3275. 491 B hgatt@uta.edu
GATTI, Robert, M ... 614-823-1250. 387 K rgatti@otterbein.edu
GATTIN, Tom ... 870-230-5135... 21 D gattint@hsu.edu
GATTIS, Tom ... 614-222-3237. 378 A tgattis@ccad.edu
GATTON, Pam ... 903-983-8207. 475 E pgatton@kilgore.edu
GATTON, Philip, S ... 618-453-4172. 159 G philg@pso.siu.edu
GATTON, Steven, J ... 903-233-4466. 475 J stevegatton@letu.edu
GATTY, Janie ... 724-335-5336. 425 F director@oaa.edu
GATTY, Janie ... 570-326-2869. 425 C director_nbi@comcast.net
GATTY, Janie ... 724-335-7127. 425 B director@nbi.edu
GATZKE, Donald ... 817-272-2801. 491 B gatzke@uta.edu
GAUBATZ, Dale ... 970-943-2244... 86 I dgaubatz@western.edu
GAUBATZ, Noreen ... 205-226-4671..... 2 C ngaubatz@bsc.edu
GAUBERT, Judith ... 985-867-2240. 206 H jgaubert@sjasc.edu
GAUCHAT, Urs, P ... 973-596-3079. 303 G urs.p.gauchat@njit.edu
GAUDINO, James, L ... 509-963-2111. 517 F gaudino@cwu.edu
GAUDIO, Arthur, R ... 413-782-2201. 238 A agaudio@law.wne.edu
GAUDIO, Melissa ... 570-408-4358. 437 F melissa.gaudio@wilkes.edu
GAUGH, Sherri ... 505-566-4007. 311 I gaughs@sanjuancollege.edu
GAUGHAN, Cheryl ... 619-849-2499... 59 L cherylgaughan@pointloma.edu
GAUGHF, Natalie, W ... 601-815-4236. 270 C nwgaughf1@umc.edu
GAUL, Julie, M ... 412-578-6042. 412 G gauljm@carlow.edu
GAULDEN, JR., Corbett, F ... 325-942-2337. 465 K corbett.gaulden@angelo.edu
GAULT, Brian, C ... 601-923-1671. 269 E bgault@rts.edu
GAULT, Carrie, J ... 724-458-2134. 417 E cjgault@gcc.edu
GAULT, Kevin ... 727-726-1153. 100 E kevingault@clearwater.edu
GAULT, Sandra ... 816-235-6234. 283 D gaults@umkc.edu
GAUME, Curtis, C ... 716-888-2300. 316 C gaume@canisius.edu
GAUMONT, Suzanne ... 408-554-4642... 64 M sgaumont@scu.edu
GAUNA, Lucy ... 210-486-4408. 464 J lgauna5@alamo.edu
GAUNCE, Lori ... 606-759-7141. 196 B
GAUNT, John, C ... 785-864-4281. 190 L jgaunt@ku.edu
GAUNT, Marianne, I ... 848-932-7505. 306 A gaunt@rci.rutgers.edu
GAUNT, Victoria, F ... 410-864-4234. 218 B vgaunt@stmarys.edu
GAURMER, Terry ... 303-458-1629... 84 M tgaurmer@regis.edu
GAUS, Gregory, J ... 630-515-7307. 153 B ggausx@midwestern.edu
GAUSS, Nancy ... 970-943-2053... 86 I ngauss@western.edu
GAUT, LaDonna ... 903-923-2477. 495 A ldgaut@wileyc.edu
GAUTAM, Mridul ... 775-327-2363. 294 J
GAUTHIER, Laureen ... 802-225-3205. 499 I laureen.gauthier@neci.edu
GAUTHIER, Raymond, C 503-682-3903. 407 B rgauthier@pioneerpacific.edu
GAUTIER, Ed, E ... 985-549-2064. 208 C egautier@selu.edu
GAUTNEY, Michael, B ... 256-765-4274..... 9 C mbgautney@una.edu
GAUTSCHI, David ... 212-636-6111. 324 G gautschi@fordham.edu

GAUVIN, Keith 203-596-4612 90 I kgauvin@post.edu
GAVAL, Kathleen, D 610-660-1204 432 E kgaval@sju.edu
GAVALETZ, Tami 618-374-5187 156 B tami.gavaletz@principia.edu
GAVANUS, Michael 610-896-1249 418 F mgavanus@haverford.edu
GAVER, Bob 402-363-5721 293 I bagaver@york.edu
GAVILLAN, Jannette 787-738-2161 554 C jannette.gavillan@upr.edu
GAVIN, Carrie 850-599-3076 114 K carrie.gavin@famu.edu
GAVIN, Jack 732-571-3536 303 C gavin@monmouth.edu
GAVIN, M. F. Chip 207-973-3335 212 A chip.gavin@maine.edu
GAVIN, Michael 414-297-6760 540 E gavinmj@matc.edu
GAVIN, Mike 828-395-1295 361 C mgavin@isothermal.edu
GAVIN, Todd 803-822-3233 445 C gavint@midlandstech.edu
GAVLICK, Christopher 914-251-6916 344 D christopher.gavlick@purchase.edu
GAVLIK, Deborah 567-661-7510 387 L deborah_gavlik@owens.edu
GAW, Kevin, E 404-413-1835 126 E kgaw@gsu.edu
GAWEHN, Julie 575-562-2115 309 H julie.gawehn@enmu.edu
GAWEL, Gary, P 912-478-5136 126 C gpgawel@georgiasouthern.edu
GAWELEK, Mary Ann 724-838-4216 433 E gawelek@setonhill.edu
GAWENDA, Matt 312-922-1884 152 C mgawenda@maccormac.edu
GAWLIK, Gail 815-740-5041 162 F ggawlik@stfrancis.edu
GAWRONSKI, JR., Michael 845-341-4284 335 H michael.gawronski@sunyorange.edu
GAWTHROP, Larry 810-762-0235 247 F larry.gawthrop@mcc.edu
GAY, Bill 760-427-2314 48 A bill.gay@imperial.edu
GAY, Cliff 478-289-2025 124 C cgay@ega.edu
GAY, John 410-386-8434 214 A jgay@carrollcc.edu
GAY, Judith, R 215-751-8000 413 I jgay@ccp.edu
GAY, Kathleen 318-678-6000 202 I kgay@bpcc.edu
GAY, Michelle 704-403-1758 352 J michelle.gay@carolinashealthcare.org
GAY, Thresa 404-270-5210 132 E tgay@spelman.edu
GAYESKI, Diane 607-274-3895 327 E gayeski@ithaca.edu
GAYHART, Terri 414-297-6663 540 E gayhartt@matc.edu
GAYLE, Barbara, M 608-796-3081 539 E bmgayle@viterbo.edu
GAYLE, Ruth, R 215-965-4002 424 D rgayle@moore.edu
GAYLEN, Nancy, I 217-424-6244 153 C ngaylen@millikin.edu
GAYLES, Jennifer 914-395-2510 340 E jgayles@sarahlawrence.edu
GAYLOR, Susan 814-332-3782 409 D sgaylor@allegheny.edu
GAYMER, Dawn 269-387-4200 252 I dawn.gaymer@wmich.edu
GAYMON, Denise 256-551-1710 4 I denise.gaymon@drakestate.edu
GAYMON, Joffery 850-474-2000 117 B
GAYNOR, Deborah 717-264-4141 437 H dgaynor@wilson.edu
GAYNOR, Dona, E 321-674-8102 104 H dgaynor@fit.edu
GAYNOR, Julie 940-397-4353 476 H julie.gaynor@mwsu.edu
GAYNOR, Kimberly 281-649-3025 473 B kgaynor@hbu.edu
GAYNOR, Michael 610-519-4000 436 F michael.gaynor@villanova.edu
GAYNOR, Suzanne 607-431-4670 325 F gaynors@hartwick.edu
GAYTON, Linda 973-684-6104 304 B lgayton@pccc.edu
GAZTAMBIDE, Fernando 787-265-3866 554 E fernando.gaztambide@upr.edu
GAZZALE, Bob 323-856-7600 27 O
GBADEGESIN, Segun 202-806-6700 95 G sgbadegesin@howard.edu
GEADELMANN, Patricia, L 319-273-6144 176 A patricia.geadelmann@uni.edu
GEAGHAN, Tom 216-687-4745 377 F t.geaghan@csuohio.edu
GEALT, Michael, A 989-774-3931 240 N gealt1ma@cmich.edu
GEAR, Jackie 215-968-8416 411 B jaclyn.gear@bucks.edu
GEAR, Lisa, L 213-738-6834 68 C admissions@swlaw.edu
GEARAN, Mark, D 315-781-3309 326 C gearan@hws.edu
GEARHART, Deb 740-593-2889 387 C gearhart@ohio.edu
GEARHART, G. David 479-575-4148 23 I gdgearh@uark.edu
GEARHART, Gregory, L 717-691-6007 423 L gearhart@messiah.edu
GEARHART, Rob 607-274-1909 327 E rgearhart@ithaca.edu
GEARHART, Trevor 715-324-6900 535 E trevor.gearhart@ni.edu
GEARHART, William, H 401-456-8200 439 F wgearhart@ric.edu
GEARIN, Christopher, A 314-434-2212 275 D
GEARY, Colette 914-654-5363 320 H cgeary@cnr.edu
GEARY, Leslie, H 203-576-4625 91 G lgeary@bridgeport.edu
GEARY, Melanie 303-534-6290 80 H melanie.geary@colostate.edu
GEARY, Wendell 303-963-3283 79 C wgeary@ccu.edu
GEARY, Wes 303-404-5024 81 N wes.geary@frontrange.edu
GEASE, Eleanor 202-885-8650 97 D egease@wesleyseminary.edu
GEASEY, David, W 607-436-3314 343 E geaseydw@oneonta.edu
GEBAUER, Philip 816-483-9600 190 D philip.gebauer@spst.edu
GEBB, Billie Anne 859-253-3637 194 A billieanne.gebb@frontier.edu
GEBEL, Karen 319-296-2320 178 J karen.gebel@hawkeyecollege.edu
GEBER, David 212-749-2802 330 A dgeber@msmnyc.edu
GEBHARDT, Charles 402-643-7411 289 B charles.gebhardt@cune.edu
GEBHARDT, Lynita 630-617-3020 145 A lynita.gebhardt@elmhurst.edu
GEBHARDT, Virginia 660-263-4110 279 B virginig@macc.edu
GEBHARDT-FUENTES, Amanda 360-475-7106 521 H agebhardtfuentes@olympic.edu
GEBHART, Daniel, L 260-481-6322 168 C gebhartd@ipfw.edu
GEBHART, Jennifer, L 937-775-5611 393 G jennifer.gebhart@wright.edu
GEBRU, Amanuel 805-378-1445 74 F agebru@vcccd.edu
GEDDES, Eva, R 845-368-7201 340 C eva.geddes@use.salvationarmy.org
GEDDES, Leonard 828-328-7024 356 B leonard.geddes@lr.edu
GEDDES, Wesley 845-368-7200 340 C wesley.geddes@use.salvationarmy.org
GEDDINGS, Scarlet 803-535-1243 446 B geddingss@octech.edu
GEDDIS, Catherine 212-854-2551 314 G cgeddis@barnard.edu
GEDDIS, Janet 610-558-5540 424 I geddisj@neumann.edu
GEDEON, Don 510-261-8500 58 G don.gedeon@patten.edu
GEDNALSKE, Julie 605-331-6683 452 D julie.gednalske@usiouxfalls.edu
GEE, Albert, R 936-261-1730 482 F argee@pvamu.edu
GEE, Henry 562-908-3489 60 I hgee@riohondo.edu
GEE, Henry 408-274-7900 63 O henry.gee@evc.edu
GEE, Jeffrey, S 434-223-6164 505 E jgee@hsc.edu
GEE, Karen, L 804-257-5628 515 F klgee@vuu.edu
GEE, Perry, M 530-226-4140 66 D pgee@simpsonu.edu
GEE, Terry 619-594-2853 35 D tgee@mail.sdsu.edu
GEEHAN, Margaret, M 518-629-7117 326 G m.geehan@hvcc.edu
GEENENS, Dave 913-360-7633 184 H dgeenens@benedictine.edu
GEER, Anne, R 585-385-8070 338 H ageer@sjfc.edu
GEER, Lyn 703-330-5398 526 B lgeer@apus.edu
GEER, Nathan 503-375-7010 403 A ngeer@corban.edu
GEER, Robert, E 315-792-7400 346 C geerre@sunyit.edu
GEFELL, Michele, D 315-786-2271 327 L mgefell@sunyjefferson.edu
GEFFERT, Bryn 413-542-2212 221 G bgeffert@amherst.edu
GEFFNER, Linda, O 860-231-5208 92 F lgeffner@usj.edu
GEGENHEIMER BALDASSARO, Sarah 202-994-5152 95 D sarahgb@gwu.edu
GEGG-LAPLUME, Tamara 314-968-6982 284 N laplume@webster.edu
GEGGIE, Steven 847-317-8178 160 M sgeggie@tiu.edu
GEHBAUER, Daryl 636-481-3120 275 I dgehbaue@jeffco.edu
GEHEBER, Leah 225-768-1746 206 D lgeheber@ololcollege.edu
GEHLER, Jan, L 480-423-6310 15 E jan.gehler@scottsdalecc.edu
GEHLER, Nick 619-388-7715 62 F ngehler@sdccd.edu
GEHLHAR, Jim 252-328-4829 367 B gehlhar@ecu.edu
GEHLHAUSEN, Keith 812-488-2943 173 H kg77@evansville.edu
GEHLING, William 617-627-3232 237 C bill.gehling@tufts.edu
GEHR, Theresa 614-287-2642 378 B tgehr@cscc.edu
GEHRET, Steve 423-636-5096 462 E sgehret@tusculum.edu
GEHRICH, Michael, D 317-381-6000 174 F mgehrich@vinu.edu
GEHRKE, Deb 715-232-2312 538 B gehrked@uwstout.edu
GEHRLS, Janet 563-441-2455 180 E jgehrls@kucampus.edu
GEHRMAN-ROTTIER, Laura 715-346-3811 538 A lgehrman@uwsp.edu
GEIB, Bethany 740-857-1311 388 I bgeib@rosedale.edu
GEIB, Christine 215-643-8458 417 F geib.c@gmc.edu
GEIBEL, Kandi 607-587-3946 345 D geibelkr@alfredstate.edu
GEIER, Cathy 202-884-9545 96 G geierc@trinitydc.edu
GEIER, Connie 605-626-2415 451 I geierc@northern.edu
GEIER, Peter, E 614-292-2635 386 E geier.10@osu.edu
GEIGER, Don 920-693-1378 540 B don.geiger@gotoltc.edu
GEIGER, Douglas 718-990-7464 339 A geigerd@stjohns.edu
GEIGER, Haley 414-326-2336 532 G hgeiger@ccon.edu
GEIGER, Robin 502-597-7014 197 A robin.geiger@kysu.edu
GEIGER, William 903-565-5515 492 D wgeiger@uttyler.edu
GEIL, Carol 641-844-5747 179 J carol.geil@iavalley.edu
GEILING, Bryan, K 610-989-1351 436 D bgeiling@vfmac.edu
GEIMAN, Ellie 410-857-2234 216 E egeiman@mcdaniel.edu
GEIMAN, Michelle 614-251-4597 386 B geimanm@ohiodominican.edu
GEIMER, Jill 312-332-0707 160 J
GEISE, Shane 406-243-2593 286 H shane.geis@umontana.edu
GEISEN, Clare 805-652-5504 74 E cgeisen@vcccd.edu
GEISER, Jeff 575-562-2153 309 H jeff.geiser@enmu.edu
GEISER, Laura 314-977-2543 281 I geiserla@slu.edu
GEISLER, Michael 802-443-5275 499 H geisler@middlebury.edu
GEISLER, Norman, L 951-698-6389 75 A
GEISSLER, Gregory, J 303-556-6819 83 D ggeissle@msudenver.edu
GEIST, Alan 937-766-7768 375 K geista@cedarville.edu
GEIST, Edward, V 203-576-4956 91 G edwgeist@bridgeport.edu
GELAYE, Enku 413-254-2300 228 F egelaye@stuaf.umass.edu
GELAYE, Enku 413-545-2684 228 F egelaye@stuaf.umass.edu
GELBKE, Konrad 517-355-9671 246 H gelbke@nscl.msu.edu
GELCH, Deborah 617-243-2390 227 K dgelch@lasell.edu
GELDENHUYS, Tammie 620-331-4100 187 G tgeldenhuys@indycc.edu
GELDER, Alvern 616-957-6045 240 M af094@calvinseminary.edu
GELDER, Minna 503-589-7870 402 E minna.gelder@chemeketa.edu
GELDWORTH, Lipa 718-853-8500 348 A
GELDZAHLER, Daniel 718-633-4715 337 E collegeoy@gmail.com
GELERNTER, Mark 303-556-5938 86 A mark.gelernter@ucdenver.edu
GELETA, Nomsa 814-732-2724 428 E ngeleta@edinboro.edu
GELFAND, Jack 315-312-2888 344 A jack.gelfand@oswego.edu
GELFAND, M 732-364-1220 299 B
GELFER, Miriam 617-682-1518 226 D mgelfer@eds.edu
GELFMAN, Arnold, J 732-224-2749 299 G agelfman@brookdalecc.edu
GELINAS, Cynthia, B 803-641-3609 448 A cindyg@usca.edu
GELINAS, Cynthia, B 803-641-2841 448 A cindyg@usca.edu
GELINAS, David 704-894-2698 353 J dagelinas@davidson.edu
GELL, Barry 518-255-5440 344 E gellbf@cobleskill.edu
GELLE, Mark 507-786-3294 264 B gelle@stolaf.edu
GELLER, Jack, M 813-253-6262 118 L jgeller@ut.edu
GELLER, James 973-596-2866 303 G jamesgeller@njit.edu
GELLER, L. Randy 541-346-3082 406 D rgeller@uoregon.edu
GELLER, Mark 800-371-6105 16 A mark@nationalparalegal.edu
GELLER, Mary, A 320-363-5601 254 J mgeller@csbsju.edu
GELLER, Steve 952-358-8954 260 B steve.geller@normandale.edu
GELLES, Richard, J 215-898-5541 435 B gelles@sp2.upenn.edu
GELLIN, Marcia, A 716-851-1113 323 I gellin@ecc.edu
GELLMAN-DANLEY, Barbara 740-245-7205 392 A bdanley@rio.edu
GELO, Daniel, J 210-458-4359 492 C daniel.gelo@utsa.edu
GELPI-RODRÍGUEZ, Phaedra 787-480-2382 548 G pgelpi@sanjuancapital.com
GELSINGER, Sue 610-372-4721 431 D sgelsinger@racc.edu
GELSTON, Tobias 802-258-9233 499 F tobiasg@marlboro.edu
GELVIN, Karen 316-323-6915 185 D kgelvin@butlercc.edu
GELY, Gilda, G 616-234-3920 243 B ggely@grcc.edu
GEMEDA, Mekbib, L 757-446-7151 504 E gemedam@evms.edu
GEMME, Terese 203-392-5499 88 A gemmet1@southernct.edu
GEMMER, Peter 513-936-1632 391 A peter.gemmer@uc.edu
GEMPERLEIN, Monica, P 919-334-1520 364 G mpgemperlein@waketech.edu
GEMPERLINE, Paul 252-328-6012 367 B gemperlinep@ecu.edu
GEMPESAW, Bobby 513-529-6721 384 G gempescm@miamioh.edu
GENANDT, James 620-431-2820 189 D jgenandt@neosho.edu
GENAO, Janet 813-879-6000 103 B jgenao@cci.edu
GENARD, Daniel, J 757-683-3090 507 N dgenard@odu.edu
GENCO, Rosemarie 973-720-2107 308 I gencor@wpunj.edu
GENDERNALIK-COOPER, Mary, L 540-654-1000 510 J mgendern@umw.edu
GENDRON, Dennis 206-296-5556 523 E gendron@seattleu.edu
GENDRON, Josee 530-242-7574 65 G jgendron@shastacollege.edu
GENECIN, Paul 203-432-0076 93 A paul.genecin@yale.edu
GENEGA, Paul 973-748-9000 299 F paul_genega@bloomfield.edu
GENERALS, Donald 609-586-4800 302 G generald@mccc.edu
GENESE, Carol 914-632-5400 331 K cgenese@monroecollege.edu
GENETTI, Carol 805-893-2013 72 B carol.genetti@graddiv.ucsb.edu
GENGARO, Nicholas 973-642-8859 307 D nicholas.gengaro@shu.edu

GENNA, Angela 602-285-7357 15 C
angela.genna@phoenixcollege.edu
GENNARO, Gwen 719-255-3153 85 M
ggennaro@uccs.edu
GENNARO, Susan 617-552-4250 224 A
susan.gennaro@bc.edu
GENO, Rita, B 802-468-1203 501 B
rita.geno@castleton.edu
GENOUS, Zandra 847-543-2420 143 A
zgenous@clcillinois.edu
GENSHAFT, Judy, L 813-974-2791 116 C
jgensha@usf.edu
GENSLER, Charlotte 505-224-4551 309 E
cgensler@cnm.edu
GENTHNER, Patricia 585-389-2002 332 D
pgenthn5@naz.edu
GENTHON, Paulette 402-556-4456 292 F
info@ucha.com
GENTILE, James 616-395-7190 244 A
gentile@hope.edu
GENTILE, James 301-431-5454 217 C
jgentile@nlc.edu
GENTILE, Kathy, J 314-516-6383 283 E
gentilek@umsl.edu
GENTILE, Lisa 801-832-2301 498 F
lgentile@westminstercollege.edu
GENTILE, Patricia 609-463-4507 299 A
pgentile@atlantic.edu
GENTILE, Shelley 407-646-2638 111 Q
sgentile@rollins.edu
GENTLES, Lori 657-278-2425 33 E
GENTLEWARRIOR, Sabrina 508-531-1429 229 D
sabrina.gentlewarrior@bridgew.edu
GENTRY, Bradley, D 217-786-2278 151 F
brad.gentry@llcc.edu
GENTRY, Gisele 601-979-6938 267 E
gisele.n.gentry@jsums.edu
GENTRY, Jerry, H 270-831-9622 195 D
jerry.gentry@kctcs.edu
GENTRY, Jodi, D 352-392-4626 116 A
jodi-gentry@ufl.edu
GENTRY, Margaret 315-859-4615 325 E
mgentry@hamilton.edu
GENTRY, Richard, E 956-326-2325 483 B
rgentry@tamiu.edu
GENTRY, Susan 252-335-0821 359 F
susan_gentry@albemarle.edu
GENTRY, Vickie 318-357-6288 208 B
gentry@nsula.edu
GENTRY, W. Marichal 203-432-2907 93 A
marichal.gentry@yale.edu
GENTRY-EPLEY, Beth 816-415-5946 285 C
gentry-epleyb@william.jewell.edu
GENTRY-WRIGHT, Susan, C 864-833-8100 446 D
sgentry-w@presby.edu
GENTSCH, James 205-652-3361 9 F
jgentsch@uwa.edu
GENTUL, Jack 973-596-3466 303 G
jack.gentul@njit.edu
GENTZLER, Randall 410-617-2345 216 A
rdgentzler@loyola.edu
GENUA, Kathy 516-918-3626 315 G
kgenua@bcl.edu
GEOCARIS, Diane, F 949-824-2880 71 B
dfgeocar@uci.edu
GEOFFRION-SCANNELL, Kathryn 978-837-5211 234 A
geoffrionsck@merrimack.edu
GEOGHEGAN, Michael 513-569-1586 376 L
michael.geoghegan@cincinnatistate.edu
GEORGALLIS, Christine 352-588-8464 112 D
christine.georgallis@saintleo.edu
GEORGE, Abraham 706-507-8111 123 D
george_abraham@columbusstate.edu
GEORGE, Archie, A 208-885-7995 139 D
archie@uidaho.edu
GEORGE, Bryant 734-432-5672 246 B
bgeorge@madonna.edu
GEORGE, Carol, S 937-766-7900 375 K
georgec@cedarville.edu
GEORGE, Chris 303-871-4883 86 B
Chris.George@du.edu
GEORGE, Christi 205-652-3840 9 F
cjw@uwa.edu
GEORGE, Dennis, K 270-745-3570 200 G
dennis.george@wku.edu
GEORGE, Douglas, J 716-652-8900 316 G
dgeorge@cks.edu
GEORGE, Ellen 309-999-4580 146 E
egeorge@icc.edu
GEORGE, Francis 847-566-6401 162 G
GEORGE, Gene 316-322-3338 185 D
ggeorge@butlercc.edu
GEORGE, Janice, S 620-421-6700 188 D
janicec@labette.edu
GEORGE, LePra 630-560-6231 148 K
lgeorge@hancocku.edu
GEORGE, Maggie 928-724-6669 13 H
mlgeorge@dinecollege.edu
GEORGE, Mertha, V 601-877-6154 265 G
mgeorge@alcorn.edu
GEORGE, Michael 419-517-8990 383 C
mgeorge@lourdes.edu
GEORGE, Michel 503-768-7850 403 K
mgeorge@lclark.edu
GEORGE, Monique 646-660-6590 316 J
Monique.George@baruch.cuny.edu
GEORGE, JR., Orlando, J 302-739-4053 93 D
pres@dtcc.edu
GEORGE, Pamela 216-397-1908 381 R
pgeorgemerrill@jcu.edu
GEORGE, Philip, J 315-445-4644 328 F
georgepj@lemoyne.edu
GEORGE, R. Dillard 757-683-4156 507 N
rdgeorge@odu.edu
GEORGE, Robert 941-756-0690 420 E
rgeorge@lecom.edu
GEORGE, Russell 970-675-3201 80 B
russell.george@cncc.edu
GEORGE, Sarah, B 801-581-6927 496 Q
sgeorge@umnh.utah.edu
GEORGE, Shanika 713-623-2040 466 G
sgeorge@aii.edu
GEORGE, Sharon, A 603-641-7084 297 G
sgeorge@anselm.edu
GEORGE, Susan 304-473-8080 531 G
george@wvwc.edu
GEORGE, Tami, B 910-272-3541 363 B
tgeorge@robeson.edu
GEORGE, Terrance, C 270-745-3978 200 G
chris.george@wku.edu
GEORGE, Thomas, F 314-516-5252 283 E
tfgeorge@umsl.edu
GEORGE, Timothy, F 205-726-2632 6 F
tfgeorge@samford.edu
GEORGE, Tom 253-680-7080 516 L
tgeorge@bates.ctc.edu
GEORGE, Viji, D 914-337-9300 321 E
viji.george@concordia-ny.edu
GEORGE, W. Michael 205-348-2857 8 D
michael.george@ua.edu
GEORGE, William, D 570-577-1228 411 A
wdgeorge@bucknell.edu
GEORGE-ROBINSON, Avril 973-877-3040 301 H
agrobinson@essex.edu
GEORGE-TAYLOR, Mosunmola 423-697-2552 460 C
GEORGENES, George 617-850-1317 227 E
gag@hchc.edu
GEORGES, Anthony, C 314-516-5508 283 E
tony_georges@umsl.edu
GEORGESON, Lance 425-249-4752 524 D
lance.georgeson@tlc.edu
GEORGIOPOULOS, Michael 407-823-5338 115 E
michaelg@ucf.edu
GEORGIOU, Tina 212-343-1234 331 D
tgeorgiou@mcny.edu
GEORGOPOULOS, Terri 707-826-3739 35 C
tmg315@humboldt.edu
GEPHART, JR., George, W 215-299-1044 415 B
presidentsoffice@ansp.org
GEPPI, Steve 410-386-8524 214 A
sgeppi@carrollcc.edu
GERA, Holly, P 973-655-5234 303 D
gerah@mail.montclair.edu
GERAC, Anna 802-728-1586 501 F
agerac@vtc.edu
GERACI, Luci 718-990-2023 339 A
geracil@stjohns.edu
GERACI, Richard, V 575-624-8400 310 H
cmdt@nmmi.edu
GERALD, Trudy 619-388-3522 62 D
tgerald@sdccd.edu
GERALL, Mina 312-935-4814 148 C
mgerall@icsw.edu
GERAMI, Keyvan 314-286-3670 280 F
kgerami@ranken.edu
GERARD, Ada 916-638-1616 47 B
ada_gerard@heald.edu
GERARD, Debra 714-480-7450 60 F
gerard_debra@rsccd.edu
GERARD, Pam 319-895-5267 177 A
pgerard@cornellcollege.edu
GERASSIMIDES, Gus 859-985-3158 192 F
gus_gerassimides@berea.edu
GERATY, Brent G, T 269-471-6530 239 D
bgeraty@andrews.edu
GERBASI, Iris 714-997-6676 38 A
gerbasi@chapman.edu
GERBER, Brian 229-333-5925 134 B
blgerber@valdosta.edu
GERBER, Cheryl 724-946-7102 437 B
gerberca@westminster.edu
GERBER, Elizabeth, L 815-599-3421 146 D
liz.gerber@highland.edu
GERBER, Linda 971-722-4357 407 D
linda.gerber@pcc.edu
GERBERRY, Jeffrey 614-947-6007 380 A
jeffrey.gerberry@franklin.edu
GERBOTH, Karen, L 937-327-6141 393 E
kgerboth@wittenberg.edu
GERBSCH, Julie 912-344-2600 120 G
julie.gerbsch@armstrong.edu
GERBSCH, Reinhold 912-650-5682 131 H
rgerbsch@southuniversity.edu
GERCH, Sheila 914-674-7339 330 J
sgersh@mercy.edu
GERDA, Joe 661-362-3452 40 E
joe.gerda@canyons.edu
GERDEMAN, Penny 419-434-4558 391 D
gerdeman@findlay.edu
GERDES, Darin 843-574-3220 441 H
dgerdes@csuniv.edu
GERDES, Neil, W 773-896-2400 141 K
ngerdes@ctschicago.edu
GERDES, Neil, W 773-256-3000 152 H
ngerdes@meadville.edu
GERDICH, Michael 724-805-2895 432 G
michael.gerdich@email.stvincent.edu
GERDING, Melissa, D 610-519-4044 436 F
melissa.gerding@villanova.edu
GERDRUM, Kacie 541-684-7288 405 C
kgerdrum@nwcu.edu
GERE, Nicholas 207-602-2011 213 A
ngere@une.edu
GEREAUX, Teresa, T 540-375-2282 509 B
gereaux@roanoke.edu
GEREMIA, Kenneth 413-528-7291 222 E
kgeremia@simons-rock.edu
GERENA, Elizabeth 787-850-9301 554 D
elizabeth.gerena@upr.edu
GERETY, RSM, Jane 401-341-2337 440 C
jane.gerety@salve.edu
GERETY, Mason 928-523-2012 16 C
mason.gerety@nau.edu
GERHARD, Karen 563-588-6444 176 F
karen.gerhard@clarke.edu
GERHARDT, Mark 605-995-7174 450 E
mark.gerhardt@mitchelltech.edu
GERHARDT, Terri, M 229-333-5701 134 B
tmgerhardt@valdosta.edu
GERHARDT, Winifred 440-826-2222 374 F
wgerhard@bw.edu
GERHART, Phillip, M 812-488-2651 173 H
pg3@evansville.edu
GERIG, Bev 541-917-4857 404 B
gerigb@linnbenton.edu
GERIGUIS, David 951-785-2002 50 B
dgerigui@lasierra.edu
GERIK, Debbie 254-659-7704 473 A
debgerik@hillcollege.edu
GERIN, Jean-Louis 802-225-3356 499 I
jean-louis.gerin@neci.edu
GERING, Jon 660-785-4248 282 L
jgering@truman.edu
GERITY, Patrick, E 724-925-4219 437 D
gerityk@wccc.edu
GERITY, Peter, F 575-835-5227 310 F
vpaa@admin.nmt.edu
GERKEN, Keith 907-796-6496 11 A
william.gerken@uas.alaska.edu
GERKEN, Robert 484-664-3110 424 H
rgerken@muhlenberg.edu
GERKEN, Stacey 715-346-3553 538 A
sgerken@uwsp.edu
GERKIN, David 623-845-4762 14 M
david.gerkin@gcmail.maricopa.edu
GERKIN, Jeffrey, G 865-974-3131 463 C
jgerkin@utk.edu
GERKO, Danielle 814-262-3825 427 C
dgerko@pennhighlands.edu
GERL, Beth, R 410-871-3199 216 E
bgerl@mcdaniel.edu
GERLACH, David, M 315-386-7082 345 F
gerlach@canton.edu
GERLACH, Jeanne, M 817-272-5476 491 B
gerlach@uta.edu
GERLACH, Karen 202-884-9203 96 G
gerlachk@trinitydc.edu
GERLICH, Bella 907-474-7224 10 I
bkgerlich@alaska.edu
GERMAIN, George, F 989-328-1275 247 D
georgeg@montcalm.edu
GERMAN, Deborah 407-266-1000 115 E
deborah.german@ucf.edu
GERMAN, Lisa 256-352-8306 9 G
lisa.german@wallacestate.edu
GERMANO, William 212-353-4274 321 F
germano@cooper.edu
GERMANY, Sylvia 256-726-8218 6 B
germany@oakwood.edu
GERN, William, A 307-766-5353 543 I
willger@uwyo.edu
GERNERT, Maureen, C 203-837-8266 88 B
gernertm@wcsu.edu
GERNES, Todd, S 508-565-1840 237 A
tgernes@stonehill.edu
GERRETSEN, Amy, L 920-748-8353 535 J
gerretsena@ripon.edu
GERRITY, Nancy 405-682-7587 397 E
ngerrity@occc.edu
GERROW, Robin 419-372-8589 374 K
robstan@bgsu.edu
GERRY, Thomas 518-828-4181 321 C
gerry@sunycgcc.edu
GERSEY, Martin, L 574-520-5522 168 E
mgersey@iusb.edu
GERSH, Geniene, M 269-387-1000 252 I
geniene.m.gersh@wmich.edu
GERSHEN, Jay, A 330-325-6263 385 E
president@neomed.edu
GERSHON, I. Richard 662-915-6900 270 B
igershon@olemiss.edu
GERSHOWITZ, Whitney 804-862-6461 508 H
wgershowitz@rbc.edu
GERSICH, Frank 309-457-2119 153 D
fgersich@monmouthcollege.edu
GERST, Bernard 410-704-3383 220 E
bgerst@towson.edu
GERSTEIN, Dean 909-607-9406 39 C
dean.gerstein@cgu.edu
GERSZEWSKI, Raymond, H 701-788-4770 371 E
Ray.Gerszewski@mayvillestate.edu
GERTH, Laura 415-422-2654 73 J
lgerth@usfca.edu
GERTS, John 231-843-5850 252 H
jkgerts@westshore.edu
GERTSMAN, Josh 253-833-9111 520 C
jgerstman@greenriver.edu
GERTSON, Katherine 212-799-5000 328 B
GERTZ, Genie 202-651-5000 95 C
genie.gertz@gallaudet.edu
GERTZ, Tanya, M 563-387-1536 180 M
gertta01@luther.edu
GERVASI, Robert 217-228-5432 156 C
gervasi@quincy.edu
GERZINA, Holly 330-325-6740 385 E
hgerzina@neomed.edu
GESO, Cristina, A 215-895-1674 415 B
cag58@drexel.edu
GESSELL, Donna 706-864-1528 133 D
donna.gessell@ung.edu
GESSLER, Klaus 845-431-8939 323 C
gessler@sunydutchess.edu
GESSNER, David 715-836-5182 536 E
gessnedp@uwec.edu
GESSNER, James, C 570-389-4105 427 H
jgessner@bloomu.edu
GESSNER, James, R 218-722-4000 255 E
jimg@dbumn.edu
GESTRINE, Beverley 360-736-9391 517 G
bgestrine@centralia.edu
GESTRING, Sheila 605-677-5255 451 F
sheila.gestring@usd.edu
GESULGA, Terry 415-485-9326 40 G
terry.gesulga@marin.edu
GETCHELL, JR., Charles, M 603-641-7320 297 G
cgetchell@anselm.edu
GETCHELL, Stephanie, L 919-530-7824 368 A
getchells@nccu.edu
GETSON, Denise 304-793-6845 530 B
dgetson@osteo.wvsom.edu
GETTING, Kris, A 651-962-6168 265 C
kagetting@stthomas.edu
GETTY, Larry, R 785-628-4513 186 F
lgetty@fhsu.edu
GETZ, Dan 715-634-4790 533 Q
dgetz@lco.edu
GETZ, Karen 724-266-3838 434 J
kgetz@tsm.edu
GETZ, Kathleen, A 312-915-6115 151 H
kgetz@luc.edu
GETZEN, Bruce 808-245-8355 136 H
bgetzen@hawaii.edu
GEU, Thomas 605-677-5443 451 F
thomas.geu@usd.edu
GEUDER, Maridith 662-329-7119 268 E
mgeuder@pa.muw.edu
GEVITZ, Norman 660-626-2522 271 A
ngevitz@atsu.edu
GEYE, Trina 254-968-9400 483 A
geye@tarleton.edu
GEYER, Dennis 916-278-3901 34 D
dgeyer@csus.edu
GEYER, Enid 518-262-6008 313 D
geyere@mail.amc.edu
GEYER, Enid 518-262-5586 313 D
geyere@mail.amc.edu
GEYER, Mariann 412-392-3805 431 B
mgeyer@pointpark.edu
GEYER, MaryK 503-552-1697 404 H
GHADIALI, Khushroo 575-234-9414 311 A
khushroo@nmsu.edu

GHAHRAMANI, Saeed .... 413-782-1218. 238 A sghahram@wne.edu

GHAMMACHI, Gabe .... 502-456-6504. 199 G gghammachi@sullivan.edu

GHAN, Mark .... 775-445-4237. 295 A mark.ghan@wnc.edu

GHANEM, Salma, I .... 989-774-1885. 240 N ghane1si@cmich.edu

GHANNADIAN, F. Frank 813-253-6221. 118 L fghannadian@ut.edu

GHARAKHANIAN, Anahid .... 213-738-6786... 68 C academicaffairs@swlaw.edu

GHARIB, Morteza .... 626-395-6365... 31 E vpr@caltech.edu

GHAZARIAN, Esther, A .. 781-768-7280. 236 A esther.ghazarian@regiscollege.edu

GHAZI-BIRRY, Hani .... 801-375-5125. 496 G hsgbirry@rmuohp.edu

GHAZVINI, Mariam .... 510-592-9688... 56 G mariam@npu.edu

GHEE, Harry .... 910-323-5614. 353 B dean@ccbs.edu

GHILANI, Mary .... 570-740-0456. 422 G mghilani@luzerne.edu

GHIO, Frederick, W .... 401-456-8201. 439 F fghio@ric.edu

GHOLSON, Shari .... 270-534-3372. 196 G shari.gholson@kctcs.edu

GHORASHI, Bahman .... 931-372-3224. 460 A bghorashi@tntech.edu

GHORAYEB, Samir .... 409-984-6484. 486 H samir.ghorayeb@lamarpa.edu

GHOSAL, Bobby .... 601-928-6213. 268 C bobby.ghosal@mgccc.edu

GHOSH, Guru .... 540-231-3205. 515 C rhodesk@vt.edu

GHOSH, Jayati .... 415-485-3238... 42 J jayati.ghosh@domincan.edu

GHOSH, Sibdas .... 914-633-2207. 327 C sghosh@iona.edu

GHOUS, Mostafa .... 707-864-7000... 66 G mostafa.ghous@solano.edu

GHYMN, Kyung-il .... 770-279-0507. 124 I Kyung.il.ghymn@gcuniv.edu

GIACCHETTI, Richard ...... 408-554-4982... 64 M rgiacchetti@scu.edu

GIACCHINO, Mike .... 305-949-9500. 102 E mgiacchino@cci.edu

GIACOBBE, Jeff .... 973-655-5373. 303 D giacobbej@mail.montclair.edu

GIACOMELLI, Marie, A ... 217-793-4201. 156 K mgiacomelli@robertmorris.edu

GIACOMINO, Dennis ...... 419-267-1356. 385 F dgiacomino@northweststate.edu

GIACONA, Nick .... 505-984-6110. 311 H ngiacona@sjcsf.edu

GIAMARTINO, Gary, A .... 215-951-1040. 420 B giamartino@lasalle.edu

GIAMBELLUCA, Russell .. 209-667-3077... 35 B rgiambelluca@csustan.edu

GIAMBRA, Leonard, M .... 860-701-6679. 545 G leonard.m.giambra@uscg.mil

GIAMPAOLI, Michael, J . 203-576-4168... 91 G gmichael@bridgeport.edu

GIAMPIETRO, Michael ... 413-565-1000. 222 F mgiampietro@baypath.edu

GIANCHETTA, Larry, D .... 406-243-4831. 286 H larry.gianchetta@business.umt.edu

GIANETTI, Natalie .... 517-750-1200. 250 E ngianetti@arbor.edu

GIANNATTASIO, Joseph 305-428-5700. 109 E giannatj@aii.edu

GIANNET, Stanley, M ..... 727-847-2727. 110 E giannes@phcc.edu

GIANNINI, Gaetan .... 610-606-4666. 412 I gtgianni@cedarcrest.edu

GIANNINI, Tula .... 718-636-3702. 336 F tgiannin@pratt.edu

GIANNOTTI, Louis, J ...... 410-293-1400. 545 J giannott@usna.edu

GIANOTTI, Margaret .... 541-278-5775. 402 C mgianotti@bluecc.edu

GIANOUSSOPOULOS, Denise .... 310-665-6962... 57 C dgianoussopoulos@otis.edu

GIAQUINTO, Thomas ..... 518-244-4547. 338 C giaqut@sage.edu

GIARDINA, Dolores .... 610-436-2728. 430 A dgiardina@wcupa.edu

GIARDINA, Nancy .... 616-331-2400. 243 C giardinn@gvsu.edu

GIARRUSSO, Denise, J .. 904-632-5007. 105 E dgiarrus@fscj.edu

GIARRUSSO, John .... 518-956-8090. 341 D jgiarrusso@albany.edu

GIAUQUE, Margie, T ...... 218-755-2038. 258 A mgiauque@bemidjistate.edu

GIBB, Julie .... 309-341-5242. 141 A jgibb@sandburg.edu

GIBB, Katharine .... 864-503-5444. 448 H kgibb@uscupstate.edu

GIBBEL, Mark .... 646-660-6067. 316 J Mark.Gibbel@baruch.cuny.edu

GIBBENS, Charlie, E .... 915-747-5352. 492 A cegibbens@utep.edu

GIBBENS, Susan .... 860-512-3680... 88 G sgibbens@manchestercc.edu

GIBBINS, Debbie .... 713-646-1889. 480 J dgibbins@stcl.edu

GIBBISON, Godfrey .... 843-953-3292. 443 A gibbisonga@lowcountrygraduatecenter.org

GIBBONS, Arthur .... 845-758-7442. 314 D gibbons@bard.edu

GIBBONS, Charlie .... 334-229-4250..... 1 D cgibbons@alasu.edu

GIBBONS, Dennis .... 315-792-5361. 331 I dgibbons@mvcc.edu

GIBBONS, Earl, F .... 360-650-3308. 525 C earl.gibbons@wwu.edu

GIBBONS, Jeremy .... 802-447-4696. 500 D jgibbons@svc.edu

GIBBONS, Kari .... 630-829-6306. 140 B kgibbons@ben.edu

GIBBONS, Michael .... 540-261-4371. 509 K michael.gibbons@svu.edu

GIBBONS, Michael, P ..... 570-348-6221. 423 B gibbons@marywood.edu

GIBBONS, Pete, W .... 304-724-3700. 526 B pgibbons@apus.edu

GIBBONS, Shari .... 818-767-0888... 76 K shari.gibbons@woodbury.edu

GIBBONS, Susan .... 203-432-1818... 93 A susan.gibbons@yale.edu

GIBBONS, Thomas, F ..... 312-503-3011. 155 D tgibbons@northwestern.edu

GIBBS, Beth, B .... 207-859-1130. 211 H gibbs@thomas.edu

GIBBS, C. Edward .... 804-828-3361. 511 F cegibbs@vcu.edu

GIBBS, Casey .... 312-935-4232. 148 C icsw.librarian@gmail.com

GIBBS, Danny, C .... 865-882-4517. 461 E gibbsdc@roanestate.edu

GIBBS, Donna .... 314-514-3101. 156 B donna.gibbs@principia.edu

GIBBS, Doug .... 314-514-3104. 156 B doug.gibbs@principia.edu

GIBBS, Heather .... 516-299-2501. 329 C heather.gibbs@liu.edu

GIBBS, Jamie .... 252-249-1851. 362 E jgibbs@pamlicocc.edu

GIBBS, Jeffery .... 863-674-6008. 101 O jgibbs3@edison.edu

GIBBS, Jeremiah .... 317-788-2058. 173 I gibbsj@uindy.edu

GIBBS, Jim .... 806-651-3289. 484 D jgibbs@mail.wtamu.edu

GIBBS, Kirsten .... 937-766-7872. 375 K gibbsk@cedarville.edu

GIBBS, Kristen .... 660-248-6246. 272 B kgibbs@centralmethodist.edu

GIBBS, Marcus .... 304-896-7419. 528 F marcus.gibbs@southernwv.edu

GIBBS, Marilyn, Y .... 803-535-5309. 442 B mgibbs@claflin.edu

GIBBS, Melissa .... 707-256-7167... 55 F lgibbs@napavalley.edu

GIBBS, Patricia, M .... 478-757-5166. 134 G pgibbs@wesleyancollege.edu

GIBBS, Patty .... 478-757-5260. 134 G pgibbs@wesleyancollege.edu

GIBBS, Raymond .... 802-773-5900. 499 B raymond.gibbs@csj.edu

GIBBS, Renisha, L .... 850-644-8082. 115 C rgibbs@admin.fsu.edu

GIBBS, Sarah, E .... 724-458-2183. 417 E sezwinger@gcc.edu

GIBELING, Jeffery, C ...... 530-752-2050... 70 J jcgibeling@ucdavis.edu

GIBERTSON, Myrna .... 617-745-3724. 225 G myrna.f.giberson@enc.edu

GIBLER, Linda .... 210-341-1366. 477 L lgibler@ost.edu

GIBLER, Rhonda .... 573-882-2094. 283 C giblerr@missouri.edu

GIBLIN, Frank .... 248-370-2395. 248 J giblin@oakland.edu

GIBLIN, Patrick .... 314-246-7174. 284 N patrickgiblin61@webster.edu

GIBLIN, Tina .... 661-654-2241... 32 H tgiblin@csub.edu

GIBRALTER, Jonathan .... 301-687-4111. 220 C jgibralter@frostburg.edu

GIBREE, Joe .... 617-873-0182. 224 G Joe.Gibree@cambridgecollege.edu

GIBSON, Amy, B .... 630-515-7198. 153 B agibso@midwestern.edu

GIBSON, Andrew .... 516-918-3628. 315 G agibson@bcl.edu

GIBSON, Betty, J .... 941-752-5452. 114 I gibsonb@scf.edu

GIBSON, Bonnie, C .... 215-898-1135. 435 B gibson@upenn.edu

GIBSON, Brandon, J .... 864-488-4371. 444 L bgibson@limestone.edu

GIBSON, Brenda .... 503-255-0332. 404 F bgibson@multnomah.edu

GIBSON, Cedric .... 772-462-7665. 106 P cgibson@irsc.edu

GIBSON, Charlie .... 912-287-5813. 130 B cgibson@okefenokeetech.edu

GIBSON, Christine .... 352-588-8273. 112 D christine.gibson@saintleo.edu

GIBSON, Christopher ..... 215-895-2928. 415 B gibsoncd@drexel.edu

GIBSON, Clayton .... 256-372-5221..... 1 A clayton.gibson@aamu.edu

GIBSON, Colleen .... 901-435-1586. 455 M colleen_gibson@loc.edu

GIBSON, Corinne, J .... 724-738-2700. 429 F corinne.gibson@sru.edu

GIBSON, Dana, L .... 936-294-1013. 487 A dgibson@shsu.edu

GIBSON, Dennis .... 301-387-3051. 214 I dennis.gibson@garrettcollege.edu

GIBSON, Diana .... 304-327-4195. 529 D dgibson@bluefieldstate.edu

GIBSON, Donald, E .... 203-254-4070... 89 I dgibson@fairfield.edu

GIBSON, Edie, B .... 731-881-7508. 463 E edgibson@utm.edu

GIBSON, Gale, E .... 973-877-4462. 301 H ggibson@essex.edu

GIBSON, Ginger .... 352-395-5211. 113 C ginger.gibson@sfcollege.edu

GIBSON, Gloria, J .... 319-273-2517. 176 A gloria.gibson@uni.edu

GIBSON, Howard, O .... 225-216-8364. 202 H gibsonh@mybrcc.edu

GIBSON, J. Murray .... 617-373-5089. 235 F

GIBSON, James .... 662-476-5078. 266 I jgibson@eastms.edu

GIBSON, James, D .... 888-777-7675. 519 K jdgibson@faithseminary.edu

GIBSON, Jeremy .... 978-837-5000. 234 A

GIBSON, Jeremy .... 918-836-6886. 400 D jgibson@mail.spartan.edu

GIBSON, John .... 918-595-7524. 400 E john.gibson@tulsacc.edu

GIBSON, Joseph .... 843-574-6311. 447 E joe.gibson@tridenttech.edu

GIBSON, Joyce .... 207-753-6594. 212 H jgibson@usm.maine.edu

GIBSON, Joyce .... 516-918-3650. 315 G jgibson@bcl.edu

GIBSON, Judy .... 972-279-6511. 465 F jgibson@amberton.edu

GIBSON, Keith, E .... 540-464-7334. 515 B gibsonke@vmi.edu

GIBSON, Ken .... 812-866-7160. 166 C gibson@hanover.edu

GIBSON, Kirk .... 541-956-7186. 407 F kgibson@roguecc.edu

GIBSON, Lauri .... 612-977-4375. 254 C

GIBSON, Lloyd, G .... 203-576-4385... 91 G llgibson@bridgeport.edu

GIBSON, Lynn .... 662-720-7239. 269 B lgibson@nemcc.edu

GIBSON, Mandi .... 713-646-1702. 480 J mgibson@stcl.edu

GIBSON, Mark, T .... 919-866-5404. 364 G mtgibson@waketech.edu

GIBSON, Michael, A .... 434-924-8838. 511 B mag3u@virginia.edu

GIBSON, Nola, R .... 601-974-1132. 267 I gibsonk@millsaps.edu

GIBSON, Polly .... 480-990-3773... 14 H

GIBSON, Rick .... 310-506-4125... 58 H rick.gibson@pepperdine.edu

GIBSON, Robert, L .... 301-405-5611. 219 B rgibson@umd.edu

GIBSON, Ross .... 802-258-3116. 500 C ross.gibson@worldlearning.org

GIBSON, Ryan .... 606-368-6130. 191 J ryangibson@alc.edu

GIBSON, Sandra, S .... 803-934-3419. 445 F sangibson@morris.edu

GIBSON, Sara .... 207-699-3052. 210 H sgibson@meca.edu

GIBSON, Scott .... 919-684-3945. 354 A gibso022@mc.duke.edu

GIBSON, Sheri .... 212-346-1619. 335 J sgibson@pace.edu

GIBSON, Stacey .... 208-282-3973. 138 E gibssta2@isu.edu

GIBSON, Steve, T .... 843-953-5635. 443 A gibsont@cofc.edu

GIBSON, Susan .... 404-880-8757. 122 J sgibson@cau.edu

GIBSON, Tammy .... 706-379-3111. 134 L tgibson@yhc.edu

GIBSON, Thomas .... 718-262-2415. 319 F tgibson@york.cuny.edu

GIBSON-HAIGLER, Patricia .... 803-536-7104. 446 G phaigler@scsu.edu

GIBSON-SHREVE, Lada .. 330-494-6170. 389 F lgibson@starkstate.edu

GIDDENS, Jean .... 804-828-0100. 511 F jgiddens@vcu.edu

GIDDIS, Rayanne .... 352-854-2322. 100 K giddisr@cf.edu

GIDEON, Amy, C .... 615-868-6503. 457 D amy@mtsa.edu

GIDEON, Heather .... 760-480-8474... 76 C hgideon@wscal.edu

GIE, Lori .... 504-520-5730. 209 D lgie@xula.edu

GIEBEL, Joe .... 212-785-0111. 426 X

GIELISSE, Victor .... 845-451-1294. 322 D v_gielis@culinary.edu

GIELOW, Bob .... 603-623-0313. 297 E bobgielow@nhia.edu

GIELOW, Curt .... 734-995-7588. 241 E curt.gielow@cuw.edu

GIERI, Joe .... 505-224-3037. 309 E jgieri@cnm.edu

GIEROK, Ed .... 503-554-2090. 403 C egierok@georgefox.edu

GIERYN, Thomas .... 812-855-2809. 167 F gieryn@indiana.edu

GIES, Jason .... 814-254-0564. 413 C jgies@pa.gov

GIESCHEN, Charles, A .... 260-452-2104. 165 D charles.gieschen@ctsfw.edu

GIESE, Ralph .... 719-255-4327... 85 M rgiese@uccs.edu

GIESE, Richard, F .... 330-823-6050. 391 E gieserf@mountunion.edu

GIESELMAN, Tammy .... 812-488-2260. 173 H tg85@evansville.edu

GIESEMAN, Mark .... 913-758-6526. 191 B giesemanm@stmary.edu

GIESON, Sandi .... 309-796-5345. 140 E gieson@bhc.edu

GIESSMAN, Michelle ...... 636-949-4848. 276 D mgiessman@lindenwood.edu

GIFFIN, Ralph, G .... 201-216-8541. 307 E rgiffin@stevens.edu

GIFFORD, Darcy .... 734-487-5375. 242 D dgiffor2@emich.edu

GIFFORD, Denise, D .... 610-499-1265. 437 E ddgifford@widener.edu

GIFFORD, Julie-Angela .. 561-297-3693. 114 L agifford@fau.edu

GIFFORD, Rachel .... 870-838-2902... 19 K rgifford@smail.anc.edu

GIFFORD, Rhonda .... 724-938-4413. 428 A gifford@calu.edu

GIFT, Charles .... 937-512-2534. 388 O charles.gift@sinclair.edu

GIFT, Helen, C .... 828-884-8319. 352 I hgift@brevard.edu

GIGGLEMAN, Gene .... 972-438-6932. 478 C ggiglman@parkercc.edu

GIGLIOTTI, Peter .... 717-477-1202. 429 E pmgigl@ship.edu

GIGLIOTTI-GURIDI, Chandra, M .... 410-822-5400. 214 C cGigliotti-Guridi@chesapeake.edu

GIGUERE, Marlene .... 770-538-4722. 122 A mgiguere@brenau.edu

GIGUETTE, Marguerite .... 504-520-7525. 209 D mgiguett@xula.edu

GIILBERT, Michael .... 860-486-6137... 92 A michael.gilbert@uconn.edu

GIL, Andres .... 305-348-2494. 115 B andres.gil@fiu.edu

GIL, Betty .... 401-874-2310. 440 D betty@uri.edu

GIL, Karen .... 919-962-3082. 368 D kgil@email.unc.edu

GILBEAUX, Kristi .... 254-867-8780. 486 B kristi.gilbeaux@systems.tstc.edu

GILBERT, Aerin .... 703-821-8570. 510 B agilbert@stratford.edu

GILBERT, Alan .... 718-951-5102. 317 C agilbert@brooklyn.cuny.edu

GILBERT, Bentley .... 541-440-4600. 408 D bentley.gilbert@umpqua.edu

GILBERT, Carl .... 254-295-4537. 490 B cgilbert@umhb.edu

GILBERT, Carol, S .... 703-330-5398. 526 B cgilbert@apus.edu

GILBERT, Cherryl .... 770-229-3409. 132 B cgilbert@sctech.edu

GILBERT, David, H .... 414-906-4670. 537 A dhg@uwm.edu

GILBERT, Dianna .... 225-675-8270. 203 G dgilbert@rpcc.edu

GILBERT, Douglas .... 719-442-0505... 86 F
douglas.gilbert@rockies.edu
GILBERT, Faye .... 601-266-4659. 270 E
faye.gilbert@usm.edu
GILBERT, Fred .... 928-757-0854... 15 L
fgilbert@mohave.edu
GILBERT, Fredrick .... 718-960-8350. 318 A
fredrick.gilbert@lehman.cuny.edu
GILBERT, Glen .... 252-328-9595. 367 B
gilbertg@ecu.edu
GILBERT, Glen, G .... 252-328-4630. 367 B
gilbertg@ecu.edu
GILBERT, Jan .... 308-367-5252. 293 B
jgilbert3@unl.edu
GILBERT, Jerome, A .... 662-325-3742. 268 D
jgilbert@provost.msstate.edu
GILBERT, Karen .... 404-471-6435. 119 I
kgilbert@agnesscott.edu
GILBERT, Karen .... 303-273-3541... 80 E
KGilbert@mines.edu
GILBERT, Karen .... 815-965-8616. 157 B
kgilbert@rockfordcareercollege.edu
GILBERT, Kat .... 414-382-6306. 531 I
kat.gilbert@alverno.edu
GILBERT, Kyle .... 606-539-4236. 200 B
kyle.gilbert@ucumberlands.edu
GILBERT, Larry .... 916-278-7702... 34 D
lgilbert@csus.edu
GILBERT, Larry .... 940-498-6282. 477 I
lgilbert@nctc.edu
GILBERT, Lynda .... 205-348-4530..... 8 D
lgilbert@uasystem.ua.edu
GILBERT, Mary .... 215-641-5506. 417 F
gilbert.m@gmc.edu
GILBERT, Michael .... 213-624-1200... 44 D
mgilbert@fidm.edu
GILBERT, Nancy .... 419-448-3413. 389 J
ngilbert@tiffin.edu
GILBERT, Paula, E .... 919-684-5383. 354 A
pgilbert@duke.edu
GILBERT, Peter, J .... 920-832-7353. 533 S
peter.j.gilbert@lawrence.edu
GILBERT, Peter, M .... 610-758-3034. 422 A
pmg207@lehigh.edu
GILBERT, Peter, N .... 410-706-7004. 219 C
pgilbert@umaryland.edu
GILBERT, Regina .... 615-383-4848. 464 D
rgilbert@watkins.edu
GILBERT, Sharon .... 603-542-7744. 296 D
sgilbert@ccsnh.edu
GILBERT, Susan, M .... 530-752-3383... 70 J
smvgilbert@ucdavis.edu
GILBERT, Susan, P .... 678-547-6438. 128 H
gilbert_sp@mercer.edu
GILBERT, Teresa .... 423-478-7702. 458 B
tgilbert@ptseminary.edu
GILBERT, Timothy .... 804-204-1221. 502 F
tgilbert@btsr.edu
GILBERT, Trent, R .... 423-266-4574. 458 F
tgilbert@richmont.edu
GILBERTI, Anthony, F ..... 304-367-4642. 529 F
anthony.gilberti@fairmontstate.edu
GILBERTSON, Eric, R ..... 989-964-4041. 249 G
erg@svsu.edu
GILBERTSON, Rita .... 641-585-8140. 183 D
gilbertsr@waldorf.edu
GILBREATH, Bill .... 972-279-6511. 465 F
bgilbreath@amberton.edu
GILCHRIST, Bryan .... 305-809-3279. 104 I
bryan.gilchrist@fkcc.edu
GILCHRIST, Cheryl, B ..... 502-852-8139. 200 D
cbgilc01@louisville.edu
GILCHRIST, Debbie .... 956-665-2140. 492 B
gilchrist@utpa.edu
GILCHRIST, Debra .... 253-964-6584. 522 C
dgilchrist@pierce.ctc.edu
GILCHRIST, James, A ..... 269-387-2382. 252 I
james.gilchrist@wmich.edu
GILCHRIST, Joseph .... 239-513-1122. 106 O
jgilchrist@hodges.edu
GILCHRIST, Lou Ann ...... 660-785-4111. 282 L
lcg@truman.edu
GILCHRIST, Stephan .... 608-262-0277. 538 E
stephan.gilchrist@uwex.uwc.edu
GILCREASE, Kathy, J ...... 936-294-1012. 487 A
gilcrease@shsu.edu
GILDAWIE, Janice .... 413-528-7698. 222 E
jgildawie@simons-rock.edu
GILDEHAUS, Goldie .... 636-584-6583. 273 M
gagildeh@eastcentral.edu
GILDEN, Bruce, F .... 858-499-0202... 40 C
bgilden@coleman.edu
GILDERHUS, Kiki .... 303-753-6046... 85 B
kgilderhus@rmcad.edu
GILDERSLEEVE,
Elizabeth, T .... 781-283-2376. 237 F
egilders@wellesley.edu
GILDERSLEEVE,
Susan, M .... 402-472-3886. 292 I
sgildersleeve1@unl.edu

GILE, Shelby .... 802-485-2658. 500 A
sgile@norwich.edu
GILER, Will .... 516-877-3900. 313 A
bookstore@adelphi.edu
GILES, Cameron .... 415-282-7600... 27 L
media@actcm.edu
GILES, Don .... 859-336-5082. 198 J
dongiles@sccky.edu
GILES, JR., Henry, C ..... 864-592-4616. 447 A
gilesh@sccsc.edu
GILES, Marsha .... 617-537-6803. 152 G
magiles@mckendree.edu
GILES, Pam .... 276-523-2400. 513 A
pgiles@me.vccs.edu
GILES, Roger, W .... 870-235-4008... 23 F
rwgiles@saumag.edu
GILES, Timothy, W .... 904-620-4200. 116 B
timothy.giles@unf.edu
GILES-GEE, Helen .... 215-596-8972. 435 H
president@usciences.edu
GILFILLAN, Margaret .... 412-392-3994. 431 B
mgilfillan@pointpark.edu
GILGOUR, Joe .... 660-596-7393. 282 G
jgilgour@sfccmo.edu
GILIO, Brenda, R .... 610-499-4345. 437 E
brgilio@widener.edu
GILION, Millie .... 417-455-5480. 273 E
MillieGilion@crowder.edu
GILKER, Bill .... 817-760-5504. 473 A
wmgilker@hillcollege.edu
GILKERSON, Tammeil ...... 510-235-7800... 41 K
tgilkerson@contracosta.edu
GILKEY, Shane, L .... 740-593-9813. 387 C
gilkeys@ohio.edu
GILL, Allison .... 978-837-5174. 234 A
gilla@merrimack.edu
GILL, Ann, M .... 970-491-5421... 80 I
ann.gill@colostate.edu
GILL, Anne, M .... 617-989-4193. 237 G
gilla@wit.edu
GILL, Barbara, A .... 301-314-8350. 219 B
bgill@umd.edu
GILL, Barbara, J .... 850-201-6570. 117 D
gillb@tcc.fl.edu
GILL, Casey .... 937-327-7800. 393 E
cgill@wittenberg.edu
GILL, Chris, G .... 509-313-3836. 520 A
gill@its.gonzaga.edu
GILL, D. Christopher .... 573-288-6322. 273 F
cgill@culver.edu
GILL, Dennis .... 541-881-5915. 408 C
dgill@tvcc.cc
GILL, Jamie, W .... 727-864-8337. 101 N
gilljw@eckerd.edu
GILL, Janet .... 712-274-6400. 183 G
janet.gill@witcc.edu
GILL, Jason .... 847-866-3987. 145 E
jason.gill@garrett.edu
GILL, Jeffery, A .... 574-372-5100. 166 B
gillja@grace.edu
GILL, Keith .... 804-289-8345. 510 L
kgill@richmond.edu
GILL, Lanae .... 313-993-1230. 250 K
gilla@udmercy.edu
GILL, Lee, A .... 330-972-7522. 390 E
lee16@uakron.edu
GILL, Michele .... 308-345-8109. 290 J
gillm@mpcc.edu
GILL, Nancy .... 805-437-8456... 32 I
nancy.gill@csuci.edu
GILL, Nicholas .... 207-216-4467. 211 C
ngill@yccc.edu
GILL, Rebecca .... 828-884-8233. 352 I
rebecca.gill@brevard.edu
GILL, Russell .... 602-749-7311. 144 A
rgill@devry.edu
GILL, Ruth .... 410-334-2928. 221 D
rgill@worwic.edu
GILL, Sandra .... 630-829-6216. 140 B
sgill@ben.edu
GILL, Sean .... 951-827-6063... 71 E
sean.gill@ucr.edu
GILL, Sean, P .... 860-444-8201. 545 G
sean.p.gill@uscg.mil
GILL, Stevon .... 609-258-3466. 304 E
sgill@princeton.edu
GILL, Tom .... 503-338-2368. 402 G
tgill@clatsopcc.edu
GILL-JACOBSON,
Roseanne .... 419-824-3829. 383 C
rgill-jacobson@lourdes.edu
GILLAHAN, Sheilah .... 731-286-3316. 460 F
gillahan@dscc.edu
GILLAM WEIR, Linda ...... 501-244-5110... 19 J
linda.gillam@arkansasbaptist.edu
GILLAN, Christine .... 302-259-6100... 93 E
cgillan1@dtcc.edu
GILLAN, Maria .... 973-684-5904. 304 B
mgillan@pccc.edu
GILLARD, Natalie .... 575-461-4413. 309 M
natalieg@mesalands.edu

GILLARDI, Michael .... 401-598-1450. 439 B
mgillardi@jwu.edu
GILLASPIE, Ray .... 270-824-8592. 196 A
ray.gillaspie@kctcs.edu
GILLASPY, Art .... 501-450-3122... 25 H
artg@uca.edu
GILLE, Chaudron .... 678-717-3835. 133 D
chaudron.gille@ung.edu
GILLECE, Nancy, E .... 301-696-3710. 215 D
gillece@hood.edu
GILLEN, Ann .... 209-946-2135... 73 A
agillen@pacific.edu
GILLEN, Dan .... 319-296-4268. 178 J
daniel.gillen@hawkeyecollege.edu
GILLEN, Edward .... 203-582-8471... 91 A
edward.gillen@quinnipiac.edu
GILLEN, Jonathan .... 541-881-5842. 408 C
jgillen@tvcc.cc
GILLEN-CARYL, Shawn ... 315-498-2537. 335 G
gillencs@sunyocc.edu
GILLES, Barbara, L .... 412-578-6123. 412 G
gillesbl@carlow.edu
GILLESPIE, Barbara .... 276-326-4237. 502 H
bgillespie@bluefield.edu
GILLESPIE, Bart .... 678-839-6582. 133 I
bgillesp@westga.edu
GILLESPIE, SJ, C. Kevin 610-660-1200. 432 E
cgillesp@sju.edu
GILLESPIE, Christine ...... 201-612-7488. 299 C
cgillespie@bergen.edu
GILLESPIE, Dave .... 402-941-6545. 290 K
gillespie@midlandu.edu
GILLESPIE, David, M ...... 301-687-4396. 220 C
dgillespie@frostburg.edu
GILLESPIE, Greg .... 805-289-6460... 74 H
ggillespie@vcccd.edu
GILLESPIE, Joseph, E ..... 610-558-5641. 424 I
gillespj@neumann.edu
GILLESPIE, Melanie .... 864-644-5504. 446 I
mlgillespie@swu.edu
GILLESPIE, Michael .... 212-220-8323. 317 A
mgillespie@bmcc.cuny.edu
GILLESPIE, Pamela .... 212-650-7271. 317 D
prgcc@sci.ccny.cuny.edu
GILLESS, J. Keith .... 510-642-7171... 70 I
gilless@berkeley.edu
GILLETT, Charisse, L ...... 859-252-0361. 197 C
cgillett@lextheo.edu
GILLETT, William .... 603-668-2211. 297 I
w.gillett@snhu.edu
GILLETTE, Donna .... 207-947-4591. 209 G
dgillette@bealcollege.edu
GILLETTE, Emily .... 203-365-7671... 91 C
gillettee2@sacredheart.edu
GILLETTE, Jack .... 617-349-8401. 228 B
jgillett@lesley.edu
GILLETTE, Kimberly .... 218-282-8442. 264 E
gillette@umn.edu
GILLETTE, Lynn .... 775-831-7509. 295 F
lgillette@sierranevada.edu
GILLETTE, Maureen, D .... 773-442-5500. 154 H
m-gillette@neiu.edu
GILLETTE, Susan .... 410-706-5353. 219 C
sgillett@umaryland.edu
GILLEY, Michael .... 276-523-2400. 513 A
mgilley@me.vccs.edu
GILLIAM, Cynthia .... 832-813-6512. 476 A
cynthia.f.gilliam@lonestar.edu
GILLIAM, Dara .... 405-273-5331. 395 I
dgilliam@familyoffaithcollege.edu
GILLIAM, JR.,
Franklin, D .... 310-206-7568... 71 C
fgilliam@conet.ucla.edu
GILLIAM, Janice, H .... 423-323-0201. 461 C
jhgilliam@northeaststate.edu
GILLIAM, Kevin, E .... 616-538-2330. 243 A
kgilliam@gbcol.edu
GILLIAM, Thomas, J .... 850-484-1690. 110 G
tgilliam@pensacolastate.edu
GILLIAM, Tom .... 850-484-1500. 110 G
tgilliam@pensacolastate.edu
GILLICK, Megan .... 410-617-2290. 216 A
mgillick@loyola.edu
GILLIGAN, Patrick, K .... 740-427-5643. 382 J
gilliganp@kenyon.edu
GILLIGAN, Thomas, J .... 402-466-4774. 289 E
thomas.gilligan@doane.edu
GILLIGAN, Thomas, W ... 512-471-5058. 491 C
dean.gilligan@mccombs.utexas.edu
GILLIGAN, William .... 617-824-8190. 226 A
william_gilligan@emerson.edu
GILLILAND, Christie .... 253-833-9111. 520 C
cgilliland@greenriver.edu
GILLILAND, Drew .... 541-552-6319. 406 C
gilliland@sou.edu
GILLILAND, Jane, A .... 607-587-3979. 345 D
gillilja@alfredstate.edu
GILLILAND, William .... 301-295-3017. 545 C
william.gilliland@usuhs.edu
GILLIN, Gary .... 507-537-6253. 261 F
Gary.Gillin@smsu.edu

GILLING RAYNOR,
Beatrice .... 718-951-6545. 317 C
braynor@brooklyn.cuny.edu
GILLIS, Arthur .... 225-771-5050. 206 J
arthur_gillis@subr.edu
GILLIS, Chester .... 202-687-4259... 95 E
gillisc@georgetown.edu
GILLIS, Graham .... 501-450-3181... 25 H
ggillis@uca.edu
GILLIS, Ida .... 219-980-6853. 168 B
ilgillis@iun.edu
GILLIS, Rick, D .... 414-955-6333. 534 C
rgillis@mcw.edu
GILLISPIE, James .... 910-592-8081. 363 E
jgillispie@sampsoncc.edu
GILLISS, Buster .... 701-224-5512. 372 B
buster.gilliss@bismarckstate.edu
GILLISS, Catherine .... 919-684-3786. 354 A
catherine.gilliss@duke.edu
GILLMAN, Howard .... 949-824-6296... 71 B
provost@uci.edu
GILLMAN, Rick .... 219-464-6718. 174 E
rick.gillman@valpo.edu
GILLMING, Kenneth, D .. 617-364-3510. 223 G
kgillming@boston.edu
GILLOOLY, Patrick .... 617-258-9276. 233 B
GILLUM, Danny .... 620-227-9269. 186 B
dgillum@dc3.edu
GILLUM, Deborah .... 574-807-7015. 164 D
gillumd@bethelcollege.edu
GILLUS, Raynaldo .... 937-376-6205. 376 E
rgillus@centralstate.edu
GILMAN, Frederick, J ..... 412-268-5124. 412 H
gilman@andrew.cmu.edu
GILMAN, Jean .... 314-977-3415. 281 I
jgilman2@slu.edu
GILMAN, Josephine .... 301-387-3091. 214 I
josephine.gilman@garrettcollege.edu
GILMAN, Mary, A .... 864-597-4010. 449 I
gilmanaf@wofford.edu
GILMAN, Regis, M .... 217-581-6644. 144 E
rmgilman@eiu.edu
GILMAN, Sarah, S .... 808-689-2700. 136 C
sgilman@hawaii.edu
GILMAN, Sharon .... 520-515-5382... 12 R
gilmans@cochise.edu
GILMARTIN, Anne .... 914-674-7337. 330 J
agilmartin@mercy.edu
GILMARTIN, Maureen, A 410-827-5842. 214 C
mgilmartin@chesapeake.edu
GILMARTIN, Michael ...... 831-646-4039... 54 I
mgilmartin@mpc.edu
GILMER, Elizabeth .... 478-289-2037. 124 C
egilmer@ega.edu
GILMER, Francene .... 859-257-2746. 200 C
francene.gilmer@uky.edu
GILMER, Garrett .... 419-372-2081. 374 K
ggilmer@bgsu.edu
GILMER, Larry .... 910-843-5304. 357 J
GILMER, Leigh Ann .... 206-296-6140. 523 E
gilmerl@seattleu.edu
GILMER, Shannon .... 404-237-7573. 121 F
sgilmer@bauder.edu
GILMORE, Calvin, L .... 336-272-7102. 354 E
gilmorec@greensboro.edu
GILMORE, Chris .... 603-577-6381. 296 F
cgilmore@dwc.edu
GILMORE, Dan .... 856-256-4684. 305 E
gilmore@rowan.edu
GILMORE, David .... 401-254-3843. 440 B
dgilmore@rwu.edu
GILMORE, Denise .... 620-431-2820. 189 D
dgilmore@neosho.edu
GILMORE, Don .... 661-362-2811... 53 G
dgilmore@masters.edu
GILMORE, George .... 603-535-2846. 298 G
gtgilmore@plymouth.edu
GILMORE, Grover, C .... 216-368-2270. 375 J
gcg@case.edu
GILMORE, Jennifer, D .... 812-888-5332. 174 F
jgilmore@vinu.edu
GILMORE, Jessica .... 253-833-9111. 520 C
jgilmore@greenriver.edu
GILMORE, John, W .... 609-497-7705. 304 D
john.gilmore@ptsem.edu
GILMORE, Kevin, P .... 913-971-3294. 188 H
kgilmore@mnu.edu
GILMORE, Laurie, A .... 518-438-3111. 330 C
laurieg@mariacollege.edu
GILMORE, Maureen .... 585-266-0430. 324 A
mgilmore@cci.edu
GILMORE, Robert .... 914-323-5357. 330 B
robert.gilmore@mville.edu
GILMORE, Sherri .... 802-485-2001. 500 A
sgilmore@norwich.edu
GILMOUR, Davie, J .... 570-320-2400. 426 A
djg120@psu.edu
GILMOUR, Davie Jane .... 570-326-3761. 427 B
dgilmour@pct.edu
GILNER, David .... 513-487-3273. 325 G
dgilner@huc.edu

GILNETT, Jennifer, J .... 206-281-2974. 523 C
jgilnett@spu.edu
GILORMINI, Dominique . 787-763-3393. 549 J
dgilormini@inter.edu
GILOT, Sandra .... 973-618-3353. 300 A
sgilot@caldwell.edu
GILPIN, Sue .... 309-268-8139. 146 B
sue.gilpin@heartland.edu
GILROY, Janice .... 914-606-6610. 350 F
janice.gilroy@sunywcc.edu
GILROY, Maryellen .... 518-783-2328. 340 J
mgilroy@siena.edu
GILSON, Corinna .... 561-912-2166. 103 C
cgilson@evergladesuniversity.edu
GILSON, David .... 216-791-5000. 377 E
david.gilson@case.edu
GILSON, Jannie .... 508-588-9100. 232 A
GILSON, Ken .... 562-903-4870... 29 L
ken.gilson@biola.edu
GILSTRAP, Don .... 316-978-3586. 191 F
don.gilstrap@wichita.edu
GILSTRAP, Linda .... 619-216-6614... 68 B
GILTZ, Scott .... 503-594-3440. 402 F
scottg@clackamas.edu
GILYARD, Reginald .... 714-997-6684... 38 A
gilyard@chapman.edu
GIMA, Wesley, T .... 671-735-3025. 546 C
wesley.gima@guamcc.edu
GINDELE, Linda, K .... 513-556-1301. 390 G
linda.gindele@uc.edu
GINDER, Bernice .... 848-445-7149. 306 B
ginder@rutgers.edu
GINDER, Greg .... 317-955-6018. 170 V
gginder@marian.edu
GINDER, Terry .... 212-217-4260. 324 C
terry_ginder@fitnyc.edu
GINES, Joan .... 801-585-9144. 496 Q
joan.gines@utah.edu
GINES, Joan, E .... 801-585-9144. 496 Q
joan.gines@utah.edu
GINES, Scott .... 361-593-2414. 484 A
david.gines@tamuk.edu
GINEVAN, Douglas, W .... 207-786-6093. 209 F
dginevan@bates.edu
GINGERELLA, David .... 978-556-3924. 232 E
dgingerella@necc.mass.edu
GINGERICH, Jeffrey .... 610-902-8302. 411 E
jeff.p.gingerich@cabrini.edu
GINGERICH, Samuel ...... 605-773-3455. 451 E
sam.gingerich@sdbor.edu
GINGERICH, Willard, P .. 973-655-4383. 303 D
gingerichw@mail.montclair.edu
GINGRAS, Gregory .... 510-869-1589... 61 I
ggingras@samuelmerritt.edu
GINN, Brian .... 601-477-4240. 267 F
brian.ginn@jcjc.edu
GINN, Bryan .... 678-225-7500. 430 D
bginn@pcom.edu
GINNEY, Monica .... 859-344-3346. 199 H
monica.ginney@thomasmore.edu
GINOTTI, Melissa .... 559-278-2741... 33 D
melissa_ginotti@csufresno.edu
GINSBERG, Mark, R .... 703-993-2004. 505 C
mginsber@gmu.edu
GINSBERG, Rick .... 785-864-4297. 190 L
ginsberg@ku.edu
GINSBURG, Charles, M . 214-648-8597. 493 E
charles.ginsburg@utsouthwestern.edu
GINTER, Earl .... 706-542-7575. 133 C
eginter@uga.edu
GINTER, Judy .... 912-344-3231. 120 G
judy.ginter@armstrong.edu
GINTHER, John .... 253-680-7123. 516 L
jginther@bates.ctc.edu
GINTHER, Randy .... 325-649-8036. 473 F
rginther@hputx.edu
GINZBERG, Michael, J ... 202-885-1985... 94 F
ginzberg@aeerican.edu
GIOGLIO, Thomas .... 570-422-3642. 428 D
tgioglio@po-box.esu.edu
GIOIELLI, Brian .... 612-874-3787. 257 B
bgioielli@mcad.edu
GIORDANI, Robert .... 410-704-2096. 220 E
rgiordani@towson.edu
GIORDANO, Anthony .... 617-422-7286. 235 B
agiordano@nesl.edu
GIORDANO, Chris .... 567-661-7129. 387 L
christopher_giordano@owens.edu
GIORDANO, George .... 315-268-7722. 320 A
ggiordan@clarkson.edu
GIORDANO, Matthew ...... 716-896-0700. 350 A
giordano@villa.edu
GIORDANO, Nicholas, J 334-844-5737..... 1 G
njg0003@auburn.edu
GIORDANO, Nick .... 575-538-6109. 312 N
GIORDANO, Sandra, M .. 610-861-1487. 424 E
mesmg02@moravian.edu
GIORGIO, Cynthia, R ..... 951-827-7884... 71 E
cynthia.giorgio@ucr.edu
GIORLANDO, Michael ..... 504-864-7787. 205 H
giorland@loyno.edu
GIOVANNELLI, Joseph ... 718-951-5116. 317 C
jgiovannelli@brooklyn.cuny.edu
GIOVANNELLI, Tony ...... 724-964-8811. 425 A
tgiovannelli@ncstrades.edu
GIOVANNETTI, Robert ... 806-742-0012. 487 D
robert.giovannetti@ttu.edu
GIOVANNINI, Joanne ..... 570-288-8400. 416 H
GIPE, Jason .... 252-399-6360. 352 F
jmgipe@barton.edu
GIPP, David .... 701-255-3285. 373 C
dmgipp@aol.com
GIPP, Freda .... 785-749-8407. 187 B
freda.gipp@bie.edu
GIPSON, Brian .... 770-426-2730. 128 D
brian.gipson@life.edu
GIPSON, Lourdes .... 817-210-0755. 131 H
lgipson@southuniversity.edu
GIPSON, William .... 215-898-0809. 435 B
wgipson@exchange.upenn.edu
GIRARD, Christine, L ..... 480-970-0000... 17 P
c.girard@scnm.edu
GIRARD, Don .... 310-434-4287... 65 A
girard_donald@smc.edu
GIRARD, John .... 701-328-2960. 371 B
GIRARD, Matthew .... 617-369-3871. 236 F
mgirard@smfa.edu
GIRAU, Adolfo .... 504-671-5447. 203 A
agirau@dcc.edu
GIRAUD, Gerald .... 307-754-6235. 543 G
Gerald.Giraud@northwestcollege.edu
GIRELLI, Carl, A .... 434-947-8126. 508 D
cgirelli@randolphcollege.edu
GIRKINS, Margaret, L .... 406-756-3884. 286 B
mgirkins@fvcc.edu
GIROD, Arty, E .... 601-984-1365. 270 C
agirod@umc.edu
GIROD, Mark .... 503-838-8471. 406 E
girodm@wou.edu
GIROIR, Brett .... 979-458-6054. 482 E
brett.giroir@tamus.edu
GIRON, Jenny .... 915-831-6571. 472 B
jgiron6@epcc.edu
GIROUX, Jennifer .... 401-456-8990. 439 F
jgiroux@ric.edu
GIRRES, Raymond .... 574-936-8898. 163 K
ray.girres@ancilla.edu
GIRVEN, Wendy .... 207-326-2260. 211 D
wendy.girven@mma.edu
GIRVIN, Steven, M .... 203-432-4448... 93 A
steve.girvin@yale.edu
GISCHIA, Arthur, J .... 906-227-2360. 248 A
agischia@nmu.edu
GISH, Joanne .... 805-565-6066... 76 D
jgish@westmont.edu
GISSY, Cindy .... 304-424-8314. 530 E
cindy.gissy@wvup.edu
GIST, Bobby, D .... 803-777-3854. 447 G
bgist@mailbox.sc.edu
GIST, Sylvia .... 773-995-3988. 141 J
sgist@csu.edu
GIST, Vicki .... 406-265-3706. 287 D
gist@msun.edu
GITAU, Peter .... 859-572-6447. 198 I
gitau@nku.edu
GITCHELL, David .... 620-242-0455. 188 G
gitcheld@mcpherson.edu
GITENSTEIN, R. Barbara . 609-771-2101. 300 E
rbgit@tcnj.edu
GITHENS, Misty .... 620-331-4100. 187 G
mgithens@indycc.edu
GITHENS, Travis .... 620-331-4100. 187 G
tgithens@indycc.edu
GITKIND, Kristi .... 303-273-3280... 80 E
kgitkind@mines.edu
GITTELL, Ross .... 603-230-3501. 295 J
rgittell@ccsnh.edu
GITTENS, Robert, P .... 617-373-5805. 235 F
GITTINGS, Carl, W .... 304-457-6368. 526 A
gittingscw@ab.edu
GITTLEMAN, John, L ...... 706-542-2968. 133 C
ecohead@uga.edu
GIUGNI, Terry .... 714-992-7031... 56 F
tgiugni@fullcoll.edu
GIULLI, Gail .... 425-640-1557. 519 D
gail.giulli@edcc.edu
GIUMETTE, Peter, M .... 781-736-3703. 224 F
giumette@brandeis.edu
GIUSTI, Stacey, J .... 509-527-5980. 525 E
giustis@whitman.edu
GIVAN, Natalie .... 212-757-1190. 313 H
ngivan@funeraleducation.org
GIVEN, Christopher .... 203-576-6193... 91 D
Christopher.Given@stvincents.org
GIVEN, Steve .... 415-282-9603... 27 L
stevegiven@actcm.edu
GIVENS, Chaney .... 303-458-3529... 84 M
cgivens@regis.edu
GIVENS, Corey .... 920-693-1118. 540 B
corey.givens@gotoltc.edu
GIVENS, Doris, F .... 913-288-7123. 187 L
dgivens@kckcc.edu
GIVENS, Emily .... 417-873-6894. 273 H
egivens@drury.edu
GIVENS, Hal .... 907-822-3201... 10 A
hgivens@akbible.edu
GIVENS, Hali .... 251-442-2212..... 9 A
hgivens@umobile.edu
GIVENS, Patrick .... 732-987-2736. 302 B
givensp@georgian.edu
GIVENS, Richard .... 850-412-5480. 114 K
richard.givens@famu.edu
GIVENS, Steven .... 850-718-2377... 99 N
givenss@chipola.edu
GIVENS, Steven, J .... 314-935-5127. 284 L
sjgivens@wustl.edu
GIVENS, Will .... 816-995-2818. 280 G
william.givens@researchcollege.edu
GIVHAN, Mary .... 859-344-3531. 199 H
mary.givhan@thomasmore.edu
GIVHAN, Waldo, D .... 334-953-7442. 544 D
GIVLER, Sharon, M .... 717-867-6235. 421 H
givler@lvc.edu
GIVNER, Christine, E ...... 716-673-3311. 342 A
christine.givner@fredonia.edu
GIWA, Tunde .... 212-799-5000. 328 B
GIZZI, Zane .... 717-815-6521. 438 D
zgizzi@ycp.edu
GJERDE, Michelle, B ...... 719-549-2512... 80 K
michelle.gjerde@colostate-pueblo.edu
GJERTSON, Sarah .... 303-871-3263... 86 B
sgjertso@du.edu
GLAB, Nancy .... 319-398-5566. 180 J
nglab@kirkwood.edu
GLADCHUK, Chet .... 410-293-2429. 545 J
gladchuk@usna.edu
GLADDEN, Calvin .... 410-337-6133. 215 A
cgladden@goucher.edu
GLADDEN, James, M ..... 317-278-2826. 168 D
jamglad@iupui.edu
GLADDEN, Tina .... 662-846-4640. 266 G
SM8031@bncollege.com
GLADEN, Dennis .... 701-671-2217. 372 E
dennis.gladen@ndscs.edu
GLADFELTER, Donald, L 309-457-2124. 153 D
don@monmouthcollege.edu
GLADIS, Alex, J .... 724-772-5520. 411 C
alex.gladis@bc3.edu
GLADSTONE, Hannah ..... 207-859-1243. 211 H
gladstoneh@thomas.edu
GLADSTONE, Kevin .... 440-646-8355. 392 D
kgladstone@ursuline.edu
GLADU, Frank .... 931-598-3397. 458 H
fxgladu@sewanee.edu
GLADUE, Angel .... 701-477-7862. 373 B
agladue@tm.edu
GLADWIN, Ryan, R .... 215-684-7400. 423 L
rgladwin@messiah.edu
GLAESER, Doug, P .... 909-869-4944... 32 G
dglaeser@csupomona.edu
GLANCY, John, L .... 206-281-2325. 523 C
jglancy@spu.edu
GLANCY, Marian .... 937-769-1827. 373 I
mglancy@antioch.edu
GLANCY, Susan .... 212-851-0627. 321 D
GLANDER, Mindy .... 706-439-6313. 129 G
mglander@northgatech.edu
GLANDON, Bert .... 208-562-3000. 138 C
GLANDON,
Constance, J .... 641-422-4332. 181 D
glandcon@niacc.edu
GLANDT, Eduardo, D .... 215-898-7244. 435 B
eglandt@seas.upenn.edu
GLANNER, Marnie .... 317-429-3100. 380 A
marnie.glanner@franklin.edu
GLANZ, Melissa, A .... 330-494-6170. 389 F
mglanz@starkstate.edu
GLANZER, Chris .... 620-947-3121. 190 J
chrisg@tabor.edu
GLANZER, Joshua .... 561-237-7761. 108 X
jglanzer@lynn.edu
GLANZER, Jules .... 620-947-3121. 190 J
julesg@tabor.edu
GLAPA-GROSSKLAG,
James .... 661-362-3632... 40 E
james.glapa-grossklag@canyons.edu
GLAROS, Alan, G .... 816-654-7523. 275 K
aglaros@kcumb.edu
GLAS, Rich .... 218-299-4231. 255 A
glas@cord.edu
GLASCO, Gerald .... 810-762-3480. 251 E
gglasco@umflint.edu
GLASENER, Jacquelyn .... 559-278-2586... 33 D
jacquelyn_glasener@csufresno.edu
GLASER, Barton, G .... 512-448-8657. 479 C
bartong@stedwards.edu
GLASER, Brendan .... 360-442-2503. 521 A
bglaser@lowercolumbia.edu
GLASER, Brian .... 309-796-5238. 140 E
glaserb@bhc.edu
GLASER, Karen .... 215-503-0704. 434 C
karen.glaser@jefferson.edu
GLASER, Milton .... 212-592-2000. 340 H
GLASER, Thomas, J .... 630-942-2218. 142 G
glasert@cod.edu
GLASER, Thomas, J .... 443-518-4442. 215 E
tglaser@howardcc.edu
GLASGOW,
Mary Ellen, S .... 412-396-6554. 415 F
glasgowm@duq.edu
GLASGOW, Michael .... 203-785-3680... 93 A
michael.glasgow@yale.edu
GLASGOW, Sara .... 619-644-7600... 46 E
sara.glasgow@gcccd.edu
GLASGOW, Terri .... 269-749-7623. 249 A
tglasgow@olivetcollege.edu
GLASGOW, Wayne, C ..... 478-301-2024. 128 H
glasgow_wc@mercer.edu
GLASMAN, Yvonne .... 270-707-3722. 195 E
yvonne.glasman@kctcs.edu
GLASPER, Rufus .... 480-731-8100... 14 I
r.glasper@domail.maricopa.edu
GLASPIE, Tamara .... 910-296-2400. 361 D
tglaspie@jamessprunt.edu
GLASS, Alan, I .... 314-935-9626. 284 L
aglass@wustl.edu
GLASS, Arthur .... 215-489-6378. 414 E
Arthur.Glass@delval.edu
GLASS, Carrie .... 504-865-3231. 205 H
ceglass@loyno.edu
GLASS, Carrie .... 617-732-2199. 233 E
carrie.glass@mcphs.edu
GLASS, Fred .... 812-856-1196. 167 E
athldir@indiana.edu
GLASS, Fred .... 812-855-2794. 167 F
athldir@indiana.edu
GLASS, Jennifer .... 731-352-4259. 453 D
glassj@bethelu.edu
GLASS, Jim .... 229-217-4140. 129 F
jglass@moultrietech.edu
GLASS, JR., Robert .... 706-776-0111. 130 E
bglass@piedmont.edu
GLASS, Tony .... 309-467-6382. 145 C
arglass@eureka.edu
GLASS, Wendy, G .... 207-786-6096. 209 F
wglass@bates.edu
GLASSCOCK, Darrell, R .. 210-434-6711. 477 N
drglasscock@lake.ollusa.edu
GLASSCOCK, Vicki .... 423-614-8059. 455 L
vglasscock@leeuniversity.edu
GLASSER, Joanne, K ...... 309-677-3167. 140 I
jglasser@bumail.bradley.edu
GLASSES, Euegene .... 505-786-4187. 310 D
eglasses@navajotech.edu
GLASSMAN, Danny .... 404-364-8427. 130 A
dglassman@oglethorpe.edu
GLASSMAN, David .... 309-677-3152. 140 I
dglassman@bradley.edu
GLASSMAN, Edward .... 312-332-0707. 160 J
GLASSMAN, Joel, N .... 314-516-5753. 283 E
jglassman@umsl.edu
GLASSMAN, Paul .... 201-559-6070. 302 A
glassmanp@felician.edu
GLASSNER, Barry .... 503-768-7680. 403 K
president@lclark.edu
GLATT, Camilla .... 509-542-5548. 518 C
GLATT, Laura .... 701-328-4116. 371 B
laura.glatt@ndus.edu
GLATT, Robert .... 206-934-6790. 523 A
robert.glatt@seattlecolleges.edu
GLATTER, Bryan, E .... 985-448-7915. 203 B
bryan.glatter@fletcher.edu
GLATTER, Jill .... 516-877-3321. 313 A
registrar@adelphi.edu
GLAVIN, Anne, P .... 818-677-2201... 34 C
anne.glavin@csun.edu
GLAVIN, JR., John, A .... 610-359-5105. 414 D
jglavin@dccc.edu
GLAWE, Laura .... 414-229-6444. 537 A
glawe@uwm.edu
GLAZE, Randy .... 205-929-6445..... 5 D
rglaze@lawsonstate.edu
GLAZER, Greer, L .... 513-558-5330. 390 G
greer.glazer@uc.edu
GLAZER, Meir .... 718-268-4700. 337 F
GLAZER, Randy .... 212-678-3724. 347 G
glazer@tc.edu
GLAZIER, Larry, C .... 308-398-7315. 288 I
lglazier@cccneb.edu
GLAZIER, Steve .... 918-465-1811. 395 G
sglazier@eosc.edu
GLAZIER, Steve, G .... 918-465-1811. 395 G
sglazier@eosc.edu
GLAZIER-MCDONALD,
Beth .... 859-238-5205. 193 E
beth.glazier@centre.edu
GLAZIER-SMITH, Laura .. 718-368-6725. 318 E
laura.glazier-smith@kbcc.cuny.edu
GLEAN, Randy .... 940-397-4568. 476 H
randy.glean@mwsu.edu
GLEASON, Amy, S .... 608-796-3182. 539 E
asgleason@viterbo.edu
GLEASON, Ann, C .... 919-760-8521. 356 G
gleasona@meredith.edu

GLEASON, Brian .... 616-647-4803... 18 I
brian.gleason@phoenix.edu
GLEASON, David .... 410-455-2709. 219 D
gleason@umbc.edu
GLEASON, Jamie .... 215-702-4393. 411 F
jgleason@cairn.edu
GLEASON, Jan .... 404-727-0639. 124 E
jan.gleason@emory.edu
GLEASON, Joseph, K ..... 417-268-6001. 271 I
jgleason@gobbc.edu
GLEASON, Katie .... 310-660-3593... 43 B
kgleason@elcamino.edu
GLEASON, Katie .... 310-660-3670... 43 B
kgleason@elcamino.edu
GLEASON, Katie .... 310-660-3593... 43 B
kgleason@elcamino.edu
GLEASON, Mark .... 507-222-4046. 254 D
mgleason@carleton.edu
GLEASON, Matthew .... 918-540-6311. 396 G
matthew.gleason@neo.edu
GLEASON, Timothy, W ... 541-346-3739. 406 D
tgleason@uoregon.edu
GLEAVES, Scott .... 334-386-7154..... 3 H
sgleaves@faulkner.edu
GLEESON, Larry .... 937-484-1220. 392 C
uusafety@urbana.edu
GLEETON, Claude .... 662-252-8090. 269 F
cgleeton@rustcollege.edu
GLEIM, Jeffery, T .... 412-624-8277. 435 C
jeff.gleim@ia.pitt.edu
GLEJZER, Richard .... 802-258-9234. 499 F
rglejzer@marlboro.edu
GLEN, Dorsie .... 618-374-5162. 156 B
dorsie.glen@principia.edu
GLEN, Will .... 949-451-5201... 67 B
wglen@ivc.edu
GLENDENING, Andrew ... 909-748-8014... 73 H
andrew_glendening@redlands.edu
GLENMAYE, Linnea .... 316-978-5054. 191 F
linnea.glenmay@wichita.edu
GLENN, Amanda .... 301-624-2851. 214 H
aglenn@frederick.edu
GLENN, Ashley .... 540-362-6609. 505 G
cdc@hollins.edu
GLENN, Barbara, M .... 804-523-5263. 512 F
bglenn@reynolds.edu
GLENN, Brian .... 806-651-2105. 484 D
bglenn@mail.wtamu.edu
GLENN, Chance .... 256-372-5725..... 1 A
chance.glenn@aamu.edu
GLENN, Christy .... 931-393-1682. 461 A
cglenn@mscc.edu
GLENN, Crystal .... 828-327-7000. 359 A
cglenn@cvcc.edu
GLENN, Darrell .... 212-217-4075. 324 C
darrell_glenn@fitnyc.edu
GLENN, Daymond .... 503-517-1056. 408 H
dglenn@warnerpacific.edu
GLENN, Dennis, E .... 706-385-1064. 130 F
dennis.glenn@point.edu
GLENN, Doris .... 304-260-4380. 527 N
dglenn@blueridgectc.edu
GLENN, Idella, G .... 864-294-3104. 444 C
idella.glenn@furman.edu
GLENN, Jason .... 386-226-6209. 102 B
glennj1@erau.edu
GLENN, Jenna .... 630-889-6620. 154 E
jglenn@nuhs.edu
GLENN, Jonathan, A .... 501-450-3126... 25 H
jona@uca.edu
GLENN, Katie .... 205-226-7737..... 2 C
kglenn@bsc.edu
GLENN, Lane, A .... 978-556-3855. 232 E
lglenn@necc.mass.edu
GLENN, Laverne .... 610-527-0200. 432 B
laverne.glenn@rosemont.edu
GLENN, Michael .... 303-282-3427... 85 D
GLENN, Robert, K .... 256-233-8201..... 1 F
bob.glenn@athens.edu
GLENN, Tenika .... 336-315-7800... 96 F
GLENN, Thane .... 267-502-4844. 410 I
thane.glenn@anc-gc.org
GLENN-SUMMITT,
Peggy .... 918-456-5511. 396 H
glennsum@nsuok.edu
GLENSHAW, Peter .... 802-831-1318. 500 H
pglenshaw@vermontlaw.edu
GLESSNER, Lisa .... 724-805-2933. 432 G
lisa.glessner@email.stvincent.edu
GLEW, Karen .... 207-453-5820. 210 L
kglew@kvcc.me.edu
GLEZERMAN, David, R ... 215-204-7269. 433 K
david.glezerman@temple.edu
GLICK, Carol .... 313-593-6751. 251 D
cglick@umich.edu
GLICK, Michael, L .... 716-829-2836. 341 F
sdm-dean@buffalo.edu
GLICK, Steven .... 330-263-2590. 377 H
sglick@wooster.edu
GLICK, William, H .... 713-348-5928. 479 A
glickb@rice.edu
GLICKMAN, Gena .... 860-512-3100... 88 G
gglickman@manchestercc.edu
GLIDDEN, Stacey, T .... 978-468-7111. 227 A
sglidden@gcts.edu
GLIDEWELL, Chris .... 618-536-3345. 159 F
cglide@siu.edu
GLIDWELL, Bob .... 417-328-1550. 282 C
bglidwell@sbuniv.edu
GLIEM, Valerie .... 727-864-8408. 101 N
gliemvm@eckerd.edu
GLIMCHER, Laurie .... 212-746-6005. 322 A
glimche@med.cornell.edu
GLINDEMANN, Kent, E .. 276-223-4885. 514 F
kglindemann@wcc.vccs.edu
GLINES, Carey .... 603-668-2211. 297 I
c.glines@snhu.edu
GLINES, Carol, A .... 563-333-6329. 182 B
GlinesCarolA@sau.edu
GLINIECKI, Anita .... 203-332-5224... 88 F
agliniecki@hcc.commnet.edu
GLISCH, John .... 321-433-7017. 101 M
glischj@easternflorida.edu
GLISSON, Michael .... 337-521-8951. 203 I
michael.glisson@southlouisiana.edu
GLISSON, Tony, L .... 270-745-5360. 200 G
tony.glisson@wku.edu
GLOBIS, Roxanne .... 609-633-9658. 308 A
rglobis@tesc.edu
GLOCK, Jon, W .... 563-588-8000. 178 D
jglock@emmaus.edu
GLOD, Carol, A .... 978-542-7044. 230 E
cglod@salemstate.edu
GLOGOWSKI,
Maryruth, F .... 716-878-6314. 343 A
glogowmf@buffalostate.edu
GLORE, Susan, J .... 410-871-3305. 216 E
sglore@mcdaniel.edu
GLORIA, Jackie .... 858-566-1200... 42 G
jgloria@disd.edu
GLORIA SAWYER, Rita .. 323-563-4922... 38 B
ritasawyer@cdrewu.edu
GLOSSER, Wade, W .... 816-654-7717. 275 K
bglosser@kcumb.edu
GLOSTER, Sandra .... 803-780-1019. 449 E
sdgloster@voorhees.edu
GLOTZBACH, Philip, A ... 518-580-5700. 341 A
pglotzba@skidmore.edu
GLOVEN, Gates .... 303-765-3109... 82 E
ggloven@iliff.edu
GLOVER, David .... 501-812-2318... 22 G
dglover@pulaskitech.edu
GLOVER, David .... 757-727-5259. 505 F
david.glover@hamptonu.edu
GLOVER, Devon, H .... 208-524-3000. 138 D
devon.glover@my.eitc.edu
GLOVER, Diane, F .... 919-718-7231. 359 B
dglover@cccc.edu
GLOVER, Jamie, L .... 580-581-2987. 394 G
jglover@cameron.edu
GLOVER, Joseph .... 352-392-2404. 116 A
jglover@aa.ufl.edu
GLOVER, Joseph, M .... 812-941-2028. 168 F
joglover@ius.edu
GLOVER, Katie .... 703-370-6600. 508 B
GLOVER, Nathaniel .... 904-470-8010. 102 A
n.glover@ewc.edu
GLOVER, Paula .... 660-263-4110. 279 B
paulag@macc.edu
GLOVER, Shirley .... 478-988-6890. 122 G
sglover@centralgatech.edu
GLOWKA, Arthur, W .... 770-720-5628. 130 G
awg@reinhardt.edu
GLUCK, Daniel .... 916-577-2200... 76 J
dgluck@jessup.edu
GLUCKOWSKY,
Moshe, M .... 718-774-3430. 316 F
GLUSKER, Marjorie .... 914-606-6585. 350 F
marge.glusker@sunywcc.edu
GLYNN, Amy, C .... 413-545-8500. 228 F
aglynn@admin.umass.edu
GLYNN, Graham .... 914-674-7125. 330 J
gglynn@mercy.edu
GLYNN, Joan, M .... 336-272-7102. 354 E
joan.glynn@greensboro.edu
GLYNN, John, B .... 414-410-4313. 532 B
jbglynn@stritch.edu
GLYNN, Terry, S .... 858-499-0202... 40 C
tglynn@coleman.edu
GMEINER, Mary, L .... 989-686-9042. 242 C
marygmeiner@delta.edu
GMEINER, Rebecca .... 678-466-4145. 123 A
rebeccagmeiner@clayton.edu
GNADE, Bruce .... 972-883-6636. 491 E
gnade@utdallas.edu
GNADINGER, Cindy, G .. 502-272-8259. 192 E
cgnadinger@bellarmine.edu
GNAN, Peter, D .... 708-209-3192. 143 E
pete.gnan@cuchicago.edu
GNASSO, Emil, A .... 610-758-3200. 422 A
emg3@lehigh.edu
GNECCO, Donald .... 706-776-0117. 130 E
dgnecco@piedmont.edu
GNIOT, Phillip, E .... 606-783-2097. 198 A
p.gniot@moreheadstate.edu
GOAD, Philip .... 256-766-6610..... 4 B
pgoad@hcu.edu
GOAD, William .... 405-425-5180. 397 D
bill.goad@oc.edu
GOAN, Bradley, L .... 859-233-8300. 199 I
bgoan@transy.edu
GOAR, Michele .... 575-492-2161. 312 M
mgoar@usw.edu
GOBAR, Angela .... 601-979-0663. 267 E
angela.m.gobar@jsums.edu
GOBBI, Laura .... 510-430-2112... 54 F
lgobbi@mills.edu
GOBBLE, Sheryl .... 619-388-7428... 62 F
sgobble@sdccd.edu
GOBER, Chris, G .... 636-922-8211. 280 J
cgober@stchas.edu
GOBER, T. Kale .... 870-230-5072... 21 D
gobertk@hsu.edu
GOBER, Teresa .... 703-257-5515. 502 E
dcaamm@aviationmaintenance.edu
GOBERISH, John, S .... 724-480-3450. 413 H
john.goberish@ccbc.edu
GOBLE, Bryen .... 606-886-3863. 194 K
bryen.goble@kctcs.edu
GOBLE, Daniel .... 203-837-8851... 88 B
gobled@wcsu.edu
GOBLE, David, S .... 843-953-1267. 442 A
dgoble@citadel.edu
GOBLET, Lois .... 518-255-5524. 344 E
gobletle@cobleskill.edu
GOBLET, Lois, E .... 518-255-5524. 344 E
goblette@cobleskill.edu
GOCHENAUR,
Heather, K .... 260-982-5873. 170 U
hkgochenaur@manchester.edu
GOCHENAUR, Jack, A .... 260-982-5245. 170 U
jagochenaur@manchester.edu
GOCHNAUER,
Richard, D .... 302-356-6795... 94 E
richard.d.gochnauer@wilmu.edu
GOCIAL, Tammy .... 314-529-6893. 276 G
tgocial@maryville.edu
GODAR, Susan .... 973-720-2964. 308 I
godars@wpunj.edu
GODBOLD, Heidi .... 719-638-6580... 81 K
hgodbold@cci.edu
GODBOUT, Muriel .... 315-364-3356. 350 E
mgodbout@wells.edu
GODDARD, Deanna .... 507-457-2493. 262 A
dgoddard@winona.edu
GODDARD, Diane, H .... 785-864-4904. 190 L
dgoddard@ku.edu
GODDARD, Robert .... 802-773-5900. 499 B
robert.goddard@csj.edu
GODDARD, Scott, D .... 304-637-1352. 526 E
goddards@dewv.edu
GODDING, Jesse .... 972-825-4811. 481 F
jgodding@sagu.edu
GODEK, Jim .... 949-376-6000... 50 C
jgodek@lagunacollege.edu
GODENZI, Alberto, A ..... 617-552-6399. 224 A
alberto.godenzi@bc.edu
GODES, Iris .... 508-854-4260. 232 F
igodes@qcc.mass.edu
GODFREY, Blanton .... 919-515-6500. 368 B
blanton_godfrey@ncsu.edu
GODFREY, Christian, J ... 208-524-3000. 138 D
christian.godfrey@my.eitc.edu
GODFREY, Christine .... 808-544-1189. 135 F
cgodfrey@hpu.edu
GODFREY, Michael .... 757-873-1111. 504 J
GODFREY, W. Robert ..... 760-480-8474... 76 C
bvansolkema@wscal.edu
GODFREY-DAWSON,
Angela, R .... 252-335-0821. 359 F
adawson@albemarle.edu
GODIN, Norm .... 951-571-6341... 60 K
norm.godin@mvc.edu
GODIN, Patricia, A .... 919-866-5170. 364 G
pagodin@waketech.edu
GODIN, Roger, A .... 717-291-3989. 416 J
roger.godin@fandm.edu
GODINA, Estela .... 312-226-6294. 151 A
busofc1@lexingtoncollege.edu
GODLESKI, Mark, G .... 315-445-4520. 328 F
godlesmg@lemoyne.edu
GODO, James .... 630-637-5809. 154 F
jwgodo@noctrl.edu
GODSEY, Jim .... 507-288-4563. 255 C
library@crossroadscollege.edu
GODSEY, Lisa .... 312-777-8659. 147 D
lgodsey@aii.edu
GODSEY, R. Kirby .... 478-330-5609. 128 H
godsey_rk@mercer.edu
GODSOE, Kim .... 781-736-3474. 224 F
godsoe@brandeis.edu
GODWIN, Angeline, D .... 276-656-0201. 513 D
agodwin@patrickhenry.edu
GODWIN, Donald, R ...... 619-260-4588... 73 I
donald.godwin@sandiego.edu
GODWIN, Jack .... 916-278-6686... 34 D
jgodwin@csus.edu
GODWIN, Joseph, H ...... 616-331-2400. 243 C
godwinj@gvsu.edu
GODWIN, Lewis .... 678-891-3960. 125 G
lewis.godwin@gpc.edu
GODWIN, Ronald, S .... 434-582-7600. 506 I
rgodwin@liberty.edu
GODWIN, Wendell .... 580-559-5274. 395 F
wgodwin@ecok.edu
GODZWA, Alicia .... 540-362-6660. 505 G
agodzwa@hollins.edu
GOEBEL, Jeffrey, D .... 218-477-2069. 259 H
goebelj@mnstate.edu
GOEBEL, Ken .... 603-358-2378. 298 F
kgoebel@keene.edu
GOEBEL, Rob .... 217-228-5432. 156 C
goebero@quincy.edu
GOECKER, James, A .... 812-877-8894. 172 C
james.goecker@rose-hulman.edu
GOEDDE, Tony, G .... 419-434-4556. 391 D
goedde@findlay.edu
GOEDEKE, Allen .... 336-841-9191. 355 C
agoedeke@highpoint.edu
GOEDERT, JoAnn .... 301-445-1921. 219 A
sansbury@usmd.edu
GOEL, Meeta .... 970-945-8691... 79 G
GOELDNER, Jason .... 715-365-4534. 540 G
jgoeldner@nicoletcollege.edu
GOELLNER, Marilyn .... 814-732-1778. 428 E
mgoellner@edinboro.edu
GOELOE-ALSTON,
Hendrina .... 718-270-1191. 342 D
hgoeloe-alston@downstate.edu
GOELZHAUSER,
Michael, J .... 812-464-1717. 174 D
mjgoelzh@usi.edu
GOEN, Jennifer .... 239-590-1020. 115 A
jgoen@fgcu.edu
GOEPPINGER,
Kathleen, H .... 630-515-7300. 153 B
drgoeppinger@midwestern.edu
GOERING, Doug .... 907-474-7730... 10 I
djgoering@alaska.edu
GOERING, Fred .... 316-284-5250. 184 J
fgoering@bethelks.edu
GOERING, Wynn, M .... 505-277-7601. 312 F
wgoering@unm.edu
GOERTEMILLER, Paul ..... 903-510-2389. 488 E
pgoe@tjc.edu
GOERTZ, Christine .... 563-884-5159. 182 A
christine.goertz@palmer.edu
GOERTZEN, Leroy .... 253-759-6104. 403 A
lgoertzen@nbs.edu
GOERTZEN, Ryan .... 918-836-6886. 400 D
rgoertzen@mail.spartan.edu
GOERZEN, Les .... 316-284-5261. 184 J
lgoerzen@bethelks.edu
GOETHE, Corey .... 989-386-6622. 247 B
cgoethe@midmich.edu
GOETRA, Robert .... 620-223-2700. 186 G
GOETSCH, Lori, A .... 785-532-7402. 188 A
lgoetsch@ksu.edu
GOETSCH, Steven, E .... 201-355-1462. 302 A
goetschs@felician.edu
GOETSCHIUS, Susan, C . 607-871-2144. 313 E
goetshcius@alfred.edu
GOETZ, Bruce, P .... 303-273-3225... 80 E
bgoetz@mines.edu
GOETZ, Michael, A .... 414-847-3305. 534 F
mikegoetz@miad.edu
GOETZE, David .... 810-989-5761. 249 H
dpgoetze@sc4.edu
GOEWERT, Ed .... 618-374-5109. 156 B
ed.goewert@principia.edu
GOFF, Anton .... 301-860-3571. 220 A
agoff@bowiestate.edu
GOFF, David .... 303-724-7304... 86 A
david.goff@ucdenver.edu
GOFF, David, W .... 870-236-6901... 20 K
dgoff@crc.edu
GOFF, Jay .... 314-977-8191. 281 I
goffjw@slu.edu
GOFF, Karen .... 732-987-2601. 302 B
kgoff@georgian.edu
GOFF, Kathleen .... 413-542-2226. 221 G
kgoff@amherst.edu
GOFF, Michelle .... 478-289-2095. 124 C
mgoff@ega.edu
GOFF, Mike .... 214-818-1334. 470 A
mgoff@criswell.edu
GOFF, Patricia, A .... 401-865-1031. 439 E
pgoff@providence.edu
GOFF, Susan .... 707-468-3131... 54 B
sgoff@mendocino.edu

GOFF-CREWS, Kimberly, M .... 203-432-6602... 93 A
kimberly.goff-crews@yale.edu
GOFFENEY, Robert .... 313-593-5454. 251 D
rgoffene@umich.edu
GOFFNETT, Chris .... 989-386-6622. 247 B
cgoffnett@midmich.edu
GOFORTH, Craig .... 828-689-1405. 356 F
cgoforth@mhc.edu
GOGA, Nedzad .... 718-636-3599. 336 F
ngoga@pratt.edu
GOGGIN, Trudi .... 708-524-6824. 144 C
tgoggin@dom.edu
GOGNAT, Tim .... 937-327-7457. 393 E
tgognat@wittenberg.edu
GOGOL, Miriam .... 914-674-7875. 330 J
mgogol@mercy.edu
GOGUE, Jay .... 334-844-4650..... 1 G
president@auburn.edu
GOH, Phan .... 408-260-0208... 44 J
sjextension@fivebranches.edu
GOHLKE, Brian, B .... 608-757-7773. 539 I
bgohlke@blackhawk.edu
GOHMANN, Jennifer ...... 502-585-9911. 199 C
jgohmann@spalding.edu
GOHN, Sherry .... 360-442-2216. 521 A
sgohn@lowercolumbia.edu
GOIN, JR., Randy, A ...... 850-245-0466. 114 J
randy.goin@flbog.edu
GOINES, Janice .... 979-230-3395. 468 A
janice.goines@brazosport.edu
GOINES, Shirley, M .... 479-968-0399... 20 E
sgoines@atu.edu
GOINGS, Amy, M .... 425-739-8200. 520 K
amy.goings@lwtech.edu
GOINGS, Eric .... 918-335-6257. 398 F
egoings@okwu.edu
GOINS, David .... 409-882-3367. 486 G
david.goins@lsco.edu
GOINS, Deb .... 740-374-8716. 392 I
dgoins@wscc.edu
GOINS, Jessica, D .... 864-488-4590. 444 L
jgoins@limestone.edu
GOINS, Scott, E .... 337-475-5329. 207 G
sgoins@mcneese.edu
GOITIA PADILLA, Francisco, J .... 787-763-6700. 549 A
javiergoitia@aol.com
GOKE, Evelyn .... 906-487-7272. 242 G
evelyn.goke@finlandia.edu
GOKE-PARIOLA, Abiodun .... 704-337-2492. 365 G
g-p@queens.edu
GOKEL, George, W .... 314-516-5321. 283 E
gokelg@umsl.edu
GOLABEK, Sue .... 843-208-8144. 448 B
sgolabek@uscb.edu
GOLATO, Andrea .... 512-245-2581. 487 C
a_g554@txstate.edu
GOLBA, Gina .... 816-802-3397. 275 J
ggolba@kcai.edu
GOLD, Artie, L .... 920-923-8750. 534 A
algold16@marianuniversity.edu
GOLD, Cheryl .... 727-864-8058. 101 N
goldcc@eckerd.edu
GOLD, Ellen .... 734-487-1107. 242 D
ellen.gold@emich.edu
GOLD, Harriet, B .... 270-384-8017. 197 D
goldh@lindsey.edu
GOLD, Jeffrey .... 419-383-5320. 392 B
jeffrey.gold@utoledo.edu
GOLD, Jeffrey, P .... 419-383-4243. 392 B
jeffrey.gold@utoledo.edu
GOLD, Kathleen, E .... 802-626-4860. 501 E
kathleen.gold@lyndonstate.edu
GOLD, Kim .... 828-395-1663. 361 C
kgold@isothermal.edu
GOLD, Mark .... 718-951-5861. 317 C
mark@brooklyn.cuny.edu
GOLD, Steven, J .... 714-816-0366... 70 A
steven.gold@trident.edu
GOLD, Victor, J .... 213-736-1062... 53 E
victor.gold@lls.edu
GOLDAMMER, Diana ...... 605-995-2160. 450 A
digoldam@dwu.edu
GOLDBART, Paul .... 404-894-3300. 125 D
paul.goldbart@cos.gatech.edu
GOLDBERG, Barbara ...... 818-947-2647... 52 E
goldbeba@lavc.edu
GOLDBERG, Carole, E .... 310-206-9345... 71 C
cgoldberg@conet.ucla.edu
GOLDBERG, Donald .... 310-660-3200... 43 B
dgoldberg@elcamino.edu
GOLDBERG, Ellen, J ...... 630-844-5147. 140 A
egoldbrg@aurora.edu
GOLDBERG, Glenn .... 904-819-6305. 103 E
GGoldberg@flagler.edu
GOLDBERG, Jane, F .... 360-538-4005. 520 B
jgoldber@ghc.edu
GOLDBERG, Jeanette ...... 603-668-2211. 297 I
j.goldberg@snhu.edu
GOLDBERG, Jeffrey, B ... 520-621-6594... 18 F
jgoldberg@arizona.edu
GOLDBERG, Jerold, S .... 216-368-3266. 375 J
jsg@case.edu
GOLDBERG, Marc .... 503-491-7019. 404 E
marc.goldberg@mhcc.edu
GOLDBERG, Milton .... 303-784-8264... 82 Q
mgoldberg@jiu.edu
GOLDBERG, Robert .... 646-981-4500. 348 B
rgoldberg@touro.edu
GOLDBERG, Velda .... 201-761-6033. 306 L
vgoldberg@saintpeters.edu
GOLDBERG, Yisroel .... 973-267-9404. 304 G
sgrca1213@gmail.com
GOLDBERGBELLE, Jonathan .... 217-206-8319. 161 E
goldbergbelle.jonathan@uis.edu
GOLDEN, Andrew, K ...... 609-258-4136. 304 E
agolden@princeton.edu
GOLDEN, Beverley .... 903-566-7303. 492 D
bgolden@uttyler.edu
GOLDEN, Bryan, A .... 229-391-5060. 119 H
bgolden@abac.edu
GOLDEN, Carolyn .... 334-244-3369..... 2 A
cgolden2@aum.edu
GOLDEN, Cheryl .... 901-435-1201. 455 M
cheryl_golden@loc.edu
GOLDEN, Chris .... 423-614-8020. 455 L
cgolden@leeuniversity.edu
GOLDEN, Clarence .... 301-687-4759. 220 C
cgolden@frostburg.edu
GOLDEN, Cynthia .... 412-624-3335. 435 C
goldenc@pitt.edu
GOLDEN, Dan .... 303-986-2320... 80 D
dan@csha.net
GOLDEN, Denise .... 814-871-7663. 416 K
golden007@gannon.edu
GOLDEN, Dennis, C .... 314-889-1419. 274 E
dgolden@fontbonne.edu
GOLDEN, Elisabeth, I ..... 304-877-6428. 526 C
lisa.golden@abc.edu
GOLDEN, Gary, A .... 856-225-2828. 306 C
Gary.Golden@rutgers.edu
GOLDEN, James, R .... 757-221-1190. 503 N
jrgold@wm.edu
GOLDEN, Kendra, J .... 509-527-4952. 525 E
golden@whitman.edu
GOLDEN, Robert, N .... 608-263-4910. 536 D
rngolden@wisc.edu
GOLDEN, Timothy, P .... 540-464-7184. 515 B
goldentp@vmi.edu
GOLDENBERG, David, H 860-768-4055... 92 D
goldenber@hartford.edu
GOLDENBERG, Isabel ..... 202-741-2656... 95 D
iag@gwu.edu
GOLDENBERG, Mary ...... 847-491-3541. 155 D
m-goldenberg@northwestern.edu
GOLDENBERG, Richard .. 212-594-4000. 347 H
rgoldenberg@tcicollege.edu
GOLDFARB, Donald .... 212-854-8011. 321 D
gold@ieor.columbia.edu
GOLDFARB, Ronald .... 732-906-2515. 303 B
rgoldfarb@middlesexcc.edu
GOLDFEIZ, Emanuel .... 410-653-0433. 217 D
GOLDGEIER, Eileen .... 919-515-3071. 368 B
eileen_goldgeier@ncsu.edu
GOLDGEIER, James .... 202-885-1603... 94 F
jgoldei@american.edu
GOLDHABER, Yochanan . 718-232-7800. 351 C
GOLDING, Stephen, D ... 215-898-1005. 435 B
sgolding@upenn.edu
GOLDING, Stephen, M ... 214-887-5191. 471 F
sgolding@dts.edu
GOLDING, Stephen, T ..... 740-593-2555. 387 C
golding@ohio.edu
GOLDIZEN, Debora .... 907-852-3333... 10 F
debora.goldizen@ilisagvik.edu
GOLDMAN, Aryeh .... 718-268-4700. 337 F
GOLDMAN, Larry .... 908-709-7130. 308 B
goldman@ucc.edu
GOLDMAN, Lee .... 212-305-2752. 321 D
lg2379@columbia.edu
GOLDMAN, Lynn, R .... 202-994-1000... 95 D
GOLDMAN, Michael .... 513-529-3842. 384 G
goldmam3@miamioh.edu
GOLDMAN, Moses .... 919-546-8256. 366 E
mgoldman@shawu.edu
GOLDNER, Lauren .... 310-824-1586... 26 B
lgoldner@ajrca.org
GOLDRING, William, J .... 419-289-5959. 374 C
wgoldrin@ashland.edu
GOLDSBERRY, Kimberlie, L .... 740-368-3139. 387 J
klgoldsb@owu.edu
GOLDSBERRY, Mark .... 402-554-3083. 293 A
mgoldsberry@unomaha.edu
GOLDSBY, Jimmie .... 334-876-9325..... 4 A
jgoldsby@wccs.edu
GOLDSCHMID, Steven ... 520-626-4555... 18 F
sgoldsch@email.arizona.edu
GOLDSCHMIDT, Barbara 212-924-5900. 347 B
pr@swedishinstitute.edu
GOLDSCHMIDT, Pascal, J .... 305-243-6545. 118 F
pgoldschmidt@miami.edu
GOLDSCHMIDT, Robert .. 212-463-0400. 348 B
robertgo@touro.edu
GOLDSMITH, Carole .... 559-934-2200... 75 H
carolegoldsmith@whccd.edu
GOLDSMITH, Carolee ..... 970-204-8360... 81 N
carolee.goldsmith@frontrange.edu
GOLDSMITH, Clair .... 956-882-7900. 491 D
clair.goldsmith@utb.edu
GOLDSMITH, Diane .... 401-874-4128. 440 D
dgoldsmith@uri.edu
GOLDSMITH, Helen .... 415-338-2206... 35 E
hgold@sfsu.edu
GOLDSMITH, Pete .... 812-855-8188. 167 F
hdgoldsm@indiana.edu
GOLDSMITH, Rae .... 618-453-2518. 159 G
rae.goldsmith@siu.edu
GOLDSMITH, Sandra .... 917-422-7203. 235 B
sgoldsmith@nesl.edu
GOLDSMITH, Steve .... 903-813-2342. 466 H
sgoldsmith@austincollege.edu
GOLDSMITH, Steve .... 503-491-7365. 404 E
steve.goldsmith@mhcc.edu
GOLDSTEIN, Arthur .... 508-531-2418. 229 D
arthur.goldstein@bridgew.edu
GOLDSTEIN, Bill .... 641-472-7000. 180 N
bgoldstein@mum.edu
GOLDSTEIN, Brian .... 215-951-1432. 420 B
goldstein@lasalle.edu
GOLDSTEIN, Chip, B ...... 415-575-6100... 31 D
cgoldstein@ciis.edu
GOLDSTEIN, Howard ...... 724-938-5930. 428 A
goldstein@calu.edu
GOLDSTEIN, Jeffrey, E ... 610-330-5001. 420 D
goldstej@lafayette.edu
GOLDSTEIN, Jill .... 212-924-5900. 347 B
library@swedishinstitute.edu
GOLDSTEIN, Jody .... 978-934-4574. 229 B
Jody_Goldstein@uml.edu
GOLDSTEIN, Joy, W .... 215-635-7300. 417 C
jgoldstein@gratz.edu
GOLDSTEIN, Mary Ellen . 704-878-3351. 362 B
mgoldstein@mitchellcc.edu
GOLDSTEIN, Peter, A ..... 415-241-2229... 38 L
pgoldste@ccsf.edu
GOLDSTEIN, Robert, S ... 502-852-6169. 200 D
rsgold03@louisville.edu
GOLDSTEIN, Serge, J ..... 609-258-6059. 304 E
serge@princeton.edu
GOLDSTEIN, Sharon .... 973-684-6919. 304 B
sgoldstein@pccc.edu
GOLDSTEIN, Sharon .... 973-278-5400. 299 D
sfg@berkeleycollege.edu
GOLDSTEIN, Steve .... 781-736-2101. 224 F
goldstein@brandeis.edu
GOLDSTEIN, Steven .... 973-353-5568. 306 D
steven.goldstein@rutgers.edu
GOLDSTEIN, Stuart .... 973-720-2110. 308 I
goldsteins@wpunj.edu
GOLDSTEIN, Wendy .... 907-834-1690... 11 B
wgoldstein@pwscc.edu
GOLDSTINE, Susan .... 240-895-4366. 218 A
sgoldstine@smcm.edu
GOLDWATER, Joanne, A 240-895-4207. 218 A
jagoldwater@smcm.edu
GOLDWIRE, Diana .... 706-880-8185. 128 A
dgoldwire@lagrange.edu
GOLEN, Harriet, S .... 215-670-9328. 425 J
hsgolen@peirce.edu
GOLEZ, Reno .... 415-282-7600... 27 L
renogolez@actcm.edu
GOLIAS, David, P .... 651-286-7446. 263 A
dpgolias@nwc.edu
GOLICH, Vicki .... 303-556-3040... 83 D
vgolich@msudenver.edu
GOLISCH, Paul .... 602-787-7789... 15 B
paul.golisch@paradisevalley.edu
GOLLADAY, Dennis .... 443-412-2475. 215 C
dgolladay@harford.edu
GOLLAHALLI, Anil .... 405-325-4124. 401 B
agollahalli@ou.edu
GOLLETTE, Tonya .... 251-442-2917..... 9 A
tgollette@umobile.edu
GOLLEY, Jessica .... 716-488-3022. 327 I
jessicagolley@jamestownbusinesscollege.edu
GOLMAN, Bridgett .... 803-327-8016. 449 J
BGolman@yorktech.edu
GOLOGOR, Ethan .... 718-270-4852. 319 A
ethan@mec.cuny.edu
GOLSHANI, Forouzan ..... 562-985-1512... 33 F
coe-dean@csulb.edu
GOLSON, Randy .... 254-442-5162. 468 I
randy.golson@cisco.edu
GOLTERMANN, John, M 310-287-4579... 52 F
golterjm@wlac.edu
GOLTSER, Zhanna .... 410-532-5735. 217 E
zgoltser@ndm.edu
GOLUB, Andrew .... 207-602-2319. 213 A
agolub@une.edu
GOLZ, Carolyn .... 847-735-5202. 150 B
golz@lakeforest.edu
GOMBERG, Barry, G .... 801-626-6240. 497 D
bgomberg@weber.edu
GOMBOSKY, Brenda, B .. 502-852-5037. 200 D
brenda.gombosky@louisville.edu
GOMES, Charles .... 718-982-3149. 317 E
charles.gomes@csi.cuny.edu
GOMES, Farrahmarie ...... 808-974-7664. 136 A
fmgomes@hawaii.edu
GOMES, Lyle .... 661-632-6105. 342 C
lyle.gomes@stonybrook.edu
GOMES, JR., Miguel ...... 508-531-1207. 229 D
mgomes@bridgew.edu
GOMES, Roxanne .... 401-874-2442. 440 D
roxanne@uri.edu
GOMES, Stacy .... 619-574-6909... 57 E
sgomes@pacificcollege.edu
GOMEZ, Aguilda .... 787-744-1060. 551 J
aguilda@mechtech.edu
GOMEZ, Alicia .... 956-872-5529. 480 I
agomez@southtexascollege.edu
GOMEZ, Angelo .... 541-737-4381. 406 A
angelo.gomez@oregonstate.edu
GOMEZ, Angelo .... 541-737-3556. 406 A
angelo.gomez@oregonstate.edu
GOMEZ, Bellegran .... 562-860-2451... 37 I
bgomez@cerritos.edu
GOMEZ, Beth .... 951-372-7157... 60 L
beth.gomez@norcocollege.edu
GOMEZ, David .... 718-368-5650. 318 E
dgomez@kbcc.cuny.edu
GOMEZ, Elba .... 559-244-5973... 68 H
elba.gomez@scccd.edu
GOMEZ, Elizabeth .... 213-252-5100... 26 A
GOMEZ, Fernando, C ..... 512-463-1808. 486 D
fernando.gomez@tsus.edu
GOMEZ, Gabe .... 505-984-6102. 311 H
gabe.gomez@sjcsf.edu
GOMEZ, Grace .... 787-279-1912. 550 B
ggomez@bayamon.inter.edu
GOMEZ, Gregorio .... 410-462-8539. 213 F
ggomez@bccc.edu
GOMEZ, Jaime .... 860-465-5293... 87 L
GOMEZ, Johanna .... 718-518-6556. 318 B
jgomez@hostos.cuny.edu
GOMEZ, Jose .... 323-343-3615... 34 A
jgomez22@cslanet.calstatela.edu
GOMEZ, Luis .... 215-951-1201. 420 B
gomez@lasalle.edu
GOMEZ, Milady .... 787-758-2525. 554 F
milady.gomez@upr.edu
GOMEZ, Robert .... 949-824-4645... 71 B
rgomez@uci.edu
GOMEZ, Robert .... 312-922-1884. 152 C
rgomez@maccormac.edu
GOMEZ-HEITZEBERG, Nan .... 661-395-4305... 49 N
ngomez@bakersfieldcollege.edu
GOMEZ-JOINS, Constanza .... 919-536-7200. 360 B
gomezc@durhamtech.edu
GOMILA, Sol, A .... 787-728-1515. 555 D
sgomila@sagrado.edu
GOMOLL, Brian .... 563-588-6343. 176 F
brian.gomoll@clarke.edu
GONDEK, Gretchen .... 712-274-6400. 183 G
gretchen.gondek@witcc.edu
GONG, Changzhen .... 651-631-0204. 253 D
tcmhealth@aol.com
GONG-GUY, Elizabeth .... 310-825-0768... 71 C
egongguy@sps.ucla.edu
GONGRE, Charles .... 409-984-6229. 486 H
charles.gongre@lamarpa.edu
GONLAG, Mari .... 864-644-5229. 446 I
mgonlag@swu.edu
GONSALVES-MCCABE, Kristi .... 303-458-4153... 84 M
kgonsalv@regis.edu
GONSOULIN, Sid .... 601-266-5767. 270 E
sidney.gonsoulin@usm.edu
GONTHIER, Sheri .... 603-271-6484. 296 C
sgonthier@ccsnh.edu
GONYA, Cindy, D .... 708-216-9949. 151 H
cgonya@lumc.edu
GONYEA, David .... 207-755-5251. 210 J
dgonyea@cmcc.edu
GONZÁLEZ, Angela .... 787-264-1912. 551 A
angela_gonzalez_mederos@intersg.edu
GONZÁLEZ, Samuel .... 787-738-2161. 554 C
GONZÁLEZ DE RESENDE, María, A .... 787-993-8872. 554 A
maria.gonzalez34@upr.edu
GONZÁLEZ-GONZÁLEZ, Orlando .... 787-993-0000. 553 G
orlando.gonzalez8@upr.edu

GONZÁLEZ-GONZÁLEZ, Orlando ... 787-993-8850. 554 A
orlando.gonzalez8@upr.edu
GONZALES, Adrian ... 760-744-1150... 58 D
adgonzales@palomar.edu
GONZALES, Adrian ... 760-773-7453... 40 F
agonzales@collegeofthedesert.edu
GONZALES, Adrian ... 760-773-2522... 40 F
agonzales@collegeofthedesert.edu
GONZALES, Al ... 623-845-3035... 14 M
al.gonzales@gcmail.maricopa.edu
GONZALES, Alfredo, M .. 616-395-7785. 244 A
gonzales@hope.edu
GONZALES, Ana ... 210-829-3937. 490 A
anagonza@uiwtx.edu
GONZALES, Carmen ... 505-428-1000. 311 J
carmen.gonzales@sfccc.edu
GONZALES, Casey ... 817-272-2099. 491 B
gonzales@uta.edu
GONZALES, Christina ... 303-492-8476... 85 L
christina.gonzales@colorado.edu
GONZALES, Dianna ... 209-954-5059... 63 C
dgonzales@deltacollege.edu
GONZALES, Gilbert ... 505-277-8125. 312 F
gonzgil@unm.edu
GONZALES, Heather ... 623-245-4600... 18 D
hgonzales@uti.edu
GONZALES, Hector ... 830-591-7281. 481 C
hegonzales@swtjc.edu
GONZALES, Jackie ... 951-343-4239... 30 H
jgonzale@calbpatist.edu
GONZALES, Jenni ... 520-494-5420... 12 P
jenni.gonzales@centralaz.edu
GONZALES, Joe ... 209-954-5139... 63 C
jgonzales@deltacollege.edu
GONZALES, JR., Joseph, M ... 312-329-4202. 153 E
joe.gonzales@moody.edu
GONZALES, Junius ... 915-747-5725. 492 A
jjxgonzales@utep.edu
GONZALES, Leticia ... 432-837-8193. 487 B
lgonzales@sulross.edu
GONZALES, Louis ... 432-335-6848. 477 M
lgonzales@odessa.edu
GONZALES, Mario ... 559-638-3641... 69 A
mario-gonzales@reedleycollege.edu
GONZALES, Mark ... 408-274-7900... 63 O
mark.gonzales@evc.edu
GONZALES, Mary, J ... 401-874-2101. 440 D
mjgonzales@mail.uri.edu
GONZALES, Mona ... 785-749-8448. 187 B
mona.gonzales@bie.edu
GONZALES, Oscar ... 713-718-7561. 473 C
oscar.gonzales@hccs.edu
GONZALES, Rhonda ... 719-549-2315... 80 K
rhonda.gonzales@colostate-pueblo.edu
GONZALES, Robert ... 719-549-2943... 80 K
robert.gonzales@colostate-pueblo.edu
GONZALES, Ron ... 505-454-5305. 309 L
rgonzales@luna.edu
GONZALES, Roxanne ... 303-458-1844... 84 M
rmgonzales@regis.edu
GONZALES, Rudy ... 337-521-8949. 203 I
rudy.gonzales@southlouisiana.edu
GONZALES, Samuel ... 210-458-4595. 492 C
sam.gonzales@utsa.edu
GONZALES, Sandra, M .. 602-944-3335... 11 D
sgonzales@aicag.edu
GONZALES, Steven ... 520-494-5213... 12 P
steven.gonzales@centralaz.edu
GONZALES, Veronica ... 956-665-5301. 492 B
gonzalesv@utpa.edu
GONZALES-MCKOSKY, Latricia ... 505-438-8884. 312 A
latricia@acupuncturecollege.edu
GONZALES-TAPIA, Sarah ... 626-914-8556... 38 K
sgonzales-tapia@citruscollege.edu
GONZALEZ, Alex ... 505-277-4792. 312 F
agonzale@unm.edu
GONZALEZ, Alexander ... 916-278-7737... 34 D
alexg@csus.edu
GONZALEZ, Amilcar ... 939-292-2223. 555 C
amilcar.gonzalez2@upr.edu
GONZALEZ, Anna ... 503-768-7110. 403 K
annag@lclark.edu
GONZALEZ, Beatriz ... 909-593-3511... 72 E
bgonzalez@laverne.edu
GONZALEZ, Belen ... 787-744-1060. 551 J
belengonzalez@mechtech.edu
GONZALEZ, Bethaida ... 315-443-3259. 347 C
bgonzale@syr.edu
GONZALEZ, Blanca ... 787-780-5134. 551 L
bgonzalez@nuc.edu
GONZALEZ, Blanca, M ... 787-250-1912. 550 E
bmgonzalez@metro.inter.edu
GONZALEZ, Carla ... 313-664-1533. 241 C
cgonzalez@collegeforcreativestudies.edu
GONZALEZ, Carmen ... 787-841-2000. 552 B
cgonzalez@pucpr.edu
GONZALEZ, Carolina, E . 973-290-4345. 300 F
cgonzalez01@cse.edu
GONZALEZ, Caroline ... 787-786-3030. 547 F
cagonzalez@ucb.edu.pr
GONZALEZ, Cheryl, N ... 904-620-2507. 116 B
cheryl.gonzalez@unf.edu
GONZALEZ, Chuck ... 209-667-3298... 35 B
cegonzalez@csustan.edu
GONZALEZ, Debra ... 939-292-8914. 555 C
debra.gonzalez1@upr.edu
GONZALEZ, Diana ... 515-242-6116. 175 G
GONZALEZ, Eladio ... 787-664-0353. 555 C
eladio.gonzalez1@upr.edu
GONZALEZ, Eleazar ... 956-721-5142. 475 F
elegon@laredo.edu
GONZALEZ, Elidine ... 787-891-0925. 549 K
egonzale@aguadilla.inter.edu
GONZALEZ, Elizabeth ... 787-761-0640. 553 F
GONZALEZ, Elma, D ... 936-261-2124. 482 F
edgonzalez@pvamu.edu
GONZALEZ, Esther ... 336-917-5579. 366 D
esther.gonzalez@salem.edu
GONZALEZ, Evelyn ... 787-844-9231. 555 A
evelyn.gonzalez2@upr.edu
GONZALEZ, Fernando ... 787-884-6000. 549 D
fgonzalez@icprjc.edu
GONZALEZ, Francisco ... 787-891-0925. 549 K
fgonzale@aguadilla.inter.edu
GONZALEZ, Gerardo ... 812-856-8001. 167 F
gonzalez@indiana.edu
GONZALEZ, Griselda ... 212-217-3363. 324 C
griselda_gonzalez@fitnyc.edu
GONZALEZ, Griselda ... 212-217-4000. 324 C
griselda_gonzalez@fitnyc.edu
GONZALEZ, Hector ... 609-894-9311. 299 I
hgonzale@bcc.edu
GONZALEZ, Herman ... 623-845-3562... 14 M
herman.gonzalez@gcmail.maricopa.edu
GONZALEZ, Herman ... 602-787-6601... 15 B
herman.gonzalez@paradisevalley.edu
GONZALEZ, J, E ... 727-873-4716. 116 D
jegon@usfsp.edu
GONZALEZ, Jaime ... 787-620-2040. 547 C
trodriguez@aupr.edu
GONZALEZ, Jean ... 714-867-5009... 66 J
GONZALEZ, Jeffery ... 305-348-2731. 115 B
jeff@fiu.edu
GONZALEZ, Jemilis ... 787-882-2065. 553 A
recursoshumanos@unitecpr.net
GONZALEZ, Jorge ... 323-259-2634... 56 I
jgonzale@oxy.edu
GONZALEZ, Jose ... 914-323-5445. 330 B
jose.gonzalez@mville.edu
GONZALEZ, Judith ... 787-766-1717. 552 J
jugonzalez@suagm.edu
GONZALEZ, Karen ... 787-766-1717. 552 J
um_kgonzalez@suagm.edu
GONZALEZ, Linda ... 915-831-2566. 472 B
lgonz265@epcc.edu
GONZALEZ, Lizbeth ... 603-882-6923. 296 B
lgonzalez@ccsnh.edu
GONZALEZ, Lori, S ... 828-262-2070. 367 A
gonzalezls@appstate.edu
GONZALEZ, Luis ... 787-815-0000. 553 I
luis.gonzalez38@upr.edu
GONZALEZ, Luis ... 724-357-2330. 428 F
Luis.Gonzalez@iup.edu
GONZALEZ, Luz ... 559-278-3013... 33 D
luz_gonzalez@csufresno.edu
GONZALEZ, Mara ... 305-220-4120. 111 E
GONZALEZ, Mari, G ... 787-743-7979. 552 I
mggonzalez@suagm.edu
GONZALEZ, Maria ... 305-273-4499. 100 H
registrar@cbt.edu
GONZALEZ, Marilyn ... 787-882-2065. 553 A
secretaria_ejecutiva@unitecpr.net
GONZALEZ, Marisol ... 787-264-1912. 551 A
margonza@sg.inter.edu
GONZALEZ, Mary ... 361-593-2494. 484 A
kamlp00@tamuk.edu
GONZALEZ, Mauricio ... 904-620-2600. 116 B
mgonzale@unf.edu
GONZALEZ, Miguel ... 956-665-3510. 492 B
gonzalezma@utpa.edu
GONZALEZ, Monica, D .. 787-723-4481. 548 A
mgonzalez@ceaprc.edu
GONZALEZ, Nichole ... 716-375-2572. 338 E
ngonzalez@sbu.edu
GONZALEZ, Noelia ... 209-667-3337... 35 B
ngonzalez@csustan.edu
GONZALEZ, Patricia ... 787-250-1912. 550 E
pgonzalez@metro.inter.edu
GONZALEZ, Raul, D ... 818-947-2606... 52 E
gonzalrd@lavc.edu
GONZALEZ, Reina, M ... 787-840-8108. 555 A
reina.gonzalez@upr.edu
GONZALEZ, Reinaldo ... 787-744-8519. 548 L
rgonzalez@ediccollege.edu
GONZALEZ, Reyes ... 414-256-1228. 535 A
gonzaler@mtmary.edu
GONZALEZ, Roberto ... 310-434-4912... 65 A
gonzalez_roberto@smc.edu
GONZALEZ, Rocelia, T ... 904-620-2870. 116 B
rrgonz@unf.edu
GONZALEZ, Rosa ... 787-891-0925. 549 K
rgonzale@aguadilla.inter.edu
GONZALEZ, Ruben, L ... 516-876-3275. 343 D
gonzalezr@oldwestbury.edu
GONZALEZ, Ruth ... 860-738-6315... 89 C
rgonzalez@nwcc.commnet.edu
GONZALEZ, Sandra ... 787-882-2065. 553 A
administracion_empresas@unitecpr.net
GONZALEZ, Sarai ... 787-746-1400. 549 B
sgonzalez@huertas.edu
GONZALEZ, Saraliz ... 787-857-3600. 550 A
sgonzalez@br.inter.edu
GONZALEZ, Sergio, M ... 305-284-4111. 118 F
smgonzalez@miami.edu
GONZALEZ, Sophia ... 210-486-2247. 465 B
fklein@alamo.edu
GONZALEZ, Stacy ... 515-244-2209. 338 C
gonzas@sage.edu
GONZALEZ, Steven ... 602-286-8008... 14 L
steven.gonalez@gatewaycc.edu
GONZALEZ, Thomasa ... 609-652-4724. 305 C
t.gonzalez@stockton.edu
GONZALEZ, Tina ... 212-799-5000. 328 B
GONZALEZ, Urania ... 787-720-1022. 547 E
Administracion@atlanticcollege.edu
GONZALEZ, Virginia ... 787-743-7979. 552 I
ut_vgonzalez@suagm.edu
GONZALEZ, Yanira ... 787-891-0925. 549 K
ygonzalez@aguadilla.inter.edu
GONZALEZ-BOHNERT, Jennifer ... 727-873-4808. 116 D
gonzalezbohn@usfsp.edu
GONZALEZ-DE JESUS, Naydeen ... 201-612-5467. 299 C
ngonzalezdejesus@bergen.edu
GONZALEZ DE SCOLLARD, Edith ... 212-817-7520. 317 F
egonzalez@gc.cuny.edu
GONZALEZ-GENERALS, Joann ... 973-618-3589. 300 A
jgonzalez@caldwell.edu
GONZALEZ-MENDEZ, Ricardo, C ... 787-758-2525. 554 F
ricardo.gonzalez7@upr.edu
GONZALEZ-RODRIGUEZ, Mariamelia ... 787-480-2351. 548 G
GONZALEZ-SCARANO, Francisco ... 210-567-4432. 493 A
scarano@uthscsa.edu
GOOCH, Cheryl Renee ... 484-365-7664. 422 D
cgooch@lincoln.edu
GOOCH, Cynthia ... 402-457-2649. 290 G
cgooch@mccneb.edu
GOOCH, Gene ... 254-299-8679. 476 D
ggooch@mclennan.edu
GOOCH, Janet ... 660-785-4383. 282 L
jquinzek@truman.edu
GOOD, Barry ... 406-243-7811. 286 H
barry.good@umontana.edu
GOOD, Claire ... 859-622-1721. 193 P
claire.good@eku.edu
GOOD, Glenn ... 352-392-3261. 116 A
ggood@coe.ufl.edu
GOOD, Jennifer ... 251-380-2278... 7 D
jgood@shc.edu
GOOD, Joseph, C ... 843-792-4063. 445 B
goodj@musc.edu
GOOD, Kathy ... 864-596-9082. 443 D
kathy.good@converse.edu
GOOD, Laura, E ... 330-823-6050. 391 E
goodle@mountunion.edu
GOOD, Lee Anna ... 432-552-2800. 493 D
good_l@utpb.edu
GOOD, Michael, L ... 352-273-7500. 116 A
mgood@ufl.edu
GOOD, Niki ... 757-873-1111. 504 J
GOOD, Rhonda ... 717-337-6015. 417 B
rgood@gettysburg.edu
GOOD, Rhonda, L ... 717-766-2511. 423 L
rgood@messiah.edu
GOOD, William ... 309-854-1831. 140 E
goodb@bhc.edu
GOOD LUCK, Aldean ... 406-638-3118. 286 D
goodluckav@lbhc.edu
GOODALE, Brian ... 518-587-2100. 346 A
brian.goodale@esc.edu
GOODARZI, Shirin, M ... 410-777-2148. 213 D
smgoodarzi@aacc.edu
GOODCUFF, Esther ... 516-877-3681. 313 A
goodcuff@adelphi.edu
GOODE, Debbie ... 580-581-2255. 394 G
debbieg@cameron.edu
GOODE, Gail ... 513-772-9888. 386 C
gail.goode@omw.edu
GOODE, Greg, J ... 812-237-7778. 167 A
greg.goode@indstate.edu
GOODE, Gregg, R ... 785-309-3100. 190 E
gregg.goode@salinatech.edu
GOODE, Mark ... 714-432-5898... 39 K
mgoode@occ.cccd.edu
GOODE, Tammy ... 423-585-6845. 462 A
tammy.goode@ws.edu
GOODE, Tracy ... 229-317-6929. 124 A
tracy.goode@darton.edu
GOODE, Tyler ... 828-339-4000. 364 B
tylerg@southwesterncc.edu
GOODELL-LACKEY, Shirley, J ... 802-654-2586. 500 B
sgoodell-lackey@smcvt.edu
GOODEN, Charles, H ... 314-340-5030. 275 A
goodenc@hssu.edu
GOODEN, Winston, E ... 626-584-5501... 45 E
gooden@fuller.edu
GOODER, Kellee ... 307-532-8336. 542 a
kellee.gooder@ewc.wy.edu
GOODFELLOW, Sandy ... 615-844-5280. 464 E
alex@welch.edu
GOODGAME, Henry ... 404-215-2658. 129 D
hgoodgame@morehouse.edu
GOODGE, Samuel ... 304-829-7905. 526 D
sgoodge@bethanywv.edu
GOODHEART, Harriet, K . 610-660-1532. 432 E
hgoodhea@sju.edu
GOODHUE, Bill ... 607-436-2532. 343 E
goodhucw@oneonta.edu
GOODHUE LYNCH, Mary ... 508-588-9100. 232 A
GOODIN, Ruth ... 925-439-2181... 42 A
rgoodin@losmedanos.edu
GOODING, Betsy ... 903-434-8137. 477 J
bgooding@ntcc.edu
GOODING, Mary, B ... 229-333-7444. 134 B
mbgooding@valdosta.edu
GOODLING, Barry, G ... 717-796-5064. 423 L
bgoodlin@messiah.edu
GOODLING, Eileen, J ... 716-338-1025. 327 J
eileengoodling@mail.sunyjcc.edu
GOODLIVE, Kathy ... 707-476-4151... 40 H
kathy-goodlive@redwoods.edu
GOODMAN, Brent ... 619-849-2371... 59 L
brentgoodman@pointloma.edu
GOODMAN, Brittney, G .. 218-477-2923. 259 H
brittney.goodman@mnstate.edu
GOODMAN, Catie ... 850-201-8281. 117 D
goodmanc@tcc.fl.edu
GOODMAN, Clay ... 623-935-8456... 14 K
clay.goodman@estrellamountain.edu
GOODMAN, Debbie ... 229-225-3978. 132 D
dgoodman@southwestgatech.edu
GOODMAN, Grayson ... 407-303-1631... 97 H
grayson.goodman@adu.edu
GOODMAN, Guy ... 309-694-8970. 146 E
ggoodman@icc.edu
GOODMAN, Jacque ... 641-844-5640. 179 H
Jacque.Goodman@iavalley.edu
GOODMAN, Jacque ... 641-844-7106. 179 J
jacque.goodman@iavalley.edu
GOODMAN, Jacqueline, K ... 315-267-2116. 344 C
goodmajk@potsdam.edu
GOODMAN, James ... 808-455-0228. 137 A
goodmanj@hawaii.edu
GOODMAN, Jeremy ... 781-292-2373. 226 G
jeremy.goodman@olin.edu
GOODMAN, Jerry, C ... 713-798-7234. 467 F
jgoodman@bcm.edu
GOODMAN, Julie ... 308-432-6487. 291 D
jgoodman@csc.edu
GOODMAN, Larry, J ... 312-942-7073. 157 G
larry_j_goodman@rush.edu
GOODMAN, Lena, C ... 920-433-6630. 531 L
lena.goodman@bellincollege.edu
GOODMAN, Marc, P ... 310-506-4670... 58 H
marc.goodman@pepperdine.edu
GOODMAN, Mark ... 914-632-5400. 331 K
mgoodman@monroecollege.edu
GOODMAN, Michael ... 504-865-5725. 207 C
mgoodman@tulane.edu
GOODMAN, Patricia ... 859-442-1173. 195 B
patricia.goodman@kctcs.edu
GOODMAN, Patricia ... 603-882-6923. 296 B
pgoodman@ccsnh.edu
GOODMAN, Patricia ... 254-298-8321. 482 C
patricia.goodman@templejc.edu
GOODMAN, Rachel ... 641-472-7000. 180 N
rgoodman@mum.edu
GOODMAN, Richard, H .. 503-494-5078. 405 I
goodmanr@ohsu.edu
GOODMAN, Robert, M ... 848-932-3600. 306 B
execdean@cook.rutgers.edu
GOODMAN, Sharon ... 910-410-1734. 362 I
sharong@richmondcc.edu
GOODMAN, Sylvia ... 405-789-6400. 399 K
sgoodman@snu.edu
GOODMAN, Timothy, D . 478-289-2034. 124 C
goodman@ega.edu

GOODMAN, Veronica 803-535-5540. 442 B vgoodman@claflin.edu
GOODMAN, Wille 404-527-5735. 127 I sfgoodman@itc.edu
GOODNER, Jason 229-732-5929. 120 D jasongoodner@andrewcollege.edu
GOODNOUGH, Doug 517-264-7141. 250 B dgoodnou@sienaheights.edu
GOODNOW, Jean 989-686-9201. 242 C jeangoodnow@delta.edu
GOODRICH, Curtis Jason 409-880-8305. 486 F jason.goodrich@lamar.edu
GOODRICH, Deborah 607-587-3945. 345 D goodridj@alfredstate.edu
GOODRICH, James, A 323-343-2800... 34 A jgoodri7@calstatela.edu
GOODRICH, Joy, P 804-354-5210. 515 F jgoodrich@vuu.edu
GOODRICH, Larry 972-825-4820. 481 F lgoodrich@sagu.edu
GOODRICH, Mark 415-338-2723... 35 E goodrich@sfsu.edu
GOODRICH PELLETIER, Monica 508-213-2108. 235 E monica.goodrich-pelletier@nichols.edu
GOODRUM, OP, Mary Cecilia 615-297-7545. 452 J srmcecilia@aquinascollege.edu
GOODSON, Kenneth 903-434-8260. 477 J kgoodson@ntcc.edu
GOODSTEIN, Eban 845-758-7067. 314 D ebangood@bard.edu
GOODSTEIN, Richard, E .. 864-656-3084. 442 C regst@clemson.edu
GOODWIN, Alan 805-493-3573... 31 H agoodwin@clunet.edu
GOODWIN, Amie, M 978-542-6241. 230 E agoodwin@salemstate.edu
GOODWIN, Ann 860-685-2200... 92 H agoodwin@wesleyan.edu
GOODWIN, Anna 540-362-6223. 505 G agoodwin@hollins.edu
GOODWIN, Candace 773-929-8500. 144 B cgoodwin@devry.edu
GOODWIN, Cheryl 206-876-6100. 523 D cgoodwin@theseattleschool.edu
GOODWIN, Christy 251-578-1313.... 6 D cgoodwin@rstc.edu
GOODWIN, Cindi, J 336-633-4475. 362 H cjgoodwin@randolph.edu
GOODWIN, Dale 509-313-6133. 520 A goodwin@gonzaga.edu
GOODWIN, Darrell 206-296-6060. 523 E goodwind@seattleu.edu
GOODWIN, David 205-726-2337.... 6 F dbgoodwi@samford.edu
GOODWIN, David 505-583-1074. 236 D dgoodwin@salter.edu
GOODWIN, Erika, A 937-382-6661. 393 B erika_goodwin@wilmington.edu
GOODWIN, Jennifer 516-299-3759. 329 C jennifer.goodwin@liu.edu
GOODWIN, Jerome 919-530-6739. 368 A jgoodwin@nccu.edu
GOODWIN, Ken 971-722-4980. 407 D kgoodwin@pcc.edu
GOODWIN, Kristine, C ... 401-865-2144. 439 E kgoodwi2@providence.edu
GOODWIN, Larry 218-723-6033. 254 K lgoodwin@css.edu
GOODWIN, Laura 303-556-2279... 86 A laura.goodwin@ucdenver.edu
GOODWIN, Laura 303-315-2105... 86 A laura.goodwin@ucdenver.edu
GOODWIN, LouAnn 989-386-6622. 247 B lrgoodwin@midmich.edu
GOODWIN, Mark 972-721-4068. 488 F mgoodwin@udallas.edu
GOODWIN, Mary Ann 509-533-3820. 518 F maryann.goodwin@spokanefalls.edu
GOODWIN, Michael 802-447-6343. 500 D mgoodwin@svc.edu
GOODWIN, Michelle 301-934-7635. 214 D michellg@csmd.edu
GOODWIN, Mike 541-737-3288. 406 A mike.goodwin@oregonstate.edu
GOODWIN, Naomi 310-243-3303... 33 B ngoodwin@csudh.edu
GOODWIN, Stephen, D .. 859-846-5782. 197 I sgoodwin@midway.edu
GOODWIN, Steve 413-545-2766. 228 F sgoodwin@cns.umass.edu
GOODWIN, Virginia 317-543-3672. 171 A vgoodwin@martin.edu
GOODWIN, Wayne 601-979-2522. 267 E wayne.goodwin@jsums.edu
GOODWIN, Wendell, B .. 919-866-5148. 364 G wbgoodwin@waketech.edu
GOODWIN, Whittington . 281-649-3238. 473 B wgoodwin@hbu.edu
GOODWIN-GOMEZ, Gale 401-456-8005. 439 F ggoodwin@ric.edu
GOODYEAR, Anne 207-798-4352. 209 H agoodyea@bowdoin.edu
GOODYEAR, Frank 207-725-3673. 209 H fgoodyea@bowdoin.edu
GOODYEAR, Jack 214-333-5238. 470 D jackg@dbu.edu
GOOKIN, Kathleen 502-410-6200. 194 B kgookin@galencollege.edu
GOOLSBY, Edwin, G 727-816-3264. 110 E goolsbe@phcc.edu
GOON, Arthur 215-637-7700. 418 G
GOOR, Mark 909-593-3511... 72 E mgoor@laverne.edu
GOORIS, Daniel 773-244-5222. 154 G dgooris@northpark.edu
GOOS, Karen 816-604-2326. 277 F karen.goos@mcckc.edu
GOOSBY, Marlayna 850-729-4974. 109 I goosbym@nwfsc.edu
GOOSEN, Rebecca 281-459-7667. 479 G rebecca.goosen@sjcd.edu
GOPLIN, Scott 701-252-3467. 373 D
GOPP, Jeff 408-848-4705... 45 F jgopp@gavilan.edu
GORA, Jo Ann, M 765-285-5555. 164 B president@bsu.edu
GORAB, Beth 973-618-3204. 300 A bgorab@caldwell.edu
GORAIEB, Janis, A 818-779-8040... 50 A jgoraieb@kingsuniversity.edu
GORBANDT, Donald, A .. 859-572-5487. 198 I gorbandtd@nku.edu
GORBANDT, Melissa 859-572-5744. 198 I gorbandt@nku.edu
GORBY, Lesley 605-331-6611. 452 D lesley.gorby@usiouxfalls.edu
GORDIEN CASE, Lori, K 909-593-3511... 72 E lgordien@laverne.edu
GORDIER, Paige 906-635-2749. 245 G pgordier@lssu.edu
GORDIN, Sandy 864-596-9029. 443 D sandy.gordin@converse.edu
GORDON, Andrea 603-542-7744. 296 D agordon@ccsnh.edu
GORDON, Andrew, R 212-998-1212. 334 D andrew.gordon.hr@nyu.edu
GORDON, Carl 409-933-8246. 469 E cgordon@com.edu
GORDON, Charles, J 201-684-7091. 305 A cgordon7@ramapo.edu
GORDON, Daniel, L 413-577-3902. 228 F dean@honors.umass.edu
GORDON, David 810-237-6503. 251 E dgordon@umich.edu
GORDON, David, E 804-257-5783. 515 F degordon@vuu.edu
GORDON, David, F 585-245-5531. 343 C gordon@geneseo.edu
GORDON, Debra 404-297-9522. 126 A gordond@gptc.edu
GORDON, Donette 941-907-2262. 103 C dogordon@evergladesuniversity.edu
GORDON, Elaine 251-580-2112.... 4 L elaine.gordon@faulknerstate.edu
GORDON, Eloisa 787-766-1717. 552 J elgordon@suagm.edu
GORDON, Fannie 732-906-2546. 303 B FGordon@middlesexcc.edu
GORDON, Glenda 541-684-7225. 405 C ggordon@nwcu.edu
GORDON, Howard 315-312-2213. 344 A howard.gordon@oswego.edu
GORDON, III, James, D 801-422-4919. 495 D jim_gordon@byu.edu
GORDON, Jan, M 502-447-1000. 199 E jgordon@spencerian.edu
GORDON, Jeffrey 518-262-5486. 313 D gordonj@mail.amc.edu
GORDON, Jessica 989-386-6622. 247 B jmgordon@midmich.edu
GORDON, Joan 415-503-6229... 62 H jgordon@sfcm.edu
GORDON, Joel 707-527-4671... 65 B jgordon@santarosa.edu
GORDON, Joseph, W 203-432-2900... 93 A joseph.gordon@yale.edu
GORDON, Kevin 727-344-8062. 112 E gordon.kevin@spcollege.edu
GORDON, Lynn 602-429-4921... 16 O lgordon@ps.edu
GORDON, Mark 402-494-2311. 290 O mgordon@thenicc.edu
GORDON, Mark, C 419-783-2300. 379 C mgordon@defiance.edu
GORDON, Mary, J 785-827-5541. 188 C mary.gordon@kwu.edu
GORDON, Melissa 706-646-6188. 132 B mgordon@sctech.edu
GORDON, Monica 692-625-3291. 546 F cmiregistrar@ntamar.net
GORDON, Myra, E 785-532-6276. 188 A mygordon@ksu.edu
GORDON, Paul 573-876-7106. 282 H pgordon@stephens.edu
GORDON, Richard 313-593-5333. 251 D rfgordon@umich.edu
GORDON, Robert 617-587-5631. 234 H gordonb@neco.edu
GORDON, Robert, W 517-264-7152. 250 B rgordon@sienaheights.edu
GORDON, Ronald 937-328-7819. 377 A gordonr@clarkstate.edu
GORDON, Sally 814-886-6395. 424 G SGordon@mtaloy.edu
GORDON, Samantha 954-308-2218... 98 G sagordon@aii.edu
GORDON, Sandra 718-473-8701. 319 B sgordon@citytech.cuny.edu
GORDON, Saundra, E 812-941-2394. 168 F gordonse@ius.edu
GORDON, Scott, A 812-464-1701. 174 D sgordon@usi.edu
GORDON, Scott, S 270-745-8831. 200 G scott.gordon@wku.edu
GORDON, Steve 614-292-4132. 386 E sgordon@osc.edu
GORDON, T. Scott 724-458-3352. 417 E stgordon@gcc.edu
GORDON, Timothy 414-229-4632. 537 A gordont@uwm.edu
GORDON, Tonia, J 814-886-6390. 424 G tgordon@mtaloy.edu
GORDON, Wade 218-733-7656. 259 A w.gordon@lsc.edu
GORDY, Reggie 334-291-4947..... 2 H reggie.gordy@cv.edu
GORDY-WATKINS, Anita 918-293-5156. 398 B anita.gordy_watkins@okstate.edu
GORDZICA, Theresa, K .. 785-864-4868. 190 L tgordzica@ku.edu
GORE, Erin, S 510-642-5737... 70 I esgore@berkeley.edu
GORE, Frederick, S 863-667-5729. 113 P fsgore@seu.edu
GORE, James, A 813-257-3095. 118 L jgore@ut.edu
GORE, Mike 301-314-0415. 219 B mgore@ubcmail.umd.edu
GORE, Paul, A 801-581-3286. 496 Q paul.gore@utah.edu
GORE, Vennie 517-355-7457. 246 H gore@msu.edu
GOREHAM, Beth 617-369-3684. 236 F egoreham@mfa.org
GORES, Connie, J 507-537-6272. 261 F President@smsu.edu
GORES, Greg 507-538-5027. 254 F gores.greg@mayo.edu
GORES, Julie, C 608-246-6633. 540 C jgores@madisoncollege.edu
GORHAM, James, C 757-569-6769. 513 E jgorham@pdc.edu
GORIN, Beth 908-709-7039. 308 B gorin@ucc.edu
GORINI, Cathy 641-472-1161. 180 N dof@mum.edu
GORINSHTEYN, Dasha ... 718-368-4975. 318 E dasha.gorinshteyn@kbcc.cuny.edu
GORKA, Barbara, C 215-898-1651. 435 B bgorka@pobox.upenn.edu
GORKA, Gary 415-482-3524... 42 J gary.gorka@dominican.edu
GORLAND, Gary 206-934-4585. 522 I gary.gorland@seattlecolleges.edu
GORMAN, Bonnie 906-487-2212. 247 A
GORMAN, Deb 920-996-2813. 539 K gorman@fvtc.edu
GORMAN, Joseph 610-558-5504. 424 I gormanj@neumann.edu
GORMAN, Kimberly 828-227-7469. 369 E ksgorman@wcu.edu
GORMAN, Lawrence, J ... 312-939-0111. 144 D larry@eastwest.edu
GORMAN, Leah 903-988-7521. 475 E lgorman@kilgore.edu
GORMAN, Mary 646-312-3315. 316 J Mary.Gorman@baruch.cuny.edu
GORMAN, Raymond, F .. 513-529-1799. 384 G gormanrf@miamioh.edu
GORMAN, Robin 724-357-2410. 428 F rgorman@iup.edu
GORMAN, Susan 443-334-2279. 218 E sgorman@stevenson.edu
GORMAN, Susan, L 617-558-1788. 235 C sgorman@nesa.edu
GORMAN, Tom 620-223-2700. 186 G tomg@fortscott.edu
GORMAN, Wil 573-651-2297. 282 B wgorman@semo.edu
GORMAN, William, P 617-989-4147. 237 G gormanb@wit.edu
GORMAN, Yolanda, J 818-386-5650... 59 E ygorman@pgi.edu
GORMICAN, Mary Ellen . 920-923-8725. 534 A mgormican@marianuniversity.edu
GORMLEY, Christina, L .. 717-337-6611. 417 B cgormley@gettysburg.edu
GORMLEY, Eloise 203-932-7449... 92 E egormley@newhaven.edu
GORMLEY, Jack 718-862-7944. 329 M jack.gormley@manhattan.edu
GORMLEY, Ken 412-396-6281. 415 F gormley@duq.edu
GORNE, Ivan 253-680-7005. 516 L igorne@bates.ctc.edu
GORNEAULT, Gregg 860-701-5043... 90 G gorneault_g@mitchell.edu
GORNEY, Linda 516-299-3256. 329 C linda.gorney@liu.edu
GORNICK, Frank, P 559-934-2107... 75 G frankgornick@whccd.edu
GORNTO, Mary, M 910-962-3626. 369 C gorntom@uncw.edu
GORR, Alan 630-829-6566. 140 B agorr@ben.edu
GORR, Nathan 612-330-1390. 253 H gorr@augsburg.edu
GORRELL, Cathy 303-458-4117... 84 M cgorrell@regis.edu
GORRELL, John 304-424-8269. 530 E john.gorrell@wvup.edu
GORRELL, Renee 314-454-8171. 274 G rgorrell@bjc.org
GORRELL, Victoria 970-351-1886... 86 C victoria.gorrell@unco.edu
GORRILLA, Adele, N 740-587-8646. 379 D gorrilla@denison.edu
GORSKI, Holly 253-964-6519. 522 C hgorski@pierce.ctc.edu
GORSLINE, Denise, M ... 218-477-4623. 259 H gorsline@mnstate.edu
GORT, Amy 612-330-1041. 253 H gort@augsburg.edu
GORT, Karla 336-917-5595. 366 D karla.gort@salem.edu
GORTON, Holly 240-895-4204. 218 A hlgorton@smcm.edu
GORTON, Holly, J 231-995-1012. 248 B hgorton@nmc.edu
GORUD, Mary, E 715-833-6250. 539 J mgorud@cvtc.edu
GORZ, Christine 312-329-2016. 153 E christine.gorz@moody.edu
GOSCH, Judy 865-539-7233. 461 D jagosch@pstcc.edu
GOSDECK, David, M 507-354-8221. 256 M gosdecdm@mlc-wels.edu
GOSE, Pilar 831-582-3595... 34 B pgose@csumb.edu
GOSLIN, Elaine 309-694-5282. 146 E elaine.goslin@icc.edu
GOSNELL, Kelly 202-884-9401... 96 G gosnellk@trinitydc.edu
GOSNELL, Victor 434-947-8138. 508 D vgosnell@randolphcollege.edu
GOSPODARCZYK, Tom .. 715-346-3386. 538 A Tom.Gospodarczyk@uwsp.edu
GOSS, Barbara 205-853-1200..... 5 B bgoss@jeffstateonline.com
GOSS, Christopher 617-353-2288. 224 D cgoss@bu.edu
GOSS, David 828-227-7170. 369 E dgoss@wcu.edu
GOSS, David 828-227-7127. 369 E dgoss@wcu.edu
GOSS, Jonathan, D 315-268-2290. 320 A jgoss@clarkson.edu
GOSS, Leah 225-308-4410. 202 G lgoss@lctcs.edu
GOSS, Marion 845-687-5075. 348 H gossm@sunyulster.edu
GOSS, Nathan, R 770-534-6162. 122 A ngoss@brenau.edu
GOSS, Ronald 541-956-7119. 407 F rgoss@roguecc.edu
GOSSELIN, Grant, M 781-239-5250. 222 D ggosselin@babson.edu
GOSSELIN, Karen 603-448-2445. 297 A kgosselin@lebanoncollege.edu
GOSSELIN, Marc 207-755-5261. 210 J mgosselin@cmcc.edu
GOSSEN, Douglas 920-693-1221. 540 B doug.gossen@gotoltc.edu
GOSSEN, Ronald, H 314-516-5776. 283 E ron@umsl.edu
GOSSEN, Tim 507-457-1409. 264 A tgossen@smumn.edu
GOSSETT, Angie 303-245-4797... 83 F agossett@naropa.edu

GOSSETT, Charles ... 916-278-6331 ... 34 D
gossettc@csus.edu
GOSWAMI, Jaya ... 361-593-4411. 484 A
jaya.goswami@tamuk.edu
GOSWAMI, Utpal ... 816-604-3044. 277 G
utpal.goswami@mcckc.edu
GOSWICK, Barbara ... 501-686-2500 ... 23 H
bgoswic@uasys.edu
GOSZ, Michael ... 312-567-3198. 147 F
gosz@iit.edu
GOTANDA, John ... 610-519-7005. 436 F
gotanda@law.villanova.edu
GOTHAM, Kerry ... 585-395-2068. 342 F
kgotham@brockport.edu
GOTHARD, Mathew, J ... 303-963-3223 ... 79 C
mgothard@ccu.edu
GOTLIEB, Peter, M ... 201-761-6412. 306 L
pgotlieb@saintpeters.edu
GOTSCH, Ken ... 312-369-7215. 143 D
kgotsch@colum.edu
GOTSCHALL, Matt, R ... 402-562-1211. 288 I
mgotschall@cccneb.edu
GOTSCHALL, Nichole ... 251-981-3771 ... 2 I
nichole.gotschall@columbiasouthern.edu
GOTSHALL, Kathy ... 812-535-5162. 172 F
kgotshal@smwc.edu
GOTTDIENER, Yitzchok .. 718-941-8000. 331 C
GOTTFREDSON,
Michael, R ... 541-346-3036. 406 D
pres@uoregon.edu
GOTTFRIED, Bradley ... 301-934-7625. 214 D
bgottfried@csmd.edu
GOTTFRIED, Randy ... 406-243-2857. 286 H
randy.gottfried@umontana.edu
GOTTLIEB, Jane ... 212-799-5000. 328 B
GOTTLIEB, Rachelle ... 904-620-2903. 116 B
r.gottlieb@unf.edu
GOTTLIEB, Tracy, T ... 973-761-9074. 307 C
tracy.gottlieb@shu.edu
GOTTSCHALK, Glenn, F . 410-293-1911. 545 J
gotts@usna.edu
GOTTSCHALK, Sandy ... 785-623-6155. 189 F
sgottschalk@ncktc.edu
GOTTULA, Todd ... 308-865-8454. 292 H
GOTZON, Mary, A ... 610-282-1100. 414 F
mary.gotzon@desales.edu
GOUDEAU, Arthur ... 281-487-1170. 484 H
agoudeau@txchiro.edu
GOUDEAU, LaTasha ... 713-221-8162. 489 D
goudeaul@uhd.edu
GOUGH, Annette ... 732-571-3402. 303 C
gough@monmouth.edu
GOUGH, Christopher ... 203-332-5022 ... 88 F
cgough@hcc.commnet.edu
GOUGH, Darby ... 816-501-3660. 271 H
darby.gough@avila.edu
GOUGH, Paul ... 605-773-3455. 451 E
paul.gough@sdbor.edu
GOUGH, Richard ... 910-695-3703. 363 F
goughr@sandhills.edu
GOUIN, Dean ... 303-846-1700 ... 87 A
GOUKER, Dan ... 702-651-4163. 294 E
dan.gouker@csn.edu
GOUKER, Toby ... 301-654-7267. 218 C
GOULD, Amanda ... 413-565-1000. 222 F
agould@baypath.edu
GOULD, Bryan ... 360-867-6170. 519 J
gouldb@evergreen.edu
GOULD, Holly ... 617-369-4041. 236 F
hgould@smfa.edu
GOULD, Ingrid ... 773-782-8846. 161 B
i-gould@uchicago.edu
GOULD, Jerry ... 757-826-1883. 502 G
GOULD, Jessica ... 617-730-7091. 235 D
jessica.gould@newbury.edu
GOULD, Karen, L ... 718-951-5671. 317 C
bcpresident@brooklyn.cuny.edu
GOULD, Larry ... 928-317-6475 ... 16 C
larry.gould@nau.edu
GOULD, Lawrence, V ... 785-628-4241. 186 F
lgould@fhsu.edu
GOULD, Mark ... 978-837-5072. 234 A
gouldm@merrimack.edu
GOULD, Robert, J ... 802-287-8369. 499 D
gouldr@greenmtn.edu
GOULD, Thomas, E ... 919-536-7200. 360 B
gouldt@durhamtech.edu
GOULDING, Laurel ... 701-662-1513. 372 D
laurel.goulding@lrsc.edu
GOULDING, Ruth ... 619-239-0391 ... 36 D
rgoulding@cwsl.edu
GOULET, Camille, A ... 213-891-2188 ... 51 E
gouletca@laccd.edu
GOULET, Richard ... 978-556-3981. 232 E
rgoulet@necc.mass.edu
GOULET, Stephen, P ... 508-793-7598. 225 A
sgoulet@clarku.edu
GOULETTE, Thomas ... 603-524-3207. 295 L
tgoulette@ccsnh.edu
GOUNARD, Jean, F ... 716-878-5331. 343 A
gounarjf@buffalostate.edu

GOUNDIE, Tedd ... 207-786-6219. 209 F
tgoundie@bates.edu
GOUPIL, Sharon ... 951-781-2727 ... 61 C
srgoupil@sagecollege.edu
GOURD, David ... 206-934-4349. 522 J
david.gourd@seattlecolleges.edu
GOURDINE, Raji ... 334-876-9292 ... 4 A
rgourdine@wccs.edu
GOURJI, Konstantin ... 650-685-6616 ... 46 F
GOURLEY, Kristin ... 865-981-8194. 456 D
kristin.gourley@maryvillecollege.edu
GOURLEY, Pamela, L ... 276-944-6122. 504 H
pgourley@ehc.edu
GOURNEAU, Haven ... 406-768-6329. 286 C
hgourneau@fpcc.edu
GOUSE, Richard, I ... 401-739-5000. 439 D
GOUSE, Valerie ... 856-691-8600. 301 A
vgouse@cccnj.edu
GOUSHA, Sean ... 858-513-9240. 175 F
sean.gousha@ashford.edu
GOUTTIERRE,
Thomas, E ... 402-554-2376. 293 A
teg@unomaha.edu
GOVAN, Shawn, L ... 708-709-3518. 156 A
sgovan@prairiestate.edu
GOVAN, JR., Tom ... 708-596-2000. 159 C
tgovan@ssc.edu
GOVE, Marilyn ... 949-480-4131 ... 66 F
mgove@soka.edu
GOVEA, Sam ... 972-860-4216. 470 G
sgovea@dcccd.edu
GOVEN, Arthur ... 940-565-3590. 490 C
arthur.goven@unt.edu
GOVER, Bruce ... 606-679-8501. 196 D
bruce.gover@kctcs.edu
GOVER, Kristie ... 904-256-7070. 107 Q
kgover1@ju.edu
GOVINDAN, Indira ... 201-692-2060. 301 J
govindan@fdu.edu
GOVITZ, Leanne ... 989-686-9490. 242 C
leannegovitz@delta.edu
GOVITZ, Scott ... 989-386-6624. 247 B
sgovitz@midmich.edu
GOVONI, Mark ... 215-951-2700. 430 E
govonim@philau.edu
GOW, Joe ... 608-785-8004. 536 G
jgow@uwlax.edu
GOWAN, Mary ... 540-568-3254. 506 F
gowanma@jmu.edu
GOWER, J. Michael ... 212-960-5475. 351 M
gower@yu.edu
GOWER, Michael, E ... 615-898-2540. 459 D
mike.gower@mtsu.edu
GOWER, Paula ... 405-585-5410. 397 C
paula.gower@okbu.edu
GOWER, Stephanie ... 205-453-6300 ... 96 F
GOYAK, Antone ... 715-324-6900. 535 E
antone.goyak@ni.edu
GOYETTE, Barbara ... 410-295-5554. 217 G
barbara.goyette@sjca.edu
GOZIK, Nick ... 617-552-3827. 224 A
nick.gozik@bc.edu
GOZON, Richard, C ... 215-955-6617. 434 C
richard.gozon@jefferson.edu
GOZUM, Allan ... 630-829-6418. 140 B
agozum@ben.edu
GOZZO, James ... 518-694-7255. 313 B
james.gozzo@acphs.edu
GRAAGE, Eric ... 401-454-6525. 440 A
egraage@risd.edu
GRABAN, Jennifer, L ... 812-488-1178. 173 H
jg54@evansville.edu
GRABE, David ... 314-977-3923. 281 I
dgrabe@slu.edu
GRABE, William ... 928-523-4340 ... 16 C
william.grabe@nau.edu
GRABER, David ... 402-375-7257. 291 F
dagrabe1@wsc.edu
GRABER, Doug ... 620-947-3121. 190 J
dougg@tabor.edu
GRABER, Thomas ... 570-208-5900. 419 P
thomasgraber@kings.edu
GRABER, Tony ... 316-284-5233. 184 J
tgraber@bethelks.edu
GRABLE, Lynda ... 478-445-7305. 125 A
lynda.grable@gcsu.edu
GRABOWSKA, Lynette ... 605-367-6122. 452 C
lynette.grabowska@southeasttech.edu
GRABOWSKI, Janice, T .. 724-925-4123. 437 D
grabowskij@wccc.edu
GRABOWSKI, John, F ... 410-777-2231. 213 D
jfgrabowski@aacc.edu
GRABOWSKI, Mark ... 417-328-1556. 282 C
mgrabowski@sbuniv.edu
GRABOWSKI, Rod, M ... 513-556-6703. 390 G
grabowrd@ucmail.uc.edu
GRABUS, Scott ... 215-572-8515. 409 H
grabuss@arcadia.edu
GRACA, Michael ... 508-286-3503. 238 B
mgraca@wheatonma.edu

GRACA, Thomas, J ... 972-860-7218. 470 I
TomGraca@dcccd.edu
GRACE, Chris ... 562-903-4708 ... 29 L
chris.grace@biola.edu
GRACE, Coy, F ... 870-633-4480 ... 21 A
cgrace@eacc.edu
GRACE, Dennis ... 239-304-7093 ... 98 K
dennis.grace@avemaria.edu
GRACE, Ellen ... 561-868-3135. 110 C
gracee@palmbeachstate.edu
GRACE, Glenda ... 718-518-4154. 318 B
ggrace@hostos.cuny.edu
GRACE, Martin ... 617-541-5352. 232 G
mgrace@rcc.mass.edu
GRACE, Michelle, M ... 847-543-2274. 143 A
mgrace@clcillinois.edu
GRACE, Nabil, F ... 248-204-2500. 245 I
ngrace@ltu.edu
GRACE, Ted, W ... 618-453-4485. 159 G
tgrace@siu.edu
GRACIA, Hector ... 787-780-0070. 547 G
graciah@caribbean.edu
GRACIA, Jessica, L ... 508-565-1301. 237 A
jlgracia@stonehill.edu
GRACIA, Zaida ... 787-728-1515. 555 D
zgracia@sagrado.edu
GRACIE, Larry, W ... 252-249-1851. 362 E
lgracie@pamlicocc.edu
GRACYALNY, David ... 410-225-2220. 216 C
dgracyal@mica.edu
GRACYK, June ... 440-684-6083. 392 D
jgracyk@ursuline.edu
GRACZKOWSKI, Eric ... 641-844-5690. 179 J
eric.graczkowski@iavalley.edu
GRADER, Timothy ... 413-205-3050. 221 F
timothy.grader@aic.edu
GRADOWSKI, Charles ... 484-365-7404. 422 D
cgradowski@lincoln.edu
GRADY, Amber ... 870-512-7890 ... 20 B
amber_grady@asun.edu
GRADY, Bruce ... 919-546-8574. 366 E
bgrady@shawu.edu
GRADY, Carole ... 453-879-4802. 497 E
grady@dixie.edu
GRADY, Christine ... 815-753-1311. 154 I
cgrady@niu.edu
GRADY, David, L ... 319-335-3114. 175 I
david-grady@uiowa.edu
GRADY, Dennis, O ... 540-831-5187. 508 C
dgrady4@radford.edu
GRADY, Helene ... 443-997-3359. 215 H
hgrady1@jhu.edu
GRADY, J. Thomas ... 508-678-2811. 231 B
tom.grady@bristolcc.edu
GRADY, Lynne ... 706-379-3111. 134 L
lbgrady@yhc.edu
GRADY, Meghan ... 610-606-4612. 412 I
megrady@cedarcrest.edu
GRADY, Sarah ... 718-409-7262. 346 D
sgrady@sunymaritime.edu
GRADY, Suzanne ... 845-257-3245. 342 B
gradys@newpaltz.edu
GRAEBERT, James, K ... 414-288-3048. 534 B
james.graebert@marquette.edu
GRAEM, David ... 903-675-6364. 488 D
dgraem@tvcc.edu
GRAF, Bob ... 651-696-6280. 256 L
rgraf@macalester.edu
GRAF, Debby ... 208-376-7731. 137 F
dgraf@boisebible.edu
GRAF, Elizabeth ... 219-866-6195. 172 E
bethg@saintjoe.edu
GRAF, Katie, M ... 716-839-8364. 322 E
kgraf@daemen.edu
GRAF, Nancy ... 316-295-5888. 186 H
ngraf@friends.edu
GRAFF, Irene ... 310-660-3515 ... 43 B
igraff@elcamino.edu
GRAFF, Jonathan ... 575-624-8291. 310 H
graff@nmmi.edu
GRAFFAM, JoAnn, K ... 417-625-3072. 278 D
graffam-j@mssu.edu
GRAFFICE, Anne ... 330-823-2030. 391 E
graffiaz@mountunion.edu
GRAFFIUS, Jeff ... 740-753-6336. 380 K
graffiusj@hocking.edu
GRAFTON, David ... 215-248-6347. 422 F
dgrafton@ltsp.edu
GRAFTON, Ken ... 701-231-7655. 371 G
k.grafton@ndsu.edu
GRAFTON, Steve, C ... 734-763-9730. 251 C
sgrafton@umich.edu
GRAGG, Derrick ... 918-631-2181. 401 F
teresa-moyer@utulsa.edu
GRAGG, T. Dewayne ... 903-875-7376. 477 G
dewayne.gragg@navarrocollege.edu
GRAHAM, Amanda ... 619-201-8711 ... 62 B
Amanda.Graham@sdcc.edu
GRAHAM, Amie, E ... 757-594-7672. 503 M
amie.graham@cnu.edu

GRAHAM, Angela ... 540-863-2806. 512 B
agraham@dslcc.edu
GRAHAM, Archie ... 414-297-6870. 540 E
grahama@matc.edu
GRAHAM, Bernard ... 570-408-4280. 437 F
bernard.graham@wilkes.edu
GRAHAM, Bruce ... 312-996-1040. 161 D
bgraham@uic.edu
GRAHAM, Carlos ... 573-681-5971. 276 C
grahamc@lincolnu.edu
GRAHAM, Carole ... 540-857-7273. 514 E
cgraham@virginiawestern.edu
GRAHAM, Catherine ... 310-338-2753 ... 53 E
cgraham@lmu.edu
GRAHAM, Charles, W ... 405-325-2444. 401 B
cwgraham@ou.edu
GRAHAM, Chuck ... 352-335-2332 ... 97 E
GRAHAM, Frances, D ... 919-530-6738. 368 A
fdgraham@nccu.edu
GRAHAM, Jack ... 970-491-3350 ... 80 I
jack.graham@colostate.edu
GRAHAM, James, F ... 660-543-4279. 283 A
graham@ucmo.edu
GRAHAM, Janielle ... 773-995-2067. 141 J
jgraham@csu.edu
GRAHAM, Jean ... 251-580-2293 ... 4 L
jgraham@faulknerstate.edu
GRAHAM, Jeanne ... 906-932-4231. 242 I
jeanneg@gogebic.edu
GRAHAM, Jeffrey ... 956-665-2112. 492 B
grahamja@utpa.edu
GRAHAM, Jennifer ... 254-298-8592. 482 C
jennifer.graham@templejc.edu
GRAHAM, Joan, E ... 585-475-6079. 337 L
jegirp@rit.edu
GRAHAM, Joe, M ... 704-233-8148. 370 G
graham@wingate.edu
GRAHAM, John ... 845-938-5868. 545 I
John.Graham@usma.edu
GRAHAM, III, John ... 412-346-2100. 430 F
jgrahamiii@pia.edu
GRAHAM, John, D ... 812-855-1432. 167 F
grahamjd@indiana.edu
GRAHAM, John, M ... 512-471-4716. 491 C
john.graham@athletics.utexas.edu
GRAHAM, John-Bauer ... 256-782-5255 ... 4 K
jgraham@jsu.edu
GRAHAM, Kate ... 281-929-4653. 479 H
kate.graham@sjcd.edu
GRAHAM, Kathleen ... 570-577-3607. 411 A
kathy.graham@bucknell.edu
GRAHAM, Keith ... 570-740-0307. 422 G
kgraham@luzerne.edu
GRAHAM, Kevin ... 321-674-8111. 104 H
kgraham@fit.edu
GRAHAM, Kevin, C ... 217-424-6360. 153 C
kgraham@millikin.edu
GRAHAM, Ladd ... 818-299-5500 ... 75 E
lgraham@westcoastuniversity.edu
GRAHAM, LeRoy ... 802-443-5415. 499 H
leroyg@middlebury.edu
GRAHAM, JR., Lewis, P 803-934-3404. 445 F
lgraham@morris.edu
GRAHAM, Lindsey ... 304-637-1803. 526 E
grahaml@dewv.edu
GRAHAM, Lori ... 910-410-1737. 362 I
ljgraham1273@richmondcc.edu
GRAHAM, JR.,
Louis, W ... 617-253-2808. 233 B
GRAHAM, Margaret, P ... 434-223-6167. 505 E
bgraham@hsc.edu
GRAHAM, MariAnn ... 651-962-5000. 265 C
magraham@stthomas.edu
GRAHAM, Mark, R ... 276-944-6104. 504 H
mgraham@ehc.edu
GRAHAM, Mary, S ... 601-928-6280. 268 C
mary.graham@mgccc.edu
GRAHAM, SJ,
Michael, J ... 513-745-3502. 393 H
GRAHAM, Mickey ... 580-477-7782. 401 J
mckey.graham@wosc.edu
GRAHAM, Nancy, D ... 724-847-6550. 417 A
ngraham@geneva.edu
GRAHAM, Philip ... 858-795-5210 ... 64 E
pgraham@sanfordburnham.org
GRAHAM, Robert ... 575-562-2125. 309 H
robert.graham@enmu.edu
GRAHAM, Robert, J ... 724-458-2187. 417 E
rjgraham@gcc.edu
GRAHAM, Roy ... 803-934-3298. 445 F
roygraham@morris.edu
GRAHAM, Sandra ... 414-382-6366. 531 I
sandra.graham@alverno.edu
GRAHAM, Stephanie ... 608-663-4861. 532 I
srgraham@edgewood.edu
GRAHAM, Stephanie ... 909-607-6722 ... 46 H
stephanie_graham@hmc.edu
GRAHAM, Stephen, A ... 973-761-9011. 307 C
stephen.graham@shu.edu
GRAHAM, Steve ... 252-492-2061. 364 F
grahams@vgcc.edu

GRAHAM, Steven, W ...... 573-884-3360. 283 B
grahams@umsystem.edu
GRAHAM, Terri .... 402-461-7431. 289 I
tgraham@hastings.edu
GRAHAM, Wray .... 901-375-4400. 457 C
wraygraham@midsouthcc.org
GRAHAM-ROBEY,
Judith .... 617-228-3296. 231 C
jgraham@bhcc.mass.edu
GRAHEK, Matthew .... 817-923-8459. 469 F
matt.grahek@fishermore.edu
GRAINGER, Kristen .... 503-370-6209. 408 J
kgrainge@willamette.edu
GRAJEK, Michael, A .... 330-569-5272. 380 I
GrajekMA@hiram.edu
GRAMBERG,
Anne-Katrin .... 334-844-4026..... 1 G
gramban@auburn.edu
GRAMENZ, Gary .... 559-453-2291... 45 D
gary.gramenz@fresno.edu
GRAMLICH, Annalisa ...... 816-501-4122. 280 I
annalisa.gramlich@rockhurst.edu
GRAMLICH, Nicole .... 314-768-7806. 278 C
ngramlich@missouricollege.com
GRAMLING, Jennifer ...... 865-251-1800. 458 I
jgramling@southcollegetn.edu
GRAMLING, Keith, E ...... 504-865-3240. 205 H
gramling@loyno.edu
GRAMLING, Kelly .... 937-294-6155. 382 A
kgramling@kaplan.edu
GRAMLING, P.J .... 325-649-8406. 473 F
pgramling@hputx.edu
GRAMLING, Tim .... 719-590-6797... 81 B
GRAMOPADHYE, Anand 864-656-5540. 442 C
agramop@clemson.edu
GRAMS, Kathyrn .... 678-839-6552. 133 I
kgrams@westga.edu
GRAN, Tracey .... 651-690-6566. 263 O
tlgran@stkate.edu
GRANA, Joe .... 714-879-3901... 47 K
jgrana@hiu.edu
GRANADE, Ray .... 870-245-5121... 22 D
granade@obu.edu
GRANADO, Esequiel .... 956-665-2701. 492 B
zeke@utpa.edu
GRANADOS, Alex .... 661-362-2626... 53 G
agranados@masters.edu
GRANADOS, Patricia ...... 708-456-0300. 161 A
pgranado@triton.edu
GRANATA, Brian .... 215-572-2194. 409 H
granatab@arcadia.edu
GRANATOWSKI, Doris ... 480-212-1704... 17 N
GRANBERRY,
Jacqueline, M .... 601-857-3363. 267 A
jgranberry@hindscc.edu
GRANBERRY-RUSSELL,
Paulette .... 517-353-3922. 246 H
prussell@msu.edu
GRAND PRE, Paul, D ..... 914-337-9300. 321 E
paul.grandpre@concordia-ny.edu
GRANDALL, Jerolyn, R ... 608-785-9576. 541 E
grandallj@westerntc.edu
GRANDCHAMP,
Michael, N .... 401-341-2142. 440 C
grandchm@salve.edu
GRANDGEORGE, Cindy .. 661-362-3420... 40 E
cindy.grandgeorge@canyons.edu
GRANDNER, Deborah, F 301-314-7343. 219 B
dgrandne@umd.edu
GRANDY, E. Ann .... 757-683-4132. 507 N
egrandy@odu.edu
GRANEY, Carol .... 215-717-6281. 435 A
graney@uarts.edu
GRANEY-MULHOLLAND,
Michael .... 925-969-3319... 49 B
mgraney@jfku.edu
GRANFIELD, Cathy .... 414-955-8566. 534 C
mcw@matthewsstores.com
GRANGER, Earl, T .... 757-221-1188. 503 N
earl.granger@wm.edu
GRANGER, Gary .... 503-771-1112. 407 E
ggranger@reed.edu
GRANGER, Heidi .... 703-993-2349. 505 C
hgranger@gmu.edu
GRANGER, Jennifer .... 617-243-2475. 227 K
jgranger@lasell.edu
GRANGER, Jill .... 434-381-6166. 510 F
granger@sbc.edu
GRANGER, Joey .... 601-984-1199. 270 C
jgranger@umc.edu
GRANGER, Ron .... 307-855-2025. 542 Y
rgranger@cwc.edu
GRANGER, Vern .... 614-292-3324. 386 E
GRANHOLD, Kevin, B ..... 713-500-3624. 492 E
kevin.b.granhold@uth.tmc.edu
GRANITTO, Joseph .... 516-299-4002. 329 D
joseph.granitto@liu.edu
GRANLUND, Shirley, M . 952-446-4112. 255 D
granlunds@crown.edu
GRANT, Alan .... 540-231-4152. 515 C
algrant@vt.edu
GRANT, Andrew .... 212-824-2294. 325 G
agrant@huc.edu
GRANT, Andrew .... 330-490-7334. 392 H
agrant@walsh.edu
GRANT, Andrew, D .... 419-372-3905. 374 K
agrant@bgsu.edu
GRANT, Armada .... 443-885-3195. 217 A
armada.grant@morgan.edu
GRANT, Barry .... 860-512-3403... 88 G
bgrant@manchestercc.edu
GRANT, Beth, A .... 813-988-5131. 104 A
registrar@floridacollege.edu
GRANT, Bob .... 937-775-2771. 393 G
bob.grant@wright.edu
GRANT, Brad .... 912-525-5000. 131 B
bgrant@scad.edu
GRANT, Bradford, C .... 202-806-7420... 95 G
bcgrant@howard.edu
GRANT, Brian, T .... 315-268-6480. 320 A
bgrant@clarkson.edu
GRANT, Brid .... 860-486-3016... 92 A
brid.grant@uconn.edu
GRANT, Bud .... 563-333-6419. 182 B
GrantRobert@sau.edu
GRANT, Christa, J .... 518-783-2330. 340 J
cgrant@siena.edu
GRANT, Christy .... 402-354-7077. 291 B
christy.grant@methodistcollege.edu
GRANT, Dale, E .... 308-432-6202. 291 D
dgrant@csc.edu
GRANT, Debby .... 956-665-2500. 492 B
debbygrant@utpa.edu
GRANT, Deborah, L .... 504-865-5210. 207 C
dgrant@tulane.edu
GRANT, Diane .... 717-764-9550. 413 J
dgrant@csb.edu
GRANT, Donna .... 504-286-5040. 206 K
dgrant@suno.edu
GRANT, Gary, B .... 410-778-2800. 221 C
GRANT, George .... 616-331-6850. 243 C
grantg@gvsu.edu
GRANT, James .... 660-263-4110. 279 B
jamesg@macc.edu
GRANT, Jamie .... 920-686-6206. 536 A
Jamie.Grant@sl.edu
GRANT, Janet .... 860-701-5166... 90 G
grant_j@mitchell.edu
GRANT, Jeff .... 229-245-3852. 134 B
jgrant@valdosta.edu
GRANT, Jim .... 503-768-7628. 403 K
grant@lclark.edu
GRANT, Johnny .... 478-445-5852. 125 A
johnny.grant@gcsu.edu
GRANT, Jordan, L .... 206-281-2469. 523 C
grantj@spu.edu
GRANT, Karen .... 508-854-4275. 232 F
kgrant@qcc.mass.edu
GRANT, Keith .... 513-671-1920. 192 D
kgrant@beckfield.edu
GRANT, Kizuwanda .... 214-379-5407. 478 D
kgrant@pqc.edu
GRANT, Kizuwanda .... 214-379-5500. 478 D
kgrant@pqc.edu
GRANT, Louise, G .... 207-941-7176. 211 F
grantl@nescom.edu
GRANT, Lowe .... 706-419-1411. 123 F
grant.lowe@covenant.edu
GRANT, Lyman, W .... 512-223-3352. 466 I
lgrant@austincc.edu
GRANT, Marta .... 254-526-1302. 468 G
ctc.international@ctcd.edu
GRANT, Marvin .... 904-470-8892. 102 A
marvin.grant@ewc.edu
GRANT, Mary, K .... 413-662-5201. 230 C
mary.grant@mcla.edu
GRANT, Michael .... 212-592-2000. 340 H
mgrant@sva.edu
GRANT, Michelle .... 904-332-0910. 106 K
GRANT, Ralph, T .... 973-803-5000. 304 C
rgrant@pillar.edu
GRANT, Ray .... 312-427-2737. 148 L
rgrant@jmls.edu
GRANT, Robert .... 816-501-4418. 280 I
bob.grant@rockhurst.edu
GRANT, S. G .... 607-777-7329. 341 E
sggrant@binghamton.edu
GRANT, Sabrina .... 973-720-2754. 308 I
grants@wpunj.edu
GRANT, Sharone, V .... 410-651-6597. 219 E
svgrant@umes.edu
GRANT, Steve .... 229-430-4623. 119 J
steve.grant@asurams.edu
GRANT, Terry .... 304-724-3700. 526 B
tgrant@apus.edu
GRANT, Terry, H .... 605-394-1204. 452 A
terry.grant@asu.edu
GRANT, Velvet, L .... 757-683-3159. 507 N
vlgrant2@odu.edu
GRANT BAHAN,
Rebecca .... 314-889-4509. 274 E
rgrantbahan@fontbonne.edu
GRANTHAM, Brittney ...... 417-865-2815. 274 B
granthamb@evangel.edu
GRANVILLE, Andrea, L ... 212-752-1530. 328 G
andrea.granville@limcollege.edu
GRAPES, Jody .... 212-353-4160. 321 F
grapes@cooper.edu
GRAPPO, Ann Marie ...... 212-217-3900. 324 C
ann_grappo@fitnyc.edu
GRASSADONIA,
Jane, M .... 814-886-6472. 424 G
jgrassadonia@mtaloy.edu
GRASSEL, OSB, Martin .. 503-845-3326. 404 D
martin.grassel@mtangel.edu
GRASSEL, Nancy .... 605-642-6545. 451 G
nancy.grassel@bhsu.edu
GRASSETTI, J. Vincent ... 413-755-4061. 233 A
vgrassetti@stcc.edu
GRASSINI, Dennis, J ...... 401-825-2151. 439 A
dgrassini@ccri.edu
GRASSLER, Frank, P .... 214-648-8188. 493 E
frank.grassler@utsouthwestern.edu
GRASSO, Domenico .... 302-831-2101... 94 B
dg@udel.edu
GRASSO, Maureen .... 706-425-2933. 133 C
mgrasso@uga.edu
GRASSO, Nick .... 410-752-4710. 510 B
ngrasso@stratford.edu
GRATE, Sheresa .... 918-333-6830. 398 F
sgrate@okwu.edu
GRATEROLE-ROSARIO,
Agustin .... 787-993-8886. 554 A
agustin.graterole@upr.edu
GRATTAN, Matthew .... 518-381-1314. 340 G
grattamj@sunysccc.edu
GRATTON, John .... 575-234-9210. 311 A
jgratton@nmsu.edu
GRATZ, Robert, D .... 512-245-2121. 487 C
rg02@txstate.edu
GRATZ, T, R .... 360-736-9391. 517 G
trgratz@centralia.edu
GRAU, Frances .... 787-720-1022. 547 E
fgrau@atlanticcollege.edu
GRAU, Isidro .... 713-221-8494. 489 D
Graul@uhd.edu
GRAU, Leeann .... 740-389-4636. 383 F
graul@mtc.edu
GRAU, Monica, C .... 607-436-2255. 343 E
graumc@oneonta.edu
GRAUMAN, Gregory .... 202-855-6063... 94 F
grauman@american.edu
GRAUMLICH, Lisa .... 206-221-0907. 524 G
graumlic@uw.edu
GRAUNKE, Jan .... 920-686-6180. 536 A
Jan.Graunke@sl.edu
GRAVDAHL, Jeanette ...... 605-698-3966. 451 D
jgravdahl@swc.tc
GRAVEL, Matthew .... 413-755-4623. 233 A
mgravel@stcc.edu
GRAVELY, Archer, R .... 828-232-5118. 368 C
gravely@unca.edu
GRAVENBERG, Eric .... 510-748-2200... 59 B
egravenberg@peralta.edu
GRAVES, Aaron .... 919-684-6571. 354 A
aaron.graves@duke.edu
GRAVES, Becky .... 256-352-8159..... 9 G
becky.graves@wallacestate.edu
GRAVES, Ben .... 270-247-8521. 197 H
bgraves@midcontinent.edu
GRAVES, Diane, J .... 210-999-8121. 488 C
diane.graves@trinity.edu
GRAVES, Finley .... 940-565-3097. 490 C
gravesf@unt.edu
GRAVES, Frank .... 254-299-8126. 476 D
fgraves@mclennan.edu
GRAVES, Harold, B .... 719-884-5000... 83 K
hbgraves@nbc.edu
GRAVES, Kevin .... 504-280-6266. 205 G
kgraves@uno.edu
GRAVES, Larry .... 608-262-9652. 538 E
larry.graves@uwc.edu
GRAVES, Loreatha, D ...... 336-334-7551. 367 E
loretha@ncat.edu
GRAVES, Matt .... 208-792-2247. 138 G
mlgraves@lcsc.edu
GRAVES, Peter, E .... 512-463-1823. 486 D
peter.graves@tsus.edu
GRAVES, Randy, K .... 269-471-3854. 239 D
gravesr@andrews.edu
GRAVES, Rita .... 318-357-5178. 208 B
gravesr@nsula.edu
GRAVES, Robbie .... 731-661-5008. 462 F
rgraves@uu.edu
GRAVES, Robert .... 413-528-7316. 222 E
rgraves@simons-rock.edu
GRAVES, Sara, J .... 256-824-6064..... 8 F
Sara.Graves@uah.edu
GRAVES, Susan .... 270-534-3155. 196 G
susan.graves@kctcs.edu
GRAVES, Veronica .... 301-736-3631. 216 B
veronica.graves@msbbcs.edu
GRAVES, William, T .... 318-342-1961. 208 E
graves@ulm.edu
GRAVETT, Erika .... 478-825-6301. 124 H
gravette@fvsu.edu
GRAVETT, Sharon, L .... 229-333-5993. 134 B
sgravett@valdosta.edu
GRAVETT, Sharron .... 229-333-5950. 134 B
sgravett@valdosta.edu
GRAVIETTE, Kimberly, K 402-461-7387. 289 I
kgraviette@hastings.edu
GRAVLEY, John .... 913-667-5700. 185 J
jgravley@cbts.edu
GRAVO, Daniel .... 330-244-4752. 392 H
dgravo@walsh.edu
GRAY, Aaron .... 816-531-5223. 272 I
agray@concorde.edu
GRAY, Alicia .... 409-882-3343. 486 G
alicia.gray@lsco.edu
GRAY, Amy .... 630-844-5467. 140 A
lamphere@aurora.edu
GRAY, Anita .... 260-359-4063. 166 O
agray@huntington.edu
GRAY, Anita .... 703-897-1972. 510 B
agray@stratford.edu
GRAY, Betty .... 252-940-6387. 358 A
bettyg@beaufortccc.edu
GRAY, Bo .... 828-835-4222. 364 E
bgray@tricountycc.edu
GRAY, Chad .... 501-882-4432... 19 M
cdgray@asub.edu
GRAY, Charlotte .... 417-967-5466. 282 J
GRAY, Christopher .... 309-694-5132. 146 E
christopher.gray@icc.edu
GRAY, Corey .... 402-643-3651. 289 B
corey.gray@cune.edu
GRAY, Craig .... 336-316-2426. 355 A
graycr@guilford.edu
GRAY, David .... 575-624-8078. 310 H
david@nmmi.edu
GRAY, David, J .... 814-865-6574. 426 A
djg36@psu.edu
GRAY, David, R .... 540-868-7154. 512 H
dgray@lfcc.edu
GRAY, David, W .... 615-898-2414. 459 D
david.gray@mtsu.edu
GRAY, Deborah .... 229-225-4087. 132 D
dgray@southwestgatech.edu
GRAY, Donna .... 501-205-8805... 20 I
dgray@cbc.edu
GRAY, Douglass, P .... 410-827-5830. 214 C
dgray@chesapeake.edu
GRAY, Erin .... 312-567-3720. 147 F
grayi@iit.edu
GRAY, Gary .... 907-474-7780... 10 I
GRAY, Gary, E .... 618-235-2700. 160 A
gary.gray@swic.edu
GRAY, Gary, W .... 714-449-7481... 67 D
ggray@scco.edu
GRAY, Glenn .... 319-273-2333. 176 A
glenn.gray@uni.edu
GRAY, Gregory, S .... 334-727-8011..... 8 A
gsgray@tuskegee.edu
GRAY, Gregory, W .... 860-493-0011... 87 J
grayg@ct.edu
GRAY, III, James, A .... 252-985-5140. 365 D
jgray@ncwc.edu
GRAY, Jeff .... 478-387-4781. 125 E
GRAY, Jeffrey .... 515-271-1506. 177 H
jeffrey.gray@dmu.edu
GRAY, Jeffrey, L .... 718-817-4750. 324 G
gray@fordham.edu
GRAY, Jennifer .... 817-272-2776. 491 B
jgray@uta.edu
GRAY, Joe .... 615-547-1255. 454 A
jgray@cumberland.edu
GRAY, John, C .... 302-295-1139... 94 E
john.c.gray@wilmu.edu
GRAY, Kelly .... 575-769-4179. 309 F
kelly.gray@clovis.edu
GRAY, Kelly .... 419-755-4823. 385 D
kgray@ncstatecollege.edu
GRAY, Kenneth, D .... 304-293-5811. 530 D
ken.gray@mail.wvu.edu
GRAY, Kilen .... 502-895-3411. 197 F
kgray@lpts.edu
GRAY, Kristen .... 706-778-0100. 130 E
kgray@piedmont.edu
GRAY, Kristen .... 616-395-7945. 244 A
gray@hope.edu
GRAY, Leah .... 731-425-2606. 460 G
lgray@jscc.edu
GRAY, Lisa, G .... 410-546-6390. 220 D
lggray@salisbury.edu
GRAY, Lydia, E .... 718-862-7231. 329 M
lydia.gray@manhattan.edu
GRAY, Martha, D .... 607-274-3164. 327 E
mgray@ithaca.edu
GRAY, Maryann, J .... 310-825-5573... 71 C
mgray@conet.ucla.edu
GRAY, Megan .... 419-251-1784. 383 G
megan.gray@mercycollege.edu

GRAY, Michaelle ... 580-371-2371. 396 E mgray@mscok.edu
GRAY, Nancy ... 970-339-6392... 78 C nancy.gray@aims.edu
GRAY, Nancy, O ... 540-362-6321. 505 G presoffc@hollins.edu
GRAY, Nyree ... 213-738-6871... 68 C deanofstudents@swlaw.edu
GRAY, Rebecca ... 254-968-9473. 483 A rgray@tarleton.edu
GRAY, Rebecca ... 843-953-5633. 443 A grayrj@cofc.edu
GRAY, Reginald ... 214-379-5409. 478 D rgray@pqc.edu
GRAY, Richard, D ... 860-486-3455... 92 A richard.gray@uconn.edu
GRAY, Robert, R ... 804-257-5842. 515 F rrgray@vuu.edu
GRAY, Sandra, C ... 859-858-3511. 192 B president@asbury.edu
GRAY, Sarah ... 309-649-6265. 160 E sarah.gray@src.edu
GRAY, Seneca ... 503-768-6781. 403 K seneca@lclark.edu
GRAY, Shashuna ... 540-891-3046. 512 E dgray@germanna.edu
GRAY, Shaun ... 207-741-5580. 211 A sgray@smccme.edu
GRAY, Shawn ... 409-880-8466. 486 F shawn.gray@lamar.edu
GRAY, Sheryl ... 865-471-3240. 453 F sgray@cn.edu
GRAY, Shonda ... 443-885-3430. 217 A shonda.gray@morgan.edu
GRAY, Susan ... 478-289-2027. 124 C sgray@ega.edu
GRAY, Tim ... 319-208-5022. 182 G tgray@scciowa.edu
GRAY, Toni ... 806-354-6083. 465 E tbgray@actx.edu
GRAY, Warren ... 606-589-3070. 196 F warren.gray@kctcs.edu
GRAY, Warren, S ... 401-865-1602. 439 E wgray@providence.edu
GRAY, Wilbur, E ... 717-728-2511. 412 J billgray@centralpenn.edu
GRAY-DEVINE, Sherry ... 580-371-2371. 396 E
GRAY KOGEN, Elizabeth 212-472-1500. 334 B giving@nysid.edu
GRAY-LACKEY, Denise ... 502-213-7202. 195 F denise.graylackey@kctcs.edu
GRAY-LITTLE, Bernadette 785-864-3131. 190 L graylittle@ku.edu
GRAY PAYTON, Pamela . 619-260-4681... 73 I grayp@sandiego.edu
GRAYBEAL, Clay ... 207-221-4509. 213 A cgraybeal@une.edu
GRAYBEAL, Jerry, G ... 801-626-8114. 497 D jgraybeal@weber.edu
GRAYBEAL, Susan, E ... 423-354-2471. 461 C segraybeal@northeaststate.edu
GRAYS, Shantay ... 713-718-5053. 473 C shantay.grays@hccs.edu
GRAYSON, Chinester ... 334-874-5700..... 3 A cgrayson@ccal.edu
GRAYSON, Denise, R ... 605-256-5152. 451 H denise.grayson@dsu.edu
GRAYSON, Lorenzo ... 251-405-7170..... 2 D lgrayson@bishop.edu
GRAYSON, Paul ... 212-774-0727. 330 E pgrayson@mmm.edu
GRAZIANO, Joanne ... 516-299-2999. 329 D joanne.graziano@liu.edu
GRAZIANO, Judith ... 651-793-1368. 259 C judith.graziano@metrostate.edu
GRAZIANO, Vincent, S ... 412-391-6710. 410 H vgraziano@bradfordpittsburgh.edu
GREALISH, William ... 617-578-7178. 236 E wgrealish@sbboston.com
GREANEY, KC ... 707-521-7940... 65 B kgreaney@santarosa.edu
GREAR, Nancy, C ... 585-389-2801. 332 D ngrear2@naz.edu
GREATHOUSE, Jan ... 615-248-7782. 462 D jgreathouse@trevecca.edu
GREATHOUSE, Jane ... 507-389-7408. 261 E jane.greathouse@southcentral.edu
GREATHOUSE, Maren ... 973-353-5568. 306 D maren.greathouse@rutgers.edu
GREAVES, Christopher ... 718-997-3930. 319 C christopher.greaves@qc.cuny.edu
GREB, Christine ... 215-951-2808. 430 E grebc@philau.edu
GREBEL, David, A ... 817-257-7130. 484 I d.grebel@tcu.edu
GREBING, Karen ... 573-651-2433. 282 B kgrebing@semo.edu
GRECO, Anne ... 215-751-8217. 413 I agreco@ccp.edu
GRECO, Frank, M ... 412-365-1133. 412 K greco@chatham.edu
GRECO, Juneann ... 570-340-6004. 423 B greco@marywood.edu
GRECO, Michelle ... 504-671-6001. 203 A mgreco@dcc.edu
GRECO, Peter ... 925-631-4747... 61 F peter.greco2@stmarys-ca.edu
GRECO, Sal ... 516-299-3796. 329 C sal.greco@liu.edu
GREDEN, Leigh ... 734-487-7048. 242 D lgreden@emich.edu
GREDER, Darcy, L ... 309-556-3541. 148 B dgreder@iwu.edu
GREDY, John, W ... 937-766-3200. 375 K jgredy@cedarville.edu
GREEAR, Amy ... 276-523-7480. 513 A agreear@mecc.edu
GREEAR, Marisa ... 360-442-2391. 521 A mgreear@lowercolumbia.edu
GREEN, Allen ... 914-395-2249. 340 E agreen@sarahlawrence.edu
GREEN, Alus ... 201-360-4047. 302 D agreen@hccc.edu
GREEN, Andrew ... 516-726-6182. 545 H greena@usmma.edu
GREEN, Andy ... 256-782-5268..... 4 K agreen@jsu.edu
GREEN, Anita ... 313-593-5190. 251 D ujima@umich.edu
GREEN, Ann, F ... 828-694-1709. 358 C anng@blueridge.edu
GREEN, Audrey ... 661-362-3424... 40 E audrey.green@canyons.edu
GREEN, Barbara, C ... 626-395-6351... 31 E barbarag@caltech.edu
GREEN, Betti ... 315-781-3600. 326 C bgreen@hws.edu
GREEN, Bevley, W ... 251-460-6188..... 9 E bwgreen@southalabama.edu
GREEN, Cathy ... 603-513-5101. 298 D cathy.green@law.unh.edu
GREEN, Charles, D ... 319-335-5026. 175 I charles-green@uiowa.edu
GREEN, Chris ... 859-985-3727. 192 F greenchr@berea.edu
GREEN, Christopher ... 805-546-3902... 42 C cgreen@cuesta.edu
GREEN, Clarence ... 660-562-1254. 279 I cgreen@nwmissouri.edu
GREEN, Constance, C ... 503-842-8222. 408 B green@tillamookbay.cc
GREEN, Danny ... 919-760-8026. 356 G greend@meredith.edu
GREEN, David, A ... 217-786-2406. 151 F david.green@llcc.edu
GREEN, David, M ... 818-947-2679... 52 E greendm@lavc.edu
GREEN, Don ... 657-278-2413... 33 E dgreen@fullerton.edu
GREEN, Donald ... 973-290-4290. 300 F security@cse.edu
GREEN, Donald ... 231-591-2548. 242 F greend@ferris.edu
GREEN, Donald ... 616-643-5737. 242 F greend@ferris.edu
GREEN, Donna ... 562-985-8403... 33 F dgreen4@csulb.edu
GREEN, Ed ... 408-855-5021... 75 K ed.green@wvm.edu
GREEN, Elaine ... 215-248-7063. 413 A greene@chc.edu
GREEN, Eleanor, M ... 979-845-5051. 483 C emgreen@tamu.edu
GREEN, Ellen ... 843-574-6147. 447 E ellen.green@tridenttech.edu
GREEN, Ellen, R ... 806-371-5131. 465 E ergreen@actx.edu
GREEN, Elna ... 408-924-2450... 36 A elna.green@sjsu.edu
GREEN, Gary, M ... 336-734-7200. 360 E ggreen@forsythtech.edu
GREEN, Hope ... 773-380-6840. 163 D hgreen@westwood.edu
GREEN, Jean, M ... 217-228-5432. 156 C greenje@quincy.edu
GREEN, Jeff, W ... 256-549-8317..... 3 M jgreen@gadsdenstate.edu
GREEN, Jeffrey ... 312-662-4401. 139 F jgreen@adler.edu
GREEN, Jennifer ... 909-621-8000... 46 H jgreen@hmc.edu
GREEN, Jennifer, K ... 434-395-2944. 506 J mailto:greenjk@longwood.edu
GREEN, Jenny ... 607-729-1581. 322 F jgreen@davisny.edu
GREEN, Jerry ... 718-817-4170. 324 G jgreen@fordham.edu
GREEN, Joel ... 626-584-5298... 45 E cats@fuller.edu
GREEN, John ... 312-369-7291. 143 D jgreen@colum.edu
GREEN, John, C ... 610-683-4114. 429 A jgreen@kutztown.edu
GREEN, Jonathan, D ... 309-556-3101. 148 B provost@iwu.edu
GREEN, Judith ... 201-684-7523. 305 A jgreen2@ramapo.edu
GREEN, Julia ... 207-941-7129. 210 B greenj@husson.edu
GREEN, Karen ... 484-664-3182. 424 H green@muhlenberg.edu
GREEN, Karen ... 336-517-2159. 352 H kagreen@bennett.edu
GREEN, Kathy, W ... 717-736-4163. 417 I kwgreeni@hacc.edu
GREEN, Keith, A ... 717-901-5123. 418 E KGreen@HarrisburgU.edu
GREEN, Kristina ... 207-893-7998. 211 G kgreen@sjcme.edu
GREEN, Kurt ... 530-541-4660... 50 D green@ltcc.edu
GREEN, Latrelle, A ... 804-257-5662. 515 F lagreen@vuu.edu
GREEN, Lawrence ... 610-399-2137. 428 B lgreen@cheyney.edu
GREEN, Lillie, F ... 757-727-5057. 505 F lillie.green@hamptonu.edu
GREEN, Lina ... 757-455-2115. 515 H lgreen@vwc.edu
GREEN, Lisa ... 315-792-3736. 349 F lcgreen@utica.edu
GREEN, Lorry ... 864-977-7124. 445 H lorry.green@ngu.edu
GREEN, Mark, A ... 618-235-2700. 160 A mark.green@swic.edu
GREEN, Mary ... 269-965-3931. 244 O greenm@kellogg.edu
GREEN, Mary Beth ... 334-222-6591..... 5 E mbgreen@lbwcc.edu
GREEN, Mary Jo ... 715-422-5504. 540 D maryjo.green@mstc.edu
GREEN, Matthew ... 805-546-3924... 42 C mgreen@cuesta.edu
GREEN, Matthew ... 845-688-1568. 348 H greenm@sunyulster.edu
GREEN, Melanie, H ... 804-627-5300. 502 I
GREEN, Melissa ... 315-498-2912. 335 G m.a.green2@sunyocc.edu
GREEN, Melissa ... 567-429-3535. 387 L melissa_green3@owens.edu
GREEN, Michael, R ... 717-867-6208. 421 H mgreen@lvc.edu
GREEN, Michael, S ... 518-629-4554. 326 G m.green@hvcc.edu
GREEN, Mike ... 615-966-6000. 456 B mike.green@lipscomb.edu
GREEN, Moishe ... 845-352-5852. 350 I
GREEN, Monica ... 951-372-7082... 60 L monica.green@norcollege.edu
GREEN, Myrtes ... 205-929-6305..... 5 D mdgreen@lawsonstate.edu
GREEN, Nancy ... 704-403-3599. 352 J nancy.green@carolinashealthcare.org
GREEN, Nichol ... 601-928-6264. 268 C nichol.green@mgccc.edu
GREEN, O. Jerome ... 501-374-6305... 23 C
GREEN, Paula ... 626-914-8873... 38 K pgreen@citruscollege.edu
GREEN, Paula, L ... 508-849-3344. 222 B pgreen@annamaria.edu
GREEN, Rachel ... 570-662-4815. 429 C rgreen@mansfield.edu
GREEN, Rachel, T ... 904-819-6223. 103 E rgreen@flagler.edu
GREEN, Ragan ... 478-275-7865. 129 I rgreen@oftc.edu
GREEN, Ramona ... 903-223-3058. 484 C ramona.green@tamut.edu
GREEN, Ray ... 903-468-3005. 483 E raymond.green@tamuc.edu
GREEN, Rebecca ... 760-355-6499... 48 A becky.green@imperial.edu
GREEN, Renee, R ... 850-201-6564. 117 D greenr@tcc.fl.edu
GREEN, Rhonda, T ... 209-575-6664... 77 J greenr@yosemite.cc.ca.us
GREEN, Richard ... 229-430-4635. 119 J richard.green@asurams.edu
GREEN, Robert, L ... 540-464-7321. 515 B greenrl@vmi.edu
GREEN, Ronnie ... 402-472-2871. 292 G rgreen@nebraska.edu
GREEN, Ronnie, D ... 402-472-2871. 292 I rgreen2@unl.edu
GREEN, Ruvain ... 845-352-5852. 350 I
GREEN, Sandy, B ... 864-488-8348. 444 L sgreen@limestone.edu
GREEN, Satasha ... 516-686-7706. 333 H slgreen@nyit.edu
GREEN, Sharon, F ... 318-670-9337. 207 A sgreen@susla.edu
GREEN, Shirley ... 602-787-6604... 15 B shirley.green@paradisevalley.edu
GREEN, Stanton ... 732-571-3419. 303 C sgreen@monmouth.edu
GREEN, Susan ... 802-635-1308. 501 D susan.green@jsc.edu
GREEN, Teresa ... 806-894-9611. 480 H
GREEN, Tica, D ... 336-272-7102. 354 E tica.green@greensboro.edu
GREEN, Tim ... 256-549-8601..... 3 M tgreen@gadsdenstate.edu
GREEN, Timothy, M ... 615-248-1387. 462 D tgreen@trevecca.edu
GREEN, Tracey ... 315-498-2532. 335 G
GREEN, Tracy, A ... 440-365-5222. 383 B
GREEN, Tracy, S ... 804-523-5789. 512 F tgreen@reynolds.edu
GREEN, Valerie ... 404-880-8041. 122 J vgreen@cau.edu
GREEN, Vannessa ... 718-951-5842. 317 C vgreen@brooklyn.cuny.edu
GREEN, Vashba ... 813-880-8013. 107 C vgreen@academy.edu
GREEN, Walter ... 312-850-7167. 142 C wgreen21@ccc.edu
GREEN, Wayne ... 334-974-5700..... 3 A wgreen@ccal.edu
GREEN, William ... 423-614-8240. 455 L wgreen@leeuniversity.edu
GREEN, William, S ... 305-284-2006. 118 F wgreen@miami.edu
GREEN COWLES, Maria . 301-696-3811. 215 D cowles@hood.edu
GREEN POWELL, Patricia ... 850-561-2989. 114 K patricia.greenpowell@famu.edu
GREEN-QUARLES, Ryanne ... 916-361-1660... 36 H rgreen@carrington.edu
GREENAN, Jennie ... 309-692-4092. 152 J jgreenan@midstate.edu
GREENAN, Martin ... 317-543-4890. 171 A mgreenan@martin.edu
GREENBERG, Erik ... 703-376-6150... 18 I erik.greenberg@phoenix.edu
GREENBERG, Kenneth, S ... 617-573-8265. 237 B kgreenbe@suffolk.edu
GREENBERG, Mark ... 360-650-3051. 525 C mark.greenberg@wwu.edu
GREENBERG, Mark, L ... 215-895-2200. 415 B mlg25@drexel.edu
GREENBERG, Penelope, S ... 610-499-4475. 437 E psgreenberg@widener.edu
GREENBERG, Raymond, S ... 512-499-4201. 491 A
GREENBERG, Roberta ... 718-933-6700. 331 K rgreenbe@monroecollege.edu
GREENBERG, Scott, B ... 508-626-4550. 230 A sgreenberg@framingham.edu
GREENBERG, Stephen, B ... 713-798-8878. 467 F stepheng@bcm.edu
GREENBERG, Wendy ... 610-409-3329. 436 B wgreenberg@ursinus.edu
GREENBERG, Yeshaya ... 305-534-7050. 117 E
GREENBURGER, Roxanne ... 847-574-5236. 150 C rgreenburger@lfgsm.edu
GREENE, Bary ... 718-933-6700. 331 K bgreene@monroecollege.edu
GREENE, Brian ... 541-506-6080. 402 H bgreene@cgcc.cc.or.us
GREENE, Carol ... 606-326-2142. 194 J Carol.Greene@kctcs.edu
GREENE, Cary ... 910-695-3781. 363 F greenec@sandhills.edu
GREENE, D. Gayle ... 919-532-5522. 364 G dggreene@waketech.edu
GREENE, David, A ... 773-702-1377. 161 B davidgreene@uchicago.edu
GREENE, Doug ... 641-782-1324. 182 I greene@swcciowa.edu
GREENE, Eric ... 269-965-3931. 244 O greenee@kellogg.edu
GREENE, Gloria ... 256-824-6000..... 8 F gloria.green@uah.edu
GREENE, Heidi ... 302-736-2300... 94 C greene@cchs.k12.de.us
GREENE, James ... 386-506-4429. 101 G greenej@DaytonaState.edu
GREENE, James ... 202-319-5247... 94 G greene@cua.edu
GREENE, Jeff, W ... 606-474-3298. 194 H jgreene@kcu.edu
GREENE, Jessica, A ... 617-552-3111. 224 A jessica.greene.2@bc.edu
GREENE, John, W ... 615-322-0480. 463 G john.greene@vanderbilt.edu

GREENE, Joseph, J .... 401-598-1038. 439 B
jgreene@jwu.edu
GREENE, Karen, L .... 614-234-5685. 384 J
kgreene@mccn.edu
GREENE, Ken, S .... 252-334-2019. 357 A
ken.greene@macuniversity.edu
GREENE, Kimberly .... 714-556-3610... 74 D
kimberly.greene@vanguard.edu
GREENE, Linda, S .... 858-822-3542... 71 F
vcedi@ucsd.edu
GREENE, Lori, A .... 773-508-3079. 151 H
lgreene@luc.edu
GREENE, Maggie .... 828-328-7109. 356 B
maggie.greene@lr.edu
GREENE, Marcia .... 239-590-7781. 115 A
mgreene@fgcu.edu
GREENE, Mark .... 808-983-4163. 135 G
mgreene@tokai.edu
GREENE, Mark .... 307-766-2474. 543 I
mgreene@uwyo.edu
GREENE, Mike .... 480-732-7146... 14 J
mike.greene@cgc.edu
GREENE, Moshe .... 516-239-9002. 340 I
GREENE, Myra .... 864-388-8351. 444 K
mgreene@lander.edu
GREENE, Patricia .... 843-521-4117. 448 B
pagreene@uscb.edu
GREENE, Perry .... 516-877-4041. 313 A
greene@adelphi.edu
GREENE, Randy .... 201-216-8761. 307 E
Rgreene@stevens.edu
GREENE, Roger .... 212-410-8147. 333 E
rgreene@nycpm.edu
GREENE, Ryan .... 206-296-6260. 523 E
greener@seattleu.edu
GREENE, Shelley, W .... 336-633-0174. 362 H
swgreene@randolph.edu
GREENE, Steve .... 918-495-7040. 398 H
sgreene@oru.edu
GREENE, Teresa .... 253-589-4520. 518 B
teresa.greene@cptc.edu
GREENE, Thomas .... 530-541-4660... 50 D
greene@ltcc.edu
GREENE, Thomas, G ...... 503-943-7105. 408 F
greene@up.edu
GREENE,
Thomas Christopher ..... 802-828-8613. 500 G
thomas.greene@vcfa.edu
GREENE, Timothy, J .... 269-387-2378. 252 I
tim.greene@wmich.edu
GREENE, Tom .... 718-636-3787. 336 F
tgreene@pratt.edu
GREENE, Tommy .... 704-669-4084. 359 D
greene@clevelandcc.edu
GREENE, Travis .... 641-269-3700. 178 H
greenet@grinnell.edu
GREENE, Vanessa .... 616-395-7800. 244 A
greene@hope.edu
GREENE-RAINEY, Velva . 484-365-7335. 422 D
vgrainey@lincoln.edu
GREENER, Gary, J .... 213-738-6834... 68 C
ggreener@swlaw.edu
GREENFELD, Shia .... 718-782-7070. 349 B
swg@utsny.edu
GREENFIELD, Brenda, T . 315-470-6683. 345 B
bgreenfield@esf.edu
GREENFIELD, Derek .... 601-877-6700. 265 G
dgreenfield@alcorn.edu
GREENFIELD, Helga .... 404-270-6425. 132 E
hgreenfield@spelman.edu
GREENFIELD, Ilene .... 201-291-1111. 314 K
igl@berkeleycollege.edu
GREENFIELD, Ilene .... 201-291-1111. 299 D
igl@berkeleycollege.edu
GREENFIELD, Meg .... 504-278-6424. 203 F
mgreenfield@nunez.edu
GREENFIELD, Wendy, M 610-526-5221. 410 J
wgreenfi@brynmawr.edu
GREENGART, Eli .... 410-484-7200. 217 D
GREENHALGH, Jill .... 651-779-3338. 258 C
jill.greenhalgh@century.edu
GREENHALGH, Mark .... 714-992-7042... 56 F
mgreenhalgh@fullcoll.edu
GREENHALGH, Mark ...... 714-992-7044... 56 F
mgreenhalgh@fullcoll.edu
GREENHAW, David, M ... 314-918-2620. 274 A
dgreenhaw@eden.edu
GREENHAW, Eric .... 479-524-7285... 21 G
EGreenhaw@jbu.edu
GREENHOUSE, Jeremy ... 413-755-4524. 233 A
jgreenhouse@stcc.edu
GREENING, Doug, J .... 936-294-1910. 487 A
ppl_djg@shsu.edu
GREENING, Kris .... 870-743-3000... 22 B
kgreening@northark.edu
GREENLAW, David, E ..... 407-303-7894... 97 H
dave.greenlaw@adu.edu
GREENLEE, Carmen, M ... 207-725-3286. 209 H
cgreenle@bowdoin.edu
GREENLEE, Daniel, D ..... 906-487-2436. 247 A
ddgreen@mtu.edu
GREENLEE, Lisa .... 580-477-7702. 401 J
lisa.greenlee@wosc.edu
GREENO, Jimmie .... 215-972-2303. 426 Y
jgreeno@pafa.edu
GREENSLADE, Ernestine . 978-556-3862. 232 E
egreenslade@necc.mass.edu
GREENSTEIN, Amy .... 212-875-4402. 314 C
gradcourses@bankstreet.edu
GREENSTEIN, Benjamin . 319-895-4251. 177 A
bgreenstein@cornellcollege.edu
GREENSTEIN, David .... 212-353-4198. 321 F
davidg@cooper.edu
GREENSTREET,
Robert, C .... 414-229-4016. 537 A
bobg@uwm.edu
GREENTHAL, Joseph, T .. 607-587-3938. 345 D
greentjt@alfredstate.edu
GREENUP, Troy .... 562-907-4287... 76 I
greenup@whittier.edu
GREENWADE, Gabrielle .. 281-487-1170. 484 H
ggreenwade@txchiro.edu
GREENWALD, J. Patrick . 716-888-8216. 316 C
greenwal@canisius.edu
GREENWALD, Nicole ...... 206-876-6100. 523 D
ngreenwald@theseattleschool.edu
GREENWALD, Reesa ...... 973-275-2828. 307 C
reesa.greenwald@shu.edu
GREENWALD, Richard .... 718-940-5900. 339 B
rgreenwald@sjcny.edu
GREENWALT, Riane, B ... 618-650-2852. 159 H
rgreenw@siue.edu
GREENWAY, Adam .... 502-897-4043. 199 B
agreenway@sbts.edu
GREENWAY, Janet .... 605-995-7136. 450 E
janet.greenway@mitchelltech.edu
GREENWAY, Kimberly .... 256-765-4248..... 9 C
kagreenway@una.edu
GREENWELL, Joseph, D . 415-338-3885... 35 E
joey@sfsu.edu
GREENWELL, Randall ..... 309-649-6251. 160 E
randy.greenwell@src.edu
GREENWICH, Grace .... 509-963-2885. 517 F
GreenwichG@cwu.edu
GREENWOOD, Anita .... 978-934-4605. 229 B
anita_greenwood@uml.edu
GREENWOOD, Gail .... 423-472-7141. 460 D
ggreenwood@clevelandstatecc.edu
GREENWOOD, Kevin .... 614-947-6095. 380 A
kevin.greenwood@franklin.edu
GREENWOOD, M. R. C .. 808-956-9704. 135 L
mrcgreenwood@hawaii.edu
GREENWOOD, Mark, D .. 641-422-4395. 181 D
greenmar@niacc.edu
GREENWOOD, Nichole ... 801-832-2027. 498 F
nhg@westminstercollege.edu
GREENWOOD, Paul, G ... 207-859-4776. 209 J
pggreenw@colby.edu
GREENWOOD, Teresa .... 336-315-7800... 96 F
GREENY, Erik .... 707-664-2563... 36 B
erik.greeny@sonoma.edu
GREER, Bobby, T .... 864-488-8251. 444 L
bgreer@limestone.edu
GREER, Christine, G .... 906-227-1700. 248 A
cgreer@nmu.edu
GREER, Colleen .... 218-755-2988. 258 A
cgreer@bemidjistate.edu
GREER, James .... 325-793-4882. 476 E
jgreer@mcm.edu
GREER, Jody .... 260-665-4105. 173 E
greerj@trine.edu
GREER, Karla, J .... 972-860-7173. 470 I
KGreer@dcccd.edu
GREER, Kevin .... 417-626-1234. 279 J
greer.kevin@occ.edu
GREER, Kimberly .... 507-389-5717. 259 G
kimberly.greer@mnsu.edu
GREER, Linda, L .... 704-922-6266. 360 F
greer.linda@gaston.edu
GREER, M. Bradley .... 864-429-8728. 448 G
greerm@mailbox.sc.edu
GREER, Michael, A .... 814-886-6425. 424 G
mgreer@mtaloy.edu
GREER, Rebecca, M .... 540-224-4696. 506 G
rmgreer@jchs.edu
GREER, Sherman, D .... 901-333-4101. 461 F
sdgreer@southwest.tn.edu
GREER, William, B .... 423-461-8710. 457 H
bgreer@milligan.edu
GREER, JR., William, T .. 757-455-3215. 515 H
wtgreer@vwc.edu
GREGERSON, Robert ...... 912-344-2617. 120 G
Robert.Gregerson@armstrong.edu
GREGG, Cody .... 956-872-2528. 480 I
cgregg@southtexascollege.edu
GREGG, Daniel .... 706-754-7728. 129 G
dgregg@northgatech.edu
GREGG, Ellen .... 970-351-2877... 86 C
ellen.gregg@unco.edu
GREGG, Gerald, A .... 503-943-7161. 408 F
gregg@up.edu
GREGG, Heidi .... 973-300-2232. 307 F
hgregg@sussex.edu
GREGG, Karla .... 417-447-6966. 279 K
greggk@otc.edu
GREGG, Michael, J .... 818-779-8040... 50 A
lpyun@kingsuniversity.edu
GREGG, Michael, J .... 818-779-8503... 50 A
mgregg@kingsuniversity.edu
GREGG, Patti .... 678-891-2571. 125 G
patricia.gregg@gpc.edu
GREGG, Robert, S .... 609-652-4542. 305 C
robert.gregg@stockton.edu
GREGG, Thomas, W .... 724-458-3795. 417 E
twgregg@gcc.edu
GREGG, Virginia .... 518-276-6524. 337 I
greggv@rpi.edu
GREGOIRE, David, P ...... 518-564-2090. 344 B
gregoidp@plattsburgh.edu
GREGOIRE, JR., Paul, E 504-282-4455. 206 A
pgregoire@nobts.edu
GREGOIRE, Ronald, J ..... 217-786-2243. 151 F
ron.gregoire@llcc.edu
GREGOIRE, Tom .... 614-292-9426. 386 E
gregoire.5@osu.edu
GREGORI-GAHAN, Heidi 812-465-1248. 174 D
gahan@usi.edu
GREGOROWICZ,
Stephen .... 609-586-4800. 302 G
gregoros@mccc.edu
GREGORY, Alison .... 570-321-4082. 422 H
gregory@lycoming.edu
GREGORY, Annette, K .... 512-414-9820. 466 I
agregory@austincc.edu
GREGORY, Brent .... 662-246-6302. 268 B
bgregory@msdelta.edu
GREGORY, Carolyn .... 216-368-5276. 375 J
carolyn.gregory@case.edu
GREGORY, Charles .... 630-829-6009. 140 B
cgregory@ben.edu
GREGORY, Cheryl .... 850-478-8496. 110 F
GREGORY, Christopher .. 508-626-4510. 230 A
cgregory@framingham.edu
GREGORY, Dan .... 320-308-4932. 261 B
ddgregory@stcloudstate.edu
GREGORY, Darlene .... 334-386-7108..... 3 H
dgregory@faulkner.edu
GREGORY, David, B .... 615-366-4430. 459 A
david.gregory@tbr.edu
GREGORY, David, D .... 413-585-3770. 236 H
dgregory@smith.edu
GREGORY, David, L .... 606-783-5100. 198 A
d.gregory@moreheadstate.edu
GREGORY, Denise .... 205-726-2725..... 6 F
djgregor@samford.edu
GREGORY, Denise .... 740-351-3182. 388 N
dgregory@shawnee.edu
GREGORY, Ellen, D .... 859-846-6046. 197 I
egregory@midway.edu
GREGORY, J. Roy .... 931-221-7127. 459 B
gregoryr@apsu.edu
GREGORY, John, H .... 207-581-1609. 212 B
jgregory@maine.edu
GREGORY, Lisa .... 217-875-7200. 156 J
lgregory@richland.edu
GREGORY, Melissa .... 240-567-5036. 216 F
melissa.gregory@montgomerycollege.edu
GREGORY, Michelle .... 503-491-7210. 404 E
michelle.gregory@mhcc.edu
GREGORY, Paula .... 678-225-7483. 430 D
paulagr@pcom.edu
GREGORY, Richard .... 281-618-5508. 476 A
richard.b.gregory@lonestar.edu
GREGORY, Sadie, R .... 410-951-3010. 220 B
sgregory@coppin.edu
GREGORY, Tom, F .... 570-326-3761. 427 B
tgregory@pct.edu
GREGORY, Travis .... 760-355-6212... 48 A
travis.gregory@imperial.edu
GREGORY, Trisha .... 301-687-4201. 220 C
tgregory@frostburg.edu
GREGORYK, Michael, D . 909-274-4230... 55 A
mgregoryk@mtsac.edu
GREIFE, Alice, L .... 660-543-4450. 283 A
greife@ucmo.edu
GREIFE, Steve, B .... 816-604-2221. 277 F
steve.greife@mcckc.edu
GREIG, Carl .... 903-223-3062. 484 C
carl.greig@tamut.edu
GREIG, Judith, M .... 650-508-3503... 56 H
jgreig@ndnu.edu
GREIL, Stan .... 405-733-7488. 399 F
sgreil@rose.edu
GREIM, Jeffrey .... 413-565-1000. 222 F
jgreim@baypath.edu
GREINER, Stephen .... 606-436-5721. 195 C
steve.greiner@kctcs.edu
GREISOFE, Jennifer .... 516-299-4053. 329 D
jennifer.greisofe@liu.edu
GRELL, Vince .... 602-557-1937... 18 I
vince.grell@phoenix.edu
GRELLE, Elaine .... 978-837-5947. 234 A
grellee@merrimack.edu
GRELLE, Michael .... 660-543-4116. 283 A
grelle@ucmo.edu
GRELLSON, Mona, S ...... 651-631-5390. 263 A
msgrellson@nwc.edu
GREMILLION, Henry .... 504-619-8500. 205 C
hgremi@lsuhsc.edu
GREMMELS,
Gillian (Jill), S .... 704-894-2160. 353 J
jigremmels@davidson.edu
GREMMELS, Luther .... 205-652-3768..... 9 F
gremmels@uwa.edu
GRENDA, Katherine .... 586-445-7315. 246 A
grendak@macomb.edu
GRENDER, Teresa .... 606-368-6044. 191 J
teresagrender@alc.edu
GRENNAN, Jon .... 845-434-5750. 347 A
jgrennan@sullivan.suny.edu
GRENNAN, Kim .... 619-961-4291... 69 I
kimg@tjsl.edu
GRENNIER, Dana .... 414-277-6765. 534 G
grennier@msoe.edu
GRENON, Jamie .... 401-254-4847. 440 B
jgrenon@rwu.edu
GRENOT, Teresa .... 707-826-3441... 35 C
Teresa.Grenot@humboldt.edu
GRENOT-SCHEYER,
Marquita .... 562-985-4513... 33 F
mgrenot@csulb.edu
GREPPIN, Monica .... 615-366-4417. 459 A
monica.greppin@tbr.edu
GRESE, Susan .... 734-995-7457. 241 E
greses@cuaa.edu
GRESH, Charles, E .... 215-951-1539. 420 B
gresh@lasalle.edu
GRESHAM, Jerry .... 731-881-7250. 463 E
jgresham@utm.edu
GRESHAM, John .... 314-792-6308. 275 L
gresham@kenrick.edu
GRESHAM, Loren, P .... 405-491-6300. 399 K
lgresham@snu.edu
GRESHAM, Susan .... 812-535-5121. 172 F
sgresham@smwc.edu
GRESS, JR., Mark .... 215-572-2972. 409 H
gressm@arcadia.edu
GRESS, Michael, E .... 812-888-4506. 174 F
mgress@vinu.edu
GRESSETT, Chris .... 305-644-1171. 100 P
cgressett@dademedical.edu
GRESSLEY, Jerry, A .... 260-359-4052. 166 O
jgressley@huntington.edu
GRETCH, Jim .... 406-791-5320. 288 E
jgretch@ugf.edu
GRETCH-CARTER,
Michele .... 317-274-7602. 168 D
mgretch@iupui.edu
GREUFE, Sandra .... 641-648-4611. 179 I
sandra.greufe@iavalley.edu
GREULICH, William .... 760-245-4271... 75 B
Bill.Greulich@vvc.edu
GREVA, Suzanne .... 415-442-7859... 45 I
sgreva@ggu.edu
GREVE, Debbie .... 620-235-4206. 189 L
dgreve@pittstate.edu
GREVING, John .... 402-465-2486. 291 G
jgreving@nebrwesleyan.edu
GREWAL, Harpal, S .... 803-535-5202. 442 B
hgrewal@claflin.edu
GREY, Kimberly .... 314-392-2241. 278 B
grey@mobap.edu
GREY, Margaret .... 203-785-2393... 93 A
margaret.grey@yale.edu
GREY, Thomasina .... 505-786-4186. 310 D
tgrey@navajotech.edu
GREYDANUS, John .... 541-737-9099. 406 A
john.greydanus@oregonstate.edu
GRIBBEN, Les .... 212-817-7470. 317 F
lgribben@gc.cuny.edu
GRIBBIN, David .... 478-289-2047. 124 C
dgribbin@ega.edu
GRIBBLE, Kari .... 608-663-2305. 532 I
kgribble@edgewood.edu
GRIBBLE, Shannon, L .... 301-687-4161. 220 C
slgribble@frostburg.edu
GRIBBONS, Barry .... 661-362-5500... 40 E
barry.gribbons@canyons.edu
GRIBOU, Julius, M .... 210-458-4110. 492 C
julius.gribou@utsa.edu
GRICE, Anne .... 314-340-3649. 275 A
gricea@hssu.edu
GRICE, Sharon .... 319-895-4167. 177 A
sgrice@cornellcollege.edu
GRICE, Vivian, D .... 803-641-3550. 448 A
viviang@usca.edu
GRIDLEY, Madison .... 206-592-3212. 520 E
mgridley@highline.edu
GRIEGER, Ingrid .... 914-633-2038. 327 C
igrieger@iona.edu
GRIEGO, Brenda .... 702-968-1619. 295 E
bgriego@roseman.edu

GRIEP, Mary ... 507-786-3055. 264 B griep@stolaf.edu
GRIER, Douglas, L ... 630-466-7900. 162 J dgrier@waubonsee.edu
GRIER, Ed, A ... 804-827-0072. 511 F egrier@vcu.edu
GRIER, Frank, O ... 334-833-4005. 4 D fgrier@huntingdon.edu
GRIER, Judith, M ... 757-789-1753. 512 D jgrier@es.vccs.edu
GRIER, Tricia, S ... 334-833-4534. 4 D tgrier@huntingdon.edu
GRIESBACH, Scott ... 715-232-1334. 538 B griesbachs@uwstout.edu
GRIESSE, Sarah ... 612-330-1489. 253 H griesse@augsburg.edu
GRIEVE, Cathy ... 303-871-2397. 86 B cgrieve@du.edu
GRIEVE, Kimberly ... 605-677-5331. 451 F kimberly.grieve@nsd.edu
GRIFFENBERG, Bill ... 843-661-8261. 443 G bill.griffenberg@fdtc.edu
GRIFFES, Michael ... 910-843-5304. 357 J
GRIFFES, Michelle Rae ... 910-843-5304. 357 J
GRIFFEY, JR., David ... 718-429-6600. 349 H david.griffey@aughn.edu
GRIFFIIN-SOBEL, Joyce . 315-464-3921. 342 E griffinj@upstate.edu
GRIFFIN, Adrian ... 718-260-5050. 319 B agriffin@citytech.cuny.edu
GRIFFIN, Angela ... 806-457-4200. 472 G agriffin@fpctx.edu
GRIFFIN, Archie ... 614-292-9820. 386 E griffin@ohiostatealumni.org
GRIFFIN, Barbara ... 202-806-2100. 95 G bgriffin@howard.edu
GRIFFIN, Brent ... 706-295-6306. 125 C bgriffin@highlands.edu
GRIFFIN, Brian ... 919-658-7763. 357 I bgriffin@moc.edu
GRIFFIN, Bruce ... 510-659-6514. 57 A bgriffin@ohlone.edu
GRIFFIN, Cathy ... 908-526-1200. 305 B cgriffin@raritanval.edu
GRIFFIN, Cindy ... 352-365-3521. 108 S griffinc@lssc.edu
GRIFFIN, Clifton, P ... 410-677-0050. 220 D cpgriffin@salisbury.edu
GRIFFIN, D. Joseph ... 617-373-2121. 235 F
GRIFFIN, Dale, M ... 405-585-5700. 397 C dale.griffin@okbu.edu
GRIFFIN, Daniel ... 706-886-6831. 133 A dgriffin@tfc.edu
GRIFFIN, Daniel ... 315-312-2250. 344 A daniel.griffin@oswego.edu
GRIFFIN, David ... 206-239-4500. 517 M dgriffin@cityu.edu
GRIFFIN, Deborah ... 510-659-6151. 57 A dgriffin@ohlone.edu
GRIFFIN, Donitha ... 334-876-9302. 4 A dgriffin@wccs.edu
GRIFFIN, Elaine ... 615-966-5818. 456 B elaine.griffin@lipscomb.edu
GRIFFIN, Ellen ... 415-338-1666. 35 E elleng@sfsu.edu
GRIFFIN, SR., Ervin, V ... 252-536-7217. 361 A egriffin518@halifaxcc.edu
GRIFFIN, Gary ... 815-939-5296. 155 H ggriffin@olivet.edu
GRIFFIN, Heather ... 502-895-3411. 197 F hgriffin@lpts.edu
GRIFFIN, Jacquelyn, H ... 864-977-7081. 445 H jackie.griffin@ngu.edu
GRIFFIN, Janie ... 503-491-6701. 404 E janic.griffin@mhcc.edu
GRIFFIN, Jeff ... 765-455-9339. 168 A griffon0@purdue.edu
GRIFFIN, Jeff, D ... 504-816-8018. 206 A jgriffin@nobts.edu
GRIFFIN, Jennie ... 601-979-2522. 267 E jennie.b.griffin@jsums.edu
GRIFFIN, Jennifer, S ... 724-589-2069. 434 B jgriffin@thiel.edu
GRIFFIN, Joan ... 805-493-3555. 31 H griffin@clunet.edu
GRIFFIN, Joel ... 864-941-8446. 446 C griffin.j@ptc.edu
GRIFFIN, John ... 757-221-2498. 503 N dean-ugs@wm.edu
GRIFFIN, John ... 401-841-6594. 545 A
GRIFFIN, Joseph, E ... 530-226-4157. 66 D jgriffin@simpsonu.edu
GRIFFIN, Karen ... 813-253-7002. 106 M kgriffin@hccfl.edu
GRIFFIN, Karen ... 636-584-6575. 273 M kgriffin@eastcentral.edu
GRIFFIN, Larry ... 901-375-4400. 457 C larrygriffin@midsouthcc.org
GRIFFIN, Lee, G ... 225-578-3811. 204 O lgriffin@lsufoundation.org
GRIFFIN, Leslie ... 662-846-4400. 266 G lgriffin@deltastate.edu
GRIFFIN, Linner ... 252-328-1418. 367 B griffinl@ecu.edu
GRIFFIN, Lisa ... 229-217-4144. 129 F lgriffin@moultrietech.edu
GRIFFIN, Lori ... 253-912-3633. 522 C lgriffin@pierce.ctc.edu
GRIFFIN, Lynn ... 843-383-8071. 442 F lgriffin@coker.edu
GRIFFIN, Mark ... 973-353-1458. 306 D markg@andromeda.rutgers.edu
GRIFFIN, Matthew ... 678-915-4288. 132 C jgriffin@spsu.edu
GRIFFIN, Michael ... 415-575-6154. 31 D admissions@ciis.edu
GRIFFIN, Michael ... 212-636-6520. 324 G mgriffinl@fordham.edu
GRIFFIN, Monique ... 209-473-5200. 47 F monique_griffin@heald.edu
GRIFFIN, Patricia ... 610-660-1266. 432 E pgriffin@sju.edu
GRIFFIN, Patricia, L ... 785-628-5377. 186 F pgriffin@fhsu.edu
GRIFFIN, Patrick ... 845-431-8924. 323 C griffin@sunydutchess.edu
GRIFFIN, Patsy ... 770-531-6326. 128 B pgriff@laniertech.edu
GRIFFIN, Paul, F ... 315-684-6081. 345 A griffipf@morrisville.edu
GRIFFIN, Ragan ... 814-393-2315. 428 C rwatson@clarion.edu
GRIFFIN, Randy, R ... 541-881-5595. 408 C rgriffin@tvcc.cc
GRIFFIN, Sallie ... 601-877-6377. 265 G sgriffin@alcorn.edu
GRIFFIN, Susan ... 513-745-3311. 393 H 0565mgr@fheg.follett.com
GRIFFIN, Tamara ... 870-612-2022. 25 A tamara.griffin@uaccb.edu
GRIFFIN, Terrie, E ... 434-528-5276. 515 G tgriffin@vul.edu
GRIFFIN, Thomas, H ... 919-515-5036. 368 B thgriffi@ncsu.edu
GRIFFIN, Timothy ... 201-216-5325. 307 E tgriffin@stevens.edu
GRIFFIN, Walt, R ... 864-488-4616. 444 L wgriffin@limestone.edu
GRIFFIN, William ... 910-678-8564. 360 D griffinw@faytechcc.edu
GRIFFIN-DONALDSON, Michelle ... 513-569-1515. 376 L michelle.donaldson@cincinnstate.edu
GRIFFIS, Teresa ... 912-525-5000. 131 B tgriffis@scad.edu
GRIFFITH, Becki, S ... 281-425-6399. 475 I bgriffit@lee.edu
GRIFFITH, Cynthia ... 979-209-7206. 467 I
GRIFFITH, David ... 903-813-2587. 466 H dgriffith@austincollege.edu
GRIFFITH, Debbie ... 828-232-5066. 368 C dgriffit@unca.edu
GRIFFITH, Denise ... 618-634-3277. 158 M deniseg@shawneecc.edu
GRIFFITH, Dennis, J ... 330-369-3200. 390 B tbcmail@tbc-trumbullbusiness.com
GRIFFITH, Dennis, R ... 937-393-3431. 389 B dgriffith@soucc.sscc.edu
GRIFFITH, Dennison, W . 614-222-3220. 378 A dgriffith@ccad.edu
GRIFFITH, Ivelaw, L ... 478-825-6211. 124 H
GRIFFITH, Jeffrey ... 505-272-2321. 312 F jkgriffith@salud.unm.edu
GRIFFITH, John ... 610-526-5160. 410 J jgriffith@brynmawr.edu
GRIFFITH, Jolene ... 641-782-1456. 182 I griffith@swcciowa.edu
GRIFFITH, Julie ... 406-377-3396. 286 A jgriffith@dawson.edu
GRIFFITH, Julie, K ... 765-494-6838. 171 M jgriff@purdue.edu
GRIFFITH, Kathy ... 740-392-6868. 384 K kathy.griffity@mvnu.edu
GRIFFITH, Larry ... 765-361-6212. 175 B griffitl@wabash.edu
GRIFFITH, Larry, K ... 724-847-6585. 417 A lkgriffith@geneva.edu
GRIFFITH, Maxine, F ... 212-854-6524. 321 D mfg30@columbia.edu
GRIFFITH, Roger, D ... 304-647-6563. 528 D rgriffith@newriver.edu
GRIFFITH, Ross, A ... 336-758-5244. 370 D
GRIFFITH, Steven, J ... 515-961-1720. 182 E steve.griffith@simpson.edu
GRIFFITHS, Andy ... 207-801-5605. 210 A agriffiths@coa.edu
GRIFFITHS, Geoffrey ... 217-351-2273. 155 J GGriffiths@parkland.edu
GRIFFITHS, Jose-Marie .. 401-232-6060. 438 K jgriffiths@bryant.edu
GRIFFITHS, Slade ... 620-441-6584. 186 A griffiths@cowley.edu
GRIFFUS, Randall ... 706-272-4440. 123 G rgriffus@daltonstate.edu
GRIGG, Daniel, J ... 336-334-4822. 360 G djgrigg@gtcc.edu
GRIGG, Eddie, G ... 704-334-6882. 357 K egrigg@nlts.edu
GRIGG, James, J ... 843-953-7962. 442 A james.grigg@citadel.edu
GRIGGS, Carmen, S ... 617-912-9121. 224 B cgriggs@bostonconservatory.edu
GRIGGS, Donald, R ... 843-953-5540. 443 A griggsd@cofc.edu
GRIGGS, Gary, B ... 831-459-2464. 72 C griggs@es.ucsc.edu
GRIGGS, Judith, R ... 412-396-6661. 415 F griggs@duq.edu
GRIGGS, Robert, J ... 218-755-2097. 258 A rgriggs@bemidjistate.edu
GRIGGS, Ronald, K ... 740-427-5632. 382 J griggs@kenyon.edu
GRIGGS, Tanya ... 510-869-6131. 61 I tgriggs@samuelmerritt.edu
GRIGGS, Thomas, J ... 906-786-5802. 240 K griggst@baycollege.edu
GRIGGS-GRIFFIN, Ebony ... 859-344-4069. 199 H ebony.griggs-griffin@thomasmore.edu
GRIGSBY, Beth ... 712-279-5504. 176 B beth.grigsby@briarcliff.edu
GRIGSBY, Bryon, L ... 610-861-1364. 424 E grigsbyb@moravian.edu
GRIGSBY, Lindle, D ... 972-860-7199. 470 I LGrigsby@dcccd.edu
GRIGSBY, Mark ... 918-540-6275. 396 G mgrigsby@neo.edu
GRIJALVA, Norma ... 575-646-6030. 310 I norma@nmsu.edu
GRIJALVA, Sara ... 575-835-5133. 310 F sjgrijalva@admin.nmt.edu
GRILL, Joshua, L ... 570-577-3223. 411 A josh.grill@bucknell.edu
GRILL, Stephen, A ... 574-372-5100. 166 B grillsa@grace.edu
GRILLI, Eugene, P ... 330-941-1331. 394 A epgrilli@ysu.edu
GRILLO, Mary Ann ... 212-226-5500. 314 A mgrillo@aii.edu
GRILLO, Robert ... 305-348-2738. 115 B robert.grillo@fiu.edu
GRILLOT, Larry, R ... 405-325-3821. 401 B lrgrillot@ou.edu
GRILLOT, Suzette, R ... 405-325-6003. 401 B sgrillot@ou.edu
GRIM, Sandy ... 304-384-5290. 529 E counseling_center@concord.edu
GRIMES, Charles, R ... 330-471-8438. 383 D cgrimes@malone.edu
GRIMES, Deborah ... 252-527-6223. 361 F dgrimes@lenoircc.edu
GRIMES, Donnie ... 606-539-4197. 200 B donnie.grimes@ucumberlands.edu
GRIMES, Howard ... 208-282-3134. 138 E grimhow@isu.edu
GRIMES, Judith ... 816-271-5991. 279 A grimes@missouriwestern.edu
GRIMES, Kathryn ... 952-885-5436. 263 B kgrimes@nwhealth.edu
GRIMES, Larry ... 304-829-7420. 526 D lgrimes@bethanywv.edu
GRIMES, Lee ... 956-872-7271. 480 I lgrimes@southtexascollege.edu
GRIMES, Mark ... 812-749-1368. 171 K mgrimes@oak.edu
GRIMES, Paul ... 620-235-4598. 189 L paul.grimes@pittstate.edu
GRIMES, Robert ... 212-636-6300. 324 G rgrimes@fordham.edu
GRIMES, Robert (Bud), D ... 731-881-7615. 463 E bgrimes@utm.edu
GRIMES, Steve ... 918-540-6226. 396 G sgrimes@neo.edu
GRIMES, Terri, A ... 815-599-3514. 146 D terri.grimes@highland.edu
GRIMES, Tresmaine ... 914-633-2206. 327 C tgrimes@iona.edu
GRIMES, William, S ... 512-505-3021. 473 G wsgrimes@htu.edu
GRIMLEY, Janet ... 206-934-5488. 522 J janet.grimley@seattlecolleges.edu
GRIMM, Carol, M ... 218-477-2327. 259 H grimm@mnstate.edu
GRIMM, Gary ... 503-370-6814. 408 J ggrimm@willamette.edu
GRIMM, Keith ... 503-370-6210. 408 J kgrimm@willamette.edu
GRIMM, Randy ... 816-322-0110. 271 O randy.grimm@calvary.edu
GRIMM, Rich ... 731-661-5102. 462 F rgrimm@uu.edu
GRIMM, Robert, J ... 610-683-4120. 429 A grimm@kutztown.edu
GRIMM, Tony ... 815-935-4992. 155 H tgrimm@olivet.edu
GRIMMER, Karen, D ... 618-374-5152. 156 B karen.grimmer@principia.edu
GRIMMER, Kevin, M ... 315-792-7520. 346 C grimmek@sunyit.edu
GRIMMER, Nick ... 315-792-7110. 346 C nick.grimmer@sunyit.edu
GRIMMETT, Branden ... 507-786-3268. 264 B grimmett@stolaf.edu
GRIMSHAW-CLARK, Maria ... 315-312-4416. 344 A maria.grimshaw@oswego.edu
GRIMSLEY, Deloris ... 973-877-3056. 301 H dgrimsle@essex.edu
GRIMSLEY, Linda ... 229-430-4635. 119 J linda.grimsley@asurams.edu
GRIMSON, W. Eric, L ... 617-253-9742. 233 B
GRINDELL, Monique ... 503-352-1566. 407 A grindelm@pacificu.edu
GRINNAN, Susan ... 804-706-5035. 512 G sgrinnan@jtcc.edu
GRINNELL, Mike ... 509-542-4898. 518 C mgrinnell@columbiabasin.edu
GRINO, Placido ... 713-798-8085. 467 F grino@bcm.edu
GRIPP, Kristine ... 216-791-5000. 377 E kristine.gripp@case.edu
GRIPPIN, Margaret ... 518-255-5516. 344 E grippim@cobleskill.edu
GRISCOM, William, E ... 717-299-7722. 434 A griscom@stevenscollege.edu
GRISHAM, Bob ... 360-438-4372. 522 G bgrisham@stmartin.edu
GRISHAM, Linda ... 781-239-3147. 231 G lgrisham@massbay.edu
GRISI, Mark, P ... 215-968-8391. 411 B grisim@bucks.edu
GRISSOM, Cytha, D ... 717-477-1444. 429 E cdgris@ship.edu
GRISSOM, Randy ... 505-428-1252. 311 J randy.grissom@sfcc.edu
GRISSOM, Randy ... 505-428-1301. 311 J randy.grissom@sfcc.edu
GRISWOLD, Al ... 206-934-5482. 522 J alfred.griswold@seattlecolleges.edu
GRISWOLD, Anna, M ... 814-863-0507. 426 A amg5@psu.edu
GRISWOLD, Emmett ... 229-430-3396. 120 A egriswold@albanytech.edu
GRISWOLD, Mac ... 713-348-6163. 479 A griswold@rice.edu
GRISWOLD, Richard, M . 617-262-5000. 223 F richard.griswold@the-bac.edu
GRISWOLD, William ... 334-285-5177. 4 J bill.griswold@istc.edu
GRITTON, Mark ... 559-934-2455. 75 H markgritton@whccd.edu
GRIZANTI, Vincent ... 716-896-0700. 350 A vgrizanti@villa.edu
GRIZZARD, Juanita Nita . 434-949-1017. 513 H juanita.grizzard@southside.edu
GRIZZLE, Debra, F ... 706-245-7226. 124 D dgrizzle@ec.edu
GRIZZLE, Jeff ... 870-512-7866. 20 B jeff_grizzle@asun.edu
GRIZZLE, Jerry, W ... 575-624-8001. 310 H supt@nmmi.edu
GRMELA, Sylvia ... 716-896-0700. 350 A grmela@villa.edu
GROAT, Gary ... 415-380-1330. 45 H garygroat@ggbts.edu
GROBINS, Mary Alice ... 360-416-7719. 523 G maryalice.grobins@skagit.edu
GRODE-HANKS, Carol ... 605-995-7103. 450 E carol.grode-hanks@mitchelltech.edu
GRODSKY, Jennifer ... 202-434-8718. 224 D jgrodsky@bu.edu
GROELING, Jeff ... 765-998-5246. 173 C jfgroeling@taylor.edu
GROENER, Michael ... 323-259-2646. 56 I groenerm@oxy.edu
GROENER, Michael ... 973-408-3501. 301 C mgroener@drew.edu
GROENINGER, Sandra ... 847-543-2345. 143 A sgroeninger@clcillinois.edu
GROENWALD, Susan ... 877-751-5783. 141 F
GROENWALD, Susan, L . 630-512-8882. 141 G sgroenwald@chamberlain.edu
GROESBECK, John ... 417-625-9348. 278 D groesbeck-j@mssu.edu
GROFF, Keith ... 614-947-6122. 380 A keith.groff@franklin.edu
GROFF, Rodney ... 717-728-2258. 412 J rodgroff@centralpenn.edu
GROGAN, Angela ... 573-592-5245. 285 B angela.grogan@westminster-mo.edu

GROGAN, Anne 617-349-8155. 228 B agrogan@lesley.edu
GROGAN, Rita 408-855-5072... 75 K rita.grogan@wvm.edu
GROGAN LAVIN, Bernadette 718-990-1980. 339 A lavinb@stjohns.edu
GROGG, Pete 812-855-6511. 167 F pgrogg@indiana.edu
GROGG, Sam, L 516-877-4125. 313 A sgrogg@adelphi.edu
GROH, Sara 315-228-6134. 320 F sgroh@colgate.edu
GROH BECK, Genelle 507-457-1421. 264 A ggroh@smumn.edu
GROHMAN, Adam 516-299-2256. 329 D adam.grohman@liu.edu
GROLEAU, Dan 715-365-4450. 540 G dgroleau@nicoletcollege.edu
GROLEAU, Ron, W 815-224-0482. 148 A ron_groleau@ivcc.edu
GROMAN, Elizabeth, A ... 260-399-7700. 174 C bgroman@sf.edu
GROMATZKY, Steven 913-360-7511. 184 H sgromatzky@benedictine.edu
GRONA, Marion 940-552-6291. 493 F mgrona@vernoncollege.edu
GRONBECK-TEDESCO, Susan 785-864-6161. 190 L slgt@ku.edu
GRONDAHL, Mary, M 518-454-5150. 321 A grondahm@strose.edu
GRONER, Steve 618-532-2049. 149 D sgroner@kaskaskia.edu
GRONEWALD, Kate 903-233-3291. 475 J kategronewald@letu.edu
GRONNIGER, Eileen, C .. 785-442-6010. 187 E egronniger@highlandcc.edu
GRONO, Anthony 718-817-4943. 324 G grono@fordham.edu
GROOM, David 503-255-0332. 404 F dgroomjr@multnomah.edu
GROOME, Jean, M 336-734-7292. 360 E jgroome@forsythtech.edu
GROOMS, Craig 814-732-2761. 428 E eup_admissions@edinboro.edu
GROOMS, David 808-984-3376. 137 B grooms@hawaii.edu
GROOMS, Jean, M 843-792-3433. 445 B groomsj@musc.edu
GROOMS, Jerri, H 931-540-2538. 460 E jgrooms@columbiastate.edu
GROOP, Judith, M 717-691-6035. 423 L jgroop@messiah.edu
GROOT, Joycelyn 714-241-6323... 39 I
GROOTERS, Stacy 508-565-1324. 237 A sgrooters@stonehill.edu
GROOVER, Diane 520-206-4592... 17 A dgroover@pima.edu
GROOVER, Joann, V 803-938-3789. 448 F groover@vm.sc.edu
GROOVER, John 912-486-7602. 129 J jgroover@ogeecheetech.edu
GROOVER, R. Edwin 404-669-2065. 130 F eddie.groover@point.edu
GROPEN, Laura 760-744-1150... 58 D lgropen@palomar.edu
GROPP, Douglas, M 214-528-8600. 478 I
GROPP, Jonathan 864-622-6011. 441 B jgropp@andersonuniversity.edu
GROPPER, Daniel 561-297-3629. 114 L dgropper@fau.edu
GROPPER, Nancy 212-875-4703. 314 C ngropper@bankstreet.edu
GRORUD, Kelly 608-663-2200. 532 I KGrorud@edgewood.edu
GROS, Kathy, R 504-865-3237. 205 H kgros@loyno.edu
GROSBY, Karen 954-262-5701. 109 K grosby@nova.edu
GROSETH, Rolf, S 406-657-2300. 287 C rolf.groseth@msubillings.edu
GROSHANS, David, E 308-635-6105. 293 E groshans@wncc.edu
GROSHONG, Matt 425-564-5608. 517 A matt.groshong@bellevuecollege.edu
GROSLAND, David, E 515-574-1149. 179 D grosland@iowacentral.edu
GROSOVSKY, Andrew 617-287-5775. 228 G andrew.grosovsky@umb.edu
GROSPITCH, Eric 816-235-8955. 283 D grospitche@umkc.edu
GROSS, Anne 303-871-3382... 86 B agross@du.edu
GROSS, Barbara, L 818-677-2121... 34 C barbara.gross@csun.edu
GROSS, Bernard, M 301-459-8686. 218 D rbernard@host.sdc.edu
GROSS, Bill 605-274-4311. 449 K bill.gross@augie.edu
GROSS, Bob 715-682-1347. 535 D bgross@northland.edu
GROSS, Candace 870-512-7716... 20 B candance_gross@asun.edu
GROSS, Carla, E 717-691-6027. 423 L cgross@messiah.edu
GROSS, Dana 507-786-3624. 264 B grossd@stolaf.edu
GROSS, Daryl, J 315-443-8705. 347 C djgross@syr.edu
GROSS, Dolores 915-831-2122. 472 B dgross2@epcc.edu
GROSS, Jim 507-285-7256. 261 A jim.gross@rctc.edu
GROSS, Karen 802-447-6319. 500 D kgross@svc.edu
GROSS, Karli 952-563-1250. 450 G kgross@national.edu
GROSS, Laura 518-255-5626. 344 E grossll@cobleskill.edu
GROSS, Linda 517-884-1350. 246 H grossl@msu.edu
GROSS, Michael 732-987-2373. 302 B gross@georgian.edu
GROSS, Michael 508-362-2131. 231 D mgross@capecod.edu
GROSS, Michelle, R 410-951-3610. 220 B mgross@coppin.edu
GROSS, Monika 301-860-4091. 220 A mgross@bowiestate.edu
GROSS, Natalie 914-337-0700. 340 E ngross@sarahlawrence.edu
GROSS, Peter 503-251-5709. 408 G pgross@uws.edu
GROSS, Scott 606-436-5721. 195 C scott.gross@kctcs.edu
GROSS, Susan 201-692-2823. 301 J swgross@fdu.edu
GROSS, Tim 770-426-2611. 128 D tim.gross@life.edu
GROSS METHNER, Sara, E 651-962-5000. 265 C gross6968@stthomas.edu
GROSSBERG, Richard 718-951-5296. 317 C richardg@brooklyn.cuny.edu
GROSSE, Mike 502-456-0004. 199 F mgrosse@sullivan.edu
GROSSE, Mike 502-451-0815. 199 G mgrosse@sullivan.edu
GROSSET, Jane, M 215-751-8085. 413 I jgrosset@ccp.edu
GROSSI, OSB, Anthony .. 724-537-4554. 432 G anthony.grossi@email.stvincent.edu
GROSSI, Deann 312-777-8665. 147 D dgrossi@aii.edu
GROSSINGER, Harvey 202-651-5000... 95 C harvey.grossinger@gallaudet.edu
GROSSKOPF, John 850-973-1601. 109 H grosskopfj@nfcc.edu
GROSSMAN, Alan 201-200-3344. 303 F agrossman@njcu.edu
GROSSMAN, Claudio 202-274-4004... 94 F grossman@american.edu
GROSSMAN, David 714-992-7046... 56 F dgrossman@fullcoll.edu
GROSSMAN, Divina 508-999-8004. 229 A chancellor@umassd.edu
GROSSMAN, LuAnn 605-331-6738. 452 D luann.grossman@usiouxfalls.edu
GROSSMAN, Miriam 845-425-1370. 335 F
GROSSMAN, Richard, G . 603-535-2425. 298 G rggrossman@plymouth.edu
GROSSMAN, Ruth 732-414-2834. 308 K ytcbks@gmail.com
GROSZ, Dale 701-671-2188. 372 E dale.grosz@ndscs.edu
GROSZ, Ken 701-228-5431. 372 C ken.grosz@dakotacollege.edu
GROSZ, Kenneth 701-228-5431. 371 F ken.grosz@dakotacollege.edu
GROSZ, Tanya, L 651-286-7453. 263 A tlgrosz@nwc.edu
GROTGEN, John 229-333-5940. 134 B jgrotgen@valdosta.edu
GROTH, Clayton 608-249-6611. 533 I cgroth@herzing.edu
GROTH, Sue 360-442-2110. 521 A sgroth@lowercolumbia.edu
GROTHE, Malcom, P 206-934-6808. 523 A malcolm.grothe@seattlecolleges.edu
GROTJAN, Gayle 512-313-3000. 469 L gayle.grotjan@concordia.edu
GROTRIAN, James 402-457-2335. 290 G jgrotrian@mccneb.edu
GROUSOSKY, David, P .. 412-396-6699. 415 F grousosk@duq.edu
GROUT, David 574-372-5100. 166 B groutd@grace.edu
GROUT, John 706-236-2233. 121 G jgrout@berry.edu
GROVE, Amber 208-376-7731. 137 F agrove@boisebible.edu
GROVE, Dana 708-656-8000. 153 H dana.grove@morton.edu
GROVE, Daryl 563-425-5311. 183 B groved@uiu.edu
GROVE, Doug 949-214-3434... 41 I doug.grove@cui.edu
GROVE, Kathryne 303-871-7436... 86 B Kathryne.Grove@du.edu
GROVE, Kathy, M 641-422-4382. 181 D grovekat@niacc.edu
GROVE, Laurie 717-396-7188. 434 A grove@stevenscollege.edu
GROVE, Luke, J 515-574-1062. 179 D grove@iowacentral.edu
GROVE, Russell 208-376-7731. 137 F russellg@boisebible.edu
GROVE, Shannon, D 814-886-6391. 424 G sgrove@mtaloy.edu
GROVE, Susan, M 972-860-7040. 470 I SGrove@dcccd.edu
GROVE, Warren 513-244-4200. 377 G warren_grove@mail.msj.edu
GROVE-MARKWOOD, Robert 207-942-6781. 209 E rgrove-markwood@bts.edu
GROVER, Arthur 215-951-1300. 420 B grover77@lasalle.edu
GROVER, Barbara 801-957-4434. 498 B barbara.grover@slcc.edu
GROVER, Carol, N 315-279-5252. 328 D cgrover@mail.keuka.edu
GROVER, Herbert 806-291-1118. 494 F groverh@wbu.edu
GROVER, Rajiv 901-678-3633. 460 B rgrover@memphis.edu
GROVER-BISKER, Edna .. 573-341-6170. 284 A egroverb@mst.edu
GROVER-ROOSA, Janice 307-382-1701. 543 J jgrover@wwcc.wy.edu
GROVES, Allen, W 434-924-7429. 511 B awg8vd@virginia.edu
GROVES, Christine 614-251-4613. 386 B grovesc@ohiodominican.edu
GROVES, Danford, F 910-272-3335. 363 B dgroves@robeson.edu
GROVES, Denise 432-837-8432. 487 B dgroves@sulross.edu
GROVES, Doris 309-438-7304. 147 J dfgrove@ilstu.edu
GROVES, Eric 619-849-2520... 59 L ericgroves@pointloma.edu
GROVES, Jason 325-674-2646. 464 H jason.groves@acu.edu
GROVES, Jay 309-438-5631. 147 J jrgrove@ilstu.edu
GROVES, Jeffrey 909-621-8122... 46 H groves@hmc.edu
GROVES, Kathleen, H 585-395-2317. 342 F kgroves@brockport.edu
GROVES, Kathy 573-592-1106. 285 D kathy.groves@williamwoods.edu
GROVES, Monica, R 651-631-5380. 263 A mrgroves@nwc.edu
GROVES, Robert 517-884-1008. 246 H grovesr@msu.edu
GROVES, Robert, M 202-687-6400... 95 E provost@georgetown.edu
GROVES, Shelley 405-789-7661. 400 A shelley.groves@swcu.edu
GROW, David 801-274-3280. 498 E dgrow@wgu.edu
GROWDEN, Melissa, A .. 517-264-7614. 250 B mgrowden@sienaheights.edu
GROWDON, James, F 610-785-6252. 432 C jgrowdon@scs.edu
GROWNEY, Kathy 603-668-2211. 297 I k.growney@snhu.edu
GROWNS, Richard, O 501-977-2024... 25 C growns@uaccm.edu
GROZA, Adam 415-380-1448... 45 H adamgroza@ggbts.edu
GRUBB, Autumn 252-638-2039. 359 G grubbc@cravencc.edu
GRUBB, Dan 910-592-8081. 363 E dgrubb@sampsoncc.edu
GRUBB, David 504-286-5343. 206 K dgrubb@suno.edu
GRUBB, Derek 970-542-3158... 83 E derek.grubb@morgancc.edu
GRUBB, Geoffrey 419-824-3818. 383 C ggrubb@lourdes.edu
GRUBB, Lillie 620-223-2700. 186 G lillieg@fortscott.edu
GRUBE, Dave 616-222-1412. 241 F dave.grube@cornerstone.edu
GRUBE, M. Marshall 423-439-4219. 459 C grube@etsu.edu
GRUBE, Sean 816-235-8719. 283 D grubes@umkc.edu
GRUBER, Carol 215-646-7300. 417 F gruber.c@gmc.edu
GRUBER, Christopher, J 704-894-2710. 353 J chgruber@davidson.edu
GRUBER, Jay 202-687-7014... 95 E jg1502@georgetown.edu
GRUBER, Thomas 504-671-6480. 203 A tgrube@dcc.edu
GRUBY, Elizabeth 773-878-3752. 158 B egruby@staugustine.edu
GRUEN, Kris 802-322-1721. 499 C kris.gruen@goddard.edu
GRUENDLER, Donny 323-860-1188... 55 E donnyg@mi.edu
GRUENDYKE, Randall 765-998-5205. 173 C rngruendyke@taylor.edu
GRUENIG, Gwen 907-450-8190... 10 G gdgruenig@alaska.edu
GRUENING, Jennifer 309-677-4939. 140 I jgruening@bradley.edu
GRUENING, Kyle 715-365-4481. 540 G gruening@nicoletcollege.edu
GRUETZEMACHER, Richard, R 423-425-4007. 463 D richard-gruetzemacher@utc.edu
GRUHLER, Sarah 360-992-2406. 518 A sgruhler@clark.edu
GRUICHICH, Dawn 480-732-7050... 14 J dawn.gruichich@cgc.edu
GRULKE, Kimmi 928-226-4343... 13 B kimmi.grulke@coconino.edu
GRUMBLES, Owen Kent . 336-316-2499. 355 A grumblesok@gulford.edu
GRUMET, Barbara 718-260-5345. 319 B bgrumet@citytech.cuny.edu
GRUNBLATT, Akiva 718-268-4700. 337 F
GRUND, Faye 419-520-2602. 374 C fgrund@ashland.edu
GRUNDBERG, Andy 202-639-1847... 95 B agrundberg@corcoran.org
GRUNDEN, Jennifer, J ... 302-857-1040... 93 G jgrunden@dtcc.edu
GRUNDEN, Pauline 513-772-9888. 386 C pauline.grunden@omw.edu
GRUNDER, Mark 989-358-7317. 239 C grunderm@alpenacc.edu
GRUNDHAUSER, Tony ... 651-523-2219. 256 A agrundhauser01@hamline.edu
GRUNDIG, John 863-680-6212. 105 D jgrundig@flsouthern.edu
GRUNDMAN, Stephen 703-416-1441. 505 I sgrundman@ipsciences.edu
GRUNDY, Jeffrey, W 973-596-2451. 303 G jeffrey.w.grundy@njit.edu
GRUNDY, Marc, A 423-236-2834. 458 J magrundy@southern.edu
GRUNER, Bradley, W 702-651-5920. 294 E bradley.gruner@csn.edu
GRUNER, Celeste, A 704-216-3459. 363 D celeste.gruner@rccc.edu
GRUNINGER, Sandra 212-686-9040. 350 G sgruninger@woodtobecoburn.edu
GRUNOW, Tamie 231-591-3879. 242 F grunowt@ferris.edu
GRUNTMEIR, Laura 405-422-1253. 399 B gruntmeirl@redlandscc.edu
GRUNWALD, Gerald 215-503-8982. 434 C gerald.grunwald@jefferson.edu
GRUNWALD, James, R .. 507-354-8221. 256 M grunwajr@mlc-wels.edu
GRUPP-PATRUTZ, Deborah 617-373-8838. 235 F
GRUS, Shannon, M 636-584-6505. 273 M smgrus@eastcentral.edu
GRUSHINSKI, Alberta 570-945-8373. 419 N alberta.grushinski@keystone.edu
GRUSKA, Julie 320-363-3395. 263 P jgruska@csbsju.edu
GRUSKA, Julie, E 320-363-3395. 254 J jgruska@csbsju.edu
GRUSZKA, William 404-413-4469. 126 E billgruszka@gsu.edu
GRUVER, Wendy 903-886-5140. 483 E wendy.gruver@tamuc.edu
GRUWELL, Mark, A 712-362-0439. 179 E mgruwell@iowalakes.edu
GRZESIAK, Michael, P ... 724-503-1001. 436 G mgrzesiak@washjeff.edu
GRZYBOWSKI, Mark, J .. 815-224-0437. 148 A mark_grzybowski@ivcc.edu
GSCHWEND, Richard 217-875-7200. 156 J rqschwend@richland.edu
GSTALDER, Steven 203-773-0129... 87 G sgstalder@albertus.edu
GUADAGNINO, Beatrice . 954-545-4500. 113 F cfo@sfbc.edu
GUADAGNINO, Joseph .. 954-545-4500. 113 F jguadagnino@sfbc.edu
GUADALUPE, Ana, R 787-763-3877. 555 B rectoria@uprrp.edu

GUADALUPE, Sarahi ...... 787-769-9965. 554 B
sarahi.guadalupe@upr.edu
GUADALUPE, Yvonne ..... 787-766-1717. 552 J
yguadalupe@suagm.edu
GUADAMUZ, Tatiana ...... 510-261-8500... 58 G
tatiana.Gaudamuz@patten.edu
GUAGLIANONE, Curtis .. 509-865-8530. 520 D
guaglianone_c@heritage.edu
GUAJARDO, Dan .... 918-495-7707. 398 H
dguajardo@oru.edu
GUAJARDO, George .... 405-224-3140. 401 E
gguajardo@usao.edu
GUAN, Sharon .... 773-325-7726. 143 H
xguan@depaul.edu
GUANCI-THERRIEN, Patricia .... 603-641-7202. 297 G
pguanci@anselm.edu
GUANG, Virginia .... 787-743-4041. 548 H
vguang@columbiaco.edu
GUARASCI, Richard .... 718-390-3131. 350 B
guarasci@wagner.edu
GUARDIA, Juan, R .... 773-442-5445. 154 H
j-guardia@neiu.edu
GUARDINO, Richard, V .. 516-463-4069. 326 D
richard.v.guardino@hofstra.edu
GUARIGLIA, Carolyn, L .. 315-255-1743. 316 D
guarigliac@cayuga-cc.edu
GUARIGLIA, Daniel, M ... 716-286-8431. 334 F
dmg@niagara.edu
GUASCONI, Joseph .... 973-378-2643. 307 C
joseph.guasconi@shu.edu
GUAY, Sheila .... 401-323-6324. 438 K
sguay@bryant.edu
GUBAN, Philip .... 440-943-7600. 388 J
pguban@dioceseofcleveland.org
GUBBINS, Jean, E .... 216-368-5557. 375 J
jeg2@case.edu
GUBLER, Seth .... 435-652-7571. 497 E
sgubler@dixie.edu
GUC, Jeremy .... 248-689-8282. 251 I
jguc@walshcollege.edu
GUCKERT, Donald, J ...... 319-335-1201. 175 I
don-guckert@uiowa.edu
GUDBRANSON, Margaret .... 216-421-8016. 377 C
mgudbranson@cia.edu
GUDENA, Chandragupta . 432-837-8702. 487 B
cgudena@sulross.edu
GUDMUNDSON, Donald 970-351-2764... 86 C
donald.gudmundson@unco.edu
GUDUR, Jaganmohan ..... 303-458-4050... 84 M
jgudur@regis.edu
GUDVANGEN, John .... 860-685-2543... 92 H
jgudvangen@wesleyan.edu
GUEDEA CARRENO, Lisa, G .... 574-535-7425. 166 A
lisagc@goshen.edu
GUELICH, Julie .... 952-358-8156. 260 B
julie.guelich@normandale.edu
GUELL, Steven .... 702-567-1920. 293 N
GUENARD, Erik, M .... 906-932-4231. 242 I
erikg@gogebic.edu
GUENARD, Hayward .... 985-448-4479. 208 A
hayward.guenard@nicholls.edu
GUENGERICH, Colleen .... 575-835-5525. 310 F
cguengerich@admin.nmt.edu
GUENTER-SCHLESINGER, Sue .... 360-650-3307. 525 C
sue.guenter-schlesinger@wwu.edu
GUENTHER, Thomas ...... 847-543-2264. 143 A
tguenther@clcillinois.edu
GUENTTER, Robert .... 740-695-9500. 374 H
rguentter@belmontcollege.edu
GUERIN, David .... 318-257-4854. 207 F
dguerin@latech.edu
GUERIN, Fae .... 908-835-2302. 308 G
guerin@warren.edu
GUERIN, Keith .... 908-526-1200. 305 B
kguerin@raritanval.edu
GUERIN, Thomas, B .... 513-556-2389. 390 G
tom.guerin@uc.edu
GUERNICA, Angela .... 312-553-5901. 141 N
grazo@ccc.edu
GUERNSEY, Thomas, F .. 619-961-4272... 69 I
guernsey@tjsl.edu
GUERRA, Blanca .... 210-567-2621. 493 A
guerrabe@uthscsa.edu
GUERRA, Dahlia .... 956-665-2175. 492 B
guerrad@utpa.edu
GUERRA, Elizabeth .... 909-469-5418... 76 B
guerra@westernu.edu
GUERRA, Esmeralda .... 956-665-2103. 492 B
engd5dc@utpa.edu
GUERRA, Jorge .... 305-237-6034. 109 D
jguerra3@mdc.edu
GUERRA, Juan, M .... 512-245-2820. 487 C
jg76@txstate.edu
GUERRA, Luis .... 510-436-1516... 47 J
guerra@hnu.edu
GUERRA, Manuel .... 503-365-4684. 402 E
manuel.guerra@chemeketa.edu
GUERRA, Michael .... 510-628-8031... 51 A
mguerra@lincolnuca.edu
GUERRA, Michael .... 209-575-6867... 77 J
guerram@mjc.edu
GUERRA, Nancy .... 302-831-2852... 94 B
nguerra@udel.edu
GUERRA, Olivia .... 972-860-8065. 470 H
oguerra@dcccd.edu
GUERRA, Ron .... 336-841-9363. 355 C
rguerra@highpoint.edu
GUERRA, Sabra .... 254-968-9770. 483 A
sguerra@tarleton.edu
GUERRA GAIER, Norma 512-245-2645. 487 C
ng14@txstate.edu
GUERRERO, Bertha, M ... 671-735-5638. 546 C
boardoftrustees@guamcc.edu
GUERRERO, Carmen ...... 805-986-5824... 74 G
cguerrero@vcccd.edu
GUERRERO, Daniel, G .... 310-206-6382... 71 C
dguerrero@athletics.ucla.edu
GUERRERO, Dolores ...... 361-593-4410. 484 A
dolores.guerrero@tamuk.edu
GUERRERO, Jennifer ...... 609-984-1588. 308 A
jguerrero@tesc.edu
GUERRERO, John .... 670-234-5498. 547 A
johng@nmcnet.edu
GUERRERO, Larry, M ..... 432-837-8134. 487 B
lguerrero2@sulross.edu
GUERRERO, Sherrie, L ... 909-652-6131... 37 M
sherrie.guerrero@chaffey.edu
GUERRERO, Tammy .... 219-989-2675. 171 N
guerrero@purduecal.edu
GUERRERO, Tim .... 303-464-2320... 84 K
tguerrero@redstone.edu
GUERRERO, Tracy .... 670-234-5498. 547 A
tracyg@nmcnet.edu
GUERRERO-LONGORIA, Marissa .... 956-721-5416. 475 F
marissa.longoria@laredo.edu
GUERRETTE, Leslie, R .... 207-834-7550. 212 E
leslieg@maine.edu
GUERRIERI, Joe .... 213-763-3683... 52 D
guerrierij@lattc.edu
GUERRIERO, Steven .... 215-248-7022. 413 A
guerrieros@chc.edu
GUERRIERO, William ..... 480-732-7012... 14 J
william.guerriero@cgc.edu
GUERRISI, Theresa, L .... 717-780-2576. 417 I
tlguerri@hacc.edu
GUERTIN, Donna .... 413-565-1000. 222 F
dguertin@baypath.edu
GUEST, Charles .... 251-460-6447..... 9 E
cguest@southalabama.edu
GUEST, Denise .... 540-891-3040. 512 E
dguest@germanna.edu
GUEST, James .... 402-472-7488. 292 I
jguest2@unl.edu
GUEST, James .... 845-368-7200. 340 C
james.guest@use.salvationarmy.org
GUEST, Joshua .... 662-472-2312. 267 B
jguest@holmescc.edu
GUETTI, Joan .... 973-761-9018. 307 C
joan.guetti@shu.edu
GUEUERRA, Jonathan .... 305-809-3204. 104 I
jonathan.gueuerra@fkcc.edu
GUEVARA, Carla .... 631-244-3220. 323 B
guevara@dowling.edu
GUEVARA, Christine .... 505-473-6652. 311 K
christine.guevara@santafeuniversity.edu
GUEVARA, Julia .... 616-331-2400. 243 C
guevaraj@gvsu.edu
GUEVARA, Yamil .... 813-663-0100... 96 F
GUFFEY, Larry, D .... 256-228-6001..... 5 H
ldguffey@nacc.edu
GUFFEY, Paula, J .... 606-679-8501. 196 D
paula.guffey@kctcs.edu
GUFFEY, Ryan .... 636-949-4475. 276 D
rguffey@lindenwood.edu
GUGELCHUK, Gary .... 909-469-5381... 76 B
gugelchuk@westernu.edu
GUGENHEIMER, Yirmiya 718-853-8500. 348 A
GUGERTY, SSND, Catherine .... 410-617-2997. 216 A
cgugerty@loyola.edu
GUGGENHEIM, Joan ...... 609-586-4800. 302 G
guggenhj@mccc.edu
GUGGENMOS, Karl, J .... 401-598-2244. 439 B
kguggenmos@jwu.edu
GUGLIELMO, B. Joseph . 415-476-8010... 72 A
guglielmoj@pharmacy.ucsf.edu
GUGLIELMO, David .... 757-822-1177. 514 C
dguglielomo@tcc.edu
GUGLIELMONI, Mark, J . 203-254-4080... 89 I
mguglielmoni@fairfield.edu
GUICE, Leslie, K .... 318-257-3785. 207 F
guice@latech.edu
GUICHARD-ASHBROOK, Danielle .... 617-253-3795. 233 B
GUIDA, Nancy, J .... 212-431-2325. 333 I
nguida@nyls.edu
GUIDO, Deana .... 252-451-8244. 362 D
dguido@nashcc.edu
GUIDO, Diane .... 626-812-3034... 29 H
dguido@apu.edu
GUIDRY, Stephen .... 954-783-7339. 102 M
sguidry@cci.edu
GUILBAULT, Melodi .... 863-638-7122. 119 C
melodi.guilbault@warner.edu
GUILBAULT, Susie .... 909-607-7821... 39 C
susie.guilbault@cgu.edu
GUILBEAULT, Nancy, G . 612-330-1169. 253 H
guilbeau@augsburg.edu
GUILBERT, Debra, A .... 740-368-3394. 387 J
daguilbe@owu.edu
GUILBERT, Fred .... 318-487-7135. 202 F
fred.guilbert@lacollege.edu
GUILD, Richard, L .... 920-403-3216. 535 L
rick.guild@snc.edu
GUILER, Douglas .... 352-365-3526. 108 S
guilerd@lssc.edu
GUILER, Jeff .... 614-236-6508. 375 H
jguiler@capital.edu
GUILFOIL, Kacey .... 818-386-5606... 59 E
kguilfoil@pgi.edu
GUILFOILE, Patrick, G .... 218-755-2016. 258 A
pguilfoile@bemidjistate.edu
GUILFORD, Arthur, M .... 941-359-4200. 117 A
GUILFORD, Arthur, M .... 941-359-4340. 116 C
aguilford@sar.usf.edu
GUILFORD, Renate, H .... 703-993-2299. 505 C
rguilfor@gmu.edu
GUILIANO, Edward .... 516-686-7650. 333 H
edwardg@nyit.edu
GUILLAUME, Cindy .... 928-541-7777... 16 B
cguillaume@ncu.edu
GUILLEN, George .... 281-283-3950. 489 C
guillen@uhcl.edu
GUILLEN, Patrick .... 310-243-3893... 33 B
pguillen@csudh.edu
GUILLETTE, Natalie, L .... 802-656-4183. 500 F
natalie.guillette@uvm.edu
GUILLIANI, Melissa .... 787-766-1717. 552 J
mguilliani@suagm.edu
GUILLIOM, Allison .... 313-577-2230. 252 G
dy9063@wayne.edu
GUILLIOT, Jessie .... 650-543-3896... 54 C
jguilliot@menlo.edu
GUILLORY, Angela .... 225-578-2171. 204 O
angelagu@lsu.edu
GUILLORY, Ann, V .... 201-559-6154. 302 A
guillorya@felician.edu
GUILLORY, Justin .... 360-676-2772. 521 D
jguillory@nwic.edu
GUILLORY, Tonya, L .... 202-806-5990... 95 G
tguillory@howard.edu
GUILLOT, Sheila .... 409-984-6381. 486 H
guillsr@lamarpa.edu
GUILMETTE, Winfield, L . 610-409-3591. 436 B
wguilmette@ursinus.edu
GUIM, George .... 408-273-2765... 55 H
gguim@nhu.edu
GUIMOND, Kathy, A ...... 505-277-1933. 312 F
kguimo@unm.edu
GUINAN, JR., Mark, A .. 607-871-2909. 313 E
guinan@alfred.edu
GUINAN, Mary .... 702-895-5090. 294 I
mary.guinan@unlv.edu
GUINARA, Angel .... 713-780-9777. 465 G
info@acaom.edu
GUINN, Raines .... 303-457-2757... 81 L
rguinn@cci.edu
GUINN, Stephen .... 913-667-5700. 185 J
sguinn@cbts.edu
GUINN, Traci, L .... 989-774-3700. 240 N
guinn1tl@cmich.edu
GUION, John .... 916-278-7322... 34 D
jguion@csus.edu
GUION, Kent .... 706-721-9273. 126 B
wguion@gru.edu
GUION, Martin .... 252-638-7283. 359 G
guionm@cravencc.edu
GUISE, John .... 540-563-8000. 509 F
jguise@skyline.edu
GUIZADO, Roy .... 909-469-5445... 76 B
roygpac@westernu.edu
GUKENBERGER, Vickie .. 630-942-8425. 142 G
gukenbergerv@cod.edu
GUKICH, Doris, B .... 863-638-7261. 119 C
doris.gukich@warner.edu
GULARTE, Mary Anne .... 562-860-2451... 37 I
mgularte@cerritos.edu
GULAS, Charles .... 314-529-9625. 276 G
cgulas@maryville.edu
GULDBRANDSEN, Thad . 603-535-2525. 298 G
tcguldbrandsen@plymouth.edu
GULEFF, Virginia .... 707-468-3068... 54 B
vguleff@mendocino.edu
GULICK, Joseph, G .... 217-333-3303. 162 A
ggulick@illinois.edu
GULINO, Tracy .... 858-566-1200... 42 G
tgulino@disd.edu
GULIUZZA, Frank .... 540-338-1776. 508 A
academicdean@phc.edu
GULLEDGE, Jim, E .... 704-463-3366. 365 E
jim.gulledge@fsmail.pfeiffer.edu
GULLEY, Cheryl .... 615-383-4848. 464 D
cgulley@watkins.edu
GULLEY, S. Beverly .... 773-298-3221. 158 E
gulley@sxu.edu
GULLEY, Shawn, M .... 504-286-5348. 206 K
sgulley@suno.edu
GULLEY, Yancey .... 706-355-5175. 120 J
ygulley@athenstech.edu
GULLICKSON, Janet .... 509-533-3535. 518 D
janet.gullickson@spokanefalls.edu
GULLICKSON, Janet .... 509-533-3535. 518 F
janet.gullickson@spokanefalls.edu
GULLICKSON, Marcia, A 563-387-1400. 180 M
gullicma@luther.edu
GULLION, Christy, D ...... 202-624-1424. 524 G
cgullion@uw.edu
GULLO, Safawo .... 256-726-7054..... 6 B
sgullo@oakwood.edu
GULLY, Constance, G ..... 314-340-3321. 275 A
gullyc@hssu.edu
GULSTAD, Rita .... 660-248-6211. 272 B
rgulstad@centralmethodist.edu
GUMA, Susan .... 914-395-2371. 340 E
sguma@sarahlawrence.edu
GUMBRIS, Janet .... 508-531-1341. 229 D
jgumbris@bridgew.edu
GUMBS, Jean .... 718-270-6434. 319 A
jgumbs@mec.cuny.edu
GUMBS, Marva .... 202-994-6495... 95 D
mgumbs@gwu.edu
GUMM, Eric .... 325-674-2300. 464 H
gummj@acu.edu
GUMPPER, Marianne, L . 203-254-4184... 89 I
mgumpper@fairfield.edu
GUMZ, Diane .... 503-777-7560. 407 E
diane.gumz@reed.edu
GUNASEKARAN, Angappa .... 508-999-9187. 229 A
agunasekaran@umassd.edu
GUNASEKARAN, Suresh 214-633-1500. 493 E
suresh.gunasekaran@utsouthwestern.edu
GUNDERMAN, Lisa .... 501-977-2025... 25 C
gunderman@uaccm.edu
GUNDERSON, Garth, M . 208-496-3000. 137 H
gundersong@byui.edu
GUNDERSON, Gayle, C .. 303-963-3252... 79 C
ggunderson@ccu.edu
GUNDERSON, Greg .... 314-246-7406. 284 N
greggunderson86@webster.edu
GUNDERSON, Jeff .... 415-749-4559... 62 G
jgunderson@sfai.edu
GUNDERSON, Shirley ..... 402-399-2435. 289 A
sgunderson@csm.edu
GUNDRUM, Peggy .... 847-214-7399. 144 F
pgundrum@elgin.edu
GUNEY, Stacey .... 512-223-7000. 466 I
stacey.guney@austincc.edu
GUNKEL, John .... 973-353-5213. 306 D
jgunkel@andromeda.rutgers.edu
GUNKEL, John .... 973-353-5541. 306 A
jgunkel@andromeda.rutgers.edu
GUNN, Daniel, P .... 207-778-7276. 212 D
dpgunn@maine.edu
GUNN, E. Anthony .... 336-342-4261. 363 C
gunnt@rockinghamcc.edu
GUNN, George, A .... 530-221-4275... 65 F
ggunn@shasta.edu
GUNN, J. Martyn .... 209-664-6635... 35 B
jgunn@csustan.edu
GUNN, Karen .... 801-957-4366. 498 B
karen.gunn@slcc.edu
GUNN, Michael, C .... 605-394-2414. 452 A
michael.gunn@sdsmt.edu
GUNN, Stanley, T .... 512-223-1200. 466 I
sgunn@austincc.edu
GUNN, Tim .... 972-438-6932. 478 C
tgunn@parkercc.edu
GUNNELS, Robert .... 870-574-4541... 23 G
rgunnels@sautech.edu
GUNNER, Jeanne .... 714-744-7627... 38 A
gunner@chapman.edu
GUNNING, Mary Jo .... 570-961-4724. 423 B
gunning@marywood.edu
GUNNINK, Brett .... 406-994-2111. 287 B
bgunnink@montana.edu
GUNNOE, JR., Charles .. 616-632-2151. 239 E
gunnocha@aquinas.edu
GUNS, Michael .... 608-663-6714. 532 I
mguns@edgewood.edu
GUNSALUS, Robert .... 818-677-4400... 34 C
robert.gunsalus@csun.edu
GUNSELMAN, Ken, D ..... 252-334-2046. 357 A
ken.gunselman@macuniversity.edu
GUNSOLLEY, Joanne ...... 785-227-3380. 184 I
gunsolleyj@bethanylb.edu
GUNTER, Gail, P .... 662-329-7333. 268 E
ggunter@library.muw.edu

GUNTER, Joan .... 985-549-2301. 208 C
joan.gunter@selu.edu
GUNTER, Kathy .... 334-244-3343..... 2 A
kgunter1@aum.edu
GUNTER, Mary .... 479-968-0398... 20 E
mgunter@atu.edu
GUNTER, Michael .... 870-850-4826... 23 E
mgunter@seark.edu
GUNTER, Randy .... 910-576-6222. 362 C
gunterr@montgomery.edu
GUNTER, Steve .... 828-766-1320. 361 H
sgunter@mayland.edu
GUNTER-SMITH,
Pamela, J .... 717-815-1221. 438 D
collegepresident@ycp.edu
GUNTHER, Janet .... 270-707-3833. 195 E
janet.gunther@kctcs.edu
GUNTHORPE,
Sydney, D .... 505-224-4427. 309 E
sydney@cnm.edu
GUNZENHAUSER,
Bonnie .... 312-341-3500. 157 D
GUO, Lan .... 816-415-5032. 285 C
guol@william.jewell.edu
GUPCHUP, Gireesh, V .... 618-650-5153. 159 H
ggupchu@siue.edu
GUPTA, Mahendra, R ..... 314-935-6344. 284 L
guptam@wustl.edu
GUPTA, Sunil .... 212-346-8449. 317 A
sbgupta@bmcc.cuny.edu
GURA, Daniel, T .... 813-253-6277. 118 L
dgura@ut.edu
GURANOWSKI, Vicki ...... 212-217-4100. 324 C
vicki_guranowski@fitnyc.edu
GUREK, Shannon .... 413-538-2040. 234 D
sgurek@mtholyoke.edu
GURLAND, Jerome, S ..... 413-782-1508. 238 A
jgurland@wne.edu
GURLER, Dan .... 415-575-6125... 31 D
dgurler@ciis.edu
GURLEY, LaShonda .... 419-772-3145. 386 D
l-gurley@onu.edu
GURLEY-ALLOWAY,
Tiffany .... 214-379-5518. 478 D
talloway@pqc.edu
GURNON, R, G .... 508-830-5001. 230 D
rgurnon@maritime.edu
GURROLA, Jeannette ...... 909-607-8632... 39 C
jeanette.gurrola@cgu.edu
GURSKIS, Daniel, A .... 973-655-5104. 303 D
gurskisd@mail.montclair.edu
GUSKOS, Nick .... 310-287-4314... 52 F
guskosn@wlac.edu
GUSSIN, Louise .... 410-888-9048. 216 D
lgussin@muih.edu
GUST, Jonathan .... 610-519-6508. 436 F
jonathan.gust@villanova.edu
GUSTAFSON, Crandon ...... 617-262-5000. 223 F
Crandon.Gustafson@the-bac.edu
GUSTAFSON, Donna, J .. 812-877-8275. 172 C
donna.gustafson@rose-hulman.edu
GUSTAFSON, Eric .... 508-626-4012. 230 A
egustafson1@framingham.edu
GUSTAFSON, Eric, T ...... 704-847-5600. 366 J
egustafson@ses.edu
GUSTAFSON, Liz .... 510-580-6750... 77 C
lgustafson@cci.edu
GUSTAFSON, Peter, A .... 812-877-8230. 172 C
peter.a.gustafson@rose-hulman.edu
GUSTAFSON, Ralph .... 651-638-6122. 253 K
r-gustafson@bethel.edu
GUSTAFSON, Rita .... 661-654-3405... 32 H
rgustafson@csub.edu
GUSTAFSON, Thomas, J 802-656-4450. 500 F
thomas.gustafson@uvm.edu
GUSTAFSON, William ..... 516-299-2824. 329 D
william.gustafson@liu.edu
GUSTAVSON, Julie .... 206-264-9100. 516 J
julieg@bgu.edu
GUSTIN, Joseph .... 216-221-8584. 392 G
jgustin@vmcad.edu
GUSTIN, Luigidge .... 813-935-5700. 111 N
luigidge_gustin@remingtoncollege.edu
GUSTITUS, Carole, R ...... 570-348-6247. 423 B
gustitusc@marywood.edu
GUSTWILLER, Douglas ... 812-488-2678. 173 H
dg57@evansville.edu
GUSZCZA, Susie, C .... 617-373-2101. 235 F
GUTELIUS, Harry .... 610-341-1729. 415 G
hguteliu@eastern.edu
GUTENBERGER,
Thomas, C .... 804-287-8052. 510 L
tgutenbe@richmond.edu
GUTER, Donald, J .... 713-646-1819. 480 J
dguter@stcl.edu
GUTERMAN, Neil .... 773-702-1420. 161 B
nguterman@uchicago.edu
GUTFREUND, Dina .... 718-252-6333. 351 K
GUTFREUND,
Meir Chaim .... 718-252-6333. 351 K
GUTFREUND,
Mordechai .... 718-252-6333. 351 K
GUTH, Virginia .... 847-628-1151. 149 B
gguth@judsonu.edu
GUTH, Wendee .... 309-999-4656. 146 E
wguth@icc.edu
GUTHIER, Mark, C .... 608-262-4463. 536 D
mcguthier@wisc.edu
GUTHMAN, John, C .... 516-463-6791. 326 D
john.c.guthman@hofstra.edu
GUTHRIE, Anne Marie .... 315-279-5412. 328 D
aguthrie@mail.keuka.edu
GUTHRIE, Charles .... 360-992-2268. 518 A
cguthrie@clark.edu
GUTHRIE, Chris .... 615-322-9800. 463 G
chris.guthrie@vanderbilt.edu
GUTHRIE, David, S .... 724-847-5565. 417 A
dguthrie@geneva.edu
GUTHRIE, Edward, L ...... 302-356-6870... 94 E
edward.l.guthrie@wilmu.edu
GUTHRIE, Grant .... 601-318-6193. 270 I
grant.guthrie@wmcarey.edu
GUTHRIE, Gregory .... 641-472-1125. 180 N
gguthrie@mum.edu
GUTHRIE, Lauren .... 877-248-6724... 14 A
lguthrie@hmu.edu
GUTHRIE, Tara .... 919-718-7245. 359 B
tguthrie@cccc.edu
GUTHRO, Clement, P ..... 207-859-5104. 209 J
cpguthro@colby.edu
GUTIERREZ, Amanda ...... 620-242-0424. 188 G
gutierra@mcpherson.edu
GUTIERREZ, Angie .... 305-220-4120. 111 E
GUTIERREZ, Anthony ..... 805-546-3289... 42 C
agutierr@cuesta.edu
GUTIERREZ, Brian, G ..... 817-257-7815. 484 I
brian.gutierrez@tcu.edu
GUTIERREZ, Diana .... 989-686-9434. 242 C
dvgutier@delta.edu
GUTIERREZ, Edna, I .... 787-720-1022. 547 E
registrador@atlanticcollege.edu
GUTIERREZ, Eduardo ...... 305-271-6555... 97 L
GUTIERREZ, Elias, R ...... 787-764-0000. 555 B
eliasgutierrez@yahoo.com
GUTIERREZ, Estela .... 775-336-7564. 294 H
elevario@tmcc.edu
GUTIERREZ, Isela .... 208-524-3000. 138 D
isela.gutierrez@my.eitc.edu
GUTIERREZ, Jaime, P ...... 520-621-1501... 18 F
jaimeg@email.arizona.edu
GUTIERREZ, Juan, F .... 626-585-7264... 58 F
jfgutierrez@pasadena.edu
GUTIERREZ, Luis .... 509-574-4702. 525 G
lgutierrez@yvcc.edu
GUTIERREZ, Mary .... 650-738-4202... 64 D
gutierrezm@smccd.edu
GUTIERREZ, Mary .... 361-593-2601. 484 A
sm698@bncollege.com
GUTIERREZ, Michael, J .. 972-860-7196. 470 I
MGutierrez@dcccd.edu
GUTIERREZ, Muriel .... 786-972-9083. 103 L
mgutierrez@careercollege.edu
GUTIERREZ, Nancy, A .... 704-687-0081. 368 E
ngutierr@uncc.edu
GUTIERREZ, Olivia .... 509-865-8697. 520 D
gutierrez_o@heritage.edu
GUTIERREZ, Olivia .... 509-865-8508. 520 D
gutierrez_o@heritage.edu
GUTIERREZ, Roberto ...... 541-880-2210. 403 H
gutierrezr@klamathcc.edu
GUTIERREZ, Silvia .... 626-584-5579... 45 E
silviagutierrez@fuller.edu
GUTIERREZ, Susan .... 707-664-2287... 36 B
susan.gutierrez@sonoma.edu
GUTIERREZ, Tiffany .... 518-694-7254. 313 B
tiffany.gutierrez@acphs.edu
GUTIERREZ, Tim .... 505-277-0963. 312 F
tguiterr@unm.edu
GUTIERREZ-KEETON,
Rebecca, L .... 909-869-3305... 32 G
rgkeeton@csupomona.edu
GUTIERREZ-LOPEZ,
Leticia .... 657-278-3040... 33 E
lgutierrez-lopez@fullerton.edu
GUTKIND, Susan .... 650-949-7741... 44 N
gutkindsusan@foothill.edu
GUTKNECHT, Leah, K ..... 319-273-2846. 176 A
leah.gutknecht@uni.edu
GUTMAN, Gretchen .... 765-285-1020. 164 B
gkgutman@bsu.edu
GUTMANN, Amy .... 215-898-7221. 435 B
president@upenn.edu
GUTMANN, Mark .... 813-620-1446. 105 O
GUTOSKEY, David, P ..... 410-543-6040. 220 D
dpgutoskey@salisbury.edu
GUTSTEIN, Daniel .... 410-225-4254. 216 C
dgutstein@mica.edu
GUTTENTAG,
Christoph, O .... 919-684-2898. 354 A
christoph.guttentag@duke.edu
GUTTERIDGE, Thomas ... 419-530-4391. 392 B
thomas.gutteridge@utoledo.edu
GUTTERMAN, David, D .. 414-955-8495. 534 C
dgutte@mcw.edu
GUTTMAN, Minerva .... 201-692-2890. 301 J
minerva_guttman@fdu.edu
GUTTMAN, Stephen, J ... 610-758-4204. 422 A
sjg2@lehigh.edu
GUVENDIREN, Ali .... 781-239-2557. 231 G
aguvendiren@massbay.edu
GUY, Elmer .... 505-786-4112. 310 D
eguy@navajotech.edu
GUY, Kristen .... 650-433-3874... 58 B
kguy@paloaltou.edu
GUY, Renee .... 914-606-7612. 350 F
renee.guy@sunywcc.edu
GUY-SHEFTALL, Beverly . 404-270-5624. 132 E
bsheftall@spelman.edu
GUYDEN, Janet, A .... 318-274-7374. 207 E
guydenj@gram.edu
GUYDOSH, Raymond, M 518-564-3185. 344 B
guydosrm@plattsburgh.edu
GUYER, Kathy, M .... 570-577-3307. 411 A
kathy.guyer@bucknell.edu
GUYER, Kim .... 402-898-1000. 289 C
kim_g@creativecenter.edu
GUYETTE, Daniel .... 269-387-5811. 252 I
daniel.guyette@wmich.edu
GUYETTE, Daniel, G .... 360-650-6144. 525 C
dan.guyette@wwu.edu
GUYMON, Ronald, E ...... 801-524-8113. 495 O
guymonre@ldsbc.edu
GUYN, Kathy .... 606-589-3098. 196 F
kathy.guyn@kctcs.edu
GUYNES, Del .... 972-923-5437. 481 F
dguynes@sagu.edu
GUYOL, Kate .... 314-792-7435. 275 L
guyol@kenrick.edu
GUYONNEAU, Christine . 317-788-3431. 173 I
guyonneau@uindy.edu
GUYTON, Deirdre .... 304-327-4569. 529 D
dguyton@bluefieldstate.edu
GUYTON, Don .... 713-743-8000. 489 A
dguyton@uh.edu
GUYTON, Duffy .... 901-751-8453. 457 B
dguyton@mabts.edu
GUZDAR, Farida .... 443-518-3823. 215 E
fguzdar@howardcc.edu
GUZELIMIAN, Ara .... 212-799-5000. 328 B
GUZICK, David, S .... 352-733-1700. 116 A
dguzick@ufl.edu
GUZMAN, Ana (Cha) ...... 505-428-1201. 311 J
ana.guzman@sfcc.edu
GUZMAN, Ariel .... 787-751-0160. 548 J
aguzman@cmpr.pr.gov
GUZMAN, Evelyn .... 718-951-4796. 317 C
eguzman@brooklyn.cuny.edu
GUZMAN, Fernando .... 303-273-3021... 80 E
fguzman@mines.edu
GUZMAN, Gabriel .... 708-456-0300. 161 A
gguzman@triton.edu
GUZMAN, John .... 718-782-2200. 315 E
jguzman@boricuacollege.edu
GUZMAN, Juan .... 308-865-8127. 292 H
guzmanj@unk.edu
GUZMAN,
Juan Johnny, C .... 830-591-7264. 481 C
jcguzman@swtjc.edu
GUZMAN, Ruben .... 949-451-5409... 67 B
rguzman@ivc.edu
GUZMAN, Sandra, Q ...... 956-665-2741. 492 B
sandraq@utpa.edu
GUZMAN, Tobias .... 970-351-1944... 86 C
tobias.guzman@unco.edu
GUZMAN-LOPEZ,
Evelyn .... 787-480-2453. 548 G
eguzman@sanjuancapital.com
GUZZARDO, Joseph .... 609-777-3083. 308 A
jguzzardo@tesc.edu
GUZZI, Martin .... 607-778-5245. 315 I
guzzimj@sunybroome.edu
GUZZO, Linda .... 860-906-5132... 88 D
lguzzo@ccc.commnet.edu
GWALTNEY, Darrell .... 615-460-6405. 453 C
darrell.gwaltney@belmont.edu
GWYTHER, Chelsea .... 802-387-6870. 499 E
chelseagwyther@landmark.edu
GYLLIN, John .... 407-708-4722. 113 E
gyllinj@seminolestate.edu
GYOLAI, Kevin .... 651-450-3526. 258 H
kgyolai@inverhills.edu

H

HA, Jee Won .... 714-517-1945... 29 K
admission@buc.edu
HA, Kevin .... 760-328-5554... 54 A
HAACK, Joel .... 319-273-2725. 176 A
joel.haack@uni.edu
HAACK, Julie, A .... 563-333-6314. 182 B
HaackJulieA@sau.edu
HAACK, Kim .... 617-912-9150. 224 B
khaack@bostonconservatory.edu
HAACK, Kristen .... 617-521-2917. 236 G
kristen.haack@simmons.edu
HAAG, Brandon .... 678-717-3885. 133 D
brandon.haag@ung.edu
HAAGENSON, Heidi .... 763-576-4910. 257 Q
hhaagenson@anokatech.edu
HAAK, Robert .... 330-569-5125. 380 I
haakrd@hiram.edu
HAAKENSON,
Thomas, O .... 612-874-3858. 257 B
thaakenson@mcad.edu
HAAKONSEN, Alexis ...... 203-392-5644... 88 A
haakonsena1@southernct.edu
HAAN, Andrea .... 563-884-5447. 182 A
andrea.haan@palmer.edu
HAAN, Fred .... 712-722-6050. 177 J
fred.haan@dordt.edu
HAAN, Stanley, L .... 616-526-6442. 240 L
haan@calvin.edu
HAAR, Jean .... 507-389-5445. 259 G
jean.haar@mnsu.edu
HAAR, Scott .... 417-862-5700. 271 N
shaar@bryancolleges.edu
HAAS, Brenda .... 740-351-3299. 388 N
bhaas@shawnee.edu
HAAS, Carol, A .... 989-774-5251. 240 N
haas1ca@cmich.edu
HAAS, Evelyn .... 612-861-7554. 253 C
ev@alfredadler.edu
HAAS, Frank .... 808-734-9518. 136 E
fhaas@hawaii.edu
HAAS, Fritz .... 610-358-4541. 424 I
haasf@neumann.edu
HAAS, Jan, M .... 215-702-4312. 411 F
jhaas@cairn.edu
HAAS, Julie .... 913-469-8500. 187 J
jhaas@jccc.edu
HAAS, Mark .... 517-355-5014. 246 H
hass@finance.msu.edu
HAAS, Mitch .... 503-251-5728. 408 G
mhaas@uws.edu
HAAS, Nate .... 970-351-1763... 86 C
nate.haas@unco.edu
HAAS, Nicole .... 718-951-5671. 317 C
nicole@brooklyn.cuny.edu
HAAS, Ocki .... 417-865-2815. 274 B
haaso@evangel.edu
HAAS, Patricia .... 215-503-5511. 434 C
patricia.haas@jefferson.edu
HAAS, Sarah .... 573-518-2307. 278 A
shaas@mineralarea.edu
HAAS, Stephen .... 800-371-6105... 16 A
shaas@nationalparalegal.edu
HAAS, Thomas, J .... 616-331-2100. 243 C
president@gvsu.edu
HAASE, Arthur, H .... 812-888-4448. 174 F
ahaase@vinu.edu
HAASE, Ryan .... 620-862-5252. 184 E
rhaase@barclaycollege.edu
HAASE, Ted .... 206-546-4704. 523 F
thaase@shoreline.edu
HAATVEDT, Chad .... 218-322-2444. 258 I
chad.haatvedt@itascacc.edu
HABA, Jerry .... 972-721-5018. 488 F
dhaba@udallas.edu
HABBEN, Dorothy, E .... 718-990-1611. 339 A
habbend@stjohns.edu
HABECKER, Eugene, B ... 765-998-5201. 173 C
president@taylor.edu
HABEGER, Christian, M . 864-379-8813. 443 F
habeger@erskine.edu
HABEGGER, Toni .... 509-359-6373. 519 C
thabegger@ewu.edu
HABEL, Leah .... 406-771-4327. 287 E
lhabel@gfcmsu.edu
HABER, Carole .... 504-865-5225. 207 C
chaber@tulane.edu
HABER, Jessica .... 914-674-7457. 330 J
jhaber@mercy.edu
HABER, Melanie .... 860-512-2803... 88 G
mhaber@manchestercc.edu
HABER, Sheldon, R .... 425-602-3040. 516 K
shaber@bastyr.edu
HABERAECKER,
Heather, J .... 312-996-2860. 161 D
hjh2@uic.edu
HABERER, Kathy .... 618-468-4126. 150 G
khaberer@lc.edu
HABERER, Ronald, J ...... 716-888-2812. 316 C
habererr@canisius.edu
HABERER, Ronald, J ...... 716-888-8527. 316 C
habererr@canisius.edu
HABERICH, Klaus .... 614-947-6026. 380 A
klaus.haberich@franklin.edu
HABERKORN, Connie .... 608-822-2314. 541 C
chaberkorn@swtc.edu
HABERLE, Charles, J ...... 401-865-1154. 439 E
chaberle@providence.edu

HABERMAS, Mary .... 479-524-7153... 21 G
mhaberma@jbu.edu
HABETZ, Pauline, M ...... 713-500-8425. 492 E
pauline.m.habetz@uth.tmc.edu
HABIB, A. Frank .... 414-277-7259. 534 G
habib@msoe.edu
HABIB, Claudia .... 559-638-3641... 69 A
claudia.habib@reedleycollege.edu
HABLE, Jim .... 415-282-7600... 27 L
jimhable@actcm.edu
HABSCHMIDT, Cathy ..... 765-983-1772. 165 G
habscca@earlham.edu
HABTEMARIAM,
Tsegaye .... 334-727-8174.... 8 A
thabtemariam@tuskegee.edu
HABUCHMAI, Joseph ...... 691-320-2480. 546 B
jhabuchmai@comfsm.fm
HABUKI, Daniel, Y .... 949-480-4005... 66 F
habuki@soka.edu
HACHT, Blake .... 904-470-8050. 102 A
c.hacht@ewc.edu
HACHTEL, John .... 478-445-6804. 125 A
john.hachtel@gcsu.edu
HACK, Mary, C .... 609-984-1661. 308 A
mhack@tesc.edu
HACKEMER, Kurt, B .... 605-677-6497. 451 F
kurt.hackemer@usd.edu
HACKEN, Francis .... 570-208-5954. 419 P
franceshacken@kings.edu
HACKER, Carl .... 692-625-3394. 546 F
HACKER, Carol, J .... 781-239-4220. 222 D
hackerc@babson.edu
HACKER, Cheryl .... 740-351-3283. 388 N
chacker@shawnee.edu
HACKER, David .... 909-469-5408... 76 B
dhacker@westernu.edu
HACKET, JR.,
William, C .... 863-667-5004. 113 P
wchacket@seu.edu
HACKETT, Amy, E .... 253-879-3140. 524 F
ahackett@pugetsound.edu
HACKETT, Gail .... 816-235-1107. 283 D
hackettg@umkc.edu
HACKETT, Matthew .... 859-572-5198. 198 I
hackettm2@nku.edu
HACKETT, Royce .... 229-931-2074. 126 D
royce.hackett@gsw.edu
HACKETT, Timothy .... 510-436-2464... 59 D
thackett@peralta.edu
HACKETT, Tom .... 706-507-8968. 123 D
hackett_tom@columbusstate.edu
HACKING, George, B ..... 802-626-6200. 501 E
george.hacking@lyndonstate.edu
HACKLE, Dale .... 850-973-1616. 109 H
hackled@nfcc.edu
HACKLER, Ken .... 785-670-1010. 191 D
HADALLER, David .... 718-289-5139. 317 B
david.hadaller@bcc.cuny.edu
HADDAD, Abdallah .... 843-349-2938. 442 E
abdallah@coastal.edu
HADDAN, Susan .... 620-431-2820. 189 D
shaddan@neosho.edu
HADDAWAY-WILLIAMS,
Chelsea .... 410-455-6830. 219 D
chelseah@umbc.edu
HADDEN, Diane .... 701-777-6284. 371 C
diane.hadden@und.edu
HADDOCK, Greg .... 660-562-1145. 279 I
haddock@nwmissouri.edu
HADDOCK, Gregory .... 660-562-1145. 279 I
haddock@nwmissouri.edu
HADDOCK, Jennifer .... 870-743-3000... 22 B
jhaddock@northark.edu
HADDON, Phoebe, A ..... 410-706-2041. 219 C
phaddon@law.umaryland.edu
HADDOW, Deb .... 607-733-2300. 349 D
dhaddow@uscny.edu
HADEN, David, W .... 617-824-8620. 226 A
david_haden@emerson.edu
HADEN, Patrick, C .... 213-740-4154... 74 A
phaden@usc.edu
HADENFELDT, Sharon .... 402-481-8606. 288 H
sharon.hadenfeldt@bryanhealthcollege.edu
HADER, John .... 312-553-5962. 141 N
jhader@ccc.edu
HADFIELD, Christopher .. 218-894-5172. 258 B
chadfield@clcmn.edu
HADFIELD, Janice, M .... 402-466-4774. 289 E
janice.hadfield@doane.edu
HADGIS, Nicholas, J ...... 610-499-1103. 437 E
njhadgis@widener.edu
HADJEZ, Claudia .... 305-899-3970... 98 O
chadjez@barry.edu
HADLEY, Craig .... 207-992-1953. 210 B
hadleyc@husson.edu
HADLEY, H. Roger .... 909-558-4481... 51 C
rhadley@llu.edu
HADLEY, Herbert .... 904-256-7484. 107 Q
hhadley@ju.edu
HADLEY, June, M .... 818-779-8424... 50 A
jhadley@kingsuniversity.edu
HADLEY, Kim .... 479-524-7117... 21 G
KHadley@jbu.edu
HADLEY, Linda .... 706-568-2044. 123 D
hadley_linda@columbusstate.edu
HADLEY, Pamela .... 610-399-2260. 428 B
phadley@cheyney.edu
HADLEY, Richard .... 508-588-9100. 232 A
HADLOCK, Eddie, L .... 940-668-7731. 477 I
ehadlock@nctc.edu
HADLOCK, Heather .... 214-333-5340. 470 D
heather@dbu.edu
HADSELL, Heidi .... 860-509-9502... 90 B
hadsell@hartsem.edu
HADWIN, Julie .... 803-584-3446. 448 D
jhadwin@mailbox.sc.edu
HAECKER, Ryan .... 512-444-8082. 485 B
library@thsu.edu
HAEFNER, Jeremy, A ...... 585-475-6399. 337 L
jahpro@rit.edu
HAEFNER, Ronald, I .... 920-748-8320. 535 J
haefnerr@ripon.edu
HAEGER, John, D .... 928-523-3232... 16 C
john.haeger@nau.edu
HAEGER, Loredana, C .... 901-572-2772. 453 B
loredana.haeger@bchs.edu
HAEHL, Sherry, L .... 910-814-5582. 352 K
haehl@campbell.edu
HAELEN, Robert .... 518-320-1100. 341 C
Robert.Haele@suny.edu
HAEN, Rich, N .... 920-565-1213. 533 R
haenrn@lakeland.edu
HAERENS, Joy .... 909-652-6840... 37 M
joy.haerens@chaffey.edu
HAESLOOP, Mary .... 650-508-3651... 56 H
mhaesloop@ndnu.edu
HAEUSER, Patricia, N ..... 928-523-7777... 16 C
patricia.haeuser@nau.edu
HAFFAR, Warren .... 215-572-4094. 409 H
haffarw@arcadia.edu
HAFFEY, Jim .... 662-226-0830. 267 B
jhaffey@holmescc.edu
HAFFNER,
Christopher, D .... 904-819-6225. 103 E
haffnerc@flagler.edu
HAFFORD, Patrick .... 617-989-4870. 237 G
haffordp@wit.edu
HAFKEMEYER, Susan, P 563-588-7769. 180 L
sue.hafkemeyer@loras.edu
HAFNER, Arthur, W .... 765-285-5277. 164 B
ahafner@bsu.edu
HAFNER, Donald, L .... 617-552-4173. 224 A
donald.hafner@bc.edu
HAFNER, Erin .... 419-517-8971. 383 C
ehafner@lourdes.edu
HAFNER, Greg .... 641-673-2168. 183 H
hafnerg@wmpenn.edu
HAFT, Jennifer .... 702-992-2354. 294 G
jennifer.haft@nsc.edu
HAFT, Tami .... 208-769-7729. 138 I
tami_haft@nic.edu
HAGAN, Abdalla, F .... 903-927-3343. 495 A
afhagan@wileyc.edu
HAGAN, Bruce .... 949-451-5254... 67 B
bhagan@ivc.edu
HAGAN, Dara .... 763-488-2465. 258 F
dara.hagan@hennepintech.edu
HAGAN, G. Michael .... 605-336-6588. 451 C
gmhagan@sfseminary.edu
HAGAN, Linda .... 248-689-8282. 251 I
lhagan@walshcollege.edu
HAGAN, Michael .... 217-351-2457. 155 J
mhagan@parkland.edu
HAGAN, Rick .... 619-260-4624... 73 I
rhagan@sandiego.edu
HAGAN, Willie, J .... 310-243-3301... 33 B
presidenthagan@csudh.edu
HAGANS, Karen .... 419-289-5067. 374 C
khagans@ashland.edu
HAGANS, Lori, R .... 405-878-2708. 397 C
lori.hagans@okbu.edu
HAGARA, Kimberly, K .... 409-747-3277. 493 C
kkhagara@utmb.edu
HAGBERG, Stewart .... 801-818-8900. 496 F
stewarth@provocollege.edu
HAGE, Gloria .... 734-487-1055. 242 D
ghage@emich.edu
HAGEDORN, Christine ... 215-968-8034. 411 B
hagedorn@bucks.edu
HAGEDORN, Valerie, A .. 412-531-4433. 414 C
info@deantech.edu
HAGEMAN, Diane .... 320-363-5748. 254 J
dhageman@csbsju.edu
HAGEMAN, Kristin .... 651-773-1780. 258 C
kristin.hageman@century.edu
HAGEMANN, Ryan .... 503-725-6555. 405 G
ryan_hagemann@ous.edu
HAGEMEYER, Gwen .... 812-535-5285. 172 F
ghagemeyer@smwc.edu
HAGEN, Berta .... 218-285-2207. 260 G
berta.hagen@rainyriver.edu
HAGEN, Cheryl, M .... 734-462-4400. 250 A
chagen@schoolcraft.edu
HAGEN, Gary, D .... 701-788-4754. 371 E
Gary.Hagen@mayvillestate.edu
HAGEN, Mike .... 641-683-5243. 179 A
michael.hagen@indianhills.edu
HAGEN, Patrick .... 608-647-6186. 538 E
patrick.hagen@uwc.edu
HAGEN, Peter .... 609-652-4504. 305 C
hagenp@stockton.edu
HAGEN, Stan .... 503-838-8174. 406 E
hagens@wou.edu
HAGEN, Susan .... 205-226-4660..... 2 C
shagen@bsc.edu
HAGEN-FOLEY, Deb, L ... 920-565-1345. 533 R
hagenfoleydl@lakeland.edu
HAGEN-SWANSON,
Cherish .... 218-755-4096. 258 A
chagenswanson@bemidjistate.edu
HAGENBAUGH, Jamie ..... 610-647-4400. 418 I
jhagenbaugh@immaculata.edu
HAGENBAUGH, Stacie ... 413-585-2582. 236 H
shagenba@smith.edu
HAGENBUCH, Brian .... 607-431-4518. 325 F
hagenbuchb@hartwick.edu
HAGER, Amy .... 660-263-4110. 279 B
amyh@macc.edu
HAGER, Melissa .... 609-652-4295. 305 C
melissa.hager@stockton.edu
HAGER, Michael, A .... 319-273-2382. 176 A
michael.hager@uni.edu
HAGER, Tim .... 515-964-6409. 177 B
tjhager@dmacc.edu
HAGERMAN, Brandi, F ... 336-633-0213. 362 H
bfhagerman@randolph.edu
HAGERMAN,
Elizabeth, M .... 812-877-1511. 172 C
HAGERMAN, Reis .... 207-893-6601. 211 G
rhagerman@sjcme.edu
HAGERMANN,
P. Donald .... 302-356-6844... 94 E
p.donald.hagermann@wilmu.edu
HAGERTY, George, J ...... 352-787-7660... 99 B
jhagerty@beaconcollege.edu
HAGERTY, Michael .... 617-266-1400. 223 D
HAGG, Scott .... 760-750-4826... 35 A
shagg@csusm.edu
HAGGARD, Bill .... 828-251-6474. 368 C
bhaggard@unca.edu
HAGGARD, Cynthia .... 785-442-6002. 187 E
chaggard@highlandcc.edu
HAGGARD, David, L .... 423-775-7207. 453 E
david.haggard@bryan.edu
HAGGERTY, Angela .... 203-773-8538... 87 G
shaggerty@albertus.edu
HAGGERTY, Christina ..... 815-455-8727. 152 F
chaggerty@mchenry.edu
HAGGERTY, Dennis .... 609-894-9311. 299 I
dhaggert@bcc.edu
HAGGERTY, Gary .... 617-266-1400. 223 D
HAGGERTY, Janet, A ...... 918-631-2304. 401 F
janet-haggerty@utulsa.edu
HAGGINS, Debra, L .... 757-727-5340. 505 F
debra.haggins@hamptonu.edu
HAGGINS, Isaac .... 216-201-9025. 383 A
HAGGINS, Summer .... 216-201-9025. 383 A
HAGGINS, Tanya .... 216-201-9025. 383 A
HAGGRAY, M. Annette ... 443-412-2244. 215 C
ahaggray@harford.edu
HAGGRAY, Shelby, M .... 202-885-8614... 97 D
shaggray@wesleyseminary.edu
HAGHIGHI, Shawn .... 636-949-4726. 276 D
shaghighi@lindenwood.edu
HAGON, Sean, P .... 617-585-1100. 234 I
sean.hagon@necmusic.edu
HAGOOD, Matthew .... 305-348-2820. 115 B
matthew.hagood@fiu.edu
HAGOVSKY, Beth .... 610-660-1072. 432 E
bhagovsk@sju.edu
HAGSTROM, Fred .... 507-222-5488. 254 D
fhagstro@carleton.edu
HAGSTROM, Steven, W .. 817-515-5186. 482 B
steven.hagstrom@tccd.edu
HAGUE, Barth, A .... 316-978-6288. 191 F
barth.hague@wichita.edu
HAGUE, Stephen, T .... 410-323-6211. 214 F
sthague@faiththeological.org
HAGUE-PALMER, T .... 937-708-5777. 393 A
thague-palmer@wilberforce.edu
HAHKA, Curt .... 906-487-7380. 242 G
curt.hahka@finlandia.edu
HAHN, Audrey .... 765-677-2389. 169 B
audrey.hahn@indwes.edu
HAHN, Greg .... 208-426-5391. 137 G
greghahn@boisestate.edu
HAHN, Jack .... 760-744-1150... 58 D
jhahn@palomar.edu
HAHN, Kathy .... 828-328-7402. 356 B
kathy.hahn@lr.edu
HAHN, Kelli .... 269-927-6701. 245 D
khahn@lakemichigancollege.edu
HAHN, Lenell .... 573-986-6012. 282 B
lhahn@semo.edu
HAHN, Marc, B .... 816-654-7203. 275 K
HAHN, Mary Joan .... 509-313-6095. 520 A
hahn@gonzaga.edu
HAHN, Richard .... 814-866-8160. 420 E
rhahn@lecom.edu
HAHN, Roger .... 816-268-5412. 279 G
rlhahn@nts.edu
HAHN, Sarah .... 530-752-0871... 70 J
shahn@shcs.ucdavis.edu
HAHN, Stephen .... 973-720-2565. 308 I
hahns@wpunj.edu
HAHN, Steven .... 240-895-2000. 536 D
HAHN, Terence .... 312-777-8705. 147 D
thahn@aii.edu
HAHS, Sharon, K .... 773-442-5400. 154 H
s-hahs@neiu.edu
HAID, William, R .... 858-534-5448... 71 F
whaid@ucsd.edu
HAIDER, Rita .... 740-351-3127. 388 N
rhaider@shawnee.edu
HAIDERER, Virginia .... 757-825-2895. 514 B
haidererv@tncc.edu
HAIDLE, Shirley, J .... 208-467-8523. 139 A
sjhaidle@nnu.edu
HAIGHT, Larry, L .... 530-226-4110... 66 D
lhaight@simpsonu.edu
HAIGLER, Anna, D .... 803-536-7047. 446 G
ahaigler@scsu.edu
HAIL, Amy .... 207-221-4228. 213 A
ahail@une.edu
HAIL, Joyce .... 501-569-3110... 24 B
jahail@ualr.edu
HAILE, Bob, A .... 309-649-6331. 160 E
bob.haile@src.edu
HAILE, Christine, E .... 518-956-8080. 341 D
chaile@albany.edu
HAILE, Gregory, A .... 954-201-7410... 99 D
ghaile@broward.edu
HAILEY, Maryann .... 903-875-7305. 477 G
maryann.hailey@navarrocollege.edu
HAILEY, Robert, C .... 504-862-8064. 207 C
rhailey@tulane.edu
HAILU, Elias .... 713-313-7879. 485 F
hailu_ex@tsu.edu
HAIN, C. Stuart .... 610-328-8575. 433 I
chain1@swarthmore.edu
HAIN, Peggy, S .... 402-465-2137. 291 G
phain@nebrwesleyan.edu
HAIN, Tom .... 432-552-2782. 493 D
hain_t@utpb.edu
HAINAJ, Rosa .... 440-365-5222. 383 B
HAINES, Chris .... 602-285-7800... 15 C
chris.haines@phoenixcollege.edu
HAINES, Chuck .... 805-893-8541... 72 B
chuck.haines@bap.ucsb.edu
HAINES, Ena .... 212-678-3486. 347 G
ena@tc.columbia.edu
HAINES, George .... 405-585-5504. 397 C
george.haines@okbu.edu
HAINES, Gerald, C .... 240-500-2000. 215 B
gchaines@hagerstowncc.edu
HAINES, Lynne .... 912-650-5673. 131 H
lhaines@southuniversity.edu
HAINES, Malcolm .... 757-727-5477. 505 F
malcolm.haines@hamptonu.edu
HAINES, Rachel .... 252-335-3744. 367 C
rmhaines@mail.ecsu.edu
HAINES, Terry .... 913-266-8601. 189 I
terry.haines@ottawa.edu
HAINEY, Dale, E .... 817-202-6519. 481 E
haineyd@swau.edu
HAINGRAY, Donald .... 585-567-9287. 326 F
donald.haingray@houghton.edu
HAINLINE, Benjamin .... 580-628-6250. 396 M
ben.hainline@noc.edu
HAINRICK, Jennifer .... 691-320-2480. 546 B
jenniferh@comfsm.fm
HAINSTOCK, Brian .... 215-717-6614. 435 A
bhainstock@uarts.edu
HAIR, Shannon .... 434-797-8495. 512 C
shair@dcc.vccs.edu
HAIRSTON, Creasie .... 312-996-3219. 161 D
cfh@uic.edu
HAIRSTON, Demond .... 704-463-3408. 365 E
demond.hairston@fsmail.pfeiffer.edu
HAIRSTON, Gregory, G .. 336-750-2125. 370 A
hairstong@wssu.edu
HAIRSTON, Jewel, E .... 804-524-5871. 515 D
jhairston@vsu.edu
HAIRSTON, Lathan .... 870-862-8131... 23 D
lhairston@southark.edu
HAIRSTON, Marie .... 415-565-4703... 71 A
hairston@uchastings.edu
HAIRSTON, Tali .... 206-281-2455. 523 C
tali@spu.edu
HAISCH, Craig .... 503-883-2217. 404 A
chaisch@linfield.edu
HAISEN, Michael .... 808-735-4785. 135 D
mhaisen@chominade.edu

HAISLETT, Judith .... 575-562-2221. 309 H judith.haislett@enmu.edu
HAISMA, Dale .... 616-632-3037. 239 E haismdal@aquinas.edu
HAITCH, Russell .... 800-287-8822. 164 C haitcru@bethanyseminary.edu
HAITH, Carolyn .... 213-738-6705... 68 C registrar@swlaw.edu
HAJELA, Prabhat .... 518-276-6624. 337 I hajelap@rpi.edu
HAJEWSKI, Vicki .... 715-394-8241. 538 C vhajewsk@uwsuper.edu
HAJOVSKY, Ted .... 979-209-7211. 467 I thajovsky@blinn.edu
HAKA, Clifford, H .... 517-355-2341. 246 H hakac@msu.edu
HAKANSON, David .... 314-977-7221. 281 I hakanson@slu.edu
HAKER, Catherine, A ...... 518-454-5158. 321 A hakerc@strose.edu
HAKIM, George .... 810-762-3223. 251 E heohak@umflint.edu
HAKIM, Iman, A .... 520-626-7083... 18 F ihakim@email.arizona.edu
HAKKAKIAN, Eliyahu ..... 410-484-7200. 217 D
HAKKENBERG, Michael, A .... 540-375-2379. 509 B hakkenberg@roanoke.edu
HAKL, Roberta, H .... 605-667-5651. 451 F roberta.hakl@usd.edu
HAKLIN, Joseph, R .... 765-361-6233. 175 B haklinj@wabash.edu
HALAKAN, Cathy .... 518-262-4019. 313 D halakac@mail.amc.edu
HALARIS, Dimitris .... 914-633-2649. 327 C dhalaris@iona.edu
HALASZ, Thomas .... 803-777-3971. 447 G halasztj@mailbox.sc.edu
HALAUFIA, Patty .... 435-797-2053. 497 B patty.halaufia@usu.edu
HALBERSTADT, Joseph .. 718-438-1002. 331 A yhalberstadt@yeshivanet.com
HALBERT, Jay .... 325-942-2355. 465 K jay.halbert@angelo.edu
HALBERT, Martin .... 940-565-3025. 490 C martin.halbert@unt.edu
HALBROOK, David, W .... 540-338-1776. 508 A
HALCOMB, Jonda .... 361-698-1210. 471 G jhalcomb@delmar.edu
HALCUMB, Cambrea ...... 573-840-9658. 282 K chalcumb@trcc.edu
HALDEMAN, Pam .... 310-954-4366... 54 J phaldeman@msmc.la.edu
HALE, Barry .... 903-923-2020. 471 J bhale@etbu.edu
HALE, Brian .... 334-683-2367..... 5 F bhale@marionmilitary.edu
HALE, Christi .... 580-349-1556. 397 G chale@opsu.edu
HALE, David, B .... 804-289-8150. 510 L dhale2@richmond.edu
HALE, Don .... 404-413-3025. 126 E dhale@gsu.edu
HALE, Duke .... 704-847-5600. 366 J dhale@ses.edu
HALE, Ed .... 478-445-3350. 125 A ed.hale@gcsu.edu
HALE, Georgia .... 479-788-7721... 24 A georgia.hale@uafs.edu
HALE, Jeffery, L .... 918-540-6201. 396 G jhale@neo.edu
HALE, Jeffrey .... 605-688-5148. 452 B jeffrey.hale@sdstate.edu
HALE, Kara, B .... 620-431-2820. 189 D khale@neosho.edu
HALE, Kenneth .... 216-987-4251. 378 D kenneth.hale@tri-c.edu
HALE, Lloyd .... 816-604-4062. 277 H lloyd.hale@mcckc.edu
HALE, Mark .... 717-564-4112. 419 I mhale@kaplan.edu
HALE, Nora, M .... 704-847-5600. 366 J nhale@ses.edu
HALE, Nori .... 785-242-5200. 189 I nori.hale@ottawa.edu
HALE, Philip, P .... 312-915-6494. 151 H phale@luc.edu
HALE, Susie .... 863-784-7132. 113 G susie.hale@southflorida.edu
HALE, Ted .... 860-906-5053... 88 D thale@ccc.commnet.edu
HALE-SMITH, Margaret .. 269-467-9945. 242 H mhalesmith@glenoaks.edu
HALER, Jennifer .... 317-573-8946. 527 G jhaler@salemu.edu
HALES, Christie, C .... 434-949-1068. 513 H christie.hales@southside.edu
HALEVY, Julia .... 617-262-5000. 223 F julia.halevy@the-bac.edu
HALEY, Alyssa .... 903-223-3060. 484 C alyssa.haley@tamut.edu
HALEY, Brian .... 916-660-7202... 66 B bhaley@sierracollege.edu
HALEY, Donna .... 678-839-6438. 133 I dhaley@westga.edu
HALEY, Gene .... 863-784-7112. 113 G GHaley@neeboo.com
HALEY, John, R .... 315-445-4689. 328 F haleyjr@lemoyne.edu
HALEY, Ken .... 903-785-7661. 478 B khaley@parisjc.edu
HALEY, Tannis .... 303-629-8200... 87 F
HALEY, Ted .... 508-767-7215. 222 C thaley@assumption.edu
HALEY-BROWN, Perry Kay .... 325-793-4894. 476 E pkbrown@mcm.edu
HALEY-THOMSON, Lisa . 518-454-5102. 321 A thomsonl@strose.edu
HALEYALIG, Eddie .... 691-320-2481. 546 B eddieh@comfsm.fm
HALFHILL, Kim .... 850-973-1623. 109 H halfhill@nfcc.edu
HALFMANN, Tina .... 612-375-1900. 256 E thalfmann@ipr.edu
HALFORD, Sharon .... 602-285-7434... 15 C sharon.halford@phoenixcollege.edu
HALGREN, Cara .... 701-777-2664. 371 C cara.halgren@und.edu
HALIBURTON, Tori, L ..... 731-426-7595. 455 J thaliburton@lanecollege.edu
HALIEMUN, Cynthia .... 217-228-5432. 156 C haliecy@quincy.edu
HALL, Amber, L .... 501-450-5371... 25 H amberh@uca.edu
HALL, Amy, J .... 540-674-3601. 513 B ahall@nr.edu
HALL, Andy .... 423-585-6801. 462 A andy.hall@ws.edu
HALL, Andy .... 423-585-6801. 462 A robert.hall@ws.edu
HALL, Ann .... 989-463-7411. 239 B hall@alma.edu
HALL, Barbara .... 603-358-2111. 298 F bhall@keene.edu
HALL, Becky .... 404-364-8469. 130 A bhall1@oglethorpe.edu
HALL, Bobbie .... 404-527-5264. 127 I bhall@itc.edu
HALL, Bobby, L .... 806-291-3410. 494 F hallb@wbu.edu
HALL, Bonnie .... 508-831-6645. 238 F bjhall@wpi.edu
HALL, C. Rick .... 706-771-4020. 121 D chall@augustatech.edu
HALL, Cassie .... 406-447-4572. 285 G chall@carroll.edu
HALL, Cathy .... 605-229-8453. 450 J cathy.hall@presentation.edu
HALL, Charles, F .... 310-506-4532... 58 H charles.hall@pepperdine.edu
HALL, Charles, W .... 386-752-1822. 104 G charles.hall@fgc.edu
HALL, Cheryl .... 985-549-5312. 208 C chall@selu.edu
HALL, Chezra .... 334-876-9284..... 4 A chezra.hall@wccs.edu
HALL, Chris .... 352-638-9703... 99 B chall@beaconcollege.edu
HALL, Chris .... 618-537-6833. 152 G chall@mckendree.edu
HALL, Christopher .... 207-216-4311. 211 C chall@yccc.edu
HALL, Cindy .... 419-559-2371. 389 I chall02@terra.edu
HALL, Clover, W .... 718-990-1924. 339 A hallc@stjohns.edu
HALL, Cynthia, B .... 814-863-5680. 426 A cbh3@psu.edu
HALL, Daniel .... 763-424-0817. 260 C dhall@nhcc.edu
HALL, Daniel .... 502-852-6026. 200 D daniel.hall@louisville.edu
HALL, Darrin .... 832-842-9064. 489 B dhall3@central.uh.edu
HALL, Darrin .... 832-842-9064. 489 A dmhall@uh.edu
HALL, David .... 931-540-2622. 460 E rhall12@Columbiastate.edu
HALL, David .... 340-693-1000. 555 E dhall@live.uvi.edu
HALL, David, L .... 814-865-3528. 426 A dlh28@psu.edu
HALL, Deborah, P .... 828-884-8262. 352 I dphall@brevard.edu
HALL, Delores .... 216-421-7425. 377 C dhall@cia.edu
HALL, Dennis, G .... 615-322-2809. 463 G dennis.hall@vanderbilt.edu
HALL, Derek, J .... 904-256-7045. 107 Q dhall3@ju.edu
HALL, Dessie .... 478-240-5162. 129 H dhall@oftc.edu
HALL, Diana .... 903-434-8121. 477 J dhall@ntcc.edu
HALL, Donald .... 580-581-2293. 394 G dhall@cameron.edu
HALL, Donald, E .... 610-758-4570. 422 A deh211@lehigh.edu
HALL, Donny .... 508-854-4515. 232 F dhall@qcc.mass.edu
HALL, Dorothy, J .... 540-985-8491. 506 G DJHall@jchs.edu
HALL, Earl, W .... 540-338-1776. 508 A campusservices@phc.edu
HALL, Elizabeth .... 856-415-2228. 302 C ehall@gccnj.edu
HALL, Ellen, W .... 937-769-1850. 373 I ehall2@antioch.edu
HALL, Ellis, F .... 317-738-8080. 165 I ehall@franklincollege.edu
HALL, Faith, M .... 904-620-4723. 116 B fhall@unf.edu
HALL, Frank .... 508-929-8304. 230 G fhall2@worcester.edu
HALL, Frank, L .... 603-428-2203. 297 D fhall@nec.edu
HALL, Gail .... 304-236-7619. 528 F gail.hall@southernwv.edu
HALL, Gary .... 252-399-6517. 352 F ghall@barton.edu
HALL, George .... 859-442-4188. 195 B george.hall@kctcs.edu
HALL, Gregory, V .... 863-638-7209. 119 C greg.hall@warner.edu
HALL, Gwen .... 304-724-3700. 526 B ghall@apus.edu
HALL, H. Michael .... 864-503-5140. 448 H mhall@uscupstate.edu
HALL, Heather .... 630-617-3576. 145 A heatherh@elmhurst.edu
HALL, Heather .... 616-632-2457. 239 E heather.hall@aquinas.edu
HALL, Hollie, M .... 607-587-4200. 345 D hallhm@alfredstate.edu
HALL, Jackie .... 606-487-3180. 195 C jackie.hall@kctcs.edu
HALL, James .... 251-381-3491..... 7 D jhall@shc.edu
HALL, James .... 320-589-6378. 264 F jhall@morris.umn.edu
HALL, James (Bo) .... 520-417-4050... 12 R bohall@cochise.edu
HALL, Jami .... 706-272-4428. 123 G jhall@daltonstate.edu
HALL, Janice .... 828-898-8841. 356 A hallj@lmc.edu
HALL, Jason .... 910-893-1291. 352 K hallj@campbell.edu
HALL, Jeffrey, B .... 706-419-1121. 123 F hall@covenant.edu
HALL, Jennifer .... 330-829-6644. 391 E halljene@mountunion.edu
HALL, Jill .... 863-297-1072. 110 H jhall@polk.edu
HALL, Jim .... 479-619-4182... 22 C jhall@nwacc.edu
HALL, Jim .... 631-420-2457. 346 B jim.hall@farmingdale.edu
HALL, III, Jim .... 405-325-1700. 401 B tripp@ou.edu
HALL, John, A .... 214-768-3518. 481 A jhall@smu.edu
HALL, John, D .... 817-272-2102. 491 B jhall@uta.edu
HALL, John, E .... 601-984-1801. 270 C jehall@umc.edu
HALL, Jon Mark .... 812-464-1846. 174 D jmhall@usi.edu
HALL, Juanita .... 805-493-3951... 31 H jahall@clunet.edu
HALL, Judy, H .... 334-493-3573..... 5 E jhall@lbwcc.edu
HALL, Karla .... 502-213-2507. 195 F karla.hall@kctcs.edu
HALL, Karyn .... 936-468-3806. 482 A khall@sfasu.edu
HALL, Kathleen .... 419-289-5030. 374 C khall5@ashland.edu
HALL, Kathy .... 319-398-5498. 180 J khall@kirkwood.edu
HALL, Kelli .... 606-886-3863. 194 K kelli.hall@kctcs.edu
HALL, Kellie .... 701-477-7862. 373 B khall@tm.edu
HALL, Ken .... 254-710-2561. 467 G Ken_Hall@baylor.edu
HALL, Kenneth, C .... 570-577-3143. 411 A ken.hall@bucknell.edu
HALL, Kenneth, L .... 570-484-2598. 429 B khall@lhup.edu
HALL, Kim .... 360-416-7601. 523 G kim.hall@skagit.edu
HALL, Kim, B .... 865-251-1800. 458 I khall@southcollegetn.edu
HALL, Kimberly .... 614-287-2838. 378 B khall46@cscc.edu
HALL, Kimlin, A .... 318-274-6201. 207 E hallk@gram.edu
HALL, Krista .... 559-438-4222... 46 K krista_hall@heald.edu
HALL, Kristin, E .... 845-758-7531. 314 D hall@bard.edu
HALL, Kristy .... 276-523-2400. 513 A khall@me.vccs.edu
HALL, Lanny .... 325-670-1227. 472 O lhall@hsutx.edu
HALL, Larretta .... 701-477-7862. 373 B lhall@tm.edu
HALL, Larry .... 828-328-7112. 356 B larry.hall@lr.edu
HALL, Lataria .... 559-925-3338... 75 I latariahall@whccd.edu
HALL, Laurie .... 716-829-7640. 323 D hallla@dyc.edu
HALL, Lawrence .... 860-832-2298... 87 K halllaw@ccsu.edu
HALL, Lindy .... 206-296-5852. 523 E hallli@seattleu.edu
HALL, Lori .... 419-448-3433. 389 J hallla@tiffin.edu
HALL, Louis, J .... 662-254-3384. 269 A ljhall@mvsu.edu
HALL, Lynn .... 520-247-4364... 18 I lynn.hall@phoenix.edu
HALL, Lynn .... 812-866-7385. 166 C hall@hanover.edu
HALL, Marion .... 270-789-5069. 193 D mthall@campbellsville.edu
HALL, Mark .... 918-495-7742. 398 H mhall@oru.edu
HALL, Mark .... 734-384-4261. 247 C mhall@monroeccc.edu
HALL, Mark .... 615-297-7545. 452 J hallm@aquinascollege.edu
HALL, Marlon, R .... 530-251-8820... 50 F mhall@lassencollege.edu
HALL, Mary Lee .... 731-881-7125. 463 E mlhall@utm.edu
HALL, Matthew .... 502-897-4205. 199 B mhall@sbts.edu
HALL, Mavis .... 718-631-6391. 319 D mhall@qcc.cuny.edu
HALL, Megan .... 828-898-8729. 356 A hallm@lmc.edu
HALL, Michael .... 302-736-2483... 94 C halljmic@wesley.edu
HALL, Michael, R .... 336-841-9235. 355 C mhall@highpoint.edu
HALL, Michelle .... 620-278-4211. 190 I mhall@sterling.edu
HALL, Michelle .... 985-549-2077. 208 C mhall@selu.edu
HALL, Michelle .... 404-364-8336. 130 A mhall@oglethorpe.edu
HALL, Michelle .... 301-846-2493. 214 H mhall@frederick.edu
HALL, Michelle .... 662-685-4771. 266 C mhall@bmc.edu
HALL, Norman, D .... 618-664-7119. 145 G norm.hall@greenville.edu
HALL, Pamela .... 313-845-6410. 243 H phall@hfcc.edu
HALL, Pat .... 620-862-5252. 184 E pat.hall@barclaycollege.edu
HALL, Patricia .... 479-394-7622... 23 B phall@rmcc.edu
HALL, Patricia .... 402-280-2702. 289 D patriciahall@creighton.edu
HALL, Paulakay .... 423-775-7308. 453 E phall7036@bryan.edu
HALL, Philip, D .... 843-792-8979. 445 B hallpd@musc.edu
HALL, Ralph, G .... 972-758-3831. 469 G rhall@collin.edu
HALL, Randolph, W .... 213-740-6709... 74 A rwhall@usc.edu
HALL, Randy .... 864-597-4351. 449 I halljr@wofford.edu
HALL, Raymond, D .... 810-762-3335. 251 E raydhall@umflint.edu
HALL, Rebecca .... 304-326-1304. 527 G rhall@salemu.edu
HALL, Renardo .... 404-653-7858. 129 D rhall@morehouse.edu
HALL, Ricardo, D .... 305-284-5353. 118 F rdhall@miami.edu
HALL, Richard .... 405-208-5050. 397 F rhall@okcu.edu
HALL, Richard (Bubba) ... 520-515-5380... 12 R hallr@cochise.edu

HALL, Robert .... 716-829-7657. 323 D
hallrm@dyc.edu
HALL, Ron .... 865-251-1800. 458 I
rhall@southcollegetn.edu
HALL, Russell .... 806-894-9611. 480 H
rhall@southplainscollege.edu
HALL, Ruth .... 757-340-2121. 503 I
dcacvab@centura.edu
HALL, Ryan .... 513-732-5301. 391 B
hallrn@email.uc.edu
HALL, Sandra Betts .... 334-833-4349..... 4 D
shall@huntingdon.edu
HALL, Sandy .... 325-674-2273. 464 H
halls@acu.edu
HALL, Sarah, S .... 859-238-5471. 193 E
sarah.hall@centre.edu
HALL, Sigrid .... 336-750-3148. 370 A
allensh@wssu.edu
HALL, Stacy .... 706-865-2134. 133 B
shall@truett.edu
HALL, Steven .... 309-341-7823. 150 A
shall@knox.edu
HALL, Steven, A .... 617-353-2251. 224 D
sahall@bu.edu
HALL, Susan .... 214-378-1609. 470 F
shall@dcccd.edu
HALL, Susan .... 856-415-2185. 302 C
shall@gccnj.edu
HALL, Tara, D .... 580-327-8601. 396 N
tdhall@nwosu.edu
HALL, Teresa .... 410-704-2332. 220 E
thall@towson.edu
HALL, Terry .... 415-561-1908... 38 L
thall@ccsf.edu
HALL, Tim .... 410-455-2207. 219 D
HALL, Tim .... 308-535-3612. 290 J
hallt@mpcc.edu
HALL, Timothy, L .... 931-221-7566. 459 B
hallt@apsu.edu
HALL, Tom .... 904-256-7715. 107 Q
thall5@ju.edu
HALL, Tom .... 806-291-3750. 494 F
hallt@wbu.edu
HALL, Tracy .... 314-644-9280. 281 E
thall80@stlcc.edu
HALL, Tracy .... 845-434-5750. 347 A
thall@sullivan.suny.edu
HALL, Tracy .... 360-867-6205. 519 J
hallt@evergreen.edu
HALL, Tracy, A .... 336-316-2349. 355 A
thall@guilford.edu
HALL, Trevor .... 863-638-7286. 119 C
trevor.hall@warner.edu
HALL, Walter .... 404-364-8543. 130 A
whall@oglethorpe.edu
HALL, Wayne .... 502-852-6111. 200 D
whall@louisville.edu
HALL, Wendy .... 360-442-2491. 521 A
whall@lowercolumbia.edu
HALL, William .... 714-997-6891... 38 A
whall@chapman.edu
HALL, JR., William .... 859-858-3511. 192 B
bill.hall@asbury.edu
HALL, William, B .... 401-341-2132. 440 C
hallb@salve.edu
HALL, William, C .... 617-984-1760. 235 I
whall@quincycollege.edu
HALL, William, M .... 256-824-2302..... 8 F
William.Hall@uah.edu
HALL CARNES, Ginger ... 210-486-3884. 465 A
vcarnes@alamo.edu
HALL-JONES, Jenny .... 740-593-1800. 387 C
hallj1@ohio.edu
HALL-NUZUM,
Deidra, R .... 304-829-7115. 526 D
dhall-nuzum@bethanywv.edu
HALL SMITH, Willa .... 202-797-3670..... 8 A
HALL-YATES, Joyce .... 419-448-3049. 389 J
hallyatesjc@tiffin.edu
HALLADAY, Choi .... 253-964-6506. 522 C
challaday@pierce.ctc.edu
HALLAHAN, Kerry, R ...... 314-505-7000. 272 J
hallahank@csl.edu
HALLAM, Donna .... 813-874-0094. 100 O
HALLAM, Steve .... 315-279-5213. 328 D
shallam@mail.keuka.edu
HALLANGER, Nathan ...... 612-330-1674. 253 H
hallange@augsburg.edu
HALLAS, Vicki .... 718-405-3332. 320 G
vicki.hallas@mountsaintvincent.edu
HALLBERG, Robert .... 773-298-3109. 158 E
hallberg@sxu.edu
HALLBLADE, Shirley .... 904-620-2616. 116 B
shirley.hallblade@unf.edu
HALLE, Kevin .... 402-375-7234. 291 F
kehalle1@wsc.edu
HALLEEN, Jan .... 952-888-4777. 263 B
jhalleen@nwhealth.edu
HALLER, Amy .... 815-455-8768. 152 F
aheller@mchenry.edu
HALLER, Bryan .... 212-220-8013. 317 A
bhaller@bmcc.cuny.edu
HALLER, John, G .... 610-660-1305. 432 E
jhaller@sju.edu
HALLER, John, R .... 320-308-5922. 261 C
jhaller@sctcc.edu
HALLER, Pam .... 715-833-6397. 539 J
phaller1@cvtc.edu
HALLERAN, Donna .... 608-265-3443. 536 D
dhalleran@vc.wisc.edu
HALLERAN, Michael .... 757-221-1993. 503 N
halleran@wm.edu
HALLETT, David .... 503-399-5172. 402 E
david.hallett@chemeketa.edu
HALLETT, Tom .... 708-209-3350. 143 E
tom.hallett@cuchicago.edu
HALLGREN, Martyne ...... 402-557-7199. 288 G
martyne.hallgren@bellevue.edu
HALLICK, Lesley, M .... 503-352-2123. 407 A
president@pacificu.edu
HALLIDAY, Chris .... 660-626-2800. 271 A
challiday@atsu.edu
HALLIDAY, Clayton .... 530-754-1073... 70 J
clhalliday@ucdavis.edu
HALLIDAY, Robert, M .... 315-792-3122. 349 F
rhalliday@utica.edu
HALLIGAN, Meg, F .... 563-333-6311.. 182 B
HalliganMegF@sau.edu
HALLINAN, Marie .... 877-751-5783. 141 F
HALLIS, John .... 419-448-3300. 389 J
hallisj@tiffin.edu
HALLISEY, L. Ann .... 510-204-0716... 38 J
ahallisey@cdsp.edu
HALLMAN, Janet, S .... 253-879-8620. 524 F
jhallman@pugetsound.edu
HALLMARK, James .... 979-458-6070. 482 E
jhallmark@tamus.edu
HALLOCK, Meghan .... 603-428-2211. 297 D
mhallock@nec.edu
HALLORAN, Beth .... 641-269-3200. 178 H
halloran@grinnell.edu
HALLORAN, Sybil, C ...... 804-828-6125. 511 F
schallor@vcu.edu
HALLORAN, Tom .... 781-595-6768. 228 C
thalloran@mariancourt.edu
HALLQUIST, Carrie, L .... 715-833-6670. 539 J
challquist1@cvtc.edu
HALLSTROM, Lilian .... 808-543-8088. 135 F
lhallstrom@hpu.edu
HALLSTROM, Peggy .... 605-626-3011. 451 I
hallstrp@northern.edu
HALLUM, Ann .... 415-338-2231... 35 E
glider@sfsu.edu
HALMON, Judy .... 803-793-5170. 443 E
holmanj@denmarktech.edu
HALONEN, Jane, S .... 850-474-2688. 117 B
jhalonen@uwf.edu
HALPERIN, Edward, C .... 914-594-4900. 334 A
edward_halperin@nymc.edu
HALPERIN, Michael .... 607-735-1895. 323 H
registrar@elmira.edu
HALPERN, Avrohom .... 516-239-9002. 340 I
HALPERN, Jane, L .... 410-704-2466. 220 E
jhalpern@towson.edu
HALPERN, Linda, C .... 540-568-2852. 506 F
halperlc@jmu.edu
HALPERN, Mike .... 208-769-3310. 138 I
mike_halpern@nic.edu
HALPIN, Eamon .... 318-473-6545. 205 A
ehalpin@lsua.edu
HALPIN, Eamon .... 318-427-4469. 205 A
ehalpin@lsua.edu
HALPIN-ROBBINS,
Kathleen .... 413-565-1000. 222 F
khrobbins@baypath.edu
HALPRIN, Janet .... 845-434-5750. 347 A
jhalprin@sunysullivan.edu
HALSEY, Cindy .... 843-470-8396. 447 C
chalsey@tcl.edu
HALSEY, Glenn .... 307-755-9820. 544 B
ghalsey@wyotechstaff.edu
HALSEY, Mark, D .... 845-758-7267. 314 D
halsey@bard.edu
HALSTEAD, Barbara .... 407-582-3250. 118 M
bhalstead@valenciacollege.edu
HALSTEAD, John, R .... 585-395-2361. 342 F
halstead@brockport.edu
HALSTEAD, Joyce .... 229-225-5062. 132 D
jhalstead@southwestgatech.edu
HALSTEAD, Lois, A .... 312-942-7117. 157 G
lois_a_halstead@rush.edu
HALSTEAD, Michele .... 845-257-3295. 342 B
halsteam@newpaltz.edu
HALSTEAD, Sarah .... 541-684-7250. 405 C
khalstead@nwcu.edu
HALSTED, Steve .... 406-771-4367. 287 E
shalsted@gfcmsu.edu
HALTER, Robert .... 317-274-7746. 168 D
rhalter@iupui.edu
HALTERMAN, Lauren, C . 410-827-5818. 214 C
lhalterman@chesapeake.edu
HALTERMAN, Rick .... 423-236-2871. 458 J
halterman@southern.edu
HALTERMAN, Virginia .... 660-626-2272. 271 A
vhalterman@atsu.edu
HALUSCHAK, Rich .... 626-396-2308... 28 P
rich.haluschak@artcenter.edu
HALUSHKA, Lisa .... 248-751-7800. 250 G
halushkl@cooley.edu
HALUSHKA, Perry, V ...... 843-792-3012. 445 B
halushpv@musc.edu
HALUSKA, Jan .... 423-236-2738. 458 J
haluska@southern.edu
HALUZAK, Jennifer, L .... 414-955-8246. 534 C
jhaluzak@mcw.edu
HALVERSON, Andrea, R . 651-631-5121. 263 A
arhalverson@nwc.edu
HALVERSON, Paul, K ...... 317-274-3126. 168 D
pkhalver@iupui.edu
HALVERSON, Tom, L ...... 605-256-5165. 451 H
tom.halverson@dsu.edu
HALVERSTADT, David ..... 360-538-4234. 520 B
dhalverst@ghc.edu
HALVORSON, Daisy .... 563-588-6315. 176 F
daisy.halvorson@clarke.edu
HALVORSON, J. Derek ... 706-419-1117. 123 F
derek.halvorson@covenant.edu
HALVORSON, Lloyd .... 701-662-1681. 372 D
Lloyd.Halvorson@lrsc.edu
HAM, Clay .... 217-732-3168. 151 B
cham@lincolnchristian.edu
HAM, Frederic .... 321-674-7318. 104 H
fmh@fit.edu
HAM, Gary .... 978-762-4000. 232 D
gham@northshore.edu
HAM, Jeoung, H .... 636-327-4645. 277 K
reg@midwest.edu
HAM, Karen, L .... 315-267-2344. 344 C
hamkl@potsdam.edu
HAM, Marsha, K .... 203-932-7386... 92 E
mham@newhaven.edu
HAM, Paige .... 919-735-5151. 364 H
peham@waynecc.edu
HAM, Scott, D .... 317-940-8112. 164 J
sdham@butler.edu
HAM, Yoo, J .... 636-327-4645. 277 K
seoul@midwest.edu
HAMAD, James .... 630-844-4910. 140 A
jhamad@aurora.edu
HAMADA, Larisa .... 562-985-8256... 33 F
larisa.hamada@csulb.edu
HAMAKER, Michelle .... 308-865-8517. 292 H
hamakerm@unk.edu
HAMAKER, Steve .... 805-690-7680... 30 A
shamaker@brooks.edu
HAMAN, Linda .... 636-227-2100. 276 F
linda.haman@logan.edu
HAMANN, Andrew .... 507-529-2789. 261 A
andrew.hamann@rctc.edu
HAMANN, Dick, T .... 407-708-2258. 113 E
hamannd@seminolestate.edu
HAMANN, Gregory, J ...... 541-917-4200. 404 B
hamanng@linnbenton.edu
HAMANN, Melanie .... 573-840-9767. 282 K
mhamann@trcc.edu
HAMBERGER,
Barnett, W .... 212-998-2310. 334 D
bwh1@nyu.edu
HAMBEY, Anthony .... 205-226-4850..... 2 C
ahambey@bsc.edu
HAMBLEN, Jon .... 916-660-7382... 66 B
jhamblen@sierracollege.edu
HAMBLIN, Carolyn .... 928-875-9116... 15 L
chamblin@mohave.edu
HAMBLIN, John .... 503-491-7384. 404 E
john.hamblin@mhcc.edu
HAMBLIN, Veronica .... 660-263-3900. 272 A
vhamblin@cccb.edu
HAMBLY, Raine .... 714-432-5628... 39 K
rhambly@occ.cccd.edu
HAMBROCK, Daniel .... 651-793-1712. 259 C
daniel.hambrock@metrostate.edu
HAMBURG, Gail .... 509-793-2002. 517 C
gailh@bigbend.edu
HAMBURG, Gary .... 773-834-2059. 160 I
ghamburg@ttic.edu
HAMBURG, Jo Ann .... 845-341-4903. 335 H
joann.hamburg@sunyorange.edu
HAMBURGER, Daniel ..... 630-725-1930. 144 A
dhamburger@devry.edu
HAMBY, Dale .... 717-901-5100. 418 E
dhamby@harrisburgu.edu
HAMBY, Dan .... 270-707-3790. 195 E
dan.hamby@kctcs.edu
HAMBY, David .... 918-343-7771. 399 C
dhamby@rsu.edu
HAMBY, Edwina, H .... 615-329-8768. 454 F
ehamby@fisk.edu
HAMBY, Eileen .... 386-506-3939. 101 G
hambye@DaytonaState.edu
HAMBY, Karen, G .... 205-726-2643..... 6 F
kghamby@samford.edu
HAMEL, Dale, M .... 508-626-4580. 230 A
dhamel@framingham.edu
HAMEL, James .... 978-665-3584. 229 E
jhamel@fitchburgstate.edu
HAMEL, John .... 617-573-8460. 237 B
jhamel@suffolk.edu
HAMEL, Kayte .... 815-825-2086. 149 F
kayte.hamel@kishwaukeecollege.edu
HAMEL, Thomas .... 847-635-1660. 155 F
thamel@oakton.edu
HAMELINE, Walter .... 718-390-3488. 350 B
whamelin@wagner.edu
HAMEN, Laurie, M .... 630-637-5155. 154 F
lahamen@noctrl.edu
HAMER, Ronald, J .... 518-454-2060. 321 A
hamerj@strose.edu
HAMEROFF, Lee .... 860-727-2073... 90 A
lhameroff@goodwin.edu
HAMES, Anne .... 731-352-4066. 453 D
hamesa@bethelu.edu
HAMES, Becky .... 731-352-4046. 453 D
hamesb@bethelu.edu
HAMES, Joe .... 731-352-4000. 453 D
hamesj@bethelu.edu
HAMIDY, Wahid .... 619-388-7702... 62 F
whamidy@sdccd.edu
HAMIL, Bobby .... 678-466-4050. 123 A
bobbyhamil@clayton.edu
HAMILL, Amy .... 740-392-6868. 384 K
amy.hamill@mvnu.edu
HAMILL, Anne .... 410-837-5753. 221 A
ahamill@ubalt.edu
HAMILL, Nancy, G .... 510-987-9720... 72 B
nancy.hamill@ucop.edu
HAMILL, Robert, P .... 740-392-6868. 384 K
robert.hamill@mvnu.edu
HAMILTON, Alice .... 785-442-6025. 187 E
ahamilton@highlandcc.edu
HAMILTON, Allana, R .... 423-279-7632. 461 C
arhamilton@northeaststate.edu
HAMILTON, Barbara .... 870-837-4003... 23 G
bhamilto@sautech.edu
HAMILTON, Barbara .... 601-318-6524. 270 I
barbara.hamilton@wmcarey.edu
HAMILTON, Bennyce ...... 937-382-6661. 393 B
bennyce_hamilton@wilmington.edu
HAMILTON, Bill .... 850-484-1304. 110 G
bhamilton@pensacolastate.edu
HAMILTON, Billy Jo .... 813-974-3039. 116 C
BJHamilton@usf.edu
HAMILTON, Bob .... 412-237-3108. 413 D
rhamilton@ccac.edu
HAMILTON, Brandon ...... 503-552-1664. 404 H
bhamilton@ncnm.edu
HAMILTON, Cara .... 864-646-1797. 447 D
chamilt5@tctc.edu
HAMILTON, Cecilia .... 305-348-2560. 115 B
cecilia.hamilton@fiu.edu
HAMILTON, Cheresa, Y .. 904-620-2455. 116 B
chamilto@unf.edu
HAMILTON, Cheryl .... 336-917-5329. 366 D
cheryl.hamilton@salem.edu
HAMILTON, Chris .... 352-365-3592. 108 S
hamiltonc@lssc.edu
HAMILTON, Dana .... 828-328-7080. 356 B
dana.hamilton@lr.edu
HAMILTON, Donna, B .... 301-405-9354. 219 B
dhamil@umd.edu
HAMILTON, Dwight .... 616-331-2242. 243 C
hamiltdw@gvsu.edu
HAMILTON, JR., Elbert .. 713-629-8940. 493 G
HAMILTON, Eldrie .... 318-274-6321. 207 E
hamiltoneb@gram.edu
HAMILTON, Eric .... 843-574-6272. 447 E
eric.hamilton@tridenttech.edu
HAMILTON, Ethan .... 619-849-2621... 59 L
ethanhamilton@pointloma.edu
HAMILTON, Eugene, J ... 989-964-4069. 249 G
hamilton@svsu.edu
HAMILTON, Fred .... 212-226-5500. 314 A
fhamilton@aii.edu
HAMILTON, Gary .... 909-869-4426... 32 G
gahamilton@csupomona.edu
HAMILTON, Glenn .... 708-524-6795. 144 C
hamilton@dom.edu
HAMILTON, Glenn, R ..... 859-858-3511. 192 B
glenn.hamilton@asbury.edu
HAMILTON, Jackie .... 314-918-2627. 274 A
jhamilton@eden.edu
HAMILTON, Jeff .... 910-576-6222. 362 C
hamiltonj@montgomery.edu
HAMILTON, Jeff .... 740-351-3263. 388 N
jhamilton@shawnee.edu
HAMILTON, Judy .... 714-556-3610... 74 D
jhamilton@vanguard.edu
HAMILTON, Kate .... 517-264-7142. 250 B
khamilton@sienaheights.edu
HAMILTON, Kathleen ..... 718-260-3792. 336 E
hamilton@poly.edu
HAMILTON, Kathleen, M 607-733-7177. 323 F
khamilton@ebi-college.com

HAMILTON, Kerry-Ann ... 202-238-2338... 95 G
k_hamilton@howard.edu
HAMILTON, Kevin .... 501-370-5354... 22 F
khamilton@philander.edu
HAMILTON, Kevin .... 585-345-6950. 325 C
kphamilton@genesee.edu
HAMILTON, Larry .... 702-895-1229. 294 I
larry.hamilton@unlv.edu
HAMILTON, Laura .... 585-271-3657. 338 D
lhamilton@stbernards.edu
HAMILTON, Laura, Y ...... 832-252-4612. 468 L
laura.hamilton@cbshouston.edu
HAMILTON, Lesley .... 512-492-3040. 466 B
lhamilton@aoma.edu
HAMILTON, Lisa .... 724-503-1001. 436 G
lhamilton@washjeff.edu
HAMILTON, Margaret ..... 856-227-7200. 300 B
mhamilton@camdencc.edu
HAMILTON, Marty .... 423-236-2806. 458 J
mlhamil@southern.edu
HAMILTON, Mary Jane .. 361-825-2649. 483 F
mary.hamilton@tamucc.edu
HAMILTON, Maryanne ... 563-386-3570. 178 I
HAMILTON, Matt .... 405-325-8481. 401 B
mhamilton@ou.edu
HAMILTON, Mike .... 205-226-7790..... 2 C
mhamilto@bsc.edu
HAMILTON, Monica .... 863-638-2775. 119 C
monica.hamilton@warner.edu
HAMILTON, Pat .... 605-721-5200. 450 G
phamilton@national.edu
HAMILTON, Priscilla ...... 210-295-9604. 545 C
HAMILTON, Rhoda .... 281-899-1240. 478 J
HAMILTON, Richard .... 516-299-3609. 329 D
richard.hamilton@liu.edu
HAMILTON, Richard .... 360-442-2263. 521 A
rhamilton@lowercolumbia.edu
HAMILTON, Rick .... 601-477-4025. 267 F
rick.hamilton@jcjc.edu
HAMILTON, Robert .... 802-735-2612. 313 B
robert.hamilton@acphs.edu
HAMILTON, Roy .... 219-989-2779. 171 N
hamilton@purduecal.edu
HAMILTON, Scott .... 276-523-7469. 513 A
shamilton@me.vccs.edu
HAMILTON, Shaan .... 651-846-1694. 261 D
shaan.hamilton@saintpaul.edu
HAMILTON, Shelley .... 760-921-5483... 58 C
shamilton@paloverde.edu
HAMILTON, Susan .... 425-352-8583. 517 E
shamilton@cascadia.edu
HAMILTON, Sylvia .... 609-984-7188. 308 A
shamilton@tesc.edu
HAMILTON, Theresa .... 601-857-3250. 267 A
THHamilton@hindscc.edu
HAMILTON, Wallace, O .. 405-789-7661. 400 A
wallace.hamilton@swcu.edu
HAMILTON, Wayne, T .... 802-626-6410. 501 E
wayne.hamilton@lyndonstate.edu
HAMILTON, William, P .. 803-536-7060. 446 G
whamilton@scsu.edu
HAMILTON-CHANDLER,
Beverly .... 609-258-6355. 304 E
hamilton@princeton.edu
HAMILTON-DAVIS, Jody 919-546-8415. 366 E
jhamiltondavis@shawu.edu
HAMILTON-GOLDEN,
Barbara .... 201-447-7113. 299 C
bagolden@bergen.edu
HAMILTON SLANE,
Sandra .... 530-242-7799... 65 G
sslane@shastacollege.edu
HAMLET, Michael .... 931-221-7179. 459 B
hamletm@apsu.edu
HAMLETT, Adele .... 916-660-7160... 66 B
ahamlett@sierracollege.edu
HAMLETT, Melvin, R ...... 731-426-7539. 455 J
hamlett@lanecollege.edu
HAMLETT, Willie .... 626-815-3890... 29 H
whamlett@apu.edu
HAMLIN, John .... 337-550-1233. 205 B
HAMLIN, Kelly .... 828-652-0629. 362 A
khamlin@mcdowelltech.edu
HAMLIN, Lyn .... 201-200-3525. 303 F
lhamlin@njcu.edu
HAMLIN, Toby .... 518-608-8218. 324 B
thamlin@excelsior.edu
HAMM, Annette .... 609-652-4325. 305 C
annette.hamm@stockton.edu
HAMM, Bradley, J .... 847-491-2045. 155 D
bradely.hamm@northwestern.edu
HAMM, Dede .... 479-899-6928... 22 C
chamm@nwacc.edu
HAMM, Jolene, D .... 540-365-4323. 504 L
jdhamm@ferrum.edu
HAMM, Joy .... 334-214-4860..... 2 H
joy.hamm@cv.edu
HAMM, L, L .... 504-988-5462. 207 C
lhamm@tulane.edu
HAMM, Leonard .... 410-951-3906. 220 B
lhamm@coppin.edu
HAMM, Margo .... 606-679-8501. 196 D
margo.hamm@kctcs.edu
HAMM, Marilyn .... 386-752-1822. 104 G
marilyn.hamm@fgc.edu
HAMM, Tammy, S .... 423-439-4457. 459 C
hammt@etsu.edu
HAMMACK, Becky .... 325-674-2265. 464 H
rsh12a@acu.edu
HAMMACK, Mike .... 325-670-1278. 472 O
mhammack@hsutx.edu
HAMMACK, R, C .... 850-263-3261... 98 N
rchammack@baptistcollege.edu
HAMMAKER, Michelle .... 570-586-2400. 410 D
mhammaker@bbc.edu
HAMME, Gary .... 321-674-8832. 104 H
gary@fit.edu
HAMMEL, Nicole .... 484-664-3190. 424 H
hammel@muhlenberg.edu
HAMMER, Amanda .... 575-461-4413. 309 M
amandah@mesalands.edu
HAMMER, Ann, E .... 573-288-6388. 273 F
ahammer@culver.edu
HAMMER, Bradley, C ...... 419-434-6922. 391 D
hammer@findlay.edu
HAMMER, Joyce .... 253-833-9111. 520 C
jhammer@greenriver.edu
HAMMER, Kimberley ...... 412-397-6413. 431 I
hammerk@rmu.edu
HAMMER, Larry .... 828-227-7232. 369 E
hammer@wcu.edu
HAMMER, Lila, D .... 260-982-5234. 170 U
ldhammer@manchester.edu
HAMMERSCHMIDT,
David .... 734-432-5441. 246 B
dhammerschmidt@madonna.edu
HAMMERSMITH, Sue, K 651-793-1900. 259 C
sue.hammersmith@metrostate.edu
HAMMETT, Amy, S .... 216-368-4318. 375 J
registrar@case.edu
HAMMETT, Hugh, B .... 518-587-2100. 346 A
hugh.hammett@esc.edu
HAMMETT, John .... 256-782-5445..... 4 K
jhammett@jsu.edu
HAMMETT, Maria, A .... 478-301-2670. 128 H
hammett_ma@mercer.edu
HAMMILL, Viv .... 406-444-0325. 286 G
vhammill@montana.edu
HAMMITT, Norman .... 865-251-1800. 458 I
nhammitt@southcollegetn.edu
HAMMITT, Stephanie ...... 218-879-0810. 258 E
shammitt@fdltcc.edu
HAMMON, Denise .... 781-595-6768. 228 C
dhammon@mariancourt.edu
HAMMON, Denise .... 781-309-6768. 228 C
dhammon@mariancourt.edu
HAMMON, Gary .... 617-730-7135. 235 D
gary.hammon@newbury.edu
HAMMON, Kyle .... 360-442-2551. 521 A
khammon@lowercolumbia.edu
HAMMOND, Ben .... 781-283-2305. 237 F
HAMMOND, Brad .... 307-754-6400. 543 G
Brad.Hammond@northwestcollege.edu
HAMMOND, Brian, J ...... 443-412-2379. 215 C
bhammond@harford.edu
HAMMOND, Caroline ..... 207-942-6781. 209 E
chammond@bts.edu
HAMMOND, Charles, A . 302-225-6352... 93 H
hammond@gbc.edu
HAMMOND, Christine ..... 231-348-6660. 247 H
chammond@ncmich.edu
HAMMOND, Denise .... 870-584-4471... 24 F
dhammond@cccua.edu
HAMMOND, Edward, H .. 785-628-4231. 186 F
ehammond@fhsu.edu
HAMMOND,
Elizabeth, D .... 478-301-2964. 128 H
hammond_bd@mercer.edu
HAMMOND, Erin .... 314-256-8808. 271 F
registrar@ai.edu
HAMMOND, James .... 803-323-2148. 449 G
hammondj@winthrop.edu
HAMMOND, Jamie .... 203-575-8022... 89 B
jhammond@nvcc.commnet.edu
HAMMOND, Jane, F ...... 607-844-8222. 347 I
hammonj@tc3.edu
HAMMOND, Jeff .... 601-266-5422. 270 E
jeff.hammond@usm.edu
HAMMOND, Jerome .... 423-614-8310. 455 L
jhammond@leeuniveristy.edu
HAMMOND, Jessica, L .. 315-445-4130. 328 F
hammonjl@lemoyne.edu
HAMMOND, Karen, S .... 240-500-2000. 215 B
kshammond@hagerstowncc.edu
HAMMOND, Laura .... 951-827-5531... 71 E
laura.hammond@ucr.edu
HAMMOND, Lesa .... 415-355-2007... 26 L
lhammond@alliant.edu
HAMMOND, Lesa .... 510-430-2034... 54 F
lhammond@mills.edu
HAMMOND, Lynne, B ..... 334-844-4145..... 1 G
hammolb@auburn.edu
HAMMOND, Mark, L ...... 910-893-1275. 352 K
hammond@campbell.edu
HAMMOND, Mary Ann .. 610-436-2509. 430 A
mhammond@wcupa.edu
HAMMOND, Mike .... 803-535-1267. 446 B
hammondm@octech.edu
HAMMOND, Pamela .... 276-466-7876. 514 G
phammond@vic.edu
HAMMOND, Pamela, V .. 757-727-5201. 505 F
pamela.hammond@hamptonu.edu
HAMMOND, Randy .... 717-477-1256. 429 E
rphamm@ship.edu
HAMMOND, Sally, J ...... 864-596-9218. 443 D
sally.hammond@converse.edu
HAMMOND, Shane .... 413-775-1804. 231 E
hammonds@gcc.mass.edu
HAMMOND, Sue-Anne ... 207-893-6633. 211 G
shammond@sjcme.edu
HAMMOND, Thomas ...... 630-844-6850. 140 A
thammond@aurora.edu
HAMMOND, Troy, D ...... 630-637-5454. 154 F
tdhammond@noctrl.edu
HAMMOND,
Ulyssess, B .... 860-439-2046... 89 H
ubham@conncoll.edu
HAMMOND, Vanessa ..... 423-614-8511. 455 L
vhammond@leeuniversity.edu
HAMMOND NASS,
Holly .... 207-602-2306. 213 A
hnass@une.edu
HAMMONDS, Dave .... 936-294-2709. 487 A
david.hammonds@shsu.edu
HAMMONDS, Diane, M . 610-526-1407. 409 F
diane.hammonds@theamericancollege.edu
HAMMONDS, Kathy .... 509-467-1727. 520 F
kathyh@interface.edu
HAMMONS, Chris .... 281-649-3600. 473 B
chammons@hbu.edu
HAMMONS, Steve .... 606-679-8501. 196 D
steve.hammons@kctcs.edu
HAMMONTREE, Tonya ... 501-205-8809... 20 I
thammontree@cbc.edu
HAMNER, Deon .... 540-374-4300... 96 F
HAMNER, Mark .... 940-898-3039. 488 B
mhamner@twu.edu
HAMP, Herlisa .... 408-741-4616... 75 L
herlisa.hamp@westvalley.edu
HAMPSHIRE-COWAN,
Artis, G .... 202-806-2250... 95 G
ahampshire-cowan@howard.edu
HAMPTON, Andre .... 210-436-3716. 479 D
ahampton@stmarytx.edu
HAMPTON, Anita .... 319-385-6220. 179 K
anita.hampton@iwc.edu
HAMPTON, Brenda .... 712-325-3402. 179 L
bhampton@iwcc.edu
HAMPTON, Connie .... 318-274-3278. 207 E
hamptonc@gram.edu
HAMPTON, Franki .... 540-234-9261. 511 H
hamptonf@brcc.edu
HAMPTON, Gary, W .... 512-223-6076. 466 I
ghampton@austincc.edu
HAMPTON, Hayes, D ...... 803-938-3860. 448 F
hhampton@uscsumter.edu
HAMPTON, Jarvis, D ...... 806-651-3451. 484 D
jhampton@mail.wtamu.edu
HAMPTON, Jennifer .... 630-752-5327. 163 F
jennifer.hampton@wheaton.edu
HAMPTON, Joyce .... 413-265-2343. 225 C
hamptonj@elms.edu
HAMPTON, Julie .... 309-649-6201. 160 E
julie.hampton@src.edu
HAMPTON, Kay .... 912-279-5853. 123 B
khampton@ccga.edu
HAMPTON, Lacy .... 210-486-2178. 465 B
lhampton14@alamo.edu
HAMPTON, Logan, C ..... 501-569-3328... 24 B
lchampton@ualr.edu
HAMPTON, Michael .... 503-883-2442. 404 A
mhampton@linfield.edu
HAMPTON, Mike .... 305-919-4018. 115 B
mike.hampton@fiu.edu
HAMPTON, Mike .... 319-385-6303. 179 K
mhampton@iwc.edu
HAMPTON, Rene .... 514-287-5299. 378 B
rhampton@cscc.edu
HAMPTON, Renee .... 614-287-5353. 378 B
rhampton@cscc.edu
HAMPTON, Renee .... 417-667-8181. 273 A
rhampton@cottey.edu
HAMPTON, Sherill .... 704-378-1194. 355 K
shampton@jcsu.edu
HAMPTON, Terri .... 626-585-7361... 58 F
tlhampton@pasadena.edu
HAMPTON, Valerie, J ..... 607-777-4775. 341 E
vhampton@binghamton.edu
HAMPTON, Vickie .... 404-507-8647. 129 D
vhampton@morehouse.edu
HAMPTON, William .... 386-226-4811. 102 B
hamptonw@erau.edu
HAMPTON, William .... 903-730-4890. 474 O
william_hampton@jarvis.edu
HAMRA, Jena .... 903-434-8359. 477 J
jhamra@ntcc.edu
HAMRE, Laurie, B .... 651-696-6220. 256 L
hamre@macalester.edu
HAMRE, Lynne .... 218-723-5966. 254 K
lhamre@css.edu
HAMRIC, Mark .... 540-231-4000. 504 G
HAMRICK, Carolyn .... 678-872-8069. 125 C
chamrick@highlands.edu
HAMRICK, David, S .... 512-232-7604. 491 C
dhamrick@utpress.utexas.edu
HAMRICK, Mark, W .... 706-721-6900. 126 B
mhamrick@gru.edu
HAMRICK, Mike .... 304-696-5408. 529 H
hamrickm@marshall.edu
HAMRICK, Robin, G .... 704-406-3996. 354 C
rhamrick@gardner-webb.edu
HAMRICK, Sarah .... 202-651-5214... 95 C
sarah.hamrick@gallaudet.edu
HAMRICK, Stephen, A .... 678-915-4200. 132 C
shamrick@spsu.edu
HAMSTRA, Pete .... 708-239-4709. 160 K
pete.hamstra@trnty.edu
HAMZAVI, Maria .... 858-499-0202... 40 C
mhamzavi@coleman.edu
HAN, Jenjen .... 407-888-8689. 104 B
jhan@fcim.edu
HAN, Joseph .... 216-687-5343. 377 F
joseph.han@csuohio.edu
HAN, Ki Hyung .... 213-386-0080... 54 E
HAN, Ki Won .... 714-527-0691... 43 H
HAN, Peter .... 303-273-3131... 80 E
phan@mines.edu
HAN, Sang-Ehil .... 423-478-7524. 458 B
shan@ptseminary.edu
HAN, Woo Jin .... 703-244-4251... 36 C
whan@calums.edu
HAN, Younghee .... 770-279-0507. 124 I
financial.aid@gcuniv.edu
HAN, Younghee .... 770-279-0507. 124 I
admissions@gcuniv.edu
HANADA,
Tamone Karen .... 808-984-3527. 137 B
tkhanada@hawaii.edu
HANAK, Donald .... 575-624-8480. 310 H
hanak@nmmi.edu
HANAK, Lesley .... 912-525-5000. 131 B
lhanak@scad.edu
HANBURY, II,
George, L .... 954-262-7575. 109 K
hanbury@nova.edu
HANBURY, James, T ...... 401-456-8684. 439 F
jhanbury@ric.edu
HANBURY, John .... 276-656-0205. 513 D
jhanbury@patrickhenry.edu
HANCE, Kent .... 806-742-0012. 487 D
kent.hance@ttu.edu
HANCOCK, Barry .... 618-985-3741. 148 J
barryhancock@jalc.edu
HANCOCK, JR., Ben, E .. 910-630-7000. 356 H
bhancock@methodist.edu
HANCOCK, Blair, M .... 336-838-6230. 365 B
blair.hancock@wilkescc.edu
HANCOCK, Cheryl .... 507-453-2419. 259 E
chancock@southeastmn.edu
HANCOCK, John .... 713-500-2401. 492 E
john.hancock@uth.tmc.edu
HANCOCK, John .... 503-768-7160. 403 K
hancock@lclark.edu
HANCOCK, Jory, L .... 520-626-8030... 18 F
jory@email.arizona.edu
HANCOCK, Lori .... 810-762-0321. 247 F
lori.hancock@mcc.edu
HANCOCK, Lua .... 386-822-7343. 117 C
lhancock@stetson.edu
HANCOCK, Mara .... 510-594-5080... 30 K
mhancock@cca.edu
HANCOCK, Merodie .... 518-587-2100. 346 A
president@esc.edu
HANCOCK, Priscilla .... 502-852-5667. 200 D
pahanc01@louisville.edu
HANCOCK, Richard, R .... 501-450-5284... 25 H
russh@mail.uca.edu
HANCOCK, Wanda .... 229-225-5089. 132 D
whancock@southwestgatech.edu
HANCOVA, Marketa .... 619-265-0107... 59 K
mhancova@platt.edu
HANCOX, Robert, E .... 610-892-1578. 427 E
rhancox@pit.edu
HAND, Courtney .... 304-473-8163. 531 G
hand_c@wvwc.edu
HAND, Greg .... 513-556-3001. 390 G
greg.hand@uc.edu
HAND, Jason .... 973-353-1640. 306 D
jhand@ugadm.rutgers.edu
HAND, Jeffrey .... 856-256-5186. 305 E
handj@rowan.edu
HAND, Natalie .... 484-664-3804. 424 H
nhand@muhlenberg.edu

HAND, Robert .... 207-893-7721. 211 G
rhand@sjcme.edu
HANDCOX, Jenelle .... 910-521-6255. 369 B
jenelle.handcox@uncp.edu
HANDEL, Tom .... 617-585-1310. 234 I
thomas.handel@necmusic.edu
HANDFIELD, Sandy .... 321-433-5502. 101 M
handfields@easternflorida.edu
HANDFORD, Ann .... 262-524-7211. 532 C
ahandfor@carrollu.edu
HANDLER, Jan .... 319-368-6482. 181 C
handler@mtmercy.edu
HANDLER, Janet, R .... 319-363-6482. 181 C
handler@mtmercy.edu
HANDLER, Jeffrey .... 201-761-7101. 306 L
jhandler@saintpeters.edu
HANDLER-HUTCHINSON,
Simone .... 973-642-8863. 307 D
simone.handler-hutchinson@shu.edu
HANDLEY, Scott .... 417-626-1234. 279 J
handley.scott@occ.edu
HANDOJO, Jeanne .... 626-584-5366... 45 E
jeanne@fuller.edu
HANDS, Ashanti .... 619-388-2699... 62 E
ahands@sdccd.edu
HANDS, Colette .... 847-635-1767. 155 F
chands@oakton.edu
HANDY, Cromwell .... 334-229-4309..... 1 D
chandy@alasu.edu
HANDY, Cynthia, H .... 404-752-1654. 129 E
cynthia@msm.edu
HANDY, James, L .... 214-860-2067. 470 J
jhandy@dcccd.edu
HANDY, Jennifer .... 336-721-2831. 366 D
jennifer.handy@salem.edu
HANDY, Linda, B .... 317-788-3349. 173 I
handy@uindy.edu
HANDY, Ty .... 850-729-5360. 109 I
handyt@nwfsc.edu
HANDZLIK, Deborah ...... 716-896-0700. 350 A
dhandzlik@villa.edu
HANDZLIK, Diane, M ..... 716-896-0700. 350 A
dianeh@villa.edu
HANE, Jennifer .... 719-255-3180... 85 M
jhane@uccs.edu
HANEBUTTE, Shema ...... 253-566-5352. 524 C
shanebutte@tacomacc.edu
HANEFIELD, Robert .... 580-581-2415. 394 G
rhanefield@cameron.edu
HANELLY, William .... 570-484-2002. 429 B
whanelly@lhup.edu
HANES, Carol .... 903-875-7380. 477 G
carol.hanes@navarrocollege.edu
HANES, David .... 304-214-8827. 528 G
dhanes@wvncc.edu
HANES, Madlyn .... 814-863-0327. 426 A
mqh3@psu.edu
HANEWICH, Sheila, K ..... 219-866-6157. 172 E
sheilah@saintjoe.edu
HANEY, David, P .... 276-944-6168. 504 H
dhaney@ehc.edu
HANEY, Frank .... 913-234-0788. 185 L
frank.haney@cleveland.edu
HANEY, Joyce, A .... 814-863-0274. 426 A
jzh8@psu.edu
HANEY, Lee Anna .... 828-694-1885. 358 C
leeannah@blueridge.edu
HANEY, Michele .... 303-914-6215... 84 I
Michele.Haney@rrcc.edu
HANEY, Neil .... 512-476-2772. 466 J
HANEY, Pamela .... 708-974-5204. 153 F
haney@morainevalley.edu
HANEY, Regina .... 806-457-4200. 472 G
rhaney@fpctx.edu
HANEY, Rich .... 301-846-2477. 214 H
rhaney@frederick.edu
HANEY, Richard, J .... 847-543-2635. 143 A
rhaney@clcillinois.edu
HANFOR, Rita .... 662-621-4144. 266 D
rhanfor@coahomacc.edu
HANFORD, Karen .... 909-469-5243... 76 B
khanford@westernu.edu
HANFORD, Thomas .... 607-753-4702. 343 B
thomas.hanford@cortland.edu
HANG, Foua .... 920-693-1387. 540 B
foua.hang@gotoltc.edu
HANGER, Rex .... 262-472-1296. 538 D
rhangerr@uww.edu
HANIFIN, Martin .... 719-549-2320... 80 K
marty.hanifin@colostate-pueblo.edu
HANIGAN, Sherri .... 402-826-8586. 289 E
sherri.hanigan@doane.edu
HANINCIK, Amanda .... 610-921-7529. 409 A
ahanincik@alb.edu
HANK, Jack, L .... 210-434-6711. 477 N
jlhank@lake.ollusa.edu
HANKE, Robert .... 401-454-6599. 440 A
rhanke@risd.edu
HANKERSON, Brian .... 954-486-7728. 118 E
HANKIN, Brette .... 785-460-5509. 185 P
brette.hankin@colbycc.edu

HANKIN, Joseph, N .... 914-606-6707. 350 F
joseph.hankin@sunywcc.edu
HANKINS, Deborah .... 501-569-3137... 24 B
dshankins@ualr.edu
HANKINS, Jeff .... 501-660-1004... 19 L
jhankins@asusystem.edu
HANKINS, Kim .... 815-455-8778. 152 F
khankins@mchenry.edu
HANKINS, Lori .... 904-826-0084. 118 I
lhankins@usa.edu
HANKINS, Orlando, E ..... 919-516-4860. 366 C
oehankins@st-aug.edu
HANKINS, Stephen, J ..... 864-242-5100. 441 D
HANKS, Bob .... 928-541-7777... 16 B
bhanks@ncu.edu
HANKS, Martha .... 803-822-3434. 445 C
hanksm@midlandstech.edu
HANKS, Robert .... 251-460-7051..... 9 E
rbhanks@southalabama.edu
HANLEIN, Jeanette .... 973-655-7066. 303 D
hanleinj@mail.montclair.edu
HANLEY, Darla, S .... 617-266-1400. 223 D
HANLEY, Glenn .... 512-245-2392. 487 C
gh18@txstate.edu
HANLEY, Jim .... 215-204-4494. 433 K
jim.hanley@temple.edu
HANLEY, Peggy .... 318-274-6546. 207 E
peggy@gram.edu
HANLIN, Shawn .... 541-888-1546. 407 H
shanlin@socc.edu
HANLON, Christopher .... 610-921-7264. 409 A
chanlon@alb.edu
HANLON, Erin .... 617-296-8300. 227 I
erin_hanlon@laboure.edu
HANLON, Joyce .... 617-730-7074. 235 D
joyce.hanlon@newbury.edu
HANLON, Philip, J .... 603-646-2223. 296 G
philip.j.hanlon@dartmouth.edu
HANLON, Rob .... 479-936-5116... 22 C
rhanlon@nwacc.edu
HANN, Julia .... 478-445-1549. 125 A
julia.hann@gcsu.edu
HANN, Lindsey .... 717-334-6286. 422 E
lhann@ltsg.edu
HANNA, Aaron .... 210-436-3335. 479 D
ahanna1@stmarytx.edu
HANNA, Bashar, W .... 215-489-2324. 414 E
bashar.hanna@delval.edu
HANNA, C. Phil .... 270-384-8102. 197 D
hannap@lindsey.edu
HANNA, Cheryl .... 802-831-1282. 500 H
channa@vermontlaw.edu
HANNA, Jeffery, G .... 540-458-8459. 516 A
jhanna@wlu.edu
HANNA, Kimberly .... 575-461-4413. 309 M
kimberlyh@mesalands.edu
HANNA, Mae .... 513-732-5332. 391 B
hannamh@email.uc.edu
HANNA, Mark .... 806-371-5401. 465 E
mlhanna@actx.edu
HANNA, Michael .... 315-781-3574. 326 C
hanna@hws.edu
HANNA, Peter .... 562-947-8755... 67 H
peterhanna@scuhs.edu
HANNA, Roger .... 970-675-3212... 80 B
roger.hanna@cncc.edu
HANNA, Sean .... 585-275-2354. 349 C
sean.hanna@rochester.edu
HANNABURY,
Stephen, P .... 781-292-2401. 226 G
stephen.hannabury@olin.edu
HANNAFIN, Robert .... 516-299-2210. 329 D
robert.hannafin@liu.edu
HANNAH, Marcus .... 334-876-9360..... 4 A
mhannah@wccs.edu
HANNAH, Mary .... 218-751-8670. 263 C
registrar@oakhills.edu
HANNAH, Roddy .... 570-586-2400. 410 D
rhannah@bbc.edu
HANNAH, Russ .... 870-972-3303... 19 N
rhannah@astate.edu
HANNAH-BENNETT,
Connie .... 903-730-4890. 474 O
channah-bennett@jarvis.edu
HANNAHS, Mitch .... 618-544-8657. 147 A
hannahsm@iecc.edu
HANNAM, Paula, A .... 610-799-1718. 421 I
phannam@lccc.edu
HANNAM, Susan, E .... 724-738-2982. 429 F
susan.hannam@sru.edu
HANNAN, John, L .... 202-319-6910... 94 G
hannan@cua.edu
HANNAN, Michael .... 814-732-2729. 428 E
hannan@edinboro.edu
HANNAN, Steven, M .... 419-289-5007. 374 C
shannan@ashland.edu
HANNAR, Christine .... 636-949-4965. 276 D
channar@lindenwood.edu
HANNEMAN, Richard .... 402-457-2739. 290 G
rhanneman@mccneb.edu

HANNER, Mary Beth ...... 518-464-8500. 324 B
mhanner@excelsior.edu
HANNIGAN, Jennifer ...... 903-675-6327. 488 D
jhannigan@tvcc.edu
HANNIGAN, Jim .... 610-566-1776. 437 G
jhannigan@williamson.edu
HANNIGAN, Terence ...... 718-862-8000. 329 M
terence.hannigan@manhattan.edu
HANNO, Barbara .... 406-586-3585. 286 F
barbara.hanno@montanabiblecollege.edu
HANNO, Dennis .... 781-239-5660. 222 D
dhanno@babson.edu
HANNON, Bernard .... 765-285-1186. 164 B
bmhannon@bsu.edu
HANNON, Charles .... 724-503-1001. 436 G
channon@washjeff.edu
HANNON, Jim, M .... 563-333-6359. 182 B
HannonJamesM@ambrose.sau.edu
HANNON, Kristin .... 330-966-5459. 389 F
khannon@starkstate.edu
HANNON, Patrick, K .... 678-664-0527. 134 H
pat.hannon@westgatech.edu
HANNON, Ron .... 408-848-4895... 45 F
rhannon@gavilan.edu
HANNUM, Judy, A .... 508-793-2431. 225 B
jhannum@holycross.edu
HANNUM, Julie .... 413-236-5201. 231 A
jhannum@berkshirecc.edu
HANNUM, Natalie .... 925-439-2181... 42 A
nhannum@losmedanos.edu
HANOFEE, Rose .... 845-434-5750. 347 A
rhanofee@sullivan.suny.edu
HANOLD, John, W .... 814-863-0768. 426 A
jhh6@psu.edu
HANOUSEK, Mandy .... 208-885-5369. 139 D
hanousek@uidaho.edu
HANRAHAN, Mark .... 740-284-5247. 379 N
mhanrahan@franciscan.edu
HANRAHAN, Susan, N ... 870-972-3112... 19 N
hanrahan@astate.edu
HANRAHAN, Thomas ...... 718-399-4308. 336 F
hanrahan@pratt.edu
HANRAHAN,
Thomas, M .... 717-867-6030. 421 H
hanrahan@lvc.edu
HANRON-SANFORD,
Maia .... 802-287-8376. 499 D
hanronsanfordm@greenmtn.edu
HANS, John .... 651-905-3474. 254 B
jhans@browncollege.edu
HANSARD, Joanna .... 303-542-7000. 450 G
jhansard@national.edu
HANSBURY, Kevin .... 302-736-2586... 94 C
hansbuke@wesley.edu
HANSEL, Marie, C .... 708-709-3766. 156 A
mhansel@prairiestate.edu
HANSELL, Phyllis .... 973-761-9015. 307 C
phyllis.hansell@shu.edu
HANSEN, Allan .... 310-287-4307... 52 F
hansenas@wlac.edu
HANSEN, Andrew, C .... 307-766-4286. 543 I
hansen@uwyo.edu
HANSEN, Anne, P .... 775-445-3235. 295 A
anne.hansen@wnc.edu
HANSEN, Beverly .... 262-564-3160. 540 A
hansenb@gtc.edu
HANSEN, Carl, F .... 707-826-3731... 35 C
ch1@humboldt.edu
HANSEN, Carl, K .... 575-624-8011. 310 H
hansenc@nmmi.edu
HANSEN, Carrie .... 507-537-6221. 261 F
Carrie.Hansen@smsu.edu
HANSEN, Chelsea .... 561-912-2166. 103 C
chehansen@evergladesuniversity.edu
HANSEN, Cheryl .... 503-534-4005. 404 C
chansen@marylhurst.edu
HANSEN, Chris .... 423-236-2915. 458 J
chansen@southern.edu
HANSEN, Christian .... 203-576-4642... 91 G
registrar@bridgeport.edu
HANSEN, Corinne .... 605-642-6215. 451 G
corinne.hansen@bhsu.edu
HANSEN, Courtney .... 719-590-8302. 450 G
chansen@national.edu
HANSEN, D. Alton .... 208-496-3535. 137 H
hansena@byui.edu
HANSEN, David .... 605-367-7568. 451 E
dave.hansen@sdbor.edu
HANSEN, David .... 843-574-6021. 447 E
david.hansen@tridenttech.edu
HANSEN, Douglas .... 801-957-4084. 498 B
douglas.hansen@slcc.edu
HANSEN, Dwight .... 605-642-6146. 451 G
dwight.hansen@bhsu.edu
HANSEN, Eric .... 619-594-2941... 35 D
ehansen@mail.sdsu.edu
HANSEN, Erica, L .... 516-671-7373. 350 C
ehansen@webb.edu
HANSEN, Ginger .... 828-898-8944. 356 A
hanseng@lmc.edu

HANSEN, Gregg .... 978-468-7111. 227 A
ghansen@gcts.edu
HANSEN, Heather .... 907-564-8275... 10 C
hhansen@alaskapacific.edu
HANSEN, James .... 706-886-6831. 133 A
jhansen@tfc.edu
HANSEN, Jessica .... 515-244-4221. 175 C
hansenj@aib.edu
HANSEN, Julie .... 641-673-1096. 183 H
hansenj@wmpenn.edu
HANSEN, Kathy .... 909-537-5142... 34 E
hansen@csusb.edu
HANSEN, Kaylyn, L .... 580-327-8439. 396 N
klhansen@nwosu.edu
HANSEN, Kenneth .... 402-559-5301. 292 J
hansenkl@unmc.edu
HANSEN, Kent, A .... 909-558-2644... 51 C
khansen@claysonlaw.com
HANSEN, Kevin .... 801-626-8022. 497 D
khansen@weber.edu
HANSEN, Kinsey .... 432-264-5015. 473 E
khansen@howardcollege.edu
HANSEN, Lauren .... 262-551-5816. 532 D
lhansen@carthage.edu
HANSEN, Linda, L .... 406-768-6331. 286 C
lhansen@fpcc.edu
HANSEN, Lynn .... 407-823-2362. 115 E
lynn.hansen@ucf.edu
HANSEN, Marianne, W ... 509-777-4347. 525 F
mhansen@whitworth.edu
HANSEN, Marie .... 207-973-1081. 210 B
hansenm@my.husson.edu
HANSEN, Mary Mincer ... 515-271-1424. 177 H
mary.hansen@dmu.edu
HANSEN, Matt, B .... 563-333-6258. 182 B
HansenMattB@sau.edu
HANSEN, Patricia .... 212-774-0748. 330 E
phansen@mmm.edu
HANSEN, Peter .... 210-436-3324. 479 D
phansen@stmarytx.edu
HANSEN, Richard .... 225-342-6950. 207 D
Rich.Hansen@la.gov
HANSEN, Terry .... 432-264-5160. 473 E
thansen@howardcollege.edu
HANSEN, Tiffany .... 619-574-6909... 57 E
thansen@pacificcollege.edu
HANSEN, Timothy .... 925-288-5800... 46 J
timothy_hansen@heald.edu
HANSEN, Timothy, R ...... 847-578-8734. 157 F
tim.hansen@rosalindfranklin.edu
HANSEN, Vagn, K .... 256-765-4288..... 9 C
vkhansen@una.edu
HANSEN, Victor .... 617-422-7252. 235 B
vhansen@nesl.edu
HANSEN-KIEFFER,
Kristin, M .... 717-796-5234. 423 L
khansen@messiah.edu
HANSEN-MCCRORY,
Heidi .... 434-381-6164. 510 F
hmccrory@sbc.edu
HANSHEW, Daniel, S ..... 304-877-6428. 526 C
dan.hanshew@abc.edu
HANSHUMAKER, David . 978-478-3400. 235 G
dhanshumaker@northpoint.edu
HANSOM, Connie .... 615-297-7545. 452 J
hansomc@aquinascollege.edu
HANSON, Andrew .... 208-792-2218. 138 G
ahanson@lcsc.edu
HANSON, Brenda .... 406-756-3812. 286 B
bhanson@fvcc.edu
HANSON, Catherine .... 979-230-3632. 468 A
cathie.hanson@brazosport.edu
HANSON, Charlene .... 401-841-6541. 545 A
HANSON, Charles, D ...... 810-762-7812. 244 Q
chanson@kettering.edu
HANSON, Christina, R ... 717-766-2511. 423 L
chanson@messiah.edu
HANSON, Christy, L .... 651-696-6332. 256 L
chanson5@macalester.edu
HANSON, Clint .... 603-880-8308. 298 A
tmc@thomasmorecc.edu
HANSON, Daniel .... 402-872-2239. 291 E
dhanson@peru.edu
HANSON, David, K .... 701-355-8244. 373 E
dkhanson@umary.edu
HANSON, David, W .... 804-828-6116. 511 F
dwhanson@vcu.edu
HANSON, Denise .... 319-226-2012. 175 D
Denise.Hanson@AllenCollege.edu
HANSON, Gail, S .... 202-885-3484... 94 F
gsher@american.edu
HANSON, Gary, A .... 310-506-4607... 58 H
gary.hanson@pepperdine.edu
HANSON, Glenn .... 910-642-7141. 364 A
Glenn.Hanson@sccnc.edu
HANSON, Janet, K .... 715-394-8014. 538 C
jhanson@uwsuper.edu
HANSON, Karen .... 612-625-0051. 264 G
karhan@umn.edu
HANSON, Kent .... 763-576-4700. 257 Q

HANSON, Kent .... 763-433-1179. 257 P
kent.hanson@anokaramsey.edu
HANSON, Kirk, O .... 408-554-7898... 64 M
kohanson@scu.edu
HANSON, Kristina .... 281-487-1170. 484 H
khanson@txchiro.edu
HANSON, Laurie, R .... 563-336-3351. 177 L
lhanson@eicc.edu
HANSON, Linda .... 641-844-5731. 179 J
linda.hanson@iavalley.edu
HANSON, Linda .... 507-389-2986. 259 G
linda.hanson@mnsu.edu
HANSON, Linda, N .... 651-523-2202. 256 A
president@hamline.edu
HANSON, Lisa .... 309-341-5212. 141 A
lhanson@sandburg.edu
HANSON, Mark .... 920-206-2373. 533 U
mark.hanson@mbbc.edu
HANSON, Melissa, S ..... 901-321-3399. 453 H
mhanson@cbu.edu
HANSON, Patricia .... 701-777-4361. 371 C
pat.hanson@und.edu
HANSON, Paula .... 903-886-5890. 483 E
paula.hanson@tamuc.edu
HANSON, Richard, A ...... 218-755-2011. 258 A
rhanson@bemidjistate.edu
HANSON, Rick, D .... 816-501-4275. 280 I
rick.hanson@rockhurst.edu
HANSON, Sara .... 402-354-7111. 291 B
sara.hanson@methodistcollege.edu
HANSON, Shirley, M ...... 701-788-4767. 371 E
Shirley.M.Hanson@mayvillestate.edu
HANSON, Stephen, E ..... 757-221-3590. 503 N
sehanson@wm.edu
HANSON, Steven, D .... 517-355-2350. 246 H
ispdean@msu.edu
HANSON, Steven, J .... 425-235-2235. 522 F
shanson@rtc.edu
HANSON, Susan .... 909-469-5329... 76 B
shanson@westernu.edu
HANSON, Susanah .... 724-266-3838. 434 J
shanson@tsm.edu
HANSON, Terry .... 432-264-5095. 473 E
tlhanson@howardcollege.edu
HANSON HUBER,
Tonya .... 952-358-8213. 260 B
tonya.huber@normandale.edu
HANSS, Patrick, G .... 315-386-7222. 345 F
hanssp@canton.edu
HANSTEIN, Andrea .... 714-992-7014... 56 F
ahanstein@fullcoll.edu
HANTEN, Joan .... 360-475-7120. 521 H
jhanten@olympic.edu
HANTZ, Joan .... 406-477-6215. 285 H
jhantz@cdkc.edu
HANTZSCHEL, Linda, J .. 516-463-6903. 326 D
linda.j.hantzschel@hofstra.edu
HANUSCIN, R. Douglas . 419-755-4871. 385 D
dhanusci@ncstatecollege.edu
HANYPSIAK, Krista, L .... 716-645-3020. 341 F
klh5@buffalo.edu
HANZLIK, Gilbertt .... 804-524-3698. 515 D
ghanzik@vsu.edu
HANZLIK, Jodie, R .... 970-491-6817... 80 I
jodie.hanzlik@colostate.edu
HAO, Lan .... 626-914-8521... 38 K
lhao@citruscollege.edu
HAPEMAN, Barbara .... 570-961-7837. 420 C
hapemanb@lackawanna.edu
HAPPE, Doyle .... 713-529-2778. 468 F
happe@paralegal.edu
HAPPOLD, Jennifer .... 402-844-7045. 291 I
jennifer@northeast.edu
HAPSMITH, Linda, M ..... 907-474-1849... 10 I
lhapsmith@alaska.edu
HARA, Jimmy .... 323-563-9326... 38 B
jimmyhara@cdrewu.edu
HARADA, Margaret .... 425-564-2064. 517 A
maggie.harada@bellevuecollege.edu
HARARI-RAFUL, Joseph 347-394-1036. 315 A
HARBAUGH, Martha .... 314-529-9360. 276 G
mharbaugh@maryville.edu
HARBER, Dan .... 507-433-0609. 260 I
dharber@riverland.edu
HARBER, Debra, J .... 540-654-2468. 510 J
dharber@umw.edu
HARBER, Linda .... 703-993-2600. 505 C
lharber@gmu.edu
HARBERT, Robert, E .... 706-419-1116. 123 F
harbert@covenant.edu
HARBIN, Eddie .... 580-745-2843. 399 J
eharbin@se.edu
HARBIN, Samuel, L .... 215-368-7538. 412 A
sharbin@cbs.edu
HARBIN, Suzanne .... 256-352-8144..... 9 G
suzanne.harbin@wallacestate.edu
HARBISON, Amanda .... 205-391-5878...... 6 H
aharbison@sheltonstate.edu
HARBISON, John .... 909-335-8863... 41 C
jharbison@cccollege.edu
HARBOUT, Ellen, K .... 740-427-5121. 382 J
harboute@kenyon.edu
HARDASH, Peter .... 714-480-7340... 60 F
hardash_peter@rsccd.edu
HARDAWAY, Patricia, L . 937-708-5704. 393 A
phardaway@wilberforce.edu
HARDAWAY, Rex .... 404-727-4332. 124 E
rex.hardaway@emory.edu
HARDAWAY, Thelria .... 615-963-5137. 459 E
thardaway@tnstate.edu
HARDCASTLE, Bob .... 610-359-5182. 414 D
bhardcastle@dccc.edu
HARDCASTLE, Louis, B .. 770-484-1204. 128 E
lru@lru.edu
HARDECKE, John, M ...... 636-584-6656. 273 M
hardecj@eastcentral.edu
HARDEE, Jerry .... 770-426-2775. 128 D
jhardee@life.edu
HARDEE, John .... 870-230-5320... 21 D
hardeej@hsu.edu
HARDEE, Terrence .... 609-894-9311. 299 I
thardee@bcc.edu
HARDEE, Tim .... 803-778-6640. 441 F
hardeebt@cctech.edu
HARDEGREE, JR.,
Lester .... 816-604-4832. 277 H
lester.hardegree@mcck.edu
HARDEMAN, Patricia, R . 478-757-5192. 134 G
phardeman@wesleyancollege.edu
HARDEN, Burshunda ...... 706-821-8251. 130 C
bharden@paine.edu
HARDEN, Derrick .... 847-543-2225. 143 A
dharden@clcillinois.edu
HARDEN, Erica .... 478-553-2068. 129 H
eharden@oftc.edu
HARDEN, Jim .... 906-487-7307. 242 G
jim.harden@finlandia.edu
HARDEN, Mark .... 617-427-7293. 227 A
mharden@gcts.edu
HARDEN, Michelle .... 614-508-7219. 381 E
mharden@hondros.edu
HARDEN, Robert .... 972-825-4814. 481 F
rharden@sagu.edu
HARDEN, Ronald, W ...... 916-348-4689... 43 F
rharden@epic.edu
HARDEN, Thomas, K ...... 920-465-2207. 536 F
hardent@uwgb.edu
HARDEN, Yoshiko .... 425-564-2300. 517 A
yoshiko.harden@bellevuecollege.edu
HARDEN SMITH, Lisa .... 336-770-3314. 369 D
smithl@uncsa.edu
HARDER, James, M .... 419-358-3324. 374 J
harderj@bluffton.edu
HARDER, Maria, D .... 605-256-5129. 451 H
maria.harder@dsu.edu
HARDER, Mike .... 254-867-3940. 485 G
mike.harder@systems.tstc.edu
HARDER, Natalie .... 337-521-8953. 203 I
natalie.harder@southlouisiana.edu
HARDERS, Michael .... 770-423-6533. 127 N
mharders@kennesaw.edu
HARDERSEN, Al .... 920-459-6610. 538 E
al.hardersen@uwc.edu
HARDESTY, Amy .... 806-720-7178. 476 B
amy.hardesty@lcu.edu
HARDESTY, Jon .... 972-377-1725. 469 G
jhardesty@collin.edu
HARDESTY, Larry, E .... 724-458-2700. 417 E
lehardesty@gcc.edu
HARDGRAVE, Bill .... 334-844-4030..... 1 G
bch0014@auburn.edu
HARDGROVE, David .... 201-761-6454. 306 L
dhardgrove@saintpeters.edu
HARDGROVE, Mark .... 404-627-2681. 121 H
mark.hardgrove@beulah.org
HARDGROVE, Mark .... 404-627-2681. 121 H
Mark.Hardgrove@beulah.org
HARDIE, Jeff .... 510-436-1681... 47 J
hardie@hnu.edu
HARDIMAN, Michael, R . 608-262-8721. 536 D
mhardiman@bussvc.wisc.edu
HARDIN, Barbara .... 210-436-3135. 479 D
bhardin@stmarytx.edu
HARDIN, Belinda, F .... 256-539-0834..... 4 E
reg@hbc1.edu
HARDIN, Dan .... 575-492-2771. 310 G
dhardin@nmjc.edu
HARDIN, David .... 910-362-7020. 358 F
dhardin@cfcc.edu
HARDIN, David, M .... 910-362-7020. 358 F
dhardin@cfcc.edu
HARDIN, Elizabeth .... 828-689-1148. 356 F
ehardin@mhc.edu
HARDIN, Elizabeth, A ..... 704-687-5750. 368 E
eahardin@uncc.edu
HARDIN, Fred .... 864-388-8340. 444 K
fhardin@lander.edu
HARDIN, J. Michael .... 205-348-8935..... 8 D
mhardin@cba.ua.edu
HARDIN, Jeanie .... 903-463-8634. 472 M
hardinj@grayson.edu
HARDIN, Joe .... 479-788-7291... 24 A
joe.hardin@uafs.edu
HARDIN, III, John, B .... 940-552-6291. 493 F
jhardin@vernoncollege.edu
HARDIN, Karen .... 480-461-7584... 15 A
karen.hardin@mcmail.maricopa.edu
HARDIN, Mike, W .... 704-406-4280. 354 C
mhardin@gardner-webb.edu
HARDIN, Phil .... 870-245-5400... 22 D
hardinp@obu.edu
HARDIN, Philip, W .... 870-245-5400... 22 D
hardinp@obu.edu
HARDIN, Richard, H .... 636-481-3130. 275 I
rhardin@jeffco.edu
HARDIN, Sally, B .... 619-260-4550... 73 I
shardin@sandiego.edu
HARDIN, Sandy .... 575-492-4735. 310 G
shardin@nmjc.edu
HARDIN, Steve, D .... 317-447-6126. 166 I
Steve.Hardin@harrison.edu
HARDIN, Tammie .... 662-720-7594. 269 B
twhardin@nemcc.edu
HARDIN, Walter, A .... 803-323-2261. 449 G
hardinw@winthrop.edu
HARDING, Ann .... 309-556-3251. 148 B
iwualum@iwu.edu
HARDING, Blane .... 785-864-4350. 190 L
bharding@ku.edu
HARDING, Harry .... 434-924-0812. 511 B
hh7b@Virginia.EDU
HARDING, Jim .... 617-745-5704. 225 G
james.harding@enc.edu
HARDING, Kelly .... 660-263-3900. 272 A
bookstore@cccb.edu
HARDING, Marc, L .... 412-624-7164. 435 C
mharding@pitt.edu
HARDING, Mary .... 989-686-9226. 242 C
maryharding@delta.edu
HARDING, Sally .... 212-431-2319. 333 I
sharding@nyls.edu
HARDING, Samuel .... 217-854-3231. 140 G
shard@blackburn.edu
HARDING, Tayloe .... 803-777-4336. 447 G
tharding@sc.edu
HARDING, Terry, M .... 716-878-6112. 343 A
hardintm@buffalostate.edu
HARDISON, Brad .... 805-964-0581 ... 64 I
hardison@sbcc.edu
HARDISON, John .... 910-296-2433. 361 D
jhardison@jamessprunt.edu
HARDISON, R. Karol ...... 270-809-4388. 198 B
khardison@murraystate.edu
HARDISON, Roshanna ... 832-252-0728. 468 L
roshanna.hardison@cbshouston.edu
HARDLEY, Michelle .... 805-565-7263... 76 D
mhardley@westmont.edu
HARDMAN,
Alton (Tony) .... 580-349-1542. 397 G
ahardman@opsu.edu
HARDMAN, John .... 870-245-5189... 22 D
hardmanj@obu.edu
HARDMAN, John .... 404-420-5100. 124 E
jhardm@emory.edu
HARDMAN, Michael, L ... 801-581-7200. 496 Q
michael.hardman@utah.edu
HARDMAN, II,
Robert, O .... 304-462-4107. 529 G
robert.hardman@glenville.edu
HARDRICK, Jaffus .... 305-348-2190. 115 B
jaffus.hardrick@fiu.edu
HARDT, Jennifer .... 405-682-1611. 397 E
jharrison@occc.edu
HARDT, Jim .... 412-392-6186. 431 B
jhardt@pointpark.edu
HARDT, John .... 773-274-3000. 151 H
jhardt@lumc.edu
HARDT, John, P .... 570-577-1232. 411 A
john.hardt@bucknell.edu
HARDT, William, M .... 609-258-3379. 304 E
whardt@princeton.edu
HARDWICK, James .... 813-253-6209. 118 L
jhardwick@ut.edu
HARDWICK, James, D .... 406-447-4530. 285 G
jhardwic@carroll.edu
HARDWIDGE, Sue, C ..... 630-515-7600. 153 B
shardw@midwestern.edu
HARDWRICK, Vikita, B ... 870-230-5028... 21 D
hardwrv@hsu.edu
HARDY, Alison, B .... 253-752-2020. 519 K
communications@faithseminary.edu
HARDY, Anthony .... 251-809-1531..... 5 A
anthony.hardy@jdcc.edu
HARDY, Beatriz, B .... 410-543-6130. 220 D
bbhardy@salisbury.edu
HARDY, Catherine .... 203-575-8080... 89 B
chardy@nvcc.commnet.edu
HARDY, Charles .... 910-962-3317. 369 C
hardyc@uncw.edu
HARDY, Daniel, R .... 330-337-6403. 373 F
college@awc.edu
HARDY, SR., Daniel, R .. 330-337-6403. 373 F
president@awc.edu
HARDY, Deborah, L .... 440-525-7828. 382 M
dhardy@lakelandcc.edu
HARDY, Deborah, L .... 440-525-7446. 382 M
dhardy@lakelandcc.edu
HARDY, Deirdre .... 954-762-5654. 114 L
dhardy@fau.edu
HARDY, Heather .... 775-784-6805. 294 J
hhardy@unr.edu
HARDY, James .... 402-935-9400. 290 N
jhardy@nechristian.edu
HARDY, Karen .... 760-245-4271... 75 B
karen.hardy@vvc.edu
HARDY, Karin, S .... 801-585-6220. 496 Q
karin.hardy@utah.edu
HARDY, Kevin .... 207-947-4591. 209 G
khardy@bealcollege.edu
HARDY, Leroy .... 775-831-1314. 295 F
lhardy@sierranevada.edu
HARDY, JR., Lonza .... 870-575-8000... 24 E
hardyl@uapb.edu
HARDY, Mark, G .... 615-963-5301. 459 E
mhardy@tnstate.edu
HARDY, Pamela .... 619-239-0391... 36 D
phardy@cwsl.edu
HARDY, Pollye .... 205-348-3952..... 8 D
phardy@fa.ua.edu
HARDY, Rebekah, L .... 410-778-7865. 221 C
rhardy2@washcoll.edu
HARDY, Richard, J .... 309-298-2228. 162 K
rj-hardy@wiu.edu
HARDY, Robert, M .... 203-396-8390... 91 C
hardyr@sacredheart.edu
HARDY, Sarah .... 207-778-7124. 212 D
sarah.hardy@maine.edu
HARDY, Scott, E .... 678-891-3965. 125 G
scott.hardy@gpc.edu
HARDY, Stacia .... 225-216-8247. 202 H
hardys@mybrcc.edu
HARDY, Stephen, R .... 972-985-3751. 469 G
shardy@collin.edu
HARDY, Thomas, P .... 217-333-6400. 161 C
hardyt@uillinois.edu
HARDY, Thomas, W .... 229-333-5920. 134 B
twhardy@valdosta.edu
HARDY, Tyrone, M .... 253-752-2020. 519 K
registrar@faithseminary.edu
HARDY, Tyrrell .... 505-786-4183. 310 D
thardy@navajotech.edu
HARDY, Virginia .... 252-328-6541. 367 B
Hardyv@ecu.edu
HARDY-LUCAS, Faye ...... 757-727-5233. 505 F
faye.hardy-lucas@hamptonu.edu
HARE, George, W .... 619-201-8994... 67 G
ghare@socalsem.edu
HARE, Sara .... 605-256-7321. 451 H
sara.hare@dsu.edu
HARE-PAYNTER,
Jodi, M .... 262-472-1570. 538 D
harej@uww.edu
HARELIK, Harry .... 254-299-8606. 476 D
hharelik@mclennan.edu
HAREWOOD, Wayne, H . 718-368-5681. 318 E
wharewood@kbcc.cuny.edu
HARF, James .... 314-529-6851. 276 G
jharf@maryville.edu
HARFORD, Ellen .... 207-216-4435. 211 C
eharford@yccc.edu
HARFST, Terry .... 618-453-3102. 159 G
terriw@siu.edu
HARGAN, Denise .... 617-348-6558. 237 E
hargan@urbancollege.edu
HARGER, Kathy .... 815-455-8695. 152 F
kharger@mchenry.edu
HARGETT, Doug .... 256-331-5415..... 6 A
dhargett@nwscc.edu
HARGETT, Jack .... 901-321-3315. 453 H
jhargett@cbu.edu
HARGIS, James .... 828-884-8282. 352 I
hargisje@brevard.edu
HARGIS, Joe .... 507-222-4327. 254 D
jhargis@carleton.edu
HARGIS, Michael .... 501-450-3106... 25 H
mhargis@uca.edu
HARGIS, Randall .... 318-487-7129. 202 F
randall.hargis@lacollege.edu
HARGIS, V. Burns .... 405-744-6384. 397 H
osupres@okstate.edu
HARGRAVE, Alan, L .... 765-285-8011. 164 B
ahargrav@bsu.edu
HARGRAVE, Carolyn, H . 225-578-6118. 204 N
chargrave@lsu.edu
HARGRAVE, Gary .... 319-656-2447. 182 D
HARGRAVE, Jaime .... 713-500-3476. 492 E
Jaime.N.Hargrave@uth.tmc.edu
HARGRAVE, John, R ...... 580-559-5212. 395 F
jhargrave@ecok.edu
HARGRAVE, Michael .... 503-654-8000. 407 B
mhargrave@pioneerpacific.edu

HARGRAVE,
Stephanie, J .... 316-295-5886. 186 H
stephanie_hargrave@friends.edu
HARGRAVE MEISLAHN,
Nancy .... 860-685-2269... 92 H
nmeislahn@wesleyan.edu
HARGRAVES, Stanley ..... 804-355-0671. 510 G
shargraves@upsem.edu
HARGROVE, Demond ..... 201-200-3507. 303 F
dhargrove@njcu.edu
HARGROVE, Jesse .... 501-370-5216... 22 F
jhargrove@philander.edu
HARGROVE, Jesse .... 501-370-5286... 22 F
jhargrove@philander.edu
HARGROVE, Kristi .... 615-383-4848. 464 D
khargrove@watkins.edu
HARGROVE, S. Keith ...... 615-963-5451. 459 E
skhargrove@tnstate.edu
HARGROVE,
Samantha, V .... 336-256-0863. 367 E
svhargro@ncat.edu
HARICHANDRAN,
Ronald .... 203-932-7167... 92 E
rharichandran@newhaven.edu
HARICOMBE,
Lorraine, J .... 785-864-3601. 190 L
ljharic@ku.edu
HARING, Peter .... 219-473-4323. 164 K
pharing@ccsj.edu
HARING-SMITH, Tori ..... 724-503-1001. 436 G
taringsmith@washjeff.edu
HARISH, Steve .... 701-662-1542. 372 D
Steve.Harish@lrsc.edu
HARITOS, George, K ...... 330-972-6978. 390 E
haritos@uakron.edu
HARKAVY, Ira .... 215-898-5351. 435 B
harkavy@upenn.edu
HARKENRIDER, Tom ...... 949-480-4091... 66 F
harkenrider@soka.edu
HARKER, Alan, R .... 801-422-5995. 495 D
alan_harker@byu.edu
HARKER, Patrick, T .... 302-831-2111... 94 B
harker@udel.edu
HARKER, Perry, L .... 252-222-6205. 358 G
harkerp@carteret.edu
HARKER, Phillip .... 802-225-3201. 499 I
phillip.harker@neci.edu
HARKEY, Betsy .... 940-552-6291. 493 F
bharkey@vernoncollege.edu
HARKEY, Cindy .... 501-812-2233... 22 G
charkey@pulaskitech.edu
HARKEY, Dina .... 704-216-3470. 363 D
dina.harkey@rccc.edu
HARKEY, Gary Don .... 940-552-6291. 493 F
gdharkey@vernoncollege.edu
HARKEY, Penny .... 806-743-7424. 487 E
penny.harkey@ttuhsc.edu
HARKINS, Amanda .... 256-215-4273..... 2 G
aharkins@cacc.edu
HARKINS, Dennis .... 714-432-5712... 39 K
dharkins@occ.cccd.edu
HARKINS,
Gerald "Bob", R .... 512-471-5767. 491 C
bharkins@austin.utexas.edu
HARKLEROAD,
Laralee, F .... 423-652-4784. 455 I
lfharkleroad@king.edu
HARKLESS, Lawrence ..... 909-706-3498... 76 B
lharkless@westernu.edu
HARKNESS, Charles .... 440-826-2426. 374 F
charkness@bw.edu
HARKNESS, Kim .... 603-358-2496. 298 F
kharkness@keene.edu
HARKNESS, M. Frances . 610-902-8546. 411 E
mfrances.harkness@cabrini.edu
HARLAN, Brian .... 661-255-1050... 31 C
bharlan@calarts.edu
HARLAN, Cathy .... 954-262-5366. 109 K
charlan@nova.edu
HARLAN, Don .... 501-207-6201... 19 M
dharlan@searcy.asub.edu
HARLAND, Teresa, L ...... 218-299-3733. 255 A
harland@cord.edu
HARLAND-WHITE,
Faith, A .... 410-777-2961. 213 D
faharlandwhite@aacc.edu
HARLANDER, Heidi .... 320-363-2724. 254 J
hharlander@csbsju.edu
HARLANDER, Heidi .... 320-363-2724. 263 P
hharlander@csbsju.edu
HARLE, Bill .... 423-775-7185. 453 E
bharle@hssu.edu
HARLESS, Cleta, M .... 304-357-4736. 527 H
cletaharless@ucwv.edu
HARLESS, Debra .... 651-638-6371. 253 K
d-harless@bethel.edu
HARLEY, Jay .... 214-333-6812. 470 D
jay@dbu.edu
HARLEY, Joyce, W .... 973-877-4347. 301 H
harley@essex.edu
HARLEY, Tracie, M .... 904-264-2172. 111 P
tracie.harley@iws.edu

HARLOW, Angie, D .... 770-720-5603. 130 G
adh@reinhardt.edu
HARLOW, Cheri .... 816-501-4555. 280 I
cheri.harlow@rockhurst.edu
HARLOW, Jessica .... 804-290-4231. 510 B
jharlow@stratford.edu
HARLOW, Susan .... 773-380-7042. 140 D
susan.harlow@seabury.edu
HARM, Joseph .... 912-247-4431. 131 H
jharm@southuniversity.edu
HARMAN, Bruce .... 201-200-3127. 303 F
bharman@njcu.edu
HARMAN, Elizabeth .... 619-260-4682... 73 I
harman@sandiego.edu
HARMAN, Joany .... 916-608-6500... 53 C
HARMAN, SJ, Paul, F .... 508-793-2011. 225 B
pharman@holycross.edu
HARMAN, William .... 801-878-1403. 295 E
wharman@roseman.edu
HARMEL, Lori .... 605-229-8531. 450 J
lori.harmel@presentation.edu
HARMON, Bruce .... 719-590-6852... 81 B
bharmon@coloradotech.edu
HARMON, Carolyn .... 252-399-6357. 352 F
charmon@barton.edu
HARMON, Christopher .... 717-337-6810. 417 B
charmon@gettysburg.edu
HARMON, Debbie .... 503-883-2607. 404 A
dharmon@linfield.edu
HARMON, Debra, J .... 217-732-3155. 151 C
dharmon@lincolncollege.edu
HARMON, Eva .... 828-726-2715. 358 E
eharmon@cccti.edu
HARMON, Jeff .... 479-788-7125... 24 A
jeff.harmon@uafs.edu
HARMON, Jeff, M .... 208-732-6210. 138 B
jharmon@csi.edu
HARMON, Justin .... 603-862-1463. 298 C
justin.harmon@unh.edu
HARMON, Kate .... 503-244-0726. 401 M
kateharmon@achs.edu
HARMON, Kathy, M .... 937-229-4303. 391 C
KHarmon1@udayton.edu
HARMON, Kevin .... 701-858-4363. 371 F
kevin.harmon@minotstateu.edu
HARMON, Ladelle .... 828-652-0626. 362 A
ladelleh@mcdoweltech.edu
HARMON, LaVerne, T ..... 302-356-6938... 94 E
laverne.t.harmon@wilmu.edu
HARMON, Lindsay .... 312-461-0600. 139 H
lharmon@aaart.edu
HARMON, Martino .... 515-294-0754. 175 H
mharmon@iastate.edu
HARMON, Martino .... 513-569-4215. 376 L
martino.harmon@cincinnatistate.edu
HARMON, Mary, R .... 989-964-7117. 249 G
mharmon@svsu.edu
HARMON, Nathaniel, S .. 417-268-6403. 271 I
nharmon@gobbc.edu
HARMON, Patricia .... 304-929-5460. 528 D
pharmon@newriver.edu
HARMON, Steve, K .... 956-326-2180. 483 B
harmon@tamiu.edu
HARMON, W. Ken .... 770-423-6023. 127 N
wharmon3@kennesaw.edu
HARMON, William .... 713-718-6041. 473 C
william.harmon@hccs.edu
HARMS, JR., Alfred .... 407-823-2232. 115 E
alfred.harms@ucf.edu
HARMS, Jeff .... 507-223-7252. 260 A
jeff.harms@mnwest.edu
HARMS, Mason .... 641-585-8137. 183 D
harmsm@waldorf.edu
HARMS, Steve .... 513-721-7944. 380 D
sharms@gbs.edu
HARMS ROSE, Scott ...... 312-935-4240. 148 C
srose@icsw.edu
HARMSEN, Dee .... 920-923-8530. 534 A
dharmsen@marianuniversity.edu
HARMSEN,
Frederika (Fraka) .... 530-898-6121... 33 A
fharmsen@csuchico.edu
HARMSEN, Mark .... 254-526-1365. 468 G
mark.harmsen@ctcd.edu
HARN, Angela .... 912-478-6397. 126 C
aharn@georgiasouthern.edu
HARN, William .... 409-880-8229. 486 F
william.harn@lamar.edu
HARNAGE, David, F .... 757-683-3159. 507 N
dharnage@odu.edu
HARNER, Holly, M .... 215-951-1865. 420 B
harner@lasalle.edu
HARNER, Kristy .... 423-614-8110. 455 L
kharner@leeuniversity.edu
HARNER, Mike .... 517-607-2303. 243 I
mike.harner@hillsdale.edu
HARNEY, Joseph, M .... 212-854-1540. 321 D
jh2087@columbia.edu
HARNISCH, Antje .... 860-486-3994... 92 A
antje.harnisch@uconn.edu

HARNISH, Eric .... 661-362-3400... 40 E
eric.harnish@canyons.edu
HARNUM, Donald, P ...... 609-896-5054. 305 D
harnum@rider.edu
HAROLD, Martin .... 858-653-6740... 49 C
HARP, Brittaney .... 859-371-9393. 192 D
bharp@beckfield.edu
HARP, Debbie .... 606-539-4259. 200 B
debbie.harp@ucumberlands.edu
HARP, Jeff .... 405-974-2800. 400 K
jharp@uco.edu
HARP, John, W .... 319-895-4234. 177 A
jharp@cornellcollege.edu
HARP-STEPHENS, Becky 859-246-6498. 194 L
becky.harp@kctcs.edu
HARPER, Allyson, R .... 612-874-3775. 257 B
allyson_harper@mcad.edu
HARPER, Cheri .... 502-895-3411. 197 F
cvharper@lpts.edu
HARPER, David .... 229-209-5239. 120 D
dahar@andrewcollege.edu
HARPER, David .... 828-298-3325. 370 E
dharper@warren-wilson.edu
HARPER, David .... 937-229-2973. 391 C
Dharper1@udayton.edu
HARPER, Deborah .... 607-274-3136. 327 E
dharper@ithaca.edu
HARPER, Derry .... 850-245-0466. 114 J
derry.harper@flbog.edu
HARPER, Donna, L .... 540-568-3705. 506 F
harperdl@jmu.edu
HARPER, Doreen, C .... 205-934-5360..... 8 E
dcharper@uab.edu
HARPER, E. Royster .... 734-764-5132. 251 C
harperer@umich.edu
HARPER, Elizabeth .... 703-323-3398. 513 C
eharper@nvcc.edu
HARPER, Heather .... 615-230-3519. 461 G
heather.harper@volstate.edu
HARPER, Jane .... 817-515-5391. 482 B
jane.harper@tccd.edu
HARPER, Janice, A .... 919-530-5216. 368 A
jharper@nccu.edu
HARPER, Jimmy .... 423-614-8420. 455 L
jharper@leeuniversity.edu
HARPER, Joann .... 706-245-7226. 124 D
jharper@ec.edu
HARPER, Katherine .... 304-766-3142. 530 C
harperkl@wvstateu.edu
HARPER, Kristin .... 205-226-4720..... 2 C
kharper@bsc.edu
HARPER, Kyle .... 405-325-2216. 401 B
kyle@ou.edu
HARPER, Larisa .... 740-588-1252. 394 C
lharper@zanestate.edu
HARPER, Lisa .... 405-974-2553. 400 K
lharper@uco.edu
HARPER, Lisa, D .... 859-858-3511. 192 B
lisa.harper@asbury.edu
HARPER, Lisa, M .... 903-510-2147. 488 E
lhar@tjc.edu
HARPER, Marilyn, A .... 865-694-6700. 461 D
maharper@pstcc.edu
HARPER, Marjoree .... 318-678-6000. 202 I
mharper@bpcc.edu
HARPER, Mary, J .... 812-464-1767. 174 D
mjharper@usi.edu
HARPER, Mary Ann .... 501-337-5000... 20 J
mharper@coto.edu
HARPER, Norma .... 706-233-7268. 131 E
nharper@shorter.edu
HARPER, Pam .... 270-706-8434. 195 A
pam.harper@kctcs.edu
HARPER, Patricia .... 816-654-7162. 275 K
pharper@kcumb.edu
HARPER, Randy .... 870-574-4590... 23 G
rharper@sautech.edu
HARPER, Ridge .... 229-248-2502. 121 E
ridge.harper@bainbridge.edu
HARPER, Robert .... 559-278-2482... 33 D
roberth@csufresno.edu
HARPER, Robert .... 903-593-8311. 485 A
rharper@texascollege.edu
HARPER, Rosie .... 601-977-7818. 270 A
rharper@tougaloo.edu
HARPER, Sandra .... 325-793-3800. 476 E
HARPER, Therese .... 307-778-5222. 543 D
tharper@lccc.wy.edu
HARPER, Vernon .... 610-436-1000. 430 A
vharper@wcupa.edu
HARPER, William .... 704-971-8500. 353 F
HARPER, Yvonne .... 564-587-4278. 447 B
harpery@smcsc.edu
HARPER HAGAN,
Mary, T .... 718-990-2505. 339 A
harperm@stjohns.edu
HARPER-MARINICK,
Maria .... 480-731-8101... 14 I
maria.harper@domail.maricopa.edu
HARPHAM, Jennifer .... 757-822-1360. 514 C
jharpham@tcc.edu

HARPINE, Layne .... 252-444-7289. 359 G
harpinel@cravencc.edu
HARPOLE, Jessica .... 662-329-7352. 268 E
jharpole@sa.muw.edu
HARPS, Trynette Lottie ... 231-777-0559. 247 G
trynette.lottie-harps@muskegoncc.edu
HARPST, Steve .... 845-341-4230. 335 H
steve.harpst@sunyorange.edu
HARPSTER, G. F. (Jody) 717-477-1030. 429 E
gfharp@ship.edu
HARPSTER, George, F .... 717-477-1301. 429 E
gfharp@ship.edu
HARR, Kathleen .... 785-354-5853. 184 C
kharr@stormontvail.org
HARR, Lois .... 718-862-7142. 329 M
lois.harr@manhattan.edu
HARRADINE, Andy, A .... 315-267-3011. 344 C
andy@potsdam.edu
HARRAH, Scott .... 301-784-5000. 213 B
sharrah@allegany.edu
HARRAL, Judy .... 361-825-2495. 483 F
judy.harral@tamucc.edu
HARRAL, Kevin .... 650-949-7223... 44 N
harralkevin@foothill.edu
HARRAR, William, R ...... 570-389-4255. 427 H
wharrar@bloomu.edu
HARREL, Erin .... 239-489-9319. 101 O
eharrel@edison.edu
HARRELL, Bryant, L .... 860-727-6756... 90 A
bharrell@goodwin.edu
HARRELL, Charlie, R ...... 252-823-5166. 360 C
harrellc@edgecombe.edu
HARRELL, Diana .... 512-245-1555. 487 C
dh32@txstate.edu
HARRELL, Frank (Doug) . 504-865-5352. 207 C
fharrel@tulane.edu
HARRELL, Ivan, L .... 410-777-2830. 213 D
ilharrell@aacc.edu
HARRELL, Jerry, H .... 317-921-4447. 169 L
jeharrel@ivytech.edu
HARRELL, Jessica .... 336-506-4113. 357 M
jessica.harrell@alamancecc.edu
HARRELL, John (Lee) ...... 775-445-3259. 295 A
john.harrell@wnc.edu
HARRELL, P. Randy .... 252-398-6209. 353 H
harrer@chowan.edu
HARRELL, Pamela, J .... 919-209-2048. 361 E
pjharrell@johnstoncc.edu
HARRELL, Robin .... 404-627-2681. 121 H
robin.harrell@beulah.org
HARRELL, Ronald .... 270-706-8580. 195 A
ron.harrell@kctcs.edu
HARRELL, Wanda .... 423-585-6976. 462 A
wanda.harrell@ws.edu
HARRELSON, Jerry, W .... 336-316-2333. 355 A
jharrelson@guilford.edu
HARRES, JR., Burt, H .... 727-816-3490. 110 E
harresb@phcc.edu
HARREYS, M. Seamus .... 617-373-4095. 235 F
HARRI, Ed .... 360-383-3220. 525 D
eharri@whatcom.ctc.edu
HARRI, Robert .... 563-387-2103. 180 M
harrro01@luther.edu
HARRICK, Kristie .... 205-970-9244..... 7 B
kharrick@sebc.edu
HARRIENDORF, SC,
Cecilia .... 718-405-3215. 320 G
cecilia.harriendorf@mountsaintvincent.edu
HARRIGER, Sherill .... 863-638-7235. 119 C
sherill.harriger@warner.edu
HARRILL, Thad .... 828-395-1624. 361 C
tharrill@isothermal.edu
HARRIMAN, Mark .... 661-654-2635... 32 H
mharriman@csub.edu
HARRIMAN, Scott .... 207-454-1012. 211 B
sharriman@wccc.me.edu
HARRING, Kathleen, E ... 484-664-3424. 424 H
harring@muhlenberg.edu
HARRING-HENDON,
Janice .... 773-442-4000. 154 H
j-harringhendon@neiu.edu
HARRINGTON, Anne, E .. 603-641-7465. 297 G
aharrington@anselm.edu
HARRINGTON, Bonnie ... 215-751-8253. 413 I
bharrington@ccp.edu
HARRINGTON, Charles .. 864-503-5483. 448 H
charrington@uscupstate.edu
HARRINGTON, Daphne .. 617-521-2754. 236 G
daphne.harrington@simmons.edu
HARRINGTON, David ..... 603-641-7020. 297 G
dharrington@anselm.edu
HARRINGTON,
James, W .... 253-692-5646. 524 G
jwh@uw.edu
HARRINGTON, John ...... 603-524-3207. 295 L
jharrington@ccsnh.edu
HARRINGTON,
L. Katharine .... 213-740-7849... 74 A
vpap@usc.edu
HARRINGTON, Lizzie ..... 630-743-0681. 163 C
lharrington01@westwood.edu

HARRINGTON, Lynn ...... 708-974-5704. 153 F
harrington@morainevalley.edu
HARRINGTON, Mary, M 662-915-7387. 270 B
ccmary@olemiss.edu
HARRINGTON, Maurice . 541-463-5306. 403 I
harringtonm@lanecc.edu
HARRINGTON, Melissa .. 406-496-4108. 287 F
mharrington@mtech.edu
HARRINGTON, Melody .. 405-878-5310. 399 G
maharrington@stgregorys.edu
HARRINGTON, Michael .. 631-420-2053. 346 B
michael.harrington@farmingdale.edu
HARRINGTON,
Michael, J ...... 415-422-2790... 73 J
Harrington@usfca.edu
HARRINGTON, Pamela ... 401-454-6318. 440 A
pharring@risd.edu
HARRINGTON, Robert .... 417-625-3191. 278 D
harrington-r@mssu.edu
HARRINGTON, Sharon ... 704-330-1437. 355 K
sharrington@jcsu.edu
HARRINGTON,
Shawn, M ...... 860-231-5314... 92 F
sharrington@usj.edu
HARRINGTON,
Sherre Lee ...... 706-236-2285. 121 G
sharrington@berry.edu
HARRINGTON, Thea ...... 570-945-8516. 419 N
thea.harrington@keystone.edu
HARRINGTON, Thomas .. 520-206-4772... 17 A
teharrington@pima.edu
HARRINGTON, Thomas .. 504-280-1154. 205 G
trharrin@uno.edu
HARRINGTON WILSON,
Alice, E ...... 585-292-2304. 332 A
awilson@monroecc.edu
HARRIS, Alex ...... 208-769-7156. 138 I
afharris@nic.edu
HARRIS, Allatia ...... 281-459-7140. 479 E
allatia.harris@sjcd.edu
HARRIS, Amelia, J ...... 276-376-4557. 511 C
ajh7a@uvawise.edu
HARRIS, Andrew ...... 603-358-2772. 298 F
aharris5@keene.edu
HARRIS, Andrew, M ...... 940-565-2055. 490 C
aharris@unt.edu
HARRIS, Angela ...... 706-272-4476. 123 G
aharris@daltonstate.edu
HARRIS, Anjour, B ...... 804-828-2021. 511 F
abharris@vcu.edu
HARRIS, Ann ...... 573-681-5074. 276 C
harrisa@lincolnu.edu
HARRIS, Anthony ...... 610-341-5840. 415 G
aharris8@eastern.edu
HARRIS, April ...... 256-824-6085..... 8 F
april.harris@uah.edu
HARRIS, Bennie, L ...... 615-966-5687. 456 B
bennie.harris@lipscomb.edu
HARRIS, Bernice ...... 303-556-3786... 81 D
bernice.harris@ccd.edu
HARRIS, Beth ...... 203-287-3023... 90 H
paierartlibrary@snet.net
HARRIS, Beth, A ...... 773-702-7243. 161 B
ba-harris@uchicago.edu
HARRIS, Bethany, W ...... 434-949-1007. 513 H
bethany.harris@southside.edu
HARRIS, Betsy, A ...... 207-768-2791. 210 M
bharris@nmcc.edu
HARRIS, Beverly ...... 620-331-4100. 187 G
bharris@indycc.edu
HARRIS, Beverly ...... 757-823-2409. 507 M
bbharris@nsu.edu
HARRIS, Beverly Jo ...... 304-734-6601. 527 O
jharris@bridgemont.edu
HARRIS, Brent ...... 254-295-8642. 490 B
bharris@umhb.edu
HARRIS, Camille ...... 312-939-4975. 146 A
charris@harrington.edu
HARRIS, Celia, D ...... 781-736-3015. 224 F
cdharris@brandeis.edu
HARRIS, Charles ...... 334-420-4232..... 7 G
charris@trenholmstate.edu
HARRIS, Charles, S ...... 434-791-5701. 502 D
csharris@averett.edu
HARRIS, Charlotte ...... 937-775-2821. 393 G
charlotte.harris@wright.edu
HARRIS, Charlotte, M ...... 205-348-6690..... 8 D
charris@fa.ua.edu
HARRIS, Chelsy ...... 719-502-3033... 84 A
chelsy.harris@ppcc.edu
HARRIS, Chris ...... 949-214-3169... 41 I
chris.harris@cui.edu
HARRIS, Chris ...... 440-375-7000. 382 L
charris1@lec.edu
HARRIS, Chris ...... 601-635-2111. 266 H
charris@eccc.edu
HARRIS, Chriss ...... 419-755-4753. 385 D
charris@ncstatecollege.edu
HARRIS, Christina ...... 215-568-9215. 423 M
chharris@phmc.org
HARRIS, Clark ...... 810-762-0500. 247 F
clark.harris@mcc.edu
HARRIS, Clayton ...... 216-987-4325. 378 D
clayton.harris@tri-c.edu
HARRIS, Cliff ...... 313-664-7403. 241 C
charris@collegeforcreativestudies.edu
HARRIS, Connie, L ...... 419-448-2000. 380 G
HARRIS, Craig ...... 716-926-8888. 326 B
charris@hilbert.edu
HARRIS, Craig ...... 540-857-6479. 514 E
charris@virginiawestern.edu
HARRIS, Crystal ...... 252-862-1246. 363 A
harrisc@roanokechowan.edu
HARRIS, D. Steve ...... 229-317-6780. 124 A
steve.harris@darton.edu
HARRIS, Dan, I ...... 414-277-7230. 534 G
harris@msoe.edu
HARRIS, Darrell, A ...... 904-264-2172. 111 P
dharris@iws.edu
HARRIS, David ...... 718-268-4700. 337 F
HARRIS, David, P ...... 909-558-7600... 51 C
dpharris@llu.edu
HARRIS, David, R ...... 617-627-3310. 237 C
david.harris@tufts.edu
HARRIS, David, W ...... 505-277-7520. 312 F
dwharris@unm.edu
HARRIS, Debbie ...... 804-751-9191. 503 K
dharris@rsht.edu
HARRIS, Delphia ...... 901-435-1380. 455 M
delphia_harris@loc.edu
HARRIS, Denise ...... 716-926-8727. 326 B
dharris@hilbert.edu
HARRIS, Dennis ...... 405-422-1283. 399 B
harrisd@redlandscc.edu
HARRIS, Dina ...... 574-520-4131. 168 E
dlharris@iusb.edu
HARRIS, Duncan ...... 307-766-4110. 543 I
dharris@uwyo.edu
HARRIS, Edwin ...... 860-465-5775... 87 L
harrised@easternct.edu
HARRIS, Erica ...... 606-539-4250. 200 B
erica.harris@ucumberlands.edu
HARRIS, SR., Forrest, E . 615-256-1463. 452 G
harrisfe@abcnash.edu
HARRIS, Freda, J ...... 608-262-6423. 536 C
fharris@uwsa.edu
HARRIS, G. Duncan ...... 860-512-3203... 88 G
gharris@manchestercc.edu
HARRIS, Gail ...... 423-746-5208. 462 C
gharris@twcnet.edu
HARRIS, Gary, L ...... 202-806-6800... 95 G
gharris@howard.edu
HARRIS, Gheretta, R ...... 248-341-2081. 248 D
grharris@oaklandcc.edu
HARRIS, Greg ...... 770-426-2836. 128 D
gharris@life.edu
HARRIS, Greg ...... 503-584-7153. 402 E
greg.harris@chemeketa.edu
HARRIS, Gregory ...... 617-573-8406. 237 B
gharris@suffolk.edu
HARRIS, Gregory ...... 803-533-3740. 446 G
gharri17@scsu.edu
HARRIS, Gregory, C ...... 704-378-1101. 355 K
gcharris@jcsu.edu
HARRIS, Helen ...... 225-216-8287. 202 H
harrish@mybrcc.edu
HARRIS, Hubert, B ...... 804-524-8989. 515 D
hharris@vsu.edu
HARRIS, Hugh, W ...... 610-330-5330. 420 D
harrish@lafayette.edu
HARRIS, James ...... 903-593-8311. 485 A
jharris@texascollege.edu
HARRIS, III, James, T ... 610-499-4101. 437 E
jtharris@widener.edu
HARRIS, Jay, H ...... 260-481-6785. 168 C
harrishj@ipfw.edu
HARRIS, Jerry ...... 307-778-1280. 543 D
jharris@lccc.wy.edu
HARRIS, Jo-Anne ...... 610-399-2247. 428 B
jharris@cheyney.edu
HARRIS, Joel, C ...... 843-953-6841. 442 A
joel.harris@citadel.edu
HARRIS, John ...... 515-961-1626. 182 E
john.harris@simpson.edu
HARRIS, John ...... 903-923-2181. 471 J
jharris@etbu.edu
HARRIS, Kathy ...... 618-544-8657. 147 A
harrisk@iecc.edu
HARRIS, Kendall, T ...... 936-261-9900. 482 F
ktharris@pvamu.edu
HARRIS, Kim ...... 865-882-4695. 461 E
harriskb@roanestate.edu
HARRIS, Kip, B ...... 208-496-9200. 137 H
harrisk@byui.edu
HARRIS, Kristin ...... 940-855-2203. 493 F
kharris@vernoncollege.edu
HARRIS, Lakecia ...... 334-244-3903..... 2 A
lharri18@aum.edu
HARRIS, Lamel ...... 408-288-3731... 63 P
lamel.harris@sjcc.edu
HARRIS, Lesa, C ...... 270-809-3750. 198 B
lharris@murraystate.edu
HARRIS, Lisa ...... 208-426-1630. 137 G
lisaharris@boisestate.edu
HARRIS, Lisa ...... 763-433-1292. 257 P
lisa.harris@anokaramsey.edu
HARRIS, Margie, R ...... 402-552-3470. 288 L
harris@clarksoncollege.edu
HARRIS, Marie Joan ...... 816-501-3758. 271 H
marie.harris@avila.edu
HARRIS, Martha ...... 785-594-8338. 184 C
martha.harris@bakeru.edu
HARRIS, Marty ...... 562-902-3341... 67 H
martyharris@scuhs.edu
HARRIS, Mary ...... 317-931-2300. 165 B
mharris@cts.edu
HARRIS, Mary, A ...... 202-274-5498... 97 A
mharris@udc.edu
HARRIS, Mary, E ...... 512-223-7705. 466 I
mharris3@austincc.edu
HARRIS, Mary, M ...... 309-298-1888. 162 K
mm-harris@wiu.edu
HARRIS, Mary, R ...... 575-492-2162. 312 M
mharris@usw.edu
HARRIS, Michael, E ...... 336-734-7764. 360 E
mharris@forsythtech.edu
HARRIS, Michelle ...... 404-872-3593. 121 C
mharris@johnmarshall.edu
HARRIS, Nancy ...... 323-856-7600... 27 O
HARRIS, Nick, L ...... 504-816-4704. 201 K
nharris@dillard.edu
HARRIS, Obadiah ...... 323-663-2167... 73 B
HARRIS, Ozzie ...... 404-727-2616. 124 E
ozzie.harris@emory.edu
HARRIS, Patricia ...... 662-252-8000. 269 F
pharris@rustcollege.edu
HARRIS, Patricia, R ...... 616-222-3000. 245 C
pharris@kuyper.edu
HARRIS, Patrick ...... 406-447-4380. 285 G
pharris@carroll.edu
HARRIS, Patty ...... 651-290-6358. 265 F
patty.harris@wmitchell.edu
HARRIS, Paul ...... 585-475-4992. 337 L
pahdar@rit.edu
HARRIS, Peggy ...... 850-973-1621. 109 H
harrisp@nfcc.edu
HARRIS, Peggy ...... 785-594-8492. 184 C
peggy.harris@bakeru.edu
HARRIS, Peter ...... 860-512-3213... 88 G
pharris@manchestercc.edu
HARRIS, Randall ...... 601-857-3280. 267 A
Randall.Harris@hindscc.edu
HARRIS, JR., Rerrance ... 407-628-5870. 102 K
rharris@cci.edu
HARRIS, Rhonda, L ...... 757-683-4003. 507 N
rlharris@odu.edu
HARRIS, Richard ...... 877-804-1424. 266 A
rharris@belhaven.edu
HARRIS, Richard, C ...... 516-671-2215. 350 C
rharris@webb.edu
HARRIS, Rob ...... 417-328-1827. 282 C
rharris@sbuniv.edu
HARRIS, Robin ...... 252-335-0821. 359 F
robin_harris@albemarle.edu
HARRIS, Rotesha ...... 404-880-6917. 122 J
rharris@cau.edu
HARRIS, Sara ...... 620-331-4100. 187 G
sharris@indycc.edu
HARRIS, Scott ...... 309-298-1949. 162 K
sd-harris@wiu.edu
HARRIS, Sedgwick ...... 815-825-2086. 149 F
sedgwick.harris@kishwaukeecollege.edu
HARRIS, Sharlene, J ...... 340-693-1361. 555 E
sharris@live.uvi.edu
HARRIS, Simone ...... 985-448-4521. 208 A
simone.harris@nicholls.edu
HARRIS, Stephen, A ...... 615-248-1245. 462 D
sharris@trevecca.edu
HARRIS, Susan ...... 901-381-3939. 464 C
susan@visible.edu
HARRIS, Susan, G ...... 434-924-7081. 511 B
sgh4c@virginia.edu
HARRIS, Suzann ...... 615-248-1201. 462 D
sharris@trevecca.edu
HARRIS, Terral ...... 912-279-5726. 123 B
tharris@ccga.edu
HARRIS, JR., Thomas ...... 229-430-4650. 119 J
thomas.harris@asurams.edu
HARRIS, Thomas, W ...... 859-257-1933. 200 C
tom.harris@uky.edu
HARRIS, Todd, D ...... 910-630-7155. 356 H
toharris@methodist.edu
HARRIS, Tonya ...... 870-838-2913... 19 K
tharris@smail.anc.edu
HARRIS, Tosca ...... 620-365-5116. 183 I
harris@allencc.edu
HARRIS, Tracy ...... 240-725-5300. 214 D
tracy.harris@csmd.edu
HARRIS, Troy ...... 805-565-6848... 76 D
tharris@westmont.edu
HARRIS, Troy ...... 313-596-0210. 250 K
harristl2@udmercy.edu
HARRIS, Valorie ...... 618-468-4100. 150 G
vharris@lc.edu
HARRIS, Virginia, M ...... 203-371-7958... 91 C
harrisv@sacredheart.edu
HARRIS, Wayne ...... 757-727-5071. 505 F
wayne.harris@hamptonu.edu
HARRIS,
Whitney Stewart ...... 651-201-1746. 257 N
whitney.harris@so.mnscu.edu
HARRIS, William, H ...... 334-229-6944..... 1 D
wharris@alasu.edu
HARRIS, William, L ...... 859-257-9101. 200 C
harriswl@uky.edu
HARRIS, Wilma, K ...... 479-979-1215... 25 J
wkharris@ozarks.edu
HARRIS, Yolanda ...... 719-502-4689... 84 A
yolanda.harris@ppcc.edu
HARRIS, Yonie ...... 805-893-2771... 72 B
yonie.harris@sa.ucsb.edu
HARRIS BANE, Holly ..... 330-972-7508. 390 E
harrisb@uakron.edu
HARRIS-HOOKER,
Sandra ...... 404-752-1725. 129 E
sharris-hooker@msm.edu
HARRIS-JOLLY,
Stephanie ...... 229-430-4667. 119 J
stephanie.harris-jolley@asurams.edu
HARRIS-LUMPKINS,
Deidra ...... 704-971-8500. 353 F
HARRIS PAOLILLO,
Linda ...... 212-752-1530. 328 G
linda.harris@limcollege.edu
HARRISON, Antione ...... 518-381-1449. 340 G
harrisaw@sunysccc.edu
HARRISON, B. Keith ...... 251-460-6261..... 9 E
kharrison@southalabama.edu
HARRISON, B. Timothy .. 618-537-6962. 152 G
btharrison@mckendree.edu
HARRISON, Bobbie, J ...... 972-238-6130. 471 C
bjharrison@dcccd.edu
HARRISON, Carol ...... 301-934-7552. 214 D
carolh@csmd.edu
HARRISON, Cheryl ...... 718-862-7862. 329 M
cheryl.harrison@manhattan.edu
HARRISON, Crystal ...... 920-498-5541. 541 B
crystal.harrison@nwtc.edu
HARRISON, David, T ...... 614-287-2402. 378 B
dth@cscc.edu
HARRISON, Dianne, F .... 818-677-2121... 34 C
dianne.harrison@csun.edu
HARRISON, Don ...... 770-534-6136. 122 A
dharrison@brenau.edu
HARRISON, Fred, H ...... 501-686-2515... 23 H
fhharrison@uasys.edu
HARRISON, Hope, S ...... 864-379-6546. 443 F
harrison@erskine.edu
HARRISON, James, H ...... 920-206-2327. 533 U
jharrison@mbbc.edu
HARRISON, James, M ... 228-897-7131. 270 I
james.harrison@wmcarey.edu
HARRISON, Janice ...... 508-565-1096. 237 A
jharrison@stonehill.edu
HARRISON, Jim ...... 478-553-2108. 129 H
jharrison@oftc.edu
HARRISON, Jim, H ...... 920-206-2327. 533 U
jharrison@mbbc.edu
HARRISON, Judy ...... 870-230-5358... 21 D
harrisj@hsu.edu
HARRISON, Karen, D ...... 918-465-1829. 395 G
kdharrison@eosc.edu
HARRISON, Kelly, G ...... 904-620-1707. 116 B
n00874366@unf.edu
HARRISON, Kenneth ...... 334-291-4963..... 2 H
kenneth.harrison@cv.edu
HARRISON, Kim, W ...... 931-363-9876. 456 C
kharrison@martinmethodist.edu
HARRISON, Lacey ...... 229-226-1621. 132 F
lharrison@thomasu.edu
HARRISON, Lisa ...... 205-226-4912..... 2 C
lharriso@bsc.edu
HARRISON, Lonnie ...... 575-492-2168. 312 M
lharrison@usw.edu
HARRISON, Mark ...... 360-475-7700. 521 H
mharrison@olympic.edu
HARRISON, Matthew ...... 773-995-2867. 141 J
mharri42@csu.edu
HARRISON, Melissa ...... 509-527-4675. 524 H
melissa.harrison@wwcc.edu
HARRISON, Monnie ...... 660-626-2325. 271 A
mharrison@atsu.edu
HARRISON, Paul, D ...... 740-245-7200. 392 A
harrison@rio.edu
HARRISON, Richard ...... 402-872-2257. 291 E
rharrison@peru.edu
HARRISON, Richard ...... 903-983-8212. 475 E
rharrison@kilgore.edu
HARRISON, Robert ...... 269-927-8600. 245 D
harrison@lakemichigancollege.edu

HARRISON, JR., Robert, L ... 304-766-3313. 530 C harrisonr@wvstateu.edu

HARRISON, Rodney, A ... 816-414-3700. 277 L rharrison@mbts.edu

HARRISON, Ruth ... 928-776-2163... 19 H ruth.harrison@yc.edu

HARRISON, Ruth, G ... 413-597-3166. 238 D ruth.g.harrison@williams.edu

HARRISON, Scot ... 360-438-8808. 522 G sharrison@stmartin.edu

HARRISON, Scott ... 517-371-5140. 250 G harrisos@cooley.edu

HARRISON, Sheryl, E ... 404-872-3593. 121 C sharrison@johnmarshall.edu

HARRISON, Steve ... 843-349-6405. 442 E harrison@coastal.edu

HARRISON, Suzan ... 727-864-8212. 101 N harrisms@eckerd.edu

HARRISON, Tamara ... 928-523-6962... 16 C Tamara.Harrison@nau.edu

HARRISON, Tammiko ... 601-979-2345. 267 E tammiko.l.harrison@jsums.edu

HARRISON, Tammy ... 501-569-3492... 24 B twharrison@ualr.edu

HARRISON, Teresa ... 757-925-6782. 513 E tharrison@pdc.edu

HARRISON, Thomas ... 904-256-7347. 107 Q tharris7@ju.edu

HARRISON, Thomas ... 304-327-4011. 529 D tharrison@bluefieldstate.edu

HARRISON, Tim ... 805-289-6121... 74 H tharrison@vcccd.edu

HARRISON, Tracey ... 601-925-3239. 268 A tharriso@mc.edu

HARRISON, Valerie ... 215-517-2383. 409 H harrisonv@arcadia.edu

HARRISON, Valerie, E ... 803-535-5225. 442 B vharrison@claflin.edu

HARRISON, W. Darryl ... 706-385-1098. 130 F darryl.harrison@point.edu

HARRISON, Walter ... 860-768-4417... 92 D horky@hartford.edu

HARRISON, Wendy ... 757-569-6792. 513 E wharrison@pdc.edu

HARROD, John ... 608-263-3077. 536 D jharrod@fpm.wisc.edu

HARROD, Joseph, C ... 502-897-4215. 199 B jharrod@sbts.edu

HARROD, Robert, C ... 937-382-6661. 393 B chip_harrod@wilmington.edu

HARROL, Jackie ... 405-422-1406. 399 B harrolj@redlandscc.edu

HARROLD, Cindy ... 620-429-3896. 185 O cindyh@coffeyville.edu

HARROLD, Frank ... 801-626-6232. 497 D frankharrold@weber.edu

HARROZ, JR., Joseph ... 405-325-4699. 401 B jharroz@ou.edu

HARSHA, Brad ... 419-783-2365. 379 C bharsha@defiance.edu

HARSHBARGER, Bruce ... 478-445-5169. 125 A bruce.harshbarger@gcsu.edu

HARSHBARGER, John ... 440-775-8470. 385 H John.Harshbarger@oberlin.edu

HARSHMAN, Cheryl, R ... 304-336-8035. 530 A harshmac@westliberty.edu

HARSHMAN, Cris ... 828-254-1921. 357 N charshman@abtech.edu

HARSHMAN, Ellen, F ... 314-977-3833. 281 I harshman@slu.edu

HARSTINE, Stan ... 316-295-5871. 186 H harstine@friends.edu

HART, Aaron ... 317-274-7200. 168 D aarohart@iupui.edu

HART, Anne ... 239-280-1669... 98 K anne.hart@avemaria.edu

HART, Bill ... 251-442-2223... 9 A bhart@umobile.edu

HART, Brad ... 912-538-3121. 132 A brhart@southeasterntech.edu

HART, Caroline ... 828-898-8777. 356 A hartc@lmc.edu

HART, Charlene ... 775-784-4040. 294 J crhart@unr.edu

HART, Charles ... 601-643-8358. 266 F charles.hart@colin.edu

HART, Chris ... 502-585-9911. 199 C chart@spalding.edu

HART, Chris ... 410-837-5739. 221 A chart@ubalt.edu

HART, Christi ... 503-491-6961. 404 E christi.hart@mhcc.edu

HART, Christina ... 772-462-4703. 106 P chart@irsc.edu

HART, Craig, H ... 801-422-3567. 495 D craig_hart@byu.edu

HART, Curt ... 605-995-2152. 450 A cuhart@dwu.edu

HART, Darrell, E ... 435-797-1952. 497 B darrell.hart@usu.edu

HART, Dave ... 865-974-1224. 463 C

HART, Deanna ... 562-860-2451... 37 I dhart@cerritos.edu

HART, Debra ... 304-696-2597. 529 H hart70@marshall.edu

HART, Erick ... 585-395-2579. 342 F ehart@brockport.edu

HART, Eyvonne ... 912-486-7784. 129 J ehart@ogeecheetech.edu

HART, George ... 978-934-4556. 229 B George_Hart@uml.edu

HART, James, R ... 904-264-2172. 111 P president@iws.edu

HART, James, T ... 804-863-2107. 508 H jhart@rbc.edu

HART, Jana, D ... 479-979-1221... 25 J jhart@ozarks.edu

HART, Jeffery ... 509-313-4150. 520 A hart@gonzaga.edu

HART, Jimmy, W ... 615-898-2919. 459 D jimmy.hart@mtsu.edu

HART, Jodi ... 561-868-3465. 110 C hartj@palmbeachstate.edu

HART, John ... 937-766-4898. 375 K johnhart@cedarville.edu

HART, Karen ... 248-218-2011. 249 D khart@rc.edu

HART, Kathleen ... 209-954-5047... 63 C khart@deltacollege.edu

HART, Kelly ... 413-572-8519. 230 F khart@westfield.ma.edu

HART, Kerry ... 970-542-3105... 83 E kerry.hart@morgancc.edu

HART, Kristy ... 916-608-6500... 53 C flc-pio@flc.losrios.edu

HART, Latoya ... 601-877-2336. 265 G lhart@alcorn.edu

HART, Lauren ... 313-664-1162. 241 C lhart@collegeforcreativestudies.edu

HART, Mary ... 619-388-7614... 62 F mhart@sdccd.edu

HART, Mickey ... 614-222-3294. 378 A mhart@ccad.edu

HART, Peter, L ... 978-232-2058. 226 C lehart@endicott.edu

HART, Quentin ... 319-296-4463. 178 J quentin.hart@hawkeyecollege.edu

HART, Rahmon ... 412-396-1117. 415 F hartr1214@duq.edu

HART, Richard, H ... 909-558-4540... 51 C rhart@llu.edu

HART, Richard, L ... 214-768-4301. 481 A rlhart@smu.edu

HART, Robert ... 508-793-2224. 225 B rhart@holycross.edu

HART, Roderick, P ... 512-471-5646. 491 C rod.hart@austin.utexas.edu

HART, Sharon, Y ... 670-234-5498. 547 A president@nmcnet.edu

HART, Susan ... 615-343-2388. 463 G susan.hart@vanderbilt.edu

HART, Susan, L ... 205-934-5816... 8 E slhart@uab.edu

HART, Tara ... 973-761-9593. 307 C tara.hart@shu.edu

HART, Thomas ... 412-396-6004. 415 F hartt1@duq.edu

HART, Tom ... 314-246-7576. 284 N harttr@webster.edu

HART, Trois, K ... 260-399-7700. 174 C thart@sf.edu

HART-SCHUTTE, Julie ... 605-995-7135. 450 E julie.schutte@mitchelltech.edu

HART-THORE, Dawn ... 504-278-6332. 203 F dhart@nunez.edu

HARTE, Meghan ... 407-646-2599. 111 Q mharte@rollins.edu

HARTENBURG, Gary ... 281-649-3630. 473 B ghartenburg@hbu.edu

HARTER, Christina ... 425-739-8225. 520 K chris.harter@lwtech.edu

HARTER, Donald, L ... 315-792-3191. 349 F dharter@utica.edu

HARTER, James ... 419-251-1786. 383 G james.harter@mercycollege.edu

HARTER, James, L ... 419-251-1786. 383 G james.harter@mercycollege.edu

HARTER, Suzanne ... 808-983-4146. 135 G sharter@tokai.edu

HARTFIELD, Colleen, C ... 601-857-3364. 267 A colleen.hartfield@hindscc.edu

HARTFORD, Linda ... 920-498-6937. 541 B linda.hartford@nwtc.edu

HARTFORD, Sharon, M ... 509-527-4323. 524 H sharon.hartford@wwcc.edu

HARTGRAVES, Stan ... 949-398-2358... 75 E sHartgraves@westcoastuniversity.edu

HARTHORN, Karen, M ... 651-962-6353. 265 C kmharthorn@stthomas.edu

HARTIG, Jeanne ... 312-567-3000. 147 F jhartig@iit.edu

HARTIGAN, Ellen ... 718-631-6351. 319 D ehartigan@qcc.cuny.edu

HARTIGAN, William, J ... 401-865-2166. 439 E hartigan@providence.edu

HARTIN, Linda, A ... 334-222-6591... 5 E lhartin@lbwcc.edu

HARTING, William ... 317-955-6015. 170 V bharting@marian.edu

HARTING, William ... 317-955-6016. 170 V bharting@marian.edu

HARTKE, Emily ... 217-234-5259. 150 D ehartke@lakeland.cc.il.us

HARTLEROAD, LeAnn ... 618-393-2982. 146 H hartleroadl@iecc.edu

HARTLESS, Sharon ... 434-582-7600. 506 I shartles@liberty.edu

HARTLEY, Brian ... 618-664-6821. 145 G brian.hartley@greenville.edu

HARTLEY, Carolyn ... 219-980-6971. 168 B cjhartle@iun.edu

HARTLEY, Christina ... 401-454-6794. 440 A chartley@risd.edu

HARTLEY, Christopher ... 617-682-1532. 226 D chartley@eds.edu

HARTLEY, Gary ... 916-608-6500... 53 C

HARTLEY, Greg, L ... 916-348-4689... 43 F ghartley@epic.edu

HARTLEY, Laura ... 503-554-2143. 403 C lhartley@georgefox.edu

HARTLEY, Lorraine ... 216-987-2424. 378 D lorraine.hartley@tri-c.edu

HARTLEY, Meredith ... 504-861-5888. 205 H mhartley@loyno.edu

HARTLEY, Stephanie, J ... 601-923-1657. 269 E shartley@rts.edu

HARTLEY, William ... 972-721-5194. 488 F whartley@udallas.edu

HARTLINE, Beverly ... 406-496-4456. 287 F bhartline@mtech.edu

HARTMAN, Brandi, P ... 864-488-4604. 444 L bhartman@limestone.edu

HARTMAN, Bruce ... 559-442-8201... 68 H bruce.hartman@scccd.edu

HARTMAN, Bryan, G ... 518-564-2280. 344 B hartmabg@plattsburgh.edu

HARTMAN, Cheryl, J ... 605-221-3100. 450 C chartman@kilian.edu

HARTMAN, Christine, M 717-337-6276. 417 B chartman@gettysburg.edu

HARTMAN, Dean, A ... 706-880-8246. 128 A dhartman@lagrange.edu

HARTMAN, Eric, G ... 931-598-1229. 458 H ehartman@sewanee.edu

HARTMAN, Fred, W ... 919-515-7159. 368 B fred_hartman@ncsu.edu

HARTMAN, Freda ... 480-557-3049... 18 I freda.hartman@phoenix.edu

HARTMAN, Jackie, L ... 785-532-6221. 188 A jlh1980@ksu.edu

HARTMAN, James, P ... 215-951-2966. 430 E hartmanj@philau.edu

HARTMAN, Joel, L ... 407-823-6778. 115 E joel.hartman@ucf.edu

HARTMAN, Joseph ... 978-934-2576. 229 B joseph_hartman@uml.edu

HARTMAN, Joseph ... 972-825-4774. 481 F jhartman@sagu.edu

HARTMAN, Laurie ... 315-792-7400. 346 C laurie.hartman@sunyit.edu

HARTMAN, Luke ... 540-432-4000. 504 D luke.hartman@emu.edu

HARTMAN, Melissa ... 619-961-2164. 463 J mhartman@victory.edu

HARTMAN, Nancy ... 513-244-8447. 376 J nancy.hartman@ccuniversity.edu

HARTMAN, Nathan ... 859-344-3602. 199 H nathan.hartman@thomasmore.edu

HARTMAN, Phil ... 817-257-7727. 484 I p.hartman@tcu.edu

HARTMAN, Regina ... 513-585-2773. 376 I regina.hartman@thechristhospital.com

HARTMAN, Robert ... 740-477-7843. 385 L rhartman@ohiochristian.edu

HARTMAN, Robin ... 714-879-3901... 47 K rhartman@hiu.edu

HARTMAN, Sherry, L ... 208-467-8588. 139 A slhartman@nnu.edu

HARTMANN, Bruce ... 630-466-7900. 162 J bhartmann@waubonsee.edu

HARTMANN, Kimberly, D ... 203-582-8679... 91 A kimberly.hartmann@quinnipiac.edu

HARTMANN, Patricia ... 414-382-6072. 531 I pat.hartmann@alverno.edu

HARTMANN, Wendy ... 636-584-6712. 273 M wahartm@eastcentral.edu

HARTNETT, Deborah ... 212-650-8638. 317 D dhartnett@ccny.cuny.edu

HARTOG, John ... 712-324-5066. 181 G jhartog@nwicc.edu

HARTOG, II, John ... 515-964-0601. 178 E hartogj2@faith.edu

HARTOG, Paul ... 515-064-0601. 178 E hartogp@faith.edu

HARTOG, William, M ... 540-458-8710. 516 A bhartog@wlu.edu

HARTON, Mary Kay ... 928-344-7580... 11 L marykay.harton@azwestern.edu

HARTS, Stanley, H ... 910-962-3057. 369 C hartss@uncw.edu

HARTSELL, Angela ... 239-489-9427. 101 O ahartsell1@edison.edu

HARTSFIELD, LaTanya ... 404-237-7573. 121 F lhartsfield@bauder.edu

HARTSHORN, Tricia ... 785-227-3380. 184 I hartshornt@bethanylb.edu

HARTSOE, Janice ... 678-717-3671. 133 D janice.hartsoe@ung.edu

HARTUNG, Jason ... 661-362-2207... 53 G jhartung@masters.edu

HARTUNIAS, Vaughn ... 225-248-1015. 202 A

HARTWELL, Robert, E ... 516-877-4231. 313 A hartwell@adelphi.edu

HARTZ, James ... 270-686-4630. 196 C jim.hartz@kctcs.edu

HARTZ, Jan ... 949-753-4774... 29 M hartz@brandman.edu

HARTZ, Jason ... 304-829-7516. 526 D jhartz@bethanywv.edu

HARTZ, Jason, M ... 517-265-5161. 238 G shelfer@adrian.edu

HARTZ, Wayne ... 603-358-2220. 298 F whartz@keene.edu

HARTZEL, Ruth Ann ... 724-847-5673. 417 A rhartzel@geneva.edu

HARTZLER, Christi ... 407-823-4663. 115 E christi.hartzler@ucf.edu

HARTZLER, Murray, G ... 843-661-1237. 444 B mhartzler@fmarion.edu

HARTZOG, Gail, C ... 850-718-2342... 99 N hartzogg@chipola.edu

HARVEY, Addie ... 901-435-1704. 455 M addie_harvey@loc.edu

HARVEY, Andre ... 404-527-4520. 122 E

HARVEY, Barron, H ... 202-806-1500... 95 G bharvey@howard.edu

HARVEY, Bryan, C ... 413-545-6238. 228 F harvey@provost.umass.edu

HARVEY, David ... 941-487-4511. 115 D dharvey@ncf.edu

HARVEY, Diana ... 801-957-4278. 498 B diana.harvey@slcc.edu

HARVEY, Iris, E ... 330-672-7882. 382 B iharvey1@kent.edu

HARVEY, Jenny ... 540-234-9261. 511 H harveyj@brcc.edu

HARVEY, John ... 803-754-4100. 443 C

HARVEY, John ... 325-793-4751. 476 E jharvey@mcm.edu

HARVEY, Karen ... 276-935-4349. 502 A kharvey@asl.edu

HARVEY, Kelly ... 252-536-6348. 361 A kharvey951@halifaxcc.edu

HARVEY, Kim, M ... 636-481-3207. 275 I kharvey@jeffco.edu

HARVEY, Laurie ... 516-686-7711. 333 H lharve05@nyit.edu

HARVEY, Leah ... 651-793-1777. 259 C leah.harvey@metrostate.edu

HARVEY, Linda ... 718-780-7966. 315 H linda.harvey@brooklaw.edu

HARVEY, Lydia ... 907-564-8218... 10 C lydiah@alaskapacific.edu

HARVEY, Marcus ... 816-604-4121. 277 H marcus.harvey@mcckc.edu

HARVEY, Mary, J ... 773-702-8806. 161 B mharvey@uchicago.edu

HARVEY, Pauline ... 907-442-3400... 10 I pharvey1@alaska.edu

HARVEY, Peter, W ... 509-527-5145. 525 E harvey@whitman.edu

HARVEY, Richard, C ... 304-367-4395. 529 F richard.harvey@fairmontstate.edu

HARVEY, Roberta ... 856-256-5140. 305 E harvey@rowan.edu

HARVEY, Rodger ... 757-683-3460. 507 N rharvey@odu.edu

HARVEY, Sarah, J ... 260-359-4010. 166 O sharvey@huntington.edu

HARVEY, Scott ... 864-646-1556. 447 D sharvey@tctc.edu

HARVEY, Shannon, S ... 717-339-3503. 417 I ssharvey@hacc.edu

HARVEY, Steven ... 603-645-9611. 297 I s.harvey@snhu.edu

HARVEY, Stewart, A ... 207-581-2638. 212 B stewarth@maine.edu

HARVEY, Stu ... 405-682-7849. 397 E sharvey@occc.edu

HARVEY, Valtroud ... 410-923-4500... 96 F valtroud.harvey@strayer.edu

HARVEY, William, B .... 336-334-7757. 367 E
wbharvey@ncat.edu
HARVEY, William, R .... 757-727-5231. 505 F
presidentsoffice@hamptonu.edu
HARVEY-JACOBS, Pam .. 920-465-2111. 536 F
harveyp@uwgb.edu
HARVEY-LEE, Peggy, A .. 585-292-2252. 332 A
pharvey-lee@monroecc.edu
HARVEY-SAHAK,
Judy, B .... 909-621-8973... 65 D
judy.harveysahak@scrippscollege.edu
HARVEY-SMITH, Alicia ... 603-542-7744. 296 D
HARVIN, Lillian .... 510-869-8785... 61 I
lharvin@samuelmerritt.edu
HARVIN, Peter, B .... 864-231-2017. 441 B
pharvin@andersonuniversity.edu
HARVITH, John .... 412-624-4380. 435 C
harvith@pitt.edu
HARWARD, Brian .... 814-332-3027. 409 D
bharward@allegheny.edu
HARWOOD, Debra .... 704-991-0206. 364 C
dharwood5544@stanly.edu
HARWOOD, Scott .... 518-891-2915. 335 A
sharwood@nccc.edu
HASAN, Rashidah .... 973-877-3260. 301 H
hasan@essex.edu
HASAN, Zia .... 803-535-5219. 442 B
hasan@claflin.edu
HASBROUCK,
Norman, G .... 724-938-1561. 428 A
hasbrouck@calu.edu
HASELBARTH, Jared .... 610-785-6267. 432 C
jhaselbarth@scs.edu
HASELDEN, Gregory, W . 864-379-8812. 443 F
haselden@erskine.edu
HASELOFF, Gregory, K ... 859-858-3511. 192 B
greg.haseloff@asbury.edu
HASELTON, Blake .... 502-852-5597. 200 D
blake.haselton@louisville.edu
HASENOEHRL, Mary .... 208-792-2458. 138 G
mlhasenoehrl@lcsc.edu
HASFURTHER, Victor ...... 435-879-4801. 497 E
hasfurther@dixie.edu
HASH, Jennifer .... 303-722-5724... 83 A
jhash@lincolntech.com
HASH, Joseph .... 707-476-4212... 40 H
joe-hash@redwoods.edu
HASHEMIPOUR,
Mohammad .... 516-364-0808. 333 D
mhashemipour@nycollege.edu
HASHIZUME, John .... 650-306-3276... 64 B
hashizumej@smccd.edu
HASINGER, Guenther ..... 808-956-8566. 136 B
hasinger@hawaii.edu
HASKA, Christine, M ...... 831-656-3411. 544 M
cmhaska@nps.edu
HASKAJ, Tatjana .... 617-588-1358. 223 B
thaskaj@bfit.edu
HASKAMP, Misty .... 573-875-7582. 272 G
mrhaskamp@ccis.edu
HASKELL, Benjamin, E ... 207-941-7176. 211 F
haskellb@nescom.edu
HASKELL, Richard .... 781-239-3191. 231 G
rhaskell@massbay.edu
HASKETT, Tammy .... 828-227-7222. 369 E
haskett@wcu.edu
HASKEY, Glennita .... 928-724-6723... 13 H
ghaskey@dinecollege.edu
HASKINS, Brenda .... 985-448-4518. 208 A
brenda.haskins@nicholls.edu
HASKINS, Dana, R .... 972-860-7269. 470 I
DRHaskins@dcccd.edu
HASKINS, Dennis .... 931-363-9889. 456 C
dhaskins@martinmethodist.edu
HASKINS, Eileen, T .... 401-598-1035. 439 B
ehaskins@jwu.edu
HASKINS, Jamie .... 573-592-5262. 285 B
jamie.haskins@westminster-mo.edu
HASKINS, Michael, R ...... 843-953-6461. 443 A
haskinsm@cofc.edu
HASKINS, Nena .... 574-936-8898. 163 K
nena.haskins@ancilla.edu
HASKINS, Richard .... 412-392-8097. 431 B
rhaskins@pointpark.edu
HASKVITZ, Esther .... 518-244-4590. 338 C
haskev@sage.edu
HASLAG, Daniel .... 573-592-5282. 285 B
dan.haslag@westminster-mo.edu
HASLAM, Kent .... 406-243-5370. 286 H
kent.haslam@umontana.edu
HASLANGER, Sally .... 617-253-8844. 233 B
HASLEM, Lori .... 309-341-7214. 150 A
lhaslem@knox.edu
HASLER, Paul .... 715-346-3059. 538 A
phasler@uwsp.edu
HASLIM, Hue .... 602-943-2311... 19 C
Hue.Haslim@west.edu
HASS, Marjorie .... 903-813-3001. 466 H
mhass@austincollege.edu
HASS, Martha .... 518-694-7238. 313 B
martha.hass@acphs.edu

HASSAN, Nidia .... 903-510-2883. 488 E
nhas@tjc.edu
HASSAN, Sharon, E .... 301-322-0749. 217 F
hassanse@pgcc.edu
HASSEL, George, E .... 610-499-4182. 437 E
gehassel.sr@widener.edu
HASSELER, Susan, S ...... 605-274-4113. 449 K
susan.hasseler@augie.edu
HASSELL, Adalecia .... 787-841-2000. 552 B
ahassell@pucpr.edu
HASSELL, Dayna .... 973-748-9000. 299 F
dayna_hassell@bloomfield.edu
HASSELL, Robert .... 615-256-1463. 452 G
rhassell@abcnash.edu
HASSELTINE, Donald ...... 507-222-4199. 254 D
dhasseltine@carleton.edu
HASSEN, Marjorie .... 207-725-3000. 209 H
HASSENZAHL, David ...... 412-365-1842. 412 K
dhassenzahl@chatham.edu
HASSENZAHL, Roger ...... 765-285-1532. 164 B
rahassenzahl@bsu.edu
HASSETT, A. Tracy .... 508-831-5473. 238 F
thassett@wpi.edu
HASSEVOORT, Darrin ..... 423-697-3383. 460 C
HASSINGER, Steven .... 717-728-2262. 412 J
stevehassinger@centralpenn.edu
HASSLER, Ardoth .... 202-687-1973... 95 E
hasslera@georgetown.edu
HASSON, Amy, S .... 410-548-3316. 220 D
ashasson@salisbury.edu
HASTAD, Doug, N .... 262-524-7246. 532 C
dhastad@carrollu.edu
HASTED, Grigor .... 517-437-7341. 243 I
grigor.hasted@hillsdale.edu
HASTINGS, Brian .... 402-458-1100. 292 I
bhastings@nufoundation.org
HASTINGS, Dana, M ...... 785-532-6221. 188 A
dhasting@ksu.edu
HASTINGS, Donald, B .... 518-580-5768. 341 A
dhasting@skidmore.edu
HASTINGS, Jan .... 818-401-1030... 41 B
jhastings@columbiacollege.edu
HASTINGS, Jennifer, D ... 253-879-2460. 524 F
jhastings@pugetsound.edu
HASTINGS, Michael, M .. 207-581-1484. 212 B
mhastings@maine.edu
HASTINGS, Nancy .... 312-329-4415. 153 E
nancy.hastings@moody.edu
HASTINGS, Rebecca .... 425-352-8256. 517 E
rhastings@cascadia.edu
HASTINGS, Susan .... 651-255-6120. 264 C
shastings@unitedseminary.edu
HASTLER, Samantha, R .. 718-390-4500. 339 A
hastlers@stjohns.edu
HASTRITER, Michael, L .. 937-255-3636. 544 C
michael.hastriter@afit.edu
HATAIER, Maria .... 212-678-3779. 347 G
mrt2112@tc.columbia.edu
HATANAKA, Janice .... 562-985-5252... 33 F
jhatanak@csulb.edu
HATCH, Adam .... 808-544-0839. 135 F
ahatch@hpu.edu
HATCH, Blaine .... 928-524-7440... 16 E
blaine.hatch@npc.edu
HATCH, SHCJ,
Jeanne Marie .... 610-527-0200. 432 B
jhatch@rosemont.edu
HATCH, Jennifer .... 717-764-9550. 414 A
jhatch@csb.edu
HATCH, Joy, A .... 804-819-4990. 511 G
jhatch@vccs.edu
HATCH, Mark .... 719-389-6805... 79 D
mhatch@coloradocollege.edu
HATCH, Mary .... 847-214-7421. 144 F
mhatch@elgin.edu
HATCH, Nathan, O .... 336-758-5211. 370 D
hatch@wfu.edu
HATCH, Paul .... 218-262-6731. 258 G
paulhatch@hibbing.edu
HATCHER, Barb .... 540-365-4231. 504 L
bhatcher@ferrum.edu
HATCHER, Betty, K .... 252-638-3745. 359 G
hatcherb@cravencc.edu
HATCHER, Brian .... 410-617-5026. 216 A
bhatcher@loyola.edu
HATCHER, George .... 919-546-8353. 366 E
ghatcher@shawu.edu
HATCHER, Kevin, L .... 909-537-5011... 34 E
khatcher@csusb.edu
HATCHER, Lisa, M .... 304-929-6737. 528 D
lhatcher@newriver.edu
HATCHER, Oeida .... 434-544-8344. 506 K
hatcher@lynchburg.edu
HATCHER, Robert .... 212-817-7020. 317 F
rhatcher@gc.cuny.edu
HATCHER, Wayne .... 870-248-4000... 20 G
wayne.hatcher@blackrivertech.edu
HATER, Karen .... 407-646-2345. 111 Q
khater@rollins.edu
HATFIELD, Amy .... 360-475-7841. 521 H
ahatfield@olympic.edu

HATFIELD, Barbara, S .... 318-473-6446. 205 A
bhatfield@lsua.edu
HATFIELD, Chad .... 914-961-8313. 340 B
hatfield@svots.edu
HATFIELD, Heather .... 865-539-7331. 461 D
hrhatfield@pstcc.edu
HATFIELD, Karen .... 352-588-8460. 112 D
karen.hatfield@saintleo.edu
HATFIELD, Mark .... 662-720-7270. 269 B
mahatfield@nemcc.edu
HATFIELD, Misty .... 803-938-3728. 448 F
hatfielm@uscsumter.edu
HATFIELD, Renee .... 503-222-3225. 403 B
rhatfiel@cci.edu
HATFIELD, Sharon, L ..... 540-985-8263. 506 G
slhatfield@jchs.edu
HATFIELD, Tish .... 419-995-8230. 381 Q
hatfield.t@rhodesstate.edu
HATHAWAY, Gretchel, L 518-388-8327. 348 J
hathawag@union.edu
HATHAWAY, Jeffrey .... 516-463-6750. 326 D
jeffrey.hathaway@hofstra.edu
HATHAWAY, Joel .... 314-434-4044. 273 C
joel.hathaway@covenantseminary.edu
HATHAWAY, Karry, L ..... 443-412-2401. 215 C
khathaway@harford.edu
HATHAWAY, Nick .... 405-325-3916. 401 B
nhathaway@ou.edu
HATHAWAY, Tom .... 513-569-1493. 376 L
tom.hathaway@cincinnatistate.edu
HATHAWAY, William ...... 757-352-4294. 508 G
willhat@regent.edu
HATHAWAY-CLARK, Bill 303-458-4066... 84 M
whathawa@regis.edu
HATHCOCK, Michele ...... 828-398-7203. 357 N
mhathcock@abtech.edu
HATHCOTE, Jan, M .... 706-542-4907. 133 C
hathcote@uga.edu
HATHMAN, Laurie, E ...... 816-501-4144. 280 I
laurie.hathman@rockhurst.edu
HATHORN, Janine, M .... 540-458-8671. 516 A
jhathorn@wlu.edu
HATLEY, Anita .... 501-370-5314... 22 F
ahatley@philander.edu
HATMAN, Lonnie .... 360-596-5300. 524 A
lhatman@spscc.edu
HATNEY, Taura .... 706-396-7606. 130 C
thatney@paine.edu
HATRAK, Gregory .... 914-961-8313. 340 B
ghatrak@svots.edu
HATTAUER, Edward, A ... 718-990-6384. 339 A
hattauee@stjohns.edu
HATTAWAY, Trey .... 903-983-8218. 475 E
thattaway@kilgore.edu
HATTEBERG, Gregory, A 214-887-5101. 471 F
alumni@dts.edu
HATTEN, Angie .... 309-692-4092. 152 J
ahatten@midstate.edu
HATTEN, LaRue .... 504-286-3275. 270 I
larue.hatten@wmcarey.edu
HATTERMAN, Dawn, K ... 816-604-3223. 277 G
HATTERMANN, Troy .... 309-694-5156. 146 E
troy.hattermann@icc.edu
HATTMAN, Melissa .... 314-516-5708. 283 E
hattmanm@umsl.edu
HATTO, Susan .... 989-328-1254. 247 D
susanf@montcalm.edu
HATTON, Jay .... 703-784-4037. 544 J
jay.hatton@usmc.mil
HATTON, John .... 314-577-8600. 281 I
hattonjf@slu.edu
HATTON, Karl .... 270-247-8521. 197 H
khatton@midcontinent.edu
HATTON, Martin .... 662-329-7138. 268 E
mhatton@as.muw.edu
HATTON, Martin .... 662-329-7110. 268 E
mhatton@as.muw.edu
HATZENBUEHLER,
Linda .... 208-282-4899. 138 E
hatzlind@isu.edu
HAU, Hoang .... 562-907-4244... 76 I
hhau@whittier.edu
HAUB, Elaine .... 812-941-2284. 168 F
ehaub@ius.edu
HAUB, Mark .... 865-251-1800. 458 I
mhaub@southcollegetn.edu
HAUCK, Gary .... 989-328-1234. 247 D
garyh@montcalm.edu
HAUCK, Steven .... 605-882-5284. 450 D
haucks@lakeareatech.edu
HAUF, Todd .... 701-483-2570. 371 D
todd.hauf@dickinsonstate.edu
HAUFF, Joel, S .... 520-621-1417... 18 F
hauff@email.arizona.edu
HAUG, Amy .... 765-658-4181. 165 F
amyhaug@depauw.edu
HAUG, Christopher .... 503-943-7205. 408 F
haug@up.edu
HAUG, Marsha, L .... 610-436-3411. 430 A
mhaug@wcupa.edu

HAUGABROOK,
Adrian, K .... 617-879-2008. 238 C
ahaugabrook@wheelock.edu
HAUGABROOK,
Brian, A .... 229-333-7447. 134 B
bahaugab@valdosta.edu
HAUGE, Todd, W .... 410-293-1600. 545 J
hauge@usna.edu
HAUGEN,
Catherine (Kate) .... 701-231-7052. 371 G
kate.haugen@ndsu.edu
HAUGEN, Daniel .... 612-861-7554. 253 C
haugen@alfredadler.edu
HAUGEN, Dolores .... 253-566-6090. 524 C
dhaugen@tacomacc.edu
HAUGEN, Donna, M .... 516-572-7809. 332 C
donna.haugen@ncc.edu
HAUGEN, Doris .... 847-628-1510. 149 B
dhaugen@judsonu.edu
HAUGEN, Doug .... 530-938-5295... 41 A
haugend@siskiyous.edu
HAUGEN, Jay .... 314-977-2350. 281 I
haugenjp@slu.edu
HAUGEN, Nancy .... 510-869-6511... 61 I
nhaugen@samuelmerritt.edu
HAUGEN, Regina .... 270-384-8300. 197 D
haugenr@lindsey.edu
HAUGHT, Kenneth .... 701-483-2149. 371 D
ken.haught@dickinsonstate.edu
HAUGHT, Paul, A .... 901-321-3579. 453 H
phaught@cbu.edu
HAUGSLAND, Judy, M ... 414-410-4202. 532 B
jmhaugsland@stritch.edu
HAUK, Gary, S .... 404-727-6021. 124 E
gary.hauk@emory.edu
HAUKE, Raymond, A ...... 620-341-5173. 186 D
rhauke@emporia.edu
HAULOTTE, Erin .... 847-947-5491. 153 I
erin.haulotte@nl.edu
HAUNGS, Megan .... 510-666-8248... 26 F
mhaungs@aimc.edu
HAUPERT, Vincent, D ..... 260-359-4089. 166 O
vhaupert@huntington.edu
HAUPT, Benjamin .... 314-505-7040. 272 J
hauptb@csl.edu
HAURY, Clifford, W .... 434-961-5380. 513 F
chaury@pvcc.edu
HAUS, Teri .... 970-943-2196... 86 I
thaus@western.edu
HAUSAMMANN, Marilyn 617-495-8635. 227 C
marilyn_hausammann@harvard.edu
HAUSCARRIAGUE,
Elizabeth .... 925-969-2085... 41 L
ehauscarriague@dvc.edu
HAUSCHILD, Karen .... 843-953-5404. 443 A
hauschildkb@cofc.edu
HAUSCHILDT, Jim .... 816-932-6739. 281 J
jhaushildt@saintlukescollege.edu
HAUSE, Jeffrey .... 402-280-3581. 289 D
jeffreyhause@creighton.edu
HAUSER, Carol .... 513-529-3131. 384 G
hauserca@miamioh.edu
HAUSER, John .... 336-838-6149. 365 B
john.hauser@wilkescc.edu
HAUSER, Joseph, H .... 901-722-3228. 458 K
jhauser@sco.edu
HAUSER, LuAnn .... 620-431-2820. 189 D
lhauser@neosho.edu
HAUSER, Robert .... 217-244-2807. 162 A
r-hauser@illinois.edu
HAUSER, Stephen, C ...... 608-246-2101. 540 C
shauser@madisoncollege.edu
HAUSFATHER, Sam .... 314-529-9466. 276 G
shausfather@maryville.edu
HAUSINGER, Shannon .... 281-290-2832. 476 A
shannon.hausinger@lonestar.edu
HAUSKNECHT, Robert .... 708-456-0300. 161 A
rhauskne@triton.edu
HAUSLADEN, Stephanie . 559-438-4222... 46 K
stephanie_hausladen@heald.edu
HAUSLER, Jackie .... 716-827-4347. 348 G
hauslerj@trocaire.edu
HAUSMAN, Amy .... 973-290-4214. 300 F
bookstore@cse.edu
HAUSMANN, Tom, L .... 608-796-3860. 539 E
tlhausmann@viterbo.edu
HAUSS, Kevin .... 212-237-8512. 318 D
khauss@jjay.cuny.edu
HAUSSMANN, Robert ..... 928-541-7777... 16 B
rhaussmann@ncu.edu
HAUTANEN, David .... 978-837-5000. 234 A
hautanend@merrimack.edu
HAUVER, Dottie .... 508-793-2327. 225 B
dhauver@holycross.edu
HAVARD, Mary, G .... 409-772-2618. 493 C
mghavard@utmb.edu
HAVEARD, Melanie, J .... 850-474-2540. 117 B
mhaveard@uwf.edu
HAVELY, Candace .... 319-296-4229. 178 J
candace.havely@hawkeyecollege.edu

HAVENS, Brandi .... 806-874-3571. 468 J
brandi.havens@clarendoncollege.edu
HAVENS, Luisa .... 305-348-7596. 115 B
luisa.havens@fiu.edu
HAVERKAMPF, Kelly ...... 715-365-4917. 540 G
khaverkampf@nicoletcollege.edu
HAVERLACK, Sandra, J .. 540-863-2822. 512 B
shaverlack@dslcc.edu
HAVERLY, Mark .... 660-596-7407. 282 G
mhaverly@sfccmo.edu
HAVERSTICK, III,
Henry, W .... 718-780-7906. 315 H
henry.haverstick@brooklaw.edu
HAVERTY, April .... 414-955-4844. 534 C
ahaverty@mcw.edu
HAVERTY, Dan .... 574-239-8350. 166 N
dhaverty@hcc-nd.edu
HAVERTY, Terry .... 276-669-6101. 514 G
terryhaverty@vic.edu
HAVHOLM, Karen, G ...... 715-836-3405. 536 E
havholkg@uwec.edu
HAVIG, Dee .... 307-754-6412. 543 G
Dee.Havig@northwestcollege.edu
HAVIGHORST,
Deborah, S .... 708-709-7918. 156 A
dhavighorst@prairiestate.edu
HAVILAND, Bobbie .... 620-365-5116. 183 I
haviland@allencc.edu
HAVIS, Allan .... 858-534-4004... 71 F
ahavis@ucsd.edu
HAVIS, Joe .... 217-424-6251. 153 C
jhavis@millikin.edu
HAVRAN, Natalie, M ...... 609-652-4384. 305 C
natalie.havran@stockton.edu
HAWES, Heather .... 404-270-5068. 132 E
hhawes@spelman.edu
HAWES, Matthew .... 315-866-0300. 326 A
hawesmr@herkimer.edu
HAWES, Vanessa .... 910-642-7141. 364 A
Vanessa.Hawes@sccnc.edu
HAWGOOD, Samuel .... 415-476-2342... 72 A
sam.hawgood@ucsf.edu
HAWK, Cheryl .... 636-227-2100. 276 F
HAWK, Jeanine .... 415-355-2000... 26 L
jhawk@alliant.edu
HAWK, Linda .... 760-750-4950... 35 A
lhawk@csusm.edu
HAWK, Thomas, R .... 215-751-8029. 413 I
thawk@ccp.edu
HAWKES, Nicole .... 617-353-2230. 224 D
nhawkes@bu.edu
HAWKES, Peter .... 570-422-3494. 428 D
phawkes@po-box.esu.edu
HAWKEY, Christina .... 928-344-1723... 11 L
christina.hawkey@azwestern.edu
HAWKEY, Earl, W .... 402-472-2025. 292 I
ehawkey1@unl.edu
HAWKEY, Philip, A .... 909-593-3511... 72 E
phawkey@laverne.edu
HAWKIN, Chris .... 541-463-5547. 403 I
hawkinc@lanecc.edu
HAWKINS, Amanda, B ... 253-535-7667. 521 I
hawkinab@plu.edu
HAWKINS, Andre .... 772-462-7100. 106 P
ahawkins@irsc.edu
HAWKINS, Angela .... 415-476-5997... 72 A
Angela.Hawkins@ucsf.edu
HAWKINS, Audrey .... 903-675-6357. 488 D
ahawkins@tvcc.edu
HAWKINS, Ben .... 910-893-1380. 352 K
hawkinsb@campbell.edu
HAWKINS, Billy, C .... 256-761-6212..... 7 F
bhawkins@talladega.edu
HAWKINS, Bob .... 352-854-2322. 100 K
hawkinsb@cf.edu
HAWKINS, Carson .... 731-661-5018. 462 F
chawkins@uu.edu
HAWKINS, Charles .... 951-487-3073... 55 B
chawkins@msjc.edu
HAWKINS, Cheryl .... 734-462-4400. 250 A
chawkins@schoolcraft.edu
HAWKINS, Christie .... 405-744-4244. 397 H
christie.hawkins@okstate.edu
HAWKINS, Daryl .... 610-341-5822. 415 G
dhawkins@eastern.edu
HAWKINS, DeLores .... 515-964-6514. 177 B
dwhawkins@dmacc.edu
HAWKINS, Don .... 205-970-9213..... 7 B
dhawkins@sebc.edu
HAWKINS, Donna .... 215-646-7300. 417 F
hawkins.d@gmc.edu
HAWKINS, Greg .... 901-986-5969. 266 A
stlife@belhaven.edu
HAWKINS, Irene .... 302-857-6261... 93 C
ihawkins@desu.edu
HAWKINS, J. Barney ...... 703-370-6600. 508 B
HAWKINS, JR., Jack ...... 334-670-3200..... 7 H
jhawkins@troy.edu
HAWKINS, Jacqueline .... 270-706-8538. 195 A
jhawkins0045@kctcs.edu
HAWKINS, JoAnn .... 443-518-4974. 215 E
jhawkins@howardcc.edu
HAWKINS, Jodi .... 401-874-2141. 440 D
jhawk@uri.edu
HAWKINS, John .... 802-862-9616. 498 I
jhawkins@burlington.edu
HAWKINS, Jonathan .... 615-547-1239. 454 A
jhawkins@cumberland.edu
HAWKINS, Julia, L .... 606-783-5189. 198 A
j.hawkins@moreheadstate.edu
HAWKINS, Katherine ...... 540-831-6514. 508 C
khawkins3@radford.edu
HAWKINS, Marcia .... 606-546-1211. 200 A
mhawkins@unionky.edu
HAWKINS, Mark .... 312-362-5562. 143 H
mhawkin1@depaul.edu
HAWKINS, Mary, B .... 402-557-7005. 288 G
mary.hawkins@bellevue.edu
HAWKINS, Mary, M .... 303-871-4758... 86 B
mhawkins@du.edu
HAWKINS, JR.,
Melvin, O .... 307-778-1154. 543 D
mhawkins@lccc.wy.edu
HAWKINS, Michele .... 561-297-3245. 114 L
mhawkins@fau.edu
HAWKINS, Mike .... 816-414-3700. 277 L
registrar@mbts.edu
HAWKINS, Paul, M .... 386-312-4134. 112 C
mikehawkins@sjrstate.edu
HAWKINS, Philip .... 678-839-5000. 133 I
phawkins@westga.edu
HAWKINS, Ronald, E ..... 434-592-4030. 506 I
rehawkin@liberty.edu
HAWKINS, Tara .... 775-673-7206. 294 H
thawkins@tmcc.edu
HAWKINS, Vernon, L ..... 922-860-4221. 470 G
vhawkins@dcccd.edu
HAWKINS, Warren, H ..... 903-927-3390. 495 A
whawkins@wileyc.edu
HAWKINS, William .... 860-231-5405... 92 F
bhawkins@usj.edu
HAWKINSON, Kenneth ... 309-298-1066. 162 K
ks-hawkinson@wiu.edu
HAWKS, Sue, W .... 910-642-7141. 364 A
Sue.Hawks@sccnc.edu
HAWKSHEAD, Richard ... 256-378-2022..... 2 G
rhawkshead@cacc.edu
HAWLEY, Dennis, W ...... 570-577-1911. 411 A
dennis.hawley@bucknell.edu
HAWLEY, Eric .... 435-797-8146. 497 B
eric.hawley@usu.edu
HAWLEY, Harold .... 843-349-5279. 444 F
harold.hawley@hgtc.edu
HAWLEY, Katie .... 802-865-6424. 499 A
hawley@champlain.edu
HAWLEY, Kent .... 217-641-4570. 148 M
khawley@jwcc.edu
HAWLEY, Logan .... 731-989-6672. 454 J
lhawley@fhu.edu
HAWLEY, Michael, E ...... 314-286-4846. 280 F
mehawley@ranken.edu
HAWLEY, Michelle .... 323-343-5969... 34 A
mhawley@calstatela.edu
HAWLEY, Stephanie .... 512-223-7637. 466 I
shawley@austincc.edu
HAWLEY, Tamela .... 408-223-6471... 63 N
tamela.hawley@sjeccd.org
HAWLEY, Thomas .... 605-626-2524. 451 I
thawley@northern.edu
HAWLEY, Thomas, A ...... 231-843-5803. 252 H
tahawley@westshore.edu
HAWORTH, Karen .... 847-947-5246. 153 I
khaworth@nl.edu
HAWS, Pamela, M .... 817-272-3365. 491 B
haws@uta.edu
HAWSEY, David, S .... 276-944-6133. 504 H
dhawsey@ehc.edu
HAWSEY, Vicki .... 256-352-8180..... 9 G
vicki.hawsey@wallacestate.edu
HAWTIN, Mary, L .... 810-989-5546. 249 H
mhawtin@sc4.edu
HAWXHURST, Joan .... 269-337-7384. 244 K
Joan.Hawxhurst@kzoo.edu
HAXTON, Lori .... 660-626-2236. 271 A
lhaxton@atsu.edu
HAY, Alexandra .... 610-861-1350. 424 E
registrar@moravian.edu
HAY, April .... 812-237-2020. 167 A
april.hay@indstate.edu
HAY, Judy .... 307-778-1217. 543 D
jhay@lccc.wy.edu
HAY, Kuni .... 408-741-2052... 75 L
kuni.hay@westvalley.edu
HAY, Rod .... 310-243-2547... 33 B
rhay@csudh.edu
HAY, Sharon, L .... 401-865-2750. 439 E
sharhay@providence.edu
HAY, William .... 605-856-5880. 451 B
william.hay@sintegleska.edu
HAYASHI, Adam .... 847-635-1862. 155 F
ahayashi@oakton.edu
HAYASHI-PETERSEN,
Elaine .... 360-867-5195. 519 J
peach@evergreen.edu
HAYASHIDA, Peter, A .... 951-827-5203... 71 E
peter.hayashida@ucr.edu
HAYDEN, Brian .... 724-480-3460. 413 H
brian.hayden@ccbc.edu
HAYDEN, Cathy, C .... 601-857-3322. 267 A
cchayden@hindscc.edu
HAYDEN, Christopher .... 617-912-9125. 224 B
chayden@bostonconservatory.edu
HAYDEN, Dolph .... 918-293-4809. 398 B
dolph.hayden@okstate.edu
HAYDEN, Donna, G .... 601-877-6182. 265 G
dhayden@alcorn.edu
HAYDEN, Hart .... 803-822-3676. 445 C
haydenh@midlandstech.edu
HAYDEN, John, D .... 215-836-2222. 409 G
john.hayden@antonelli.edu
HAYDEN, Julie, M .... 619-201-8964... 67 G
jmhayden@socalsem.edu
HAYDEN, Roger .... 410-704-2487. 220 E
rhayden@towson.edu
HAYDEN, Ruby .... 425-739-8208. 520 K
ruby.hayden@lwtech.edu
HAYDEN-MILES, Marie .. 631-420-2012. 346 B
marie.hayden-miles@farmingdale.edu
HAYDN, Stephanie .... 907-564-8346... 10 C
shaydn@alaskapacific.edu
HAYE, Erin .... 207-216-4311. 211 C
ehaye@yccc.edu
HAYE, Melissa .... 304-327-4145. 529 D
mhaye@bluefieldstate.edu
HAYEK, Cheryl .... 800-955-2527. 274 I
chayek@grantham.edu
HAYEN, Christopher .... 518-388-6911. 348 J
hayenc@union.edu
HAYES, Ann, C .... 717-867-6416. 421 H
hayes@lvc.edu
HAYES, Ann, K .... 573-651-2552. 282 B
ahayes@semo.edu
HAYES, Anne, M .... 610-566-1776. 437 G
ahayes@williamson.edu
HAYES, Bethany .... 740-588-1397. 394 C
bhayes@zanestate.edu
HAYES, Billy .... 251-981-3771..... 2 I
billy.hayes@columbiasouthern.edu
HAYES, Blair .... 301-985-7940. 219 F
diversity-initiatives@umuc.edu
HAYES, Charlene, M .... 410-516-8113. 215 H
chayes13@jhu.edu
HAYES, Clint, R .... 606-679-8501. 196 D
clint.hayes@kctcs.edu
HAYES, Collette, M .... 302-454-3959... 93 F
cmhayes@dtcc.edu
HAYES, Dale .... 772-462-7809. 106 P
dhayes@irsc.edu
HAYES, Dan .... 434-791-7252. 502 D
dhayes@averett.edu
HAYES, Daniel, J .... 315-267-2147. 344 C
hayesdj@potsdam.edu
HAYES, Deborah, L .... 302-831-3358... 94 B
dlhayes@udel.edu
HAYES, Debra, L .... 330-972-7210. 390 E
dlhayes@uakron.edu
HAYES, Denise .... 909-621-8355... 39 B
denise_hayes@cuc.claremont.edu
HAYES, Diane .... 802-831-1308. 500 H
dhayes@vermontlaw.edu
HAYES, Erik, Z .... 812-877-8230. 172 C
erik.hayes@rose-hulman.edu
HAYES, Gaye .... 229-928-1273. 126 D
gaye.hayes@gsw.edu
HAYES, Gaynelle, H .... 409-944-1206. 472 I
ghayes@gc.edu
HAYES, George .... 212-431-2836. 333 I
ghayes@nyls.edu
HAYES, George .... 212-431-2837. 333 I
ghayes@nyls.edu
HAYES, Greg .... 816-235-1015. 283 D
hayesgr@umkc.edu
HAYES, Homer, M .... 903-510-3203. 488 E
bhay2@tjc.edu
HAYES, Ingrid .... 256-824-6857..... 8 F
ingrid.hayes@uah.edu
HAYES, Jack .... 401-863-2972. 438 J
HAYES, Jacqueline .... 802-322-1719. 499 C
jacqueline.hayes@goddard.edu
HAYES, Jeff .... 863-638-1426. 119 C
jeff.hayes@warner.edu
HAYES, Jeff .... 678-359-5008. 127 A
jeff@gordonstate.edu
HAYES, Jessica .... 516-299-1451. 329 D
jessica.hayes@liu.edu
HAYES, Joe .... 907-474-7081... 10 I
uaf-fyalum@alaska.edu
HAYES, Joe, F .... 864-977-1367. 445 H
joe.hayes@ngu.edu
HAYES, John .... 352-392-1784. 116 A
hayesj@ufl.edu
HAYES, Julie, C .... 413-545-4169. 228 F
jhayes@hfa.umass.edu
HAYES, Lance, R .... 512-448-8750. 479 C
lanceh@stedwards.edu
HAYES, Linda .... 650-306-3201... 64 B
hayes@smccd.edu
HAYES, Linda .... 513-862-3571. 380 E
HAYES, Margaret .... 928-314-9515... 11 L
peggy.hayes@azwestern.edu
HAYES, Marshall .... 815-825-2086. 149 F
marshall.hayes@kishwaukeecollege.edu
HAYES, Matthew, D .... 304-696-2523. 529 H
HAYES, Michael .... 860-434-5232... 90 F
mhayes@lymeacademy.edu
HAYES, Mike .... 423-614-8406. 455 L
mhayes@leeuniversity.edu
HAYES, Ray .... 205-348-8343..... 8 C
crhayes@uasystem.ua.edu
HAYES, Rhonda, M .... 252-335-3103. 367 C
rmhayes@mail.ecsu.edu
HAYES, Richard, L .... 251-380-2738..... 9 E
rlhayes@southalabama.edu
HAYES, Rob .... 617-266-1400. 223 D
HAYES, Robert .... 708-209-3007. 143 E
robert.hayes@cuchicago.edu
HAYES, Robin, A .... 501-882-8936... 19 M
rahayes@asub.edu
HAYES, Samantha .... 270-852-3130. 197 B
shays@kwc.edu
HAYES, Sandra, J .... 207-725-3770. 209 H
shayes@bowdoin.edu
HAYES, Sandra, L .... 408-554-1784... 64 M
shayes@scu.edu
HAYES, Stephanie, A ...... 804-524-5997. 515 D
shayes@vsu.edu
HAYES, Susan .... 859-246-6381. 194 L
susan.hayes@kctcs.edu
HAYES, Susan .... 973-300-2116. 307 F
shayes@sussex.edu
HAYES, Suzanne .... 518-587-2100. 346 A
suzanne.hayes@esc.edu
HAYES, Tony .... 217-228-5432. 156 C
hayesto@quincy.edu
HAYES, Valerie, O .... 814-732-2167. 428 E
vhayes@edinboro.edu
HAYES, Wendy .... 937-376-6470. 376 E
whayes@centralstate.edu
HAYES, William .... 336-750-2142. 370 A
hayeswl@wssu.edu
HAYES-MORRISON,
Ruth .... 352-371-2833. 101 K
admissions@dragonrises.edu
HAYGOOD, Jennifer .... 919-807-7100. 357 L
haygoodj@nccommunitycolleges.edu
HAYHURST, David, T .... 619-594-6061... 35 D
dhayhurs@mail.sdsu.edu
HAYHURST, Neil .... 225-216-8169. 202 H
hayhurstn@mybrcc.edu
HAYMAN, Gregory .... 916-558-2544... 53 D
haymang@scc.losrios.edu
HAYMORE, Teresa .... 706-865-2134. 133 B
HAYNER, Kate .... 510-869-4780... 61 I
khayner@samuelmerritt.edu
HAYNER, Leon .... 407-646-2649. 111 Q
lhayner@rollins.edu
HAYNER, Stephen, A .... 404-687-4514. 123 C
hayners@ctsnet.edu
HAYNES, Alexis .... 315-279-5674. 328 D
ahaynes@mail.keuka.edu
HAYNES, Amy, M .... 330-684-8932. 390 F
hamy@uakron.edu
HAYNES, Angela .... 706-233-7464. 131 E
ahaynes@shorter.edu
HAYNES, Angela, N .... 919-516-4127. 366 C
anhaynes@st-aug.edu
HAYNES, Anthony .... 615-741-8220. 463 B
anthony.haynes@tennessee.edu
HAYNES, Brian .... 678-466-5433. 123 A
brianhaynes@clayton.edu
HAYNES, Brian, L .... 909-537-5185... 34 E
HAYNES, Calvin .... 816-279-7000. 271 B
faid@acot.edu
HAYNES, Carl, E .... 607-844-8222. 347 I
haynesc@tc3.edu
HAYNES, Carolyn, A .... 513-529-6722. 384 G
haynesca@miamioh.edu
HAYNES, David, A .... 540-985-4020. 506 G
dahaynes@jchs.edu
HAYNES, David, S .... 906-227-2242. 248 A
dhaynes@nmu.edu
HAYNES, Douglas, M ...... 949-824-2798... 71 B
dhaynes@uci.edu
HAYNES, John, G .... 806-743-7387. 487 E
john.g.haynes@ttuhsc.edu
HAYNES, John, K .... 404-215-2609. 129 D
jhaynes@morehouse.edu
HAYNES, Karen, S .... 760-750-4040... 35 A
pres@csusm.edu
HAYNES, Kimberly .... 304-865-6003. 527 F
kimberly.haynes@ovu.edu

HAYNES, Lisa .... 616-331-7204. 243 C haynesl@gvsu.edu
HAYNES, Martha, B .... 906-227-2610. 248 A haynes@nmu.edu
HAYNES, Melesa .... 304-776-6290. 526 F mhaynes@cci.edu
HAYNES, Mike .... 254-968-9354. 483 A rhaynes@tarleton.edu
HAYNES, Pamela, J .... 336-888-9055. 355 C phaynes@highpoint.edu
HAYNES, Patricia, A .... 636-922-8427. 280 J phaynes@stchas.edu
HAYNES, Penny, A .... 518-381-1374. 340 G haynespa@sunysccc.edu
HAYNES, Peter, F .... 225-578-9903. 204 O pfhaynes@vetmed.lsu.edu
HAYNES, Sandra .... 303-556-2978... 83 D hayness@msudenver.edu
HAYNES, Scott .... 870-245-5220... 22 D hayness@obu.edu
HAYNES, Sonja .... 828-339-4251. 364 B sonjah@southwesterncc.edu
HAYNES, Stephanie, C ... 304-637-1335. 526 E hayness@dewv.edu
HAYNES, Susan .... 325-649-8043. 473 F shaynes@hputx.edu
HAYNES, Thomas .... 850-599-3491. 114 K thomas.haynes@famu.edu
HAYNES, Tina .... 704-216-3461. 363 D tina.haynes@rccc.edu
HAYNES, Victoria .... 816-995-2831. 280 G victoria.haynes@researchcollege.edu
HAYNIE, Glenda, D .... 804-333-6719. 513 G ghaynie@rappahannock.edu
HAYNIE, Janice .... 910-672-1211. 367 D jhaynie@uncfsu.edu
HAYNIE, Todd .... 928-428-8320... 13 J todd.haynie@eac.edu
HAYS, Antoinette, M .... 781-768-7122. 236 A antoinette.hays@regiscollege.edu
HAYS, Cheryl, M .... 412-268-6382. 412 H chays@andrew.cmu.edu
HAYS, Danny .... 870-245-5526... 22 D haysd@obu.edu
HAYS, Ina, R .... 636-584-6565. 273 M haysir@eastcentral.edu
HAYS, Joel .... 602-386-4127... 11 G joel.hays@arizonachristian.edu
HAYS, Karen, L .... 410-777-2332. 213 D klhays@aacc.edu
HAYS, Larry .... 314-529-9390. 276 G lhays@maryville.edu
HAYS, Mark .... 918-293-5130. 398 B mark.hays@okstate.edu
HAYS, Regina, M .... 618-650-3324. 159 H rmhays@siue.edu
HAYS, Rex .... 913-469-8500. 187 J rhays@jccc.edu
HAYS, Richard .... 919-660-3411. 354 A richard.hays@duke.edu
HAYS, Ryan .... 513-556-2201. 390 G ryan.hays@uc.edu
HAYS, Stacie .... 712-274-5254. 181 B hays@morningside.edu
HAYS, Wm. Randy .... 859-238-5471. 193 E randy.hays@centre.edu
HAYS-MUSSOINI, Stephanie .... 765-973-8331. 167 G shaysmus@iue.edu
HAYSBERT, JoAnn .... 757-727-5693. 505 F joann.haysbert@hamptonu.edu
HAYTER, Christopher, A . 614-823-1348. 387 K chayter@otterbein.edu
HAYTER, Richard .... 972-721-5227. 488 F rhayter@udallas.edu
HAYTER, Sonya .... 417-269-3469. 273 D sonya.hayter@coxcollege.edu
HAYTER, Sonya .... 417-269-3469. 273 D shayter@coxcollege.edu
HAYTON, Heather .... 336-316-2397. 355 A hhayton@guilford.edu
HAYWARD, Craig .... 949-451-5766... 67 B chayward@ivc.edu
HAYWARD, Dawn .... 215-646-7300. 417 F hayward.d@gmc.edu
HAYWARD, Jayanne .... 717-867-6321. 421 H hayward@lvc.edu
HAYWARD, John .... 419-251-1314. 383 G john.hayward@mercycollege.edu
HAYWARD, Maysa .... 732-255-0400. 304 A mhayward@ocean.edu
HAYWARD-WYZIK, Lisa 603-542-7744. 296 D lwyzik@ccsnh.edu
HAYWOOD, Carl .... 210-829-3935. 490 A carl@uiwtx.edu
HAYWOOD, Chanta .... 229-430-3690. 119 J chanta.haywood@asurams.edu
HAYWOOD, Jerry .... 478-825-6211. 124 H haywoodj@fvsu.edu
HAYWOOD, Michele .... 910-576-6222. 362 C haywoodm@montgomery.edu
HAYWOOD, Nikki .... 402-461-7393. 289 I nhaywood@hastings.edu
HAYWOOD, Zina .... 262-564-3104. 540 A haywoodz@gtc.edu
HAYWORTH, Kimberly, K .... 517-750-1200. 250 E kimh@arbor.edu
HAZAM, Bruce .... 207-801-5645. 210 A bhazam@coa.edu
HAZARD, Laurie, L .... 401-232-6746. 438 K lhazard@bryant.edu
HAZARD, Victor, A .... 859-257-3754. 200 C vahaz@uky.edu
HAZEL, Julie .... 719-502-3005... 84 A julie.hazel@ppcc.edu
HAZELBAKER, Chato ...... 360-992-2921. 518 A chazelbaker@clark.edu
HAZELBAKER, Nicole ..... 406-683-7900. 286 I n_hazelbaker@umwestern.edu
HAZELKORN, Michael .... 912-279-5720. 123 B mhazelkorn@ccga.edu
HAZELTON, Janet .... 802-468-1208. 501 B janet.hazelton@castleton.edu
HAZELWOOD, Renita ...... 336-386-3392. 364 D hazelwoodr@surry.edu
HAZELWOOD, Rhonda, L .... 336-386-3397. 364 D hazelwoodr@surry.edu
HAZELWOOD, Sonia, H . 501-569-3302... 24 B shhazelwood@ualr.edu
HAZEN, Ian .... 315-268-6439. 320 A ihazen@clarkson.edu
HAZEN, Ron .... 615-297-7545. 452 J hazenr@aquinascollege.edu
HAZEN, Verna, J .... 585-475-5520. 337 L vjhsfa@rit.edu
HAZEN, Virginia, S .... 603-646-2451. 296 G virginia.s.hazen@dartmouth.edu
HAZEWINKEL, Sue .... 334-683-2378..... 5 F shazewinkel@marionmilitary.edu
HAZLETT, Brian .... 717-872-3371. 429 D brian.hazlett@millersville.edu
HAZLETT, Brian .... 717-872-3024. 429 D
HAZLETT, Laura .... 510-594-3688... 30 K lhazlett@cca.edu
HAZZARD, Douglas .... 904-256-7100. 107 Q dhazzar@ju.edu
HAZZARD, Mike .... 270-706-8686. 195 A mikew.hazzard@kctcs.edu
HAZZARD, Terry .... 251-405-7285..... 2 D thazzard@bishop.edu
HA'O, Melanie .... 401-841-7367. 545 A
HE, Huot .... 301-548-5500... 96 F
HE, Joyce .... 408-260-8868... 44 J sjclinic@fivebranches.edu
HE, Phil .... 617-373-6817. 235 F
HE, Yuxin .... 512-454-1188. 466 B info@aoma.edu
HEACOCK, Maureen .... 937-769-1846. 373 I mheacock@antioch.edu
HEAD, Elizabeth .... 904-620-2111. 116 B ehead@unf.edu
HEAD, Elizabeth, M .... 904-620-2111. 116 B ehead@unf.edu
HEAD, Janet .... 801-333-8100. 495 J
HEAD, John .... 678-839-6423. 133 I jhead@westg.edu
HEAD, Linda .... 832-813-6816. 476 A linda.head@lonestar.edu
HEAD, Robert, L .... 815-226-4010. 157 C rhead@rockford.edu
HEAD, Steve .... 281-618-5440. 476 A steve.head@lonestar.edu
HEAD, Susan .... 315-792-7342. 346 C susan.head@sunyit.edu
HEADING-GRANT, Wanda, R .... 802-656-8426. 500 F wanda.heading-grant@uvm.edu
HEADINGS, Ronald .... 419-358-3660. 374 J headingsr@bluffton.edu
HEADLEY, Larry .... 816-414-3700. 277 L lheadley@mbts.edu
HEADLEY, Sarah .... 502-205-8811... 20 I sheadley@cbc.edu
HEADLEY, Scot .... 503-554-2836. 403 C sheadley@georgefox.edu
HEADRICK, Darrell, L ..... 804-752-7374. 508 E dheadric@rmc.edu
HEADRICK, Dennis .... 402-323-3427. 292 C dheadric@southeast.edu
HEADRICK, Robert .... 479-248-7236... 21 B bheadrick@ecollege.edu
HEADY, Nancy .... 325-649-8069. 473 F nheady@hputx.edu
HEAFNER, Lori .... 843-349-7871. 444 F lori.heafner@hgtc.edu
HEAGLE, Leanne .... 937-255-6565. 544 C leanne.heagle@afit.edu
HEALD, Donna .... 518-244-2466. 338 C healdd@sage.edu
HEALD, James, W .... 414-955-4400. 534 C jheald@mcw.edu
HEALEY, Maureen .... 219-866-6161. 172 E maureenh@saintjoe.edu
HEALEY, Stephen, E .... 203-576-4271... 91 G healey@bridgeport.edu
HEALEY, Tom .... 810-762-0417. 247 F thomas.healey@mcc.edu
HEALY, Amy .... 518-255-5111. 344 E healyak@cobleskill.edu
HEALY, Diane .... 312-942-6849. 157 G diane_healy@rush.edu
HEALY, Gayle .... 518-629-7326. 326 G g.healy@hvcc.edu
HEALY, James .... 508-856-2007. 229 C james.healy@umassmed.edu
HEALY, Joanne .... 313-664-1474. 241 C jhealy@collegeforcreativestudies.edu
HEALY, John .... 210-832-2198. 490 A jhealy@uiwtx.edu
HEALY, Kevin .... 612-338-6537. 253 H healyk@augsburg.edu
HEALY, Mary .... 812-749-1277. 171 K mhealy@oak.edu
HEALY, Patrick, J .... 203-582-8643... 91 A patrick.healy@quinnipiac.edu
HEALY, Paul, F .... 215-717-6161. 435 A phealy@uarts.edu
HEALY, Rose Mary .... 973-278-5400. 299 D rmh@berkeleycollege.edu
HEALY, Rose Mary .... 973-278-5400. 314 K rmh@berkeleycollege.edu
HEALY, William, L .... 863-680-4140. 105 D whealy@flsouthern.edu
HEANEY, Roma, E .... 313-593-5353. 251 D rheaney@umich.edu
HEAP, Jeffrey .... 815-280-2401. 149 A jheap@jjc.edu
HEARD, DeNorris .... 770-454-9270... 96 F
HEARD, JR., Ernest, W .. 615-460-6424. 453 C ernest.heard@belmont.edu
HEARD, Jeanne, K .... 501-686-5572... 24 C heardjeannek@uams.edu
HEARD, John .... 660-626-2397. 271 A jheard@atsu.edu
HEARD, Michael .... 229-217-4207. 129 F mheard@moultrietech.edu
HEARD, Sasha .... 888-384-0849... 27 E sheard@allied.edu
HEARD-JOHNSON, Cessa .... 206-934-6749. 523 A cessa.heard.johnson@seattlecolleges.edu
HEARN, Deyna .... 310-434-4435... 65 A hearn_deyna@smc.edu
HEARN, Kevin .... 716-286-8405. 334 F khearn@niagara.edu
HEARN, JR., Robert, W . 302-259-6110... 93 E rhearn@dtcc.edu
HEARN, Sabrina, B .... 205-934-9176..... 8 C shearn@uasystem.ua.edu
HEARNS, Rene .... 814-732-1052. 428 E rhearns@edinboro.edu
HEAROD, Marguerite ...... 405-382-9950. 399 I m.hearod@sscok.edu
HEARTFIELD, Judy .... 254-526-1472. 468 G judy.heartfield@ctcd.edu
HEARTLEIN, Karrie .... 309-341-7340. 150 A kheartle@knox.edu
HEARTT, Justine .... 916-278-5992... 34 D hearttj@csus.edu
HEASLEY, Christopher .... 215-895-6155. 415 B clh344@drexel.edu
HEASLEY, Ronald, P .... 717-361-1558. 415 H heasleyrp@etown.edu
HEASTON, Amy .... 912-344-2505. 120 G amy.heaston@armstrong.edu
HEATER, Deborah .... 614-287-2408. 378 B dheater@cscc.edu
HEATER, Margaret .... 585-343-0055. 325 C meheater@genesee.edu
HEATH, Aaron .... 816-322-0110. 271 O aaron.heath@calvary.edu
HEATH, Ann .... 610-647-4400. 418 I aheath@immaculata.edu
HEATH, Bill .... 863-638-2953. 119 D heathwl@webber.edu
HEATH, Bob .... 417-626-1234. 279 J heath.bob@occ.edu
HEATH, Cheryl, A .... 307-674-6446. 543 F cheath@sheridan.edu
HEATH, David, A .... 212-938-5650. 345 C dheath@sunyopt.edu
HEATH, Diann .... 785-825-5422. 185 B dheath@brownmackie.edu
HEATH, Eric .... 703-993-3840. 505 C eheath2@gmu.edu
HEATH, Fred, M .... 512-495-4350. 491 C fheath@austin.utexas.edu
HEATH, Gregory .... 616-538-2330. 243 A gheath@gbcol.edu
HEATH, Hildy .... 415-405-4256... 35 E hheath@sfsu.edu
HEATH, Jason .... 502-897-4106. 199 B jheath@sbts.edu
HEATH, Jeffrey, D .... 864-242-5100. 441 D
HEATH, Joan, L .... 512-245-2133. 487 C jh06@txstate.edu
HEATH, Kathy .... 207-326-2339. 211 D kathy.heath@mma.edu
HEATH, Marie .... 904-470-8141. 102 A
HEATH, Mary-Teresa ...... 518-828-4181. 321 C mary-teresa.heath@sunycgcc.edu
HEATH, Raymond, P .... 570-348-6246. 423 B heath@marywood.edu
HEATH, Richard, C .... 410-777-2204. 213 D rcheath@aacc.edu
HEATH, Robert .... 205-366-8851..... 7 E rheath@stillman.edu
HEATH-THORNTON, Debra .... 610-225-5055. 415 G dheath@eastern.edu
HEATHERLY, David, L .... 910-938-6789. 359 E heatherlyd@coastalcarolina.edu
HEATHERSHAW, Leslie .. 605-455-6000. 450 I lheathershaw@olc.edu
HEATON, Dennis .... 641-472-7000. 180 N dheaton@mum.edu
HEATON, Karick .... 801-302-2879. 496 B karick.heaton@neumont.edu
HEATON, Monica .... 563-425-5773. 183 B heatonm@uiu.edu
HEATON, Scott .... 209-946-2541... 73 A sheaton@pacific.edu
HEATON, Tim .... 605-688-5117. 452 B tim.heaton@sdstate.edu
HEATON, JR., William ... 714-449-7464... 67 D wheaton@scco.edu
HEATON-DUNLAP, Anne 650-543-3804... 54 C adunlap@menlo.edu
HEATOR, Martin .... 734-462-4400. 250 A mheator@schoolcraft.edu
HEATWOLE, Deirdre .... 617-287-5324. 228 E dheatwole@umassp.edu
HEATWOLE, Deirdre .... 774-455-7300. 228 G DHeatwole@umassp.edu
HEAVENER, Mac .... 904-596-2400. 117 H macheavener@tbc.edu
HEAVY RUNNER, Joely . 701-255-3285. 373 C jheavyrunner@uttc.edu
HEBARD, John .... 907-474-6831... 10 I jahebard@alaska.edu
HEBBARD, Don .... 972-279-6511. 465 F dhebbard@amberton.edu
HEBBARD, Matthew .... 956-872-2147. 480 I mshebbar@southtexascollege.edu
HEBERLE, Julia, F .... 610-921-7581. 409 A jheberle@alb.edu
HEBERLING, Michael ..... 810-766-4374. 239 G mike.heberling@baker.edu
HEBERT, Barbara, B .... 985-549-3894. 208 C bhebert@selu.edu
HEBERT, Carol .... 318-487-5443. 202 M carolhebert@cltc.edu
HEBERT, Carolyn .... 860-515-3880... 87 I chebert@charteroak.edu
HEBERT, Deborrah .... 707-654-1182... 31 I dhebert@csum.edu
HEBERT, Dustin .... 334-475-5424. 207 G
HEBERT, Helen, D .... 336-334-5371. 369 A helen_dennison@uncg.edu
HEBERT, Jaimie .... 936-294-1001. 487 A hebert@shsu.edu
HEBERT, Jeanne .... 401-863-2206. 438 J jeanne_hebert@brown.edu
HEBERT, Joseph .... 281-998-6150. 479 H joseph.hebert@sjcd.edu
HEBERT, Mark .... 502-852-3133. 200 D mark.hebert@louisville.edu
HEBERT, Rudolph .... 413-572-5699. 230 F rudy@westfield.ma.edu
HECHT, Boruch .... 973-267-9404. 304 G boruch.hecht@gmail.com
HECHT, George, E .... 541-346-2290. 406 D ghecht@uoregon.edu
HECHT, Laura .... 661-654-2124... 32 H lhecht@csub.edu
HECHT, Pinchas .... 718-645-0536. 331 G phecht@thejnet.com
HECK, Barbara, H .... 410-778-7805. 221 C bheck2@washcoll.edu
HECK, Catherine, J .... 740-283-6498. 379 N check@franciscan.edu
HECK, Corrie .... 309-467-6345. 145 C check@eureka.edu
HECK, Paul .... 773-878-3194. 158 B pheck@staugustine.edu
HECK, Rafael .... 847-628-1546. 149 B rafael.heck@judsonu.edu
HECK, Thomas, R .... 701-252-3467. 373 D theck@jc.edu

HECK, Traci .... 918-595-8634. 400 E
traci.heck@tulsacc.edu
HECKAMAN, Daniel, A ... 218-477-2300. 259 H
daniel.heckaman@mnstate.edu
HECKAMAN, Judith, M .. 717-560-8278. 421 A
jheckaman@lbc.edu
HECKARD, Bonnie .... 734-462-4400. 250 A
bheckard@schoolcraft.edu
HECKEL, David .... 704-463-3124. 365 E
david.heckel@fsmail.pfeiffer.edu
HECKENDORN, Miles, J 320-308-3453. 261 B
mjheckendorn@stcloudstate.edu
HECKENLAIBLE, Anna ..... 605-331-6651. 452 D
anna.heckenlaible@usiouxfalls.edu
HECKER, Jeffrey, E .... 207-581-1954. 212 B
jhecker@maine.edu
HECKER, Laurel, A .... 340-692-3160. 555 E
lhecker@live.uvi.edu
HECKERT, L. Randall ...... 330-471-8280. 383 D
rheckert@malone.edu
HECKLER, Casey .... 812-866-6740. 166 C
heckler@hanover.edu
HECKLER, Mark, A .... 219-464-5115. 174 E
mark.heckler@valpo.edu
HECKMAN, Mary Ellen ... 610-372-4721. 431 D
mheckman@racc.edu
HECKMAN, Richard, A ... 717-245-1308. 414 H
heckman@dickinson.edu
HECTOR, Gerald .... 607-274-3118. 327 E
ghector@ithaca.edu
HEDAYAT, Nasser .... 407-582-3326. 118 M
nhedayat@valenciacollege.edu
HEDBERG, Rick .... 701-858-3042. 371 F
rick.hedberg@minotstateu.edu
HEDBERG, Ulf .... 202-250-2642... 95 C
ulf.hedberg@gallaudet.edu
HEDDERICK, Malgorzata 617-253-9358. 233 B
HEDDLESTON, George ... 937-775-7098. 393 G
george.heddleston@wright.edu
HEDDLESTON,
Patrick, D .... 330-823-6572. 391 E
heddlepd@mountunion.edu
HEDEEN, Deborah, L ...... 208-282-2783. 138 E
hededebo@isu.edu
HEDEEN, Paul .... 734-384-4152. 247 C
phedeen@monroeccc.edu
HEDGE, Clarence, A .... 405-466-3419. 395 N
cahedge@langston.edu
HEDGE, Dennis .... 605-688-6197. 452 B
dennis.hedge@sdstate.edu
HEDGEMAN, Denita .... 901-435-1729. 455 M
denita_hedgeman@loc.edu
HEDGER, Mark .... 417-268-6023. 271 I
mhedger@gobbc.edu
HEDGES, Denise, C .... 417-667-8181. 273 A
dhedges@cottey.edu
HEDGES, Douglas .... 609-343-4911. 299 A
hedges@atlantic.edu
HEDGES, Jerris, R .... 808-692-0881. 136 B
jerris@hawaii.edu
HEDGES, Mark, C .... 270-852-3242. 197 B
mhedges@kwc.edu
HEDGES, Tammy, L .... 901-678-5314. 460 B
thedges@memphis.edu
HEDLIN, Carol .... 907-796-6016... 11 A
carol.hedlin@uas.alaska.edu
HEDMAN, Shawn .... 507-537-6292. 261 F
Shawn.Hedman@smsu.edu
HEDRICK, Erica .... 978-927-2217. 226 C
ehedrick@endicott.edu
HEDRICK, Jennifer .... 303-457-2757... 81 L
jhedrick@cci.edu
HEDRICK, Van .... 940-668-7347. 477 I
vhedrick@nctc.edu
HEEKE, JR., David, W .... 989-774-1711. 240 N
heeke1dw@cmich.edu
HEEN, Shellee .... 808-544-0290. 135 F
sheen@hpu.edu
HEENAN, Christine .... 617-495-1703. 227 C
christine_heenan@harvard.edu
HEENAN, Elizabeth, A .... 215-951-1240. 420 B
heenan@lasalle.edu
HEER, Angela .... 816-501-3727. 271 H
angela.heer@avila.edu
HEEREN, Matthew .... 660-626-2064. 271 A
mheeren@atsu.edu
HEERMAN, Heather .... 508-565-1325. 237 A
hheerman@stonehill.edu
HEERMANN, Keith .... 417-862-9533. 274 F
kheermann@globaluniversity.edu
HEERSINK, Heather .... 719-587-7759... 78 B
heather_heersink@adams.edu
HEETER-BASS, Janet, A .. 740-826-8080. 384 L
jheeter@muskingum.edu
HEETLAND, David, L .... 847-866-3970. 145 E
david.heetland@garrett.edu
HEFFELFINGER, Scott .... 610-372-4721. 431 D
sheffelfinger@racc.edu
HEFFERIN, Cathy, D .... 336-633-0208. 362 H
cdhefferin@randolph.edu
HEFFERNAN, Gloria, C ... 315-445-5438. 328 F
heffergc@lemoyne.edu
HEFFERNAN, Robert, J ... 848-932-7305. 306 B
heffernan@instlres.rutgers.edu
HEFFERNAN, Robert, J ... 848-932-7305. 306 A
heffernan@instlres.rutgers.edu
HEFFERNAN, Thomas, J 561-237-7270. 108 X
theffernan@lynn.edu
HEFFLEY, David, P .... 215-699-5700. 421 E
dheffley@LSB.edu
HEFFNER, David, B .... 570-321-4278. 422 H
heffner@lycoming.edu
HEFFRON, Jay .... 949-480-4028... 66 F
heffron@soka.edu
HEFLEY, Jacqueline, D ... 512-404-4826. 467 A
jhefley@austinseminary.edu
HEFLIN, Sherry .... 717-815-1257. 438 D
sheflin@ycp.edu
HEFNER, David, S .... 706-721-6569. 126 B
dhefner@gru.edu
HEFNER, Dennis, L .... 315-267-2100. 344 C
hefnerdl@potsdam.edu
HEFNER, James, A .... 404-880-8753. 122 J
jhefner@cau.edu
HEGAB, Hisham .... 318-257-4647. 207 F
hhegab@latech.edu
HEGARTY, Kevin, P .... 512-471-1422. 491 C
hegarty@mail.utexas.edu
HEGDE, Raju .... 909-389-3362... 61 K
rhegde@craftonhills.edu
HEGEDUS, George, C ..... 610-799-1132. 421 I
ghegedus@lccc.edu
HEGEDUS, Mary Ellen ... 574-239-8391. 166 N
mhegedus@hcc-nd.edu
HEGEL, Barbara .... 907-796-6457... 11 A
barbara.hegel@uas.alaska.edu
HEGEMAN, Diane .... 303-797-5702... 78 F
diane.hegeman@arapahoe.edu
HEGEMAN, Jay .... 301-687-4000. 220 C
HEGERTY, Staci .... 303-861-1151... 81 E
shegerty@concorde.edu
HEGGEMEYER, Terri .... 402-844-7263. 291 I
terrih@northeast.edu
HEGGOY, Liv .... 540-868-4091. 512 H
lheggoy@lfcc.edu
HEGLAND, Paul, R .... 262-551-5858. 532 D
paul@carthage.edu
HEGMAN, John, P .... 404-471-6109. 119 I
jhegman@agnesscott.edu
HEGRANES, Colleen .... 651-690-8844. 263 O
cahegranes@stkate.edu
HEGYES, Louis, L .... 610-799-1575. 421 I
admissions@lccc.edu
HEIBER, Ali .... 540-891-3016. 512 E
aheiber@germanna.edu
HEICHELBECK, Tamie ...... 618-664-7000. 145 G
tamie.heichelbeck@greenville.edu
HEIDA, Debbie .... 706-236-2207. 121 G
dheida@berry.edu
HEIDBREDER, Kay, K ..... 540-231-6293. 515 C
heidbred@vt.edu
HEIDE, Gale .... 406-586-3585. 286 F
gale.heide@montanabiblecollege.edu
HEIDEMAN, Carl, E .... 616-395-7670. 244 A
heideman@hope.edu
HEIDER, Cindy .... 816-271-4364. 279 A
heider@missouriwestern.edu
HEIDER, Donald, B .... 312-915-6548. 151 H
dheider@luc.edu
HEIDER, Mary Jane .... 585-345-6813. 325 C
mjheider@genesee.edu
HEIDICK, Venesa, A .... 979-845-1059. 483 C
vheidick@tamu.edu
HEIDINGSFIELD,
Michael, J .... 512-499-4688. 491 A
mheidingsfield@utsystem.edu
HEIDKE, Stephen .... 314-392-2372. 278 B
heidkesj@mobap.edu
HEIDRICH, Mark, W .... 240-895-4208. 218 A
mwheidrich@smcm.edu
HEIDRICK, Judy .... 785-738-9058. 189 F
jheidrick@ncktc.edu
HEIDT, Loretta, A .... 701-483-2418. 371 D
loretta.heidt@dickinsonstate.edu
HEIDTKE, Staci, L .... 715-836-5358. 536 E
heidtksl@uwec.edu
HEIER, Greg .... 402-826-8583. 289 E
greg.heier@doane.edu
HEIFETZ, Harry, S .... 262-554-2010. 534 D
harryh.21stcentury@rcn.com
HEIFNER, Bryan .... 432-335-6512. 477 M
bheifner@odessa.edu
HEIGHES, Robert .... 734-487-1222. 242 D
rheighes@emich.edu
HEIGHT, Linda, L .... 248-204-2128. 245 I
lheight@ltu.edu
HEIGLE, Christopher, A .. 870-633-4480... 21 A
cheigle@eacc.edu
HEIKEL, Karen .... 920-424-1463. 537 B
heikelk@uwosh.edu
HEIKKILA, Christina .... 910-362-7313. 358 F
cheikkila@cfcc.edu
HEIL, Elissa .... 479-979-1338... 25 J
eheil@ozarks.edu
HEIL, Lina .... 619-388-2759... 62 E
lheil@sdccd.edu
HEIL, Marti .... 812-855-7137. 167 F
heilm@indiana.edu
HEIL, Marti .... 804-828-0100. 511 F
HEIL, Mary Colleen .... 717-396-7833. 427 A
mcheil@pcad.edu
HEILE, Judi .... 513-244-4824. 377 G
judi_heile@mail.msj.edu
HEILEMAN, Gregory .... 505-277-2611. 312 F
heileman@unm.edu
HEILGEIST, Peter, J .... 435-586-7732. 497 A
heilgeist@suu.edu
HEILKE, Thomas, W .... 785-864-8040. 190 L
heilke@ku.edu
HEILLE, Gregory .... 314-256-8881. 271 F
heille@ai.edu
HEILMAN, Carl, R .... 620-792-9301. 184 F
heilmanc@bartonccc.edu
HEILMAN,
Timothy Bruce .... 804-204-1211. 502 F
theilman@btsr.edu
HEILMAN, Valerie .... 701-228-5437. 372 C
valerie.heilman@dakotacollege.edu
HEILPERN, Jerry .... 770-394-8300. 120 H
jheilpern@aii.edu
HEIM, Peggy, M .... 610-799-1532. 421 I
pheim@lccc.edu
HEIMAN, Kelly, J .... 262-524-7695. 532 C
kheiman@carrollu.edu
HEIMAN, Scott, R .... 608-243-4890. 540 C
sheiman@madisoncollege.edu
HEIMANN, Anne .... 402-481-3908. 288 H
anne.heimann@bryanhealthcollege.edu
HEIMANN, B. Sue .... 419-289-5324. 374 C
sheimann@ashland.edu
HEIMARCK, Heather .... 617-262-5000. 223 F
Heather.Heimarck@the-bac.edu
HEIMBROCK, Kimberly ... 859-572-5139. 198 I
heimbrockk@nku.edu
HEIMBURGER, David ...... 314-977-2233. 281 I
dheimbu1@slu.edu
HEIMERL, Marc, D .... 920-923-8796. 534 A
mdheimerl78@marianuniversity.edu
HEIMMERMANN, Dan ..... 662-329-7142. 268 E
dheimmermann@vpaa.muw.edu
HEIMOVITZ, Issac .... 718-438-1002. 331 A
HEIN, Audrey, D .... 563-333-6364. 182 B
HeinAudreyD@sau.edu
HEIN, Beth, A .... 715-426-8225. 539 J
bhein1@cvtc.edu
HEIN, Candy .... 956-326-4483. 483 B
candy.hein@tamiu.edu
HEIN, Denise .... 517-265-5161. 238 G
dhein@adrian.edu
HEIN, Holly, A .... 207-948-9244. 211 I
hein@unity.edu
HEIN, Maria .... 314-246-7546. 284 N
mariahein01@webster.edu
HEIN, Steven, M .... 912-478-0831. 126 C
shein@georgiasouthern.edu
HEINDL, Michael, J .... 601-928-6234. 268 C
michael.heindl@mgccc.edu
HEINE, Greg .... 605-668-1500. 450 F
greg.heine@mtmc.edu
HEINEMAN, Pete .... 402-557-7146. 288 G
pete.heineman@bellevue.edu
HEINEMAN, William .... 978-556-3327. 232 E
wheineman@necc.mass.edu
HEINEMANN, Brian .... 760-366-5278... 42 B
bhelnemann@cmccd.edu
HEINEMANN, Dovid .... 732-367-4259. 303 A
HEINEMANN, Ken .... 813-935-5700. 111 N
kenheinemann@remingtoncollege.edu
HEINEN, Judith, A .... 313-927-1256. 246 D
jheinen@marygrove.edu
HEINEN, Terry .... 615-230-3227. 461 G
terry.heinen@volstate.edu
HEINES, Katherine .... 410-626-2512. 217 G
katherine.heines@sjca.edu
HEINLE, Dennis, P .... 717-736-4134. 417 I
dpheinle@hacc.edu
HEINLE, Sharon .... 703-726-1087... 95 D
sheinle@gwu.edu
HEINOLD, Sandra .... 361-570-4286. 489 E
heinolds@uhv.edu
HEINRICH, Carl .... 913-469-8500. 187 J
heinrich@jccc.edu
HEINRICH, Heike .... 216-687-2051. 377 F
h.heinrich@csuohio.edu
HEINRICH, Matt, W .... 816-501-4064. 280 I
matt.heinrich@rockhurst.edu
HEINRICH, Peggy .... 847-214-6911. 144 F
pheinrich@elgin.edu
HEINRICH, Sam .... 916-577-2200... 76 J
sheinrich@jessup.edu
HEINRICHS, Abby .... 262-551-6100. 532 D
aheinrichs@carthage.edu
HEINS, Donald .... 607-962-9264. 322 B
dheins1@corning-cc.edu
HEINSELMAN, Gregg ..... 715-425-4444. 537 E
gregg.heinselman@uwrf.edu
HEINSELMAN, Gregg, M 715-425-4444. 537 E
gregg.heinselman@uwrf.edu
HEINSOHN, Lori .... 701-224-5690. 372 B
lori.heinsohn@bismarckstate.edu
HEINTER, Amy .... 570-586-2400. 410 D
aheitner@bbc.edu
HEINTZ, Jill .... 315-792-5584. 331 I
jheintz@mvcc.edu
HEINTZE, Michael, R ...... 512-245-1977. 487 C
mh63@txstate.edu
HEINTZELMAN,
Jonathan, R .... 312-915-7262. 151 H
jheintz@luc.edu
HEINZ, Anne, K .... 303-492-2202... 85 L
anne.heinz@colorado.edu
HEINZ, Heidi .... 217-854-3231. 140 G
hhein@blackburn.edu
HEINZ, Kartha .... 206-876-6100. 523 D
kheinz@theseattleschool.edu
HEINZMAN, Mary, B .... 563-333-6241. 182 B
HeinzmanMaryB@sau.edu
HEISER, Andrew .... 712-274-5493. 181 B
heiser@morningside.edu
HEISER, Donna .... 239-687-5402... 98 J
dheiser@avemarialaw.edu
HEISER, Gregory, M .... 405-325-3221. 401 B
gheiser@ou.edu
HEISER, Mary, C .... 570-321-4246. 422 H
heiser@lycoming.edu
HEISEY, Donald .... 252-493-7289. 362 G
dheisey@email.pittcc.edu
HEISEY, Terry, M .... 717-866-5775. 416 E
theisey@evangelical.edu
HEISLER, John, F .... 614-885-5585. 388 C
jheisler@pcj.edu
HEISSERER, Nick .... 218-855-8038. 258 B
nheisserer@clcmn.edu
HEIST, Daniel, P .... 814-865-1359. 426 A
dph3@psu.edu
HEIST, Richard .... 386-226-6216. 102 B
richard.heist@erau.edu
HEITHAUS, Peter, A .... 314-516-5809. 283 E
peter_heithaus@umsl.edu
HEITKAMP, Michael .... 218-755-2040. 258 A
mheitkamp@bemidjistate.edu
HEITKEMPER, Mary .... 509-313-4231. 520 A
heitkemper@gonzaga.edu
HEITNER, Douglas .... 570-586-2400. 410 D
dheitner@bbc.edu
HEITZ, Tim .... 717-560-8211. 421 A
theitz@lbc.edu
HEITZENRATER, Kim, D . 931-598-1121. 458 H
kheitzen@sewanee.edu
HEITZMANN, Dennis, E . 814-865-0966. 426 A
deh8@psu.edu
HEJL, Cindy .... 303-556-4741... 83 D
hejlc@msudenver.edu
HEKKEL, Jerry .... 206-726-5111. 518 G
jhekkel@cornish.edu
HELBERT, Lee, A .... 708-709-3639. 156 A
lhelbert@prairiestate.edu
HELBIG, Tuesdi .... 270-745-3250. 200 G
tuesdi.helbig@wku.edu
HELBING, Shirley .... 570-702-8918. 419 G
shelbing@johnson.edu
HELBLE, Joseph .... 603-646-2238. 296 G
joseph.helble@dartmouth.edu
HELDEROP, Sue .... 248-364-6135. 248 J
helderop@oakland.edu
HELEKAR, Andrea .... 213-624-1200... 44 D
ahelekar@fidm.edu
HELENS, Joyce, M .... 320-308-5017. 261 C
jhelens@sctcc.edu
HELFGOT, Steven .... 480-731-8098... 14 I
steve.helfgot@domail.maricopa.edu
HELFRICH, Christine .... 301-846-2518. 214 H
chelfrich@frederick.edu
HELFRICH, Glenda .... 806-743-2986. 487 E
glenda.helfrich@ttuhsc.edu
HELFRICH, Stephen, P ... 812-464-1782. 174 D
shelfric@usi.edu
HELGERSON, Carolyn .... 605-221-3108. 450 C
chelgerson@kilian.edu
HELGESEN, Paul .... 978-867-4730. 226 H
paul.helgesen@gordon.edu
HELGESEN, Pete .... 913-360-7476. 184 H
phelgesen@benedictine.edu
HELGESON, Danyel .... 507-433-0526. 260 I
danyel.helgeson@riverland.edu
HELGESON, Grant .... 808-455-0645. 137 A
helgeson@hawaii.edu
HELGESON, Richard, J ... 731-881-7380. 463 E
helgeson@utm.edu
HELGESTAD, Chris .... 612-861-7554. 253 C
chris.helgestad@alfredadler.edu

HELIS, James 516-726-5815. 545 H helisj@usmma.edu
HELLA, Lori, L 989-774-7194. 240 N hella1l@cmich.edu
HELLAND, Carol 218-749-7715. 259 B c.helland@mr.mnscu.edu
HELLDOBLER, Richard ... 773-442-5420. 154 H r-helldobler@neiu.edu
HELLENBRAND, Harry .... 818-677-2957... 34 C harry.hellenbrand@csun.edu
HELLER, Adam 623-245-4600... 18 D aheller@uti.edu
HELLER, Donald, E 517-355-1734. 246 H dheller@msu.edu
HELLER, James 262-595-2455. 537 C james.heller@uwp.edu
HELLER, Jennifer 913-360-7431. 184 H jheller@benedictine.edu
HELLER, Joshua, W 585-785-1335. 324 D hellerjw@flcc.edu
HELLER, Mary 406-265-4198. 287 D mary.heller@msun.edu
HELLER, Tracy 858-635-4763... 26 M theller@alliant.edu
HELLER, William 727-873-4979. 116 D wheller@mail.usf.edu
HELLER-ROSS, Holly 518-564-5180. 344 B hellerhb@plattsburgh.edu
HELLERSTEIN, Laurel 978-232-2153. 226 C lhellers@endicott.edu
HELLERUD, Nancy 314-246-7440. 284 N nancyhellerud@webster.edu
HELLIE, Thomas 503-883-2408. 404 A thellie@linfield.edu
HELLIGE, Joseph 310-338-2733... 53 E jhellige@lmu.edu
HELLING, Mary Kay 605-688-4173. 452 B mary.helling@sdstate.edu
HELLING, Nathan, M 605-336-6588. 451 C nhelling@sfseminary.edu
HELLMICH, David, M 859-246-4649. 194 L david.hellmich@kctcs.edu
HELLMUND, Paul, C 413-369-4044. 225 D hellmund@csld.edu
HELLUMS, Duane 502-410-6200. 194 B dhellums@galencollege.edu
HELLWIG, Beth, A 715-836-5992. 536 E hellwiba@uwec.edu
HELLYER, Brenda 281-998-6100. 479 E brenda.hellyer@sjcd.edu
HELM, Hunt, C 502-272-8046. 192 E hhelm@bellarmine.edu
HELM, Jennifer 304-724-3700. 526 B jhelm@apus.edu
HELM, Jonathan, C 254-710-8824. 467 G Jonathan_Helm@baylor.edu
HELM, Karen, P 919-515-6648. 368 B karen_helm@ncsu.edu
HELM, Lloyd 503-594-6793. 402 F lloydh@clackamas.edu
HELM, Peyton, R 484-664-3125. 424 H pres@muhlenberg.edu
HELM, Ron, C 870-368-2027... 22 E rhelm@ozarka.edu
HELM, Scott 641-782-1481. 182 I helm@swcciowa.edu
HELM, Steven, P 540-831-5471. 508 C shelm@radford.edu
HELM, Thomas 603-668-2211. 297 I t.helm@snhu.edu
HELMER, Robert, C 440-826-2424. 374 F rhelmer@bw.edu
HELMER, Shannon 610-799-1857. 421 I shelmer@lccc.edu
HELMICH, Doris 520-494-5200... 12 P doris.helmich@centralaz.edu
HELMICK, Michael, S 336-342-4261. 363 C
HELMICK, Tom 724-852-3210. 437 A thelmick@waynesburg.edu
HELMING, Jay 202-685-3909. 544 K jay.helming@ndu.edu
HELMS, Chris 828-766-1291. 361 H chelms@mayland.edu
HELMS, Doris, R 864-656-3243. 442 C biol110@clemson.edu
HELMS, James, B 256-306-2545..... 2 F jbh@calhoun.edu
HELMS, Lance 912-538-3207. 132 A lhelms@southeasterntech.edu
HELMS, Mark 704-330-6127. 359 C mark.helms@cpcc.edu
HELMS, Sherrie 478-289-2360. 124 C shelms@ega.edu
HELMS, Steve 334-222-6591..... 5 E shelms@lbwcc.edu
HELMSING, Debra, F 260-665-4240. 173 E helmsingd@trine.edu
HELMSTETTER, Donald, W 651-641-8227. 255 B helmstetter@csp.edu
HELMUS, D. Mark 317-940-9332. 164 J mhelmus@butler.edu
HELMUTH, Andrea 574-807-7351. 164 D andrea.helmuth@bethelcollege.edu
HELOU, Ibrahim (Abe) .... 909-593-3511... 72 E ahelou@laverne.edu
HELSEL, Dennis 252-398-6484. 353 H helsel@chowan.edu
HELSETH, Joe 423-697-2606. 460 C
HELSHAM, Irene 684-699-9155. 546 A i.helsham@amsamoa.edu
HELSPER, Nancy 320-589-6012. 264 F helsper@morris.umn.edu
HELTON, Karen 903-927-3369. 495 A khelton@wileyc.edu
HELTON, Kasey 678-915-3998. 132 C khelton@spsu.edu
HELTON, Patti 303-871-3289... 86 B phelton@du.edu
HELTON, Richard, E 812-888-4208. 174 F president@vinu.edu
HELTON, Tom 706-507-8909. 123 D helton_tom@columbusstate.edu
HELTSLEY, Susan, D 360-438-4534. 522 G sheltsley@stmartin.edu
HELVERING, Christal, R . 765-641-4205. 163 L crhelvering@anderson.edu
HELVIE-MASON, Lora 254-968-9488. 483 A helviemason@tarleton.edu
HELVY, Eric 256-761-6277..... 7 F ehelvy@talladega.edu
HELWIG, Christine, A 518-629-7343. 326 G c.helwig@hvcc.edu
HELWIG, Daniel, S 717-815-1502. 438 D dhelwig@ycp.edu
HELWIG, Denice 707-826-3300... 35 C dh7003@humboldt.edu
HELWIG, Susan, M 570-674-6368. 424 A shelwig@misericordia.edu
HEMANS, Peter 828-694-1723. 358 C peterh@blueridge.edu
HEMBREE, Lois, D 620-421-6700. 188 D loish@labette.edu
HEMED, Ruslan 318-342-1043. 208 E hemed@ulm.edu
HEMESATH, Michael 320-363-2882. 263 P sjpresident@csbsju.edu
HEMINGWAY, Sally, A ... 478-757-5212. 134 G shemingway@wesleyancollege.edu
HEMLICK, Lisa, M 610-341-5830. 415 G lhemlick@eastern.edu
HEMMASI, Harriette 401-863-2162. 438 J harriette_hemmasi@brown.edu
HEMMESCH, Michael 320-363-2595. 263 P mhemmesch@csbsju.edu
HEMMING, Erik G, C 414-229-4201. 537 A hemmingc@aux.uwm.edu
HEMMINGER, John, C ... 949-824-5796... 71 B jchemmin@uci.edu
HEMMINGSEN, Jens 614-236-6105. 375 H jhemming@capital.edu
HEMMITT, Ernita 404-880-6128. 122 J ehemmitt@cau.edu
HEMPE, Laura, J 414-410-4194. 532 B ljhempe@stritch.edu
HEMPEL, Lamont, C 909-748-8589... 73 H monty_hempel@redlands.edu
HEMPHILL, Brian, O 304-766-3111. 530 C bhemphill@wvstateu.edu
HEMPHILL, Constance ... 704-334-6882. 357 K chemphill@nlts.edu
HEMPHILL, Michael, R ... 318-869-5104. 201 H mhemphill@centenary.edu
HEMPHILL, Teale 719-336-1591... 82 R teale.hemphill@lamarcc.edu
HEMPHILL, Valory 800-438-6932. 478 C vhemphill@parkercc.edu
HEMPILL, Geoffrey 718-420-4269. 350 B Geoffrey.Hempill@wagner.edu
HEMPSTEAD, Laurie, A .. 518-381-1271. 340 G hempstla@sunysccc.edu
HEMPTON, David, N 617-495-4513. 227 C dhempton@hds.harvard.edu
HEMRICK, Robert, D 731-425-2636. 460 G dhemrick@jscc.edu
HEMSEY, Charles 516-796-4800. 333 C chemsey@nycc.edu
HEMWALL, Lara 412-291-6275. 410 B lhemwall@aii.edu
HENAHAN, David 518-587-2100. 346 A david.henahan@esc.edu
HENAN, Carmen 505-424-2302. 309 J chenan@iaia.edu
HENARD, Kevin 817-760-5831. 473 A khenard@hillcollege.edu
HENAULT, Cheri 860-701-5052... 90 G henault_c@mitchell.edu
HENBERG, Marvin 208-459-5502. 138 A
HENCHY, Alexandra 859-858-2049. 192 A
HENCHY, Dolores 201-355-1133. 302 A henchyd@felician.edu
HENCK, Anita 626-815-5348... 29 H ahenck@apu.edu
HENDEL, Kurt 774-256-0776. 152 B khendel@lstc.edu
HENDERSHOT, Debra 256-306-2581..... 2 F ddg@calhoun.edu
HENDERSHOT, Lewis 407-303-8192... 97 H lewis.hendershot@adu.edu
HENDERSHOT, Mike, W . 816-604-6766. 277 D mike.hendershot@mcckc.edu
HENDERSHOT, Stephanie, N 412-262-6251. 431 I hendershot@rmu.edu
HENDERSON, Allen 817-531-4405. 488 A ahenderson@txwes.edu
HENDERSON, Amanda ... 210-410-9159. 148 D ahenderson@careered.com
HENDERSON, Andrea 309-298-1977. 162 K ad-henderson@wiu.edu
HENDERSON, Angela 773-995-2411. 141 J ahende22@csu.edu
HENDERSON, Ann, S 212-817-7215. 317 F ahenderson@gc.cuny.edu
HENDERSON, Barbara, J 512-448-8532. 479 C barbarah@stedwards.edu
HENDERSON, Carl, E 443-412-2300. 215 C chenderson@harford.edu
HENDERSON, Carol 607-274-3837. 327 E cghenderson@ithaca.edu
HENDERSON, Castella 314-539-5354. 281 D chenderson@stlcc.edu
HENDERSON, III, Charles, M 401-874-4763. 440 D chad@uri.edu
HENDERSON, Christine .. 773-371-5402. 141 D chenderson@ctu.edu
HENDERSON, Cindy 815-753-4405. 154 I chenderson@niu.edu
HENDERSON, Cynthia 903-223-3053. 484 C cynthia.henderson@tamut.edu
HENDERSON, Cynthia, L 202-884-1723... 95 G cynthia.henderson@howard.edu
HENDERSON, Darren 219-473-4346. 164 K dhenderson@ccsj.edu
HENDERSON, Dee 731-424-3520. 460 G dhenderson@jscc.edu
HENDERSON, Eddie, W . 806-651-2600. 484 D ehenderson@mail.wtamu.edu
HENDERSON, Eric 928-524-7350... 16 E eric.henderson@npc.edu
HENDERSON, Floyd 843-525-8271. 447 C fhenderson@tcl.edu
HENDERSON, George, A 252-257-1900. 364 F henderson@vgcc.edu
HENDERSON, Gregg 626-395-4701... 31 E gregg.henderson@caltech.edu
HENDERSON, Harlan 937-376-6304. 376 E hhenderson@centralstate.edu
HENDERSON, Howard 580-349-1380. 397 G howardh@opsu.edu
HENDERSON, Jack 847-925-6000. 145 H jhenders@harpercollege.edu
HENDERSON, James 856-256-4175. 305 E henderson@rowan.edu
HENDERSON, James, B . 318-678-6000. 202 I jhenderson@bpcc.edu
HENDERSON, James, P . 323-343-2000... 34 A jhender3@calstatela.edu
HENDERSON, Janet 706-754-7761. 129 G jhenders@northgatech.edu
HENDERSON, Janice 850-729-5392. 109 I hendersonj@nwfsc.edu
HENDERSON, Joseph 215-635-7300. 417 C jhenderson@gratz.edu
HENDERSON, Kathy 408-855-5113... 75 K kathy.henderson@wvm.edu
HENDERSON, Kyle, W 740-427-5729. 382 J hendersonk@kenyon.edu
HENDERSON, Laura 413-755-4057. 233 A lahenderson@stcc.edu
HENDERSON, Lennijo 972-238-6107. 471 C lhenderson@dcccd.edu
HENDERSON, Lisle 718-636-3664. 336 F lhenderson@pratt.edu
HENDERSON, Mantra 662-254-3495. 269 A mlhenderson@mvsu.edu
HENDERSON, Mark 216-368-1025. 375 J mark.henderson@case.edu
HENDERSON, Mark 713-525-3155. 490 L hendermk@stthom.edu
HENDERSON, Maureen, E 816-501-4063. 280 I maureen.henderson@rockhurst.edu
HENDERSON, Melisha 219-473-4229. 164 K mhenderson@ccsj.edu
HENDERSON, Michelle .. 760-252-2411... 29 I mhenderson@barstow.edu
HENDERSON, Mitchell 718-482-5534. 318 F mhenderson@lagcc.cuny.edu
HENDERSON, Nancy 319-296-4448. 178 J nancy.henderson@hawkeyecollege.edu
HENDERSON, Necedah .. 256-233-8151..... 1 F necedah.henderson@athens.edu
HENDERSON, Pamela 251-460-6133..... 9 E phenderson@southalabama.edu
HENDERSON, Paul 207-602-2302. 213 A phenderson@une.edu
HENDERSON, Peter 410-455-3263. 219 D phenders@umbc.edu
HENDERSON, Ron, R 618-235-2700. 160 A ronald.henderson@swic.edu
HENDERSON, Sandra 205-929-6333..... 5 D shenderson@lawsonstate.edu
HENDERSON, Sandra 845-569-3112. 332 B sandra.cefaloni-henderson@msmc.edu
HENDERSON, Sean 559-265-5711... 68 I sean.henderson@fresnocitycollege.edu
HENDERSON, Sherri 919-760-8139. 356 G hendersh@meredith.edu
HENDERSON, Stanley, E 313-593-5151. 251 D sehender@umich.edu
HENDERSON, Sue 201-200-3111. 303 F shenderson@njcu.edu
HENDERSON, Tammy 850-484-1766. 110 G thenderson@pensacolastate.edu
HENDERSON, Thomas, W 601-974-1070. 267 I hendetw@millsaps.edu
HENDERSON, Timothy, G 605-394-2371. 452 A tim.henderson@sdsmt.edu
HENDERSON, Toni 910-296-2438. 361 D thenderson@jamessprunt.edu
HENDERSON, Trennis 870-245-5206... 22 D hendersont@obu.edu
HENDERSON, Virginia 601-968-5903. 266 A vhenderson@belhaven.edu
HENDLER, Catherine 269-965-3931. 244 O hendlerc@kellogg.edu
HENDLER, Gail 708-216-9192. 151 H ghendler@lumc.edu
HENDREY, Elizabeth 718-997-5441. 319 C elizabeth.hendrey@qc.cuny.edu
HENDREY, Elizabeth 718-997-5900. 319 C elizabeth.hendrey@qc.cuny.edu
HENDRICK, Larry 724-537-4555. 432 G larry.hendrick@email.stvincent.edu
HENDRICK, Robert, B 215-503-3403. 434 C robert.hendrick@jefferson.edu
HENDRICK, Ruth 434-832-7610. 512 A hendrickr@cvcc.vccs.edu
HENDRICKS, Cynthia, L . 651-696-6145. 256 L chendric@macalester.edu
HENDRICKS, Daniel, L ... 256-765-5018..... 9 C dhendricks@una.edu
HENDRICKS, Denisha 502-597-6014. 197 A denisha.hendricks@kysu.edu
HENDRICKS, Francis, L .. 570-662-4046. 429 C fhendricks@mansfield.edu
HENDRICKS, J. Gary 254-867-4898. 485 G gary.hendricks@systems.tstc.edu
HENDRICKS, Jeff 336-278-5580. 354 B jhendrick4@elon.edu
HENDRICKS, Joan, C 215-898-8841. 435 B vetdean@vet.upenn.edu
HENDRICKS, Julie 805-965-0581... 64 L hendrick@sbcc.edu
HENDRICKS, Laurie, M .. 515-574-1145. 179 D hendricks@iowacentral.edu
HENDRICKS, Linda 865-974-8170. 463 B Linda.Hendricks@tennessee.edu
HENDRICKS, JR., Lynn .. 305-348-3661. 115 B llynn.hendricks@fiu.edu
HENDRICKS, Mark, S 512-245-2925. 487 C mh06@txstate.edu
HENDRICKS, Martha, S .. 937-382-6661. 393 B martha_hendricks@wilmington.edu
HENDRICKS, Michael 202-319-5305... 94 G hendricks@cua.edu
HENDRICKS, Michelle 515-294-5802. 175 H mh2@iastate.edu
HENDRICKS, Nancy 956-364-4708. 485 H nancy.henricks@itstc.edu
HENDRICKS, Randy 678-839-5450. 133 I rhendric@westga.edu
HENDRICKS, Scott 708-209-3505. 143 E scott.hendricks@cuchicago.edu
HENDRICKS, Steve 808-236-5809. 135 F shendricks@hpu.edu
HENDRICKS, Sylvia 520-383-8401... 18 B shendricks@tocc.cc.az.us
HENDRICKSON, Anthony 402-280-2852. 289 D anthonyhendrickson@creighton.edu
HENDRICKSON, Avis, D 203-332-5183... 88 F ahendrickson@hcc.commnet.edu
HENDRICKSON, Brooke . 909-621-8807... 59 G brooke_hendrickson@pitzer.edu
HENDRICKSON, Charles 575-624-8379. 310 H hendrick@nmmi.edu

HENDRICKSON, Karen ... 701-231-8356. 371 G karen.hendrickson@ndsu.edu

HENDRICKSON, Kristen . 309-438-3430. 147 J khendri@ilstu.edu

HENDRICKSON, Kristine 401-341-2148. 440 C hendrick@salve.edu

HENDRICKSON, Mary .... 717-262-2018. 437 H mhendrickson@wilson.edu

HENDRICKSON, Philip ... 402-643-7358. 289 B philip.hendrickson@cune.edu

HENDRICKSON, Sandy .. 425-889-5232. 521 G sandy.hendrickson@northwestu.edu

HENDRICKSON, Vicki, A 918-631-2526. 401 F vicki-hendrickson@utulsa.edu

HENDRIETH, Emma .... 815-479-8584. 152 F ehendrieth@mchenry.edu

HENDRIKSMA, Jane, E .. 616-526-6116. 240 L jhendrik@calvin.edu

HENDRIX, Andrew .... 803-641-3490. 448 A andrewh@usca.edu

HENDRIX, Frances .... 405-733-7394. 399 F fhendrix@rose.edu

HENDRIX, Joan .... 601-766-6425. 268 C joan.hendrix@mgccc.edu

HENDRIX, Kristie, F ...... 336-734-7051. 360 E khendrix@forsythtech.edu

HENDRIX, Mary .... 903-468-8706. 483 E mary.hendrix@tamuc.edu

HENDRIX, Sherri .... 405-789-7661. 400 A sherri.hendrix@swcu.edu

HENDRY, Christopher .... 978-665-4933. 229 E chendry@fitchburgstate.edu

HENDRY, Daryle .... 915-831-2580. 472 B dhendry@epcc.edu

HENDRY, David .... 850-201-6100. 117 D hendryd@tcc.fl.edu

HENDRY, William .... 517-787-0800. 244 J hendrywilliaml@jccmi.edu

HENDRYX, Julie, A .... 260-359-4002. 166 O jhendryx@huntington.edu

HENEGAR, Kellie .... 618-545-3025. 149 D khenegar@kaskaskia.edu

HENFER, Marsha .... 715-346-2727. 538 A mhenfer@uwsp.edu

HENFER, Marsha .... 608-263-6012. 538 E marsha.henfer@uwc.edu

HENGEL, Crystal, L .... 619-239-0391... 36 D chengel@cwsl.edu

HENGEL, Madeline .... 612-375-1900. 256 E mhengel@ipr.edu

HENGGLER, Josh .... 573-876-7105. 282 H jhenggler@stephens.edu

HENGSTERMAN, Stacey . 518-320-1148. 341 C stacey.hengsterman@suny.edu

HENICK, Steven, T .... 410-777-2429. 213 D sthenick@aacc.edu

HENIK, John .... 319-398-5518. 180 J jhenik@kirkwood.edu

HENK, William, A .... 414-288-7376. 534 B william.henk@marquette.edu

HENKE, Holger .... 718-262-5338. 319 F hhenke@york.cuny.edu

HENKEL, David .... 805-969-3626... 57 K dhenkel@pacifica.edu

HENKEL, Scott .... 612-977-5410. 254 C scott.henkel@capella.edu

HENKING, Susan .... 312-235-3552. 159 A s.henking@shimer.edu

HENLEY, Barbara .... 312-996-7654. 161 D bhenley@uic.edu

HENLEY, Blair .... 423-636-7300. 462 E bhenley@tusculum.edu

HENLEY, Brian, L .... 423-439-4213. 459 C henleybl@etsu.edu

HENLEY, Keldon .... 870-245-4188... 22 D henleyk@obu.edu

HENLEY, Kyle .... 303-376-2635... 80 H kyle.henley@colostate.edu

HENLEY, Marilynn, D ..... 602-614-2337... 11 C

HENLEY, Marsia .... 215-751-8902. 413 I mhenley@ccp.edu

HENLINE, Branden, H .... 928-541-7777... 16 B bhenline@ncu.edu

HENNARD, Cynthia .... 802-635-1424. 501 D cynthia.hennard@jsc.edu

HENNEN, Jack .... 513-562-6262. 373 K jhennen@artacademy.edu

HENNES, Doug, E .... 651-962-6402. 265 C dehennes@stthomas.edu

HENNESSEY, David .... 617-243-2478. 227 K dhennessey@lasell.edu

HENNESSEY, Patrick ...... 914-606-6638. 350 F patrick.hennessey@sunywcc.edu

HENNESSEY, Richard ..... 203-332-5079... 88 F rhennessey@hcc.commnet.edu

HENNESSY, Andrea .... 845-675-4414. 335 C andrea.hennessy@nyack.edu

HENNESSY, Catherine .... 516-463-6820. 326 D catherine.hennessy@hofstra.edu

HENNESSY, James .... 212-636-6470. 324 G hennessy@fordham.edu

HENNESSY, John, L .... 650-723-4074... 68 E hennessy@stanford.edu

HENNESSY, Michael .... 512-245-2317. 487 C mh17@txstate.edu

HENNESSY, Shirell .... 503-517-1369. 408 H shennessy@warnerpacific.edu

HENNIG, Gloria .... 402-643-7270. 289 B finaid@cune.edu

HENNIG, Kathy .... 415-487-2413... 38 L khenning@ccsf.edu

HENNIGAN, Paul .... 412-392-3990. 431 B phennigan@pointpark.edu

HENNIGES, Amy .... 920-465-2380. 536 F hennigea@uwgb.edu

HENNING, Amy .... 215-895-1415. 415 B amyh@drexel.edu

HENNING, Arnold .... 847-866-3920. 145 E arnold.henning@garrett.edu

HENNING, Cindy .... 706-507-8774. 123 D henning_cindy@columbusstate.edu

HENNING, Florence .... 330-369-3200. 390 B tbcmail@tbc-trumbullbusiness.com

HENNING, Jacqueline .... 954-201-6455... 99 D jhenning@broward.edu

HENNING, Kent, L .... 515-263-2802. 178 G khenning@grandview.edu

HENNING, Patti .... 906-786-5802. 240 K henningp@baycollege.edu

HENNING, Stephanie ..... 641-628-5343. 176 E hennings@central.edu

HENNING, Volker .... 423-236-2912. 458 J henning@southern.edu

HENNINGER, Edward, A 570-326-3761. 427 B ehenninger@pct.edu

HENNINGSEN, James, D .... 352-873-5835. 100 K jim.henningsen@cf.edu

HENNIS, Anne, R .... 336-386-3451. 364 D hennisa@surry.edu

HENRICH, Brad .... 605-394-4034. 452 E brad.henrich@wdt.edu

HENRICH, William, L ..... 210-567-2050. 493 A henrich@uthscsa.edu

HENRICHS, Susan, M .... 907-474-7096... 10 I smhenrichs@alaska.edu

HENRICKSEN, Melanie ... 503-552-1848. 404 H mhenriksen@ncnm.edu

HENRICKSON, Gary .... 218-736-1506. 259 F gary.henrickson@minnesota.edu

HENRICKSON, Jay, A ..... 701-788-4899. 371 E Jay.Henrickson@mayvillestate.edu

HENRIE, Kimberly .... 801-957-4782. 498 B kimberly.henrie@slcc.edu

HENRIE, M. Elaine .... 620-341-5211. 186 D ehenrie@emporia.edu

HENRIE, M. Elaine .... 620-341-5457. 186 D ehenrie@emporia.edu

HENRIKSEN, Curtis .... 406-338-5441. 285 F smokeyh@bfcc.edu

HENRIKSEN, Deb .... 605-642-6581. 451 G deb.henriksen@bhsu.edu

HENRIKSEN, JL .... 509-533-7295. 518 E JL.Henriksen@scc.spokane.edu

HENRIKSEN, Rebecca ..... 602-978-7118... 18 A rebecca.henriksen@thunderbird.edu

HENRIKSON, Bruce .... 217-351-2435. 155 J bhenrikson@parkland.edu

HENRIQUES, Richard ..... 402-486-2511. 292 E rihenriq@ucollege.edu

HENRIQUES, Shilo .... 508-678-2811. 231 B shilo.henriques@bristolcc.edu

HENRIS, Dan .... 989-463-7144. 239 B henris@alma.edu

HENRISS, Silvia, H .... 330-287-1253. 386 F henriss.1@osu.edu

HENRY, Alanna, L .... 423-478-7705. 458 B ahenry@ptseminary.edu

HENRY, Alison .... 609-652-4831. 305 C alison.henry@stockton.edu

HENRY, Amy .... 404-894-7475. 125 D amy.henry@oie.gatech.edu

HENRY, Audrey .... 813-695-6296. 148 D ahenry@careered.com

HENRY, Barbara .... 404-364-8476. 130 A bhenry@oglethorpe.edu

HENRY, Barbara, L .... 419-372-4825. 374 K bhenry@bgsu.edu

HENRY, Bill .... 559-791-2459... 49 P bhenry@portervillecollege.edu

HENRY, Charles, E .... 713-313-4343. 485 F henryce@tsu.edu

HENRY, David .... 813-974-4150. 116 C dhenry@usf.edu

HENRY, Debbie .... 832-842-5786. 489 B daherman@central.uh.edu

HENRY, Deena, H .... 919-209-2017. 361 E dhhenry@johnstoncc.edu

HENRY, Dolph .... 865-981-8141. 456 D dolph.henry@maryvillecollege.edu

HENRY, Donna, P .... 276-328-0122. 511 C dph3p@uvawise.edu

HENRY, Eugene .... 434-528-5276. 515 G ehenry@vul.edu

HENRY, Frank .... 406-395-4313. 288 D fghenry_9@hotmail.com

HENRY, Jamie .... 618-544-8657. 147 A henryj@iecc.edu

HENRY, Jeffery .... 406-395-4875. 288 D jhenry@stonechild.edu

HENRY, Jennifer .... 314-529-9552. 276 G jhenry@maryville.edu

HENRY, Jerlynn .... 505-786-4180. 310 D jhenry@navajotech.edu

HENRY, Jonathan .... 727-726-1153. 100 E jonathanhenry@clearwater.edu

HENRY, Katie .... 501-450-5007... 25 H khenry@uca.edu

HENRY, Kevin, C .... 717-866-5775. 416 E khenry@evangelical.edu

HENRY, Kimberly .... 712-325-3207. 179 L khenry@iwcc.edu

HENRY, Larry .... 701-477-7862. 373 B lhenry@tm.edu

HENRY, Linda .... 913-360-7500. 184 H lhenry@benedictine.edu

HENRY, Marci .... 970-521-6617... 83 L marci.henry@njc.edu

HENRY, Margaret .... 303-871-3740... 86 B mhenry@du.edu

HENRY, Matthew .... 903-233-3510. 475 J MatthewHenry@letu.edu

HENRY, Melanie .... 985-380-2483. 203 H melaniehenry@scl.edu

HENRY, Melissa .... 610-647-4400. 418 I mhenry@immaculata.edu

HENRY, Melody .... 903-434-8148. 477 J mhenry@ntcc.edu

HENRY, Melody .... 406-395-4313. 288 D mrbhenry@hotmail.com

HENRY, Nick .... 706-272-4435. 123 G nhenry@daltonstate.edu

HENRY, Patrick, J .... 304-336-8250. 530 A phenry@westliberty.edu

HENRY, Philip, W .... 717-477-1481. 429 E pwhenr@ship.edu

HENRY, Richard .... 951-222-8000... 61 A

HENRY, Rita .... 402-554-2779. 293 A rhenry@unomaha.edu

HENRY, Robert .... 585-395-2408. 342 F rhenry@brockport.edu

HENRY, Robert, H .... 405-208-5032. 397 F rhenry@okcu.edu

HENRY, Ronnie .... 229-317-6700. 124 A ronnie.henry@darton.edu

HENRY, Ronnie, A .... 229-317-6700. 124 A ronnie.henry@darton.edu

HENRY, Shannon, B .... 336-750-2020. 370 A henrysb@wssu.edu

HENRY, Susan, P .... 802-865-4422. 501 C henrys@ccv.edu

HENRY, TOR, Terence ... 740-283-3771. 379 N thenry@franciscan.edu

HENRY, Terrence .... 914-674-7607. 330 J thenry@mercy.edu

HENRY, Thad .... 704-463-3034. 365 E thad.henry@fsmail.pfeiffer.edu

HENRY, Veronica .... 631-420-2622. 346 B veronica.henry@farmingdale.edu

HENRY-CROWE, Susan .. 404-727-6226. 124 E shenryc@emory.edu

HENRY-DAVENPORT, Jannette .... 706-821-8636. 130 C jhenrydavenport@paine.edu

HENRY-MITCHELL, Kim . 856-691-8600. 301 A kmitchell@cccnj.edu

HENRY-QUINN, Barbara 877-442-0505... 86 F barbara.henry-quinn@rockies.edu

HENRY ROBINSON, Shanelle .... 914-773-3775. 335 J shenryrobinson@pace.edu

HENSAL, Nathan .... 815-599-3599. 146 D nathan.hensal@highland.edu

HENSCHEL, Paul, D .... 440-525-7060. 382 M phenschel@lakelandcc.edu

HENSEL, Chester .... 610-876-7300. 437 E cahensel@widener.edu

HENSEL, Julie .... 706-233-7308. 131 E jhensel@shorter.edu

HENSGEN, Brian, C .... 217-442-3044. 143 G bhensgen@dacc.edu

HENSHAW, Debbie .... 706-649-1888. 123 E dhenshaw@columbustech.edu

HENSHAW, Rodney, N ... 515-271-3993. 177 K rod.henshaw@drake.edu

HENSLER, Douglas, A .... 831-656-2371. 544 M dhensler@nps.edu

HENSLEY, Glenn, S .... 540-224-6752. 506 G gshensley@jchs.edu

HENSLEY, Kimberly, S ... 815-753-8494. 154 I khensley@niu.edu

HENSLEY, Linda .... 619-421-6700... 68 B lhensley@swccd.edu

HENSLEY, Mary .... 512-223-7618. 466 I mhensley@austincc.edu

HENSLEY, Michele, R ..... 540-432-4139. 504 D michele.hensley@emu.edu

HENSLEY, Mike .... 704-216-3651. 363 D mike.hensley@rccc.edu

HENSLEY, Ron .... 417-255-7255. 278 F ronhensley@missouristate.edu

HENSLEY, Scott .... 580-745-3198. 399 J shensley@se.edu

HENSLEY, Stephen, W .... 304-696-2269. 529 H hensley@marshall.edu

HENSLEY, Steve, L .... 864-242-5100. 441 D

HENSLEY, Wanda, F .... 501-977-2028... 25 C hensley@uaccm.edu

HENSON, Alexander, L ... 804-828-0138. 511 F alhenson@vcu.edu

HENSON, Emily .... 618-252-5400. 159 E emily.henson@sic.edu

HENSON, Greg .... 630-705-8112. 155 A ghenson@seminary.edu

HENSON, Jena .... 312-752-2182. 149 E jena.henson@kendall.edu

HENSON, Joel .... 805-482-2755... 61 E jhenson@stjohnsem.edu

HENSON, Kevin .... 650-574-6581... 64 C hensonk@smccd.edu

HENSON, Mark .... 618-985-3741. 148 J markhenson@jalc.edu

HENSON, Pamella, A ...... 314-935-5277. 284 L hensonp@wustl.edu

HENSON, Travis .... 618-545-3177. 149 D thenson@kaskaskia.edu

HENSON-WILLIAMS, Paula .... 253-864-3229. 522 C phenson@pierce.ctc.edu

HENSRUD, Faith .... 715-394-8449. 538 C fhensrud@uwsuper.edu

HENSS, Mark .... 217-206-7796. 161 E henss.mark@uis.edu

HENTHORN, Becky .... 580-371-2371. 396 E bhenthorn@mscok.edu

HENTHORN, Janet .... 312-235-3507. 159 A j.henthorn@shimer.edu

HENTHORNE, Michael .... 541-737-2416. 406 A michael.henthorne@oregonstate.edu

HENTON, June, M .... 334-844-4790..... 1 G hentoju@auburn.edu

HENTSCHEL, Alain, R ..... 386-312-4302. 112 C alainhentschel@sjrstate.edu

HENZEL, JR., John, R ... 706-245-7226. 124 D jhenzel@ec.edu

HEOS, Pamela .... 517-371-5140. 250 G heosp@cooley.edu

HEPBURN, Deborah, G .. 814-371-2090. 434 H dhepburn@triangle-tech.edu

HEPBURN, Deborah, G .. 814-371-2090. 434 I dhepburn@triangle-tech.edu

HEPERI, Vernon, L .... 801-422-7254. 495 D vernon_heperi@byu.edu

HEPHNER-LABANC, Brandi .... 662-915-5050. 270 B bhl@olemiss.edu

HEPLER, Lisa, L .... 814-393-2229. 428 C lhepler@clarion.edu

HEPLER, Robin .... 614-222-6163. 378 A rhepler@ccad.edu

HEPNER, Mickey .... 405-974-2809. 400 K mhepner@uco.edu

HEPPNER, Angela .... 417-624-7070. 476 F aheppner@messengercollege.edu

HEPPNER, Gloria .... 313-577-5600. 252 G heppnerg@wayne.edu

HEPPNER, Harold, H ...... 406-353-2607. 285 E hheppner@ancollege.edu

HERALD, John .... 606-886-3863. 194 K john.herald@kctcs.edu

HERALD, Sara, B .... 305-899-3080... 98 O sherald@barry.edu

HERANANDEZ, Eldra ...... 787-257-0000. 554 B eldra.hernandez@upr.edu

HERB, Amanda, K .... 740-374-8716. 392 I aherb@wscc.edu

HERBERT, Derek .... 970-521-6714... 83 L derek.herbert@njc.edu

HERBERT, George, E ...... 319-335-3179. 175 I george-herbert@uiowa.edu

HERBERT, Jim .... 678-915-6824. 132 C jherbert@spsu.edu

HERBERT, Mike .... 541-888-7208. 407 H mherbert@socc.edu

HERBERT, Tom .... 513-529-4029. 384 G herbertw@miamioh.edu

HERBERT-ASHTON, Marilyn, J .... 540-857-6372. 514 E mherbert-ashton@virginiawestern.edu

HERBERTZ, Anita .... 317-955-6021. 170 V aherbertz@marian.edu

HERBRAND, Laurie .... 209-228-2741... 71 D LHerbrand@UCMerced.edu

HERBST, Adam .... 320-363-3819. 263 P
aherbst@csbsju.edu
HERBST, Chet .... 208-792-2240. 138 G
cgherbst@lcsc.edu
HERBST, Daniel .... 480-732-7120... 14 J
daniel.herbst@cgc.edu
HERBST, Gordon, J .... 814-732-2585. 428 E
herbst@edinboro.edu
HERBST, Jeffrey .... 315-228-7444. 320 F
jherbst@colgate.edu
HERBST, Joel .... 561-297-3970. 114 L
jherbst1@fau.edu
HERBST, John, H .... 859-257-5781. 200 C
herbst@uky.edu
HERBST, Susan .... 860-486-2337... 92 A
president@uconn.edu
HERBSTER, David .... 605-677-5309. 451 F
david.herbster@usd.edu
HERCULES, Tim .... 314-977-3434. 281 I
hercultp@slu.edu
HERDEA, Eve .... 312-662-4403. 139 F
eherdea@adler.edu
HERDLICK, Michael .... 419-448-3582. 389 J
herdlickm@tiffin.edu
HERDLICK, Mike .... 419-448-3421. 389 J
herdlickm@tiffin.edu
HERDLITZKA, Roxana .... 740-753-7032. 380 K
herdlitzka_r@hocking.edu
HERENCIA, Ada .... 787-844-8181. 555 A
ada.herencia@upr.edu
HERENDEEN, Steve, A ... 260-422-5561. 167 B
saherendeen@indianatech.edu
HERGAN, Mark, J .... 443-352-4400. 218 E
mhergan@stevenson.edu
HERGENROTHER,
Diane, S .... 718-990-1428. 339 A
hergenrd@stjohns.edu
HERGERT, Erin .... 719-549-3053... 84 G
erin.hergert@pueblocc.edu
HERGERT, Erin .... 719-549-3226... 84 G
erin.hergert@pueblocc.edu
HERGERT, Travis, J .... 641-422-4990. 181 D
hergetra@niacc.edu
HERGOTT, Lori .... 402-461-7370. 289 I
lhergott@hastings.edu
HERINGER, Chris .... 701-224-5631. 371 D
Chris.Heringer@dickinsonstate.edu
HERINGER, David, L ...... 870-307-7290... 21 H
david.heringer@lyon.edu
HERKELRATH, William ... 909-793-4263... 29 G
HERLE, Jeff .... 617-951-2350. 234 G
jeff.herle@necb.edu
HERLIHY, James, E .... 205-665-6600..... 9 B
herlihyj@montevallo.edu
HERLIHY, Joseph, M ...... 617-552-2855. 224 A
joseph.herlihy@bc.edu
HERLOCKER, Linda, K .... 407-582-1388. 118 M
lherlocker@valenciacollege.edu
HERMAN, Amber .... 336-838-6292. 365 B
amber.herman@wilkescc.edu
HERMAN, Anne .... 503-352-2777. 407 A
hermana@pacificu.edu
HERMAN, Annette .... 435-797-1158. 497 B
annette.herman@usu.edu
HERMAN, Barbara, B ...... 817-257-7855. 484 I
b.herman@tcu.edu
HERMAN, Brian .... 612-624-5054. 264 G
herman@umn.edu
HERMAN, Bruce .... 410-455-2460. 219 D
bherman@umbc.edu
HERMAN, Catherine .... 518-956-8151. 341 D
cherman@albany.edu
HERMAN, David, E .... 716-673-3271. 342 A
david.herman@fredonia.edu
HERMAN, Deborah .... 860-512-2872... 88 G
dherman@manchestercc.edu
HERMAN, Fran .... 248-414-6900. 246 F
fherman@mji.edu
HERMAN, Harry .... 516-323-3503. 331 J
hherman@molloy.edu
HERMAN, Harvey .... 605-856-5880. 451 B
harvey.herman@sintegleska.edu
HERMAN, Jeanne .... 330-941-2264. 394 A
jmherman@ysu.edu
HERMAN, Sharon, S .... 816-654-7177. 275 K
sherman@kcumb.edu
HERMAN, Terry .... 740-588-1290. 394 C
therman@zanestate.edu
HERMAN, Vanessa, J ..... 212-346-1025. 335 J
vherman@pace.edu
HERMAN-BARLOW,
Janet .... 440-365-5222. 383 B
HERMANN, David .... 815-802-8524. 149 C
dhermann@kcc.edu
HERMANN, Julie, K .... 732-445-8610. 306 A
julie.hermann@rutgers.edu
HERMANN-ARTIM,
Diane .... 802-388-5371. 501 C
diane.hermann-artim@ccv.edu
HERMANNY, Danielle, E 503-943-8715. 408 F
hermannd@up.edu
HERMANSEN, Beckie ..... 435-283-7346. 498 A
beckie.hermansen@snow.edu
HERMANSTON, Fran ...... 509-335-3942. 525 A
HERMES, John .... 405-425-1815. 397 D
john.hermes@oc.edu
HERMES, Joseph .... 312-996-3490. 161 D
jhermes@uic.edu
HERMES, Wayne, J .... 970-247-7432... 81 M
hermes_w@fortlewis.edu
HERMON, Vada .... 620-227-9213. 186 B
vhermon@dc3.edu
HERMOSILLO, Gilbert .... 760-757-2121... 54 G
ghermosillo@miracosta.edu
HERMSEN, Cindy, L .... 248-370-3370. 248 J
hermsen@oakland.edu
HERNÁNDEZ, Olga .... 787-834-5151. 552 B
HERN, Marcia, J .... 502-852-8300. 200 D
m.hern@louisville.edu
HERNANDEZ, Abraham .. 956-882-8281. 491 D
abraham.hernandez@utb.edu
HERNANDEZ, Albert .... 303-765-3183... 82 E
ahernandez@iliff.edu
HERNANDEZ, Alex .... 915-831-6383. 472 B
aherna78@epcc.edu
HERNANDEZ, Ana .... 813-974-4041. 116 C
ahernandez@usf.edu
HERNANDEZ, Ana .... 787-764-0000. 555 B
ana.hernandez@upr.edu
HERNANDEZ, Annette .... 717-560-8240. 421 A
ahernandez@lbc.edu
HERNANDEZ, Aracely, C 956-326-2732. 483 B
achernandez@tamiu.edu
HERNANDEZ, Arnold ...... 208-459-5868. 138 A
ahernandez@collegeofidaho.edu
HERNANDEZ, Arthur ...... 361-825-2661. 483 F
art.hernandez@tamucc.edu
HERNANDEZ, Axel, N .... 858-499-0202... 40 C
ahernandez@coleman.edu
HERNANDEZ, Ayana, D .. 919-530-7266. 368 A
ahernandez@nccu.edu
HERNANDEZ, Caridad .... 305-821-3333. 105 A
csanchez@fnu.edu
HERNANDEZ, Carlos ...... 972-780-3600. 490 D
HERNANDEZ, Cathy .... 602-286-8028... 14 L
cathleen.hernandez@gwmail.maricopa.edu
HERNANDEZ, Christine ... 916-558-2438... 53 D
hernana2@scc.losrios.edu
HERNANDEZ, Christine .. 787-786-3030. 547 F
chernandez@ucb.edu.pr
HERNANDEZ, Cledia ...... 956-364-4530. 485 H
cledia.hernandez@tstc.edu
HERNANDEZ, Daisy .... 801-840-4800. 495 K
dhernandez@cci.edu
HERNANDEZ, David .... 805-565-6164... 76 D
dhernand@westmont.edu
HERNANDEZ, Dino .... 775-831-1314. 295 F
dhernandez@sierranevada.edu
HERNANDEZ, Edwin .... 787-881-1212. 552 B
edwin_hernandez@pucpr.edu
HERNANDEZ, Eliza .... 210-486-4913. 464 J
ehernandez716@alamo.edu
HERNANDEZ, Felix .... 805-922-6966... 26 K
fhernandez@hancockcollege.edu
HERNANDEZ, Francisco . 787-840-8894. 555 A
francisco.hernandez7@upr.edu
HERNANDEZ,
Francisco, J .... 808-956-3290. 136 B
fjh@hawaii.edu
HERNANDEZ, Frank .... 847-214-7442. 144 F
fhernandez@elgin.edu
HERNANDEZ, Frank .... 432-552-2120. 493 D
hernandez_f@utpb.edu
HERNANDEZ, Grace .... 806-742-2121. 487 D
grace.hernandez@ttu.edu
HERNANDEZ, Harry .... 787-738-2161. 554 C
harry.hernandez2@upr.edu
HERNANDEZ, Ilsamar ..... 787-751-0160. 548 J
ihernandez@cmpr.pr.gov
HERNANDEZ, Isabel .... 305-237-6151. 109 D
ihernand@mdc.edu
HERNANDEZ, Jean .... 425-640-1515. 519 D
jean.hernandez@edcc.edu
HERNANDEZ, Jelenny ..... 305-821-3333. 105 A
jhernandez@fnu.edu
HERNANDEZ, Jocceline . 818-386-5632... 59 E
jhernandez@pgi.edu
HERNANDEZ, Joe .... 281-487-1170. 484 H
jhernandez@txchiro.edu
HERNANDEZ, John .... 714-628-4886... 60 H
hernandez_john@sccollege.edu
HERNANDEZ, John .... 212-678-3379. 347 G
jlh2172@tc.columbia.edu
HERNANDEZ, Jorge .... 808-739-4640. 135 D
jhernand@chaminade.edu
HERNANDEZ, Jose .... 813-974-4373. 116 C
HERNANDEZ, Jose, E .... 910-962-7104. 369 C
hernandezj@uncw.edu
HERNANDEZ, Josephine 973-341-1600. 304 B
hernandez@pccc.edu
HERNANDEZ,
Juan Carlos .... 787-751-0160. 548 J
jhernandez@cmpr.pr.gov
HERNANDEZ, Justin, J .. 660-944-2851. 272 H
justin@conception.edu
HERNANDEZ, Lino .... 787-738-2161. 554 C
lino.hernandez@upr.edu
HERNANDEZ, Lisa .... 773-907-4700. 142 A
lhernandez@ccc.edu
HERNANDEZ, Luz, S ...... 787-620-2040. 547 C
lhernandez@aupr.edu
HERNANDEZ, Maria .... 715-422-5469. 540 D
maria.hernandez@mstc.edu
HERNANDEZ, Martin ...... 903-823-3450. 482 D
martin.hernandez@texarkanacollege.edu
HERNANDEZ, Michelle ... 212-616-7278. 325 H
michelle.hernandez@heleneculd.edu
HERNANDEZ, Nina .... 908-709-7127. 308 B
hernandez@ucc.edu
HERNANDEZ, Noe .... 432-837-8603. 487 B
noeh@sulross.edu
HERNANDEZ, Oscar .... 956-872-2522. 480 I
oscarh@southtexascollege.edu
HERNANDEZ, Oscar .... 361-593-2303. 484 A
oscar.hernandez2@tamuk.edu
HERNANDEZ, Otto .... 606-343-4978. 299 A
hernande@atlantic.edu
HERNANDEZ, JR., Paul . 956-872-8372. 480 I
phernan@southtexascollege.edu
HERNANDEZ, Paul, R .... 937-775-4001. 393 G
paul.hernandez@wright.edu
HERNANDEZ, Phil .... 641-844-5668. 179 J
phil.hernandez@iavalley.edu
HERNANDEZ, Raul .... 787-746-1400. 549 B
rahernandez@huertas.edu
HERNANDEZ, Raul .... 787-284-1912. 550 F
rhernand@ponce.inter.edu
HERNANDEZ, Raymond . 650-738-4221... 64 D
hernandezr@smccd.edu
HERNANDEZ, Rebecca ... 574-535-7775. 166 A
rhernandez@goshen.edu
HERNANDEZ, Richard .... 760-252-2411... 29 I
rhernandez@barstow.edu
HERNANDEZ, Richard .... 843-574-6350. 447 E
richard.hernandez@tridenttech.edu
HERNANDEZ, Ruth, E .... 787-279-1912. 550 B
rehernandez@bayamon.inter.edu
HERNANDEZ, Samuel ..... 787-882-2065. 553 A
asistencia_economica@unitecpr.net
HERNANDEZ, Sandra ..... 787-757-1520. 554 B
sandrahernandez@upr.edu
HERNANDEZ, Shalyn, J . 770-720-9202. 130 G
sjh@reinhardt.edu
HERNANDEZ, Sheila ...... 831-582-3632... 34 B
shernandez@csumb.edu
HERNANDEZ,
Thomas, J .... 585-395-2510. 342 F
thernand@brockport.edu
HERNANDEZ, Todd .... 419-267-1445. 385 F
thernandez@northweststate.edu
HERNANDEZ, Tracy .... 801-878-1035. 295 E
thernandez@roseman.edu
HERNANDEZ, Victoria .... 305-237-3221. 109 D
vhernand@mdc.edu
HERNANDEZ, Wanda ..... 212-463-0400. 348 B
wandau@touro.edu
HERNANDEZ, Wendie .... 254-659-7503. 473 A
whernandez@hillcollege.edu
HERNANDEZ, Wilfredo .. 787-754-7120. 549 I
HERNANDEZ, Yezmin ..... 787-728-1515. 555 D
yhernandez@sagrado.edu
HERNANDEZ, Yvette ...... 830-591-7318. 481 C
yvetteh@swtjc.edu
HERNANDEZ BONILLA,
Edna, E .... 787-890-2681. 553 H
edna.hernandez@upr.edu
HERNANDEZ-HUNTER,
Anna .... 503-838-8195. 406 E
hernana@wou.edu
HERNANDEZ-MERGAL,
Lui .... 787-763-7005. 548 J
lhernandez@cmpr.pr.gov
HERNANDEZ NUNEZ,
Maria, L .... 787-884-3838. 547 D
directora_ejecutiva@atenascollege.edu
HERNANDEZ-SANCHEZ,
Wanda .... 787-620-2040. 547 C
whernandez@aupr.edu
HERNDON, Craig .... 804-819-4782. 511 G
cherndon@vccs.edu
HERNDON, Godfrey, B ... 919-530-5063. 368 A
gherndon@nccu.edu
HERNDON, Jim .... 602-978-7986... 18 A
jim.herndon@thunderbird.edu
HERNDON, Jim .... 602-978-7234... 18 A
jim.herndon@thunderbird.edu
HERNDON,
Kimmetha, D .... 205-726-2198..... 6 F
kherndon@samford.edu
HERNDON, OSB, Linda . 913-360-7553. 184 H
lherndon@benedictine.edu
HERNDON, Linda, M ...... 229-226-1621. 132 F
lherndon@thomasu.edu
HERNDON,
Michael (Mike) .... 817-515-5331. 482 B
michael.herndon@tccd.edu
HERNDON, Steven, T ..... 937-229-3317. 391 C
SHerndon1@udayton.edu
HERNE, Jaclyn .... 716-839-8245. 322 E
0134mgr@fheg.follett.com
HERNEY, Susan .... 562-908-3445... 60 I
sherney@riohondo.edu
HERNON, Michael .... 740-283-6447. 379 N
mhernon@franciscan.edu
HEROLD, Brent .... 504-568-2412. 205 C
bherol@lsuhsc.edu
HEROLD, Irene .... 808-956-7205. 136 B
heroldi@hawaii.edu
HEROLD, Paul, A .... 330-972-7873. 390 E
BoardOffice@uakron.edu
HEROLD, Paul, A .... 330-972-7873. 390 E
paulherold@uakron.edu
HERON-BURKE, Alice .... 516-686-7683. 333 H
aburke@nyit.edu
HERR, Audrey .... 717-872-3263. 429 D
audrey.herr@millersville.edu
HERR, Robert .... 718-420-4242. 350 B
robert.herr@wagner.edu
HERR-VALBURG,
Melissa .... 605-995-2600. 450 A
meherr@dwu.edu
HERRARA, La Nae .... 202-462-2101... 96 A
financialaid@iwp.edu
HERRELKO, III,
Edward, J .... 619-201-8996... 67 G
eherrelko@socalsem.edu
HERRELKO, III,
Edward, J .... 619-201-8981... 67 G
eherrelko@socalsem.edu
HERREN, James .... 310-825-1633... 71 C
jherren@ucpd.ucla.edu
HERREN, Melissa .... 405-945-3297. 398 C
HERRERA, Antoinette ...... 408-270-6448... 63 O
antoinette.herrera@evc.edu
HERRERA, Antonio .... 410-462-8563. 213 F
aherrera@bccc.edu
HERRERA, Cynthia .... 805-986-5944... 74 G
cherrera@vcccd.edu
HERRERA, Gilberto .... 787-890-2681. 553 H
gilberto.herrera@upr.edu
HERRERA, Jennifer .... 828-627-4507. 361 B
jherrera@haywood.edu
HERRERA, Linda .... 503-589-7720. 402 E
linda.herrera@chemeketa.edu
HERRERA, Rick .... 956-364-4052. 485 G
rick.herrera@harlingen.tstc.edu
HERRERA, Rick .... 956-364-4052. 485 H
rick.herrera@systems.edu
HERRERA, William .... 832-813-6589. 476 A
william.herrera@lonestar.edu
HERRERA LINDSTROM,
Cynthia, E .... 312-413-2495. 161 D
cynthiar@uic.edu
HERRICK, Alice .... 207-326-2445. 211 D
alice.herrick@mma.edu
HERRICK, Bryan, D .... 636-481-3168. 275 I
bherrick@jeffco.edu
HERRICK, James, S .... 619-594-0213... 35 D
herrick1@mail.sdsu.edu
HERRICK, Laura .... 704-463-3439. 365 E
laura.herrick@fsmail.pfeiffer.edu
HERRICK, P. Douglas ..... 215-503-0264. 434 C
doug.herrick@jefferson.edu
HERRIFORD, Steven, R .. 317-781-5767. 173 I
sherriford@uindy.edu
HERRIN, Brice .... 229-732-5980. 120 D
briceherrin@andrewcollege.edu
HERRIN, Carl .... 508-929-8263. 230 G
cherrin@worcester.edu
HERRIN, Jodi .... 843-521-4137. 448 B
herrinj@uscb.edu
HERRIN, Kari .... 912-525-5000. 131 B
kherrin@scad.edu
HERRIN, Mark .... 405-974-3141. 400 K
mherrin@uco.edu
HERRIN, Mary, L .... 316-978-3030. 191 F
mary.herrin@wichita.edu
HERRIN, Scott .... 619-660-4452... 46 D
scott.herrin@gcccd.edu
HERRIN, Timothy, D .... 704-233-8150. 370 G
herrin@wingate.edu
HERRIN, William .... 209-946-2259... 73 A
wherrin@pacific.edu
HERRING, Barry, O .... 757-823-8275. 507 M
boherring@nsu.edu
HERRING, Cassandra ...... 757-727-2072. 505 F
cassandra.herring@hamptonu.edu
HERRING, David .... 505-277-4700. 312 F
herring@law.unm.edu
HERRING, Donald, R .... 910-938-6236. 359 E
herringd@coastalcarolina.edu

HERRING, George .... 972-860-4634. 470 G
gtherring@dcccd.edu
HERRING, Jack .... 928-350-2010... 17 K
jherring@prescott.edu
HERRING, Jack .... 360-650-3779. 525 C
jack.herring@wwu.edu
HERRING, Jayne .... 262-564-3092. 540 A
herringj@gtc.edu
HERRING, Jeff .... 801-585-0928. 496 Q
jeff.herring@utah.edu
HERRING, Jimmy, G ...... 706-880-8237. 128 A
jherring@lagrange.edu
HERRING, Mark, Y .... 803-323-2232. 449 G
herringm@winthrop.edu
HERRING, Patrick, C ...... 352-294-0963. 116 A
pherring@ufl.edu
HERRING, Trellie .... 919-735-5151. 364 H
wcc-bookstore@waynecc.edu
HERRING, Vanessa .... 816-501-3780. 271 H
vanessa.herring@avila.edu
HERRINGER, Gretchen ... 315-228-7676. 320 F
gherringer@colgate.edu
HERRINGTON, Glenda ...... 936-468-2304. 482 A
gherrington@sfasu.edu
HERRINGTON, Jere .... 662-562-3214. 269 C
recruiting@northwestms.edu
HERRINGTON, Katie .... 601-477-4087. 267 F
katie.herrington@jcjc.edu
HERRINGTON, Laurie ..... 912-443-5519. 131 D
lherrington@savannahtech.edu
HERRINGTON-HALL, Glen .... 651-255-6107. 264 C
gherrington-hall@unitedseminary.edu
HERRINGTON-PERRY, Mary, C .... 217-581-3514. 144 E
mhperry@eiu.edu
HERRINTON, Dick .... 559-453-2252... 45 D
dick.herrinton@fresno.edu
HERRINTON, Thomas, R 619-260-4553... 73 I
herrinton@sandiegoe.edu
HERRIOTT, Scott .... 641-472-1219. 180 N
sherriott@mum.edu
HERRLINGER, Timothy, J .... 610-799-1711. 421 I
therrlinger@lccc.edu
HERRMANN, Anthony .... 914-323-5406. 330 B
anthony.herrmann@mville.edu
HERRMANN, Bryan .... 320-589-6038. 264 F
herrmanb@morris.umn.edu
HERRMANN, Jane .... 618-545-3220. 149 D
jherrmann@kaskaskia.edu
HERRMANN, John, L ..... 740-284-5215. 379 N
jherrmann@franciscan.edu
HERRMANN, Marilyn, M 909-558-4517... 51 C
mherrmann@llu.edu
HERRMANN, Mark .... 907-474-7116... 10 I
mlherrmann@alaska.edu
HERRMANN, Nira .... 212-346-1517. 335 J
nherrmann@pace.edu
HERRMANN, Tim .... 812-357-6501. 173 A
therrmann@saintmeinrad.edu
HERRMANN, William ..... 718-409-2882. 346 D
wherrmann@sunymaritime.edu
HERRNDON, Jessica ...... 704-406-2297. 354 C
jherndon@gardner-webb.edu
HERROD, Lorinda .... 432-264-5028. 473 E
lherrod@howardcollege.edu
HERRON, Alberta, H .... 336-841-9198. 355 C
aherron@highpoint.edu
HERRON, Anne, J .... 315-255-1743. 316 D
anne.herron@cayuga-cc.edu
HERRON, Crystal .... 314-286-0236. 280 F
cherron@ranken.edu
HERRON, Jerry .... 313-577-3030. 252 G
ad5017@wayne.edu
HERRON, Larry .... 425-564-2282. 517 A
larry.herron@bellevuecollege.edu
HERRON, Margaret .... 660-785-4143. 282 L
mherron@truman.edu
HERRON, Marla .... 859-572-5225. 198 I
herronm1@nku.edu
HERRON-WILLIAMS, Sharron .... 334-229-4232..... 1 D
sherron@alasu.edu
HERSCHEDE, Kathryn, J . 859-572-5172. 198 I
herschede@nku.edu
HERSH, Doug .... 805-965-0581... 64 L
hersh@sbcc.edu
HERSH, Melissa .... 802-865-5402. 499 A
hersh@champlain.edu
HERSH-TUDOR, Andrew . 509-682-6715. 525 B
ehersh-tudor@wvc.edu
HERSHBELL, Anne .... 434-947-8158. 508 D
ahershbell@randolphcollege.edu
HERSHBERGER, Bernie .. 207-725-3069. 209 H
bhershbe@bowdoin.edu
HERSHBERGER, Bryn ..... 303-986-2320... 80 D
bryn@csha.net
HERSHENSON, Jay .... 646-664-9041. 316 I
jay.hershenson@cuny.edu
HERSHEY, J. David .... 717-396-7833. 427 A
dhershey@pcad.edu
HERSHEY, Jonathan .... 706-368-7639. 125 C
jhershey@highlands.edu
HERSHEY, Roger .... 816-584-6540. 280 C
roger.hershey@park.edu
HERSHKOWITZ, M .... 203-325-4351... 87 H
HERSHOCK, Martin .... 313-593-5490. 251 D
mhershoc@umich.edu
HERSKOWITZ, Issac .... 212-463-0400. 348 B
issac.herskowitz@touro.edu
HERSKOWITZ, Mordechai .... 732-367-1060. 299 E
HERSON, Moshe .... 973-267-9404. 304 G
rca069@aol.com
HERT, Fiona .... 616-234-3744. 243 B
fhert@grcc.edu
HERTEL, Tina, L .... 484-664-3550. 424 H
thertel@muhlenberg.edu
HERTENBERGER, Patricia .... 281-756-3789. 465 D
phertenberger@alvincollege.edu
HERTERICH, Werner .... 312-899-1294. 158 L
wherterich@saic.edu
HERTIK, Vince .... 406-477-6215. 285 H
vhertik@cdkc.edu
HERTS, George .... 870-575-8316... 24 E
hertsg@uapb.edu
HERTZ, Adam .... 610-328-8325. 433 I
ahertz1@swarthmore.edu
HERTZ, Amy .... 828-884-8124. 352 I
hertzae@brevard.edu
HERTZ, Matthew .... 716-888-2436. 316 C
hertzm@canisius.edu
HERTZFELD, Patricia, A .. 508-213-2382. 235 E
patricia.hertzfeld@nichols.edu
HERTZOG, Janet .... 607-778-5203. 315 I
hertzogjm@sunybroome.edu
HERTZOG, Matthew .... 309-672-5533. 152 I
mhertzog@methodistcol.edu
HERVAS, Kevin .... 212-217-4126. 324 C
kevin_hervas@fitnyc.edu
HERVEY, Llyod .... 501-370-5286... 22 F
lhervey@philander.edu
HERZ, Carol, A .... 561-237-7821. 108 X
cherz@lynn.edu
HERZBERG, Tina .... 864-503-5572. 448 H
therzberg@uscupstate.edu
HERZBERGER, Sharon, D .... 562-907-4201... 76 I
president@whittier.edu
HERZEK, Farley .... 310-233-4010... 51 H
herzekf@lahc.edu
HERZIG, Brenda, H .... 218-726-8532. 264 D
bherzig@d.umn.edu
HERZING, Renee .... 608-249-6611. 533 I
rherzing@herzing.edu
HERZOG, Jennifer .... 925-631-4108... 61 F
jgh3@stmarys-ca.edu
HERZOG, Michael .... 509-313-6104. 520 A
herzog@gonzaga.edu
HERZOG, Serge .... 775-784-4546. 294 J
serge@unr.edu
HESBROOK, Mechele ..... 505-428-1664. 311 J
mechele.hesbrook@sfcc.edu
HESCH, Kim .... 701-845-7403. 372 A
kim.hesch@vcsu.edu
HESELIUS, Helen, S .... 757-446-6065. 504 E
heselihs@evms.edu
HESHEL, Alan .... 213-427-2200... 37 G
HESLEP, Debbie .... 662-846-4020. 266 G
dheslep@deltastate.edu
HESLEP, Debbie, S .... 662-846-4655. 266 G
dheslep@deltastate.edu
HESLEPH, Jack .... 801-957-4013. 498 B
jack.hesleph@slcc.edu
HESLIN, Joseph .... 802-258-9209. 499 F
jheslin@gradcenter.marlboro.edu
HESPE, David, C .... 609-894-9311. 299 I
dhespe@bcc.edu
HESS, Allison, B .... 801-626-7948. 497 D
ahess@weber.edu
HESS, Ann .... 928-536-6257... 16 E
ann.hess@npc.edu
HESS, Cindy .... 502-852-1105. 200 D
cindy.hess@louisville.edu
HESS, Cindy, K .... 314-644-9743. 281 E
chess17@stlcc.edu
HESS, Clayton .... 423-869-6377. 456 A
clayton.hess@lmunet.edu
HESS, Craig, E .... 803-822-3216. 445 C
hessc@midlandstech.edu
HESS, Cynthia .... 254-968-9125. 483 A
hess@tarleton.edu
HESS, Daniel .... 651-641-8252. 255 B
hess@csp.edu
HESS, Danielle .... 509-335-2636. 525 A
danielleh@wsu.edu
HESS, Donald .... 692-625-5903. 546 F
cmihess@yahoo.com
HESS, Donald .... 692-625-3394. 546 F
HESS, Eleanor, B .... 207-834-7541. 212 E
eleanor.hess@maine.edu
HESS, Gregory, D .... 765-361-6221. 175 B
hessg@wabash.edu
HESS, Janet .... 692-625-3994. 546 F
cmihess@yahoo.com
HESS, Jay .... 317-274-8416. 167 E
HESS, Jay, L .... 317-274-8157. 168 D
jayhess@iu.edu
HESS, Kristine, M .... 402-354-7260. 291 B
kris.hess@methodistcollege.edu
HESS, Pam .... 440-375-8005. 382 L
phess@lec.edu
HESS, Pat .... 507-786-3000. 264 B
hessp@stolaf.edu
HESS, Patrice .... 309-694-5295. 146 E
phess@icc.edu
HESS, Resa .... 559-791-2457... 49 P
resa.hess@portervillecollege.edu
HESS, Shimon .... 718-259-2525. 315 C
HESS, Stephen .... 352-395-5926. 112 D
stephen.hess@saintleo.edu
HESS, Thomas, R .... 606-218-5475. 200 F
thomashess@upike.edu
HESS, William .... 510-628-8013... 51 A
whess@lincolnuca.edu
HESS, Wilson, G .... 207-834-7504. 212 E
wilson.hess@maine.edu
HESS MOLL, Sandra .... 815-455-8987. 152 F
smoll@mchenry.edu
HESSE, Allison .... 714-556-3610... 74 D
allison.hesse@vanguard.edu
HESSE, Carla .... 510-642-5195... 70 I
chesse@berkeley.edu
HESSE, Cindy .... 303-360-4752... 81 C
cindy.hesse@ccaurora.edu
HESSE-BIBER, Sharlene . 617-552-4130. 224 A
sharlene.hesse-biber@bc.edu
HESSEE, Jennifer .... 918-540-6250. 396 G
jennifer.hessee@neo.edu
HESSELL, Debra .... 617-578-7100. 236 E
dhessell@sbboston.com
HESSER, Kevin .... 605-331-6895. 452 D
kevin.hesser@usiouxfalls.edu
HESSLER, James .... 231-591-3947. 242 F
hesslej@ferris.edu
HESSLER, Robert, L .... 308-635-6030. 293 E
hesslerr@wncc.edu
HESTAND, Phil .... 870-972-2318... 19 N
phestand@astate.edu
HESTER, Barry, C .... 318-670-6414. 207 A
bhester@susla.edu
HESTER, Clyda .... 740-377-2520. 389 K
clydasteacup@windstream.net
HESTER, Colleen .... 217-479-7025. 152 D
president@mac.edu
HESTER, Cynthia, L .... 318-670-6236. 207 A
chester@susla.edu
HESTER, D. Jean .... 503-821-8926. 406 F
jhester@pnca.edu
HESTER, Dana .... 626-914-8870... 38 K
dhester@citruscollege.edu
HESTER, David .... 502-895-3411. 197 F
dhester@lpts.edu
HESTER, Kerri .... 916-660-7603... 66 B
khester@sierracollege.edu
HESTER, Kevin .... 615-844-5098. 464 E
khester@welch.edu
HESTER, Lynda .... 252-473-2264. 359 F
lynda_hester@albemarle.edu
HESTER, Malcolm .... 606-337-1114. 193 F
mhester@ccbbc.edu
HESTER, Mary .... 620-242-0487. 188 G
hesterm@mcpherson.edu
HESTER, Michael, D .... 678-839-0626. 133 I
mhester@westga.edu
HESTER, Ranan .... 501-279-4331... 21 C
rhester@harding.edu
HESTER, Ray .... 252-536-7250. 361 A
wgester956@halifaxcc.edu
HESTER, Rebeckah .... 765-973-8585. 167 G
rrieder@iue.edu
HESTNESS, Gregory, S ... 612-626-4734. 264 G
hestness@umn.edu
HESTON, Dave .... 602-429-4927... 16 O
dheston@ps.edu
HESTON, Grant .... 407-823-5988. 115 E
grant.heston@ucf.edu
HETH, Justin .... 630-752-5022. 163 F
justin.heth@wheaton.edu
HETHERINGTON, Kathleen, B .... 443-518-4820. 215 E
khetherington@howardcc.edu
HETRICK, Barbara .... 904-620-2560. 116 B
barbara.hetrick@unf.edu
HETRICK, Fran .... 719-502-3261... 84 A
fran.hetrick@ppcc.edu
HETRICK, Janice .... 215-637-7700. 418 G
jhetrick@holyfamily.edu
HETTLEMAN, Thomas ..... 410-617-1120. 216 A
tdhettleman@loyola.edu
HETTRICK, Allyson .... 828-298-3325. 370 E
ahettrick@warren-wilson.edu
HETU, Marcel .... 559-334-2960... 75 H
marcelhetu@whccd.edu
HETZEL, Bob .... 608-785-6491. 536 G
bhetzel@uwlax.edu
HETZEL, June .... 562-903-6000... 29 L
june.hetzel@bioloa.edu
HEU, Nancy .... 808-235-7435. 137 C
heu@hawaii.edu
HEUBLER, Deborah, T .... 808-956-0768. 136 B
dhuebler@hawaii.edu
HEUER, John, J .... 215-898-6884. 435 B
heuer@upenn.edu
HEUER, Timothy .... 773-508-3254. 151 H
theuer@luc.edu
HEUGEL, Jim .... 425-889-4098. 521 G
jim.heugel@northwestu.edu
HEULITT, Ken .... 312-329-2070. 153 E
ken.heulitt@moody.edu
HEUPEL, Jaelee .... 808-983-4187. 135 G
jae@tokai.edu
HEURING, Curt .... 609-771-3269. 300 E
heuring@tcnj.edu
HEURING, Michael .... 406-243-2022. 286 H
michael.heuring@umontana.edu
HEUSCHELE, Joel .... 715-425-3265. 537 E
joel.heuschele@uwrf.edu
HEUSNER, Warren .... 718-270-6048. 319 A
wheusner@mec.cuny.edu
HEUTON, Mary Ellen ...... 304-696-6603. 529 H
heuton@marshall.edu
HEVRON, Danelle .... 617-544-8657. 147 A
hevrond@iecc.edu
HEWELL, Sherry, D .... 270-824-8666. 196 A
sherry.hewell@kctcs.edu
HEWERDINE, Kevin, L .... 812-877-8184. 172 C
kevin.l.hewerdine@rose-hulman.edu
HEWES, Pollyanne .... 207-947-4591. 209 G
phewes@bealcollege.edu
HEWETSON, Hank .... 812-855-6169. 167 F
hhewetso@indiana.edu
HEWETT, James, E .... 712-749-2248. 176 D
hewettj@bvu.edu
HEWETT, Kelly .... 410-334-2908. 221 D
khewett@worwic.edu
HEWETT, Lamar .... 803-549-6314. 448 D
dlhewett@mailbox.sc.edu
HEWITT, Bradley, L .... 618-650-2871. 159 H
bhewitt@siue.edu
HEWITT, Dawn .... 718-262-2060. 319 F
hewittd@york.cuny.edu
HEWITT, Diane .... 978-934-2355. 229 B
diane_hewitt@uml.edu
HEWITT, Emma .... 712-274-6400. 183 G
emma.hewitt@witcc.edu
HEWITT, Gordon, J .... 315-859-4084. 325 E
ghewitt@hamilton.edu
HEWITT, JR., Harold, W 714-997-6815... 38 A
hewitt@chapman.edu
HEWITT, Mark, S .... 781-736-2010. 224 F
mhewitt@brandeis.edu
HEWITT, Maureen, A ..... 312-935-4235. 148 C
mhewitt@icsw.edu
HEWITT, Michael .... 718-951-5131. 317 C
mhewitt@brooklyn.cuny.edu
HEWITT, Nathaniel .... 903-923-2404. 495 A
nhewitt@wileyc.edu
HEWITT, Russ .... 402-826-8295. 289 E
russ.hewitt@doane.edu
HEWITT, Stephany .... 843-574-6922. 447 E
stephany.hewitt@tridenttech.edu
HEWITT, Thomas .... 650-738-4313... 64 D
hewitt@smccd.edu
HEWITT BOYD, Kimberly .... 612-624-9547. 264 G
boyd009@umn.edu
HEWITT-CLARKE, Gail .... 301-295-1667. 545 C
gail.hewitt-clarke@usuhs.edu
HEWITT WATKINS, Sharon .... 718-990-3369. 339 A
hewittws@stjohns.edu
HEWLETT, Fannie .... 423-697-4456. 460 C
HEXTER, Ralph, J .... 530-752-4964... 70 J
provost@ucdavis.edu
HEY, Jeanne .... 207-602-2371. 213 A
Jhey@une.edu
HEYDARI, Shahryar .... 706-778-8500. 130 E
sheydari@piedmont.edu
HEYE, Nick .... 858-653-6740... 49 C
HEYER, Cary, R .... 608-246-6443. 540 C
cheyer@madisoncollege.edu
HEYER, Doreen, E .... 213-738-6801... 68 C
academicadmin@swlaw.edu
HEYING, Lori .... 319-363-8213. 181 C
lheying@mtmercy.edu
HEYING, Steve .... 210-829-6023. 490 A
lindaw@uiwtx.edu
HEYMAN, George .... 585-271-3657. 338 D
gheyman@stbernards.edu

HEYMAN, Jeffrey 510-466-7369 58 I jheyman@peralta.edu
HEYMAN, Jeffrey 510-466-7369 59 A jheyman@peralta.edu
HEYMAN, Jeffrey 510-436-2419 59 D jheyman@peralta.edu
HEYMANN, Jody 310-825-6381 71 C jheymann@ucla.edu
HEYNDERICKX, Roy, F 360-438-4307 522 G president@stmartin.edu
HEYNING, Katharina, E 262-472-1101 538 D heyningk@uww.edu
HEYWARD, Elijah 703-812-4757 506 H eheyward@leland.edu
HEYWARD, ILene 340-693-1101 555 E iheywar@live.uvi.edu
HEYWARD, Kerry, L 404-413-0500 126 E kheyward@gsu.edu
HEYWARD, Loretta 912-358-3049 131 C heywardl@savannahstate.edu
HIATT, Aaron 415-433-9200 65 C ahiatt@saybrook.edu
HIATT, Edwin, L 229-333-5886 134 B elhiatt@valdosta.edu
HIATT, Elaine 614-825-6255 373 G ehiatt@aiam.edu
HIATT, Jim 615-248-1256 462 D Jhiatt@trevecca.edu
HIATT, Jon 605-331-6636 452 D jon.hiatt@usiouxfalls.edu
HIBBARD, Steve, V 262-243-5700 532 H steve.hibbard@cuw.edu
HIBBARD, Susan 239-489-9013 101 O shibbard@edison.edu
HIBBERD, Charles 402-472-2966 292 I hibberd@unl.edu
HIBBERT-JONES, Karla 937-512-4573 388 O karla.hibbert-jones@sinclair.edu
HIBBS, Anthony 216-485-0900 381 S
HIBBS, Joseph, L 856-691-8600 301 A jhibbs@cccnj.edu
HIBBS, Randy 920-206-2318 533 U rhibbs@mbbc.edu
HIBBS, Thomas, S 254-710-7689 467 G thomas_hibbs@baylor.edu
HIBLER, Dirk 904-819-6336 103 E dhibler@flagler.edu
HIBNER, Lisa 225-216-8244 202 H hibnerl@mybrcc.edu
HICE, Muriel 269-488-4410 244 L mhice@kvcc.edu
HICHWA, Richard, D 319-335-2106 175 I richard-hichwa@uiowa.edu
HICKE, Linda, A 512-471-3285 491 C cnsdean@austin.utexas.edu
HICKERSON, Amanda 502-447-1000 199 E ahickerson@spencerian.edu
HICKERSON, Jim 812-866-6741 166 C hickerson@hanover.edu
HICKEY, Bill 320-363-5480 254 J whickey@csbsju.edu
HICKEY, David 513-569-1448 376 L david.hickey@cincinnatistate.edu
HICKEY, Dean 617-243-2141 227 K dhickey@lasell.edu
HICKEY, Dean, J 508-373-9520 223 A dean.hickey@becker.edu
HICKEY, Diane 678-891-2304 125 G diane.hickey@gpc.edu
HICKEY, Jay 401-841-6515 545 A
HICKEY, John, M 253-879-3203 524 F hickey@pugetsound.edu
HICKEY, Lynn 210-458-4444 492 C lynn.hickey@utsa.edu
HICKEY, Melissa 845-675-4424 335 C melissa.hickey@nyack.edu
HICKEY, JR., Robert, E 937-775-3326 393 G robert.hickey@wright.edu
HICKEY, Thomas, F 312-915-7796 151 H thickey@luc.edu
HICKL, Frank 979-230-3157 468 A frank.hickl@brazosport.edu
HICKMAN, Carla 314-889-1416 274 E chickman@fontbonne.edu
HICKMAN, Heather 415-749-4540 62 G hhickman@sfai.edu
HICKMAN, Lauren 916-961-8727 61 B
HICKMAN, Melissa 317-931-2311 165 B mhickman@cts.edu
HICKMAN, Randall 586-445-7866 246 A hickmanr@macomb.edu
HICKMAN, Saeedah 718-960-8357 318 A saeedah.hickman@lehman.cuny.edu
HICKMAN, Thomas, N 803-323-2129 449 G hickmant@winthrop.edu
HICKMAN, Tim 909-558-4532 51 C thickman@llu.edu
HICKMAN, Tom 701-671-2354 372 E tom.hickman@ndscs.edu
HICKMAN, Tracy 386-752-1822 104 G tracy.hickman@fgc.edu
HICKMAN, Wesley 803-777-7440 447 G whickman@mailbox.sc.edu
HICKMAN, Wesley, T 803-777-3478 447 G whickman@mailbox.sc.edu
HICKOX, Chad, E 206-934-5201 523 A chad.hickox@seattlecolleges.edu
HICKS, Ali 505-565-1290 237 A ahicks@stonehill.edu
HICKS, Barbara 928-541-7777 16 B bhicks@ncu.edu
HICKS, Brenda, D 620-229-6387 190 G brenda.hicks@sckans.edu
HICKS, Brian, A 336-734-7191 360 E bhicks@forsythtech.edu
HICKS, Bruce 310-287-4307 52 F hicksbr@wlac.edu
HICKS, Bryan 256-372-4014 1 A byran.hicks@aamu.edu
HICKS, Cheryl 816-414-3700 277 L chicks@mbts.edu
HICKS, David, L 610-292-9852 431 F bishophicks@comcast.net
HICKS, Deanita 870-762-3146 19 K dhicks@smail.anc.edu
HICKS, Debbie, L 757-455-3338 515 H dlhicks@vwc.edu
HICKS, Dennis 765-973-8456 167 G dehicks@iue.edu
HICKS, Douglas 315-228-7222 320 F dhicks@colgate.edu
HICKS, Ed 334-386-7309 3 H ehicks@faulkner.edu
HICKS, Elena 410-617-2251 216 A ehicks@loyola.edu
HICKS, Elizabeth, M 617-253-4090 233 B
HICKS, George 740-588-1379 394 C ghicks@zanestate.edu
HICKS, J. David 423-652-4782 455 I jdhicks@king.edu
HICKS, Janine, M 815-740-2272 162 F jhicks@stfrancis.edu
HICKS, Jim 423-425-4246 463 D jim-hicks@utc.edu
HICKS, Jimmy 691-320-2480 546 B jhicks@comfsm.fm
HICKS, Juanita 678-839-6424 133 I jhicks@westga.edu
HICKS, Jud 806-457-4200 472 G jhicks@fpctx.edu
HICKS, Julia 860-685-2100 92 H jhicks@wesleyan.edu
HICKS, Kelly 918-343-7553 399 C kellyhicks@rsu.edu
HICKS, Kenneth 215-248-7103 413 A hicksk@chc.edu
HICKS, Larry 919-962-2056 368 D larry_hicks@unc.edu
HICKS, LaTosha 828-726-2705 358 E lhicks@cccti.edu
HICKS, Loretta 404-297-9522 126 A hicksl@gptc.edu
HICKS, Marcus 404-297-9522 126 A hicksm@gptc.edu
HICKS, Michael 706-821-8350 130 C mhicks@paine.edu
HICKS, Minora 803-327-7402 442 D mhicks@clintonjuniorcollege.edu
HICKS, Mona, L 561-803-2174 110 B mona_hicks@pba.edu
HICKS, Nancy, W 609-652-4693 305 C nancy.hicks@stockton.edu
HICKS, Ramona 314-977-5028 281 I rhicks1@slu.edu
HICKS, Renee, G 985-493-2556 208 A renee.hicks@nicholls.edu
HICKS, Ronald 847-566-6401 162 G rhicks@usml.edu
HICKS, Sara 978-837-5502 234 A hickss@merrimack.edu
HICKS, Scott, M 434-592-4808 506 I smhicks@liberty.edu
HICKS, Stacey 209-384-6100 54 D stacey.hicks@mccd.edu
HICKS, Terence 936-261-3600 482 F tlhicks@pvamu.edu
HICKS, Terri, L 205-226-4625 2 C thicks@bsc.edu
HICKS, Timothy, J 315-859-4790 325 E thicks@hamilton.edu
HICKS, Virginia 304-876-5712 529 I vhicks@shepherd.edu
HICKS, Wanda 706-355-5160 120 J whicks@athenstech.edu
HICKS, Willie 501-244-5104 19 J willie.hicks@arkansasbaptist.edu
HICKS-GOLDSTEIN, Regan 302-454-3998 93 F regan@dtcc.edu
HICKSON, Cheryl, E 443-412-2129 215 C chickson@harford.edu
HICSWA, Stefani 307-754-6200 543 G Stefani.Hicswa@northwestcollege.edu
HIDALGO, Jeannie 305-220-4120 111 E hrdir@ptcmatt.com
HIDALGO, Lisa 985-448-7939 203 B lisa.hidalgo@fletcher.edu
HIDY, Steve 952-888-4777 263 B shidy@nwhealth.edu
HIEDEMAN, Ann 701-671-2904 372 E ann.hiedeman@ndscs.edu
HIEL, Edwin 619-388-3036 62 D ehiel@sdccd.edu
HIELEMA, Leslie 407-629-7359 104 H lhielema@fit.edu
HIEMENZ, Karen, A 320-308-5017 261 C khiemenz@sctcc.edu
HIEMSTRA, Tricia 805-893-2489 72 B tricia.hiemstra@hr.ucsb.edu
HIERONYMUS, Bob 208-882-1566 138 H bobh@nsa.edu
HIERS, Richard 314-434-4044 273 C richard.hiers@covenantseminary.edu
HIESIGER, Linda 413-585-2231 236 H lhiesige@smith.edu
HIETALA, David 507-431-2250 260 I david.hietala@riverland.edu
HIETALA, Robert 406-994-5523 287 B robert.hietala@montana.edu
HIETAPELTO, Amy 218-726-7281 264 D lsbe@d.umn.edu
HIETSCH, Stephen, C 717-245-1891 414 H hietschs@dickinson.edu
HIETT, David 617-746-1990 227 F david.hiett@hult.edu
HIGA, Jane, H 805-565-6028 76 D jhiga@westmont.edu
HIGA, Milton 808-734-9572 136 E miltonh@hawaii.edu
HIGASHI, Guy 541-485-1780 405 B guyhigashi@newhope.edu
HIGASHI, Lori 541-485-1780 405 B lorihigashi@enewhope.edu
HIGDEM, Julie 763-488-2453 258 F julie.higdem@hennepintech.edu
HIGDON, Albert 573-629-3011 274 J ahigdon@hlg.edu
HIGDON, Hal, L 417-447-2602 279 K higdonh@otc.edu
HIGDON, Jo Ann 310-660-3107 43 B jhigdon@elcamino.edu
HIGDON, Jo Ann 310-660-3670 43 B jhigdon@elcamino.edu
HIGDON, JR., Leo, I 860-439-2666 89 H lhigdon@conncoll.edu
HIGGINBOTHAM, Debra 940-397-4120 476 H debra.higginbotham@mwsu.edu
HIGGINBOTHAM, Karen 212-472-1500 334 B khigginbotham@nysid.edu
HIGGINBOTHOM, Jessica 870-633-4480 21 A jhigginbothom@eacc.edu
HIGGINS, Brenda 660-785-4562 282 L bhiggins@truman.edu
HIGGINS, Dalton 918-335-6865 398 F dhiggins@okwu.edu
HIGGINS, Dawn 603-271-6484 296 C dhiggins@ccsnh.edu
HIGGINS, Elizabeth 518-262-5831 313 D higgine@mail.amc.edu
HIGGINS, Elizabeth 207-780-4632 212 H bhiggins@maine.maine.edu
HIGGINS, Garland 502-597-6760 197 A garland.higgins@kysu.edu
HIGGINS, Kacey 325-670-1368 472 O Kacey.Higgins@hsutx.edu
HIGGINS, Kelly 603-641-7107 297 G khiggins@anselm.edu
HIGGINS, Lisa 716-829-7542 323 D higginsl@dyc.edu
HIGGINS, Margaret 401-341-2205 440 C margaret.higgins@salve.edu
HIGGINS, Mark, M 401-874-4244 440 D markhiggins@uri.edu
HIGGINS, Michael 314-434-4044 273 C mike.higgins@covenantseminary.edu
HIGGINS, Michael, J 203-371-7902 91 C higginsmw@sacredheart.edu
HIGGINS, Peter, J 678-359-5156 127 A phiggins@gordonstate.edu
HIGGINS, Richard, J 518-564-2040 344 B higginrj@plattsburgh.edu
HIGGINS, Ronnell, A 203-432-9455 93 A ronnell.higgins@yale.edu
HIGGINS, Sandra 718-260-5700 319 B shiggins@citytech.cuny.edu
HIGGINS, Sharon 410-617-5025 216 A sbhiggins@loyola.edu
HIGGINS, Tammy 620-235-4240 189 L thiggins@pittstate.edu
HIGGINS, Terri 641-782-1431 182 I thiggins@swcciowa.edu
HIGGINS, Thomas, J 518-564-3013 344 B higgintj@plattsburgh.edu
HIGGINS, Wendy 845-451-1311 322 D w_higgin@culinary.edu
HIGGS, David 601-643-8376 266 F david.higgs@colin.edu
HIGGS, Jessica 309-677-2700 140 I jhiggs@bradley.edu
HIGGS, John 715-422-5356 540 D john.higgs@mstc.edu
HIGGS, Richard 864-596-9021 443 D richard.higgs@converse.edu
HIGGS, Ronnie 831-582-4363 34 B rhiggs@csumb.edu
HIGH, Jon 612-343-3544 262 X jahigh@northcentral.edu
HIGH, Katherine, N 865-974-3843 463 B khigh@tennessee.edu
HIGH, Kaye 606-759-7141 196 B kaye.high@kctcs.edu
HIGH, Sherine 443-627-7808 265 D Sherine.High@waldenu.edu
HIGHAM, Pamela, S 814-332-3576 409 D phigham@allegheny.edu
HIGHERS, Michael 408-270-6490 63 O michael.highers@evc.edu
HIGHLEY, Melinda, C 606-783-2033 198 A m.highley@moreheadstate.edu
HIGHLEY, Tonda, S 845-257-3236 342 B highleyt@newpaltz.edu
HIGHSMITH, Manique 631-370-3300 340 F MHighsmith@sbmelville.edu
HIGHSTREET, Eve 856-227-7200 300 B ehighstreet@camdencc.edu
HIGHTOWER, Barbara 334-244-3202 2 A bhighto1@aum.edu
HIGHTOWER, Darlene 405-744-3555 397 H darlene.hightower@okstate.edu
HIGHTOWER, Diane, D 724-925-4050 437 D higtowerd@wccc.edu
HIGHTOWER, Jennifer 713-221-8978 489 D hightowerj@uhd.edu
HIGHTOWER, Kenneth, R 248-370-3562 248 J hightowe@oakland.edu
HIGHTOWER, Maggie, W 904-632-3357 105 E mhightow@fscj.edu
HIGHTOWER, JR., William, H 276-223-4794 514 F bhightower@wcc.vccs.edu
HIGINBOTHAM, Lynn, E 212-998-4444 334 D lynn.higinbotham@nyu.edu
HIGLEY, David 203-591-5042 90 I dhigley@post.edu
HIGLEY, Natalie 315-386-7014 345 F higleyn@canton.edu
HIGLEY, Natalie, L 315-267-2146 344 C higleynl@potsdam.edu
HIGLEY, Tony 509-434-5123 518 F thigley@ccs.spokane.edu
HIGLEY, Tony 509-434-5123 518 E tony.higley@ccs.spokane.edu
HIGLEY, Tony, D 509-434-5123 518 D thigley@ccs.spokane.edu
HIJLEH, Mark 585-567-9315 326 F mark.hijleh@houghton.edu
HILBERT, Diane 972-238-6250 471 C dhilbert@dcccd.edu
HILBERT, Pamela 910-272-3230 363 B philbert@robeson.edu
HILBRANDS, Steve 616-538-2330 243 A shilbrands@gbcol.edu
HILBUN, Christy 601-477-4058 267 F christy.hilbun@jcjc.edu
HILBURN, Julius 405-325-1826 401 B jhilburn@ou.edu
HILBY, Jim 414-382-6327 531 I jim.hilby@alverno.edu
HILDEBRAND, Jane 563-387-1008 180 M hildebja@luther.edu
HILDEBRAND, Kathryn 334-670-3365 7 H khildebrand@troy.edu
HILDRETH, Holly 304-296-8282 531 F hhildreth@wvjcmorgantown.edu
HILDRETH, James, E 530-752-4460 70 J jekhildreth@ucdavis.edu
HILEMAN, Jeffrey 814-732-1333 428 E jhileman@edinboro.edu
HILES, Dawn 417-873-7614 273 H dhiles@drury.edu
HILES, Dawn 417-873-7303 273 H dhiles@drury.edu
HILES, Jason 602-639-7500 13 S
HILES, Tom 573-882-7703 283 C hilest@missouri.edu
HILGENBRINK, Robert, J 618-235-2700 160 A robert.hilgenbrink@swic.edu
HILGERSOM, Karin, M 845-434-5750 347 A khilgersom@sunysullivan.edu

HILKE, David .... 412-536-1104. 420 A
david.hilke@laroche.edu
HILKE, Jurgen .... 301-846-2401. 214 H
jhilke@frederic.edu
HILL, Alan, P .... 317-738-8062. 165 I
ahill@franklincollege.edu
HILL, Allan .... 610-436-1050. 430 A
ahill@wcupa.edu
HILL, Angeline .... 707-476-4364... 40 H
angeline-hill@redwoods.edu
HILL, Art .... 541-278-5863. 402 C
ahill@bluecc.edu
HILL, Ashley .... 601-477-4039. 267 F
ashley.hill@jcjc.edu
HILL, Breanne .... 405-878-5102. 399 G
bhill@stgregorys.edu
HILL, Brian, W .... 540-231-4000. 504 G
HILL, Calvin .... 508-929-8784. 230 G
chill@worcester.edu
HILL, Catharine, B .... 845-437-7200. 349 G
hill@vassar.edu
HILL, Chris .... 801-581-5605. 496 Q
chill@huntsman.utah.edu
HILL, Christopher, R .... 303-871-2539... 86 B
Christopher.R.Hill@du.edu
HILL, Craig .... 585-389-2591. 332 D
chill0@naz.edu
HILL, Curtis .... 435-865-8621. 497 A
hillc@suu.edu
HILL, Curtis .... 903-785-7661. 478 B
chill@parisjc.edu
HILL, David, R .... 903-566-7028. 492 D
dhill@uttyler.edu
HILL, Deana .... 570-484-2014. 429 B
dhill@lhup.edu
HILL, Deborah .... 435-865-8628. 497 A
hilld@suu.edu
HILL, Deidra, W .... 212-650-5310. 317 D
dhill@ccny.cuny.edu
HILL, Deidra, W .... 301-322-0916. 217 F
dhill@pgcc.edu
HILL, Dennis .... 479-394-7622... 23 B
dhill@rmcc.edu
HILL, Diana .... 770-394-8300. 120 H
diahill@aii.edu
HILL, Diane .... 973-353-1630. 306 D
dianeh@andromeda.rutgers.edu
HILL, Donna .... 501-337-5000... 20 J
dhill@coto.edu
HILL, Donna .... 502-213-2184. 195 F
donna.hill@kctcs.edu
HILL, Doris .... 651-450-3372. 258 H
dhill@inverhills.edu
HILL, Edward .... 478-825-6211. 124 H
HILL, Edward .... 216-687-2135. 377 F
e.hill@urban.csuohio.edu
HILL, Elizabeth .... 360-596-5416. 524 A
bhill@spscc.edu
HILL, Elizabeth, A .... 718-940-5989. 339 B
sehill@sjcny.edu
HILL, Emily .... 503-228-6528. 402 A
ehill@aii.edu
HILL, Erin .... 302-857-6351... 93 C
ehill@desu.edu
HILL, Fitz .... 501-370-4000... 19 J
fitzhill@hotmail.com
HILL, G. Richard .... 801-626-7313. 497 D
grhill@weber.edu
HILL, Gladys .... 205-391-2457..... 6 H
ghill@sheltonstate.edu
HILL, Henderson .... 931-221-6274. 459 B
hillh@apsu.edu
HILL, Ira .... 305-534-7050. 117 E
ryhill@talmudicu.edu
HILL, Janeen .... 714-628-7318... 38 A
jhill@chapman.edu
HILL, Jean .... 505-454-3562. 310 E
jlhill@nmhu.edu
HILL, Jeannie .... 309-268-8061. 146 B
jeannie.hill@heartland.edu
HILL, Jeff .... 630-743-0710. 163 C
jhill@westwood.edu
HILL, Jennifer .... 256-352-8032..... 9 G
jennifer.hill@wallacestate.edu
HILL, Joanna .... 813-620-1446. 105 O
HILL, John .... 256-726-7346..... 6 B
jhill@oakwood.edu
HILL, Karen .... 252-577-6223. 361 F
khill@lenoircc.edu
HILL, Kelly .... 352-588-7560. 112 D
kelly.hill02@saintleo.edu
HILL, Ken .... 207-801-5630. 210 A
khill@coa.edu
HILL, Ken .... 678-915-6827. 132 C
khill@spsu.edu
HILL, Kirby .... 580-628-6789. 396 M
kirby.tickel@noc.edu
HILL, Laqueta .... 870-850-8632... 23 E
lhill@seark.edu
HILL, Laura .... 208-769-3272. 138 I
ljhill2@nic.edu
HILL, Leah .... 252-985-5291. 365 D
lhill@ncwc.edu
HILL, Leon .... 215-641-6674. 424 B
hlhill@mc3.edu
HILL, Linda .... 207-941-7154. 210 B
hilll@husson.edu
HILL, Marie .... 617-587-5678. 234 H
hillm@neco.edu
HILL, Marion, A .... 214-333-5261. 470 D
marion@dbu.edu
HILL, Marty .... 336-887-3000. 355 N
mhill@laureluniversity.edu
HILL, Mary .... 202-806-5431... 95 G
marhill@howard.edu
HILL, Mathew, B .... 651-631-5362. 263 A
mbhill@nwc.edu
HILL, Melissa .... 509-865-0411. 520 D
hill_m@heritage.edu
HILL, Michael .... 610-328-8067. 433 I
mhill1@swarthmore.edu
HILL, Michelle, D .... 757-823-8531. 507 M
mdhill@nsu.edu
HILL, Mike .... 661-824-2977... 55 I
HILL, Nelson, W .... 585-594-6944. 337 K
hill_nelson@roberts.edu
HILL, Nicole .... 707-654-1275... 31 I
nhill@csum.edu
HILL, Pamela .... 978-665-3515. 229 E
phill@fitchburgstate.edu
HILL, Patricia, L .... 334-271-1670..... 6 C
phill@princeinstitute.edu
HILL, Paul, L .... 304-558-0699. 529 C
paul.hill@hepc.wvnet.edu
HILL, Ralph .... 870-762-3159... 19 K
rhill@smail.anc.edu
HILL, Reinhold .... 708-534-4101. 145 F
rhill@govst.edu
HILL, Ricardo .... 513-772-9888. 386 C
ricardo.hill@omw.edu
HILL, Rick .... 252-222-6153. 358 G
hillr@carteret.edu
HILL, Robert .... 701-777-2674. 371 C
robert.hill@und.edu
HILL, Robert, A .... 617-353-3560. 224 D
rahill@bu.edu
HILL, Robert, R .... 716-888-2758. 316 C
hill52@canisius.edu
HILL, Robert, W .... 936-468-3501. 482 A
rhill@sfasu.edu
HILL, S. Trent .... 361-825-5749. 483 F
trent.hill@tamucc.edu
HILL, Sam .... 703-878-5778. 513 C
shill@nvcc.edu
HILL, Scott .... 540-985-4693. 506 G
bshill@jchs.edu
HILL, Sean .... 618-468-6000. 150 G
shill@lc.edu
HILL, Seddrick .... 919-719-8850. 366 E
shill@shawu.edu
HILL, Shannon .... 805-546-3279... 42 C
shannon_hill@cuesta.edu
HILL, Sharon, F .... 781-891-2108. 223 C
shill@bentley.edu
HILL, Sheila .... 706-771-4840. 121 D
shill@augustatech.edu
HILL, Sherry, A .... 334-271-1670..... 6 C
shill@princeinstitute.edu
HILL, Shirley .... 901-435-1450. 455 M
shirley_hill@loc.edu
HILL, Stephanie, C .... 702-651-3144. 294 E
stephanie.hill@csn.edu
HILL, Stephen, E .... 801-422-4104. 495 D
steve_hill@byu.edu
HILL, Thomas, L .... 515-294-4420. 175 H
tomhill@iastate.edu
HILL, Travis, R .... 315-859-4023. 325 E
thill@hamilton.edu
HILL, Valerie, D .... 512-505-3060. 473 G
vdhill@htu.edu
HILL, Vicki .... 918-647-1373. 394 I
vhill@carlalbert.edu
HILL, W. Timothy .... 801-422-7011. 495 D
wthill@byu.edu
HILL, W. Weldon .... 804-524-5997. 515 D
whill@vsu.edu
HILL, Walter, A .... 334-727-8157..... 8 A
hillwa@mytu.tuskegee.edu
HILL, Wanda .... 513-921-9856. 376 H
wanda.hill@chatfield.edu
HILL, Wayne, R .... 330-972-2148. 390 E
whill@uakron.edu
HILL, Wendy, L .... 610-330-5066. 420 D
hillw@lafayette.edu
HILL, William .... 732-571-3580. 303 C
hill@monmouth.edu
HILL, William, E .... 904-256-7345. 107 Q
whill@ju.edu
HILL, II, William, L .... 215-965-4022. 424 D
whill@moore.edu
HILL, Willie, L .... 413-545-3517. 228 F
drwhill@aol.com
HILL, Wynn, N .... 208-496-9204. 137 H
hillw@byui.edu
HILL-CHEATOM, Petrina . 716-851-1120. 323 I
cheatom@ecc.edu
HILL-CLARKE, Kandi ...... 812-237-2919. 167 A
kandi.hill-clarke@indstate.edu
HILL-FLANAGAN,
LaVerne, M .... 202-274-6069... 97 A
lflanagan@udc.edu
HILL GETZ, Janet .... 309-268-8175. 146 B
janet.hill-getz@heartland.edu
HILL-MILLER, Katherine . 516-299-2234. 329 D
katherine.hill-miller@liu.edu
HILLARD, Jan .... 859-572-7528. 198 I
hillardj1@nku.edu
HILLE, Jim .... 817-257-7031. 484 I
j.hille@tcu.edu
HILLEARY, Sherry .... 816-322-0110. 271 O
sherry.hilleary@calvary.edu
HILLEBRAND, Karen .... 248-689-8282. 251 I
khillebr@walshcollege.edu
HILLENBRAND, Bruce .... 845-451-1286. 322 D
b_hillen@culinary.edu
HILLER, Jerry .... 315-279-5244. 328 D
jhiller@mail.keuka.edu
HILLER, Melissa .... 301-687-4341. 220 C
HILLER-FREUND,
Darby, L .... 231-995-1084. 248 B
dhiller@nmc.edu
HILLERMAN, Donnie .... 660-359-3948. 279 H
dhillerman@mail.ncmissouri.edu
HILLERY, Barbara .... 516-876-3915. 343 D
hilleryb@oldwestbury.edu
HILLES, Sharon .... 909-869-3261... 32 G
shilles@csupomona.edu
HILLESHEIM, Gwen .... 312-752-2094. 149 E
gwen.hillesheim@kendall.edu
HILLIAR, Mara, M .... 804-594-1570. 512 G
mhilliar@jtcc.edu
HILLIARD, Aaron .... 231-777-0447. 247 G
aaronhilliard@muskegoncc.edu
HILLIARD, Beth .... 859-256-3100. 194 I
beth.hilliard@kctcs.edu
HILLIARD, Colette .... 903-675-6306. 488 D
chilliard@tvcc.edu
HILLIARD, Danny, C .... 405-325-0311. 401 B
dhilliard@ou.edu
HILLIARD, Dianne .... 775-445-3288. 295 A
dianne.hilliard@wnc.edu
HILLIS, Greg .... 575-439-3624. 310 J
ghillis@nmsu.edu
HILLMAN, Amy .... 480-965-3402... 11 K
amy.hillman@asu.edu
HILLMAN, Brenda .... 925-631-4457... 61 F
bhillman@stmarys-ca.edu
HILLMAN, Elizabeth, L ... 415-565-4682... 71 A
hillmane@uchastings.edu
HILLMAN, Melinda .... 865-481-2000. 461 E
hillmanmk@roanestate.edu
HILLS, Fred .... 254-299-8000. 476 D
fhills@mclennan.edu
HILLS, Jim .... 206-546-4634. 523 F
jhills@shoreline.edu
HILLS, Stacey .... 802-442-5427. 500 D
shills@svc.edu
HILLS, Warren .... 269-387-3895. 252 I
warren.hills@wmich.edu
HILLSTOCK, Laurie .... 864-644-5038. 446 I
lhillstock@swu.edu
HILLYER, Jill .... 336-334-4079. 369 A
jill_hillyer@uncg.edu
HILPERTS, Jeffrey .... 251-380-2290..... 7 D
jhilperts@shc.edu
HILSABECK, Alison .... 847-947-5065. 153 I
ahilsabeck@nl.edu
HILT, Elizabeth .... 650-433-3818... 58 B
ehilt@paloaltou.edu
HILTERBRAN, Stephen ... 870-543-5907... 23 E
shilterbran@seark.edu
HILTON, Adriel .... 616-331-5051. 243 C
hiltona@gvsu.edu
HILTON, Carol .... 949-582-4872... 67 C
chilton@saddleback.edu
HILTON, Don .... 254-647-3234. 478 H
dhilton@rangercollege.edu
HILTON, III, Earl, M ...... 336-334-7686. 367 E
hiltone@ncat.edu
HILTON, Eric .... 610-399-2100. 428 B
ehilton@cheyney.edu
HILTON, James, L .... 434-924-1432. 511 B
jlh5mc@virginia.edu
HILTON, Linda .... 802-224-3000. 501 A
hiltonl@lsc.vsc.edu
HILTON, Linwood .... 404-752-1663. 129 E
lhilton@msm.edu
HILTON, Richard, H .... 315-697-2300. 349 D
rhilton@uscny.edu
HILTON, Robert, C .... 479-979-1203... 25 J
rchilton@mail.ozarks.edu
HILTON, Stacey .... 928-717-7775... 19 H
stacey.hilton@yc.edu
HILTS, Deb, B .... 607-431-4171. 325 F
hiltsd@hartwick.edu
HILVO, Wendy .... 414-326-2337. 532 G
wendy.hilvo@ccon.edu
HILYER, Billy, D .... 334-386-7103..... 3 H
bhilyer@faulkner.edu
HIMBEAULT-TAYLOR,
Simone .... 734-764-5132. 251 C
shtaylor@umich.edu
HIMBER, David .... 212-960-5330. 351 M
himber@yu.edu
HIMES, A.C. (Buddy) ...... 936-468-2801. 482 A
himesac@sfasu.edu
HIMES, Shane, D .... 814-641-3141. 419 H
himess@juniata.edu
HIMLER, Kim, A .... 724-925-4116. 437 D
himlerk@wccc.edu
HIMLEY, Margaret, R ...... 315-443-1137. 347 C
mrhimley@syr.edu
HIMMELBERGER, Jeffrey 508-793-7374. 225 A
jhimmelberer@clarku.edu
HIMMELBERGER,
Stacey, J .... 315-859-4416. 325 E
shimmelb@hamilton.edu
HIMMELSTEIN, Amos ..... 323-259-1347... 56 I
himmelstein@oxy.edu
HIMMELSTEIN, Bree .... 212-517-0540. 330 E
bhimmelstein@mmm.edu
HIMSEL, Christian .... 262-243-5700. 532 H
christian.himsel@cuw.edu
HIMSTEDT, Lucy .... 812-488-2625. 173 H
lh133@evansville.edu
HINCH, Virginia .... 509-359-2329. 519 C
vhinch@ewu.edu
HINCHEE, Jeanne .... 423-697-4721. 460 C
HINCK, Wolfgang .... 212-986-4343. 314 K
wlh@berkeleycollege.edu
HINCK, Wolfgang .... 212-986-4343. 299 D
wlh@berkeleycollege.edu
HINCKER, Larry .... 540-231-5396. 515 C
hincker@vt.edu
HINCKLEY, Richard .... 702-651-7488. 294 E
richard.hinckley@csn.edu
HINCKLEY, Shane .... 979-845-2217. 483 C
shane.hinckley@tamu.edu
HIND, Jonathan, T .... 315-859-4116. 325 E
jhind@hamilton.edu
HINDELEH, Nitsa .... 314-392-2319. 278 B
hindeleh@mobap.edu
HINDERS, Sally .... 208-769-3349. 138 I
sally_hinders@nic.edu
HINDES, Victoria .... 408-741-2020... 75 L
victoria.hindes@westvalley.edu
HINDS, Blayne, E .... 405-530-7507. 395 N
behinds@langston.edu
HINDS, David .... 301-784-5000. 213 B
dhinds@allegany.edu
HINDS, M. Ray .... 813-988-5131. 104 A
hindsr@floridacollege.edu
HINDS, Randy, C .... 770-423-6755. 127 N
rhinds@kennesaw.edu
HINDS, Steven .... 479-619-2220... 22 C
schinds1@nwacc.edu
HINDUS, Myra .... 617-266-1400. 223 D
HINE, Christopher .... 661-336-5040... 49 M
christopher.hine@kccd.edu
HINE, James .... 415-502-3037... 72 A
jhine@finance.ucsf.edu
HINE, Mark, L .... 434-592-3240. 506 I
mhine@liberty.edu
HINE, Suzanne, A .... 423-746-5205. 462 C
shine@twcnet.edu
HINE, Terry .... 203-576-5072... 91 D
thine@stvincentscollege.edu
HINES, Alexander .... 507-457-5597. 262 A
ahines@winona.edu
HINES, Bonnie .... 318-473-6438. 205 A
hines@lsua.edu
HINES, Bradford .... 414-297-6990. 540 E
hinesbe@matc.edu
HINES, Clay, T .... 919-866-5699. 364 G
cthines@waketech.edu
HINES, Cory .... 214-333-5628. 470 D
coryh@dbu.edu
HINES, Craig .... 312-662-4111. 139 F
chines@adler.edu
HINES, Deborah-Harmon 508-856-2444. 229 C
deborah-harmon.hines@umassmed.edu
HINES, Florence, W .... 410-857-2273. 216 E
fhines@mcdaniel.edu
HINES, Jean, C .... 804-289-8181. 510 L
jhines@richmond.edu
HINES, Joseph .... 908-497-4317. 308 B
joseph.hines@ucc.edu
HINES, Kenneth, D .... 919-658-7783. 357 I
dhines@moc.edu
HINES, Lara .... 314-392-2242. 278 B
robeyl@mobap.edu
HINES, Mark .... 978-934-4000. 229 B
Mark_Hines@uml.edu

HINES, Melvin ..... 334-229-4505 ..... 1 D mhines@alasu.edu
HINES, Michelle ..... 661-763-7870 ..... 69 D mhines@taftcollege.edu
HINES, Nancy, A ..... 563-333-6377 ..... 182 B HinesNancyA@sau.edu
HINES, Nancy, G ..... 509-777-4638 ..... 525 F nhines@whitworth.edu
HINES, Odessa ..... 919-546-8268 ..... 366 E ohines@shawu.edu
HINES, Patrick ..... 919-536-7220 ..... 360 B hinesp@durhamtech.edu
HINES, Patti ..... 619-574-6909 ..... 57 E phines@pacificcollege.edu
HINES, Resche ..... 773-995-2549 ..... 141 J rhines@csu.edu
HINES, Ruth ..... 617-427-0600 ..... 232 G rhines@rcc.mass.edu
HINES, JR., Samuel, M ..... 843-953-5007 ..... 442 A sam.hines@citadel.edu
HINES, Scott ..... 650-433-3855 ..... 58 B shines@paloaltou.edu
HINES, Susan ..... 208-459-5826 ..... 138 A shines@collegeofidaho.edu
HINES-FRITTS, Mary Lou, A ..... 816-235-1107 ..... 283 D hinesml@umkc.edu
HINEY, Delaine, S ..... 712-362-0428 ..... 179 E dhiney@iowalakes.edu
HINGA, Gilbert ..... 402-461-7305 ..... 289 I ghinga@hastings.edu
HINGELBERG, Julie ..... 313-664-7494 ..... 241 C julieh@collegeforcreativestudies.edu
HINKEN, Michele ..... 415-458-3726 ..... 42 J michele.hinken@dominican.edu
HINKLE, Adrian ..... 405-789-7661 ..... 400 A Adrian.Hinkle@swcu.edu
HINKLE, Ana ..... 907-834-1623 ..... 11 B ahinkle@pwscc.edu
HINKLE, Barbara ..... 724-838-4206 ..... 433 E hinkle@setonhill.edu
HINKLE, Barbara, C ..... 724-838-4206 ..... 433 E hinkle@setonhill.edu
HINKLE, Bernadette ..... 610-436-2961 ..... 430 A bhinkle@wcupa.edu
HINKLE, Charles, R ..... 407-823-6432 ..... 115 E rhinkle@ucf.edu
HINKLE, Keith ..... 310-506-4893 ..... 50 H keith.hinkle@pepperdine.edu
HINKLE, Lance ..... 405-744-5237 ..... 397 H lance.hinkle@okstate.edu
HINKLE, M, L ..... 620-665-3526 ..... 187 F hinklem@hutchcc.edu
HINKLE, Sandy, L ..... 573-651-2250 ..... 282 B shinkle@semo.edu
HINKLEY, Lisa ..... 847-735-5235 ..... 150 B hinkley@lakeforest.edu
HINKLEY, Richard ..... 434-592-3077 ..... 506 I rdhinkle@liberty.edu
HINKSMAN, Paul ..... 610-543-2500 ..... 96 F
HINKSON, Avis ..... 212-854-3075 ..... 314 G ahinkson@barnard.edu
HINNEN, Jack ..... 205-226-4761 ..... 2 C jhinnen@bsc.edu
HINNEN, Marsha ..... 251-981-3771 ..... 2 I marsha.hinnen@columbiasouthern.edu
HINNERS, Gordon ..... 828-689-1208 ..... 356 F ghinners@mhc.edu
HINOJOSA, Maggie ..... 956-665-2321 ..... 492 B hinojosam@utpa.edu
HINSDALE, Eric ..... 845-451-1323 ..... 322 D e_hinsda@culinary.edu
HINSHAW, Ada Sue ..... 301-295-9002 ..... 545 C adasue.hinshaw@usuhs.edu
HINSHAW, Dana ..... 620-665-3322 ..... 187 F hinshawd@hutchcc.edu
HINSHAW, Garrett, D ..... 828-327-7000 ..... 359 A ghinshaw@cvcc.edu
HINSHAW, Lynn ..... 828-898-3473 ..... 356 A hinshawl@lmc.edu
HINSON, Bobby ..... 850-201-6071 ..... 117 D hinsonb@tcc.fl.edu
HINSON, Danny ..... 865-471-3310 ..... 453 F dhinson@cn.edu
HINSON, David ..... 704-991-0183 ..... 364 C hinsonld@stanly.edu
HINSON, David, J ..... 501-450-1340 ..... 21 E
HINSON, Dianne, B ..... 919-747-0007 ..... 364 G dbhinson@waketech.edu
HINSON, Jane ..... 478-445-4546 ..... 125 A jane.hinson@gcsu.edu
HINSON, Shirley, R ..... 843-953-3096 ..... 443 A hinsons@cofc.edu
HINTERLONG, James, E ..... 804-828-1036 ..... 511 F jehinterlong@vcu.edu
HINTON, Amy, E ..... 601-426-6346 ..... 269 G ahinton@southeasternbaptist.edu
HINTON, Billy, C ..... 713-500-8444 ..... 492 E william.c.hinton@uth.tmc.edu
HINTON, Cheryl ..... 443-352-4489 ..... 218 E chinton@stevenson.edu
HINTON, Don ..... 435-652-7651 ..... 497 E hinton@dixie.edu
HINTON, H. Scott ..... 435-797-2776 ..... 497 B hinton@engineering.usu.edu
HINTON, John, A ..... 252-398-6376 ..... 353 H hintoj@chowan.edu
HINTON, Mary, D ..... 845-569-3203 ..... 332 B mary.hinton@msmc.edu
HINTON, Neil ..... 740-753-7212 ..... 380 K hintonn@hocking.edu
HINTON, Toby, R ..... 770-534-6257 ..... 122 A thinton@brenau.edu
HINTON-RIVERA, Jake ..... 928-524-7662 ..... 16 E jake.hinton-rivera@npc.edu
HINTY, Danny ..... 614-222-3224 ..... 378 A dhinty@ccad.edu
HINTZ, Carol ..... 816-235-1621 ..... 283 D hintzc@umkc.edu
HINTZ, Debra ..... 704-406-3973 ..... 354 C dhintz@gardner-webb.edu
HINTZ, Lynn ..... 863-784-7105 ..... 113 G lynn.hintzl@southflorida.edu
HINTZ, Nancy, L ..... 920-748-8346 ..... 535 J hintzn@ripon.edu
HINTZ, Sharon ..... 908-835-2356 ..... 308 G hintz@warren.edu
HINZ, James ..... 770-593-2257 ..... 127 B jahinz@gupton-jones.edu
HINZ, Laurence, A ..... 505-473-6234 ..... 311 K president@santafeuniversity.edu
HINZMAN, Larry ..... 907-474-7331 ..... 10 I ldhinzman@alaska.edu
HIPES, Mark ..... 276-326-4208 ..... 502 H mhipes@bluefield.edu
HIPOL, Ana ..... 408-848-4720 ..... 45 F ahipol@gavilan.edu
HIPOLITO, Veronica ..... 928-226-4334 ..... 13 B veronica.hipolito@coconino.edu
HIPONIA, Lorenzo, S ..... 202-231-8785 ..... 544 L lorenzo.hiponia@dodiis.mil
HIPP, Joye, G ..... 803-786-3178 ..... 443 B joyehipp@columbiasc.edu
HIPP, Kathleen ..... 603-577-6659 ..... 296 F hipp@dwc.edu
HIPPLE, Andrew ..... 717-757-1100 ..... 438 H andy.hipple@yti.edu
HIPPLER, Stanley ..... 337-475-5181 ..... 207 G stan@mcneese.edu
HIPPOLITE WRIGHT, Debbie ..... 808-675-3799 ..... 135 C debbie.hippolite.wright@byuh.edu
HIPPS, OSB, Norman, W ..... 724-805-2271 ..... 432 G norman.hipps@email.stvincent.edu
HIPPS, Suzanne ..... 602-243-8153 ..... 15 F suzanne.hipps@smcmail.maricopa.edu
HIRA, Tahira, K ..... 515-294-2745 ..... 175 H tkhira@iastate.edu
HIRAK, Joe ..... 802-728-1283 ..... 501 F
HIRALDO, Rafael ..... 787-863-2390 ..... 550 C rafael.hiraldo@fajardo.inter.edu
HIRAMOTO, Patti ..... 831-582-3366 ..... 34 B phiramoto@csumb.edu
HIRATA, Heather ..... 808-974-7636 ..... 136 A hiratah@hawaii.edu
HIRD, Lon ..... 605-367-7284 ..... 452 C lon.hird@southeasttech.edu
HIRDLER, Joy, L ..... 707-965-6232 ..... 57 J jhirdler@puc.edu
HIRE, Jack ..... 740-587-5698 ..... 379 D hire@denison.edu
HIRLEMAN, E. Daniel ..... 209-228-4021 ..... 71 D dhirleman@UCMerced.edu
HIRNEISEN, Deborah ..... 610-917-2003 ..... 436 C dghirneisen@vfcc.edu
HIRNER, Leo, J ..... 816-604-4501 ..... 277 C leo.hirner@mcckc.edu
HIROKAWA, Randy ..... 808-974-7300 ..... 136 A randyh@hawaii.edu
HIROKO, Tezuko ..... 269-927-8100 ..... 245 D tezuko@lakemichigancollege.edu
HIRONAKA-JUTEAU, Jody ..... 559-278-4004 ..... 33 D jhironak@csufresno.edu
HIRSCH, Andrew, H ..... 570-577-3698 ..... 411 A andy.hirsch@bucknell.edu
HIRSCH, Deborah ..... 408-554-4113 ..... 64 M dhirsch@scu.edu
HIRSCH, Deborah ..... 563-876-3353 ..... 177 I dhirsch@dwci.edu
HIRSCH, Deborah ..... 617-928-4730 ..... 234 E dhirsch@mountida.edu
HIRSCH, Glenn ..... 612-624-4390 ..... 264 G ghirsch@umn.edu
HIRSCH, Jerry, A ..... 413-782-1247 ..... 238 A jhirsch@wne.edu
HIRSCH, Linda, R ..... 563-333-6296 ..... 182 B HirschLindaR@sau.edu
HIRSCH, Michele ..... 718-489-5202 ..... 338 G mhirsch@sfc.edu
HIRSCH, Robert ..... 941-405-1500 ..... 420 E rhirsch@lecom.edu
HIRSCH, Samuel ..... 215-751-8160 ..... 413 I shirsch@ccp.edu
HIRSCH, Tom ..... 641-472-1170 ..... 180 N thirsch@mum.edu
HIRSCHBECK, Denise, R ..... 314-935-5320 ..... 284 L dhirschbeck@wustl.edu
HIRSCHFIELD, Michael, T ..... 262-472-1633 ..... 538 D hirschfm@uww.edu
HIRSCHY, Margaret ..... 419-434-4260 ..... 393 D hirschym@findlay.edu
HIRSH, Barbara ..... 215-576-0800 ..... 431 E bhirsh@rrc.edu
HIRSH, Deborah, D ..... 714-438-4707 ..... 39 H dhirsh@mail.cccd.edu
HIRSH, Haym ..... 607-255-9188 ..... 322 A cis-dean@cornell.edu
HIRSHMAN, Elliot ..... 619-594-5201 ..... 35 D presidents.office@sdsu.edu
HIRSHON, Arnold ..... 216-368-5292 ..... 375 J arnold.hirshon@case.edu
HIRST, Martha, K ..... 718-990-3250 ..... 339 A hirstm@stjohns.edu
HIRST, Thomas, M ..... 845-451-1904 ..... 322 D t_hirst@culinary.edu
HIRT, E. Jill ..... 610-861-5421 ..... 425 D jhirt@northampton.edu
HIRTLE, Christopher ..... 413-572-5455 ..... 230 F chris@westfield.ma.edu
HISAMOTO, Masashi ..... 773-834-2500 ..... 160 I hisamoto@ttic.edu
HISCANO, Lisa ..... 908-965-2358 ..... 308 B hiscano@ucc.edu
HISE, Paul ..... 806-720-7279 ..... 476 B paul.hise@lcu.edu
HISER, Larry, R ..... 740-376-4665 ..... 383 E larry.hiser@marietta.edu
HISEY, Richard, M ..... 617-266-1400 ..... 223 D
HISKES, Anne ..... 616-331-8655 ..... 243 C hiskesa@gvsu.edu
HISLE, W. Lee ..... 860-439-2650 ..... 89 H wlhis@conncoll.edu
HISLOP, Charli ..... 888-384-0849 ..... 27 E charli@allied.edu
HISRICH, Matt ..... 765-983-1523 ..... 165 G hisrima@earlham.edu
HISS, Nancy ..... 503-699-6242 ..... 404 C nhiss@marylhurst.edu
HISSONG, Kimberly ..... 315-229-5837 ..... 339 F khissong@stlawu.edu
HISTAND, James, L ..... 574-535-7456 ..... 166 A jimlh@goshen.edu
HISTAND, Phillip, C ..... 541-737-9355 ..... 406 A phillip.histand@oregonstate.edu
HITCH, Elizabeth, J ..... 801-321-7122 ..... 496 P ehitch@ushe.edu
HITCHCOCK, Cheryl, Y ..... 443-885-3535 ..... 217 A cheryl.hitchcock@morgan.edu
HITCHCOCK, Claude, E ..... 443-885-3938 ..... 217 A claude.hitchcock@morgan.edu
HITCHCOCK, Eloise ..... 615-547-1351 ..... 454 A ehitchcock@cumberland.edu
HITCHCOCK, Susan ..... 607-255-5147 ..... 322 A sh54@cornell.edu
HITCHCOCK, Walter, T ..... 575-624-8183 ..... 310 H hitchcock@nmmi.edu
HITCHELL, Dan, J ..... 740-368-3351 ..... 387 J djhitche@owu.edu
HITE, Carl ..... 423-478-6200 ..... 460 D chite@clevelandstatecc.edu
HITE, Elinor ..... 312-662-4415 ..... 139 F ehite@adler.edu
HITE, Griffin ..... 256-765-4400 ..... 9 C una@bkstr.com
HITE, Joe ..... 940-552-6291 ..... 493 F jhite@vernoncollege.edu
HITE, Patrick ..... 214-768-2146 ..... 481 A phite@smu.edu
HITE, Robert, D ..... 415-442-7058 ..... 45 I bhite@ggu.edu
HITE, Trudy, E ..... 302-356-6965 ..... 94 E trudy.e.hite@wilmu.edu
HITES, Michael ..... 217-244-0102 ..... 161 C hites@uillinois.edu
HITESMAN, Bill ..... 402-461-2400 ..... 288 I bhitesman@cccneb.edu
HITLIN, Amy ..... 919-760-8521 ..... 356 G hitlina@meredith.edu
HITT, John, C ..... 407-823-1823 ..... 115 E john.hitt@ucf.edu
HITT, Richard, J ..... 863-784-7036 ..... 113 G richard.hitt@southflorida.edu
HITTENBERGER, Jeff ..... 714-556-3610 ..... 74 D officeoftheprovost@vanguard.edu
HITTENMILLER, David ..... 847-543-2824 ..... 143 A dhittenmiller@clcillinois.edu
HITTLE, Dennis, M ..... 309-794-7370 ..... 139 L dennishittle@augustana.edu
HITZ, Randy ..... 503-725-4697 ..... 406 B hitz@pdx.edu
HITZEMAN, John ..... 936-294-1900 ..... 487 A pur_jch@shsu.edu
HIX, Patty ..... 803-754-4100 ..... 443 C
HIXON, Jennifer ..... 413-565-1000 ..... 222 F jhixon@baypath.edu
HIXON, Sharon ..... 706-272-4594 ..... 123 G shixon@daltonstate.edu
HIXSON, Carla ..... 701-224-5580 ..... 372 B carla.hixson@bismarckstate.edu
HIXSON, Carol ..... 727-873-4400 ..... 116 D carol.hixson@nelson.usf.edu
HIXSON, Jana ..... 254-710-1421 ..... 467 G jana_hixson@baylor.edu
HIXSON, John ..... 479-619-4341 ..... 22 C jhixson@nwacc.edu
HIXSON, Paul ..... 217-244-6227 ..... 162 A pch@mx.uillinois.edu
HIYANE-BROWN, Kathi ..... 360-383-3330 ..... 525 D khiyane-brown@whatcom.ctc.edu
HJELLUM, Wilma ..... 402-457-2723 ..... 290 G whjellum@mccneb.edu
HLADEK, Thomas ..... 718-482-5510 ..... 318 F tomhl@lagcc.cuny.edu
HLADIO, Patricia, A ..... 724-738-2044 ..... 429 F patricia.hladio@sru.edu
HLADIS, Jirka ..... 303-245-4702 ..... 83 F jirka@naropa.edu
HLAVENKA, Lawrence ..... 201-689-7057 ..... 299 C lhlavenka@bergen.edu
HLAVIN, Karen ..... 847-543-2384 ..... 143 A khlavin@clcillinois.edu
HLEBOWITSH, Peter ..... 205-348-6052 ..... 8 D peter.hleb@ua.edu
HLINAK, Matthew, J ..... 708-524-6812 ..... 144 C mhlinak@dom.edu
HLINKA, Karen ..... 270-534-3236 ..... 196 G karen.hlinka@kctcs.edu
HLUBB, Emma ..... 931-424-7366 ..... 456 C ehlubb@martinmethodist.edu
HLUBB, James, R ..... 931-424-7379 ..... 456 C jhlubb@martinmethodist.edu
HMIELESKI, Kristin ..... 413-265-2340 ..... 225 C hmieleskik@elms.edu
HMIELEWSKI, Christopher ..... 507-537-7984 ..... 261 F Christopher.Hmielewski@smsu.edu
HMIELEWSKI, Thomas ..... 715-682-1208 ..... 535 D thmielewski@northland.edu
HO, Co ..... 714-992-7020 ..... 56 F cho@fullcoll.edu
HO, John, T ..... 716-645-3786 ..... 341 F proho@buffalo.edu
HO, Katy ..... 808-845-9235 ..... 136 G katyho@hawaii.edu
HO, Peggy ..... 773-442-5143 ..... 154 H k-ho1@neiu.edu
HO, Sam ..... 408-298-2181 ..... 63 N sam.ho@sjeccd.org
HO, Sandra ..... 603-427-7614 ..... 295 K sho@ccsnh.edu
HO, Sue ..... 212-659-3605 ..... 328 E sho@tkc.edu
HOABY, Candy ..... 402-354-7137 ..... 291 B candance.hoaby@methodistcollege.edu
HOADLEY, Diane ..... 715-836-2500 ..... 536 E hoadled@uwec.edu
HOAG, David ..... 847-317-7128 ..... 160 M dhoag@tiu.edu
HOANG, Linh ..... 808-734-9570 ..... 136 E lhoang@hawaii.edu
HOANG, Minh-Ha ..... 619-260-4506 ..... 73 I hoangm@sandiego.edu
HOAR, Robert ..... 608-785-8039 ..... 536 G rhoar@uwlax.edu
HOAR, Tanya, L ..... 906-786-5802 ..... 240 K tanya.hoar@baycollege.edu
HOARD, David ..... 601-979-2282 ..... 267 E david.hoard@jsums.edu
HOARE, William, D ..... 262-551-6200 ..... 532 D whoare@carthage.edu
HOBAN, Elizabeth ..... 973-328-5160 ..... 300 G ehoban@ccm.edu
HOBAN, Kristi, M ..... 817-257-7803 ..... 484 I k.hoban@tcu.edu
HOBAN, Patricia, K ..... 503-375-5477 ..... 408 J phoban@willamette.edu
HOBAN, Theresa, M ..... 315-568-3216 ..... 333 C thoban@nycc.edu
HOBAUGH, Greg ..... 215-572-3848 ..... 437 C ghobaugh@wts.edu
HOBBIE, Lawrence ..... 516-877-3165 ..... 313 A hobbie@adelphi.edu
HOBBS, Clinton, G ..... 706-379-3111 ..... 134 L clinth@yhc.edu
HOBBS, Evelyn ..... 575-527-7630 ..... 311 B erhobbs@nmsu.edu
HOBBS, Harriet ..... 704-378-3572 ..... 355 K hhobbs@jcsu.edu

HOBBS, Harriet ... 910-879-5516. 358 B
hhobbs@bladencc.edu
HOBBS, Henry ... 912-588-2579. 120 B
hhobbs@altamahatech.edu
HOBBS, Jeanie ... 817-598-6267. 494 G
hobbs@wc.edu
HOBBS, Jeremy ... 415-351-3536... 62 G
jhobbs@sfai.edu
HOBBS, Marcia, B ... 270-809-2196. 198 B
mhobbs4@murraystate.edu
HOBBS, Nancy, A ... 734-764-7254. 251 C
hobbsn@umich.edu
HOBBS, Pamelia, C ... 336-322-2120. 362 F
Pam.Hobbs@piedmontcc.edu
HOBBS, Patrick, E ... 973-642-8750. 307 D
patrick.hobbs@shu.edu
HOBBS, Patrick, J ... 973-642-8750. 307 C
patrick.hobbs@shu.edu
HOBBS, Phillip, M ... 205-853-1200... 5 B
mhobbs@jeffstateonline.com
HOBBS, Rose ... 518-438-3111. 330 C
roseh@mariacollege.edu
HOBBY, Angela ... 229-333-5365. 134 K
angela.hobby@wiregrass.edu
HOBBY-MEARS,
Michelle ... 949-480-4134... 66 F
mhobby@soka.edu
HOBDY, Gerri ... 225-216-8401. 202 H
hobdyg@mybrcc.edu
HOBERMAN, Chaim ... 516-225-4700. 337 C
HOBIN, Caron, T ... 413-565-1333. 222 F
chobin@baypath.edu
HOBIN, Gail ... 617-287-5310. 228 G
gail.hobin@umb.edu
HOBLER, Dean ... 419-227-3141. 391 F
dahobler@unoh.edu
HOBLET, Kent, H ... 662-325-1418. 268 D
hoblet@cvm.msstate.edu
HOBLICK, Dave ... 303-753-6046... 85 B
dhoblick@rmcad.edu
HOBSON, James ... 703-284-1617. 507 B
bing.hobson@marymount.edu
HOBSON, Lynn, M ... 620-341-5267. 186 D
lhobson@emporia.edu
HOBSON, Paula Lee ... 775-674-7686. 294 H
phobson@tmcc.edu
HOBSON, Sheila ... 301-860-3451. 220 A
shobson@bowiestate.edu
HOBSON, Tricia ... 405-422-1263. 399 B
hobsont@redlandscc.edu
HOBYAK, Michael, S ... 215-785-0111. 426 X
HOCHANADEL, Gery ... 972-438-6932. 478 C
ghochanadel@parkercc.edu
HOCHRADEL, Ted ... 662-846-4745. 266 G
thochradel@deltastate.edu
HOCHSCHILD, Joshua ... 301-447-7435. 217 B
hochschild@msmary.edu
HOCHSTEIN, Dale ... 201-761-7827. 306 L
dhochstein@saintpeters.edu
HOCK, Amy ... 402-471-2505. 291 C
ahock@nscs.edu
HOCK, Joan ... 215-489-2975. 414 E
Joan.Hock@delval.edu
HOCKENBERRY,
Frederick ... 301-846-2544. 214 H
fhockenberry@frederick.edu
HOCKENHULL,
Benjamin, R ... 512-448-8688. 479 C
ben@stedwards.edu
HOCKENSMITH, William 805-922-6966... 26 K
whockensmith@hancockcollege.edu
HOCKETT, Anne, B ... 336-633-0218. 362 H
abhockett@randolph.edu
HOCKING, Eileen ... 860-231-5308... 92 F
ehocking@usj.edu
HOCKMAN, Joan ... 814 371 2090. 434 F
jhockman@triangle-tech.edu
HOCKSTRA, Dale ... 650-543-3874... 54 C
dhockstra@menlo.edu
HOCQUARD, Stephen, L 989-964-4081. 249 G
shoc@svsu.edu
HOCUTT, Kirby ... 806-742-3355. 487 D
kirby.hocutt@ttu.edu
HOCUTT, Martha ... 205-652-3675... 9 F
mhocutt@uwa.edu
HODGE, Brad, K ... 215-670-9210. 425 J
bkhodge@peirce.edu
HODGE, Charles ... 937-484-1256. 392 C
chodge@urbana.edu
HODGE, David ... 513-529-2345. 384 G
president@miamioh.edu
HODGE, David ... 334-291-4928... 2 H
david.hodge@cv.edu
HODGE, David ... 978-478-3400. 235 G
dhodge@northpoint.edu
HODGE, Evelyn ... 334-229-4139... 1 D
ehodge@alasu.edu
HODGE, Gary, B ... 972-881-5897. 469 G
ghodge@collin.edu
HODGE, Jessica ... 212-752-1530. 328 G
jessica.hodge@limcollege.edu
HODGE, Jimmer ... 218-262-6705. 258 G
jimmerhodge@hibbing.edu
HODGE, Johnesa ... 313-496-2796. 252 B
jdimick1@wcccd.edu
HODGE, Marilyn ... 757-822-7244. 514 C
mhodge@tcc.edu
HODGE, Michel, A ... 718-262-2707. 319 F
mahodge@york.cuny.edu
HODGE, Mildred ... 860-885-2344... 89 F
mhodge@trcc.commnet.edu
HODGE, Tiffani ... 404-523-8520. 132 E
thodge3@spelman.edu
HODGE-HENRY, Harriet . 617-282-9798. 272 D
harriet@techmission.org
HODGEN, Danielle ... 509-527-4301. 524 H
danielle.hodgen@wwcc.edu
HODGES, Carolyn, R ... 865-974-3694. 463 C
chodges@utk.edu
HODGES, Christopher ... 215-893-5262. 414 B
christopher.hodges@curtis.edu
HODGES, Dale, B ... 269-471-3321. 239 D
dbhodges@andrews.edu
HODGES, Daniel, K ... 540-365-4365. 504 L
dhodges@ferrum.edu
HODGES, Dawn ... 770-229-3293. 132 B
dhodges@sctech.edu
HODGES, Elaine ... 843-661-8020. 443 G
elaine.hodges@fdtc.edu
HODGES, Greg ... 276-656-0213. 513 D
ghodges@patrickhenry.edu
HODGES, Heath ... 918-463-2931. 395 D
heath.hodges@connorsstate.edu
HODGES, Jeff ... 540-362-6503. 505 G
jhodges@hollins.edu
HODGES, Jill ... 906-487-3310. 247 A
jhodges@mtu.edu
HODGES, Jimmy ... 256-352-8229... 9 G
jimmy.hodges@wallacestate.edu
HODGES, Mike ... 423-472-7141. 460 D
MHodges@clevelandstatecc.edu
HODGES, Omega ... 828-298-3325. 370 E
ohodges@warren-wilson.edu
HODGES, Rhonda ... 276-656-0256. 513 D
rhodges@patrickhenry.edu
HODGES, Richard ... 757-825-2868. 514 B
hodgesr@tncc.edu
HODGES, Ricky, C ... 336-734-7272. 360 E
rhodges@forsythtech.edu
HODGES, Stacey ... 601-276-3708. 269 H
slee@smcc.edu
HODGES, Stephen ... 617-746-1990. 227 F
stephen.hodges@hult.edu
HODGES, Tim ... 785-594-8365. 184 C
tim.hodges@bakeru.edu
HODGES, Tina ... 731-352-4032. 453 D
hodgest@bethelu.edu
HODGES, YLonne ... 912-688-6922. 129 J
yhodges@ogeecheetech.edu
HODGES, Zachary ... 713-718-5721. 473 C
zachary.hodges@hccs.edu
HODGES MOORE, Sue .. 859-572-5349. 198 I
moores4@nku.edu
HODGINS, Diane, W ... 850-729-6485. 109 I
hodginsd@nwfsc.edu
HODGINS, Randy ... 206-221-5670. 524 G
rhodgins@uw.edu
HODGSON, Matt ... 707-826-3321... 35 C
matthodson@humboldt.edu
HODGSON, Regina ... 813-879-6000. 103 B
rhodgson@cci.edu
HODNETT, James ... 478-387-4715. 125 E
HODOWANEC, Michael .. 610-372-4721. 431 D
mhodowanec@racc.edu
HODOWNES, Stephen ... 603-645-9730. 297 I
s.hodownes@snhu.edu
HODSDON, Roger ... 626-815-5080... 29 H
rhodsdon@apu.edu
HODSON, April ... 860-701-5027... 90 G
hodson_a@mitchell.edu
HODSON, J. Bradford ... 620-235-4757. 189 L
bhodson@pittstate.edu
HODSON, Luke ... 859-985-3503. 192 F
hodsonl@berea.edu
HODUM, Robert ... 931-372-3888. 460 A
rhodum@tntech.edu
HOECK, Andreas ... 303-715-3218... 85 D
HOEF, Ted ... 314-968-6980. 284 N
hoeftl@webster.edu
HOEFFNER, Denise ... 785-309-3100. 190 E
denise.hoeffner@salinatech.edu
HOEFLER, William ... 479-968-0353... 20 E
whoeflerjr@atu.edu
HOEFT, Robert ... 217-333-9480. 162 A
rhoeft@illinois.edu
HOEG, Portia ... 814-332-3350. 409 D
phoeg@allegheny.edu
HOEGE, Jennifer, L ... 608-246-6944. 540 C
jlhoege@madisoncollege.edu
HOEH, Susan ... 407-888-8689. 104 B
shoeh@fcim.edu
HOEHN, Alex, J ... 718-990-2998. 339 A
hoehna@stjohns.edu
HOEHNKE, Diane ... 414-443-8627. 539 F
diane.hoehnke@wlc.edu
HOEKSTRA, Erik ... 712-722-6002. 177 J
erik.hoekstra@dordt.edu
HOEKSTRA, Jonathan ... 254-867-4892. 485 G
jonathan.hoekstra@systems.tstc.edu
HOEL, Aaron ... 301-687-3101. 220 C
ahoel@frostburg.edu
HOEL, Monica, S ... 276-944-6126. 504 H
mshoel@ehc.edu
HOELLEN, Kathy, L ... 803-981-7150. 449 J
khoellen@yorktech.edu
HOELSCHER, Ronda ... 325-793-4857. 476 E
hoelscher.ronda@mcm.edu
HOELTGE, Patricia ... 212-752-1530. 328 G
patricia.hoeltge@limcollege.edu
HOELTING, Floyd, B ... 512-471-8631. 491 C
floydh@austin.utexas.edu
HOELTZEL, Susan ... 718-960-8731. 318 A
susan.hoeltzel@lehman.cuny.edu
HOEMANN, D. Lee ... 360-867-6300. 519 J
hoemannl@evergreen.edu
HOEMANN, George ... 217-228-5432. 156 C
hoemage@quincy.edu
HOEPFER, Maureen, G ... 717-780-1157. 417 I
mhoepfer@hacc.edu
HOEPP, Michael ... 315-781-3309. 326 C
hoepp@hws.edu
HOEPPNER, Stephen, A . 651-962-6949. 265 C
sahoeppner@stthomas.edu
HOERITZ, Kim ... 412-396-6213. 415 F
hoeritzk@duq.edu
HOERSCH, Alice, L ... 215-951-1010. 420 B
hoersch@lasalle.edu
HOERST, Barbara ... 215-951-1386. 420 B
hoerst@lasalle.edu
HOERTH, Richard ... 920-693-1237. 540 B
rich.hoerth@gotoltc.edu
HOETING, Mark ... 678-891-2830. 125 G
mark.hoeting@gpc.edu
HOEWING, Rodney, E ... 217-333-2034. 162 A
rhoewing@illinois.edu
HOEY, John, T ... 508-999-8002. 229 A
jhoey@umassd.edu
HOEY, Joseph ... 858-513-9240. 175 F
joseph.hoey@ashford.edu
HOFEMANN, Neva ... 408-273-2718... 55 H
nhofemann@nhu.edu
HOFER, Jeanie, H ... 573-341-4208. 284 A
jeanie@mst.edu
HOFER, Linda ... 605-995-2956. 450 A
lihofer@dwu.edu
HOFF, Andrew ... 559-278-2636... 33 D
andrewh@csufresno.edu
HOFF, Brad ... 507-786-3310. 264 B
hoff@stolaf.edu
HOFF, Darren ... 763-433-1159. 257 P
darren.hoff@anokaramsey.edu
HOFF, Dianne ... 678-839-6570. 133 I
dhoff@westga.edu
HOFF, Michael, B ... 423-439-4236. 459 C
HOFF, Reno, R ... 503-375-7000. 403 A
rhoff@corban.edu
HOFFACKER, Thomas, E 270-809-2146. 198 B
thoffacker@murraystate.edu
HOFFARD, Dwight ... 618-985-3741. 148 J
dwighthoffard@jalc.edu
HOFFBAUER, Claudia ... 509-574-4612. 525 G
choffbauer@yvcc.edu
HOFFER, Wallace, C ... 330-966-5450. 389 F
whoffer@starkstate.edu
HOFFMAN, A, P ... 334-556-2225... 3 N
ahoffman@wallace.edu
HOFFMAN, Angela ... 859-336-5082. 198 J
ahoffman@sccky.edu
HOFFMAN, Barbara ... 319-399-8540. 176 G
bhoffman@coe.edu
HOFFMAN, Bart ... 714-564-6800... 60 G
hoffman_bart@sac.edu
HOFFMAN, Beth ... 301-687-4101. 220 C
bhoffman@frostburg.edu
HOFFMAN, Brad ... 513-244-4230. 377 G
brad_hoffman@mail.msj.edu
HOFFMAN, Bryce, T ... 518-564-2090. 344 B
bhoff003@plattsburgh.edu
HOFFMAN, Carolyn, F ... 301-322-0561. 217 F
hoffmacf@pgcc.edu
HOFFMAN, David ... 540-665-5457. 509 E
dhoffman@su.edu
HOFFMAN, Deborah ... 813-935-5700. 111 N
deborahhoffman@remingtoncollege.edu
HOFFMAN, Derek, M ... 717-872-3820. 429 D
derek.hoffman@millersville.edu
HOFFMAN, Donna ... 909-389-3333... 61 K
dhoffman@sbccd.edu
HOFFMAN, Ed ... 402-471-2505. 291 C
ehoffman@nscs.edu
HOFFMAN, Erin ... 847-735-5207. 150 B
hoffman@lakeforest.edu
HOFFMAN, Gail ... 212-854-1079. 321 D
gh2116@columbia.edu
HOFFMAN, Jaime ... 323-259-2500... 56 I
jhoffman@oxy.edu
HOFFMAN, Jay ... 309-438-5677. 147 J
jchoffm@ilstu.edu
HOFFMAN, Jeffrey ... 626-396-2325... 28 P
jeffrey.hoffman@artcenter.edu
HOFFMAN, Jeffrey, L ... 315-255-1743. 316 D
foundation@cayuga-cc.edu
HOFFMAN, John, R ... 215-572-2195. 409 H
hoffmanj@arcadia.edu
HOFFMAN, Joseph, C ... 315-386-7204. 345 F
president@canton.edu
HOFFMAN, Joseph, M ... 301-687-4120. 220 C
jhoffman@frostburg.edu
HOFFMAN, Kyle, D ... 209-228-4400... 71 D
khoffman@UCMerced.edu
HOFFMAN, Larry ... 914-395-2384. 340 E
lhoffman@sarahlawrence.edu
HOFFMAN, Linda, K ... 330-471-8145. 383 D
lhoffman@malone.edu
HOFFMAN, Lorraine, B .. 530-898-6231... 33 A
lbhoffman@csuchico.edu
HOFFMAN, Louis ... 410-484-7200. 217 D
HOFFMAN, Marcia, K ... 570-577-1631. 411 A
marcia.hoffman@bucknell.edu
HOFFMAN, Marion, S ... 850-488-2447. 116 A
marionh@ufl.edu
HOFFMAN, Mark ... 610-341-5935. 415 G
hoffman@eastern.edu
HOFFMAN, SR.,
Martin, A ... 609-894-9311. 299 I
mhoffman@bcc.edu
HOFFMAN, Mary ... 719-587-7372... 78 B
mchoffma@adams.edu
HOFFMAN, Melissa ... 402-354-7212. 291 B
melissa.hoffman@methodistcollege.edu
HOFFMAN, Michael ... 716-375-2530. 338 E
mhoffman@sbu.edu
HOFFMAN, Michael ... 515-965-7130. 177 B
mjhoffman@dmacc.edu
HOFFMAN, Micki, D ... 636-584-6532. 273 M
mdhoffma@eastcentral.edu
HOFFMAN, Mika ... 518-464-8773. 324 B
mhoffman@excelsior.edu
HOFFMAN, Molly ... 740-362-3373. 383 H
mhoffman@mtso.edu
HOFFMAN, Neil, J ... 414-847-3210. 534 F
neilhoffman@miad.edu
HOFFMAN, Paula ... 320-629-5180. 260 F
hoffmanp@pinetech.edu
HOFFMAN, Peter ... 912-877-1906. 120 G
peter.hoffman@armstrong.edu
HOFFMAN, Robert ... 507-389-5566. 259 G
robert.hoffman@mnsu.edu
HOFFMAN, Sandra ... 856-415-2220. 302 C
shoffma2@gccnj.edu
HOFFMAN, Sharon, L ... 802-287-8215. 499 D
hoffmans@greenmtn.edu
HOFFMAN, Sharon, L ... 802-287-8216. 499 D
hoffmans2@greenmtn.edu
HOFFMAN, Sonia ... 336-272-7102. 354 E
sonia.hoffman@greensboro.edu
HOFFMAN, Steven, A ... 859-236-6688. 193 E
steven.hoffman@centre.edu
HOFFMAN, Thomas ... 507-453-2770. 259 E
thoffman@southeastmn.edu
HOFFMAN, Wendy ... 859-846-5364. 197 I
whoffman@midway.edu
HOFFMANN, Len ... 563-589-0322. 183 F
lhoffmann@wartburgseminary.edu
HOFFMANN, Lowell ... 731-286-3307. 460 F
hoffmann@dscc.edu
HOFFMANN, Mark ... 701-777-2492. 371 C
mark.hoffmann@und.edu
HOFFMANN, Pauline ... 716-375-2578. 338 E
hoffmann@sbu.edu
HOFFMANN, Phylis ... 501-205-8813... 20 I
phoffmann@cbc.edu
HOFFMANN, Susie ... 785-670-1643. 191 D
susie.hoffmann@washburn.edu
HOFFMANN HARDING,
Erin ... 574-631-7394. 174 A
eharding@nd.edu
HOFFMANS, Kim ... 805-378-1459... 74 F
khoffmans@vcccd.edu
HOFFMEYER, Tom ... 254-710-1561. 467 G
tom_hoffmeyer@baylor.edu
HOFFNUNG, Michele ... 203-582-8903... 91 A
michele.hoffnung@quinnipiac.edu
HOFHERR, Michael ... 614-292-6553. 386 E
hofherr3@osu.edu
HOFMANN, John ... 650-493-4430... 66 E
john.hofmann@sofia.edu
HOFMEISTER, David ... 316-295-5685. 186 H
david_hofmeister@friends.edu
HOFMEYER, Karna ... 712-324-5061. 181 G
khofmeyer@nwicc.edu
HOFNER, Amyjo ... 617-262-5000. 223 F
amyjo.hofner@the-bac.edu

HOFRENNING, Dan .... 507-786-3128. 264 B
dhofrenn@stolaf.edu
HOFRENNING, Ilene .... 508-626-4900. 230 A
ihofrenning@framingham.edu
HOFSTEDT, Petra .... 715-682-1983. 535 D
phofstedt@northland.edu
HOFSTETTER, Dale .... 513-745-8308. 391 A
hofsteda@uc.edu
HOFSTETTER, Martha, J . 302-857-1124... 93 G
mhofste1@dtcc.edu
HOFSTETTER, Shirley, A . 636-584-6704. 273 M
sahofste@eastcentral.edu
HOFTIEZER, David .... 609-984-1164. 308 A
dhoftiezer@tesc.edu
HOGAN, Amy .... 785-242-5200. 189 I
amy.hogan@ottawa.edu
HOGAN, Andrea .... 203-582-5215... 91 A
andrea.hogan@quinnipiac.edu
HOGAN, Barbara .... 215-248-7120. 413 A
hoganb@chc.edu
HOGAN, Beverly, W .... 601-977-7730. 270 A
bhogan@tougaloo.edu
HOGAN, Bill .... 206-296-5451. 523 E
hoganw@seattleu.edu
HOGAN, Brenda .... 478-471-6684. 128 I
brenda.hogan@maconstate.edu
HOGAN, Carrie .... 518-783-2554. 340 J
chogan@siena.edu
HOGAN, Cheryl .... 231-843-5864. 252 H
clhogan@westshore.edu
HOGAN, Christopher ...... 617-287-6800. 228 G
christopher.hogan@umb.edu
HOGAN, Dave .... 334-386-7152..... 3 H
dhogan@faulkner.edu
HOGAN, Heather .... 440-775-8410. 385 H
heather.hogan@oberlin.edu
HOGAN, Jennifer .... 810-767-2150. 251 E
jhogan@umflint.edu
HOGAN, Joan, P .... 828-448-6041. 365 A
jhogan@wpcc.edu
HOGAN, John, T .... 401-865-2676. 439 E
jhogan@providence.edu
HOGAN, Judith .... 781-280-3816. 232 B
hoganj@middlesex.mass.edu
HOGAN, Kay .... 850-973-9422. 109 H
hogank@nfcc.edu
HOGAN, Lesley .... 253-833-9111. 520 C
lhogan@greenriver.edu
HOGAN, Lesley .... 425-235-7872. 522 F
lhogan@rtc.edu
HOGAN, Marianna .... 212-431-2173. 333 I
mhogan@nyls.edu
HOGAN, Martha, A .... 972-238-6210. 471 C
mhogan@dcccd.edu
HOGAN, Pat .... 910-362-7009. 358 F
phogan@cfcc.edu
HOGAN, Patrick, D .... 434-924-3252. 511 B
pdh9t@virginia.edu
HOGAN, Patrick, J .... 301-445-1927. 219 A
pjhogan@usmd.edu
HOGAN, Paul .... 603-271-6484. 296 C
phogan@ccsnh.edu
HOGAN, Phyllis, E .... 317-466-2121. 167 B
pehogan@indianatech.edu
HOGAN, Sean .... 847-543-2419. 143 A
shogan@clcillinois.edu
HOGAN, CSSP, Sean ..... 412-396-5069. 415 F
hogan@duq.edu
HOGAN, Susan, S .... 413-597-4204. 238 D
susan.s.hogan@williams.edu
HOGAN, Terrance, E .... 305-474-6018. 112 F
thogan@stu.edu
HOGAN, Terrence .... 319-273-2332. 176 A
terry.hogan@uni.edu
HOGAN, Tracy .... 415-482-3507... 42 J
tracy.hogan@dominican.edu
HOGAN, William .... 907-786-4407... 10 H
whhogan@uaa.alaska.edu
HOGARTH-SMITH,
Heather .... 340-693-1151. 555 E
hhogart@live.uvi.edu
HOGARTY, Lisa .... 617-495-1512. 227 C
lisa_hogarty@harvard.edu
HOGEBOOM, Cindi .... 510-261-8500... 58 G
cindi.hogeboom@patten.edu
HOGELAND, Beth .... 541-917-4211. 404 B
hogelab@linnbenton.edu
HOGENCAMP, Kelly .... 909-621-8273... 65 D
registrar@ad.scrippscol.edu
HOGENSON, Deborah ..... 952-888-4777. 263 B
dhogenson@nwhealth.edu
HOGG, Matt .... 215-572-3838. 437 C
mhogg@wts.edu
HOGGE, Jane Curley ...... 410-617-2131. 216 A
jchogge@loyola.edu
HOGLUND, Carol .... 307-778-1281. 543 D
choglund@lccc.wy.edu
HOGLUND, Susan .... 740-826-8081. 384 L
shoglund@muskingum.edu
HOGREFE, Richard .... 909-389-3205... 61 K
rhogrefe@craftonhills.edu
HOGSETT, Denise .... 304-696-2370. 529 H
hogsettd@marshall.edu
HOGUE, Belinda .... 334-727-8763..... 8 A
bahoque@mytu.tuskegee.edu
HOGUE, Eileen .... 719-502-2419... 84 A
eileen.hogue@ppcc.edu
HOGUE, Eric .... 916-577-2200... 76 J
ehogue@jessup.edu
HOGUE, Gina .... 870-972-2030... 19 N
ghogue@astate.edu
HOGUE, Jeffery, H .... 417-328-1591. 282 C
jhogue@sbuniv.edu
HOGUE, Michael .... 205-726-2820..... 6 F
mdhogue@samford.edu
HOGUE, Stacey, L .... 501-569-3318... 24 B
slhogue@ualr.edu
HOGUE, William, F .... 803-777-0707. 447 G
hogue@sc.edu
HOGYA, Tiffany .... 330-823-2030. 391 E
hogyata@mountunion.edu
HOHBERG, Tonian .... 213-624-1200... 44 D
thohberg@fidm.edu
HOHENSTEIN, Janet, M . 218-477-2956. 259 H
hohenst@mnstate.edu
HOHIEMER, Victoria .... 270-686-4512. 196 C
vickie.hohiemer@kctcs.edu
HOHL, Kathleen .... 414-297-6208. 540 E
hohlk@matc.edu
HOHMAN, Adam .... 260-982-5228. 170 U
arhohman@manchester.edu
HOHMANN, Mark .... 502-585-9911. 199 C
mhohmann@spalding.edu
HOI, Samuel .... 310-665-6935... 57 C
shoi@otis.edu
HOIDA, Will .... 775-881-1314. 295 F
whoida@sierranevada.edu
HOILMAN, Sandra, K ..... 828-448-6020. 365 A
shoilman@wpcc.edu
HOING, Joe, W .... 479-979-1321... 25 J
jhoing@ozarks.edu
HOINS, Dennis .... 315-279-5251. 328 D
dhoins@mail.keuka.edu
HOISINGTON, Gloria ...... 760-355-6244... 48 A
gloria.carmona@imperial.edu
HOIT, Marc, I .... 919-515-0141. 368 B
mark_hoit@ncsu.edu
HOJAN, Elizabeth, M ...... 262-554-2010. 534 D
mwcfinancialaid@aol.com
HOJAN-CLARK, Jane .... 414-229-6300. 537 A
jhojan@uwm.edu
HOJSACK, Dana .... 619-849-2678... 59 L
danahojsack@pointloma.edu
HOKANSON, Sharon .... 928-524-7471... 16 E
sharon.hokanson@npc.edu
HOKE, Cheryl .... 650-493-4430... 66 E
cheryl.hoke@sofia.edu
HOKE, Mary .... 210-829-3982. 490 A
mhoke@uiwtx.edu
HOL, Dick .... 509-533-8018. 518 E
dick.hol@ccs.spokane.edu
HOLAK, Susan, L .... 718-982-2464. 317 E
susan.holak@csi.cuny.edu
HOLAWAY, Rick .... 615-966-6133. 456 B
rick.holaway@lipscomb.edu
HOLBERG, Connie .... 315-786-2402. 327 L
cholberg@sunyjefferson.edu
HOLBERT, Carolyn .... 704-216-7223. 363 D
carolyn.holbert@rccc.edu
HOLBERT, Woodrow .... 734-995-7598. 241 E
woodrow.holbert@cuaa.edu
HOLBROOK, Adam .... 937-393-3431. 389 B
aholbrook@sscc.edu
HOLBROOK, Carl .... 334-347-2623..... 3 G
cholbrook@escc.edu
HOLBROOK, Catherine ... 508-531-1276. 229 D
cholbrook@bridgew.edu
HOLBROOK, Christine .... 413-552-2299. 231 F
cholbrook@hcc.edu
HOLBROOK, Eddie .... 704-669-4223. 359 D
holbrook@clevelandcc.edu
HOLBROOK, Jennifer ..... 870-230-5275... 21 D
holbroj@hsu.edu
HOLBROOK, Mary Anne 276-466-7887. 514 G
maryanneholbrook@vic.edu
HOLBROOK, Peter, J ...... 414-410-4004. 532 B
pjholbrook@stritch.edu
HOLBROOKS,
Johnnie, L .... 432-837-8100. 487 B
johnnieh@sulross.edu
HOLCOMB, David .... 254-295-4184. 490 B
dholcomb@umhb.edu
HOLCOMB, Grant .... 585-276-8902. 349 C
gholcomb@mag.rochester.edu
HOLCOMB, J. David .... 713-798-4613. 467 F
jholcomb@bcm.edu
HOLCOMB, Jeffrey, R ..... 605-367-8355. 452 C
jeff.holcomb@southeasttech.edu
HOLCOMB, Mark .... 815-939-5236. 155 H
mholcomb@olivet.edu
HOLCOMB, Richard, E ... 248-341-2054. 248 D
reholcomb@oaklandcc.edu
HOLCOMB, Todd, R .... 308-635-6101. 293 E
holcombt@wncc.edu
HOLCOMBE, Annalisa .... 801-832-2551. 498 F
asteggell@westminstercollege.edu
HOLCOMBE, Bridget .... 336-841-9470. 355 C
bholcomb@highpoint.edu
HOLCOMBE, Robert .... 864-429-8728. 448 G
reholcom@mailbox.sc.edu
HOLCOMBE, Willis .... 904-632-3224. 105 E
wholcomb@fscj.edu
HOLDA, William, M .... 903-983-8100. 475 E
bholda@kilgore.edu
HOLDEN, Camille .... 928-757-0838... 15 L
cholden@mohave.edu
HOLDEN, Charles, J .... 240-895-4393. 218 A
cjholden@smcm.edu
HOLDEN, Dave .... 618-664-6750. 145 G
dave.holden@greenville.edu
HOLDEN, Eileen .... 863-297-1098. 110 H
eholden@polk.edu
HOLDEN, Elaine, P .... 704-637-4402. 353 E
epholden@catawba.edu
HOLDEN, Howard .... 610-902-8240. 411 E
howard.holden@cabrini.edu
HOLDEN, Joseph, M .... 951-698-6389... 75 A
HOLDEN, Larry .... 615-327-6339. 456 E
lholden@mmc.edu
HOLDEN, Nina .... 313-664-7864. 241 C
nholden@collegeforcreativestudies.edu
HOLDEN, Ronnie, E .... 410-651-6229. 219 E
reholden@umes.edu
HOLDEN, Scott, A .... 212-799-5000. 328 B
HOLDEN, Wesley .... 772-546-5534. 106 N
wesleyholden@hsbc.edu
HOLDEN-DUFFY, Cheryl 410-651-6460. 219 E
clduffy@umes.edu
HOLDER, Ann, H .... 936-294-1613. 487 A
lib_ahh@shsu.edu
HOLDER, Arthur .... 510-649-2440... 46 B
aholder@gtu.edu
HOLDER, Beth .... 336-841-9279. 355 C
bholder@highpoint.edu
HOLDER, Candace .... 336-386-3382. 364 D
holderc@surry.edu
HOLDER, Eugene .... 972-825-4762. 481 F
eholder@sagu.edu
HOLDER, Gerald, D .... 412-624-9811. 435 C
holder@engr.pitt.edu
HOLDER, Jayne .... 423-425-4785. 463 D
jayne-holder@utc.edu
HOLDER, Karen, G .... 214-887-5221. 471 F
kholder@dts.edu
HOLDER, Mary .... 704-403-2026. 352 J
mary.holder@carolinashealthcare.org
HOLDER, Mike .... 405-744-7231. 397 H
mike.holder@okstate.edu
HOLDER, William, W ...... 213-740-4838... 74 A
wholder@marshall.usc.edu
HOLDERBY, Amy .... 937-766-7700. 375 K
holderby@cedarville.edu
HOLDING-JORDAN,
Karen, R .... 919-866-5838. 364 G
khjordan@waketech.edu
HOLDREN, Susan .... 740-588-1243. 394 C
sholdren@zanestate.edu
HOLDSTEIN, Deborah ..... 312-369-8219. 143 D
dholdstein@colum.edu
HOLEMAN, Gary .... 304-896-7436. 528 F
gary.holeman@southernwv.edu
HOLESTINE, Dan .... 214-210-4079. 163 I
HOLEY, Linka .... 612-728-5123. 264 A
lholey@smumn.edu
HOLFORD, K. Chris .... 219-785-5735. 172 A
cholford@pnc.edu
HOLGATE, Randy, L .... 312-893-7110. 145 B
rholgate@erikson.edu
HOLGER, David, K .... 515-294-7184. 175 H
holger@iastate.edu
HOLGUIN, Emilsen .... 518-608-8356. 324 B
eholguin@excelsior.edu
HOLIFIELD, Brenda .... 870-780-1227... 19 K
bholifield@smail.anc.edu
HOLL, Lynn .... 609-586-4800. 302 G
holll@mccc.edu
HOLLAAR, Jean, R .... 218-477-2336. 259 H
hollaar@mnstate.edu
HOLLADAY, Kelly .... 575-492-2801. 310 G
kholladay@nmjc.edu
HOLLAND, Alex .... 520-322-6330... 13 T
info@hanuniversity.edu
HOLLAND, Ann, T .... 270-707-3724. 195 E
ann.holland@kctcs.edu
HOLLAND, Bill .... 573-651-2203. 282 B
bholland@semo.edu
HOLLAND, Carol, L .... 724-738-2034. 429 F
carol.holland@sru.edu
HOLLAND, Colleen .... 417-455-5588. 273 E
ColleenHolland@crowder.edu
HOLLAND, Curt .... 405-912-9470. 395 K
cholland@hc.edu
HOLLAND, Dan .... 864-646-1552. 447 D
dhollan1@tctc.edu
HOLLAND, Dana .... 903-875-7355. 477 G
dana.holland@navarrocollege.edu
HOLLAND, Deana, K .... 828-689-1275. 356 F
dholland@mhc.edu
HOLLAND, Gregory, K .... 713-313-7446. 485 F
hollandgk@tsu.edu
HOLLAND, Heather, E .... 423-461-1521. 454 E
hholland@ecs.edu
HOLLAND, Jann .... 417-873-7276. 273 H
jholland@drury.edu
HOLLAND, Jennifer, L .... 580-581-2244. 394 G
jennifer@cameron.edu
HOLLAND, Jenny .... 860-297-2139... 91 F
jenny.holland@trincoll.edu
HOLLAND, Julie, E .... 704-403-3207. 352 J
juliette.holland@carolinashealthcare.org
HOLLAND, Kathy .... 704-878-4395. 362 B
kholland@mitchellcc.edu
HOLLAND, Lawson .... 843-349-2010. 442 E
lawsonh@coastal.edu
HOLLAND, LeeAnne .... 305-809-3178. 104 I
leeanne.holland@fkcc.edu
HOLLAND, Leslie .... 901-272-5131. 456 F
lholland@mca.edu
HOLLAND, Linda .... 501-354-7565... 25 C
holland@uaccm.edu
HOLLAND, Lynne .... 270-745-3095. 200 G
lynne.holland@wku.edu
HOLLAND, Matthew, S ... 801-863-3000. 497 C
matthew.holland@uvu.edu
HOLLAND, Melissa .... 303-546-3597... 83 F
mholland@naropa.edu
HOLLAND, Michaelle ...... 816-412-5501. 450 G
mholland@national.edu
HOLLAND, Paul, D .... 203-254-4050... 89 I
pholland@fairfield.edu
HOLLAND, Richard, D .... 205-652-3527...... 9 F
rholland@uwa.edu
HOLLAND, Sally, C .... 603-535-2212. 298 G
scholland@plymouth.edu
HOLLAND, Scott .... 800-287-8822. 164 C
hollasc@bethanyseminary.edu
HOLLAND, Steven, C .... 520-621-1556... 18 F
sholland@email.arizona.edu
HOLLAND, Teresa .... 509-574-4667. 525 G
tholland@yvcc.edu
HOLLAND, Tina, S .... 574-239-8372. 166 N
tsholland@hcc-nd.edu
HOLLAND, Tony .... 334-556-2214..... 3 N
tholland@wallace.edu
HOLLAND, W. Stan .... 973-642-3888. 299 D
sh@berkeleycollege.edu
HOLLANDER, Lisa .... 219-464-6882. 174 E
lisa.hollander@valpo.edu
HOLLANDER, Teri .... 301-445-1909. 219 A
tholland@usmd.edu
HOLLANDSWORTH,
Heather .... 540-365-4282. 504 L
hhollandsworth@ferrum.edu
HOLLAR, Paula .... 828-327-7000. 359 A
phollar@cvcc.edu
HOLLARS, Mary, L .... 812-888-5965. 174 F
mhollars@vinu.edu
HOLLATZ, Gary .... 318-678-6000. 202 I
ghollatz@bpcc.edu
HOLLDORF, Barry .... 206-878-3710. 520 E
bholldorf@highline.edu
HOLLEMS, Diane .... 805-965-0581... 64 L
hollems@sbcc.edu
HOLLENBECK, Dean .... 620-343-4600. 186 E
dhollenbeck@fhtc.edu
HOLLENBECK, Pat .... 713-646-1824. 480 J
phollenbeck@stcl.edu
HOLLENHORST, Steven .. 360-650-3521. 525 C
HOLLER, Juanita, M .... 413-545-1581. 228 F
jholler@admin.umass.edu
HOLLER, Richard, G .... 724-925-4129. 437 D
hollerr@wccc.edu
HOLLERAN, Lisa .... 512-404-4803. 467 A
lholleran@austinseminary.edu
HOLLERAN, Theresa .... 614-251-4730. 386 B
Hollerat@ohiodominican.edu
HOLLERN, Denny .... 740-366-9301. 376 A
dhollern@cotc.edu
HOLLEY, Connie .... 270-444-9676. 193 N
cholley@daymarcollege.edu
HOLLEY, Dannye .... 713-313-7388. 485 F
dholley@tsulaw.edu
HOLLEY, Debra, S .... 252-246-1311. 365 C
dholley@wilsoncc.edu
HOLLEY, Earle .... 843-208-8140. 448 B
eholley@uscb.edu
HOLLEY, Lucretia, C .... 860-255-3500... 89 G
HOLLEY, Stephanie .... 903-886-5101. 483 E
stephanie.holley@tamuc.edu
HOLLEY, Tara .... 512-472-4133. 480 G
tholley@ssw.edu
HOLLEY, Tracy, S .... 540-365-4216. 504 L
tholley@ferrum.edu

HOLLIDAY, Corey .... 937-328-3858. 377 A
hollidayc@clarkstate.edu
HOLLIDAY, Jeff .... 828-669-8012. 357 H
jholliday@montreat.edu
HOLLIDAY, Lisa, C .... 503-370-6574. 408 J
lcjones@willamette.edu
HOLLIDAY, Matthew .... 239-489-9052. 101 O
mholliday@edison.edu
HOLLIDAY, Paul .... 213-613-2200... 67 E
paul_holliday@sciarc.edu
HOLLIDAY, Shawn, P ..... 580-327-8410. 396 N
spholliday@nwosu.edu
HOLLIDAY, Theresa .... 913-288-7110. 187 L
tholliday@kckcc.edu
HOLLIER, Larry, H .... 504-568-4800. 205 C
lhholl@lsuhsc.edu
HOLLIFIELD, Jim .... 901-722-3264. 458 K
jhollifield@sco.edu
HOLLIMAN, Stephanie ... 641-683-5751. 179 A
stephanie.holliman@indianhills.edu
HOLLIMON, Mike .... 770-531-3123. 122 A
mhollimon@brenau.edu
HOLLINGDALE, Linda ..... 802-654-2310. 500 B
lhollingdale@smcvt.edu
HOLLINGER, Dennis .... 978-468-7111. 227 A
dhollinger@gcts.edu
HOLLINGER, John .... 603-314-7983. 297 I
j.hollinger@snhu.edu
HOLLINGER, LaShannon 251-575-8271..... 1 C
lhollinger@ascc.edu
HOLLINGSWORTH,
Gabe .... 704-233-8368. 370 G
g.hollingsworth@wingate.edu
HOLLINGSWORTH,
Kimberly .... 312-850-7301. 142 C
khollingsworth@ccc.edu
HOLLINGSWORTH,
Marge .... 973-684-5920. 304 B
mhollingsworth@pccc.edu
HOLLINGSWORTH,
Rusty .... 270-789-5009. 193 D
rhollingsworth@campbellsville.edu
HOLLINGSWORTH,
Stacey .... 601-635-2111. 266 H
sholling@eccc.edu
HOLLINGWORTH, Lilyne 860-509-9525... 90 B
lilyne@hartsem.edu
HOLLINS, JR.,
Thomas, N .... 804-523-5296. 512 F
thollins@reynolds.edu
HOLLIS, Debra .... 704-378-1128. 355 K
dhollis@jcsu.edu
HOLLIS, Keith .... 978-837-5356. 234 A
hollisk@merrimack.edu
HOLLIS, Mark .... 440-943-7600. 388 J
mhollis@dioceseofcleveland.org
HOLLIS, Mark, J .... 517-432-2607. 246 H
hollis@msu.edu
HOLLIS, Sara .... 504-284-5511. 206 K
shollis@suno.edu
HOLLISTER, Jim .... 570-389-4047. 427 H
jhollist@bloomu.edu
HOLLMAN-STANCIL,
Cynthia .... 903-730-4890. 474 O
CHollman-Stancil@jarvis.edu
HOLLOMAN, Anthony ...... 205-247-8164..... 7 E
aholloman@stillman.edu
HOLLOMAN, Darryl, B ... 404-413-1503. 126 E
dholloman@gsu.edu
HOLLOMAN, Suzanne .... 215-619-7397. 424 B
sholloman@mc3.edu
HOLLOWAY, Amy .... 478-757-3510. 122 F
aholloway@centragatech.edu
HOLLOWAY, Amy, L ...... 478-988-6849. 122 G
aholloway@centralgatech.edu
HOLLOWAY, Anna .... 478-825-6338. 124 H
hollowaa@fvsu.edu
HOLLOWAY, Antonio ...... 512-505-3031. 473 G
aholloway@htu.edu
HOLLOWAY, C. Allen ..... 501-977-2031... 25 C
holloway@uaccm.edu
HOLLOWAY, Claire .... 701-328-4159. 371 B
claire.holloway@ndus.edu
HOLLOWAY, David, J ..... 304-877-6428. 526 C
dave.holloway@abc.edu
HOLLOWAY, DeAira .... 972-273-3163. 471 B
dholloway@dcccd.edu
HOLLOWAY, Denise, W . 478-757-5211. 134 G
dholloway@wesleyancollege.edu
HOLLOWAY, Jackie .... 501-337-5000... 20 J
jholloway@coto.edu
HOLLOWAY, James, P ... 734-763-0395. 251 C
hagar@umich.edu
HOLLOWAY, Jerry, R ..... 918-631-2539. 401 F
jerry-holloway@utulsa.edu
HOLLOWAY, Jessica ...... 479-968-0269... 20 E
jholloway@atu.edu
HOLLOWAY, John .... 718-960-8242. 318 A
john.holloway@lehman.cuny.edu
HOLLOWAY, Karen .... 229-931-2151. 126 D
karen.holloway@gsw.edu

HOLLOWAY, Kendra .... 510-780-4500... 50 I
khollowa@lifewest.edu
HOLLOWAY, Mary .... 803-822-3529. 445 C
hollowaym@midlandstech.edu
HOLLOWAY, Richard, L . 414-955-8256. 534 C
holloway@mcw.edu
HOLLOWAY, Stacy .... 618-985-3741. 148 J
stacyholloway@jalc.edu
HOLLOWELL, Lorna .... 218-281-8580. 264 E
lholl0we@umn.edu
HOLLOWELL,
Meghan, E .... 513-585-4841. 376 I
meghan.hollowell@thechristcollege.edu
HOLLOWELL, Stephen .... 212-237-8521. 318 D
shollowell@jjay.cuny.edu
HOLLY, Gordon, K .... 330-684-8740. 390 F
gholly@uakron.edu
HOLLY, Marty .... 208-459-5850. 138 A
mholly@collegeofidaho.edu
HOLLY, Richard .... 815-753-1138. 154 I
rholly@niu.edu
HOLLY, Shelly .... 918-631-2550. 401 F
shelly-holly@utulsa.edu
HOLLY, Yvette, A .... 402-559-5678. 292 J
yholly@unmc.edu
HOLM, Carl, D .... 906-227-2622. 248 A
cholm@nmu.edu
HOLM, Cyndi .... 507-537-7854. 261 F
Cyndi.Holm@smsu.edu
HOLM, Janet .... 253-589-5545. 518 B
janet.holm@cptc.edu
HOLMAN, Cheri .... 734-462-4400. 250 A
cholman@schoolcraft.edu
HOLMAN, Dena .... 828-726-2737. 358 E
dnholman@cccti.edu
HOLMAN, Fred, B .... 775-784-4853. 294 J
fholman@unr.edu
HOLMAN, James .... 414-443-8566. 539 F
james.holman@wlc.edu
HOLMAN, John .... 606-218-5194. 200 F
johnholman@upike.edu
HOLMAN, Lucy .... 606-218-5265. 200 F
lucyholman@upike.edu
HOLMAN, Lucy .... 410-837-4333. 221 A
lholman@ubalt.edu
HOLMAN, Mark .... 701-854-8024. 372 J
markh@sbci.edu
HOLMAN, Neil .... 847-574-5230. 150 C
nholman@lfgsm.edu
HOLMAN, Pat .... 505-984-6144. 311 H
pat.holman@sjcsf.edu
HOLMAN, Sara, C .... 920-832-6583. 533 S
sara.b.holman@lawrence.edu
HOLMAN, Steven .... 847-543-2444. 143 A
sholman@clcillinois.edu
HOLMANS, Jim .... 325-674-4974. 464 H
holmansj@acu.edu
HOLMBOE, Janelle .... 413-205-3275. 221 F
janelle.holmboe@aic.edu
HOLMES, Annie .... 805-756-2250... 32 F
aholmes@calpoly.edu
HOLMES, Barbara, A ...... 651-255-6106. 264 C
bholmes@unitedseminary.edu
HOLMES, Barbara, J ...... 202-274-6156... 97 A
bholmes@udc.edu
HOLMES, Bert .... 757-727-5315. 505 F
bert.holmes@hamptonu.edu
HOLMES, Betsy .... 603-623-0313. 297 E
betsyholmes@nhia.edu
HOLMES, Beverly .... 309-341-7755. 150 A
bholmes@knox.edu
HOLMES, Carlos .... 302-857-6062... 93 C
cholmes@desu.edu
HOLMES, Charley .... 903-586-2501. 467 D
holmes@bmats.edu
HOLMES, Claire .... 510-642-6436... 70 I
claireholmes@berkeley.edu
HOLMES, Debra .... 912-279-5787. 123 B
dholmes@ccga.edu
HOLMES, Donna .... 412-365-1262. 412 K
dholmes@chatham.edu
HOLMES, Edward, J .... 716-851-1016. 323 I
holmese@ecc.edu
HOLMES, Ella .... 601-979-6858. 267 E
ella.b.holmes@jsums.edu
HOLMES, Erica .... 773-602-5020. 142 B
HOLMES, Erin .... 907-786-4517... 10 H
ejholmes@uaa.alaska.edu
HOLMES, Frank, R .... 936-294-3625. 487 A
holmes@shsu.edu
HOLMES, Gilbert .... 909-460-2000... 72 E
gholmes@laverne.edu
HOLMES, Harold, R .... 336-758-5226. 370 D
holmes@wfu.edu
HOLMES, Heather, W ...... 410-677-4850. 220 D
hwholmes@salisbury.edu
HOLMES, Heidi .... 314-768-7808. 278 C
hholmes@missouricollege.com
HOLMES, Jeanne, E .... 804-862-6224. 508 H
jholmes@rbc.edu

HOLMES, Joan .... 813-253-7043. 106 M
jholmes16@hccfl.edu
HOLMES, John, D .... 402-449-2873. 289 H
jholmes@graceu.edu
HOLMES, Johnny, B .... 901-321-3445. 453 H
jholmes@cbu.edu
HOLMES, Judy .... 785-825-5422. 185 B
jholmes@brownmackie.edu
HOLMES, Kenneth .... 212-237-8211. 318 D
kholmes@jjay.cuny.edu
HOLMES, Kristen .... 256-352-8118..... 9 G
kristen.holmes@wallacestate.edu
HOLMES, Kristiana, L ..... 509-777-4563. 525 F
kholmes@whitworth.edu
HOLMES, Kurt .... 330-263-2011. 377 H
kholmes@wooster.edu
HOLMES, Lloyd, A .... 978-762-4000. 232 D
lholmes@northshore.edu
HOLMES, Malcolm .... 540-654-1617. 510 J
mholmes3@umw.edu
HOLMES, Malcolm, T ..... 804-523-5230. 512 F
mholmes@reynolds.edu
HOLMES, Matthew .... 610-902-8228. 411 E
matthew.holmes@cabrini.edu
HOLMES, Megan .... 314-529-9343. 276 G
HOLMES, Michael .... 281-899-1240. 478 J
HOLMES, Michelle, M ..... 510-841-1905... 27 H
mmholmes@absw.edu
HOLMES, Myioshi, U ..... 972-860-8237. 470 H
muh3310@dcccd.edu
HOLMES, Owen .... 657-278-5403... 33 E
oholmes@fullerton.edu
HOLMES, Phillip, M .... 478-387-4904. 125 E
mholmes@gmc.cc.ga.us
HOLMES, R.J .... 319-895-4574. 177 A
rjholmes@cornellcollege.edu
HOLMES, Robert .... 602-243-8062... 15 F
bear.holmes@southmountaincc.edu
HOLMES, JR., Robert ..... 407-882-1250. 115 E
robert.holmes@ucf.edu
HOLMES, Robin, H .... 541-346-1137. 406 D
rhholmes@uoregon.edu
HOLMES, Rodney .... 480-461-7315... 15 A
rodney.holmes@mesacc.edu
HOLMES, Ron .... 325-793-4631. 476 E
rholmes@mcm.edu
HOLMES, Ronald .... 606-487-3198. 195 C
rholmes0022@kctcs.edu
HOLMES, Sharon, N .... 920-924-6326. 540 F
sholmes@morainepark.edu
HOLMES, Susan .... 956-364-4107. 485 H
susan.holmes@tstc.edu
HOLMES, Terrell .... 302-857-6375... 93 C
tholmes@desu.edu
HOLMES, Tiffany .... 312-345-3760. 158 L
tholmes@saic.edu
HOLMES, Wanda .... 662-621-4853. 266 D
wholmes@coahomacc.edu
HOLMES, Wendy .... 845-341-4662. 335 H
wendy.holmes@sunyorange.edu
HOLMES, William .... 859-622-1478. 193 P
william.holmes@eku.edu
HOLMES BACZKOWSKI,
Helene .... 215-951-1817. 420 B
holmes@lasalle.edu
HOLMGREN, Marilyn ...... 605-721-5275. 450 G
mholmgren@national.edu
HOLMGREN, Richard, A . 814-332-2898. 409 D
richard.holmgren@allegheny.edu
HOLMQUIST, David .... 562-903-4886... 29 L
dave.holmquist@biola.edu
HOLMQUIST, Eric .... 712-279-5435. 176 B
eric.holmquist@briarcliff.edu
HOLMQUIST, Jake .... 718-862-7449. 329 M
jake.holmquist@manhattan.edu
HOLODICK, Nicholas, A . 570-208-5895. 419 P
naholodi@kings.edu
HOLOMAN,
Christopher, L .... 716-926-8854. 326 B
choloman@hilbert.edu
HOLOPIREK, Darnell ...... 620-792-9367. 184 F
holopirekd@bartonccc.edu
HOLOWICKI, Linda .... 708-209-3170. 143 E
linda.holowicki@cuchicago.edu
HOLPER, Mark .... 651-779-5834. 258 C
mark.holper@century.edu
HOLS, Eric .... 703-284-1601. 507 B
eric.hols@marymount.edu
HOLSCLAW, Mick .... 916-568-3017... 52 K
holsclm@losrios.edu
HOLSCLAW, Scott .... 870-245-5129... 22 D
holsclaws@obu.edu
HOLSCLAW, Sheila, K .... 859-846-5310. 197 I
sholsclaw@midway.edu
HOLSENBECK, Daniel ..... 407-823-2387. 115 E
daniel.holsenbeck@ucf.edu
HOLSINGER, Kent .... 860-486-2182... 92 A
kent.holsinger@uconn.edu
HOLSINGER-FUCHS,
Pamela .... 715-232-2639. 538 B
holsinger-fuchsp@uwstout.edu

HOLST, Tim .... 218-726-7571. 264 D
tholst@umn.edu
HOLSTAD, Deb .... 320-308-3277. 261 C
dholstad@sctcc.edu
HOLSTAD, Deb, A .... 320-308-3227. 261 C
dholstad@sctcc.edu
HOLSTEIN, David .... 561-868-3004. 110 C
holsteid@palmbeachstate.edu
HOLSTEN, Robert, D ...... 252-246-1258. 365 C
rholsten@wilsoncc.edu
HOLSTER, Melissa .... 617-228-2271. 231 C
mholster@bhcc.mass.edu
HOLSTON, Tavarez .... 229-217-4202. 129 F
tholston@moultrietech.edu
HOLSTON, William .... 336-841-9221. 355 C
bookstor@highpoint.edu
HOLT, Amy .... 575-562-2467. 309 H
amy.holt@enmu.edu
HOLT, Brooke .... 479-619-4298... 22 C
bholt@nwacc.edu
HOLT, Bruce .... 865-981-8035. 456 D
bruce.holt@maryvillecollege.edu
HOLT, Debbie .... 859-246-6286. 194 L
debbie.holt@kctcs.edu
HOLT, Dennis .... 573-651-2249. 282 B
dholt@semo.edu
HOLT, Diann .... 757-822-1069. 514 C
dholt@tcc.edu
HOLT, Gail, W .... 413-542-2296. 221 G
financialaid@amherst.edu
HOLT, Jerry .... 219-785-5200. 172 A
jholt@pnc.edu
HOLT, Joseph .... 559-734-9000... 63 D
HOLT, Joseph, L .... 410-778-7201. 221 C
jholt2@washcoll.edu
HOLT, Lynda .... 518-608-8171. 324 B
lholt@excelsior.edu
HOLT, Raymond .... 229-931-2001. 131 G
rholt@southgatech.edu
HOLT, Roslyn, J .... 318-670-6436. 207 A
rholt@susla.edu
HOLT, Russ .... 925-439-2181... 42 A
rholt@losmedanos.edu
HOLT, Ryan, C .... 828-884-8217. 352 I
holtrc@brevard.edu
HOLT, Shari .... 870-743-3000... 22 B
sholt@northark.edu
HOLT, Wilford .... 334-420-4400..... 7 G
wholt@trenholmstate.edu
HOLTAN, Sarah, E .... 262-243-5700. 532 H
sarah.holtan@cuw.edu
HOLTE, Terri .... 404-237-7573. 121 F
tholte@khec.com
HOLTEN, Kathryn .... 803-323-2275. 449 G
holtenk@winthrop.edu
HOLTER, Emily .... 507-288-4563. 255 C
eholter@crossroadscollege.edu
HOLTER, Joan .... 218-723-6041. 254 K
jholer@css.edu
HOLTER, Sherer .... 509-963-2111. 517 F
holters@cwu.edu
HOLTFRETER, David .... 217-875-7200. 156 J
dholt@richland.edu
HOLTGREIVE, Shaun .... 989-774-3111. 240 N
holtg1s@cmich.edu
HOLTGREN, Shawn, M ... 574-807-7215. 164 D
holtgrs@bethelcollege.edu
HOLTHAUS, Barbara .... 217-641-4104. 148 M
bholthaus@jwcc.edu
HOLTHOUSER,
David, M .... 704-894-2220. 353 J
daholthouser@davidson.edu
HOLTMANN, Ruth Ann ... 314-421-0949. 282 I
holtmann@siba.edu
HOLTON, Nick .... 989-275-5000. 245 B
nick.holton@kirtland.edu
HOLTON, Simone .... 802-387-6753. 499 E
sholton@landmark.edu
HOLTROP, Stephen, D ... 260-359-4166. 166 O
sholtrop@huntington.edu
HOLTSCHNEIDER,
Dennis, H .... 312-362-8890. 143 H
president@depaul.edu
HOLTZ, Daniel, F .... 320-222-5205. 260 H
daniel.holtz@ridgewater.edu
HOLTZ, Eddie .... 712-325-3426. 179 L
eholtz@iwcc.edu
HOLTZCLAW, Mike .... 510-659-6191... 57 A
Mholtzclaw@ohlone.edu
HOLTZCLAW, Rhonda ..... 239-590-1037. 115 A
rholtzcl@wgcu.edu
HOLTZEN, Wende .... 714-879-3901... 47 K
wholtzen@hiu.edu
HOLUBIK, Donna .... 567-661-7288. 387 L
donna_holubik@owens.edu
HOLVEY, Amy .... 215-596-7485. 435 H
a.holvey@usciences.edu
HOLWICK, Jana .... 440-375-7252. 382 L
jholwick@lec.edu
HOLYCROSS, Robert, L .. 205-652-3601..... 9 F
rlh@uwa.edu

HOLZ, Doris 212-220-8021. 317 A dholz@bmcc.cuny.edu
HOLZ, Richard 414-288-7700. 534 B richard.holz@marquette.edu
HOLZ-CLAUSE, Mary 860-486-4792... 92 A mary.holz-clause@uconn.edu
HOLZBERLEIN, Anne 405-974-2770. 400 K aholzberlein@uco.edu
HOLZEM, Madeline 608-785-8013. 536 G mholzem@uwlax.edu
HOLZEMER, William, L .. 973-353-5149. 306 D holzemer@andromeda.rutgers.edu
HOLZEMER, William, L .. 732-932-1770. 306 B holzemer@andromeda.rutgers.edu
HOLZER, Charlotte 718-871-6187. 348 B charloth@touro.edu
HOLZER, Marc 973-353-5268. 306 D mholzer@rutgers.edu
HOLZHEUSER, Christina 361-825-5975. 483 F christina.holzheuser@tamucc.edu
HOLZMAN, Terri, L 920-748-8351. 535 J holzmant@ripon.edu
HOLZMER, OSF, M. Anita 260-399-7700. 174 C mholzmer@sf.edu
HOM, Kevin 718-260-5525. 319 B khom@citytech.cuny.edu
HOMAN, David 847-233-7700. 155 B dhoman@nc.edu
HOMAN, Elizabeth 240-567-7970. 216 F elizabeth.homan@montgomerycollege.edu
HOMAN, J. Michael 507-284-9595. 254 F homan.michael@mayo.edu
HOMAN, J. Michael 507-284-9595. 254 G
HOMAN, Patricia 513-875-3344. 376 H patricia.homan@chatfield.edu
HOMAN, Richard, V 757-446-5800. 504 E homanrv@evms.edu
HOMAN, Thomas 218-723-2214. 254 K thoman@css.edu
HOMANN, Gordon 617-912-9154. 224 B ghomann@bostonconservatory.edu
HOMBURGER, John, R 518-564-2130. 344 B homburjr@plattsburgh.edu
HOMEIER, Debra, L 906-227-2092. 248 A dhomeier@nmu.edu
HOMER, Jessica 781-768-7049. 236 A jessica.homer@regiscollege.edu
HOMESLEY, Diane 678-839-6582. 133 I dhomesle@westga.edu
HOMFELDT, Mike 541-880-2244. 403 H homfeldt@klamathcc.edu
HOMIAK, JR., Albert, J . 302-831-7285... 94 B homiak@udel.edu
HOMKOW, Gary 516-572-7304. 332 C gary.homkow@ncc.edu
HOMOLKA, Jessica 785-242-5200. 189 I jessica.homolka@ottawa.edu
HOMOLKA, Karen, K 217-245-3094. 146 F khomolk@ic.edu
HOMSHER, Betsy, E 810-762-9540. 244 Q bhomsher@kettering.edu
HOMSTED, Gillian 800-862-9616. 498 I ghomsted@burlington.edu
HOMZA, Lu Ann 757-221-2469. 503 N dean-ep@wm.edu
HONAKER, Evelyn, J 423-585-6972. 462 A evelyn.honaker@ws.edu
HONAKER, Lisa 609-652-4505. 305 C lisa.honaker@stockton.edu
HONAN, Molly 617-735-9876. 226 B honanm@emmanuel.edu
HONDA, Jacqueline 707-826-5339... 35 C jacqueline.honda@humboldt.edu
HONDROS, Jack 610-526-1445. 409 F jack.hondros@theamericancollege.edu
HONDROS, Linda 614-508-7203. 381 E
HONEA, Scott 979-436-0900. 484 B shonea@tamhsc.edu
HONEGAN, Rhonda 404-270-5075. 132 E rhonegan@spelman.edu
HONEGGER, Rose 337-482-6819. 208 D oia@louisiana.edu
HONEMAN, Donald 508-793-7419. 225 A dhoneman@clarku.edu
HONEY, Delores 417-625-9696. 278 D honey-d@mssu.edu
HONEYCUTT, Alan 858-642-8190... 55 J ahoneycutt@nu.edu
HONEYCUTT, Tony, L 606-679-8501. 196 D tony.honeycutt@kctcs.edu
HONEYWOOD, Omega 803-327-7402. 442 D ohoneywood@clintonjuniorcollege.edu
HONG, E-Sing 408-260-0208... 44 J chinesedoctoral@fivebranches.edu
HONG, Luoluo 808-974-7334. 136 A luoluo@hawaii.edu
HONG, Steven 800-463-8990. 313 G
HONG, Tran 951-343-3907... 30 H thong@calbaptist.edu
HONIG, Selila 202-639-1791... 95 B shonig@corcoran.org
HONKE, Mary, J 402-844-7124. 291 I maryh@northeast.edu
HONNELL, Cherie 503-494-7800. 405 I regohsu@ohsu.edu
HONSBERGER, Dean 269-387-4280. 252 I dean.honsberger@wmich.edu
HONTS, Arlen 316-295-5800. 186 H ahonts@friends.edu
HOOD, Brent 919-735-5151. 364 H wbhood@waynecc.edu
HOOD, Donna 828-395-1404. 361 C dhood@isothermal.edu
HOOD, IV, Edward 912-650-5607. 131 H ehood@southuniversity.edu
HOOD, Gwendolyn, D 205-348-5855..... 8 D ghood@aalan.ua.edu
HOOD, Jean 817-272-5554. 491 B jmhood@uta.edu
HOOD, Jeremiah 314-595-3400. 271 D
HOOD, Jon 402-449-2928. 289 H jhood@graceu.edu
HOOD, Mary, D 408-554-2732... 64 M mhood@scu.edu
HOOD, Michael, J 724-357-2397. 428 F mhood@iup.edu
HOOD, Mike 903-233-4115. 475 J mikehood@letu.edu
HOOD, Nan, S 610-989-1456. 436 D nhood@vfmac.edu
HOOD, Pam 317-917-3370. 171 A phood@martin.edu
HOOD, Patricia 706-649-1883. 123 E phood@columbustech.edu
HOOD, Philip 847-735-6003. 150 B hood@lakeforest.edu
HOOD, Robert 650-306-3340... 64 B hoodr@smccd.edu
HOOD, Robin 931-363-9800. 456 C rhood@martinmethodist.edu
HOOD, Scott, W 207-725-3256. 209 H shood@bowdoin.edu
HOOD, Sonya 931-393-1765. 461 A shood@mscc.edu
HOOD, Steven 205-348-9364..... 8 D shood1@sa.ua.edu
HOOD, Tim 815-599-3417. 146 D tim.hood@highland.edu
HOOD, W.C. (Chip) 864-656-3414. 442 C chip@clemson.edu
HOOGAKKER, John 540-458-8446. 516 A jhoogakker@wlu.edu
HOOK, Amy 617-353-2399. 224 D amyhook@bu.edu
HOOK, Randall 540-828-5358. 502 J rhook@bridgewater.edu
HOOK, Rebecca 610-436-6973. 430 A rhook@wcupa.edu
HOOK, Samuel, S 864-592-4630. 447 A hooks@sccsc.edu
HOOK, Talbort 808-455-0611. 137 A talbort@hawaii.edu
HOOKER, Dianna 406-638-3142. 286 D dianna@lbhc.edu
HOOKER-HARING, Christopher 484-664-3245. 424 H hookerh@muhlenberg.edu
HOOKS, Beth 919-735-5151. 364 H bhooks@waynecc.edu
HOOKS, Brenda 502-456-6504. 199 G bhooks@sullivan.edu
HOOKS, Gerald, D 478-289-2036. 124 C jhooks@ega.edu
HOOKS, Haley 229-317-6746. 124 A haley.hooks@darton.edu
HOOLE, Thomas 978-934-3509. 229 B thomas_hoole@uml.edu
HOOPER, Celia, R 336-334-5744. 369 A crhooper@uncg.edu
HOOPER, Debra, A 919-488-8500. 356 C dhooper@living-arts-college.edu
HOOPER, John 940-565-3858. 490 C john.hooper@unt.edu
HOOPER, Julie 512-232-2129. 491 C jhooper@austin.utexas.edu
HOOPER, Lynn 405-425-5157. 397 D lynn.looper@oc.edu
HOOPER, Robert, D 740-427-5109. 382 J hooperr@kenyon.edu
HOOPER, Stephanie, L ... 304-336-8990. 530 A stephanie.hooper@westliberty.edu
HOOPES, Robbin 513-569-1616. 376 L robbin.hoopes@cincinnatistate.edu
HOOPES, Tom 913-360-7529. 184 H thoopes@benedictine.edu
HOOPS, Dan 248-689-8282. 251 I dhoops@walshcollege.edu
HOOTEN, Al 936-294-1016. 487 A ahooten@shsu.edu
HOOTEN, Jennifer 909-447-2506... 39 E jhooten@cst.edu
HOOTEN, Jon 909-447-2558... 39 E jhooten@cst.edu
HOOTEN, Michael 806-354-5589. 487 E michael.hooten@ttuhsc.edu
HOOTON, Linda, J 205-853-1200..... 5 B lhooton@jeffstateonline.com
HOOTS, Cathy 336-750-2265. 370 A hoots@wssu.edu
HOOVER, Chris 620-341-5337. 186 D choover@emporia.edu
HOOVER, Christine 561-433-2330. 113 J
HOOVER, Douglas 724-938-4096. 428 A hoover@calu.edu
HOOVER, James, W 214-887-5347. 471 F jhoover@dts.edu
HOOVER, Jean, B 717-262-2007. 437 H jhoover@wilson.edu
HOOVER, Jeffrey 717-560-8258. 421 A jhoover@lbc.edu
HOOVER, Jonathan 214-333-5821. 470 D jonh@dbu.edu
HOOVER, Kathleen 610-558-5560. 424 I hooverk@neumann.edu
HOOVER, Kim 601-984-6200. 270 C khoover@umc.edu
HOOVER, Linda 806-742-3031. 487 D linda.hoover@ttu.edu
HOOVER, Lisa 214-637-3530. 494 E lhoover@wadecollege.edu
HOOVER, Lisa, D 570-577-3757. 411 A lisa.hoover@bucknell.edu
HOOVER, Lorette, M 706-649-1837. 123 E lhoover@columbustech.edu
HOOVER, Myrna 850-644-6089. 115 C mhoover@fsu.edu
HOOVER, Nancy 503-699-6261. 404 C nhoover@marylhurst.edu
HOOVER, Nancy, Z 740-587-6629. 379 D hoover@denison.edu
HOOVER, Samantha 212-472-1500. 334 B shoover@nysid.edu
HOOVER, Sara 205-226-4989..... 2 C shoover@bsc.edu
HOOVER, Tom 423-425-5300. 463 D tom-hoover@utc.edu
HOOVLER, David 216-987-4854. 378 D david.hoovler@tri-c.edu
HOOYMAN, Jamie 660-359-3948. 279 H jhooyman@mail.ncmissouri.edu
HOPE, Laura 909-652-6113... 37 M laura.hope@chaffey.edu
HOPE, Marilyn 909-335-8863... 41 C mhope@verizon.net
HOPE, Maury, M 515-294-0323. 175 H mmhope@iastate.edu
HOPE, Oral 212-431-2300. 333 I ohope@nyls.edu
HOPE, Thomas 407-646-1580. 111 Q thope@rollins.edu
HOPE, Wilbert 718-270-6961. 319 A wilbert@mec.cuny.edu
HOPEWELL, Mitch 605-642-6011. 451 G mitch.hopewell@bhsu.edu
HOPEWELL, JR., Woodson, H 757-727-5303. 505 F woodson.hopewell@hamptonu.edu
HOPEY, Christopher, E ... 978-837-5110. 234 A christopher.hopey@merrimack.edu
HOPKINS, Amanda 407-646-2124. 111 Q ahopkins@rollins.edu
HOPKINS, Becky 323-343-3200... 34 A bhopkins@cslanet.calstatela.edu
HOPKINS, Bill 650-543-3935... 54 C bill.hopkins@menlo.edu
HOPKINS, Christi 620-242-0414. 188 G hopkinsc@mcpherson.edu
HOPKINS, Darlene 910-630-7150. 356 H dhopkins@methodist.edu
HOPKINS, David, R 937-775-2312. 393 G david.hopkins@wright.edu
HOPKINS, Denise, C 718-990-1323. 339 A hopkinsd@stjohns.edu
HOPKINS, Drew, W 609-984-3430. 308 A dhopkins@tesc.edu
HOPKINS, Dustin 918-781-7400. 394 D hopkinsd@bacone.edu
HOPKINS, Gena 260-459-4500. 169 C ghopkins@ibcfortwayne.edu
HOPKINS, Glenn, W 662-915-7177. 270 B ghopkins@olemiss.edu
HOPKINS, Hunter, H 412-338-4770. 419 M hhopkins@kaplan.edu
HOPKINS, Jane, L 618-664-6600. 145 G jane.hopkins@greenville.edu
HOPKINS, Jayne, S 270-384-8033. 197 D hopkinsj@lindsey.edu
HOPKINS, Jim 405-224-3140. 401 E jhopkins@usao.edu
HOPKINS, John 330-263-2082. 377 H jhopkins@wooster.edu
HOPKINS, LC, John 703-416-1441. 505 I jhopkins@ipsciences.edu
HOPKINS, Joseph 205-726-2778..... 6 F jhopkins@samford.edu
HOPKINS, Kathryn 870-777-5722... 25 B kathryn.hopkins@uacch.edu
HOPKINS, Laurie, B 803-786-3669. 443 B lhopkins@columbiasc.edu
HOPKINS, Marilyn 707-638-5276... 69 K marilyn.hopkins@tu.edu
HOPKINS, Mark 706-236-2231. 121 G mhopkins@berry.edu
HOPKINS, Nicole 509-574-6870. 525 G nhopkins@yvcc.edu
HOPKINS, Paulette 619-388-7750... 62 F phopkins@sdccd.edu
HOPKINS, Robert, P 212-353-4350. 321 F bob@cooper.edu
HOPKINS, Sara 615-248-1653. 462 D shopkins@trevecca.edu
HOPKINS, Shelli 918-781-7344. 394 D hopkinss@bacone.edu
HOPKINS, Shirley, L 804-523-5896. 512 F shopkins@reynolds.edu
HOPKINS, Stacy 724-357-2218. 428 F stacy.hopkins@iup.edu
HOPKINS, T. Hampton ... 704-355-5585. 353 D hampton.hopkins@carolinascollege.edu
HOPKINS, Thomas, F 540-464-7228. 515 B hopkinstf@vmi.edu
HOPKINS, Tony 740-588-1409. 394 C thopkins@zanestate.edu
HOPKINS, Willie 718-951-3166. 317 C WHopkins@brooklyn.cuny.edu
HOPKINS-BEST, Mary .... 715-232-1168. 538 B hopkinsbestm@uwstout.edu
HOPKINS GROSS, Anne, M 802-447-6323. 500 D ahopkinsgross@svc.edu
HOPP, Melissa 443-840-3176. 214 E mhopp@ccbcmd.edu
HOPP, Susan 503-883-2278. 404 A shopp@linfield.edu
HOPPA, Anthony, T 585-245-5516. 343 C thoppa@geneseo.edu
HOPPE, Elizabeth 909-706-3497... 76 B shoppe@westernu.edu
HOPPE, Heather 419-251-8989. 383 G heather.hoppe@mercycollege.edu
HOPPE, Jim 651-696-6220. 256 L hoppe@macalester.edu
HOPPE, Ken 870-236-6901... 20 K khoppe@crc.edu
HOPPER, Darla 812-535-5110. 172 F dhopper@smwc.edu
HOPPER, David, R 757-455-3415. 515 H dhopper@vwc.edu
HOPPER, George, M 662-325-2953. 268 D ghopper@cfr.msstate.edu
HOPPER, Jack 409-880-8741. 486 F jack.hopper@lamar.edu
HOPPER, Karen, S 870-508-6110... 20 A khopper@asumh.edu
HOPPER, Lisa 501-760-4241... 22 A lhopper@npcc.edu
HOPPER, Richard 207-453-5129. 210 L president@kvcc.me.edu
HOPPER, Susan 731-661-5078. 462 F shopper@uu.edu
HOPPER, William, E 305-626-3701. 104 J William.Hopper@fmuniv.edu
HOPPES, Cherron 415-442-6510... 45 I choppes@ggu.edu
HOPPLE, Dennis, M 570-577-1201. 411 A dennis.hopple@bucknell.edu
HOPPLE, Stephnie 928-541-7777... 16 B shopple@ncu.edu
HOPPMANN, Richard, A 803-733-1531. 447 G richard.hoppmann@uscmed.sc.edu
HOPSON, Anthony 607-274-3111. 327 E ahopson@ithaca.edu
HOPSON, George, A 864-977-2194. 445 H george.hopson@ngu.edu
HOPSON, Pamela, F 812-465-7188. 174 D pfhopson@usi.edu
HOPWOOD, Dennis, T ... 509-527-5172. 525 E hopwoodt@whitman.edu
HOPWOOD, Julie, D 207-581-1512. 212 B julie.hopwood@maine.edu
HOR, Annie, Y 209-667-3709... 35 B ahor@csustan.edu
HORADAN, Lloyd 478-553-2060. 129 H lhoradan@oftc.edu
HORADAN, Lloyd 478-553-2060. 129 I lhoradan@oftc.edu
HORAK, Janice 254-968-9075. 483 A jhorak@tarleton.edu
HORAK, Janice 254-968-9890. 483 A jhorak@tarleton.edu

HORAK, Maureen ... 413-662-5205. 230 C
m.horak@mcla.edu
HORAK, Michael, D ... 972-860-8344. 470 I
MHorak@dcccd.edu
HORAN, Kevin ... 925-439-2181... 42 A
khoran@losmedanos.edu
HORAN, Michael, D ... 404-364-8322. 130 A
mhoran@oglethorpe.edu
HORAN, Thomas ... 909-607-9302... 39 C
thomas.horan@cgu.edu
HORBACEWICZ, Jill ... 212-463-0400. 348 B
jillh@touro.edu
HORGAN, Elizabeth ... 508-213-2289. 235 E
elizabeth.horgan@nichols.edu
HORGAN, Joan ... 518-454-5296. 321 A
horganj@strose.edu
HORGAN, Louise, M ... 732-224-2202. 299 G
lhorgan@brookdalecc.edu
HORGAN, Ralph, R ... 412-268-6156. 412 H
rh44@andrew.cmu.edu
HORINE, Troy ... 316-942-4291. 189 E
horinet@newmanu.edu
HORINEK, Jon ... 405-682-1611. 397 E
jhorinek@occc.edu
HORISSIAN, Kevork, T ... 570-577-3623. 411 A
kevork.horissian@bucknell.edu
HORN, Allison ... 503-883-2323. 404 A
ahorn@linfield.edu
HORN, Brian, S ... 727-816-3458. 110 E
hornb@phcc.edu
HORN, Carla ... 717-757-1100. 438 H
carla.horn@yti.edu
HORN, Christy, A ... 605-394-1604. 452 A
christy.horn@sdsmt.edu
HORN, Cindy ... 231-591-5309. 242 F
hornc@ferris.edu
HORN, David, G ... 978-468-7111. 227 A
dhorn@gcts.edu
HORN, David, G ... 614-292-6359. 386 E
horn.5@osu.edu
HORN, George ... 912-478-2897. 126 C
ghorn@georgiasouthern.edu
HORN, Herman ... 512-245-2539. 487 C
hh18@txstate.edu
HORN, Jamie ... 334-386-7168... 3 H
jhorn@faulkner.edu
HORN, Jay ... 817-272-2355. 491 B
horn@uta.edu
HORN, John, F ... 215-898-7593. 435 B
horn3@upenn.edu
HORN, S.J., John, P ... 314-792-6152. 275 L
horn@kenrick.edu
HORN, Jonathon ... 419-995-8302. 381 Q
horn.j@rhodesstate.edu
HORN, Josh ... 518-828-4181. 321 C
josh.horn@sunycgcc.edu
HORN, Kristin ... 717-728-2288. 412 J
kristinhorn@centralpenn.edu
HORN, Larry, S ... 812-488-2775. 173 H
lh6@evansville.edu
HORN, Mark ... 479-788-7006... 24 A
mark.horn@uafs.edu
HORN, Mary ... 304-766-3239. 530 C
maryhorn@wvstateu.edu
HORN, Michael ... 704-330-5963. 359 C
michael.horn@cpcc.edu
HORN, Paul, M ... 212-998-3228. 334 D
paul.horn@nyu.edu
HORN, Samuel, E ... 763-417-8250. 254 E
HORN, Sonia ... 530-741-6989... 77 M
shorn@yccd.edu
HORN, Tammy ... 859-246-6637. 194 L
tammy.horn@kctcs.edu
HORN BUNK, Sheri ... 661-763-7936... 69 D
shornbunk@taftcollege.edu
HORNBACHER, Noel ... 313-593-5410. 251 D
noelhorn@umich.edu
HORNBEAK, Joe, N ... 405-466-3265. 395 N
jnhornbeak@langston.edu
HORNBECK, Billi ... 605-455-6037. 450 I
bhornbeck@olc.edu
HORNBERGER,
Cynthia, A ... 785-670-1213. 191 D
cynthia.hornberger@washburn.edu
HORNBERGER, Lois ... 503-352-2240. 407 A
lhornberger@pacificu.edu
HORNBERGER, Rob ... 417-836-6444. 278 E
robhornberger@missouristate.edu
HORNBERGER, Tiffany ... 502-863-8027. 194 C
tiffany_hornberger@georgetowncollege.edu
HORNBUCKLE, Jami, M ... 606-783-2372. 198 A
j.hornbuckle@moreheadstate.edu
HORNBURG, Trisha, L ... 262-691-5446. 541 D
thornburg@wctc.edu
HORNDT, Christin ... 989-275-5000. 245 B
christin.horndt@kirtland.edu
HORNE, Arlene ... 903-886-5159. 483 E
arlene.horne@tamuc.edu
HORNE, Bart ... 502-863-8182. 194 C
bart_horne@georgetowncollege.edu
HORNE, Cathy ... 704-272-5337. 363 G
chorne@spcc.edu
HORNE, David ... 410-704-6242. 220 E
dhorne@towson.edu
HORNE, Hadie, C ... 252-246-1221. 365 C
hhorne@wilsoncc.edu
HORNE, J. Douglas ... 801-524-8110. 495 O
d-horne@ldsbc.edu
HORNE, Pamela, T ... 765-494-9116. 171 M
pamhorne@purdue.edu
HORNE, JR., Rex, M ... 870-245-5400... 22 D
president@obu.edu
HORNE, Valerie ... 601-403-1211. 269 D
vhorne@prcc.edu
HORNE, Walter ... 330-325-6558. 385 E
wih@neomed.edu
HORNER, Andrew ... 617-353-2290. 224 D
ahorner@bu.edu
HORNER, Jeff ... 719-502-2011... 84 A
jeffrey.horner@ppcc.edu
HORNER, Jeffrey, T ... 423-798-7952. 462 A
jeff.horner@ws.edu
HORNER, Jennifer ... 860-768-4296... 92 D
horner@hartford.edu
HORNER, Kenneth, R ... 931-540-2533. 460 E
khorner@columbiastate.edu
HORNER, Rick ... 610-527-2912. 432 B
rosemont_store@fheg.follett.com
HORNER, Sherri ... 419-372-7343. 374 K
shorner@bgsu.edu
HORNER, Stacy ... 269-782-1220. 250 C
shorner@swmich.edu
HORNER, Taylor ... 617-369-3620. 236 F
thorner@smfa.edu
HORNER, Theresa ... 716-827-2485. 348 G
hornert@trocaire.edu
HORNICK, Robert ... 510-567-6174... 69 C
bhornick@sum.edu
HORNING, Kirsten ... 503-338-2341. 402 G
khorning@clatsopcc.edu
HORNS, Phyllis, N ... 252-744-2265. 367 B
hornsp@ecu.edu
HORNSBY, Jacob ... 415-518-5396... 71 A
hornsbyj@uchastings.edu
HORNSHUH KENT, Jan ... 541-485-1780. 405 B
jankent@newhope.edu
HOROWITZ, Anne, B ... 215-596-7518. 435 H
a.horowitz@usciences.edu
HOROWITZ, Avery ... 718-252-7800. 348 B
averymh@touro.edu
HOROWITZ,
Boruch Avrohom ... 718-438-2018. 337 A
rcby26@aol.com
HOROWITZ, Elias ... 845-783-0833. 349 E
HOROWITZ, Samuel, L ... 904-264-2172. 111 P
shorowitz@iws.edu
HOROWITZ, Sara ... 212-678-8838. 328 A
sahorowitz@jtsa.edu
HORRAS, Danielle ... 208-377-8080. 137 K
dhorras@carrington.edu
HORRELL, Jeffrey, L ... 603-646-2235. 296 G
jeffrey.l.horrell@dartmouth.edu
HORSCH, Ellen, S ... 906-487-1737. 247 A
eshorsch@mtu.edu
HORSEY, Cheryl ... 215-641-5546. 417 F
horsey.c@gmc.edu
HORSEY, Dwight, G ... 717-872-3026. 429 D
dwight.horsey@millersville.edu
HORSEY, Earlie, P ... 757-823-2392. 507 M
ephorsey@nsu.edu
HORSLEY, Darrell ... 513-772-9888. 386 C
dr.horsley@omw.edu
HORSLEY, Jeff, O ... 714-808-4822... 56 D
jhorsley@nocccd.edu
HORSMAN, Karen ... 317-931-2315. 165 B
khorsman@cts.edu
HORST, Pamela ... 907-822-3201... 10 A
phorst@akbible.edu
HORSTMEYER, Mark ... 708-974-5275. 153 F
horstmeyer@morainevalley.edu
HORTON, Amy ... 847-317-7152. 160 M
ahorton@tiu.edu
HORTON, C, R ... 864-488-4586. 444 L
chorton@limestone.edu
HORTON, Carol, R ... 626-914-8886... 38 K
chorton@citruscollege.edu
HORTON, Claudia ... 816-833-0524. 178 F
horton@graceland.edu
HORTON, Connie ... 310-506-4210... 58 H
connie.horton@pepperdine.edu
HORTON, Dan ... 414-382-6238. 531 I
dan.horton@alverno.edu
HORTON, Gretchen ... 503-253-3443. 405 E
ghorton@ocom.edu
HORTON, Howard, E ... 617-951-2350. 234 G
howard.horton@necb.edu
HORTON, Jana ... 251-575-8252... 1 C
jhorton@ascc.edu
HORTON, Jane, T ... 540-458-8401. 516 A
jhorton@wlu.edu
HORTON, Jeannine ... 918-495-7575. 398 H
jhorton@oru.edu
HORTON, Jeff ... 916-649-2400... 30 C
HORTON, Johnna ... 507-389-7223. 261 E
johnna.horton@southcentral.edu
HORTON, Joseph, M ... 603-641-7600. 297 G
jhorton@anselm.edu
HORTON, Julian, K ... 240-500-2000. 215 B
jkhorton@hagerstowncc.edu
HORTON, Kelley, R ... 910-775-4403. 369 B
kelley.horton@uncp.edu
HORTON, Kimberly ... 937-778-7806. 379 G
khorton@edisonohio.edu
HORTON, Kimberly ... 937-769-1837. 373 I
khorton2@antioch.edu
HORTON, Larry, N ... 650-725-3324... 68 E
larry.horton@stanford.edu
HORTON, Leslie ... 508-854-2798. 232 F
lhorton@qcc.mass.edu
HORTON, Mac ... 251-380-2272... 7 D
horton@shc.edu
HORTON, Michele ... 850-471-4639. 110 G
mhorton@pensacolastate.edu
HORTON, Muriel ... 843-574-6138. 447 E
muriel.horton@tridenttech.edu
HORTON, Peter ... 412-536-1050. 420 A
peter.horton@laroche.edu
HORTON, Stanley, W ... 360-538-4051. 520 B
shorton@ghc.edu
HORTON, Steve ... 318-357-5851. 208 B
hortons@nsula.edu
HORTON, Steve ... 318-357-4330. 208 B
hortons@nsula.edu
HORTON, Susan ... 845-434-5750. 347 A
shorton@sullivan.suny.edu
HORTON, JR., Walter, E 330-325-6499. 385 E
wehj@neomed.edu
HORTON, JR., Walter, E 330-325-6290. 385 E
wehj@neomed.edu
HORVATH, Cathy ... 701-858-4444. 371 F
cathy.horvath@minotstateu.edu
HORVATH, Fran ... 831-656-2228. 544 M
rfhorvat@nps.edu
HORVATH, John, K ... 413-545-2125. 228 F
jhorvath@admin.umass.edu
HORVATH, Karl ... 215-646-7300. 417 F
horvath.k@gmc.edu
HORVATH, Michael ... 678-839-6445. 133 I
mhorvath@westga.edu
HORVATH, Rebecca, L ... 215-951-1898. 420 B
horvath@lasalle.edu
HORVATH, Virginia, S ... 716-673-3456. 342 A
virginia.horvath@fredonia.edu
HORVATH-PLYMAN,
Melissa ... 201-684-7081. 305 A
mhorvath@ramapo.edu
HORWATH, Amy ... 814-536-5168. 412 C
ahorwath@crbc.net
HORWITZ, Pamela ... 314-529-9418. 276 G
phorwitz@maryville.edu
HOSACK, Susan, E ... 314-935-5567. 284 L
sue.hosack@wustl.edu
HOSCH, Jason ... 504-278-6281. 203 F
jhosch@nunez.edu
HOSEA, Walter ... 865-251-1800. 458 I
whosea@southcollegetn.edu
HOSEI, Huan, F ... 671-735-5595. 546 C
huan.hosei@guamcc.edu
HOSELTON, Steven, A ... 312-341-2442. 157 D
shoselton@roosevelt.edu
HOSENEY, Jason ... 651-450-3692. 258 H
jhosene@inverhills.edu
HOSHIKO, Carol ... 808-734-9568. 136 E
hoshiko@hawaii.edu
HOSKEY, Lisa ... 607-274-3011. 327 E
HOSKINS, Deb ... 970-641-2237... 86 I
dhoskins@western.edu
HOSKINS, Sheila ... 252-823-5166. 360 C
hoskinss@edgecombe.edu
HOSKINS, Steve ... 606-546-4151. 200 A
shoskins@unionky.edu
HOSKINSON, Heidi ... 316-295-5861. 186 H
heidi_hoskinson@friends.edu
HOSKOWITZ, Joel, M ... 410-386-8412. 214 A
jhoskowitz@carrollcc.edu
HOSS, Cindy ... 620-665-3507. 187 F
hossc@hutchcc.edu
HOSS, Neal ... 760-750-4400... 35 A
nhoss@csusm.edu
HOSSENLOPP, Jeanne ... 414-288-5322. 534 B
jeanne.hossenlopp@marquette.edu
HOSSLER, Charles ... 912-650-5674. 131 H
chossler@southuniversity.edu
HOSTELLER, Mayme ... 212-228-1888. 337 H
HOSTER, Robert, L ... 570-577-3342. 411 A
bob.hoster@bucknell.edu
HOSTETLER, Bumper, R ... 812-888-4510. 174 F
bhostetler@vinu.edu
HOSTETLER, Chad ... 304-457-6320. 526 A
hostetlercs@ab.edu
HOSTETLER, James, D ... 570-577-1911. 411 A
jim.hostetler@bucknell.edu
HOSTETLER, Lori, J ... 812-888-4121. 174 F
lhostetler@vinu.edu
HOSTETLER, Marna, M ... 812-464-1834. 174 D
mmhostetle@usi.edu
HOSTETLER,
Theodore, J ... 434-947-8133. 508 D
thostetler@randolphcollege.edu
HOSTETLER, Timothy, J ... 423-775-7262. 453 E
hostetti@bryan.edu
HOSTETTER, Julie, M ... 800-287-8822. 164 C
hosteju@bethanyseminary.edu
HOSTETTER, Larry ... 270-686-4236. 192 G
larry.hostetter@brescia.edu
HOSTETTER, Steve, J ... 218-751-8670. 263 C
stevehostetter@oakhills.edu
HOSTINA, Michael ... 907-450-8080... 10 G
mike.hostina@alaska.edu
HOSTLER, Sharon, L ... 434-924-9030. 511 B
slh2m@virginia.edu
HOTALING, Diane, E ... 757-455-3216. 515 H
dhotaling@vwc.edu
HOTALING, Marcus, S ... 518-388-6161. 348 J
hotalinm@union.edu
HOTCHKISS, Carolyn ... 781-239-5528. 222 D
hotchkiss@babson.edu
HOTCHKISS, Charles ... 617-989-4831. 237 G
hotchkissc@wit.edu
HOTCHKISS, Pat ... 520-515-5420... 12 R
hotchkis@cochise.edu
HOTEZ, Peter, J ... 713-798-4951. 467 F
hotez@bcm.edu
HOTTEL, Haven ... 910-893-1421. 352 K
hottelh@campbell.edu
HOTTON, Bob ... 661-362-2696... 53 G
bhotton@masters.edu
HOTZFIELD, Brian ... 773-298-3096. 158 E
hotzfield@sxu.edu
HOTZLER, Russell, K ... 718-260-5400. 319 B
rhotzler@citytech.cuny.edu
HOU, Feng ... 941-752-5694. 114 I
houf@scf.edu
HOUBECK, JR.,
Robert, L ... 810-762-3410. 251 E
rhoubeck@umflint.edu
HOUCHINS, Shelia, E ... 270-745-4493. 200 G
shelia.houchins@wku.edu
HOUCK, Brenda ... 757-340-2121. 503 I
careercvab@centura.edu
HOUCK, Clarence, M ... 803-934-3235. 445 F
chouck@morris.edu
HOUCK, James, W ... 814-865-4294. 426 A
jwh32@psu.edu
HOUCK, Keith, W ... 407-582-3465. 118 M
khouck@valenciacollege.edu
HOUCK, Laurie ... 330-263-2583. 377 H
lhouck@wooster.edu
HOUCK, Maureen, B ... 516-463-6745. 326 D
maureen.b.houck@hofstra.edu
HOUCK, Susan ... 803-738-7610. 445 C
houcks@midlandstech.edu
HOUDEK, Rob ... 605-642-6562. 451 G
robert.houdek@bhsu.edu
HOUDESHELL, Tara ... 740-366-9223. 376 A
thoudesh@cotc.edu
HOUDYSHELL, Michael ... 308-635-6123. 293 E
HOUFER, Michael ... 651-747-4085. 258 C
michael.houfer@century.edu
HOUGH, Bradley ... 636-227-2100. 276 F
brad.hough@logan.edu
HOUGH, David ... 417-836-5254. 278 E
davidhough@missouristate.edu
HOUGH, David, K ... 540-464-7094. 515 B
houghdk@vmi.edu
HOUGH, John ... 304-724-3700. 526 B
jhough@apus.edu
HOUGH, Mark ... 336-770-3329. 369 D
houghm@uncsa.edu
HOUGH, Melanie ... 419-772-2027. 386 D
m-hough@onu.edu
HOUGH, Tony ... 803-738-7695. 445 C
hought@midlandstech.edu
HOUGH, Twyla ... 210-999-8321. 488 C
Twyla.Hough@trinity.edu
HOUGHTON, David, C ... 405-585-4400. 397 C
david.houghton@okbu.edu
HOUGHTON, James ... 212-799-5000. 328 B
HOUGHTON, Susan ... 510-659-6441... 57 A
shoughton@ohlone.edu
HOUGLAND, Dawm ... 312-341-3531. 157 D
dhougland@roosevelt.edu
HOUK, Christopher ... 270-686-4241. 192 G
chris.houk@brescia.edu
HOUK, Suzanne, N ... 724-458-2208. 417 E
snhouk@gcc.edu
HOULE, Greg ... 212-938-5607. 345 C
ghoule@sunyopt.edu
HOULE, Linda ... 508-362-2131. 231 D
lhoule@capecod.edu

HOULE, Pamela .... 508-580-5550. 341 A
phoule@skidmore.edu
HOULETTE, Forrest .... 502-456-6504. 199 G
fhoulette@sullivan.edu
HOULIHAN, Janet, M ..... 714-895-8307... 39 J
jhoulihan@gwc.cccd.edu
HOULIHAN, Robert .... 516-323-3456. 331 J
rhoulihan@molloy.edu
HOULIHAN, Timothy, J .. 718-489-5290. 338 G
thoulihan@sfc.edu
HOULKER, Megan .... 781-239-5264. 222 D
mhoulker@babson.edu
HOULT, Kevin .... 256-782-8122..... 4 K
khoult@jsu.edu
HOUPIS, James .... 510-885-3711... 33 C
james.houpis@csueastbay.edu
HOURIGAN,
Christopher, P .... 401-456-8998. 439 F
chourigan@ric.edu
HOURIGAN, Gerard .... 216-987-4706. 378 D
gerard.hourigan@tri-c.edu
HOUSE,
Charles (Chuck) .... 408-541-0100... 40 A
HOUSE, Cheryl .... 520-206-4646... 17 A
chouse@pima.edu
HOUSE, Christopher .... 847-566-6401. 162 G
chouse@usml.edu
HOUSE, J. Daniel .... 815-753-6002. 154 I
jhouse@niu.edu
HOUSE, Janice, M .... 805-546-3248... 42 C
jhouse@cuesta.edu
HOUSE, Jess .... 203-837-9500... 88 B
housej@wcsu.edu
HOUSE, Seymour .... 503-845-3507. 404 D
seymour.house@mtangel.edu
HOUSE, Steven, D .... 336-278-6647. 354 B
shouse@elon.edu
HOUSE, Vicki .... 325-670-5892. 472 O
vhouse@hsutx.edu
HOUSE, Vicki, D .... 325-670-5892. 472 O
vhouse@hsutx.edu
HOUSEKNECHT, Rick ...... 215-368-5000. 410 F
rhouseknecht@biblical.edu
HOUSENICK, Joseph ...... 570-408-4631. 437 F
joseph.housenick@wilkes.edu
HOUSER, Frieda .... 406-444-6570. 286 G
fhouser@montana.edu
HOUSER, Gary .... 530-242-7590... 65 G
ghouser@shastacollege.edu
HOUSER, Gerald, B .... 503-370-6413. 408 J
jhouser@willamette.edu
HOUSER, Janet .... 303-458-4174... 84 M
jhouser@regis.edu
HOUSER, Kay .... 910-642-7141. 364 A
Kay.Houser@sccnc.edu
HOUSER, Kristin .... 661-362-3245... 40 E
kristin.houser@canyons.edu
HOUSER, Samuel .... 717-291-4271. 416 J
sam.houser@fandm.edu
HOUSEWORTH, Julie ...... 573-592-4260. 285 D
julie.houseworth@williamwoods.edu
HOUSHMAND, Ali, A ...... 856-256-4100. 305 E
houshmand@rowan.edu
HOUSHOWER, Hans .... 419-358-3234. 374 J
houshowerh@bluffton.edu
HOUSKA, Nila .... 712-749-2233. 176 D
houskan@bvu.edu
HOUSLEY, Harold .... 903-875-7307. 477 G
harold.housley@navarrocollege.edu
HOUSLEY, Heather, L ..... 404-413-2070. 126 E
heatherh@gsu.edu
HOUSLEY, La Royce .... 310-954-4191... 54 J
ldodd@msmc.la.edu
HOUSTON, A. Glen .... 281-283-3000. 489 C
houston@uhcl.edu
HOUSTON, Adam .... 760-921-5463... 58 C
ahouston@paloverde.edu
HOUSTON, Alan .... 858-534-4370... 71 F
vcsa@ucsd.edu
HOUSTON, Alan, C .... 858-534-2247... 71 F
ahouston@ucsd.edu
HOUSTON, Chrystal .... 402-363-5607. 293 I
chrystal.houston@york.edu
HOUSTON, Don .... 408-855-5428... 75 K
don.houston@wvm.edu
HOUSTON, Douglas, B ... 530-741-6971... 77 K
dhouston@yccd.edu
HOUSTON, Kristen .... 206-876-6100. 523 D
khouston@theseattleschool.edu
HOUSTON, M. Sue .... 419-372-5387. 374 K
shousto@bgsu.edu
HOUSTON, Michael .... 662-621-4205. 266 D
mhouston@coahomacc.edu
HOUSTON, Michelle .... 631-499-7100. 329 B
mhouston@libi.edu
HOUSTON, Nainsi .... 419-448-2108. 380 G
nhouston@heidelberg.edu
HOUSTON, Rachel .... 704-403-1228. 352 J
rachel.houston@carolinashealthcare.org
HOUSTON, Richard .... 662-846-4694. 266 G
rhouston@deltastate.edu
HOUSTON, Teresa .... 662-846-4698. 266 G
thouston@deltastate.edu
HOUSTON, Teresa, L .... 601-635-6202. 266 H
thouston@eccc.edu
HOUSTON, Tim .... 740-695-9500. 374 H
thouston@belmontcollege.edu
HOUSTON, Vinson .... 256-782-5993..... 4 K
vhouston@jsu.edu
HOUSTON, Whitney, C ... 972-860-7396. 470 I
WhitneyHouston@dcccd.edu
HOUSTON, William .... 662-621-4226. 266 D
whouston@coahomacc.edu
HOUSTON, Willie .... 937-376-6631. 376 E
whouston@centralstate.edu
HOUSTON-BLACK,
Barbaina, M .... 252-335-3279. 367 C
bmhouston-black@mail.ecsu.edu
HOUSTON-BROWN,
Clive, K .... 909-593-3511... 72 E
chouston-brown@laverne.edu
HOUSTON-PHILPOT,
Kimberly, R .... 989-774-2085. 240 N
houst1kr@cmich.edu
HOUTMAN, Anne .... 661-654-3450... 32 H
ahoutman@csub.edu
HOUTSMA, Lisa .... 605-336-4602. 450 G
lhoutsma@national.edu
HOVATTER, Angela, L .... 301-687-4301. 220 C
ahovatter@frostburg.edu
HOVEKAMP, Tina .... 541-383-7563. 402 D
thovekamp@cocc.edu
HOVERSTEN, Mark, E ..... 208-885-5423. 139 D
hoverstm@uidaho.edu
HOVESTOL, Daniel .... 218-751-8670. 263 C
ohfinaid@oakhills.edu
HOVEY, Ann .... 714-992-7033... 56 F
ahovey@fullcoll.edu
HOVEY, Jeff .... 314-977-8375. 281 I
hoveyj@slu.edu
HOVEY, Roger, S .... 308-635-6012. 293 E
rhovey@wncc.edu
HOWARD, Andrew .... 806-743-7103. 487 E
andrew.howard@ttuhsc.edu
HOWARD, Angelita .... 404-627-2681. 121 H
angelita.howard@beulah.org
HOWARD, Barbara, C ...... 352-365-3520. 108 S
howardb@lssc.edu
HOWARD, Burgwell .... 847-467-0301. 155 D
b-howard@northwestern.edu
HOWARD, Carol .... 828-298-3325. 370 E
choward@warren-wilson.edu
HOWARD, Catherine, W . 804-828-8790. 511 F
choward@vcu.edu
HOWARD, Charles, L ...... 215-898-8457. 435 B
choward@pobox.upenn.edu
HOWARD, Cheryl .... 617-521-2131. 236 G
cheryl.howard@simmons.edu
HOWARD, Christie .... 903-593-8311. 485 A
choward@texascollege.edu
HOWARD,
Christopher, B .... 434-223-6110. 505 E
choward@hsc.edu
HOWARD, Dale, S .... 330-490-7303. 392 H
dhoward@walsh.edu
HOWARD, Dan, J .... 303-556-2624... 86 A
dan.howard@ucdenver.edu
HOWARD, Doris .... 415-503-6214... 62 H
finaid@sfcm.edu
HOWARD, Drema, K .... 813-974-9718. 116 C
dhoward@usf.edu
HOWARD, Eddie, J .... 706-771-4035. 121 D
ehoward@augustatech.edu
HOWARD, Elizabeth .... 215-646-7300. 417 F
howard.e@gmc.edu
HOWARD, Gary, E .... 859-858-3511. 192 B
gary.howard@asbury.edu
HOWARD, Gena .... 610-921-7859. 409 A
ghoward@alb.edu
HOWARD, Genevieve ...... 360-992-2936. 518 A
ghoward@clark.edu
HOWARD, Herman .... 803-705-4567. 441 C
howardh@benedict.edu
HOWARD, James .... 573-681-5275. 276 C
jhoward@nebook.com
HOWARD, Jane .... 620-792-9208. 184 F
howardj@bartonccc.edu
HOWARD, Jay, R .... 317-940-9874. 164 J
jrhoward@butler.edu
HOWARD, Jeff .... 325-235-7396. 486 C
jeff.howard@tstc.edu
HOWARD, Jennifer, L ..... 425-388-9232. 519 I
jhoward@everettcc.edu
HOWARD, Jessica .... 971-722-6268. 407 D
jessica.howard@pcc.edu
HOWARD, Jim .... 541-349-7471. 405 C
jhoward@nwcu.edu
HOWARD, Jonathan .... 202-319-5232... 94 G
howardjr@cua.edu
HOWARD, Katrina .... 912-427-5876. 120 B
khoward@altamahatech.edu
HOWARD, Kevin .... 478-825-6300. 124 H
howardk@fvsu.edu
HOWARD, Kimberly, A ... 802-656-4296. 500 F
kimberly.howard@uvm.edu
HOWARD, Lallah, M .... 361-593-3612. 484 A
lallah.howard@tamuk.edu
HOWARD, Lelia .... 267-502-2680. 410 I
lelia.howard@brynathyn.edu
HOWARD, Leon .... 662-252-8000. 269 F
lhoward@rustcollege.edu
HOWARD, Margaret .... 973-408-3071. 301 C
phoward@drew.edu
HOWARD, Martin, J .... 617-353-2290. 224 D
mjhoward@bu.edu
HOWARD, Mary Ann .... 478-757-5137. 134 G
mhoward@wesleyancollege.edu
HOWARD, Maureen .... 575-646-3221. 310 I
mhoward@nmsu.edu
HOWARD, Megan .... 605-882-5284. 450 D
megan.howard@lakeareatech.edu
HOWARD, Michael, W ... 617-324-8142. 233 B
HOWARD, Michelle, L ... 989-774-7506. 240 N
howar1ml@cmich.edu
HOWARD, Patricia .... 913-345-8288. 191 B
howardp@stmary.edu
HOWARD, Patricia .... 859-323-6332. 200 C
pbhowa00@uky.edu
HOWARD, Penny, G .... 434-395-2034. 506 J
howardpg@longwood.edu
HOWARD, Phil .... 847-214-7835. 144 F
phoward@elgin.edu
HOWARD, Philip .... 706-721-4551. 126 B
phoward@gru.edu
HOWARD, Phillip, D .... 404-215-2659. 129 D
phoward@morehouse.edu
HOWARD, Randy, B .... 765-285-1033. 164 B
rbhoward@bsu.edu
HOWARD, Robert .... 252-335-0821. 359 F
robert_howard@albemarle.edu
HOWARD, Robert, P .... 919-344-2650. 120 G
robert.howard@armstrong.edu
HOWARD, Ronald .... 601-925-3203. 268 A
howard@mc.edu
HOWARD, Rosetta .... 662-621-4244. 266 D
rhoward@coahomacc.edu
HOWARD, Sally .... 916-608-6500... 53 C
HOWARD, Sandra .... 205-929-6397..... 5 D
showard@lawsonstate.edu
HOWARD, Sarah .... 219-989-2417. 171 N
howard@purduecal.edu
HOWARD, Sharon, L .... 304-647-6369. 530 B
showard@osteo.wvsom.edu
HOWARD, Shawanda, M 504-286-5388. 206 K
showard@suno.edu
HOWARD, Steve .... 601-403-1219. 269 D
swhoward@prcc.edu
HOWARD, Tammy, M .... 414-410-4225. 532 B
tmhoward@stritch.edu
HOWARD, Tim .... 717-755-2300. 410 C
thoward@aii.edu
HOWARD, Traci, D .... 619-239-0391... 36 D
thoward@cwsl.edu
HOWARD, Trish .... 801-863-8440. 497 C
howardpa@uvu.edu
HOWARD, Walter, C .... 706-396-7639. 130 C
whoward@paine.edu
HOWARD, William .... 520-206-4568... 17 A
whoward@pima.edu
HOWARD, William, F ...... 518-320-1100. 341 C
HOWARD, Yaffa .... 215-635-7300. 417 C
yhoward@gratz.edu
HOWARD, Yelitza Marie . 956-326-2171. 483 B
yelitza.howard@tamiu.edu
HOWARD-UBELHOER,
Tracey .... 732-987-2765. 302 B
howardt@georgian.edu
HOWARD-VITAL,
Michelle, R .... 610-399-2220. 428 B
president@cheyney.edu
HOWARTH, James, R ...... 860-465-4418... 87 L
howarthj@easternct.edu
HOWARTH, Joan, W .... 517-432-6804. 246 H
howarth@law.msu.edu
HOWARTH, Michael .... 417-625-3051. 278 D
howarth-m@mssu.edu
HOWDEN, Norman .... 214-860-2176. 470 J
norman@dcccd.edu
HOWDEN, Tonya .... 269-467-9945. 242 H
thowden@glenoaks.edu
HOWDYSHELL,
Cynthia, K .... 540-828-5314. 502 J
chowdysh@bridgewater.edu
HOWDYSHELL, Linda ...... 954-201-7426... 99 D
lhowdysh@broward.edu
HOWE, Derek .... 617-353-6500. 224 D
dhowe@bu.edu
HOWE, Gregory .... 216-791-5000. 377 E
gxh36@case.edu
HOWE, Jodi, L .... 607-871-2128. 313 E
howe@alfred.edu
HOWE, Ken, D .... 985-549-2240. 208 C
khowe@selu.edu
HOWE, Mark .... 951-343-4299... 30 H
mhowe@calbaptist.edu
HOWE, Nanci .... 650-725-3104... 68 E
nanhowe@stanford.edu
HOWE, William .... 626-571-8811... 74 B
williamc@uwest.edu
HOWE, Zane .... 208-459-5599. 138 A
zhowe@collegeofidaho.edu
HOWE-VEENSTRA,
Carol, L .... 320-363-5201. 254 J
choweveenstr@csbsju.edu
HOWELL, Aaron, D .... 541-737-3031. 406 A
aaron.howell@oregonstate.edu
HOWELL, Amy .... 229-391-4980. 119 H
ahowell@abac.edu
HOWELL, Billy .... 606-337-1072. 193 F
bhowell@ccbbc.edu
HOWELL, Candice .... 402-465-2149. 291 G
chowell@nebrwesleyan.edu
HOWELL, Carla .... 704-216-3452. 363 D
carla.howell@rccc.edu
HOWELL, Charles .... 330-941-3265. 394 A
clhowell01@ysu.edu
HOWELL, Cheryl, A .... 718-489-5315. 338 G
chowell@sfc.edu
HOWELL, Diane .... 785-242-2067. 189 D
dhowell@neosho.edu
HOWELL, Dianne, B .... 318-797-5190. 205 F
dianne.howell@lsus.edu
HOWELL, Eleanor, V .... 402-280-2004. 289 D
howell@creighton.edu
HOWELL, James, R .... 252-398-6313. 353 H
howelj@chowan.edu
HOWELL, Jonathan .... 860-701-5161... 90 G
howell_s@mitchell.edu
HOWELL, Karen .... 904-826-0084. 118 I
khowell@usa.edu
HOWELL, Kathryn .... 414-410-4003. 532 B
khowell@stritch.edu
HOWELL, Kevin .... 919-515-9340. 368 B
kevin_howell@ncsu.edu
HOWELL, Kevin, A .... 813-257-7777. 118 L
khowell@ut.edu
HOWELL, La Donna .... 918-302-3617. 395 G
lhowell@eosc.edu
HOWELL, Laura .... 662-846-4624. 266 G
lhowell@deltastate.edu
HOWELL, LaVerne, B ...... 864-977-7013. 445 H
laverne.howell@ngu.edu
HOWELL, Lawrence, W ... 985-448-4148. 208 A
larry.howell@nicholls.edu
HOWELL, Lenni .... 330-287-1275. 386 F
howell.444@osu.edu
HOWELL, Linda .... 828-835-4259. 364 E
lhowell@tricountycc.edu
HOWELL, Liz .... 501-279-4276... 21 C
lhowell@harding.edu
HOWELL, Marie .... 803-535-1207. 446 B
howellm@octech.edu
HOWELL, Martie .... 716-286-8300. 334 F
meh@niagara.edu
HOWELL, Marya, L .... 704-894-2642. 353 J
mahowell@davidson.edu
HOWELL, R. Edward .... 434-924-8324. 511 B
reh2u@virginia.edu
HOWELL, Rohan .... 973-720-2125. 308 I
howellr5@wpunj.edu
HOWELL, Rose Mary ...... 973-655-4118. 303 D
howellr@mail.montclair.edu
HOWELL, Rosemarie .... 916-348-4689... 43 F
rhowell@epic.edu
HOWELL, Shelly .... 650-433-3858... 58 B
showell@paloaltou.edu
HOWELL, Shirley .... 773-252-5125. 156 I
shirley.howell@resu.edu
HOWELL, Stephen, C ...... 419-289-5944. 374 C
showell@ashland.edu
HOWELL, Steven .... 209-946-3066... 73 A
showell@pacific.edu
HOWELL, Verna, G .... 864-656-5444. 442 C
howell@clemson.edu
HOWELL, Wendy .... 229-430-3816. 120 A
whowell@albanytech.edu
HOWER, Michelle .... 205-970-9253..... 7 B
mhower@sebc.edu
HOWERTER, Wendy, L .... 217-786-2283. 151 F
wendy.howerter@llcc.edu
HOWERTON, Bruce .... 706-867-2876. 133 D
bruce.howerton@ung.edu
HOWERTON, Carol, A .... 304-896-7337. 528 F
carol.howerton@southernwv.edu
HOWERTON, Cheryl, L ... 217-424-6317. 153 C
chowerton@millikin.edu
HOWERTON, Karol .... 337-521-8955. 203 I
karol.howerton@southlouisiana.edu
HOWERTON, Lisa, A .... 270-824-8582. 196 A
lisa.howerton@kctcs.edu
HOWERTON, Michael, P 740-374-8716. 392 I
mhowerton1@wscc.edu

HOWERTON, Mike .... 740-374-8716. 392 I
mhowerton1@wscc.edu
HOWEY, Debbie .... 573-334-6825. 282 A
dhowey@sehealth.org
HOWIE, Dennis, J .... 248-204-2304. 245 I
dhowie@ltu.edu
HOWIE, Douglas .... 972-524-3341. 481 H
HOWIE, Michael .... 402-461-7743. 289 I
mhowie@hastings.edu
HOWINGTON, Channing 205-391-2256..... 6 H
chowington@sheltonstate.edu
HOWLAND, Kristine .... 210-999-8058. 488 C
khowland@trinity.edu
HOWLAND, Michael .... 904-256-7021. 107 Q
mhowlan@ju.edu
HOWLE, David .... 808-488-8570. 494 F
howled@wbu.edu
HOWLE, Jonathan .... 718-779-1430. 336 D
jhowle@plazacollege.edu
HOWLE, Meg .... 843-574-6356. 447 E
meg.howle@tridenttech.edu
HOWLETT, Jeffrey .... 919-760-8828. 356 G
howlettj@meredith.edu
HOWLETT, Katherine .... 516-299-2264. 329 D
kate.howlett@liu.edu
HOWLETT, Lucy, J .... 540-674-3619. 513 B
lhowlett@nr.edu
HOWLETT, Sophia .... 908-737-0300. 302 F
sohowlett@kean.edu
HOWLEY, Kathleen .... 717-720-4200. 427 G
khowley@passhe.edu
HOWRIGAN, Penny .... 802-635-1219. 501 D
penny.howrigan@jsc.edu
HOXIE, David, E .... 304-457-6306. 526 A
hoxiede@ab.edu
HOXIE, Hal .... 620-241-0723. 185 K
hal.hoxie@centeralchristian.edu
HOXIE, Saundra, E .... 304-457-6278. 526 A
hoxiese@ab.edu
HOXSIE, Patti, D .... 706-880-8327. 128 A
phoxsie@lagrange.edu
HOXTER, Laney .... 410-287-1043. 214 B
lhoxter@cecil.edu
HOY, Cliff .... 423-636-7307. 462 E
choy@tusculum.edu
HOY, David .... 610-896-1350. 418 F
dhoy@haverford.edu
HOY, Leah .... 817-272-2185. 491 B
hoy@uta.edu
HOY, Murray, K .... 410-334-2810. 221 D
rhoy@worwic.edu
HOY, Patricia .... 617-912-9103. 224 B
phoy@bostonconservatory.edu
HOYACK, Chuck .... 520-417-4060... 12 R
hoyackc@cochise.edu
HOYER, Erik .... 920-686-6113. 536 A
Erik.Hoyer@sl.edu
HOYERT, Mark .... 219-980-6731. 168 B
mhoyert@iun.edu
HOYLE, Bobby .... 870-460-1036... 24 D
hoyle@uamont.edu
HOYLE, Ken, R .... 919-718-7436. 359 B
khoyle@cccc.edu
HOYLE, Michael .... 617-243-2100. 227 K
mhoyle@lasell.edu
HOYNE, Susan, H .... 206-533-6638. 523 F
shoyne@shoreline.edu
HOYOS, Denise .... 520-417-4148... 12 R
hoyosd@cochise.edu
HOYT, Bill .... 717-764-9550. 414 A
bhoyt@csb.edu
HOYT, Brad .... 217-641-4777. 148 M
bhoyt@jwcc.edu
HOYT, Carol, A .... 563-884-5635. 182 A
carol.hoyt@palmer.edu
HOYT, David, R .... 972-599-3133. 469 G
dhoyt@collin.edu
HOYT, Jeff, E .... 615-494-8803. 459 D
jeff.hoyt@mtsu.edu
HOYT, Jennith, E .... 831-656-2288. 544 M
jehoyt@nps.edu
HOYT, William .... 617-349-8593. 228 B
whoyt@lesley.edu
HOYT, William .... 717-394-6211. 413 J
bhoyt@csb.edu
HOZDIK, Elaine .... 239-590-7931. 115 A
ehozdik@fgcu.edu
HRABEC, Erika, J .... 734-764-6270. 251 C
erikah@umich.edu
HRABOSKY, James, A .... 724-287-8711. 411 C
james.hrabosky@bc3.edu
HRABOWSKI,
Freeman, A .... 410-455-2274. 219 D
hrabowski@umbc.edu
HRADSKY, Robert .... 202-885-3318... 94 F
hradsky@american.edu
HRANITZ, John, M .... 570-389-4208. 427 H
jhranitz@bloomu.edu
HRDLICKA, Rick .... 909-384-8656... 62 A
rhrdlicka@sbccd.cc.ca.us
HRIBAR, Frank, J .... 517-265-5161. 238 G
fhribar@adrian.edu
HRISHENKO, Michael, S 330-941-3520. 394 A
mshrishenko@ysu.edu
HRITZAK, Susan, A .... 570-408-4850. 437 F
susan.hritzak@wilkes.edu
HRNCIR, Duane .... 605-394-2256. 452 A
duane.hrncir@sdsmt.edu
HROMISIN, Ronald, S .... 570-674-6312. 424 A
rhromisi@misericordia.edu
HRON, Stacey .... 218-683-8584. 260 D
stacey.hron@northlandcollege.edu
HRUSKA, Amanda .... 920-924-3193. 540 F
ahruska@morainepark.edu
HRUSKA, Amanda .... 920-465-2155. 536 F
hruskaa@uwgb.edu
HRUSKA, Sheryl .... 413-775-1811. 231 E
hruskas@gcc.mass.edu
HSIAO, Benjamin .... 631-632-6265. 342 C
HSIAO, Grace .... 626-571-8811... 74 B
graceh@uwest.edu
HSIAO, Lily .... 510-592-9688... 56 G
hsiaosf@npu.edu
HSIAO, Terrence .... 425-352-8870. 517 E
thsiao@cascadia.edu
HSIEH, Cheng-Yuan .... 847-679-3135. 149 G
cyhsieh@ksi.edu
HSIEH, Chialin .... 415-485-9545... 40 G
chialin.hsieh@marin.edu
HSIEH, George .... 510-592-9688... 56 G
georgeh@npu.edu
HSIEH, Jeanette .... 847-317-8191. 160 M
jhsieh@tiu.edu
HSIEH, Patricia .... 619-388-7834... 62 F
phsieh@sdccd.edu
HSIEH, Wen .... 510-592-9688... 56 G
wen@npu.edu
HSING, Danny .... 619-298-1829... 68 A
dshing@ssu.edu
HSIUNG, Anna .... 516-739-1545. 333 F
financial_aid@nyctcm.edu
HSU, Andrew .... 408-924-3800... 36 A
andrew.hsu@sjsu.edu
HSU, Becky .... 617-287-5152. 228 G
becky.hsu@umb.edu
HSU, Kwei .... 979-532-6350. 494 L
kweih@wcjc.edu
HSU, Lily .... 617-732-2064. 233 E
lily.hsu@mcphs.edu
HSU, Pochang .... 510-657-5913... 56 G
phsu@npu.edu
HSU, Stephen .... 517-355-0306. 246 H
hsu@msu.edu
HSU, Tai .... 510-592-9709... 56 G
taihsu@npu.edu
HU, Gigi .... 415-355-1601... 27 L
development@actcm.edu
HU, Mi .... 847-214-7137. 144 F
mhu@elgin.edu
HUA, Maggie .... 510-628-8029... 51 A
maggiehua@lincolnuca.edu
HUA, Susan .... 818-677-2077... 34 C
susan.hua@csun.edu
HUANG, Aileen .... 415-355-1601... 27 L
ailinghuang@actcm.edu
HUANG, Betsy .... 508-793-7145. 225 A
bhuang@clarku.edu
HUANG, Che-Tsao .... 718-262-2750. 319 F
huang@york.cuny.edu
HUANG, Christopher ...... 708-534-4503. 145 F
chuang@govst.edu
HUANG, Gina .... 408-260-0208... 44 J
sjstudentservices@fivebranches.edu
HUANG, Guiyou .... 802-485-2025. 500 A
vpaa@norwich.edu
HUANG, Jasmine .... 408-260-0208... 44 J
jasmine@fivebranches.edu
HUANG, Jefferson .... 909-621-8114... 39 D
jefferson.huang@cmc.edu
HUANG, Lixin .... 415-282-7600... 27 L
lixinhuang@actcm.edu
HUANG, Mimi .... 973-642-8747. 307 D
mimi.huang@shu.edu
HUANG, Roger, D .... 574-631-1691. 174 A
huang.31@nd.edu
HUANG, Wen .... 713-780-9777. 465 G
info@acaom.edu
HUARD, Jenny .... 660-944-2823. 272 H
communications@conception.edu
HUARD, Susan, D .... 603-206-8002. 296 A
shuard@ccsnh.edu
HUBAND, David, E .... 757-446-8474. 504 E
hubandde@evms.edu
HUBBARD, Ann .... 772-462-7570. 106 P
ahubbard@irsc.edu
HUBBARD, Annie .... 618-634-3228. 158 M
annieh@shawneecc.edu
HUBBARD, Brittany .... 812-941-2246. 168 F
bchubbar@ius.edu
HUBBARD, Dean, L .... 816-932-6743. 281 J
dlhubbard@saintlukescollege.edu
HUBBARD, Francis .... 207-941-7144. 210 B
hubbardfj@husson.edu
HUBBARD, James .... 309-268-8453. 146 B
jim.hubbard@heartland.edu
HUBBARD, Janet .... 248-689-8282. 251 I
jhubbard@walshcollege.edu
HUBBARD, Jeannette .... 726-946-7199. 437 B
hubbarj@westminster.edu
HUBBARD, Joan .... 801-626-6403. 497 D
jhubbard@weber.edu
HUBBARD, Laura, E .... 716-645-5124. 341 F
laurahub@buffalo.edu
HUBBARD, R. Glenn ...... 212-854-2888. 321 D
rgh1@columbia.edu
HUBBARD, Robert .... 203-773-8563... 87 G
hubbard@albertus.edu
HUBBARD, Ruth .... 443-334-2203. 218 E
rhubbard@stevenson.edu
HUBBARD, Stacey .... 217-424-6383. 153 C
shubbard@millikin.edu
HUBBARD, William .... 920-465-2510. 536 F
hubbardw@uwgb.edu
HUBBARD, Yvonne, B .... 434-982-6000. 511 B
yhs@virginia.edu
HUBBARD GIVEN, Mary 626-584-5691... 45 E
mgiven@fuller.edu
HUBBELL, Kent, L .... 607-255-1115. 322 A
klh4@cornell.edu
HUBBERT, Daron .... 951-552-8000... 30 H
dhubbert@calbaptist.edu
HUBBS, Janet .... 732-255-0400. 304 A
jhubbs@ocean.edu
HUBBS, Jocelyn .... 541-684-7345. 405 C
jhubbs@nwcu.edu
HUBENER, James .... 214-860-8695. 471 A
jhubener@dcccd.edu
HUBER, Amy .... 973-803-5000. 304 C
ahuber@pillar.edu
HUBER, Bettina .... 818-677-3277... 34 C
bettina.huber@csun.edu
HUBER, Chip .... 616-222-1423. 241 F
chip.huber@cornerstone.edu
HUBER, Gary .... 239-280-2573... 98 K
gary.huber@avemaria.edu
HUBER, Gary .... 309-796-5602. 140 E
huberg@bhc.edu
HUBER, Lane .... 701-224-5714. 372 B
lane.huber@bismarckstate.edu
HUBER, Laurie, G .... 248-232-4513. 248 D
lghuber@oaklandcc.edu
HUBER, Lydia .... 361-572-6461. 493 H
lydia.huber@victoriacollege.edu
HUBER, Margaret .... 605-229-8405. 450 J
margaret.huber@presentation.edu
HUBER, Mark, D .... 570-372-4247. 433 H
huber@susqu.edu
HUBER, Matthew .... 304-876-5212. 529 I
mhuber@shepherd.edu
HUBER, Michael .... 484-664-3150. 424 H
huber@muhlenberg.edu
HUBER, Patricia, B .... 540-674-3631. 513 B
phuber@nr.edu
HUBER, Peter .... 920-206-2347. 533 U
peter.huber@mbbc.edu
HUBER, Susan, J .... 651-962-6720. 265 C
sjhuber@stthomas.edu
HUBERMAN, Jeffrey, H .. 309-677-2360. 140 I
huberman@bradley.edu
HUBERMAN, Steven .... 212-463-0400. 348 B
stevenh@touro.edu
HUBERS, Todd, K .... 616-526-6495. 240 L
thubers@calvin.edu
HUBERT, Anthony .... 910-678-8244. 360 D
huberta@faytechcc.edu
HUBIN, David, R .... 541-346-3036. 406 D
hubin@uoregon.edu
HUBINGER, Amy, M ...... 906-227-2626. 248 A
ahubinge@nmu.edu
HUBLER, Barbara .... 415-338-2611... 35 E
bhubler@sfsu.edu
HUBLER, Grant .... 541-956-7235. 407 F
grant@roguecc.edu
HUBREGTSE, Joyce .... 605-221-3113. 450 C
jhubregtse@kilian.edu
HUCH, Robert, E .... 540-261-8413. 509 K
bob.huch@svu.edu
HUCK, Jack, J .... 402-323-3415. 292 C
jhuck@southeast.edu
HUCKABA, Sam .... 850-644-4404. 115 C
shuckaba@fsu.edu
HUCKABAY, Sonia .... 559-791-2403... 49 P
shuckaba@portervillecollege.edu
HUCKABY, Henry, M ...... 404-656-2202. 134 A
chancellor@usg.edu
HUCKEBY, Ed .... 405-789-7661. 400 A
ed.huckeby@swcu.edu
HUCKESTEIN, Jim .... 541-917-4331. 404 B
jim.huckestein@linnbenton.edu
HUCKESTEIN, Julie, A .... 503-399-6575. 402 E
julie.huckestein@chemeketa.edu
HUCKINS, Heather .... 603-535-2249. 298 G
hhuckins@plymouth.edu
HUCKMAN, Beverly, B ... 312-942-7093. 157 G
beverly_b_huckman@rush.edu
HUCKS, Cheri, A .... 864-592-4931. 447 A
hucksc@sccsc.edu
HUDACK, John, J .... 716-827-2512. 348 G
hudackj@trocaire.edu
HUDACK, Jon .... 716-827-2547. 348 G
hudackj@trocaire.edu
HUDAK, DeDe .... 916-577-2200... 76 J
dhudak@jessup.edu
HUDAK, Jane, E .... 484-664-3300. 424 H
hudak@muhlenberg.edu
HUDAK, Randy .... 304-293-3944. 530 D
randy.hudak@mail.wvu.edu
HUDAK, Sharon .... 570-674-6295. 424 A
shudak@misericordia.edu
HUDDLESTON, Gwen ..... 805-289-6388... 74 H
ghuddleston@vcccd.edu
HUDDLESTON, Mark, W 603-862-2450. 298 C
presidents.office@unh.edu
HUDDLESTON, Sean ...... 616-331-5034. 243 C
huddless@gvsu.edu
HUDDLESTON,
Tracey, R .... 615-898-5191. 459 D
tracey.huddleston@mtsu.edu
HUDEC, Susan .... 718-940-5854. 339 B
shudec@sjcny.edu
HUDELSON-PUTNAM,
Cece .... 209-575-6131... 77 J
hudelsonputnam@mjc.edu
HUDGENS, Lisa .... 618-985-3741. 148 J
lisahudgens@jalc.edu
HUDGIN, Denise .... 419-251-1324. 383 G
denise.hudgin@mercycollege.edu
HUDGINGS, Janice .... 909-621-8137... 60 A
janice.hudgings@pomona.edu
HUDGINS, Chris .... 702-895-0301. 294 I
chris.hudgins@unlv.edu
HUDGINS, Jim .... 870-460-1018... 24 D
hudgins@uamont.edu
HUDGINS, John, L .... 410-951-3528. 220 B
jhudgins@coppin.edu
HUDGINS, V. Lavoyed ... 859-985-3240. 192 F
hudginsv@berea.edu
HUDLUN, Randy .... 417-862-9533. 274 F
rhedlun@globaluniversity.edu
HUDNUT-BEUMLER,
James .... 615-343-3960. 463 G
james.hudnut-beumler@vanderbilt.edu
HUDOK, Cynthia, K .... 304-367-4213. 529 F
cynthia.hudok@fairmontstate.edu
HUDSON, Angela .... 501-686-2504... 23 H
ahudson@uasys.edu
HUDSON, Blake, W .... 423-285-1689. 453 E
blake.hudson@bryan.edu
HUDSON, Bobby .... 615-230-3445. 461 G
bobby.hudson@volstate.edu
HUDSON, Danny .... 404-527-4537. 122 E
dhudson@carver.edu
HUDSON, David, D .... 714-895-8907... 39 J
dhudson@gwc.cccd.edu
HUDSON, Dean, P .... 843-349-2739. 442 E
dhudson@coastal.edu
HUDSON, Debra .... 270-247-8521. 197 H
dhudson@midcontinent.edu
HUDSON, Delaphine .... 562-907-4223... 76 I
dhudson@whittier.edu
HUDSON, Donald .... 812-488-2452. 173 H
dh104@evansville.edu
HUDSON, Donald .... 609-894-9311. 299 I
dhudson@bcc.edu
HUDSON, Earnest .... 828-227-7301. 369 E
ehudson@wcu.edu
HUDSON, Garien, I .... 260-399-7700. 174 C
ghudson@sf.edu
HUDSON, Gregory .... 662-621-4153. 266 D
ghudson@coahomacc.edu
HUDSON, Harold .... 937-529-2201. 390 D
hhudson@united.edu
HUDSON, Jackie .... 205-929-1401..... 5 G
jhudson@miles.edu
HUDSON, Jennifer, M .... 713-646-1899. 480 J
jhudson@stcl.edu
HUDSON, Jerry .... 503-636-8141. 404 C
president@marylhurst.edu
HUDSON, Karen .... 615-771-7821. 464 G
karen.hudson@williamsoncc.edu
HUDSON, Kathy .... 434-961-5446. 513 F
khudson@pvcc.edu
HUDSON, Keith .... 270-686-4261. 192 G
keith.hudson@brescia.edu
HUDSON, Lea Ann .... 404-471-6402. 119 I
lhudson@agnesscott.edu
HUDSON, Lyla .... 843-792-8721. 445 B
hudsonly@musc.edu
HUDSON, Mark, A .... 217-581-3923. 144 E
mahudson@eiu.edu
HUDSON, Maureen .... 781-280-3506. 232 B
hudsonm@middlesex.mass.edu

HUDSON, Melissa, A ..... 530-226-4974... 66 D
mhudson@simpsonu.edu
HUDSON, Michael, J ..... 630-637-5661. 154 F
mjhudson@noctrl.edu
HUDSON, Pam ..... 417-455-5506. 273 E
phudson@crowder.edu
HUDSON, Pat ..... 816-414-3700. 277 L
phudson@mbts.edu
HUDSON, Richard ..... 502-585-9911. 199 C
rhudson@spalding.edu
HUDSON, Richard, B ..... 479-575-7964... 23 I
rhudson@uark.edu
HUDSON, Robert ..... 617-353-3710. 224 D
rhudson@bu.edu
HUDSON, Rodeny, B ..... 803-535-5470. 442 B
rhudson@claflin.edu
HUDSON, Stacy ..... 208-769-7819. 138 I
stacy_hudson@nic.edu
HUDSON, Tijuana, R ..... 803-535-5197. 442 B
thudson@claflin.edu
HUDSON, Tim ..... 870-972-3030... 19 N
timhudson@astate.edu
HUDSON, JR., William .. 850-599-3183. 114 K
william.hudson@famu.edu
HUDSON, William, B ..... 608-342-1561. 537 D
hudsonw@uwplatt.edu
HUDSPETH, Donald ..... 585-475-7077. 337 L
HUDSPETH, Harvey, L .... 806-651-2116. 484 D
hhudspeth@mail.wtamu.edu
HUDSPETH, Larry ..... 503-821-8943. 406 F
hudspeth@pnca.edu
HUDY, Karen ..... 216-421-7321. 377 C
khudy@cia.edu
HUEBER, Charlie ..... 830-792-7277. 480 F
cmhueber@schreiner.edu
HUEBNER, Janet ..... 319-352-8227. 183 E
janet.huebner@wartburg.edu
HUEBNER, Thomas ..... 205-391-2999..... 6 H
thuebner@sheltonstate.edu
HUEBOTTER, Chris ..... 573-288-6542. 273 F
chuebotter@culver.edu
HUEBSCH, Pat ..... 541-956-7163. 407 F
phuebsch@roguecc.edu
HUEG, Kurt ..... 650-949-7394... 44 N
huegkurt@foothill.edu
HUEGEL, Mary ..... 978-232-2084. 226 C
mhuegel@endicott.edu
HUELSBECK, David, R .... 253-535-7645. 521 I
huelsdr@plu.edu
HUELSBECK, Tom, A ..... 253-535-7200. 521 I
tom.huelsbeck@plu.edu
HUELSMAN, Shelly ..... 620-227-9285. 186 B
shuelsman@dc3.edu
HUENEMANN, Kurt ..... 419-448-2351. 380 G
keh@heidelberg.edu
HUENINK, Richard ..... 262-551-6200. 532 D
rhuenink@carthage.edu
HUENNEKE, Laura ..... 928-523-2230... 16 C
laura.huenneke@nau.edu
HUERTA, David ..... 559-278-8400... 33 D
davidhu@csufresno.edu
HUERTA, Patricia ..... 312-362-8601. 143 H
phuerta@depaul.edu
HUERTAS, Belmarie ..... 787-743-4041. 548 H
bhuertas@columbiaco.edu
HUERTAS, Linda ..... 773-481-8434. 142 F
lhuertas@ccc.edu
HUERTAS, Mildred ..... 787-257-7373. 552 H
ue_mhuertas@suagm.edu
HUERTAS, Orlando ..... 305-626-3798. 104 J
orlando.huertas@fmuniv.edu
HUERTAS-BERMÚDEZ,
Antonio ..... 787-993-8862. 554 A
antonio.huertas@upr.edu
HUESER, Kyle ..... 712-274-6400. 183 G
kyle.hueser@witcc.edu
HUESING, Alan ..... 903-923-2172. 471 J
ahuesing@etbu.edu
HUEY, Lindley ..... 617-253-6162. 233 B
HUFF, Alexandra ..... 617-369-3659. 236 F
ahuff@mfa.org
HUFF, Amy ..... 931-393-1629. 461 A
ahuff@mscc.edu
HUFF, Betty ..... 901-678-5218. 460 B
bjhuff@memphis.edu
HUFF, Cassandra ..... 515-244-4221. 175 C
huffc@aib.edu
HUFF, Eugene, C ..... 925-229-6851... 41 J
ehuff@4cd.edu
HUFF, Glenda ..... 325-649-8014. 473 F
ghuff@hputx.edu
HUFF, III, Joseph, E ..... 409-944-1302. 472 I
jhuff@gc.edu
HUFF, Kim ..... 803-535-1210. 446 B
huffk@octech.edu
HUFF, Kim, R ..... 803-535-1204. 446 B
huffk@octech.edu
HUFF, Lester ..... 301-295-1210. 545 C
lester.huff@usuhs.edu
HUFF, Marie ..... 828-227-7271. 369 E
mhuff@wcu.edu
HUFF, Phyllis ..... 919-718-7405. 359 B
phuff@cccc.edu
HUFF, Thomas, F ..... 804-827-5600. 511 F
tfhuff@vcu.edu
HUFF, Tim, T ..... 405-744-5459. 397 H
tim.huff@okstate.edu
HUFFAKER, John ..... 806-742-2155. 487 D
john.huffaker@ttu.edu
HUFFARD, Lorri, M ..... 276-223-4829. 514 F
lhuffard@wcc.vccs.edu
HUFFCUTT, Tom, G ..... 715-833-6661. 539 J
thuffcutt@cvtc.edu
HUFFMAN, Amanda ..... 443-518-4773. 215 E
ahuffman@howardcc.edu
HUFFMAN, Debbie ..... 940-668-4475. 477 I
dhuffman@nctc.edu
HUFFMAN, Don ..... 312-662-4236. 139 F
dhuffman@adler.edu
HUFFMAN, Gerald ..... 206-296-5869. 523 E
huffmanje@seattleu.edu
HUFFMAN, Jeffery ..... 419-559-2257. 389 I
jhuffman01@terra.edu
HUFFMAN, Jessamine .... 256-840-4151..... 6 I
jhuffman@snead.edu
HUFFMAN, Laurene, K ... 740-374-8716. 392 I
lhuffman@wscc.edu
HUFFMAN, Maggie ..... 503-491-7145. 404 E
maggie.huffman@mhcc.edu
HUFFMAN, Mari, L ..... 419-866-0261. 389 H
mlhuffman@stautzenberger.com
HUFFMAN, Monica, R .... 660-543-4106. 283 A
mhuffman@ucmo.edu
HUFFMAN, Pat ..... 425-640-1002. 519 D
phuffman@edcc.edu
HUFFMAN, Rebecca ..... 276-328-0139. 511 C
reg5a@uvawise.edu
HUFFMAN, Robin ..... 260-399-7700. 174 C
rhuffman@sf.edu
HUFFMAN, Sherri, H ..... 434-797-8576. 512 C
shuffman@dcc.vccs.edu
HUFFMAN, Tammy, S .... 740-588-1212. 394 C
thuffman@zanestate.edu
HUFFMAN, Virginia, A ... 212-327-8300. 338 A
huffman@rockefeller.edu
HUFFSTETLER,
Edward, W ..... 540-828-5332. 502 J
ehuffste@bridgewater.edu
HUFFT, Anita, G ..... 229-333-5959. 134 B
ahufft@valdosta.edu
HUFNAGEL, Michele ..... 724-503-1001. 436 G
mhufnagel@washjeff.edu
HUFSTETLER, Catrice ..... 770-975-4000. 122 I
HUFTALIN, Deneece ..... 801-957-4285. 498 B
deneece.huftalin@slcc.edu
HUFTEL, Joe ..... 715-246-6561. 541 F
joe.huftel@witc.edu
HUG-ENGLISH, Cheryl ... 775-784-6122. 294 J
cherylh@med.unr.edu
HUGETZ, Edward ..... 713-221-8003. 489 D
hugetze@uhd.edu
HUGGETT, Monica ..... 212-799-5000. 328 B
HUGGINS, Brian ..... 314-340-3335. 275 A
hugginsb@hssu.edu
HUGGINS, Cynthia, E ..... 207-255-1210. 212 F
chuggins@maine.edu
HUGGINS, Jonathan ..... 706-236-2217. 121 G
jhuggins@berry.edu
HUGGINS, Regina, M ..... 919-866-5408. 364 G
rmhuggins@waketech.edu
HUGHES, A. LeAnn ..... 423-652-4706. 455 I
lhughes@king.edu
HUGHES, Ally ..... 912-650-6230. 131 H
ahughes@southuniversity.edu
HUGHES, Andrew ..... 775-673-7240. 294 H
ahughes@tmcc.edu
HUGHES, Angela ..... 219-473-4227. 164 K
ahughes2@ccsj.edu
HUGHES, Ann ..... 912-583-3230. 122 B
HUGHES, B. Hilles ..... 740-376-4645. 383 E
hilles.hughes@marietta.edu
HUGHES, Barbara, J ..... 814-641-3311. 419 H
hughesb@juniata.edu
HUGHES, Bernice ..... 229-391-5130. 119 H
bhughes@abac.edu
HUGHES, Billy ..... 205-665-6130..... 9 B
hugheswl@montevallo.edu
HUGHES, Bonnie ..... 506-865-8588. 520 D
hughes_b@heritage.edu
HUGHES, C. Raymond ..... 860-906-5012... 88 D
rhughes@ccc.commnet.edu
HUGHES, Carol ..... 312-362-8592. 143 H
chughe23@depaul.edu
HUGHES, Chad ..... 313-883-8673. 249 E
hughes.chad@shms.edu
HUGHES, Charles, F ..... 417-690-2211. 272 E
hughes@cofo.edu
HUGHES, Christine ..... 617-824-8908. 226 A
christine_hughes@emerson.edu
HUGHES, Craig ..... 716-839-8246. 322 E
HUGHES, David ..... 785-738-9008. 189 F
dhughes@ncktc.edu
HUGHES, David ..... 501-760-4311... 22 A
dhughes@npcc.edu
HUGHES, DeVetta ..... 843-574-6199. 447 E
devetta.hughes@tridenttech.edu
HUGHES, Dianna ..... 662-252-8000. 269 F
dr_hughes@rustcollege.edu
HUGHES, Ed ..... 859-442-1175. 195 B
ed.hughes@kctcs.edu
HUGHES, Edwin ..... 973-278-5400. 299 D
ejh@berkeleycollege.edu
HUGHES, Edwin ..... 973-278-5400. 314 K
ejh@berkeleycollege.edu
HUGHES, Elizabeth ..... 312-567-5045. 147 F
hughes@iit.edu
HUGHES, Elizabeth, B ..... 417-690-2212. 272 E
ehughes@cofo.edu
HUGHES, Erinn ..... 281-649-3213. 473 B
erhughes@hbu.edu
HUGHES, Ernie, T ..... 225-771-3911. 206 I
ernie_hughes@sus.edu
HUGHES, Frank ..... 605-274-4325. 449 K
frank.hughes@augie.edu
HUGHES, Gail, D ..... 501-569-3113... 24 B
gdhughes@ualr.edu
HUGHES, George ..... 805-756-6650... 32 F
grhughes@calpoly.edu
HUGHES, Jacqueline ..... 909-537-5029... 34 E
HUGHES, James, J ..... 860-297-2376... 91 F
james.hughes@trincoll.edu
HUGHES, James, L ..... 410-706-1935. 219 C
jhughes@umaryland.edu
HUGHES, James, W ..... 848-932-2828. 306 B
jwhughes@rci.rutgers.edu
HUGHES, Jason ..... 608-363-2137. 531 M
hughesj@beloit.edu
HUGHES, Jay ..... 870-460-1053... 24 D
hughesj@uamont.edu
HUGHES, Jennifer ..... 650-574-6118... 64 C
hughesj@smccd.edu
HUGHES, Jerry, M ..... 660-543-4250. 283 A
hughes@ucmo.edu
HUGHES, Jim ..... 620-235-4154. 189 L
jhughes@pittstate.edu
HUGHES, Joe Pat ..... 580-371-2371. 396 E
jhughes@mscok.edu
HUGHES, John ..... 661-362-2223... 53 G
jhughes@masters.edu
HUGHES, Joseph, B ..... 215-895-2210. 415 B
engineering@coe.drexel.edu
HUGHES, Juliana ..... 620-223-2700. 186 G
julianah@fortscott.edu
HUGHES, Kevin, M ..... 757-594-7335. 503 M
kmhughes@cnu.edu
HUGHES, Korey ..... 804-330-0111. 503 G
finaidcrim@centura.edu
HUGHES, Laura ..... 870-460-1454... 24 D
hughesl@uamont.edu
HUGHES, Laura ..... 208-792-2224. 138 G
lhughes@lcsc.edu
HUGHES, Lecia ..... 325-793-4998. 476 E
hughes.lecia@mcm.edu
HUGHES, Leslie ..... 601-635-2111. 266 H
lhughes@eccc.edu
HUGHES, Linda ..... 402-354-7049. 291 B
linda.hughes@methodistcollege.edu
HUGHES, Louise ..... 870-612-2013... 25 A
louise.hughes@uaccb.edu
HUGHES, Lucille ..... 215-717-6144. 435 A
lhughes@uarts.edu
HUGHES, Mark ..... 301-925-3800. 268 A
rmhughes@mc.edu
HUGHES, Mark ..... 512-245-2501. 487 C
mh66@txstate.edu
HUGHES, Marshall ..... 617-541-5381. 232 G
mhughes@rcc.mass.edu
HUGHES, Martha ..... 972-273-3590. 471 B
mhughes@dcccd.edu
HUGHES, Martin ..... 616-222-1497. 241 F
martin.hughes@cornerstone.edu
HUGHES, Mary, E ..... 614-235-4136. 390 A
mhughes@TLSohio.edu
HUGHES, Matthew ..... 334-347-2623..... 3 G
mhughes@escc.edu
HUGHES, Melany ..... 308-432-6415. 291 D
mhughes@csc.edu
HUGHES, Michael ..... 415-422-2465... 73 J
hughesm@usfca.edu
HUGHES, Michael, J ..... 740-351-3539. 388 N
mhughes@shawnee.edu
HUGHES, Michelle ..... 508-588-9100. 232 A
HUGHES, Michelle ..... 610-683-4822. 429 A
hughes@kutztown.edu
HUGHES, Mike ..... 231-591-2924. 242 F
hughesm@ferris.edu
HUGHES, Mike, C ..... 817-923-1921. 481 G
mhughes@swbts.edu
HUGHES, Myron ..... 513-556-4344. 390 G
myron.hughes@uc.edu
HUGHES, Nancy ..... 405-224-3140. 401 E
nhughes@usao.edu
HUGHES, Nancy, B ..... 607-746-4573. 345 G
hughesnb@delhi.edu
HUGHES, Pennie, D ..... 864-488-4544. 444 L
phughes@limestone.edu
HUGHES, Peter, D ..... 518-244-2200. 338 C
hughep@sage.edu
HUGHES, Randy ..... 361-593-3209. 484 A
j.hughes@tamuk.edu
HUGHES, Robert ..... 615-963-1836. 459 E
rhughes@tnstate.edu
HUGHES, Robert, A ..... 402-398-5527. 288 F
robert.hughes@alegent.org
HUGHES, Sandra ..... 843-863-7933. 441 H
shughes@csuniv.edu
HUGHES, Sandra, E ..... 870-235-4041... 23 F
sandrahughes@saumag.edu
HUGHES, Scott ..... 352-638-9745... 99 B
shughes@beaconcollege.edu
HUGHES, Sherri, L ..... 703-284-1550. 507 B
sherri.hughes@marymount.edu
HUGHES, Stacy ..... 312-915-6740. 151 H
shughe2@luc.edu
HUGHES, Tamara, J ..... 803-536-8103. 446 G
thughes@scsu.edu
HUGHES, Tanya, G ..... 432-335-6750. 477 M
thughes@odessa.edu
HUGHES, Tom ..... 928-776-2205... 19 H
tom.hughes@yc.edu
HUGHES, Tom ..... 800-962-7682. 285 A
athletics@wma.edu
HUGHES, W. William ..... 909-558-1300... 51 C
bhughes@llu.edu
HUGHES HANDLEY,
Allyson ..... 207-621-3403. 212 C
allyson.handley@maine.edu
HUGHES HARRIS,
Cynthia ..... 850-599-3818. 114 K
cynthia.hughes@famu.edu
HUGHEY, Andrew, C ..... 713-313-7470. 485 F
hugheyac@tsu.edu
HUGHEY, Richard ..... 831-459-4908... 72 C
vpdue@ucsc.edu
HUGHEY, Willie, M ..... 903-927-3211. 495 A
wmhughey@wileyc.edu
HUGHSTON, Patty ..... 251-580-2101..... 4 L
phughston@faulknerstate.edu
HUGINE, JR., Andrew .... 256-372-5230..... 1 A
andrew.hugine@aamu.edu
HUGLE, Shelbie ..... 859-246-6216. 194 L
shelbie.hugle@kctcs.edu
HUGUENIN, Sanders ..... 276-328-0120. 511 C
jsh4ew@uvawise.edu
HUGULEY, John ..... 843-953-2060. 443 A
huguleyj@cofc.edu
HUHRA, Lourdene ..... 847-543-2514. 143 A
lhuhra@clcillinois.edu
HUI, Andrew ..... 215-702-4203. 411 F
ahui@cairn.edu
HUI, Timothy, K ..... 215-702-4377. 411 F
thui@cairn.edu
HUIATT, Ron ..... 724-938-5775. 428 A
huiatt@calu.edu
HUIDEKOPER, Elizabeth . 401-863-9400. 438 J
elizabeth_huidekoper@brown.edu
HUISH, David ..... 928-524-7888... 16 E
david.huish@npc.edu
HUISKAMP, Julie, G ..... 563-562-3263. 181 E
huiskamj@nicc.edu
HUIZINGA, Dorota ..... 657-278-4831... 33 E
dhuizinga@fullerton.edu
HUKE, Theresa ..... 610-361-5249. 424 I
huket@neumann.edu
HUKILL, Lezlie ..... 806-291-3440. 494 F
hukill@wbu.edu
HUKILL, Lezlie ..... 806-291-3446. 494 F
lezlieh@wbu.edu
HUKOWICZ, Elizabeth .... 413-265-2360. 225 C
hukowicze@elms.edu
HULETT, Kevin ..... 918-293-5476. 398 B
kevin.hulett@okstate.edu
HULETT, Matt ..... 505-277-0385. 312 F
mhulett@unm.edu
HULETT, Tom ..... 816-604-3063. 277 G
tom.hulett@mcckc.edu
HULIN, Alicia ..... 337-521-8920. 203 I
alicia.hulin@solacc.edu
HULIN, Christopher, P ... 615-868-6503. 457 D
chris.hulin@mtsa.edu
HULKE, Carla, J ..... 507-354-8221. 256 M
hulkecj@mlc-wels.edu
HULL, Anne ..... 904-826-0084. 118 I
ahull@usa.edu
HULL, Brian ..... 479-979-1421... 25 J
bhull@ozarks.edu
HULL, Brooks, A ..... 903-813-2419. 466 H
bhull@austincollege.edu
HULL, Deborah ..... 323-731-2383... 57 I
dhull@psuca.edu
HULL, Edward, C ..... 413-545-1964. 228 F
ehull@gw.housing.umass.edu

HULL, James, L ... 419-755-4850. 385 D
jhull@ncstatecollege.edu
HULL, Jim ... 217-234-5225. 150 D
jhull17327@lakeland.cc.il.us
HULL, JR., Joe ... 843-953-5546. 443 A
hullj@cofc.edu
HULL, Judy, M ... 931-372-3491. 460 A
jmhull@tntech.edu
HULL, Mark ... 719-208-3800. 450 G
mhull@national.edu
HULL, Shawn ... 573-592-4389. 285 D
shull@williamwoods.edu
HULL, Stephen, E ... 863-297-1026. 110 H
shull@polk.edu
HULL, Teresa ... 909-652-7653... 37 M
teresa.hull@chaffey.edu
HULL, Thomas, A ... 212-346-1200. 335 J
thull@pace.edu
HULL, William ... 269-749-7535. 249 A
bjhull@olivetcollege.edu
HULL ANDERSON,
Carolyn ... 410-462-7799. 213 F
HULLETT, Lisa ... 256-352-8267... 9 G
lisa.hullett@wallacestate.edu
HULON, Jane ... 601-643-8310. 266 F
jane.hulon@colin.edu
HULS, Jack ... 360-417-6246. 522 A
jhuls@pencol.edu
HULSE, Debra ... 325-793-4761. 476 E
hulse.debra@mcm.edu
HULSEBOSCH, Patricia ... 202-448-7036... 95 C
patricia.hulsebosch@gallaudet.edu
HULSEY, Janet ... 706-419-1262. 123 F
hulsey@covenant.edu
HULSEY, Tara ... 843-863-7075. 441 H
thulsey@csuniv.edu
HULSEY, Timothy, L ... 804-828-1803. 511 F
tlhulsey@vcu.edu
HULST, Mary ... 616-526-7617. 240 L
msh4@calvin.edu
HULST, Shani ... 541-956-7158. 407 F
shulst@roguecc.edu
HULSTEIN, Pamela, L ... 712-722-6689. 177 J
pam.hulstein@dordt.edu
HULSTINE, Thomas ... 717-544-5395. 421 C
tjhulsti@lancastergeneralcollege.edu
HULT, Alexander, R ... 304-345-2820. 531 E
admin@wvjc.edu
HULTBERG, Jane ... 207-801-5660. 210 A
jhultberg@coa.edu
HULTIN, Steve, R ... 970-491-0006... 80 I
steve.hultin@colostate.edu
HULTMAN, Ken ... 402-554-3514. 293 A
khultman@unomaha.edu
HULTZ, Rachel ... 502-897-4121. 199 B
rehultz@sbts.edu
HULVEY, Matt ... 931-393-1602. 461 A
mhulvey@mscc.edu
HUMBERGER, Laura ... 406-994-4361. 287 B
lhumberger@montana.edu
HUMBERT, Mark ... 315-312-2248. 344 A
mark.humbert@oswego.edu
HUMBLE, Dina ... 562-938-4446... 51 D
dhumble@lbcc.edu
HUME, Richard ... 631-420-2080. 346 B
richard.hume@farmingdale.edu
HUMERICK,
Rosalind, M ... 386-312-4212. 112 C
rosalindhumerick@sjrstate.edu
HUMES, Cynthia ... 909-607-8713... 39 D
cynthia.humes@cmc.edu
HUMESTON, Howard, D ... 305-899-3139... 98 O
dhumeston@barry.edu
HUMISTON, Dolores, J ... 509-777-4320. 525 F
dhumiston@whitworth.edu
HUMME, Larryl ... 708-239-3977. 160 K
larryl.humme@trnty.edu
HUMMEL, Mandi ... 419-448-3422. 389 J
hummelas@tiffin.edu
HUMMEL, Scott ... 601-318-6497. 270 I
shummel@wmcarey.edu
HUMMEL, Scott, R ... 610-330-5403. 420 D
hummels@lafayette.edu
HUMMER, Alissa ... 805-893-4091... 72 B
alissa.hummer@planning.ucsb.edu
HUMMER, Jim ... 760-773-2561... 40 F
jhummer@collegeofthedesert.edu
HUMMER, Judith, G ... 717-290-8718. 421 D
jhummer@lancasterseminary.edu
HUMMERT, Mary Lee ... 785-864-4904. 190 L
mlhummert@ku.edu
HUMMINGBIRD,
Edward ... 505-922-6506. 312 E
edward.hummingbird@bie.edu
HUMMONS, Tina ... 937-512-3120. 388 O
tina.hummons@sinclair.edu
HUMPHREY, Bonnie ... 660-831-4108. 278 I
humphreyb@moval.edu
HUMPHREY, Dana, N ... 207-581-2213. 212 B
danah@maine.edu
HUMPHREY, George, D ... 520-626-7301... 18 F
ghumphre@email.arizona.edu
HUMPHREY, George, E ... 617-732-2292. 233 E
george.humphrey@mcphs.edu
HUMPHREY, Jim ... 615-966-7600. 456 B
jim.humphrey@lipscomb.edu
HUMPHREY, Kathy, W ... 412-648-1006. 435 C
kathyh@pitt.edu
HUMPHREY, Keith ... 805-756-1521... 32 F
humphrey@calpoly.edu
HUMPHREY, Lynn ... 208-426-2948. 137 G
lynnhumphrey@boisestate.edu
HUMPHREY, Richard, A ... 423-775-6596. 458 A
HUMPHREY, Scott ... 315-792-3835. 349 F
shumphrey@utica.edu
HUMPHREY, Shawn ... 904-448-9499. 113 K
HUMPHREY, Twila ... 719-502-2052... 84 A
twila.humphrey@ppcc.edu
HUMPHREYS, Amy ... 309-268-8194. 146 B
amy.humphreys@heartland.edu
HUMPHREYS, Bryce ... 509-882-7049. 525 G
bhumphreys@yvcc.edu
HUMPHREYS,
George, G ... 270-824-1723. 196 A
george.humphreys@kctcs.edu
HUMPHREYS, Joe ... 361-485-4485. 489 E
humphreysj@uhv.edu
HUMPHREYS, Robert, G ... 209-478-0800... 47 M
rgh@humphreys.edu
HUMPHREYS, JR.,
Robert, G ... 209-478-0800... 47 M
rhumphreys@humphreys.edu
HUMPHRIES, Brian, L ... 651-286-7620. 263 A
blhumphries@nwc.edu
HUMPHRIES, Corey ... 706-233-7231. 131 E
chumphries@shorter.edu
HUMPHRIES, Karl ... 903-875-7600. 477 G
karl.humphries@navarrocollege.edu
HUMPHRIES, Kelly ... 864-250-7000... 96 F
kyh@strayer.edu
HUMPHRIES, Lou ... 619-388-3473... 62 D
lhumphri@sdccd.edu
HUMPHRIES, Tara ... 919-735-5151. 364 H
tarah@waynecc.edu
HUMPRES, Patricia ... 714-484-7309... 56 E
phumpres@cypresscollege.edu
HUNCHBERGER, Mary ... 360-417-6535. 522 A
mhunchberger@pencol.edu
HUNDLEY, Patrick ... 618-650-2345. 159 H
phundle@siue.edu
HUNDRIESER, James ... 603-535-2240. 298 G
jmhundrieser@plymouth.edu
HUNEYCUTT, Richy ... 252-527-6223. 361 F
rhuneycutt@lenoircc.edu
HUNG, Lily ... 212-220-8141. 317 A
lhung@bmcc.cuny.edu
HUNGER, Suzanne ... 406-447-6938. 287 A
hungers@umhelena.edu
HUNGERFORD, Dan ... 740-376-4720. 383 E
dan.hungerford@marietta.edu
HUNKER, Kurt ... 619-684-8787... 56 C
khunker@newschoolarch.edu
HUNN, Martha, S ... 843-349-2962. 442 E
mhunn@coastal.edu
HUNN, II, Marvin, T ... 214-887-5281. 471 F
mhunn@dts.edu
HUNNICUTT, Lew ... 806-648-1450. 472 G
lunnicutt@fpctx.edu
HUNNICUTT, Marianne ... 630-942-4306. 142 G
hunnicutt@cod.edu
HUNSAKER, Deanna ... 660-626-2356. 271 A
dhunsaker@atsu.edu
HUNSAKER, Miles ... 801-524-8108. 495 O
mhunsaker@ldsbc.edu
HUNSBERGER, Jill ... 734-481-2324. 242 D
jhunsberg1@emich.edu
HUNSBERGER, Susan ... 208-459-5407. 138 A
shunsberger@collegeofidaho.edu
HUNSICKER, Donald ... 617-262-5000. 223 F
don.hunsicker@the-bac.edu
HUNSINGER, Fred ... 215-340-8401. 411 B
hunsinge@bucks.edu
HUNSINGER PATTEN,
Rachael ... 518-743-2243. 345 E
pattenr@sunyacc.edu
HUNSUCKER, Jeremy ... 847-467-2152. 155 D
jhunsucker@northwestern.edu
HUNSUCKER, Scott, E ... 704-233-8220. 370 G
scotth@wingate.edu
HUNT, Alice ... 773-896-2400. 141 K
ahunt@ctschicago.edu
HUNT, Alisa ... 203-596-4512... 90 I
ahunt@post.edu
HUNT, Altavese ... 803-327-7402. 442 D
ahunt@clintonjuniorcollege.edu
HUNT, Cathy ... 270-831-9723. 195 D
cathy.hunt@kctcs.edu
HUNT, D. Bradford ... 312-281-3145. 157 D
dbhunt@roosevelt.edu
HUNT, Daphne ... 254-968-1852. 483 A
djhunt@tarleton.edu
HUNT, Darla ... 606-759-7141. 196 B
darla.hunt@kctcs.edu
HUNT, David, A ... 801-422-3868. 495 D
david_hunt@byu.edu
HUNT, Delores ... 704-406-2361. 354 C
dhunt@gardner-webb.edu
HUNT, Denise ... 760-921-5510... 58 C
dhunt@paloverde.edu
HUNT, Dennis ... 812-866-7017. 166 C
huntd@hanover.edu
HUNT, Gregory, K ... 570-340-6063. 423 B
gkhunt@marywood.edu
HUNT, J. Steven ... 503-375-7591. 403 A
shunt@corban.edu
HUNT, James, W ... 512-863-1567. 481 I
huntj@southwestern.edu
HUNT, Jeffrey ... 808-235-7442. 137 C
jwhunt@hawaii.edu
HUNT, Jennifer ... 617-912-9130. 224 B
jhunt@bostonconservatory.edu
HUNT, Jill ... 270-809-3763. 198 B
thunt2@murraystate.edu
HUNT, John ... 254-526-1402. 468 G
john.hunt@ctcd.edu
HUNT, Judith, L ... 973-655-4301. 303 D
huntjl@mail.montclair.edu
HUNT, Karen ... 937-327-6377. 393 E
khunt@wittenberg.edu
HUNT, Kathy ... 206-546-4741. 523 F
khunt@shoreline.edu
HUNT, Lawrence ... 413-585-2260. 236 H
lhunt@smith.edu
HUNT, Lisa, O ... 910-272-3501. 363 B
lohunt@robeson.edu
HUNT, Liz ... 701-252-3467. 373 D
lhunt@jc.edu
HUNT, Lori ... 509-533-7378. 518 E
lori.hunt@scc.spokane.edu
HUNT, Louis, D ... 919-515-1428. 368 B
ldhunt@ncsu.edu
HUNT, Mark ... 334-386-7140... 3 H
mhunt@faulkner.edu
HUNT, Marsha, D ... 301-937-8448. 218 H
mhunt@tesst.com
HUNT, Marvin ... 913-288-7659. 187 L
mhunt@kckcc.edu
HUNT, Mary ... 312-226-6294. 151 A
mhunt@lexingtoncollege.edu
HUNT, Melany, L ... 626-395-6249... 31 E
hunt@caltech.edu
HUNT, Patricia ... 304-734-6611. 527 O
phunt@bridgemont.edu
HUNT, Patricia ... 304-205-6623. 528 B
phunt@kvctc.edu
HUNT, Patrick, G ... 240-895-4307. 218 A
pghunt@smcm.edu
HUNT, Paul, M ... 517-432-4499. 246 H
pmhunt@msu.edu
HUNT, Peter, G ... 434-949-1005. 513 H
peter.hunt@southside.edu
HUNT, Rene ... 662-325-0610. 268 D
rch2@its.msstate.edu
HUNT, Roe, B ... 803-535-5471. 442 B
rhunt@claflin.edu
HUNT, Ruston ... 678-915-7338. 132 C
rhunt@spsu.edu
HUNT, Rusty ... 336-249-8186. 360 A
rthunt@davidsonccc.edu
HUNT, Ryan ... 513-569-1756. 376 L
ryan.hunt@cincinnatistate.edu
HUNT, Steven ... 910-521-6401. 369 B
steven.hunt@uncp.edu
HUNT, Todd, A ... 407-582-1463. 118 M
thunt3@valenciacollege.edu
HUNT, Virginia ... 570-504-7291. 413 B
HUNT BULL, Nicholas ... 603-668-2211. 297 I
n.hunt-bull@snhu.edu
HUNT-CARTER, Pamela ... 831-459-2749... 72 C
phcarter@ucsc.edu
HUNT-WEST, Jessica ... 916-638-1616... 47 B
jessica_west@heald.edu
HUNTER, Amber, S ... 402-472-0671. 292 I
ahunter3@unl.edu
HUNTER, Amelia ... 615-329-8537. 454 F
HUNTER, Ben, D ... 317-940-9982. 164 J
bdhunter@butler.edu
HUNTER, Bill ... 850-201-6556. 117 D
hunterb@tcc.fl.edu
HUNTER, Bill ... 850-973-9448. 109 H
hunterb@nfcc.edu
HUNTER, Bonnie, L ... 219-464-5411. 174 E
bonnie.hunter@valpo.edu
HUNTER, Brandon ... 404-756-1652. 129 E
bhunter@msm.edu
HUNTER, Carolyn, A ... 513-585-2068. 376 I
carolyn.hunter@thechristcollege.edu
HUNTER, Cynthia ... 941-752-5290. 114 I
hunterc@scf.edu
HUNTER, Donna, L ... 304-766-4146. 530 C
hunterdl@wvstateu.edu
HUNTER, Edith, T ... 212-280-1342. 349 A
ehunter@uts.columbia.edu
HUNTER, Gary ... 970-247-7224... 81 M
ghunter@fortlewis.edu
HUNTER, Gayle ... 386-752-1822. 104 G
gayle.hunter@fgc.edu
HUNTER, Gerald, E ... 336-750-2703. 370 A
hunterge@wssu.edu
HUNTER, Jack, M ... 417-836-5636. 278 E
jackhunter@missouristate.edu
HUNTER, JR., Jairy, C ... 843-863-7500. 441 H
jhunter@csuniv.edu
HUNTER, James ... 952-446-4138. 255 D
hunterj@crown.edu
HUNTER, James, E ... 804-524-5997. 515 D
jhunter@vsu.edu
HUNTER, Janet ... 563-387-2229. 180 M
hunterja@luther.edu
HUNTER, Janice ... 760-872-2000... 42 E
jhunter@deepsprings.edu
HUNTER, Jim ... 928-645-6681... 13 B
Jim.Hunter@coconino.edu
HUNTER, John ... 417-626-1234. 279 J
library@occ.edu
HUNTER, Kim ... 870-245-5185... 22 D
hunterk@obu.edu
HUNTER, Kim ... 513-244-4248. 377 G
kim_hunter@mail.msj.edu
HUNTER, Kymm ... 803-705-4519. 441 C
hunterk@benedict.edu
HUNTER, Larry, T ... 614-236-6641. 375 H
lhunter2@capital.edu
HUNTER, Lori ... 865-981-8121. 456 D
lori.hunter@maryvillecollege.edu
HUNTER, Lynn ... 508-270-4005. 231 G
lhunter@massbay.edu
HUNTER, Maria ... 480-994-9244... 17 Q
mariah@swiha.edu
HUNTER, Mark, A ... 805-756-5222... 32 F
mhunter@calpoly.edu
HUNTER, Mary ... 925-969-3466... 49 B
mhunter@jfku.edu
HUNTER, Melissa ... 931-221-7315. 459 B
hunterm@apsu.edu
HUNTER, Pam ... 760-773-2508... 40 F
phunter@collegeofthedesert.edu
HUNTER, Patricia ... 425-739-8361. 520 K
patricia.hunter@lwtech.edu
HUNTER, Rebecca ... 508-793-7561. 225 A
rhunter@clarku.edu
HUNTER, Robert, D ... 325-674-2495. 464 H
hunterr@acu.edu
HUNTER, Rosemarie ... 801-972-3596. 496 Q
r.hunter@partners.utah.edu
HUNTER, Steve ... 360-867-6310. 519 J
hunters@evergreen.edu
HUNTER, Susan ... 503-552-1512. 404 H
shunter@ncnm.edu
HUNTER, Susan, J ... 207-581-1547. 212 B
hunter@maine.edu
HUNTER, Susan, S ... 804-523-5375. 512 F
shunter@reynolds.edu
HUNTER, Teressa ... 405-466-2915. 395 N
thunter@langston.edu
HUNTER, Tim, W ... 814-332-2755. 409 D
tim.hunter@allegheny.edu
HUNTER, Tracie, N ... 252-335-3283. 367 C
tnhunter@mail.ecsu.edu
HUNTER, W, B ... 602-429-4431... 16 O
bhunter@ps.edu
HUNTER-GOLDSWORTHY,
Heidi ... 570-484-2344. 429 B
hgh4845@lhup.edu
HUNTINGTON, Judith, A ... 914-654-5430. 320 H
president@cnr.edu
HUNTINGTON, Mark, W ... 260-982-5051. 170 U
mwhuntington@manchester.edu
HUNTINGTON, Robert ... 419-448-2202. 380 G
president@heidelberg.edu
HUNTLEY, Daniel ... 641-844-5670. 179 J
daniel.huntley@iavalley.edu
HUNTLEY, Deborah ... 989-964-4144. 249 G
dhuntley@svsu.edu
HUNTLEY, Edelma, D ... 828-262-2130. 367 A
huntleyed@appstate.edu
HUNTLEY, Steve, E ... 904-264-2172. 111 P
steve.huntley@iws.edu
HUNTLEY-SMITH, Jen ... 775-784-8262. 294 J
jhuntleysmith@unr.edu
HUNTON, Ladonna, L ... 270-745-6867. 200 G
ladonna.hunton@wku.edu
HUNTOON, JR.,
David, H ... 845-938-2610. 545 I
8sgs@usma.edu
HUNTOON,
Jacqueline, E ... 906-487-2327. 247 A
jeh@mtu.edu
HUNTSINGER, Trish ... 828-395-1297. 361 C
thuntsing@isothermal.edu

HUNTSMAN, Deborah, C ... 330-672-3237. 382 B
dhuntsm1@kent.edu
HUNTSMAN, Kent ... 512-863-1235. 481 I
huntsmak@southwestern.edu
HUO, Xiaoming (Sharon) ... 931-372-3463. 460 A
xhuo@tntech.edu
HUOPPI, Jennifer ... 860-465-4357... 87 L
huoppij@easternct.edu
HUOT, Anne, E ... 603-358-2000. 298 F
ahuot@keene.edu
HUPACH, Laura ... 316-942-4291. 189 E
nicholasla@newmanu.edu
HUPFER, Mary, A ... 812-464-1627. 174 D
mhupfer@usi.edu
HUPKE, Doug ... 415-405-3824... 35 E
dhupke@sfsu.edu
HUPP, Mark ... 419-755-5665. 385 D
mhupp@ncstatecollege.edu
HUPP, Stephen ... 304-424-8273. 530 E
stephen.hupp@wvup.edu
HUPPE, Alicia, L ... 972-377-1749. 469 G
ahuppe@collin.edu
HUPPERT, Susan ... 515-271-1384. 177 H
susan.huppert@dmu.edu
HURD, Cathy ... 704-378-1181. 355 K
churd@jcsu.edu
HURD, Clifton ... 407-277-0311. 103 C
churd@evergladesuniversity.edu
HURD, James, R ... 850-474-2384. 117 B
jhurd@uwf.edu
HURD, Janice ... 501-279-4403... 21 C
jhurd@harding.edu
HURD, Roy ... 707-546-4000... 43 E
rhurd@empcol.edu
HURD, Sherie ... 707-546-4000... 43 E
shurd@empcol.edu
HURDLE, Bill ... 478-757-4024. 134 G
bhurdle@wesleyancollege.edu
HURDLE-WINSLOW, B. Lynn ... 252-335-0821. 359 F
lynnhw@albemarle.edu
HURDT, Emily ... 704-669-4321. 359 D
hurdte@clevelandcc.edu
HURLBUT, L, E ... 540-464-7292. 515 B
hurlbutle@vmi.edu
HURLEIGH, Barbara ... 718-405-3733. 320 G
barbara.hurleigh@mountsaintvincent.edu
HURLEY, Alicia ... 212-998-6859. 334 D
alicia.hurley@nyu.edu
HURLEY, Ann ... 708-524-6829. 144 C
ahurley@dom.edu
HURLEY, Celia ... 919-718-7360. 359 B
churley@cccc.edu
HURLEY, Charles, T ... 574-631-7495. 174 A
hurley.32@nd.edu
HURLEY, Deanne ... 440-646-8108. 392 D
dhurley@ursuline.edu
HURLEY, Deanne ... 440-646-8320. 392 D
dhurley@ursuline.edu
HURLEY, Elizabeth ... 212-799-5000. 328 B
HURLEY, Gail, A ... 814-865-5423. 426 A
gah5@psu.edu
HURLEY, James, B ... 601-923-1630. 269 E
jhurley@rts.edu
HURLEY, James, L ... 606-218-5261. 200 F
jhurley@upike.edu
HURLEY, James, M ... 847-491-4286. 155 D
j-hurley2@northwestern.edu
HURLEY, John ... 360-867-6500. 519 J
hurleyj@evergreen.edu
HURLEY, John, J ... 716-888-2100. 316 C
hurleyj@canisius.edu
HURLEY, Leah, A ... 214-648-7986. 493 E
leah.hurley@utsouthwestern.edu
HURLEY, Patricia ... 818-240-1000... 45 G
phurley@glendale.edu
HURLEY, Richard, V ... 540-654-1301. 510 J
president@umw.edu
HURLEY, Rose ... 928-776-2211... 19 H
rose.hurley@yc.edu
HURLEY, Sam ... 903-928-3288. 488 D
shurley@tvcc.edu
HURLEY, Travis ... 417-626-1234. 279 J
hurley.travis@occ.edu
HURLEY, Wanda ... 601-635-2111. 266 H
whurley@eccc.edu
HURRELL, Rockie ... 719-502-2007... 84 A
rockie.hurrell@ppcc.edu
HURRIN, Jeffrey ... 973-655-5188. 303 D
hurrinj@mail.montclair.edu
HURST, Andrew ... 412-518-4504. 131 H
ahurst@southuniversity.edu
HURST, Dan ... 727-726-1153. 100 E
danhurst@clearwater.edu
HURST, DeWayne ... 909-607-8509... 39 C
dewayne.hurst@cgu.edu
HURST, Fred ... 928-523-6598... 16 C
fred.hurst@nau.edu
HURST, James ... 574-520-4125. 168 E
jhurst@iusb.edu
HURST, Jason ... 850-718-2260... 99 N
hurstj@chipola.edu
HURST, Jeffrey, J ... 801-626-7256. 497 D
jhurst@weber.edu
HURST, Laura ... 610-660-1175. 432 E
lannhurs@sju.edu
HURST, Mark ... 423-585-2629. 462 A
mark.hurst@ws.edu
HURST, Richard, S ... 773-508-7465. 151 H
rhurst@luc.edu
HURST, Susan ... 870-245-5567... 22 D
hursts@obu.edu
HURST, Thomas, R ... 410-864-3613. 218 B
thurst@stmarys.edu
HURST, Timothy ... 931-221-7671. 459 B
hurstt@apsu.edu
HURT, Lynn ... 540-857-6244. 514 E
lhurt@virginiawestern.edu
HURTADO, Geoffrey ... 414-229-5390. 537 A
ghurtado@uwm.edu
HURTADO, Jose ... 707-256-7225... 55 F
jhurtado@napavalley.edu
HURTE, Vernon ... 757-221-2300. 503 N
vjhurt@wm.edu
HURTIG, Juliet, K ... 419-772-2032. 386 D
j-hurtig@onu.edu
HURWITZ, T. Alan ... 202-651-5005... 95 C
president@gallaudet.edu
HUSAIN, Naveed ... 718-997-3009. 319 C
naveed.husain@qc.cuny.edu
HUSAK, William ... 310-338-5940... 53 E
whusak@lmu.edu
HUSCHLE, Brian ... 218-793-2592. 260 D
brian.huschle@northlandcollege.edu
HUSEIN, Lori, A ... 310-338-7552... 53 E
lhusein@lmu.edu
HUSELTON, Ken ... 412-323-4000. 410 G
khuselton@mcg-btc.org
HUSHON, Kate ... 814-868-9900. 416 C
kateh@erieit.edu
HUSK, Mark, A ... 317-921-4723. 169 K
mhusk@ivytech.edu
HUSK, Stephanie ... 503-375-7010. 403 A
shusk@corban.edu
HUSKEY, Dana, K ... 336-342-4261. 363 C
huskeyd@rockinghamcc.edu
HUSKEY, Jeffrey ... 605-688-6895. 452 B
jeffrey.huskey@sdstate.edu
HUSKEY, Robin ... 903-983-8620. 475 E
rhuskey@kilgore.edu
HUSKINS, Steve ... 423-697-4466. 460 C
HUSMANN, Calvin, D ... 920-832-6517. 533 S
calvin.d.husmann@lawrence.edu
HUSS, Greg ... 262-551-5701. 532 D
ghuss@carthage.edu
HUSS, H. Fenwick ... 404-413-7000. 126 E
hfhuss@gsu.edu
HUSS, Larry, F ... 803-754-4100. 443 C
HUSSAIN, Asif ... 718-368-6674. 318 E
ahussain@kbcc.cuny.edu
HUSSAIN, Nayyer ... 845-574-4242. 338 B
rondell@sunyrockland.edu
HUSSEY, LeighAnn ... 601-928-6225. 268 C
leighann.hussey@mgccc.edu
HUSSEY, Mark, A ... 979-862-4384. 483 C
mhussey@tamu.edu
HUSSON, James, J ... 617-552-3441. 224 A
james.husson@bc.edu
HUST, Ryan ... 847-317-7152. 160 M
rhust@tiu.edu
HUSTED, David, S ... 972-881-5684. 469 G
dhusted@collin.edu
HUSTED, Jean, L ... 203-582-8645... 91 A
jean.husted@quinnipiac.edu
HUSTED, Joy Lin ... 918-343-7545. 399 C
jhusted@rsu.edu
HUSTOLES, Carol L, J ... 269-387-1900. 252 I
carol.hustoles@wmich.edu
HUSTON, Daniel ... 480-517-8401... 15 D
daniel.huston@riosalad.edu
HUSTON, Gina ... 360-475-7766. 521 H
ghuston@olympic.edu
HUSTON, Jayne ... 724-830-4612. 433 E
huston@setonhill.edu
HUSTON, Jennifer ... 651-905-3420. 254 B
jennifer.huston@browncollege.edu
HUSTON, Richard ... 858-653-6740... 49 C
HUSTON, Robert, H ... 304-766-3261. 530 C
hustonrh@wvstateu.edu
HUSTON, Susan, A ... 716-645-5300. 341 F
huston@buffalo.edu
HUSTON, William, D ... 859-336-5082. 198 J
whuston@sccky.edu
HUTCHCRAFT, Joy, D ... 309-438-8041. 147 J
jdhutch@ilstu.edu
HUTCHENS, Sue ... 513-562-8749. 373 K
shutchens@artacademy.edu
HUTCHENS, III, William, H ... 304-293-5841. 530 D
whhutchens@mail.wvu.edu
HUTCHERSON, Annette ... 863-297-1039. 110 H
ahutcherson@polk.edu
HUTCHERSON, Cecil, L ... 864-592-4693. 447 A
hutchersonc@sccsc.edu
HUTCHERSON, James ... 910-642-7141. 364 A
James.Hutcherson@sccnc.edu
HUTCHERSON, Patricia, J ... 318-274-3242. 207 E
jenkinsp@gram.edu
HUTCHESON, Donna, R ... 770-420-4421. 127 N
dhutches@kennesaw.edu
HUTCHESON, Patty, S ... 770-593-2257. 127 B
gjcfs@gupton-jones.edu
HUTCHESON, Philip ... 615-966-5850. 456 B
philip.hutcheson@lipscomb.edu
HUTCHINGS, Hayden ... 864-596-9744. 443 D
hayden.hutchings@converse.edu
HUTCHINGS, Robert, L ... 512-471-3200. 491 C
rhutchings@austin.utexas.edu
HUTCHINS, Andrew ... 207-778-7360. 212 D
hutchins-andrew@aramark.com
HUTCHINS, Carin ... 832-813-6737. 476 A
carin.a.hutchins@lonestar.edu
HUTCHINS, Donald, L ... 410-276-0306. 218 D
dhutchins@host.sdc.edu
HUTCHINS, Greg ... 608-262-6151. 538 E
greg.hutchins@uwex.edu
HUTCHINS, Mark ... 931-372-3206. 460 A
mhutchins@tntech.edu
HUTCHINS, Mittie, D ... 903-923-3206. 486 A
mittie.hutchins@tstc.edu
HUTCHINS, Paul, C ... 910-592-8081. 363 E
phutchins@sampsoncc.edu
HUTCHINS, Terrel, F ... 269-488-4244. 244 L
thutchins@kvcc.edu
HUTCHINS, Thelma, J ... 304-367-4122. 529 F
thelma.hutchins@fairmontstate.edu
HUTCHINS, Thomas ... 931-221-7456. 459 B
hutchinst@apsu.edu
HUTCHINS, Wesley, D ... 336-757-3053. 360 E
whutchins@forsythtech.edu
HUTCHINSON, Adriane ... 815-479-7829. 152 F
ahutchinson@mchenry.edu
HUTCHINSON, Andre ... 503-943-7371. 408 F
hutchina@up.edu
HUTCHINSON, Brian, A ... 606-783-2088. 198 A
b.hutchinson@moreheadstate.edu
HUTCHINSON, Corrie ... 537-442-2211. 282 H
HUTCHINSON, Diane, L ... 315-255-1743. 316 D
diane.hutchinson@cayuga-cc.edu
HUTCHINSON, Gayle ... 805-437-8441... 32 I
gayle.hutchinson@csuci.edu
HUTCHINSON, James ... 256-726-7145..... 6 B
jhutchinson@oakwood.edu
HUTCHINSON, John, S ... 713-348-4996. 479 A
hutchinson@rice.edu
HUTCHINSON, Kathryn, T ... 718-990-6820. 339 A
hutchink@stjohns.edu
HUTCHINSON, Laura ... 765-983-1317. 165 G
hutchla@earlham.edu
HUTCHINSON, Lisa ... 215-248-6393. 422 F
lhutchinson@ltsp.edu
HUTCHINSON, Natalie, N ... 641-628-5220. 176 E
hutchinsonn@central.edu
HUTCHINSON, Paulette ... 610-527-0200. 432 B
phutchinson@rosemont.edu
HUTCHINSON, Ryan ... 919-761-2100. 366 I
rhutchinson@sebts.edu
HUTCHINSON, Steve ... 402-461-7339. 289 I
shutchinson@hastings.edu
HUTCHINSON, Vanessa ... 903-233-3100. 475 J
vanessahutchinson@letu.edu
HUTCHINSON BELL, Robin ... 614-234-1372. 384 J
rhutchinsonbell@mccn.edu
HUTCHISON, Adam ... 956-364-4600. 485 H
adam.hutchison@tstc.edu
HUTCHISON, Bill ... 818-785-2726... 37 F
bill.hutchison@casalomacollege.edu
HUTCHISON, Chris ... 714-628-7321... 38 A
hutchiso@chapman.edu
HUTCHISON, David ... 541-440-4600. 408 D
david.hutchison@umpqua.edu
HUTCHISON, Donna ... 217-732-3155. 151 C
dhutchison@lincolncollege.edu
HUTCHISON, Elizabeth ... 615-771-7821. 464 G
e.hutchison@williamsoncc.edu
HUTCHISON, Jane ... 973-720-2980. 308 I
hutchisonj@wpunj.edu
HUTCHISON, Karen ... 717-396-7833. 427 A
khutchison@pcad.edu
HUTCHISON, Kathleen ... 601-925-3870. 268 A
khutchis@mc.edu
HUTCHISON, Michael ... 601-974-1024. 267 I
hutchmv@millsaps.edu
HUTCHISON, Nancy ... 610-902-8305. 411 E
nancy.c.hutchison@cabrini.edu
HUTCHISON, Theresa, R ... 817-598-6271. 494 G
thutchison@wc.edu
HUTH, F. Robert ... 386-822-7015. 117 C
fhuth@stetson.edu
HUTH, Laura, L ... 218-477-2142. 259 H
laura.huth@mnstate.edu
HUTH, Steven, K ... 412-268-2649. 412 H
huth@cmu.edu
HUTH, Tracy, A ... 248-370-2669. 248 J
huth@oakland.edu
HUTSELL, Richard ... 903-923-2048. 471 J
rhutsell@etbu.edu
HUTSLAR, Karen, E ... 989-774-3261. 240 N
karen.e.hutslar@cmich.edu
HUTSON, Carol, A ... 903-510-3225. 488 E
chut@tjc.edu
HUTSON, Eva ... 239-936-5822. 106 J
HUTSON, Jerome ... 610-436-3273. 430 A
jhutson@wcupa.edu
HUTSON, Jim ... 806-743-2700. 487 E
jim.hutson@ttuhsc.edu
HUTSON, Kristin, E ... 319-399-8546. 176 G
khutson@coe.edu
HUTSON, Lora ... 248-218-2036. 249 D
lhutson@rc.edu
HUTT, Guy ... 216-987-5008. 378 D
guy.hutt@tri-c.edu
HUTTENHOWER, Edward, R ... 814-472-3200. 432 D
ehuttenhower@francis.edu
HUTTENLOCHER, Daniel, P ... 212-255-8587. 322 A
dph2@cornell.edu
HUTTER, Jeffery, W ... 617-638-4780. 224 D
jhutter@bu.edu
HUTTI, Deb ... 217-234-5273. 150 D
dhutti@lakeland.cc.il.us
HUTTO, Dena ... 503-777-7572. 407 E
dhutto@reed.edu
HUTTO, Jimmy ... 334-493-3573..... 5 E
jhutto@lbwcc.edu
HUTTO-HARRIS, LaShanda ... 864-578-8770. 446 F
lhutto@sherman.edu
HUTTON, Bob, C ... 573-875-7300. 272 G
bchutton@email.ccis.edu
HUTTON, Gina ... 618-393-2982. 146 H
huttong@iecc.edu
HUTTON, Todd, S ... 315-792-3222. 349 F
thutton@utica.edu
HUTTON, Tom ... 719-255-3439... 85 M
thutton@uccs.edu
HUTTON-LOPEZ, Karen ... 909-469-5650... 76 B
klopez@westernu.edu
HUTZEL-BATESON, Alice ... 740-366-9420. 376 A
abateson@cotc.edu
HUTZLEY, Brian ... 518-320-1281. 341 C
brian.hutzley@suny.edu
HUVAL, Barbara ... 409-984-6330. 486 H
barbara.huval@lamarpa.edu
HUXEL, Mary, B ... 636-584-6613. 273 M
huxelmb@eastcentral.edu
HUXFORD, Wye ... 706-385-1012. 130 F
wye.huxford@point.edu
HUYBRECHT, Melissa ... 612-874-3764. 257 B
mhubrecht@mcad.edu
HUYCK, Becky ... 909-599-5433... 50 J
bhuyck@lifepacific.edu
HUYSER, Kent ... 816-604-1411. 277 C
kent.huyser@mcckc.edu
HUYSER, Mackenzi ... 708-239-4809. 160 K
mackenzi.huyser@trnty.edu
HWANG, Delphine ... 510-649-8252... 57 H
dhwang@psr.edu
HWANG, Jenny ... 631-632-6720. 342 C
jenny.hwang@stonybrook.edu
HWANG, Leo ... 413-775-1221. 231 E
hwang@gcc.mass.edu
HWU, Alex ... 707-826-3731... 35 C
sh1911@humboldt.edu
HYATT, Chad ... 256-824-6813..... 8 F
chad.hyatt@uah.edu
HYATT, Danny ... 903-463-8622. 472 M
hyattdan@grayson.edu
HYATT, Garey ... 410-951-3366. 220 B
ghyatt@coppin.edu
HYATT, Gwen ... 503-699-3316. 404 C
registrar@marylhurst.edu
HYATT, James, A ... 520-621-5977... 18 F
HYATT, Katherine, E ... 770-720-5591. 130 G
keh@reinhardt.edu
HYATT, Regina, G ... 256-824-6700..... 8 F
regina.hyatt@uah.edu
HYATT, Tom ... 410-225-2291. 216 C
thyatt@mica.edu
HYBLE, Carol, F ... 989-463-7081. 239 B
hyble@alma.edu

HYCLAK, Thomas, J ... 610-758-6725. 422 A
tjh7@lehigh.edu

HYDE, Anne ... 617-228-3290. 231 C
ahyde@bhcc.mass.edu

HYDE, Barbara ... 907-796-6494... 11 A
barbara.hyde@uas.alaska.edu

HYDE, Carliss ... 254-867-4843. 486 B
carliss.hyde@tstc.edu

HYDE, Fred ... 931-424-9007. 456 C
fhyde@martinmethodist.edu

HYDE, Gerald ... 828-766-1220. 361 H
ghyde@mayland.edu

HYDE, Holly ... 828-835-4219. 364 E
hhyde@tricountycc.edu

HYDE, John ... 516-686-7527. 333 H
jmhyde@nyit.edu

HYDE, Les ... 800-955-2527. 274 I
lhyde@grantham.edu

HYDE, Matthew ... 610-330-5100. 420 D
hydem@lafayette.edu

HYDE, Richard, D ... 979-532-6346. 494 L
richardh@wcjc.edu

HYDE, Truell ... 254-710-3763. 467 G
truell_hyde@baylor.edu

HYDEN, John, P ... 330-941-3235. 394 A
jphyden@ysu.edu

HYDER, Bret ... 952-446-4347. 255 D
hyderb@crown.edu

HYDER, Mark ... 423-236-2155. 458 J
markhyder@southern.edu

HYDRO, Susan ... 609-771-2997. 300 E
berksus@tcnj.edu

HYELER, Maral ... 310-434-3551... 65 A
hyeler_maral@smc.edu

HYER, Joel ... 308-432-6359. 291 D
jhyer@csc.edu

HYLAND, Cheryl ... 615-223-7801. 461 A
chyland@mscc.edu

HYLAND, Patricia ... 650-949-7389... 44 N
hylandpatricia@foothill.edu

HYLAND-MURR,
Mary Ann ... 502-213-2424. 195 F
mary.hyland-murr@kctcs.edu

HYLTON, Gary ... 304-384-5233. 529 E
ghylton@concord.edu

HYLTON, Jessica ... 704-233-8246. 370 G
jhylton@wingate.edu

HYMAN, Cheryl ... 312-553-2500. 141 M

HYMAN, Eric, C ... 979-845-1159. 483 C
ehyman@tamu.edu

HYMAN, Susan ... 410-704-2097. 220 E
shyman@towson.edu

HYMANS, Diane, J ... 614-235-4136. 390 A
dhymans@TLSohio.edu

HYMON, Carolyn ... 662-252-8000. 269 F
chymon@rustcollege.edu

HYND, George, W ... 843-953-5527. 443 A
hyndg@cofc.edu

HYNDMAN, Steve ... 502-410-6200. 194 B
shyndman@galencollege.edu

HYNES, Andy ... 901-751-8453. 457 B
ahynes@mabts.edu

HYNES, Jeff ... 708-209-3444. 143 E
jeff.hynes@cuchicago.edu

HYNES, Kevin, P ... 630-515-6073. 153 B
khynes@midwestern.edu

HYNES, Peter ... 973-684-6602. 304 B
phynes@pccc.edu

HYNES, Robert ... 978-665-3152. 229 E
rhynes@fitchburgstate.edu

HYNES, Thomas ... 678-466-4300. 123 A
thomashynes@clayton.edu

HYNES, William, J ... 510-436-1520... 47 J
hynes@hnu.edu

HYNES-WILSON,
Mentha ... 410-543-6080. 220 D
mahynes-wilson@salisbury.edu

HYPES, George ... 304-734-6663. 527 O
ghypes@bridgemont.edu

HYSLOP, Daniel ... 310-338-2881... 53 E
dhyslop@lmu.edu

HYSON, Ronald ... 214-459-2217... 28 M
rhyson@argosy.edu

HYTCHE, William, P ... 334-229-4233..... 1 D
whytche@alasu.edu

HYUN, Eunsook ... 323-343-4300... 34 A
eunsook.hyun@calstatela.edu

HYUN, Timothy ... 253-752-2020. 519 K
librarian@faithseminary.edu

I

IACAMPO, Beth ... 860-297-2273... 91 F
beth.iacampo@trincoll.edu

IACONO, Anthony ... 772-462-7215. 106 P
tiacono@irsc.edu

IACOVELLI, John ... 609-652-4833. 305 C
john.iacovelli@stockton.edu

IACUESSA, Michelle, A ... 845-569-3217. 332 B
michelle.iacuessa@msmc.edu

IACULLO, Stephen ... 561-912-1211. 103 C
siacullo@evergladesuniversity.edu

IADEVAIA, Norma ... 310-506-4149... 58 H
norma.iadevaia@pepperdine.edu

IALENTI, Vincent ... 978-632-6600. 232 C
v_ialenti@mwcc.mass.edu

IAMUNNO, Janine ... 910-962-2445. 369 C
iamunnoj@uncw.edu

IANNAZZI, Michael, L ... 203-371-7899... 91 C
iannazzim@sacredheart.edu

IANNELLI, Clare ... 281-998-6150. 479 G
clare.iannelli@sjcd.edu

IANNO, Daniel ... 315-792-5356. 331 I
dianno@mvcc.edu

IANNUZZI, Patricia ... 702-895-2226. 294 I
patricia.iannuzzi@unlv.edu

IBARRA, Rudy ... 305-628-6633. 112 F
ribarra@stu.edu

IBEANUSI, Victor ... 850-599-3550. 114 K
victor.ibeanusi@famu.edu

ICE, Brenda ... 315-228-7367. 320 F
bice@colgate.edu

ICE, Phil ... 304-724-3700. 526 B
pice@apus.edu

ICE, Richard ... 320-363-5401. 254 J
rice@csbsju.edu

ICE, Richard ... 320-363-3147. 263 P
rice@csbsju.edu

ICENHOWER, Nathan ... 541-485-1780. 405 B
nathanicenhower@newhope.edu

ICHON, Eric ... 310-287-4305... 52 F
ichone@wlac.edu

ICHSAN, Tony ... 707-527-4432... 65 B
aichsan@santarosa.edu

ICKES, Jessica ... 574-284-4574. 172 G
jickes@saintmarys.edu

IDA, Rick ... 916-558-2097... 53 D
idar@scc.losrios.edu

IDDINGS, Keith ... 864-644-5002. 446 I
kiddings@swu.edu

IDE, Andrea ... 425-425-4723. 524 D
andrea.ide@tlc.edu

IDE, Melissa ... 570-702-8910. 419 G
mide@johnson.edu

IDLE, Bonnie, L ... 703-323-3023. 513 C
bidle@nvcc.edu

IDOHL-CORWIN, Carla .. 360-596-5235. 524 A
ccorwin@spscc.edu

IENUSO, Joe, A ... 212-854-3291. 321 D
ji4@columbia.edu

IERARDI, Kristina ... 508-362-2131. 231 D
kierardi@capecod.edu

IERIEN, Kim ... 503-281-4181. 402 I

IETTO, Domenick ... 949-376-6000... 50 C
dietto@lagunacollege.edu

IFILL, Roberto ... 240-895-4208. 218 A
rnifill@smcm.edu

IGE, Joanne, A ... 671-735-5555. 546 C
joanne.ige@guamcc.edu

IGE, John ... 808-544-1123. 135 F
jige@hpu.edu

IGHODARO, Osaro ... 602-243-8036... 15 F
osaro.ighodaro@southmountaincc.edu

IGLICH, Esther ... 410-857-2405. 216 E
eiglich@mcdaniel.edu

IGNASH, Jan ... 850-245-0466. 114 J
jan.ignash@flbog.edu

IGUCHI, Martin, Y ... 202-687-3118... 95 E
iguchi@georgetown.edu

IGYARTO, Mia ... 630-942-3410. 142 G
igyartom@cod.edu

IHDE, Rick ... 402-643-7422. 289 B
rick.ihde@cune.edu

IHEKWEAZU, Stanley, N 803-536-8392. 446 G
sihekwea@scsu.edu

IHRKE, Barbara ... 765-677-2389. 169 B
barbara.ihrke@indwes.edu

IJIRI, Lisa ... 617-349-8426. 228 B
lijiri@lesley.edu

IJIRI, Lisa ... 617-349-8706. 228 B
lijiri@lesley.edu

IKEDA, Deborah ... 559-325-5200... 69 B

IKEDA, Gary, L ... 206-543-4150. 524 G
ikedagl@uw.edu

IKEDA, Kimi, M ... 805-756-2186... 32 F
kikeda@calpoly.edu

IKEN, Mark ... 678-407-5400. 125 B
miken@ggc.edu

IKEN, Stacie ... 701-224-5491. 372 B
stacie.iken@bismarckstate.edu

IKENBERRY, David, L ... 303-492-1809... 85 L
david.ikenberry@colorado.edu

IKEOKWU, Francis ... 904-470-8000. 102 A
fikeokwu@ewc.edu

IKHARO, Sadiq ... 510-466-7336... 59 D
sikharo@peralta.edu

IKHARO, Sadiq ... 510-466-7336... 59 A
sikharo@peralta.edu

ILER, Susan ... 216-791-5000. 377 E
susan.iler@cim.edu

ILES, Linda ... 530-221-4275... 65 F
finaid@shasta.edu

ILIAKIS-DOHERTY,
Sophia ... 360-417-6219. 522 A
sdoherty@pencol.edu

ILICETO, Thomas ... 212-229-5101. 332 E
ilicetot@newschool.edu

ILLICH, Paul ... 254-299-8636. 476 D
pillich@mclennan.edu

ILLIES, Diane ... 218-755-2448. 258 A
dillies@bemidjistate.edu

ILLINGWORTH, Kendra .. 219-866-6428. 172 E
kendra@saintjoe.edu

ILLO, Joseph ... 805-525-4417... 69 H
jillo@thomasaquinas.edu

ILOWITE, Patricia ... 410-706-7355. 219 C
pilowite@af.umaryland.edu

ILSE, Thomas ... 304-327-4022. 529 D
tilse@bluefieldstate.edu

ILYAS, Mohammad ... 302-225-6234... 93 H
ilyasm@gbc.edu

ILYAS, Mohammad ... 561-297-3426. 114 L
ilyas@fau.edu

IMAI, Geri ... 808-235-7430. 137 C
gerii@hawaii.edu

IMAI, Peggy, H ... 802-654-2222. 500 B
pimai@smcvt.edu

IMASUEN, Edwin ... 810-762-9642. 244 Q
eimasuen@kettering.edu

IMBIMBO, Patricia ... 646-312-4683. 316 J
Patricia.Imbimbo@baruch.cuny.edu

IMBLER, John, M ... 918-610-8303. 398 I
john.imbler@ptstulsa.edu

IMBRAGULIO, Lisa ... 205-726-4172..... 6 F
lcimbrag@samford.edu

IMBRESCIA, Jeffrey, D ... 724-653-2200. 415 A
jimbrescia@dec.edu

IMBRIALE, William ... 212-752-1530. 328 G
william.imbriale@limcollege.edu

IMES, Jean ... 352-854-2322. 100 K
imesj@cf.edu

IMES, Melissa ... 717-262-2000. 437 H
melissa.imes@wilson.edu

IMHOF, Howard ... 740-366-9379. 376 A
himhof@cotc.edu

IMHOFF, Donna ... 412-237-2770. 413 D
dimhoff@ccac.edu

IMHOFF, Jacquelyn ... 270-247-8521. 197 H
jimhoff@midcontinent.edu

IMHOFF, Kevin ... 270-247-8521. 197 H
kevin.imhoff@midcontinent.edu

IMHOFF, Maren, E ... 212-327-8682. 338 A
imhoff@rockefeller.edu

IMHOFF, Robert, J ... 270-247-8521. 197 H
bimhoff@midcontinent.edu

IMLER, Mary Elizabeth ... 815-740-3415. 162 F
mimler@stfrancis.edu

IMLER, Sylvia ... 330-941-3370. 394 A
sjimler@ysu.edu

IMMERMAN, Stephen, D 978-921-4242. 234 C
steve.immerman@montserrat.edu

IMPERATO, Anthony ... 718-368-5902. 318 E
aimperato@kbcc.cuny.edu

IMPERATO, Pamela ... 402-557-7125. 288 G
pamela.imperato@bellevue.edu

IMWALLE, Todd, W ... 937-229-3299. 391 C
TImwalle1@udayton.edu

INABINET, Chad, E ... 231-843-5965. 252 H
ceinabinet@westshore.edu

INAFUKU, Derek ... 808-845-9103. 136 G
dinafuku@hawaii.edu

INBODY, Brian, L ... 620-431-2820. 189 D
binbody@neosho.edu

INCANDELA, Marybeth ... 631-420-2107. 346 B
marybeth.incandela@farmingdale.edu

INCH, Edward ... 916-278-7674... 34 D
edward.inch@csus.edu

INDVIK, Julie ... 530-898-6189... 33 A
jindvik@scuchico.edu

INFANTI, Steven, M ... 717-901-5146. 418 E
SInfanti@harrisburgu.edu

INFINGER, Kim ... 425-739-8274. 520 K
kim.infinger@lwtech.edu

INGALLS, Keith ... 413-748-3946. 236 I
kingalls@springfieldcollege.edu

INGARGIOLA, Janet, M .. 217-443-8760. 143 G
jingarg@dacc.edu

INGBER, Marc ... 303-556-8270... 86 A
marc.ingber@ucdenver.edu

INGELSON, Jeannine ... 563-441-4046. 178 C
jingleson@eicc.edu

INGERMAN, Bret ... 850-201-6082. 117 D
ingermab@tcc.fl.edu

INGERSOLL, Chris ... 989-774-1850. 240 N
inger1c@cmich.edu

INGERSOLL, Julia ... 610-526-6132. 417 H
jingersoll@harcum.edu

INGERSOLL, Pat ... 616-234-3869. 243 B
pingerso@grcc.edu

INGHAM, Joanne ... 212-431-2876. 333 I
jingham@nyls.edu

INGHAM, Lester, A ... 661-824-2977... 55 I

INGHRAM, Scott ... 304-384-5271. 529 E
inghramcs@concord.edu

INGLE, Andrea ... 765-285-5974. 164 B
akingle@bsu.edu

INGLE, Brooke ... 970-247-7421... 81 M
bookstoremgr@fortlewis.edu

INGLE, Jeff, S ... 704-406-4654. 354 C
jingle@gardner-webb.edu

INGLE, Kent ... 863-667-5002. 113 P
kingle@seu.edu

INGLE, Pam ... 417-624-7070. 476 F
pingle@messengercollege.edu

INGLE, Vernell ... 417-624-7070. 476 F
vingle@messengercollege.edu

INGLES, Roger, D ... 740-368-3738. 387 J
rdingles@owu.edu

INGLES, Susan, L ... 414-410-4236. 532 B
slingles@stritch.edu

INGLI, Robin ... 603-228-1541. 298 D
robin.ingli@law.unh.edu

INGLI, Robin, C ... 651-523-2461. 256 A
ringli@hamline.edu

INGLIS, Mark ... 216-421-7403. 377 C
minglis@cia.edu

INGLISH, Darla ... 940-397-4321. 476 H
darla.inglish@mwsu.edu

INGMIRE, Randall, L ... 785-539-3571. 188 F
ringmire@mccks.edu

INGOLD, Barbara, S ... 815-740-3369. 162 F
bingold@stfrancis.edu

INGOLD, Scott ... 305-284-4206. 118 F
singold@miami.edu

INGOLFSLAND, Dennis .. 952-446-4239. 255 D
ingolfsland@crown.edu

INGRAHAM, Barry ... 207-768-2702. 210 M
bingraham@nmcc.edu

INGRAHAM, Timothy ... 978-468-7111. 227 A
tingraham@gcts.edu

INGRAM, Archinya ... 803-327-7402. 442 D
aingram@clintonjuniorcollege.edu

INGRAM, Beth ... 319-335-3565. 175 I
beth-ingram@uiowa.edu

INGRAM, Beverly ... 318-487-7694. 202 F
beverly.ingram@lacollege.edu

INGRAM, Charles, E ... 609-652-4381. 305 C
charles.ingram@stockton.edu

INGRAM, Charlotte ... 276-466-7868. 514 G
charlotteingram@vic.edu

INGRAM, Earl ... 334-670-3104..... 7 H
ingram@troy.edu

INGRAM, Geoff ... 951-785-2000... 50 B
gingram@lasierra.edu

INGRAM, Gregory ... 301-891-4017. 221 B
gingram@wau.edu

INGRAM, Iris ... 805-378-1412... 74 F
iingram@vcccd.edu

INGRAM, J. Kevin ... 785-539-3571. 188 F
kingram@mccks.edu

INGRAM, Jim ... 662-862-8047. 267 C
jingram@iccms.edu

INGRAM, Joyce, A ... 850-644-7950. 115 C
jingram@admin.fsu.edu

INGRAM,
Lashawanda, T ... 315-386-7128. 345 F
ingraml@canton.edu

INGRAM, Mike ... 423-746-5292. 462 C
mingram@twcnet.edu

INGRAM, Ozzie ... 214-333-6875. 470 D
ozzie@dbu.edu

INGRAM, Sherry ... 704-406-4303. 354 C
singram@gardner-webb.edu

INGRAM, Shirley, M ... 956-872-5051. 480 I
singram@southtexascollege.edu

INGRAM, Sue ... 417-255-7911. 278 F
sueingram@missouristate.edu

INGRAM, Victoria, L ... 540-828-5393. 502 J
vingram@bridgewater.edu

INGRAM, Wanda Rhea ... 334-244-3476..... 2 A
wingram4@aum.edu

INGRAM, William, G ... 919-536-7250. 360 B
ingramb@durhamtech.edu

INGRAM-WALLACE,
Brenda, J ... 610-921-7585. 409 A
bingramwallace@alb.edu

INGS, Margaret Ann ... 617-824-8299. 226 A
margaret_ann_ings@emerson.edu

INIGUEZ-JIMENEZ,
J. Alfredo ... 956-764-5798. 475 F
ainiguez@laredo.edu

INKSTER, Larry ... 606-546-1233. 200 A
linkster@unionky.edu

INMAN, Ann ... 812-866-7013. 166 C
inmana@hanover.edu

INMAN, Barbara, L ... 757-727-5264. 505 F
barbara.inman@hamptonu.edu

INMAN, Dan ... 270-926-1188. 193 M
dinman@daymargroup.com

INMAN, Dan ... 270-926-1188. 378 J
dinman@daymargroup.com

INMAN, Dean 870-862-8131 23 D dinman@southark.edu
INMAN, Gerald 617-989-4252 237 G inmang@wit.edu
INMAN, James, P 540-464-7104 515 B inmanjp@vmi.edu
INMAN, John, G 724-458-2176 417 E jginman@gcc.edu
INMAN, Keith 502-852-6924 200 D akinma01@louisville.edu
INMAN, Leigh 619-961-4278 69 I glinman@tjsl.edu
INMAN, Linda, D 336-334-7708 367 E ldinman@ncat.edu
INMAN, Lisa 919-536-7200 360 B inmanl@durhamtech.edu
INMAN, Stan, D 801-585-5028 496 Q sinman@sa.utah.edu
INNIS, Daniel, E 603-862-1983 298 C dan.innis@unh.edu
INNISS, Courtney 973-877-3268 301 H coinniss@essex.edu
INOA, Luis 845-437-5862 349 G inoa@vassar.edu
INOUYE, Carolyn 805-986-5803 74 G cinouye@vcccd.edu
INOUYE, Jon 949-794-9090 68 D jinouye@stanbridge.edu
INOUYE, Susan, K 808-956-8155 135 L susani@hawaii.edu
INOWAY-RONNIE, Eden 608-265-5975 536 D etinoway@wisc.edu
INSANALLI, Dawn 914-637-2726 327 C dinsanalli@iona.edu
INSERTO, Fathiah 909-396-6090 31 F
INSLER, Gayle, D 516-877-3167 313 A insler@adelphi.edu
INSLEY, Andrea 206-587-3899 522 J ainsley@sccd.ctc.edu
INSLEY, Lynn 201-216-8927 307 E linsley@stevens.edu
INTILLE, Amy 617-989-4885 237 G intillea@wit.edu
INTROCASO, CDP, Candace 412-536-1204 420 A cintrocaso@laroche.edu
INZER, Monica, C 315-859-4421 325 E minzer@hamilton.edu
IOANNOU, Carin 336-770-3301 369 D Ioannouc@uncsa.edu
IOCANO, Lynn 302-857-6250 93 C liocano@desu.edu
IODICE, Emilio 773-508-2760 151 H eiodice@luc.edu
IOLI, Christine 412-809-5100 430 H ioli.christine@pti.edu
IORG, Jeff 415-380-1322 45 H jeffiorg@ggbts.edu
IORIO, Richard, F 773-702-4488 161 B richiorio@uchicago.edu
IOSSI, Lora 402-557-7343 288 G lora.iossi@bellevue.edu
IOVANNONE, Jeffry, J 716-673-4747 342 A jeffry.iovannone@fredonia.edu
IPACH, Nichole 805-437-8893 32 I nichole.ipach@csuci.edu
IPPINECA, Carey, L 607-735-1812 323 H cippineca@elmira.edu
IPPOLITO, Andrew 201-692-2531 301 J andrew_ippolito@fdu.edu
IRBY, Matthew 714-241-6104 39 I 1180mgr@follett.com
IRBY, Michele 573-651-5120 282 B mirby@semo.edu
IRBY, Sharon 770-229-3454 132 B sirby@sctech.edu
IRBY, Xaviere, J 334-874-5700 3 A xirby@ccal.edu
IRELAND, Alan 336-750-2935 370 A irelandag@wssu.edu
IRELAND, Chris, M 801-581-3402 496 Q cireland@deans.pharm.utah.edu
IRELAND, Jim, D 620-792-9339 184 F irelandj@bartonccc.edu
IRELAND, Timothy 716-286-8060 334 F toi@niagara.edu
IRICK, Troy, D 260-359-4066 166 O tirick@huntington.edu
IRIS, Michael 908-852-1400 300 D irism@centenarycollege.edu
IRISH, Allyson 617-521-2324 236 G allyson.irish@simmons.edu
IRISH, Bridget 970-382-6940 81 M irish_b@fortlewis.edu
IRISH, Edward, P 757-221-2425 503 N epiris@wm.edu
IRIZARRY, Elba, T 787-264-1912 551 A elbatirizarry@sg.inter.edu
IRIZARRY, Jose, R 787-296-1101 224 G Jose.Irizarry@cambridgecollege.edu
IRIZARRY, Margarita 787-758-2525 554 F margarita.irizarry@upr.edu
IRIZARY, Herminio 787-841-2000 552 B hirizary@pucpr.edu
IRLA-CHESNEY, Kathy 603-862-2120 298 C kathy.irla-chesney@unh.edu
IROFF, Jayson 954-201-7423 99 D jiroff@broward.edu
IROFF, Steven 770-576-4498 131 A
IRUDAYAM, Irene 508-849-3410 222 B iirudayam@annamaria.edu
IRVIN, Camilla 334-833-4577 4 D cirvin@huntingdon.edu
IRVIN, Cynthia 904-680-7653 103 Q cirvin@fcsl.edu
IRVIN, Dale, T 212-870-1223 334 C dirvin@nyts.edu
IRVIN, Dan 972-829-2150 450 G dirvin@national.edu
IRVIN, Dave 865-974-2178 463 C irvin@utk.edu
IRVIN, Dexter 808-974-7762 136 A ldirvin@hawaii.edu
IRVIN, Hal 540-231-7784 515 C hirvin@vt.edu
IRVIN, Michael, E 864-503-5217 448 H mirvin@uscupstate.edu
IRVIN, ValaRay 225-771-2480 206 J valaray_irvin@subr.edu
IRVIN, Zoe, A 443-518-4742 215 E zirvin@howardcc.edu
IRVINE, Angela 802-654-2396 500 B airvine@smcvt.edu
IRVINE, David 518-262-5251 313 D irvined@mail.amc.edu
IRVINE, Dianne 225-342-6950 207 D Dianne.Irvinne@la.gov
IRVINE, Shelly 540-887-7367 507 A sirvine@mbc.edu
IRVING, Jacqueline 610-341-5872 415 G jirving@eastern.edu
IRVING, Jean, H 530-898-5944 33 A jirving@csuchico.edu
IRVING, Merrill 847-635-2604 155 F mirving@oakton.edu
IRWIN, Bonnie 217-581-2917 144 E dbirwin@eiu.edu
IRWIN, Dennis 740-593-1479 387 C irwind@ohio.edu
IRWIN, Holly 619-849-2706 59 L hollyirwin@pointloma.edu
IRWIN, Joseph 404-894-0771 125 D joe.irwin@alumni.gatech.edu
IRWIN, Kathy 810-762-0415 247 F kathy.irwin@mcc.edu
IRWIN, Lorry 845-434-5750 347 A lirwin@sullivan.suny.edu
IRWIN, Raymond 216-987-2341 378 D raymond.irwin@tri-c.edu
IRWIN, Robert 864-578-8770 446 F rirwin@sherman.edu
IRWIN, Suzy 903-823-3095 482 D suzy.irwin@texarkanacollege.edu
IRWIN, Ursula 503-491-7469 404 E ursula.irwin@mhcc.edu
ISAAC, Bina 760-862-1333 40 F bisaac@collegeofthedesert.edu
ISAAC, Nancy 620-431-2820 189 D nisaac@neosho.edu
ISAAC, Wolde-Ab 951-222-8155 61 A
ISAAC, Wolde-Ab 951-222-8000 60 J Wolde-Ab.Isaac@rcc.edu
ISAACS, Becky 580-559-5243 395 F bisaacs@ecok.edu
ISAACS, Carol, B 260-481-6147 168 C isaacs@ipfw.edu
ISAACS, Jerry 918-495-7750 398 H jisaacs@oru.edu
ISAACS, Mona 859-622-1986 193 P mona.isaacs@eku.edu
ISAACS, Yolanda 815-280-6691 149 A yisaacs@jjc.edu
ISAACSON, Jeff, A 402-465-7525 291 G jai@nebrwesleyan.edu
ISAACSON, Lyn, R 641-628-5266 176 E isaacsonl@central.edu
ISAACSON, Melvin 212-346-1366 335 J misaacson@pace.edu
ISAACSON, Michael, L 605-642-6788 451 G michael.isaacson@bhsu.edu
ISAAK, Don 626-815-6000 29 H disaak@apu.edu
ISABELLE, Callista, S 484-664-3120 424 H cisabelle@muhlenberg.edu
ISABELLE, Geoffrey, S 315-684-6070 345 A isabelgs@morrisville.edu
ISACKMAN, Brigid, K 215-596-8701 435 H b.isackman@usciences.edu
ISACSON, Barbara 973-748-9000 299 F barbara_isacson@bloomfield.edu
ISAK, Misty 609-984-1588 308 A misak@tesc.edu
ISAKOFF, Louis, A 757-352-2794 508 G isakoff@regent.edu
ISBELL, Corey 785-738-9055 189 F cisbell@ncktc.edu
ISBELL, Monica 336-506-4130 357 M monica.isbell@alamancecc.edu
ISBELL, Teresa, S 214-860-2017 470 J tisbell@dcccd.edu
ISCH, Larry, A 479-979-1420 25 J laisch@ozarks.edu
ISCHAY, Maureen 216-373-5335 385 G mischay@ndc.edu
ISEKENEGBE, Thomas, A 856-691-8600 301 A thomasi@cccnj.edu
ISELI, Madeline 937-512-2510 388 O madeline.iseli@sinclair.edu
ISEMINGER, Ernie 909-621-8096 39 D Ernie.Iseminger@cmc.edu
ISEMINGER, Jeff 507-389-2823 259 G jeffrey.iseminger@mnsu.edu
ISEMINGER, Jeff 507-389-6830 259 G jeffrey.iseminger@mnsu.edu
ISENBERG, Jerold 847-982-2500 146 C isenberg@htc.edu
ISENHOUR, John, L 770-423-6620 127 N jisenhou@kennesaw.edu
ISENHOWER, Robert, W 864-587-4117 447 B isenhowerb@smcsc.edu
ISENSEE, Paul 215-702-4432 411 F pisensee@cairn.edu
ISERMANN, Sue, L 815-224-0408 148 A sue_isermann@ivcc.edu
ISGETT, J. Samuel 864-877-3052 445 H sam.isgett@ngu.edu
ISH, Cheryl, J 570-208-5855 419 P cjish@kings.edu
ISHEE, Jimmy 940-898-2852 488 B jishee@twu.edu
ISHERWOOD, J. Thomas 770-720-5502 130 G jti@reinhardt.edu
ISHIDA, Kevin 808-235-7403 137 C kevini@hawaii.edu
ISHIDA, Yoshiharu 808-946-3773 135 B
ISHIDA-BABINEAU, Ellen 808-235-7339 137 C ellenib@hawaii.edu
ISHII, Debra 808-956-6855 135 L debrai@hawaii.edu
ISHIMOTO, Lester 808-689-2689 136 C lishimot@hawaii.edu
ISHIYAMA, Howard, J 412-536-1282 420 A howard.ishiyama@laroche.edu
ISHMAEL, Amy 918-540-6212 396 G aishmael@neo.edu
ISHMAEL, Derek 217-424-6350 153 C dishmael@millikin.edu
ISHOP, Kedra, B 512-475-7326 491 C kedra.ishop@austin.utexas.edu
ISKRA, Theresa 571-371-5140 250 G iskrat@cooley.edu
ISLE, Wendy 620-331-4100 187 G wisle@indycc.edu
ISLEY, MJ 515-965-7120 177 B
ISMAIL, Amid 215-707-2799 433 K amid.ismail@temple.edu
ISMAIL, Lizah 864-488-4610 444 L lismail@limestone.edu
ISMAIL, Shaik 503-883-2228 404 A sismail@linfield.edu
ISOM, Andy 501-882-4428 19 M adisom@asub.edu
ISOM, Darryl 404-653-7806 129 D disom@morehouse.edu
ISOM, Roger 410-293-1881 545 J isom@usna.edu
ISOMOTO, Robert, G 310-434-4201 65 A isomoto_robert@smc.edu
ISOZAKI, Peggy 415-883-2211 40 G peggy.isozaki@marin.edu
ISPIR, Sheri 401-598-1872 439 B sispir@jwu.edu
ISRAEL, Adrienne, M 336-316-2181 355 A aisrael@guilford.edu
ISRAEL, Cary, A 972-758-3801 469 G cisrael@collin.edu
ISRAEL, OSB, Jude 985-867-2249 206 H
ISRAEL, Richard 714-556-3610 74 D rich.israel@vanguard.edu
ISRAEL, Susan, H 860-515-3839 87 I sisrael@charteroak.edu
ISSELMANN, Sandy 920-832-6541 533 S sandy.isselmann@lawrence.edu
ISSOD, Cheryl 410-225-2310 216 C cissod@mica.edu
ITALIANO, Christina 414-326-2306 532 G christina.italiano@ccon.edu
ITTLEMAN, Leona, R 413-755-4055 233 A ittleman@stcc.edu
IULIANO, Robert, W 617-496-4179 227 C robert_iuliano@harvard.edu
IUSO, Kenneth, J 848-445-2620 306 A iuso@rci.rutgers.edu
IUSO, Kenneth, J 848-445-2620 306 B iuso@rci.rutgers.edu
IVAN, Elaine, R 719-365-8291 85 J elaine.ivan@uchealth.org
IVANKOVIC, John 845-341-4190 335 H john.ivankovic@sunyorange.edu
IVANKOVIC, Judith 845-575-3000 330 D judith.ivankovic@marist.edu
IVANY, Robert 713-525-2160 490 L president@stthom.edu
IVERSEN, Jerre 903-566-7110 492 D jiversen@uttyler.edu
IVERSON, Amy 386-506-3240 101 G iversoa@DaytonaState.edu
IVERSON, Ann 612-374-5800 255 F aiverson@dunwoody.edu
IVERSON, Carrie 719-638-6580 81 K civerson@cci.edu
IVERSON, Chuck 605-668-1529 450 F civerson@mtmc.edu
IVERSON, Daryl, A 864-231-2005 441 B diverson@andersonuniversity.edu
IVERSON, Ed 208-882-1566 138 H eiverson@nsa.edu
IVERSON, Robert 626-914-8888 38 K riverson@citruscollege.edu
IVERSON, Scott 219-989-4151 171 N scott.iverson@purduecal.edu
IVERSON, Terrie 406-657-2155 287 C tiverson@msubillings.edu
IVERSON, William 817-202-6229 481 E wiverson@swau.edu
IVERY, Curtis, L 313-496-2510 252 B civery1@wcccd.edu
IVES, Richard 269-488-4865 244 L rives@kvcc.edu
IVES, Richard 518-783-3285 340 J rives@siena.edu
IVES, Stephanie 215-204-6556 433 K stephanie.ives@temple.edu
IVESTER, Kathie 706-754-7750 129 G kivester@northgatech.edu
IVESTER, Mark 706-754-7736 129 G mivester@northgatech.edu
IVESTER, Steve 630-752-5088 163 F Steve.Ivester@wheaton.edu
IVEY, Carolyn 713-221-8681 489 D iveyc@uhd.edu
IVEY, Diane 919-735-5151 364 H dtivey@waynecc.edu
IVEY, Garry, M 918-647-1210 394 I givey@carlalbert.edu
IVEY, Michelle 334-683-2359 5 F mivey@marionmilitary.edu
IVEY, Pat 478-218-3306 122 F pivey@centralgatech.edu
IVEY, Paul 225-578-2870 204 O pivey1@lsu.edu
IVEY, R. Paul 225-578-2870 204 O pivey1@lsu.edu
IVEY, Ryan 903-886-5568 483 E ryan.ivey@tamuc.edu
IVEY, Tracey 919-735-5151 364 H ivey@waynecc.edu
IVIE, Wendy 541-885-1539 405 J wendy.ivie@oit.edu
IVIS, Dan 515-965-7029 177 B drivis@dmacc.edu
IVORY, Joanne 773-291-6410 142 D jivory1@ccc.edu
IVY, William 620-231-7000 189 L wivy@pittstate.edu
IWAMA, Kenichi 718-982-2400 317 E kenichi.iwama@csi.cuny.edu
IWAMOTO, Dawn 480-557-3228 18 I dawn.iwamoto@phoenix.edu
IWAMURA, Jane 626-571-8811 74 B janei@uwest.edu
IWANOWICZ, Sue 518-694-7217 313 B susan.iwanowicz@acphs.edu
IWASA, Mark 916-278-6851 34 D m.iwasa@csus.edu
IWATA, Chris 916-558-2552 53 D iwatac@scc.losrios.edu
IYENGAR, Sundararaj 305-348-3549 115 B undararaj.iyengar@fiu.edu
IYER, Nalini 206-296-6161 523 E niyer@seattleu.edu
IYER, Savitri, V 585-245-5541 343 C iyer@geneseo.edu
IYERE, Peter 402-481-8863 288 H peter.iyere@bryanhealthcollege.edu
IZADI, Mahyar 217-581-3526 144 E mizadi@eiu.edu

IZADIAN, Ali .... 916-278-6241... 34 D
aizadian@csus.edu
IZAGUIRRE, Alexander ... 713-798-1103. 467 F
alex@bcm.edu
IZAGUIRRE, Ceferino ..... 956-721-5323. 475 F
cizaguirre@laredo.edu
IZBRAND, Joe .... 210-458-8754. 492 C
joe.izbrand@utsa.edu
IZQUIERDO, Aileen .... 954-201-7540... 99 D
aizquier@broward.edu
IZVONAR, Ivana .... 650-543-3787... 54 C
iizvonar@menlo.edu
IZZARD, Marilyn .... 803-938-3709. 448 F
maizzard@uscsumter.edu
IZZI, Michael, A .... 949-824-6932... 71 B
mizzi@uci.edu

J

JAASMA, Marjorie, A ...... 209-667-3203... 35 B
mjaasma@csustan.edu
JABAR, Abdul .... 212-346-1521. 335 J
ajabar@pace.edu
JABBAAR-GYAMBRAH,
Tara .... 716-926-8835. 326 B
tjabbaar-gyambrah@hilbert.edu
JABER, A.J .... 312-980-9257. 148 D
ajaber@iadtchicago.com
JABLONSKI, Erin, L .... 570-577-1644. 411 A
erin.jablonski@bucknell.edu
JABLONSKI, John, E .... 518-562-4101. 320 B
john.jablonski@clinton.edu
JABLONSKI, Suzanne ..... 212-678-7452. 347 G
sj2487@tc.columbia.edu
JABLONSKY, Carol .... 516-686-1014. 333 H
cjablons@nyit.edu
JABRASSIAN, Vic .... 213-613-2200... 67 E
vic@sciarc.edu
JABS, Carol, A .... 708-209-3145. 143 E
carol.jabs@cuchicago.edu
JABUSCH, Diann .... 815-921-4802. 157 A
d.jabusch@rockvalleycollege.edu
JACAMAN, Mark, D .... 512-448-8728. 479 C
markj@stedwards.edu
JACCARINO, David .... 305-626-3766. 104 J
david.jaccarino@fmuniv.edu
JACCUZZO, Craig, M ..... 985-448-7131. 208 A
craig.jaccuzzo@nicholls.edu
JACHIM-MOORE,
Darrell, K .... 585-292-2185. 332 A
djachim-moore@monroecc.edu
JACK, Danielle .... 310-233-4011... 51 H
jackdt@lahc.edu
JACK, Eric .... 205-934-8800..... 8 E
ejack@uab.edu
JACK, Grilly .... 691-320-3795. 546 B
gjack@comfsm.fm
JACK, Jill .... 319-399-8023. 176 G
jjack@coe.edu
JACK, Jo Ann .... 617-627-2000. 237 C
joann.jack@tufts.edu
JACKIEWICZ, Rachel ...... 845-398-4067. 340 A
rjackiew@stac.edu
JACKIEWICZ, Thomas, E 323-442-9775... 74 A
thomas.jackiewicz@med.usc.edu
JACKLIN, Michele, J ...... 860-297-4285... 91 F
michele.jacklin@trincoll.edu
JACKMAN, Deborah .... 414-277-7302. 534 G
jackman@msoe.edu
JACKMAN, Diane, H .... 217-581-2524. 144 E
dhjackman@eiu.edu
JACKO, Mariusz .... 787-250-1912. 550 E
mjacko@intermetro.com
JACKOWSKI, Barbara ..... 843-383-8013. 442 F
bjackowski@coker.edu
JACKS, Benjamin .... 404-527-4540. 122 E
bjacks@carver.edu
JACKS, Olive .... 404-527-4520. 122 E
ojacks@carver.edu
JACKSON, Addie, R .... 530-226-4788... 66 D
ajackson@simpsonu.edu
JACKSON, Alan .... 423-442-2001. 454 L
jackson@hiwassee.edu
JACKSON, Alan, D .... 903-927-3217. 495 A
adjackson@wileyc.edu
JACKSON, Alexa .... 617-824-8133. 226 A
alexa_jackson@emerson.edu
JACKSON, Alfred, B .... 601-979-2300. 267 E
alfred.b.jackson@jsums.edu
JACKSON, Allen, M .... 803-535-5348. 442 B
allen.jackson@claflin.edu
JACKSON, Amy .... 620-672-5641. 190 A
amyj@prattcc.edu
JACKSON, Andrew .... 615-327-6894. 456 E
aljackson@mmc.edu
JACKSON, Arthur, R .... 704-687-2206. 368 E
ajacks90@uncc.edu
JACKSON, Athena .... 305-626-3782. 104 J
Athena.Jackson@fmuniv.edu
JACKSON, Betty .... 706-649-1813. 123 E
bjackson@columbustech.edu
JACKSON, Brenda .... 910-695-3718. 363 F
jacksonbr@sandhills.edu
JACKSON, Brenda, W ..... 504-586-5274. 206 K
bjackson@suno.edu
JACKSON, Brian, K .... 609-652-4521. 305 C
brian.jackson@stockton.edu
JACKSON, Buddy .... 334-386-7293..... 3 H
bjackson@faulkner.edu
JACKSON, Byron, H .... 412-924-1380. 431 A
bjackson@pts.edu
JACKSON, Caesar, R ...... 919-530-7395. 368 A
crjackson@nccu.edu
JACKSON, Candice Love 601-977-7889. 270 A
cljackson@tougaloo.edu
JACKSON, Carol .... 212-517-0756. 330 E
cjackson@mmm.edu
JACKSON, Catrina .... 336-334-7593. 367 E
sm8093@bncollege.com
JACKSON, Celia .... 414-382-6022. 531 I
celia.jackson@alverno.edu
JACKSON, Charles .... 940-565-3992. 490 C
jacksonc@unt.edu
JACKSON, Charles, C ..... 240-895-4413. 218 A
ccjackson@smcm.edu
JACKSON, Chauncey, J .. 405-466-2957. 395 N
cjjackson@langston.edu
JACKSON, Chip .... 337-482-6287. 208 D
axj0653@louisiana.edu
JACKSON, Christin .... 859-371-9393. 192 D
cjackson@beckfield.edu
JACKSON, Christine .... 402-472-4455. 292 I
cjackson3@unl.edu
JACKSON, Christy .... 434-381-6262. 510 F
cjackson@sbc.edu
JACKSON, Claudia .... 361-698-1247. 471 G
cjackson@delmar.edu
JACKSON, Corey, D .... 703-993-8730. 505 C
cjacksol@gmu.edu
JACKSON, Craig .... 478-757-3508. 122 F
cjackson@centralgatech.edu
JACKSON, Craig .... 478-988-6800. 122 G
cjackson@centralgatech.edu
JACKSON, Craig .... 828-669-8012. 357 H
cjackson@montreat.edu
JACKSON, Craig, R .... 909-558-4545... 51 C
cjackson@llu.edu
JACKSON, Darryl .... 256-372-5060..... 1 A
darryl.jackson1@aamu.edu
JACKSON, David .... 941-309-0166. 111 O
djackson@ringling.edu
JACKSON, David, H .... 941-309-4719. 111 O
djackson@ringling.edu
JACKSON, Deanne .... 573-341-4362. 284 A
registrar@mst.edu
JACKSON, Debbie .... 202-319-5044... 94 G
jacksond@cua.edu
JACKSON, Deborah .... 617-873-0172. 224 G
deborah.jackson@cambridgecollege.edu
JACKSON, Debra .... 864-656-4592. 442 C
dbj@clemson.edu
JACKSON, Dexter .... 334-874-5700..... 3 A
djackson@ccal.edu
JACKSON, Dionne, V ...... 340-693-1041. 555 E
djackso@live.uvi.edu
JACKSON, Donald .... 402-461-7326. 289 I
djackson@hastings.edu
JACKSON, Edison, O .... 386-481-2001... 99 C
jacksone@cookman.edu
JACKSON, Elizabeth .... 806-720-7486. 476 B
disabilityservices@lcu.edu
JACKSON, Elizabeth .... 432-837-8145. 487 B
ejackson@sulross.edu
JACKSON, Emily, S .... 302-225-6271... 93 H
emily@gbc.edu
JACKSON, Equilla .... 936-261-1890. 482 F
eqjackson@pvamu.edu
JACKSON, Eric .... 334-874-5700..... 3 A
ejackson@ccal.edu
JACKSON, Flossie .... 772-462-7467. 106 P
fjackson@irsc.edu
JACKSON, Frances, L ..... 617-333-2970. 225 E
fjackson@curry.edu
JACKSON, G. Smith .... 336-278-7220. 354 B
jacksons@elon.edu
JACKSON, Gary .... 662-325-3036. 268 D
gary@ext.msstate.edu
JACKSON, III,
George, E .... 309-556-3412. 148 B
mcaffairs@iwu.edu
JACKSON, Governor, E ... 940-898-3050. 488 B
gjackson@twu.edu
JACKSON, Gregory .... 256-372-8653..... 1 A
gregory.jackson@aamu.edu
JACKSON, Gregory, S ..... 848-932-7865. 306 A
greg.jackson@rutgers.edu
JACKSON, Harvey .... 973-328-5553. 300 G
hjackson@ccm.edu
JACKSON, Heather .... 508-831-5211. 238 F
hjackson@wpi.edu
JACKSON, Henry .... 732-255-0400. 304 A
hjackson@ocean.edu
JACKSON, Henry .... 910-521-6883. 369 B
tom.jackson@uncp.edu
JACKSON, Hollie .... 661-362-2209... 53 G
hgjackson@masters.edu
JACKSON, Jacob .... 541-245-7802. 407 F
JAjackson@roguecc.edu
JACKSON, JR.,
James, T .... 410-777-2529. 213 D
jjackson@aacc.edu
JACKSON, Jan .... 225-922-1635. 202 G
jjackson@lctcs.edu
JACKSON, Jean .... 919-760-8556. 356 G
jacksonj@meredith.edu
JACKSON, Jean, R .... 336-334-4822. 360 G
rjjackson@gtcc.edu
JACKSON, Jeff .... 419-372-9487. 374 K
jacksjl@bgsu.edu
JACKSON, Jerry .... 423-746-5285. 462 C
jgjackson@twcnet.edu
JACKSON, Jessica .... 814-641-3331. 419 H
jacksoj@juniata.edu
JACKSON, Jim .... 518-891-2915. 335 A
jjackson@nccc.edu
JACKSON, Jim, C .... 580-581-2460. 394 G
jjackson@cameron.edu
JACKSON, Jodie .... 304-293-6999. 530 D
jjackson2@hsc.wvu.edu
JACKSON, John .... 916-577-2200... 76 J
JACKSON, John, A .... 508-541-1814. 225 F
jjackson@dean.edu
JACKSON, Johnny .... 937-376-6522. 376 E
jjackson@centralstate.edu
JACKSON, Joseph, R ...... 937-328-6003. 377 A
jacksonj@clarkstate.edu
JACKSON, Joyce, M .... 623-935-8055... 14 K
joyce.jackson@estrellamountain.edu
JACKSON, Judi .... 504-282-4455. 206 A
jjackson@nobts.edu
JACKSON, Judy, J .... 859-257-9293. 200 C
jj@uky.edu
JACKSON, Judy, T .... 256-765-4896...... 9 C
jtjackson@una.edu
JACKSON, Julie .... 662-846-4151. 266 G
jjackson@deltastate.edu
JACKSON, Karen .... 323-469-3300... 27 F
info@amda.edu
JACKSON, Karima .... 203-932-7338... 92 E
kjackson@newhaven.edu
JACKSON, Kashanta .... 601-928-6267. 268 C
kashanta.jackson@mgccc.edu
JACKSON, Katherine .... 334-244-3704..... 2 A
kjackson@outreach.aum.edu
JACKSON, Keith .... 443-885-3350. 217 A
keith.jackson@morgan.edu
JACKSON, Keith .... 414-326-2335. 532 G
kjackso4@ccon.edu
JACKSON, Kenneth .... 219-989-2366. 171 N
kjackson@purduecal.edu
JACKSON, Kevin .... 254-710-1314. 467 G
kevin_jackson@baylor.edu
JACKSON, Kim .... 509-793-2067. 517 C
kimj@bigbend.edu
JACKSON, Kimberly .... 252-940-6252. 358 A
kimj@beaufortccc.edu
JACKSON, L. Judy .... 413-748-5555. 236 I
ljackson@springfieldcollegel.edu
JACKSON, Lauren .... 318-357-5961. 208 B
potterl@nsula.edu
JACKSON, Lee, F .... 214-752-8585. 490 C
chancellor@unt.edu
JACKSON, Lemario .... 312-850-7090. 142 C
jackson400@ccc.edu
JACKSON, Lenora .... 404-270-5209. 132 E
lenoraj@spelman.edu
JACKSON, Linda, Y .... 512-505-3006. 473 G
lyjackson@htu.edu
JACKSON, Lisa .... 225-675-8270. 203 G
ljackson@rpcc.edu
JACKSON, Lisa, D .... 740-368-3002. 387 J
ldjackso@owu.edu
JACKSON, Lorraine .... 516-323-3051. 331 J
ljackson@molloy.edu
JACKSON, Lynn, E .... 309-794-7347. 139 L
ljackson@augustana.edu
JACKSON, III, Mack .... 985-732-6640. 203 D
JACKSON, Margaret, W .. 931-363-9836. 456 C
mjackson@martinmethodist.edu
JACKSON, Marian, D ...... 903-510-2759. 488 E
mjac@tjc.edu
JACKSON, Marsha, D ..... 716-851-1205. 323 I
jacksonm@ecc.edu
JACKSON, Martin .... 253-879-3207. 524 F
mjackson@pugetsound.edu
JACKSON, Melanie, M ..... 863-784-7018. 113 G
melanie.jackson@southflorida.edu
JACKSON, Melika .... 803-780-1259. 449 E
mjackson@voorhees.edu
JACKSON, Miles .... 360-992-2934. 518 A
mjackson@clark.edu
JACKSON, Minor .... 217-353-2119. 155 J
mjackson@parkland.edu
JACKSON, Natalie .... 406-338-5441. 285 F
njackson@bfcc.edu
JACKSON, Natalie .... 567-661-2647. 387 L
natalie_jackson3@owens.edu
JACKSON, Newton, N ..... 904-620-2700. 116 B
newton.jackson@unf.edu
JACKSON, Pamela .... 318-342-5230. 208 E
pjackson@ulm.edu
JACKSON, Paul .... 603-880-8308. 298 A
tmc@thomasmorecollege.edu
JACKSON, Paula .... 281-290-2722. 476 A
paula.jackson@lonestar.edu
JACKSON, Peggy .... 870-612-2030... 25 A
peggy.jackson@uaccb.edu
JACKSON, Raymond, L .. 817-272-3186. 491 B
jackson@uta.edu
JACKSON, Rhalanda .... 318-670-9328. 207 A
rjackson@susla.edu
JACKSON, Rickey .... 928-289-6530... 16 E
rickey.jackson@npc.edu
JACKSON, Robert .... 715-682-1207. 535 D
rjackson@northland.edu
JACKSON, Robert, D ...... 847-578-3248. 157 F
robert.jackson@rosalindfranklin.edu
JACKSON, Robert, L .... 270-809-3978. 198 B
rjackson@murraystate.edu
JACKSON, Roberta .... 212-463-0400. 348 B
roberta.jackson@touro.edu
JACKSON, Ron .... 864-592-4817. 447 A
jacksonr@sccsc.edu
JACKSON, Ronald .... 513-556-5858. 390 G
ronald.jackson@uc.edu
JACKSON, Ronald, C .... 215-751-8876. 413 I
rcjackson@ccp.edu
JACKSON, Rose Mary ..... 501-882-8855... 19 M
rmjackson@asub.edu
JACKSON, Rosemary ...... 423-585-2614. 462 A
rosemary.jackson@ws.edu
JACKSON, Sally .... 509-533-3123. 518 F
sally.jackson@spokanefalls.edu
JACKSON, Shanna .... 615-790-4419. 460 E
sjackson@columbiatate.edu
JACKSON, Sharon, S ...... 804-752-3747. 508 E
sjackson@rmc.edu
JACKSON, Sherry .... 904-256-7212. 107 Q
sjackso@ju.edu
JACKSON, Shirley, A .... 518-276-6211. 337 I
president@rpi.edu
JACKSON, Starlene .... 919-718-7216. 359 B
sjackson@cccc.edu
JACKSON, Summer .... 606-546-1709. 200 A
sjackson@unionky.edu
JACKSON, Susan .... 406-586-3585. 286 F
susan.jackson@montanabiblecollege.edu
JACKSON, Tamika .... 704-971-8500. 353 F
JACKSON, Tammi .... 510-430-3322... 54 F
tajackson@mills.edu
JACKSON, Theron .... 318-670-6000. 207 A
tjackson@susla.edu
JACKSON, JR.,
Thomas, H .... 706-542-8090. 133 C
tjackson@uga.edu
JACKSON, Tim .... 713-348-4052. 479 A
timothy.j.jackson@rice.edu
JACKSON, Tom .... 918-456-5511. 396 H
jacks009@nsuok.edu
JACKSON, JR., Tom .... 502-852-6933. 200 D
trjack02@louisville.edu
JACKSON, Tondaleya ...... 803-705-4479. 441 C
jacksont@benedict.edu
JACKSON, Twana .... 304-929-6716. 528 D
tjackson@newriver.edu
JACKSON, Tyrone .... 601-857-3232. 267 A
Tyrone.Jackson@hindscc.edu
JACKSON, Tysus .... 256-761-6201..... 7 F
tdjackson@talladega.edu
JACKSON, Vanessa .... 312-777-8562. 147 D
vjackson@aii.edu
JACKSON, Vera .... 601-979-2326. 267 E
vera.j.jackson@jsums.edu
JACKSON, Vincent .... 213-763-7035... 52 D
vjackson@lattc.edu
JACKSON, Wayne .... 407-823-2716. 115 E
wayne.jackson@ucf.edu
JACKSON, Weldon .... 301-860-3462. 220 A
wjackson@bowiestate.edu
JACKSON, Wendy .... 704-216-6158. 356 D
wjackson@livingstone.edu
JACKSON, William .... 301-891-4133. 221 B
news@wau.edu
JACKSON, Willie, J .... 334-727-8514..... 8 A
jacksonw@tuskegee.edu
JACKSON, Wilma .... 402-826-8620. 289 E
wilma.jackson@doane.edu
JACKSON, Zena .... 972-273-3482. 471 B
zjackson@dcccd.edu
JACKSON-ELMOORE,
Cynthia .... 517-355-2326. 246 H
jacks174@msu.edu

JACKSON-HAMMOND, Cynthia ... 937-376-6332. 376 E chammond@centralstate.edu
JACKSON HOLLOWAY, Melissa ... 919-530-6105. 368 A jacksonm@nccu.edu
JACKSON-LEE, Sophia ... 318-670-9355. 207 A slee@susla.edu
JACOB, Alan, B ... 509-777-3250. 525 F ajacob@whitworth.edu
JACOB, Mary ... 805-893-3753... 72 B mary.jacob@sa.ucsb.edu
JACOB, Mary, J ... 805-893-3753... 72 B jacob-m@sa.ucsb.edu
JACOB, Shirley ... 985-549-2217. 208 C Shirley.Jacob@selu.edu
JACOB, Travis ... 208-376-7731. 137 F tjacob@boisebible.edu
JACOBI, Judy, N ... 219-785-5593. 172 A jjacobi@pnc.edu
JACOBOWITZ, Chanie ... 732-367-1060. 299 E cjacobowitz@bmg.edu
JACOBOWITZ, Sharon ... 516-239-9002. 340 I
JACOBS, Alice, M ... 217-443-8848. 143 G amjacobs@dacc.edu
JACOBS, Andrew, C ... 207-834-7671. 212 E andrew.jacobs@maine.edu
JACOBS, Bonita ... 706-864-1993. 133 D president@ung.edu
JACOBS, Bret ... 504-865-3979. 205 H bljacobs@loyno.edu
JACOBS, Bruce ... 812-855-5650. 167 F jacobsb@indiana.edu
JACOBS, Carolyn ... 413-585-7950. 236 H cjacobs@smith.edu
JACOBS, Craig, M ... 610-892-1509. 427 E cjacobs@pit.edu
JACOBS, Danny, O ... 409-772-4793. 493 C djacobs@utmb.edu
JACOBS, Dawn Ellen ... 951-343-4275... 30 H djacobs@calbaptist.edu
JACOBS, Dennis ... 408-554-4533... 64 M dcjacobs@scu.edu
JACOBS, Derya ... 412-397-3851. 431 I jacobs@rmu.edu
JACOBS, D'Naie ... 419-530-7970. 392 B DNaie.Jacobs@utoledo.edu
JACOBS, Elisa ... 828-398-2536. 366 G ejacobs@southcollegenc.edu
JACOBS, Holly, A ... 330-941-2340. 394 A hajacobs@ysu.edu
JACOBS, James ... 586-445-7241. 246 A jacobsj@macomb.edu
JACOBS, Jane ... 973-761-9181. 307 C jane.jacobs@shu.edu
JACOBS, Jeanne ... 305-237-5006. 109 D jfjacobs@mdc.edu
JACOBS, Jeff ... 701-224-5441. 372 B jeffrey.jacobs@bismarckstate.edu
JACOBS, Jennifer ... 573-897-5000. 276 E
JACOBS, JR., John, O ... 334-844-9891... 1 G jacobjo@auburn.edu
JACOBS, Joshua, E ... 270-809-3763. 198 B jjacobs@murraystate.edu
JACOBS, Junoesque ... 601-977-7765. 270 A jjacobs@tougaloo.edu
JACOBS, Ken ... 785-628-4259. 186 F kjacobs@fhsu.edu
JACOBS, Kerri ... 617-824-8655. 226 A kerri_jacobs@emerson.edu
JACOBS, Kevin ... 303-315-2727... 86 A kevin.jacobs@ucdenver.edu
JACOBS, Kim ... 402-826-8111. 289 E kim.jacobs@doane.edu
JACOBS, LerVerne ... 352-854-2322. 100 K jacobsj@cf.edu
JACOBS, Linda ... 517-265-5161. 238 G
JACOBS, Lloyd, A ... 419-530-2211. 392 B lloyd.jacobs@utoledo.edu
JACOBS, Lori, A ... 757-594-7961. 503 M lori.jacobs@cnu.edu
JACOBS, Mark ... 480-965-2354... 11 K mark.jacobs@asu.edu
JACOBS, Mary, R ... 513-875-3344. 376 H mary.jacobs@chatfield.edu
JACOBS, Mary Ellen ... 210-486-3915. 465 A mjacobs@alamo.edu
JACOBS, Pat ... 661-654-2483... 32 H pjacobs@csub.edu
JACOBS, Patricia ... 615-460-6490. 453 C patricia.jacobs@belmont.edu
JACOBS, Patti ... 617-327-6777. 233 D patti_jacobs@mspp.edu
JACOBS, Phillip ... 479-968-0320... 20 E pjacobs@atu.edu
JACOBS, Ralph ... 719-549-2256... 80 K ralph.jacobs@colostate-pueblo.edu
JACOBS, Steve ... 303-458-3560... 84 M jjacobs@regis.edu
JACOBS, Todd ... 231-591-3817. 242 F jacobst@ferris.edu
JACOBS, Wayne ... 903-233-3860. 475 J waynejacobs@letu.edu
JACOBS ANDERSON, Laura ... 503-370-6206. 408 J ljacobsa@willamette.edu
JACOBS ASTLE, Karen ... 215-503-1040. 434 C karen.astle@jefferson.edu
JACOBS ELSON, Claire ... 609-258-4131. 304 E celson@princeton.edu
JACOBS-WILKE, Alexandra, M ... 315-267-2918. 344 C jacobsam@potsdam.edu
JACOBSEN, Brandy ... 318-670-9371. 207 A bjacobsen@susla.edu
JACOBSEN, Cheryl, R ... 563-588-7107. 180 L cheryl.jacobsen@loras.edu
JACOBSEN, Gabe ... 206-281-2043. 523 C
JACOBSEN, Jackie, S ... 308-635-6175. 293 E jacobse2@wncc.edu
JACOBSEN, Jeffrey ... 406-994-3681. 287 B agdean@montana.edu
JACOBSEN, Jim ... 605-367-5461. 452 C james.jacobsen@southeasttech.edu
JACOBSEN, Stan ... 828-884-8381. 352 I jacobssf@brevard.edu
JACOBSMA, Kelly, G ... 616-395-7790. 244 A jacobsma@hope.edu
JACOBSMEYER, Adam, R ... 808-675-3368. 135 C adam.jacobsmeyer@byuh.edu
JACOBSON, Adela ... 619-388-7313... 62 F ajacobson@sdccd.edu
JACOBSON, Adele ... 605-352-2662. 450 A adjacobs@dwu.edu
JACOBSON, Anne, D ... 804-828-1223. 511 F adjacobson@vcu.edu
JACOBSON, Beatrice, F ... 563-333-6100. 182 B JacobsonBeatriceF@sau.edu
JACOBSON, Bert ... 815-802-8242. 149 C bjacobson@kcc.edu
JACOBSON, Betsy ... 218-733-7618. 259 A b.jacobson@lsc.edu
JACOBSON, Carl ... 302-831-6070... 94 B carlj@udel.edu
JACOBSON, Carol ... 978-630-9306. 232 C c_jacobson@mwcc.mass.edu
JACOBSON, Cynthia ... 620-365-5116. 183 I jacobson@allencc.edu
JACOBSON, Dan ... 715-675-3331. 541 A jacobson@ntc.edu
JACOBSON, Gloria ... 773-298-3706. 158 E jacobson@sxu.edu
JACOBSON, Jennifer ... 218-846-3769. 259 F Jennifer.Jacobson@minnesota.edu
JACOBSON, John, E ... 765-285-5251. 164 B jejacobson@bsu.edu
JACOBSON, Karen ... 610-372-4721. 431 D kjacobson@racc.edu
JACOBSON, Larry, P ... 585-385-8256. 338 H ljacobson@sjfc.edu
JACOBSON, Mary ... 763-433-1315. 257 Q mary.jacobson@anokaramsey.edu
JACOBSON, Mary ... 763-433-1315. 257 P mary.jacobson@anokaramsey.edu
JACOBSON, Renee, R ... 231-995-1256. 248 B jacobsr@nmc.edu
JACOBSON, Ron ... 718-817-1000. 324 G rjacobson@fordham.edu
JACOBSON, Shane, M ... 802-656-0518. 500 F shane.jacobson@uvm.edu
JACOBSON, Stacy ... 651-690-6526. 263 O ssjacobson@stkate.edu
JACOBSON, Steven ... 209-946-2331... 73 A sjacobson@pacific.edu
JACOBSON, Tim ... 952-995-1471. 258 F tim.jacobson@hennepintech.edu
JACOBSON, Timothy, K ... 262-691-5221. 541 D tjacobson9@wctc.edu
JACOBSON, Vicky ... 203-576-5869... 91 D vjacobson@stvincentscollege.edu
JACOBSON-BERG, Judy ... 320-308-5096. 261 C jjacobsonberg@sctcc.edu
JACOBSON-SCHULTE, Patrick ... 320-308-0121. 261 B
JACOBY, Anne ... 617-296-8300. 227 I anne_jacoby@laboure.edu
JACOBY, Brian ... 612-375-1900. 256 E bjacoby@ipr.edu
JACOBY, Jeremy ... 304-865-6135. 527 F jeremy.jacoby@ovu.edu
JACOBY, Robin, M ... 214-648-2288. 493 E robin.jacoby@utsouthwestern.edu
JACQUES, Angelo ... 505-747-2139. 311 E ajacques@nnmc.edu
JACQUES, Ed ... 617-879-2446. 238 C ejacques@wheelock.edu
JACQUES, Kathleen, C ... 207-795-2858. 209 I jacqueka@cmhc.org
JACQUES, Paul ... 323-856-7643... 27 O pjacques@afi.com
JACQUES, Theresa, K ... 906-487-2936. 247 A tjacques@mtu.edu
JACQUET, Roberta ... 610-902-8260. 411 E roberta.c.jacquet@cabrini.edu
JACQUEZ, Ricardo ... 575-646-2914. 310 I rjacquez@nmsu.edu
JACQUIN, Kristine ... 805-898-2949... 44 I kjacquin@fielding.edu
JACZYNSKI, Linda ... 610-519-4080. 436 F linda.jaczynski@villanova.edu
JADALLAH, Edward ... 843-349-2773. 442 E ejadalla@coastal.edu
JADAV, Ameeta ... 770-394-8300. 120 H ajadav@aii.edu
JADHAV, Esther ... 859-858-3511. 192 B esther.jadhav@asbury.edu
JADLOS, Melissa ... 585-385-8164. 338 H mjadlos@sjfc.edu
JADUSHLEVER, Renee ... 510-430-2033... 54 F reneejad@mills.edu
JAECKEL, Andrea ... 734-487-3328. 242 D ajaeckel@emich.edu
JAECKEL, Roger ... 707-654-1127... 31 I rjaeckel@csum.edu
JAECQUES, Chad ... 660-263-4110. 279 B ChadJaecques@macc.edu
JAEGER, Alberta ... 973-300-2176. 307 F ajaeger@sussex.edu
JAEGER, David ... 239-590-2315. 115 A djaeger@fgcu.edu
JAEGER, Naftalie ... 515-239-9002. 340 I
JAEGER, Steven, C ... 507-344-7330. 253 J sjaeger@blc.edu
JAEGER, Timothy, J ... 949-214-3179... 41 I tim.jaeger@cui.edu
JAEHNE, Dennis ... 408-924-5360... 36 A dennis.jaehne@sjsu.edu
JAFARI, Marzie, A ... 718-960-8666. 318 A marzie.jafar@lehman.cuny.edu
JAFERIAN, Warren ... 978-232-2272. 226 C wjaferia@endicott.edu
JAFFE, David, L ... 561-237-7099. 108 X djaffe@lynn.edu
JAFFE, Hyla ... 603-668-2211. 297 I h.jaffe@snhu.edu
JAFFE, John, G ... 434-381-6139. 510 F jgjaffe@sbc.edu
JAFFE, Leslie, R ... 413-585-2806. 236 H ljaffe@smith.edu
JAFFE, Steven ... 562-947-8755... 67 H stevenjaffe@scuhs.edu
JAFFE, Susan ... 336-770-1478. 369 D jaffes@uncsa.edu
JAFFEE, Victoria ... 949-214-3042... 41 I victori.jaffe@cui.edu
JAFFRAY, Shelly ... 714-564-6500... 60 G jaffray_shelly@sac.edu
JAFFRY, John-Herbert ... 636-227-2100. 276 F john.jaffry@logan.edu
JAGENDORF, Susan ... 518-255-5558. 344 E jagends@cobleskill.edu
JAGER, Donna ... 612-343-4488. 262 X dmjager@northcentral.edu
JAGER, Tim ... 712-274-5313. 181 B jager@morningside.edu
JAGERS, J. Lee ... 214-887-5370. 471 F ljagers@dts.edu
JAGGER, Kathleen ... 859-233-8121. 199 I kjagger@transy.edu
JAGGERS, Karen ... 928-428-8308... 13 J karen.jaggers@eac.edu
JAGODZINSKI, Paul ... 928-523-2701... 16 C paul.jagodzinski@nau.edu
JAGORD, Mary-Jo ... 716-878-6001. 343 A jagordmj@buffalostate.edu
JAHAN, Mina ... 408-855-5360... 75 K mina.jahan@wvm.edu
JAHANGIR, Rashed ... 312-939-0111. 144 D rashed@eastwest.edu
JAHNKE, Eileen ... 920-403-3251. 535 L eileen.jahnke@snc.edu
JAHNKE, Tamera, S ... 417-836-5249. 278 E tamerajahnke@missouristate.edu
JAIME, Mark ... 281-425-6489. 475 I mjaime@lee.edu
JAIME, Victor ... 760-355-6219... 48 A victor.jaime@imperial.edu
JAIN, Anil ... 323-953-4000... 51 G jainak@lacitycollege.edu
JAIN, Arun ... 713-743-1422. 489 B ajain@uh.edu
JAIN, Madhu ... 312-939-0111. 144 D madhu@eastwest.edu
JAKUB, William ... 740-283-6366. 379 N wjakub@franciscan.edu
JAKUBIAK, Laura ... 770-537-5720. 134 H laura.jakubiak@westgatech.edu
JAKUBOW, Sandra ... 561-297-3534. 114 L sjakubow@fau.edu
JAKUBOWICZ, OFM, Gregory ... 518-783-2332. 340 J gregj@siena.edu
JAKUBOWSKI, Gerald ... 707-654-1020... 31 I gjakubowski@csum.edu
JAKUBOWSKI, Jason ... 716-286-8566. 334 F jjakubowski@niagara.edu
JAKUBS, Deborah ... 919-660-5800. 354 A deborah.jakubs@duke.edu
JAKWAY, Julie ... 941-752-5000. 114 I
JALALI, Reza ... 207-753-6653. 212 H reza@usm.maine.edu
JALOMO, Romero ... 831-755-6822... 46 G rjalomo@hartnell.edu
JALOVICK, Dana ... 215-702-4301. 411 F bookstore@cairn.edu
JALSEVAC, Paul ... 540-636-2900. 503 L pjalsevac@christendom.edu
JAMBHEKAR, Sunil ... 941-782-5692. 420 E sjambhekar@lecom.edu
JAMERSON, James ... 606-546-2553. 200 A jjamerson@unionky.edu
JAMERSON, Paula ... 903-983-8187. 475 E pjamerson@kilgore.edu
JAMES, A, D ... 334-727-8213... 8 A jamesad@mytu.tuskegee.edu
JAMES, Aaron ... 909-794-2161. 207 E
JAMES, Alicia ... 248-414-6900. 246 F ajames@mji.edu
JAMES, Anisa ... 606-546-1704. 200 A ajames@unionky.edu
JAMES, Ann ... 513-569-1512. 376 L ann.james@cincinnatistate.edu
JAMES, Arthur ... 972-860-4417. 471 B ajames@dcccd.edu
JAMES, Barbara ... 423-236-2942. 458 J bjames@southern.edu
JAMES, Blake ... 305-284-6381. 118 F bjames@miami.edu
JAMES, Bobby ... 870-777-5722... 25 B bobby.james@uacch.edu
JAMES, Bruce ... 501-975-6066... 22 F bjames@philander.edu
JAMES, Buckley ... 386-506-4414. 101 G jamesb@DaytonaState.edu
JAMES, Carley ... 904-819-6459. 103 E Cjames@flagler.edu
JAMES, Catherine ... 269-965-3931. 244 O jamesc@kellogg.edu
JAMES, Charles ... 859-246-6393. 194 L charles.james@kctcs.edu
JAMES, Conley ... 718-270-6137. 319 A conley@mec.cuny.edu
JAMES, David ... 617-573-8148. 237 B djames@suffolk.edu
JAMES, Donna ... 701-845-7276. 372 A donna.james@vcsu.edu
JAMES, III, Frank ... 215-368-5000. 410 F fjames@biblical.edu
JAMES, Glenn ... 210-829-3940. 490 A gjames@uiwtx.edu
JAMES, Glenn, W ... 931-372-6144. 460 A gjames@tntech.edu
JAMES, Henry, D ... 704-687-8454. 368 E hjames1@uncc.edu
JAMES, Hollis ... 423-236-2002. 458 J hjames@southern.edu
JAMES, Jacqueline ... 404-270-5111. 132 E jjames@spelman.edu
JAMES, Janet, C ... 972-238-6974. 471 C jjames@dcccd.edu
JAMES, Jeremy ... 334-556-2361... 3 N jjames@wallace.edu
JAMES, Jesse, L ... 563-589-3214. 182 J jjames@dbq.edu
JAMES, Jim ... 404-962-3155. 134 A jim.james@usg.edu
JAMES, John ... 502-585-9911. 199 C jjames@spalding.edu
JAMES, Joy, L ... 804-706-5214. 512 G jjames@jtcc.edu
JAMES, Kathy ... 325-649-8409. 473 F kjames@hputx.edu
JAMES, Kelly ... 815-394-5045. 157 C KJames@rockford.edu
JAMES, Kevin, L ... 312-662-4213. 139 F kjames@adler.edu
JAMES, Larry, C ... 937-775-3494. 393 G larry.james@wright.edu
JAMES, Larry, K ... 501-450-3111... 25 H larryj@uca.edu
JAMES, Latisha ... 216-368-3909. 375 J latisha.james@case.edu
JAMES, Leroy, K ... 202-806-1073... 95 G l_k_james@howard.edu
JAMES, Lori ... 860-832-2525... 87 K jamesloa@ccsu.edu
JAMES, Margaret ... 814-871-7238. 416 K james015@gannon.edu
JAMES, Mark, S ... 816-604-1011. 277 C mark.james@mcckc.edu

JAMES, Melinda, L .... 630-466-7900. 162 J
mjames@waubonsee.edu
JAMES, Michael .... 850-599-3560. 114 K
michael.james@famu.edu
JAMES, Michael .... 360-676-2772. 521 D
mjames@nwic.edu
JAMES, Michael, F .... 402-449-2817. 289 H
mjames8054@graceu.edu
JAMES, Pansy .... 212-594-4000. 347 H
pjames@tcicollege.edu
JAMES, Patricia .... 425-564-3152. 517 A
patricia.james@bellevuecollege.edu
JAMES, Patricia .... 951-639-5440... 55 B
pjames@msjc.edu
JAMES, Patrick .... 312-629-6600. 158 L
pjames@saic.edu
JAMES, Patrick .... 601-974-1220. 267 I
jamespg@millsaps.edu
JAMES, Penny .... 402-354-7225. 291 B
penny.james@methodistcollege.edu
JAMES, Randall .... 404-237-7573. 121 F
rjames@bauder.edu
JAMES, Reginald .... 334-271-1670..... 6 C
rjames@princeinstitute.edu
JAMES, Richard, L .... 801-585-5690. 496 Q
rljames@usa.utah.edu
JAMES, Scott .... 978-542-6243. 230 E
jscott@salemstate.edu
JAMES, Sean .... 661-395-4221... 49 N
sjames@bakersfieldcollege.edu
JAMES, Sean, P .... 661-336-5165... 49 M
sjames@kccd.edu
JAMES, Shauna .... 256-331-5368..... 6 A
sjames@nwscc.edu
JAMES, Steven .... 865-981-8802. 456 D
steven.james@maryvillecollege.edu
JAMES, Sujaya .... 404-527-4520. 122 E
sjames@carver.edu
JAMES, Sujaya .... 404-527-4688. 122 E
sjames@carver.edu
JAMES, Tessa .... 800-567-2344. 532 E
tjames@menominee.edu
JAMES, Thomas .... 212-678-3050. 347 G
james@tc.edu
JAMES, Timmy .... 256-331-6281..... 6 A
timmy.james@nwscc.edu
JAMES, Tracy .... 636-481-3187. 275 I
tjames@jeffco.edu
JAMES, Vernon .... 706-880-8979. 128 A
vjames@lagrange.edu
JAMES, W. Brian .... 706-245-7226. 124 D
bjames@ec.edu
JAMES BLACKWELL,
Leanna .... 413-565-1000. 222 F
ljamesblackwell@baypath.edu
JAMES-MOORE, Annette 901-272-5153. 456 F
amoore@mca.edu
JAMES PRYOR, Jennifer 914-323-5299. 330 B
jj.pryor@mville.edu
JAMES-WHIDBEE,
Donna .... 252-335-3785. 367 C
dmjameswhidbee@mail.ecsu.edu
JAMESON, Deborah .... 800-818-2261. 296 F
djameson@dwc.edu
JAMESON, Dennis .... 916-577-2200... 76 J
djameson@jessup.edu
JAMESON, J, L .... 215-898-6796. 435 B
ljameson@mail.med.upenn.edu
JAMESON, Maisha .... 510-464-3236... 59 C
mjameson@peralta.edu
JAMESON, Sean .... 914-395-2494. 340 E
sjameson@sarahlawrence.edu
JAMESON, Stacey .... 212-924-5900. 347 B
sjameson@swedishinstitute.edu
JAMIESON, Leah, H .... 765-494-5346. 171 M
lhj@purdue.edu
JAMIESON, Michelle, E .. 724-287-8711. 411 C
michelle.jamieson@bc3.edu
JAMIESON, Richard, J ... 216-368-3720. 375 J
rjj@case.edu
JAMIESON-DRAKE,
David .... 919-684-3501. 354 A
david.jamieson.drake@duke.edu
JAMIL, Hasan .... 713-313-1953. 485 F
jamil_hx@tsu.edu
JAMISON, Artie .... 561-297-3904. 114 L
ajamiso5@fau.edu
JAMISON, Calvin, D .... 972-883-2213. 491 E
cjamison@utdallas.edu
JAMISON, Charles .... 610-409-3607. 436 B
cjamison@ursinus.edu
JAMISON, David, L .... 412-397-6225. 431 I
jamison@rmu.edu
JAMISON, Kristin, E .... 217-245-3046. 146 F
kristin.jamison@ic.edu
JAMISON, Matt .... 303-678-3845... 81 N
matt.jamison@frontrange.edu
JAMISON, Steven, A .... 859-238-5455. 193 E
steve.jamison@centre.edu
JAMISON, Todd, M .... 740-587-5712. 379 D
jamisont@denison.edu
JAMMER, Veronica .... 281-476-1501. 479 F
veronica.jammer@sjcd.edu
JAMROGOWICZ, John ... 843-574-6136. 447 E
john.jamrogowicz@tridenttech.edu
JANAIRO, Ed .... 920-693-1871. 540 B
ed.janairo@gotoltc.edu
JANAK, Bickram .... 443-885-3333. 217 A
bickram.janak@morgan.edu
JANAK, Kenneth .... 817-257-5712. 484 I
k.janak@tcu.edu
JANARO, Walter, A .... 540-636-2900. 503 L
walter@christendom.edu
JANDA, Kenneth, C .... 949-824-6022... 71 B
kcjanda@uci.edu
JANDOVITZ, Tom .... 301-846-2501. 214 H
tjandovitz@frederick.edu
JANDRIS, Thomas .... 708-209-3597. 143 E
thomas.jandris@cuchicago.edu
JANDT, Fred, E .... 909-473-8118... 34 E
fjandt@csusb.edu
JANES, Brian .... 401-454-6651. 440 A
bjanes@risd.edu
JANESCH, Cynthia, D ..... 570-577-3763. 411 A
cindy.janesch@bucknell.edu
JANG, Jeanie .... 562-903-4875... 29 L
jeanie.jang@biola.edu
JANG, Michelle .... 714-533-1495... 66 H
michelle@southbaylo.edu
JANIK, Julie .... 972-721-4127. 488 F
jjanik@udallas.edu
JANIS, Anita .... 707-465-2300... 40 H
anita-janis@redwoods.edu
JANIS, Brad .... 562-624-9530... 77 D
bjanis@cci.edu
JANIS, Robert, J .... 312-362-8762. 143 H
bjanis@depaul.edu
JANITZ, Suzanne .... 607-431-4244. 325 F
janitzs@hartwick.edu
JANKE, Louise, L .... 608-785-8604. 536 G
ljanke@uwlax.edu
JANKO, Karen .... 312-777-8666. 147 D
kjanko@aii.edu
JANKOVIAK,
Michael, W .... 989-386-6603. 247 B
mjankoviak@midmich.edu
JANKOWSKI, Cheryl ...... 440-934-3101. 385 K
cjankowski@ohiobusinesscollege.edu
JANKOWSKI, Phillip, E .. 219-785-5404. 172 A
pjankowski@pnc.edu
JANKOWSKI,
Stephen, E .... 618-650-2760. 159 H
sjankow@siue.edu
JANNE, Rex .... 979-845-4570. 483 C
r-janne@tamu.edu
JANNEY, Craig .... 252-398-6298. 353 H
jannec@chowan.edu
JANNEY, Dell Ann .... 573-288-6388. 273 F
djanney@culver.edu
JANNEY, Suzanne, L ...... 941-487-4110. 115 D
janney@ncf.edu
JANOSIK, Daniel .... 704-847-5600. 366 J
djanosik@ses.edu
JANOT, Melissa .... 617-349-8755. 228 B
mjanot@lesley.edu
JANOW, Susan .... 360-331-0307. 521 E
registrar@nila.edu
JANOWIAK, Diane, J ...... 708-709-3603. 156 A
djanowiak@prairiestate.edu
JANSEN, James .... 206-546-4651. 523 F
jjansen@shoreline.edu
JANSEN, James, S .... 402-280-5589. 289 D
jimjansen@creighton.edu
JANSEN, Mark .... 815-599-3455. 146 D
mark.jansen@highland.edu
JANSEN, Matthew .... 217-234-5549. 150 D
mjansen57335@lakeland.cc.il.us
JANSEN, Sandy .... 865-974-6611. 463 B
sjansen@utk.edu
JANSEN, Wendy .... 605-221-3100. 450 C
wjansen@kilian.edu
JANSMA, Pamela .... 817-272-3491. 491 B
pjansma@uta.edu
JANSSEN, Jill, M .... 815-599-3412. 146 D
jill.janssen@highland.edu
JANSSEN, Michelle .... 859-985-3007. 192 F
janssenm@berea.edu
JANSSON, Jimilea .... 580-628-6771. 396 M
jimilea.jansson@noc.edu
JANULIS, Jeffrey .... 773-481-8816. 142 F
jjanulis@ccc.edu
JANUS, Eric, S .... 651-290-6310. 265 F
eric.janus@wmitchell.edu
JANUSZESKI, Carol, A ... 512-448-8414. 479 C
carolj@stedwards.edu
JANUTOLO, D. Blake ...... 765-641-4541. 163 L
dbjanutolo@anderson.edu
JANVIER, Kathy, A .... 302-454-3973... 93 F
kathy.janvier@dtcc.edu
JANZ, Curtis .... 405-425-5358. 397 D
curtis.janz@oc.edu
JANZ, Kenneth .... 507-457-2299. 262 A
kjanz@winona.edu
JANZEN, Amy .... 405-425-5907. 397 D
amy.janzen@oc.edu
JANZEN, Dennis .... 559-453-2000... 45 D
djanzen@fresno.edu
JANZEN, Rod .... 559-453-2210... 45 D
rjanzen@fresno.edu
JANZEN, Scott .... 574-296-6213. 163 J
registrar@ambs.edu
JANZEN, Teresa .... 616-222-3000. 245 C
tjanzen@kuyper.edu
JANZER, Todd .... 215-785-0111. 426 X
JAQUES, Kate .... 916-484-8654... 53 A
jaquesk@arc.losrios.edu
JAQUILLARD, Jenny .... 800-869-7223. 131 B
jjaquill@scad.edu
JARA, Amna .... 562-860-2451... 37 I
ajara@cerritos.edu
JARACZEWSKI, John ...... 262-595-2591. 537 C
john.jaraczewski@uwp.edu
JARAMILLO, Brooke .... 229-333-2100. 134 K
brooke.jaramillo@wiregrass.edu
JARAMILLO, Fernan .... 507-222-4301. 254 D
fjaramil@carleton.edu
JARAMILLO, Ray .... 806-665-8801. 468 J
ray.jaramillo@clarendoncollege.edu
JARAMILLO, Rick .... 505-454-2561. 309 L
rjaramillo@luna.edu
JARAMILLO FLEMING,
Melissa .... 575-835-5880. 310 F
mjaramillo@admin.nmt.edu
JARBOE, Dan .... 870-245-5591... 22 D
jarboed@obu.edu
JARED, Tim .... 864-622-6011. 441 B
tjared@andersonuniversity.edu
JARETT, Sadie .... 334-874-5700..... 3 A
sjarret@ccal.edu
JARGO, Jeralyn .... 651-779-3235. 258 C
jeralyn.jargo@century.edu
JARICH, Amy .... 510-642-3175... 70 I
awjarich@berkeley.edu
JARLEY, Paul .... 407-823-2181. 115 E
pjarley@bus.ucf.edu
JARMAN, Chet .... 252-940-6241. 358 A
chetj@beaufortccc.edu
JARMIN MILLER,
Catherine .... 503-883-2494. 404 A
cjarmin@linfield.edu
JARMUZ, Nick .... 312-935-2005. 156 K
njarmuz@robertmorris.edu
JARNAGIN, Lea .... 657-278-3211... 33 E
ljarnagin@fullerton.edu
JARNAGIN, Missy .... 805-437-3282... 32 I
missy.jarnagin@csuci.edu
JARONSKI, Ann .... 813-974-3598. 116 C
atj1@usf.edu
JAROSZ, John .... 402-354-7065. 291 B
john.jarosz@methodistcollege.edu
JAROSZ, Jonathan .... 810-424-5486. 251 E
jarosz@umflint.edu
JAROT, Lisa .... 847-628-1572. 149 B
ljarot@judsonu.edu
JARR, William .... 770-426-2632. 128 D
wdjarr@life.edu
JARRELL, Bruce, E .... 410-706-2304. 219 C
brucejarrell@som.umaryland.edu
JARRELL, Karen .... 214-379-5412. 478 D
kjarrell@pqc.edu
JARRELL, Michelle .... 205-391-2328..... 6 H
mjarrell@sheltonstate.edu
JARRELL, Sasha .... 850-729-5363. 109 I
jarrells@nwfsc.edu
JARRELL, Sheila .... 928-776-2188... 19 H
sheila.jarrell@yc.edu
JARRET, Ronald .... 508-793-2541. 225 B
rjarret@holycross.edu
JARRETT, Courtney .... 540-535-3461. 509 E
cjarrett1@su.edu
JARRETT, Jessica .... 918-335-6334. 398 F
founders@okwu.edu
JARRETT, Juan, A .... 413-545-0360. 228 F
jjarrett@admin.umass.edu
JARRETT, Kathy .... 413-565-1000. 222 F
kjarrett@baypath.edu
JARRETT, Robert .... 713-221-8191. 489 D
jarrettr@uhd.edu
JARRETT-HORTIS,
Frances, L .... 864-503-5195. 448 H
fjarrett-hortis@uscupstate.edu
JARRY, Timothy .... 508-793-2515. 225 B
tjarry@holycross.edu
JARSTFER, Amiel .... 423-869-6203. 456 A
amiel.jarstfer@lmunet.edu
JARVIE, Greg, I .... 330-672-9494. 382 B
gjarvie@kent.edu
JARVIS, Jeffrey, A .... 419-227-3141. 391 F
jjarvis@unoh.edu
JARVIS, Keith .... 307-532-8255. 542 a
keith.jarvis@ewc.wy.edu
JARVIS, Sam .... 610-841-3333. 427 F
sjarvis@psb.edu
JARVIS, Sarah .... 802-322-1751. 499 C
sarah.jarvis@goddard.edu
JARVIS, Shelli, W .... 703-323-3361. 513 C
sjarvis@nvcc.edu
JARZABSKI, Kerri, P ...... 413-782-1312. 238 A
kjarzabs@wne.edu
JASEK, Michael, D .... 575-646-1722. 310 I
mjasek@nmsu.edu
JASHINSKI, Michelle, L . 814-371-2090. 434 F
mjashinski@triangle-tech.edu
JASHO, Gay-linn .... 404-880-8892. 122 J
gjasho@cau.edu
JASIENIECKI, Darren ...... 219-473-4292. 164 K
djasieniecki@ccsj.edu
JASINSKI, John .... 660-562-1110. 279 I
johnj@nwmissouri.edu
JASMAN, Troy .... 712-274-6400. 183 G
troy.jasman@witcc.edu
JASON, Hoerr, U .... 610-921-7221. 409 A
jhoerr@alb.edu
JASON, Karen .... 508-531-2750. 229 D
kjason@bridgew.edu
JASS, Lori, K .... 503-517-1320. 408 H
ljass@warnerpacific.edu
JASTORFF, Mark .... 303-556-8320... 83 D
mjastorf@msudenver.edu
JASTORFF, Michael .... 605-642-6279. 451 G
michael.jastorff@bhsu.edu
JASUR, Andela .... 631-420-2717. 346 B
angela.jasur@farmingdale.edu
JASWAL, Faisal .... 425-564-6151. 517 A
fjaswal@bellevuecollege.edu
JASZKA, Michael, S .... 716-286-8343. 334 F
msj@niagara.edu
JATTKOWSKI-HUDSON,
Anna, J .... 815-226-3392. 157 C
ajattkowski-hudson@rockford.edu
JATULIS, Viltis, A .... 805-525-4417... 69 H
vjatulis@thomasaquinas.edu
JAUNARAJS, Imants .... 740-593-2909. 387 C
jaunaraj@ohio.edu
JAUREGUY, Steven, P .... 209-667-3114... 35 B
sjaureguy@csustan.edu
JAURON, Les .... 530-895-2266... 30 F
jauronle@butte.edu
JAVAHERIPOUR, G, H ... 760-245-4271... 75 B
GH.Javaheripour@vvc.edu
JAVARIZ, Gerardo .... 787-890-2681. 553 H
gerardo.javariz@upr.edu
JAVDEKAR, Chitra .... 781-239-2703. 231 G
cjavdekar@massbay.edu
JAVIER, Byron, A .... 312-850-7140. 142 C
bjavier@ccc.edu
JAVIER, Pedro .... 787-264-1912. 551 A
pj.javier@intersg.edu
JAVINAR, Jan .... 808-689-2689. 136 C
javinar@hawaii.edu
JAVINAR, Jan, M .... 808-956-5283. 135 L
javinar@hawaii.edu
JAVOR, Seta .... 818-767-0888... 76 K
seta.javor@woodbury.edu
JAVOREK, Mary Beth, E . 216-397-4943. 381 R
javorek@jcu.edu
JAVOROSKI, Alan .... 715-422-5402. 540 D
al.javoroski@mstc.edu
JAWAHAR, Jim .... 309-438-7018. 147 J
jimoham@ilstu.edu
JAY, Andrea .... 305-348-7347. 115 B
andrea.jay@fiu.edu
JAY, Ben .... 808-956-7301. 136 B
athdir@hawaii.edu
JAYARAMAN, Ruki .... 312-505-0705... 28 M
rjayaraman@argosy.edu
JAYASURIYA, Kumara .... 219-785-5201. 172 A
kjayasur@pnc.edu
JAYAWICKREMA,
Arosha .... 860-768-4276... 92 D
jaya@hartford.edu
JAYE, Marilyn .... 617-559-8642. 227 D
mjaye@hebrewcollege.edu
JAYNE, Billie Jo .... 315-279-5684. 328 D
bjjayne@keuka.edu
JAYNE, Joanne .... 718-429-6600. 349 H
joanne.jayne@vaughn.edu
JAYNE, Lisa .... 928-524-7418... 16 E
lisa.jayne@npc.edu
JAYNE, Lorrie .... 828-298-3325. 370 E
ljayne@warren-wilson.edu
JAYNES, Jamie .... 630-353-7049. 144 A
jjaynes@devry.edu
JAYNES, Kathy .... 406-265-4147. 287 D
kjaynes@msun.edu
JAYNES, Lorene .... 406-771-4305. 287 E
ljaynes@gfcmsu.edu
JAYNES, Tom .... 919-536-7250. 360 B
jaynest@durhamtech.edu
JAZDZEWSKI,
Richard, L .... 262-472-1305. 538 D
jazdzewr@uww.edu

JAZWIECKI, Gabrielle, E 203-837-8281... 88 B
jazwieckig@wcsu.edu
JAZZABI, Monica .... 323-343-3342... 34 A
mjazzabi@cslanet.calstatela.edu
JEAN, Kevin .... 405-789-7661. 400 A
kevin.jean@swcu.edu
JEAN, Kevin, J .... 919-658-7750. 357 I
kjean@moc.edu
JEAN, Libby .... 269-749-7655. 249 A
ljean@olivetcollege.edu
JEAN, Martin, D .... 203-432-9681... 93 A
martin.jean@yale.edu
JEAN-LOUIS, Patrick ...... 617-541-5388. 232 G
pjeanlouis@rcc.mass.edu
JEAN-PIERRE, Paul .... 718-631-6314. 319 D
pjean-pierre@qcc.cuny.edu
JEANCAKE, Chris .... 912-427-1958. 120 B
cjeancake@altamahatech.edu
JEANES, Opey .... 919-734-8585. 357 I
ojeanes@moc.edu
JEANES, Opey, D .... 919-734-8585. 357 I
ojeanes@moc.edu
JEANPIERRE, Letha .... 408-864-8976... 44 M
jeanpierreletha@deanza.edu
JEARDOE, Amanda .... 785-825-5422. 185 B
ajeardoe@brownmackie.edu
JEBALI, Lisa .... 978-837-5109. 234 A
lisa.jebali@merrimack.edu
JEBSEN, Chris .... 419-995-8020. 381 Q
jebsen.c@rhodesstate.edu
JECH, Sue .... 507-433-0610. 260 I
sue.jech@riverland.edu
JECHURA, Kacey .... 303-300-8740... 78 M
kacey.jechura@collegeamerica.com
JEELANI, Shaik .... 334-727-8970..... 8 A
jeelanis@mytu.tuskegee.edu
JEFFERS, Brenda, R .... 217-544-6464. 158 D
JEFFERS, Carrie .... 586-286-2187. 246 A
jeffersc@macomb.edu
JEFFERS, Karen .... 918-595-7441. 400 E
karen.jeffers@tulsacc.edu
JEFFERS, Leta .... 724-589-2042. 434 B
ljeffers@thiel.edu
JEFFERSON, Adriene ...... 772-462-7606. 106 P
ajeffers@irsc.edu
JEFFERSON, Arthur .... 601-979-2484. 267 E
arthur.jefferson@jsums.edu
JEFFERSON, Barbie, F .... 864-597-4237. 449 I
jeffersonbf@wofford.edu
JEFFERSON, Curtis .... 352-395-5175. 113 C
curtis.jefferson@sfcollege.edu
JEFFERSON, Debrah .... 773-995-3586. 141 J
djeffers@csu.edu
JEFFERSON, Doug .... 817-598-6247. 494 G
djefferson@wc.edu
JEFFERSON, Henry .... 606-759-7141. 196 B
henry.jefferson@kctcs.edu
JEFFERSON, Jennifer ...... 781-239-2629. 231 G
jjefferson@massbay.edu
JEFFERSON, Joy .... 757-727-4012. 505 F
joy.jefferson@hamptonu.edu
JEFFERSON, Karyl .... 360-676-2772. 521 D
kjefferson@nwic.edu
JEFFERSON, Michael .... 707-965-7080... 57 J
mjeffereson@puc.edu
JEFFERSON, Patrick .... 323-241-5280... 52 C
jefferpd@lasc.edu
JEFFERSON, Richard, P .. 617-552-3334. 224 A
richard.jefferson@bc.edu
JEFFERSON, Shirley .... 802-831-1333. 500 H
sjefferson@vermontlaw.edu
JEFFERSON, Venessa, F . 803-934-3175. 445 F
vjefferson@morris.edu
JEFFERSON, Vivian .... 409-880-8188. 486 E
vgjefferson@lit.edu
JEFFERSON, Willie .... 803-780-1049. 449 E
williej@voorhees.edu
JEFFERY, Charles, F .... 623-845-4001... 14 M
charles.jeffery@gcmail.maricopa.edu
JEFFERY, James, E .... 570-586-2400. 410 D
jjeffery@bbc.edu
JEFFERY, James, R .... 269-471-3481. 239 D
jimjeff@andrews.edu
JEFFERY, John, A .... 610-660-1060. 432 E
jjeffery@sju.edu
JEFFERY, Kathryn .... 916-558-2100... 53 D
jefferk@scc.losrios.edu
JEFFERY, Penny .... 936-468-4008. 482 A
jefferype@sfasu.edu
JEFFES, Annette, S .... 413-662-5416. 230 C
annette.jeffes@mcla.edu
JEFFORD, Janet, L .... 860-727-6904... 90 A
jjefford@goodwin.edu
JEFFRESS, Conway, A .... 734-462-4400. 250 A
jeffress@schoolcraft.edu
JEFFREY, Dave .... 620-241-0723. 185 K
JEFFREY, David, K .... 540-568-7044. 506 F
jeffredk@jmu.edu
JEFFREY, Don .... 334-983-6556..... 7 H
djeffr@troy.edu
JEFFREY, Douglas .... 517-607-2518. 243 I
doug.jeffrey@hillsdale.edu
JEFFREY, Douglas .... 517-437-7341. 243 I
doug.jeffrey@hillsdale.edu
JEFFREY, Russell .... 512-313-3000. 469 L
russell.jeffrey@concordia.edu
JEFFRIES, Frankie .... 901-435-1530. 455 M
frankie_jeffries@loc.edu
JEFFRIES, Mammie .... 904-470-8055. 102 A
m.jeffries@ewc.edu
JEFFRIES, Michael .... 660-543-8203. 283 A
jeffries@ucmo.edu
JEFFRIES, Rosemary .... 732-987-2252. 302 B
jeffries@georgian.edu
JEFFRIES, Shellie .... 616-632-2130. 239 E
jeffrmic@aquinas.edu
JEFFRIES, Susan, K .... 580-327-8570. 396 N
skjeffries@nwosu.edu
JEFFRION, William .... 504-520-6780. 209 D
wjeffrio@xula.edu
JEFIMENKO, Otto .... 219-981-4291. 168 B
ojefimen@iun.edu
JEFREMOW, George .... 212-217-4420. 324 C
george_jefremow@fitnyc.edu
JEHNINGS, Marcia .... 860-512-2703... 88 G
mjehnings@manchestercc.edu
JEKA, Mary, R .... 617-627-4220. 237 C
mary.jeka@tufts.edu
JELINEK, John, A .... 312-329-4185. 153 E
john.jelinek@moody.edu
JELLEMA, Jon, A .... 616-331-2400. 243 C
jellemaj@gvsu.edu
JELLERSON, George .... 804-862-6212. 508 H
gjellerson@rbc.edu
JELLINGHAUS, Fritz .... 860-434-5232... 90 F
fjellinghaus@lymeacademy.edu
JELLISON, Rebecca .... 269-782-1241. 250 C
rjellison@swmich.edu
JELLY, Katherine .... 518-587-2100. 346 A
katherine.jelly@esc.edu
JEMIOLA, Richard .... 757-352-4028. 508 G
richjem@regent.edu
JEMISON, Jan .... 415-565-4723... 71 A
jemisonj@uchastings.edu
JEN, Ezbon .... 707-524-1591... 65 B
ejen@santarosa.edu
JEN, Tien-Chien .... 907-786-1900... 10 H
tjen@uaa.alaska.edu
JENAL, Robert, F .... 508-856-3892. 229 C
robert.jenal@umassmed.edu
JENCKS, Doyle .... 580-477-7736. 401 J
doyle.jencks@wosc.edu
JENDA, Overtoun .... 334-844-4184..... 1 G
jendaov@auburn.edu
JENE, Beverly .... 802-322-1650. 499 C
beverly.jene@goddard.edu
JENERETTE, Kim .... 937-766-3640. 375 K
kimjenerette@cedarville.edu
JENIK, Jeff .... 803-641-3455. 448 A
jeffj@usca.edu
JENIOUS, Anita .... 615-322-4705. 463 G
anita.jenious@vanderbilt.edu
JENKINS, Allen .... 718-933-6700. 331 K
ajenkins@monroecollege.edu
JENKINS, Anne .... 252-737-1133. 367 B
jenkinsa@ecu.edu
JENKINS, Anthony, L .... 410-651-2200. 219 E
aljenkins@umes.edu
JENKINS, Ashley .... 617-739-1700. 235 A
ajenkins@aii.edu
JENKINS, Betty, A .... 803-705-4808. 441 C
jenkinsb@benedict.edu
JENKINS, Bobby .... 580-349-1376. 397 G
bjenkins@opsu.edu
JENKINS, Bonita .... 706-771-4019. 121 D
bjenkins@augustatech.edu
JENKINS, Brandon .... 919-735-5151. 364 H
bmjenkins@waynecc.edu
JENKINS, Brian .... 657-278-2423... 33 E
bjenkins@fullerton.edu
JENKINS, Briar .... 580-477-7700. 401 J
briar.jenkins@wosc.edu
JENKINS, Bryan .... 919-807-7100. 357 L
jenkinsb@nccommunitycolleges.edu
JENKINS, Cara .... 610-436-3513. 430 A
cjenkins@wcupa.edu
JENKINS, Carolyn .... 404-237-7573. 121 F
cjenkins@bauder.edu
JENKINS, Carri, P .... 801-422-1166. 495 D
carri_jenkins@byu.edu
JENKINS, Cheryl, S .... 919-760-8338. 356 G
jenkinsc@meredith.edu
JENKINS, Daniel .... 334-874-5700..... 3 A
djenkins@ccal.edu
JENKINS, Deborah, D ...... 410-334-2904. 221 D
djenkins@worwic.edu
JENKINS, Debra .... 262-524-7120. 532 C
djenkins@carrollu.edu
JENKINS, Edward .... 205-781-7471..... 5 G
JENKINS, G. Scott .... 336-334-7006. 367 E
gsjenkin@ncat.edu
JENKINS, Gerald .... 440-525-7248. 382 M
gjenkins@lakelandcc.edu
JENKINS, Geraldine, M .. 440-646-8322. 392 D
gerri.jenkins@ursuline.edu
JENKINS, H.E .... 512-313-3000. 469 L
he.jenkins@concordia.edu
JENKINS, Helen .... 713-646-1887. 480 J
hjenkins@stcl.edu
JENKINS, J. Marshall ..... 706-236-2259. 121 G
mjenkins@berry.edu
JENKINS, Jan .... 479-968-0456... 20 E
ejenkins@atu.edu
JENKINS, Jane, E .... 614-235-4136. 390 A
jjenkins@TLSohio.edu
JENKINS, Jeffrey, L .... 812-877-8209. 172 C
jenkins@rose-hulman.edu
JENKINS, Jessika .... 281-873-0262. 469 H
j.jenkins@commonwealth.edu
JENKINS, Jim .... 909-274-4570... 55 A
jjenkins@mtsac.edu
JENKINS, SR.,
Jimmy, R .... 704-216-6098. 356 D
jjenkins@livingstone.edu
JENKINS, John .... 404-527-4520. 122 E
jjenkins@carver.edu
JENKINS, CSC, John, I .. 574-631-3903. 174 A
jenkins.1@nd.edu
JENKINS, Joyce, O .... 501-492-0619... 19 J
joyce.jenkins@arkansasbaptist.edu
JENKINS, Katrina, E .... 217-245-3060. 146 F
katrina.jenkins@ic.edu
JENKINS, Kevin .... 870-307-7220... 21 H
kevin.jenkins@lyon.edu
JENKINS, Malia .... 619-201-8728... 62 B
Malia.Jenkins@sdcc.edu
JENKINS, Mark .... 713-348-4966. 479 A
jenky@rice.edu
JENKINS, Matt .... 304-263-0979. 527 J
JENKINS, Mike .... 903-983-8189. 475 E
mjenkins@kilgore.edu
JENKINS, Morris .... 573-651-2178. 282 B
mjenkins@semo.edu
JENKINS, Nichelle .... 212-280-1317. 349 A
njenkins@uts.columbia.edu
JENKINS, Paul .... 513-244-4351. 377 G
paul_jenkins@mail.msj.edu
JENKINS, Rebecca .... 419-434-5692. 391 D
jenkinsr1@findlay.edu
JENKINS, Richard, J .... 701-858-3299. 371 F
dick.jenkins@minotstateu.edu
JENKINS, Robert .... 713-500-3334. 492 E
robert.jenkins@uth.tmc.edu
JENKINS, Rod .... 972-708-7369. 472 L
rod_jenkins@gial.edu
JENKINS, Rodney .... 570-484-2253. 429 B
rj2253@lhup.edu
JENKINS, Sam .... 770-537-6012. 134 H
sam.jenkins@westgatech.edu
JENKINS, Scott .... 810-762-0502. 247 F
scott.jenkins@mcc.edu
JENKINS, Sharon .... 575-439-3806. 310 J
djenkins@nmsu.edu
JENKINS, Sonja .... 478-218-3308. 122 F
sjenkins@centralgatech.edu
JENKINS, Sonja .... 478-988-6800. 122 G
sjenkins@centralgatech.edu
JENKINS, Stephen .... 541-962-3553. 405 H
stephen.jenkins@eou.edu
JENKINS, Sterling .... 719-296-6106... 84 G
sterling.jenkins@pueblocc.edu
JENKINS, Steve .... 619-201-8720... 62 B
Steve.Jenkins@sdcc.edu
JENKINS, Steven .... 740-392-6868. 384 K
steven.jenkins@mvnu.edu
JENKINS, Sylvia .... 708-974-5201. 153 F
jenkins@morainevalley.edu
JENKINS, Tara, F .... 508-854-4249. 232 F
tarafj@qcc.mass.edu
JENKINS, Terry .... 217-641-4960. 148 M
tjenkins@jwcc.edu
JENKINS, Timothy, S ...... 219-464-5304. 174 E
tim.jenkins@valpo.edu
JENKINS, Vanessa, C ...... 757-823-8173. 507 M
vcjenkins@nsu.edu
JENKINS-CARTER,
D'Lonika .... 510-567-6174... 69 C
djenkins@sum.edu
JENKINS-SCOTT, Jackie . 617-879-2161. 238 C
jjenkins-scott@wheelock.edu
JENKS, Dean .... 503-517-1093. 408 H
djenks@warnerpacific.edu
JENKS, Debra .... 414-277-4516. 534 G
jenks@msoe.edu
JENKS, Paul .... 402-486-2536. 292 E
pajenks@ucollege.edu
JENLINK, Christee .... 918-449-6000. 396 H
jenlink@nsuok.edu
JENNEMAN, Eugene, A .. 231-995-1572. 248 B
ejenneman@nmc.edu
JENNERJOHN, Julie .... 906-487-7352. 242 G
julie.jennerjohn@finlandia.edu
JENNESS, Valerie .... 949-824-6094... 71 B
jenness@uci.edu
JENNETT, Charles .... 804-828-0190. 511 F
cjennett@vcu.edu
JENNINGS, Arbolina, L .. 713-313-7661. 485 F
jennings_al@tsu.edu
JENNINGS, Barbara .... 641-844-5522. 179 H
barb.jennings@iavalley.edu
JENNINGS, Bret .... 256-765-4658..... 9 C
nmjennings@una.edu
JENNINGS, Charla .... 870-743-3000... 22 B
charlam@northark.edu
JENNINGS, Charles .... 209-954-5040... 63 C
cjennings@deltacollege.edu
JENNINGS, Chris .... 213-624-1200... 44 D
cjennings@fidm.edu
JENNINGS, Christal .... 610-225-5102. 415 G
cjenning@eastern.edu
JENNINGS, David, C .... 845-675-4616. 335 C
david.jennings@nyack.edu
JENNINGS, Diana, E ...... 508-531-1382. 229 D
diana.jennings@bridgew.edu
JENNINGS, Donna .... 630-353-9069. 144 A
djennings@devry.edu
JENNINGS,
George-Harold .... 973-408-3392. 301 C
gjenning@drew.edu
JENNINGS, Hope .... 937-775-4818. 393 G
hope.jennings@wright.edu
JENNINGS, John, L .... 903-813-2410. 466 H
jjennings@austincollege.edu
JENNINGS, Patricia, L .... 302-295-1163... 94 E
pattie.l.jennings@wilmu.edu
JENNINGS, Patti .... 203-596-4693... 90 I
pjennings@post.edu
JENNINGS, Rita, O .... 252-335-0821. 359 F
rjennings@albemarle.edu
JENNINGS, Robert, R ...... 484-365-7400. 422 D
rjennings@lincoln.edu
JENNINGS, Ross .... 253-833-9111. 520 C
rjennings@greenriver.edu
JENNINGS, Sandra .... 718-405-3260. 320 G
sandra.jennings@mountsaintvincent.edu
JENNINGS, Sarah, E .... 870-235-4040... 23 F
sejennings@saumag.edu
JENNINGS, Susan .... 423-697-2576. 460 C
JENNINGS, Suzanne .... 843-661-8161. 443 G
suzanne.jennings@fdtc.edu
JENNINGS, Thomas, W .. 850-645-9655. 115 C
tjennings@fsu.edu
JENNINGS, Todd .... 909-537-5655... 34 E
tjennin@csusb.edu
JENNISON, Barry .... 423-697-2614. 460 C
JENNUM, Joe .... 909-274-4630... 55 A
jjennum@mtsac.edu
JENNY, Paul .... 206-543-6277. 524 G
pjenny@uw.edu
JENSEN, Betty .... 850-201-8235. 117 D
jensenb@tcc.fl.edu
JENSEN, Bruce .... 612-343-4417. 262 X
bajensen@northcentral.edu
JENSEN, Carol .... 406-657-1022. 288 B
jensenc@rocky.edu
JENSEN, Chuck .... 406-756-3808. 286 B
cjensen@fvcc.edu
JENSEN, Clyde .... 503-256-3180. 408 G
cjensen@uws.edu
JENSEN, Dale .... 417-865-2815. 274 B
jensend@evangel.edu
JENSEN, Dan .... 817-735-2500. 490 E
Danny.Jensen@unthsc.edu
JENSEN, Darlene .... 714-992-7096... 56 F
djensen@fullcoll.edu
JENSEN, Doug .... 661-722-6300... 28 F
djensen@avc.edu
JENSEN, Douglas, J .... 724-925-5974. 437 D
jensend@wccc.edu
JENSEN, Eric .... 651-523-2576. 256 A
ejensen07@hamline.edu
JENSEN, Gail .... 402-280-2870. 289 D
gailjensen@creighton.edu
JENSEN, Gail .... 210-458-4105. 492 C
gail.jensen@utsa.edu
JENSEN, Genevieve, M ... 718-357-4522. 339 G
gjensen@edaff.com
JENSEN, Jed .... 307-686-0254. 543 F
jjensen@sheridan.edu
JENSEN, Jeffrey .... 305-899-3250... 98 O
jjensen@barry.edu
JENSEN, Kathleen, M ..... 520-626-5620... 18 F
kmjensen@email.arizona.edu
JENSEN, Katie .... 425-388-9581. 519 I
JENSEN, Laura .... 239-590-1155. 115 A
ljensen@fgcu.edu
JENSEN, Laura .... 970-491-5939... 80 I
l.jensen@colostate.edu
JENSEN, Leigh .... 662-325-2091. 268 D
ljensen@saffairs.msstate.edu
JENSEN, Patricia .... 414-382-6321. 531 I
patricia.jensen@alverno.edu

JENSEN, Paul ... 708-456-0300. 161 A pjensen@triton.edu

JENSEN, Peter, E ... 605-677-5341. 451 F pete.jensen@usd.edu

JENSEN, Robert ... 714-992-7035... 56 F rjensen@fullcoll.edu

JENSEN, Robert ... 619-201-8698... 62 B Robert.Jensen@sdcc.edu

JENSEN, Sol ... 701-777-3000. 371 C sol.jensen@und.edu

JENSEN, Stan, C ... 313-845-9650. 243 H sjenson@hfcc.edu

JENSEN, Steve, M ... 563-588-8000. 178 D smjensen@emmaus.edu

JENSEN, Terri ... 641-628-5427. 176 E jensent@central.edu

JENSEN, Tom, P ... 618-537-6959. 152 G tpjensen@mckendree.edu

JENSEN, Travis ... 763-852-7502. 450 G tjensen@national.edu

JENSEN-MARTIN, Lisa ... 530-741-6766... 77 M ljensen@yccd.edu

JENSKI, Laura ... 605-677-5370. 451 F laura.jenski@usd.edu

JENSKI, Laura, J ... 605-677-5370. 451 F laura.jenski@usd.edu

JENSON, Douglas ... 619-477-6310... 70 D djenson@usuniversity.edu

JENSON, Hal, B ... 269-353-5530. 252 I hal.jenson@wmich.edu

JENSON, Linda ... 817-515-4521. 482 B linda.jenson@tccd.edu

JENT, Laura ... 931-393-1544. 461 A ljent@mscc.edu

JEONG, Peter ... 973-748-9000. 299 F peter_jeong@bloomfield.edu

JEONG, Wooseob ... 414-229-4709. 537 A wjj8612@uwm.edu

JEPSON, Darla ... 815-802-8832. 149 C djepson@kcc.edu

JEREBKO, Peter, J ... 716-851-1221. 323 I jerebko@ecc.edu

JEREZ, Antonio ... 201-327-8877. 301 G ajerez@eastwick.edu

JERGINS, Rusty ... 254-968-9890. 483 A jergins@tarleton.edu

JERGOVIC, Diana ... 773-702-4261. 161 B jergovic@uchicago.edu

JERIES, John ... 651-690-6533. 263 O jjeries@stkate.edu

JERMAN, Rita, H ... 919-866-5701. 364 G whjerman@waketech.edu

JERMAN LIGUORI, Denise ... 201-447-7480. 299 C djerman@bergen.edu

JERNIGAN, Paula ... 850-471-4679. 110 G pjernigan@pensacolastate.edu

JERNIGAN, Ron ... 505-566-3035. 311 I jerniganr@sanjuancollege.edu

JERNIGAN, Tony ... 301-934-7715. 214 D tjernigan@csmd.edu

JERNIGAN, William ... 918-495-6723. 398 H wjernigan@oru.edu

JEROME, Allison ... 808-735-4718. 135 D ajerome@chaminade.edu

JEROME, Evan ... 914-632-6700. 331 K ejerome@monroecollege.edu

JEROME, Leslie ... 914-632-5400. 331 K ljerome@monroecollege.edu

JEROME, Marc, M ... 914-632-5400. 331 K mjerome@monroecollege.edu

JEROME, Priya ... 619-482-6557... 68 B pjerome@swccd.edu

JEROME, Stephen, J ... 718-933-6700. 331 K sjerome@monroecollege.edu

JERRY, Lisa ... 516-726-5799. 545 H jerryl@usmma.edu

JERRY, Robert, H ... 352-273-0600. 116 A jerryr@law.ufl.edu

JERSKY, Brian ... 909-869-3600... 32 G bjersky@csupomona.edu

JESKO, Rhonda ... 575-769-4043. 309 F rhonda.jesko@clovis.edu

JESME, Shannon ... 218-683-8577. 260 D shannon.jesme@northlandcollege.edu

JESPERSEN, Christopher 706-864-1771. 133 D christopher.jespersen@ung.edu

JESSE, Hugh, A ... 406-243-2788. 286 H hugh.jesse@umontana.edu

JESSELL, Kenneth ... 305-348-2101. 115 B kenneth.jessell@fiu.edu

JESSEN-MARSHALL, Amy ... 434-381-6205. 510 F ajessen-marshall@sbc.edu

JESSIE, Jason ... 918-456-5511. 396 H jessiejb@nsuok.edu

JESSOGNE, Cheryl ... 312-499-4186. 158 L cjessogne@saic.edu

JESSOP, Craig ... 435-797-3046. 497 B craig.jessop@usu.edu

JESSUP, James ... 401-739-5000. 439 D jjessup@neit.edu

JESSUP, Jim ... 916-577-2200... 76 J jjessup@jessup.edu

JESSUP, Leonard, M ... 520-621-2125... 18 F len@eller.arizona.edu

JESSUP, Rhonda, E ... 919-658-7754. 357 I rjessup@moc.edu

JESSUP, Tracy, C ... 704-406-4279. 354 C tjessup@gardner-webb.edu

JESTER, Chris ... 302-736-2468... 94 C chris.jester@wesley.edu

JESUS CESAREO, Lourdes ... 787-763-6700. 549 A ldjesus@se-pr.edu

JETER, Everett, M ... 919-536-7209. 360 B jetere@durhamtech.edu

JETER, Kaye ... 937-376-6210. 376 E kjeter@centralstate.edu

JETT, Andy ... 913-344-1247. 184 C andy.jett@bakeru.edu

JETT, Melissa ... 417-255-7955. 278 F melissajett@missouristate.edu

JETT, Susan, P ... 864-429-8728. 448 G jettsp@mailbox.sc.edu

JETTE, Tracey ... 406-265-3708. 287 D tracey.jette@msun.edu

JETTON, Kent ... 731-286-3250. 460 F jetton@dscc.edu

JEW, Carl ... 415-561-1875... 38 L cjew@ccsf.edu

JEWEL, Marion ... 210-297-9630. 467 B

JEWELL, JoAnn, I ... 814-866-8106. 420 E jjewell@lecom.edu

JEWELL, Kirk ... 405-385-5112. 397 H kjewell@osugiving.com

JEWELL, Richard, G ... 724-458-2500. 417 E rgjewell@gcc.edu

JEWELL, Scott ... 617-349-8714. 228 B sjewell@lesley.edu

JEWELL, Steve ... 303-245-4686... 83 F sjewell@naropa.edu

JEWETT, Darla ... 207-741-5584. 211 A djewett@smccme.edu

JEWETT, John ... 386-752-1822. 104 G john.jewett@fgc.edu

JEWETT, Robin ... 615-248-1504. 462 D rjewett@trevecca.edu

JEWETT, Ronald ... 614-837-4088. 392 E jewettr@valorcollege.com

JEWSBURY, Evan ... 918-540-6378. 396 G evan.jewsbury@neo.edu

JEZAK, Patricia ... 567-661-2650. 387 L patricia_jezak@owens.edu

JEZEK, Kenda ... 918-495-6198. 398 H kjezek@oru.edu

JEZEK-TAUSSIG, Jennifer ... 314-968-5944. 284 N jezekjk@webster.edu

JEZIORSKI, Jennifer ... 847-735-5242. 150 B jeziorski@lakeforest.edu

JEZUIT, Deborah ... 847-543-2339. 143 A djezuit@clcillinois.edu

JHA, Mona ... 646-312-4542. 316 J Mona.Jha@baruch.cuny.edu

JHAJ, Sukhwant, S ... 503-725-8996. 406 B jhaj@pdx.edu

JHANJI, Andy, A ... 850-644-4747. 115 C ajhanji@foundation.fsu.edu

JIACOMETTI, Judy ... 888-897-3222... 50 G jjiacometti@sf.chefs.edu

JIAMBALVO, Jim ... 206-543-9132. 524 G jjiambal@uw.edu

JIANG, Jerome ... 626-289-7719... 26 J

JIANG, Shaojie ... 608-796-3172. 539 E sjiang@viterbo.edu

JIE, Yiyun ... 334-229-6859..... 1 D yjiek@alasu.edu

JIGA, Anthony ... 212-998-2278. 334 D anthony.jiga@nyu.edu

JILBERT, Deborah ... 262-691-5210. 541 D djilbert@wctc.edu

JILES, Michael ... 678-664-0534. 134 H michael.jiles@westgatech.edu

JIMÉNEZ-PÉREZ, Nancy . 787-993-8877. 554 A nancy.jimenez1@upr.edu

JIMENEZ, Annie ... 480-732-7391... 14 J a.jimenez@cgc.edu

JIMENEZ, Araceli ... 661-726-1911... 70 G araceli.jimenez@uav.edu

JIMENEZ, Asdrubal ... 787-891-0925. 549 K ajimenez@aguadilla.inter.edu

JIMENEZ, Carlos ... 787-890-2681. 553 H c.jimenez@upr.edu

JIMENEZ, Elena ... 773-896-2400. 141 K ejimenez@ctschicago.edu

JIMENEZ, Eva ... 530-242-7560... 65 G ejimenez@shastacollege.edu

JIMENEZ, Irma ... 787-878-6000. 549 D ijimenez@icprjc.edu

JIMENEZ, Ivelisse ... 787-725-8120. 548 O ijimenez0027@eap.edu

JIMENEZ, Maria ... 954-322-4460. 107 V library@jmvu.edu

JIMENEZ, Misael ... 787-834-9595. 553 B mjimenez@uaa.edu

JIMENEZ, Obed ... 787-834-9595. 553 B ojimenez@uaa.edu

JIMENEZ, Oscar ... 432-837-8042. 487 B ojimenez@sulross.edu

JIMENEZ, Sharon ... 510-567-6174... 69 C sjimenez@sum.edu

JIMENEZ, Silverio ... 787-882-2065. 553 A dispensario@unitecpr.net

JIMENEZ, Tomas, M ... 787-751-1459. 549 J tjimenez@inter.edu

JIMENEZ-TORRES, Aida . 787-725-6500. 547 H ajimenez@sju.albizu.edu

JIMENO, Cheri, A ... 575-439-3640. 310 J cjimeno@nmsu.edu

JIMINEZ, Johanna ... 305-220-4120. 111 E

JIMISON, Nancy, M ... 804-706-5024. 512 G njiminson@jtcc.edu

JIMMERSON, Judy ... 229-430-3514. 120 A jjimmerson@albanytech.edu

JIN, Xudong ... 252-493-7354. 362 G xjin@email.pittcc.edu

JINDARYAN, Liana ... 818-767-0888... 76 K liana.jindaryan@woodbury.edu

JINDRA, Barbara ... 972-758-3821. 469 G bjindra@collin.edu

JINKINS, Michael ... 502-895-3411. 197 F mjinkins@lpts.edu

JINKS, Mary ... 865-974-6621. 463 B mary.jinks@tennessee.edu

JINRIGHT, Dwight ... 205-358-8543..... 9 B jinrightd@montevallo.edu

JIRA, Pamela, A ... 740-588-1205. 394 C pjira@zanestate.edu

JIRAK, Randy ... 785-227-3380. 184 I jirakr@bethanylb.edu

JIROUSEK, Nancy ... 440-826-2298. 374 F njirouse@bw.edu

JIROVEC, Kelly ... 402-826-8265. 289 E kelly.jirovec@doane.edu

JIWANJI, Insiya ... 240-684-2124. 219 F admissions@umuc.edu

JO, Yong Soo ... 770-279-0507. 124 I lustiadei@gmail.com

JOACHIM, Gisele ... 973-642-8747. 307 D gisele.joachim@shu.edu

JOACHIM KITZMAN, Patricia ... 641-628-5271. 176 E kitzmanp@central.edu

JOANIS, Jessica, L ... 920-748-8186. 535 J joanisj@ripon.edu

JOBE, Deanna, L ... 319-399-8741. 176 G djobe@coe.edu

JOBE, Jarrett ... 405-974-5560. 400 K jjobe@uco.edu

JOBE, Steve ... 812-866-7005. 166 C jobe@hanover.edu

JOBIN, Amy ... 650-508-3761... 56 H ajobin@ndnu.edu

JOBSON, John, E ... 616-395-7800. 244 A jobson@hope.edu

JOCHEMS, Jeff ... 417-447-7932. 279 K jochemsj@otc.edu

JOCHEMS, Judith ... 954-308-2434... 98 G jjochems@aii.edu

JODELKA, Edward ... 708-709-3795. 156 A ejodelka@prairiestate.edu

JODIS, Stephen, M ... 724-805-2358. 432 G stephen.jodis@email.stvincent.edu

JOECKEL, Brooke ... 512-651-4700. 450 G bjoeckel@national.edu

JOEL, Harry ... 650-358-6767... 64 A joelh@smccd.edu

JOEL, Richard, M ... 212-960-5300. 351 M rjoel@yu.edu

JOENSEN, William ... 563-588-7104. 180 L william.joensen@loras.edu

JOERSCHKE, Bonnie, C .. 706-542-8208. 133 C bonniej@uga.edu

JOERZ, Lorilee ... 914-337-9300. 321 E lorilee.joerz@concordia-ny.edu

JOERZ, LoriLee ... 914-337-9300. 321 E lorilee.joerz@concordia-ny.edu

JOHANNES, Cheri ... 406-657-2158. 287 C cjohannes@msubillings.edu

JOHANNESEN, Christine 518-255-5522. 344 E johanncm@cobleskill.edu

JOHANNSEN, Danelle, D ... 712-279-3377. 182 C johanndd@stlukescollege.edu

JOHANSEN, Alfred, W ... 801-832-2127. 498 F ajohansen@westminstercollege.edu

JOHANSEN, Bob, L ... 626-815-4603... 29 H bjohansen@apu.edu

JOHANSON, Ingrid ... 561-297-3288. 114 L johanson@fau.edu

JOHANSON, Michael ... 808-675-3669. 135 C michael.johanson@byuh.edu

JOHANSON, Rod ... 503-517-1010. 408 H rjohanson@warnerpacific.edu

JOHANSON, Rosanne ... 716-664-5100. 327 I rosannejohnson@jamestownbusinesscollege.edu

JOHHSON, Quentin ... 363-334-4822. 360 G qrjohnson@gtcc.edu

JOHN, Beth ... 608-663-2334. 532 I bjohn@edgewood.edu

JOHN, Joby ... 337-482-6491. 208 D jjohn@louisiana.edu

JOHN, Kathy ... 937-769-1840. 373 I kjohn@antioch.edu

JOHN, JR., Leon ... 570-348-6257. 423 B ljohn@marywood.edu

JOHN, Rebecca ... 612-330-1482. 253 H rjohn@augsburg.edu

JOHN, Rowan ... 219-989-2654. 171 N jrowan@purduecal.edu

JOHN, Samuel ... 201-447-7868. 299 C sjohn@bergen.edu

JOHN, Stephen, S ... 806-894-9611. 480 H sjohn@southplainscollege.edu

JOHNDROW, David, A ... 570-674-6762. 424 A djohndro@misericordia.edu

JOHNOSON, April ... 301-860-3831. 220 A ajohnson@bowiestate.edu

JOHNS, David ... 606-546-4151. 200 A djohns@unionky.edu

JOHNS, Lolita ... 727-784-0003... 99 J ljohns@cfi.edu

JOHNS, Marci ... 334-386-7100..... 3 H mjohns@faulkner.edu

JOHNS, Patrick ... 218-733-5997. 259 A p.johns@lsc.edu

JOHNS, Priscilla, C ... 671-735-6013. 546 C priscilla.johns@guamcc.edu

JOHNS, Sheila, R ... 308-635-6366. 293 E johnss23@wncc.edu

JOHNS, Xenia ... 770-228-7348. 132 B xjohns@sctech.edu

JOHNSEN, David, C ... 319-335-7144. 175 I david-johnsen@uiowa.edu

JOHNSEN, John, H ... 315-792-3120. 349 F jjohnsen@utica.edu

JOHNSON, Aaron ... 303-762-6933... 81 G aaron.johnson@denverseminary.edu

JOHNSON, Abe ... 972-548-6677. 469 G ajohnson@collin.edu

JOHNSON, Adam ... 405-974-2385. 400 K adjohnson@uco.edu

JOHNSON, Alan, D ... 812-482-3030. 174 F ajohnson@vinu.edu

JOHNSON, JR., Albert, D ... 580-581-2999. 394 G ajohnson@cameron.edu

JOHNSON, Alex ... 216-987-4851. 378 D alex.johnson@tri-c.edu

JOHNSON, Alex, F ... 617-726-8008. 234 B ajohnson@mghihp.edu

JOHNSON, Alice ... 210-486-0902. 465 C ajohnson235@alamo.edu

JOHNSON, Alisa, M ... 207-859-4140. 209 J ajohnson@colby.edu

JOHNSON, Allan ... 202-806-5042... 95 G ajohnson@howard.edu

JOHNSON, Allen ... 951-343-4477... 30 H ajohnson@calbaptist.edu

JOHNSON, Alton, B ... 936-261-5125. 482 F abjohnson@pvamu.edu

JOHNSON, Amy ... 610-861-1304. 424 E johnsona@moravian.edu

JOHNSON, Amy ... 731-286-3398. 460 F ajohnson@dscc.edu

JOHNSON, Amy ... 509-359-2292. 519 C ajohnson20@ewu.edu

JOHNSON, Andrea ... 870-236-6901... 20 K ajohnson@crc.edu

JOHNSON, Andy ... 912-260-4430. 131 F andy.johnson@sgsc.edu

JOHNSON, Angela ... 216-987-4213. 378 D angela.johnson@tri-c.edu

JOHNSON, Anna ... 740-753-6553. 380 K johnson_a@hocking.edu

JOHNSON, Anne ... 651-450-3642. 258 H ajohnson@inverhills.edu

JOHNSON, Annette, M ... 906-786-5802. 240 K johnsona@baycollege.edu

JOHNSON, Annie ... 213-624-1200... 44 D ajohnson@fidm.edu

JOHNSON, Anthony ... 401-454-6638. 440 A ajohnson@risd.edu

JOHNSON, Arvid, C ... 815-740-3369. 162 F ajohnson@stfrancis.edu

JOHNSON, Ashlee ... 314-392-2305. 278 B JohnsonA@mobap.edu

JOHNSON, Barbara ... 609-777-4351. 308 A bjohnson@tesc.edu

JOHNSON, Barbara ... 615-327-6435. 456 E

JOHNSON, Barbara, G .... 412-578-6021. 412 G johnsonbg@carlow.edu
JOHNSON, Barbara, L .... 308-865-8205. 292 H johnsonbl@unk.edu
JOHNSON, Barbara, L .... 802-656-4490. 500 F barbara.johnson@uvm.edu
JOHNSON, Barry .... 408-864-5678... 44 M
JOHNSON, Barry .... 704-406-4440. 354 C bjohnson@gardner-webb.edu
JOHNSON, Bart .... 218-322-2388. 258 I bart.johnson@itascacc.edu
JOHNSON, Bernard .... 973-754-7192. 304 B bjohnson@pccc.edu
JOHNSON, Bernard, A ... 240-500-2000. 215 B bajohnson@hagerstowncc.edu
JOHNSON, Bernice .... 919-530-6230. 368 A bjohnson@nccu.edu
JOHNSON, Beth Ann, H . 203-392-5250... 88 A johnsonb3@southernct.edu
JOHNSON, Betsy .... 567-661-7883. 387 L betsy_johnson@owens.edu
JOHNSON, Bonnie .... 641-673-1036. 183 H johnsonb@wmpenn.edu
JOHNSON, Brad .... 859-858-3511. 192 B bjohnson@asbury.edu
JOHNSON, Brad .... 417-328-1805. 282 C bjohnson@sbuniv.edu
JOHNSON, Brad .... 901-751-8453. 457 B bjohnson@mabts.edu
JOHNSON, Brad, W .... 903-434-8102. 477 J bjohnson@ntcc.edu
JOHNSON, Brandon .... 816-501-2400. 271 H brandon.johnson@avila.edu
JOHNSON, Brenda .... 812-855-3403. 167 F johnbren@indiana.edu
JOHNSON, Brenda .... 510-981-2830... 59 A bjohnson@peralta.edu
JOHNSON, Brenda, R ..... 510-780-4500... 50 I bjohnson@lifewest.edu
JOHNSON, Brian .... 931-221-7992. 459 B johnsonb@apsu.edu
JOHNSON, Brian, D .... 208-885-6246. 139 D johnsonb@uidaho.edu
JOHNSON, Brian, T .... 219-464-6732. 174 E brian.johnson1@valpo.edu
JOHNSON, Brodie, I .... 901-320-9700. 463 J bjohnson@victory.edu
JOHNSON, Bryan, M ...... 205-726-4036...... 6 F bmjohnso@samford.edu
JOHNSON, C. Lynn .... 320-222-5208. 260 H lynn.johnson@ridgewater.edu
JOHNSON, Calvin .... 870-575-8471... 24 E johnsonc@uapb.edu
JOHNSON, Calvin, M ..... 334-844-4546...... 1 G johncal@auburn.edu
JOHNSON, Candace .... 810-766-4109. 239 H candace.johnson@baker.edu
JOHNSON, Carl .... 847-317-8138. 160 M cjohnson@tiu.edu
JOHNSON, Carl .... 303-871-3111... 86 B cdjohnson@du.edu
JOHNSON, Carl, E .... 704-687-7217. 368 E cjohns1@uncc.edu
JOHNSON, Carol .... 606-783-2022. 198 A c.johnson@moreheadstate.edu
JOHNSON, Carol .... 704-878-3225. 362 B cjohnson@mitchellcc.edu
JOHNSON, Carol, B .... 386-481-2075... 99 C johnsonc@cookman.edu
JOHNSON, Casie .... 507-453-2663. 259 E cjohnson@southeastmn.edu
JOHNSON, Cassandra ..... 706-233-7208. 131 E cjohnson@shorter.edu
JOHNSON, Catherine, W 336-506-4237. 357 M cathy.johnson@alamancecc.edu
JOHNSON, Cathi .... 901-334-5811. 457 A chjohnson@memphisseminary.edu
JOHNSON, Cecelia .... 931-540-2762. 460 E cjohnson@columbiastate.edu
JOHNSON, Chad .... 651-290-6475. 265 F chad.johnson@wmitchell.edu
JOHNSON, Charlene, M . 803-536-7243. 446 G cmjohnson@scsu.edu
JOHNSON, JR., Charles, R .... 812-888-4262. 174 F provost@vinu.edu
JOHNSON, Charlie .... 405-974-2315. 400 K chjohnson@uco.edu
JOHNSON, Charlotte ...... 870-584-4471... 24 F cjohnson@cccua.edu
JOHNSON, Charlotte, H . 603-646-2243. 296 G charlotte.h.johnson@dartmouth.edu
JOHNSON, Chauncy .... 307-268-2025. 542 X cjohnson@caspercollege.edu
JOHNSON, Cheryl .... 618-545-3091. 149 D cjohnson@kaskaskia.edu
JOHNSON, Chris .... 303-762-6924... 81 G chris.johnson@denverseminary.edu
JOHNSON, Chris .... 478-757-3400. 122 F cjjohnson@centralgatech.edu
JOHNSON, Chris .... 336-342-4261. 363 C johnsonc@rockinghamcc.edu
JOHNSON, Chris .... 434-592-3017. 506 I cjohnson@liberty.edu
JOHNSON, Christana ..... 304-876-5453. 529 I cjohns12@shepherd.edu
JOHNSON, Christina ...... 510-783-2100... 46 L christina_johnson@heald.edu
JOHNSON, Christine ...... 509-434-5006. 518 D cjohnson@ccs.spokane.edu
JOHNSON, Christine ...... 509-434-5006. 518 E christine.johnson@ccs.spokane.edu
JOHNSON, Christopher .. 253-833-9111. 520 C cjohnson@greenriver.edu
JOHNSON, Christopher .. 203-254-4332... 89 I cjohnson@fairfield.edu
JOHNSON, Christy .... 206-726-5045. 518 G cjohnson@cornish.edu
JOHNSON, Cindi Beth ... 651-255-6137. 264 C cbjohnson@unitedseminary.edu
JOHNSON, Cindy .... 620-235-4185. 189 L cjohnso1@pittstate.edu
JOHNSON, Cindy, K ...... 816-604-1011. 277 C cindy.johnson@mcckc.edu
JOHNSON, Clara, E .... 757-594-8801. 503 M clara.johnson@cnu.edu
JOHNSON, JR., Clyde ... 443-552-1659. 216 C cjohnson01@mica.edu
JOHNSON, Colleen .... 916-608-6500... 53 C
JOHNSON, Cornelia .... 302-454-3944... 93 F cornelia@dtcc.edu
JOHNSON, Craig .... 813-253-7051. 106 M cjohnson@hccfl.edu
JOHNSON, Craig .... 773-244-5637. 154 G crjohnson@northpark.edu
JOHNSON, Craig .... 870-972-2852... 19 N crjohnso@astate.edu
JOHNSON, Croslena ...... 864-646-1568. 447 D cjohnso5@tctc.edu
JOHNSON, Curtis .... 501-244-5111... 19 J curtis.johnson@arkansasbaptist.edu
JOHNSON, Cuthrell .... 336-750-2230. 370 A johnsonc@wssu.edu
JOHNSON, Cynda Ann ... 540-526-2500. 515 E
JOHNSON, Cynthia .... 360-486-8131. 522 G cjohnson@stmartin.edu
JOHNSON, D. Nichole ... 614-236-6945. 375 H njohnson@capital.edu
JOHNSON, Dacia .... 218-736-1512. 259 F dacia.johnson@minnesota.edu
JOHNSON, Dale .... 510-780-4500... 50 I djohnson@lifewest.edu
JOHNSON, Danae .... 229-226-1621. 132 F djohnson@thomasu.edu
JOHNSON, Daniel .... 701-662-1515. 372 D dan.johnson@lrsc.edu
JOHNSON, Daniel .... 803-584-3446. 448 D johns943@mailbox.sc.edu
JOHNSON, Daniel .... 918-456-5511. 396 H johnso89@nsuok.edu
JOHNSON, Daniel, R ...... 203-582-8930... 91 A dan.johnson@quinnipiac.edu
JOHNSON, Daniel, W ..... 414-443-8952. 539 F daniel.johnson@wlc.edu
JOHNSON, Darren .... 518-381-1320. 340 G johnsod@sunysccc.edu
JOHNSON, Daryl .... 651-793-1303. 259 C daryl.johnson@metrostate.edu
JOHNSON, Daryl .... 651-793-1227. 259 C daryl.johnson@metrostate.edu
JOHNSON, David .... 716-338-1002. 327 J davejohnson@mail.sunyjcc.edu
JOHNSON, David .... 812-855-8908. 167 F dj44@indiana.edu
JOHNSON, David .... 256-824-6288...... 8 F david.johnson@uah.edu
JOHNSON, David .... 606-368-6031. 191 J davidjohnson@alc.edu
JOHNSON, David .... 650-306-3336... 64 B johnsond@smccd.edu
JOHNSON, David, A .... 330-494-6170. 389 F djohnson@starkstate.edu
JOHNSON, David, E .... 804-828-6611. 511 F dejohnson2@vcu.edu
JOHNSON, David, J .... 513-745-3202. 393 H johnsond8@xavier.edu
JOHNSON, David, N .... 919-209-2050. 361 E dnjohnson@johnstoncc.edu
JOHNSON, Deborah .... 419-251-1327. 383 G deborah.johnson@mercycollege.edu
JOHNSON, Deborah .... 713-798-5263. 467 F djohnson@bcm.edu
JOHNSON, Debra .... 318-274-2560. 207 E johnsond@gram.edu
JOHNSON, Debra, J .... 540-985-8492. 506 G djjohnson@jchs.edu
JOHNSON, Deirdra, G .... 410-334-2902. 221 D djohnson@worwic.edu
JOHNSON, Denis .... 913-971-3279. 188 H ddjohnson@mnu.edu
JOHNSON, Dennis .... 719-549-3035... 84 G dennis.johnson@pueblocc.edu
JOHNSON, Dennis .... 314-889-1452. 274 E djohnson@fontbonne.edu
JOHNSON, Derrick .... 951-222-8000... 61 A
JOHNSON, Deshawn ...... 248-204-2117. 245 I djohnson@ltu.edu
JOHNSON, DeWayne ...... 213-637-1376... 76 G dejohnson@westwood.edu
JOHNSON, Dexter .... 425-564-4261. 517 A dexter.johnson@bellevuecollege.edu
JOHNSON, Diana .... 479-936-5135... 22 C djohnson@nwacc.edu
JOHNSON, Diane .... 415-813-6024... 56 A djohnson@new.edu
JOHNSON, Diane .... 518-828-4181. 321 C diane.johnson@sunycgcc.edu
JOHNSON, Diane, S .... 515-263-6149. 178 G djohnson@grandview.edu
JOHNSON, Dion .... 770-612-2170... 96 F
JOHNSON, Don .... 603-848-9904. 422 F djohnson@ltsp.edu
JOHNSON, Donna .... 845-431-8682. 323 C djohnson@sunydutchess.edu
JOHNSON, Doris .... 972-524-3341. 481 H
JOHNSON, Doris, W ...... 803-705-4536. 441 C johnsond@benedict.edu
JOHNSON, Doug .... 662-846-4654. 266 G djohnson@deltastate.edu
JOHNSON, Doug .... 404-460-2467. 130 F doug.johnson@point.edu
JOHNSON, Douglas, P .... 207-581-1392. 212 B douglasj@maine.edu
JOHNSON, Earl .... 918-631-3142. 401 F earl-johnson@utulsa.edu
JOHNSON, Edward .... 716-829-7636. 323 D
JOHNSON, Edwin .... 406-243-2995. 286 H edwin.johnson@umontana.edu
JOHNSON, Elise .... 586-498-4119. 246 A johnsonem@macomb.edu
JOHNSON, Elizabeth ...... 813-253-7449. 106 M bjohnson@hccfl.edu
JOHNSON, Elizabeth ...... 203-596-8598... 90 I ejohnson@post.edu
JOHNSON, Elizabeth ...... 330-823-2030. 391 E johnsoec@mountunion.edu
JOHNSON, Elizabeth, J .. 415-422-6534... 73 J johnson@usfca.edu
JOHNSON, Eric .... 318-487-7134. 202 F eric.johnson@lacollege.edu
JOHNSON, Eric .... 219-464-5085. 174 E eric.johnson@valpo.edu
JOHNSON, Eric .... 402-844-7236. 291 I eric@northeast.edu
JOHNSON, Eric, C .... 617-627-5484. 237 C eric.johnson@tufts.edu
JOHNSON, Eric, P .... 218-299-3447. 255 A johnson@cord.edu
JOHNSON, Eric, W .... 985-549-3860. 208 C ejohnson@selu.edu
JOHNSON, Erica .... 404-270-5189. 132 E ESJohnson@spelman.edu
JOHNSON, Estelle .... 605-668-1363. 450 F ejohnson@mtmc.edu
JOHNSON, Eva, R .... 253-535-7159. 521 I johnsoer@plu.edu
JOHNSON, Ezra .... 916-577-2200... 76 J ejohnson@jessup.edu
JOHNSON, Fatima, R ...... 585-245-5620. 343 C johnsonf@geneseo.edu
JOHNSON, Faye, R .... 229-226-1621. 132 F fjohnson@thomasu.edu
JOHNSON, Floretha, J ... 636-922-8365. 280 J fjohnson@stchas.edu
JOHNSON, Frank .... 620-947-3121. 190 J frankj@tabor.edu
JOHNSON, Frank .... 404-756-4013. 121 A frankjohnson@atlm.edu
JOHNSON, Freddie .... 404-756-4442. 121 A fjohnson@atlm.edu
JOHNSON, Frederick ...... 412-392-6132. 431 B fjohnson@pointpark.edu
JOHNSON, Fredrick, P ... 443-412-2407. 215 C rjohnson@harford.edu
JOHNSON, G. David ...... 251-460-6261...... 9 E djohnson@southalabama.edu
JOHNSON, Gail .... 903-886-5180. 483 E gail.johnson@tamuc.edu
JOHNSON, Gary .... 704-878-3250. 362 B gjohnson@mitchellcc.edu
JOHNSON, Gary, C .... 402-461-7407. 289 I gcjohnson@hastings.edu
JOHNSON, Gary, K .... 815-224-0378. 148 A gary_johnson@ivcc.edu
JOHNSON, George .... 336-279-9237. 354 B gjohnson8@elon.edu
JOHNSON, George .... 937-376-2946. 388 B gjohnson@payne.edu
JOHNSON, Gerry .... 502-213-7276. 195 F gerald.johnson@kctcs.edu
JOHNSON, Gina .... 303-871-2287... 86 B gina.johnson@du.edu
JOHNSON, Gladys .... 859-622-1571. 193 P gladys.johnson@eku.edu
JOHNSON, Glen .... 205-391-2327...... 6 H gjohnson@sheltonstate.edu
JOHNSON, Glen .... 276-739-2467. 514 D gjohnson@vhcc.edu
JOHNSON, Glenn .... 304-929-1495. 527 H glennjohnson@ucwv.edu
JOHNSON, Gloria .... 615-963-7518. 459 E gjohnson@tnstate.edu
JOHNSON, Gloria, M ..... 972-860-7001. 470 I GloriaJohnson@dcccd.edu
JOHNSON, Gordon, L .... 270-745-6455. 200 G gordon.johnson@wku.edu
JOHNSON, Gregory, A ... 562-988-2278... 28 B gjohnson@auhs.edu
JOHNSON, Gregory, W .. 757-221-3952. 503 N gwjohnson@wm.edu
JOHNSON, Harold .... 940-898-3130. 488 B hjohnson@twu.edu
JOHNSON, Irma .... 502-597-6634. 197 A irma.johnson@kysu.edu
JOHNSON, Iryna, Y .... 334-844-4765...... 1 G iyj0001@auburn.edu
JOHNSON, J. Lee .... 517-264-7108. 250 B ljohnson@sienaheights.edu
JOHNSON, J. Theodore . 704-233-8105. 370 G tjohnson@wingate.edu
JOHNSON, J.I .... 405-466-3260. 395 N jijohnson@langston.edu
JOHNSON, Jacqueline .... 320-589-6020. 264 F jrjohnso@morris.umn.edu
JOHNSON, James .... 620-235-4389. 189 L jjohnson@pittstate.edu
JOHNSON, James, F ...... 215-898-2173. 435 B johnsonj@isc.upenn.edu
JOHNSON, James, J ...... 507-453-2721. 259 E jjohnson@southeastmn.edu
JOHNSON, James, K ...... 651-286-7773. 263 A jkjohnson2@nwc.edu
JOHNSON, James, M ...... 630-752-5113. 163 F james.johnson@wheaton.edu
JOHNSON, James, R ...... 717-477-1373. 429 E jrjohnson@ship.edu
JOHNSON, Jamie .... 502-585-9911. 199 C jjohnson16@spalding.edu
JOHNSON, Janet, L .... 812-464-1928. 174 D jljohnson@usi.edu
JOHNSON, Jason .... 580-628-6240. 396 M jason.johnson@noc.edu
JOHNSON, Jason, L .... 970-491-6270... 80 I jason.johnson@colostate.edu
JOHNSON, Jean .... 773-838-7544. 142 E jjohnson2@ccc.edu
JOHNSON, Jean .... 785-594-8384. 184 C jean.johnson@bakeru.edu
JOHNSON, Jean .... 202-994-3725... 95 D sonjej@gwumc.edu
JOHNSON, Jean, A .... 319-399-8561. 176 G jjohnson@coe.edu
JOHNSON, Jeff, A .... 757-446-6100. 504 E johnsonja@evms.edu
JOHNSON, Jeffrey, C ..... 561-237-7333. 108 X jjohnson@lynn.edu
JOHNSON, Jeffrey, W .... 515-294-6561. 175 H jjohnsn@iastate.edu
JOHNSON, Jennifer .... 559-442-8281... 68 I jennifer.johnson@fresnocitycollege.edu
JOHNSON, Jennifer .... 330-941-3515. 394 A jljohnson03@ysu.edu
JOHNSON, Jenny .... 731-989-6378. 454 J jjohnson@fhu.edu
JOHNSON, Jerry .... 812-866-7364. 166 C johnsonj@hanover.edu
JOHNSON, Jerry .... 214-821-5433. 470 A jjohnson@criswell.edu
JOHNSON, Jeryl .... 843-863-8080. 441 H jjohnson@csuniv.edu
JOHNSON, Jill .... 515-961-1595. 182 E jill.johnson@simpson.edu
JOHNSON, Jill .... 501-760-4324... 22 A jjohnson@npcc.edu
JOHNSON, Jill, R .... 864-587-4232. 447 B johnsoj@smcsc.edu
JOHNSON, Jo .... 309-796-5005. 140 E johnsonjo@bhc.edu
JOHNSON, Jo Ann .... 580-559-5246. 395 F jajohnsn@ecok.edu
JOHNSON, Jodi, S .... 706-272-4475. 123 G jjohnson@daltonstate.edu
JOHNSON, John .... 937-708-5721. 393 A admission@wilberforce.edu
JOHNSON, John .... 605-455-6044. 450 I jjohnson@olc.edu
JOHNSON, John, F .... 708-209-3004. 143 E john.johnson@cuchicago.edu
JOHNSON, John, J .... 361-698-1269. 471 G jjohnson@delmar.edu

JOHNSON, John, P .... 386-226-6200. 102 B
john.p.johnson@erau.edu
JOHNSON, Jonathan ...... 706-529-6752. 123 G
jljohnson@daltonstate.edu
JOHNSON, JR., Joseph . 619-594-1424... 35 D
jjohnson@mail.sdsu.edu
JOHNSON, Joyce .... 229-430-6442. 119 J
joyce.johnson@asurams.edu
JOHNSON, Joyce .... 951-639-5439... 55 B
jajohnso@msjc.edu
JOHNSON, Joyce .... 757-825-2827. 514 B
johnsonj@tncc.edu
JOHNSON, Judy .... 309-438-7611. 147 J
jjohns4@ilstu.edu
JOHNSON, Julie .... 801-462-1056... 28 M
jljohnson@argosy.edu
JOHNSON, Julie .... 360-736-9391. 517 G
jjohnson@centralia.edu
JOHNSON, Julie, A .... 209-667-3006... 35 B
jjohnson34@csustan.edu
JOHNSON, Julie, A .... 901-678-3951. 460 B
juljohn@memphis.edu
JOHNSON, Julie, H .... 920-748-8772. 535 J
johnsonj@ripon.edu
JOHNSON, Karen .... 507-457-5300. 262 A
kjohnson@winona.edu
JOHNSON, Karen .... 906-487-7348. 242 G
karen.johnson@finlandia.edu
JOHNSON, Karen .... 402-354-7038. 291 B
karen.johnson@methodistcollege.edu
JOHNSON, Karen, A .... 229-245-4329. 134 B
kjohnson@valdosta.edu
JOHNSON, Karen, A .... 574-284-4571. 172 G
kjohnson@saintmarys.edu
JOHNSON, Karen, D .... 630-515-7268. 153 B
kjohns@midwestern.edu
JOHNSON, Karen, L .... 607-871-2346. 313 E
kjohnson@alfred.edu
JOHNSON, Katherine, M 727-816-3400. 110 E
johnsonk@phcc.edu
JOHNSON, Kathleen .... 219-785-5288. 172 A
kjohnson@pnc.edu
JOHNSON, Kathleen .... 404-215-2660. 129 D
kljohnso@morehouse.edu
JOHNSON, Kathleen, L .. 651-696-6551. 256 L
johnsonkl@macalester.edu
JOHNSON, Kathryn, B .... 315-268-3943. 320 A
kjohnson@clarkson.edu
JOHNSON, Kathy .... 269-488-4223. 244 L
kjohnson@kvcc.edu
JOHNSON, Kathy .... 317-278-0033. 168 D
kjohnso@iupui.edu
JOHNSON, Kathy .... 954-492-5353. 100 A
kjohnson@citycollege.edu
JOHNSON, Kathy .... 434-200-3070. 503 B
JOHNSON, Kathy, J .... 605-642-6512. 451 G
kathy.johnson@bhsu.edu
JOHNSON, Kathy, Y .... 615-230-3580. 461 G
kathy.y.johnson@volstate.edu
JOHNSON, Kaytie .... 215-965-4044. 424 D
kjohnson@moore.edu
JOHNSON, Keesha .... 501-337-5000... 20 J
kjohnson@coto.edu
JOHNSON, Keith .... 785-242-5200. 189 I
keith.johnson@ottawa.edu
JOHNSON, Keith .... 408-855-5457... 75 K
keith.johnson@wvm.edu
JOHNSON, Keith .... 270-706-8413. 195 A
keith.johnson@kctcs.edu
JOHNSON, Keith .... 701-671-2218. 372 E
keith.johnson@ndscs.edu
JOHNSON, Kelley .... 760-245-4271... 75 B
Kelley.Johnson@vvc.edu
JOHNSON, Kelly .... 312-362-5067. 143 H
kjohnson@depaul.edu
JOHNSON, Kellye .... 405-789-7661. 400 A
Kellye.johnson@swcu.edu
JOHNSON, Ken, L .... 214-860-2113. 470 J
kenljohnson@dcccd.edu
JOHNSON, Kenneth .... 850-644-9396. 115 C
ken.johnson@fsu.edu
JOHNSON, Kenneth .... 740-593-2247. 387 C
Johnsok9@ohio.edu
JOHNSON, Kent, M .... 319-273-2122. 176 A
kent.johnson@uni.edu
JOHNSON, Kent, R .... 219-785-5249. 172 A
kjohnson@pnc.edu
JOHNSON, Kersten .... 605-677-6713. 451 F
kersten.johnson@usd.edu
JOHNSON, Kevin .... 620-341-5667. 186 D
kjohnson@emporia.edu
JOHNSON, Kevin, R .... 530-752-0243... 70 J
krjohnson@ucdavis.edu
JOHNSON, Kim .... 319-398-5525. 180 J
kjohnso@kirkwood.edu
JOHNSON, Kim .... 714-556-3610... 74 D
OfficeVPEM@vanguard.edu
JOHNSON, Kim, S .... 402-465-2551. 291 G
kjohnso2@nebrwesleyan.edu
JOHNSON, Kimberlee ...... 215-769-3128. 415 G
kjohnso2@eastern.edu

JOHNSON, Kirk .... 712-274-5116. 181 B
johnson@morningside.edu
JOHNSON, Kirk .... 509-963-1866. 517 F
johnsonk@cwu.edu
JOHNSON, Kristie .... 802-773-5900. 499 B
kristie.johnson@csj.edu
JOHNSON, Kyle .... 808-739-8552. 135 D
kyle.johnson@chaminade.edu
JOHNSON, LaKenya .... 229-931-2057. 131 G
ljohnson@southgatech.edu
JOHNSON, Landy, C ...... 580-767-7666. 222 C
lajohnson@assumption.edu
JOHNSON, LaRhonda, K 252-514-6715. 359 G
johnsonl@cravencc.edu
JOHNSON, Larry .... 601-977-7758. 270 A
ljohnson@tougaloo.edu
JOHNSON, Larry .... 706-272-4571. 123 G
ljohnson@daltonstate.edu
JOHNSON, Larry .... 870-236-6901... 20 K
ljohnson@crc.edu
JOHNSON, Larry .... 202-685-2128. 544 K
johnsonl@ndu.edu
JOHNSON, Latasha .... 312-850-7016. 142 C
ljohnson02@ccc.edu
JOHNSON, LaTrina .... 317-632-5553. 170 T
ljohnson@lincolntech.com
JOHNSON, Laura .... 870-574-4513... 23 G
ljohnson@sautech.edu
JOHNSON, Laura .... 704-216-6029. 356 D
ljohnson@livingstone.edu
JOHNSON, Laura, T .... 520-621-3175... 18 F
ltj@email.arizona.edu
JOHNSON, Lawrence, J . 513-556-2322. 390 G
lawrence.johnson@uc.edu
JOHNSON, Lea .... 518-438-3111. 330 C
ljohnson@mariacollege.edu
JOHNSON, Leda .... 623-935-8868... 14 K
leda.johnson@estrellamountain.edu
JOHNSON, Lena, H .... 757-455-3116. 515 H
ljohnson@vwc.edu
JOHNSON, Les .... 218-281-8345. 264 E
ljohnson@umn.edu
JOHNSON, Levester .... 317-940-9381. 164 J
ljohnson@butler.edu
JOHNSON, Lisa .... 617-287-6020. 228 G
lisa.johnson@umb.edu
JOHNSON, Lisa .... 423-636-7305. 462 E
ljohnson@tusculum.edu
JOHNSON, Lisa .... 701-858-3494. 371 B
lisa.a.johnson@ndus.edu
JOHNSON, Lisa, A .... 252-335-0821. 359 F
lajohnson@albemarle.edu
JOHNSON, Lois, M .... 717-720-4122. 427 G
ljohnson@passhe.edu
JOHNSON, Lonnie .... 816-271-4417. 279 A
johnsonl@missouriwestern.edu
JOHNSON, Lora, A .... 302-283-3115... 93 F
lora.johnson@dtcc.edu
JOHNSON, Lori .... 615-230-3526. 461 G
lori.johnson@volstate.edu
JOHNSON, Louise .... 215-248-7313. 422 F
ljohnson@ltsp.edu
JOHNSON, Lucia .... 972-860-8016. 470 H
ljohnson@dcccd.edu
JOHNSON, Lynda, K .... 770-423-6033. 127 N
ljohnson@kennesaw.edu
JOHNSON, Lynn .... 970-491-1550... 80 I
lynn.johnson@colostate.edu
JOHNSON, Lynn .... 218-755-2068. 258 A
ljohnson@bemidjistate.edu
JOHNSON, Lynn .... 631-632-6151. 342 C
lynn.johnson@stonybrook.edu
JOHNSON, Lynn .... 216-791-5000. 377 E
lynn.m.johnson@cim.edu
JOHNSON, Lynne .... 907-796-6416... 11 A
lynne.johnson@uas.alaska.edu
JOHNSON, Maggie .... 972-708-7573. 472 L
admissions@gial.edu
JOHNSON, Marc .... 763-422-6112. 257 P
marc.johnson@anokaramsey.edu
JOHNSON, Marc .... 775-784-4805. 294 J
marc.johnson@unr.edu
JOHNSON, Marcia .... 803-750-2500... 96 F
JOHNSON, Marco .... 661-726-1911... 70 G
marco.johnson@uav.edu
JOHNSON, Marcus .... 702-651-4148. 294 E
maracus.johnson@csn.edu
JOHNSON, Marguerite ... 617-732-2277. 233 E
peg.johnson@mcphs.edu
JOHNSON, Marianne, H . 215-699-5700. 421 E
mjohnson@LSB.edu
JOHNSON, Marie, D ...... 802-656-5700. 500 F
marie.johnson@uvm.edu
JOHNSON, Marilyn .... 479-968-0271... 20 E
mjohnson@atu.edu
JOHNSON, Marjorie, R .. 206-281-2650. 523 C
mjohnson@spu.edu
JOHNSON, Mark .... 425-235-2352. 522 F
mark.johnson@rtc.edu
JOHNSON, Mark .... 314-889-1467. 274 E
mjohnson@fontbonne.edu

JOHNSON, Mark .... 248-218-2080. 249 D
mjohnson@rc.edu
JOHNSON, Mark, R .... 919-735-5151. 364 H
mrjohnson@waynecc.edu
JOHNSON, Mark, S .... 202-806-6270... 95 G
mark.johnson@howard.edu
JOHNSON, Martha .... 252-473-5936. 359 F
martha_johnson@albemarle.edu
JOHNSON, Marty .... 831-646-4191... 54 I
mljohnson@mpc.edu
JOHNSON, Mary .... 618-262-8641. 147 C
johnsonm@iecc.edu
JOHNSON, Mary .... 910-678-8372. 360 D
johnsoma@faytechcc.edu
JOHNSON, Mary .... 507-453-2745. 259 E
mjohnson@southeastmn.edu
JOHNSON, Mary Jean .... 419-358-3272. 374 J
johnsonmj@bluffton.edu
JOHNSON, Matthew .... 701-349-5780. 373 A
mjohnson@trinitybiblecollege.edu
JOHNSON, McCeil, J ..... 312-261-3935. 153 I
mjohnson@nl.edu
JOHNSON, Melissa .... 701-671-2520. 372 E
melissa.j.johnson@ndscs.edu
JOHNSON, Melody .... 479-979-1219... 25 J
mjohnson@ozarks.edu
JOHNSON, Merrill, L ..... 503-554-2411. 403 C
mjohnson@georgefox.edu
JOHNSON, Michael .... 660-562-1212. 279 I
mikej@nwmissouri.edu
JOHNSON, Michael, C .... 214-860-2167. 470 J
mcjohnson@dcccd.edu
JOHNSON, Michael, D .... 607-255-5106. 322 A
mdj27@cornell.edu
JOHNSON, Michael, D .... 407-823-1911. 115 E
michael.johnson@ucf.edu
JOHNSON, Michael, J .... 717-245-1019. 414 H
johnsomi@dickinson.edu
JOHNSON, Michael, J .... 913-684-3357. 545 E
michael.johnson@leavenworth.army.mil
JOHNSON, Michael, L .... 270-824-8567. 196 A
michael.johnson@kctcs.edu
JOHNSON, Michele .... 253-864-3100. 522 C
mjohnson@pierce.ctc.edu
JOHNSON, Michelle .... 626-969-3434... 29 H
mmjohnson@apu.edu
JOHNSON, Michelle .... 309-796-5370. 140 E
johnsonm@bhc.edu
JOHNSON, Mike .... 479-575-6601... 23 I
mrj03@uark.edu
JOHNSON, Mike .... 503-352-2871. 407 A
johnsong@pacificu.edu
JOHNSON, Mike .... 405-585-5130. 397 C
mike.johnson@okbu.edu
JOHNSON, Mildred .... 540-231-6267. 515 C
mildredj@vt.edu
JOHNSON, Mimi .... 334-420-4243..... 7 G
mjohnson@trenholmstate.edu
JOHNSON, Mindy .... 816-604-4339. 277 H
mindy.johnson@mcckc.edu
JOHNSON, Mitchell .... 336-334-4822. 360 G
mjohnson@gtcc.edu
JOHNSON, Molly, B .... 785-227-3380. 184 I
johnsonm@bethanylb.edu
JOHNSON, Monir .... 763-488-2415. 258 F
monir.johnson@hennepintech.edu
JOHNSON, Monty .... 218-631-7812. 259 F
monty.johnson@minnesota.edu
JOHNSON, Nadja .... 701-845-7306. 372 A
nadja.johnson@vcsu.edu
JOHNSON, Nancy .... 606-886-3863. 194 K
nancy.johnson@kctcs.edu
JOHNSON, Nancy .... 903-875-7385. 477 G
nancy.johnson@navarrocollege.edu
JOHNSON, Nancy, N .... 713-646-1751. 480 J
njohnson@stcl.edu
JOHNSON, Nathan .... 616-538-2330. 243 A
njohnson@gbcol.edu
JOHNSON, Nial, L .... 309-677-2333. 140 I
nial@bradley.edu
JOHNSON, Nick .... 801-818-8900. 496 F
nick.johnson@provocollege.edu
JOHNSON, Nicole .... 718-260-3151. 336 E
njohnson@poly.edu
JOHNSON, Norman .... 937-708-5685. 393 A
njohnson@wilberforce.edu
JOHNSON, JR., P. Kelly 919-508-2329. 370 F
pkjohnsonjr@peace.edu
JOHNSON, Pam .... 256-835-5456...... 3 M
pjohnson@gadsdenstate.edu
JOHNSON, Pamela .... 903-233-3140. 475 J
pamjohnson@letu.edu
JOHNSON, Pamela, D .... 937-766-7765. 375 K
johnsonp@cedarville.edu
JOHNSON, Patricia, A .... 607-254-1590. 322 A
paj5@cornell.edu
JOHNSON, Patrick .... 240-567-5288. 216 F
patrick.johnson@montgomerycollege.edu
JOHNSON, Paul .... 478-757-2641. 128 I
paul.johnson@maconstate.edu

JOHNSON, Paul, C .... 480-965-9235... 11 K
paul.c.johnson@asu.edu
JOHNSON,
Paula "Tendai" .... 919-719-5060. 366 E
tejohnson@shawu.edu
JOHNSON, CRM,
Paula, J .... 858-534-2552... 71 F
pjjohnson@ucsd.edu
JOHNSON, Paulette .... 256-726-7250..... 6 B
pjohnson@oakwood.edu
JOHNSON, Paulette .... 314-644-9228. 281 E
pjohnson@stlcc.edu
JOHNSON, Peg .... 505-428-1506. 311 J
peg.johnson@sfcc.edu
JOHNSON, Penny .... 408-855-5195... 75 K
penny.johnson@wvm.edu
JOHNSON, Peter, B .... 701-777-4317. 371 C
peter.johnson@und.edu
JOHNSON, Philip .... 906-487-7201. 242 G
philip.johnson@finlandia.edu
JOHNSON, Philip, M .... 503-255-0332. 404 F
pjohnson@multnomah.edu
JOHNSON, Phillip .... 471-667-8181. 273 A
pjohnson@cottey.edu
JOHNSON, Phillip .... 205-391-2665..... 6 H
pjohnson@sheltonstate.edu
JOHNSON, Phillip, A ...... 574-631-8338. 174 A
johnson.30@nd.edu
JOHNSON, Phyllis, E ...... 701-777-6736. 371 C
phyllis.e.johnson@research.und.edu
JOHNSON, Ralph .... 504-486-7411. 209 D
JOHNSON, Ralph .... 864-977-2077. 445 H
ralph.johnson@ngu.edu
JOHNSON, Ralph, F .... 706-542-7369. 133 C
rfj@uga.edu
JOHNSON, Rebecca .... 770-467-6037. 132 B
rajohnson@sctech.edu
JOHNSON, Rebecca .... 901-321-4208. 453 H
rebecca.johnson@cbu.edu
JOHNSON, Rebecca .... 541-322-3100. 406 A
rebecca.johnson@osucascades.edu
JOHNSON, Rebecca, D .. 203-932-7176... 92 E
rjohnson@newhaven.edu
JOHNSON, Rhonda .... 817-598-6283. 494 G
rjohnson@wc.edu
JOHNSON, Richard .... 870-236-6901... 20 K
rjohnson@crc.edu
JOHNSON, Richard, A .... 864-597-4090. 449 I
johnsonra@wofford.edu
JOHNSON, Richard, W .... 315-268-7718. 320 A
rjohnson@clarkson.edu
JOHNSON, Richelle .... 703-897-1972. 510 B
rjohnson@stratford.edu
JOHNSON, Rick .... 239-590-7072. 115 A
rjohnson@wgcu.edu
JOHNSON, Rick .... 806-651-2080. 484 D
rjohnson@mail.wtamu.edu
JOHNSON, Rita .... 828-328-7235. 356 B
rita.johnson@lr.edu
JOHNSON, Robert .... 916-691-7390... 53 B
johnsor@crc.losrios.edu
JOHNSON, Robert .... 516-726-5646. 545 H
johnsonr@usmma.edu
JOHNSON, Robert, E ...... 508-373-1900. 223 A
robert.johnson@becker.edu
JOHNSON, Robert, E ...... 913-667-5700. 185 J
rjohnson@cbts.edu
JOHNSON, Robert, E ...... 704-687-8242. 368 E
robejohn@uncc.edu
JOHNSON, JR.,
Robert, M .... 901-843-3745. 458 E
johnsonb@rhodes.edu
JOHNSON, Roberta, L .... 515-294-0109. 175 H
rljohns@iastate.edu
JOHNSON, Robin .... 440-375-7251. 382 L
rjohnson@lec.edu
JOHNSON, Rodney .... 937-766-4114. 375 K
johnsnr@cedarville.edu
JOHNSON, Rodney .... 803-934-3226. 445 F
johnsonrod@morris.edu
JOHNSON, JR., Rodney 225-675-8270. 203 G
rojohnson@rpcc.edu
JOHNSON, Roger .... 870-248-4000... 20 G
rogerj@blackrivertech.edu
JOHNSON, Roger .... 218-733-5935. 259 A
r1.johnson@lsc.edu
JOHNSON, Ronald .... 713-500-3455. 492 E
ronald.johnson@uth.tmc.edu
JOHNSON, Ronald, A ..... 713-313-7922. 485 F
johnsonra@tsu.edu
JOHNSON, Ronald, D ..... 701-231-8804. 371 G
ronald.d.johnson@ndsu.edu
JOHNSON, Ronald, W ..... 310-206-0404... 71 C
rojohnso@saonet.ucla.edu
JOHNSON, Ruben .... 972-860-8160. 470 H
rjohnson@dcccd.edu
JOHNSON, Rushton .... 404-225-4444. 121 B
rjohnson@atlantatech.edu
JOHNSON, Ryan .... 501-205-8815... 20 I
rjohnson@cbc.edu

JOHNSON, Sabrina, C ... 540-654-1046. 510 J
sjohnson@umw.edu
JOHNSON, Samuel .... 215-568-9215. 423 M
sjohnson@phmc.org
JOHNSON, Sandra .... 661-726-1911... 70 G
sandra.johnson@uav.edu
JOHNSON, Sandra .... 516-463-6933. 326 D
sandra.johnson@hofstra.edu
JOHNSON, Sandra .... 646-717-9760. 325 B
sjohnson@gts.edu
JOHNSON, Sara .... 315-265-9260. 320 A
clarkson@bkstr.com
JOHNSON, Sara .... 662-862-8050. 267 C
scjohnson@iccms.edu
JOHNSON, Sara, S .... 803-786-3029. 443 B
sjohnson@columbiasc.edu
JOHNSON, Sarah .... 303-837-0825... 78 H
sljohnson@aii.edu
JOHNSON, Sarah .... 781-309-5242. 228 C
sjohnson@mariancourt.edu
JOHNSON, Scott .... 701-228-5474. 372 C
scott.johnson@dakotacollege.edu
JOHNSON, Scott .... 336-838-6141. 365 B
scott.johnson@wilkescc.edu
JOHNSON, Scott, L .... 716-878-5906. 343 A
johnsosl@buffalostate.edu
JOHNSON, Sean .... 707-664-2790... 36 B
sean.johnson@sonoma.edu
JOHNSON, Sean .... 325-942-2264. 465 K
sean.johnson@angelo.edu
JOHNSON, Sharon .... 903-468-8707. 483 E
sharon.johnson@tamuc.edu
JOHNSON, Sharon .... 440-775-8430. 385 H
Sharon.Johnson@oberlin.edu
JOHNSON, Sheila .... 731-668-7240. 464 F
sheila.johnson@wtbc.edu
JOHNSON, Sheila, G ...... 405-744-6321. 397 H
sheila.johnson@okstate.edu
JOHNSON, Shelia .... 304-327-4040. 529 D
sjohnson@bluefieldstate.edu
JOHNSON, Shemila .... 707-864-7000... 66 G
shemila.johnson@solano.edu
JOHNSON, Sherie .... 410-951-3846. 220 B
shejohnson@coppin.edu
JOHNSON, Sherrick, L ... 706-771-4008. 121 D
sjohnson@augustatech.edu
JOHNSON, Sonia .... 870-236-6901... 20 K
sjohnson@crc.edu
JOHNSON, Sonja .... 616-331-6811. 243 C
johnsoso@gvsu.edu
JOHNSON, Stacey .... 718-939-5100. 329 B
sjohnson@libi.edu
JOHNSON, Stacey, R ..... 407-582-2822. 118 M
srjohnson@valenciacollege.edu
JOHNSON, Stefanie .... 407-303-9498... 97 H
stefanie.johnson@adu.edu
JOHNSON, Stephanie ..... 410-455-1517. 219 D
sjohn@umbc.edu
JOHNSON, Stephen .... 626-812-3020... 29 H
sjohnson@apu.edu
JOHNSON, Stephen .... 560-860-2451... 37 I
sjohnson@cerritos.edu
JOHNSON, Stephen .... 325-674-3791. 464 H
scj98d@acu.edu
JOHNSON, Stephen, P ... 607-255-9029. 322 A
spj2@cornell.edu
JOHNSON, Steve .... 504-280-6303. 205 G
sgjohnso@uno.edu
JOHNSON, Steve .... 913-360-7415. 184 H
stevej@benedictine.edu
JOHNSON, Steve .... 435-652-7544. 497 E
johnsons@dixie.edu
JOHNSON, Steve .... 503-552-2001. 404 H
sjohnson@ncnm.edu
JOHNSON, Steven .... 215-489-2905. 414 E
Steven.Johnson@delval.edu
JOHNSON, Steven .... 212-346-1835. 335 J
sjohnson@pace.edu
JOHNSON, Steven, C ..... 208-885-7372. 139 D
stevejohnson@uidaho.edu
JOHNSON, Steven, L ..... 212-346-1835. 335 J
sjohnson@pace.edu
JOHNSON, Steven, L ..... 989-774-1169. 240 N
johns1sl@cmich.edu
JOHNSON, Steven, L ..... 973-655-7677. 303 D
johnsonst@mail.montclair.edu
JOHNSON, Steven, L ..... 937-512-2525. 388 O
president@sinclair.edu
JOHNSON, Susan .... 775-831-1314. 295 F
JOHNSON, Susie .... 863-784-7108. 113 G
susie.johnson@southflorida.edu
JOHNSON, Sylvester, C . 504-865-5300. 207 C
sylj@tulane.edu
JOHNSON, Tammy .... 304-696-3161. 529 H
johnson73@marshall.edu
JOHNSON, Tasha .... 252-527-6223. 361 F
tjohnson@lenoircc.edu
JOHNSON, Ted .... 847-543-2247. 143 A
bld320@clcillinois.edu
JOHNSON, Ted .... 858-822-5949... 71 F
edjohnson@ucsd.edu
JOHNSON, Teisha .... 312-949-7407. 146 G
tjohnson@ico.edu
JOHNSON, Tera .... 216-373-5274. 385 G
tjohnson@ndc.edu
JOHNSON, Teresa .... 573-840-9660. 282 K
tjohnson@trcc.edu
JOHNSON, Terri .... 248-213-1614. 144 A
tjohnson@devry.edu
JOHNSON, Terri .... 512-863-1342. 481 I
tjohnson@southwestern.edu
JOHNSON, Terry, L .... 937-382-6661. 393 B
terry_johnson@wilmington.edu
JOHNSON, Theodore ...... 630-889-6512. 154 E
tjohnson@nuhs.edu
JOHNSON, Thomas .... 712-325-3227. 179 L
tjohnson@iwcc.edu
JOHNSON, Thomas .... 323-343-3480... 34 A
tjohnson@cslanet.calstatela.edu
JOHNSON, Thomas, A .... 903-510-2950. 488 E
tjoh@tjc.edu
JOHNSON, Thomasine ... 202-319-6065... 94 G
johnsotn@cua.edu
JOHNSON, Tim, P .... 937-766-7777. 375 K
johnsont@cedarville.edu
JOHNSON, Timothy .... 336-334-5636. 369 A
tjjohns3@uncg.edu
JOHNSON, Timothy .... 617-731-7116. 235 H
johnsontim@pmc.edu
JOHNSON, Todd .... 757-683-3462. 507 N
tjohnso@odu.edu
JOHNSON, Tom .... 314-246-7975. 284 N
thomasjohnson18@webster.edu
JOHNSON, Tom .... 910-221-2224. 354 D
tjohnson@gcd.edu
JOHNSON, Tonjanita ...... 865-974-8184. 463 B
tonjanita.johnson@tennessee.edu
JOHNSON, Tony .... 903-983-8102. 475 E
tjohnson@kilgore.edu
JOHNSON, Tonya, L ...... 678-359-5011. 127 A
tonyaj@gordonstate.edu
JOHNSON, Tracey .... 618-634-3271. 158 M
traceyj@shawneecc.edu
JOHNSON, Tracie .... 615-383-4848. 464 D
tjohnson@watkins.edu
JOHNSON, Travis .... 704-334-6882. 357 K
tjohnson@nlts.edu
JOHNSON, Troy .... 309-438-2157. 147 J
JOHNSON, Trygve, D .... 616-395-7145. 244 A
johnsont@hope.edu
JOHNSON, Veronica .... 773-947-6319. 152 E
vjohnson@mccormick.edu
JOHNSON, Vicki .... 731-989-6095. 454 J
vjohnson@fhu.edu
JOHNSON, Victoria, D .... 504-865-5591. 207 C
victoria@tulane.edu
JOHNSON, Walter .... 864-977-7068. 445 H
walter.johnson@ngu.edu
JOHNSON, Walter .... 601-979-2522. 267 E
walter.l.johnson@jsums.edu
JOHNSON, Warner, O ..... 412-397-6409. 431 I
johnsonw@rmu.edu
JOHNSON, Wayne, E ..... 704-406-4331. 354 C
wjohnson@gardner-webb.edu
JOHNSON, Wendy .... 225-675-8270. 203 G
wjohnson@rpcc.edu
JOHNSON, Wendy .... 937-393-3431. 389 B
wjohnson@sscc.edu
JOHNSON, William, H .... 203-254-4000... 89 I
wjohnson@fairfield.edu
JOHNSON-BAILEY,
Juanita .... 706-542-2846. 133 C
jjb@uga.edu
JOHNSON-BLAKE,
Deborah .... 404-225-4491. 121 B
djohnsonblake@atlantatech.edu
JOHNSON-CRAFT,
Shirley .... 928-757-0857... 15 L
sjohnsoncraft@mohave.edu
JOHNSON-CRAMER,
Michael, E .... 570-577-1756. 411 A
m.johnson-cramer@bucknell.edu
JOHNSON-FANNIN,
Arcelia .... 210-883-1015. 490 A
johnsonf@uiwtx.edu
JOHNSON HADLEY,
Erma, C .... 817-515-5201. 482 B
erma.johnson-hadley@tccd.edu
JOHNSON-HAWKINS,
Alma .... 818-710-2911... 52 B
johnsoal@piercecollege.edu
JOHNSON-HOUSTON,
Debbie, L .... 337-475-5716. 207 G
djohnsonhouston@mcneese.edu
JOHNSON JONES,
Sylvia, M .... 847-543-2404. 143 A
cps086@clcillinois.edu
JOHNSON-ODIM,
Cheryl .... 708-524-6813. 144 C
cjohnson-odim@dom.edu
JOHNSON RENVALL,
Poppy .... 505-224-4435. 309 E
pjohnsonrenvall@cnm.edu
JOHNSON-ROSS,
Debora .... 410-386-4632. 216 E
djohnson@mcdaniel.edu
JOHNSON-SHAHEED,
Karen .... 301-860-3555. 220 A
kshaheed@bowiestate.edu
JOHNSON-TAYLOR,
Don, W .... 803-321-5112. 445 G
don.johnson-taylor@newberry.edu
JOHNSON-WEEKS,
Demetria .... 713-313-7940. 485 F
weeks_dj@tsu.edu
JOHNSON WILLIAMS,
Nikki .... 540-362-6217. 505 G
nwilliams@hollins.edu
JOHNSRUD, Courtney .... 406-771-4387. 287 E
cjohnsrud@gfcmsu.edu
JOHNSRUD, Linda, K ..... 808-956-7075. 135 L
johnsrud@hawaii.edu
JOHNSTON, Alysia .... 620-251-7700. 185 O
alysiaj@coffeyville.edu
JOHNSTON, Angela .... 330-263-2313. 377 H
ajohnston@wooster.edu
JOHNSTON, Bonnie .... 415-451-2812... 63 A
bjohnston@sfts.edu
JOHNSTON, Brian .... 216-373-5252. 385 G
bjohnston@ndc.edu
JOHNSTON, Brian, A ...... 202-319-6425... 94 G
johnston@cua.edu
JOHNSTON, Cheryl, L .... 724-847-6577. 417 A
cljohnst@geneva.edu
JOHNSTON,
Christine, D .... 309-457-2327. 153 D
cjohnsto@monmouthcollege.edu
JOHNSTON, Daniel .... 402-354-7080. 291 B
dan.johnston@methodistcollege.edu
JOHNSTON, Danielle .... 702-992-2621. 294 G
danielle.johnston@nsc.edu
JOHNSTON, Daryl .... 352-271-2905. 113 C
daryl.johnston@sfcollege.edu
JOHNSTON, Deborah ..... 907-564-8204... 10 C
debj@alaskapacific.edu
JOHNSTON, Dusty, R ..... 940-552-6291. 493 F
drj@vernoncollege.edu
JOHNSTON, E. Bubby .... 601-635-2111. 266 H
bjohnston@eccc.edu
JOHNSTON, Elizabeth .... 214-637-3530. 494 E
ejohnston@wadecollege.edu
JOHNSTON, Emily .... 251-460-6231..... 9 E
ejohnston@southalabama.edu
JOHNSTON, F. Bruce ..... 870-307-7247... 21 H
bruce.johnston@lyon.edu
JOHNSTON, James .... 940-397-4594. 476 H
james.johnston@mwsu.edu
JOHNSTON, James, K .... 219-989-2232. 171 N
johnston@purduecal.edu
JOHNSTON, Jed .... 402-826-8604. 289 E
jed.johnston@doane.edu
JOHNSTON, Jeff .... 574-520-4454. 168 E
jjohnsto@iusb.edu
JOHNSTON, Jeffrey .... 907-747-7704... 11 A
jeff.johnston@uas.alaska.edu
JOHNSTON, John .... 212-217-3600. 324 C
john_johnston@fitnyc.edu
JOHNSTON, John, E ...... 517-265-5161. 238 G
jjohnston@adrian.edu
JOHNSTON, Judy .... 912-279-5705. 123 B
jjohnston@ccga.edu
JOHNSTON, Judy .... 502-895-3411. 197 F
jjohnston@lpts.edu
JOHNSTON, Julie, L .... 530-251-8820... 50 F
jjohnston@lassencollege.edu
JOHNSTON, Justin .... 716-839-8468. 322 E
jjohnsto@daemen.edu
JOHNSTON, Kathy .... 636-481-3280. 275 I
kjohnsto@jeffco.edu
JOHNSTON, Kathy .... 620-421-6700. 188 D
kathyj@labette.edu
JOHNSTON, Kerri .... 978-934-3948. 229 B
kerri_johnston@uml.edu
JOHNSTON, Kimberly ...... 309-672-5583. 152 I
kajohnston@methodistcol.edu
JOHNSTON, Laine .... 360-383-3126. 525 D
ljohnston@whatcom.ctc.edu
JOHNSTON, Laurel, A .... 808-956-7323. 135 L
laurel.johnston@hawaii.edu
JOHNSTON, Mary .... 618-842-3711. 146 I
johnstonm@iecc.edu
JOHNSTON, Matthew ..... 661-835-1111... 64 F
JOHNSTON, Matthew ..... 805-339-2999... 64 J
JOHNSTON, Matthew ..... 805-922-8256... 64 I
JOHNSTON, Michelle ..... 205-665-6392..... 9 B
johnstonmr@montevallo.edu
JOHNSTON, Michelle ..... 203-392-6501... 88 A
johnstonm2@southerct.edu
JOHNSTON, Michelle ..... 231-591-3648. 242 F
michelle_johnston@ferris.edu
JOHNSTON, Pamela .... 210-999-7507. 488 C
pamela.johnston@trinity.edu
JOHNSTON, Paul, E .... 207-859-4252. 209 J
pejohnst@colby.edu
JOHNSTON, Peter .... 508-588-9100. 232 A
JOHNSTON, Raschelle .... 816-414-3700. 277 L
financialaid@mbts.edu
JOHNSTON, Robert, C .... 315-445-4321. 328 F
johnstrc@lemoyne.edu
JOHNSTON, Robin .... 850-201-8580. 117 D
johnstor@tcc.fl.edu
JOHNSTON, Roxanne ..... 585-395-2309. 342 F
rjohnsto@brockport.edu
JOHNSTON, Sally .... 702-651-5664. 294 E
sally.johnston@csn.edu
JOHNSTON, Sandra .... 815-455-9793. 152 F
sjohnston@mchenry.edu
JOHNSTON, Sandra .... 386-752-1822. 104 G
sandra.johnston@fgc.edu
JOHNSTON, Susan .... 703-784-2884. 544 J
susan.johnston@usmc.mil
JOHNSTON, Thomas, C . 207-941-7176. 211 F
thom@nescom.edu
JOHNSTON, Tim .... 760-245-4271... 75 B
Tim.Johnston@vvc.edu
JOHNSTON, Tim .... 903-434-8175. 477 J
tjohnston@ntcc.edu
JOHNSTON, Timothy .... 530-242-7669... 65 G
tjohnston@shastacollege.edu
JOHNSTON, Timothy, D . 336-334-5607. 369 A
johnston@uncg.edu
JOHNSTON, William, N .. 302-736-2508... 94 C
wnj@wesley.edu
JOHNSTON, William, S .. 406-243-5211. 286 H
bill.johnston@umontana.edu
JOHNSTON-ORTIZ, Eric . 575-624-7121. 309 I
eric.johnston-ortiz@roswell.enmu.edu
JOINER, Erin .... 502-897-4206. 199 B
ejoiner@sbts.edu
JOINER, Haywood .... 318-473-6466. 205 A
hjoiner@lsua.edu
JOINER, Karen .... 360-442-2861. 521 A
kjoiner@lowercolumbia.edu
JOINER, Steve .... 615-966-7141. 456 B
steve.joiner@lipscomb.edu
JOINER, Wayne .... 919-546-8251. 366 E
wjoiner@shawu.edu
JOKELA, Roxana .... 402-559-4385. 292 J
rjokela@unmc.edu
JOKERST-HARTER, Jill .... 314-367-8700. 281 C
jill.harter@stlcop.edu
JOLER-LABBE, Michelle . 207-859-1240. 211 H
hr@thomas.edu
JOLINE, Mary Lou .... 717-560-8215. 421 A
mjoline@lbc.edu
JOLIVETTE, Thomas .... 651-641-3528. 256 J
tjolivet@luthersem.edu
JOLL, Ray .... 727-784-0003... 99 J
rjoll@cfi.edu
JOLLEY, JR., Edward, B . 912-358-3000. 131 C
jolleye@savannahstate.edu
JOLLEY, Kassandra .... 404-270-5323. 132 E
kjolley@spelman.edu
JOLLEY, Kate .... 707-527-4413... 65 B
kjolley@santarosa.edu
JOLLEY, Rick .... 864-587-4260. 447 B
jolleyr@smcsc.edu
JOLLEY, Tammy .... 870-612-2027... 25 A
tammy.jolley@uaccb.edu
JOLLIFFE, Vicki, M .... 724-439-4900. 421 F
vjolliffe@laurel.edu
JOLLY, Connie .... 843-574-6150. 447 E
connie.jolly@tridenttech.edu
JOLLY, Jim, L .... 256-549-8256..... 3 M
jjolly@gadsdenstate.edu
JOLLY, Julia, A .... 916-558-2407... 53 D
jollyj@scc.losrios.edu
JOLLY, Laura, D .... 706-583-0690. 133 C
ljolly@uga.edu
JOLLY, Lawson .... 352-588-8354. 112 D
lawson.jolly@saintleo.edu
JOLLY, Melody .... 714-850-4800... 69 E
jolly@taftu.edu
JOLLY, Michael .... 719-846-5691... 85 H
michael.jolly@trinidadstate.edu
JOLLY, Randy .... 337-421-6903. 204 E
randy.jolly@sowela.edu
JOLLY, Richard, C .... 432-685-4524. 476 G
rjolly@midland.edu
JOLLY-SMITH, Sue .... 662-329-7175. 268 E
sjolly@edhs.muw.edu
JOLY, Jennifer .... 303-937-4232... 79 E
jjoly@chu.edu
JONAITIS, Aldona .... 907-474-6939... 10 I
ajonaitis@alaska.edu
JONAS-MORRISON,
Carol .... 719-502-3383... 84 A
carol.jonas-morrison@ppcc.edu
JONES, Aaron .... 417-873-7301. 273 H
aaronjones@drury.edu

JONES, Albert, W .... 570-484-2322. 429 B
ajones@lhup.edu
JONES, Alesia, M .... 250-934-5321..... 8 E
amjones@uab.edu
JONES, Allison .... 323-953-4000... 51 G
jonessa@lacitycollege.edu
JONES, Allison .... 918-495-6912. 398 H
ajones@oru.edu
JONES, Almarie .... 856-415-2154. 302 C
ajones@gccnj.edu
JONES, Alonzo .... 434-791-4773. 502 D
ajones@averett.edu
JONES, Alvena .... 903-927-3318. 495 A
ajones@wileyc.edu
JONES, Amy .... 734-462-4400. 250 A
ajones2@schoolcraft.edu
JONES, Amy .... 425-889-7823. 521 G
amy.jones@northwestu.edu
JONES, Amy, J .... 712-749-2101. 176 D
jonesa@bvu.edu
JONES, Andrew, C .... 714-438-4888... 39 H
ajones@mail.cccd.edu
JONES, Andy .... 562-951-4500... 32 E
ajones@calstate.edu
JONES, Angie .... 504-278-6427. 203 F
ajones@nunez.edu
JONES, Annie .... 434-381-6346. 510 F
anniejones@sbc.edu
JONES, Anthony .... 256-761-8571..... 7 F
amjones@talladega.edu
JONES, Anthony .... 850-201-8103. 117 D
jonesa@tcc.fl.edu
JONES, April .... 704-330-6190. 359 C
april.jones@cpcc.edu
JONES, Art .... 605-642-6245. 451 G
art.jones@bhsu.edu
JONES, Barbara .... 870-862-8131... 23 D
brjones@southark.edu
JONES, Barbara .... 617-552-2052. 224 A
barbara.jones@bc.edu
JONES, Barbara .... 601-484-8804. 267 G
bjones@meridiancc.edu
JONES, Barbara, E .... 607-746-4440. 345 G
jonesbe@delhi.edu
JONES, Ben .... 440-775-8624. 385 H
ben.jones@oberlin.edu
JONES, Benjamin, F .... 605-256-5270. 451 H
benjamin.jones@dsu.edu
JONES, Bert .... 804-819-4920. 511 G
bjones@vccs.edu
JONES, Beverly .... 512-863-1527. 481 I
jonesb@southwestern.edu
JONES, Bill .... 209-543-7000... 49 J
bjones@kaplancollege.edu
JONES, III, Bob .... 864-242-5100. 441 D
JONES, Bobby, G .... 870-230-5090... 21 D
jonesb@hsu.edu
JONES, Bonnie .... 941-359-4200. 117 A
JONES, Brad .... 317-738-8033. 165 I
bjones@franklincollege.edu
JONES, Brenda .... 281-922-3403. 479 H
brenda.jones@sjcd.edu
JONES, Brenda .... 281-998-6150. 479 E
brenda.jones@sjcd.edu
JONES, Brenda .... 414-847-3231. 534 F
brendajones@miad.edu
JONES, Brian .... 310-544-6442... 61 H
brian.jones@usw.salvationarmy.org
JONES, Brian .... 704-378-1238. 355 K
bjones@jcsu.edu
JONES, Brian .... 507-389-2422. 259 G
brian.jones@mnsu.edu
JONES, Brian .... 813-879-6000. 103 B
brjones@cci.edu
JONES, Brian .... 915-779-8031. 494 C
bjones@computercareercenter.com
JONES, Brinda, A .... 843-661-1131. 444 B
bjones@fmarion.edu
JONES, Britt, E .... 325-670-1317. 472 O
brittj@hsutx.edu
JONES, Bronte .... 410-626-2514. 217 G
bronte.jones@sjca.edu
JONES, Bryan .... 503-222-3225. 403 B
bjones1@cci.edu
JONES, Byron .... 602-557-9322... 18 I
Byron.Jones@phoenix.edu
JONES, Candace, L .... 919-497-3237. 356 E
cjones@louisburg.edu
JONES, Carl .... 404-880-8787. 122 J
cjones@cau.edu
JONES, Carl .... 318-357-4254. 208 B
jonesc@nsula.edu
JONES, Carnell .... 401-874-7280. 440 D
carnell@mail.uri.edu
JONES, Carol .... 478-218-3700. 122 F
cjones@centralgatech.edu
JONES, Carol .... 706-272-4545. 123 G
cjones@daltonstate.edu
JONES, Carol, F .... 478-988-6800. 122 G
cjones@centralgatech.edu
JONES, Carolyn, D .... 973-655-5194. 303 D
jonesc@mail.montclair.edu
JONES, Carolyn, J .... 412-924-1404. 431 A
cjones@pts.edu
JONES, Carolyn, K .... 812-888-4182. 174 F
cjones@vinu.edu
JONES, Catherine .... 815-479-7752. 152 F
cjones@mchenry.edu
JONES, Cathy .... 704-330-1461. 355 K
cjones2@jcsu.edu
JONES, Cecelia, K .... 903-593-8311. 485 A
ckjones@texascollege.edu
JONES, Charles, E .... 270-745-3253. 200 G
charles.jones2@wku.edu
JONES, Cheri .... 530-541-4660... 50 D
jones@ltcc.edu
JONES, Chris .... 606-589-3003. 196 F
chris.jones@kctcs.edu
JONES, Chrissy .... 509-533-3743. 518 F
chrissy.davis@spokanefalls.edu
JONES, Christopher .... 978-867-4500. 226 H
chris.jones@gordon.edu
JONES, Christopher, M .. 315-445-4310. 328 F
jonescm@lemoyne.edu
JONES, Cindy, M .... 417-873-7330. 273 H
cjones@drury.edu
JONES, Clayton, H .... 662-915-7431. 270 B
chj1@olemiss.edu
JONES, Cliff .... 870-733-6722... 21 I
cejones@midsouthcc.edu
JONES, Clifton .... 803-641-3340. 448 A
cliftonj@usca.edu
JONES, Courtney .... 405-382-9204. 399 I
c.jones@sscok.edu
JONES, Cravor .... 304-327-4016. 529 D
cjones@bluefieldstate.edu
JONES, Curtis .... 912-201-6123. 131 H
cejones@southuniversity.edu
JONES, D.B .... 215-895-1267. 415 B
d.b.jones@drexel.edu
JONES, Dan .... 903-886-5011. 483 E
dan.jones@tamuc.edu
JONES, Dan, L .... 828-262-3180. 367 A
jonesdl@appstate.edu
JONES, Daniel .... 315-792-7234. 346 C
daniel.jones@sunyit.edu
JONES, Daniel, W .... 662-915-7111. 270 B
chancllr@olemiss.edu
JONES, Danneal .... 305-626-3711. 104 J
Danneal.Jones@fmuniv.edu
JONES, Danny, L .... 601-977-7870. 270 A
dljones@tougaloo.edu
JONES, Danson .... 979-532-6975. 494 L
jonesd@wcjc.edu
JONES, Darcy .... 814-824-2233. 423 J
djones@mercyhurst.edu
JONES, Darin .... 801-832-2573. 498 F
djones@westminstercollege.edu
JONES, Darnell .... 816-501-4117. 280 I
darnell.jones@rockhurst.edu
JONES, Darren .... 501-977-2191... 25 C
jones@uaccm.edu
JONES, Darren .... 301-736-3631. 216 B
darren.jones@msbbcs.edu
JONES, Darryl .... 510-231-5000... 49 D
JONES, Darryl .... 914-654-5522. 320 H
djones@cnr.edu
JONES, David .... 573-592-5288. 285 B
david.jones@westminster-mo.edu
JONES, David .... 507-389-2121. 259 G
david.jones@mnsu.edu
JONES, David .... 251-809-1592..... 5 A
david.jones@jdcc.edu
JONES, David .... 904-256-7267. 107 Q
djones1@ju.edu
JONES, David .... 650-725-3334... 68 E
david.jones@stanford.edu
JONES, David .... 931-363-9816. 456 C
djones@martinmethodist.edu
JONES, David, E .... 831-459-3700... 72 C
dej@ucsc.edu
JONES, David, R .... 301-784-5000. 213 B
djones@allegany.edu
JONES, Deborah .... 757-727-5251. 505 F
deborah.jones@hamptonu.edu
JONES, Deborah, A .... 859-238-5286. 193 E
deb.jones@centre.edu
JONES, Debra .... 229-430-3605. 120 A
djones@albanytech.edu
JONES, Debra .... 360-752-8313. 517 B
djones@btc.ctc.edu
JONES, Deneese .... 515-271-3623. 177 K
deneese.jones@drake.edu
JONES, Dennis .... 510-436-1049... 47 J
jones@hnu.edu
JONES, Dennis, H .... 256-766-6610..... 4 B
djones@hcu.edu
JONES, Dennis, L .... 727-341-3152. 112 E
jones.dennisl@spcollege.edu
JONES, Diana .... 641-784-5412. 178 F
dianaj@gracelend.edu
JONES, Dianna .... 781-768-7291. 236 A
dianna.jones@regiscollege.edu
JONES, DiOnetta .... 617-253-5010. 233 B
JONES, Don .... 617-585-1154. 234 I
don.jones@necmusic.edu
JONES, Donald .... 860-768-4751... 92 D
djones@hartford.edu
JONES, Donald .... 812-488-1209. 173 H
dj29@evansville.edu
JONES, Donald, A .... 502-371-8330. 192 C
djones@ata.edu
JONES, Donald, E .... 803-754-4100. 443 C
JONES, Dorothy, D .... 904-743-1122. 107 T
vjones@jones.edu
JONES, Doug .... 910-893-1235. 352 K
jones@campbell.edu
JONES, Douglas, W .... 805-565-6048... 76 D
vpfinance@westmont.edu
JONES, Ed .... 434-791-5684. 502 D
ejones@averett.edu
JONES, JR., Edward .... 202-274-7441... 97 A
ejones@udc.edu
JONES, Eli .... 479-575-5949... 23 I
ejones@walton.uark.edu
JONES, Elizabeth, R .... 404-413-3003. 126 E
bethjones@gsu.edu
JONES, Ellen .... 517-483-9871. 245 H
jonese14@lcc.edu
JONES, Elwin .... 251-981-3771..... 2 I
elwin.jones@columbiasouthern.edu
JONES, Eric .... 641-628-5249. 176 E
jonese@central.edu
JONES, Eric .... 312-915-7452. 151 H
ejones6@luc.edu
JONES, Eric, C .... 860-444-8286. 545 G
eric.c.jones@uscg.mil
JONES, Erica .... 406-683-7511. 286 I
e_jones@umwestern.edu
JONES, Ericka, D .... 512-505-3040. 473 G
edjones@htu.edu
JONES, Erytheia .... 301-891-4542. 221 B
eljones@wau.edu
JONES, Faye .... 615-353-3556. 461 B
faye.jones@nscc.edu
JONES, Frances .... 309-677-2646. 140 I
fjc@bradley.edu
JONES, Garry .... 407-679-0100. 106 D
gjones@fullsail.com
JONES, Garry .... 662-243-2643. 266 I
gjones@eastms.edu
JONES, Gary .... 618-252-5400. 159 E
gary.jones@sic.edu
JONES, Gary .... 405-425-5904. 397 D
gary.jones@oc.edu
JONES, Gena .... 806-743-2865. 487 E
gena.jones@ttuhsc.edu
JONES, George, A .... 606-759-7141. 196 B
george.jones@kctcs.edu
JONES, Gerald .... 334-386-7600..... 3 H
gjones@faulkner.edu
JONES, Geraldine .... 724-938-4400. 428 A
jones_gm@calu.edu
JONES, Gina, G .... 803-323-2194. 449 G
jonesg@winthrop.edu
JONES, Gladys, J .... 601-977-7821. 270 A
gjones@tougaloo.edu
JONES, Glendell .... 870-230-5091... 21 D
president@hsu.edu
JONES, Glenn .... 973-720-2950. 308 I
jonesg13@wpunj.edu
JONES, Glenna, S .... 815-224-0230. 148 A
glenna_jones@ivcc.edu
JONES, Gloria .... 803-323-3900. 449 G
jonesg@winthrop.edu
JONES, Grace, S .... 860-383-5201... 89 F
gjones@trcc.commnet.edu
JONES, Grady, B .... 724-946-7368. 437 B
jonesgb@westminster.edu
JONES, Gwen .... 937-512-4294. 388 O
gwendolyn.jones2518@sinclair.edu
JONES, Gwen .... 262-595-2151. 537 C
gaines@uwp.edu
JONES, Harold .... 903-675-6256. 488 D
hjones@tvcc.edu
JONES, Harold, P .... 205-934-5149..... 8 E
jonesh@uab.edu
JONES, Harriett, S .... 706-821-8219. 130 C
hjones@paine.edu
JONES, Ingrid .... 561-297-3959. 114 L
ijones7@fau.edu
JONES, J. Pernell .... 610-341-5948. 415 G
pjones1@eastern.edu
JONES, J. Preston .... 954-262-5127. 109 K
prestonj@nova.edu
JONES, Jacquelyn, K .... 573-882-4097. 283 C
jonesjk@missouri.edu
JONES, JR., James, F .... 860-297-2086... 91 F
james.f.jones@trincoll.edu
JONES, James, M .... 812-888-5555. 174 F
jjones@vinu.edu
JONES, James, V .... 716-888-2475. 316 C
jones11@canisius.edu
JONES, Jane, M .... 423-439-4211. 459 C
jonesj@etsu.edu
JONES, Janet .... 256-331-5310..... 6 A
janetj@nwscc.edu
JONES, Janet .... 937-512-2514. 388 O
janet.jones@sinclair.edu
JONES, Jay .... 870-460-1022... 24 D
jonesj@uamont.edu
JONES, Jayne, W .... 479-968-0400... 20 E
jjones@atu.edu
JONES, Jean .... 814-732-2981. 428 E
jjones@edinboro.edu
JONES, Jeannine .... 541-343-1641. 405 C
jjones@nwcu.edu
JONES, Jeff .... 407-823-1582. 115 E
jeffrey.jones@ucf.edu
JONES, Jeffrey .... 570-422-3833. 428 D
jjones@po-box.esu.edu
JONES, Jeffrey, A .... 724-847-6512. 417 A
jajones@geneva.edu
JONES, Jennifer .... 815-455-8770. 152 F
jjones@mchenry.edu
JONES, Jennifer .... 606-546-1205. 200 A
jjones@unionky.edu
JONES, Jennifer .... 201-200-3005. 303 F
jjones@njcu.edu
JONES, Jenny .... 859-246-6653. 194 L
jenny.jones@kctcs.edu
JONES, Jenny .... 704-687-7799. 368 E
Jenny.Jones@uncc.edu
JONES, Jenny, E .... 512-542-7834. 484 B
jjones@tamhsc.edu
JONES, Jessica .... 815-921-4755. 157 A
j.jones@rockvalleycollege.edu
JONES, Jessica .... 505-747-2241. 311 E
jjones@nnmc.edu
JONES, Jessica, S .... 252-246-1216. 365 C
jjones@wilsoncc.edu
JONES, Jim .... 706-721-0011. 126 B
jjones@gru.edu
JONES, Jim .... 325-670-1207. 472 O
jjones@hsutx.edu
JONES, John .... 765-677-2387. 169 B
john.jones@indwes.edu
JONES, John, D .... 662-254-3800. 269 A
john.jones@mvsu.edu
JONES, John, D .... 432-837-8585. 487 B
jjones4@sulross.edu
JONES, John, P .... 520-621-1112... 18 F
jpjones@email.arizona.edu
JONES, John, R .... 479-788-7912... 24 A
john.jones@uafs.edu
JONES, John, R .... 910-521-6304. 369 B
jrjones@uncp.edu
JONES, John, S .... 772-546-5534. 106 N
johnjones@hsbc.edu
JONES, Johnny, D .... 402-878-2380. 290 D
president@littlepriest.edu
JONES, Joli .... 251-580-2271..... 4 L
joli.jones@faulknerstate.edu
JONES, Jon .... 417-268-6110. 271 I
jjones@gobbc.edu
JONES, Joree .... 334-291-4913..... 2 H
joree.jones@cv.edu
JONES, Joseph .... 773-244-5648. 154 G
jjones@northpark.edu
JONES, Joshua .... 309-677-1000. 140 I
jjones@bradley.edu
JONES, Judy .... 870-245-5578... 22 D
jonesj@obu.edu
JONES, Judy .... 979-532-6561. 494 L
judyj@wcjc.edu
JONES, Karen .... 636-922-8258. 280 J
kjones@stchas.edu
JONES, Karen .... 828-395-1429. 361 C
kjones@isothermal.edu
JONES, Karen .... 717-815-1787. 438 D
kjones@ycp.edu
JONES, Karen, S .... 478-289-2012. 124 C
kjones@ega.edu
JONES, Katherine .... 410-334-2892. 221 D
kjones@worwic.edu
JONES, Katherine .... 919-735-5151. 364 H
kathyj@waynecc.edu
JONES, Kathryn .... 803-705-4865. 441 C
jonesk@benedict.edu
JONES, Kathryn, C .... 870-972-3027... 19 N
kjones@astate.edu
JONES, Katie .... 413-565-1000. 222 F
kjones@baypath.edu
JONES, Katie, P .... 864-488-4597. 444 L
kjones@limestone.edu
JONES, Ken .... 818-767-0888... 76 K
ken.jones@woodbury.edu
JONES, Ken, A .... 918-595-7029. 400 E
ken.jones@tulsacc.edu
JONES, Kenneth, E .... 662-252-8000. 269 F
kjones@rustcollege.edu
JONES, Kent .... 256-228-6001..... 5 H
jonesk@nacc.edu

JONES, Kevin, M .... 919-530-5436. 368 A
kjones151@nccu.edu
JONES, Kim .... 903-823-3004. 482 D
kim.jones@texarkanacollege.edu
JONES, Kim .... 361-593-2187. 484 A
krkdy00@tamuk.edu
JONES, Kim .... 731-668-7240. 464 F
kim.jones@wtbc.edu
JONES, Kona .... 217-875-7200. 156 J
kona@richland.edu
JONES, Kristen .... 406-756-3894. 286 B
kjones@fvcc.edu
JONES, Kushi .... 951-343-4344... 30 H
kjones@calbaptist.edu
JONES, Lance .... 307-268-2672. 542 X
ljones@caspercollege.edu
JONES, Larry .... 334-222-6591..... 5 E
ljones@lbwcc.edu
JONES, Larry .... 334-874-5700..... 3 A
ljones@ccal.edu
JONES, Larry, W .... 662-329-7282. 268 E
ljones@its.muw.edu
JONES, Laura, B .... 734-764-7423. 251 C
laurabj@umich.edu
JONES, Laurel .... 831-479-6302... 30 G
lajones@cabrillo.edu
JONES, Laurene .... 609-586-4800. 302 G
jonesl@mccc.edu
JONES, Laurie, S .... 706-568-2005. 123 D
jones_laurie@columbusstate.edu
JONES, Leonard .... 360-650-2953. 525 C
leonard.jones@wwu.edu
JONES, Leslie .... 985-448-4325. 208 A
leslie.jones@nicholls.edu
JONES, Linda, E .... 607-871-2767. 313 E
jones@alfred.edu
JONES, Linda, M .... 254-968-9104. 483 A
ljones@tarleton.edu
JONES, Linda Kay .... 575-538-6133. 312 N
jonesl6@wnmu.edu
JONES, Lirse .... 973-720-2101. 308 I
jonesl@wpunj.edu
JONES, Lisa .... 845-257-3216. 342 B
jonesl@newpaltz.edu
JONES, Lisa .... 252-335-0821. 359 F
lisa_jones@albemarle.edu
JONES, Lisa .... 801-832-2237. 498 F
ljones@westminstercollege.edu
JONES, Lisa, R .... 785-670-1712. 191 D
lisa.jones@washburn.edu
JONES, Marcia .... 678-466-4250. 123 A
marciajones@clayton.edu
JONES, Marcus .... 318-357-5701. 208 B
marcusj@nsula.edu
JONES, Margaret .... 914-422-4043. 335 J
mjones@pace.edu
JONES, Marian .... 704-378-1074. 355 K
myjones@jcsu.edu
JONES, Mark, W .... 540-362-6363. 505 G
jonesmw@hollins.edu
JONES, Marlene .... 410-276-0306. 218 D
mjones@host.sdc.edu
JONES, Marvin, L .... 410-651-6144. 219 E
mljones@umes.edu
JONES, Mary .... 870-575-8461... 24 E
jonesm@uapb.edu
JONES, Mary .... 913-971-3393. 188 H
maryjones@mnu.edu
JONES, Mary .... 805-289-6346... 74 H
mjones@vcccd.edu
JONES, Mary, C .... 502-213-2200. 195 F
maryc.jones@kctcs.edu
JONES, Mary, O .... 814-371-6920. 415 C
mainc@dbcollege.edu
JONES, Matteel .... 864-250-8177. 444 E
matteel.jones@gvltec.edu
JONES, Maurice .... 510-748-2234... 59 B
majones@peralta.edu
JONES, Megan .... 423-323-0201. 461 C
majones@northeaststate.edu
JONES, Melanie, E .... 803-327-8012. 449 J
mjones@yorktech.edu
JONES, Melinda, L .... 901-678-2690. 460 B
mljones6@memphis.edu
JONES, Melissa, A .... 910-678-8474. 360 D
jonesma@faytechcc.edu
JONES, Melvin .... 304-766-3061. 530 C
mjones55@wvstateu.edu
JONES, Michelle, M .... 570-577-2404. 411 A
michelle.jones@bucknell.edu
JONES, Mike .... 601-925-3819. 268 A
jones01@mc.edu
JONES, Mike .... 325-649-8830. 473 F
mjones@hputx.edu
JONES, Monica .... 859-985-3795. 192 F
jonesmo@berea.edu
JONES, Murel, M .... 252-335-3944. 367 C
mmjones@mail.ecsu.edu
JONES, Nancy .... 714-241-6209... 39 I
njones@coastline.edu
JONES, Nancy, A .... 816-654-7039. 275 K
njones@kcumb.edu
JONES, Ned, J .... 518-783-2423. 340 J
jones@siena.edu
JONES, Nicholas, P .... 814-865-2505. 426 A
npj1@psu.edu
JONES, Nikki .... 912-583-3287. 122 B
njones@bpc.edu
JONES, Nolan .... 972-825-7970. 481 F
nojones@sagu.edu
JONES, Norm .... 970-247-2929... 84 G
norm.jones@pueblocc.edu
JONES, Norman .... 256-372-8653..... 1 A
norman.jones@aamu.edu
JONES, Pamela .... 225-771-5763. 206 J
pamela_jones@subr.edu
JONES, Pamela, R .... 716-880-2451. 330 F
pamela.r.jones@medaille.edu
JONES, Para, M .... 330-494-6170. 389 F
pjones@starkstate.edu
JONES, Patricia .... 301-736-3631. 216 B
patricia.jones@msbbcs.edu
JONES, Patricia .... 863-297-1025. 110 H
pjones@polk.edu
JONES, Patricia, C .... 636-227-2100. 276 F
patricia.jones@logan.edu
JONES, Patrick .... 518-464-8500. 324 B
pjones@excelsior.edu
JONES, Patty .... 727-341-3141. 112 E
jones.patty@spcollege.edu
JONES, Paul, A .... 478-445-5148. 125 A
paul.jones@gcsu.edu
JONES, Paulette .... 405-912-9020. 395 K
pjones@hc.edu
JONES, Peter .... 215-204-2044. 433 K
peter.jones@temple.edu
JONES, Phil .... 772-546-5534. 106 N
philjones@hsbc.edu
JONES, Philip .... 717-245-1740. 414 H
jonesph@dickinson.edu
JONES, JR., Philip, M ... 704-687-0514. 368 E
pmjones@uncc.edu
JONES, Phillip .... 773-291-6245. 142 D
pjones140@ccc.edu
JONES, Pocahantas .... 252-862-1222. 363 A
jonesp@roanokechowan.edu
JONES, R. Channing .... 910-272-3600. 363 B
cjones@robeson.edu
JONES, Rachel .... 413-755-4480. 233 A
rejones@stcc.edu
JONES, Randall, F .... 214-648-6846. 493 E
randall.jones@utsouthwestern.edu
JONES, Randy .... 302-857-6230... 93 C
ljones@desu.edu
JONES, Randy .... 805-565-7048... 76 D
rjones@westmont.edu
JONES, Randy .... 304-384-5385. 529 E
rjones@concord.edu
JONES, Rauchelle .... 281-283-2536. 489 C
jonesrau@uhcl.edu
JONES, Rene .... 870-733-6722... 21 I
rjones@midsouthcc.edu
JONES, Richard .... 718-270-5128. 319 A
richardj@mec.cuny.edu
JONES, Richard .... 856-256-4040. 305 E
jonesri@rowan.edu
JONES, Robert .... 903-823-3315. 482 D
robert.jones@texarkanacollege.edu
JONES, Robert .... 303-762-6913... 81 G
robert.jones@denverseminary.edu
JONES, Robert .... 239-732-3753. 101 O
rrjones@edison.edu
JONES, Robert .... 401-232-6027. 438 K
rjones10@bryant.edu
JONES, Robert, A .... 317-788-3304. 173 I
rjones@uindy.edu
JONES, Robert, H .... 304-293-4611. 530 D
robert.jones@mail.wvu.edu
JONES, Robert, J .... 518-956-8010. 341 D
presmail@albany.edu
JONES, Robert, P .... 915-831-3112. 472 B
rjones35@epcc.edu
JONES, Robin .... 575-769-4921. 309 F
robin.jones@clovis.edu
JONES, Rockwell, F .... 740-368-3000. 387 J
rfjones@owu.edu
JONES, Ronald, L .... 901-272-5100. 456 F
rjones@mca.edu
JONES, Rosalie, I .... 215-596-8697. 435 H
r.jones@usciences.edu
JONES, Rose .... 256-331-5313..... 6 A
jonesr@nwscc.edu
JONES, Sam .... 850-729-4929. 109 I
joness@nwfsc.edu
JONES, Sam .... 601-477-4038. 267 F
sam.jones@jcjc.edu
JONES, Samuel .... 731-989-6992. 454 J
sjones@fhu.edu
JONES, Samuel, B .... 843-953-6367. 443 A
jonessa@cofc.edu
JONES, Samuel, E .... 757-221-2565. 503 N
sejone@wm.edu
JONES, Sarah, L .... 540-464-7667. 515 B
jonessl10@vmi.edu
JONES, Scott .... 765-455-9380. 168 A
scotjone@iuk.edu
JONES, Serene .... 212-280-1403. 349 A
sjones@uts.columbia.edu
JONES, Sha-Ron .... 704-216-6001. 356 D
shajones@livingstone.edu
JONES, Shalonda .... 972-773-8650. 450 G
sjones@national.edu
JONES, Sharon .... 760-921-5428... 58 C
sheri.jones@paloverde.edu
JONES, Sharon .... 503-943-7314. 408 F
joness@up.edu
JONES, Sheba .... 312-662-4131. 139 F
sjones@adler.edu
JONES, Sheila Dove .... 570-389-4027. 427 H
sjones@bloomu.edu
JONES, Sheri .... 610-861-5451. 425 D
sjones@northampton.edu
JONES, Sheri .... 858-513-9240. 175 F
Sheri.Jones@ashford.edu
JONES, Sloan .... 678-717-3836. 133 D
sloan.jones@ung.edu
JONES, Stacey .... 479-788-7302... 24 A
stacey.jones@uafs.edu
JONES, Stanley .... 229-333-5727. 134 B
sjones@valdosta.edu
JONES, Stanton, L .... 630-752-5004. 163 F
stanton.jones@wheaton.edu
JONES, Stephen .... 864-242-5100. 441 D
JONES, Stephen, M .... 801-422-8271. 495 D
stephen_jones@byu.edu
JONES, Stephen, W .... 330-569-5128. 380 I
jonessw@hiram.edu
JONES, Steve .... 904-826-0084. 118 I
sjones@usa.edu
JONES, Steven .... 323-343-3830... 34 A
sjones@calstatela.edu
JONES, Stuart .... 260-665-4365. 173 E
joness@trine.edu
JONES, Stuart .... 435-586-7775. 497 A
jones@suu.edu
JONES, Sue .... 936-633-3209. 465 J
sjones@angelina.edu
JONES, Susan .... 573-592-1107. 285 D
susan.jones@williamwoods.edu
JONES, Tami, B .... 606-783-2080. 198 A
t.jones@moreheadstate.edu
JONES, Tamica .... 404-880-8126. 122 J
tjones@cau.edu
JONES, Teresa .... 225-216-8053. 202 H
jonest@mybrcc.edu
JONES, Thomas .... 765-998-5204. 173 C
thjones@taylor.edu
JONES, Thomas, H .... 704-406-4369. 354 C
tjones@gardner-webb.edu
JONES, Tim .... 850-245-0466. 114 J
tim.jones@flbog.edu
JONES, Tim .... 334-493-3573..... 5 E
twjones@lbwcc.edu
JONES, Tim .... 870-230-5117... 21 D
jonest@hsu.edu
JONES, Tim .... 501-812-2760... 22 G
thjones@pulaskitech.edu
JONES, Tim .... 410-827-5704. 214 C
tjones@chesapeake.edu
JONES, Tim .... 412-536-1139. 420 A
tim.jones@laroche.edu
JONES, Timothy Paul .... 502-897-4347. 199 B
tjones@sbts.edu
JONES, Tina, N .... 205-652-3497..... 9 F
tnj@uwa.edu
JONES, Todd .... 706-295-6339. 125 C
tjones@highlands.edu
JONES, Todd .... 515-964-6242. 177 B
tgjones@dmacc.edu
JONES, Todd .... 215-751-8167. 413 I
tjones@ccp.edu
JONES, Tom, O .... 870-759-4101... 25 K
tjones@wbcoll.edu
JONES, Tony .... 312-899-5136. 158 L
tonyjones@saic.edu
JONES, Tony .... 804-706-5235. 512 G
tjones@jtcc.edu
JONES, Tori .... 802-831-1237. 500 H
tjones@vermontlaw.edu
JONES, Trevor, H .... 410-334-2828. 221 D
tjones@worwic.edu
JONES, Trina .... 757-569-6720. 513 E
tjones@pdc.edu
JONES, V. Dale .... 434-223-6116. 505 E
djones@hsc.edu
JONES, Valerie .... 432-335-6412. 477 M
vjones@odessa.edu
JONES, Verma .... 870-575-8476... 24 E
jonesv@uapb.edu
JONES, Victoria .... 206-296-6363. 523 E
jonesv@seattleu.edu
JONES, Virgil, E .... 507-933-7449. 255 I
vjones@gustavus.edu
JONES, Virginia .... 972-273-3171. 471 B
vjones@dcccd.edu
JONES, W. Terrell .... 814-865-5906. 426 A
wtj1@psu.edu
JONES, Walter .... 562-908-3467... 60 I
walter.jones@riohondo.edu
JONES, Wayne .... 405-733-7450. 399 F
wzjones@rose.edu
JONES, Wendy .... 325-674-2359. 464 H
jonesw@acu.edu
JONES, William .... 706-880-8257. 128 A
wjones@lagrange.edu
JONES, William, H .... 803-754-4100. 443 C
JONES, Wilma .... 718-982-4001. 317 E
wilma.jones@csi.cuny.edu
JONES, Winfred .... 318-274-6344. 207 E
jones@gram.edu
JONES, Yolanda .... 622-254-3528. 269 A
yjones@mvsu.edu
JONES, Yvette, M .... 504-865-5259. 207 C
yjones@tulane.edu
JONES-HENDRICKSON,
Simon, B .... 340-692-4020. 555 E
sjonesh@live.uvi.edu
JONES JOHNSON,
Yosette .... 212-817-7700. 317 F
yjonesjohnson@gc.cuny.edu
JONES-MALONE,
Dionne .... 219-473-4305. 164 K
djonesmalone@ccsj.edu
JONES-SCHENK, Jan .... 801-274-3280. 498 E
jjonesschenk@wgu.edu
JONES SCHWEITZER,
Sharon .... 210-999-8406. 488 C
sjones@trinity.edu
JONES-SEARLE, Donna .. 860-253-3030... 88 C
djones-searle@asnuntuck.edu
JONES-VARNELL,
Karla (Page) .... 252-672-1751. 359 G
jonesp@cravencc.edu
JONES WATKINS,
Brenda .... 708-456-0300. 161 A
bwatkins@triton.edu
JONES-WILCOX,
Youlanda .... 731-286-3345. 460 F
ywilcox@dscc.edu
JONES-WILCOX,
Youlanda .... 731-286-3346. 460 F
ywilcox@dscc.edu
JONES-WILCOX,
Youlanda .... 731-286-3265. 460 F
ywilcox@dscc.edu
JONES-WILKINS,
Brenda .... 979-209-7264. 467 I
brendawilkins@blinn.edu
JONES-WOODIN,
Beryl, R .... 718-780-7957. 315 H
beryl.jones@brooklaw.edu
JONESHILL, Nancy .... 870-236-6901... 20 K
njoneshill@crc.edu
JONGEWARD, David, W 503-255-0332. 404 F
jongeward@multnomah.edu
JONGSMA KNAUSS,
Sonya .... 712-722-6024. 177 J
sonya.knauss@dordt.edu
JONSE, Paula .... 903-813-2059. 466 H
pjonse@austincollege.edu
JONTE-PACE, Diane, E ... 408-554-4751... 64 M
djontepace@scu.edu
JOO, Kay .... 213-487-0150... 42 K
aromc@dula.edu
JOPLIN, David .... 405-945-3317. 398 C
JORDAHL, Ronald, I .... 704-847-5600. 366 J
rjordahl@ses.edu
JORDAN, A. Dane .... 704-233-8026. 370 G
djordan@wingate.edu
JORDAN, Amanda .... 276-326-4348. 502 H
ajordan@bluefield.edu
JORDAN, Amber .... 706-295-6768. 125 F
ajordan@gntc.edu
JORDAN, Andy .... 803-508-7241. 440 G
jordana@atc.edu
JORDAN, Angela .... 843-661-8341. 443 G
angela.jordan@fdtc.edu
JORDAN, Angela .... 312-935-2002. 156 K
ajordan@robertmorris.edu
JORDAN, Augustus .... 802-443-5141. 499 H
jordan@middlebury.edu
JORDAN, Austina .... 706-245-7226. 124 D
ajordan@ec.edu
JORDAN, Belva Brown ... 918-610-8303. 398 I
belva.jordan@ptstulsa.edu
JORDAN, Ben .... 256-395-2211..... 7 C
benjordan@suscc.edu
JORDAN, Brian .... 718-489-5493. 338 G
bjordan@sfc.edu
JORDAN, Carol, W .... 704-337-2400. 365 G
jordanc@queens.edu

JORDAN, Cheryl ... 256-395-2211 ... 7 C
cjordan@suscc.edu
JORDAN, Cordell ... 405-682-1611. 397 E
cjordan@occc.edu
JORDAN, Corey ... 315-386-7319. 345 F
jordanc@canton.edu
JORDAN, Dave ... 443-518-3801. 215 E
djordan@howardcc.edu
JORDAN, Debi ... 281-425-6453. 475 I
djordan@lee.edu
JORDAN, Diane ... 573-334-9181. 276 I
diane@metrobusinesscollege.edu
JORDAN, Donald, K ... 212-650-7278. 317 D
djordan@aol.com
JORDAN, Edward, K ... 386-312-4083. 112 C
edwardjordan@sjrstate.edu
JORDAN, Elizabeth, P ... 302-295-1186 ... 94 E
elizabeth.p.jordan@wilmu.edu
JORDAN, Ellen ... 919-658-7755. 357 I
ejordan@moc.edu
JORDAN, Ellen, S ... 919-658-7755. 357 I
ejordan@moc.edu
JORDAN, Gillian ... 207-581-7700. 212 C
gillian@maine.edu
JORDAN, Gregory, D ... 423-652-4784. 455 I
gdjordan@king.edu
JORDAN, Herb ... 251-405-7135 ... 2 D
hjordan@bishop.edu
JORDAN, Holly ... 254-526-1128. 468 G
holly.jordan@ctcd.edu
JORDAN, Jane ... 404-712-1512. 124 E
jane.jordan@emory.edu
JORDAN, Jeffrey, C ... 206-281-2123. 523 C
jordaj2@spu.edu
JORDAN, Jessica ... 415-422-5455 ... 73 J
jgjordan@usfca.edu
JORDAN, John ... 425-889-7788. 521 G
john.jordan@northwestu.edu
JORDAN, Judy, G ... 615-547-1249. 454 A
jjordan@cumberland.edu
JORDAN, Katina ... 877-442-0505 ... 86 F
katina.jordan@rockies.edu
JORDAN, Katrina ... 513-556-3471. 390 G
katrina.jordan@uc.edu
JORDAN, Ken ... 610-420-6765. 153 C
kjordan@millikin.edu
JORDAN, Larry, W ... 301-736-3631. 216 B
larry.jordan@msbbcs.edu
JORDAN, Laurel ... 802-443-5626. 499 H
ljordan@middlebury.edu
JORDAN, Lorrie ... 714-628-4933 ... 60 H
jordan_lorrie@sccollege.edu
JORDAN, Lucille, A ... 603-882-6923. 296 B
ljordan@ccsnh.edu
JORDAN, Mary, V ... 423-439-4211. 459 C
jordanm@etsu.edu
JORDAN, Megan, K ... 781-283-3795. 237 F
mjordan@wellesley.edu
JORDAN, Melissa ... 336-278-7243. 354 B
mjordan@elon.edu
JORDAN, Michael ... 864-977-7058. 445 H
mike.jordan@ngu.edu
JORDAN, Michael, J ... 252-823-5166. 360 C
jordanm@edgecombe.edu
JORDAN, Michael, R ... 304-637-1311. 526 E
jordanm@dewv.edu
JORDAN, Nancy, E ... 908-526-1200. 305 B
njordan@raritanval.edu
JORDAN, Percy ... 409-984-6335. 486 H
jordanpj@lamarpa.edu
JORDAN, Peter ... 817-515-4501. 482 B
peter.jordan@tccd.edu
JORDAN, Richard ... 806-354-5401. 487 E
richard.jordan@ttuhsc.edu
JORDAN, Ronald ... 714-997-6815 ... 38 A
JORDAN, Sandra ... 803-641-3434. 448 A
JORDAN, Stephen ... 918-587-6789. 400 J
sjordan@twsweld.com
JORDAN, Stephen, M ... 303-556-3022 ... 83 D
smjordan@msudenver.edu
JORDAN, Susan ... 870-862-8131 ... 23 D
sjordan@southark.edu
JORDAN, Terry, J ... 601-977-7720. 270 A
tjordan@tougaloo.edu
JORDAN, Tiffany ... 918-587-6789. 400 J
tjordan@twsweld.com
JORDAN, Tim ... 937-769-1304. 373 H
tjordan@antioch.edu
JORDAN, Tracy ... 912-427-5861. 120 B
tjordan@altamahatech.edu
JORDAN, Tuajuanda, C ... 503-768-7100. 403 K
casdean@lclark.edu
JORDAN, Willis ... 312-980-9293. 148 D
wjordan@iadtchicago.com
JORDAN WAGNER,
James ... 931-372-3372. 460 A
jordanwagner@tntech.edu
JORDANO, Mark ... 814-871-7438. 416 K
jordan001@gannon.edu
JORDE, Brad ... 507-288-4563. 255 C
bjorde@crossroadscollege.edu
JORDEN, Steven ... 660-626-2529. 271 A
sjorden@atsu.edu
JORDON, Christina ... 863-638-2944. 119 D
cmjordon@webber.edu
JORDRE, Todd ... 605-626-3005. 451 I
todd.jordre@northern.edu
JORDT, Mary ... 406-756-3362. 286 B
mjordt@fvcc.edu
JORE, Katie ... 715-346-3710. 538 A
kjore@uwsp.edu
JORGENSEN, Colleen ... 303-914-6241 ... 84 I
JORGENSEN, Harlan, R ... 712-707-7333. 181 H
harlan@nwciowa.edu
JORGENSEN, Janice, E ... 701-788-4762. 371 E
Janice.Jorgensen@mayvillestate.edu
JORGENSEN, Jennifer ... 402-826-8261. 289 E
jennifer.jorgensen@doane.edu
JORGENSEN, Jerry ... 816-584-6445. 280 C
jerry.jorgensen@park.edu
JORGENSEN, Laurie ... 630-942-2755. 142 G
jorgensenl@cod.edu
JORGENSEN, Lin ... 727-864-8886. 101 N
jorgenly@eckerd.edu
JORGENSEN, Michael ... 435-283-7262. 498 A
michael.jorgensen@snow.edu
JORGENSEN, Patti ... 920-735-5649. 539 K
jorgensp@fvtc.edu
JORGENSEN, Ronald, A ... 712-274-5128. 181 B
jorgensenr@morningside.edu
JORGENSEN,
Stephen, R ... 573-882-6227. 283 C
jorgensens@missouri.edu
JORGENSEN-FUNK,
Sandy ... 619-594-6410 ... 35 D
jorgens1@mail.sdsu.edu
JORGENSON, Donald ... 701-662-1521. 372 D
donald.jorgenson@lrsc.edu
JORGENSON, Evelyn ... 479-619-4191 ... 22 C
ejorgenson@nwacc.edu
JORGENSON, Jan ... 360-538-4243. 520 B
jjorgens@ghc.edu
JORGENSON, Jo ... 480-517-8538 ... 15 D
jo.jorgenson@riosalado.edu
JOSAY, Ashley ... 724-838-7832. 433 E
josay@setonhill.edu
JOSCHKO, Brian ... 309-677-1002. 140 I
bjoschko@bradley.edu
JOSE, Jorge ... 317-856-1079. 167 E
jjv@iu.edu
JOSE, Jorge ... 812-856-2408. 167 F
jjv@indiana.edu
JOSE, Juana Clare ... 520-383-8401 ... 18 B
jjose@tocc.cc.az.us
JOSEPH, Beatriz ... 210-481-3936. 465 A
ijospeh@alamo.edu
JOSEPH, JR.,
Cheney, C ... 225-578-8491. 205 E
JOSEPH, Daniel, P ... 410-951-3549. 220 B
djoseph@coppin.edu
JOSEPH, Gerard ... 217-206-6724. 161 E
joseph.gerard@uis.edu
JOSEPH, Jann ... 734-487-1414. 242 D
jjosep10@emich.edu
JOSEPH, Josh ... 212-960-0083. 351 M
jjoseph@yu.edu
JOSEPH, Laurel ... 281-756-3500. 465 D
ljoseph@alvincollege.edu
JOSEPH, Mark ... 740-284-5870. 379 N
mjoseph@franciscan.edu
JOSEPH, Michael ... 219-464-6896. 174 E
michael.joseph@valpo.edu
JOSEPH, Mitch ... 937-484-1262. 392 C
jmjoseph@urbana.edu
JOSEPH, Noson ... 718-601-3523. 351 L
noson.jo@juno.com
JOSEPH, Patricia, A ... 484-365-8259. 422 D
joseph@lincoln.edu
JOSEPH, Richard ... 617-746-1990. 227 F
richard.joseph@hult.edu
JOSEPH, Sonya, F ... 407-582-7734. 118 M
sjoseph@valenciacollege.edu
JOSEPH, Stephen, M ... 724-287-8711. 411 C
steve.joseph@bc3.edu
JOSEPH, Susan ... 423-697-3136. 460 C
JOSEPH, Wendy ... 253-589-5822. 518 B
wendy.joseph@cptc.edu
JOSEPH MATTISON,
Sue ... 920-465-2050. 536 F
mattisons@uwgb.edu
JOSEPHS, Mell ... 610-436-2955. 430 A
mjosephs@wcupa.edu
JOSEPHS, Nadine, W ... 412-291-6298. 410 B
njosephs@aii.edu
JOSEPHSON, David ... 973-655-6956. 303 D
josephsond@mail.montclair.edu
JOSEY, Peige ... 334-222-6591 ... 5 E
pjosey@lbwcc.edu
JOSHEE, Jeet ... 562-985-4106 ... 33 F
jeet.joshee@csulb.edu
JOSHEE, Jeet ... 562-985-8330 ... 33 F
jeet.joshee@csulb.edu
JOSHI, Anupama ... 310-243-2046 ... 33 B
ajoshi@csudh.edu
JOSHUA, Kazi ... 814-332-3353. 409 D
kjoshua@allegheny.edu
JOSLIN, Dennis, A ... 402-354-7257. 291 B
dennis.joslin@methodistcollege.edu
JOSLIN, Mike ... 661-362-3260 ... 40 E
michael.joslin@canyons.edu
JOSLIN, Monica ... 413-662-5242. 230 C
m.joslin@mcla.edu
JOSS, Jamie ... 503-517-1261. 408 H
jjoss@warnerpacific.edu
JOST, Bruce ... 502-213-7264. 195 F
bruce.jost@kctcs.edu
JOST, Jenifer ... 402-941-6241. 290 K
jostj@midlandu.edu
JOST, Patricia, A ... 812-888-4225. 174 F
pjost@vinu.edu
JOST, Steve, A ... 301-860-4212. 220 A
sjost@bowiestate.edu
JOTHEN, Karen, G ... 651-690-6666. 263 O
kgjothen@stkate.edu
JOUGANATOS, Brandon ... 415-264-6635 ... 55 J
bjouganatos@nu.edu
JOVANOVICH, Donna ... 804-594-1576. 512 G
djovanovich@jtcc.edu
JOVELL, Kristi ... 802-865-5728. 499 A
kjovell@champlain.edu
JOWERS, Angel ... 205-652-3547 ... 9 F
ajowers@uwa.edu
JOWERS, Jeff ... 601-679-3570. 266 I
jjowers@eastms.edu
JOWI, Doreen ... 570-389-5247. 427 H
djowi@bloomu.edu
JOY, Frank ... 505-428-1225. 311 J
frank.joy@sfcc.edu
JOY, John ... 937-393-3431. 389 B
jjoy@sscc.edu
JOY, John, A ... 734-384-4226. 247 C
jjoy@monroeccc.edu
JOYCE, Charles ... 740-284-5327. 379 N
cjoyce@franciscan.edu
JOYCE, David, C ... 828-884-8264. 352 I
president@brevard.edu
JOYCE, Gerard ... 610-282-1100. 414 F
gerard.joyce@desales.edu
JOYCE, Jane ... 617-349-8785. 228 B
ajoyce5@lesley.edu
JOYCE, Kevin ... 239-280-1695 ... 98 K
kevin.joyce@avemaria.edu
JOYCE, Kevin ... 914-674-7775. 330 J
kjoyce@mercy.edu
JOYCE, Kimberly, L ... 302-739-3732 ... 93 D
kimjoyce@dtcc.edu
JOYCE, Mary ... 228-896-2517. 268 C
mary.joyce@mgccc.edu
JOYCE, Maureen ... 239-280-1516 ... 98 K
mauren.joyce@avemaia.edu
JOYCE, Paul ... 208-885-6338. 139 D
joyce@uidaho.edu
JOYCE, Teresa, M ... 770-423-6023. 127 N
tjoyce@kennesaw.edu
JOYCE-BRADY, Jean ... 617-732-2178. 233 E
jean.joyce-brady@mcphs.edu
JOYE, Teresa ... 510-649-2410 ... 46 B
tjoye@gtu.edu
JOYNER, Barry ... 912-478-5322. 126 C
joyner@georgiasouthern.edu
JOYNER, David, M ... 814-865-1086. 426 A
dmj14@psu.edu
JOYNER, Deborah ... 828-726-2311. 358 E
djoyner@cccti.edu
JOYNER, Jennifer ... 706-507-8956. 123 D
joyner_jennifer@columbusstate.edu
JOYNER, Jill ... 704-847-5600. 366 J
jjoyner@ses.edu
JOYNER, Laurie, M ... 937-327-7916. 393 E
ljoyner@wittenberg.edu
JOYNER, Mandy ... 864-225-7653. 444 A
mandyjoyner@forrestcollege.edu
JOYNER, Scott ... 803-321-5617. 445 G
scott.joyner@newberry.edu
JOYNER, SR., Stephen ... 704-330-1406. 355 K
sjoyner@jcsu.edu
JOYNER, Stephen, E ... 718-951-5114. 317 C
sjoyner@brooklyn.cuny.edu
JOYNER-GRAHAM,
JoAnn ... 718-270-4832. 319 A
jjoyner@mec.cuny.edu
JOYNTON, Olin ... 989-358-7246. 239 C
joyntono@alpenacc.edu
JOZAITIS, Judy ... 217-786-2200. 151 F
judy.jozaitis@llcc.edu
JROSKI, Linda, L ... 610-330-5017. 420 D
jroskil@lafayette.edu
JUARBE, Lorraine ... 787-763-6425. 549 J
ljuarbe@inter.edu
JUARBE, Myriam ... 787-720-4476. 553 D
asistenciaeconomica@mizpa.edu
JUAREZ, Benjamin ... 617-353-3334. 224 D
bjuarez@bu.edu
JUAREZ, David ... 210-434-6711. 477 N
djuarez4090@lake.ollusa.edu
JUAREZ, Elisa ... 520-494-5426 ... 12 P
elisa.juarez@centralaz.edu
JUAREZ, Reina ... 858-534-3755 ... 71 F
rjuarez@ucsd.edu
JUCHAU, Adrian ... 801-524-8158. 495 O
AJuchau@ldsbc.edu
JUCHEMS, Jane, J ... 319-352-8521. 183 E
jane.juchems@wartburg.edu
JUCHT, Craig ... 605-221-3110. 450 C
cjucht@kilian.edu
JUCKIEWICZ, Robert, W ... 516-463-6900. 326 D
robert.w.juckiewicz@hofstra.edu
JUDD, Cristle Collins ... 207-725-3578. 209 H
cjudd@bowdoin.edu
JUDD, Deborah ... 304-876-5287. 529 I
djudd@shepherd.edu
JUDD, Kimberly ... 802-387-6723. 499 E
kjudd@landmark.edu
JUDD, Matthew ... 909-274-4425 ... 55 A
mjudd@mtsac.edu
JUDD, Maureen ... 617-726-6069. 234 B
mjudd@mghihp.edu
JUDD, Philip, H ... 304-766-3333. 530 C
pjudd@wvstateu.edu
JUDD, Summer ... 731-989-6662. 454 J
sjudd@fhu.edu
JUDD, T. Randy ... 435-652-7641. 497 E
judd@dixie.edu
JUDD, Tim ... 270-789-5027. 193 D
tmjudd@campbellsville.edu
JUDE, China ... 718-997-2795. 319 C
china.jude@qc.cuny.edu
JUDGE, Anne Marie ... 518-445-3209. 313 C
ajudg@albanylaw.edu
JUDGE, Jeff ... 952-358-7272. 260 B
jeff.judge@normandale.edu
JUDGE, Joseph ... 609-896-5121. 305 D
jjudge@rider.edu
JUDGE, Laurie, L ... 765-641-3787. 163 L
lljudge@anderson.edu
JUDGE, Mark ... 321-253-2929. 102 K
mjudge@cci.edu
JUDGE, Michael ... 937-708-5743. 393 A
mjudge@wilberforce.edu
JUDGE, Peter ... 803-323-2160. 449 G
judgep@winthrop.edu
JUDGE, William ... 617-682-1553. 226 D
wjudge@eds.edu
JUDKINS, Brooke ... 877-314-2380 ... 57 G
bjudkins@pacificoaks.edu
JUDKINS, Fred ... 334-727-8011 ... 8 A
fjudkins@mytu.tuskegee.edu
JUDY, Joyce, M ... 802-828-2800. 501 C
judyj@ccv.edu
JUDY, Thomas, L ... 775-784-6662. 294 J
tomj@unr.edu
JUE, Jeffrey, K ... 215-887-5511. 437 C
jjue@wts.edu
JUEDES, Scott ... 781-283-1000. 237 F
sjuedes@wellesley.edu
JUEHNE, Elizabeth ... 618-537-6529. 152 G
bjuehne@mckendree.edu
JUERGENS, Valorie ... 269-467-9945. 242 H
vjuergens@glenoaks.edu
JUHL, Lavonne ... 501-812-2293 ... 22 G
ljuhl@pulaskitech.edu
JUKOSKI, Mary Ellen ... 860-701-5027 ... 90 G
jukoski_m@mitchell.edu
JULIA, Jake ... 847-491-2912. 155 D
jjulia@northwestern.edu
JULIAN, Augusta, A ... 859-246-6501. 194 L
augusta.julian@kctcs.edu
JULIAN, Carol ... 386-822-7738. 117 C
cjulian@stetson.edu
JULIAN, Charity ... 812-749-1235. 171 K
cjulian@oak.edu
JULIAN, Elizabeth, A ... 706-771-4049. 121 D
ejulian@augustatech.edu
JULIAN, James ... 617-287-7050. 228 E
jjulian@umassp.edu
JULIAN, Jeff ... 847-214-7823. 144 F
jjulian@elgin.edu
JULIAN, Kimberly ... 404-727-8782. 124 E
kjulian@emory.edu
JULIAN, Kris, N ... 336-629-2758. 362 H
knjulian@randolph.edu
JULIAN, Leisa ... 765-285-1104. 164 B
lijulian@bsu.edu
JULIAN, Tijuana, S ... 417-873-7215. 273 H
tjulian@drury.edu
JULIAN, Tracey ... 423-636-7300. 462 E
tjulian@tusculum.edu
JULIANO, Ben ... 530-898-5963 ... 33 A
bjuliano@csuchico.edu
JULIEN, Earlye, A ... 563-884-5476. 182 A
earlye.julien@palmer.edu
JULIEN, Heidi ... 205-348-4610 ... 8 D
hjulien@slis.ua.edu

JULIN, Paul .... 315-268-7718. 320 A
pjulin@clarkson.edu
JULIO, Elizabeth .... 906-353-4600. 245 A
liz@kbocc.org
JULIO, Liz .... 906-353-4600. 245 A
liz@kbocc.org
JULIUS, Daniel, J .... 212-317-3558. 341 C
dan.julius@levininstitute.org
JULIUS, David .... 815-967-7322. 157 B
djulius@rockfordcareercollege.edu
JULIUS, James .... 760-757-2121... 54 G
jjulius@miracosta.edu
JULIUS, Peg .... 319-398-1274. 180 J
pjulius@kirkwood.edu
JULIUS, Peg .... 319-398-1274. 180 J
peg.julius@kirkwood.edu
JUMP, Jonathan, D .... 740-362-3440. 383 H
jjump@mtso.edu
JUMP, Jonathon, D .... 765-361-6206. 175 B
jumpj@wabash.edu
JUMPER, Barbara .... 202-274-5140... 97 A
bjumper@udc.edu
JUMPER, G. Robin .... 850-263-3261... 98 N
grjumper@baptistcollege.edu
JUMPS, Tressa .... 623-845-3809... 14 M
tressa.jumps@gcmail.maricopa.edu
JUNE, Jan, J .... 585-785-1273. 324 D
juneje@flcc.edu
JUNE, Jane .... 508-854-4517. 232 F
jjune@qcc.mass.edu
JUNE, Vincent .... 678-891-2340. 125 G
vincent.june@gpc.edu
JUNEJA, Renu .... 219-464-6880. 174 E
renu.juneja@valpo.edu
JUNG, Barnabas .... 415-371-0002... 57 B
JUNG, Holly .... 512-313-3000. 469 L
holly.jung@concordia.edu
JUNG, Hyun Shim .... 636-327-4645. 277 K
librarian@midwest.edu
JUNG, Jimmy .... 207-581-1591. 212 B
JUNG WHANG, Eui .... 323-643-0301... 27 N
JUNGKUNTZ, David .... 360-752-8355. 517 B
djungkun@btc.ctc.edu
JUNGO, Rene .... 918-293-5026. 398 B
rene.jungo@okstate.edu
JUNISBAI, Barbara .... 909-607-7304... 59 G
barbara_junisbai@pitzer.edu
JUNKER, Linda, K .... 301-447-5306. 217 B
junker@msmary.edu
JUNKER, Tercio, B .... 317-937-9336. 165 B
tjunker@cts.edu
JUNKERMAN,
Charles, L .... 650-723-6866... 68 E
clj@stanford.edu
JUNKIN, Lawrence .... 410-857-2256. 216 E
cjunkin@mcdaniel.edu
JUNN, Ellen .... 408-924-2400... 36 A
ellen.junn@sjsu.edu
JUNOR, Bill .... 914-251-6460. 344 D
bill.junor@purchase.edu
JURASEK, Richard, T ...... 716-880-2202. 330 F
richard.t.jurasek@medaille.edu
JURENOVICH, David, M . 210-829-6007. 490 A
davidj@uiwtx.edu
JURGELA, Linda .... 617-735-9920. 226 B
jurgela@emmanuel.edu
JURGENS, Ronald .... 800-567-2344. 532 E
rjurgens@menominee.edu
JURGENS, William, K ...... 321-674-8032. 104 H
bjurgens@fit.edu
JURICH, Tom .... 502-852-5732. 200 D
jurich@louisville.edu
JURICK, Donna, M .... 512-448-8412. 479 C
donnaj@stedwards.edu
JURMA, William .... 308-865-8521. 292 H
jurmaw@unk.edu
JUSKEVICE, Leigh .... 207-948-9208. 211 I
ljuskevice@unity.edu
JUSKIEWICZ,
Mary Kathryn .... 802-728-1319. 501 F
mjuskiewicz@vtc.edu
JUSSEAUME, Richard ...... 330-490-7102. 392 H
rjusseaume@walsh.edu
JUSTER, Fern, R .... 914-594-4507. 334 A
fern_juster@nymc.edu
JUSTICE, Brooke .... 270-901-1001. 196 E
brooke.justice@kctcs.edu
JUSTICE, George .... 573-884-4178. 283 C
justiceg@missouri.edu
JUSTICE, Josh .... 276-376-4517. 511 C
jvj6e@uvawise.edu
JUSTICE, Joshua .... 276-376-4514. 511 C
jvj6e@uvawise.edu
JUSTICE, Katherine .... 281-283-2160. 489 C
justice@uhcl.edu
JUSTICE, Lorraine .... 585-475-5436. 337 L
lxjpgd@rit.edu
JUSTICE, Melinda .... 606-886-3863. 194 K
melinda.justice@kctcs.edu
JUSTICE, Stephen, C ...... 949-451-5212... 67 B
cjustice@ivc.edu
JUSTICE, Teresa, R .... 803-323-2460. 449 G
justicet@winthrop.edu
JUSTIS, Janet .... 757-789-1723. 512 D
jjustis@es.vccs.edu
JUSTIZ, Manuel, J .... 512-471-7255. 491 C
mjustiz@mail.utexas.edu
JUUSELA, Kari .... 617-266-1400. 223 D

K

KAAI, Elmer .... 808-956-4153. 136 B
elmerk@hawaii.edu
KAANOI, Aulani .... 808-739-8394. 135 D
akaanoi@chaminade.edu
KAASA, Teri, L .... 919-536-7249. 360 B
kaasat@durhamtech.edu
KAATRUDE, Peter, B ...... 409-984-6216. 486 H
peter.kaatrude@lamarpa.edu
KAATZ, Forrest .... 575-461-4413. 309 M
forrestk@mesalands.edu
KAAZ, Barry .... 785-460-5429. 185 P
barry.kaaz@colbycc.edu
KAAZ, Lisa .... 408-741-2065... 75 L
lisa.kaaz@westvalley.edu
KABAT LENSCH, Ellen ... 563-336-3331. 177 L
ekabat@eicc.edu
KABBAZ, Michael, S ...... 513-529-2075. 384 G
mkabbaz@miamioh.edu
KABENGELE, Blanche ..... 513-618-1926. 376 K
bkabengele@ccms.edu
KABETZKE, Donald .... 214-333-5305. 470 D
donaldk@dbu.edu
KABISATPATHY, Ashok .. 803-793-5105. 443 E
kabisatpathya@denmarktech.edu
KABISATPATHY,
Bijayalaxmi .... 803-793-5196. 443 E
kabisatpathyk@denmark.edu
KACERIK, Amy .... 860-412-7268... 89 E
akacerik@qvcc.commnet.edu
KACHEL, Tim .... 701-252-3467. 373 D
kachel@jc.edu
KACHUR, John .... 412-434-6626. 415 F
bksduquesne@bncollege.com
KACZMAR, Debra .... 831-770-6145... 46 G
dkaczmar@hartnell.edu
KACZMARCZYK, Joseph 215-871-6652. 430 D
josephk@pcom.edu
KACZMAREK, Christine .. 518-580-5813. 341 A
ckaczmar@skidmore.edu
KACZOR, Adrian .... 561-912-2166. 103 C
akaczor@evergladesuniversity.edu
KACZOROWSKI, Robert .. 856-227-7200. 300 B
rkaczorowski@camdencc.edu
KACZVINSKY, Don .... 318-257-4805. 207 F
dkaczv@latech.edu
KADA, Solange .... 707-256-7186... 55 F
skada@napavalley.edu
KADAVY, Matthew, T ...... 402-465-2323. 291 G
mtk@nebrwesleyan.edu
KADDEN, Jerome, H ...... 410-484-7200. 217 D
KADEL, Andrew .... 646-717-9744. 325 B
kadel@gts.edu
KADEL, Jim .... 740-351-3270. 388 N
jkadel@shawnee.edu
KADISH, Alan .... 212-463-0400. 348 B
alan.kadish@touro.edu
KADISH, Alan .... 212-463-0400... 69 K
alan.kadish@touro.edu
KADISH, Alan .... 212-463-0400... 69 J
alan.kadish@touro.edu
KADISH, Alan, H .... 914-594-4600. 334 A
alan_kadish@nymc.edu
KADISH, Steven .... 617-373-2226. 235 F
KADUC, Maria .... 701-671-2616. 372 E
maria.kaduc@ndscs.edu
KAEGI, Keli, A .... 413-597-4233. 238 D
keli.a.kaegi@williams.edu
KAEPPNER, Jenny .... 513-244-4298. 377 G
jenny_kaeppner@mail.msj.edu
KAESER, Martha .... 636-227-2100. 276 F
martha.kaeser@logan.edu
KAESS, Almabeth .... 719-384-6857... 83 M
almabeth.kaess@ojc.edu
KAFF, Pinches .... 718-854-2290. 315 B
rabbikaff@bhsy.org
KAFTAN, John .... 315-792-3102. 349 F
jkaftan@utica.edu
KAGAN, Aaron .... 303-629-8200... 87 F
KAGAN, Aleksandra .... 718-261-5800. 315 F
akagan@bramsonort.edu
KAGAN, Israel .... 303-629-8200... 87 F
KAHALAS, Harvey .... 312-906-6596. 147 F
kahalas@stuart.iit.edu
KAHALAS, Judith .... 617-427-0060. 232 G
jkahalas@rcc.mass.edu
KAHAN, Miriam .... 818-299-5500... 75 E
mkahan@westcoastuniversity.edu
KAHKEDJIAN, George .... 480-731-8102... 14 I
george.kahkedjian@domail.maricopa.edu
KAHKOLA, Shane .... 606-337-1512. 193 F
skahkola@ccbbc.edu
KAHL, Michael, D .... 585-389-2890. 332 D
mkahl6@naz.edu
KAHLE, David, J .... 617-627-3435. 237 C
david.kahle@tufts.edu
KAHLE, Lisa .... 607-753-5793. 343 B
lisa.kahle@cortland.edu
KAHLER, Dean, R .... 501-683-7302... 24 B
drkahler@ualr.edu
KAHLER, Jay, L .... 402-465-2169. 291 G
jlk@nebrwesleyan.edu
KAHLER, Josephine .... 304-357-4835. 527 H
josephinekahler@ucwv.edu
KAHLER, Kari, L .... 231-995-1228. 248 B
kkahler@nmc.edu
KAHLER, Ken .... 413-545-2619. 228 F
umass@bkstr.com
KAHLER, Lewis .... 315-792-5537. 331 I
lkahler@mvcc.edu
KAHLER, Mark .... 731-661-5543. 462 F
mkahler@uu.edu
KAHLER, William .... 619-239-0391... 36 D
wkahler@cwsl.edu
KAHLIG, Charla .... 254-295-5436. 490 B
ckahlig@umhb.edu
KAHN, Alfred .... 281-283-2600. 489 C
kahn@uhcl.edu
KAHN, Amy .... 877-798-0584... 86 F
amy.kahn@rockies.edu
KAHN, Amy .... 585-395-2126. 342 F
akahn@brockport.edu
KAHN, Avi .... 718-382-8702. 351 B
KAHN, Carrie, W .... 716-270-5167. 323 I
kahn@ecc.edu
KAHN, Fito .... 512-472-4133. 480 G
fito.kahn@ssw.edu
KAHN, Henry .... 415-476-1683... 72 A
henry.kahn@ucsf.edu
KAHN, Jay, V .... 603-358-2114. 298 F
jkahn@keene.edu
KAHN, Patricia .... 732-224-2061. 299 G
pkahn@brookdalecc.edu
KAHN, Shirley, S .... 205-934-0177..... 8 E
kahn@uab.edu
KAHN-JETTER, Zella .... 360-491-4700. 522 G
zkahnjetter@stmartin.edu
KAHNE, Stephanie .... 405-974-2335. 400 K
skahne@uco.edu
KAHOL, Pawan .... 620-235-4223. 189 L
pkahol@pittstate.edu
KAHR, Audra .... 610-606-4630. 412 I
ajhoffma@cedarcrest.edu
KAHRL, Sarah, H .... 740-427-5154. 382 J
kahrls@kenyon.edu
KAHWAJIAN, Z. Greg ..... 626-873-2181... 55 C
KAHWAJY-ANDERSON,
Joan .... 434-791-5624. 502 D
jkahwajy@averett.edu
KAI KAI, Deborah .... 410-752-4710. 510 B
dkaikai@stratford.edu
KAIL, Pam .... 870-933-7903... 19 L
pkail@asusystem.edu
KAIN, Douglas .... 209-384-6344... 54 D
kain.d@mccd.edu
KAIN, Kassi .... 509-313-4100. 520 A
kain@gonzaga.edu
KAIN GRAY, Karol .... 919-962-3795. 368 D
kkgray@unc.edu
KAINTH, Pritpal .... 516-876-3207. 343 D
kainthp@oldwestbury.edu
KAIO, Christopher .... 713-221-8430. 489 D
kaioc@uhd.edu
KAIRO, Moses, T .... 410-651-6072. 219 E
mkairo@umes.edu
KAISER, Chris, A .... 617-253-4500. 233 B
KAISER, David, M .... 305-237-7445. 109 D
dkaiser@mdc.edu
KAISER, Joyce .... 716-827-2445. 348 G
kaiserj@trocaire.edu
KAISER, Kenneth, H .... 215-204-6545. 433 K
ken.kaiser@temple.edu
KAISER, Larry .... 215-707-8773. 433 K
larry.kaiser@temple.edu
KAISER, Larry, R .... 215-707-8773. 433 K
larry.kaiser@temple.edu
KAISER, Melissa, D .... 215-972-2002. 426 Y
mkaiser@pafa.edu
KAISER, Nancy .... 618-468-3315. 150 G
nkaiser@lc.edu
KAISER, William .... 209-575-6835... 77 J
kaiserw@yosemite.cc.ca.us
KAISRLIK, Linda .... 407-628-5870. 102 K
lkaisrlik@cci.edu
KAIVOLA, Karen .... 612-330-1024. 253 H
kaivola@augsburd.edu
KAJIWARA, Robert .... 808-245-8236. 136 H
kajiwara@hawaii.edu
KAKAR, Casandra .... 602-285-7607... 15 C
casandra.kakar@phoenixcollege.edu
KAKOULIDIS, Sofia .... 516-463-6810. 326 D
sofia.kakoulidis@hofstra.edu
KAKUGAWA-LEONG,
Alyson, Y .... 808-974-7642. 136 A
alyson@hawaii.edu
KALAFATIS, Lara, A .... 216-368-4244. 375 J
lara.kalafatis@case.edu
KALAKONAS, Dia .... 603-428-2417. 297 D
dkalakonas@nec.edu
KALANTZIS, Mary .... 217-333-0960. 162 A
kalantzi@illinois.edu
KALB, Melanie, T .... 740-368-3377. 387 J
mtkalb@owu.edu
KALBERER, Neal .... 701-355-8222. 373 E
nkalberer@umary.edu
KALBFLEISCH, Gary .... 206-546-5813. 523 F
garyk@shoreline.edu
KALBFLEISCH, Pamela ... 708-209-3255. 143 E
pamela.kalbfleisch@cuchicago.edu
KALBRENER, Kristen ...... 508-910-6503. 229 A
kkalbrener@umassd.edu
KALDAHL, Tim .... 402-554-2762. 293 A
tkaldahl@unomaha.edu
KALDENBERG, Tom .... 319-398-5561. 180 J
tom.kaldenberg@kirkwood.edu
KALDIS, Paula .... 978-681-0800. 233 C
paulad@mslaw.edu
KALE, Kathy .... 408-554-5021... 64 M
kkale@scu.edu
KALEMBA, Lena .... 815-455-8581. 152 F
lkalemba@mchenry.edu
KALER, Eric, W .... 612-626-1616. 264 G
upres@umn.edu
KALER, Robin .... 217-333-5010. 162 A
rkaler@illinois.edu
KALERT, David .... 210-341-1366. 477 L
dkalert@ost.edu
KALEVITCH, Maria, V ..... 412-397-4020. 431 I
kalevitch@rmu.edu
KALFAYAN, Stephanie .... 650-725-2788... 68 E
kalfayan@stanford.edu
KALIAN, Heidi .... 703-658-4304. 503 L
kalian@christendom.edu
KALICKI, Scott .... 603-524-3207. 295 L
skalicki@ccsnh.edu
KALIKOW, Theodora, J .. 207-780-4480. 212 H
kalikow@usm.maine.edu
KALINOWSKI, Teresa ..... 716-851-1051. 323 I
kalinowski@ecc.edu
KALIS, Michelle .... 860-231-5229... 92 F
mkalis@usj.edu
KALISA, Marie-Chantal ... 402-472-3747. 292 I
mkalisa2@unl.edu
KALK, Jonathan .... 808-245-8272. 136 H
kalk@hawaii.edu
KALKBRENNER, John ...... 641-269-4300. 178 H
kalkbren@grinnell.edu
KALKBRENNER,
Suzanne, K .... 518-629-4530. 326 G
s.kalkbrenner@hvcc.edu
KALKHORAN, Iraj .... 718-260-3619. 336 E
iraj@poly.edu
KALLIERIS, Nick, C .... 847-543-2476. 143 A
nkallieris@clcillinois.edu
KALLIN, Robert .... 717-337-6301. 417 B
rkallin@gettysburg.edu
KALLINA, Wendy .... 478-387-4746. 125 E
KALLSEN, Tammy .... 970-521-6730... 83 L
tammy.kallsen@njc.edu
KALM, Stephen .... 406-243-4970. 286 H
stephen.kalm@umontana.edu
KALMANOWITZ, Osher .. 718-645-0536. 331 G
mirrer@thejnet.com
KALMANSON, Dan, P ..... 973-378-9856. 307 C
daniel.kalmanson@shu.edu
KALOOSTIAN, Damita .... 602-243-8021... 15 F
damita.kaloostian@smcmail.maricopa.edu
KALOUPEK, W. Thomas . 540-231-6221. 515 C
kals@vt.edu
KALOUS, Annie .... 641-648-4611. 179 I
annie.kalous@iavalley.edu
KALOUSEK, Kay .... 480-219-6111. 271 A
kkalousek@atsu.edu
KALOYEROS, Alain .... 518-442-4533. 341 D
akaloyeros@albany.edu
KALSBEEK, David, H ...... 312-362-8706. 143 H
dkalsbee@depaul.edu
KALSKI, Lynn .... 940-696-8752. 493 F
lkalski@vernoncollege.edu
KALSOW, Susan .... 712-749-2250. 176 D
kalsow@bvu.edu
KALSOW, Susan .... 605-668-1584. 450 F
susan.kalsow@mtmc.edu
KALTCHEV, Matey .... 414-277-7544. 534 G
kaltchev@msoe.edu
KALTEFLEITER, Caroline . 607-753-4203. 343 B
caroline.kaltefleiter@cortland.edu
KALTENBAUGH, Louise . 504-286-5019. 206 K
lkaltenb@suno.edu
KALTHOFF, Theodore, J . 501-882-8830... 19 M
tjkalthoff@asub.edu
KALU, Mma .... 919-546-8350. 366 E
mkalu@shawu.edu

KALUSH, Paul 213-738-6818 68 C
accounting@swlaw.edu
KALWEIT, Clayton 847-566-6401 162 G
ckalweit@usml.edu
KALYN, Andrea 440-775-8200 385 H
Andrea.Kalyn@oberlin.edu
KAMAHELE, Ron 907-786-4680 10 H
afrck@uaa.alaska.edu
KAMALI, Reza 209-667-3153 35 B
rkamali@csustan.edu
KAMATH, Cecile, E 843-792-2252 445 B
kamath@musc.edu
KAMATH, Kiran 925-439-2181 42 A
kkamath@losmedanos.edu
KAMEDA, Stephen 808-984-3517 137 B
skameda@hawaii.edu
KAMENETSKIY, Boris 212-349-4330 325 D
borisk@globe.edu
KAMENETSKY, Shmuel 215-473-1212 433 J
talmudicalyeshiva@yahoo.com
KAMENETSKY, Sholom 215-477-1000 433 J
talmudicalyeshvia@yahoo.com
KAMIAB, Jane 336-770-3297 369 D
kamiabj@uncsa.edu
KAMIENIECKI, Sheldon 831-459-3212 72 C
sk1@ucsc.edu
KAMINSHINE, Steven, J 404-413-9040 126 E
skaminshine@gsu.edu
KAMINSKI, Charles 413-236-2105 231 A
ckaminsk@berkshirecc.edu
KAMINSKI, Donald 304-243-8152 531 H
dkaminski@wju.edu
KAMINSKI, Janice, M 724-480-3423 413 H
jan.kaminski@ccbc.edu
KAMINSKI, Linda 509-574-4635 525 G
lkaminski@yvcc.edu
KAMINSKI, Marie 414-847-3334 534 F
mkaminski@miad.edu
KAMINSKY, Frances, R 203-596-4580 90 I
fkaminsky@post.edu
KAMIONKOWSKI, Tamar 215-576-0800 431 E
tkamionkowski@rrc.edu
KAMLET, Lee 203-582-3641 91 A
lee.kamlet@quinnipiac.edu
KAMLET, Mark, S 412-268-6684 412 H
kamlet@andrew.cmu.edu
KAMM, Judy 781-891-2867 223 C
jkamm@bentley.edu
KAMMER, Roy 651-213-4863 256 B
rkammer@hazelden.edu
KAMMERER, Joe 417-255-7240 278 F
joekammerer@missouristate.edu
KAMMERZELL, Joan 360-752-8436 517 B
jkammerz@btc.ctc.edu
KAMOCHE, Njambi 847-925-6764 145 H
nkamoche@harpercollege.edu
KAMPF, Stephen 419-372-7485 374 K
skampf@bgsu.edu
KAMPS, Anne 920-498-6367 541 B
anne.kamps@nwtc.edu
KAMPS, Larissa 866-323-0233 60 E
KAMWITHI, Gina 419-755-4711 385 D
gkamwithi@ncstatecollege.edu
KAN-SHAGHAGHI, Kazem 704-886-6500 96 F
kazem.khan-shaghaghi@strayer.edu
KANACH, Nancy, A 609-258-5524 304 E
nkanach@princeton.edu
KANAREK, Berel 914-736-1500 335 E
KANAREK, E 914-736-1500 335 E
KANAREK, Robin 617-627-5902 237 C
robin.kanarek@tufts.edu
KANAWADA, Christine 518-694-7355 313 B
christine.kanawada@acphs.edu
KANDEL, David 636-949-4970 276 D
dkandel@lindenwood.edu
KANDUS-FISHER, Christopher 386-822-7200 117 C
ckandus@stetson.edu
KANE, Andrew 609-258-3469 304 E
kane@princeton.edu
KANE, Barry, S 212-854-1458 321 D
barry@columbia.edu
KANE, JR., Edward 518-437-4570 341 D
ekane@albany.edu
KANE, Elizabeth 201-761-6046 306 L
ekane@saintpeters.edu
KANE, Gerald, J 434-924-4274 511 B
gjk5y@virginia.edu
KANE, Janet 610-647-4400 418 I
jkane@immaculata.edu
KANE, Jeffrey 516-299-2917 329 C
jeffrey.kane@liu.edu
KANE, Jesse 605-256-5124 451 H
jesse.kane@dsu.edu
KANE, Kevin, M 610-660-3020 432 E
kevin.kane@sju.edu
KANE, Luanne 763-433-1297 257 P
luanne.kane@anokaramsey.edu
KANE, Marion, J 352-323-3617 108 S
kanem@lssc.edu
KANE, Melissa 951-222-8589 61 A
melissa.kane@rccd.edu
KANE, Melissa 951-222-8589 60 J
melissa.kane@rcc.edu
KANE, Michael 281-476-1501 479 F
michael.kane@sjcd.edu
KANE, Sara, F 863-638-7602 119 C
sara.kane@warner.edu
KANE, Scott, D 401-456-8061 439 F
skane@ric.edu
KANE, Teresa, L 336-841-9166 355 C
tkane@highpoint.edu
KANE, Terrence 607-777-2131 341 E
tkane@binghamton.edu
KANE, Terrence 607-777-5014 341 E
tkane@binghamton.edu
KANE, Thomas 401-254-3531 440 B
tkane@rwu.edu
KANE, Thomas, F 570-674-6223 424 A
tkane@misericordia.edu
KANE, Thomas, W 781-891-2340 223 C
tkane@bentley.edu
KANELOS, Gwen, E 708-209-3101 143 E
gwen.kanelos@cuchicago.edu
KANELOS, Peter 219-464-5022 174 E
peter.kanelos@valpo.edu
KANG, Soonhae 714-527-0691 43 H
KANGAS, Christie 319-273-2281 176 A
christie.kangas@uni.edu
KANGAS, Michelle 218-855-8034 258 B
mkangas@clcmn.edu
KANIA, Edward, A 704-894-2125 353 J
edkania@davidson.edu
KANIPE, H. Dean 828-652-0634 362 A
deank@mcdowelltech.edu
KANIS, David, R 773-995-2339 141 J
dkanis@csu.edu
KANJIRATHINKAL, Mathew 563-876-3353 177 I
mathewk@dwci.edu
KANKE, Frederick, W 936-639-1301 465 J
fkanke@angelina.edu
KANN, Stephanie, J 847-808-8444 163 G
skann@worshamcollege.com
KANNAN, Jack 919-735-5151 364 H
jek@waynecc.edu
KANNENWISCHER, Susan, E 614-236-6511 375 H
skannenwischer@capital.edu
KANNON, Gavindarajan 478-825-6320 124 H
kannong@fvsu.edu
KANNWISCHER, Kelly 714-556-3610 74 D
OfficeVPUA@vanguard.edu
KANOSKY, Joe, M 815-599-3513 146 D
joe.kanosky@highland.edu
KANOTZ, Ashley 304-829-7411 526 D
akanotz@bethanywv.edu
KANTARDJIEFF, Katherine 760-750-7204 35 A
kkantard@csusm.edu
KANTER, Connie 206-296-6148 523 E
kanterc@seattleu.edu
KANTER, Joshua 847-982-2500 146 C
jkanter@htc.edu
KANTNER, Joanne 815-825-2086 149 F
joanne.kantner@kishwaukeecollege.edu
KANTNER, Michael 856-256-4566 305 E
kantner@rowan.edu
KANTO, Kind 691-330-2620 546 B
kank@comfsm.fm
KANTOR, Ali 617-521-1038 236 G
ali.kantor@simmons.edu
KANTOR, Jeffrey 210-431-3996 477 N
jekantor@lake.ollusa.edu
KANTOR, Rebecca 303-315-6343 86 A
rebecca.kantor@ucdenver.edu
KANU, Andrew 804-524-5769 515 D
akanu@vsu.edu
KANWISCHER, Wanda, L 952-358-8123 260 B
wanda.kanwischer@normandale.edu
KAO, Chi-Chang 650-723-2300 68 E
KAO, Monica 628-448-0023 48 L
vp-admin@itsla.edu
KAOUDIS, Kathy 303-914-6341 84 I
kathy.koaudis@rrcc.edu
KAPALKA, Christopher 305-222-2815 103 L
ckapalka@careercollege.edu
KAPARTHI, Shashidhar 319-273-3050 176 A
shashi.kaparthi@uni.edu
KAPCSOS, Kathy 610-861-5499 425 D
kkapcsos@northampton.edu
KAPENSKI, Mark 973-408-3250 301 C
mkapenski@drew.edu
KAPFER, Mark 563-336-3315 177 L
mkapfer@eicc.edu
KAPLA, Dale, P 906-227-2920 248 A
KAPLAN, Anne, C 815-753-9503 154 I
akaplan@niu.edu
KAPLAN, Beth 617-879-2250 238 C
bkaplan@wheelock.edu
KAPLAN, Cary 510-436-1430 47 J
kaplan@hnu.edu
KAPLAN, John 315-386-7777 345 F
kaplanj@canton.edu
KAPLAN, John, A 315-267-2222 344 C
kaplanja@potsdam.edu
KAPLAN, Jonathan, A 410-843-6878 265 D
jonathan.kaplan@waldenu.edu
KAPLAN, Karen, K 713-500-3045 492 E
karen.k.kaplan@uth.tmc.edu
KAPLAN, Leonard, I 973-596-3638 303 G
leonard.i.kaplan@njit.edu
KAPLAN, Leslie, G 904-620-2649 116 B
leslie.kaplan@unf.edu
KAPLAN, Richard 617-732-2808 233 E
richard.kaplan@mcphs.edu
KAPLAN, Ronald, S 847-578-8840 157 F
ronald.kaplan@rosalindfranklin.edu
KAPLAN, Shelley 781-239-5840 222 D
skaplan1@babson.edu
KAPLAN, Steven, H 203-932-7276 92 E
skaplan@newhaven.edu
KAPLINSKY, Yoheved 212-799-5000 328 B
KAPLOWITZ, Craig 847-628-1126 149 B
ckaplowitz@judsonu.edu
KAPP, Alisha 217-854-3231 140 G
alisha.kapp@blackburn.edu
KAPP, John 704-403-1326 352 J
john.kapp@carolinashealthcare.org
KAPPAS, Constance 309-796-4845 140 E
Kappasc@bhc.edu
KAPPAUF, Linda 704-290-5215 363 G
lkappauf@spcc.edu
KAPPLAN, Bethany 727-726-1153 100 E
bethanykaplan@clearwater.edu
KAPPUS, Sheryl, S 254-659-7501 473 A
skappus@hillcollege.edu
KAPRIVE, Mark 561-803-2542 110 B
mark_kaprive@pba.edu
KAPTAIN, Laurence 225-578-9959 204 D
kaptain@lsu.edu
KAPTIK, Michael, W 808-956-8177 136 B
kaptik@hawaii.edu
KAPUR, Anup 484-384-2931 425 I
akapur@eastern.edu
KAPUR, Bobby 713-798-4951 467 F
kapur@bcm.edu
KARABETSOS, Michael, L 517-264-7109 250 B
mkarabet@sienaheights.edu
KARAHADIAN, Milton 619-849-2649 59 L
miltonkarahadian@pointloma.edu
KARAM, Robert 318-473-6475 205 A
rkaram@lsua.edu
KARAM, Vanessa 626-571-8811 74 B
vanessak@uwest.edu
KARAMAN, Ana 415-422-6263 73 J
takaraman@usfca.edu
KARAMARGIN, C.J 520-206-4850 17 A
ckaramargin@pima.edu
KARAMOL, Mark 567-661-7988 387 L
mark_karamol@owens.edu
KARANJA, Benson, M 404-627-2681 121 H
benson.karanja@beulah.org
KARANJA, Peter 404-627-2681 121 H
Peter.Karanja@beulah.org
KARAS, Gregory 617-236-8800 226 F
gkaras@fisher.edu
KARAS, Jane, A 406-756-3800 286 B
jkaras@fvcc.edu
KARAS, Jennifer 303-871-6793 86 B
jkaras@du.edu
KARAS, Tara 941-487-5001 115 D
tkaras@ncf.edu
KARAS, Tim 408-855-5167 75 K
tim.karas@wvm.edu
KARASINSKI, Tracy 401-825-2305 439 A
tkarasinski@ccri.edu
KARBHARI, Vistasp, M 817-272-2101 491 B
vkarbhari@uta.edu
KARBOWSKI, Suzanne 308-635-6067 293 E
karbowsk@wncc.edu
KARCHER, Jeff 715-346-3901 538 A
jkarcher@uwsp.edu
KARDAN, Sel 213-621-2200 40 B
KARGBO, Mariatu 703-212-7410 505 D
KARGES, Teri 843-863-7050 441 H
tkarges@csuniv.edu
KARIM, Ata 425-564-2206 517 A
ata.karim@bellevuecollege.edu
KARIM, Mohammad 508-999-8024 229 A
provost@umassd.edu
KARIMKHANI, Denise 254-295-4636 490 B
karimkhani@umhb.edu
KARIMPOR, Mehdi 562-408-6969 26 G
KARIMPOUR, Mehdi 562-408-6969 26 G
KARIUKI, Cheryl 601-629-3568 265 G
cheryl@alcorn.edu
KARKI, Bhagbat 716-888-2336 316 C
karkib@canisius.edu
KARL, Debbie 325-734-3640 486 C
debbie.karl@tstc.edu
KARLBERG, Anne Marie 360-383-3302 525 D
amkarlberg@whatcom.ctc.edu
KARLIN, Angela, L 660-543-4040 283 A
karlin@ucmo.edu
KARLIN, Barbara, H 415-442-7882 45 I
bkarlin@ggu.edu
KARLIN, Bree 928-505-3314 15 L
bkarlin@mohave.edu
KARLIN, Craig, E 785-628-4408 186 F
ckarlin@fhsu.edu
KARLIN, Jane 212-824-2212 325 G
jkarlin@huc.edu
KARLIN, Lisa, M 785-628-4232 186 F
lkarlin@fhsu.edu
KARLOFF, Michael 402-461-7473 289 I
mkarloff@hastings.edu
KARLOUTSOS, James, D 617-850-1290 227 E
jkarloutsos@hchc.edu
KARLSSON, Anette 216-687-2558 377 F
a.karlsson@csuohio.edu
KARLSTAD, Amanda 612-332-3361 253 G
KARMANN, Jason 717-545-4747 419 O
KARMANOVA, Tatiana 909-537-3986 34 E
tkarma@csusb.edu
KARMIS, Beth 312-949-7415 146 G
bkarmis@ico.edu
KARN, Samantha 317-791-5612 173 I
karns@uindy.edu
KARNES, Melinda Ann 716-673-3717 342 A
melinda.karnes@fredonia.edu
KARNES, Michael, S 585-753-3700 332 A
mkarnes@monroecc.edu
KARNES, Susan, J 816-415-5973 285 C
armstrongs@william.jewell.edu
KARNES, Valerie 760-384-6258 49 O
vkarnes@cerrocoso.edu
KARNS, Jennifer, E 703-416-1441 505 I
jkarns@ipsciences.edu
KARNS, Julie, A 609-896-5016 305 D
karns@rider.edu
KARNS, Leslie 801-878-1402 295 E
lkarns@roseman.edu
KAROL, Diana 903-510-2127 488 E
dkar@tjc.edu
KAROLLE-BERG, Julia 216-397-4193 381 R
jkarolle@jcu.edu
KAROW, Thomas, R 312-341-3512 157 D
tkarow@roosevelt.edu
KARP, Adam 916-484-8050 53 A
karpa@arc.losrios.edu
KARP, David 518-580-5779 341 A
dkarp@skidmore.edu
KARP, Emily 212-237-8488 318 D
ekarp@jjay.cuny.edu
KARP, Jeff 913-234-0634 185 L
jeff.karp@cleveland.edu
KARP, Robert, M 518-564-4106 344 B
karprm@plattsburgh.edu
KARP, Roberta 518-891-2915 335 A
bkarp@nccc.edu
KARPALO, Nikolay 610-526-6012 417 H
facilities@harcum.edu
KARPEL, Michael 760-252-2411 29 I
mkarpel@barstow.edu
KARPER, Barbara, M 315-445-4530 328 F
karperbm@lemoyne.edu
KARPF, Michael 859-323-5126 200 C
mkarpf@uky.edu
KARPILO, Lacy 907-786-1015 10 H
lnkarpilo@uaa.alaska.edu
KARPOVICH, Jeff, A 336-841-9011 355 C
jkarpovi@highpoint.edu
KARPP, Edward 818-240-1000 45 G
ekarpp@glendale.edu
KARR, Amanda 617-369-3391 236 F
akarr@smfa.edu
KARR, Charles, L 205-348-6405 8 D
ckarr@eng.ua.edu
KARR, Forrest 906-227-1826 248 A
fkarr@nmu.edu
KARR, Jason 301-295-3028 545 C
jason.carr@usuhs.edu
KARR, Mary 414-256-1251 535 A
karrm@mtmary.edu
KARR, Susan 281-351-3644 476 A
susan.karr@lonestar.edu
KARRAKER, Katherine 304-293-4611 530 D
katherine.karraker@mail.wvu.edu
KARRICK, Cathy 618-545-3182 149 D
ckarrick@kaskaskia.edu
KARRIKER, W. Keith 864-833-8220 446 D
kkarriker@presby.edu
KARRY, Cathy 626-396-2321 28 P
cathy.karry@artcenter.edu
KARSHMER, Judith 415-422-2959 73 J
jfkarshmer@usfca.edu

KARSON, Kimberly, M ... 330-972-7608. 390 E
kmorgan@uakron.edu
KARSTEN, Suzanne ... 773-477-4822... 57 E
skarsten@pacificcollege.edu
KARTJE, Jean, V ... 630-942-4516. 142 G
kartjej@cod.edu
KARVIA, Nick ... 714-992-7009... 56 F
nkarvia@fullcoll.edu
KARWOCKI, Michele ... 603-271-6484. 296 C
mkarwocki@ccsnh.edu
KARWOWSKI, Sharon ... 607-844-8222. 347 I
karwows@TC3.edu
KASBOHM, Kristine, E ... 716-888-8407. 316 C
kasbohmk@canisius.edu
KASDIN, Robert ... 212-854-9967. 321 D
rk2052@columbia.edu
KASDORF, Michael ... 217-234-5431. 150 D
mkasdorf@lakeland.cc.il.us
KASE, Robert ... 815-740-3367. 162 F
rkase@stfrancis.edu
KASE, Ronald ... 201-684-7287. 305 A
rkase@ramapo.edu
KASELOUSKAS, Mary ... 413-265-2306. 225 C
kaselouskasm@elms.edu
KASEM, Shahed ... 708-237-5000. 155 B
skasem@nc.edu
KASEY, Jay, D ... 614-293-9701. 386 E
kasey.3@osu.edu
KASEY, Tina ... 270-686-2110. 192 G
tina.kasey@brescia.edu
KASH, Elizabeth, F ... 516-877-3247. 313 A
kash@adelphi.edu
KASHACK, Susan ... 707-664-2122... 36 B
susan.kashack@sonoma.edu
KASHAN, Cindy ... 845-434-5750. 347 A
ckashan@sunysullivan.edu
KASHIMA, Stephanie ... 408-741-2119... 75 L
stephanie.kashima@westvalley.edu
KASHIWADA, Keith ... 808-734-9578. 136 E
kashiwad@hawaii.edu
KASIMATIS, Margaret ... 310-338-3790... 53 E
mkasimat@lmu.edu
KASKEL, Roberta ... 504-865-3860. 205 H
rekaskel@loyno.edu
KASLER, Brian ... 217-757-1190. 313 H
bkasler@funeraleducation.org
KASLYN, SJ, Robert, J ... 202-319-5492... 94 G
kaslyn@cua.edu
KASNICK, Pat ... 315-279-5228. 328 D
pkasnick@mail.keuka.edu
KASPER, Beverly ... 773-508-7478. 151 H
bkasper@luc.edu
KASPER, Chet ... 906-248-8431. 240 J
ckasper@bmcc.edu
KASPER, Lisa, A ... 973-655-6911. 303 D
kasperl@mail.montclair.edu
KASPRZAK, Ken ... 847-947-5575. 153 I
kkasprzak@nl.edu
KASSA, Adane, G ... 708-709-7916. 156 A
akassa@prairiestate.edu
KASSA, Zewdnesh ... 973-877-3107. 301 H
zkassa@essex.edu
KASSEBAUM, Denise ... 303-724-7100... 86 A
denise.kassebaum@ucdenver.edu
KASSEBAUM,
Elizabeth, W ... 843-953-5747. 443 A
kassebaume@cofc.edu
KASSEL, Paul ... 845-257-3860. 342 B
kasselp@newpaltz.edu
KASSNER, Scott ... 805-893-8000... 72 B
skassner@ltsc.ucsb.edu
KAST, Christina ... 304-204-4341. 530 C
ckast@wvstateu.edu
KASTAN, Shira ... 305-284-2618. 118 F
skastan@miami.edu
KASTER, James, D ... 540-458-8720. 516 A
jdkaster@wlu.edu
KASTL, Camille ... 402-461-7439. 289 I
ckastl@hastings.edu
KASTNER, Marc, A ... 617-253-8900. 233 B
KASTOR, Lisa ... 330-263-2496. 377 H
lkastor@wooster.edu
KASYAN, Linda ... 910-362-7054. 358 F
lkasyan@cfcc.edu
KATCHER, Marcie ... 516-726-6048. 545 H
katcherm@usmma.edu
KATCHMAR, Paul ... 314-792-5510. 331 I
pkatchmar@mvcc.edu
KATEHI, Linda, P ... 530-752-2065... 70 J
chancellor@ucdavis.edu
KATEMAN, Mike ... 573-875-7563. 272 G
mwkateman@ccis.edu
KATEN-BAHENSKY,
Donna ... 608-263-8025. 536 D
dkaten-bahensky@uwhealth.org
KATER, Charles ... 816-584-6567. 280 C
Charles.kater@park.edu
KATER, Sue ... 480-731-8121... 14 I
sue.kater@domail.maricopa.edu
KATES, Donald ... 215-780-1240. 433 A
don@salus.edu
KATES, Jonathan, A ... 434-924-3721. 511 B
jak7g@virginia.edu
KATES, Kenneth ... 319-356-3155. 175 I
ken-kates@uiowa.edu
KATHMAN, Mary Jo ... 513-862-2743. 380 E
KATHOL, Diane ... 402-481-8847. 288 H
diane.kathol@bryanhealthcollege.edu
KATHOL, Lyle, J ... 402-844-7215. 291 I
lylek@northeast.edu
KATHRINS, Bess ... 609-652-4870. 305 C
bess.kathrins@stockton.edu
KATHURIA, Navneet ... 713-798-4951. 467 F
kathuria@bcm.edu
KATINAS, James ... 617-850-1303. 227 E
jkatinas@hchc.edu
KATIP, William, J ... 574-372-5100. 166 B
bill.katip@grace.edu
KATIS, David, J ... 814-393-1997. 428 C
dkatis@clarion.edu
KATKANANT, Chanida ... 201-360-4014. 302 D
ckatkanant@hccc.edu
KATO, Stephen ... 908-709-7045. 308 B
kato@ucc.edu
KATOS, Demetrios ... 617-850-1253. 227 E
dkatos@hchc.edu
KATOSANG, Dahlia, M ... 680-488-2471. 547 B
dahliapcc@palaunet.com
KATRENICZ, Laura ... 570-740-0384. 422 G
lkatrenicz@luzerne.edu
KATS, Lee ... 310-506-4501... 58 H
lee.kats@pepperdine.edu
KATSCHKE, Richard, N ... 414-955-4748. 534 C
rkatschk@mcw.edu
KATSIAFICAS, Charles ... 909-621-8016... 60 A
charles.katsiaficas@pomona.edu
KATSILOMETES, Bessie ... 208-373-1708. 138 E
katsbess@isu.edu
KATSKY, Patricia ... 805-969-3626... 57 K
pkatsky@pacifica.edu
KATSOULEAS, Thomas ... 919-660-5386. 354 A
tom.katsouleas@duke.edu
KATT, Donald, C ... 845-687-5050. 348 H
kattd@sunyulster.edu
KATTELMANN, Dean ... 605-688-4136. 452 B
dean.kattelmann@sdstate.edu
KATTERMAN, Sharon ... 708-974-5271. 153 F
katterman@morainevalley.edu
KATZ, Avi ... 800-371-6105... 16 A
avi@nationalparalegal.edu
KATZ, Ben ... 617-928-4777. 234 E
bkatz@mountida.edu
KATZ, Bernard ... 718-782-7070. 349 B
bkatz@utsny.edu
KATZ, Brit ... 601-974-1200. 267 I
katzrb@millsaps.edu
KATZ, Clifford, H ... 401-874-4402. 440 D
chkatz@uri.edu
KATZ, Craig ... 201-200-3022. 303 F
ckatz@njcu.edu
KATZ, Daniel ... 301-431-5402. 217 C
dkatz@nlc.edu
KATZ, David ... 315-792-5307. 331 I
dkatz@mvcc.edu
KATZ, David, G ... 843-953-5572. 443 A
katzd@cofc.edu
KATZ, Edward, J ... 828-250-3872. 368 C
ekatz@unca.edu
KATZ, Elya ... 718-941-8000. 331 C
KATZ, Harry, C ... 607-255-2185. 322 A
hck2@cornell.edu
KATZ, Jeffrey ... 845-758-7501. 314 D
katz@bard.edu
KATZ, Jeffrey ... 270-745-6311. 200 G
jeffrey.katz@wku.edu
KATZ, Jonathan, N ... 626-395-4068... 31 E
jkatz@caltech.edu
KATZ, Louis, H ... 202-994-6600... 95 D
lkatz@gwu.edu
KATZ, Martin, J ... 303-871-6301... 86 B
mkatz@du.edu
KATZ, Matthew ... 909-469-5567... 76 B
mkatz@westernu.edu
KATZ, Milton ... 816-802-3373. 275 J
mkatz@kcai.edu
KATZ, Paul ... 856-361-2800. 305 E
katzp@rowan.edu
KATZ, Saul, W ... 718-368-5051. 318 E
bkatz@kbcc.cuny.edu
KATZENMEYER, Scott ... 216-781-9400. 377 D
scottk@cie-wc.edu
KATZENMEYER, Scott ... 757-464-4600. 516 E
instruct@cie-wc.edu
KATZMAN, Carol ... 212-854-5768. 314 G
ckatzman@barnard.edu
KATZMAN, Gerald ... 518-694-7298. 313 B
gerald.katzman@acphs.edu
KATZMARK, Gina ... 218-726-6141. 264 D
katzmark@d.umn.edu
KAUCHER, Ellie ... 626-529-8419... 57 G
ekaucher@pacificoaks.edu
KAUFFMAN, Dana ... 703-323-3750. 513 C
tkauffman@nvcc.edu
KAUFFMAN, JR.,
John, M ... 910-893-1776. 352 K
kauffmanj@campbell.edu
KAUFFMAN, Peg ... 717-872-3402. 429 D
peg.kauffman@millersville.edu
KAUFFMAN, Steve ... 312-369-7383. 143 D
skauffman@colum.edu
KAUFFMAN, Wendy ... 910-695-3814. 363 F
kauffmanw@sandhills.edu
KAUFFMAN, William, R . 314-977-3719. 281 I
kauffman@slu.edu
KAUFMAN, Angela ... 817-257-7830. 484 I
a.kaufman@tcu.edu
KAUFMAN, Donald, E ... 812-888-5343. 174 F
dkaufman@vinu.edu
KAUFMAN, Geof ... 253-680-7180. 516 L
gkaufman@bates.ctc.edu
KAUFMAN, Helena ... 507-222-4349. 254 D
hkaufman@carleton.edu
KAUFMAN, Jason ... 651-450-3768. 258 H
dkaufma@inverhills.edu
KAUFMAN, Kris, A ... 716-878-3000. 343 A
kaufmaka@buffalostate.edu
KAUFMAN, Lon ... 312-413-3450. 161 D
lkaufman@uic.edu
KAUFMAN, Norman ... 561-297-3061. 114 L
nkaufman@fau.edu
KAUFMAN, Paulette ... 303-751-8700... 78 J
kaufman@bel-rea.com
KAUFMAN, Steven ... 734-462-4400. 250 A
skaufman@schoolcraft.edu
KAUFMAN-OSBORN,
Timothy ... 509-527-5397. 525 E
kaufmatv@whitman.edu
KAUFMANN, Marta ... 215-968-8242. 411 B
kaufmann@bucks.edu
KAUFMANN, Sandra ... 516-876-2715. 343 D
kaufmanns@oldwestbury.edu
KAUGARS, Karlis ... 607-436-3663. 343 E
karlis.kaugars@oneonta.edu
KAUKE, Donna ... 815-599-3688. 146 D
donna.kauke@highland.edu
KAUKUS, Arlene, F ... 716-645-2231. 341 F
arleneks@buffalo.edu
KAUL, Gitanjali ... 561-297-1333. 114 L
gkaul@fau.edu
KAUL, Terri, S ... 262-243-5700. 532 H
terri.kaul@cuw.edu
KAULFUS, John ... 903-886-5086. 483 E
john.kaulfus@tamuc.edu
KAUNITZ, Carol ... 732-255-0400. 304 A
ckaunitz@ocean.edu
KAUR, Kuldeep ... 530-741-6723... 77 K
kkaur@yccd.edu
KAUS, Annette ... 575-835-5333. 310 F
akaus@admin.nmt.edu
KAUS, Cheryl ... 609-652-4512. 305 C
cheryl.kaus@stockton.edu
KAUSHAL, Janice ... 312-935-4852. 156 K
jkaushal@robertmorris.edu
KAUSHANSKY, Kenneth . 631-444-9011. 342 C
kenneth.kashansky@stonybrook.edu
KAUSHIK, Suresh, C ... 334-420-4244..... 7 G
skaushik@trenholmstate.edu
KAUTZ, Barbara, K ... 413-748-3222. 236 I
bkautz@springfieldcollege.edu
KAUTZ, III, John ... 561-803-2084. 110 B
john_kautz@pba.edu
KAUTZ DE ARANGO,
Kathy ... 610-341-5870. 415 G
kkautz2@eastern.edu
KAUTZER, Julie ... 920-686-6190. 536 A
Julie.Kautzer@sl.edu
KAVAJECZ, Kenneth, A ... 315-443-9494. 347 C
kakavaje@syr.edu
KAVALIER, Barbara ... 903-875-7308. 477 G
barbara.kavalier@navarrocollege.edu
KAVANAGH, Kathy, J ... 914-594-4487. 334 A
kathy_johnston@nymc.edu
KAVANAGH, Kenneth ... 239-590-7007. 115 A
kavanagh@fgcu.edu
KAVANAUGH, Maria, A .. 508-565-1331. 237 A
mkavanaugh@stonehill.edu
KAVANAUGH, Michael ... 714-484-7108... 56 E
mkavanaugh@cypresscollege.edu
KAVANAUGH, Steven ... 610-896-1141. 418 F
skavanau@haverford.edu
KAVERMAN, Don ... 314-340-3534. 275 A
kavermad@hssu.edu
KAVLIE, Lucas, B ... 912-650-6233. 131 H
lkavlie@southuniversity.edu
KAVOURIS, John ... 312-369-8646. 143 D
jkavouris@colum.edu
KAVRAN, Elizabeth ... 440-449-2015. 392 D
ekavran@ursuline.edu
KAWA, Steve ... 714-628-4717... 60 H
kawa_steve@sccollege.edu
KAWAI`AE`A, Keiki ... 808-974-7794. 136 A
KAWAKAMI, Alice, K ... 323-343-3950... 34 A
akawaka@calstatela.edu
KAWALL, Scott ... 773-777-4220. 155 B
skawall@nc.edu
KAWAMOTO, Barbara, K 808-956-7161. 135 L
barbk@hawaii.edu
KAWAMOTO, Judy ... 401-232-6046. 438 K
jkawamot@bryant.edu
KAWANNA, JR., Ronald 708-596-2000. 159 C
rkawanna@ssc.edu
KAY, Carol ... 915-831-2854. 472 B
ckay@epcc.edu
KAY, Gilmary ... 610-785-6235. 432 C
gkay@scs.edu
KAY, James, F ... 609-497-7815. 304 D
academic.dean@ptsem.edu
KAY, Kent ... 314-539-5291. 281 D
kentkay@stlcc.edu
KAY, R. David ... 570-327-4770. 427 B
dkay@pct.edu
KAY, Sabrina ... 213-355-7777... 45 B
KAY, Steve, A ... 858-534-4281... 71 F
skay@ucsd.edu
KAY, Steve, A ... 213-740-2531... 74 A
dean@dornsife.usc.edu
KAYE, Arlene, E ... 714-992-7865... 67 D
akaye@scco.edu
KAYE, Leslie, J ... 617-912-9276. 224 B
lkaye@bostonconservatory.edu
KAYE, Ted ... 925-424-1013... 37 L
tkaye@laspositascollege.edu
KAYES, Christopher ... 202-994-1000... 95 D
KAYLOR, Alice, J ... 724-537-4566. 432 G
alice.kaylor@email.stvincent.edu
KAYLOR, Christine ... 508-999-8620. 229 A
ckaylor@umassd.edu
KAYLOR, Doug ... 937-512-2107. 388 O
douglas.kaylor@sinclair.edu
KAYLOR, Sean, P ... 845-575-3000. 330 D
sean.kaylor@marist.edu
KAYNAMA, Shohreh ... 410-704-3342. 220 E
skaynama@towson.edu
KAYNARD, Meryl ... 718-997-5725. 319 C
meryl.kaynard@qc.cuny.edu
KAYNE, Susan, W ... 212-346-1200. 335 J
skayne@pace.edu
KAYS, Brenda ... 704-991-0220. 364 C
bkays2651@stanly.edu
KAYSEN-LUZBETAK,
Angie ... 815-280-6679. 149 A
akaysen@jjc.edu
KAZANECKI-KEMPTER,
Diane ... 631-420-2065. 346 B
diane.kazanecki-kempter@farmingdale.edu
KAZANJIAN, Victor, H ... 781-283-2685. 237 F
vkazanji@wellesley.edu
KAZARIAN, Julie ... 508-929-8650. 230 G
jkazarian@worcester.edu
KAZDA, Kathleen ... 262-691-5464. 541 D
kkazda@wctc.edu
KAZEE, Thomas, A ... 812-488-2151. 173 H
president@evansville.edu
KAZEN, James, D ... 210-567-0390. 493 A
kazen@uthscsa.edu
KAZEROUNIAN, Kazem .. 860-486-2221... 92 A
kazem.kazerounian@uconn.edu
KAZIN, Robert ... 315-859-4340. 325 E
rkazin@hamilton.edu
KAZLO WATSON, Jaime 518-562-4161. 320 B
jaime.kazlo@clinton.edu
KAZMAREK, Shannon ... 325-674-6341. 464 H
srb04a@acu.edu
KAZMIR, Darin ... 361-582-2417. 493 H
darin.kazmir@victoriacollege.edu
KAZUMA, Clement ... 680-488-2471. 547 B
KEA, Jerry ... 707-642-8188... 66 G
thomas.kea@solano.edu
KEABLES, Mike ... 303-871-2621... 86 B
mkeables@du.edu
KEADY, Thomas, J ... 617-552-6795. 224 A
thomas.keady@bc.edu
KEAGY, Thomas, A ... 215-951-1042. 420 B
keagy@lasalle.edu
KEAL, Aaron, J ... 620-421-6700. 188 D
aaronk@labette.edu
KEALA, David ... 808-675-3572. 135 C
david.keala@byuh.edu
KEALEY, Michelle, L ... 814-393-2352. 428 C
mkealey@clarion.edu
KEAN, Betsy ... 415-338-2687... 35 E
bkean@sfsu.edu
KEAN, Cheryl ... 269-471-3288. 239 D
kean@andrews.edu
KEAN, Linda ... 781-239-4284. 222 D
kean@babson.edu
KEANE-DAWES,
Jennifer, M ... 410-651-6507. 219 E
jmkeanedawes@umes.edu
KEARNEY, Anne, E ... 315-445-4195. 328 F
kearneae@lemoyne.edu
KEARNEY, Catherine ... 209-468-9155... 69 F

KEARNEY, Janice ... 870-575-8283... 24 E kearneyj@uapb.edu
KEARNEY, John ... 570-504-7000. 413 B
KEARNEY, Joseph, D ... 414-288-1955. 534 B joseph.kearney@marquette.edu
KEARNEY, Margaret ... 585-275-9093. 349 C margaret.kearney@rochester.edu
KEARNS, Joanne ... 973-328-5044. 300 G jkearns@ccm.edu
KEARNS, Kevin ... 716-673-3111. 342 A kevin.kearns@fredonia.edu
KEARNS, Michael ... 928-757-0801... 15 L mkearns@mohave.edu
KEARNS, Tom ... 765-983-1465. 165 G kearnto@earlham.edu
KEARNS-BARRETT, Marybeth ... 508-793-2448. 225 B mkearns@holycross.edu
KEAS, Lenora ... 361-698-1208. 471 G lkeas@delmar.edu
KEASEY, Rosemary, C ... 724-287-8711. 411 C rosemary.keasey@bc3.edu
KEASLER, Robert, L ... 859-238-5451. 193 E robert.keasler@centre.edu
KEASLING, Diane ... 423-461-8968. 457 H dlkeasling@milligan.edu
KEAST, Cindy ... 620-665-3565. 187 F keastc@hutchcc.edu
KEATHLEY, Gwynne ... 410-669-9200. 216 C gkeathley@mica.edu
KEATHLEY, Naymond ... 254-710-2657. 467 G naymond_keathley@baylor.edu
KEATING, Dana ... 618-252-5400. 159 E dana.keating@sic.edu
KEATING, Frederick ... 856-415-2100. 302 C fkeating@gccnj.edu
KEATING, Jeff ... 909-469-5205... 76 B jkeating@westernu.edu
KEATING, Joseph ... 740-588-1396. 394 C jkeating@zanestate.edu
KEATING, Kathy ... 616-234-4953. 243 B kkeating@grcc.edu
KEATING, MaryJo ... 860-297-5110... 91 F maryjo.keating@trincoll.edu
KEATING, Patrick, C ... 605-256-5222. 451 H pat.keating@dsu.edu
KEATING, Patrick, J ... 617-552-3255. 224 A patrick.keating@bc.edu
KEATING, Richard, S ... 413-782-1473. 238 A rkeating@wne.edu
KEATING, Sarah ... 570-945-8112. 419 N sarah.keating@keystone.edu
KEATON, Angela ... 423-636-7300. 462 E akeaton@tusculum.edu
KEATS, Patrick ... 540-636-2900. 503 L pkeats@christendom.edu
KEATY, Anthony ... 781-899-5500. 223 E
KEATY, Anthony ... 781-899-5500. 223 E akeaty@blessedjohnxxiii.edu
KEBAETSE, Masego ... 484-384-2968. 425 I mkebaets@eastern.edu
KEBISEK, Kris ... 503-297-5544. 405 D kkebisek@ocac.edu
KECHICHIAN, Avedis (Avo) ... 909-593-3511... 72 E akechichian@laverne.edu
KECK, Amy ... 630-375-8260. 156 K akeck@robertmorris.edu
KECK, David, A ... 434-223-6269. 505 E dkeck@hsc.edu
KECK, Kathleen, A ... 518-327-6223. 336 B kkeck@paulsmiths.edu
KECK, Kay ... 269-965-3931. 244 O keckk@kellogg.edu
KECK, Michael ... 315-279-5267. 328 D mkeck@mail.keuka.edu
KECK, III, Ray, M ... 956-326-2320. 483 B president@tamiu.edu
KECK, Sara, E ... 573-629-3014. 274 J SKeck@hlg.edu
KECSKÉS, Gary ... 630-466-7900. 162 J gkecskes@waubonsee.edu
KEDDO, Dwain ... 239-489-9205. 101 O dkeddo@edison.edu
KEDROSKI, Cristie ... 850-729-5357. 109 I kedroskc@nwfsc.edu
KEDROWSKI, Jeff ... 630-617-3042. 145 A jeffk@elmhurst.edu
KEDSKI, Cathy ... 508-830-5042. 230 D ckedski@maritime.edu
KEEBAUGH, Joseph, E ... 920-433-6631. 531 L joe.keebaugh@bellincollege.edu
KEEBLER, David ... 805-289-6354... 74 H dkeebler@vcccd.edu
KEEBLER, Joel ... 503-399-6565. 402 E joel.keebler@chemeketa.edu
KEECH, Brian ... 215-895-2100. 415 B brian.keech@drexel.edu
KEEDY, Thomas, E ... 765-361-6227. 175 B keedyt@wabash.edu
KEEFAUVER, Timothy ... 309-457-2210. 153 D tkeefauver@monmouthcollege.edu
KEEFE, Kathleen, A ... 724-925-4101. 437 D keefek@wccc.edu
KEEFE, Kevin ... 973-328-5064. 300 G kkeefe@ccm.edu
KEEFE, Maureen ... 617-879-7705. 230 B mkeefe@massart.edu
KEEFE, Terri, K ... 610-799-1580. 421 I tkeefe@lccc.edu
KEEFE, Thomas, W ... 972-721-5203. 488 F
KEEFE, Tim ... 480-732-7033... 14 J tim.keefe@cgc.edu
KEEFE, Timothy, C ... 603-535-2206. 298 G timk@plymouth.edu
KEEFER, Elizabeth ... 216-368-4286. 375 J elizabeth.keefer@case.edu
KEEFER, Maureen, H ... 412-397-4334. 431 I keefer@rmu.edu
KEEFER, Michael, R ... 814-393-1610. 428 C mkeefer@cuf-inc.org
KEEFER, Sue ... 719-384-6882... 83 M sue.keefer@ojc.edu
KEEGAN, Bridget, M ... 402-280-2431. 289 D bmkeegan@creighton.edu
KEEGAN, Kim ... 603-206-8005. 296 A kkeegan@ccsnh.edu
KEEGAN, Michael ... 605-394-2336. 452 A michael.keegan@sdsmt.edu
KEEGAN, Thomas ... 360-416-7997. 523 G thomas.keegan@skagit.edu
KEEHLWETTER, F. Stanley ... 724-458-2142. 417 E fskeehlwetter@gcc.edu
KEEHNER, Julia ... 304-473-8440. 531 G keehner@wvwc.edu
KEEL, Barry ... 800-422-2418... 99 A bkeel@baymedical.org
KEEL, Brooks, A ... 912-478-5211. 126 C bkeel@georgiasouthern.edu
KEEL, Kimberly ... 803-323-2211. 449 G keelk@winthrop.edu
KEELER, Anne, B ... 540-828-5386. 502 J akeeler@bridgewater.edu
KEELER, John, T ... 412-624-7605. 435 C keeler@pitt.edu
KEELEY, Brian ... 360-383-3375. 525 D bkeeley@whatcom.ctc.edu
KEELEY, Edward, J ... 608-663-2223. 532 I ekeeley@edgewood.edu
KEELEY, Eileen, M ... 704-894-2422. 353 J eikeeley@davidson.edu
KEELS, Carl ... 301-736-3631. 216 B genekeels@aol.com
KEELY, Donna, J ... 802-626-6344. 501 E donna.keely@lyndonstate.edu
KEEN, Cathy ... 352-395-5829. 113 C cathy.keen@sfcollege.edu
KEEN, Hubert ... 631-420-2239. 346 B hubert.keen@farmingdale.edu
KEEN, Larry ... 910-678-8321. 360 D keenl@faytechcc.edu
KEEN, Russell ... 912-478-1583. 126 C russellkeen@georgiasouthern.edu
KEEN, Suzanne, P ... 540-458-8400. 516 A keens@wlu.edu
KEENAN, Bernard ... 617-573-8120. 237 B bkeenan@suffolk.edu
KEENAN, Claudia ... 757-446-520 . 504 E Keenance@evms.edu
KEENAN, Claudine ... 609-652-3593. 305 C claudine.keenan@stockton.edu
KEENAN, Kathleen ... 617-879-7065. 230 B kkeenan@massart.edu
KEENAN, Maura ... 215-780-1266. 433 A mkeenan@salus.edu
KEENAN, Robert ... 518-631-9848. 348 K keenanr@uniongraduatecollege.edu
KEENE, David ... 859-276-4357. 199 G dkeene@sullivan.edu
KEENE, Sheila ... 515-244-4221. 175 C sheilak@aib.edu
KEENER, Barb ... 419-755-4539. 385 D bkeener@ncstatecollege.edu
KEENER, Dauthan ... 734-995-7461. 241 E keened@cuaa.edu
KEENER, Donna ... 813-253-7132. 106 M
KEENER, Gary, S ... 540-863-2900. 512 B gkeener@dslcc.edu
KEENER, John, F ... 434-947-8367. 508 D jkeener@randolphcollege.edu
KEENER, Roger, E ... 716-375-2354. 338 E rkeener@sbu.edu
KEENEY, Donald ... 512-472-4133. 480 G donald.keeney@ssw.edu
KEENEY, Leroy, M ... 717-815-1360. 438 D lkeeney@ycp.edu
KEENEY, Madonna ... 815-599-3449. 146 D madonna.keeney@highland.edu
KEENEY, Mary Ellen, R ... 518-587-2100. 346 A maryellen.keeney@esc.edu
KEENEY, Robert ... 919-536-7201. 360 B keeneyr@durhamtech.edu
KEENUM, Mark, E ... 662-325-3221. 268 D president@msstate.edu
KEEP, John ... 609-771-3255. 300 E keep@tcnj.edu
KEEPERS, Beverly, C ... 502-585-7121. 199 C bkeepers@spalding.edu
KEES, Tedd, C ... 517-321-0242. 243 F tkees@glcc.edu
KEESE, Russelle ... 256-761-6132... 7 F rkeese@talladega.edu
KEESLING, Donna ... 765-993-1341. 165 G keesldo@earlham.edu
KEETER, Brian, C ... 334-844-4650... 1 G bck0001@auburn.edu
KEETER, Howell, W ... 417-690-2370. 272 E hkeeter@cofo.edu
KEETER, Tara ... 252-536-7223. 361 A tkeeter618@halifaxcc.edu
KEETON, Cheryl, L ... 919-866-5611. 364 G clkeeton@waketech.edu
KEETON, James, E ... 601-984-1010. 270 C jkeeton@umc.edu
KEETON, Kristi ... 913-971-3544. 188 H kkeeton@mnu.edu
KEETON, Tim ... 913-971-3607. 188 H tkeeton@mnu.edu
KEGEL, Gregory ... 406-265-3740. 287 D kegel@msun.edu
KEGELMAN, Nancy ... 732-224-2221. 299 G nkegelman@brookdalecc.edu
KEGLER, Jason ... 620-431-2820. 189 D jkegler@neosho.edu
KEHL, Maria ... 760-922-8714... 58 C mkehl@paloverde.edu
KEHOE, Clare ... 718-940-5579. 339 B ckehoe@sjcny.edu
KEHOE, Joseph ... 925-631-4286... 61 F jkehoe@stmarys-ca.edu
KEHOE, Robert, J ... 585-395-2226. 342 F rkehoe@brockport.edu
KEHOE, Sharon, A ... 208-882-2536. 139 D skehoe@uidaho.edu
KEHRBERG, Robert ... 828-227-7028. 369 E rkehrberg@wcu.edu
KEHRER, Sharon, K ... 636-227-2100. 276 F sharon.kehrer@logan.edu
KEHRES, Larry, T ... 330-823-4880. 391 E kehreslt@mountunion.edu
KEIGHER, Craig ... 815-802-8402. 149 C ckeigher@kcc.edu
KEILERS, Vikki ... 903-233-4141. 475 J vikkikeilers@letu.edu
KEILITZ, Craig, D ... 336-841-9057. 355 C ckeilitz@highpoint.edu
KEILLER, James, B ... 404-627-2681. 121 H james.keiller@beulah.org
KEILLOR, Robin ... 503-352-2081. 407 A keillor@pacificu.edu
KEILSON, Suzanne ... 410-617-2608. 216 A skeilson@loyola.edu
KEIM, Howard ... 620-327-8233. 187 D howardk@hesston.edu
KEIN, Chris ... 207-948-9283. 211 I ckein@unity.edu
KEINO, Leah ... 403-375-7112. 291 F lekeino1@wsc.edu
KEIRN, Christy, C ... 870-508-6107... 20 A ckeirn@asumh.edu
KEIRSTEAD, Carol, A ... 864-242-5100. 441 D
KEISER, Arthur ... 954-776-4476. 108 C artk@keiseruniversity.edu
KEISER, Pamela, G ... 570-577-1238. 411 A pamela.keiser@bucknell.edu
KEISER, Sue, T ... 662-915-7111. 270 B stkeiser@olemiss.edu
KEISER, Thomas ... 757-479-3706. 503 C tkeiser@baptistseminary.edu
KEISLER, Ruben ... 501-337-5000... 20 J rkeisler@coto.edu
KEISLING, Bruce, L ... 502-897-4807. 199 B bkeisling@sbts.edu
KEISTER, Shaun, B ... 530-754-4438... 70 J sbkeister@ucdavis.edu
KEITA, Alma, G ... 229-931-2708. 126 D alma.keita@gsw.edu
KEITES, Jim ... 352-395-5536. 113 C jim.keites@sfcollege.edu
KEITGES, David ... 513-529-5623. 384 G dkeitges@miamioh.edu
KEITH, C. David ... 478-301-5639. 128 H keith_cd@mercer.edu
KEITH, Colleen, P ... 864-587-4236. 447 B keithc@smcsc.edu
KEITH, Dana, S ... 205-348-4530... 8 D dkeith@fa.ua.edu
KEITH, Frank ... 856-222-9311. 299 I fskeith@bcc.edu
KEITH, Heather ... 908-709-7514. 308 B keith@ucc.edu
KEITH, Jamie, L ... 352-392-1358. 116 A jlkeith@ufl.edu
KEITH, Jeffrey ... 813-626-8008... 96 F jeffrey.keith@strayer.edu
KEITH, Jeffrey, D ... 801-422-4331. 495 D jeff_keith@byu.edu
KEITH, Joe ... 704-825-6272. 360 F keith.joe@gaston.edu
KEITH, Lisa, M ... 706-233-7250. 131 E lkeith@shorter.edu
KEITH, Marcia ... 219-473-4375. 164 K mkeith@ccsj.edu
KEITH, Nancy ... 806-291-3766. 494 F keithn@wbu.edu
KEITH, Paul ... 832-252-4673. 468 L paul.keith@cbshouston.edu
KEITH, Paula, S ... 618-536-3471. 159 F pkeith@siu.edu
KEITH, Scott ... 949-214-3046... 41 I scott.keith@cui.edu
KEITH, Shelby, C ... 318-797-5221. 205 F shelby.keith@lsus.edu
KEITH, Shelley ... 540-654-2266. 510 J tkeith@umw.edu
KEITH, Shena ... 312-915-7283. 151 H smcnama@luc.edu
KEITH, Tammy ... 740-753-6356. 380 K keitht@hocking.edu
KEIZS, Marcia, V ... 718-262-2350. 319 F mkeizs@york.cuny.edu
KELAHER, James, E ... 713-798-7880. 467 F jkelaher@bcm.edu
KELCHNER, Alan ... 510-649-2425... 46 B akelchner@gtu.edu
KELCHNER, Dana ... 660-596-7250. 282 G dkelchner@sfccmo.edu
KELCHNER, Loretta, L ... 660-263-3900. 272 A lkelchner@cccb.edu
KELCHNER, Mark ... 660-596-7402. 282 G mkelchner@sfccmo.edu
KELEMEN, Frank ... 517-629-0236. 239 A fkelemen@albion.edu
KELEMEN, Mary, E ... 206-546-4733. 523 F mkelemen@shoreline.edu
KELEMEN, Paul ... 972-273-3590. 471 B pkelemen@dcccd.edu
KELIN, Shebon ... 303-861-1151... 81 E skelin@concorde.edu
KELL, Christine ... 814-866-8169. 420 E ckell@lecom.edu
KELL, Gwen ... 707-256-7335... 55 F gkell@napavalley.edu
KELLAM, James, W ... 410-651-6174. 219 E jwkellam@umes.edu
KELLAR, Deborah ... 303-762-6881... 81 G debbie.kellar@denverseminary.edu
KELLAR, Doug ... 419-448-2000. 380 G
KELLAR, Katharine, E ... 724-653-2221. 415 A kkellar@dec.edu
KELLAR, Michelle ... 641-628-5431. 176 E kellarm@central.edu
KELLARIS, William, K ... 540-338-1776. 508 A admissions@phc.edu
KELLEHER, Audrey ... 877-804-1424. 266 A akelleher@belhaven.edu
KELLEHER, Christopher ... 402-935-9400. 290 N ckelleher@nechristian.edu
KELLEHER, Daniel ... 212-749-2802. 330 A finaid@msmnyc.edu
KELLEHER, Erin, C ... 978-665-3150. 229 E ekelleher@fitchburgstate.edu
KELLEHER, Maureen, E ... 617-373-2333. 235 F
KELLEHER, Paul, D ... 212-749-2802. 330 A pkelleher@msmnyc.edu
KELLEHER, William, J ... 413-782-1288. 238 A bkelleher@wne.edu
KELLEN, Jim ... 251-405-7086... 2 D jkellen@bishop.edu
KELLEN, Vincent, J ... 859-257-3609. 200 C vincent.kellen@uky.edu
KELLEPOURIS, Nikos ... 913-971-3687. 188 H nskellepouris@mnu.edu
KELLER, Alison ... 248-218-2268. 249 D akeller@rc.edu
KELLER, Barbara ... 906-635-2267. 245 G bkeller@lssu.edu
KELLER, Bill ... 718-368-5028. 318 E bkeller@kbcc.cuny.edu
KELLER, Bruce ... 215-572-2922. 409 H kellerb@arcadia.edu
KELLER, Chaim, D ... 773-463-7738. 160 H cdkeller@telshe.gov
KELLER, Charlotte ... 928-757-0852... 15 L ckeller@mohave.edu
KELLER, Christopher ... 570-389-4070. 427 H ckeller@bloomu.edu
KELLER, Cindy ... 276-656-0337. 513 D ckeller@patrickhenry.edu
KELLER, David ... 248-218-2150. 249 D dkeller@rc.edu

KELLER, Diane, W 570-340-6047. 423 B
keller@marywood.edu
KELLER, Harrison 512-232-8277. 491 C
harrison.keller@austin.utexas.edu
KELLER, James, W 650-358-6790... 64 A
kellerj@smccd.edu
KELLER, Joe 661-362-2226... 53 G
jkeller@masters.edu
KELLER, John 413-265-2210. 225 C
kellerj@elms.edu
KELLER, John, C 319-335-2142. 175 I
john-keller@uiowa.edu
KELLER, Jonathan 617-994-6941. 228 D
jkeller@bhe.mass.edu
KELLER, Kara 828-398-7870. 357 N
kkeller@abtech.edu
KELLER, Kerri, D 785-532-6506. 188 A
kdkeller@ksu.edu
KELLER, Kristina 320-308-5538. 261 C
kkeller@sctcc.edu
KELLER, Linda 619-961-4282... 69 I
lkeller@tjsl.edu
KELLER, Linda, B 270-852-3110. 197 B
lkeller@kwc.edu
KELLER, Lise, K 336-334-5243. 369 A
lise_keller@uncg.edu
KELLER, Loreen 812-455-8947. 152 F
lkeller@mchenry.edu
KELLER, Mae 734-995-7378. 241 E
kellem@cuaa.edu
KELLER, Marlon, D 215-699-5700. 421 E
mkeller@LSB.edu
KELLER, Michael, A 650-723-5553... 68 E
michael.keller@stanford.edu
KELLER, Michael, J 605-677-5455. 451 F
mike.keller@usd.edu
KELLER, Mike 325-236-8253. 486 C
mike.keller@tstc.edu
KELLER, Peter 570-662-4804. 429 C
pkeller@mansfield.edu
KELLER, Rebecca 518-262-8105. 313 D
kellerr@mail.amc.edu
KELLER, Richard 518-262-6008. 313 D
KELLER, Rod 541-888-7292. 407 H
rod.keller@socc.edu
KELLER, Scott 610-358-4547. 424 I
kellersc@neumann.edu
KELLER, Scott 815-280-2775. 149 A
skeller@jjc.edu
KELLER, Stephen, H 413-755-4440. 233 A
keller@stcc.edu
KELLER, Tammy, S 270-686-4246. 192 G
tammy.keller@brescia.edu
KELLER, Thomas 636-227-2100. 276 F
thomas.keller@logan.edu
KELLER, Travis 740-392-6868. 384 K
travis.keller@mvnu.edu
KELLER, Wayne 301-846-2548. 214 H
wkeller@frederick.edu
KELLER, William 718-997-5557. 319 C
william.keller@qc.cuny.edu
KELLER-GILTNER,
Heather 573-288-6536. 273 F
hkeller@culver.edu
KELLERHOUSE, James 518-445-3219. 313 C
jkell@albanylaw.edu
KELLERMANN, Arthur 301-295-3017. 545 C
KELLERSBERGER, Gail 713-221-8047. 489 D
kellersbergerg@uhd.edu
KELLETT, Chris 206-726-5180. 518 G
ckellett@cornish.edu
KELLETT, Earle 706-233-7821. 131 E
ekellett@shorter.edu
KELLETT, Lucas, C 207-778-7344. 212 D
luke.kellett@maine.edu
KELLEWAY, Nancy 703-897-1972. 510 B
nkelleway@stratford.edu
KELLEY, Amber, L 512-223-2012. 466 I
amberk@austincc.edu
KELLEY, Aundrea 617-994-6979. 228 D
akelley@bhe.mass.edu
KELLEY, Betty 863-667-5249. 113 P
bkelley@seu.edu
KELLEY, Brenda 334-214-4815..... 2 H
brenda.kelley@cv.edu
KELLEY, JR., Charles, S 504-282-4455. 206 A
ckelley@nobts.edu
KELLEY, Cindy 304-205-6614. 528 B
ckelley@kvctc.edu
KELLEY, Dale 731-352-4000. 453 D
kelleyd@bethelu.edu
KELLEY, Danny, R 926-261-3180. 482 F
drkelley@pvamu.edu
KELLEY, David 541-485-1780. 405 B
davidkelley@newhope.edu
KELLEY, Debbie, D 417-625-9805. 278 D
kelley-d@mssu.edu
KELLEY, Ella 225-771-2360. 206 J
ella_kelley@subr.edu
KELLEY, Ella 225-771-4845. 206 J
ella_kelley@aol.com
KELLEY, Gary, F 978-232-2048. 226 C
gkelley@endicott.edu
KELLEY, Gloria 704-330-6441. 359 C
gloria.kelley@cpcc.edu
KELLEY, Holly 904-743-1122. 107 T
hkelley@jones.edu
KELLEY, James, W 336-633-0049. 362 H
jwkelley@randolph.edu
KELLEY, Jan 541-485-1780. 405 B
jankelley@newhope.edu
KELLEY, Jane 518-737-3622. 325 A
jkelley@fmcc.suny.edu
KELLEY, Janet 918-444-2204. 396 H
kelleyje@nsuok.edu
KELLEY, Jeanne 617-353-3565. 224 D
jkelley@bu.edu
KELLEY, Katherine, M 423-439-4224. 459 C
kelleyk@etsu.edu
KELLEY, Kathleen 860-253-3011... 88 C
kkelley@asnuntuck.edu
KELLEY, Kelvin, J 325-670-5898. 472 O
kjkelley@hsutx.edu
KELLEY, Kevin 417-328-1536. 282 C
kkelley@sbuniv.edu
KELLEY, Kim 706-754-7726. 129 G
kkelley@northgatech.edu
KELLEY, Kimberly 309-268-8057. 146 B
kim.kelley@heartland.edu
KELLEY, Kimberly 262-595-2553. 537 C
kelleyk@uwp.edu
KELLEY, Larry, H 252-985-5138. 365 D
lkelley@ncwc.edu
KELLEY, Laurie, C 503-943-8332. 408 F
kelleyl@up.edu
KELLEY, Lisa 859-622-2101. 193 P
lisa.kelley@eku.edu
KELLEY, Mark 541-485-1780. 405 B
markkelley@newhope.edu
KELLEY, Michael 402-280-2733. 289 D
michaelk@creighton.edu
KELLEY, Mildred 972-860-4195. 470 G
mkelley1@dcccd.edu
KELLEY, Richard, D 631-656-2130. 324 F
richard.kelley@ftc.edu
KELLEY, Ritch 570-586-2400. 410 D
rkelley@bbc.edu
KELLEY, Robert, O 701-777-2121. 371 C
robert.kelley@und.edu
KELLEY, Robinette 515-294-0123. 175 H
kelley@iastate.edu
KELLEY, Rosa 646-312-2050. 316 J
Rosa.Kelley@baruch.cuny.edu
KELLEY, Scott, C 512-499-4560. 491 A
skelley@utsystem.edu
KELLEY, Sylvia 541-552-6127. 406 C
KelleySy@sou.edu
KELLEY, Thomas 508-626-4614. 230 A
tkelley@framingham.edu
KELLEY, Todd, D 262-551-5900. 532 D
tkelley@carthage.edu
KELLEY, Tom 301-934-7822. 214 D
tkelley@csmd.edu
KELLIHER, Marsha 570-372-4455. 433 H
kelliher@susqu.edu
KELLLY, Sarah, M 937-327-7800. 393 E
smkelly@wittenberg.edu
KELLMAN, Jordan 337-482-6219. 208 D
kellman@louisiana.edu
KELLO, Christopher 209-228-4104... 71 D
ckello@UCMerced.edu
KELLOGG, Angie 715-346-4323. 538 A
akellogg@uwsp.edu
KELLOGG, Dan 715-346-2046. 538 A
dkellogg@uwsp.edu
KELLOGG, Gary 530-221-4275... 65 F
gkellogg@shasta.edu
KELLOGG, John 612-625-3387. 264 G
j-kell@umn.edu
KELLOGG, Leslie 269-927-8167. 245 D
souden@lakemichigancollege.edu
KELLOGG, Tonia 405-585-5802. 397 C
tonia.kellogg@okbu.edu
KELLOGG-BRADLEY,
Polly 507-288-4563. 255 C
pkelloggbradley@crossroadscollege.edu
KELLOGG PITTMAN,
Tiffany 804-204-1210. 502 F
tpittman@btsr.edu
KELLOUGH, Stephen, B 630-752-5087. 163 F
stephen.kellough@wheaton.edu
KELLT, Kirk 503-725-6246. 406 B
kkelly@pdx.edu
KELLY, Alan, J 516-463-5027. 326 D
alan.j.kelly@hofstra.edu
KELLY, Anita 484-664-3178. 424 H
akelly@muhlenberg.edu
KELLY, Anna 401-739-5000. 439 D
akelly@neit.edu
KELLY, Audrey 908-737-7000. 302 F
aukelly@kean.edu
KELLY, OSB, Augustine 603-641-7250. 297 G
akelly@anselm.edu
KELLY, Barbara 334-386-7299..... 3 H
bkelly@faulkner.edu
KELLY, Benji 270-789-5211. 193 D
jbkelly@campbellsville.edu
KELLY, Bill 570-702-8984. 419 G
bkelly@johnson.edu
KELLY, Brendan 850-474-3306. 117 B
bkelly@uwf.edu
KELLY, Brendan, B 850-474-2332. 117 B
bkelly@uwf.edu
KELLY, Brian 805-525-4417... 69 H
bkelly@thomasaquinas.edu
KELLY, Brian 508-541-1622. 225 F
bkelly@dean.edu
KELLY, Brian 510-780-4500... 50 I
bkelly@lifewest.edu
KELLY, Chris 620-235-4122. 189 L
ckelly@pittstate.edu
KELLY, OSB, David 724-805-2644. 432 G
david.kelly@email.stvincent.edu
KELLY, Debra 609-771-2161. 300 E
dkelly@tcnj.edu
KELLY, Diane 312-788-1123. 162 H
dkelly@vandercook.edu
KELLY, Donald 203-591-7394... 90 I
dkelly@post.edu
KELLY, Donald 901-272-5796. 456 F
dkelly@mca.edu
KELLY, Drew 610-526-6669. 417 H
dkelly@harcum.edu
KELLY, Edward, J 423-439-8550. 459 C
kellye@etsu.edu
KELLY, Evelyn 252-527-6223. 361 F
ekelly@lenoircc.edu
KELLY, Gary, E 781-891-2360. 223 C
gkelly@bentley.edu
KELLY, George 610-282-1100. 414 F
george.kelly@desales.edu
KELLY, George, N 615-327-6800. 456 E
gkelly@mmc.edu
KELLY, Grace, A 802-654-2568. 500 B
gkelly@smcvt.edu
KELLY, Hank 740-420-5924. 385 L
hkelly@ohiochristian.edu
KELLY, Heather, A 302-831-2021... 94 B
hkelly@udel.edu
KELLY, Inesha 773-697-2093. 144 B
ikelly@devry.edu
KELLY, Jacinta 301-628-5605. 217 C
jkelly@nlc.edu
KELLY, Jack 617-732-2143. 233 E
jack.kelly@mcphs.edu
KELLY, Jack 717-262-2013. 437 H
jkelly@wilson.edu
KELLY, James 650-543-3860... 54 C
jkelly@menlo.edu
KELLY, James 401-841-3674. 545 A
KELLY, Jamie 617-989-4668. 237 G
kellyj8@wit.edu
KELLY, Janet, H 478-988-6800. 122 G
jkelly@centralgatech.edu
KELLY, Jeffrey, M 443-352-4012. 218 E
jkelly@stevenson.edu
KELLY, Jennifer 516-686-1254. 333 H
jkelly16@nyit.edu
KELLY, Jennifer 412-338-4770. 419 M
jennifer.kelly@kaplan.edu
KELLY, JR., John, W 864-656-3015. 442 C
jkelly@clemson.edu
KELLY, Judith 518-454-5211. 321 A
kellyj@strose.edu
KELLY, Karen 334-291-4938..... 2 H
karen.kelly@cv.edu
KELLY, Kathryn 973-596-3305. 303 G
kelly@njit.edu
KELLY, Kathy 513-244-4418. 377 G
kathy_kelly@mail.msj.edu
KELLY, Kevin 413-545-0222. 228 F
kk@admissions.umass.edu
KELLY, Kevin, P 860-701-5079... 90 G
kelly_k@mitchell.edu
KELLY, Kevin, R 937-229-3557. 391 C
kellyker@udayton.edu
KELLY, Kristi 815-836-5332. 150 H
kellykr@lewisu.edu
KELLY, Lee 516-299-3092. 329 D
lee.kelly@liu.edu
KELLY, Leslie, E 207-834-7522. 212 E
lesliek@maine.edu
KELLY, Leslie, G 540-868-7134. 512 H
lkelley@lfcc.edu
KELLY, Lois, M 805-756-5893... 32 F
lkelly@calpoly.edu
KELLY, Lori 305-428-5909. 109 E
lkelly@aii.edu
KELLY, Louise 615-230-3400. 461 G
louise.kelly@volstate.edu
KELLY, Lyn 585-475-2946. 337 L
lyn.kelly@rit.edu
KELLY, M. Genevra 864-938-3831. 446 D
gkelly@presby.edu
KELLY, Marcia, J 603-646-3113. 296 G
marcia.j.kelly@dartmouth.edu
KELLY, DC, Margaret, J 718-990-6470. 339 A
kellymj@stjohns.edu
KELLY, Margaret, S 215-637-7700. 418 G
mkelly@holyfamily.edu
KELLY, Marisa 607-274-3113. 327 E
provost@ithaca.edu
KELLY, Marjorie 518-743-2257. 345 E
kellym@sunyacc.edu
KELLY, Mark 269-927-8100. 245 D
kelly@lakemichigancollege.edu
KELLY, Mark 312-369-7650. 143 D
mkelly@colum.edu
KELLY, Mark, L 864-294-2151. 444 C
mark.kelly@furman.edu
KELLY, Mary Ellen 413-775-1335. 231 E
kelly@gcc.mass.edu
KELLY, Mary Knopp 914-674-7809. 330 J
mkkelly@mercy.edu
KELLY, Matthew 908-852-1400. 300 D
kellym@centenarycollege.edu
KELLY, Matthew 740-364-9644. 376 A
mkelly@cotc.edu
KELLY, Michael 810-762-0455. 247 F
michael.kelly@mcc.edu
KELLY, Michelle 608-663-3256. 532 I
registrar@edgewood.edu
KELLY, Mike 360-538-4011. 520 B
mkelly@ghc.edu
KELLY, Paul 202-651-5075... 95 C
paul.kelly@gallaudet.edu
KELLY, SCJ, Paul 414-425-8300. 535 K
pkelly@shst.edu
KELLY, Peggy 909-869-2307... 32 G
pkelly@csupomona.edu
KELLY, Robert 773-508-3890. 151 H
rkelly1@luc.edu
KELLY, Robert 620-665-3417. 187 F
kellyr@hutchcc.edu
KELLY, Rod 478-445-5596. 125 A
rod.kelly@gcsu.edu
KELLY, Rosemary 910-678-8325. 360 D
kellyr@faytechcc.edu
KELLY, Roxanne 541-440-4662. 408 D
Roxanne.Kelly@umpqua.edu
KELLY, Scott 410-225-2256. 216 C
skelly@mica.edu
KELLY, Scott, A 979-458-6120. 483 C
s-kelly@tamus.edu
KELLY, Sean 239-590-7440. 115 A
skelly@fgcu.edu
KELLY, Stephanie 317-788-6099. 173 I
spkelly@uindy.edu
KELLY, Stephen 212-220-8261. 317 A
skelly@bmcc.cuny.edu
KELLY, Susan 617-287-7050. 228 E
skelly@umassp.edu
KELLY, T. Liisa 910-843-5304. 357 J
KELLY, Terence 207-834-7557. 212 E
terence.kelly@maine.edu
KELLY, Terence 207-834-7500. 212 E
terence.kelly@maine.edu
KELLY, Thomas 607-431-4111. 325 F
kellyt2@hartwick.edu
KELLY, Thomas 601-857-3237. 267 A
twkelly@hindscc.edu
KELLY, Thomas, J 646-888-6639. 329 J
tkelly@sloankettering.edu
KELLY, Thomas, M 312-915-6400. 151 H
tkelly4@luc.edu
KELLY, Todd 719-549-2380... 80 K
todd.kelly@colostate-pueblo.edu
KELLY, Tonya 352-854-2322. 100 K
kellyt@cf.edu
KELLY, William, P 646-664-9100. 316 I
chancellor@cuny.edu
KELLY, Yvan, J 904-819-6392. 103 E
kellyyj@flagler.edu
KELLY-ALBERTSON,
Lynn 269-387-2745. 252 I
lynn.kelly-albertson@wmich.edu
KELLY BATES, Martha 847-578-8582. 157 F
martha.bates@rosalindfranklin.edu
KELLY-BOWRY, Tanya 303-831-6192... 85 K
Tanya.KellyBowry@cu.edu
KELSCH, Anne 701-777-3325. 371 C
anne.kelsch@und.edu
KELSCH, Tyler 970-521-6615... 83 L
tyler.kelsch@njc.edu
KELSEN, Iris 513-793-1337. 393 B
iris_kelsen@wilmington.edu
KELSER, Sandra, B 334-833-4409..... 4 D
skelser@huntingdon.edu
KELSEY, Craig 661-952-5071... 32 H
ckelsey@csub.edu
KELSEY, Craig 661-654-2441... 32 H
ckelsey@csub.edu

KELSEY, Jane .... 217-854-3231. 140 G
jkels@blackburn.edu
KELSEY, Jane, M .... 814-824-2038. 423 J
jkelsey@mercyhurst.edu
KELSEY, Kimberly, R .... 717-736-4190. 417 I
krkelsey@hacc.edu
KELSEY, Madelaine .... 203-596-4624... 90 I
mkelsey@post.edu
KELSEY, Marty .... 307-382-1609. 543 J
mkelsey@wwcc.wy.edu
KELSHEIMER, Bradley, A .... 765-658-4161. 165 F
bradkelsheimer@depauw.edu
KELSHIAN, Patricia, L .... 202-885-3284... 94 F
pat@american.edu
KELSO, Kent .... 903-223-3063. 484 C
kent.kelso@tamut.edu
KELSO, Linda, M .... 863-667-5010. 113 P
lmkelso@seu.edu
KELSO, William .... 912-344-2541. 120 G
william.kelso@armstrong.edu
KELSON, Brandon .... 801-622-1573. 496 I
clint.kelson@stevenshenager.edu
KELTNER, Tom .... 417-865-2815. 274 B
keltnert@evangel.edu
KELTY, Edward .... 480-517-8630... 15 D
edward.kelty@riosalado.edu
KELTY, Jennifer .... 217-641-4201. 148 M
jkelty@jwcc.edu
KEMBLE, Karen, D .... 207-581-1226. 212 B
karen.kemble@maine.edu
KEMERER, John, J .... 740-593-0465. 387 C
kemerer@ohio.edu
KEMMER, Corby .... 218-281-8434. 264 E
ckemmer@umn.edu
KEMMY, Dave .... 401-254-3428. 440 B
dkemmy@rwu.edu
KEMNA, Betty .... 573-681-5953. 276 C
kemnab@lincolnu.edu
KEMNITZ, Carl .... 661-654-3420... 32 H
ckemnitz@csub.edu
KEMP, Ann .... 501-686-2500... 23 H
pakemp@uasys.edu
KEMP, Dale, A .... 630-752-5085. 163 F
dale.kemp@wheaton.edu
KEMP, Danny, M .... 540-831-5167. 508 C
dmkemp@radford.edu
KEMP, Gloria .... 501-686-6728... 24 C
kempgloriad@uams.edu
KEMP, Jamie .... 808-544-0276. 135 F
jkemp@hpu.edu
KEMP, Jerylle .... 212-237-8964. 318 D
jkemp@jjay.cuny.edu
KEMP, John .... 864-294-3717. 444 C
john.kemp@furman.edu
KEMP, Karl .... 870-307-7398... 21 H
karl.kemp@lyon.edu
KEMP, Katie .... 847-317-8177. 160 M
katiek@tiu.edu
KEMP, Lisa .... 714-816-0366... 70 A
lisa.kemp@trident.edu
KEMP, Rick .... 480-517-8508... 15 D
rick.kemp@riosalado.edu
KEMP, Shelley .... 901-320-9777. 463 J
skemp@victory.edu
KEMP, Shirley .... 304-829-7485. 526 D
skemp@bethanywv.edu
KEMP, Stephen .... 515-292-9694. 175 E
stephen.kemp@antiochschool.edu
KEMP, Steve .... 760-366-5283... 42 B
skemp@cmccd.edu
KEMP, Vandy .... 865-981-8111. 456 D
vandy.kemp@maryvillecollege.edu
KEMPA, Richard .... 307-382-1731. 543 J
rkempa@wwcc.wy.edu
KEMPEL, Leo .... 517-355-5133. 246 H
kempel@egr.msu.edu
KEMPER, Brad .... 575-562-2425. 309 H
brad.kemper@enmu.edu
KEMPER, Cathy .... 281-425-6867. 475 I
ckemper@lee.edu
KEMPER, Dan .... 636-949-4501. 276 D
dkemper@lindenwood.edu
KEMPER, James .... 740-588-1209. 394 C
jkemper@zanestate.edu
KEMPER, Kenneth, B .... 616-538-2330. 243 A
preskemper@gbcol.edu
KEMPER, Terry .... 262-695-3459. 541 D
tkemper1@wctc.edu
KEMPF, Emily, J .... 816-501-3571. 280 I
emily.kempf@rockhurst.edu
KEMPF, Gary .... 620-278-4469. 190 I
gkempf@sterling.edu
KEMPIAK, Robert .... 815-838-0500. 150 H
kempiaro@lewisu.edu
KEMPSTER, Jan .... 928-350-3213... 17 K
jkempster@prescott.edu
KEMPTON, Daniel .... 740-283-6228. 379 N
dkempton@franciscan.edu
KENDALL, Bruce .... 254-526-3101. 468 G
bruce.kendall@ctcd.edu
KENDALL, Chris .... 507-457-1640. 264 A
ckendall@smumn.edu
KENDALL, Christopher, W .... 734-764-0584. 251 C
ckndll@umich.edu
KENDALL, Curtis, L .... 540-828-5476. 502 J
ckendall@bridgewater.edu
KENDALL, Deborah .... 408-554-2717... 64 M
dkendall@scu.edu
KENDALL, Donna, M .... 781-891-2913. 223 C
dkendall@bentley.edu
KENDALL, Justin .... 620-862-5252. 184 E
jkendall@barclaycollege.edu
KENDALL, Kathy .... 970-247-7399... 81 M
kendall_k@fortlewis.edu
KENDALL, Laura .... 717-872-3265. 429 D
laura.kendall@millersville.edu
KENDALL, Matt .... 740-695-9500. 374 H
mkendall@belmontcollege.edu
KENDALL, Peter .... 828-328-7100. 356 B
peter.kendall@lr.edu
KENDALL, Rex .... 812-514-8446. 167 A
rkendall@indstatefoundation.org
KENDALL, Susan .... 412-924-1421. 431 A
skendall@pts.edu
KENDALL-JOHNSTON, Kathy, A .... 503-943-8004. 408 F
kendall@up.edu
KENDELL, Richard, E .... 435-586-7702. 497 A
richkendell@suu.edu
KENDER, JR., Joseph, P .... 610-758-5535. 422 A
jkender@lehigh.edu
KENDIG, P. Tysen .... 860-486-2240... 92 A
tysen.kendig@uconn.edu
KENDIG, Tysen .... 860-486-6713... 92 A
tysen.kendig@uconn.edu
KENDJORIA, Barrett .... 864-656-2354. 442 C
bkendjo@clemson.edu
KENDREX, Bradley .... 480-732-7379... 14 J
bradley.kendrex@cgc.edu
KENDRICK, Becky .... 660-248-6680. 272 B
bkendrick@centralmethodist.edu
KENDRICK, Bethany .... 620-421-6700. 188 D
bethanyk@labette.edu
KENDRICK, Dorsey, L .... 203-285-2060... 88 E
dkendrick@gwcc.commnet.edu
KENDRICK, Douglas, S .. 906-786-5802. 240 K
kendricd@baycollege.edu
KENDRICK, Leroy .... 504-671-6469. 203 A
lkendr@dcc.edu
KENDRICK, Mike .... 615-966-5773. 456 B
mike.kendrick@lipscomb.edu
KENDRICK, Mildred .... 706-821-8248. 130 C
mkendrick@paine.edu
KENERSON, Laura .... 401-874-5271. 440 D
kenerson@uri.edu
KENERSON, Murle .... 615-963-5212. 459 E
mkenerson@tnstate.edu
KENESSON, Alexander .... 253-680-7150. 516 L
akenesson@bates.ctc.edu
KENESSON, Summer .... 253-680-7204. 516 L
skenesson@bates.ctc.edu
KENIMER, Ann .... 979-845-3210. 483 C
a-kenimer@tamu.edu
KENIREY, Margo, S .... 478-757-2519. 122 F
mkenirey@centralgatech.edu
KENKEL, Kevin .... 605-995-2617. 450 A
kekenkel@dwu.edu
KENKEL, Mary Beth .... 321-674-8142. 104 H
mkenkel@fit.edu
KENMILLE, Cleo .... 406-275-4864. 288 C
cleo_kenmille@skc.edu
KENNA, Robert, F .... 315-655-7265. 316 E
rkenna@cazenovia.edu
KENNAMER, Mike .... 256-228-6001..... 5 H
kennamerm@nacc.edu
KENNAN, William, R .... 540-831-6415. 508 C
bkennan@radford.edu
KENNARD, Douglas .... 304-876-5330. 529 I
dkennard@shepherd.edu
KENNARD, Janet .... 713-942-9505. 473 D
jkennard@hgst.edu
KENNARD, Mary, E .... 202-885-3285... 94 F
mekesq@american.edu
KENNEDAY, Mark, A .... 501-686-5674... 24 C
kennedaymark@uams.edu
KENNEDY, Aaron .... 575-461-4413. 309 M
aaronk@mesalands.edu
KENNEDY, Alexis .... 708-534-7096. 145 F
akennedy@govst.edu
KENNEDY, Andrea .... 336-841-9283. 355 C
amoller@highpoint.edu
KENNEDY, April .... 216-373-5238. 385 G
akennedy@ndc.edu
KENNEDY, Brenda, J .... 251-580-2185..... 4 L
bkennedy@faulknerstate.edu
KENNEDY, Brett, E .... 706-236-2215. 121 G
bkennedy@berry.edu
KENNEDY, C. Ted .... 252-451-8275. 362 D
tkennedy@nashcc.edu
KENNEDY, Carol, M .... 570-577-1511. 411 A
carol.kennedy@bucknell.edu
KENNEDY, Catherine, B . 401-739-5000. 439 D
ckennedy@neit.edu
KENNEDY, Catherine, C . 727-394-6202. 112 E
kennedy.catherine@spcollege.edu
KENNEDY, Charles .... 206-685-1428. 524 G
kennec@uw.edu
KENNEDY, Craig, H .... 706-542-6446. 133 C
chk@uga.edu
KENNEDY, Dale .... 623-245-4600... 18 D
dkennedy@uti.edu
KENNEDY, Dana .... 410-626-2502. 217 G
dana.kennedy@sjca.edu
KENNEDY, Danielle .... 334-229-6969..... 1 D
dkennedylamar@alasu.edu
KENNEDY, David .... 919-760-8888. 356 G
kennedyd@meredith.edu
KENNEDY, Deborah .... 316-978-3830. 191 F
deborah.kennedy@wichita.edu
KENNEDY, Deborah, D .... 540-674-3690. 513 B
dkennedy@nr.edu
KENNEDY, Dennis .... 518-629-8085. 326 G
d.kennedy1@hvcc.edu
KENNEDY, Ellen .... 413-236-1003. 231 A
ekennedy@berkshirecc.edu
KENNEDY, Helen .... 724-357-2431. 428 F
helen.kennedy@iup.edu
KENNEDY, James .... 714-241-5708... 60 G
kennedy_james@sac.edu
KENNEDY, Jay, S .... 617-266-1400. 223 D
KENNEDY, Jeanne .... 252-527-6223. 361 F
jkennedy@lenoircc.edu
KENNEDY, Jeremy .... 419-783-2312. 379 C
jkennedy@defiance.edu
KENNEDY, John .... 413-545-8500. 228 F
jkennedy@admin.umass.edu
KENNEDY, John .... 641-472-1194. 180 N
personnel@mum.edu
KENNEDY, John .... 516-726-5589. 545 H
kennedyj@usmma.edu
KENNEDY, John, F .... 415-485-3282... 42 J
kennedy@dominican.edu
KENNEDY, John, M .... 315-386-7513. 345 F
kennedyjm@canton.edu
KENNEDY, Julie, A .... 910-576-6222. 362 C
kennedyj@montgomery.edu
KENNEDY, Katherine .... 617-353-4745. 224 D
kkennedy@bu.edu
KENNEDY, Kathleen .... 504-520-7421. 209 D
kkenned1@xula.edu
KENNEDY, Keith .... 386-506-3562. 101 G
kennedk@DaytonaState.edu
KENNEDY, Kerry, L .... 210-458-4201. 492 C
kerry.kennedy@utsa.edu
KENNEDY, Kevin .... 708-456-0300. 161 A
kkennedy@triton.edu
KENNEDY, Kim .... 814-732-1248. 428 E
kennedy@edinboro.edu
KENNEDY, Kristabell .... 828-766-1271. 361 H
kkennedy@mayland.edu
KENNEDY, Laurel, B .... 740-587-6208. 379 D
kennedy@denison.edu
KENNEDY, Leroy, E .... 312-567-8851. 147 F
kennedy@iit.edu
KENNEDY, Linda .... 949-480-4072... 66 F
lkennedy@soka.edu
KENNEDY, Marianne .... 203-392-5350... 88 A
kennedym4@southernct.edu
KENNEDY, Mark .... 810-762-0596. 247 F
mark.kennedy@mcc.edu
KENNEDY, Mary, M .... 207-725-3067. 209 H
mkennedy@bowdoin.edu
KENNEDY, Matthew .... 732-255-0400. 304 A
mkennedy@ocean.edu
KENNEDY, Matthew .... 267-502-4566. 410 I
matthew.kennedy@brynathyn.edu
KENNEDY, Norma .... 478-289-2002. 124 C
nwoods@ega.edu
KENNEDY, Patricia .... 914-674-3065. 330 J
pkennedy@mercy.edu
KENNEDY, Patrick .... 906-779-8547. 240 K
kennedyp@baycollege.edu
KENNEDY, Paul, W .... 585-594-6469. 337 K
kennedy_paul@roberts.edu
KENNEDY, Peggy .... 218-736-1503. 259 F
peggy.kennedy@minnesota.edu
KENNEDY, Rebecca, E .... 850-474-2420. 117 B
rkennedy@uwf.edu
KENNEDY, Richard .... 708-216-8434. 151 H
rkennedy@lumc.edu
KENNEDY, Shannon .... 704-669-4002. 359 D
kennedy@clevelandcc.edu
KENNEDY, SSJ, Sheila ... 215-248-7023. 413 A
kennedys@chc.edu
KENNEDY, Thomas, D .... 706-236-2297. 121 G
tkennedy@berry.edu
KENNEDY, Tim .... 910-576-6222. 362 C
kennedyt@montgomery.edu
KENNEDY, Tim .... 325-793-4775. 476 E
tkennedy@mcm.edu
KENNEDY, Timothy, R .... 507-933-6395. 255 I
tkennedy@gustavus.edu
KENNEDY, Treva .... 918-465-1761. 395 G
tkennedy@eosc.edu
KENNEDY, Treva .... 918-465-1786. 395 G
tkennedy@eosc.edu
KENNEDY, Valerie .... 718-270-5000. 319 A
vkennedy@mec.cuny.edu
KENNEDY, Vernal, L .... 859-246-6507. 194 L
vernal.kennedy@kctcs.edu
KENNEDY, Vicki, D .... 864-587-4236. 447 B
kennedyv@smcsc.edu
KENNEDY-DYGAS, Margaret .... 740-593-1808. 387 C
kennedm1@ohio.edu
KENNEDY-WITTHAR, Shawna, J .... 806-651-2227. 484 D
switthar@mail.wtamu.edu
KENNELL, Deena .... 308-432-6388. 291 D
dkennell@csc.edu
KENNELL, Janine, W .... 757-594-7754. 503 M
janine@cnu.edu
KENNELL, Scott, E .... 570-326-3761. 427 B
sek3@pct.edu
KENNELLY, Raymond .... 815-836-5521. 150 H
kennelra@lewisu.edu
KENNER, Corry, G .... 701-662-1505. 372 D
corry.kenner@lrsc.edu
KENNERLY, A. Chris .... 740-427-5160. 382 J
kennerlyc@kenyon.edu
KENNERLY, John, F .... 864-379-8747. 443 F
kennerly@erskine.edu
KENNEY, Anne, R .... 607-255-3393. 322 A
ark3@cornell.edu
KENNEY, Beth .... 301-687-4244. 220 C
bkenney@frostburg.edu
KENNEY, Daniel .... 910-521-6227. 369 B
daniel.kenney@uncp.edu
KENNEY, Debra .... 914-674-7891. 330 J
dkenney@mercy.edu
KENNEY, Dianne .... 412-268-5075. 412 H
dkenney@andrew.cmu.edu
KENNEY, Michael .... 734-432-5343. 246 B
mkenney@madonna.edu
KENNEY, Patrick .... 480-965-4222... 11 K
pkenney@asu.edu
KENNEY, Sue .... 443-334-2547. 218 E
skennney@stevenson.edu
KENNINGTON, Janet, S . 410-334-2942. 221 D
jkennington@worwic.edu
KENNISON, Kimberly .... 860-768-5516... 92 D
kennison@hartford.edu
KENNON, John (Gil) .... 573-518-2127. 278 A
gil@mineralarea.edu
KENNON, Paul .... 314-340-3351. 275 A
kennonp@hssu.edu
KENNY, Cathleen .... 845-569-3210. 332 B
cathleen.kenny@msmc.edu
KENNY, Edmond .... 352-588-8994. 112 D
edmond.kenny@saintleo.edu
KENNY, Edward, N .... 540-863-2880. 512 B
ekenny@dslcc.edu
KENNY, John .... 702-254-7577. 295 B
KENNY, Keith (Dallas) .... 308-865-8246. 292 H
kennyd2@unk.edu
KENNY, Kevin .... 510-783-2100... 46 L
kevin_kenny@heald.edu
KENNY, Maureen, E .... 617-552-4030. 224 A
maureen.kenny@bc.edu
KENNY, Robert .... 732-987-2416. 302 B
kennyr@georgian.edu
KENSER, Idalene .... 812-855-2707. 167 F
ikesner@indiana.edu
KENT, Carolyn .... 608-249-6611. 533 I
ckent@herzing.edu
KENT, Caryn .... 518-244-2391. 338 C
kentc@sage.edu
KENT, David .... 414-277-7350. 534 G
kent@msoe.edu
KENT, Jonathan .... 207-859-1111. 211 H
kentj@thomas.edu
KENT, Leigh .... 360-992-2101. 518 A
lkent@clark.edu
KENT, Linda .... 425-249-4758. 524 D
linda.kent@tlc.edu
KENT, Ronald, H .... 313-577-3390. 252 G
rkent@wayne.edu
KENT, Tom .... 518-793-5250. 345 E
kentt@sunyacc.edu
KENT-DAVIS, Linda, S ... 401-456-8031. 439 F
lkent@ric.edu
KENTON, Jay .... 541-737-3646. 405 G
jay_kenton@ous.edu
KENTOPP, Timothy .... 803-780-1219. 449 E
tkentopp@voorhees.edu
KENTOR, Jeffrey .... 734-487-0042. 242 D
jkentor@emich.edu
KENWORTHY, Anne .... 901-321-4213. 453 H
anne.kenworthy@cbu.edu
KENYON, Charles, B .... 716-878-4618. 343 A
kenyoncb@buffalostate.edu

KENYON, Kevin, S .... 765-285-8988. 164 B
kkenyon@bsu.edu
KENYON, Mark .... 617-287-5519. 228 G
mark.kenyon@umb.edu
KENYON, Steven .... 508-678-2811. 231 B
steve.kenyon@bristolcc.edu
KENZOR, Jennifer .... 812-877-8217. 172 C
jennifer.seddelmeyer@rose-hulman.edu
KEOHANE, Edward, J ..... 508-856-2900. 229 C
edward.keohane@umassmed.edu
KEOHANE, Ellen, J .... 508-793-2477. 225 B
ekeohane@holycross.edu
KEON, Thomas, L .... 219-989-2204. 171 N
tkeon@purduecal.edu
KEOUGH, Edward .... 718-862-7178. 329 M
edward.keough@manhattan.edu
KEOUGH, Vicki, A .... 708-216-5448. 151 H
vkeough@luc.edu
KEPHART, Kevin .... 605-688-5642. 452 B
kevin.kephart@sdstate.edu
KEPHAS, Kalwin .... 691-370-3191. 546 B
dirksa@comfsm.fm
KEPPLER, Kurt, J .... 225-578-3607. 204 O
kkeppler@lsu.edu
KEPPNER, Dana .... 217-228-5432. 156 C
keppnda@quincy.edu
KERBS, Nancy .... 417-667-8181. 273 A
nkerbs@cottey.edu
KERBUSCH, William .... 440-826-2233. 374 F
bkerbusc@bw.edu
KERBY, Debra .... 660-785-4346. 282 L
dkerby@truman.edu
KERBY, Diane .... 859-985-3110. 192 F
kerbyd@berea.edu
KERDA, Stephen, J .... 202-231-3068. 544 L
stephen.kerda@dodiis.mil
KERDOLFF, Russell, A ... 859-572-6455. 198 I
kerdolff@nku.edu
KERESTLY, Ed .... 325-674-2546. 464 H
ed.kerestly@acu.edu
KERFELD, Sally .... 320-222-5977. 260 H
sally.kerfeld@ridgewater.edu
KERICH, Julie, A .... 717-358-4743. 416 J
julie.kerich@fandm.edu
KERKAERT, Debra .... 507-537-6093. 261 F
Deb.Kerkaert@smsu.edu
KERKER, R. Michael .... 512-471-2694. 491 C
mkerker@austin.utexas.edu
KERKHOFF, Tom .... 217-540-3555. 150 D
tkerkhof@lakeland.cc.il.us
KERKIAN, Glen, R .... 603-526-3000. 295 I
glen.kerkian@colby-sawyer.edu
KERLEY, Jim .... 850-872-3800. 106 H
jkerley@gulfcoast.edu
KERLIN, Julia, M .... 404-413-1405. 126 E
jkerlin1@gsu.edu
KERLIN, Matthew, S ...... 205-726-2825..... 6 F
mskerlin@samford.edu
KERLIN, Scott .... 415-433-9200... 65 C
skerlin@saybrook.edu
KERMAN, Lucy, E .... 215-895-2123. 415 B
lucy.e.kerman@drexel.edu
KERMAN, Ron .... 615-297-7545. 452 J
kermanr@aquinascollege.edu
KERMES, Anita .... 916-278-6082... 34 D
anita.kermes@csus.edu
KERN, Alexander .... 617-373-2728. 235 F
KERN, Kim .... 912-583-3221. 122 B
kkern@bpc.edu
KERN, Ralph, M .... 208-496-1188. 137 H
kernr@byui.edu
KERNAN, William .... 503-838-8154. 406 E
kernanb@wou.edu
KERNEK, Lee .... 407-823-3812. 115 E
lee.kernek@ucf.edu
KERNER, Kelly .... 207-725-3808. 209 H
kkerner@bowdoin.edu
KERNER, Kelly, K .... 207-725-3808. 209 H
kkerner@bowdoin.edu
KERNER, Martha .... 608-262-0063. 536 D
mkerner@bussvc.wisc.edu
KERNICK, Rhonda .... 432-264-5101. 473 E
rkernick@howardcollege.edu
KERNIN, Richard, P .... 716-286-8044. 334 F
rpk@niagara.edu
KERNS, Connie, M .... 620-792-9273. 184 F
kernsc@bartonccc.edu
KERNS, David .... 970-247-7427... 81 M
kerns_d@fortlewis.edu
KERNS, Michael .... 209-954-5632... 63 C
mkerns@deltacollege.edu
KERP, Lauri .... 860-444-8308. 545 G
bookstore@uscga.edu
KERR, Andre .... 864-592-4774. 447 A
kerra@sccsc.edu
KERR, Anne, B .... 863-680-4100. 105 D
akerr@flsouthern.edu
KERR, Chad .... 620-241-0723. 185 K
chad.kerr@centralchristian.edu
KERR, Colleen .... 206-219-2408. 525 A
colleen.kerr@wsu.edu
KERR, Deeann .... 801-304-4224. 495 H
dkerr@broadviewuniversity.edu
KERR, Greg .... 620-278-4217. 190 I
gkerr@sterling.edu
KERR, Johnathan, C .... 706-886-6831. 133 A
jkerr@tfc.edu
KERR, Kathleen, G .... 302-831-1201... 94 B
kkerr@udel.edu
KERR, Marcel, S .... 817-531-7587. 488 A
mskerr@txwes.edu
KERR, Marcus .... 817-531-4237. 488 A
mkerr@txwes.edu
KERR, Maria .... 513-732-5204. 391 B
maria.kerr@euc.edu
KERR, Mary, E .... 216-368-2544. 375 J
mary.kerr@case.edu
KERR, Samuel .... 605-721-5214. 450 G
skerr@national.edu
KERR, Shelly, K .... 541-346-3227. 406 D
skerr@uoregon.edu
KERR, Steve .... 801-626-7587. 497 D
skerr1@weber.edu
KERRICK, Sandra .... 804-751-9191. 503 K
skerrick@rsht.edu
KERRIGAN, John, E .... 408-554-4968... 64 M
jekerrigan@scu.edu
KERRIGAN, JR.,
John, F .... 503-883-2443. 404 A
kerrigan@linfield.edu
KERRIGAN, Patrick, G .... 608-796-3041. 539 E
pgkerrigan@viterbo.edu
KERRY, Susan .... 218-726-8475. 264 D
se.kerry@d.umn.edu
KERSCHNER, Joseph, E . 414-955-8213. 534 C
jkerschner@mcw.edu
KERSCHNER-TAPPAN,
Alexis .... 505-224-4669. 309 E
akerschner@cnm.edu
KERSENBROCK,
Angela, M .... 407-708-2483. 113 E
kersenbrocka@seminolestate.edu
KERSEY, Elizabeth, A ...... 757-683-3152. 507 N
ekersey@odu.edu
KERSEY-MATUSIAK,
Gloria .... 215-637-7700. 418 G
gkmatusiak@holyfamily.edu
KERSH, Rogan .... 336-758-3128. 370 D
kersh@wfu.edu
KERSTEN, Andrew .... 920-465-2033. 536 F
kerstena@uwgb.edu
KERSTEN, Davide, W ...... 773-244-6214. 154 G
dwkersten@northpark.edu
KERSTEN, James, B .... 515-574-1132. 179 D
kersten@iowacentral.edu
KERSTETTER, Philip, P ... 919-658-7746. 357 I
pkerstetter@moc.edu
KERSTIENS, Michael, J .. 812-941-2596. 168 F
mjkersti@ius.edu
KERSTING, Monica, R .... 218-299-4557. 255 A
kersting@cord.edu
KERTULIS-TARTAR, Gina 706-272-4516. 123 G
gkertulistartar@daltonstate.edu
KERWIN, Cornelius, M ... 202-885-2121... 94 F
president@american.edu
KERWIN, Linda .... 716-827-2454. 348 G
kerwinl@trocaire.edu
KERWIN, Mark .... 617-369-3281. 236 F
mkerwin@mfa.org
KERWITZ, Ann .... 815-921-4001. 157 A
a.kerwitz@rockvalleycollege.edu
KERWOOD, Jennifer .... 413-236-2188. 231 A
jkerwood@berkshirecc.edu
KESERAUSKIS,
Elizabeth, M .... 618-650-3605. 159 H
ekesera@siue.edu
KESICKI, Michael .... 814-871-5873. 416 K
kesicki001@gannon.edu
KESKULA, Douglas, R ..... 828-227-7271. 369 E
KESLER, Michael .... 802-773-5900. 499 B
michael.kesler@csj.edu
KESSEL, Joyce .... 716-896-0700. 350 A
jkessel@villa.edu
KESSELMAN, Harvey ...... 609-652-4514. 305 C
harvey.kesselman@stockton.edu
KESSIN, Janet .... 212-799-5000. 328 B
KESSINGER, Kevin, S ..... 765-658-4175. 165 F
kevinkessinger@depauw.edu
KESSLER, Gene .... 219-473-4299. 164 K
gkessler@ccsj.edu
KESSLER, Jeanne, D .... 785-670-1629. 191 D
jeanne.kessler@washburn.edu
KESSLER, Jeffrey, A .... 516-877-3660. 313 A
kessler@adelphi.edu
KESSLER, Karen .... 850-484-1673. 110 G
kkessler@pensacolastate.edu
KESSLER, Kathleen .... 802-839-8317. 499 I
kathleen.kessler@neci.edu
KESSLER, Nevin, E .... 848-445-4636. 306 A
KESSLER, Richard .... 212-580-0210. 332 E
kesslerr@newschool.edu
KESSLER, Susan, B .... 386-312-4021. 112 C
susankessler@sjrstate.edu
KESSLER, Suzanne .... 914-251-6600. 344 D
suzanne.kessler@purchase.edu
KESSLER-CLEARY,
Timothy .... 973-618-3484. 300 A
tcleary@caldwell.edu
KESTEN, Philip, R .... 408-554-4311... 64 M
pkesten@scu.edu
KESTER, Karen, A .... 941-752-5329. 114 I
kesterk@scf.edu
KESTER, Kelly .... 360-383-3245. 525 D
kkester@whatcom.ctc.edu
KESTER, Lori .... 303-556-2906... 81 D
lori.kester@ccd.edu
KESTERSON, Ronald, L .. 865-694-6608. 461 D
rkesterson@pstcc.edu
KESTNER, Carly .... 276-326-4243. 502 H
ckestner@bluefield.edu
KESTNER, Laura, F .... 414-288-7424. 534 B
laura.kestner@marquette.edu
KETCHESON, Kathi, A ..... 503-725-3432. 406 B
ketchesonk@pdx.edu
KETCHUM, William .... 678-915-7479. 132 C
wketchum@spsu.edu
KETELS, Margo .... 563-589-3131. 182 J
mketels@dbq.edu
KETNER, Annette .... 619-260-2925... 73 I
aketner@sandiego.edu
KETO, Stephen, W .... 919-515-9224. 368 B
steve_keto@ncsu.edu
KETTEMAN, Paul, G .... 615-844-5000. 464 E
gketteman@welch.edu
KETTENBEIL, Kenneth ..... 313-593-5140. 251 D
kketten@umich.edu
KETTERER, John, J .... 256-782-5303..... 4 K
jkettere@jsu.edu
KETTERER, Kathleen .... 229-248-2530. 121 E
kathleen.ketterer@bainbridge.edu
KETTERER, Patricia .... 212-237-8516. 318 D
pketterer@jjay.cuny.edu
KETTERMAN, Dave, V ..... 417-667-8181. 273 A
dketterman@cottey.edu
KETTERMAN, Jesse .... 301-687-4226. 220 C
jketterman@frostburg.edu
KETTING-WELLER,
Ginger .... 951-785-2266... 50 B
gketting@lasierra.edu
KETTL, Donald, F .... 301-405-6355. 219 B
kettl@umd.edu
KETTLEWELL, Charles, L 214-648-3606. 493 E
charles.kettlewell@utsouthwestern.edu
KETTNER, Valrey, V .... 701-231-9608. 371 G
val.kettner@ndsu.edu
KETTNER-POLLEY, Rick .. 617-759-1700. 235 A
rketner-polley@aii.edu
KETTS, Amy .... 636-651-1600. 281 K
aketts@sbc-fenton.com
KETTYLE, William, M ...... 617-253-1774. 233 B
KEUFFEL, Elizabeth .... 603-641-7203. 297 G
ekeuffel@anselm.edu
KEUP, Mike .... 309-677-2677. 140 I
mkeup@bradley.edu
KEVIL, Tim .... 903-875-7443. 477 G
tim.kevil@navarrocollege.edu
KEY, Charlet .... 309-796-5143. 140 E
keyc@bhc.edu
KEY, Dan .... 641-844-5741. 179 J
dan.key@iavalley.edu
KEY, Elizabeth .... 801-832-2202. 498 F
ekey@westminstercollege.edu
KEY, Henry .... 908-709-7151. 308 B
key@ucc.edu
KEY, John .... 205-652-5456..... 9 F
jkey@uwa.edu
KEY, Monica .... 617-989-4125. 237 G
keym@wit.edu
KEY, Rand .... 832-813-6522. 476 A
rand.key@lonestar.edu
KEY, Roby, V .... 817-257-7706. 484 I
r.key@tcu.edu
KEY, Spencer .... 607-729-1581. 322 F
skey@davisny.edu
KEY, Stacy .... 479-979-1360... 25 J
skey@ozarks.edu
KEY, Stan .... 859-257-8907. 200 C
srkey@email.uky.edu
KEYES, Beth, H .... 937-229-3769. 391 C
bkeyes@udayton.edu
KEYES, Danny .... 318-628-4342. 202 K
dkeyes@ltc.edu
KEYES, James, R .... 802-443-5523. 499 H
jkeyes@middlebury.edu
KEYES, Judy .... 617-287-6300. 228 G
judy.keyes@umb.edu
KEYES, Robert .... 575-234-9216. 311 A
rkeyes@nmsu.edu
KEYS, Carolyn .... 909-274-4525... 55 A
ckeys@mtsac.edu
KEYS, James, A .... 910-843-5304. 357 J
KEYS, Margo, A .... 715-858-1825. 539 J
mkeys@cvtc.edu
KEYS, Marina .... 503-845-3550. 404 D
marina.keys@mtangel.edu
KEYS, Terrance .... 585-292-3432. 332 A
tkeys@monroecc.edu
KEZIRIAN, Wayne, M ..... 401-598-1900. 439 B
wkezirian@jwu.edu
KHACHATRYAN, Davit .... 949-451-5326... 67 B
dkhachatryan@ivc.edu
KHACHIKIAN, Crist .... 818-677-2138... 34 C
crist.khachikian@csun.edu
KHADANGA, Dave .... 334-386-7113..... 3 H
dkhadanga@faulkner.edu
KHALDEN, Jeff .... 817-598-6485. 494 G
jkhalden@wc.edu
KHALEEL, Tasneem .... 406-657-2177. 287 C
tkhaleel@msubillings.edu
KHAMIS, Bill .... 814-371-2090. 434 F
bkhamis@triangle-tech.edu
KHAN, Adil .... 636-227-2100. 276 F
adil.khan@logan.edu
KHAN, Akhande .... 330-941-3394. 394 A
askhan@ysu.edu
KHAN, Ali, A .... 252-335-3291. 367 C
aakhan@mail.ecsu.edu
KHAN, Andrea .... 816-802-3466. 275 J
akhan@kcai.edu
KHAN, Farooq, A .... 678-839-6027. 133 I
fkhan@westga.edu
KHAN, Feroze .... 703-539-6890. 510 B
fkhan@stratford.edu
KHAN, Jehana .... 320-222-5986. 260 H
jehana.khan@ridgewater.edu
KHAN, Kamran .... 713-348-3500. 479 A
kamran@rice.edu
KHAN, M. Wasiullah .... 312-939-0111. 144 D
chancellor@eastwest.edu
KHAN, Rehan .... 617-373-2752. 235 F
KHAN-MARCUS,
Zaveeni .... 805-893-8411... 72 B
zaveeni.khan-marcus@sa.ucsb.edu
KHANDKE, Kailash .... 864-294-3316. 444 C
kailash.khandke@furman.edu
KHANEJA, Gurvinder .... 201-684-7766. 305 A
gkhaneja@ramapo.edu
KHANI, Anthony .... 646-717-9743. 325 B
khani@gts.edu
KHANNA, Pradeep .... 217-333-9525. 162 A
pkhanna@illinois.edu
KHANNA, Ranjana .... 919-668-2548. 354 A
rkhanna@duke.edu
KHANOYAN, Gayane .... 818-988-2300... 55 G
KHARASCH, Evan, D .... 314-362-8796. 284 L
kharasch@wustl.edu
KHARTABIL, Basim .... 312-935-6214. 156 K
bkhartabil@robertmorris.edu
KHASAWNEH, Rami .... 815-836-5360. 150 H
khasawra@lewisu.edu
KHATOR, Renu .... 713-743-8820. 489 B
rkhator@uh.edu
KHATOR, Renu .... 713-743-8820. 489 A
rkhator@uh.edu
KHATTARI, Karen .... 610-606-4632. 412 I
klkhatta@cedarcrest.edu
KHAWAJA, Ikram .... 330-941-3103. 394 A
ikhawaja@ysu.edu
KHAWAR, Mariam .... 607-735-1932. 323 H
mkhawar@elmira.edu
KHAYUM, Mohammed ... 812-464-1718. 174 D
mkhayum@usi.edu
KHEHRA, Harry .... 281-290-6576. 476 A
harry.khehra@lonestar.edu
KHLEIF, Samir .... 706-721-0570. 126 B
skhleif@gru.edu
KHOSLA, Pradeep, K .... 858-534-3135... 71 F
chancellor@ucsd.edu
KHOSRAVANI, Mariam ... 714-241-6159... 39 I
mkhosravani@coastline.edu
KHOSROWPANAH,
Shahram .... 671-735-2694. 546 E
khosrow@uguam.uog.edu
KHOURY, Melik Peter .... 207-948-9122. 211 I
mkhoury@unity.edu
KHOURY, Philip, S .... 617-253-0887. 233 B
KHOURY, Terry, L .... 814-371-6920. 415 C
admissions@dbcollege.edu
KHURANA, Nikki .... 909-621-8054... 65 D
nkhurana@scrippscollege.edu
KIA, Norman .... 575-769-4074. 309 F
norman.kia@clovis.edu
KIAH, Jude .... 309-298-1931. 162 K
jl-kiah@wiu.edu
KIAN, David .... 561-297-3007. 114 L
david.kian@fau.edu
KIANI, Tanya .... 805-756-7507... 32 F
tkiani@calpoly.edu
KIBBE, Anne .... 352-588-7373. 112 D
anne.kibbe@saintleo.edu
KIBLER, Michele .... 614-222-4009. 378 A
mkibler@ccad.edu

KIBLER, William, L .... 662-325-3045. 268 D
billk@saffairs.msstate.edu
KIBOTA, Travis .... 360-992-2282. 518 A
tkibota@clark.edu
KICKLIGHTER, Jeremy .... 314-434-4044. 273 C
jeremy.kicklighter@covenantseminary.edu
KICKLITER, Holly .... 727-873-4455. 116 D
hkicklit@mail.usf.edu
KICKNER, Robert .... 253-833-9111. 520 C
rkickner@greenriver.edu
KICKUL, Gerard, H .... 815-740-3432. 162 F
gkickul@stfrancis.edu
KIDD, Aixa, L .... 508-793-7666. 225 A
akidd@clarku.edu
KIDD, Jane .... 706-369-6833. 130 E
jkidd@piedmont.edu
KIDD, Lisa, L .... 920-923-8115. 534 A
llkidd@marianuniversity.edu
KIDD, Mary .... 615-514-2787. 457 P
financialaid@nossi.edu
KIDD, Meredith .... 785-670-2100. 191 D
meredith.kidd@washburn.edu
KIDD, Mike .... 828-327-7000. 359 A
mkidd@cvcc.edu
KIDD, Richard .... 757-352-4840. 508 G
rkidd@regent.edu
KIDD, Windy .... 859-280-1237. 197 C
wkidd@lextheo.edu
KIDDER, Ralph .... 703-284-3847. 507 B
ralph.kidder@marymount.edu
KIDESS LUCEY, Tamie ... 413-748-3161. 236 I
tkidessl@springfieldcollege.edu
KIDWELL, Debra .... 573-681-5418. 276 C
purchasing@lincolnu.edu
KIDWELL, Eric, A .... 334-833-4420..... 4 D
ekidwell@huntingdon.edu
KIDWELL, Martin .... 503-253-3443. 405 E
mkidwell@ocom.edu
KIEBA-TOLKSDORF, Helen, C .... 248-689-8282. 251 I
hkieba@walshcollege.edu
KIEC, Michael .... 216-373-5227. 385 G
mkiec@ndc.edu
KIECKHAFER, David, S .. 608-342-1321. 537 D
kieckhaferd@uwplatt.edu
KIEDA, David, B .... 801-581-8796. 496 Q
dave.kieda@utah.edu
KIEF, Bob .... 253-879-2820. 524 F
bkief@pugetsound.edu
KIEFER, Cindy .... 406-756-3843. 286 B
ckiefer@fvcc.edu
KIEFER, David, E .... 626-584-5409... 45 E
dkiefer@fuller.edu
KIEFER, Irene .... 800-567-2344. 532 E
ikiefer@menominee.edu
KIEFER, Jane .... 203-857-7261... 89 D
jkiefer@norwalk.edu
KIEFER, Michael .... 229-317-6558. 124 A
michael.kiefer@darton.edu
KIEFER, Michael .... 610-896-1142. 418 F
mkiefer@haverford.edu
KIEFER, Theodore, E ...... 610-785-6207. 432 C
tkiefer@scs.edu
KIEFFER, Barb .... 920-735-5734. 539 K
kieffer@fvtc.edu
KIEFFER, Don .... 212-986-4343. 314 K
dmk@berkeleycollege.edu
KIEFFER, Don .... 212-986-4343. 299 D
dmk@Berkeleycollege.edu
KIEFFER, Linda .... 509-359-6345. 519 C
lkieffer@ewu.edu
KIEFFER, Regina .... 316-322-3104. 185 D
rkieffer@butlercc.edu
KIEFFER, Roger, L .... 847-317-7055. 160 M
rkieffer@tiu.edu
KIEFFER, Shelly .... 318-473-6508. 205 A
skieffer@lsua.edu
KIEFT, Robert .... 323-259-2832... 56 I
kieft@oxy.edu
KIEHART, Dan .... 919-668-2728. 354 A
natscidean@duke.edu
KIEHL, Gregg .... 607-844-8222. 347 I
kiehlg@TC3.edu
KIEHNE, Rolfe, E .... 636-327-4645. 277 K
sil@midwest.edu
KIEL, Cindy, M .... 530-754-1184... 70 J
cmkiel@ucdavis.edu
KIEL, Mark .... 847-635-7122. 155 F
mkiel@oakton.edu
KIELB, Mitch .... 815-753-1083. 154 I
mkielb@niu.edu
KIELBASA, Jody, K .... 434-982-5326. 511 B
jkk8j@virginia.edu
KIELT, Chris .... 919-962-3444. 368 D
chris_kielt@unc.edu
KIELTY, Megan .... 413-265-2211. 225 C
kieltym@elms.edu
KIELY, Douglas, W .... 202-231-3280. 544 L
douglas.kiely@dodiis.mil
KIELY, Maurice, J .... 804-412-2026. 508 E
mkiely@rmc.edu
KIENER, Dan, W .... 412-397-5263. 431 I
kiener@rmu.edu
KIENHOLZ JURCEVICH, Ann .... 509-533-3535. 518 F
ann.jurcevich@spokanefalls.edu
KIENITZ, Kelli, S .... 320-222-5215. 260 H
kelli.kienitz@ridgewater.edu
KIENLE-GRANZO, Beth .. 718-260-3486. 336 E
ekienleg@poly.edu
KIENOW, Sharon .... 605-626-2640. 451 I
kienows@northern.edu
KIERALDO, John .... 312-553-5761. 141 N
jkieraldo@ccc.edu
KIERAN, OP, Helen .... 203-773-8515... 87 G
hkieran@albertus.edu
KIERAN, Robert .... 541-346-5758. 405 G
bob_kieran@ous.edu
KIERNAN, Catherine, A .. 973-761-9191. 307 C
catherine.kiernan@shu.edu
KIERNAN, Jo, A .... 540-831-6222. 508 C
jakiernan@radford.edu
KIERNAN, Joseph .... 201-692-2460. 301 J
kiernan@fdu.edu
KIES, Susan, M .... 217-333-1920. 161 C
kies@uillinois.edu
KIESER, Bruce .... 206-934-6020. 522 I
bruce.kieser@seattlecolleges.edu
KIESLER, Dolores .... 270-686-4259. 192 G
dolores.kiesler@brescia.edu
KIESLING, Gay .... 425-235-7863. 522 F
gkiesling@rtc.edu
KIESSLING, Marcia, K .... 812-464-1757. 174 D
kiessling@usi.edu
KIEST, Diane, M .... 217-351-2283. 155 J
dkiest@parkland.edu
KIETZMANN, David, L .... 217-443-8771. 143 G
dkietz@dacc.edu
KIEWIET, D, R .... 626-395-6351... 31 E
drk@caltech.edu
KIFER, Ruth .... 408-808-2020... 36 A
ruth.kifer@sjsu.edu
KIGER, Nicole, C .... 757-683-3446. 507 N
nkiger@odu.edu
KIGGINS, Maureen .... 718-429-6600. 349 H
maureen.kiggins@vaughn.edu
KIGHT, Brian .... 325-641-3918. 486 C
brian.kight@tstc.edu
KIGHT, Kurtis, L .... 252-334-2007. 357 A
kurtis.kight@macuniversity.edu
KIGHT, Walda .... 912-260-4274. 131 F
walda.kight@sgsc.edu
KIGHTLINGER, Linda ..... 814-732-2770. 428 E
lkightlinger@edinboro.edu
KIGHTLINGER, Paul, B .. 814-732-1266. 428 E
pkightliner@edinboro.edu
KIHL, Brenda, K .... 972-377-1551. 469 G
bkihl@collin.edu
KIJANCA, Lori, N .... 954-322-4460. 107 V
graduatestudies@jmvu.edu
KIJEWSKI, Megan .... 206-239-2299. 516 H
mkijewski@aii.edu
KIJINSKI, John, L .... 716-673-3174. 342 A
john.kijinski@fredonia.edu
KIKENDALL, Alison .... 215-702-4334. 411 F
akikendall@cairn.edu
KIKWEBATI, Muleka .... 757-547-6063... 96 F
muleka.kikwebati@strayer.edu
KIL RYU, Jong .... 323-643-0301... 27 N
KILBER REBMAN, Kerry 619-660-4400... 46 D
kerry.kilberrebman@gcccd.edu
KILBOURNE, Kathleen .... 704-945-7315. 365 E
kathleen.kilbourne@fsmail.pfeiffer.edu
KILBURG, Lynn, J .... 563-333-6352. 182 B
KilburgLynnJ@sau.edu
KILBURG, Peggy, L .... 503-554-2182. 403 C
pkilburg@georgefox.edu
KILBURN, Ericka .... 773-907-4457. 142 A
ekilburn@ccc.edu
KILBURN, Todd .... 305-546-3517... 83 F
tkilburn@naropa.edu
KILBURN, Todd .... 303-546-3557... 83 F
KILBY, Melonie .... 336-838-6489. 365 B
melonie.kilby@wilkescc.edu
KILCHENSTEIN, Lynn ..... 603-271-6484. 296 C
lkilchenstein@ccsnh.edu
KILCREASE, Daniel .... 801-626-6968. 497 D
dwkilcrease@weber.edu
KILCREASE, Dawn .... 603-882-6923. 296 B
dkilcrease@ccsnh.edu
KILCREASE, Mitch .... 405-744-5231. 397 H
mitch.kilcrease@okstate.edu
KILCULLEN, Peter .... 570-340-6044. 423 B
kilcullen@marywood.edu
KILDAL, Lori .... 831-770-7090... 46 G
lkildal@hartnell.edu
KILEDJIAN, Michael .... 866-323-0233... 60 E
KILEN, Ray Ann .... 701-483-2470. 371 D
rayann.kilen@dsu.nodak.edu
KILEY, Maeve, M .... 312-915-7712. 151 H
mkiley2@luc.edu
KILEY, Maryellen, M .... 617-333-2124. 225 E
mcollito0606@curry.edu
KILGALLIN, Michael .... 507-288-4563. 255 C
mkilgallin@crossroadscollege.edu
KILGALLON, J. Scott ...... 715-836-5858. 536 E
kilgals@uwec.edu
KILGORE, Janelle .... 701-777-3121. 371 C
janelle.kilgore@und.edu
KILGORE, Jeff .... 254-867-3984. 485 G
jeff.kilgore@tstc.edu
KILGORE, Jeffrey, L .... 254-710-1121. 467 G
jeff_kilgore@baylor.edu
KILGORE, Kimberly, J .... 314-367-8700. 281 C
kimberly.kilgore@stlcop.edu
KILGOUR, Dean .... 213-477-2746... 54 J
dkilgour@msmc.la.edu
KILKENNY, Rosemary ..... 202-687-4798... 95 E
kilkennr@georgetown.edu
KILLACKEY, Herbert .... 949-824-7371... 71 B
hkillack@uci.edu
KILLAM, Gary, A .... 904-808-7492. 112 C
garykillam@sjrstate.edu
KILLEBREW, Flavius, C .. 361-825-2621. 483 F
flavius.killebrew@tamucc.edu
KILLEBREW, Veronica .... 313-927-1427. 246 D
KILLEEN, Donald .... 440-525-7261. 382 M
dkilleen@lakelandcc.edu
KILLEEN, Suzanne Valle . 770-394-8300. 120 H
skilleen@aii.edu
KILLEEN, Timothy .... 518-434-7120. 341 C
timothy.killeen@rfsuny.org
KILLEN, Anne .... 315-279-5416. 328 D
akillen@mail.keuka.edu
KILLEY, Joshua, D .... 317-274-5693. 168 D
jkilley@iupui.edu
KILLIAN, Darnita .... 404-270-5130. 132 E
dkillian@spelman.edu
KILLIAN, Michael .... 419-824-3730. 383 C
mkillian@lourdes.edu
KILLIAN, Peggy .... 630-617-3625. 145 A
peggyk@elmhurst.edu
KILLIAN, Peter, S .... 315-445-4555. 328 F
killiaps@lemoyne.edu
KILLIAN, Susan .... 828-327-7000. 359 A
skillian@cvcc.edu
KILLIN, Jim, P .... 408-453-9900... 47 H
jkillin@henley-putnam.edu
KILLINGSWORTH, Blake 214-333-5175. 470 D
blake@dbu.edu
KILLINGSWORTH, Patrick .... 707-864-7000... 66 G
patrick.killingsworth@solano.edu
KILLION, Kathleen .... 941-487-5000. 115 D
kkillion@ncf.edu
KILLORAN, Margaret, A . 315-255-1743. 316 D
maggie.killoran@cayuga-cc.edu
KILLOUGH, April .... 828-694-1805. 358 C
a_killough@blueridge.edu
KILLOUGH, Jay .... 806-742-2210. 487 D
jay.killough@ttu.edu
KILLPACK, Marian .... 641-784-5106. 178 F
killpack@graceland.edu
KILLPATRICK, Paul .... 206-934-4144. 522 J
paul.killpatrick@seattlecolleges.edu
KILLPATRICK, Paul .... 206-934-4144. 522 H
paul.killpatrick@seattlecolleges.edu
KILMARX, John, N .... 724-357-7507. 428 F
john.kilmarx@iup.edu
KILMER, Alisa .... 612-436-7541. 257 J
akilmer@msbcollege.edu
KILMISTER, Mairim .... 603 526 3715. 295 I
mkilmister@colby-sawyer.edu
KILPATRICK, Andrew, W 570-321-4349. 422 H
kilpatri@lycoming.edu
KILPATRICK, Kirk .... 901-751-8453. 457 B
kkilpatrick@mabts.edu
KILPATRICK, Peter, K ..... 574-631-5534. 174 A
peter.kilpatrick.4@nd.edu
KILPINEN, Jon, T .... 219-464-5314. 174 E
jon.kilpinen@valpo.edu
KILROY, John .... 559-453-2284... 45 D
john.kilroy@fresno.edu
KILTY, Duane .... 765-677-2605. 169 B
duane.kilty@indwes.edu
KILZER, Rebekah .... 740-351-3267. 388 N
rkilzer@shawnee.edu
KIM, Albert .... 213-487-0110... 42 K
info@dula.edu
KIM, Bokin .... 215-884-8942. 438 A
president@woninstitute.edu
KIM, Brian, H .... 213-413-9500... 67 I
president@scusoma.edu
KIM, Dae, G .... 636-327-4645. 277 K
dgkim@midwest.edu
KIM, Daniel, D .... 770-279-0507. 124 I
danielkim@gcuniv.edu
KIM, David .... 704-330-6828. 359 C
david.kim@cpcc.edu
KIM, Davis, S .... 703-333-5904. 516 B
KIM, Diane .... 916-577-2200... 76 J
dkim@missouri.edu
KIM, Eunice .... 770-279-0507. 124 I
daltting@gmail.com
KIM, Eunice .... 312-662-4215. 139 F
eukim@adler.edu
KIM, Haeryon .... 970-382-6977... 81 M
kim_h@fortlewis.edu
KIM, Hanjik .... 714-533-1495... 66 H
hjk@southbaylo.edu
KIM, Heather .... 602-386-4136... 11 G
heather.kim@arizonachristian.edu
KIM, Heather, H .... 608-262-2321. 536 C
hkim@uwsa.edu
KIM, Hyo In .... 714-517-1945... 29 K
chiefacademic@buc.edu
KIM, Hyun Wan .... 714-525-0088... 46 A
dean@gm.edu
KIM, Jake, J .... 609-497-7756. 304 D
alumni@ptsem.edu
KIM, James .... 714-533-3946... 36 C
jameskim@calums.edu
KIM, James .... 714-533-1495... 66 H
james@southbaylo.edu
KIM, Jin Song .... 323-731-2383... 57 I
KIM, John .... 619-684-8841... 56 C
jkim@newschoolarch.edu
KIM, John, J .... 415-405-4155... 35 E
johnjkim@sfsu.edu
KIM, Jongchai .... 662-254-3600. 269 A
mvsukim@gmail.com
KIM, Julius .... 760-480-8474... 76 C
jjkim@wscal.edu
KIM, Jung .... 415-282-7600... 27 L
jungkim@actcm.edu
KIM, Keith, K .... 323-731-2383... 57 I
keith@psuca.edu
KIM, Kwang-Wu .... 480-965-8561... 11 K
kwang-wu.kim@asu.edu
KIM, Kwang-Wu .... 312-369-7200. 143 D
kwkim@colum.edu
KIM, Kwangsin .... 714-525-0088... 46 A
KIM, Melissa .... 412-536-1109. 420 A
melissa.kim@laroche.edu
KIM, Min Sang .... 323-731-2383... 57 I
mskim@psuca.edu
KIM, Min Soo .... 770-279-0507. 124 I
soo729@hotmail.com
KIM, Moonsik .... 323-731-2383... 57 I
mkim@psuca.edu
KIM, Myeong .... 213-252-5100... 26 A
KIM, Paul, C .... 770-279-0507. 124 I
drpaul@gcuniv.edu
KIM, Rebecca .... 847-574-5264. 150 C
rkim@lfgsm.edu
KIM, Richard, K .... 703-206-0508. 504 A
KIM, Sammuel .... 310-243-3657... 33 B
skim@csudh.edu
KIM, Samuel .... 770-279-0507. 124 I
38317muel@hanmail.net
KIM, Sang Jo .... 714-535-3886... 66 H
sjkim@southbaylo.edu
KIM, Sara .... 770-279-0507. 124 I
sarakim@gcuniv.edu
KIM, Shalom, Y .... 323-550-8888... 66 A
KIM, Stacey .... 503-777-7590. 407 E
kims@reed.edu
KIM, Uriah .... 860-509-9516... 90 B
ukim@hartsem.edu
KIM, Young Joon .... 714-517-1945... 29 K
chieffinancial@buc.edu
KIM, Yun .... 310-453-8300... 43 D
yun@emperors.edu
KIM, Yun .... 201-447-7100. 299 C
yunkim@bergen.edu
KIM, Zukweon .... 323-731-2383... 57 I
zkim@psuca.edu
KIMATA, Stephen, A .... 434-924-4241. 511 B
sak@virginia.edu
KIMBALL, Amber, M .... 919-508-2028. 370 F
amkimball@peace.edu
KIMBALL, Christopher .... 805-493-3100... 31 H
ckimball@clunet.edu
KIMBALL, Curtis .... 603-668-2211. 297 I
c.kimball@snhu.edu
KIMBALL, Elmer .... 802-654-0505. 501 C
elmer.kimball@ccv.edu
KIMBALL, Jon .... 617-521-2411. 236 G
jon.kimball@simmons.edu
KIMBALL, Joseph .... 814-824-2559. 423 J
jkimball@mercyhurst.edu
KIMBALL, Kevin .... 541-383-7209. 402 D
kekimball@cocc.edu
KIMBALL, Ranch .... 781-239-5075. 222 D
rckimball@babson.edu
KIMBARK, Kris .... 409-933-8131. 469 E
kkimbark@com.edu
KIMBAROVSKY, Jennifer 815-280-2357. 149 A
KIMBER, Brady .... 801-524-8171. 495 O
BKimber@ldsbc.edu
KIMBERLING, Charles, L .... 413-662-5099. 230 C
charles.kimberling@mcla.edu

KIMBLE, Darius, Z .... 903-927-3316. 495 A
dkimble@wileyc.edu
KIMBRO, K. Sean .... 919-530-7025. 368 A
kkimbro@nccu.edu
KIMBROUGH, Ann .... 850-599-3379. 114 K
ann.kimbrough@famu.edu
KIMBROUGH,
Michael, J .... 913-288-7161. 187 L
kimbr@kckcc.edu
KIMBROUGH, Scott .... 904-256-7118. 107 Q
skimbro@ju.edu
KIMBROUGH, Walter, M 504-816-4640. 201 K
wkimbrough@dillard.edu
KIMBROUGH-WALLS,
Vickie .... 619-216-6670... 68 B
vkimbrough@swccd.edu
KIMBROW, Terry .... 501-205-8904... 20 I
tkimbrow@cbc.edu
KIMES, Althea .... 757-352-4047. 508 G
akimes@regent.edu
KIMLIN, Ernie .... 847-925-6225. 145 H
ekimlin@harpercollege.edu
KIMMEL, Howard, S .... 973-596-3574. 303 G
howard.kimmel@njit.edu
KIMMEL, Margaret .... 207-786-6328. 209 F
mkimmel@bates.edu
KIMMEL, Rhonda .... 262-595-2281. 537 C
rhonda.kimmel@uwp.edu
KIMMEL, William .... 212-229-5762. 332 E
kimmelw@newschool.edu
KIMMELBLATT, Rachel ... 518-629-7736. 326 G
r.kimmelblatt@hvcc.edu
KIMMELMAN, Eric .... 518-736-3622. 325 A
ekimmelm@fmcc.suny.edu
KIMMELMAN, Scott .... 772-462-7760. 106 P
skimmelm@irsc.edu
KIMMENS, Randy .... 480-731-8202... 14 I
randy.kimmens@domail.maricopa.edu
KIMMERLE, Robert, S .... 518-580-5733. 341 A
bkimmerl@skidmore.edu
KIMMERLY, Ian .... 415-641-1241... 62 G
ikimmerly@sfai.edu
KIMMINS, William, P ..... 516-876-3179. 343 D
kimminsw@oldwestbury.edu
KIMMITT, Francis .... 423-493-4260. 462 B
kimmittf@tntemple.edu
KIMREY, Donna .... 704-991-0285. 364 C
dkimrey5073@stanly.edu
KIMREY, Phil .... 205-726-2736..... 6 F
ppkimrey@samford.edu
KIMSEY, James .... 520-494-5200... 12 P
jim.kimsey@centralaz.edu
KIMSEY, Phillip .... 706-295-6350. 125 C
pkimsey@highlands.edu
KIMURA, Keiko .... 408-298-2181... 63 P
keiko.kimura@sjcc.edu
KIMURA, Melissa .... 562-947-8755... 67 H
melissakimura@scuhs.edu
KINANE, Denis, F .... 215-898-1038. 435 B
dean@dental.upenn.edu
KINANE, Michael, G .... 516-876-3162. 343 D
kinanem@oldwestbury.edu
KINANE, Michael, G .... 516-876-3212. 343 D
kinanem@oldwestbury.edu
KINARD, Patricia, M ...... 843-953-7777. 442 A
pat.kinard@citadel.edu
KINARD, Sylvia .... 718-270-6936. 319 A
skinard@mec.cuny.edu
KINARD, Sylvia, G .... 718-270-6136. 319 A
sthompson@mec.cuny.edu
KINARD, Trent .... 803-584-3446. 448 D
tkinard@mailbox.sc.edu
KINARD, Zeolean, F .... 864-941-8688. 446 C
kinard.z@ptc.edu
KINCADE, Luis .... 432-264-5092. 473 E
wkincade@howardcollege.edu
KINCADE, Susan .... 209-575-6058... 77 J
kincades@mjc.edu
KINCAID, Paul, K .... 417-836-5139. 278 E
paulkincaid@missouristate.edu
KINCAID, Rachel, A .... 504-280-7049. 205 G
rakincai@uno.edu
KINCAID, Ramona .... 808-245-8336. 136 H
rkincaid@hawaii.edu
KINCAID, Scott, A .... 317-940-9700. 164 J
kincaid@butler.edu
KINCAID, Tim .... 419-559-2211. 389 I
tkincaid@terra.edu
KINCAID, William .... 317-931-2330. 165 B
bkincaid@cts.edu
KINCHEN, Thomas, A ...... 850-263-3261... 98 N
takinchen@baptistcollege.edu
KINCHERLOW-MARTIN,
Janet .... 256-306-2561..... 2 F
jkm@calhoun.edu
KIND, Jule .... 765-677-2980. 169 B
jule.kind@indwes.edu
KIND, Larry .... 715-675-3331. 541 A
Kind@ntc.edu
KIND-KEPPEL, Heather ... 217-875-7200. 156 J
hkindkep@richland.edu
KINDE, Haragewen .... 909-384-8265... 62 A
hkinde@sbccd.cc.ca.us
KINDE, Wayne .... 858-695-8587... 47 L
wkinde@horizonuniversity.edu
KINDER, Angie, M .... 304-260-4380. 527 N
akinder@blueridgectc.edu
KINDER, Jim .... 330-287-1212. 386 F
kinder.15@osu.edu
KINDER, L. Chad .... 580-774-7036. 400 B
chad.kinder@swosu.edu
KINDERS, Mark .... 405-974-5560. 400 K
mkinders@uco.edu
KINDL, Christine .... 724-938-5492. 428 A
kindl@calu.edu
KINDLE, Carolyn .... 618-634-3364. 158 M
carolynk@shawneecc.edu
KINDLE, Derek .... 202-806-2864... 95 G
dkindle@howard.edu
KINDLE, Joan .... 847-925-6738. 145 H
jkindle@harpercollege.edu
KINEAVY, Jacqueline ...... 973-684-6300. 304 B
jkineavy@pccc.edu
KINERSON, Sara .... 802-635-1257. 501 D
sara.kinerson@jsc.edu
KINES, Teresa .... 336-249-8186. 360 A
tkines@davidsonccc.edu
KINESKEY, Jessica .... 407-628-5870. 102 K
jkineskey@cci.edu
KING, Alissa .... 601-318-6474. 270 I
aking@wmcarey.edu
KING, Amanda .... 601-266-5000. 270 E
amanda.king@usm.edu
KING, Amy .... 303-871-7420... 86 B
amking@du.edu
KING, Amy, L .... 304-457-6354. 526 A
kingal@ab.edu
KING, Andrew, B .... 618-650-2197. 159 H
andking@siue.edu
KING, Angelynn .... 302-259-6193... 93 E
angelynn.king@dtcc.edu
KING, B, J .... 423-439-4414. 459 C
kingbj@etsu.edu
KING, Barbara .... 405-682-1611. 397 E
bking@occc.edu
KING, Barbara, E .... 570-408-4107. 437 F
barbara.king@wilkes.edu
KING, Baron .... 215-702-4224. 411 F
baronking@cairn.edu
KING, Becky, L .... 254-710-4566. 467 G
becky_king@baylor.edu
KING, Beverly .... 910-521-6295. 369 B
beverly.king@uncp.edu
KING, Bobby .... 707-654-1245... 31 I
rking@csum.edu
KING, Brenda, M .... 304-336-8076. 530 A
kingbren@westliberty.edu
KING, Brian .... 916-568-3021... 52 K
kingb@losrios.edu
KING, Brian .... 814-866-6641. 420 E
bking@lecom.edu
KING, Bruce .... 510-235-7800... 41 K
bking@contracosta.edu
KING, Bruce .... 507-786-3334. 264 B
kingb@stolaf.edu
KING, Carole .... 202-884-9120... 96 G
kingc@trinitydc.edu
KING, Carolee .... 409-772-1904. 493 C
caaking@utmb.edu
KING, Caroline .... 941-907-2262. 103 C
caking@evergladesuniversity.edu
KING, Catherine .... 508-457-1313. 234 F
cking@ngs.edu
KING, Charles, G .... 423-652-4700. 455 I
gregking1@king.edu
KING, Charles, W .... 540-568-6434. 506 F
kingcw@jmu.edu
KING, Cheryl .... 301-295-3045. 545 C
cheryl.king@usuhs.edu
KING, Christopher .... 956-665-2221. 492 B
kingca@utpa.edu
KING, Christy .... 407-708-2103. 113 E
kingc@seminolestate.edu
KING, Chuck .... 303-753-6046... 85 B
cking@rmcad.edu
KING, Curt .... 413-662-5062. 230 C
curt.king@mcla.edu
KING, Cynthia .... 202-651-5865... 95 C
cynthia.king@gallaudet.edu
KING, Cynthia, L .... 610-861-5510. 425 D
cking@northampton.edu
KING, Cynthia, P .... 617-726-2947. 234 B
cking@mghihp.edu
KING, D. Wayne .... 859-238-5550. 193 E
wayne.king@centre.edu
KING, Daniel, P .... 334-844-4810..... 1 G
dpk0002@auburn.edu
KING, David .... 315-312-3692. 344 A
david.king@oswego.edu
KING, David, A .... 541-737-2676. 406 A
ecampus@oregonstate.edu
KING, David, A .... 540-432-4440. 504 D
david.king@emu.edu
KING, David, A .... 330-471-8121. 383 D
dking@malone.edu
KING, David, S .... 203-582-3213... 91 A
david.king@quinnipiac.edu
KING, David, W .... 805-565-6036... 76 D
dking@westmont.edu
KING, Deborah .... 870-338-6474... 24 G
KING, Deborah .... 410-276-0306. 218 D
dking@host.sdc.edu
KING, Dee .... 248-204-2127. 245 I
dking@ltu.edu
KING, Denise .... 423-472-7141. 460 D
DKing05@clevelandstatecc.edu
KING, Dennis .... 785-628-4291. 186 F
dking@fhsu.edu
KING, Diane .... 603-427-7630. 295 K
djking@ccsnh.edu
KING, Don .... 508-999-8575. 229 A
dking@umassd.edu
KING, Donald (Jr.) .... 765-285-1478. 164 B
jking@bsu.edu
KING, Donna .... 903-463-8735. 472 M
donnaking@grayson.edu
KING, Donna, J .... 606-783-2000. 198 A
d.king@moreheadstate.edu
KING, Dottie .... 812-535-5296. 172 F
president@smwc.edu
KING, Duane .... 918-596-2710. 401 F
duane-king@utulsa.edu
KING, E. Thayne .... 918-456-5511. 396 H
king21@nsuok.edu
KING, Eddie .... 843-208-8135. 448 B
eking@uscb.edu
KING, Elizabeth .... 316-978-3510. 191 F
elizabeth.king@witchita.edu
KING, Elizabeth .... 636-949-4975. 276 D
eking@lindenwood.edu
KING, Elizabeth, C .... 513-558-8547. 390 G
elizabeth.king@uc.edu
KING, Elston, H .... 504-286-5197. 206 K
eking@suno.edu
KING, Fred, L .... 304-293-3449. 530 D
fking@mail.wvu.edu
KING, Gordon, B .... 617-557-1520. 237 B
gking@suffolk.edu
KING, Greg .... 423-236-2983. 458 J
gking@southern.edu
KING, Gregory .... 330-823-2282. 391 E
kinggl@mountunion.edu
KING, JR., H. Lee .... 434-223-7258. 505 E
lking@hsc.edu
KING, Herbert .... 651-773-1794. 258 C
herbert.king@century.edu
KING, Irene .... 610-519-4080. 436 F
irene.king@villanova.edu
KING, Jackie, E .... 585-275-1051. 349 C
jking@admin.rochester.edu
KING, James .... 615-336-4470. 459 A
james.king@tbr.edu
KING, CSC, James, B ..... 574-631-7800. 174 A
king.61@nd.edu
KING, Janice .... 530-754-1388... 70 J
janking@ucdavis.edu
KING, Janice .... 775-753-2361. 294 F
janice.king@gbcnv.edu
KING, Jeannie .... 704-337-2509. 365 G
kingj@queens.edu
KING, Jeff .... 706-764-3530. 125 F
jking@gntc.edu
KING, Jennifer .... 413-559-5427. 227 B
KING, Jerry .... 903-675-6210. 488 D
jking@tvcc.edu
KING, Jim .... 318-257-2445. 207 F
king@latech.edu
KING, Jim, M .... 318-257-2445. 207 F
king@latech.edu
KING, Joan .... 509-335-9681. 525 A
joank@wsu.edu
KING, Jodie .... 215-248-7004. 413 A
kingj@chc.edu
KING, Joe .... 334-244-3600..... 2 A
jking25@aum.edu
KING, John .... 218-726-8821. 264 D
jking@d.umn.edu
KING, John, C .... 806-720-7211. 476 B
john.king@lcu.edu
KING, John, J .... 401-254-3042. 440 B
jjking@rwu.edu
KING, John, M .... 617-552-4445. 224 A
john.king.2@bc.edu
KING, John, W .... 423-652-4832. 455 I
jwking@king.edu
KING, Jovanna, J .... 864-656-0663. 442 C
jovanna@clemson.edu
KING, Joy, S .... 512-505-3015. 473 G
jsking@htu.edu
KING, Julie, A .... 803-786-3871. 443 B
juking@columbiasc.edu
KING, Karen, D .... 423-439-5654. 459 C
kingk@etsu.edu
KING, Katherine .... 949-480-4161... 66 F
kking@soka.edu
KING, Katie .... 405-491-6350. 399 K
kking@snu.edu
KING, Kelli, B .... 574-535-7563. 166 A
kellibk@goshen.edu
KING, Kimberly .... 425-558-0299. 519 B
kimking@digipen.edu
KING, Kristin .... 267-502-2579. 410 I
kristin.king@brynathyn.edu
KING, Kristy .... 251-343-8200..... 6 E
kristy.king@remingtoncollege.edu
KING, Kristyn .... 815-394-5061. 157 C
kking@rockford.edu
KING, Kwanna .... 918-463-2931. 395 D
kwanna.king@connorsstate.edu
KING, L. Dianne .... 864-231-2026. 441 B
ldking@andersonuniversity.edu
KING, Laura .... 870-512-7850... 20 B
laura_king@asun.edu
KING, Laura, C .... 814-393-1926. 428 C
lking@clarion.edu
KING, Laura, M .... 651-201-1732. 257 N
laura.king@so.mnscu.edu
KING, Libby .... 423-869-6358. 456 A
libby.king@lmunet.edu
KING, Linda, L .... 541-346-2966. 406 D
llking@uoregon.edu
KING, Lonnie .... 614-688-8749. 386 E
king.1518@osu.edu
KING, Lynn .... 910-879-5520. 358 B
lking@bladencc.edu
KING, Lynne, O .... 518-381-1240. 340 G
kinglo@sunysccc.edu
KING, Manny .... 785-749-8447. 187 B
manford.king@bie.edu
KING, Marella .... 954-923-4440. 108 P
mking@keycollege.edu
KING, Mari, P .... 570-674-6218. 424 A
mking@misericordia.edu
KING, Mary .... 334-285-5177..... 4 J
mary.king@istc.edu
KING, Mary .... 940-552-6291. 493 F
mking@vernoncollege.edu
KING, Mary, B .... 336-734-7901. 360 E
mking@forsythtech.edu
KING, Mary Jo .... 270-706-8530. 195 A
maryjo.king@kctcs.edu
KING, Maura .... 845-451-1429. 322 D
m_king@culinary.edu
KING, Michael .... 706-754-7711. 129 G
mking@northgatech.edu
KING, Michael .... 817-923-8459. 469 F
michael.king@fishermore.edu
KING, Michael, A .... 540-432-4261. 504 D
michael.king@emu.edu
KING, Michelle .... 310-434-3323... 65 A
king_michelle@smc.edu
KING, Miriam, E .... 410-837-4612. 221 A
mking@ubalt.edu
KING, Neal .... 650-493-4430... 66 E
neal.king@sofia.edu
KING, Pat .... 215-884-8942. 438 A
librarian@woninstitute.edu
KING, Patricia .... 512-394-9766. 118 I
pking@usa.edu
KING, Peggy .... 630-752-5246. 163 F
peggy.king@wheaton.edu
KING, Peter .... 843-661-1362. 444 B
pking@fmarion.edu
KING, Phillip .... 503-594-3430. 402 F
phillipk@clackamas.edu
KING, Phyllis .... 414-229-6175. 537 A
pking@wm.edu
KING, Piper .... 505-438-8884. 312 A
piper@acupuncturecollege.edu
KING, R. Wayne .... 304-284-4040. 530 D
wking@wvuf.org
KING, Rebecca .... 870-612-2071... 25 A
rebecca.king@uaccb.edu
KING, Rhonda .... 504-671-5051. 203 A
rking1@dcc.edu
KING, Richard .... 520-494-5296... 12 P
richard.king@centralaz.edu
KING, Robin, L .... 724-852-3333. 437 A
rlking@waynesburg.edu
KING, Rochelle .... 919-546-8565. 366 E
acarter@shawu.edu
KING, Rochelle .... 919-546-8240. 366 E
rking@shawu.edu
KING, Ronan .... 276-466-7988. 514 G
ronanking@vic.edu
KING, S. Bruce .... 336-758-5774. 370 D
kingsb@wfu.edu
KING, Sarah .... 843-792-3621. 445 B
kingsara@musc.edu
KING, Shauna .... 203-432-1094... 93 A
shauna.king@yale.edu

KING, Shawn .... 509-359-6878. 519 C
sking@ewu.edu

KING, Shelly .... 816-415-5963. 285 C
kings@william.jewell.edu

KING, Stephanie .... 413-565-1000. 222 F
sking@baypath.edu

KING, Steven .... 413-662-5410. 230 C
steven.king@mcla.edu

KING, Sue .... 816-501-3759. 271 H
sue.king@avila.edu

KING, Susan .... 919-962-1204. 368 D
susanking@unc.edu

KING, Susan, L .... 207-780-4681. 212 H
susank@usm.maine.edu

KING, Teresa .... 540-831-6200. 508 C
tking54@radford.edu

KING, Terry .... 765-285-1333. 164 B
tsking@bsu.edu

KING, Theresa .... 201-684-7800. 305 A
0396mgr@fheg.follett.com

KING, Thomas .... 610-896-1111. 418 F
tking@haverford.edu

KING, Tim .... 256-782-5020..... 4 K
tbking@jsu.edu

KING, Tim .... 256-782-5400..... 4 K
tbking@jsu.edu

KING, Tom .... 610-896-1111. 410 J
tking01@brynmawr.edu

KING, Tom .... 216-881-1700. 387 B
tking@ohiotechnicalcollege.com

KING, Tommy .... 601-318-6495. 270 I
pres@wmcarey.edu

KING, Toni, C .... 740-587-6469. 379 D
kingt@denison.edu

KING, Valarie, G .... 407-823-6479. 115 E
valarie.king@ucf.edu

KING, Veda .... 620-417-1400. 190 F
veda.king@sccc.edu

KING, Venita .... 256-372-5248..... 1 A
venita.king@aamu.edu

KING, Victor, I .... 323-343-3054... 34 A
vking@cslanet.calstatela.edu

KING, W. Cody .... 229-931-2045. 126 D
cody.king@gsw.edu

KING, Wayne .... 815-280-2210. 149 A
wking@jjc.edu

KING, Wendell, C .... 913-684-3280. 545 E
wendell.king@leavenworth.army.mil

KING, Wendy, L .... 304-293-7304. 530 D
wking@hsc.wvu.edu

KING, William .... 540-231-4000. 504 G

KING, William, L .... 903-510-2252. 488 E
bkin@tjc.edu

KING-LEROY,
Cynthia, B .... 518-783-2420. 340 J
kingleroy@siena.edu

KING SANDERS, Nancy . 361-593-3290. 484 A
nancy.kingsanders@tamuk.edu

KING-TODD, Catherine .. 602-978-7888... 18 A
catherine.king-todd@thunderbird.edu

KINGCADE, Fawn, M .... 580-327-8533. 396 N
fmkingcade@nwosu.edu

KINGHAM, Margaret, T .. 610-566-1776. 437 G
mkingham@williamson.edu

KINGKADE, H.K .... 502-863-8209. 194 C
hk_kingkade@georgetowncollege.edu

KINGMA, Bruce .... 315-443-4525. 347 C
brkingma@syr.edu

KINGRY, Kelly .... 910-642-7141. 364 A
Kelly.Kingry@sccnc.edu

KINGSBURY, Judy .... 507-285-7216. 261 A
judy.kingsbury@rctc.edu

KINGSFORD, Laura .... 562-985-5559... 33 F
lking@csulb.edu

KINGSFORD, Peter .... 251-442-2355..... 9 A
pkingsford@umobile.edu

KINGSLEY, Hal .... 716-827-2558. 348 G
kingsleyh@trocaire.edu

KINGSLEY, Margery .... 580-581-2331. 394 G
margeryk@cameron.edu

KINGSLIEN, Gene .... 785-784-6606. 184 F
kingslieng@bartonccc.edu

KINGSOLVER, Robert ..... 502-272-3628. 192 E
kingsolver@bellarmine.edu

KINGSTON, Chris .... 419-372-7052. 374 K

KINGSTON, Jeffrey .... 925-485-5244... 37 L
jkingston@clpccd.org

KINGSTON, Jeffrey .... 925-485-5244... 37 J
jkingston@clpccd.org

KINGSTON, Laura .... 206-934-7959. 523 A
laura.kingston@seattlecolleges.edu

KINGSTON, Linda .... 651-846-1411. 261 D
linda.kingston@saintpaul.edu

KINGTON, Raynard, S .... 641-269-3000. 178 H
kington@grinnell.edu

KINKADE, Mark .... 618-985-3741. 148 J
markkinkade@jalc.edu

KINKADE, Mike .... 870-584-4471... 24 F
mkinkade@cccua.edu

KINKEAD, Angela Gay .... 304-473-8007. 531 G
kinkead@wvwc.edu

KINKEL, Anthony, G .... 316-677-9400. 191 E

KINKELA, David .... 716-673-3529. 342 A
david.kinkela@fredonia.edu

KINKELLA, John .... 775-445-3271. 295 A
john.kinkella@wnc.edu

KINKLEY, Matthew, J ..... 419-995-8283. 381 Q
kinkley.m@rhodesstate.edu

KINLAW, Mark, O .... 910-272-3300. 363 B
mkinlaw@robeson.edu

KINLEY, Naomi .... 718-489-5260. 338 G
nkinley@sfc.edu

KINN, Harold .... 419-448-3276. 389 J
bkinn@tiffin.edu

KINNAMON, Joel, L .... 760-773-2500... 40 F
jkinnamon@collegeofthedesert.edu

KINNE, III, Harry, C ...... 603-646-2234. 296 G
harry.c.kinne@dartmouth.edu

KINNE, Mary .... 315-786-2327. 327 L
mkinne@sunyjefferson.edu

KINNERSLEY, Ruth .... 615-248-1491. 462 D
rkinnersley@trevecca.edu

KINNEY, Dan .... 712-325-3201. 179 L
dkinney@iwcc.edu

KINNEY, Daniel .... 631-632-7100. 342 C

KINNEY, Daniel, P .... 515-574-1150. 179 D
kinney@iowacentral.edu

KINNEY, Denise .... 715-422-5502. 540 D
denise.kinney@mstc.edu

KINNEY, Dorado, M .... 512-223-5129. 466 I
dkinney@austincc.edu

KINNEY, Douglas .... 315-498-2478. 335 G
kinneyd@sunyocc.edu

KINNEY, Frank .... 321-674-8960. 104 H
fkinney@fit.edu

KINNEY, John, W .... 804-257-5717. 515 F
jwkinney@vuu.edu

KINNEY, Kathy .... 510-780-4500... 50 I
kkinney@lifewest.edu

KINNEY, Lee, M .... 575-439-3605. 310 J
kinney@nmsu.edu

KINNEY, Mark .... 906-786-5802. 240 K
kinneym@baycollege.edu

KINNEY, Megan .... 303-360-4740... 81 C
megan.kinney@ccaurora.edu

KINNEY, Michael .... 607-778-5031. 315 I
kinneym@sunybroome.edu

KINNEY, Michael, J .... 203-371-7872... 91 C
mike.kinney@sacredheart.edu

KINNEY, Paula .... 319-385-6315. 179 K
pkinney@iwc.edu

KINNEY, Peter .... 516-686-7474. 333 H
pkinney@nyit.edu

KINNEY, Phillip .... 740-377-2520. 389 K

KINNEY, Sandra .... 225-308-4415. 202 G
skinney@lctcs.edu

KINNEY, Sandy .... 715-365-4689. 540 G
skinney@nicoletcollege.edu

KINNEY, Scott .... 888-227-3552. 254 C
scott.kinney@capella.edu

KINNEY, Susan, E .... 205-226-4646..... 2 C
skinney@bsc.edu

KINSELLA, Denise .... 310-434-3466... 65 A
kinsella_denise@smc.edu

KINSELLA, Frederick, W . 717-337-6970. 417 B
fkinsell@gettysburg.edu

KINSELLA, Joseph, J ...... 509-313-3667. 520 A
kinsella@gonzaga.edu

KINSELLA, Michael .... 216-421-7412. 377 C
mkinsella@cia.edu

KINSELLA, Steven, M ..... 408-848-4712... 45 F
skinsella@gavilan.edu

KINSER, April .... 845-758-7177. 314 D
kinser@bard.edu

KINSER, Rhonda, L .... 620-417-1106. 190 F
rhonda.kinser@sccc.edu

KINSEY, Barry, C .... 734-384-4124. 247 C
bkinsey@monroeccc.edu

KINSEY, Gary .... 805-437-2002... 32 I
gary.kinsey@csuci.edu

KINSEY, Nancy .... 618-545-3020. 149 D
nkinsey@kaskaskia.edu

KINSINGER, Janice .... 309-694-5758. 146 E
jkinsinger@icc.edu

KINSLER, Jeffrey, S .... 615-460-6320. 453 C
jeff.kinsler@belmont.edu

KINSLEY, Betsy .... 805-756-6000... 32 F
ekinsley@calpoly.edu

KINTZI, Audrey .... 507-457-1486. 264 A
akintzi@smumn.edu

KINUCAN, Robert, J .... 432-837-8201. 487 B
kinucan@sulross.edu

KINYATTI, Njoki .... 718-262-2021. 319 F
nkinyatti@york.cuny.edu

KINYON, Kim, J .... 573-875-7420. 272 G
kjkinyon@ccis.edu

KINZEL, Erin .... 574-807-7382. 164 D
erin.kinzel@bethelcollege.edu

KINZER, Esther .... 951-785-2175... 50 B
ekinzer@lasierra.edu

KINZER, Jay .... 903-675-6220. 488 D
jkinzer@tvcc.edu

KINZER, Kathy, Y .... 724-847-5559. 417 A
kykinzer@geneva.edu

KINZER, Marlin, L .... 605-394-2374. 452 A
marlin.kinzer@sdsmt.edu

KINZER, Steve .... 260-459-4513. 169 C
skinzer@ibcfortwayne.edu

KINZLER, Debra .... 212-749-2802. 330 A
pr@msmnyc.edu

KINZLER, Robert, J .... 215-951-1048. 420 B
kinzler@lasalle.edu

KIP, Margaret .... 215-717-6415. 435 A
mkip@uarts.edu

KIPER, Dawn .... 217-854-3231. 140 G
dawn.kiper@blackburn.edu

KIPETZ, Sharon .... 920-424-3100. 537 B
kipetzs@uwosh.edu

KIPFER, Julie .... 406-994-5737. 287 B
jkipfer@montana.edu

KIPHART, Jan, A .... 410-857-2217. 216 E
jkiphart@mcdaniel.edu

KIPHART, Michael .... 410-386-8217. 214 A
mkiphart@carrollcc.edu

KIPP, Billie Jo .... 406-338-5441. 285 F
drkipp@bfcc.edu

KIPP, Deborah, J .... 484-664-3223. 424 H
kipp@muhlenberg.edu

KIPP, Rita .... 732-987-2617. 302 B
kippr@georgian.edu

KIPP, Tom, E .... 414-410-4157. 532 B
tekipp@stritch.edu

KIPPENHAN, Heidi .... 218-333-6646. 260 E
heidi.kippenham@ntcmn.edu

KIRALLA, Laura .... 310-665-6961... 57 C
lkiralla@otis.edu

KIRBY, Claire, J .... 704-687-7292. 368 E
ckirby@uncc.edu

KIRBY, Henry .... 850-599-3183. 114 K
henry.kirby@famu.edu

KIRBY, Jack, R .... 304-367-4101. 529 F
Jack.Kirby@fairmontstate.edu

KIRBY, John .... 401-874-2957. 440 D
jdkirby@uri.edu

KIRBY, Kevin .... 859-572-6544. 198 I
kirby@nku.edu

KIRBY, Kevin .... 713-348-6040. 479 A
kevin.kirby@rice.edu

KIRBY, Marie .... 979-209-7337. 467 I
marie.kirby@blinn.edu

KIRBY, Melanie .... 603-271-6484. 296 C
mkirby@ccsnh.edu

KIRBY, Vickie, S .... 903-813-2414. 466 H
vkirby@austincollege.edu

KIRBY, Yvonne .... 860-832-1784... 87 K
vkirby@ccsu.edu

KIRCH, Michael .... 952-358-8164. 260 B
michael.kirch@normandale.edu

KIRCHER, Anna .... 707-826-6101... 35 C
anna.kircher@humboldt.edu

KIRCHER COLE, Elsa ..... 505-277-5035. 312 F
ekcole@salud.unm.edu

KIRCHMEYER-BATTAGLIA,
Elizabeth .... 716-896-0700. 350 A
kirchmeyerea@villa.edu

KIRCHNER, Lisa .... 419-559-2163. 389 I
lkirchner01@terra.edu

KIRCHNER, Tom, A .... 440-525-7138. 382 M
tkirchner@lakelandcc.edu

KIREGIAN, Nazaret .... 631-499-7100. 329 B
nkiregian@libi.edu

KIRIN, Jenifer .... 410-888-9048. 216 D
jkirin@muih.edu

KIRITSIS, Nikos .... 337-475-5875. 207 G
nikosk@mcneese.edu

KIRK, Artemis, G .... 202-687-7425... 95 E
agk3@georgetown.edu

KIRK, JR., Arthur, F .... 352-588-8242. 112 D
arthur.f.kirk.jr@saintleo.edu

KIRK, Barrie .... 803-732-3875. 445 C
kirkb@midlandstech.edu

KIRK, Donna .... 503-838-8684. 406 E
kirkd@wou.edu

KIRK, Earl, D .... 812-488-1040. 173 H
ek43@evansville.edu

KIRK, Ellis, I .... 717-866-5775. 416 E
ekirk@evangelical.edu

KIRK, James .... 404-894-7162. 125 D
jim.kirk@business.gatech.edu

KIRK, Jeff .... 301-784-5000. 213 B
jkirk@allegany.edu

KIRK, Jennifer .... 978-762-4000. 232 D
jkirk@northshore.edu

KIRK, Kerri .... 425-388-9578. 519 I
kkirk@everettcc.edu

KIRK, Kevin .... 325-649-8022. 473 F
kkirk@hputx.edu

KIRK, Kevin, L .... 918-610-0027. 395 C
kkirk@communitycarecollege.edu

KIRK, Kristi .... 512-313-3000. 469 L
kristi.kirk@concordia.edu

KIRK, Mary, P .... 910-576-6222. 362 C
kirkm@montgomery.edu

KIRK, Melissa .... 718-289-5193. 317 B
melissa.kirk@bcc.cuny.edu

KIRK, Michael .... 860-486-0715... 92 A
michael.kirk@uconn.edu

KIRK, Nina .... 970-339-6622... 78 C
nina.kirk@aims.edu

KIRK, Rich .... 541-956-7040. 407 F
rkirk@roguecc.edu

KIRK, Tim .... 870-862-8131... 23 D
wtkirk@southark.edu

KIRK, William .... 239-280-2544... 98 K
william.kirk@avemaria.edu

KIRKEBY, Lori .... 763-424-0713. 260 C
lkirkeby@nhcc.edu

KIRKEN, Robert .... 915-747-5000. 492 A
rakirken@utep.edu

KIRKER, Elizabeth .... 302-225-6256... 93 H
kirkere@gbc.edu

KIRKER, William .... 516-299-2278. 329 D
william.kirker@liu.edu

KIRKHAM, Stephen, W .. 719-255-3075... 85 M
skirkham@uccs.edu

KIRKHOLM, Mark .... 712-749-2500. 176 D
kirkholmm@bvu.edu

KIRKLAND, Cecil, E .... 304-326-1519. 527 G
ekirkland@salemu.edu

KIRKLAND, Cecil, E .... 304-326-1344. 527 G
ekirkland@salemu.edu

KIRKLAND, Debbie .... 503-725-5878. 406 B
kirkladd@pdx.edu

KIRKLAND, Jennifer, E ... 540-458-8929. 516 A
jkirkland@wlu.edu

KIRKLAND, Joe .... 828-669-8012. 357 H
kirkland@montreat.edu

KIRKLAND, Joe .... 828-669-8012. 357 H
jkirkland@montreat.edu

KIRKLAND, Joseph .... 409-882-3926. 486 G
joe.kirkland@lsco.edu

KIRKLAND, Kim, D .... 317-274-2306. 168 D
kirkland@iupui.edu

KIRKLAND, Lee Ann ...... 919-344-2614. 120 G
leeann.kirkland@armstrong.edu

KIRKLAND, Sandra .... 804-594-1556. 512 G
skirkland@jtcc.edu

KIRKLAND, Sara, G .... 570-372-4108. 433 H
kirkland@susqu.edu

KIRKLAND, Susan, M .... 336-278-5428. 354 B
skirkland3@elon.edu

KIRKLAND, Willie .... 504-816-4428. 201 K
wkirkland@dillard.edu

KIRKLAND-GORDON,
Sharon, E .... 301-314-7675. 219 B
skirklan@umd.edu

KIRKLAND-HARRIS,
Linda .... 757-727-5617. 505 F
linda.kirkland-harri@hamptonu.edu

KIRKLEY, James .... 919-546-8399. 366 E
jkirkley@shawu.edu

KIRKLIN, Anlatear .... 504-816-4170. 201 K
akirklin@dillard.edu

KIRKLIN, Kathleen .... 916-608-6500... 53 C

KIRKMAN, Dawayne .... 937-512-5805. 388 O
dawayne.kirkman@sinclair.edu

KIRKMAN, Duane .... 828-328-7028. 356 B
duane.kirkman@lr.edu

KIRKMAN, Susan .... 805-690-7601... 30 A
sue.kirkman@brooks.edu

KIRKPATRICK, Dana .... 510-436-1601... 47 J
kirkpatrick@hnu.edu

KIRKPATRICK,
Elizabeth, L .... 240-500-2000. 215 B
elkirkpatrick@hagerstowncc.edu

KIRKPATRICK, Holly, R .. 215-572-4475. 409 H
kirkpath@arcadia.edu

KIRKPATRICK, Judith, A 315-792-3122. 349 F
jkirkpatrick@utica.edu

KIRKPATRICK,
Kenneth, J .... 765-658-4141. 165 F
kjkirk@depauw.edu

KIRKPATRICK, Laura ...... 931-363-9864. 456 C
lkirkpatrick@martinmethodist.edu

KIRKPATRICK, Lisa, L ..... 512-448-8408. 479 C
lisak@stedwards.edu

KIRKPATRICK, Nancy ...... 317-955-6223. 170 V
nkirkpatrick@marian.edu

KIRKPATRICK, R. James 517-355-4473. 246 H
cnsdean@msu.edu

KIRKPATRICK, Randy ..... 940-397-4278. 476 H
randy.kirkpatrick@mwsu.edu

KIRKPATRICK, Stephen .. 516-876-3156. 343 D
kirkpatricks@oldwestbury.edu

KIRKPATRICK, Stephen .. 901-321-4036. 453 H
skirkpat@cbu.edu

KIRKSEY, Jason .... 405-744-9154. 397 H
jason.kirksey@okstate.edu

KIRKSEY, Jeff .... 617-745-3717. 225 G
jeff.kirksey@enc.edu

KIRKSEY, Jennifer .... 740-593-1804. 387 C
kirkseyj@ohio.edu

KIRKSEY, Kirk, A .... 214-645-8404. 493 E
kirk.klrksey@utsouthwestern.edu

KIRKTON, Vicki, S .... 574-535-7376. 166 A
vickysk@goshen.edu
KIRKWOOD, J Burton .... 603-526-3761. 295 I
burton.kirkwood@colby-sawyer.edu
KIRKWOOD, Valerie .... 509-793-2371. 517 C
valeriek@bigbend.edu
KIRKWOOD, William, G . 423-439-4219. 459 C
kirkwood@etsu.edu
KIRMER, Lisa .... 620-343-4600. 186 E
lkirmer@fhtc.edu
KIRSCH, Lloyd .... 480-990-3773... 14 H
KIRSCH, OSB, Myron .... 724-805-2111. 432 G
myron.kirsch@email.stvincent.edu
KIRSCH, Rodney, P .... 814-863-4826. 426 A
rpk6@psu.edu
KIRSCHENMANN,
Sandra, G .... 916-325-4600. 415 B
sandra.g.kirschenmann@drexel.edu
KIRSCHLING, Jane, M ... 410-706-6741. 219 C
kirschling@son.umaryland.edu
KIRSCHNER, Kelly .... 727-864-8965. 101 N
kirschkm@eckerd.edu
KIRSH, Bruce, M .... 603-899-4080. 296 H
kirshb@franklinpierce.edu
KIRSON, Donald .... 619-594-1156... 35 D
dkirson@mail.sdsu.edu
KIRSTEIN, Frank, W .... 716-888-8361. 316 C
kirstein@canisius.edu
KIRSTEIN, Kurt .... 206-239-4500. 517 M
kdkirstein@cityu.edu
KIRSTEN, Jan .... 732-255-0400. 304 A
jkirsten@ocean.edu
KIRTLEY, Adam, M .... 509-522-4449. 525 E
kirtleam@whitman.edu
KIRTLEY, Brad, J .... 931-221-7561. 459 B
kirtleyb@apsu.edu
KIRTLEY, Karen .... 304-696-3328. 529 H
kirtley@marshall.edu
KIRTMAN, Janet .... 212-346-1700. 335 J
jkirtman@pace.edu
KIRVES, Carol .... 270-707-3751. 195 E
carol.kirves@kctcs.edu
KIRWAN, William .... 301-445-1901. 219 A
bkirwan@usmd.edu
KIRWIN, Luanne .... 617-373-2520. 235 F
KIRWIN, Margaret, M ..... 518-454-5120. 321 A
kirwinm@strose.edu
KIRZNER, Yehudis .... 718-252-6333. 351 K
KISCADEN, Elizabeth ...... 641-585-8672. 183 D
elizabeth.kiscaden@waldorf.edu
KISELYUK, Ella .... 212-817-7700. 317 F
ekiselyuk@gc.cuny.edu
KISER, Dan .... 828-328-7154. 356 B
dan.kiser@lr.edu
KISER, Holly .... 817-531-4495. 488 A
hkiser@txwes.edu
KISER, Joseph, B .... 276-328-0143. 511 C
jbk5b@uvawise.edu
KISER, Kristy .... 276-328-0220. 511 C
kej5c@uvawise.edu
KISER, Lee .... 828-448-6707. 365 A
lkiser@wpcc.edu
KISER, Leonard, R .... 336-734-7313. 360 E
lkiser@forsythtech.edu
KISER, Lyda .... 540-869-0623. 512 H
lkiser@lfcc.edu
KISER, Michael, D .... 207-859-4356. 209 J
mdkiser@colby.edu
KISER, Ronnie .... 276-964-7221. 514 A
ronnie.kiser@sw.edu
KISH-GOODLING,
Donna, M .... 484-664-3479. 424 H
kishgood@muhlenberg.edu
KISLING, Reid .... 503-517-1820. 408 I
rkisling@westernseminary.edu
KISNER, Dawn .... 410-287-1025. 214 B
dkisner@cecil.edu
KISPERT, Craig, G .... 206-281-2536. 523 C
ckispert@spu.edu
KISPERT, John, J .... 843-661-1110. 444 B
jkispert@fmarion.edu
KISS, Elizabeth .... 404-471-6280. 119 I
president@agnesscott.edu
KISS, Nikki .... 920-693-1136. 540 B
nikki.kiss@gotoltc.edu
KISSACK, Heather .... 254-659-7731. 473 A
hkissack@hillcollege.edu
KISSEL, Karen .... 708-534-4054. 145 F
kkissel@govst.edu
KISSELL, Joseph .... 570-389-4263. 427 H
jkissell@bloomu.edu
KISSELL, Juanita .... 615-547-1397. 454 A
jkissell@cumberland.edu
KISSICK, Sharon .... 910-521-6298. 369 B
sharon.kissick@uncp.edu
KISSINGER, John .... 937-298-3399. 382 K
john.kissinger@kc.edu
KISSIS, Leonora .... 718-951-5861. 317 C
lkissis@brooklyn.cuny.edu
KISTLER, Kevin .... 209-384-6105... 54 D
kevin.kistler@mccd.edu
KISTLER, Ron .... 580-928-5533. 400 B
ron.kistler@swosu.edu
KISTNER, Angie .... 618-437-5321. 156 H
kistner@rlc.edu
KISTNER, Warren .... 309-556-3071. 148 B
wkistner@iwu.edu
KITAJIMA, Lorraine, N ... 650-949-7117... 44 N
kitajimalorraine@fhda.edu
KITCHEN, Augusta .... 803-780-1159. 449 E
akitchen@voorhees.edu
KITCHEN, Cheryl .... 419-772-2220. 386 D
c-kitchen@onu.edu
KITCHEN, Clifford .... 719-549-3121... 84 G
clifford.kitchen@pueblocc.edu
KITCHEN, Darrell, B .... 937-327-7009. 393 E
dkitchen@wittenberg.edu
KITCHEN, Janie .... 606-326-2163. 194 J
janie.kitchen@kctcs.edu
KITCHEN, Kimberly .... 814-641-3114. 419 H
kitchek@juniata.edu
KITCHEN, Mark .... 307-754-6405. 543 G
Mark.Kitchen@northwestcollege.edu
KITCHEN, Steve .... 678-915-3929. 132 C
skitchen@spsu.edu
KITCHEN, Todd .... 479-619-4232... 22 C
tkitchen@nwacc.edu
KITCHENFLINT, Athena .. 412-578-6164. 412 G
carlow@bkstr.com
KITCHENS, Joann .... 701-662-1502. 372 D
joann.kitchens@lrsc.edu
KITCHENS, Joseph, H .... 770-720-5966. 130 G
jhk@reinhardt.edu
KITCHENS, Larry, E .... 817-257-7121. 484 I
l.kitchens@tcu.edu
KITCHENS, Penny .... 478-553-2060. 129 H
pkitchens@oftc.edu
KITCHENS, Ronnie .... 601-426-6346. 269 G
rkitchens@southeasternbaptist.edu
KITCHENS, Tempie .... 770-233-6170. 132 B
tkitchens@sctech.edu
KITCHEYAN, Tori .... 402-878-2380. 290 D
tkitcheyan@littlepriest.edu
KITCHINGS, Dorcas, A ... 803-822-3584. 445 C
kitchingsd@midlandstech.edu
KITCHNER, Russell .... 304-724-3700. 526 B
rkitchner@apus.edu
KITE, Bruce .... 575-646-2446. 310 I
bkite@nmsu.edu
KITE, Joy, A .... 608-822-2319. 541 C
jkite@swtc.edu
KITE, Michelle .... 269-782-1302. 250 C
mkite@swmich.edu
KITEI, Susan, C .... 610-758-3870. 422 A
sck0@lehigh.edu
KITHCART, Jane .... 845-687-5111. 348 H
kithcarj@sunyulster.edu
KITTEL, Jane .... 715-675-3331. 541 A
kittelj@ntc.edu
KITTELL, Gary .... 315-464-4448. 342 E
kittelg@upstate.edu
KITTINGER, Fred .... 407-823-1208. 115 E
fred.kittinger@ucf.edu
KITTLE, Aaron, P .... 304-457-6342. 526 A
kittleap@ab.edu
KITTLE, Paul .... 336-841-9107. 355 C
pkittle@highpoint.edu
KITTO, Kathleen .... 360-650-5929. 525 C
kathleen.kitto@wwu.edu
KITTRELL-MIKELL,
Deborah .... 478-289-2161. 124 C
dkittrell@ega.edu
KITTS, Kenneth, D .... 910-521-6224. 369 B
ken.kitts@uncp.edu
KITZINGER, Denis .... 603-880-8308. 298 A
dkitzinger@thomasmorecollege.edu
KITZINGER, Sara .... 603-880-8308. 298 A
skitzinger@thomasmorecollege.edu
KITZMAN, Judy .... 206-934-7791. 522 I
judy.kitzman@seattlecolleges.edu
KIUHARA, Sharon .... 718-390-3158. 350 B
skiuhara@wagner.edu
KIVEL, Andy .... 925-969-2586... 41 L
akivel@dvc.edu
KIVETZ, Robert .... 212-998-4611. 334 D
rsk1@nyu.edu
KIYOSAKI, Donna .... 808-689-2500. 136 C
donnafay@hawaii.edu
KIYOSHI, Jack, O .... 670-234-5498. 547 A
jackk@nmcnet.edu
KIZINA, Terrence, R .... 814-871-5759. 416 K
kizina002@gannon.edu
KJARTANSON, Mary .... 619-221-2144... 62 F
mkjartan@sdccd.edu
KJONAAS, Wayne .... 970-247-7525... 81 M
kjonaas_w@fortlewis.edu
KLAAREN, Jon .... 334-285-5177..... 4 J
jon.klaaren@istc.edu
KLAAS, Alan .... 928-692-3085... 15 L
aklaas@mohave.edu
KLAAS, Carlene .... 312-362-8146. 143 H
cklaas@depaul.edu
KLAAS, Gerry .... 314-659-0816. 275 L
klaas@kenrick.edu
KLAASSEN, Sara .... 816-322-0110. 271 O
sara.klaassen@calvary.edu
KLABECHEK, IV, John ... 262-551-5911. 532 D
jklabechek@carthage.edu
KLADIVKO, Deborah .... 803-641-3577. 448 A
debk@usca.edu
KLAFFKE, David .... 208-467-8641. 139 A
dklaffke@nnu.edu
KLAG, Michael, J .... 410-955-3540. 215 H
mklag@jhsph.edu
KLAGGE, Jay .... 480-446-5022... 18 I
jay.klagge@phoenix.edu
KLAHR, Sabine .... 801-581-8876. 496 Q
s.klahr@ic.utah.edu
KLAIBER, James, S .... 440-775-5603. 385 H
Jim.Klaiber@oberlin.edu
KLAICH, Daniel, J .... 775-784-4901. 294 D
chancellor@nevada.edu
KLAPPER, Robert .... 770-729-8400. 120 I
KLASEN, James .... 617-588-1344. 223 B
jklasen@bfit.edu
KLASKO, Stephen, K .... 813-974-2196. 116 C
sklasko@health.usf.edu
KLASS, Stephen, P .... 413-597-3118. 238 D
stephen.p.klass@williams.edu
KLATT, Colleen .... 802-468-1344. 501 B
colleen.klatt@castleton.edu
KLAUBER, James, S .... 270-686-4508. 196 C
jim.klauber@kctcs.edu
KLAUDER, Mark, J .... 802-447-6322. 500 D
mklauder@svc.edu
KLAUS, Allen, R .... 210-434-6711. 477 N
arklaus@lake.ollusa.edu
KLAUS, Chad, L .... 609-258-5498. 304 E
klaus@princeton.edu
KLAUS, Dennis .... 801-957-4250. 498 B
dennis.klaus@slcc.edu
KLAUS, Eric .... 315-781-3304. 326 C
klaus@hws.edu
KLAUS, John Mark .... 814-472-3391. 432 D
jklaus@francis.edu
KLAUS, Katie .... 920-433-6651. 531 L
katie.klaus@bellincollege.edu
KLAUSER, Patricia, A .... 203-371-7978... 91 C
klauserp@sacredheart.edu
KLAUSMEYER, Robert .... 573-875-7304. 272 G
rklausmeyer@ccis.edu
KLAWE, Maria, M .... 909-921-8120... 46 H
klawe@hmc.edu
KLAWITTER, Christina .... 608-363-2660. 531 M
klawitterc@beloit.edu
KLAWUNN, Margaret, M 401-863-1800. 438 J
margaret_klawunn@brown.edu
KLAY, Kathy, A .... 937-328-6085. 377 A
klayk@clarkstate.edu
KLEBE, Kelli .... 719-255-3417... 85 M
kklebe@uccs.edu
KLEBESADEL, Shirley ...... 715-232-2190. 538 B
klebesadels@uwstout.edu
KLEDZIK, Eric .... 321-674-8107. 104 H
ekledzik@fit.edu
KLEE, John .... 606-759-7141. 196 B
john.klee@kctcs.edu
KLEEMAN, Amy .... 407-582-1238. 118 M
akleeman@valenciacollege.edu
KLEEMAN, Beverly, S ...... 509-777-4548. 525 F
bkleeman@whitworth.edu
KLEICH, Tammie .... 308-635-6072. 293 E
kleicht@wncc.edu
KLEIN, Andrew, O .... 508-849-3313. 222 B
aklein@annamaria.edu
KLEIN, Andrew, R .... 317-274-2581. 168 D
anrklein@iupui.edu
KLEIN, Barb .... 641-648-4611. 179 I
barb.klein@iavalley.edu
KLEIN, Barbara, A .... 410-269-5087. 219 C
bklein@umaryland.edu
KLEIN, Bob, P .... 518-783-2432. 340 J
rklein@siena.edu
KLEIN, Craig .... 801-863-5063. 497 C
cklein@uvu.edu
KLEIN, Cynthia .... 412-809-5100. 430 H
klein.cynthia@pti.edu
KLEIN, David, A .... 434-223-6129. 505 E
dklein@hsc.edu
KLEIN, Edward .... 970-943-2101... 86 I
eklein@western.edu
KLEIN, Eileen .... 512-223-5766. 466 I
eklein@austincc.edu
KLEIN, Gary, L .... 608-796-3074. 539 E
glklein@viterbo.edu
KLEIN, James .... 541-552-6114. 406 C
kleinj@sou.edu
KLEIN, Janie .... 925-631-4572... 61 F
mminguil@stmarys-ca.edu
KLEIN, Jim .... 502-456-6508. 199 G
jklein@sullivan.edu
KLEIN, Joanne, R .... 240-895-4251. 218 A
jrklein@smcm.edu
KLEIN, Joy .... 480-994-9244... 17 Q
joyk@swiha.edu
KLEIN, June .... 650-433-3849... 58 B
jklein@paloaltou.edu
KLEIN, Lori .... 907-796-6529... 11 A
lori.klein@uas.alaska.edu
KLEIN, Marjorie, S .... 814-332-5910. 409 D
marjorie.klein@allegheny.edu
KLEIN, Mendel .... 718-384-5460. 351 H
KLEIN, Michael .... 215-204-9570. 433 K
michael.klein@temple.edu
KLEIN, Michael .... 718-368-5087. 318 E
mklein@kbcc.cuny.edu
KLEIN, Michelle, W .... 504-866-7426. 206 B
finance@nds.edu
KLEIN, Paul .... 415-749-4589... 62 G
paulklein@sfai.edu
KLEIN, Sandy, L .... 701-483-2371. 371 D
sandy.klein@dickinsonstate.edu
KLEIN, Sara .... 718-390-3423. 350 B
sara.klein@wagner.edu
KLEIN, Scott .... 812-866-7061. 166 C
klein@hanover.edu
KLEIN, Shelley .... 661-763-7711... 69 D
sklein@taftcollege.edu
KLEIN, Steve .... 503-352-2822. 407 A
kleinsk@pacificu.edu
KLEIN, Steven .... 316-295-5237. 186 H
steven_klein@friends.edu
KLEIN, Steven, J .... 765-361-6253. 175 B
kleins@wabash.edu
KLEIN, Stuart .... 212-431-2170. 333 I
Stuart.Klein@nyls.edu
KLEIN, Susan .... 816-802-3435. 275 J
sklein@kcai.edu
KLEIN, Terry .... 715-468-2815. 541 F
Terry.Klein@witc.edu
KLEINDL, Brad .... 816-584-6308. 280 C
brad.kleindl@park.edu
KLEINE, Patricia, A .... 715-836-2320. 536 E
kleinepa@uwec.edu
KLEINER, Stephen .... 937-529-2201. 390 D
sjkleiner@united.edu
KLEINER, Zev .... 347-394-1036. 315 A
KLEINHANS, Randy .... 574-372-5100. 166 B
kleinhrp@grace.edu
KLEINKAUFMAN, Dovid . 718-327-7600. 350 J
yfr1@verizon.net
KLEINLEIN, Tom .... 912-478-5047. 126 C
tkleinlein@georgiasouthern.edu
KLEINMAN, Ilene .... 201-447-7160. 299 C
ikleinman@bergen.edu
KLEINMAN, Kent .... 607-255-9110. 322 A
aapdean@cornell.edu
KLEINMAN, Naftaly .... 212-343-1234. 331 D
nkleinman@mcny.edu
KLEINMAN, Yisroel .... 718-853-8500. 348 A
KLEINPETER, Jennifer ...... 225-675-8270. 203 G
jkleinpeter@rpcc.edu
KLEINSORGE, Ilene, K .... 541-737-6024. 406 A
ilene.kleinsorge@bus.oregonstate.edu
KLEINTOP, Douglas .... 610-660-1219. 432 E
dkleinto@sju.edu
KLEINWORTH, Tom .... 713-798-6297. 467 F
tklein@bcm.edu
KLEM, Janikke .... 408-924-1143... 36 A
janikke.klem@sjsu.edu
KLEM, John, F .... 727-726-1153. 100 E
president@clearwater.edu
KLEMANN, M. Adam .... 330-471-8308. 383 D
aklemann@malone.edu
KLEMENT, Emily .... 940-872-4002. 477 I
eklement@nctc.edu
KLEMENT, Kathryn .... 708-209-3337. 143 E
cathryn.klement@cuchicago.edu
KLEMPA, Richard, M .... 304-243-2394. 531 H
rklempa@wju.edu
KLEMPNER, Mark, D .... 508-856-8000. 229 C
mark.klempner@umassmed.edu
KLENIEWSKI, Nancy .... 607-436-2500. 343 E
klenien@oneonta.edu
KLENK, Debbie .... 410-287-6060. 214 B
dklenk@cecil.edu
KLENKE, James, W .... 618-650-2020. 159 H
jklenke@siue.edu
KLEPCYK, Ronald, A .... 336-278-5560. 354 B
klepcyk@elon.edu
KLEPITSCH, Heather, A ... 815-227-2446. 158 A
heatherklepitsch@sacn.edu
KLEPONIS, Stephen .... 610-526-6017. 417 H
skleponis@harcum.edu
KLESCHICK, Paul .... 610-660-1018. 432 E
pkleschi@sju.edu
KLESGES, Lisa, M .... 901-678-4637. 460 B
lmklsges@memphis.edu
KLESTINEC, Cynthia .... 513-529-2021. 384 G
klestic@miamioh.edu
KLETZER, Lori, G .... 207-859-4770. 209 J
Lori.Kletzer@colby.edu
KLEVA, Barbara .... 609-984-1124. 308 A
bkleva@tesc.edu

KLIEBHAN, Camille .... 414-410-4014. 532 B
ckliebhan@stritch.edu
KLIER, Jody .... 701-845-7297. 372 A
jody.klier@vcsu.edu
KLIEWONEIT, Chris .... 989-386-6652. 247 B
ckliewon@midmich.edu
KLIJEWSKI, Chuck .... 303-953-3435... 79 C
ctklijewski@ccu.edu
KLIKA, William .... 201-443-8972. 301 J
helen_bajek@fdu.edu
KLIMA, Kris .... 785-670-1030. 191 D
kris.klima@washburn.edu
KLIMCZAK, Craig .... 314-539-5426. 281 D
cklimczak@stlcc.edu
KLIMCZYK, Karen .... 219-464-5015. 174 E
karen.klimczyk@valpo.edu
KLIMITAS, Paul .... 215-596-8916. 435 H
p.klimitas@usciences.edu
KLIMITCHEK, Michelle ... 361-572-6407. 493 H
missy.klimitchek@victoriacollege.edu
KLIMKOWSKI,
Ann Francis .... 419-885-3211. 383 C
aklimkowski@lourdes.edu
KLIMOFF, Dodi .... 215-635-7300. 417 C
dklimoff@gratz.edu
KLIMPT, Kelly .... 409-944-1356. 472 I
kklimpt@gc.edu
KLIMSCHOT, Patricia ...... 910-296-2474. 361 D
pklimschot@jamessprunt.edu
KLINCAR, Thomas, D ..... 254-526-1214. 468 G
thomas.klincar@ctcd.edu
KLINDT, Kenneth, C .... 850-474-2938. 117 B
kklindt@uwf.edu
KLINE, Amy .... 212-875-4504. 314 C
akline@bankstreet.edu
KLINE, Frank, M .... 253-535-7272. 521 I
klinefm@plu.edu
KLINE, Joseph .... 575-562-2733. 309 H
joseph.kline@enmu.edu
KLINE, Julie .... 909-593-3511... 72 E
jkline@laverne.edu
KLINE, Kenneth .... 859-572-6626. 198 I
klinek1@nku.edu
KLINE, Loni, N .... 570-577-3661. 411 A
loni.kline@bucknell.edu
KLINE, Mae .... 407-328-2096. 113 E
kline@seminolestate.edu
KLINE, Meredith .... 978-468-7111. 227 A
mmkline@gcts.edu
KLINE, Patricia .... 701-671-2106. 372 E
patty.kline@ndscs.edu
KLINE, Rebecca .... 573-876-7111. 282 H
rkline@stephens.edu
KLINE, Rhonda, K .... 309-298-2010. 162 K
r-kline@wiu.edu
KLINE, Richard .... 440-375-7512. 382 L
rkline@lec.edu
KLINE, Richard, L .... 724-938-4074. 428 A
kline@calu.edu
KLINE, Ronald, J .... 610-861-1510. 424 E
merjk01@moravian.edu
KLINE, William .... 812-877-8136. 172 C
william.kline@rose-hulman.edu
KLINE, William .... 978-837-5134. 234 A
klinew@merrimack.edu
KLINE, William .... 808-356-5256. 135 F
bkline@hpu.edu
KLINESMITH, Jerry .... 740-264-5591. 379 F
jklinesmith@egcc.edu
KLING, Deron .... 608-663-4420. 532 I
dkling@edgewood.edu
KLINGBEIL, Marsha .... 419-473-2700. 378 I
mklingbeil@daviscollege.edu
KLINGBEIL, Nathan, W ... 937-775-5007. 393 G
nathan.klingbeil@wright.edu
KLINGBORG, Anne, K .... 217 544 6464. 158 D
KLINGENBERG, Erin .... 701-845-7424. 372 A
erin.klingenberg@vcsu.edu
KLINGENSMITH, John ... 972-860-4190. 470 G
jklingensmith@dcccd.edu
KLINGENSMITH, Lynn ... 610-436-3511. 430 A
lklingensmith@wcupa.edu
KLINGENSMITH, Ron, D 858-499-0202... 40 C
rklingensmith@coleman.edu
KLINGER, Brian .... 920-424-0317. 537 B
klingerb@uwosh.edu
KLINGER, John .... 314-505-7384. 272 J
klingerj@csl.edu
KLINGSHIRN, Connie ..... 419-267-1329. 385 F
cklingshirn@northweststate.edu
KLINK, Charles, J .... 804-828-7525. 511 F
cjklink@vcu.edu
KLINKE, Gene .... 218-935-0417. 265 E
gene.klinke@wetcc.edu
KLINKE, Gene .... 218-683-8554. 260 D
gene.klinke@northlandcollege.edu
KLINKE, Vance .... 916-361-1660... 36 H
vklinke@carrington.edu
KLINKENBERG, Laurel ... 319-296-4041. 178 J
laurel.klinkenberg@hawkeyecollege.edu

KLINKENBERG, Russell .. 619-594-5904... 35 D
rklinkenberg@shsmail.sdsu.edu
KLINKHAMMER, Lucy .... 702-895-0096. 294 I
lucy.klinkhammer@unlv.edu
KLINKNER, Melvin .... 262-595-2076. 537 C
klinkner@uwp.edu
KLIPEL, Gene .... 906-487-3555. 247 A
reklippe@mtu.edu
KLIPP, Todd L, C .... 617-353-2326. 224 D
tklipp@bu.edu
KLIPPENSTEIN, Stacy ..... 406-657-2307. 287 C
sklippenstein@msubillings.edu
KLITSNER, John .... 818-364-7886... 52 A
klitsnjn@lamission.edu
KLOBA, Joseph, A .... 561-803-2051. 110 B
joe_kloba@pba.edu
KLOBERDANZ, Jennifer .. 815-280-2414. 149 A
jkloberd@jjc.edu
KLOBERDANZ, Mark .... 515-271-4526. 177 K
mark.kloberdanz@drake.edu
KLOCK, David .... 305-348-2751. 115 B
David.Klock@fiu.edu
KLOCKE, John, J .... 701-788-4787. 371 E
John.J.Klocke@mayvillestate.edu
KLOCKMAN, Mary .... 605-221-3100. 450 C
mklockman@kilian.edu
KLOEPPEL, Beverly .... 505-277-3432. 312 F
bkloeppe@unm.edu
KLOEPPEL, Michael .... 575-835-5424. 310 F
mkloeppel@admin.nmt.edu
KLOFT, Craig .... 563-589-3251. 182 J
ckloft@dbq.edu
KLOHA, Jeffrey .... 314-505-7756. 272 J
klohaj@csl.edu
KLOMPARENS, Karen, L 517-353-3220. 246 H
kklompar@msu.edu
KLONIS, Suzanne, C ...... 828-689-1360. 356 F
sklonis@mhc.edu
KLONOFF, Robert .... 503-768-6602. 403 K
klonoff@lclark.edu
KLONOSKI, Edward .... 860-515-3888... 87 I
eklonoski@charteroak.edu
KLOOS, Lori .... 320-308-5026. 261 C
lkloos@sctcc.edu
KLOPFER, Jerome, J ...... 575-624-8380. 310 H
klopfer@nmmi.edu
KLOPPENBERG, Lisa ...... 408-554-4362... 64 M
lkloppenberg@scu.edu
KLOPSCH, Vicki, P .... 909-621-8180... 65 D
vicki.klopsch@scrippscollege.edu
KLOS, Elizabeth .... 313-664-7861. 241 C
eklos@collegeforcreativestudies.edu
KLOS, Hank, M .... 608-785-5092. 536 G
hklos@uwlax.edu
KLOSKA, Robert, L .... 574-239-8365. 166 N
rkloska@hcc-nd.edu
KLOSTERMANN, Jill .... 618-545-3235. 149 D
jklostermann@kaskaskia.edu
KLOTMAN, Paul .... 713-798-6363. 467 F
pklotman@bcm.edu
KLOTZBACH, Daniel, P .. 309-556-3527. 148 B
dklotzba@iwu.edu
KLUCK, Linda, A .... 512-223-7503. 466 I
lkluck@austincc.edu
KLUCK, Wesley .... 870-245-5220... 22 D
kluckw@obu.edu
KLUDING, Tom .... 419-755-5659. 385 D
tkluding@ncstatecollege.edu
KLUENDER, Theresa .... 352-588-8857. 112 D
theresa.kluender@saintleo.edu
KLUEVER, Al .... 507-389-7412. 261 E
al.kluever@southcentral.edu
KLUG, Dan .... 218-793-2465. 260 D
dan.klug@northlandcollege.edu
KLUG, Jane .... 605-642-6080. 451 G
jane.klug@bhsu.edu
KLUIN, Rich .... 605-367-5692. 452 C
rich.kluin@southeasttech.edu
KLUKA, Darlene .... 305-899-3549... 98 O
dkluka@barry.edu
KLUKAS, Carol, K .... 262-646-6547. 535 B
cklukas@nashotah.edu
KLUMP, Philip .... 248-414-6900. 246 F
pklump@mji.edu
KLUTH, David .... 503-493-6538. 402 J
ckunert@cu-portland.edu
KLUTTZ, Joy .... 507-222-4013. 254 D
jkluttz@carleton.edu
KLUTTZ, Kendell, M .... 530-226-4770... 66 D
kkluttz@simpsonu.edu
KLUTTZ, Margaret .... 704-636-6545. 355 D
mkluttz@hoodseminary.edu
KLUTTZ, Matthew, B .... 530-226-4475... 66 D
mkluttz@simpsonu.edu
KLUTTZ, Sandy .... 423-697-4475. 460 C
KLUTTZ-LEACH, Camille 336-750-2105. 370 A
leachck@wssu.edu
KLUVER, Erica, L .... 515-263-2816. 178 G
ekluver@grandview.edu
KLUVER, Kirk .... 205-934-8221..... 8 E
kluver@uab.edu

KLYCZEK, James .... 716-614-5905. 334 E
klyczek@niagaracc.suny.edu
KLYMENKO, Anthony ..... 201-559-6100. 302 A
klymenkoa@felician.edu
KLYN, Jeremy .... 866-874-6463. 160 K
jeremy.klyn@trnty.edu
KNAB, Andrew, R .... 302-831-1175... 94 B
drewknab@udel.edu
KNAFF, Mary .... 423-697-3371. 460 C
KNAPP, Charles, B .... 706-542-8100. 133 C
cknapp@terry.uga.edu
KNAPP, Clair, W .... 574-807-7877. 164 D
clair.knapp@bethelcollege.edu
KNAPP, Elizabeth .... 540-458-8705. 516 A
knappe@wlu.edu
KNAPP, Jeffrey .... 518-454-5374. 321 A
knappj@strose.edu
KNAPP, Jennifer, A .... 615-353-3237. 461 B
jennifer.knapp@nscc.edu
KNAPP, John, C .... 616-395-7780. 244 A
knapp@hope.edu
KNAPP, John, C .... 205-726-4362..... 6 F
jknapp@samford.edu
KNAPP, Karl .... 317-788-3232. 173 I
knappk@uindy.edu
KNAPP, Katherine .... 707-638-5221... 69 K
katherine.knapp@tu.edu
KNAPP, Lori .... 516-299-4030. 329 C
lori.knapp@liu.edu
KNAPP, Scott, E .... 207-755-5230. 210 J
sknapp@cmcc.edu
KNAPP, Steven .... 202-994-6500... 95 D
sknapp@gwu.edu
KNAPP, Tom, E .... 301-322-0409. 217 F
tknapp@pgcc.edu
KNAPP, William .... 440-525-7716. 382 M
wknapp@lakelandcc.edu
KNAPP-GROSZ, Tamara . 912-525-5000. 131 B
tknappgr@scad.edu
KNAPPER, Logan .... 918-463-2931. 395 D
logan.knapper@connorsstate.edu
KNAPPER, William, D .... 308-635-6102. 293 E
knapperw@wncc.edu
KNAUER, Christopher, B 704-687-5703. 368 E
cknauer@uncc.edu
KNAUS, Kelli .... 440-646-8316. 392 D
kknaus@ursuline.edu
KNAUTH, Michael .... 631-420-2040. 346 B
michael.knauth@farmingdale.edu
KNECHT, Jennifer .... 956-872-6445. 480 I
jatwood@southtexascollege.edu
KNECHT, Mike, A .... 270-831-9761. 195 D
mike.knecht@kctcs.edu
KNECHT, Mike, W .... 270-831-9760. 195 D
mike.knecht@kctcs.edu
KNEEBONE, Elaine .... 870-230-5820... 21 D
kneebone@hsu.edu
KNEELEY, Steve .... 804-289-6010. 510 L
skneeley@richmond.edu
KNEEPKENS, Elizabeth ... 218-723-6391. 254 K
ekneepke@css.edu
KNEFEL, Mary Anne .... 563-589-3215. 182 J
mknefel@dbq.edu
KNELLY, Ken .... 570-586-2400. 410 D
kknelly@bbc.edu
KNEPFLE, Chuck .... 864-656-3311. 442 C
knepfle@clemson.edu
KNEPP, Marcia .... 301-387-3056. 214 I
marcia.knepp@garrettcollege.edu
KNEPPER, Brenda .... 310-243-3849... 33 B
bknepper@csudh.edu
KNERR, Amanda .... 812-237-3993. 167 A
amanda.knerr@indstate.edu
KNERR, Doug .... 312-341-3615. 157 D
dknerr@roosevelt.edu
KNESAL, Amanda .... 228-377-0090. 270 I
amanda.knesal@wmcarey.edu
KNESEK, Gerald .... 586-286-2172. 246 A
knesekg@macomb.edu
KNESER, Greg .... 507-786-3503. 264 B
kneser@stolaf.edu
KNESTRICK, Joyce .... 606-672-2312. 194 A
joyce.knestrick@frontier.edu
KNETEN, Norval, C .... 252-399-6309. 352 F
nkneten@barton.edu
KNETL, Brian .... 847-925-6773. 145 H
bknetl@harpercollege.edu
KNETTER, Michael, M .... 608-265-9953. 536 D
mike.knetter@supportuw.org
KNEUBUEHL, Erik .... 212-217-3800. 324 C
erik_kneubuel@fitnyc.edu
KNEUBUHL, James .... 684-699-7832. 546 A
j.kneubuhl@amsamoa.edu
KNICELEY, Allen .... 704-669-4037. 359 D
kniceleya@clevelandcc.edu
KNICK, Gary, R .... 540-464-7215. 515 B
knickgr@vmi.edu
KNIER, Carey, A .... 920-565-1527. 533 R
knierca@lakeland.edu
KNIERIM, Jeff .... 304-336-8301. 530 A
jknierim@westliberty.edu

KNIERING, John .... 860-768-4288... 92 D
kniering@hartford.edu
KNIGHT, Antonia .... 716-286-8204. 334 F
abk@niagara.edu
KNIGHT, Arlinda .... 334-420-4235..... 7 G
aknight@trenholmstate.edu
KNIGHT, Ashley .... 847-925-6462. 145 H
aknight@harpercollege.edu
KNIGHT, Brenda, L .... 270-831-9652. 195 D
brenda.knight@kctcs.edu
KNIGHT, Brent .... 517-483-9647. 245 H
knightb4@lcc.edu
KNIGHT, Cindi .... 304-647-6299. 530 B
cknight@osteo.wvsom.edu
KNIGHT, Darryl .... 847-925-6350. 145 H
dknight@harpercollege.edu
KNIGHT, David .... 256-726-7389..... 6 B
dknight@oakwood.edu
KNIGHT, David .... 252-985-5169. 365 D
dknight@ncwc.edu
KNIGHT, Debra, L .... 217-443-8865. 143 G
dknight@dacc.edu
KNIGHT, Erin .... 580-371-2371. 396 E
eknight@mscok.edu
KNIGHT, Gary, E .... 803-705-4559. 441 C
knightg@benedict.edu
KNIGHT, Gayle .... 601-318-6197. 270 I
gayle.knight@wmcarey.edu
KNIGHT, Griena .... 205-929-1455..... 5 G
gknight@mail.miles.edu
KNIGHT, Heather, J .... 707-965-6211... 57 J
hknight@puc.edu
KNIGHT, Holly .... 508-830-5029. 230 D
hknight@maritime.edu
KNIGHT, Jacob, E .... 317-738-8080. 165 I
jknight@franklincollege.edu
KNIGHT, James .... 774-354-0658. 223 A
james.knight@becker.edu
KNIGHT, Jessie .... 954-731-8880. 100 M
KNIGHT, Jim, D .... 815-939-5201. 155 H
jdknight@olivet.edu
KNIGHT, John, E .... 832-252-4603. 468 L
john.knight@cbshouston.edu
KNIGHT, JR., John, F .... 334-229-4286..... 1 D
jknight@alasu.edu
KNIGHT, Keller Anne ...... 828-298-3325. 370 E
bookstore@warren-wilson.edu
KNIGHT, Kelly .... 337-521-8934. 203 I
kelly.knight@southlouisiana.edu
KNIGHT, Kelly .... 937-948-0333. 203 J
kelly.knight@solacc.edu
KNIGHT, Kelly .... 337-348-0333. 204 B
kelly.knight@solacc.edu
KNIGHT, Kelly .... 337-948-0333. 204 C
kelly.knight@solacc.edu
KNIGHT, Kerri .... 229-226-1621. 132 F
kknight@thomasu.edu
KNIGHT, Lea Ann .... 601-643-8342. 266 F
leaann.knight@colin.edu
KNIGHT, Leonard .... 760-245-4271... 75 B
Leonard.Knight@vvc.edu
KNIGHT, Lori .... 504-816-4797. 201 K
lknight@dillard.edu
KNIGHT, Lydia .... 706-272-4527. 123 G
lknight@daltonstat.edu
KNIGHT, Mary .... 847-925-6278. 145 H
mknight@harpercollege.edu
KNIGHT, Mary, E .... 512-471-3727. 491 C
bd.knightme@austin.utexas.edu
KNIGHT, Melvin .... 973-877-3301. 301 H
knight@essex.edu
KNIGHT, Renee .... 317-738-8595. 165 I
rknight@franklincollege.edu
KNIGHT, Robert .... 530-898-5351... 33 A
KNIGHT, Robert .... 715-836-4353. 536 E
knightrm@uwec.edu
KNIGHT, Robert .... 360-992-2101. 518 A
rknight@clark.edu
KNIGHT, Robin .... 478-387-4890. 125 E
KNIGHT, Roger, A .... 601-403-1206. 269 D
rknight@prcc.edu
KNIGHT, Sheri .... 620-343-4600. 186 E
sknight@fhtc.edu
KNIGHT, Sherry, S .... 989-774-6107. 240 N
knigh1s@cmich.edu
KNIGHT, Steven, H .... 601-318-6111. 270 I
steve.knight@wmcarey.edu
KNIGHT, Tim .... 870-245-5216... 22 D
knightt@obu.edu
KNIGHT, Tim .... 202-884-9133... 96 G
knightt@trinitydc.edu
KNIGHT, Unita .... 910-296-2460. 361 D
uknight@jamessprunt.edu
KNIGHT, W. Hal .... 423-439-7627. 459 C
knighth@etsu.edu
KNIGHT, Wendy, S .... 563-557-8271. 181 E
knightw@nicc.edu
KNIGHTON, Denise .... 662-915-7792. 270 B
denisek@olemiss.edu
KNIGHTON, Diana, W .... 205-929-1442..... 5 G
diana@mail.miles.edu

KNIGHTON, Joy .... 229-430-3602. 120 A
jknighton@albanytech.edu
KNIPSCHIELD, Debbie .... 253-833-9111. 520 C
DKnipschield@greenriver.edu
KNISELY, Bertie .... 610-861-1345. 424 E
bertiek@moravian.edu
KNISLEY, Joel .... 828-251-6100. 368 C
jknisley@unca.edu
KNISPEL, Todd .... 406-377-9413. 286 A
knispelt@dawson.edu
KNISS, Fred, L .... 540-432-4105. 504 D
fred.kniss@emu.edu
KNOBEL, David .... 954-535-8820. 103 L
dknobel@careercollege.edu
KNOBLAUCH, Laura .... 309-438-8658. 147 J
lmknobl@ilstu.edu
KNOBLICH, Julie, A .... 620-792-9275. 184 F
knoblichj@bartonccc.edu
KNOCH, Daniel, L .... 517-437-7341. 243 I
dan.knoch@hillsdale.edu
KNOCHE, Charlotte, M ... 651-641-8240. 255 B
knoche@csp.edu
KNODLE-BRAGIEL, Lisa . 503-883-2214. 404 A
lbragiel@linfield.edu
KNOEBEL, Ann, G .... 210-999-7601. 488 C
aknoebel@trinity.edu
KNOELL, Karen .... 605-995-2647. 450 A
kaknoell@dwu.edu
KNOETTGEN, Suzi .... 785-243-1435. 185 M
sknoettgen@cloud.edu
KNOFF, Gregory .... 313-664-7650. 241 C
gknoff@collegeforcreativestudies.edu
KNOLHOFF, Wayne .... 314-505-7170. 272 J
knolhoffw@csl.edu
KNOLL, Joseph .... 617-824-8112. 226 A
joseph_knoll@emerson.edu
KNOLLMAN, Paul, L ...... 734-384-4282. 247 C
pknollman@monroeccc.edu
KNOOR, Robert .... 616-957-6039. 240 M
rknoor@calvinseminary.edu
KNOP, Joachim, W .... 202-994-6506... 95 D
knop@gwu.edu
KNOP-COX, Barbara .... 405-422-1401. 399 B
knopcoxb@redlandscc.edu
KNORR, Stephen, C .... 573-882-2726. 283 B
knorrs@umsystem.edu
KNORR, Walter .... 312-413-9097. 161 C
wknorr@uillinois.edu
KNORTZ, Geraldine .... 802-654-2200. 500 B
gknortz@smcvt.edu
KNOST, Julie .... 812-855-7559. 167 F
jknost@indiana.edu
KNOST, Julie .... 812-855-7559. 167 E
knost@indiana.edu
KNOTHE, Thomas, E ...... 608-796-3376. 539 E
teknothe@viterbo.edu
KNOTT, Allan .... 214-860-8531. 471 A
aknott@dcccd.edu
KNOTT, Brenda .... 405-974-3561. 400 K
KNOTT, Gregory .... 305-237-0825. 109 D
gknott@mdc.edu
KNOTT, Jack, H .... 213-740-0350... 74 A
jhknott@usc.edu
KNOTT, Kevin .... 217-351-2239. 155 J
kknott@parkland.edu
KNOTT, Ronald .... 812-357-6544. 173 A
rknott@saintmeinrad.edu
KNOTT, William .... 616-222-1918. 241 F
bill.knott@cornerstone.edu
KNOTTS, Ann .... 386-312-4022. 112 C
annknotts@sjrstate.edu
KNOTTS, Bradley .... 815-226-3398. 157 C
bknotts@rockford.edu
KNOTTS, Cecil .... 318-357-5965. 208 B
knottsc@nsula.edu
KNOTTS, David .... 636-798-2166. 276 D
dknotts@lindenwood.edu
KNOTTS, Debby .... 505-277-5765. 312 F
debby@unm.edu
KNOUSE, Christine .... 717-262-2016. 437 H
cknouse@wilson.edu
KNOWLES, Harley .... 423-746-5201. 462 C
hknowles@twcnct.edu
KNOWLES, Melody .... 703-370-6600. 508 B
KNOWLES, Monica .... 360-992-2904. 518 A
mknowles@clark.edu
KNOWLES, Susan .... 315-268-6633. 320 A
sknowles@clarkson.edu
KNOWLTON,
Douglas, D .... 651-201-1652. 257 N
douglas.knowlton@so.mnscu.edu
KNOWLTON, Eloise .... 508-767-7487. 222 C
eknowlton@assumption.edu
KNOX, Arlene .... 239-489-9234. 101 O
amknox@edison.edu
KNOX, Chrisanne .... 925-969-2048... 41 L
cknox@dvc.edu
KNOX, Darby .... 585-395-5160. 342 F
dknox@brockport.edu
KNOX, Edwin .... 973-877-4473. 301 H
knox@essex.edu
KNOX, George, C .... 620-421-6700. 188 D
georgek@labette.edu
KNOX, Linda .... 219-989-2337. 171 N
Linda.Knox@purduecal.edu
KNOX, Marg .... 512-322-3774. 491 A
mknox@utsystem.edu
KNOX, Pamela .... 615-366-4411. 459 A
pamela.knox@tbr.edu
KNOX, Ramon .... 714-532-6039... 38 A
rknox@chapman.edu
KNOX, Ronnie .... 256-233-8186..... 1 F
ronnie.knox@athens.edu
KNOX, Ruth, A .... 478-757-5212. 134 G
rknox@wesleyancollege.edu
KNOX, Teresa, L .... 918-610-0027. 395 C
tknox@communitycarecollege.edu
KNOX, Tracey .... 970-521-6643... 83 L
tracey.knox@njc.edu
KNUDSEN, Alice, B .... 510-430-2350... 54 F
aknudsen@mills.edu
KNUDSEN, H. Peter .... 406-496-4395. 287 F
pknudsen@mtech.edu
KNUDSEN, J. Todd .... 562-902-3358... 67 H
toddknudsen@scuhs.edu
KNUDSEN, Ross .... 208-376-7731. 137 F
rknudsen@boisebible.edu
KNUDSON, Dan .... 218-299-6521. 259 F
dan.knudson@minnesota.edu
KNUDSON, Edward, T .... 661-722-6300... 28 F
eknudson@avc.edu
KNUDSON, Kari .... 701-224-5604. 372 B
kari.l.knudson@bismarckstate.edu
KNUDSON, Paula, M ...... 608-785-8150. 536 G
pknudson@uwlax.edu
KNUDSON-CARL, Tara ... 402-399-2449. 289 A
tknudsoncarl@csm.edu
KNUESEL, Rita .... 320-363-5503. 254 J
rknuesel@csbsju.edu
KNUESEL, Rita .... 320-363-5503. 263 P
rknuesel@csbsju.edu
KNUEVE, Donald, S .... 419-783-2581. 379 C
dknueve@defiance.edu
KNUTEL, Phillip, G .... 781-891-3422. 223 C
pknutel@bentley.edu
KNUTESON, Catherine .... 414-326-2304. 532 G
catherine.knuteson@ccon.edu
KNUTH, Barbara, A .... 607-255-5864. 322 A
bak3@cornell.edu
KNUTH, Doug .... 775-784-6900. 294 J
dknuth@unr.edu
KNUTSEN, John, D .... 510-883-2073... 42 I
jknutsen@dspt.edu
KNUTSEN, Mark .... 740-755-7302. 376 A
mknutsen@cotc.edu
KNUTSON, Craig .... 405-208-5000. 397 F
crknutson@okcu.edu
KNUTSON, Julie .... 734-487-0427. 242 D
jknutson@emich.edu
KNUTSON, Karen .... 320-363-5922. 254 J
kknutson@csbsju.edu
KNUTSON, Karen, G .... 320-363-5922. 263 P
kknutson@csbsju.edu
KNUTSON, Sherry .... 415-749-4571... 62 G
sknutson@sfai.edu
KNUTZEN, Gary .... 360-416-7714. 523 G
gary.knutzen@skagit.edu
KNUTZEN, Kathleen .... 661-654-2210... 32 H
kknutzen@csub.edu
KO, Jeanne .... 212-472-1500. 334 B
jko@nysid.edu
KO, Vivien .... 323-343-2730... 34 A
vko@calstatela.edu
KO, Yoo, K .... 571-730-4750. 277 K
wdc@midwest.edu
KOAL, Penny .... 360-596-5227. 524 A
pkoal@spscc.edu
KOAN, Mark .... 602-285-7855... 15 C
mark.koan@phoenixcollege.edu
KOBALLA, Thomas .... 912-478-5648. 126 C
tkoballa@georgiasouthern.edu
KOBAYASHI, Frank .... 916-485-6028... 53 A
kobayaf@arc.losrios.edu
KOBAYASHI, Vivian .... 408-541-0100... 40 A
vkobayashi@cogswell.edu
KOBERNA, Sharon .... 480-517-8220... 15 D
sharon.koberna@riosalado.edu
KOBES, Patricia .... 845-574-4280. 338 B
pkobes@sunyrockland.edu
KOBLER, Wendy .... 256-372-8344..... 1 A
wendy.kobler@aamu.edu
KOBOLAKIS, Evan .... 212-410-8008. 333 E
ekbolakis@nycpm.edu
KOBRITZ, Richard .... 818-345-7921... 41 B
rkobritz@columbiacollege.edu
KOBUS, Gloria .... 330-941-3142. 394 A
gjkobus@ysu.edu
KOBUS, Lee .... 732-255-0400. 304 A
lkobus@ocean.edu
KOBYLSKI, Janet .... 570-408-4501. 437 F
janet.kobylski@wilkes.edu
KOCAR, Deb .... 617-349-8800. 228 B
ugadm@lesley.edu
KOCER, Ken .... 605-668-1589. 450 F
kkocer@mtmc.edu
KOCH, Amelia .... 617-266-1400. 223 D
KOCH, Bill .... 252-328-6166. 367 B
kochb@ecu.edu
KOCH, Bradley .... 610-902-8571. 411 E
bradley.r.koch@cabrini.edu
KOCH, Connie .... 314-362-6289. 274 G
ckoch@bjc.org
KOCH, Deborah .... 413-755-4479. 233 A
DSKoch@stcc.edu
KOCH, Dennis .... 903-886-5796. 483 E
dennis.koch@tamuc.edu
KOCH, Don .... 618-634-3289. 158 M
donk@shawneecc.edu
KOCH, James .... 651-638-6415. 253 K
j-koch@bethel.edu
KOCH, Keith .... 612-977-5322. 254 C
keith.koch@capella.edu
KOCH, Kelly .... 989-386-6639. 247 B
kkoch@midmich.edu
KOCH, Lindsey .... 361-570-4136. 489 E
kochl@uhv.edu
KOCH, Paul .... 831-459-5861... 72 C
plkoch@ucolick.org
KOCH, Paul .... 563-333-6212. 182 B
KochPaulC@sau.edu
KOCH, Paul, C .... 563-333-6196. 182 B
KochPaulC@sau.edu
KOCH, Robert .... 657-278-2638... 33 E
rkoch@fullerton.edu
KOCH, Susan .... 217-206-6634. 161 C
koch@uis.edu
KOCH, Susan .... 217-206-6634. 161 E
koch@uis.edu
KOCH, Thomas, L .... 520-621-2448... 18 F
tlkoch@email.arizona.edu
KOCHAN, Julie .... 518-454-5121. 321 A
kochanj@strose.edu
KOCHAN, Roman .... 562-985-4047... 33 F
rkochan@csulb.edu
KOCHANCZYK, Kristin ... 617-262-5000. 223 F
kristin.kochanczyk@the-bac.edu
KOCHANEK, Lea .... 210-341-1366. 477 L
lkochanek@ost.edu
KOCHARD, Dale, A .... 610-758-5801. 422 A
dak304@lehigh.edu
KOCHARD, Lawrence, E . 434-924-4245. 511 B
lek8e@virginia.edu
KOCHER, Andy, M .... 317-788-3493. 173 I
akocher@uindy.edu
KOCHER, Betty, A .... 269-387-2360. 252 I
betty.kocher@wmich.edu
KOCHER, Craig, T .... 804-289-8500. 510 L
ckocher@richmond.edu
KOCHER, Edward, W ...... 412-396-6082. 415 F
kocher@duq.edu
KOCHERA, Melissah .... 203-596-4652... 90 I
mkochera@post.edu
KOCHEVAR, Brenda .... 218-749-0314. 259 B
b.kochevar@mr.mnscu.edu
KOCHEVAR, Deborah ...... 508-887-4700. 237 C
deborah.kochevar@tufts.edu
KOCHIEN, Kenneth, G .... 603-526-3627. 295 I
kkochien@colby-sawyer.edu
KOCHIN, Frank, S .... 314-516-6311. 283 E
kochinf@umsl.edu
KOCHIS, Stephen, J .... 845-575-3000. 330 D
stephen.kochis@marist.edu
KOCHON, Barbara .... 413-565-1000. 222 F
bkochon@baypath.edu
KOCIAN, Bryce .... 979-532-6308. 494 L
brycek@wcjc.edu
KOCIAN, Justin .... 402-494-2311. 290 O
jkocian@thenicc.edu
KOCIOLEK, Patrick .... 303-492-8464... 85 L
patrick.kociolek@colorado.edu
KOCOUR, Bruce .... 865-471-3240. 453 F
bkocour@cn.edu
KOCZON, Lenore .... 701-858-3310. 371 F
lenore.koczon@minotstateu.edu
KODAMA, Be-Jay .... 808-739-8526. 135 D
bkodama@chaminade.edu
KODAT, Catherine .... 215-717-6260. 435 A
ckodat@uarts.edu
KOEBEL, Dave .... 402-457-2391. 290 G
dkoebel@mccneb.edu
KOECHIG, Donna .... 541-463-5307. 403 I
koechigd@lanecc.edu
KOEGEL, Warren .... 256-782-5368..... 4 K
wkoegel@jsu.edu
KOEGLER, Jason, W .... 304-336-8302. 530 A
jkoegler@westliberty.edu
KOEHLER, Al .... 636-922-8452. 280 J
alkoehler@stchas.edu
KOEHLER, David .... 308-635-6021. 293 E
koehlerd@wncc.edu
KOEHLER, Donna .... 253-589-5588. 518 B
donna.koehler@cptc.edu
KOEHLER, Jeri .... 918-343-7533. 399 C
jkoehler@rsu.edu
KOEHLER, John .... 406-791-5330. 288 E
jkoehler01@ugf.edu
KOEHLER, Larry .... 810-232-8153. 247 F
larry.koehler@mcc.edu
KOEHLER, Martha Kaye .. 813-253-7007. 106 M
mkoehler@hccfl.edu
KOEHLER, Randy .... 513-244-8449. 376 J
randy.koehler@ccuniversity.edu
KOEHN, David .... 918-444-2186. 396 H
koehn@nsuok.edu
KOEHN, Effie, F .... 406-243-6413. 286 H
effie.koehn@umontana.edu
KOEHN, Jack .... 224-293-5961... 81 B
KOEHN, Michelle .... 316-226-2002. 175 D
Michelle.Koehn@AllenCollege.edu
KOEHN, Suzie .... 307-855-2148. 542 Y
suzie@cwc.edu
KOEHNKE, Paul .... 704-330-6121. 359 C
paul.koehnke@cpcc.edu
KOELBL, James .... 207-602-2678. 213 A
jkoelbl@une.edu
KOELBL, James .... 207-221-4701. 213 A
jkoelbl@une.edu
KOELKER, June .... 817-257-7106. 484 I
j.koelker@tcu.edu
KOELLEIN, David .... 615-794-4254. 457 Q
dkoellein@omorecollege.edu
KOELLER, Martin, E .... 973-761-9782. 307 C
martin.koeller@shu.edu
KOELLIKER, Marilynn ..... 785-670-1450. 191 D
marilynn.koelliker@washburn.edu
KOELTZOW, Dawn .... 309-677-2510. 140 I
dkoeltzow@bradley.edu
KOENECKE, David .... 660-626-2410. 271 A
dkoenecke@atsu.edu
KOENIG, Eric .... 415-476-4318... 72 A
ekoenig@ucsf.edu
KOENIG, Jerry, L .... 317-921-4491. 169 L
jkoenig@ivytech.edu
KOENIG, Jim .... 815-836-5206. 150 H
koenigji@lewisu.edu
KOENIG, Jim .... 320-363-5563. 263 P
jkoenig@csbsju.edu
KOENIG, Jim, J .... 320-363-5563. 254 J
jkoenig@csbsju.edu
KOENIG, Lucas .... 920-433-6621. 531 L
lucas.koenig@bellincollege.edu
KOENIGSKNECHT,
Cindy, J .... 734-462-4400. 250 A
ckoenigs@schoolcraft.edu
KOEP, Jeffrey .... 702-895-4210. 294 I
jeffrey.koep@unlv.edu
KOEPKE, Andrea .... 419-434-4677. 391 D
koepke@findlay.edu
KOEPKE, Mark .... 701-252-3467. 373 D
mkoepke@jc.edu
KOEPPEL, Edmund .... 516-572-7126. 332 C
edmund.koeppel@ncc.edu
KOEPPEN, Bruce .... 203-528-5301... 91 A
bruce.koeppen@quinnipiac.edu
KOERBER, Brent .... 614-236-7167. 375 H
bkoerber@capital.edu
KOERMER, Kelly, A .... 410-777-7432. 213 D
kkoermer@aacc.edu
KOERNER, Mari, E .... 602-543-6352... 11 K
mari.koerner@asu.edu
KOESER, Bryan .... 920-693-1731. 540 B
bryan.koeser@gotoltc.edu
KOESTER, Craig .... 651-641-3471. 256 J
ckoester@luthersem.edu
KOETT, Kevin, S .... 606-783-2014. 198 A
k.koett@moreheadstate.edu
KOETTING, Sandy .... 573-681-5071. 276 C
koettings@lincolnu.edu
KOETZNER, John .... 707-468-3000... 54 B
jkoetzne@mendocino.edu
KOEVEN, Gary, J .... 435-652-7770. 497 E
koeven@dixie.edu
KOFFLER, Jeromy .... 503-943-7470. 408 F
koffler@up.edu
KOFNOVEC, David .... 254-867-3791. 486 B
david.kofnovec@tstc.edu
KOFRON, Cheryl, L .... 563-884-5670. 182 A
cheryl.kofron@palmer.edu
KOGA, Laura, A .... 815-740-5084. 162 F
lkoga@stfrancis.edu
KOGAN, Alexander .... 212-327-8001. 338 A
kogana@rockefeller.edu
KOGAN, Linda .... 719-255-3757... 85 M
lkogan@uccs.edu
KOGER, Ron, R .... 678-915-3720. 132 C
rkoger@spsu.edu
KOGUT, Leonard .... 616-632-2885. 239 E
lvk001@aquinas.edu
KOGUT, Leonard, V .... 276-964-7500. 514 A
len.kogut@sw.edu
KOHAN, Eileen, B .... 213-740-5679... 74 A
kohan@usc.edu

KOHL, Erin, K ... 920-565-1256. 533 R kohlEK@lakeland.edu
KOHL, James ... 978-934-2108. 229 B James_Kohl@uml.edu
KOHL, Jay ... 732-932-4716. 306 A jkohl@aps.rutgers.edu
KOHL, Marie ... 315-792-5340. 331 I mkohl@mvcc.edu
KOHL, Troy ... 920-735-5766. 539 K kohlt@fvtc.edu
KOHLER, David, L ... 253-535-7380. 521 I kohlerdl@plu.edu
KOHLER, Donald ... 712-325-3262. 179 L dkohler@iwcc.edu
KOHLER, Patti ... 435-797-0174. 497 B patti.kohler@usu.edu
KOHLI, Cathy, L ... 419-995-8060. 381 Q kohli.c@rhodesstate.edu
KOHLMAN, Shawn ... 757-873-4235. 510 B skohlman@stratford.edu
KOHLMEYER, Bill ... 503-399-6505. 402 E bill.kohlmeyer@chemeketa.edu
KOHN, David ... 845-341-4388. 335 H david.kohn@sunyorange.edu
KOHN, Gary ... 608-757-7769. 539 I gkohn@blackhawk.edu
KOHN, Gregory, N ... 406-657-1160. 288 B greg.kohn@rocky.edu
KOHN, Marilyn, F ... 212-678-8997. 328 A makohn@jtsa.edu
KOHN, Melissa ... 920-236-6100. 539 K kohn@fvtc.edu
KOHN, Paul ... 404-385-3708. 125 D paul.kohn@ssc.gatech.edu
KOHN, Shayeh ... 718-327-7600. 350 J yfr1@verizon.net
KOHN SANDERS, Courtney ... 708-534-5000. 145 F csanders5@govst.edu
KOHNEN-CAHALL, Nan .. 513-569-5807. 376 L nan.cahall@cincinnatistate.edu
KOHNKE, Maria ... 805-493-3105... 31 H kohnke@clunet.edu
KOHR, Lesa, J ... 585-594-6966. 337 K kohrl@roberts.edu
KOHRMAN, Robert ... 313-577-2001. 252 G dt9443@wayne.edu
KOHRN, Lynn ... 203-932-7131... 92 E lkohrn@newhaven.edu
KOHRS, Becky ... 402-471-2505. 291 C bkohrs@nscs.edu
KOHRT, Carl, F ... 864-294-2100. 444 C carl.kohrt@furman.edu
KOIVISTO, Rex ... 503-255-0332. 404 F rexk@multnomah.edu
KOJIMA, Glenn, Y ... 714-449-7465... 67 D gkojima@scco.edu
KOJIRO, Angela ... 239-687-5332... 98 J amkojiro@avemarialaw.edu
KOK, Cynthia ... 616-526-6125. 240 L ckok@calvin.edu
KOK, John, H ... 712-722-6210. 177 J john.kok@dordt.edu
KOKAJKO, Hillary, C ... 336-841-9118. 355 C hkokajko@highpoint.edu
KOKER, John, J ... 920-424-1210. 537 B koker@uwosh.edu
KOKER, Michelle ... 612-624-2941. 264 G koker@umn.edu
KOKINOVA, Margarita, D ... 330-325-6333. 385 E mkokinov@neomed.edu
KOKKALA, Irene ... 706-864-1862. 133 D irene.kokkala@ung.edu
KOKOLUS, Cait ... 610-785-6280. 432 C ckokolus@scs.edu
KOKOLUS, John ... 717-361-1291. 415 H kokolusj@etown.edu
KOKONAS, Georgios ... 914-961-8313. 340 B gkokonas@svots.edu
KOKOSKA, Stephen ... 570-389-4713. 427 H skokoska@bloomu.edu
KOLACINSKI, John ... 213-484-8850... 30 D
KOLAJO, Ebenezer, F ... 540-831-2469. 508 C ekolajo@radford.edu
KOLANDER, John, D ... 414-443-8816. 539 F john.kolander@wlc.edu
KOLB, Daniel ... 812-357-6566. 173 A dkolb@saintmeinrad.edu
KOLB, Edward, W ... 773-702-7950. 161 B rocky.kolb@uchicago.edu
KOLB, George, R ... 610-519-4580. 436 F george.kolb@villanova.edu
KOLB, John, E ... 518-276-2122. 337 I kolbj@rpi.edu
KOLB, Mike ... 501-337-5000... 20 J mkolb@coto.edu
KOLB, Susan ... 605-455-6051. 450 I sheathershaw@olc.edu
KOLBE, Donald, A ... 262-595-2228. 537 C donald.kolbe@uwp.edu
KOLBE, Rick ... 859-572-5551. 198 I kolber1@nku.edu
KOLCHARNO, Julia ... 570-504-9614. 413 B
KOLENBRANDER, Kirk, D ... 617-253-3365. 233 B
KOLENDA, Richard ... 315-312-2246. 344 A richard.kolenda@oswego.edu
KOLENO, Jeff ... 440-365-5222. 383 B
KOLENOVIC, Zeke ... 212-472-1500. 334 B zkolenovic@nysid.edu
KOLESAR, James, G ... 413-597-4233. 238 D james.g.kolesar@williams.edu
KOLESAR-LYNCH, Marilyn, K ... 972-860-4181. 470 G mklynch@dcccd.edu
KOLHOFF, Kathleen ... 684-699-9155. 546 A k.kolhoff@amsamoa.edu
KOLIMAGA, Karen ... 978-632-6600. 232 C k_kolimaga@mwcc.mass.edu
KOLINS, Craig ... 971-722-6268. 407 D ckolins@pcc.edu
KOLISZ, Karin ... 219-757-6132. 172 D
KOLJENOVIC, Denis ... 718-261-5800. 315 F dkoljenovic@ortopsusa.org
KOLL, Nancy ... 773-481-8663. 142 F nkoll@ccc.edu
KOLLAR, Kristen ... 216-791-5000. 377 E kristen.kollar@case.edu
KOLLAR, OSB, Rene ... 724-805-2343. 432 G rene.kollar@email.stvincent.edu
KOLLATH, Carissa ... 402-844-7159. 291 I carissa@northeast.edu
KOLLBAUM, Kristin, E ... 712-324-5061. 181 G kkollbaum@nwicc.edu
KOLLER, Bobbie ... 510-723-6923... 37 K bkoller@chabotcollege.edu
KOLLER, Rebecca, H ... 402-472-3917. 292 G rkoller@nebraska.edu
KOLLIEN, Mike ... 989-358-7339. 239 C kollienm@alpenacc.edu
KOLLIGIAN, John ... 609-258-3285. 304 E jkjr@princeton.edu
KOLLMEYER, Will ... 662-862-8274. 267 C wakollmeyer@iccms.edu
KOLLMORGEN, Terry ... 918-495-6175. 398 H tmk@oru.edu
KOLLOCK, Chenita, R ... 410-651-8045. 219 E crkollock@umes.edu
KOLLROSS, Crystal ... 626-585-7759... 58 F cakollross@pasadena.edu
KOLLURU, Ramesh ... 337-482-6541. 208 D rxk6962@louisiana.edu
KOLMAN, Mark ... 740-427-5000. 382 J kolmanm@kenyon.edu
KOLODZIEJSKI, Gwynne 610-796-8325. 409 E gwynne.kolodziejski@alvernia.edu
KOLOMITZ, Kara ... 781-768-7055. 236 A kara.kolomitz@regiscollege.edu
KOLPACK, Bryce ... 715-675-3331. 541 A Kolpack@ntc.edu
KOLTON, Russell ... 401-874-4515. 440 D rkolton@advance.uri.edu
KOLVOORD, Robert ... 540-568-2752. 506 F kolvoora@jmu.edu
KOM, Sheila ... 208-792-2288. 138 G sheilak@lcsc.edu
KOMACEK, Stan ... 724-938-4187. 428 A komacek@calu.edu
KOMACK, Julie ... 781-239-2661. 231 G jkomack@massbay.edu
KOMANECKY, Sharon ... 912-260-4427. 131 F sharon.Komanecky@sgsc.edu
KOMARNY, Phil ... 724-830-1850. 433 E komarny@setonhill.edu
KOMATSUBARA, Carole 808-544-0200. 135 F
KOMDAT, Mark ... 845-687-5051. 348 H komdatm@sunyulster.edu
KOMLYN, Lorie ... 617-369-3665. 236 F lkomlyn@smfa.edu
KOMORA, Melissa ... 518-244-2325. 338 C komorm@sage.edu
KOMOTO, Cary ... 952-358-8428. 260 B cary.komoto@normandale.edu
KOMP, Chuck ... 715-365-4537. 540 G ckomp@nicoletcollege.edu
KOMPARE, Lou ... 440-365-5222. 383 B
KOMPELIEN, Ken ... 701-671-2297. 372 E ken.kompelien@ndscs.edu
KOMUNIECKI, Patricia, R ... 419-530-4968. 392 B patricia.komuniecki@utoledo.edu
KONAN, Denise, E ... 808-956-6570. 136 B konan@hawaii.edu
KONANGI, Vijaya ... 216-687-3588. 377 F v.konangi@csuohio.edu
KONAR-STEENBERG, Mehmet ... 651-290-6456. 265 F mehmet.konar-steenberg@wmitchell.edu
KONCSOL, Carol ... 848-932-7454. 306 A koncsol@oldqueens.rutgers.edu
KONCZAL, Timothy, J ... 330-672-9192. 382 B tkonczal@kent.edu
KONDA, Kevin, J ... 316-978-3490. 191 F kevin.konda@wichita.edu
KONDRACH, Carol, S ... 609-895-5196. 305 D kondrach@rider.edu
KONDRAK, Mark ... 651-523-2512. 256 A mkondrak01@hamline.edu
KONDRAT, Mary Ellen ... 785-864-4720. 190 L maryek@ku.edu
KONDRATENKO, Svetlana ... 619-298-1829... 68 A skondratenko@ssu.edu
KONDRATH, William ... 617-682-1510. 226 D bkondrath@eds.edu
KONEN, Judee, L ... 402-461-7434. 289 I jkonen@hastings.edu
KONESCO, Jason, T ... 317-447-6022. 166 I Jason.Konesco@harrison.edu
KONG, Xiangping ... 609-626-6025. 305 C xiangping.kong@stockton.edu
KONIG, Angela, A ... 641-422-1521. 181 D angela.konig@iwd.iowa.gov
KONIG, Michael ... 413-565-1000. 222 F mkonig@baypath.edu
KONIN, Jeff ... 860-465-4509... 87 L koninj@easternct.edu
KONING, Shawnn ... 951-343-4224... 30 H skoning@calbaptist.edu
KONKLE, Lance, R ... 716-851-1868. 323 I konkle@ecc.edu
KONKLE, Thomas, E ... 812-888-4451. 174 F tkonkle@vinu.edu
KONKOL, Brian, E ... 507-933-7446. 255 I
KONKOLESKI, RJ ... 740-695-9500. 374 H rkonkoleski@belmontcollege.edu
KONKOLY, Thomas, H ... 440-826-3460. 374 F tkonkoly@bw.edu
KONNY, Sharon ... 847-214-7260. 144 F skonny@elgin.edu
KONO, Kim ... 971-722-4387. 407 D kim.kono@pcc.edu
KONOPKA, Daniel ... 914-633-2069. 327 C dkonopka@iona.edu
KONRAD, Jim ... 847-491-8121. 155 D j-konrad@northwestern.edu
KONSCHAK, Norma ... 320-308-5382. 261 C nkonschak@sctcc.edu
KONSTALID, Daniel, T ... 717-337-6200. 417 B dkonstal@gettysburg.edu
KONUWA, Alfred, B ... 530-661-5712... 77 L akonuwa@yccd.edu
KONWERSKI, Peter, A ... 202-994-7210... 95 D peterk@gwu.edu
KONYA, Jeffrey ... 661-654-2200... 32 H jkonya@csub.edu
KONYAOLE, Cedric ... 501-370-5336... 22 F cronyaole@philander.edu
KONZ, Jeff ... 828-251-6570. 368 C jkonz@unca.edu
KONZEM, Gail ... 785-227-3380. 184 I konzemg@bethanylb.edu
KOO, James ... 714-525-0088... 46 A administration@gm.edu
KOOB, Sondra ... 215-785-0111. 426 X
KOOHANG, Alex ... 478-471-2801. 128 I alex.koohang@maconstate.edu
KOOI, Jana ... 904-997-2649. 105 E janakooi@fscj.edu
KOOI, Janeen, W ... 260-982-5219. 170 U jwkooi@manchester.edu
KOOI, Shelly ... 219-464-5212. 174 E shelly.kooi@valpo.edu
KOOIMAN, Florence ... 219-864-2400. 171 F fkooiman@midamerica.edu
KOOK, Kathleen ... 510-649-2464... 46 B kkook@gtu.edu
KOON, Ann, M ... 740-264-5591. 379 F akoon@egcc.edu
KOON, Chi ... 718-270-6107. 319 A chi@mec.cuny.edu
KOON, J. Michael ... 304-723-7500. 528 G mkoon@wvncc.edu
KOON, J. Michael ... 304-214-8967. 528 G mkoon@wvncc.edu
KOONCE, Kenneth, L ... 225-578-2080. 204 O kkoonce@lsu.edu
KOONSE, Cyndi ... 573-592-4358. 285 D cyndi.koonse@williamwoods.edu
KOONTZ, David ... 562-903-4760... 29 L dave.koontz@biola.edu
KOONTZ, Sondra ... 316-284-5341. 184 J skoontz@bethelks.edu
KOONZ, Peter ... 518-454-5182. 321 A koonzp@strose.edu
KOOP, Stuart ... 510-436-1250... 47 J koop@hnu.edu
KOOP LIECHTY, Dan ... 574-535-7002. 166 A dankl@goshen.edu
KOOPMAN, Douglas ... 616-526-6554. 240 L dkoopman@calvin.edu
KOOPMAN, Jan ... 402-643-7341. 289 B alumni@cune.edu
KOOPMANS, Sue, M ... 573-875-7668. 272 G smkoopmans@ccis.edu
KOOPMANS, Tina, M ... 340-693-1540. 555 E tkoopma@live.uvi.edu
KOOTI, John ... 717-477-1435. 429 E JGKooti@ship.edu
KOPACH, Christopher, M ... 520-241-6482... 18 F ckopach@email.arizona.edu
KOPAS, Michael ... 973-408-3609. 301 C mkopas@drew.edu
KOPENEC, Rose, M ... 414-425-8300. 535 K rkopenec@shst.edu
KOPERA, Ken ... 864-646-1770. 447 D kkopera@tctc.edu
KOPERSKI, Kate ... 716-286-8288. 334 F kjk@niagara.edu
KOPERSKI, Mike ... 415-442-7082... 45 I mkoperski@ggu.edu
KOPICKO, Ronald, L ... 517-750-1200. 250 E rkopicko@arbor.edu
KOPISCHKE, Kevin ... 320-762-4404. 257 O kevink@alextech.edu
KOPLOWITZ, Stephan ... 661-255-1050... 31 C skoplowitz@calarts.edu
KOPONEN, Angela ... 713-221-5913. 489 D koponena@uhd.edu
KOPONEN, Glenn ... 845-675-4691. 335 C glenn.koponen@nyack.edu
KOPP, Courtney, A ... 515-574-1020. 179 D kopp@iowacentral.edu
KOPP, Stephen, J ... 304-696-2300. 529 H kopp@marshall.edu
KOPP, Sue ... 503-517-1032. 408 H skopp@warnerpacific.edu
KOPP, Will ... 614-287-2412. 378 B wkopp@cscc.edu
KOPPEL, Sheree ... 502-456-6509. 199 F skoppel@sctd.edu
KOPPELL, Jonathan ... 602-496-0402... 11 K koppel@asu.edu
KOPPER, Beverly ... 262-472-1672. 538 D kopperb@uww.edu
KOPPI, Steve ... 508-831-5260. 238 F skoppi@wpi.edu
KORAN, Noel ... 541-552-6522. 406 C korann@sou.edu
KORB, Judy ... 913-469-8500. 187 J jkorb@jccc.edu
KORB, Leigh, S ... 662-846-4000. 266 G lkorb@deltastate.edu
KORB, Leslie ... 270-384-8030. 197 D korbl@lindsey.edu
KORB, Scott ... 906-635-2032. 245 G skorb@lssu.edu
KORB, Scott, M ... 906-635-2032. 245 G skorb@lssu.edu
KORB-NICE, Jobe, S ... 206-281-2564. 523 C jobe@spu.edu
KORBEL, Linda ... 847-635-1952. 155 F lkorbel@oakton.edu
KORD, JoLanna ... 620-341-6839. 186 D jkord@emporia.edu
KORDENBROCK, Jeffrey . 859-344-3321. 199 H jeff.kordenbrock@thomasmore.edu
KOREEN, Michael ... 952-358-7007. 260 B michael.koreen@normandale.edu
KOREN, Christina ... 814-886-6407. 424 G CKoren@mtaloy.edu
KORESKI, Debbie ... 503-725-5040. 406 B debbie.koreski@pdx.edu
KORETOFF, Lisa, A ... 336-334-4822. 360 G lakoretoff@gtcc.edu
KORETSKY, Carla, M ... 269-387-3230. 252 I carla.koretsky@wmich.edu
KOREY, Christopher, A ... 843-953-7178. 443 A koreyc@cofc.edu
KOREY, Eileen ... 330-972-8589. 390 E korey@uakron.edu
KORF, Abraham ... 305-673-5664. 119 G rabbikorf@hotmail.com
KORF, Benzion ... 305-653-8770. 119 G bkorf@lecfl.com
KORFIATIS, George, P ... 201-216-5263. 307 E gkorfiat@stevens.edu
KORINEK, Clare, M ... 312-915-7235. 151 H ckorine@luc.edu
KORINKE, Kim ... 805-378-1463... 74 F kkorinke@vcccd.edu
KORMAN, Thomas, P ... 517-750-1200. 250 E tkorman@arbor.edu
KORN, Jane ... 509-313-3700. 520 A jkorn@lawschool.gonzaga.edu
KORNBERG, Judith ... 212-986-4343. 314 K jdk@berkeleycollege.edu
KORNBERG, Judith ... 973-278-5400. 299 D
KORNBERG, Mindy ... 206-685-4730. 524 G mindyk@uw.edu

KORNBLUH, Mark .... 859-257-8354. 200 C
kornbluh@uky.edu
KORNBLUH, Rebecca ..... 909-621-8000... 59 G
rebecca_kornbluh@cucmail.claremont.edu
KORNEGAY, Anne .... 804-758-6731. 513 G
akornegay@rappahannock.edu
KORNEGAY, Arthur .... 910-296-2575. 361 D
akornegay@jamessprunt.edu
KORNEGAY, Barbara, R .. 919-658-7756. 357 I
bkornegay@moc.edu
KORNEGAY, Jeffrey .... 910-879-5574. 358 B
jeffkornegay@bladencc.edu
KORNEGAY, Jeri, S .... 260-982-5285. 170 U
jskornegay@manchester.edu
KORNEGAY, Joy .... 919-735-5151. 364 H
jkornegay@waynecc.edu
KORNER, Barbara, O ...... 814-865-2591. 426 A
bok2@psu.edu
KORNFELD, Harriet, S .... 617-724-6399. 234 B
hkornfeld@mghihp.edu
KORNIEWICZ, Denise ..... 701-777-4555. 371 C
denise.korniewicz@und.edu
KORNKVEN, Kelly .... 701-788-4816. 371 E
Kelly.Kornkven@mayvillestate.edu
KORNMILLER,
Brenda, L .... 740-374-8716. 392 I
bkornmiller@wscc.edu
KORNOWSKI, Andrew ...... 502-213-4162. 195 F
andrew.kornowski@kctcs.edu
KOROCH, Greg, A .... 269-927-8161. 245 D
koroch@lakemichigancollege.edu
KOROLOFF, Nancy .... 503-725-9675. 406 B
koroloff@pdx.edu
KOROMA, Joseph .... 559-934-2306... 75 H
josephkoroma@whccd.edu
KORONKIEWICZ, Talia ... 815-455-8734. 152 F
tkoronkiewicz@mchenry.edu
KORPELA, Doreen .... 906-487-7201. 242 G
doreen.korpela@finlandia.edu
KORPI, Ray .... 360-992-2932. 518 A
rkorpi@clark.edu
KORR, Wynne, S .... 217-333-2261. 162 A
wkorr@illinois.edu
KORSCHGEN, Ann, J ...... 573-882-7651. 283 C
korschgena@missouri.edu
KORSTAD, Donna .... 509-542-4401. 518 C
dkorstad@columbiabasin.edu
KORSTAD, John .... 918-495-6942. 398 H
jkorstad@oru.edu
KORTE, Andi .... 910-695-3767. 363 F
kortea@sandhills.edu
KORVAS, Ronald .... 407-646-2174. 111 Q
rkorvas@rollins.edu
KORVER, Bill .... 910-323-5614. 353 B
president@ccbs.edu
KORVER, Marcia .... 910-323-5614. 353 B
admissions@ccbs.edu
KORZAN, Loren .... 419-227-3141. 391 F
lkorzan@unoh.edu
KORZINEK, Sue .... 616-331-2035. 243 C
korzines@gvsu.edu
KOSAK, Robbee .... 412-268-2136. 412 H
rkosak@andrew.cmu.edu
KOSANOVIC, David .... 614-251-4512. 386 B
kosanovd@ohiodominican.edu
KOSARUE, Lori .... 517-264-7132. 250 B
lshearer@sienaheights.edu
KOSBOTH, Michele .... 617-243-2227. 227 K
mkosboth@lasell.edu
KOSCHMEDER, Douglas . 563-387-1167. 180 M
registrar@luther.edu
KOSEL, Paul .... 402-554-2648. 293 A
pkosel@unomaha.edu
KOSELUK, William .... 805-893-5252... 72 B
william.koseluk@ic.ucsb.edu
KOSH, Jamie .... 814-472-3372. 432 D
jkosh@francis.edu
KOSHEWA, Angela, D .... 502-852-6981. 200 D
adkosh01@louisville.edu
KOSHORK, Lori .... 206-726-5027. 518 G
lkoshork@cornish.edu
KOSHUT, Thomas, M ...... 256-824-6100..... 8 F
tom.koshut@uah.edu
KOSHUTE, Daniel .... 814-472-3222. 432 D
dkoshute@francis.edu
KOSIN, Mary .... 570-740-0395. 422 G
mkosin@luzerne.edu
KOSINSKI, Mark .... 203-285-2077... 88 E
mkosinski@gwcc.commnet.edu
KOSINSKY, James, A ..... 708-209-3519. 143 E
jim.kosinsky@cuchicago.edu
KOSKI, Lynne, D .... 402-844-7036. 291 I
lynne@northeast.edu
KOSKO, Lisa .... 412-281-2600. 433 B
lkosko@western-school.com
KOSLOSKI, James .... 516-877-3974. 313 A
kosloski@adelphi.edu
KOSLOW MARTIN, Jodi 773-244-5740. 154 G
jkoslow@northpark.edu
KOSMER, Mary, K .... 920-923-8089. 534 A
mkkosmer09@marianuniversity.edu
KOSMOSKI, Kathleen ..... 912-486-7409. 129 J
kkosmoski@ogeecheetech.edu
KOSOWSKY, Vicki .... 812-535-5216. 172 F
vkosowsk@smwc.edu
KOSS, Michelle .... 734-462-4400. 250 A
mkoss@schoolcraft.edu
KOSSE, Glenn, F .... 502-272-8328. 192 E
gkosse@bellarmine.edu
KOSSES, Jennifer .... 617-732-2866. 233 E
jennifer.kosses@mcphs.edu
KOSSO, Cynthia .... 928-523-9305... 16 C
cynthia.kosso@nau.edu
KOSSUTH, Joanne .... 781-292-2431. 226 G
joanne.kossuth@olin.edu
KOST, Carrie .... 920-686-6141. 536 A
carrie.kost@sl.edu
KOSTELL, Stacey .... 217-333-0302. 162 A
skostell@illinois.edu
KOSTELNIK, Marjorie ..... 402-472-2913. 292 I
mkostelnik2@unl.edu
KOSTER, Ed .... 605-668-1367. 450 F
edward.koster@mtmc.edu
KOSTRAB, Lynn, M .... 330-569-5109. 380 I
kostrablm@hiram.edu
KOSTRUBANIC,
Robert, M .... 260-481-6196. 168 C
kostrubr@ipfw.edu
KOSTRZEWA, Waldemar . 203-575-8297... 89 B
wkostrzewa@nvcc.commnet.edu
KOSTYUKOV, Victoria ..... 718-522-9073. 314 B
victoria_kostyukov@asa.edu
KOTAGAL, Nirmala .... 507-285-7143. 261 A
nirmala.kotagal@rctc.edu
KOTAJARVI, Kathy .... 920-693-1163. 540 B
kathy.kotajarvi@gotoltc.edu
KOTARSKI, Beth .... 610-328-8058. 433 I
bkotars1@swarthmore.edu
KOTCAMP, Butch .... 740-351-3429. 388 N
bkotcamp@shawnee.edu
KOTECKI, Kathy .... 406-657-1660. 287 C
kkotecki@msubillings.edu
KOTESKEY, Kerri .... 406-791-5207. 288 E
kkoteskey01@ugf.edu
KOTH, Tara .... 402-449-2831. 289 H
tkoth@graceu.edu
KOTHENBEUTEL, Nancy . 563-336-3328. 177 L
nkothenbeutel@eicc.edu
KOTLER, A. Malkiel .... 732-367-1060. 299 E
KOTLER, Aaron .... 732-367-1060. 299 E
akotler@bmg.edu
KOTLER, Yitzchok, S ...... 732-367-1060. 299 E
KOTLIKOFF, Michael, I ... 607-253-3771. 322 A
mik7@cornell.edu
KOTLINSKI, Michael, J .. 717-337-6363. 417 B
mkotlinski@gettysburg.edu
KOTONIAS, Nancy .... 914-654-5914. 320 H
nkotonias@cnr.edu
KOTOWICZ, Keith, A .... 414-847-3301. 534 F
keithkotowicz@miad.edu
KOTSIOPULOS, Peter ..... 308-865-8474. 292 H
pkotsiopulos@nufoundation.org
KOTSIOPULOS, Peter ..... 308-698-5270. 292 H
pkotsiopulos@nufoundation.org
KOTTAS, Kathy .... 620-792-9355. 184 F
kottask@bartonccc.edu
KOTTER, Ronald, L .... 812-888-4124. 174 F
rkotter@vinu.edu
KOTTICH, Sarah .... 402-399-2427. 289 A
skottich@csm.edu
KOTTON, Stevenson .... 692-625-4931. 546 F
KOTTOYIL, Joseph .... 305-223-4561. 112 B
josephpothen@hotmail.com
KOTULSKI, Bob, L .... 417-268-6036. 271 I
bkotulski@gobbc.edu
KOUA, Deb .... 515-965-7025. 177 B
dkkoua@dmacc.edu
KOUBEK, Richard .... 225-578-5701. 204 O
rkoubek@lsu.edu
KOUCOUMARIS,
John, S .... 740-695-9500. 374 H
jkoucoumaris@belmontcollege.edu
KOUDELIK-JONES,
Rachelle .... 540-857-6187. 514 E
rkoudelikjones@virginiawestern.edu
KOUDOU, Nick .... 816-559-6182. 280 C
nick.koudou@park.edu
KOUGH, Katherine .... 717-262-2006. 437 H
kkough@wilson.edu
KOUKARI, Ray .... 262-619-6712. 540 A
koukarir@gtc.edu
KOUKOLA, Christine, H . 573-882-4523. 283 C
koukolac@missouri.edu
KOULIK, Chester .... 845-451-1347. 322 D
c_koulik@culinary.edu
KOUMARIANOS, Dee .... 603-577-6570. 296 F
ykoumarianos@dwc.edu
KOURY, Kevin, A .... 724-938-4125. 428 A
koury@calu.edu
KOUTSOUTIS, Kalli .... 718-429-6600. 349 H
kalli.koutsoutis@vaughn.edu
KOUTSOVITIS,
Christopher, S .... 914-337-9300. 321 E
christopher.koutsovitis@concordia-ny.edu
KOVAC, Matt .... 724-287-8711. 411 C
matt.kovac@bc3.edu
KOVACH, Kathy .... 912-427-1963. 120 B
kkovach@altamahatech.edu
KOVACH-ALLEN,
Katharina, E .... 585-345-6831. 325 C
kekovachallen@genesee.edu
KOVACICH, Christine ...... 330-325-6551. 385 E
ckovacich@neomed.edu
KOVACS, Anita, A .... 863-784-7123. 113 G
anita.kovacs@southflorida.edu
KOVACS, Charles .... 941-359-7650. 111 O
ckovacs@ringling.edu
KOVACS, Mark, C .... 315-792-3025. 349 F
mkovacs@utica.edu
KOVAL, Volga .... 707-826-4143... 35 C
volga.koval@humboldt.edu
KOVALA, Irene .... 623-845-3012... 14 M
irene.kovala@gcmail.maricopa.edu
KOVALCHICK, Mary .... 610-799-1957. 421 I
mkovalchick@lccc.edu
KOVALCIK, Andrew, B ..... 412-648-0233. 435 C
kandrew@pitt.edu
KOVANES, Tera, D .... 540-654-1042. 510 J
tkovanes@umw.edu
KOVATCH, John, E .... 330-972-6922. 390 E
kovatch@uakron.edu
KOVATCH, Richard, A ..... 434-982-5166. 511 B
rak3e@virginia.edu
KOVATCHITCH, Marian .. 315-798-8125. 338 F
mkovatch@secon.edu
KOVERMAN, Robert .... 312-369-6543. 143 D
rkoverman@colum.edu
KOVEROLA, Catherine .... 617-349-8317. 228 B
koverola@lesley.edu
KOVIC, Hong Yu .... 860-383-5284... 89 F
hkovic@trcc.commnet.edu
KOVLER, Allen .... 518-828-4181. 321 C
kovler@sunycgcc.edu
KOWAL, Donna, M .... 585-395-5400. 342 F
dkowal@brockport.edu
KOWALCHUK, Elizabeth . 785-864-3661. 190 L
kowalchu@ku.edu
KOWALESKI, Curt .... 920-403-3117. 535 L
curt.kowaleski@snc.edu
KOWALEWSKI, John, L .. 801-626-7212. 497 D
jkowalewski@weber.edu
KOWALEWSKY, Lyn .... 989-358-7280. 239 C
kowalewl@alpenacc.edu
KOWALIK, Thomas .... 607-777-2792. 341 E
kowalik@binghamton.edu
KOWALSKI, JR.,
Edward, J .... 315-255-1743. 316 D
kowalskie@cayuga-cc.edu
KOWALSKI, Gerard, J .... 706-542-8318. 133 C
kowalski@uga.edu
KOWALSKI, JR.,
Jonathan, V .... 414-277-4510. 534 G
kowalski@msoe.edu
KOWALSKI, Karl .... 907-450-8383... 10 I
karl.kowalski@alaska.edu
KOWALSKI, Karl .... 907-450-8383... 10 G
kekowalski@alaska.edu
KOWALSKI, Melanie .... 570-504-1583. 420 C
kowalskim@lackawanna.edu
KOWALSKI, Timothy, J .. 540-231-4000. 504 G
KOWAR, Pamela .... 860-255-3603... 89 G
pkowar@txcc.commnet.edu
KOWEEK, Joan .... 518-828-4181. 321 C
joan.koweek@sunycgcc.edu
KOWICH, Colleen .... 816-271-5650. 279 A
ckowich@missouriwestern.edu
KOWNACKI, James .... 570-484-2460. 429 B
jkownack@lhup.edu
KOWPAK, Corinne .... 207-216-4399. 211 C
ckowpak@yccc.edu
KOWTA, Mayumi .... 805-437-3107... 32 I
mayumi.kowta@csuci.edu
KOYE, Diane .... 609-984-1110. 308 A
dkoye@tesc.edu
KOZACHYN, Karen .... 610-359-5362. 414 D
kkozachy@dccc.edu
KOZAK, Diane .... 907-786-4513... 10 H
andhk1@uaa.alaska.edu
KOZAK, Gregory .... 847-574-5194. 150 C
gkozak@lfgsm.edu
KOZAK, Laura, A .... 410-706-8138. 219 C
lkoza001@umaryland.edu
KOZAKIEWICZ, Patricia .. 201-684-7610. 305 A
pkozakie@ramapo.edu
KOZERA, Mark .... 706-368-6945. 121 G
mkozera@berry.edu
KOZERACKI, Carol .... 323-415-5374... 51 F
kozeraca@elac.edu
KOZIATEK, Caroline .... 203-932-7479... 92 E
ckoziatek@newhaven.edu
KOZIEK, Timothy, J .... 708-709-3702. 156 A
tkoziek@prairiestate.edu
KOZIK, Bob .... 518-631-9881. 348 K
kozikr@uniongraduatecollege.edu
KOZIKOWSKI, Mitch .... 724-938-5706. 428 A
kozikowski@calu.edu
KOZIL, Cindy, T .... 508-541-1552. 225 F
ckozil@dean.edu
KOZIMOR, Renee .... 847-635-1761. 155 F
rkozimor@oakton.edu
KOZISEK, Kelly, L .... 541-737-4261. 406 A
kelly.kozisek@oregonstate.edu
KOZISEK, Sue .... 402-421-7410. 290 L
KOZLOWSKI, Gerald, F .. 972-860-7143. 470 I
GeraldKozlowski@dcccd.edu
KOZLOWSKI, Jean Ann .. 225-922-1643. 202 G
jeanannkozlowski@lctcs.edu
KOZLOWSKI, Lynn, T ..... 716-829-3434. 341 F
sphhp@buffalo.edu
KOZLOWSKI, Michelle ... 559-934-2240... 75 G
michellekozlowski@whccd.edu
KOZOJED, Bob, J .... 701-788-4872. 371 E
bob.kozojed@mayvillestate.edu
KOZOMAN, Robert .... 312-362-6695. 143 H
bkozoman@depaul.edu
KOZUMA, Hikaru .... 215-898-6081. 435 B
kozuma@upenn.edu
KRAAL, Steven, A .... 512-475-6976. 491 C
sakraal@mail.utexas.edu
KRACKER, Christie .... 330-263-2498. 377 H
ckracker@wooster.edu
KRAEGEL, Josh .... 262-243-5700. 532 H
josh.kraegel@cuw.edu
KRAEMER, David .... 212-678-8075. 328 A
dakraemer@jtsa.edu
KRAEMER, Ronald, D ...... 574-631-9700. 174 A
kraemer.5@nd.edu
KRAEUCHI, Bob .... 314-719-8024. 274 E
rkraeuch@fontbonne.edu
KRAFT, Deborah .... 443-334-2337. 218 E
dkraft@stevenson.edu
KRAFT, Deborah .... 281-756-3509. 465 D
dkraft@alvincollege.edu
KRAFT, Gary, L .... 402-472-3609. 292 I
gary.kraft@uln.edu
KRAFT, John .... 352-392-2398. 116 A
john.kraft@warrington.ufl.edu
KRAFT, John .... 912-344-2589. 120 G
john.kraft@armstrong.edu
KRAFT, Patricia .... 912-279-5858. 123 B
pkraft@ccga.edu
KRAFT, Paul .... 541-881-5599. 408 C
pkraft@tvcc.cc
KRAFT, Ronald, D .... 707-256-7160... 55 F
rkraft@napavalley.edu
KRAFT, Walter .... 734-487-6895. 242 D
walter.kraft@emuch.edu
KRAFT-MEYER, Kelly ...... 434-381-6205. 510 F
kraft_meyer@sbc.edu
KRAGT, Donna .... 616-234-4040. 243 B
dkragt@grcc.edu
KRAGULJEVIC, Nev .... 520-494-5471... 12 P
nev.kraguljevic@centralaz.edu
KRAH, Stephanie, L .... 410-651-8420. 219 E
skrah@umes.edu
KRAHE, Sharon, A .... 814-871-7670. 416 K
krahe@gannon.edu
KRAHL, Tracy .... 312-362-5577. 143 H
tkrahl@depaul.edu
KRAIMER, Paul .... 651-905-3509. 254 B
pkraimer@browncollege.edu
KRAJEWSKI, Scott .... 612-330-1471. 253 H
krajewsk@augsburg.edu
KRAJNIAK, Chris, A .... 262-554-2010. 534 D
chriskrajn@aol.com
KRAKLAU, Laura .... 269-927-8198. 245 D
kraklau@lakemichigancollege.edu
KRAKOFF, Steve, P .... 419-372-7127. 374 K
skrakof@bgsu.edu
KRAKORA, Edward, M ..... 419-289-5401. 374 C
ekrakora@ashland.edu
KRAL, Kathy .... 678-839-6585. 133 I
kkral@westga.edu
KRAL, Martin, J .... 309-298-1838. 162 K
mj-kral@wiu.edu
KRALEVICH, Richard, C . 302-857-1754... 93 D
richardk@dtcc.edu
KRALICEK, James .... 816-531-5223. 272 I
jkralicek@concorde.edu
KRALL, Jason .... 412-578-6152. 412 G
jkrall@carlow.edu
KRALL, Jim .... 479-524-7145... 21 G
jkrall@jbu.edu
KRALL, Julia .... 304-876-5526. 529 I
jkrall@shepherd.edu
KRALL, Lisi .... 607-753-4827. 343 B
lisi.krall@cortland.edu
KRALLMAN, Denise, A .... 513-529-7095. 384 G
krallmda@miamioh.edu
KRAM, Lauri .... 425-640-1522. 519 D
lkram@edcc.edu
KRAMBUHL, Scott .... 541-917-4722. 404 B
krambus@linnbenton.edu

KRAMER, Alan .... 229-391-4928. 119 H
akramer@abac.edu
KRAMER, Alan .... 860-913-2032... 90 A
akramer@goodwin.edu
KRAMER, Arthur .... 201-200-3073. 303 F
akramer@njcu.edu
KRAMER, Benjamin .... 540-674-3600. 513 B
bkramer@nr.edu
KRAMER, Cathy .... 828-298-3325. 370 E
service@warren-wilson.edu
KRAMER, Cecil .... 434-582-2077. 506 I
cvkramer@liberty.edu
KRAMER, Chris .... 217-234-5475. 150 D
ckramer@lakeland.cc.il.us
KRAMER, Eric .... 413-528-7476. 222 E
ekramer@simons-rock.edu
KRAMER, Gene .... 513-618-1923. 376 K
gkramer@ccms.edu
KRAMER, Jill .... 317-921-4569. 169 K
jkramer5@ivytech.edu
KRAMER, John .... 305-220-4120. 111 E
acadir@ptcmatt.com
KRAMER, Kathleen, A ..... 619-260-6832... 73 I
kramer@sandiego.edu
KRAMER, Kirk, A .... 810-989-5503. 249 H
kkramer@sc4.edu
KRAMER, Kyle .... 812-357-6678. 173 A
kkramer@saintmeinrad.edu
KRAMER, Mark .... 757-825-2815. 514 B
kramerm@tncc.edu
KRAMER, Matt .... 617-327-6777. 233 D
matt_kramer@mspp.edu
KRAMER, Monte .... 605-773-3455. 451 E
monte.kramer@sdbor.edu
KRAMER, Nancy .... 319-226-2040. 175 D
Nancy.Kramer@AllenCollege.edu
KRAMER, Nikki, A .... 920-923-8142. 534 A
nakramer22@marianuniversity.edu
KRAMER, Pamela .... 239-687-5305... 98 J
pkramer@avemarialaw.edu
KRAMER, Scott, E .... 270-852-3286. 197 B
scottkr@kwc.edu
KRAMER, Steve .... 620-223-2700. 186 G
stevek@fortscott.edu
KRAMER, Sue .... 610-902-8781. 411 E
susan.m.kramer@cabrini.edu
KRAMER, Terry .... 781-239-2431. 231 G
tkramer1@massbay.edu
KRAMER-ERTEL, Pamela 570-422-3377. 428 D
pkramer@po-box.esu.edu
KRAMER-JEFFERSON,
Kate .... 301-846-2409. 214 H
kkramerjefferson@frederick.edu
KRAMLICH, Carol .... 209-478-0800... 47 M
ckramlich@humphreys.edu
KRAMPF, Harry .... 507-389-6315. 259 G
harry.krampf@mnsu.edu
KRAN, Paul .... 212-678-4106. 347 G
kran@tc.columbia.edu
KRANE, Barbara .... 954-969-9771. 104 F
barbaraw@steinerleisure.com
KRANE, Maria, C .... 402-280-2221. 289 D
mkrane@creighton.edu
KRANSBERGER,
M. Elizabeth (Beth) .... 619-961-4330... 69 I
bkransberger@tjsl.edu
KRANTZ, Margaret .... 812-866-7126. 166 C
krantzm@hanover.edu
KRANZLER, Michael .... 212-960-5277. 351 M
kranzler@yu.edu
KRAPF, Audrey .... 631-420-2009. 346 B
audrey.krapf@farmingdale.edu
KRAPOHL, Robert, H ...... 847-317-4004. 160 M
rkrapohl@tiu.edu
KRAPP, Peter .... 949-824-8213... 71 B
chair@uci.edu
KRAPPES, Frank .... 970-491-5105... 80 I
louis.krappes@colostate.edu
KRASNY, Peter .... 413-265-2395. 225 C
krasnyp@elms.edu
KRASOWSKI, Marilyn ..... 952-488-2465. 258 F
mkrasowski@hennepintech.edu
KRATKY, Rita .... 406-247-3016. 287 C
rkratky@msubillings.edu
KRATOCHVIL, Bob .... 925-439-2181... 42 A
bkratochvil@losmedanos.edu
KRATOCHVIL,
Christopher .... 402-559-8490. 292 J
ckrotoch@unmc.edu
KRATTENMAKER, Tom .... 503-768-7975. 403 K
tkratt@lclark.edu
KRATZ, JR., Charles, E .. 570-941-4008. 436 A
charles.kratz@scranton.edu
KRATZ, David .... 212-966-0300. 333 A
info@nyaa.edu
KRATZ, Dennis .... 972-883-2984. 491 E
dkratz@utdallas.edu
KRATZ, Ken .... 504-568-4970. 205 C
kkratz@lsuhsc.edu
KRATZER, David .... 352-392-1265. 116 A
kratzerd@ufl.edu

KRAUS, Brian .... 615-230-3428. 461 G
brian.kraus@volstate.edu
KRAUS, Colt .... 402-461-7394. 289 I
ckraus@hastings.edu
KRAUS, Edwin .... 719-632-7626... 82 J
ekraus@intellitec.edu
KRAUS, Jeffrey .... 718-390-3254. 350 B
jkraus@wagner.edu
KRAUS, Jeffrey .... 718-390-3173. 350 B
jkraus@wagner.edu
KRAUS, Jeffrey .... 718-390-3254. 350 B
jkraus@wagner.edu
KRAUS, Jes, S .... 802-656-3368. 500 F
jes.kraus@uvm.edu
KRAUS, John .... 417-865-2815. 274 B
krausj@evangel.edu
KRAUS, John, D .... 603-862-2411. 298 C
john.kraus@unh.edu
KRAUS, Kevin .... 563-387-1005. 180 M
krauske@luther.edu
KRAUS, Larry .... 818-719-6420... 52 B
krausl@piercecollege.edu
KRAUS, Marcy .... 585-275-2354. 349 C
marcy.kraus@rochester.edu
KRAUS, Pamela .... 410-626-2511. 217 G
pamela.kraus@sjca.edu
KRAUS, William .... 440-525-7828. 382 M
wkraus@lakelandcc.edu
KRAUSE, Ann Marie .... 715-422-5421. 540 D
annmarie.krause@mstc.edu
KRAUSE, Aric .... 240-684-2476. 219 F
aric.krause@umuc.edu
KRAUSE, Carolyn .... 513-861-6400. 390 C
carolyn.krause@myunion.edu
KRAUSE, Chris .... 254-710-6672. 467 G
chris_krause@baylor.edu
KRAUSE, David, H .... 708-524-6994. 144 C
dkrause@dom.edu
KRAUSE, David, R .... 210-436-3141. 479 D
dkrause@stmarytx.edu
KRAUSE, Debbie .... 757-340-2121. 503 I
bursarcvab@centura.edu
KRAUSE, Deborah .... 314-918-2587. 274 A
dkrause@eden.edu
KRAUSE, Karen .... 507-457-5632. 262 A
kkrause@winona.edu
KRAUSE, Karen .... 817-272-3561. 491 B
kkrause@uta.edu
KRAUSE, Kassy .... 423-236-2900. 458 J
kkrause@southern.edu
KRAUSE, Kate .... 505-277-2631. 312 F
kkrause@unm.edu
KRAUSE, Laura .... 802-440-4714. 498 G
lkrause@bennington.edu
KRAUSE, Mark .... 402-935-9400. 290 N
mkrause@nechristian.edu
KRAUSE, Teresa .... 213-487-2211... 28 D
KRAUSHAAR, Robert .... 518-320-1278. 341 C
robert.kraushaar@suny.edu
KRAUTH, Stephanie .... 573-592-5240. 285 B
stephanie.krauth@westminster-mo.edu
KRAVAS, Connie .... 206-685-1980. 524 G
ckravas@uw.edu
KRAVCAK, Jamison .... 215-643-8458. 417 F
kravcak.j@gmc.edu
KRAVITZ, Merryl .... 408-274-7900... 63 O
merryl.kravitz@evc.edu
KRAY, Helga .... 909-537-5185... 34 E
hkray@csusb.edu
KRAYNAK, Carrie .... 724-964-8811. 425 A
ckraynak@ncstrades.edu
KREAGH, CM, Kevin .... 716-286-8400. 334 F
kreagh@niagara.edu
KREBS, Becky .... 979-830-4112. 467 I
becky.krebs@blinn.edu
KREBS, Julianne .... 937-393-3431. 389 B
jkrebs@sscc.edu
KREBS, Katharine .... 607-777-2150. 341 E
kkrebs@binghamton.edu
KREBS, Paul, R .... 505-925-5510. 312 F
pkrebs@unm.edu
KREBS, Paula, M .... 508-531-6131. 229 D
pkrebs@bridgew.edu
KREBS, Phil .... 530-749-3868... 77 K
pkrebs@yccd.edu
KREBS, Stephanie, R ...... 813-253-6204. 118 L
srkrebs@ut.edu
KRECH, Donald, A .... 570-577-1242. 411 A
donald.krech@bucknell.edu
KREHBIEL, Brenda .... 620-242-0415. 188 G
krehbieb@mcpherson.edu
KREHBIEL, Erika, M .... 773-442-4223. 154 H
e-krehbiel@neiu.edu
KREHBIEL, Lee .... 479-788-7304... 24 A
lee.krehbiel@uafs.edu
KREIDER, Paul, K .... 304-293-4841. 530 D
paul.kreider@mail.wvu.edu
KREIDLER, Mickie, L ...... 605-256-5100. 451 H
mickie.kreidler@dsu.edu
KREIDLER, Steve .... 405-974-2251. 400 K
skreidler@uco.edu

KREINER, Thane .... 408-551-6058... 64 M
tkreiner@scu.edu
KREISBERG, Robert .... 304-336-8062. 530 A
kreisbob@westliberty.edu
KREISER, Valerie .... 610-740-3785. 412 I
valerie@cedarcrest.edu
KREITL, Bethany .... 206-296-6082. 523 E
kreitlb@seattleu.edu
KREITZ, Patricia .... 925-631-4525... 61 F
pak2@stmarys-ca.edu
KREITZER, Joseph, L ..... 651-962-6032. 265 C
jlkreitzer@stthomas.edu
KREJCI, Janet .... 309-438-2174. 147 J
jkrejci@ilstu.edu
KREJCI, Teresa .... 641-782-1336. 182 I
tkrejci@swcciowa.edu
KREKE, Toni, L .... 660-543-4069. 283 A
kreke@ucmo.edu
KREMENEK, Amy .... 315-498-7252. 335 G
kremenea@sunyocc.edu
KREMER, Edward .... 913-288-7111. 187 L
ekremer@kckcc.edu
KREMER, Peter, W .... 502-272-8334. 192 E
pkremer@bellarmine.edu
KREMER, Timothy .... 563-589-3396. 182 J
finaid@univ.dbq.edu
KREMINSKI, Rick .... 719-549-2340... 80 K
rick.kreminski@colostate-pueblo.edu
KREMINSKI, Rick .... 719-549-2110... 80 K
rick.kreminski@colostate-pueblo.edu
KREMS, Carol .... 617-349-8624. 228 B
ckrems@lesley.edu
KREMS, Ruth .... 860-906-5141... 88 D
rkrems@ccc.commnet.edu
KRENDL, Kathy, A .... 614-823-1420. 387 K
kkrendl@otterbein.edu
KRENT, Harold, J .... 312-906-5010. 147 F
hkrent@kentlaw.edu
KRENTZ, Kenneth, L .... 252-335-0821. 359 F
kkrentz@albemarle.edu
KRENTZ, Peter, M .... 704-894-2270. 353 J
pekrentz@davidson.edu
KRENTZ, Shelby .... 859-815-7648. 195 B
shelby.krentz@kctcs.edu
KRESCH, Thomas .... 570-389-4748. 427 H
tkresch@bloomu.edu
KRESL-HOTZ, Peggie ..... 307-778-1258. 543 D
peggiekreslhotz@lccc.wy.edu
KRESS, Anne, M .... 585-292-2100. 332 A
akress@monroecc.edu
KRESS, Cathann, A .... 515-294-5390. 175 H
cathann@iastate.edu
KRESS, Debra, G .... 512-475-8029. 491 C
debra.kress@austin.utexas.edu
KRESS, Lisa, P .... 785-864-3911. 190 L
lpkress@ku.edu
KRESS, Michael .... 718-982-2350. 317 E
michael.kress@csi.cuny.edu
KRESS, Ruth .... 812-357-6561. 173 A
rkress@saintmeinrad.edu
KRESSAL, Linda .... 828-835-4288. 364 E
lkressal@tricountycc.edu
KRETA, Steve .... 707-654-1019... 31 I
skreta@csum.edu
KRETSCHMER, Mark .... 805-525-4417... 69 H
mkretschmer@thomasaquinas.edu
KRETSCHMER, Mark, R .. 805-525-4417... 69 H
mkretschmer@thomasaquinas.edu
KRETZ, Heather .... 715-836-5188. 536 E
kretzhm@uwec.edu
KREUTZER, Linda .... 620-441-5214. 186 A
kreutzerl@cowley.edu
KREUZMAN, Henry, B .... 330-263-2008. 377 H
hkreuzman@wooster.edu
KREVH, Janet, M .... 216-397-4349. 381 R
jkrevh@jw.edu
KREY, Maria .... 206-239-4500. 517 M
mariakrey@cityu.edu
KREY, Philip, D .... 215-248-6310. 422 F
pkrey@ltsp.edu
KRHIN, Daniel, J .... 920-748-8394. 535 J
krhind@ripon.edu
KRIARAS, Dimitrios .... 847-233-7700. 155 B
dkriaras@nc.edu
KRICHMAR, Lee .... 562-860-2451... 37 I
lkrichmar@cerritos.edu
KRICKX, Guido .... 916-278-3583... 34 D
krickx@csus.edu
KRIDELBAUGH, Linda .... 541-888-7402. 407 H
lkridelbaugh@socc.edu
KRIDER, Jack .... 719-549-2067... 80 K
jack.krider@colostate-pueblo.edu
KRIEB, Dennis .... 618-468-4300. 150 G
dkrieb@lc.edu
KRIEBEL, Denise A, T .... 765-641-4133. 163 L
dakriebel@anderson.edu
KRIEDER, Eric, W .... 330-972-5303. 390 E
ewk@uakron.edu
KRIEDLER, Steve .... 303-556-3022... 83 D
KRIEG, Katherine .... 225-490-1674. 206 D
kkrieg@ololcollege.edu

KRIEG, Randall .... 585-385-8116. 338 H
rkrieg@sjfc.edu
KRIEGBAUM, Chrissy .... 910-892-3178. 355 B
CKriegbaum@heritagebiblecollege.edu
KRIEGER, Nora .... 973-748-9000. 299 F
nora_krieger@bloomfield.edu
KRIEGERMEIER, Pat .... 815-455-8726. 152 F
pkriegermeier@mchenry.edu
KRIEGH, David .... 650-321-5655... 61 G
info@stpatricksseminary.org
KRIEPS, Kevin .... 219-473-4330. 164 K
kkrieps@ccsj.edu
KRIER, Jacob, C .... 507-344-7519. 253 J
jake.krier@blc.edu
KRIESE, Theresa .... 605-995-2621. 450 A
thkriese@dwu.edu
KRIGEL, Belinda .... 256-233-8104..... 1 F
belinda.krigel@athens.edu
KRIKAU, Paul .... 920-923-7666. 534 A
KRIKORIAN, Gregory, H 717-867-6238. 421 H
krikoria@lvc.edu
KRIMMEL, Bob, S .... 814-472-3276. 432 D
bkrimmel@francis.edu
KRIMMEL, J. Thomas ..... 781-292-2291. 226 G
thomas.krimmel@olin.edu
KRIMPELBEIN, Kristi .... 715-232-2441. 538 B
krimpelbeink@uwstout.edu
KRIOFSKY, Richard .... 757-493-6909. 131 H
rkriofsky@southuniversity.edu
KRIPPEL, Nancy, F .... 770-534-6119. 122 A
nkrippel@brenau.edu
KRISAK, Wendy .... 610-282-1100. 414 F
wendy.krisak@desales.edu
KRISE, Thomas, W .... 253-535-7101. 521 I
tkrise@plu.edu
KRISHNAMOORTI,
Ramanan .... 713-743-4307. 489 B
rkrishna@central.uh.edu
KRISHNAMURTHY, K ...... 573-341-4154. 284 A
kkrishna@mst.edu
KRISHNAMURTI,
Praveen .... 414-256-0238. 535 A
krishnap@mtmary.edu
KRISHNAN, G, V .... 713-221-8478. 489 D
krishnang@uhd.edu
KRISHNAN, Kris .... 609-652-4514. 305 C
kris.krishnan@stockton.edu
KRISHNAN, Ramayya ...... 412-268-2159. 412 H
rk2x@andrew.cmu.edu
KRISHNASWAMY, Vidya 972-860-8152. 470 H
KRISLOV, Marvin .... 440-775-8400. 385 H
marvin.krislov@oberlin.edu
KRISS, George .... 618-537-6425. 152 G
gnkriss@mckendree.edu
KRISS, OSF, M. Elise ..... 260-399-7700. 174 C
ekriss@sf.edu
KRIST, Paula, S .... 619-260-7878... 73 I
pkrist@sandiego.edu
KRISTENSEN,
Douglas, A .... 308-865-8208. 292 H
kristensend@unk.edu
KRISTOF, Leslie .... 954 382-5303... 18 I
leslie.kristof@phoenix.edu
KRISTOFCO, Clare, M .... 858-534-6861... 71 F
ckristofco@ucsd.edu
KRISTOFCO, Clare, M .... 858-534-6861... 71 F
ckristofco@ucsd.edu
KRISTOFF, Tricia .... 904-819-6311. 103 E
tkristoff@flagler.edu
KRITSCHER, Matt .... 510-723-6716... 37 K
mkritscher@chabotcollege.edu
KRIVDA, Ronald, A .... 724-925-4278. 437 D
krivdar@wccc.edu
KRIVESTI, Robin .... 740-593-2665. 387 C
krivesti@ohio.edu
KRIVOSKI, James, F ...... 610-330-5200. 420 D
krivoskj@lafayette.edu
KRIZMANIC, Nick .... 217-641-4521. 148 M
nkrizmanic@jwcc.edu
KRNA, Karan .... 800-955-2527. 274 I
kkrna@grantham.edu
KROB, Jay, C .... 785-827-5541. 188 C
jayk@kwu.edu
KROBER, Alfred, C .... 585-594-6501. 337 K
krobera@roberts.edu
KROBER, Kent .... 314-516-4115. 283 E
kroberk@umsl.edu
KROBOTH, Patricia, D .... 412-624-3270. 435 C
pkroboth@pitt.edu
KROC, Richard, J .... 520-621-8543... 18 F
kroc@email.arizona.edu
KROEGER, Laura .... 859-442-1177. 195 B
laura.kroeger@kctcs.edu
KROEGER, Lillian .... 254-526-1114. 468 G
admissions.registrar@ctcd.edu
KROEKER, Dean .... 620-241-0770. 185 K
dean.kroeker@centralchristian.edu
KROENING, Mike .... 507-453-2752. 259 E
mkroening@southeastmn.edu
KROENKE, Joel .... 800-567-2344. 532 E
jkroenke@menominee.edu

KROENKE, Paul ... 309-677-2325. 140 I
pkroenke@bradley.edu
KROEZE, Nicholas, V ... 616-988-3624. 245 C
nvk@kuyper.edu
KROGER, John ... 503-777-7500. 407 E
krogerj@reed.edu
KROGH, Nancy ... 208-885-2020. 139 D
nkrogh@uidaho.edu
KROGH, Nancy, A ... 208-885-2020. 139 D
nkrogh@uidaho.edu
KROGMAN, Mark, A ... 207-741-5629. 211 A
mkrogman@smccme.edu
KROH, Lynne ... 417-862-9533. 274 F
enroll@globaluniversity.edu
KROH, JR., Robert, C ... 215-951-1315. 420 B
kroh@lasalle.edu
KROHN, Paul ... 630-617-3142. 145 A
paulk@elmhurst.edu
KROLL, Jason ... 732-571-3400. 303 C
KROLL, John, R ... 773-702-1941. 161 B
xjrk@uchicago.edu
KROLL, Mark ... 956-882-7304. 491 D
mark.kroll@utb.edu
KROLOFF, Reed ... 248-645-3301. 241 G
rkroloff@cranbrook.edu
KRONDAK, Anita, M ... 913-288-7274. 187 L
akrondak@kckcc.edu
KRONEMAN, Ann ... 517-483-1604. 245 H
kronemaa@lcc.edu
KRONENBURGER, John . 630-942-3614. 142 G
kronenburgerj@cod.edu
KRONENFIELD, Michael . 480-219-6091. 271 A
mkronenfield@atsu.edu
KRONSTEIN, Krista ... 330-263-2498. 377 H
kkronstein@wooster.edu
KROOK, Darrell ... 603-668-2211. 297 I
d.krook@snhu.edu
KROOK, Scott ... 507-285-7205. 261 A
scott.krook@rctc.edu
KROOT, Irwin ... 212-229-5671. 332 E
krooti@newschool.edu
KROPF, Kevin ... 785-594-8327. 184 C
Kevin.Kropf@bakeru.edu
KROPFF, Robert ... 330-972-7048. 390 E
bobk@uakron.edu
KROPP, Vicky ... 989-358-7317. 239 C
kroppv@alpenacc.edu
KROPP-ANDERSON,
Pamela ... 207-973-1048. 210 B
kroppandersonp@husson.edu
KROSCH, Brandon ... 651-255-6136. 264 C
bkrosch@unitedseminary.edu
KROTSENG, Martha, V ... 304-327-4000. 529 D
mkrotseng@bluefieldstate.edu
KROTZER, Mary Jane ... 205-366-8929... 7 E
mkrotzer@stillman.edu
KROUSE, Alisa ... 713-963-8979. 131 H
akrouse@southuniversity.edu
KROV, Matthew ... 903-813-2370. 466 H
mkrov@austincollege.edu
KROVI, Ravi ... 330-972-7442. 390 E
krovi@uakron.edu
KRSTIC, Miroslav ... 858-534-5556... 71 F
mkrstic@ucsd.edu
KRUCHOWSKI, Gary ... 218-733-7649. 259 A
g.kruchowski@lsc.edu
KRUCZEK, Thomas ... 561-237-7458. 108 X
tkruczek@lynn.edu
KRUDOP, James, D ... 334-382-2133... 5 E
jkrudop@lbwcc.edu
KRUEGER, Bryon, D ... 651-631-5392. 263 A
bdkrueger@nwc.edu
KRUEGER, Cheryl ... 937-775-2556. 393 G
cheryl.krueger@wright.edu
KRUEGER, Cindy ... 419-267-1233. 385 F
ckrueger@northweststate.edu
KRUEGER, Conrad ... 210-486-0915. 465 C
ckrueger@alamo.edu
KRUEGER, James, M ... 314-516-6539. 283 E
jimkrueger@umsl.edu
KRUEGER, Jim ... 402-399-2332. 289 A
jkrueger@csm.edu
KRUEGER, Joni ... 605-274-4015. 449 K
joni.krueger@augie.edu
KRUEGER, Justin ... 815-226-4006. 157 C
JKrueger@rockford.edu
KRUEGER, Karl ... 215-248-6330. 422 F
kkrueger@ltsp.edu
KRUEGER, Kurt, J ... 949-214-3194... 41 I
kurt.krueger@cui.edu
KRUEGER, Linda ... 715-833-6433. 539 J
lkrueger@cvtc.edu
KRUEGER, Mablene ... 312-935-6645. 156 K
mkrueger@robertmorris.edu
KRUEGER, Mary, M ... 419-372-8034. 374 K
mkruege@bgsu.edu
KRUEGER PARK,
Kathleen ... 415-257-1309... 42 J
kathleen.kruegerpark@dominican.edu
KRUEZER, Norbert ... 612-375-1900. 256 E
nkreuzer@ipr.edu
KRUG, Anna ... 312-427-2737. 148 L
akrug@jmls.edu
KRUG, Bryce ... 314-918-2568. 274 A
bkrug@eden.edu
KRUG, Cherie ... 301-387-3100. 214 I
cherie.krug@garrettcollege.edu
KRUG, Christopher ... 858-642-8145... 55 J
ckrug@nu.edu
KRUG, Sheila, R ... 620-229-6368. 190 G
sheila.krug@sckans.edu
KRUG, Stefan ... 617-521-3929. 236 G
stefan.krug@simmons.edu
KRUGER, Darrell ... 504-280-1278. 205 G
dkruger@uno.edu
KRUGER, Michael, J ... 704-366-5066. 269 E
KRUGMAN, Richard, D .. 303-724-0882... 86 A
richard.krugman@ucdenver.edu
KRUHLY, Leslie, L ... 215-898-7005. 435 B
kruhly@upenn.edu
KRUKONES, James, H ... 216-397-4762. 381 R
jkrukones@jcu.edu
KRUKOWSKA, Justyna ... 510-883-2071... 42 I
jkrukowska@dspt.edu
KRULAK, Charles, C ... 205-226-4620... 2 C
ckrulak@bsc.edu
KRULL, Kimberly ... 316-322-3100. 185 D
kim.krull@butlercc.edu
KRULL, Kimberly ... 785-243-1435. 185 M
kkrull@cloud.edu
KRULL, Lucille ... 503-251-6115. 524 I
lucy.krull@wallawalla.edu
KRUMHANSL, Ezra ... 502-585-9911. 199 C
ekrumhansl@spalding.edu
KRUML, Susan ... 217-424-6285. 153 C
skruml@millikin.edu
KRUMM, Brenda, L ... 620-431-2820. 189 D
bkrumm@neosho.edu
KRUMM, Javier ... 951-785-2295... 50 B
jkrumm@lasierra.edu
KRUMMRICH, Philip ... 606-783-2726. 198 A
p.krummrich@moreheadstate.edu
KRUMPE, Keith ... 828-250-3880. 368 C
kkrumpe@unca.edu
KRUPANSKY, Sharla ... 270-534-3275. 196 G
sharla.krupansky@kctcs.edu
KRUPICA, Glen ... 217-854-3231. 140 G
glen.krupica@blackburn.edu
KRUPICA, Suzanne ... 217-854-3231. 140 G
suzanne.krupica@blackburn.edu
KRUPIN, Maria ... 201-684-7621. 305 A
mkrupin@ramapo.edu
KRUPKA, Moshe ... 212-463-0400. 348 B
moshe.krupka@touro.edu
KRUPP, Jason ... 727-341-3050. 112 E
krupp.jason@spcollege.edu
KRUPP, Robert, A ... 503-517-1838. 408 I
rakrupp@westernseminary.edu
KRUPSKI, Eric, A ... 617-422-7232. 235 B
ekrupski@nesl.edu
KRUSE, Amy ... 320-629-5115. 260 F
krusea@pinetech.edu
KRUSE, Emily ... 563-588-6436. 176 F
emily.kruse@clarke.edu
KRUSE, Janetta ... 817-598-6391. 494 G
jkruse@wc.edu
KRUSE, Kristen ... 541-962-3512. 405 H
kristen.kruse@eou.edu
KRUSE, Mary ... 517-264-7112. 250 B
mkruse@sienaheights.edu
KRUSE, Robert ... 304-336-8252. 530 A
rkruse@westliberty.edu
KRUSE, Tracy, L ... 402-844-7056. 291 I
tracyk@northeast.edu
KRUSEE, Kelly ... 310-377-5501... 53 F
kkrusee@marymountcalifornia.edu
KRUSEMARK, Stacy, L ... 605-256-5127. 451 H
stacy.krusemark@dsu.edu
KRUSEN, Cynthia ... 978-840-0176. 232 C
c_krusen@mwcc.mass.edu
KRUSHINSKI, Lynn ... 570-702-8955. 419 G
lkrushinski@johnson.edu
KRUSLING, James ... 415-442-7248... 45 I
jkrusling@ggu.edu
KRUSNIAK, Bryan ... 660-626-2364. 271 A
bkrusniak@atsu.edu
KRUTKY, Judith, B ... 440-826-2257. 374 F
jkrutky@bw.edu
KRUTZ, Ellen ... 610-519-4237. 436 F
ellen.krutz@villanova.edu
KRUZEL, Douglas ... 734-973-3497. 252 A
kruzel@wccnet.edu
KRYLOWICZ, Brian ... 413-748-3345. 236 I
Bkrylowicz@springfieldcollege.edu
KRYSIAK, Richard ... 405-744-7147. 397 H
rick.krysiak@okstate.edu
KRZAK, Chris ... 909-593-3511... 72 E
ckrzak@laverne.edu
KRZYSTOFIAK, Susan ... 716-645-2642. 341 F
krzystof@buffalo.edu
KRZYWICKI, Tricia ... 617-327-6777. 233 D
tricia_krzywicki@mspp.edu
KTUL, Kathy ... 252-492-2061. 364 F
ktul@vgcc.edu
KU, OP, John Baptist ... 202-495-3846... 96 C
jbku@dhs.edu
KU, Kelly ... 410-752-4710. 510 B
kku@stratford.edu
KUAN, Jeffrey ... 909-447-2552... 39 E
jkuan@cst.edu
KUBA, Jodie, M ... 808-956-3993. 136 B
jodiek@hawaii.edu
KUBA, Lori, P ... 602-944-3335... 11 D
lpryor-kuba@aicag.edu
KUBA, Michael ... 304-473-8090. 531 G
kuba_m@wvwc.edu
KUBA, Shawn ... 304-473-8560. 531 G
kuba_s@wvwc.edu
KUBACAK, James ... 254-299-8608. 476 D
jkubacak@mclennan.edu
KUBAT, Laural ... 507-389-7219. 261 E
laural.kubat@southcentral.edu
KUBAT, Robert, A ... 814-863-3681. 426 A
rak28@psu.edu
KUBATZKE, Trevor ... 414-297-6279. 540 E
kubatzkt@matc.edu
KUBB, Richard ... 314-529-9606. 276 G
rkubb@maryville.edu
KUBEJA, Judy ... 814-732-2729. 428 E
kubeja@edinboro.edu
KUBERSKI, Chris ... 618-437-5321. 156 H
kuberski@rlc.edu
KUBERSKY, Edward ... 201-559-6117. 302 A
kuberskye@felician.edu
KUBIC, Craig ... 816-414-3700. 277 L
ckubic@mbts.edu
KUBINAK, Lois, A ... 610-921-7612. 409 A
lkubinak@alb.edu
KUBO, Takeo ... 408-288-3733... 63 P
takeo.kubo@sjcc.edu
KUBOW, Stephen ... 732-255-0356. 302 F
skubow@kean.edu
KUCERA, Kevin ... 734-487-2390. 242 D
kkucera@emich.edu
KUCHEL, Michele ... 432-552-2371. 493 D
kuchel_m@utpb.edu
KUCIA, John, F ... 513-745-3997. 393 H
kucia@xavier.edu
KUCIK, Maggie ... 317-955-6213. 170 V
mkucik@marian.edu
KUCINSKI, Colleen ... 413-775-1208. 231 E
kucinski@gcc.mass.edu
KUCINSKI, Nancy ... 325-670-1298. 472 O
nkicinski@hsutx.edu
KUCKO, Jane ... 817-257-7473. 484 I
j.kucko@tcu.edu
KUCYNDA, Steve ... 660-596-7282. 282 G
skucynda@sfccmo.edu
KUDLAC, John ... 412-392-3920. 431 B
jkudlac@pointpark.edu
KUDRAVETZ, Douglas ... 202-885-3283... 94 F
doug@american.edu
KUEBLER, Alan, S ... 314-935-5727. 284 L
alan_kuebler@wustl.edu
KUEHL, William ... 405-878-5161. 399 G
wmkuehl@stgregorys.edu
KUEHLER, Robert ... 303-837-2112... 85 K
Robert.Kuehler@cu.edu
KUEHN, Lisa ... 620-252-7137. 185 O
lisak@coffeyville.edu
KUEHNER, Megan, R ... 904-620-2523. 116 B
mkuehner@unf.edu
KUENSTLER, Donna ... 432-837-8361. 487 B
dkuenstl@sulross.edu
KUERBIS, Matt ... 503-223-2245. 403 J
mkuerbis@portland.chefs.edu
KUERZI, Kenneth ... 856-256-4138. 305 E
kuerzi@rowan.edu
KUEWA, Jubilee ... 808-933-0824. 136 A
jkuewa@hawaii.edu
KUFFELL, Lorne ... 205-348-7204... 8 D
lkuffel@ua.edu
KUGELMANN DEKAT,
Laurie ... 972-721-5322. 488 F
ldekat@udallas.edu
KUGLER, Adriana ... 202-687-5716... 95 E
ak659@georgetown.edu
KUGLER, Angela ... 425-558-0299. 519 B
akugler@digipen.edu
KUGLER, Sharon ... 203-432-1128... 93 A
sharon.kugler@yale.edu
KUHL, Colleen, M ... 563-588-7650. 180 L
colleen.kuhl@loras.edu
KUHL, Sara ... 262-472-1194. 538 D
kuhls@uww.edu
KUHLHORST,
Michelle, L ... 260-399-7700. 174 C
mkuhlhorst@sf.edu
KUHLMAN, Ann ... 203-432-2305... 93 A
ann.kuhlman@yale.edu
KUHLMAN, Gregory ... 718-951-5174. 317 C
kuhlman@brooklyn.cuny.edu
KUHLMANN, Diana, E ... 620-341-5304. 186 D
dkuhlman@emporia.edu
KUHLMANN, Kristin ... 575-562-2321. 309 H
kristin.kuhlmann@enmu.edu
KUHN, Bill ... 952-446-4227. 255 D
kuhnb@crown.edu
KUHN, Charles ... 301-447-5244. 217 B
ckuhn@msmary.edu
KUHN, Helen ... 217-245-3013. 146 F
registrar@ic.edu
KUHN, Jane ... 928-523-7732... 16 C
jane.kuhn@nau.edu
KUHN, Kathryn, A ... 414-955-8217. 534 C
kkuhn@mcw.edu
KUHN, Kevin ... 601-477-4106. 267 F
kevin.kuhn@jcjc.edu
KUHN, Robert ... 225-578-1231. 204 O
rkuhn@lsu.edu
KUHN, Robert ... 814-824-2104. 423 J
rkuhnn@mercyhurst.edu
KUHN, Sean ... 937-433-3410. 379 J
skuhn@edaff.com
KUHN, Stephen ... 262-524-7132. 532 C
skuhn@carrollu.edu
KUHR, Peggy ... 406-243-2311. 286 H
peggy.kuhr@umontana.edu
KUIPER, Dale ... 616-222-3000. 245 C
dkuiper@kuyper.edu
KUIPER, Jeff ... 507-537-6225. 261 F
Kuiperjb@smsu.edu
KUIPERS, David ... 229-931-2001. 131 G
dkuipers@southgatech.edu
KUJAWA, Edward ... 415-485-3245... 42 J
ekujawa@dominican.edu
KUJAWA, Lisa, R ... 248-204-2403. 245 I
lkujawa@ltu.edu
KUJAWA, Rose Marie ... 734-432-5315. 246 B
srosemarie@madonna.edu
KUJAWA, Thomas ... 920-465-2300. 536 F
kujawat@uwgb.edu
KUJAWA, Tricia, A ... 217-786-2211. 151 F
tricia.kujawa@llcc.edu
KUKAINIS, Maris ... 856-227-7200. 300 B
mkukainis@camdencc.edu
KUKER, Ronald ... 937-529-2201. 390 D
rkuker@united.edu
KUKOR, Jerome, J ... 848-932-7275. 306 B
kukor@aesop.rutgers.edu
KUKREJA, Anil ... 504-520-7652. 209 D
akukreja@xula.edu
KUKREJA, Sunil ... 253-879-3207. 524 F
skukreja@pugetsound.edu
KUKULIES, Emily Ann ... 808-845-9219. 136 G
kukulies@hawaii.edu
KULA, Jarrod ... 909-599-5433... 50 J
jkula@lifepacific.edu
KULAGA, Jon, S ... 859-858-3511. 192 B
jon.kulaga@asbury.edu
KULBICKI, OFM CONV,
Timothy, A ... 410-864-3602. 218 B
tkulbicki@stmarys.edu
KULBISKI, Neil ... 785-594-4791. 184 C
neil.kulbiski@bakeru.edu
KULECK, Gary ... 313-993-1216. 250 K
gary.kuleck@udmercy.edu
KULESZA, Darrell ... 508-541-1864. 225 F
dkulesza@dean.edu
KULHOWVICK, John, P ... 802-654-2445. 500 B
jkulhowvick@smcvt.edu
KULICH, James ... 630-617-6472. 145 A
jimk@elmhurst.edu
KULICK, Liz, M ... 215-968-8123. 411 B
kulicke@bucks.edu
KULICK, Steven, W ... 315-445-4560. 328 F
kulicksw@lemoyne.edu
KULICS, Jennifer ... 330-672-9494. 382 B
jkulics@kent.edu
KULIK, Dmitry ... 202-462-2101... 96 A
kulik@iwp.edu
KULK, Allyn ... 914-964-4282. 320 C
KULKE, Erik ... 262-551-5916. 532 D
ekulke@carthage.edu
KULL, F. Jon ... 603-646-1552. 296 G
f.jon.kull@dartmouth.edu
KULL, Michael ... 219-989-2231. 171 N
mjkull@purduecal.edu
KULPA, Brian ... 734-487-4192. 242 D
bkulpa@emich.edu
KULWICKI, Anahid ... 617-287-7500. 228 G
anahid.kulwicki@umb.edu
KUMAR, Mukul ... 617-619-1900. 227 F
mukul.kumar@hult.edu
KUMAR, Neeraj ... 312-341-3587. 157 D
neeraj.kumar@roosevelt.edu
KUMAR, Nikhil ... 914-323-5129. 330 B
nikhil.kumar@mville.edu
KUMAR, Shashi ... 516-726-5832. 545 H
kumars@usmma.edu
KUMAR, Sunil ... 646-386-6481. 336 E
skumar@poly.edu

KUMAR, Sunil .... 773-702-1680. 161 B
Sunil.kumar@chicagobooth.edu
KUMAR, Thulsai .... 860-486-4240... 92 A
thulasi.kumar@uconn.edu
KUMARASAMY, Sundar . 937-229-3725. 391 C
sundar@udayton.edu
KUMASHIRO, Kevin, K ... 415-422-2108... 73 J
kkumashiro@usfca.edu
KUMFER, Earl, T .... 260-399-7700. 174 C
ekumfer@sf.edu
KUMI, Ina .... 212-659-7200. 328 E
ikumi@tkc.edu
KUMLER, Kurt .... 412-268-2922. 412 H
kkumler@andrew.cmu.edu
KUMM, David .... 402-643-7222. 289 B
david.kumm@cune.edu
KUMMER, Maryann, S ... 313-927-1373. 246 D
mkummer@marygrove.edu
KUMMERMAN, Howard .. 562-908-3476... 60 I
foundation@riohondo.edu
KUMNICK, Stephen .... 860-231-5363... 92 F
skumnick@usj.edu
KUMPF, Dan .... 805-289-6339... 74 H
dkumpf@vcccd.edu
KUMPF, Robert .... 732-255-0400. 304 A
rkumpf@ocean.edu
KUNA, Gerri .... 701-858-3497. 371 F
gerri.kuna@minotstateu.edu
KUNCE, Kim, M .... 708-709-3684. 156 A
kkunce@prairiestate.edu
KUNCL, Ralph, W .... 909-748-8390... 73 H
ralph_kuncl@redlands.edu
KUNG, Susanna .... 212-594-4000. 347 H
skung@tcicollege.edu
KUNIYOSHI, Tammy ...... 808-956-3028. 136 B
tammyk@hawaii.edu
KUNKEL, Bruce .... 619-849-2571... 59 L
brucekunkel@pointloma.edu
KUNKEL, Cheryl, A .... 859-371-9393. 192 D
ckunkel@beckfield.edu
KUNKEL, Glenn .... 510-261-8500... 58 G
glenn.kunkel@patten.edu
KUNKEL, Karl .... 620-235-4684. 189 L
kkunkel@pittstate.edu
KUNKEL, Marita .... 503-352-1401. 407 A
marita.kunkel@pacificu.edu
KUNKEL, Ronald, T .... 847-566-6401. 162 G
rkunkel@usml.edu
KUNKEL, Sharon, L .... 518-276-6233. 337 I
kunkes@rpi.edu
KUNKEL, Thomas .... 920-403-3165. 535 L
thomas.kunkel@snc.edu
KUNKO, Bill .... 575-492-2501. 310 G
bkunko@nmjc.edu
KUNKO, Christina .... 575-492-2782. 310 G
ckunko@nmjc.edu
KUNO, Dan .... 701-349-3621. 373 A
dkuno@trinitybiblecollege.edu
KUNO, Phyllis .... 701-349-5407. 373 A
phylliskuno@trinitybiblecollege.edu
KUNSMANN, Jill, F .... 414-847-3335. 534 F
jillkunsmann@miad.edu
KUNTZ, Daniel .... 805-493-3855... 31 H
kuntz@clunet.edu
KUNTZ, F. Douglas .... 570-321-4116. 422 H
kuntz@lycoming.edu
KUNTZ, Jason .... 717-391-7322. 434 A
kuntz@stevenscollege.edu
KUNTZ, John .... 973-300-2231. 307 F
jkuntz@sussex.edu
KUNTZ, Lisa, M .... 610-398-5300. 422 B
lkuntz@lincolntech.com
KUNTZ, Wayne .... 228-897-4361. 268 C
wayne.kuntz@mgccc.edu
KUNTZELMAN, Ken .... 928-344-7699... 11 L
kenneth.kuntzelman@azwestern.edu
KUNZ, Kent .... 208-241-2900. 138 E
kunzkent@isu.edu
KUNZE, Joel .... 563-425-5259. 183 B
kunzej@uiu.edu
KUO, David .... 215-871-7128. 430 D
davidku@pcom.edu
KUO, Ling Ling .... 626-571-8811... 74 B
linglingk@uwest.edu
KUO, Mason .... 808-974-7333. 136 A
mkuo@hawaii.edu
KUO, Wai-Lan .... 512-444-8082. 485 B
wkuo@thsu.edu
KUPCZYNSKI, Bonnie, L 218-722-4000. 255 E
bonniek@dbumn.edu
KUPER, Jane, T .... 605-274-4110. 449 K
jane.kuper@augie.edu
KUPER, Tom .... 713-623-2040. 466 G
tkuper@aii.edu
KUPERMAN, Eli .... 732-367-1060. 299 E
ekuperman@bmg.edu
KUPERSHTEYN, Jacob ... 212-349-4330. 325 D
jkupershteyn@globe.edu
KUPERSMITH, Peter, A .. 215-489-2254. 414 E
Peter.Kupersmith@delval.edu

KUPKA, Alyssa .... 312-362-6585. 143 H
akupka@depaul.edu
KUPP, Terry, L .... 315-255-1743. 316 D
Terry.Kupp@cayuga-cc.edu
KUPPINGER, Karen .... 585-389-2100. 332 D
kkuppin9@naz.edu
KURAPATI, Raaj .... 907-474-5866... 10 I
rkurapati@alaska.edu
KURAS, James .... 603-535-2436. 298 G
jmjuras@plymouth.edu
KURIMAY, Mary Beth ..... 610-436-6931. 430 A
mkurimay@wcupa.edu
KURKOWSKI, Bridget ..... 712-749-2235. 176 D
kurkowskib@bvu.edu
KURLAND, Michael .... 860-486-0744... 92 A
michael.kurland@uconn.edu
KURN, Seth, A .... 401-739-5000. 439 D
skurn@neit.edu
KUROKAWA, Linda .... 760-757-2121... 54 G
lkorokawa@miracosta.edu
KUROWSKI, Mark .... 630-829-6029. 140 B
mkurowski@ben.edu
KURPIUS, David .... 225-578-3113. 204 O
kurpius@lsu.edu
KURTINITIS, Sandra, L ... 443-840-1015. 214 E
skurtinitis@ccbcmd.edu
KURTYKA, Steve .... 973-761-9454. 307 C
steve.kurtyka@shu.edu
KURTZ, Diane, L .... 517-750-1200. 250 E
dkurtz@arbor.edu
KURTZ, Edward, J .... 810-766-4224. 239 G
ed.kurtz@baker.edu
KURTZ, Eldon .... 540-432-4390. 504 D
kurtze@emu.edu
KURTZ, Jan .... 503-777-7578. 407 E
kurtzj@reed.edu
KURTZ, Maija .... 719-549-3014... 84 G
Maija.Kurtz@pueblocc.edu
KURTZ, Rebecca .... 740-695-9500. 374 H
bkurtz@belmontcollege.edu
KURTZ, Rick .... 231-591-3667. 242 F
Rick_Kurtz@ferris.edu
KURTZ, Steve .... 573-518-2146. 278 A
skurtz@mineralarea.edu
KURTZ, Terri .... 361-572-6463. 493 H
terri.kurtz@victoriacollege.edu
KURTZ, Terry, J .... 440-826-3170. 374 F
tkurtz@bw.edu
KURTZ, William .... 269-749-7700. 249 A
bkurtz@olivetcollege.edu
KURUVILLA, Mohan .... 281-649-3325. 473 B
mkuruvilla@hbu.edu
KURZ, Katie .... 207-255-1203. 212 F
kkurz@maine.edu
KURZ, Matt .... 309-556-3181. 148 B
mkurz@iwu.edu
KURZ, Richard .... 817-735-2323. 490 E
Richard.Kurz@unthsc.edu
KUSANO, Ellen, I .... 808-974-7499. 136 A
ekusano@hawaii.edu
KUSE, Tammy .... 815-836-5216. 150 H
kuseta@lewisu.edu
KUSER, Janet .... 617-236-8800. 226 F
jkuser@fisher.edu
KUSH, Michael .... 914-337-9300. 321 E
michael.kush@concordia-ny.edu
KUSHIBAB, Debbie .... 623-935-8812... 14 K
debbie.kushibab@estrellamountain.edu
KUSHIGIAN, Elise, J ...... 317-940-9620. 164 J
ekushigi@butler.edu
KUSHINO, Karen .... 773-697-2002. 144 B
kkushino@devry.edu
KUSHMEREK, Michael ... 978-665-3441. 229 E
mkushmerek@fitchburgstate.edu
KUSHNER, Cathy .... 518-464-8543. 324 B
ckushner@excelsior.edu
KUSHNER, Melissa .... 610-607-6212. 431 D
mkushner@racc.edu
KUSNIERZ, Zbigniew ...... 773-252-5316. 156 I
zbigniew.kusnierz@resu.edu
KUSPA, Adam .... 713-798-4951. 467 F
akuspa@bcm.edu
KUSS, Vincent .... 315-464-4361. 342 E
kussv@upstate.edu
KUSSE, Debra .... 585-475-3947. 337 L
dskpur@rit.edu
KUSSMAN, Kevin .... 360-992-2356. 518 A
kkussman@clark.edu
KUSTER, Brian .... 270-745-2037. 200 G
brian.kuster@wku.edu
KUSTER, Daniel .... 602-978-7593... 18 A
daniel.kuster@thunderbird.edu
KUSTER, Frank .... 508-213-2101. 235 E
frank.kuster@nichols.edu
KUSTRA, Robert, W .... 208-426-1491. 137 G
bobkustra@boisestate.edu
KUSZYNSKI,
Lawrence, J .... 352-854-2322. 100 K
larry.kuszynski@cf.edu
KUTATELADZE, Andrei ... 303-871-2693... 86 B
akutatel@du.edu

KUTCH, Keith .... 443-334-2090. 218 E
kkutch@stevenson.edu
KUTCH, Roxanne .... 417-864-7220. 274 D
rkutch@cci.edu
KUTCHNER, Wendy .... 561-297-2429. 114 L
kutchner@fau.edu
KUTI, Morakinyo .... 937-376-6547. 376 E
mkuti@centralstate.edu
KUTLENIOS, Rose .... 304-336-8108. 530 A
rose.kutlenios@westliberty.edu
KUTNER, Sender .... 847-982-2500. 146 C
kutner@htc.edu
KUTTENKULER, Scott ..... 870-460-1110... 24 D
kuttenkuler@uamont.edu
KUTZ, Ellen, M .... 330-490-7302. 392 H
ekutz@walsh.edu
KUTZKE, Mike .... 320-222-5218. 260 H
mike.kutzke@ridgewater.edu
KUWASAKI, L. Michelle . 206-878-3710. 520 E
mkuwasaki@highline.edu
KUWITZKY, Chris .... 405-325-5161. 401 B
ckuwitzky@ou.edu
KUYKENDALL, Francis ... 870-862-8131... 23 D
fkuykendall@southark.edu
KUYKENDALL, John .... 870-575-8498... 24 E
kuykendallj@uapb.edu
KUYKENDALL, Randy ..... 915-532-3737. 494 J
rkuykendall@westerntech.edu
KUYKENDALL, Todd .... 575-769-4919. 309 F
todd.kuykendall@clovis.edu
KUZAK, Michael, J .... 906-227-1126. 248 A
mkuzak@nmu.edu
KUZMA, Lynn .... 207-780-4347. 212 H
kuzma@usm.maine.edu
KUZUOKA, Gina .... 502-588-7185. 199 C
gkuzuoka@spalding.edu
KVAAL, Kimberly, L .... 415-422-6732... 73 J
klkvaal@usfca.edu
KVAM, Robert, A .... 765-285-5495. 164 B
rkvam@bsu.edu
KVISTAD, Gregg, O .... 303-871-2966... 86 B
gkvistad@du.edu
KWAI, CK .... 207-581-3433. 212 B
ck.kwai@maine.edu
KWAN, Cecilia .... 213-763-7088... 52 D
kwancw@lattc.edu
KWAN, Phoebe .... 415-338-6810... 35 E
pkwan@sfsu.edu
KWANDRANS, Karen ...... 716-829-8449. 323 D
kwandrans@dyc.edu
KWENDA, Maxwell .... 605-642-6011. 451 G
maxwell.kwenda@bhsu.edu
KWESKIN, Amy, B .... 314-935-5608. 284 L
amy.b.kweskin@wustl.edu
KWIECHIEN, Garth .... 775-784-1641. 294 J
gkwiechien@unr.edu
KWOK, Borree .... 910-893-1460. 352 K
kwokb@campbell.edu
KWOLEK-FOLLAND,
Angel .... 352-392-4792. 116 A
akf@aa.ufl.edu
KWON, David .... 213-738-0712... 66 H
kwon@southbaylo.edu
KWONG, Joanne .... 212-854-2037. 314 G
jkwong@barnard.edu
KYLE, Lorrie .... 407-646-1540. 111 Q
lkyle@rollins.edu
KYLE, Michael .... 507-786-3025. 264 B
kylem@stolaf.edu
KYLE, Paul .... 913-469-8500. 187 J
pkyle@jccc.edu
KYLE, Penelope, W .... 540-831-5401. 508 C
pwkyle@radford.edu
KYLE, Roberta .... 508-929-8811. 230 G
rkyle@worcester.edu
KYLE, Theresa .... 310-660-3281... 43 B
tkyle@elcamino.edu
KYLES, Vanessa, M .... 251-809-1516..... 5 A
vanessa.kyles@jdcc.edu
KYPRIOS, Linda .... 972-881-5726. 469 G
lkyprios@collin.edu
KYRIAKAKIS, Alana .... 678-915-3021. 132 C
akyriaka@spsu.edu
KYSOR, Darwin, V .... 814-641-3351. 419 H
kysord@juniata.edu
KYTE, Richard, L .... 608-796-3704. 539 E
rlkyte@viterbo.edu
KYZER, Melany .... 405-789-6400. 399 K
mkyzer@snu.edu

L

LÓPEZ, Brunilda .... 787-850-9342. 554 D
brunilda.lopez@upr.edu
LÓPEZ, Héctor, L .... 787-894-2828. 555 C
hector.lopez975@upr.edu
LÓPEZ, José .... 787-850-9376. 554 D
jose.lopez33@upr.edu
LÓPEZ, Maribel .... 787-857-3600. 550 A
mlopez@br.inter.edu

LÓPEZ, Vilmari .... 787-894-2828. 555 C
vilmari.lopez@upr.edu
LÓPEZ-FUENTES,
Ana, N .... 787-250-0000. 553 G
ana.lopez6@upr.edu
LÓPEZ GARRIGA, Juan . 787-265-3828. 554 E
juan.lopez16@upr.edu
LA BELLE, Heather .... 213-627-2580... 38 G
LA BRANCHE, Mark, D .. 919-497-3226. 356 E
mdl@louisburg.edu
LA BRIE, Mary Anne ...... 603-623-0313. 297 E
maryannelabrie@nhia.edu
LA CHAPELLE,
Jacqueline .... 337-550-1282. 205 B
LA DUKE, John, C .... 308-865-8518. 292 H
ladukejc@unk.edu
LA FLEUR, Mary Ann ..... 703-416-1441. 505 I
mlafleur@ipsciences.edu
LA PERLA-MORALES,
Joann .... 732-906-2517. 303 B
jlaperla@middlesexcc.edu
LA POINT, Kristine, L .... 262-975-1295. 534 D
krisbob1@cs.com
LA RUE, Lacie .... 541-737-4218. 406 A
lacie.larue@oregonstate.edu
LA SERNA, Jennifer .... 559-730-3823... 40 I
jenniferl@cos.edu
LAACKMAN, Donald, J ... 312-553-5901. 141 N
dlaackman@ccc.edu
LAAGER, Melinda .... 912-427-5835. 120 B
mlaager@altamahatech.edu
LAAKSO, Kathleen .... 901-843-3885. 458 E
laakso@rhodes.edu
LAANAN, Frankie, S .... 671-735-2444. 546 E
laanan@uguam.uog.edu
LABAO, Nida .... 562-947-8755... 67 H
nidalabao@scuhs.edu
LABARBERA, Mark .... 219-464-6894. 174 E
mark.labarbera@valpo.edu
LABARBERA, Paul .... 845-758-7819. 314 D
labarbera@bard.edu
LABAT, Tony .... 415-641-1241... 62 G
tlabat@sfai.edu
LABATE, William .... 310-206-7323... 71 C
labate@ats.ucla.edu
LABAUGH, Amy, R .... 208-496-9810. 137 H
labaugha@byui.edu
LABAUVE-MAHER,
Laura .... 847-925-6522. 145 H
llabauve@harpercollege.edu
LABBADIA, Gail .... 860-253-3015... 88 C
glabbadia@asnuntuck.edu
LABBERTON, Mark, A .... 626-584-5201... 45 E
LABE, Paul, E .... 443-412-2291. 215 C
plabe@harford.edu
LABEFF, Toni .... 903-434-8105. 477 J
tlabeff@ntcc.edu
LABELLE, Alyssa .... 603-271-6484. 296 C
alabelle@ccsnh.edu
LABELLE-HAMER, Nettie 907-474-6167... 10 I
nettie.labellehamer@alaska.edu
LABERGE, Mark .... 313-845-9770. 243 H
mplaberge@hfcc.edu
LABINE, Nancy .... 423-478-6227. 460 D
nlabine@clevelandstatecc.edu
LABKOWSKI, Zalman ...... 718-434-0784. 316 F
LABOE, Mark .... 773-325-4004. 143 H
mlaboe@depaul.edu
LABOE, Timothy .... 313-883-8556. 249 E
laboe.timothy@shms.edu
LABONTE, Gene, R .... 978-542-6542. 230 E
glabonte@salemstate.edu
LABONTE, Kim .... 618-650-2789. 159 F
klabont@siue.edu
LABONTE, Robert .... 978-632-6600. 232 C
r_labonte@mwcc.mass.edu
LABOR, Jennifer .... 918-465-1814. 395 G
jlabor@eosc.edu
LABORDO, Darwin .... 909-869-2008... 32 G
dlabordo@csupomona.edu
LABOY, Esther, N .... 787-834-9595. 553 B
elaboy@uaa.edu
LABOY, Lilliam .... 787-284-1912. 550 F
llaboy@ponce.inter.edu
LABOY, Rafael .... 787-720-4476. 553 D
relacionespublicas@mizpa.edu
LABRANCHE, Michael ..... 504-398-2241. 206 C
mlabranche@olhcc.edu
LABRIE, John, G .... 617-373-2400. 235 F
LABRIE, Joseph .... 310-338-5238... 53 E
jlabrie@lmu.edu
LABRIE, Lori, A .... 713-313-7040. 485 F
labrie_la@tsu.edu
LABRIE, Lynn .... 928-317-6178... 11 L
lynn.labrie@azwestern.edu
LABRIOLA, Elisabeth, S . 860-439-2064... 89 H
elisabeth.labriola@conncoll.edu
LABRON, Wendy .... 617-735-9778. 226 B
labronw@emmanuel.edu
LABROSSE, Tonya, B ...... 603-899-4097. 296 H
labrosset@franklinpierce.edu

LABRUZZO, Anne ... 928-350-4006... 17 K
alabruzzo@prescott.edu

LABUDE, Mark, S ... 318-342-3610. 208 E
labude@ulm.edu

LABYAK, Gregory ... 618-545-3015. 149 D
glabyak@kaskaskia.edu

LACAY, Phebe ... 973-328-5056. 300 G
placay@ccm.edu

LACEK, Steven ... 304-896-7357. 528 F
steven.lacek@southernwv.edu

LACEY, Aaron ... 314-264-1802. 293 D
aaron.lacey@vatterott-college.edu

LACEY, Aaron ... 314-264-1802. 162 I
aaron.lacey@vatterott-college.edu

LACEY, Kasi ... 573-592-5269. 285 B
kasi.lacey@westminster-mo.edu

LACEY, Pete ... 810-989-5561. 249 H
placey@sc4.edu

LACEY, R. Alton ... 314-392-2355. 278 B
president@mobap.edu

LACEY, Tracey ... 202-408-2400... 96 F

LACEY-HAUN, Lora ... 816-235-1700. 283 D
lacey-haunc@umkc.edu

LACH, Peter ... 304-367-4219. 529 F
peter.lach@fairmontstate.edu

LACHANCE, Andrea ... 607-753-5430. 343 B
andrea.lachance@cortland.edu

LACHANCE, Beatrice ... 615-547-1244. 454 A
blachance@cumberland.edu

LACHANCE, Elizabeth, A . 585-385-8410. 338 H
llachance@sjfc.edu

LACHANCE, Laurie, G ... 207-859-1201. 211 H
president@thomas.edu

LACHAPELLE, Laurie ... 978-762-4000. 232 D
llachape@northshore.edu

LACHER, Candis ... 509-793-2063. 517 C
candyl@bigbend.edu

LACHER, Henry ... 615-460-6670. 453 C
henry.lacher@belmont.edu

LACHICA-CHAVEZ,
Cassandra, M ... 915-747-7354. 492 A
cmlachica@utep.edu

LACK, Paul, D ... 443-334-2205. 218 E
cvanrensselaer@stevenson.edu

LACKEY, Amy ... 785-442-6023. 187 E
alackey@highlandcc.edu

LACKEY, Charles ... 956-882-6552. 491 D
charles.lackey@utb.edu

LACKEY, David, A ... 570-586-2400. 410 D
dlackey@bbc.edu

LACKEY, Fred, G ... 251-442-2482..... 9 A
wbchurch@bellsouth.net

LACKEY, Mary Lou ... 209-946-2011... 73 A

LACKEY, Miles ... 515-294-2220. 175 H
mlackey@iastate.edu

LACKEY, Polly, R ... 806-291-3702. 494 F
lackeyp@wbu.edu

LACKEY, Russell, L ... 515-263-6004. 178 G
rlackey@grandview.edu

LACKEY, Sharon ... 803-321-5113. 445 G
sharon.lackey@newberry.edu

LACKNER, Andrew ... 985-871-6201. 207 C
alackner@tulane.edu

LACKNER, Elisabeth ... 718-631-6279. 319 D
elackner@qcc.cuny.edu

LACKNER, Sandra ... 252-246-1435. 365 C
slackner@wilsoncc.edu

LACOLA, Chris ... 803-786-3012. 443 B

LACOMBA, AJ ... 518-587-2100. 346 A
aj.lacomba@esc.edu

LACOUR, Joseph ... 318-670-9378. 207 A
jlacour@susla.edu

LACOUR, Mary ... 985-549-2244. 208 C
mlacour@selu.edu

LACOUR, Melissa ... 504-671-6219. 203 A
mlacou@dcc.edu

LACOURSE, Peter, W ... 231-995-1198. 248 B
placourse@nmc.edu

LACOURSE, William ... 410-455-2598. 219 D
lacourse@umbc.edu

LACOVARA, Vincent, A ... 202-319-6735... 94 G
lacovara@cua.edu

LACRO, Erika ... 808-845-9225. 136 G
lacro@hawaii.edu

LACROIX, Michael, J ... 402-280-2217. 289 D
lacroix@creighton.edu

LACROIX, Mike ... 419-755-4048. 385 D
lacroix.12@osu.edu

LACROIX, Roland, J ... 207-581-4053. 212 B
roland.j.lacroix@maine.edu

LACY, Charles, F ... 702-968-2016. 295 E
clacy@roseman.edu

LACY, Gary ... 914-948-6206. 346 A
gary.lacy@esc.edu

LACY, Linda, L ... 562-860-2451... 37 I
llacy@cerritos.edu

LACY, Russell ... 503-255-0332. 404 F
rlacy@Multnomah.edu

LACY, William, B ... 530-752-6376... 70 J
wblacy@ucdavis.edu

LADAGE, Marcia ... 816-932-6742. 281 J
mladage@saintlukescollege.edu

LADANY, Nicholas ... 408-551-3074... 64 M
nladany@scu.edu

LADD, Dan ... 307-855-2143. 542 Y
dladd@cwc.edu

LADD, Darin ... 937-255-6565. 544 C
darin.ladd@afit.edu

LADD, Jack ... 432-552-2170. 493 D
ladd_j@utpb.edu

LADD, Sheilah, M ... 802-626-6697. 501 E
sheilah.ladd@lyndonstate.edu

LADD, Susan, K ... 515-271-3048. 177 K
susan.ladd@drake.edu

LADE, Becky ... 515-271-1485. 177 H
becky.lade@dmu.edu

LADENDECKER, Rob ... 213-388-9950... 30 E

LADEWIG, Patricia, A ... 303-458-1843... 84 M
pladewig@regis.edu

LADHA, Amin ... 734-973-3400. 252 A
amin@wccnet.edu

LADINO, Pedro ... 312-553-5600. 141 N
pladino@ccc.edu

LADISCH, Christine, M ... 765-494-8210. 171 M
ladischc@purdue.edu

LADITKA, Doug ... 330-263-2310. 377 H
dladitka@wooster.edu

LADITKA, Robyn ... 330-263-2545. 377 H
rladitka@wooster.edu

LADNER, Barbara ... 304-766-4113. 530 C
ladnerbe@wvstateu.edu

LADNER, Gayle ... 985-732-6640. 203 D

LADNER, Hilda ... 320-589-6095. 264 F
hladner@morris.umn.edu

LADNER, Marilyn ... 352-854-2322. 100 K
ladnerm@cf.edu

LADNER, Pam ... 228-497-7642. 268 C
pamela.ladner@mgccc.edu

LADNER-MATHIS,
Jocelyn ... 216-987-4537. 378 D
jocelyn.ladner-mathis@tri-c.edu

LADUCA, Bonnie ... 651-690-8664. 263 O
bsladuca@stkate.edu

LADUCER, Wanda ... 701-477-7862. 373 B
wladucer@tm.edu

LADUSAW, William ... 831-459-2696... 72 C
humdean@ucsc.edu

LADWIG, Steven ... 707-826-4402... 35 C
ladwig@humboldt.edu

LAFATA-JOHNSON,
Paulette ... 219-980-6769. 168 B
plafataj@iun.edu

LAFAVE, Alan ... 605-626-2497. 451 I
lafavea@northern.edu

LAFAVOR, Jeff ... 712-279-1634. 176 B
jeff.lafavor@briarcliff.edu

LAFAYETTE, Jack ... 610-921-6652. 409 A
jlafayette@alb.edu

LAFERLA, Chris ... 712-325-3293. 179 L
claferla@iwcc.edu

LAFEVER, Steven, D ... 316-978-3070. 191 F
steve.lafever@wichita.edu

LAFFERTY, Carolyn ... 732-255-0400. 304 A
clafferty@ocean.edu

LAFFERTY, T. Kevin ... 813-258-7456. 118 L
klafferty@ut.edu

LAFFERTY, William, J ... 717-337-6912. 417 B
wlaffert@gettysburg.edu

LAFFEY, Brian ... 312-567-3677. 147 F
blaffey1@iit.edu

LAFFITTE, Ron ... 864-587-4002. 447 B
laffitter@smcsc.edu

LAFLAMME, Martha ... 603-752-1113. 296 E
mlaflamme@ccsnh.edu

LAFLASH, Debra, A ... 508-854-4551. 232 F
dal@qcc.mass.edu

LAFLEN, Jody ... 206-934-5566. 522 J
jody.laflen@seattlecolleges.edu

LAFLER, Lisa ... 319-368-6473. 181 C
llafler@mtmercy.edu

LAFLEUR, Joyce ... 616-632-2106. 239 E
laflejoy@aquinas.edu

LAFONTAINE, Joni ... 701-477-7862. 373 B
jlafontaine@tm.edu

LAFORCE, Gail ... 970-521-6603... 83 L
gail.laforce@njc.edu

LAFORGE, Daniel ... 207-948-9287. 211 I
dlaforge@unity.edu

LAFORGE, William (Bill) . 662-846-4000. 266 G
wlaforge@deltastate.edu

LAFORGIA, John, W ... 507-284-2073. 254 G
john.laforgia@mayo.edu

LAFRANCE, Mark ... 617-243-2178. 227 K
mlafrance@lasell.edu

LAFROMEOISE, Tanya ... 605-698-3966. 451 D
tlafromeoise@swc.tc

LAFUZE, Alice ... 765-983-1677. 165 G
lafuzal@earlham.edu

LAGASSE, Ray ... 701-777-6438. 371 C
raymond.lagasse@und.edu

LAGATTA, James, J ... 518-629-4523. 326 G
j.lagatta@hvcc.edu

LAGATTA, Regina ... 518-255-5524. 344 E
lagattrm@cobleskill.edu

LAGATTA, Regina, M ... 607-746-4556. 345 G
lagattrm@delhi.edu

LAGEORGE, Lisa ... 661-362-2205... 53 G
llageorge@masters.edu

LAGER, Carol ... 360-752-8323. 517 B
clager@btc.ctc.edu

LAGESON, David ... 541-962-3114. 405 H
dlageson@eou.edu

LAGGNER, Laurie ... 802-586-7711. 500 E
llaggner@sterlingcollege.edu

LAGRANGE, Janet ... 337-521-8900. 203 I
janet.lagrange@southlouisiana.edu

LAGRANGE, Linda ... 505-454-3578. 310 E
lagrange_l@nmhu.edu

LAGRANGE, Teresa ... 216-523-7402. 377 F
t.lagrange@csuohio.edu

LAGRASSA, Michael ... 508-999-9180. 229 A
mlagrassa@umassd.edu

LAGROW, Patricia ... 405-974-3371. 400 K
plagrow@uco.edu

LAGUARDIA, John, A ... 330-972-5328. 390 E
jlaguardia@uakron.edu

LAGUERRE, Jowel, C ... 707-864-7112... 66 G
jowel.laguerre@solano.edu

LAGUERRE-BROWN,
Caroline ... 410-516-8075. 215 H
clbrown@jhu.edu

LAGUNA, Robert ... 512-492-3010. 466 B
rlaguna@aoma.edu

LAHARGOUE, Brian ... 785-841-9640. 189 K

LAHART, Amy ... 570-674-6340. 424 A
alahart@misericordia.edu

LAHART, Edward ... 570-504-7000. 413 B

LAHER, Ron ... 307-532-8218. 542 a
ron.laher@ewc.wy.edu

LAHEY, John, L ... 203-582-8700... 91 A
john.lahey@quinnipiac.edu

LAHM, Chris ... 417-626-1234. 279 J
lahm.chris@occ.edu

LAHM, Terry, D ... 614-236-6800. 375 H
tlahm@capital.edu

LAHODA, Anne, L ... 412-397-5235. 431 I
lahoda@rmu.edu

LAHR, Sheri, K ... 580-327-8550. 396 N
sklahr@nwosu.edu

LAHTI, Michele ... 209-667-3131... 35 B
mlahti@csustan.edu

LAI, Chun ... 215-572-3850. 437 C
clai@wts.edu

LAI, James, S ... 408-554-5760... 64 M
jlai@scu.edu

LAI, Mary, M ... 516-299-2502. 329 C
mary.lai@liu.edu

LAI HING, Kenneth ... 256-726-7112..... 6 B
laihing@oakwood.edu

LAIBLE, Jim ... 815-967-7307. 157 B
jlaible@rockfordcareercollege.edu

LAIDACKER, Crystal ... 972-241-3371. 470 E
claidacker@dallas.edu

LAINE, Glen, A ... 979-845-8585. 483 C
glaine@tamu.edu

LAING, Katherine ... 217-333-1086. 161 C
klaing@illinois.edu

LAING, Kimberly ... 203-392-5301... 88 A
laingk1@southernct.edu

LAING, Steve ... 360-867-6189. 519 J
laings@evergreen.edu

LAINO, Nicholas ... 315-866-0300. 326 A
lainonf@herkimer.edu

LAIPSON, Peter ... 413-528-7239. 222 E
plaipson@simons-rock.edu

LAIR, Patrick ... 651-423-8399. 258 D
pat.lair@dctc.edu

LAIRD, Allan ... 208-459-5454. 138 A
alaird@collegeofidaho.edu

LAIRD, Brenda ... 307-778-1372. 543 D
blaird@lcccfoundation.edu

LAIRD, Kim ... 903-468-3039. 483 E
kim.laird@tamuc.edu

LAIRD, Melissa ... 503-297-5544. 405 D
mlaird@ocac.edu

LAIRD, Richard ... 321-433-7032. 101 M
lairdr@easternflorida.edu

LAIRD, William, G ... 312-915-7797. 151 H
wlaird@luc.edu

LAIRMORE, Michael, D .. 530-752-1361... 70 J
mdlairmore@ucdavis.edu

LAISURE, Sharon ... 919-530-5214. 368 A
slaisure@nccu.edu

LAJEUNESSE, Deb ... 419-824-3733. 383 C

LAJEUNESSE,
Mary Ellen ... 518-629-7292. 326 G
m.lajeunesse@hvcc.edu

LAJINESS, Todd ... 313-883-8501. 249 E
lajiness.todd@shms.edu

LAKE, Amber ... 641-673-1078. 183 H
lakea@wmpenn.edu

LAKE, Diana ... 360-475-7831. 521 H
dlake@olympic.edu

LAKE, Doris, J ... 270-831-9617. 195 D
doris.lake@kctcs.edu

LAKE, Gashaw ... 502-597-6117. 197 A
gashaw.lake@kysu.edu

LAKE, James, G ... 334-683-2300..... 5 F
jlake@marionmilitary.edu

LAKE, Kathy ... 231-591-2113. 242 F
lakek@ferris.edu

LAKE, Kathy ... 414-382-6084. 531 I
kathy.lake@alverno.edu

LAKE, Lyndon, J ... 315-267-3274. 344 C
lakelj@potsdam.edu

LAKE, Marjean ... 801-524-8163. 495 O
mlake@ldsbc.edu

LAKE, Michael, P ... 850-644-2478. 115 C
mlake@admin.fsu.edu

LAKE, Patrick, R ... 270-707-3705. 195 E
pat.lake@kctcs.edu

LAKE, Stephanie, S ... 919-866-5927. 364 G
sslake@waketech.edu

LAKE, Todd ... 615-460-6628. 453 C
todd.lake@belmont.edu

LAKE, Tracy ... 860-231-5447... 92 F
tlake@usj.edu

LAKE-KING, Shirley ... 340-693-1400. 555 E
sking@live.uvi.edu

LAKEN, Elizabeth, A ... 815-740-3372. 162 F
elaken@stfrancis.edu

LAKEN, Michael, J ... 630-515-6148. 153 B
mlaken@midwestern.edu

LAKER, Craig ... 260-665-4862. 173 E
lakerc@trine.edu

LAKES, Steven ... 859-371-9393. 192 D
slakes@beckfield.edu

LAKETA, Dave ... 815-740-3464. 162 F
dlaketa@stfrancis.edu

LAKHANI, Vikash ... 661-654-3934... 32 H
vlakhani@csub.edu

LAKHANI, Vikash ... 707-826-4402... 35 C
vikash.lakhani@humboldt.edu

LAKIS, James ... 570-321-4141. 422 H
lakis@lycoming.edu

LAKURIQI, Elona ... 215-951-2186. 430 E
lakuriqie@philau.edu

LALIBERTE, Jean ... 334-670-3608..... 7 H
jlaliber@troy.edu

LALIBERTE, Michael, R .. 414-229-1122. 537 A
lalibert@uwm.edu

LALLY, Jay ... 321-674-8225. 104 H
jlally@fit.edu

LALLY, Mary ... 617-573-8430. 237 B
mlally@suffolk.edu

LALLY, Shiela ... 617-236-8800. 226 F
slally@fisher.edu

LALOR, Melinda, M ... 205-934-8420..... 8 E
mlalor@uab.edu

LALOVIC-HAND, Mira ... 856-256-4146. 305 E
lalovic-hand@rowan.edu

LALUZERNE, Joseph ... 651-638-6879. 253 K
j-laluzerne@bethel.edu

LALUZERNE,
Shannon, S ... 920-923-7661. 534 A
slaluzerne@marianuniversity.edu

LAM, Clement ... 408-855-5332... 75 K
clement.lam@wvm.edu

LAM, Edward ... 888-488-4968... 48 K

LAM, Felix ... 212-650-8173. 317 D
flam@ccny.cuny.edu

LAM, Kenneth ... 718-420-4164. 350 B
kenneth.lam@wagner.edu

LAM, Nathan ... 310-824-1586... 26 B

LAM, Nicole ... 503-493-6456. 402 J
nlam@cu-portland.edu

LAM, Simon, Y ... 415-338-2541... 35 E
slam@sfsu.edu

LAM YUEN, Peteru ... 684-699-9155. 546 A
p.lamyuen@amsamoa.edu

LAMADANIE, Mahmoud . 209-667-3122... 35 B

LAMADANIE, Mahmoud . 318-274-7798. 207 E
lamadaniem@gram.edu

LAMADE, Dawn ... 706-379-3526. 134 L
dlamade@yhc.edu

LAMADRID, Eduardo ... 787-766-1912. 549 J
elamadrid@inter.edu

LAMADRID, Edward ... 773-477-4822... 57 E
elamadrid@pacificcollege.edu

LAMADRID, Lupe ... 225-578-1175. 204 O
glamadrid@lsu.edu

LAMAR, Charlene ... 912-688-6039. 129 J
clamar@ogeecheetech.edu

LAMAR, Sharmaine ... 610-690-5675. 433 I
slamar1@swarthmore.edu

LAMAR, Sondra ... 479-788-7025... 24 A
sondra.lamar@uafs.edu

LAMARCHE, Paul ... 609-258-4999. 304 E
lamarche@princeton.edu

LAMARRE, Wayne ... 207-602-2412. 213 A
wlamarre@une.edu

LAMAS, Frank 817-272-6080. 491 B lamas@uta.edu
LAMASCUS, Scott 405-425-5469. 397 D scott.lamascus@oc.edu
LAMB, Bill 319-398-5509. 180 J blamb@kirkwood.edu
LAMB, Colin 620-276-9640. 187 A colin.lamb@gcccks.edu
LAMB, Craig 585-345-6969. 325 C
LAMB, Curtis, S 864-488-8354. 444 L
LAMB, David 716-829-7652. 323 D kavinokytheater@dyc.edu
LAMB, Duane 205-348-8092. 8 D dlamb@fa.ua.edu
LAMB, Jimmie 972-825-4636. 481 F jlamb@sagu.edu
LAMB, John, C 414-288-1671. 534 B john.lamb@marquette.edu
LAMB, Keith 940-397-4291. 476 H keith.lamb@mwsu.edu
LAMB, Kevin, D 740-376-4712. 383 E kevin.lamb@marietta.edu
LAMB, Linda 315-866-0300. 326 A lamblc@herkimer.edu
LAMB, Mark 618-664-6801. 145 G mark.lamb@greenville.edu
LAMB, Martha 508-286-3905. 238 B mlamb@wheatonma.edu
LAMB, Marybeth 508-531-1353. 229 D marybeth.lamb@bridgew.edu
LAMB, Melissa 912-427-5841. 120 B mlamb@altamahatech.edu
LAMB, Michael 706-649-1821. 123 E mlamb@columbustech.edu
LAMB, Sophie, A 785-827-5541. 188 C sophie.lamb@kwu.edu
LAMB, Sue 757-388-2900. 509 D salamb@sentara.com
LAMB, Susan, E 925-969-2003. 41 L slamb@dvc.edu
LAMBA, Ram 787-725-6500. 547 H rlamba@albizu.edu
LAMBA, Sandy 209-473-5200. 47 F sandy_lamba@heald.edu
LAMBE, Joan 212-772-5462. 318 C joan.lambe@hunter.cuny.edu
LAMBERT, Ame 802-860-2784. 499 A alambert@champlain.edu
LAMBERT, Angela 304-327-4480. 529 D alambert@bluefieldstate.edu
LAMBERT, Bill 909-274-4215. 55 A wlambert@mtsac.edu
LAMBERT, Bryan, S 312-939-0111. 144 D
LAMBERT, Collin 312-329-4290. 153 E collin.lambert@moody.edu
LAMBERT, Connie 509-963-1411. 517 F lambertc@cwu.edu
LAMBERT, Donovan 701-255-3285. 373 C dlambert@uttc.edu
LAMBERT, Edward 617-287-5300. 228 G edward.lambert@umb.edu
LAMBERT, Elaine, J 570-326-3761. 427 B elambert@pct.edu
LAMBERT, Elizabeth, A 607-735-1825. 323 H elambert@elmira.edu
LAMBERT, Huntington, D 617-495-2930. 227 C lambert@fas.harvard.edu
LAMBERT, James 419-372-9970. 374 K jlamber@bgsu.edu
LAMBERT, Jay 361-570-4290. 489 E lambertj1@uhv.edu
LAMBERT, Kevin 606-633-3305. 196 F kevin.lambert@kctcs.edu
LAMBERT, Kim, D 315-792-3341. 349 F klambert@utica.edu
LAMBERT, Lake 478-301-2915. 128 H lambert_l@mercer.edu
LAMBERT, Lee, D 520-206-4747. 17 A llambert@pima.edu
LAMBERT, Leo, M 336-278-7900. 354 B lambert@elon.edu
LAMBERT, Linda 360-383-3295. 525 D llambert@whatcom.ctc.edu
LAMBERT, Lori, A 513-745-4884. 393 H lambert@xavier.edu
LAMBERT, Mark, A 540-985-9031. 506 G malambert@jchs.edu
LAMBERT, Matthew 315-786-2271. 327 L mlambert@sunyjefferson.edu
LAMBERT, Matthew, T 757-221-1001. 503 N mtlambert@wm.edu
LAMBERT, Michael 419-473-2700. 378 I
LAMBERT, Michelin 903-730-4890. 474 O michelin.lambert@jarvis.edu
LAMBERT, Patrick 845-398-4396. 340 A plambert@stac.edu
LAMBERT, Peggy, E 330-287-1376. 386 F lambert.133@osu.edu
LAMBERT, Rebecca 479-524-7493. 21 G blambert@jbu.edu
LAMBERT, Stacey 617-327-6777. 233 D stacey_lambert@mspp.edu
LAMBETH, Christopher 513-721-7944. 380 D clambeth@gbs.edu
LAMBIE-SIMPSON, Yasmin 650-543-3976. 54 C ylambie-simpson@menlo.edu
LAMBLA, Kenneth, A 704-687-0090. 368 E kalambla@uncc.edu
LAMBORGHINI, Nita 978-556-3818. 232 E nlamborghini@necc.mass.edu
LAMBORN, John, E 765-361-6327. 175 B lambornj@wabash.edu
LAMBOY, Maritza 787-834-9595. 553 B mlamboy@uaa.edu
LAMBRAKIS, Christine 602-286-8227. 14 L christine.lambrakis@gwmail.maricopa.edu
LAMBRECHT, Anne, K 989-463-7225. 239 B lambrechtak@alma.edu
LAMBRECHT, Jennifer 763-424-0909. 260 C jsummer-lambrecht@nhcc.edu
LAMBRECHT, John 708-456-0300. 161 A jlambrec@triton.edu
LAMBRECHTSEN, Karen 916-577-2200. 76 J klambrechtsen@jessup.edu
LAMBRIGHT, Jonathan 912-358-3269. 131 C lambrij@savannahstate.edu
LAMBROS, Mary Ann 410-225-2262. 216 C mlambros@mica.edu
LAME BULL, Crystal 509-865-8653. 520 D lamebull_c@heritage.edu
LAMERSON, Cindy 581-803-2013. 110 B cynthia_lamerson@pba.edu
LAMHAOUAR, Said 718-429-6600. 349 H said.lamhaouar@vaughn.edu
LAMICA, Victoria 925-485-5287. 37 K vlamica@clpccd.cc.ca.us
LAMIMAN, Lynne 972-708-7536. 472 L
LAMKIN, Corbet, J 870-574-4501. 23 G clamkin@sautech.edu
LAMM, Deborah, L 252-823-5166. 360 C lammd@edgecombe.edu
LAMM, Edward 920-403-3007. 535 L edward.lamm@snc.edu
LAMM, Gary 254-295-4545. 490 B glamm@umhb.edu
LAMM, Laura 503-251-5742. 408 G llamm@uws.edu
LAMM, Peggy 970-248-1020. 79 F plamm@coloradomesa.edu
LAMMERS, Glenda 334-683-2372. 5 F glammers@marionmilitary.edu
LAMMERS, Keith 215-780-1260. 433 A keith@salus.edu
LAMMERS, Kim 419-783-2563. 379 C klammers@defiance.edu
LAMMERS, Michael 503-699-6252. 404 C mlammers@marylhurst.edu
LAMMERS, Paul 605-668-1544. 450 F plammers@mtmc.edu
LAMMONS, Anthony 951-343-4217. 30 H alammons@calbaptist.edu
LAMOE, Jeff, P 913-684-2905. 545 E jeff.lamoe@leavenworth.army.mil
LAMONTAGNE, Gregory, A 401-825-2142. 439 A glamontagne@ccri.edu
LAMONTAGNE, Michael 253-833-9111. 520 C MLaMontagne@greenriver.edu
LAMONTAGNE, Ramona 815-836-5291. 150 H lamontra@lewisu.edu
LAMONTAGNE, Susan 413-572-5425. 230 F slamontagne@westfield.ma.edu
LAMOREAUX, Barbara 330-287-1214. 386 F lamoreaux.1@osu.edu
LAMOREAUX, Marilyn 435-652-7502. 497 E lamoreaux@dixie.edu
LAMORTE, Debra, A 212-998-6411. 334 D debra.lamorte@nyu.edu
LAMORTE, JR., Louis, A 215-951-1075. 420 B lamorte@lasalle.edu
LAMOTHE, Vivian 808-934-2713. 136 F vlamothe@hawaii.edu
LAMOTT, Eric, E 651-641-8729. 255 B lamott@csp.edu
LAMOTTE, Steve 302-736-2485. 94 C steve.lamotte@wesley.edu
LAMOUNTAIN, Kevin 602-759-2258. 11 H klamountain@arizonacollege.edu
LAMPARELLI, Kimberly 518-458-5354. 321 A lamparek@strose.edu
LAMPE, Emily, A 712-749-2103. 176 D lampee@bvu.edu
LAMPE, Gregory, P 608-263-1794. 538 E greg.lampe@uwc.edu
LAMPE, Mary Beth 803-822-3251. 445 C lampem@midlandstech.edu
LAMPHERE, Sue 740-362-3344. 383 H slamphere@mtso.edu
LAMPKIN, Alison 706-802-5473. 125 C alampkin@highlands.edu
LAMPKIN, Patricia, M 434-924-7984. 511 B pml@virginia.edu
LAMPKIN-WILLIAMS, Ann 313-593-5321. 251 D lampkin@umich.edu
LAMPLEY, Paul, C 662-252-8000. 269 F plampley@rustcollege.edu
LAMPROPOULOS, Cindy 801-524-8169. 495 O CLampropoulos@ldsbc.edu
LAMPUS, Rita 239-513-1122. 106 O rlampus@hodges.edu
LAMURAGLIA, Rose 619-388-3488. 62 D rlamurag@sdccd.edu
LAMWERS, Linda, L 610-436-3405. 430 A llamwers@wcupa.edu
LAMY, Patrick, J 973-748-9000. 299 F patrick_lamy@bloomfield.edu
LAN, Larry, L 407-888-8689. 104 B llan@fcim.edu
LANA, Peter 585-389-2344. 332 D plana0@naz.edu
LANAGAN, Keni 865-981-8308. 456 D keni.lanagan@maryvillecollege.edu
LANASA, Steven, M 913-621-6070. 186 C slanasa@donnelly.edu
LANCASTER, Adrianna 580-559-5368. 395 F alancaster@ecok.edu
LANCASTER, Andrea 425-235-2352. 522 F alancaster@rtc.edu
LANCASTER, Beth 864-596-9704. 443 D beth.lancaster@converse.edu
LANCASTER, Carol 202-687-0468. 95 E lancastc@georgetown.edu
LANCASTER, Dennis 417-255-7272. 278 F dennislancaster@missouristate.edu
LANCASTER, James 626-852-6403. 38 K jlancaster@citruscollege.edu
LANCASTER, Lindsay 405-733-7311. 399 F llancaster@rose.edu
LANCASTER, Loren 406-874-6171. 286 E lancastral@milescc.edu
LANCASTER, Robin 501-882-4547. 19 M rglancaster@asub.edu
LANCASTER, Sydney 440-365-5222. 383 B
LANCE, Ann, H 507-284-2915. 254 G ann.lance@mayo.edu
LANCE, Charlene 330-684-8755. 390 F clance@uakron.edu
LANCE, Charles, A 828-669-8012. 357 H clance@montreat.edu
LANCE, Regena 620-223-2700. 186 G regenal@fortscott.edu
LANCHESTER, Judy 209-588-5366. 77 I lanchesterj@yosemite.cc.ca.us
LANCI, John 508-565-1239. 237 A jlanci@stonehill.edu
LAND, Lauren 870-245-5283. 22 D landl@obu.edu
LAND, Mark 812-855-0850. 167 E mdland@iu.edu
LAND, Matt 260-665-4143. 173 E landm@trine.edu
LAND, Mitch 757-352-4916. 508 G mland@regent.edu
LAND, Patricia 941-637-5656. 101 O pland@edison.edu
LAND, Richard, D 704-847-5600. 366 J cwoodside@ses.edu
LAND, Sabrina 773-821-4976. 141 J sland20@csu.edu
LAND, Steven, J 423-478-7702. 458 B president@ptseminary.edu
LANDA, Michelle 541-881-5583. 408 C mlanda@tvcc.cc
LANDAU, Barbara 410-516-8094. 215 H landau@jhu.edu
LANDE, Richard 507-457-5045. 262 A rlande@winona.edu
LANDEN, Jenny 505-428-1653. 311 J jenny.landen@sfcc.edu
LANDEN, Robyn 307-268-2362. 542 X rlanden@caspercollege.edu
LANDEN, William 307-268-2667. 542 X blanden@caspercollege.edu
LANDER, Laura 413-565-1000. 222 F llander@baypath.edu
LANDER, Maria 704-290-5267. 363 G mlander@spcc.edu
LANDERS, Joanne 216-421-7327. 377 C jlanders@cia.edu
LANDERS, Mary 816-501-4199. 280 I mary.landers@rockhurst.edu
LANDERS, Sharon 615-771-7821. 464 G sharon.landers@williamsoncc.edu
LANDERS, Stephanie 313-993-1549. 250 K landerss@udmercy.edu
LANDERS, Thomas, L 405-325-2621. 401 B landers@ou.edu
LANDERS, Timothy, M 585-343-0055. 325 C tmlanders@genesee.edu
LANDES, Marie, C 540-665-4516. 509 E mlandes@su.edu
LANDES, Mark 620-327-8219. 187 D markl@hesston.edu
LANDEY, Sena 765-983-1468. 165 G landse@earlham.edu
LANDGAARD, Jodi 507-372-3403. 260 A jodi.landgaard@mnwest.edu
LANDGRAF, Tanya 712-749-2212. 176 D landgraft@bvu.edu
LANDGREN, Peter 513-556-3737. 390 G peter.landgren@uc.edu
LANDI, Pamela 561-297-2003. 114 L plandi@fau.edu
LANDIS, Ann 229-226-1621. 132 F alandis@thomasu.edu
LANDIS, Justin 517-264-7172. 250 B jlandis@sienaheights.edu
LANDIS, SCC, Marie Cecelia 973-543-6528. 298 I spmcl@juno.com
LANDIS, Shirley, A 215-951-2717. 430 E landiss@philau.edu
LANDON, Deborah 515-244-4221. 175 C landond@aib.edu
LANDPHAIR, Juliette, L 804-289-8468. 510 L jlandpha@richmond.edu
LANDRAU, Barbara 787-993-8856. 554 A barbara.landrau@upr.edu
LANDREBE, Robert, S 859-858-2192. 192 A
LANDRITH, J. Wayne 864-977-7017. 445 H wayne.landrith@ngu.edu
LANDRON, Carmen, T 787-620-2040. 547 C clandron@aupr.edu
LANDRUM, Kay 616-222-1402. 241 F kay.landrum@cornerstone.edu
LANDRUM, Kay 817-598-6499. 494 G klandrum@wc.edu
LANDRUM, Kristin 276-656-0259. 513 D klandrum@patrickhenry.edu
LANDRUM, Paul 575-538-6488. 312 N landrump@wumu.edu
LANDRUM, Thomas, S 706-542-2002. 133 C tlandrum@uga.edu
LANDRUM, Treina 318-342-5305. 208 E landrum@ulm.edu
LANDRUM, Wes 704-922-6462. 360 F landrum.wes@gaston.edu
LANDRUM-SIMS, Alonzetta 334-347-2623. 3 G alandrum-sims@escc.edu
LANDRY, Abbie 318-357-4403. 208 B landry@nsula.edu
LANDRY, Bill 843-574-6745. 447 E bill.landry@tridenttech.edu
LANDRY, Cara 225-675-8270. 203 G clandry@rpcc.edu
LANDRY, Debbie 918-456-5511. 396 H landry@nsuok.edu
LANDRY, Fred 318-869-5136. 201 H flandry@centenary.edu
LANDRY, Karen 425-267-0153. 519 I klandry@everettcc.edu
LANDRY, Lisa, C 337-482-5430. 208 D ldlandry@louisiana.edu
LANDRY, Lisa, L 337-482-6471. 208 D housing@louisiana.edu
LANDRY, Madelaine 337-550-1257. 205 B
LANDRY, Patrick 337-482-6402. 208 D pml@louisiana.edu
LANDRY, Ruth 337-482-5811. 208 D rwl@louisiana.edu
LANDRY, Shawntel, D 214-210-4050. 163 I
LANDRY, Shawntel, D 317-829-9366. 163 I
LANDRY, Stephen 973-275-2299. 307 C stephen.landry@shu.edu
LANDSAW, Christy 918-456-5511. 396 H landsaw@nsuok.edu
LANDSMARK, Theodore, C 617-262-5000. 223 F ted.landsmark@the-bac.edu
LANDSTROM, Corey 563-387-1020. 180 M clandstrom@luther.edu
LANDWEHR, Brynn 630-844-7861. 140 A landwehr@aurora.edu
LANDWER, Allan, J 325-670-2222. 472 O alandwer@hsutx.edu
LANE, Amy 715-232-1469. 538 B lanea@uwstout.edu
LANE, Austin 936-273-7222. 476 A austin.lane@lonestar.edu
LANE, Barbara 573-329-5160. 276 C laneb@lincolnu.edu
LANE, Bradley 206-934-2926. 522 J bradley.lane@seattlecolleges.edu
LANE, Charles, E 213-740-3649. 74 A clane@caps.usc.edu
LANE, David 207-621-3448. 212 C dlane@maine.edu
LANE, Deborah 205-348-8089. 8 D dlane@ur.ua.edu

LANE, Deborah .... 405-744-6384. 397 H
debbie.lane@okstate.edu
LANE, Deborah .... 865-573-4517. 455 G
dlane@johnsonU.edu
LANE, Diane, C .... 410-287-6060. 214 B
dlane@cecil.edu
LANE, Diane, L .... 217-362-6416. 153 C
dlane@millikin.edu
LANE, Edwin, H .... 816-415-7643. 285 C
lanee@william.jewell.edu
LANE, Eric .... 516-463-5854. 326 D
eric.lane@hofstra.edu
LANE, Greg .... 619-574-6909... 57 E
glane@pacificcollege.edu
LANE, Jason .... 518-320-1356. 341 C
jason.lane@suny.edu
LANE, Jennifer .... 808-675-4971. 135 C
jennifer.lane@byuh.edu
LANE, Jill .... 618-468-4900. 150 G
jlane@lc.edu
LANE, Jill .... 678-466-4194. 123 A
jilllane@clayton.edu
LANE, John .... 713-221-8292. 489 D
lanej@uhd.edu
LANE, Kimberly .... 216-373-5290. 385 G
klane@ndc.edu
LANE, Laura .... 248-476-1122. 246 G
llane@mispp.edu
LANE, Marguerite .... 516-323-4014. 331 J
mlane@molloy.edu
LANE, Mark .... 808-455-0213. 137 A
marklane@hawaii.edu
LANE, Mary .... 363-334-4822. 360 G
mslane@gtcc.edu
LANE, Matt .... 304-776-6290. 526 F
mlane@cci.edu
LANE, Michael .... 516-686-7723. 333 H
mlane@nyit.edu
LANE, Natalie .... 307-382-1673. 543 J
nlane@wwcc.wy.edu
LANE, Nicole .... 724-222-5330. 425 K
nlane@penncommercial.edu
LANE, Phyllis .... 360-867-6034. 519 J
lanep@evergreen.edu
LANE, Robert, J .... 515-961-1417. 182 E
bob.lane@simpson.edu
LANE, Roberta .... 847-578-8309. 157 F
roberta.lane@rosalindfranklin.edu
LANE, Russ .... 402-557-7452. 288 G
russ.lane@bellevue.edu
LANE, Shannon .... 318-487-7498. 202 F
shannon.lane@lacollege.edu
LANE, Shelese .... 404-270-5110. 132 E
sjlane@spelman.edu
LANE, Tamara, N .... 806-743-6429. 487 E
tamara.lane@ttuhsc.edu
LANE, Tiletha .... 843-383-8082. 442 F
tlane@coker.edu
LANE COBB, Michelle .... 252-789-0244. 361 G
mlane@martincc.edu
LANE-MARTIN, Tanya .... 585-345-6800. 325 C
tmlanemartin@genesee.edu
LANEY, Mary, A .... 386-312-4069. 112 C
maryannelaney@sjrstate.edu
LANEY, Miriam .... 803-778-7825. 441 F
laneymt@cctech.edu
LANFEAR, Jeffery .... 773-325-8308. 143 H
jlanfear@depaul.edu
LANG, Anita .... 201-216-5163. 307 E
alang@stevens.edu
LANG, Ashley .... 319-352-8486. 183 E
ashley.lang@wartburg.edu
LANG, Christine .... 843-574-6162. 447 E
chris.lang@tridenttech.edu
LANG, Cyndi .... 574-520-4490. 168 E
clang@iusb.edu
LANG, George .... 401-841-2245. 545 A
LANG, Heather .... 971-722-4532. 407 D
heather.lang@pcc.edu
LANG, Jean .... 808-544-0272. 135 F
jlang@hpu.edu
LANG, Jennifer .... 718-780-0383. 315 H
jennifer.lang@brooklaw.edu
LANG, Kathy, J .... 414-288-1782. 534 B
kathy.lang@marquette.edu
LANG, Mandy .... 715-422-5446. 540 D
mandy.lang@mstc.edu
LANG, Melissa, W .... 757-446-6054. 504 E
langmw@evms.edu
LANG, Michelle .... 503-517-1190. 408 H
mlang@warnerpacific.edu
LANG, Natasha .... 925-424-1634... 37 L
nlang@laspositascollege.edu
LANG, Paul, L .... 906-227-2920. 248 A
plang@nmu.edu
LANG, Sherrie .... 210-486-2252. 465 B
slang14@alamo.edu
LANG, Stephen, W .... 432-837-8061. 487 B
slang@sulross.edu
LANGAN, Sally .... 920-498-5688. 541 B
sally.langan@nwtc.edu
LANGAN, Terrence, G ..... 651-962-6001. 265 C
tglangan@stthomas.edu
LANGDON, Deb .... 740-389-4636. 383 F
langdond@mtc.edu
LANGDON, Steven, D ..... 515-643-6716. 181 A
slangdon@mercydesmoines.org
LANGDON, Tennille .... 660-831-4157. 278 I
langdont@moval.edu
LANGE, Andrea .... 410-778-7776. 221 C
alange2@washcoll.edu
LANGE, Andrea, G .... 410-778-7776. 221 C
alange2@washcoll.edu
LANGE, Chris, J .... 414-410-4207. 532 B
cjlange@stritch.edu
LANGE, Christine, M ..... 941-359-7594. 111 O
clange@ringling.edu
LANGE, Dan .... 541-278-5891. 402 C
dlange@bluecc.edu
LANGE, Douglas, J .... 606-218-5988. 200 F
douglaslange@upike.edu
LANGE, Janet .... 309-677-2523. 140 I
lange@bradley.edu
LANGE, Jean .... 203-582-8444... 91 A
jean.lange@quinnipiac.edu
LANGE, Karen .... 307-778-1204. 543 D
klange@lccc.wy.edu
LANGE, Karen, M .... 651-962-6050. 265 C
kmlange@stthomas.edu
LANGE, Mike .... 928-776-2067... 19 H
mike.lange@yc.edu
LANGE, Mindy, W .... 717-691-6024. 423 L
mlange@messiah.edu
LANGE, Peter .... 919-684-2631. 354 A
peter.lange@duke.edu
LANGE, Robert .... 757-594-8070. 503 M
robert.lange@cnu.edu
LANGE, Steven .... 320-629-5155. 260 F
langes@pinetech.edu
LANGE, Tom, J .... 715-831-7285. 539 J
tlange8@cvtc.edu
LANGE, Tyana .... 570-484-2087. 429 B
tsl400@lhup.edu
LANGEMO, Bree .... 719-502-3008... 84 A
bree.langemo@ppcc.edu
LANGENBACK, Timothy . 941-752-5342. 114 I
langent@scf.edu
LANGER, Nathan .... 218-723-6010. 254 K
nlanger@css.edu
LANGER, Peter .... 617-287-5611. 228 G
peter.langer@umb.edu
LANGERBEIN, Helmut .... 870-235-4200... 23 F
helmetlangerbein@saumag.edu
LANGEVIN, John .... 207-602-2549. 213 A
jlangevin@une.edu
LANGFORD, Allison .... 417-328-2093. 282 C
alangford@sbuniv.edu
LANGFORD, David .... 201-692-9867. 301 J
david_langford@fdu.edu
LANGFORD, Debra .... 304-876-5216. 529 I
dlangfor@shepherd.edu
LANGFORD, George, M . 315-443-3949. 347 C
glangfor@syr.edu
LANGFORD, James, D ... 325-674-2855. 464 H
langford@acu.edu
LANGFORD, Joel, C .... 770-720-5585. 130 G
jcl@reinhardt.edu
LANGFORD, Pamela .... 909-537-7454... 34 E
plangfor@csusb.edu
LANGHAM, Gay .... 601-643-8307. 266 F
gay.langham@colin.edu
LANGHAM, Julie .... 706-595-0166. 121 D
jlangham@augustatech.edu
LANGHAM, Lynda .... 936-468-2503. 482 A
llangham@sfasu.edu
LANGHAMMER, Paul ..... 401-874-9500. 440 D
langhammer@uri.edu
LANGINESTRA, Jaime .... 212-431-2843. 333 I
Jaime.Laginestra@nyls.edu
LANGIS, Gayle .... 207-893-7850. 211 G
glangis@sjcme.edu
LANGKILDE, Jared .... 480-461-7396... 15 A
jared.langkilde@mesacc.edu
LANGLAND, Elizabeth .... 602-543-4506... 11 K
elizabeth.langland@asu.edu
LANGLAND, Meg .... 573-592-5381. 285 B
meg.langland@westminster-mo.edu
LANGLEY, Amy .... 256-840-4185..... 6 I
alangley@snead.edu
LANGLEY, Angie .... 662-720-7249. 269 B
alangle@nemcc.edu
LANGLEY, Dawn, E .... 336-322-2207. 362 F
Dawn.Langley@piedmontcc.edu
LANGLEY, Dorothy .... 903-730-4890. 474 O
dorothy_langley@jarvis.edu
LANGLEY, Goldie .... 614-947-6509. 380 A
goldie.langley@franklin.edu
LANGLEY, Janet .... 623-845-3155... 14 M
janet.langley@gccaz.edu
LANGLEY, Janet, R .... 601-974-1134. 267 I
langljr@millsaps.edu
LANGLEY, Pamela .... 603-271-6484. 296 C
plangley@ccsnh.edu
LANGLEY, Winston .... 617-287-5600. 228 G
winston.langley@umb.edu
LANGLEY-TURNBAUGH,
Samantha .... 207-780-5361. 212 H
langley@usm.maine.edu
LANGLIE, Mary, L .... 516-876-3175. 343 D
langliem@oldwestbury.edu
LANGLOIS, John .... 508-767-7045. 222 C
jlanglois@assumption.edu
LANGLOIS, OP, John ..... 202-495-3831... 96 C
president@dhs.edu
LANGLOIS, Judith, H ..... 512-232-3600. 491 C
jlanglois@austin.utexas.edu
LANGLOIS, Mary Ann .... 716-888-2103. 316 C
langloim@canisius.edu
LANGMADE, Mary .... 612-343-4776. 262 X
malangma@northcentral.edu
LANGRELL, Ron .... 253-680-7103. 516 L
rlangrell@bates.ctc.edu
LANGRIDGE, Nick .... 540-568-3197. 506 F
langrinl@jmu.edu
LANGSDORF, John .... 336-272-7102. 354 E
john.langsdorf@greensboro.edu
LANGSETH, Roger .... 507-535-3309. 255 C
rlangseth@crossroadscollege.edu
LANGSETH, Roger, W ..... 507-288-4563. 255 C
rlangseth@crossroadscollege.edu
LANGSFORD, Marcus .... 516-745-5769. 391 A
marcus.langsford@uc.edu
LANGSTAFF, Kris, A .... 606-474-3153. 194 H
klangstaff@kcu.edu
LANGSTON, II, Bill, C .... 863-680-4209. 105 D
blangston@flsouthern.edu
LANGSTON, Carol .... 870-368-2006... 22 E
carol.langston@ozarka.edu
LANGSTON, Diane .... 706-295-6357. 125 C
dlangston@highlands.edu
LANGSTON, Ginna, V .... 918-631-2641. 401 F
ruth-langston@utulsa.edu
LANGSTON, Randall .... 585-395-2772. 342 F
rlangsto@brockport.edu
LANGSTON, Randall .... 585-395-2751. 342 F
rlangston@brockport.edu
LANGSTON-SMITH,
Sanette .... 601-977-4458. 270 A
slsmith@tougaloo.edu
LANGSTRAAT, Nate .... 360-383-3350. 525 D
nlangstraat@whatcom.ctc.edu
LANGTEAU, Paula .... 715-735-4339. 538 E
paula.langteau@uwc.edu
LANGUTH, Christine .... 860-383-5211... 89 F
clanguth@trcc.commnet.edu
LANHAM, Allen, K .... 217-581-6061. 144 E
aklanham@eiu.edu
LANHAM, Heather .... 937-778-7803. 379 G
hlanham@edisonohio.edu
LANHAM, Jeff .... 740-245-7485. 392 A
jlanham@rio.edu
LANIAK, Timothy, S .... 704-527-9909. 227 A
tlaniak@gcts.edu
LANIER, Amy, S .... 803-786-3927. 443 B
alanier@columbiasc.edu
LANIER, Carolyn .... 203-837-8277... 88 B
lanierc@wcsu.edu
LANIER, Gregory, W .... 850-474-2934. 117 B
glanier@uwf.edu
LANIER, Marilyn .... 415-405-3838... 35 E
mlanier@sfsu.edu
LANIER, Percy .... 205-929-1665..... 5 G
plani@mail.miles.edu
LANIER, Stephen, M .... 843-792-2211. 445 B
lanier@musc.edu
LANKA, Greg .... 330-494-6170. 389 F
glanka@starkstate.edu
LANKER, Jason .... 716-926-8933. 326 B
jlanker@hilbert.edu
LANKES, Susan .... 716-652-8900. 316 G
slankes@cks.edu
LANKFORD, Eric .... 740-374-8716. 392 I
elankford@wscc.edu
LANKFORD, Peggy .... 575-538-6629. 312 N
lankfordp@wnmu.edu
LANN, Jennifer .... 802-387-6764. 499 E
jlann@landmark.edu
LANNERT, Mary .... 406-447-6944. 287 A
mary.lannert@umhelena.edu
LANNING, Gale .... 507-453-1443. 259 E
glanning@southeastmn.edu
LANNING, Patrick .... 503-399-5144. 402 E
patrick.lanning@chemeketa.edu
LANNING, Stephanie .... 620-227-9409. 186 B
slg@dc3.edu
LANNON, SJ,
Timothy, R .... 402-280-2770. 289 D
tlannon@creighton.edu
LANNUTTI, Pamela .... 215-951-1935. 420 B
lannuttip@lasalle.edu
LANPHER, Jim .... 803-754-4100. 443 C
LANSER, Michael .... 920-693-1123. 540 B
michael.lanser@gotoltc.edu
LANTAGNE, Douglas, O . 802-656-2990. 500 F
doug.lantagne@uvm.edu
LANTING, Mark .... 815-802-8709. 149 C
mlanting@kcc.edu
LANTIS, Jeffrey, S .... 517-437-7341. 243 I
jeff.lantis@hillsdale.edu
LANTZ, Dona .... 215-568-4012. 424 D
dlantz@moore.edu
LANTZ, Glen .... 563-588-6784. 176 F
glen.lantz@clarke.edu
LANTZ, James, D .... 989-328-1220. 247 D
jlantz@montcalm.edu
LANTZ, Mary Jan .... 409-944-1281. 472 I
mlantz@gc.edu
LANTZ, Melody .... 423-746-5327. 462 C
mlantz@twcnet.edu
LANTZ, Susan, L .... 570-577-1601. 411 A
susan.lantz@bucknell.edu
LANTZY, Robert .... 719-638-6580... 81 K
rlantzy@cci.edu
LANZA-KADUCE, Linda .. 352-395-5493. 113 C
linda.lanza-kaduce@sfcollege.edu
LANZALACO, Joseph, M 585-385-8367. 338 H
jlanzalaco@sjfc.edu
LANZI, Lesley .... 518-736-3622. 325 A
lesley.lanzi@fmcc.suny.edu
LANZILLO, Lee-Ann .... 617-349-8875. 228 B
llanzill@lesley.edu
LANZILLO, Susan .... 508-626-4534. 230 A
slanzillo@framingham.edu
LANZILOTTI, Salvatore ... 808-734-9520. 136 E
ssl@hawaii.edu
LAOS, Joel .... 303-762-6903... 81 G
joel.laos@denverseminary.edu
LAP, James .... 718-260-5565. 319 B
jlap@citytech.cuny.edu
LAPAGLIA, Karen .... 814-838-7673. 416 G
klapaglia@fortisinstitute.edu
LAPALOMBARA,
Catherine .... 301-322-0414. 217 F
lapalocx@pgcc.edu
LAPARY, Allison .... 202-495-3820... 96 C
assistant@dhs.edu
LAPENNA, Alan, G .... 860-444-8322. 545 G
Alan.G.Lapenna@uscg.mil
LAPENTA, Thomas .... 302-831-8306... 94 B
lapenta@udel.edu
LAPERUTA, Domenick .... 718-960-8593. 318 A
domenick.laperuta@lehman.cuny.edu
LAPETINO, Kelly .... 815-740-3384. 162 F
klapetino@stfrancis.edu
LAPHAM, Steve .... 301-891-4161. 221 B
slapham@wau.edu
LAPIDUS, Chaim, D .... 410-484-7200. 217 D
cdl@nirc.edu
LAPIDUS, Richard, S .... 909-869-2400... 32 G
rslapidus@csupomona.edu
LAPIER, Terry .... 561-381-4990... 99 F
LAPIERRE, Jonathan .... 617-879-2427. 238 C
jlapierre@wheelock.edu
LAPIKAS, Sonya, L .... 724-589-2172. 434 B
slapikas@thiel.edu
LAPINSKAS, Connie, L ... 765-494-7537. 171 M
clapinsk@purdue.edu
LAPINSKI, Jason .... 216-373-6352. 385 G
jlapinski@ndc.edu
LAPLACE, Bobbi .... 412-536-1087. 420 A
bobbi.laplace@laroche.edu
LAPLANT, James, T .... 229-333-5694. 134 B
jtlaplant@valdosta.edu
LAPLANTE, Brian .... 518-445-2381. 313 C
blapl@albanylaw.edu
LAPLANTE, Glenn .... 802-287-8236. 499 D
laplanteg@greenmtn.edu
LAPLANTE, Kim .... 920-498-5487. 541 B
kim.laplante@nwtc.edu
LAPLANTE, Larry .... 207-768-2707. 210 M
llaplante@nmcc.edu
LAPOINTE, Gregory .... 207-621-3240. 212 C
glapointe@maine.edu
LAPOINTE, Laurence .... 860-465-5113... 87 L
lapointel@easternct.edu
LAPOINTE, Michael .... 219-980-7106. 168 B
mslapoin@iun.edu
LAPOLT, Philip .... 323-343-3810... 34 A
plapolt@calstatela.edu
LAPORTE, Laura .... 518-736-3622. 325 A
llporte@fmcc.suny.edu
LAPORTE, Sandra .... 312-567-5199. 147 F
laporte@iit.edu
LAPOS, Christopher .... 570-389-4740. 427 H
clapos@bloomu.edu
LAPP, Katherine, N .... 617-495-9877. 227 C
katie_lapp@harvard.edu
LAPPLE, James, H .... 212-327-8371. 338 A
james.lapple@rockefeller.edu
LAPRADE, Kimberly .... 602-639-7500... 13 S
LAPRADE, Susan .... 508-854-4368. 232 F
slaprade@qcc.mass.edu

LAPREZIOSA, Mark .... 215-572-2833. 409 H laprezim@arcadia.edu
LAPRISE, John, P .... 423-585-6882. 462 A john.laprise@ws.edu
LAQUEY, Karen .... 806-291-3526. 494 F laqueyk@wbu.edu
LARA, Cynthia .... 210-999-8290. 488 C clara@trinity.edu
LARA, Ernest .... 623-935-8010... 14 K ernie.lara@estrellamountain.edu
LARA, Helen .... 213-613-2200... 67 E helen_lara@sciarc.edu
LARA, Jessika .... 214-379-5494. 478 D jlara@pqc.edu
LARCOM, Geoffrey .... 734-487-4400. 242 D glarcom@emich.edu
LARD, Carter .... 718-270-1133. 342 D clard@downstate.edu
LAREAU, Joel .... 417-447-7551. 279 K lareauj@otc.edu
LAREAU, Martin .... 708-596-2000. 159 C mlareau@ssc.edu
LAREY, Keith, L .... 903-813-2431. 466 H klarey@austincollege.edu
LARGE, Donald, L .... 334-844-4650..... 1 G largedl@auburn.edu
LARGE, Ron .... 509-313-6767. 520 A large@gonzaga.edu
LARGENT, Liz .... 405-682-7834. 397 E llargent@occc.edu
LARGENT, Michael .... 205-329-7945..... 3 B mike.largent@ecacolleges.com
LARGENT, Trudy .... 510-466-7296... 59 D tlargent@peralta.edu
LARGENT, Trudy .... 510-466-7252... 59 A tlargent@peralta.edu
LARIA, Miriam .... 201-200-3484. 303 F mlaria@njcu.edu
LARICK, Duane, K .... 919-515-2196. 368 B duane_larick@ncsu.edu
LARIMORE, James, A ..... 413-542-2337. 221 G deanstudents@amherst.edu
LARIOS, Jose .... 706-245-7226. 124 D jlarios@ec.edu
LARIOS, Liza .... 718-631-6356. 319 D llarios@qcc.cuny.edu
LARK, Catherine .... 603-646-2441. 296 G catherine.lark@dartmouth.edu
LARKAN-SKINNER, Kara 210-434-6711. 477 N klarkan-skinner@lake.ollusa.edu
LARKIN, Bob .... 775-770-2528... 18 I robert.larkin@phoenix.edu
LARKIN, Conal .... 203-575-8173... 89 B clarkin@nvcc.commnet.edu
LARKIN, Earlene .... 334-876-9394..... 4 A earlene.larkin@wccs.edu
LARKIN, Jon .... 541-962-3740. 405 H jlarkin@eou.edu
LARKIN, Josh .... 802-828-2835. 501 C josh.larkin@ccv.edu
LARKIN, Kim .... 813-879-6000. 103 B klarkin@cci.edu
LARKIN, Linda .... 860-515-3841... 87 I llarkin@charteroak.edu
LARKIN, Linda .... 716-338-1125. 327 J lindalarkin@mail.sunyjcc.edu
LARKIN, SSJ, Mary Josephine .... 215-248-7055. 413 A mjlarkin@chc.edu
LARKIN, Michael, F .... 512-448-8452. 479 C michaell@stedwards.edu
LARKIN, Patti .... 619-482-6325... 68 B plarkin@swccd.edu
LARKIN, Thomas, F .... 413-748-3458. 236 I tlarkin@springfieldcollege.edu
LARKIN, Willie .... 443-885-3035. 217 A willie.larkin@morgan.edu
LARKIN-BEENE, Bridgett 815-280-2476. 149 A blarkin@jjc.edu
LARKINS, Wendolyn .... 404-237-7573. 121 F wlarkins@kaplan.edu
LARNER, Eve .... 914-606-6562. 350 F Eve.Larner@sunywcc.edu
LAROBINA, Michael, D .. 203-371-7859... 91 C larobinam@sacredheart.edu
LAROCCA MEYER, Theresa .... 718-940-5820. 339 B tlaroccameyer@sjcny.edu
LAROCHELLE, Josee .... 408-924-1550... 36 A josee.larochelle@sjsu.edu
LAROCHELLE, Therese .... 603-897-8241. 297 F tlarochelle@rivier.edu
LAROCK, J.D .... 617-373-2101. 235 F
LAROCQUE, Monique ..... 207-780-5422. 212 H mlarocque@usm.maine.edu
LAROCQUE, Sandra .... 701-477-7862. 373 B salrocqu@tm.edu
LAROSA, Angela .... 607-778-5187. 315 I larosaam@sunybroome.edu
LAROSA, George, P .... 631-420-2170. 346 B larosa@farmingdale.edu
LAROSE, Patrick, S .... 828-398-2566. 366 G plarose@southcollegenc.edu
LAROSEE, Howie .... 617-879-7938. 230 B hlarosee@massart.edu
LARRABEE, Kate .... 607-274-1082. 327 E klarrabee@ithaca.edu
LARRAT, Paul .... 401-874-5011. 440 D larrat@uri.edu
LARSEN, Carl .... 423-636-7313. 462 E clarsen@tusculum.edu
LARSEN, Chris .... 417-690-2373. 272 E larsen@cofo.edu
LARSEN, Christian, P ..... 404-727-5631. 124 E clarsen@emory.edu
LARSEN, Dianna .... 360-475-7208. 521 H
LARSEN, Erin .... 651-423-8433. 258 D erin.larsen@dctc.edu
LARSEN, Geri .... 410-532-5866. 217 E glarsen@ndm.edu
LARSEN, Jacque .... 208-524-3000. 138 D jacque.larsen@my.eitc.edu
LARSEN, Jacque .... 540-423-9050. 512 E jlarsen@germanna.edu
LARSEN, Jay, A .... 605-688-4695. 452 B jay.larsen@sdstate.edu
LARSEN, Jennifer .... 402-559-4837. 292 J jlarsen@unmc.edu
LARSEN, Jon-Erik .... 503-352-7221. 407 A larsenj@pacificu.edu
LARSEN, Juliana, P .... 801-626-6459. 497 D jlarsen@weber.edu
LARSEN, Katrina .... 715-425-3350. 537 E katrina.larsen@uwrf.edu
LARSEN, Kerstin .... 609-258-9289. 304 E klarsen@princeton.edu
LARSEN, Kevin, W .... 252-334-2009. 357 A kevin.larsen@macuniversity.edu
LARSEN, Kevin, W .... 252-334-2044. 357 A kevin.larsen@macuniversity.edu
LARSEN, Kristina, L .... 858-534-3133... 71 F klarseni@ucsd.edu
LARSEN, Lauralyn .... 707-778-3930... 65 B llarsen@santaorsa.edu
LARSEN, Naomi .... 865-471-3471. 453 F nlarsen@cn.edu
LARSEN, Philip .... 727-726-1153. 100 E phillarsen@clearwater.edu
LARSEN, Rance .... 218-477-2549. 259 H rance.larsen@mnstate.edu
LARSEN, III, Randolph, K .... 240-895-4597. 218 A rklarsen@smcm.edu
LARSEN, Robert .... 507-537-7150. 261 F Robert.Larsen@smsu.edu
LARSEN, Ron .... 406-994-4371. 287 B ronl@montana.edu
LARSEN, Ronald .... 406-994-3790. 287 B ronl@montana.edu
LARSEN, Ronald, L .... 412-624-5139. 435 C rlarsen@pitt.edu
LARSEN, Susan .... 435-283-7317. 498 A susan.larsen@snow.edu
LARSEN, Whitney .... 540-261-8530. 509 K whitney.larsen@svu.edu
LARSON, Ann .... 513-529-5040. 384 G ann.larson@miamioh.edu
LARSON, Barb .... 308-398-7359. 288 I blarson@cccneb.edu
LARSON, Barbara .... 813-253-7015. 106 M blarson2@hccfl.edu
LARSON, Bruce, R .... 507-284-8541. 254 F larson.bruce@mayo.edu
LARSON, Carol .... 434-961-6546. 513 F clarson@pvcc.edu
LARSON, Craig .... 763-424-0733. 260 C clarson@nhcc.edu
LARSON, Cynthia .... 619-261-7245... 28 M clarson-daugherty@argosy.edu
LARSON, Dale, C .... 214-887-5021. 471 F dlarson@dts.edu
LARSON, Daniel .... 302-857-1595... 93 D dlarson@dtcc.edu
LARSON, Daniel, J .... 814-865-9591. 426 A djl18@psu.edu
LARSON, Daniel, L .... 309-341-7492. 150 A dlarson2@knox.edu
LARSON, Debra .... 618-537-6816. 152 G dlarson@mckendree.edu
LARSON, Debra .... 805-756-2131... 32 F dslarson@calpoly.edu
LARSON, Don, A .... 858-534-0386... 71 F dlarson@ucsd.edu
LARSON, Donna .... 503-338-2440. 402 G dlarson@clatsopcc.edu
LARSON, Doreen, M .... 304-367-4933. 528 E Doreen.Larson@pierpont.edu
LARSON, Gary, N .... 630-752-5990. 163 F gary.larson@wheaton.edu
LARSON, Gayle .... 651-423-8395. 258 D gayle.larson@dctc.edu
LARSON, Gloria, C .... 781-891-2101. 223 C glarson@bentley.edu
LARSON, Jennifer .... 701-845-7401. 372 A jennifer.larson@vcsu.edu
LARSON, Jon, H .... 732-255-0330. 304 A jlarson@ocean.edu
LARSON, Joyce .... 603-535-2806. 298 G jlarson@plymouth.edu
LARSON, Kalynn .... 435-652-7535. 497 E larson@dixie.edu
LARSON, Kent, D .... 208-282-2981. 138 E larskent@isu.edu
LARSON, Kristin .... 906-635-2453. 245 G klarsen1@lssu.edu
LARSON, Lisa .... 763-424-0820. 260 C llarson@nhcc.edu
LARSON, Lisa, M .... 319-895-4219. 177 A llarson@cornellcollege.edu
LARSON, Lois .... 651-793-1414. 259 C lois.larson@metrostate.edu
LARSON, Matthew .... 860-486-2616... 92 A matthew.larson@uconn.edu
LARSON, Melanie .... 617-243-2050. 227 K mlarson@lasell.edu
LARSON, Melinda .... 509-777-4392. 525 F mlarson@whitworth.edu
LARSON, Mike .... 515-244-4221. 175 C larsonm@aib.edu
LARSON, Nathan .... 303-300-8740... 78 M nathan.larson@collegeamerica.edu
LARSON, Paul, V .... 805-565-6286... 76 D plarson@westmont.edu
LARSON, Rick .... 952-446-4190. 255 D larsonr@crown.edu
LARSON, Rob, K .... 563-387-1568. 180 M larsro01@luther.edu
LARSON, Rodney .... 207-941-7122. 210 B larsonr@husson.edu
LARSON, Sandy .... 229-931-2450. 131 G slarson@southgatech.edu
LARSON, Shane .... 618-545-3146. 149 D slarson@kaskaskia.edu
LARSON, Steve .... 406-756-3821. 286 B slarson@fvcc.edu
LARSON, Steve, M .... 316-978-6612. 191 F steve.larson@wichita.edu
LARSON, Susan .... 913-971-3698. 188 H slarson@mnu.edu
LARSON, Susan .... 706-355-5034. 120 J slarson@athenstech.edu
LARSON, Susan .... 575-562-2211. 309 H susan.larson@enmu.edu
LARSON, Thomas, R .... 423-652-4765. 455 I trlarson@king.edu
LARSON, Trina .... 480-732-7222... 14 J trina.larson@cgc.edu
LARSON, Vernon, C .... 607-436-3369. 343 E vernon.larson@oneonta.edu
LARSON-COONEY, Kim .. 303-797-5723... 78 F kim.larson-cooney@arapahoe.edu
LARSON-DIAZ, Mary .... 913-344-6090. 184 C mary.larsondiaz@bakeru.edu
LARTEY, Charles, R .... 330-471-8469. 383 D clartey@malone.edu
LARUE, Carol .... 830-591-7324. 481 C cllarue@swtjc.edu
LARUE, Clint .... 405-425-5191. 397 D clint.larue@oc.edu
LARUE, Rita .... 215-895-1534. 415 B larue@drexel.edu
LARUE, Shanda .... 270-686-4252. 192 G shanda.larue@brescia.edu
LARVICK, Steve .... 541-552-6594. 406 C larvick@sou.edu
LASALDE DOMINICCI, José, A .... 787-250-0000. 553 G jose.lasalde@upr.edu
LASALDE-DOMINICCI, José, A .... 787-250-0000. 553 G jose.lasalde@upr.edu
LASALLE, Patti .... 214-768-7660. 481 A plasalle@smu.edu
LASANEN, Raymond, E .. 906-487-2510. 247 A relasane@mtu.edu
LASANTA, Miriam .... 787-850-9345. 554 D mirian.lasanta@upr.edu
LASCANO, Rey .... 432-552-2108. 493 D lascano_r@utpb.edu
LASCEK-SPEAKMAN, Natalie .... 717-396-7833. 427 A nlascek@pcad.edu
LASCH, Jacqueline, D ..... 407-582-3302. 118 M jlasch@valenciacollege.edu
LASCHER, Ted .... 916-278-6504... 34 D tedl@csus.edu
LASER KIGER, Amy .... 540-234-9261. 511 H kigera@brcc.edu
LASEY, Brian .... 479-968-0261... 20 E blasey@atu.edu
LASH, Gail, D .... 937-708-5734. 393 A glash@wilberforce.edu
LASH, Jeff .... 330-494-6170. 389 F jlash@starkstate.edu
LASH, Jonathan .... 413-559-5521. 227 B president@hampshire.edu
LASH, Julie .... 317-274-2548. 168 D jlash@iupui.edu
LASHAWAY, Robert, V ... 406-994-2001. 287 B rvl@facilities.montana.edu
LASHBROOK, Jeffrey, T . 585-395-5028. 342 F jlashbro@brockport.edu
LASHER, John .... 315-792-7265. 346 C john.lasher@sunyit.edu
LASHER, Katherine, M .... 989-774-3253. 240 N lashe1km@cmich.edu
LASHER, Robert, W .... 603-646-3095. 296 G robert.w.lasher@dartmouth.edu
LASHIN-CUREWITZ, Sandy .... 508-373-9529. 223 A sandy.curewitz@becker.edu
LASHLEY, Bob .... 405-425-5120. 397 D bob.lashley@oc.edu
LASHLEY, Brian, R .... 860-465-5306... 87 L lashleyb@easternct.edu
LASHLEY, Edwin, L .... 410-543-6007. 220 D ellashley@salisbury.edu
LASHLEY, Jeffery .... 660-263-4110. 279 B jeffl@macc.edu
LASHLEY, Kent .... 405-733-7490. 399 F klashley@rose.edu
LASHLEY, Marsha .... 660-831-4115. 278 I lashleym@moval.edu
LASHLEY, Sarah, E .... 859-238-5573. 193 E sarah.lashley@centre.edu
LASHURE, Faith .... 630-466-7900. 162 J flashure@waubonsee.edu
LASICH, Deb .... 303-273-3097... 80 E dlasich@mines.edu
LASIEWSKI, Doreen .... 401-739-5000. 439 D dlasiewski@neit.edu
LASITER, Paul, B .... 310-506-4497... 58 H paul.lasiter@pepperdine.edu
LASKA-NIXON, Diane ..... 508-767-7026. 222 C dlaska@assumption.edu
LASKARIS, Maria .... 603-646-2604. 296 G maria.laskaris@dartmouth.edu
LASKARIS, Theodore .... 802-860-2757. 499 A tlaskaris@champlain.edu
LASKE, Lori, L .... 719-587-7867... 78 B lllaske@adams.edu
LASKER, Y. Mayer .... 718-377-0777. 336 I
LASKOWSKI-SACHNOFF, Marilyn .... 732-906-2502. 303 B MLaskowski-Sachnoff@middlesexcc.edu
LASKY, Melodee, S .... 848-932-9064. 306 A mlasky@echo.rutgers.edu
LASLEY, Roger .... 507-222-4289. 254 D rlasley@carleton.edu
LASLEY, Steven, T .... 615-460-6404. 453 C steve.lasley@belmont.edu
LASSEN, Gregg .... 504-280-6207. 205 G glassen@uno.edu
LASSILA, Deborah, L ...... 906-487-3112. 247 A dlassila@mtu.edu
LASSITER, Colleen .... 706-233-7337. 131 E classiter@shorter.edu
LASSITER, Donald, L ...... 910-630-7081. 356 H lassiter@methodist.edu
LASSITER, Fred .... 614-251-4513. 386 B lassitef@ohiodominican.edu
LASSITER, Jack .... 870-460-1020... 24 D lassiter@uamont.edu
LASSITER, John .... 706-295-6511. 125 F jlassiter@gntc.edu
LASSITER, Pamela .... 203-392-5491... 88 A lassiterp1@southernct.edu
LASSITER, Pamela .... 920-424-0330. 537 B lassitep@uwosh.edu
LASSITER, JR., Wright, L .... 214-378-1601. 470 F wlassiter@dcccd.edu
LASSLEY, Joan, K .... 559-323-2100... 63 B jlassley@sjcl.edu
LASSNER, David, K .... 808-956-3501. 135 L david@hawaii.edu
LASSNER, Jennifer .... 319-335-2123. 175 I jennifer-lassner@uiowa.edu
LASTER, Jill, L .... 817-257-7790. 484 I j.laster@tcu.edu
LASTINGER, Michael ...... 304-293-6955. 530 D michael.lastinger@mail.wvu.edu
LASTORIA, Michael, D ... 585-567-9622. 326 F michael.lastoria@houghton.edu
LASTRA, Sarai .... 787-743-7979. 552 I ut_slastra@suagm.edu
LASURE, Keith .... 864-941-8687. 446 C lasure.k@ptc.edu
LATANE, Jane .... 520-383-8401... 18 B jlatane@tocc.cc.az.us
LATCHAW HIRSH, Sharon .... 610-527-0200. 432 B shirsh@rosemont.edu

LATCHUM, Lucy, L ... 757-594-7702. 503 M
llatchum@cnu.edu
LATCOVICH, Mark, A ... 440-943-7600. 388 J
mal@dioceseofcleveland.org
LATEER, Deborah ... 805-652-5539... 74 E
dlateer@vcccd.edu
LATERRA BELLINO,
Frank ... 718-940-5852. 339 B
flaterra@sjcny.edu
LATHAM, Adrienne ... 615-329-8632. 454 F
alatham@fisk.edu
LATHAM, Amy ... 662-562-3201. 269 C
a_latham@northwestms.edu
LATHAM, Angela ... 708-534-4376. 145 F
alatham@govst.edu
LATHAM, Brenda ... 209-381-6410... 54 D
latham.b@mccd.edu
LATHAM, Clara ... 940-397-4757. 476 H
clara.latham@mwsu.edu
LATHAM, Eric ... 937-484-1346. 392 C
elatham@urbana.edu
LATHAM, Karen, K ... 701-323-6734. 372 I
karen.latham@sanfordcollege.edu
LATHAM, Linda, H ... 334-734-7582. 360 E
llatham@forsythtech.edu
LATHAM, Marilae ... 618-664-7110. 145 G
marilae.latham@greenville.edu
LATHAM, Mark ... 912-260-4300. 131 F
mark.latham@sgsc.edu
LATHAM, Mark ... 802-831-1327. 500 H
mlatham@vermontlaw.edu
LATHAM, Michael ... 718-817-4700. 324 G
latham@fordham.edu
LATHAM, Mike ... 252-443-4011. 362 D
mlatham@nashcc.edu
LATHAM, Sarah ... 831-459-3778... 72 C
sclatham@ucsc.edu
LATHAM, Sheila ... 701-858-4145. 371 F
sheila.latham@minotstateu.edu
LATHAM, Tricia ... 580-477-7725. 401 J
tricia.latham@wosc.edu
LATHROP, Alison, S ... 802-626-6497. 501 E
alison.lathrop@lyndonstate.edu
LATHROP, Sam ... 217-228-5432. 156 C
lathrsa@quincy.edu
LATIF, Niaz ... 219-989-3251. 171 N
nlatif@purduecal.edu
LATIGO, Ben ... 603-577-6610. 296 F
blatigo@dwc.edu
LATIMER, Dewana ... 731-425-2624. 460 G
dlatimer@jscc.edu
LATIMER, Loretta ... 904-470-8100. 102 A
m.latimer@ewc.edu
LATIMER, Tanisha ... 864-941-8363. 446 C
latimer.t@ptc.edu
LATIMORE, Debra ... 919-546-8223. 366 E
dlatimore@shawu.edu
LATIMORE, Leatrice, D ... 504-284-5435. 206 K
llatimor@suno.edu
LATIMORE, Nancy, J ... 717-361-1407. 415 H
latimonj@etown.edu
LATIN, Quinton ... 903-730-4890. 474 O
quinton.latin@jarvis.edu
LATINO, Jennifer, A ... 910-814-5577. 352 K
latinoj@campbell.edu
LATINVILLE, Darlene ... 213-624-1200... 44 D
dlatinville@fidm.edu
LATIOLAIS, Perry ... 281-487-1170. 484 H
platiolais@txchiro.edu
LATIOLAIS, Scott ... 425-235-2409. 522 F
slatiolais@rtc.edu
LATORELLA, Jacqueline ... 813-253-6219. 118 L
jlatorella@ut.edu
LATORRE, Daria ... 610-796-8264. 409 E
daria.latorre@alvernia.edu
LATORRE, Luis ... 787-738-2161. 554 C
luis.latorre1@upr.edu
LATORTUE, Paul ... 787-751-7410. 555 B
prlatortue@aol.com
LATOUF, Christina ... 646-660-6114. 316 J
Christina.Latouf@baruch.cuny.edu
LATOUR, Bill ... 217-641-4290. 148 M
blatour@jwcc.edu
LATOUR, Mickey, A ... 618-453-2469. 159 G
mlatour@siu.edu
LATOUR, Terry, S ... 814-393-2343. 428 C
tlatour@clarion.edu
LATSHAW, Todd, M ... 717-867-6330. 421 H
latshaw@lvc.edu
LATTA, Bruce, J ... 410-293-1801. 545 J
latta@usna.edu
LATTA, Dionne ... 909-558-4567... 51 C
sm8026@BNcollege.com
LATTA, Mark, A ... 402-280-2860. 289 D
marklatta@creighton.edu
LATTA, Michael ... 812-877-8975. 172 C
michael.latta@rose-hulman.edu
LATTA, Stanley ... 814-865-5423. 426 A
sxl1@psu.edu
LATTEN, Erin ... 507-453-1462. 259 E
elatten@southeastmn.edu
LATTER, Deborah ... 863-784-7251. 113 G
latterd@southflorida.edu
LATTER, George ... 619-849-2317... 59 L
georgelatter@pointloma.edu
LATTER, Gerald ... 212-327-8925. 338 A
latter@rockefeller.edu
LATTIMORE, Dan, L ... 901-678-2991. 460 B
dlattimr@memphis.edu
LATTIMORE, John ... 704-669-4020. 359 D
lattimorej@clevelandcc.edu
LATTIMORE, Mark ... 478-825-6296. 124 H
lattimorem@fvsu.edu
LATTIMORE, Michael, P . 973-353-1670. 306 D
mikelatt@andromeda.rutgers.edu
LATTIMORE, Vergel, L ... 704-636-6823. 355 D
vlattiimore@hoodseminary.edu
LATTING, John ... 404-727-6036. 124 E
john.latting@emory.edu
LATUSZEK, Doty, A ... 260-422-5561. 167 B
dalatuszek@indianatech.edu
LATVIS, Mike ... 313-436-9152. 251 D
latvism@umich.edu
LATZ, Gil ... 317-278-1265. 168 D
glatz@iupui.edu
LAU, Allison ... 206-878-3710. 520 E
alau@highline.edu
LAU, Bradley, A ... 503-554-2312. 403 C
blau@georgefox.edu
LAU, Jason ... 415-485-9316... 40 G
jason.lau@marin.edu
LAU, John ... 760-355-6235... 48 A
john.lau@imperial.edu
LAU, Kimberly ... 831-459-2418... 72 C
lau@ucsc.edu
LAU, Lawrence ... 310-577-3000... 77 G
lau@yosan.edu
LAU, Stuart ... 808-956-8010. 136 B
stuartl@hawaii.edu
LAUB, David, J ... 513-875-3344. 376 H
dave.laub@chatfield.edu
LAUB, James, A ... 561-803-2302. 110 B
james_laub@pba.edu
LAUB, Jeffrey, W ... 434-832-7707. 512 A
laubj@cvcc.vccs.edu
LAUB, Joe ... 212-484-1108. 318 D
jlaub@jjay.cuny.edu
LAUB, Marty ... 312-935-4245. 148 C
LAUBAUCH, Harold ... 954-262-1303. 109 K
harold@nova.edu
LAUBE, Irene, H ... 919-536-7211. 360 B
laubei@durhamtech.edu
LAUBE, Philip ... 740-826-8101. 384 L
plaube@muskingum.edu
LAUBERSHEIMER,
David, E ... 217-786-2240. 151 F
david.laubersheimer@llcc.edu
LAUDADIO, John ... 858-695-8587... 47 L
jlaudadio@horizonuniversity.edu
LAUDE, David, A ... 512-232-3317. 491 C
dalaude@austin.utexas.edu
LAUDER, Frank ... 617-873-0137. 224 G
finaid@cambridgecollege.edu
LAUDER, Sue, M ... 978-665-3313. 229 E
slauder@fitchburgstate.edu
LAUDERBACK, Cindy ... 360-417-6233. 522 A
clauderback@pencol.edu
LAUDERDALE, Wendy ... 985-549-5544. 208 C
wlauderdale@selu.edu
LAUER, Andrew, J ... 212-790-0310. 351 M
andrewlauer@yu.edu
LAUER, Bonnie ... 570-740-0734. 422 G
blauer@luzerne.edu
LAUER, Brenda ... 719-502-2403... 84 A
brenda.lauer@ppcc.edu
LAUER, John ... 719-389-6618... 79 D
jlauer@coloradocollege.edu
LAUER, Jonathan, D ... 717-766-2511. 423 L
jlauer@messiah.edu
LAUER, Larry, D ... 817-257-7808. 484 I
l.lauer@tcu.edu
LAUER, Theresa ... 909-607-2760... 46 H
theresa_lauer@hmc.edu
LAUERMAN, Meg ... 402-472-0088. 292 I
mlauerman1@unl.edu
LAUFENBERG, Helen ... 608-822-2308. 541 C
hlaufenberg@swtc.edu
LAUFER, Marilyn ... 334-844-1486..... 1 G
laufema@auburn.edu
LAUFFENBURGER,
Linda, M ... 937-327-7811. 393 E
llauffenburger@wittenberg.edu
LAUGEL, JoAnn, E ... 812-488-2364. 173 H
jl25@evansville.edu
LAUGHLIN, Ed ... 978-478-3400. 235 G
elaughlin@northpoint.edu
LAUGHLIN, Frederick, L . 231-995-1197. 248 B
flaughlin@nmc.edu
LAUGHLIN, Janet ... 434-791-5630. 502 D
jlaughlin@averett.edu
LAUGHLIN, Judith ... 724-938-4430. 428 A
laughlin@calu.edu
LAUGHLIN, Karen, L ... 850-644-2740. 115 C
klaughlin@admin.fsu.edu
LAUGHLIN, Lynn ... 217-732-3168. 151 B
llaughli@lincolnchristian.edu
LAUGHLIN, Patricia ... 312-567-3827. 147 F
plaughli@iit.edu
LAUGHLIN, Ronda ... 360-752-8334. 517 B
rlaughlin@btc.ctc.edu
LAUGHLIN, Russ ... 817-202-6462. 481 E
laughlinr@swau.edu
LAUGHLIN, Sherry ... 601-318-6170. 270 I
slaughlin@wmcarey.edu
LAUGHRAN, Patrick ... 508-626-4357. 230 A
plaughran@framingham.edu
LAUGHREY, James, C ... 202-231-3351. 544 L
james.laughrey@dodiis.mil
LAUGHTER, Ray ... 832-813-6621. 476 A
ray.laughter@lonestar.edu
LAUGHTON, John ... 609-771-2278. 300 E
jlaughto@tcnj.edu
LAUINGER, Curt ... 605-394-4034. 452 E
curt.lauinger@wdt.edu
LAUNIUS, Michael ... 509-963-3612. 517 F
launiusm@cwu.edu
LAURANZON,
Anne Marie ... 804-752-7317. 508 E
alauranz@rmc.edu
LAURENCE, David ... 928-776-7666... 19 H
david.laurence@yc.edu
LAURENT, Joyce ... 574-807-7233. 164 D
laurenj@bethelcollege.edu
LAURENT, Timothy ... 406-791-5302. 288 E
tlaurent01@ugf.edu
LAURENZ, Jamie ... 575-562-2312. 309 H
jamie.laurenz@enmu.edu
LAURENZI, Kellie, L ... 412-397-5201. 431 I
laurenzi@rmu.edu
LAURETANO, Angela ... 914-632-5400. 331 K
alauretano@monroecollege.edu
LAURIA, Dorothy, M ... 203-582-8258... 91 A
dorothy.lauria@quinnipiac.edu
LAURIA, James ... 412-809-5100. 430 H
lauria.james@pti.edu
LAURIE, Sean ... 516-323-4820. 331 J
slaurie@molloy.edu
LAURIN, Janet ... 714-533-3946... 36 C
jlaurin@calums.edu
LAURITZEN, Rhonda ... 801-627-8388. 496 D
lauritzr@owatc.edu
LAUSCH, Mark, C ... 608-243-4508. 540 C
mlausch@madisoncollege.edu
LAUSELL, Ana, C ... 787-891-0925. 549 K
amelon@aguadilla.inter.edu
LAUX, Carolyn ... 850-729-5360. 109 I
lauxc@nwfsc.edu
LAUX, Dan ... 402-461-7301. 289 I
dlaux@hastings.edu
LAUZON CLABO, Laurie 617-643-0605. 234 B
llauzonclabo@mghihp.edu
LAVALLÉE-WELCH,
Catherine ... 608-785-8805. 536 G
clavallee-welch@uwlax.edu
LAVALLA, Daniel, N ... 215-368-5000. 410 F
dlavalla@biblical.edu
LAVANIA, Ambrish ... 803-793-5263. 443 E
lavaniaa@denmarktech.edu
LAVELLE, Helen ... 312-942-2030. 157 G
helen_lavelle@rush.edu
LAVELLI, Lucinda ... 352-392-0207. 116 A
llavelli@arts.ufl.edu
LAVENDER, Earl ... 615-966-5834. 456 B
earl.lavender@lipscomb.edu
LAVENDER, Julie ... 989-275-5000. 245 B
julie.lavender@kirtland.edu
LAVENDER, Laryssa ... 217-228-5432. 156 C
lavenla@quincy.edu
LAVENDER, Melissa ... 850-747-3211. 106 H
mlavender@gulfcoast.edu
LAVENDER, Michael, K ... 828-652-0681. 362 A
michaell@mcdowelltech.edu
LAVERNIA, Enrique, J ... 530-752-0554... 70 J
lavernia@ucdavis.edu
LAVERRIERE, Robert, J ... 937-255-6234. 544 C
robert.laverriere@afit.edu
LAVERY, Jim ... 740-389-4636. 383 F
laveryj@mtc.edu
LAVERY, Roger ... 765-285-6000. 164 B
rlavery@bsu.edu
LAVES, Beth ... 270-745-1900. 200 G
beth.laves@wku.edu
LAVIAL, Pierre ... 772-466-4822... 98 L
pierre.lavial@aviator.edu
LAVIGNA, Lisa ... 518-608-8252. 324 B
llavigna@excelsior.edu
LAVIGNA, Robert ... 608-890-3888. 536 D
rlavigna@ohr.wisc.edu
LAVIGNE, JR., F. Travis 985-448-7909. 203 B
travis.lavigne@fletcher.edu
LAVIGNE, Robert, W ... 508-213-2217. 235 E
robert.lavigne@nichols.edu
LAVIN, Marjorie, W ... 518-587-2100. 346 A
marjorie.lavin@esc.edu
LAVIN, Thomas, J ... 401-456-8094. 439 F
tlavin@ric.edu
LAVINE, Danielle ... 860-509-9511... 90 B
dlavine@hartsem.edu
LAVINE, Danielle, R ... 207-942-6781. 209 E
dlavine@bts.edu
LAVINE, Steven, D ... 661-255-1050... 31 C
slavine@calarts.edu
LAVIOLETTE, Marc ... 239-590-7891. 115 A
mlaviole@fgcu.edu
LAVIT, Daniel, A ... 270-809-2160. 198 B
dlavit@murraystate.edu
LAVITT, Melissa ... 208-426-3776. 137 G
melissalavitt@boisestate.edu
LAVNER, Lilly ... 610-896-1228. 418 F
llavner@haverford.edu
LAVOIE, Chuck ... 802-468-1250. 501 B
chuck.lavoie@castleton.edu
LAVOIE, Lisa ... 860-255-3805... 89 G
LAVOIE, Rocky ... 541-888-7425. 407 H
rlavoie@socc.edu
LAVORATA, Christina, M 304-367-4101. 529 F
Chris.Lavorata@fairmontstate.edu
LAW, John ... 413-236-3001. 231 A
jlaw@berkshirecc.edu
LAW, John, W ... 630-844-5438. 140 A
jlaw@aurora.edu
LAW, Nancy ... 903-983-8101. 475 E
nlaw@kilgore.edu
LAW, William, D ... 727-341-3241. 112 E
law.bill@spcollege.edu
LAW, William, R ... 219-989-2468. 171 N
William.Law@purduecal.edu
LAWERENCE, Gail ... 325-235-7333. 485 G
gail.lawerence@sweetwater.tstc.edu
LAWERENCE, JR.,
Kenneth ... 215-204-4455. 433 K
kenneth.lawrence@temple.edu
LAWHON, John ... 940-898-3250. 488 B
jlawhon@twu.edu
LAWHON, R. Lynn ... 864-488-8277. 444 L
llawhon@limestone.edu
LAWHON, William ... 941-487-4323. 115 D
wlawhon@ncf.edu
LAWHORN, Janice ... 928-428-8509... 13 J
janice.lawhorn@eac.edu
LAWHORNE, Sara ... 205-552-1284..... 3 B
sara.lawhorne@ecacolleges.com
LAWING, Kim ... 910-362-7003. 358 F
klawing@cfcc.edu
LAWING, Martha, A ... 603-862-2053. 298 C
anne.lawing@unh.edu
LAWLER, Greg ... 805-966-3888... 30 A
glawler@brooks.edu
LAWLER, Hannah ... 310-434-3472... 65 A
lawler_hannah@smc.edu
LAWLER, Nicola ... 256-761-6207..... 7 F
Nllawler@talladega.edu
LAWLESS, Daniel, M ... 843-349-2021. 442 E
dan@coastal.edu
LAWLESS, J. Alan ... 918-343-7715. 399 C
alawless@rsu.edu
LAWLESS, Richard ... 516-572-7317. 332 C
richard.lawless@ncc.edu
LAWLIS, Philip, J ... 717-796-5357. 423 L
plawlis@messiah.edu
LAWLOR, Andrew ... 215-968-8408. 411 B
andrew.lawlor@bucks.edu
LAWLOR, David, D ... 202-994-9487... 95 D
ddlawlor@gwu.edu
LAWLOR, Edward, F ... 314-935-6693. 284 L
elawlor@wustl.edu
LAWLOR, Jill ... 508-286-8207. 238 B
lawlor_jill@wheatonma.edu
LAWLOR, Kevin, P ... 203-254-4000... 89 I
klawlor@fairfield.edu
LAWLOR, Susan ... 415-451-2853... 63 A
slawlor@sfts.edu
LAWRENCE, Alexander ... 801-626-8940. 497 D
alexanderlawrence@weber.edu
LAWRENCE, Alfred, C ... 915-831-4463. 472 B
alawren4@epcc.edu
LAWRENCE, Barbara ... 646-660-6530. 316 J
Barbara.Lawrence@baruch.cuny.edu
LAWRENCE, Charles ... 206-296-6384. 523 E
lawrence@seattleu.edu
LAWRENCE, Craig ... 205-929-3427..... 5 D
clawrence@lawsonstate.edu
LAWRENCE, Dana, J ... 563-884-5302. 182 A
dana.lawrence@palmer.edu
LAWRENCE, Dave ... 707-965-6699... 57 J
jcollins@puc.edu
LAWRENCE, David ... 740-245-7407. 392 A
lawrence@rio.edu
LAWRENCE, Deborah, A . 240-895-4224. 218 A
dalawrence@smcm.edu
LAWRENCE, Frank ... 518-255-5317. 344 E
lawrenfj@cobleskill.edu

LAWRENCE, Frederick, M 781-736-2000. 224 F lawrence@brandeis.edu
LAWRENCE, Gabrielle, S 651-696-6315. 256 L lawrence@macalester.edu
LAWRENCE, Gail 325-235-7333. 486 C gail.lawrence@tstc.edu
LAWRENCE, Gary 805-893-3781... 72 B gary.lawrence@ucen.ucsb.edu
LAWRENCE, Greg 708-596-2000. 159 C glawrence@ssc.edu
LAWRENCE, Jane, F 209-228-4490... 71 D JLawrence@UCMerced.edu
LAWRENCE, Jason 870-368-2058... 22 E jason.lawrence@ozarka.edu
LAWRENCE, Jaye 507-222-4438. 254 D jlawrenc@carleton.edu
LAWRENCE, Jill 760-872-2000... 42 E jlawrence@deepsprings.edu
LAWRENCE, Jodie 312-777-8667. 147 D jlawrence@aii.edu
LAWRENCE, Karen, R 914-395-2201. 340 E president@sarahlawrence.edu
LAWRENCE, Kim 903-434-8132. 477 J klawrence@ntcc.edu
LAWRENCE, Lara 660-263-3900. 272 A laral@cccb.edu
LAWRENCE, Larry, D 501-450-3196... 25 H larryl@pplant.uca.edu
LAWRENCE, Laura 870-368-2010... 22 E llawrence@ozarka.edu
LAWRENCE, Laurie 808-696-6378. 137 A lauriejl@hawaii.edu
LAWRENCE, Leslie 518-276-6287. 337 I lawrel@rpi.edu
LAWRENCE, Luanne, M 530-752-6888... 70 J lmlawrence@ucdavis.edu
LAWRENCE, Lynn 360-442-2371. 521 A llawrence@lowercolumbia.edu
LAWRENCE, Mark 617-541-5357. 232 G mlawrence@rcc.mass.edu
LAWRENCE, Maureen 732-224-2219. 299 G mlawrence@brookdalecc.edu
LAWRENCE, Melissa 770-531-2569. 128 B mlawrence@laniertech.edu
LAWRENCE, Melody, L 828-339-4224. 364 B mlawrence@southwesterncc.edu
LAWRENCE, Pareena, G 309-794-7000. 139 L pareenalawrence@augustana.edu
LAWRENCE, Robin, P 864-388-8234. 444 K rlawrence@lander.edu
LAWRENCE, Ross 406-874-6172. 286 E lawrencer@milescc.edu
LAWRENCE, Sharee 478-825-6282. 124 H lawrencs@fvsu.edu
LAWRENCE, Stephen, P 989-774-7473. 240 N lawre1sp@cmich.edu
LAWRENCE, Tena 701-252-3467. 373 D tlawrenc@jc.edu
LAWRENCE, Thomas, J 718-990-6647. 339 A lawrenct@stjohns.edu
LAWRENCE, Vanessa 850-201-8519. 117 D lawrencv@tcc.fl.edu
LAWRENCE, William, B 214-768-2534. 481 A wblawren@smu.edu
LAWRENCE, Yvonne, D 340-693-1424. 555 E ylawren@live.uvi.edu
LAWRENCE KEANE, Loretta 212-217-4700. 324 C loretta_keane@fitnyc.edu
LAWRENCE-MARKARIAN, Bob 360 417-6344. 522 A blawrence@pencol.edu
LAWRENCE-PHILLIPS, Teresa 615-963-1545. 459 E tphillips@tnstate.edu
LAWRENCE-RAMAEKER, Janice 715-232-2114. 538 B ramaekerj@uwstout.edu
LAWRENSON, Lisa 916-484-8406... 53 A lawrenl@arc.losrios.edu
LAWRENZ, Frances 612-625-2048. 264 G lawrenz@umn.edu
LAWS, Michaele, D 423-439-8611. 459 C lawsm@etsu.edu
LAWS, Paige 870-633-4480... 21 A plaws@eacc.edu
LAWSON, Angela 712-274-6400. 183 G angela.lawson@witcc.edu
LAWSON, Angela, Y 276-223-4757. 514 F alawson@wcc.vccs.edu
LAWSON, Christopher 617-333-2929. 225 E clawson0307@curry.edu
LAWSON, Cynthia 312-362-7730. 143 H clawso12@depaul.edu
LAWSON, Dan, L 419-289-5480. 374 C dlawson@ashland.edu
LAWSON, Dan, R 423-461-1530. 454 E dlawson@ecs.edu
LAWSON, Daniel 415-422-4222... 73 J lawson@usfca.edu
LAWSON, Danny, L 423-323-0234. 461 C dllawson@northeaststate.edu
LAWSON, Darren, P 864-242-5100. 441 D
LAWSON, Deneen 864-242-5100. 441 D
LAWSON, Diana 320-308-3213. 261 B dlawson@stcloudstate.edu
LAWSON, Donald, S 724-938-4535. 428 A lawson@calu.edu
LAWSON, Earl 831-582-3062... 34 B elawson@csumb.edu
LAWSON, Elizabeth 212-686-9244. 313 G
LAWSON, Eric, L 864-488-4603. 444 L elawson@limestone.edu
LAWSON, Gary 256-761-6324..... 7 F glawson@talladega.edu
LAWSON, Irene 301-962-5111. 221 E ilawson@yeshiva.edu
LAWSON, Joanne 870-633-4480... 21 A jlawson@eacc.edu
LAWSON, John, D 360-650-3480. 525 C john.lawson@wwu.edu
LAWSON, Linda 423-461-8712. 457 H llawson@milligan.edu
LAWSON, Lisa 215-596-8878. 435 H l.lawson@usciences.edu
LAWSON, Mary, W 276-964-7348. 514 A mary.lawson@sw.edu
LAWSON, Murray, J 206-281-2188. 523 C mlawson@spu.edu
LAWSON, Nikki 256-726-7356..... 6 B nlawson@oakwood.edu
LAWSON, Patricia, A 717-337-6805. 417 B plawson@gettysburg.edu
LAWSON, Randal, R 310-434-4360... 65 A lawson_randal@smc.edu
LAWSON, Raymond 815-479-7573. 152 F rlawson@mchenry.edu
LAWSON, Rebecca, L 843-673-1828. 444 B rlawson@fmarion.edu
LAWSON, Regina, G 336-758-6066. 370 D lawsonrg@wfu.edu
LAWSON, Scott 276-328-0211. 511 C msl6r@uvawise.edu
LAWSON, Sheeler 336-770-3264. 369 D lawson@uncsa.edu
LAWSON, Thomas 661-255-1050... 31 C tlawson@calarts.edu
LAWSON, Tonia 386-752-1822. 104 G tonia.lawson@fgc.edu
LAWSON, Valerie 276-376-4528. 511 C vas7k@uvawise.edu
LAWSON, Wendy 734-973-3329. 252 A wlawson@wccnet.edu
LAWSON, Wesley, S 434-223-6127. 505 E wlawson@hsc.edu
LAWSON-BORDERS, Gracie 202-806-7694... 95 G gracie.lawsonborders@howard.edu
LAWTER, JR., Vernon 352-746-6721. 100 K lawterv@cf.edu
LAWTON, III, Boyce, M 864-597-4020. 449 I lawtonbm@wofford.edu
LAWTON, Jennifer, G 413-559-5484. 227 B
LAWTON, Margaret, M 843-377-2423. 441 G mlawton@charlestonlaw.edu
LAWVER, Miranda 906-932-4231. 242 I mirandal@gogebic.edu
LAWYER, Becky 952-888-4777. 263 B blawyer@nwhealth.edu
LAWYER, Mary, K 518-783-4288. 340 J mlawyer@siena.edu
LAWYER, Scott 901-321-3104. 453 H mlawyer@cbu.edu
LAX, William 802-254-0152. 390 C bill.lax@myunion.edu
LAY, Bethany 931-540-2837. 460 E blay@columbiastate.edu
LAY, Brian, K 734-384-4188. 247 C blay@monroeccc.edu
LAY, Doreen 860-768-5565... 92 D lay@hartford.edu
LAY, John 617-582-4443. 235 A jlay@aii.edu
LAY, Karen, D 304-462-4103. 529 G karen.lay@glenville.edu
LAY, Kim 620-252-7067. 185 O kimlay@coffeyville.edu
LAY, Robert, S 617-552-2371. 224 A robert.lay@bc.edu
LAY, Robin 423-636-7300. 462 E rlay@tusculum.edu
LAYDEN, James, E 614-251-4758. 386 B laydenj@ohiodominican.edu
LAYDEN, Susan 518-580-8150. 341 A slayden@skidmore.edu
LAYER, Paul 907-474-7608... 10 I pwlayer@alaska.edu
LAYMAN, Susan 918-631-3244. 401 F susan-layman@utulsa.edu
LAYNE, Barbara 603-428-2410. 297 D blayne@nec.edu
LAYNE, Barbara 603-228-3000. 298 E barbara.layne@granite.edu
LAYNE, Rosemary 321-674-8137. 104 H rlayne@fit.edu
LAYNE, Tiffany 303-986-2320... 80 D tiffany@csha.net
LAYNOR, Barbara 856-227-7200. 300 B blaynor@camdencc.edu
LAYTHAM, D. Brent 410-864-4202. 218 B blaytham@stmarys.edu
LAYTON, Bruce 847-491-8396. 155 D b-layton@northwestern.edu
LAYTON, Christopher 281-873-0262. 469 H c.layton@commonwealth.edu
LAYTON, David, B 724-847-6508. 417 A dblayton@geneva.edu
LAYTON, Erin, C 423-461-1536. 454 E elayton@ecs.edu
LAYTON, Peg, A 830-895-7156. 480 F palayton@schreiner.edu
LAYTON, Susan 303-458-1638... 84 M slayton@regis.edu
LAYZELL, Daniel 309-438-2143. 147 J dlayzel@ilstu.edu
LAZA-SCHMITZ, Roselle 973-618-3907. 300 A rlazaschmitz@caldwell.edu
LAZAR, Colleen 419-448-3438. 389 J lazarc@tiffin.edu
LAZAR, Kathleen 716-880-2362. 330 F kathleen.lazar@medaille.edu
LAZARAKIS, Pam 978-867-4275. 226 H pam.lazarakis@gordon.edu
LAZARO, Felix 787-848-5265. 552 B flazaro@pucpr.edu
LAZART, Kathleen 219-942-1459. 165 C klazart@ccr.edu
LAZARUS, Francis, M 508-767-7312. 222 C flazarus@assumption.edu
LAZARUS, IV, Fred 410-225-2237. 216 C flazarus@mica.edu
LAZARUS, Stephen 954-969-9771. 104 F stephenl@steinerleisure.com
LAZOWSKI, Stephen 478-445-6284. 125 A steve.lazowski@gcsu.edu
LAZZELL, Greg 928-350-4302... 17 K glazzell@prescott.edu
LE, Ba 619-684-8886... 56 C ble@newschoolarch.edu
LE, Bao 626-529-8403... 57 G ble@pacificoaks.edu
LE, Hung, V 310-506-4307... 58 H hung.le@pepperdine.edu
LE, Rebecca 918-335-6829. 398 F rle@okau.edu
LE DOUX, Debra 320-762-4482. 257 O debral@alextech.edu
LE GENDRE, Glenda, G 443-352-4482. 218 E glegendre@stevenson.edu
LE GRANDE, Harry 510-642-6727... 70 I vcsa@berkeley.edu
LE MASTERS, Philip 325-793-3898. 476 E plemasters@mcm.edu
LE ROY, Michael, K 616-526-6100. 240 L
LE SAUX, Catherine 812-866-7399. 166 C lesaux@hanover.edu
LEA, Brette, E 512-223-7611. 466 I blea@austincc.edu
LEA, Deborah, R 504-671-5420. 203 A drlea@dcc.edu
LEA, Jernice 484-365-7250. 422 D jlea@lincoln.edu
LEA, Kizzy 704-216-7235. 363 D kizzy.lea@rccc.edu
LEACH, Adria 978-542-7524. 230 E adria.leach@salemstate.edu
LEACH, Frances, H 302-454-3962... 93 F leach@dtcc.edu
LEACH, Karen, L 315-859-4524. 325 E kleach@hamilton.edu
LEACH, Karla, N 307-382-1602. 543 J kleach@wwcc.wy.edu
LEACH, R. Gavin 906-227-2200. 248 A gleach@nmu.edu
LEACH, Rachel 615-297-7545. 452 J leachr@aquinascollege.edu
LEACH, Stephanie 602-943-2311... 19 C Stephanie.Leach@west.edu
LEACH, Stephen, E 304-367-4692. 528 E Stephen.Leach@pierpont.edu
LEACH, Steven 214-645-5439. 493 E steven.leach@utsouthwestern.edu
LEACH, Timothy 207-326-2276. 211 D timothy.leach@mma.edu
LEACH, Todd, J 603-862-0918. 298 B todd.leach@usnh.edu
LEACH, Todd, J 603-513-1307. 298 E gsc.president@granite.edu
LEADER, Jeanne 425-388-9502. 519 I jleader@everettcc.edu
LEADER, Liv 773-834-2500. 160 I lleader@ttic.edu
LEADLEY, Robert 734-462-4400. 250 A rleadley@schoolcraft.edu
LEADON, Priscilla 510-235-7800... 41 K pleadon@contracosta.edu
LEAGUE, Timothy 410-386-8052. 214 A tleague@carrollcc.edu
LEAHEY, James, P 859-238-5224. 193 E jamey.leahey@centre.edu
LEAHY, Debra 617-951-2350. 234 G debra.leahy@necb.edu
LEAHY, Mindy, S 563-884-5647. 182 A mindy.leahy@palmer.edu
LEAHY, Patrick, F 570-408-4000. 437 F patrick.leahy@wilkes.edu
LEAHY, Thomas 515-643-6621. 181 A tleahy@mercydesmoines.org
LEAHY, SJ, William, P 617-552-3250. 224 A william.leahy@bc.edu
LEAK, Angela 336-334-4822. 360 G acleak@gtcc.edu
LEAK, Arthur, J 765-641-4162. 163 L ajleak@anderson.edu
LEAK, Monica 703-812-4757. 506 H mleak@leland.edu
LEAK, Shanna 269-471-6346. 239 D shannal@andrews.edu
LEAKS, Ileka, L 864-488-4557. 444 L ileaks@limestone.edu
LEAL, Juan 956-364-4607. 485 H juan.leal@tstc.edu
LEAL, Sylvia 956-882-8213. 491 D sylvia.leal@utb.edu
LEAL-SOTELO, Margaret 310-267-5439... 71 C mlealsotelo@conet.ucla.edu
LEAMER, Thomas, C 610-799-1517. 421 I tleamer@lccc.edu
LEAO, Katie 775-445-3240. 295 A katie.leao@wnc.edu
LEAR, Doug 603-899-4123. 296 H leard@franklinpierce.edu
LEAR, Shelly 315-781-3388. 326 C lear@hws.edu
LEARCH, Chad, N 904-620-2414. 116 B clearch@unf.edu
LEARN, Linda 570-702-8956. 419 G llearn@johnson.edu
LEARNED, Betsy, P 401-254-3625. 440 B blearned@rwu.edu
LEARSON, Nicole 337-893-4984. 204 B nicole.learson@solacc.edu
LEARY, Alison, L 212-998-4217. 334 D alison.leary@nyu.edu
LEARY, Carol, A 413-565-1000. 222 F cleary@baypath.edu
LEARY, Dennis 252-335-3388. 367 C deleary@mail.ecsu.edu
LEARY, James 508-856-8200. 229 C james.leary@umassmed.edu
LEARY, Russell, J 920-433-6635. 531 L russell.leary@bellincollege.edu
LEARY, Sharon 214-648-0100. 493 E sharon.leary@utsouthwestern.edu
LEARY, Thomas, P 570-740-0388. 422 G tleary@luzerne.edu
LEARY, JR., Thomas, S 213-821-6251... 74 A lear442@usc.edu
LEARY, Tim 206-296-6160. 523 E tleary@seattleu.edu
LEAS, Terry 509-793-2001. 517 C terryl@bigbend.edu
LEASE BUTTS, Jennifer 860-486-4223... 92 A jennifer.lease@uconn.edu
LEATH, Randy 325-794-4407. 468 I randy.leath@cisco.edu
LEATH, Steven 515-294-2042. 175 H sleath@iastate.edu
LEATHERBARROW, Ronald 360-383-3230. 525 D rleatherbarrow@whatcom.ctc.edu
LEATHERBURY, JR., Ernest 410-651-6589. 219 E eleatherbury@umes.edu
LEATHERMAN, Dale 870-759-4124... 25 K dleatherman@wbcoll.edu
LEATHERS, Barb 309-268-8148. 146 B barb.leathers@heartland.edu
LEATHERS, Debra, L 213-738-6814... 68 C advancement@swlaw.edu
LEATHERS, Ed, C 972-881-5142. 469 G eleathers@collin.edu
LEATHERS, Evelyn 919-546-8368. 366 E eleathers@shawu.edu
LEATHERS, Walt 509-467-1727. 520 F wleather@interface.edu
LEATHERWOOD, Cynthia, D 205-247-8038..... 7 E cleatherwood@stillman.edu
LEATHERWOOD, Laura 828-565-4220. 361 B lbleatherwood@haywood.edu
LEAU, Michael 684-699-9155. 546 A m.leau@amsamoa.edu

LEAVENWORTH, Geoff, M ... 512-471-6080. 491 C goeff@po.utexas.edu
LEAVER, Betty Lou ... 831-242-4404. 544 F betty.l.leaver.civ@mail.mil
LEAVER, Harold, L ... 989-964-4047. 249 G hlleaver@svsu.edu
LEAVER, Walt ... 615-966-7653. 456 B walt.leaver@lipscomb.edu
LEAVITT, Andrew ... 706-864-1547. 133 D andy.leavitt@ung.edu
LEAVITT, Daniel ... 312-777-8583. 147 D dleavitt@aii.edu
LEAVITT, David ... 650-433-3839... 58 B support@paloaltou.edu
LEAVITT, Lorretta ... 619-594-5901... 35 D leavitt@mail.sdsu.edu
LEAVITT, Stephen, C ... 518-388-6116. 348 J leavitts@union.edu
LEBAR, Peter, M ... 814-332-5369. 409 D pete.lebar@allegheny.edu
LEBBE, Duane ... 504-568-4832. 205 C dlebbe@lsuhsc.edu
LEBEAU, Bryan ... 913-758-6115. 191 B lebeau87@stmary.edu
LEBEAU, Mandie, A ... 617-422-7499. 235 B mlebeau@nesl.edu
LEBEAU, Michael ... 205-226-4719..... 2 C mlebeau@bsc.edu
LEBEDEFF, Alex ... 510-659-6263... 57 A alebedeff@ohlone.edu
LEBEL, Richard ... 631-244-3480. 323 B
LEBER, Frank, W ... 312-329-4388. 153 E fleber@moody.edu
LEBER, Sally, S ... 740-368-3080. 387 J ssleber@owu.edu
LEBESCH, Anna, M ... 386-312-4061. 112 C annalebesch@sjrstate.edu
LEBESCO, Kathleen ... 212-774-4861. 330 E klebesco@mmm.edu
LEBHERZ, Joe ... 301-682-8315. 217 B lebherz@msmary.edu
LEBICA, John ... 508-362-2131. 231 D jlebica@capecod.edu
LEBIODA, Ed ... 805-437-8547... 32 I ed.lebioda@csuci.edu
LEBLANC, Ann ... 757-352-4222. 508 G aleblanc@regent.edu
LEBLANC, Barbara ... 603-641-7243. 297 G bleblanc@anselm.edu
LEBLANC, Bruce ... 309-796-5431. 140 E leblancb@bhc.edu
LEBLANC, Debbie ... 207-947-4591. 209 G dleblanc@bealcollege.edu
LEBLANC, Elva, C ... 817-515-7750. 482 B elva.leblanc@tccd.edu
LEBLANC, Erica ... 310-434-4227... 65 A leblanc_erica@smc.edu
LEBLANC, Jacqueline ... 212-752-1530. 328 G jacqueline.leblanc@limcollege.edu
LEBLANC, Jerry, L ... 337-482-6235. 208 D jerrylukeleblanc@louisiana.edu
LEBLANC, Linda ... 409-880-8921. 486 F linda.leblanc@lamar.edu
LEBLANC, Nina ... 337-439-5765. 201 J nina@deltatech.edu
LEBLANC, Paul ... 603-645-9631. 297 I p.leblanc@snhu.edu
LEBLANC, Robert ... 713-525-3540. 490 L leblancr@stthom.edu
LEBLANC, Thomas, J ... 305-284-3356. 118 F leblanc@miami.edu
LEBLANC, William ... 401-825-2225. 439 A leblanc@ccri.edu
LEBLEU BURNS, Michele ... 408-864-8218... 44 M lebleuburnsmichele@deanza.edu
LEBO, Cathy, J ... 410-516-4107. 215 H lebo@jhu.edu
LEBO, Russ ... 559-734-9000... 63 D russl@sjvc.edu
LEBON, Nathalie ... 717-337-6781. 417 B nlebon@gettysburg.edu
LEBRON, Hector ... 787-744-1060. 551 J hectorlebron@mechtech.edu
LEBRON, Maria ... 312-226-6294. 151 A finaid@lexingtoncollege.edu
LEBRON, Nestor, A ... 787-864-2222. 550 D nalebron@inter.edu
LEBRUN, Kathy ... 512-472-4133. 480 G kathy.lebrun@ssw.edu
LEBSOCK, Gale ... 760-384-6215... 49 O glebsock@cerrocoso.edu
LECHE, Adrian ... 252-536-7260. 361 A aleche096@halifaxcc.edu
LECHLER, Terry ... 254-299-8652. 476 D tlechler@mclennan.edu
LECHNER, David ... 402-472-2191. 292 G dlechner@nebraska.edu
LECHTENBERG, Melanie . 217-641-4310. 148 M mlechtenberg@jwcc.edu
LECK, Kathleen, M ... 847-574-5196. 150 C kleck@lfgsm.edu
LECKONBY, Larry, W ... 843-953-5030. 442 A larry.leckonby@citadel.edu
LECKRONE, Michael, J ... 260-982-5004. 170 U mjleckrone@manchester.edu
LECLERC, Robin ... 248-204-2203. 245 I rleclerc@ltu.edu
LECOUNT, Heidi ... 919-760-8633. 356 G lecounth@meredith.edu
LECOURT, Nancy ... 707-965-6234... 57 J nlecourt@puc.edu
LECRONE, Jeffrey, L ... 570-321-4112. 422 H lecrone@lycoming.edu
LEDBETTER, Beverly, E ... 401-863-9900. 438 J beverly_ledbetter@brown.edu
LEDBETTER, Bonnie ... 251-343-8200..... 6 E bonnie.ledbetter@remingtoncollege.edu
LEDBETTER, Cathy ... 678-946-1103. 125 C cledbett@highlands.edu
LEDBETTER, Cathy ... 678-872-4201. 125 C cledbett@highlands.edu
LEDBETTER, Kate ... 828-669-8012. 357 H kledbetter@montreat.edu
LEDBETTER, Kim, M ... 828-652-0602. 362 A kims@mcdowelltech.edu
LEDBETTER, Lisa ... 704-216-3620. 363 D lisa.ledbetter@rccc.edu
LEDBETTER, Mary, L ... 828-659-6001. 362 A maryl@mcdowelltech.edu
LEDBETTER, Neal ... 251-442-2429..... 9 A nledbetter@umobile.edu
LEDBETTER, Sislena ... 202-274-5373... 97 A sledbetter@udc.edu
LEDBETTER, Spencer ... 405-789-7661. 400 A spencer.ledbetter@swcu.edu
LEDBETTER, William, B .. 828-652-0674. 362 A bradl@mcdowelltech.edu
LEDDY, Michael ... 401-341-2195. 440 C mike.leddy@salve.edu
LEDERER, Benjamin ... 718-851-0183. 337 G
LEDERMANN, Stacy, A ... 585-385-8142. 338 H sledermann@sjfc.edu
LEDESMA, Amadeo ... 575-527-7530. 311 B amadeol@nmsu.edu
LEDESMA, Mark ... 206-726-5028. 518 G mledesma@cornish.edu
LEDFORD, Howard ... 706-335-9337. 128 B hledford@laniertech.edu
LEDFORD, Julia ... 270-686-4627. 196 C julia.ledford@kctcs.edu
LEDFORD, Julie ... 360-736-9391. 517 G jledford@centralia.edu
LEDFORD, Kristin ... 304-205-6612. 528 B kledford@kvctc.edu
LEDFORD, Laura ... 217-362-6499. 153 C lledford@millikin.edu
LEDFORD, Randy ... 336-386-3279. 364 D ledfordr@surry.edu
LEDFORD, Robert ... 407-971-5010. 113 E ledford@seminolestate.edu
LEDFORD, Terry ... 864-941-8559. 446 C ledford.t@ptc.edu
LEDFORD, Tommy, R ... 828-766-1190. 361 H tledford@mayland.edu
LEDLOW, Susan, E ... 407-582-3423. 118 M sledlow@valenciacollege.edu
LEDMAN, Robert ... 520-383-8401... 18 B rledman@tocc.cc.az.us
LEDONNE, Patricia, N ... 540-375-2500. 509 B ledonne@roanoke.edu
LEDONNE, Peter ... 201-447-7159. 299 C pledonne@bergen.edu
LEDUC, Don ... 517-371-5140. 250 G leducd@cooley.edu
LEDUC, Laura ... 517-371-5140. 250 G leducl@cooley.edu
LEDUC, Paul, D ... 518-564-2090. 344 B leducpd@plattsburgh.edu
LEDVINA, Anne ... 205-226-7722..... 2 C aledvina@bsc.edu
LEDWIN, Richard ... 323-259-2613... 56 I ledwin@oxy.edu
LEDYARD, Christopher, L ... 740-283-6437. 379 N cledyard@franciscan.edu
LEE, Alberta, G ... 585-292-2106. 332 A alee@monroecc.edu
LEE, Allisha ... 270-707-3958. 195 E allisha.lee@kctcs.edu
LEE, Amanda ... 910-362-7475. 358 F alee@cfcc.edu
LEE, Amy ... 510-748-2288... 59 B ahlee@peralta.edu
LEE, Amy ... 207-741-5644. 211 A alee@smccme.edu
LEE, Amy, H ... 510-464-3124... 59 C ahlee@peralta.edu
LEE, IHM, Andrea, J ... 651-690-6525. 263 O ajlee@stkate.edu
LEE, Andrew ... 908-737-4850. 302 F jilee@kean.edu
LEE, Angelo, C ... 615-327-6223. 456 E aclee@mmc.edu
LEE, Ann, B ... 812-941-2356. 168 F alee@ius.edu
LEE, Anyork ... 626-289-7719... 26 J
LEE, Barbara ... 831-646-4014... 54 I blee@mpc.edu
LEE, Bert ... 410-276-0306. 218 D blee@host.sdc.edu
LEE, Brenda ... 419-530-7730. 392 B brenda.lee@utoledo.edu
LEE, Brian, K ... 626-395-6307... 31 E brian.lee@caltech.edu
LEE, Carla ... 314-340-3307. 275 A leec@hssu.edu
LEE, Carol ... 269-782-1305. 250 C clee02@swmich.edu
LEE, Catherine ... 334-844-1350..... 1 G leecath@auburn.edu
LEE, Catherine ... 910-362-7033. 358 F clee@cfcc.edu
LEE, Charley ... 714-527-0691... 43 H
LEE, Chenetta ... 334-876-9303..... 4 A chenetta.lee@wccs.edu
LEE, Chris ... 270-706-8622. 195 A chris.lee@kctcs.edu
LEE, Christopher ... 804-819-4685. 511 G clee@vccs.edu
LEE, Chul ... 413-265-2294. 225 C leec@elms.edu
LEE, Cindy ... 352-588-8869. 112 D cindy.lee@saintleo.edu
LEE, Crystal ... 225-675-8270. 203 G clee@rpcc.edu
LEE, Curtis ... 253-964-6595. 522 C clee@pierce.ctc.edu
LEE, D. Lynn ... 443-412-2258. 215 C llee@harford.edu
LEE, Dana ... 914-594-4567. 334 A dana_lee@nymc.edu
LEE, Darin, N ... 208-496-2311. 137 H leed@byui.edu
LEE, David ... 303-273-3155... 80 E dlee@mines.edu
LEE, David, C ... 706-542-5969. 133 C dclee@uga.edu
LEE, David, D ... 270-745-2344. 200 G david.lee@wku.edu
LEE, David, S ... 609-258-9548. 304 E davidlee@princeton.edu
LEE, David, Y ... 703-333-5904. 516 B
LEE, Debra, A ... 330-471-8406. 383 D dlee@malone.edu
LEE, Delores ... 310-243-3691... 33 B dslee@csudh.edu
LEE, Dennis ... 229-225-5087. 132 D dlee@southwestgatech.edu
LEE, Dewain ... 907-786-1214... 10 H dllee@uaa.alaska.edu
LEE, Diana ... 405-491-6310. 399 K dlee@snu.edu
LEE, Diane ... 212-226-7300. 336 G dlee@pbcny.edu
LEE, Diane, M ... 410-455-2859. 219 D dlee@umbc.edu
LEE, Donald ... 334-874-5700..... 3 A dlee@ccal.edu
LEE, Donald, E ... 252-493-7262. 362 G dlee@email.pittcc.edu
LEE, Donna, A ... 404-471-6391. 119 I dlee@agnesscott.edu
LEE, Donzell ... 601-877-6122. 265 G dlee@alcorn.edu
LEE, Donzell ... 601-877-3922. 265 G dlee@alcorn.edu
LEE, Doug ... 724-852-3212. 437 A dlee@waynesburg.edu
LEE, Elaine ... 808-689-2315. 136 C elainel@hawaii.edu
LEE, Elwyn, C ... 832-842-5090. 489 B eclee@uh.edu
LEE, Frieda ... 415-338-2356... 35 E friedale@sfsu.edu
LEE, Gloria ... 203-392-5200... 88 A leeg1@southernct.edu
LEE, Grayce ... 504-468-2900. 207 B drlee@southwest.edu
LEE, Harlan ... 425-564-2212. 517 A harlan.lee@bellevuecollege.edu
LEE, Hee, C ... 636-327-4645. 277 K hclee@midwest.edu
LEE, Herbert ... 831-459-2351... 72 C vpaa@ucsc.edu
LEE, Ho Woo ... 770-279-0507. 124 I howard.hw.lee@gcuniv.edu
LEE, Holly ... 580-628-6274. 396 M holly.lee@noc.edu
LEE, Humphrey ... 256-331-5214..... 6 A hlee@nwscc.edu
LEE, Ingrid ... 928-226-4315... 13 B ingrid.lee@coconino.edu
LEE, J. Steve ... 251-442-2390..... 9 A slee@umobile.edu
LEE, Jaekyung ... 716-645-6640. 341 F gscdean@buffalo.edu
LEE, James, S ... 562-926-1023... 60 B jameslee@ptsa.edu
LEE, Janet ... 303-458-3552... 84 M jlee@regis.edu
LEE, Jay ... 970-521-6607... 83 L jay.lee@njc.edu
LEE, Jayre ... 620-276-9508. 187 A jayre.lee@gcccks.edu
LEE, Jennifer ... 213-621-2200... 40 B
LEE, Joel ... 512-651-4730. 450 G jlee@national.edu
LEE, John ... 707-826-3961... 35 C john.lee@humboldt.edu
LEE, Jonathan ... 860-509-9556... 90 B jlee@hartsem.edu
LEE, Jonathan ... 310-233-4471... 51 H leej@lahc.edu
LEE, Jonathan ... 508-626-4697. 230 A jlee8@framingham.edu
LEE, Jonathan, E ... 540-375-2237. 509 B jelee@roanoke.edu
LEE, Joni, C ... 501-569-3186... 24 B jclee@ualr.edu
LEE, Joseph ... 617-731-7101. 235 H jlee@pmc.edu
LEE, K, W ... 401-874-2695. 440 D lee@egr.uri.edu
LEE, Kathleen, F ... 317-917-5935. 169 L klee@ivytech.edu
LEE, Katrina, K ... 919-658-2502. 357 I klee@moc.edu
LEE, Keum Hee ... 213-385-2322... 77 A khlee@wmu.edu
LEE, Kevin ... 620-862-5252. 184 E kevin.lee@barclaycollege.edu
LEE, Kim ... 601-923-1681. 269 E klee@rts.edu
LEE, Kimberly ... 229-420-1284. 120 A klee@albanytech.edu
LEE, Kyu, H ... 253-752-2020. 519 K revkhlee@faithseminary.edu
LEE, Larry ... 361-698-1700. 471 G llee@delmar.edu
LEE, Lauralyn, B ... 202-687-5177... 95 E leb27@georgetown.edu
LEE, Lenetta ... 484-365-7253. 422 D llee@lincoln.edu
LEE, Leon ... 212-226-7300. 336 G llee@pbcny.edu
LEE, Linda, J ... 414-288-7206. 534 B linda.j.lee@marquette.edu
LEE, Linda, S ... 657-725-7789... 68 E lslee@stanford.edu
LEE, Lisa ... 714-533-3946... 36 C lisa@calums.edu
LEE, Lisa ... 212-410-8032. 333 E llee@nycpm.edu
LEE, Lisa ... 610-328-8402. 433 I llee2@swarthmore.edu
LEE, Marc, D ... 202-806-6131... 95 G mdlee2@howard.edu
LEE, Margaret, B ... 847-635-1801. 155 F plee@oakton.edu
LEE, Marsha ... 662-246-6314. 268 B mlee@msdelta.edu
LEE, Marty ... 707-527-4689... 65 B mlee@santarosa.edu
LEE, Mary, Y ... 617-627-4733. 237 C mary.lee@tufts.edu
LEE, SSJ, Mary Esther ... 215-248-7062. 413 A leem@chc.edu
LEE, Mary Margaret ... 802-860-2721. 499 A mlee@champlain.edu
LEE, Mary Margaret ... 802-860-2721. 499 A
LEE, Mary W, L ... 630-515-7311. 153 B mleexx@midwestern.edu
LEE, Maurice ... 704-357-2541. 131 H mlee@southuniversity.edu
LEE, Maurice, A ... 501-450-3167... 25 H mauricel@uca.edu
LEE, Mei-Lin ... 210-436-3414. 479 D mlee@stmarytx.edu
LEE, Michael ... 859-815-7799. 195 B michael.lee@kctcs.edu
LEE, Michael ... 678-225-7336. 430 D michaellee@pcom.edu
LEE, Michael, D ... 229-226-1621. 132 F mlee@thomasu.edu
LEE, Michael, E ... 814-860-5141. 420 E elee@lecom.edu
LEE, Michele, S ... 864-429-8728. 448 G michele@mailbox.sc.edu
LEE, Mike ... 386-752-1822. 104 G mike.lee@fgc.edu

LEE, Ming-Tung "Mike" .. 916-278-6312... 34 D
mikelee@csus.edu
LEE, Mona ...... 808-734-9522. 136 E
monal@hawaii.edu
LEE, Myung-Soo ...... 646-312-3030. 316 J
Myung-Soo.Lee@baruch.cuny.edu
LEE, Norma ...... 423-697-2478. 460 C
LEE, Otto ...... 619-388-6965... 62 C
olee@sdccd.edu
LEE, Pamela ...... 512-313-3000. 469 L
pamela.lee@concordia.edu
LEE, Patricia, A ...... 843-355-4127. 449 F
leepa@wiltech.edu
LEE, Peter ...... 888-897-3222... 50 G
plee@sf.chefs.edu
LEE, Raeann ...... 614-416-6239. 375 B
rlee@bradfordschoolcolumbus.edu
LEE, Randall ...... 601-635-6375. 266 H
rlee@eccc.edu
LEE, Randolph ...... 860-297-2413... 91 F
randolph.lee@trincoll.edu
LEE, Rebecca ...... 909-621-8277... 65 D
rebecca.lee@scrippscollege.edu
LEE, Rebecca ...... 478-757-3551. 122 F
blee@centralgatech.edu
LEE, Richard ...... 607-436-2541. 343 E
richard.lee@oneonta.edu
LEE, Robert, E ...... 563-884-5123. 182 A
robert.lee@palmer.edu
LEE, Robert, L ...... 575-835-5143. 310 F
lee@prrc.nmt.edu
LEE, Robert, W ...... 260-399-7700. 174 C
rlee@sf.edu
LEE, Robin ...... 785-227-3380. 184 I
leert@bethanylb.edu
LEE, Roger, R ...... 770-720-5537. 130 G
rrl@reinhardt.edu
LEE, Sally ...... 423-439-4210. 459 C
lees@etsu.edu
LEE, Samuel ...... 626-914-8855... 38 K
slee@citruscollege.edu
LEE, Sandra ...... 650-508-3516... 56 H
slee@ndnu.edu
LEE, Sang Meyng ...... 562-926-1023... 60 B
sangmeynglee@msn.com
LEE, Seong Heon ...... 425-249-4715. 524 D
Seongheon.lee@tlc.edu
LEE, Seong Heon ...... 425-249-4732. 524 D
seongheon.lee@tlc.edu
LEE, Sheng Chien ...... 561-297-2718. 114 L
lees@fau.edu
LEE, Sophie ...... 508-588-9100. 232 A
LEE, Stephen ...... 413-565-1000. 222 F
slee@baypath.edu
LEE, Stephen, E ...... 304-293-2121. 530 D
stephen.lee@mail.wvu.edu
LEE, Steven ...... 757-446-5221. 504 E
leect@evms.edu
LEE, Susan ...... 330-263-2434. 377 H
slee@wooster.edu
LEE, Teresa ...... 913-758-4359. 191 B
hr@stmary.edu
LEE, Theresa ...... 865-974-4337. 463 C
artscidean@utk.edu
LEE, Timothy ...... 323-643-0301... 27 N
LEE, Todd, G ...... 805-893-2169... 72 B
todd.lee@bap.ucsb.edu
LEE, Tom ...... 515-433-5020. 177 B
tlee@dmacc.edu
LEE, Traci ...... 602-383-8228... 18 E
LEE, Treva, A ...... 504-520-7566. 209 D
tlee@xula.edu
LEE, Tyjaun, A ...... 301-322-0412. 217 F
leeta@pgcc.edu
LEE, Valerie ...... 614-292-4355. 386 E
lee.89@osu.edu
LEE, Vincent ...... 901-381-3939. 464 C
vincent@visible.edu
LEE, Vivian, S ...... 801-581-7480. 496 Q
vivian.lee@hsc.utah.edu
LEE, Wai-Fong ...... 206-934-4062. 522 J
wai-fong.lee@seattlecolleges.edu
LEE, Wendy ...... 415-257-1365... 42 J
wendy.lee@dominican.edu
LEE, Wendy ...... 909-447-2535... 39 E
wlee@cst.edu
LEE, Wes ...... 405-491-6455. 399 K
wlee@snu.edu
LEE, Wynetta ...... 919-530-5327. 368 A
wynetta.lee@nccu.edu
LEE, Y. Ben ...... 260-422-5561. 167 B
yblee@indianatech.edu
LEE, Youngwoo ...... 770-279-0507. 124 I
LEE, Yuet ...... 909-621-8243... 59 G
yuet_lee@pitzer.edu
LEE, Yung Jae ...... 925-631-4610... 61 F
ylee@stmarys-ca.edu
LEE-BARBER, Jill ...... 404-413-1640. 126 E
jleebarber@gsu.edu
LEE-CLARK, Margaret ...... 215-619-7413. 424 B
plee@mc3.edu
LEE-GLAUSER, Gina ...... 315-443-2492. 347 C
leeglaug@syr.edu
LEE ISBARA, Jiseon ...... 503-297-5544. 405 D
jlee@ocac.edu
LEE KADIRIFU, Pamela .. 312-362-8464. 143 H
plee14@depaul.edu
LEE-LEWIS, Sherri ...... 310-434-4419... 65 A
lee-lewis_sherri@smc.edu
LEE-SADDUL, Claudia .... 714-895-8178... 39 J
clee-saddul@gwc.cccd.edu
LEE SANG, Brian ...... 202-885-6108... 94 F
leesang@american.edu
LEEBRON, David, W ...... 713-348-5050. 479 A
president@rice.edu
LEEBRON TUTELMAN,
Elizabeth ...... 215-204-7188. 433 K
elizabeth.leebron@temple.edu
LEECH, David ...... 304-647-6326. 530 B
dleech@osteo.wvsom.edu
LEEDER, Elaine, A ...... 707-664-2120... 36 B
elaine.leeder@sonoma.edu
LEEDS, Mark ...... 817-923-1921. 481 G
mleeds@swbts.edu
LEEDS, Stacy ...... 479-575-4504... 23 I
sleeds@uark.edu
LEEDY, David ...... 212-659-0741. 328 E
LEEK, Linda ...... 859-985-3205. 192 F
leekl@berea.edu
LEEK, Marilyn, J ...... 515-961-1675. 182 E
marilyn.leek@simpson.edu
LEEMAN, Julia ...... 314-949-2620. 281 K
jleeman@sbc-stpeters.com
LEEMON, Donna ...... 334-683-2362..... 5 F
dleemon@marionmilitary.edu
LEENEY-PANAGROSSI,
Anne ...... 203-773-8595... 87 G
panagrossi@albertus.edu
LEENHOUTS, David ...... 979-532-6905. 494 L
leenhoutsd@wcjc.edu
LEENHOUTS, Peter ...... 360-385-4948. 521 F
peterl@nwboatschool.org
LEEPER, Greg, J ...... 612-343-4457. 262 X
gjleeper@northcentral.edu
LEEPER, Karla ...... 254-710-3555. 467 G
karla_leeper@baylor.edu
LEES, David ...... 610-660-1773. 432 E
lees@sju.edu
LEES, Elizabeth, M ...... 484-664-3116. 424 H
lees@muhlenberg.edu
LEES, Melissa ...... 410-532-5565. 217 E
mlees@ndm.edu
LEES, Merlinda ...... 304-829-7131. 526 D
mlees@bethanywv.edu
LEET, Gregory, R ...... 949-824-5011... 71 B
gregory.leet@uci.edu
LEET, Thomas, R ...... 858-534-0286... 71 F
tleet@ucsd.edu
LEETH, Blake ...... 256-840-4170..... 6 I
bleeth@snead.edu
LEFAUVE, Linda, M ...... 704-894-2124. 353 J
lilefauve@davidson.edu
LEFEBVRE, Bob ...... 573-986-6191. 282 B
rlefebvre@semo.edu
LEFEBVRE, Carol ...... 706-721-8611. 126 B
clefebvr@gru.edu
LEFEBVRE, Lora ...... 518-320-1660. 341 C
lora.lefebvre@suny.edu
LEFEBVRE, Raymond ...... 508-531-2247. 229 D
raymond.lefebvre@bridgew.edu
LEFEVER, Stephen ...... 413-748-3252. 236 I
slafever@springfieldcollege.edu
LEFEVER DAVIS, Shirley . 316-978-3301. 191 F
shirley.lefever-davis@wichita.edu
LEFEVERS, William, L ...... 828-448-3125. 365 A
wlefevers@wpcc.edu
LEFEVRE, Linda ...... 215-489-2933. 414 E
linda.lefevre@delval.edu
LEFEVRE, Richard, J ...... 704-878-3202. 362 B
rlefevre@mitchellcc.edu
LEFFARD, Mary Ellen ...... 770-426-2971. 128 D
maryellen.leffard@life.edu
LEFFEL, Lisa ...... 414-443-8796. 539 F
lisa.leffel@wlc.edu
LEFFLER, Charles, D ...... 919-515-2155. 368 B
charles_leffler@ncsu.edu
LEFFLER, Ernest, H ...... 781-891-2552. 223 C
eleffler@bentley.edu
LEFLER, James, C ...... 423-354-2425. 461 C
jclefler@northeaststate.edu
LEFLORE, Larry ...... 940-898-3415. 488 B
lleflore@twu.edu
LEFOE, Grant ...... 704-290-5269. 363 G
cglefoe@spcc.edu
LEFORT, Donna, P ...... 256-765-4252..... 9 C
dpjacobs@una.edu
LEFRANCOIS, Paul, R ...... 864-488-4527. 444 L
plefrancois@limestone.edu
LEFT HAND, Frederica ... 406-638-3131. 286 D
lefthandfv@lbhc.edu
LEFTON, Lester, A ...... 330-672-2210. 382 B
lefton@kent.edu
LEFTWICH, Edrice ...... 334-727-8505..... 8 A
leftwich@tuskegee.edu
LEFTWICH, Michael ...... 417-823-3466. 281 M
mleftwich@forest.edu
LEFTWICH, Shawn, B ...... 630-752-5011. 163 F
shawn.leftwich@wheaton.edu
LEGAKO, Jana ...... 405-682-7850. 397 E
jana.k.legako@occc.edu
LEGASPI, Lorenzo ...... 925-485-5203... 37 J
llegaspi@clpccd.org
LEGER-HORNBY, Tracey 508-831-5058. 238 F
tlh@wpi.edu
LEGG, David ...... 865-573-4517. 455 G
dlegg@johnsonU.edu
LEGG, Elizabeth ...... 540-365-4255. 504 L
elegg@ferrum.edu
LEGG, Hal, S ...... 607-436-2748. 343 E
legghs@oneonta.edu
LEGG, Jamie, W ...... 910-630-7028. 356 H
jlegg@methodist.edu
LEGG, Margaret, A ...... 423-775-7201. 453 E
leggma@bryan.edu
LEGGAT, Barbara ...... 570-674-8144. 424 A
bleggat@misericordia.edu
LEGGE, Jerome, S ...... 706-425-3340. 133 C
jlegge@uga.edu
LEGGE, Karen ...... 570-961-7886. 420 C
leggek@lackawanna.edu
LEGGETT, Connie ...... 229-430-1917. 119 J
connie.leggett@asurams.edu
LEGGETT, Ida, F ...... 615-898-5910. 459 D
ida.fazillah@mtsu.edu
LEGGETT, Mia, S ...... 540-868-7087. 512 H
mlegget@lfcc.edu
LEGGETT, Tricia ...... 740-588-1271. 394 C
tleggett@zanestate.edu
LEGGETT, Vi ...... 330-363-6183. 374 E
vleggett@aultman.com
LEGGETTE, Evelyn ...... 601-979-2127. 267 E
evelyn.j.leggette@jsums.edu
LEGGETTE, Priscilla ...... 315-386-7315. 345 F
leggettep@canton.edu
LEGGIO, Karyl ...... 410-617-2301. 216 A
kbleggio@loyola.edu
LEGGITT, Dan ...... 618-544-8657. 147 A
leggittd@iecc.edu
LEGRANDE, Tomikia, P .. 713-221-8100. 489 D
legrandet@uhd.edu
LEGREID, Ann, M ...... 304-876-5011. 529 I
alegreid@shepherd.edu
LEGRO, Jeffrey, w ...... 434-924-6835. 511 B
legro@virginia.edu
LEGROW, Lori ...... 727-298-8685. 118 B
LEGROW, Maryanne ...... 860-515-3846... 87 I
mlegrow@charteroak.edu
LEGURIA, Gina, B ...... 209-667-3351... 35 B
gleguria@csustan.edu
LEHDE, Wade ...... 314-454-7547. 274 G
walehde@bjc.org
LEHMAN, Ann ...... 716-375-2435. 338 E
alehman@sbu.edu
LEHMAN, Ann ...... 814-865-8753. 426 A
axw14@psu.edu
LEHMAN, Bruce ...... 301-687-4025. 220 C
blehman@frostburg.edu
LEHMAN, DeWayne ...... 617-287-5302. 228 G
deWayne.lehman@umb.edu
LEHMAN, Douglas, K ...... 937-327-7016. 393 E
dlehman@wittenberg.edu
LEHMAN, John, B ...... 906-487-1832. 247 A
jblehman@mtu.edu
LEHMAN, Joseph ...... 814-472-3054. 432 D
jlehman@francis.edu
LEHMAN, Josh ...... 580-581-2211. 394 G
jlehman@cameron.edu
LEHMAN, Theresa ...... 317-738-8176. 165 I
tlehman@franklincollege.edu
LEHMAN, Tracey, A ...... 541-885-1291. 405 J
tracey.lehman@oit.edu
LEHMAN, William, H ...... 262-554-2010. 534 D
lehmannw@yahoo.com
LEHMAN-FELTS, Juliana . 940-397-4193. 476 H
juliana.felts@mwsu.edu
LEHMANN, Craig ...... 631-444-2253. 342 C
craig.lehmann@stonybrook.edu
LEHMANN, Daniel ...... 617-559-8773. 227 D
dlehmann@hebrewcollege.edu
LEHMANN, Donna ...... 212-217-4710. 324 C
donna_lehmann@fitnyc.edu
LEHMANN, Jay ...... 904-680-7671. 103 Q
jlehmann@fcsl.edu
LEHN, Patty ...... 217-353-2683. 155 J
plehn@parkland.edu
LEHNER, Eric, J ...... 757-479-3706. 503 C
elehner@baptistseminary.edu
LEHNER, Kathryn, G ...... 707-476-4170... 40 H
kathy-lehner@redwoods.edu
LEHNERT, Charles ...... 419-530-1447. 392 B
charles.lehnert@utoledo.edu
LEHOCKY, John, F ...... 847-566-6401. 162 G
jlehocky@usml.edu
LEHOCZKY, John, P ...... 412-268-2832. 412 H
jl16@andrew.cmu.edu
LEHOTAK, Ed ...... 402-557-7050. 288 G
ed.lehotak@bellevue.edu
LEHR, Christine ...... 309-343-4212. 150 D
christine.lehr@doc.illionis.gov
LEHR, Kirk, A ...... 989-317-4611. 247 B
klehr@midmich.edu
LEHR, Louis ...... 504-278-6474. 203 F
llehr@nunez.edu
LEHR, Valerie, D ...... 315-229-5993. 339 F
vlehr@stlawu.edu
LEHRBERGER, Paula ...... 215-596-8891. 435 H
p.lehrbe@usciences.edu
LEHRE, Elaine ...... 906-248-8422. 240 J
elehre@bmcc.edu
LEHRLING, Tony ...... 580-745-2918. 399 J
tlehrling@se.edu
LEHRMAN, III,
Kenneth, F ...... 814-863-0471. 426 A
kfl2@psu.edu
LEHRMAN, Sue ...... 215-951-2810. 430 E
Lehrmans@philau.edu
LEI, Joy ...... 909-593-3511... 72 E
jlei@laverne.edu
LEIBLE, Arthur ...... 302-857-6060... 93 C
aleible@desu.edu
LEIBOLD, Susanne ...... 563-588-6580. 176 F
susanne.leibold@clarke.edu
LEIBOWITZ, Adrienne ...... 716-286-8339. 334 F
ael@niagara.edu
LEIBOWITZ, J. Michael .. 402-559-6438. 292 J
mleibowitz@unmc.edu
LEICHLITER, Christine .... 202-639-1813... 95 B
cleichliter@corcoran.org
LEICHLITER, Kirk ...... 970-351-2446... 86 C
kirk.leichliter@unco.edu
LEICHT, Sandra ...... 262-595-2640. 537 C
leicht@uwp.edu
LEICHTNAM, Marky ...... 614-885-5585. 388 C
mleichtnam@pcj.edu
LEICHTY, Jeff, S ...... 260-422-5561. 167 B
jsleichty@indianatech.edu
LEIDA, Mary ...... 712-274-5252. 181 B
leidam@morningside.edu
LEIDERMAN, Roni ...... 954-262-6930. 109 K
roni@nova.edu
LEIDIG, Julie ...... 703-450-2517. 513 C
jleidig@nvcc.edu
LEIDIG, Mary ...... 865-471-3402. 453 F
mleidig@cn.edu
LEIDINGER, Angie ...... 864-656-5615. 442 C
angiel@clemson.edu
LEIFELD, Martin, F ...... 314-516-4151. 283 E
leifeldm@umsl.edu
LEIGH, Anthony, J ...... 334-833-4528..... 4 D
aleigh@huntingdon.edu
LEIGH, Bradley, K ...... 419-372-2238. 374 K
bleigh@bgsu.edu
LEIGH, Steven, R ...... 303-492-7294... 85 L
steven.leigh@colorado.edu
LEIGH, Thomas ...... 719-590-6774... 81 B
tleigh@coloradotech.edu
LEIGHTON, Erin ...... 207-947-4591. 209 G
eleighton@bealcollege.edu
LEIGHTON, Jackie ...... 609-258-5006. 304 E
jleighto@princeton.edu
LEIKER, Jeff ...... 620-252-7147. 185 O
jeffl@coffeyville.edu
LEIKER, Meg ...... 619-265-0107... 59 K
mleiker@platt.edu
LEIKER, Robert, D ...... 619-265-0107... 59 K
rleiker@platt.edu
LEIMBACH, Bill ...... 410-337-6138. 215 A
bleimbach@goucher.edu
LEIMBACH, Bridget, S ... 410-386-8032. 214 A
bleimbach@carrollcc.edu
LEIMBEK, Melissa ...... 763-424-0946. 260 C
mleimbek@nhcc.edu
LEIMER, Christina ...... 858-513-9240. 175 F
christina.leimer@ashford.edu
LEIMER, Jennifer ...... 601-928-6211. 268 C
jennifer.leimer@mgccc.edu
LEIN, Laura ...... 734-764-5347. 251 C
leinl@umich.edu
LEINBERRY, Beth ...... 401-841-4448. 545 A
LEINEN, Margaret ...... 772-465-2400. 114 L
mleinen@fau.edu
LEININGER, Earl ...... 704-406-3522. 354 C
eleininger@gardner-webb.edu
LEININGER, Jeffrey ...... 708-209-3470. 143 E
jeff.leininger@cuchicago.edu
LEINWALL, Checka ...... 319-368-6469. 181 C
cleinwall@mtmercy.edu
LEINWEBER, Laura ...... 619-849-2856... 59 L
lauraleinweber@pointloma.edu
LEIPERTZ, Rosemary ...... 724-339-7542. 425 B
financialaid@nbi.edu
LEIPHEIMER, Jack ...... 724-589-2212. 434 B
jleipheimer@thiel.edu

LEISINGER, Scott, C 319-352-8495. 183 E scott.leisinger@wartburg.edu
LEIST, Terry 406-994-4361. 287 B tleist@montana.edu
LEISTIKOW, Patricia 218-322-2403. 258 I patricia.leistikow@itascacc.edu
LEITE, Randy 740-593-9336. 387 C leite@ohio.edu
LEITER, Dena 908-709-7622. 308 B leiter@ucc.edu
LEITHNER STAUFFER, Andrea, C 570-577-1331. 411 A andrea.leithner.stauffer@bucknell.edu
LEITNAKER, Gary, E 785-532-6277. 188 A geleit@ksu.edu
LEITNER, Jennifer 603-882-6923. 296 B jleitner@ccsnh.edu
LEITNER, Lewis 609-652-4298. 305 C lewis.leitner@stockton.edu
LEITSON, Cynthia 216-987-3510. 378 D cynthia.leitson@tri-c.edu
LEITZEL, Thomas, C 863-784-7110. 113 G leitzelt@southflorida.edu
LEIVAS, Chris 925-969-2017... 41 L cleivas@dvc.edu
LEJA, Ann 651-793-1333. 259 C ann.leja@metrostate.edu
LEJTER, Nelly 603-428-2217. 297 D nlejter@nec.edu
LEKANG, Laurie 701-671-2871. 372 E laurie.lekang@ndscs.edu
LELACHEUR, Brendan 541-485-1780. 405 B brendanlelacheur@newhop.edu
LELACK, Connie 503-399-5016. 402 E connie.lelack@chemeketa.edu
LELAND, Chris 405-733-7350. 399 F cleland@rose.edu
LELAND, Dorothy 209-228-4417... 71 D Chancellor@UCMerced.edu
LELAND, Mary 916-558-2198... 53 D lelandm@scc.losrios.edu
LELAND, Melinda, T 276-739-2548. 514 D mleland@vhcc.edu
LELAND, Ted 209-946-2392... 73 A tleland@pacific.edu
LELCHOOK, Heather 970-667-4611... 78 C heather.lelchook@aims.edu
LELE, Pradeep 281-618-7123. 476 A pradeep.m.lele@lonestar.edu
LELIAERT, Deborah, S 940-565-2108. 490 C leliaert@unt.edu
LELIK, Mary 312-996-3254. 161 D lelik@uic.edu
LELONG, Kristine, D 504-865-3858. 205 H klelong@loyno.edu
LELOUDIS, James, L 919-966-5110. 368 D leloudis@unc.edu
LEMA, Barbara 508-286-8206. 238 B blema@wheatoncollege.edu
LEMAHIEU, Dan 847-735-5083. 150 B lemahieu@lakeforest.edu
LEMAHIEU, Keith 219-864-2400. 171 F klemahieu@midamerica.edu
LEMAIRE, Renee 334-222-6591..... 5 E rlemaire@lbwcc.edu
LEMANN, Nicholas 212-854-6056. 321 D nl2124@columbia.edu
LEMANSKI, Ken 413-572-8178. 230 F klemanski@westfield.ma.edu
LEMARBE, Thomas, P 248-370-2445. 248 J lemarbe@oakland.edu
LEMASTER, Charles 254-647-3214. 478 H clemaster@rangercollege.edu
LEMASTER, Courtney 270-852-3107. 197 B
LEMASTER, J. Michael 937-258-8251. 381 F
LEMASTERS, Michael 724-357-2696. 428 F michael.lemasters@iup.edu
LEMASTERS, Phil 325-793-3898. 476 E plemasters@mcm.edu
LEMAY, Aaron 936-294-3899. 487 A caaronlemay@shsu.edu
LEMAY, Eileen 563-589-0300. 183 F elemay@wartburgseminary.edu
LEMAY, Elaine 510-869-6739... 61 I elemay@samuelmerritt.edu
LEMAY, Jerret 315-312-2237. 344 A jerret.lemay@oswego.edu
LEMAY, Mitch 415-485-9467... 40 G mitchell.lemay@marin.edu
LEMBKE, Roberta 507-786-3097. 264 B lembke@stolaf.edu
LEMBO, Vincent, J 617-373-2157. 235 F
LEMBURG, Mary 713-718-8505. 473 C mary.lemburg@hccs.edu
LEMCOE, Diane 908-526-1200. 305 B dlemcoe@raritanval.edu
LEMERY, Cynthia 518-327-6399. 336 B clemery@paulsmiths.edu
LEMIERE, Donna 617-928-4519. 234 E dlemiere@mountida.edu
LEMIESZ, Linda 212-353-4115. 321 F lemiesz@cooper.edu
LEMIEUX, Carlene, P 207-893-7754. 211 G clemieux@sjcme.edu
LEMING, Heidi 912-279-5970. 123 B hleming@ccga.edu
LEMISCH, Jamie 215-780-1391. 433 A jlemisch@salus.edu
LEMISH, Dafna, P 618-453-7708. 159 G dafnalemish@siu.edu
LEMKE, Chris 616-222-1360. 241 F chris.lemke@cornerstone.edu
LEMKE, Gregory, J 218-477-5869. 259 H greg.lemke@mnstate.edu
LEMKE, Steve, W 504-282-4455. 206 A slemke@nobts.edu
LEMLEY, David 310-506-4275... 58 H david.lemley@pepperdine.edu
LEMMA, Paulette 860-832-2364... 87 K lemma@ccsu.edu
LEMME, Gary, D 334-844-4444..... 1 G gdl0003@aces.edu
LEMMER, Nick 507-457-6649. 264 A nlemmer@smumn.edu
LEMMON, Ann 919-962-4592. 366 K awlemmon@northcarolina.edu
LEMMON, John 650-508-3605... 56 H jlemmon@ndnu.edu
LEMMONS, Crystal 417-625-9394. 278 D lemmons-c@mssu.edu
LEMOINE, Sandra, M 318-342-1235. 208 E slemoine@ulm.edu
LEMON, Jason 619-260-4585... 73 I jasonlemon@sandiego.edu
LEMON, Ronald, E 304-896-7425. 528 F ronald.lemon@southernwv.edu
LEMON, William, J 314-824-2002. 283 E lemonj@umsl.edu
LEMOND, Charles 901-843-3890. 458 E lemond@rhodes.edu
LEMONIS, Samuel 601-857-3204. 267 A splemonis@hindscc.edu
LEMONNIER, Janet 973-642-8583. 307 D janet.wagman-lemonnier@shu.edu
LEMONS, James 434-832-7680. 512 A lemonsj@cvcc.vccs.edu
LEMONS, L. Jay 570-372-4130. 433 H supres@susqu.edu
LEMUEL, Robert, L 989-964-4393. 249 G lemuel@svsu.edu
LEMURA, Linda, M 315-445-4312. 328 F lemuralm@lemoyne.edu
LEMUS, Maria De Jesus . 773-371-5453. 141 D mlemus@ctu.edu
LENA, Hugh, F 401-865-2155. 439 E hlena@providence.edu
LENAHAN, Robert 631-632-6350. 342 C robert.lenahan@stonybrook.edu
LENARD, Mary 262-595-2644. 537 C mary.lenard@uwp.edu
LENART, Deborah 205-552-1257..... 3 B deborah.lenart@ecacolleges.com
LENCHAK, Timothy, A 563-876-3353. 177 I tlenchak@dwci.edu
LENCZOWSKI, John 202-462-2101... 96 A lenczowski@iwp.edu
LENDIO, Darolyn 808-956-9901. 135 L lendio@hawaii.edu
LENFEST, Richard 413-572-5405. 230 F rlenfest@westfield.ma.edu
LENGA, Kirk 516-299-4209. 329 C kirk.lenga@liu.edu
LENIG, Joni, L 931-540-2752. 460 E jlenig@columbiastate.edu
LENIHAN, Bernard 908-709-7605. 308 B lenihan@ucc.edu
LENIHAN, Deb 402-891-9411. 293 D deb.lenihan@vatterott-college.edu
LENIHAN, Gerald 973-642-8252. 307 D gerald.lenihan@shu.edu
LENIO, Jim 612-312-1295. 265 D jim.lenio@waldenu.edu
LENITNI, James, P 248-370-2193. 248 J jlentini@oakland.edu
LENKER, Michael 509-533-8280. 518 E mike.lenker@scc.spokane.edu
LENNEMAN, Marc 406-447-4336. 285 G mlenneman@carroll.edu
LENNERTZ, Reid 239-590-7960. 115 A rlennert@fgcu.edu
LENNEY, Raina 202-885-5936... 94 F lenney@american.edu
LENNIE, Peter 585-275-5931. 349 C lennie@rochester.edu
LENNIHAN, Louise 212-817-7200. 317 F llennihan@gc.cuny.edu
LENNON, Gerald, P 610-758-3165. 422 A gpl0@lehigh.edu
LENNON, John 845-848-4061. 322 G john.lennon@dc.edu
LENO, Melissa 218-733-5903. 259 A m.leno@lsc.edu
LENO, Tom 701-224-5497. 372 B thomas.leno@bismarckstate.edu
LENORE-JENKINS, Shani 314-529-9350. 276 G slenore@maryville.edu
LENOX, John, G 609-896-5192. 305 D jlenox@rider.edu
LENROW, Jon 215-670-9359. 425 J jlenrow@peirce.edu
LENSING, Peggy 563-387-1015. 180 M lensinpe@luther.edu
LENT, Scott 903-223-3087. 484 C scott.lent@tamut.edu
LENTING, Amy, L 312-788-1120. 162 H alenting@vandercook.edu
LENTINO, Nicholas 860-727-6765... 90 A nlentino@goodwin.edu
LENTNER, Nikolaus 914-251-6070. 344 D nikolaus.lentner@purchase.edu
LENTO, Joseph 718-260-5430. 319 B jlento@citytech.cuny.edu
LENTSNER, Dina 614-236-6952. 375 H dlentsne@capital.edu
LENTZ, Alice 828-726-2234. 358 E alentz@cccti.edu
LENTZ, Heather 605-995-7227. 450 E heather.lentz@mitchelltech.edu
LENTZ, Kristi, L 701-788-4772. 371 E kristi.lentz@mayvillestate.edu
LENTZ, Lynette 402-375-7241. 291 F lylentz1@wsc.edu
LENWAY, Stefanie, A 517-355-8377. 246 H lenway@msu.edu
LENZ, Christopher 323-343-3237... 34 A clenz@cslanet.calstatela.edu
LENZ, Craig, J 334-699-2266..... 1 B
LENZ, Joseph 515-271-3939. 177 K joe.lenz@drake.edu
LENZ, Mary 320-762-4648. 257 O maryl@alextech.edu
LENZ, Patrick, J 510-987-9101... 70 H patrick.lenz@ucop.edu
LENZ, Suzanne 603-623-0313. 297 E suzannelenz@nhia.edu
LENZI, John 413-545-2313. 228 F jlenzi@registrar.umass.edu
LENZI, Patrick 610-436-1048. 430 A plenzi@wcupa.edu
LENZO, Daniel 212-226-5500. 314 A dlenzo@aii.edu
LEON, Christine 714-564-6230... 60 G leon_christine@sac.edu
LEON, Dante, J 425-235-5831. 522 F dleon@rtc.edu
LEON, Gloria 914-606-6744. 350 F gloria.leon@sunywcc.edu
LEON, Juan, C 787-844-8812. 555 A juan.leon1@upr.edu
LEON, Nelson 212-752-1530. 328 G nelson.leon@limcollege.edu
LEON, Way 415-422-2868... 73 J leon@usfca.edu
LEON, Wayne 203-932-7416... 92 E wleon@newhaven.edu
LEON GUERRERO, Barbara, B 671-735-5519. 546 C csi@guamcc.edu
LEON GUERRERO, Deborah, D 671-735-2585. 546 E deborah@uguam.uog.edu
LEONARD, Brenda 704-330-6626. 359 C brenda.leonard@cpcc.edu
LEONARD, David, M 540-458-8752. 516 A dleonard@wlu.edu
LEONARD, Debbie 305-809-3203. 104 I debbie.leonard@fkcc.edu
LEONARD, Dianne 515-244-4221. 175 C leonardd@aib.edu
LEONARD, III, Edward, F 785-227-3380. 184 I president@bethanylb.edu
LEONARD, Gloria, J 314-516-5362. 283 E gloria_leonard@umsl.edu
LEONARD, J. Rich 919-865-5878. 352 K leonardjr@campbell.edu
LEONARD, Jacqueline 908-709-7610. 308 B leonard@ucc.edu
LEONARD, Jesse, W 814-641-3162. 419 H leonarj@juniata.edu
LEONARD, Joseph, G 202-296-5254... 95 D gleonard@gwu.edu
LEONARD, Katie 570-702-8925. 419 G kleonard@johnson.edu
LEONARD, Katy 205-226-4647..... 2 C kleonard@bsc.edu
LEONARD, Kimberly 618-453-2466. 159 G kleonard@siu.edu
LEONARD, Lawrence 318-257-3712. 207 F lleonard@latech.edu
LEONARD, Michael 215-951-6858. 430 E leonardm@philau.edu
LEONARD, Nora 757-388-2900. 509 D neleonar@sentara.com
LEONARD, Patricia, L 910-962-3117. 369 C leonard@uncw.edu
LEONARD, Patricia, Y 810-989-5523. 249 H pleonard@sc4.edu
LEONARD, OSFS, Peter . 610-282-1100. 414 F peter.leonard@desales.edu
LEONARD, Robert 256-824-2233..... 8 F robert.leonard@uah.edu
LEONARD, Robert 724-589-2024. 434 B rleonard@thiel.edu
LEONARD, Steve 317-738-8316. 165 I sleonard@franklincollege.edu
LEONARD, Thomas, C 510-642-3773... 70 I toml@berkeley.edu
LEONARD, Vee 239-590-1101. 115 A vleonard@fgcu.edu
LEONARD, William 617-735-9883. 226 B leonard@emmanuel.edu
LEONARD-HINDS, Hannah 404-237-7573. 121 F hleonardhinds@bauder.edu
LEONARD-MARTIN, Peg 615-460-6856. 453 C peg.leonardmartin@belmont.edu
LEONARD-RAY, Pamela . 843-574-6411. 447 E Pamela.Leonard-Ray@tridenttech.edu
LEONE, John 518-828-4181. 321 C john.leone@sunycgcc.edu
LEONG, Jodi 808-956-9437. 135 L jleong@hawaii.edu
LEONHARDT, Chuck 970-351-1890... 86 C charles.leonhardt@unco.edu
LEONOR, JR., Samuel, E 951-785-2090... 50 B sleonor@lasierra.edu
LEONOWICH, Donna 860-343-5762... 89 A dleonowich@mxcc.commnet.edu
LEOPARD, David 706-379-3111. 134 L
LEOPARD, Tim 205-348-8157..... 8 D tleopard@fa.ua.edu
LEOPARDI, Dino 607-844-8222. 347 I leopard@tc3.edu
LEOPOLD, Lillian 619-482-6564... 68 B lleopold@swccd.edu
LEOUSIS, Kim 251-442-2290..... 9 A kleousis@umobile.edu
LEPAGE, Bob 413-755-4477. 233 A rglepage@stcc.edu
LEPAGE, Francoise 415-485-3284... 42 J flepage@dominican.edu
LEPAGE, Greg 425-739-8108. 520 K greg.lepage@lwtech.edu
LEPAGE, Joe 512-863-1915. 481 I lepagej@southwestern.edu
LEPAGE, Sharon 808-440-4263. 135 D slepage@chaminade.edu
LEPLEY, Pamela, D 804-828-6057. 511 F pdlepley@vcu.edu
LEPPANEN, Hannu 906-487-7285. 242 G hannu.leppanen@finlandia.edu
LEPPELLERE, Terry 312-777-8594. 147 D tleppellere@aii.edu
LEPPER, Charles, W 757-822-1066. 514 C clepper@tcc.edu
LEPPERT, Glenn, W 620-862-5252. 184 E registrar@barclaycollege.edu
LEPPMAN, Erika 541-552-8484. 406 C leppmane@sou.edu
LEPUS, Jennifer 410-455-3751. 219 D jlepus@umbc.edu
LERBINGER, Jan 617-585-1284. 234 I jan.lerbinger@necmusic.edu
LERCH, Carol 508-929-8119. 230 G clerch@worcester.edu
LERCH, Derek 530-283-0202... 44 H dlerch@frc.edu
LERCH, Maureen, T 330-684-8951. 390 F mlerch@uakron.edu
LERER, Nava 516-877-3236. 313 A lerer@adelphi.edu
LERER, Seth 858-534-6270... 71 F slerer@ucsd.edu
LERMA, Raul, H 915-831-2565. 472 B rlerma23@epcc.edu
LERMAN, Linda 203-857-7211... 89 D llerman@norwalk.edu
LERMAN, Steven 202-994-6510... 95 D Lerman@gwu.edu
LERME, Keith 502-456-6504. 199 G klerme@sullivan.edu
LERNER, Bart 602-216-3114... 28 M blerner@argosy.edu
LERNER, Sandra 718-960-6959. 318 A sandra.lerner@lehman.cuny.edu
LERNER, Sharon 212-817-7400. 317 F slerner@gc.cuny.edu
LEROSEN, Genene, D 804-523-5550. 512 F glerosen@reynolds.edu

LEROY, Antonio .... 229-430-3635. 119 J
antonio.leroy@asurams.edu
LEROY, Francois .... 859-572-7976. 198 I
leroy@nku.edu
LEROY, Glen, S .... 248-204-2803. 245 I
gleroy@ltu.edu
LERUD, Theodore .... 630-617-3661. 145 A
tedl@elmhurst.edu
LERUD-HECK, Joanne, V 303-273-3690... 80 E
jvlerud@mines.edu
LESAGE, Jasper .... 712-707-7102. 181 H
lesage@nwciowa.edu
LESAN, Thomas, L .... 641-782-1443. 182 I
lesan@swcciowa.edu
LESAVOY, Barbara .... 585-395-5700. 342 F
blesavoy@brockport.edu
LESCAULT, JR.,
Maurice, A .... 434-971-3291. 544 I
moe.lescault@us.army.mil
LESCH, William .... 701-328-2965. 371 B
LESCHES, Elchonon .... 718-363-2034. 347 F
LESCINSKI, CSJ, Joan ...... 563-333-6213. 182 B
officeofthepresident@sau.edu
LESEANE, Reginald .... 912-358-3389. 131 C
leseaner@savannahstate.edu
LESESNE, David, L .... 804-752-7305. 508 E
davidlesesne@rmc.edu
LESGOLD, Alan, M .... 412-648-1738. 435 C
al@pitt.edu
LESH, Aja .... 626-815-6000... 29 H
alesh@apu.edu
LESHAN, Tim, E .... 617-373-8528. 235 F
LESHIN, Laurie .... 518-276-6305. 337 I
leshl@rpi.edu
LESHINSKIE, Eric .... 623-845-3692... 14 M
eric.leshinskie@gcmail.maricopa.edu
LESHKEVICH, Pete .... 734-973-3729. 252 A
pleshkev@wccnet.edu
LESHOK, Paul .... 414-443-3658. 535 A
leshokp@mtmary.edu
LESHT, Faye .... 217-333-3061. 162 A
flesht@illinois.edu
LESHT, Scott .... 312-752-2120. 149 E
scott.lesht@kendall.edu
LESICK, Lawrence, T .... 419-772-2261. 386 D
l-lesick@onu.edu
LESLIE, Abigail .... 314-744-7695. 278 B
lesliea@mobap.edu
LESLIE, Andrea .... 513-569-1746. 376 L
andrea.leslie@cincinnatistate.edu
LESLIE, Benjamin, C .... 704-406-4239. 354 C
bleslie@gardner-webb.edu
LESLIE, Betty .... 251-662-5363..... 2 D
bleslie@bishop.edu
LESLIE, Bruce .... 210-485-0020. 464 I
bleslie@alamo.edu
LESLIE, Deidre Lynn .... 940-898-2950. 488 B
dleslie@twu.edu
LESLIE, Donald .... 434-528-5276. 515 G
dleslie@vul.edu
LESLIE, Frances, M .... 949-824-6351... 71 B
fmleslie@uci.edu
LESLIE, Howard .... 973-278-5400. 314 K
hdl@berkeleycollege.edu
LESLIE, Julie .... 419-251-1598. 383 G
julie.leslie@mercycollege.edu
LESLIE, Paul, L .... 336-272-7102. 354 E
lesliep@greensboro.edu
LESLIE, Sandra .... 770-531-3172. 122 A
sleslie1@brenau.edu
LESLIE, Shirley, Y .... 617-541-5350. 232 G
sleslie@rcc.mass.edu
LESLIE, Steven, W .... 512-232-3301. 491 C
sleslie@mail.utexas.edu
LESNIAK, Stephen, L .... 909-593-3511... 72 E
slesniak@laverne.edu
LESS, Karen .... 704-922-6315. 360 F
less.karen@gaston.edu
LESSANE JENKINS,
Wanda .... 910-672-1145. 367 D
wljenkins@uncfsu.edu
LESSARD, Richard, J .... 617-732-2132. 233 E
richard.lessard@mcphs.edu
LESSEIG, Lisa .... 912-279-5737. 123 B
llesseig@ccga.edu
LESSEM, Louis, A .... 313-577-2268. 252 G
ac6001@wayne.edu
LESSER, Edward, R .... 617-585-1211. 234 I
ed.lesser@necmusic.edu
LESSER, Mary .... 828-328-7078. 356 B
mary.lesser@lr.edu
LESSUN, Walter .... 906-932-4231. 242 I
waltl@gogebic.edu
LESTARJETTE, Steve .... 281-425-6336. 475 I
slestarjette@lee.edu
LESTER, Candie .... 614-251-4690. 386 B
lesterc@ohiodominican.edu
LESTER, Dyan, E .... 276-964-7677. 514 A
dyan.lester@sw.edu
LESTER, Ellyn .... 619-684-8775... 56 C
elester@newschoolarch.edu
LESTER, John .... 706-562-1652. 123 D
lester_john@columbusstate.edu
LESTER, Karen, K .... 218-477-2062. 259 H
lesterka@mnstate.edu
LESTER, III, Robert, A .... 931-598-3227. 458 H
ralester@sewanee.edu
LESTER, Ron .... 405-491-6356. 399 K
rlester@snu.edu
LESTER, Tammy .... 252-451-8296. 362 D
tlester@nashcc.edu
LESWICK, Brenda .... 909-607-1403... 39 C
brenda.leswick@cgu.edu
LETENDRE, Diane .... 406-994-5326. 287 B
dletendre@montana.edu
LETENDRE, Donald, E .... 319-335-8794. 175 I
donald-letendre@uiowa.edu
LETH, Carl .... 815-939-5268. 155 H
cleth2@olivet.edu
LETH-STEENSEN, Ted ..... 413-565-1000. 222 F
tlethsteensen@baypath.edu
LETO, Michael, A .... 413-545-4200. 228 F
mleto@admin.umass.edu
LETSON, Dierdre .... 908-852-1400. 300 D
letsond@centenarycollege.edu
LETSOU, Peter, V .... 901-678-2421. 460 B
pvletsou@memphis.edu
LETT, Rita .... 334-876-9240..... 4 A
rita.lett@wccs.edu
LETTINI, Gabriella .... 510-549-4714... 68 G
glettini@sksm.edu
LETTMAN, Dennis .... 419-530-3303. 392 B
dennis.lettman@utoledo.edu
LETTS, John .... 217-641-4101. 148 M
letts@jwcc.edu
LEUENBERGER, Donald .. 402-559-6300. 292 J
dleuenbe@unmc.edu
LEUM, Kay .... 307-382-1639. 543 J
kleum@wwcc.wy.edu
LEUNER, Jean .... 407-823-5496. 115 E
jean.leuner@ucf.edu
LEUNG, Michael .... 510-885-3441... 33 C
michael.leung@csueastbay.edu
LEUNG, Stanley .... 415-282-7600... 27 L
stanleyleung@actcm.edu
LEUSCH, Lucy .... 404-364-8309. 130 A
lleusch@oglethorpe.edu
LEUTH, Sophia .... 303-837-0825... 78 H
sleuth@aii.edu
LEVALLEY, Angela .... 303-556-6930... 83 D
alevalle@msudenver.edu
LEVAN, Kent, G .... 314-977-7143. 281 I
levankg@slu.edu
LEVANDER, Caroline ...... 717-348-4228. 479 A
clevande@rice.edu
LEVAO, Richard, A .... 973-748-9000. 299 F
rlevao@bloomfield.edu
LEVASHEFF, Drake .... 714-556-3610... 74 D
dlevasheff@vanguard.edu
LEVATO, Peggy, S .... 315-379-3871. 345 F
levatop@canton.edu
LEVEN, Carol .... 212-217-4700. 324 C
carol_leven@fitnyc.edu
LEVEN, Scott .... 417-447-6985. 279 K
levens@otc.edu
LEVENE, Donna .... 602-749-3191. 189 I
donna.levene@otawa.edu
LEVENS, Michael .... 248-689-8282. 251 I
mlevens@walshcollege.edu
LEVENSON, Stephanie ..... 630-617-3354. 145 A
slevenson@elmhurst.edu
LEVENTHAL, Mitchel ...... 212-317-3546. 341 C
mitch.leventhal@suny.edu
LEVERENZ, Jeffrey .... 262-691-5301. 541 D
jleverenz@wctc.edu
LEVERETTE, Chad .... 803-641-3291. 448 A
chadl@usca.edu
LEVERGOOD, Bill, J .... 417-268-6042. 271 I
blevergoodl@gobbc.edu
LEVERING, E, H .... 305-237-0777. 109 D
eleverin@mdc.edu
LEVERINGTON, Paul ...... 512-505-3041. 473 G
ptleverington@htu.edu
LEVERS, David, W .... 718-289-5157. 317 B
david.levers@bcc.cuny.edu
LEVERSEE, Gordon .... 603-358-2545. 298 F
gleverse@keene.edu
LEVERT, Martin .... 954-783-7339. 102 M
mlevert@cci.edu
LEVERTON, Kathryn .... 609-771-2881. 300 E
leverton@tcnj.edu
LEVERTOV, Hannah .... 617-730-7021. 235 D
hannah.levertov@newbury.edu
LEVESQUE, Jacqueline ... 713-798-3356. 467 F
levesque@bcm.edu
LEVESQUE, Jeanne .... 617-552-4787. 224 A
jeanne.levesque@bc.edu
LEVESQUE, CM,
Joseph, L .... 718-990-6301. 339 A
pres@stjohns.edu
LEVESQUE, Keli .... 773-602-5016. 142 B
LEVESQUE, Lynne .... 972-860-4121. 470 G
llevesque@dcccd.edu
LEVETT, Ann .... 478-757-2544. 128 I
ann.levett@maconstate.edu
LEVETT, Kerry .... 541-463-5315. 403 I
levettk@lanecc.edu
LEVEY, Steve .... 713-718-5261. 473 C
stephen.levey@hccs.edu
LEVI, David, F .... 919-613-7001. 354 A
david.levi@law.duke.edu
LEVI, Dennis, M .... 510-642-3414... 70 I
dlevi@berkeley.edu
LEVICK, Cheryl, L .... 404-413-4000. 126 E
clevick@gsu.edu
LEVIN, Avrohom, C .... 773-463-7738. 160 H
aclevin@telshe.gov
LEVIN, Donald, E .... 313-927-1205. 246 D
dlevin@marygrove.edu
LEVIN, Gary, M .... 702-968-5248. 295 E
glevin@roseman.edu
LEVIN, Jason .... 801-274-3280. 498 E
jason.levin@wgu.edu
LEVIN, Jonathan .... 540-654-1241. 510 J
jlevin@umw.edu
LEVIN, Lubbe .... 310-794-0810... 71 C
llevin@chr.ucla.edu
LEVIN, Marc .... 410-888-9048. 216 D
mlevin@muih.edu
LEVIN, Sarah .... 802-728-1302. 501 F
slevin@vtc.edu
LEVIN, Yitzchok .... 773-463-7738. 160 H
yzlevin@telshe.gov
LEVIN-STANKEVICH,
Brian, L .... 801-832-2550. 498 F
bstankevich@westminstercollege.edu
LEVINE, Alan, M .... 570-348-6232. 423 B
levine@marywood.edu
LEVINE, Alan, M .... 570-348-6230. 423 B
levine@marywood.edu
LEVINE, Allen .... 612-624-1234. 264 G
aslevine@umn.edu
LEVINE, Arthur, S .... 412-648-8975. 435 C
alevine@pitt.edu
LEVINE, Barbara, J .... 412-397-2591. 431 I
levine@rmu.edu
LEVINE, Berinthia .... 216-687-5522. 377 F
berinthia.levine@csuohio.edu
LEVINE, Beth, F .... 718-951-2023. 317 C
bflevine@brooklyn.cuny.edu
LEVINE, Bryan .... 503-223-2245. 403 J
blevine@portland.chefs.edu
LEVINE, Eric .... 212-464-0400. 348 B
eric.levine@touro.edu
LEVINE, Harold, G .... 530-752-4663... 70 J
hlevine@ucdavis.edu
LEVINE, Heidi .... 319-895-4234. 177 A
hlevine@cornellcollege.edu
LEVINE, Helen .... 727-873-4744. 116 D
hlevine@mail.usf.edu
LEVINE, Isaac .... 732-367-1060. 299 E
ilevine@bmg.edu
LEVINE, Joe .... 212-678-3176. 347 G
jlevine@tc.columbia.edu
LEVINE, Joel .... 619-482-6349... 68 B
jlevine@swccd.edu
LEVINE, Laurie .... 561-237-7181. 108 X
llevine@lynn.edu
LEVINE, Lawrence, M ...... 303-492-4691... 85 L
larry.levine@colorado.edu
LEVINE, Linda .... 212-678-8007. 328 A
registrar@jtsa.edu
LEVINE, Linda .... 212-678-8007. 328 A
financialaid@jtsa.edu
LEVINE, Louis, L .... 212-410-8023. 333 E
llevine@nycpm.edu
LEVINE, Marilyn .... 509-963-1400. 517 F
levinem@cwu.edu
LEVINE, Mark .... 208-282-3620. 138 E
levimark@isu.edu
LEVINE, Martin, L .... 213-740-2101... 74 A
levine@usc.edu
LEVINE, Matt .... 530-251-8890... 50 F
mlevine@lassencollege.edu
LEVINE, Michael, F .... 716-878-4311. 343 A
levinmf@buffalostate.edu
LEVINE, Mona .... 301-405-0141. 219 B
mona1@umd.edu
LEVINE, Ned .... 801-302-2800. 496 B
ned.levine@neumont.edu
LEVINE, Richard .... 301-295-3303. 545 C
richard.levine@usuhs.edu
LEVINE, Susan .... 212-875-4657. 314 C
slevine@bankstreet.edu
LEVINE, Vikki .... 434-395-2921. 506 J
levinevj@longwood.edu
LEVINE, Virginia .... 607-753-2201. 343 B
virginia.levine@cortland.edu
LEVINE LAUFGRABEN,
Jodi .... 215-204-7000. 433 K
jodi.levine@temple.edu
LEVINESS, Peter, O .... 804-289-8119. 510 L
plevines@richmond.edu
LEVINO, Evelyn .... 614-947-6765. 380 A
evelyn.levino@franklin.edu
LEVINSON, David .... 203-857-7024... 87 J
dlevinson@ncc.commnet.edu
LEVINSON, David, L .... 203-857-7024... 89 D
dlevinson@norwalk.edu
LEVINSTEIN, Edward ...... 585-343-0055. 325 C
ejlevenstein@genesee.edu
LEVINTHAL, Keith .... 914-323-7277. 330 B
keith.levinthal@mville.edu
LEVIS, Kelly .... 603-623-0313. 297 E
kellylevis@nhia.edu
LEVISEUR, Jacquelyn ..... 330-941-2136. 394 A
jmleviseur@ysu.edu
LEVISON, Dan .... 510-654-2934... 44 B
dlevison@expression.edu
LEVISTER, Jason, O .... 910-272-3533. 363 B
jlevister@robeson.edu
LEVISTER, JR.,
Joseph, W .... 910-678-8327. 360 D
levistej@faytechcc.edu
LEVIT, Janet .... 918-631-2400. 401 F
janet-levit@utulsa.edu
LEVITT, Bart .... 412-809-5100. 430 H
levitt.bart@pti.edu
LEVY, Alan .... 312-935-4242. 148 C
alevy@icsw.edu
LEVY, Audre .... 281-290-3940. 476 A
audre.levy@lonestar.edu
LEVY, Ben .... 201-684-7533. 305 A
blevy1@ramapo.edu
LEVY, Dessie .... 414-297-6392. 540 E
levyd@matc.edu
LEVY, Donald .... 773-702-1383. 161 B
d-levy@uchicago.edu
LEVY, Douglas .... 586-445-7535. 246 A
levyd@macomb.edu
LEVY, Gary .... 410-704-2124. 220 E
glevy@towson.edu
LEVY, Kenneth, R .... 401-598-1007. 439 B
klevy@jwu.edu
LEVY, Laura .... 504-988-3291. 207 C
llevy@tulane.edu
LEVY, Samuel, J .... 651-962-6390. 265 C
sjlevy@stthomas.edu
LEVY, Sarah .... 845-574-4472. 338 B
slevy@sunyrockland.edu
LEVY, Shelley .... 718-289-5114. 317 B
shelley.levy@bcc.cuny.edu
LEVY CRUZ, Madeline ..... 570-558-1818. 416 I
LEW, Gary, B .... 716-888-2255. 316 C
lew@canisius.edu
LEW, Tom .... 310-660-3316... 43 B
tlew@elcamino.edu
LEW YAN VOON,
Lok, C .... 843-953-6682. 442 A
llewyanv@citadel.edu
LEWALLEN, Rhonda .... 432-335-6405. 477 M
rlewallen@odessa.edu
LEWALLEN, Willard .... 831-755-6900... 46 G
wlewallen@hartnell.edu
LEWANDOWSKI,
Joseph, D .... 660-543-4633. 283 A
lewandowski@ucmo.edu
LEWANDOWSKI, Ken ...... 610-789-6700. 431 C
klewandowski@prismcareerinstitute.edu
LEWELLEN, Phyllis .... 928-776-2190... 19 H
phyllis.lewellen@yc.edu
LEWELLEN, Randy .... 903-983-8130. 475 E
rlewellen@kilgore.edu
LEWELLYN, Tricia .... 313-845-9670. 243 H
tnllewellyn@hfcc.edu
LEWICKI, Denise .... 860-628-4751... 90 D
dlewicki@lincolncollegene.edu
LEWIN, Harris, A .... 530-754-7764... 70 J
lewin@ucdavis.edu
LEWIN, Jason .... 315-792-3282. 349 F
jmlewin@utica.edu
LEWIN, Lisa, M .... 414-410-4230. 532 B
lmlewin@stritch.edu
LEWIN, Luis, E .... 765-494-7395. 171 M
luislewin@purdue.edu
LEWIN, Ross .... 301-405-4772. 219 B
rdlewin@umd.edu
LEWINSKI, Chris .... 920-693-1277. 540 B
chris.lewinski@gotoltc.edu
LEWIS, Alana .... 706-821-8253. 130 C
alewis@paine.edu
LEWIS, Albert .... 708-974-5407. 153 F
lewisjra@morainevalley.edu
LEWIS, Alex, O .... 405-962-1663. 395 N
aolewis@langston.edu
LEWIS, Alicia .... 425-640-1020. 519 D
alicia.lewis@edcc.edu
LEWIS, Alisha .... 870-584-4471... 24 F
alewis@cccua.edu
LEWIS, Andre .... 831-582-3044... 34 B
alewis@csumb.edu

LEWIS, Andrew ... 304-829-7645. 526 D
alewis@bethanywv.edu
LEWIS, Ann ... 208-769-7812. 138 I
ann_lewis@nic.edu
LEWIS, April ... 864-596-9040. 443 D
april.lewis@converse.edu
LEWIS, Beth ... 409-933-8271. 469 E
blewis@com.edu
LEWIS, Beverly, N ... 336-734-7512. 360 E
blewis@forsythtech.edu
LEWIS, Bill ... 505-566-3339. 311 I
lewisb@sanjuancollege.edu
LEWIS, Bill, E ... 314-434-2212. 275 D
LEWIS, Blaine, D ... 330-823-7365. 391 E
lewisbd@mountunion.edu
LEWIS, Brenda, N ... 757-683-4885. 507 N
blewis@odu.edu
LEWIS, Brian ... 765-677-2188. 169 B
brian.lewis@indwes.edu
LEWIS, Brien ... 704-637-4414. 353 E
wblewis@catawba.edu
LEWIS, Bruce ... 847-491-4933. 155 D
balewis@northwestern.edu
LEWIS, C. Jasper ... 870-235-4065... 23 F
cjlewis@saumag.edu
LEWIS, Carol, E ... 907-474-7083... 10 I
celewis@alaska.edu
LEWIS, Carolyn ... 201-559-3560. 302 A
lewisc@felician.edu
LEWIS, Cassandra, B ... 601-877-3905. 265 G
cblewis@alcorn.edu
LEWIS, Charles, R ... 256-782-5003... 4 K
crlewis@jsu.edu
LEWIS, Christopher ... 517-371-5140. 250 G
lewisch@cooley.edu
LEWIS, Chuck ... 918-647-1450. 394 I
cllewis@carlalbert.edu
LEWIS, Cindy ... 805-493-3199... 31 H
clewis@clunet.edu
LEWIS, Crissy ... 864-578-8770. 446 F
clewis@sherman.edu
LEWIS, Daniel, G ... 925-631-4616... 61 F
dlewis@stmarys-ca.edu
LEWIS, Daphne ... 704-216-3463. 363 D
daphne.lewis@rccc.edu
LEWIS, David, A ... 808-675-4783. 135 C
david.lewis@byuh.edu
LEWIS, David, E ... 585-275-5240. 349 C
david.lewis@rochester.edu
LEWIS, David, R ... 802-356-6824... 94 E
david.r.lewis@wilmu.edu
LEWIS, David, W ... 317-274-0462. 168 D
dlewis@iupui.edu
LEWIS, Dawanna ... 713-221-8974. 489 D
lewisd@uhd.edu
LEWIS, Dewey, H ... 910-938-6225. 359 E
lewisd@coastalcarolina.edu
LEWIS, Don ... 763-433-1116. 257 P
donald.lewis@anokaramsey.edu
LEWIS, Donald ... 763-433-1116. 257 Q
donald.lweis@anokaramsey.edu
LEWIS, Donald, M ... 651-523-2941. 256 A
dlewis02@gw.hamline.edu
LEWIS, Donna ... 601-925-3967. 268 A
dlewis@mc.edu
LEWIS, Donna, M ... 304-647-6566. 528 D
dlewis@newriver.edu
LEWIS, Doris ... 269-965-3931. 244 O
lewisd@kellogg.edu
LEWIS, E. Charles ... 817-202-6720. 481 E
lewis@swau.edu
LEWIS, Eleanor ... 717-867-6302. 421 H
lewis@lvc.edu
LEWIS, Eva ... 423-697-2659. 460 C
LEWIS, Felicia ... 502-597-6286. 197 A
felicia.lewis@kysu.edu
LEWIS, Fred ... 423-279-7665. 461 C
fdlewis@northeaststate.edu
LEWIS, Georj ... 219-980-6824. 168 B
gllewis@iun.edu
LEWIS, Gillian, O ... 206-546-4780. 523 F
glewis@shoreline.edu
LEWIS, Goldene ... 718-270-6121. 319 A
goldene@mec.cuny.edu
LEWIS, Gregory ... 804-257-5750. 515 F
gelewis@vuu.edu
LEWIS, Gregory, V ... 661-824-2977... 55 I
LEWIS, Hal, M ... 312-322-1715. 160 D
LEWIS, Jack, M ... 540-674-3601. 513 B
jlewis@nr.edu
LEWIS, James ... 484-365-8096. 422 D
jlewis@lincoln.edu
LEWIS, James, E ... 206-934-5157. 523 A
james.lewis@seattlecolleges.edu
LEWIS, III, James, E ... 812-941-2430. 168 F
lewisjae@ius.edu
LEWIS, Jan ... 541-737-4605. 405 G
jan_lewis@ous.edu
LEWIS, Jan ... 252-328-6514. 367 B
lewisja@ecu.edu
LEWIS, Jan, P ... 253-535-7283. 521 I
lewisjp@plu.edu
LEWIS, Jan Ellen ... 973-353-5213. 306 D
janlewis@andromeda.rutgers.edu
LEWIS, Jane, L ... 209-946-2125... 73 A
jlewis@pacific.edu
LEWIS, Jeanne ... 609-652-4201. 305 C
jeanne.lewis@stockton.edu
LEWIS, Jeannie, M ... 559-323-2100... 63 B
jlewis@sjcl.edu
LEWIS, Jennifer ... 619-660-4670... 46 D
jennifer.lewis@gcccd.edu
LEWIS, Jerry ... 817-272-0979. 491 B
jerrylewis@uta.edu
LEWIS, Jill ... 843-661-8003. 443 G
jill.lewis@fdtc.edu
LEWIS, Jim ... 806-743-2530. 487 E
jim.lewis@ttuhsc.edu
LEWIS, Jim ... 817-272-2584. 491 B
jimlewis@uta.edu
LEWIS, Jim, D ... 704-637-4720. 353 E
jdlewis@catawba.edu
LEWIS, John ... 518-464-8560. 324 B
jlewis@excelsior.edu
LEWIS, John ... 901-321-3227. 453 H
john.lewis@cbu.edu
LEWIS, John, C ... 801-422-2533. 495 D
john_lewis@byu.edu
LEWIS, Joseph, S ... 949-824-8792... 71 B
jslewis@uci.edu
LEWIS, Judith ... 716-829-7776. 323 D
lewisj@dyc.edu
LEWIS, Judith, H ... 914-323-5279. 330 B
judith.lewis@mville.edu
LEWIS, Julie ... 315-866-1550. 326 A
LEWIS, Karen ... 515-271-7498. 177 H
Karen.Lewis@dmu.edu
LEWIS, Katherine, P ... 570-340-6094. 423 B
kplewis@marywood.edu
LEWIS, Kayli ... 407-277-0311. 103 C
kalewis@evergladesuniversity.edu
LEWIS, Keisha ... 205-929-1810... 5 G
klewis@miles.edu
LEWIS, JR., Kenneth, A . 252-492-2061. 364 F
lewis@vgcc.edu
LEWIS, Kent ... 270-852-3289. 197 B
klewis@kwc.edu
LEWIS, Lamar ... 757-340-2121. 503 I
directoredcvab@centura.edu
LEWIS, Leontye ... 910-672-1265. 367 D
llewis8@uncfsu.edu
LEWIS, Leslie ... 607-274-3533. 327 E
llewis@ithaca.edu
LEWIS, Lindsey, C ... 781-891-2551. 223 C
llewis@bentley.edu
LEWIS, Lisa ... 805-898-4010... 44 I
llewis@fielding.edu
LEWIS, Lisa ... 612-624-6142. 264 G
lrlewis@umn.edu
LEWIS, Lori ... 410-857-2250. 216 E
llewis@mcdaniel.edu
LEWIS, Lori ... 336-917-5577. 366 D
lori.lewis@salem.edu
LEWIS, Lynn ... 864-646-1437. 447 D
llewis@tctc.edu
LEWIS, Lynn ... 434-381-6106. 510 F
llewis@sbc.edu
LEWIS, Mark ... 325-674-2867. 464 H
mark.lewis@acu.edu
LEWIS, Marsha, L ... 716-829-2533. 341 F
UBNursingDean@buffalo.edu
LEWIS, Mary ... 651-641-8892. 255 B
lewis@csp.edu
LEWIS, Mary ... 772-462-7444. 106 P
mlewis@irsc.edu
LEWIS, Melissa ... 505-473-6404. 311 K
melissa.lewis@santafeuniversity.edu
LEWIS, Michael ... 785-749-8451. 187 B
michael.lewis@bie.edu
LEWIS, Michael ... 785-749-8497. 187 B
president@haskell.edu
LEWIS, Michael ... 614-251-4589. 386 B
lewism2@ohiodominican.edu
LEWIS, Michele ... 406-353-2607. 285 E
mlewis@ancollege.edu
LEWIS, Michelle ... 314-977-3065. 281 I
lewisml@slu.edu
LEWIS, Nichole, R ... 919-516-5082. 366 C
nrlewis@st-aug.edu
LEWIS, Nora, E ... 215-746-1172. 435 B
nlewis@sas.upenn.edu
LEWIS, Orlando ... 903-730-4890. 474 O
olewis@jarvis.edu
LEWIS, Patricia ... 404-297-9522. 126 A
lewisp@gptc.edu
LEWIS, Phil ... 405-425-5560. 397 D
phil.lewis@oc.edu
LEWIS, Preston ... 325-942-2248. 465 K
preston.lewis@angelo.edu
LEWIS, Rebecca ... 585-245-5546. 343 C
lewis@geneseo.edu
LEWIS, Rebecca, B ... 423-439-6155. 459 C
bakerr@etsu.edu
LEWIS, Richard ... 330-325-2511. 385 E
rwl@neomed.edu
LEWIS, Richard ... 928-350-1307... 17 K
rlewis@prescott.edu
LEWIS, Rita, F ... 704-461-6726. 352 G
ritalewis@bac.edu
LEWIS, Rob ... 859-985-3323. 192 F
lewisro@berea.edu
LEWIS, Robin ... 606-326-2423. 194 J
Robin.Lewis@kctcs.edu
LEWIS, Rosalyn ... 318-247-0430. 207 E
lewisros@gram.edu
LEWIS, Russ ... 951-827-3009... 71 E
russ.lewis@ucr.edu
LEWIS, S. Kay ... 206-543-6107. 524 G
sklewis@uw.edu
LEWIS, Shaun, M ... 504-286-5292. 206 K
slewis@suno.edu
LEWIS, Shirley ... 707-864-7000... 66 G
shirley.lewis@solano.edu
LEWIS, Steven ... 207-942-6781. 209 E
slewis@bts.edu
LEWIS, Susan ... 325-674-2024. 464 H
lewiss@acu.edu
LEWIS, Susan, A ... 617-262-5000. 223 F
susan.lewis@the-bac.edu
LEWIS, Ted, A ... 865-694-6523. 461 D
talewis@pstcc.edu
LEWIS, Terry, W ... 731-881-7890. 463 E
tlewis@utm.edu
LEWIS, Thomas ... 443-287-9900. 215 H
tomlewis@jhu.edu
LEWIS, Thomas, C ... 404-413-1404. 126 E
tomlewis@gsu.edu
LEWIS, Tiffany ... 765-677-2102. 169 B
tiffany.lewis@indwes.edu
LEWIS, Trevor ... 305-626-3750. 104 J
trevor.lewis@fmuniv.edu
LEWIS, Urick ... 610-526-6080. 417 H
ulewis@harcum.edu
LEWIS, Victoria ... 831-479-6406... 30 G
vilewis@cabrillo.edu
LEWIS, Vivian ... 585-273-2760. 349 C
vivian.lewis@rochester.edu
LEWIS, Walter ... 518-587-2100. 346 A
walter.lewis@esc.edu
LEWIS, Wendy ... 330-823-6045. 391 E
lewisws@mountunion.edu
LEWIS, William, A ... 601-403-1201. 269 D
wlewis@prcc.edu
LEWIS, SR., William, T .. 540-231-3811. 515 C
wtlewiss@vt.edu
LEWIS-ANTHONY,
Justin ... 703-370-6600. 508 B
LEWIS-BOYD, Janice ... 313-593-5200. 251 D
jckboyd@umich.edu
LEWIS-JASPER, Vera ... 409-944-1496. 472 I
vlewis@gc.edu
LEWIS LOGUE, Judith ... 619-260-4720... 73 I
jllogue@sandiego.edu
LEWIS-MOTTS, Irene ... 330-494-6170. 389 F
imotts@starkstate.edu
LEWIS SAULO, Mileva ... 650-292-5579... 61 I
msaulo@samuelmerritt.edu
LEWIS-THOMAS, Janice . 256-726-7840... 6 B
jthomas@oakwood.edu
LEWIS-WHITE, Yasmin ... 202-885-8552... 97 D
ylwhite@wesleyseminary.edu
LEWISTON, Linda ... 619-594-5211... 35 D
llewisto@mail.sdsu.edu
LEWIT, Jonathan, D ... 845-257-3130. 342 B
lewit@newpaltz.edu
LEWKIEWICZ, Debra ... 845-434-5750. 347 A
dlewkiew@sullivan.suny.edu
LEWTER, Andy ... 478-445-5169. 125 A
andy.lewter@gcsu.edu
LEWTHWAITE,
Barbara-Jayne ... 908-852-1400. 300 D
lewthwaiteb@centenarycollege.edu
LEWY, MariLynn, J ... 941-752-5383. 114 I
lewym@scf.edu
LEX, Andrea, A ... 301-322-0723. 217 F
lexaa@pgcc.edu
LEXOW, Les ... 636-227-2100. 276 F
les.lexow@logan.edu
LEYBA, Marylou ... 415-239-3291... 38 L
mleyba@ccsf.edu
LEYDEN, John, J ... 401-865-2390. 439 E
jleyden@providence.edu
LEYDON, John ... 919-962-4908. 366 K
jleydon@northcarolina.edu
LEYDON, Pamela, F ... 904-819-6423. 103 E
pleydon@flagler.edu
LEYKAM, Scott ... 503-943-7117. 408 F
leykam@up.edu
LEYSER, Becky ... 510-549-4704... 68 G
bleyser@sksm.edu
LEYVA-PUEBLA, Ricardo 206-934-6455. 523 A
ricardo.leyva-puebla@seattlecolleges.edu
LEZAK JANOW,
Roseann ... 860-509-9501... 90 B
rlezak@hartsem.edu
LE'I, Emilia ... 684-699-9155. 546 A
e.lei@amsamoa.edu
LI, Al ... 314-434-4044. 273 C
al.li@covenantseminary.edu
LI, Benn ... 212-924-5900. 347 B
bli@swedishinstitute.edu
LI, Christine ... 212-650-6849. 317 D
cli@sci.ccny.cuny.edu
LI, Dai ... 602-235-4179. 189 L
dli@pittstate.edu
LI, Joanne ... 937-775-4859. 393 G
joanne.li@wright.edu
LI, Kevin ... 773-481-8250. 142 F
kli@ccc.edu
LI, Liz ... 888-488-4968... 48 K
LI, Luchen ... 812-877-8810. 172 C
li2@rose-hulman.edu
LI, Ming ... 740-593-1889. 387 C
lim1@ohio.edu
LI, Peter, B ... 330-972-6493. 390 E
peter8@uakron.edu
LI, Rui ... 610-430-4959. 430 A
rli@wcupa.edu
LI, Shaozhi ... 512-444-8082. 485 B
sli@thsu.edu
LI, Sharon, F ... 415-422-2790... 73 J
lis@usfca.edu
LI, Sheng ... 714-533-1495... 66 H
sli@southbaylo.edu
LI, Xin ... 425-558-0299. 519 B
xli@digipen.edu
LI, Yan ... 415-355-1601... 27 L
yanli@actcm.edu
LI, Yi ... 937-775-2611. 393 G
yi.li@wright.edu
LI, Zhan ... 925-631-4604... 61 F
zgl1@stmarys-ca.edu
LI-BUGG, Cherry ... 707-527-4392... 65 B
wli-bugg@santarosa.edu
LIANG, Bryan, A ... 619-239-0391... 36 D
bliang@cwsl.edu
LIANG, John Paul ... 713-780-9777. 465 G
info@acaom.edu
LIANG, Mark ... 714-564-6040... 60 G
liang_mark@sac.edu
LIANG, Sherry ... 510-628-8027... 51 A
controller@lincolnuca.edu
LIBBY, Betsy ... 207-755-5334. 210 J
blibby@cmcc.edu
LIBBY, Elizabeth ... 847-735-6011. 150 B
libby@lakeforest.edu
LIBBY, James ... 207-859-1420. 211 H
libbyj@thomas.edu
LIBBY, John ... 240-567-7951. 216 F
john.libby@montgomerycollege.edu
LIBBY, Wendy, B ... 386-822-7250. 117 C
wlibby@stetson.edu
LIBEN, Lucy ... 212-924-5900. 347 B
lucy@swedishinstitute.edu
LIBERATORE,
Anthony, F ... 217-424-6338. 153 C
aliberatore@millikin.edu
LIBERATORE, Debra ... 518-454-5145. 321 A
liberatd@strose.edu
LIBERATOS, James, D ... 318-257-4287. 207 F
schisto@latech.edu
LIBERATOSCIOLI, Daniel 215-222-4200. 431 H
president@walnuthillcollege.edu
LIBERATOSCIOLI, Peggy 215-222-4200. 431 H
pl@walnuthillcollege.edu
LIBERMAN, Ira ... 718-438-1002. 331 A
yliberman@yeshivanet.com
LIBERTELLA, Anthony ... 516-877-4607. 313 A
libertella@adelphi.edu
LIBERTELLI, Joseph ... 202-274-7338... 97 A
jlibertelli@udc.edu
LIBERTY, Bob ... 254-526-1310. 468 G
bob.liberty@ctcd.edu
LIBERTY, Paul ... 703-993-8860. 505 C
pliberty@gmu.edu
LIBET, Alice, Q ... 843-792-4930. 445 B
libeta@musc.edu
LIBMAN, Peter ... 516-463-6913. 326 D
peter.libman@hofstra.edu
LIBURD, Kenrick ... 423-493-4220. 462 B
liburdk@tntemple.edu
LIBURD, Tina ... 423-493-4417. 462 B
liburdt@tntemple.edu
LIBUTTI, Dean ... 401-874-4405. 440 D
dean@uri.edu
LICAR, Jason ... 918-836-6886. 400 D
jlicar@mail.spartan.edu
LICARI, Frank ... 702-990-4433. 295 E
LICARI, Michael, J ... 319-273-2518. 176 A
michael.licari@uni.edu
LICATA, Betty Jo ... 330-941-3064. 394 A
bjlicata@ysu.edu

LICATA, Christine, M ...... 585-475-2953. 337 L cmlnbt@rit.edu
LICCIARDI, Anne .... 916-558-2201... 53 D licciaa@scc.losrios.edu
LICHT, Daniel .... 914-395-2301. 340 E dlicht@sarahlawrence.edu
LICHT, Jodi, N .... 212-752-1530. 328 G jodi.licht@limcollege.edu
LICHTBLAU, Jobey, L ..... 701-231-9581. 371 G jobey.lichtblau@ndsu.edu
LICHTENBERG, Tami ...... 218-625-4921. 254 K tlichten@css.edu
LICHTENBERGER, Lynn .. 856-691-8600. 301 A llichtenberger@cccnj.edu
LICHTENFELD, Randy ..... 505-349-2150... 18 I randy.lichtenfeld@phoenix.edu
LICHTENSTEIN, Art .... 501-450-5202... 25 H artl@uca.edu
LICHTENSTEIN, Gregg .... 619-594-7351... 35 D lichtens@mail.sdsu.edu
LICHTLE, Richard .... 419-358-3314. 374 J lichtler@bluffton.edu
LICHTSINN, Jill .... 260-982-5015. 170 U jslichtsinn@manchester.edu
LICHTY, Dennis .... 402-375-7389. 291 F delicht1@wsc.edu
LICKISS, Steve .... 619-388-7455... 62 F slickiss@sdccd.edu
LICKTIEG, Elaine .... 203-285-2389... 88 E elicktieg@gwcc.commnet.edu
LIDDELL, Alan, C .... 908-526-1200. 305 B aliddell@raritanval.edu
LIDDELL, Marilynn .... 970-339-6210... 78 C marsi.liddell@aims.edu
LIDDELL, Peter, E .... 315-255-1743. 316 D pliddell@twcny.rr.com
LIDDELL, Robert .... 352-588-8346. 112 D robert.liddell@saintleo.edu
LIDDICOAT, Al .... 805-756-2844... 32 F aliddico@calpoly.edu
LIDDLE, Trevor, C .... 956-326-1300. 483 B tliddle@tamiu.edu
LIDDY, Colette .... 973-618-3209. 300 A cliddy@caldwell.edu
LIDDY, Elizabeth, D .... 315-443-2736. 347 C liddy@syr.edu
LIDERS, Gunta .... 585-275-4031. 349 C gliders@orpa.rochester.edu
LIDGUS, Jonathan, A ..... 314-516-5537. 283 E lidgusj@umsl.edu
LIDSTONE, Rhonda, W ... 478-301-2005. 128 H lidstone_rw@mercer.edu
LIDSTROM, Mary, E .... 206-616-0804. 524 G lidstrom@uw.edu
LIDY, Paul .... 217-362-6410. 153 C plidy@millikin.edu
LIEB, James, F .... 814-824-2276. 423 J jlieb@mercyhurst.edu
LIEBAU, Linda, B .... 513-244-4593. 377 G linda_liebau@mail.msj.edu
LIEBER, Barbara .... 217-641-4535. 148 M blieber@jwcc.edu
LIEBERMAN, Devorah, A 909-593-3511... 72 E dlieberman@laverne.edu
LIEBERMAN, Ilene .... 610-499-4275. 437 E idlieberman@widener.edu
LIEBERMAN, Jethro, K ... 212-431-2378. 333 I jlieberman@nyls.edu
LIEBERMAN, Robert .... 410-516-3355. 215 H rlieberman@jhu.edu
LIEBERMAN, Robert, C .. 212-854-4604. 321 D rcl15@columbia.edu
LIEBERT, Elizabeth .... 415-451-2859... 63 A eliebert@sfts.edu
LIEBERT, Jane .... 913-758-6126. 191 B Jane.Liebert@stmary.edu
LIEBERT, June .... 312-427-2737. 148 L 8liebert@jmls.edu
LIEBOVITCH, Larry .... 718-997-4105. 319 C larry.liebovitch@qc.cuny.edu
LIEBOWITZ, Ronald, D ... 802-443-5400. 499 H liebowit@middlebury.edu
LIEBRECHT, Alan, J .... 816-584-6234. 280 C alan.liebrecht@park.edu
LIEBROCK, Lorie .... 575-835-5481. 310 F liebrock@cs.nmt.edu
LIEBSCHER, Kim, K .... 580-774-3776. 400 B kim.liebscher@swosu.edu
LIECHTY, Dennis, G .... 812-888-2890. 174 F dliechty@vinu.edu
LIECHTY, Jeanne, M .... 574-535-7401. 166 A jeannem@goshen.edu
LIEDTKA, Theresa .... 423-425-4506. 463 D theresa-liedtka@utc.edu
LIEDTKE, Richard, W ...... 785-670-1812. 191 D richard.liedtke@washburn.edu
LIEF, Charles, G .... 303-546-3517... 83 F president@naropa.edu
LIEFELD, Julie .... 203-392-5475... 88 A liefeldj1@southernct.edu
LIEGEL, Angela .... 312-915-6191. 151 H aliegel@luc.edu
LIEGLER, Rose .... 626-812-3085... 29 H rliegler@apu.edu
LIERMAN, Michael .... 800-962-7682. 285 A mlierman@wma.edu
LIERZ, Rachel .... 816-501-4866. 280 I rachel.lierz@rockhurst.edu
LIES, CSC, James .... 508-565-1551. 237 A jlies@stonehill.edu
LIES, CSC, William, M ... 574-631-9800. 174 A lies.7@nd.edu
LIESCH, Ed .... 717-728-2273. 412 J edliesch@centralpenn.edu
LIESEN, Joseph .... 573-288-6480. 273 F jliesen@culver.edu
LIESEN, Kristen .... 217-228-5432. 156 C liesekr@quincy.edu
LIESKE, Brian .... 650-493-4430... 66 E brian.lieske@sofia.edu
LIESMAN, Laura .... 732-987-2685. 302 B liesmanl@georgian.edu
LIETO, Mary .... 914-923-2690. 335 J mlieto@pace.edu
LIEU, Mark .... 510-659-6173... 57 A mlieu@ohlone.edu
LIEURANCE, Lorissa .... 515-271-3781. 177 K lorissa.lieurance@drake.edu
LIGEIKIS, Kelli .... 607-778-5089. 315 I ligeikiskh@sunybroome.edu
LIGGETT, Shawn .... 541-888-7221. 407 H sliggett@socc.edu
LIGGINGS, Elena .... 915-351-8100. 465 I
LIGHT, Brad .... 336-334-4355. 369 A uncg@bkstore.com
LIGHT, Cathy, A .... 412-268-5345. 412 H calight@andrew.cmu.edu
LIGHT, Joanne .... 978-762-4000. 232 D jlight@northshore.edu
LIGHT, Kathleen .... 210-829-3943. 490 A light@uiwtx.edu
LIGHTBOURN, Andre, M 305-628-6712. 112 F alightbourn@stu.edu
LIGHTBURN, Arifah .... 504-278-6421. 203 F alightburn@nunez.edu
LIGHTCAP, Stephen .... 215-717-6375. 435 A slightcap@uarts.edu
LIGHTFIELD, Nancy, R ... 608-757-7750. 539 I nlightfield@blackhawk.edu
LIGHTFOOT, Bill .... 770-718-5326. 122 A blightfoot@brenau.edu
LIGHTFOOT, Carolyn, A . 281-425-6455. 475 I clightfo@lee.edu
LIGHTFOOT, Connie .... 765-998-5105. 173 C cnlightfoot@taylor.edu
LIGHTFOOT, Douglas ..... 816-604-1061. 277 C douglas.lightfoot@mcckc.edu
LIGHTFOOT, James, D ... 434-832-7643. 512 A lightfootd@cvcc.vccs.edu
LIGHTFOOT, Justine .... 574-807-7420. 164 D justine.lightfot@bethelcollege.edu
LIGHTHILL, M. Joyce ..... 641-784-5222. 178 F lighthil@graceland.edu
LIGHTNER, Sharon .... 760-750-4211... 35 A slightner@csusm.edu
LIGHTSY, Spencer .... 713-222-5391. 489 D lightsys@uhd.edu
LIGIOSO, Yulian .... 707-864-7000... 66 G yulian.ligioso@solano.edu
LIGMAN, Scott .... 509-527-2431. 524 I scott.ligman@wallawalla.edu
LIGNOWSKI, Beth .... 201-559-6027. 302 A 0267mgr@sheg.follett.com
LIIMATTA, Michael, K ..... 816-960-2008. 272 D mliimatta@cityvision.edu
LIKENS, Erin .... 601-643-8316. 266 F erin.likens@colin.edu
LILES, Jeffrey, R .... 606-783-2000. 198 A j.liles@moreheadstate.edu
LILES, Joel, O .... 740-389-4636. 383 F lilesj@mtc.edu
LILES, Kevin .... 803-641-3581. 448 A kevinl@usca.edu
LILES, Stewart .... 202-685-7375. 544 K stewart.liles@ndu.edu
LILES, Tammy .... 859-246-6449. 194 L tammy.liles@kctcs.edu
LILIENTHAL, Ronda .... 615-248-1245. 462 D rlilienthal@trevecca.edu
LILLBACK, Peter, A .... 215-572-3811. 437 C plillback@wts.edu
LILLEBO, Troy .... 816-235-6585. 283 D lillebot@umkc.edu
LILLER, Karen, D .... 813-974-2846. 116 C kliller@usf.edu
LILLESTON, Judith .... 914-831-0369. 321 B jlilleston@cw.edu
LILLEY, Jeffrey .... 734-462-4400. 250 A jlilley@schoolcraft.edu
LILLEY, Richard .... 443-840-4698. 214 E rlilley@ccbcmd.edu
LILLEY, Todd, D .... 540-828-5759. 502 J tlilley@bridgewater.edu
LILLIBRIDGE, Fred .... 575-527-7728. 311 B flillibr@nmsu.edu
LILLIE, Sandra .... 720-890-8922... 82 I president@itea.edu
LILLIS, John, R .... 651-582-8188. 253 K j-lillis@bethel.edu
LILLQUIST, Erik, R .... 973-642-8844. 307 D erik.lillquist@shu.edu
LILLQUIST, Mark .... 941-487-4570. 115 D mlillquist@ncf.edu
LILLY, Claude, C .... 864-833-8222. 446 D clilly@presby.edu
LILLY, Donald .... 864-977-7122. 445 H donald.lilly@ngu.edu
LILLY, Flavius, R .... 410-706-7767. 219 C flilly@umaryland.edu
LILLY, Gary, D .... 724-946-7250. 437 B glilly@westminster.edu
LILLY, Kenneth, E .... 304-877-6428. 526 C ken.lilly@abc.edu
LILLY, Mary .... 617-732-2144. 233 E mary.lilly@mcphs.edu
LILLY, Renee .... 330-494-6170. 389 F rlilly@starkstate.edu
LILLY, Vivian, C .... 210-733-3056. 194 B vlilly@galencollege.edu
LIM, Adriene, I .... 248-370-2486. 248 J ailim@oakland.edu
LIM, Ben .... 620-229-6388. 190 G ben.lim@sckans.edu
LIM, Bob .... 785-864-4999. 190 L blim@ku.edu
LIM, Chong, W .... 636-327-4645. 277 K jwlim44@hotmail.com
LIM, Colleen .... 650-723-2300... 68 E
LIM, Dan .... 407-303-9473... 97 H dan.lim@adu.edu
LIM, Dong Hwan .... 714-517-1945... 29 K president@buc.edu
LIM, Eunjoo .... 714-533-3946... 36 C
LIM, Gim .... 215-751-8275. 413 I glim@ccp.edu
LIM, Janine .... 269-471-6546. 243 G janine@andrews.edu
LIM, Kyung, C .... 770-484-1204. 128 E lru@lru.edu
LIM, Mercy .... 415-442-7080... 45 I mlim@ggu.edu
LIM, Morris .... 210-341-1366. 477 L mlim@ost.edu
LIM, Paul .... 213-385-2322... 77 A paul1911@wmu.edu
LIM, Sung Jin .... 213-385-2322... 77 A sunglim@wmu.edu
LIM, Teik, C .... 513-556-4450. 390 G teik.lim@uc.edu
LIM-THOMPSON, Soo-Yin .... 218-281-6510. 264 E
LIMA, Brad .... 508-830-5012. 230 D blima@maritime.edu
LIMA, Judy, E .... 205-329-7904..... 3 B judy.lima@ecacolleges.com
LIMA-JONES, Paula, M .. 717-245-1559. 414 H limap@dickinson.edu
LIMAYEM, Moez .... 813-974-3229. 116 C mlimayem@usf.edu
LIMBAUGH, James .... 406-265-3720. 287 D james.limbaugh@msun.edu
LIMBIRD, Lee .... 615-329-1907. 454 F llimbird@fisk.edu
LIMEGROVER, Eric .... 740-376-4477. 383 E el002@marietta.edu
LIMON, Frank .... 773-843-7553. 142 E flimon@ccc.edu
LIMONCELLI, Jerry .... 516-686-7815. 333 H jlimonce@nyit.edu
LIMPER, Leslie .... 503-777-7224. 407 E leslie.limper@reed.edu
LIMTUATCO, Edwin, E .... 671-735-5560. 546 C edwin.limtuatco@guamcc.edu
LIN, Alecia .... 269-927-8108. 245 D lin@lakemichigancollege.edu
LIN, Anne .... 410-532-5545. 217 E alin@ndm.edu
LIN, Ellen .... 408-924-5940... 36 A ellen.lin@sjsu.edu
LIN, Kuoliang .... 626-571-5110... 51 B klin@les.edu
LIN, Lisa .... 512-444-8082. 485 B lisalin@thsu.edu
LIN, Paul .... 512-444-8082. 485 B thsu@thsu.edu
LIN, Yi-Chun Tricia .... 203-392-6864... 88 A lyny4@southernct.edu
LIN-COOK, Wendy, W .... 973-275-2498. 307 C wendy.lincook@shu.edu
LINAMEN, Larry .... 951-552-8744... 30 H llinamen@calbaptist.edu
LINARES, Rachel .... 859-846-5856. 197 I rmlinares@midway.edu
LINBACK, John .... 574-936-8898. 163 K john.linback@ancilla.edu
LINBERG, Kurt .... 218-723-5930. 254 K klinberg@css.edu
LINBURG, Kurt .... 303-991-1575... 78 D kurt.linburg@americansentinel.edu
LINCKE, James .... 610-353-7630. 419 L jlincke@kaplan.edu
LINCOLN, III, George, A 570-577-1037. 411 A george.lincoln@bucknell.edu
LINCOLN, Greg .... 212-472-1500. 334 B glincoln@nysid.edu
LINCOLN, Jonathan .... 570-389-5333. 427 H jlincoln@bloomu.edu
LINCOLN, Judy .... 314-837-6777. 280 K jlincoln@slcconline.edu
LINCOLN, Timothy .... 512-404-4873. 467 A tlincoln@austinseminary.edu
LINCOLN-PENZEL, Brenda .... 314-264-1000. 284 G
LINCOURT, Carrie .... 212-592-2000. 340 H clincourt@sva.edu
LIND, Curt, D .... 541-346-1228. 406 D clind@uoregon.edu
LIND, Daniel, G .... 319-335-2645. 175 I daniel-lind@uiowa.edu
LIND, Jan .... 812-877-8297. 172 C lind@rose-hulman.edu
LIND, Louise .... 218-879-0879. 258 E llind@fdltcc.edu
LIND, Steven .... 415-442-7261... 45 I slind@ggu.edu
LIND-GONZALEZ, Patricia .... 631-420-2298. 346 B patricia.lind-gonzalez@farmingdale.edu
LINDAHL, Roberta .... 503-943-7321. 408 F lindahl@up.edu
LINDAHL, Susan .... 785-594-8375. 184 C susan.lindahl@bakeru.edu
LINDAHL, Wesley .... 773-244-5667. 154 G wlindahl@northpark.edu
LINDAU, Buff, L .... 802-654-2536. 500 B blindau@smcvt.edu
LINDBERG, Brad .... 507-786-3446. 264 B lindberg@stolaf.edu
LINDBERG, Kevin, D ...... 956-326-2601. 483 B klindberg@tamiu.edu
LINDBERG, Maryann ...... 603-358-2181. 298 F mlindberg1@keene.edu
LINDELL, Belinda, S .... 218-755-2043. 258 A blindell@bemidjistate.edu
LINDELL, Gretchen .... 716-488-3020. 327 I gretchenlindell@jamestownbusinesscollege.edu
LINDELL, P. Griffith .... 503-375-7034. 403 A glindell@corban.edu
LINDELL, TyAnn .... 906-487-7301. 242 G tyann.lindell@finlandia.edu
LINDEMAN, Brian .... 651-696-6214. 256 L lindeman@macalester.edu
LINDEMAN, Craig .... 316-978-7282. 191 F craig.lindeman@wichita.edu
LINDEMAN, Randy .... 361-354-2271. 468 K randyl@coastalbend.edu
LINDEMANN, Deborah ..... 510-780-4500... 50 I dlindemann@lifewest.edu
LINDEMER, Geoffrey .... 802-728-1232. 501 F glindemer@vtc.edu
LINDEMEYER, Donna, M .... 973-290-4442. 300 F dlindemeyer@cse.edu
LINDEMUTH, Gregory, L 610-566-1776. 437 G glindemuth@williamson.edu
LINDEN, Eric .... 718-252-7800. 348 B elinden@touro.edu
LINDEN, Erika .... 515-271-1526. 177 H erika.linden@dmu.edu
LINDEN, James .... 215-489-2446. 414 E James.Linden@delval.edu
LINDEN, Peter .... 815-455-8996. 152 F plinden@mchenry.edu
LINDEN, Stephen, M .... 248-341-2186. 248 D smlinden@oaklandcc.edu
LINDENBAUM, Sharon ... 816-235-2650. 283 D lindenbaums@umkc.edu
LINDENBERG, David, A . 802-447-6360. 500 D dlindenberg@svc.edu
LINDENMEYER, Kriste .... 856-225-2809. 306 C kriste.lindenmeyer@camden.rutgers.edu
LINDENMEYER, Mark, L 410-617-2576. 216 A lindenmeyer@loyola.edu
LINDENMEYR, Adele .... 610-519-7090. 436 F adele.lindenmeyr@villanova.edu
LINDENMUTH, Susan, E 610-799-1151. 421 I slindenmuth@lccc.edu
LINDER, Chad .... 717-815-1346. 438 D clinder@ycp.edu
LINDER, Cynthia .... 912-287-4098. 130 B clinder@okefenokeetech.edu

LINDER, Jim 402-554-2373. 292 G jlinder@nebraska.edu
LINDER, Keith, D 602-496-0789... 11 K keith.linder@asu.edu
LINDER, Mark 256-765-4397... 9 C mdlinder@una.edu
LINDER, Vincent, P 517-586-3007. 241 A vlinder@cleary.edu
LINDGREN, Dianne 828-339-4268. 364 B diannel@southwesterncc.edu
LINDGREN, Katherine, S 423-425-4646. 463 D kay-lindgren@utc.edu
LINDGREN, Rita 701-224-5427. 372 B rita.lindgren@bismarckstate.edu
LINDGREN, Robert, R 804-752-7211. 508 E rlindgren@rmc.edu
LINDGREN, Sheri 414-464-9777. 539 G sherilindgren@wspp.edu
LINDGREN, Teresa, C 606-783-2449. 198 A t.lindgren@moreheadstate.edu
LINDLEY, Carolyn, V 847-491-8557. 155 D c-lindley@northwestern.edu
LINDLEY, Georgia 662-325-1810. 268 D georgia@saffairs.msstate.edu
LINDLEY, Patricia 620-235-4132. 189 L plindley@pittstate.edu
LINDLEY, Stu 314-744-7623. 278 B lindleys@mobap.edu
LINDNER, Bill 850-644-7572. 115 C blindner@fsu.edu
LINDNER, Hollie, M 208-467-8531. 139 A hmlindner@nnu.edu
LINDNER, Janet, E 203-432-2188... 93 A janet.lindner@yale.edu
LINDNER, Rosalyn, A 716-878-6939. 343 A lindera@buffalostate.edu
LINDNER, Susan 718-262-2272. 319 F slindner@york.cuny.edu
LINDO, Patricia 860-512-3100... 88 G plindo@manchestercc.edu
LINDON, Jeniffer 606-436-5721. 195 C jennifer.lindon@kctcs.edu
LINDQUIST, Cynthia, A 701-766-4055. 370 H president@littlehoop.edu
LINDQUIST, Joyce 970-207-4500... 86 G JoyceL@uscareerinstitute.edu
LINDQUIST, Joyce 970-207-4550... 83 B
LINDQUIST, Kathy 918-335-6234. 398 F klindquist@okwu.edu
LINDQUIST, Kimberly 734-384-4101. 247 C klindquist@monroeccc.edu
LINDQUIST, Stefanie, A 706-542-2059. 133 C slindquist@uga.edu
LINDSAY, Cecile 562-985-4128... 33 F clindsay@csulb.edu
LINDSAY, Charles, W 607-735-1798. 323 H clindsay@elmira.edu
LINDSAY, Cheryl, A 315-255-1743. 316 D cheryl.lindsay@cayuga-cc.edu
LINDSAY, Creighton 503-845-3508. 404 D creighton.lindsay@mtangel.edu
LINDSAY, D. Michael 978-867-4800. 226 H president@gordon.edu
LINDSAY, Dane 619-388-7823... 62 F dlindsay@sdccd.edu
LINDSAY, Dawn 410-777-2222. 213 D
LINDSAY, Dennis 541-684-7253. 405 C dennisl@nwcu.edu
LINDSAY, John 401-232-6154. 438 K jlindsay@bryant.edu
LINDSAY, Jonathan 614-222-3234. 378 A jlindsay@ccad.edu
LINDSAY, Kristen 419-448-2301. 380 G klindsay@heidelberg.edu
LINDSAY, Larry 765-677-2103. 169 B larry.lindsay@indwes.edu
LINDSAY, Nathan 816-235-6084. 283 D lindsayn@umkc.edu
LINDSAY, Shawn 417-626-1234. 279 J lindsay.shawn@occ.edu
LINDSAY, Terry 773-244-4588. 154 G tlindsay@northpark.edu
LINDSAY, Twila 410-923-4585... 96 F twila.lindsay@strayer.edu
LINDSETH, Becky 218-683-8630. 260 D becky.lindseth@northlandcollege.edu
LINDSETH, Becky 218-793-2476. 260 D becky.lindseth@northlandcollege.edu
LINDSETH, Lori 602-787-7102... 15 B lori.lindseth@paradisevalley.edu
LINDSETH, Paul, G 218-755-4143. 258 A plindseth@bemidjistate.edu
LINDSEY, April 336-887-3000. 355 N alindsey@laureluniversity.edu
LINDSEY, Beverly 662-846-4648. 266 G blindsey@deltastate.edu
LINDSEY, Bruce, M 314-935-6200. 284 L blindsey@wustl.edu
LINDSEY, Carolyn 909-384-8282... 62 A clindse@sbccd.cc.ca.us
LINDSEY, DeLois 860-768-5122... 92 D lindsey@hartford.edu
LINDSEY, Earlene 205-652-3528..... 9 F elindsey@uwa.edu
LINDSEY, Heidie 337-482-6272. 208 D hlindsey@louisiana.edu
LINDSEY, John, L 336-887-3000. 355 N jlindsey@laureluniversity.edu
LINDSEY, Larry, J 989-837-4376. 248 C larryl@northwood.edu
LINDSEY, Lee 707-476-4100... 40 H lee-lindsey@redwoods.edu
LINDSEY, Patrick, O 313-577-4228. 252 G cz5360@wayne.edu
LINDSEY, Shannon 785-628-4462. 186 F sdlindsey@fhsu.edu
LINDSTAEDT, William 415-502-2422... 72 A bill.lindstaedt@ucsf.edu
LINDSTROM, Richard 559-442-8277... 68 I richard.lindstrom@fresnocitycollege.edu
LINDSTROM, Richard, W 323-563-5832... 38 B richardlindstrom@cdrewu.edu
LINDSTROM, Ryan 801-863-8303. 497 C lindstry@uvu.edu
LINDTORTH, Scott, A 919-684-0539. 354 A scott.lindroth@duke.edu
LINDUSKA, Kim 515-964-6628. 177 B kjlinduska@dmacc.edu
LINDVALL, Sherie, J 651-638-6233. 253 K s-lindvall@bethel.edu
LINDZEY, Jonathan 570-484-2987. 429 B jlindzey@lhup.edu
LINE, Robert 419-434-4528. 391 D link@findlay.edu
LINEBAUGH, Jonathan 954-771-0376. 108 Q
LINEBERG, Kimberly 304-260-4380. 527 N klineberg@blueridgectc.edu
LINEBERGER, Marilyn 404-880-8049. 122 J mlineberger@cau.edu
LINEBERGER, Susanne, B 386-312-4050. 112 C susannelineberger@sjrstate.edu
LINEBERRY, Forrest 336-757-3396. 360 E flineberry@forsythtech.edu
LINEBERRY, Gene, T 859-323-6589. 200 C gt.lineberry@uky.edu
LINEBURG, Robert 540-831-5228. 508 C rlineburg@radford.edu
LINEHAN, Rob 765-998-4905. 173 C rblinehan@taylor.edu
LINEHAN, Sarah, J 518-743-2263. 345 E linehans@sunyacc.edu
LINER, Andrea 979-830-4413. 467 I andrea.liner@blinn.edu
LINFANTE, Felix 973-877-3070. 301 H linfante@essex.edu
LINFANTE, Patrick 973-761-9328. 307 C patrick.linfante@shu.edu
LING, Jack, T 937-229-2541. 391 C jling1@udayton.edu
LING, Stan 740-362-3130. 383 H sling@mtso.edu
LINGEFELT, Jeff 803-938-3784. 448 F jdlingef@uscsumter.edu
LINGEN, BVM, Joan 563-588-6406. 176 F joan.lingen@clarke.edu
LINGER, Frederick, S 740-427-5250. 382 J lingerf@kenyon.edu
LINGER, JR., Jerry 859-371-9393. 192 D jlinger@beckfield.edu
LINGER, Rob 304-367-4692. 528 E rob.linger@pierpont.edu
LINGERFELT, Harley, W 405-878-5100. 399 G hwlingerfelt@stgregorys.edu
LINGLE, Ronald, K 910-938-6211. 359 E lingler@coastalcarolina.edu
LINGRELL, Scott 678-839-6423. 133 I slingrel@westga.edu
LINGUA, Jane 310-954-4132... 54 J jlingua@msmc.la.edu
LINHART, Lisa 303-762-6980... 81 G lisa.linhart@denverseminary.edu
LINIO, Richard, T 606-783-2066. 198 A r.linio@moreheadstate.edu
LINK, Harvey 701-671-2112. 372 E harvey.link@ndscs.edu
LINK, Johnson 864-656-7389. 442 C jwl@clemson.edu
LINK, Laura 612-874-3700. 257 B laura_link@mcad.edu
LINK, Lisa 616-222-1426. 241 F lisa.link@cornerstone.edu
LINK, Rebecca, C 717-815-1336. 438 D rlink@ycp.edu
LINK, Robert 419-434-4528. 391 D link@findlay.edu
LINK, Rosemary, J 515-961-1615. 182 E rosemary.link@simpson.edu
LINKER, Timothy, L 336-841-9313. 355 C tlinker@highpoint.edu
LINKINS, Arthur 903-334-6650. 484 C arthur.linkins@tamut.edu
LINKS, Jonathan 410-516-8070. 215 H jlinks1@jhu.edu
LINN, Brent 901-375-4400. 457 C brentlinn@midsouthcc.org
LINN, Jeffrey, S 724-589-2757. 434 B jlinn@thiel.edu
LINN, Joseph, G 785-628-4222. 186 F jlinn@fhsu.edu
LINN, Reid, J 540-568-6131. 506 F linnrj@jmu.edu
LINN, Richard, T 716-827-3451. 348 G linnr@trocaire.edu
LINN, Richard, T 716-827-4351. 348 G linnr@trocaire.edu
LINN, Timon 410-626-6931. 217 G timon.linn@sjca.edu
LINNANE, SJ, Brian, F 410-617-2201. 216 A president@loyola.edu
LINNE, Gil 860-628-4751... 90 D glinne@lincolncollegene.edu
LINNEBUR, Michael 316-942-4291. 189 E linneburm@newmanu.edu
LINNEHAN, Francis 215-895-2122. 415 B francis.linnehan@drexel.edu
LINNEHAN, JR., James, F 978-656-3151. 232 B linnehanj@middlesex.mass.edu
LINNENBURGER, Jane, C 309-677-2515. 140 I jane@bradley.edu
LINNEVERS, David 831-582-3094... 34 B dlinnevers@csumb.edu
LINNEY, Jean, A 610-519-4606. 436 F jean.linney@villanova.edu
LINO, Paulette 510-723-2665... 37 K plino@chabotcollege.edu
LINOS, Megan, W 812-465-1061. 174 D mwlinos@usi.edu
LINSCHEID, David 316-284-5251. 184 J dlin@bethelks.edu
LINSEY, Troy 706-265-7515. 128 B tlinsey@laniertech.edu
LINSON, Marci 417-690-2636. 272 E linson@cofo.edu
LINSON, Phil 323-856-7792... 27 O plinson@afi.com
LINTHICUM, David 410-287-6060. 214 B dlinthicum@cecil.edu
LINTHICUM, Glen 615-248-1243. 462 D glinthicum@trevecca.edu
LINTON, Josh 918-610-8303. 398 I josh.linton@ptstulsa.edu
LINTON, Leon, E 847-229-9595. 159 B
LINTON, Meg 310-665-6907... 57 C mlinton@otis.edu
LINTON, Pamela 212-752-1530. 328 G pamela.linton@limcollege.edu
LINTON, Peggy 334-493-3573..... 5 E plinton@lbwcc.edu
LINTON, Richard, H 919-515-2668. 368 B richard_linton@ncsu.edu
LINTS, Richard 978-468-7111. 227 A rlints@gcts.edu
LINZER, Daniel, I 847-491-5117. 155 D dlinzer@northwestern.edu
LINZEY, Scott 912-525-5000. 131 B slinzey@scad.edu
LINZMEYER, Kathryn 510-723-6751... 37 K klinzmeyer@chabotcollege.edu
LIOUDAKIS, Angelo 213-252-5100... 26 A
LIPAN, Petruta 314-977-3571. 281 I lipanp@slu.edu
LIPE, Leslie 503-338-2450. 402 G llipe@clatsopcc.edu
LIPHART, Jodi 904-826-0084. 118 I jliphart@usa.edu
LIPHART, Kristy 715-682-1496. 535 D kliphart@northland.edu
LIPIEC, Susan 216-373-5211. 385 G slipiec@ndc.edu
LIPINSKI, Marion, A 410-706-0025. 219 C mlipinski@umaryland.edu
LIPIRA, Pat 417-625-9394. 278 D lipira-p@mssu.edu
LIPKEY, Debra 202-651-5000... 95 C debra.lipkey@gallaudet.edu
LIPMAN, Howard 305-348-6298. 115 B howard.lipman@fiu.edu
LIPMAN, Sheryl, H 901-678-2155. 460 B slipman@memphis.edu
LIPMAN, Steven 617-266-1400. 223 D
LIPOLD, Tony 949-582-4547... 67 C tlipold@saddleback.edu
LIPORTO, Charles 603-513-1354. 298 E charles.liporto@granite.edu
LIPP, Evan, E 508-767-7285. 222 C elipp@assumption.edu
LIPP, Jacob 713-226-5585. 489 D lippp@uhd.edu
LIPPARD, Rodney 704-216-3686. 363 D rodney.lippard@rccc.edu
LIPPE, Diane 954-262-4870. 109 K lipped@nova.edu
LIPPE, Karen, M 561-868-3735. 110 C lippek@palmbeachstate.edu
LIPPENS, Nancy 319-273-7738. 176 A nancy.lippens@uni.edu
LIPPENS, Susan, M 419-866-0261. 389 H smlippens@stautzenberger.com
LIPPERT, Rebecca, M 215-887-5511. 437 C rlippert@wts.edu
LIPPERT, Wendy, S 717-766-2511. 423 L wlippert@messiah.edu
LIPPIELLO, Stephen 304-214-8809. 528 G slippiello@wvncc.edu
LIPPIN, Carol, A 732-987-2360. 302 B lippin@georgian.edu
LIPPINCOTT, Andi 315-279-5313. 328 D alippinc@keuka.edu
LIPPINCOTT, Doug 315-279-5641. 328 D dlippinc@mail.keuka.edu
LIPPINCOTT, James 503-375-5304. 408 J jlippinc@willamette.edu
LIPPMAN, Fred 954-262-1508. 109 K flippman@nova.edu
LIPPMAN, Stuart 212-463-0400. 348 B stuartl@touro.edu
LIPPMANN, Frances 559-442-4600... 68 I
LIPSCHUTZ, Ronnie 831-459-3275... 72 C rligsch@ucsc.edu
LIPSCOMB, Benjamin 585-567-9374. 326 F benjamin.lipscomb@houghton.edu
LIPSCOMB, Donnie 423-869-6353. 456 A donnie.lipscomb@lmunet.edu
LIPSCOMB, Natasha 704-216-3622. 363 D natasha.lipscomb@rccc.edu
LIPSCOMB, Sharyon 225-578-8833. 204 N slipsc1@lsu.edu
LIPSCOMB, Tamra 540-863-2905. 512 B tlipscomb@dslcc.edu
LIPSETT, Teresa 787-743-7979. 552 I
LIPSHITZ, Rita 773-973-0241. 146 C lipshitz@htc.edu
LIPSKIER, Hershel 973-267-9404. 304 G
LIPSTREU, Tiffany 614-947-6556. 380 A tiffany.lipstreu@franklin.edu
LIPTAK, M. Victoria 818-767-0888... 76 K vic.liptak@woodbury.edu
LIPTON, Ethan 302-343-4500... 34 A elipton@exchange.calstate.edu
LIPTON, Jeffrey 631-656-2122. 324 F jeffrey.lipton@ftc.edu
LIPTON, Mitchell 212-353-4121. 321 F lipton@cooper.edu
LIRA, Ken 760-776-7428... 40 F klira@collegeofthedesert.edu
LIRLEY, Sean 719-336-1543... 82 R sean.lirley@lamarcc.edu
LISBERGER, Jody 401-874-4620. 440 D jlisberger@uri.edu
LISBOA, Sandra 787-738-2161. 554 C sandra.lisboa@upr.edu
LISCHKA, Rosemary, L 913-288-7246. 187 L rlischka@kckcc.edu
LISCHWE, Sheila, T 864-656-1661. 442 C slischw@clemson.edu
LISENBY, Sadie 901-321-3527. 453 H slisenby@cbu.edu
LISI, Peter 860-768-2446... 92 D lisi@hartford.edu
LISLE, Kristy 352-323-3630. 108 S lislek@lssc.edu
LISS, Donna 660-785-4163. 282 L dliss@truman.edu
LISS, Ron 216-987-5125. 378 D ron.liss@tri-c.edu
LIST, Kathleen, L 941-359-7587. 111 O klist@ringling.edu
LISTER, Basil 816-604-6748. 277 D basil.lister@mcckc.edu
LISTER, Carole, B 864-597-4230. 449 I listercb@wofford.edu
LISTER, Charlotte, T 302-857-1290... 93 G clister@dtcc.edu
LISTER, Renae 281-851-0156. 469 L renae.lister@concordia.edu
LISTON, Brenda 614-947-6532. 380 A brenda.liston@franklin.edu
LISTON, Jed 406-243-2361. 286 H jed.liston@umontana.edu
LISTON, Sunny 503-534-4007. 404 C sliston@marylhurst.edu
LISTWAK, Jeffrey, A 412-397-5277. 431 I listwak@rmu.edu
LISZKA, James 518-564-5402. 344 B jlisz001@plattsburgh.edu
LITCHFIELD, Greg 802-862-9616. 498 I glitchfield@burlington.edu
LITCHFIELD, Randy, I 740-362-3482. 383 H rlitchfield@mtso.edu

LITCHKE, Gwen .... 218-322-2329. 258 I
gwen.litchke@itascacc.edu
LITCHMAN, Jennifer, B .. 410-706-3477. 219 C
jlitchman@umaryland.edu
LITKE, Russell .... 505-566-3253. 311 I
litker@sanjuancollege.edu
LITOLFF, Edwin .... 225-342-6950. 207 D
Edwin.Litolff@la.gov
LITT, Jacquelyn, S .... 732-932-9721. 306 B
jacquelyn.litt@rutgers.edu
LITT, Jacquelyn, S .... 573-882-0647. 283 C
littj@missouri.edu
LITTERAL, Samuel .... 304-896-7426. 528 F
samuel.litteral@southernwv.edu
LITTLE, Albert, P .... 386-312-4116. 112 C
allittle@sjrstate.edu
LITTLE, Andrew, P .... 410-777-2227. 213 D
aplittle1@aacc.edu
LITTLE, Anthony .... 480-732-7313... 14 J
anthony.little@cgc.edu
LITTLE, Bert .... 254-968-9463. 483 A
little@tarleton.edu
LITTLE, Colleen .... 802-447-6319. 500 D
clittle@svc.edu
LITTLE, Daniel .... 313-593-5500. 251 D
delittle@umich.edu
LITTLE, Ellen, B .... 325-674-2625. 464 H
ellen.little@acu.edu
LITTLE, Glenn, W .... 863-784-7218. 113 G
glenn.little@southflorida.edu
LITTLE, Jill, M .... 586-445-7576. 246 A
littlej@macomb.edu
LITTLE, Judith, W .... 510-643-6644... 70 I
jwlittle@berkeley.edu
LITTLE, Karen .... 513-244-8437. 376 J
karen.little@ccuniversity.edu
LITTLE, Karen, A .... 419-289-5032. 374 C
klittle@ashland.edu
LITTLE, Kevin, K .... 831-656-2508. 544 M
kllittle@nps.edu
LITTLE, Lee .... 706-721-4018. 126 B
llittle@gru.edu
LITTLE, Lynn .... 940-397-4198. 476 H
lynn.little@mwsu.edu
LITTLE, Martha .... 850-729-4901. 109 I
littlem@nwfsc.edu
LITTLE, Michael, S .... 757-683-3189. 507 N
mlittle@odu.edu
LITTLE, Pamela, M .... 919-866-5805. 364 G
pmlittle@waketech.edu
LITTLE, Patricia, L .... 330-471-8359. 383 D
plittle@malone.edu
LITTLE, Philip .... 312-752-2110. 149 E
philip.little@kendall.edu
LITTLE, Ralph .... 801-524-8131. 495 O
rkl28@ldsbc.edu
LITTLE, Rebecca, K .... 812-888-4220. 174 F
rlittle@vinu.edu
LITTLE, II, Ron .... 510-659-7307... 57 A
rlittle@ohlone.edu
LITTLE, Scott .... 601-968-5956. 266 A
slittle@belhaven.edu
LITTLE, Shanon .... 415-257-1302... 42 J
shanon.little@dominican.edu
LITTLE, Ted, A .... 336-334-7555. 367 E
talittle@ncat.edu
LITTLE, Trace .... 336-334-4104. 369 A
tjlittle@uncg.edu
LITTLE, Verna, S .... 334-727-8503..... 8 A
little@mytu.tuskegee.edu
LITTLE, William .... 607-962-9458. 322 B
wlittle@corning-cc.edu
LITTLE-BERRY, Teri .... 352-854-2322. 100 K
berryt@cf.edu
LITTLE OWL, Barbara ..... 701-255-3285. 373 C
blittleowl@uttc.edu
LITTLE-VANN, Darla .... 904-256-7500. 107 Q
dlitte2@ju.edu
LITTLE WHITEMAN,
Iona .... 701-627-4738. 371 A
llittl@fbcc.bia.edu
LITTLEBEAR, Richard ...... 406-477-6215. 285 H
rlbear@cdkc.edu
LITTLEFIELD,
Elizabeth, S .... 804-523-5181. 512 F
blittlefield@reynolds.edu
LITTLEFIELD, Julie .... 979-230-3576. 468 A
julie.littlefield@brazosport.edu
LITTLEFIELD, Marisa ...... 918-343-6816. 399 C
mlittlefield@rsu.edu
LITTLEJOHN, Sylvia .... 803-738-7764. 445 C
littlejohns@midlandstech.edu
LITTLEPAGE, Craig, K ..... 434-982-5100. 511 B
ckl9e@virginia.edu
LITTLES, Douglas, M ...... 251-578-1313..... 6 D
dlittles@rstc.edu
LITTLES, James, A .... 314-921-9290. 284 D
jlittles@ugst.edu
LITTLETON, Christine, A . 310-206-7411... 71 C
clittleton@conet.ucla.edu
LITTLETON, Robert, A ..... 423-652-6022. 455 I
ralittle@king.edu
LITTMAN, Jared, E .... 718-990-2920. 339 A
littmanj@stjohns.edu
LITTON, Ashley .... 513-244-4979. 377 G
ashley_litton@mail.msj.edu
LITTON, Freddie .... 361-570-4261. 489 E
littonf@uhv.edu
LITTRELL, Beth .... 402-461-7372. 289 I
blittrell@hastings.edu
LITVINOV, Dimitri .... 713-743-4168. 489 B
litvinov@central.uh.edu
LITWILLER, Jennifer, L ... 540-432-4131. 504 D
careerservices@emu.edu
LITYNSKI, Daniel, M ...... 269-387-8294. 252 I
dan.litynski@wmich.edu
LITZ, Kerri .... 410-225-2277. 216 C
klitz@mica.edu
LITZIN, Louise .... 928-724-6633... 13 H
louise@dinecollege.edu
LIU, Alan .... 626-289-7719... 26 J
LIU, Felix .... 626-571-5110... 51 B
felixliu@les.edu
LIU, Juanita, C .... 808-956-7166. 136 B
liujuani@hawaii.edu
LIU, Jun .... 404-413-2536. 126 E
junliu@gsu.edu
LIU, Lan .... 860-343-5833... 89 A
lliu@mxcc.commnet.edu
LIU, Lawrence .... 909-599-5433... 50 J
lliu@lifepacific.edu
LIU, Lena .... 415-282-7600... 27 L
lenaliu@actcm.edu
LIU, Monika .... 415-452-5730... 38 L
mliu@ccsf.edu
LIU, Shuang .... 410-532-5544. 217 E
sliu@ndm.edu
LIU, Victor .... 734-973-3379. 252 A
vliu@wccnet.edu
LIU, Yuxing .... 512-454-1188. 466 B
LIVELSBERGER, Patricia . 410-857-2223. 216 E
plivelsberger@mcdaniel.edu
LIVELY, Alisa .... 304-473-8441. 531 G
lively_a@wvwc.edu
LIVELY, Don .... 704-971-8500. 353 F
LIVELY, Julie .... 903-675-6233. 488 D
jlively@tvcc.edu
LIVELY, Lisa, A .... 304-293-8638. 530 D
lisa.lively@mail.wvu.edu
LIVELY, Robert, L .... 207-778-7277. 212 D
lively@maine.edu
LIVENGOOD, Jacob .... 508-626-4625. 230 A
jlivengood@framingham.edu
LIVENGOOD, Jim .... 702-895-4729. 294 I
don.livengood@unlv.edu
LIVENGOOD, Lori .... 316-394-5227. 184 J
llivengood@bethelks.edu
LIVERNOIS, Jim .... 972-721-5128. 488 F
livernois@udallas.edu
LIVERPOOL, Patrick, R ... 336-334-7233. 367 E
pliverp@ncat.edu
LIVERS, Elaine, D .... 337-482-6391. 208 D
livers@louisiana.edu
LIVERS, John, T .... 812-888-4301. 174 F
jlivers@vinu.edu
LIVESAY, Brandi .... 540-828-5336. 502 J
LIVESAY, Bruce .... 931-553-0071. 457 F
bruce.livesay@miller-motte.com
LIVESAY, Stephen, D ...... 423-775-7201. 453 E
livesast@bryan.edu
LIVINGOOD,
Susannah, B .... 405-325-3681. 401 B
slivingood@ou.edu
LIVINGS-EASSA, Libby ... 772-462-7402. 106 P
elivings@irsc.edu
LIVINGSTON, Carolyn .... 404-727-7195. 124 E
chlivin@emory.edu
LIVINGSTON, David, J ... 419-824-3809. 383 C
dlivingston@lourdes.edu
LIVINGSTON, Joe, A ...... 407-582-8069. 118 M
jlivingston@valenciacollege.edu
LIVINGSTON, Kathy .... 308-865-8204. 292 H
livingstonke@unk.edu
LIVINGSTON, Kay .... 229-248-2611. 121 E
kay.livingston@bainbridge.edu
LIVINGSTON, Linda .... 310-568-5539... 58 H
linda.livingston@pepperdine.edu
LIVINGSTON, Lynette ...... 715-833-6669. 539 J
livingston3@cvtc.edu
LIVINGSTON, Nancy .... 651-779-3222. 258 C
nancy.livingston@century.edu
LIVINGSTON, Pam .... 702-579-3512. 294 B
plivingston@kaplan.edu
LIVINGSTON, Randy .... 650-724-0213... 68 E
livingston@stanford.edu
LIVINGSTON, Sarah, M .. 402-399-2430. 289 A
slivingston@csm.edu
LIVINGSTON, Shannon .. 715-675-3331. 541 A
livingst@ntc.edu
LIVINGSTON, Stan .... 601-477-4006. 267 F
stan.livingston@jcjc.edu
LIVINGSTON, Tina .... 903-886-5667. 483 E
tina.livingston@tamuc.edu
LIWAG, Jonathan .... 670-234-3690. 547 A
jonathanl@nmcnet.edu
LIZARDI, David .... 787-738-2161. 554 C
david.lizardi@upr.edu
LIZER, Shannon, K .... 815-227-2444. 158 A
shannonlizer@sacn.edu
LIZOTTE, Alan, J .... 518-442-5214. 341 D
a.lizotte@albany.edu
LIZOTTE, Edmund .... 203-596-4604... 90 I
elizotte@post.edu
LJUBICIC, Amanda .... 860-629-6115... 90 G
ljubicic_a@mitchell.edu
LJUTIC, Peter .... 201-200-3045. 303 F
pljutic@njcu.edu
LLANA, James .... 212-237-8110. 318 D
jllana@jjay.cuny.edu
LLANOS, Keren .... 787-620-2040. 547 C
kllanos@aupr.edu
LLANOS, Rafael .... 787-764-0000. 555 B
rafael.llanos@upr.edu
LLERANDI, Joanne, A ..... 718-990-1487. 339 A
llerandj@stjohns.edu
LLERANDI, Mariel .... 787-878-5475. 549 L
mllerandi@arecibo.inter.edu
LLERENA, Fernando, N ... 305-273-4499. 100 H
fllerena@cbt.edu
LLERENA, Gladys, P ...... 305-273-4499. 100 H
gladys@cbt.edu
LLERENA, Luis, E .... 305-273-4499. 100 H
luis@cbt.edu
LLERENA, Monica .... 305-273-4499. 100 H
monica@cbt.edu
LLESES, Wilbert .... 650-508-3441... 56 H
finaid@ndnu.edu
LLEWELLYN, Donna, C ... 404-894-2340. 125 D
donna.llewellyn@oars.gatech.edu
LLEWELLYN, Jean, M ..... 973-596-5546. 303 G
jean.llewellyn@njit.edu
LLOPIZ, Maria .... 773-481-8323. 142 F
mllopiz@ccc.edu
LLORENS, James .... 225-771-5020. 206 J
james_llorens@subr.edu
LLOVIO, Kay .... 916-577-2200... 76 J
kllovio@jessup.edu
LLOYD, Andrea .... 802-443-5908. 499 H
lloyd@middlebury.edu
LLOYD, Celia .... 212-650-7859. 317 D
clloyd@ccny.cuny.edu
LLOYD, Charles .... 603-271-6484. 296 C
clloyd@ccsnh.edu
LLOYD, Chris .... 215-702-4339. 411 F
clloyd@cairn.edu
LLOYD, Christine .... 239-590-1425. 115 A
clloyd@fgcu.edu
LLOYD, Christine, M ...... 610-499-4182. 437 E
cmlloyd@widener.edu
LLOYD, Curtis .... 518-320-1192. 341 C
curtis.lloyd@suny.edu
LLOYD, Daniel .... 630-942-2865. 142 G
lloydd@cod.edu
LLOYD, David .... 765-998-4634. 173 C
dvlloyd@taylor.edu
LLOYD, Don .... 573-897-5000. 276 E
LLOYD, Giovina .... 607-871-2966. 313 E
lloydgm@alfred.edu
LLOYD, Gweneth .... 845-257-2920. 342 B
lloydg@newpaltz.edu
LLOYD, James .... 315-792-7300. 346 C
jim.lloyd@sunyit.edu
LLOYD, James, H .... 513-244-8138. 376 J
jim.lloyd@ccuniversity.edu
LLOYD, James, W .... 352-392-2213. 116 A
lloydjw@ufl.edu
LLOYD, Jan .... 407-708-2144. 113 E
lloydj@seminolestate.edu
LLOYD, Julie .... 415-394-6235... 65 C
jlloyd@saybrook.edu
LLOYD, Mary, J .... 815-599-3418. 146 D
mary.lloyd@highland.edu
LLOYD, Patrick, M .... 614-292-9755. 386 E
lloyd.256@osu.edu
LLOYD, Rachel .... 918-540-6971. 396 G
rlloyd@neo.edu
LLOYD, Richard, B .... 802-776-5236. 499 B
richard.lloyd@csj.edu
LLOYD, Rodie, F .... 207-725-3963. 209 H
rlloyd@bowdoin.edu
LLOYD, Sharon .... 678-359-5133. 127 A
sharonl@gordonstate.edu
LLOYD, Tricia .... 202-462-2101... 96 A
lloyd@iwp.edu
LLOYD, Willie, L .... 248-232-4142. 248 D
wllloyd@oaklandcc.edu
LO, Deborah .... 907-796-6123... 11 A
deborah.lo@uas.alaska.edu
LO, Jim .... 765-677-1771. 169 B
jim.lo@indwes.edu
LO SASSO, Joseph .... 609-652-4235. 305 C
joe.losasso@stockton.edu
LO SCHIAVO, SJ,
John, J .... 415-422-6215... 73 J
loschiavo@usfca.edu
LOAR, Peggy .... 202-639-1736... 95 B
ploar@corcoran.org
LOBASSO, Lisa, M .... 570-941-7459. 436 A
lisa.lobasso@scranton.edu
LOBASSO, Thomas .... 386-506-3257. 101 G
lobasst@DaytonaState.edu
LOBATO, Ana .... 831-476-9424... 44 K
studentservices@fivebranches.edu
LOBATO, Richard, L ...... 915-831-3391. 472 B
rlobato@epcc.edu
LOBB, Barry .... 434-544-8521. 506 K
lobb@lynchburg.edu
LOBB, William, K .... 414-288-7485. 534 B
william.lobb@marquette.edu
LOBBAN-VIRAVONG,
Heather .... 641-269-4349. 178 H
lobbanvh@grinnell.edu
LOBDELL, James .... 716-614-5982. 334 E
jlobdell@niagaracc.suny.edu
LOBE, Robert .... 212-592-2661. 340 H
rlobe@sva.edu
LOBERTINI, Jo .... 316-295-5682. 186 H
jo_lobertini@friends.edu
LOBLAND, Brad .... 907-474-7700... 10 I
balobland@alaska.edu
LOBUONO, Joseph .... 978-665-4614. 229 E
jlobuono@fitchburgstate.edu
LOCANDER, William ...... 504-864-7946. 205 H
locander@loyno.edu
LOCASCIO, Patti, P .... 352-395-5169. 113 C
patti.locascio@sfcollege.edu
LOCATELLI, Dominic ...... 914-633-2245. 327 C
dlocatelli@iona.edu
LOCH, OSB, Killian .... 724-805-2350. 432 G
killian.loch@email.stvincent.edu
LOCHBAUM, Doug .... 770-394-8300. 120 H
dlochbaum@aii.edu
LOCHER, Linda, L .... 570-577-1604. 411 A
linda.locher@bucknell.edu
LOCHHEAD, Michael ...... 508-793-2327. 225 B
mlochhea@holycross.edu
LOCHNER, Elizabeth ...... 215-951-5123. 420 B
lochnere@lasalle.edu
LOCHNER, Mary Ann ..... 828-227-7116. 369 E
lochner@wcu.edu
LOCHSTAMPFOR, Mike .. 770-534-6230. 122 A
mlochstampfor@brenau.edu
LOCICERO, Jack .... 336-721-2625. 366 D
jack.locicero@salem.edu
LOCK, Ben, W .... 806-742-0012. 487 D
ben.lock@ttu.edu
LOCK, Cory .... 512-448-8720. 479 C
julial@stedwards.edu
LOCK, Vickie .... 920-498-5447. 541 B
victoria.lock@nwtc.edu
LOCKABY, Charlotte ...... 606-589-3020. 196 F
charlotte.lockaby@kctcs.edu
LOCKARD, Angela .... 270-247-8521. 197 H
alockard@midcontinent.edu
LOCKARD, Scott .... 864-225-7653. 444 A
scottlarkard@forrestcollege.edu
LOCKE, Carolyn .... 617-726-3177. 234 B
clocke1@mghihp.edu
LOCKE, Cindy .... 512-863-1584. 481 I
daviesc@southwestern.edu
LOCKE, Don .... 601-925-3250. 268 A
locke@mc.edu
LOCKE, Dot, M .... 662-685-4771. 266 C
dlocke@bmc.edu
LOCKE, Edward .... 718-631-6320. 319 D
elocke@qcc.cuny.edu
LOCKE, Heidi .... 503-821-8972. 406 F
hlocke@pnca.edu
LOCKE, Helen .... 949-451-5364... 67 B
vlocke@ivc.edu
LOCKE, Jason .... 607-255-2000. 322 A
jcl31@cornell.edu
LOCKE, Lisa .... 517-629-0206. 239 A
llocke@albion.edu
LOCKE, Mamie, E .... 757-727-5400. 505 F
mamie.locke@hamptonu.edu
LOCKE, Mary, G .... 772-462-4702. 106 P
mlocke@irsc.edu
LOCKERBY, Thomas, P .. 617-552-9076. 224 A
thomas.lockerby@bc.edu
LOCKETT, JR.,
Eugene, D .... 301-985-7330. 219 F
cfo@umuc.edu
LOCKETT, Tina .... 724-266-3838. 434 J
tlockett@tsm.edu
LOCKETT, Tom .... 217-224-0600. 162 I
tom.lockett@vatterott-college.edu
LOCKHART, Anne, A ...... 318-342-5426. 208 E
lockhart@ulm.edu
LOCKHART, Elaine .... 828-726-2241. 358 E
elockhart@cccti.edu
LOCKHART, Heidi .... 909-274-4510... 55 A
hlockhart@mtsac.edu

LOCKHART, Janet 310-506-4301 58 H
janet.lockhart@pepperdine.edu
LOCKHART, Janet, M 915-831-2676. 472 B
jlockha2@epcc.edu
LOCKHART, Tom 651-255-6113. 264 C
tlockhart@unitedseminary.edu
LOCKLEAR, Amy 409-933-8229. 469 E
alocklear@com.edu
LOCKLEAR, Chris 252-328-6105. 367 B
locklearc@ecu.edu
LOCKLEAR, Kindra 910-775-4471. 369 B
kindra.locklear@uncp.edu
LOCKLEAR, Marla, K 910-521-6201. 369 B
marla.locklear@uncp.edu
LOCKLEAR, William, L 910-272-3304. 363 B
wlocklea@robeson.edu
LOCKLEAR, Zoe 910-775-4041. 369 B
zoe.locklear@uncp.edu
LOCKMAN, Merlita 763-433-1298. 257 P
merlita.lockman@anokaramsey.edu
LOCKREM, Michael 605-688-6161. 452 B
michael.lockrem@sdstate.edu
LOCKRIDGE, Anita 502-597-6343. 197 A
anita.lockridge@kysu.edu
LOCKRIDGE, Jeanne 312-893-7140. 145 B
jlockridge@erikson.edu
LOCKTON, Barry 559-453-2089 45 D
bhl@fresno.edu
LOCKWARD, Ana, C 516-323-4209. 331 J
alockward@molloy.edu
LOCKWOOD, Barbara 630-844-5139. 140 A
lockwood@aurora.edu
LOCKWOOD, Catherine 312-935-6640. 156 K
clockwood@robertmorris.edu
LOCKWOOD, Charles, J 614-292-2600. 386 E
lockwood.59@osu.edu
LOCKWOOD, Daniel, R 503-255-0332. 404 F
dlockwood@multnomah.edu
LOCKWOOD,
Lawrence, J 319-335-0217. 175 I
larry-lockwood@uiowa.edu
LOCKWOOD,
Matthew, T 313-577-9098. 252 G
mlockwood@wayne.edu
LOCOCO, Nina 406-447-4388. 285 G
nlococo@carroll.edu
LOCURTO, Chuck 401-232-6196. 438 K
clocurto@bryant.edu
LOCUST, JR.,
Jonathan, E 419-207-5504. 374 C
jlocust@ashland.edu
LOCUST, Wayne 860-486-1463 92 A
wayne.locust@uconn.edu
LODATO, Michelle 864-379-6606. 443 F
lodato@erskine.edu
LODDER, Diane, E 919-866-5198. 364 G
delodder@waketech.edu
LODGE, Danielle 478-757-5180. 134 G
dlodge@wesleyancollege.edu
LODGE, Danielle 478-757-5205. 134 G
dlodge@wesleyancollege.edu
LODGE, Helen 417-667-8181. 273 A
hlodge@cottey.edu
LODGE, Pat 937-529-2201. 390 D
plodge@united.edu
LODOVICO, John 860-255-3420 89 G
jlodovico@txcc.commnet.edu
LOE, Meika 315-228-7546. 320 F
mloe@colgate.edu
LOECHNER, Randy 314-889-1450. 274 E
rloechner@fontbonne.edu
LOEDING, David 808-934-2705. 136 F
loeding@hawaii.edu
LOEFFEL, Linda, L 414-443-8842. 539 F
linda.loeffel@wlc.edu
LOEFFELHOLZ, Mary 617-373-4774. 235 F
LOEFFLER, Lauren 215-968-8017. 411 B
loeffler@bucks.edu
LOEHER, Larry, L 310-825-9149 71 C
lloeher@ucla.edu
LOEHFELM, Courtney 303-797-5914 78 F
courtney.loehfelm@arapahoe.edu
LOERA, Daniel, L 909-593-3511 72 E
dloera@laverne.edu
LOERS, Deborah, L 319-352-8745. 183 E
deb.loers@wartburg.edu
LOESCH, Richard 847-578-3225. 157 F
rick.loesch@rosalindfranklin.edu
LOESCH, Rick 847-578-3225. 157 F
rick.loesch@rosalindfranklin.edu
LOESCHKE, Maravene, S 410-704-2356. 220 E
presidentsoffice@towson.edu
LOESER, Diane 614-236-6159. 375 H
dloeser@capital.edu
LOESSBERG-ZAHL,
Robert, J 530-752-5728 70 J
rjloessb@ucdavis.edu
LOESSIN, Bruce, A 216-368-4352. 375 J
bruce.loessin@case.edu
LOETHEN, Laurie 913-621-8765. 186 C
lloethen@donnelly.edu
LOETTERLE, Jon 402-461-7424. 289 I
jloetterle@hastings.edu
LOETZ, Devon 443-627-7511. 265 D
Devon.Loetz@laureate.net
LOEWEN, Howard, J 626-584-5304 45 E
hloewen@fuller.edu
LOEWEN, Steve 620-343-4600. 186 E
sloewen@fhtc.edu
LOEWENSTEIN, Karna 712-325-3400. 179 L
kloewenstein@iwcc.edu
LOF, Gregory 617-724-6313. 234 B
glof@mghihp.edu
LOFALD, Dan 904-826-0084. 118 I
dlofald@usa.edu
LOFFLER, Alicia 847-491-4647. 155 D
a-loffler@kellogg.northwestern.edu
LOFFREDO, Joe 585-475-2829. 337 L
jjlrgr@rit.edu
LOFLAND, Jessica 580-349-1362. 397 G
jlofland@opsu.edu
LOFLIN, Gene 828-398-7240. 357 N
williamgloflin@abtech.edu
LOFQUIST, Beth 828-227-7495. 369 E
AcademicAffairsOffice@wcu.edu
LOFQUIST, Vicki 651-795-1810. 259 C
vicki.lofquist@metrostate.edu
LOFSTEAD, Rebecca, B 304-293-9358. 530 D
becky.lofstead@mail.wvu.edu
LOFT, Jan 507-537-6218. 261 F
Jan.Loft@smsu.edu
LOFTHOUSE, David, R 951-785-2938 50 B
dlofthou@lasierra.edu
LOFTIN, Lynn 580-559-5252. 395 F
lloftin@ecok.edu
LOFTIN, R. Bowen 979-845-2217. 483 C
president@tamu.edu
LOFTON, Antwan 202-806-6077 95 G
antwan.lofton@howard.edu
LOFTUS, Bill 863-638-2941. 119 D
loftuswj@webber.edu
LOFTUS, Edward, J 570-577-1458. 411 A
edward.loftus@bucknell.edu
LOFTUS, James, P 414-410-4003. 532 B
jploftus@stritch.edu
LOFTUS, Kate 262-472-1392. 538 D
loftusk@uww.edu
LOFTUS, Marie 718-933-6700. 331 K
mloftus@monroecollege.edu
LOFTUS, Roger 507-786-3068. 264 B
loftus@stolaf.edu
LOFTUS-BERLIN, Eileen 973-278-5400. 314 K
eml@berkeleyCollege.edu
LOGAN, Barry 207-725-3290. 209 H
blogan@bowdoin.edu
LOGAN, Bert 971-722-4490. 407 D
bert.logan@pcc.edu
LOGAN, David, A 401-254-4509. 440 B
dlogan@law.rwu.edu
LOGAN, Doug 509-527-2074. 524 I
doug.logan@wallawalla.edu
LOGAN, Elaine 313-593-5400. 251 D
loganem@umich.edu
LOGAN, Erin 405-682-1611. 397 E
elogan@occc.edu
LOGAN, Ethan 806-742-1480. 487 D
ethan.logan@ttu.edu
LOGAN, Gary 210-999-7306. 488 C
glogan@trinity.edu
LOGAN, Irene, F 804-524-5902. 515 D
ilogan@vsu.edu
LOGAN, Jill, B 601-643-5101. 266 F
jill.logan@colin.edu
LOGAN, Linda 269-749-6669. 249 A
llogan@olivetcollege.edu
LOGAN, Mark 562-860-2451 37 I
mlogan@cerritos.edu
LOGAN, Mike 712-274-6400. 183 G
mike.logan@witcc.edu
LOGAN, Robin 210-829-3933. 490 A
rlogan@uiwtx.edu
LOGAN, Ruth 585-594-6260. 337 K
loganr@roberts.edu
LOGAN, Timothy, M 254-710-6665. 467 G
tim_logan@baylor.edu
LOGAN, Tonya 740-264-5591. 379 F
tlogan@egcc.edu
LOGAN, Traci, A 781-891-3472. 223 C
tlogan@bentley.edu
LOGAN-BENNETT, Lorie 410-704-2386. 220 E
lloganbennett@towson.edu
LOGEL, Mark, J 812-488-2941. 173 H
ml44@evansville.edu
LOGEVALL, Fredrick 607-255-8933. 322 A
fl57@cornell.edu
LOGGAN, Todd 503-251-2836. 408 G
tloggan@uws.edu
LOGGINS, Jeff 662-254-3325. 269 A
jloggins@mvsu.edu
LOGGINS, Penny 706-778-8500. 130 E
ploggins@piedmont.edu
LOGHIN, Sarah 512-313-3000. 469 L
sarah.loghin@concordia.edu
LOGRASSO, Thomas 515-294-2770. 175 H
lograsso@ameslab.gov
LOGSDON, Michael 301-387-3333. 214 I
michael.logsdon@garrettcollege.edu
LOGSDON, Paul 417-865-2815. 274 B
logsdonp@evangel.edu
LOGSDON, Paul, M 419-772-2180. 386 D
p-logsdon@onu.edu
LOGSDON, Penelope 270-706-8649. 195 A
penelope.logsdon@kctcs.edu
LOGUE, Alexandra 664-646-8075. 316 I
academicaffairs@cuny.edu
LOGUE, Mary 805-565-6251 76 D
mlogue@westmont.edu
LOH, Wallace, D 301-405-1000. 219 B
wdloh@umd.edu
LOHDEN, Bethany, L 636-584-6503. 273 M
lohdenb@eastcentral.edu
LOHIDE, Kurt, D 707-654-1038 31 I
klohide@csum.edu
LOHMANN, Carl 315-792-3285. 349 F
calohman@utica.edu
LOHMANN, Steven, L 580-327-8406. 396 N
sllohmann@nwosu.edu
LOHR, Joel 209-946-2325 73 A
jlohr@pacific.edu
LOHRENZ, Steven 508-910-6550. 229 A
slohrenz@umassd.edu
LOHRI-POSEY, Brenda 740-695-9500. 374 H
bposey@belmontcollege.edu
LOHRMEYER, Robert 208-792-2225. 138 G
rlohrmey@lcsc.edu
LOHSANDT, Marie, A 605-256-5122. 451 H
marie.lohsandt@dsu.edu
LOHSE, MaryPat 617-349-8669. 228 B
mlohse@lesley.edu
LOHSTROH, Tracy 618-634-3203. 158 M
tracyl@shawneecc.edu
LOILAND, Chen 253-680-7464. 516 L
cloiland@bates.ctc.edu
LOILAND, Cheri 253-680-7206. 516 L
cloiland@bates.ctc.edu
LOILAND, Sharon 701-777-3178. 371 C
sharon.loiland@und.edu
LOISEAU, Marvin 617-588-1337. 223 B
mloiseau@bfit.edu
LOISELLE, Helene 407-582-1701. 118 M
hloiselle@valenciacollege.edu
LOIZEAUX, Elizabeth 617-353-2138. 224 D
ebloiz@bu.edu
LOIZZO, Joseph, A 740-284-7217. 379 N
jloizzo@franciscan.edu
LOJKO, Frank 435-652-7511. 497 E
lojko@dixie.edu
LOKEY, Cheryl, P 318-323-2889. 201 F
cheryl.lokey@careertc.edu
LOKEY, Pat 480-423-6653 15 E
pat.lokey@scottsdalecc.edu
LOKKEN, Jay, M 608-785-8017. 536 G
jlokken@uwlax.edu
LOKKEN, Pamela, S 314-935-5752. 284 L
lokken@wustl.edu
LOKMAN, Lawrence, H 310-825-9045 71 C
llokman@support.ucla.edu
LOKUTA, Sharon 260-422-5561. 167 B
slokuta@indianatech.edu
LOLATTE, Richard, J 203-773-8501 87 G
rjlolatte@albertus.edu
LOLLAND, Sonja 916-660-7800 66 B
slolland@sierracllege.edu
LOLLAR, Cay 662-862-8032. 267 C
cllollar@iccms.edu
LOMANTO, Andrea 518-454-5196. 321 A
lomantoa@strose.edu
LOMAS, Mark 704-499-9200 96 F
LOMAX, Terri, L 919-515-2117. 368 B
terri_lomax@ncsu.edu
LOMBARD, Amy 724-938-4418. 428 A
lombard@calu.edu
LOMBARD, Anne, E 315-470-6658. 345 B
aelombard@esf.edu
LOMBARD, J. Anthony 423-478-7716. 458 B
alombard@ptseminary.edu
LOMBARD, Karen, L 515-574-1140. 179 D
lombard@iowacentral.edu
LOMBARDI, George, J 203-371-1252 91 C
lombardi@sacredheart.edu
LOMBARDI, Mark 314-529-9330. 276 G
president@maryville.edu
LOMBARDI, Phillip 401-232-6374. 438 K
plombardi@bryant.edu
LOMBARDI, Ryan 740-593-2561. 387 C
lombardi@ohio.edu
LOMBARDO,
Dominic, P 260-422-5561. 167 B
dplombardo@indianatech.edu
LOMBARDO, Joann 860-486-5519 92 A
joann.lombardo@uconn.edu
LOMBARDO, John 631-851-6225. 346 E
lombarj@sunysuffolk.edu
LOMBARDO, Michael 503-777-7542. 407 E
lombardm@reed.edu
LOMBARDO, Natalie 814-944-5643. 438 H
natalie.lombardo@yti.edu
LOMBARDO, Natalie 814-944-5643. 438 F
natalie.lombardo@yti.edu
LOMBARDO, Pam 805-893-2040 72 B
pam.lombardo@ehs.ucsb.edu
LOMBARDO, Roberto 386-506-3159. 101 G
lombarr@DaytonaState.edu
LOMBARDO, Tony 225-578-5603. 204 O
lombardo@lsu.edu
LOMBELLA, James 860-253-3048 88 C
jlombella@asnuntuck.edu
LOMELI, Cristina 818-386-5608 59 E
clomeli@pgi.edu
LOMELINO, Josh 615-794-4254. 457 Q
jlomelino@omorecollege.edu
LOMENA, Sandra 305-821-3333. 105 A
slomena@fnu.edu
LOMETTI, Guy 718-405-3343. 320 G
guy.lometti@mountsaintvincent.edu
LOMONACO, Barbara 859-233-8215. 199 I
blomonaco@transy.edu
LONABOCKER,
Louise, M 617-552-3300. 224 A
louise.lonabocker@bc.edu
LONDA, Ivan 212-962-0002. 333 B
ilonda@nyci.edu
LONDON, Howard 508-531-1295. 229 D
hlondon@bridgew.edu
LONDON, Manuel 631-632-8304. 342 C
manuel.london@stonybrook.edu
LONDON, Michael 415-422-4400 73 J
melondon@usfca.edu
LONDON, Samuel 256-726-7223 6 B
slondon@oakwood.edu
LONDON-JONES, Emily 504-520-7517. 209 D
LONDRIGAN, Michael 212-752-1530. 328 G
michael.londrigan@limcollege.edu
LONE HILL, Karen 605-455-6100. 450 I
klonehill@olc.edu
LONEKER, Ronald 973-290-4235. 300 F
rloneker@cse.edu
LONERGAN, Dennis 718-862-7349. 329 M
dennis.lonergan@manhattan.edu
LONERGAN, Joel, C 256-824-6414 8 F
joel.lonergan@uah.edu
LONERGAN, Penny 913-758-6111. 191 B
longergan@stmary.edu
LONERGAN, Thomas 616-698-7111. 241 H
tlongeran1@davenport.edu
LONEY, Carl, E 937-327-7307. 393 E
cloney@wittenberg.edu
LONEY, Teresa, A 816-604-1517. 277 C
teresa.loney@mcckc.edu
LONG, Andrew 205-652-3400. 290 J
LONG, Antonio 404-756-4477. 121 A
along@atlm.edu
LONG, Aubrey, E 386-481-2800 99 C
longa@cookman.edu
LONG, Bobbie 972-548-6866. 469 G
blong@collin.edu
LONG, Brenda, J 252-222-6151. 358 G
longb@carteret.edu
LONG, Brittney 402-399-2454. 289 A
blong@csm.edu
LONG, C. Adam 864-488-4583. 444 L
along@limestone.edu
LONG, Carol, S 585-245-5531. 343 C
long@geneseo.edu
LONG, Catherine, E 607-255-2946. 322 A
cel3@cornell.edu
LONG, Charla 615-966-2501. 456 B
charla.long@lipscomb.edu
LONG, Charles 412-281-2600. 433 B
clong@western-school.com
LONG, Christina 620-665-3521. 187 F
longc@hutchcc.edu
LONG, Curt 563-588-6657. 176 F
curt.long@clarke.edu
LONG, Daniel 313-664-7675. 241 C
dlong@collegeforcreativestudies.edu
LONG, Deborah 336-278-5900. 354 B
dlong@elon.edu
LONG, Dennis 425-739-8313. 520 K
dennis.long@lwtech.edu
LONG, Donald 651-748-2626. 258 C
donald.long@century.edu
LONG, Durwin 715-836-4899. 536 E
longd@uwec.edu
LONG, Faith 518-564-2090. 344 B
long9194@plattsburgh.edu
LONG, II, Gardner 478-757-3498. 122 F
gardner@centralgatech.edu
LONG, Gerard, E 210-562-6285. 493 A
longg@uthscsa.edu
LONG, Gladys 919-572-1625. 352 C
doc_long@apexsot.edu

LONG, Hosea .... 501-686-7085... 24 C
longhoseaw@uams.edu
LONG, Jaime .... 815-825-2086. 149 F
jaime.long@kishwaukeecollege.edu
LONG, Jeanine .... 229-227-2668. 132 D
jlong@southwestgatech.edu
LONG, Jeff, C .... 570-389-4198. 427 H
jlong@bloomu.edu
LONG, Jennifer .... 405-224-3140. 401 E
jlong@usao.edu
LONG, Jesse .... 806-720-7657. 476 B
jesse.long@lcu.edu
LONG, Jewel, B .... 757-727-5486. 505 F
jewel.long@hamptonu.edu
LONG, Jim .... 573-592-4225. 285 D
jim.long@williamwoods.edu
LONG, Joanne .... 845-437-5255. 349 G
long@vassar.edu
LONG, Joyce .... 704-290-5281. 363 G
jlong@spcc.edu
LONG, K, O .... 325-793-3850. 476 E
longk@mcm.edu
LONG, Kenneth, A .... 570-422-3201. 428 D
kenlong@po-box.esu.edu
LONG, Kim .... 215-489-2314. 414 E
Kim.Long@delval.edu
LONG, Kimberly .... 870-512-7827... 20 B
kimberly_long@asun.edu
LONG, Larry .... 501-279-4335... 21 C
llong@harding.edu
LONG, Laurel .... 256-824-2259..... 8 F
laurel.long@uah.edu
LONG, Lauren .... 703-993-2909. 505 C
llong3@gmu.edu
LONG, Lisa .... 256-761-6466..... 7 F
lelong@talladega.edu
LONG, Marcus .... 314-367-8700. 281 C
marcus.long@stlcop.edu
LONG, Matthew .... 336-272-7102. 354 E
matt.long@greensboro.edu
LONG, Nathan, A .... 513-585-2051. 376 I
nathan.long@thechristcollege.edu
LONG, Patricia, N .... 785-594-8311. 184 C
president@bakeru.edu
LONG, Paul, D .... 816-604-1080. 277 C
paul.long@mcckc.edu
LONG, Rebecca .... 740-992-1880. 392 A
rlong@rio.edu
LONG, Richard .... 802-860-2755. 499 A
rlong@champlain.edu
LONG, Ronald, B .... 770-484-1204. 128 E
lru@lru.edu
LONG, Sally .... 410-386-8110. 214 A
slong@carrollcc.edu
LONG, Shane .... 207-741-5544. 211 A
slong@smccme.edu
LONG, Sherry .... 606-368-6091. 191 J
sherrylong@alc.edu
LONG, Susan .... 909-274-5200... 55 A
slong@mtsac.edu
LONG, Terri .... 909-274-5429... 55 A
tlong@mtsac.edu
LONG, Tim .... 312-369-7282. 143 D
tlong@colum.edu
LONG, Vicki .... 316-322-3152. 185 D
vlong@butlercc.edu
LONG, III, William .... 518-743-2273. 345 E
longw@sunyacc.edu
LONG, William, J .... 404-413-5100. 126 E
long@gsu.edu
LONG-COFFEE, Michelle 310-287-4597... 52 F
longcofm@wlac.edu
LONG-JACOBS, Anade ... 507-389-7219. 261 E
anade.long-jacobs@southcentral.edu
LONGACRE, Jeffrey .... 301-295-1917. 545 C
jeffrey.longacre@usuhs.edu
LONGACRE, Teri, E .... 713 743 4669. 489 B
elkins@central.uh.edu
LONGAKER, Frank .... 540-986-1800. 198 E
frank@national-college.edu
LONGAKER, Frank, E .... 540-986-1800. 501 H
frank@national-college.edu
LONGATAN, Nancy .... 503-760-3131. 402 B
nancy@birthingway.edu
LONGENECKER, Jack, R . 717-361-1263. 415 H
longenjr@etown.edu
LONGENECKER, Lyn .... 717-544-5711. 421 C
jllongen@lancastergeneralcollege.edu
LONGENECKER, Penni ... 717-544-5668. 421 C
pelongen@lancastergeneralcollege.edu
LONGFIELD, Bradley, J .. 563-599-3122. 182 J
blongfie@dbq.edu
LONGHTA, Karie, L .... 217-786-2263. 151 F
karie.longhta@llcc.edu
LONGJOHN, Gerald .... 616-222-1423. 241 F
gerald.longjohn@cornerstone.edu
LONGLEY, S. Catherine .. 207-725-3242. 209 H
clongley@bowdoin.edu
LONGO, Laura .... 732-224-2259. 299 G
llongo@brookdalecc.edu
LONGO, Rick .... 978-921-4242. 234 C
rick.longo@montserrat.edu
LONGO, Thomas, F .... 813-974-2628. 116 C
tlongo@admin.usf.edu
LONGORIA, Roxanne .... 617-928-4554. 234 E
rlongoria@mountida.edu
LONGSTON, Susan .... 203-285-2187... 88 E
Slogston@gwcc.commnet.edu
LONGWELL, B. Thomas . 812-461-1901. 174 D
btlongwell@usi.edu
LONGYEAR, JR.,
George, E .... 203-436-4899... 93 A
george.longyear@yale.edu
LONON, Justin, H .... 214-378-1824. 470 F
justin.lonon@dcccd.edu
LONOWSKI, Jerrold .... 575-624-8421. 310 H
lonowsk@nmmi.edu
LONQUIST, Jackie .... 773-481-8625. 142 F
jlonquist@ccc.edu
LONSINGER, Linda .... 740-593-1636. 387 C
lonsinge@ohio.edu
LOO, Chih .... 256-824-2243..... 8 F
chih.loo@uah.edu
LOOCHTAN, Anne .... 419-251-1785. 383 G
anne.loochtan@mercycollege.edu
LOOKADOO, Dan, A .... 540-674-3607. 513 B
dlookadoo@nr.edu
LOOKER, Michael, E .... 716-839-8218. 322 E
mlooker@daemen.edu
LOOMIS, Grace, H .... 585-785-1451. 324 D
loomisgh@flcc.edu
LOOMIS, Marnie .... 503-552-1625. 404 H
mloomis@ncnm.edu
LOOMIS, Michael, J .... 724-847-5321. 417 A
mjloomis@geneva.edu
LOOMIS, Nancy, G .... 509-777-4524. 525 F
nloomis@whitworth.edu
LOOMIS, Robin .... 716-827-4332. 348 G
loomisr@trocaire.edu
LOOMIS, Susan .... 951-639-5212... 55 B
sloomis@msjc.edu
LOONAN, John, F .... 570-389-4115. 427 H
jloonan@bloomu.edu
LOONEY, JoAnn .... 845-675-4542. 335 C
joann.looney@nyack.edu
LOONEY, Ken .... 615-963-1845. 459 E
klooney@tnstate.edu
LOONEY, CSC, Thomas .. 570-208-5900. 419 P
LOOP, Quentin, C .... 405-912-9478. 395 K
qloop@hc.edu
LOOPE, David, R .... 804-523-5547. 512 F
dloope@reynolds.edu
LOOPE, William, J .... 304-929-5494. 528 D
wloope@newriver.edu
LOOS, Christopher .... 816-584-6226. 280 C
christopher.loos@park.edu
LOOS, Tal .... 912-443-4140. 131 D
tloos@savannahtech.edu
LOOSER, Bob .... 217-479-7214. 152 D
bob.looser@mac.edu
LOOSER, Jackie .... 217-479-7007. 152 D
jackie.looser@mac.edu
LOOSMAN, Sharon .... 919-513-4206. 368 B
sharon_loosman@ncsu.edu
LOPARDO, Gina .... 206-296-6460. 523 E
glopardo@seattleu.edu
LOPATTO, David .... 641-269-3100. 178 H
lopatto@grinnell.edu
LOPER, Marianne .... 585-567-9328. 326 F
marianne.loper@houghton.edu
LOPER, Michelle, D .... 810-762-7434. 244 Q
mloper@kettering.edu
LOPER, Thomas .... 413-565-1000. 222 F
tloper@baypath.edu
LOPES, Anne .... 212-484-1347. 318 D
alopes@jjay.cuny.edu
LOPES, Joyce .... 707 826 3351... 35 C
Joyce.Lopes@humboldt.edu
LOPEZ, Alberto .... 787-765-3560. 548 M
lopeza@edpuniversity.edu
LOPEZ, Ana .... 504-865-5261. 207 C
lopez@tulane.edu
LOPEZ, Antonio .... 202-526-3799... 96 D
LOPEZ, Arthur .... 760-245-4271... 75 B
arthur.lopez@vvc.edu
LOPEZ, Beto .... 915-747-8244. 492 A
alopez@utep.edu
LOPEZ, Carlos .... 760-757-2121... 54 G
clopez@miracosta.edu
LOPEZ, Carmen, J .... 787-258-1501. 548 H
clopez@columbiaco.edu
LOPEZ, Chas .... 503-725-4453. 406 B
chlopez@pdx.edu
LOPEZ, Chris .... 915-747-5526. 492 A
cvlopez3@utep.edu
LOPEZ, Consuelo, G .... 580-591-0203. 395 B
LOPEZ, Coral .... 775-445-4230. 295 A
coral.lopez@wnc.edu
LOPEZ, Dana .... 310-665-6862... 57 C
dlopez@otis.edu
LOPEZ, JR., Daniel .... 773-442-4600. 154 H
d-lopez@neiu.edu
LOPEZ, Daniel, H .... 575-835-5600. 310 F
lalagarcia@admin.nmt.edu
LOPEZ, David, P .... 408-273-2697... 55 H
dlopez@nhu.edu
LOPEZ, Derek .... 719-549-2535... 80 K
derek.lopez@colostate-pueblo.edu
LOPEZ, Desi .... 787-780-5134. 551 L
dlopez@nuc.edu
LOPEZ, Don .... 559-442-4600... 68 I
don.lopez@fresnocitycollege.edu
LOPEZ, Ed .... 337-521-8901. 203 I
elopez@solacc.edu
LOPEZ, Edgar .... 949-214-3073... 41 I
edgar.lopez@cui.edu
LOPEZ, Elias, S .... 530-752-3619... 70 J
eslopez@ucdavis.edu
LOPEZ, Estela .... 203-575-8116... 89 B
elopez@nvcc.commnet.edu
LOPEZ, Felix, M .... 719-502-2541... 84 A
felix.lopez@ppcc.edu
LOPEZ, Gene .... 304-734-6616. 527 O
glopez@bridgemont.edu
LOPEZ, Gersom .... 914-632-5400. 331 K
glopez@monroecollege.edu
LOPEZ, Gilma .... 909-621-8055... 46 H
gilma_lopez@hmc.edu
LOPEZ, Heather .... 509-335-2001. 525 A
hlopez@wsu.edu
LOPEZ, Jane .... 757-221-3965. 503 N
jalope@wm.edu
LOPEZ, Jerry .... 415-439-2411... 27 M
jlopez@act-sf.org
LOPEZ, Jim, H .... 602-944-3335... 11 D
jlopez@aicag.edu
LOPEZ, Jose .... 559-925-3149... 75 I
joselopez@whccd.edu
LOPEZ, Jose Israel .... 347-964-8600. 315 E
jilopez@boricuacollege.edu
LOPEZ, Juan .... 956-364-4206. 485 H
juan.lopez@tstc.edu
LOPEZ, Keila .... 787-882-2065. 553 A
presidentutc@yahoo.com
LOPEZ, Kim .... 650-306-3236... 64 B
lopezk@smccd.edu
LOPEZ, Lorena .... 830-591-7352. 481 C
lmlopez@swtjc.edu
LOPEZ, Luis .... 787-743-4041. 548 H
llopez@columbiaco.edu
LOPEZ, Lynda .... 956-364-4114. 485 H
lynda.lopez@tstc.edu
LOPEZ, Maria .... 504-861-5550. 205 H
mlopez@loyno.edu
LOPEZ, Maribel .... 203-285-2000... 88 E
LOPEZ, Mario .... 620-331-0815. 187 G
mlopez@indycc.edu
LOPEZ, Matthew .... 801-585-9453. 496 Q
matthew.lopez@utah.edu
LOPEZ, Mayra, I .... 787-754-8000. 553 E
mlopez@pupr.edu
LOPEZ, Melissa, H .... 203-576-4712... 91 G
melissal@bridgeport.edu
LOPEZ, Michael .... 860-383-5202... 89 F
mlopez@trcc.commnet.edu
LOPEZ, Mike .... 651-201-1673. 257 N
mike.lopez@so.mnscu.edu
LOPEZ, Myriam, D .... 787-841-2000. 552 B
mdlopez@pucpr.edu
LOPEZ, Oscar .... 972-860-4837. 470 G
olopez@dcccd.edu
LOPEZ, Paulette .... 509-574-4901. 525 G
plopez@yvcc.edu
LOPEZ, Roberto .... 212-686-9244. 313 G
LOPEZ, Roger .... 305-644-1171. 100 P
rlopez@dademedical.edu
LOPEZ, Sam, T .... 704 687 4759. 368 E
slopez7@uncc.edu
LOPEZ, Santa .... 209-478-0800... 47 M
slopez@humphreys.edu
LOPEZ, Sergio .... 760-355-6457... 48 A
sergio.lopez@imperial.edu
LOPEZ, Sonia .... 323-267-3794... 51 F
lopezms@elac.edu
LOPEZ, Stacey .... 787-738-2161. 554 C
stacey.lopez@upr.edu
LOPEZ, Stacey, J .... 215-573-5836. 435 B
staceylo@upenn.edu
LOPEZ, Stephen .... 281-478-2712. 479 F
stephen.lopez@sjcd.edu
LOPEZ, Sue Ann .... 806-894-9611. 480 H
slopez@southplainscollege.edu
LOPEZ, Sylvia .... 787-725-6500. 547 H
slopez@albizu.edu
LOPEZ, Syvia .... 787-725-6500. 547 H
slopez@albizu.edu
LOPEZ, Tammy, L .... 719-587-7122... 78 B
tllopez@adams.edu
LOPEZ, Teresa .... 787-725-8120. 548 O
tlopez@eap.edu
LOPEZ, Theresa .... 562-860-2451... 37 I
tmlopez@cerritos.edu
LOPEZ, Thomas .... 407-582-1455. 118 M
tlopez@valenciacollege.edu
LOPEZ, Tom .... 818-947-2988... 52 E
lopezt@lavc.edu
LOPEZ, Vince .... 323-343-6190... 34 A
vlopez@cslanet.calstatela.edu
LOPEZ, Vinicio .... 714-241-6184... 39 I
vlopez@coastline.edu
LOPEZ-AVILES,
Maria del Mar .... 787-746-1400. 549 B
mlopez@huertas.edu
LOPEZ-CEPERO,
Maria, C .... 787-720-1022. 547 E
orientador@atlanticcollege.edu
LOPEZ-CORDOVA,
Nanet .... 787-725-6500. 547 H
nlopez@albizu.edu
LOPEZ HAUGEN,
Denise .... 503-517-1119. 408 H
dhaugen@warnerpacific.edu
LOPEZ-MATTHEWS,
Amy, L .... 937-229-3333. 391 C
AMatthews1@udayton.edu
LOPEZ-MEDERO,
Lilliana, M .... 787-765-4210. 548 E
llopez@cempr.edu
LOPEZ-MOLINA,
Generosa .... 312-261-3149. 153 I
generosa.lopez-molina@nl.edu
LOPEZ-PHILLIPS,
Matthew .... 707-664-2839... 36 B
matthew.lopez-phillips@sonoma.edu
LOPEZ-ROSADO, Jorge .. 239-590-1210. 115 A
jlopez@fgcu.edu
LOPEZ-STRONG, Maria .. 806-894-9611. 480 H
mstrong@southplainscollege.edu
LOPEZ-WAGNER, Muriel 909-537-3067... 34 E
mclopez@csusb.edu
LOPIAN, David .... 718-339-1090. 351 G
LOPIANSKY, Aaron .... 301-649-7077. 221 E
alopiansky@yeshiva.edu
LOPUCKI, Carol .... 616-331-7480. 243 C
lopuckic@gvsu.edu
LOR, Kia .... 262-243-5700. 532 H
kia.lor@cuw.edu
LORAINE, Donna .... 630-353-7001. 144 A
dloraine@devry.edu
LORAN, Roberto .... 787-743-7979. 552 I
rloran@suagm.edu
LORANCE, Beth .... 714-556-3610... 74 D
beth.lorance@vanguard.edu
LORBER, Jeffrey, D .... 217-206-7822. 161 E
jlorber@uis.edu
LORCH, Teddi .... 949-582-4850... 67 C
tlorch@socccd.org
LORD, Blair, M .... 217-581-2121. 144 E
blord@eiu.edu
LORD, David .... 304-294-2010. 528 F
david.lord@southernwv.edu
LORD, George, F .... 256-782-5455..... 4 K
glord@jsu.edu
LORD, Harold, W .... 585-567-9645. 326 F
harold.lord@houghton.edu
LORD, Jess .... 610-896-1350. 418 F
jlord@haverford.edu
LORD, Kenneth, M .... 810-989-5536. 249 H
klord@sc4.edu
LORD, Kenneth, R .... 818-677-2455... 34 C
kenneth.lord@csun.edu
LORD, Lisa .... 337-482-6863. 208 D
lisa@louisiana.edu
LORD, Mara .... 414-955-8298. 534 C
mlord@mcw.edu
LORD, Marianne, E .... 617-521-2328. 236 G
marianne.lord@simmons.edu
LORD, Mark .... 828-227-7495. 369 E
mlord@wcu.edu
LORD, Patty, R .... 818-677-3776... 34 C
patty.lord@csun.edu
LORD, Resa .... 334-214-4843..... 2 H
resa.lord@cv.edu
LORDAN, John, J .... 718-817-3120. 324 G
lordan@fordham.edu
LORDEN, Joan, F .... 704-687-5962. 368 E
jflorden@uncc.edu
LORE, Peggy .... 303-352-3526... 86 A
peggy.lore@ucdenver.edu
LOREEN, Susan .... 425-640-1489. 519 D
s.loreen@edcc.edu
LORENSON, James, A .... 906-932-4231. 242 I
LORENTZ, Gerald, F .... 518-783-6203. 346 A
gerald.lorentz@esc.edu
LORENTZEN, Carol .... 707-826-5728... 35 C
carol.lorentzen@humboldt.edu
LORENTZEN, Marcia, H .. 203-576-4139... 91 G
marcia@bridgeport.edu
LORENZ, Chuck .... 610-527-0200. 432 B
clorenz@rosemont.edu

LORENZ, Georgia 310-434-4277 65 A lorenz_georgia@smc.edu
LORENZ, Gina 425-352-8880 517 E glorenz@cascadia.edu
LORENZ, Heather 603-668-2211 297 I h.lorenz@snhu.edu
LORENZ, Tracy 602-943-2311 19 C Tracy.Lorenz@west.edu
LORENZANA, Ruth, G 818-767-0888 76 K ruth.lorenzana@woodbury.edu
LORENZEN, Michael 309-298-2762 162 K mg-lorenzen@wiu.edu
LORENZET, Steven, J 609-896-5152 305 D slorenzet@rider.edu
LORENZO, Jerilyn 808-734-9899 136 E jilorenz@hawaii.edu
LORENZO, JR., Joseph 303-797-5711 78 F joe.lorenzo@arapahoe.edu
LORENZO, Lorisa 727-864-7810 101 N lorenzll@eckerd.edu
LORGAN, Jason 530-752-9075 70 J jplorgan@ucdavis.edu
LORIA, Sal 713-743-9092 489 B sloria@uh.edu
LORIG, Beverly, T 540-458-8595 516 A blorig@wlu.edu
LORIMER, David, W 606-693-5000 196 H dlorimer@kmbc.edu
LORIMER, Linda, K 203-432-2321 93 A linda.lorimer@yale.edu
LORIMER, Stephen, A 606-693-5000 196 H slorimer@kmbc.edu
LORIMER, Susan, L 916-568-3031 52 K lorimes@losrios.edu
LORIMER, Thomas, H 606-693-5000 196 H tlorimer@kmbc.edu
LORING, Christopher 413-585-2902 236 H cloring@smith.edu
LORING, Trish 603-271-6984 296 C tloring@ccsnh.edu
LORINO, Anthony, P 504-862-8698 207 C alorino@tulane.edu
LORION, Raymond 410-704-2571 220 E rlorion@towson.edu
LORKOVICH, Malinda 312-996-4350 161 D mlork@uic.edu
LORTON-ROWLAND, Julie 317-921-4715 169 K jlorton@ivytech.edu
LORTZ, Peter 206-934-3746 522 I peter.lortz@seattlecolleges.edu
LOSCHEIDER, Paul, H 630-637-5678 154 F phloscheider@noctrl.edu
LOSCHIAVO, Linda 718-817-3570 324 G
LOSEY, Teri, L 616-331-2100 243 C loseyt@gvsu.edu
LOSHIN, David 954-262-1402 109 K loshin@nova.edu
LOSINGER, Regina 607-778-5040 315 I losingerr@sunybroome.edu
LOSKOT, SDS, Donald 414-425-8300 535 K dloskot@shst.edu
LOSO, Hilary 304-829-7064 526 D
LOSS, Amy 618-842-3711 146 I lossa@iecc.edu
LOSSING, David, E 810-766-6647 251 E dalossin@umflint.edu
LOSTETTER, Ron 262-524-7200 532 C rlosett@carrollu.edu
LOSTRACCO, Joe, M 512-223-7607 466 I lostracc@austincc.edu
LOTFI, Vahid 810-762-3164 251 E vahid@umflint.edu
LOTFI, Vahid 810-762-3171 251 E vahid@umflint.edu
LOTH, Karen, M 616-331-6000 243 C lothk@gvsu.edu
LOTHAMER, Mary Ellen 615-383-4848 464 D mlothamer@watkins.edu
LOTHRINGER, Bobby 940-898-3036 488 B rlothringer@twu.edu
LOTHRINGER, Rebecca 940-565-3793 490 C rebecca.lothringer@unt.edu
LOTICH, Lynda 336-770-1432 369 D lotichl@uncsa.edu
LOTITO, Tom 757-493-6000 96 F
LOTRIONTE, John, D 901-321-3550 453 H jlotrion@cbu.edu
LOTT, Donalyn, L 504-286-5244 206 K dlott@suno.edu
LOTT, Patricia, D 850-474-3419 117 B plott@uwf.edu
LOTT, Vicki, V 512-505-3076 473 G vvlott@htu.edu
LOTT, Wayne, J 801-422-4147 495 D wayne_lott@byu.edu
LOTURCO, Jennifer 518-320-1805 341 C jennifer.loturco@suny.edu
LOTYCZEWSKI, Halina 315-792-3087 349 F halotycz@utica.edu
LOU, Kris 503-370-5328 408 J klou@willamette.edu
LOUALLEN, Cheryl 937-382-6661 393 B cheryl_louallen@wilmington.edu
LOUCHE, Suzee, S 321-674-8099 104 H slouche@fit.edu
LOUCKS, Bill 573-592-5163 285 B bill.loucks@westminster-mo.edu
LOUCKS, C. Melvin 626-448-0023 48 L president@itsla.edu
LOUCY, Brian, M 315-445-4174 328 F loucyb@lemoyne.edu
LOUDEN, Sandy 731-352-4095 453 D loudens@bethelu.edu
LOUDEN, William, F 812-488-2376 173 H bl9@evansville.edu
LOUDENSLAGER, Anne 570-662-4809 429 C aloudens@mansfield.edu
LOUDER, Corey 660-626-2203 271 A clouder@atsu.edu
LOUDIN, Rose Ellen 304-473-8600 531 G loudin_r@wvwc.edu
LOUDON, Tina 360-650-3240 525 C tina.loudon@wwu.edu
LOUGEE, Wendy, P 612-624-1807 264 G wlougee@umn.edu
LOUGH, Krista, L 785-827-5541 188 C krista.lough@kwu.edu
LOUGHERY, James, F 215-968-8041 411 B loughery@bucks.edu
LOUGHLEY, Heather 614-433-0095 18 I heather.loughley@phoenix.edu
LOUGHLIN, Monica 504-520-7469 209 D mloughli@xula.edu
LOUGHMAN, Ann 518-262-5435 313 D loughma@mail.amc.edu
LOUGHRAN, Kristine 513-732-5218 391 B loughrke@ucmail.uc.edu
LOUGHRAN, Sean 203-837-9330 88 B loughrans@wcsu.edu
LOUIE, Larry 415-869-2900 227 F larry.louie@hult.edu
LOUIE, Sharon 949-451-5226 67 B slouie@ivc.edu
LOUIS, Michael 314-505-7301 272 J louism@csl.edu
LOUIS, Naomi 937-778-7814 379 G nlouis@edisonohio.edu
LOUMA, David, M 906-227-2355 248 A daluoma@nmu.edu
LOUREIRO, Rita, D 561-237-7035 108 X rloureiro@lynn.edu
LOURO, Jeffrey 508-999-8171 229 A jlouro@umassd.edu
LOUSTAUNAU, Jeffery 207-326-2230 211 D jeff.loustaunau@mma.edu
LOUTH, Richard, L 212-998-2118 334 D richard.louth@nyu.edu
LOUTHERBACK, George 254-295-4698 490 B gloutherback@umhb.edu
LOUTTIT, Julianne, E 724-287-8711 411 C julianne.louttit@bc3.edu
LOUWAGIE, Vincent 210-349-9928 477 L vince.louwagie@ost.edu
LOVALLO, Charles, G 973-877-3401 301 H lovallo@essex.edu
LOVE, Anne 718-420-4212 350 B alove@wagner.edu
LOVE, Arlyn 541-962-3496 405 H alove@eou.edu
LOVE, David 814-393-2334 428 C dlove@clarion.edu
LOVE, Deborah, A 757-221-1306 503 N dalove@wm.edu
LOVE, Deborah, E 504-862-8083 207 C dlove1@tulane.edu
LOVE, Hannah 325-236-8277 486 C hannah.love@tstc.edu
LOVE, Jamica 617-731-7195 235 H jlove@pmc.edu
LOVE, Jan 404-727-6324 124 E jlove3@emory.edu
LOVE, Jane 864-294-2248 444 C jane.love@furman.edu
LOVE, Julie, N 970-247-7503 81 M studenthousing@fortlewis.edu
LOVE, Kathryn 239-687-5430 98 J klove@avemarialaw.edu
LOVE, Kathy, S 912-443-3024 131 D klove@savannahtech.edu
LOVE, Kensey 740-753-7007 380 K love_k@hocking.edu
LOVE, Louise 312-369-7495 143 D llove@colum.edu
LOVE, Malinda, C 570-326-3761 427 B
LOVE, Mike 262-551-5900 532 D mlove@carthage.edu
LOVE, Patty 970-943-7052 86 I plove@western.edu
LOVE, Ronald 662-254-3624 269 A rlove@mvsu.edu
LOVE, Tommy 503-838-8281 406 E lovet@wou.edu
LOVE, Tony 432-552-2633 493 D love_t@utpb.edu
LOVEDAY, Joyce 253-589-5788 518 B joyce.loveday@cptc.edu
LOVELACE, Everett 209-384-6192 54 D everett.lovelace@mccd.edu
LOVELACE, Everett 209-384-6185 54 D everett.lovelace@mcc.edu
LOVELACE, Rhonda 501-370-5297 22 F rlovelace@philander.edu
LOVELACE-ROSS, Betty, M 614-236-6611 375 H blovelaceross@capital.edu
LOVELADY, III, Artis 832-252-4617 468 L artis@cbshouston.edu
LOVELAND, David, A 607-746-4013 345 G lovelada@delhi.edu
LOVELAND, George 252-399-6501 352 F gwloveland@barton.edu
LOVELESS, Cecelia 360-596-5204 524 A cloveless@spscc.edu
LOVELESS, Elizabeth, B 563-333-6271 182 B LovelessElizabethB@sau.edu
LOVELESS, Jill 928-757-0806 15 L jloveless@mohave.edu
LOVELIDGE, Robert 979-830-4194 467 I rlovelidge@blinn.edu
LOVELIS, Buffy 580-559-5651 395 F blovelis@ecok.edu
LOVELL, Cheryl 303-373-2008 85 C president@rvu.edu
LOVELL, Ellen 719-336-1541 82 R library@lamarcc.edu
LOVELL, Ellen, M 802-258-9245 499 F emlovell@marlboro.edu
LOVELL, JR., Ernest, L 601-403-1183 269 D elovell@prcc.edu
LOVELL, Kim 706-778-3000 130 E klovell@piedmont.edu
LOVELL, Michael, R 414-229-4331 537 A mlovell@uwm.edu
LOVELL, Sharon 540-568-2705 506 F lovellse@jmu.edu
LOVELL, Susan 706-562-1681 123 D lovell_susan@columbusstate.edu
LOVELL, Susan 212-472-1500 334 B slovell@nysid.edu
LOVELY, Christine, D 916-278-6078 34 D clovely@csus.edu
LOVERIDGE, Robert 801-863-8161 497 C loveriro@uvu.edu
LOVERIN, Mat 616-538-2330 243 A mhloverin@gbcol.edu
LOVERING, James 802-387-6795 499 E jlovering@landmark.edu
LOVETT, Christopher, M 814-886-6400 424 G clovett@mtaloy.edu
LOVETT, David, L 717-477-1164 429 E dllove@ship.edu
LOVETT, Leslie 304-367-4786 528 E Leslie.Lovett@pierpont.edu
LOVETT, Michael 256-215-4247 2 G mlovett@cacc.edu
LOVETT, Rod, M 217-351-2409 155 J rlovett@parkland.edu
LOVICK, Reed 252-527-6223 361 F rlovick@lenoircc.edu
LOVIG, Kristin 641-269-4974 178 H lovigkk@grinnell.edu
LOVIK, Eric 252-335-0821 359 F eric_lovik@albemarle.edu
LOVIN, Eddie 615-547-1231 454 A elovin@cumberland.edu
LOVINCE, Thomas 504-671-5627 203 A tlovin@dcc.edu
LOVING, Julie 434-832-7630 512 A lovingj@cvcc.vccs.edu
LOVINGOOD, Deborah, F 630-466-7900 162 J dlovingood@waubonsee.edu
LOVINS, Greg, M 828-262-2030 367 A lovinsgm@appstate.edu
LOVINS, Sandy 813-974-8063 116 C slovins@usf.edu
LOVITT, Carl, R 860-832-2228 87 K lovittcar@ccsu.edu
LOVSTUEN, Brenda, C 319-895-4292 177 A blovstuen@cornellcollege.edu
LOVVORN, Judi 229-217-4163 129 F jlovvorn@moultrietech.edu
LOW, Beverly 315-228-7368 320 F balow@colgate.edu
LOW, Catherine Yu-Ling 808-371-5443 135 I cfo@orientalmedicine.edu
LOW, Douglas 812-749-1298 171 K dlow@oak.edu
LOW, Joanne 415-239-3322 38 L jlow@ccsf.edu
LOW, Kathryn, G 207-786-6066 209 F klow@bates.edu
LOW, Ryan 207-623-3344 212 A ryan.low@maine.edu
LOW, Stephanie 831-755-6764 46 G slow@hartnell.edu
LOW, Wai Hoa 808-521-2288 135 I whlow@orientalmedicine.edu
LOW-HOGAN, Nancy 973-761-9000 307 C nancy.lowhogan@shu.edu
LOWBRIDGE, John 270-824-1835 196 A john.lowbridge@kctcs.edu
LOWDEN, Don 419-227-3141 391 F dmlowden@unoh.edu
LOWDEN, Paul 616-732-1194 241 H plowden@davenport.edu
LOWDER, Diane, M 804-752-7218 508 E dianelowder@rmc.edu
LOWDERMILK, Robert, S 336-342-4261 363 C lowdermilkr@rockinghamcc.edu
LOWE, Adam 423-478-6206 460 D ALowe04@clevelandstatecc.edu
LOWE, Brenda 806-720-7307 476 B brenda.lowe@lcu.edu
LOWE, Carmen 617-627-4239 237 C carmen.lowe@tufts.edu
LOWE, Carrie, B 865-573-4517 455 G cblowe@johnsonU.edu
LOWE, Charles 561-297-3500 114 L clowe@fau.edu
LOWE, Ellen 760-591-3012 118 I elowe@usa.edu
LOWE, JR., Eugene, Y 847-491-5255 155 D eyljr@northwestern.edu
LOWE, JR., James 251-405-7130 2 D jlowe@bishop.edu
LOWE, James, R 860-486-0566 92 A jim.lowe@uconn.edu
LOWE, Janet, S 307-766-3307 543 I jlowe@uwyo.edu
LOWE, Judy 423-697-2686 460 C
LOWE, Kathy 205-665-6100 9 B lowek@montevallo.edu
LOWE, Kathy 707-638-5806 69 K kathy.lowe@tu.edu
LOWE, Kayarda 334-872-2533 6 G
LOWE, Keri 616-988-1000 241 D
LOWE, Mark, S 701-483-2532 371 D mark.lowe@dickinsonstate.edu
LOWE, Myra 304-293-0305 530 D mlowe@mail.wvu.edu
LOWE, OFM, Philip, J 610-358-4241 424 I lowep@neumann.edu
LOWE, Rick, D 910-630-7027 356 H rlowe@methodist.edu
LOWE, Sharon 772-462-7476 106 P slowe@irsc.edu
LOWE, Susan, G 620-229-6334 190 G susan.lowe@sckans.edu
LOWE, Tamara, A 330-684-8931 390 F lowe@uakron.edu
LOWE, Verna 859-622-3515 193 P verna.lowe@eku.edu
LOWE, William, J 219-980-6701 168 B wjlowe@iun.edu
LOWE-SCHNEIDER, Katy 812-866-7081 166 C lowe@hanover.edu
LOWEN, Wayne 785-827-5541 188 C wayne.lowen@kwu.edu
LOWENBERG, Jaime 505-589-3158 465 I
LOWENBERG, James 312-942-2275 157 G james_lowenberg@rush.edu
LOWENBERG, Ron 714-895-8369 39 J rlowenberg@gwc.cccd.edu
LOWENGRUB, Morton 212-960-5217 351 M lowengru@yu.edu
LOWENSTEIN, Noah 415-394-5062 65 C nlowenstein@saybrook.edu
LOWENSTEIN, Tamara 415-749-4523 62 G tlowenstein@sfai.edu
LOWENTHAL, Benjamin 410-455-1720 219 D blowenth@umbc.edu
LOWENTHAL, Cynthia, J 843-953-0760 443 A lowenthalc@cofc.edu
LOWENTHAL, Tina 626-395-2758 31 E tina.lowenthal@caltech.edu
LOWERY, Anne, B 251-442-2270 9 A alowery@umobile.edu
LOWERY, Anne, B 251-422-2270 9 A alowery@umobile.edu
LOWERY, Anne, B 251-442-2270 9 A alowery@umobile.edu
LOWERY, Carla 662-329-8543 268 E clowery@ir.muw.edu
LOWERY, Daniel 219-473-4333 164 K dlowery@ccsj.edu
LOWERY, Juliet, J 540-375-2099 509 B lowery@roanoke.edu
LOWERY, Kathryn 601-266-6775 270 E kathryn.lowery@usm.edu

LOWERY, LaTanya .... 512-505-3035. 473 G
llowery@htu.edu
LOWERY, Lisa .... 508-588-9100. 232 A
LOWERY, Sara .... 410-548-2341. 220 D
salowery@salisbury.edu
LOWERY, Wendy .... 910-521-6252. 369 B
wendy.lowery@uncp.edu
LOWERY-HART, Russell . 806-371-5226. 465 E
rdloweryhart@actx.edu
LOWERY-MOORE, Hollis 409-880-8661. 486 F
hollis.moore@lamar.edu
LOWES, JR., Guy .... 304-236-7633. 528 F
guy.lowes@southernwv.edu
LOWMAN, Stacey, L .... 240-500-2000. 215 B
sllowman@hagerstowncc.edu
LOWMAN, Tony .... 856-256-5300. 305 E
chin@rowan.edu
LOWN, Maris .... 908-709-7006. 308 B
maris.lown@ucc.edu
LOWRANCE, Jeffrey .... 704-330-6666. 359 C
jeff.lowrance@cpcc.edu
LOWRANCE, Vicki .... 254-647-3234. 478 H
vlow@rangercollege.edu
LOWRY, David .... 405-425-1941. 397 D
david.lowry@oc.edu
LOWRY, Douglas .... 585-274-1010. 349 C
dlowry@esm.rochester.edu
LOWRY, Elisabeth .... 415-503-6258... 62 H
elowry@sfcm.edu
LOWRY, Gail .... 317-738-8040. 165 I
glowry@franklincollege.edu
LOWRY, Jenny .... 410-617-2451. 216 A
jlowry@loyola.edu
LOWRY, John .... 615-966-5951. 456 B
john.lowry@lipscomb.edu
LOWRY, III,
L. Randolph .... 615-966-1787. 456 B
randy.lowry@lipscomb.edu
LOWRY, Rebekah .... 910-272-3235. 363 B
relowry@robeson.edu
LOWRY, Rebekah, R .... 910-272-3235. 363 B
relowry@robeson.edu
LOWRY, Sharon .... 661-722-6300... 28 F
salowry@avc.edu
LOWY, Esther .... 323-822-9700... 69 J
tourola@touro.edu
LOWY, Laurence .... 212-410-8007. 333 E
llowy@nycpm.edu
LOWY, Vivien .... 213-624-1200... 44 D
vlowy@fidm.edu
LOY, Barry, J .... 978-867-4263. 226 H
barry.loy@gordon.edu
LOY, Marty .... 715-346-3169. 538 A
mloy@uwsp.edu
LOYACK, John .... 570-208-5832. 419 P
johnloyack@kings.edu
LOYD, Bill .... 706-776-0104. 130 E
bloyd@piedmont.edu
LOYD, James .... 706-649-1449. 123 E
jloyd@columbustech.edu
LOYD, Jo Lynn .... 972-279-6511. 465 F
jloyd@amberton.edu
LOYD, Marta .... 479-788-7021... 24 A
marta.loyd@uafs.edu
LOYD, Nicole, L .... 610-861-1502. 424 E
LOYD, Nicole, L .... 610-861-1502. 424 E
loyd@moravian.edu
LOYD-PAIGE, Michelle ... 616-526-8703. 240 L
lopa@calvin.edu
LOYNAZ, Oscar .... 305-348-6796. 115 B
oscar.loynaz@fiu.edu
LOYOLA, David .... 956-380-8196. 479 B
dloyola@riogrande.edu
LOZA, Frank .... 325-670-1461. 472 O
floza@hsutx.edu
LOZADA, Josc .... 787 727 7020. 555 D
jlozada@sagrado.edu
LOZANO, Fran .... 408-848-4702... 45 F
flozano@gavilan.edu
LOZANO, Franz .... 415-338-1463... 35 E
franz@sfsu.edu
LOZEN, Stephen .... 617-588-1367. 223 B
slozen@bfit.edu
LOZINA, Mary .... 914-674-7651. 330 J
mlozina@mercy.edu
LOZOYA, Lynnette .... 909-599-5433... 50 J
llozoya@lifepacific.edu
LS SHANA, Jim .... 620-862-5252. 184 E
jim.leshana@barclaycollege.edu
LTAIF, Nicholas, G .... 518-381-1274. 340 G
ltaifng@sunysccc.edu
LU, Gail .... 415-451-2824... 63 A
glu@sfts.edu
LU, Kuang Kai .... 323-731-2383... 57 I
LU, Wel .... 305-595-9500... 97 G
LU, Yubin .... 651-631-0204. 253 D
yubinlu39@yahoo.com
LU, Yue .... 626-289-7719... 26 J
LUAN, Jing .... 650-358-6880... 64 A
luan@smccd.edu

LUBBE, Veronica, A .... 859-344-3522. 199 H
veronica.lubbe@thomas.more.edu
LUBBERDEN, Mike .... 641-628-5346. 176 E
lubberdenm@central.edu
LUBBERTS, Rhonda .... 616-331-2525. 243 C
lubbertr@gvsu.edu
LUBCKER, Donna .... 903-923-2272. 471 J
dlubcker@etbu.edu
LUBECK, Eileen .... 973-720-2450. 308 I
lubecke@wpunj.edu
LUBIENECKI, Teresa .... 716-652-8940. 316 G
tlubienecki@cks.edu
LUBINSKY, Hindy .... 718-787-1602. 348 B
hindy.lubinsky@touro.edu
LUBRANO, Ann .... 718-818-6470. 339 H
LUBRANO, Carmelo .... 973-642-8878. 307 D
carmelo.lubrano@shu.edu
LUCAS, Audrey, O .... 336-335-5090. 369 A
audrey_daniel@uncg.edu
LUCAS, Beverly, R .... 713-785-5995. 468 L
beverly.lucas@cbshouston.edu
LUCAS, Bonnie .... 847-635-1711. 155 F
blucas@oakton.edu
LUCAS, Bryan .... 817-257-7682. 484 I
b.lucas@tcu.edu
LUCAS, Catherine .... 303-556-5122... 83 D
lucascat@msudenver.edu
LUCAS, Cecilia .... 808-455-0325. 137 A
cblucas@hawaii.edu
LUCAS, Dawn .... 704-463-3207. 365 E
dawn.lucas@fsmail.pfeiffer.edu
LUCAS, Doreen .... 443-394-3339... 96 F
LUCAS, Dwayne .... 315-781-3304. 326 C
lucas@hws.edu
LUCAS, Frances .... 228-867-8795. 270 E
frances.lucas@usm.edu
LUCAS, Glenn, E .... 805-893-2126... 72 B
gene.lucas@evc.ucsb.edu
LUCAS, Hakim, J .... 386-481-2929... 99 C
lucash@cookman.edu
LUCAS, James .... 336-770-3317. 369 D
lucasj@uncsa.edu
LUCAS, Jennifer, R .... 717-337-6211. 417 B
jlucas@gettysburg.edu
LUCAS, Joan .... 662-325-8131. 268 D
jlucas@legal.msstate.edu
LUCAS, John .... 802-258-3266. 500 C
john.lucas@worldlearning.org
LUCAS, Kathy, A .... 765-285-5289. 164 B
klucas@bsu.edu
LUCAS, LaTanya, V .... 336-744-0900. 353 A
latanya@carolina.edu
LUCAS, Linda, C .... 205-934-0622..... 8 E
lucas@uab.edu
LUCAS, Lois .... 304-766-3050. 530 C
lucasml@wvstateu.edu
LUCAS, Mark, L .... 573-882-3621. 283 C
lucasm@missouri.edu
LUCAS, Matthew .... 503-375-7019. 403 A
mlucas@corban.edu
LUCAS, Megan .... 563-588-6315. 176 F
megan.lucas@clarke.edu
LUCAS, Mona .... 860-486-2819... 92 A
mona.lucas@uconn.edu
LUCAS, Pam, A .... 214-860-2097. 470 J
plucas@dcccd.edu
LUCAS, Paul, M .... 724-287-8711. 411 C
paul.lucas@bc3.edu
LUCAS, JR., Richard .... 301-860-4303. 220 A
rlucas@bowiestate.edu
LUCAS, Sandra .... 520-383-8401... 18 B
slucas7578@aol.com
LUCAS, Sheri .... 614-222-3220. 378 A
slucas@ccad.edu
LUCAS, Vern .... 215-785-0111. 426 X
LUCAS, Virginia, S .... 910-592-8081. 363 E
vlucas@sampsoncc.edu
LUCAS-YOUMANS,
Tasha .... 386-481-2181... 99 C
lucast@cookman.edu
LUCCHESI, Michael .... 718-270-2407. 342 D
michael.lucchesi@downstate.edu
LUCE, Monica .... 206-878-3710. 520 E
mluce@highline.edu
LUCE, Richard, E .... 405-325-2611. 401 B
rluce@ou.edu
LUCENTA, Christine .... 630-889-6532. 154 E
clucenta@nuhs.edu
LUCERO, Gabe .... 307-742-9375. 544 B
glucero@wyotechstaff.edu
LUCERO, Kathy .... 909-652-6620... 37 M
kathy.lucero@chaffey.edu
LUCERO, Louis .... 661-722-6300... 28 F
llucero@avc.edu
LUCERO, Marie .... 925-631-8631... 61 F
gmw1@stmarys-ca.edu
LUCERO-MILLER,
Denise .... 940-898-3801. 488 B
dluceromiller@twu.edu
LUCEY, Carol, A .... 775-445-4450. 295 A
carol.lucey@wnc.edu

LUCHS, Jason .... 212-229-5626. 332 E
luchsj@newschool.edu
LUCHSINGER, Andrew ..... 651-638-6055. 253 K
andrew-luchsinger@bethel.edu
LUCIA, Jonathan .... 706-568-2026. 123 D
lucia_jonathan@columbusstate.edu
LUCIA, Joseph .... 215-204-8231. 433 K
joseph.lucia@temple.edu
LUCIANI, Michael .... 802-387-6713. 499 E
mluciani@landmark.edu
LUCIANO, Jennifer, K ..... 212-752-1530. 328 G
jennifer.luciano@limcollege.edu
LUCIANO, Joseph .... 570-344-7101. 420 C
lucianoj@lackawanna.edu
LUCIANO, Linda .... 973-278-5400. 299 D
lml@berkeleycollege.edu
LUCIANO, Linda .... 973-278-5400. 314 K
lml@berkeleycollege.edu
LUCIANO-FIGUEROA,
Yomarachaliff .... 787-265-3884. 554 E
egresados@uprm.edu
LUCID, Robert .... 973-408-3379. 301 C
rlucid@drew.edu
LUCIDO, Samuel, C .... 248-370-3000. 248 J
lucido@oakland.edu
LUCIER, Christopher, H .. 802-656-1394. 500 F
christopher.lucier@uvm.edu
LUCIO, Robert .... 352-588-8252. 112 D
robert.lucio@saintleo.edu
LUCK, Cathy .... 616-632-2916. 239 E
cathleen.luck@aquinas.edu
LUCK, Deborah, S .... 336-633-0272. 362 H
dsluck@randolph.edu
LUCK, Edward, C .... 619-260-7919... 73 I
luck@sandiego.edu
LUCK, Janice, J .... 610-921-7824. 409 A
jluck@alb.edu
LUCK, Oliver, F .... 304-293-5621. 530 D
oliver.luck@mail.wvu.edu
LUCKADOO, Timothy, R . 919-515-3088. 368 B
trluckad@ncsu.edu
LUCKE, Peggy .... 701-777-2015. 371 C
peggy.lucke@und.edu
LUCKETT, Jenni .... 503-352-3006. 407 A
jluckett@pacificu.edu
LUCKETT, Robin .... 502-410-6200. 194 B
rluckett@galencollege.edu
LUCKEY, Rhonda, H .... 724-357-4040. 428 F
rluckey@iup.edu
LUCKEY, JR., William, T 270-384-8001. 197 D
luckeyw@lindsey.edu
LUCKIE, Sandra .... 419-755-4727. 385 D
sluckie@ncstatecollege.edu
LUCKIE, Sharon .... 718-289-5800. 317 B
sharon.luckie@bcc.cuny.edu
LUCKIESH, Ann .... 415-433-9200... 65 C
aluckiesh@saybrook.edu
LUCKING, Rachel .... 508-626-4615. 230 A
rlucking@framingham.edu
LUCKY, Jana .... 318-357-4503. 208 B
luckyj@nsula.edu
LUCUMI, Ana, M .... 787-780-5134. 551 L
alucumi@nuc.edu
LUCY, Cecil .... 334-727-8531..... 8 A
LUCZAK, Greg .... 989-686-3616. 242 C
gpluczak@delta.edu
LUDDEN, Paul, W .... 214-768-1491. 481 A
pludden@smu.edu
LUDE, Judith .... 740-264-5591. 379 F
jlude@egcc.edu
LUDEMAN, Angela .... 301-846-2452. 214 H
aludeman@frederick.edu
LUDFORD, Deborah .... 714-808-4868... 56 D
dludford@nocccd.edu
LUDLAM, Laura .... 717-477-1201. 429 E
LJLudlam@ship.edu
LUDLOW, Cynthia .... 716-851-1166. 323 I
ludlow@ecc.edu
LUDMAN, Naomi .... 269-782-1329. 250 C
nludman@swmich.edu
LUDMAN, Ronald .... 617-824-8640. 226 A
ronald_ludman@emerson.edu
LUDWICK, Carol .... 620-278-4273. 190 I
cludwick@sterling.edu
LUDWIG, Amy .... 479-397-7622... 23 B
aludwig@rmcc.edu
LUDWIG, Amy .... 479-394-7622... 23 B
aludwig@rmcc.edu
LUDWIG, Dean .... 419-824-3686. 383 C
dludwig@lourdes.edu
LUDWIG, Dee .... 307-532-8221. 542 a
dee.ludwig@ewc.wy.edu
LUDWIG, Glenn .... 717-334-6286. 422 E
gludwig@ltsg.edu
LUDWIG, Michael, R ...... 765-494-1063. 171 M
mrludwig@purdue.edu
LUDWIG, Nancy, M .... 617-373-5038. 235 F
LUDWIG, Petra .... 732-571-3526. 303 C
pludwig@monmouth.edu
LUDWIG, Thomas .... 989-358-7202. 239 C
ludwigt@alpenacc.edu

LUDWIG-JOHNSON,
Stacey .... 801-274-3280. 498 E
sludwig@wgu.edu
LUEB, Cindy .... 970-248-1424... 79 F
clueb@coloradomesa.edu
LUEBBERT, Paula, J .... 217-782-1086. 151 F
paula.luebbert@llcc.edu
LUEBKE, Linda .... 804-706-5202. 512 G
lluebke@jtcc.edu
LUEBKE, Miriam, E .... 651-641-8825. 255 B
luebke@csp.edu
LUEBKE, Susan .... 870-673-4201... 24 G
LUECK, Terrie .... 507-457-6921. 264 A
tlueck@smumn.edu
LUECKE, Chris .... 435-797-2452. 497 B
chris.luecke@usu.edu
LUEDER, Billie .... 808-845-9187. 136 G
bktakaki@hawaii.edu
LUEKEN, Paul, A .... 724-738-2021. 429 F
paul.lueken@sru.edu
LUEKENGA, Chris .... 970-943-2616... 86 I
cluekenga@western.edu
LUESSE, Amy .... 952-446-4122. 255 D
luessea@crown.edu
LUETKEHANS, Lara .... 724-357-2480. 428 F
lara.luetkehans@iup.edu
LUETSCHWAGER,
Julie, A .... 920-923-8094. 534 A
jaluetschwager25@marianuniversity.edu
LUETTGER, Michele .... 607-436-2514. 343 E
luettgme@oneonta.edu
LUETZEN, Leigh Ann ...... 617-912-9118. 224 B
lluetzen@bostonconservatory.edu
LUFF, Debra .... 916-558-2139... 53 D
luffd@scc.losrios.edu
LUFF, Paula .... 312-362-8091. 143 H
pluff@depaul.edu
LUFKIN, Daniel .... 757-825-3810. 514 B
Lufkind@tncc.edu
LUFKIN, Mary Beth .... 603-513-1328. 298 E
mb.lufkin@granite.edu
LUFT, John, P .... 717-766-2511. 423 L
jluft@messiah.edu
LUGEMBE, Farida .... 310-453-8300... 43 D
farida@emperors.edu
LUGG, Linda, L .... 603-513-5101. 298 D
linda.lugg@law.unh.edu
LUGG, Thomas, W .... 610-359-5336. 414 D
tlugg@dccc.edu
LUGO, Daniel, G .... 717-291-3953. 416 J
daniel.lugo@fandm.edu
LUGO, Efrain .... 787-620-2040. 547 C
elugo@aupr.edu
LUGO, Eric .... 646-660-6095. 316 J
Eric.Lugo@baruch.cuny.edu
LUGO, Ivette .... 407-447-7300. 105 I
ilugo@ftccollege.edu
LUGO, Javier .... 787-600-2819. 555 C
javier.lugo3@upr.edu
LUGO, Josue .... 787-600-4124. 555 C
josue.lugo@upr.edu
LUGO, Lester .... 336-334-7595. 367 E
llugo@ncat.edu
LUGO, Maria de los, A .. 787-766-1717. 552 J
um_mlugo@suagm.edu
LUGO, Maria Ines .... 787-264-1912. 551 A
milugo@sg.inter.edu
LUGO, Ruth, E .... 212-343-1234. 331 D
rlugo@mcny.edu
LUGO, Udeth .... 407-646-2573. 111 Q
ulugo@rollins.edu
LUGO, Victoria .... 805-289-6455... 74 H
vlugo@vcccd.edu
LUGO-DEJESUS,
Waleska .... 413-572-5272. 230 F
wlugodejesus@westfield.ma.edu
LUHTALA, Erik .... 619-684-8801... 56 C
eluhtala@newschoolarch.edu
LUIKART, Nancy .... 563-288-6073. 178 B
nluikart@eicc.edu
LUING, Kevin, L .... 973-278-5400. 314 K
kevin@berkeleycollege.edu
LUING, Kevin, L .... 973-278-5400. 299 D
kevin@berkeleycollege.edu
LUJAN, Annette .... 719-846-5679... 85 H
annette.lujan@trinidadstate.edu
LUJAN, Linda .... 480-732-7010... 14 J
linda.lujan@cgc.edu
LUJAN, Manuel .... 361-593-4060. 484 A
manuel.lujan@tamuk.edu
LUJAN, Nereida .... 620-417-1104. 190 F
nereida.lujan@sccc.edu
LUKAC, Dan .... 513-244-4617. 377 G
dan_lukac@mail.msj.edu
LUKACSKO, Debbie .... 201-684-7535. 305 A
dlukacsk@ramapo.edu
LUKAS, Veronica .... 718-631-6367. 319 D
vlukas@qcc.cuny.edu
LUKASIK, Douglas, S ..... 607-778-5028. 315 I
lukasikds@sunybroome.edu

LUKASKIEWICZ, Robert, P 802-773-5900. 499 B rob.lukaskiewicz@csj.edu
LUKASZEWSKI, Patricia, L 919-508-2220. 370 F pllukaszewski@peace.edu
LUKE, Jonathan, H 973-596-5836. 303 G jonathan.h.luke@njit.edu
LUKE, Kristie 580-745-2176. 399 J kluke@se.edu
LUKE, Learie, B 803-536-7185. 446 G lluke@scsu.edu
LUKE, Sarah 207-801-5670. 210 A sluke@coa.edu
LUKEHART, Debra 515-271-2169. 177 K debra.lukehart@drake.edu
LUKEN, James, O 843-349-2783. 442 E joluken@coastal.edu
LUKHAUP, Walter, P 724-480-3376. 413 H walter.lukhaup@ccbc.edu
LUKMAN, Roy 407-303-8520... 97 H roy.lukman@adu.edu
LUKOSHUS, Wes, K 219-989-2217. 171 N lukoshus@purduecal.edu
LULJAK, Thomas, L 414-229-4035. 537 A tluljak@uwm.edu
LULLI, Linda, S 401-232-6011. 438 K lslulli@bryant.edu
LUM-AKANA, Aileen 808-455-0606. 137 A aileenla@hawaii.edu
LUMETTA, Joanne 734-432-5689. 246 B jlumetta@madonna.edu
LUMM, John 734-487-2031. 242 D jlumm@emich.edu
LUMM, Werner 920-390-2820. 533 U werner.lumm@mbbc.edu
LUMMUS, John 864-646-1548. 447 D jlummus@tctc.edu
LUMPKIN, Ann 985-732-6640. 203 D
LUMPKIN, James 318-257-4526. 207 F jlumpkin@latech.edu
LUMPKIN, Scott, R 303-871-2647... 86 B slumpkin@du.edu
LUMPP, David, A 651-641-8217. 255 B lumpp@csp.edu
LUMPP, Marycate 303-458-4058... 84 M mlumpp@regis.edu
LUNA, Andrew, L 256-765-4221..... 9 C alluna@una.edu
LUNA, Carmen 787-766-1717. 552 J
LUNA, Edna 931-363-9824. 456 C eluna@martinmethodist.edu
LUNA, Gene 803-777-4283. 447 G genel@sc.edu
LUNA, J. Nikky 304-457-1700. 526 A lunajn@ab.edu
LUNA, Leslie 520-383-8401... 18 B lluna@tocc.cc.az.us
LUNA, Marlene 801-878-1062. 295 E mluna@roseman.edu
LUNA, Olga 787-766-1912. 549 J oluna@inter.edu
LUNA, Rita 608-822-2701. 541 C rluna@swtc.edu
LUNA, Shirley 936-468-2605. 482 A sluna@sfasu.edu
LUNAN, Kathy 314-529-9332. 276 G klunan@maryville.edu
LUNARDI, Joseph, M 610-660-1221. 432 E jlunardi@sju.edu
LUNBECK, Jo 870-972-3593... 19 L jlunbeck@asusystem.edu
LUNCEFORD, Casey 772-462-7693. 106 P cluncefo@irsc.edu
LUND, Bob 719-502-2040... 84 A bob.lund@ppcc.edu
LUND, Eric 507-786-3069. 264 B lund@stolaf.edu
LUND, James 760-480-8474... 76 C jlund@wscal.edu
LUND, Jon 563-387-1428. 180 M lundjon@luther.edu
LUND, Karla 406-874-6186. 286 E lundk@milescc.edu
LUND, Kristen 812-488-2241. 173 H kl147@evansville.edu
LUND, Lisa 989-328-1219. 247 D lisal@montcalm.edu
LUND, Stephen, R 608-263-5722. 536 D slund@ohr.wisc.edu
LUNDAHL, Deb 402-375-7209. 291 F delunda1@wsc.edu
LUNDAY, Herbert 417-255-7225. 278 F herblunday@missouristate.edu
LUNDBERG, Cliff 805-565-7188... 76 D clundber@westmont.edu
LUNDBERG, Erik 734-615-4445. 251 C lerikl@umich.edu
LUNDBLAD, Larry, A 218-855-8053. 258 B llundblad@clcmn.edu
LUNDBLAD, Tracey 302-736-2372... 94 C luncbltr@wesley.edu
LUNDBURG, P. Wesley 508-678-2811. 231 B wesley.lundburg@bristolcc.edu
LUNDE MARUYAMA, Aimee 937-327-7433. 393 E maruyamaa@wittenberg.edu
LUNDEEN, Bruce 810-766-4017. 239 G bruce.lundeen@baker.edu
LUNDEEN, Kate 414-382-6103. 531 I kate.lundeen@alverno.edu
LUNDEEN, Sally 414-229-4189. 537 A slundeen@uwm.edu
LUNDEN, Steve, M 509-313-5624. 520 A slunden@plant.gonzaga.edu
LUNDERMAN, Dedria 850-729-5361. 109 I lundermand@nwfsc.edu
LUNDGREN, LaRae 951-827-2587... 71 E larae.lundgren@ucr.edu
LUNDGREN, LouAnne 505-224-4000. 309 E llundgren1@cnm.edu
LUNDQUIST, Daniel 518-244-2018. 338 C 1lundqd@sage.edu
LUNDQUIST, Lisa, M 678-547-6308. 128 H lundquist_lm@mercer.edu
LUNDQUIST, Sara 714-564-6085... 60 G lundquist_sara@sac.edu
LUNDQUIST, Travis 605-394-4034. 452 E travis.lundquist@wdt.edu
LUNDRIGAN, Kathleen 513-244-4330. 377 G kathleen_lundrigan@mail.msj.edu
LUNDSTREM, Karen 718-260-5140. 319 B klundstrem@citytech.cuny.edu
LUNDSTROM, Joel 785-320-4502. 188 E joellundstrom@matc.net
LUNDSTROM, Linda 781-595-6768. 228 C llundstrom@mariancourt.edu
LUNDY, Constance, L 484-365-7785. 422 D lundy@lincoln.edu
LUNDY, Elizabeth 503-594-3020. 402 F elizabethl@clackamas.edu
LUNDY, Jennifer 412-365-1145. 412 K jlundy@chatham.edu
LUNGSTRUM, Anthony 573-592-1638. 285 D anthony.lungstrum@williamwoods.edu
LUNIN, Jeanne 212-353-4107. 321 F lunin@cooper.edu
LUNK, Ron 678-915-4101. 132 C rlunk@spsu.edu
LUNN, D. Paul 919-513-6210. 368 B dplunn@ncsu.edu
LUNNERMON, JR., James, G 410-651-6434. 219 E jglunnermonii@umes.edu
LUNSFORD, Dale, A 903-233-3100. 475 J dalelunsford@letu.edu
LUNSFORD, Dan, G 828-689-1141. 356 F dlunsford@mhc.edu
LUNSFORD, Larry 305-348-2797. 115 B Larry.Lunsford@fiu.edu
LUNT, Ruth, M 920-832-6528. 533 S ruth.m.lunt@lawrence.edu
LUONG, Carmen 718-482-5511. 318 F carmenl@lagcc.cuny.edu
LUONG, Huan 972-860-8102. 470 H hluong@dcccd.edu
LUOTTO, John, A 304-326-1234. 527 G jluotto@salemu.edu
LUPE, Mark 239-433-6948. 101 O mlupe@edison.edu
LUPIEN, Alfred 605-322-8090. 450 F alfred.lupien@mtmc.edu
LUPO, Bernadette 413-662-5203. 230 C bernadette.lupo@mcla.edu
LUPOLE, Barbara, H 610-799-1510. 421 I blupole@lccc.edu
LUPTAK, Andrew, J 262-243-5700. 532 H andrew.luptak@cuw.edu
LUPTON, Deborah 410-337-6135. 215 A dlupton@goucher.edu
LUPTON, Mark 704-272-5406. 363 G mlupton@spcc.edu
LURIA, J 845-731-3700. 352 A yv@ksrnet.com
LURSEN, Cara 704-403-1614. 352 J cara.lursen@carolinashealthcare.org
LUSBY, Mary Lee 402-354-7058. 291 B marylee.lusby@methodistcollege.edu
LUSE, Kimberly 919-530-7601. 368 A kluse@nccu.edu
LUSH, Mary Jean 662-332-8500. 268 B mjlush@msdelta.edu
LUSH, Susan 617-369-3870. 236 F slush@mfa.org
LUSHBAUGH, Jeffery 609-777-3083. 308 A jlushbaugh@tesc.edu
LUSIGNAN, Susan, C 585-389-2147. 332 D slusign6@naz.edu
LUSK, D. Claude 806-291-3436. 494 F luskc@wbu.edu
LUSK, David 252-493-7260. 362 G dlusk@email.pittcc.edu
LUSK, Ju-Hsin 423-697-3338. 460 C
LUSK, Kent 312-553-5628. 141 N klusk1@ccc.edu
LUSK, Kevin 304-243-2389. 531 H klusk@wju.edu
LUSK, Susan 310-954-4037... 54 J slusk@msmc.la.edu
LUSSKIN, Elizabeth 718-260-3392. 336 E elusskin@poly.edu
LUST, Kevin 217-789-1017. 151 F kevin.lust@llcc.edu
LUSTER, Pamela, T 619-388-2721... 62 E pluster@sdccd.edu
LUSTIG, Derek 315-781-3000. 326 C lustig@hws.edu
LUSTIG, Kevin 928-541-7777... 16 B klustig@ncu.edu
LUTCHEN, Kenneth, R 617-353-2800. 224 D klutch@bu.edu
LUTER, Gary, S 813-253-3333. 118 L gluter@ut.edu
LUTES, Jean 610-519-6518. 436 F jean.lutes@villanova.edu
LUTGEN, Roxanne, M 715-365-4413. 540 G rlutgen@nicoletcollege.edu
LUTGRING, Ray 812-488-2589. 173 H rl5@evansville.edu
LUTHER, Judith 502-585-9911. 199 C jluther@spalding.edu
LUTHER, Nikol 208-792-5272. 138 G ncluther@lcsc.edu
LUTHER, Patricia 760-245-4271... 75 B Pat.Luther@vvc.edu
LUTHI, John, R 570-577-3332. 411 A john.luthi@bucknell.edu
LUTHMAN-TURNBULL, Nicole 973-278-5400. 299 D nll@berkeleycollege.edu
LUTOMSKI, Robert 212-229-5459. 332 E lutomskr@newschool.edu
LUTRICK, Candee 972-825-4612. 481 F clutrick@sagu.edu
LUTRICK, Donny 972-825-4824. 481 F dlutrick@sagu.edu
LUTTENBERGER, CM, Gerard, H 718-990-6570. 339 A luttenbg@stjohns.edu
LUTTRELL, Curt 503-768-6036. 403 K luttrell@lclark.edu
LUTY, Paul, J 503-943-7308. 408 F luty@up.edu
LUTZ, JR., Ben 865-573-4517. 455 G blutz@johnsonU.edu
LUTZ, Cathleen, A 570-321-4069. 422 H lutz@lycoming.edu
LUTZ, Charles 419-448-3351. 389 J clutz@tiffin.edu
LUTZ, Dan 765-285-8984. 164 B dlutz@bsu.edu
LUTZ, Debra, K 989-686-9386. 242 C dklutz@delta.edu
LUTZ, J. Gary 610-758-3708. 422 A jgl3@lehigh.edu
LUTZ, Kim, L 810-766-4271. 239 G kim.lutz@baker.edu
LUTZ, Mitzi 660-562-1119. 279 I mitzi@nwmissouri.edu
LUTZ, Natalie 816-654-7032. 275 K nlutz@kcumb.edu
LUTZ, Nate, K 612-874-3780. 257 B nate_lutz@mcad.edu
LUTZ, Paula 307-766-4106. 543 I plutz@uwyo.edu
LUTZ, Robert 516-739-1545. 333 F studentservices@nyctcm.edu
LUTZ, Susan 303-871-2118... 86 B susan.lutz@du.edu
LUTZ-DAVIDSON, Stacy 719-389-6953... 79 D sdavidson@coloradocollege.edu
LUTZKA, David 218-722-4000. 255 E davidl@dbumn.edu
LUTZKA, David, R 218-722-4000. 255 E davidl@dbumn.edu
LUTZKY, Raymond 718-637-5984. 336 E rlutzky@poly.edu
LUU, Khien 563-876-3353. 177 I kluu@dwci.com
LUUKKONEN, John 212-594-4000. 347 H jluukkonen@tcicollege.edu
LUVERA, Michael 509-963-2959. 517 F luveram@cwu.edu
LUX, David 401-232-6433. 438 K dlux@bryant.edu
LUXNER, Catherine 570-961-4703. 423 B luxner@marywood.edu
LUXTON, Andrea, T 269-471-3404. 239 D aluxton@andrews.edu
LUY, Peg 616-233-3413. 241 H pluy@davenport.edu
LUYMES, Robyn 616-732-1157. 241 H rluymes3@davenport.edu
LUZADER, Timothy, B 765-494-3981. 171 M tluzader@purdue.edu
LUZAR, E. Jane 317-278-5082. 168 D ejluzar@iupui.edu
LUZURIAGA, Katherine 508-856-6282. 229 C Katherine.Luzuriaga@umassmed.edu
LUZURIAGA, Susana 513-745-3461. 393 H luzuriagas@xavier.edu
LU'UWAI, Maile 808-739-8597. 135 D maile.luuwai@chaminade.edu
LY, Geisce 415-267-6521... 38 L jly@ccsf.edu
LY, Vi 323-265-6793... 51 F lyv@elac.edu
LYALL, James 303-556-3892... 83 D jlyall1@msudenver.edu
LYBYER, Debra 208-792-2313. 138 G dlybyer@lcsc.edu
LYDDON, Jerri, L 620-417-1151. 190 F jerrilynn.lyddon@sccc.edu
LYDDON, Susan 718-482-5010. 318 F slyddon@lagcc.cuny.edu
LYDEN, Elizabeth 715-394-6677. 541 F elizabeth.lyden@witc.edu
LYDEN, Michael, P 814-824-3652. 423 J mlyden@mercyhurst.edu
LYDER, Courtney 310-825-9621... 71 C clyder@sonnet.ucla.edu
LYDIC, R. Jeffrey 724-847-6581. 417 A jlydic@geneva.edu
LYDON, Carol Ann 828-694-1882. 358 C ca_lydon@blueridge.edu
LYDON, Christopher 508-565-1801. 237 A clydon@stonehill.edu
LYDON, John 504-394-7744. 206 C jlydon@olhcc.edu
LYDON, JR., Theodore, M 415-422-6396... 73 J lydon@usfca.edu
LYDY, Kenneth, A 937-382-6661. 393 B kenneth_lydy@wilmington.edu
LYKE, Alan, D 719-884-5000... 83 K adlyke@nbc.edu
LYKE, Heather 734-487-1849. 242 D hlyke@emich.edu
LYKINS, Jason 660-263-3900. 272 A jlykins@cccb.edu
LYKINS, Karen 931-372-3214. 460 A klykins@tntech.edu
LYKOUDIS, Michael, N 574-631-7473. 174 A lykoudis.1@nd.edu
LYLE, Donald, L 724-458-2122. 417 E dllyle@gcc.edu
LYLE, J. Gary 410-777-2836. 213 D jglyle@aacc.edu
LYLE, William 215-489-4987. 414 E William.Lyle@delval.edu
LYLES, Carol, S 256-765-4201..... 9 C cslyles@una.edu
LYM, Brian 516-877-3250. 313 A blym@adelphi.edu
LYMAN, Barbara, G 717-477-1371. 429 E bglyman@ship.edu
LYMAN, Kristin 320-363-5233. 254 J klyman@csbsju.edu
LYMPANY, John 859-985-3990. 192 F john_lympany@berea.edu
LYN, Janice 334-244-3028..... 2 A jlyn@aum.edu
LYNCH, Amy 956-364-4500. 485 H amy.lynch@tstc.edu
LYNCH, Bruce, G 336-334-4556. 369 A bglynch@uncg.edu
LYNCH, Christopher 251-460-7725..... 9 E clynch@southalabama.edu
LYNCH, Christopher 251-460-6494..... 9 E clynch@southalabama.edu
LYNCH, Cynthia 414-847-3340. 534 F cynthialynch@miad.edu
LYNCH, Cynthia, D 414-847-3340. 534 F cynthialynch@miad.edu
LYNCH, Darlene 219-980-6614. 168 B darlynch@iun.edu
LYNCH, Deborah 407-708-2144. 113 E lynchd@seminolestate.edu
LYNCH, Dianne 573-876-7210. 282 H dlynch@stephens.edu
LYNCH, Eileen 773-838-7984. 142 E elynch4@ccc.edu
LYNCH, James 912-279-5713. 123 B jlynch@ccga.edu
LYNCH, James 315-792-5316. 331 I jlynch@mvcc.edu
LYNCH, Janet, D 815-288-5511. 158 K lynchj@svcc.edu
LYNCH, Joe 717-337-6518. 417 B jlynch@gettysburg.edu
LYNCH, Julie 512-499-4309. 491 A jlynch@utsystem.edu

LYNCH, Kathryn .... 781-283-3583. 237 F
klynch@wellesley.edu
LYNCH, Kelly .... 781-239-6350. 222 D
klynch@babson.edu
LYNCH, Kevin .... 315-228-6611. 320 F
kplynch@colgate.edu
LYNCH, Kim .... 763-433-1865. 257 P
kimberly.lynch@anokaramsey.edu
LYNCH, Kris .... 252-399-6329. 352 F
klynch@barton.edu
LYNCH, Lisa .... 781-736-3883. 224 F
lisalynch@brandeis.edu
LYNCH, Melinda .... 859-336-5082. 198 J
melindalynch@sccky.edu
LYNCH, Michael .... 508-999-8845. 229 A
mlynch4@umassd.edu
LYNCH, Michael .... 315-568-3052. 333 C
mlynch@nycc.edu
LYNCH, Michelle .... 502-863-7061. 194 C
michelle_lynch@georgetowncollege.edu
LYNCH, Mike .... 617-353-1905. 224 D
mlynch@bu.edu
LYNCH, Paul .... 703-284-1608. 507 B
paul.lynch@marymount.edu
LYNCH, Paul, F .... 315-445-4551. 328 F
lynchpf@lemoyne.edu
LYNCH, Richard, E .... 972-708-7340. 472 L
dick_lynch@gial.edu
LYNCH, Robert .... 240-567-7306. 216 F
bob.lynch@montgomerycollege.edu
LYNCH, Robert, P .... 407-888-8689. 104 B
blynch@fcim.edu
LYNCH, Rose .... 908-835-2306. 308 G
lynchr@warren.edu
LYNCH, Scott .... 970-207-4500... 86 G
ScottL@uscareerinstitute.edu
LYNCH, Stephanie, J .... 202-687-4056... 95 E
sjl28@georgetown.edu
LYNCH, Stephen, J .... 401-865-2233. 439 E
sjlynch@providence.edu
LYNCH, Timothy, G .... 734-764-0304. 251 C
timlynch@umich.edu
LYNCH, William, F .... 215-895-2167. 415 B
wfl27@drexel.edu
LYNCH-CARIS, Terri .... 810-762-9859. 244 Q
tlynch@kettering.edu
LYNCH MAESTAS,
Michael .... 785-864-2277. 190 L
mvlm@ku.edu
LYNDGAARD, David .... 320-363-3350. 263 P
dlyndgaard@csbsju.edu
LYNEMA, Dawn, A .... 616-988-3624. 245 C
dlynema@kuyper.edu
LYNES, Rich .... 918-465-1802. 395 G
rlynes@eosc.edu
LYNG, Heather .... 802-287-8231. 499 D
gmc@bkstr.com
LYNG-GLIDDI, Diana, L . 518-327-6314. 336 B
dlyngglidd@paulsmiths.edu
LYNN, Angela .... 309-298-1891. 162 K
an-lynn@wiu.edu
LYNN, Crystal .... 540-828-5356. 502 J
clynn@bridgewater.edu
LYNN, Dahlia .... 207-780-4524. 212 H
dlynn@usm.maine.edu
LYNN, Kathy .... 802-865-6485. 499 A
lynn@champlain.edu
LYNN, Ken .... 281-998-6306. 479 E
ken.lynn@sjcd.edu
LYNN, Kerrie .... 423-746-5206. 462 C
klynn@twcnet.edu
LYNN, Laura .... 410-662-2797. 265 D
laura.lynn@waldenu.edu
LYNN, Marvin .... 574-520-4845. 168 E
lynnm@iusb.edu
LYNN, Michael .... 219-785-5380. 172 A
mlynn@pnc.edu
LYNN, Rexton .... 201-684-7627. 305 A
rlynn@ramapo.edu
LYNN, Richard .... 251-809-1556..... 5 A
richard.lynn@jdcc.edu
LYNN, Richardson, R .... 404-872-3593. 121 C
rlynn@johnmrshall.edu
LYNN, Terence .... 413-775-1440. 231 E
LynnT@gcc.mass.edu
LYNN, Tristan .... 515-244-4221. 175 C
lynnt@aib.edu
LYNN, Vicki .... 501-450-1494... 21 E
lynn@hendrix.edu
LYNN, William .... 570-208-5946. 419 P
williamlynn@kings.edu
LYNNE, Christopher .... 928-541-7777... 16 B
clynne@ncu.edu
LYNNERUP, Rasmus .... 312-553-2500. 141 M
rlynnerup@ccc.edu
LYNOTT, Patricia .... 603-645-9596. 297 I
p.lynott@snhu.edu
LYON, Alison .... 650-508-3503... 56 H
alyon@ndnu.edu
LYON, Bob .... 423-425-4717. 463 D
bob-lyon@utc.edu
LYON, Doug .... 970-247-7010... 81 M
lyon_d@fortlewis.edu
LYON, JR., James, C .... 773-442-4100. 154 H
j-lyonjr@neiu.edu
LYON, Larry .... 254-710-3588. 467 G
larry_lyon@baylor.edu
LYON, Larry .... 919-761-2372. 366 I
llyon@sebts.edu
LYON, Mary Eilleen .... 616-331-2221. 243 C
lyonme@gvsu.edu
LYON, Misty .... 309-341-5422. 141 A
mlyon@sandburg.edu
LYON, Robert .... 256-824-6127..... 8 F
robert.lyon@uah.edu
LYON, Tammy .... 910-938-6247. 359 E
lyont@coastalcarolina.edu
LYON, Wade .... 620-417-1064. 190 F
wade.lyon@sccc.edu
LYONS, Anthony .... 620-227-9203. 186 B
alyons@dc3.edu
LYONS, Becky .... 406-657-2144. 287 C
blyons@msubillings.edu
LYONS, Cheryl, C .... 501-450-3140... 25 H
clyons@uca.edu
LYONS, Cindy .... 239-590-7904. 115 A
clyons@fgcu.edu
LYONS, James .... 408-554-4000... 64 M
LYONS, SR., James, E ... 202-274-6016... 97 A
james.lyons@udc.edu
LYONS, Joan .... 510-580-6716... 77 C
jlyons@cci.edu
LYONS, Katherine, M .... 985-732-6640. 203 D
LYONS, Kyra, A .... 202-319-5608... 94 G
lyonsk@cua.edu
LYONS, Larry .... 309-438-5626. 147 J
lelyons@ilstu.edu
LYONS, Mary, E .... 619-260-4520... 73 I
president@sandiego.edu
LYONS, Marybeth .... 315-792-7505. 346 C
smbl@sunyit.edu
LYONS, Melinda .... 928-541-7777... 16 B
mlyons@ncu.edu
LYONS, Michael .... 781-239-2443. 231 G
mlyons@massbay.edu
LYONS, Nicholas, A .... 315-312-2222. 344 A
nicholas.lyons@oswego.edu
LYONS, Patrick, G .... 973-761-9498. 307 C
patrick.lyons@shu.edu
LYONS, Pattyanne .... 617-349-8178. 228 B
plyons@lesley.edu
LYONS, Peter .... 404-413-2578. 126 E
lyonsp@gsu.edu
LYONS, Phil .... 715-232-1683. 538 B
lyonsp@uwstout.edu
LYONS, Richard, K .... 510-643-2027... 70 I
lyons@haas.berkeley.edu
LYONS, Sharon, K .... 563-588-7829. 180 L
sharon.lyons@loras.edu
LYONS, Shawn .... 859-238-5500. 193 E
shawn.lyons@centre.edu
LYONS, Sheila .... 601-352-9666. 266 A
bookstore@belhaven.edu
LYONS, Steve .... 218-723-6167. 254 K
slyons@css.edu
LYONS, Steven, J .... 937-775-5745. 393 G
steven.lyons@wright.edu
LYONS, Theresa .... 907-786-1240... 10 H
LYONS, Yolanda .... 719-389-6245... 79 D
yolanda.lyons@ColoradoCollege.edu
LYSENG, Brenda .... 651-779-3447. 258 C
brenda.lyseng@century.edu
LYSIONEK, Christine .... 610-902-8416. 411 E
christine.lysionek@cabrini.edu
LYSLE, Jane, H .... 302-225-6274... 93 H
lyslej@gbc.edu
LYSNE, Marit .... 507-222-4080. 254 D
mlysne@carleton.edu
LYTCH, Carol, E .... 717-290-8701. 421 D
president@lancasterseminary.edu
LYTLE, Anne .... 212-772-4242. 318 C
alytle@hunter.cuny.edu
LYTLE, Carol, J .... 712-749-2440. 176 D
lytlec@bvu.edu
LYTLE, David .... 210-434-6711. 477 N
dlytle@lake.ollusa.edu
LYTLE, James, R .... 570-586-2400. 410 D
jlytle@bbc.edu
LYTLE, Jesse .... 610-896-1000. 418 F
jlytle@haverford.edu
LYTLE, Rick, S .... 325-674-2503. 464 H
lytler@acu.edu
LYTLE, Rodney .... 828-298-3325. 370 E
rlytle@warren-wilson.edu
LYTTLE, Marsha, J .... 810-762-9660. 244 Q
mlyttle@kettering.edu
LYTTLE, Mary Jo .... 724-357-7942. 428 F
mjlyttle@iup.edu
LYTTLE, Sonya .... 843-525-8248. 447 C
slyttle@tcl.edu
LYTTON, Billy .... 704-922-6480. 360 F
lytton.billy@gaston.edu
L'ALLIER, Kristi .... 218-235-2153. 261 G
k.laillier@vcc.edu
L'ETOILE, Michelle .... 617-422-7210. 235 B
mletoile@nesl.edu
L'HEUREUX, Robert, W .. 712-362-0421. 179 E
rl'heureux@iowalakes.edu

M

MA, Dongxin .... 512-454-1188. 466 B
info@aoma.edu
MA, Duc, D .... 520-626-1188... 18 F
mad2@email.arizona.edu
MA, Elise .... 516-739-1545. 333 F
executive_asst@nyctcm.edu
MA, Jennifer .... 510-235-7800... 41 K
jma@contracosta.edu
MA, Jim .... 630-942-4034. 142 G
maj127@cod.edu
MA, Michelle .... 714-241-6186... 39 I
mma@coastline.edu
MA, Qing .... 626-289-7719... 26 J
MA, Qingyun .... 213-740-2083... 74 A
archdean@usc.edu
MA, Stephen .... 831-646-4040... 54 I
sma@mpc.edu
MA, Yongli, C .... 678-915-7473. 132 C
yma@spsu.edu
MAAG, Traci .... 605-886-3450. 450 G
tmaag@national.edu
MAALOUF, Kathy .... 757-822-1298. 514 C
kmaalouf@tcc.edu
MAANUM, Jeanne .... 612-659-6251. 259 D
jeanne.maanum@minneapolis.edu
MAAS, Bruce .... 608-262-5381. 536 D
bruce.mass@cio.wisc.edu
MAAS, Paula .... 212-229-8947. 332 E
maasp@neschool.edu
MAASJO, Bryan .... 212-772-4582. 318 C
MAATSCH, Darrell .... 210-567-2890. 493 A
maatsch@uthscsa.edu
MABE, Mark .... 816-271-4261. 279 A
mabe@missouriwestern.edu
MABERRY, Sue .... 310-665-6925... 57 C
maberry@otis.edu
MABERY, Dam .... 870-230-5101... 21 D
mayberb@hsu.edu
MABEUS, Amy .... 319-385-6478. 179 K
iwcbookstore@iwc.edu
MABINI, Shirley, A .... 671-734-1812. 546 D
smabini@piu.edu
MABRY, Dawn, M .... 260-399-7700. 174 C
dmabry@sf.edu
MABRY, James .... 480-461-7325... 15 A
james.mabry@mesacc.edu
MABRY, Rodney, H .... 903-566-7119. 492 D
president@uttyler.edu
MABUCHI, Julia .... 617-558-1788. 235 C
jmabuchi@nesa.edu
MAC EWAN, Peter .... 216-987-4702. 378 D
peter.macewan@tri-c.edu
MACADAM, Martha, P .... 717-872-3820. 429 D
martha.macadam@millersville.edu
MACALUSO, Anthony .... 718-990-2452. 339 A
macalusa@stjohns.edu
MACALUSO, Daniel .... 909-621-8335... 46 H
dmacaluso@hmc.edu
MACAN, Drew .... 802-443-5261. 499 H
cmacan@middlebury.edu
MACAPINLAC, Jonas, D . 671-735-2944. 546 E
jmacapinlac@uguam.uog.edu
MACARI, Emir, J .... 916-278-6366... 34 D
emacari@ecs.csus.edu
MACARTHUR, John .... 661-362-2220... 53 G
sstaats@masters.edu
MACAULAY, Barbara .... 617-732-2800. 233 E
MACCARTHY,
Stephen, J .... 215-898-8724. 435 B
smaccar@upenn.edu
MACCHI, Thomas, J .... 215-572-2942. 409 H
macchit@arcadia.edu
MACCLAREN, Jon .... 802-387-6721. 499 E
jonmacclaren@landmark.edu
MACCORQUODALE,
Patricia .... 520-621-2848... 18 F
pmac@email.arizona.edu
MACCUISH, Spencer .... 805-581-1233... 43 G
MACCULLOCH, Heather .. 718-409-7331. 346 D
hmacculloch@sunymaritime.edu
MACCULLOUGH,
Deborah .... 215-702-4360. 411 F
dmaccullough@cairn.edu
MACDONALD, Ann .... 507-457-2773. 262 A
amacdonald@winona.edu
MACDONALD, Brian .... 802-654-2588. 500 B
bmacdonald@smcvt.edu
MACDONALD,
Christopher .... 912-478-5406. 126 C
cmacdonald@georgiasouthern.edu
MACDONALD, David .... 419-772-2200. 386 D
d-macdonald@onu.edu
MACDONALD, Dick .... 928-681-5562... 15 L
dmacdonald@mohave.edu
MACDONALD, Duncan ... 607-431-4032. 325 F
macdonaldd@hartwick.edu
MACDONALD, Elizabeth . 636-949-4396. 276 D
emacdonald@lindenwood.edu
MACDONALD, Eric .... 207-974-4685. 210 K
emacdonald@emcc.edu
MACDONALD, Gordon ... 303-762-6890... 81 G
gordon.macdonald@denverseminary.edu
MACDONALD, Gregory ... 610-330-5069. 420 D
macdonag@lafayette.edu
MACDONALD, Gregory ... 540-868-7275. 512 H
gmacdonald@lfcc.edu
MACDONALD, Ida .... 903-566-7064. 492 D
ida_macdonald@uttyler.edu
MACDONALD, James .... 978-921-4242. 234 C
james.macdonald@montserrat.edu
MACDONALD, Jean .... 716-926-8932. 326 B
jmacdonald@hilbert.edu
MACDONALD, Nancy .... 518-454-2161. 321 A
macdonan@strose.edu
MACDONALD,
Randall, M .... 863-680-4165. 105 D
rmacdonald1@flsouthern.edu
MACDONALD,
William, L .... 740-366-3321. 386 E
macdonald.24@osu.edu
MACDONALD-DENNIS,
Chris, A .... 651-696-6210. 256 L
cmacdona@macalester.edu
MACDONELL, Chuck, C . 402-552-2693. 288 L
macdonell@clarksoncollege.edu
MACDONNELL, Lisa .... 313-993-1455. 250 K
macdonnl@udmercy.edu
MACE, Paul .... 410-334-2932. 221 D
pmace@worwic.edu
MACEACHRAN, Joanne .. 352-588-8462. 112 D
joanne.maceachran@saintleo.edu
MACEDO, Maria .... 425-739-8255. 520 K
maria.macedo@lwtech.edu
MACELROY, Molly .... 518-388-6117. 348 J
macelrom@union.edu
MACENCZAK,
Kimberly, C .... 706-385-1442. 130 F
kim.macenczak@point.edu
MACEO, Brenda, K .... 213-740-5371... 74 A
maceo@usc.edu
MACEWAN, Bonnie .... 334-844-1714..... 1 G
macewbj@auburn.edu
MACFARLAND,
Randolph, M .... 303-762-6900... 81 G
randy.macfarland@denverseminary.edu
MACFARLANE, Lisa .... 603-862-3290. 298 C
lisa.macfarlane@unh.edu
MACFIE, Thomas, E .... 931-598-1274. 458 H
tmacfie@sewanee.edu
MACGILLIVRAY,
Diane, N .... 617-373-2520. 235 F
MACH, Stella .... 312-935-4180. 156 K
smach@robertmorris.edu
MACHACEK, Jennifer .... 920-748-8185. 535 J
machacekj@ripon.edu
MACHADO, Diane .... 718-405-3262. 320 G
diane.machado@mountsaintvincent.edu
MACHALA, Janis .... 425-564-2732. 517 A
janis.machala@bellevuecollege.edu
MACHALSKI, Thomas .... 248-683-0311. 250 F
tmachalski@sscms.edu
MACHARG, Janie .... 310-243-3818... 33 B
jmacharg@csudh.edu
MACHELL, James .... 405-974-5701. 400 K
jmachell@uco.edu
MACHEN, James, B .... 352-392-1311. 116 A
president@ufl.edu
MACHEN, Paul .... 210-486-2157. 465 B
pmachen@alamo.edu
MACHI, Jeffrey .... 212-650-7125. 317 D
jmachi@ccny.cuny.edu
MACHIA, Michael .... 580-628-6291. 396 M
michael.machia@noc.edu
MACHIELSON, Allen, J ... 260-982-5052. 170 U
ajmachielson@manchester.edu
MACHLIS, Gedelyah .... 718-232-7800. 351 C
MACHNIK, Michael, E .... 908-526-1200. 305 B
mmachnik@raritanval.edu
MACHON, Margaret .... 708-974-5708. 153 F
machon@morainevalley.edu
MACHT, Barbara, E .... 240-500-2000. 215 B
bemacht@hagerstowncc.edu
MACHTLEY, Ronald, K .... 401-232-6008. 438 K
rmac@bryant.edu
MACHUCA, Melilssa .... 602-943-2311... 19 C
Melissa.Machuca@west.edu
MACHUSAK, Janice, M .. 313-927-1301. 246 D
jmachusak@marygrove.edu
MACIAG, Clark .... 704-971-8500. 353 F
MACIAG, Gary .... 716-375-2032. 338 E
gmaciag@sbu.edu
MACIAS, Anita .... 412-563-6673. 131 H
amacias@southuniversity.edu

MACIAS, Benjamin 626-914-8611 38 K
bmacias@citruscollege.edu
MACIAS, Erica 509-865-0420 520 D
macias_e@heritage.edu
MACIAS, Paige, L 949-824-5108 71 B
plmacias@uci.edu
MACIAS, Sandy 650-961-9300 58 B
smacias@paloaltou.edu
MACIAS, Tom 760-757-2121 54 G
tmacias@miracosta.edu
MACIAS, Trisha 719-549-2951 80 K
trisha.macias@colostate-pueblo.edu
MACIEJ-HINER, Marian, G 608-342-1314 537 D
maciejhm@uwplatt.edu
MACIEJEWSKI, Felice, E 708-524-6873 144 C
fmaciejewski@dom.edu
MACIEL, Rene 210-924-4338 467 E
rene.maciel@bua.edu
MACIK, Lillian 254-867-4893 485 G
lillian.macik@systems.tstc.edu
MACINNIS, Stewart, D 540-464-7207 515 B
macinnissd@vmi.edu
MACINTOSH, Kay, H 410-810-7408 221 C
kmacintosh2@washcoll.edu
MACINTYRE, Bennett 406-447-4374 285 G
bmacintyre@carroll.edu
MACIONUS, Joseph 203-576-5616 91 D
jmacionus@stvincentscollege.edu
MACIULAITIS, Mark 631-632-6090 342 C
mark.maciulaitis@stonybrook.edu
MACK, Bill 570-326-3761 427 B
wem1@pct.edu
MACK, Carol 503-725-3419 406 B
mackc@pdx.edu
MACK, Carol 843-525-8250 447 C
cmack@tcl.edu
MACK, Craig 781-239-3157 231 G
cmack@massbay.edu
MACK, Jeffrey, A 813-974-2539 116 C
jmack@admin.usf.edu
MACK, Johnny 503-399-6243 402 E
johnny.mack@chemeketa.edu
MACK, Jon 610-917-1467 436 C
jmack@vfcc.edu
MACK, Joseph 607-431-4209 325 F
mackj@hartwick.edu
MACK, Joseph, J 570-674-6336 424 A
jmack@misericordia.edu
MACK, Kari 845-687-5214 348 H
mackk@sunyulster.edu
MACK, Kimberly, J 252-536-6399 361 A
kmack219@halifaxcc.edu
MACK, Lesley, A 414-955-8733 534 C
lmack@mcw.edu
MACK, Linda 336-517-2109 352 H
lmack@bennett.edu
MACK, Marie 701-777-2746 371 C
marie.mack@email.und.edu
MACK, Marva 973-877-3346 301 H
mack@essex.edu
MACK, Melvin 803-934-3401 445 F
mmack@morris.edu
MACK, Qing, L 860-253-3008 88 C
qmack@asnuntuck.edu
MACK, Teresa 803-793-5106 443 E
mackt@denmarktech.edu
MACK, Timothy, P 724-357-2244 428 F
tmack@iup.edu
MACK, Tom 803-641-3479 448 A
tomm@usca.edu
MACK-HISGEN, Maura 518-262-5033 313 D
mmack@mail.amc.edu
MACKAY, Danielle 845-398-4102 340 A
dmackay@stac.edu
MACKAY, Danielle 845-398-4016 340 A
dmackay@stac.edu
MACKAY, Jeff 503-883-2436 404 A
jmackay@linfield.edu
MACKAY, Tara 480-212-1704 17 N
MACKAY, William, M 617-266-1400 223 D
MACKE, Charles 931-372-3414 460 A
cmacke@tntech.edu
MACKEL, Carol 814-254-0400 413 C
cmackel@pa.gov
MACKEL, Thomas, J 678-839-6252 133 I
tmackel@westga.edu
MACKEN, Jennifer 303-914-6600 84 I
MACKENZIE, Donald 616-234-4000 243 B
MACKENZIE, Lorie 315-229-5600 339 F
lmackenzie@stlawu.edu
MACKERETH, Anne 952-885-5417 263 B
amackereth@nwhealth.edu
MACKERSIE, Chris 253-912-3655 522 C
cmackers@pierce.ctc.edu
MACKEY, Angela 305-949-9500 102 E
amackey@cci.edu
MACKEY, Craig 973-300-2344 307 F
cmackey@sussex.edu
MACKEY, Peter, F 570-577-3260 411 A
pete.mackey@bucknell.edu
MACKEY, Roberta 850-872-3866 106 H
rmackey@gulfcoast.edu
MACKEY, Thomas 518-587-2100 346 A
thomas.mackey@esc.edu
MACKEY, Thomas, A 713-500-3267 492 E
thomas.a.mackey@uth.tmc.edu
MACKIE, Keith 828-327-7000 359 A
kmackie@cvcc.edu
MACKIE-MASON, Jeffrey, K 734-647-3576 251 C
jmm@umich.edu
MACKILLOP, Jane 718-482-5302 318 F
jmackillop@lagcc.cuny.edu
MACKIN, Brian, W 205-975-8221 8 E
bmackin@uab.edu
MACKIN, Janet 212-614-6110 336 C
jmackin@chpnet.org
MACKIN, Jim 402-461-7482 289 I
jmackin@hastings.edu
MACKIN, OFM, Kevin 845-569-3202 332 B
kevin.mackin@msmc.edu
MACKIN, Mary Beth 262-472-1533 538 D
mackinm@uww.edu
MACKINNON, George 847-619-7290 157 D
gmackinnon@roosevelt.edu
MACKINNON, Neil, J 513-558-3326 390 G
neil.mackinnon@uc.edu
MACKINNON, Thomas, S 414-288-8020 534 B
thomas.mackinnon@marquette.edu
MACKINTOSH, Carol 315-792-3228 349 F
cmackintosh@utica.edu
MACKLIN, James, F 518-629-7353 326 G
j.macklin@hvcc.edu
MACKSEY-ETHIER, Jennifer 413-662-5210 230 C
j.ethier@mcla.edu
MACLACHLAN, Scott 561-207-5325 110 C
maclachs@palmbeachstate.edu
MACLAREN, James 504-865-5225 207 C
maclaren@tulane.edu
MACLEAN, Roger 406-243-2900 286 H
roger.maclean@umontana.edu
MACLEISH, Padraic 760-872-2000 42 E
padraicm@deepsprings.edu
MACLENNAN, Kevin, L 303-492-6694 85 L
kevin.maclennan@colorado.edu
MACLENNAN, Richard 301-387-3056 214 I
rick.maclennan@garrettcollege.edu
MACLEOD, Catherine 212-431-2833 333 I
cmacleod@nyls.edu
MACLEOD, David, J 563-588-8000 178 D
dmacleod@emmaus.edu
MACLEOD, Ian 508-830-5269 230 D
imacleod@maritime.edu
MACLEOD, Kelly 727-726-1153 100 E
kellymacleod@clearwater.edu
MACLEOD, Kimberly, M 607-746-4603 345 G
macleokm@delhi.edu
MACLEOD, Melissa, A 724-458-2050 417 E
mamacleod@gcc.edu
MACLEOD, Robert 813-974-6015 116 C
rmacleod@usf.edu
MACLEOD, Stephen, C 978-867-4068 226 H
steve.macleod@gordon.edu
MACLIN, Sharonda 620-242-0501 188 G
maclins@mcpherson.edu
MACMAHON, James 435-797-2478 497 B
jim.macmahon@usu.edu
MACMASTER, Donald 989-358-7344 239 C
macmastd@alpenacc.edu
MACMILLAN, Cynthia 609-984-1130 308 A
cmacmillan@tesc.edu
MACMILLAN, David, F 415-422-2047 73 J
macmillan@usfca.edu
MACMILLAN, Douglas, B 478-757-5155 134 G
dmacmillan@wesleyancollege.edu
MACMINN, Linda 305-809-3285 104 I
linda.macminn@fkcc.edu
MACMORRIS, Anne 609-771-2674 300 E
macmorri@tcnj.edu
MACNAMARA, Timothy 307-778-1256 543 D
tmacnama@lccc.wy.edu
MACNAUGHTON, Kevin, J 919-515-2732 368 B
kevin_macnaughton@ncsu.edu
MACNEIL, Jacqueline 727-864-7856 101 N
macneijm@eckerd.edu
MACNEIL, M. A. J. Lex 630-515-7275 153 B
lmacne@midwestern.edu
MACNEIL, R. Lamont 860-679-2808 92 A
MacNeil@nso.uchc.edu
MACNEILL, Andrew, J 619-388-2797 62 E
amacneil@sdccd.edu
MACNEW, James 215-637-7700 418 G
jmacnew@holyfamily.edu
MACONACHY, W. Vic 301-369-2800 213 G
wvmaconachy@capitol-college.edu
MACOPSON, Elmer, R 828-652-0603 362 A
elmerm@mcdowelltech.edu
MACOSKO, Ron 830-792-7421 480 F
rpmacosko@schreiner.edu
MACPHEE, Donna, H 212-851-7487 321 D
dhm18@columbia.edu
MACPHERSON, Andy 903-463-8777 472 M
macphersona@grayson.edu
MACPHERSON, Corey 617-745-3525 225 G
corey.s.macpherson@enc.edu
MACPHERSON, Heidi 608-785-8042 536 G
hmacpherson@uwlax.edu
MACQUEEN, William, J 248-341-2027 248 D
wjmacque@oaklandcc.edu
MACRAE, Tom 831-656-2441 544 M
tmacrae@navy.edu
MACREADY, Neil, A 909-748-8049 73 H
neil_macready@redlands.edu
MACRINA, Francis, L 804-827-2262 511 F
macrina@vcu.edu
MACRITCHIE, Andrea 508-854-4461 232 F
amacritchie@qcc.mass.edu
MACRO, Venessa 515-271-3133 177 K
venessa.macro@drake.edu
MACTAGGART, Julie 563-589-3619 182 J
jmactaggart@dbq.edu
MACTAGGART, Melissa 563-425-5959 183 B
mactaggartm@uiu.edu
MACUILA, Terry 606-242-0974 196 F
terry.macuila@kctcs.edu
MACUMBER, Linda, K 563-333-6336 182 B
MacumberLindaK@sau.edu
MACUR, Kenneth, M 785-227-3380 184 I
macurk@bethanylb.edu
MACVARISH, Greg 312-662-4141 139 F
gmacvarish@adler.edu
MACVEY, Mark 760-480-8474 76 C
mmacvey@wscal.edu
MACWILLIAMS, Erika 305-809-3155 104 I
erika.macwilliams@fkcc.edu
MADAIO-O'BRIEN, Melanie 617-353-2256 224 D
asmelmad@bu.edu
MADAMA, Patrick 732-906-2551 303 B
PMadama@middlesexcc.edu
MADANIPOUR, Manouche 617-928-7376 234 E
mmadanipour@mountida.edu
MADDALI, Ramesh 601-877-6146 265 G
rmaddali@alcorn.edu
MADDEN, Beverly 650-574-6538 64 C
maddenb@smccd.edu
MADDEN, Charles, E 478-387-4804 125 E
emadden@gmc.cc.ga.us
MADDEN, Christopher 214-648-0702 493 E
christopher.madden@utsouthwestern.edu
MADDEN, Deanna 808-983-4152 135 G
dmadden@tokai.edu
MADDEN, Fred, H 856-415-2272 302 C
fmadden@gccnj.edu
MADDEN, Joe 936-639-1301 465 J
jmadden@angelina.edu
MADDEN, John 575-624-7111 309 I
john.madden@roswell.enmu.edu
MADDEN, Margaret, E 315-267-2108 344 C
maddenme@potsdam.edu
MADDEN, Mike 417-447-8170 279 K
maddenm@otc.edu
MADDEN, Paul 740-351-3421 388 N
pmadden@shawnee.edu
MADDEN, Richard 931-363-9844 456 C
rmadden@martinmethodist.edu
MADDEN, Susan 240-567-5274 216 F
susan.madden@montgomerycollege.edu
MADDEN, Warren, R 515-294-6162 175 H
wmadden@iastate.edu
MADDIGAN, Susan 508-362-2131 231 D
smaddigan@capecod.edu
MADDIN, Brent 212-228-1888 337 H
MADDOCKS, Ami 918-463-2931 395 D
ami.maddocks@connorsstate.edu
MADDOCKS, Peter 617-989-4328 237 G
maddocksp@wit.edu
MADDOX, David 619-201-8700 62 B
MADDOX, Gregory, H 713-313-7889 485 F
maddox_gh@tsu.edu
MADDOX, Julie, A 219-464-5333 174 E
julie.maddox@valpo.edu
MADDOX, Kelley, L 770-534-6270 122 A
kmaddox@brenau.edu
MADDOX, Kenneth 256-372-4871 1 A
kenneth.maddox@aamu.edu
MADDOX, Lori, B 615-353-3305 461 B
lori.maddox@nscc.edu
MADDOX, Nedra 704-669-4142 359 D
maddox@clevelandcc.edu
MADDOX, Richard 402-643-7408 289 B
Richard.Maddox@cune.edu
MADDOX, Ronald, W 910-893-1686 352 K
maddox@campbell.edu
MADDOX, Tangella 312-341-3584 157 D
tmaddox@roosevelt.edu
MADDOX, Winston 609-586-4800 302 G
maddoxw@mccc.edu
MADDUX, Gary 256-824-2679 8 F
gary.maddux@us.army.mil
MADDUX, Susan, A 864-833-8205 446 D
smaddux@presby.edu
MADDY, Angela, M 620-792-9322 184 F
maddya@bartonccc.edu
MADELONE, Laura 607-436-2526 343 E
madelolm@oneonta.edu
MADELUNG, Donald, G 608-663-2000 533 T
dmadelung@mediainstitute.edu
MADER, Louis 212-772-4521 318 C
lmader@hunter.cuny.edu
MADER, Mary 978-542-6390 230 E
mary.mader@salemstate.edu
MADER, Sharon, B 504-280-6556 205 G
smader@uno.edu
MADHAVARAU, Leela 909-748-8285 73 H
leela_madhavarau@redlands.edu
MADIGAN, David 212-854-8296 321 D
MADIGAN, Kay 330-652-9919 379 I
kaymadigan@eticollege.edu
MADIN, Laurence, P 508-289-2515 238 E
lmadin@whoi.edu
MADISON, Anna 617-287-7232 228 G
anna.madison@umb.edu
MADISON, Jennifer 940-898-3103 488 B
jmadison@twu.edu
MADISON, Katheryn 541-684-4644 407 B
kmadison@pioneerpacific.edu
MADISON, Olivia, M 515-294-1443 175 H
omadison@iastate.edu
MADISON, S. (Sean) 954-201-8800 99 D
smadison@broward.edu
MADISON, Sandra 305-899-4933 98 O
smadison@barry.edu
MADLUCK, Calvin 510-466-5398 58 I
MADONNA, JR., Richard, A 212-280-7100 349 A
rmadonna@uts.columbia.edu
MADORE, Keith, L 207-768-9568 212 G
keith.madore@umpi.edu
MADRAY, Van 252-493-7750 362 G
vmadray@email.pittcc.edu
MADRID, Maria, E 787-728-1515 555 D
mmadrid@sagrado.edu
MADSEN, Alice 206-878-3710 520 E
amadsen@highline.edu
MADSEN, Gary, L 512-223-7087 466 I
gmadsen@austincc.edu
MADSEN, Jan, D 402-280-3386 289 D
janmadsen@creighton.edu
MADSEN, Lois 785-827-5541 188 C
lois.madsen@kwu.edu
MADSEN, Patrick, O 336-334-5454 369 A
pomadsen@uncg.edu
MADSEN, Stephanie, D 410-382-4674 216 E
smadsen@mcdaniel.edu
MADSEN, Thor 816-414-3700 277 L
academicdean@mbts.edu
MADSON, Greg 406-791-5359 288 E
gmadson01@ugf.edu
MADSON, Gregory 406-791-5359 288 E
gmadson01@ugf.edu
MADSON, Jerome 860-628-4751 90 D
jmadson@lincolncollegene.edu
MADULI, Ed 408-741-2082 75 J
ed_maduli@wvm.edu
MADURO, Milca 787-834-9595 553 B
mmaduro@uaa.edu
MAEDA, John 401-454-6764 440 A
president@risd.edu
MAEDA, Sandy 808-455-0462 137 A
smaeda@hawaii.edu
MAEL, Laura 608-663-2000 533 T
lmael@mediainstitute.edu
MAELSON, Diane, C 215-204-3745 433 K
diane.maleson@temple.edu
MAENE, Sara 304-876-5112 529 I
smaene@shepherd.edu
MAERTINS, Bryan 903-923-3442 486 A
bryan.maertins@tstc.edu
MAES, Sue, C 785-532-5644 188 A
scmaes@ksu.edu
MAESTAS, Belen 719-587-7321 78 B
bmaestas@adams.edu
MAESTAS, Joseph 970-945-8691 79 G
MAESTAS, Ricardo 432-837-8032 487 B
rmaestas@sulross.edu
MAESTAS, Richard 303-360-4751 81 C
richard.maestas@ccaurora.edu
MAESTAS, Stacy 307-778-1240 543 D
smaestas@lccc.wy.edu
MAFAHER, Ziaeddin 202-319-5373 94 G
mafaher@cua.edu
MAFFEI, Melody 209-667-3623 35 B
mmaffei@csustan.edu
MAFFUCCI, Michael 704-290-5864 363 G
mmaffucci@spcc.edu

MAFICO, Temba, L .... 404-527-7704. 127 I
tmafico@itc.edu
MAFREDI, Juan, J .... 412-624-0790. 435 C
manfredi@pitt.edu
MAGALONG, Mariles ..... 510-235-7800... 41 K
mmagalong@contracosta.edu
MAGDALENO, Jose .... 718-960-8241. 318 A
joseph.magdaleno@lehman.cuny.edu
MAGDZIARZ, Wayne ...... 312-915-6403. 151 H
wmagdzi@luc.edu
MAGEE, JR., David, E .... 423-439-4441. 459 C
magee@etsu.edu
MAGEE, Edward .... 304-558-0281. 529 C
emagee@hepc.wvnet.edu
MAGEE, Francy .... 516-686-7996. 333 H
fmagee@nyit.edu
MAGEE, Gwen .... 601-477-4028. 267 F
gwen.magee@jcjc.edu
MAGEE, Jennifer .... 214-637-3530. 494 E
jmagee@wadecollege.edu
MAGEE, Jim .... 610-341-1720. 415 G
jmagee@eastern.edu
MAGEE, Maggie .... 207-947-4591. 209 G
mmagee@bealcollege.edu
MAGEE, Patricia .... 504-568-4800. 205 C
pmagee@lsuhsu.edu
MAGEE, Rosemary .... 404-727-6020. 124 E
rosemary.magee@emory.edu
MAGEE, Rosie .... 717-262-2006. 437 H
rmagee@wilson.edu
MAGEE, Tiffany .... 225-768-1701. 206 D
tiffany.magee@ololcollege.edu
MAGEE, Vicki .... 815-802-8258. 149 C
vmagee@kcc.edu
MAGEEAN, Deirdre .... 216-687-3588. 377 F
d.mageean@csuohio.edu
MAGER, Marlowe .... 828-565-4077. 361 B
mmager@haywood.edu
MAGERS, Dwight, E .... 423-236-2992. 458 J
magers@southern.edu
MAGET, Douglas .... 212-854-6991. 314 G
dmaget@barnard.edu
MAGGARD, Bradley .... 517-265-5161. 238 G
MAGGELAKIS, Sophia .... 585-475-2483. 337 L
sxmsma@rit.edu
MAGGERT, Jerry .... 800-962-7682. 285 A
MAGGIO, Chris .... 318-357-4414. 208 B
maggioc@nsula.edu
MAGGIO, Evelyn .... 718-270-5103. 319 A
emaggio@mec.cuny.edu
MAGGIO, Marielena .... 216-368-2519. 375 J
mxm346@case.edu
MAGGIOTTO,
Michael, A .... 765-285-1042. 164 B
mmaggiotto@bsu.edu
MAGGITTI, Patrick, G ..... 610-519-4331. 436 F
patrick.maggitti@villanova.edu
MAGGITTI, Sara .... 610-902-8561. 411 E
sara.t.maggitti@cabrini.edu
MAGGS, Gregory, E .... 202-994-6288... 95 D
gmaggs@gwu.edu
MAGGS, Mark .... 814-234-7755. 433 G
mmaggs@southhills.edu
MAGHROORI, Ray .... 951-222-8043... 60 J
ray.maghroori@rcc.edu
MAGHSOUD, Amanda, F 803-323-4891. 449 G
maghsouda@winthrop.edu
MAGID, Bruce, R .... 781-736-2256. 224 F
bmagid@brandeis.edu
MAGIDA, David .... 802-485-2145. 500 A
davem@norwich.edu
MAGIE, CM, Sandra, C .. 713-686-4345. 490 L
smagie@stthom.edu
MAGIERA, Steve, L .... 239-590-1119. 115 A
smagiera@fgcu.edu
MAGILL, Jim .... 828-298-3325. 370 E
jmagill@warren-wilson.edu
MAGILL, M. Elizabeth ..... 650-723-2300... 68 E
MAGINN, Julie .... 908-526-1200. 305 B
jmaginn@raritanval.edu
MAGLION, Joyce .... 973-408-3631. 301 C
jmaglion@drew.edu
MAGLIULO, Sabrina .... 201-360-4181. 302 D
smagliulo@hccc.edu
MAGNAN, Carolyn .... 860-832-3715... 87 K
magnanc@ccsu.edu
MAGNER, Brent .... 402-363-5636. 293 I
brent.magner@york.edu
MAGNER, Kevin .... 714-867-5009... 66 J
MAGNUS, Keith, B .... 317-940-9385. 164 J
kmagnus@butler.edu
MAGNUSON, Kelly, J ...... 320-222-6094. 260 H
kelly.magnuson@ridgewater.edu
MAGNUSON, Kendyl ...... 760-744-1150... 58 D
kmagnuson@palomar.edu
MAGNUSON, Mark .... 218-733-7628. 259 A
m.magnuson@lsc.edu
MAGNUSON, Nancy .... 410-337-6364. 215 A
nmagnuso@goucher.edu
MAGNUSON, Nancy .... 509-335-6412. 525 A
magnuson@vetmed.wsu.edu
MAGNUSON, Nancy, M . 314-516-5671. 283 E
magnuson@umsl.edu
MAGNUSSON, Selena .... 706-295-6866. 125 F
smagnussen@gntc.edu
MAGNUSSON DURHAM,
Nancy .... 615-966-5275. 456 B
nancy.durham@lipscomb.edu
MAGOON, Don .... 919-735-5151. 364 H
djmagoon@waynecc.edu
MAGOON, Maggie .... 989-386-6622. 247 B
mmagoon@midmich.edu
MAGRETTA, Dawn .... 586-445-7302. 246 A
magrettad@macomb.edu
MAGUET, Kathryn, L ...... 570-577-3700. 411 A
kathryn.maguet@bucknell.edu
MAGUIRE, Chris .... 715-422-5322. 540 D
chris.maguire@mstc.edu
MAGUIRE, Eric .... 607-274-1555. 327 E
emaguire@ithaca.edu
MAGUIRE, James, C ...... 859-985-3020. 192 F
maguirej@berea.edu
MAGUIRE, Karen .... 212-355-1501. 316 H
kmaguire@christies.edu
MAGUIRE, Kevin, C .... 617-627-3502. 237 C
kevin.maguire@tufts.edu
MAGUIRE, Trish .... 575-562-2165. 309 H
trish.maguire@enmu.edu
MAGUIRE-BECK,
Michele .... 641-784-5029. 178 F
mbeck@graceland.edu
MAGUS, Sue .... 512-892-2835. 469 A
MAHACHEK, Jim .... 610-282-1100. 414 F
jim.mahachek@desales.edu
MAHAFFEY, Danielle, L .. 336-841-4683. 355 C
dmahaffe@highpoint.edu
MAHAFFEY, Danny .... 225-578-3962. 204 N
dmahaf1@lsu.edu
MAHAFFEY, Dean .... 205-329-7950..... 3 B
dean.mahaffey@ecacolleges.com
MAHALINGAM, Shankar 256-824-6474..... 8 F
Shankar.Mahalingam@uah.edu
MAHAN, Amy, J .... 501-882-8880... 19 M
ajmahan@asub.edu
MAHAN, Christine, P ..... 610-341-1706. 415 G
cmahan@eastern.edu
MAHAN, David .... 718-862-7597. 329 M
david.mahan@manhattan.edu
MAHAN, Elizabeth .... 860-486-3152... 92 A
elizabeth.mahan@uconn.edu
MAHAN, Forest .... 843-921-6919. 446 A
fmahan@netc.edu
MAHAN, Karl .... 806-720-7122. 476 B
karl.mahan@lcu.edu
MAHAN, Kim, B .... 806-371-5050. 465 E
kbmahan@actx.edu
MAHAN, Lisa, E .... 317-738-8148. 165 I
lmahan@franklincollege.edu
MAHAN, Marilyn .... 785-320-4501. 188 E
marilynmahan@matc.net
MAHAN, Mickie .... 417-455-5536. 273 E
MickieMahan@crowder.edu
MAHAN, Nicholas .... 701-483-2340. 371 D
Nicholas.Mahan@dickinsonstate.edu
MAHAR, Valerie .... 603-542-7744. 296 D
vmahar@ccsnh.edu
MAHARAJ, Peter .... 714-241-6297... 39 I
pmaharaj@coastline.edu
MAHARAJ,
Sandhya (Sandy), G ..... 304-766-3236. 530 C
smaharaj@wvstateu.edu
MAHARAS, Marian .... 303-404-5285... 81 N
marian.maharas@frontrange.edu
MAHDI, Johnni, F .... 315-792-3209. 349 F
jmahdi@utica.edu
MAHDI, Syed .... 803-705-4576. 441 C
mahdis@benedict.edu
MAHER, Brian .... 973-278-5400. 299 D
bdm@berkeleycollege.edu
MAHER, Brian .... 973-278-5400. 314 K
bdm@berkeleycollege.edu
MAHER, Brian .... 631-420-2507. 346 B
brian.maher@farmingdale.edu
MAHER, Cathy .... 313-831-5200. 242 E
cmaher@etseminary.edu
MAHER, Hannah .... 309-457-2286. 153 D
hmaher@monmouthcollege.edu
MAHER, James .... 989-964-2222. 249 G
jimmaher@svsu.edu
MAHER, CM, James .... 716-286-8350. 334 F
jjm@niagara.edu
MAHER, Jeremiah, J ...... 530-752-7596... 70 J
jeremiah.maher@ucdavis.edu
MAHER, John .... 304-696-4748. 529 H
maherj@marshall.edu
MAHER, Judith .... 724-805-2900. 432 G
judith.maher@email.stvincent.edu
MAHER, Mary .... 410-837-5392. 221 A
mmaher@ubalt.edu
MAHER, Nadine, M .... 215-670-9236. 425 J
nmmaher@peirce.edu
MAHER, Susan .... 218-726-8981. 264 D
smaher@umn.edu
MAHER, Tracy .... 701-854-8039. 372 J
tracym@sbci.edu
MAHER, Walter .... 210-829-3939. 490 A
maher@uiwtx.edu
MAHER, William, J .... 716-888-2970. 316 C
maherw@canisius.edu
MAHER-GARCIA, Martha 585-292-2114. 332 A
mmaher-garcia@monroecc.edu
MAHI, Linda .... 650-949-6193... 44 M
mahilinda@fhda.edu
MAHL, Aaron .... 847-317-7074. 160 M
amahl@tiu.edu
MAHLBERG, James, A ... 712-325-3218. 179 L
jmahlberg@iwcc.edu
MAHLBERG, Lynn, M ..... 775-753-2282. 294 F
lynn.mahlberg@gbcnv.edu
MAHLER, Craig .... 615-844-5000. 464 E
cmahler@welch.edu
MAHLER, Greg .... 765-983-1318. 165 G
gregm@earlham.edu
MAHLER, Stephen, J ...... 337-482-6418. 208 D
mahler@louisiana.edu
MAHLER, Steve .... 337-482-6780. 208 D
mahler@louisiana.edu
MAHLMEISTER,
Kenneth, J .... 718-990-5883. 339 A
mahlmeik@stjohns.edu
MAHN, Jerry .... 937-298-3399. 382 K
jerry.mahn@kc.edu
MAHON, Cathryn, A .... 843-953-5432. 443 A
mahonc@cofc.edu
MAHON, Edward, G .... 330-672-4704. 382 B
emahon@kent.edu
MAHON, James, L .... 409-772-6015. 493 C
jlmahon@utmb.edu
MAHON, Mariann .... 732-987-2600. 302 B
mahonm@georgian.edu
MAHON, Marveen .... 210-829-6017. 490 A
marveenm@uiwtx.edu
MAHON, Patricia, G .... 605-394-2416. 452 A
patricia.mahon@sdsmt.edu
MAHON, Steven .... 318-342-5350. 208 E
smahon@ulm.edu
MAHON, Tom .... 605-394-5045. 450 G
tmahon@national.edu
MAHONE-LEIWS, Gerald 254-526-1166. 468 G
gerald.mahone-lewis@ctcd.edu
MAHONEY, Deirdre, M ... 231-995-1184. 248 B
dmahoney@nmc.edu
MAHONEY, Jack .... 518-276-6790. 337 I
mahonj@rpi.edu
MAHONEY, Janet .... 732-571-5271. 303 C
jmahoney@monmouth.edu
MAHONEY, Janet, L .... 218-477-2070. 259 H
jan.mahoney@mnstate.edu
MAHONEY, John .... 530-898-3276... 33 A
jmahoney@csuchico.edu
MAHONEY, John .... 940-552-6291. 493 F
jmahoney@vernoncollege.edu
MAHONEY, JR.,
John, L .... 617-552-3100. 224 A
john.mahoney.2@bc.edu
MAHONEY, Maureen, A . 413-585-4900. 236 H
mmahoney@smith.edu
MAHONEY, Michael .... 714-816-0366... 70 A
michael.mahoney@trident.edu
MAHONEY, Michelle, L .. 815-740-3372. 162 F
mmahoney@stfrancis.edu
MAHONEY, Oluyemi .... 603-656-6028. 297 G
omahoney@anselm.edu
MAHONEY, Paul, G .... 434-924-7343. 511 B
pgm9h@Virginia.EDU
MAHONEY, Peter, E .... 724-805-2241. 432 G
peter.mahoney@email.stvincent.edu
MAHONEY, Thomas .... 609-771-2734. 300 E
tmahoney@tcnj.edu
MAHONEY, Wayne .... 213-738-6719... 68 C
finaid@swlaw.edu
MAHONY, Daniel, F .... 330-672-2202. 382 B
dmahony@kent.edu
MAHONY, James .... 517-264-3525. 238 G
jmahony@adrian.edu
MAHTANI, Dinesh .... 845-675-4402. 335 C
dinesh.mahtani@nyack.edu
MAI, Brent .... 503-493-6560. 402 J
bmai@cu-portland.edu
MAIELI, Kathryn, J .... 802-626-6492. 501 E
kathryn.maieli@lyndonstate.edu
MAIER, Mark .... 517-437-7341. 243 I
mark.maier@hillsdale.edu
MAIER, Michael, M .... 815-280-2289. 149 A
mmaier@jjc.edu
MAIER, Richard, P .... 478-757-2083. 134 G
rmaier@wesleyancollege.edu
MAIERHOFER, Jean .... 763-488-2633. 258 F
jean.maierhofer@hennepintech.edu
MAIETTA, Heather .... 978-837-5000. 234 A
maiettah@merrimack.edu
MAIGAARD, Brenda .... 785-864-4700. 190 L
bmaigaard@ku.edu
MAILEN, Debbie .... 423-697-4400. 460 C
MAILHOT, John .... 413-748-3145. 236 I
jmailhot@springfieldcollege.edu
MAILLET, Becky .... 504-278-6477. 203 F
bmaillet@nunez.edu
MAILLET, Pierrette .... 678-915-7702. 132 C
pmaillet@spsu.edu
MAILLOUX, Mark, R .... 608-342-1785. 537 D
maillouxm@uwplatt.edu
MAIMON, Elaine, P .... 708-534-4130. 145 F
emaimon@govst.edu
MAIMONE, Charles .... 910-962-3067. 369 C
maimonec@uncw.edu
MAIN, Gregory .... 405-878-5422. 399 G
president@stgregorys.edu
MAIN, Jim, E .... 323-563-4874... 38 B
jamesmain@cdrewu.edu
MAIN, Marie Andre .... 716-827-2489. 348 G
mainm@trocaire.edu
MAIN, Mary .... 207-786-6140. 209 F
mmain@bates.edu
MAIN, Nathan .... 269-927-8169. 245 D
nmain@lakemichigancollege.edu
MAIN, Sajid .... 708-534-4515. 145 F
smain@govst.edu
MAINCA, Daniel .... 213-383-8999... 26 H
MAINE, Kate .... 706-864-1950. 133 D
kate.maine@ung.edu
MAINENTI, David .... 516-299-4212. 329 C
David.Mainenti@liu.edu
MAINENTI, Raymond ...... 304-367-4081. 528 E
raymond.mainenti@pierpont.edu
MAINIERO, Michael, A ... 718-260-3060. 336 E
mmainier@poly.edu
MAINRIDGE, Valerie .... 503-517-1832. 408 I
vmainridge@westernseminary.edu
MAIO, James .... 315-792-5401. 331 I
jmaio@mvcc.edu
MAIORISI, Stephen, M ... 401-863-1297. 438 J
stephen_maiorisi@brown.edu
MAIR, Bernard, A .... 352-846-1761. 116 A
bamair@ufl.edu
MAIR, Dave .... 804-819-4929. 511 G
dmair@vccs.edu
MAISEL, Jacqueline, M .. 410-543-6150. 220 D
jmmaisel@salisbury.edu
MAISNER, Roger, N .... 570-662-4636. 429 C
rmaisner@mansfield.edu
MAISON, Amy .... 229-225-3977. 132 D
amaison@southwestgatech.edu
MAISONNEUVE,
John, N .... 315-386-7035. 345 F
maisonnj@canton.edu
MAISTO, Jeremy, A .... 717-867-6215. 421 H
maisto@lvc.edu
MAITLAND, Jason, R ..... 585-785-1437. 324 D
maitlajr@flcc.edu
MAITLAND, Tina, A .... 313-993-1005. 250 K
maitlata@udmercy.edu
MAIURI, Geary .... 586-445-7579. 246 A
maiurig@macomb.edu
MAIZE, Kay .... 402-481-8602. 288 H
kay.maize@bryanhealthcollege.edu
MAJEBE, Mary Cissy ...... 828-225-3993. 353 I
president@daoisttraditions.edu
MAJEROWITZ,
Mordechai .... 718-851-8721. 350 K
MAJEWSKI, Deborah ...... 508-999-9293. 229 A
dmajewski@umassd.edu
MAJID, Anouar .... 206-221-4447. 213 A
amajid@une.edu
MAJKA, David, R .... 412-397-5443. 431 I
majka@rmu.edu
MAJOR, Adrienne .... 802-387-7143. 499 F
amajor@landmark.edu
MAJOR, Brenda, L .... 217-581-2223. 144 E
bmajor@eiu.edu
MAJOR, Charles, H .... 715-836-5387. 536 E
majorch@uwec.edu
MAJOR, James .... 309-438-8322. 147 J
jmajor@ilstu.edu
MAJOR, Michael .... 989-964-7130. 249 G
mmajor@svsu.edu
MAJOR, Patricia .... 210-485-0391. 464 I
pmajor@alamo.edu
MAJOR, Phillip .... 561-803-2034. 110 B
phillip_major@pba.edu
MAJOR, Samantha .... 828-835-4203. 364 E
smajor@tricountycc.edu
MAJOR, Wayne .... 785-272-0889. 185 C
MAJORS, Christy .... 704-337-2512. 365 G
majorsc@queens.edu
MAJORS, Courtney .... 417-667-8181. 273 A
cmajors@cottey.edu
MAJORS, Joe .... 704-378-1226. 355 K
jmajors@jcsu.edu
MAJOVSKI, Laura, F .... 253-535-7191. 521 I
majovslf@plu.edu

MAJZNER, Kathy ... 903-233-4381. 475 J
kathymajzner@letu.edu
MAKARECHI, Pejman ... 215-503-7841. 434 C
pejman.makarechi@jefferson.edu
MAKER, Laurie ... 508-588-9100. 232 A
MAKEVICH, John ... 661-362-3102... 40 E
john.makevich@canyons.edu
MAKI, David, W ... 906-227-1262. 248 A
dmaki@nmu.edu
MAKI, Jackie ... 817-515-5379. 482 B
jackie.maki@tccd.edu
MAKI, William ... 218-755-2012. 260 E
wmaki@bemidjistate.edu
MAKI, William, D ... 218-755-2012. 258 A
wmaki@bemidjistate.edu
MAKIN, Linda ... 801-863-8457. 497 C
linda.makin@uvu.edu
MAKOFSKE, Rose ... 215-619-7383. 424 B
rmakofske@mc3.edu
MAKOWSKI, Sharon ... 203-576-5478... 91 D
smakowski@stvincentscollege.edu
MAKREZ, Heather ... 978-934-4809. 229 B
heather_makrez@uml.edu
MAKSYMICZ, Kathy, E ... 330-287-1283. 386 F
maksymicz.1@osu.edu
MAKSYMIK, Michelle ... 814-262-3820. 427 C
mmaksymik@pennhighlands.edu
MALAFA, Jeanette ... 217-652-6467. 162 K
j-malafa@wiu.edu
MALARA, Kathleen ... 718-817-4160. 324 G
kmalara@fordham.edu
MALARET, Frank ... 916-558-2402... 53 D
malarej@scc.losrios.edu
MALARTE-FELDMAN,
Claire, L ... 603-862-2398. 298 C
clmf@cisunix.unh.edu
MALASKA, Amy ... 330-490-7321. 392 H
amalaska@walsh.edu
MALASKA, Amy, K ... 330-490-7321. 392 H
amalaska@walsh.edu
MALASPINA, Margaret ... 860-906-5096... 88 D
mmalaspina@ccc.commnet.edu
MALAT, Heide ... 651-690-6805. 263 O
hlmalat@stkate.edu
MALATESTA, Addy ... 570-408-4020. 437 F
adelene.malatesta@wilkes.edu
MALATESTA, Matthew, J 518-388-6112. 348 J
malatesm@union.edu
MALATRAS, Jim ... 518-320-1311. 341 C
jim.malatras@suny.edu
MALAVE, Sarah ... 787-738-2161. 554 C
sarah.malave@upr.edu
MALAVE-LASSO, Mara ... 787-480-2402. 548 G
mamalave@sanjuancapital.com
MALAVEZ, Jessica ... 718-260-5006. 319 B
jmalavez@citytech.cuny.edu
MALAVOLTI, TOR,
Nathan ... 740-283-6406. 379 N
nmalavolti@franciscan.edu
MALCHOW, Larry, P ... 920-748-8347. 535 J
malchowl@ripon.edu
MALCOLM, III,
Everett, J ... 904-620-2600. 116 B
emalcolm@unf.edu
MALCOLM, John, M ... 413-597-4057. 238 D
john.m.malcolm@williams.edu
MALCOLM, Joshua ... 910-521-6201. 369 B
joshua.malcolm@uncp.edu
MALCOLM, Kathy ... 309-796-5038. 140 E
malcolmk@bhc.edu
MALCOLM, Kim ... 309-694-8815. 146 E
kmalcolm@icc.edu
MALCOLM, Ward ... 304-434-8000. 528 A
wmalcolm@eastern.wvnet.edu
MALCOLM, Yvonnie ... 508-849-3427. 222 B
ymalcolm@annamaria.edu
MALCONIAN, Sara ... 617-324-4538. 233 B
MALDONADO, Amelia ... 787-850-9327. 554 D
junta-senado.uprh@upr.edu
MALDONADO, Cesar ... 956-364-4020. 485 G
cesar.maldonado@harlingen.tstc.edu
MALDONADO, Cesar ... 956-364-4020. 485 H
cesar.maldonado@tstc.edu
MALDONADO, Gilda ... 619-388-2817... 62 E
gmaldona@sdccd.edu
MALDONADO, Ileana ... 787-725-8120. 548 O
imaldonado@eap.edu
MALDONADO, Jo Ann ... 973-642-8578. 307 D
joann.maldonado@shu.edu
MALDONADO, Juan, L ... 956-721-5101. 475 F
president@laredo.edu
MALDONADO, Kenneth .. 787-751-0178. 552 G
kenmaldona@suagm.edu
MALDONADO, Lourdes .. 787-766-1717. 552 J
lmaldonado@suagm.edu
MALDONADO, Monique 504-286-5118. 206 K
mmaldonado@suno.edu
MALDONADO, Robert ... 585-389-2840. 332 D
rmaldon0@naz.edu
MALDONADO,
Rosemarie ... 212-237-8911. 318 D
rmaldonado@jjay.cuny.edu
MALDONADO, Victor ... 787-878-5475. 549 L
vmaldonado@arecibo.inter.edu
MALDONADO, Wanda ... 787-758-2525. 554 F
wanda.maldonado1@upr.edu
MALDONADO-RUIZ,
Alberto ... 787-257-7373. 552 H
ue_amaldona@suagm.edu
MALECHA, Marvin, J ... 919-515-8302. 368 B
marvin_malecha@ncsu.edu
MALECKE, Kenneth ... 313-927-1445. 246 D
kmalecke@marygrove.edu
MALEK, Casey ... 620-227-9349. 186 B
dcccgolf@dc3.edu
MALEK, Debby ... 620-227-9260. 186 B
dmalek@dc3.edu
MALEKZADEH, Ali, R ... 785-532-7227. 188 A
MALEPEAI, Alexis ... 606-487-3178. 195 C
alexis.malepeai@kctcs.edu
MALEWSKI, Erik ... 678-794-7575. 127 N
emalewsk@kennesaw.edu
MALEY, Beth ... 859-344-3614. 199 H
beth.maley@thomasmore.edu
MALEY, Brian ... 513-745-3315. 393 H
maley@xavier.edu
MALEY, Daniel ... 269-488-4298. 244 L
dmaley@kvcc.edu
MALEY, David, C ... 607-274-3480. 327 E
maley@ithaca.edu
MALEY, Robert ... 215-968-8116. 411 B
maleyr@bucks.edu
MALEY, Sandra, J ... 609-497-7720. 304 D
human.resources@ptsem.edu
MALFITANO, Gregory, J . 561-237-7277. 108 X
gmalfitano@lynn.edu
MALHAS, Faris, A ... 419-372-2438. 374 K
fmalhas@bgsu.edu
MALHOTRA, Devinder ... 320-308-4909. 261 B
dmmalhotra@stcloudstate.edu
MALHOTRA, Rajiv ... 617-732-2791. 233 E
rajiv.malhotra@mcphs.edu
MALHUS, Faris ... 860-832-1801... 87 K
fm4241@ccsu.edu
MALIEKAL, Jose ... 585-395-2394. 342 F
jmalieka@brockport.edu
MALIG, Jannet ... 562-860-2451... 37 I
jmalig@cerritos.edu
MALIK, Christopher, P ... 716-839-8332. 322 E
cmalik@daemen.edu
MALIK, David, J ... 219-980-6966. 168 B
dmalik@iun.edu
MALIK, Melinda ... 603-206-8151. 296 A
mmalik@ccsnh.edu
MALIK, Rick ... 312-788-1188. 162 H
rmalik@vandercook.edu
MALIK, Zafar, A ... 312-939-0111. 144 D
zafar@eastwest.edu
MALIN, Burke ... 650-685-6616... 46 F
MALIN, John ... 217-854-3231. 140 G
jmali@blackburn.edu
MALINOWSKI, Lisa ... 229-317-6729. 124 A
lisa.malinowski@darton.edu
MALINOWSKI, Sarah ... 201-761-6239. 306 L
smalinowski@saintpeters.edu
MALISCH, Susan, M ... 773-508-7750. 151 H
smalisc@luc.edu
MALIWESKY, Martin ... 614-287-3669. 378 B
mmaliwes@cscc.edu
MALKEMES, Janet ... 704-330-4806. 359 C
janet.malkemes@cpcc.edu
MALKERSON, Elizabeth .. 612-624-2854. 264 G
beckym@umn.edu
MALKIEWICZ, OFM,
Stephen ... 414-425-8300. 535 K
smalkiewicz@shst.edu
MALKOWSKI, Brenda ... 417-255-7966. 278 F
brendamalkowski@missouristate.edu
MALKOWSKI, Keith ... 989-686-9449. 242 C
keithmalkowski@delta.edu
MALLABO, Jose ... 912-525-5000. 131 B
jmallabo@scad.edu
MALLACH, Sachi ... 610-526-6005. 417 H
smallach@harcum.edu
MALLARD, Jessica ... 806-651-2777. 484 D
jmallard@mail.wtamu.edu
MALLARD, Kina, S ... 865-471-3219. 453 F
kmallard@cn.edu
MALLER, Jennifer ... 847-543-2375. 143 A
jmaller@clcillinois.edu
MALLERY, Mike ... 503-352-2258. 407 A
mallerym@pacificu.edu
MALLET, Colleen ... 845-437-5276. 349 G
MALLETT, Chris ... 801-274-3280. 498 E
chris.mallett@wgu.edu
MALLETT, Justin ... 217-245-3271. 146 F
justin.mallett@ic.edu
MALLETT, Kristi ... 918-343-7796. 399 C
kmallett@rsu.edu
MALLETTE, Richard ... 847-735-5277. 150 B
mallette@lakeforest.edu
MALLIA, Maria ... 201-559-6072. 302 A
malliam@felician.edu
MALLO, Ted, A ... 330-972-6021. 390 E
tamallo@uakron.edu
MALLOL, Ramon ... 787-765-3560. 548 M
arivera@edpuniversity.edu
MALLORY, Brian ... 864-503-5796. 448 H
mallory-brian@uscupstate.edu
MALLORY, Carolyn, R ... 361-570-4130. 489 E
malloryc@uhv.edu
MALLORY, Dale, E ... 585-292-3040. 332 A
dmallory@monroecc.edu
MALLORY, Kristen ... 909-621-8267... 39 D
kristen.mallory@cmc.edu
MALLORY, Kristin ... 304-734-6605. 527 O
kmallory@bridgemont.edu
MALLORY, Sarah Beth ... 706-880-8338. 128 A
smallory@lagrange.edu
MALLOY, Jeffrey ... 812-535-5219. 172 F
jmalloy@smwc.edu
MALLOY, Kathleen, A ... 724-925-4028. 437 D
malloyka@wccc.edu
MALLOY, Leanne ... 317-955-6150. 170 V
lmalloy@marian.edu
MALLOY, Michael, J ... 508-373-5611. 233 E
michael.malloy@mcphs.edu
MALLOY, SJ, Richard, G 570-941-6153. 436 A
richard.malloy@scranton.edu
MALLOY, Thomas, K ... 610-499-4174. 437 E
tkmalloy@widener.edu
MALM, Betsy ... 312-935-4404. 156 K
bmalm@robertmorris.edu
MALM, James ... 719-549-2940... 80 K
james.malm@colostate-pueblo.edu
MALMGREN, Betty, M ... 707-256-7112... 55 F
bmalmgren@napavalley.edu
MALMGREN, Irene ... 909-274-5414... 55 A
imalmgren@mtsac.edu
MALMROSE, John ... 843-792-2721. 445 B
malmrose@musc.edu
MALONE, Allison ... 870-574-4544... 23 G
amalone@sautech.edu
MALONE, Anne, B ... 412-924-1379. 431 A
amalone@pts.edu
MALONE, Brenda, R ... 919-962-1554. 368 D
brenda_malone@unc.edu
MALONE, Brian ... 505-277-8900. 312 F
bmalone@unm.edu
MALONE, Casey ... 610-225-5462. 415 G
cmalone2@eastern.edu
MALONE, Dan ... 214-333-6883. 470 D
dan@dbu.edu
MALONE, Dean, P ... 630-515-7145. 153 B
dmalon@midwestern.edu
MALONE, Deborah ... 610-282-1100. 414 F
debbie.malone@desales.edu
MALONE, Elbert, R ... 803-536-8213. 446 G
malone@scsu.edu
MALONE, Jennifer ... 318-342-5397. 208 E
jmalone@ulm.edu
MALONE, Jill ... 727-725-2688. 102 I
mmalone@cci.edu
MALONE, John ... 651-962-6925. 265 C
j9malone@stthomas.edu
MALONE, Judith, A ... 781-891-2016. 223 C
jmalone@bentley.edu
MALONE, Kathy ... 219-980-6701. 168 B
kalmalon@iun.edu
MALONE, Lora ... 817-272-2594. 491 B
lmalone@uta.edu
MALONE, Mary Frances . 203-254-4000... 89 I
malone@fairfield.edu
MALONE, Maureen ... 610-989-1453. 436 D
mmalone@vfmac.edu
MALONE, Michael ... 815-753-6065. 154 I
mmalone@niu.edu
MALONE, Michael, F ... 413-545-5270. 228 F
mmalone@umass.edu
MALONE, Michael, P ... 815-753-6065. 154 I
mmalone@niu.edu
MALONE, Michelle ... 718-818-6470. 339 H
MALONE, Pamela ... 528-587-2100. 346 A
pamela.malone@esc.edu
MALONE, Ted, E ... 765-494-4600. 171 M
temalone@purdue.edu
MALONE, Virginia, J ... 314-340-3339. 275 A
malonev@hssu.edu
MALONE-FENNER,
Shirley ... 617-879-2248. 238 C
smalone-fenner@wheelock.edu
MALONEY, Barry, M ... 508-929-8020. 230 G
bmaloney@worcester.edu
MALONEY, Catherine ... 617-984-1787. 235 I
cmaloney@quincycollege.edu
MALONEY, Cordelia ... 312-996-8586. 161 D
cordelia@uic.edu
MALONEY, Dena ... 661-763-7710... 69 D
dmaloney@taftcollege.edu
MALONEY, Gerald, J ... 404-894-0881. 125 D
jerry.maloney@bks.gatech.edu
MALONEY, Heather ... 513-745-5710. 391 A
heather.maloney@uc.edu
MALONEY, Kathryn, A ... 530-752-2396... 70 J
kamaloney@ucdavis.edu
MALONEY, Kevin ... 206-934-6875. 523 A
kevin.maloney@seattlecolleges.edu
MALONEY, Krisellen ... 210-458-7506. 492 C
krisellen.maloney@utsa.edu
MALONEY, Layne ... 517-371-5140. 250 G
maloneyl@cooley.edu
MALONEY, Marcy ... 805-756-1281... 32 F
mmaloney@calpoly.edu
MALONEY, Maureen, L .. 203-358-0700... 91 G
mmaureen@bridgeport.edu
MALONEY, Michael ... 212-280-1530. 349 A
mmaloney@uts.columbia.edu
MALONEY, Michelle ... 610-917-1406. 436 C
mmmaloney@vfcc.edu
MALONEY, Rebecca, S ... 504-866-7426. 206 B
rmaloney@nds.edu
MALONEY, Shari ... 320-762-4466. 257 O
sharim@alextech.edu
MALONEY, Vicky, G ... 803-778-6612. 441 F
maloneyvg@cctech.edu
MALONEY, Vincent, U ... 802-626-6413. 501 E
vincent.maloney@lyndonstate.edu
MALOOF, Lisa ... 770-868-4069. 128 B
lmaloof@laniertech.edu
MALOSH, Ann ... 541-917-4923. 404 B
malosha@linnbenton.edu
MALOTT, Michelle, L ... 218-477-2574. 259 H
michelle.malott@mnstate.edu
MALOTT, Pat ... 719-384-6841... 83 M
pat.malott@ojc.edu
MALOY, Frances, J ... 518-388-6739. 348 J
maloyf@union.edu
MALOY, Michael, T ... 610-436-3309. 430 A
mmaloy@wcupa.edu
MALOY, Stanley ... 619-594-5142... 35 D
smaloy@mail.sdsu.edu
MALOY, Vicky ... 319-368-6465. 181 C
vmaloy@mtmercy.edu
MALPASS, Scott, C ... 574-631-8877. 174 A
malpass.1@nd.edu
MALSHEIMER, Cheryl ... 305-809-3201. 104 I
cheryl.malsheimer@fkcc.edu
MALSON, Don, G ... 573-875-7421. 272 G
dgmalson@ccis.edu
MALTA, Anthony ... 318-342-3547. 208 E
malta@ulm.edu
MALTBIE, Randy ... 256-840-4112... 6 I
rmaltbie@snead.edu
MALTBY, Lee ... 773-878-3728. 158 B
lmaltby@staugustine.edu
MALTBY, Marc ... 270-686-4544. 196 C
marc.maltby@kctcs.edu
MALTESE, Vincent ... 734-384-4128. 247 C
vmaltese@monroeccc.edu
MALTINO, Frank ... 973-408-3955. 301 C
fmaltino@drew.edu
MALTZ, Mara ... 631-656-2131. 324 F
mara.maltz@ftc.edu
MALTZMAN, Forrest ... 202-994-6510... 95 D
forrest@gwu.edu
MALUTICH, Stephen, M . 602-275-7133... 17 L
Stephen.Malutich@rsiaz.edu
MALVERS, Dennis ... 978-656-3116. 232 B
malversd@middlesex.mass.edu
MALY, Lonn, D ... 651-641-8203. 255 B
maly@csp.edu
MALZACHER, Valerie, I .. 715-425-3224. 537 E
valerie.i.malzacher@uwrf.edu
MAMA, Robin ... 732-571-3543. 303 C
rmama@monmouth.edu
MAMARCHEV, Helen ... 239-590-1022. 115 A
hmamarchev@fgcu.edu
MAMI, Gwendolyn ... 303-352-7004... 83 D
gmami@msudenver.edu
MAMMEN, Ellen ... 413-528-7297. 222 E
emammen@simons-rock.edu
MAMON, Troy ... 404-527-4520. 122 E
tmamon@carver.edu
MAN, Gordon ... 808-734-9124. 136 E
goman@hawaii.edu
MANAHAN, Jamie ... 773-298-3329. 158 E
manahan@sxu.edu
MANARO, James, V ... 410-778-7204. 221 C
jmanaro2@washcoll.edu
MANASERI, Christopher . 808-455-0260. 137 A
cmanaser@hawaii.edu
MANASSAH, Michele ... 815-836-5455. 150 H
manassmi@lewisu.edu
MANAUTOU, Teresa ... 787-864-2222. 550 D
tmantou@inter.edu
MANAZIR, Theodore ... 802-728-1275. 501 F
tmanazir@vtc.edu
MANCE, Charles ... 724-938-1535. 428 A
mance@calu.edu

MANCE, Jerry .... 757-455-3349. 515 H
jmance@vwc.edu
MANCHESTER-MOLAK, Ann .... 401-865-2406. 439 E
ammolak@providence.edu
MANCHION, Jody .... 816-584-6272. 280 C
jody.manchion@park.edu
MANCIAZ, Jesse .... 915-747-7925. 492 A
jmanciaz@utep.edu
MANCINI, Donna .... 610-896-1230. 418 F
dmancini@haverford.edu
MANCINI, Nicholas .... 610-785-6263. 432 C
nmancini@scs.edu
MANCINI-BROWN, Darlene .... 860-512-3660... 88 G
dmancini_brown@manchestercc.edu
MANCONE, Nichole .... 617-989-4962. 237 G
manconen@wit.edu
MANCOSH, Bridget .... 412-392-3992. 431 B
bmancosh@pointpark.edu
MANCUSO, Angela .... 414-256-1223. 535 A
mancusoa@mtmary.edu
MANCUSO, Mary .... 607-436-3573. 343 E
mary.mancuso@oneonta.edu
MANCUSO, Tracy .... 928-532-6170... 16 E
tracy.mancuso@npc.edu
MANDAKOVIC, Tomislav .... 305-899-3532... 98 O
tmandakovic@barry.edu
MANDALA, Jim .... 973-408-3395. 301 C
jmandala@drew.edu
MANDARINO, James ..... 505-454-3199. 310 E
jfmandarino@nmhu.edu
MANDAYAM, Shreekanth .... 856-256-5150. 305 E
shreek@rowan.edu
MANDEL, Christine .... 315-655-7887. 316 E
cmandel@cazenovia.edu
MANDEL, Christine .... 315-655-7174. 316 E
cmandel@cazenovia.edu
MANDEL, Jeffrey .... 570-389-4311. 427 H
jmandel@bloomu.edu
MANDEL, Larry .... 562-951-4430... 32 E
lmandel@calstate.edu
MANDEL, Robert .... 323-856-7741... 27 O
rmandel@afi.com
MANDELKERN, Michael . 714-432-5786... 39 K
mmandelkern@occ.cccd.edu
MANDELL, Charlotte .... 978-934-3954. 229 B
Charlotte_Mandell@uml.edu
MANDEREN, Michael, C 440-775-8413. 385 H
michael.manderen@oberlin.edu
MANDERSCHEID, David, C .... 614-292-1677. 386 E
manderscheid.1@osu.edu
MANDERSCHEID, David, C .... 402-472-6262. 292 I
dmanderschied2@unl.edu
MANDEVILLE, Kenneth ... 304-327-4067. 529 D
kmandeville@bluefieldstate.edu
MANDEVILLE, Richard, G .... 509-777-4536. 525 F
rmandeville@whitworth.edu
MANDEVILLE, Steven ..... 314-529-6849. 276 G
shmandeville@maryville.edu
MANDL, Michael, J .... 404-727-6018. 124 E
michael.mandl@emory.edu
MANDOLESE, Jennifer .... 617-670-4468. 226 F
jmandolese@fisher.edu
MANDRACHIA, Florence 718-409-7342. 346 D
0858mgr@fheg.follett.com
MANDRELL, Jon .... 815-288-5511. 158 K
mandrej@svcc.edu
MANDY, Lisa .... 408-864-8403... 44 M
mandylisa@deanza.edu
MANDYAM, Raja .... 512-454-1188. 466 B
info@aoma.edu
MANER, Edward .... 863-667-5777. 113 P
elmaner@seu.edu
MANERI, Wendy, L .... 315-568-3262. 333 C
wmaneri@nycc.edu
MANES, Matthew .... 301-649-7077. 221 E
mmanes@yeshiva.edu
MANESS, Joseph, D .... 580-774-7152. 400 B
joseph.maness@swosu.edu
MANESS, Terry, S .... 254-710-1211. 467 G
terry_maness@baylor.edu
MANESS, Thomas .... 541-737-4279. 406 A
thomas.maness@oregonstate.edu
MANETAS, Magda .... 609-771-2466. 300 E
mmanetas@tcnj.edu
MANETAS, Pete .... 609-771-2393. 300 E
MANEV, Ivan, M .... 207-581-1968. 212 B
imanev@maine.edu
MANEY, Robert, L .... 814-863-6188. 426 A
rlm1@psu.edu
MANFRA, Matt .... 970-351-2551... 86 C
matthew.manfra@unco.edu
MANFREDO, Francis, A .. 315-859-4144. 325 E
fmanfred@hamilton.edu
MANGAN, DeWayne .... 512-313-3000. 469 L
dewayne.mangan@concordia.edu
MANGAN, Kathryn .... 510-567-6174... 69 C
kmangan@sum.edu
MANGAN, William .... 712-279-5402. 176 B
william.mangan@briarcliff.edu
MANGAN-FLOOD, Mary . 920-923-7166. 534 A
mmanganflood@marianuniversity.edu
MANGANARO, Marc ...... 504-865-3034. 205 H
manganar@loyno.edu
MANGELS, Andrew, P .... 413-545-2141. 228 F
amangels@admin.umass.edu
MANGELS, Kathy, M ..... 573-651-2570. 282 B
kmangels@semo.edu
MANGELS, Susan .... 636-949-4939. 276 D
smangels@lindenwood.edu
MANGELSDORF, Sarah, C .... 847-491-3276. 155 D
dean@wcas.northwestern.edu
MANGIACAPRA, Vincent, P .... 203-932-7058... 92 E
vmangiacapra@newhaven.edu
MANGINE, John, J .... 814-332-4356. 409 D
johnmangine@allegheny.edu
MANGINI, William .... 860-913-2005... 90 A
bmangini@goodwin.edu
MANGINO, Christine ...... 718-518-6753. 318 B
smangino@hostos.cuny.edu
MANGIONE, Robert, A ... 718-990-6308. 339 A
mangionr@stjohns.edu
MANGIONE, Terri, L ...... 716-888-2130. 316 C
mangiont@canisius.edu
MANGLES, Lenore .... 715-365-4637. 540 G
lmangles@nicoletcollege.edu
MANGLITZ, Elaine .... 678-466-5448. 123 A
elainemanglitz@clayton.edu
MANGLITZ, Marci .... 706-213-2116. 120 J
mmanglitz@athenstech.edu
MANGLONA, Gregorio, T .... 671-777-5591. 546 C
safety@guamcc.edu
MANGLONA, Ross .... 670-234-5498. 547 A
rossm@nmcnet.edu
MANGLONA-PROPST, Daisy .... 670-243-5498. 547 A
daisym@nmcnet.edu
MANGO, Peter .... 703-416-1441. 505 I
jmango@ipsciences.edu
MANGO, Peter .... 703-416-1441. 505 I
pmango@ipsciences.edu
MANGOLD, Melissa .... 636-651-1600. 281 K
mmangold@sbc-fenton.com
MANGOLD, Thomas .... 401-841-2074. 545 A
MANGRO, Nelly .... 408-934-4900... 47 A
nelly_mangro@heald.edu
MANGUM, Elmira .... 607-255-0155. 322 A
em443@cornell.edu
MANGUM, R. Todd .... 215-368-5000. 410 F
tmangum@biblical.edu
MANGUM, Steve .... 865-974-5061. 463 C
smangum@utk.edu
MANGUN, George, R ..... 530-754-8925... 70 J
mangun@lsdo.ucdavis.edu
MANGUS, Christy .... 269-782-1473. 250 C
cmangus@swmich.edu
MANHARDT, Joseph ...... 207-741-5598. 211 A
jmanhardt@smccme.edu
MANIACI, Vincent, M ..... 413-205-3202. 221 F
vincent.maniaci@aic.edu
MANIATIS, Marc .... 203-932-7218... 92 E
mmaniatis@newhaven.edu
MANIER, Tracy, L .... 512-448-8602. 479 C
tracym@stedwards.edu
MANIGAULT, Kimberly ... 937-376-6018. 376 E
kmanigault@centralstate.edu
MANIGO, Venis .... 803-777-4115. 447 G
venis.manigo@sc.edu
MANINGER, Catherine ... 405-878-5128. 399 G
camaninger@stgregorys.edu
MANION, Andrew, P .... 630-844-5252. 140 A
amanion@aurora.edu
MANION, Anne .... 617-296-8300. 227 I
anne_manion@laboure.edu
MANION, Shawna .... 618-437-5321. 156 H
manions@rlc.edu
MANIS, Janice, A .... 213-738-6800... 68 C
administrativeservices@swlaw.edu
MANISCALCO, Steven, J 607-436-2735. 343 E
maniscsj@oneonta.edu
MANKEY, Richanne, C ... 716-839-8519. 322 E
rmankey@daemen.edu
MANKO, Tammy .... 724-357-2235. 428 F
tammy.manko@iup.edu
MANKOWICH, James ..... 205-929-3498..... 5 D
jmankowich@lawsonstate.edu
MANLEY, Anna .... 541-956-7104. 407 F
amanley@roguecc.edu
MANLEY, Colleen .... 315-229-5988. 339 F
cmanley@stlawu.edu
MANLEY, Hannah, J .... 802-626-6433. 501 E
hannah.manley@lyndonstate.edu
MANLEY, Jen .... 253-566-5322. 524 C
jmanley@tacomacc.edu
MANLEY, Kelly .... 706-310-6203. 133 D
kelly.manley@ung.edu
MANLEY, Kyle .... 212-650-5040. 317 D
kmanley@ccny.cuny.edu
MANLEY, Thomas .... 503-821-8880. 406 F
tom@pnca.edu
MANLEY-ROOK, Stephanie .... 252-493-7383. 362 G
sgmrook@email.pittcc.edu
MANN, Charles, G .... 301-696-3611. 215 D
mann@hood.edu
MANN, Christy .... 870-512-7867... 20 B
christy_mann@asun.edu
MANN, Daniel, R .... 217-333-0100. 162 A
danmann@illinois.edu
MANN, Douglas .... 410-225-2352. 216 C
dmann@mica.edu
MANN, Gary .... 678-915-7290. 132 C
gmann@spsu.edu
MANN, Gwendolyn .... 334-229-4436..... 1 D
gmann@alasu.edu
MANN, Henrietta .... 406-994-7431. 287 B
henrim@montana.edu
MANN, Janet .... 202-687-1307... 95 E
mannj2@georgetown.edu
MANN, Jason .... 205-329-7875..... 3 B
jason.mann@ecacolleges.com
MANN, Jeanne, E .... 203-773-8516... 87 G
mann@albertus.edu
MANN, Jeffery .... 610-789-6700. 431 C
jmann@prismeducation.edu
MANN, Karen .... 502-585-9911. 199 C
kmann@spalding.edu
MANN, Kevin .... 509-313-6803. 520 A
mann@gonzaga.edu
MANN, Kevin, J .... 410-543-6202. 220 D
kjmann@salisbury.edu
MANN, Lara, G .... 317-781-5760. 173 I
mannlg@uindy.edu
MANN, Mark .... 619-849-2359... 59 L
markmann@pointloma.edu
MANN, Nelson, T .... 816-654-7112. 275 K
nmann@kcumb.edu
MANN, Randy .... 254-295-4618. 490 B
rmann@umhb.edu
MANN, Suellen .... 561-868-3450. 110 C
manns@palmbeachstate.edu
MANN, Thomas .... 802-860-2751. 499 A
tmann@champlain.edu
MANN, Warrenetta, C .... 757-221-3620. 503 N
MANN, FSC, William ...... 507-457-1503. 264 A
wmann@smumn.edu
MANN FAULKNER, Kenya .... 513-556-3483. 390 G
faulknka@ucmail.uc.edu
MANNELLA, Charles, J .. 856-225-6329. 306 C
chuck219@camden.rutgers.edu
MANNELLA, Stephen ...... 610-436-2242. 430 A
smannella@wcupa.edu
MANNERING, Susan, M 302-225-6232... 93 H
manners@gbc.edu
MANNETTI, Michael ...... 203-596-4531... 90 I
mmannetti@post.edu
MANNEY, Bill .... 218-262-6734. 258 G
williammanney@hibbing.edu
MANNING, Andrea .... 410-276-0306. 218 D
amanning@host.sdc.edu
MANNING, Dan .... 704-878-3281. 362 B
dmanning@mitchellcc.edu
MANNING, Danielle .... 617-573-8400. 237 B
dmanning@suffolk.edu
MANNING, Dianne, M ... 413-662-5249. 230 C
dianne.manning@mcla.edu
MANNING, Don .... 708-596-2000. 159 C
dmanning@ssc.edu
MANNING, Gaye .... 870-574-4509... 23 G
gmanning@sautech.edu
MANNING, Gerald .... 870-574-4516... 23 G
gbmannin@sautech.edu
MANNING, Jason .... 518-458-5303. 321 A
manningj@strose.edu
MANNING, Jean .... 513-569-1519. 376 L
jean.manning@cincinnatistate.edu
MANNING, Joanne .... 617-682-1521. 226 D
jmanning@eds.edu
MANNING, John .... 912-583-3108. 122 B
MANNING, Josh .... 870-307-7416... 21 H
josh.manning@lyon.edu
MANNING, Karen .... 910-695-3995. 363 F
manningk@sandhills.edu
MANNING, Kevin, J .... 443-334-2203. 218 E
rhubbard@stevenson.edu
MANNING, Kim, B .... 402-280-2738. 289 D
kmanning@creighton.edu
MANNING, Kimberly, M 848-932-1769. 306 A
kim.manning@rutgers.edu
MANNING, Kirk .... 845-398-4066. 340 A
kmanning@stac.edu
MANNING, Lynn Etta, G 214-887-5366. 471 F
lmanning@dts.edu
MANNING, Marcus .... 314-529-9313. 276 G
mmanning@maryville.edu
MANNING, Mark .... 315-498-2268. 335 G
m.r.manning@sunyocc.edu
MANNING, Noel, T .... 704-406-4631. 354 C
ntmanning@gardner-webb.edu
MANNING, Patricia .... 850-201-8994. 117 D
manningp@tcc.fl.edu
MANNING, Qy-Ana .... 360-736-9391. 517 G
qmanning@centralia.edu
MANNING, Robert .... 217-228-5432. 156 C
manniro@quincy.edu
MANNING, Scott .... 570-372-4256. 433 H
manning@susqu.edu
MANNING, Sherron, K ... 580-928-5533. 400 B
sherron.manning@swosu.edu
MANNING, Stephen .... 773-896-2400. 141 K
smanning@ctschicago.edu
MANNING, Terri .... 704-330-6592. 359 C
terri.manning@cpcc.edu
MANNING, Tina .... 912-427-5814. 120 B
tmanning@altamahatech.edu
MANNING, Wayne .... 580-349-1402. 397 G
wemann@opsu.edu
MANNING-MILLER, Donald .... 662-252-8000. 269 F
manningmiller@rustcollege.edu
MANNINO, Sam .... 502-459-3535. 199 G
smannino@sullivan.edu
MANNION, Joe .... 503-493-6233. 402 J
jmannion@cu-portland.edu
MANNION, Tom, N .... 626-395-6174... 31 E
mannion@caltech.edu
MANNIX, William .... 413-236-3036. 231 A
wmannix@berkshirecc.edu
MANNLE, Frank .... 212-346-1743. 335 J
fmannle@pace.edu
MANNO, Mechele .... 215-965-8569. 424 D
mmanno@moore.edu
MANNO, Vincent, P .... 781-292-2509. 226 G
vincent.manno@olin.edu
MANNOLINI, III, Lawrence, P .... 570-321-4118. 422 H
mannolin@lycoming.edu
MANNS, Derrick .... 225-308-4422. 202 G
dmanns@lctcs.edu
MANOGIN, Esther, M ..... 828-262-2190. 367 A
manoginem@appstate.edu
MANOHAR, Aruna, S ..... 410-323-6211. 214 F
aruna.manohar@gmail.com
MANOHAR, Namita .... 718-951-5476. 317 C
nmanohar@brooklyn.cuny.edu
MANOHAR, Norman, J ... 410-323-6211. 214 F
nmanohar@faiththeological.org
MANOLIS, Lilly .... 617-327-6777. 233 D
lilly_manolis@mspp.edu
MANOOSINGH, Celine ... 561-912-2166. 103 C
cmanoosingh@evergladesuniversity.edu
MANORD, Wayne .... 256-352-8116..... 9 G
wayne.manord@wallacestate.edu
MANOS, Dennis, M .... 757-871-9581. 503 N
dmanos@wm.edu
MANOS, Steve .... 781-736-4404. 224 F
ssmanos@brandeis.edu
MANOTTI, Ken .... 773-702-0686. 161 B
kmanotti@uchicago.edu
MANRIQUE, Santos .... 620-768-2908. 186 G
santosm@fortscott.edu
MANRIQUEZ, Chris .... 310-243-3702... 33 B
cmanriquez@csudh.edu
MANRY, J. Mark .... 248-218-2120. 249 D
mmanry@rc.edu
MANS, Sandra .... 518-445-2377. 313 C
smans@albanylaw.edu
MANSAPIT, Felix .... 671-735-2365. 546 E
safety@uguam.uog.edu
MANSDOERFER, Steve ... 503-517-1813. 408 I
smansdoerfer@westernseminary.edu
MANSER, Jacqueline, M . 330-490-7117. 392 H
jmanser@walsh.edu
MANSFIELD, Tim .... 315-228-7433. 320 F
tmansfield@colgate.edu
MANSHEIM, Bill .... 719-587-7727... 78 B
billmansheim@adams.edu
MANSHIP, James .... 651-690-8631. 263 O
jlmanship@stkate.edu
MANSON, Michael, L ..... 202-885-2416... 94 F
mmanson@american.edu
MANSON, Robert .... 714-564-6247... 60 G
manson_robert@sac.edu
MANSON, Sharon .... 817-531-5004. 488 A
smanson@txwes.edu
MANSOUR, Joe .... 318-345-9130. 203 C
jmansour@ladelta.edu
MANSOUR, Nick .... 602-222-9300... 11 H
nmansour@arizonacollege.edu
MANSPERGER, Thomas . 740-245-5353. 392 A
thomasm@rio.edu

MANSTROM, Paul, W ..... 269-337-7308. 244 K
Paul.Manstrom@kzoo.edu
MANSUR, Jay ..... 859-858-2305. 192 A
MANTELLA,
Philomena, V ..... 617-373-4798. 235 F
MANTELLI, Louis ..... 719-846-5619... 85 H
louis.mantelli@trinidadstate.edu
MANTHE, Theodore, E .... 507-344-7745. 253 J
tmanthe@blc.edu
MANTHEI, Peter ..... 505-454-5351. 309 L
pmanthei@luna.edu
MANTIA, Deborah ..... 312-893-7170. 145 B
dmantia@erikson.edu
MANTLE-BROMLEY,
Corinne ..... 208-885-6773. 139 D
cmantle@uidaho.edu
MANTONI, Thomas ..... 610-282-1100. 414 F
thomas.mantoni@desales.edu
MANTOOTH, Brooks, E .. 620-665-3497. 187 F
mantoothb@hutchcc.edu
MANUEL, Barbara ..... 718-262-2362. 319 F
bmanuel@york.cuny.edu
MANUEL, David ..... 417-873-7201. 273 H
dmanuel@drury.edu
MANUEL, Jeff ..... 205-652-3682..... 9 F
jmanuel@uwa.edu
MANUEL, Kamran ..... 323-822-9700... 69 J
kamran.manuel@touro.edu
MANUEL, Marilyn, G ..... 504-286-5020. 206 K
mmanuel@suno.edu
MANUEL, Mark ..... 859-246-6673. 194 L
mark.manuel@kctcs.edu
MANUEL, Robert, L ..... 317-788-3211. 173 I
rmanuel@uindy.edu
MANUEL, Shenethia ..... 573-341-4241. 284 A
manuels@mst.edu
MANUEL, Warde, J ..... 860-486-2725... 92 A
warde.manuel@uconn.edu
MANUEL-CORTEZ,
Dorinna ..... 808-934-2710. 136 F
dorinna@hawaii.edu
MANY LIGHTNINGS,
Janel ..... 605-698-3966. 451 D
jmanylightnings@swc.tc
MANZANARES, Ed ..... 505-454-3351. 310 E
edmanz@nmhu.edu
MANZANO, Anna ..... 310-665-6951... 57 C
amanzano@otis.edu
MANZANO, Florentino .. 818 947 2691... 52 E
manzanf@lavc.edu
MANZANO, Lynn ..... 714-628-4930... 60 H
manzano_lynn@sccollege.edu
MANZANO-BROWN,
Yvonne ..... 575-835-5533. 310 F
ymanzano@admin.nmt.edu
MANZIONE, Lara ..... 301-431-5450. 217 C
lmanzione@nlc.edu
MANZIONE, Louis ..... 860-768-5015... 92 D
manzione@hartford.edu
MANZKE, Rob ..... 715-346-3738. 538 A
rmanzke@uwsp.edu
MANZO, Pablo ..... 916-856-3400... 52 K
manzop@losrios.edu
MAO, Ruixuan ..... 847-214-7440. 144 F
rmao@elgin.edu
MAPES, Kim ..... 570-961-7810. 420 C
mapesk@lackawanna.edu
MAPHUMULO, Peter ..... 760-245-4271... 75 B
peter.maphumulo@vvc.edu
MAPLES, Cathy ..... 956-364-4300. 485 H
cathy.maples@tstc.edu
MAPLES, Christopher ..... 541-885-1100. 405 J
chris.maples@oit.edu
MAPLES, Stephen ..... 775-784-4700. 294 J
smaples@unr.edu
MAPLES-STERRY,
Brenda ..... 513-569-1555. 376 L
brenda.maples-sterry@cincinnatistate.edu
MAPLEY, Gordon ..... 816-271-4100. 279 A
gmapley@missouriwestern.edu
MAR, Pansy ..... 415-565-8902... 71 A
marp@uchastings.edu
MARA, Glenn, L ..... 510-987-9405... 70 H
glenn.mara@ucop.edu
MARA, Mary ..... 206-239-4500. 517 M
mmara@cityu.edu
MARA, Stacy, J ..... 920-832-7486. 533 S
stacy.j.mara@lawrence.edu
MARABETI, Hilary, B ..... 615-230-3355. 461 G
hilary.marabeti@volstate.edu
MARABLE, Shelia ..... 205-929-6437..... 5 D
smarable@lawsonstate.edu
MARAGAKIS, Emmanuel 775-784-6925. 294 J
maragaki@ce.unr.edu
MARAK, Randy ..... 713-646-2912. 480 J
rmarak@stcl.edu
MARANA, Jennifer ..... 410-857-2791. 216 E
MARANDE, Robert, P ..... 570-389-4805. 427 H
rmarande@bloomu.edu
MARANDO, Anne ..... 781-736-8782. 224 F
marando@brandeis.edu
MARANO, Jeanne ..... 973-655-5333. 303 D
maranoj@mail.montclair.edu
MARANO, Nicole ..... 443-334-2509. 218 E
nmarano@stevenson.edu
MARANTO-PHILLIPS,
Tracy ..... 318-869-5191. 201 H
tmphillips@centenary.edu
MARAVETZ, Sarah ..... 410-225-2219. 216 C
smaravetz@mica.edu
MARAVIGLIA, James, L . 805-756-2311... 32 F
jmaravig@calpoly.edu
MARBACH, Joseph, R .... 215-951-1015. 420 B
marbach@lasalle.edu
MARBERRY, Thomas, L . 405-912-9004. 395 K
tmarberry@hc.edu
MARBERT, Larry, D ..... 305-284-5660. 118 F
lmarbert@miami.edu
MARBLE, Alan ..... 417-625-9395. 278 D
MARBLE, Amanda, F ..... 208-467-8402. 139 A
afmarble@nnu.edu
MARBLE, Dexter ..... 405-224-3140. 401 E
dmarble@usao.edu
MARBLE, Jan ..... 507-389-5120. 259 G
janice.marble@mnsu.edu
MARBLE, Julie ..... 318-678-6865... 18 I
julie.marble@phoenix.edu
MARBURGER, Ann, M ... 937-255-6565. 544 C
ann.marburger@afit.edu
MARBUT, Terry ..... 256-782-5034..... 4 K
tmarbut@jsu.edu
MARCANTONIO, James . 573-681-5018. 276 C
marcantonioj@lincolnu.edu
MARCE, Harvey ..... 605-698-3966. 451 D
hmarce@swc.tc
MARCEL, Gina ..... 985-448-7929. 203 B
gina.marcel@fletcher.edu
MARCEL, Yorgun ..... 712-749-1227. 176 D
marcely@bvu.edu
MARCEL, Yorgun ..... 330-263-2262. 377 H
ymarcel@wooster.edu
MARCELLA, Aimee, R ..... 203-576-4466... 91 G
amarcell@bridgeport.edu
MARCELLA, Pat ..... 413-528-7204. 222 E
pmarcella@simons-rock.edu
MARCELLAIS, Alexsis ..... 701-477-7862. 373 B
amarcellais@tm.edu
MARCELLO, Kathleen, A . 717-245-1554. 414 H
marcellk@dickinson.edu
MARCH, Priscilla ..... 978-934-2355. 229 B
priscilla_march@uml.edu
MARCHAL, Jerry ..... 859-858-3511. 192 B
jmarchal@asbury.edu
MARCHAND, William ..... 516-686-7904. 333 H
wmarchan@nyit.edu
MARCHANT, Karen ..... 605-626-7781. 451 I
Karen.Marchang@northern.edu
MARCHANT, Lloyd ..... 660-263-4110. 279 B
lloydm@macc.edu
MARCHANT, T. Eston ..... 919-718-7246. 359 B
bmarchant@cccc.edu
MARCHASE, Richard, B .. 205-934-1294..... 8 E
marchase@uab.edu
MARCHBANKS, Pete ..... 979-845-8423. 483 C
pete-marchbanks@tamu.edu
MARCHELLETTA,
Barbara ..... 207-947-4591. 209 G
bmarchelletta@bealcollege.edu
MARCHELLO, Sara, L ..... 757-221-2801. 503 N
sallie.marchello@wm.edu
MARCHESCHI, Graziano . 773-298-3419. 158 E
marcheschi@sxu.edu
MARCHESE, Cynthia, C .. 212-687-4303. 299 D
ccm@berkeleycollege.edu
MARCHESE, Cynthia, C .. 212-687-3730. 314 K
ccm@berkeleycollege.edu
MARCHESE, Paul, J ..... 718-631-6690. 319 D
pmarchese@qcc.cuny.edu
MARCHETTA, Jon ..... 971-722-8486. 407 D
jonathan.marchetta@pcc.edu
MARCHILDON, Scott ..... 207-221-4230. 213 A
smarchildon@une.edu
MARCHIONE, Susan, M . 716-839-8447. 322 E
smarchio@daemen.edu
MARCHIONINI, Gary ..... 919-962-8363. 368 D
gary@ils.unc.edu
MARCHIORI, Dennis, M . 563-884-5500. 182 A
dennis.marchiori@palmer.edu
MARCHU, Gene ..... 760-773-2567... 40 F
gmarchu@collegeofthedesert.edu
MARCI, Mark ..... 412-281-2600. 433 B
mmarci@western-school.com
MARCIAL, Myriam ..... 787-891-0925. 549 K
mmarcial@aguadilla.inter.edu
MARCIAL VEGA,
Ivonne, M ..... 787-945-7010. 548 O
rectoria@eap.edu
MARCILLE, Andrea, M .... 868-701-6393. 545 G
Andrea.M.Marcille@uscg.mil
MARCIN, Heidi, C ..... 585-785-1609. 324 D
marcinhc@flcc.edu
MARCINEK, Myron ..... 570-961-4786. 423 B
mmarcinek@marywood.edu
MARCO, Rachel ..... 815-288-5511. 158 K
marcor@svcc.edu
MARCO SCANLON,
Cynthia ..... 216-397-1699. 381 R
cmarco@jcu.edu
MARCOCCIA, Louis, G ... 315-443-3037. 347 C
lmarcocc@syr.edu
MARCOE, Timothy ..... 570-784-3123. 427 H
frtim@bloomu.edu
MARCOGLIESE, Marie .... 651-450-3546. 258 H
mmarcog@inverhills.edu
MARCOLINE, Beverly, J . 315-792-3041. 349 F
bmarcoline@utica.edu
MARCONE, Luigi ..... 203-837-9314... 88 B
marconel@wcsu.edu
MARCOTTE, Sharon ..... 218-335-4253. 256 I
sharon.marcotte@lltc.edu
MARCUCCILLI,
Christine, M ..... 260-481-6106. 168 C
marcuccc@ipfw.edu
MARCUM, Marie ..... 603-542-7744. 296 D
mmarcum@ccsnh.edu
MARCUM, Roger, L ..... 859-336-5082. 198 J
rmarcum@sccky.edu
MARCUS, Jamie, E ..... 207-778-7000. 212 D
jaime.marcus@maine.edu
MARCUS, John ..... 508-541-1508. 225 F
jmarcus@dean.edu
MARCUS, Lynn ..... 978-762-4000. 232 D
lmarcus@northshore.edu
MARCUS, Nancy ..... 850-644-3500. 115 C
nmarcus@fsu.edu
MARCUS, Robert, J ..... 317-940-9910. 164 J
rmarcus@butler.edu
MARCUS, W. Andrew ..... 541-346-3902. 406 D
marcus@uoregon.edu
MARCUS, William ..... 406-243-4154. 286 H
william.marcus@umontana.edu
MARCUS-NEWHALL,
Amy ..... 909-607-2822... 65 D
amy.marcus-newhall@scrippscollege.edu
MARCUSE, Adrian, G ..... 212-752-1530. 328 G
adrian.marcuse@limcollege.edu
MARCUSE, Elizabeth, S .. 212-752-1530. 328 G
elizabeth.marcuse@limcollege.edu
MARCUSSEN, Thomas ..... 414-229-4537. 537 A
marcusse@uwm.edu
MARCY, Mary, B ..... 415-485-3200... 42 J
president@dominican.edu
MARCZYNSKI, Jerry ..... 775-784-4898. 294 J
marczyns@unr.edu
MARDEN, Rose ..... 210-341-1366. 477 L
rmarden@ost.edu
MARDIROSIAN, Haig ..... 813-253-6100. 118 L
hmardirosian@ut.edu
MARDIS, Michael ..... 502-852-5787. 200 D
mike.mardis@louisville.edu
MAREK, Diane ..... 847-233-7700. 155 B
dmarek@nc.edu
MAREK, Kate ..... 708-524-6648. 144 C
kmarek@dom.edu
MAREK, Robin ..... 401-232-6804. 438 K
rmarek@bryant.edu
MAREK, Robin ..... 731-425-2654. 460 G
rmarek@jscc.edu
MAREK, Sandra ..... 660-263-4110. 279 B
sandram@macc.edu
MAREK, Thomas ..... 901-320-9700. 463 J
tmarek@victory.edu
MARELICK, Lin ..... 408-741-4084... 75 L
lin.marelick@westvalley.edu
MARES, Maria ..... 787-864-2222. 550 D
mmares@inter.edu
MARFELL, Julie ..... 859-253-3637. 194 A
julie.marfell@frontier.edu
MARFISE, Larry, J ..... 813-253-6240. 118 L
lmarfise@ut.edu
MARGERUM, Eric, W ..... 812-888-5127. 174 F
emargerum@vinu.edu
MARGHEIM, Jeffrey ..... 386-822-7020. 117 C
jmarghei@stetson.edu
MARGISON, Richard, L .. 205-934-5493..... 8 E
margison@uab.edu
MARGLIOTTI, Garrett, D . 412-578-6010. 412 G
gdmargliotti@carlow.edu
MARGOLIS, Liza ..... 340-693-1053. 555 E
lmargol@live.uvi.edu
MARGUIS, Jack ..... 814-944-5643. 438 F
john.marguis@yti.edu
MARGULES, Gary, S ..... 954-262-7507. 109 K
margules@nova.edu
MARGULIES, Anne ..... 617-495-9092. 227 C
anne_margulies@harvard.edu
MARGULIES, L ..... 718-853-8500. 348 A
MARGULIES, Mordechai . 718-854-2290. 315 B
MARI, Mike ..... 707-468-3165... 54 B
mari@mendocino.edu
MARIANI, Elsa ..... 787-257-7373. 552 H
emariani@suagm.edu
MARIANI, William ..... 716-829-8194. 323 D
marianiw@dyc.edu
MARIANO, Anthony, A ... 802-485-2230. 500 A
tmariano@norwich.edu
MARIANS, Kenneth, J .... 646-888-6639. 329 J
kmarians@sloankettering.edu
MARICHAL-LUGO,
Carlos ..... 787-993-8866. 554 A
carlos.marichal@upr.edu
MARIN, Anthony, S ..... 575-646-1631. 310 I
amarin@nmsu.edu
MARIN, Gerardo ..... 415-422-2199... 73 J
marin@usfca.edu
MARIN, Noemi ..... 561-297-3850. 114 L
nmarin@fau.edu
MARIN-HILL, Angelica ... 214-648-3684. 493 E
angelica.marin-hill@utsouthwestern.edu
MARINACCIO, Jessica .... 212-854-1222. 321 D
jm996@columbia.edu
MARINACE, Betsy ..... 973-684-6861. 304 B
bmarinace@pccc.edu
MARINCH, Maria ..... 702-651-7546. 294 E
maria.marinch@csn.edu
MARINELLI, Bryan, D ..... 401-865-1822. 439 E
bmarinel@providence.edu
MARINELLI, Nicholas ..... 678-891-3953. 125 G
nicholas.marinelli@gpc.edu
MARINI, Jacob ..... 212-237-8449. 318 D
jmarini@jjay.cuny.edu
MARINI, Janice, K ..... 215-955-2244. 434 C
janice.marini@jefferson.edu
MARINI, Mario ..... 724-589-2022. 434 B
mmarini@thiel.edu
MARINI, Stephen, T ..... 508-854-4272. 232 F
smarini@qcc.mass.edu
MARINIS, Jeremy ..... 419-448-3301. 389 J
marinisjj@tiffin.edu
MARINO, Chris ..... 864-646-1836. 447 D
cmarino@tctc.edu
MARINO, James ..... 856-225-6046. 306 C
jmarino@camden.rutgers.edu
MARINO, Kathy ..... 973-290-4089. 300 F
kmarino@cse.edu
MARINO, Lucille ..... 785-864-7431. 190 L
lmarino@ku.edu
MARINO, Michael ..... 717-295-1100. 438 H
michael.marino@yti.edu
MARINO, Michael ..... 717-767-0303. 438 H
michael.marino@yti.edu
MARINO, Patricia ..... 518-262-9550. 313 D
marinop@mail.amc.edu
MARINO, Robert ..... 585-389-2604. 332 D
rmarino9@naz.edu
MARINUCCI, Dorothy ..... 718-817-3000. 324 G
marinucci@fordham.edu
MARION, D. Keith ..... 803-754-4100. 443 C
MARION, Joseph ..... 504-286-5389. 206 K
jmarion@suno.edu
MARION, Lucy, N ..... 706-721-3771. 126 B
lumarion@gru.edu
MARION, Michael ..... 916-691-7738... 53 B
marionm@crc.losrios.edu
MARION, Paul ..... 978-934-3107. 229 B
paul_marion@uml.edu
MARION, Paul ..... 419-448-3413. 389 J
marionp@tiffin.edu
MARION, Phyllis, C ..... 619-239-0391... 36 D
pmarion@cwsl.edu
MARIS, Charles ..... 678-839-4760. 133 I
cmaris@westga.edu
MARIUCCI, Robert ..... 805-546-3210... 42 C
rmariucc@cuesta.edu
MARIX, Amy ..... 225-578-3486. 204 O
amarix@lsu.edu
MARIZ, George ..... 360-650-3446. 525 C
george.mariz@wwu.edu
MARK, Gregory, A ..... 312-362-5595. 143 H
gmark@depaul.edu
MARK, ASC, JoAnn ..... 316-942-4291. 189 E
markj@newmanu.edu
MARK, Joy ..... 620-947-3121. 190 J
joym@tabor.edu
MARK JONES, John ..... 903-468-8144. 483 E
john.jones@tamuc.edu
MARKEL, Mark, D ..... 608-263-6716. 536 D
markelm@svm.vetmed.wisc.edu
MARKELL, Dawn ..... 517-338-3048. 241 A
dmarkell@cleary.edu
MARKER, David ..... 631-244-3395. 323 B
markerd@dowling.edu
MARKER, David ..... 850-474-3386. 117 B
dmarker@uwf.edu
MARKER, John ..... 831-582-4796... 34 B
jmarker@csumb.edu
MARKERT, Stephen ..... 713-221-8946. 489 D
markerts@uhd.edu
MARKEY, John ..... 210-341-1366. 477 L
eowens@ost.edu
MARKEY, Nanette ..... 301-696-3620. 215 D
markey@hood.edu

MARKEY-GRABILL,
Mindy .... 937-393-3431. 389 B
mmarkey@sscc.edu
MARKGRAF, Karl, F ...... 715-836-4411. 536 E
markgraf@uwec.edu
MARKHAM, Ian, S .... 703-370-6600. 508 B
MARKHAM, Joseph .... 770-962-7580. 127 D
jmarkham@gwinnetttech.edu
MARKIEWICZ, Renee, J . 508-849-3291. 222 B
rmarkiewicz@annamaria.edu
MARKIN, Karen .... 401-874-5971. 440 D
kmarkin@uri.edu
MARKIN, Rodney .... 402-559-7687. 292 J
rmarkin@unmc.edu
MARKLAND, Scott .... 937-512-5502. 388 O
scott.markland@sinclair.edu
MARKLE, Chris, A .... 570-372-4425. 433 H
marklec@susqu.edu
MARKLE, Elizabeth .... 775-831-1314. 295 F
emarkle@sierranevada.edu
MARKLE, Suzanne .... 412-346-2100. 430 F
smarkle@pia.edu
MARKLE, William, J .... 610-359-5113. 414 D
wmarkle@dccc.edu
MARKLEY, Bradley, A ..... 717-766-2511. 423 L
bmarkley@messiah.edu
MARKLEY, Neil .... 707-664-4068... 36 B
neil.markley@sonoma.edu
MARKLEY, Rebecca .... 800-962-7682. 285 A
bmarkley@wma.edu
MARKOV, Kornelia .... 928-776-2087... 19 H
kornelia.markov@yc.edu
MARKOVICH, Matt .... 415-485-9591... 40 G
matt.markovich@marin.edu
MARKOWITZ, Marianne . 315-448-5040. 339 D
MARKOWITZ, Martin, S . 848-445-3600. 306 B
markowitz@business.rutgers.edu
MARKOWSKI, Vincent .... 201-684-7432. 305 A
vmarkows@ramapo.edu
MARKS, Andrea, M .... 210-567-7020. 493 A
marksa@uthscsa.edu
MARKS, Debra, J .... 714-449-7463... 67 D
dmarks@scco.edu
MARKS, Ellen .... 906-487-2500. 247 A
ebmarks@mtu.edu
MARKS, Erica .... 718-260-3298. 336 E
emarks@poly.edu
MARKS, Janice, L .... 443-518-4617. 215 E
jmarks@howardcc.edu
MARKS, Leota .... 913-288-7200. 187 L
lmarks@kckcc.edu
MARKS, Lilly .... 303-724-5369... 86 A
lilly.marks@ucdenver.edu
MARKS, Lisa, M .... 618-453-1067. 159 G
marks04@siu.edu
MARKS, Michelle .... 703-993-8705. 505 C
mmarks@gmu.edu
MARKS, Patrice .... 908-526-1200. 305 B
pmarks@raritanval.edu
MARKS, Ronald .... 504-865-5314. 207 C
rmarks@tulane.edu
MARKS, Rondah .... 601-984-1012. 270 C
rmarks@umc.edu
MARKS, Sandra .... 562-860-2451... 37 I
smarks@cerritos.edu
MARKSBERRY, Annette .. 513-745-4261. 393 H
marksberrya@xavier.edu
MARKSBURY, Nancy ...... 516-299-2281. 329 D
nancy.marksbury@liu.edu
MARKSBURY, Rick .... 504-865-5555. 207 C
rmarksby@tulane.edu
MARKSON, Alison, W .... 617-333-2120. 225 E
amarkson1109@curry.edu
MARKULY, Mark .... 206-296-5330. 523 E
markulym@seattleu.edu
MARKUM, Grace .... 814-262-3812. 427 C
gmarkum@pennhighlands.edu
MARKUM, Michael .... 254-298-8291. 482 C
mmarkum@templejc.edu
MARKWOOD,
Christopher, L .... 361-825-2722. 483 F
chris.markwood@tamucc.edu
MARKWORD, Theresa .... 530-242-7510... 65 G
tmarkword@shastacollege.edu
MARLAIRE, Natalyn, M .. 715-852-1399. 539 J
nmarlaire@cvtc.edu
MARLAND, Jaime .... 401-427-6954. 440 A
jmarland@risd.edu
MARLER, Dan .... 970-542-3157... 83 E
dan.marler@morgancc.edu
MARLER, Eric .... 808-675-3708. 135 C
eric.marler@byuh.edu
MARLEY, Bernard .... 812-749-1404. 171 K
bmarley@oak.edu
MARLEY, Chad .... 307-778-1346. 543 D
cmarley@lccc.wy.edu
MARLEY, Phillip .... 660-263-3900. 272 A
pmarley@cccb.edu
MARLEY, Robert .... 406-994-2452. 287 B
MARLIN, Nancy, A .... 619-594-6881... 35 D
nmarlin@mail.sdsu.edu
MARLING, Janet .... 706-864-1574. 133 D
janet.marling@ung.edu
MARLOWE, Bethany .... 803-323-4503. 449 G
marloweb@winthrop.edu
MARLOWE, June .... 314-991-6220. 141 G
jmarlowe@chamberlain.edu
MARLOWE, June .... 877-751-5783. 141 F
MARLOWE, Robert, W .... 843-953-2502. 443 A
marlower@cofc.edu
MARMARELLI, Beth .... 313-593-5542. 251 D
bethmar@umich.edu
MARMOLEJO, William .... 323-953-4000... 51 G
marmolwa@lacitycollege.edu
MARMON, Richard .... 623-935-8075... 14 K
rich.marmon@estrellamountain.edu
MARMUR, Michael .... 212-824-2215. 325 G
mmarmur@huc.edu
MARNEN, Ted .... 814-871-7599. 416 K
marnen001@gannon.edu
MARNICH, Darlene .... 412-392-3474. 431 B
dmarnich@pointpark.edu
MAROHL, Matthew .... 507-786-3092. 264 B
marohl@stolaf.edu
MAROLDO, Brian .... 516-686-7449. 333 H
bmaroldo@nyit.edu
MARONE, Phillip, J .... 215-955-7750. 434 C
phillip.marone@jefferson.edu
MARONEY, Wesley .... 805-922-6966... 26 K
wmaroney@hancockcollege.edu
MARONI, Paul, L .... 860-439-2044... 89 H
plmar@conncoll.edu
MAROTTA, Marsha .... 413-572-5374. 230 F
mmarotta@westfield.ma.edu
MAROVICH, Diana .... 219-785-5373. 172 A
dmarovich@pnc.edu
MARPLE, Bradley .... 214-648-2646. 493 E
bradley.marple@utsouthwestern.edu
MARQUARDT,
Christopher .... 315-229-5250. 339 F
cmarquardt@stlawu.edu
MARQUARDT,
Clifford, L .... 740-377-2520. 389 K
cmark@zoominternet.net
MARQUARDT, Larry .... 515-271-1430. 177 H
larry.marquardt@dmu.edu
MARQUARDT, Richard ... 570-465-2344. 420 C
marquardtr@lackawanna.edu
MARQUARDT, Scott, E ... 608-342-1584. 537 D
marquars@uwplatt.edu
MARQUARDT, Shelly ...... 714-547-9625... 30 J
smarquardt@calcoast.edu
MARQUES, Javier .... 305-348-2111. 115 B
javier.marques@fiu.edu
MARQUES, Jeffrey .... 413-775-1700. 231 E
marquesj@gcc.mass.edu
MARQUEZ, Dianne .... 575-492-2841. 310 G
dmarquez@nmjc.edu
MARQUEZ, Edward .... 913-621-8713. 186 C
emarquez@donnelly.edu
MARQUEZ, JR., Felix, J 407-251-0007. 110 A
MARQUEZ, Ivan .... 914-337-9300. 321 E
ivan.marquez@concordia-ny.edu
MARQUEZ, Kenneth, L ... 719-587-7227... 78 B
klmarque@adams.edu
MARQUEZ, Krishna .... 787-746-1400. 549 B
kmarquez@huertas.edu
MARQUEZ, Lonnie, G .... 575-835-5606. 310 F
lmarquez@admin.nmt.edu
MARQUEZ, Moses .... 505-454-5312. 309 L
mmarquez@luna.edu
MARQUEZ, Nitza .... 787-786-3030. 547 F
nimarquez@ucb.edu.pr
MARQUEZ, Nora .... 650-433-3850... 58 B
nmarquez@paloaltou.edu
MARQUEZ BELL, Mary .. 516-876-3082. 343 D
bellm@oldwestbury.edu
MARQUEZ-SCALLY,
Marline .... 505-984-6075. 311 H
registrar@sjcsf.edu
MARQUIS, Lauren .... 617-879-2328. 238 C
lmarquis@wheelock.edu
MARQUIS, Susan .... 310-393-0411... 58 E
smarquis@rand.org
MARQUSEE, Steven, J .... 315-267-2231. 344 C
marqussj@potsdam.edu
MARR, J, R .... 704-820-0726. 352 G
jrmarr@bac.edu
MARR, Jay .... 502-456-6506. 199 G
jmarr@sullivan.edu
MARR, Jena .... 405-422-1265. 399 B
marrj@redlandscc.edu
MARR, JR., John, W ...... 216-987-4000. 378 D
john.marr-jr@tri-c.edu
MARR, Michael .... 603-230-3505. 295 J
mmarr@ccsnh.edu
MARR, Ronda .... 209-946-2206... 73 A
rmarr@pacific.edu
MARRA, Angelina .... 718-261-5800. 315 F
amarra@bramsonort.edu
MARRANT, Dale .... 913-234-0612. 185 L
dale.marrant@cleveland.edu
MARRERO, Keyla, O .... 780-250-1912. 550 E
kmarrero@metro.inter.edu
MARRERO, Kyle .... 678-839-6442. 133 I
MARRERO, Milagros ...... 787-850-9375. 554 D
milagros.marrero1@upr.edu
MARRERO, Wilma .... 787-765-1915. 551 C
wmarrero@inter.edu
MARRERO, Yari, M .... 787-740-1611. 553 C
yari.marrero@uccaribe.edu
MARRETT, Clifford .... 860-465-5577... 87 L
marrettc@easternct.edu
MARRIN, John .... 719-336-1511... 82 R
john.marrin@lamarcc.edu
MARRIOTT, Carol .... 585-343-0055. 325 C
cmarriott@genesee.edu
MARRIOTT, Donna, M .... 240-500-2000. 215 B
dmmarriott@hagerstowncc.edu
MARRIOTT, Karin .... 951-487-3060... 55 B
kmarriott@msjc.edu
MARRIOTT, Martin .... 920-206-2310. 533 U
mmarriott@mbbc.edu
MARRIOTT, Russell .... 214-818-1318. 470 A
rmarriott@criswell.edu
MARROCCO, Susan .... 941-752-5201. 114 I
marrocs@scf.edu
MARROCCO, Therese ..... 203-857-7311... 89 D
tmarrocco@norwalk.edu
MARRON, Ariana, V .... 858-499-0202... 40 C
amarron@coleman.edu
MARRON, Timothy .... 206-296-5990. 523 E
marront@seattleu.edu
MARRONE, Joseph .... 203-576-5515... 91 D
jmarrone@stvincentscollege.edu
MARRONE, Michelle .... 603-899-4221. 296 H
Marronem@franklinpierce.edu
MARRONGELLE, Karen ... 503-725-5718. 405 G
karen_marrongelle@ous.edu
MARROTT, Ann .... 845-687-5070. 348 H
marrotta@sunyulster.edu
MARROW, Cary .... 806-894-9611. 480 H
cmarrow@southplainscollege.edu
MARRS, Gianna, F .... 207-581-1324. 212 B
gianna@maine.edu
MARRS, Rick, R .... 310-506-4280... 58 H
rick.marrs@pepperdine.edu
MARRS, Stuart, L .... 207-581-1547. 212 B
marrs@maine.edu
MARRS DE BARRON,
Keri .... 219-785-5479. 172 A
kmarrs@pnc.edu
MARSALEK, Lisa .... 419-783-2366. 379 C
lmarsalek@defiance.edu
MARSCH, III, Andrew, J 205-934-4175..... 8 E
marsch@uab.edu
MARSCH, Charlotte .... 417-328-1803. 282 C
cmarsch@sbuniv.edu
MARSCHKE, Robyn .... 719-255-3640... 85 M
rmarschk@uccs.edu
MARSDEN, Janet, L .... 802-440-4303. 498 G
jmarsden@bennington.edu
MARSDEN, John .... 252-399-6343. 352 F
jmarsden@barton.edu
MARSDEN, John, P .... 859-846-5310. 197 I
jmarsden@midway.edu
MARSH, Bonnie Jean ..... 724-439-4900. 421 F
bmarsh@laurel.edu
MARSH, Brent, A .... 325-649-8613. 473 F
bmarsh@hputx.edu
MARSH, Cecilia .... 660-359-3948. 279 H
cmarsh@mail.ncmissouri.edu
MARSH, Cheryl .... 704-216-3503. 363 D
cheryl.marsh@rccc.edu
MARSH, Dawn .... 517-265-5161. 238 G
dmarsh@adrian.edu
MARSH, Douglas, K .... 574-631-4200. 174 A
marsh.14@nd.edu
MARSH, Elinor .... 517-629-0247. 239 A
emarsh@albion.edu
MARSH, Geoff, A .... 517-750-1200. 250 E
gmarsh@arbor.edu
MARSH, Gregory .... 409-880-2100. 486 F
gregory.marsh@lamar.edu
MARSH, Heather, A .... 214-860-3611. 471 A
hmarsh@dcccd.edu
MARSH, James, G .... 254-710-2467. 467 G
jim_marsh@baylor.edu
MARSH, Janet .... 517-437-7341. 243 I
janet.marsh@hillsdale.edu
MARSH, Jed .... 609-258-7860. 304 E
jmarsh@princeton.edu
MARSH, John .... 315-792-7125. 346 C
john.marsh@sunyit.edu
MARSH, Julie .... 913-758-6146. 191 B
marsh50@stmary.edu
MARSH, Kathleen .... 989-358-7458. 239 C
marshk@alpenacc.edu
MARSH, Kent .... 970-248-1465... 79 F
kmarsh@coloradomesa.edu
MARSH, Mae .... 907-474-6600... 10 I
mmarsh36@alaska.edu
MARSH, Marti, F .... 502-895-3411. 197 F
mmarsh@lpts.edu
MARSH, Mecca .... 757-822-1227. 514 C
mmarsh@tcc.edu
MARSH, Nicole, Y .... 510-628-8011... 51 A
librarian@lincolnuca.edu
MARSH, Robert .... 231-439-6353. 247 H
rmarsh@ncmich.edu
MARSH, Scott .... 253-566-5124. 524 C
smarsh@tacomacc.edu
MARSH, Spencer .... 631-444-3100. 342 C
spencer.marsh@stonybrook.edu
MARSH-WILLIAMS,
Pamela, R .... 413-545-6493. 228 F
marshwil@acad.umass.edu
MARSHALL, Alan, G .... 660-248-6260. 272 B
agmarsha@centralmethodist.edu
MARSHALL, Angela .... 985-543-4120. 203 D
MARSHALL, Ave .... 404-270-5288. 132 E
amarshall@spelman.edu
MARSHALL, Ben .... 813-253-7125. 106 M
rmarshall10@hccfl.edu
MARSHALL, Beth, A .... 978-542-6022. 230 E
bmarshall@salemstate.edu
MARSHALL, Bonnie .... 610-527-0200. 432 B
bonnie.marshall@rosemont.edu
MARSHALL, Bryon .... 609-586-4800. 302 G
marshalb@mccc.edu
MARSHALL, Cheryl, A .... 909-389-3200... 61 K
cmarshal@craftonhills.edu
MARSHALL, Connie .... 423-354-2533. 461 C
cmarshall@northeaststate.edu
MARSHALL, Darryl .... 850-644-5716. 115 C
dmarshall@admin.fsu.edu
MARSHALL, Dave .... 218-235-2125. 261 G
d.marshall@vcc.edu
MARSHALL, David .... 773-291-6100. 142 D
dmarshall39@ccc.edu
MARSHALL, David, B ..... 805-893-4327... 72 B
dmarshall@ltsc.ucsb.edu
MARSHALL, Deborah, A . 434-832-7812. 512 A
marshalld@cvcc.vccs.edu
MARSHALL, Edwin .... 812-856-5700. 167 E
marshall@indiana.edu
MARSHALL, Edwin .... 812-856-5700. 167 F
marshall@indiana.edu
MARSHALL, George .... 802-447-4001. 500 D
gmarshall@svc.edu
MARSHALL, JaNice .... 216-987-3260. 378 D
janice.marshall@tri-c.edu
MARSHALL, Jay .... 765-983-1687. 165 G
marshja@earlham.edu
MARSHALL, Jim .... 303-360-4754... 81 C
jim.marshall@ccaurora.edu
MARSHALL, Jo .... 606-679-8501. 196 D
jo.marshall@kctcs.edu
MARSHALL, Joe .... 301-846-2824. 214 H
jmarshall@frederick.edu
MARSHALL, Joe .... 817-923-8459. 469 F
joe.marshall@fishermore.edu
MARSHALL, John .... 970-248-1366... 79 F
marshall@coloradomesa.edu
MARSHALL, Jon .... 620-365-5116. 183 I
marshall@allencc.edu
MARSHALL, Juanita .... 731-426-7539. 455 J
jmarshall@lanecollege.edu
MARSHALL, Judith .... 618-536-2626. 159 G
jmarshal@siu.edu
MARSHALL, Kent .... 708-974-5390. 153 F
marshallk34@morainevalley.edu
MARSHALL, Kirstin .... 309-672-5740. 152 I
kamarshall@methodistcol.edu
MARSHALL, Larry .... 724-852-3230. 437 A
lmarshal@waynesburg.edu
MARSHALL, Larry, W ...... 606-474-3277. 194 H
lmarshall@kcu.edu
MARSHALL, Lori .... 856-256-4197. 305 E
marshall@rowan.edu
MARSHALL, Lynette, L ... 319-335-3305. 175 I
lynette-marshall@uiowa.edu
MARSHALL, MacArthur .. 718-631-6202. 319 D
mmarshall@qcc.cuny.edu
MARSHALL, Maura .... 603-641-7028. 297 G
mmarshall@anselm.edu
MARSHALL, Molly, T ...... 913-667-5700. 185 J
mtmarshall@cbts.edu
MARSHALL, Patricia, A .. 508-929-8938. 230 G
pmarshall@worcester.edu
MARSHALL, Peter .... 812-357-6280. 173 A
pmarshall@saintmeinrad.edu
MARSHALL, Phyllis .... 609-633-6460. 308 A
pmarshall@tesc.edu
MARSHALL, Richard .... 608-899-4241. 296 H
marshallr@franklinpierce.edu
MARSHALL, Rick .... 828-694-1746. 358 C
rickm@blueridge.edu
MARSHALL, Rob .... 540-868-7050. 512 H
rmarshall@lfcc.edu
MARSHALL, Robert .... 859-341-4867. 199 H
robert.marshall@thomasmore.edu

MARSHALL, Rosita .... 606-693-5000. 196 H finaid@kmbc.edu
MARSHALL, Sheila, M ... 315-267-2184. 344 C marshasm@potsdam.edu
MARSHALL, Stacey .... 503-760-3131. 402 B stacey@birthingway.edu
MARSHALL, Steven .... 610-282-1100. 414 F steven.marshall@desales.edu
MARSHALL, Susan .... 870-733-6722... 21 I smarshall@midsouthcc.edu
MARSHALL, Susan, D .... 423-652-6006. 455 I sdmarsha@king.edu
MARSHALL, Tim .... 212-229-8947. 332 E provost@newschool.edu
MARSHALL, Timothy (Tim) .... 817-515-5389. 482 B timothy.marshall@tccd.edu
MARSHALL, Todd .... 517-750-1200. 250 E marshall@arbor.edu
MARSHALL, Toni .... 803-508-7242. 440 G marshalt@atc.edu
MARSHALL-BIGGINS, Cynthia .... 903-593-8311. 485 A cmarshall-biggins@texascollege.edu
MARSHALL-BRADLEY, Tina .... 706-396-7596. 130 C tmarshallbradley@paine.edu
MARSHBURN, Roxann ... 847-376-7099. 155 F rmarshbu@oakton.edu
MARSHEL, Kimberly .... 360-992-2358. 518 A kmarshel@clark.edu
MARSICANO, Leslie, M .. 704-894-2804. 353 J lemarsicano@davidson.edu
MARSICO, Richard, J ..... 330-941-3767. 394 A rjmarsico@ysu.edu
MARSICO, Richard, J ..... 330-941-3036. 394 A rjmarsico@ysu.edu
MARSILI, Amanda .... 401-254-3774. 440 B amarsili@rwu.edu
MARSILIO, Maria, S .... 610-660-1798. 432 E marsilio@sju.edu
MARSON, Wendy .... 651-450-3392. 258 H wmarson@inverhills.edu
MARSOW, Mendel .... 718-774-5050. 347 F
MARSTELLER, Diane .... 330-652-9919. 379 I dianemarsteller@eticollege.edu
MARSTELLER, Jill, A .... 610-409-3582. 436 B jmarsteller@ursinus.edu
MARSTON, Mike, B .... 208-467-8950. 139 A mmarston@nnu.edu
MARTAINDALE, Ward ...... 281-283-2255. 489 C martaindale@uhcl.edu
MARTE, Benjamin .... 518-276-6287. 337 I marteb2@rpi.edu
MARTE, Carolina .... 305-386-9900. 102 D cmarte@cci.edu
MARTEL, Ronald .... 401-598-2848. 439 B rmartel@jwu.edu
MARTELL, Donna .... 315-268-6486. 320 A dmartell@clarkson.edu
MARTELL, Kathryn .... 509-963-1955. 517 F martellk@cwu.edu
MARTELLARO, John .... 816-235-1592. 283 D martellaroj@umkc.edu
MARTELLO, John, S .... 410-594-3832. 219 D martello@umbc.edu
MARTENS, Daniel, R ...... 812-464-1799. 174 D dmartens@usi.edu
MARTENS, John .... 360-736-9391. 517 G jmartens@centralia.edu
MARTENSEN, Carsten, P 607-274-3184. 327 E cmertensen@ithaca.edu
MARTERER, Aaron, C ..... 803-777-1006. 447 G marterer@sc.edu
MARTHERS, Paul .... 518-276-6143. 337 I marthp@rpi.edu
MARTI, Dennis, N .... 216-221-8584. 392 G dmarti@vmcad.edu
MARTI, Quinn, E .... 216-221-8584. 392 G qmarti@vmcad.edu
MARTI, Tammy, S .... 563-588-7142. 180 L tammy.marti@loras.edu
MARTI, Vionet .... 787-738-2161. 554 C vionet.marti@upr.edu
MARTI-VEITH, Virginia .... 216-221-8584. 392 G vmv@vmcad.edu
MARTIN, Aaron .... 337-482-6397. 208 D aaronmartin@louisiana.edu
MARTIN, Adrienne .... 530-752-0860... 70 J almartin@ucdavis.edu
MARTIN, Alan .... 405-425-5371. 397 D alan.martin@oc.edu
MARTIN, Alan, B .... 304-293-7398. 530 D alan.martin@mail.wvu.edu
MARTIN, Allison .... 912-525-5000. 131 B amartin@scad.edu
MARTIN, Andrea .... 713-348-4661. 479 A andrea@rice.edu
MARTIN, Angela, A .... 515-574-1064. 179 D martin_a@iowacentral.edu
MARTIN, Angela, S .... 859-257-9830. 200 C angelam@uky.edu
MARTIN, Ann .... 303-964-5718... 84 M amartin@regis.edu
MARTIN, Ann .... 660-562-1570. 279 I amartin@nwmissouri.edu
MARTIN, Anna, B .... 757-221-2553. 503 N martin@wm.edu
MARTIN, Anthony .... 281-649-3152. 473 B amartin@hbu.edu
MARTIN, SR., Anthony .. 219-989-2220. 171 N anthony.martin@purduecal.edu
MARTIN, Barbara .... 802-828-2800. 501 C martinb@ccv.edu
MARTIN, Barry .... 303-273-3900... 80 E bemartin@mines.edu
MARTIN, Bethany, A .... 315-386-7555. 345 F martinb@canton.edu
MARTIN, Bobby .... 405-491-6339. 399 K bgmartin@snu.edu
MARTIN, Bonnie .... 518-255-5402. 344 E martinbg@cobleskill.edu
MARTIN, Bonnie .... 678-891-2406. 125 G bonnie.martin@gpc.edu
MARTIN, Bonnie, G .... 607-746-4495. 345 G martinbg@delhi.edu
MARTIN, Brandon .... 818-677-3208... 34 C brandon.martin@csun.edu
MARTIN, Bridgit .... 920-403-3963. 535 L bridgit.martin@snc.edu
MARTIN, Brock .... 219-785-5225. 172 A bmartin@pnc.edu
MARTIN, JR., C. Vernon .... 305-626-3714. 104 J vmartin@fmuniv.edu
MARTIN, Cameron .... 717-560-8206. 421 A cmartin@lbc.edu
MARTIN, Cameron, K ..... 801-863-8514. 497 C cameron.martin@uvu.edu
MARTIN, Carla .... 870-575-8577... 24 E martinc@uapb.edu
MARTIN, Carla .... 318-487-7750. 202 F carla.martin@lacollege.edu
MARTIN, Carmella .... 904-470-8081. 102 A carmella.martin0906@ewc.edu
MARTIN, Carolyn, R .... 804-289-8088. 510 L cmartin@richmond.edu
MARTIN, Carolyn (Biddy), A .... 413-542-2234. 221 G president@amherst.edu
MARTIN, Cecelia .... 251-460-6591..... 9 E cgmartin@southalabama.edu
MARTIN, Charles .... 340-693-1511. 555 E cmartin@live.uvi.edu
MARTIN, Charlie .... 727-376-6911. 117 I cmartin@trinitycollege.edu
MARTIN, Chonte' .... 803-705-4539. 441 C cmartin@gcaservices.com
MARTIN, Chris .... 316-677-9507. 191 E cmartin@watc.edu
MARTIN, Christa, S .... 931-540-2644. 460 E cmartin@columbiastate.edu
MARTIN, Christopher, L . 318-869-5149. 201 H cmartin@centenary.edu
MARTIN, Clara .... 843-574-6326. 447 E clara.martin@tridenttech.edu
MARTIN, Cleo .... 843-525-8203. 447 C ctmartin@tcl.edu
MARTIN, Curt .... 970-248-1396... 79 F cumartin@coloradomesa.edu
MARTIN, Curtis .... 256-372-8214..... 1 A curtis.martin@aamu.edu
MARTIN, D. Michael .... 415-380-1504... 45 H michaelmartin@ggbts.edu
MARTIN, Dale .... 318-357-4496. 208 B dale@nsula.edu
MARTIN, Dan, J .... 412-268-2349. 412 H djmartin@cmu.edu
MARTIN, Daniel .... 312-935-2016. 156 K dmartin@robertmorris.edu
MARTIN, Daniel, J .... 978-656-3134. 232 B martind@middlesex.mass.edu
MARTIN, Daniel, J .... 206-281-2114. 523 C dmartin@spu.edu
MARTIN, Dave .... 724-852-3463. 437 A dmartin@waynesburg.edu
MARTIN, David .... 423-636-7319. 462 E dmartin@tusculum.edu
MARTIN, David .... 212-787-5300. 313 F
MARTIN, David .... 414-847-3213. 534 F davidmartin@miad.edu
MARTIN, David .... 570-674-6294. 424 A dmartin@misericordia.edu
MARTIN, David .... 502-852-4653. 200 D dcmart02@louisville.edu
MARTIN, David .... 502-852-8220. 200 D dcmart02@louisville.edu
MARTIN, David .... 323-469-3300... 27 F
MARTIN, David .... 718-420-4341. 350 B dmartin@wagner.edu
MARTIN, David .... 910-893-1610. 352 K dmartin@campbell.edu
MARTIN, David, G .... 585-385-8079. 338 H dmartin@sjfc.edu
MARTIN, David, J .... 979-845-0532. 483 C david-j-martin@tamu.edu
MARTIN, David, W .... 605-394-2400. 452 A david.martin@sdsmt.edu
MARTIN, Debbie .... 973-290-4208. 300 F dmartin@cse.edu
MARTIN, Deborah .... 312-629-6800. 158 L dmartin@saic.edu
MARTIN, Deborah .... 717-477-1121. 429 E dkmart@ship.edu
MARTIN, Deidre .... 803-641-3448. 448 A deidrem@usca.edu
MARTIN, Deshun, T .... 601-979-3950. 267 E deshun.t.martin@jsums.edu
MARTIN, Desiree .... 718-409-7271. 346 D dmartin@sunymaritime.edu
MARTIN, Dewey .... 314-246-7560. 284 N deweymartin21@webster.edu
MARTIN, Diane .... 704-463-3052. 365 E diane.martin@fsmail.pfeiffer.edu
MARTIN, Diane, C .... 202-994-0513... 95 D dmartin@gwu.edu
MARTIN, Donald, L .... 706-233-7203. 131 E dmartin@shorter.edu
MARTIN, Donna, P .... 270-901-1116. 196 E donna.martin@kctcs.edu
MARTIN, Dorothy .... 229-430-4610. 119 J dorothy.martin@asurams.edu
MARTIN, Dorothy .... 207-768-2806. 210 M dmartin@nmcc.edu
MARTIN, Dorothy .... 718-429-6600. 349 H dorothy.martin@vaughn.edu
MARTIN, Dorothy, J .... 205-348-4894..... 8 D dot@ua.edu
MARTIN, Dustin .... 765-641-4150. 163 L dlmartin@anderson.edu
MARTIN, Earl, F .... 509-313-6289. 520 A martine@gonzaga.edu
MARTIN, III, Earl Joe .... 225-752-4230. 202 C jmartin@iticollege.edu
MARTIN, Edd .... 254-295-4524. 490 B emartin@umhb.edu
MARTIN, Edward .... 931-363-9832. 456 C emartin@martinmethodist.edu
MARTIN, Elaine, R .... 508-856-2399. 229 C elaine.martin@umassmed.edu
MARTIN, Elizabeth .... 906-487-7253. 242 G beth.martin@finlandia.edu
MARTIN, Emily .... 251-580-2101..... 4 L emartin@faulknerstate.edu
MARTIN, Eric .... 212-752-1530. 328 G eric.martin@limcollege.edu
MARTIN, Etienne .... 614-287-2491. 378 B emarti10@cscc.edu
MARTIN, G. Steven .... 510-642-5716... 70 I gsm@berkeley.edu
MARTIN, Geoffrey .... 419-530-1242. 392 B geoffrey.martin@utoledo.edu
MARTIN, George, E .... 512-448-8411. 479 C georgem@stedwards.edu
MARTIN, George, M .... 716-888-8208. 316 C martin@canisius.edu
MARTIN, Gerardina .... 610-738-0496. 430 A gmartin@wcupa.edu
MARTIN, Greg .... 515-964-6368. 177 B gcmartin@dmacc.edu
MARTIN, Gregg, F .... 202-685-3924. 544 K gregg.martin@ndu.edu
MARTIN, Harold, L .... 336-334-7940. 367 E hmartin@ncat.edu
MARTIN, Irene .... 860-343-5740... 89 A imartin@mxcc.commnet.edu
MARTIN, Jack .... 815-967-7302. 157 B jmartin@rockfordcareercollege.edu
MARTIN, James .... 409-747-9055. 493 C j5martin@utmb.edu
MARTIN, James, J .... 501-882-8851... 19 M jjmartin@asub.edu
MARTIN, Jan .... 323-469-3300... 27 F
MARTIN, Jan .... 212-787-5300. 313 F
MARTIN, Jana .... 918-293-5339. 398 B jana.s.martin@okstate.edu
MARTIN, Jeania .... 704-991-0114. 364 C
MARTIN, Jeanne .... 210-366-2701. 478 G
MARTIN, Jenni .... 509-279-6212. 518 E jenni.martin@scc.spokane.edu
MARTIN, Jennifer .... 940-898-3415. 488 B jmartin@twu.edu
MARTIN, Jerry .... 334-387-3877..... 1 E jerrymartin@amrdigeuniversity.edu
MARTIN, Jill .... 800-567-2344. 532 E jmartin@menominee.edu
MARTIN, Jim David .... 415-575-6165... 31 D jmartin@ciis.edu
MARTIN, Jimmy .... 832-813-6680. 476 A james.d.martin@lonestar.edu
MARTIN, Joanne .... 253-833-9111. 520 C jmartin@greenriver.edu
MARTIN, Joel, W .... 413-545-6330. 228 F jmartin@provost.umass.edu
MARTIN, John .... 916-631-8108... 32 C
MARTIN, John, A .... 585-594-6100. 337 K presidentsoffice@roberts.edu
MARTIN, John, A .... 585-594-6100. 335 B presidentsoffice@roberts.edu
MARTIN, John, O .... 413-545-0361. 228 F jomartin@admin.umass.edu
MARTIN, JR., John, R ... 817-515-7765. 482 B john.martin@tccd.edu
MARTIN, John, U .... 941-487-4444. 115 D jmartin@ncf.edu
MARTIN, Joshua .... 508-854-7513. 232 F jmartin@qcc.mass.edu
MARTIN, Joshua .... 612-343-4469. 262 X jdmartin@northcentral.edu
MARTIN, Juanita, K .... 330-972-7082. 390 E juanita@uakron.edu
MARTIN, Jules, A .... 212-998-1300. 334 D jules.martin@nyu.edu
MARTIN, Karen, O .... 912-279-5750. 123 B kmartin@ccga.edu
MARTIN, Kathleen .... 413-565-1000. 222 F kmartin@baypath.edu
MARTIN, Kathy .... 712-274-5148. 181 B martink@morningside.edu
MARTIN, Kathy .... 208-792-2282. 138 G kmartin@lcsc.edu
MARTIN, Kathy .... 704-406-4636. 354 C kmartin@gardner-webb.edu
MARTIN, Kathy .... 615-963-5254. 459 E kmartin@tnstate.edu
MARTIN, Keith .... 716-338-1261. 327 J keithmartin@mail.sunyjcc.edu
MARTIN, Keith .... 918-343-7631. 399 C kmartin@rsu.edu
MARTIN, Kelley .... 316-295-5568. 186 H kelley_martin@friends.edu
MARTIN, Kenneth .... 972-937-7612. 477 G kenneth.martin@navarrocollege.edu
MARTIN, Kenneth, M ...... 717-815-1211. 438 D kmartin@ycp.edu
MARTIN, Kevin .... 618-650-2345. 159 H kemarti@siue.edu
MARTIN, Kevin .... 302-225-6241... 93 H martink@gbc.edu
MARTIN, Kevin .... 215-407-0584. 426 Y kmartin@pafa.edu
MARTIN, Kim .... 949-794-9090... 68 D kmartin@stanbridge.edu
MARTIN, Kyle, R .... 208-496-1010. 137 H martink@byui.edu
MARTIN, Lara .... 561-237-7459. 108 X lmartin@lynn.edu
MARTIN, Laura .... 404-471-6054. 119 I lmartin@agnesscott.edu
MARTIN, Leandra .... 408-855-5182... 75 K leandra.martin@wvm.edu
MARTIN, Lee .... 419-448-2169. 380 G lmartin@heidelberg.edu
MARTIN, Linda .... 609-586-4800. 302 G martinl@mccc.edu
MARTIN, Lisa .... 504-865-3428. 205 H lmartin@loyno.edu
MARTIN, Lisa .... 918-343-7614. 399 C lmartin@rsu.edu
MARTIN, Lizbeth, J .... 510-436-1040... 47 J martin@hnu.edu
MARTIN, Lois .... 612-977-5307. 254 C lois.martin@capella.edu
MARTIN, Lonnie .... 717-560-8254. 421 A lmartin@lbc.edu
MARTIN, Louisa .... 603-668-2211. 297 I l.martin@snhu.edu
MARTIN, Louisa, A .... 210-431-5005. 479 D lmartin@stmarytx.edu
MARTIN, Luke .... 714-542-8086... 29 N lmartin@bristoluniversity.edu
MARTIN, Lynn .... 515-271-1681. 177 H lynn.martin@dmu.edu
MARTIN, Lynn .... 734-973-3507. 252 A lgmartin@wccnet.edu
MARTIN, Maggie .... 229-391-5135. 119 H mmartin@abac.edu
MARTIN, Marcus, L .... 434-243-2079. 511 B mlm8n@Virginia.EDU
MARTIN, Marie .... 651-604-4131. 257 A
MARTIN, Marie .... 803-780-1229. 449 E martin@voorhees.edu
MARTIN, Mariel, L .... 518-580-8212. 341 A mariel@skidmore.edu
MARTIN, Mark, A .... 989-837-4497. 248 C martinm@northwood.edu
MARTIN, Mary .... 802-635-1360. 501 D mary.martin@jsc.edu
MARTIN, Michael .... 408-541-0100... 40 A mmartin@cogswell.edu

MARTIN, Michael .... 212-636-6875. 324 G
mimartin@law.fordham.edu
MARTIN, Michael .... 918-647-1360. 394 I
mmartin@carlalbert.edu
MARTIN, Michaeld .... 303-534-6290... 80 H
chancellor@colostate.edu
MARTIN, Michele .... 802-586-7711. 500 E
mmartin@sterlingcollege.edu
MARTIN, Mirta, M .... 804-524-5166. 515 D
mmartin@vsu.edu
MARTIN, Mona .... 310-434-4692... 65 A
martin_mona@smc.edu
MARTIN, Nanci .... 401-456-8105. 439 F
nmartin@ric.edu
MARTIN, Pam .... 903-566-7043. 492 D
pmartin@uttyler.edu
MARTIN, Pamela .... 641-673-1182. 183 H
martinp@wmpenn.edu
MARTIN, Patrick .... 860-231-5311... 92 F
pmartin@usj.edu
MARTIN, Paul .... 510-841-1905... 27 H
pmartin@absw.edu
MARTIN, Paul .... 617-730-7155. 235 D
paul.martin@newbury.edu
MARTIN, Paul .... 518-276-8711. 337 I
martip@rpi.edu
MARTIN, Peggy Murray . 305-626-3749. 104 J
pmartin@fmuniv.edu
MARTIN, Quincy .... 708-456-0300. 161 A
qmartin@triton.edu
MARTIN, R. Brad .... 901-678-2234. 460 B
president@memphis.edu
MARTIN, Rafael .... 972-883-4824. 491 E
rafael.martin@utdallas.edu
MARTIN, Randy .... 870-972-2093... 19 N
rmartin@astate.edu
MARTIN, Ray .... 254-295-4590. 490 B
rmartin@umhb.edu
MARTIN, Richard, D .... 706-776-0105. 130 E
dmartin@piedmont.edu
MARTIN, Robert .... 202-885-8611... 97 D
rmartin@wesleyseminary.edu
MARTIN, Robert .... 508-626-4575. 230 A
rmartin@framingham.edu
MARTIN, Robert .... 810-766-8756. 239 H
robert.martin@baker.edu
MARTIN, Robert .... 505-424-2302. 309 J
rmartin@iaia.edu
MARTIN, Robert .... 845-758-7419. 314 D
martin@bard.edu
MARTIN, Robert, E .... 303-233-4697... 80 F
rm@schooloftrades.edu
MARTIN, Robert, K .... 217-581-5983. 144 E
rmartin@eiu.edu
MARTIN, Ron .... 618-262-8641. 147 C
martinr@iecc.edu
MARTIN, Ron .... 417-690-3248. 272 E
martin@cofo.edu
MARTIN, Ronald, C .... 814-732-2743. 428 E
martinr@edinboro.edu
MARTIN, Roneida .... 847-543-2641. 143 A
rmartin@clcillinois.edu
MARTIN, Rosalynn .... 256-782-5007..... 4 K
martin@jsu.edu
MARTIN, Roy, J .... 225-578-2284. 204 O
rjmartin@lsu.edu
MARTIN, Ruth .... 619-201-8685... 62 B
Ruth.Martin@sdcc.edu
MARTIN, Ryan .... 201-360-4024. 302 D
rmartin@hccc.edu
MARTIN, Ryan .... 360-779-9993. 521 C
rmartin@ncad.edu
MARTIN, Sally, L .... 920-498-6866. 541 B
sally.martin@nwtc.edu
MARTIN, Scott .... 706-355-5037. 120 J
smartin@athenstech.edu
MARTIN, Shana .... 714-556-3610... 74 D
shana.martin@vanguard.edu
MARTIN, Shane .... 310-338-7457... 53 E
smartin@lmu.edu
MARTIN, Sharon, L .... 304-293-0111. 530 D
MARTIN, Shirley .... 901-320-9700. 463 J
smartin@victory.edu
MARTIN, Staci .... 903-983-8200. 475 E
smartin@kilgore.edu
MARTIN, Susan .... 415-749-4533... 62 G
smartin@sfai.edu
MARTIN, Susan .... 502-863-8407. 194 C
susan_martin@georgetowncollege.edu
MARTIN, Susan, D .... 865-974-2445. 463 C
sdmartin@utk.edu
MARTIN, Susan, M .... 630-942-3324. 142 G
martinsu@cod.edu
MARTIN, Susan, W .... 734-487-2211. 242 D
sue.martin@emich.edu
MARTIN, Susie .... 310-377-5501... 53 F
smartin@marymountcalifornia.edu
MARTIN, Suzanne .... 985-448-7945. 203 B
suzanne.martin@fletcher.edu
MARTIN, Terry .... 225-675-8270. 203 G
tmartin@rpcc.edu
MARTIN, Terry .... 318-487-7201. 202 F
terry.martin@lacollege.edu
MARTIN, Thomas, K .... 972-758-3817. 469 G
tmartin@collin.edu
MARTIN, Timothy, J .... 515-574-1097. 179 D
martin@iowacentral.edu
MARTIN, Timothy, R .... 508-767-7373. 222 C
timartin@assumption.edu
MARTIN, Tod, J .... 402-363-5678. 293 I
tjmartin@york.edu
MARTIN, Tom .... 361-593-3419. 484 A
katdm00@tamuk.edu
MARTIN, Tony, L .... 336-386-3222. 364 D
martint@surry.edu
MARTIN, Traci .... 410-337-6191. 215 A
tmartin@goucher.edu
MARTIN, Traycee, F .... 229-333-5708. 134 B
tmartin@valdosta.edu
MARTIN, Troy .... 716-375-2373. 338 E
MARTIN, Valerie, G .... 570-372-4288. 433 H
vmartin@susqu.edu
MARTIN, Vicki, J .... 414-297-7269. 540 E
martinv@matc.edu
MARTIN, Victor .... 661-654-2222... 32 H
vmartin4@csub.edu
MARTIN, Walter .... 919-866-5385. 364 G
wmartin@waketech.edu
MARTIN, Wayne .... 540-453-2347. 511 H
martinw@brcc.edu
MARTIN, Wendy .... 207-859-1101. 211 H
martinw@thomas.edu
MARTIN, Wendy .... 909-607-0723... 39 C
wendy.martin@cgu.edu
MARTIN, William .... 225-675-8270. 203 G
bmartin@rpcc.edu
MARTIN-HALL, Margaret 870-575-8702... 24 E
hallm@uapb.edu
MARTIN II, Ralph, C .... 617-373-2101. 235 F
MARTIN-OSORIO,
Carol, J .... 615-353-3268. 461 B
carol.martin-osorio@nscc.edu
MARTIN PALMER,
Barbara .... 301-447-5371. 217 B
palmer@msmary.edu
MARTIN-REND, Jill .... 814-653-8265. 411 C
jill.martin-rend@bc3.edu
MARTIN-SCHRAMM,
Karen, B .... 563-387-1527. 180 M
marschka@luther.edu
MARTIN TSE, Jennifer .... 315-464-4604. 342 E
martinj@upstate.edu
MARTIN-VEGA, Louis, A 919-515-2311. 368 B
louis_martin-vega@ncsu.edu
MARTINEAU, Jim .... 503-594-3271. 402 F
jmartineau@clackamas.edu
MARTINEAU, Tammy ...... 386-752-1822. 104 G
tammy.martineau@fgc.edu
MARTINELLI, Joseph, I .. 301-336-6000. 217 F
jmartinelli@pgcc.edu
MARTINELLI, Joseph, L . 301-322-0417. 217 F
martinjl@pgcc.edu
MARTINELLI, Robert, J .. 916-558-2120... 53 D
martinr@scc.losrios.edu
MARTINELLI-FERNANDEZ,
Susan .... 309-298-1828. 162 K
martinelli-fernandez@wiu.edu
MARTINESI, Anthony ...... 718-390-3165. 350 B
tmartine@wagner.edu
MARTINETTI, Roseann .... 570-702-8919. 419 G
rmartinetti@johnson.edu
MARTINEZ, Abelardo ...... 787-276-8240. 554 B
abelardo.martinez@upr.edu
MARTINEZ, Carla .... 714-432-5741... 39 K
cmartinez@occ.cccd.edu
MARTINEZ, Carlos .... 817-531-4959. 488 A
cmartinez@txwes.edu
MARTINEZ, Carmella ...... 505-747-2118. 311 E
carmella@nnmc.edu
MARTINEZ, Carriann ...... 719-549-3056... 84 G
carriann.martinez@pueblocc.edu
MARTINEZ, Carriann ...... 719-549-3080... 84 G
carriann.martinez@pueblocc.edu
MARTINEZ, Cristina .... 830-792-7281. 480 F
cimartinez@schreiner.edu
MARTINEZ, Daniel .... 951-222-8000... 61 A
MARTINEZ, David .... 718-960-8545. 318 A
david.martinez@lehman.cuny.edu
MARTINEZ, Debra .... 787-284-1912. 550 F
dmartinez@ponce.inter.edu
MARTINEZ, Denise .... 920-735-5795. 539 K
martinez@fvtc.edu
MARTINEZ, Didit .... 806-743-2900. 487 E
didit.martinez@ttuhsc.edu
MARTINEZ, Dolly .... 718-518-4300. 318 B
dmartinez@hostos.cuny.edu
MARTINEZ, Dominic .... 303-724-8004... 86 A
dominic.martinez@ucdenver.edu
MARTINEZ, Elena, M ...... 956-326-2433. 483 B
emartinez@tamiu.edu
MARTINEZ, Elizabeth ...... 956-326-2335. 483 B
elizabeth@tamiu.edu
MARTINEZ, Elizabeth, N . 956-326-2380. 483 B
enmartinez@tamiu.edu
MARTINEZ, Erlinda, J .... 714-564-6975... 60 G
martinez_erlinda@sac.edu
MARTINEZ, Everardo ...... 928-314-9422... 11 L
everardo.martinez@azwestern.edu
MARTINEZ, JR., Frank ... 610-341-5934. 415 G
eastern@bkstr.com
MARTINEZ, Freddie .... 787-841-2000. 552 B
fmartinez@pucpr.edu
MARTINEZ, Geraldine ...... 575-527-7710. 311 B
gerri66@nmsu.edu
MARTINEZ, German .... 609-497-7778. 304 D
facilities-security@ptsem.edu
MARTINEZ, Heather .... 806-742-7017. 487 D
heather.martinez@ttu.edu
MARTINEZ, Hector .... 787-284-1912. 550 F
hmartin@ponce.inter.edu
MARTINEZ, Hiram, G ...... 717-872-3787. 429 D
hiram.martinez@millersville.edu
MARTINEZ, Javier .... 787-863-2390. 550 C
javier.martinez@fajardo.inter.edu
MARTINEZ, Javier .... 956-882-8252. 491 D
javier.martinez@utb.edu
MARTINEZ, Jeffrey .... 909-748-8411... 73 H
jeffrey_martinez@redlands.edu
MARTINEZ, Jeremy .... 432-685-5523. 476 G
jmartinez@midland.edu
MARTINEZ, Jerry .... 970-943-3026... 86 I
jMartinez@western.edu
MARTINEZ, Jesus .... 787-738-2161. 554 C
jesus.martinez5@upr.edu
MARTINEZ, Jesus, J ...... 830-591-7234. 481 C
jjmartinez1060@swtjc.edu
MARTINEZ, Jody .... 574-807-7345. 164 D
martinj@bethelcollege.edu
MARTINEZ, Jose .... 417-624-7070. 476 F
jmartinez@messengercollege.edu
MARTINEZ, Juan, F .... 787-279-2220. 550 B
jmartinez@bayamon.inter.edu
MARTINEZ, Kara .... 806-894-9611. 480 H
kmartinez@southplainscollege.edu
MARTINEZ, Karol .... 410-225-2284. 216 C
kmartinez@mica.edu
MARTINEZ, Kim .... 303-457-2757... 81 L
kmartinez@cci.edu
MARTINEZ, Leticia .... 928-344-7644... 11 L
leticia.martinez@azwestern.edu
MARTINEZ, Leticia .... 817-272-2099. 491 B
martinezlc@uta.edu
MARTINEZ, Leticia .... 787-264-1912. 551 A
letmarti@sg.inter.edu
MARTINEZ, Liane .... 305-348-2790. 115 B
liane.martinez@fiu.edu
MARTINEZ, Lisa .... 903-468-8175. 483 E
lisa.martinez@tamuc.edu
MARTINEZ, Loretta, P .... 303-556-3022... 83 D
lpmartin@msudenver.edu
MARTINEZ, Lorna .... 787-766-1717. 552 J
lomartinez@suagm.edu
MARTINEZ, Luis .... 787-766-1717. 552 J
um_lmartinez@suagm.edu
MARTINEZ, Luis .... 520-494-5446... 12 P
luis.martinez@centralaz.edu
MARTINEZ, Luz .... 787-664-0489. 555 C
luz.martinez6@upr.edu
MARTINEZ, Marco .... 915-532-3737. 494 J
mmartinez@westerntech.edu
MARTINEZ, Maria .... 407-646-2003. 111 Q
mmartinez@rollins.edu
MARTINEZ, Maria .... 787-751-0178. 552 G
ac_mmartinez@suagm.edu
MARTINEZ, Maria .... 918-465-1711. 395 G
mmartinez@eosc.edu
MARTINEZ, Maria, D ...... 860-486-4040... 92 A
maria.d.martinez@uconn.edu
MARTINEZ, Maria, L ...... 909-869-2373... 32 G
mlmartinez@csupomona.edu
MARTINEZ, Maria Gil ...... 787-264-1912. 551 A
magil@sg.inter.edu
MARTINEZ, Marilyn .... 787-863-2390. 550 C
marilyn.martinez@fajardo.inter.edu
MARTINEZ, Martha .... 615-297-7545. 452 J
martinezm@aquinascollege.edu
MARTINEZ, Marvin .... 323-265-8662... 51 F
martinmr@elac.edu
MARTINEZ, Melba .... 787-764-0000. 555 B
melba.martinez@upr.edu
MARTINEZ, Michael .... 610-896-1293. 418 F
mmartinez@haverford.edu
MARTINEZ, Mike .... 575-624-7116. 309 I
mike.martinez@roswell.enmu.edu
MARTINEZ, Miriam .... 787-284-1912. 550 F
mmartine@ponce.inter.edu
MARTINEZ, Nina .... 502-456-6505. 199 G
nmartinez@sullivan.edu
MARTINEZ, Paula .... 303-556-3991... 83 D
martipau@msudenver.edu
MARTINEZ, Pedro, I .... 787-844-8181. 555 A
pedro.imartinez@upr.edu
MARTINEZ, Phil .... 951-343-4346... 30 H
pmartine@calbaptist.edu
MARTINEZ, Ramiro, V .... 956-721-5111. 475 F
ramiro.martinez@laredo.edu
MARTINEZ, Ramon .... 787-738-2161. 554 C
ramon.martinez2@upr.edu
MARTINEZ, Renee, D ...... 323-953-4000... 51 G
martinrd@lacitycollege.edu
MARTINEZ, Richard .... 626-812-3002... 29 H
rsmartinez@apu.edu
MARTINEZ, Robert .... 719-589-7035... 85 H
robert.martinez@trinidadstate.edu
MARTINEZ, Roman .... 305-237-0012. 109 D
rmartin9@mdc.edu
MARTINEZ, Rosa, J .... 787-864-2222. 550 D
rjmartin@inter.edu
MARTINEZ, Rosalia .... 787-841-2000. 552 B
rosalia.martinez@pucpr.edu
MARTINEZ, Rosemary ...... 956-882-8240. 491 D
rosemary.martinez@utb.edu
MARTINEZ, Ruben, O ...... 407-303-9372... 97 H
ruben.martinez@adu.edu
MARTINEZ, Santos .... 702-651-5750. 294 E
santos.martinez@csn.edu
MARTINEZ, Sara .... 787-720-4476. 553 D
registraduria@mizpa.edu
MARTINEZ, Sara .... 915-831-7792. 472 B
smart237@epcc.edu
MARTINEZ, Sonia .... 303-300-8740... 78 M
sonia.martinez@collegeamerica.com
MARTINEZ, Tara .... 612-659-6761. 259 D
tara.martinez@minneapolis.edu
MARTINEZ, Veronica ...... 408-848-4725... 45 F
vmartinez@gavilan.edu
MARTINEZ, Vesta, M ...... 817-515-7795. 482 B
vesta.martinez@tccd.edu
MARTINEZ, Vidal .... 505-454-5378. 309 L
vmartinez@luna.edu
MARTINEZ, Xochitl, E .... 909-593-3511... 72 E
xmartinez@laverne.edu
MARTINEZ, Yuli .... 619-201-8953... 67 G
Yuli.Martinez@socalsem.edu
MARTINEZ, Yvonne .... 480-990-3773... 14 H
MARTINEZ, Yvonne .... 505-224-3232. 309 E
ymartinez@cnm.edu
MARTINEZ-ABREU,
Heriberto .... 787-720-1022. 547 E
martinezabreu@atlanticcollege.edu
MARTINEZ-BROOKS,
Jessica .... 405-682-1611. 397 E
jmbrooks@occc.edu
MARTINEZ-DE DIOS,
Heriberto .... 787-720-0596. 547 E
hmartinez@atlanticcollege.edu
MARTINEZ-LASSO,
Miguel, A .... 915-831-2847. 472 B
mmart722@epcc.edu
MARTINEZ-LUGO,
Miguel .... 787-725-6500. 547 H
mmartinez@albizu.edu
MARTINEZ-SANCHEZ,
Mary Ann .... 520-206-4684... 17 A
mamsanchez@pima.edu
MARTINEZ STLUKA,
Rena .... 714-992-7077... 56 F
rmartinezstluka@fullcoll.edu
MARTINEZ-YADEN,
Camille .... 520-383-8401... 18 B
MARTINI, Barbara, M ...... 814-371-6920. 415 C
mainc@dbcollege.edu
MARTINI, Louis .... 609-777-5696. 308 A
lmartini@tesc.edu
MARTINO, Andrew .... 603-668-2211. 297 I
a.martino@snhu.edu
MARTINO, Bill .... 212-592-2000. 340 H
wmartino@sva.edu
MARTINO, Dolores, E .... 610-359-7349. 414 D
dmartino@dccc.edu
MARTINO, Gregory .... 215-972-2079. 426 Y
gmartino@pafa.edu
MARTINOV, William .... 914-674-7318. 330 J
wmartinov@mercy.edu
MARTINSEN, Daniel .... 254-299-8333. 476 D
dmartinsen@mclennan.edu
MARTINSEN, Michael ...... 937-775-2056. 393 G
michael.martinsen@wright.edu
MARTINSEN, Sarah .... 907-852-3333... 10 F
sarah.martinsen@ilisagvik.edu
MARTINSON, Caroline .... 502-213-5010. 195 F
caroline.martinson@kctcs.edu
MARTINSON, David, O .... 479-575-6291... 23 I
dom@uark.edu
MARTLAND, Paul .... 860-412-7381... 89 E
pmartland@qvcc.commnet.edu
MARTLEW, Jeffre .... 813-419-5100. 250 G
martlewj@cooley.edu
MARTNER, James, E ...... 630-942-2543. 142 G
martner@cod.edu
MARTON, Nate, R .... 716-880-2549. 330 F
nathan.r.marton@medaille.edu

MARTONE, John ... 973-720-2179. 308 I
martonej@wpunj.edu
MARTONI, Charles ... 724-325-6650. 413 D
cmartoni@ccac.edu
MARTORANA,
Anne Marie ... 617-879-2231. 238 C
amartorana@wheelock.edu
MARTORANA, Lorraine .. 410-287-1030. 214 B
lmartorana@cecil.edu
MARTS, Chad ... 757-490-1241. 501 G
cmarts@auto.edu
MARTUCCI, Ronald ... 201-684-7758. 305 A
rmartucc@ramapo.edu
MARTY, Angela, L ... 630-515-6120. 153 B
amarty@midwestern.edu
MARTYN, Margaret ... 312-553-5922. 141 N
mmartyn1@ccc.edu
MARTYN, Nancy ... 503-375-7590. 403 A
nmartyn@corban.edu
MARTZ, Jill ... 406-994-3293. 287 B
jmartz@montana.edu
MARTZ, Scott ... 909-599-5433... 50 J
maintenance@lifepacific.edu
MARTZ, Thomas ... 207-973-1065. 210 B
martzt@husson.edu
MARTZ, Tim ... 517-483-1813. 245 H
martzt@lcc.edu
MARTZEN, Mark ... 425-602-3162. 516 K
mmartzen@bastyr.edu
MARTÍNEZ, Luz, E ... 787-894-2828. 555 C
luz.martinez6@upr.edu
MARTÍNEZ, Miriam, D ... 787-250-0000. 553 G
miriam.martinez3@upr.edu
MARTÍNEZ-BARRIOS,
Abdiel ... 787-993-8881. 554 A
abdiel.martinez1@upr.edu
MARUCHA, Phillip, T ... 503-494-8801. 405 I
marucha@ohsu.edu
MARUS, Elisa ... 901-321-4417. 453 H
emarus@cbu.edu
MARUSCHOCK, George .. 412-747-7800... 96 F
MARVEL, Debra ... 352-365-3571. 108 S
marveld@lssc.edu
MARVIN, Benjamin ... 518-454-5102. 321 A
marvinb@strose.edu
MARVIN, Corey ... 760-384-6201... 49 O
cmarvin@cerrocoso.edu
MARVIN, Kerry, A ... 913-360-7621. 184 H
kmarvin@benedictine.edu
MARVIN, Kim ... 817-461-8741. 466 D
kmarvin@arlingtonbaptistcollege.edu
MARVUGLIO, Matt ... 617-266-1400. 223 D
MARWICK, Judith ... 847-925-6290. 145 H
jmarwick@harpercollege.edu
MARX, Christopher ... 845-802-7167. 348 H
marxc@sunyulster.edu
MARX, Lew, D ... 563-333-6186. 182 B
MarxLewisD@sau.edu
MARX, Lisa ... 410-778-7261. 221 C
lmarx2@washcoll.edu
MARX, Ronald, W ... 520-621-1081... 18 F
ronmarx@email.arizona.edu
MARX, Tracy, W ... 502-231-5221. 197 E
president@myLBC.us
MARYANSKI, Elizabeth ... 850-644-1000. 115 C
lizm@fsu.edu
MARZANO, Maria ... 212-517-0428. 330 E
mmarzano@mmm.edu
MARZANO, William ... 630-466-7900. 162 J
wmarzano@waubonsee.edu
MARZCAK, Kelly ... 906-932-4231. 242 I
kellym@gogebic.edu
MARZION, Michael, J ... 414-229-4627. 537 A
marzion@uwm.edu
MARZITELLI, Ronald ... 518-464-8500. 324 B
marzitelli@excelsor.edu
MARZOLF, Donna ... 507-389-7326. 261 E
donna.marzolf@southcentral.edu
MAS, Desander ... 212-410-8086. 333 E
Dmas@nycpm.edu
MAS, Nestor ... 787-257-7373. 552 H
ue_nestor@suagm.edu
MASAR, Patrick ... 620-241-0723. 185 K
MASCARO, Juan ... 828-884-8108. 352 I
mascarjc@brevard.edu
MASCARO, Maria, S ... 787-841-2000. 552 B
exaluminos@pucpr.edu
MASCH, Michael ... 718-862-7356. 329 M
michael.masch@manhattan.edu
MASCHMAN, Greg, D ... 402-465-2116. 291 G
gdm@nebrwesleyan.edu
MASCIANTONIO, John ... 215-596-8531. 435 H
j.mascia@usciences.edu
MASCOLO, Marc ... 912-344-2506. 120 G
marc.mascolo@armstrong.edu
MASEK, Phyllis, J ... 573-592-5213. 285 B
phyllis.masek@westminster-mo.edu
MASELBAS, Amanda ... 303-477-7240... 82 C
amandam@heritage-education.com
MASELLA, Joanne ... 561-803-2827. 110 B
joanne_masella@pba.edu
MASENTHIN, Kim ... 262-243-5700. 532 H
kim.masenthin@cuw.edu
MASER, Jill ... 302-736-2521... 94 C
maserjil@wesley.edu
MASH, David ... 617-266-1400. 223 D
MASH, David ... 864-388-8320. 444 K
dmash@lander.edu
MASH, Ron ... 740-753-6079. 380 K
mash_r@hocking.edu
MASHBURN, Scott ... 423-746-5203. 462 C
smashburn@twcnet.edu
MASHETT, Jayne ... 215-248-7020. 413 A
mashettj@chc.edu
MASHLAN, Alexa ... 405-682-1611. 397 E
amashlan@occc.edu
MASI, Jessica ... 207-216-4401. 211 C
jmasi@yccc.edu
MASICH, David ... 843-953-1835. 443 A
masichd@cofc.edu
MASINI, Blase, E ... 773-442-4890. 154 H
b-masini@neiu.edu
MASINI, Marco ... 630-829-6006. 140 B
mmasini@ben.edu
MASIUK, Wendy ... 413-755-4211. 233 A
wmasiuk@stcc.edu
MASKEY, Cynthia, L ... 217-786-2436. 151 F
cynthia.maskey@llcc.edu
MASLAR, David, R ... 607-778-5033. 315 I
maslardr@sunybroome.edu
MASLIN, Adrienne ... 860-343-5759... 89 A
amaslin@mxcc.commnet.edu
MASLOWSKY, Craig ... 518-464-8500. 324 B
cmaslowsky@excelsior.edu
MASLYN, Dave ... 401-874-4602. 440 D
dcm@uri.edu
MASO, Marta, E ... 773-442-5210. 154 H
m-maso@neiu.edu
MASO-FLEISHMAN,
Roberta ... 619-477-6310... 70 D
rmaso-fleishman@usuniversity.edu
MASON, Amy ... 304-457-1700. 526 A
masonar@ab.edu
MASON, Andrea ... 585-340-9632. 320 E
amason@crcds.edu
MASON, April, C ... 785-532-6224. 188 A
masona@ksu.edu
MASON, Brenda, A ... 304-457-6385. 526 A
masonba@ab.edu
MASON, Cameran ... 781-283-2223. 237 F
cmason@wellesley.edu
MASON, Chip ... 601-968-8945. 266 A
cmason@belhaven.edu
MASON, Cyndi ... 724-222-5330. 425 K
cmason@penncommercial.edu
MASON, Dan, J ... 641-422-4281. 181 D
masondan@niacc.edu
MASON, Deborah, P ... 513-529-2346. 384 G
masonda@miamioh.edu
MASON, Doug, R ... 208-496-3405. 137 H
masond@byui.edu
MASON, Geri ... 402-557-7020. 288 G
geri.mason@bellevue.edu
MASON, Gregory ... 410-986-3220. 213 F
gmason@bccc.edu
MASON, Holly ... 740-366-9172. 376 A
hmason@cotc.edu
MASON, J. Mike ... 208-732-6203. 138 B
mmason@csi.edu
MASON, Jeff ... 678-359-5573. 127 A
jeffreym@gordonstate.edu
MASON, Jenifer, R ... 870-972-3964... 19 N
jrmason@astate.edu
MASON, Jeremy ... 601-877-6114. 265 G
jmason@alcorn.edu
MASON, John, M ... 334-844-4784... 1 G
jmm0027@auburn.edu
MASON, Linda ... 423-585-6809. 462 A
linda.mason@ws.edu
MASON, Mary Ellen ... 410-777-2707. 213 D
memason@aacc.edu
MASON, Mary Jo ... 203-371-7955... 91 C
masonm@sacredheart.edu
MASON, Matthew ... 717-560-8254. 421 A
mmason@lbc.edu
MASON, Orenthia ... 903-593-8311. 485 A
omason@texascollege.edu
MASON, Phil ... 912-279-5710. 123 B
pmason@ccga.edu
MASON, Rachel ... 562-860-2451... 37 I
rmason@cerritos.edu
MASON, Rick ... 606-242-0138. 196 F
rick.mason@kctcs.edu
MASON, Rochelle ... 719-389-6800... 79 D
rmason@coloradocollege.edu
MASON, Ron ... 203-837-8736... 88 B
masonr@wcsu.edu
MASON, Ronald, E ... 203-582-3950... 91 A
ronaldv.p.mason@quinnipiac.edu
MASON, JR., Ronald, F . 225-771-4680. 206 I
ronald_mason@sus.edu
MASON, JR., Russell, D 701-627-4738. 371 A
rmason@fbcc.bia.edu
MASON, Sally ... 319-335-3549. 175 I
sally-mason@uiowa.edu
MASON, Stephen ... 502-597-6260. 197 A
stephen.mason@kysu.edu
MASON, Stephen ... 803-793-5155. 443 E
masons@denmarltech.edu
MASON, Steven, D ... 903-233-3230. 475 J
stevenmason@letu.edu
MASON, Tamra ... 505-224-4000. 309 E
tmason@cnm.edu
MASON, Terry, W ... 515-294-0153. 175 H
oriole@iastate.edu
MASON, Thelma ... 212-650-5816. 317 D
tmason@ccny.cuny.edu
MASON, Tisa ... 785-628-4277. 186 F
tmason@fhsu.edu
MASON, Traci ... 352-873-5808. 100 K
masont@cf.edu
MASON, Zed ... 562-985-5314... 33 F
zed.mason@csulb.edu
MASON JENNINGS,
Martha ... 269-749-7644. 249 A
mjennings@olivetcollege.edu
MASON-KINSEY,
Natalie, L ... 718-951-4128. 317 C
nmasonkinsey@brooklyn.cuny.edu
MASOUM, Nazi ... 949-794-9090... 68 D
nazim@stanbridge.edu
MASS, Gregory ... 973-596-5745. 303 G
mass@njit.edu
MASSA, Gary, R ... 513-745-3335. 393 H
massag@xavier.edu
MASSA, Laurie ... 216-397-4661. 381 R
lmassa@jcu.edu
MASSA, Robert, J ... 610-330-5120. 420 D
massar@lafayette.edu
MASSA, Tina ... 518-587-2100. 346 A
tina.massa@esc.edu
MASSANO, Donna, R ... 508-999-8043. 229 A
dmassano@umassd.edu
MASSARI, Lydia, I ... 787-751-0178. 552 G
ac_lmassari@suagm.edu
MASSARI, Mark ... 805-893-3400... 72 B
mark.massari@athletics.ucsb.edu
MASSARO, Chris, J ... 615-898-2450. 459 D
chris.massaro@mtsu.edu
MASSARO, Patrick, W ... 724-287-8711. 411 C
patrick.massaro@bc3.edu
MASSARO, SJ, Thomas . 510-549-5040... 64 M
tmassaro@jstb.edu
MASSARO, Vincent ... 914-395-2314. 340 E
vmassaro@sarahlawrence.edu
MASSARONI, Larry ... 914-606-7895. 350 F
larry.massaroni@sunywcc.edu
MASSE, Carol ... 414-847-3270. 534 F
carolmasse@miad.edu
MASSE, Raymond ... 207-755-5258. 210 J
rmasse@cmcc.edu
MASSE, Thomas, G ... 386-822-8950. 117 C
thomas.masse@stetson.edu
MASSE, Wendy ... 860-434-5232... 90 F
wmasse@lymeacademy.edu
MASSELL, Laura ... 802-654-0532. 501 C
laura.massell@mail.ccv.vsc.edu
MASSENA, Deborah ... 618-235-2700. 160 A
deborah.massena@swic.edu
MASSENA, James, R ... 269-471-3307. 239 D
massenaj@andrews.edu
MASSENA, John ... 618-664-7130. 145 G
john.massena@greenville.edu
MASSENBURG, Gerald ... 973-353-5541. 306 D
geraldm@andromeda.rutgers.edu
MASSEY, Anne ... 812-855-1610. 167 F
amassey@indiana.edu
MASSEY, April ... 202-274-5194... 97 A
amassey@udc.edu
MASSEY, David ... 503-883-2259. 404 A
dmassey@linfield.edu
MASSEY, Dennis ... 252-493-7220. 362 G
dmassey@email.pittcc.edu
MASSEY, Diane ... 610-647-4400. 418 I
dmassey@immaculata.edu
MASSEY, Edwin, R ... 772-462-4701. 106 P
emassey@irsc.edu
MASSEY, Gary ... 573-875-7756. 272 G
gamassey@ccis.edu
MASSEY, Janet ... 610-358-4260. 424 I
jmassey@neumann.edu
MASSEY, Jeff ... 318-487-7386. 202 F
jeff.massey@lacollege.edu
MASSEY, Laura ... 971-722-7700. 407 D
laura.massey@pcc.edu
MASSEY, Marge ... 972-279-6511. 465 F
mmassey@amberton.edu
MASSEY, Michael ... 919-209-2087. 361 E
mtmassey@johnstoncc.edu
MASSEY, Pamela, L ... 501-450-3237... 25 H
pamm@uca.edu
MASSEY, Perry, A ... 910-672-1475. 367 D
pmassey@uncfsu.edu
MASSEY, Rufus ... 706-368-6945. 121 G
wmassey@berry.edu
MASSEY, Sandra ... 870-512-7841... 20 B
sandra_massey@asun.edu
MASSEY, Therisa ... 281-873-0262. 469 H
library@commonwealth.edu
MASSEY, Thomas, P ... 508-793-7408. 225 A
tmassey@clarku.edu
MASSEY, Walter, E ... 312-899-5136. 158 L
wmassey@saic.edu
MASSEY, Walter, T ... 404-413-3407. 126 E
wmassey@gsu.edu
MASSI, Christopher, A ... 301-846-2479. 214 H
cmassi@frederick.edu
MASSIE, Chase ... 580-581-2245. 394 G
cmassie@cameron.edu
MASSIE, Laura ... 330-972-6476. 390 E
massie1@uakron.edu
MASSIE, Maribeth ... 207-221-4519. 213 A
bmassie@une.edu
MASSIE, Patricia ... 606-759-7141. 196 B
patee.massie@kctcs.edu
MASSIS, Bruce ... 614-287-2461. 378 B
bmassis@cscc.edu
MASSMAN, Joseph ... 816-654-7105. 275 K
jmassman@kcumb.edu
MASSOELS, William ... 219-866-6184. 172 E
billm@saintjoe.edu
MASSOGLIA, Mike ... 336-734-7177. 360 E
mmassoglia@forsythtech.edu
MASSON, Mary ... 802-654-2234. 500 B
mmasson@smcvt.edu
MAST, Amy, H ... 330-684-8982. 390 F
amast1@uakron.edu
MAST, Brian ... 615-966-1052. 456 B
brian.mast@lipscomb.edu
MAST, Gregg, A ... 732-247-5241. 303 E
gmast@nbts.edu
MAST, Maura ... 617-287-6330. 228 G
maura.mast@umb.edu
MAST, Russell, F ... 229-333-5941. 134 B
rmast@valdosta.edu
MAST HEWITT, Marilyn . 630-620-2136. 155 A
registrar@seminary.edu
MAST HEWITT,
Marilyn, R ... 630-620-2196. 155 A
registrar@seminary.edu
MASTANDUNO, Michael 603-646-3999. 296 G
michael.mastanduno@dartmouth.edu
MASTELLER, John, Q ... 805-525-4417... 69 H
jmasteller@thomasaquinas.edu
MASTELLER, Rod ... 318-487-7118. 202 F
rod.masteller@lacollege.edu
MASTER, Jonathan, L ... 215-702-4358. 411 F
jmaster@cairn.edu
MASTERNAK, Donald ... 517-629-0350. 239 A
dmasternak@albion.edu
MASTERS, Bradley ... 318-345-9239. 203 C
bmasters@ladelta.edu
MASTERS, Brenda ... 405-744-7135. 397 H
brenda.masters@okstate.edu
MASTERS, Carolynn, B ... 814-871-7401. 416 K
masters004@gannon.edu
MASTERS, Deborah, C ... 415-338-1681... 35 E
dmasters@sfsu.edu
MASTERS, Debra, G ... 405-466-2952. 395 N
dgmasters@langston.edu
MASTERS, Janelle ... 701-224-5525. 372 B
janelle.masters@bismarckstate.edu
MASTERS, Karen ... 617-296-8300. 227 I
karen_masters@laboure.edu
MASTERS, Michael ... 706-272-4461. 123 G
mmasters@daltonstate.edu
MASTERS, Rebecca ... 803-323-2225. 449 G
mastersr@winthrop.edu
MASTERS, Sarah, L ... 818-364-7788... 52 A
masterss@lamission.edu
MASTERSON, Ana ... 928-757-0803... 15 L
amasterson@mohave.edu
MASTERSON, Anne ... 313-664-7463. 241 C
amasterson@collegeforcreativestudies.edu
MASTERSON, Christine .. 425-602-3015. 516 K
cmasters@bastyr.edu
MASTERSON, John, A ... 620-365-5116. 183 I
masterson@allencc.edu
MASTERSON, Lisanne ... 828-694-1806. 358 C
lmasterson@blueridge.edu
MASTERSON, Michael, J 334-953-8126. 544 D
michael.masterson.4@us.af.mil
MASTERSON, Robert ... 559-730-3862... 40 I
bobm@cos.edu
MASTERTON, Bob ... 603-623-0313. 297 E
bobmasterton@nhia.edu
MASTRANGELO, Joseph 212-799-5000. 328 B
MASTRE, Tom, M ... 831-656-1095. 544 M
tmastre@nps.edu
MASTRO, Steve ... 707-654-1074... 31 I
smastro@csum.edu

MASTROIANNI, Michael 815-921-2195. 157 A
m.mastroianni@rockvalleycollege.edu
MASTROMONICO, Jeff ... 803-641-2837. 448 A
jeffm@usca.edu
MASUCCI, Michele .... 215-204-6875. 433 K
michele.masucci@temple.edu
MASUD, Abu .... 316-978-3285. 191 F
abu.masud@wichita.edu
MASUDA, Walter .... 530-741-6761... 77 M
wmasuda@yccd.edu
MASULLO, Sharon .... 215-567-7080. 410 A
smasullo@edmc.edu
MASUTANI, Carol .... 808-734-9528. 136 E
masutani@hawaii.edu
MATA, Armando .... 773-907-4350. 142 A
amata@ccc.edu
MATA, Cindy .... 956-364-4647. 485 H
cindy.mata@tstc.edu
MATA, Heloise .... 831-443-1700... 47 D
heloise_mata@heald.edu
MATA, Margaret .... 325-942-2012. 465 K
margaret.mata@angelo.edu
MATA, Margot .... 830-591-7223. 481 C
mhmata@swtjc.edu
MATACHEK, John .... 651-523-2252. 256 A
jmatachek@hamline.edu
MATAGI, Lorraine .... 808-675-3542. 135 C
matagil@byuh.edu
MATANYI, Eric .... 708-209-3255. 143 E
eric.mantanyi@cuchicago.edu
MATASAR, Richard, A .... 212-998-7041. 334 D
richard.matasar@nyu.edu
MATASSINO, Dana .... 610-409-3188. 436 B
dmatassino@ursinus.edu
MATCHETT, Clay .... 318-487-7157. 202 F
clay.matchett@lacollege.edu
MATCHETT, Jill .... 715-634-4790. 533 Q
jmatchett@lco.edu
MATE, Robert, L .... 765-494-5860. 171 M
rmate@purdue.edu
MATEJKOVIC,
Edward, M .... 610-436-3555. 430 A
ematejkovic@wcupa.edu
MATEN, Lionel .... 662-915-7328. 270 B
lmaten@olemiss.edu
MATEO, Robin .... 407-646-2258. 111 Q
rmateo@rollins.edu
MATERN, Cindy .... 253-879-3369. 524 F
cmatern@pugetsound.edu
MATERNOWSKI, Peter .... 608-243-4587. 540 C
pmaternowski@madisoncollege.edu
MATHAY, Patti, J .... 412-624-7512. 435 C
mathay@pitt.edu
MATHENA, Cindy .... 904-826-0084. 118 I
cmathena@usa.edu
MATHENEY, H. Scott ...... 630-617-3025. 145 A
hscottm@elmhurst.edu
MATHENY, Christopher .. 920-735-2401. 539 K
matheny@fvtc.edu
MATHENY, Jacqueline .... 716-827-2450. 348 G
mathenyj@trocaire.edu
MATHENY, Kevin .... 503-493-6521. 402 J
kmatheny@cu-portland.edu
MATHENY, Samuel .... 215-871-6170. 430 D
samuelmat@pcom.edu
MATHENY, Stephen .... 828-395-1293. 361 C
smatheny@isothermal.edu
MATHER, Bruce, J .... 630-617-3178. 145 A
brucem@elmhurst.edu
MATHER, Jannah, H .... 801-581-6194. 496 Q
jmather@socwk.utah.edu
MATHER, Kim .... 978-867-4246. 226 H
kim.mather@gordon.edu
MATHER, Sharon .... 573-592-6050. 285 B
sharon.mather@westminster-mo.edu
MATHERLY, Cheryl .... 918-631-3225. 401 F
cheryl-matherly@utulsa.edu
MATHERN, Rebecca .... 541-737-4331. 406 A
rebecca.mathern@oregonstate.edu
MATHES, Cassie, M .... 417-625-9365. 278 D
mathes-c@mssu.edu
MATHES, Dennis .... 717-477-1463. 429 E
dhm@ship.edu
MATHES, James .... 850-644-8360. 115 C
jmathes@fsu.edu
MATHES, Leon .... 504-865-3148. 205 H
mathes@loyno.edu
MATHESON, Marian, F .... 413-542-5187. 221 G
mfmatheson@amherst.edu
MATHESON, Regina, M .. 563-333-5838. 182 B
MathesonReginaM@sau.edu
MATHEW, Bruce, E .... 608-785-9214. 541 E
mathewb@westerntc.edu
MATHEW, Prakash, C ..... 701-231-7701. 371 G
prakash.mathew@ndsu.edu
MATHEW, Roy .... 915-747-5117. 492 A
rmathew@utep.edu
MATHEW, Thomson .... 918-495-7016. 398 H
tmathew@oru.edu
MATHEW, Usha .... 281-283-2135. 489 C
mathew@uhcl.edu

MATHEWS, Bill .... 334-683-5156..... 5 C
bmathews@judson.edu
MATHEWS, Bruce .... 808-974-7393. 136 A
bmathews@hawaii.edu
MATHEWS, Carla, R .... 248-341-2197. 248 D
crmathew@oaklandcc.edu
MATHEWS, Darren .... 970-247-7428... 81 M
mathews_d@fortlewis.edu
MATHEWS, David .... 269-782-1270. 250 C
president@swmich.edu
MATHEWS, Jeanne .... 706-236-2226. 121 G
jmathews@berry.edu
MATHEWS, Jennifer .... 508-565-1915. 237 A
jmathews@stonehill.edu
MATHEWS, Karen .... 937-376-6076. 376 E
kmathews@centralstate.edu
MATHEWS, Marc .... 859-233-8100. 199 I
mmathews@transy.edu
MATHEWS, Rebecca, B .. 618-537-6940. 152 G
rbmathews@mckendree.edu
MATHEWS, Tracy .... 870-633-4480... 21 A
tmathews@eacc.edu
MATHIAS, Suzi .... 715-675-3331. 541 A
mathias@ntc.edu
MATHIASEN, Rebecca .... 402-354-7034. 291 B
rebecca.mathiasen@methodistcollege.edu
MATHIE, Craig .... 435-893-2216. 498 A
craig.mathie@snow.edu
MATHIES, Bonnie .... 419-586-0341. 393 G
bonnie.mathies@wright.edu
MATHIES, Richard .... 510-642-4192... 70 I
cocdean@berkeley.edu
MATHIESEN, Gaylan .... 218-739-3375. 256 K
gmathiesen@lbs.edu
MATHIEU, Dickens .... 315-443-9732. 347 C
dmathieu@syr.edu
MATHIOS, Alan, D .... 607-255-2138. 322 A
adm5@cornell.edu
MATHIS, Bob, D .... 512-863-1425. 481 I
bmathis@southwestern.edu
MATHIS, Carolyn .... 626-529-8437... 57 G
cmathis@pacificoaks.edu
MATHIS, Claude .... 915-831-2857. 472 B
cmathis1@epcc.edu
MATHIS, Clay, P .... 361-593-5401. 484 A
clay.mathis@tamuk.edu
MATHIS, Dixie .... 801-622-1573. 496 I
dixie.mathis@stevenhenager.edu
MATHIS, Elizabeth .... 215-965-4017. 424 D
emathis@moore.edu
MATHIS, Jennifer, M ...... 864-388-8307. 444 K
jmathis@lander.edu
MATHIS, Jim .... 239-939-4766. 114 F
jmathis@swfc.edu
MATHIS, Jon .... 503-255-0332. 404 F
jmathis@multnomah.edu
MATHIS, Kala .... 931-553-0071. 457 F
kala.mathis@miller-motte.com
MATHIS, Martha .... 802-485-2640. 500 A
martham@norwich.edu
MATHIS, Maureen .... 610-660-1306. 432 E
mmathis@sju.edu
MATHIS, Shawn .... 501-450-1333... 21 E
mathis@hendrix.edu
MATHIS, Teri .... 229-391-5045. 119 H
tmathis@abac.edu
MATHIS, Tina .... 559-438-4222... 46 K
tina_mathis@heald.edu
MATHIS-STUMP,
Becky, D .... 304-865-6021. 527 F
becky.mathis-stump@ovu.edu
MATHO, Diego, L .... 617-262-5000. 223 F
diego.matho@the-bac.edu
MATHUR, Ambika .... 313-577-1324. 252 G
au1432@wayne.edu
MATHWEG, Cathy, M ..... 920-923-8138. 534 A
cmathweg@marianuniversity.edu
MATIENZO-CARRERO,
Ivonne .... 787-764-0000. 555 B
ivonne.matienzo@upr.edu
MATIER, Michael .... 254-710-2414. 467 G
michael_matier@baylor.edu
MATIJEVIC, Patricia .... 970-339-6374... 78 C
pat.matijevic@aims.edu
MATILDA, Mecca .... 831-476-9424... 44 K
finaid@fivebranches.edu
MATIS, Michael .... 207-255-1237. 212 F
mmatis@maine.edu
MATIS, Michelle, D .... 407-582-3130. 118 M
mmatis@valenciacollege.edu
MATISON, Kim .... 253-566-5194. 524 C
kmatison@tacomacc.edu
MATISTA, Theresa .... 916-568-3164... 52 K
matistt@losrios.edu
MATITIA, Abraham .... 440-943-5300. 388 F
MATKIN, Gary, W .... 949-824-5525... 71 B
gmatkin@uci.edu
MATKIN, Neil .... 225-922-2373. 202 G
nmatkin@lctcs.edu
MATLAK, Richard, E .... 508-793-2497. 225 B
rmatlak@holycross.edu

MATLOCK, Bianca .... 214-379-5530. 478 D
bmatlock@pqc.edu
MATLOCK, David, N .... 276-739-2473. 514 D
dmatlock@vhcc.edu
MATLOCK, Eugene, M .... 515-964-0601. 178 E
matlockg@faith.edu
MATLOCK, Jack .... 501-975-8522... 22 F
jmatlock@philander.edu
MATLOCK, John .... 405-425-5500. 397 D
john.matlock@oc.edu
MATLOCK, John, H .... 734-936-1055. 251 C
matlock@umich.edu
MATLOCK, Kathy .... 910-642-7141. 364 A
Kathy.Matlock@sccnc.edu
MATLOCK, Mark .... 814-732-1301. 428 E
mmatlock@edinboro.edu
MATNEY, Paul .... 806-371-5123. 465 E
jpmatney@actx.edu
MATOLA, Erich .... 719-549-2566... 80 K
erich.matola@colostate-pueblo.edu
MATONAK, Andrew, J ..... 518-629-4530. 326 G
a.matonak@hvcc.edu
MATOS, Awilda .... 787-834-9595. 553 B
amatos@uaa.edu
MATOS, Carol .... 212-749-2802. 330 A
administration@msmnyc.edu
MATOS, Daniel .... 212-650-8150. 317 D
dmatos@ccny.cuny.edu
MATOS, Emily .... 787-844-8181. 555 A
emily.matos@upr.edu
MATOS, Felix .... 718-518-4300. 318 B
fmatos@hostos.cuny.edu
MATOS, Lillian .... 787-780-0070. 547 G
lmatos@caribbean.edu
MATOS, Thomas .... 651-846-1362. 261 D
thomas.matos@saintpaul.edu
MATOS FLORES,
Angel, L .... 787-265-3869. 554 E
decadmi@uprm.edu
MATOSO, Michael .... 209-667-3566... 35 B
mmatoso@csustan.edu
MATSEN, Maureen, R ..... 757-594-7571. 503 M
maureen.matsen@cnu.edu
MATSON, Christine, B .... 671-735-0231. 546 C
christine.matson@guamcc.edu
MATSON, Elizabeth .... 610-375-1212. 425 H
ematson@paceinstitute.com
MATSON, Jack .... 315-445-4155. 328 F
matsojoe@lemoyne.edu
MATSON, Karen .... 541-888-7345. 407 H
kmatson@socc.edu
MATSON, Laurel, L .... 719-884-5000... 83 K
llmatson@nbc.edu
MATSON, Laurel, L .... 719-884-5000... 83 K
LLmatson@nbc.edu
MATSON, Pamela, A .... 650-723-2750... 68 E
pamela.matson@stanford.edu
MATSON, Ronald, R .... 316-978-6152. 191 F
ron.matson@wichita.edu
MATSON, Steven, W .... 919-962-3251. 368 D
smatson@bio.unc.edu
MATSUDA, Matthew, K ... 848-932-2300. 306 B
mmatsuda@rci.rutgers.edu
MATSUO, Monica .... 626-396-2268... 28 P
monica.matsuo@artcenter.edu
MATT, Kathleen, S .... 302-831-8370... 94 B
ksmatt@udel.edu
MATT, Laura .... 563-425-5225. 183 B
mattl@uiu.edu
MATTEI, Teresita .... 787-894-2828. 555 C
teresita.mattei@upr.edu
MATTERN, Carolyn .... 303-914-6372... 84 I
carolyn.mattern@rrcc.edu
MATTES, Bill, S .... 717-901-5134. 418 E
BMattes@HarrisburgU.edu
MATTES, Marty .... 253-680-7156. 516 L
mmattes@bates.ctc.edu
MATTESON, Bill .... 401-874-4275. 440 D
matteson@uri.edu
MATTEY, Melissa .... 443-518-4208. 215 E
mmattey@howardcc.edu
MATTHEIS, Bernd .... 203-575-8234... 89 B
bmattheis@nvcc.commnet.edu
MATTHES, Bruce .... 619-684-8871... 56 C
bmatthes@newschoolarch.edu
MATTHEW, Erica .... 305-222-2822. 103 L
ematthew@careercollege.edu
MATTHEWS, Adrienne .... 301-891-4177. 221 B
amatthew@wau.edu
MATTHEWS, Al .... 740-753-6590. 380 K
matthewsa11702@hocking.edu
MATTHEWS, Beverly .... 903-785-7661. 478 B
bmatthews@parisjc.edu
MATTHEWS, Brad .... 845-451-1309. 322 D
b_matthews@culinary.edu
MATTHEWS, Bryan, L ..... 410-778-7231. 221 C
bmatthews2@washcoll.edu
MATTHEWS, Cassandra .. 205-929-6393..... 5 D
cmatthews@lawsonstate.edu
MATTHEWS, Cissy .... 409-944-1203. 472 I
amatthew@gc.edu

MATTHEWS, Daniel .... 405-273-5331. 395 I
dmatthews@familyoffaithcollege.edu
MATTHEWS, Daniel, J .... 405-273-5331. 395 I
dmatthews@familyoffaithcollege.edu
MATTHEWS, Dennis, W .. 215-968-8301. 411 B
matthews@bucks.edu
MATTHEWS, Donnajean .. 714-449-7438... 67 D
djmatthews@scco.edu
MATTHEWS, Douglas, K . 859-858-2206. 192 A
MATTHEWS, Gary, C ...... 858-534-6820... 71 F
gcmatthews@ucsd.edu
MATTHEWS, JR.,
George, E .... 336-758-4016. 370 D
matthews@wfu.edu
MATTHEWS, Gregory ...... 802-387-6716. 499 E
gmatthews@landmark.edu
MATTHEWS, Harold, P .... 812-488-2051. 173 H
hm3@evansville.edu
MATTHEWS, Hazel .... 502-413-8880. 199 F
hmatthews@sullivan.edu
MATTHEWS, Hazel .... 502-413-8880. 199 G
hmatthews@sullivan.edu
MATTHEWS, Hewitt .... 678-547-6306. 128 H
matthews_h@mercer.edu
MATTHEWS, Jacque .... 702-651-7924. 294 E
jacque.matthews@csn.edu
MATTHEWS, Jacqueline .. 610-758-3900. 422 A
jamh@lehigh.edu
MATTHEWS, Janet .... 828-328-7254. 356 B
janet.matthews@lr.edu
MATTHEWS, John .... 660-596-7295. 282 G
jmatthews@sfccmo.edu
MATTHEWS, John, D ...... 864-242-5100. 441 D
MATTHEWS, Lavonne ..... 336-334-7683. 367 E
lavonne@ncat.edu
MATTHEWS, Lawrence .... 419-358-3246. 374 J
matthewsl@bluffton.edu
MATTHEWS, Lea, W .... 910-296-1812. 361 D
lmatthews@jamessprunt.edu
MATTHEWS, Mary .... 907-474-5655... 10 I
mcmatthews@alaska.edu
MATTHEWS, Pamela, R .. 979-845-4016. 483 C
p-matthews@tamu.edu
MATTHEWS, Robin .... 252-447-3818. 359 G
matthewsr@cravencc.edu
MATTHEWS, Ron .... 704-378-1023. 355 K
rmatthews@jcsu.edu
MATTHEWS, Ross, D ...... 504-864-7914. 205 H
rdmatthews@loyno.edu
MATTHEWS, Ruth .... 507-457-1481. 264 A
rmatthews@smumn.edu
MATTHEWS, Samuel, W . 405-273-5331. 395 I
smatthews@familyoffaithcollege.edu
MATTHEWS, Sharon .... 617-262-5000. 223 F
Sharon.Matthews@the-bac.edu
MATTHEWS, Stephen, P . 518-564-3282. 344 B
matthesp@plattsburgh.edu
MATTHEWS, Thomas ...... 216-368-4446. 375 J
careers@case.edu
MATTHEWS, Todd .... 719-596-7400... 82 M
tmatthews@intellitecmedical.edu
MATTHEWS, Valencia, E . 850-599-3430. 114 K
valencia.matthews@famu.edu
MATTHEWS, Victor .... 417-836-5529. 278 E
victormatthews@missouristate.edu
MATTHEWS, Wesley .... 701-858-3352. 371 F
wes.matthews@minotstateu.edu
MATTHEWSON, Donald ... 661-255-1050... 31 C
dmatthewson@calarts.edu
MATTHEWSON,
Mansfield .... 616-234-3851. 243 B
mmatthew@grcc.edu
MATTHIAS, Ryan .... 402-643-7374. 289 B
ryan.matthias@cune.edu
MATTHIES, Brad .... 307-268-2036. 542 X
bmatthies@caspercollege.edu
MATTIA, Antonio .... 305-220-4120. 111 E
ceo@ptcmatt.com
MATTIA, Cynthia .... 732-987-2757. 302 B
mattiac@georgian.edu
MATTIA, Marc .... 305-220-4120. 111 E
MATTIACCI, John, A .... 215-629-0300. 433 K
john.mattiacci@temple.edu
MATTIACE, Lisa, C .... 419-372-6780. 374 K
lmattia@bgsu.edu
MATTIES, A. Joseph .... 518-828-4181. 321 C
matties@sunycgcc.edu
MATTILA, Lisa .... 413-236-1609. 231 A
lmattila@berkshirecc.edu
MATTINGLY, Bruce .... 607-753-4312. 343 B
bruce.mattingly@cortland.edu
MATTINGLY, Bruce, A .... 606-783-2544. 198 A
b.mattingly@moreheadstate.edu
MATTINGLY, Catherine ... 215-572-2086. 409 H
mattingly@arcadia.edu
MATTINGLY, Gerald, L ... 865-573-4517. 455 G
gmattingly@johnsonU.edu
MATTINGLY, Keith, E ..... 269-471-3411. 239 D
matt@andrews.edu
MATTIOLI, Kathy, L .... 740-283-6267. 379 N
kmattioli@franciscan.edu

MATTIOLI, Monica .... 716-375-2302. 338 E
mmattioli@sbu.edu
MATTIS, JR., George, E . 276-223-4744. 514 F
gmattis@wcc.vccs.edu
MATTISON, Debra .... 651-213-4282. 256 B
dmattison@hazelden.edu
MATTISON, Gwen, M ..... 937-775-2475. 393 G
gwen.mattison@wright.edu
MATTISON, Michael .... 207-255-1320. 212 F
michael.mattison@maine.edu
MATTIX, Larry .... 757-823-8180. 507 M
lmattix@nsu.edu
MATTOCKS, Vicki, S .... 417-836-5262. 278 E
vickimattocks@missouristate.edu
MATTOX, Bennie .... 229-732-5908. 120 D
benniemattox@andrewcollege.edu
MATTOX, Robert, J .... 770-423-6600. 127 N
bmattox@kennesaw.edu
MATTSON, Craig .... 708-239-4881. 160 K
craig.mattson@trnty.edu
MATTSON, Jean .... 308-865-8202. 292 H
mattsonj@unk.edu
MATTSON, Jo .... 314-862-3456. 274 E
jmattson@fontbonne.edu
MATTSON, Paul, R .... 563-387-1717. 180 M
paul.mattson@luther.edu
MATTY, David .... 801-626-6159. 497 D
davidmatty@weber.edu
MATTY, Joseph .... 815-753-8821. 154 I
jmatty@niu.edu
MATULIA, Michael, K ..... 352-323-3643. 108 S
matuliam@lssc.edu
MATURANA SENDOYA,
Ines .... 617-552-3358. 224 A
ines.maturana@bc.edu
MATUS, David .... 602-787-7872... 15 B
david.matus@paradisevalley.edu
MATUSIAK, Joseph .... 914-961-8313. 340 B
jmatusiak@svots.edu
MATUSICK, Robert .... 386-822-7300. 117 C
rmatusic@stetson.edu
MATUSOW-AYRES,
Helen .... 718-636-3639. 336 F
hmayres@pratt.edu
MATWEYCHUK, Karen .... 610-647-4980. 418 I
kmatweychuk@immaculata.edu
MATYE EDWARDS, Lisa 360-442-2301. 521 A
lmatyeedwards@lowercolumbia.edu
MATYSTIK, Walter, F ...... 718-862-7268. 329 M
walter.matystik@manhattan.edu
MATZ, Christopher .... 808-455-0673. 137 A
cmatz@hawaii.edu
MATZ, Jeannine .... 515-643-6703. 181 A
jmatz@mercydesmoines.org
MATZ, Jesse, E .... 740-427-5926. 382 J
matzj@kenyon.edu
MATZA, Diane .... 315-792-3259. 349 F
dmatza@utica.edu
MATZKE, Brian .... 616-632-2073. 239 E
matzkbri@aquinas.edu
MATZKE, William .... 989-358-7259. 239 C
matzkew@alpenacc.edu
MAUCERI, Philip .... 845-257-3280. 342 B
maucerip@newpaltz.edu
MAUCH, Elizabeth .... 570-389-4005. 427 H
emauch@bloomu.edu
MAUCH, Tom .... 909-274-4380... 55 A
tmauch@mtsac.edu
MAUCH AMIR, Carol ..... 213-740-7922... 74 A
cmauch@usc.edu
MAUE, Lea .... 618-235-2700. 160 A
lea.maue@swic.edu
MAUER, J. David .... 740-245-7322. 392 A
dmauer@rio.edu
MAUERMEYER,
Henry, A .... 973-596-3124. 303 G
henry.mauermeyer@njit.edu
MAUGE, Lucille .... 404-880-6662. 122 J
lmauge@cau.edu
MAUGER, Alana .... 215-641-6359. 424 B
amauger@mc3.edu
MAUGHAN, Doug, L ...... 208-732-6262. 138 B
dmaughan@csi.edu
MAUGHON, Sandra .... 706-754-7852. 129 G
smaughon@northgatech.edu
MAUHS-PUGH,
Thomas, J .... 802-287-8393. 499 D
mauhs-pught@greenmtn.edu
MAUK, Jean .... 305-809-3266. 104 I
jean.mauk@fkcc.edu
MAUK, Teresa .... 508-999-8042. 229 A
tmauk@umassd.edu
MAUL, Diana .... 212-678-4055. 347 G
maul@tc.edu
MAUL, Jeffrey .... 814-262-6431. 427 C
jmaul@pennhighlands.edu
MAULDIN, Angela .... 704-378-3578. 355 K
amauldin@jcsu.edu
MAULDIN, Brad .... 575-562-2393. 309 H
bradley.mauldin@enmu.edu
MAULDIN, Kim .... 256-765-4608..... 9 C
komauldin@una.edu
MAULDIN, Shawn .... 985-448-4170. 208 A
shawn.mauldin@nicholls.edu
MAULDIN, Teena, P .... 704-463-3031. 365 E
teena.mauldin@fsmail.pfeiffer.edu
MAULDIN, Walter .... 585-275-3340. 349 C
walter.mauldin@rochester.edu
MAULDIN, Walter .... 423-614-8400. 455 L
wmauldin@leeuniversity.edu
MAULL, Perry .... 812-855-8961. 167 F
pjmaull@indiana.edu
MAULTSBY, Bill .... 910-642-7141. 364 A
Bill.Maultsby@sccnc.edu
MAUN, Duane, F .... 717-901-5120. 418 E
DMaun@HarrisburgU.edu
MAUN, Robin .... 717-477-1302. 429 E
rmmaun@ship.edu
MAUNEY, Billy, L .... 910-272-3330. 363 B
bmauney@robeson.edu
MAUPIN, JR., John, E ... 404-752-1740. 129 E
jmaupin@msm.edu
MAUPIN, Ron .... 417-328-1511. 282 C
rmaupin@sbuniv.edu
MAURANO, Steven, J ..... 401-865-2775. 439 E
smaurano@providence.edu
MAURER, Amybeth .... 847-214-7423. 144 F
amaurer@elgin.edu
MAURER, Bobby Jo .... 309-341-7315. 150 A
bmaurer@knox.edu
MAURER, Carmen, K ...... 402-472-3906. 292 G
cmaurer@nebraska.edu
MAURER, Carolyn .... 717-766-2511. 423 L
cmaurer@messiah.edu
MAURER, Charles .... 212-757-1190. 313 H
cmaurer@funeraleducation.org
MAURER, Erin, C .... 864-622-6074. 441 B
emaurer@andersonuniversity.edu
MAURER, Harold, M .... 402-559-4200. 292 J
hmmaurer@unmc.edu
MAURER, Joseph .... 541-885-1389. 405 J
joseph.maurer@oit.edu
MAURER, Linda .... 314-889-1423. 274 E
lmaurer@fontbonne.edu
MAURER, Michael, S ...... 217-581-7568. 144 E
msmaurer@eiu.edu
MAURER, Nancy .... 518-472-5836. 313 C
nmaur@albanylaw.edu
MAURER, Paul .... 978-867-4900. 226 H
paul.maurer@gordon.edu
MAURER, Paulette, A ..... 708-709-3630. 156 A
pmaurer@prairiestate.edu
MAURER, Roy, E .... 708-709-3580. 156 A
rmaurer@prairiestate.edu
MAURER, Ryan, S .... 937-327-6114. 393 E
rmaurer@wittenberg.edu
MAURER, William, M ...... 949-824-6802... 71 B
wmmaurer@uci.edu
MAURIELLO, Thomas ..... 718-862-7241. 329 M
thomas.mauriello@manhattan.edu
MAURIN, Kay .... 985-549-2118. 208 C
kmaurin@selu.edu
MAURO, Laurie .... 304-263-6262. 527 B
lmauro@martinsburginstitute.edu
MAURO, Steven, A .... 814-871-7618. 416 K
mauro003@gannon.edu
MAUSSER, Richard, F ..... 216-397-1630. 381 R
rmausser@jcu.edu
MAUST, Amy .... 248-218-2059. 249 D
amaust@rc.edu
MAUST, Scott .... 309-341-7892. 150 A
smaust@knox.edu
MAVI, Pam .... 513-732-5229. 391 B
pam.mavi@uc.edu
MAVRINAC, Mary Ann ... 585-275-4461. 349 C
maryann.mavrinac@rochester.edu
MAVROGIANNIS,
Sophia .... 646-230-1360. 346 A
sophia.mavrogiannis@esc.edu
MAVROS, Jeffrey .... 309-556-3024. 148 B
jmavros@iwu.edu
MAVROUDHIS,
Athina-Eleni .... 617-850-1289. 227 E
amavroudhis@hchc.edu
MAX, Barbara .... 303-333-4224... 78 I
bmax@aspen.edu
MAX, Sheryl .... 816-995-2842. 280 G
sheryl.max@researchcollege.edu
MAXEINER, Amy .... 815-455-8717. 152 F
amaxeiner@mchenry.edu
MAXEINER, Maddy .... 320-589-6386. 264 F
maxeinme@morris.umn.edu
MAXEY, Larry .... 619-388-3498... 62 D
lmaxey@sdccd.edu
MAXEY, Michael, C .... 540-375-2200. 509 B
maxey@roanoke.edu
MAXFIELD, Judith .... 620-227-9253. 186 B
maxfield@dc3.edu
MAXFIELD, Sylvia .... 401-865-1224. 439 E
maxfield@providence.edu
MAXIE-ASHFORD,
Leslie, M .... 502-272-3101. 192 E
lmaxie-ashford@bellarmine.edu
MAXIN, Leslie .... 724-503-1001. 436 G
lmaxin@washjeff.edu
MAXON, John .... 256-824-6108..... 8 F
john.maxon@uah.edu
MAXSON, Carol .... 615-248-1258. 462 D
cmaxson@trevecca.edu
MAXSON, Robert .... 785-243-1435. 185 M
bmaxson@cloud.edu
MAXWELL, Alice .... 850-201-6049. 117 D
maxwella@tcc.fl.edu
MAXWELL, Barbara, A .... 509-527-5208. 525 E
maxwelba@whitman.edu
MAXWELL, Bruce .... 509-682-6835. 525 B
bmaxwell@wvc.edu
MAXWELL, Chris .... 706-245-7226. 124 D
cmaxwell@ec.edu
MAXWELL, Daniel .... 713-743-5390. 489 B
dmmaxwell@central.uh.edu
MAXWELL, David, E .... 515-271-2191. 177 K
david.maxwell@drake.edu
MAXWELL, Jack .... 785-242-5200. 189 I
jack.maxwell@ottawa.edu
MAXWELL, James .... 217-479-7047. 152 D
james.maxwell@mac.edu
MAXWELL, James .... 972-524-3341. 481 H
MAXWELL, III,
James, D .... 515-964-0601. 178 E
maxwellj@faith.edu
MAXWELL, Jewerl .... 937-766-3616. 375 K
jmaxwell@cedarville.edu
MAXWELL, Jim .... 402-557-7786. 288 G
jim.maxwell@bellevue.edu
MAXWELL, JR., John, B 205-348-1202..... 8 D
jmaxwell@cchs.ua.edu
MAXWELL, Kim .... 970-542-3169... 83 E
kim.maxwell@morgancc.edu
MAXWELL, Lafayette ...... 919-572-1625. 352 C
lmaxwell@apexsot.edu
MAXWELL, Laura .... 678-407-5726. 125 B
lmaxwell@ggc.edu
MAXWELL, Lourena .... 850-201-8911. 117 D
maxwelll@tcc.fl.edu
MAXWELL, Melody .... 903-923-2175. 471 J
mmaxwell@etbu.edu
MAXWELL, Richard .... 662-254-3412. 269 A
rmax@mvsu.edu
MAXWELL, Rick .... 972-860-4722. 470 G
rmaxwell@dcccd.edu
MAXWELL, Sharon .... 630-844-5630. 140 A
smaxwel@aurora.edu
MAXWELL, Valarie .... 940-397-4346. 476 H
valarie.maxwell@mwsu.edu
MAXWELL, Veda .... 501-370-5284... 22 F
vmaxwell@philander.edu
MAXWELL-DOHERTY,
Melissa .... 805-493-3330... 31 H
revmmmd@clunet.edu
MAXWELL-DOHERTY,
Scott .... 805-493-3230... 31 H
revsjmd@clunet.edu
MAXWELL-FRIEDEN,
Lisa .... 765-658-4216. 165 F
lisamaxwellfrieden@depauw.edu
MAY, Bobbie Jo, C .... 919-496-1567. 364 F
may@vgcc.edu
MAY, Brian, J .... 325-942-2073. 465 K
president@angelo.edu
MAY, Bruce .... 608-785-8095. 536 G
bmay@uwlax.edu
MAY, Bryan .... 803-778-7841. 441 F
maybw@cctech.edu
MAY, Carol .... 920-735-2542. 539 K
mayc@fvtc.edu
MAY, Chad, L .... 215-637-7700. 418 G
cmay@holyfamily.edu
MAY, Christopher, V .... 314-977-3185. 281 I
cmay8@slu.edu
MAY, Daniel .... 203-932-7267... 92 E
dmay@newhaven.edu
MAY, David, J .... 603-862-2727. 298 C
david.may@unh.edu
MAY, Gary, S .... 404-894-6825. 125 D
gary.may@coe.gatech.edu
MAY, Gordon, F .... 248-232-4500. 248 D
gfmay@oaklandcc.edu
MAY, Grace .... 973-275-2725. 307 C
grace.may@shu.edu
MAY, Janet .... 520-206-4740... 17 A
jmay3@pima.edu
MAY, Janet .... 712-279-5227. 176 B
janet.may@briarcliff.edu
MAY, Janet .... 713-718-8570. 473 C
may.janet@hccs.edu
MAY, Janet, B .... 205-934-8132..... 8 E
jmay@uab.edu
MAY, Jefferson, J .... 864-388-8314. 444 K
jmay@lander.edu
MAY, Jerry, A .... 734-647-6030. 251 C
jamay@umich.edu
MAY, Joe .... 225-922-1643. 202 G
jmay@lctcs.edu
MAY, Katharyn, A .... 608-263-9725. 536 D
kamay@wisc.edu
MAY, Mariani .... 310-577-3000... 77 G
slmay@yosan.edu
MAY, Mel, A .... 216-987-2204. 378 D
mel.may@tri-c.edu
MAY, Michael .... 724-738-4573. 429 F
michael.may@sru.edu
MAY, Michelle .... 605-455-6064. 450 I
mmay@olc.edu
MAY, Nancy, S .... 617-373-2700. 235 F
MAY, Nina .... 609-586-4800. 302 G
mayn@mccc.edu
MAY, Paul, A .... 508-213-2377. 235 E
paul.may@nichols.edu
MAY, Robert, E .... 276-739-2432. 514 D
rmay@vhcc.edu
MAY, Ron .... 574-936-8898. 163 K
ron.may@ancilla.edu
MAY, Ronald .... 253-964-6736. 522 C
rmay@pierce.ctc.edu
MAY, Sarah, E .... 478-301-2413. 128 H
may_se@mercer.edu
MAY, Susan, A .... 920-735-5731. 539 K
may@fvtc.edu
MAY, Tobi .... 518-562-4170. 320 B
tobi.may@clinton.edu
MAY, Walter, P .... 770-720-5540. 130 G
wpm@reinhardt.edu
MAY, William, V .... 254-710-1221. 467 G
william_may@baylor.edu
MAY-RICCIUTI, Heather .. 304-829-7335. 526 D
hricciuti@bethanywv.edu
MAYABB, Patricia .... 214-887-5022. 471 F
pmayabb@dts.edu
MAYATT, Darlene .... 601-484-8724. 267 G
dmayatt@meridiancc.edu
MAYBANK, Denise, B ..... 517-355-7535. 246 H
maybank@msu.edu
MAYBELL, Steven, A ...... 206-281-2824. 523 C
maybes@spu.edu
MAYBURY, Greg .... 616-395-7671. 244 A
maybury@hope.edu
MAYDEN, Kimberly, A .... 618-537-6825. 152 G
kamayden@mckendree.edu
MAYDEN, Sharrie .... 702-895-0970. 294 I
sharrie.mayden@unlv.edu
MAYER, Brenna, S .... 914-654-5289. 320 H
bmayer@cnr.edu
MAYER, Charles .... 336-249-8186. 360 A
cmayer@davidsonccc.edu
MAYER, Christine .... 615-452-8600. 461 G
christine.mayer@volstate.edu
MAYER, Ed .... 440-375-7223. 382 L
emayer@lec.edu
MAYER, Erin .... 713-221-8543. 489 D
mayere@uhd.edu
MAYER, Louis, J .... 610-660-1321. 432 E
lmayer@sju.edu
MAYER, Marni Saling ..... 360-752-8325. 517 B
msmayer@btc.ctc.edu
MAYER, Russell .... 978-837-3507. 234 A
mayerr@merrimack.edu
MAYER, Sara .... 602-279-9700... 11 E
MAYERS, Darryl .... 617-287-5458. 228 G
darryl.mayers@umb.edu
MAYERS, Ronnie .... 662-846-4300. 266 G
rmayers@deltastate.edu
MAYES, Brent .... 770-229-3327. 132 B
bmayes@sctech.edu
MAYES, David, M .... 501-882-4420... 19 M
dmmayes@asub.edu
MAYES, Florence .... 803-738-7512. 445 C
maysf@midlandstech.edu
MAYES, John, A .... 203-432-3503... 93 A
john.mayes@yale.edu
MAYES, Lakeisha, E .... 757-823-8396. 507 M
lemayes@nsu.edu
MAYES, Michara, N .... 713-313-6815. 485 F
mayesmn@tsu.edu
MAYES, Rick .... 479-936-5162... 22 C
rmayes@nwacc.edu
MAYES, JR., Robert, G .. 251-981-3771..... 2 I
robert@columbiasouthern.edu
MAYEUX, Liza .... 225-768-1737. 206 D
neetu.mayeux@ololcollege.edu
MAYEWSKI, Raymond ..... 585-275-4786. 349 C
Raymond_Mayewski@URMC.Rochester.
edu
MAYFIELD, Amanda, B ... 860-439-2088... 89 H
amanda.mayfield@conncoll.edu
MAYFIELD, Andrea .... 662-476-5025. 266 I
ascott@eastms.edu
MAYFIELD, Donny .... 423-746-5253. 462 C
dmayfield@twcnet.edu
MAYFIELD, Mike, W .... 828-262-7660. 367 A
mayfldmw@appstate.edu

MAYFIELD, Panny ... 662-621-4157. 266 D
pmayfield@coahomacc.edu
MAYHER, Michael, E ... 440-525-7255. 382 M
mmayher@lakelandcc.edu
MAYHEW, Glen, R ... 540-985-8539. 506 G
Grmayhew@jchs.edu
MAYHEW, Kelly ... 619-388-3136... 62 D
kmayhew@sdccd.edu
MAYHEW, Marty ... 520-206-6661... 17 A
mmayhew@pima.edu
MAYHEW, Sally, A ... 618-537-6838. 152 G
samayhew@mckendree.edu
MAYHEW, Sam ... 229-248-3946. 121 E
sam.mayhew@bainbridge.edu
MAYHEW, Steven ... 620-231-7000. 189 L
smayhew@pittstate.edu
MAYHEW, Susan, L ... 276-498-4190. 501 I
MAYHORNE, John, F ... 443-412-2382. 215 C
jmayhorne@harford.edu
MAYHUE, Richard, L ... 818-909-5517... 53 G
rmayhue@tms.edu
MAYLE, David ... 804-290-4231. 510 B
dmayle@stratford.edu
MAYLE, Glenn ... 928-344-7500... 11 L
glenn.mayle@azwestern.edu
MAYLE, Teresa ... 252-536-7207. 361 A
tmayle426@halifaxcc.edu
MAYLONE, Theresa, M ... 718-990-2517. 339 A
maylonet@stjohns.edu
MAYNARD, Barbara ... 314-256-8858. 271 F
maynard@ai.edu
MAYNARD, Francyenne .. 972-273-3109. 471 B
fmaynard@dcccd.edu
MAYNARD, Jennifer ... 937-769-1826. 373 I
jmaynard@antioch.edu
MAYNARD, Kimberly, L . 304-896-7345. 528 F
kimberly.maynard@southernwv.edu
MAYNARD, Nelly ... 773-821-2453. 141 J
nmaynard@csu.edu
MAYNARD, Pamela ... 973-877-3115. 301 H
maynard@essex.edu
MAYNARD, Rebecca, A .. 207-768-2715. 210 M
bmaynard@nmcc.edu
MAYNARD, Scott ... 662-325-3344. 268 D
smaynard@career.msstate.edu
MAYNARD NELSON,
Jeanette ... 612-861-7554. 253 C
jeanette@alfredadler.edu
MAYNARD-REID,
Pedrito ... 509-527-2028. 524 I
pedrito.maynard-reid@wallawalla.edu
MAYNE, Florence, P ... 512-499-4517. 491 A
fmayne@utsystem.edu
MAYNE, Kevin ... 508-373-9400. 223 A
kevin.mayne@becker.edu
MAYO, Bob ... 518-276-8300. 337 I
mayor@rpi.edu
MAYO, Cindy ... 870-743-3000... 22 B
cmayo@northark.edu
MAYO, Dan ... 252-493-7304. 362 G
dmayo@email.pittcc.edu
MAYO, Donna ... 706-864-1620. 133 D
donna.mayo@ung.edu
MAYO, Doug ... 701-231-6825. 371 G
doug@ndsualumni.com
MAYO, Lindsey ... 978-556-3621. 232 E
lmayo@necc.mass.edu
MAYO, Louis ... 803-793-5214. 443 E
mayol@denmarktech.edu
MAYO, Michael ... 501-205-8826... 20 I
mmayo@cbc.edu
MAYO, Sandra ... 951-571-6160... 60 J
sandra.mayo@mvc.edu
MAYO, Sandra ... 951-571-6160... 60 K
sandra.mayo@mvc.edu
MAYO, Sandra ... 512-245-2361. 487 C
sm37@txstate.edu
MAYO, Stephen, L ... 626-395-4951... 31 E
steve@mayo.caltech.edu
MAYO, Tom ... 239-590-1520. 115 A
tmayo@fgcu.edu
MAYORGA, Oscar ... 508-849-3368. 222 B
omayorga@annamaria.edu
MAYRAND, Leslie ... 325-486-6247. 465 K
leslie.mayrand@angelo.edu
MAYROSE, Julie ... 920-686-6125. 536 A
Julie.Mayrose@sl.edu
MAYROSE, William ... 413-775-1212. 231 E
mayroseb@gcc.mass.edu
MAYS, Anna ... 972-860-8261. 470 H
amays@dcccd.edu
MAYS, Beth, A ... 410-777-2480. 213 D
bamays@aacc.edu
MAYS, Jon ... 513-861-6400. 390 C
jon.mays@myunion.edu
MAYS, Marilyn ... 972-273-3501. 471 B
mmays@dccd.edu
MAYS, Nathaniel ... 617-349-8539. 228 B
nmays@lesley.edu
MAYS, Pamela ... 972-273-3116. 471 B
pmays@dcccd.edu
MAYS, Shirley, L ... 602-682-6870... 16 N
smays@phoenixlaw.edu
MAYS, Susan ... 615-771-7821. 464 G
susan.mays@williamsoncc.edu
MAYS, Wendy ... 903-675-6371. 488 D
wmays@tvcc.edu
MAYS-JACKSON, Debra . 601-885-7002. 267 A
Debra.Mays-Jackson@hindscc.edu
MAYSAMI, Ramin ... 910-521-6466. 369 B
ramin.maysami@uncp.edu
MAYSILLES, Michael, E .. 973-596-5642. 303 G
michael.maysilles@njit.edu
MAYSON, Adrianna ... 845-434-5750. 347 A
amayson@sullivan.suny.edu
MAZA-DUERTO,
Aristides ... 786-331-1000. 109 F
amaza@maufl.edu
MAZA-MOSS, Orianna ... 786-331-1000. 109 F
omaza@maufl.edu
MAZACHEK, Juliann ... 785-670-4483. 191 D
jmazachek@wufoundation.org
MAZE, Mary ... 248-341-2053. 248 D
momaze@oaklandcc.edu
MAZEL, David ... 719-587-7771... 78 B
dbmazel@adams.edu
MAZER, Vickie ... 301-687-7053. 220 C
vmmazer@frostburg.edu
MAZEY, Mary Ellen ... 419-372-2211. 374 K
mmazey@bgsu.edu
MAZGULSKI, Judy ... 860-343-5868... 89 A
jmazgulski@mxcc.commnet.edu
MAZIAR, Christine, M ... 574-631-8052. 174 A
maziar.1@nd.edu
MAZIAR, Christine, M ... 574-631-2749. 174 A
maziar.1@nd.edu
MAZIAR, Lucia ... 860-444-8517. 545 G
Lucia.Maziar@uscga.edu
MAZICH, OSB, Edward .. 724-805-2845. 432 H
edward.mazich@email.stvincent.edu
MAZOR, Sandy ... 561-912-1211. 103 C
smazor@evergladesuniversity.edu
MAZOROL, Patrick ... 651-635-8050. 253 K
p-mazorol@bethel.edu
MAZUR, III, Francis, J .. 352-873-5822. 100 K
mazurf@cf.edu
MAZUR, JoAnne ... 440-684-6129. 392 D
jmazur@ursuline.edu
MAZUR, Joe ... 772-462-7340. 106 P
fmazur@irsc.edu
MAZUR, Paul ... 973-300-2120. 307 F
pmazur@sussex.edu
MAZURAK, Kristina ... 208-459-5170. 138 A
kmazurak@collegeofidaho.edu
MAZZA, Diane ... 203-392-5405... 88 A
boutaughd1@southernct.edu
MAZZA, James, A ... 607-255-1989. 322 A
jam16@cornell.edu
MAZZA, Jennifer ... 845-398-4034. 340 A
jmazza@stac.edu
MAZZA, Joseph ... 760-757-2121... 54 G
jmazza@miracosta.edu
MAZZA, Maralyn ... 814-234-7755. 433 G
MAZZA, Nicholas ... 850-644-4752. 115 C
nfmazza@fsu.edu
MAZZA, Rachelle, E ... 617-730-7111. 235 D
rachelle.mazza@newbury.edu
MAZZA, Stephen, W ... 785-864-4550. 190 L
smazza@ku.edu
MAZZARELLA, Janet ... 619-482-6344... 68 B
MAZZARELLI, Carla ... 631-451-4244. 346 E
mazzarc@sunysuffolk.edu
MAZZARELLLI, Judi ... 419-995-8479. 381 Q
mazzarelli.j@rhodesstate.edu
MAZZARESE, John, A ... 412-359-1000. 434 H
jmazzarese@triangle-tech.edu
MAZZEI, Robert, W ... 607-746-4647. 345 G
mazzeirw@delhi.edu
MAZZOCCO, Lisa ... 213-740-6426... 74 A
lisa.mazzocco@usc.edu
MAZZOLA, Frank ... 603-358-2242. 298 F
fmazzola@keene.edu
MAZZOLA, Gregg ... 603-645-9635. 297 I
g.mazzola@snhu.edu
MAZZOLA, Joseph ... 216-687-6952. 377 F
MAZZUCA-PESCE,
Colleen ... 708-456-0300. 161 A
cmazzuca@triton.edu
MBOMEH, Gabriel, A ... 240-895-4305. 218 A
gambomeh@smcm.edu
MBUWAYESANGO,
Dora, R ... 704-636-6077. 355 D
dmbuwayesango@hoodseminary.edu
MBYIRUKIRA, James ... 256-726-7157... 6 B
mbyirukira@oakwood.edu
MC CAIG, Robert ... 732-571-3413. 303 C
rmccaig@monmouth.edu
MC DONALD, Molly ... 408-554-6993... 64 M
mmcdonald@scu.edu
MC GINTY, Sabrina ... 518-244-6891. 338 C
mcgins@sage.edu
MC GOVERN, Michael ... 516-323-3030. 331 J
mmcgovern@molloy.edu
MC SHEA, Bob ... 661-824-2977... 55 I
MCABEE, Linda, R ... 336-334-7862. 367 E
lrmcabee@ncat.edu
MCABEE, Sarah ... 256-233-8102... 1 F
sarah.mcabee@athens.edu
MCADAM DONEGAN,
Lisa ... 508-531-2294. 229 D
lisa.mcadamdonegan@bridgew.edu
MCADAMS, Beverly, R ... 864-231-2100. 441 B
bmcadams@andersonuniversity.edu
MCADAMS, Charles ... 660-562-1197. 279 I
mcadams@nwmissouri.edu
MCAFEE, Kurt ... 620-672-5641. 190 A
kurtm@prattcc.edu
MCALARY, Chris ... 310-954-4030... 54 J
cmcalary@msmc.la.edu
MCALEER, Brenda ... 207-621-3425. 212 C
mcaleer@maine.edu
MCALEXANDER, Dan ... 706-880-8230. 128 A
dmcalexander@lagrange.edu
MCALISTER, Becky ... 773-697-2031. 144 B
bmcalister@devry.edu
MCALISTER, Meree ... 803-778-6646. 441 F
mcalistermm@cctech.edu
MCALISTER, Richie ... 601-484-8779. 267 G
rmcalist@mcc.cc.ms.us
MCALLASTER, Craig ... 407-646-2249. 111 Q
cmcallaster@rollins.edu
MCALLESTER, David ... 773-702-5562. 160 I
mcallester@ttic.edu
MCALLISTER, Bruce ... 864-242-5100. 441 D
MCALLISTER, Carol ... 760-750-4802... 35 A
cmcallis@csusm.edu
MCALLISTER, Charles ... 573-651-2112. 282 B
cdmcallister@semo.edu
MCALLISTER, Eugene, J . 406-791-5300. 288 E
emcallister01@ugf.edu
MCALLISTER, Gary ... 501-205-8827... 20 I
gmcallister@cbc.edu
MCALLISTER, Kirk ... 907-796-6473... 11 A
kirk.mcallister@uas.alaska.edu
MCALLISTER, Latrelle, P . 704-378-1230. 355 K
lmcallister@jcsu.edu
MCALLISTER, Linda ... 510-981-2998... 59 A
lmcallister@peralta.edu
MCALLISTER, Peter ... 323-343-4001... 34 A
peter.mcallister2@calstatela.edu
MCALLISTER, Steven, G . 540-458-8740. 516 A
smcallister@wlu.edu
MCALLISTER-WILSON,
David ... 202-885-8601... 97 D
president@wesleyseminary.edu
MCALMOND, Barb ... 406-447-6907. 287 A
barb.mcalmond@umhelena.edu
MCALONAN, Jenny ... 313-993-3343. 250 K
mcalonjl@udmercy.edu
MCALOOSE, Carl ... 678-466-4672. 123 A
carlmcaloose@clayton.edu
MCALPIN, David, M ... 816-414-3700. 277 L
dmcalpin@mbts.edu
MCALPIN, Michael ... 925-631-4222... 61 F
mdm5@stmarys-ca.edu
MCALPINE, Helen, T ... 256-551-3117... 4 I
helen.mcalpine@drakestate.edu
MCALPINE, Suzy ... 270-384-8236. 197 D
mcalpins@lindsey.edu
MCANALLY, Danita, L ... 806-371-5495. 465 E
dlmcanally@actx.edu
MCANALLY, David ... 903-675-6232. 488 D
dmcanally@tvcc.edu
MCANALLY, Kent ... 785-670-1938. 191 D
kent.mcanally@washburn.edu
MCANDREW, John ... 570-208-5958. 419 P
johnmcandrew@kings.edu
MCANDREW, Kristin ... 574-284-4587. 172 G
mcandrew@saintmarys.edu
MCANELLEY, Becky, J ... 409-882-3318. 486 G
becky.mcanelley@lsco.edu
MCANUFF, Courtney ... 732-445-6601. 306 A
cmcanuff@rci.rutgers.edu
MCANUFF, Courtney, O . 848-445-6601. 306 B
cmcanuff@rci.rutgers.edu
MCARDELL, James ... 218-855-8136. 258 B
jmcardell@clcmn.edu
MCARDLE, Eliza ... 413-549-4600. 227 B
MCARDLE, John ... 541-917-4210. 404 B
mcardlj@linnbenton.edu
MCARDLE, Kate ... 818-401-1034... 41 B
kmcardle@columbiacollege.edu
MCARDLE, Molly ... 216-397-1904. 381 R
mmcrdle@jcu.edu
MCARDLE, William, F ... 401-598-1024. 439 B
wmcardle@jwu.edu
MCAREAVEY, Julie ... 605-331-6644. 452 D
julie.mcareavey@usiouxfalls.edu
MCARTHUR, Douglas ... 517-437-7341. 243 I
douglas.mcarthur@hillsdale.edu
MCARTHUR, Jennifer ... 307-674-6446. 543 F
jmcarthur@sheridan.edu
MCARTHUR, John, M ... 580-581-2201. 394 G
jmcarthur@cameron.edu
MCARTHUR, Neil ... 478-757-3548. 122 F
nmcarthur@centralgatech.edu
MCARTHUR, Phillip ... 808-675-3907. 135 C
phillip.mcarthur@byuh.edu
MCARTHUR, Rachel ... 859-371-9393. 192 D
rmcarthur@beckfield.edu
MCARTHUR, Ronald ... 609-343-5007. 299 A
mcarthur@atlantic.edu
MCASEY, Veronica ... 402-872-2218. 291 E
vmcasey@peru.edu
MCATEE, Christopher ... 847-566-6401. 162 G
cmcatee@usml.edu
MCATEE, Jim ... 765-285-2420. 164 B
jfmcatee@bsu.edu
MCAULAY, Brian, J ... 972-438-6932. 478 C
bmcaulay@parkercc.edu
MCAULEY, Germaine ... 404-270-5711. 132 E
gmcauley@spelman.edu
MCAULIFF, Kimberly, B .. 315-445-4553. 328 F
mcaulikb@lemoyne.edu
MCAULIFFE, John ... 732-987-2764. 302 B
mcauliffej@georgian.edu
MCAULIFFE, Lynne ... 307-855-2206. 542 Y
lynne@cwc.edu
MCAULIFFE, Margaret ... 718-997-5787. 319 C
margaret.mcauliffe@qc.cuny.edu
MCAULIFFE, Richard, J .. 402-280-2104. 289 D
rmcaulif@creighton.edu
MCAVOY, Eugene ... 425-388-9031. 519 I
MCAVOY, John ... 304-876-5374. 529 I
jmcavoy@shepherd.edu
MCAVOY, William ... 508-831-5337. 238 F
wjmcavoy@wpi.edu
MCBEATH, Trish ... 918-465-1804. 395 G
tmcbeath@eosc.edu
MCBEE, Barry ... 512-322-3715. 491 A
bmcbee@utsystem.edu
MCBEE, Lori, A ... 479-979-1413... 25 J
lamcbee@ozarks.edu
MCBEE, Misty ... 573-288-6507. 273 F
mmcbee@culver.edu
MCBEE, Russ ... 620-227-9313. 186 B
rmcbee@dc3.edu
MCBETH, Valerie ... 360-676-2772. 521 D
vmcbeth@nwic.edu
MCBREEN, William ... 507-457-5122. 262 A
wmcbreen@winona.edu
MCBRIDE, Andrew, S ... 804-289-8964. 510 L
amcbride@richmond.edu
MCBRIDE, JR., Bill ... 706-721-8106. 126 B
wmcbride@gru.edu
MCBRIDE, Catherine ... 562-947-8755... 67 H
catherinemcbride@scuhs.edu
MCBRIDE, Christy ... 618-985-3741. 148 J
christymcbride@jalc.edu
MCBRIDE, David ... 731-668-1818. 462 F
dmcbride@uu.edu
MCBRIDE, David, R ... 617-353-3575. 224 D
dmcbride@bu.edu
MCBRIDE, Dwight, A ... 847-491-8502. 155 D
dwight-mcbride@northwestern.edu
MCBRIDE, JR.,
James, L ... 434-924-8900. 511 B
jlm5qw@virginia.edu
MCBRIDE, Jeanette ... 910-576-6222. 362 C
mcbridej@montgomery.edu
MCBRIDE, John, E ... 512-245-2557. 487 C
jm05@txstate.edu
MCBRIDE, Lisa ... 215-871-6178. 430 D
lisamcb@pcom.edu
MCBRIDE, Lisa ... 724-938-4014. 428 A
mcbride@calu.edu
MCBRIDE, Michael, J ... 973-642-8872. 307 D
michael.mcbride@shu.edu
MCBRIDE, Neal ... 951-343-4925... 30 H
nmcbride@calbaptist.edu
MCBRIDE, Noel ... 206-934-3869. 522 J
noel.mcbride@seattlecolleges.edu
MCBRIDE, Okang ... 201-692-7004. 301 J
okang_mcbride@fdu.edu
MCBRIDE, Phil ... 928-428-8404... 13 J
phil.mcbride@eac.edu
MCBRIDE, Regina ... 618-650-2712. 159 H
rmcbrid@siue.edu
MCBRIDE, Robert ... 201-200-3057. 303 F
rmcbride@njcu.edu
MCBRIDE, Scott ... 606-783-2650. 198 A
s.mcbride@moreheadstate.edu
MCBRIDE GATES, Jane .. 203-837-8400... 88 B
gatesj@wcsu.edu
MCBRINE, Paul ... 617-236-8800. 226 F
pmcbrine@fisher.edu
MCBROOM, Michael ... 806-651-4400. 484 D
mmcbroom@mail.wtamu.edu
MCBRYAN, Jamie ... 406-265-3515. 287 D
jamie.mcbryan@msun.edu
MCBRYDE, Tennie, S ... 334-420-4306... 7 G
tmcbryde@trenholmstate.edu

MCBURNETT, David ... 706-295-6933. 125 F
dmcburnett@gntc.edu
MCBURNEY, Melissa ... 509-542-4832. 518 C
mmcburney@columbiabasin.edu
MCCABE, Cynthia ... 215-641-6562. 424 B
cmccabe@mc3.edu
MCCABE, Diana ... 309-796-5268. 140 E
Mccabed@bhc.edu
MCCABE, Eileen ... 718-405-3240. 320 G
eileen.mccabe@mountsaintvincent.edu
MCCABE, John ... 315-464-4223. 342 E
mccabej@upstate.edu
MCCABE, Kenneth ... 410-825-2111. 439 A
kfmccabe@ccri.edu
MCCABE, Kim ... 434-544-8690. 506 K
mccabe@lynchburg.edu
MCCABE, Margaret, S ... 603-513-5261. 298 D
margaret.mccabe@law.unh.edu
MCCABE, Michael, M ... 828-884-8248. 352 I
mmccabe@brevard.edu
MCCABE, Michael, V ... 937-229-3515. 391 C
mmccabe1@udayton.edu
MCCABE, Philip, J ... 203-371-7934... 91 C
mccabep@sacredheart.edu
MCCABE, Robert, G ... 802-626-6210. 501 E
robert.mccabe@lyndonstate.edu
MCCABE, Sunnie ... 304-243-2412. 531 H
smccabe@wju.edu
MCCABE-SMITH, Linda .. 618-453-1186. 159 G
lsmith@siu.edu
MCCADDEN, Brian, M ... 401-865-2503. 439 E
bmccadde@providence.edu
MCCADDEN, Kevin ... 610-436-2223. 430 A
kmccadden@wcupa.edu
MCCADEN, Dorothy ... 215-612-6600. 419 J
dmccaden@chicareers.com
MCCAFFERTY, Coreen ... 610-921-7274. 409 A
cmccafferty@alb.edu
MCCAFFERTY, Mike ... 404-387-0345. 130 F
mike.mccafferty@point.edu
MCCAFFERTY, Pamela ... 978-665-3435. 229 E
pmccafferty@fitchburgstate.edu
MCCAFFERTY, Patricia ... 978-934-3238. 229 B
patricia_mccafferyt@uml.edu
MCCAFFREY, Dena ... 636-481-3400. 275 I
dmccaffr@jeffco.edu
MCCAFFREY, Kathryn, E . 508-286-8381. 238 B
mccaffrey_kate@wheatoncollege.edu
MCCAFFREY, Matthew ... 267-502-2798. 410 I
matthew.mccaffrey@brynathyn.edu
MCCAFFREY, Michael, H 260-399-7700. 174 C
mmccaffrey@sf.edu
MCCAHAN, Jason ... 570-372-4107. 433 H
mccahan@susqu.edu
MCCAIG, Gerald ... 409-880-8108. 486 F
gerald.mccaig@lamar.edu
MCCAIN, Gail, C ... 212-772-4000. 318 C
gmccain@hunter.cuny.edu
MCCAIN, Lindy ... 662-472-2312. 267 B
lmccain@holmescc.edu
MCCALEB, Cathy ... 972-721-5203. 488 F
mccaleb@udallas.edu
MCCALEB, Colin ... 517-630-8169. 244 O
mccalebc@kellogg.edu
MCCALEB, Gary, D ... 325-674-2156. 464 H
mccalebg@acu.edu
MCCALEB, George ... 956-872-8396. 480 I
gmccaleb@southtexascollege.edu
MCCALL, Andy, K ... 865-981-8113. 456 D
andy.mccall@maryvillecollege.edu
MCCALL, Angela, R ... 636-227-2100. 276 F
angela.mccall@logan.edu
MCCALL, Anne ... 607-777-2144. 341 E
amccall@binghamton.edu
MCCALL, Brian ... 512-463-3280. 486 D
chancellor@tsus.edu
MCCALL, Chris ... 713-221-8030. 489 D
mccallc@uhd.edu
MCCALL, Courtney ... 314-340-3391. 275 A
mccallc@hssu.edu
MCCALL, Kris ... 602-943-2311... 19 C
Kris.McCall@west.edu
MCCALL, Michael ... 269-488-4207. 244 L
mmccall@kvcc.edu
MCCALL, Michael, B ... 859-256-3132. 194 I
president@kctcs.edu
MCCALL, Michele ... 660-263-4110. 279 B
michelem@macc.edu
MCCALL, Mike ... 303-871-2562... 86 B
mike.mccall@du.edu
MCCALL, Ryan ... 937-393-3431. 389 B
rmccall@sscc.edu
MCCALL, Sam ... 850-644-6031. 115 C
smmccall@fsu.edu
MCCALL, Sara ... 704-406-2118. 354 C
smccall@gardner-webb.edu
MCCALLA, Connie, L ... 610-359-5301. 414 D
cmccalla@dccc.edu
MCCALLA, Kelly ... 218-855-8184. 258 B
kmccalla@clcmn.edu
MCCALLEY, Greg ... 651-423-8281. 258 D
greg.mccalley@dctc.edu
MCCALLIE, Kathleen, D .. 918-270-6441. 398 I
kathleen.mccallie@ptstulsa.edu
MCCALLIN, Julia, M ... 626-395-3230... 31 E
julia.mccallin@caltech.edu
MCCALLISTER, Emilie ... 815-280-1321. 149 A
emccalli@jjc.edu
MCCALLON, Melanie, C . 270-809-4152. 198 B
mmccallon@murraystate.edu
MCCALLUM, Arminda ... 816-604-2631. 277 F
mindy.mccallum@mcckc.edu
MCCALLUM, SJ,
David, C ... 315-445-6110. 328 F
mccaldac@lemoyne.edu
MCCALLUM, SJ,
David, C ... 315-445-4280. 328 F
mccaldac@lemoyne.edu
MCCALLUM, James ... 919-546-8311. 366 E
jmccallum@shawu.edu
MCCALLUM, Jeannie ... 864-388-8053. 444 K
jmccallum@lander.edu
MCCALLUM, Mark ... 704-463-3307. 365 E
mark.mccallum@fsmail.pfeiffer.edu
MCCALLUM, Rex, M ... 409-772-3639. 493 C
remccall@utmb.edu
MCCALLUM-BEATTY,
Krista ... 740-593-4330. 387 C
mccallum@ohio.edu
MCCALOP, Larry, J ... 404-413-3156. 126 E
lmccalop@gsu.edu
MCCAMBRIDGE, Greg ... 704-687-7683. 368 E
gmccambr@uncc.edu
MCCAMEY, Wade, B ... 423-585-6770. 462 A
wade.mccamey@ws.edu
MCCAMISH, Daniel ... 252-398-6246. 353 H
mccamd@chowan.edu
MCCAMPBELL, Martha ... 423-869-7070. 456 A
matha.mccampbell@lmunet.edu
MCCAMPBELL, Tiffany ... 605-394-2643. 452 A
tiffany.mastin@sdsmt.edu
MCCANCE, John ... 575-492-2141. 312 M
jmccance@usw.edu
MCCANDLESS, Amy, T ... 843-953-1436. 443 A
mccandlessa@cofc.edu
MCCANDLESS, Ann ... 724-287-8711. 411 C
ann.mccandless@bc3.edu
MCCANDLESS, Beverly ... 270-686-4255. 192 G
beverly.mccandless@brescia.edu
MCCANDLESS, John ... 513-529-2223. 384 G
mccandjm@miamioh.edu
MCCANDLESS, Mike ... 209-381-6489... 54 D
mccandless.m@mccd.edu
MCCANDLESS, N. Jane .. 678-839-5170. 133 I
jmccandl@westga.edu
MCCANDLESS, Raymond 419-434-4565. 391 D
mccandless@findlay.edu
MCCANE, Latitia ... 251-405-7013..... 2 D
lmccane@bishop.edu
MCCANN, Bonnie ... 614-947-6017. 380 A
bonnie.mccann@franklin.edu
MCCANN, Diane ... 410-532-5393. 217 E
dmccann@ndm.edu
MCCANN, Heidi ... 978-632-6600. 232 C
MCCANN, Jack ... 423-869-6298. 456 A
jack.mccann@lmunet.edu
MCCANN, James ... 804-627-5300. 502 I
MCCANN, James, D ... 910-962-7410. 369 C
mccannj@uncw.edu
MCCANN, Jean, A ... 636-584-6601. 273 M
mccannja@eastcentral.edu
MCCANN, John ... 512-863-1752. 481 I
mccannj@southwestern.edu
MCCANN, Linda ... 215-968-8003. 411 B
mccannl@bucks.edu
MCCANN, Paul, A ... 217-581-2979. 144 E
pmccann@eiu.edu
MCCANN, Ralph, J ... 770-484-1204. 128 E
lru@lru.edu
MCCANNON, Mindy ... 706-295-6846. 125 F
mmccannon@gntc.edu
MCCARDELL, JR.,
John, M ... 931-598-1101. 458 H
jmmccard@sewanee.edu
MCCAREL, Lori, L ... 757-455-8786. 515 H
MCCARN, Sarah ... 912-525-5000. 131 B
smccarn@scad.edu
MCCARRAHER, Charlotte 609-894-9311. 299 I
cmccarra@bcc.edu
MCCARRICK, Richard, G 914-594-4503. 334 A
richard_mccarrick@nymc.edu
MCCARROLL, Colleen ... 312-235-3531. 159 A
c.mccarroll@shimer.edu
MCCARROLL, John, F ... 515-294-6137. 175 H
jmccarol@iastate.edu
MCCARRON, Anne ... 414-382-6068. 531 I
anne.mccarron@alverno.edu
MCCARRON, Tom ... 619-594-5631... 35 D
tmccarron@mail.sdsu.edu
MCCARRON-BURNS,
Ann, K ... 716-673-3333. 342 A
ann.burns@fredonia.edu
MCCARRY, Tim ... 325-670-1434. 472 O
facilities@hsutx.edu
MCCARTER, Debbie, L ... 423-585-6844. 462 A
debbie.mccarter@ws.edu
MCCARTER, Kevin ... 215-972-2097. 426 Y
kmccarter@pafa.edu
MCCARTER, Rachel ... 610-902-8256. 411 E
rachel.mccarter@cabrini.edu
MCCARTHY, Anne ... 651-523-2335. 256 A
MCCARTHY, Ashley ... 607-431-4990. 325 F
mccarthya3@hartwick.edu
MCCARTHY, Barbara ... 914-773-3741. 335 J
bmccarthy@pace.edu
MCCARTHY, Barbara ... 860-253-3102... 88 C
bmccarthy@asnuntuck.edu
MCCARTHY, Carla, M ... 401-841-2220. 545 A
MCCARTHY, Casey, J ... 218-755-3888. 258 A
cmccarthy@bemidjistate.edu
MCCARTHY, Christian ... 508-767-7424. 222 C
cmccarthy@assumption.edu
MCCARTHY, Colby ... 610-861-1330. 424 E
mectm01@moravian.edu
MCCARTHY, Daniel ... 985-549-2055. 208 C
dmccarthy@selu.edu
MCCARTHY, David, B ... 402-461-7397. 289 I
dmccarthy@hastings.edu
MCCARTHY, Douglas ... 602-285-7245... 15 C
douglas.mccarthy@phoenixcollege.edu
MCCARTHY, Elizabeth, K 508-678-2811. 231 B
elizabeth.mccarthy@bristolcc.edu
MCCARTHY, Faith ... 530-221-4275... 65 F
shastaonline@clearwire.net
MCCARTHY, Faith ... 530-221-4275... 65 F
registrar@shasta.edu
MCCARTHY, Hannah, M . 617-730-7035. 235 D
hannah.mccarthy@newbury.edu
MCCARTHY, James ... 617-573-8000. 237 B
jmccarthy@suffolk.edu
MCCARTHY, James ... 609-652-4335. 305 C
james.mccarthy@stockton.edu
MCCARTHY, James ... 610-861-5506. 425 D
jmccarthy@northampton.edu
MCCARTHY, Joan ... 402-461-7700. 289 I
jmccarthy@hastings.edu
MCCARTHY, John, C ... 202-319-5259... 94 G
mccartjc@cua.edu
MCCARTHY, John, H ... 617-373-2240. 235 F
MCCARTHY, John, J ... 413-545-5220. 228 F
jmccarthy@grad.umass.edu
MCCARTHY, Katherine ... 304-766-3039. 530 C
kmccarthy@wvstateu.edu
MCCARTHY, Kelly ... 708-235-3966. 145 F
kmccarthy@govst.edu
MCCARTHY, Kevin ... 518-255-5217. 344 E
mccartk@cobleskill.edu
MCCARTHY, Kevin ... 315-568-3267. 333 C
kmccarthy@nycc.edu
MCCARTHY, Kevin ... 757-822-5121. 514 C
kmccarthy@tcc.edu
MCCARTHY, Kevin ... 425-564-2191. 517 A
kevin.mccarthy@bellevuecollege.edu
MCCARTHY, Kevin ... 704-355-2000. 353 D
kevin.mccarthy@carolinashealthcare.org
MCCARTHY, Kevin ... 704-330-6907. 359 C
kevin.mccarthy@cpcc.edu
MCCARTHY, Kevin, E ... 630-637-5134. 154 F
kemccarthy@nactrl.edu
MCCARTHY, Lisa ... 609-771-2082. 300 E
mccarthy@tcnj.edu
MCCARTHY, Margaret ... 716-888-2120. 316 C
mmccarth@canisius.edu
MCCARTHY, Margaret ... 716-888-3745. 316 C
mmccarth@canisius.edu
MCCARTHY, Margo, M ... 203-576-5556... 91 D
mmccarthy@stvincentscollege.edu
MCCARTHY, Mark, D ... 216-397-4213. 381 R
mmccarthy@jcu.edu
MCCARTHY, Marsha ... 973-877-3053. 301 H
mccarthy@essex.edu
MCCARTHY, Mary ... 607-778-5210. 315 I
mccarthyma@sunybroome.edu
MCCARTHY, Maureen ... 770-499-3545. 127 N
mmccar10@kennesaw.edu
MCCARTHY, Melissa ... 401-874-2599. 440 D
melissa@uri.edu
MCCARTHY, SJ, Michael 408-554-4715... 64 M
mcmccarthy@scu.edu
MCCARTHY, Monique ... 239-687-5423... 98 J
mmccarthy@avemarialaw.edu
MCCARTHY, Pamela ... 413-585-2840. 236 H
pmccarth@smith.edu
MCCARTHY, Paul, J ... 214-860-2010. 470 J
pmccarthy@dcccd.edu
MCCARTHY, Peter, X ... 386-506-3107. 101 G
mccartp@DaytonaState.edu
MCCARTHY, Rosemary ... 412-536-1173. 420 A
rosemary.mccarthy@laroche.edu
MCCARTHY, Sean ... 312-777-8726. 147 D
smccarthy@aii.edu
MCCARTHY, Sherry ... 573-592-4368. 285 D
smccarth@williamwoods.edu
MCCARTHY, Suzanne ... 908-852-1400. 300 D
library@centenarycollege.edu
MCCARTHY, Thomas ... 718-862-7977. 329 M
thomas.mccarthy@manhattan.edu
MCCARTNEY, Kathleen ... 413-585-2100. 236 H
kmccartney@smith.edu
MCCARTNEY, Patrick, S . 913-288-7166. 187 L
MCCARTNEY, William, G 765-496-2270. 171 M
mccart@purdue.edu
MCCARTNEY, JR.,
William, L ... 252-328-6050. 367 B
mccartneyw@ecu.edu
MCCARTY, Alison ... 617-964-1100. 222 A
amccarty@ants.edu
MCCARTY, II, Gerald ... 810-766-4206. 239 H
gerald.mccartyii@baker.edu
MCCARTY, Josh ... 870-759-4143... 25 K
jmccarty@wbcoll.edu
MCCARTY, Kyla ... 417-690-3292. 272 E
mccarty@cofo.edu
MCCARTY, Lori ... 276-656-0212. 513 D
lmccarty@patrickhenry.edu
MCCARTY, Michael ... 715-324-6900. 535 E
michael.mccarty@ni.edu
MCCARTY, Richard, C ... 615-322-4219. 463 G
richard.mccarty@vanderbilt.edu
MCCARTY, Susan ... 212-772-4850. 318 C
susan.mccarty@hunter.cuny.edu
MCCARTY, Therese, A ... 518-388-6102. 348 J
mccartyt@union.edu
MCCARTY, Thomas ... 415-276-8143... 18 I
thomas.mccarty@phoenix.edu
MCCARTY-HARRIS,
Yulanda ... 216-687-2223. 377 F
y.mccartyharris@csuohio.edu
MCCARVEL, Thomas, J ... 406-447-4409. 285 G
tmccarve@carroll.edu
MCCARY, Sylvia ... 610-353-7630. 419 L
MCCASKILL, Angela ... 202-651-5000... 95 C
angela.mccaskill@gallaudet.edu
MCCASKILL, Donna ... 407-831-9816... 99 O
dmccaskill@citycollege.edu
MCCASKILL, Rock ... 864-644-5538. 446 I
rmccaskill@swu.edu
MCCASKILL, Sharrell ... 202-651-5642... 95 C
sharrell.mccaskill@gallaudet.edu
MCCASLIN, John ... 931-553-0071. 457 F
john.mccaslin@miller-motte.com
MCCASLIN, Julie ... 423-746-5214. 462 C
jmccaslin@twcnet.edu
MCCASLIN, Randall ... 814-732-1346. 428 E
rmccaslin@edinboro.edu
MCCASLIN, Sharon ... 314-889-4567. 274 E
smccaslin@fontbonne.edu
MCCAUGHTRY,
Samuel, L ... 814-456-7504. 416 A
mccaughtrys@eriebc.edu
MCCAULEY, Brian ... 618-374-5180. 156 B
brian.mccauley@principia.edu
MCCAULEY, Dennis ... 215-968-8394. 411 B
mccauley@bucks.edu
MCCAULEY, Howard ... 816-271-4266. 279 A
admissn@missouriwestern.edu
MCCAULEY, James, L ... 860-444-8280. 545 G
james.l.mccauley@uscg.mil
MCCAULEY, Kevin, R ... 805-893-8182... 72 B
kevin.mccauley@chancellor.ucsb.edu
MCCAULEY, Laurie, K ... 734-763-3311. 251 C
mccauley@umich.edu
MCCAULEY, Linda ... 404-727-7976. 124 E
linda.mccauley@emory.edu
MCCAULEY, Terry, L ... 248-232-4550. 248 D
tlmccaul@oaklandcc.edu
MCCAUSLAND, Bill ... 813-974-1868. 116 C
mccausland@usf.edu
MCCAUSLAND, Randy ... 850-644-2129. 115 C
rmccausland@admin.fsu.edu
MCCAUSLIN, Lauren ... 617-243-2139. 227 K
lmccauslin@lasell.edu
MCCAW, Ian, J ... 254-710-1222. 467 G
ian_mccaw@baylor.edu
MCCAW, Matt, S ... 312-939-0111. 144 D
matt@eastwest.edu
MCCAWLEY, Loree ... 831-479-6234... 30 G
lomccawl@cabrillo.edu
MCCAY, Bill ... 509-865-8520. 520 D
mccay_b@heritage.edu
MCCAY, Julie ... 828-884-8264. 352 I
mccayjp@brevard.edu
MCCAY, T. Dwayne ... 321-674-8889. 104 H
tdmccay@fit.edu
MCCHESNEY, Rob ... 309-467-6396. 145 C
rmcchesney@eureka.edu
MCCLAFFERTY, Joseph .. 406-496-4804. 287 F
jmcclafferty@mtech.edu
MCCLAIN, Beth ... 309-694-5323. 146 E
bmcclain@icc.edu

MCCLAIN, Davina .... 318-357-4592. 208 B
mcclaind@nsula.edu

MCCLAIN, Elman .... 206-934-5437. 522 J
elman.mcclain@seattlecolleges.edu

MCCLAIN, James .... 626-914-8794... 38 K
jmcclain@citruscollege.edu

MCCLAIN, James, W ...... 870-838-2910... 19 K
jmcclain@smail.anc.edu

MCCLAIN, Jason .... 304-829-7601. 526 D
jmcclain@bethanywv.edu

MCCLAIN, Mark .... 937-766-7933. 375 K
mcclain@cedarville.edu

MCCLAIN, Paula, D .... 919-681-1560. 354 A
pmmclain@duke.edu

MCCLAIN, Samantha, E .. 515-574-1080. 179 D
mcclain@iowacentral.edu

MCCLAIN, Tim .... 360-486-8875. 522 G
tmc@stmartin.edu

MCCLANAHAN, Ana, M .. 919-513-2311. 364 G
ammcclanahan@waketech.edu

MCCLANAHAN, Keith ..... 501-882-8811... 19 M
mkmcclanahan@asub.edu

MCCLANAHAN, Ronda ... 423-442-2001. 454 L
mcclanahan@hiwassee.edu

MCCLANAHAN,
Thomas, H .... 559-278-0840... 33 D
thomas_mcclanahan@csufresno.edu

MCCLANE, Curtis .... 865-599-0203. 458 A
curtismcclane@gmail.com

MCCLAY, Diana, D .... 423-439-5890. 459 C
mcclayd@etsu.edu

MCCLAY, Kelly .... 609-343-4939. 299 A
mcclay@atlantic.edu

MCCLEAN, Freda .... 212-220-8316. 317 A
fmcclean@bmcc.edu

MCCLEAN, Kevin .... 602-639-7500... 13 S

MCCLEARY, Kathryn, S ... 410-778-7470. 221 C
kmccleary2@washcoll.edu

MCCLEARY, Tim .... 406-638-3121. 286 D
baaxpaa@lbhc.edu

MCCLEERY, Steve .... 575-392-5004. 310 G
smccleery@nmjc.edu

MCCLEISH, Joan, M .... 515-643-6625. 181 A
jmccleish@mercydesmoines.org

MCCLELLAN, Cissy .... 802-860-2711. 499 A
mcclella@champlain.edu

MCCLELLAN, Craig .... 304-326-1465. 527 G
cmcclellan@salemu.edu

MCCLELLAN, Debralee .... 843-525-8210. 447 C
dmcclellan@tcl.edu

MCCLELLAN, Edie .... 414-847-3233. 534 F
ediemcclellan@miad.edu

MCCLELLAN, Fletcher ..... 717-361-1555. 415 H
mcclelef@etown.edu

MCCLELLAN, George, S .. 260-481-6844. 168 C
mcclellg@ipfw.edu

MCCLELLAN, Jane .... 201-200-3196. 303 F
jmcclellan@njcu.edu

MCCLELLAN, Laura .... 276-739-2425. 514 D
lMcClellan@vhcc.edu

MCCLELLAN, Mack .... 405-585-4426. 397 C
mark.mcclellan@okbu.edu

MCCLELLAN, Mia, C .... 619-482-6369... 68 B
mmcclellan@swccd.edu

MCCLELLAN, Patricia ...... 828-251-6001. 368 C
pmcclell@unca.edu

MCCLELLAN, Scott .... 206-220-8229. 523 E
mcclells@seattleu.edu

MCCLELLAN, Steven, J .... 501-569-3202... 24 B
sjmcclellan@ualr.edu

MCCLELLAND,
Charles, F .... 713-313-7216. 485 F
mcclellandcf@tsu.edu

MCCLELLAND, Janet .... 763-424-0902. 260 C
jmcclelland@nhcc.edu

MCCLELLAND, II,
Thomas, H .... 318-257-0211. 207 F

MCCLELLON, Leslie .... 303-352-3786... 81 D
leslie.mcclellon@ccd.edu

MCCLENAGAN,
Cindy, M .... 806-291-1106. 494 F
cindym@wbu.edu

MCCLENDON, Bev .... 479-788-7082... 24 A
bev.mcclendon@uafs.edu

MCCLENDON, Karen .... 916-631-8108... 32 C

MCCLENDON, Mark .... 817-515-5203. 482 B
mark.mcclendon@tccd.edu

MCCLENDON, Mark .... 940-397-4567. 476 H
mark.mcclendon@mwsu.edu

MCCLENDON, Rick .... 540-665-5445. 509 E
rmcclend@su.edu

MCCLENDON,
Rodney, P .... 979-862-1065. 483 C
rpm@tamu.edu

MCCLENDON, Vivienne .. 707-654-1283... 31 I
vmcclendon@csum.edu

MCCLEON, Mitch .... 601-635-2111. 266 H
mmcleon@eccc.edu

MCCLINTOCK, Kate .... 707-527-4797... 65 B
kmcclintock@santarosa.edu

MCCLINTOCK, Marta ...... 724-938-4251. 428 A
mcclintock@calu.edu

MCCLINTOCK, Melvin, A 240-895-4309. 218 A
mamcclintock@smcm.edu

MCCLINTOCK, Patty .... 812-237-2305. 167 A
patty.mcclintock@indstate.edu

MCCLINTON, JR.,
Flandus .... 225-771-5021. 206 J
flandus_mcclinton@subr.edu

MCCLINTON, Martin .... 518-743-2337. 345 E
mcclintonm@sunyacc.edu

MCCLOSKEY, Erin, E ...... 814-472-3100. 432 D
emccloskey@francis.edu

MCCLOSKEY, James, M . 302-356-6880... 94 E
james.m.mccloskey@wilmu.edu

MCCLOSKEY, JR.,
John, R .... 610-796-3005. 409 E
john.mccloskey@alvernia.edu

MCCLOUD, Alyssa .... 973-313-6146. 307 C
alyssa.mccloud@shu.edu

MCCLOUD, Clarence .... 386-506-6301. 101 G
mcclouc@DaytonaState.edu

MCCLOUD, Elizabeth, K .. 717-361-1404. 415 H
mcclouek@etown.edu

MCCLOUD, Michael .... 816-604-4332. 277 H
micky.mccloud@mcckc.edu

MCCLOY, Eric .... 215-572-8521. 409 H
mccloy@arcadia.edu

MCCLUNEY, Alice .... 828-395-1495. 361 C
amccluney@isothermal.edu

MCCLUNG, Alan .... 423-614-8410. 455 L
amcclung@leeuniversity.edu

MCCLUNG, Alex .... 973-684-6741. 304 B
amcclung@pccc.edu

MCCLUNG, Denise .... 304-424-8230. 530 E
denise.mcclung@wvup.edu

MCCLUNG, Hugh .... 281-649-3308. 473 B
hmcclung@hbu.edu

MCCLUNG, Philip, L .... 336-734-7212. 360 E
pmcclung@forsythtech.edu

MCCLURE, A. Glann .... 610-917-1453. 436 C
agmcclure@vfcc.edu

MCCLURE, Amber .... 575-461-4413. 309 M
amberm@mesalands.edu

MCCLURE, Amy .... 740-368-3562. 387 J
aamcclur@owu.edu

MCCLURE, Dan .... 503-821-8970. 406 F
dan@pnca.edu

MCCLURE, Danielle .... 419-227-3141. 391 F
dmcclure@unoh.edu

MCCLURE, David .... 254-526-1166. 468 G
david.mcclure@ctcd.edu

MCCLURE, Erin .... 361-593-2795. 484 A
erin.mcclure@tamuk.edu

MCCLURE, Guy .... 256-233-8296..... 1 F
guy.mcclure@athens.edu

MCCLURE, H. Lawrence .. 215-780-1331. 433 A
larry@salus.edu

MCCLURE, Jennifer .... 847-214-7319. 144 F
jmcclure@elgin.edu

MCCLURE, John .... 773-602-5000. 142 B

MCCLURE, Joy .... 312-332-0707. 160 J

MCCLURE, Kelly .... 215-991-3573. 420 B
mcclure@lasalle.edu

MCCLURE, Ken .... 417-836-5233. 278 E
kmcclure@missuristate.edu

MCCLURE, Lawrence .... 215-780-1331. 433 A
larry@salus.edu

MCCLURE, Mike .... 541-956-7237. 407 F
mmclure@roguecc.edu

MCCLURE, Robert .... 845-446-1522. 545 I
Robert.McClure@wpaog.org

MCCLURE, Tonya .... 478-757-3467. 122 F
tmcclure@centralgatech.edu

MCCLURE, Wesley, C ...... 731-426-7595. 455 J
mcclure@lanecollege.edu

MCCLURE, William .... 718-997-5790. 319 C
william.mcclure@qc.cuny.edu

MCCLURE, William, S ...... 413-545-2111. 228 F
billmcclure@contined.umass.edu

MCCLUSKEY, Don .... 360-676-2772. 521 D
dmccluskey@nwic.edu

MCCLUSKEY, Eugene ...... 207-768-2786. 210 M
emccluskey@nmcc.edu

MCCLUSKEY, Jennifer ..... 314-529-9561. 276 G
jmccluskey@maryville.edu

MCCLUSKEY, Peter .... 860-255-3510... 89 G
pmccluskey@txcc.commnet.edu

MCCLUSKEY-FAWCETT,
Kathleen, A .... 785-864-2768. 190 L
kamf@ku.edu

MCCLYMONT, Jay, W ..... 717-766-2511. 423 L
jmcclymont@messiah.edu

MCCOEY, Margaret .... 215-951-1222. 420 B
mccoey@lasalle.edu

MCCOLGIN, Cathleen, C 315-498-2790. 335 G
mccolgic@sunyocc.edu

MCCOLLETT, Sherry .... 207-621-3141. 212 C
umafa@maine.edu

MCCOLLOCH, Mark .... 443-840-1021. 214 E
mmocolloch@ccbcmd.edu

MCCOLLOUGH, Gary ...... 501-450-3124... 25 H
gmccollough@uca.edu

MCCOLLOUGH, Laura, L 907-474-1886... 10 I
lcmccollough@alaska.edu

MCCOLLUM, Alonzo, L ... 516-876-3068. 343 D
mccolluma@oldwestbury.edu

MCCOLLUM, Estella .... 785-864-2468. 190 L
estellam@ku.edu

MCCOLLUM, James .... 717-871-5955. 429 D
james.mccollum@millersville.edu

MCCOLLUM, Julie .... 816-584-6206. 280 C
julie.mccollum@park.edu

MCCOLLUM, Kenneth ..... 718-940-5952. 339 B
kmccollum@sjcny.edu

MCCOLLUM, Rick, L .... 501-450-3132... 25 H
rickm@uca.edu

MCCOLLUM, Scott .... 937-512-3068. 388 O
scott.mccullum@sinclair.edu

MCCOLSKEY, Erin, S ...... 561-868-3139. 110 C
mccolske@palmbeachstate.edu

MCCOMAS, Richard .... 580-581-2524. 394 G
richardm@cameron.edu

MCCOMB, Brenda .... 541-737-4881. 406 A
brenda.mccomb@oregonstate.edu

MCCOMBS, Ed .... 928-724-6635... 13 H
emccombs@dinecollege.edu

MCCOMBS, Gary .... 864-388-8305. 444 K
gmccombs@lander.edu

MCCOMBS, Gillian, M .... 214-768-2400. 481 A
gmccombs@smu.edu

MCCOMBS, Laurie .... 216-687-3606. 377 F
l.mccombs11@csuohio.edu

MCCOMBS, Tyrone .... 856-756-5400. 305 E
mccombs@rowan.edu

MCCONAHAY, Mark .... 812-855-2654. 167 F
mcconaha@indiana.edu

MCCONATHY, Jamie .... 870-862-8131... 23 D
jmcconathy@southark.edu

MCCONATHY, Terry, M .. 318-257-4262. 207 F
tmm@latech.edu

MCCONNELL, Blake .... 618-658-8331. 150 D
james.mcconnell@doc.illinois.gov

MCCONNELL,
C. Douglas .... 626-584-5205... 45 E
provost@fuller.edu

MCCONNELL, Cary .... 617-573-8575. 237 B
cmcconnell@suffolk.edu

MCCONNELL, Cheryl, M 816-501-4087. 280 I
cheryl.mcconnell@rockhurst.edu

MCCONNELL, David .... 336-272-7102. 354 E
dmcconnell@greensboro.edu

MCCONNELL, Frank, J ... 706-864-1606. 133 D
mac.mcconnell@ung.edu

MCCONNELL, Gaye .... 704-216-3600. 363 D
gaye.mcconnell@rccc.edu

MCCONNELL, Jason .... 423-869-6333. 456 A
jason.mcconnell@lmunet.edu

MCCONNELL, Joyce, E .... 304-293-3199. 530 D
joyce.mcconnell@mail.wvu.edu

MCCONNELL, Judy, A .... 940-565-2741. 490 C
judith.mcconnell@unt.edu

MCCONNELL, Kathy .... 619-849-2412... 59 L
kathymcconnell@pointloma.edu

MCCONNELL, Marcia ...... 706-232-5374. 121 G

MCCONNELL, Penny, J .. 217-443-8747. 143 G
pmcconn@dacc.edu

MCCONNELL,
Richard, W .... 260-359-4043. 166 O
rmcconnell@huntington.edu

MCCONNELL, Robert .... 334-876-9270..... 4 A
rmcconnell@wccs.edu

MCCONNELL, Savannah . 304-296-8282. 531 F
smcconnell@wvjcmorgantown.edu

MCCONNELLOGUE, Ken . 303-860-5600... 85 K
ken.mcconnellogue@cu.edu

MCCONOUGHEY, Gina ... 608-757-7723. 539 I
gmcconoughey@blackhawk.edu

MCCOO, Myron, S .... 603-646-0007. 296 G
myron.s.mccoo@dartmouth.edu

MCCOOL, Bobby .... 606-886-3863. 194 K
bobby.mccool@kctcs.edu

MCCOOL, Jeffery .... 575-492-4711. 310 G
jmccool@nmjc.edu

MCCOOL, Joan, L .... 716-878-4436. 343 A
mccooljl@buffalostate.edu

MCCORD, Carol .... 812-856-2291. 167 F
camccord@indiana.edu

MCCORD, Christopher .... 815-753-1061. 154 I
mccord@niu.edu

MCCORD, Elizabeth .... 415-451-2832... 63 A
emccord@sfts.edu

MCCORD, Jeff, D .... 423-354-5207. 461 C
jdmccord@northeaststate.edu

MCCORD, S. Alan .... 248-204-2400. 245 I
amccord@ltu.edu

MCCORD-FITHIAN,
Regina, L .... 812-888-5848. 174 F
rmccord-fithian@vinu.edu

MCCORMACK, Amy .... 708-524-6770. 144 C
amccormack@dom.edu

MCCORMACK, Bridey ..... 806-457-4200. 472 G
bmccormack@fpctx.edu

MCCORMACK, Corky ...... 417-447-8172. 279 K
mccormac@otc.edu

MCCORMACK, Erin .... 801-302-2800. 496 B
erin.mccormack@neumont.edu

MCCORMACK, Gary .... 713-942-3400. 490 L
mccormack@stthom.edu

MCCORMACK, Jeff .... 615-966-7167. 456 B
jeff.mccormack@lipscomb.edu

MCCORMACK, John .... 708-596-2000. 159 C
jmccormack@ssc.edu

MCCORMACK, Laurie ..... 816-584-6210. 280 C
laurie.mccormack@park.edu

MCCORMACK, Mike .... 205-726-2916...... 6 F
hmmccorm@samford.edu

MCCORMICK, Adrienne ... 716-673-3111. 342 A
adrienne.mccormick@fredonia.edu

MCCORMICK, Al .... 800-962-7682. 285 A
amccormick@wma.edu

MCCORMICK, Bobbie ..... 209-473-5200... 47 F
bobbie_mccormick@heald.edu

MCCORMICK, Brad .... 618-985-8340. 148 J
bradmccormick@jalc.edu

MCCORMICK, Brad .... 423-697-3264. 460 C

MCCORMICK, Charlie, T 830-792-7371. 480 F
ctmccormick@schreiner.edu

MCCORMICK,
Christine, B .... 413-545-2705. 228 F
cmccormick@educ.umass.edu

MCCORMICK, David .... 312-567-4972. 147 F
dmccormick@iitri.org

MCCORMICK, Deanna ..... 410-435-0100. 217 E
dmccormick@ndm.edu

MCCORMICK, Gordon ..... 831-656-2484. 544 M
gmccormick@navy.edu

MCCORMICK, Heidi, A ... 330-263-2533. 377 H
hmccormick@wooster.edu

MCCORMICK, Jim, S ...... 303-963-3363... 79 C
jimmccormick@ccu.edu

MCCORMICK, John .... 801-957-4024. 498 B
john.mccormick@slcc.edu

MCCORMICK, Kelly, L .... 303-765-3121... 82 E
kmccormick@iliff.edu

MCCORMICK, Kevin, M .. 630-515-6053. 153 B
kmccor@midwestern.edu

MCCORMICK, Kimberly .. 423-697-2647. 460 C

MCCORMICK,
Kirsten, M .... 714-879-3901... 47 K
kmmccormick@hiu.edu

MCCORMICK, Mark .... 205-247-8831..... 7 E
mmccormick@stillman.edu

MCCORMICK, Mark .... 856-351-2670. 307 B
mmccormick@salemcc.edu

MCCORMICK, OSU,
Mary .... 440-943-7600. 388 J
mmccormick@dioceseofcleveland.org

MCCORMICK, Megan ...... 310-377-5501... 53 F
mmccormick@marymountcalifornia.edu

MCCORMICK,
Michael, R .... 315-386-7222. 345 F
mccormic@canton.edu

MCCORMICK, Patrick, T . 509-313-6715. 520 A
mccormick@calvin.gonzaga.edu

MCCORMICK, Reenie ...... 410-334-2939. 221 D
rmccormick@worwic.edu

MCCORMICK, Reid, W .... 714-879-3901... 47 K
rwmccormick@hiu.edu

MCCORMICK, Robert ...... 312-362-6627. 143 H
bmccormi@depaul.edu

MCCORMICK, Stanley ..... 229-430-4754. 119 J
stanley.McCormick@asurams.edu

MCCORMICK, Susan .... 979-230-3423. 468 A
susan.mccormick@brazosport.edu

MCCORMICK, Vicky .... 626-396-2456... 28 P
vicky.mccormick@artcenter.edu

MCCORRY, Laurie, K ...... 617-228-2465. 231 C
lkmccorry@bhcc.mass.edu

MCCORRY-ANDALIS,
Catherine, M .... 915-747-5648. 492 A
cmandalis@utep.edu

MCCORVEY, Angela, E .... 850-474-7448. 117 B
amccorv0@uwf.edu

MCCORY, Denise .... 216-987-5544. 378 D
denise.mccory@tri-c.edu

MCCOULLUM, Valarie, S 215-898-5337. 435 B
cade@upenn.edu

MCCOURT,
Mary Frances .... 812-855-7618. 167 E
mmmccour@indiana.edu

MCCOURT, MaryFrances 812-855-7114. 167 F
vpcfo@indiana.edu

MCCOURT, MaryFrances 812-855-3565. 167 E
mmmccour@indiana.edu

MCCOWAN, Carla .... 217-333-3701. 162 A
cmccowan@illinois.edu

MCCOWAN, Thema .... 865-273-8851. 456 D
thema.mccowan@maryvillecollege.edu

MCCOWN, Rachel .... 417-864-7220. 274 D
rmccown@cci.edu

MCCOWN, William ... 318-342-1036. 208 E mccown@ulm.edu
MCCOY, Amy ... 509-533-7015. 518 E Amy.McCoy@scc.spokane.edu
MCCOY, Amy ... 509-533-7015. 518 D amy.mccoy@scc.spokane.edu
MCCOY, Avis, M ... 954-201-7401... 99 D amccoy@broward.edu
MCCOY, Carole, A ... 315-786-2230. 327 L cmccoy@sunyjefferson.edu
MCCOY, Chris ... 651-201-1454. 257 N chris.mccoy@so.mnscu.edu
MCCOY, Dara ... 903-813-2335. 466 H dmccoy@austincollege.edu
MCCOY, David, M ... 804-289-8718. 510 L dmccoy2@richmond.edu
MCCOY, Elizabeth, W ... 801-581-5701. 496 Q liz.mccoy@utah.edu
MCCOY, Holly, M ... 724-738-2650. 429 F holly.mccoy@sru.edu
MCCOY, Hugh ... 715-324-6900. 535 E hugh.mccoy@ni.edu
MCCOY, J. Kelly ... 229-931-2320. 126 D kellly.mccoy@gsw.edu
MCCOY, James ... 203-932-7306... 92 E jmccoy@newhaven.edu
MCCOY, Janee ... 914-964-4282. 320 C
MCCOY, Jeff ... 504-394-7744. 206 C jmccoy@olhcc.edu
MCCOY, John ... 423-236-2444. 458 J jmccoy@southern.edu
MCCOY, Jolie, A ... 605-394-1924. 452 A jolie.mccoy@sdsmt.edu
MCCOY, Julie ... 803-938-3753. 448 F jmccoy@uscsumter.edu
MCCOY, Keith ... 773-838-7514. 142 E kmccoy@ccc.edu
MCCOY, Marilyn ... 847-491-4335. 155 D mmccoy@northwestern.edu
MCCOY, Mark ... 765-658-6732. 165 F markmccoy@depauw.edu
MCCOY, Mary ... 409-882-3080. 486 G mary.mccoy@lsco.edu
MCCOY, Mary ... 405-682-1611. 397 E mmccoy@occc.edu
MCCOY, Matthew, J ... 541-383-7210. 402 D mmccoy@cocc.edu
MCCOY, Mike ... 515-244-4221. 175 C mccoym@aib.edu
MCCOY, Mike ... 256-216-3300... 1 F mike.mccoy@athens.edu
MCCOY, Myron, F ... 816-483-9600. 190 D myron@spst.edu
MCCOY, Paddy ... 509-527-2343. 524 I paddy.mccoy@wallawalla.edu
MCCOY, Patrick, J ... 828-262-3187. 367 A mccoypj@appstate.edu
MCCOY, Peggy, S ... 406-496-4404. 287 F pmccoy@mtech.edu
MCCOY, Robert ... 907-474-7500... 10 I rpmccoy@alaska.edu
MCCOY, Shelly ... 931-393-1600. 461 A smccoy@mscc.edu
MCCOY, Stephen, L ... 276-328-2677. 511 C slm4u@uvawise.edu
MCCOY, Sue ... 212-353-4167. 321 F mccoy@cooper.edu
MCCOY, Thomas, J ... 940-369-8249. 490 C thomas.mccoy@unt.edu
MCCOY, William, K ... 570-577-1609. 411 A bill.mccoy@bucknell.edu
MCCRACKEN, Carolyn ... 423-354-2509. 461 C cgmccracken@northeaststate.edu
MCCRACKEN, Fawn ... 952-446-4325. 255 D mccrackenf@crown.edu
MCCRACKEN, Jeff, B ... 919-966-5730. 368 D jeff_mccracken@unc.edu
MCCRACKEN, Joann ... 610-989-1450. 436 D jbmiller@vfmac.edu
MCCRACKEN, Larry ... 503-517-1879. 408 I lmccracken@westernseminary.edu
MCCRACKEN, Mike ... 620-235-4624. 189 L mmccrack@pittstate.edu
MCCRAE, Byron ... 413-559-5412. 227 B
MCCRANEY, Michelle ... 386-506-4110. 101 G mccranm@DaytonaState.edu
MCCRANEY, Steven ... 601-925-3204. 268 A smccraney@mc.edu
MCCRARY, Betty, M ... 318-797-5364. 205 F betty.mccrary@lsus.edu
MCCRARY, Brian ... 678-839-6619. 133 I bmccrary@westga.edu
MCCRARY, Kevin ... 386-506-3475. 101 G mccrark@DaytonaState.edu
MCCRAW, Bethany, J ... 254-710-1715. 467 G bethany_mccraw@baylor.edu
MCCRAW, Ed ... 903-785-7661. 478 B emccraw@parisjc.edu
MCCRAW, Patti, H ... 864-488-4571. 444 L pmccraw@limestone.edu
MCCRAW, Sasha ... 706-821-8167. 130 C smccraw@paine.edu
MCCRAY, Allison ... 912-650-5677. 131 H amccray@southuniversity.edu
MCCRAY, Carie ... 573-592-4317. 285 D carrie.mccray@williamwoods.edu
MCCRAY, JR., John, H ... 401-277-5489. 440 D drmccray@uri.edu
MCCRAY, Suzanne ... 479-575-4883... 23 I smccray@uark.edu
MCCREADIE, Maureen ... 215-968-8004. 411 B mccreadi@bucks.edu
MCCREADY, Peggy, A ... 203-432-2038... 93 A peggy.mccready@yale.edu
MCCREADY, Randall ... 262-595-2004. 537 C randall.mccready@uwp.edu
MCCREARY, Lynn ... 940-565-2378. 490 C mccreary@unt.edu
MCCREARY, Sherry ... 423-869-6467. 456 A sherry.mccreary@lmunet.edu
MCCREDIE, Wendy ... 310-954-4015... 54 J wmccredie@msmc.la.edu
MCCREE, Bernard, L ... 610-683-4032. 429 A mccree@kutztown.edu
MCCREE, Ray ... 410-837-6807. 221 A rmccree@ubalt.edu
MCCREE, Robin ... 704-991-0252. 364 C mmccree5540@stanly.edu
MCCREE, Robin ... 704-991-0252. 364 C
MCCREERY, Deborah, M 973-290-4455. 300 F dmccreery@cse.edu
MCCREERY, Shane ... 309-438-3383. 147 J msmccre@ilstu.edu
MCCRILLIS, Neal, R ... 706-565-4036. 123 D mccrillis_neal@columbusstate.edu
MCCRIMMON, Donald, A ... 315-655-7117. 316 E damccrimmon@cazenovia.edu
MCCROHAN, Betty, A ... 979-532-6304. 494 L bettym@wcjc.edu
MCCRORY, Cynthia ... 704-922-6406. 360 F mccrory.cynthia@gaston.edu
MCCRORY, Eric ... 903-233-3810. 475 J ericmccrory@letu.edu
MCCRORY, Robert, L ... 585-275-4973. 349 C rmcc@lle.rochester.edu
MCCROW, Rich ... 661-720-2002... 49 N rmccrow@bakersfieldcollege.edu
MCCROY, Shirley ... 719-532-1234... 85 A
MCCROY-HEINS, Michelle ... 201-692-2190. 301 J michelle_mccroy@fdu.edu
MCCRYSTAL, Mary ... 216-373-5331. 385 G mmccrystal@ndc.edu
MCCUBBIN, Jeff ... 970-491-5841... 80 I jeff.mccubbin@colostate.edu
MCCUBBIN, Todd, A ... 573-882-6017. 283 C mccubbint@missouri.edu
MCCUE, Brian ... 773-907-4856. 142 A bmccue@ccc.edu
MCCUE, Cindy ... 631-420-2319. 346 B cynthia.mccue@farmingdale.edu
MCCUE, James ... 914-674-7880. 330 J jmccue@mercy.edu
MCCUE, Jennie ... 949-582-4320... 67 C jmccue@saddleback.edu
MCCUE, Mary, E ... 419-559-2204. 389 I mmccue@terra.edu
MCCUEN, Jan ... 714-997-6701... 38 A mccuen@chapman.edu
MCCUIEN-SMITH, Cassandra ... 501-450-3173... 25 H cmccuien@uca.edu
MCCULLAR, Douglas, D ... 405-878-5141. 399 G ddmccullar@stgregorys.edu
MCCULLAR, Ron ... 706-245-7226. 124 D rmccullar@ec.edu
MCCULLEN, Ann, S ... 904-620-2100. 116 B amccullen@unf.edu
MCCULLEN, Ann, S ... 904-620-2109. 116 B amccullen@unf.edu
MCCULLEY, Becky ... 214-645-5482. 493 E becky.mcculley@utsouthwestern.edu
MCCULLOCH, Dave ... 770-962-7580. 127 D dmcculloch@gwinnetttech.edu
MCCULLOCH, Greg ... 618-252-5400. 159 E greg.mcculloch@sic.edu
MCCULLOCH, Joseph ... 318-675-5000. 205 D jmccul@lsuhsc.edu
MCCULLOCH, Lisa ... 505-224-4688. 309 E lmcculloch2@cnm.edu
MCCULLOCH, Sonja ... 912-260-4402. 131 F sonja.mcculloch@sgsc.edu
MCCULLOH, Edna ... 330-490-7191. 392 H emcculloh@walsh.edu
MCCULLOH, Julie, A ... 509-313-6572. 520 A mcculloh@gu.gonzaga.edu
MCCULLOH, Thayne, M ... 509-313-6102. 520 A president@gonzaga.edu
MCCULLOH, Waylyn, C ... 563-333-6078. 182 B McCullohWaylynC@sau.edu
MCCULLOUGH, Barbara ... 360-538-4034. 520 B bmccullo@ghc.edu
MCCULLOUGH, Barbara ... 423-614-8567. 455 L mccullough@leeuniversity.edu
MCCULLOUGH, Bryan ... 336-249-4688. 360 A
MCCULLOUGH, Catherine ... 802-728-1247. 501 F cmccull@vtc.edu
MCCULLOUGH, Desiree, A ... 731-881-7014. 463 E dmccull1@utm.edu
MCCULLOUGH, Doreen ... 802-773-5900. 499 B dmccullough@csj.edu
MCCULLOUGH, James ... 918-293-5068. 398 B james.mccullough@okstate.edu
MCCULLOUGH, John, P ... 304-336-8000. 530 A mcculljp@westliberty.edu
MCCULLOUGH, Jonathan, W ... 903-434-8115. 477 J jmccullough@ntcc.edu
MCCULLOUGH, Laura, C ... 301-687-4068. 220 C lcmccullough@frostburg.edu
MCCULLOUGH, Laura, L 304-205-6611. 528 B lmccullough@kvctc.edu
MCCULLOUGH, Lois, N ... 419-783-2317. 379 C lmccullough@defiance.edu
MCCULLOUGH, Randy ... 419-559-2355. 389 I rmccullough01@terra.edu
MCCULLOUGH, Robert, R ... 216-368-5445. 375 J robert.mccullough@case.edu
MCCULLOUGH, Willie ... 606-326-2068. 194 J willie.mccullough@kctcs.edu
MCCULLUM, B. J ... 309-854-1723. 140 E mccullumb@bhc.edu
MCCULLUM, Juan ... 601-877-6380. 265 G jmccullum@alcorn.edu
MCCULLY, Clare ... 617-730-7089. 235 D clare.mccully@newbury.edu
MCCUNE, John ... 781-239-2527. 231 G jmccune@massbay.edu
MCCUNE, John ... 716-673-3373. 342 A thomas.mccune@fredonia.edu
MCCUNE, Mary ... 315-312-3443. 344 A mary.mccune@oswego.edu
MCCUNE, Ryan ... 620-252-7180. 185 O ryanm@coffeyville.edu
MCCURDY, Clantha ... 617-727-9420. 228 D cmccurdy@osfa.mass.edu
MCCURDY, Debra, L ... 419-995-8200. 381 Q mccurdy.d@rhodesstate.edu
MCCURDY, Eugene, M ... 608-796-3921. 539 E emmccurdy@viterbo.edu
MCCURDY, Lyndon, C ... 937-327-7325. 393 E lmccurdy@wittenberg.edu
MCCURLEY, Steve ... 918-540-6196. 396 G smccurley@neo.edu
MCCURREN, Cynthia ... 616-331-3558. 243 C mccurrec@gvsu.edu
MCCURRY, David ... 619-849-2370... 59 L davidmccurry@pointloma.edu
MCCURRY, Faith ... 803-535-1424. 446 B mccurryf@octech.edu
MCCURRY, Rickey, N ... 812-877-8211. 172 C rickey.mccurry@rose-hulman.edu
MCCURTY, Kenyetta ... 334-387-3877... 1 E kenyettamccurty@amridgeuniversity.edu
MCCUSKEY, Beth, M ... 765-494-1022. 171 M bmccuske@purdue.edu
MCCUTCHAN, Molly, M ... 734-384-4245. 247 C mmccutchan@monroeccc.edu
MCCUTCHEN, Michael ... 731-989-6901. 454 J mmccutchen@fhu.edu
MCCUTCHEON, Bruce, E 610-330-5530. 420 D mccutchb@lafayette.edu
MCCUTCHEON, John, F ... 413-545-9682. 228 F jmccutch@admin.umass.edu
MCCUTCHEON, Ron ... 541-885-1120. 405 J ron.mccutcheon@oit.edu
MCDADE, Linda ... 570-348-6249. 423 B lmcdade@marywood.edu
MCDADE, Lucinda ... 909-625-8767... 39 C lucinda.mcdade@cgu.edu
MCDADE, William ... 773-834-3861. 161 B wmcdade@bsd.uchicago.edu
MCDADE-CLAY, W. Thomas ... 585-340-9648. 320 E tmcdadeclay@crcds.edu
MCDAID, James ... 617-879-7960. 230 B jmcdaid@massart.edu
MCDANIEL, Anna, M ... 352-273-6324. 116 A annammcdaniel@ufl.edu
MCDANIEL, C. Joan ... 846-846-5781. 197 I jmcdaniel@midway.edu
MCDANIEL, Cindy ... 810-762-5620. 247 F cindy.mcdanie@mcc.edu
MCDANIEL, Cliff ... 817-461-8741. 466 D cmcdaniel@arlingtonbaptistcollege.edu
MCDANIEL, Diane ... 765-677-2117. 169 B diane.mcdaniel@indwes.edu
MCDANIEL, Donna ... 903-823-3451. 482 D donna.mcdaniel@texarkanacollege.edu
MCDANIEL, Donna, N ... 402-557-7184. 288 G donna.mcdaniel@bellevue.edu
MCDANIEL, Gary, R ... 949-214-3055... 41 I gary.mcdaniel@cui.edu
MCDANIEL, Jervaise ... 618-842-3711. 146 I mcdanielj@iecc.edu
MCDANIEL, Joy ... 580-371-2371. 396 E jmcdaniel@mscok.edu
MCDANIEL, Juley ... 620-223-2700. 186 G juleym@fortscott.edu
MCDANIEL, Julie ... 937-484-1337. 392 C jmcdaniel@urbana.edu
MCDANIEL, Kimberly ... 916-558-2376... 53 D mcdanik@scc.losrios.edu
MCDANIEL, Kristina, D ... 573-840-9695. 282 K mcdank@trcc.edu
MCDANIEL, Lance ... 304-384-5258. 529 E mcdaniell26@mycu.concord.edu
MCDANIEL, Laura ... 701-231-8330. 371 G laura.mcdaniel@ndsu.edu
MCDANIEL, Lucinda ... 870-933-7906... 19 L lmcdaniel@asusystem.edu
MCDANIEL, Mary, W ... 864-388-8242. 444 K mmcdaniel@lander.edu
MCDANIEL, Mary Lee ... 601-857-3395. 267 A mlmcdaniel@hindscc.edu
MCDANIEL, Mick, R ... 607-844-8222. 347 I mcdanim@tc3.edu
MCDANIEL, Peter ... 864-250-7000... 96 F
MCDANIEL, Thomas ... 864-596-9015. 443 D tom.mcdaniel@converse.edu
MCDANIEL, Thomas ... 610-921-7672. 409 A tmcdaniel@alb.edu
MCDANIEL, Yvette ... 803-793-5109. 443 E mcdaniely@denmarktech.edu
MCDANIELS, Lisa ... 207-741-5545. 211 A lmcdaniels@smccme.edu
MCDANIELS, Tammy ... 918-781-7263. 394 D mcdanielsta@bacone.edu
MCDANIELS WILSON, Cathy ... 614-236-6114. 375 H cmcdanielswilson@capital.edu
MCDAVID, Courtney ... 860-832-3003... 87 K mcdavidc@ccsu.edu
MCDAVIS, Roderick, J ... 740-593-1804. 387 C mcdavis@ohio.edu
MCDERMOTT, Patrick ... 941-377-4880. 109 B
MCDERMOTT, A. Keith ... 617-541-2454. 232 G kmcderm@rcc.mass.edu
MCDERMOTT, Ann, B ... 508-793-2443. 225 B amcdermo@holycross.edu
MCDERMOTT, Anne ... 978-922-8222. 234 C anne.mcdermott@montserrat.edu
MCDERMOTT, Beth ... 617-552-4400. 224 A beth.mcdermott@bc.edu
MCDERMOTT, Brian ... 308-398-7387. 288 I bmcdermott@cccneb.edu
MCDERMOTT, Christine ... 315-568-3105. 333 C cmcdermott@nycc.edu
MCDERMOTT, Christine ... 302-736-2491... 94 C mcdermch@wesley.edu
MCDERMOTT, Colleen ... 714-703-1900... 41 E
MCDERMOTT, Daniel ... 216-987-2340. 378 D daniel.mcdermott@tri-c.edu
MCDERMOTT, David ... 617-287-7128. 228 E dmcdermott@umassp.edu
MCDERMOTT, Dennis ... 718-489-5362. 338 G dmcdermott@sfc.edu
MCDERMOTT, Diane ... 312-226-6294. 151 A busofc@lexingtoncolleg.edu
MCDERMOTT, Emily ... 617-287-6500. 228 G emily.mcdermott@umb.edu
MCDERMOTT, Harry ... 520-621-7428... 18 F mcdermott@email.arizona.edu
MCDERMOTT, Joan ... 303-556-8300... 83 D mcdermoj@msudenver.edu
MCDERMOTT, John, R ... 563-588-7132. 180 L john.mcdermott@loras.edu
MCDERMOTT, Marty ... 231-777-0462. 247 G marty.mcdermott@muskegoncc.edu
MCDERMOTT, Patrice ... 410-455-3150. 219 D mcdermot@umbc.edu
MCDERMOTT, Richard, L ... 713-500-4963. 492 E richard.l.mcdermott@uth.tmc.edu
MCDERMOTT, Teresa ... 360-475-7480. 521 H tmcdermott@olympic.edu
MCDERMOTTE, John ... 803-777-4939. 447 G dynamo@moore.sc.edu
MCDEVITT, Brigid ... 206-934-6314. 522 J brigid.mcdevitt@seattlecolleges.edu
MCDEVITT, Jenna ... 740-587-6655. 379 D mcdevitts@denison.edu
MCDIARMID, Bill ... 919-966-1356. 368 D bmcd@email.unc.edu
MCDIFFETT, Tim ... 907-786-1800... 10 H
MCDILL, M. Augustus ... 843-661-1128. 444 B mmcdill@fmarion.edu

MCDILL, Sandy .... 602-787-7352... 15 B
sandy.mcdill@paradisevalley.edu
MCDOLE, Rob .... 803-754-4100. 443 C
MCDONAGH, David .... 212-749-2802. 330 A
dmcdonagh@msmnyc.edu
MCDONALD, Ann, M ...... 978-632-6600. 232 C
a_mcdonald@mwcc.mass.edu
MCDONALD, Barbara ..... 218-322-2402. 258 I
barbara.mcdonald@itascacc.edu
MCDONALD, Becky .... 937-298-3399. 382 K
becky.mcdonald@kc.edu
MCDONALD, Cathy .... 701-328-4111. 371 B
cathy.mcdonald@ndus.edu
MCDONALD,
Christopher .... 949-582-4820... 67 C
cmcdonald@saddleback.edu
MCDONALD, Clay .... 636-227-2100. 276 F
Clay.McDonald@logan.edu
MCDONALD, Dalene .... 620-229-6271. 190 G
dalene.mcdonald@sckans.edu
MCDONALD, Dana .... 301-846-2458. 214 H
dmcdonald@frederick.edu
MCDONALD, David .... 503-838-8211. 406 E
mcdonald@wou.edu
MCDONALD, David .... 608-757-7759. 539 I
dmcdonald@blackhawk.edu
MCDONALD, Debbie ...... 626-966-4576... 27 P
info@agu.edu
MCDONALD, Deborah .... 845-938-5706. 545 I
addimssion@usma.edu
MCDONALD, Denise ...... 434-544-8665. 506 K
mcdonald@lynchburg.edu
MCDONALD, Dennis ...... 518-454-5170. 321 A
mcdonald@strose.edu
MCDONALD, Dotty .... 337-550-1357. 205 B
MCDONALD, Eric .... 864-587-4200. 447 B
mcdonalde@smcsc.edu
MCDONALD, Frank .... 212-346-1800. 335 J
fmcdonald@pace.edu
MCDONALD, Gary .... 415-422-2699... 73 J
mcdonald@usfca.edu
MCDONALD, Ginger .... 978-478-3400. 235 G
gmcdonald@northpoint.edu
MCDONALD, Jack, J ...... 203-582-8621... 91 A
jack.mcdonald@quinnipiac.edu
MCDONALD, James .... 435-586-7898. 497 A
mcdonaldj@suu.edu
MCDONALD, James, L ... 415-451-2810... 63 A
jmcdonald@sfts.edu
MCDONALD, Jan .... 864-977-7151. 445 H
jan.mcdonald@ngu.edu
MCDONALD, Jason .... 503-943-7147. 408 F
mcdonaja@up.edu
MCDONALD, Jennifer ..... 714-241-6163... 39 I
jmcdonald@coastline.edu
MCDONALD, Jessyna ..... 202-274-5533... 97 A
jmcdonald@udc.edu
MCDONALD, Joan, T ..... 215-895-2902. 415 B
mcdonajt@drexel.edu
MCDONALD, Johnny .... 662-252-8000. 269 F
jbmcdonald@rustcollege.edu
MCDONALD, Joseph ...... 518-631-9869. 348 K
mcdonalj@uniongraduatecollege.edu
MCDONALD, Joseph ...... 256-761-6443..... 7 F
jmcdonald@talladega.edu
MCDONALD, Joseph ...... 239-590-1102. 115 A
jmcdonald@fgcu.edu
MCDONALD, Julia, J ...... 270-745-4346. 200 G
julia.mcdonald@wku.edu
MCDONALD, Kevin .... 585-475-6795. 337 L
kgmpro@rit.edu
MCDONALD, Kurt .... 417-690-3200. 272 E
purch@cofo.edu
MCDONALD, Latrice .... 601-928-6206. 268 C
latrice.mcdonald@mgccc.edu
MCDONALD, Leander ...... 701-766-1133. 370 H
leander.mcdonald@littlehoop.edu
MCDONALD, Loretta .... 615-329-8503. 454 F
lmcdonald@fisk.edu
MCDONALD, Lori .... 949-214-3074... 41 I
lori.mcdonald@cui.edu
MCDONALD, Martha .... 626-914-8602... 38 K
mmcdonald@citruscollege.edu
MCDONALD, Mary .... 510-231-5000... 49 D
MCDONALD, Matt, C ..... 507-786-3255. 264 B
mcdonamc@stolaf.edu
MCDONALD, Michael ..... 567-661-7203. 387 L
michael_mcdonald6@owens.edu
MCDONALD, Michael, A 269-337-7162. 244 K
Michael.McDonald@kzoo.edu
MCDONALD, Patrick, S .. 716-880-2345. 330 F
patrick.s.mcdonald@medaille.edu
MCDONALD, Paul, R ...... 626-966-4576... 27 P
paulmcdonald@agu.edu
MCDONALD, Pete .... 706-295-6928. 125 F
pmcdonald@gntc.edu
MCDONALD, Pete .... 706-295-6960. 125 F
pmcdonald@gntc.edu
MCDONALD, Peter .... 559-278-2403... 33 D
pmcdonald@csufresno.edu

MCDONALD, Riley .... 814-536-5168. 412 C
rmcdonald@crbc.net
MCDONALD, Sallie .... 671-735-2233. 546 E
salliemcd@uguam.uog.edu
MCDONALD, Scott .... 979-458-0996. 483 C
smcdonald@tamu.edu
MCDONALD, Steven .... 401-277-4955. 440 A
smcdonal@risd.edu
MCDONALD, Tammy .... 361-698-2177. 471 G
tmcdonal1@delmar.edu
MCDONALD, Tim .... 256-726-8399..... 6 B
tmcdonald@oakwood.edu
MCDONALD, Tim .... 770-531-6339. 128 B
tmcdonal@laniertech.edu
MCDONALD, Timothy ..... 816-501-4077. 280 I
timothy.mcdonald@rockhurst.edu
MCDONALD, Todd .... 231-348-6603. 247 H
tmcdonald@ncmich.edu
MCDONALD, Tom .... 212-229-5900. 332 E
mcdonalt@newschool.edu
MCDONALD, William ...... 315-866-0300. 326 A
mcdonaldwh@herkimer.edu
MCDONALD, William ...... 617-951-2350. 234 G
bill.mcdonald@necb.edu
MCDONALD, William, A . 973-748-9000. 299 F
bill_mcdonald@bloomfield.edu
MCDONALD, William, M 706-542-7774. 133 C
bmcdonal@uga.edu
MCDONALD-RASH,
Jean .... 848-932-7057. 306 A
jrash@rci.rutgers.edu
MCDONALD-RASH,
Jean .... 848-932-7057. 306 B
jean.rash@ofa.rutgers.edu
MCDONEL, James, L ...... 540-224-4515. 506 G
JLMcDonel@jchs.edu
MCDONNEL, Wendy .... 605-221-3100. 450 C
wmcdonnel@kilian.edu
MCDONNELL, Brian, A ... 401-341-2185. 440 C
mcdonneb@salve.edu
MCDONNELL,
Constance, F .... 570-941-7640. 436 A
constance.mcdonnell@scranton.edu
MCDONNELL, Heidi .... 908-852-1400. 300 D
0553txt@fheg.follett.com
MCDONNELL, Jason .... 480-245-7970... 14 B
jason.mcdonnell@ibcs.edu
MCDONNELL, John .... 801-581-5791. 496 Q
john.mcdonnell@utah.edu
MCDONNELL, John .... 716-270-5612. 323 I
mcdonnellj@ecc.edu
MCDONNELL, John .... 773-481-8253. 142 F
jmcdonnell@ccc.edu
MCDONNELL, John .... 215-991-3778. 420 B
mcdonnell72@lasalle.edu
MCDONNELL, Joseph ..... 207-780-4020. 212 H
jmcdonnell@usm.maine.edu
MCDONNELL, Lauren ...... 610-527-0200. 432 B
lmcdonnell@rosemont.edu
MCDONNELL, Tessa, H .. 603-513-1308. 298 E
tessa.mcdonnell@granite.edu
MCDONOUGH, Ann .... 702-774-4619. 294 I
ann.mcdonough@unlv.edu
MCDONOUGH, David ...... 207-786-6231. 209 F
dmcdonou@bates.edu
MCDONOUGH, Eileen ..... 305-899-3085... 98 O
emcdonough@barry.edu
MCDONOUGH,
Jennifer, N .... 330-569-5957. 380 I
mcdonoughjn@hiram.edu
MCDONOUGH, Michael 802-447-4658. 500 D
mmcdonough@svc.edu
MCDONOUGH,
Michael, J .... 585-292-2170. 332 A
mmcdonough@monroecc.edu
MCDONOUGH, Patrick ... 610-807-9221. 418 J
MCDONOUGH, Peter, G . 609-258-2511. 304 E
pmcd@princeton.edu
MCDONOUGH, JR.,
Peter, J .... 848-932-7741. 306 A
mcdonough@oldqueens.rutgers.edu
MCDONOUGH, Shawna . 630-889-6701. 154 E
smcdonough@nuhs.edu
MCDORMAN, Heather .... 636-922-8277. 280 J
hmcdorman@stchas.edu
MCDOUGAL, Tammy ...... 731-426-7526. 455 J
tmcdougal@lanecollege.edu
MCDOUGALD, Sherlock . 919-546-8423. 366 E
sherlock@shawu.edu
MCDOUGALL, Gerald ..... 573-651-2063. 282 B
gmcdougall@semo.edu
MCDOUGALL,
Gordon, A .... 804-828-8192. 511 F
gamcdougall@vcu.edu
MCDOUGLE, James .... 304-205-6600. 527 O
jmcdougle@kvctc.edu
MCDOWALL-LONG,
Kimberly .... 701-355-8021. 373 E
kmcdowalllong@umary.edu
MCDOWELL, Amy .... 802-763-7170. 500 H
amcdowell@vermontlaw.edu

MCDOWELL, Brooke .... 215-702-4306. 411 F
bmcdowell@cairn.edu
MCDOWELL, Chad .... 318-798-4107. 205 F
chad.mcdowell@lsus.edu
MCDOWELL, Charles, E . 608-243-4137. 540 C
cemcdowell@madisoncollege.edu
MCDOWELL, Denise .... 913-288-7299. 187 L
dmcdowell@kckcc.edu
MCDOWELL, Jackie .... 706-236-2202. 121 G
jmcdowell@berry.edu
MCDOWELL, James .... 860-512-3603... 88 G
jmcdowell@manchestercc.edu
MCDOWELL, Jennifer ..... 972-883-6301. 491 E
jpazik@utdallas.edu
MCDOWELL, Joann .... 910-962-3712. 369 C
mcdowellj@uncw.edu
MCDOWELL, Katie .... 913-360-7578. 184 H
kmcdowell@benedictine.edu
MCDOWELL, N. Renee ... 724-653-2212. 415 A
rmcdowell@dec.edu
MCDOWELL, Pamela ...... 507-786-3011. 264 B
mcdowell@stolaf.edu
MCDOWELL, Richard, L . 405-878-5350. 399 G
rlmcdowell@stgregorys.edu
MCDOWELL, Salim .... 423-869-6674. 456 A
salim.mcdowell@lmunet.edu
MCDOWELL, Scott .... 615-966-5690. 456 B
scott.mcdowell@lipscomb.edu
MCDOWELL, Stephanie .. 785-227-3380. 184 I
mcdowells@bethanylb.edu
MCDOWN, Linda .... 405-422-1203. 399 B
mcdownl@redlandscc.edu
MCDUFF, Nancy, G .... 706-542-2112. 133 C
nmcduff@uga.edu
MCDUFFIE, Hinfred .... 502-597-6760. 197 A
hinfred.mcduffie@kysu.edu
MCDUFFIE, Jack .... 910-879-5596. 358 B
jmcduffie@bladencc.edu
MCDUGLE, Darin .... 918-360-2737. 394 D
mcduglem@bacone.edu
MCEACHERN, Daniel ...... 704-330-6395. 359 C
jj.mceachern@cpcc.edu
MCELANEY-JOHNSON,
Ann .... 310-954-4011... 54 J
MCELFRESH, Dwight ..... 419-289-6995. 374 C
dmcelfre@ashland.edu
MCELHANEY, Patrick ...... 706-233-7225. 131 E
pmcelhaney@shorter.edu
MCELHANY, Ryan .... 972-825-4701. 481 F
rmcelhany@sagu.edu
MCELHOE, Dennis .... 704-687-1280. 368 E
dmcelhoe@uncc.edu
MCELMURRY, Chauvette 314-340-3600. 275 A
mcelmurc@hssu.edu
MCELRATH, Ann .... 423-614-8105. 455 L
amcelrath@leeuniversity.edu
MCELRATH, Kay .... 619-398-4902... 47 I
MCELRATH, William .... 732-571-4444. 303 C
wmcelrat@monmouth.edu
MCELROY, Annie .... 229-225-5200. 132 D
amcelroy@southwestgatech.edu
MCELROY, Catherine ...... 215-968-8213. 411 B
cmcelroy@bucks.edu
MCELROY, Catherine, C . 215-968-8213. 411 B
mcelroyc@bucks.edu
MCELROY, Clint .... 704-330-6339. 359 C
clint.mcelroy@cpcc.edu
MCELROY, Coleetta .... 408-924-6086... 36 A
coleetta.mcelroy@sjsu.edu
MCELROY, Diana .... 816-584-6465. 280 C
diana.mcelroy@park.edu
MCELROY, Doug .... 270-745-7009. 200 G
doug.mcelroy@wku.edu
MCELROY, Edith .... 704-330-4386. 359 C
edith.mcelroy@cpcc.edu
MCELROY, Janine .... 516-323-3458. 331 J
jmcelroy@molloy.edu
MCELROY, Kevin .... 650-949-6202... 44 L
mcelroykevin@fhda.edu
MCELROY, Lee .... 518-442-2562. 341 D
lmcelroy@albany.edu
MCELROY, Neil, J .... 610-330-5150. 420 D
mcelroyn@lafayette.edu
MCELROY, Tim .... 918-683-0641. 396 H
mcelroyt@nsuok.edu
MCELVEEN, John .... 706-507-5341. 123 D
mcelveen_john@columbusstate.edu
MCELWEE, Kay, E .... 217-581-5313. 144 E
kemcelwee@eiu.edu
MCELWEE, Timothy, A .... 610-921-7501. 409 A
tmcelwee@alb.edu
MCENEANY, Barbara ...... 845-848-4031. 322 G
barbara.mceneany@dc.edu
MCENERNEY, Gerard, A . 718-390-4588. 339 A
mcenerng@stjohns.edu
MCENERNEY, Kathleen ... 615-963-4937. 459 E
kmcenerney@tnstate.edu
MCENTERGART, Rory ...... 302-793-1101... 94 A
MCENTIRE, Cheryl .... 713-646-1794. 480 J
cmcentire@stcl.edu

MCENTIRE, Mary .... 530-221-4275... 65 F
mmcentire09@shasta.edu
MCENTIRE, Tina, M .... 704-687-7019. 368 E
tmmcenti@uncc.edu
MCENTIRE, Tracy, D ...... 336-838-6422. 365 B
tracy.mcentire@wilkescc.edu
MCEUEN, Brent .... 928-428-8201... 13 J
brent.mceuen@eac.edu
MCEVER, Howar .... 352-588-8432. 112 D
howard.mcever@saintleo.edu
MCEVOY, Anita .... 215-895-2100. 415 B
aam42@drexel.edu
MCEVOY, Arthur, F .... 213-738-6808... 68 C
facultyresearch@swlaw.edu
MCEVOY, Ed, M .... 610-526-1286. 409 F
ed.mcevoy@theamericancollege.edu
MCEVOY, Kathleen .... 724-503-1001. 436 G
kmcevoy@washjeff.edu
MCEVOY, Pam .... 910-630-7043. 356 H
pmcevoy@methodist.edu
MCEVOY, Robert, T .... 910-630-7182. 356 H
mcevoy@methodist.edu
MCEWAN, Anna, E .... 205-665-6360..... 9 B
mcewanae@montevallo.edu
MCEWEN, Jessie .... 312-939-4975. 146 A
jmcewen@harrington.edu
MCEWEN, Jill .... 920-996-2847. 539 K
mcewen@fvtc.edu
MCEWEN, Randy .... 971-722-4335. 407 D
rmcewen@pcc.edu
MCEWEN, Ruth .... 305-348-3264. 115 B
ruthann.mcewen@fiu.edu
MCEWEN, Wendy .... 909-748-8187... 73 H
wendy_mcewan@redlands.edu
MCFADDEN, Brown .... 252-940-6302. 358 A
brownmcf@beaufortccc.edu
MCFADDEN, Calvin .... 508-678-2811. 231 B
calvin.mcfadden@bristolcc.edu
MCFADDEN, David, F ..... 260-982-5226. 170 U
dfmcfadden@manchester.edu
MCFADDEN, Deborah ..... 973-300-2209. 307 F
dmcfadden@sussex.edu
MCFADDEN, Harry .... 914-251-6196. 344 D
harry.mcfadden@purchase.edu
MCFADDEN, John .... 305-899-3208... 98 O
jmcfadden@barry.edu
MCFADDEN, Judy .... 970-521-6660... 83 L
judy.mcfadden@njc.edu
MCFADDEN, Mark .... 607-871-2164. 313 E
mcfaddenm@alfred.edu
MCFADDEN, Mary .... 845-848-7809. 322 G
mary.mcfadden@dc.edu
MCFADDEN, Mary Kay ... 206-296-6100. 523 E
mcfadden@seattleu.edu
MCFADDEN, Michael ...... 202-806-1280... 95 G
michael.mcfadden@howard.edu
MCFADDEN, Pam .... 817-735-2581. 490 E
Pam.McFadden@unthsc.edu
MCFADDEN, Paul .... 870-236-6901... 20 K
pmcfadden@crc.edu
MCFADDEN, Sandy .... 252-940-6353. 358 A
SandyMcF@beaufortccc.edu
MCFADDEN, Scott .... 509-527-2205. 524 I
scott.mcfadden@wallawalla.edu
MCFADDEN, Thomas .... 540-636-2900. 503 L
tmcfadden@christendom.edu
MCFADDEN, Toney, C .... 423-624-0077. 453 G
tonym@chattanoogacollege.edu
MCFADDIN, David .... 859-622-6220. 193 P
david.mcfaddin@eku.edu
MCFARLAND, Darrin ...... 620-331-4100. 187 G
darrinm@indycc.edu
MCFARLAND, Dave .... 812-749-1218. 171 K
dmcfarland@oak.edu
MCFARLAND, James ...... 412-731-1177. 431 G
rptrustees@aol.com
MCFARLAND, JoAnne, Y 307-855-2101. 542 Y
jmcfarla@cwc.edu
MCFARLAND, Kathryn .... 813-226-4983. 112 D
kathryn.mcfarland@saintleo.edu
MCFARLAND, Marielle ... 870-777-5722... 25 B
marielle.mcfarland@uacch.edu
MCFARLAND,
Michael, S .... 570-389-4050. 427 H
mcfarland@bloomu.edu
MCFARLAND, Mike .... 919-962-2011. 368 D
Mike_McFarland@unc.edu
MCFARLAND,
Reoungeneria .... 901-435-1213. 455 M
reo_mcfarland@loc.edu
MCFARLAND, Robie .... 252-222-6021. 358 G
mcfarlandr@carteret.edu
MCFARLAND, Ruth, E .... 484-384-2950. 425 I
rmcfarla@eastern.edu
MCFARLAND,
Stephen, L .... 910-962-3867. 369 C
mcfarlands@uncw.edu
MCFARLAND, Steven ...... 630-844-5496. 140 A
smcfarla@aurora.edu
MCFARLAND, Steven, W 518-327-6436. 336 B
smcfarland@paulsmiths.edu

MCFARLAND, Thomas .... 435-586-7785. 497 A thomasmcfarland@suu.edu
MCFARLANE, Alison .... 801-957-4103. 498 B alison.mcfarlane@lscc.edu
MCFARLANE, Allen, M ... 212-998-4345. 334 D allen.mcfarlane@nyu.edu
MCFARLANE, Edwin, O .. 503-777-7506. 407 E edwin.mcfarlane@reed.edu
MCFARLANE, Maureen ... 352-395-5932. 113 C maureen.mcfarlane@sfcollege.edu
MCFARLANE, Mike .... 775-753-2266. 294 F mike.mcfarlane@gbcnv.edu
MCFARLIN, Dean, B .... 412-396-1372. 415 F mcfarlind@duq.edu
MCFARLIN, Diane, H ...... 352-392-0466. 116 A dmcfarlin@ufl.edu
MCFARLING, Patricia, G . 270-852-3257. 197 B patmc@kwc.edu
MCFEE, Brenda .... 828-766-1330. 361 H bmcfee@mayland.edu
MCFRAZIER, Michael, L . 936-261-2111. 482 F mlmcfrazier@pvamu.edu
MCFRY, Benjamin .... 706-233-7641. 131 E bmcfry@shorter.edu
MCGADNEY, C. Andrew . 508-793-7569. 225 A cmcgadney@clarku.edu
MCGAHA, SR., Gary, A .. 404-756-4440. 121 A gmcgaha@atlm.edu
MCGAHEY, Julia .... 303-871-4528... 86 B jmcgahey@du.edu
MCGALLIARD, Anna .... 207-948-9250. 211 I amcgalliard@unity.edu
MCGANN, Robert P, H .... 603-862-1360. 298 C admissions@unh.edu
MCGANNON, Heather ..... 651-846-4118. 261 D heather.mcgannon@saintpaul.edu
MCGAREY, Tracy .... 316-942-4291. 189 E mcgareyt@newmanu.edu
MCGARITY, William, G ... 706-542-9037. 133 C gmcgarity@sports.uga.edu
MCGARRITY, Maureen .... 215-637-7700. 418 G mmcgarrity@holyfamily.edu
MCGARRY, Craig .... 712-279-5423. 176 B craig.mcgarry@briarcliff.edu
MCGARRY, Eileen, M ..... 520-621-6734... 18 F emcgarry@email.arizona.edu
MCGARRY, Maureen .... 401-333-7102. 439 A mmcgarry@ccri.edu
MCGARRY, Timothy .... 516-876-3303. 343 D mcgarryt@oldwestbury.edu
MCGARVEY, Betty, S ...... 901-572-2585. 453 B bettysue.mcgarvey@bchs.edu
MCGARVEY, Brian, F ...... 518-381-1353. 340 G mcgarvbf@sunysccc.edu
MCGARVEY, Scott .... 660-263-4110. 279 B scottm@macc.edu
MCGARVEY, Vicki Lewis 215-204-8874. 433 K mcgarvey@temple.edu
MCGAUGH, Becky, E ...... 928-523-6415... 16 C becky.mcgaugh@nau.edu
MCGAUGHEY, Kevin, B .. 651-631-5318. 263 A kbmcgaughey@nwc.edu
MCGAUGHEY, Scott .... 573-288-6395. 273 F smcgaughey@culver.edu
MCGEACHY, Neill .... 828-328-7128. 356 B neill.mcgeachy@lr.edu
MCGEE, Bonita .... 812-237-8954. 167 A bonita.mcgee@indstate.edu
MCGEE, Brenda, L .... 716-375-2017. 338 E bmcgee@sbu.edu
MCGEE, Brian .... 843-953-5500. 443 A mcgeeb@cofc.edu
MCGEE, Byron .... 318-487-7259. 202 F byron.mcgee@lacollege.edu
MCGEE, Christine .... 414-297-7997. 540 E mcgeecm@matc.edu
MCGEE, Cindy, R .... 304-336-8233. 530 A mcgeecin@westliberty.edu
MCGEE, Corlis, A .... 617-745-3702. 225 G corlis.mcgee@enc.edu
MCGEE, Deborah .... 217-875-7200. 156 J dmcgee@richland.edu
MCGEE, E. Ann .... 407-708-2009. 113 E mcgeea@seminolestate.edu
MCGEE, James .... 708-534-4900. 145 F jmcgee@govst.edu
MCGEE, James .... 847-214-7359. 144 F jmcgee@elgin.edu
MCGEE, Janice .... 205-929-6313...... 5 D jmcgee@lawsonstate.edu
MCGEE, Jerry, E .... 704-233-8111. 370 G mcgee@wingate.edu
MCGEE, Joan .... 702-651-5966. 294 E joan.mcgee@csn.edu
MCGEE, Jon .... 320-363-5287. 263 P jmcgee@csbsju.edu
MCGEE, Jon, D .... 320-363-5287. 254 J jmcgee@csbsju.edu
MCGEE, Laura .... 847-925-6686. 145 H lmcgee@harpercollege.edu
MCGEE, Linda .... 409-984-6237. 486 H linda.mcgee@lamarpa.edu
MCGEE, Lynn .... 843-208-8240. 448 B lmcgee@uscb.edu
MCGEE, Marc .... 707-654-1331... 31 I mmcgee@csum.edu
MCGEE, Marjorie .... 352-854-2322. 100 K mcgeem@cf.edu
MCGEE, Mary .... 607-871-2171. 313 E mcgee@alfred.edu
MCGEE, Mary, A .... 217-786-2766. 151 F mary.mcgee@llcc.edu
MCGEE, Mary, E .... 678-915-7451. 132 C mmcgee@spsu.edu
MCGEE, Robert .... 910-362-7191. 358 F rmcgee@cfcc.edu
MCGEE, Sean .... 907-474-6215... 10 I semcgee@alaska.edu
MCGEE, Shawn .... 229-248-2611. 121 E shawn.mcgee@bainbridge.edu
MCGEE, Stacey .... 325-674-2539. 464 H slm03h@acu.edu
MCGEE, Steve, G .... 817-257-7930. 484 I s.mcgee@tcu.edu
MCGEE, Steve, R .... 512-245-2533. 487 C srm18@txstate.edu
MCGEE, Tammy .... 612-330-1027. 253 H mcgee@augsburg.edu
MCGEE, Thomas, W .... 314-837-6777. 280 K
MCGEE, Vince .... 636-227-2100. 276 F vince.mcgee@logan.edu
MCGEE-YUROF, Carrie ... 203-857-7040... 89 D cmcgee-yurof@norwalk.edu
MCGEEHAN, Catherine ... 610-499-4396. 437 E cmcgeehan@widener.edu
MCGEHEE, JR., Robert, E .... 501-686-5454... 24 C rem@uams.edu
MCGETTIGAN, Glenn ...... 801-524-8112. 495 O Glenn@ldsbc.edu
MCGHEE, Angela .... 340-693-1013. 555 E amcghee@live.uvi.edu
MCGHEE, JR., James, D 804-752-3736. 508 E jamesmcghee@rmc.edu
MCGHEE, Janet .... 269-660-8021. 249 C mcgheeja@millercollege.edu
MCGHEE, Lisa .... 870-762-3174... 19 K lmchgee@smail.anc.edu
MCGHEE, Marianne, S .... 804-523-5810. 512 F mmcghee@reynolds.edu
MCGHEE, Sandra, W .... 540-375-2287. 509 B mcghee@roanoke.edu
MCGHEE, Tim .... 423-697-4400. 460 C
MCGHEE, Tony .... 276-964-7648. 514 A tony.mcghee@sw.edu
MCGHEE JOHNSON, Kassandra .... 773-291-6100. 142 D kmcgheejohnson@ccc.edu
MCGILL, Bret .... 256-306-2861..... 2 F jbm@calhoun.edu
MCGILL, Duncan .... 202-231-4082. 544 L duncan.mcgill@dodiis.mil
MCGILL, Jennifer .... 601-925-7782. 268 A McGill@mc.edu
MCGILL, Jenny .... 214-887-5368. 471 F jmcgill@dts.edu
MCGILL, Shawna .... 575-769-4954. 309 F shawna.mcgill@clovis.edu
MCGILL, Shelia .... 405-466-3283. 395 N sheliamcgill2@langston.edu
MCGILL, Tracy .... 318-678-6190. 202 I tmcgill@bpcc.edu
MCGILLAN, Mary Ellen .. 808-687-7065. 135 F mmcgillan@hpu.edu
MCGILLIN, Victoria .... 614-823-1556. 387 K vmcgillin@otterbein.edu
MCGILLIVRAY, Kristin .... 503-228-6528. 402 A kmcgillivray@aii.edu
MCGILVRAY, Amy .... 254-295-5077. 490 B amcgilvray@umhb.edu
MCGILVRAY, Mary, E ...... 918-270-6405. 398 I mary.mcgilvay@ptstulsa.edu
MCGIMPSEY, Jason .... 406-657-2197. 287 C
MCGIMPSEY, W. Grant ... 330-672-6501. 382 B wmcgimps@kent.edu
MCGINITY, Richard .... 732-571-3400. 543 I
MCGINLEY, Anne, M .... 856-227-7200. 300 B amcginley@camdencc.edu
MCGINLEY, Barbara .... 617-587-5620. 234 H mcginleyb@neco.edu
MCGINLEY, Lisa .... 715-682-1249. 535 D lmcginley@northland.edu
MCGINLEY, Lynn, M .... 410-706-2889. 219 C lmcginley@af.umaryland.edu
MCGINLEY, Patricia .... 914-633-2201. 327 C pmcginley@iona.edu
MCGINLEY, Patricia .... 845-620-1350. 327 C pmcginley@iona.edu
MCGINN, Jayne .... 508-929-8110. 230 G jmcginn@worcester.edu
MCGINN, Joseph .... 410-704-4677. 220 E jmcginn@towson.edu
MCGINN, Marifrances .... 401-865-2774. 439 E mfmcginn@providence.edu
MCGINN, III, Thomas, J 410-777-2240. 213 D tjmcginn@aacc.edu
MCGINNIS, Blake .... 870-759-4170... 25 K bmcginnis@wbcoll.edu
MCGINNIS, David .... 406-657-2363. 287 C dmcginnis@msubillings.edu
MCGINNIS, Erik .... 704-463-3001. 365 E erik.mcginnis@fsmail.pfeiffer.edu
MCGINNIS, Grace .... 708-709-3519. 156 A gmcginnis@prairiestate.edu
MCGINNIS, Kathy .... 619-388-3489... 62 D kmcginni@sdccd.edu
MCGINNIS, Kelly .... 325-574-7609. 494 K kmcginnis@wtc.edu
MCGINNIS, Mara .... 718-636-3471. 336 F mmcginnis@pratt.edu
MCGINNIS, Maurice (Max) .... 585-594-6409. 337 K mcginnis_max@roberts.edu
MCGINNIS, Michael .... 802-485-2327. 500 A
MCGINNIS, Odette .... 909-384-8909... 62 A omcginnis@sbccd.cc.ca.us
MCGINNIS, Renae, R ...... 304-929-6736. 528 D rmcginnis@newriver.edu
MCGINNIS, Sharon, R .... 910-938-6231. 359 E mcginniss@coastalcarolina.edu
MCGINNISS, Jeremy .... 570-586-2400. 410 D JeMcGinniss@bbc.edu
MCGINNISS, Michael, J . 215-951-1010. 420 B mcginnis@lasalle.edu
MCGINTY, Daniel, E .... 715-425-3505. 537 E daniel.e.mcginty@uwrf.edu
MCGINTY, Evelyn, J .... 936-261-1725. 482 F ejmcginty@pvamu.edu
MCGINTY, Jack .... 412-809-5100. 430 H mcginty.john@pti.edu
MCGINTY, James, J .... 732-255-0400. 304 A jmcginty@ocean.edu
MCGINTY, Jill .... 312-935-4860. 156 K jmcginty@robertmorris.edu
MCGINTY, Louis, L .... 804-523-2280. 512 F mmcginty@ccwa.vccs.edu
MCGINTY, Mac, L .... 804-523-2280. 512 G mmcginty@ccwa.vccs.edu
MCGINTY, Mary Kate ..... 215-596-8719. 435 H m.mcginty@usciences.edu
MCGIRR, Kathleen .... 215-641-6603. 424 B kmcgirr@mc3.edu
MCGIRT, David .... 910-893-1265. 352 K mcgirt@campbell.edu
MCGIVNEY, R, J .... 860-768-4401... 92 D rmcgivney@hartford.edu
MCGIVNEY, Sean .... 719-549-2753... 80 K sean.mcgivney@colostate-pueblo.edu
MCGLADDERY, Nicole .... 805-581-1233... 43 G
MCGLAMERY, Matt .... 970-247-7065... 81 M mcglamery_m@fortlewis.edu
MCGLASSON, Robert .... 417-328-1535. 282 C bmcglasson@sbuniv.edu
MCGLONE, John .... 606-326-2400. 194 J john.mcglone@kctcs.edu
MCGLOTHIN, Kris .... 302-735-7696... 94 C bkwesley@bncollege.edu
MCGLOTHIN-ELLER, Vince .... 847-866-3907. 145 E vince.mcglothin-eller@garrett.edu
MCGLOTHLAN, Mary ...... 503-255-0332. 404 F mmcglothlan@multnomah.edu
MCGLOTHLIN, Michael, G .... 276-498-4190. 501 I
MCGLOTHLIN, Sandy ..... 559-934-2324... 75 H sandymcglothlin@whccd.edu
MCGLOUGHLIN, Stephen .... 916-691-7589... 53 B mcglous@crc.losrios.edu
MCGLYNN, Ken .... 443-518-4802. 215 E kmcglynn@howardcc.edu
MCGOFF, Michael, F .... 607-777-2143. 341 E mmcgoff@binghamton.edu
MCGOLDRICK, John .... 215-951-1015. 420 B mcgoldri@lasalle.edu
MCGONIGAL, Terry, P ..... 509-777-4345. 525 F tmcgonigal@whitworth.edu
MCGONIGLE, Gregory ..... 440-775-5191. 385 H greg.mcgonigle@oberlin.edu
MCGONIGLE, Mary .... 610-519-4070. 436 F mary.mcgonigle@villanova.edu
MCGONIGLE, Robert, B .. 570-208-5875. 419 P rbmcgoni@kings.edu
MCGONIGLE, Steve .... 215-951-1075. 420 B mcgonigle@lasalle.edu
MCGOOKIN, Yvonne .... 425-564-2195. 517 A yvonne.mcgookin@bellevuecollege.edu
MCGORDY, Sandra .... 817-515-7463. 482 B sandra.mcgordy@tccd.edu
MCGOUGH, David .... 802-635-1323. 501 D david.mcgough@jsc.edu
MCGOUGH, Lucy .... 276-935-4349. 502 A lmcgough@asl.edu
MCGOUGH, Marsha .... 425-602-3036. 516 K mmcgough@bastyr.edu
MCGOVERN, Bruce .... 713-646-2920. 480 J bmcgovern@stcl.edu
MCGOVERN, Daniel .... 516-686-7533. 333 H dmcgover@nyit.edu
MCGOVERN, Lorrie .... 352-588-7869. 112 D lorrie.mcgovern@saintleo.edu
MCGOVERN, Mark, S ..... 401-865-2702. 439 E mmcgovrn@providence.edu
MCGOVERN, Martin, P ... 508-565-1321. 237 A mmcgovern@stonehill.edu
MCGOVERN, Mary Grace .... 707-476-4264... 40 H marygrace-mcgovern@redwoods.edu
MCGOVERN, Terry .... 615-230-3352. 461 G terry.mcgovern@volstate.edu
MCGOVERN, Thomas ..... 617-236-8800. 226 F tmcgovern@fisher.edu
MCGOVERN, Tina, L .... 570-961-4596. 423 B tmcgovern@marywood.edu
MCGOWAN, Bill .... 828-898-8776. 356 A mcgowanb@lmc.edu
MCGOWAN, Bruce, W .... 918-877-8116. 395 N bwmcgowan@langston.edu
MCGOWAN, Charlotte .... 269-782-1347. 250 G cmcgowan@swmich.edu
MCGOWAN, Chris .... 573-651-2163. 282 B cwmcgowan@semo.edu
MCGOWAN, Cynthia .... 978-837-5139. 234 A mcgowanc@merrimack.edu
MCGOWAN, James .... 516-877-3162. 313 A mcgowan2@adelphi.edu
MCGOWAN, Jeanne .... 215-641-5571. 417 F mcgowan.j@gmc.edu
MCGOWAN, John .... 205-348-5610..... 8 D john.mcgowan@ua.edu
MCGOWAN, Joseph, J ... 502-272-8234. 192 E jmcgowan@bellarmine.edu
MCGOWAN, Joumana ...... 909-274-4600... 55 A jmcgowan@mtsac.edu
MCGOWAN, Kent .... 406-243-5373. 286 H kent.mcgowan@umontana.edu
MCGOWAN, Kevin .... 239-687-5335... 98 J kmcgowan@avemarialaw.edu
MCGOWAN, Lisa .... 717-846-5000. 438 E
MCGOWAN, Paul .... 617-552-3055. 224 A paul.mcgowan.2@bc.edu
MCGOWAN, Richard .... 217-875-7200. 156 J rmcgowan@richland.edu
MCGOWAN, Sindi .... 770-537-5746. 134 H sindi.mcgowan@westgatech.edu
MCGOY, Jeff .... 618-634-3236. 158 M jeffm@shawneecc.edu
MCGRADY, Patricia .... 973-543-6528. 298 I treasurer@acs350.org
MCGRADY, Ronald, L ..... 330-325-6799. 385 E rmcgrady@neomed.edu
MCGRAIL, Annmarie .... 914-773-3741. 335 J amcgrail@pace.edu
MCGRAIL, Frederick, J ... 610-758-4487. 422 A fjm208@lehigh.edu
MCGRAIL, III, James, J . 740-264-5591. 379 F jmcgrail@egcc.edu
MCGRAIL, Jennifer .... 580-581-2988. 394 G jbowen@cameron.edu
MCGRAIL, Margaret .... 914-674-3031. 330 J mmcgrail@mercy.edu
MCGRANAHAN, Mary, S 617-552-3300. 224 A mary.mcgranahan@bc.edu
MCGRANE, Jack, V .... 973-748-9000. 299 F jack_mcgrane@bloomfield.edu
MCGRANE, Wendy .... 417-625-9386. 278 D mcgrane-w@mssu.edu
MCGRANN, Loretta, A .... 718-940-5980. 339 B lmcgrann@sjcny.edu
MCGRATH, Abigail .... 312-567-3497. 147 F amcgrat1@iit.edu
MCGRATH, Andrew, S .... 608-757-7764. 539 I amcgrath@blackhawk.edu
MCGRATH, Cheryl .... 508-565-1111. 237 A cmcgrath1@stonehill.edu
MCGRATH, Deborah, F ... 603-526-3609. 295 I dmcgrath@colby-sawyer.edu
MCGRATH, Debra .... 312-369-7151. 143 D dmcgrath@colum.edu
MCGRATH, Elisabeth ...... 201-216-3389. 307 E cos.mcgrath@stevens.edu
MCGRATH, Jamie, M ..... 260-399-7700. 174 C jmcgrath@sf.edu
MCGRATH, Janet .... 716-827-2428. 348 G mcgrath@trocaire.edu
MCGRATH, John .... 212-594-4000. 347 H jmcgrath@tcicollege.edu
MCGRATH, John, J .... 989-774-3094. 240 N mcgra2jj@cmich.edu
MCGRATH, Joseph, C .... 800-955-2527. 274 I jmcgrath@grantham.edu

MCGRATH, Karen, P .... 716-880-2200. 330 F
karen.p.mcgrath@medaille.edu
MCGRATH, Laurie .... 503-552-1694. 404 H
lmcgrath@ncnm.edu
MCGRATH, Mark .... 215-242-1501. 413 A
mcgrathm@chc.edu
MCGRATH, Patti .... 803-641-3569. 448 A
pattim@usca.edu
MCGRATH, Robert .... 404-407-7401. 125 D
robert.mcgrath@gtri.gatech.edu
MCGRATH, Thomas .... 508-565-1086. 237 A
tmcgrath@stonehill.edu
MCGRATH, Tim .... 619-388-2600... 62 E
tmcgrath@sdccd.edu
MCGRATH, William .... 212-346-1200. 335 J
wmcgrath@pace.edu
MCGRAW, Annette .... 716-375-2234. 338 E
amcgraw@sbu.edu
MCGRAW, Darryl, D .... 919-866-5108. 364 G
ddmcgraw@waketech.edu
MCGRAW, Hesse .... 415-749-4580... 62 G
hmcgraw@sfai.edu
MCGRAW, Matthew .... 540-863-2866. 512 B
mmcgraw@dslcc.edu
MCGRAW, Packy .... 518-694-7257. 313 B
packy.mcgraw@acphs.edu
MCGREAL, Paul, E .... 937-229-3795. 391 C
pmcgreal1@udayton.edu
MCGREEVEY, Michael ..... 315-364-3275. 350 E
mmcgreevey@wells.edu
MCGREEVY, Bill .... 303-914-6634... 84 I
bill.mcgreevy@rrcc.edu
MCGREEVY, John, T .... 574-631-6642. 174 A
mcgreevy.5@nd.edu
MCGREGOR, Kyle, W ..... 254-968-9464. 483 A
mcgregor@tarleton.edu
MCGREGOR, Patricia .... 860-297-2120... 91 F
patricia.mcgregor@trincoll.edu
MCGREGOR, Tiffany .... 610-361-2487. 424 I
mcgregot@neumann.edu
MCGREGOR, Wilson, E .. 254-710-2663. 467 G
bud_mcgregor@baylor.edu
MCGREGORY, Richard ... 262-472-4985. 538 D
mcgregor@uww.edu
MCGREW, Kevin .... 218-723-6198. 254 K
kmcgrew@css.edu
MCGREW, Mackenzie ..... 843-525-8218. 447 C
mmcgrew@tcl.edu
MCGREW, Paula .... 304-473-8461. 531 G
mcgrew_p@wwc.edu
MCGREW, Shea .... 419-372-7706. 374 K
smcgrew@bgsu.edu
MCGRIFF, Ilona .... 336-517-2201. 352 H
imcgriff@bennett.edu
MCGRIFF, Sheryl .... 313-993-1017. 250 K
mcgrifsj@udmercy.edu
MCGRIFF-POWERS,
Kathleen .... 716-851-1017. 323 I
mcgrifpowers@ecc.edu
MCGRISKEN, June .... 718-489-5352. 338 G
jmcgrisken@sfc.edu
MCGUCKIN, Denis .... 516-686-7791. 333 H
dmcgucki@nyit.edu
MCGUCKIN, Tammy .... 262-595-2571. 537 C
mcguckin@uwp.edu
MCGUFFEY, Michael, J .. 304-696-3648. 529 H
mcguffey@marshall.edu
MCGUFFIN, Kurt .... 816-271-5623. 279 A
kmcguffin@missouriwestern.edu
MCGUINESS, Ilona .... 410-617-5547. 216 A
imcguiness@loyola.edu
MCGUINN, Ellen .... 215-248-7163. 413 A
mcguinne@chc.edu
MCGUINNESS, Mary ...... 914-654-5441. 320 H
mmcguinness@cnr.edu
MCGUINNESS, Maureen . 940-565-2648. 490 C
moe@unt.edu
MCGUINNESS, Paul, M .. 219-785-5730. 172 A
mcguinpm@pnc.edu
MCGUINNESS,
Thomas, P .... 617-552-3310. 224 A
thomas.mcguinness@bc.edu
MCGUIRE, Ann .... 216-421-7417. 377 C
amcguire@cia.edu
MCGUIRE, Christine .... 617-353-4176. 224 D
chmcguir@bu.edu
MCGUIRE, David .... 561-697-9200. 131 H
dmcguire@southuniversity.edu
MCGUIRE, David, T .... 435-586-7755. 497 A
mcguire@suu.edu
MCGUIRE, Ellen .... 570-504-7000. 413 B
MCGUIRE, Jamie .... 336-838-6482. 365 B
jamie.mcguire@wilkescc.edu
MCGUIRE, Jane .... 615-230-3204. 461 G
jane.mcguire@volstate.edu
MCGUIRE, Jim .... 206-239-2302. 516 H
jmcguire@aii.edu
MCGUIRE, Josh .... 479-248-7236... 21 B
jmcguire@ecollege.edu
MCGUIRE, Katherine .... 404-471-6176. 119 I
kmcguire@agnesscott.edu

MCGUIRE, Kathleen .... 508-541-1615. 225 F
kmcguire@dean.edu
MCGUIRE, Mark, T .... 740-284-5249. 379 N
mmcguire@franciscan.edu
MCGUIRE, Maureen .... 509-313-6137. 520 A
mcguirem@gonzaga.edu
MCGUIRE, Michael .... 303-871-3518... 86 B
mmcguire@du.edu
MCGUIRE, Michael, J ..... 785-670-1763. 191 D
michael.mcguire@washburn.edu
MCGUIRE, Nancy .... 712-279-5455. 176 B
nancy.mcguire@briarcliff.edu
MCGUIRE, Nona, S .... 614-236-6908. 375 H
nmcguire@capital.edu
MCGUIRE, Patricia, A ..... 202-884-9050... 96 G
mcguirep@trinitydc.edu
MCGUIRE, Rachel, L .... 641-422-4104. 181 D
mcguirac@niacc.edu
MCGUIRE, Ruth, A .... 651-631-5343. 263 A
ramcguire@nwc.edu
MCGUIRE, Sharon .... 208-426-4062. 137 G
sharonmcguire@boisestate.edu
MCGUIRE, Tara .... 402-280-3973. 289 D
taramcguire@creighton.edu
MCGUIRE-CLOSSON,
Margaret .... 610-861-4558. 425 D
mclosson@northampton.edu
MCGURGAN, Susan .... 513-231-2223. 374 D
smcgurgan@athenaeum.edu
MCGURIK, Paul .... 972-660-5701. 475 L
MCGURIMAN, Joseph .... 215-641-6605. 424 B
jmcgurim@mc3.edu
MCGURIMAN, Timothy .. 312-915-7802. 151 H
tmcguri@luc.edu
MCGURK, Mark, A .... 520-626-1677... 18 F
mcgurkm@email.arizona.edu
MCGURN, Joseph, P .... 740-283-6278. 379 N
jmcgurn@franciscan.edu
MCGURR, Paul .... 714-542-8086... 29 N
pmcgurr@bristoluniversity.edu
MCGURREN, Cynthia ...... 978-542-7591. 230 E
cmcgurren@salemstate.edu
MCGURTY, Thomas, S ... 617-627-3264. 237 C
thomas.mcgurty@tufts.edu
MCGUTHRY, John, W ..... 909-869-6442... 32 G
jwmcguthry@csupomona.edu
MCGWIN, Michael .... 585-389-2830. 332 D
mmcgwin6@naz.edu
MCHALE, Barbara .... 215-641-5521. 417 F
mchale.b@gmc.edu
MCHAN, Kaye .... 941-309-4731. 111 O
kmchan@ringling.edu
MCHARGUE, Jackie .... 828-250-2370. 368 C
jmchargu@unca.edu
MCHARRIS, Michael .... 315-792-5489. 331 I
mmcharris@mvcc.edu
MCHENRY, Bart .... 949-582-4907... 67 C
bmchenry@saddleback.edu
MCHENRY, Lepaine .... 405-585-4450. 397 C
lepaine.mchenry@okbu.edu
MCHENRY, Pat .... 706-568-2056. 123 D
mchenry_patrick@columbusstate.edu
MCHENRY, Renee .... 417-823-3448. 281 M
rmchenry@forest.edu
MCHENRY, Stephanie ..... 216-687-3673. 377 F
s.y.mchenry@csuohio.edu
MCHONE, Michael, L ..... 276-223-4798. 514 F
mmchone@wcc.vccs.edu
MCHUGH, Carol, G .... 203-285-2061... 88 E
cmchugh@gwcc.commnet.edu
MCHUGH, Elizabeth .... 360-867-6808. 519 J
mchughe@evergreen.edu
MCHUGH, John .... 704-748-1055. 360 F
mchugh.john@gaston.edu
MCHUGH, Kevin .... 207-786-6341. 209 F
kmchugh@batcs.edu
MCHUGH, Mary .... 978-837-5125. 234 A
mary.mchugh@merrimack.edu
MCHUGH, Mary .... 865-251-1800. 458 I
library@southcollegetn.edu
MCHUGH, Shelley .... 402-465-2123. 291 G
smchugh@nebrwesleyan.edu
MCHUGH, Tracy .... 630-889-6607. 154 E
tmchugh@nuhs.edu
MCILLECE, Michelle .... 319-399-8844. 176 G
mmcillec@coe.edu
MCILNAY, Sandy .... 816-604-4616. 277 H
sandy.mcilnay@mcckc.edu
MCILROY, Julia .... 208-885-6123. 139 D
juliam@uidaho.edu
MCILVANE, Amy .... 770-426-2648. 128 D
mcilvane@life.edu
MCILVRIED, John .... 317-788-3274. 173 I
jmcilvried@uindy.edu
MCINALLY, David, W ...... 319-399-8686. 176 G
dmcinally@coe.edu
MCINERNEY, Claire, R ... 848-932-8796. 306 B
claire.mcinerney@rutgers.edu
MCINERNEY, Tammy .... 203-837-8290... 88 B
hammershoyt@wcsu.edu

MCINNES, Robert .... 704-334-6882. 357 K
rmcinnes@nlts.edu
MCINNIS, Dion .... 281-283-2021. 489 C
mcinnis@uhcl.edu
MCINNIS, Maurie, D ...... 434-982-2334. 511 B
mdm6n@virginia.edu
MCINNIS, Robert, L .... 704-216-6400. 356 D
rmcinnis@livingstone.edu
MCINNIS, W. Dale .... 910-410-1806. 362 I
mcinnisd@richmondcc.edu
MCINTIRE, Dennis, K ..... 770-720-9221. 130 G
dkm@reinhardt.edu
MCINTIRE, Mary .... 713-348-2599. 479 A
maryb@rice.edu
MCINTIRE, OSFS,
Timothy .... 610-282-1100. 414 F
Timothy.McIntire@desales.edu
MCINTOSH, Allison .... 405-789-7661. 400 A
allison.mcintosh@swcu.edu
MCINTOSH, Becky, R ..... 864-941-8358. 446 C
mcintosh.b@ptc.edu
MCINTOSH, Bedford .... 909-621-8025... 39 C
bedford.mcintosh@cgu.edu
MCINTOSH, Carl, R .... 803-938-3733. 448 F
mcintocr@uscsumter.edu
MCINTOSH, Cecilia, A .... 423-439-4221. 459 C
mcintosc@etsu.edu
MCINTOSH, Craig .... 518-276-3992. 337 I
mcintc@rpi.edu
MCINTOSH, Gary .... 425-889-7790. 521 G
gary.mcintosh@northwestu.edu
MCINTOSH, Gayle .... 253-879-3905. 524 F
gmcintosh@pugetsound.edu
MCINTOSH, Glenn .... 248-370-4200. 248 J
mcintosh@oakland.edu
MCINTOSH, James .... 314-773-0083. 271 K
MCINTOSH, Joe .... 817-515-5377. 482 B
joe.mcintosh@tccd.edu
MCINTOSH, Joe, E .... 336-734-7297. 360 E
jmcintosh@forsythtech.edu
MCINTOSH, John .... 574-520-4183. 168 E
jmcintos@iusb.edu
MCINTOSH, John .... 256-331-5323..... 6 A
jmcintosh@nwscc.edu
MCINTOSH, Jonathan ..... 208-882-1566. 138 H
jmcintosh@nsa.edu
MCINTOSH, Julie .... 419-434-4062. 391 D
mcintosh@findlay.edu
MCINTOSH, Keith .... 520-206-4809... 17 A
kwmcintosh@pima.edu
MCINTOSH, Nicole .... 701-349-5403. 373 A
nicolemcintosh@trinitybiblecollege.edu
MCINTOSH, Tanisha .... 734-432-5755. 246 B
tmcintosh@madonna.edu
MCINTOSH, Tim .... 541-683-5141. 403 D
tmcintosh@gutenberg.edu
MCINTOSH-DOTY,
Mikail .... 512-313-3000. 469 L
mikail.doty@concordia.edu
MCINTURF, Rob .... 910-962-2681. 369 C
mcinturfr@uncw.edu
MCINTYRE, Ashley .... 912-538-3129. 132 A
amcintyre@southeasterntech.edu
MCINTYRE, Ellen, C .... 704-687-8722. 368 E
Ellen.McIntyre@uncc.edu
MCINTYRE, Faye, S .... 678-839-6467. 133 I
fmcintyr@westga.edu
MCINTYRE, Jacqueline ... 516-364-0808. 333 D
jmcintyre@nycollege.edu
MCINTYRE, Jacqueline ... 516-364-0808. 333 D
jmclntyre@nycollege.edu
MCINTYRE, James .... 513-244-8616. 376 J
james.mcintyre@ccuniversity.edu
MCINTYRE, James, P ..... 617-552-3246. 224 A
james.mcintyre@bc.edu
MCINTYRE, Janet .... 503-491-7589. 404 E
janet.mcintyre@mhcc.edu
MCINTYRE, Julie .... 518-244-2255. 338 C
mcinitj@sage.edu
MCINTYRE, Karen .... 412-392-3976. 431 B
kmcintyre@pointpark.edu
MCINTYRE, Kevin .... 806-743-7425. 487 E
kevin.mcintyre@ttuhsc.edu
MCINTYRE, Kevin, M ...... 610-527-0200. 432 B
kmcintyre@rosemont.edu
MCINTYRE, Leonard, A .. 803-536-7173. 446 G
lamcintyre@scsu.edu
MCINTYRE, Mary, F .... 412-396-6668. 415 F
mcintyre@duq.edu
MCINTYRE, Richard .... 401-874-4126. 440 D
mcintyre@uri.edu
MCINTYRE, Susan, H ..... 252-222-6230. 358 G
mcintyres@carteret.edu
MCINTYRE, William, A ... 603-882-6923. 296 B
bmcintyre@ccsnh.edu
MCINTYRE, Willie .... 910-672-1157. 367 D
wmcintyre@uncfsu.edu
MCISAAC, Penny, J .... 561-868-3583. 110 C
mcisaacp@palmbeachstate.edu

MCISAAC-TRACY,
Jeannie .... 406-657-2387. 287 C
jmtracy@msubillings.edu
MCIVER, John .... 208-885-6651. 139 D
jmciver@uidaho.edu
MCJANNET, Cathy .... 619-216-6762... 68 B
cmcjannet@swccd.edu
MCJUNKIN, Gayle .... 507-222-4335. 254 D
gmcjunki@carleton.edu
MCKAIN, Joshua .... 617-236-8800. 226 F
jmckain@fisher.edu
MCKAMEY, Sheldon .... 406-994-6342. 287 B
smckamey@montana.edu
MCKANE, Heather, L ...... 630-844-5448. 140 A
hmckane@aurora.edu
MCKANN, Helen .... 804-594-1523. 512 G
hmckann@jtcc.edu
MCKAY, Alan, B .... 540-665-1280. 509 E
amckay@su.edu
MCKAY, Bill .... 509-542-5531. 518 C
bmckay@columbiabasin.edu
MCKAY, Darlene .... 864-225-7653. 444 A
darlenemckay@forrestcollege.edu
MCKAY, David .... 617-266-1400. 223 D
MCKAY, Emily .... 701-224-2410. 372 B
emily.mckay@bismarckstate.edu
MCKAY, Eugene .... 501-882-8956... 19 M
emckay@asub.edu
MCKAY, Kerri .... 313-664-7441. 241 C
kmckay@collegeforcreativestudies.edu
MCKAY, Kevin .... 425-640-1547. 519 D
kevin.mckay@edcc.edu
MCKAY, Kimberly .... 956-872-2096. 480 I
kjmckay@southtexascollege.edu
MCKAY, Kimberly .... 432-335-6683. 477 M
kmckay@odessa.edu
MCKAY, Michael, E .... 609-258-5491. 304 E
mckay@princeton.edu
MCKAY, Patricia .... 301-295-3155. 545 C
patricia.mckay@usuhs.edu
MCKAY, Richard .... 281-998-6150. 479 H
richard.mckay@sjcd.edu
MCKAY, Sally .... 615-460-6456. 453 C
sally.mckay@belmont.edu
MCKAY, Scott .... 870-235-4290... 23 F
semckay@saumag.edu
MCKAY, Shaun, L .... 631-451-4736. 346 E
mckays@sunysuffolk.edu
MCKAYLE-STOLZ,
Camille .... 340-693-1201. 555 E
cmckayl@uvi.edu
MCKEAN, Debbie .... 602-943-2311... 19 C
Debbie.McKean@west.edu
MCKEAN, Gerry .... 309-438-7651. 147 J
gwmckea@ilstu.edu
MCKEARNEY, James, L .. 650-325-5621... 61 G
frjamesmck@gmail.com
MCKECHNIE, Janna .... 701-858-3373. 371 F
janna.mckechnie@minotstateu.edu
MCKECHNIE, Sally .... 360-650-3340. 525 C
sally.mckechnie@wwu.edu
MCKECHNIE, Susan, E ... 410-706-7776. 219 C
smckechnie@af.umaryland.edu
MCKEE, Andrew .... 260-399-7700. 174 C
amckee@sf.edu
MCKEE, Anne .... 865-981-8298. 456 D
anne.mckee@maryvillecollege.edu
MCKEE, Bruce, G .... 641-422-4348. 181 D
mckeebru@niacc.edu
MCKEE, Diann, E .... 812-237-2372. 167 A
diann.mckee@indstate.edu
MCKEE, Eugenia .... 314-529-9509. 276 G
gmckee@maryville.edu
MCKEE, J, P .... 803-323-2205. 449 G
mckeej@winthrop.edu
MCKEE, John, C .... 409-747-9080. 493 C
jcmckee@utmb.edu
MCKEE, Jonathon .... 808-984-3213. 137 B
jvmckee@hawaii.edu
MCKEE, Kasey .... 636-922-8472. 280 J
kmckee@stchas.edu
MCKEE, Kathrine .... 937-327-7811. 393 E
kmckee@wittenberg.edu
MCKEE, Lauren .... 408-274-7900... 63 O
lauren.mckee@evc.edu
MCKEE, Lori .... 419-755-4828. 385 D
lmckee@ncstatecollege.edu
MCKEE, Lori .... 575-646-2172. 310 I
lomckee@nmsu.edu
MCKEE, Melinda .... 919-497-3330. 356 E
mmckee@louisburg.edu
MCKEE, Mike .... 386-752-1822. 104 G
mike.mckee@fgc.edu
MCKEE, Richard .... 432-685-4734. 476 G
rmckee@midland.edu
MCKEE, Suzanne .... 334-683-2347..... 5 F
smckee@marionmilitary.edu
MCKEE-LEONE, Virginia . 951-222-8250... 61 A
virginia.mckee-leone@rcc.edu
MCKEEGAN, John .... 503-883-2202. 404 A
jmckeeg@linfield.edu

MCKEEN, Jerry .... 505-566-3322. 311 I
mckeenj@sanjuancollege.edu
MCKEEVER, Diane, M ..... 312-942-6830. 157 G
diane_m_mckeever@rush.edu
MCKEEVER, Kerry .... 603-899-4303. 296 H
mckeeverk@franklinpierce.edu
MCKEEVER, Matt .... 303-797-5859... 78 F
matt.mckeever@arapahoe.edu
MCKEEVER, Stephen, W . 405-744-6501. 397 H
stephen.mckeever@okstate.edu
MCKEEVER, William, P ... 716-829-7807. 323 D
mckeever@dyc.edu
MCKELLIPS, Stephen ...... 901-678-5140. 460 B
sjmckllp@memphis.edu
MCKELLOGG, James, M . 859-344-3302. 199 H
jim.mckellogg@thomasmore.edu
MCKELVEY, C. Richard ... 512-863-1484. 481 I
mckelver@southwestern.edu
MCKELVEY, Scott .... 970-204-8255... 81 N
scott.mckelvey@frontrange.edu
MCKELVIE, OSF,
Roberta .... 610-796-5509. 409 E
roberta.mckelvie@alvernia.edu
MCKENDALL, Keith .... 504-816-4375. 201 K
kmckendall@dillard.edu
MCKENDREE, Lynda .... 713-525-2151. 490 L
mckendla@stthom.edu
MCKENNA, Catherine ..... 718-405-3233. 320 G
catherine.mckenna@mountsaintvincent.edu
MCKENNA, Heidi .... 510-883-7160... 42 I
hmckenna@dspt.edu
MCKENNA, Joann, C ...... 781-891-2455. 223 C
jmckenna@bentley.edu
MCKENNA, John .... 518-587-2100. 346 A
john.mckenna@esc.edu
MCKENNA, Kevin, M ...... 508-793-7468. 225 A
kmckenna@clarku.edu
MCKENNA, Megan .... 440-375-7508. 382 L
mmckenna@lec.edu
MCKENNA, Patrick .... 404-894-6088. 125 D
pat.mckenna@carnegie.gatech.edu
MCKENNA, Sheila .... 412-392-3450. 431 B
smckenna@pointpark.edu
MCKENNA-FRAZIER,
Lynnette .... 260-399-7700. 174 C
lfrazier@sf.edu
MCKENNA-GRANT,
Patricia .... 860-768-5433... 92 D
mckenna@hartford.edu
MCKENZIE, Amanda .... 478-289-2088. 124 C
amckenzie@ega.edu
MCKENZIE, Andre, A ...... 718-990-1892. 339 A
mckenzia@stjohns.edu
MCKENZIE, Bobby .... 334-874-5700..... 3 A
bmckenzie@ccal.edu
MCKENZIE, Connie, L .... 757-446-6070. 504 E
mckenzcl@evms.edu
MCKENZIE, Elizabeth ...... 617-573-8705. 237 B
emckenzi@suffolk.edu
MCKENZIE, Fred, R .... 630-844-5420. 140 A
mckenzie@aurora.edu
MCKENZIE, JoAnn .... 404-727-6052. 124 E
jmckenz@emory.edu
MCKENZIE, Joy .... 615-383-4848. 464 D
jmckenzie@watkins.edu
MCKENZIE, Justin, D ..... 336-750-3044. 370 A
mckenziej@wssu.edu
MCKENZIE, Laura .... 208-282-2661. 138 E
mckelaur@isu.edu
MCKENZIE, Lester .... 931-372-3073. 460 A
lmckenzie@tetech.edu
MCKENZIE, Lisa .... 518-454-5114. 321 A
mckenzil@strose.edu
MCKENZIE, Patricia, M .. 936-639-1301. 465 J
mckenzie@angelina.edu
MCKENZIE, Peter, C ...... 617-552-8740. 224 A
peter.mckenzie@bc.edu
MCKENZIE, Pia .... 919-807-7100. 357 L
mckenziep@nccommunitycolleges.edu
MCKENZIE, Scott .... 714-992-7052... 56 F
smckenzie@fullcoll.edu
MCKENZIE, Sheri .... 415-703-9535... 30 K
smckenzie@cca.edu
MCKENZIE, Vandeen ...... 575-439-3711. 310 J
vmckenzi@nmsu.edu
MCKENZIE, W. Shelby ... 225-578-4126. 204 N
wmcken1@lsu.edu
MCKEON, Judith, O .... 540-985-9083. 506 G
jomckeon@jchs.edu
MCKEON, Meg .... 712-749-2123. 176 D
mckeonm@bvu.edu
MCKEON, Michael .... 925-631-4552... 61 F
mfm4@stmarys-ca.edu
MCKEON, Thomas, K ...... 918-595-7868. 400 E
tom.mckeon@tulsacc.edu
MCKEOWN, Patricia .... 360-752-8333. 517 B
pmckeown@btc.ctc.edu
MCKERNAN, Steve .... 505-272-2071. 312 F
smckernan@salud.unm.edu
MCKESSON, Leslie .... 828-448-3156. 365 A
lmckesson@wpcc.edu

MCKETHAN, Lisa, H .... 254-710-1011. 467 G
lisa_mckethan@baylor.edu
MCKEVER, Ted .... 928-692-3076... 15 L
tmckever@mohave.edu
MCKEVITT, Sallie .... 301-369-2800. 213 G
sjmckevitt@capitol-college.edu
MCKEY, Jim .... 765-983-1636. 165 G
jimmckey@earlham.edu
MCKEY, Marites .... 808-687-7015. 135 F
mckey@hpu.edu
MCKIBBENS, Donna .... 617-879-2242. 238 C
dmckibbens@wheelock.edu
MCKIBBIN, Barbara .... 704-669-4116. 359 D
mckibbin@clevelandcc.edu
MCKIE, Betty .... 970-542-3208... 83 E
betty.mckie@morgancc.edu
MCKIEL, Allen .... 503-838-8886. 406 E
mckiela@wou.edu
MCKIERNAN, Gavin .... 305-809-3281. 104 I
gavin.mckiernan@fkcc.edu
MCKIM, Dana .... 704-463-3409. 365 E
dana.mckim@fsmail.pfeiffer.edu
MCKINION, Randall, L .... 800-672-3060. 366 F
MCKINLEY, Cathy .... 620-276-9627. 187 A
catherine.mckinley@gcccks.edu
MCKINLEY, Kathy .... 919-536-7244. 360 B
mckinleyk@durhamtech.edu
MCKINLEY, Patricia .... 713-525-3575. 490 L
mckinley@stthom.edu
MCKINLEY, Randy .... 574-251-3250. 166 N
rmckinley@holycrossvillage.com
MCKINLEY, Ronald, B .... 409-772-2636. 493 C
rbmckinl@utmb.edu
MCKINNEY, Andre .... 404-880-6791. 122 J
amckinney@cau.edu
MCKINNEY, Bryan .... 870-245-5250... 22 D
mckinneyb@obu.edu
MCKINNEY, Bryan .... 870-245-5513... 22 D
mckinneyb@obu.edu
MCKINNEY, Cathy .... 301-937-8448. 218 H
cmckinney@tesst.com
MCKINNEY, David, C ..... 828-398-7124. 357 N
dmckinney@abtech.edu
MCKINNEY, Dee .... 478-289-2062. 124 C
dmckinney@ega.edu
MCKINNEY, Destiny, S ... 512-505-3037. 473 G
dsmckinney@htu.edu
MCKINNEY, Donald, W .. 252-334-2084. 357 A
don.mckinney@macuniversity.edu
MCKINNEY, Frances, H .. 410-651-6668. 219 E
fhmckinney@umes.edu
MCKINNEY, Joan, C .... 270-789-5214. 193 D
jmckinney@campbellsville.edu
MCKINNEY, Marion .... 610-436-3307. 430 A
mmckinney@wcupa.edu
MCKINNEY, Mary .... 407-823-2827. 115 E
mary.mckinney@ucf.edu
MCKINNEY, Michael .... 724-589-2193. 434 B
mmckinney@thiel.edu
MCKINNEY, Nancy .... 360-596-5268. 524 A
nmckinney@spscc.edu
MCKINNEY, Paul .... 662-325-7428. 268 D
kpm137@msstate.edu
MCKINNEY, Richard, L .... 785-864-3136. 190 L
rlm@ku.edu
MCKINNEY, Robert .... 734-995-7328. 241 E
mckinr@cuaa.edu
MCKINNEY, Roger .... 443-627-7421. 265 D
roger.mckinney@laureate.net
MCKINNEY, Scott .... 828-398-7111. 357 N
smckinney@abtech.edu
MCKINNEY, Shortie .... 978-934-4460. 229 B
Shortie_McKinney@uml.edu
MCKINNEY, Stephen .... 610-861-1442. 424 E
mckinney@moravian.edu
MCKINNEY, Veronica .... 251-809-1532..... 5 A
veronica.mckinney@jdcc.edu
MCKINNEY, William .... 229-333-5952. 134 B
wjmckinney@valdosta.edu
MCKINNEY, William, J ... 813-988-5131. 104 A
bj@floridacollege.edu
MCKINNIES, Magi .... 617-349-8546. 228 B
mmckinni@lesley.edu
MCKINNON, Brad .... 256-766-6610..... 4 B
bmckinnon@hcu.edu
MCKINNON, Brenda .... 740-389-4636. 383 F
mckinnonb@mtc.edu
MCKINNON, Maureen ...... 816-501-4831. 280 I
maureen.mckinnon@rockhurst.edu
MCKINNON, Robert, G ... 770-720-5516. 130 G
rgm@reinhardt.edu
MCKINNON, Sarah .... 617-369-4054. 236 F
smckinnon@smfa.edu
MCKINNON, Ted, M .... 512-245-2396. 487 C
tm02@txstate.edu
MCKINNON, Theresa ...... 615-327-6185. 456 E
tmckinnon@mmc.edu
MCKINNON, Will .... 801-863-8922. 497 C
will.mckinnon@uvu.edu

MCKINSEY-MABRY,
Kimberly .... 585-262-1616. 332 A
kmckinseymabry@monroecc.edu
MCKINZIE, Deborah .... 607-735-1770. 323 H
MCKINZIE, Steve .... 704-637-4666. 353 E
smckinzie@catawba.edu
MCKINZIE, Wes .... 405-425-5132. 397 D
wes.mckinzie@oc.edu
MCKIRNAN, Lori .... 614-236-6814. 375 H
lmckirna@capital.edu
MCKISSICK, Milton, E .... 803-536-8938. 446 G
mckissick@scsu.edu
MCKISSON, Kevin .... 281-476-1501. 479 F
kevin.mckisson@sjcd.edu
MCKNIGHT, Avery .... 850-599-3591. 114 K
avery.mcknight@famu.edu
MCKNIGHT, Carrie .... 650-508-3717... 56 H
cmknight@ndnu.edu
MCKNIGHT, Cynthia .... 440-684-6102. 392 D
cmcknigh@ursuline.edu
MCKNIGHT, Frank .... 330-490-7226. 392 H
fmcknight@walsh.edu
MCKNIGHT, Irby .... 972-825-4662. 481 F
imcknight@sagu.edu
MCKNIGHT, Janet .... 414-410-4079. 532 B
jmcknight@stritch.edu
MCKNIGHT, Sandra .... 216-987-4832. 378 D
sandra.mcknight@tri-c.edu
MCKONE, Kevin .... 601-643-8369. 266 F
kevin.mckone@colin.edu
MCKOWN, Charles .... 620-441-5264. 186 A
mckown@cowley.edu
MCKOWN, Johnette .... 254-299-8649. 476 D
jmckown@mclennan.edu
MCKOWN, Richard, A .... 919-536-7200. 360 B
mckownr@durhamtech.edu
MCKOY, Dana .... 910-362-7029. 358 F
dmckoy@cfcc.edu
MCKULA, Patrick, R .... 724-925-4085. 437 D
mckulap@wccc.edu
MCKUSICK, James .... 406-243-2541. 286 H
james.mckusick@umontana.edu
MCLACKEN, Susan .... 401-232-6881. 438 K
smcdonal@bryant.edu
MCLAIN, Charles .... 215-368-7538. 412 A
cmclain@cbs.edu
MCLAIN, Katherine .... 916-691-7411... 53 B
mclaink@crc.losrios.edu
MCLAIN, Mandy .... 715-324-6900. 535 E
mandy.mclain@ni.edu
MCLAIN, Tony, L .... 906-635-2202. 245 G
tmclain@lssu.edu
MCLANE, Anne, P .... 214-648-5617. 493 E
anne.mclane@utsouthwestern.edu
MCLANE, Curren .... 202-639-1835... 95 B
cmclane@corcoran.org
MCLARAN, Diane .... 503-316-3229. 402 E
diane.mclaran@chemeketa.edu
MCLARTY, Bruce, D .... 501-279-4274... 21 C
president@harding.edu
MCLAUGHLIN, Carrie ..... 716-286-8405. 334 F
cmclaughlin@niagara.edu
MCLAUGHLIN, David ...... 212-998-2415. 334 D
david.mclaughlin@nyu.edu
MCLAUGHLIN, Deborah . 508-999-8051. 229 A
dmclaughlin@umassd.edu
MCLAUGHLIN, Ed .... 541-684-4644. 407 B
emclaughlin@pioneerpacific.edu
MCLAUGHLIN,
Edward, K .... 804-828-6692. 511 F
athleticsdir@vcu.edu
MCLAUGHLIN,
Francis, X .... 718-817-4300. 324 G
mclaughlin@fordham.edu
MCLAUGHLIN, Gerald .... 215-641-5550. 417 F
mclaughlin.g@gmc.edu
MCLAUGHLIN, Henry, J . 646-660-6000. 316 J
Henry.Mclaughlin@baruch.cuny.edu
MCLAUGHLIN, James .... 518-388-6284. 348 J
mclaughj@union.edu
MCLAUGHLIN, Jeff .... 507-786-3775. 264 B
mclaughj@stolaf.edu
MCLAUGHLIN, John .... 401-456-8235. 439 F
jmclaughlin@ric.edu
MCLAUGHLIN, Joyce ..... 978-934-4237. 229 B
Joyce_McLaughlin@uml.edu
MCLAUGHLIN,
Kelly Anne .... 315-781-3000. 326 C
mclaughlin@hws.edu
MCLAUGHLIN, Kevin ...... 415-503-6253... 62 H
kmclaughlin@sfcm.edu
MCLAUGHLIN, Kevin ...... 401-863-9525. 438 J
kevin_mclaughlin@brown.edu
MCLAUGHLIN, Larry ...... 617-552-3622. 224 A
larry.mclaughlin@bc.edu
MCLAUGHLIN, Laura ...... 636-227-2100. 276 F
Laura.McLaughlin@logan.edu
MCLAUGHLIN, Laurie ..... 951-487-6410... 55 B
lmclaugh@msjc.edu
MCLAUGHLIN, Laurie, L 612-626-1499. 264 G
mclau001@umn.edu

MCLAUGHLIN, LaVerne .. 229-430-4799. 119 J
laverne.mclaughlin@asurams.edu
MCLAUGHLIN, Leah .... 918-647-1370. 394 I
lmclaughlin@carlalbert.edu
MCLAUGHLIN, Margaret 386-752-1822. 104 G
maggie.mclaughlin@fgc.edu
MCLAUGHLIN,
Margaret, K .... 412-578-6071. 412 G
mclaughlinmk@carlow.edu
MCLAUGHLIN, Mark ...... 513-745-3409. 393 H
mclaughlin@xavier.edu
MCLAUGHLIN, Mark, W . 860-832-0065... 87 K
mclaughlinm@ccsu.edu
MCLAUGHLIN, Mary ...... 603-526-3755. 295 I
mmclaughlin@colby-sawyer.edu
MCLAUGHLIN, Mary, R .. 518-454-5170. 321 A
mclaughr@strose.edu
MCLAUGHLIN, Mike .... 319-398-4947. 180 J
mclaug@kirkwood.edu
MCLAUGHLIN, Nora .... 503-777-7774. 407 E
nora.mclaughlin@reed.edu
MCLAUGHLIN,
Patrick, A .... 260-481-6128. 168 C
mclaughp@ipfw.edu
MCLAUGHLIN, Polly ...... 973-353-1236. 306 D
pollymc@newark.rutgers.edu
MCLAUGHLIN, Sabrina .. 850-474-2433. 117 B
smclaughlin2@uwf.edu
MCLAUGHLIN, Sandee ... 805-546-3116... 42 C
smclaugh@cuesta.edu
MCLAUGHLIN,
Timothy, G .... 315-655-7244. 316 E
tmclaughlin@cazenovia.edu
MCLAUGHLIN,
Timothy, G .... 315-655-7368. 316 E
tmclaughlin@cazenovia.edu
MCLAURIN, Lisa, H .... 919-209-2178. 361 E
lhmclaurin@johnstoncc.edu
MCLAWHORN, Toni, D .. 540-375-2303. 509 B
mclawhorn@roanoke.edu
MCLAY, Deidre .... 831-656-2511. 544 M
dmclay@nps.edu
MCLAY, Melody, H .... 607-871-2612. 313 E
mclaym@alfred.edu
MCLEAN, Amber .... 906-635-2382. 245 G
amclean@lssu.edu
MCLEAN, Anita .... 609-258-3285. 304 E
amclean@princeton.edu
MCLEAN, Brandon .... 402-844-7102. 291 I
brandon@northeast.edu
MCLEAN, David .... 970-491-3366... 80 I
david.mclean@colostate.edu
MCLEAN, Deborah .... 907-842-5109... 10 I
dlmclean@alaska.edu
MCLEAN, Donna, D .... 612-330-1556. 253 H
mclean@augsburg.edu
MCLEAN, Edward .... 910-672-1315. 367 D
emclean@uncfsu.edu
MCLEAN, Jack .... 773-508-3912. 151 H
jmclean@luc.edu
MCLEAN, Janna .... 815-939-5231. 155 H
jmclean@olivet.edu
MCLEAN, Jennifer .... 570-326-3761. 427 B
jmclean@pct.edu
MCLEAN, Karen, P .... 515-271-1463. 177 H
karen.mclean@dmu.edu
MCLEAN, Mary .... 773-838-7883. 142 E
mmclean2@ccc.edu
MCLEAN, Michael, F ...... 805-525-4417... 69 H
mmclean@thomasaquinas.edu
MCLEAN, Natalie .... 336-273-4431. 352 H
nmclean@bennett.edu
MCLEAN, Pat .... 417-690-3441. 272 E
mclean@cofu.edu
MCLEAN, Roger .... 706-821-8232. 130 C
rmclean@paine.edu
MCLEAN, Sandra .... 972-438-6932. 478 C
smclean@parkercc.edu
MCLEAN, Valis .... 620-365-5116. 183 I
mclean@allencc.edu
MCLEAN, William, H ...... 847-491-7050. 155 D
wmclean@northwestern.edu
MCLEAN-SCANLON,
Mary .... 708-456-0300. 161 A
MCLEANE, David .... 870-574-4458... 23 G
dmcleane@sautech.edu
MCLELLAN, Carolyn .... 757-822-7124. 514 C
cmclellan@tcc.edu
MCLELLAN, Holly, H ...... 251-626-3303..... 8 B
hmclellan@ussa.edu
MCLELLAN, Mark, R .... 435-797-1180. 497 B
mark.mclellan@usu.edu
MCLELLAND, Brandy ...... 310-243-3569... 33 B
bmclelland@csudh.edu
MCLEMORE, Larry, A ...... 620-417-1651. 190 F
rry.mclemore@sccc.edu
MCLEMORE, Maria, R ..... 651-201-1745. 257 N
maria.mclemore@so.mnscu.edu
MCLENDON, Catrenia ..... 404-297-9522. 126 A
mclendon@gptc.edu

MCLENDON, George, L .. 713-348-4026. 479 A
mclendon@rice.edu
MCLENDON, Ginny .... 252-823-5166. 360 C
mclendong@edgecombe.edu
MCLENDON, Joan, S ...... 919-209-2079. 361 E
jsmclendon@johnstoncc.edu
MCLENDON, Kathi .... 704-330-6976. 359 C
kathi.mclendon@cpcc.edu
MCLENDON, Paul .... 870-235-4013... 23 F
PaulMcLendon@saumag.edu
MCLENDON, Sandra .... 864-644-5353. 446 I
smclendon@swu.edu
MCLENNAN, Dale .... 978-232-2101. 226 C
dmclenna@endicott.edu
MCLENNAN, William, L .. 650-723-1762... 68 E
mclennan@stanford.edu
MCLEOD, Allan .... 215-871-6652. 430 D
allanm@pcom.edu
MCLEOD, Carol .... 504-278-6418. 203 F
cmcleod@nunez.edu
MCLEOD, Gregory, K ...... 904-808-7400. 112 C
gregmcleod@sjrstate.edu
MCLEOD, Kimberly, R .... 713-313-1857. 485 F
mcleodkr@tsu.edu
MCLEOD, Mark .... 404-727-7457. 124 E
rmcleod@emory.edu
MCLEOD, Martha .... 860-253-3001... 88 C
mmcleod@asnuntuck.edu
MCLEOD, Michael .... 863-784-7441. 113 G
michael.mcleod@southflorida.edu
MCLEOD, Michael, J ...... 516-877-3177. 313 A
mcleod@adelphi.edu
MCLEOD, Susan .... 910-576-6222. 362 C
mcleods@montgomery.edu
MCLESKEY, Stephanie .... 828-689-1128. 356 F
smcleskey@mhc.edu
MCLIN, SR., Kevin, J ..... 334-727-4553..... 8 A
kjones2056@mytu.tuskegee.edu
MCLLWAIN, Daryl .... 207-780-5510. 212 H
darylmc@usm.maine.edu
MCLOAD, Steve .... 706-864-1915. 133 D
steve.mcleod@ung.edu
MCLOGAN, Matthew, E .. 616-331-2190. 243 C
mcloganm@gvsu.edu
MCLOUGHLIN, II,
Paul, J .... 610-330-5082. 420 D
mcloughp@lafayette.edu
MCLOUGHLIN, Suzanne . 516-876-3109. 343 D
mcloughlins@oldwestbury.edu
MCLURE, Amanda .... 954-783-7339. 102 M
amclure@cci.edu
MCMAHAN, Carla .... 864-977-7090. 445 H
carla.mcmahan@ngu.edu
MCMAHAN, David .... 423-636-7315. 462 E
dmcmahan@tusculum.edu
MCMAHAN, Kerrin .... 323-415-4135... 51 F
mcmahakm@elac.edu
MCMAHAN, Mendi, M ... 214-333-5119. 470 D
mendi@dbu.edu
MCMAHAN, Oliver, L ..... 423-478-7037. 458 B
omcmahan@ptseminary.edu
MCMAHAN, Richard .... 304-647-6410. 530 B
rmcmahan@osteo.wvsom.edu
MCMAHAN, Robert, K .... 810-762-9864. 244 Q
mcmahan@kettering.edu
MCMAHAN, Shari .... 657-278-7000... 33 E
smcmahan@fullerton.edu
MCMAHILL, Janet, M ..... 515-271-3726. 177 K
janet.mcmahill@drake.edu
MCMAHON,
Bernadette, B .... 312-369-7436. 143 D
bmcmahon@colum.edu
MCMAHON, Charles, P .. 504-988-8555. 207 C
cpm@tulane.edu
MCMAHON, Christa .... 239-304-7344... 98 K
christa.mcmahon@avemaria.edu
MCMAHON, Cindy .... 212-962-0002. 333 B
cmcmahon@nyci.edu
MCMAHON, David .... 413-748-3210. 236 I
dmcmahon@springfieldcollege.edu
MCMAHON, Doug .... 727-864-8587. 101 N
mcmahodh@eckerd.edu
MCMAHON, Ellen .... 847-574-5212. 150 C
emcmahon@lfgsm.edu
MCMAHON, James, P .... 414-288-7208. 534 B
james.mcmahon@marquette.edu
MCMAHON, Jessica .... 252-527-6223. 361 F
jmcmahon@lenoircc.edu
MCMAHON, Kathleen, N 401-254-3161. 440 B
kmcmahon@rwu.edu
MCMAHON, Kevin .... 213-613-2200... 67 E
kevin_mcmahon@sciarc.edu
MCMAHON, Marie .... 619-388-7497... 62 F
mmcmahon@sdccd.edu
MCMAHON, Mary Pat ..... 207-725-3225. 209 H
mmcmahon@bowdoin.edu
MCMAHON, Melody, L ... 773-371-5460. 141 D
mmcmahon@ctu.edu
MCMAHON, Michael, S . 701-355-8130. 373 E
msmcmahon@umary.edu

MCMAHON, Natalie .... 601-276-3865. 269 H
nmcmahon@smcc.edu
MCMAHON, Patricia .... 513-862-2743. 380 E
MCMAHON, Renee, M ... 406-447-5501. 285 G
rmcmahon@carroll.edu
MCMAHON, Roberta .... 708-524-6790. 144 C
rmcmahon@dom.edu
MCMAHON, Shelly, A .... 740-368-3201. 387 J
samcmaho@owu.edu
MCMAHON, Stephen ...... 802-654-2516. 500 B
smcmahon@smcvt.edu
MCMAHON, Timothy, J .. 412-359-1000. 434 H
tmcmahon@triangle-tech.edu
MCMAHON, Timothy, J .. 412-359-1000. 434 I
tmcmahon@triangle-tech.edu
MCMAINS, III,
Robert, E .... 205-934-4427..... 8 E
mmains@uab.edu
MCMAKIN, Sandy .... 210-805-3005. 490 A
mcmakin@uiwtx.edu
MCMANIGLE, John .... 301-295-3016. 545 C
john.mcmanigle@usuhs.edu
MCMANIS, Michael .... 660-626-2522. 271 A
mcmanis@atsu.edu
MCMANNESS, Matthew .. 215-951-1050. 420 B
mcmanness@lasalle.edu
MCMANUS, Bill .... 864-977-2094. 445 H
bill.mcmanus@ngu.edu
MCMANUS, Cecil .... 919-546-8417. 366 E
cmcmanus@shawu.edu
MCMANUS, D. Kim .... 804-758-6705. 513 G
kmcmanus@rappahannock.edu
MCMANUS, Janet .... 816-501-3618. 271 H
janet.mcmanus@avila.edu
MCMANUS, Jeffrey .... 239-348-4715... 98 K
jeff.mcmanus@avemaria.edu
MCMANUS, Michael .... 303-797-5654... 78 F
michael.mcmanus@arapahoe.edu
MCMASTER, Dennis .... 724-503-1001. 436 G
dmcmaster@washjeff.edu
MCMASTER, Jeff .... 617-217-9036. 222 G
jmcmaster@baystate.edu
MCMASTER, Pam .... 402-481-8718. 288 H
pam.mcmaster@bryanhealthcollege.edu
MCMASTER, Robert .... 612-625-9883. 264 G
mcmaster@umn.edu
MCMATH, Robert .... 479-575-7678... 23 I
rmcmath@uark.edu
MCMEANS, Orlando, F ... 304-766-4300. 530 C
mcmeanso@wvstateu.edu
MCMENAMIN,
Margaret, M .... 908-709-7100. 308 B
mcmenamin@ucc.edu
MCMICHAEL, Cyndi .... 248-204-4109. 245 I
cmcmichae@ltu.edu
MCMICHAEL, Robert .... 717-560-8240. 421 A
bmcmichael@lbc.edu
MCMICKLE, Marvin, A .... 585-340-9680. 320 E
mmcmickle@crcds.edu
MCMILLAN, Caroline ...... 912-486-7056. 124 C
cmcmillan@ega.edu
MCMILLAN, Cindy .... 251-343-8200..... 6 E
cindy.mcmillan@remingtoncollege.edu
MCMILLAN, Douglas ...... 580-745-2206. 399 J
dmcmillan@se.edu
MCMILLAN, Forrest .... 325-670-1250. 472 O
fmcmill@hsutx.edu
MCMILLAN, Jacqueline .. 937-775-4271. 393 G
jacqueline.mcmillan@wright.edu
MCMILLAN, Jane .... 580-745-2604. 399 J
jmcmillan@se.edu
MCMILLAN, Joseph .... 512-444-8082. 485 B
jtmcmillan@thsu.edu
MCMILLAN, Judy .... 210-486-4567. 464 J
jmcmillan@alamo.edu
MCMILLAN, Karon .... 601-925-3212. 268 A
kmcmilla@mc.edu
MCMILLAN, Laura .... 770-499-3056. 127 N
lmcmilla@kennesaw.edu
MCMILLAN, III, Lex, O .. 610-921-7600. 409 A
lmcmillan@alb.edu
MCMILLAN, Marilyn, A .. 212-998-2001. 334 D
marilyn.mcmillan@nyu.edu
MCMILLAN, Mary .... 310-303-7302... 53 F
dhall@marymountcalifornia.edu
MCMILLAN, Michelle ...... 918-495-6013. 398 H
mmcmillan@oru.edu
MCMILLAN, Minnie .... 334-874-5700..... 3 A
mmcmillan@ccal.edu
MCMILLAN, Sally, J .... 865-974-0684. 463 C
sjmcmill@utk.edu
MCMILLEN, Jeremy, P ... 903-463-8600. 472 M
mcmillenj@grayson.edu
MCMILLIAN, Anthony ..... 281-618-5524. 476 A
anthony.mcmillian@lonestar.edu
MCMILLIAN, Carey .... 816-271-4582. 279 A
mcmilli@missouriwestern.edu
MCMILLIN, Barbara, C ... 662-685-4771. 266 C
bmcmillin@bmc.edu
MCMILLIN, David .... 417-626-1234. 279 J
dmcmillin@occ.edu

MCMILLIN, Donna .... 870-972-3700... 19 N
mcmillin@astate.edu
MCMILLIN, Jennifer .... 417-626-1234. 279 J
jmcmillin@occ.edu
MCMILLIN, Lisa .... 601-635-2111. 266 H
lmcmillan@eccc.edu
MCMILLIN, Nicole .... 605-367-4821. 452 C
nicole.mcmillin@southeasttech.edu
MCMILLIN, Renee .... 303-292-0015... 81 F
r.mcmillin@denverschoolofnursing.edu
MCMILLION, David .... 706-776-0114. 130 E
dmcmillion@piedmont.edu
MCMILLION, Eric, C ...... 859-858-3511. 192 B
eric.mcmillion@asbury.edu
MCMILLON, Avis .... 732-224-2967. 299 G
amcmillon@brookdalecc.edu
MCMINIMY, Gisele .... 316-295-5377. 186 H
mcminimy@friends.edu
MCMINN, Jamie, G .... 724-946-7031. 437 B
mcminnjg@westminster.edu
MCMOY, Johnny .... 256-352-8117..... 9 G
johnny.mcmoy@wallacestate.edu
MCMULLAN, Martin, H .. 601-815-4700. 270 C
mhmcmullan@umc.edu
MCMULLEN, David, S .... 202-319-6907... 94 G
mcmulled@cua.edu
MCMULLEN, Eileen .... 215-567-7080. 410 A
emcmullen@aii.edu
MCMULLEN, Judith .... 216-987-4836. 378 D
judith.mcmullen@tri-c.edu
MCMULLEN, Michael ...... 315-498-2566. 335 G
mcmullem@sunyocc.edu
MCMULLEN, Patricia ...... 202-319-5403... 94 G
mcmullep@cua.edu
MCMULLEN, Ruth .... 707-524-1721... 65 B
rmcmullen@santarosa.edu
MCMULLEN, Sylvia .... 979-830-4000. 467 I
MCMULLEN, William .... 817-515-1268. 482 B
william.mcmullen@tccd.edu
MCMULLIN, Angeline ...... 423-614-8357. 455 L
amcmullin@leeuniversity.edu
MCMULLIN, Sallie, D ..... 434-395-2598. 506 J
mcmullinsd@longwood.edu
MCMURDOCK, Linda .... 310-338-3756... 53 E
lmcmurdock@lmu.edu
MCMURPHY, Elizabeth ... 580-349-1566. 397 G
MCMURRAY, Aaron .... 503-517-1220. 408 H
amcmurray@warnerpacific.edu
MCMURRAY, Aaron, P ... 509-777-3730. 525 F
amcmurray@whitworth.edu
MCMURRAY, Brock .... 661-763-7811... 69 D
bmcmurray@taftcollege.edu
MCMURRAY, Jeffrey .... 903-886-5852. 483 E
jeffrey.mcmurray@tamuc.edu
MCMURRAY, Kelly .... 301-934-7624. 214 D
kmcmurray@csmd.edu
MCMURRY, Alice .... 717-872-3820. 429 D
alice.mcmurry@millersville.edu
MCMURRY, Marna, R ..... 910-256-0255. 357 I
mdavenport@moc.edu
MCMURTRY, Craig .... 254-298-8524. 482 C
craig.mcmurtry@templejc.edu
MCNABB, Ann, M .... 773-442-5110. 154 H
a-mcnabb@neiu.edu
MCNABB, David .... 970-521-6655... 83 L
david.mcnabb@njc.edu
MCNABB, Deana, M .... 406-338-5421. 285 F
deana_mcnabb@bfcc.edu
MCNABB, Jeffrey .... 812-749-1239. 171 K
jmnnabb@oak.edu
MCNABB, Kathleen, J ..... 218-477-4321. 259 H
mcnabb@mnstate.edu
MCNABB, Terry .... 319-399-8870. 176 G
tmcnabb@coe.edu
MCNABB, Theresa, P 434-381-6210. 510 F
tmcnabb@sbc.edu
MCNAIR, Betty-Ann, W .. 832-252-4691. 468 L
bettyann.mcnair@cbshouston.edu
MCNAIR, Christopher, L . 325-670-1401. 472 O
cmcnair@hsutx.edu
MCNAIR, Lily, D .... 718-390-3211. 350 B
lily.mcnair@wagner.edu
MCNAIR, Phil .... 304-724-3700. 526 B
pmcnair@apus.edu
MCNAIR, Sheila .... 804-524-6948. 515 D
smcnair@vsu.edu
MCNALL, Mike .... 309-457-2122. 153 D
mike@monmouthcollege.edu
MCNALLY, Beth .... 712-749-2052. 176 D
mcnallyb@bvu.edu
MCNALLY, Elizabeth, B ... 740-376-4683. 383 E
beth.mcnally@marietta.edu
MCNALLY, Minta, A .... 336-758-4237. 370 D
mcnallma@wfu.edu
MCNALLY, Neal, P .... 330-941-2489. 394 A
npmcnally@ysu.edu
MCNALLY, Patrick .... 313-496-2689. 252 B
pmcnall1@wcccd.edu
MCNALLY, Robin .... 508-793-7467. 225 A
rmcnally@clarku.edu

MCNALLY, Steven, L ...... 303-492-5489... 85 L
steve.mcnally@colorado.edu
MCNALLY, Susanne .... 315-781-3467. 326 C
banks@hws.edu
MCNALLY, Tom .... 803-777-3142. 447 G
tom@mailbox.sc.edu
MCNAMARA, Anne .... 602-639-7500... 13 S
MCNAMARA, Bob .... 800-686-7022... 90 D
bmcnamara@lincolncollegene.edu
MCNAMARA, Bob, H ...... 843-953-2072. 442 A
bob.mcnamara@citadel.edu
MCNAMARA, Connie .... 717-245-1813. 414 H
mcnamarc@dickinson.edu
MCNAMARA, John .... 862-906-5102... 88 D
jmcnamara@ccc.commnet.edu
MCNAMARA, John .... 815-394-5152. 157 C
jmcnamara@rockford.edu
MCNAMARA, Julia, M ..... 203-773-8529... 87 G
mcnamara@albertus.edu
MCNAMARA, Kristine, E . 401-598-1565. 439 B
kmcnamara@jwu.edu
MCNAMARA, Paul, D ..... 904-779-4141. 105 E
pmcnamara@fscj.edu
MCNAMARA, Ryan .... 727-726-1153. 100 E
ryanmcnamara@clearwater.edu
MCNAMARA, Thomas ..... 508-929-8033. 230 G
tmcnamara@worcester.edu
MCNAMARA, Thomas ..... 610-282-1100. 414 F
tom.mcnamara@desales.edu
MCNAMEE, Anoush .... 305-237-0656. 109 D
amcnamee@mdc.edu
MCNAMEE, Barbara .... 734-384-4244. 247 C
bmcnamee@monroeccc.edu
MCNAMEE, Kathleen .... 870-612-2081... 25 A
kathleen.mcnamee@uaccb.edu
MCNAMEE, Mark, G ...... 540-231-6123. 515 C
mmcnamee@vt.edu
MCNAMEE, Stephen .... 910-962-3660. 369 C
mcnamee@uncw.edu
MCNANEY, Duane .... 903-983-8107. 475 E
dmcnaney@kilgore.edu
MCNEAL, Deborah .... 662-621-4124. 266 D
dmcneal@coahomacc.edu
MCNEAL, Gloria, J .... 858-642-8107... 55 J
gmcneal@nu.edu
MCNEAL, Lewatis .... 270-852-8607. 196 C
lewatis.mcneal@kctcs.edu
MCNEAL, Nadine .... 731-989-6644. 454 J
nmcneal@fhu.edu
MCNEALEY, Ernest .... 205-366-8800..... 7 E
emcnealey@stillman.edu
MCNEALY, Tara, F .... 843-953-5336. 442 A
tara.mcnealy@citadel.edu
MCNEAR, Jack .... 502-597-5853. 197 A
jack.mcnear@kysu.edu
MCNEECE, Brian .... 760-355-6438... 48 A
brian.mcneece@imperial.edu
MCNEEL, Jon, T .... 402-449-2858. 289 H
deanofmen@graceu.edu
MCNEELEY, Wendy .... 325-649-8619. 473 F
wmcneeley@hputx.edu
MCNEELY, Bonnie .... 405-974-2883. 400 K
bmcneely@uco.edu
MCNEELY, Nate .... 847-628-2521. 149 B
nmcneely@judsonu.edu
MCNEELY, Shelley .... 608-785-9880. 541 E
mcneelys@westerntc.edu
MCNEELY, Stanton .... 985-448-7936. 203 B
stanton.mcneely@fletcher.edu
MCNEELY, Timothy, A .... 304-367-4937. 529 F
Tim.McNeely@fairmontstate.edu
MCNEESE, Margaret .... 713-500-5116. 492 E
margaret.c.mcneese@uth.tmc.edu
MCNEESE, Tim, D .... 402-363-5683. 293 I
tdmcneese@york.edu
MCNEICE-STALLARD,
Barbara .... 909-274-4109... 55 A
bmcneice-stallard@mtsac.edu
MCNEIL, Denise, M .... 810-989-5571. 249 H
dmcneil@sc4.edu
MCNEIL, J. Derek .... 206-876-6105. 523 D
dmcneil@theseattleschool.edu
MCNEIL, Jacquelyn .... 941-752-5231. 114 I
mcneilj@scf.edu
MCNEIL, Marilyn .... 732-571-3415. 303 C
mmcneil@monmouth.edu
MCNEIL, Mary Anne .... 805-652-5547... 74 E
mmcneil@vcccd.edu
MCNEIL, Roger, R .... 606-783-2158. 198 A
r.mcneil@moreheadstate.edu
MCNEIL, Ronald, D .... 217-206-6533. 161 E
mcneil.ron@uis.edu
MCNEIL, Sybil .... 478-757-5200. 134 G
smcneil@wesleyancollege.edu
MCNEIL, Teresa .... 619-660-4301... 46 D
teresa.mcneil@gcccd.edu
MCNEIL, Teronda .... 910-642-7141. 364 A
Teronda.McNeil@sccnc.edu
MCNEIL, Vickie, J .... 336-334-5099. 369 A
vlmcnei2@uncg.edu

MCNEIL, Wanda ... 314-340-3511. 275 A mcneilj@hssu.edu
MCNEILL, Denise ... 806-720-7527. 476 B denise.mcneill@lcu.edu
MCNEILL, Janette, N ... 336-454-1126. 360 G jnmcneill@gtcc.edu
MCNEILL, Kevin ... 910-576-6222. 362 C mcneillk@montgomery.edu
MCNEILL, Savonne ... 704-922-6420. 360 F mcneill.savonne@gaston.edu
MCNEILL, William, T ... 336-506-4157. 357 M terry.mcneill@alamancecc.edu
MCNERNEY, David ... 515-271-1408. 177 H david.mcnerney@dmu.edu
MCNERNEY, Norma, L ... 203-857-7020... 89 D nmcnerney@norwalk.edu
MCNESBY, Gerard, M ... 302-739-4057... 93 D gmcnesby@dtcc.edu
MCNEW, Regina ... 865-694-6650. 461 D rdmcnew@pstcc.edu
MCNICHOL, David, K ... 973-761-9621. 307 C David.mcnichol@shu.edu
MCNICOL, Greg, L ... 915-747-7182. 492 A gmcnicol@utep.edu
MCNIER, Michelle ... 989-463-7423. 239 B mcnierml@alma.edu
MCNIVEN, Spencer ... 860-628-4751... 90 D smcniven@lincolncollegene.edu
MCNULTY, Edward, J ... 312-629-9159. 158 L emcnulty@saic.edu
MCNULTY, Mary Kate ... 215-572-2877. 409 H mcnultym@arcadia.edu
MCNULTY, Priscilla ... 612-977-5901. 254 C priscilla.mcnulty@capella.edu
MCNULTY, Ray ... 570-342-7701... 16 L ray.mcnulty@pennfoster.edu
MCNULTY, Sean, J ... 602-386-4117... 11 G sean.mcnulty@arizonachristian.edu
MCNULTY, Sharon ... 973-290-4134. 300 F mcnulty@cse.edu
MCNUTT, Anne ... 205-387-0511..... 2 B amcnutt@bscc.edu
MCNUTT, Paula ... 406-447-4404. 285 G pmcnutt@carroll.edu
MCPARTLAN, Edward, J . 914-337-9300. 321 E ed.mcpartlan@concordia-ny.edu
MCPEAK, Charlene ... 586-286-2097. 246 A mcpeakc@macomb.edu
MCPEAK, Ronie ... 615-444-2462. 454 A rmcpeak@cumberland.edu
MCPHAIL, Brenda, M ... 314-516-6503. 283 E bmcphail@umsl.edu
MCPHAIL, Craig ... 828-898-2483. 356 A mcphail@lmc.edu
MCPHAIL, Mark ... 262-472-1221. 538 D mcphailm@uww.edu
MCPHATTER, Anna ... 443-885-4325. 217 A anna.mcphatter@morgan.edu
MCPHEARSON, Petra, R . 731-881-7805. 463 E prencher@utm.edu
MCPHEE, Gary, R ... 781-280-3530. 232 B mcpheeg@middlesex.mass.edu
MCPHEE, Kelly ... 602-286-8186... 14 L kelly.mcphee@gwmail.maricopa.edu
MCPHEE, Scott ... 765-674-6901. 169 B scott.mcphee@indwes.edu
MCPHEE, Sidney, A ... 615-898-2623. 459 D sidney.mcphee@mtsu.edu
MCPHEETERS, Andrew ... 503-768-7936. 403 K mcpheete@lclark.edu
MCPHERON, Bruce ... 614-292-6164. 386 E mcpheron.24@osu.edu
MCPHERREN, Ann, C ... 260-359-4225. 166 O amcpherren@huntington.edu
MCPHERSON, Dawn ... 906-932-4231. 242 I dawnm@gogebic.edu
MCPHERSON, Evelyn ... 806-743-2860. 487 D evelyn.mcpherson@ttuhsc.edu
MCPHERSON, John ... 765-285-5600. 164 B jmcphers@bsu.edu
MCPHERSON, Lindsey ... 713-525-3639. 490 L guthmanl@stthom.edu
MCPHERSON, Mary, L ... 972-860-5097. 470 J lmcpherson@dcccd.edu
MCPHERSON, Robert ... 713-743-5003. 489 B bmcph@uh.edu
MCPHERSON, Sean ... 570-586-2400. 410 D smacpherson@bbc.edu
MCPHERSON, Terry ... 704-378-1237. 355 K tmcpherson@jcsu.edu
MCPHERSON-BARNES, Penny ... 856-256-4086. 305 E barnesp@rowan.edu
MCPHIE-OLIVEIRA, Laura, E ... 401-341-2103. 440 C mcphiel@salve.edu
MCPHILIMY, Betty, L ... 847-491-2622. 155 D b-mcphilimy@northwestern.edu
MCPIKE, Brian ... 719-255-3211... 85 M bmcpike@uccs.edu
MCPIKE, Julie ... 618-468-3600. 150 G jmcpike@lc.edu
MCQUADE, Robert, K ... 574-631-6161. 174 A mcquade.10@nd.edu
MCQUADE, Shauna, N ... 301-784-5000. 213 B smcquade@allegany.edu
MCQUARIE, Audra ... 602-557-6151... 18 I audra.mcquarie@phoenix.edu
MCQUARRIE, Laurie ... 207-942-6781. 209 E lmcquarrie@bts.edu
MCQUARRIE, Michael ... 410-626-2558. 217 G michael.mcquarrie@sjca.edu
MCQUATE, Craig ... 617-369-3252. 236 F cmcquate@mfa.org
MCQUAY-PENINGER, Laurel ... 310-434-3718... 65 A mcquay-peninger_laurel@smc.edu
MCQUE, Buffie ... 207-941-7027. 210 B alumni@husson.edu
MCQUEEN, Angus ... 540-887-7012. 507 A amcqueen@mbc.edu
MCQUEEN, Candice ... 615-966-5708. 456 B candice.mcqueen@lipscomb.edu
MCQUEEN, Elaine ... 803-754-4582. 449 H emcqueen@wlbc.edu
MCQUEEN, Lee ... 308-865-1700. 292 H mcqueenlv@unk.edu
MCQUEEN, Mary ... 361-698-1317. 471 G mmcqueen2@delmar.edu
MCQUEEN, Rebecca ... 704-463-3404. 365 E rebecca.mcqueen@fsmail.pfeiffer.edu
MCQUEEN, Sylvia ... 910-642-7141. 364 A Sylvia.McQueen@sccnc.edu
MCQUEENY, Jane ... 785-864-3687. 190 L jane.mcqueeny@ku.edu
MCQUERRY, Marcia ... 405-585-5101. 397 C marcia.mcquerry@okbu.edu
MCQUESTEN, Pam ... 512-863-1300. 481 I pmcquesten@southwestern.edu
MCQUESTEN, Pamela ... 323-259-1451... 56 I pmcquesten@oxy.edu
MCQUILKIN, Scott, A ... 509-777-4386. 525 F smcquilkin@whitworth.edu
MCQUILLAN, Mark ... 603-668-2211. 297 I m.mcquillan@snhu.edu
MCQUILLAN, Pat ... 651-423-8318. 258 D patrick.mcQuillan@dctc.edu
MCQUILLAN, Pat ... 651-450-3655. 258 H pmcquil@inverhills.edu
MCQUINN, Robert ... 847-467-2469. 155 D r.mcquinn@northwestern.edu
MCQUISTION, Chris ... 615-383-4848. 464 D cmcquistion@watkins.edu
MCQUOWN, Daniel ... 517-629-0492. 239 A dmcquown@albion.edu
MCRAE, Alphonzo ... 910-272-3500. 363 B mcrae@robeson.edu
MCRAE, Alphonzo ... 910-272-3500. 363 B amcrae@robeson.edu
MCRAE, Georgia, D ... 414-288-7596. 534 B georgia.mcrae@marquette.edu
MCRAE, Jim ... 206-780-6214. 516 I jim.mcrae@bgi.edu
MCRAE, Kevin ... 406-444-0328. 286 G kmcrae@montana.edu
MCRAE, Mary ... 972-881-5771. 469 G mmcrae@collin.edu
MCRAE, Mary ... 215-572-2781. 409 H mcraem@arcadia.edu
MCRAE, Maureen ... 323-259-2548... 56 I mmclevy@oxy.edu
MCRELL, Michael ... 620-341-5214. 186 D mcrellmi@emporia.edu
MCREYNOLDS, Betsy, A . 417-667-8181. 273 A bmcreynolds@cottey.edu
MCREYNOLDS, Karla ... 573-288-6544. 273 F kmcreynolds@culver.edu
MCREYNOLDS, Shawn ... 276-223-4810. 514 F smcreynolds@wcc.vccs.edu
MCROBBIE, Michael ... 812-855-4613. 167 F iupres@iu.edu
MCROBBIE, Michael, A .. 812-855-4613. 167 E iupres@iu.edu
MCROBIE, Karen ... 415-442-6599... 45 I kmcrobie@ggu.edu
MCRORIE, Sally, E ... 850-644-6876. 115 C smcrorie@fsu.edu
MCSHAN, Jim, C ... 713-313-1382. 485 F mcshanjc@tsu.edu
MCSHANE, Bridget ... 860-439-2314... 89 H bamcs@conncoll.edu
MCSHANE, SJ, Joseph, M ... 718-817-3000. 324 G
MCSHEA, Anitra, M ... 570-941-7680. 436 A anitra.mcshea@scranton.edu
MCSHEEHY, Diane, M ... 303-458-4223... 84 M dmcsheehy@regis.edu
MCSHURLEY, Mark, C ... 540-636-2900. 503 L markm@christendom.edu
MCSPADDEN, Galen, W . 620-417-1550. 190 F galen.mcspadden@sccc.edu
MCSPADDEN, Jean ... 903-675-6304. 488 D jmcspadden@tvcc.edu
MCSWAIN, Garry ... 704-406-3923. 354 C gmcswain@gardner-webb.edu
MCSWAIN, Michael ... 704-669-4115. 359 D mcswainm@clevelandcc.edu
MCSWAIN, Roderick ... 251-665-4139..... 2 D rmcswain@bishop.edu
MCSWEENEY, Frances ... 509-335-5581. 525 A fkmcs@wsu.edu
MCSWEENEY, Kevin, D .. 608-262-2748. 536 D kmcsweeney@wisc.edu
MCTERNAN, Edmund ... 518-464-8500. 324 B mmcternan@excelsior.edu
MCTIERNAN, Kerri-Ann .. 212-217-4210. 324 C kerriann_mctiernan@fitnyc.edu
MCVAY, Janine ... 413-565-1000. 222 F jmcvay@baypath.edu
MCVAY, John ... 509-527-2186. 524 I john.mcvay@wallawalla.edu
MCVAY, John, R ... 575-624-8150. 310 H mcvay@nmmi.edu
MCVEAN, Aaron ... 530-541-4660... 50 D mcvean@ltcc.edu
MCVEARRY, Kenneth ... 301-447-5274. 217 B mcvearry@msmary.edu
MCVEETY, Cassie ... 503-352-3096. 407 A mcveety@pacificu.edu
MCVEIGH, Paul, J ... 703-323-4224. 513 C pmcveigh@nvcc.edu
MCVETY, Paul, J ... 401-598-1775. 439 B pmcvety@jwu.edu
MCVEY, Greg ... 573-288-6424. 273 F gmcvey@culver.edu
MCVEY, Lindsay ... 740-374-8716. 392 I lmcvey@wscc.edu
MCWADE, Patricia, A ... 202-687-4547... 95 E mcwadep@georgetown.edu
MCWHERTER, Karen ... 731-661-5337. 462 F kmcwhert@uu.edu
MCWHERTER, Lisa ... 864-644-5013. 446 I lmcwherter@swu.edu
MCWHORTER, Lois, A ... 606-878-4801. 196 D lois.mcwhorter@kctcs.edu
MCWHORTER, Shirlyon, J ... 305-348-2785. 115 B shirlyon.mcwhorter@fiu.edu
MCWHORTER, Thomas ... 213-740-5445... 74 A faodean@usc.edu
MCWILLIAMS, Mary ... 740-389-4636. 383 F mcwilliamsm@mtc.edu
MCWILLIAMS, Stephen, T ... 610-519-4095. 436 F stephen.mcwilliams@villanova.edu
MCZEE, Taran ... 812-866-7076. 166 C mczee@hanover.edu
MEA, William ... 718-390-3315. 350 B william.mea@wagner.edu
MEAD, Alicia ... 303-220-1200... 78 K alicia.mead@cffp.edu
MEAD, Dana, G ... 717-361-1359. 415 H meaddg@etown.edu
MEAD, David, B ... 817-515-6604. 482 B david.mead@tccd.edu
MEAD, Doug ... 567-661-7277. 387 L douglas_mead@owens.edu
MEAD, JR., George, F ... 337-475-5785. 207 G mead@mcneese.edu
MEAD, K. Ann ... 270-745-2434. 200 G ann.mead@wku.edu
MEAD, Steven ... 860-255-3473... 89 G smead@txcc.commnet.edu
MEAD, Susan ... 845-431-8036. 323 C mead@sunydutchess.edu
MEAD, Tom ... 858-513-9240. 175 F Thomas.mead@ashford.edu
MEAD-ROACH, Amanda . 314-644-9099. 281 E amead2@stlcc.edu
MEADE, Elizabeth ... 610-606-4637. 412 I emeade@cedarcrest.edu
MEADE, Linda, B ... 724-946-7339. 437 B meadelb@westminster.edu
MEADE, Marianne ... 610-989-1240. 436 D mmeade@vfmac.edu
MEADOR, Diane ... 907-796-6457... 11 A diane.meador@uas.alaska.edu
MEADOR, JR., John, M . 607-777-2346. 341 E jmeador@binghamton.edu
MEADOR, Mark ... 615-966-6223. 456 B mark.meador@lipscomb.edu
MEADOR, Michele ... 775-673-7249. 294 H mmeador@tmcc.edu
MEADOR, Roy ... 515-643-6612. 181 A rmeador@mercydesmoines.org
MEADOR, Ruby ... 870-762-3125... 19 K rmeador@smail.anc.edu
MEADOR, Vernie ... 870-633-4480... 21 A vmeador@eacc.edu
MEADORS, Mark ... 918-343-7860. 399 C mmeadors@rsu.edu
MEADOWS, Dan ... 304-357-4881. 527 H danmeadows@ucwv.edu
MEADOWS, David, D ... 814-641-0714. 419 H meadowd@juniata.edu
MEADOWS, David, J ... 804-524-5995. 515 D pbullock@vsu.edu
MEADOWS, Dawn ... 863-638-7246. 119 C dawn.meadows@warner.edu
MEADOWS, Dean ... 863-638-7255. 119 C dean.meadows@warner.edu
MEADOWS, Ed ... 850-484-1700. 110 G emeadows@pensacolastate.edu
MEADOWS, Mark ... 619-482-6569... 68 B mmeadows@swccd.edu
MEADOWS, Steve ... 304-384-5180. 529 E meadows@concord.edu
MEADOWS, Wanda ... 334-244-3260..... 2 A wmeadow2@aum.edu
MEAGHER, Paula, G ... 915-831-4530. 472 B pmeagher@epcc.edu
MEALER, Donna ... 731-286-3312. 460 F mealer@dscc.edu
MEALY, Robert ... 212-799-5000. 328 B
MEANA, Marta ... 702-895-2267. 294 I marta.meana@unlv.edu
MEANER, Christopher, M ... 412-578-6069. 412 G meanercm@carlow.edu
MEANEY, Heather, L ... 518-381-1250. 340 G meaneyhl@sunysccc.edu
MEANS, Ben ... 217-228-5432. 156 C meansbe@quincy.edu
MEANS, Gary, A ... 724-925-4061. 437 D meansg@wccc.edu
MEANS, Jennifer ... 623-845-3289... 14 M jennifer.means@gccaz.edu
MEANS, John ... 918-335-6892. 398 F jmeans@okwu.edu
MEANS, Margie ... 706-776-0123. 130 E mmeans@piedmont.edu
MEANY, Birgit ... 907-852-3333... 10 F birgit.meany@ilisagvik.edu
MEANY, David ... 509-359-6335. 519 C dmeany@ewu.edu
MEANY, John ... 508-929-8746. 230 G jmeany@worcester.edu
MEANY, Mary, T ... 920-832-6561. 533 S mary.t.meany@lawrence.edu
MEARA, Mark ... 609-894-9311. 299 I mmeara@bcc.edu
MEARINI, Mary Ann ... 516-877-3265. 313 A mearini@adelphi.edu
MEARNS, Geoffrey, S ... 859-572-5123. 198 I mearns@nku.edu
MEARNS, Raiana ... 847-543-2402. 143 A rmearns@clcillinois.edu
MEARS, Bobby ... 757-789-1747. 512 D bmears@es.vccs.edu
MEARS, Laura ... 301-846-2429. 214 H lmears@frederick.edu
MEARS, Michael, J ... 941-752-5267. 114 I mearsm@scf.edu
MEARS, Ted ... 320-252-1489. 261 B husky@bkstr.com
MEASAMER, Ronnie ... 919-718-7409. 359 B rmeasamer@cccc.edu
MEASE, Ervin, J ... 610-799-1112. 421 I emease@lccc.edu
MEASE, Stephen ... 802-865-6432. 499 A smease@champlain.edu
MECCA, Kim ... 570-504-0920. 420 C meccak@lackawanna.edu
MECH, Terrence, F ... 570-208-5943. 419 P tfmech@kings.edu
MECHAM, Melissa, E ... 206-239-4500. 517 M mmecham@cityu.edu
MECHAM, Steven, J ... 435-797-1967. 497 B steve.mecham@usu.edu
MECHE, Eddie, P ... 337-475-5501. 207 G emeche@mcneese.edu
MECHE, Lance ... 972-825-4747. 481 F LMeche@sagu.edu
MECHNIG, Virginia ... 630-353-7049. 144 A vmechnig@devry.edu
MECK, Bill ... 641-683-5106. 179 A bill.meck@indianhills.edu
MECK, Bill ... 319-208-5069. 182 G bmeck@scciowa.edu
MECK, Heather, J ... 814-472-3264. 432 D hmeck@francis.edu
MECKEL, David ... 415-703-9561... 30 K dmeckel@cca.edu
MEDA, Pat ... 626-529-8261... 57 G pmeda@pacificoaks.edu
MEDA-POLLACK, Andro . 407-843-3984. 105 P careers@fortiscollege.edu
MEDAGLIA, Frank ... 804-594-1414. 512 G fmedaglia@jtcc.edu
MEDAGLIA, Kimberly ... 630-752-5729. 163 F kimberly.Medaglia@wheaton.edu

MEDALEN, Brenda, L ..... 605-336-6588. 451 C
bmedalen@sfseminary.edu
MEDBURY, Doug .... 425-235-2352. 522 F
dmedbury@rtc.edu
MEDCALF, Elizabeth .... 301-687-4161. 220 C
emedcalf@frostburg.edu
MEDDERS, Alan .... 706-507-8954. 123 D
medders_alan@columbusstate.edu
MEDDERS, Mike, W .... 903-566-7393. 492 D
mmedders@uttyler.edu
MEDDINGS, Nancy .... 805-922-6966... 26 K
nmeddings@hancockcollege.edu
MEDEARIS, Cheryl .... 605-856-5880. 451 B
cheryl.medearis@sintegleska.edu
MEDEARIS, Ellen .... 919-385-3100. 354 A
ellen.medearis@duke.edu
MEDEIROS, Brad .... 508-626-4911. 230 A
bmedeiros@framingham.edu
MEDEIROS, Dave .... 803-786-3007. 443 B
dave@columbiasc.edu
MEDEIROS, Denis, M ..... 816-235-1301. 283 D
medeirosd@umkc.edu
MEDEIROS, Denise, V .... 704-687-7781. 368 E
dvmedei@uncc.edu
MEDEMA, Pam .... 815-288-5511. 158 K
medemap@svcc.edu
MEDENBLIK, Julius, T ... 616-957-6024. 240 M
jmedenblik@calvinseminary.edu
MEDFORD, Adriane .... 215-567-7080. 410 A
amedford@aii.edu
MEDFORD, Mike .... 404-687-4576. 123 C
medfordm@ctsnet.edu
MEDINA, JR., Alfredo .... 518-782-6558. 340 J
amedina@siena.edu
MEDINA, Carlos .... 518-320-1176. 341 C
carlos.medina@suny.edu
MEDINA, Cynthia .... 303-751-8700... 78 J
medina@bel-rea.com
MEDINA, Deborah, M .... 716-851-1828. 323 I
medina@ecc.edu
MEDINA, Fernendo .... 787-815-0000. 553 I
fernando.medina1@upr.edu
MEDINA, Mara .... 787-780-0070. 547 G
mmedina@caribbean.edu
MEDINA, Maria .... 973-684-5651. 304 B
mmedina@pccc.edu
MEDINA, Nancy .... 773-442-5240. 154 H
n-medina4@neiu.edu
MEDINA, Raúl .... 787-264-0406. 551 A
rimedina@intersg.edu
MEDINA, Reinalda .... 718-997-4455. 319 C
reinalda.medina@qc.cuny.edu
MEDINA, Widylia .... 787-890-2681. 553 H
widylia.medina@upr.edu
MEDLEY, Brenda .... 504-520-7392. 209 D
bdmedley@xula.edu
MEDLEY, Dawn .... 828-298-3325. 370 E
dmedley@warren-wilson.edu
MEDLEY, Lara .... 303-273-3200... 80 E
lara.medley@is.mines.edu
MEDLEY, Linda, S .... 502-895-3411. 197 F
lsmedley@lpts.edu
MEDLEY, Mike .... 435-896-9714. 498 A
michael.medley@snow.edu
MEDLEY-WEEKS, Clarice 214-379-5565. 478 D
cweeks@pqc.edu
MEDLIN, Melissa, T .... 256-765-4276..... 9 C
mtmedlin@una.edu
MEDLOCK, Vicky .... 540-665-4936. 509 E
vmedlock@su.edu
MEDRANO, Jennifer .... 801-832-2126. 498 F
jmedrano@westminstercollege.edu
MEDRO, Alfred .... 619-265-0107... 59 K
amedro@platt.edu
MEDWICK, Peter .... 215-972-2017. 426 Y
pmedwick@pafa.edu
MEE, Christine, L .... 843-349-2091. 442 E
christin@coastal.edu
MEE, David .... 615-460-6785. 453 C
david.mee@belmont.edu
MEECE, Jeffrey, S .... 414-229-3634. 537 A
meece@uwm.edu
MEECE, Jill, N .... 606-679-8501. 196 D
jill.meece@kctcs.edu
MEEHAN, Gabriel, M ...... 916-484-8354... 53 A
meehang@arc.losrios.edu
MEEHAN, Linda, M .... 609-984-1105. 308 A
meehan@tesc.edu
MEEHAN, Martin, T .... 978-934-4744. 229 B
martin_meehan@uml.edu
MEEHAN, Mary, J .... 414-382-6064. 531 I
mary.meehan@alverno.edu
MEEHAN, Nicole .... 312-915-7266. 151 H
nleduc@luc.edu
MEEHAN, Patricia .... 856-227-7200. 300 B
pmeehan@camdencc.edu
MEEHAN, Paula, T .... 616-632-2852. 239 E
meehapau@aquinas.edu
MEEHAN, William, A ...... 256-782-5881..... 4 K
pres@jsu.edu

MEEK, James, A .... 864-379-8880. 443 F
meek@erskine.edu
MEEK, Laura .... 614-251-4642. 386 B
meekl@ohiodominican.edu
MEEK, Leslie .... 320-589-6200. 264 F
meekles@morris.umn.edu
MEEK, Michelle .... 606-886-3863. 194 K
michelle.meek@kctcs.edu
MEEK, Scott .... 602-787-7902... 15 B
scott.meek@paradisevalley.edu
MEEK, Tequecie .... 903-730-4890. 474 O
tequecie.meek@jarvis.edu
MEEKER, April, M .... 605-642-6092. 451 G
april.meeker@bhsu.edu
MEEKER, Steve, L .... 605-642-6385. 451 G
steve.meeker@bhsu.edu
MEEKMA, Glenn, A .... 269-471-3484. 239 D
meekma@andrews.edu
MEEKS, Andy .... 859-572-5575. 198 I
meeksa@nku.edu
MEEKS, Harry, L .... 812-888-4511. 174 F
hmeeks@vinu.edu
MEEKS, J. Duane .... 561-803-2610. 110 B
duane_meeks@pba.edu
MEEKS, Kimela, A .... 812-888-4377. 174 F
kmeeks@vinu.edu
MEEKS, Laura, M .... 740-264-5591. 379 F
lmeeks@egcc.edu
MEEKS, Mark .... 478-445-5851. 125 A
mark.meeks@gcsu.edu
MEEKS, Matthew .... 972-241-3371. 470 E
mmeeks@dallas.edu
MEEKS, Susan .... 478-387-4801. 125 E
MEEKS, Tom .... 216-373-5206. 385 G
tmeeks@ndc.edu
MEEKS, Tony .... 606-679-8501. 196 D
tony.meeks@kctcs.edu
MEENAN, Robert, F .... 617-638-4640. 224 D
rmeenan@bu.edu
MEER, Jonathan, D .... 609-896-5167. 305 D
jmeer@rider.edu
MEERTS, John .... 860-685-3800... 92 H
jmeerts@wesleyan.edu
MEESE, JoAnna .... 724-439-4900. 421 F
jmeese@laurel.edu
MEESE, Paul .... 303-678-3707... 81 N
paul.meese@frontrange.edu
MEESKE, Susan .... 402-461-7398. 289 I
smeeske@hastings.edu
MEGAHED, Nivine .... 312-261-3232. 153 I
nivine.megahed@nl.edu
MEGALE, Nicole .... 517-264-3850. 238 G
MEGORDEN,
Timothy, M .... 218-299-4161. 255 A
megorden@cord.edu
MEGREDY, Jill .... 785-227-3380. 184 I
megredyj@bethanylb.edu
MEHA, Arapata .... 808-675-3739. 135 C
mehaa@byuh.edu
MEHDIZADEH, Mojden .. 925-229-6849... 41 J
mmehdizadeh@4cd.edu
MEHL, Jason .... 706-886-6831. 133 A
jmehl@tfc.edu
MEHL, Shelley .... 501-450-3127... 25 H
shelleym@uca.edu
MEHLER, Mark .... 609-771-2186. 300 E
mehler@tcnj.edu
MEHLHOFF, Monte .... 605-626-7781. 451 I
mehlhofm@northern.edu
MEHLIG, Lisa .... 815-921-4070. 157 A
l.mehlig@rockvalleycollege.edu
MEHNERT-MELAND,
Karen, B .... 218-477-2447. 259 H
meland@mnstate.edu
MEHRINGER, Marty .... 317-805-1791. 527 G
mmehringer@salemu.edu
MEHTA, Apurva .... 617-287-5220. 228 G
apurva.mehta@umb.edu
MEHTA, Chander, S .... 713-313-1895. 485 F
mehta_cs@tsu.edu
MEI, Jeffrey .... 617-731-7170. 235 H
meijeffery@pmc.edu
MEIER, Beth, A .... 919-760-8427. 356 G
meierb@meredith.edu
MEIER, Harvey .... 402-486-2502. 292 E
hameier@ucollege.edu
MEIER, Jared .... 970-248-1698... 79 F
jmeier@coloradomesa.edu
MEIER, Jay .... 701-224-5666. 372 B
jay.meier@bismarckstate.edu
MEIER, Karen, F .... 757-683-5026. 507 N
kmeier@odu.edu
MEIER, Marina .... 208-524-3000. 138 D
marina.meier@my.eitc.edu
MEIER, Neal .... 513-487-1174. 390 C
neal.meier@myunion.edu
MEIER WELTZIEN, Lynn 406-683-7180. 286 I
l_weltzien1@umwestern.edu
MEIERGERD, Joseph ...... 314-792-6140. 275 L
meiergerd@kenrick.edu

MEIGHEN, Mark, A .... 724-946-7191. 437 B
meighema@westminster.edu
MEIKLEJOHN, Scott, A .. 207-725-3148. 209 H
smeiklej@bowdoin.edu
MEIKSINS, Peter .... 216-687-5559. 377 F
p.meiksins@csuohio.edu
MEILMAN, Philip, W ...... 202-687-6985... 95 E
pwm9@georgetown.edu
MEINE, Laurel .... 712-279-5433. 176 B
laurel.meine@briarcliff.edu
MEINEKE, John .... 309-796-5053. 140 E
meinekej@bhc.edu
MEINERTS, Marita, K ...... 651-631-5168. 263 A
mkmeinerts@nwc.edu
MEINHARDT, Stephanie . 972-881-5847. 469 G
smeinhardt@collin.edu
MEINHOLD, Patricia .... 843-383-8267. 442 F
pmeinhold@coker.edu
MEINTANIS, Maria .... 312-261-3092. 153 I
maria.meintanis@nl.edu
MEIR, Michael .... 212-594-4000. 347 H
mmeir@tcicollege.edu
MEIS, Aaron .... 513-745-2941. 393 H
meisa@xavier.edu
MEIS, Darrell .... 719-587-7912... 78 B
djmeis@adams.edu
MEIS, Gail, N .... 404-471-6306. 119 I
gmeis@agnesscott.edu
MEISCHEID, Michelle ..... 252-862-1252. 363 A
meischei@roanokechowan.edu
MEISEL, Joseph, S .... 401-863-9499. 438 J
joseph_meisel@brown.edu
MEISELES, Gary .... 502-597-6438. 197 A
gary.meiseles@kysu.edu
MEISENZAHL, Dan .... 808-956-5941. 135 L
dmeisenz@hawaii.edu
MEISER, Michelle .... 717-728-2312. 412 J
michellemeiser@centralpenn.edu
MEISER, Patricia .... 860-768-4989... 92 D
pmeiser@hartford.edu
MEISNER, Jane .... 515-244-4221. 175 C
meisnerj@aib.edu
MEISSNER, Ken .... 712-749-2111. 176 D
meissnerk@bvu.edu
MEISTER, Barbara .... 740-477-7858. 385 L
bmeister@ohiochristian.edu
MEISTER, Bobbi .... 712-274-5606. 181 B
meisterb@morningside.edu
MEISTER, Debra .... 312-915-7244. 151 H
dmeiste@luc.edu
MEISTER, Tony .... 660-944-2899. 272 H
tmeister@conception.edu
MEISTERLING,
Richard, E .... 319-399-8555. 176 G
rmeister@coe.edu
MEITZ, Mark, G .... 434-223-6242. 505 E
mmeitz@hsc.edu
MEITZNER, June .... 507-285-7213. 261 A
june.meitzner@rctc.edu
MEIXSEL-CORDERO,
Terri .... 623-245-4600... 18 D
tmeixsell@uti.edu
MEJEUR, Sharon, K .... 260-399-7700. 174 C
smejeur@sf.edu
MEJIA, Gary .... 559-453-7103... 45 D
gary.mejia@fresno.edu
MEJIA KRUG, Miroslava 312-341-3583. 157 D
mmkrug@roosevelt.edu
MEJIAS, Angel .... 787-858-3668. 547 G
amejias@vegabaja.caribbean.edu
MEJIAS, Ida, A .... 787-250-1912. 550 E
iamejias@metro.inter.edu
MEJIAS, Nelson .... 787-753-6335. 549 D
nmejias@icprjc.edu
MELADY, Thomas, P ...... 973-313-6174. 307 C
ambmelady@aol.com
MELANA, Johnny .... 225-216-8360. 202 H
melanaj@mybrcc.edu
MELANSON, Chris .... 207-948-9141. 211 I
cmelanson@unity.edu
MELANSON, Leigh Anne 603-862-3290. 298 C
leigh-anne.melanson@unh.edu
MELARAGNI, Robert .... 617-670-4401. 226 F
rmelaragni@fisher.edu
MELARAGNO, Steven ..... 401-254-3667. 440 B
smelaragno@rwu.edu
MELBY, Darlene .... 805-378-1550... 74 F
dmelby@vcccd.edu
MELBY, Laurie .... 714-241-6110... 39 I
lmelby@coastline.edu
MELCHER, Jan .... 912-588-2578. 120 B
jmelcher@altamahatech.edu
MELCHER, Mike .... 806-291-3425. 494 F
melcherp@wbu.edu
MELCHER, Rick, W .... 610-921-7748. 409 A
rmelcher@alb.edu
MELCHERT, Russell, B ... 816-235-1607. 283 D
melchertr@umkc.edu
MELCHIOR, Vonda .... 813-253-7107. 106 M
vmelchior@hccfl.edu

MELDREM, Joyce, A .... 563-588-7164. 180 L
joyce.meldrem@loras.edu
MELDRUM, John .... 313-883-8512. 249 E
meldrum.john@shms.edu
MELE, Donald .... 956-665-2711. 492 B
meledj@utpa.edu
MELECKI, Thomas, G ..... 512-475-6203. 491 C
tom.melecki@austin.utexas.edu
MELEG, Mike .... 309-796-5002. 140 E
melegm@bhc.edu
MELEIS, Afaf, I .... 215-898-8283. 435 B
meleis@nursing.upenn.edu
MELEN, Pia .... 714-533-1495... 66 H
pmelen@southbaylo.edu
MELENDEZ, Briseida ...... 787-265-3813. 554 E
registro@uprm.edu
MELENDEZ, Ciara .... 787-751-0160. 548 J
cmelendez@cmpr.pr.gov
MELENDEZ, David .... 661-654-2136... 32 H
dmelendez2@csub.edu
MELENDEZ, Georgianna . 617-287-4818. 228 G
georgianna.melendez@umb.edu
MELENDEZ, Jessica .... 610-841-3333. 427 F
jmelendez@psb.edu
MELENDEZ, John .... 201-200-3507. 303 F
jmelendez@njcu.edu
MELENDEZ, Leonardo .... 787-720-4476. 553 D
decanatoacademico@mizpa.edu
MELENDEZ, Marina .... 860-685-3927... 92 H
mmelendez@wesleyan.edu
MELENDEZ, Mercedes .... 212-343-1234. 331 D
mmelendez@mcny.edu
MELENDEZ, Nildalee ...... 787-852-1430. 549 C
nmelendez@hccpr.edu
MELENDEZ, Nitza .... 787-725-8120. 548 O
nmelendez@eap.edu
MELENDEZ, Rosa .... 787-754-7597. 549 J
rmelendez@inter.edu
MELENDEZ, Ruben .... 908-709-7085. 308 B
ruben.melendez@ucc.edu
MELENDEZ, Yahaira .... 787-620-2040. 547 C
melendezy@aupr.edu
MELENDRES, Andrew ..... 651-793-1521. 259 C
andrew.melendres@metrostate.edu
MELENDY, Lisa, M .... 413-597-2477. 238 D
lisa.m.melendy@williams.edu
MELETIES, Panayiotis .... 718-262-2780. 319 F
pmeleties@york.cuny.edu
MELHART, Bonnie .... 817-257-7729. 484 I
b.melhart@tcu.edu
MELIAN, Carlos .... 773-442-4470. 154 H
c-melian@neiu.edu
MELIKECHI, Noureddine . 302-857-6656... 93 C
nmelikechi@desu.edu
MELILLO, SR.,
Thomas, V .... 216-707-8200. 382 B
tmelillo@kent.edu
MELINA, Livio .... 202-526-3799... 96 D
MELINE, Doug .... 530-242-7990... 65 G
dmeline@shastacollege.edu
MELINE, Randy .... 641-784-5213. 178 F
meline@graceland.edu
MELISI, Mary Ann .... 610-558-5611. 424 I
melisim@neumann.edu
MELKONIAN, Madeleine 718-405-3236. 320 G
madeleine.melkonian@mountsaintvincent.edu
MELKY, Huda, N .... 270-745-5121. 200 G
huda.melky@wku.edu
MELL, Doug .... 715-232-1198. 538 B
melld@uwstout.edu
MELLAND, Helen .... 406-657-3784. 287 B
helen.melland@montana.edu
MELLEGAARD, Corey ...... 605-995-2648. 450 A
comelleg@dwu.edu
MELLEMA, Barbara, J ..... 712-722-6020. 177 J
barb.mellema@dordt.edu
MELLER, Brenda .... 248-689-8282. 251 I
bmeller@walshcollege.edu
MELLICHAMP, James, F 706-776-0100. 130 E
president@piedmont.edu
MELLING, Alice .... 206-934-3693. 522 I
alice.melling@seattlecolleges.edu
MELLINGER, Laurie, A ... 717-866-7581. 416 E
lemllinger@evangelical.edu
MELLO, James, A .... 860-768-5365... 92 D
jmello@hartford.edu
MELLO, Jeffrey, A .... 518-783-2321. 340 J
jmello@siena.edu
MELLON, Edward, J .... 703-323-3083. 513 C
emellon@nvcc.edu
MELLON, James, P .... 808-974-7313. 136 A
mellon@hawaii.edu
MELLON, Suzanne, K ..... 412-578-6123. 412 G
skmellon@carlow.edu
MELLONI, Suzanne .... 508-999-9299. 229 A
smelloni@umassd.edu
MELLOTT, David, M .... 717-290-8723. 421 D
rgawn@lancasterseminary.edu
MELLOTT, Ramona, N ..... 928-523-6534... 16 C
ramona.mellott@nau.edu

MELLOW, Gail, O .... 718-482-5050. 318 F gmellow@lagcc.cuny.edu
MELMED, Shlomo .... 310-423-8171... 37 H
MELNICK, Julie .... 402-844-7123. 291 I juliem@northeast.edu
MELNICK, Marie .... 215-637-7700. 418 G mmelnick@holyfamily.edu
MELNIK, JoAnn .... 724-964-8811. 425 A jmelnik@ncstrades.edu
MELNYK, Bernadette .... 614-292-4844. 386 E melnyk.15@osu.edu
MELO, Manuel .... 787-523-6000. 549 D mmelo@icprjc.edu
MELOAN, Andrea .... 816-415-7831. 285 C meloana@william.jewell.edu
MELOAN, Ross, B .... 270-809-3735. 198 B rmeloan@murraystate.edu
MELOCHE, Kyle .... 410-857-2275. 216 E kmeloche@mcdaniel.edu
MELOY, Joseph, P .... 414-277-7227. 534 G meloy@msoe.edu
MELOY, William .... 850-484-1476. 110 G wmeloy@pensacolastate.edu
MELSON, Rick .... 585-567-9340. 326 F rick.melson@houghton.edu
MELTON, Amye .... 317-845-0100. 171 D amelton@medtechcollege.edu
MELTON, Chris .... 206-546-4613. 523 F cmelton@shoreline.edu
MELTON, David, V .... 617-364-3510. 223 G dmelton@boston.edu
MELTON, Judi .... 206-264-9100. 516 J judim@bgu.edu
MELTON, Lori .... 252-985-5404. 365 D lmelton@ncwc.edu
MELTON, Marie, C .... 434-961-5209. 513 F mmelton@pvcc.edu
MELTON, Mark, A .... 919-516-4029. 366 C mamelton@st-aug.edu
MELTON, Matthew .... 423-614-8115. 455 L mmelton@leeuniversity.edu
MELTON, Melissa .... 251-380-2271..... 7 D mmelton@shc.edu
MELTON, Michelle .... 336-917-5721. 366 D michelle.melton@salem.edu
MELTON, Nancy .... 859-985-3313. 192 F meltonn@berea.edu
MELTON, Randall .... 269-927-8139. 245 D melton@lakemichigancollege.edu
MELTON, Rita, A .... 864-592-4836. 447 A meltonr@sccsc.edu
MELTON, Ron .... 912-583-3238. 122 B rmelton@bpc.edu
MELTON, Steve .... 828-297-3811. 358 E smelton@cccti.edu
MELTON PAGES, Joyce . 817-598-6245. 494 G jpages@wc.edu
MELUSKY, Marie, B .... 814-472-3126. 432 D mmelusky@francis.edu
MELVIN, Cruse .... 409-880-8395. 486 F cruse.melvin@lamar.edu
MELVIN, Cynthia .... 601-977-7716. 270 A cmelvin@tougaloo.edu
MELVIN, Dana .... 412-304-0738. 416 F damelvin@cci.edu
MELVIN, Lee, H .... 716-645-6003. 341 F
MELVIN, Marilee, A .... 630-752-5517. 163 F marilee.melvin@wheaton.edu
MELVIN, Matt .... 785-864-4381. 190 L mattmelvin@ku.edu
MELZ-JENNINGS, Lisa .... 309-298-1106. 162 K la-melz@wiu.edu
MEMBRINO, Charles .... 617-585-1239. 234 I itshelp@necmusic.edu
MEMOLI, Phil .... 239-513-1122. 106 O pmemoli@hodges.edu
MEN, Su-hua .... 941-752-5250. 114 I mens@scf.edu
MENA, Clara .... 203-285-2123... 88 E cmena@gwcc.commnet.edu
MENA, Robert .... 213-738-6716... 68 C studentaffairs@swlaw.edu
MENA, Salvador, B .... 718-982-2335. 317 E salvador.mena@csi.cuny.edu
MENA, Terry .... 561-297-3547. 114 L tmena@fau.edu
MENADIER, Judy .... 352-854-2322. 100 K menadiej@cf.edu
MENANTEAUX, Kathleen, A .... 309-649-6222. 160 E kathleen.menanteaux@src.edu
MENARD, Connie .... 940-898-3826. 488 B cmenard@twu.edu
MENARD, Michael .... 860-570-9208... 92 A michael.menard@uconn.edu
MENARD, Richard, O .... 509-313-3583. 520 A menardr@gonzaga.edu
MENARD, Richard, R .... 401-841-7004. 545 A richard.menard@usnwc.edu
MENASCHE, Kathleen, T . 410-386-8108. 214 A kmenasche@carrollcc.edu

MENCER, James .... 405-425-5260. 397 D book.store@oc.edu
MENCHACA, Leticia .... 520-206-4973... 17 A lmenchaca@pima.edu
MENCHACA, Ron .... 843-953-3395. 443 A menchacar@cofc.edu
MENDEDO, Tilahun, M .. 334-874-5700..... 3 A tmendedo@ccal.edu
MENDEL, Maurice, I .... 901-678-5877. 460 B mmendel@memphis.edu
MENDELL, Sean, M .... 513-751-1206. 374 A sean@aic.arts.edu
MENDELSOHN, Kathy .... 831-755-6700... 46 G kmendelsohn@hartnell.edu
MENDELSON, Eleonor .... 831-476-9424... 44 K admissions@fivebranches.edu
MENDENHALL, Beverly, A .... 817-202-6232. 481 E bevm@swau.edu
MENDENHALL, Diane .... 402-472-2841. 292 I dmendenhall@huskeralum.org
MENDENHALL, Leslie .... 816-995-2820. 280 G leslie.mendenhall@researchcollege.edu
MENDENHALL, Robert, W .... 801-274-3280. 498 E rwm@wgu.edu
MENDES, Godfrey .... 614-947-6027. 380 A godfrey.mendes@frankli.edu
MENDES, Wendy .... 559-734-9000... 63 D wendym@sjvc.edu
MENDEZ, Ana .... 312-935-4080. 156 K amendez@robertmorris.edu
MENDEZ, Ariel .... 787-766-1717. 552 J armendez@suagm.edu
MENDEZ, Celestino .... 605-626-2601. 451 I tino.mendez@northern.edu
MENDEZ, Celia .... 787-276-0130. 554 B celia.mendez@upr.edu
MENDEZ, José, F .... 787-766-1717. 552 J ac_jmendez@suagm.edu
MENDEZ, Jose, F .... 787-751-2262. 552 G ac_jmendez@suagm.edu
MENDEZ, JR., Jose, F ... 787-751-0178. 552 G jmendez@suagm.edu
MENDEZ, Larry .... 903-510-2281. 488 E lmen@tjc.edu
MENDEZ, Magaly .... 787-815-0000. 553 I magaly.mendez@upr.edu
MENDEZ, Maria .... 562-860-2451... 37 I mmendez@cerritos.edu
MENDEZ, Pedro .... 209-575-6498... 77 J mendezp@yosemite.cc.ca.us
MENDEZ, Rafael .... 787-257-0000. 554 B rafael.mendez@upr.edu
MENDEZ, Rolando, J .... 787-284-1912. 550 F rmendez@ponce.inter.edu
MENDEZ, Sheri .... 775-784-4176. 294 J smendez@unr.edu
MENDIAS, Lauren .... 432-837-8140. 487 B lmendias@sulross.edu
MENDICK, Kay .... 701-777-4300. 371 C kay.mendick@und.edu
MENDIETA, Juan .... 305-237-7611. 109 D jmendiet@mdc.edu
MENDIETTA, Dorianna .... 559-730-3821... 40 I doriannam@cos.edu
MENDINI, Shauna .... 435-865-8185. 497 A mendini_s@suu.edu
MENDIOLA, Emma .... 210-486-0373. 465 C emendiola@alamo.edu
MENDIOLA, Francisco .... 691-320-2480. 546 B mendiolaf@comfsm.fm
MENDIOLA, Mark, B .... 671-735-2957. 546 E funduog@gmail.com
MENDOLA, Richard, A ... 404-727-7879. 124 E rich.mendola@emory.edu
MENDONEZ RUSSELL, Bernadette .... 561-862-4400. 110 C russellb@palmbeachstate.edu
MENDOZA, Beth, A .... 920-929-2137. 540 F bmendoza@morainepark.edu
MENDOZA, Eric .... 559-791-2460... 49 P emendoza@portervillecollege.edu
MENDOZA, Graciano .... 831-479-6279... 30 G grmendoz@cabrillo.edu
MENDOZA, Pablo .... 724-357-2200. 428 F social-equity@iup.edu
MENDOZA, Robert .... 714-432-5045... 39 K rmendoza@occ.cccd.edu
MENDOZA, Sandra .... 219-980-6954. 168 B sleone@iun.edu
MENDOZA-WELCH, Maxine .... 903-886-5851. 483 E maxine.Mmendo@tamu.edu
MENEAR, Anne, P .... 660-263-3900. 272 A arm@cccb.edu
MENEFEE, Jeannine .... 303-678-3664... 81 N jeannine.menefee@frontrange.edu
MENEGHIN, Cindy, L .... 973-655-7917. 303 D meneghinc@mail.montclair.edu

MENENDEZ, Jacqueline, R .... 305-284-5505. 118 F jmenendez@miami.edu
MENENDEZ, Marco .... 510-464-3221... 59 C mmenendez@peralta.edu
MENESES, Jilma .... 503-725-4432. 406 B jmeneses@pdx.edu
MENG, William .... 718-940-5884. 339 B wmeng@sjcny.edu
MENG, Xiao-Li .... 617-496-1464. 227 C xlmeng@fas.harvard.edu
MENGHINI, Becci .... 608-262-8967. 536 D menghini@chancellor.wisc.edu
MENGHINI, Charles, T ... 312-225-6288. 162 H cmenghini@vandercook.edu
MENGINE, Tina .... 814-732-1732. 428 E tmengine@edinboro.edu
MENGLER, Thomas, M .... 210-436-3722. 479 D tmengler@stmarytx.edu
MENITOFF, Michael .... 310-824-1586... 26 B
MENJARES, Pete .... 562-777-4048... 29 L pete.menjares@biola.edu
MENJARES, Pete, C .... 559-453-2010... 45 D fpupres@fresno.edu
MENJIVAR, Claudia .... 718-357-0500. 339 G cmenjivar@edaff.com
MENJIVAR, Claudia, I .... 650-574-6146... 64 C menjivarc@smccd.edu
MENK, David, A .... 507-933-6539. 255 I dmenk@gustavus.edu
MENKE, Brandi .... 314-768-7851. 278 C bmenke@missouricollege.com
MENKE, Scott .... 262-595-2155. 537 C scott.menke@uwp.edu
MENKING, Cornell .... 575-646-3199. 310 I cmenking@nmsu.edu
MENLOVE, Ronda, R .... 435-797-3728. 497 B ronda.menlove@usu.edu
MENN, Esther .... 773-256-0762. 152 B emenn@lstc.edu
MENNE, Renee, A .... 563-588-7130. 180 L renee.menne@loras.edu
MENNECHEY, Pamela .... 407-708-2380. 113 E mennechey@seminolestate.edu
MENNEKE, Beth, R .... 314-505-7761. 272 J mennekeb@csl.edu
MENNICKE, Sue .... 717-291-3911. 416 J susan.mennicke@fandm.edu
MENNINGER, Gaynia .... 785-242-5200. 189 I gaynia.menninger@ottawa.edu
MENNINGER, Jay, E .... 802-656-3290. 500 F jay.menninger@uvm.edu
MENNS, Melvin .... 202-722-8111... 96 F melvin.menns@strayer.edu
MENOGAN, Kelle .... 601-977-7828. 270 A kmenogan@tougaloo.edu
MENON, Ajay .... 970-491-2398... 80 I ajay.menon@colostate.edu
MENSAH, Michael, O .... 570-941-4049. 436 A michael.mensah@scranton.edu
MENSAH, Vincent .... 304-424-8223. 530 E vincent.mensah@wvup.edu
MENSAH-DARTEY, Virgil 678-422-4100... 96 F
MENSCHING, Ron .... 630-889-6606. 154 E rmensching@nuhs.edu
MENSHOUSE, Nancy .... 606-326-2199. 194 J nancy.menshouse@kctcs.edu
MENTE, Patrick, J .... 607-436-2596. 343 E mentepj@oneonta.edu
MENTZER, Cathy .... 717-264-4141. 437 H cmentzer@wilson.edu
MENZ, Harald .... 304-829-7915. 526 D hmenz@bethanywv.edu
MENZ, Leslie, E .... 309-655-2180. 158 C leslie.menz@osfhealthcare.org
MENZEL, Carol, A .... 410-334-2946. 221 D cmenzel@worwic.edu
MENZER, Paul .... 540-887-7058. 507 A pmenzer@mbc.edu
MEONSKE, Kali .... 330-325-6492. 385 E kmeonske@neomed.edu
MERCADANTE, Richard .. 727-791-2527. 112 E Mercadante.Richard@spcollege.edu
MERCADO, Caroline .... 570-372-4753. 433 H mercado@susqu.edu
MERCADO, Carolyn .... 787-894-2828. 555 C carolyn.mercado@upr.edu
MERCADO, Elizabeth .... 856-351-2910. 307 B emercado@salemcc.edu
MERCADO, Frank .... 201-360-4043. 302 D fmercado@hccc.edu
MERCADO, Harry .... 787-740-3555. 553 C harry.mercado@uccaribe.edu
MERCADO, Juan Carlos . 212-925-6625. 317 D jmercado@ccny.cuny.edu
MERCADO, Lemuel .... 770-228-7383. 132 B lmercado@sctech.edu
MERCADO, Leo, A .... 843-953-3020. 442 A leo.mercado@citadel.edu
MERCADO, Maritza E, M 212-247-3434. 329 L mmercado@mandl.edu

MERCED, Randolph .... 215-717-6827. 435 A rmerced@uarts.edu
MERCER, Bobby .... 740-377-2520. 389 K mercer.tsbc@gmail.com
MERCER, Brenda, D .... 919-735-5151. 364 H bdmercer@waynecc.edu
MERCER, David, M .... 585-567-9322. 326 F david.mercer@houghton.edu
MERCER, Debbie, K .... 785-532-5525. 188 A dmercer@ksu.edu
MERCER, Ellen .... 920-923-8112. 534 A emercer@marianuniversity.edu
MERCER, Frank .... 386-506-4461. 101 G mercerf@DaytonaState.edu
MERCER, John .... 760-384-6353... 49 O john.mercer@cerrocoso.edu
MERCER, John .... 513-745-4890. 393 H mercerjl@xavier.edu
MERCER, JR., John .... 704-463-3352. 365 E john.mercer@fsmail.pfeiffer.edu
MERCER, John, D .... 850-872-3807. 106 H jmercer@gulfcoast.edu
MERCER, Judith, R .... 757-446-5841. 504 E mercerjr@evms.edu
MERCER, Karen .... 319-895-4342. 177 A kmercer@cornellcollege.edu
MERCER, Laura .... 937-512-4571. 388 O laura.mercer@sinclair.edu
MERCER, Leneil .... 313-487-7420. 202 F leneil.mercer@lacollege.edu
MERCER, Leslie, K .... 651-201-1862. 257 N leslie.mercer@so.mnscu.edu
MERCER, Molly .... 724-738-2179. 429 F molly.mercer@sru.edu
MERCER, Paul .... 207-326-2337. 211 D paul.mercer@mma.edu
MERCER, Peter, P .... 201-684-7607. 305 A pmercer@ramapo.edu
MERCHANT, Betty .... 210-458-4370. 492 C betty.merchant@utsa.edu
MERCHANT, Debra, S .... 513-556-4119. 390 G debra.merchant@uc.edu
MERCHANT, Janie .... 575-646-6014. 310 I jpence@nmsu.edu
MERCHANT, Joshua .... 517-629-0242. 239 A jmerchant@albion.edu
MERCHANT, Joshua, D .. 517-629-0321. 239 A jdmerchant@albion.edu
MERCHANT, Susan, C .... 315-267-2162. 344 C merchasc@potsdam.edu
MERCHANT, Walter .... 757-499-5447. 505 A
MERCHLEWITZ, Ann, E .. 507-457-1587. 264 A amerchle@smumn.edu
MERCIER, Casey .... 601-477-4223. 267 F casey.mercier@jcjc.edu
MERCIER, Collette .... 801-627-8304. 496 D mercierc@owatc.edu
MERCIER, William, C .... 812-237-7829. 167 A william.mercier@indstate.edu
MERCINCAVAGE, Janet, E .... 570-208-5878. 419 P jemercin@kings.edu
MERCK, II, William, F .... 407-823-2351. 115 E william.merck@ucf.edu
MERCOGLIANO, Amy .... 609-771-2495. 300 E mercogli@tcnj.edu
MERCOMES, Brenda, W . 617-541-5383. 232 G bmercomes@rcc.mass.edu
MERCURIO, Gloria .... 201-761-6125. 306 L gmercurio@saintpeters.edu
MERCURIO, Sherry .... 614-947-6581. 380 A sherry.mercurio@franklin.edu
MEREDITH, Brian .... 270-745-6169. 200 G brian.meredith@wku.edu
MEREDITH, Cynthia, L ... 731-661-5202. 462 F cmeredit@uu.edu
MEREDITH, Daniel .... 864-941-8442. 446 C meredith.d@ptc.edu
MEREDITH, Dave .... 504-280-7013. 205 G
MEREDITH, Gloria .... 847-578-3270. 157 F gloria.meredith@rosalindfranklin.edu
MEREDITH, Janette, T .... 603-899-4077. 296 H Meridethj@franklinpierce.edu
MEREDITH, Joyce .... 740-587-6515. 379 D meredithj@denison.edu
MEREDITH, Kelly .... 405-208-5088. 397 F kmeredith@okcu.edu
MEREDITH, Marc .... 310-665-6815... 57 C marcm@otis.edu
MEREDITH, Patricia .... 813-463-7163... 28 M pmeredith@argosy.edu
MERESSI, Tesfay .... 508-999-8542. 229 A tmeressi@umassd.edu
MERFALEN, Barbara, K ... 670-234-5498. 547 A barbaram@nmcnet.edu
MERFELD, Laura, L .... 641-422-4355. 181 D merfelau@niacc.edu
MERGEN, Amy .... 419-824-3677. 383 C amergen@lourdes.edu
MERGENER, Jodi .... 608-249-6611. 533 I jmergener@herzing.edu

MERGENTHAL, James .... 215-895-0476. 415 B
jem38@drexel.edu
MERGET, Kathleen .... 845-451-1776. 322 D
k_merget@culinary.edu
MERGIOTTI, James, J .... 215-670-9494. 425 J
president@peirce.edu
MERGL, Francine, R .... 716-888-8211. 316 C
merglf@canisius.edu
MERGLER, Nancy, L .... 405-325-3221. 401 B
nmergler@ou.edu
MERICA, Michael .... 928-226-4212... 13 B
Michael.Merica@coconino.edu
MERICKEL, Mark .... 707-664-2394... 36 B
mark.merickel@sonoma.edu
MERICLE, Margaret, E .... 559-442-8210... 68 I
margaret.mericle@fresnocitycollege.edu
MERIDITH, Pamela .... 870-759-4139... 25 K
pmeridith@wbcoll.edu
MERIGOLD, Mary .... 716-896-0700. 350 A
merigoldm@villa.edu
MERILAT, Meliinda .... 832-252-0745. 468 L
melinda.merilat@cbshouston.edu
MERILLAT, Jason, C .... 610-566-1776. 437 G
jmerillat@williamson.edu
MERIMEE, Nancy, S .... 913-971-3427. 188 H
nsmerimee@mnu.edu
MERINAR, Whitney, A .... 570-321-4144. 422 H
merinar@lycoming.edu
MERINGOLO,
Salvatore, M .... 540-654-1372. 510 J
tmeringo@umw.edu
MERITT, Necole .... 404-752-1761. 129 E
nmerritt@msm.edu
MERIWETHER, Jan .... 434-947-8127. 508 D
jmeriwether@randolphcollege.edu
MERIWETHER, Jason ..... 615-329-8854. 454 F
jmeriwether@fisk.edu
MERIWETHER, Jason, L . 812-941-2420. 168 F
Jlmeriwe@ius.edu
MERJIL, Mark .... 909-384-8990... 62 A
mmerjil@sbccd.cc.ca.us
MERKEL, Cynthia, F .... 906-635-2674. 245 G
cmerkel@lssu.edu
MERKEL, Diane .... 518-564-2195. 344 B
dmerk001@plattsburgh.edu
MERKEL, Luz, I .... 509-777-4225. 525 F
lmerkel@whitworth.edu
MERKEL-VEER, Chelly .... 701-766-1302. 370 H
chelly.merkel@littlehoop.edu
MERKIN, Yitzchok .... 301-962-5111. 221 E
ymerkin@yeshiva.edu
MERKLE, Ben .... 208-882-1566. 138 H
bmerkle@nsa.edu
MERKLE, H. Bart .... 616-331-3585. 243 C
merkleb@gvsu.edu
MERKLE, Jean .... 563-425-5765. 183 B
merklej@uiu.edu
MERKLE, Joseph, F .... 717-815-1460. 438 D
jmerkle@ycp.edu
MERKLE, Karen, L .... 410-386-8107. 214 A
kmerkle@carrollcc.edu
MERKLE, Patricia .... 315-568-3277. 333 C
pmerkle@nycc.edu
MERKLEY, Brett .... 801-524-8132. 495 O
bmerkley@idsbc.edu
MERKLIN, Lynn .... 269-471-6066. 239 D
merklin@andrews.edu
MERKT, Mary Lou .... 864-294-2140. 444 C
marylou.merkt@furman.edu
MERKX, Gilbert .... 919-684-5830. 354 A
gilbert.merkx@duke.edu
MERL, Jill .... 808-544-9364. 135 F
jmerl@hpu.edu
MERLE, Dan .... 704-290-5219. 363 G
dmerle@spcc.edu
MERLINO, Keith .... 412-809-5100. 430 H
merlino.keith@pti.edu
MERLO, Barbara .... 254-526-1223. 468 G
barbara.merlo@ctcd.edu
MERMANN-JOZWIAK,
Elisabeth .... 509-313-5522. 520 A
mermann-jozwiak@gonzaga.edu
MERMELSTEIN, Joanne .. 978-837-5117. 234 A
mermelsteinj@merrimack.edu
MERRELL, Donna .... 660-248-6214. 272 B
dmerrell@centralmethodist.edu
MERRELL, Frances .... 501-882-8824... 19 M
flmerrell@asub.edu
MERRELL, Melinda, M ... 425-235-5846. 522 F
mmerrell@rtc.edu
MERRELL, Sue .... 937-512-2917. 388 O
sue.merrell@sinclair.edu
MERRICK, Bernard, D ..... 412-365-1231. 412 K
merrick@chatham.edu
MERRICK, Jocelyn .... 413-662-5193. 230 C
j.merrick@mcla.edu
MERRICK, Robyn .... 225-771-5361. 206 J
robyn_merrick@sus.edu
MERRICK, Robyn .... 225-771-4200. 206 I
robyn_merrick@sus.edu

MERRICK, Sara .... 601-984-2300. 270 C
smerrick@umc.edu
MERRICK, Vallyn .... 410-951-6300. 220 B
vmerrick@coppin.edu
MERRIFIELD, Mary .... 314-529-9510. 276 G
mmerrifield@maryville.edu
MERRIGAN, John .... 660-543-4233. 283 A
merrigan@ucmo.edu
MERRIGAN, Kathleen ...... 912-443-5500. 131 D
kmerrigan@savannahtech.edu
MERRIHEW, Mark, W ..... 620-417-1202. 190 F
mark.merrihew@sccc.edu
MERRILL, Brendy .... 417-864-7220. 274 D
bmerrill@cci.edu
MERRILL, Chad .... 828-694-1704. 358 C
chadm@blueridge.edu
MERRILL, Dale .... 714-997-6849... 38 A
merrill@chapman.edu
MERRILL, H. Donald ...... 704-233-8284. 370 G
dmerrill@wingate.edu
MERRILL, Joanne .... 603-897-8257. 297 F
jmerrill@rivier.edu
MERRILL, Kristin .... 513-244-8151. 376 J
kristin.merrill@ccuniversity.edu
MERRILL, Martha, C .... 860-439-2200... 89 H
mcmer@conncoll.edu
MERRILL, Melvin .... 229-391-4894. 119 H
mmerrill@abac.edu
MERRILL, Michael .... 212-647-7801. 346 A
michael.merrill@esc.edu
MERRILL, Paul .... 256-331-5223...... 6 A
merrill@nwscc.edu
MERRILL, Scott, M .... 508-793-2438. 225 B
smerrill@holycross.edu
MERRILL, Timothy, W .... 804-752-7212. 508 E
timothymerrill@rmc.edu
MERRILL-DOSS, Jean ..... 573-518-2262. 278 A
jeanmer@mineralarea.edu
MERRIMAN, Gary .... 909-599-5433... 50 J
gmerriman@lifepacific.edu
MERRIMAN, Karen .... 704-330-6796. 359 C
karen.merriman@cpcc.edu
MERRIMAN, William, J .. 718-862-7374. 329 M
william.merriman@manhattan.edu
MERRIMAN, JR.,
William, R .... 620-229-6223. 190 G
dick.merriman@sckans.edu
MERRIS, Justin .... 309-636-8608. 156 K
jmerris@robertmorris.edu
MERRITT, Bert .... 850-484-1140. 110 G
bmerritt@pensacolastate.edu
MERRITT, Christine, C .... 315-859-4111. 325 E
cmerritt@hamilton.edu
MERRITT, Ed .... 909-869-2269... 32 G
eamerritt@csupomona.edu
MERRITT, Jaci, M .... 903-434-8103. 477 J
jmerritt@ntcc.edu
MERRITT, James, A .... 608-246-6330. 540 C
jamerritt1@madisoncollege.edu
MERRITT, Judy, M .... 205-853-1200..... 5 B
jmerritt@jeffstateonline.com
MERRITT, Maribea .... 432-552-2809. 493 D
merritt_m@utpb.edu
MERRITT, Scott .... 318-869-5708. 201 H
smerritt@centenary.edu
MERRITT, Stephen, R ..... 610-519-7499. 436 F
stephen.merritt@villanova.edu
MERRITT, Susan .... 804-290-4231. 510 B
smerritt@stratford.edu
MERRITT, Susan, M .... 212-346-1810. 335 J
smerritt@pace.edu
MERRYMAN, Ed .... 408-554-5076... 64 M
emerryman@scu.edu
MERRYMAN, Jon .... 870-245-5506... 22 D
merrymanj@obu.edu
MERRYMAN, Marjorie .... 212-749-2002. 330 A
mmerryman@msmnyc.edu
MERRYMAN, Susan .... 614-236-6831. 375 H
MERSETH, Juel, O .... 507-344-7854. 253 J
juel.merseth@blc.edu
MERSMANN, Tina .... 513-244-4232. 377 G
tina_mersmann@mail.msj.edu
MERSON, Michael, H ..... 919-681-7760. 354 A
michael.merson@duke.edu
MERTEN, Elizabeth .... 712-749-2062. 176 D
mertenl@bvu.edu
MERTES, Scott .... 989-773-6622. 247 B
smertes@midmich.edu
MERTH, Paula, B .... 651-290-6376. 265 F
paula.merth@wmitchell.edu
MERTLER, Craig .... 561-237-7441. 108 X
cmertler@lynn.edu
MERTZ, Jennifer, L .... 610-758-3181. 422 A
jlm207@lehigh.edu
MERVAR, Megan .... 860-701-6540. 545 G
Megan.K.Sullivan@uscga.edu
MERVINE, Ed .... 310-577-3000... 77 G
financialaid@yosan.edu
MERVYN, Frances .... 617-327-6777. 233 D
frances_mervyn@mspp.edu

MERY, Pam .... 415-239-3227... 38 L
pmery@ccsf.edu
MERYHEW, Barb .... 307-268-2249. 542 X
bmeryhew@caspercollege.edu
MERZ, Nancy .... 816-235-1154. 283 D
merzn@umkc.edu
MERZ, Sarah .... 563-588-6307. 176 F
sarah.merz@clarke.edu
MERZ, Soon, O .... 512-223-7035. 466 I
smerz@austincc.edu
MESA, Tina .... 210-486-3901. 465 A
tmesa@alamo.edu
MESAROS, Cyndi .... 805-922-6966... 26 K
cmesaros@hancockcollege.edu
MESCH, Barry .... 617-559-8613. 227 D
bmesch@hebrewcollege.edu
MESCHIEVITZ, Catherine 561-297-3282. 114 L
cmeschie@fau.edu
MESCON, Timothy, S ..... 706-507-8950. 123 D
mescon_timothy@columbusstate.edu
MESECAR, Christopher ... 919-317-3052. 131 H
cjmesecar@southuniversity.edu
MESEROLE, Brooke .... 910-362-7062. 358 F
bmeserole@cfcc.edu
MESERVE, Mary .... 207-786-6097. 209 F
mmeserve@bates.edu
MESERVEY, Patricia, M .. 978-542-6134. 230 E
pmeservey@salemstate.edu
MESHKATY, Shahra .... 619-260-2298... 73 I
meshkaty@sandiego.edu
MESICS, Linda, L .... 610-799-1585. 421 I
lmesics@lccc.edu
MESINA, Irene .... 808-845-9195. 136 G
imesina@hawaii.edu
MESLER, Cecelia .... 616-632-2868. 239 E
meslecec@aquinas.edu
MESONAS, Lenny .... 908-526-1200. 305 B
lmesonas@raritanval.edu
MESQUITA, Cezar .... 208-885-6163. 139 D
cezarm@uidaho.edu
MESQUITA, Joseph .... 860-512-3215... 88 G
jmesquita@manchestercc.edu
MESSA, Emily .... 832-842-8184. 489 B
eamessa@uh.edu
MESSA, Emily .... 832-842-8184. 489 A
eamessa@uh.edu
MESSAC, Achille .... 662-325-2270. 268 D
MESSAROS, Jean .... 570-674-6320. 424 A
srjean@misericordia.edu
MESSER, Brian .... 913-344-6020. 184 C
brian.messer@bakeru.edu
MESSER, Emily .... 706-233-7342. 131 E
emesser@shorter.edu
MESSER, J, B .... 405-682-7812. 397 E
jmesser@occc.edu
MESSER, Kirk, D .... 414-410-4425. 532 B
kdmesser@stritch.edu
MESSER, Stanley, B .... 848-445-2000. 306 B
smesser@rci.rutgers.edu
MESSER, Thomas, C .... 904-596-2411. 117 H
tmesser@tbc.org
MESSER-ROY, Stephanie 228-897-3886. 268 C
stephanie.roy@mgccc.edu
MESSERE, Fritz .... 315-312-2285. 344 A
fritz.messere@oswego.edu
MESSERVY, Steven .... 256-824-6343..... 8 F
steven.messervy@uah.edu
MESSICK, Fred .... 626-584-5367... 45 E
fmessick@fuller.edu
MESSICK, Gary, A .... 260-422-5561. 167 B
gamessick@indianatech.edu
MESSIER, David, H .... 508-831-5216. 238 F
dmessier@wpi.edu
MESSIER, Jake .... 617-912-9108. 224 B
jmessier@bostonconservatory.edu
MESSINA, Cliff .... 757-340-2121. 503 I
adirectorcvab@centura.edu
MESSINA, John, A .... 330-972-7800. 390 E
jam125@uakron.edu
MESSINA, Kimberlee ...... 650-949-7209... 44 N
messinakimberlee@foothill.edu
MESSINA, Marianne .... 812-877-8840. 172 C
messina@rose-hulman.edu
MESSINA, Susan, G .... 704-463-3040. 365 E
susan.messina@fsmail.pfeiffer.edu
MESSINA, Tom .... 407-823-2849. 115 E
thomas.messina@ucf.edu
MESSINA-DYSERT, Gina . 440-646-8120. 392 D
gina.messina-dysert@ursuline.edu
MESSING, Robert, O .... 512-471-1735. 491 C
romessing@austin.utexas.edu
MESSINGER, Jacquelyn .. 903-510-2305. 488 E
jmes@tjc.edu
MESSITT, Todd .... 845-938-2715. 545 I
Todd.Messitt@usma.edu
MESSITTE, Zachariah, P .. 920-748-8118. 535 J
messittez@ripon.edu
MESSNER, Leonard, V .... 312-949-7108. 146 G
lmessner@ico.edu
MESSNER, Robert, H ...... 717-780-2333. 417 I
rhmessne@hacc.edu

MESSNER, Stephanie ...... 312-949-7013. 146 G
smessner@ico.edu
MESSNER, Thomas .... 305-899-4062... 98 O
tmessner@barry.edu
MESSNER, William, F ..... 413-552-2700. 231 F
wmessner@hcc.edu
MESTAN, Michael, A ...... 315-568-3226. 333 C
mmestan@nycc.edu
MESTAS, Richard .... 202-231-8650. 544 L
richard.mestas@dodiis.mil
MESTETH, Leslie .... 605-455-6033. 450 I
lmesteth@olc.edu
MESTLER, Nathan .... 480-245-7979... 14 B
nathan.mestler@ibcs.edu
METAL, Autre .... 804-330-0111. 503 G
a.metal@centura.edu
METCALF, Christine .... 603-271-6484. 296 C
cmetcalf@ccsnh.edu
METCALF, Eleanor, S ...... 301-295-1104. 545 C
eleanor.metcalf@usuhs.edu
METCALF, Jeff, K .... 606-474-3258. 194 H
jmetcalf@kcu.edu
METCALF, Jon .... 859-985-3828. 192 F
jon_metcalf@berea.edu
METCALF, Kelly .... 828-395-1432. 361 C
kmetcalf@isothermal.edu
METCALF, Robert .... 907-443-8402... 10 I
rgmetcalf@alaska.edu
METCALF, Shirley .... 541-383-7700. 402 D
smetcalf@cocc.edu
METCALFE, Dorothy .... 714-546-0930... 44 D
dmetcalfe@fidm.edu
METE, T.J .... 772-466-4822... 98 L
METESH, John, J .... 406-496-4159. 287 F
jmetesh@mtech.edu
METHVIN, Jennifer .... 870-777-5722... 25 B
jennifer.methvin@uacch.edu
METIANU, Mihaela .... 561-297-3049. 114 L
mmetianu@fau.edu
METILLY, Paul .... 617-254-2610. 236 B
METIVIER SCOTT, Shelly 508-910-6402. 229 A
sscott1@umassd.edu
METKE, L. Michael .... 903-510-2380. 488 E
mmet@tjc.edu
METRESS, Heather .... 706-721-5052. 126 B
hmetress@gru.edu
METRO, Joseph .... 717-361-1408. 415 H
metroj@etown.edu
METS, Lisa, A .... 727-864-8221. 101 N
metsla@eckerd.edu
METTAUER, Janice, L ..... 608-246-6174. 540 C
jmettauer@madisoncollege.edu
METTILLE, Teege .... 715-682-1224. 535 D
tmettille@northland.edu
METTLEN, Susan .... 908-709-7538. 308 B
susan.mettlen@ucc.edu
METTS, Amanda .... 252-399-6315. 352 F
ahmetts@barton.edu
METTS, Deanna .... 931-372-3045. 460 A
dmetts@tntech.edu
METZ, Catherine, A .... 765-361-6418. 175 B
metzc@wabash.edu
METZ, David .... 614-287-2617. 378 B
dmetz@cscc.edu
METZ, George .... 843-863-7765. 441 H
gmet@csuniv.edu
METZ, Gregory .... 513-745-5720. 391 A
gregory.metz@uc.edu
METZ, Linda, D .... 740-588-1386. 394 C
lmetz@zanestate.edu
METZ, Lorraine .... 716-829-7502. 323 D
metzla@dyc.edu
METZ, Perry .... 812-855-8000. 167 F
metz@indiana.edu
METZ, Ray .... 313-593-5253. 251 D
remetz@umich.edu
METZ, Robert, C .... 517-264-7117. 250 B
rmetz@sienaheights.edu
METZ, Starla .... 727-341-4368. 112 E
metz.starla@spcollege.edu
METZ, Susan .... 201-216-5245. 307 E
smetz@stevens.edu
METZ, Timothy, D .... 910-893-1907. 352 K
metz@campbell.edu
METZELAARS, Gretchen . 614-688-8011. 386 E
metzelaars.1@osu.edu
METZGAR, Albert, C .... 757-594-7294. 503 M
metzgar@cnu.edu
METZGAR, Johanna .... 415-254-6033... 70 I
jmetzgar@berkeley.edu
METZGER, David, D .... 757-683-3260. 507 N
dmetzger@odu.edu
METZGER, David, D .... 757-683-4865. 507 N
dmetzger@odu.edu
METZGER, Elizabeth .... 505-277-3389. 312 F
emetzger@unm.edu
METZGER, Jeanie .... 574-520-4383. 168 E
jmetzger@iusb.edu
METZGER, Kris .... 414-443-8925. 539 F
kris.metzger@wlc.edu

METZGER, Nan ... 414-258-4810. 535 A
metzgern@mtmary.edu
METZGER, Nate ... 309-248-8418. 146 B
nate.metzger@heartland.edu
METZGER, Peggy ... 707-826-4321... 35 C
mam7001@humboldt.edu
METZGER, Richard, A ... 814-332-2755. 409 D
rich.metzger@allegheny.edu
METZGER, Thomas ... 702-968-2013. 295 E
tmetzger@roseman.edu
METZGER HARE, Erica .. 802-828-8545. 500 G
erica.hare@vcfa.edu
METZINGER, Michelle ... 605-229-8379. 450 J
michelle.metzinger@presentation.edu
METZINGER, Ryland ... 408-924-1800... 36 A
ryland.metzinger@sjsu.edu
METZLER, Christopher ... 717-391-1349. 434 A
metzler@stevenscollege.edu
METZLER, Christopher ... 717-299-7794. 434 A
metzler@stevenscollege.edu
METZLER, Madeleine, A . 401-865-2499. 439 E
mmetzler@providence.edu
METZNER, Sue ... 802-447-6358. 500 D
smetzner@svc.edu
MEUKAM, Kirstan ... 708-534-5000. 145 F
kneukam@govst.edu
MEULEMANS, Nicole ... 651-423-8462. 258 D
nicole.meulemans@dctc.edu
MEUNIER, LaVonda ... 305-809-3248. 104 I
lavonda.meunier@fkcc.edu
MEUNINGHOFF, OP,
Mary Ann ... 708-524-6521. 144 C
mmeuninghoff@dom.edu
MEUSCHKE, Daylene ... 661-362-5329... 40 E
daylene.meuschke@canyons.edu
MEUSER, John ... 713-525-3813. 490 L
meuserj@stthom.edu
MEUWISSEN, Daniel, J .. 651-962-5100. 265 C
djmeuwissen@stthomas.edu
MEVS, Osei ... 615-327-6251. 456 E
omevs@mmc.edu
MEW, Ashley ... 423-614-8390. 455 L
amew@leeuniversity.edu
MEY, Craig, A ... 715-836-3263. 536 E
meyca@uwec.edu
MEYDAM, Mark, R ... 715-425-3500. 537 E
mark.r.meydam@uwrf.edu
MEYER, Aaron, J ... 914-337-9300. 321 E
aaron.meyer@concordia-ny.edu
MEYER, Adam ... 212-799-5000. 328 B
MEYER, Alan, E ... 708-209-3468. 143 E
alan.meyer@cuchicago.edu
MEYER, Andy ... 706-272-4420. 123 G
ameyer@daltonstate.edu
MEYER, Angela ... 573-651-2292. 282 B
admeyer@semo.edu
MEYER, Ann ... 312-329-4417. 153 E
ameyer@moody.edu
MEYER, Bale ... 303-427-5292... 84 F
MEYER, Bruce ... 805-756-2511... 32 F
brmeyer@calpoly.edu
MEYER, Bruce ... 419-372-6821. 374 K
bameyer@bgsu.edu
MEYER, Bruce, A ... 214-648-9794. 493 E
bruce.meyer@utsouthwestern.edu
MEYER, Carrie ... 260-744-8747. 173 C
crmeyer@taylor.edu
MEYER, Chris ... 405-733-7913. 399 F
cmeyer@rose.edu
MEYER, Chuck ... 415-405-3835... 35 E
cmeyer@sfsu.edu
MEYER, Cindy ... 660-263-3900. 272 A
cmeyer@cccb.edu
MEYER, Colleen, D ... 970-491-6533... 80 I
colleen.meyer@colostate.edu
MEYER, Courtney ... 414-258-4810. 535 A
meyerc@mtmary.edu
MEYER, Dale, A ... 314-505-7010. 272 J
meyerd@csl.edu
MEYER, Daniel, L ... 765-658-4108. 165 F
danmeyer@depauw.edu
MEYER, Daniel, R ... 920-832-6607. 533 S
daniel.r.meyer@lawrence.edu
MEYER, Danielle ... 330-941-3582. 394 A
dlmeyer@ysu.edu
MEYER, David ... 701-671-2212. 372 E
david.m.meyer@ndscs.edu
MEYER, David, A ... 860-685-2345... 92 H
dmeyer@wesleyan.edu
MEYER, David, D ... 504-865-5930. 207 C
meyer@tulane.edu
MEYER, Donald, C ... 757-446-5615. 504 E
meyerdc@evms.edu
MEYER, Donald, G ... 610-917-1402. 436 C
president@vfcc.edu
MEYER, Donald, J ... 319-352-8517. 183 E
donald.meyer@wartburg.edu
MEYER, Doug ... 503-493-6471. 402 J
dmeyer@cu-portland.edu
MEYER, Edward ... 718-405-3320. 320 G
edward.meyer@mountsaintvincent.edu
MEYER, Elise ... 805-893-5050... 72 B
elise.meyer@ucsb.edu
MEYER, Ellen ... 615-383-4848. 464 D
emeyer@watkins.edu
MEYER, Evie ... 610-917-1417. 436 C
eemeyer@vfcc.edu
MEYER, Francis, P ... 603-271-6484. 296 C
fmeyer@ccsnh.edu
MEYER, Gary ... 414-288-6350. 534 B
gary.meyer@marquette.edu
MEYER, Greg ... 616-632-2802. 239 E
greg.meyer@aquinas.edu
MEYER, Greg ... 208-792-2200. 138 G
gameyer@lcsc.edu
MEYER, Gregg, A ... 508-531-1237. 229 D
gmeyer@bridgew.edu
MEYER, Heidi ... 217-228-5432. 156 C
meyerhe@quincy.edu
MEYER, Irene ... 216-987-4469. 378 D
irene.meyer@tri-c.edu
MEYER, Jan ... 325-674-6802. 464 H
meyerj@acu.edu
MEYER, Jay ... 847-543-2717. 143 A
jmeyer@clcillinois.edu
MEYER, Jill ... 414-258-4810. 535 A
meyerj@mtmary.edu
MEYER, John ... 414-443-8910. 539 F
john.meyer@wlc.edu
MEYER, John ... 239-985-3451. 101 O
jmeyer9@edison.edu
MEYER, John ... 605-626-2379. 451 I
meyerj@northern.edu
MEYER, John, A ... 530-752-7941... 70 J
jameyer@ucdavis.edu
MEYER, John, E ... 507-354-8221. 256 M
meyerjd@mlc-wels.edu
MEYER, Joseph, M ... 512-245-2386. 487 C
jm01@txstate.edu
MEYER, Josh ... 540-857-6311. 514 E
jmeyer@virginiawestern.edu
MEYER, Kathy ... 701-483-2535. 371 D
Kathleen.Meyer@dickinsonstate.edu
MEYER, Kelly ... 518-458-5402. 321 A
meyerk@strose.edu
MEYER, Kevin, C ... 402-826-2161. 289 E
MEYER, Kingsley ... 740-245-7365. 392 A
kmeyer@rio.edu
MEYER, Kyle ... 402-559-7428. 292 J
kpmeyer@unmc.edu
MEYER, Larry ... 859-572-6117. 198 I
meyerl3@nku.edu
MEYER, Laura ... 617-578-7100. 236 E
lmeyer@sbboston.com
MEYER, Lisa ... 503-768-7056. 403 K
lmeyer@lclark.edu
MEYER, Mark, S ... 507-344-7740. 253 J
msmeyer@blc.edu
MEYER, Mary, J ... 402-844-7030. 291 I
maryjm@northeast.edu
MEYER, Merry ... 845-758-7005. 314 D
sm568@bncollege.com
MEYER, Michele ... 715-682-1674. 535 D
mmeyer@northland.edu
MEYER, Nancy, L ... 616-526-6224. 240 L
meyn@calvin.edu
MEYER, Nicole ... 309-677-4200. 140 I
ndmeyer@bradley.edu
MEYER, Pamela ... 504-280-6159. 205 G
pameyer@uno.edu
MEYER, Patricia ... 513-745-1996. 393 H
meyerp@xavier.edu
MEYER, Paul ... 361-825-3996. 483 F
paul.meyer@tamucc.edu
MEYER, Paul, W ... 215-247-5777. 435 B
pmeyer@upenn.edu
MEYER, Peter, E ... 863-680-4264. 105 D
pmeyer@flsouthern.edu
MEYER, Ralph ... 512-245-8336. 487 C
rm22@txstate.edu
MEYER, Robert, M ... 715-468-2815. 541 F
Bob.Meyer@witc.edu
MEYER, Sabrina ... 707-527-4821... 65 B
smeyer@santarosa.edu
MEYER, Sandy ... 480-557-1081... 18 I
sandy.meyer@phoenix.edu
MEYER, Shana ... 816-271-4432. 279 A
slmeyer@missouriwestern.edu
MEYER, Shelly ... 503-768-7976. 403 K
smeyer@lclark.edu
MEYER, Stan ... 602-639-7500... 13 S
MEYER, Susan ... 320-308-5512. 261 C
smeyer@sctcc.edu
MEYER, Thomas ... 605-274-5330. 449 K
thomas.meyer@augie.edu
MEYER, Timothy, R ... 248-341-2115. 248 D
trmeyer@oaklandcc.edu
MEYER, Tina ... 909-469-5586... 76 B
tmeyer@westernu.edu
MEYER, Wanda ... 701-774-4275. 372 F
wanda.meyer@willistonstate.edu
MEYER REIMER,
Kathryn ... 574-535-7443. 166 A
kathymr@goshen.edu
MEYEROWICH, Drew ... 913-684-7316. 545 E
drew.meyerowich@leavenworth.army.mil
MEYEROWITZ, Beth, E ... 213-740-6715... 74 A
meyerow@usc.edu
MEYERS, Andrew, W ... 901-678-2590. 460 B
ameyers@memphis.edu
MEYERS, Bonnie ... 651-779-3346. 258 C
bonnie.meyers@century.edu
MEYERS, Carolyn ... 601-979-2323. 267 E
carolyn.meyers@jsums.edu
MEYERS, Ernest, G ... 864-488-4367. 444 L
emeyers@limestone.edu
MEYERS, Gene ... 504-865-5353. 207 C
gmeyers@tulane.edu
MEYERS, Larry ... 763-424-0772. 260 C
lmeyers@nhcc.edu
MEYERS, Lynda ... 717-846-5000. 438 E
MEYERS, Lynda, R ... 717-846-5000. 438 E
MEYERS, Mark ... 513-745-3119. 393 H
meyersd3@xavier.edu
MEYERS, Michael ... 810-766-4062. 239 H
michael.meyers@baker.edu
MEYERS, Paul ... 281-283-3016. 489 C
meyers@uhcl.edu
MEYERS, Rick ... 859-572-6565. 198 I
meyersr@nku.edu
MEYERS, Ruth ... 510-204-0720... 38 J
rmeyers@cdsp.edu
MEYERS, Shelly, A ... 864-488-8207. 444 L
smeyers@limestone.edu
MEYERS, Tom, J ... 574-535-7346. 166 A
tomjm@goshen.edu
MEZA, Jose ... 787-769-9965. 554 B
jose.meza1@upr.edu
MEZA, Juan ... 209-228-4487... 71 D
jmeza@ucmerced.edu
MEZA, Lorena ... 760-750-4056... 35 A
lmeza@csusm.edu
MEZA, Narcisa ... 787-257-0000. 554 B
narcisa.meza1@upr.edu
MEZIERE, Kevin ... 858-653-6740... 49 C
MEZYNSKI, David ... 914-961-8313. 340 B
dmezynski@svots.edu
MHLANGA, Fortune ... 615-966-5073. 456 B
fortune.mhlanga@lipscomb.edu
MI, Hanfu ... 217-206-6512. 161 E
MIARKA-GRZELAK,
Anna ... 518-587-2100. 346 A
anna.miarka-grzelak@esc.edu
MIAZGA, John ... 325-942-2212. 465 K
john.miazga@angelo.edu
MICA, Christine ... 202-319-5304... 94 G
mica@cua.edu
MICCO, Melissa, A ... 412-397-5264. 431 I
micco@rmu.edu
MICEK, Tyler ... 843-383-8173. 442 F
tmicek@coker.edu
MICELI, Anthony ... 617-726-8439. 234 B
amiceli@mghihp.edu
MICELI, Lynne ... 757-457-8101. 502 C
lynne.miceli@atlanticuniv.edu
MICELI, Tara ... 248-689-8282. 251 I
tmiceli@walshcollege.edu
MICHAEL, Bernardo, A ... 717-766-2511. 423 L
bmichael@messiah.edu
MICHAEL, Bob ... 706-864-1998. 133 D
bob.michael@ung.edu
MICHAEL, Cheryl ... 410-334-2884. 221 D
cmichael@worwic.edu
MICHAEL, Donohue ... 312-777-8582. 147 D
mdonohue@aii.edu
MICHAEL, Gage ... 719-549-3006... 84 G
Michael.Gage@pueblocc.edu
MICHAEL, Jennifer ... 617-732-2871. 233 E
jennifer.michael@bos.mcphs.edu
MICHAEL, Jennifer ... 315-364-3312. 350 E
jmichael@wells.edu
MICHAEL, Jim ... 559-278-3923... 33 D
jim_michael@csufresno.edu
MICHAEL, Jody ... 810-762-0048. 247 F
jody.michael@mcc.edu
MICHAEL, Lloyd, H ... 713-798-4842. 467 F
lmichael@bcm.edu
MICHAEL, Marge, M ... 701-252-3467. 373 D
mmichael@jc.edu
MICHAEL, III, Max ... 205-934-7730... 8 E
maxm@uab.edu
MICHAEL, Robert ... 706-864-7998. 133 D
bob.michael@ung.edu
MICHAEL, Sandra ... 215-637-7700. 418 G
smichael@holyfamily.edu
MICHAEL, Steve, O ... 215-572-2924. 409 H
michaels@arcadia.edu
MICHAEL, Timothy ... 313-577-2116. 252 G
ea3307@wayne.edu
MICHAEL-PICKETT,
Stephanie ... 704-922-6215. 360 F
michael.stephanie@gaston.edu
MICHAELIDES, Anthony . 661-362-3253... 40 E
anthony.michaelides@canyons.edu
MICHAELIDES, Barbara .. 318-342-5550. 208 E
michaelides@ulm.edu
MICHAELIS, Jim ... 801-863-8996. 497 C
michaeji@uvu.edu
MICHAELIS, Randall, B .. 509-777-4303. 525 F
rmichaelis@whitworth.edu
MICHAELS, Alan, C ... 614-292-2631. 386 E
michaels.23@osu.edu
MICHAELS, Andrea, P ... 508-793-7773. 225 A
amichaels@clarku.edu
MICHAELS, Brent ... 910-678-8209. 360 D
michaelb@faytechcc.edu
MICHAELS, Cathy ... 718-262-2238. 319 F
ctsia@york.cuny.edu
MICHAELS, Craig ... 718-997-5220. 319 C
craig.michaels@qc.cuny.edu
MICHAELS, Debbie ... 541-552-6590. 406 C
michaeld@sou.edu
MICHAELS, George, H ... 805-893-2378... 72 B
george@id.ucsb.edu
MICHAELS, Jeff, A ... 717-477-1171. 429 E
jamich@ship.edu
MICHAELS, Lynda ... 570-389-4061. 427 H
lmichael@bloomu.edu
MICHAELS, Meredith ... 949-824-4923... 71 B
m.michaels@uci.edu
MICHAELS, Sheri ... 319-385-6229. 179 K
sheri.michaels@iwc.edu
MICHAELS, Sue ... 916-660-7272... 66 B
smichaels@sierracollege.edu
MICHAELSEN, Kevin ... 919-760-8565. 356 G
michaelsen@meredith.edu
MICHAELSON,
Dorcas, M ... 651-523-2210. 256 A
dmichaelson01@hamline.edu
MICHAELSON FISHER,
Bonnie ... 410-778-7261. 221 C
bfisher2@washcoll.edu
MICHAJLA, Patty ... 425-640-1516. 519 D
pmichajl@edcc.edu
MICHAL, Barbara, M ... 706-419-1275. 123 F
michal@covenant.edu
MICHALAK, Sarah ... 919-962-1301. 368 D
smichala@email.unc.edu
MICHALEK, Laurie ... 406-496-4119. 287 F
lmichalek@mtech.edu
MICHALENKO, John ... 412-397-4399. 431 I
michalenko@rmu.edu
MICHALERYA,
William, D ... 610-758-5802. 422 A
wdm1@lehigh.edu
MICHALSKI, Greg ... 904-632-3017. 105 E
gmichals@fscj.edu
MICHALSKI, Monica ... 718-489-5274. 338 G
mmichalski@sfc.edu
MICHALSKI, Tim ... 361-570-4820. 489 E
michalskit@uhv.edu
MICHAUD, Joanne ... 305-237-3008. 109 D
jmichau1@mdc.edu
MICHAUD, Paul ... 912-478-5468. 126 C
pmichaud@georgiasouthern.edu
MICHAUD, Paul ... 908-526-1200. 305 B
pmichaud@raritanval.edu
MICHEALS, Deborah ... 724-480-3515. 413 H
deb.micheals@ccbc.edu
MICHEL, Francisco ... 773-878-7950. 158 B
fmichel@staugustine.edu
MICHEL, Mike ... 410-293-1901. 545 J
michel@usna.edu
MICHEL, Pamela ... 315-312-2102. 344 A
pamela.michel@oswego.edu
MICHEL, R. Keith ... 516-671-2277. 350 C
kmichel@webb.edu
MICHEL, William ... 773-702-2673. 161 B
wmichel@uchicago.edu
MICHELINI, Debra ... 847-543-2383. 143 A
dmichelini@clcillinois.edu
MICHELINI, Rick, H ... 724-287-8711. 411 C
rick.michelini@bc3.edu
MICHELL, Peter ... 925-631-4571... 61 F
pmichell@stmarys-ca.edu
MICHELSON, Peggy ... 314-529-6543. 276 G
pmichelson@maryville.edu
MICKANIS, Judith, L ... 570-577-3171. 411 A
mickanis@bucknell.edu
MICKELSEN, Scott, R ... 308-367-5253. 293 B
smickelsen4@unl.edu
MICKELSON, Carrie ... 608-663-3317. 532 I
cmickelson@edgewood.edu
MICKELSON, Doug ... 414-256-1252. 535 A
mickelsd@mtmary.edu
MICKENS, Charles ... 517-371-5140. 250 G
mickensc@cooley.edu
MICKENS, George ... 623-245-4600... 18 D
gmickens@uti.edu
MICKENS, Helen ... 517-371-5140. 250 G
mickensh@cooley.edu
MICKENS, Kendrick ... 610-359-5340. 414 D
kmickens@dccc.edu

MICKEY, Marty .... 847-947-5580. 153 I
mmickey@nl.edu
MICKEY-BOGGS, Shari ... 513-745-3657. 393 H
mickeyboggss@xavier.edu
MICKLES, Muriel, B .... 434-832-7656. 512 A
micklesm@cvcc.vccs.edu
MICKOOL, Richard .... 937-525-3811. 393 E
rmickool@wittenberg.edu
MICUS, David .... 307-766-5272. 543 I
dmicus@uwyo.edu
MIDCAP, Richard, D .... 410-827-5858. 214 C
rmidcap@chesapeake.edu
MIDDEKER, Vicki .... 303-464-2308... 84 K
vmiddeker@westwood.edu
MIDDENDORF, Sandra ... 651-641-3599. 256 J
smiddendorf001@luthersem.edu
MIDDENDORF, Terry ...... 651-523-2302. 256 A
tmiddendorf@hamline.edu
MIDDENDORF, Tom .... 615-248-1237. 462 D
tmiddendorf@trevecca.edu
MIDDLEBROOK, Sharon 254-659-7502. 473 A
smiddlebrook@hillcollege.edu
MIDDLEMIST,
George, M .... 303-556-5043... 83 D
middlemi@msudenver.edu
MIDDLESWARTH,
Jean, E .... 336-575-3901. 360 E
jmiddleswarth@forsythtech.edu
MIDDLETON, Antoinette . 212-220-1267. 317 A
amiddleton@bmcc.cuny.edu
MIDDLETON, Charles, R 312-341-3800. 157 D
cmiddleton@roosevelt.edu
MIDDLETON, Dewayne ... 601-849-0112. 266 F
dewayne.middleton@colin.edu
MIDDLETON, Jacqueline 330-263-2580. 377 H
jkmiddleton@wooster.edu
MIDDLETON, James, E .. 541-383-7201. 402 D
jmiddleton@cocc.edu
MIDDLETON, Joan .... 301-934-7568. 214 D
joanm@csmd.edu
MIDDLETON, Joan .... 301-934-7853. 214 D
joanm@csmd.edu
MIDDLETON, Joseph ...... 718-960-8421. 318 A
joseph.middleton@lehman.cuny.edu
MIDDLETON, Kenna .... 859-622-1515. 193 P
kenna.middleton@eku.edu
MIDDLETON, Lowell .... 757-727-5640. 505 F
lowell.middleton@hamptonu.edu
MIDDLETON, Lyle .... 501-205-8830... 20 I
lmiddleton@cbc.edu
MIDDLETON, Melinda, L 812-877-8259. 172 C
melinda.l.middleton@rose-hulman.edu
MIDDLETON, Michael, A 573-882-3394. 283 C
middletonm@missouri.edu
MIDDLETON, Nigel, T .... 303-273-3327... 80 E
nmiddlet@mines.edu
MIDDLETON, Norma, L .. 336-316-2151. 355 A
nmiddlet@guilford.edu
MIDDLETON, Renee, A ... 740-593-4400. 387 C
middletr@ohio.edu
MIDDLETON, Rodney, C 989-328-1202. 247 D
rodm@montcalm.edu
MIDDLETON,
Whittaker, V .... 803-535-5347. 442 B
wmiddleton@claflin.edu
MIDEI, Ron .... 954-262-5224. 109 K
ronmidei@nova.edu
MIDGETT, Pam .... 940-397-4182. 476 H
pam.midgett@mwsu.edu
MIDGETTE, Juanita .... 252-335-3586. 367 C
jmidgette@mail.ecsu.edu
MIDGLEY, Michael, T ..... 512-223-7579. 466 I
midgley@austincc.edu
MIDHA, Chand .... 330-972-7857. 390 E
cmidha@uakron.edu
MIDKIFF, Kittridge .... 270-686-4508. 196 C
kitt.midkiff@kctcs.edu
MIDKIFF, Lindsay .... 870-633-4480... 21 A
lindsay.midkiff@eacc.edu
MIDKIFF, Lori, A .... 304-929-5472. 528 D
lmidkiff@newriver.edu
MIDKIFF, Mike .... 903-923-2136. 471 J
mmidkiff@etbu.edu
MIDKIFF, JR.,
Robert, M .... 570-577-1561. 411 A
robert.midkiff@bucknell.edu
MIDKIFF, Scott, F .... 540-231-4227. 515 C
midkiff@vt.edu
MIDTHUN, Steve .... 414-277-7224. 534 G
midthun@msoe.edu
MIEDEMA, Linda .... 321-433-7380. 101 M
miedemal@easternflorida.edu
MIEDEMA, Linda, L .... 321-433-7380. 101 M
miedemal@easternflorida.edu
MIELKE, Dan .... 541-962-3399. 405 H
dmielke@eou.edu
MIERA, Joseph .... 505-277-2511. 312 F
jmiera@unm.edu
MIERS, Michael .... 508-849-3326. 222 B
mmiers@annamaria.edu

MIERTSCHIN, Charla ...... 507-457-5299. 262 A
cmiertschin@winona.edu
MIGLAW, Kari, L .... 831-656-2077. 544 M
klmiglaw@nps.edu
MIGLER, Jerome .... 520-206-4999... 17 A
jmigler@pima.edu
MIGLIO, Joseph .... 617-873-0471. 224 G
joseph.miglio@cambridgecollege.edu
MIGNAULT, Richard .... 845-451-1369. 322 D
r_mignau@culinary.edu
MIGNOGNA, Janice .... 215-780-1235. 433 A
janice@salus.edu
MIGUEL, George .... 520-383-8401... 18 B
gmiguel@tocc.cc.az.us
MIGYANKO,
Stephanie, M .... 724-439-4900. 421 F
smigyanko@laurel.edu
MIHAL, Deborah, F .... 843-953-1431. 443 A
mihaldf@cofc.edu
MIHAL, Roxanne .... 617-984-1695. 235 I
rmihal@quincycollege.edu
MIHAL, Ruthie .... 704-355-5316. 353 D
ruthie.mihal@carolinashealthcare.org
MIHALAKIS, Marina .... 401-454-6764. 440 A
mmihalak@risd.edu
MIHALCIN, Patricia .... 724-287-8711. 411 C
patricia.mihalcin@bc3.edu
MIHALEVICH, Rick .... 573-897-5000. 276 E
MIHALIC, Angela .... 214-648-2168. 493 E
angela.mihalic@utsouthwestern.edu
MIHALIK, Brian .... 803-777-4290. 447 G
bmahalik@hrsm.sc.edu
MIHALY, Christine .... 734-973-3477. 252 A
cmihaly@wccnet.edu
MIHALY, Marc .... 802-831-1237. 500 H
mmihaly@vermontlaw.edu
MIHALYO, JR.,
Michael, P .... 304-637-1243. 526 E
mihalyom@dewv.edu
MIHALYOV, David .... 585-395-2577. 342 F
dmihalyo@brockport.edu
MIHEL, George, J .... 815-288-5511. 158 K
mihelg@svcc.edu
MIHLBACHLER, Dennis .. 217-532-6961. 150 D
dennis.mihlbachler@doc.illinois.gov
MIHM-HEROLD,
Wendy, A .... 563-562-3263. 181 E
mihm-heroldw@portal.nicc.edu
MIHOPULOS, Sheryl, L .. 516-877-3365. 313 A
mihopulos@adelphi.edu
MIKALSON, Joan .... 518-608-8144. 324 B
jmikalson@excelsior.edu
MIKE, James .... 717-477-1151. 429 E
jhmike@ship.edu
MIKEL, Benjy .... 662-325-5508. 268 D
wbm50@msstate.edu
MIKESCH, Gregory .... 314-792-6119. 275 L
mikesch@kenrick.edu
MIKESELL, Blake .... 319-363-8213. 181 C
bmikesell@mtmercy.edu
MIKESELL, Brian .... 413-528-7274. 222 E
bmikesell@simons-rock.edu
MIKESELL, Leslie .... 530-283-0202... 44 H
lmikesell@frc.edu
MIKESIC, Patrick .... 785-594-8447. 184 C
patrick.mikesic@bakeru.edu
MIKEWORTH, Becky, L .. 618-544-8657. 147 A
mikeworthb@iecc.edu
MIKHAIL, Michael, B ..... 312-413-3375. 161 D
mmikhail@uic.edu
MIKHAIL, Mona .... 626-812-3013... 29 H
mmikhail@apu.edu
MIKHAIL, Osama, I .... 713-500-3047. 492 E
osama.i.mikhail@uth.tmc.edu
MIKKELSEN, Andrea .... 507-457-5024. 262 A
amikkelsen@winona.edu
MIKKELSEN, Carmelita ... 251-580-2213..... 4 L
cmikkelsen@faulknerstate.edu
MIKKELSEN, Morris, E ... 319-273-2611. 176 A
morris.mikkelsen@uni.edu
MIKLUSAK, Courtney ..... 619-239-0391... 36 D
cmiklusak@cwsl.edu
MIKNAVICH, Marie .... 315-866-0300. 326 A
miknavimt@herkimer.edu
MIKO, Matthew .... 202-408-2400... 96 F
MIKOWSKI, Thomas .... 616-632-2853. 239 E
mikowtho@aquinas.edu
MIKSA, Tony .... 815-455-8673. 152 F
tmiksa@mchenry.edu
MIKULAY, Jennifer .... 414-382-6395. 531 I
jennifer.mikulay@alverno.edu
MIKUS, Robert, L .... 717-867-6234. 421 H
mikus@lvc.edu
MIKUSZEWSKI, Barbara . 216-987-4497. 378 D
barbara.mikuszewski@tri-c.edu
MILADIN, Judith, G .... 315-255-1743. 316 D
miladin@cayuga-cc.edu
MILAM, B. Hofler .... 336-758-3121. 370 D
bhm@wfu.edu
MILAM, John, H .... 540-868-7249. 512 H
jmilam@lfcc.edu

MILAM, Kathy, L .... 937-382-6661. 393 B
kathy_milam@wilmington.edu
MILAM, Linda .... 918-781-7247. 394 D
milaml@bacone.edu
MILANO, Joy .... 616-222-3000. 245 C
jmilano@kuyper.edu
MILARDOVICH, Julia ...... 916-278-6322... 34 D
juliam@csus.edu
MILASINOVIC, Milan ...... 212-752-1530. 328 G
milan.milasinovic@limcollege.edu
MILAVETZ, Barry .... 701-777-4278. 371 C
barry.milavetz@und.edu
MILBAUER, Barbara .... 313-993-1025. 250 K
barbara.milbauer@udmercy.edu
MILBERG, William .... 212-229-5901. 332 E
milbergw@newschool.edu
MILBOURNE, John, M ... 321-674-7160. 104 H
jmilbour@fit.edu
MILBURN, Milo, C .... 740-283-3771. 379 N
mmilburn@franciscan.edu
MILBURN, Tim, R .... 208-467-8644. 139 A
trmilburn@nnu.edu
MILBY, Kevin, S .... 859-238-5534. 193 E
kevin.milby@centre.edu
MILBY, Megan, H .... 859-238-5516. 193 E
megan.milby@centre.edu
MILDON, Todd, B .... 206-616-6811. 524 G
tmildon@uw.edu
MILEHAM, Mardi .... 503-883-2217. 404 A
mmileham@linfield.edu
MILEM, Jill .... 936-468-2401. 482 A
jmilem@sfasu.edu
MILES, Alicia, C .... 770-720-5542. 130 G
acm1@reinhardt.edu
MILES, Arletha .... 914-773-3856. 335 J
lmiles@pace.edu
MILES, Belinda .... 216-987-4787. 378 D
belinda.miles@tri-c.edu
MILES, Candice .... 202-274-5000... 97 A
cmiles@udc.edu
MILES, Chris .... 562-985-4376... 33 F
chris.miles@csulb.edu
MILES, Cindy .... 619-644-7569... 46 C
cindy.miles@gcccd.edu
MILES, David .... 802-225-3240. 499 I
david.miles@neci.edu
MILES, David, A .... 201-692-2227. 301 J
dmiles@fdu.edu
MILES, Donald .... 814-472-3360. 432 D
dmiles@francis.edu
MILES, Donald .... 814-472-3029. 432 D
dmiles@francis.edu
MILES, Frank .... 334-244-3467..... 2 A
fmiles1@aum.edu
MILES, Herb, E .... 979-230-3474. 468 A
herb.miles@brazosport.edu
MILES, Jason .... 425-889-7800. 521 G
jason.miles@northwestu.edu
MILES, Jennifer .... 662-329-7129. 268 E
jmiles@vpss.muw.edu
MILES, Jessica .... 973-642-8700. 307 D
jessica.miles@shu.edu
MILES, Kenneth, O .... 225-578-5736. 204 O
komiles@lsu.edu
MILES, Kevin, J .... 610-799-1169. 421 I
kmiles@lccc.edu
MILES, Kim .... 626-585-7400... 58 F
kxmiles@pasadena.edu
MILES, Linda .... 252-398-6505. 353 H
milesl@chowan.edu
MILES, Lora .... 618-650-2020. 159 H
lflamm@siue.edu
MILES, Martin .... 757-727-5635. 505 F
martin.miles@hamptonu.edu
MILES, Mary, E .... 502-852-6688. 200 D
maryelizabeth.miles@louisville.edu
MILES, Ray .... 337-475-5192. 207 G
rmiles@mcneese.edu
MILES, Rebecca .... 903-823-3200. 482 D
rebecca.miles@texarkanacollege.edu
MILES, Richard .... 513-721-7944. 380 D
rmiles@gbs.edu
MILES, Stephannie .... 704-461-6873. 352 G
stephanniemiles@bac.edu
MILES, Stephen .... 941-487-4200. 115 D
miles@ncf.edu
MILES, Tom .... 478-445-4027. 125 A
tom.miles@gcsu.edu
MILES, Vickie .... 334-670-3732..... 7 H
vmiles@troy.edu
MILES, Wendy .... 508-373-9544. 223 A
wendy.miles@becker.edu
MILETTI, Linnette .... 787-841-2000. 552 B
lmiletti@pucpr.edu
MILEWICZ, Mark .... 910-521-6630. 369 B
mark.milewicz@uncp.edu
MILEY, Abigail .... 812-488-2272. 173 H
am275@evansville.edu
MILEY, Melinda .... 843-953-5426. 443 A
mileym@cofc.edu

MILFORD, William .... 516-299-2345. 329 D
william.milford@liu.edu
MILHAM, Donna .... 616-451-3511. 241 H
dmilham@davenport.edu
MILHAUSEN, Michael .... 503-399-6527. 402 E
michael.milhausen@chemeketa.edu
MILHIZER, Eugene, R ..... 239-687-5301... 98 J
ermilhizer@avemarialaw.edu
MILHOLLAND, Tom, A ... 325-674-2918. 464 H
milholland@acu.edu
MILICH, Marianne .... 219-980-6618. 168 B
mmilich@iun.edu
MILICI, Roger .... 212-636-6545. 324 G
milici@fordham.edu
MILIONI, Mark, L .... 417-268-6008. 271 I
mmilioni@gobbc.edu
MILIONIS, Daren .... 503-375-7012. 403 A
dmilionis@corban.edu
MILJEVICH, Greg .... 715-365-4486. 540 G
gmiljevidh@nicoletcollege.edu
MILKOWSKI, Rose .... 312-629-6182. 158 L
rmilkowski@saic.edu
MILLA, Rosalinda .... 619-477-6310... 70 D
rmilla@usuniversity.edu
MILLAGE, Mark .... 605-221-3114. 450 C
mmillage@kilian.edu
MILLAN, Brett .... 956-872-7263. 480 I
bmillan@southtexascollege.edu
MILLANE, Maureen .... 716-839-8334. 322 E
mmillane@daemen.edu
MILLAR, Janet .... 661-654-3366... 32 H
jmillar@csub.edu
MILLAR, John .... 419-448-3406. 389 J
jmillar@tiffin.edu
MILLAR, Kenneth .... 562-985-4691... 33 F
kmillar@csulb.edu
MILLAR, Norman .... 818-767-0888... 76 K
norman.millar@woodbury.edu
MILLARD, Bill .... 765-677-2520. 169 B
bill.millard@indwes.edu
MILLARD, Cristi .... 801-957-4145. 498 B
cristi.millard@slcc.edu
MILLARD, James .... 816-501-4370. 280 I
james.millard@rockhurst.edu
MILLARD, James, R .... 252-638-7283. 359 G
millardj@cravencc.edu
MILLARD, Jill .... 704-290-5887. 363 G
jmillard@spcc.edu
MILLARD, Timothy, R ..... 540-985-9781. 506 G
trmillard@jchs.edu
MILLAY, David .... 501-569-3390... 24 B
dlmillay@ualr.edu
MILLAY, David, L .... 501-569-3390... 24 B
dlmillay@ualr.edu
MILLENBACH, Judy .... 503-699-6266. 404 C
jmillenbach@marylhurst.edu
MILLENDER, Angelia ...... 954-201-7486... 99 D
amillender@broward.edu
MILLER, Adam .... 509-527-5778. 525 E
millera@whitman.edu
MILLER, Al .... 251-442-2357..... 9 A
amiller@umobile.edu
MILLER, Alex .... 864-977-7010. 445 H
alex.miller@ngu.edu
MILLER, Amy .... 765-983-1498. 165 G
amymul@earlham.edu
MILLER, Amy .... 215-568-9215. 423 M
amiller@phmc.org
MILLER, Amy .... 215-568-9215. 423 M
ammiller@phmc.org
MILLER, Andrea, L .... 225-216-8402. 202 H
chancellorsoffice@mybrcc.edu
MILLER, Andrew .... 863-667-5703. 113 P
aemiller@seu.edu
MILLER, Andrew, T .... 607-255-6384. 322 A
atm65@cornell.edu
MILLER, Angela, M .... 608-342-1555. 537 D
millerang@uwplatt.edu
MILLER, Anita, L .... 814-871-5847. 416 K
miller064@gannon.edu
MILLER, Ann, M .... 336-841-9021. 355 C
amiller@highpoint.edu
MILLER, Ann, S .... 530-226-4733... 66 D
amiller@simpsonu.edu
MILLER, Anne .... 212-217-4190. 324 C
anne_miller@fitnyc.edu
MILLER, Antoinette .... 216-791-5000. 377 E
axm120@case.edu
MILLER, Arnold, R .... 304-696-2677. 529 H
miller@marshall.edu
MILLER, Ashley .... 270-384-8065. 197 D
MILLER, Ave .... 770-962-7580. 127 D
amiller@gwinnetttech.edu
MILLER, Barbara .... 443-352-4369. 218 E
blmiller@stevenson.edu
MILLER, Barbara, A .... 215-968-8409. 411 B
millerb@bucks.edu
MILLER, Barbara, R .... 301-447-5372. 217 B
brmiller@msmary.edu
MILLER, Becky .... 913-360-7410. 184 H
beckymiller@benedictine.edu

MILLER, Beth .... 409-880-2292. 486 E
bbmiller@lit.edu
MILLER, Betsy .... 575-538-6118. 312 N
millerb@wnmu.edu
MILLER, Bill .... 314-539-5220. 281 D
wmiller129@stlcc.edu
MILLER, Bill .... 830-372-8120. 485 C
bmiller@tlu.edu
MILLER, BJ .... 540-432-4304. 504 D
bj.miller@emu.edu
MILLER, Bo .... 601-968-8797. 266 A
bmiller@belhaven.edu
MILLER, Bob .... 610-526-7878. 410 J
rmiller03@brynmawr.edu
MILLER, Brian .... 501-244-5129... 19 J
brian.miller@arkansasbaptist.edu
MILLER, Brian .... 616-451-3511. 241 H
bmiller@davenport.edu
MILLER, Brian .... 252-493-7241. 362 G
bmiller@email.pittcc.edu
MILLER, Bridget .... 315-655-7225. 316 E
bmmiller@cazenovia.edu
MILLER, Carla .... 231-591-3825. 242 F
millerc@ferris.edu
MILLER, Carol, A .... 262-472-1130. 538 D
millerc@uww.edu
MILLER, Carol, J .... 701-231-7761. 371 G
carol.miller@ndsu.edu
MILLER, Caroline, B .... 513-556-3379. 390 G
caroline.miller@uc.edu
MILLER, Carolyn .... 740-284-5822. 379 N
cmiller@franciscan.edu
MILLER, Cary Beth .... 615-383-4848. 464 D
cmiller@watkins.edu
MILLER, Catherine .... 203-857-3342... 89 D
cmiller@norwalk.edu
MILLER, Cecile .... 478-274-7643. 129 I
cmiller@oftc.edu
MILLER, Chad .... 859-253-3637. 194 A
chad.miller@frontier.edu
MILLER, Chandra .... 918-293-5266. 398 B
chandra.miller@okstate.edu
MILLER, Chani .... 908-354-6057. 308 M
MILLER, Charles .... 337-521-8990. 203 I
charles.miller@southlouisiana.edu
MILLER, Cheryl .... 503-552-1510. 404 H
cmiller@ncnm.edu
MILLER, Cheryl .... 540-857-7201. 514 E
ccmiller@virginiawestern.edu
MILLER, Cheryl, L .... 860-439-2085... 89 H
cheryl.miller@conncoll.edu
MILLER, Chris .... 760-744-1150... 58 D
cmiller@palomar.edu
MILLER, Chris .... 847-317-7036. 160 M
cmiller@tiu.edu
MILLER, Chris .... 740-392-6868. 384 K
chris.miller@mvnu.edu
MILLER, Chris, E .... 570-326-3761. 427 B
cmiller@pct.edu
MILLER, Christine .... 507-292-5130. 261 A
christinem.miller@rctc.edu
MILLER, Christine, A .... 724-946-7148. 437 B
millerca@westminster.edu
MILLER,
Clarence (Hank) .... 845-687-5065. 348 H
millerh@sunyulster.edu
MILLER, Colleen .... 320-589-6006. 264 F
mille593@morris.umn.edu
MILLER, Colleen .... 419-383-6805. 392 B
colleen.miller@utoledo.edu
MILLER, Craig .... 314-246-7773. 284 N
craigmiller29@webster.edu
MILLER, Craig .... 484-384-2953. 425 I
semregis@eastern.edu
MILLER, Dan .... 505-473-6706. 311 K
dan.miller@santafeuniversity.edu
MILLER, Daniel, P .... 570-321-4139. 422 H
millerda@lycoming.edu
MILLER, Darlene .... 973-877-3101. 301 H
dmiller@essex.edu
MILLER, David .... 402-935-9400. 290 N
dmiller@nechristian.edu
MILLER, David .... 563-425-5293. 183 B
millerd@uiu.edu
MILLER, David .... 606-546-1291. 200 A
dkmiller@unionky.edu
MILLER, David .... 312-362-8720. 143 H
miller@cdm.depaul.edu
MILLER, David .... 608-262-4048. 536 C
dmiller@uwsa.edu
MILLER, David, J .... 515-294-2631. 175 H
djmille@iastate.edu
MILLER, David, L .... 501-686-7609... 24 C
dlmiller2@uams.edu
MILLER, Davlon .... 662-846-4336. 266 G
dmiller@deltastate.edu
MILLER, Debbie .... 262-564-3220. 540 A
millerd@gtc.edu
MILLER, Deborah .... 714-997-6603... 38 A
dmiller@chapman.edu
MILLER, Deborah .... 419-772-2464. 386 D
d-miller@onu.edu
MILLER, Debra .... 217-357-3129. 141 A
dmiller@sandburg.edu
MILLER, Debra, M .... 570-326-3761. 427 B
dmiller2@pct.edu
MILLER, Dennis, L .... 414-443-8853. 539 F
dennis.miller@wlc.edu
MILLER, Dennis, R .... 570-662-4846. 429 C
dmiller@mansfield.edu
MILLER, Derrick .... 573-840-9666. 282 K
dmiller@trcc.edu
MILLER, Derrick .... 573-840-9675. 282 K
dmiller@trcc.edu
MILLER, Dianna, L .... 956-721-5820. 475 F
vpi@laredo.edu
MILLER, Dolores, M .... 563-562-3263. 181 E
millerd@nicc.edu
MILLER, Donna .... 502-213-5333. 195 F
donna.miller@kctcs.edu
MILLER, Donna .... 603-513-5118. 298 D
donna.miller@law.unh.edu
MILLER, Doug .... 417-626-1234. 279 J
miller.doug@occ.edu
MILLER, Draco .... 575-562-2631. 309 H
draco.miller@enmu.edu
MILLER, Drew .... 936-294-1720. 487 A
adm007@shsu.edu
MILLER, Drucilla, W .... 423-798-7942. 462 A
drucilla.miller@ws.edu
MILLER, Dyan .... 925-424-1275... 37 L
dmiller@laspositascollege.edu
MILLER, E. John .... 701-231-7933. 371 G
ej.miller@ndsu.edu
MILLER, Earl .... 845-675-4790. 335 C
earl.miller@nyack.edu
MILLER, Edgar .... 803-777-8134. 447 G
ewmiller@mailbox.sc.edu
MILLER, Elinor .... 303-964-5758... 84 M
emiller@regis.edu
MILLER, Elizabeth .... 805-922-6966... 26 K
emiller@hancockcollege.edu
MILLER, Elizabeth .... 920-832-7164. 533 S
elizabeth.miller@lawrence.edu
MILLER, Elizabeth, K .... 651-638-6215. 253 K
e-miller@bethel.edu
MILLER, Ellen, B .... 540-828-5755. 502 J
emiller@bridgewater.edu
MILLER, Elvert .... 718-270-6002. 319 A
miller@mec.cuny.edu
MILLER, Erin .... 570-321-4231. 422 H
millerer@lycoming.edu
MILLER, Faith .... 706-272-4462. 123 G
fmiller@daltonstate.edu
MILLER, Fayneese, S .... 802-656-3424. 500 F
fayneese.miller@uvm.edu
MILLER, Fred .... 907-852-3333... 10 F
fred.miller@ilisagvik.edu
MILLER, Fred .... 864-294-3800. 444 C
fred.miller@furman.edu
MILLER, Frederick .... 805-493-3960... 31 H
fdmiller@clunet.edu
MILLER, Galen, P .... 989-386-6644. 247 B
gpmiller@midmich.edu
MILLER, Gary .... 732-987-2533. 302 B
millerg@georgian.edu
MILLER, Gary .... 478-825-6228. 124 H
millerg@fvsu.edu
MILLER, Gary .... 415-451-2806... 63 A
maintenance@sfts.edu
MILLER, Gary, L .... 910-962-3030. 369 C
millerg@uncw.edu
MILLER, George, P .... 224-293-5609. 139 I
MILLER, Gina .... 412-536-1085. 420 A
gina.miller@laroche.edu
MILLER, Glen .... 503-399-5210. 402 E
glen.miller@chemeketa.edu
MILLER, Glenn .... 800-962-7682. 285 A
gmiller@wma.edu
MILLER, Gretchen .... 260-665-4312. 173 E
millerg@trine.edu
MILLER, H. Michael .... 303-629-8200... 87 F
MILLER, H. Samuel .... 828-227-7147. 369 E
sammiller@wcu.edu
MILLER, Harry, E .... 484-664-3464. 424 H
hmiller@muhlenberg.edu
MILLER, Henry .... 580-559-5760. 395 F
bmiller@ecok.edu
MILLER, Holly, N .... 508-289-7632. 238 E
hmiller@whoi.edu
MILLER, Jack .... 619-574-6909... 57 E
jmiller@pacificcollege.edu
MILLER, Jack .... 334-448-5129..... 7 H
jmiller@troy.edu
MILLER, Jaclyn .... 303-300-8740... 78 M
jaclyn.miller@collegeamerica.com
MILLER, Jacqueline .... 781-899-5500. 223 E
srmiller@blessedjohnxxiii.edu
MILLER, Jaime, M .... 708-709-3513. 156 A
jmmiller@prairiestate.edu
MILLER, James .... 630-637-5500. 154 F
jlmiller@noctrl.edu
MILLER, James .... 201-447-7124. 299 C
jmiller@bergen.edu
MILLER, James .... 814-732-2826. 428 E
jbmiller@edinboro.edu
MILLER, James, A .... 256-824-2846..... 8 F
James.Miller@uah.edu
MILLER, James, G .... 585-475-6637. 337 L
jgm6527@rit.edu
MILLER, James, P .... 573-629-2003. 274 J
jmiller@hlg.edu
MILLER, James, S .... 401-863-7940. 438 J
james_s_miller@brown.edu
MILLER, Janathin .... 858-653-3000... 32 A
jmiller@calmu.edu
MILLER, Jay .... 610-409-3790. 436 B
jmiller@ursinus.edu
MILLER, Jean, M .... 314-516-4570. 283 E
MILLER, Jeanne, C .... 607-436-2513. 343 E
millerjc@oneonta.edu
MILLER, Jeanne, Y .... 570-669-7010. 421 I
jmiller@lccc.edu
MILLER, Jeff .... 803-754-4100. 443 C
MILLER, Jeff .... 937-512-4848. 388 O
jeff.miller@sinclair.edu
MILLER, Jeff .... 574-296-6206. 163 J
jmiller@ambs.edu
MILLER, Jeff .... 541-956-7270. 407 F
jmiller@roguec.edu
MILLER, Jeffrey .... 314-529-9350. 276 G
jeffmiller@maryville.edu
MILLER, Jeffrey, A .... 412-396-5081. 415 F
millerjeff@duq.edu
MILLER, Jennifer .... 805-437-8516... 32 I
jennifer.miller@csuci.edu
MILLER, Jess .... 541-440-4600. 408 D
jess.miller@umpqua.edu
MILLER, Jessica, K .... 608-796-3013. 539 E
jkmiller@viterbo.edu
MILLER, Jim .... 603-513-1338. 298 E
jim.miller@granite.edu
MILLER, Jim .... 828-227-7124. 369 E
jimmiller@wcu.edu
MILLER, Joanne .... 508-793-7320. 225 A
jmiller@clarku.edu
MILLER, Joel, C .... 319-895-4107. 177 A
jmiller@cornellcollege.edu
MILLER, John .... 256-840-4195..... 6 I
jmiller@snead.edu
MILLER, John .... 503-352-2215. 407 A
jmiller@pacificu.edu
MILLER, John, S .... 208-732-6280. 138 B
jmiller@csi.edu
MILLER, John, W .... 860-832-3000... 87 K
millerjw@ccsu.edu
MILLER, Jonathan .... 508-854-4334. 232 F
jmiller@qcc.mass.edu
MILLER, Jonathan .... 407-646-2306. 111 Q
jxmiller@rollins.edu
MILLER, Jonathan, L .... 413-755-4230. 233 A
jmiller@stcc.edu
MILLER, Joseph, C .... 706-880-8253. 128 A
jcmiller@lagrange.edu
MILLER, Joshua .... 205-665-6245..... 9 B
millerjd@montevallo.edu
MILLER, Judith, E .... 904-620-2720. 116 B
j.miller@unf.edu
MILLER, Judy .... 989-686-9472. 242 C
jamiller@delta.edu
MILLER, Julie, H .... 313-577-2034. 252 G
aa6560@wayne.edu
MILLER, K, C .... 480-994-9244... 17 Q
kc@swiha.edu
MILLER, Karen .... 404-215-2645. 129 D
kmiller@morehouse.edu
MILLER, Karen .... 507-223-7252. 260 A
karen.miller@mnwest.edu
MILLER, Karen .... 216-987-3471. 378 D
karen.miller@tri-c.edu
MILLER, Kate .... 605-995-2901. 450 A
kamiller1@dwu.edu
MILLER, Kate, C .... 979-845-3651. 483 C
kcmiller@tamu.edu
MILLER, Katherine .... 845-451-1261. 322 D
k_miller@culinary.edu
MILLER, Kathleen .... 239-590-7600. 115 A
kmiller@fgcu.edu
MILLER, SSJ, Kathryn .... 215-248-7167. 413 A
kmiller@chc.edu
MILLER, Kathy .... 847-628-1088. 149 B
kmiller@judsonu.edu
MILLER, Keith .... 864-250-8175. 444 E
keith.miller@gvltec.edu
MILLER, Keith, T .... 804-524-5070. 515 D
ktmiller@vsu.edu
MILLER, Kelly, M .... 317-788-3437. 173 I
kmiller@uindy.edu
MILLER, Ken .... 407-646-2999. 111 Q
kmiller@rollins.edu
MILLER, Ken .... 502-456-6506. 199 G
kmiller@sullivan.edu
MILLER, Kenneth .... 740-857-1311. 388 I
kmiller@rosedale.edu
MILLER, Kent .... 573-288-6373. 273 F
kmiller@culver.edu
MILLER, Kevin .... 239-489-9135. 101 O
ksmiller3@edison.edu
MILLER, Kevin .... 800-686-7022... 90 D
kmiller@lincolncollegene.edu
MILLER, Kevin, D .... 973-408-3109. 301 C
theoadm@drew.edu
MILLER, Kieron .... 562-907-4236... 76 I
kmiller@whittier.edu
MILLER, Kilohana .... 808-984-3518. 137 B
kilohana@hawaii.edu
MILLER, Kimberly, A .... 410-822-5400. 214 C
kmiller@chesapeake.edu
MILLER, Kimberly, D .... 812-877-8176. 172 C
kimberly.miller@rose-hulman.edu
MILLER, Kimela .... 575-835-5888. 310 F
kmiller@admin.nmt.edu
MILLER, Kris .... 775-753-2135. 294 F
kris.miller@gbcnv.edu
MILLER, Kristin .... 402-935-9400. 290 N
kmiller@nechristian.edu
MILLER, L. Christopher .. 414-288-7206. 534 B
l.christopher.miller@marquette.edu
MILLER, Larry .... 228-896-2506. 268 C
larry.miller@mgccc.edu
MILLER, Larry, S .... 270-686-4502. 196 C
larry.miller@kctcs.edu
MILLER, Laura, M .... 717-766-2511. 423 L
lmiller@messiah.edu
MILLER, Lauren .... 312-935-6026. 156 K
lmiller@robertmorris.edu
MILLER, Leilani, M .... 408-554-4439... 64 M
lmiller@scu.edu
MILLER, Lester .... 908-526-1200. 305 B
lmiller@raritanval.edu
MILLER, Lewis, R .... 317-940-9714. 164 J
lmiller@butler.edu
MILLER, Linda .... 618-395-1169. 147 B
millerli@iecc.edu
MILLER, Linda, G .... 270-809-2154. 198 B
lmiller@murraystate.edu
MILLER, Linda, J .... 262-691-5526. 541 D
lmiller@wctc.edu
MILLER, Lisa .... 708-210-5767. 159 C
lmiller@ssc.edu
MILLER, Lisa .... 563-244-7002. 178 A
lmiller@eicc.edu
MILLER, Lisa .... 620-672-5641. 190 A
lisam@prattcc.edu
MILLER, Lisa .... 516-323-3046. 331 J
lmiller@molloy.edu
MILLER, Lisa, R .... 318-342-5431. 208 E
lmiller@ulm.edu
MILLER, Lori .... 412-338-4770. 419 M
lmiller@kaplan.edu
MILLER, Lucy, T .... 727-816-3448. 110 E
millerl@phcc.edu
MILLER, Marc .... 706-737-1418. 126 B
mmiller3@gru.edu
MILLER, Marc, L .... 520-621-1498... 18 F
marc.miller@law.arizona.edu
MILLER, Marcia, K .... 316-284-5315. 184 J
mmiller@bethelks.edu
MILLER, Margaret, C .... 847-543-2101. 143 A
ecd185@clcillinois.edu
MILLER, Margaret, L .... 423-439-4300. 459 C
millerml@etsu.edu
MILLER, Margaret, M ...... 609-258-5813. 304 E
mmmiller@princeton.edu
MILLER, Marie .... 620-341-5278. 186 D
mmiller@emporia.edu
MILLER, Marilynn .... 406-657-2244. 287 C
mmiller@msubillings.edu
MILLER, Mark .... 318-869-5117. 201 H
mmiller@centenary.edu
MILLER, Mark, A .... 303-245-4775... 83 F
markm@naropa.edu
MILLER, Mark, A .... 740-376-4741. 383 E
mark.miller@marietta.edu
MILLER, Marlene, R .... 702-968-2023. 295 E
mmiller@roseman.edu
MILLER, Marty, L .... 757-823-9539. 507 M
mlmiller@nsu.edu
MILLER, Martyn, J .... 215-204-7708. 433 K
martyn.miller@temple.edu
MILLER, Mary .... 612-977-5736. 254 C
mary.miller@capella.edu
MILLER, Mary .... 203-432-2900... 93 A
mary.miller@yale.edu
MILLER, Marylou .... 559-453-7104... 45 D
marylou.miller@fresno.edu
MILLER, Matt .... 989-386-6600. 247 B
mmiller@midmich.edu
MILLER, Matthew .... 678-839-5500. 133 I
mmiller@westga.edu

MILLER, Megan .... 410-225-2420. 216 C
memiller@mica.edu
MILLER, Megan .... 978-542-6000. 230 E
MILLER, Melinda .... 615-248-1650. 462 D
mmiller@trevecca.edu
MILLER, Melinda, A .... 315-386-7085. 345 F
millerm@canton.edu
MILLER, Melissa .... 843-661-8104. 443 G
melissa.miller@fdtc.edu
MILLER, Melissa, A .... 585-785-1639. 324 D
millerma@flcc.edu
MILLER, Melissa, C .... 386-312-4106. 112 C
melissamiller@sjrstate.edu
MILLER, Melvin .... 802-485-2134. 500 A
miller@norwich.edu
MILLER, Merrill .... 315-228-1000. 320 F
mmiller@colgate.edu
MILLER, Michael .... 406-683-7636. 286 I
m_miller@umwestern.edu
MILLER, Michael .... 805-893-2118... 72 B
Mike.Miller@sa.ucsb.edu
MILLER, Michael .... 715-425-0629. 537 E
michael.miller@uwrf.edu
MILLER, Michael .... 715-682-1202. 535 D
mmiller@northland.edu
MILLER, Michael .... 715-425-0629. 537 E
michael.miller@uwrf.edu
MILLER, Michael .... 715-425-3843. 537 E
honors@uwrf.edu
MILLER, Michael, A .... 512-471-4110. 491 C
mike.miller@austin.utexas.edu
MILLER, Michael, C .... 704-463-3030. 365 E
mike.miller@fsmail.pfeiffer.edu
MILLER, Michael, D .... 805-756-2344... 32 F
mdmiller@calpoly.edu
MILLER, Michael, H .... 410-293-1500. 545 J
millerm@usna.edu
MILLER, Michael, J .... 718-289-5548. 317 B
michael.miller@bcc.cuny.edu
MILLER, Michael, R .... 330-471-8205. 383 D
mimiller@malone.edu
MILLER, Michael, S .... 510-436-1360... 47 J
mmiller@hnu.edu
MILLER, Michael Patrick 708-524-5921. 144 C
mmiller@dom.edu
MILLER, Michelle .... 802-860-2729. 499 A
miller@champlain.edu
MILLER, Michelle, R .... 757-727-5447. 505 F
michelle.miller@hamptonu.edu
MILLER, Mike .... 951-827-3658... 71 E
mike.miller@ucr.edu
MILLER, Mike .... 229-430-4646. 119 J
mike.miller@asurams.edu
MILLER, Mike .... 918-683-4581. 394 D
millerm@bacone.edu
MILLER, Mike, B .... 336-386-3235. 364 D
millerm@surry.edu
MILLER, Miryom, R .... 845-434-5240. 352 B
mmiller@yg2m.edu
MILLER, Morris .... 253-589-5565. 518 B
morris.miller@cptc.edu
MILLER, Nancy .... 530-938-5404... 41 A
millern@siskiyous.edu
MILLER, Nancy .... 517-787-0800. 244 J
millernancya@jccmi.edu
MILLER, Nancy, W .... 323-226-6301... 52 G
MILLER, Nelson .... 616-301-6800. 250 G
millern@cooley.edu
MILLER, Nora, R .... 662-329-7145. 268 E
nmiller@vpfa.muw.edu
MILLER, Pam .... 985-380-2483. 203 H
pamelamiller@scl.edu
MILLER, Pamela .... 402-241-6405. 291 I
pamm@northeast.edu
MILLER, Parks .... 706-776-0102. 130 E
parksmiller@piedmont.edu
MILLER, Pat .... 517-629-0318. 239 A
pmiller@albion.edu
MILLER, Patricia, A .... 816-322-0110. 271 O
pat.miller@calvary.edu
MILLER, Patrick .... 817-257-7825. 484 I
p.miller@tcu.edu
MILLER, Paul .... 662-243-1902. 266 I
pmiller@eastms.edu
MILLER, Peggy .... 806-834-3850. 487 D
peggy.miller@ttu.edu
MILLER, Peter .... 508-849-3586. 222 B
pmiller@annamaria.edu
MILLER, Phil .... 803-754-4100. 443 C
MILLER, Rachel, S .... 620-327-8213. 187 D
rachelsm@hesston.edu
MILLER, Randall, C .... 304-260-4380. 527 N
rmiller@blueridgectc.edu
MILLER, Randi .... 201-360-4073. 302 D
rmiller@hccc.edu
MILLER, Ray .... 402-449-2920. 289 H
rmiller6053@graceu.edu
MILLER, Remy .... 901-272-5107. 456 F
rmiller@mca.edu
MILLER, Richard, A .... 970-247-7426... 81 M
miller_r@fortlewis.edu
MILLER, Richard, B .... 417-625-9565. 278 D
miller-r@mssu.edu
MILLER, Richard, C .... 270-745-5468. 200 G
richard.c.miller@wku.edu
MILLER, Richard, H .... 732-571-3400. 543 I
MILLER, Richard, K .... 781-292-2301. 226 G
richard.miller@olin.edu
MILLER, Richard, L .... 713-500-3603. 492 E
richard.l.miller@uth.tmc.edu
MILLER, Rick .... 518-320-1646. 341 C
rick.miller@suny.edu
MILLER, Rick .... 262-691-5323. 541 D
rmiller@wctc.edu
MILLER, Rob .... 913-758-6160. 191 B
millerr@stmary.edu
MILLER, Robert .... 860-412-7327... 89 E
rmiller@qvcc.commnet.edu
MILLER, Robert .... 352-392-1336. 116 A
rmiller@admin.ufl.edu
MILLER, Robert .... 908-852-1400. 300 D
millerr@centenarycollege.edu
MILLER, Robert .... 269-387-2073. 252 I
bob.miller@wmich.edu
MILLER, Robert, B .... 626-585-7170... 58 F
rbmiller@pasadena.edu
MILLER, Robert, B .... 626-585-7178... 58 F
rbmiller@pasadena.edu
MILLER, Robert, G .... 901-333-4368. 461 F
rgmiller1@southwest.tn.edu
MILLER, Robert, H .... 225-771-5170. 206 J
rhmillerjr@aol.com
MILLER, Robert, H .... 216-368-6269. 375 J
robert.miller@case.edu
MILLER, Robert, L .... 217-581-7249. 144 E
rlmiller@eiu.edu
MILLER, Robert, R .... 540-828-5383. 502 J
rmiller@bridgewater.edu
MILLER, Rodney, E .... 706-419-1134. 123 F
rmiller@covenant.edu
MILLER, Rodney, E .... 316-978-3389. 191 F
rodney.miller@wichita.edu
MILLER, Roger .... 269-488-4257. 244 L
rmiller@kvcc.edu
MILLER, Roland, G .... 847-543-2551. 143 A
com624@clcillinois.edu
MILLER, Ross .... 973-642-3888. 299 D
rem@berkeleycollege.edu
MILLER, Roy .... 609-894-9311. 299 I
rmiller@bcc.edu
MILLER, Ruby .... 480-517-8152... 15 D
ruby.miller@riosalado.edu
MILLER, Rush, G .... 412-648-7747. 435 C
rgmiller@mail.pitt.edu
MILLER, Ruth .... 785-594-4530. 184 C
ruth.miller@bakeru.edu
MILLER, Ruth .... 650-306-3125... 64 B
miller@smccd.edu
MILLER, Sally .... 707-664-4444... 36 B
sally.miller@sonoma.edu
MILLER, Samira .... 323-822-9700... 69 J
samira.miller@touro.edu
MILLER, Samuel, T .... 229-928-1387. 126 D
sam.miller@gsw.edu
MILLER, Sandra .... 716-827-4348. 348 G
millers@trocaire.edu
MILLER, Sandra .... 973-720-2659. 308 I
millers@wpunj.edu
MILLER, Sarah .... 772-546-5534. 106 N
admissions@hsbc.edu
MILLER, Sarah, A .... 218-477-2968. 259 H
sarah.miller@mnstate.edu
MILLER, Scott .... 814-732-2460. 428 E
millerse@edinboro.edu
MILLER, Scott, D .... 304-829-7111. 526 D
smiller@bethanywv.edu
MILLER, Shametra .... 256-761-6415..... 7 F
skmiller@talladega.edu
MILLER, Shari, K .... 716-673-3438. 342 A
shari.miller@fredonia.edu
MILLER, Sharon .... 248-341-2131. 248 D
semiller@oaklandcc.edu
MILLER, Sharon .... 863-297-1093. 110 H
smiller@polk.edu
MILLER, Sharyne .... 201-612-5499. 299 C
smiller@bergen.edu
MILLER, Sherri .... 757-352-4843. 508 G
sstocks@regent.edu
MILLER, Stacey, A .... 802-656-3434. 500 F
stacey.miller@uvm.edu
MILLER, Stan, W .... 574-535-7515. 166 A
stanreg@goshen.edu
MILLER, Stephanie .... 417-328-1797. 282 C
smiller@sbuniv.edu
MILLER, Stephen .... 925-631-4970... 61 F
scmiller@stmarys-ca.edu
MILLER, Stephen .... 240-684-2037. 219 F
smiller@umuc.edu
MILLER, Steve .... 912-871-1801. 129 J
smiller@ogeecheetech.edu
MILLER, Steve .... 206-934-6075. 522 I
steve.miller@seattlecolleges.edu
MILLER, Steve, S .... 419-995-8457. 381 Q
miller.s@rhodesstate.edu
MILLER, Steve, T .... 573-629-3123. 274 J
smiller@hlg.edu
MILLER, Steven .... 303-963-3353... 79 C
stemiller@ccu.edu
MILLER, Stuart, C .... 626-395-6393... 31 E
scmiller@caltech.edu
MILLER, Susan .... 508-362-2131. 231 D
smiller@capecod.edu
MILLER, Susan .... 610-436-2442. 430 A
smiller2@wcupa.edu
MILLER, Susan, S .... 901-272-5152. 456 F
smiller@mca.edu
MILLER, Susan, T .... 219-785-5300. 172 A
smiller@pnc.edu
MILLER, Tamara, D .... 913-288-7136. 187 L
tmiller@kckcc.edu
MILLER, Tamsin .... 865-882-4730. 461 E
miller@roanestate.edu
MILLER, Tana, J .... 806-651-4911. 484 D
tmiller@mail.wtamu.edu
MILLER, Tara .... 641-648-4611. 179 I
tara.miller@iavalley.edu
MILLER, Terence .... 414-288-3208. 534 B
terence.miller@marquette.edu
MILLER, Terry, W .... 253-535-7674. 521 I
millertw@plu.edu
MILLER, Theresa .... 413-662-5106. 230 C
t.miller@mcla.edu
MILLER, Thomas .... 541-956-7147. 407 F
tmiller@roguecc.edu
MILLER, Thomas, D .... 812-877-8210. 172 C
thomas.miller@rose-hulman.edu
MILLER, Thomas, E .... 813-974-9084. 116 C
millert@usf.edu
MILLER, Thomas, I .... 270-809-3763. 198 B
tmiller@murraystate.edu
MILLER, Thomas, K .... 919-513-5006. 368 B
tkm@ncsu.edu
MILLER, Thomas, P .... 520-626-0202... 18 F
tpm@email.arizona.edu
MILLER, Tina .... 906-248-3354. 240 J
tinamiller@bmcc.edu
MILLER, Todd .... 908-852-1400. 300 D
millert02@centenarycollege.edu
MILLER, Tracy, L .... 330-471-8238. 383 D
tmiller@malone.edu
MILLER, Troy .... 516-686-7742. 333 H
tmille02@nyit.edu
MILLER, Troy .... 901-320-9700. 463 J
tmiller@victory.edu
MILLER, Tyrus .... 831-459-5079... 72 C
tyrus@ucsc.edu
MILLER, Valerie .... 740-593-4141. 387 C
millerv@ohio.edu
MILLER, Van .... 254-298-8456. 482 C
van.miller@templejc.edu
MILLER, Vernease .... 704-945-7313. 365 E
vernease.miller@fsmail.pfeiffer.edu
MILLER, Vince .... 208-282-1045. 138 E
millvince@isu.edu
MILLER, Walter .... 877-248-6724... 14 A
wmiller@hmu.edu
MILLER, Walter, C .... 505-277-2331. 312 F
wcmiller@unm.edu
MILLER, Wayne, C .... 614-947-6153. 380 A
wayne.miller@franklin.edu
MILLER, Wendy .... 847-214-7308. 144 F
wmiller@elgin.edu
MILLER, Will .... 904-819-6322. 103 E
wmiller@flagler.edu
MILLER, William .... 561-297-3165. 114 L
miller@fau.edu
MILLER, William, D .... 419-434-4605. 391 D
miller@findlay.edu
MILLER, William, L .... 724-287-8711. 411 C
william.miller@bc3.edu
MILLER-BOREN, Joyce ... 217-641-4528. 148 M
millerj@jwcc.edu
MILLER-HERNANDEZ,
Leangela .... 559-730-3795... 40 I
leangelam@cos.edu
MILLER HOLST, Sandra . 602-787-7668... 15 B
sandra.miller.holst@paradisevalley.edu
MILLER-KERMANI,
Donn .... 321-674-7648. 104 H
dkermani@fit.edu
MILLER-PARKER, Donna 206-934-6827. 523 A
donna.miller-parker@seattlecolleges.edu
MILLER-REID, M. Susan 925-631-4352... 61 F
msm9@stmarys-ca.edu
MILLER START, Roni ... 213-624-1200... 44 D
rmiller@fidm.edu
MILLER-SUBER,
Evelyn, V .... 516-463-6473. 326 D
evelyn.v.miller-suber@hofstra.edu
MILLER-YOW, Ronnie .... 501-370-5344... 22 F
miller-yow@philander.edu
MILLERICK, Frank, E ...... 774-354-0481. 223 A
frank.millerick@becker.edu
MILLERICK, Timothy, P .. 903-813-2228. 466 H
tmillerick@austincollege.edu
MILLET, Matthew, B .... 412-397-6406. 431 I
millet@rmu.edu
MILLET, Michelle .... 216-397-3053. 381 R
mmillet@jcu.edu
MILLET, Peter .... 205-366-8951..... 7 E
pmillet@stillman.edu
MILLETTE, Paul .... 802-287-8224. 499 D
millettep@greenmtn.edu
MILLETTE, Paulette .... 207-216-4342. 211 C
pmillette@yccc.edu
MILLHORN, David, E ..... 865-974-8913. 463 B
millhorn@tennessee.edu
MILLHORN, David, E ..... 865-974-4048. 463 B
millhorn@tennessee.edu
MILLICAN, Edward .... 909-384-8587... 62 A
emillica@sbccd.cc.ca.us
MILLICAN, Valorie, L ..... 816-654-7332. 275 K
vmillican@kcumb.edu
MILLIGAN, Laura .... 573-840-9607. 282 K
lmilligan@trcc.edu
MILLIGAN, Margaret, J .. 812-888-4277. 174 F
pmilligan@vinu.edu
MILLIGAN, Tom .... 970-491-6621... 80 I
tom.milligan@colostate.edue.edu
MILLIGAN, Troy .... 405-422-1206. 399 B
milligant@redlandscc.edu
MILLIGAN,
Yuri Rodgers .... 757-727-5253. 505 F
yuri.milligan@hamptonu.edu
MILLIKAN, Jessica .... 707-256-7205... 55 F
jmillikan@napavalley.edu
MILLIKEN, James, B ...... 402-472-8636. 292 G
president@nebraska.edu
MILLIKEN, Richard .... 402-935-9400. 290 N
rmilliken@nechristian.edu
MILLIKEN, Ronald, P ..... 207-778-7105. 212 D
milliken@maine.edu
MILLIKEN, Stephanie ...... 270-534-3394. 196 G
stephanie.milliken@kctcs.edu
MILLIKIN, Mary .... 918-343-7615. 399 C
mmillikin@rsu.edu
MILLIMAN, Nick .... 269-467-9945. 242 H
nmilliman@glenoaks.edu
MILLINGTON, Anne .... 919-735-5151. 364 H
annemill@waynecc.edu
MILLION, Christina, C ... 404-413-1430. 126 E
cmillion@gsu.edu
MILLIRONS, Anna, S ...... 540-985-8530. 506 G
asmillirons@jchs.edu
MILLIS, Jack .... 714-532-6049... 38 A
millis@chapman.edu
MILLMAN, Sheila, U .... 310-233-4321... 51 H
millmasu@lahc.edu
MILLNER, Timothy .... 410-225-4251. 216 C
tmillner@mica.edu
MILLNER, Vaughn, S ...... 251-460-6283..... 9 E
vmillner@southalabama.edu
MILLOY, Gretchen .... 651-255-6162. 264 C
gmilloy@unitedseminary.edu
MILLOY, Phyllis .... 757-822-1063. 514 C
pmilloy@tcc.edu
MILLS, Andrew .... 212-659-7200. 328 E
MILLS, Barry .... 207-725-3221. 209 H
bmills@bowdoin.edu
MILLS, Bernice .... 207-221-4314. 213 A
bmills@une.edu
MILLS, Brian .... 217-732-3168. 151 B
bmills@lincolnchristian.edu
MILLS, Chris .... 610-896-1039. 418 F
cmills@haverford.edu
MILLS, Crystal .... 717-290-8719. 421 D
cmills@lancasterseminary.edu
MILLS, Dan .... 616-222-1444. 241 F
dan.mills@cornerstone.edu
MILLS, David .... 937-766-7986. 375 K
millsd@cedarville.edu
MILLS, Dora .... 207-221-4621. 213 A
dmills2@une.edu
MILLS, Ed .... 785-890-3641. 189 H
emills@nwktc.edu
MILLS, Edward .... 916-278-6060... 34 D
emills@csus.edu
MILLS, Edward, D .... 912-478-1193. 126 C
edmills@georgiasouthern.edu
MILLS, F. Joe .... 931-221-7444. 459 B
millsj@apsu.edu
MILLS, Frank .... 340-693-1067. 555 E
fmills@live.uvi.edu
MILLS, JR., Gordon, E ... 251-460-7859..... 9 E
gmills@southalabama.edu
MILLS, Janie, A .... 319-368-6461. 181 C
jmills@mtmercy.edu
MILLS, Jessica, M .... 203-576-4506... 91 G
jemills@bridgeport.edu
MILLS, Jock, S .... 541-737-4514. 406 A
jock.mills@oregonstate.edu
MILLS, John .... 606-368-6121. 191 J
johnmills@alc.edu

MILLS, John, W .... 518-327-6223. 336 B
jmills@paulsmiths.edu

MILLS, Jonathan .... 415-575-6283... 31 D
jmills@ciis.edu

MILLS, Katherine .... 574-936-8898. 163 K
kathy.mills@ancilla.edu

MILLS, Kelly .... 863-638-7254. 119 C
kelly.mills@warner.edu

MILLS, Kevin .... 828-398-7200. 357 N
kevinsmills@abtech.edu

MILLS, Kim .... 307-754-6404. 543 G
Kim.Mills@northwestcollege.edu

MILLS, Laura, J .... 912-344-3073. 120 G
laura.mills@armstrong.edu

MILLS, Linda, G .... 212-998-9712. 334 D
linda.mills@nyu.edu

MILLS, Martha .... 530-741-6757... 77 M
mmills@yccd.edu

MILLS, Marvin .... 912-478-5558. 120 C
mmills@georgiasouthern.edu

MILLS, Matthew .... 912-650-6218. 131 H
mmills@southuniversity.edu

MILLS, Michael .... 918-631-2510. 401 F
michael-mills@utulsa.edu

MILLS, Michael .... 940-397-4428. 476 H
michael.mills@mwsu.edu

MILLS, Michael, E .... 847-491-4477. 155 D
michael-mills@northwestern.edu

MILLS, Nancy .... 914-633-2625. 327 C
nmills@iona.edu

MILLS, Nancy .... 320-308-4913. 261 B
nfmills@stcloudstate.edu

MILLS, Ossie .... 918-495-7312. 398 H
omills@oru.edu

MILLS, Patti .... 201-692-2132. 301 J
patti_mills@fdu.edu

MILLS, Patty .... 513-244-1646. 377 G
patty_mills@mail.msj.edu

MILLS, Priscilla, L .... 928-523-7855... 16 C
priscilla.mills@nau.edu

MILLS, R. Dean .... 573-882-6686. 283 C
millsr@missouri.edu

MILLS, Randy, W .... 336-750-2706. 370 A
millsrw@wssu.edu

MILLS, Sandra, M .... 513-487-3206. 325 G
smills@huc.edu

MILLS, Sandy .... 262-646-6508. 535 B
smills@nashotah.edu

MILLS, Susan .... 951-222-8000... 61 A

MILLS, Tom .... 405-382-9745. 399 I
t.mills@sscok.edu

MILLS, William, R .... 617-552-8661. 224 A
william.mills@bc.edu

MILLS WOOLSEY, Linda 585-567-9315. 326 F
lindamills.woolsey@houghton.edu

MILLSAP, Byron .... 405-325-5161. 401 B
bmillsap@ou.edu

MILLSAP, Pam .... 409-933-8192. 469 E
pmillsap@com.edu

MILLSAPPS, Michael ...... 970-339-6376... 78 C
michael.millsapps@aims.edu

MILLSAPS, Brooke .... 828-298-3325. 370 E
bmillsaps@warren-wilson.edu

MILLSAPS, John .... 404-962-3053. 134 A
john.millsaps@usg.edu

MILLSON-MARTULA,
Christopher, A .... 434-544-8204. 506 K
millsonmartula@lynchburg.edu

MILLSTONE, Linda, H .... 512-471-2437. 491 C
lindam@austin.utexas.edu

MILLUSH, Mary Ann ...... 630-942-2269. 142 G
millush@cod.edu

MILLWOOD, Kent, A ...... 864-231-2049. 441 B
kmillwood@andersonuniversity.edu

MILNARICH, Sarah ...... 361-354-2741. 468 K
sarahm@coastalbend.edu

MILNE, Sheila .... 252-399-6326. 352 F
smilne@barton.edu

MILNER, Eric .... 401-341-2218. 440 C
eric.milner@salve.edu

MILNER, Jocelyn, L .... 608-263-5658. 536 D
jlmilner@wisc.edu

MILNER, Wesley .... 812-488-2686. 173 H
wm23@evansville.edu

MILNES, Robert, W .... 940-565-4003. 490 C
milnes@unt.edu

MILON, Ronald .... 201-447-7125. 299 C
rmilon@bergen.edu

MILONE-NUZZO,
Paula, F .... 814-863-0245. 426 A
pxm36@psu.edu

MILROY, James, B .... 585-245-5601. 343 C
milroy@geneseo.edu

MILSO, Lisa .... 978-762-4000. 232 D
lmilso@northshore.edu

MILSOM, Penny .... 443-840-5426. 214 E
mmilsom@ccbcmd.edu

MILSTEIN, Marc .... 212-960-5233. 351 M
mmilstei@yu.edu

MILSTONE, David, M ..... 508-999-8640. 229 A
dmilstone@umassd.edu

MILTENBERGER, Susan . 410-225-2201. 216 C
smiltenb@mica.edu

MILTON, Alice .... 205-929-6306..... 5 D
amilton@lawsonstate.edu

MILTON, Barbara, J .... 973-655-4349. 303 D
miltonb@mail.montclair.edu

MILTON, Erika .... 337-948-0239. 204 C
erika.milton@solacc.edu

MILTON, Shirlette, G ...... 713-313-7551. 485 F
milton_sg@tsu.edu

MILTON, Suzanne .... 509-359-2333. 519 C
smilton@ewu.edu

MILZ, George .... 713-646-1864. 480 J
gmilz@stcl.edu

MIMMS, Jacqueline .... 661-654-2160... 32 H
jmimms@csub.edu

MIMMS, Lee, S .... 818-779-8040... 50 A
lmimms@kingsuniversity.edu

MIMS, Janet .... 843-863-8004. 441 H
jmims@csuniv.edu

MIMS, Jason .... 432-264-5008. 473 E
jmims@howardcollege.edu

MIMS, Lloyd .... 561-803-2400. 110 B
lloyd_mims@pba.edu

MIMS, Yolanda, L .... 504-286-5335. 206 K
ymims@suno.edu

MIN, Sangki .... 913-288-7686. 187 L
smin@kckcc.edu

MINAAI, Brian .... 808-956-7935. 135 L
bminaai@hawaii.edu

MINAR, Thomas .... 202-885-3424... 94 F
tjm@american.edu

MINARDI, Judy .... 617-573-8415. 237 B
jminardi@suffolk.edu

MINATOYA, Lydia .... 206-934-3712. 522 I
lydia.minatoya@seattlecolleges.edu

MINCH, Kevin .... 660-785-5384. 282 L
kminch@truman.edu

MINCHEFF, Chris .... 303-753-6046... 85 B
cmincheff@rmcad.edu

MINCHELLO, Brian .... 617-879-2205. 238 C
bminchello@wheelock.edu

MINCKLER, Tye .... 254-968-9877. 483 A
minckler@tarleton.edu

MINCKS, Kathy .... 907-564-8272... 10 C
kmincks.akpacprop@gci.net

MINDEMAN, Tad .... 706-419-1434. 123 F
mindeman@covenant.edu

MINDERMAN, James, W 812-888-4227. 174 F
jwminderman@vinu.edu

MINE, Jodi .... 808-934-2742. 136 F
mine@hawaii.edu

MINEHAN, Cathy .... 617-521-3806. 236 G
cathy.minehan@simmons.edu

MINEO, Michael .... 718-817-4931. 324 G
mineo@fordham.edu

MINER, Judy, C .... 650-949-7200... 44 N
minerjudy@fhda.edu

MINER, Madonne .... 801-626-6424. 497 D
madonneminer@weber.edu

MINER, Marlene, R .... 513-745-5660. 391 A
marlene.miner@uc.edu

MINER, R. Clinton .... 508-457-1313. 234 F
cminer@ngs.edu

MINERVINI, Ron .... 617-730-7222. 235 D
ron.minervini@newbury.edu

MINFORD, Joell .... 412-392-3422. 431 B
jminford@pointpark.edu

MING, Amanda .... 248-476-1122. 246 G
aming@mispp.edu

MINGEE, Sheila .... 217-709-0923. 150 E
smingee@lakeviewcol.edu

MINGENBACK, Mary ...... 620-341-5413. 186 D
mmingenb@emporia.edu

MINGLE, James, J .... 607-255-3903. 322 A
jjm19@cornell.edu

MINGO, Rhonda .... 864-596-9016. 443 D
rhonda.mingo@converse.edu

MINGO, Susan .... 207-454-1032. 211 B
smingo@wccc.me.edu

MINGO, Tracey, K .... 608-342-1836. 537 D
mingot@uwplatt.edu

MINHAS, Omer .... 419-772-2529. 386 D
o-minhas@onu.edu

MINI, Susan .... 815-753-0495. 154 I
smini@niu.edu

MINICK, Evelyn .... 610-660-1905. 432 E
minick@sju.edu

MINICK, Thomas .... 610-790-1901. 409 E
thomas.minick@alvernia.edu

MINICKIELLO, Maria, F .. 845-569-3634. 332 B
maria.minickiello@msmc.edu

MINIER-DELGADO,
Jesenia .... 718-289-5288. 317 B
jesenia.minier-delgado@bcc.cuny.edu

MINK, Randy, L .... 412-397-4901. 431 I
mink@rmu.edu

MINK, Rose .... 901-751-8453. 457 B
rmink@mabts.edu

MINK-SALAS, Kandy ...... 657-278-3211... 33 E
kmink@fullerton.edu

MINKIEWICZ,
Jennifer, V .... 216-221-8584. 392 G
jennifermink@vmcad.edu

MINKLER, James .... 509-533-3764. 518 F
jim.minkler@spokanefalls.edu

MINKLER, Jim .... 509-533-3764. 518 D
jimm@spokanefalls.edu

MINKLER, Steven .... 860-343-5706... 89 A
sminkler@mxcc.commnet.edu

MINKS, Larry .... 580-745-2500. 399 J
lminks@se.edu

MINNE, Erin .... 309-438-7681. 147 J
eminne@ilstu.edu

MINNER, Sam, H .... 540-831-5404. 508 C
sminner@radford.edu

MINNICH, Bryan, K .... 785-827-5541. 188 C
bryan.minnich@kwu.edu

MINNICH, Donna .... 973-596-3603. 303 G
donna.minnich@njit.edu

MINNICH, Peggy .... 513-244-4531. 377 G
peggy_minnich@mail.msj.edu

MINNICH, Thomas .... 304-734-6699. 527 O
tminnich@bridgemont.edu

MINNICK, Ann, M .... 651-696-6036. 256 L
aminnick@macalester.edu

MINNICK, Susan .... 262-691-5392. 541 D
sminnick@wctc.edu

MINNICK, William, C ..... 712-707-7226. 181 H
bminnick@nwciowa.edu

MINNIEFIELD, Angela, L 323-563-4897... 38 B
angelaminniefield@cdrewu.edu

MINNIS, Phil .... 618-985-3741. 148 J
philminnis@jalc.edu

MINNIS, Sarah, L .... 919-536-7200. 360 B
minniss@durhamtech.edu

MINNIS, Stephen, D .... 913-360-7400. 184 H
sminnis@benedictine.edu

MINNITI, Lea .... 513-745-2872. 393 H
minnitil@xavier.edu

MINNIX, Roy .... 914-337-9300. 321 E
roy.minnix@concordia-ny.edu

MINOR, Diana, Y .... 909-869-3704... 32 G
dyminor@csupomona.edu

MINOR, Diane .... 312-553-2500. 141 M
dminor1@ccc.edu

MINOR, Frankie, D .... 573-882-7275. 283 C
minorf@missouri.edu

MINOR, Karen .... 770-531-6347. 128 B
kminor@laniertech.edu

MINOR, Lloyd .... 650-723-2300... 68 E
lminor@stanford.edu

MINOR, Lottie .... 901-369-0835... 96 F
lottie.minor@strayer.edu

MINOR, Scott .... 916-631-8108... 32 C

MINOR, Tamra .... 518-956-8110. 341 D
tminor@albany.edu

MINOW, Martha .... 617-495-4601. 227 C
minow@law.harvard.edu

MINTEN, Sam, L .... 615-868-6503. 457 D
sam@mtsa.edu

MINTER, Doug .... 309-268-8385. 146 B
doug.minter@heartland.edu

MINTER, Doug, O .... 507-933-7527. 255 I
dminter@gustavus.edu

MINTER, Michelle .... 609-258-6110. 304 E
mminter@princeton.edu

MINTER, Penny .... 731-426-7550. 455 J
pminter@lanecollege.edu

MINTERN, Janet .... 252-493-7286. 362 G
jmintern@email.pittcc.edu

MINTON, Randy, F .... 912-583-3109. 122 B
rminton@bpc.edu

MINUS, Daryl .... 252-638-7200. 359 G
minusd@cravencc.edu

MINUS, Molly, E .... 512-448-8581. 479 C
mollym@stedwards.edu

MIRABAL, Larry .... 505-424-2316. 309 J
lmirabal@iaia.edu

MIRABAL-RIVERA,
Gloria .... 787-480-2355. 548 G
gmirabal@sanjuancapital.com

MIRABILE, Kathleen .... 800-231-3803... 12 D

MIRABILE, Kathleen .... 602-212-0501... 16 K
kmirabile@theparalegalinstitute.edu

MIRABITO, Michael .... 570-348-6209. 423 B
mirabito@marywood.edu

MIRACKY, SJ, James, F 410-617-2327. 216 A
jjmiracky@loyola.edu

MIRACLE, William, D ..... 540-828-5380. 502 J
wmiracle@bridgewater.edu

MIRAGLIA, Gregory .... 707-256-3035... 55 F
gmiraglia@napavalley.edu

MIRANDA, Albert .... 714-484-7394... 56 E
amiranda@cypresscollege.edu

MIRANDA, Candida .... 312-567-3134. 147 F
miranda@iit.edu

MIRANDA, Carmen, A .... 787-850-9375. 554 D
carmen.miranda1@upr.edu

MIRANDA, Deana .... 312-935-6657. 156 K
dmiranda@robertmorris.edu

MIRANDA,
Edmund (Rick) .... 562-860-2451... 37 I
ermiranda@cerritos.edu

MIRANDA, Elizabeth .... 787-250-1912. 550 E
emiranda@metro.inter.edu

MIRANDA, Enid .... 787-841-2000. 552 B
emiranda@pucpr.edu

MIRANDA, Gloria .... 310-660-3735... 43 B
gmiranda@elcamino.edu

MIRANDA, Marie, L .... 734-764-2550. 251 C
mlmirand@umich.edu

MIRANDA, Mark .... 732-571-3593. 303 C
mmiranda@monmouth.edu

MIRANDA, Nelson .... 787-738-2161. 554 C
nelson.miranda1@upr.edu

MIRANDA, Paul .... 718-429-6600. 349 H
paul.miranda@vaughn.edu

MIRANDA, Rick .... 970-491-6614... 80 H
rick.miranda@colostate.edu

MIRANDA, Rick .... 970-491-6614... 80 I
rick.miranda@colostate.edu

MIRANDA, Robert .... 714-992-7090... 56 F
bmiranda@fullcoll.edu

MIRANDA, Rowan, A ...... 734-764-7270. 251 C
rowanm@umich.edu

MIRANDA RIVERA,
Carmen, A .... 787-850-0000. 553 G
rectora.uprh@upr.edu

MIRANTE, Aida .... 401-341-2140. 440 C
mirantea@salve.edu

MIRCH, Mary .... 818-240-1000... 45 G
mmirch@glendale.edu

MIRECKI, Julie .... 920-693-1193. 540 B
julie.mirecki@gotoltc.edu

MIRELES, Rod .... 936-261-1905. 482 F
rmireles@pvamu.edu

MIRENDA, Rosalie, M .... 610-558-5501. 424 I
rmirenda@neumann.edu

MIRES, Mike .... 208-769-7783. 138 I

MIRIZZI, Ray .... 859-572-6421. 198 I
mirizzir1@nku.edu

MIRMIRAN, Amir .... 305-348-2522. 115 B
amir.mirmiran@fiu.edu

MIROCHA, Ken .... 563-441-4116. 178 C
kmirocha@eicc.edu

MIROTZNIK, Jerrold .... 718-951-5024. 317 C
jerrym@brooklyn.cuny.edu

MIRRO, Roberta .... 631-249-3048. 346 B
sm711/bncollege@bncollege.com

MIRSHAB, Bahman .... 248-204-3050. 245 I
bmirshab@ltu.edu

MIRUS, Tarrah .... 229-430-4638. 119 J
tarrah.mirus@asurams.edu

MIRZA, Zoaib .... 312-662-4233. 139 F
zmirza@adler.edu

MISAK, M. David .... 580-774-3275. 400 B
david.misak@swosu.edu

MISANTONE, Louis .... 781-762-1211. 226 E
drlou@fine-ne.com

MISCAVAGE, Denise .... 570-674-6248. 424 A
dmiscava@misericordia.edu

MISCH, Donald .... 303-492-0025... 85 L
donald.misch@colorado.edu

MISCHE, Jenny .... 816-331-5700. 280 D
jmische@pcitraining.edu

MISCHE, Terri .... 320-308-6675. 261 B
tamische@stcloudstate.edu

MISCHKE, Joel, P .... 414-443-8812. 539 F
joel.mischke@wlc.edu

MISCHKE, Trevor .... 402-972-4250. 450 G
tmischke@national.edu

MISERENDINO, Peter ..... 203-287-3026... 90 H
paier.admin@snet.net

MISGEN, Sherry .... 312-899-5216. 158 L
smisgen@saic.edu

MISHEK, Mark .... 651-213-4006. 256 B
mmishek@hazelden.edu

MISHLER, Brent .... 989-386-6622. 247 B
bmishler@midmich.edu

MISHLER, Jeremy .... 231-591-2345. 242 F
mishlerj@ferris.edu

MISHLER, Richard .... 814-886-6339. 424 G
RMishler@mtaloy.edu

MISHOE, Cindy .... 410-287-6060. 214 B
cmishoe@cecil.edu

MISHOE, Shelley, C .... 757-683-4960. 507 N
smishoe@odu.edu

MISHRA, Sharda, D .... 615-327-6156. 456 E
smishra@mmc.edu

MISHRA, Tara .... 479-788-7002... 24 A
tara.mishra@uafs.edu

MISIANO, Chris .... 434-592-3144. 506 I
cjmisiano@liberty.edu

MISKELL, Jane .... 305-273-4499. 100 H
jane.miskell@cbt.edu

MISKO, Elaine, J .... 412-578-6137. 412 G
miskoej@carlow.edu

MISKOVIC, Linda .... 714-628-4901... 60 H
miskovic_linda@sccollege.edu

MISKUS, Lynn .... 219-473-4310. 164 K
lmiskus@ccsj.edu

MISKY, Allison .... 860-727-2117... 90 A
amisky@goodwin.edu
MISNER, John .... 706-778-8500. 130 E
jmisner@piedmont.edu
MISNER, John .... 706-776-0115. 130 E
jmisner@piedmont.edu
MISRA, Hara, P .... 540-231-4000. 504 G
MISRA, Kalpana .... 918-631-2547. 401 F
kalpana-misra@utulsa.edu
MISRA, Ravi, P .... 414-955-8778. 534 C
rmisra@mcw.edu
MISS, Stephen .... 704-461-6802. 352 G
StephenMiss@bac.edu
MISSAKIAN, Anais .... 401-454-6184. 440 A
amissaki@risd.edu
MISSEL, Chris .... 912-588-2580. 120 B
cmissel@altamahatech.edu
MISSELL, Katherine .... 619-260-4551... 73 I
kmissell@sandiego.edu
MISSURELLI, David, S ... 630-637-5680. 154 F
dsmissurelli@noctrl.edu
MISTICK, Barbara, K .... 717-262-2000. 437 H
barbara.mistick@wilson.edu
MISTO, RSM, Leona .... 401-341-2229. 440 C
mistol@salve.edu
MITCHAM, Aaron .... 412-396-5098. 415 F
mitchama@duq.edu
MITCHAM, Larry, G .... 678-359-5059. 127 A
larrym@gordonstate.edu
MITCHELL, Alan .... 256-331-5362..... 6 A
mitchell@nwscc.edu
MITCHELL, Amanda .... 706-754-7724. 129 G
amitchell@northgatech.edu
MITCHELL, Andrea .... 954-783-7339. 102 M
amitchell@cci.edu
MITCHELL, Audrey .... 256-765-4124..... 9 C
admitchell@una.edu
MITCHELL, Bede .... 912-478-5116. 126 C
wbmitch@georgiasouthern.edu
MITCHELL, Beth .... 828-766-1301. 361 H
bmitchell@mayland.edu
MITCHELL, Betsy .... 626-395-6148... 31 E
betsy.mitchell@caltech.edu
MITCHELL, Bonnie .... 508-626-4651. 230 A
bmitchell@framingham.edu
MITCHELL, Bradley, J ..... 937-382-6661. 393 B
brad_mitchell@wilmington.edu
MITCHELL, Brenda .... 479-788-7519... 24 A
brenda.mitchell@uafs.edu
MITCHELL, Brenda, S ..... 301-322-0858. 217 F
bmitchell@pgcc.edu
MITCHELL, Brian, S .... 504-865-5261. 207 C
brian@tulane.edu
MITCHELL, Brian, S .... 504-314-2818. 207 C
brian@tulane.edu
MITCHELL, Bryan .... 404-756-4025. 121 A
bmitchell@atlm.edu
MITCHELL, Carl .... 910-678-8373. 360 D
mitchelc@faytechcc.edu
MITCHELL, Cassandra .... 919-719-8880. 366 E
c.mitchell@shawu.edu
MITCHELL, Cathryn .... 912-538-3101. 132 A
cmitchell@southeasterntech.edu
MITCHELL, Cathy .... 806-894-9611. 480 H
cmitchell@southplainscollege.edu
MITCHELL, Charles .... 607-735-1937. 323 H
cmitchell@elmira.edu
MITCHELL, Chase .... 435-283-7340. 498 A
chase.mitchell@snow.edu
MITCHELL, Chris .... 501-205-8919... 20 I
cmitchell@cbc.edu
MITCHELL, Chrisie .... 845-431-8976. 323 C
chrisie.mitchell@sunydutchess.edu
MITCHELL, Connie .... 803-754-4100. 443 C
MITCHELL, Darren .... 815-753-9679. 154 I
dmitchell@niu.edu
MITCHELL, David .... 415-503-6218... 62 H
dlmitchell@sfcm.edu
MITCHELL, David, B .... 301-405-5726. 219 B
chief@umpd.umd.edu
MITCHELL, David, C .... 360-475-7100. 521 H
dmitchell@olympic.edu
MITCHELL, Dawn, P .... 336-734-7207. 360 E
dmitchell@forsythtech.edu
MITCHELL, Debbie .... 760-921-5408... 58 C
dmitchell@paloverde.edu
MITCHELL, Debbie .... 734-432-4076. 246 B
doffman@madonna.edu
MITCHELL, Denise .... 843-953-5822. 443 A
mitchellda@cofc.edu
MITCHELL, Don .... 602-386-4183... 11 G
don.mitchell@arizonachristian.edu
MITCHELL, Donald .... 217-206-6690. 161 E
mitchell.donald@uis.edu
MITCHELL, Donna .... 740-245-7302. 392 A
mitchell@rio.edu
MITCHELL, Douglas .... 951-827-5802... 71 E
douglas.mitchell@ucr.edu
MITCHELL, III,
Earnest, L .... 731-426-7604. 455 J
ernest@lanecollege.edu

MITCHELL, Emanuel .... 770-537-6065. 134 H
emanuel.mitchell@westgatech.edu
MITCHELL, IV, Enzley .... 312-567-7124. 147 F
emitche2@iit.edu
MITCHELL, Eyvon .... 678-891-2784. 125 G
eyvon.mitchell@gpc.edu
MITCHELL, Franklin, L .... 864-488-8239. 444 L
fmitchell@limestone.edu
MITCHELL, Gary .... 575-763-0535. 494 F
mitchellg@wbu.edu
MITCHELL, Geoffrey .... 601-984-1115. 270 C
gmitchell@umc.edu
MITCHELL, Gerald, A ...... 919-866-5143. 364 G
gamitchell@waketech.edu
MITCHELL, Gregory .... 843-477-2032. 444 F
greg.mitchell@hgtc.edu
MITCHELL, Gregory .... 903-886-5719. 483 E
gregory.mitchell@tamuc.edu
MITCHELL, Horace .... 661-654-2241... 32 H
hmitchell@csub.edu
MITCHELL, James .... 212-678-4084. 347 G
jm331@tc.columbia.edu
MITCHELL, James, M ..... 334-876-9231..... 4 A
jmitchell@wccs.edu
MITCHELL, Jeff .... 319-398-4983. 180 J
jmitche@kirkwood.edu
MITCHELL, Jennifer, E .... 757-455-8785. 515 H
jemitchell@vwc.edu
MITCHELL, Joan .... 801-274-3280. 498 E
jmitchell@wgu.edu
MITCHELL, Joann .... 215-898-6630. 435 B
joannm@upenn.edu
MITCHELL, John .... 912-344-2529. 120 G
john.mitchell@armstrong.edu
MITCHELL, Johnica .... 704-437-6808. 121 D
jmitchel@augustatech.edu
MITCHELL, Judy .... 815-280-6640. 149 A
jmitchel@jjc.edu
MITCHELL, Karen .... 615-230-3505. 461 G
karen.mitchell@volstate.edu
MITCHELL, Kathy, J .... 276-739-2440. 514 D
kmitchell@vhcc.edu
MITCHELL, Kemper .... 650-433-3835... 58 B
kmitchell@paloaltou.edu
MITCHELL, Ken, H .... 919-209-2112. 361 E
khmitchell@johnstoncc.edu
MITCHELL, Kent, H .... 781-280-3571. 232 B
mitchellk@middlesex.mass.edu
MITCHELL, Kerrie .... 575-492-2560. 310 G
kmitchell@nmjc.edu
MITCHELL, Kim .... 502-456-6508. 199 G
kmitchell@sullivan.edu
MITCHELL, Larry, K .... 252-451-8224. 362 D
lkm@nashcc.edu
MITCHELL, Lawrence, E .. 216-368-3283. 375 J
lawrence.e.mitchell@case.edu
MITCHELL, Lorraine, C ... 252-862-1272. 363 A
lcmitchell@roanokechowan.edu
MITCHELL, Lynn .... 215-884-8942. 438 A
academicdean@woninstitute.edu
MITCHELL, M. Ellen .... 312-567-3362. 147 F
mitchelle@iit.edu
MITCHELL, Margaret .... 773-702-8221. 161 B
mmm17@uchicago.edu
MITCHELL, Maria .... 610-372-4721. 431 D
mmitchell@racc.edu
MITCHELL, Marionette .... 713-525-3120. 490 L
marion@stthom.edu
MITCHELL, Mary Lou ..... 619-239-0391... 36 D
mmitchell@cwsl.edu
MITCHELL, Matt .... 573-592-5301. 285 B
matt.mitchell@westminster-mo.edu
MITCHELL, Melissa .... 308-432-6221. 291 D
mmitchell@csc.edu
MITCHELL, Michael .... 405-425-5065. 397 D
michael.mitchell@oc.edu
MITCHELL, Monique .... 252-862-1262. 363 A
mitchellm@roanokechowan.edu
MITCHELL, Nancy, L .... 509-527-5168. 525 E
mitchenl@whitman.edu
MITCHELL, Natalie .... 703-284-6861. 507 B
natalie.mitchell@marymount.edu
MITCHELL, Patrice .... 843-574-6010. 447 E
patrice.mitchell@tridenttech.edu
MITCHELL, Patrice, B ..... 912-344-2590. 120 G
patrice.mitchell@armstrong.edu
MITCHELL, Patricia .... 301-860-3416. 220 A
pmitchell@bowiestate.edu
MITCHELL, Patricia .... 601-979-2282. 267 E
patricia.b.mitchell@jsums.edu
MITCHELL, Paula .... 915-831-4030. 472 B
pmitche8@epcc.edu
MITCHELL, Peg, P .... 302-356-6810... 94 E
peg.p.mitchell@wilmu.edu
MITCHELL, Randolph .... 904-470-8150. 102 A
randolph.mitchell@ewc.edu
MITCHELL, Renee, D ...... 773-995-2040. 141 J
rmitch26@csu.edu
MITCHELL, Rick, L .... 330-287-1277. 386 F
mitchell.246@osu.edu

MITCHELL, Robert .... 504-816-4864. 201 K
rmitchell@dillard.edu
MITCHELL, Robert .... 502-456-6509. 199 F
rmitchell@sctd.edu
MITCHELL, Robin .... 563-288-6103. 178 B
rmitchell@eicc.edu
MITCHELL, Ronald, S ..... 417-625-9531. 278 D
mitchell-r@mssu.edu
MITCHELL, Rose .... 973-748-9000. 299 F
rose_mitchell@bloomfield.edu
MITCHELL, Rose .... 815-802-8110. 149 C
rmitchell@kcc.edu
MITCHELL, Sandra, L ..... 303-964-5304... 84 M
smitchell@regis.edu
MITCHELL, Saralyn .... 256-233-8146..... 1 F
saralyn.mitchell@athens.edu
MITCHELL, Sharon, L ..... 716-645-2720. 341 F
smitch@buffalo.edu
MITCHELL, Sheila .... 731-661-5953. 462 F
smitchell@uu.edu
MITCHELL, Stephen .... 845-434-5750. 347 A
smitchell@sullivan.suny.edu
MITCHELL, Stephen, R .... 202-687-3922... 95 E
mitchelr@georgetown.edu
MITCHELL, Steve .... 225-216-8404. 202 H
mitchells@mybrcc.edu
MITCHELL, Tedd .... 806-743-2900. 487 E
tedd.mitchell@ttuhsc.edu
MITCHELL, Tee .... 678-407-5880. 125 B
rmitche1@ggc.edu
MITCHELL, Thomas .... 401-397-3302. 440 D
mitchell@uri.edu
MITCHELL, Thomas, J .... 352-392-5407. 116 A
tmitchell@uff.ufl.edu
MITCHELL, Thomas, R .... 956-326-2460. 483 B
tmitchell@tamiu.edu
MITCHELL, Todd .... 270-534-3256. 196 G
todd.mitchell@kctcs.edu
MITCHELL, Tucker .... 843-661-1225. 444 B
tmitchell@fmarion.edu
MITCHELL, Venita .... 573-592-4239. 285 D
vmitchel@williamwoods.edu
MITCHELL, William .... 508-588-9100. 232 A
MITCHELL-CRUMP,
Pamela .... 860-512-2605... 88 G
pmitchell-crump@manchestercc.edu
MITCHELSON, Ron .... 252-328-9471. 367 B
mitchelsonr@ecu.edu
MITCHLEY, Jill .... 570-484-2526. 429 B
jmitchle@lhup.edu
MITCHUM, Lori, A .... 270-809-2596. 198 B
lori.mitchum@murraystate.edu
MITJANS, Dolores .... 787-882-2065. 553 A
compras@unitecpr.net
MITRA, Brian .... 718-368-5115. 318 E
bmitra@kbcc.cuny.edu
MITSUI, Mark .... 206-934-3601. 522 H
mark.mitsui@seattlecolleges.edu
MITTA, Ave, M .... 540-985-4097. 506 G
ammitta@jchs.edu
MITTELHAMMER,
Ronald .... 509-335-4561. 525 A
mittelha@wsu.edu
MITTELMEIER, Ashley, E 304-457-6323. 526 A
mittelmeierae@ab.edu
MITTELSTAEDT, John ..... 732-571-3400. 543 I
MITTEN, Edeline .... 718-270-2422. 342 D
emitten@downstate.edu
MITTERNDORFER,
Sylvia .... 757-221-3595. 503 N
smmitt@wm.edu
MITTLEMAN, Michael, H 215-780-1280. 433 A
president@salus.edu
MITTLESTEAD, Eric .... 559-730-3908... 40 I
ericm@cos.edu
MITTMAN, Paul, A .... 480-858-9100... 17 P
p.mittman@scnm.edu
MITTON, Gregory, S .... 484-664-3175. 424 H
mitton@muhlenberg.edu
MITTUCH, Maggie, A ...... 253-879-3673. 524 F
mmittuch@pugetsound.edu
MITZE, Marne, D .... 310-506-4451... 58 H
marne.mitze@pepperdine.edu
MITZEL, Thomas .... 860-297-2130... 91 F
thomas.mitzel@trincoll.edu
MIX, Kerry .... 281-998-6150. 479 H
kerry.mix@sjcd.edu
MIXNER, Mark, P .... 610-436-2731. 430 A
mmixner@wcupa.edu
MIXON, Bill .... 205-853-1200..... 5 B
bmixon@jeffstateonline.com
MIXON, Janine .... 415-442-7284... 45 I
jmixon@ggu.edu
MIXON, Margie .... 318-345-9270. 203 C
margiemixon@ladelta.edu
MIXTER, John .... 401-341-2334. 440 C
mixterj@salve.edu
MIYAMOTO, Michael, H . 563-589-3270. 182 J
mmiyamoto@dbq.edu
MIYAMOTO, Norma .... 760-744-1150... 58 D
nmiyamoto@palomar.edu

MIYARES, Javier .... 301-985-7077. 219 F
president-office@umuc.edu
MIYASAKI, Kevin, T .... 208-496-1155. 137 H
miyasakik@byui.edu
MIYASHIRO, Ross .... 562-938-4130... 51 D
rmiyashiro@lbcc.edu
MIZE, Charles .... 478-301-2951. 128 H
mize_c@mercer.edu
MIZE, Kyle, C .... 325-649-8049. 473 F
kmize@hputx.edu
MIZE, Lewis .... 620-227-9376. 186 B
lmize@dc3.edu
MIZE, Matt .... 478-445-5771. 125 A
matt.mize@gcsu.edu
MIZE, Nancy .... 252-328-6387. 367 B
mizen@ecu.edu
MIZELL, Catherine, S ..... 865-974-3245. 463 B
cmizell@tennessee.edu
MIZELL, Paul .... 912-871-1645. 129 J
pmizell@ogeecheetech.edu
MIZELLE, Angela, J .... 919-866-5825. 364 G
ajmizelle@waketech.edu
MIZEN, Al .... 317-931-3324. 165 B
amizen@cts.edu
MIZERA, Peter, J .... 708-235-2210. 145 F
pmizera@govst.edu
MLADENOVIC, Jeanette .. 503-494-4460. 405 I
provost@ohsu.edu
MLODZIK, Leigh, D .... 920-748-8704. 535 J
mlodzikl@ripon.edu
MMEJE, Kenechukwu ..... 773-508-8840. 151 H
kmmeje@luc.edu
MNCUBE-BARNES,
Fatima .... 615-327-5770. 456 E
fbarnes@mmc.edu
MOAK, JR., James, A .... 502-863-7970. 194 C
james_moak@georgetowncollege.edu
MOATS, Nancy, I .... 405-224-3140. 401 E
nmoats@usao.edu
MOATS, Scott .... 952-446-4210. 255 D
moatss@crown.edu
MOBASSERI, Maria .... 217-403-4599. 155 J
mmobasseri@parkland.edu
MOBBS, Kevin .... 912-279-4505. 123 B
kmobbs@ccga.edu
MOBERG, Bret .... 847-578-8308. 157 F
bret.moberg@rosalindfranklin.edu
MOBERG, Kathleen .... 408-864-8292... 44 M
mobergkathleen@deanza.edu
MOBLEY, Bob .... 863-638-7213. 119 C
bob.mobley@warner.edu
MOBLEY, Cathryn .... 434-832-7635. 512 A
mobleyc@cvcc.vccs.edu
MOBLEY, Cedric .... 410-225-2343. 216 C
cmobley@mica.edu
MOBLEY, Cheryl .... 601-925-3310. 268 A
cmobley@mc.edu
MOBLEY, Karen .... 912-871-1638. 129 J
kmobley@ogeecheetech.edu
MOBLEY, Marilyn, S .... 216-368-8877. 375 J
marilyn.mobley@case.edu
MOBLEY, Ralph .... 404-894-3754. 125 D
ralph.mobley@success.gatech.edu
MOBLEY, Wanda .... 336-517-2267. 352 H
wmobley@bennett.edu
MOBLEY-SMITH, Miriam 773-821-2589. 141 J
msmith56@csu.edu
MOCABEE, Norma .... 626-815-4550... 29 H
nmocabee@apu.edu
MOCARSKY, Michelle ..... 215-248-7036. 413 A
mocarskym@chc.edu
MOCCIA, Mario, L .... 618-453-7250. 159 G
mmoccia@siu.edu
MOCK, Ashley .... 229-391-5055. 119 H
amock@abac.edu
MOCK, Diana .... 559-453-5505... 45 D
dbmock@fresno.edu
MOCK, Gerald, L .... 772-462-7315. 106 P
gmock@irsc.edu
MOCK, Keith .... 334-386-7876..... 3 H
kmock@faulkner.edu
MOCK, Kelly .... 314-529-9579. 276 G
kmock@maryville.edu
MOCK, Raymond, F .... 513-529-6023. 384 G
mockrf@miamioh.edu
MOCK, JR., Robert, C .... 859-257-1911. 200 C
robert.mock@uky.edu
MOCNIK, Joe .... 478-445-0980. 125 A
joe.mocnik@gcsu.edu
MODELANE, Dan .... 508-541-1614. 225 F
dmodelane@dean.edu
MODENE, Kathleen, R .... 314-991-6229. 141 G
kmodene@chamberlain.edu
MODENSTEIN, Susan ..... 212-592-2000. 340 H
smodenstein@sva.edu
MODERSOHN, Ellen, E .. 563-387-1350. 180 M
ellen.modersohn@luther.edu
MODESTOU, Jennifer, A . 319-335-0705. 175 I
jennifer-modestou@uiowa.edu
MODICA, Joseph, B .... 610-341-5826. 415 G
jmodica@eastern.edu

MODICA-NAPOLITANO, Josephine .... 978-837-5115. 234 A
josephine.modicanapolitano@merrimack.edu
MODIG, James, E .... 785-864-3431. 190 L
jmodig@ku.edu
MODLIN, Andrew .... 540-887-7260. 507 A
amodlin@mbc.edu
MODLIN, Jason, E .... 919-497-3210. 356 E
jmodlin@louisburg.edu
MODRCIN, Mary Anne ... 423-869-6319. 456 A
maryanne.modrcin@lmunet.edu
MODRZAKOWSKI, Malcolm .... 304-647-6302. 530 B
mmodrzakowski@osteo.wvsom.edu
MOE, Marie .... 701-483-2560. 371 D
Marie.Moe@dickinsonstate.edu
MOE, Peggy .... 425-235-2285. 522 F
pmoe@rtc.edu
MOE, Warren .... 503-654-8000. 407 B
wmoe@pioneerpacific.edu
MOEDER, Lawrence, E ... 785-532-6250. 188 A
larrym@ksu.edu
MOEDER, Lawrence, E ... 785-532-6420. 188 A
larrym@ksu.edu
MOEGENBURG, Stacey .. 845-341-4286. 335 H
stacey.moegenburg@sunyorange.edu
MOEGGENBERG, Richard .... 517-437-7341. 243 I
richard.moeggenberg@hillsdale.edu
MOEGLIN, Maureen .... 402-457-2236. 290 G
mmoeglin@mccneb.edu
MOELLER, Bret .... 617-228-2293. 231 C
bmoeller@bhcc.mass.edu
MOELLER, Darin .... 712-274-6400. 183 G
darin.moeller@witcc.edu
MOELLER, Ginger .... 605-668-1566. 450 F
ginger.moeller@mtmc.edu
MOEN, Matthew, C .... 605-677-5221. 451 F
matthew.moen@usd.edu
MOEN, Stuart .... 281-873-0262. 469 H
s.moen@commonwealth.edu
MOENKHAUS, Kevin, P .. 515-271-3902. 177 K
kevin.moenkhaus@drake.edu
MOERLAND, Timothy, S 724-357-2219. 428 F
tim.moerland@iup.edu
MOERSCHBAECHER, Joseph, M .... 504-568-4804. 205 C
jmoers@lsuhsc.edu
MOESER, James .... 336-770-3200. 369 D
moeserj@uncsa.edu
MOESSNER, Phillip .... 208-282-4229. 138 E
moesphil@isu.edu
MOEZ, Chrystal .... 262-619-6830. 540 A
moezc@gtc.edu
MOFFAT, Heather .... 812-888-4120. 174 F
hmoffat@vinu.edu
MOFFATT, Tammy, L .... 603-646-2846. 296 G
tammy.l.moffatt@dartmouth.edu
MOFFETT, Danielle .... 575-538-6675. 312 N
moffettd@wnmu.edu
MOFFETT, Rafael .... 405-466-3446. 395 N
rmoffett@langston.edu
MOFFITT, Clinton .... 559-278-3902... 33 D
clinton_moffitt@csufresno.edu
MOFFITT, Jamie, H .... 541-346-3003. 406 D
jmoffitt@uoregon.edu
MOFFITT, Lisa .... 615-327-3927. 455 F
moffitt@guptoncollege.edu
MOFFITT, Michael .... 765-677-2201. 169 B
michael.moffitt@indwes.edu
MOFFITT, Michael, L ...... 541-346-3836. 406 D
mmoffitt@uoregon.edu
MOFFITT, Thomas, J ...... 610-566-1776. 437 G
tmoffitt@williamson.edu
MOGCK, Steven, A .... 312-329-4131. 153 E
steve.mogck@moody.edu
MOGFORD, Jon .... 979-458-5598. 482 E
JMogford@tamus.edu
MOHAJIR, Terry .... 870-972-3880... 19 N
tmohajir@astate.edu
MOHAMADIAN, Habib, P .... 225-771-5290. 206 J
mohamad@engr.subr.edu
MOHAMED, Carol, W ..... 412-648-7861. 435 C
pauca5@pitt.edu
MOHAMMADI, Aghajan . 718-262-2333. 319 F
aghajan@york.cuny.edu
MOHAMMADI, Amir .... 302-857-6200... 93 C
amohammadi@desu.edu
MOHAMMADI, Rameen .. 315-312-2232. 344 A
rameen.mohammadi@oswego.edu
MOHAMMED, Abdul, K .. 919-530-7082. 368 A
amohammed@nccu.edu
MOHANTY, Bidhu, D ...... 757-823-8005. 507 M
bbmohanty@nsu.edu
MOHAR, Gregory, D .... 513-556-3483. 390 G
gregory.mohar@uc.edu
MOHDZAIN, Zaidy .... 870-235-4057... 23 F
azmohdzain@saumag.edu
MOHIYEDDINI, Sohila ... 714-533-1495... 66 H
soh@southbaylo.edu
MOHLER, JR., R. Albert . 502-897-4121. 199 B
mohler@sbts.edu
MOHLER-FARIA, Dana ... 508-531-1201. 229 D
dmohlerfaria@bridgew.edu
MOHN, Kate .... 612-874-3737. 257 B
kmohn@mcad.edu
MOHNEY, Len .... 661-362-3207... 40 E
len.mohney@canyons.edu
MOHNING, David, D ...... 615-343-5931. 463 G
d.mohning@vanderbilt.edu
MOHR, James .... 360-475-7230. 521 H
jmohr@olympic.edu
MOHR, James, R .... 724-946-7115. 437 B
mohrjr@westminister.edu
MOHR, Jean Marie .... 845-398-4106. 340 A
jmohr@stac.edu
MOHR, Joan, I .... 203-582-8959... 91 A
joan.isaacmohr@quinnipiac.edu
MOHR, Karl, F .... 530-752-2063... 70 J
kfmohr@ucdavis.edu
MOHR, Rick .... 937-529-2201. 390 D
mohr@united.edu
MOHR, Sharon .... 763-488-2525. 258 F
sharon.mohr@hennepintech.edu
MOHR, Terry .... 910-755-8517. 358 D
mohrt@brunswickcc.edu
MOHR, Thomas .... 303-373-2008... 85 C
tmohr@rvu.edu
MOHR, Wayne, C .... 570-389-4303. 427 H
wmohr@bloomu.edu
MOHRBACHER, Bob .... 509-793-2055. 517 C
Bobm@bigbend.edu
MOHRBUTTER, Trent, L . 252-451-8336. 362 D
tlmohrbutter@nashcc.edu
MOHS, Marlene .... 651-690-6932. 263 O
mmohn@stkate.edu
MOHSEN, Bashir .... 201-216-9901. 301 E
eicollege@verizon.net
MOHSINI, Virga .... 617-824-7858. 226 A
virga_mohsini@emerson.edu
MOIANI, Thomas .... 215-596-7532. 435 H
t.moiani@usciences.edu
MOINESTER, Eli .... 610-526-6197. 417 H
emoinester@harcum.edu
MOIOLA, Tena .... 858-566-1200... 42 G
tmoiola@disd.edu
MOIR, Chris .... 216-987-3492. 378 D
chris.moir@tri-c.edu
MOISEY, Neil .... 406-444-0314. 286 G
nmoisey@montana.edu
MOIST, Kirk, L .... 715-833-6224. 539 J
kmoist@cvtc.edu
MOJICA, Agnes .... 787-892-4320. 551 A
amojica@sg.inter.edu
MOJICA, Francis, J .... 787-723-4481. 548 A
fmojica@ceaprc.edu
MOJICA, Jorge, E .... 787-852-1430. 549 C
jmojica@hccpr.edu
MOJOCK, Charles, R ...... 352-365-3523. 108 S
mojockc@lssc.edu
MOKEL, Haroon .... 202-408-2400... 96 F
haroon.mokel@strayer.edu
MOKOSSO, Henry, E ...... 504-286-5250. 206 K
hmokosso@suno.edu
MOKUAU, Noreen, K ...... 808-956-6300. 136 B
noreen@hawaii.edu
MOLALENGE, Teshome, H .... 540-828-5751. 502 J
tmolalen@bridgewater.edu
MOLAND, Millie .... 970-248-1304... 79 F
mmoland@coloradomesa.edu
MOLCHANY, Jim .... 610-282-1100. 414 F
jim.molchany@desales.edu
MOLD, Jean .... 435-722-6900. 496 M
jean@ubatc.edu
MOLDENHAUER, Susan . 307-766-6620. 543 I
amsm@uwyo.edu
MOLDER, Kandi .... 918-335-6237. 398 F
kmolder@okwu.edu
MOLDER, Mark .... 918-335-6843. 398 F
mmolder@okwu.edu
MOLDOVAN, Randi .... 614-947-6543. 380 A
randi.moldovan@franklin.edu
MOLDSTAD, Donald, L ... 507-344-7312. 253 J
donm@blc.edu
MOLEN, Brent .... 801-426-8234. 496 O
president@ucdh.edu
MOLEN, Kenneth .... 801-226-1081. 496 O
director@ucdh.edu
MOLENAAR, James, H .... 320-222-5211. 260 H
jim.molenaar@ridgewater.edu
MOLENKAMP, Kathy, L .. 616-538-2330. 243 A
kmolenkamp@gbcol.edu
MOLER, Delanie, S .... 848-445-3787. 306 A
delanie.moler@rutgers.edu
MOLER, Misty .... 704-216-3623. 363 D
misty.moler@rccc.edu
MOLESWORTH, Mark, D 608-342-1567. 537 D
moleswom@uwplatt.edu
MOLEY, Linda .... 620-252-7115. 185 O
lmoley@coffeyville.edu
MOLIFE, Brenda .... 508-531-1201. 229 D
bmolife@bridgew.edu
MOLIKEN, Laura .... 610-409-3606. 436 B
lmoliken@ursinus.edu
MOLINA, Alejandra .... 315-781-3000. 326 C
molina@hws.edu
MOLINA, Carlos .... 718-518-6658. 318 B
cmolina@hostos.cuny.edu
MOLINA, Carlos .... 202-495-3876... 96 C
cmolina@dhs.edu
MOLINA, Michael .... 806-742-2116. 487 D
michael.molina@ttu.edu
MOLINA, Pablo .... 203-392-5004... 88 A
molina@southernct.edu
MOLINAR, Anthony .... 415-749-4524... 62 G
amolinar@sfai.edu
MOLINARO, Brian .... 315-792-5545. 331 I
bmolinaro@mvcc.edu
MOLITIERNO, Jason, J .. 203-371-7775... 91 C
molitiernoj@sacredheart.edu
MOLIVER, Donald .... 732-571-3422. 303 C
dmoliver@monmouth.edu
MOLL, Amy .... 208-426-5719. 137 G
amoll@boisestate.edu
MOLL, John .... 480-654-7777... 15 A
john.moll@mesacc.edu
MOLL, Jonathan .... 781-239-4022. 222 D
jmoll@babson.edu
MOLL, Joseph .... 215-646-7300. 417 F
moll.j@gmc.edu
MOLL, Monica, M .... 419-372-2346. 374 K
mmoll@bgsu.edu
MOLL, Stephen .... 305-919-5700. 115 B
molls@fiu.edu
MOLLA, Mike .... 410-225-2215. 216 C
mmolla@mica.edu
MOLLAHAN, David, J ..... 334-683-2301..... 5 F
dmollahan@marionmilitary.edu
MOLLARD, Tikhon .... 570-561-1818. 432 F
MOLLBERG, Barbara, J .. 507-285-7111. 261 A
barb.mollberg@rctc.edu
MOLLEN, Elizabeth .... 607-778-5008. 315 I
mollenes@sunybroome.edu
MOLLENKOPF, Robert .... 724-480-3387. 413 H
robert.mollenkopf@ccbc.edu
MOLLER, Amanda .... 312-752-2170. 149 E
amanda.mollor@kendall.edu
MOLLER, Edward .... 617-928-4515. 234 E
enmoller@mountida.edu
MOLLER, Jerry, E .... 806-371-5297. 465 E
jemoller@actx.edu
MOLLER, Mark .... 740-587-6668. 379 D
moller@denison.edu
MOLLER, Mary .... 503-725-9818. 406 B
mollerm@pdx.edu
MOLLER, Steffen .... 503-594-3390. 402 F
steffenm@clackamas.edu
MOLLEUR, Sherri .... 802-322-1626. 499 C
sherri.molleur@goddard.edu
MOLLIS, Kristi, L .... 561-912-1211. 103 C
kmollis@evergladesuniversity.edu
MOLLNER, Daniel .... 507-933-7569. 255 I
dmollner@gustavus.edu
MOLLO, Peter .... 508-541-1664. 225 F
pmollo@dean.edu
MOLLOY, Christopher .... 848-932-5663. 306 A
molloy@oldqueens.rutgers.edu
MOLLOY, Christopher .... 848-932-5663. 306 B
molloy@oldqueens.rutgers.edu
MOLLOY, Christopher, H .... 317-788-3360. 173 I
cmolloy@uindy.edu
MOLLOY, Marcie, A .... 410-822-5400. 214 C
mamolloy@chesapeake.edu
MOLNAR, James .... 610-660-1295. 432 E
jmolnar@sju.edu
MOLONEY, Jacqueline ... 978-934-2943. 229 B
jacqueline_moloney@uml.edu
MOLS, Frank .... 717-867-6118. 421 H
mols@lvc.edu
MOLTA, Phyllis .... 617-588-1347. 223 B
pmolta@bfit.edu
MOLYNEUX, Annette ...... 215-895-1415. 415 B
ajm26@drexel.edu
MOLZ, Chris .... 215-222-4200. 431 H
cmolz@walnuthillcollege.edu
MOMAN, Frank .... 317-921-4396. 169 L
fmoman@ivytech.edu
MOMAN, Orthella, P ...... 601-977-7778. 270 A
omoman@tougaloo.edu
MOMAN, Tim .... 602-432-8414... 11 C
MOMANY, Christopher, P .... 517-265-5161. 238 G
cmomany@adrian.edu
MOMAYEZI, Betty .... 678-466-4143. 123 A
bettymomayezi@clayton.edu
MOMAYEZI, Nasser .... 678-466-4700. 123 A
nassermomayezi@clayton.edu
MOMBERG, Joel .... 813-974-1899. 116 C
jmomberg@usf.edu
MOMINEY, Michael .... 954-262-8252. 109 K
mominey@nova.edu
MONACO, A, G .... 225-578-8200. 204 O
amonaco@lsu.edu
MONACO, Anthony, P .... 617-627-3300. 237 C
anthony.monaco@tufts.edu
MONACO, Dennis .... 978-232-2357. 226 C
dmonaco@endicott.edu
MONACO, Pamela .... 316-684-5335. 190 G
pamela.monaco@sckans.edu
MONACO, Salvatore .... 415-354-5714... 56 A
smonaco@unow.com
MONACO, Tana .... 510-261-8500... 58 G
tana.monaco@patten.edu
MONAGAN, Paul, R .... 903-510-2130. 488 E
pmon@tjc.edu
MONAGHAN, Thomas, S .... 239-280-2522... 98 K
tmonaghan@avemaria.edu
MONAHAN, JR., Charles, F .... 617-732-2880. 233 E
charles.monahan@mcphs.edu
MONAHAN, Daniel .... 508-565-1373. 237 A
dmonahan@stonehill.edu
MONAHAN, Mark .... 734-487-5386. 242 D
mmonahan@emich.edu
MONAHAN, Michael, D . 717-245-1341. 414 H
monahanm@dickinson.edu
MONAHAN, Susanne ..... 503-838-8226. 406 E
monahans@wou.edu
MONAN, SJ, J. Donald .. 617-552-2128. 224 A
j.donald.monan@bc.edu
MONASCH, Chris, P .... 718-990-6223. 339 A
monaschc@stjohns.edu
MONAST, Louise .... 401-847-6650. 440 C
louise.monast@salve.edu
MONCHUSIE, David .... 816-584-6434. 280 C
david.monchusie@park.edu
MONCK-MARCELLINO, Caitlin .... 718-780-0322. 315 H
caitlin.monck-marcellino@brooklaw.edu
MONCRIFFE, Pritchard ... 405-466-3253. 395 N
pmoncriffe@langston.edu
MONCURE, Anna .... 540-362-6490. 505 G
moncurea@hollins.edu
MONCURE, Betty .... 601-979-2227. 267 E
betty.j.moncure@jsums.edu
MONCURE, Thomas, M .. 703-993-2619. 505 C
tmoncure@gmu.edu
MONDAY, JR., Elden, R 206-239-2315. 516 H
emonday@aii.edu
MONDAY, Eric, N .... 859-257-1841. 200 C
emonday@uky.edu
MONDAY, Kathryn, J ..... 804-289-8771. 510 L
kmonday@richmond.edu
MONDEH, Sama .... 205-247-8070..... 7 E
smondeh@stillman.edu
MONDEIK, Shelly .... 715-675-3331. 541 A
mondeik@ntc.edu
MONDELLI, Robert .... 973-684-6626. 304 B
rmondelli@pccc.edu
MONDLOCK, Ali .... 703-821-8570. 510 B
amondloch@stratford.edu
MONDOU, Sherry, B .... 253-879-3204. 524 F
smondou@pugetsound.edu
MONDROS, Jacqueline ... 212-452-7085. 318 C
jmondros@hunter.cuny.edu
MONDZIEL, Marlene ...... 804-819-4902. 511 G
mmondziel@vccs.edu
MONE, Jennifer .... 516-463-7310. 326 D
jennifer.mone@hofstra.edu
MONESTIME, Carrie, L .... 617-427-0060. 232 G
cmonestime@rcc.mass.edu
MONETA, Larry .... 919-684-3737. 354 A
larry.moneta@duke.edu
MONETA, Raymond, J .... 814-393-2676. 428 C
rmoneta@clarion.edu
MONEY, Barbara .... 972-599-3151. 469 G
bmoney@collin.edu
MONEY, Ken .... 601-366-8880. 270 H
kmoney@wbs.edu
MONEY, Royce .... 325-674-4974. 464 H
moneyr@acu.edu
MONEYHAM, Valerie, Z . 850-474-2041. 117 B
vmoneyha@uwf.edu
MONFETTE, Francine ...... 401-341-2231. 440 C
monfettf@salve.edu
MONG, Scott .... 740-753-7203. 380 K
mongs@hocking.edu
MONGAN, Jeremiah James .... 970-352-1181... 78 A
MONGE, Eduardo .... 714-997-6847... 38 A
monge@chapman.edu
MONGELLI, Antoinette .... 310-983-3525... 71 C
mongelli@volunteer.ucla.edu
MONGEON, Mike .... 508-373-9458. 223 A
michael.mongeon@becker.edu
MONGER, Todd .... 612-343-3513. 262 X
tjmonger@northcentral.edu

MONGILLO, Anne, M ..... 516-463-6776. 326 D
anne.mongillo@hofstra.edu
MONGO, Karen .... 214-860-2235. 470 J
kmongo@dcccd.edu
MONHEIT, Yidel .... 718-853-2442. 351 F
MONHOLLON, Michael .. 325-670-5870. 472 O
mmonholl@hsutx.edu
MONIACI, Steve, C .... 281-649-3096. 473 B
smoniaci@hbu.edu
MONIODIS, Paul .... 410-837-5270. 221 A
pmoniodis@ubalt.edu
MONK, David, H .... 814-865-2526. 426 A
dhm6@psu.edu
MONK, Matthew .... 802-828-8556. 500 G
matthew.monk@vcfa.edu
MONK, Suzanne .... 662-476-5014. 266 I
smonk@eastms.edu
MONK, Tammy .... 304-384-5325. 529 E
tmonk@concord.edu
MONKS, Birgit .... 909-652-6876... 37 M
birgit.monks@chaffey.edu
MONKS, Laura .... 931-438-0028. 461 A
lmonks@mscc.edu
MONNAT, Angela, B .... 585-385-8042. 338 H
amonnat@sjfc.edu
MONNES, Mark, J .... 419-755-4824. 385 D
mmonnes@ncstatecollege.edu
MONNOT, Charles .... 405-208-5295. 397 F
cmonnot@okcu.edu
MONOD, Kelly .... 941-752-5491. 114 I
monodk@scf.edu
MONROE, Dennis .... 334-420-4266..... 7 G
dmonroe@trenholmstate.edu
MONROE, J.P .... 541-346-2085. 406 D
jpmonroe@uoregon.edu
MONROE, Jill .... 619-849-2298... 59 L
jillmonroe@pointloma.edu
MONROE, Joseph, W ...... 859-257-5770. 200 C
joe.monroe@uky.edu
MONROE, Murphy .... 312-369-7133. 143 D
mmonroe@colum.edu
MONROE, Randall, L ...... 570-326-3761. 427 B
rmonroe@pct.edu
MONROE, Taunya, N ...... 336-517-2161. 352 H
tmonroe@bennett.edu
MONROE, W. Sam .... 409-984-6100. 486 H
sam.monroe@lamarpa.edu
MONROE, Walter .... 386-481-2497... 99 C
monroew@cookman.edu
MONROE, William .... 713-743-9007. 489 B
wmonroe@uh.edu
MONS, Marie .... 404-894-4582. 125 D
marie.mons@finaid.gatech.edu
MONSERRATE, Julio ...... 787-744-1060. 551 J
jmonserrate@mechtech.edu
MONSON, Terry .... 906-487-7338. 242 G
terry.monson@finlandia.edu
MONTAG, Jerry .... 815-753-1747. 154 L
jerry.montag@niu.edu
MONTAGNINO, Chris ...... 608-249-6611. 533 I
cmontagnino@msn.herzing.edu
MONTAGUE, Evan .... 517-483-1046. 245 H
montage@lcc.edu
MONTAGUE, Krista .... 406-657-2061. 287 C
MONTAGUE, Marlena, O 671-735-5612. 546 C
marlena.montague@guamcc.edu
MONTAGUE, Orinthia ...... 952-358-8283. 260 B
orinthia.montague@normandale.edu
MONTALBAN, Silvia .... 646-557-4409. 318 D
smontalban@jjay.cuny.edu
MONTALBANO, Ivonne .. 713-221-8060. 489 D
montalbanoi@uhd.edu
MONTALVO, Carmen ...... 787-878-5475. 549 L
cmontalv@arecibo.inter.edu
MONTALVO, Cynthia ...... 201-559-6036. 302 A
montalvoc@felician.edu
MONTALVO, Francisco ... 787-279-1912. 550 B
fmontalvo@bayamon.inter.edu
MONTALVO, Janette, G .. 919-536-7250. 360 B
montalvoj@durhamtech.edu
MONTALVO, Luis .... 617-262-5000. 223 F
luis.montalvo@the-bac.edu
MONTALVO, Provi .... 787-878-5475. 549 L
pmontalvo@arecibo.inter.edu
MONTALVO, Veronica .... 203-596-6164... 90 I
vmontalvo@post.edu
MONTANARI, James ...... 815-836-5222. 150 H
montanja@lewisu.edu
MONTANEZ, John .... 212-220-8011. 317 A
jmontanez@bmcc.cuny.edu
MONTANEZ, Robert .... 916-691-7204... 53 B
montanr@crc.losrios.edu
MONTANEZ-LOPEZ,
Nilda .... 787-740-3001. 553 C
nilda.montanez@uccaribe.edu
MONTANO-CORDOVA,
Ruby, S .... 909-593-3511... 72 E
rmontano-cordova@laverne.edu
MONTE, Renee .... 415-338-3982... 35 E
rmonte@sfsu.edu

MONTEAU, Shannon ...... 406-395-4313. 288 D
smonteau@stonechild.edu
MONTECALVO, Frank ..... 814-472-3002. 432 D
fmontecalvo@francis.edu
MONTEFUSCO, Anthony . 401-254-3023. 440 B
amontefusco@rwu.edu
MONTEIRO, F. Marconi . 210-924-4338. 467 E
marconi.monteiro@bua.edu
MONTEIRO, Kenneth, P . 415-338-1693... 35 E
monteiro@sfsu.edu
MONTEITH, Delos, D ..... 828-339-4236. 364 B
delos@southwesterncc.edu
MONTEITH, Kellie .... 828-227-7147. 369 E
monteith@wcu.edu
MONTEITH, Monte .... 505-346-2340. 312 E
monte.monteith@bie.edu
MONTELEONE, Paul .... 318-473-6477. 205 A
pmonteleone@lsua.edu
MONTELONGO, Angie .... 713-525-3572. 490 L
montela@stthom.edu
MONTEMURRO,
Kimberly .... 914-633-2246. 327 C
Kmontemurro@iona.edu
MONTENEGRO, Luis ...... 718-289-5497. 317 B
luis.montenegro@bcc.cuny.edu
MONTERECY, Monty .... 206-934-3628. 522 I
orestes.monterecy@seattlecolleges.edu
MONTERO, Grecia .... 609-771-3132. 300 E
montero@tcnj.edu
MONTERO, Janina .... 310-825-1404... 71 C
jmontero@saonet.ucla.edu
MONTES, Bruce, A .... 773-508-7601. 151 H
bmontes@luc.edu
MONTES, Darlene .... 818-364-7792... 52 A
montesd@lamission.edu
MONTES, Porfirio .... 787-863-2390. 550 C
porfirio.montes@fajardo.inter.edu
MONTES, Susan, R .... 305-284-6021. 118 F
smontes@miami.edu
MONTES-BURGOS,
Carmen .... 787-993-8952. 554 A
carmen.montes1@upr.edu
MONTES-MORALES,
Maria .... 347-964-8600. 315 E
mmontes@boricuacollege.edu
MONTESINO,
María del C .... 787-720-1022. 547 E
recaudaciones@atlanticcollege.edu
MONTESINOS, Rene .... 904-620-2602. 116 B
r.monteagudo@unf.edu
MONTEVIRGEN, Alexis ... 510-748-2205... 59 B
amontevirgen@peralta.edu
MONTEZON, Juíce .... 612-343-4188. 262 X
jjmontez@northcentral.edu
MONTGOMERY,
Adrienne .... 978-837-5196. 234 A
montgomerya@merrimack.edu
MONTGOMERY,
Candace .... 312-553-2500. 141 M
cmontgomery30@ccc.edu
MONTGOMERY, Carol .... 312-362-5361. 143 H
cmontgo1@depaul.edu
MONTGOMERY, Cathy ... 912-427-6265. 120 B
cmontgomery@altamahatech.edu
MONTGOMERY, Cindy ... 229-226-1621. 132 F
cmontgomery@thomasu.edu
MONTGOMERY, Clyde ... 405-466-3636. 395 N
cmontgomery@langston.edu
MONTGOMERY, Dale ..... 479-619-4234... 22 C
dmontgom@nwacc.edu
MONTGOMERY, Isalene . 386-506-3961. 101 G
montgoi@DaytonaState.edu
MONTGOMERY, Jacque . 303-315-2120... 86 A
jacque.montgomery@ucdenver.edu
MONTGOMERY, Joe ...... 509-544-4935. 518 C
jmontgomery@columbiabasin.edu
MONTGOMERY, John .... 951-343-4963... 30 H
jmontgomery@calbaptist.edu
MONTGOMERY, John .... 575-562-4002. 309 H
john.montgomery@enmu.edu
MONTGOMERY,
Karen, L .... 817-531-6579. 488 A
kmontgomery@txwes.edu
MONTGOMERY, Keith .... 715-261-6223. 538 E
keith.montgomery@uwc.edu
MONTGOMERY, Kit, P ... 214-333-5242. 470 D
kit@dbu.edu
MONTGOMERY,
Laura, M .... 630-752-5227. 163 F
Laura.Montgomery@wheaton.edu
MONTGOMERY, Lisa ...... 312-567-3777. 147 F
montgomeryl@iit.edu
MONTGOMERY, Lisa, P . 843-792-5050. 445 B
montgoml@musc.edu
MONTGOMERY, Martha . 254-442-5114. 468 I
martha.montgomery@cisco.edu
MONTGOMERY,
Maureen .... 559-791-2209... 49 P
maureen.montgomery@portervillecollege.edu

MONTGOMERY, Nancy .. 562-860-2451... 37 I
nmontgomery@cerritos.edu
MONTGOMERY, Nancy .. 575-439-3798. 310 J
nmontgom@nmsu.edu
MONTGOMERY, Roark ... 903-875-7487. 477 G
roark.montgomery@navarrocollege.edu
MONTGOMERY, Robert .. 248-341-2305. 248 D
rjmontgo@oaklandcc.edu
MONTGOMERY,
Soncerey, L .... 336-750-2314. 370 A
montgomerysl@wssu.edu
MONTGOMERY, Tammy . 916-484-8101... 53 A
montgot2@arc.losrios.edu
MONTGOMERY,
Toni-Marie .... 847-491-3959. 155 D
t-montgomery@northwestern.edu
MONTGOMERY, Tony .... 662-476-5062. 266 I
tmontgomery@eastms.edu
MONTGOMERY, Tonya ... 502-597-6434. 197 A
tonya.montgomery@kysu.edu
MONTGOMERY RICE,
Valerie .... 404-752-1194. 129 E
vmontgomeryrice@msm.edu
MONTI, Joseph .... 407-644-1408. 111 Q
jmonti@rollins.edu
MONTICINO, Michael ..... 940-565-2010. 490 C
michael.monticino@unt.edu
MONTIEL, Arthuro .... 956-488-5808. 480 I
amontiel@southtexascollege.edu
MONTIJO, Minerva .... 716-896-0700. 350 A
montijom@villa.edu
MONTMINY, Ann .... 978-656-3200. 232 B
montminya@middlesex.mass.edu
MONTNEY, Kevin .... 920-206-2312. 533 U
kevin.montney@mbbc.edu
MONTOGMERY,
Nash, D .... 757-823-8462. 507 M
ndmontgomery@nsu.edu
MONTONE, Richard .... 413-644-4776. 222 E
rmontone@simons-rock.edu
MONTOYA, Adrian .... 210-486-3135. 465 A
amontoya@alamo.edu
MONTOYA, Bernadette ... 575-646-2447. 310 I
bermonto@nmsu.edu
MONTOYA, Debra .... 818-401-1282... 41 B
dmontoya@columbiacollege.edu
MONTOYA, Denise .... 505-224-4000. 309 E
montoyad@cnm.edu
MONTOYA, Loretta .... 505-224-3457. 309 E
lmontoya@cnm.edu
MONTOYA, Michael .... 505-454-2534. 309 L
mimontoya@luna.edu
MONTOYA, Mitzi, M ...... 480-727-1955... 11 K
mitzi.montoya@asu.edu
MONTOYA, Rolando .... 305-237-3872. 109 D
rmontoya@mdc.edu
MONTOYA, Valerie .... 505-346-2330. 312 E
valerie.montoya@bie.edu
MONTRALLO, Pamela ..... 435-652-7522. 497 E
montrallo@dixie.edu
MONTREAL, Steven .... 734-995-7325. 241 E
steven.montreal@cuw.edu
MONTREAL, Steven .... 262-243-5700. 532 H
steve.montreal@cuw.edu
MONTS, Lester, P .... 734-764-3982. 251 C
lmonts@umich.edu
MONTZ, Ruth .... 330-287-1247. 386 F
montz.11@osu.edu
MOO-YOUNG, Keith .... 509-372-7258. 525 A
MOODY, Ashley .... 336-633-0156. 362 H
camoody@randolph.edu
MOODY, Barbara .... 207-941-7000. 210 B
moodyb@husson.edu
MOODY, Bill .... 678-717-3630. 133 D
bill.moody@ung.edu
MOODY, Brad .... 501-760-4213... 22 A
bmoody@npcc.edu
MOODY, Brad .... 501-760-4222... 22 A
MOODY, Chip .... 602-429-4919... 16 O
cmoody@ps.edu
MOODY, Christopher, M 302-259-6315... 93 E
cmoody@dtcc.edu
MOODY, D. L .... 817-461-8741. 466 D
dlmoody@arlingtonbaptistcollege.edu
MOODY, Donna .... 618-235-2700. 160 A
donna.moody@swic.edu
MOODY, Jan .... 601-928-6207. 268 C
janet.moody@mgccc.edu
MOODY, Jeff, T .... 219-942-1459. 165 C
jmoody@ccr.edu
MOODY, Josh .... 817-461-8741. 466 D
jmoody@arlingtonbaptistcollege.edu
MOODY, Kari .... 920-465-2226. 536 F
moodyk@uwgb.edu
MOODY, Kay .... 219-942-1459. 165 C
kay.moody@ccr.edu
MOODY, Krystal .... 903-927-3312. 495 A
kmoody@wileyc.edu
MOODY, Linda .... 213-477-2560... 54 J
lmoody@msmc.la.edu

MOODY, Lisa .... 302-857-6120... 93 C
lmoody@desu.edu
MOODY, Marilyn .... 503-725-4616. 406 B
marilynmoody@pdx.edu
MOODY, Marla .... 417-447-4842. 279 K
moodym@otc.edu
MOODY, Mary .... 615-366-4437. 459 A
mary.moody@tbr.edu
MOODY, Michelle, L ...... 757-594-8819. 503 M
mlmoody@cnu.edu
MOODY, Monica .... 478-757-5224. 134 G
mmoody@wesleyancollege.edu
MOODY, Nancy, B .... 423-636-7301. 462 E
nmoody@tusculum.edu
MOODY, Tim .... 912-279-5762. 123 B
tmoody@ccga.edu
MOOLENAR-WIRSY,
Pamela .... 678-891-2433. 125 G
Pamela.Moolenar-Wirsy@gpc.edu
MOON, Beverly .... 662-846-4873. 266 G
bmoon@deltastate.edu
MOON, David .... 719-255-3566... 85 M
cmoon@uccs.edu
MOON, Don .... 434-592-3237. 506 I
donmoon@liberty.edu
MOON, Freddie, P .... 256-766-6610..... 4 B
pmoon@hcu.edu
MOON, Gary, W .... 404-233-3949. 458 F
gmoon@richmont.edu
MOON, Greg .... 503-517-1880. 408 I
gmoon@westernseminary.edu
MOON, Greta .... 760-245-4271... 75 B
Greta.Moon@vvc.edu
MOON, Hope .... 440-365-5222. 383 B
MOON, Hyon .... 949-480-4139... 66 F
hmoon@soka.edu
MOON, Jessica .... 803-508-7262. 440 G
moonj@atc.edu
MOON, Joshua .... 605-626-3336. 451 I
Joshua.Moom@northern.edu
MOON, Kevin .... 847-317-7023. 160 M
kmoon@tiu.edu
MOON, Lee, L .... 904-620-2833. 116 B
l.moon@unf.edu
MOON, Mary .... 212-757-1190. 313 H
mmoon@funeraleducation.org
MOON, Michael, J .... 503-370-6017. 408 J
mmoon@willamette.edu
MOON, Randy .... 251-460-6121..... 9 E
rmoon@southalabama.edu
MOON, Susan .... 573-288-6441. 273 F
smoon@culver.edu
MOONEY, Carol Ann ...... 574-284-4602. 172 G
mooney@saintmarys.edu
MOONEY, Cathryn .... 631-244-3273. 323 B
mooneyc@dowling.edu
MOONEY, Debra .... 513-745-3204. 393 H
mooney@xavier.edu
MOONEY, Dee .... 575-492-2115. 312 M
dmooney@usw.edu
MOONEY, Denise .... 617-353-9814. 224 D
dmooney@bu.edu
MOONEY, Ken .... 704-669-4030. 359 D
mooneyk@clevelandcc.edu
MOONEY, Kim .... 603-899-4284. 296 H
mooneyk@franklinpierce.edu
MOONEY, Mary, K .... 806-371-5311. 465 E
mkmooney@actx.edu
MOONEY, Sandra, N ...... 281-649-3256. 473 B
smooney@hbu.edu
MOONEY, Thelma .... 936-294-4047. 487 A
tgm001@shsu.edu
MOONEYHAN, Allen ...... 870-512-7864... 20 B
allen_mooneyhan@asun.edu
MOONO, Steady .... 610-819-2070. 424 B
smoono@mc3.edu
MOORADIAN,
Ronald, G .... 562-903-4757... 29 L
ron.mooradian@biola.edu
MOORE, Albert .... 408-741-2060... 75 J
albert.moore@wvm.edu
MOORE, Albert .... 408-741-2060... 75 L
albert.moore@wvm.edu
MOORE, Alicia .... 541-383-7262. 402 D
amoore@cocc.edu
MOORE, Allison, O .... 816-654-7204. 275 K
aomoore@kcumb.edu
MOORE, Anita, W .... 662-252-8000. 269 F
amoore@rustcollege.edu
MOORE, Ann .... 601-403-1250. 269 D
amoore@prcc.edu
MOORE, Anne .... 413-236-1641. 231 A
amoore@berkshirecc.edu
MOORE, Anne, C .... 618-453-2522. 159 G
amoore@lib.siu.edu
MOORE, Anthony .... 270-384-8108. 197 D
moorea@lindsey.edu
MOORE, A'kilah .... 925-439-2181... 42 A
amoore@losmedanos.edu
MOORE, Barbara .... 718-997-5421. 319 C
barbara.moore@qc.cuny.edu

MOORE, Barbara .... 585-340-9593. 320 E
bmoore@crcds.edu
MOORE, Barbara .... 914-251-6018. 344 D
barbara.moore@purchase.edu
MOORE, Barbara, C .... 803-705-4604. 441 C
mooreb@benedict.edu
MOORE, Barbara, E .... 207-859-4250. 209 J
barbara.moore@colby.edu
MOORE, Barbe .... 724-357-4077. 428 F
bmoore@iup.edu
MOORE, Barry, L .... 561-993-1134. 110 C
mooreb@palmbeachstate.edu
MOORE, Becky .... 706-865-2134. 133 B
bmoore@truett.edu
MOORE, III, Berrien .... 405-325-3095. 401 B
berrien@ou.edu
MOORE, Bert, S .... 972-883-2355. 491 E
bmoore@utdallas.edu
MOORE, Beverly .... 714-556-3610... 74 D
beverly.moore@vanguard.edu
MOORE, Beverly .... 845-434-5750. 347 A
bmoore@sullivan.suny.edu
MOORE, Billy .... 662-846-4200. 266 G
bmoore@deltastate.edu
MOORE, Brad .... 505-224-4423. 309 E
bmoore28@cnm.edu
MOORE, Brad, D .... 336-278-5490. 354 B
bmoore6@elon.edu
MOORE, Brett, C .... 607-735-1724. 323 H
bmoore@elmira.edu
MOORE, Brian .... 845-569-3275. 332 B
brian.moore@msmc.edu
MOORE, Brianna .... 415-703-9522... 30 K
bmoore@cca.edu
MOORE, Bridget .... 325-670-1482. 472 O
bmoore@jsutx.edu
MOORE, Calvin .... 918-595-7000. 400 E
calvin.moore@tulsacc.edu
MOORE, Carl, C .... 251-460-6419..... 9 E
ccmoore@southalabama.edu
MOORE, Carlos .... 605-718-6551. 450 G
cmoore@national.edu
MOORE, Carol .... 805-922-6966... 26 K
cvanname@hancockcollege.edu
MOORE, Caroline .... 805-756-2945... 32 F
cmoore36@calpoly.edu
MOORE, Catherine .... 732-987-2602. 302 B
moorec@georgian.edu
MOORE, Charlette .... 501-882-8876... 19 M
camoore@asub.edu
MOORE, Chris .... 205-802-1594..... 3 C
chris.moore@vc.edu
MOORE, Christine .... 619-961-4323... 69 I
cmoore@tjsl.edu
MOORE, Christopher, W 208-496-3526. 137 H
moorec@byui.edu
MOORE, Claire, E .... 443-352-4306. 218 E
cmoore@stevenson.edu
MOORE, Cynthia .... 310-434-4305... 65 A
moore_cynthia@smc.edu
MOORE, Dan .... 580-745-2006. 399 J
dmoore@se.edu
MOORE, Dana .... 217-972-0839. 426 Y
dmoore@pafa.edu
MOORE, Danae .... 580-349-1356. 397 G
danaem@opsu.edu
MOORE, Danny, B .... 252-398-6448. 353 H
moored@chowan.edu
MOORE, Daryl .... 973-720-2232. 308 I
moored@wpunj.edu
MOORE, David, C .... 562-860-2451... 37 I
dcmoore@cerritos.edu
MOORE, David, J .... 602-944-3335... 11 D
dmoore@aicag.edu
MOORE, David, P .... 256-824-6285..... 8 F
david.moore@uah.edu
MOORE, Davis .... 314-644-9196. 281 E
dfmoore@stlcc.edu
MOORE, Debbie .... 706-886-6831. 133 A
dmoore@tfc.edu
MOORE, Deborah, D ...... 785-670-1538. 191 D
deborah.moore@washburn.edu
MOORE, Denise .... 913-469-8500. 187 J
dmoore56@jccc.edu
MOORE, Dennis, T .... 585-785-1294. 324 D
mooredt@flcc.edu
MOORE, Dirk, S .... 276-944-6810. 504 H
dsmoore@ehc.edu
MOORE, Donald .... 856-256-4199. 305 E
moored@rowan.edu
MOORE, Edward .... 773-508-8928. 151 H
emoore@luc.edu
MOORE, Edwin .... 707-965-7103... 57 J
emoore@puc.edu
MOORE, Elinore .... 773-838-7528. 142 E
emoore20@ccc.edu
MOORE, Erin, B .... 847-866-3902. 145 E
erin.moore@garrett.edu
MOORE, Ernest .... 404-880-6423. 122 J
emoore@cau.edu
MOORE, Evelyn, J .... 319-399-8526. 176 G
emoore@coe.edu
MOORE, Faye .... 570-586-2400. 410 D
fmoore@bbc.edu
MOORE, Frank, X .... 253-535-7504. 521 I
moorefx@plu.edu
MOORE, Frederick, V ...... 712-749-2103. 176 D
mooref@bvu.edu
MOORE, Garret .... 740-587-6482. 379 D
moore@denison.edu
MOORE, Gary .... 615-329-8881. 454 F
gmoore@fisk.edu
MOORE, George, E .... 215-204-6542. 433 K
george.moore@temple.edu
MOORE, Gina .... 803-705-4358. 441 C
mooreg@benedict.edu
MOORE, Glen .... 601-928-6297. 268 C
glen.moore@mgccc.edu
MOORE, Gordon .... 404-894-3959. 125 D
gordon.moore@omed.gatech.edu
MOORE, Gregory .... 404-894-1420. 125 D
gregory.moore@health.gatech.edu
MOORE, Gregory, R .... 859-323-5823. 200 C
grmoor2@uky.edu
MOORE, Gwendolyn .... 912-443-5711. 131 D
gmoore@savannahtech.edu
MOORE, Hallie .... 216-791-5000. 377 E
hallie.moore@case.edu
MOORE, Harry .... 215-751-8800. 413 I
hmoore@ccp.edu
MOORE, Holly .... 206-934-6867. 523 A
holly.moore@seattlecolleges.edu
MOORE, Hsiao-Ping, H .. 248-204-3500. 245 I
hmoore@ltu.edu
MOORE, Jacques .... 207-859-4732. 209 J
jrmoore@colby.edu
MOORE, James .... 520-494-5406... 12 P
james.moore7@centralaz.edu
MOORE, James, E .... 215-951-1017. 420 B
mooreje@lasalle.edu
MOORE, James, K .... 814-866-6641. 420 E
jkmoore@lecom.edu
MOORE, James, R .... 847-317-8036. 160 M
jmoore@tiu.edu
MOORE, Jamillah .... 805-652-5502... 74 E
jmoore@vcccd.edu
MOORE, Jana .... 928-317-6052... 11 L
jana.moore@azwestern.edu
MOORE, Janice .... 717-728-2219. 412 J
janicemoore@centralpenn.edu
MOORE, Jason .... 205-391-5809..... 6 H
jmoore@sheltonstate.edu
MOORE, Jay .... 805-289-6340... 74 H
jmooret@vcccd.edu
MOORE, Jeanie .... 704-216-3500. 363 D
jeanie.moore@rccc.edu
MOORE, Jennie .... 617-670-4427. 226 F
jmoore@fisher.edu
MOORE, Jim, H .... 520-621-1483... 18 F
Jim.Moore@uafoundation.org
MOORE, John .... 585-475-2154. 337 L
jfmfms@rit.edu
MOORE, John, F .... 540-231-8991. 515 C
jmoore1@vt.edu
MOORE, Johnnie .... 434-582-2250. 506 I
jrmoore@liberty.edu
MOORE, Johnny, M .... 501-370-5275... 22 F
jmoore@philander.edu
MOORE, Joseph .... 630-942-2371. 142 G
moorej7718@cod.edu
MOORE, Joseph, B .... 617-349-8500. 228 B
jbmoore@lesley.edu
MOORE, Joy, A .... 740-389-4636. 383 F
moorej@mtc.edu
MOORE, Judy .... 815-599-3457. 146 D
judy.moore@highland.edu
MOORE, Karen .... 816-604-5229. 277 E
karen.moore@mcckc.edu
MOORE, Kathy, J .... 740-826-8114. 384 L
moore@muskingum.edu
MOORE, Keirsten .... 614-236-6679. 375 H
kmoore@capital.edu
MOORE, Keith, E .... 757-455-3354. 515 H
kmoore@vwc.edu
MOORE, Kevin .... 603-577-6529. 296 F
kmoore@dwc.edu
MOORE, Kimberly .... 850-201-8760. 117 D
mooreki@tcc.fl.edu
MOORE, Kimberly, M ..... 972-860-7028. 470 I
KimberlyMoore@dcccd.edu
MOORE, Kyle .... 806-651-2006. 484 D
kmoore@mail.wtamu.edu
MOORE, Lara .... 541-962-3773. 405 H
lmoore@eou.edu
MOORE, Lara .... 541-962-3368. 405 H
lmoore@eou.edu
MOORE, Laura .... 567-661-7410. 387 L
laura_moore@owens.edu
MOORE, Lee .... 361-593-2153. 484 A
lee.moore@tamuk.edu
MOORE, Leeshawn .... 909-593-3511... 72 E
lmoore@laverne.edu
MOORE, Lesa .... 251-442-2207..... 9 A
lmoore@umobile.edu
MOORE, Leslie .... 253-833-9111. 520 C
lmoore@greenriver.edu
MOORE, Lew .... 501-279-4347... 21 C
lmoore@harding.edu
MOORE, Lew Rita .... 513-861-6400. 390 C
lewrita.moore@munion.edu
MOORE, Linda .... 309-671-2734. 152 I
lmoore@methodistcol.edu
MOORE, Linda, H .... 217-351-2551. 155 J
lmoore@parkland.edu
MOORE, Linda, L .... 217-581-2412. 144 E
llmoore@eiu.edu
MOORE, Lisa .... 925-631-4328... 61 F
lmoore@stmarys-ca.edu
MOORE, Lisa, J .... 904-632-3326. 105 E
limoore@fscj.edu
MOORE, Lisia .... 702-579-3518. 294 B
lmoore@kaplan.edu
MOORE, Loretta, A .... 601-979-0552. 267 E
loretta.a.moore@jsums.edu
MOORE, Lorna, G .... 336-758-5301. 370 D
moore@wfu.edu
MOORE, Lynn .... 603-752-1113. 296 E
lmoore@ccsnh.edu
MOORE, Lynn .... 606-589-3001. 196 F
lynn.moore@kctcs.edu
MOORE, Mable .... 912-358-4400. 131 C
mooremj@savannahstate.edu
MOORE, Margie .... 405-262-2552. 399 B
moorem@redlandscc.edu
MOORE, Marilyn .... 402-481-8781. 288 H
marilyn.moore@bryanhealthcollege.edu
MOORE, Marilyn, A .... 814-871-7614. 416 K
moore037@gannon.edu
MOORE, Mark .... 405-974-2499. 400 K
mmoore@uco.edu
MOORE, Mark .... 402-363-5600. 293 I
dmark.moore@gmail.com
MOORE, Mark .... 740-351-3207. 388 N
mmoore@shawnee.edu
MOORE, Marlene .... 503-370-6285. 408 J
moorem@willamette.edu
MOORE, Martha .... 734-372-4900. 250 G
moorem@cooley.edu
MOORE, Mary .... 410-287-1053. 214 B
mmoore@cecil.edu
MOORE, Mary, C .... 317-788-6150. 173 I
moore@uindy.edu
MOORE, Mary, E .... 617-353-3050. 224 D
mmoore@bu.edu
MOORE, Mary Pat .... 319-296-4255. 178 J
mary.moore@hawkeyecollege.edu
MOORE, Mary Rita .... 708-456-0300. 161 A
mpatrice@triton.edu
MOORE, Matt .... 504-280-6218. 205 G
msmoore2@uno.edu
MOORE, Matt .... 605-995-2187. 450 A
mamoore@dwu.edu
MOORE, Matthew .... 718-951-3136. 317 C
matthewm@brooklyn.cuny.edu
MOORE, Matthew .... 937-512-2960. 388 O
matthew.moore157@sinclair.edu
MOORE, Maureen .... 352-588-8121. 112 D
maureen.moore@saintleo.edu
MOORE, May .... 317-578-7353. 171 I
MOORE, Mazie .... 314-889-1421. 274 E
mmoore@fontbonne.edu
MOORE, Mea .... 509-865-8652. 520 D
Moore_mea@heritage.edu
MOORE, Melody, L .... 804-706-5122. 512 G
mmoore@jtcc.edu
MOORE, Michael .... 941-359-7674. 111 O
mmoore@ringling.edu
MOORE, Michael .... 701-777-6772. 371 C
michael.moore@research.und.edu
MOORE, Michael, A .... 231-843-5900. 252 H
mamoore@westshore.edu
MOORE, Michael, K .... 501-686-2533... 23 H
mmoore@uasys.edu
MOORE, Michael, P .... 509-865-8585. 520 D
moore_m@heritage.edu
MOORE, Michael, R .... 317-274-0622. 168 D
mmoore1@iupui.edu
MOORE, Mickey .... 423-614-8430. 455 L
mmoore@leeuniversity.edu
MOORE, Mike .... 949-480-4155... 66 F
mmoore@soka.edu
MOORE, Mike, K .... 701-788-4706. 371 E
Mike.Moore@mayvillestate.edu
MOORE, Mitchell, L .... 540-665-1298. 509 E
mmoore7@su.edu
MOORE, Nancy .... 908-526-1200. 305 B
nmoore@raritanval.edu
MOORE, Nicole .... 314-889-1496. 274 E
nmoore@fontbonne.edu
MOORE, Paige .... 803-758-2700. 441 A
pmoore@allenuniversity.edu
MOORE, Pamela .... 541-684-4644. 407 B
pmoore@pioneerpacific.edu
MOORE, Patrice .... 504-671-6535. 203 A
pmoore@dcc.edu
MOORE, Paul .... 229-732-5910. 120 D
paulmoore@andrewcollege.edu
MOORE, Perry .... 512-463-7281. 486 D
perry.moore@tsus.edu
MOORE, Phil .... 860-727-6941... 90 A
pmoore@goodwin.edu
MOORE, Philip, S .... 803-777-2814. 447 G
philmoore@sc.edu
MOORE, R. Bartley .... 202-687-0454... 95 E
rbm9@georgetown.edu
MOORE, Ray .... 334-876-9248..... 4 A
rmoore@wccs.edu
MOORE, Reggie .... 504-456-3141. 201 C
MOORE, Renee .... 210-805-5864. 490 A
reneem@uiwtx.edu
MOORE, Renee, R .... 865-639-6604. 461 D
rmoore@pstcc.edu
MOORE, Robert, G .... 719-389-6693... 79 D
robert.moore@coloradocollege.edu
MOORE, Robert, M .... 207-859-1104. 211 H
moorer@thomas.edu
MOORE, Robin .... 402-761-8270. 292 C
rmoore@southeast.edu
MOORE, Robin .... 757-822-1724. 514 C
rmoore@tcc.edu
MOORE, Rochelle .... 337-521-8957. 203 I
rochelle.moore@southlouisiana.edu
MOORE, Rodney .... 936-261-9311. 482 F
rvmoore@pvamu.edu
MOORE, Roger .... 501-882-8906... 19 M
rlmoore@asub.edu
MOORE, Russell .... 303-492-2890... 85 L
rmoore@colorado.edu
MOORE, Sandra .... 859-622-6587. 193 P
sandra.moore@eku.edu
MOORE, Sandra .... 803-535-1237. 446 B
mooresj@octech.edu
MOORE, Sandy .... 757-388-2900. 509 D
snmoore1@sentara.com
MOORE, Scott .... 781-239-4218. 222 D
smoore@babson.edu
MOORE, Sean .... 603-862-3827. 298 C
sean.moore@unh.edu
MOORE, Shanee', S .... 214-860-2138. 470 J
ksmoore@dcccd.edu
MOORE, Sharamie, T ..... 337-475-5493. 207 G
strahan@mcneese.edu
MOORE, Sharon .... 860-412-7273... 89 E
smoore@qvcc.commnet.edu
MOORE, Sharyn .... 650-543-3798... 54 C
smoore@menlo.edu
MOORE, Shirley .... 937-778-7861. 379 G
smoore@edisonohio.edu
MOORE, Stacey .... 330-972-5770. 390 E
staceyjm@uakron.edu
MOORE, Stan .... 817-274-4284. 467 H
smoore@bhcarroll.edu
MOORE, Stephany .... 575-835-5128. 310 F
smoore@admin.nmt.edu
MOORE, Steve .... 979-458-6018. 482 E
steve.moore@tamus.edu
MOORE, Steven, C .... 239-590-1919. 115 A
cmoore@fgcu.edu
MOORE, Stuart .... 251-380-2240..... 7 D
smoore@shc.edu
MOORE, Tammie, L .... 985-380-2957. 203 H
tammiemoore1@scl.edu
MOORE, Teresa .... 806-291-3752. 494 F
teresam@wbu.edu
MOORE, Teri, D .... 540-674-3600. 513 B
tmoore@nr.edu
MOORE, Theresa .... 608-796-3172. 539 E
trmoore@viterbo.edu
MOORE, Thomas .... 510-659-6105... 57 A
tmoore@ohlone.edu
MOORE, Thomas .... 864-503-5200. 448 H
tmoore@uscupstate.edu
MOORE, Thomas, J .... 989-774-3500. 240 N
thomas.j.moore@cmich.edu
MOORE, Tim .... 706-379-5166. 134 L
tsmoore@yhc.edu
MOORE, Timothy .... 617-353-0750. 224 D
mooretj@bu.edu
MOORE, Timothy .... 847-214-7651. 144 F
tmoore@elgin.edu
MOORE, Timothy .... 518-255-5323. 344 E
mooretw@cobleskill.edu
MOORE, Timothy, J .... 919-530-7420. 368 A
tmoore@nccu.edu
MOORE, Tina .... 417-865-2815. 274 B
mooret@evangel.edu
MOORE, Tina .... 217-234-5346. 150 D
tmoore@lakeland.cc.il.us
MOORE, Todd, H .... 316-284-5230. 184 J
tmoore@bethelks.edu
MOORE, JR., Tom, A ..... 205-329-7871..... 3 B
tom.moore@ecacolleges.com

MOORE, Tonja 305-348-2168. 115 B
tonja.moore@fiu.edu

MOORE, Tony 225-771-3201. 206 I
tony_moore@sus.edu

MOORE, Torin, Y 413-542-2161. 221 G
tmoore@amherst.edu

MOORE, Wayne 956-882-6567. 491 D
wayne.moore@utb.edu

MOORE, William (Joe) 605-688-4678. 452 B
william.moore@sdstate.edu

MOORE, Winifred, B 843-953-7477. 442 A
bo.moore@citadel.edu

MOORE-ASSEM, Carolyn, D 919-530-5294. 368 A
cmoore@nccu.edu

MOORE BERTRAND, Denise 404-215-3486. 129 D
dmbertrand@morehouse.edu

MOORE-JONES, Yolanda, V 919-536-7201. 360 B
jonesym@durhamtech.edu

MOORE-LINN, Cathleen 671-735-2600. 546 E
cmoore@uguam.uog.edu

MOORER, Glynda, M 517-355-2488. 246 H
moorerg@msu.edu

MOORES, Lisa 301-295-3188. 545 C
lisa.moores@usuhs.edu

MOORHEAD, Tracey, A 219-299-3654. 255 A
moorhead@cord.edu

MOORMAN, Annorrah 309-556-3052. 148 B
amoorman@iwu.edu

MOORMAN, Cathy 765-998-5123. 173 C
ctmoorman@taylor.edu

MOORMAN, Jack, W 919-515-3000. 368 B
jack_moorman@ncsu.edu

MOORMAN, Thomas, D 817-735-2505. 490 E
Thomas.Moorman@unthsc.edu

MOORMANN, Kay 815-455-8783. 152 F
lmoormann@mchenry.edu

MOORS, Dean 402-462-4000. 288 I
dmoors@cccneb.edu

MOORWOOD, Woody 626-815-3855... 29 H
wmoorwood@apu.edu

MOOS, Michael 317-917-3623. 171 A
mmoos@martin.edu

MOOS, William, H 509-335-0200. 525 A
bill.moos@wsu.edu

MOOSE, Richard, E 315-267-2377. 344 C
moosere@potsdam.edu

MOOSMANN, Gloria 216-987-4788. 378 D
gloria.moosmann@tri-c.edu

MOOT, Bradley 212-678-8035. 328 A
brmoot@jtsa.edu

MOOTHART, Kathy 319-385-6209. 179 K
kathy.moothart@iwc.edu

MOOTZ, Jay 916-739-7151... 73 A
jmootz@pacific.edu

MOPPERT, Jan 610-499-4177. 437 E
jamoppert@widener.edu

MORA, Aracely 714-628-4880... 60 H
mora_aracely@sccollege.edu

MORA, Francisco 503-845-3110. 404 D
francisco.mora@mtangel.edu

MORA, Isabelle 360-438-4463. 522 G
imora@stmartin.edu

MORA, Michelle 818-240-1000... 45 G
mmora@glendale.edu

MORA, Peter, L 609-343-4901. 299 A
mora@atlantic.edu

MORA, Victoria 505-984-6109. 311 H
vmora@sjcsf.edu

MORADILLOS, Alicia 787-834-9595. 553 B
amoradillos@uaa.edu

MORAH, Emeka, O 937-708-5705. 393 A
emorah@wilberforce.edu

MORAIN, Tom 641-784-5053. 178 F
tmorain@gracelend.edu

MORALE, Joseph, L 903-927-3232. 495 A
jmorale@wileyc.edu

MORALE, Mary 937-708-5782. 393 A
mmorale@wilberforce.edu

MORALE, Sonja 903-566-7059. 492 D
smorale@uttyler.edu

MORALES, Ada 787-882-2065. 553 A
colocaiones@unitecpr.net

MORALES, Adelina, C 325-942-2073. 465 K
adelina.morales@angelo.edu

MORALES, Aurea 718-963-4112. 315 E
amorales@boricuacollege.edu

MORALES, Carlos 817-515-5021. 482 B
carlos.morales@tccd.edu

MORALES, David 713-221-8513. 489 D
MoralesD@uhd.edu

MORALES, Edwin 787-786-3030. 547 F
emorales@ucb.edu.pr

MORALES, Edwin 787-265-3864. 554 E
edwin.morales3@upr.edu

MORALES, George 806-743-2952. 487 E
george.morales@ttuhsc.edu

MORALES, George 336-917-5405. 366 D
george.morales@salem.edu

MORALES, Honorio 773-878-3256. 158 B
hmorales@staugustine.edu

MORALES, Ileana 787-878-5475. 549 L
imorales@arecibo.inter.edu

MORALES, Irma 787-863-2390. 550 C
irma.morales@fajardo.inter.edu

MORALES, James 435-797-1712. 497 B
james.morales@usu.edu

MORALES, Jesus 408-254-6900... 55 H
jmorales@nhu.edu

MORALES, Jossue 787-891-0925. 549 K
jomorales@aguadilla.inter.edu

MORALES, Karen, G 787-841-2000. 552 B
karen_morales@pucpr.edu

MORALES, Luis 787-744-1060. 551 J
lmorales@mechtech.edu

MORALES, Marisol 909-593-3511... 72 E
mmorales3@laverne.edu

MORALES, Milga 718-951-5352. 317 C
milga@brooklyn.cuny.edu

MORALES, Milsa 787-264-1912. 551 A
mmorales@sg.inter.edu

MORALES, Nora 361-354-2239. 468 K
moralesn@coastlbend.edu

MORALES, Rachel 207-780-5670. 212 H
rmorales@usm.maine.edu

MORALES, Robert 805-965-0581... 64 L
moralesr@sbcc.edu

MORALES, Rosalia 787-864-2222. 550 D
rmorales@inter.edu

MORALES, Rosalie 787-780-0070. 547 G
rmorales@caribbean.edu

MORALES, Sandra, M 787-857-3600. 550 A
smorales@br.inter.edu

MORALES, Tomas 909-537-5002... 34 E
tmorales@csusb.edu

MORALES-MARTINEZ, Maria 787-264-1912. 551 A
marimo@sg.inter.edu

MORAMARCO, Jacques 310-453-8300... 43 D
jacques@emperors.edu

MORAN, Alan 216-987-3484. 378 D
alan.moran@tri-c.edu

MORAN, OP, Allen 202-495-3836... 96 C
registrar@dhs.edu

MORAN, Carmella 630-844-5132. 140 A
cmoran@aurora.edu

MORAN, Christine 616-222-3000. 245 C
cmoran@kuyper.edu

MORAN, Christyn 610-527-0200. 432 B
christyn@rosemont.edu

MORAN, Francis, J 540-234-9261. 511 H
moranf@brcc.edu

MORAN, James 314-977-3873. 281 I

MORAN, III, James, D 717-720-4200. 427 G
jmoran@passhe.edu

MORAN, James, J 615-353-3249. 461 B
josh.moran@nscc.edu

MORAN, James, M 203-576-4735... 91 G
jmoran@bridgeport.edu

MORAN, Kathryn, A 317-788-3367. 173 I
kmoran@uindy.edu

MORAN, Ken 502-456-6504. 199 G
kmoran@sullivan.edu

MORAN, Lauren, E 386-226-7024. 102 B
lauren.moran@erau.edu

MORAN, Maggie 662-562-3277. 269 C
mmoran@northwestms.edu

MORAN, Michael 413-565-1000. 222 F
mmoran@baypath.edu

MORAN, Parker 252-222-6243. 358 G
moranp@carteret.edu

MORAN, Patricia 212-650-3733. 318 C

MORAN, Patricia 979-830-4157. 467 I
pmoran@blinn.edu

MORAN, Patrick 307-766-4175. 543 I
therock@uwyo.edu

MORAN, Paul, J 570-208-5948. 419 P
pjmoran@kings.edu

MORAN, Rachel 310-825-8202... 71 C
moran@law.ucla.edu

MORAN, Sam, E 540-365-4250. 504 L
semoran@ferrum.edu

MORAN, Tracy 585-389-2030. 332 D
tmoran8@naz.edu

MORAN, Virginia 760-245-4271... 75 B
Virginia.Moran@vvc.edu

MORAN, Yvette 602-274-1885... 16 M
ymoran@pihma.edu

MORAN-BROWN, Carol 802-865-6426. 499 A
moran@champlain.edu

MORANO, Joseph 845-451-1314. 322 D
j_morano@culinary.edu

MORANO, Lori 518-464-8648. 324 B
lmorano@excelsior.edu

MORANSKI, Karen 217-206-7440. 161 E
moranski.karen@uis.edu

MORANT, Blake 336-758-5430. 370 D
morantbd@wfu.edu

MORAVEC, Todd, A 518-564-2072. 344 B
moraveta@plattsburgh.edu

MORAZ, Kristen, L 561-237-7602. 108 X
kmoraz@lynn.edu

MORBER, Timothy, T 330-471-8279. 383 D
tmorber@malone.edu

MORCIGLIO, Jean 517-483-1862. 245 H
morcigj@lcc.edu

MORDACH, John 312-942-5600. 157 G
john_mordach@rush.edu

MORDI, John 787-765-1915. 551 C
jmordi@inter.edu

MORE, George 412-281-2600. 433 B
gmore@western-school.com

MOREAU, Donald 603-641-7350. 297 G
dmoreau@anselm.edu

MOREAU, Joseph 650-949-6119... 44 L
moreaujoe@fhda.edu

MOREAU, Sandra, E 619-239-0391... 36 D
sem@cwsl.edu

MOREFIELD, Bill, R 423-318-2735. 462 A
bill.morefield@ws.edu

MOREHEAD, Jere, W 706-542-3000. 133 C

MOREHEAD, Kaleybra 870-543-5963... 23 E
kmorehead@seark.edu

MOREHEAD, Kaleybra, M 870-543-5963... 23 E
kmorehead@seark.edu

MOREHEAD, Michael, A 575-646-5858. 310 I
mmorehea@nmsu.edu

MOREHOUSE, JR., Percy, A 303-556-3022... 83 D
morehoup@msudenver.edu

MOREIRA, Antonio, R 410-455-6576. 219 D
moreira@umbc.edu

MOREL, Derek 504-280-6102. 205 G
dmorel@uno.edu

MORELAND, Jeremy 480-557-3231... 18 I
jeremy.moreland@phoenix.edu

MORELAND, Mark 503-654-8000. 407 B
mmoreland@pioneerpacific.edu

MORELAND, Robert 260-665-4111. 173 E
morelandr@trine.edu

MORELL-MARRERO, Idalia 787-993-8897. 554 A
idalia.morell1@upr.edu

MORELLI, Brad 405-974-3573. 400 K
bmorelli@uco.edu

MORELLO, Chanell 828-327-7000. 359 A
cmorello@cvcc.edu

MORELLO, Debra 607-778-5199. 315 I
morelloda@sunybroome.edu

MORELLO, John, T 540-654-1269. 510 J
jmorello@umw.edu

MORELLO, Joseph 650-738-4271... 64 D
morelloj@smccd.edu

MORELOCK, Luann 309-655-7353. 158 C
luann.morelock@osfhealthcare.org

MORELOCK, Tommy 352-854-2322. 100 K
moreloct@cf.edu

MORENA, Pat 718-368-5069. 318 E
pmorena@kbcc.cuny.edu

MORENCY, Maurice 212-752-1530. 328 G
maurice.morency@limcollege.edu

MORENO, Amy, R 717-291-3989. 416 J
amy.moreno@fandm.edu

MORENO, Francisco 787-738-2161. 554 C

MORENO, Gertrud 903-875-7315. 477 G
gettie.moreno@navarrocollege.edu

MORENO, Linda 773-298-3379. 158 E
moreno@sxu.edu

MORENO, Luis, S 815-288-5511. 158 K
morenol@svcc.edu

MORENO, Marta 941-487-4230. 115 D
mmoreno@ncf.edu

MORENO, Monica 818-364-7863... 52 A
morenomm@lamission.edu

MORENO, Patricia 281-873-0262. 469 H
p.moreno@commonwealth.edu

MORENO-RIANO, Gerson 757-352-4500. 508 G
gmorenoriano@regent.edu

MORENO-WEINERT, Inez 602-243-8134... 15 F
inez.moreno-weinert@smcmail.maricopa.edu

MORENZ, Angela 217-854-3231. 140 G
angela.morenz@blackburn.edu

MORERA-GONZÁLEZ, Angel 787-993-8871. 554 A
angel.morera1@upr.edu

MORESCHI, Tracy, L 503-255-0332. 404 F
tmoreschi@multnomah.edu

MOREST, Vanessa 203-857-3368... 89 D
vmorest@norwalk.edu

MORETTI, James 215-567-7080. 410 A
jmoretti@edmc.edu

MORETTI, James, A 610-799-1128. 421 I
jmoretti1@lccc.edu

MORETTI, JoAnn 561-297-0853. 114 L
jmoretti@fau.edu

MORETTI, Linda 716-829-7811. 323 D
moretti@dyc.edu

MORETZ, Drew 919-962-7096. 366 K
agmoretz@northcarolina.edu

MOREY, Ann, N 818-677-2878... 34 C
ann.morey@csun.edu

MOREY, Megan 413-542-2985. 221 G
mmorey@amherst.edu

MOREY, Robin 202-687-3124... 95 E
rm1469@georgetown.edu

MORGAN, Alikhan 914-606-6745. 350 F
Alikhan.Morgan@sunywcc.edu

MORGAN, Allen 865-471-3372. 453 F
amorgan@cn.edu

MORGAN, Andre 832-252-0722. 468 L
andre.morgan@cbshouston.edu

MORGAN, Andy, L 618-453-7524. 159 G
amorgan@sdev.siu.edu

MORGAN, Anna, B 731-661-5410. 462 F
amorgan@uu.edu

MORGAN, Annette 903-983-8217. 475 E
amorgan@kilgore.edu

MORGAN, Barbara 617-879-2118. 238 C
bmorgan@wheelock.edu

MORGAN, Betsy, S 269-467-9945. 242 H
bmorgan@glenoaks.edu

MORGAN, Brian, J 858-499-0202... 40 C
netadmin@coleman.edu

MORGAN, Bronwyn 870-762-3172... 19 K
bmorgan@anc.edu

MORGAN, Bruce 423-775-7233. 453 E
bruce.morgan@bryan.edu

MORGAN, Bryant 802-251-7690. 499 F
bmorgan@marlboro.edu

MORGAN, Camella 253-833-9111. 520 C
cmorgan@greenriver.edu

MORGAN, Candice 919-854-2121... 18 I
candice.morgan@phoenix.edu

MORGAN, Catherine 239-433-8047. 101 O
cmorgan@edison.edu

MORGAN, Chris 951-343-4369... 30 H
cmorgan@calbaptist.edu

MORGAN, Chris 908-737-0600. 302 F
cmorgan@kean.edu

MORGAN, David 765-361-6382. 175 B
morgand@wabash.edu

MORGAN, David 423-775-2041. 453 E
morganda@bryan.edu

MORGAN, Deborah 918-540-6312. 396 G
demorgan@neo.edu

MORGAN, Derek 303-273-3288... 80 E
dmorgan@mines.edu

MORGAN, Edward 508-999-8485. 229 A
emorgan1@umassd.edu

MORGAN, Elizabeth 909-621-8101... 39 D
elizabeth.morgan@cmc.edu

MORGAN, Elizabeth, M 207-768-2700. 210 M
emorgan@nmcc.edu

MORGAN, Eloise, L 914-337-9300. 321 E
eloise.morgan@concordia-ny.edu

MORGAN, Erin 509-359-6685. 519 C
emorgan@ewu.edu

MORGAN, Gilbert 443-885-3125. 217 A
gilbert.morgan@morgan.edu

MORGAN, Ginny 510-841-9230... 77 B
vmorgan@wi.edu

MORGAN, Greg 541-463-5516. 403 I
morgang@lanecc.edu

MORGAN, Heath 660-831-4087. 278 I
morganh@moval.edu

MORGAN, Helen 912-525-5000. 131 B
hmorgan@scad.edu

MORGAN, J. Reid 336-758-5122. 370 D
jrm@wfu.edu

MORGAN, James, F 609-497-7705. 304 D
james.morgan@ptsem.edu

MORGAN, Jason 734-477-8992. 252 A
jtmorgan@wccnet.edu

MORGAN, Jason 256-352-8225..... 9 G
jason.morgan@wallacestate.edu

MORGAN, Jay 270-809-3744. 198 B
jmorgan@murraystate.edu

MORGAN, Jeff 713-743-3455. 489 B
jjmorgan@central.uh.edu

MORGAN, Jim 575-461-4413. 309 M
jimm@mesalands.edu

MORGAN, Joanne, L 919-658-8558. 357 I
jmorgan@moc.edu

MORGAN, John 973-684-5402. 304 B
jmorgan@pccc.edu

MORGAN, John 928-717-7721... 19 H
john.morgan@yc.edu

MORGAN, John, G 615-366-4403. 459 A
chancellor@tbr.edu

MORGAN, Joshua 575-492-2769. 310 G
jmorgan@nmjc.edu

MORGAN, Julie 585-245-5704. 343 C
morgan@geneseo.edu

MORGAN, Karrie 605-331-6672. 452 D
karrie.morgan@usiouxfalls.edu

MORGAN, Kathleen 617-353-7464. 224 D
kmorgan@bu.edu

MORGAN, Ken .... 478-825-6304. 124 H
morgank@fvsu.edu
MORGAN, Leigh .... 415-476-8039... 72 A
leigh.morgan@ucsf.edu
MORGAN, Lily .... 620-331-4100. 187 G
lmorgan@indycc.edu
MORGAN, Linda .... 276-466-7998. 514 G
lindamorgan@vic.edu
MORGAN, Lissa .... 901-572-2441. 453 B
lissa.morgan@bchs.edu
MORGAN, Marji .... 509-963-1858. 517 F
mmorgan@cwu.edu
MORGAN, Mark .... 407-708-2224. 113 E
morganm@seminolestate.edu
MORGAN, Mary .... 757-340-2121. 503 I
stuadvcvab@centura.edu
MORGAN, Melanie .... 979-830-4146. 467 I
melanie.morgan@blinn.edu
MORGAN, Melissa .... 215-574-9600. 418 H
mmorgan@hussianart.edu
MORGAN, Mia .... 781-595-6768. 228 C
mmorgan@mariancourt.edu
MORGAN, Michael, D .... 205-726-2727..... 6 F
mmorgan@samford.edu
MORGAN, Michael, D .... 518-564-3066. 344 B
morganmd@plattsburgh.edu
MORGAN, Michele .... 206-855-9559. 516 I
michele.morgan@bgi.edu
MORGAN, Mike .... 510-666-8248... 26 F
mmorgan@aimc.edu
MORGAN, Nancy .... 386-506-4579. 101 G
morgann@DaytonaState.edu
MORGAN, Ophelia .... 201-360-4198. 302 D
omorgan@hccc.edu
MORGAN, Pamela .... 940-397-4785. 476 H
pamela.morgan@mwsu.edu
MORGAN, Patricia .... 207-221-4273. 213 A
pmorgan1@une.edu
MORGAN, Patricia .... 707-256-7305... 55 F
pmorgan@napavalley.edu
MORGAN, Paul .... 970-943-3087... 86 I
pmorgan@western.edu
MORGAN, Peggy .... 303-914-6337... 84 I
peggy.morgan@rrcc.edu
MORGAN, R. Gregory .... 617-452-2082. 233 B
MORGAN, Randy .... 559-791-2232... 49 P
rmorgan@portervillecollege.edu
MORGAN, Scott .... 509-533-7042. 518 D
scott.morgan@scc.spokane.edu
MORGAN, Scott .... 509-533-7042. 518 E
scott.morgan@scc.spokane.edu
MORGAN, Scott .... 360-867-6913. 519 J
sustainabilitydirector@evergreen.edu
MORGAN, Sharon, E ...... 973-596-5560. 303 G
sharon.e.morgan@njit.edu
MORGAN, Stephen .... 626-571-8811... 74 B
presidentoffice@uwest.edu
MORGAN, Stephen, R .... 801-832-2750. 498 F
smorgan@westminstercollege.edu
MORGAN, Steve .... 206-934-6424. 523 A
steve.morgan@seattlecolleges.edu
MORGAN, Steve .... 740-695-9500. 374 H
smorgan@belmontcollege.edu
MORGAN, Steven .... 304-424-8289. 530 E
steven.morgan@wvup.edu
MORGAN, Tom .... 770-394-8300. 120 H
tmorgan@aii.edu
MORGAN, Tyler, S .... 801-524-8161. 495 O
tmorgan@ldsbc.edu
MORGAN, Warren, H ..... 413-542-2267. 221 G
whmorgan@amherst.edu
MORGAN-CLEMENT,
Linda .... 330-263-2602. 377 H
lclement@wooster.edu
MORGAN FOSTER,
Stacey .... 509-359-6015. 519 C
sfoster@ewu.edu
MORGAN-HOLDER,
Davetta Ann .... 212-563-6647. 348 I
MORGAN RIGGS, Janet . 717-337-6010. 417 B
jriggs@gettysburg.edu
MORGAN-RUSSELL,
Simon .... 419-372-2340. 374 K
smorgan@bgsu.edu
MORGAN-RUSSELL,
Simon, N .... 419-372-2340. 374 K
simorgan@bgsu.edu
MORGANLANDER, Beth . 718-261-5800. 315 F
jobplacement@bramsonort.edu
MORGANSTEIN, Penny .. 212-472-1500. 334 B
pmorganstein@mysid.edu
MORGANTI, Danielle ...... 856-415-2113. 302 C
dmorganti@gccnj.edu
MORGEN, Sandra .... 541-346-2800. 406 D
smorgen@uoregon.edu
MORGENSTERN, Patricia 269-467-9945. 242 H
pmorgenstern@glenoaks.edu
MORGENSTERN, Teresa . 239-489-9061. 101 O
tmorgenstern@edison.edu
MORGENTHALER,
Diane, S .... 203-392-6300... 88 A
morgenthald1@southernct.edu
MORGESE, James .... 270-745-6519. 200 G
james.morgese@wku.edu
MORI, Darryl .... 626-396-4288... 28 P
darryl.mori@artcenter.edu
MORIARTY, Beth .... 508-531-1277. 229 D
bmoriarty@bridgew.edu
MORIARTY, Christy, A ... 302-259-6031... 93 E
cmoriart@dtcc.edu
MORIARTY, Debra .... 410-704-2055. 220 E
dmoriarty@towson.edu
MORIARTY, Donna, E ..... 914-594-4536. 334 A
donna_moriarty@nymc.edu
MORIARTY, George .... 978-659-1224. 232 E
gmoriarty@necc.mass.edu
MORIARTY, Joan .... 973-618-3394. 300 A
jmoriarty@caldwell.edu
MORIARTY, John .... 305-899-3957... 98 O
jmoriarty@barry.edu
MORIARTY, Maureen ...... 802-831-1265. 500 H
mmoriarty@vermontlaw.edu
MORIARTY, Sean .... 315-312-5500. 344 A
sean.moriarty@oswego.edu
MORICONI, Jill .... 814-254-0404. 413 C
jmoriconi@pa.gov
MORICONI, Kimberly, A . 816-604-6544. 277 D
kim.moriconi@mcckc.edu
MORIN, Christine .... 207-755-5215. 210 J
cmorin@cmcc.edu
MORIN, Erin .... 336-770-3296. 369 D
morine@uncsa.edu
MORIN, III,
Frederick, C .... 802-656-2156. 500 F
frederick.morin@uvm.edu
MORIN, Jeff .... 715-346-4920. 538 A
jmorin@uwsp.edu
MORIN, Jodie .... 712-749-2097. 176 D
morinj@bvu.edu
MORIN, Jose Luis .... 646-313-8000. 319 E
MORIN, Kevin .... 414-277-7129. 534 G
morin@msoe.edu
MORIN, Kevin, A .... 414-277-7129. 534 G
morin@msoe.edu
MORIN, Regina .... 660-785-7468. 282 L
rmorin@truman.edu
MORIN, Stephen .... 617-994-6486. 237 B
smorin@suffolk.edu
MORIN, William .... 914-337-9300. 321 E
william.morin@concordia-ny.edu
MORINEC, Maire .... 707-864-7000... 66 G
maire.morinec@solano.edu
MORISHITA, Leroy, M .... 510-885-3877... 33 C
leroy.morishita@csueastbay.edu
MORISTON, Shelley .... 303-292-0015... 81 F
s.moriston@denverschoolofnursing.edu
MORIWAKI, Sharene ...... 808-847-9843. 136 G
snmm@hawaii.edu
MORLAN, Tom .... 503-255-0332. 404 F
tmorlan@multnomah.edu
MORLEY, Del .... 660-562-1363. 279 I
dmorley@nwmissouri.edu
MORLEY, Elizabeth .... 607-431-4122. 325 F
morleye@hartwick.edu
MORLEY, John .... 312-850-7230. 142 C
jmorley@ccc.edu
MORLEY, Kathleen .... 254-710-2061. 467 G
kathleen_morley@baylor.edu
MORLEY, Mary .... 732-255-0400. 304 A
mmorley@ocean.edu
MORLEY, Mary, N .... 626-395-6354... 31 E
mmorley@caltech.edu
MORLEY, Richard, H ...... 949-451-5472... 67 B
rmorley@ivc.edu
MORLEY, Sandy .... 517-264-7193. 250 B
smorley@sienaheights.edu
MORLEY, Steve .... 765-998-5841. 173 C
stmorley@taylor.edu
MORLEY, Yvonne, Y .... 859-238-5220. 193 E
yvonne.morley@centre.edu
MORLEY-MOWER,
Cynthia .... 213-763-7072... 52 D
morleycn@lattc.edu
MORLIER, Margaret, M .. 770-720-5579. 130 G
mmm@reinhardt.edu
MORLINO, Elisabeth .... 215-596-8542. 435 H
e.morlino@usciences.edu
MORNINGSTAR, Ellen .... 585-271-3657. 338 D
registrar@stbernards.edu
MORNINGSTAR, Scott .. 406-586-3585. 286 F
scott.morningstar@montanabiblecollege.
edu
MORO, Martin .... 734-995-7589. 241 E
morom@cuaa.edu
MORODOMI, Joyce, K .... 559-323-2100... 63 B
jmorodomi@sjcl.edu
MOROI, Katsumi .... 213-613-2200... 67 E
kmoroi@sciarc.edu
MORONEY, James .... 617-254-2610. 236 B
MORONEY, Mary, F .... 401-232-6298. 438 K
mmoroney@bryant.edu
MORONG, Andrew .... 207-755-5273. 210 J
amorong@cmcc.edu
MORONY, Katelyn .... 401-949-2820. 439 C
kmorony@inteducators.org
MOROONEY, Kevin, M ... 814-865-3540. 426 A
kxm@psu.edu
MOROSKO, Linda .... 330-494-6170. 389 F
lmorosko@starkstate.edu
MOROSOFF, Wendy .... 914-251-6370. 344 D
wendy.morosoff@purchase.edu
MOROTTI, Allan .... 907-474-6440... 10 I
aamorotti@alaska.edu
MOROUKIAN,
Michael, M .... 603-513-1356. 298 E
mike.moroukian@granite.edu
MOROWSKI, James .... 701-788-4619. 371 E
james.morowski@mayvillestate.edu
MOROZOWICH, Mark ..... 202-319-5683... 94 G
morozowich@cua.edu
MORPHEW, Jeanne .... 763-488-2503. 258 F
jeanne.morphew@hennepintech.edu
MORRA, Sylvia .... 717-361-1428. 415 H
morrast@etown.edu
MORRAL, Melissa .... 585-340-9633. 320 E
morral@crcds.edu
MORREALE, John .... 812-535-5213. 172 F
jmorreale@smwc.edu
MORRELL, Erin .... 203-773-8541... 87 G
emorrell@albertus.edu
MORRELL, Nancy .... 303-546-3513... 83 F
nancym@naropa.edu
MORRELL, Sarah .... 508-678-2811. 231 B
sarah.morrell@bristolcc.edu
MORRICE, Pelema, I .... 402-554-2200. 293 A
pmorrice@unomaha.edu
MORRILL, Allen .... 724-589-2124. 434 B
amorrill@thiel.edu
MORRILL, Bill .... 575-492-2791. 310 G
bmorrill@nmjc.edu
MORRILL, Deborah, H .... 210-567-6395. 493 A
morrill@uthscsa.edu
MORRILL, Donald, D ...... 813-258-7409. 118 L
dmorrill@ut.edu
MORRIS, Adam .... 562-903-4714... 29 L
adam.morris@biola.edu
MORRIS, Andrew .... 585-389-2801. 332 D
amorris8@naz.edu
MORRIS, Ann .... 419-824-3694. 383 C
amorris@lourdes.edu
MORRIS, Ann .... 903-693-2014. 478 A
amorris@panola.edu
MORRIS, Ann .... 704-216-3542. 363 D
ann.morris@rccc.edu
MORRIS, Barbara .... 970-247-7314... 81 M
morris_b@fortlewis.edu
MORRIS, Barbara .... 410-532-5367. 217 E
bmorris@ndm.edu
MORRIS, Barry .... 601-318-6139. 270 I
bmorris@wmcarey.edu
MORRIS, Ben .... 252-940-6374. 358 A
benm@beaufortccc.edu
MORRIS, Bernadette .... 845-257-3101. 342 B
morrisb@newpaltz.edu
MORRIS, Beth .... 828-766-1257. 361 H
bmorris@mayland.edu
MORRIS, Bevan, H .... 641-472-8194. 180 N
president@mum.edu
MORRIS, Beverly .... 937-395-8551. 382 K
beverly.morris@khnetwork.org
MORRIS, Brenda .... 870-584-4471... 24 F
bmorris@cccua.edu
MORRIS, Brett .... 859-622-3840. 193 P
admissions@eku.edu
MORRIS, Carlton, E .... 334-724-4191..... 8 A
cmorris@mytu.tuskegee.edu
MORRIS, Charles .... 214-860-2392. 470 J
MORRIS, Clark .... 816-415-5997. 285 C
morrisc@william.jewell.edu
MORRIS, Clark, W .... 816-415-5997. 285 C
morrisc@william.jewell.edu
MORRIS, Claudia .... 352-365-3539. 108 S
morrisc@lssc.edu
MORRIS, Corinne .... 402-844-7361. 291 I
corinne@northeast.edu
MORRIS, Craig .... 541-552-6319. 406 C
cmorris@sou.edu
MORRIS, Cricket .... 252-985-5145. 365 D
lmorris@ncwc.edu
MORRIS, Dan .... 702-651-5500. 294 E
dan.morris@csn.edu
MORRIS, Daryl .... 334-244-3295..... 2 A
dmorris@aum.edu
MORRIS, Delesa .... 561-803-2022. 110 B
delesa_morris@pba.edu
MORRIS, Diana .... 800-567-2344. 532 E
dmorris@menominee.edu
MORRIS, Diane .... 202-639-1816... 95 B
dmorris@corcoran.org
MORRIS, Don .... 314-968-7444. 284 N
morrisdo@webster.edu
MORRIS, Dottie .... 603-358-2206. 298 F
dmorris@keene.edu
MORRIS, Emma, W .... 706-385-1058. 130 F
emma.morris@point.edu
MORRIS, Gary .... 315-312-2255. 344 A
gary.morris@oswego.edu
MORRIS, Genevieve .... 251-380-3020..... 7 D
gmorris@shc.edu
MORRIS, Geri .... 419-227-3141. 391 F
geri@unoh.edu
MORRIS, Glenn .... 352-335-2332... 97 E
MORRIS, Heather .... 740-774-6300. 378 J
hmorris@daymarcollege.edu
MORRIS, Henry .... 507-389-1150. 259 G
henry.morris@mnsu.edu
MORRIS, Jacqueline .... 205-366-8950..... 7 E
jmorris@stillman.edu
MORRIS, Jake .... 615-966-2000. 456 B
jake.morris@lipscomb.edu
MORRIS, Jeff .... 620-252-7177. 185 O
jeffm@coffeyville.edu
MORRIS, Jeffery, B .... 785-532-6415. 188 A
jbmorris@ksu.edu
MORRIS, Jennifer, M ...... 650-325-5621... 61 G
jennifer.morris@stpatricksseminary.org
MORRIS, Jeremy .... 731-265-1703. 455 J
jkmorris@lanecollege.edu
MORRIS, Joe .... 601-923-1700. 269 E
jmorris@rts.edu
MORRIS, Joe, E .... 205-853-1200..... 5 B
jmorris@jeffstateonline.com
MORRIS, John .... 928-523-6187... 16 C
john.morris@nau.edu
MORRIS, John .... 808-739-8555. 135 D
jmorris@chaminade.edu
MORRIS, John, B .... 860-486-2128... 92 A
john.morris@uconn.edu
MORRIS, John, K .... 801-581-4466. 496 Q
john.morris@legal.utah.edu
MORRIS, Jonathan .... 860-343-5779... 89 A
jmorris@mxcc.commnet.edu
MORRIS, Joseph .... 303-797-5801... 78 F
joseph.morris@arapahoe.edu
MORRIS, Juanita .... 731-426-7533. 455 J
jmorris@lanecollege.edu
MORRIS, Julia, M .... 304-457-6205. 526 A
auviljm@ab.edu
MORRIS, Karen .... 803-641-3489. 448 A
karenm@usca.edu
MORRIS, Katherine, W ... 937-775-2809. 393 G
kathy.morris@wright.edu
MORRIS, Kathryn .... 317-940-9903. 164 J
kmorris@butler.edu
MORRIS, Kenneth, W ..... 319-895-4484. 177 A
kmorris@cornellcollege.edu
MORRIS, Kevin .... 281-922-3479. 479 H
kevin.morris@sjcd.edu
MORRIS, Kevin .... 936-294-1753. 487 A
upd_khm@shsu.edu
MORRIS, Kimberly .... 770-412-4005. 132 B
kmorris@sctech.edu
MORRIS, Kizzy .... 570-422-2820. 428 D
kmorris@po-box.esu.edu
MORRIS, Kyle .... 307-755-2160. 544 B
kmorris@wyotech.edu
MORRIS, LaSonia .... 318-670-9319. 207 A
lmorris@susla.edu
MORRIS, Laura .... 832-813-6793. 476 A
laura.k.morris@lonestar.edu
MORRIS, Laura, M .... 302-295-1179... 94 E
laura.m.morris@wilmu.edu
MORRIS, Lauren .... 313-664-7462. 241 C
lmorris@collegeforcreativestudies.edu
MORRIS, Lawrence, J ..... 202-319-5142... 94 G
morrisl@cua.edu
MORRIS, Lela .... 817-598-6488. 494 G
morris@wc.edu
MORRIS, Libby, V .... 706-583-0506. 133 C
lvmorris@uga.edu
MORRIS, Lonnie .... 301-860-3427. 220 A
lmorris@bowiestate.edu
MORRIS, Loren, L .... 620-665-3523. 187 F
morrisl@hutchcc.edu
MORRIS, M. Scott .... 404-894-2499. 125 D
scott.morris@ohr.gatech.edu
MORRIS, Marie, S .... 765-641-4020. 163 L
msmorris@anderson.edu
MORRIS, Mark .... 360-438-4394. 522 G
mmorris@stmartin.edu
MORRIS, Nancy .... 615-230-3272. 461 G
nancy.morris@volstate.edu
MORRIS, Nerissa, E .... 305-284-4476. 118 F
nmorris@miami.edu
MORRIS, Nora .... 763-433-1632. 257 P
nora.morris@anokaramsey.edu
MORRIS, Paul .... 435-652-7504. 497 E
pmorris@dixie.edu
MORRIS, JR., Paul, T ..... 302-453-3096... 93 F
pmorris@dtcc.edu

MORRIS, Phil .... 803-822-3559. 445 C
morrisp@midlandstech.edu
MORRIS, Princilla, E ...... 615-329-8888. 454 F
psmart@fisk.edu
MORRIS, Rachel .... 216-373-5320. 385 G
rmorris@ndc.edu
MORRIS, Reggie .... 323-241-5200... 52 C
morrisr@lasc.edu
MORRIS, Renea .... 740-593-2563. 387 C
morrisr@ohio.edu
MORRIS, Rick .... 864-977-7777. 445 H
publicsafety@ngu.edu
MORRIS, Rita, R .... 740-351-3208. 388 N
rmorris@shawnee.edu
MORRIS, III, Robert .... 520-459-1610. 494 F
morrisb@wbu.edu
MORRIS, Robert, D .... 404-413-2502. 126 E
robinmorris@gsu.edu
MORRIS, Robert, J .... 765-285-1300. 164 B
rmorris@bsu.edu
MORRIS, Sandra, L .... 843-792-8720. 445 B
morriss@musc.edu
MORRIS, Sara, B .... 316-978-3450. 191 F
sara.morris@wichita.edu
MORRIS, Steve .... 270-789-5017. 193 D
srmorris@campbellsville.edu
MORRIS, Steve .... 606-539-4209. 200 B
steve.morris@ucumberlands.edu
MORRIS, Tammy, H .... 336-322-2150. 362 F
Tammy.Morris@piedmontcc.edu
MORRIS, Tiffany, D .... 336-342-4261. 363 C
morrist@rockinghamcc.edu
MORRIS, Tom .... 570-586-2400. 410 D
tmorris@bbc.edu
MORRIS, Tracy, L .... 815-224-0393. 148 A
tracy_morris@ivcc.edu
MORRIS, Valerie, B .... 843-953-8222. 443 A
morrisv@cofc.edu
MORRIS, Wendi .... 478-296-6179. 129 I
wmorris@oftc.edu
MORRIS, William, G .... 315-267-2579. 344 C
morriswg@potsdam.edu
MORRIS, William, R .... 512-492-3060. 466 B
wmorris@aoma.edu
MORRIS WOOD, JR.,
Dossie .... 910-843-5304. 357 J
MORRISETTE, Joanna ..... 919-735-5151. 364 H
jmmorrisette@waynecc.edu
MORRISON, Barry, F ...... 401-232-6017. 438 K
bmorriso@bryant.edu
MORRISON, Betty .... 630-829-6347. 140 B
bmorrison@ben.edu
MORRISON, Brenda, M .. 443-412-2409. 215 C
bmorrison@harford.edu
MORRISON, Carberta, A 856-225-2949. 306 C
cammor@camden.rutgers.edu
MORRISON, Carol .... 239-513-1122. 106 O
cmorrison@hodges.edu
MORRISON, Cindi .... 352-854-2322. 100 K
morrisoc@cf.edu
MORRISON, Darrell .... 479-788-7035... 24 A
darrell.morrison@uafs.edu
MORRISON, David .... 770-534-6167. 122 A
dmorrison@brenau.edu
MORRISON, Don .... 641-628-5280. 176 E
morrisond@central.edu
MORRISON, Edwina .... 406-444-6570. 286 G
emorrison@montana.edu
MORRISON, Gail .... 651-450-3512. 258 H
gmorris@inverhills.edu
MORRISON, Gale .... 805-893-2238... 72 B
gale@education.ucsb.edu
MORRISON, George, H .. 304-236-7640. 528 F
george.morrison@southernwv.edu
MORRISON, James .... 617-746-1990. 227 F
James.Morrison@hult.edu
MORRISON, Jean .... 617-353-2000. 224 D
jmorrison@bu.edu
MORRISON, Jenni .... 419-783-2380. 379 C
jmorrison@defiance.edu
MORRISON, Jennifer, K . 508-767-7007. 222 C
jemorrison@assumption.edu
MORRISON, Julie .... 734-973-5010. 252 A
jmorriso@wccnet.edu
MORRISON, Katrina .... 918-270-6421. 398 I
katrina.morrison@ptstulsa.edu
MORRISON, Kelly, S ...... 434-381-6337. 510 F
morrison@sbc.edu
MORRISON, Kirk .... 858-513-9240. 175 F
kirk.morrison@ashford.edu
MORRISON, Laura .... 252-335-0821. 359 F
laura_morrison@albemarle.edu
MORRISON, Leonard .... 781-891-2575. 223 C
lmorrison@bentley.edu
MORRISON, Lolita .... 404-297-9522. 126 A
morrisonl@gptc.org
MORRISON, Marty, G ..... 540-654-2287. 510 J
mmorris3@umw.edu
MORRISON, Michael ...... 626-650-2306... 45 K
MORRISON, Michael, L . 812-888-5736. 174 F
mmorrison@vinu.edu

MORRISON, Nancy, J .... 212-998-4924. 334 D
nancy.morrison@nyu.edu
MORRISON, Nicholas ..... 435-797-2715. 497 B
nicholas.morrison@usu.edu
MORRISON, Rebecca, L . 414-955-4949. 534 C
rmorriso@mcw.edu
MORRISON, Rhonda ...... 316-322-3124. 185 D
rmorrison@butlercc.edu
MORRISON, Ricky .... 419-227-3141. 391 F
rmorrison@unoh.edu
MORRISON, Rob .... 503-682-3903. 407 B
rmorrison@pioneerpacific.edu
MORRISON, Rodney .... 856-225-6510. 306 C
rodneymo@camden.rutgers.edu
MORRISON, Rodney .... 419-448-2391. 380 G
rmorriso@heidelberg.edu
MORRISON, Scott .... 775-445-3000. 295 A
scott.morrison@wnc.edu
MORRISON, Scott, D ...... 540-828-5376. 502 J
smorriso@bridgewater.edu
MORRISON, Shanea .... 501-337-5000... 20 J
smorrision@coto.edu
MORRISON, Sharon .... 580-745-2702. 399 J
smorrison@se.edu
MORRISON, Thomas ...... 812-855-6992. 167 E
morrison@indiana.edu
MORRISON, Tim .... 909-607-1113... 39 B
tim_morrison@cuc.claremont.edu
MORRISON, Tom .... 812-855-6992. 167 F
morrisot@indiana.edu
MORRISON, Tracy .... 909-384-8671... 62 A
tmorriso@sbccd.cc.ca.us
MORRISON-BEEDY,
Dianne .... 813-974-2191. 116 C
dmbeedy@health.usf.edu
MORRISON-FRONCKOWIAK,
Lisa, T .... 716-878-4500. 343 A
morrislt@buffalostate.edu
MORRISON-SHETLAR,
Alison .... 336-278-6490. 354 B
amorrison4@elon.edu
MORRISS-OLSON,
Melissa .... 413-565-1000. 222 F
mmolson@baypath.edu
MORRISSEY, Ann, M ...... 401-874-4846. 440 D
morrissey@uri.edu
MORRISSEY, Jeff, P .... 417-836-5770. 278 E
jeffmorrissey@missouristate.edu
MORRISSEY, Marietta ..... 973-655-4314. 303 D
morrisseym@mail.montclair.edu
MORRISSEY, Sharron ...... 919-807-7100. 357 L
morrissey@nccommunitycolleges.edu
MORRISSEY, Shawn .... 508-856-2265. 229 C
shawn.morrissey@umassmed.edu
MORRO, Robert .... 610-519-4589. 436 F
robert.morro@villanova.edu
MORROBEL-SOSA, Anny 718-960-8111. 318 A
morrobel.sosa@lehman.cuny.edu
MORRONE, Anastasia ..... 317-274-3479. 168 D
amorrone@iupui.edu
MORROW, Barbara, A .... 314-340-5763. 275 A
morrowb@hssu.edu
MORROW, Bill, J .... 302-857-1245... 93 G
bil.morrow@dtcc.edu
MORROW, Carol, K .... 212-998-4798. 334 D
carol.morrow@nyu.edu
MORROW, David .... 215-222-4200. 431 H
dmorrow@walnuthillcollege.edu
MORROW, David, M .... 518-736-3622. 325 A
dmorrow@fmcc.suny.edu
MORROW, Dorothy .... 402-557-7296. 288 G
dorothy.morrow@bellevue.edu
MORROW, Frances .... 330-490-7312. 392 H
fmorrow@walsh.edu
MORROW,
Jacqueline, R .... 717-720-4045. 428 F
MORROW, Jean .... 617-585-1250. 234 I
jean.morrow@necmusic.edu
MORROW, Jeffrey, S ...... 330-665-1084. 386 A
j.morrow@ocm.edu
MORROW, Jessica .... 918-335-6268. 398 F
jmorrow@okwu.edu
MORROW, Joyce .... 319-273-2701. 176 A
joyce.morrow@uni.edu
MORROW, Liz .... 573-681-5011. 276 C
morrowl@lincolnu.edu
MORROW, Marjann .... 325-574-7608. 494 K
mmorrow@wtc.edu
MORROW, Rebecca .... 304-793-6591. 530 B
rmorrow@osteo.wvsom.edu
MORROW, S. Rex .... 219-785-5550. 172 A
smorrow@pnc.edu
MORROW, Wanda .... 713-646-1825. 480 J
wmorrow@stcl.edu
MORROW-JENSEN,
Amanda .... 408-453-9900... 47 H
amorrow-jensen@henley-putnam.edu
MORSBERGER,
Michael, J .... 202-994-6419... 95 D
mjm@gwu.edu

MORSCHES, Michael ...... 708-974-5310. 153 F
morschesm@morainevalley.edu
MORSE, Charles, C .... 508-831-5540. 238 F
cmorse@wpi.edu
MORSE, James .... 818-767-0888... 76 K
james.morse@woodbury.edu
MORSE, Marc .... 702-651-3008. 294 E
marc.morse@csn.edu
MORSE, Mark .... 212-349-4330. 325 D
mmorse@globe.edu
MORSE, Marlane .... 530-257-6181... 50 F
mmorse@lassencollege.edu
MORSE, Rachel .... 907-786-1278... 10 H
rlmorse@uaa.alaska.edu
MORSE, Sarah .... 410-626-2522. 217 G
sarah.morse@sjca.edu
MORSE, William .... 253-879-2808. 524 F
wmorse@pugetsound.edu
MORSETTE, Clarice .... 406-395-4313. 288 D
camorsette@yahoo.com
MORSIANI, Paola .... 914-251-6105. 344 D
paola.morsiani@purchase.edu
MORSMAN, Elaine .... 607-587-4061. 345 D
morsmaem@alfredstate.edu
MORSOVILLO, Michael .. 708-524-6793. 144 C
morsomike@dom.edu
MORT, Dale .... 717-569-7071. 421 A
dmort@lbc.edu
MORTALI, Jill, M .... 603-646-3007. 296 G
jill.m.mortali@dartmouth.edu
MORTENSEN, Alan .... 815-584-2806. 150 D
alan.mortensen@doc.illinois.gov
MORTENSEN, Brad .... 801-626-6002. 497 D
bmortensen@weber.edu
MORTENSEN, Dan .... 863-667-5006. 113 P
dmortensen@seu.edu
MORTENSEN, John .... 435-797-1110. 497 B
john.mortensen@usu.edu
MORTENSEN, Larry .... 719-587-7402... 78 B
lsmorten@adams.edu
MORTENSON,
Donald, W .... 206-281-2522. 523 C
dmort@spu.edu
MORTENSON, Stacey ..... 701-627-4738. 371 A
smorte@fbcc.bia.edu
MORTHLAND, Betsey ..... 309-796-5285. 140 E
morthlandb@bhc.edu
MORTIMER, Ian .... 802-651-5911. 499 A
mortimer@champlain.edu
MORTIMER, Lee, E .... 513-556-0364. 390 G
lee.mortimer@uc.edu
MORTIMER, Theresa ...... 617-287-6800. 228 G
theresa.mortimer@umb.edu
MORTLAND, Stephen ..... 765-998-5206. 173 C
stmortlan@taylor.edu
MORTON, Amy, M .... 508-831-5874. 238 F
ammorton@wpi.edu
MORTON, Austin .... 303-477-7240... 82 C
austinm@heritage-education.com
MORTON, Brad .... 973-290-4477. 300 F
bmorton@cse.edu
MORTON, Clarresa .... 540-665-4517. 509 E
cmorton@su.edu
MORTON, Diane .... 301-846-2442. 214 H
dmorton@frederick.edu
MORTON, John .... 808-956-7038. 135 L
jmorton@hawaii.edu
MORTON, John, F .... 808-956-7038. 136 D
jmorton@hawaii.edu
MORTON, Kim .... 202-884-9053... 96 G
mortonk@trinitydc.edu
MORTON, Leo, E .... 816-235-1101. 283 D
mortonle@umkc.edu
MORTON, Lisa .... 414-276-5200. 165 C
lmorton@ccr.edu
MORTON, Lynn .... 704-337-2579. 365 G
mortonl@queens.edu
MORTON, Marcia .... 417-667-8181. 273 A
mmorton@cottey.edu
MORTON, Margaret .... 212-353-4208. 321 F
mortonnyc@cooper.edu
MORTON, Mary .... 518-587-2100. 346 A
mary.morton@esc.edu
MORTON, Nina .... 304-357-4944. 527 H
ninamorton@ucwv.edu
MORTON, Patricia .... 801-581-8262. 496 Q
patricia.morton@nurs.utah.edu
MORTON, Stephen .... 402-844-7298. 291 I
stephen@northeast.edu
MORY, Scott, M .... 213-740-2383... 74 A
mory@usc.edu
MORYAN, James .... 215-489-4889. 414 E
james.moryan@delval.edu
MOSBO, John .... 812-488-1178. 173 H
jm545@evansville.edu
MOSBURG, Calleb, N ..... 580-327-8415. 396 N
cnmosburg@nwosu.edu
MOSBY, Christel .... 602-639-7500... 13 S
MOSBY, David, C .... 301-322-0655. 217 F
dmosby@pgcc.edu

MOSBY, Gail .... 304-766-3047. 530 C
gmosby@wvstateu.edu
MOSBY, John .... 650-738-4484... 64 D
mosbyj@smccd.edu
MOSBY-WILSON,
Shatiqua, A .... 504-286-5030. 206 K
swilson@suno.edu
MOSCA, David .... 301-445-2772. 219 A
dmosca@usmd.edu
MOSCA, Joseph, L .... 330-941-3321. 394 A
jmosca@ysu.edu
MOSCARIELLO,
Dawn, M .... 610-359-5298. 414 D
dmoscariello@dccc.edu
MOSCATO, Robin, A ...... 609-258-3330. 304 E
moscato@princeton.edu
MOSCHELLA, Jayne .... 561-912-1211. 103 C
jmoschella@evergladesuniversity.edu
MOSELEY, David .... 479-968-0300... 20 E
dmoseley@atu.edu
MOSELEY, James, G .... 317-738-8010. 165 I
jmoseley@franklincollege.edu
MOSELEY, Lynne .... 707-638-5223... 69 K
lynne.moseley@tu.edu
MOSELEY-JONES, Vickie 252-638-7225. 359 G
moseleyv@cravencc.edu
MOSER, Donald, J .... 336-758-3904. 370 D
moserdj@wfu.edu
MOSER, Drew .... 765-998-5384. 173 C
drmoser@taylor.edu
MOSER, Ernest, R .... 731-881-7225. 463 E
emoser@utm.edu
MOSER, Jack, T .... 662-685-4771. 266 C
jmoser@bmc.edu
MOSER, Melissa .... 714-432-5509... 39 K
mmoser@occ.cccd.edu
MOSER, Mike .... 808-235-7361. 137 C
mikem@hawaii.edu
MOSER, Shelly .... 870-612-2034... 25 A
shelly.moser@uaccb.edu
MOSER, Steven .... 601-266-4315. 270 E
steven.moser@usm.edu
MOSER, Tina, L .... 724-738-2000. 429 F
tina.moser@sru.edu
MOSER, Tracy, S .... 662-685-4771. 266 C
tmoser@bmc.edu
MOSES, Carl, O .... 570-372-4127. 433 H
moses@susqu.edu
MOSES, Charles .... 404-880-8999. 122 J
cmoses@cau.edu
MOSES, Dyann, W .... 601-877-6230. 265 G
dmoses@alcorn.edu
MOSES, Henry .... 615-327-6266. 456 E
hmoses@mmc.edu
MOSES, M. Iyailu .... 919-516-4101. 366 C
mimoses@st-aug.edu
MOSES, Napoleon, W ..... 773-995-2400. 141 J
nmoses@csu.edu
MOSES, Orrin Douglas ... 831-656-3218. 544 M
dmoses@nps.edu
MOSES, Robert, M .... 570-422-3138. 428 D
bob.moses@po-box.esu.edu
MOSES-HOLMES,
Jeanette .... 803-934-3989. 445 F
jholmes@morris.edu
MOSESSO, Lynn .... 479-575-5869... 23 I
mosesso@uark.edu
MOSEY, Douglas, L .... 860-632-3010... 90 C
rector@holyapostles.edu
MOSHER, Cliff .... 949-480-4235... 66 F
cmo@soka.edu
MOSHER, Craig .... 785-442-6019. 187 E
cmosher@highlandcc.edu
MOSHER, Craig .... 785-442-6017. 187 E
cmosher@highlandcc.edu
MOSHER, Craig, E .... 785-442-6019. 187 E
cmosher@highlandcc.edu
MOSHER, George .... 312-329-4268. 153 E
george.mosher@moody.edu
MOSHER, Sharon .... 512-471-6048. 491 C
smosher@sg.utexas.edu
MOSHIER, Jeff .... 765-998-5203. 173 C
jfmoshier@taylor.edu
MOSIER, Greg .... 573-355-1468. 398 B
greg.a.mosier@okstate.edu
MOSIER, Gregory .... 775-784-4912. 294 J
greg.mosier@unr.edu
MOSIER, Julie .... 541-383-7779. 402 D
jmosier@cocc.edu
MOSKOVITZ, Kristin .... 313-664-7496. 241 C
kmoskovitz@collegeforcreativestudies.edu
MOSKOWITZ, Roy, P .... 212-229-5432. 332 E
moskowir@newschool.edu
MOSLEY, Cal .... 320-363-3036. 263 P
cmosley@csbsju.edu
MOSLEY, Calvin .... 320-363-3036. 254 J
cmosley@csbsju.edu
MOSLEY, Carolyn .... 479-788-7856... 24 A
carolyn.mosley@uafs.edu
MOSLEY, Crystal .... 410-951-3579. 220 B
cmosley@coppin.edu

MOSLEY, David .... 409-880-2207. 486 E
dpmosley@lit.edu
MOSLEY, Gary .... 662-562-3216. 269 C
gtmosley@northwestms.edu
MOSLEY, James .... 405-466-3259. 395 N
jmosley@langston.edu
MOSLEY, Jared .... 325-674-2353. 464 H
jared.mosley@acu.edu
MOSLEY, Juiliana .... 904-470-8216. 102 A
j.mosley@ewc.edu
MOSLEY, Julie .... 479-788-7404... 24 A
julie.mosley@uafs.edu
MOSLEY, Mary Lou .... 602-787-6607... 15 B
marylou.mosley@paradisevalley.edu
MOSLEY, Melissa .... 662-476-5074. 266 I
mmosley@eastms.edu
MOSLEY, Regina .... 734-462-4400. 250 A
rmosley@schoolcraft.edu
MOSLEY, Tom .... 281-649-3033. 473 B
tmosley@hbu.edu
MOSLEY, Walter .... 903-593-8311. 485 A
wmosley@texascollege.edu
MOSQUEDA, Margarita .. 989-686-9512. 242 C
momosque@delta.edu
MOSQUEDA, Rolando .... 702-651-4245. 294 E
rolando.mosqueda@csn.edu
MOSS, Aimi .... 810-762-3085. 251 E
aimi@umflint.edu
MOSS, Annie .... 318-274-6423. 207 E
mossa@gram.edu
MOSS, OSB, Brendan ..... 812-357-6422. 173 A
bmoss@saintmeinrad.edu
MOSS, Catherine .... 509-359-6362. 519 C
cmoss@ewu.edu
MOSS, Elizabeth, H .... 443-518-4837. 215 E
emoss@howardcc.edu
MOSS, Eric, O .... 213-613-2200... 67 E
directors_office@sciarc.edu
MOSS, Michael .... 704-330-6681. 359 C
michael.moss@cpcc.edu
MOSS, Renie .... 205-726-2116..... 6 F
rmoss@samford.edu
MOSS, Shelley .... 662-329-7106. 268 E
smoss@admissions.muw.edu
MOSS, William P. O .... 434-223-7230. 505 E
wmoss@hsc.edu
MOSSER, Daniel .... 301-934-7547. 214 D
dmosser@csmd.edu
MOSSER, Sandra, L .... 610-799-1172. 421 I
smosser@lccc.edu
MOSSEY, Christopher ..... 212-799-5000. 328 B
MOSTAFAVI, Mohsen ..... 617-495-4364. 227 C
mohsen_mostafavi@gsd.harvard.edu
MOSTARDI, OSA,
Joseph .... 610-519-4080. 436 F
joseph.mostardi@villanova.edu
MOSTASHARI, Zary .... 703-284-1673. 507 B
zary.mostashari@marymount.edu
MOSTELLER, John .... 610-896-1376. 418 F
jmostell@haverford.edu
MOSTO, Pat .... 609-896-5155. 305 D
mosto@rider.edu
MOSTOV, Julie .... 215-895-6793. 415 B
julie.mostov@drexel.edu
MOTE, Jerry .... 724-266-3838. 434 J
jmote@tsm.edu
MOTE, Marlon .... 972-860-8054. 470 H
mmote@dcccd.edu
MOTEN, Maria .... 847-925-6622. 145 H
mmoten@harpercollege.edu
MOTEN-TOLSON, Paula . 919-546-8544. 366 E
pmotentolson@shawu.edu
MOTHERWELL, Molly ...... 734-487-2229. 242 D
mmotherwe@emich.edu
MOTL, Lori .... 870-245-5110... 22 D
motll@obu.edu
MOTLEY, J. Keith .... 617-287-6800. 228 G
keith.motley@umb.edu
MOTOUAPUAKA, Hola ... 209-473-5200... 47 F
hola_motouapuaka@heald.edu
MOTT, Jeanne .... 785-594-4595. 184 C
jeanne.mott@bakeru.edu
MOTT, Molly, A .... 315-386-7425. 345 F
mottma@canton.edu
MOTT, Susan .... 269-488-4217. 244 L
smott@kvcc.edu
MOTTE, Kristin .... 617-587-5658. 234 H
mottek@neco.edu
MOTTEN, Luisa .... 206-934-6782. 523 A
luisa.motten@seattlecolleges.edu
MOTTER, Kristi .... 601-266-5020. 270 E
kristi.motter@usm.edu
MOTTET, Timothy .... 512-245-2308. 487 C
tm15@txstate.edu
MOTTOLA, Michael, A ..... 717-720-4173. 427 G
mmottola@passhe.edu
MOTTSMAN-ROSEN,
Deborah, E .... 703-323-3154. 513 C
drosen@nvcc.edu
MOTYL, Lynne, M .... 724-738-2070. 429 F
lynne.motyl@sru.edu
MOTZER, JR.,
William, G .... 847-735-5000. 150 B
motzer@lakeforest.edu
MOUA, Pa Lee .... 920-832-7030. 533 S
palee.moua@lawrence.edu
MOUA, Phong .... 907-564-8342... 10 C
pmoua@alaskapacific.edu
MOUDGIL, Virinder, K ... 248-204-2000. 245 I
president@ltu.edu
MOUDY, Quentin, J .... 260-982-5267. 170 U
qjmoudy@manchester.edu
MOUGHALIAN, David .... 212-226-5500. 314 A
dmoughalian@aii.edu
MOUGHAN, Marie .... 610-647-4400. 418 I
mmoughan@immaculata.edu
MOULD, Richard .... 256-233-8183..... 1 F
rick.mould@athens.edu
MOULTON, Cathy, B ...... 518-564-3824. 344 B
moultocb@plattsburgh.edu
MOULTON, David, A ...... 202-419-0482... 96 F
dam@strayer.edu
MOULTRIE, Anne .... 301-445-2722. 219 A
amoultrie@usmd.edu
MOULTRIE, Gloria, B ...... 504-286-5341. 206 K
gmoultrie@suno.edu
MOUNFIELD, Gina .... 843-525-8257. 447 C
gmounfield@tcl.edu
MOUNFIELD, Gina, C .... 843-525-8247. 447 C
gmounfield@tcl.edu
MOUNGA, Peni .... 605-626-3007. 451 I
moungap@northern.edu
MOUNGA, Salesi .... 605-626-2530. 451 I
Salesi.Mounga@northern.edu
MOUNGER, D. G. (Gray) 818-677-2137... 34 C
gray.mounger@csun.edu
MOUNT, Judy .... 316-677-9400. 191 E
jmount@watc.edu
MOUNT, Marianne, E ..... 540-338-2700. 503 A
mmount@cdu.edu
MOUNTAIN, Amy .... 717-361-1268. 415 H
mountaina@etown.edu
MOUNTJOY, Shane .... 402-363-5614. 293 I
mountjoy@york.edu
MOUNTJOY, Todd .... 715-365-4589. 540 G
tmountjoy@nicoletcollege.edu
MOUNTS, William .... 912-279-5851. 123 B
wmounts@ccga.edu
MOUNTY, Lauren .... 516-877-3680. 313 A
lmounty@adelphi.edu
MOURAD, Roger .... 734-677-5328. 252 A
mou@wccnet.edu
MOURTZANOS,
Emmanuel .... 661-395-4406... 49 N
emmanuel.mourtzanos@bakersfieldcollege.edu
MOUSA, Shaker .... 518-694-7575. 313 B
shaker.mousa@acphs.edu
MOUSER, Debbie .... 615-844-5222. 464 E
debbie@welch.edu
MOUSER, Lisa .... 636-922-8319. 280 J
lmouser@stchas.edu
MOUSSALLI, Samir, R ... 334-833-4509..... 4 D
samirm@huntingdon.edu
MOUSSAVI, Farzad .... 319-273-6240. 176 A
farzad.moussavi@uni.edu
MOUTON, Camille .... 409-880-8419. 486 F
camille.mouton@lamar.edu
MOUTON, Charles, P ...... 615-327-6204. 456 E
cmouton@mmc.edu
MOUTON, Phyllis .... 225-219-8068. 202 H
moutonp@mybrcc.edu
MOUTOS, Don .... 503-654-8000. 407 B
dmoutos@pioneerpacific.edu
MOUTTET, Nathan .... 773-244-5705. 154 G
nmouttet@northpark.edu
MOUTTET, Nathan .... 773-244-7505. 154 G
nmouttet@northpark.edu
MOUTZ, Dana .... 859-858-3511. 192 B
dana.moutz@asbury.edu
MOVSESIAN, David .... 858-279-4500... 49 K
dmovsesian@kaplan.edu
MOWATT, Beth .... 989-328-1217. 247 D
bethm@montcalm.edu
MOWDER, William, J ...... 610-683-4500. 429 A
mowder@kutztown.edu
MOWDY, Jennifer .... 281-458-4050. 479 G
jennifer.mowdy@sjcd.edu
MOWEN, Brenda, K .... 304-293-8450. 530 D
bkmowen@mail.wvu.edu
MOWEN, David .... 540-887-7370. 507 A
dmowen@mbc.edu
MOWERY, Chris .... 423-472-7141. 460 D
cmowery@clevelandstatecc.edu
MOWERY, Dylan .... 870-368-2013... 22 E
dmowery@ozarka.edu
MOWITZ, Marlane .... 828-251-6867. 368 C
mmowitz@unca.edu
MOWREY, J. Diane .... 704-337-2304. 365 G
mowreyd@queens.edu
MOWRY, Cynthia .... 253-589-5570. 518 B
cynthia.mowry@cptc.edu
MOXEY-INGRAHAM,
Theresa .... 242-394-8570. 218 D
tcooper@host.sdc.edu
MOY, James, S .... 813-974-7380. 116 C
moy@usf.edu
MOYANO, Angelica .... 954-607-4344. 118 D
MOYD, Greg .... 910-670-1167. 367 D
gmoyd@uncfsu.edu
MOYE, Lauren .... 802-322-1732. 499 C
lauren.moye@goddard.edu
MOYER, Carolyn, H .... 610-861-5494. 425 D
cmoyer@northampton.edu
MOYER, Christina, L ...... 610-799-1136. 421 I
cmoyer@lccc.edu
MOYER, James .... 616-331-3853. 243 C
moyerj@gvsu.edu
MOYER, James, G .... 863-638-7613. 119 C
james.moyer@warner.edu
MOYER, Michelle, L ...... 909-869-3419... 32 G
mlmoyer@csupomona.edu
MOYER, Paul .... 410-386-4660. 216 E
pmoyer@mcdaniel.edu
MOYER, R. Charles .... 502-852-6443. 200 D
charlie.moyer@louisville.edu
MOYER, Rachel .... 802-862-9616. 498 I
rmoyer@burlington.edu
MOYER, Richard .... 323-265-8678... 51 F
moyerra@elac.edu
MOYER, IV, Tilghman .... 215-926-2500. 433 K
tilghman.moyer@temple.edu
MOYERS, Penelope .... 651-690-6813. 263 O
pamoyers@stkate.edu
MOYLAN, Shannon .... 607-735-1782. 323 H
smoylan@elmira.edu
MOYNAHAN, J. Patrick .. 859-572-5379. 198 I
moynahan@nku.edu
MOYNAHAN, Joan .... 207-602-2000. 213 A
jmoynahan@une.edu
MOYNIHAN, Jack .... 617-373-2656. 235 F
MOZDZER, Alfreda .... 203-576-5479... 91 D
amozdzer@stvincentscollege.edu
MOZERSKY, Elisha .... 518-276-6000. 337 I
mozere@rpi.edu
MOZIE-ROSS, Yvette ...... 410-455-3799. 219 D
mozie@umbc.edu
MRAD, David .... 417-823-3410. 281 M
dmrad@forest.edu
MRIZEK, David, E .... 210-486-0937. 465 C
dmrizek@alamo.edu
MROZ, Donald, W .... 203-596-4666... 90 I
dmroz@post.edu
MROZ, Frank, D .... 610-799-1109. 421 I
fmroz@lccc.edu
MROZ, Glenn, D .... 906-487-2200. 247 A
gdmroz@mtu.edu
MROZEK, John .... 281-487-1170. 484 H
jmrozek@txchiro.edu
MROZIK, Jacek .... 701-858-3110. 371 F
jacek.mrozik@minotstateu.edu
MROZINSKI, Mark .... 847-925-6540. 145 H
mmrozins@harpercollege.edu
MRVOS, Dessa .... 412-396-1650. 415 F
mrvosds@duq.edu
MUBDI-BEY, Jamal .... 410-276-0306. 218 D
mubdibey@host.sdc.edu
MUCCIARONE, Paul .... 212-752-1530. 328 G
paul.mucciarone@limcollege.edu
MUCCIGROSSO, John .... 973-408-3029. 301 C
jmuccigr@drew.edu
MUCH, Kari .... 507-389-1455. 259 G
karen.much@mnsu.edu
MUCHAL, Stacey .... 570-961-7868. 420 C
muchals@lackawanna.edu
MUCHANE, Mary, W .... 704-894-2644. 353 J
mamuchane@davidson.edu
MUCHANE, Mur, K .... 704-894-2402. 353 J
mumuchane@davidson.edu
MUCK, Dan .... 605-995-3065. 450 E
dan.muck@mitchelltech.edu
MUDD, Sara .... 864-231-6062. 441 B
smudd@andersonuniversity.edu
MUDD, Stephen, B .... 314-505-7313. 272 J
mudds@csl.edu
MUDRAK, Jeff .... 859-233-8701. 199 I
jmudrak@transy.edu
MUECKE, Mary .... 718-409-7444. 346 D
mmuecke@sunymaritime.edu
MUECKE, Nancy .... 641-648-4611. 179 I
nancy.muecke@iavalley.edu
MUECKE, Nancy .... 641-648-8502. 179 H
Nancy.Muecke@iavalley.edu
MUEHSAM, Mitchell .... 936-294-1254. 487 A
mmuehsam@shsu.edu
MUELLENBACH, Joanne . 570-504-9627. 413 B
MUELLER, Al .... 815-753-6104. 154 I
amueller@niu.edu
MUELLER, Alan, C .... 336-316-2313. 355 A
muelleracc@guilford.edu
MUELLER, II, Alfred, G .. 610-558-5508. 424 I
muellera@neumann.edu
MUELLER, Andrew .... 212-966-0300. 333 A
andrew@nyaa.edu
MUELLER, Beverley, D ... 757-594-7002. 503 M
bmueller@cnu.edu
MUELLER, Brian .... 602-639-7500... 13 S
MUELLER, Carla .... 636-949-4731. 276 D
cmueller@lindenwood.edu
MUELLER, Cheryl .... 419-227-3141. 391 F
camuell@unoh.edu
MUELLER, Chris .... 715-425-3505. 537 E
chris.mueller@uwrf.edu
MUELLER, Christie, L ..... 864-833-8700. 446 D
clmueller@presby.edu
MUELLER, Donna, G ...... 585-292-2527. 332 A
dmueller@monroecc.edu
MUELLER, Edward .... 561-868-3032. 110 C
muellere@palmbeachstate.edu
MUELLER, Edward, A ..... 603-862-3220. 298 C
edward.mueller@unh.edu
MUELLER, John, L .... 773-577-8100. 143 F
MUELLER, John, P .... 414-410-4059. 532 B
jpmueller@stritch.edu
MUELLER, Joseph .... 307-382-1647. 543 J
jmueller@wwcc.wy.edu
MUELLER, Julie .... 859-344-3386. 199 H
muellej@thomasmore.edu
MUELLER, Julie .... 636-949-4901. 276 D
jmueller@lindenwood.edu
MUELLER, Lloyd .... 503-338-2412. 402 G
lmueller@clatsopcc.edu
MUELLER, Marie .... 603-577-6559. 296 F
mmueller@dwc.edu
MUELLER, Martin .... 212-229-5896. 332 E
muellerm@newschool.edu
MUELLER, Michael, R ..... 817-735-5475. 490 E
Michael.Mueller@unthsc.edu
MUELLER, Michelle .... 734-477-8976. 252 A
mimueller@wccnet.edu
MUELLER, OSU, Pam .... 270-686-4319. 192 G
pam.mueller@brescia.edu
MUELLER, Ralph .... 860-768-4648... 92 D
rmueller@hartford.edu
MUELLER, Steven, D ...... 937-229-3141. 391 C
SMueller1@udayton.edu
MUELLER, Steven, P ...... 949-214-3386... 41 I
steve.mueller@cui.edu
MUELLER, Vilma .... 973-618-3384. 300 A
vmueller@caldwell.edu
MUELLER, Vincenza .... 845-451-4368. 322 D
v_muelle@culinary.edu
MUELLER, William, J ..... 423-266-4574. 458 F
bmueller@richmont.edu
MUELLER-ROEBKE,
Jenny .... 402-643-7374. 289 B
jenny.roebke@cune.edu
MUERTZ, Julie, A .... 618-235-2700. 160 A
julie.muertz@swic.edu
MUESELER, Christine ..... 724-838-4232. 433 E
mueseler@setonhill.edu
MUETHER, John .... 407-366-9493. 269 E
jmuether@rts.edu
MUGANDA, Baraka .... 301-891-4112. 221 B
chaplain@wau.edu
MUGG, Heather .... 404-727-9326. 124 E
hmugg@emory.edu
MUGGEP, Louis .... 845-398-4174. 340 A
lmuggeo@stac.edu
MUGGLETON, Mary .... 585-271-3657. 338 D
mmuggleton@stbernards.edu
MUGLER, Dale, H .... 330-972-5365. 390 E
dmugler@uakron.edu
MUGLER, Karla .... 330-972-7066. 390 E
mugler@uakron.edu
MUGRIDGE, Philip .... 610-341-1721. 415 G
pmugridg@eastern.edu
MUGWANYA,
Edmond, M .... 818-779-8448... 50 A
emugwanya@kingsuniversity.edu
MUHA, Beth .... 202-885-2591... 94 F
beth@american.edu
MUHA, David .... 973-408-3206. 301 C
dmuha@drew.edu
MUHA, Priscilla .... 925-631-4522... 61 F
pdm2@stmarys-ca.edu
MUHA, Susan .... 216-987-3110. 378 D
susan.muha@tri-c.edu
MUHAMMED, Robert ..... 336-750-3299. 370 A
muhammedr@wssu.edu
MUHL, Erica .... 213-740-6267... 74 A
artdean@usc.edu
MUHLENBRUCH,
Kevin, D .... 641-422-4291. 181 D
muhlekev@niacc.edu
MUHLFELDER, Leslie, F . 610-330-5060. 420 D
muhlfell@lafayette.edu
MUHR, Jill .... 802-322-1652. 499 C
jill.muhr@goddard.edu
MUIR, Bernard .... 650-723-2300... 68 E
MUIR, JR., Harry, P .... 262-521-5435. 538 E
harry.muir@uwc.edu

MUIR, Janette .... 703-993-8891. 505 C
jmuir@gmu.edu
MUIR, Julie .... 916-649-8168... 49 I
jmuir@kaplan.edu
MUIR, Karen .... 614-287-2512. 378 B
kmuir@cscc.edu
MUIR, Norm .... 716-880-2240. 330 F
nmuir@medaille.edu
MUIR, Scott .... 856-256-4981. 305 E
MUIR, Thorton .... 770-426-2624. 128 D
tmuir@life.edu
MUIR, Troy .... 330-337-6403. 373 F
business@awc.edu
MUIRHEAD, Tracy .... 316-295-5814. 186 H
tracy_muirhead@friends.edu
MUITE, Paul .... 305-899-3076... 98 O
pmuite@barry.edu
MUJAHID, Ihsan, R .... 484-365-7705. 422 D
rmujahid@lincon.edu
MUKASA, Samuel .... 603-862-1781. 298 C
sam.mukasa@unh.edu
MUKES, Ora .... 850-599-3225. 114 K
ora.mukes@famu.edu
MUKHARJI, Indrani .... 312-503-2903. 155 D
indrani@northwestern.edu
MULADORE, James, G ... 989-964-4045. 249 G
jgm@svsu.edu
MULANAX, Dennis, K ..... 620-417-1181. 190 F
dennis.mulanax@sccc.edu
MULCAHEY, William .... 319-363-8213. 181 C
mulcahey@mtmercy.edu
MULCAHY, Sean .... 913-360-7500. 184 H
smulcahy@benedictine.edu
MULDER, Craig, A .... 231-995-1061. 248 B
cmulder@nmc.edu
MULDER, Lori .... 616-395-7811. 244 A
mulderl@hope.edu
MULDERICK, Thomas, J 610-799-1941. 421 I
tmulderick@lccc.edu
MULDOON GEUS,
Karen .... 215-951-1849. 420 B
geus@lasalle.edu
MULERO, Daritza .... 787-258-1501. 548 H
dmulero@columbiaco.edu
MULERO, Minerva .... 787-864-2222. 550 D
mmulero@inter.edu
MULET, Mariel .... 323-343-3040... 34 A
mariel.mulet@calstatela.edu
MULFORD, David, H .... 540-375-2290. 509 B
mulford@roanoke.edu
MULGREW, Frank .... 203-591-5040... 90 I
fmulgrew@post.edu
MULHALL, Lawrence, P .. 864-833-8300. 446 D
lmulhall@presby.edu
MULHERIN, April, C ...... 207-778-7081. 212 D
april.mulherin@maine.edu
MULHERN, Jean, K .... 937-382-6661. 393 B
jean_mulhern@wilmington.edu
MULHERN, Michelle .... 330-325-6263. 385 E
mmulhern@neomed.edu
MULHOLLAND, William . 413-236-2121. 231 A
wmulholl@berkshirecc.edu
MULINEX, Stacy .... 614-287-5128. 378 B
smulinex@cscc.edu
MULKEY, Amelia .... 850-973-1604. 109 H
mulkeya@nfcc.edu
MULKEY, Betty .... 859-572-5763. 198 I
mulkey@nku.edu
MULKEY, Stephen .... 207-948-9100. 211 I
smulkey@unity.edu
MULKEY, Tom .... 575-492-2144. 312 M
tmulkey@usw.edu
MULKIN, Matthew, J ...... 315-386-7300. 345 F
mulki104@canton.edu
MULL, Brenda .... 570-372-4451. 433 H
mullb@susqu.edu
MULL, Diane .... 803-754-4100. 443 C
MULLANE, William, S ..... 512-223-1024. 466 I
wmullane@austincc.edu
MULLANEY, Kathryn, L .. 315-229-5896. 339 F
kmullaney@stlawu.edu
MULLANEY, Kristin .... 603-228-3000. 298 E
kristin.mullaney@granite.edu
MULLANEY, Kristin .... 406-657-1007. 288 B
kristin.mullaney@rocky.edu
MULLANEY, Siri .... 928-226-4211... 13 B
siri.mullaney@coconino.edu
MULLANEY, William .... 201-447-7190. 299 C
wmullaney@bergen.edu
MULLEN, Adrienne, A ..... 323-265-8613... 51 F
mullenaa@elac.edu
MULLEN, Amber .... 540-831-5096. 508 C
amullen@radford.edu
MULLEN, Deborah, F ...... 404-687-4520. 123 C
mullend@ctsnet.edu
MULLEN, Denise .... 503-297-5544. 405 D
dmullen@ocac.edu
MULLEN, Eric .... 616-234-4164. 243 B
emullen@grcc.edu
MULLEN, Frank .... 617-266-1400. 223 D
MULLEN, James, H .... 814-332-5380. 409 D
jmullen@allegheny.edu
MULLEN, Jennifer .... 757-683-3580. 507 N
jmullen@odu.edu
MULLEN, Jim .... 252-328-9881. 367 B
mullenj@ecu.edu
MULLEN, Kate .... 518-327-6480. 336 B
kmullen@paulsmiths.edu
MULLEN, Ken .... 209-946-7372... 73 A
kmullen@pacific.edu
MULLEN, OFM, Kevin, J 518-783-2302. 340 J
kmullen@siena.edu
MULLEN, Kimberly .... 703-562-1691. 123 D
mullen_kimberly@columbusstate.edu
MULLEN, Michael .... 610-361-5222. 424 I
mullenm@neumann.edu
MULLEN, Michael, D ...... 919-515-2446. 368 B
mike.mullen@ncsu.edu
MULLEN, Patty .... 415-955-2041... 26 L
pmullen@alliant.edu
MULLEN, Sally .... 618-650-3839. 159 H
smullen@siue.edu
MULLEN, Shirley, A .... 585-567-9310. 326 F
shirley.mullen@houghton.edu
MULLEN, Steven, K .... 214-333-5170. 470 D
stevem@dbu.edu
MULLEN, William .... 612-330-1000. 253 H
mullen@augsburg.edu
MULLENIX, Elizabeth, R . 513-529-6010. 384 G
mullener@miamioh.edu
MULLENS, Rob, A .... 541-346-8835. 406 D
athleticdirector@uoregon.edu
MULLER, Andrew .... 843-355-4150. 449 F
mullera@wiltech.edu
MULLER, Christine .... 303-762-6972... 81 G
christine.muller@denverseminary.edu
MULLER, David .... 212-241-8716. 327 A
MULLER, Eugene, W ...... 973-748-9000. 299 F
eugene_muller@bloomfield.edu
MULLER, Joe .... 405-974-2502. 400 K
jmuller2@uco.edu
MULLER, Joseph .... 860-253-3055... 88 C
jmuller@asnuntuck.edu
MULLER, Joyce, D .... 410-857-2292. 216 E
jmuller@mcdaniel.edu
MULLER, Katharine .... 310-434-3701... 65 A
muller_katherine@smc.edu
MULLER, Kathy .... 304-865-6127. 527 F
kathy.muller@ovu.edu
MULLER, Kim .... 806-651-2345. 484 D
kmuller@wtamu.edu
MULLER, Nancy .... 718-818-6470. 339 H
MULLER, Ralph, W .... 215-662-2203. 435 B
ralph.muller@uphs.upenn.edu
MULLER, Susan, M .... 270-809-3590. 198 B
smuller1@murraystate.edu
MULLERY, Colleen .... 707-826-5086... 35 C
cbm1@humboldt.edu
MULLIGAN, Brendan .... 617-369-3458. 236 F
bmulligan@mfa.org
MULLIGAN, Kate, A .... 620-417-2102. 190 F
kate.mulligan@sccc.edu
MULLIGAN, Maura .... 617-989-4232. 237 G
mulliganm@wit.edu
MULLIGAN, Rob .... 916-608-6500... 53 C
MULLIGAN, Susan .... 973-877-3063. 301 H
mulligan@essex.edu
MULLIKIN, Jane .... 419-473-2700. 378 I
jmullikin@daviscollege.edu
MULLIN, Carol .... 610-359-5318. 414 D
cmullin@dccc.edu
MULLIN, OSB, Douglas . 320-363-2737. 263 P
dmullin@csbsju.edu
MULLIN, John .... 972-377-1575. 469 G
jmullin@collin.edu
MULLIN, Joseph .... 630-942-4278. 142 G
mullin@cod.edu
MULLIN, Kathleen, A ...... 603-513-1318. 298 E
kathi.mullin@granite.edu
MULLIN, Mark, E .... 573-341-4175. 284 A
memullin@mst.edu
MULLINAX, Kenneth .... 334-229-4104..... 1 D
kmullinax@alasu.edu
MULLINAX, Melissa .... 828-328-7244. 356 B
melissa.mullinax@lr.edu
MULLINGS, Jennifer .... 904-363-6221. 112 J
MULLINS, Ann, M .... 662-846-4670. 266 G
amullins@deltastate.edu
MULLINS, Brian .... 859-622-2821. 193 P
brian.mullins@eku.edu
MULLINS, Cathy .... 802-831-1037. 500 H
cmullins@vermontlaw.edu
MULLINS, Dixie .... 409-772-5302. 493 C
dimullin@utmb.edu
MULLINS, James, L .... 765-494-2900. 171 M
jmullins@purdue.edu
MULLINS, Judy .... 660-785-4150. 282 L
jmullins@truman.edu
MULLINS, Kerry .... 908-852-1400. 300 D
mullsk@centenarycollege.edu
MULLINS, Liza .... 904-256-7082. 107 Q
lmullin1@ju.edu
MULLINS, Sharon .... 281-425-6389. 475 I
smullins@lee.edu
MULLINS, Steve .... 714-879-3901... 47 K
smullins@hiu.edu
MULLINS, William .... 740-826-8120. 384 L
wmullins@muskingum.edu
MULLION, Carrie .... 760-921-5440... 58 C
carrie.mullion@paloverde.edu
MULLIS, Charles .... 478-934-3064. 128 I
cmullis@mgc.edu
MULLIS, Jay .... 478-274-7879. 129 I
jmullis@oftc.edu
MULLIS, Joe, W .... 910-678-8217. 360 D
mullisj@faytechcc.edu
MULLIS, Tres .... 540-458-8165. 516 A
tmullis@wlu.edu
MULLOWNEY,
William, J .... 407-582-3411. 118 M
bmullowney@valenciacollege.edu
MULLOY, Josetta .... 251-380-3470..... 7 D
mulloy@shc.edu
MULQUEEN, Joann .... 914-831-0418. 321 B
jmulqueen@cw.edu
MULRENAN, Holly .... 203-576-5518... 91 D
hmulrenan@stvincentscollege.edu
MULROE, Michael .... 312-942-6214. 157 G
mike_mulroe@rush.edu
MULROONEY, Bill .... 310-660-3418... 43 B
bmulroon@elcamino.edu
MULROONEY, Bill .... 310-660-3593... 43 B
bmulrooney@elcamino.edu
MULROY-BOWDEN,
Linda, A .... 601-342-1845. 537 D
mulroy@uwplatt.edu
MULROY-DEGENHART,
Carmella .... 814-865-7611. 426 A
qum11@psu.edu
MULRYAN, Michael .... 714-879-3901... 47 K
mdmulryan@hiu.edu
MULSHINE, James, L ..... 312-942-3589. 157 G
james_l_mulshine@rush.edu
MULSO, Sara, K .... 651-641-8857. 255 B
smulso@csp.edu
MULSO, William .... 507-537-6267. 261 F
William.Mulso@smsu.edu
MULTARI, James .... 516-323-3060. 331 J
jmultari@molloy.edu
MULTHAUF, Christopher 847-574-5270. 150 C
cmulthauf@lfgsm.edu
MULTOP, Kevin .... 541-383-7578. 402 D
kmultop@cocc.edu
MULVEY, Julie .... 508-588-9100. 232 A
MULVEY, Kristin .... 815-280-2353. 149 A
kmulvey@jjc.edu
MULVEY, Lisa .... 516-299-2263. 329 D
lisa.mulvey@liu.edu
MULVEY, Nick .... 262-551-5519. 532 D
nmulvey@carthage.edu
MULVILLE, Matthew, H .. 716-888-2220. 316 C
mulville@canisius.edu
MUMA, Richard, D .... 316-978-5761. 191 F
richard.muma@wichita.edu
MUMFORD, Frank .... 657-278-2423... 33 E
fmumford@fullerton.edu
MUMFORD, John, W ...... 814-641-3452. 419 H
mumford@juniata.edu
MUMMERT, John .... 650-949-7070... 44 N
mummertjohn@foothill.edu
MUMMERT, Kelly .... 304-243-2226. 531 H
kmummert@wju.edu
MUMMERT, Vernon .... 480-423-6616... 15 E
vernon.mummert@scottsdalecc.edu
MUMPER, Michael .... 719-587-7436... 78 B
mmumper@adams.edu
MUNA, Esther, A .... 671-735-5700. 546 C
gccpresident@guamcc.edu
MUNA, Joann, W .... 671-735-5539. 546 C
hr@guamcc.edu
MUNCASTER, Karen .... 617-262-5000. 223 F
Karen.Muncaster@the-bac.edu
MUNCHEL,
Christopher, T .... 765-285-5608. 164 B
cmunchel@bsu.edu
MUNCHEL, Jeff .... 410-532-5324. 217 E
jmunchel@ndm.edu
MUND, Barb .... 701-671-2204. 372 E
barb.mund@ndscs.edu
MUND, Catherine .... 443-518-1000. 215 E
MUNDAHL, Daniel, L ...... 507-344-7739. 253 J
costello@blc.edu
MUNDRANE, Michael ...... 860-486-6092... 92 A
michael.mundrane@uconn.edu
MUNDT, Mary, H .... 517-355-6527. 246 H
mundtm@msu.edu
MUNDY, Susan, R .... 516-876-3033. 343 D
mundys@oldwestbury.edu
MUNDY, Tiina .... 910-879-5556. 358 B
tmundy@bladencc.edu
MUNFORD, Michael .... 507-537-7858. 261 F
Michael.Munford@smsu.edu
MUNFORD, Teresa, L ..... 757-221-1009. 503 N
tlmunf@wm.edu
MUNGAL, Godfrey .... 408-554-2375... 64 M
mgmungal@scu.edu
MUNGER, James .... 208-426-4010. 137 G
jmunger@boisestate.edu
MUNGER, Mary Lynn ..... 816-604-3155. 277 G
marylynn.munger@mcckc.edu
MUNGO, T. Rein .... 843-349-2577. 442 E
tmungo@coastal.edu
MUNIER, Craig, D .... 402-472-2030. 292 I
cmunier1@unl.edu
MUNIFO, Rita .... 570-702-8985. 419 G
rmunifo@johnson.edu
MUNIN, Eugene .... 312-553-2500. 141 M
emunin@ccc.edu
MUNITZ, Barry .... 775-831-1314. 295 F
MUNIZ, Amanda .... 361-593-3797. 484 A
kaam003@tamuk.edu
MUNIZ, Diana .... 602-286-8031... 14 L
diana.muniz@gwmail.maricopa.edu
MUNIZ, Herman .... 787-276-0270. 554 B
herman.muniz@upr.edu
MUNKRES, Kimberli .... 909-793-2121... 73 H
kimberli_munkres@redlands.edu
MUNLEY, Anne .... 570-348-6231. 423 B
annemunley@marywood.edu
MUNN, Kathie, A .... 906-932-4231. 242 I
kathiem@gogebic.edu
MUNNELL, Barbra, M ..... 724-458-3824. 417 E
bmmunnell@gcc.edu
MUNNERLYN, Samuel .... 334-420-4216..... 7 G
smunnerlyn@trenholmstate.edu
MUNNS, Sarah .... 573-592-4296. 285 D
sarah.munns@williamwoods.edu
MUNOZ, Al .... 831-755-6914... 46 G
amunoz@hartnell.edu
MUNOZ, Candelario .... 805-546-3147... 42 C
cmunoz@cuesta.edu
MUNOZ, Carmen .... 818-401-1035... 41 B
cmunoz@columbiacollege.edu
MUNOZ, Chris .... 713-348-6271. 479 A
chris.munoz@rice.edu
MUNOZ, Ivette .... 787-725-8120. 548 O
imunoz@eap.edu
MUNOZ, Juan, S .... 806-742-7025. 487 D
juan.munoz@ttu.edu
MUNOZ, Julio, C .... 787-284-1912. 550 F
jcmunoz@ponce.inter.edu
MUNOZ, M. Angelica ..... 269-471-3251. 243 G
munozm@andrews.edu
MUNOZ, Maria .... 787-284-1912. 550 F
mmunoz@ponce.inter.edu
MUNOZ, Marisol .... 787-766-1717. 552 J
ac_mmunoz@suagm.edu
MUNOZ, Rene .... 717-872-3820. 429 D
Rene.Munoz@millersville.edu
MUNRO, Alex .... 717-299-7776. 434 A
munro@stevenscollege.edu
MUNRO, Glenn .... 301-295-0064. 545 C
glenn.munro@med.navy.mil
MUNRO, Molly .... 561-297-2114. 114 L
mmunro@fau.edu
MUNRO, Stuart, J .... 508-767-7041. 222 C
smunro@assumption.edu
MUNROE, Anthony, E ..... 312-850-7031. 142 C
amunroe@ccc.edu
MUNROE, Jane Ann .... 714-449-7446... 67 D
jmunroe@scco.edu
MUNROE, Jeffrey .... 616-392-8555. 252 J
jeff@westernsem.edu
MUNROE, Richard .... 229-226-1621. 132 F
rmunroe@thomasu.edu
MUNSCHY, Karl .... 706-729-2179. 126 B
kmunschy@gru.edu
MUNSICK, Trudy, R .... 307-674-6446. 543 F
tmunsick@sheridan.edu
MUNSIL, Len .... 602-489-5300... 11 G
len.munsil@arizonachristian.edu
MUNSON, Amy .... 309-268-8633. 146 B
amy.munson@heartland.edu
MUNSON, David, C .... 734-647-7010. 251 C
munson@umich.edu
MUNSON, Janet .... 309-649-6273. 160 E
janet.munson@src.edu
MUNSON, Leo, W .... 817-257-7104. 484 I
l.munson@tcu.edu
MUNSON, Nina .... 480-557-1712... 18 I
nina.munson@phoenix.edu
MUNSON, Ryan .... 801-622-1573. 496 I
ryan.munson@stevenhenager.edu
MUNSON, Shana .... 940-552-6291. 493 F
smunson@vernoncollege.edu
MUNSON, Steve .... 703-284-6901. 507 B
smunson@marymount.edu
MUNSON, Wanda .... 281-669-4711. 479 F
wanda.munson@sjcd.edu
MUNSON, Wanda .... 281-669-4711. 479 G
wanda.munson@sjcd.edu

MUNSON, Wanda ... 281-669-4711. 479 H
wanda.munson@sjcd.edu
MUNSON, William ... 713-743-5470. 489 B
wfmunson@central.uh.edu
MUNSTER, Charles ... 718-636-3453. 336 F
cmunster@pratt.edu
MUNT, Glada, C ... 512-863-1381. 481 I
muntg@southwestern.edu
MUNTZ, Bill ... 229-245-5147. 134 B
bmuntz@valdosta.edu
MUNTZ, Palmer ... 503-255-0332. 404 F
pmuntz@multnomah.edu
MUNZER, Pat ... 785-670-2111. 191 D
pat.munzer@washburn.edu
MURABITO, William, J ... 315-684-6044. 345 A
murabito@morrisville.edu
MURACA, Paul ... 713-798-6617. 467 F
muraca@bcm.edu
MURALI, Viji ... 509-335-8017. 525 A
vijimurali@wsu.edu
MURASKO, Donna ... 215-895-1892. 415 B
dm37@drexel.edu
MURASSO, Thomas ... 914-323-5337. 330 B
thomas.murasso@mville.edu
MURATA, Susan ... 808-734-9267. 136 E
smurata@hawaii.edu
MURDAUGH, Jim ... 850-201-8660. 117 D
murdaugj@tcc.fl.edu
MURDEN MCCLURE,
Tori ... 502-585-9911. 199 C
tmcclure@spalding.edu
MURDEN-WALDU,
Romell ... 773-481-8451. 142 F
rmurden@ccc.edu
MURDOCH, Janice, W ... 864-656-3942. 442 C
janw@clemson.edu
MURDOCH, Jessica ... 978-665-3338. 229 E
jmurdoch@fitchburgstate.edu
MURDOCH, William, G .. 909-558-6604... 51 C
wmurdoch@llu.edu
MURDOCK, Alan, K ... 336-734-7757. 360 E
amurdock@forsythtech.edu
MURDOCK, Rebecca ... 605-575-2068. 452 D
rebecca.murdock@usiouxfalls.edu
MURDOCK-TANGYE,
Annette ... 501-569-3180... 24 B
amtangye@ualr.edu
MURDZAK, Karen ... 814-732-1020. 428 E
kmurdzak@edinboro.edu
MURGA, Margaret ... 252-536-7242. 361 A
mmurga673@halifaxcc.edu
MURGA, Mario ... 617-327-6777. 233 D
mario_murga@mspp.edu
MURGUIA, Kim ... 210-732-3000. 468 E
MURGUIA, Stephanie ... 562-860-2451... 37 I
smurguia@cerritos.edu
MURIANA, Joseph, P ... 718-817-3020. 324 G
jmuriana@fordham.edu
MURIANKA, Luke ... 315-858-0940. 326 E
lmurianka@hts.edu
MURILLO, Kindred ... 530-541-4660... 50 D
murillo@ltcc.edu
MURKA, Adam ... 937-512-2947. 388 O
adam.murka@sinclair.edu
MURLEY, David ... 509-244-6851. 518 E
david.murley@scc.spokane.edu
MURLEY, James ... 954-762-5253. 114 L
jmurley@fau.edu
MURNANE, Richard, J ... 617-495-3401. 227 C
richard_murnane@gse.harvard.edu
MURNANE, Ryan ... 757-352-4891. 508 G
ryanmur@regent.edu
MURPHEY, Connie ... 912-478-5413. 126 C
cmurphey@georgiasouthern.edu
MURPHEY, Diane ... 580-349-1446. 397 G
diane@opsu.edu
MURPHREE, Danny, W .. 806-291-3635. 494 F
murphree@wbu.edu
MURPHREE, David ... 806-291-3641. 494 F
dmurphree@wbu.edu
MURPHREE, Edith, C ... 404-727-2827. 124 E
edith.murphree@emory.edu
MURPHREY,
Hiram Todd ... 252-638-7263. 359 G
murphret@cravencc.edu
MURPHY, Amy ... 508-793-3880. 225 B
amurphy@holycross.edu
MURPHY, Amy, L ... 806-742-5433. 487 D
amy.murphy@ttu.edu
MURPHY, Ann, B ... 303-556-3245... 83 D
murphann@msudenver.edu
MURPHY, Anne ... 312-942-6886. 157 G
anne_murphy@rush.edu
MURPHY, Barbara, E ... 802-635-1240. 501 D
jscpres@jsc.edu
MURPHY, Bill ... 585-275-4124. 349 C
bill.murphy@rochester.edu
MURPHY, Bonnie, D ... 805-756-1131... 32 F
bdmurphy@calpoly.edu
MURPHY, Brent, D ... 574-232-2468. 172 B
MURPHY, Bret ... 775-753-2217. 294 F
bret.murphy@gbcnv.edu
MURPHY, Brian ... 718-997-5910. 319 C
brian.murphy@qc.cuny.edu
MURPHY, Brian ... 408-864-8705... 44 M
murphybrian@deanza.edu
MURPHY, Brian ... 936-468-2803. 482 A
murphybm1@sfasu.edu
MURPHY, Britt Anne ... 501-450-1303... 21 E
johnsen@hendrix.edu
MURPHY, Bruce, T ... 334-953-5613. 544 D
bruce.murphy@maxwell.af.mil
MURPHY, Carolyn ... 402-471-2505. 291 C
cmurphy@nscs.edu
MURPHY, Catherine ... 516-299-3981. 329 C
Cathy.Murphy@liu.edu
MURPHY, Catherine ... 202-651-5019... 95 C
catherine.murphy@gallaudet.edu
MURPHY, Catherine ... 615-460-6418. 453 C
catherine.murphy@belmont.edu
MURPHY, Chad ... 309-649-6266. 160 E
chad.murphy@src.edu
MURPHY, Charles, J ... 585-275-2815. 349 C
cj.murphy@rochester.edu
MURPHY, Charles, J ... 509-313-6139. 520 A
murphyc@gonzaga.edu
MURPHY, Christine ... 516-877-3056. 313 A
murphy2@adelphi.edu
MURPHY, Christine ... 617-739-1700. 235 A
cmurphy@aii.edu
MURPHY, Colleen ... 319-895-4215. 177 A
cmurphy@cornellcollege.edu
MURPHY, JR.,
Cornelius, B ... 315-470-6681. 345 B
cbmurphy@esf.edu
MURPHY, Dan ... 803-786-3701. 443 B
dan@columbiasc.edu
MURPHY, Darin ... 617-369-3650. 236 F
dmurphy@mfa.org
MURPHY, Darlene ... 802-654-0534. 501 C
darlene.murphy@ccv.edu
MURPHY, David ... 414-288-4810. 534 B
david.murphy@marquette.edu
MURPHY, David, L ... 773-702-9466. 161 B
dlm@uchicago.edu
MURPHY, David, W ... 315-498-2213. 335 G
murphydw@sunyocc.edu
MURPHY, Denise ... 301-687-4457. 220 C
dmurphy@frostburg.edu
MURPHY, Dennis, J ... 610-361-2448. 424 I
murphydj@neumann.edu
MURPHY, Diane Lyden .. 315-443-3707. 347 C
dlmurphy@syr.edu
MURPHY, Donna, M ... 831-459-4750... 72 C
donnam@ucsc.edu
MURPHY, Douglas, L ... 501-686-5730... 24 C
dlmurphy@uams.edu
MURPHY, Frank ... 815-288-5511. 158 K
frank.j.murphy@svcc.edu
MURPHY, Frederick ... 704-378-1129. 355 K
fmurphy@jcsu.edu
MURPHY, Gaye ... 480-731-8638... 14 I
gaye.murphy@domail.maricopa.edu
MURPHY, Gene ... 601-857-3330. 267 A
TEMurphy@hindscc.edu
MURPHY, Jack ... 773-481-8124. 142 F
jmurphy@ccc.edu
MURPHY, Jacqueline ... 802-654-3000. 500 B
admissions@smcvt.edu
MURPHY, III, James, E . 704-894-2373. 353 J
jamurphy@davidson.edu
MURPHY, James, P ... 717-846-5000. 438 E
MURPHY, Janice ... 410-334-2808. 221 D
jmurphy@worwic.edu
MURPHY, Jason, J ... 920-923-7178. 534 A
jjmurphy25@marianuniversity.edu
MURPHY, Jean, D ... 313-831-5200. 242 E
jdmurphy@etseminary.edu
MURPHY, Jim ... 973-748-9000. 299 F
jim_murphy@bloomfield.edu
MURPHY, John ... 518-956-8140. 341 D
jmurphy@albany.edu
MURPHY, John ... 317-921-4243. 169 K
jmmurphy@ivytech.edu
MURPHY, John ... 708-709-7834. 156 A
jmurphy@prairiestate.edu
MURPHY, John ... 203-837-8395... 88 B
murphyj@wcsu.edu
MURPHY, John ... 210-458-3090. 492 C
john.murphy@utsa.edu
MURPHY, John, D ... 207-834-7516. 212 E
jdmurphy@maine.edu
MURPHY, John, T ... 716-829-8147. 323 D
murphyj@dyc.edu
MURPHY, SJ, Joseph, A 614-885-5585. 388 C
jmurphy@pcj.edu
MURPHY, Joseph, M ... 740-427-5120. 382 J
murphyjm@kenyon.edu
MURPHY, Josephine ... 718-368-5144. 318 E
jmurphy@kbcc.cuny.edu
MURPHY, Joyce, A ... 508-856-4842. 229 C
joyce.murphy@umassmed.edu
MURPHY, Juliann ... 231-843-5913. 252 H
jmmurphy@westshore.edu
MURPHY, Justin ... 325-649-8701. 473 F
jmurphy@hputx.edu
MURPHY, Karen ... 318-257-4205. 207 F
kmurphy@latech.edu
MURPHY, Kathleen ... 717-262-2008. 437 H
kmurphy@wilson.edu
MURPHY, Kathleen ... 216-687-3613. 377 F
kathleen.murphy@csuohio.edu
MURPHY, Kathleen, M ... 508-767-7110. 222 C
kamurphy@assumption.edu
MURPHY, Keith ... 718-409-7349. 346 D
kmurphy@sunymaritime.edu
MURPHY, Kenneth, R ... 903-510-2547. 488 E
kmur@tjc.edu
MURPHY, Kristin ... 608-246-6462. 540 C
kmmurphy@madisoncollege.edu
MURPHY, Lamar, R ... 585-276-3262. 349 C
lamar.murphy@rochester.edu
MURPHY, Laura ... 508-929-8649. 230 G
lmurphy@worcester.edu
MURPHY, Linda ... 978-837-5131. 234 A
murphyl@merrimack.edu
MURPHY, Lisa ... 480-860-2700... 13 Q
lmurphy@taliesin.edu
MURPHY, Lisa ... 307-778-1110. 543 D
lmurphy@lccc.wy.edu
MURPHY, Lisa, B ... 863-638-7690. 119 C
lisa.murphy@warner.edu
MURPHY, M. Patrick ... 336-278-7640. 354 B
murphyp@elon.edu
MURPHY, Margaret, L ... 757-446-5828. 504 E
murphyml@evms.edu
MURPHY, Marie ... 508-531-1338. 229 D
mmurphy@bridgew.edu
MURPHY, Marilyn, J ... 319-368-6465. 181 C
marilyn@mtmercy.edu
MURPHY, Mark ... 914-633-2458. 327 C
mmurphy@iona.edu
MURPHY, Mark ... 402-465-2254. 291 G
mam@nebrwesleyan.edu
MURPHY, Mary, K ... 607-753-2303. 343 B
maryk.murphy@cortland.edu
MURPHY, Marybeth ... 201-615-3469. 307 E
mmurphy4@stevens.edu
MURPHY, Maryjan ... 831-459-2120... 72 C
mjmurphy@ucsc.edu
MURPHY, Maureen ... 617-824-8575. 226 A
maureen_murphy@emerson.edu
MURPHY, Maureen ... 732-224-2204. 299 G
mmurphy@brookdalecc.edu
MURPHY, Michael ... 845-398-4118. 340 A
mmurphy@stac.edu
MURPHY, Michael ... 925-631-4366... 61 F
mmurphy@stmarys-ca.edu
MURPHY, Michael ... 412-237-4413. 413 D
MURPHY, Michael, C ... 412-268-8251. 412 H
mm1v@andrew.cmu.edu
MURPHY, Mollie ... 202-685-3933. 544 K
murphym@ndu.edu
MURPHY, Nancy ... 850-729-5365. 109 I
murphyn@nwfsc.edu
MURPHY, Neal ... 912-287-6584. 130 B
nmurphy@okefenokeetech.edu
MURPHY, Pamela ... 724-938-4427. 428 A
murphy_p@calu.edu
MURPHY, Patricia, B ... 804-484-1581. 510 L
pmurphy@richmond.edu
MURPHY, Paul ... 805-922-6966... 26 K
pmurphy@hancockcollege.edu
MURPHY, Paul ... 570-674-6272. 424 A
pmurphy@misericordia.edu
MURPHY, Paul ... 937-512-2518. 388 O
paul.murphy@sinclair.edu
MURPHY, Paul, V ... 216-397-4953. 381 R
pvmurphy@jcu.edu
MURPHY, Paul, W ... 617-726-0422. 234 B
pwmurphy@mghihp.edu
MURPHY, Peter, F ... 270-809-7064. 198 B
pmurphy@murraystate.edu
MURPHY, Peter, T ... 413-597-4351. 238 D
peter.t.murphy@williams.edu
MURPHY, Pollie ... 757-727-5201. 505 F
pollie.muphy@hamptonu.edu
MURPHY, Pollie ... 757-727-5237. 505 F
pollie.murphy@hamptonu.edu
MURPHY, Robert ... 315-781-3622. 326 C
murphy@hws.edu
MURPHY, Robert ... 508-767-7225. 222 C
rtmurphy@assumption.edu
MURPHY, Robert, P ... 716-829-8199. 323 D
murphyrp@dyc.edu
MURPHY, Stephen, C ... 203-432-8090... 93 A
stephen.murphy@yale.edu
MURPHY, Steven, J ... 773-298-3310. 158 E
murphy@sxu.edu
MURPHY, Susan, H ... 607-255-7595. 322 A
shm1@cornell.edu
MURPHY, Susan, L ... 415-422-2620... 73 J
murphy@usfca.edu
MURPHY, Suzanne ... 212-678-3755. 347 G
smurphy@tc.columbia.edu
MURPHY, Suzanne, K ... 215-596-8888. 435 H
s.murphy@usciences.edu
MURPHY, Thomas ... 516-876-3215. 343 D
murphyt@oldwestbury.edu
MURPHY, Thomas, H ... 215-898-7581. 435 B
tom.murphy@isc.upenn.edu
MURPHY, Tiffany ... 484-384-2986. 415 G
tmurphy@eastern.edu
MURPHY, Tiffany, S ... 484-384-2986. 425 I
tmurphy@eastern.edu
MURPHY, Tim ... 903-886-5550. 483 E
tim.murphy@tamuc.edu
MURPHY, Todd ... 323-343-2500... 34 A
tmurphy@cslanet.calstatela.edu
MURPHY, Wayne ... 718-289-5245. 317 B
wayne.murphy@bcc.cuny.edu
MURPHY-FREEBOLIN,
Lorie ... 563-588-6571. 176 F
lorie.murphy-freebolin@clarke.edu
MURPHY HEALEY,
Kerry ... 781-239-4263. 222 D
khealey@babson.edu
MURPHY-STETZ,
Katherine ... 312-567-3080. 147 F
murphy@iit.edu
MURR, Christopher ... 512-245-3975. 487 C
cm18@txstate.edu
MURRAH, Matt ... 214-333-6886. 470 D
matt@dbu.edu
MURRAY, Adam, L ... 270-809-5604. 198 B
amurray@murraystate.edu
MURRAY, Ann ... 307-778-1113. 543 D
amurray@lccc.wy.edu
MURRAY, Ann Marie ... 315-866-0300. 326 A
murrayam@herkimer.edu
MURRAY, Barbara, M ... 909-748-8544... 73 H
barbara_murray@redlands.edu
MURRAY, Ben ... 507-457-1443. 264 A
bmurray@smumn.edu
MURRAY, Brian ... 972-721-5008. 488 F
bmurray@udallas.edu
MURRAY, Cherry, A ... 617-495-5829. 227 C
camurray@seas.harvard.edu
MURRAY,
Christopher, D ... 208-885-6154. 139 D
chrismurray@uidaho.edu
MURRAY, David ... 732-224-2449. 299 G
dmurray@brookdalecc.edu
MURRAY, Deborah ... 423-614-8118. 455 L
debmurray@leeuniversity.edu
MURRAY, Debra, H ... 717-361-1164. 415 H
murraydh@etown.edu
MURRAY, Dennis, J ... 845-575-3000. 330 D
dennis.murray@marist.edu
MURRAY, Douglas, J ... 575-624-8020. 310 H
dmurray@nmmi.edu
MURRAY, Eric ... 425-352-8810. 517 E
emurray@cascadia.edu
MURRAY, Erin ... 336-887-3000. 355 N
emurray@laureluniversity.edu
MURRAY, Frank ... 509-542-4835. 518 C
fmurray@columbiabasin.edu
MURRAY, George, W ... 803-754-4100. 443 C
MURRAY, Gina ... 218-935-0417. 265 E
gina.murray@wetcc.edu
MURRAY, Gloria, J ... 812-941-2385. 168 F
glomurra@ius.edu
MURRAY, Harris ... 803-535-1257. 446 B
murrayh@octech.edu
MURRAY, Harris ... 803-535-1255. 446 B
murrayh@octech.edu
MURRAY, Jay ... 203-837-8286... 88 B
murrayj@wcsu.edu
MURRAY, Jen ... 617-573-8000. 237 B
jmurray@suffolk.edu
MURRAY, Jill ... 570-504-1575. 420 C
murrayj@lackawanna.edu
MURRAY, Joanne, S ... 781-283-2492. 237 F
jmurray@wellesley.edu
MURRAY, John ... 312-332-0707. 160 J
MURRAY, John ... 812-237-2785. 167 A
john.murray@indstate.edu
MURRAY, Karen ... 254-968-9103. 483 A
kmurray@tarleton.edu
MURRAY, Kathleen, M ... 651-696-6160. 256 L
kmurray@macalester.edu
MURRAY, Louise ... 973-290-4430. 300 F
lmurray@cse.edu
MURRAY, Lynne ... 202-651-5006... 95 C
lynne.murray@gallaudet.edu
MURRAY, Mallory ... 816-271-5649. 279 A
mmurray2@missouriwestern.edu
MURRAY, Mark, J ... 904-264-2172. 111 P
mark.murray@iws.edu
MURRAY, Michael ... 517-437-7341. 243 I
michael.murray@hillsdale.edu

MURRAY, Michael, D ..... 626-584-2040... 45 E mdmurray@fuller.edu
MURRAY, Michele ..... 206-296-6066. 523 E mmurray@seattleu.edu
MURRAY, Nancy, K ..... 219-464-5989. 174 E nancy.murray@valpo.edu
MURRAY, Percy ..... 903-923-2421. 495 A pmurray@wileyc.edu
MURRAY, Peter ..... 650-949-7472... 44 N murraypeter@foothill.edu
MURRAY, Peter, J ..... 410-706-2461. 219 C pmurray@umaryland.edu
MURRAY, Renae ..... 561-803-2155. 110 B renae_murray@pba.edu
MURRAY, Robert ..... 309-556-1000. 148 B bmurray@iwu.edu
MURRAY, Robert ..... 845-398-4125. 340 A rmurray@stac.edu
MURRAY, Robert ..... 860-444-8520. 545 G robert.murray@uscga.edu
MURRAY, Rose-Marie ..... 305-949-9500. 102 E rmurray@cci.edu
MURRAY, OFM, Russel . 518-783-2418. 340 J rmurray@siena.edu
MURRAY, Sharon ..... 518-292-1753. 338 C murras2@sage.edu
MURRAY, Stephen ..... 845-752-3000. 348 I s.murray@uts.edu
MURRAY, Steven ..... 870-338-6474... 24 G
MURRAY, Susan ..... 770-229-3043. 132 B smurray@sctech.edu
MURRAY, Susan ..... 509-682-6435. 525 B smurray@wvc.edu
MURRAY, Susan ..... 503-399-5145. 402 E susan.murray@chemeketa.edu
MURRAY, Suzette ..... 630-466-7900. 162 J smurray@waubonsee.edu
MURRAY, Tamsen ..... 714-879-3901... 47 K tmurray@hiu.edu
MURRAY, Thomas ..... 336-770-3277. 369 D murrayt@uncsa.edu
MURRAY, Trish ..... 704-894-2099. 353 J trmurray@davidson.edu
MURRAY, William, G ..... 516-671-2213. 350 C bmurray@webb.edu
MURRAY-JENSEN, Julie . 541-880-2221. 403 H julie@klamathcc.edu
MURRAY-LAURY, Janice 908-737-7080. 302 F jmurray@kean.edu
MURRAY-RUST, Catherine ..... 404-894-8914. 125 D catherine.rust@library.gatech.edu
MURRELL, James, T ..... 931-363-9823. 456 C jmurrell@martinmethodist.edu
MURRELL, Michele ..... 321-433-7055. 101 M murrellm@easternflorida.edu
MURRELL, Shana ..... 508-531-2009. 229 D shana.murrell@bridgew.edu
MURRELL, Terry ..... 712-274-6400. 183 G terry.murrell@witcc.edu
MURRIL, Antoinette ..... 312-567-3012. 147 F amurril@iit.edu
MURRIN, Michael ..... 716-926-8900. 326 B mmurrin@hilbert.edu
MURRY, LaKeisha ..... 901-381-3939. 464 C keisha@visible.edu
MURRY, Tracy ..... 941-487-4504. 115 D tmurry@ncf.edu
MURTAGH, Michael ..... 309-467-6315. 145 C mmurtagh@eureka.edu
MURTAUGH, Kelly ..... 651-423-8319. 258 D kelly.murtaugh@dctc.edu
MURTAUGH, Peter, T ..... 314-286-4813. 280 F ptmurtaugh@ranken.edu
MURTHA, Brenda ..... 605-274-5217. 449 K brenda.murtha@augie.edu
MURUAKO, Dominic ..... 205-366-8854..... 7 E dmuruako@stillman.edu
MURY, Hal ..... 919-209-2000. 361 E hemury@johnstoncc.edu
MUSAL, Edward ..... 914-251-6923. 344 D edward.musal@purchase.edu
MUSANTE, Nancy, M ..... 203-576-5578... 91 D nmusante@stvincentscollege.edu
MUSCARELLA, Joseph, V ..... 516-572-0605. 332 C joseph.muscarella@ncc.edu
MUSCATO, Amanda ..... 212-355-1501. 316 H amuscato@christies.edu
MUSCELLA, Matt ..... 484-365-8061. 422 D mmuscella@lincoln.edu
MUSCENTE, Catherine ..... 516-323-4200. 331 J cmuscente@molloy.edu
MUSE, Bill ..... 830-792-7355. 480 F bmuse@schreiner.edu
MUSE, Charles ..... 936-261-3860. 482 F cdmuse@pvamu.edu
MUSE, Clyde ..... 601-857-3240. 267 A vcmuse@hindscc.edu
MUSE, Douglas ..... 870-612-2167... 25 A douglas.muse@uaccb.edu
MUSE, Gail ..... 662-472-2312. 267 B gmuse@holmescc.edu
MUSE, Justin ..... 540-365-4441. 504 L jmuse@ferrum.edu
MUSEWICZ, Suellen ..... 570-961-7824. 420 C musewiczs@lackawanna.edu
MUSGRAVE, Dan ..... 575-624-8214. 310 H musgrave@nmmi.edu
MUSGROVE, Robert ..... 320-629-5120. 260 F musgrover@pinetech.edu
MUSHRUSH, Tiffany ..... 440-646-8370. 392 D tmushrush@ursuline.edu
MUSIAL, Angela ..... 661-722-6300... 28 F amusial1@avc.edu
MUSICH, Michelle ..... 828-766-1262. 361 H mmusich@mayland.edu
MUSICK, Chris ..... 614-823-1370. 387 K cmusick@otterbein.edu
MUSICK, Kelly ..... 409-933-8496. 469 E kmusick@com.edu
MUSKAVITCH, John, W . 909-389-3269... 61 K jmuskavitch@craftonhills.edu
MUSKETT, Milford ..... 319-398-4911. 180 J mmusket@kirkwood.edu
MUSKRAT, Bruce ..... 817-274-4284. 467 H
MUSOLF, Shelly, R ..... 260-422-5561. 167 B srmusolf@indianatech.edu
MUSSA-MULDOON, Carla, R ..... 310-233-4450... 51 H muldoonc@lahc.edu
MUSSELMAN, Kathy, I ..... 615-898-2929. 459 D kathy.musselman@mtsu.edu
MUSSELWHITE, Laura ..... 706-295-6331. 125 C lmusselw@highlands.edu
MUSSELWHITE, Laura ..... 706-204-2368. 125 C lmusselw@highlands.edu
MUSSER, Debra, S ..... 574-372-5100. 166 B musserds@grace.edu
MUSSER, Jeff ..... 616-331-2207. 243 C musserj@gvsu.edu
MUSSER, Steve ..... 717-560-8248. 421 A smusser@lbc.edu
MUSSO, Daniele ..... 913-360-7975. 184 H dmusso@benedictine.edu
MUSTAFA, Abeer ..... 336-750-3471. 370 A housing@wss.edu
MUSTAFA, Mustafa ..... 201-216-9901. 301 E drmustafa@eicollege.edu
MUSTAIN, Kathryn ..... 913-758-6102. 191 B Kathryn.Mustain@stmary.edu
MUSTARD, Barbara ..... 605-394-2228. 452 A barbara.mustard@sdsmt.edu
MUSTER, Robert ..... 612-659-6104. 259 D robert.muster@minneapolis.edu
MUSTERMAN, Cynthia, A ..... 314-421-0949. 282 I musterman@siba.edu
MUTCHLER, Jack, C ..... 520-621-5511... 18 F mutchler@email.arizona.edu
MUTCHLER, Jane ..... 219-989-3194. 171 N Jane.Mutchler@purduecal.edu
MUTH, Richard ..... 724-294-3300. 428 F Richard.Muth@iup.edu
MUTONE, Paul ..... 860-297-4224... 91 F paul.mutone@trincoll.edu
MUTUA, Makau, W ..... 716-645-2052. 341 F mutua@buffalo.edu
MUYET, Javier, A ..... 787-850-9318. 554 D javier.muyet@upr.edu
MUYSKENS, James, L ..... 718-997-5550. 319 C james.muyskens@qc.cuny.edu
MUYSKENS, Judy, A ..... 402-465-2110. 291 G provost@nebrwesleyan.edu
MUZIA, Raymond ..... 757-825-2900. 514 B muziar@tncc.edu
MUÑIZ, Maria ..... 787-841-2000. 552 B mmuniz@pucpr.edu
MYAZOE-DEBRUM, Diane, C ..... 692-528-5033. 546 F dcmyazoe@yahoo.com
MYAZOE-DEBRUM, Diane, C ..... 692-625-3394. 546 F dcmyazoe@cmi.edu
MYER, Bonnie ..... 360-736-9391. 517 G bmyer@centralia.edu
MYER, Marci ..... 206-934-3669. 522 I marci.myer@seattlecolleges.edu
MYERS, Alvin, B ..... 434-395-2300. 506 J myersab@longwood.edu
MYERS, Amy, A ..... 717-291-4082. 416 J amy.myers@fandm.edu
MYERS, Andrea ..... 440-375-7212. 382 L amyers@lec.edu
MYERS, Barbara, S ..... 912-358-3051. 131 C myersb@savannahstate.edu
MYERS, Beth ..... 843-863-7516. 441 H myers@csuniv.edu
MYERS, Bianca ..... 641-683-5302. 179 A bianca.myers@indianhills.edu
MYERS, Bradley, A ..... 614-292-1556. 386 E myers.7@osu.edu
MYERS, Camille ..... 843-525-8359. 447 C cmyers@tcl.edu
MYERS, Carol ..... 706-355-5080. 120 J cmeyers@athenstech.edu
MYERS, Charles ..... 215-596-8791. 435 H c.myers@usciences.edu
MYERS, Cheryl ..... 706-649-1290. 123 E cmyers@columbustech.edu
MYERS, Cheryl ..... 504-571-1290. 203 A cmyers@dcc.edu
MYERS, Cynthia ..... 360-992-6077. 518 A cmyers@clark.edu
MYERS, Dale ..... 830-792-7235. 480 F dtmyers@schreiner.edu
MYERS, Daniel, J ..... 574-631-2799. 174 A dmyers@nd.edu
MYERS, Derek, R ..... 330-471-8415. 383 D dmyers@malone.edu
MYERS, Donald ..... 202-885-2709... 94 F don@american.edu
MYERS, Donald, C ..... 901-333-5259. 461 F dmyers@southwest.tn.edu
MYERS, Eveadean ..... 701-231-7703. 371 G evie.myers@ndsu.edu
MYERS, Gary ..... 709-379-3111. 134 L glmyers@yhc.edu
MYERS, Gary ..... 573-882-3246. 283 C myers@missouri.edu
MYERS, Gary, D ..... 504-816-8003. 206 A gmeyers@nobts.edu
MYERS, Jaime ..... 661-726-1911... 70 G jaime.myers@uav.edu
MYERS, James ..... 650-325-9122... 61 G vat2ins@aol.com
MYERS, James ..... 443-334-2910. 218 E jmmyers@stevenson.edu
MYERS, James ..... 314-246-7080. 284 N jamesmyers79@webster.edu
MYERS, James, L ..... 803-536-8480. 446 G myers@scsu.edu
MYERS, Jeannette ..... 843-661-1291. 444 B jmyers@fmarion.edu
MYERS, Jennifer ..... 507-389-1515. 259 G jennifer.myers@mnsu.edu
MYERS, Jimmy ..... 239-590-7406. 115 A jimyers@fgcu.edu
MYERS, Joe ..... 931-393-1553. 461 A jmyers@mscc.edu
MYERS, Jolene ..... 406-377-9410. 286 A myers@dawson.edu
MYERS, Jonna ..... 580-774-3233. 400 B jonna.myers@swosu.edu
MYERS, Julie, K ..... 845-758-7518. 314 D myers@bard.edu
MYERS, Kelly ..... 815-802-8260. 149 C kmyers@kcc.edu
MYERS, Ken ..... 218-281-8200. 264 E kmyers@umn.edu
MYERS, Ken ..... 864-644-5215. 446 I kmyers@swu.edu
MYERS, Kevin ..... 361-570-4840. 489 E myersk@uhv.edu
MYERS, Laura ..... 740-593-2620. 387 C myersl@ohio.edu
MYERS, Lynne, M ..... 508-793-2265. 225 B lmyers@holycross.edu
MYERS, Marci ..... 620-223-2700. 186 G marcim@fortscott.edu
MYERS, Margaret ..... 701-777-2015. 371 C margaret.myers@und.edu
MYERS, Mark ..... 907-474-5837... 10 I mdmyers@alaska.edu
MYERS, Mary ..... 239-489-6768. 101 O mmyers@edison.edu
MYERS, Mary, L ..... 320-222-7534. 260 H mary.myers@ridgewater.edu
MYERS, Mary Beth ..... 317-274-1505. 168 D mbmyers@iupui.edu
MYERS, Michael ..... 847-982-2500. 146 C myers@htc.edu
MYERS, Michelle ..... 816-584-6727. 280 C michelle.meyers@park.edu
MYERS, Patricia ..... 518-587-2100. 346 A patricia.myers@esc.edu
MYERS, Patricia, T ..... 865-539-7242. 461 D pmyers@pstcc.edu
MYERS, Paul ..... 503-943-7134. 408 F myers@up.edu
MYERS, Randy, E ..... 620-665-3579. 187 F myersr@hutchcc.edu
MYERS, Robert ..... 310-434-4200... 65 A myers_robert@smc.edu
MYERS, Robert, M ..... 706-886-6831. 133 A rmyers@tfc.edu
MYERS, Robin ..... 870-508-6101... 20 A rmyers@asumh.edu
MYERS, Ronnie ..... 212-305-5199. 321 D rm36@columbia.edu
MYERS, Sara, J ..... 386-312-4037. 112 C sallymyers@sjrstate.edu
MYERS, Sherri ..... 828-627-4544. 361 B smyers@haywood.edu
MYERS, Sue Ann ..... 703-591-7042. 515 A samyers@viu.edu
MYERS, Susan ..... 979-830-4159. 467 I susan.myers@blinn.edu
MYERS, Thomas ..... 314-505-7329. 272 J myerst@csl.edu
MYERS, Tim ..... 972-825-4723. 481 F tmyers@sagu.edu
MYERS, William ..... 336-517-1540. 352 H wmyers@bennett.edu
MYETTE, Linda ..... 217-373-3789. 155 J lmyette@parkland.edu
MYHRE, Oddmund, R ..... 209-667-3652... 35 B omyhre@csustan.edu
MYHRE, Terry ..... 801-304-4224. 495 H tmyhre@globeuniversity.edu
MYKLES, Donald ..... 970-491-5679... 80 I donald.mykles@colostate.edu
MYKRIS, Michael ..... 505-428-1318. 311 J michael.mykris@sfcc.edu
MYLES, Deborah ..... 281-476-1501. 479 F deborah.myles@sjcd.edu
MYLES, Mary ..... 601-979-2321. 267 E mary.b.myles@jsums.edu
MYLETT, Bradford ..... 641-472-1110. 180 N admissions@mum.edu
MYLONA, Elza ..... 757-446-0340. 504 E mylonae@evms.edu
MYLREA, Brian ..... 260-481-6923. 168 C mylreab@ipfw.edu
MYRICK, Jessica ..... 501-205-8870... 20 I jmyrick@cbc.edu
MYRICK, Justin ..... 615-966-5887. 456 B justin.myrick@lipscomb.edu
MYRICK HARRIS, Clarissa ..... 404-507-8636. 129 D cmharris@morehouse.edu
MYROW, Steve ..... 310-434-4871... 65 A myrow_steve@smc.edu
MYRTAJ, Myftar ..... 617-588-1321. 223 B mmyrtaj@bfit.edu
MYRTLE, Jamie ..... 913-971-3513. 188 H jmyrtle@mnu.edu
MYSCOFSKI, Carole ..... 309-556-3577. 148 B myscofsk@iwu.edu
MYSLINSKI, Carienne ..... 215-965-4035. 424 D cmyslinski@moore.edu
MYSZKA, Kristine ..... 217-544-6464. 158 D
MYTON, David ..... 906-635-2349. 245 G dmyton@lssu.edu
MYVETT, Newton ..... 770-394-8300. 120 H nmyvett@aii.edu

N

NAAS, Fauzi ..... 503-399-6526. 402 E fauzi.naas@chemeketa.edu
NAATZ, Duey ..... 715-232-5243. 538 B naatzd@uwstout.edu
NABI, Lynn ..... 903-586-2518. 474 N acadean@jacksonville-college.edu
NABI, Lynn ..... 903-586-2518. 474 N lnabi@jacksonville-college.edu
NABOR, Steven, E ..... 801-626-6603. 497 D snabor@weber.edu
NABORS, Larry ..... 662-246-6301. 268 B lnabors@msdelta.edu
NABORS, Melody, L ..... 901-321-3236. 453 H mnabors@cbu.edu
NABORS, Murray ..... 816-271-4510. 279 A mnabors@missouriwestern.edu
NACCARATO, Shawn ..... 620-235-4128. 189 L snaccarato@pittstate.edu
NACCO, Stephen ..... 908-709-7005. 308 B nacco@ucc.edu
NACE, Timothy ..... 765-998-5125. 173 C tmnace@taylor.edu
NACHLAS, Rachel ..... 301-846-2836. 214 H rnachlas@frederick.edu
NACHTMANN, Robert ..... 915-747-5241. 492 A nachtmann@utep.edu
NACOS-BURDS, Kathy, J ..... 563-556-5110. 181 E nacos-burdsk@nicc.edu
NADAL, Gerrard ..... 860-632-3001... 90 C gnadal@holyapostles.edu
NADARAJAN, Gunalan, L ..... 734-763-4093. 251 C guna@umich.edu
NADAULD, Stephen, D ..... 435-652-7502. 497 E nadauld@dixie.edu
NADEAU, Evelyn ..... 563-588-6557. 176 F evelyn.nadeau@clarke.edu
NADEAU, Sharon, L ..... 207-778-7254. 212 D sharonn@maine.edu
NADELMAN, Martin, H ..... 336-506-4150. 357 M martin.nadelman@alamancecc.edu
NADENICEK, Daniel, J ..... 706-542-1365. 133 C dnadeni@uga.edu

NADER, John, S .... 607-746-4540. 345 G
naderjs@delhi.edu
NADER, Richard .... 940-565-2197. 490 C
richard.nader@unt.edu
NADICKSBERND,
Joseph, P .... 901-321-3370. 453 H
jpnadick@cbu.edu
NADLER, Burton .... 585-275-2366. 349 C
bnadler@mail.rochester.edu
NADLER, Daniel, P .... 217-581-3221. 144 E
nadler@eiu.edu
NADLER, Judith .... 773-702-8743. 161 B
j-nadler@uchicago.edu
NADOLNY, Raymond ...... 701-770-7475. 372 F
raymond.nadolny@willistonstate.edu
NAEDELE, Chris .... 605-331-6575. 452 D
chris.naedele@usiouxfalls.edu
NAEGELI, Dan .... 940-565-2105. 490 C
naegeli@unt.edu
NAFF, J. Abraham .... 540-365-4493. 504 L
anaff@ferrum.edu
NAFFAA, Nicole .... 510-849-8231... 57 H
nnaffaa@psr.edu
NAFFZIGER, Danielle ..... 312-935-4532. 156 K
dnaffziger@robertmorris.edu
NAFIE, John .... 909-558-4562... 51 C
jnafie@llu.edu
NAFUS, Shelby .... 612-436-7523. 257 J
snafus@msbcollege.edu
NAFZIGER, Kenneth, L ... 540-432-4135. 504 D
ken.l.nafziger@emu.edu
NAGANATHAN, Nagi ...... 419-530-8000. 392 B
nagi.naganathan@utoledo.edu
NAGARKATTE, Umesh .... 718-270-6425. 319 A
umesh@mec.cuny.edu
NAGARKATTI, Prakash ... 803-777-5458. 447 G
prakash@mailbox.sc.edu
NAGATA, Miles, K .... 808-974-7723. 136 A
mnagata@hawaii.edu
NAGEL, Beverly .... 507-222-4303. 254 D
bnagel@carleton.edu
NAGEL, Elizabeth .... 847-566-6401. 162 G
enagel@usml.edu
NAGEL, Lonnie .... 361-593-2420. 484 A
helpdesk@tamuk.edu
NAGEL, Michael .... 610-607-6294. 431 D
mnagel@racc.edu
NAGEL, Michele .... 212-217-4632. 324 C
michele_nagel@fitnyc.edu
NAGEL, Suzie .... 269-387-2150. 252 I
suzie.nagel@wmich.edu
NAGELKERK, Jean .... 616-331-2729. 243 C
nagelkej@gvsu.edu
NAGLE, Margaret, A .... 207-581-3743. 212 B
nagle@maine.edu
NAGLE, Ryen .... 708-974-5679. 153 F
nagler@morainevalley.edu
NAGLE, Wayne .... 724-684-8271. 415 A
wnagle@dec.edu
NAGLE-MCNAUGHTON,
Betsy .... 509-865-8586. 520 D
naglemcnaughton_b@heritage.edu
NAGURA, Cynthia, K ...... 619-216-6795... 68 B
cnagura@swccd.edu
NAGURSKI, Lisa, E .... 218-722-4000. 255 E
lisan@dbumn.edu
NAGY, Debra, A .... 304-462-4122. 529 G
debra.nagy@glenville.edu
NAGY, Ellen .... 419-448-2063. 380 G
enagy@heidelberg.edu
NAGY, Mary Anne .... 732-571-3417. 303 C
mnagy@monmouth.edu
NAGY, Paul .... 575-769-4908. 309 F
paul.nagy@clovis.edu
NAGY, Paul .... 813-253-7162. 106 M
pnagy@hccfl.edu
NAGY, Rebekah, M .... 512-637-1924. 479 C
rebekahn@stedwards.edu
NAGY, Sharon .... 864-656-1455. 442 C
snagy@clemson.edu
NAGY, Tibor, P .... 806-742-2218. 487 D
tibor.nagy@ttu.edu
NAHABEDIAN, Audrey ... 978-656-3223. 232 B
nahabedianaa@middlesex.mass.edu
NAHORNEY, Mark .... 207-602-2372. 213 A
mnahorney@une.edu
NAHRA, Diane .... 216-221-8584. 392 G
dianenahra@vmcad.edu
NAHRGANG, Rick .... 507-453-2726. 259 E
rnahrgang@southeastmn.edu
NAHUM, Rinat .... 858-499-0202... 40 C
rnahum@coleman.edu
NAIDER, Fred .... 718-982-2440. 317 E
fred.naider@csi.cuny.edu
NAIDU, Jay .... 650-543-3996... 54 C
jnaidu@menlo.edu
NAIDU, Santhana .... 812-237-8764. 167 A
santhana.naidu@indstate.edu
NAIFEH, Zeak .... 580-581-2217. 394 G
znaifeh@cameron.edu
NAIK, Datta, V .... 732-571-7550. 303 C
dnaik@monmouth.edu
NAIL, Jordyn .... 478-289-2151. 124 C
jlnail@ega.edu
NAIL, Lance .... 806-742-3171. 487 D
lance.nail@ttu.edu
NAILLER, Katie .... 202-274-5623... 97 A
knailler@udc.edu
NAILS, Dana .... 731-425-2628. 460 G
dnails@jscc.edu
NAIMPALLY, Ashok, V ... 559-442-8215... 68 I
ashok.naimpally@fresnocitycollege.edu
NAIR, Ajay .... 404-727-4364. 124 E
ajay.nair@emory.edu
NAIR, Murali .... 734-487-0077. 242 D
mnair@emich.edu
NAIRN, Roderick .... 303-315-2088... 86 A
roderick.nairn@ucdenver.edu
NAJIEB, Najla, F .... 713-313-6817. 485 F
najieb_nf@tsu.edu
NAJJAR, Joe .... 229-430-6624. 120 A
jnajjar@albanytech.edu
NAJOR, Dahlia .... 619-684-8868... 56 C
dnajor@newschoolarch.edu
NAKAGAWA, Deborah .... 808-956-0321. 136 D
debn@hawaii.edu
NAKAI, Karen .... 562-985-4121... 33 F
knakai@csulb.edu
NAKAS, Victor, B .... 202-319-5600... 94 G
nakas@cua.edu
NAKASHIMA, Deborah ... 808-544-0287. 135 F
dnakashima@hpu.edu
NAKASONE, Nancy, K .... 808-689-2525. 136 C
nancynak@hawaii.edu
NAKASONE, Ron .... 818-240-1000... 45 G
nakasone@glendale.edu
NAKAYAMA, Karen .... 970-247-7212... 81 M
nakayama_k@fortlewis.edu
NAKHAI, Mandana .... 914-337-9300. 321 E
mandana.nakhai@concordia-ny.edu
NALEPA, Laurie .... 818-947-2498... 52 E
nalepal@lavc.edu
NALES, Nereida .... 787-765-4210. 548 E
nnales@cempr.edu
NALL, Deborah .... 270-247-8521. 197 H
dnall@midcontinent.edu
NALLY, Angela, D .... 765-658-4261. 165 F
adnally@depauw.edu
NALLY, Cathy .... 610-647-4400. 418 I
cnally@immaculata.edu
NALLY, Harold .... 706-233-4062. 121 G
hnally@berry.edu
NAM, Jin Joo .... 213-385-2322... 77 A
melody@wmu.edu
NAMETZ, John .... 520-621-5200... 18 F
nametzj@email.arizona.edu
NAMIAN, Jeff .... 212-924-5900. 347 B
registrar@swedishinstitute.edu
NAMWAMBA, Grace .... 225-771-3660. 206 J
grace_namwamba@subr.edu
NAMYET, Jay .... 541-302-0308. 406 D
jnamyet@uoregon.edu
NANCE, Adam .... 206-934-5484. 522 J
adam.nance@seattlecolleges.edu
NANCE, Beverlee, S .... 910-642-7141. 364 A
Beverlee.Nance@sccnc.edu
NANCE, Damon .... 951-372-7041... 60 L
damon.nance@norcocollege.edu
NANCE, Donna, S .... 405-208-5260. 397 F
dsnance@okcu.edu
NANCE, Melissa .... 620-421-6700. 188 D
melissan@labette.edu
NANCE, Richard, E .... 757-683-3144. 507 N
rnance@odu.edu
NANCE, Stan .... 617-824-8123. 226 A
stanford_nance@emerson.edu
NANCE, Teresa, A .... 610-519-4007. 436 F
terry.nance@villanova.edu
NANCE, Wendi .... 404-752-1734. 129 E
wnance@msm.edu
NANCE, William .... 408-924-5900... 36 A
william.nance@sjsu.edu
NANCE, William, A .... 512-245-2244. 487 C
wn02@txstate.edu
NANNEY, Chris .... 704-669-4062. 359 D
nanney@clevelandcc.edu
NANNI, Louis, M .... 574-631-6123. 174 A
nanni.3@nd.edu
NANOS, Joanne .... 518-262-5521. 313 D
nanosj@mail.amc.edu
NANTAIS, David .... 313-993-1560. 250 K
nantaisd@udmercy.edu
NAPE, Steven, W .... 434-381-6142. 510 F
snape@sbc.edu
NAPIER, Anna .... 606-436-5721. 195 C
anna.napier@kctcs.edu
NAPIER, Cherie, M .... 650-738-4346... 64 D
napierc@smccd.edu
NAPIER, Crystal .... 312-553-5600. 141 N
NAPIER, LaJuana, R .... 512-505-3074. 473 G
lrnapier@htu.edu
NAPIER, Michelle .... 606-326-2011. 194 J
michelle.napier@kctcs.edu
NAPIER, William .... 216-875-9970. 377 F
w.napier@csuohio.edu
NAPLES, Bruce .... 718-631-6624. 319 D
bnaples@qcc.cuny.edu
NAPLES, Fabienne .... 415-542-5142... 38 L
fnaples@ccsf.edu
NAPLES, Robert, J .... 310-825-3894... 71 C
rnaples@saonet.ucla.edu
NAPOLEON, Jhonson ..... 305-751-0001... 98 M
NAPOLES, Gerald .... 270-901-1105. 196 E
gerald.napoles@kctcs.edu
NAPOLES, Stella .... 602-787-7029... 15 B
stella.napoles@paradisevalley.edu
NAPOLI, Kathy .... 909-652-6102... 37 M
kathy.napoli@chaffey.edu
NAPOLI-RANGEL, Sarah 651-450-3626. 258 H
snapoli@inverhills.edu
NAPOLITANO, Daniel ..... 607-871-2175. 313 E
napolitano@alfred.edu
NAPOLITANO, Janet, G .. 510-987-0700... 70 H
NAQUIN, Michael, P ...... 985-448-4060. 208 A
mike.naquin@nicholls.edu
NAQUIN, Rose .... 504-520-7301. 209 D
xubooks@xula.edu
NARANG, Anita .... 510-549-4702... 68 G
anarang@sksm.edu
NARANJO, Veronica .... 509-865-8617. 520 D
naranjo_v@heritage.edu
NARAYANAN, S .... 937-775-3035. 393 G
s.narayanan@wright.edu
NARCUM, Jeani, M .... 410-778-7214. 221 C
jnarcum2@washcoll.edu
NARDI, Joanne .... 860-738-6329... 89 C
jnardi@nwcc.commnet.edu
NARDI, Peter, A .... 410-293-1585. 545 J
nardi@usna.edu
NARDIN, Gail .... 212-752-1530. 328 G
gail.nardin@limcollege.edu
NARDO, John .... 404-364-8327. 130 A
jnardo@oglethorpe.edu
NARDONE, Mary, S .... 617-552-0346. 224 A
mary.nardone@bc.edu
NARDUCCI, Julie .... 951-785-2578... 50 B
jnarducc@lasierra.edu
NARDUZZI, James, L ..... 804-289-8135. 510 L
jnarduzz@richmond.edu
NARODOWY, Donna ...... 401-456-8101. 439 F
dnarodowy@ric.edu
NARVEKAR, Nirmal, P .... 212-851-2031. 321 D
nn2017@columbia.edu
NARY, Thomas, I .... 617-552-3225. 224 A
thomas.nary@bc.edu
NASCA, Philip .... 518-402-0281. 341 D
pnasca@albany.edu
NASH, Anna .... 313-927-1281. 246 D
anash5086@marygrove.edu
NASH, Bob .... 714-241-6143... 39 I
bnash@coastline.edu
NASH, Brittany, D .... 507-344-7321. 253 J
brittany.nash@blc.edu
NASH, Charles, R .... 205-348-8347..... 8 C
cnash@uasystem.ua.edu
NASH, David .... 308-635-6108. 293 E
dnash@wncc.edu
NASH, David .... 215-955-6969. 434 C
david.nash@jefferson.edu
NASH, Dawn, P .... 478-757-5115. 134 G
dnash@wesleyancollege.edu
NASH, Gail .... 731-989-6072. 454 J
gnash@fhu.edu
NASH, Gretchen .... 617-327-6777. 233 D
gretchen_nash@mspp.edu
NASH, Natasha .... 512-892-2640. 481 B
NASH, Richard .... 812-866-7029. 166 C
nash@hanover.edu
NASH, Robin .... 785-825-5422. 185 B
rlnashi@brownmackie.edu
NASH, Tamara .... 404-504-1976. 130 A
tnash@oglethorpe.edu
NASH, Timothy .... 718-405-3268. 320 G
tim.nash@mountsaintvincent.edu
NASH, Timothy, G .... 989-837-4129. 248 C
tgnash@northwood.edu
NASH, Vicki .... 517-437-7341. 243 I
vicki.nash@hillsdale.edu
NASH, Victoria .... 262-691-5495. 541 D
vnash@wcfc.edu
NASH-YORE, Kimberly ... 216-987-2173. 378 D
kimberly.nash-yore@tri-c.edu
NASHUA, Loy .... 714-564-6211... 60 G
nashua_loy@sac.edu
NASO, Mary Ann .... 717-262-2002. 437 H
mnaso@wilson.edu
NASON, Bradley, A .... 406-657-1018. 288 B
nasonb@rocky.edu
NASON, Mark .... 207-941-7176. 211 F
nasonm@nescom.edu
NASON, Stephen, S .... 207-948-9284. 211 I
snason@unity.edu
NASR, Nabil .... 585-475-5106. 337 L
nasr@rit.edu
NASR, Vali .... 202-663-5622. 215 H
vnasr@jhu.edu
NASRALLAH, Hany .... 916-649-8168... 49 I
hnasrallah@kaplan.edu
NASS, Allan .... 505-566-3447. 311 I
nassa@sanjuancollege.edu
NASSAR, Anne .... 315-733-2300. 349 D
anassar@uscny.edu
NASSAR, Jamal, R .... 909-537-5500... 34 E
jnassar@csusb.edu
NASSAR, Sayed .... 248-370-2697. 248 J
nassar@oakland.edu
NASSER, Dawn, S .... 217-443-8755. 143 G
dnasser@dacc.edu
NASSER, Edward, D .... 520-621-5449... 18 F
enasser@email.arizona.edu
NASSER, Mitch .... 618-537-6912. 152 G
rmnasser@mckendree.edu
NAST, Paul .... 479-524-7296... 21 G
pnast@jbu.edu
NASTANSKI, Michael ..... 352-588-8599. 112 D
michael.nastanski@saintleo.edu
NATAF, Daniel, D .... 410-777-2407. 213 D
ddnataf@aacc.edu
NATALE, J. Peter .... 513-529-5322. 384 G
natalejp@miamioh.edu
NATALE, Vickie .... 859-572-6566. 198 I
natalev1@nku.edu
NATALICCHIO, Gino .... 213-627-2580... 38 G
NATALICIO, Diana, S ..... 915-747-5555. 492 A
dnatalicio@utep.edu
NATALIE, Margaret .... 516-299-4225. 329 C
margaret.natalie@liu.edu
NATEMAN, David .... 252-222-6262. 358 G
natemand@carteret.edu
NATERA, Edmundo .... 432-837-8085. 487 B
enatera@sulross.edu
NATHAN, Eileen .... 806-742-3671. 487 D
eileen.nathan@ttu.edu
NATHAN, Vini .... 334-844-4285..... 1 G
vzn0007@auburn.edu
NATHAN, Wendy .... 419-251-1454. 383 G
wendy.nathan@mercycollege.edu
NATHAN, Yoges .... 757-873-4235. 510 B
ynathan@stratford.edu
NATHANI, Junie .... 202-687-0213... 95 E
rn44@georgetown.edu
NATHANSON, Mike .... 352-435-5027. 108 S
nathansm@lssc.edu
NATHIEL,
Most Reverend .... 914-961-8313. 340 B
NATION, Lynda .... 954-486-7728. 118 E
NATIVIDAD, Rory .... 310-660-3547... 43 B
rnatividad@elcamino.edu
NATOLI, Joseph, T .... 305-284-3800. 118 F
jnatoli@miami.edu
NATRIELLO, Gary .... 212-678-3087. 347 G
gin6@tc.columbia.edu
NATTA, Andrea .... 415-282-7600... 27 L
andreanatta@actcm.edu
NATTER, Gretchen .... 717-337-6490. 417 B
gnatter@gettysburg.edu
NATTER, Wolfgang .... 716-375-2136. 338 E
wnatter@sbu.edu
NAUGHTON, Amy .... 612-874-3799. 257 B
anaughton@mcad.edu
NAUGHTON, Randy .... 623-935-8295... 14 K
randy.naughton@estrellamountain.edu
NAUGHTON, Rosemary .. 508-929-8045. 230 G
rnaughton@worcester.edu
NAUGLE, Deemie, J .... 214-333-5291. 470 D
deemie@dbu.edu
NAUMANN, Cheryl .... 602-557-1742... 18 I
Cheryl.Naumann@phoenix.edu
NAUSER, Julie .... 816-995-2855. 280 G
julie.nauser@researchcollege.edu
NAUSER, Julie .... 816-995-2855. 280 I
Julie.Nauser@researchcollege.edu
NAVA, Esmeralda .... 626-396-2267... 28 P
esmeralda.nava@artcenter.edu
NAVA, Robert, J .... 415-338-2506... 35 E
rjnava@sfsu.edu
NAVA, Robert, J .... 415-338-2517... 35 E
rjnava@sfsu.edu
NAVANT, Yves .... 303-753-6046... 85 B
ynavant@rmcad.edu
NAVARI, Shelley .... 802-860-6405. 499 A
navari@champlain.edu
NAVARRETE, Nancy .... 602-285-7392... 15 C
nancy.navarrete@phoenixcollege.edu
NAVARRETTE, Lupe .... 325-235-7368. 486 C
jose.navarrette@tstc.edu
NAVARRETTE,
Ricardo, D .... 707-524-1651... 65 B
rnavarrette@santarosa.edu
NAVARRO, Carlos .... 408-273-2693... 55 H
cnavarro@nhu.edu
NAVARRO, David .... 619-388-7560... 62 F
dnavarro@sdccd.edu

NAVARRO, JoAnn .... 607-777-3060. 341 E
navarro@binghamton.edu
NAVARRO, Renee .... 415-514-0421... 72 A
Renee.Navarro@ucsf.edu
NAVARRO, Renee .... 415-476-7700... 72 A
renee.navarro@ucsf.edu
NAVARRO, Victor .... 480-732-7020... 14 J
victor.navarro@cgc.edu
NAVARRO-JUSINO,
Adam .... 830-372-8072. 485 C
anavarro-jusino@tlu.edu
NAVE, Felicia, M .... 926-261-2175. 482 F
fmnave@pvamu.edu
NAVE, Jeffery, W .... 504-282-4455. 206 A
jnave@nobts.edu
NAVIN, John .... 618-650-3823. 159 H
jnavin@siue.edu
NAVIN, Tom .... 802-258-3173. 500 C
tom.navin@worldlearning.org
NAVROTSKY, Alexandra . 530-754-8918... 70 J
anavrotsky@ucdavis.edu
NAWN, Ruth .... 603-513-1320. 298 E
ruth.nawn@granite.edu
NAWOICHIK, Michael .... 978-867-4500. 226 H
mike.nawoichik@gordon.edu
NAYLER, Ronald .... 847-467-5810. 155 D
r-nayler@northwestern.edu
NAYLOR, Patricia .... 973-408-3103. 301 C
pnaylor@drew.edu
NAYLOR, Richard .... 508-373-9453. 223 A
richard.naylor@becker.edu
NAYLOR, Suzette .... 816-802-3519. 275 J
snaylor@kcai.edu
NAYLOR, Tere, E .... 816-932-6744. 281 J
tnaylor@saintlukescollege.edu
NAYLOR, Tracy .... 270-686-9550. 192 G
tracy.naylor@brescia.edu
NAYLOR MOORE,
Barbara .... 662-252-8000. 269 F
bmoore@rustcollege.edu
NAYOR, Gregory .... 215-717-6606. 435 A
gnayor@uarts.edu
NAZARENKO, Tatiana ..... 805-565-6070... 76 D
tnazarenko@westmont.edu
NAZARIAN, Nick .... 909-652-6541... 37 M
nick.nazarian@chaffey.edu
NAZARIO-COLON,
Ricardo .... 606-783-9042. 198 A
r.nazariocolon@moreheadstate.edu
NAZARIO-TORRES,
Juan, C .... 787-620-2040. 547 C
jcnazario@aupr.edu
NAZZARO, Rosalyn .... 617-369-3631. 236 F
rnazzaro@mfa.org
NDIAYE, Momar .... 309-438-5276. 147 J
mndiaye@ilstu.edu
NEAD, Margaret, A .... 585-271-3778. 320 E
mnead@crcds.edu
NEAL, Bill .... 704-669-4097. 359 D
nealb@clevelandcc.edu
NEAL, Brenda .... 304-260-4380. 527 N
bneal@blueridgectc.edu
NEAL, Brigette .... 313-664-7470. 241 C
bneal@collegeforcreativestudies.edu
NEAL, Charles, V .... 607-587-4019. 345 D
nealcv@alfredstate.edu
NEAL, Donna .... 252-493-7406. 362 G
dneal@email.pittcc.edu
NEAL, Donna, V .... 252-493-7309. 362 G
dneal@email.pittcc.edu
NEAL, Gary, W .... 210-999-7411. 488 C
gneal@trinity.edu
NEAL, James, G .... 212-854-2247. 321 D
jneal@columbia.edu
NEAL, Jason .... 909-593-3511... 72 E
jneal@laverne.edu
NEAL, Kathleen .... 860-231-5271... 92 F
kneal@usj.edu
NEAL, Kurtis, R .... 325-942-2168. 465 K
kurtis.neal@angelo.edu
NEAL, JR., L. Cameron .. 972-881-5891. 469 G
cneal@collin.edu
NEAL, La Vonne .... 815-753-9055. 154 I
lneal1@niu.edu
NEAL, Lyle .... 402-761-8224. 292 C
lneal@southeast.edu
NEAL, Mary, Y .... 804-752-7259. 508 E
mneal@rmc.edu
NEAL, Michael, A .... 661-654-2287... 32 H
mneal@csub.edu
NEAL, Nicole .... 740-351-3245. 388 N
nneal@shawnee.edu
NEAL, Phillip, W .... 270-901-1114. 196 E
phil.neal@kctcs.edu
NEAL, Robin .... 916-484-8172... 53 A
nealr@arc.losrios.edu
NEAL, Rodney .... 909-558-4543... 51 C
rneal@llu.edu
NEAL, Shannon .... 504-816-4228. 201 K
sneal@dillard.edu
NEAL, Stephanie, A .... 304-710-3141. 528 C
neal@mctc.edu
NEAL, Steven, M .... 330-287-1211. 386 F
neal.2@osu.edu
NEAL, Susan .... 918-631-3246. 401 F
susan-neal@utulsa.edu
NEAL, Thomas .... 504-866-7426. 206 B
tneal@nds.edu
NEAL, Thomas, G .... 409-984-6156. 486 H
tom.neal@lamarpa.edu
NEAL, Thomas, M .... 714-547-9625... 30 J
tneal@calcoast.edu
NEAL, Tom .... 503-838-8043. 406 E
nealt@wou.edu
NEAL, Veronica .... 408-864-5338... 44 M
nealveronica@deanza.edu
NEAL, Willie .... 214-860-8784. 471 A
wneal@dcccd.edu
NEAL, Willie .... 972-860-8225. 470 H
wneal@dcccd.edu
NEAL, Zeal .... 501-279-4332... 21 C
zneal@harding.edu
NEALEIGH, Michael .... 405-224-3140. 401 E
mnealeigh@usao.edu
NEALON, Jackie .... 516-299-3717. 329 D
jackie.nealon@liu.edu
NEALON, Marisol .... 415-575-6120... 31 D
mmendoza@ciis.edu
NEALON, Michael .... 517-483-1016. 245 H
nealonm@lcc.edu
NEALON-WOODS,
Michele .... 213-627-2580... 38 G
NEANDER, Jessica .... 727-864-8148. 101 N
neandejs@eckerd.edu
NEAR, Hollis .... 206-726-5040. 518 G
hnear@cornish.edu
NEARY, Robert .... 315-866-0300. 326 A
nearyrd@herkimer.edu
NEASE, Owen .... 504-282-4455. 206 A
financialaid@nobts.edu
NEAU, George .... 510-567-6174... 69 C
chancellor@sum.edu
NEAULT, Lynn .... 619-388-3400... 62 D
NEAULT, Lynn, C .... 619-388-6922... 62 C
lneault@sdccd.edu
NEAVE, Jessica .... 617-217-9204. 222 G
jneave@baystate.edu
NEAVES, Mitchell .... 340-693-1046. 555 E
mneaves@live.uvi.edu
NEBEKER-CHRISTENSEN,
Annie .... 801-581-7066. 496 Q
anebeker@sa.utah.edu
NEBEL, Andreia .... 402-552-6178. 288 L
nebel@clarksoncollege.edu
NEBESKY, Michael .... 864-656-2390. 442 C
mnebeske@clemson.edu
NECESSARY, David .... 276-739-2448. 514 D
dnecessary@vhcc.edu
NECESSARY, Russell, D . 276-328-0322. 511 C
rdn2f@uvawise.edu
NECHIPURENKO, Erin .... 508-626-4951. 230 A
enechipurenko@framingham.edu
NECULA, Cristina .... 718-960-2416. 318 A
cristina.necula@lehman.cuny.edu
NEDBALSKI, Coleen .... 610-358-4587. 424 I
NEDBALSC@neumann.edu
NEDDERMAN,
Robert, M .... 402-461-7410. 289 I
bnedderman@hastings.edu
NEDELL, Thomas .... 617-373-2240. 235 F
NEDERHOFF, Arlan .... 712-722-6010. 177 J
arlan.nederhorff@dordt.edu
NEDWEK, Brian .... 417-823-3447. 281 M
bnedwek@forest.edu
NEEDHAM, Frankie .... 828-898-8763. 356 A
needham@lmc.edu
NEEDHAM, James .... 361-825-2778. 483 F
james.needham@tamucc.edu
NEEDHAM, Jodie .... 312-427-2737. 148 L
6needham@jmls.edu
NEEDHAM, Michele .... 630-466-7900. 162 J
mneedham@waubonsee.edu
NEEFE, Diane .... 608-785-9539. 541 E
neefed@westerntc.edu
NEEL, Buster .... 702-992-2302. 294 G
buster.neel@nsc.edu
NEEL, Ellen .... 623-845-3371... 14 M
e.neel@gcmail.maricopa.edu
NEEL, Joel .... 805-756-2193... 32 F
jneel@calpoly.edu
NEEL, Linda .... 575-624-7142. 309 I
linda.neel@roswell.enmu.edu
NEEL, Paul .... 574-807-7035. 164 D
paul.neel@bethelcollege.edu
NEELY, Chrystal .... 404-752-1782. 129 E
cneely@msm.edu
NEELY, Erin .... 740-695-9500. 374 H
eneely@belmontcollege.edu
NEELY, Jennifer .... 615-248-1237. 462 D
jneely@trevecca.edu
NEELY, Renee .... 575-562-2314. 309 H
renee.neely@enmu.edu
NEELY, Robert .... 940-898-3301. 488 B
rneely@twu.edu
NEELY-MORRIS, Felecia . 903-510-2490. 488 E
fnee@tjc.edu
NEENAN, Benedict .... 660-944-2827. 272 H
benedict@conception.edu
NEENAN, Benedict, T ..... 660-944-2859. 272 H
benedict@conception.edu
NEENAN, SJ, William, B 617-552-1640. 224 A
william.neenan@bc.edu
NEER, Stephen .... 312-261-3031. 153 I
stephen.neer@nl.edu
NEESAM, Jaci, E .... 415-422-6762... 73 J
neesam@usfca.edu
NEESE, James .... 810-989-5585. 249 H
jneese@sc4.edu
NEESE, John, M .... 325-670-1273. 472 O
jneese@hsutx.edu
NEESE, Susan .... 253-680-7025. 516 L
sneese@bates.ctc.edu
NEESMITH, Debra .... 704-216-3640. 363 D
debra.neesmith@rccc.edu
NEEVE, Tasia .... 415-442-7820... 45 I
tneeve@ggu.edu
NEF, Dennis, L .... 559-278-4468... 33 D
dennisn@csufresno.edu
NEFF, Jon .... 319-398-7195. 180 J
jneff@kirkwood.edu
NEFF, Kathryn .... 573-518-2378. 278 A
kneff@mineralarea.edu
NEFF, Sherri, A .... 913-288-7201. 187 L
sneff@kckcc.edu
NEGBENEBOR,
Anthony, I .... 704-406-4622. 354 C
anegbenebor@gardner-webb.edu
NEGIP, Marilyn .... 617-243-2244. 227 K
mnegip@lasell.edu
NEGIP, Stephanie, E .... 239-280-2500... 98 K
NEGLIA, Frank, A .... 973-290-4344. 300 F
fneglia@cse.edu
NEGLIA, Michael, S .... 904-620-2923. 116 B
mneglia@unf.edu
NEGRÓN, Luis .... 787-850-9319. 554 D
luis.negron4@upr.edu
NEGRON, Frankie .... 787-761-0640. 553 F
NEGRON, Gisela .... 787-257-7373. 552 H
gnegron@suagm.edu
NEGRÓN, Lillian .... 787-786-3030. 547 F
lnegron@ucb.edu.pr
NEGRON, Luz .... 787-743-4041. 548 H
lznegron@columbiaco.edu
NEGRÓN, Lymari .... 787-891-0825. 549 K
lynegron@aguadilla.inter.edu
NEGRÓN, Olga .... 787-832-6000. 549 D
mortiz@icprjc.edu
NEGRON, Pablo, E .... 518-629-7154. 326 G
p.negron@hvcc.edu
NEHER, Kenneth, R .... 618-650-2536. 159 H
kneher@siue.edu
NEHMER, Matt .... 213-627-2580... 38 G
NEHRA, Terese .... 313-664-7677. 241 C
tnehra@collegeforcreativestudies.edu
NEHRBAS, Mark .... 740-284-5843. 379 N
mnehrbas@franciscan.edu
NEHRING, Matthew, S ... 719-587-7504... 78 B
msnehrin@adams.edu
NEHRING, Wendy, M ..... 423-439-7051. 459 C
nehringw@etsu.edu
NEIDECK, Robert .... 765-998-5222. 173 C
rbneideck@taylor.edu
NEIDERBACH,
Michael, A .... 607-871-2329. 313 E
neiderbach@alfred.edu
NEIDORF, David .... 760-872-2000... 42 E
dneidorf@deepsprings.edu
NEIDY, Jon .... 309-677-2374. 140 I
neidy@bradley.edu
NEIFERT, Roger .... 316-322-3144. 185 D
rneifert@butlercc.edu
NEIGHBOR, Edward .... 407-823-5269. 115 E
james.neighbor@ucf.edu
NEIGHBORS, Janie .... 940-668-7333. 477 I
jneighbors@nctc.edu
NEIGLER, Peter .... 212-924-5900. 347 B
pneigler@swedishinstitute.edu
NEIHEISEL, Steve .... 208-885-5690. 139 D
steven@uidaho.edu
NEIHOF, JR., John, E .... 601-366-8880. 270 H
jneihof@wbs.edu
NEIKIRK, Mark .... 859-572-1449. 198 I
neikirkm1@nku.edu
NEIL, Amy, E .... 412-578-2090. 412 G
aeneil@carlow.edu
NEIL, Jon .... 518-580-5490. 341 A
jneil@skidmore.edu
NEIL, Linda .... 773-481-8408. 142 F
lneil@ccc.edu
NEIL, Stephanie .... 206-876-6100. 523 D
sneil@theseattleschool.edu
NEILL, Christine .... 602-243-8185... 15 F
christine.neill@smcmail.maricopa.edu
NEILL, Sarah .... 617-521-2124. 236 G
sarah.neill@simmons.edu
NEILL, Sharon .... 212-772-4460. 318 C
sharon.neill@hunter.cuny.edu
NEILS, Kathleen, A .... 603-862-2421. 298 C
kathy.neils@unh.edu
NEILSEN, Ardis .... 805-922-6966... 26 K
aneilsen@hancockcollege.edu
NEILSON, Eric, G .... 312-503-0340. 155 D
egneilson@northwestern.edu
NEILSON, Leanne .... 805-493-3145... 31 H
neilson@clunet.edu
NEILSON, Richard, P ...... 516-671-2215. 350 C
rneilson@webb.edu
NEIMAN, Gershon .... 845-731-3700. 352 A
NEIMEYER, Nicole .... 419-227-3141. 391 F
nniemeye@unoh.edu
NEIN, Daniel, F .... 207-786-6207. 209 F
dnein@bates.edu
NEINER, Catherine .... 404-471-6425. 119 I
cneiner@agnesscott.edu
NEISES, Marlene .... 414-382-6017. 531 I
marlene.neises@alverno.edu
NEITZ, Stephen .... 717-815-1924. 438 D
sneitz@ycp.edu
NEITZEL, Alan .... 405-736-0315. 399 F
aneitzel@rose.edu
NEL, Stanley, D .... 415-422-8888... 73 J
nel@usfca.edu
NELANT, Dan .... 317-805-1782. 527 G
dnelant@salemu.edu
NELKENBAUM,
Avrohom Yaakov .... 718-645-0536. 331 G
NELL, Sharon, D .... 512-448-8620. 479 C
sharonn@stedwards.edu
NELLENBACK, Marie, A .. 315-255-1743. 316 D
marie.nellenback@cayuga-cc.edu
NELLER, Irene .... 562-903-4079... 29 L
irene.neller@biola.edu
NELLESEN, Gary .... 909-274-4850... 55 A
gnellesen@mtsac.edu
NELLIS, Ginny .... 802-258-3283. 500 C
ginny.nellis@worldlearning.org
NELLIS, M. Duane .... 806-742-2121. 487 D
duane.nellis@ttu.edu
NELMS, Chad .... 864-231-2025. 441 B
cnelms@andersonuniversity.edu
NELMS, Jim, A .... 936-261-1932. 482 F
janelms@pvamu.edu
NELMS, Kristi .... 217-854-3231. 140 G
kristi.nelms@blackburn.edu
NELSEN, Erin .... 717-299-7772. 434 A
nelsen@stevenscollege.edu
NELSEN, Jeff, A .... 515-574-1115. 179 D
nelsen@iowacentral.edu
NELSEN, Robert, S .... 956-665-2100. 492 B
president@utpa.edu
NELSON, Andrew .... 830-372-8011. 485 C
anelson@tlu.edu
NELSON, Andrew, J .... 715-836-5368. 536 E
nelsonan@uwec.edu
NELSON, Angelia, J .... 252-335-3396. 367 C
adnelson@mail.ecsu.edu
NELSON, Anthony .... 301-860-3590. 220 A
anelson@bowiestate.edu
NELSON, April .... 580-477-7896. 401 J
april.nelson@wosc.edu
NELSON, Barry, C .... 979-436-9200. 484 B
nelson@tamhsc.edu
NELSON, Bill .... 573-681-5555. 276 C
nelsonb@lincolnu.edu
NELSON, Brandi .... 701-662-1509. 372 D
brandi.nelson@lrsc.edu
NELSON, Brenda .... 718-405-3223. 320 G
brenda.nelson@mountsaintvincent.edu
NELSON, Brian .... 832-813-6508. 476 A
brian.nelson@lonestar.edu
NELSON, Bruce, F .... 336-278-7280. 354 B
bnelson@elon.edu
NELSON, Camile .... 617-573-8157. 237 B
cnelson@suffolk.edu
NELSON, Carla, P .... 432-552-2100. 493 D
nelson_c@utpb.edu
NELSON, Carol .... 218-751-8670. 263 C
carolnelson@oakhills.edu
NELSON, Carolyn .... 510-885-3942... 33 C
carolyn.nelson@csueastbay.edu
NELSON, Charles .... 334-386-7220..... 3 H
cnelson@faulkner.edu
NELSON, Charles .... 425-249-4775. 524 D
chuck.nelson@tlc.edu
NELSON, Cherrie .... 801-626-7496. 497 D
cgnelson@weber.edu
NELSON, Christopher ..... 757-388-2900. 509 D
cmnelson@sentara.com
NELSON, Christopher, B 410-626-2510. 217 G
chris.nelson@sjca.edu
NELSON, Claire, N .... 207-778-7295. 212 D
claire@maine.edu

NELSON, Craig, V ... 801-524-8103. 495 O
cnelson@ldsbc.edu
NELSON, Daniel ... 651-638-6241. 253 K
dc-nelson@bethel.edu
NELSON, David, A ... 717-245-1830. 414 H
nelsond@dickinson.edu
NELSON, David, P ... 336-770-3262. 369 D
nelsond@uncsa.edu
NELSON, Deborah, L ... 773-702-8051. 161 B
dnelson@uchicago.edu
NELSON, Diane, L ... 415-422-2441... 73 J
dlnelson3@usfca.edu
NELSON, Dirk ... 806-651-2730. 484 D
jdnelson@mail.wtamu.edu
NELSON, Don ... 570-740-0750. 422 G
dnelson@luzerne.edu
NELSON, Dorothy, A ... 248-370-2552. 248 J
danelson@oakland.edu
NELSON, Doug ... 563-387-1862. 180 M
nelsondg@luther.edu
NELSON, Douglas ... 860-231-5291... 92 F
dnelson@usj.edu
NELSON, Drew ... 281-756-3500. 465 D
dnelson@alvincollege.edu
NELSON, Edwin, C ... 724-925-4003. 437 D
nelsone@wccc.edu
NELSON, Eldon ... 956-882-5000. 491 D
eldon.nelson@utb.edu
NELSON, Elizabeth, A ... 713-798-2500. 467 F
enelson@bcm.edu
NELSON, Eric ... 570-674-6725. 424 A
enelson@misericordia.edu
NELSON, Erik ... 215-572-2944. 409 H
nelson@arcadia.edu
NELSON, Evelyn, C ... 561-237-7816. 108 X
enelson@lynn.edu
NELSON, Fred ... 605-642-6848. 451 G
fred.nelson@bhsu.edu
NELSON, Garet, B ... 802-626-6446. 501 E
garet.nelson@lyndonstate.edu
NELSON, Gena, C ... 315-267-2330. 344 C
nelsongc@potsdam.edu
NELSON, Gersham ... 660-543-4750. 283 A
ganelson@ucmo.edu
NELSON, Greg ... 408-288-3723... 63 P
greg.nelson@sjcc.edu
NELSON, Gregory ... 702-579-3556. 294 B
gnelson@kaplan.edu
NELSON, James ... 903-566-7002. 492 D
jnelson@uttyler.edu
NELSON, James, A ... 304-327-4103. 529 D
jnelson@bluefieldstate.edu
NELSON, James, H ... 606-693-5000. 196 H
jnelson@kmbc.edu
NELSON, Jane, A ... 612-330-1603. 253 H
nelsonj@augsburg.edu
NELSON, Janet, A ... 315-255-1743. 316 D
helsonj@cayuga-cc.edu
NELSON, Janice ... 949-214-3334... 41 I
janice.nelson@cui.edu
NELSON, Jay ... 763-576-4773. 257 Q
jnelson@anokatech.edu
NELSON, Jeff ... 218-235-2193. 261 G
j.nelson@vcc.edu
NELSON, Jeff, A ... 952-888-4777. 263 B
jnelson@nwhealth.edu
NELSON, Jeffrey, D ... 419-372-2853. 374 K
nelsonj@bgsu.edu
NELSON, Jen ... 208-459-5121. 138 A
jnelson@collegeofidaho.edu
NELSON, Jennifer ... 770-975-4000. 122 I
NELSON, Jesse ... 509-963-1515. 517 F
nelsonje@cwu.edu
NELSON, Jim ... 606-693-5000. 196 H
jnelson@kmbc.edu
NELSON, Jim ... 479-619-3159... 22 C
jnelson3@nwacc.edu
NELSON, Joan ... 713-743-2603. 489 B
jmnelson2@uh.edu
NELSON, Joan, M ... 713-743-2603. 489 A
jmnelson2@uh.edu
NELSON, Joanne, E ... 518-564-2090. 344 B
jnels003@plattsburgh.edu
NELSON, Joseph ... 907-796-6057... 11 A
joe.nelson@uas.alaska.edu
NELSON, Joseph, D ... 706-821-8235. 130 C
jnelson@paine.edu
NELSON, Joseph, G ... 740-427-5172. 382 J
nelson@kenyon.edu
NELSON, Joy ... 617-236-8800. 226 F
jnelson@fisher.edu
NELSON, Judith, L ... 561-237-7161. 108 X
jlnelson@lynn.edu
NELSON, Karen ... 760-419-1288. 123 F
karen.nelson@covenant.edu
NELSON, Karen ... 503-943-7485. 408 F
nelsonk@up.edu
NELSON, Karen, L ... 617-262-5000. 223 F
karen.nelson@the-bac.edu
NELSON, Karen, S ... 724-653-2190. 415 A
knelson@dec.edu

NELSON, Kathleen ... 973-300-6556. 307 F
knelson@sussex.edu
NELSON, Kathleen, J ... 651-638-6126. 253 K
k-nelson@bethel.edu
NELSON, Keith, R ... 989-463-7303. 239 B
nelsonkr@alma.edu
NELSON, Kelly ... 410-617-2341. 216 A
knelson1@loyola.edu
NELSON, Kent, E ... 208-885-2272. 139 D
kentnelson@uidaho.edu
NELSON, Kevin ... 970-943-3045... 86 I
knelson@western.edu
NELSON, Kris ... 251-442-2945... 9 A
knelson@umobile.edu
NELSON, Linda ... 816-604-2250. 277 F
linda.nelson@mcckc.edu
NELSON, Linda, J ... 404-413-2567. 126 E
lnelson@gsu.edu
NELSON, Linda, J ... 404-413-3300. 126 E
lnelson@gsu.edu
NELSON, Lindsey ... 207-859-1105. 211 H
registrar@thomas.edu
NELSON, Lisa ... 570-740-0732. 422 G
lnelson@luzerne.edu
NELSON, Lisa ... 360-992-2488. 518 A
lnelson@clark.edu
NELSON, Mark ... 205-348-4893... 8 D
mnelson@ua.edu
NELSON, Mark ... 419-372-6067. 374 K
nelsonm@bgsu.edu
NELSON, Mark ... 252-940-6213. 358 A
markn@beaufortccc.edu
NELSON, Martha ... 415-257-1310... 42 J
martha.nelson@dominican.edu
NELSON, Merritt ... 402-941-6400. 290 K
NELSON, Mike ... 619-684-8771... 56 C
mnelson@newschoolarch.edu
NELSON, Murrey ... 415-503-6286... 62 H
mnelson@sfcm.edu
NELSON, Nadine ... 402-486-2504. 292 E
nanelson@ucollege.edu
NELSON, Nancy, N ... 915-831-6631. 472 B
nnelson2@epcc.edu
NELSON, Noah ... 903-886-5815. 483 E
noah.nelson@tamuc.edu
NELSON, Peggy, L ... 208-524-3000. 138 D
peggy.nelson@my.eitc.edu
NELSON, Peter, C ... 312-996-2400. 161 D
nelson@uic.edu
NELSON, Phil ... 909-469-5661... 76 B
pnelson@westernu.edu
NELSON, Phil ... 620-241-0723. 185 K
NELSON, Rebecca ... 773-244-5759. 154 G
rnelson1@northpark.edu
NELSON, Rencelly ... 691-320-2480. 546 B
rencelly@comfsm.fm
NELSON, Richard ... 518-327-6247. 336 B
rnelson@paulsmiths.edu
NELSON, Richard ... 843-953-2232. 442 A
richard.nelson@citadel.edu
NELSON, Richard, D ... 812-288-8878. 171 E
rnelson@mid-america.edu
NELSON, Samantha ... 256-306-2441... 2 F
snelson@calhoun.edu
NELSON, Sean ... 617-994-6918. 228 D
snelson@bhe.mass.edu
NELSON, Sharon ... 281-478-3656. 479 F
sharon.nelson@sjcd.edu
NELSON, Sherri ... 401-863-3476. 438 J
sherri_nelson@brown.edu
NELSON, Sheryl ... 410-209-6001. 213 F
snelson@bccc.edu
NELSON, Stephanie ... 432-837-8303. 487 B
NELSON, Steve ... 504-568-4009. 205 C
snelso1@lsuhsc.edu
NELSON, Steve ... 715-395-4619. 538 C
snelson@uwsuper.edu
NELSON, Steven ... 412-304-0723. 416 F
snelson@cci.edu
NELSON, Steven, J ... 313-993-1524. 250 K
nelsonsj@udmercy.edu
NELSON, Stuart ... 307-532-8330. 542 a
stuart.nelson@ewc.wy.edu
NELSON, Sue ... 707-256-7150... 55 F
snelson@napavalley.edu
NELSON, Sunny ... 912-525-5000. 131 B
snelson@scad.edu
NELSON, Suzy ... 315-228-7425. 320 F
snelson@colgate.edu
NELSON, Tammy ... 207-768-2747. 210 M
tnelson@nmcc.edu
NELSON, Terence ... 949-582-4473... 67 C
tnelson14@saddleback.edu
NELSON, Thomas ... 678-915-7464. 132 C
tnelson@spsu.edu
NELSON, Tim ... 301-891-4045. 221 B
tnelson@wau.edu
NELSON, Tim ... 510-723-6648... 37 K
tnelson@chabotcollege.edu
NELSON, Tim ... 803-732-6716. 445 C
nelsont@midlandstech.edu

NELSON, Timothy ... 419-267-1226. 385 F
tnelson@northweststate.edu
NELSON, Timothy, J ... 231-995-1010. 248 B
tnelson@nmc.edu
NELSON, Tommy ... 920-686-6281. 536 A
Tommy.Nelson@sl.edu
NELSON, Tonya ... 505-566-3220. 311 I
nelsont@sanjuancollege.edu
NELSON, Troy ... 417-626-1234. 279 J
occadmin@occ.edu
NELSON, Vincent, C ... 319-335-3294. 175 I
vincent-nelson@uiowa.edu
NELSON, Wilbert ... 602-285-7174... 15 C
wilbert.nelson@phoenixcollege.edu
NELSON, William, G ... 937-395-8837. 382 K
william.nelson@kc.edu
NELSON, William, L ... 800-867-2243... 57 D
NELSON-BAILEY, Robin . 781-239-3171. 231 G
nelsonbailey@massbay.edu
NELSON-HENSLEY,
Sheila ... 412-392-3498. 431 B
snelsonhensley@pointpark.edu
NELSON MOELLER,
Rachel ... 610-330-5810. 420 D
moellerr@lafayette.edu
NELSON NASH, Denise . 626-395-4638... 31 E
dnn@caltech.edu
NELSON-RUSSOM,
Lynn, A ... 610-499-1183. 437 E
lanelsonrussom@widener.edu
NELSON WINGER,
Elyse ... 309-556-3005. 148 B
enelsonw@iwu.edu
NEMCIK, Henry ... 505-277-1586. 312 F
hnemcik@unm.edu
NEMETH, Kevin ... 406-896-5872. 287 C
kevin.nemeth@msubillings.edu
NEMITZ, James, W ... 304-647-6368. 530 B
jnemitz@osteo.wvsom.edu
NENON, Thomas, J ... 901-678-2156. 460 B
tnenon@memphis.edu
NENON, Thomas, J ... 901-678-4831. 460 B
tnenon@memphis.edu
NEPHEW, Marvin ... 937-328-6125. 377 A
nephewm@clarkstate.edu
NEPOMUCENO, Tina ... 708-209-3545. 143 E
tina.nepomuceno@cuchicago.edu
NEPPER, Terry, S ... 806-651-2747. 484 D
tnepper@mail.wtamu.edu
NEPPL, Susan ... 952-888-4777. 263 B
sneppl@nwhealth.edu
NEPTUNE, Vivian ... 787-999-9531. 555 B
vneptune@law.upr.edu
NERGER, Janice, L ... 970-491-6974... 80 I
janice.nerger@colostate.edu
NERIA, Angela ... 620-235-4603. 189 L
aneria@pittstate.edu
NERO, Lut ... 610-399-2069. 428 B
lnero@cheyney.edu
NERO, Patrick ... 202-994-6650... 95 D
NERY, Annebelle ... 760-773-2519... 40 F
anery@collegeofthedesert.edu
NERY, Karen ... 910-893-1630. 352 K
nery@campbell.edu
NERZAK, J. Peter ... 865-694-6517. 461 D
pnerzak@pstcc.edu
NESBARY, Dale, K ... 231-777-0311. 247 G
dale.nesbary@muskegoncc.edu
NESBIT, Cortni ... 860-628-4751... 90 D
cnesbit@lincolncollegene.edu
NESBIT, Jim ... 937-298-3399. 382 K
jim.nesbit@kc.edu
NESBIT, Ryan, A ... 706-542-1361. 133 C
rnesbit@uga.edu
NESBITT, Jacquelyn, H ... 803-981-7195. 449 J
jnesbitt@yorktech.edu
NESBITT, Joan, M ... 573-341-4111. 284 A
nesbittj@mst.edu
NESBITT, Richard, L ... 413-597-2211. 238 D
richard.l.nesbitt@williams.edu
NESBITT, Shawna ... 214-648-2168. 493 E
shawna.nesbitt@utsouthwestern.edu
NESBITT, Thomas, W ... 315-267-2180. 344 C
nesbittw@potsdam.edu
NESBITT, Tom ... 916-734-3578... 70 J
thomas.nesbitt@ucdmc.ucdavis.edu
NESBITT, Tom, S ... 916-734-3578... 70 J
thomas.nesbitt@ucdmc.ucdavis.edu
NESHEIM-KAUFFMAN,
Rhonda, K ... 641-422-4500. 181 D
nesherho@niacc.edu
NESHIEM, Sheri ... 813-205-5166... 28 M
sneshiem@argosy.edu
NESIN, Jeffrey ... 212-592-2000. 340 H
jnesin@sva.edu
NESIUS, Elizabeth ... 201-360-4366. 302 D
enesius@hccc.edu
NESLER, Mitchell, S ... 518-587-2100. 346 A
mitchell.nesler@esc.edu
NESLER, Timothy, C ... 352-395-5160. 113 C
tim.nesler@sfcollege.edu

NESMITH, Dee ... 432-335-6429. 477 M
dnesmith@odessa.edu
NESMITH, Robert, M ... 859-238-5356. 193 E
bob.nesmith@centre.edu
NESMITH, Sylvia, L ... 843-953-6976. 442 A
sylvia.nesmith@citadel.edu
NESPOR, Vana ... 413-565-1000. 222 F
vnespor@baypath.edu
NESS, Ann ... 651-523-2963. 256 A
aness06@hamline.edu
NESS, Claudia, L ... 509-527-5040. 525 E
nesscl@whitman.edu
NESS, Craig ... 832-842-0542. 489 B
cness@central.uh.edu
NESS, Eric ... 570-389-4517. 427 H
eness@bloomu.edu
NESS, James ... 480-557-7430... 18 I
james.ness@phoenix.edu
NESS, Maurice, E ... 501-450-3138... 25 H
eness@uca.edu
NESS, Melvin, M ... 212-463-0400. 348 B
meln@touro.edu
NESS, Roberta, B ... 713-500-9052. 492 E
roberta.b.ness@uth.tmc.edu
NESS, Susan ... 701-858-3065. 371 F
susan.ness@minotstateu.edu
NESSAN, Craig, L ... 563-589-0207. 183 F
cnessan@wartburgseminary.edu
NESSEL, Lori, A ... 973-642-8700. 307 D
lori.nessel@shu.edu
NESSER, Ellen ... 724-873-2760. 428 A
nesser@calu.edu
NESTER, Joel ... 434-791-5663. 502 D
jnester@averett.edu
NESTI, CSSP, Donald ... 713-942-5069. 490 L
nesti@stthom.edu
NESTLER, George ... 914-594-4470. 334 A
george_nestler@nymc.edu
NESTMAN, Lane ... 817-735-2688. 490 E
Lane.Nestman@unthsc.edu
NESTOR, David, A ... 802-656-3380. 500 F
david.nestor@uvm.edu
NESTOR, John ... 614-287-2525. 378 B
jnestor@cscc.edu
NESTOR, Mark ... 215-596-8910. 435 H
m.nestor@usciences.edu
NESTOR, Sally ... 970-542-3151... 83 E
sally.nestor@morgancc.edu
NETHERTON, James, S .. 478-301-2710. 128 H
netherton_js@mercer.edu
NETHERTON, Shane ... 918-595-7895. 400 E
shane.netherton@tulsacc.edu
NETLAND, John ... 731-661-5519. 462 F
jnetland@uu.edu
NETTELL, Katie ... 701-662-1517. 372 D
katie.nettell@lrsc.edu
NETTLES, Evelyn ... 615-963-7004. 459 E
enettles1@tnstate.edu
NETTLES, Ronald, E ... 601-643-8300. 266 F
ronnie.nettles@colin.edu
NETTLETON, Patricia, A .. 859-371-9393. 192 D
panettleton@beckfield.edu
NETTLETON, Peter ... 859-371-9393. 192 D
pnettleton@beckfield.edu
NETZHAMMER, Mel ... 360-546-9581. 525 A
mel.netzhammer@vancouver.wsu.edu
NEU, Frances ... 727-341-3319. 112 E
neu.frances@spcollege.edu
NEUBAUER, Kirk ... 563-387-1434. 180 M
neubauki@luther.edu
NEUBAUER, Lane, B ... 215-951-5157. 420 B
neubauer@lasalle.edu
NEUBAUER, Michael ... 818-677-2957... 34 C
michael.neubauer@csun.edu
NEUBAUER, Sharon ... 954-492-5353. 100 A
sneubauer@citycollege.edu
NEUBAUER, Trish ... 563-387-1567. 180 M
neubautr@luther.edu
NEUBERGER, Boruch ... 410-484-7200. 217 D
byn@nirc.edu
NEUBERGER, Sheftel, M 410-484-7200. 217 D
sheftel@nirc.edu
NEUERBURG, Kent ... 985-549-2135. 208 C
kent.neuerburg@selu.edu
NEUFELD, Iris ... 419-358-3322. 374 J
neufeldi@bluffton.edu
NEUFELD, Jane, F ... 773-508-3852. 151 H
jneufe@luc.edu
NEUFELD, Kenley ... 805-965-0581... 64 L
neufeld@sbcc.edu
NEUFELDT, Ellen, J ... 757-683-3442. 507 N
eneufeld@odu.edu
NEUFIND, Nate ... 402-941-6009. 290 K
neufind@midlandu.edu
NEUFVILLE, Janette ... 301-576-0123. 221 B
jneufvil@wau.edu
NEUFVILLE, Mortimer, H 410-951-3838. 220 B
mneufville@coppin.edu
NEUHARD, Ian ... 772-462-7898. 106 P
ineuhard@irsc.edu

NEUHAUS, Roger .... 515-294-4077. 175 H
rneuhaus@foundation.iastate.edu
NEUHAUS, Stacie, L .... 317-788-3214. 173 I
neuhauss@uindy.edu
NEUHAUSER, Crystal ...... 860-701-5092... 90 G
neuhauser_c@mitchell.edu
NEUHAUSER, John, J .... 802-654-2212. 500 B
jneuhauser@smcvt.edu
NEUHOF, Jennifer .... 718-817-3727. 324 G
neuhof@fordham.edu
NEUHOFF, Martin, C ...... 260-422-5561. 167 B
mcneuhoff@indianatech.edu
NEUMAN, Yisroel .... 732-367-1060. 299 E
NEUMANN, Bruce .... 262-691-5226. 541 D
bneumann6@wctc.edu
NEUMANN, Gregory .... 716-645-3131. 341 F
buffalo@bkstr.com
NEUMANN, Kathleen ...... 309-298-1066. 162 K
k-neumann@wiu.edu
NEUMANN, Pamela, R ... 716-839-8325. 322 E
pneumann@daemen.edu
NEUMAYR, Mark .... 928-523-6517... 16 C
mark.neumayr@nau.edu
NEUN, Stephen .... 570-484-2133. 429 B
spn207@lhup.edu
NEUPAUER, Nicholas, C 724-287-8711. 411 C
nicholas.neupauer@bc3.edu
NEURAUTER, Janet .... 213-322-2450. 258 I
janet.neurauter@itascacc.edu
NEUVILLE, Jeff .... 828-327-7000. 359 A
jneuville@cvcc.edu
NEVAREZ, Amy .... 909-652-6020... 37 M
amy.nevarez@chaffey.edu
NEVAREZ, Augustine ...... 831-755-6825... 46 G
anevarez@hartnell.edu
NEVAREZ, Gerard .... 575-646-3635. 310 I
gerardn@nmsu.edu
NEVATT, Aaron .... 415-338-1912... 35 E
anevatt@sfsu.edu
NEVE, Nancy .... 906-635-2080. 245 G
nneve@lssu.edu
NEVEAU, Judy .... 310-434-4303... 65 A
neveau_judy@smc.edu
NEVELS, Lyle .... 510-642-4096... 70 I
lnevels@berkeley.edu
NEVES, Matthew .... 951-222-8085... 61 A
matthew.neves@rcc.edu
NEVILLE, David .... 858-642-8163... 55 J
dneville@nu.edu
NEVILLE, Frank .... 703-993-8700. 505 C
fnevill2@gmu.edu
NEVILLE, Nancy .... 216-421-7427. 377 C
nneville@cia.edu
NEVILLS, Landee .... 417-328-1826. 282 C
lnevills@sbuniv.edu
NEVIN, Amy .... 518-631-9844. 348 K
nevina@uniongraduatecollege.edu
NEVINS, Daniel .... 212-678-8067. 328 A
danevins@jtsa.edu
NEVINS, Dean .... 805-965-0581... 64 L
nevins@sbcc.edu
NEVOIS, Dana, A .... 636-481-3488. 275 I
dnevois@jeffco.edu
NEW, Amy .... 210-999-7431. 488 C
anew1@trinity.edu
NEW, Lynn .... 903-923-2093. 471 J
lnew@etbu.edu
NEW, Michael, J .... 802-654-2635. 500 B
mnew@smcvt.edu
NEWBERG, Bella .... 760-750-4444... 35 A
newberg@csusm.edu
NEWBERN, Judson .... 615-322-2715. 463 G
judson.newbern@vanderbilt.edu
NEWBERRY, Anthony ..... 502-213-2121. 195 F
tony.newberry@kctcs.edu
NEWBERRY, Beth .... 502-585-9911. 199 C
bnewberry@spalding.edu
NEWBERRY, Elizabeth .... 651-450-3654. 258 H
enewber@inverhills.edu
NEWBERRY, JR.,
James, H .... 502-863-8043. 194 C
jim_newberry@georgetowncollege.edu
NEWBERRY, Leanna, J ... 620-421-6700. 188 D
leannan@labette.edu
NEWBERRY, Robert .... 575-624-7180. 309 I
robert.newberry@roswell.enmu.edu
NEWBOLD, Pamela .... 330-823-6572. 391 E
newbolph@mountunion.edu
NEWBORN, Janis .... 256-726-7460..... 6 B
jnewborn@oakwood.edu
NEWBOULD, Ian .... 240-895-4410. 218 A
NEWBY, Belita .... 256-726-8245..... 6 B
bfleming@oakwood.edu
NEWBY, Greg .... 907-450-8663... 10 I
gbnewby@alaska.edu
NEWBY, Jennifer .... 541-383-7238. 402 D
jnewby@cocc.edu
NEWBY, Teresa .... 952-446-4484. 255 D
newbyt@crown.edu
NEWBY, Vanessa .... 708-534-4551. 145 F
vnewby@govst.edu

NEWCOMB, Mark .... 704-461-6010. 352 G
MarkNewcomb@bac.edu
NEWCOMB, Ron .... 770-975-4000. 122 I
NEWCOMB, Sherri .... 718-631-6381. 319 D
snewcomb@qcc.cuny.edu
NEWCOMB, Terry .... 315-364-3370. 350 E
tnewcomb@wells.edu
NEWCOMBE, David, A .... 540-365-4463. 504 L
dnewcombe@ferrum.edu
NEWCOMBE, Pat .... 413-782-1201. 238 A
pnewcombe@law.wne.edu
NEWCOMBE, Rodd .... 321-674-7110. 104 H
newcombe@fit.edu
NEWCOMER, Jan, A .... 501-450-3130... 25 H
jann@uca.edu
NEWELL, AJ .... 540-654-1934. 510 J
anewell@umw.edu
NEWELL, Alton, E .... 724-503-1001. 436 G
anewell@washjeff.edu
NEWELL, Bridget, M .... 570-577-1561. 411 A
bridget.newell@bucknell.edu
NEWELL, Diane .... 251-380-9090..... 3 H
dnewell@faulkner.edu
NEWELL, Glen, C .... 336-334-7731. 367 E
gcnewell@ncat.edu
NEWELL, James .... 856-256-4012. 305 E
newell@rowan.edu
NEWELL, James .... 718-270-2488. 342 D
james.newell@downstate.edu
NEWELL, Jennifer, M ...... 585-343-0055. 325 C
jmnewell@genesee.edu
NEWELL, John, H .... 843-953-7154. 443 A
newellj@cofc.edu
NEWELL, Keith .... 912-260-4377. 131 F
keith.newell@sgsc.edu
NEWELL, Mallory .... 408-864-8777... 44 M
newellmallory@deanza.edu
NEWELL, Rand, E .... 207-948-9201. 211 I
rnewell@unity.edu
NEWELL, Tamara, J .... 405-425-5475. 397 D
tammy.newell@oc.edu
NEWGARD, Debra .... 612-977-5414. 254 C
debra.newgard@capella.edu
NEWGARD, Debra .... 651-905-3400. 254 B
NEWGENT, Matt .... 405-262-2552. 399 B
newgentm@redlandscc.edu
NEWHALL, JR., Edward . 401-454-6307. 440 A
enewhall@risd.edu
NEWHOFF, Marilyn .... 619-594-6516... 35 D
mnewhoff@mail.sdsu.edu
NEWHOUSE, Dollie .... 843-661-1362. 444 B
dnewhouse@fmarion.edu
NEWHOUSE, Gary .... 847-635-1640. 155 F
garyn@oakton.edu
NEWHOUSE, Greg .... 619-388-7673... 62 F
gnewhouse@sdccd.edu
NEWHOUSE, Valerie, K .. 712-362-0434. 179 E
vnewhouse@iowalakes.edu
NEWITZ, Laurie, H .... 718-780-7503. 315 H
laurie.newitz@brooklaw.edu
NEWKIRK, Charlene .... 412-469-6300. 413 D
cnewkirk@ccac.edu
NEWKIRK, Krista, L .... 704-687-5727. 368 E
Krista.Newkirk@uncc.edu
NEWKIRK, Vann .... 256-372-5266..... 1 A
vann.newkirk@aamu.edu
NEWKIRK, Vann .... 256-372-5104..... 1 A
vann.newkirk@aamu.edu
NEWKOFSKY, Stephen ... 315-268-6620. 320 A
steve.newkofsky@clarkson.edu
NEWKOME, George, R .... 330-972-6458. 390 E
newkome@uakron.edu
NEWLAND, Carmen .... 602-285-7588... 15 C
carmen.newland@phoenixcollege.edu
NEWLAND, Jamesetta .... 212-346-1600. 335 J
jnewland@pace.edu
NEWLIN, Toni .... 765-998-5211. 173 C
tnnewlin@taylor.edu
NEWMAN, Allison .... 518-276-6000. 337 I
newmana@rpi.edu
NEWMAN, Allison .... 518-276-6359. 337 I
newmaa3@rpi.edu
NEWMAN, Carolyn .... 631-656-3191. 324 F
carolyn.newman@ftc.edu
NEWMAN, Carrie .... 814-824-3311. 423 J
cnewman@mercyhurst.edu
NEWMAN, Elizabeth .... 781-239-4538. 222 D
enewman1@babson.edu
NEWMAN, Ethel .... 321-433-5151. 101 M
newmane@easternflorida.edu
NEWMAN, Gail .... 925-439-2181... 42 A
gnewman@losmedanos.edu
NEWMAN, James .... 401-454-6394. 440 A
jnewman@risd.edu
NEWMAN, Janet .... 715-422-5476. 540 D
janet.newman@mstc.edu
NEWMAN, Janis, J .... 713-313-1183. 485 F
newmanjj@tsu.edu
NEWMAN, Jeanine .... 337-421-9615. 204 E
jeanine.newman@sowela.edu

NEWMAN, Joan .... 865-694-6453. 461 D
jnewman@pstcc.edu
NEWMAN, Kathleen .... 410-516-4065. 215 H
knewman@jhu.edu
NEWMAN, Kay, S .... 334-387-3877..... 1 E
kaynewman@amridgeuniversity.edu
NEWMAN, Keith .... 765-677-2105. 169 B
keith.newman@indwes.edu
NEWMAN, Lester, C .... 903-730-4890. 474 O
lnewman@jarvis.edu
NEWMAN, Linda, L .... 734-764-7403. 251 C
newmanll@umich.edu
NEWMAN, Lori, L .... 563-884-5408. 182 A
lori.newman@palmer.edu
NEWMAN, Louis .... 507-222-4191. 254 D
lnewman@carleton.edu
NEWMAN, Marc, A .... 919-516-4092. 366 C
manewman@st-aug.edu
NEWMAN, Michael .... 212-463-0400. 348 B
michael.newman@touro.edu
NEWMAN, Michelle .... 901-333-4217. 461 F
mnewman@southwest.tn.edu
NEWMAN, Nancy, J .... 402-465-2375. 291 G
njn@nebrwesleyan.edu
NEWMAN, Robert, D .... 801-581-8816. 496 Q
robert.newman@hum.utah.edu
NEWMAN, Russ .... 858-635-4535... 26 M
rnewman@alliant.edu
NEWMAN, Russ .... 858-635-4535... 26 L
rnewman@alliant.edu
NEWMAN, Scott .... 801-524-8167. 495 O
snewman@ldsbc.edu
NEWMAN, Scott .... 918-293-4666. 398 B
scott.newman@okstate.edu
NEWMEN, Patricia, N ..... 207-859-4460. 209 J
pnnewmen@colby.edu
NEWNHAM, David .... 916-608-6500... 53 C
NEWSCHWANDER,
Gregg .... 334-244-3658..... 2 A
gnewschw@aum.edu
NEWSCHWANDER,
Gregg .... 334-844-5662..... 1 G
gen0002@auburn.edu
NEWSOM, Deborah .... 515-271-3710. 177 K
deborah.newsom@drake.edu
NEWSOM, Lanay .... 757-683-3141. 507 N
snewsom@odu.edu
NEWSOM, Stephanie, R . 319-352-8539. 183 E
stephanie.newsom@wartburg.edu
NEWSOM, Thomas .... 469-587-1173. 131 H
tnewsom@southuniversity.edu
NEWSOM, Thomas, W ...... 575-461-4413. 309 M
thomasn@mesalands.edu
NEWSOME, Aisha .... 757-873-4235. 510 B
anewsome@stratford.edu
NEWSOME, Aisha .... 757-497-4466. 510 B
anewsome@stratord.edu
NEWSOME, Chevelle .... 916-278-6470... 34 D
cnewsome@csus.edu
NEWSOME, Gary .... 815-939-5120. 155 H
gnewsome@olivet.edu
NEWSOME, Mark .... 336-506-4121. 357 M
mark.newsome@alamancecc.edu
NEWSOME, Pam .... 612-874-3798. 257 B
pam_newsome-prochniak@mcad.edu
NEWSOME, Sarah .... 850-973-9675. 109 H
newsomes@nfcc.edu
NEWTON, Billy .... 505-566-3775. 311 I
newtonb@sanjuancollege.edu
NEWTON, Bryan .... 803-508-7245. 440 G
newtonbd@atc.edu
NEWTON, Carolyn .... 330-263-2004. 377 H
cnewton@wooster.edu
NEWTON, Christopher .... 501-370-5204... 22 F
cnewton@philander.edu
NEWTON, Deborah .... 203-392-5900... 88 A
newtond2@southernct.edu
NEWTON, Diane, D .... 501-450-3184... 25 H
dnewton@uca.edu
NEWTON, Dorian .... 510-430-2262... 54 F
newton@mills.edu
NEWTON, Dusty .... 308-865-8702. 292 H
newtond@unk.edu
NEWTON, Eric, D .... 864-242-5100. 441 D
NEWTON, H. Joseph ...... 979-845-7361. 483 C
jnewton@tamu.edu
NEWTON, Jeff .... 419-530-4484. 392 B
jeff.newton2@utoledo.edu
NEWTON, Jeffrey, L .... 617-253-3952. 233 B
NEWTON, Jimmie .... 202-231-3344. 544 L
NEWTON, Joseph, A .... 229-333-5974. 134 B
jnewton@valdosta.edu
NEWTON, Joshua .... 860-486-2709... 92 A
jnewton@foundation.uconn.edu
NEWTON, LaCresha .... 501-370-4001... 19 J
lacresha.newton@arkansasbaptist.edu
NEWTON, Lynette .... 402-826-8688. 289 E
lynette.newton@doane.edu
NEWTON, Martin .... 205-726-2131..... 6 F
cnewton@samford.edu

NEWTON, Michael, L ...... 270-384-8099. 197 D
newtonm@lindsey.edu
NEWTON, Nell, J .... 574-631-6789. 174 A
nell.newton@nd.edu
NEWTON, Sandra .... 252-492-2061. 364 F
newton@vgcc.edu
NEWTON, Steven, D .... 517-750-1200. 250 E
snewton@arbor.edu
NEWTON, Thomas .... 318-869-5701. 201 H
tnewton@centenary.edu
NEWTON, Thomas .... 630-617-6473. 145 A
tom.newton@elmhurst.edu
NEWTON, Traci .... 910-892-3178. 355 B
tnewton@heritagebiblecollege.edu
NEWTON, Verne .... 845-575-3000. 330 D
verne.newton@marist.edu
NEWTON, Warren .... 207-262-7817. 212 C
wnewton@maine.edu
NEWTOWN, Michael, J .. 315-386-7411. 345 F
newtownm@canton.edu
NEY, Cheryl, L .... 323-343-3808... 34 A
cney@cslanet.calstatela.edu
NEYENS, Richard .... 303-282-3414... 85 D
NG, Bart .... 630-829-6187. 140 B
bng@ben.edu
NG, Charles .... 800-782-2422... 32 B
cng@mail.cnuas.edu
NG, Charles .... 760-757-2121... 54 G
cng@miracosta.edu
NG, Jacob .... 907-834-1610... 11 B
jng@pwscc.edu
NG, Peh Peh .... 320-589-6300. 264 F
pehng@morris.umn.edu
NGAI, Godwin .... 626-571-5110... 51 B
ngai@les.edu
NGIRALMAU, Hilda .... 680-488-3036. 547 B
hildan@palau.edu
NGIRAMENGIOR, Todd .. 680-488-2471. 547 B
toddn@palau.edu
NGIRMERIIL,
Glendalynn .... 680-488-3036. 547 B
glendalynn@palau.edu
NGUYEN, Charles, C ...... 202-319-5160... 94 G
nguyen@cua.edu
NGUYEN, Christine .... 714-241-6144... 39 I
cnguyen@coastline.edu
NGUYEN, Dana .... 954-783-7339. 102 M
dnguyen@cci.edu
NGUYEN, Danny .... 408-855-5417... 75 K
danny.nguyen@wvm.edu
NGUYEN, Hieu .... 808-739-8577. 135 D
hnguyen@chaminade.edu
NGUYEN, Hoa .... 219-866-6151. 172 E
hnguyen@saintjoe.edu
NGUYEN, Kay .... 562-860-2451... 37 I
knguyen@cerritos.edu
NGUYEN, Loan .... 510-981-2808... 59 A
lnguyen@peralta.edu
NGUYEN, Luan, P .... 671-735-2639. 546 E
nguyen@uguam.uog.edu
NGUYEN, Minh .... 619-684-8778... 56 C
mnguyen@newschoolarch.edu
NGUYEN, Tamie .... 323-343-5808... 34 A
tnguyen10@cslanet.calstatela.edu
NGUYEN, Thy .... 312-996-2969. 161 D
thy@uic.edu
NGUYEN, Tuyen .... 714-628-4844... 60 H
nguyen_tuyen@sccollege.edu
NGWABA, Maurice, C .... 410-651-6656. 219 E
mcngwaba@umes.edu
NI, Yi .... 603-526-3648. 295 I
yni@colby-sawyer.edu
NIANOURIS, Eric .... 704-637-4463. 353 E
enianour@catawba.edu
NIAS, Danita .... 352-392-5401. 116 A
dnias@ufalumni.ufl.edu
NIBLETT, Tonie, M .... 256 228 6001..... 5 H
niblettt@nacc.edu
NICA, Claude .... 310-665-6870... 57 C
cnica@otis.edu
NICASTRO, Vincent, P .... 610-519-4110. 436 F
vincent.nicastro@villanova.edu
NICCHI, Frank, J .... 315-568-3100. 333 C
fnicchi@nycc.edu
NICE, Steve .... 239-489-9283. 101 O
snice@edison.edu
NICELY, Nancy .... 610-328-8534. 433 I
nnicely1@swarthmore.edu
NICELY, Tim .... 540-453-2371. 511 H
nicelyt@brcc.edu
NICHOL, Vicki .... 303-273-3972... 80 E
vnichol@mines.edu
NICHOLAS, Connie .... 409-984-6165. 486 H
connie.nicholas@lamarpa.edu
NICHOLAS, David, R ...... 530-221-4275... 65 F
sbcadm@shasta.edu
NICHOLAS, Jim .... 661-763-7853... 69 D
jnicholas@taftcollege.edu
NICHOLAS, Mike .... 574-807-7875. 164 D
michael.nicholas@bethelcollege.edu

NICHOLAS, Nannette ...... 607-962-9229. 322 B nicholas@corning-cc.edu
NICHOLAS, Richard, A ... 940-898-3601. 488 B rnicholas@twu.edu
NICHOLAS, Sandra .... 570-740-0730. 422 G snicholas@luzerne.edu
NICHOLES, Gary .... 510-834-5740... 59 C gnicholes@peralta.edu
NICHOLLS, Deb .... 541-888-7400. 407 H dnicholls@socc.edu
NICHOLLS, Gregory .... 610-660-1090. 432 E gnicholl@sju.edu
NICHOLLS, Tom .... 541-888-7611. 407 H tnicholls@socc.edu
NICHOLS, Aaron, F .... 802-656-3425. 500 F aaron.nichols@uvm.edu
NICHOLS, Alice .... 419-448-3416. 389 J anichols@tiffin.edu
NICHOLS, Andrew, W ..... 808-956-6594. 136 B nicholsa@hawaii.edu
NICHOLS, Anthony, J ..... 706-233-7272. 131 E anichols@shorter.edu
NICHOLS, Arlene .... 615-963-7401. 459 E anichols@tnstate.edu
NICHOLS, Beth .... 425-640-1131. 519 D bnichols@edcc.edu
NICHOLS, Bill .... 704-337-2340. 365 G nicholsb@queens.edu
NICHOLS, Brandon .... 773-602-5517. 142 B
NICHOLS, Brenda .... 409-880-8508. 486 F brenda.nichols@lamar.edu
NICHOLS, Brian .... 225-578-5295. 204 O cio@lsu.edu
NICHOLS, Brian .... 814-871-5680. 416 K nichols006@gannon.edu
NICHOLS, Carol .... 217-442-7232. 143 G cnichols1@dacc.edu
NICHOLS, Christina .... 970-351-4339... 86 C christina.nichols@unco.edu
NICHOLS, Cynthia, D ..... 217-581-5020. 144 E cdnichols@eiu.edu
NICHOLS, Dana .... 770-531-6360. 128 B dnichols@laniertech.edu
NICHOLS, Daniel .... 202-885-3458... 94 F dnichols@american.edu
NICHOLS, David .... 903-785-7661. 478 B dnichols@parisjc.edu
NICHOLS, Edward .... 814-262-6474. 427 C enichols@pennhighlands.edu
NICHOLS, Eric .... 603-641-7500. 297 G enichols@anselm.edu
NICHOLS, Fatemeh .... 636-584-6626. 273 M nichols@eastcentral.edu
NICHOLS, Gregory .... 785-460-5403. 185 P greg.nichols@colbycc.edu
NICHOLS, Harvey .... 303-546-3552... 83 F harvey@naropa.edu
NICHOLS, Jamin .... 352-371-2833. 101 K clinicdirector@dragonrises.edu
NICHOLS, Jane .... 775-673-7090. 294 H jnichols@tmcc.edu
NICHOLS, Jason, D .... 573-629-3211. 274 J jnichols@hlg.edu
NICHOLS, Jennifer .... 704-922-6223. 360 F nichols.jennifer@gaston.edu
NICHOLS, Jerry .... 662-562-3231. 269 C jnichols@northwestms.edu
NICHOLS, Karen, J .... 630-515-6159. 153 B knicho@midwestern.edu
NICHOLS, Keegan .... 785-628-5824. 186 F knichols@fhsu.edu
NICHOLS, Keith .... 304-473-8438. 531 G nichols@wvwc.edu
NICHOLS, Laurie .... 605-688-4173. 452 B laurie.nichols@sdstate.edu
NICHOLS, Leslie, A .... 937-382-6661. 393 B leslie_nichols@wilmington.edu
NICHOLS, Linda .... 307-268-2220. 542 X lnichols@caspercollege.edu
NICHOLS, Margie .... 865-974-9438. 463 C mnichols@utk.edu
NICHOLS, Marice .... 617-327-6777. 233 D marice_nichols@mspp.edu
NICHOLS, Martin .... 252-222-6155. 358 G nicholsm@carteret.edu
NICHOLS, Mary, L .... 612-645-0238. 264 G mnichols@umn.edu
NICHOLS, Pamela .... 315-268-6413. 320 A pnichols@clarkson.edu
NICHOLS, Paula .... 409-880-1847. 486 F paula.nichols@lamar.edu
NICHOLS, Rachel .... 828-328-7306. 356 B rachel.nichols@lr.edu
NICHOLS, Randall .... 207-725-3458. 209 H rnichols@bowdoin.edu
NICHOLS, Rebecca .... 724-938-4425. 428 A nichols@calu.edu
NICHOLS, Rick .... 828-328-7387. 356 B rick.nichols@lr.edu
NICHOLS, Robert .... 810-762-9828. 244 Q rnichols@kettering.edu
NICHOLS, Rosanne .... 360-438-4366. 522 G rnichols@stmartin.edu
NICHOLS, Rosemary .... 603-899-4045. 296 H nicholrm@franklinpierce.edu
NICHOLS, Ruth .... 206-239-4500. 517 M rnichols@cityu.edu
NICHOLS, Ruth, R .... 601-304-4336. 265 G rnichols@alcorn.edu
NICHOLS, Scott .... 413-662-5411. 230 C scott.nichols@mcla.edu
NICHOLS, Scott, G .... 617-353-5777. 224 D nichols@bu.edu
NICHOLS, Shane .... 847-866-3866. 145 E shane.nichols@garrett.edu
NICHOLS, Shannon .... 209-667-3693... 35 B snichols2@csustan.edu
NICHOLS, Sheila .... 850-484-1428. 110 G snichols@pensacolastate.edu
NICHOLS, Steve .... 417-269-3045. 273 D steve.nichols@coxcollege.edu
NICHOLS, Timothy .... 605-688-6361. 452 B timothy.nichols@sdstate.edu
NICHOLS, Traci .... 989-328-1285. 247 D tracin@montcalm.edu
NICHOLS, Warren .... 615-366-3937. 459 A warren.nichols@tbr.edu
NICHOLS, William, D ...... 207-581-2441. 212 B william.nichols1@maine.edu
NICHOLSON, Bonnie .... 859-246-6604. 194 L bonnie.nicholson@kctcs.edu
NICHOLSON, Brian, W ... 254-710-8400. 467 G brian_nicholson@baylor.edu
NICHOLSON, Christena .. 913-234-0644. 185 L christena.nicholson@cleveland.edu
NICHOLSON, Cindy .... 810-989-5568. 249 H cnicholson@sc4.edu
NICHOLSON, Danny .... 865-471-3459. 453 F dnicholson@cn.edu
NICHOLSON, Debra .... 719-384-6889... 83 M debra.nicholson@ojc.edu
NICHOLSON, Dennis, J .. 315-445-4300. 328 F nicholdj@lemoyne.edu
NICHOLSON, Fedearia, A .... 330-972-8289. 390 E fn@uakron.edu
NICHOLSON, Jane .... 651-779-3304. 258 C Jane.nicholson@century.edu
NICHOLSON, Judd, L ...... 202-687-4402... 95 E nicholsonj@georgetown.edu
NICHOLSON, Kim .... 765-677-2131. 169 B kim.nicholson@indwes.edu
NICHOLSON, Kristal .... 903-875-7361. 477 G kristal.nicholson@navarrocollege.edu
NICHOLSON, JR., Malverse, A .... 301-322-0853. 217 F nicholma@pgcc.edu
NICHOLSON, Marie .... 828-689-1270. 356 F mnicholson@mhc.edu
NICHOLSON, Mary .... 903-670-2664. 488 D mnicholson@tvcc.edu
NICHOLSON, Nigel .... 503-777-7257. 407 E nnicholsl@reed.edu
NICHOLSON, Robin .... 319-235-3516. 175 D Robin.Nicholson@unitypoint.org
NICHOLSON, Susie, S ..... 479-968-0402... 20 E snicholson@atu.edu
NICHOLSON, Tim .... 828-835-4261. 364 E tnicholson@tricountycc.edu
NICHOLSON, Vickie .... 251-578-1313..... 6 D vickien@rstc.edu
NICK, Sara, J .... 715-833-6275. 539 J snick1@cvtc.edu
NICKE, Glenda .... 309-796-4822. 140 E nickeg@bhc.edu
NICKEL, Kevin, A .... 419-358-3320. 374 J nickelk@bluffton.edu
NICKEL, Nancy .... 773-371-5415. 141 D nnickel@ctu.edu
NICKEL, Shelley, C .... 404-962-3241. 134 A shelley.nickel@usg.edu
NICKELL, Barbara, J .... 785-827-5541. 188 C bmarsh@kwu.edu
NICKELL, Jane Ellen .... 814-332-2800. 409 D janeellen.nickell@allegheny.edu
NICKELL, Linda .... 731-425-8820. 460 G lnickell@jscc.edu
NICKELS, Janet .... 410-386-8229. 214 A jnickels@carrollcc.edu
NICKELS, Jerrod .... 616-331-2450. 243 C nickelsj@gvsu.edu
NICKELS, Rosemerry ...... 440-934-3101. 385 K rnickels@ohiobusinesscollege.edu
NICKENS, Tawanna .... 217-351-2390. 155 J tnickens@parkland.edu
NICKERSON, Brian, J ..... 914-633-2601. 327 C bnickerson@iona.edu
NICKERSON, Edward ...... 215-951-1244. 420 B nickerso@lasalle.edu
NICKERSON, Gary .... 405-585-5210. 397 C gary.nickerson@okbu.edu
NICKERSON, Nate .... 617-258-5403. 233 B
NICKIE, Marissa .... 305-949-9500. 102 E mnickie@cci.edu
NICKLAS, Inajane .... 805-378-1443... 74 F inicklas@vcccd.edu
NICKLAUS, Megan .... 719-389-6000... 79 D megan.nicklaus@coloradocollege.edu
NICKLAUS SCHMELZER, Anastasia .... 563-588-8192. 176 F anastasia.schmelzer@clarke.edu
NICKLE, Bonny .... 888-384-0849... 27 E bnickle@allied.edu
NICKLE, Mary Anne .... 641-236-2202. 179 H maryanne.nickle@iavalley.edu
NICKLE, Stephen, R .... 210-999-7311. 488 C snickle@trinity.edu
NICKLESS, Peter .... 315-568-3310. 333 C pnickless@nycc.edu
NICKLOS, Carlee .... 405-422-1467. 399 B nocklosc@redlandscc.edu
NICKLOW, John .... 618-453-5744. 159 G nicklow@siu.edu
NICKOL, Kari .... 563-588-8137. 176 F kari.nickol@clarke.edu
NICKOLAI, Tom .... 314-968-6972. 284 N nickoltc@webster.edu
NICKOLI, Rebecca .... 317-921-4515. 169 K rnickoli@ivytech.edu
NICKSA, Gary, W .... 617-353-4468. 224 D nicksa@bu.edu
NICOL, David .... 231-591-2422. 242 F david_nicol@ferris.edu
NICOL, Patricia .... 203-392-6045... 88 A nicolp1@southernct.edu
NICOL, Thomas .... 602-243-8127... 15 F tom.nicol@southmountaincc.edu
NICOLAI, Camille .... 414-297-8875. 540 E nicolaic@matc.edu
NICOLAI, Michael .... 312-629-9411. 158 L mnicolai@saic.edu
NICOLETTE, Guy .... 352-392-1161. 116 A gnic@ufl.edu
NICOLETTI, Katherine ..... 508-213-2238. 235 E katherine.nicoletti@nichols.edu
NICOLO, Anthony, J .... 540-674-3639. 513 B tnicolo@nr.edu
NICOLS, Richard .... 386-226-6294. 102 B richard.nicols@erau.edu
NICOTERA, Phil .... 727-341-3664. 112 E nicotera.phil@spcollege.edu
NIEBERLE, Susan .... 414-256-0170. 535 A alumnae@mtmary.edu
NIEBUHR, Robert, E .... 321-674-7297. 104 H rniebuhr@fit.edu
NIECE, Andrea .... 303-986-2320... 80 D andrea@csha.net
NIECE, Becky .... 615-248-1268. 462 D bniece@trevecca.edu
NIED, Alice .... 850-201-6207. 117 D nieda@tcc.fl.edu
NIEDENS, Rosemary .... 316-942-4291. 189 E niedensr@newmanu.edu
NIEDZWIECKI, Brian, E .. 419-866-0261. 389 H beniedzwiecki@stautzenberger.com
NIEDZWIECKI, Michael .. 718-933-6700. 331 K mniedzwiedi@monroecollege.edu
NIEHOFF, Brian, A .... 785-532-4797. 188 A niehoff@ksu.edu
NIEHOFF, SJ, Robert, L . 216-397-4281. 381 R president@jcu.edu
NIEHOFF, Susan .... 410-209-6049. 213 F sniehoff@bccc.edu
NIEKRO, Cat, S .... 704-894-2533. 353 J
NIELSEN, Betty .... 541-917-4320. 404 B nielseb@linnbenton.edu
NIELSEN, David .... 860-512-3108... 88 G dnielsen@manchestercc.edu
NIELSEN, Debra, A .... 219-785-5332. 172 A dnielsen@pnc.edu
NIELSEN, Dee .... 850-873-3510. 106 H dnielsen@gulfcoast.edu
NIELSEN, Erik .... 402-461-7738. 289 I enielsen@hastings.edu
NIELSEN, Janet .... 402-878-2380. 290 D jnielsen@littlepriest.edu
NIELSEN, Jenna .... 510-848-5232... 45 A jnielsen@fst.edu
NIELSEN, Jim .... 406-657-2301. 287 C jnielsen@msubillings.edu
NIELSEN, Laura .... 805-966-3888... 30 A lnielsen@brooks.edu
NIELSEN, Leila .... 651-631-0204. 253 D lnielsen@aaaom.edu
NIELSEN, Mary .... 706-272-4403. 123 G mnielsen@daltonstate.edu
NIELSEN, Mary, F .... 414-277-7216. 534 G nielsen@msoe.edu
NIELSEN, Melore .... 206-296-2000. 523 E mnielsen@seattleu.edu
NIELSEN, Milton, C .... 512-245-1799. 487 C mn11@txstate.edu
NIELSEN, Monty, E .... 785-532-6254. 188 A nielsen@ksu.edu
NIELSEN, Norm, R .... 319-368-6464. 181 C nrnielsen@mtmercy.edu
NIELSEN, Paul, D .... 412-268-7740. 412 H nielsen@sei.cmu.edu
NIELSEN, Richard, P .... 801-375-5125. 496 G rnielsen@rmuohp.edu
NIELSEN, Scott .... 775-753-2289. 294 F scott.nielsen@gbcnv.edu
NIELSEN, Tom .... 425-564-2442. 517 A tom.nielsen@bellevuecollege.edu
NIELSON, Joel .... 330-672-3120. 382 B jnielson@kent.edu
NIELSON, Marian, J .... 315-733-2300. 349 D mnielson@uscny.edu
NIELSON, P. Douglas ...... 808-675-3510. 135 C nielsond@byuh.edu
NIELSON, Robert .... 435-283-7037. 498 A rob.nielson@snow.edu
NIEMAN, Charles, L .... 412-624-0235. 435 C cnieman@pitt.edu
NIEMAN, Donald .... 607-777-2141. 341 E dnieman@binghamton.edu
NIEMAN, James .... 773-256-0728. 152 B jnieman@lstc.edu
NIEMAN, Kenneth, F .... 765-641-4182. 163 L kfnieman@anderson.edu
NIEMAN, Larry .... 312-935-6231. 156 K lnieman@robertmorris.edu
NIEMAN, Paul .... 818-710-4121... 52 B niemanp@piercecollege.edu
NIEMANN, Kat .... 319-385-6262. 179 K kat.niemann@iwc.edu
NIEMANN, Yolanda Flores .... 940-565-3987. 490 C yolanda.niemann@unt.edu
NIEMEYER, Donna, A ...... 402-844-7351. 291 I donna@northeast.edu
NIEMI, JR., Albert, W .... 214-768-3012. 481 A aniemi@cox.smu.edu
NIEMI, Bill .... 970-943-3045... 86 I bniemi@western.edu
NIEMI, Jayne, L .... 651-696-6200. 256 L niemi@macalester.edu
NIEMIEC, Catherine .... 602-274-1885... 16 M cniemiec@pihma.edu
NIENABER, Mary .... 651-779-5837. 258 C mary.nienaber@century.edu
NIENABER, Steve .... 859-572-1366. 198 I nienabers1@nku.edu
NIENART, Marilyn .... 607-431-4104. 325 F nienartm@hartwick.edu
NIENHUIS, Nancy, E .... 617-964-1100. 222 A nnienhuis@ants.edu
NIENSTEDT, Barbara .... 856-415-2138. 302 C bnienstedt@gccnj.edu
NIES, Charles .... 209-228-7620... 71 D CNies@UCMerced.edu
NIESE, Vicki, J .... 419-772-2057. 386 D v-niese@onu.edu
NIESEN DE ABRUNA, Laura .... 203-371-7910... 91 C niesendeabrunal@sacredheart.edu
NIETERS, John .... 510-763-7787... 26 D
NIETO, Erma, M .... 940-898-3270. 488 B enieto@twu.edu
NIETO, Hollis, B .... 323-259-2598... 56 I hnieto@oxy.edu
NIETO, Linda, A .... 402-552-3039. 288 L nieto@clarksoncollege.edu
NIEUWSMA, Randal, G .. 616-526-6334. 240 L nieuwr@calvin.edu
NIEVES, Alfredo .... 787-766-1717. 552 J alnieves@suagm.edu
NIEVES, Beatriz .... 787-766-1717. 552 J um_bnieves@suagm.edu
NIEVES, Danily .... 787-882-2065. 553 A
NIEVES, Drusila, F .... 845-675-4564. 335 C drusila.nieves@nyack.edu
NIEVES, Gladys, T .... 787-765-3560. 548 M gnieves@edpuniversity.edu
NIEVES, Ivette .... 787-279-1912. 550 B inieves@bayamon.inter.edu
NIEVES, Lamberto, C ...... 201-761-6085. 306 L lnieves@saintpeters.edu
NIEVES, Liliam .... 787-725-8120. 548 O programaextension@eap.edu
NIEVES, Lourdes .... 305-821-3333. 105 A lourdes@fnu.edu
NIEVES, Lourdes, M .... 787-765-1915. 551 C lmnieves@inter.edu
NIEVES, Mayra .... 212-237-8918. 318 D mnieves@jjay.cuny.edu
NIEVES, Nancy .... 787-265-3858. 554 E placement@uprm.edu
NIEVES, Wilfredo .... 860-906-5101... 88 D wnieves@ccc.commnet.edu
NIEWENHOUS, Susan .... 208-792-2395. 138 G sniewenh@lcsc.edu

NIFONG, Mary .... 719-502-3353... 84 A
mary.nifong@ppcc.edu
NIGAGLIONI, Guillermo . 787-754-7120. 549 I
NIGGLI, Susan .... 585-275-7761. 349 C
sniggli@admin.rochester.edu
NIGHTINGALE, Charles .. 443-518-4615. 215 E
cnightingale@howardcc.edu
NIGHTINGALE, Lisa .... 972-860-8051. 470 H
lnightingale@dcccd.edu
NIGLIAZZO, Marc, A ...... 245-519-5400. 483 D
NIGRO, Frank .... 530-242-7760... 65 G
fnigro@shastacollege.edu
NIGRO, Nick .... 419-473-2700. 378 I
nnigro@daviscollege.edu
NIGRO, Richard, A .... 215-951-1360. 420 B
nigro@lasalle.edu
NIGRO, Sarah .... 402-935-9400. 290 N
snigro@nechristian.edu
NIGRO, Stephen, M .... 413-542-2101. 221 G
smnigro@amherst.edu
NIGUIDULA, Amanda ..... 305-348-3532. 115 B
amanda.niguidula@fiu.edu
NIKAS, Peter .... 262-554-2010. 534 D
dr.peter_nikas@gmx.com
NIKIAS, C. L, M .... 213-740-2111... 74 A
president@usc.edu
NIKOLAKIS, Michael ...... 251-580-2121..... 4 L
mnikolakis@faulknerstate.edu
NILA, Ed .... 818-386-5605... 59 E
enila@pgi.edu
NILAND, Eileen, A .... 716-888-2620. 316 C
nilande@canisius.edu
NILAND, Joe .... 251-442-2288..... 9 A
jniland@umobile.edu
NILES, Beau .... 919-546-8383. 366 E
bniles@shawu.edu
NILES, Maryann .... 781-280-3703. 232 B
nilesm@middlesex.mass.edu
NILES, Spencer .... 757-221-2315. 503 N
sgniles@wm.edu
NILES, Stefanie .... 540-362-6211. 505 G
nilessd@hollins.edu
NILL, Jack .... 417-862-9533. 274 F
info@globaluniversity.edu
NILSEN, Kenneth .... 201-216-5206. 307 E
knilsen@stevens.edu
NILSSON, Elizabeth .... 603-668-6660. 297 C
NIMES, Johnny, C .... 478-825-6520. 124 H
nimesj@fvsu.edu
NIMMER, Carole .... 660-543-4919. 283 A
cnimmer@ucmo.edu
NIMMO, Steven .... 706-776-0113. 130 E
snimmo@piedmont.edu
NIMOCKS DEN HERDER,
Mittie .... 608-342-1261. 537 D
denherderm@uwplatt.edu
NIMON, Opie .... 312-949-7610. 146 G
onimon@ico.edu
NIMS, Vince .... 510-848-5232... 45 A
vnims@fst.edu
NING, Bin .... 734-487-4924. 242 D
bning@emich.edu
NINI, Christy .... 901-381-3939. 464 C
christy@visible.edu
NINO-MORENO,
Eduardo .... 859-233-8777. 199 I
enino@transy.edu
NINOS, Katherine .... 505-467-6819. 312 D
NIP, Kit .... 319-385-6250. 179 K
knip@iwc.edu
NIPP, Amanda .... 402-844-7733. 291 I
amandan@northeast.edu
NIPP, Tim, J .... 731-881-7601. 463 E
timnipp@utm.edu
NIPPER, G. Edward .... 870-235-4031... 23 F
genipper@saumag.edu
NIPPERT, Karen, F .... 901-333-4283. 461 F
knippert@southwest.tn.edu
NIROOMAND, Farhang .. 361-570-4230. 489 E
niroomandf@uhv.edu
NIROUMAND, Madjid .... 714-432-5991... 39 K
mniroumand@occ.cccd.edu
NISBET, Jane, A .... 603-862-1948. 298 C
jan.nisbet@unh.edu
NISENBOYM, Svetlana ... 718-261-5800. 315 F
snisenboym@bramsonort.edu
NISH, Melinda .... 619-482-6301... 68 B
mganio@swccd.edu
NISHIGUCHI, Earl, K ...... 808-245-8274. 136 H
earln@hawaii.edu
NISHIME, Jeanie .... 310-660-3472... 43 B
jnishime@elcamino.edu
NISHIMOTO, John, H ..... 714-449-7409... 67 D
jnishimoto@scco.edu
NISHIOKA, Curtis .... 808-974-7414. 136 A
nishioka@hawaii.edu
NISSEL, Chaim .... 646-685-0115. 351 M
drnissel@yu.edu
NISSEN, Jill .... 314-367-8700. 281 C
jill.nissen@stlcop.edu
NISSEN, John .... 802-387-7145. 499 E
johnnissen@landmark.edu
NISSEN, Lindsey .... 319-296-4269. 178 J
lindsey.nissen@hawkeyecollege.edu
NISSLEY, Nick .... 513-569-1601. 376 L
nick.nissley@cincinnatistate.edu
NISWANDER, Frederick .. 252-328-6975. 367 B
niswanderf@ecu.edu
NISWONGER, Joseph, R 414-410-4504. 532 B
jrniswonger@stritch.edu
NITECKI, Danuta .... 215-895-2750. 415 B
dan44@drexel.edu
NITSCH, Wanda .... 760-591-3012. 118 I
wnitsch@usa.edu
NIX, Julie .... 256-782-5815..... 4 K
jnix@jsu.edu
NIX, Orvie .... 806-651-2345. 484 D
onix@wtamu.edu
NIX, Preston, L .... 504-282-4455. 206 A
pnix@nobts.edu
NIX, Rachel .... 870-574-1521... 23 G
rnix@sautech.edu
NIX, Sheila .... 210-431-2178. 479 D
snix@stmarytx.edu
NIX, Stephan .... 361-593-2000. 484 A
stephan.nix@tamuk.edu
NIXON, Andrea .... 507-222-4043. 254 D
anixon@carleton.edu
NIXON, Jude .... 978-542-7267. 230 E
jnixon@salemstate.edu
NIXON, Leah .... 616-234-3535. 243 B
commdept@grcc.edu
NIXON, LeAnne .... 601-477-4008. 267 F
leanne.nixon@jcjc.edu
NIXON, Monica .... 206-296-6070. 523 E
mnixon@seattleu.edu
NIXON, Russell, T .... 215-702-4392. 411 F
rnixon@cairn.edu
NIXON, Susan .... 318-487-7401. 202 F
susan.nixon@lacollege.edu
NIXON, Terry .... 325-793-4721. 476 E
tnixon@mcm.edu
NIXON, Tina, S .... 334-833-4410..... 4 D
tnixon@huntingdon.edu
NIXON, Tonia .... 410-543-6056. 220 D
tcnixon@salisbury.edu
NIXON, Valerie .... 607-587-4010. 345 D
nixonvb@alfredstate.edu
NJIE, Valerie .... 412-402-9779. 410 G
vnjie@mcg-btc.org
NJOGU, Wamucii, E .... 773-442-5700. 154 H
w-njogu@neiu.edu
NNADI, Eucharia, E .... 702-968-2038. 295 E
ennadi@roseman.edu
NNAZOR, Reginald .... 937-376-6007. 376 E
rnnazor@centralstate.edu
NNOROMELE, Patrick, C 859-622-2973. 193 P
patrick.nnoromele@eku.edu
NOACK, Kelly .... 309-794-7477. 139 L
kellynoack@augustana.edu
NOAH, Amy .... 765-494-0519. 171 M
arnoah@purdue.edu
NOAH, Tara .... 660-359-3948. 279 H
tnoah@mail.ncmissouri.edu
NOAKES, John, A .... 215-572-2897. 409 H
noakesj@arcadia.edu
NOBILE, Bryan .... 601-643-8468. 266 F
bryan.nobile@colin.edu
NOBLE, Ann .... 281-649-3304. 473 B
aanoble@hbu.edu
NOBLE, Barbara .... 314-340-3621. 275 A
nobleb@hssu.edu
NOBLE, Clay .... 605-394-2251. 452 A
clay.noble@sdsmt.edu
NOBLE, Darren .... 563-425-5208. 183 B
noblcd@uiu.edu
NOBLE, Doug .... 540-654-1235. 510 J
dnoble@umw.edu
NOBLE, Janice .... 925-424-1103... 37 L
jnoble@laspositascollege.edu
NOBLE, John, H .... 413-597-2313. 238 D
john.h.noble@williams.edu
NOBLE, Ronald, J .... 209-667-3177... 35 B
rnoble@csustan.edu
NOBLE, Ryan .... 941-487-4460. 115 D
rnoble@ncf.edu
NOBLE, Seth .... 970-542-3248... 83 E
seth.noble@morgancc.edu
NOBLE, Shlomo .... 585-473-2810. 347 D
NOBLE-GOODMAN,
Stuart .... 909-748-8142... 73 H
stuart_noblegoodman@redlands.edu
NOBLES, Daryle .... 910-678-8225. 360 D
noblesd@faytechcc.edu
NOBLES, Rodney .... 262-691-5362. 541 D
rnobles@wctc.edu
NOBLES, Susan, Q .... 252-493-7287. 362 G
snobles@email.pittcc.edu
NOBLES, Tammy .... 573-681-5271. 276 C
noblest@lincolnu.edu
NOBLET, Michael .... 207-581-2666. 212 B
noblet@maine.edu
NOBLETT, Jeffrey .... 719-389-6681... 79 D
jnoblett@coloradocollege.edu
NOBLIN, Patricia .... 973-300-2754. 307 F
pnoblin@sussex.edu
NOBLITT, Jeff .... 630-466-7900. 162 J
jnoblitt@waubonsee.edu
NOCE, Joe .... 215-780-1294. 433 A
pcobookstore@mattmccoy.com
NOCELLA, Frank .... 973-300-2115. 307 F
fnocella@sussex.edu
NOCHTA, Linda .... 724-589-2155. 434 B
lnochta@thiel.edu
NOCKUNAS, Michael ..... 413-572-5468. 230 F
mnockunas@westfield.ma.edu
NODA, Keisuke .... 845-752-3000. 348 I
dpknoda@aol.com
NODES, Jennifer .... 239-348-4710... 98 K
jennifer.nodes@avemaria.edu
NODGE, Andrea .... 734-432-5737. 246 B
anodge@madonna.edu
NODLAND, Rita .... 701-224-5692. 372 B
rita.nodland@bismarckstate.edu
NODZENSKI, Peter .... 309-796-5374. 140 E
nodzenskip@bhc.edu
NOE, Bryan, D .... 205-934-8227..... 8 E
bnoe@uab.edu
NOE, Danielle .... 904-680-7659. 103 Q
dnoe@fcsl.edu
NOEHRE, Edwin, R .... 608-258-2401. 540 C
enoehre@madisoncollege.edu
NOEL, Amy .... 910-592-8084. 363 E
anoel@sampsoncc.edu
NOEL, Cheryl, A .... 724-925-4058. 437 D
noelc@wccc.edu
NOEL, Dan .... 719-638-6580... 81 K
dnoel@cci.edu
NOEL, Erin .... 559-453-2000... 45 D
erin.noel@fresno.edu
NOEL, JR., J. Andrew .... 607-255-8832. 322 A
jan16@cornell.edu
NOEL, John, D .... 563-562-3263. 181 E
noelj@portal.nicc.edu
NOEL, Michelle .... 775-673-7000. 294 H
mnoel@tmcc.edu
NOEL, Norma .... 575-646-4986. 310 I
nnoel@nmsu.edu
NOEL, Stuart .... 678-891-3986. 125 G
stuart.noel@gpc.edu
NOEL, Terry .... 724-532-5095. 432 G
terry.noel@email.stvincent.edu
NOEL-ELKINS, Amelia .... 309-438-3217. 147 J
anoelel@ilstu.edu
NOELL, Sarah .... 860-768-4408... 92 D
snoell@hartford.edu
NOFFSINGER, Lynda, D . 336-888-6352. 355 C
lnoffsin@highpoint.edu
NOFRI, Julia, E .... 203-365-4837... 91 C
nofrij@sacredheart.edu
NOFTSINGER, Mark, P ... 540-375-2283. 509 B
noftsinger@roanoke.edu
NOGUERAS, Magdalena . 787-751-0160. 548 J
mnogueras@cmpr.pr.gov
NOH, Yoonmi .... 631-632-4418. 342 C
NOHLGREN, Bethany ...... 845-758-7099. 314 D
nohlgren@bard.edu
NOHNER, OSB, Sharon . 320-363-5285. 254 J
snohner@csbsju.edu
NOHRE, Kathy .... 320-762-4591. 257 O
kathyn@alextech.edu
NOHRIA, Nitin .... 617-495-6653. 227 C
nnohria@hbs.harvard.edu
NOISETTE, Yvonne .... 843-574-6083. 447 E
yvonne.noisette@tridenttech.edu
NOJAN, Mehran .... 315-312-2345. 344 A
mehran.nojan@oswego.edu
NOLAN, Alanna .... 718-817-3080. 324 G
anolan@fordham.edu
NOLAN, Beth .... 202-994-6503... 95 D
bnolan@gwu.edu
NOLAN, Brian .... 301-447-5223. 217 B
nolan@msmary.edu
NOLAN, Cathy, M .... 301-784-5000. 213 B
cnolan@allegany.edu
NOLAN, Charles, S .... 781-292-2201. 226 G
charles.nolan@olin.edu
NOLAN, Christina .... 973-748-9000. 299 F
christina_nolan@bloomfield.edu
NOLAN, Colleen .... 304-876-5106. 529 I
cnolan@shepherd.edu
NOLAN, Deborah .... 410-704-2452. 220 E
dnolan@towson.edu
NOLAN, Deborah, O .... 610-409-3586. 436 B
dnolan@ursinus.edu
NOLAN, Ernest .... 734-432-5313. 246 B
enolan@madonna.edu
NOLAN,
Jennifer (Jaime) .... 605-688-6361. 452 B
jennifer.nolan@sdstate.edu
NOLAN, Jim .... 505-467-6821. 312 D
pres@swc.edu
NOLAN, Judy .... 914-251-6067. 344 D
judy.nolan@purchase.edu
NOLAN, Kelly .... 310-544-6419... 61 H
kelly.nolan@usw.salvationarmy.org
NOLAN, Lisa .... 515-294-9860. 175 H
lknolan@iastate.edu
NOLAN, Tiffany .... 217-228-5432. 156 C
nolanti@quincy.edu
NOLAN-WEISS,
Sharon, E .... 716-645-2266. 341 F
senolan@buffalo.edu
NOLAN YOUNG,
Pamela .... 413-585-2141. 236 H
pnolan@smith.edu
NOLAND, Brian, E .... 423-439-4211. 459 C
president@etsu.edu
NOLAND, Josh .... 276-944-6867. 504 H
jnoland@ehc.edu
NOLAND, T. Raiford .... 205-652-3536..... 9 F
trnoland@uwa.edu
NOLDER, Deborah .... 606-759-7141. 196 B
debbie.nolder@kctcs.edu
NOLDNER, Tracy .... 605-367-7487. 452 C
tracy.noldner@southeasttech.edu
NOLDON, Denise .... 510-235-7800... 41 K
dnoldon@contracosta.edu
NOLE, Laura .... 206-878-3710. 520 E
lnole@highline.edu
NOLEN, Donald, R .... 919-530-5350. 368 A
dnolen@nccu.edu
NOLEN, Nathan .... 501-569-3345... 24 B
nxnolen@ualr.edu
NOLES, Jody .... 334-291-4922..... 2 H
jody.noles@cv.edu
NOLES, Kimberly .... 478-274-7761. 129 I
knoles@oftc.edu
NOLING, Kim .... 607-431-4106. 325 F
nolingk@hartwick.edu
NOLL, Eric .... 518-388-6108. 348 J
nolle@union.edu
NOLL SORG, Carolyn ..... 440-646-8114. 392 D
cnollsorg@ursuline.edu
NOLLEY, Dennis .... 903-675-6343. 488 D
dnolley@tvcc.edu
NOLSER, Michael .... 303-534-6290... 80 H
michael.nosler@colostate.edu
NOLTE, Beth .... 573-681-5194. 276 C
noltem@lincolnu.edu
NOLTE, Harold .... 979-830-4000. 467 I
harold.nolte@blinn.edu
NOLTE, Walter, H .... 307-268-2548. 542 X
wnolte@caspercollege.edu
NOLTEMEYER, J. Patrick 859-238-5218. 193 E
patrick.noltemeyer@centre.edu
NOMIYA, Shino .... 415-565-4616... 71 A
nomiyas@uchastings.edu
NOMURA, Cory .... 909-748-8066... 73 H
cory_nomura@redlands.edu
NONAKA, Conrad .... 808-734-9539. 136 E
conradn@hawaii.edu
NONDORF, James .... 773-702-4101. 161 B
jnondorf@uchicago.edu
NONEMAKER, Jeffrey ..... 909-593-3511... 72 E
jnonemaker@laverne.edu
NONN, Lidia .... 920-465-2565. 536 F
nonnl@uwgb.edu
NONNAMAKER, John .... 504-314-2188. 207 C
jnonnama@tulane.edu
NOOK, Mark .... 608-262-3826. 536 C
mnook@uwsa.edu
NOOKS, Kirk, A .... 816-604-2044. 277 F
kirk.nooks@mcckc.edu
NOON, Edward .... 414-443-8871. 539 F
edward.noon@wlc.edu
NOONAN, Claire .... 708-714-9107. 144 C
cnoonan@dom.edu
NOONAN, Daniel .... 860-727-6902... 90 A
dnoonan@goodwin.edu
NOONAN, Ellen, R .... 413-205-3530. 221 F
ellen.noonan@aic.edu
NOONAN, John .... 919-660-4252. 354 A
john.noonan@duke.edu
NOONAN, Mary .... 978-837-5314. 234 A
noonanm@merrimack.edu
NOONAN-TERRY, Coral . 512-813-2300. 450 G
cnoonanterry@national.edu
NOONE, Debora .... 207-948-9148. 211 I
dnoone@unity.edu
NOONE, Kate .... 714-620-3700... 28 M
knoone@argosy.edu
NOONE, Pamela, K .... 570-577-7136. 411 A
pamela.noone@bucknell.edu
NOONEN, Joe .... 740-392-6868. 384 K
joe.noonen@mvnu.edu
NOONKESTER, Myron .... 601-318-6118. 270 I
myron.noonkester@wmcarey.edu
NORBRATEN, Gary, D .... 503-777-7298. 407 E
gary.norbraten@reed.edu

NORBURY, Kerry .... 913-981-8702. 450 G
knorbury@national.edu
NORBY, Paula .... 602-286-8022... 14 L
norby@gatewaycc.edu
NORCIA, Lisa .... 201-200-2335. 303 F
lnorcia@njcu.edu
NORCINI, Heather .... 610-341-5890. 415 G
hnorcini@eastern.edu
NORCROSS, Dawn .... 607-753-2302. 343 B
dawn.norcross@cortland.edu
NORCROSS, Robert .... 760-757-2121... 54 G
rnorcross@miracosta.edu
NORD, Sheldon .... 503-375-7000. 403 A
snord@corban.edu
NORDBERG, Traci .... 615-343-3322. 463 G
traci.nordberg@vanderbilt.edu
NORDBLOM, Suzanne .... 507-389-7456. 261 E
suzanne.nordblom@southcentral.edu
NORDEEN, Mark .... 307-855-2140. 542 Y
mark.nordeen@cwc.edu
NORDENBERG, Mark, A . 412-624-4200. 435 C
norden@pitt.edu
NORDGREN, Debra, L .... 715-394-8233. 538 C
dnordgre@uwsuper.edu
NORDGREN, Peter, D ..... 715-394-8475. 538 C
pnordgre@uwsuper.edu
NORDICK, Lisa .... 701-231-8692. 371 G
lisa.nordick@ndsu.edu
NORDICK, Pat .... 218-299-6821. 259 F
pat.nordick@minnesota.edu
NORDIN, Becky .... 612-659-6712. 259 D
becky.nordin@minneapolis.edu
NORDIN, Richard, M ...... 818-767-0888... 76 K
richard.nordin@woodbury.edu
NORDLING, William .... 703-416-1441. 505 I
wnordling@ipsciences.edu
NORDONE, Jim .... 912-443-5707. 131 D
jnordone@savannahtech.edu
NORDONE, Terri .... 617-369-3688. 236 F
tnordone@smfa.edu
NORDQUIST, Neil .... 701-858-3150. 371 F
neil.nordquist@minotstateu.edu
NORDSTROM, Carolyn ... 404-237-7573. 121 F
cnordstrom@kaplan.edu
NORDSTROM, David ...... 413-369-4044. 225 D
nordstrom@csld.edu
NORDSTROM, Jennifer ... 815-226-3383. 157 C
jnordstrom@rockford.edu
NORDSTROM, Martha .... 207-948-9242. 211 I
mnordstrom@unity.edu
NORDSTROM, Terry ...... 510-869-6511... 61 I
tnordstrom@samuelmerritt.edu
NORDT, Lee, C .... 254-710-3361. 467 G
lee_nordt@baylor.edu
NORDYKE, Ann, A .... 660-543-4170. 283 A
anordyke@ucmo.edu
NOREEN, Jody .... 614-947-6077. 380 A
jody.noreen@franklin.edu
NORELIUS, Caroline .... 218-755-2876. 258 A
cnorelius@bemidjistate.edu
NOREN, Patricia .... 516-572-7087. 332 C
patricia.noren@ncc.edu
NORENBERG, David, F .. 315-386-7119. 345 F
norenbergd@canton.edu
NORIEL, Eleanor .... 707-546-4000... 43 E
enoriel@empirecollege.com
NORIN, Michele, L .... 520-621-5972... 18 F
norin@arizona.edu
NORITA, Mark .... 619-260-7556... 73 I
mnorita@sandiego.edu
NORK, Richard .... 313-577-2424. 252 G
rick.nork@wayne.edu
NORLEN, Tracy, C .... 206-281-2977. 523 C
tcnorlen@spu.edu
NORLIEN, Cheryl, A .... 320-222-5635. 260 H
cheryl.norlien@ridgewater.edu
NORMAN, Anne, S .... 920-832-6578. 533 S
anne.s.norman@lawrence.edu
NORMAN, Bruce .... 301-447-5377. 217 B
norman@msmary.edu
NORMAN, Char .... 614-222-6189. 378 A
cnorman@ccad.edu
NORMAN, Dari, L .... 518-743-2237. 345 E
normand@sunyacc.edu
NORMAN, Dax .... 301-226-9086. 544 L
NORMAN, Eric .... 617-912-9212. 224 B
enorman@bostonconservatory.edu
NORMAN, Eric, M .... 260-481-6601. 168 C
norman@ipfw.edu
NORMAN, Gary .... 801-818-8900. 496 F
gary.norman@provocollege.edu
NORMAN, Ginny, L .... 540-665-4513. 509 E
gnorman@su.edu
NORMAN, Harry .... 657-278-2937... 33 E
hnorman@fullerton.edu
NORMAN, Jason, A .... 806-371-5456. 465 E
janorman@actx.edu
NORMAN, Margie, A ...... 903-813-2247. 466 H
mnorman@austincollege.edu
NORMAN, Melora .... 207-948-9265. 211 I
mnorman@unity.edu
NORMAN, Myra, K .... 615-898-5005. 459 D
myra.norman@mtsu.edu
NORMAN, Peter, E .... 815-599-3465. 146 D
pete.norman@highland.edu
NORMAN, Robert, S .... 405-585-5805. 397 C
stan.norman@okbu.edu
NORMAN, Ross .... 605-626-2433. 451 I
normanr@northern.edu
NORMAN, Ruena .... 850-599-3017. 114 K
ruena.norman@famu.edu
NORMAN, Terry, W .... 608-796-3900. 539 E
twnorman@viterbo.edu
NORMAN, W. Ray .... 717-766-2511. 423 L
rnorman@messiah.edu
NORMAN, Yolanda .... 713-525-3836. 490 L
normany@stthom.edu
NORMAN-ARMSTRONG,
Mona Lee .... 575-769-4089. 309 F
monalee.armstrong@clovis.edu
NORMAN TILL, Danette . 260-982-5052. 170 U
dnormantill@manchester.edu
NORMANDIN, Karen ...... 207-453-5019. 210 L
knormandin@kvcc.me.edu
NORMANDY, Elizabeth ... 910-521-6000. 369 B
elizabeth.normandy@uncp.edu
NORMANN, Karen, R ...... 484-664-3496. 424 H
normann@muhlenberg.edu
NORQUIST, Bruce, R ...... 312-329-4192. 153 E
bruce.norquist@moody.edu
NORRED, Buck .... 251-442-2492..... 9 A
bnorred@umobile.edu
NORRED, J, W .... 214-648-3599. 493 E
wes.norred@utsouthwestern.edu
NORRIS, Adam .... 504-280-6939. 205 G
amnorris@uno.edu
NORRIS, Allison .... 865-981-8215. 456 D
allison.norris@maryvillecollege.edu
NORRIS, Amanda .... 617-348-6359. 237 E
amanda.norris@urbancollege.edu
NORRIS, Dawn .... 617-739-1700. 235 A
dnorris@aii.edu
NORRIS, Deb .... 937-512-5182. 388 O
deb.norris@sinclair.edu
NORRIS, Debbie .... 601-925-3225. 268 A
dnorris@mc.edu
NORRIS, Debbie .... 601-925-3260. 268 A
dnorris@mc.edu
NORRIS, Dena .... 816-604-1527. 277 C
dena.norris@mcckc.edu
NORRIS, Emily .... 502-585-9911. 199 C
enorris@spalding.edu
NORRIS, Gail .... 585-273-5824. 349 C
gnorris@admin.rochester.edu
NORRIS, John .... 704-330-1448. 355 K
jnorris@jcsu.edu
NORRIS, Joye .... 417-836-4127. 278 E
joyenorris@missouristate.edu
NORRIS, Keisha .... 740-588-4113. 394 C
knorris@zanestate.edu
NORRIS, Kenneth, A .... 913-684-2312. 545 E
norrisk@leavenworth.army.mil
NORRIS, Kisha .... 256-726-7204..... 6 B
knorris@oakwood.edu
NORRIS, LaRon .... 703-416-1441. 505 I
lnorris@ipsciences.edu
NORRIS, Lesa .... 630-801-7900. 162 J
lnorris@waubonsee.edu
NORRIS, Mark, M .... 574-372-5100. 166 B
norrismm@grace.edu
NORRIS, Mary .... 860-768-4716... 92 D
norris@hartford.edu
NORRIS, Mitzi .... 601-815-4233. 270 C
mnorris@umc.edu
NORRIS, Nancy, E .... 828-448-3150. 365 A
nnorris@wpcc.edu
NORRIS, Patricia .... 910-296-2509. 361 D
pnorris@jamessprunt.edu
NORRIS, Patricia, D ...... 336-750-2900. 370 A
norrispd@wssu.edu
NORRIS, Paul, E .... 317-274-4860. 168 D
penorris@iupui.edu
NORRIS, Robert, F .... 630-752-5559. 163 F
bob.norris@wheaton.edu
NORRIS, Sababu, C ...... 716-888-2787. 316 C
norris@canisius.edu
NORRIS, Todd .... 574-284-4560. 172 G
tnorris@saintmarys.edu
NORRIS, Veta .... 810-767-4000. 239 H
veta.norris@baker.edu
NORRIS-LANE, Virginia .. 830-896-5411. 480 F
vanorrislane@schreiner.edu
NORRIS-LITTLES,
Pamela, F .... 201-360-4201. 302 D
plittles@hccc.edu
NORS, Billy .... 254-710-2161. 467 G
baylor@bkstr.com
NORSETTER, Rhonda, D . 608-263-5510. 536 D
norsetter@chancellor.wisc.edu
NORSYM, Arlene .... 312-996-6569. 161 D
afnorsym@uic.edu
NORTELL, Bruce .... 630-637-5214. 154 F
bnortell@noctrl.edu
NORTH, Dana .... 765-983-1628. 165 G
northda@earlham.edu
NORTH, James, A .... 641-673-1065. 183 H
northj@wmpenn.edu
NORTH, Jane, D .... 717-337-6011. 417 B
jnorth@gettysburg.edu
NORTH, Jon, D .... 913-971-3600. 188 H
jonnorth@mnu.edu
NORTH, Linda .... 334-745-6437..... 7 C
lnorth@suscc.edu
NORTH, Matthew .... 412-396-4075. 415 F
northm@duq.edu
NORTH, Mike .... 865-228-2303. 461 D
mnorth@pstcc.edu
NORTH, Paula .... 918-293-5240. 398 B
paula.north@okstate.edu
NORTH, Veronica .... 312-226-6294. 151 A
pr@lexingtoncollege.edu
NORTHAM, Mark .... 307-766-2663. 543 I
mnortham@uwyo.edu
NORTHCOTT, Marshall ... 415-883-2211... 40 G
marshall.northcott@marin.edu
NORTHCROSS, Donald ... 501-244-5100... 19 J
donald.northcross@arkansasbaptist.edu
NORTHCUTT, David .... 706-419-1214. 123 F
david.northcutt@covenant.edu
NORTHCUTT,
Douglas, H .... 813-988-5131. 104 A
vpres@floridacollege.edu
NORTHERN, Norma .... 502-213-2104. 195 F
norma.northern@kctcs.edu
NORTHMAN, Esther, A .... 716-888-2784. 316 C
northman@canisius.edu
NORTHROP, Cathy .... 607-844-8222. 347 I
northrc@TC3.edu
NORTHRUP, Pamela .... 850-474-2770. 117 B
pnorthru@uwf.edu
NORTHUP, Bill .... 641-628-7645. 176 E
northupb@central.edu
NORTHUP, Lesley .... 305-348-2099. 115 B
lesley.northup@fiu.edu
NORTHWALL, Susan, F .. 717-872-3250. 429 D
susan.northwall@millersville.edu
NORTON, Alan, J .... 507-786-3016. 264 B
nortona@stolaf.edu
NORTON, Amy .... 563-588-6338. 176 F
amy.norton@clarke.edu
NORTON, Cheryl .... 724-738-2000. 429 F
cheryl.norton@sru.edu
NORTON, Daniel .... 410-337-6456. 215 A
daniel.norton@goucher.edu
NORTON, Darryl, R .... 828-689-1248. 356 F
dnorton@mhc.edu
NORTON, David, P .... 352-392-9271. 116 A
dpnorton@ufl.edu
NORTON, H. Will .... 662-915-7146. 270 B
hwnorton@olemiss.edu
NORTON, Hanna .... 479-880-4189... 20 E
hnorton@atu.edu
NORTON, Heather .... 314-889-1401. 274 E
hnorton@fontbonne.edu
NORTON, Holly .... 309-649-6050. 160 E
holly.norton@src.edu
NORTON, James .... 860-439-2268... 89 H
jwnor@conncoll.edu
NORTON, John .... 207-221-4373. 213 A
jnorton@une.edu
NORTON, Judith .... 580-477-7701. 401 J
judith.norton@wosc.edu
NORTON, Karen .... 617-228-2177. 231 C
kmnorton@bhcc.mass.edu
NORTON, Kay .... 970-351-2121... 86 C
kay.norton@unco.edu
NORTON, Kelly .... 920-924-3225. 540 F
knorton@morainepark.edu
NORTON, Lisa, M .... 812-877-8892. 172 C
lisa.norton@rose-hulman.edu
NORTON, M. Grant .... 509-335-4505. 525 A
mg_norton@wsu.edu
NORTON, Melanie .... 765-658-4216. 165 F
melanienorton@depauw.edu
NORTON, Melanie .... 601-266-4241. 270 E
melanie.norton@usm.edu
NORTON, Mitzi .... 312-662-4002. 139 F
mnorton@adler.edu
NORTON, Noelle .... 619-260-4545... 73 I
norton@sandiego.edu
NORTON, Patrick, J .... 802-443-5699. 499 H
pnorton@middlebury.edu
NORTON, Ricky .... 903-223-3012. 484 C
ricky.norton@tamut.edu
NORTON, Robert .... 928-523-6054... 16 C
robert.norton@nau.edu
NORTON, Robert, L .... 859-846-5803. 197 I
rlnorton@midway.edu
NORTON, Sheri, L .... 401-825-2311. 439 A
slnorton@ccri.edu
NORTON, Steve .... 309-341-5227. 141 A
snorton@sandburg.edu
NORTON, Susan .... 843-574-6211. 447 E
susan.norton@tridenttech.edu
NORTON, Susan, A .... 706-721-3777. 126 B
snorton@gru.edu
NORTON, Tim .... 320-308-2266. 261 B
tpnorton@stcloudstate.edu
NORVAC, Steven .... 626-256-4673... 39 A
snorvac@coh.org
NORWOOD, Donna .... 970-339-6453... 78 C
donna.norwood@aims.edu
NORWOOD, Patricia, A .. 817-202-6761. 481 E
norwoodp@swau.edu
NOSAL, Judith, S .... 860-493-0011... 87 J
nosalj@ct.edu
NOSEGBE, Isibor Joy ..... 703-891-1787. 510 A
NOSEK, Stan .... 805-756-2171... 32 F
snosek@calpoly.edu
NOSEL, Cathy .... 302-736-2317... 94 C
cathy.nosel@wesley.edu
NOSEL, Cathy .... 302-736-2317... 94 C
nosel@wesle.edu
NOSEWORTHY,
James, A .... 847-866-3952. 145 E
jim.noseworthy@garrett.edu
NOSEWORTHY, John, H 507-266-4861. 254 F
noseworthy.john@mayo.edu
NOSS, Rebecca .... 845-675-5767. 335 C
rebecca.noss@nyack.edu
NOSSER, Mike, A .... 612-343-4178. 262 X
manosser@northcentral.edu
NOSTRAND, Dennis, L ... 813-253-6211. 118 L
dnostrand@ut.edu
NOSTROM, Kim .... 607-436-2563. 343 E
kim.nostrom@oneonta.edu
NOSTRUM, Rian .... 701-231-7890. 371 G
rian.nostrum@ndsu.edu
NOTA, Michele .... 401-874-2242. 440 D
mnota@advance.uri.edu
NOTARESCHI, Rey, T ..... 330-325-6796. 385 E
rtn@neomed.edu
NOTCHICK, Thomas, K ... 570-348-6241. 423 B
notchick@marywood.edu
NOTO, Lisa .... 707-664-3019... 36 B
lisa.noto@sonoma.edu
NOTO, Robert, A .... 517-353-3530. 246 H
notor@msu.edu
NOTSON, Jeanne .... 505-566-3209. 311 I
notsonj@sanjuancollege.edu
NOTTINGHAM,
Jacqueline .... 304-384-6305. 529 E
ntnghm@concord.edu
NOTTKE, Janine .... 906-487-7267. 242 G
janine.nottke@finlandia.edu
NOURI, Imad .... 313-845-9611. 243 H
inouri@hfcc.edu
NOURSE, Chris .... 740-245-7228. 392 A
cnourse@rio.edu
NOURSE, Ryan .... 406-683-7509. 286 I
r_nourse@umwestern.edu
NOVACK, Van .... 562-985-5462... 33 F
vnovack@csulb.edu
NOVAK, JR., Albert, J ... 412-624-6800. 435 C
nalbert@pitt.edu
NOVAK, Amy, C .... 605-995-2601. 450 A
amnovak@dwu.edu
NOVAK, Bruce .... 972-883-2416. 491 E
bxn111230@utdallas.edu
NOVAK, Christina .... 773-834-2216. 160 I
cnovak@ttic.edu
NOVAK, Diane .... 832-813-6544. 476 A
diane.novak@lonestar.edu
NOVAK, J. Michael .... 563-884-5626. 182 A
michael.novak@palmer.edu
NOVAK, James .... 248-683-0504. 246 B
jnovak@madonna.edu
NOVAK, Jeffrey .... 570-702-8920. 419 G
jnovak@johnson.edu
NOVAK, Jerry .... 734-995-7340. 241 E
novakj@cuaa.edu
NOVAK, John .... 219-980-6905. 168 B
jmnovak@iun.edu
NOVAK, Joshua .... 724-287-8711. 411 C
joshua.novak@bc3.edu
NOVAK, Mark .... 408-924-2655... 36 A
mnovak@cemail.sjsu.edu
NOVAK, Mike .... 479-248-7236... 21 B
mnovak@ecollege.edu
NOVAK, Paul .... 724-738-2465. 429 F
paul.novak@sru.edu
NOVAK, Peter, J .... 415-422-2823... 73 J
novakp@usfca.edu
NOVAK, Richard, J .... 848-932-0613. 306 A
rnovak@rutgers.edu
NOVAK, Ross .... 570-348-6236. 423 B
novak@marywood.edu
NOVAK, Thomas .... 617-585-1308. 234 I
tom.novak@necmusic.edu
NOVAK, Thomas .... 207-893-6636. 211 G
tnovak@sjcme.edu
NOVAK, Wendy .... 907-277-1000... 10 D
contact@chartercollege.edu

NOVATON, Angela ... 561-391-1148. 101 J
anovaton@dmac.edu
NOVICKI, Elizabeth ... 336-917-5421. 366 D
elizabeth.novicki@salem.edu
NOVITT, Priscilla ... 413-369-4044. 225 D
novitt@csld.edu
NOVKOVIC, Meredith ... 973-290-4130. 300 F
mbeebe@cse.edu
NOVO, Frank ... 617-964-1111. 222 A
fnovo@ants.edu
NOVOTNY, April ... 614-236-6565. 375 H
anovotny@capital.edu
NOVOTNY, Dorene ... 650-949-6210... 44 L
novotnydorene@fhda.edu
NOVOTNY, Frank, J ... 719-587-7622... 78 B
fjnovotn@adams.edu
NOVOTNY, Jeanne, M ... 915-545-9724. 487 E
jeanne.novotny@ttuhsc.edu
NOVOTNY, Jodi ... 425-235-2464. 522 F
jnovotny@rtc.edu
NOVOTNY, Matthew ... 330-941-3552. 394 A
Mmnovotny@ysu.edu
NOVOTNY, Richard, J ... 440-525-7358. 382 M
rnovotny@lakelandcc.edu
NOWACZYK, Ronald ... 814-393-2223. 428 C
rnowaczyk@clarion.edu
NOWAK, Dan ... 715-675-3331. 541 A
nowakd@ntc.edu
NOWAK, Jack ... 541-880-2224. 403 H
nowak@klamathcc.edu
NOWAK, Janice ... 904-470-8192. 102 A
janice.nowak@ewc.edu
NOWAK, Linda, I ... 209-667-3288... 35 B
lnowak@csustan.edu
NOWAK, Meg ... 607-431-4501. 325 F
nowakm@hartwick.edu
NOWAK, Patricia ... 219-980-6501. 168 B
nowakpat@indiana.edu
NOWAK, Robert ... 847-635-1876. 155 F
rnowak@oakton.edu
NOWAK, Thomas, S ... 845-848-4000. 322 G
thomas.nowak@dc.edu
NOWAK, Tom ... 574-936-8898. 163 K
tom.nowak@ancilla.edu
NOWAK, Tony, J ... 414-847-3240. 534 F
tonynowak@miad.edu
NOWAKOWSKI, Adam ... 860-434-5232... 90 F
anowakowski@lymeacademy.edu
NOWAKOWSKI,
Bernadette ... 413-265-2214. 225 C
nowakowskib@elms.edu
NOWAKOWSKI, Rodney . 205-934-3036... 8 E
rnowakow@uab.edu
NOWEL, OP, Mark, D ... 401-865-2649. 439 E
mnowel@providence.edu
NOWELL, Cheryl ... 305-348-2434. 115 B
nowell@fiu.edu
NOWELL, James ... 910-893-1258. 352 K
nowell@campbell.edu
NOWICKI, Laura ... 740-593-1969. 387 C
nowicki@ohio.edu
NOWICKI, Stephen ... 919-668-2728. 354 A
snowicki@duke.edu
NOWLAN, Marilyn, L ... 860-727-6782... 90 A
mnowlan@goodwin.edu
NOWLIN, Brian ... 562-985-5537... 33 F
bnowlin@csulb.edu
NOWLIN, Steve ... 626-396-2397... 28 P
stephen.nowlin@artcenter.edu
NOWOGORSKI, Barbara . 570-961-7835. 420 C
nowogorskib@lackawanna.edu
NOYER, Rich ... 206-878-3710. 520 E
rnoyer@highline.edu
NOYES, Daniel ... 585-567-6260. 326 F
daniel.noyes@houghton.edu
NOYES, Linda ... 516-299-3281. 329 C
Linda.Noyes@liu.edu
NRI, Monique, N ... 212-229-5592. 332 E
nrim@newschool.edu
NTOKO, Alfred ... 718-262-2804. 319 F
antoko@york.cuny.edu
NUARA, Frank ... 212-875-4619. 314 C
fnuara@bankstreet.edu
NUBEL, Anna ... 402-280-2222. 289 D
annanubel@creighton.edu
NUCCI, John, A ... 617-973-1103. 237 B
jnucci@suffolk.edu
NUCCI, Lisa ... 215-567-7080. 410 A
lnucci@aii.edu
NUCCIARONE, Mary, B .. 574-631-6436. 174 A
Nucciarone.2@nd.edu
NUCCIO, Beth ... 616-777-5206. 239 G
beth.nuccio@baker.edu
NUCKOLS, Jack ... 304-734-6623. 527 O
jnuckols@bridgemont.edu
NUCKOLS, Melanie, L ... 336-734-7332. 360 E
mnuckols@forsythtech.edu
NUDELMAN, Felice ... 937-769-1351. 373 H
fnudelman@antioch.edu
NUESELL, Jerry, J ... 919-508-2314. 370 F
jnuesell@peace.edu
NUESELL, Lisa ... 919-381-6912. 357 I
lnuesell@moc.edu
NUFER, Ken ... 719-549-3220... 84 G
ken.nufer@pueblocc.edu
NUGEN, Deb ... 402-399-2442. 289 A
dnugen@csm.edu
NUGENT, Barli ... 212-799-5000. 328 B
NUGENT, Christine, R ... 828-298-3325. 370 E
cnugent@warren-wilson.edu
NUGENT, Joe ... 831-479-6140... 30 G
jonugent@cabrillo.edu
NUGENT, John, D ... 860-439-5266... 89 H
john.nugent@conncoll.edu
NUGENT, Richard ... 574-284-4542. 172 G
rnugent@saintmarys.edu
NUGENT, Timothy, M ... 860-444-8598. 545 G
timothy.m.nugent@uscg.mil
NULL, David ... 608-265-1988. 536 D
dnull@library.wisc.edu
NULL, Greg ... 800-444-1440. 430 F
gnull@pia.edu
NULL, Wesley ... 254-710-6120. 467 G
wesley_null@baylor.edu
NULPH, Wendy ... 972-438-6932. 478 C
wnulph@parkercc.edu
NUMRICH, Camille ... 401-825-2237. 439 A
cnumrich@ccri.edu
NUNAMAKER, Gail ... 989-386-6692. 247 B
gnunamaker@midmich.edu
NUNES, Grafton, J ... 216-421-7410. 377 C
gnunes@cia.edu
NUNES, Steve ... 630-829-1358. 140 B
snunes@ben.edu
NUNES, Victoria ... 650-306-3274... 64 B
nunes@smccd.edu
NUNEZ, Anilsa, R ... 718-390-4006. 339 A
nuneza@stjohns.edu
NUNEZ, Cheryl, L ... 513-745-3539. 393 H
nunezc@xavier.edu
NUNEZ, Elsa ... 860-465-5222... 87 J
nuneze@easternct.edu
NUNEZ, Elsa, M ... 860-465-5222... 87 L
nunez@easternct.edu
NUNEZ, Ivon ... 973-596-3478. 303 G
nunez@njit.edu
NUNEZ, Jessica ... 830-591-7226. 481 C
jnunez@swtjc.edu
NUNEZ, Jose ... 650-358-6836... 64 A
nunezj@smccd.edu
NUNEZ, Jose Ramon ... 562-938-4695... 51 D
jnunez@lbcc.edu
NUNEZ, Lois ... 617-928-4500. 234 E
lanunez@mountida.edu
NUNEZ, Steve ... 815-288-5511. 158 K
nunezs@svcc.edu
NUNEZ, William ... 402-472-2116. 292 I
wnunez2@unl.edu
NUNEZ, William, J ... 402-472-2097. 292 I
wnunez2@unl.edu
NUNEZ, III, William, J .. 337-550-1201. 205 B
NUNEZ, Yancy ... 806-894-9611. 480 H
ynunez@southplainscollege.edu
NUNLEY, Beth ... 815-802-8142. 149 C
bnunley@kcc.edu
NUNLEY, Ernest, L ... 276-739-2510. 514 D
enunley@vhcc.edu
NUNLEY, Gayle, R ... 802-656-8513. 500 F
gayle.nunley@uvm.edu
NUNLEY, Jeff ... 813-988-5131. 104 A
bookstore@floridacollege.edu
NUNN, Dana ... 970-248-1868... 79 F
dnunn@coloradomesa.edu
NUNN, Diane, L ... 203-773-4474... 87 G
dlnunn@albertus.edu
NUNN, Erin ... 440-375-7080. 382 L
enunn@lec.edu
NUNN, Helen, S ... 570-372-4450. 433 H
nunn@susqu.edu
NUNN, Rod ... 314-539-5302. 281 D
rodnunn@stlcc.edu
NUNNA, Ramakrishna ... 559-278-2500... 33 D
rnunna@csufresno.edu
NUNNALLY, Delecia ... 209-954-6276... 63 C
dnunnally@deltacollege.edu
NUNNELLY, Laura ... 505-473-6176. 311 K
laura.nunnelly@santafeuniversity.edu
NUNZIATIA, Ray ... 407-843-3984. 105 P
rnunziatia@fortiscollege.edu
NURNBERGER,
Charles, A ... 757-825-2717. 514 B
nurnbergerc@tncc.edu
NUSBAUM, Nancy ... 512-245-2244. 487 C
nn01@txstate.edu
NUSENBAUM, Tatiana ... 212-349-4330. 325 D
tnusenbaum@globe.edu
NUSSBAUM, Daniel ... 860-231-5770... 92 F
dnussbaum@usj.edu
NUSSBAUM, Irwin ... 860-768-7904... 92 D
nussbaum@hartford.edu
NUSSBAUM, Renee ... 419-755-4772. 385 D
rnussbau@ncstatecollege.edu
NUSSBAUMER, John ... 248-751-7800. 250 G
nussbauj@cooley.edu
NUSSBUAM, Sara Gittie . 303-629-8200... 87 F
NUSSEL, Jay ... 304-457-6581. 526 A
nusselja@ab.edu
NUSSEN, Jack ... 757-771-9978. 112 D
jack.nussen@saintleo.edu
NUSTAD, Grant ... 605-721-5200. 450 G
gnustad@national.edu
NUTEFALL, Jennifer ... 408-554-6829... 64 M
jnutefall@scu.edu
NUTI, Larry ... 925-631-4901... 61 F
lnuti@stmarys-ca.edu
NUTT, Jill ... 616-395-7765. 244 A
nutt@hope.edu
NUTT, Jill, M ... 616-234-4031. 243 B
jnutt@grcc.edu
NUTTALL, Neil ... 660-359-3948. 279 H
nnuttall@mail.ncmissouri.edu
NUTTER, Cheryl ... 419-251-1519. 383 G
cheryl.nutter@mercycollege.edu
NUTTER, Doug ... 301-860-3402. 220 A
dnutter@bowiestate.edu
NUTTER, Sarah ... 703-993-1807. 505 C
snutter@gmu.edu
NUTTER, Susan, K ... 919-515-7188. 368 B
susan_nutter@ncsu.edu
NUTTLE, Louise, C ... 423-439-6052. 459 C
nuttle@etsu.edu
NUTTY, David ... 207-780-4276. 212 H
dnutty@usm.maine.edu
NUÑEZ, Awilda ... 787-257-0000. 554 B
profanunez@yahoo.com
NUÑEZ-ACEVEDO,
Raúl, M ... 787-894-2828. 553 G
raul.nunez2@upr.edu
NWAKEZE, Peter ... 718-933-6700. 331 K
pnwakeze@monroecollege.edu
NWALA, Kingsley ... 252-335-3598. 367 C
knnwala@mail.ecsu.edu
NWANKWO, Charles ... 337-421-6925. 204 E
charles.nwankwo@sowela.edu
NWANNE, Andrew, I ... 260-422-5561. 167 B
ainwanne@indianatech.edu
NWAOGU, Eze ... 404-756-4006. 121 A
enwaogu@atlm.edu
NWARIAKU, Fiemu, E ... 214-648-9968. 493 E
fiemu.nwariaku@utsouthwestern.edu
NWOKEAFOR, Cosmos .. 301-860-3232. 220 A
cnwokeafor@bowiestate.edu
NWOSU, Peter ... 615-963-2515. 459 E
pnwosu@tnstate.edu
NYAMAPFENE, Kingston 713-313-4275. 485 F
nyamapfenek@tsu.edu
NYBERG, Christopher, L 315-684-6083. 345 A
nybergcl@morrisville.edu
NYBERG, Connie ... 307-855-2207. 542 Y
cnyberg@cwc.edu
NYBERG, Neil ... 847-317-8001. 160 M
president@tiu.edu
NYBERG-COMINS,
Laura ... 608-822-2352. 541 C
lnybergcomins@swtc.edu
NYBORG, Adam ... 760-872-2000... 42 E
anyborg@deepsprings.edu
NYCE, Douglas, J ... 540-432-4206. 504 D
douglas.nyce@emu.edu
NYCZ, Mandy ... 920-403-3181. 535 L
mandy.nycz@snc.edu
NYE, David, J ... 303-963-3197... 79 C
dnye@ccu.edu
NYE, Fumiko ... 954-783-7339. 102 M
fnye@cci.edu
NYE, Jamey ... 916-691-7226... 53 B
nyej@crc.losrios.edu
NYE, Linda, R ... 276-223-4869. 514 F
lnye@wcc.vccs.edu
NYGREEN, Ted ... 914-606-6789. 350 F
ted.nygreen@sunywcc.edu
NYHAMMER, Diane ... 608-757-7737. 539 I
dnyhammer@blackhawk.edu
NYHART, Brant ... 602-386-4154... 11 G
brant.nyhart@arizonachristian.edu
NYHUS, Orrin ... 763-433-1346. 257 P
orrin.nyhus@anokaramsey.edu
NYIRENDA, Stanley, M .. 410-651-7531. 219 E
snyirenda@umes.edu
NYKIEL, Ronald, A ... 410-651-6508. 219 E
rnykiel@umes.edu
NYMAN, Walter, D ... 570-326-3761. 427 B
wnyman@pct.edu
NYPAVER, David ... 330-972-6876. 390 E
nypaver@uakron.edu
NYQUIST, J. Paul ... 312-329-4112. 153 E
paul.nyquist@moody.edu
NYRE, Joseph, E ... 914-633-2203. 327 C
jnyre@iona.edu
NYSTROM, David, P ... 562-903-4703... 29 L
david.nystrom@biola.edu
NYSTROM, Ellen ... 210-567-2640. 493 A
nystrom@uthscsa.edu
NYUL, Renata ... 617-373-7666. 235 F
NZAMUTUNA, Issmael .. 951-785-2006... 50 B
inzamutu@lasierra.edu
NZEOGWU, Okeleke ... 702-968-1659. 295 E
onzeogwu@roseman.edu
NÚÑEZ, Raúl, M ... 939-292-8924. 555 C
raul.nunez2@upr.edu

O

O BRIEN, John, P ... 315-445-4444. 328 F
obrienjp@lemoyne.edu
OAKES, Edward, B ... 540-831-7515. 508 C
eoakes@radford.edu
OAKES, Mary ... 312-369-6802. 143 D
moakes@colum.edu
OAKES, Ronald, L ... 660-263-3900. 272 A
president@cccb.edu
OAKLEY, Christina ... 561-912-1211. 103 C
coakley@evergladesuniversity.edu
OAKLEY, Danielle ... 608-262-8350. 536 D
droakley@uhs.wisc.edu
OAKLEY, Eloy ... 562-938-4122... 51 D
eoakley@lbcc.edu
OAKLEY, Leigh ... 859-846-5395. 197 I
loakley@midway.edu
OAKLEY OCKERT,
Melissa ... 919-536-7200. 360 B
ockertm@durhamtech.edu
OAKMAN, Tommy ... 828-694-1725. 358 C
t_oakman@blueridge.edu
OAKS, Beth ... 605-642-6411. 451 G
beth.oaks@bhsu.edu
OAKS, Diane, G ... 949-451-5277... 67 B
doaks@ivc.edu
OAKS, Geneva ... 951-343-4738... 30 H
goaks@calbaptist.edu
OANES, Laura ... 507-457-1489. 264 A
loanes@smumn.edu
OATES, Bruce ... 847-635-1753. 155 F
boates@oakton.edu
OATES, Bruce ... 847-635-1705. 155 F
boates@oakton.edu
OATES, Richard ... 706-864-1840. 133 D
richard.oates@ung.edu
OATEY, J. Sue ... 218-299-3455. 255 A
joatey@cord.edu
OATMAN, Robert, R ... 860-701-6194. 545 G
robert.r.oatman@uscg.mil
OB, Fran ... 912-650-5684. 131 H
foblander@southuniversity.edu
OBARA, Daniel, J ... 724-925-4001. 437 D
obarad@wccc.edu
OBAS, Kenley ... 334-229-4308... 1 D
kobas@alasu.edu
OBBINK, Kim ... 406-994-6550. 287 B
kobbink@montana.edu
OBERBILLIG, Lynn ... 413-585-2701. 236 H
loberbil@smith.edu
OBEREM, Graham ... 760-750-4050... 35 A
oberem@csusm.edu
OBERFELDT, Kathleen ... 718-390-3158. 350 B
koberfel@wagner.edu
OBERGFELL, Ann ... 260-481-6100. 168 C
obergfea@ipfw.edu
OBERHELMAN, Don ... 805-756-1407... 32 F
obe@calpoly.edu
OBERHOLTZER, Brent ... 717-867-6111. 421 H
oberholt@lvc.edu
OBERLANDER, Cyril ... 585-245-5528. 343 C
oberland@geneseo.edu
OBERLE, George ... 540-891-3013. 512 E
goberle@germanna.edu
OBERLIN, Craig ... 714-432-5952... 39 K
coberlin@occ.cccd.edu
OBERMAN, Anne ... 320-363-5999. 254 J
aoberman@csbsju.edu
OBERMEISTER,
Tuvia, M ... 718-377-0777. 336 I
OBERMEYER, Carole ... 316-295-5779. 186 H
obermeyer@friends.edu
OBERMEYER, Larry ... 712-274-6400. 183 G
larry.obermeyer@witcc.edu
OBERQUELL, Christian ... 406-265-3761. 287 D
coberquell@msun.edu
OBERSCHLAKE, Timothy 330-490-7241. 392 H
toberschlake@walsh.edu
OBERSTEIN, Leonard ... 410-484-7200. 217 D
OBERTO, Janet ... 617-262-5000. 223 F
janet.oberto@the-bac.edu
OBILADE, Sandra, O ... 270-686-4209. 192 G
sandra.obilade@brescia.edu
OBIN, Jason ... 773-508-8643. 151 H
jobin@luc.edu
OBLANDER, Douglas ... 843-208-8256. 448 B
Oblander@uscb.edu
OBLOY, Leonard ... 248-683-0446. 250 F
lobloy@sscms.edu
OBRECHT, LeAnn ... 308-865-8248. 292 H
obrechtls@unk.edu

OBRECHT, LeAnn .... 308-865-8218. 292 H obrechtls@unk.edu
OBRENTZ, Barbara .... 678-891-2685. 125 G barbara.obrentz@gpc.edu
OBRESLEY, Amber .... 406-791-5248. 288 E aobresley01@ugf.edu
OBSNIUK, Karen .... 734-432-5648. 246 B kobsniuk@madonna.edu
OBST, Cheryl .... 619-201-8951... 67 G registrar@socalsem.edu
OBSTA, Kim .... 361-572-6410. 493 H kim.obsta@victoriacollege.edu
OBUCHAN, Peter, G .... 617-730-7255. 235 D peter.obuchan@newbury.edu
OBURN, Martha .... 713-718-8670. 473 C martha.oburn@hccs.edu
OCAMPO, Arturo .... 760-750-4309... 35 A aocampo@csusm.edu
OCASIO, Arcadio .... 787-257-0000. 554 B arcadio.ocasio@upr.edu
OCCHIOGROSSO, Paul, F ... 212-650-8276. 317 D pocchiogrosso@ccny.cuny.edu
OCHALA, Pam .... 304-647-6250. 530 B pochala@osteo.wvsom.edu
OCHALEK, Garrett .... 313-664-7815. 241 C gochalek@collegeforcreativestudies.edu
OCHANDER, Scott .... 260-982-5890. 170 U sdochander@manchester.edu
OCHELTREE, Jodi .... 304-462-4111. 529 G jodi.ocheltree@glenville.edu
OCHNIO, Carl .... 860-512-3372... 88 G cochnio@manchestercc.edu
OCHOA, Daniel .... 210-829-2707. 490 A ochoa@uiwtx.edu
OCHOA, Eduardo, M .... 831-582-3532... 34 B emochoa@csumb.edu
OCHOA, Robert, L .... 956-721-5417. 475 F rochoa@laredo.edu
OCHOA, Salvador, H ...... 956-665-3627. 492 B shochoa@utpa.edu
OCHS, Joy, E .... 319-363-8213. 181 C jochs@mtmercy.edu
OCHS, Wayne, T .... 814-732-2757. 428 E wochs@edinboro.edu
OCHSNER, Debbie .... 307-532-8238. 542 a debbie.ochsner@ewc.wy.edu
OCHSNER, Tom, J .... 402-465-2212. 291 G tjo@nebrwesleyan.edu
OCKEN, Scott .... 515-964-6364. 177 B sjocken@dmacc.edu
OCMAND, Lydia .... 504-468-2900. 207 B admissions@southwest.edu
OCONNELL KILLEN, Patricia ... 509-313-6503. 520 A killen@gonzaga.edu
OCONNER, William .... 410-293-1000. 545 J william.oconner@usna.com
ODARTEY-WILLIAMS, Edmund ... 386-226-6155. 102 B edmund.odartey@erau.edu
ODATO, David .... 415-353-4028... 72 A david.odato@hr.ucsf.edu
ODDEN, Janet .... 918-335-6879. 398 F jodden@okwu.edu
ODEGARD, Ilene .... 701-777-3904. 371 C ilene.odegard@und.edu
ODELL, David .... 805-565-6110... 76 D dodell@westmont.edu
ODELL, Kathy .... 704-463-3011. 365 E kathy.odell@fsmail.pfeiffer.edu
ODELL, Lynda .... 775-831-1314. 295 F lodell@sierranevada.edu
ODELL, Margaret .... 505-984-6066. 311 H careerservices@sjcsf.edu
ODEN, Cassandra, L ...... 412-397-4342. 431 I oden@rmu.edu
ODEN, JR., Joseph .... 304-766-3288. 530 C odenjr@wvstateu.edu
ODENBECK, Lisa .... 513-244-4475. 377 G lisa_odenbeck@mail.msj.edu
ODENWALD, Arlene, V ..... 410-455-2624. 219 D
ODENWALD, Joseph .... 601-925-3248. 268 A Odenwald@mc.edu
ODGERS, Cindy .... 602-243-8029... 15 F cindy.odgers@southmountaincc.edu
ODHNER, Carroll, C ...... 267-502-2547. 410 I carroll.odhner@brynathyn.edu
ODI, Henry, U .... 610-758-5923. 422 A huo0@lehigh.edu
ODIORNE, David, R .... 315-568-3214. 333 C dodiorne@nycc.edu
ODLE, Gary .... 785-738-9028. 189 F godle@ncktc.edu
ODOM, Amee, M .... 704-233-8096. 370 G ameeodom@wingate.edu
ODOM, Don .... 601-318-6175. 270 I dodom@wmcarey.edu
ODOM, Gale .... 318-869-5235. 201 H godom@centenary.edu
ODOM, James .... 870-762-3154... 19 K jodom@smail.anc.edu
ODOM, Julia .... 925-631-4529... 61 F jodom@stmarys-ca.edu
ODOM, Katherine .... 251-981-3771...... 2 I katherine.odom@columbiasouthern.edu
ODOM, Laura .... 219-785-5545. 172 A lodom@pnc.edu
ODOM, Leslie, R .... 972-265-5744. 488 F lodom@udallas.edu
ODOM, Lorraine .... 206-878-3710. 520 E lodom@highline.edu
ODOM, Mark, R .... 325-793-4780. 476 E modom@mcm.edu
ODOM, Megan .... 530-898-5253... 33 A modom@csuchico.edu
ODOM, III, Olin, O ...... 254-442-5130. 468 I olin.odom@cisco.edu
ODOM, Tammy .... 479-394-7622... 23 B todom@rmcc.edu
ODUCADO, Joey .... 691-320-2481. 546 B joducado@comfsm.fm
ODUTOLA, Adelaja, O .... 804-257-5697. 515 F aodutola@vuu.edu
ODUWOLE, Adeola .... 409-747-4875. 493 C aoduwole@utmb.edu
ODVODY, Dwayne, E .... 828-262-4002. 367 A odvodyde@appstate.edu
OECHSLI, Alice .... 406-275-4972. 288 C alice_oechsli@skc.edu
OECHSLI, Kori, D .... 530-226-4941... 66 D koechsli@simpsonu.edu
OEHLER, Candace .... 602-787-6606... 15 B candace.oehler@paradisevalley.edu
OEHLERKING, Kelly .... 605-394-4034. 452 E kelly.oehlerking@wdt.edu
OELKLAUS, Maurice .... 816-654-7212. 275 K moelklaus@kcumb.edu
OELSCHLAGER, Sharon, G ... 412-396-5028. 415 F goedert@duq.edu
OEN-HOXIE, Tina .... 616-234-3925. 243 B thoxie@grcc.edu
OERLY-BENNETT, Sandra ... 304-876-5470. 529 I sbennett@shepherd.edu
OERTLI, Gary .... 206-934-5311. 522 H gary.oertli@seattlecolleges.edu
OERTLI, Gary, L .... 206-934-5311. 523 A gary.oertli@seattlecolleges.edu
OESMAN, Jackie .... 908-737-4835. 302 F catholic@kean.edu
OESTER, Stephanie .... 541-881-5806. 408 C soester@tvcc.cc
OESTMANN, Deborah .... 620-252-7075. 185 O debbio@coffeyville.edu
OESTREICHER, Edina, R .. 203-576-4392... 91 G edinao@bridgeport.edu
OETTING, Stephanie, J ... 260-399-7700. 174 C soetting@sf.edu
OFE, Suellen, S .... 334-833-4515..... 4 D ofe@huntingdon.edu
OFFERMAN, Dana .... 480-517-8270... 15 D dana.offerman@riosalado.edu
OFFERMANN, Joseph .... 815-729-9020. 149 A joffermann@jjc.edu
OFFICER, Danielle .... 212-237-8185. 318 D dofficer@jjay.cuny.edu
OFFORD, Jerome .... 573-681-5483. 276 C offordj@lincolnu.edu
OFFORD, JR., Jerome .... 573-681-5502. 276 C offordj@lincolnu.edu
OFODILE, Caroline .... 201-447-9242. 299 C cofodile@bergen.edu
OFOSU, Joseph .... 860-231-5538... 92 F jofosu@usj.edu
OGAN, Belinda .... 913-621-8740. 186 C bogan@donnelly.edu
OGANS, Keith .... 405-733-7306. 399 F kogans@rose.edu
OGAWA, Michael .... 419-372-0433. 374 K mogawa@bgsu.edu
OGAWA, Michael, Y .... 419-372-0433. 374 K mogawa@bgsu.edu
OGAWA, Timothy .... 617-262-5000. 223 F tim.ogawa@the-bac.edu
OGBAA, Clara .... 203-285-2058... 88 E cogbaa@gwcc.commnet.edu
OGBAR, Jeffrey .... 860-486-5701... 92 A jeffrey.ogbar@uconn.edu
OGBURN, Shawn, D .... 701-788-4795. 371 E Shawn.Ogburn@mayvillestate.edu
OGDEN, Bernie .... 559-278-2182... 33 D bogden@csufresno.edu
OGDEN, David .... 931-540-2822. 460 E wogden@columbiastate.edu
OGDEN, Ervin .... 912-358-4350. 131 C ogdene@savannahstate.edu
OGDEN, Jodi .... 713-500-3968. 492 E jodi.ogden@uth.tmc.edu
OGDEN, Linda, J .... 740-362-3121. 383 H logden@mtso.edu
OGDEN, Paul, E .... 979-436-0202. 484 B ogden@medicine.tamhsc.edu
OGDEN, Rachel .... 814-860-5118. 420 E rogden@lecom.edu
OGDEN, Thomas, A .... 412-268-6232. 412 H togden@andrew.cmu.edu
OGEA, Reggie, R .... 504-282-4455. 206 A rogea@nobts.edu
OGEKA, Alex .... 610-683-4110. 429 A ogeka@Give2Ku.org
OGENE, Chidi .... 904-680-7630. 103 Q cogene@fcsl.edu
OGG, E. Jerald .... 731-881-7010. 463 E jogg@utm.edu
OGG, Laurie .... 707-664-2036... 36 B laurie.ogg@sonoma.edu
OGILVIE, dt .... 585-475-7181. 337 L dt@saunders.rit.edu
OGILVIE, Kristie .... 620-341-5274. 186 D kogilvie@emporia.edu
OGLE, Christophor, M .... 920-748-8111. 535 J oglec@ripon.edu
OGLE, Edward, H .... 920-923-7604. 534 A eogle@marianuniversity.edu
OGLE, Kaci .... 256-782-5405..... 4 K kogle@jsu.edu
OGLE, Robert .... 617-262-5000. 223 F Robert.Ogle@the-bac.edu
OGLES, Benjamin, M ...... 801-422-2084. 495 D ben_ogles@byu.edu
OGLESBY, Joni .... 321-674-8700. 104 H joglesby@fit.edu
OGLESBY, Lindsay .... 888-384-0849... 27 E loglesby@allied.edu
OGONJI, Gilbert .... 410-951-4124. 220 B gogonji@coppin.edu
OGOREK, Richard, W ...... 813-253-6214. 118 L rogorek@ut.edu
OGREN, Kathy .... 909-748-8359... 73 H kathy_ogren@redlands.edu
OGRODNIK, Eugene, C .. 412-362-8500. 430 G pims5808@aol.com
OGUNNAIKE, Babatunde, A ... 302-831-8017... 94 B ogunnaik@udel.edu
OGUNSOLA, Elizabeth ..... 262-472-5669. 538 D ogunsole@uww.edu
OH, Myeong, H .... 636-327-4645. 277 K mhoh@midwest.edu
OHIA, Sunny, E .... 713-313-1133. 485 F ohiase@tsu.edu
OHL, Vicki .... 419-448-2216. 380 G vohl@heidelberg.edu
OHL-GIGLIOTTI, Christine ... 304-243-2301. 531 H christineog@wju.edu
OHLANDT, George, W ...... 843-792-3281. 445 B ohlandtg@musc.edu
OHLE, Jack, R .... 507-933-7538. 255 I president@gustavus.edu
OHLEMACHER, Janet .... 410-386-8195. 214 A johlemacher@carrollcc.edu
OHLENDORF, Patricia, A 512-471-1241. 491 C pohlendorf@austin.utexas.edu
OHLES, Frederik .... 402-465-2217. 291 G president@nebrwesleyan.edu
OHLHOUS, Paula .... 518-381-1304. 340 G ohlhoup@sunysccc.edu
OHLINGER, Brian, J ...... 804-828-9647. 511 F bjohling@vcu.edu
OHLMANN, Eric, H .... 904-264-2172. 111 P eohlmann@iws.edu
OHLSON, Carl, J .... 845-938-4379. 545 I Carl.Ohlson@usma.edu
OHM, Paul .... 269-660-8021. 249 C ohmp@millercollege.edu
OHMAN, Jessica .... 316-322-3231. 185 D johman@butlercc.edu
OHNESORGE, Karen .... 785-242-5200. 189 I karen.ohnesorge@ottawa.edu
OHOTNICKY, John .... 413-572-8971. 230 F johotnicky@westfield.ma.edu
OHOTNICKY, Julianne ..... 413-585-4940. 236 H johotnic@smith.edu
OIDA, Yuzo .... 808-983-4120. 135 G oida@tokai.edu
OIE, Svein .... 706-542-1914. 133 C soie@rx.uga.edu
OIKELOME, Gloria .... 610-989-1451. 436 D goikelome@vfmac.edu
OILAR, Natasha, J .... 206-239-2311. 516 H noilar@aii.edu
OISHI, Elaine .... 808-735-4728. 135 D eoishi@chaminade.edu
OJEDA, Jessica .... 787-786-3030. 547 F jojeda@ucb.edu.pr
OJEDA-CARCAMO, Sergio ... 787-763-6700. 549 A drsojeda@se-pr.edu
OJEISEKHOBA, John, O . 562-903-4877... 29 L john.o.ojeisekhoba@biola.edu
OJEZUA, Theresa .... 501-570-5263... 22 F tojezua@philander.edu
OJIBWAY, Michael, A ..... 715-833-6343. 539 J mojibway2@cvtc.edu
OJIKUTU, Kunle .... 360-650-2926. 525 C kunle.ojikutu@wwu.edu
OKADA, Daniel, T .... 671-735-5545. 546 C daniel.okada1@guamcc.edu
OKADA, David, S .... 671-735-2902. 546 E dsokada@uguam.uog.edu
OKADA, Mary, Y .... 671-735-5700. 546 C gccpresident@guamcc.edu
OKAGAKI, Lynn .... 302-831-2394... 94 B okagaki@udel.edu
OKAMOTO, Mark .... 678-225-7340. 430 D mokamoto@pcom.edu
OKAMOTO LANE, Susan ..... 206-281-2598. 523 C solane@spu.edu
OKAMOTO-VAUGHN, Wilma ... 209-478-0800... 47 M wvaughn@humphreys.edu
OKANDA, Fred .... 731-426-7599. 455 J fokanda@lanecollege.edu
OKAY, Kathleen .... 973-300-2257. 307 F kokay@sussex.edu
OKEKE, Charles .... 702-651-7425. 294 E charles.okeke@csn.edu
OKEREKE, Augustine ...... 718-270-5135. 319 A augokereke@mec.cuny.edu
OKESSON, Gregg .... 859-858-2261. 192 A
OKLANDER, Sergio .... 760-245-4271... 75 B sergio.oklander@vvc.edu
OKOLI, Chuks .... 617-541-5343. 232 G cokoli@rcc.mass.edu
OKORONKWO, Josephine .... 504-286-5361. 206 K jokoronkwo@suno.edu
OKOYE, Stephen .... 601-979-2071. 267 E sokoye@jsums.edu
OKUDA, Alex, H .... 949-480-4159... 66 F aokuda@soka.edu
OKUN, Gail .... 973-278-5400. 314 K gso@berkeleycollege.edu
OKUN, Gail .... 973-278-5400. 299 D gso@berkeleycollege.edu
OLAN, David .... 212-817-7200. 317 F dolan@gc.cuny.edu
OLANDER, Renee .... 757-363-4108. 507 N rolander@odu.edu
OLATUNJI, Aderonke ...... 925-439-2181... 42 A aolatunji@losmedanos.edu
OLAVE, Ricardo .... 312-777-8680. 147 D rolave@aii.edu
OLBERDING, Kristina ..... 513-562-8773. 373 K kolberding@artacademy.edu
OLBERT, Doug .... 602-429-4971... 16 O dolbert@ps.edu
OLCESE, Chuck .... 785-864-3617. 190 L colcese@ku.edu
OLCOTT, Sarah .... 507-453-2516. 262 A solcott@winona.edu
OLD BEAR, Te-Atta .... 406-638-3106. 286 D oldbeart@lbhc.edu
OLDANI, John .... 636-949-4993. 276 D joldani@lindenwood.edu
OLDENKAMP, Mike .... 712-324-5061. 181 G mikeo@nwicc.edu
OLDFIELD, Curt .... 309-649-6200. 160 E curt.oldfield@src.edu
OLDFIELD, Melody, K .... 541-737-3871. 406 A university.marketing@oregonstate.edu
OLDHAM, Betty, A .... 208-496-1112. 137 H oldhamb@byui.edu
OLDHAM, Larry .... 731-989-6649. 454 J loldham@fhu.edu
OLDHAM, Philip, B .... 931-372-3241. 460 A poldham@tntech.edu
OLDHAM, Steve .... 254-295-4505. 490 B soldham@umhb.edu
OLDHAM, Todd, M .... 585-292-3057. 332 A toldham@monroecc.edu
OLDHAM, Vickie .... 229-430-4671. 119 J vickie.oldham@asurams.edu
OLDHOUSER DAVIS, Kay .... 803-938-3746. 448 F kayo@uscsumter.edu
OLDS, Carole .... 719-502-3249... 84 A carole.olds@ppcc.edu
OLDS, G. Richard .... 951-827-4564... 71 E richard.olds@ucr.edu
OLDS, Kim .... 617-217-9040. 222 G kolds@baystate.edu
OLDS, Terlynn .... 412-365-1650. 412 K tolds@chatham.edu
OLEGERIIL, Jay .... 680-488-2471. 547 B jayo@palau.edu
OLEKA, Sam .... 502-597-6411. 197 A sam.oleka@kysu.edu

OLEKSIW, Steven .... 718-780-7982. 315 H steven.oleksiw@brooklaw.edu
OLEN, Lynda .... 251-380-4195..... 7 D lolen@shc.edu
OLENCHAK, Richard .... 713-743-4984. 489 B richard0@central.uh.edu
OLENDER, Ursula, J .... 413-542-8203. 221 G uolender@amherst.edu
OLER, Elizabeth .... 312-935-4232. 148 C eoler@icsw.edu
OLER, Gregory, S .... 410-516-8000. 215 H goler@jhu.edu
OLESIUK, Sue .... 828-398-7176. 357 N sueholesiuk@abtech.edu
OLESON, Elizabeth .... 563-589-3178. 182 J eoleson@dbq.edu
OLESON, Misty .... 918-781-7225. 394 D olesonm@bacone.edu
OLESON-BRIGGS, Susan .... 704-330-6022. 359 C susan.oleson-briggs@cpcc.edu
OLESZEWSKI, Susan ...... 215-276-6070. 433 A sueo@salus.edu
OLGUIN, Javier, E .... 972-860-5306. 470 I JavierEOlguin@dcccd.edu
OLGUIN-RYAN, Elizabeth .... 915-831-6325. 472 B eolguin@epcc.edu
OLIAN, Judy, D .... 310-825-7982... 71 C judy.olian@anderson.ucla.edu
OLIARO, Paul, M .... 559-278-2541... 33 D poliaro@csufresno.edu
OLIKONG, Deikola .... 680-488-2471. 547 B olikongd@gmail.com
OLIN, Jen .... 207-948-9273. 211 I jolin@unity.edu
OLIN, Jessica .... 302-736-2455... 94 C jessica.olin@wesley.edu
OLIN, Joanna .... 413-559-5521. 227 B
OLIN, Robert, F .... 205-348-5972..... 8 D olin@as.ua.edu
OLINER, Alex .... 212-349-4330. 325 D aoliner@globe.edu
OLINER, Martin .... 212-349-4330. 325 D moliner@globe.edu
OLINGER, CSC, Gerard, J .... 503-943-8532. 408 F olinger@up.edu
OLINGER, Richard, P ..... 814-868-7767. 420 E rpolinger@mch1.org
OLINGER, Ronald, J .... 913-360-7413. 184 H rolinger@benedictine.edu
OLINICK, Erin .... 510-666-8248... 26 F eolinick@aimc.edu
OLION, LaDelle .... 910-672-1074. 367 D lolion@uncfsu.edu
OLIPHANT, Uretz, S .... 217-333-5465. 162 A uretz.oliphant@carle.com
OLIVA, Giacomo .... 212-217-4040. 324 C giacomo_oliva@fitnyc.edu
OLIVA, Joseph, E .... 718-990-6421. 339 A olivaj@stjohns.edu
OLIVA, Robert .... 718-951-5696. 317 C boliva@brooklyn.cuny.edu
OLIVARES, Carlos .... 787-279-1912. 550 B colivares@bayamon.inter.edu
OLIVARES, Jose .... 201-360-4131. 302 D jolivares@hccc.edu
OLIVAREZ, Juan .... 616-632-2880. 239 E juan.olivarez@aquinas.edu
OLIVE, David, W .... 276-326-4466. 502 H dolive@bluefield.edu
OLIVE, Kenneth, E .... 423-439-6315. 459 C olivek@etsu.edu
OLIVE, Nancy .... 605-331-6770. 452 D nancy.olive@usiouxfalls.edu
OLIVE-TAYLOR, Becky .... 336-278-6500. 354 B oliveb@elon.edu
OLIVEIRA, Sandra, J ...... 401-865-2602. 439 E solivei6@providence.edu
OLIVER, Astrid .... 970-247-7507... 81 M oliver_a@fortlewis.edu
OLIVER, Bob .... 435-283-7221. 498 A bob.oliver@snow.edu
OLIVER, Carolyne, B .... 713-313-7097. 485 F olivercb@tsu.edu
OLIVER, David, J .... 515-294-6344. 175 H doliver@iastate.edu
OLIVER, Debra .... 937-708-5748. 393 A doliver@wilberforce.edu
OLIVER, Denita .... 256-215-4290..... 2 G doliver@cacc.edu
OLIVER, Erik .... 802-383-6662. 499 A eoliver@champlain.edu
OLIVER, James .... 229-430-4702. 119 J james.oliver@asurams.edu
OLIVER, Janet, W .... 231-995-1076. 248 B joliver@nmc.edu
OLIVER, Jeanette, J .... 713-313-7104. 485 F oliver_jj@tsu.edu
OLIVER, Jeanne .... 503-352-2740. 407 A jeanne1@pacificu.edu
OLIVER, Jeannie .... 901-369-0835... 96 F
OLIVER, Jenea .... 816-235-6011. 283 D oliverj@umkc.edu
OLIVER, Jenna .... 970-339-6202... 78 C jenna.oliver@aims.com
OLIVER, Kenneth, R .... 660-248-6223. 272 B koliver@centralmethodist.edu
OLIVER, Lawrence .... 802-485-2187. 500 A loliver@norwich.edu
OLIVER, Lillian, M .... 787-723-4481. 548 A loliver@ceaprc.edu
OLIVER, OSF, M. Marilyn .... 260-399-7700. 174 C moliver@sf.edu
OLIVER, Melvin, L .... 805-893-8354... 72 B moliver@ltsc.ucsb.edu
OLIVER, Parker .... 931-598-1586. 458 H pwoliver@sewanee.edu
OLIVER, Patricia Belton .. 713-743-2400. 489 B poliver@central.uh.edu
OLIVER, Rebecca .... 870-972-2308... 19 N rsoliver@astate.edu
OLIVER, Richard, E .... 573-884-6705. 283 C oliverr@missouri.edu
OLIVER, Robert, C .... 605-274-4111. 449 K rob.oliver@augie.edu
OLIVER, Ruben, D .... 405-466-2996. 395 N rdoliver@langston.edu
OLIVER, Samuel W. "Dub" .... 903-923-2222. 471 J doliver@etbu.edu
OLIVER, Sandi .... 803-738-7699. 445 C olivers@midlandstech.edu
OLIVER, Sharon, J .... 919-530-5313. 368 A soliver@nccu.edu
OLIVER, Sharon, M .... 207-581-1561. 212 B smoliver@maine.edu
OLIVER, Shawn .... 609-497-7818. 304 D shawn.oliver@ptsem.edu
OLIVER, Thomas .... 830-372-8050. 485 C toliver@tlu.edu
OLIVER, Timothy .... 909-382-4021... 61 J toliver@sbccd.cc.ca.us
OLIVER PUTNAM, Patricia, T .... 619-260-7430... 73 I poliver@sandiego.edu
OLIVERA, Robert .... 510-261-8500... 58 G robert.olivera@patten.edu
OLIVERAS, Ivette .... 787-848-1589. 551 O ioliveras@popac.edu
OLIVERIA, Steve .... 707-468-3081... 54 B soliveria@mendocino.edu
OLIVERO, Paula .... 724-738-2683. 429 F paula.olivero@sru.edu
OLIVEROS, Jon .... 847-397-0300. 139 G
OLIVERSON, Richard ...... 316-942-4291. 189 E oliversonr@newmanu.edu
OLIVETTE, Michael .... 914-606-6912. 350 F michael.olivette@sunywcc.edu
OLIVIERI, Janies .... 787-250-1912. 550 E jolivieri@metro.inter.edu
OLIVIERI-LENAHAN, Elizabeth .... 914-633-2547. 327 C eolivieri@iona.edu
OLIVO, Cynthia, D .... 626-585-7074... 58 F cdolivo@pasadena.edu
OLIVO, Michael .... 516-323-4840. 331 J molivo@molloy.edu
OLKHOVSKAYA, Elena ... 510-436-1037... 47 J olkhovskaya@hnu.edu
OLKIEWICZ, Rose .... 920-748-8137. 535 J bookstore@ripon.edu
OLLER, Robert .... 954-262-4399. 109 K roller@nova.edu
OLLEY, Lorraine .... 847-566-6401. 162 G lolley@usml.edu
OLLIFF, Thomas .... 954-201-7693... 99 D toliff@broward.edu
OLLIVER, James .... 727-394-6111. 112 E olliver.james@spcollege.edu
OLLSON, Joanne .... 413-782-1343. 238 A jollson@wne.edu
OLMSTEAD, Audrey .... 248-689-8282. 251 I aolmstea@walshcollege.edu
OLMSTEAD, Karen, L ...... 410-543-6489. 220 D klolmstead@salisbury.edu
OLMSTEAD, Steve .... 918-293-4744. 398 B steve.olmstead@okstate.edu
OLMSTEAD, Thomas .... 505-473-6027. 311 K thomas.olmstead@santafeuniversity.edu
OLMSTED, Joanna .... 585-275-4827. 349 C joanna.olmsted@rochester.edu
OLNEY, Douglas, P .... 218-755-2764. 258 A dolney@bemidjistate.edu
OLOVSON, Matthew .... 231-591-2152. 242 F olovsom@ferris.edu
OLSCHWANG, Alana ...... 909-607-8135... 39 C alana.olschwang@cgu.edu
OLSEN, Andy .... 620-241-0723. 185 K
OLSEN, Anika .... 928-523-1428... 16 C anika.olsen@nau.edu
OLSEN, Ann, E .... 502-272-8133. 192 E aolsen@bellarmine.edu
OLSEN, Chris, W .... 608-262-5246. 536 D cwolsen@wisc.edu
OLSEN, Danny, R .... 801-422-5648. 495 D danny_olsen@byu.edu
OLSEN, Gary, R .... 570-941-7723. 436 A gary.olsen@scranton.edu
OLSEN, Jim .... 772-546-5534. 106 N jolsencpa@aol.com
OLSEN, Jo .... 218-723-7040. 254 K jolsen@css.edu
OLSEN, John, S .... 901-843-3795. 458 E olsen@rhodes.edu
OLSEN, Julene .... 435-722-6900. 496 M julene@ubatc.edu
OLSEN, Kris .... 714-628-7303... 38 A kolsen@chapman.edu
OLSEN, Matthew .... 918-495-7707. 398 H maolsen@oru.edu
OLSEN, Michelle .... 701-224-2540. 371 B michelle.olsen@ndus.edu
OLSEN, Morgan, R .... 480-727-9920... 11 K morgan.r.olsen@asu.edu
OLSEN, Pete .... 831-645-1362... 54 I polsen@mpc.edu
OLSEN, Renee .... 208-792-2151. 138 G rmolsen@lcsc.edu
OLSEN, Steven, A .... 310-825-3444... 71 C solsen@conet.ucla.edu
OLSEN, Steven, M .... 716-878-4113. 343 A olsensw@buffalostate.edu
OLSEN KELLY, Jodi .... 206-296-5405. 523 E jkelly@seattleu.edu
OLSEN KRENGEL, Jennifer .... 651-641-3516. 256 J jolsenkrengel001@luthersem.edu
OLSHINSKY, Martin .... 304-214-8800. 528 G molshinsky@wvncc.edu
OLSON, Allen .... 360-596-5283. 524 A aolson@spscc.edu
OLSON, Andrea, I .... 425-739-8127. 520 K andrea.olson@lwtech.edu
OLSON, Bette .... 402-465-7518. 291 G bolson@nebrwesleyan.edu
OLSON, Cari .... 701-858-3323. 371 F cari.olson@minotstateu.edu
OLSON, Carolyn .... 320-308-5156. 261 C colson@sctcc.edu
OLSON, Cathy .... 413-755-4419. 233 A colson@stcc.edu
OLSON, Chris .... 916-608-6500... 53 C
OLSON, Christa .... 515-271-2084. 177 K christa.olson@drake.edu
OLSON, Craige, J .... 801-581-8951. 496 Q dentaled@hsc.utah.edu
OLSON, Dawn .... 701-483-2027. 371 D Dawn.M.Olson.1@dickinsonstate.edu
OLSON, Don .... 218-723-6471. 254 K dolson@css.edu
OLSON, Doug, A .... 715-833-6237. 539 J dolson@cvtc.edu
OLSON, Douglas .... 708-456-0300. 161 A dolson@triton.edu
OLSON, Dustin .... 805-893-4151... 72 B dustin.olson@police.ucsb.edu
OLSON, Gail, M .... 651-201-1750. 257 N gail.olson@so.mnscu.edu
OLSON, Gary, A .... 716-839-8210. 322 E gaolson@daemen.edu
OLSON, Heidi, L .... 320-222-5209. 260 H heidi.olson@ridgewater.edu
OLSON, Ian .... 907-474-5317... 10 I inolson@alaska.edu
OLSON, Jeffery, D .... 651-638-6241. 253 K jeff-olson@bethel.edu
OLSON, Jeffrey .... 605-455-6055. 450 I jolson@olc.edu
OLSON, Joan, G .... 612-874-3745. 257 B joan_olson@mcad.edu
OLSON, Joe .... 541-440-4600. 408 D Joe.Olson@umpqua.edu
OLSON, John .... 425-388-9407. 519 I jolson@everettcc.edu
OLSON, Judith .... 760-591-3012. 118 I jolson@usa.edu
OLSON, Kerry, J .... 409-882-3362. 486 G kerry.olson@lsco.edu
OLSON, Ksenia .... 218-723-6139. 254 K kolson@nebook.com
OLSON, Linda .... 610-341-5930. 415 G lolson@eastern.edu
OLSON, Louise .... 401-454-6323. 440 A lolson@risd.edu
OLSON, Lynette .... 620-235-4113. 189 L lolson@pittstate.edu
OLSON, Mark, J .... 703-812-4757. 506 H molson@leland.edu
OLSON, Marlene .... 860-343-5869... 89 A molson@mxcc.commnet.edu
OLSON, MaryEllen .... 325-674-6540. 464 H meo10b@acu.edu
OLSON, Matthew .... 781-280-3802. 232 B olsonm@middlesex.mass.edu
OLSON, Megan .... 907-786-1764... 10 H msolson5@uaa.alaska.edu
OLSON, Michael .... 504-864-7051. 205 H olson@loyno.edu
OLSON, Nancy .... 641-585-8147. 183 D olsonn@waldorf.edu
OLSON, Nancy .... 217-732-3168. 151 B nolson@lincolnchristian.edu
OLSON, Neil .... 573-882-3768. 283 C olsonne@missouri.edu
OLSON, Ray, A .... 614-235-4136. 390 A rolson@TLSohio.edu
OLSON, Roberta, K .... 605-688-5178. 452 B roberta.olson@sdstate.edu
OLSON, Sandra .... 508-929-8025. 230 G solson@worcester.edu
OLSON, Sara, M .... 402-465-2185. 291 G solson@nebrwesleyan.edu
OLSON, Scott .... 906-635-2828. 245 G solson@lssu.edu
OLSON, Scott, R .... 507-457-5003. 262 A solson@winona.edu
OLSON, Shari, L .... 602-243-8035... 15 F shari.olson@southmountaincc.edu
OLSON, Shelly, Y .... 715-833-6675. 539 J solson@cvtc.edu
OLSON, Sheryl .... 763-424-0882. 260 C solson@nhcc.edu
OLSON, Stanley, N .... 563-589-0200. 183 F solson@wartburgseminary.edu
OLSON, Stephen .... 765-998-5119. 173 C stolson@taylor.edu
OLSON, Steve, J .... 253-535-7177. 521 I olsonsj@plu.edu
OLSON, Terry .... 701-572-9275. 372 F tolson@wscfoundation.com
OLSON, Todd .... 202-687-4056... 95 E tao4@georgetown.edu
OLSON, Warren .... 785-227-3380. 184 I olsonw@bethanylb.edu
OLSON, Wendy, Z .... 509-777-4306. 525 F wolson@whitworth.edu
OLSON-LOY, Sandra ...... 320-589-6013. 264 F olsonloy@morris.umn.edu
OLSSON, Jackie .... 763-424-0731. 260 C jolsson@nhcc.edu
OLSSON, Roy .... 616-331-3358. 243 C olssonr@gvsu.edu
OLSTEIN, Binyamin .... 847-982-2500. 146 C olstein@htc.edu
OLSWANG, Steven .... 206-239-4500. 517 M solswang@cityu.edu
OLSZEWSKI, Gabriel, G .. 203-432-2330... 93 A gabriel.olszewski@yale.edu
OLTMAN, Eva .... 502-213-4245. 195 F eva.oltman@kctcs.edu
OLTROGGE, Michael ...... 402-494-2311. 290 O moltrogge@thenicc.edu
OLUIC, Steven .... 440-525-7079. 382 M soluic@lakelandcc.edu
OLVERA, Eve, N .... 239-513-1135. 119 E eolvera@wolford.edu
OLZINSKI, Len .... 570-740-0370. 422 G lolzinski@luzerne.edu
OMACHONU, John, O .... 615-898-2329. 459 D john.omachonu@mtsu.edu
OMAN, Nina .... 509-865-8500. 520 D oman_n@heritage.edu
OMDAHL, Becky .... 651-793-1466. 259 C becky.omdahl@metrostate.edu
OMUNDSON, J. Andrew 864-941-8376. 446 C omundson.a@ptc.edu
ONAIFO, Greg .... 212-410-8044. 333 E gonaifo@nycpm.edu
ONARAL, Banu .... 215-895-2247. 415 B banu.onaral@drexel.edu
ONASCH, Charles .... 419-372-7197. 374 K conasch@bgsu.edu
ONDERDONK, Todd, D .. 512-637-5632. 479 C toddo@stedwards.edu
ONDRUS, Sherri .... 480-731-8014... 14 I sherri.ondrus@domail.maricopa.edu
ONEAL, Gayle .... 804-524-5087. 515 D goneal@vsu.edu
ONEAL, Susan .... 918-595-7378. 400 E susan.oneal@tulsacc.edu
ONEST, Trevor .... 304-829-7757. 526 D tonest@bethanywv.edu
ONEY, Veronica, E .... 302-259-6135... 93 E voney@dtcc.edu
ONG, Teresa .... 650-949-7549... 44 N ongteresa@fhda.edu
ONGARO, Giulio .... 209-946-2417... 73 A gongaro@pacific.edu

ONGLEY, David ... 907-852-3333... 10 F
david.ongley@ilisagvik.edu
ONION, Matthew ... 606-326-2113. 194 J
matthew.onion@kctcs.edu
ONION, Patricia ... 360-383-3070. 525 D
ponion@whatcom.ctc.edu
ONISHI, Joni ... 808-934-2514. 136 F
jonishi@hawaii.edu
ONLEY, Francesca ... 215-637-7700. 418 G
fonley@holyfamily.edu
ONLEY, Patrick ... 410-209-6040. 213 F
ponley@bccc.edu
ONO, Santa, J ... 513-556-2201. 390 G
president@uc.edu
ONOCHIE, Philip ... 817-923-8459. 469 F
philip.onochie@fishermore.edu
ONODERA, Yasushi ... 479-964-0832... 20 E
yonodera@atu.edu
ONOFRIETTI, Joseph ... 617-735-9746. 226 B
onofrij@emmanuel.edu
ONORATO, Suzanne ... 404-471-6000. 119 I
sonorato@agnesscott.edu
ONSAGER, Erin ... 303-937-4553... 79 E
eonsager@chu.edu
ONSAGER, Lawrence, W 269-471-3275. 239 D
lonsager@andrews.edu
ONTIVEROS, Mary, R ... 970-491-7197... 80 I
mary.ontiveros@colostate.edu
ONTIVEROS, Ramiro ... 916-649-2400... 30 C
ONTJES, Joe ... 316-677-9400. 191 E
jontjes@watc.edu
ONTL, Lynn ... 518-255-5225. 344 E
ontll@cobleskill.edu
ONWILER, Thomas ... 408-270-6410... 63 N
thomas.onwiler@sjeccd.org
ONWUBUARIRI, Marie ... 510-841-1905... 27 H
marieo@absw.edu
ONWUNLI, Agatha ... 850-599-3115. 114 K
agatha.onwunli@famu.edu
ONYEAGHALA, Raphael ... 507-537-6218. 261 F
Raphael.Onyeaghala@smsu.edu
OOLIE, Janis ... 973-748-9000. 299 F
janis_oolie@bloomfield.edu
OORDT, Stan ... 712-722-6401. 177 J
stan.oordt@dordt.edu
OOSTERHOUS, Karen ... 724-503-1001. 436 G
koosterhous@washjeff.edu
OPALKA, Susan ... 602-393-5900... 12 M
sopalka@carrington.edu
OPAR, Michael, E ... 563-333-6152. 182 B
OparMichaelE@sau.edu
OPATZ, Joe ... 952-358-8150. 260 B
joe.opatz@normandale.edu
OPATZ, Patrick ... 651-779-3279. 258 C
patrick.opatz@century.edu
OPAVA, William ... 617-731-7143. 235 H
wopava@pmc.edu
OPELKA, Frank ... 504-568-4769. 204 N
fopelka@lsuhsc.edu
OPENSHAW, James, N ... 843-953-7184. 442 A
james.openshaw@citadel.edu
OPGENORTH, Timothy ... 312-996-5563. 161 D
timothy1@uic.edu
OPHEIM, Cynthia, L ... 512-245-2205. 487 C
co01@txstate.edu
OPITZ, Brian, R ... 724-287-8711. 411 C
brian.opitz@bc3.edu
OPLER, Daniel ... 718-405-3235. 320 G
daniel.opler@mountsaintvincent.edu
OPP, Mike ... 651-423-8232. 258 D
mike.opp@dctc.edu
OPPEL, Amanda ... 972-773-8800. 450 G
aoppel@national.edu
OPPENHEIM, Liza ... 603-623-0313. 297 E
loppenheim@nhia.edu
OPPENHEIMER, Martin .. 212-678-8804. 328 A
maoppenheimer@jtsa.edu
OPPENHEIMER, Martin .. 617-627-3337. 237 C
martin.oppenheimer@tufts.edu
OPPENHEIMER,
Phillip, R ... 209-946-2561... 73 A
poppenhe@pacific.edu
OPPENLANDER, Fritz ... 563-425-5354. 183 B
oppenlanderf@uiu.edu
OPPERMAN,
Mary George, G ... 607-255-3621. 322 A
mgo5@cornell.edu
OPPERMANN, James ... 414-382-6120. 531 I
jim.oppermann@alverno.edu
OPPMANN, Andrew ... 615-494-7800. 459 D
andrew.oppmann@mtsu.edu
OPRISKO, George, W ... 765-361-6480. 175 B
opriskow@wabash.edu
OQUENDO, Carmen ... 787-250-1912. 550 E
coquendo@metro.inter.edu
OQUENDO, Diane ... 646-660-6154. 316 J
Diane.Oquendo@baruch.cuny.edu
OQUENDO, Migdalia ... 787-728-1515. 555 D
moquendo@sagrado.edu
OR, Scott ... 208-376-7731. 137 F
sor@boisebible.edu

ORACION, Donna ... 575-624-7403. 309 I
donna.oracion@roswell.enmu.edu
ORAM, MaryLou ... 570-622-7622. 423 G
marylou.oram@mccann.edu
ORAMALU, Lawrencina .. 651-290-6416. 265 F
lawrencina.oramalu@wmitchell.edu
ORANGE, Kathleen ... 251-380-3499..... 7 D
orange@shc.edu
ORANGE, Taur, D ... 212-217-4170. 324 C
taur_orange@fitnyc.edu
ORANTE, Newin ... 925-969-2005... 41 L
norante@dvc.edu
ORANTE, Newin, P ... 510-464-3413... 59 C
norante@peralta.edu
ORAVECZ, Joseph, A ... 308-865-8528. 292 H
oraveczja@unk.edu
ORAVETZ, Teresa ... 203-332-5014... 88 F
toravetz@hcc.commnet.edu
ORBAN, Joseph ... 318-670-9360. 207 A
jorban@susla.edu
ORBERT, Annette ... 336-272-7102. 354 E
annette.orbert@greensboro.edu
ORBIK, Jay ... 815-753-6670. 154 I
jorbik@niu.edu
ORBINATI, Albert ... 518-244-2000. 338 C
orbina@sage.edu
ORCHARD, James, P ... 651-641-8705. 255 B
orchard@csp.edu
ORCHARD, Sue ... 503-399-8111. 402 E
sue.orchard@chemeketa.edu
ORCUTT, Jo-Ann ... 570-961-7873. 420 C
orcuttj@lackawanna.edu
ORD, Kent, J ... 406-683-7301. 286 I
k_ord@umwestern.edu
ORDOYNE, Charles, R ... 985-448-4420. 208 A
charles.ordoyne@nicholls.edu
ORDUNA, Aubray ... 402-552-3100. 288 L
ORDUNA, Aubray, D ... 402-552-6118. 288 L
orduna@clarksoncollege.edu
ORDWAY, Jennifer, N ... 989-964-4917. 249 G
jnordway@svsu.edu
ORE, Dwayne ... 407-438-6000. 114 A
OREIRO, David ... 360-676-2772. 521 D
doreiro@nwic.edu
ORELLANA, Darcy ... 978-656-3558. 232 B
orellanad@middlesex.mass.edu
ORELLANA, Victoria ... 201-360-4121. 302 D
vorellana@hccc.edu
ORENSTEIN, David ... 908-835-2339. 308 G
dorenstein@warren.edu
ORENSTEIN, David ... 718-270-4883. 319 A
dorenstein@mec.cuny.edu
ORGAN, Regina ... 575-492-2761. 310 G
rorgan@nmjc.edu
ORGERA, Jeffrey, M ... 520-621-3772... 18 F
jorgera@email.arizona.edu
ORGERON, Elizabeth ... 518-255-5842. 344 E
orgeroed@cobleskill.edu
ORICK, Ron ... 479-788-7019... 24 A
ron.orick@uafs.edu
ORIDE, Leighton ... 808-245-8224. 136 H
loride@hawaii.edu
ORIHUELA, Ruthanne ... 303-556-3850... 81 D
ruthanne.orihuela@ccd.edu
ORIOLO, Michael ... 315-866-0300. 326 A
orioloma@herkimer.edu
ORIS, James, T ... 513-529-3734. 384 G
orisjt@miamioh.edu
ORITZ, Fernando ... 509-313-4054. 520 A
oritz2@gonzaga.edu
ORKIN, Michael ... 510-466-7300... 59 D
morkin@peralta.edu
ORKIN, Mike ... 510-466-7308... 59 A
morkin@peralta.edu
ORLANDO, Clara ... 978-934-3567. 229 B
clara_orlando@uml.edu
ORLANDO, Donald, A ... 724-805-2010. 432 G
don.orlando@stvincent.edu
ORLANDO, Mary ... 508-457-1313. 234 F
morlando@ngs.edu
ORLANDO, Matthew ... 207-725-3804. 209 H
morlando@bowdoin.edu
ORLANDO, Michael ... 517-264-7171. 250 B
morlando@sienaheights.edu
ORLANDO, Robert ... 203-523-4760... 18 I
robert.orlando@phoenix.edu
ORLANDO, Stephen, F ... 352-392-0186. 116 A
sfo@ufl.edu
ORLAUSKI, Brian ... 951-487-5080... 55 B
borlausk@msjc.edu
ORLE TANTILLO,
Astrida ... 312-413-7329. 161 D
tantillo@uic.edu
ORLOFF, Paige ... 413-528-7229. 222 E
porloff@simons-rock.edu
ORLOWSKI, Martin, A ... 248-522-3882. 248 D
maorlows@oaklandcc.edu
ORME, James ... 517-321-0242. 243 F
jorme@glcc.edu
ORME, Michael, R ... 801-422-3080. 137 H
mike_orme@byui.edu

ORME, Michael, R ... 801-422-3080. 495 D
mike_orme@byu.edu
ORME, Robyn ... 517-321-0242. 243 F
rorme@glcc.edu
ORMENO, Alex ... 212-924-5900. 347 B
aormeno@swedishinstitute.edu
ORMEROD, Michelle ... 617-879-2270. 238 C
mormerod@wheelock.edu
ORMISTON, Gayle, L ... 304-696-3716. 529 H
ormiston@marshall.edu
ORMOND, Tom ... 478-445-6848. 125 A
tom.ormond@gcsu.edu
ORMSBEE, Christine ... 405-744-1000. 397 H
ormsbee@okstate.edu
ORMSBEE, David ... 937-766-4547. 375 K
ormsbeed@cedarville.edu
ORMSBY, Colin ... 509-359-4217. 519 C
cormsby@ewu.edu
ORNE, Tracy ... 217-641-4106. 148 M
torne@jwcc.edu
ORNELAS, Daniel ... 323-265-8751... 51 F
ornelad@elac.edu
ORNELAS, Lynne ... 619-388-7392... 62 F
lornelas@sdccd.edu
ORNELAS, Nohemy ... 805-546-3100... 42 C
nohemy_ornelas@cuesta.edu
ORNER, Lita, J ... 240-500-2000. 215 B
ljorner@hagerstowncc.edu
ORNES, W. Harold ... 217-581-3328. 144 E
whornes@eiu.edu
ORNT, Daniel, B ... 585-475-4861. 337 L
dboihst@rit.edu
OROK, Michael ... 615-963-5139. 459 E
morok@tnstate.edu
ORONA, Edward ... 330-941-2377. 394 A
eorona@ysu.edu
ORONA, Frank ... 505-747-2161. 311 E
forona@nnmc.edu
ORONA, John ... 210-486-2510. 465 B
jorona3@alamo.edu
OROSZ, David ... 216-373-5322. 385 G
dorosz@ndc.edu
OROZA, Lourdes ... 305-237-2154. 109 D
loroza1@mdc.edu
OROZCO, Holly ... 714-816-0366... 70 A
holly.orozco@trident.edu
OROZCO, Monica ... 505-277-2215. 312 F
orozcom@unm.edu
OROZCO, Samuel ... 520-383-8401... 18 B
sorozco@tocc.cc.az.us
ORR, Brenda, B ... 601-643-5101. 266 F
brenda.orr@colin.edu
ORR, Charlotte ... 256-766-6610..... 4 B
corr@hcu.edu
ORR, Collin ... 360-867-6450. 519 J
orrc@evergreen.edu
ORR, Debra ... 617-521-2180. 236 G
debra.orr@simmons.edu
ORR, Herb ... 785-242-5200. 189 I
herb.orr@ottawa.edu
ORR, Jaimie ... 419-448-3319. 389 J
orrrj@tiffin.edu
ORR, Jeff ... 678-915-7489. 132 C
jorr@spsu.edu
ORR, Mark, C ... 925-631-4399... 61 F
morr@stmarys-ca.edu
ORR, Michael ... 847-735-5021. 150 B
morr@lakeforest.edu
ORR, Pattie ... 254-710-3200. 467 G
pattie_orr@baylor.edu
ORR, Richard ... 860-486-5796... 92 A
richard.orr@uconn.edu
ORR, Robert ... 478-445-1196. 125 A
robert.orr@gcsu.edu
ORR, Sandra ... 304-766-3381. 530 C
sorr@wvstateu.edu
ORR, Shaun ... 208-496-9340. 137 H
orrs@byui.edu
ORR, Stephanie, W ... 850-263-3261... 98 N
sworr@baptistcollege.edu
ORR, Sylvia ... 623-935-8413... 14 K
sylvia.orr@estrellamountain.edu
ORR, II, Thomas ... 530-529-8980... 65 G
torr@shastacollege.edu
ORR, Trina ... 828-227-7290. 369 E
torr@wcu.edu
ORRIS, Erika ... 630-353-7049. 144 A
eorris@devry.edu
ORRIS, Keith ... 215-571-4463. 415 B
keith.a.orris@drexel.edu
ORRISON, Russell ... 423-236-2336. 458 J
rorrison@southern.edu
ORSBORN, Ruthie, J ... 334-874-5700..... 3 A
rorsborn@ccal.edu
ORSCHELN, Paul ... 719-549-2997... 80 K
paul.orscheln@colostate-pueblo.edu
ORSCHELN, Paul ... 859-572-7852. 198 I
orschelnp1@nku.edu
ORSER, Paul, N ... 336-758-5311. 370 D
orser@wfu.edu

ORSHANSKY, Mariya ... 510-628-8010... 51 A
morshansky@lincolnuca.edu
ORSI, Michael ... 239-687-5331... 98 J
frorsi@avemarialaw.edu
ORSINI, Jamie ... 312-915-6424. 151 H
jorsini@luc.edu
ORSINI, SPHR, Teri ... 704-337-2297. 365 G
orsinit@queens.edu
ORT, Shirley, A ... 919-962-2315. 368 D
ort@email.unc.edu
ORTA, Edna ... 787-743-7979. 552 I
ut_eorta@suagm.edu
ORTA, Jose ... 305-223-4561. 112 B
ORTALE, Lynn ... 215-248-7030. 413 A
ortalel@chc.edu
ORTALO-MAGNE',
Francois ... 608-262-1234. 536 D
ORTBERG, Jennifer, L ... 714-895-8965... 39 J
jortberg@gwc.cccd.edu
ORTEGA, Bonnie ... 719-589-7131... 85 H
bonnie.ortega@trinidadstate.edu
ORTEGA, Carmen ... 787-257-7373. 552 H
ue_cortega@suagm.edu
ORTEGA, Carolyn, M ... 973-655-7327. 303 D
ortegac@mail.montclair.edu
ORTEGA, David ... 210-486-1227. 465 C
dortega@alamo.edu
ORTEGA, David, F ... 541-485-1780. 405 B
davidortega@newhope.edu
ORTEGA, J. Martin ... 210-486-0721. 465 C
jortega@alamo.edu
ORTEGA, Janet ... 602-243-8287... 15 F
janet.ortega@southmountaincc.edu
ORTEGA, Richard ... 510-436-1198... 47 J
rortega@hnu.edu
ORTEGA, Suzanne ... 919-962-4614. 366 K
stortega@northcarolina.edu
ORTEGA-RAMOS,
Luz, D ... 787-480-2407. 548 G
lortega@sanjuancapital.com
ORTELLI, Tracy, A ... 502-410-6200. 194 B
tortelli@galencollege.edu
ORTEN, Mark ... 740-587-8504. 379 D
ortenm@denison.edu
ORTH, Linda ... 423-425-4669. 463 D
linda-orth@utc.edu
ORTIZ, Abigail ... 650-508-3756... 56 H
aortiz@ndnu.edu
ORTIZ, Ann ... 910-893-1669. 352 K
ortiz@campbell.edu
ORTIZ, Ariel ... 787-766-1717. 552 J
um_aortiz@suagm.edu
ORTIZ, Blanca ... 787-767-2040. 555 B
ORTIZ, Carlos ... 787-758-2525. 554 F
carlos.ortiz33@upr.edu
ORTIZ, Christine ... 617-253-4860. 233 B
ORTIZ, Daniel ... 617-287-5910. 228 G
daniel.ortiz@umb.edu
ORTIZ, Edna ... 787-786-3030. 547 F
eortiz@ucb.edu.pr
ORTIZ, Eduardo ... 787-250-1912. 550 E
ehortiz@metro.inter.edu
ORTIZ, Elizabeth ... 818-947-2361... 52 E
ortizme@lavc.edu
ORTIZ, Elizabeth, F ... 312-362-8588. 143 H
eortiz4@depaul.edu
ORTIZ, Elvin, J ... 787-857-3600. 550 A
ejortiz@br.inter.edu
ORTIZ, Erika ... 954-322-4460. 107 V
ortize@jmvu.edu
ORTIZ, Francisco ... 860-297-2054... 91 F
francisco.ortiz@trincoll.edu
ORTIZ, Francisco ... 787-761-0640. 553 F
oficinadelpresidente@utcpr.edu
ORTIZ, Hilda, L ... 787-863-2390. 550 C
hilda.ortiz@fajardo.inter.edu
ORTIZ, Hiram ... 787-850-9312. 554 D
hiram.ortiz@upr.edu
ORTIZ, J. Michael ... 909-869-2290... 32 G
jmo@csupomona.edu
ORTIZ, Jeanne ... 562-907-4233... 76 I
jortiz@whittier.edu
ORTIZ, Jennifer ... 210-486-4208. 464 J
jortiz157@alamo.edu
ORTIZ, Johnathan ... 505-454-2596. 309 L
jortiz@luna.edu
ORTIZ, Jose, M ... 510-466-7202... 58 I
jortiz@peralta.edu
ORTIZ, Juan, M ... 787-738-2161. 554 C
rechumanos@upr.edu
ORTIZ, Judy ... 503-352-7309. 407 A
ortiz@pacificu.edu
ORTIZ, Kendra ... 787-780-0070. 547 G
kortiz@caribbean.edu
ORTIZ, Kristina ... 212-752-1530. 328 G
kristina.ortiz@limcollege.edu
ORTIZ, Laura ... 630-942-2971. 142 G
ortizl@cod.edu
ORTIZ, Lillian ... 203-575-8034... 89 B
lortiz@nvcc.commnet.edu

ORTIZ, Lourdes, Z ... 787-257-0000. 554 B
lourdes.ortiz2@upr.edu
ORTIZ, Luis, A ... 787-725-8120. 548 O
ORTIZ, Luis, A ... 787-767-4300. 555 B
luortiz@onelinkpr.net
ORTIZ, Luz ... 787-864-2222. 550 D
luzortiz@inter.edu
ORTIZ, Luz, M ... 787-832-6000. 549 D
mortiz@icprjc.edu
ORTIZ, Luz, M ... 215-503-4094. 434 C
luz.ortiz@jefferson.edu
ORTIZ, Mario ... 574-520-5511. 168 E
ortizmr@iusb.edu
ORTIZ, Maritza ... 787-264-1912. 551 A
maortiz@sg.inter.edu
ORTIZ, Mark ... 703-821-8570. 510 B
mortiz@stratford.edu
ORTIZ, Migdalia ... 787-279-1912. 550 B
morti@bayamon.inter.edu
ORTIZ, Mildred ... 787-264-1940. 551 A
mildred@sg.inter.edu
ORTIZ, Myrta ... 787-815-0000. 553 I
myrta.ortiz1@upr.edu
ORTIZ, Noel ... 787-753-6335. 549 D
nortiz@icprjc.edu
ORTIZ, Norma ... 787-620-2040. 547 C
nortiz@aupr.edu
ORTIZ, Nuria ... 650-289-3336... 61 G
nuria.ortiz@stpatrickseminary.org
ORTIZ, Rafael ... 787-725-6500. 547 H
rortiz@albizu.edu
ORTIZ, Ralph ... 559-734-9000... 63 D
ralpho@sjvc.edu
ORTIZ, Rosa ... 787-738-2161. 554 C
rosa.ortiz1@upr.edu
ORTIZ, Vivian ... 781-239-3101. 231 G
vortiz@massbay.edu
ORTIZ, Zoraida ... 787-743-7979. 552 I
zortiz@suagm.edu
ORTIZ ALVAREZ,
Lelis Antonio ... 954-322-4460. 107 V
lelisortiz@jmvu.edu
ORTIZ-CINTRÓN, Jesús . 787-993-8869. 554 A
jesus.ortiz3@upr.edu
ORTIZ-CINTRÓN, Jesús . 787-993-8878. 554 A
jesus.ortiz3@upr.edu
ORTIZ COLON, Yadira ... 787-725-8120. 548 O
yortiz@eap.edu
ORTIZ HENDRICKS,
Carmen ... 212-960-0820. 351 M
cortiz@yu.edu
ORTIZ-MORETTA, Amy ... 937-298-3399. 382 K
amy.ortiz-moretta@kc.edu
ORTIZ PARRA,
Fernando ... 954-322-4460. 107 V
ortizf@jmvu.edu
ORTIZ PARRA, Lelis ... 954-322-4460. 107 V
ortizlelis@jmvu.edu
ORTIZ-RUÍZ, Wilfredo ... 787-993-8855. 554 A
wilfredo.ortiz5@upr.edu
ORTIZ SEDA,
Darnyd, W ... 787-265-3807. 554 E
decasac@uprm.edu
ORTIZ-ZAYAS, Jose, E ... 787-857-3600. 550 A
jeortiz@br.inter.edu
ORTMAN, William, B ... 973-618-3259. 300 A
wortman@caldwell.edu
ORTMEIER, Shane ... 605-882-5284. 450 D
ortmeies@lakeareatech.edu
ORTMEYER, Rose Ann ... 573-681-5044. 276 C
ortmeyr@lincolnu.edu
ORTNER, Richard ... 617-912-9134. 224 B
rortner@bostonconservatory.edu
ORTON, Donna, J ... 641-422-4216. 181 D
ortondon@niacc.edu
ORTON, Mozelle ... 801-957-4561. 498 B
mozelle.orton@slcc.edu
ORTQUIST-AHRENS,
Leslie ... 859-985-3670. 192 F
ortquistahrensl@berea.edu
ORTSTADT, Andrew, D ... 314-935-8604. 284 L
aortstadt@wustl.edu
ORUM-ALEXANDER,
Gail ... 323-563-5851... 38 B
gailorum@cdrewu.edu
ORVIS, Arleen ... 563-387-1005. 180 M
orvisarl@luther.edu
ORWIG, Greg ... 509-777-4580. 525 F
gorwig@whitworth.edu
ORWIGHO, Godfrey ... 419-530-3955. 392 B
godfrey.ovwigho@utoledo.edu
ORZA, Deanna ... 770-781-6770. 128 B
dorza@laniertech.edu
ORZE, Carol ... 312-567-3636. 147 F
orze@iit.edu
ORZECHOWSKI, Laurie ... 419-824-3959. 383 C
lorzechowski@lourdes.edu
ORZECHOWSKI,
Michael ... 212-280-1301. 349 A
morzechowski@uts.columbia.edu
ORZOLEK, Jeffrey, P ... 540-831-5376. 508 C
jorzolek@radford.edu
ORZOLEK, Mariah ... 419-783-2358. 379 C
morzolek@defiance.edu
OSAGIE, Linda ... 214-860-8604. 471 A
losagie@dcccd.edu
OSANTOWSKI, Kimberly 248-204-3940. 245 I
kosantows@ltu.edu
OSATHANUGRAH, Vim .. 510-666-8248... 26 F
vim@aimc.edu
OSAWA, Steve ... 510-659-6111... 57 A
sosawa@ohlone.edu
OSBAHR, Diane ... 712-325-3235. 179 L
dosbahr@iwcc.edu
OSBON, Cindy ... 301-846-2593. 214 H
cosbon@frederick.edu
OSBORN, Edward, H ... 860-465-5303... 87 L
osborne@easternct.edu
OSBORN, Jeffrey ... 609-771-2724. 300 E
josborn@tcnj.edu
OSBORN, Kevin ... 626-584-5200... 45 E
kosborn@fuller.edu
OSBORN, Richard, E ... 423-439-8300. 459 C
osbornr@etsu.edu
OSBORN, Terry ... 941-359-4200. 117 A
OSBORN, William ... 928-428-8286... 13 J
bill.osborn@eac.edu
OSBORNE, Becky ... 217-353-2005. 155 J
bosborne@parkland.edu
OSBORNE, Curtis ... 510-649-2477... 46 B
cosborne@gtu.edu
OSBORNE, John ... 305-428-5700. 109 E
josborne@aii.edu
OSBORNE, John ... 405-425-5463. 397 D
john.osborne@oc.edu
OSBORNE, John ... 304-829-7395. 526 D
josborne@bethanywv.edu
OSBORNE, John, N ... 270-745-5747. 200 G
john.osborne@wku.edu
OSBORNE, Kari ... 410-837-4397. 221 A
kpsborne@ubalt.edu
OSBORNE, Kenneth, T ... 401-254-3166. 440 B
kosborne@rwu.edu
OSBORNE, Kevin ... 336-342-4261. 363 C
osbornek@rockinghamcc.edu
OSBORNE, Lynn ... 336-838-6175. 365 B
lynn.osborne@wilkescc.edu
OSBORNE, Margaret, H .. 315-255-1743. 316 D
osbornem@cayuga-cc.edu
OSBORNE, Michelle ... 518-454-5141. 321 A
osbornem@strose.edu
OSBORNE, Shelley ... 704-991-0203. 364 C
sosborne7501@stanly.edu
OSBORNE, Steven, C ... 843-953-5574. 443 A
osbornes@cofc.edu
OSBORNE, Travis, G ... 530-226-4978... 66 D
tosborne@simpsonu.edu
OSBORNE-ADAMS,
Dawn ... 607-777-2388. 341 E
ombudsman@binghamton.edu
OSBORNE-ELLIOTT,
Miriam ... 340-692-4187. 555 E
mosborn@live.uvi.edu
OSBOURN, John ... 541-956-7426. 407 F
josbourn@roguecc.edu
OSBOURNE, Jesse ... 859-336-5082. 198 J
jesseosbourne@sccky.edu
OSBURN, Jan ... 254-867-3014. 486 B
jan.osburn@tstc.edu
OSBURN, Monica ... 919-515-2423. 368 B
monica_osburn@ncsu.edu
OSBURN, Toby, W ... 337-475-5607. 207 G
tosburn@mcneese.edu
OSBURN, Wade ... 731-989-6067. 454 J
wosburn@fhu.edu
OSBY, Rachel, V ... 256-824-6549... 8 F
Rachel.Osby@uah.edu
OSEBY, Todd ... 651-779-3276. 258 C
todd.oseby@century.edu
OSEGUEDA, Roberto ... 915-747-5680. 492 A
osegueda@utep.edu
OSENGA, Annette ... 510-780-4500... 50 I
aosenga@lifewest.edu
OSGOOD, Ken ... 303-273-3596... 80 E
kosgood@mines.edu
OSHERSON, Julie ... 802-387-6732. 499 E
josherson@landmark.edu
OSHIRO, Cathie, R ... 620-792-9234. 184 F
oshiroc@bartonccc.edu
OSHIRO, James ... 503-554-2235. 403 C
joshiro@georgefox.edu
OSHIRO, Robyn ... 808-689-2900. 136 C
robyno@hawaii.edu
OSINGA, Mark, L ... 864-596-9041. 443 D
mark.osinga@converse.edu
OSIRIM, Mary, J ... 610-526-5167. 410 J
mosirim@brynmawr.edu
OSISEK, Vincent ... 803-750-2510... 96 F
OSKAMP, Shirley ... 802-287-8388. 499 D
oskamps@greenmtn.edu
OSMAN, Cathy ... 802-258-9293. 499 F
cosman@marlboro.edu
OSMANSON, Deb ... 402-449-2844. 289 H
dosmanson@graceu.edu
OSMER, Patrick, S ... 614-292-6031. 386 E
osmer.1@osu.edu
OSORIO, Jennifer ... 718-357-0500. 339 G
josorio@edaff.com
OSSORIO, Devon ... 573-288-6571. 273 F
dossorio@culver.edu
OSTASH, Heather ... 760-384-6249... 49 O
hostash@cerrocoso.edu
OSTDIEK, Donald ... 713-348-4786. 479 A
dho@rice.edu
OSTEEN, Charles ... 760-384-6115... 49 O
charles.osteen@cerrocoso.edu
OSTEN, Kevin ... 312-662-4205. 139 F
kosten@adler.edu
OSTENDARP, Timothy ... 443-352-4348. 218 E
tostendarp@stevenson.edu
OSTER, Ben Zion ... 323-937-3763... 77 F
boster@yoec.edu
OSTER, Cynthia ... 856-691-8600. 301 A
coster@cccnj.edu
OSTER, Joseph, J ... 410-704-2151. 220 E
joster@towson.edu
OSTERBIND, Kelly ... 251-460-6251... 9 E
kosterbind@southalabama.edu
OSTERHOUDT, Lori, B ... 607-746-4692. 345 G
osterhlb@delhi.edu
OSTERTHUN, Stu ... 402-323-3401. 292 C
sosterthun@southeast.edu
OSTERUD, Amelia ... 262-524-1211. 532 C
osterud@carrollu.edu
OSTLER, Jon ... 435-283-7361. 498 A
jon.ostler@snow.edu
OSTLUND, Kara ... 704-637-4111. 353 E
kostlund@catawba.edu
OSTOLAZA, Magda, E ... 787-257-7373. 552 H
ue_mostolaza@suagm.edu
OSTRANDER, Doris ... 202-298-2551... 95 B
dostrander@corcoran.org
OSTRANDER, Gary, K ... 850-644-3347. 115 C
gary@fsu.edu
OSTRANDER, Jean, M ... 641-422-4177. 181 D
ostrajea@niacc.edu
OSTRANDER, Richard ... 616-222-1589. 241 F
rick.ostrander@cornerstone.edu
OSTRANDER, Tammy ... 218-723-6173. 254 K
tostrand@css.edu
OSTROSKE, Georgette ... 516-918-3607. 315 G
gostroske@bcl.edu
OSTROW, James ... 617-243-2111. 227 K
jostrow@lasell.edu
OSTRYE, Mary, E ... 317-921-4313. 169 K
mostrye@ivytech.edu
OSTWINKLE,
Christopher, M ... 563-556-5110. 181 E
ostwinkc@nicc.edu
OSUNDE, Samuel ... 662-254-9041. 269 A
sosunde@mvsu.edu
OSVAI, Nanci ... 704-290-5251. 363 G
nosvai@spcc.edu
OSWALD, Mike, R ... 208-356-1320. 137 H
oswaldrm@byui.edu
OSWALD, P.J ... 503-517-1800. 408 I
pjoswald@westernseminary.edu
OSWALD, Peter ... 217-854-3231. 140 G
peter.oswald@blackburn.edu
OSWALD, Phil ... 920-403-3016. 535 L
phil.oswald@snc.edu
OSWALD, Sharon ... 662-325-2580. 268 D
soswald@cobilan.msstate.edu
OSWALT, Natalie ... 936-591-9075. 478 A
noswalt@panola.edu
OSWELL, Michelle ... 215-893-5265. 414 B
michelle.oswell@curtis.edu
OTAIGBE, Michael, I ... 703-878-2810... 96 F
mio@strayer.edu
OTERO, Emeterio, M ... 585-262-1610. 332 A
eotero@monroecc.edu
OTERO, Juan ... 787-766-1717. 552 J
juotero@suagm.edu
OTEY, Rex ... 704-637-4111. 353 E
OTHMAN, Saib ... 630-844-4229. 140 A
sothman@aurora.edu
OTIS, Linda ... 228-497-7649. 268 C
linda.otis@mgccc.edu
OTO, Rod, M ... 507-222-4190. 254 D
roto@carleton.edu
OTOUPAL, Vince ... 801-863-8998. 497 C
vince.otoupal@uvu.edu
OTT, Alexander ... 516-686-1037. 333 H
aott@nyit.edu
OTT, Deanna ... 501-205-8838... 20 I
dott@cbc.edu
OTT, Emlyn, A ... 614-235-4136. 390 A
eott@TLSohio.edu
OTT, Jay, W ... 719-884-5000... 83 K
jwott@nbc.edu
OTT, Luisa ... 520-494-5283... 12 P
luisa.ott@centralaz.edu
OTT, Randall ... 202-319-5188... 94 G
ott@cua.edu
OTT, Steven, H ... 704-687-7630. 368 E
SHott@uncc.edu
OTT ROWLANDS, Sue ... 540-231-6779. 515 C
sottrowlands@vt.edu
OTTAWAY, Thomas ... 208-282-3585. 138 E
ottathom@isu.edu
OTTE, Bobbi ... 406-657-1086. 288 B
otteb@rocky.edu
OTTEMAN, Marcie, M ... 989-774-1042. 240 N
ottem1mm@cmich.edu
OTTEN, Laura ... 215-951-1118. 420 B
otten@lasalle.edu
OTTEN, Valerie, A ... 626-395-6832... 31 E
votten@caltech.edu
OTTENHOFF, John ... 208-459-5334. 138 A
jottenhoff@collegeofidaho.edu
OTTERBEIN, Lesley ... 410-752-4710. 510 B
lotterbein@stratford.edu
OTTERNESS, Naomi ... 828-771-3783. 370 E
nottern@warren-wilson.edu
OTTERSON, Robert ... 605-688-4111. 452 B
robert.otterson@sdstate.edu
OTTEY, Jacqueline ... 201-447-7204. 299 C
jottey@bergen.edu
OTTINGER, Denise ... 785-670-2100. 191 D
denise.ottinger@washburn.edu
OTTINGER, Marie ... 334-386-7512... 3 H
mottinger@faulkner.edu
OTTINGER, Mary Beth ... 847-925-6000. 145 H
mottinge@harpercollege.edu
OTTINGER, Marybeth ... 636-481-3467. 275 I
mottinge@jeffco.edu
OTTINO, Julio, M ... 847-491-3195. 155 D
jm-ottino@northwestern.edu
OTTLEY, Alford, H ... 973-803-5000. 304 C
aottley@pillar.edu
OTTO, Eric, H ... 812-464-1765. 174 D
eotto@usi.edu
OTTO, Raimondi ... 732-224-2239. 299 G
craimondi@brookdalecc.edu
OTTO, Richard, H ... 312-461-0600. 139 H
ifitzgerald@aaart.edu
OTTO, Rick ... 479-979-1351... 25 J
rotto@ozarks.edu
OTTO, Robert ... 212-217-3637. 324 C
robert_otto@fitnyc.edu
OTTO, Sheryl ... 874-925-6342. 145 H
sotto@harpercollege.edu
OTTO, Tyson ... 660-359-3948. 279 H
totto@mail.ncmissouri.edu
OTTOBONI, John ... 408-554-5355... 64 M
jottoboni@scu.edu
OTTOSSON, John ... 641-673-1015. 183 H
ottossonj@wmpenn.edu
OTTS, Tonya ... 803-793-5192. 443 E
tonyao@denmarktech.edu
OTU, Emmanual ... 262-598-2973. 537 C
otu@uwp.edu
OTUONYE, Francis, O ... 931-372-3374. 460 A
fotuonye@tntech.edu
OTWELL, Michelle ... 386-386-7380... 3 H
motwell@faulkner.edu
OTY, Karla ... 580-581-7962. 394 G
koty@cameron.edu
OUART, Michael, D ... 573-882-7477. 283 C
ouartm@missouri.edu
OUBRAHAM, Ourida ... 201-216-5411. 307 E
ooubraha@stevens.edu
OUBRE, Linda ... 415-338-2670... 35 E
loubre@sfsu.edu
OUDENHOVEN, D. Arnie 847-635-1675. 155 F
aoudenho@oakton.edu
OUDENHOVEN,
Elizabeth ... 303-360-4703... 81 C
betsy.oudenhoven@ccaurora.edu
OUELLETTE, Alicia ... 518-445-3305. 313 C
aouel@albanylaw.edu
OUELLETTE, Allison ... 620-431-2820. 189 D
aouellette@neosho.edu
OUELLETTE, James ... 802-831-1209. 500 H
jouellette@vermontlaw.edu
OUELLETTE, Michelle, M 518-564-3095. 344 B
ouel8653@plattsburgh.edu
OUELLETTE, Sheila ... 314-644-9557. 281 D
souellette@stlcc.edu
OUIMET, Maurice ... 802-468-1352. 501 B
maurice.ouimet@castleton.edu
OUIMETTE, Nina ... 325-670-2357. 472 O
noiumette@hsutx.edu
OUIMETTE, Nina ... 325-671-2357. 476 E
nouimette@hsutx.edu
OULETTE, Helen ... 617-873-0689. 224 G
Helen.Oulette@cambridgecollege.edu
OURS, Alan ... 559-453-2269... 45 D
alan.ours@fresno.edu
OUSLEY, Chris ... 503-338-2326. 402 G
cousley@clatsopcc.edu

OUSLEY, Larry .... 517-750-1200. 250 E
lousley@arbor.edu
OUTEN, Jason .... 828-835-4229. 364 E
jouten@tricountycc.edu
OUTLEY, Patrice .... 318-274-2288. 207 E
outleyp@gram.edu
OUTON, Peggy, M .... 412-397-6001. 431 I
outon@rmu.edu
OUTTEN, Donnovon .... 757-727-5773. 505 F
donnovon.outten@hamptonu.edu
OUZTS, Deryl .... 229-226-1621. 132 F
douzts@thomasu.edu
OVADIA, Zak .... 904-620-2016. 116 B
zovadia@unf.edu
OVEDIA, Nicole, R .... 561-237-7237. 108 X
novedia@lynn.edu
OVEL, Steven, J .... 319-398-5466. 180 J
steve.ovel@kirkwood.edu
OVER, Lucinda .... 626-914-8538... 38 K
lover@citruscollege.edu
OVERBAUGH, Keith .... 231-995-1274. 248 B
koverbaugh@nmc.edu
OVERBY, David, B .... 605-256-5675. 451 H
david.overby@dsu.edu
OVERCASH, Shannon ..... 508-541-1841. 225 F
sovercash@dean.edu
OVEREND, Gregory .... 203-932-7430... 92 E
goverend@newhaven.edu
OVEREND, Wendy .... 805-969-3626... 57 K
woverend@pacifica.edu
OVERFIELD, Joan, T .... 203-254-4000... 89 I
jtoverfield@fairfield.edu
OVERLAND, Wanda .... 320-308-3111. 261 B
wioverland@stcloudstate.edu
OVERMAN, Jan, G .... 336-342-4261. 363 C
overmanj@rockinghamcc.edu
OVEROCKER, Josh .... 405-974-3636. 400 K
joverocker@uco.edu
OVERSTROM, Eric .... 508-831-5222. 238 F
ewo@wpi.edu
OVERTON, Chrystal .... 580-477-7831. 401 J
chrystal.overton@wosc.edu
OVERTON, James .... 617-287-5800. 228 G
james.overton@umb.edu
OVERTON, Lindi .... 573-876-7105. 282 H
loverton@stephens.edu
OVERTON, Reginald .... 412-237-3127. 413 D
roverton@ccac.edu
OVERTON, Richard .... 631-420-2700. 346 B
foundation@farmingdale.edu
OVERTON, Robert, A .... 864-488-4543. 444 L
roverton@limestone.edu
OVERTON, JR., Sam ...... 815-921-4445. 157 A
s.overton@rockvalleycollege.edu
OVERTON-HEALY, Julia . 607-871-2971. 313 E
overton@alfred.edu
OVERTURF, Kellie .... 970-332-5755... 83 E
kellie.overturf@morgancc.edu
OVERY, Lara .... 757-258-6673. 514 B
overyl@tncc.edu
OVESON, Kip, R .... 320-222-6930. 260 H
kip.oveson@ridgewater.edu
OW, Debora .... 510-559-2723... 57 F
dow@plts.edu
OWAN, Edna .... 808-675-3474. 135 C
edna.owan@byuh.edu
OWAN, Robert .... 808-675-3951. 135 C
owanb@byuh.edu
OWCZARCZAK, Kathleen 716-884-9120. 315 K
kowczarczak@bryantstratton.edu
OWCZAREK, Scott .... 608-262-3964. 536 D
owczarek@em.wisc.edu
OWEN, Amanda .... 317-921-4823. 169 L
aowen15@ivytech.edu
OWEN, Amber .... 352-365-3677. 108 S
owena@lssc.edu
OWEN, Barbara .... 207-755-5233. 210 J
bowen@cmcc.edu
OWEN, Bob .... 270-745-2243. 200 G
bob.owen@wku.edu
OWEN, David, L .... 671-734-1812. 546 D
dowen@piu.edu
OWEN, Harvey .... 717-872-3024. 429 D
harvey.owen@millersville.edu
OWEN, James (Chris) ..... 863-667-5146. 113 P
jcowen@seu.edu
OWEN, Jane, S .... 724-852-3225. 437 A
jowen@waynesburg.edu
OWEN, Janet, D .... 904-620-2500. 116 B
jowen@unf.edu
OWEN, John .... 419-448-2073. 380 G
jowen@heidelberg.edu
OWEN, Kelli, D .... 606-783-2700. 198 A
k.owen@moreheadstate.edu
OWEN, Ken .... 765-658-4634. 165 F
kowen@depauw.edu
OWEN, Kyle .... 940-397-4648. 476 H
kyle.owen@mwsu.edu
OWEN, Laurinda, A .... 574-372-5100. 166 B
owenla@grace.edu
OWEN, Michael .... 671-734-1812. 546 D
mowen@piu.edu
OWEN, Pam, D .... 715-874-4655. 539 J
powen@cvtc.edu
OWEN, Pamela .... 501-450-1358... 21 E
owen@hendrix.edu
OWEN, Patricia .... 518-891-2915. 335 A
OWEN, Ray .... 252-246-1239. 365 C
rowen@wilsoncc.edu
OWEN, Ronald, S .... 334-699-2266..... 1 B
OWEN, Samantha .... 671-734-1812. 546 D
sowen@piu.edu
OWEN, William .... 402-457-2715. 290 G
bowen@mccneb.edu
OWENBY, Judy .... 828-835-4212. 364 E
jowenby@tricountycc.edu
OWENS, Amy .... 205-934-9847..... 8 E
awowensr@uab.edu
OWENS, Anthony .... 615-329-8882. 454 F
aowens@fisk.edu
OWENS, Bertha .... 501-370-5215... 22 F
bowens@philander.edu
OWENS, Bettina .... 504-568-6130. 205 C
bowens@lsuhsc.edu
OWENS, Billy .... 501-244-6137... 19 J
billy.owens@arkansasbaptist.edu
OWENS, Casey .... 417-455-5618. 273 E
CaseyOwens@crowder.edu
OWENS, Claudia .... 740-374-8716. 392 I
cowens1@wscc.edu
OWENS, Deborah, E .... 716-829-8198. 323 D
owensde@dyc.edu
OWENS, Derek, V .... 718-990-2043. 339 A
owensd@stjohns.edu
OWENS, Don .... 254-295-4691. 490 B
dowens@umhb.edu
OWENS, Esmeralda .... 831-755-6810... 46 G
eowens@hartnell.edu
OWENS, Estelle .... 806-291-1171. 494 F
owensest@wbu.edu
OWENS, Howard .... 423-493-4224. 462 B
owensh@tntemple.edu
OWENS, Irene .... 919-530-6485. 368 A
iowens@nccu.edu
OWENS, James .... 609-633-9658. 308 A
jowens@tesc.edu
OWENS, James, R .... 859-858-3511. 192 B
jim.owens@asbury.edu
OWENS, Jeremy .... 800-818-2261. 296 F
jowens@dwc.edu
OWENS, Jessie, A .... 530-754-8920... 70 J
jaowens@ucdavis.edu
OWENS, Jossie .... 617-745-6704. 225 G
jossie.owens@enc.edu
OWENS, Kate .... 570-945-8222. 419 N
kate.owens@keystone.edu
OWENS, Kathleen, C ...... 215-641-5548. 417 F
owens.k@gmc.edu
OWENS, Kimberly .... 814-768-3430. 429 B
kowens@lhup.edu
OWENS, Kristine .... 515-643-6659. 181 A
kowens@mercydesmoines.org
OWENS, Lillian .... 205-853-1200..... 5 B
lowens@jeffstateonline.com
OWENS, Mark .... 618-664-6735. 145 G
mark.owens@greenville.edu
OWENS, O'dell .... 513-569-1515. 376 L
odell.owens@cincinnatistate.edu
OWENS, Pamela .... 815-921-4503. 157 A
p.owens@rockvalleycollege.edu
OWENS, Penny .... 816-415-5083. 285 C
owensp@william.jewell.edu
OWENS, Rick .... 252-493-7243. 362 G
rowens@email.pittcc.edu
OWENS, Rita .... 617-552-4981. 224 A
rita.long@bc.edu
OWENS, Robert .... 931-372-3392. 460 A
rowens@tntech.edu
OWENS, Roger .... 949-451-5758... 67 B
rowens@ivc.edu
OWENS, Sandra .... 920-339-6471... 78 C
sandra.owens@aims.edu
OWENS, Sharon .... 404-270-5082. 132 E
sowens5@spelman.edu
OWENS, Sheila .... 662-720-7246. 269 B
sbowens@nemcc.edu
OWENS, Stephanie .... 318-869-5012. 201 H
sowens@centenary.edu
OWENS, Stephen, J .... 573-882-3211. 283 B
owenssj@umsystem.edu
OWENS, Steve .... 870-972-3362... 19 L
sowens@asusystem.edu
OWENS, Susan .... 254-295-8686. 490 B
sowens@umhb.edu
OWENS, Thomas .... 919-681-8263. 354 A
thomas.owens@duke.edu
OWENS, Valerie .... 304-876-5465. 529 I
vowens@shepherd.edu
OWENS, Victoria .... 502-597-5960. 197 A
victoria.owens@kysu.edu
OWENS, Wanda .... 913-758-6110. 191 B
registrar@stmary.edu
OWENS, Waylan .... 817-923-1921. 481 G
wowens@swbts.edu
OWENS, William, R .... 203-329-7929..... 3 B
bill.owens@ecacolleges.com
OWENS, Wilma, G .... 760-744-1150... 58 D
wowens@palomar.edu
OWENS-PELTON,
Lesley, C .... 315-655-7287. 316 E
lcowenspelton@cazenovia.edu
OWENS-SOUTHHALL,
Mary, E .... 410-951-3090. 220 B
mowens@coppin.edu
OWENSKY, Fred .... 575-527-7543. 311 B
fowensky@nmsu.edu
OWINGS, Colleen, H ...... 916-484-8411... 53 A
owingsc@arc.losrios.edu
OWL, Diane .... 828-835-4220. 364 E
dowl@tricountycc.edu
OWSLEY, Diane .... 270-706-8406. 195 A
diane.owsley@kctcs.edu
OWSLEY, Larry, L .... 502-852-5143. 200 D
llowsl01@louisville.edu
OWSLEY, Laura .... 502-863-8007. 194 C
laura_owsley@georgetowncollege.edu
OWSLEY, Stacy .... 520-383-8401... 18 B
sowsley@tocc.cc.az.us
OWUSU-ADUEMIRI,
Kwadwo .... 850-412-7469. 114 K
kwadwo.owusuaduemiri@famu.edu
OWUSU-ANSAH,
Edward .... 570-422-3152. 428 D
eowusu-ansah@po-box.esu.edu
OWUSU-SEKYERE,
Emmanuel .... 410-951-3862. 220 B
manny@coppin.edu
OXENDINE, Ray .... 910-775-4080. 369 B
ray.oxendine@uncp.edu
OXENRIDER, Jack .... 517-607-4285. 243 I
jack.oxenrider@hillsdale.edu
OXFORD,
Mary-Catherine .... 559-730-3826... 40 I
marycat@cos.edu
OXFORD-PICKERAL,
Misti .... 352-335-2332... 97 E
info@acupuncturist.edu
OXLEY, Walter, R .... 614-885-5585. 388 C
woxley@pcj.edu
OXTOBY, David, W .... 909-621-8131... 60 A
david.oxtoby@pomona.edu
OYAMA, Jannine .... 808-845-9231. 136 G
jannine@hawaii.edu
OYEKAN, Adebayo, O ..... 713-313-4341. 485 F
oyekan_ao@tsu.edu
OYINBO, Victor .... 803-780-1086. 449 E
voyinbo@voorhees.edu
OYOLA, Elias .... 212-694-1000. 315 E
eoyola@boricuacollege.edu
OZATALAY, Savas .... 610-499-4319. 437 E
sozatalay@widener.edu
OZAYSIN, Gokhan .... 912-525-5000. 131 B
gozaysin@scad.edu
OZECHOSKI, Mary-Alice 610-606-4666. 412 I
mozechos@cedarcrest.edu
OZEE, Nancy .... 815-802-8842. 149 C
nozee@kcc.edu
OZIMEK-MAIER, Alyssa . 617-912-9213. 224 B
aozimekmaier@bostonconservatory.edu
OZMENT, Suzanne .... 205-665-6015..... 9 B
sozment@montevallo.edu
OZOLINS, Sondrea, S .... 317-940-9535. 164 J
sozolins@butler.edu
OZOLS, Ruta .... 315-229-5908. 339 F
rozols@stlawu.edu
OZTURK, Mehmet .... 559-730-3700... 40 I
OZUG, Steve .... 508-678-2811. 231 B
steven.ozug@bristolcc.edu
OZUNA, Teofilo .... 956-665-3311. 492 B
ozuna@utpa.edu
OZUROVICH, John .... 949-582-4865... 67 C
jozurovich@saddleback.edu
O'BANION, Rebecca ...... 254-295-4603. 490 B
robanion@umhb.edu
O'BANNER-JACKSON,
Marie .... 601-979-7092. 267 E
marie.obanner-jackson@jsums.edu
O'BAR, Gary .... 210-485-0102. 464 I
gobar@alamo.edu
O'BARR, Allen, H .... 919-966-3658. 368 D
allen_obarr@unc.edu
O'BEIRNE, Kirsten .... 610-526-5041. 410 J
kobeirne@brynmawr.edu
O'BEIRNE, OSF,
Marguerite .... 610-558-5511. 424 I
mobeirne@neumann.edu
O'BERRY, V. Diane .... 803-780-1142. 449 E
doberry@voorhees.edu
O'BOYLE, Andrew .... 206-296-6149. 523 E
oboylea@seattleu.edu
O'BRIEN, Alyssa .... 847-543-2409. 143 A
aobrien@clcillinois.edu
O'BRIEN, Ann .... 509-452-5100. 521 J
O'BRIEN, Brad, T .... 309-649-6294. 160 E
brad.obrien@src.edu
O'BRIEN, Colleen .... 386-481-2920... 99 C
obrienc@cookman.edu
O'BRIEN, David, J .... 850-474-2626. 117 B
dobrien@uwf.edu
O'BRIEN, David, M .... 671-735-2905. 546 E
dobrien@uguam.uog.edu
O'BRIEN, Diane, E .... 570-408-4734. 437 F
diane.obrien@wilkes.edu
O'BRIEN, Eddie .... 706-865-2134. 133 B
eobrien@truett.edu
O'BRIEN, Eileen, M .... 978-542-7529. 230 E
eobrien@salemstate.edu
O'BRIEN, Elizabeth .... 415-749-4581... 62 G
eobrien@sfai.edu
O'BRIEN, Elizabeth .... 707-664-4023... 36 B
elizabeth.obrien@sonoma.edu
O'BRIEN, Gwen .... 574-284-4595. 172 G
gobrien@saintmarys.edu
O'BRIEN, Ian .... 701-349-5405. 373 A
ianobrien@trinitybiblecollege.edu
O'BRIEN, Irene .... 973-353-5541. 306 D
jobrien@andromeda.rutgers.edu
O'BRIEN, J. Patrick .... 806-651-2100. 484 D
pobrien@mail.wtamu.edu
O'BRIEN, J. Randall .... 865-471-3200. 453 F
robrien@cn.edu
O'BRIEN, Janet, L .... 912-478-5371. 126 C
jlobrien@georgiasouthern.edu
O'BRIEN, Jennifer, E ...... 610-758-4679. 422 A
jeo211@lehigh.edu
O'BRIEN, Jim .... 480-965-9118... 11 K
james.obrien@asu.edu
O'BRIEN, John .... 740-264-5591. 379 F
jobrien@egcc.edu
O'BRIEN, John, F .... 617-422-7221. 235 B
O'BRIEN, Kathleen .... 414-382-6084. 531 I
kathleen.obrien@alverno.edu
O'BRIEN, Kelly .... 860-297-2046... 91 F
kelly.obrien@trincoll.edu
O'BRIEN, Kevin .... 865-573-4517. 455 G
kobrien@johnsonU.edu
O'BRIEN, SJ, Kevin .... 202-687-1395... 95 E
obrienkf@georgetown.edu
O'BRIEN, Margaret, A .... 605-256-5049. 451 H
peg.o'brien@dsu.edu
O'BRIEN, Mary .... 707-546-4000... 43 E
mobrien@empirecollege.com
O'BRIEN, Mary Eileen .... 845-848-7801. 322 G
mary.eileen.obrien@dc.edu
O'BRIEN, Maureen .... 310-287-4379... 52 F
obrienma@wlac.edu
O'BRIEN, Maureen .... 724-830-1075. 433 E
obrien@setonhill.edu
O'BRIEN, Michael, E .... 419-530-4987. 392 B
michael.obrien6@utoledo.edu
O'BRIEN, Michael, J .... 573-882-4421. 283 C
obrienm@missouri.edu
O'BRIEN, Michael, J ...... 610-841-3333. 427 F
mobrien@psb.edu
O'BRIEN, Paul, R .... 772-462-7376. 106 P
pobrien@irsc.edu
O'BRIEN, Stacey .... 217-641-4241. 148 M
obrien@jwcc.edu
O'BRIEN, Susan .... 256-824-6133..... 8 F
susan.obrien@uah.edu
O'BRIEN, Susan .... 301-985-7160. 219 F
susan.obrien@umuc.edu
O'BRIEN, Wayne, R .... 434-395-2409. 506 J
obrienwr@longwood.edu
O'BRIEN, William, T .... 724-287-8711. 411 C
william.obrien@bc3.edu
O'BRIEN-FOELSCH,
Molly, E .... 570-577-3624. 411 A
molly.obrien@bucknell.edu
O'BRIEN FRIEDERICHS,
Jane .... 781-239-2461. 231 G
jobrienfriederichs@massbay.edu
O'BRYAN, Dan .... 775-831-1314. 295 F
dobryan@sierranevada.edu
O'BRYANT, Theresa, M .. 413-662-5231. 230 C
theresa.obryant@mcla.edu
O'CAIN, Woody .... 704-337-2362. 365 G
ocainw@queens.edu
O'CALLAGHAN, Cecelia . 608-771-2201. 300 E
ocallagh@tcnj.edu
O'CALLAGHAN, Cindy ... 617-735-9779. 226 B
ocallac@emmanuel.edu
O'CALLAGHAN, Karen ..... 516-463-6605. 326 D
karen.ocallaghan@hofstra.edu
O'CARROLL, Theresa ...... 708-974-5248. 153 F
ocarroll@morainevalley.edu
O'CINNSEALAIGH,
Benedict .... 513-231-2223. 374 D
bocinnsealaigh@athenaeum.edu
O'CONNELL, Catharine ... 540-887-7030. 507 A
coconnell@mbc.edu

O'CONNELL, Colleen ...... 215-884-8942. 438 A
planning@woninstitute.edu
O'CONNELL, Daniel .... 978-867-4246. 226 H
daniel.oconnell@gordon.edu
O'CONNELL, Danny, J ... 330-941-3549. 394 A
djoconnell@ysu.edu
O'CONNELL, David, J .... 563-333-6092. 182 B
OConnellDavidJ@sau.edu
O'CONNELL, Erin, E .... 206-281-2175. 523 C
ocone@spu.edu
O'CONNELL, Heather, A . 302-356-6814... 94 E
heather.a.oconnell@wilmu.edu
O'CONNELL, John .... 260-481-6977. 168 C
oconnelj@ipfw.edu
O'CONNELL, Mark .... 269-965-3931. 244 O
oconnellm@kellogg.edu
O'CONNELL, Melissa, E . 386-312-4232. 112 C
melissaoconnell@sjrstate.edu
O'CONNELL, Robert, G .. 617-333-2050. 225 E
boconnel@curry.edu
O'CONNELL, Ryan .... 617-369-3617. 236 F
roconnell@smfa.edu
O'CONNELL, Sean .... 203-773-8068... 87 G
soconnell@albertus.edu
O'CONNER, Terrence, L . 305-628-6516. 112 F
toconner@stu.edu
O'CONNOR, Angela .... 773-602-5000. 142 B
O'CONNOR, Barbara ...... 860-486-4806... 92 A
barbara.o'connor@uconn.edu
O'CONNOR, OSFS,
Bernard, F .... 610-282-1100. 414 F
boconnor@desales.edu
O'CONNOR, Bill .... 425-564-5454. 517 A
bill.oconnor@bellevuecollege.edu
O'CONNOR, Brian .... 406-994-3211. 287 B
boconnor@montana.edu
O'CONNOR, Charles, D . 402-472-9339. 292 I
charles.oconnor@unl.edu
O'CONNOR, Christi .... 323-953-4000... 51 G
oconnoca@lacitycollege.edu
O'CONNOR,
Christopher, K .... 617-254-2610. 236 B
O'CONNOR, Deirdre, M . 570-577-3141. 411 A
deirdre.oconnor@bucknell.edu
O'CONNOR, Diane .... 215-641-6416. 424 B
doconnor@mc3.edu
O'CONNOR, Edward, R .. 402-280-3009. 289 D
edwardoconnor@creighton.edu
O'CONNOR, Ellen .... 617-287-5100. 228 G
ellen.oconnor@umb.edu
O'CONNOR, Ellen, M ..... 215-955-6835. 434 C
ellen.oconnor@jefferson.edu
O'CONNOR, James .... 404-894-9044. 125 D
james.oconnor@oit.gatech.edu
O'CONNOR, James .... 563-884-5294. 182 A
james.oconnor@palmer.edu
O'CONNOR, James .... 212-229-5300. 332 E
oconnorj@newschool.edu
O'CONNOR, Jeremiah .... 508-793-2564. 225 B
joconnor@holycross.edu
O'CONNOR, Jim .... 707-638-5997... 69 K
jim.oconnor@tu.edu
O'CONNOR, Jody .... 415-575-6153... 31 D
joconnor@ciis.edu
O'CONNOR, John .... 214-768-2011. 481 A
joconnor@smu.edu
O'CONNOR, Joseph .... 607-778-5379. 315 I
oconnorjt@sunybroome.edu
O'CONNOR, Kathleen ..... 816-271-5827. 279 A
koconnor5@missouriwestern.edu
O'CONNOR, Kathleen ..... 617-243-2225. 227 K
koconnor@lasell.edu
O'CONNOR, Kathleen ..... 608-663-6715. 532 I
koconnor@edgewood.edu
O'CONNOR, Kevin .... 949-582-4788... 67 C
koconnor@saddleback.edu
O'CONNOR, Marcia .... 423-473-2390. 460 D
moconnor@clevelandstatecc.edu
O'CONNOR, Mark, F ...... 617-552-3315. 224 A
mark.oconnor@bc.edu
O'CONNOR, Martin .... 570-348-6211. 423 B
oconnor@marywood.edu
O'CONNOR, Mary .... 480-731-8403... 14 I
mary.oconnor@domail.maricopa.edu
O'CONNOR, Matthew, L . 203-582-8297... 91 A
matthew.oconnor@quinnipiac.edu
O'CONNOR, Maura .... 206-296-6300. 523 E
oconnorm@seattleu.edu
O'CONNOR, Megan .... 310-577-3000... 77 G
matcm@yosan.edu
O'CONNOR, Michael ...... 815-802-8908. 149 C
moconnor@kcc.edu
O'CONNOR, Mike, J ...... 828-262-3190. 367 A
oconnormj@appstate.edu
O'CONNOR, Patrick .... 708-974-5555. 153 F
oconnorp@morainevalley.edu
O'CONNOR, Robert .... 315-781-3535. 326 C
oconnor@hws.edu
O'CONNOR, Sheila .... 402-457-2733. 290 G
soconnor7@mccneb.edu
O'CONNOR, Thomas, J .. 703-993-3256. 505 C
toconno2@gmu.edu
O'CONNOR, Timothy ..... 212-327-8080. 338 A
toconnor@rockefeller.edu
O'CONNOR, William, R .. 386-822-7500. 117 C
woconnor@stetson.edu
O'CONNOR-BENSON,
Pat .... 239-597-7101. 115 A
poconnor@fgcu.edu
O'CONNOR-GOMEZ,
Doreen .... 562-907-4352... 76 I
doconnor@whittier.edu
O'DANIEL, Carolyn .... 502-213-5333. 195 F
O'DANIEL, Rosemary ..... 309-341-5456. 141 A
rodaniel@sandburg.edu
O'DAY, Gail, R .... 336-758-4315. 370 D
odaygr@wfu.edu
O'DAY, James .... 703-416-1441. 505 I
joday@ipsciences.edu
O'DAY, Steven, P .... 717-867-6407. 421 H
oday@lvc.edu
O'DAY-STEVENS,
Tamara .... 860-231-5214... 92 F
tstevens@usj.edu
O'DELL, Cynthia .... 219-980-6509. 168 B
codell@iun.edu
O'DELL, James .... 617-912-9166. 224 B
jodell@bostonconservatory.edu
O'DELL, Tim .... 843-661-8300. 443 G
tim.odell@fdtc.edu
O'DELL MAINOUS,
Rosalie .... 937-775-3133. 393 G
rosalie.mainous@wright.edu
O'DESKY, Ryan .... 608-249-6611. 533 I
rodesky@herzing.edu
O'DONNELL, Alicia .... 402-461-7784. 289 I
aodonnell@hastings.edu
O'DONNELL, Anne .... 215-893-5272. 414 B
anne.odonnell@curtis.edu
O'DONNELL, Bill, J .... 574-520-4218. 168 E
odonnell@iusb.edu
O'DONNELL, Brennan .... 718-862-7301. 329 M
brennan.odonnell@manhattan.edu
O'DONNELL, Eileen .... 617-327-6777. 233 D
eileen_healy@mspp.edu
O'DONNELL, James .... 660-785-7777. 282 L
jodonnell@truman.edu
O'DONNELL, John .... 781-239-3101. 231 G
jodonnell@massbay.edu
O'DONNELL, Karen .... 813-880-8011. 107 C
kodonnell@academy.edu
O'DONNELL, Michael ..... 262-741-8538. 540 A
odonnellm@gtc.edu
O'DONNELL, Michael ..... 512-499-4601. 491 A
modonnell@utsystem.edu
O'DONNELL, SSJ,
Patricia .... 215-248-7125. 413 A
podonnel@chc.edu
O'DONNELL, Patrick ...... 562-860-2451... 37 I
podonnell@cerritos.edu
O'DONNELL, Ralph .... 660-944-2920. 272 H
rodonnell@conception.edu
O'DONNELL, Timothy, T 540-636-2900. 503 L
president@christendom.edu
O'DONOVAN, Stephen ... 254-526-1934. 468 G
stephen.o'donovan@ctcd.edu
O'DOWD, Kathleen .... 734-432-5300. 246 B
kodowd@madonna.edu
O'DRISCOLL, Brian .... 503-352-2917. 407 A
odriscob@pacificu.edu
O'DRISCOLL, Daniel .... 508-541-1641. 225 F
dodriscoll@dean.edu
O'DRISCOLL, Dean .... 435-865-8054. 497 A
odriscoll@suu.edu
O'DRISCOLL, Sue .... 540-545-7399. 509 E
sodrisco09@su.edu
O'DWYER, Anne .... 413-528-7240. 222 F
aodwyer@simons-rock.edu
O'DWYER, Timothy .... 503-768-7860. 403 K
odwyer@lclark.edu
O'FARRELL, Kevin, D ..... 727-376-6911. 117 I
kofarrell@trinitycollege.edu
O'FARRELL, Mark, T ...... 727-376-6911. 117 I
mofarrell@trinitycollege.edu
O'FLAHERTY, Kevin .... 215-646-7300. 417 F
oflaherty.k@gmc.edu
O'FLANNERY ANDERSON,
Jennifer .... 954-262-2100. 109 K
O'GORMAN, Deb .... 775-829-9000. 294 H
dogorman@tmcc.edu
O'GORMAN, Jane .... 706-864-2814. 133 D
janeogorman@ung.edu
O'GORMAN, Ryan .... 845-848-7600. 322 G
ryan.ogorman@dc.edu
O'GRADY, Elaine .... 845-569-3255. 332 B
elaine.ogrady@msmc.edu
O'GRADY EISENMANN,
Sharon .... 610-660-1290. 432 E
seisenma@sju.edu
O'GWYNN, Marty .... 405-208-5120. 397 F
mlogwynn@okcu.edu
O'HAGAN, Donald .... 973-618-3759. 300 A
dohagan@caldwell.edu
O'HAGAN, Jill .... 860-412-7311.... 89 E
johagan@qvcc.commnet.edu
O'HAGAN, Patricia .... 808-734-9569. 136 E
ohaganp@hawaii.edu
O'HAILEY, Tina .... 912-525-5000. 131 B
tohailey@scad.edu
O'HAIR, Dan .... 859-218-0290. 200 C
OHair@uky.edu
O'HAIR, Mary, J .... 859-257-2813. 200 C
mjohair@uky.edu
O'HALLA, Kevin .... 616-234-3638. 243 B
kohalla@grcc.edu
O'HALLORAN, Teresa .... 715-836-2387. 536 E
ohallote@uwec.edu
O'HANIAN, Hunter .... 617-879-7045. 230 B
hohanian@massart.edu
O'HANLON, James, P .... 402-472-3041. 292 I
johanlon1@unl.edu
O'HARA, Christine, S ..... 716-286-8792. 334 F
cohara@niagara.edu
O'HARA, Christine, S ..... 716-286-8776. 334 F
cso@niagara.edu
O'HARA, Colleen .... 773-298-3780. 158 E
ohara@sxu.edu
O'HARA, Edward .... 203-837-9109... 88 B
oharae@wcsu.edu
O'HARA, James, P .... 609-896-5367. 305 D
johara@rider.edu
O'HARA, Marcy .... 805-565-6114... 76 D
mohara@westmont.edu
O'HARA, Noreen .... 914-323-5165. 330 B
noreen.ohara@mville.edu
O'HARA, Patrick .... 715-732-3888. 541 B
patrick.ohara@nwtc.edu
O'HARA, Sabine .... 202-274-7174... 97 A
sabine.ohara@udc.edu
O'HARA, William, T .... 401-232-6477. 438 K
wohara@bryant.edu
O'HARE, Katie .... 617-323-6662. 233 D
katie_ohare@mspp.edu
O'HARE, Lyn .... 828-771-3012. 370 E
lohare@warren-wilson.edu
O'HARE, Susan .... 610-861-1588. 424 E
mesio01@moravian.edu
O'HERN, Susan .... 518-465-8500. 324 B
sohern@excelsior.edu
O'HERRON, Virginia, S .. 757-683-4141. 507 N
voherron@odu.edu
O'HOP, Suzanne, E .... 717-736-4279. 417 I
seohop@hacc.edu
O'KANE, Gail .... 507-285-7215. 261 A
gail.okane@rctc.edu
O'KARMA, Theodore ...... 818-345-8414... 41 B
tokarma@columbiacollege.edu
O'KEEFE, Barbara, J ...... 847-491-7023. 155 D
b-okeefe@northwestern.edu
O'KEEFE, John, L .... 610-330-5803. 420 D
okeefej@lafayette.edu
O'KEEFE, Louise .... 256-824-2445..... 8 F
Louise.OKeefe@uah.edu
O'KEEFE, Martha .... 540-891-3094. 512 E
mokeefe@germanna.edu
O'KEEFE, Michael .... 845-569-3597. 332 B
michael.okeefe@msmc.edu
O'KEEFE, Mildred .... 516-876-3247. 343 D
okeefem@oldwestbury.edu
O'KEEFE, Paterick .... 716-829-7753. 323 D
O'KEEFE, Paul .... 781-736-2120. 224 F
pokeefe@brandeis.edu
O'KEEFE, Paul .... 508-830-5063. 230 D
pokeefe@maritime.edu
O'KEEFE, Steve .... 618-985-3741. 148 J
steveokeefe@jalc.edu
O'KEEFE, Susan .... 732-571-3521. 303 C
okeefe@monmouth.edu
O'KEEFE, Tim .... 701-777-2611. 371 C
timo@undfoundation.org
O'KEEFFE, Mary Ellen .... 206-934-3701. 522 I
maryellen.okeeffe@seattlecolleges.edu
O'KEEFFE, Mary Ellen .... 206-934-3601. 522 I
maryellen.okeeffe@seattlecolleges.edu
O'KEEFFE, Michael .... 727-341-3352. 112 E
okeeffe.mike@spcollege.edu
O'KEEFFE, Phillip, D ...... 765-494-0226. 171 M
pokeeffe@purdue.edu
O'KIEF, Kristy .... 605-995-2656. 450 A
krokief@dwu.edu
O'KIEF, Mary .... 541-245-7596. 407 F
mokief@roguecc.edu
O'LARE, Russell, D .... 412-268-1001. 412 H
rdo@andrew.cmu.edu
O'LAUGHLIN, Jeanne .... 305-899-3010... 98 O
jolaughlin@barry.edu
O'LEARY, Allison .... 203-575-8276... 89 B
aoleary@nvcc.commnet.edu
O'LEARY, David .... 610-361-2330. 424 I
olearyd@neumann.edu
O'LEARY, Eileen, K .... 508-565-1347. 237 A
eoleary@stonehill.edu
O'LEARY, Kara .... 574-284-4578. 172 G
koleary@saintmarys.edu
O'LEARY, Michael .... 410-337-6501. 215 A
michael.oleary@goucher.edu
O'LEARY, Michael .... 734-995-4678. 241 E
learm@cuaa.edu
O'LEARY, Mick .... 301-846-2585. 214 H
moleary@frederick.edu
O'LEARY, Nicole .... 617-349-8888. 228 B
noleary@lesley.edu
O'LEARY, Rita .... 610-647-4400. 418 I
roleary@immaculata.edu
O'LEARY-ARCHER, Lynn 909-447-2565... 39 E
lolearyarcher@cst.edu
O'LINGER, Jennifer .... 256-551-3125..... 4 I
jennifer.o'linger@drakestate.edu
O'MAHONEY, Megan ..... 650-433-3806... 58 B
megano@paloaltou.edu
O'MALEY-LAMSON,
Patty .... 765-983-1424. 165 G
pattyo@earlham.edu
O'MALLEY, Barbara .... 314-246-7825. 284 N
barbaraomalley25@webster.edu
O'MALLEY, Deborah, A .. 617-879-5097. 233 E
deborah.omalley@mcphs.edu
O'MALLEY, Richard .... 979-830-4054. 467 I
richard.omalley@blinn.edu
O'MALLEY, Timothy, L ... 619-260-4770... 73 I
tomalley@sandiego.edu
O'MARA, Charles, A ...... 845-451-1285. 322 D
c_omara@culinary.edu
O'MEARA, Ann .... 816-501-2422. 271 H
ann.omeara@avila.edu
O'MEARA, George .... 617-266-1400. 223 D
O'MEARA, Kathy .... 802-468-1292. 501 B
kathy.omeara@castleton.edu
O'MEARA, Ron .... 229-333-2111. 134 K
ron.omeara@wiregrass.edu
O'MUIRCHEARTAIGH,
Colm .... 773-702-9693. 161 B
colm@uchicago.edu
O'NEAL, Alan .... 773-821-2897. 141 J
aoneal@csu.edu
O'NEAL, Andy .... 419-227-3141. 391 F
aoneal@unoh.edu
O'NEAL, Bruce .... 936-294-1833. 487 A
boneal@shsu.edu
O'NEAL, Christian .... 501-683-7208... 24 B
cxoneal@ualr.edu
O'NEAL, Dennis .... 254-710-3871. 467 G
dennis_oneal@baylor.edu
O'NEAL, Ginger, H .... 252-335-0821. 359 F
goneal@albemarle.edu
O'NEAL, Michelle .... 856-351-2649. 307 B
moneal@salemcc.edu
O'NEAL, Tom .... 407-882-1120. 115 E
oneal@ucf.edu
O'NEAL MOSLEY, Toni .. 404-215-2680. 129 D
tmosley@morehouse.edu
O'NEIL, Alicia, M .... 202-994-2371... 95 D
oneila@gwu.edu
O'NEIL, Burton .... 864-656-4337. 442 C
boneil@clemson.edu
O'NEIL, Christine .... 906-487-7328. 242 G
christine.oneil@finlandia.edu
O'NEIL, Laura, L .... 607-777-2131. 341 E
loneil@binghamton.edu
O'NEIL, Lisa .... 406-265-3748. 287 D
loneil@msun.edu
O'NEIL, Michael .... 617-732-2885. 233 E
michael.oneil@mcphs.edu
O'NEIL, Patricia, A .... 413-585-2550. 236 H
toneil@smith.edu
O'NEIL, Tabitha .... 773-602-5125. 142 B
toneil@ccc.edu
O'NEIL, Tom .... 661-722-6300... 28 F
loneil@avc.edu
O'NEIL-GARRETT, Mary . 360-417-6225. 522 A
mogarrett@pencol.edu
O'NEILL, Bettyann .... 706-236-2261. 121 G
boneill@berry.edu
O'NEILL, Charles .... 724-830-1144. 433 E
oneill@setonhill.edu
O'NEILL, Dale, A .... 919-209-2106. 361 E
daoneill@johnstoncc.edu
O'NEILL, Daniel .... 978-762-4000. 232 D
Daoneill@northshore.edu
O'NEILL, Denise .... 609-652-4332. 305 C
denise.oneill@stockton.edu
O'NEILL, Gerry, J .... 252-246-1337. 365 C
goneill@wilsoncc.edu
O'NEILL, Jennifer .... 603-577-6000. 296 F
joneill@dwc.edu
O'NEILL, Jerry, F .... 412-731-8690. 431 G
joneill@rpts.edu
O'NEILL, Maureen .... 978-762-4000. 232 D
moneill@northshore.edu
O'NEILL, Meggan .... 201-355-1421. 302 A
oneillm@feliciabn.edu
O'NEILL, Michael .... 610-519-7926. 436 F
mike.oneill@villanova.edu

O'NEILL, Molly .... 919-668-6330. 354 A
molly.oneill@duke.edu
O'NEILL, Patrick .... 303-404-5400... 81 N
patrick.o'neill@frontrange.edu
O'NEILL, Priscilla .... 262-595-2233. 537 C
oneillp@uwp.edu
O'NEILL, Russ .... 330-966-5455. 389 F
roneill@starkstate.edu
O'NEILL, Shannon .... 518-782-5830. 340 J
soneill@siena.edu
O'NEILL, Shawn .... 201-216-8143. 307 E
shawn.oneill@stevens.edu
O'NEILL, Stephen .... 507-786-3062. 264 B
oneill@stolaf.edu
O'NEILL, Thomas .... 315-228-7418. 320 F
toneill@colgate.edu
O'NEILL, Walter .... 616-554-5827. 241 H
woneill1@davenport.edu
O'NEILL, William .... 402-559-1952. 292 J
woneill@unmc.edu
O'NEILL, JR.,
William, J .... 617-573-8300. 237 B
woneill@suffolk.edu
O'NIELL, Claudia .... 720-890-8922... 82 I
registrar@itea.edu
O'QUINN, Doretha .... 562-777-4048... 29 L
doretha.oquinn@biola.edu
O'QUINN, Michael .... 979-845-2217. 483 C
irishmike@tamu.edu
O'QUINN, Monica, S ..... 912-427-5840. 120 B
moquinn@altamahatech.edu
O'RAND, Angela, M .... 919-668-2746. 354 A
aorand@soc.duke.edu
O'REAR, Randy, G .... 254-295-4500. 490 B
rorear@umhb.edu
O'REGAN, Danny .... 808-440-4226. 135 D
daniel.oregan@chaminade.edu
O'REGGIO, Elizabeth ...... 352-395-5486. 113 C
elizabeth.oreggio@sfcollege.edu
O'REILLY, Jane .... 617-369-3477. 236 F
joreilly@mfa.org
O'REILLY, Kevin, P .... 914-968-6200. 339 E
O'REILLY, Lillian .... 718-951-5184. 317 C
loreilly@brooklyn.cuny.edu
O'REILLY, Paul, J .... 805-525-4417... 69 H
poreilly@thomasaquinas.edu
O'REILLY, Sharon .... 239-280-1654... 98 K
sharon.oreilly@avemaria.edu
O'REILLY, Tricia .... 510-841-9230... 77 B
toreilly@wi.edu
O'RILEY, Jane .... 318-670-9400. 207 A
joriley@susla.edu
O'RILEY, Shawn .... 516-877-3404. 313 A
oriley@adelphi.edu
O'RIORDAN, Steven .... 978-934-3463. 229 B
Steven_Oriordan@uml.edu
O'RORKE, Kevin .... 530-242-7629... 65 G
kororke@shastacollege.edu
O'ROURKE, Bernard, C .. 973-618-3409. 300 A
borourke@caldwell.edu
O'ROURKE, Brian .... 908-526-1200. 305 B
borourke@raritanval.edu
O'ROURKE, Brian .... 510-430-2133... 54 F
borourke@mills.edu
O'ROURKE, Brian, J .... 864-656-4248. 442 C
orourke@clemson.edu
O'ROURKE, Elizabeth, B 315-443-5195. 347 C
eorourke@syr.edu
O'ROURKE, John .... 413-552-2203. 231 F
jorourke@hcc.edu
O'ROURKE, Joseph .... 413-585-3000. 236 H
jorourke@smith.edu
O'ROURKE, Joyce .... 225-771-5260. 206 J
joyce_orourke@subr.edu
O'ROURKE, Kevin .... 718-489-5496. 338 G
korourke@sfc.edu
O'ROURKE, Maureen, A . 617-353-3112. 224 D
morourke@bu.edu
O'ROURKE, Pat .... 303-860-5600... 85 K
patrick.orourke@cu.edu
O'ROURKE, Raymond .... 617-541-5308. 232 G
rorourke@rcc.mass.edu
O'ROURKE, Shaun .... 617-262-5000. 223 F
Shaun.ORourke@the-bac.edu
O'ROURKE, Sheila, N ..... 973-618-3341. 300 A
sorourke@caldwell.edu
O'ROURKE, Timothy, C . 215-204-7077. 433 K
timothy.orourke@temple.edu
O'ROURKE, Timothy, G . 757-455-3210. 515 H
torourke@vwc.edu
O'SABEN, Carol .... 928-523-2261... 16 C
carol.osaben@nau.edu
O'SHAUGHNESSY,
Brian, J .... 413-205-3247. 221 F
brian.oshaughnessy@aic.edu
O'SHEA, Dennis .... 443-287-9908. 215 H
doshea@jhu.edu
O'SHEA, Donal, E .... 941-487-4100. 115 D
doshea@ncf.edu
O'SHEA, Gregory, M ...... 856-225-6475. 306 C
osheag@camden.rutgers.edu
O'SHEA, Maureen .... 508-362-2131. 231 D
moshea@capecod.edu
O'SHEA, Patrick, G .... 301-405-6499. 219 B
poshea@umd.edu
O'SHEA, William .... 503-352-1419. 407 A
osheawa@pacificu.edu
O'SHIELDS, Shannon ..... 714-879-3901... 47 K
soshields@hiu.edu
O'SULLIVAN, Eileen .... 508-531-2921. 229 D
eosullivan@bridgew.edu
O'SULLIVAN, Elaine .... 617-879-7906. 230 B
eo'sullivan@massart.edu
O'SULLIVAN, Gerard, P . 610-558-5507. 424 I
osullivg@neumann.edu
O'SULLIVAN, Joseph ..... 314-516-6800. 283 E
osullivanj@umsl.edu
O'SULLIVAN, Kevin .... 914-323-5125. 330 B
kevin.osullivan@mville.edu
O'SULLIVAN, Leighton ... 404-880-8067. 122 J
losullivan@cau.edu
O'SULLIVAN, Meg .... 718-270-2487. 342 D
mosullivan@downstate.edu
O'SULLIVAN, Michael, J 310-338-3015... 53 E
michael.osullivan@lmu.edu
O'SULLIVAN, Patrick ...... 516-876-3135. 343 D
osullivanp@oldwestbury.edu
O'SULLIVAN, Richard ..... 715-422-5325. 540 D
richard.osullivan@mstc.edu
O'TOOLE, Diana .... 605-394-1288. 452 A
diana.otoole@sdsmt.edu
O'TOOLE, Laura, L .... 401-341-3183. 440 C
laura.otoole@salve.edu
O'TOOLE, Lynne, B .... 978-232-2030. 226 C
lynne@endicott.edu
O'TOOLE, Patty .... 540-362-6588. 505 G
potoole@hollins.edu
O'CARROLL, Dottie .... 480-860-2700... 13 Q
docarroll@taliesin.edu

P

PÉREZ, José .... 787-857-3600. 550 A
japerez@br.inter.edu
PÉREZ, Maritza .... 787-764-0000. 555 B
maritza.perez@upr.edu
PÉREZ, Yolanda .... 787-892-5400. 551 A
myperez@sg.inter.edu
PÉREZ-SÁNCHEZ, María . 787-993-8887. 554 A
maria.perez29@upr.edu
PAANANEN, Marian .... 425-640-1680. 519 D
mpaanane@edcc.edu
PAAP, Beth .... 715-634-4790. 533 Q
bpaap@lco.edu
PAAVOLA, Cindy, L .... 906-227-2720. 248 A
cipaavol@nmu.edu
PABÓN-BATLE, Luis, H .. 787-993-8867. 554 A
luis.pabon4@upr.edu
PABÓN-BATLLE, Luis ..... 787-993-8870. 554 A
luis.pabon4@upr.edu
PABÓN-BATLLE, Luis, H 787-993-8868. 554 A
luis.pabon4@upr.edu
PABST, Kathy .... 573-681-5206. 276 C
pabstk@lincolnu.edu
PACCHIANA, Patricia ...... 845-398-4044. 340 A
ppacchia@stac.edu
PACE, Derek .... 601-635-2111. 266 H
dpace@eccc.edu
PACE, Duane .... 423-614-8104. 455 L
dpace@leeuniversity.edu
PACE, JR., G. Michael ... 540-375-2047. 509 B
gpace@roanoke.edu
PACE, Gay .... 870-460-1140... 24 D
pace@uamont.edu
PACE, Harold .... 336-758-5206. 370 D
hpace@wfu.edu
PACE, Julie .... 210-486-4932. 464 J
jpace@alamo.edu
PACE, Lisa, L .... 843-953-4823. 442 A
lisa.pace@citadel.edu
PACE, Roger, C .... 619-260-7847... 73 I
honors@sandiego.edu
PACE, Terry, G .... 256-765-4225..... 9 C
tgpace@una.edu
PACENTI, Elena .... 619-684-8800... 56 C
epacenti@newschoolarch.edu
PACHECO, Andrea .... 505-467-6809. 312 D
registrar@swc.edu
PACHECO, Anthony, R .... 718-990-2663. 339 A
pachecoa@stjohns.edu
PACHECO, Caryn, L .... 405-325-5505. 401 B
cpacheco@ou.edu
PACHECO, Cathy .... 757-253-4900. 503 N
cpacheco@wm.edu
PACHECO, Federico .... 510-549-4711... 68 G
fpacheco@sksm.edu
PACHECO, Jacob .... 505-747-2122. 311 E
jpacheco@nnmc.edu
PACHECO, Jennifer .... 508-531-1221. 229 D
jennifer.pacheco@bridgew.edu
PACHECO, Joanie .... 415-749-4576... 62 G
jpacheco@sfai.edu
PACHECO, Ken .... 360-992-2413. 518 A
kpacheco@clark.edu
PACHECO, Philicia .... 508-678-2811. 231 B
philicia.pacheco@bristolcc.edu
PACHECO, Randy .... 505-327-5705. 311 I
pachecor@sanjuancollege.edu
PACHECO, Sandra, L ...... 512-448-8408. 479 C
sandrap@stedwards.edu
PACHECO DUNN,
Tanhena .... 845-257-3172. 342 B
pachecot@newpaltz.edu
PACHEO, Diane .... 816-604-1341. 277 C
diane.pacheco@mcckc.edu
PACHUAU, Lalsangkima . 859-858-3581. 192 A
PACIEJ-WOODRUFF,
Amy .... 570-340-6016. 423 B
apaciej@marywood.edu
PACINI, Christine .... 313-993-1208. 250 K
pacinicm@udmercy.edu
PACK, C. Gail .... 803-938-3771. 448 F
pack@uscsumter.edu
PACK, Della .... 606-886-3863. 194 K
della.pack@kctcs.edu
PACK, Kathy, P .... 828-298-3325. 370 E
kpack@warren-wilson.edu
PACKARD, James .... 573-341-4252. 284 A
jpackard@mst.edu
PACKER-MUTI, Barbara .. 954-262-5398. 109 K
packerb@nova.edu
PACKER-WILLIAMS,
Catherine .... 251-809-1500..... 5 A
catherine.williams@jdcc.edu
PACKETT, Felicia, B .... 804-758-6742. 513 G
fpackett@rappahannock.edu
PACKEY, Matthew .... 704-337-2375. 365 G
packeym@queens.edu
PACKHAM, Jo .... 831-459-5806... 72 C
jpackham@ucsc.edu
PACKHAM, Larry .... 310-287-4424... 52 F
packhald@wlac.edu
PACTOL, Monica .... 916-608-6500... 53 C
PADASH, Ali .... 916-608-6500... 53 C
PADDIO, Jacqueline .... 256-761-6231..... 7 F
jpaddio@talladega.edu
PADDOCK, Ericka .... 909-389-3457... 61 K
epaddock@craftonhills.edu
PADDOCK, Jean .... 330-363-5205. 374 E
jpaddock@aultman.com
PADDOCK, John .... 315-498-2299. 335 G
paddockj@sunyocc.edu
PADDOCK, Suzanne .... 315-866-0300. 326 A
paddocksm@herkimer.edu
PADDOCK, Will .... 267-620-4834. 409 H
paddockw@arcadia.edu
PADDOCK-O'REILLY,
Kimberly .... 317-573-8983. 527 G
koreilly@salemu.edu
PADEN, Marion .... 405-682-7595. 397 E
mpaden@occc.edu
PADEN, Matt .... 806-720-7233. 476 B
matt.paden@lcu.edu
PADEN, Orlando .... 662-621-4674. 266 D
opaden@coahomacc.edu
PADEN, Russ .... 480-557-2100... 18 I
russ.paden@phoenix.edu
PADGET, John .... 954-492-5353. 100 A
jpadget@citycollege.edu
PADGETT, Mary Jean ..... 601-925-3278. 268 A
padgett@mc.edu
PADGETT, Mila .... 803-641-3230. 448 A
milap@usca.edu
PADGETT, Steven .... 334-670-3267..... 7 H
padgett@troy.edu
PADIAL, Carmen .... 787-728-1515. 555 D
cpadial@sagrado.edu
PADILLA, Bernie .... 505-747-2160. 311 E
bernie.padilla@nnmc.edu
PADILLA, Christina .... 405-691-3800. 396 D
cpadilla@macu.edu
PADILLA, Eugene .... 505-224-4721. 309 E
epadilla@cnm.edu
PADILLA, Jackie .... 850-484-1721. 110 G
jpadilla@pensacolastate.edu
PADILLA, Jose, D .... 312-362-8590. 143 H
jpadill7@depaul.edu
PADILLA, Mark, W .... 757-594-7050. 503 M
mark.padilla@cnu.edu
PADILLA, Melissa .... 215-780-1382. 433 A
melissa@salus.edu
PADILLA, Miriam .... 787-264-1912. 551 A
mpadilla@sg.inter.edu
PADILLA, Rosario .... 787-856-0945. 548 H
rpadilla@columbiaco.edu
PADILLA, Sherrie .... 661-722-6300... 28 F
spadilla@avc.edu
PADILLA-COTTO,
Lymaries .... 787-725-6500. 547 H
lpadilla@sju.albizu.edu
PADIN, Carlos .... 787-766-1717. 552 J
um_cpadin@suagm.edu
PADIN, Carlos, M .... 787-766-1717. 552 J
um_cpadin@suagm.edu
PADIN, Glenda .... 787-878-6000. 549 D
onegron@icprjc.edu
PADOVANI, John, J .... 607-746-4632. 345 G
padovajj@delhi.edu
PADOW, Fran, A .... 816-604-1081. 277 C
fran.padow@mcckc.edu
PADRON, Eduardo, J ..... 305-237-3316. 109 D
epadron@mdc.edu
PADRON, Margie .... 562-938-4947... 51 D
mpadron@lbcc.edu
PADUAN, Jeffrey, D .... 831-656-3241. 544 M
jdpaduan@nps.edu
PADULA, Fernando .... 915-747-5594. 492 A
lfpadula@utep.edu
PAEPLOW, Randall, K .... 863-784-7083. 113 G
randall.paeplow@southflorida.edu
PAESE, Paul .... 765-455-9441. 168 A
jpcpaese@iuk.edu
PAFFENDORF, Nancy ..... 908-852-1400. 300 D
paffendorfn@centenarycollege.edu
PAGAN, Alba .... 617-850-1261. 227 E
apagan@hchc.edu
PAGAN, Andres .... 787-765-1915. 551 C
apagan@opto.inter.edu
PAGAN, Damaris .... 787-765-1915. 551 C
dpagan@inter.edu
PAGAN, Efren .... 787-834-9595. 553 B
epagan@uaa.edu
PAGAN, Hector .... 787-878-5475. 549 L
hpagan@arecibo.inter.edu
PAGAN, Linda .... 732-987-2255. 302 B
paganl@georgian.edu
PAGAN, Lorraine, M .... 512-448-8411. 479 C
lorraine@stedwards.edu
PAGAN, Maria .... 787-848-1520. 551 O
mpagan@popac.edu
PAGAN, Norberto .... 787-257-7373. 552 H
nopagan@suagm.edu
PAGAN, Vivian .... 212-349-4330. 325 D
vivian@globe.edu
PAGAN, Yolanda .... 787-891-0925. 549 K
ypagan@ns.inter.edu
PAGANELLI, John .... 508-531-1328. 229 D
jpaganelli@bridgew.edu
PAGANI-SOTO, Juan, C . 787-765-4210. 548 E
jcpagani@cempr.edu
PAGANO, Amy, E .... 724-458-3850. 417 E
aepagano@gcc.edu
PAGANO, Jan .... 772-462-7635. 106 P
jpagano@irsc.edu
PAGANO, Jeffrey, M .... 716-839-8254. 322 E
jpagano@daemen.edu
PAGANO, Joseph .... 716-839-8232. 322 E
jpagano1@daemen.edu
PAGANO, Mark .... 406-657-2367. 287 C
mark.pagano@msubillings.edu
PAGANO, Michael, A ..... 312-413-3375. 161 D
mapagano@uic.edu
PAGE, Beth, M .... 276-739-2506. 514 D
bpage@vhcc.edu
PAGE, Beverly .... 206-726-5004. 518 G
bpage@cornish.edu
PAGE, Cheryl .... 417-268-6412. 271 I
cpage@gobbc.edu
PAGE, Dorian .... 435-586-7721. 497 A
page@suu.edu
PAGE, Hugh, R .... 574-631-7242. 174 A
page.6@nd.edu
PAGE, James, H .... 207-973-3220. 212 A
jpage@maine.edu
PAGE, Kelli .... 209-946-2987... 73 A
kpage@pacific.edu
PAGE, Kim .... 207-255-1220. 212 F
kpage@maine.edu
PAGE, Kimberly, D .... 207-581-1293. 212 B
PAGE, Martin .... 918-631-2698. 401 F
martin-page@utulsa.edu
PAGE, Michael, J .... 781-891-2921. 223 C
mpage@bentley.edu
PAGE, Pamela .... 254-442-5121. 468 I
pam.page@cisco.edu
PAGE, Phillip .... 617-873-0256. 224 G
Phillip.Page@cambridgecollege.edu
PAGE, Richard, K .... 208-496-1121. 137 H
pager@byui.edu
PAGE, Robert .... 706-295-6300. 125 C
rpage@highlands.edu
PAGE, Robert, E .... 480-965-1288... 11 K
robert.page@asu.edu
PAGE, Scott .... 503-494-8050. 405 I
faclog@ohsu.edu
PAGE, Susan .... 708-456-0300. 161 A
spage@triton.edu
PAGE, Yolanda .... 504-816-4368. 201 K
ypage@dillard.edu
PAGE-SMITH, Julie .... 231-843-5949. 252 H
jsmith@westshore.edu
PAGE-STADLER, Jaime ... 920-424-2027. 537 B
pagestad@uwosh.edu

PAGEL, Bruce .... 352-371-2833. 101 K
director@dragonrises.edu
PAGEL, Richard .... 714-432-5024... 39 K
rpagel@occ.cccd.edu
PAGGI, Paula .... 818-710-2843... 52 B
paggipm@piercecollege.edu
PAGLIARO, Joel .... 717-262-2003. 437 H
conferences@wilson.edu
PAGLIARO, Phil .... 610-399-2418. 428 B
ppagliaro@cheyney.edu
PAGLIARULO, John .... 617-573-8115. 237 B
jpagliar@suffolk.edu
PAGNAM, Charles .... 617-287-4085. 228 E
cpagnam@umassp.edu
PAGNAM, Charles, J ...... 508-856-4340. 229 C
charles.pagnam@umassmed.edu
PAGOTTO, Louise .... 808-734-9519. 136 E
pagotto@hawaii.edu
PAHCODDY, JR., Lee .... 785-749-8467. 187 B
lpahcoddy@haskell.edu
PAHL, Jennifer .... 989-964-4011. 249 G
jkpahl@svsu.edu
PAHWA, Suchi .... 312-777-8669. 147 D
spahwa@aii.edu
PAI, Edward .... 323-953-4000... 51 G
epai@lacitycollege.edu
PAIER, Daniel, L .... 203-287-3022... 90 H
PAIER, Jonathan, E .... 203-287-3180... 90 H
paier.jep@snet.net
PAIER, Maureen, E .... 203-287-3035... 90 H
paier.fin@snet.net
PAIGE, Ellen, M .... 904-256-7024. 107 Q
epaige@ju.edu
PAIGE, CSC, John, R ..... 574-239-8375. 166 N
jpaige@hcc-nd.edu
PAIGE, Joseph, P .... 860-832-2225... 87 K
paigejop@ccsu.edu
PAIGE, Joy .... 704-378-1024. 355 K
jpaige@jcsu.edu
PAIGE, Michael .... 978-232-2259. 226 C
mpaige@endicott.edu
PAIGE, Valerie .... 717-396-7833. 427 A
vpaige@pcad.edu
PAIKOWSKI, Gary .... 903-463-8707. 472 M
paikowski@grayson.edu
PAINE, Clarke, C .... 717-291-3991. 416 J
clarke.paine@fandm.edu
PAINE, Gage .... 512-471-1133. 491 C
gage.paine@austin.utexas.edu
PAINE, James .... 636-227-2100. 276 F
james.paine@logan.edu
PAINO, Troy, D .... 660-785-4100. 282 L
tpaino@truman.edu
PAIR-CUNNINGHAM,
Stephanie, S .... 301-322-0649. 217 F
pairss@pgcc.edu
PAISANT, Julie .... 408-924-2250... 36 A
julie.paisant@sjsu.edu
PAIZ, Larry, P .... 214-350-9722. 469 M
larry.paiz@cri.edu
PAJAK, Daniel, T .... 304-829-7217. 526 D
dpajak@bethanywv.edu
PAJE-MANALO, Leila, L . 603-862-3491. 298 C
leila.paje-manalo@unh.edu
PAJIC, Natasa .... 859-233-8213. 199 I
npajic@transy.edu
PAK, Scott .... 714-816-0366... 70 A
scott.pak@trident.edu
PAKALA, James, C .... 314-434-4044. 273 C
jim.pakala@covenantseminary.edu
PAKIESER, Erik .... 763-424-0806. 260 C
epakieser@nhcc.edu
PAKOWSKI, Lawrence ..... 910-755-7324. 358 D
pakowskil@brunswickcc.edu
PAKSTIS, John .... 978-934-4331. 229 B
john_pakstis@uml.edu
PALACIO, Michelle .... 305-348-1757. 115 B
michelle.palacio@fiu.edu
PALACIOS, Elizabeth .... 254-710-3653. 467 G
liz_palacios@baylor.edu
PALACIOS, Luz, M .... 787-786-3030. 547 F
lpalacios@ucb.edu.pr
PALACIOS, Sarah .... 505-984-6103. 311 H
alumni@sjcsf.edu
PALAGONIA, Michael ..... 802-635-1205. 501 D
michael.palagonia@jsc.edu
PALAKAL, Mathew, J ...... 317-278-7689. 168 D
mpalakal@iupui.edu
PALAMIOTIS, Nikki .... 678-915-4276. 132 C
npalamio@spsu.edu
PALAMOUNTAIN,
Valerie .... 434-961-5333. 513 F
vpalamountain@pvcc.edu
PALAN, Kay .... 269-387-5050. 252 I
kay.palan@wmich.edu
PALANGI, Anthony .... 518-743-2246. 345 E
palangia@sunyacc.edu
PALANTZAS, Nicholas .... 781-821-2222. 232 A
PALARDY, William, B ..... 781-899-5500. 223 E
rev.palardy@blessedjohnxxiii.edu
PALASOTA, Joanna, E .... 713-525-3151. 490 L
palasota@stthom.edu
PALASOTA, John .... 713-525-6918. 490 L
japalaso@stthom.edu
PALATELLA, Anna Marie 724-925-4091. 437 D
palatellaa@wccc.edu
PALAZOLA, Cecelia .... 901-272-5142. 456 F
cpalazola@mca.edu
PALAZZO, Robert .... 205-934-5643..... 8 E
rpalazzo@uab.edu
PALCZEWSKI, Christine .. 716-896-0700. 350 A
cepalcz@villa.edu
PALCZEWSKI,
Christine, E .... 716-896-0700. 350 A
cepalcz@villa.edu
PALDER, Amy .... 404-364-8462. 130 A
apalder@oglethorpe.edu
PALEFSKY, Lou .... 212-875-4679. 314 C
finaid@bankstreet.edu
PALEN, Lisa .... 203-575-8100... 89 B
lpalen@nvcc.commnet.edu
PALERMO, Lisa .... 651-730-5100. 255 H
lpalermo@globeuniversity.edu
PALERMO, Marty .... 561-586-0121. 106 I
PALERMO, Pam .... 231-995-1533. 248 B
ppalermo@nmc.edu
PALERMO, Tina .... 561-586-0121. 106 I
PALESE, Rick .... 312-788-1133. 162 H
rpalese@vandercook.edu
PALEY, Laura .... 847-574-5188. 150 C
lbarnes-paley@lfgsm.edu
PALEY, Noelle .... 607-753-2336. 343 B
noelle.paley@cortland.edu
PALINKAS, Robert, D ..... 217-333-2711. 162 A
palinkas@illinois.edu
PALINSKY, David, W ...... 661-336-5147... 49 M
dpalinsk@kccd.edu
PALK, Laura .... 405-325-4124. 401 B
lpalk@ou.edu
PALLA, Joe .... 707-527-1000... 65 B
jpalla@santarosa.edu
PALLADINO, Mark .... 215-951-2700. 430 E
palladinom@philau.edu
PALLADINO, Michael ...... 732-571-3421. 303 C
mpalladi@monmouth.edu
PALLADINO, Michael ..... 212-752-1530. 328 G
michael.palladino@limcollege.edu
PALLADINO, Michael, A 215-898-9386. 435 B
mikep@isc.upenn.edu
PALLADINO, Richard ...... 914-633-2351. 327 C
rpalladino@iona.edu
PALLADINO, Robert .... 740-283-6405. 379 N
rpalladino@franciscan.edu
PALLAVICINI, Maria, G .. 209-946-2551... 73 A
mpallavicini@pacific.edu
PALLEJA, Sandra .... 212-237-8873. 318 D
spalleja@jjay.cuny.edu
PALLEMONI, Sushil .... 361-698-1207. 471 G
spallemoni@delmar.edu
PALLER, Alan .... 301-654-7267. 218 C
PALLONE, Donna, L .... 724-287-8711. 411 C
donna.pallone@bc3.edu
PALLOTO, Mike .... 805-289-6486... 74 H
mpalloto@vcccd.edu
PALM, Don .... 530-747-5220... 53 D
palmd@scc.losrios.edu
PALM, Don .... 916-375-5513... 53 D
palmd@scc.losrios.edu
PALM, Elizabeth, A .... 847-735-5107. 150 B
palm@lakeforest.edu
PALM, Matt .... 419-448-2020. 380 G
mpalm@heidelberg.edu
PALM, Risa, I .... 404-413-2574. 126 E
risapalm@gsu.edu
PALM, Ryan .... 814-824-3320. 423 J
rpalm@mercyhurst.edu
PALMA, Eugene .... 516-877-3505. 313 A
palma@adelphi.edu
PALMA, Yazmin .... 305-273-4499. 100 H
yazmin@cbt.edu
PALMER, Betty, G .... 404-627-2681. 121 H
betty.palmer@beulah.org
PALMER, Brian .... 904-256-7374. 107 Q
bpalmer@ju.edu
PALMER, Catherine .... 973-278-5400. 314 K
cat@berkeleycollege.edu
PALMER, Charles .... 813-545-4527. 444 A
charlespalmer@forrrestcollege.edu
PALMER, Colleen .... 617-585-1295. 234 I
colleen.palmer@necmusic.edu
PALMER, Dale, J .... 404-413-3434. 126 E
dpalmer@gsu.edu
PALMER, Daniel .... 605-773-3455. 451 E
daniel.palmer2@sdbor.edu
PALMER, David .... 901-321-4321. 453 H
David.Palmer@cbu.edu
PALMER, Donald, F .... 330-672-2312. 382 B
dpalmer@kent.edu
PALMER, Douglas, J ...... 979-862-6649. 483 C
dpalmer@tamu.edu
PALMER, Eric .... 810-766-4237. 239 G
ericpalmer@baker.edu
PALMER, Eric .... 810-766-4238. 239 H
eric.palmer@baker.edu
PALMER, Eric, F .... 804-287-6591. 510 L
epalmer@richmond.edu
PALMER, Gail .... 785-670-1151. 191 D
gail.palmer@washburn.edu
PALMER, Gary .... 620-223-2700. 186 G
garyp@fortscott.edu
PALMER, Gregory .... 914-323-5194. 330 B
greg.palmer@mville.edu
PALMER, Harvey, J .... 585-475-2146. 337 L
hjpeen@rit.edu
PALMER, Jacqueline .... 202-408-2400... 96 F
PALMER, James .... 706-864-1786. 133 D
james.palmer@ung.edu
PALMER, Jan, E .... 304-293-6978. 530 D
jpalmer@hsc.wvu.edu
PALMER, Janice .... 860-832-1791... 87 K
palmerj@ccsu.edu
PALMER, Jeffrey, L .... 302-831-3007... 94 B
jpalmer@udel.edu
PALMER, Jim .... 325-574-7905. 494 K
jpalmer@wtc.edu
PALMER, John .... 217-228-5432. 156 C
palmejo@quincy.edu
PALMER, John .... 651-846-1482. 261 D
john.palmer@saintpaul.edu
PALMER, John .... 320-308-3143. 261 B
jwpalmer@stcloudstate.edu
PALMER, Jonathan .... 618-374-5148. 156 B
president@principia.edu
PALMER, Joy Jimena, J . 626-448-0023... 48 L
academicdean@itsla.edu
PALMER, Joyce .... 315-792-5477. 331 I
jpalmer@mvcc.edu
PALMER, Julio .... 787-841-2000. 552 B
jpalmer@pucpr.edu
PALMER, Kevin .... 573-875-7329. 272 G
kpalmer@ccis.edu
PALMER, Kris, R .... 660-284-4800. 275 B
PALMER, Linda .... 801-422-3605. 495 D
Linda.Palmer@byu.edu
PALMER, Lisa .... 706-771-4089. 121 D
lpalmer@augustatech.edu
PALMER, Magali .... 787-279-1912. 550 B
mpalmer@bayamon.inter.edu
PALMER, Marila .... 903-886-5926. 483 E
marila.palmer@tamuc.edu
PALMER, Martha .... 660-284-4800. 275 B
PALMER, Mel .... 706-548-8505. 130 E
mpalmer@piedmont.edu
PALMER, Michael, D .... 757-352-4406. 508 G
mpalmer@regent.edu
PALMER, Nikki .... 907-822-3201... 10 A
info@akbible.edu
PALMER, Patricia .... 501-812-2210... 22 G
ppalmer@pulaskitech.edu
PALMER, Rick .... 435-879-4287. 497 E
palmer@dixie.edu
PALMER, Ron .... 304-637-1252. 526 E
palmerr@dewv.edu
PALMER, Roxanne .... 772-466-4822... 98 L
roxanne.palmer@aviator.edu
PALMER, Russell, A .... 516-877-3249. 313 A
palmer@adelphi.edu
PALMER, Sandra .... 860-512-2603... 88 G
spalmer@manchestercc.edu
PALMER, Scott .... 952-888-4777. 263 B
spalmer@nwhealth.edu
PALMER, Scott .... 541-684-7291. 405 C
spalmer@nwcu.edu
PALMER, Susan, M .... 320-363-5298. 254 J
spalmer@csbsju.edu
PALMERI, Marlan, K .... 570-208-5900. 419 P
mkpalmer@kings.edu
PALMIERI, Becky .... 518-587-2100. 346 A
becky.palmieri@esc.edu
PALMIERI, Ernie .... 914-251-5985. 344 D
ernie.palmieri@purchase.edu
PALMIERI, Kathryn .... 408-554-2377... 64 M
kpalmieri@scu.edu
PALMIERI, Robert .... 315-866-0300. 326 A
palmierrh@herkimer.edu
PALMIERI, Sherrie .... 603-594-2567. 297 H
spalmieri@sjhnh.org
PALMINI, Bill .... 415-565-4611... 71 A
palminib@uchastings.edu
PALMIRA, Arroyo .... 787-753-6335. 549 D
apalmira@icprjc.edu
PALMITER, Lia Richards . 570-961-4799. 423 B
lpalmiter@marywood.edu
PALO, Eric, E .... 425-235-2331. 522 F
epalo@rtc.edu
PALOK, Debra .... 623-845-3536... 14 M
debra.palok@gcmail.maricopa.edu
PALOMARIA, Sam .... 903-233-4171. 475 J
SamPalomaria@letu.edu
PALOMBI,
Peggy Shaddock .... 205-391-5830...... 6 H
pspalombi@sheltonstate.edu
PALOMBO, Tom, J .... 336-316-2290. 355 A
tpalombo@guilford.edu
PALOMO, Giovanni .... 212-226-5500. 314 A
gpalomo@aii.edu
PALONE, James, E .... 330-471-8255. 383 D
jpalone@malone.edu
PALONSKY, Stuart, B ..... 573-882-3893. 283 C
palonskys@missouri.edu
PALSA, Megan .... 972-860-8142. 470 H
mpalsa@dcccd.edu
PALSAK, Angela .... 269-782-1310. 250 C
apalsak@swmich.edu
PALSER, Philip, V .... 715-833-6364. 539 J
ppalser@cvtc.edu
PALTER-GILL, Dianne ..... 978-762-4000. 232 D
dpalterg@northshore.edu
PALUBNIAK, Dan .... 908-526-1200. 305 B
dpalubu@raritanval.edu
PALUMBO, Andrew, B .... 603-535-2437. 298 G
abpalumbo@plymouth.edu
PALUMBO, Carmine .... 478-289-2046. 124 C
cpalumbo@ega.edu
PALUMBO, Daniel .... 212-237-8299. 318 D
dpalumbo@jjay.cuny.edu
PALUMBO, Katey .... 508-929-8835. 230 G
kpalumbo2@worcester.edu
PALUMBO, Michelle .... 314-889-1492. 274 E
mpalumbo@fontbonne.edu
PALUMBO-OLSZANSKI,
Linda .... 706-233-7409. 131 E
lpalumbo@shorter.edu
PALZER, Jon, A .... 585-785-1224. 324 D
palzerja@flcc.edu
PAMINTUAN, Lisa .... 516-364-0808. 333 D
pamintuan@nycollege.edu
PAMMER, Andrea, M ...... 304-367-4686. 529 F
Andrea.Pammer@fairmontstate.edu
PAN, Judy .... 847-679-3135. 149 G
judy@ksi.edu
PAN, Shouan .... 480-461-7300... 15 A
shouan.pan@mesacc.edu
PANAIA, Sharon .... 724-335-5336. 425 F
spanaia@oaa.edu
PANARELLA, Pamela ...... 610-409-3163. 436 B
ppanarella@ursinus.edu
PANAS, Voytek .... 703-821-8570. 510 B
vpanas@stratford.edu
PANAYOTOVA, Evelina ... 610-790-1905. 409 E
evelina.panayotova@alvernia.edu
PANCHAL, Praveen .... 212-650-8223. 317 D
ppanchal@ccny.cuny.edu
PANCHANATHEN,
Sethuraman .... 480-965-4831... 11 K
panch@asu.edu
PANCHUCK, Paula .... 617-663-7054. 227 K
ppanchuck@lasell.edu
PANCHUK, Victor .... 404-880-8016. 122 J
vpanchuk@cau.edu
PANCIC-MEIER, Vanesa .. 503-682-3903. 407 B
vpancics-meier@pioneerpacific.edu
PANCIERA, Kathy .... 651-290-7522. 265 F
kathy.panciera@wmitchell.edu
PANCZA, Wayne .... 215-780-1402. 433 A
wpancza@salus.edu
PANDE, Sameer .... 281-283-3008. 489 C
pande@uhcl.edu
PANDELADIS, Leo .... 717-720-4030. 427 G
lpandeladis@passhe.edu
PANDEY, Bhuban, R .... 512-448-8442. 479 C
bhubanp@stedwards.edu
PANDIAN, R. Devadoss . 630-637-5354. 154 F
rdpandian@noctrl.edu
PANDIT, Kavita, K .... 706-542-2202. 133 C
pandit@uga.edu
PANDO, Paula .... 201-360-4021. 302 D
ppando@hccc.edu
PANEPINTO, Debora ...... 504-866-7426. 206 B
registrar@nds.edu
PANESAR, Paul, S .... 858-499-0202... 40 C
panesar@coleman.edu
PANETTA, Carol .... 617-277-3915. 224 C
panettac@bgsp.edu
PANFIL, Tim .... 630-617-6471. 145 A
panfilt@elmhurst.edu
PANG, Alex .... 310-506-4561... 58 H
alex.pang@pepperdine.edu
PANG, Eddie .... 808-735-4856. 135 D
epang@chaminade.edu
PANG, John .... 510-981-2849... 59 A
jpang@peralta.edu
PANG, Lily .... 310-506-4130... 58 H
lily.pang@pepperdine.edu
PANGALLO, Karen .... 978-762-4000. 232 D
kpangal@northshore.edu
PANGBORN, Joseph ...... 401-841-6555. 545 A
PANGBORN, Robert, N .. 814-865-2505. 426 A
rnp1@psu.edu

PANGBURN, William ...... 212-237-8204. 318 D bpangburn@jjay.cuny.edu
PANGELINAN, Leo .... 670-234-5498. 547 A leop@nmcnet.edu
PANGONIS, Patricia .... 440-375-7000. 382 L tpangonis@lec.edu
PANHANS, Matthew, A ... 414-277-7287. 534 G panhans@msoe.edu
PANI, Eric, A .... 318-342-1025. 208 E pani@ulm.edu
PANKEY, Bruce .... 301-628-5427. 217 C bpankey@nlc.edu
PANKEY, Susan .... 802-860-2778. 499 A pankey@champlain.edu
PANKIEVICH, Michael .... 617-989-4575. 237 G pankievichm@wit.edu
PANKRATZ, Terry .... 972-883-4802. 491 E Terry.Pankratz@utdallas.edu
PANLILIO, Carmen .... 219-989-2367. 171 N carmen.panlilio@purduecal.edu
PANNEGGIANTE, John ... 201-559-6089. 302 A pane@felician.edu
PANNELL, Melody, M ...... 804-342-3812. 515 F mmpannell@vuu.edu
PANNELL, Randall .... 864-977-7011. 445 H randall.pannell@ngu.edu
PANNELL, Vernese .... 212-410-8054. 333 E vpannel@nycpm.edu
PANNILL, W. Stephen .... 410-287-1025. 214 B spannill@cecil.edu
PANNKUK, Matthew .... 620-417-1161. 190 F matthew.pannkuk@sccc.edu
PANOFF, Virginia .... 231-348-6698. 247 H vpanoff@ncmich.edu
PANTALEO, Mark .... 251-981-3771..... 2 I mark.pantaleo@columbiasouthern.edu
PANTANO, Laura .... 603-428-2241. 297 D lpantano@nec.edu
PANTIC, Zorica .... 617-989-4476. 237 G panticz@wit.edu
PANTLIK, Sandy .... 405-208-5898. 397 F slpantlik@okcu.edu
PANTOJA, Antonio, L ..... 787-279-1912. 550 B apantoja@bayamon.inter.edu
PANTOJA, Veronica .... 818-785-2726... 37 F veronica.pantoja@casalomacollege.edu
PANTONE, Dirk .... 303-220-1200... 78 K dirk.pantone@cffp.edu
PANU, Al .... 678-717-3835. 133 D al.panu@ung.edu
PANZARELLA, Amy .... 304-724-3700. 526 B apanzarella@apus.edu
PANZECA, Linda .... 513-244-4393. 377 G linda_panzeca@mail.msj.edu
PANZER, Richard .... 845-752-3000. 348 I r.panzer@uts.edu
PAO, Roger .... 617-951-2350. 234 G roger.pao@necb.edu
PAOLELLI, Arthur .... 518-381-1202. 340 G paolela@sunysccc.edu
PAOLINI, Francine .... 616-632-2131. 239 E paolifra@aquinas.edu
PAOLUCCI, Jeff .... 719-384-6833... 83 M jeff.paolucci@ojc.edu
PAPADIMITRIOU, Dimitri .... 914-758-7426. 222 E dpb@bard.edu
PAPADIMITRIOU, Dimitri, B .... 845-758-7426. 314 D dbp@levy.bard.edu
PAPADIMOS, Peter, J .... 419-530-8411. 392 B peter.papadimos@utoledo.edu
PAPADOPOULOS, Michael .... 518-783-2376. 340 J mpapadopoulos@siena.edu
PAPAFIL, Drucie, A .... 757-446-6143. 504 E papafida@evms.edu
PAPAGEORGE, Anne ...... 215-898-7241. 435 B fresvp@upenn.edu
PAPAJOHN, Michelle ..... 631-687-5151. 339 B mpapajohn@sjcny.edu
PAPAKONSTANTINOU, Karen .... 732-255-0400. 304 A karenp@ocean.edu
PAPALEO, Stefano .... 561-237-7831. 108 X spapaleo@lynn.edu
PAPALIA, Daria .... 845-451-1359. 322 D d_papalia@culinary.edu
PAPALIA, Jean, M .... 617-627-2306. 237 C jean.papalia@tufts.edu
PAPANDREA, Vincent ..... 718-429-6600. 349 H vincent.papandrea@vaughn.edu
PAPANIKOLAOU, Constantia .... 617-994-6928. 228 D cpapanikolaou@bhe.mass.edu
PAPARO, Michael .... 315-781-3344. 326 C paparo@hws.edu
PAPATHOMAS, Thomas, V .... 848-445-6533. 306 B papathom@rci.rutgers.edu
PAPAZIAN, Mary, A .... 203-392-5250... 88 A papazianm1@southernct.edu
PAPAZIAN, Richard .... 617-873-0235. 224 G Richard.Papazian@cambridgecollege.edu
PAPE, Jim .... 270-534-3370. 196 G jim.pape@kctcs.edu
PAPE, Sabrina .... 845-437-5787. 349 G sapape@vassar.edu
PAPER, Teresa, A .... 563-441-4173. 178 C tapaper@eicc.edu
PAPESCH, Katherine .... 217-732-3155. 151 C kpapesch@lincolncollege.edu
PAPICH, Mark .... 210-829-6053. 490 A papich@uiwtx.edu
PAPILLO, Nicholas, J ..... 203-254-4000... 89 I npapillo@fairfield.edu
PAPINCHAK, John, R ..... 412-268-7404. 412 H jp7p@andrew.cmu.edu
PAPINI, Dennis .... 605-688-4723. 452 B dennis.papini@sdstate.edu
PAPP, Daniel, S .... 770-423-6033. 127 N dpapp@kennesaw.edu
PAPP, Justin .... 708-596-2000. 159 C jpapp@ssc.edu
PAPPALARDO, Faye .... 410-386-8188. 214 A fpappalardo@carrollcc.edu
PAPPALARDO, Thomas, J .... 412-924-1778. 431 A tpappalardo@pts.edu
PAPPAS, Amy .... 703-284-1681. 507 B amy.pappas@marymount.edu
PAPPAS, Domenica, G ... 312-567-3035. 147 F pappas@iit.edu
PAPPAS, Gregory, J .... 718-817-4350. 324 G pappas@fordham.edu
PAPPAS, James, P .... 405-325-6361. 401 B jpappas@ou.edu
PAPPAS, Joanna .... 773-508-7429. 151 H jpappas@luc.edu
PAPPAS, Kathrine .... 413-782-1327. 238 A kpappas@wne.edu
PAPPAS, Richard, J .... 616-698-7111. 241 H rpappas@davenport.edu
PAPPAS, Tony, A .... 641-422-4350. 181 D pappaton@niacc.edu
PAPPATHAN, Matthew ... 802-828-8740. 390 C matt.pappathan@myunion.edu
PAPROCKI, Ronald, J ..... 585-275-2800. 349 C rpaprocki@admin.rochester.edu
PAPSON, Melissa .... 724-222-5330. 425 K mpapson@penncommercial.edu
PAQUET, Casey .... 727-864-7987. 101 N paquetcd@eckerd.edu
PAQUETTE, Ashley .... 906-932-4231. 242 I ashleyp@gogebic.edu
PAQUETTE, James .... 410-617-2283. 216 A jrpaquette1@loyola.edu
PAQUETTE, Kevin .... 207-893-7797. 211 G kpaquett@sjcme.edu
PAQUETTE, Patricia .... 206-934-4105. 522 H patricia.paquette@seattlecolleges.edu
PAQUIN, Delbert .... 928-724-6772... 13 H dpaquin@dinecollege.edu
PARA, Donald .... 562-985-4121... 33 F csulb-president@csulb.edu
PARADIS, Rick .... 516-759-2040. 350 C rparadis@webb.edu
PARADIS, Ronald, S .... 541-383-7599. 402 D rparadis@cocc.edu
PARADISE, Melanie .... 865-539-7130. 461 D mmparadise@pstcc.edu
PARADISE, Richard .... 321-433-7202. 101 M paradiser@easternflorida.edu
PARADKAR, Vishvas ...... 719-389-6454... 79 D vishvas.paradkar@ColoradoCollege.edu
PARAMORE, Marcus .... 334-241-8622..... 7 H marcus@troy.edu
PARAMORE, Mary .... 252-493-7216. 362 G mparamore@email.pittcc.edu
PARAS, Ernesto .... 312-332-0707. 160 J
PARASKA, William, F ...... 404-413-4401. 126 E bparaska@gsu.edu
PARASKOS, John, A .... 508-856-2323. 229 C john.paraskos@umassmed.edu
PARCEL, Julie .... 636-922-8383. 280 J jparcel@stchas.edu
PARCELLS, Fred .... 215-785-0111. 426 X
PARCELLS, Rex .... 254-659-7821. 473 A rparcells@hillcollege.edu
PARDALES, Michael .... 207-893-6641. 211 G mpardales@sjcme.edu
PARDALES, Michael, J .... 716-888-3294. 316 C pardalem@canisius.edu
PARDEE, Joseph .... 860-701-5176... 90 G pardee_j@mitchell.edu
PARDIE, Lynn .... 217-206-6614. 161 E pardie.lynn@uis.edu
PARDIECK, David, L .... 309-677-3086. 140 I dlp@bradley.edu
PARDINI, Ron .... 775-784-1660. 294 J ronp@cabnr.unr.edu
PARDO, Kathleen .... 314-246-7698. 284 N kpardo@webster.edu
PARDO, Liane .... 407-628-5870. 102 K lpardo@cci.edu
PARDUE, Karen .... 207-221-4361. 213 A kpardue@une.edu
PARDUE, Stacy .... 919-760-8346. 356 G pardues@meredith.edu
PAREDES, Edith .... 954-322-4460. 107 V paredese@jmvu.edu
PAREDES, Esteban .... 785-827-5541. 188 C esteban.paredes@kwu.edu
PAREKH, Purvi .... 201-684-7115. 305 A purvi@ramapo.edu
PARENT, Cyrille .... 719-502-2975... 84 A cyrille.parent@ppcc.edu
PARENTE, JR., James, A .... 612-624-2535. 264 G paren001@umn.edu
PARENTI, Stefano .... 603-645-9695. 297 I s.parenti@snhu.edu
PARFITT, Mark .... 518-743-2245. 345 E parfittm@sunyacc.edu
PARFITT, Richard .... 239-489-9339. 101 O raparfitt@edison.edu
PARGE, Theodore, C .... 630-844-5262. 140 A tparge@aurora.edu
PARHAM, Dave .... 678-915-7333. 132 C dparham@spsu.edu
PARHAM, Loretta .... 404-978-2018. 132 E lparham@auctr.edu
PARHAM, Martha .... 714-438-4605... 39 H mparham@mail.cccd.edu
PARHAM, Patricia .... 805-493-3185... 31 H pparham@callutheran.edu
PARHAM, Sandra .... 310-243-3700... 33 B sparham@csudh.edu
PARHAM, Thomas, A .... 949-824-4804... 71 B taparham@uci.edu
PARHAM, Walter, H .... 803-777-7854. 447 G t.parham@sc.edu
PARIANTE, Jody .... 212-431-2137. 333 I Jody.Pariante@nyls.edu
PARINI, Shelly .... 503-594-3015. 402 F shellyp@clackamas.edu
PARIS, Kathleen, A .... 608-246-6460. 540 C kparis@madisoncollege.edu
PARIS, Lisa .... 215-670-9127. 425 J lparis@peirce.edu
PARIS, Mark, S .... 302-356-6829... 94 E mark.s.paris@wilmu.edu
PARIS, III, Oren .... 479-248-7236... 21 B oparis3@ecollege.edu
PARIS, Robin .... 615-383-4848. 464 D rparis@watkins.edu
PARIS, Susan .... 617-989-4589. 237 G pariss@wit.edu
PARIS, JR., Wendell ...... 305-626-3762. 104 J Wendell.Paris@fmuniv.edu
PARISEAU, Anita .... 719-389-6772... 79 D anita.pariseau@ColoradoCollege.edu
PARISH, Janet .... 386-506-3075. 101 G parishj@DaytonaState.edu
PARISH, Michael, C .... 906-248-8400. 240 J mparish@bmcc.edu
PARISH, Paula .... 210-434-6711. 477 N pparish@lake.ollusa.edu
PARISHER, Deborah .... 252-823-5166. 360 C parisherd@edgecombe.edu
PARISI, Dawn .... 352-588-8251. 112 D dawn.parisi@saintleo.edu
PARISI, Joseph .... 636-949-4812. 276 D jparisi@lindenwood.edu
PARISI, Michael .... 410-293-1104. 545 J parisi@usna.edu
PARISI, Rob .... 805-922-6966... 26 K rparisi@hancockcollege.edu
PARISI, Robert .... 805-922-6966... 26 K rparisi@hancockcollege.edu
PARISI, Valerie, M .... 313-577-1335. 252 G dv6552@wayne.edu
PARK, Chan, J .... 561-237-7186. 108 X cpark@lynn.edu
PARK, Choong Gi .... 562-926-1023... 60 B elpis@yahoo.com
PARK, Daniel, L .... 509-527-5999. 525 E park@whitman.edu
PARK, Daniel, W .... 858-822-1236... 71 F dwpark@ucsd.edu
PARK, David .... 714-533-3946... 36 C dpark@calums.edu
PARK, Debra, S .... 716-888-2790. 316 C parkd@canisius.edu
PARK, E.K. (Eun) .... 530-898-6880... 33 A ekpark@csuchico.edu
PARK, George .... 310-453-8300... 43 D george@emperors.edu
PARK, Heerei .... 408-260-0208... 44 J korean@fivebranches.edu
PARK, Hojin .... 215-884-8942. 438 A admissions@woninstitute.edu
PARK, Hyung .... 213-252-5100... 26 A
PARK, Jack, C .... 210-567-2020. 493 A parkjc@uthscsa.edu
PARK, James, E .... 816-654-7108. 275 K jpark@kcumb.edu
PARK, James, S .... 540-464-7390. 515 B parkjs@vmi.edu
PARK, Jessica .... 213-252-5100... 26 A
PARK, Jinsoo .... 973-877-3588. 301 H jpark@essex.edu
PARK, Julia .... 213-487-0110... 42 K financialaid@dula.edu
PARK, Kathryn .... 409-933-8201. 469 E kpark@com.edu
PARK, Kevin .... 404-687-4533. 123 C parkk@ctsnet.edu
PARK, Linda .... 315-279-5208. 328 D lpark@mail.keuka.edu
PARK, Matthew .... 940-397-4501. 476 H matthew.park@mwsu.edu
PARK, Mi .... 562-926-1023... 60 B mhpark@ptsa.edu
PARK, Michelle .... 714-533-1495... 66 H isa@southbaylo.edu
PARK, Mimi .... 714-533-1495... 66 H mimi@southbaylo.edu
PARK, Myung .... 425-739-8287. 520 K myung.park@lwtech.edu
PARK, No Hee .... 310-206-6063... 71 C npark@dent.ucla.edu
PARK, Shelley, S .... 859-622-2361. 193 P shelley.park@eku.edu
PARK, Steve .... 972-860-7771. 470 F spark@dcccd.edu
PARK, Sung Keun .... 714-517-1945... 29 K
PARK, Sunny .... 806-720-7507. 476 B sunny.park@lcu.edu
PARK, Yong Hee .... 714-533-1495... 66 H yhpark@southbaylo.edu
PARK, Yung Won .... 610-917-1457. 436 C ywpark@vfcc.edu
PARKE, Lydia .... 215-780-1417. 433 A lparke@salus.edu
PARKER, Aaron, L .... 601-426-6346. 269 G aparker@southeasternbaptist.edu
PARKER, Annette, S .... 804-862-6200. 508 H aparker@rbc.edu
PARKER, Anthony, O .... 229-430-3502. 120 A aparker@albanytech.edu
PARKER, Barbara .... 828-627-4515. 361 B bmparker@haywood.edu
PARKER, Beverly .... 318-670-9571. 207 A bparker@susla.edu
PARKER, Brent .... 215-619-7416. 424 B bparker@mc3.edu
PARKER, Brian .... 212-659-3610. 328 E bparker@tkc.edu
PARKER, Carol, A .... 864-231-2120. 441 B cparker@andersonuniversity.edu
PARKER, Cassandra .... 202-274-5323... 97 A cparker@udc.edu
PARKER, Cathy .... 601-484-8799. 267 G cparker@meridiancc.edu
PARKER, Charles, R .... 850-263-3261... 98 N crparker@baptistcollege.edu
PARKER, Charlie .... 912-433-7174. 131 H ceparker@southuniversity.edu
PARKER, Christine .... 304-865-6229. 527 F christine.parker@ovu.edu
PARKER, Christopher .... 276-656-0281. 513 D cparker@patrickhenry.edu
PARKER, Collier, B .... 570-340-6000. 423 B cbparker@marywood.edu
PARKER, Craig .... 502-897-4142. 199 B cparker@sbts.edu
PARKER, Cynthia .... 706-295-6346. 125 C cparker@highlands.edu
PARKER, Cynthia, L .... 401-598-1345. 439 B cparker@jwu.edu
PARKER, Dana .... 513-558-9964. 391 B dana.parker@uc.edu
PARKER, Dana, C .... 610-436-2627. 430 A dparker@wcupa.edu
PARKER, Danny, M .... 864-231-2145. 441 B dparker@andersonuniversity.edu
PARKER, Darnell .... 410-778-7457. 221 C dparker2@washcoll.edu
PARKER, Darrell .... 828-227-7401. 369 E dfparker@wcu.edu
PARKER, David .... 336-506-4301. 357 M dave.parker@alamancecc.edu
PARKER, Deborah .... 870-762-3151... 19 K dparker@smail.anc.edu
PARKER, Debra, O .... 919-530-5269. 368 A dparker@nccu.edu
PARKER, Diane .... 617-243-2137. 227 K dparker@lasell.edu
PARKER, Donna .... 610-399-2000. 428 B dparker@cheyney.edu
PARKER, Frank .... 936-294-1786. 487 A fparker@shsu.edu

PARKER, Gail, C ... 318-342-1961. 208 E
gparker@ulm.edu

PARKER, George ... 530-634-7643... 77 K
gparker@yccd.edu

PARKER, Gilbert, A ... 607-729-1581. 322 F
gparker@davisny.edu

PARKER, Gilda ... 713-221-8563. 489 D
parkergil@uhd.edu

PARKER, Heidi ... 641-673-1031. 183 H
parkerh@wmpenn.edu

PARKER, James ... 218-755-2075. 258 A
jparker@bemidjistate.edu

PARKER, James, T ... 801-581-6857. 496 Q
jparker@purchasing.utah.edu

PARKER, Janet ... 910-892-3178. 355 B
jparker@heritagebiblecollege.edu

PARKER, Janice, C ... 312-658-5100. 160 G
janice.parker@tbiil.edu

PARKER, Jeffrey ... 303-315-2750... 86 A
jeff.parker@ucdenver.edu

PARKER, Jerome, S ... 610-359-5100. 414 D
jparker@dccc.edu

PARKER, Jill ... 530-752-2599... 70 J
jblack@ucdavis.edu

PARKER, Jim, O ... 504-816-8592. 206 A
jparker@nobts.edu

PARKER, Jo Ellen ... 434-381-6210. 510 F
jparker@sbc.edu

PARKER, Jonathan, K ... 951-343-4213... 30 H
jparker@calbaptist.edu

PARKER, Joyce, E ... 310-233-4551... 51 H
parkerje@lahc.edu

PARKER, Juli ... 508-910-4582. 229 A
jparker@umassd.edu

PARKER, Karen, L ... 434-582-2445. 506 I
kparker@liberty.edu

PARKER, Kathleen ... 320-363-2121. 263 P
kparker@csbsju.edu

PARKER, Kathleen ... 320-363-5195. 254 J
kparker@csbsju.edu

PARKER, Keith ... 561-732-4424. 112 G
kparker@svdp.edu

PARKER, Keith, S ... 310-794-6811... 71 C
kparker@support.ucla.edu

PARKER, Kevin ... 845-758-7511. 314 D
parker@bard.edu

PARKER, Kim ... 214-637-3530. 494 E
kparker@wadecollege.edu

PARKER, Kim ... 713-646-1803. 480 J
kparker@stcl.edu

PARKER, Linda, M ... 518-388-6123. 348 J
parkerl@union.edu

PARKER, Maria ... 870-584-4471... 24 F
mparker@cccua.edu

PARKER, Maria, D ... 205-665-6050..... 9 B
parkermd@montevallo.edu

PARKER, Mark ... 405-208-5315. 397 F
mparker@okcu.edu

PARKER, Mary ... 310-393-0411... 58 E
mfparker@rand.org

PARKER, Mary, G ... 801-581-3490. 496 Q
mgparker@sa.utah.edu

PARKER, Mary Jo ... 713-221-8471. 489 D
parkerm@uhd.edu

PARKER, Melanie, L ... 617-715-5329. 233 B

PARKER, Micah ... 951-343-4318... 30 H
miparker@calbaptist.edu

PARKER, Mike ... 731-352-4239. 453 D
parkerm@bethelu.edu

PARKER, Peggy ... 910-892-3178. 355 B
pparker@heritagebiblecollege.edu

PARKER, Pennie ... 407-646-2636. 111 Q
pparker@rollins.edu

PARKER, Philip, L ... 812-464-1865. 174 D
plparker@usi.edu

PARKER, Pippin ... 212-229-5859. 332 E
parkerp@newschool.edu

PARKER, Randy ... 336-334-4822. 360 G

PARKER, Rebecca ... 510-549-4724... 68 G
rparker@sksm.edu

PARKER, Robert ... 404-471-6236. 119 I
rparker@agnesscott.edu

PARKER, Robin, L ... 513-529-6734. 384 G
parkerrl@miamioh.edu

PARKER, Rodney ... 410-617-2310. 216 A
rparker1@loyola.edu

PARKER, Ron ... 979-230-3480. 468 A
ron.parker@brazosport.edu

PARKER, Sandra ... 513-745-5736. 391 A
sandra.parker@uc.edu

PARKER, Savander ... 408-274-7900... 63 O
savander.parker@evc.edu

PARKER, Sirena ... 662-329-7127. 268 E
sparker@ss.muw.edu

PARKER, Sonia ... 801-957-4446. 498 B
sonia.parker@slcc.edu

PARKER, Stephen ... 434-961-5207. 513 F
sparker@pvcc.edu

PARKER, Tammie ... 541-278-5850. 402 C
tparker@bluecc.edu

PARKER, Teresa ... 740-389-4636. 383 F
parkert@mtc.edu

PARKER, Terry ... 303-273-3399... 80 E
tparker@mines.edu

PARKER, Thomas, H ... 413-542-2328. 221 G
admissions@amherst.edu

PARKER, Tim ... 205-879-5588..... 3 H
tparker@faulkner.edu

PARKER, Zoann, J ... 443-412-2170. 215 C
zparker@harford.edu

PARKER AMES, Gwen ... 845-675-4446. 335 C
gwen.ames@nyack.edu

PARKER-AYERS,
Jennifer ... 256-372-4735.... 1 A
martin.sherrill@aamu.edu

PARKER-BELL, Bernice ... 904-470-8261. 102 A
bparkerbell@ewc.edu

PARKER-JEFFRIES,
Terry ... 704-463-3057. 365 E
terry.jeffries@fsmail.pfeiffer.edu

PARKER-KELLY, Darlene 323-563-9340... 38 B
darleneparkerkelly@cdrewu.edu

PARKES, Martin, J ... 717-867-6038. 421 H
parkes@ivc.edu

PARKHILL, Molly ... 828-694-1706. 358 C
mollyp@blueridge.edu

PARKHURST, Abbie ... 540-828-5782. 502 J
aparkhur@bridgewater.edu

PARKIN, Janice ... 312-341-4327. 157 D
jparkin01@roosevelt.edu

PARKINSON, Alan, R ... 801-422-4327. 495 D
alan_parkinson@byu.edu

PARKINSON, Curt ... 559-278-4062... 33 D
cparkinson@csufresno.edu

PARKINSON, David ... 435-797-1645. 497 B
david.parkinson@usu.edu

PARKINSON, III,
Henry, C ... 978-665-3160. 229 E
hparkinson@fitchburgstate.edu

PARKINSON, Michael ... 314-529-9553. 276 G
mparkinson@maryville.edu

PARKINSON, Tracy ... 843-383-8012. 442 F
tparkinson@coker.edu

PARKISON, Kathy ... 765-455-9462. 168 A

PARKS, Adrian ... 803-535-5812. 442 B
adrian.parks@sodexo.com

PARKS, Amy ... 216-987-6130. 378 D
amy.parks@tri-c.edu

PARKS, Ann ... 660-263-4110. 279 B
annp@macc.edu

PARKS, Brenda ... 309-298-1944. 162 K
bs-parks@wiu.edu

PARKS, Charlotte, P ... 404-413-7064. 126 E
cparks@gsu.edu

PARKS, Cherri, S ... 303-963-3357... 79 C
cparks@ccu.edu

PARKS, Cheryl ... 410-548-2865. 220 D
caparks@salisbury.edu

PARKS, Cynthia ... 706-737-1431. 126 B
cparks1@gru.edu

PARKS, Donald, K ... 850-201-8071. 103 E
Dparks@flagler.edu

PARKS, Earl ... 202-651-5494... 95 C
earl.parks@gallaudet.edu

PARKS, Emily ... 573-840-9077. 282 K
eparks@trcc.edu

PARKS, Jason ... 318-484-2184. 208 B
parksj@nsula.edu

PARKS, Jeffrey ... 281-476-1501. 479 F
jeffrey.parks@sjcd.edu

PARKS, Joseph ... 573-875-4842. 283 E
parksj@umsl.edu

PARKS, Julie ... 616-234-3714. 243 B
jparks@grcc.edu

PARKS, Marshall ... 970-351-1814... 86 C
marshall.parks@unco.edu

PARKS, Maureen ... 217-333-2590. 161 C
mparks@uillinois.edu

PARKS, Michael ... 210-567-2791. 493 A
parksm@uthscsa.edu

PARKS, Patricia ... 714-816-0366... 70 A
patricia.parks@trident.edu

PARKS, Rodney ... 336-278-6677. 354 B
rparks4@elon.edu

PARKS, Sherrie ... 325-235-7402. 486 C
sherrie.parks@tstc.edu

PARKS, Susie, M ... 619-201-8670... 62 B
Susie.Parks@sdcc.edu

PARKS, Thomas, N ... 801-581-7236. 496 Q
tom.parks@utah.edu

PARKS, Tom ... 617-262-5000. 223 F
thomas.parks@the-bac.edu

PARKS, Valerie ... 915-779-8031. 494 C
vparks@computercareercenter.com

PARKS, Vanasia Conley . 423-425-4467. 463 D
vanasia-parks@utc.edu

PARKYN, David, L ... 773-244-5710. 154 G
dparkyn@northpark.edu

PARLE, Joseph, D ... 713-785-5995. 468 L
joe.parle@cbshouston.edu

PARLER, Branson ... 616-222-3000. 245 C
bparler@kuyper.edu

PARLETT, Ray, M ... 585-567-9333. 326 F
ray.parlett@houghton.edu

PARMANN, Maureen ... 810-767-4000. 239 H
maureen.parmann@baker.edu

PARMER, Janet ... 707-527-4679... 65 B
jparmer@santarosa.edu

PARMER, Marsha ... 503-223-2245. 403 J
mparmer@portland.chefs.edu

PARMETER, Kim ... 218-733-7607. 259 A
k.parmeter@lsc.edu

PARMETER, Kim ... 218-733-7600. 259 A
k.parmeter@lsc.edu

PARNELL, Kathleen ... 410-617-2354. 216 A
kmparnell@loyola.edu

PARNELL, Lauren ... 912-583-3211. 122 B
lparnell@bpc.edu

PARNELL, Paul ... 951-372-7015... 60 L
paul.parnell@norcocollege.edu

PARNELL, Paul ... 951-372-7015... 60 J
paul.parnell@nc.edu

PARNELL, Philip ... 701-671-2669. 372 E
philip.parnell@ndscs.edu

PARNELL, Rob Roy ... 512-463-2237. 486 D
robroy.parnell@tsus.edu

PARNES, Marvin, G ... 734-936-3933. 251 C
mgparnes@umich.edu

PARNIA, Ezat ... 626-529-8008... 57 G
eparnia@pacificoaks.edu

PARNUM CADBURY,
Sarah ... 218-951-5144. 420 B
cadbury@lasalle.edu

PAROLINI, Roger, K ... 630-844-5489. 140 A
rparolin@aurora.edu

PARPART, Amanda, L ... 605-256-5244. 451 H
amanda.parpart@dsu.edu

PARR, Ronald, G ... 901-333-4737. 461 F
rgparr@southwest.tn.edu

PARR, Tracey ... 212-431-2854. 333 I
Tracey.Parr@nyls.edu

PARR, Vanna ... 940-898-3525. 488 B
vparr@twu.edu

PARR-BARRETT,
Cindy, A ... 217-443-8759. 143 G
cparrett@dacc.edu

PARR WALKER, Diane ... 574-631-7790. 174 A
Diane.Parr.Walker@nd.edu

PARRA, Alicia, F ... 954-322-4460. 107 V
aliciafernandaparra@jmvu.edu

PARRA, Carlos, P ... 423-236-2746. 458 J
cpaarra@southern.edu

PARRA, Claudia ... 954-322-4460. 107 V
parrac@jmvu.edu

PARRENT, Condoa ... 817-515-6532. 482 B
condoa.parrent@tccd.edu

PARRENT, Jonathan, V ... 270-824-8571. 196 A
jay.parrent@kctcs.edu

PARRENT, Rick ... 615-230-3321. 461 G
rick.parrent@volstate.edu

PARRENT, Robert ... 314-246-7910. 284 N
robertparrent@webster.edu

PARRETT, Brenda, J ... 601-643-8301. 266 F
brenda.parrett@colin.edu

PARRIERA, Keri ... 360-383-3330. 525 D
kparriera@whatcom.ctc.edu

PARRILL, Jacqueline ... 740-366-9407. 376 A
parrill.9@osu.edu

PARRILLA, Arlene ... 787-863-2390. 550 C
arlene.parrilla@fajardo.inter.edu

PARRIOTT, Karen ... 307 532-8264. 542 a
karen.parriott@ewc.wy.edu

PARRIS, Gina ... 864-294-2322. 444 C
gina.parris@furman.edu

PARRISH, Austen, L ... 213-738-6710... 68 C
deansoffice@swlaw.edu

PARRISH, Clyde ... 513-487-3202. 325 G
cparrish@huc.edu

PARRISH, Dave ... 770-531-6420. 128 B
dparrish@laniertech.edu

PARRISH, Debra, J ... 906-353-4600. 245 A
dparrish@kbocc.org

PARRISH, Gretchen ... 336-342-4261. 363 C
parrishg@rockinghamcc.edu

PARRISH, J. Michael ... 408-924-4800... 36 A
mparrish@science.sjsu.edu

PARRISH, Jenni ... 415-565-4881... 71 A
parrishj@uchastings.edu

PARRISH, John ... 310-338-5810... 53 E
jparrish@lmu.edu

PARRISH, John ... 336-342-4261. 363 C
parrishj@rockinghamcc.edu

PARRISH, Paula ... 858-566-1200... 42 G
pparrish@disd.edu

PARROTT, Aaron ... 509-682-6795. 525 B
aparrott@wvc.edu

PARROTT, Mike ... 843-208-8040. 448 B
rparrot@uscb.edu

PARROTT, Rebecca ... 606-242-0256. 196 F
rebecca.parrott@kctcs.edu

PARROTT, Roger ... 601-968-5919. 266 A
president@belhaven.edu

PARRY, John ... 970-491-3939... 80 I
john.parry@colostate.edu

PARRY, John ... 216-687-4808. 377 F
john.parry@csuohio.edu

PARRY, Laura, S ... 518-783-8282. 340 J
lparry@siena.edu

PARRY, Ruth ... 620-241-0723. 185 K

PARRY, Susan ... 845-341-4251. 335 H
susan.parry@sunyorange.edu

PARSCAL, Tina ... 866-621-0124... 86 F
tina.parscal@rockies.edu

PARSHALL, William ... 267-468-8022. 433 K
william.parshall@temple.edu

PARSLEY, Nancy, L ... 847-578-8401. 157 F
nancy.parsley@rosalindfranklin.edu

PARSNIK, Pamela ... 570-674-6310. 424 A
pparsnik@misericordia.edu

PARSON, Lisa ... 620-278-4264. 190 I
lparson@sterling.edu

PARSON, Mark ... 715-232-1151. 538 B
parsonm@uwstout.edu

PARSONS, Amy ... 970-491-5257... 80 I
amy.parsons@colostate.edu

PARSONS, Brigitte ... 715-365-4406. 540 G
bparsons@nicoletcollege.edu

PARSONS, Carole, H ... 603-526-3674. 295 I
cparsons@colby-sawyer.edu

PARSONS, Cynthia ... 804-765-5800. 509 L
cynthia-parsons@chs.net

PARSONS, Duncan, A ... 423-354-2588. 461 C
daparsons@northeaststate.edu

PARSONS, Edy ... 319-363-8213. 181 C
eparsons@mtmercy.edu

PARSONS, Eric ... 802-447-6324. 500 D
eparsons@svc.edu

PARSONS, Faye ... 772-546-5534. 106 N
fayeparsons@hsbc.edu

PARSONS, JR., Frank, R 334-833-4294..... 4 D
fparsons@huntingdon.edu

PARSONS, Geoffrey, J ... 843-349-2054. 442 E
parsons@coastal.edu

PARSONS, James ... 207-859-1250. 211 H
maintenance@thomas.edu

PARSONS, Mark ... 909-447-2521... 39 E
mparsons@cst.edu

PARSONS, Nancy, P ... 309-298-1066. 162 K
np-parsons@wiu.edu

PARSONS, Pamela ... 406-771-4314. 287 E
pparsons@gfcmsu.edu

PARSONS, Paul, F ... 336-278-5724. 354 B
pparsons@elon.edu

PARSONS, Priscilla ... 409-880-7691. 486 F
priscilla.parsons@lamar.edu

PARSONS, Ray, B ... 302-857-1050... 93 G
rparsons3@dtcc.edu

PARTAIN, Julie ... 229-931-2249. 131 G
jpartain@southgatech.edu

PARTAIN, Pam ... 706-272-2985. 123 G
ppartain@daltonstate.edu

PARTCH, Nancy ... 815-825-2086. 149 F
nancy.partch@kishwaukeecollege.edu

PARTEE, Ben ... 805-965-0581... 64 L
partee@sbcc.edu

PARTEN, Janice ... 559-278-2364... 33 D
jparten@csufresno.edu

PARTON, Becky ... 217-786-2351. 151 F
becky.parton@llcc.edu

PARTON, Dwayne ... 918-683-4581. 394 D
partond@bacone.edu

PARTON, LeAnne ... 509-793-2004. 517 C
leannep@bigbend.edu

PARTON, Sabrena ... 706-233-7465. 131 E
sparton@shorter.edu

PARTON, William ... 479-968-0417... 20 E
wparton@atu.edu

PARTRIDGE, Kristen ... 405-325-3163. 401 B
kpartridge@ou.edu

PARTRIDGE, Patrick ... 801-274-3280. 498 E
ppartridge@wgu.edu

PARVIZI, Nasrin ... 607-753-5582. 343 B
nasrin.parvizi@cortland.edu

PARZIALE, Anthony ... 561-868-3239. 110 C
parziala@palmbeachstate.edu

PARZY, Robert ... 847-925-6649. 145 H
rparzy@harpercollege.edu

PASCAL, Kenneth, C ... 713-623-2040. 466 G
kpascal@aii.edu

PASCAL, Sandra, E ... 617-989-4478. 237 G
pascals@wit.edu

PASCALE, Lynn ... 203-287-3031... 90 H
paier.admission@snet.net

PASCARELL, Rose ... 703-993-8760. 505 C
rpascare@gmu.edu

PASCARELLA, John ... 936-294-1401. 487 A
jbp014@shsu.edu

PASCARIELLO,
Jacqueline ... 631-632-6840. 342 C
jacqueline.pascariello@stonybrook.edu

PASCHAL, Linda, L .... 414-955-8208. 534 C lpaschal@mcw.edu
PASCHALL, Bill .... 720-855-6014... 82 C billp@heritage-education.com
PASCHALL, Danny .... 562-903-4874... 29 L danny.paschall@biola.edu
PASCHALL, Kimberly, S . 270-809-3809. 198 B kpaschall@murraystate.edu
PASCOE, Frank, H .... 815-740-3216. 162 F fpascoe@stfrancis.edu
PASCOE, Tammie .... 903-983-8105. 475 E tpascoe@kilgore.edu
PASCOE AGUILAR, Daniel .... 541-346-6009. 406 D dpascoe@uoregon.edu
PASCUA, Vance .... 916-577-2200... 76 J vpascua@jessup.edu
PASCUA DEA, Tracy .... 925-631-4165... 61 F tjp2@stmarys-ca.edu
PASCUAL, Candice .... 727-725-2688. 102 I cpascual@cci.edu
PASCUCCI, Richard, A .... 215-871-6690. 430 D richardp@pcom.edu
PASEK, Heidi .... 406-771-4397. 287 E hpasek@gfcmsu.edu
PASENELLI, Rose .... 619-594-5677... 35 D rpasenel@mail.sdsu.edu
PASHA, Stephanie .... 508-831-6655. 238 F spasha@wpi.edu
PASKER, Mark .... 563-876-3353. 177 I mpasker@dwci.edu
PASKETT, Lindy .... 307-855-2120. 542 Y lpaskett@cwc.edu
PASKOFF, Beth, M .... 225-578-1480. 204 O bpaskoff@lsu.edu
PASKVAN, Brian .... 567-661-7742. 387 L brian_paskvan@owens.edu
PASKVAN, Kevin, F .... 740-368-3052. 387 J kfpaskva@owu.edu
PASOUR, Katherine .... 828-328-7126. 356 B katherine.pasour@lr.edu
PASQUARIELLO, Gino .... 619-201-8999... 67 G gpasquariello@socalsem.edu
PASQUERELLA, Lynn ...... 413-538-2500. 234 D commish@mtholyoke.edu
PASS-STERN, Bernice ..... 212-614-6176. 336 C bstern@chpnet.org
PASSAFIUME, Marisa ..... 718-862-7796. 329 M marisa.passafiume@manhattan.edumanhattan.edu
PASSALACQUA, Dominic .... 315-792-3393. 349 F dpassalacqua@utica.edu
PASSARO, Joanne .... 262-524-7364. 532 C jpassaro@carrollu.edu
PASSE, Jeffrey .... 609-771-2100. 300 E passej@tcnj.edu
PASSER, Christine .... 269-782-1316. 250 C cpasser@swmich.edu
PASSERINI, Katia .... 973-642-7664. 303 G katia.passerini@njit.edu
PASSIN, Cathey .... 610-647-4400. 418 I cpassin@immaculata.edu
PASSMORE, Joe .... 423-746-5333. 462 C jpassmore@twcnet.edu
PASTERIS, Marc .... 309-467-6305. 145 C mpasteris@eureka.edu
PASTERNAK, Reuven ...... 631-444-2701. 342 C
PASTIDES, Harris .... 803-777-2001. 447 G pastides@sc.edu
PASTIN, John, R .... 856-256-4550. 305 E pastin@rowan.edu
PASTOOR, Robert, A ...... 740-376-4736. 383 E bob.pastoor@marietta.edu
PASTORE, Michael, A ..... 315-255-1743. 316 D michael.pastore@cayuga-cc.edu
PASTORELLA, Mark, J .... 585-262-1509. 332 A mpastorella@monroecc.edu
PASTORINO, Mary Ellen 707-546-4000... 43 E mpastorino@empirecollege.com
PASTORIZA, Nelida .... 718-518-4412. 318 B npastoriza@hostos.cuny.edu
PASTORRES-PALFFY, Elizabeth .... 916-485-3276. 390 C beth.pastorres-palffy@myunion.edu
PASTRANA, Livia, D .... 787-728-1515. 555 D lpastrana@sagrado.edu
PASTRANA, Marie Luz ... 787-765-3560. 548 M lpastrana@edpuniversity.edu
PASTRANA, Marilyn .... 787-765-3560. 548 M mpastrana@edpuniversity.edu
PASTRANO, Ginna .... 713-646-1867. 480 J gpastrano@stcl.edu
PASTULA, Robert, G .... 256-765-4357..... 9 C rpastula@una.edu
PASZKIEWICZ, Wendy ... 312-662-4211. 139 F paszk@adler.edu
PASZTOR, Jim .... 303-220-1200... 78 K jim.pasztor@cffp.edu
PATALANO, Carla .... 617-951-2350. 234 G carla.patalano@necb.edu
PATAWARAN, Arrileen .... 773-995-2063. 141 J apatawar@csu.edu
PATBERG, Steve .... 618-262-8641. 147 C patbergs@iecc.edu
PATCH, Sara .... 802-447-4013. 500 D spatch@svc.edu
PATCHETT, Heather .... 423-636-7303. 462 E
PATCHETT, Margaret, B .. 704-403-3077. 352 J margaret.patchett@carolinashealthcare.org
PATCHNER, Michael .... 317-274-8362. 168 D patchner@iupui.edu
PATE, David, S .... 585-385-8034. 338 H dpate@sjfc.edu
PATE, Doug .... 919-209-2007. 361 E mdpate@johnstoncc.edu
PATE, Juston .... 606-759-7141. 196 B juston.pate@kctcs.edu
PATE, Kim .... 217 206-7592. 161 E kpate80@uis.edu
PATE, Nino, T .... 671-734-1812. 546 D npate@piu.edu
PATE, Susan .... 386-506-3769. 101 G pates@DaytonaState.edu
PATEE, Carla .... 620-227-9378. 186 B cpatee@dc3.edu
PATEE, Greg .... 620-227-9355. 186 B gpatee@dc3.edu
PATEGAS, Dianna .... 203-582-8797... 91 A dianna.pategas@quinnipiac.edu
PATEL, Maqbool .... 410-951-3780. 220 B mpatel@coppin.edu
PATEL, Narendra, H .... 404-880-8064. 122 J npatel@cau.edu
PATELLA, Cathleen .... 315-364-3289. 350 E cpatella@wells.edu
PATENAUDE, Craig .... 301-934-7643. 214 D cpatenaude@csmd.edu
PATERSON, Brent .... 309-438-5451. 147 J bgpater@ilstu.edu
PATERSON, Janet .... 309-438-2008. 147 J jwpater@ilstu.edu
PATERSON, Jay .... 802-728-1244. 501 F jpaterson@vtc.edu
PATERSON, John .... 802-728-1434. 501 F jpaterson@vtc.edu
PATERSON, Robert .... 516-323-4850. 331 J rpaterson@molloy.edu
PATERSON, Valerie .... 617-682-1593. 226 D vpaterson@eds.edu
PATERSON, Wendy, A .... 716-878-4214. 343 A paterswa@buffalostate.edu
PATES, Nancy .... 952-358-8200. 260 B nancy.pates@normandale.edu
PATH, Bill .... 402-379-0032. 398 B bpath@okstate.edu
PATHAK, Dushyant .... 530-752-7309... 70 J dpathak@ucdavis.edu
PATHAK, Susanna .... 414-425-8300. 535 K spathak@shst.edu
PATILLA, Shane .... 770-394-8300. 120 H spatilla@aii.edu
PATINO-MANCUELLO, Beatriz .... 508-767-7100. 222 C bpatino@assumption.edu
PATISSAL, Jeremy .... 336-725-8344. 365 F patissalj@piedmontu.edu
PATLOLLA, Babu, P .... 601-877-6120. 265 G bpatlolla@alcorn.edu
PATNAUDE, Valerie .... 603-897-8533. 297 F vpatnaude@rivier.edu
PATO, Rosevonne .... 684-699-9155. 546 A r.pato@amsamoa.edu
PATON, Jeff .... 336-322-2237. 362 F Jeff.Paton@piedmontcc.edu
PATOTA, Nancy .... 914-633-2413. 327 C npatota@iona.edu
PATOUT, Gerald .... 337-550-1380. 205 B
PATRAGNONI-SAUTER, Kirstin .... 215-951-2700. 430 E patragnonik@philau.edu
PATRIA, Patty .... 508-373-1981. 223 A ppatria@becker.edu
PATRIARCA, Linda .... 252-328-1000. 367 B patriarcal@ecu.edu
PATRICK, Beth, G .... 606-783-2053. 198 A b.patrick@moreheadstate.edu
PATRICK, Brian .... 913-288-7362. 187 L bpatrick@kckcc.edu
PATRICK, Carmel .... 518-381-1442. 340 G patricc@sunysccc.edu
PATRICK, Craig .... 718-933-6700. 331 K cpatrick@monroecollege.edu
PATRICK, Diane .... 616-234-4105. 243 B dpatrick@grcc.edu
PATRICK, Diane, D .... 616-234-4101. 243 B dpatrick@grcc.edu
PATRICK, Garry .... 707-476-4385... 40 H garry-patrick@redwoods.edu
PATRICK, Jamie .... 919-497-3245. 356 E jpatrick@louisburg.edu
PATRICK, Juletta .... 815-455-8613. 152 F jpatrick@mchenry.edu
PATRICK, Kim .... 616-331-2280. 243 C patricki@gvsu.edu
PATRICK, Lanell .... 443-412-2563. 215 C lpatrick@harford.edu
PATRICK, Laura .... 949-376-6000... 50 C lpatrick@lagunacollege.edu
PATRICK, Michelle .... 610-436-2930. 430 A mpatrick@wcupa.edu
PATRICK, Nicole .... 662-329-7114. 268 E npatrick@finaid.muw.edu
PATRICK, Paul, G .... 864-379-6675. 443 F ppatrick@erskine.edu
PATRICK, Roxann .... 937-294-0592. 388 M roxann@saa.edu
PATRICK-TURNER, Ronne .... 617-373-5416. 235 F
PATRIE, Shannon .... 315-498-2802. 335 G patries@sunyocc.edu
PATRO, Rick .... 410-843-8490. 265 D rick.patro@laureate.net
PATSALIDES, Eugene ...... 270-831-9688. 195 D eugenios.patsalides@kctcs.edu
PATSCHECK, Valerie .... 805-437-8878... 32 I valerie.patscheck@csuci.edu
PATTARINI, Stephen .... 315-792-2555. 349 F spattarini@utica.edu
PATTEE, Bob .... 254-295-4524. 490 B rpattee@umhb.edu
PATTEE, Bonnie .... 801-274-3280. 498 E bonnie.pattee@wgu.edu
PATTEE, TOR, Daniel, J . 740-283-6245. 379 N dpattee@franciscan.edu
PATTEN, David, B .... 401-825-2194. 439 A dpatten@ccri.edu
PATTEN, Diana, R .... 319-399-8844. 176 G dpatten@coe.edu
PATTEN, Don .... 570-586-2400. 410 D dpatten@bbc.edu
PATTEN, Lori .... 802-468-1211. 501 B lori.patten@castleton.edu
PATTEN-LEMONS, Rebecca .... 317-921-4667. 169 L rpatten@ivytech.edu
PATTEN WALLACE, Kaye 419-530-7963. 392 B kaye.pattenwallace@utoledo.edu
PATTENAUDE, Richard ..... 858-513-9240. 175 F richard.pattenaude@ashford.edu
PATTENGALE, Jerry .... 765-677-2170. 169 B jerry.pattengale@indwes.edu
PATTERSON, Abbie, L ..... 310-233-4031... 51 H patteral@lahc.edu
PATTERSON, Anne .... 940-552-6291. 493 F apatterson@vernoncollege.edu
PATTERSON, Anthony ...... 410-822-5400. 214 C apatterson@chesapeake.edu
PATTERSON, Barbara, A . 580-774-3261. 400 B barbara.patterson@swosu.edu
PATTERSON, Bart .... 702-992-2350. 294 G bart.patterson@nsc.edu
PATTERSON, Becky .... 502-852-3385. 200 D becky.patterson@louisville.edu
PATTERSON, Ben .... 805-565-6210... 76 D bpatters@westmont.edu
PATTERSON, Bernie .... 715-346-2123. 538 A
PATTERSON, Carrie, C .... 240-895-4252. 218 A ccpatterson@smcm.edu
PATTERSON, Charles ...... 912-478-2647. 126 C cpatterson@georgiasouthern.edu
PATTERSON, Charles ...... 912-478-5465. 126 C cpatterson@georgiasouthern.edu
PATTERSON, Charlotte ... 434-982-2961. 511 B cjp@virginia.edu
PATTERSON, Corey .... 325-674-2950. 464 H pattersonc@acu.edu
PATTERSON, Cynthia, A . 252-638-7304. 359 G pattersc@cravencc.edu
PATTERSON, Dale .... 918-540-6319. 396 G dale.patterson@neo.edu
PATTERSON, Darrin .... 330-337-6403. 373 F college@awc.edu
PATTERSON, Deborah .... 276-466-7907. 514 G deborahpatteson@vic.edu
PATTERSON, Dolly .... 510-204-0707... 38 J cdsp-advancement@cdsp.edu
PATTERSON, Donald, W . 570-484-2255. 429 B dpatters@lhup.edu
PATTERSON, Dorothy ..... 803-780-1192. 449 E pattersn@voorhees.edu
PATTERSON, Eddie .... 803-780-1249. 449 E epatterson@voorhees.edu
PATTERSON, Eric .... 757-352-4616. 508 G epatterson@regent.edu
PATTERSON, Felicia, L ... 410-777-2718. 213 D flpatterson@aacc.edu
PATTERSON, Frank .... 850-644-0453. 115 C fpatterson@fsu.edu
PATTERSON, Franklin ..... 386-481-2020... 99 C pattersonf@cookman.edu
PATTERSON, Hope .... 575-439-3729. 310 J peach@nmsu.edu
PATTERSON, Howard ...... 903-566-7316. 492 D hpatterson@uttyler.edu
PATTERSON, James .... 908-852-1400. 300 D pattersonj@centenarycollege.edu
PATTERSON, James .... 860-738-6482... 89 C jpatterson@nwcc.commnet.edu
PATTERSON, Jana Lynn, F .... 336-278-7200. 354 B patters@elon.edu
PATTERSON, Jennifer ..... 614-236-6502. 375 H jpatterson@capital.edu
PATTERSON, Joanna ...... 414-382-6009. 531 I joanna.patterson@alverno.edu
PATTERSON, John, A ..... 478-301-5537. 128 H patterson_ja@mercer.edu
PATTERSON, John, D ..... 620-235-4108. 189 L jpatters@pittstate.edu
PATTERSON, Johnny .... 318-274-6568. 207 E pattersonj@gram.edu
PATTERSON, Joi .... 219-473-4305. 164 K jpatterson@ccsj.edu
PATTERSON, Joyce, D .... 337-475-5232. 207 G alumni@mcneese.edu
PATTERSON, Kristi .... 815-479-7677. 152 F kpatterson@mchenry.edu
PATTERSON, Lametric .... 770-394-8300. 120 H lpatterson@aii.edu
PATTERSON, Laura, M ... 734-763-7109. 251 C lmpatter@umich.edu
PATTERSON, Leni, N ...... 864-833-8486. 446 D lpatters@presby.edu
PATTERSON, Lisa .... 614-823-1589. 387 K lphillips@otterbein.edu
PATTERSON, Liz .... 313-993-1254. 250 K patterew@udmercy.edu
PATTERSON, Loretta ...... 316-322-3294. 185 D lpatterson@butlercc.edu
PATTERSON, Lorna .... 360-596-5292. 524 A lpatterson@spscc.edu
PATTERSON, Michael ..... 410-225-2422. 216 C mpatters@mica.edu
PATTERSON, Michael ..... 415-503-6237... 62 H mpatterson@sfcm.edu
PATTERSON, Michael ..... 843-958-5813. 447 E michael.patterso12568@tridenttech.edu
PATTERSON, Michael, J . 570-577-1911. 411 A mike.patterson@bucknell.edu
PATTERSON, Myrna .... 808-845-9115. 136 G mpatters@hawaii.edu
PATTERSON, Nancy .... 423-697-2630. 460 C
PATTERSON, Paige .... 817-923-1921. 481 G presidentsoffice@swbts.edu
PATTERSON, Rae Lynn ... 208-524-3000. 138 D raelynn@my.eitc.edu
PATTERSON, Ralph .... 864-388-8350. 444 K rpatterson@lander.edu
PATTERSON, Roger, D ... 509-335-5524. 525 A roger.patterson@wsu.edu
PATTERSON, Ron .... 501-450-3128... 25 H rpatterson@uca.edu
PATTERSON, Sarah .... 254-867-2005. 486 B sarah.patterson@tstc.edu
PATTERSON, Sharon .... 414-443-8556. 539 F sharon.patterson@wlc.edu
PATTERSON, Stanley ...... 334-387-3877..... 1 E stanleypatterson@amridgeuniversity.edu
PATTERSON, Stephen ..... 480-965-9743... 11 K athletics.director@asu.edu
PATTERSON, Susan .... 518-458-5358. 321 A patterss@strose.edu
PATTERSON, Teresa .... 559-244-2637... 68 H teresa.patterson@scccd.edu
PATTERSON, Teresa .... 909-274-5512... 55 A tpatterson@mtsac.edu
PATTERSON, Terry, L ..... 208-732-6402. 138 B tpatterson@csi.edu
PATTERSON, Thomas ...... 334-387-3877..... 1 E thomaspatterson@amridgeuniversity.edu
PATTERSON, Tim .... 802-586-7711. 500 E tpatterson@sterlingcollege.edu
PATTERSON, Traonah ...... 404-527-4520. 122 E tpatterson@carver.edu
PATTERSON, III, U, L .... 704-669-4025. 359 D patterson@clevelandcc.edu
PATTERSON, Vanessa ..... 805-965-0581... 64 L patterson@sbcc.edu
PATTERSON, Vicki .... 832-252-4624. 468 L vicki@cbhouston.edu
PATTERSON-DIAZ, Alyce .... 304-896-7355. 528 F alyce.patterson-diaz@southernwv.edu
PATTI, Charles, H .... 303-871-6858... 86 B charles.patti@du.edu
PATTI, Christopher, M .... 510-642-7122... 70 I cpatti@berkeley.edu
PATTI, James .... 401-232-6088. 438 K jpatti@bryant.edu
PATTILLO, Andre .... 404-215-2752. 129 D apattill@morehouse.edu

PATTILLO, Baker .... 936-468-2201. 482 A
bpattillo@sfasu.edu
PATTISON, Evangeline .... 503-554-2121. 403 C
epattison@georgefox.edu
PATTISON, Peggy .... 313-593-5131. 251 D
ppatt@umich.edu
PATTON, Amy .... 570-408-4400. 437 F
amy.patton@wilkes.edu
PATTON, Barbara, L .... 615-898-2185. 459 D
barbara.patton@mtsu.edu
PATTON, Betty .... 575-624-7160. 309 I
betty.patton@roswell.enmu.edu
PATTON, Caron .... 817-531-6571. 488 A
cpatton@txwes.edu
PATTON, Chad .... 434-949-1045. 513 H
chad.patton@southside.edu
PATTON, Danny .... 662-329-7436. 268 E
dcpatton@pd.muw.edu
PATTON, James, W .... 606-474-3256. 194 H
jpatton@kcu.edu
PATTON, James, W .... 606-474-3282. 194 H
jpatton@kcu.edu
PATTON, Jeremy .... 575-439-3703. 310 J
patton@nmsu.edu
PATTON, Kathlyn .... 361-354-2221. 468 K
jfkpat@coastalbend.edu
PATTON, Kerry .... 203-582-8200... 91 A
kerry.patton2@quinnipiac.edu
PATTON, Laurie .... 919-684-4510. 354 A
laurie.patton@duke.edu
PATTON, Mary .... 817-257-7660. 484 I
m.patton@tcu.edu
PATTON, Molly .... 704-403-1755. 352 J
molly.patton@carolinashealthcare.org
PATTON, Paul, E .... 606-218-5261. 200 F
pep@upike.edu
PATTON, Philip, L .... 319-273-2241. 176 A
philip.patton@uni.edu
PATTON, Seth, H .... 740-587-6262. 379 D
patton@denison.edu
PATTON, Terry .... 940-397-4088. 476 H
terry.patton@mwsu.edu
PATTY, Jeff .... 706-295-6775. 125 C
jpatty@highlands.edu
PATTY, Stacy .... 806-720-7652. 476 B
stacy.patty@lcu.edu
PATWARY, Mohsin .... 718-270-6217. 319 A
mohsin@mec.cuny.edu
PATZ, Cecilia .... 310-243-3866... 33 B
cptaz@csudh.edu
PATZ, Thomas .... 317-738-8183. 165 I
tpatz@franklincollege.edu
PATZ, Thomas .... 317-738-8025. 165 I
tpatz@franklincollege.edu
PAUER, Staci .... 309-672-5531. 152 I
spauer@methodistcol.edu
PAUGH, Jerry .... 714-449-7487... 67 D
jpaugh@scco.edu
PAUGH, Mark .... 352-854-2322. 100 K
paughm@cf.edu
PAUKEN, Patrick .... 419-372-2226. 374 K
paukenp@bgsu.edu
PAUL, Alyson .... 706-864-1900. 133 D
alyson.paul@ung.edu
PAUL, Beth .... 386-822-7010. 117 C
bpaul@stetson.edu
PAUL, David .... 360-416-7738. 523 G
dave.paul@skagit.edu
PAUL, Emilia .... 303-556-3559... 83 D
epaul@msudenver.edu
PAUL, Ivan .... 217-641-4553. 148 M
ipaul@jwcc.edu
PAUL, Jennifer .... 714-556-3610... 74 D
jennifer.paul@vanguard.edu
PAUL, Jeremy .... 617-373-5149. 235 F
PAUL, Jina .... 402-552-3100. 288 L
PAUL, John .... 503-534-4018. 404 C
jpaul@marylhurst.edu
PAUL, Joseph, S .... 601-266-5020. 270 E
joe.paul@usm.edu
PAUL, Joy .... 606-693-5000. 196 H
jpaul@kmbc.edu
PAUL, Kelley .... 903-923-2229. 471 J
kpaul@etbu.edu
PAUL, Lisa, M .... 956-326-2383. 483 B
lisa.paul@tamiu.edu
PAUL, Mary .... 619-849-2215... 59 L
marypaul@pointloma.edu
PAUL, Michelle .... 417-455-5675. 273 E
MichellePaul@crowder.edu
PAUL, Prem, S .... 402-472-3123. 292 I
ppaul2@unl.edu
PAUL, Roberta .... 217-228-5432. 156 C
paulro@quincy.edu
PAUL, Sheilah .... 718-270-4936. 319 A
spaul@mec.cuny.edu
PAUL, Sonia .... 256-726-7134..... 6 B
spaul@oakwood.edu
PAUL, Susan .... 440-365-5222. 383 B
PAUL, Tina .... 870-612-2017... 25 A
tina.paul@uaccb.edu

PAUL, Tonya .... 419-772-3106. 386 D
t-paul@onu.edu
PAULDINE, David, J .... 630-515-4566. 144 A
dpauldine@devry.edu
PAULE, Romeo .... 415-949-7308... 44 N
pauleromeo@fhda.edu
PAULEN, Alexis .... 561-912-1211. 103 C
apaulen@evergladesuniversity.edu
PAULETTI, Daniel .... 610-436-2552. 430 A
dpauletti@wcupa.edu
PAULEY, Amy, I .... 585-785-1541. 324 D
pauleyai@flcc.edu
PAULEY, Ann .... 202-884-9725... 96 G
pauleya@trinitydc.edu
PAULEY, II, John .... 610-341-5892. 415 G
jpauley@eastern.edu
PAULI, Mary Louise .... 781-891-2660. 223 C
mpauli@bentley.edu
PAULI, Wayne, E .... 605-256-5800. 451 H
wayne.pauli@dsu.edu
PAULIEN, Jon .... 909-558-4536... 51 C
jpaulien@llu.edu
PAULIN, Christopher ...... 860-512-2753... 88 G
cpaulin@manchestercc.edu
PAULINE, Rose Lee .... 215-951-1014. 420 B
pauline@lasalle.edu
PAULISON, Wayne .... 918-631-2616. 401 F
wayne-paulison@utulsa.edu
PAULLI, OFM,
Kenneth, P .... 518-783-4290. 340 J
kpaulli@siena.edu
PAULNACK, Karl .... 607-274-3343. 327 E
kpaulnack@ithaca.edu
PAULO, Joseph .... 803-754-4100. 443 C
PAULOS, Christine .... 651-748-2619. 258 C
christine.paulos@century.edu
PAULOSKI, SP, Pam .... 773-371-5420. 141 D
presoffice@ctu.edu
PAULS, Kenton .... 712-707-7111. 181 H
kenton.pauls@nwciowa.edu
PAULS, Toni, M .... 260-399-7700. 174 C
tpauls@sf.edu
PAULSEN, Christi .... 785-227-3380. 184 I
paulsenc@bethanylb.edu
PAULSEN, John, E .... 937-327-7317. 393 E
jpaulsen@wittenberg.edu
PAULSON, Cheri .... 781-239-3845. 222 D
cpaulson@babson.edu
PAULSON, Chuck .... 612-659-6102. 259 D
chuck.paulson@minneapolis.edu
PAULSON, Dennis, J .... 630-515-7352. 153 B
dpauls@midwestern.edu
PAULSON, Don .... 208-282-2130. 138 E
pauldona@isu.edu
PAULSON, Janet .... 503-594-3162. 402 F
jpaulson@clackamas.edu
PAULSON, Jill .... 605-668-1293. 450 F
jpaulson@mtmc.edu
PAULSON, Ken, A .... 615-898-2813. 459 D
ken.paulson@mtsu.edu
PAULSON, Lawrie .... 701-252-3467. 373 D
paulson@jc.edu
PAULSON, Lynn .... 907-277-1000... 10 D
contact@chartercollege.edu
PAULSON, Nancy .... 218-855-8054. 258 B
npaulson@clcmn.edu
PAULSON, Nicole .... 612-798-3718. 257 J
npaulson@msbcollege.edu
PAULSON, Robert .... 361-593-5002. 484 A
robert.paulson@tamuk.edu
PAULSON, Stephen, M ... 423-775-7333. 453 E
steve@bryan.edu
PAULSON, Susan .... 757-373-7370. 112 D
susan.paulson@saintleo.edu
PAULSON, Veronica .... 605-626-2537. 451 I
paulsonv@northern.edu
PAULUS, Jim .... 620-947-3121. 190 J
jimp@tabor.edu
PAULUS, Michael .... 206-281-2414. 523 C
PAULUS, Michael, L .... 419-372-2891. 374 K
mpaulus@bgsu.edu
PAULY, Susan, E .... 336-721-2603. 366 D
susan.pauly@salem.edu
PAUSTENBAUGH,
Jennifer .... 801-422-2905. 495 D
jennifer_paustenbaugh@byu.edu
PAUSTIAN, Kevin .... 563-884-5721. 182 A
kevin.paustian@palmer.edu
PAUSTIAN, Tony .... 515-633-2439. 177 B
adpaustian@dmacc.edu
PAVA, Moses .... 212-960-0845. 351 M
mpava@yu.edu
PAVAN, Ron .... 615-547-1348. 454 A
rpavan@cumberland.edu
PAVAN, Tammi .... 615-547-1228. 454 A
tpavan@cumberland.edu
PAVAO, Barbara .... 707-864-7256... 66 G
barbara.pavao@solano.edu
PAVAO, Debbie .... 408-541-0100... 40 A
dpavao@cogswell.edu

PAVAO, Rod .... 408-855-5391... 75 K
rod.pavao@wvm.edu
PAVE, Adam, D .... 909-607-0109... 39 F
adam_pave@kgi.edu
PAVEGLIO, Kevin .... 757-671-7171. 504 F
kpaveglio@ecpi.edu
PAVEK, Annette .... 320-762-4411. 257 O
annettep@alextech.edu
PAVELCHAK, Mark .... 323-343-2730... 34 A
mpavelc@calstatela.edu
PAVER, Jonathan .... 541-917-4534. 404 B
paverj@linnbenton.edu
PAVEY, Carl, E .... 517-750-1200. 250 E
cpavey@arbor.edu
PAVEZA, Gregory .... 203-392-7036... 88 A
pavezag1@southernct.edu
PAVEZA, Gregory .... 203-392-5240... 88 A
pavezag1@southernct.edu
PAVIGLIANITI, Angela .... 773-371-5445. 141 D
angelap@ctu.edu
PAVIN, Anna .... 805-437-8425... 32 I
anna.pavin@csuci.edu
PAVKOVIC, Michael .... 401-841-2188. 545 A
PAVLECHKO,
Timothy, N .... 570-577-3588. 411 A
tim.pavlechko@bucknell.edu
PAVLIK, Donna .... 773-298-3258. 158 E
pavlik@sxu.edu
PAVLIK, Joni, P .... 919-718-7222. 359 B
jpavlik@cccc.edu
PAVLOCK, Tamara .... 412-291-6310. 410 B
tpavlock@aii.edu
PAVLOVICH, Dane .... 785-227-3380. 184 I
pavlovichd@bethanylb.edu
PAVLOVICH, Mark, G ..... 610-436-3303. 430 A
mpavlovich@wcupa.edu
PAVLUS, Laura .... 315-312-2258. 344 A
laura.pavlus@oswego.edu
PAVON, Tracie .... 515-961-1630. 182 E
tracie.pavon@simpson.edu
PAVONE, Cassandra .... 828-689-1196. 356 F
cpavone@mhc.edu
PAVONE, Gerri Lynn .... 586-445-7242. 246 A
pavoneg@macomb.edu
PAVONE, Joseph .... 401-825-2114. 439 A
jpavone@ccri.edu
PAVY, Edwin, C .... 270-789-5227. 193 D
ecpavy@campbellsville.edu
PAWELKO, Jennifer .... 715-425-4481. 537 E
jennifer.pawelko@uwrf.edu
PAWLAK, Katherine .... 863-680-3964. 105 D
kpawlak@flsouthern.edu
PAWLAK, Therese .... 906-932-4231. 242 I
theresep@gogebic.edu
PAWLAWSKI, Eddie .... 615-547-1225. 454 A
epawlawski@cumberland.edu
PAWLEY, Liz .... 940-898-2911. 488 B
epawley@twu.edu
PAWLICKI, Frederick, W . 785-864-4790. 190 L
fpawlick@ku.edu
PAWLOSKI, Chris, J .... 989-964-7122. 249 G
cjpawlos@svsu.edu
PAWLOW, Thomas, A ..... 618-744-0426. 152 G
tapawlow@mckendree.edu
PAWLOWSKI, Ceceile ...... 716-896-0700. 350 A
pawlowskic@villa.edu
PAWLOWSKI, Eugene ...... 212-998-2775. 334 D
gene.pawlowski@nyu.edu
PAWLUK, Steve .... 951-785-2320... 50 B
spawluk@lasierra.edu
PAXON, Barbara .... 212-616-7200. 325 H
barbara.paxon@helenefuld.edu
PAXSON, Christina, H .... 401-863-2234. 438 J
president@brown.edu
PAXTON, Helen, S .... 973-353-5262. 306 D
hs.paxton@rutgers.edu
PAXTON, Mike .... 303-546-3543... 83 F
mikep@naropa.edu
PAXTON, Pat .... 330-684-8920. 390 F
ppaxton@uakron.edu
PAXTON, Patricia, A .... 330-287-1254. 386 F
bxsosuati@bncollege.com
PAYBA, Shane .... 808-984-3496. 137 B
payba@hawaii.edu
PAYDAR, Nasser, H .... 317-274-4500. 168 D
paydar@iupui.edu
PAYLO, Keith .... 412-392-3862. 431 B
kpaylo@pointpark.edu
PAYMENT, Susan .... 843-953-5312. 443 A
payments@cofc.edu
PAYNE, Angela .... 601-481-1357. 267 G
apayne@meridiancc.edu
PAYNE, Anna Beth .... 570-372-4238. 433 H
paynea@susqu.edu
PAYNE, Betsy, P .... 828-262-6432. 367 A
paynebp@appstate.edu
PAYNE, Brandi .... 406-994-2845. 287 B
bpayne@montana.edu
PAYNE, Brian, K .... 757-683-3079. 507 N
bpayne@odu.edu

PAYNE, C. Michael .... 740-264-5591. 379 F
mpayne@egcc.edu
PAYNE, Carol .... 404-894-5596. 125 D
carol.payne@business.gatech.edu
PAYNE, Carolyn .... 606-546-1304. 200 A
cpayne@unionky.edu
PAYNE, Cathy .... 276-326-4233. 502 H
cpayne@bluefield.edu
PAYNE, Clyde .... 631-244-3404. 323 B
PAYNE, Dan .... 406-683-7142. 286 I
d_payne@umwestern.edu
PAYNE, Darnell .... 773-371-5442. 141 D
dpayne@ctu.edu
PAYNE, Darrell .... 318-487-7559. 202 F
darrell.payne@lacollege.edu
PAYNE, Deborah .... 618-985-4928. 148 J
deborahpayne@jalc.edu
PAYNE, Donna, G .... 252-328-6940. 367 B
payned@ecu.edu
PAYNE, Gail, D .... 434-381-6324. 510 F
payne@sbc.edu
PAYNE, George, M .... 240-567-2582. 216 F
george.payne@montgomerycollege.edu
PAYNE, Hal, D .... 716-878-4704. 343 A
paynehd@buffalostate.edu
PAYNE, JR., Harry, E ..... 813-988-5131. 104 A
president@floridacollege.edu
PAYNE, Harvey .... 803-754-4100. 443 C
PAYNE, Jack, M .... 352-392-1971. 116 A
jackpayne@ufl.edu
PAYNE, James .... 318-274-2504. 207 E
payneja@gram.edu
PAYNE, James .... 504-280-6723. 205 G
provost@uno.edu
PAYNE, Jamie, A .... 405-744-7420. 397 H
jamie.payne@okstate.edu
PAYNE, Jennifer .... 802-586-7711. 500 E
jpayne@sterlingcollege.edu
PAYNE, John, F .... 671-735-5565. 546 C
john.payne2@guamcc.edu
PAYNE, John, K .... 802-654-2629. 500 B
jpayne@smcvt.edu
PAYNE, June, P .... 765-285-1264. 164 B
jpayne@bsu.edu
PAYNE, Kent .... 847-214-7552. 144 F
kpayne@elgin.edu
PAYNE, Lisa .... 618-437-5321. 156 H
payne@rlc.edu
PAYNE, Lisa .... 256-233-8274..... 1 F
lisa.payne@athens.edu
PAYNE, Maggie .... 530-898-4015... 33 A
mpayne@csuchico.edu
PAYNE, Mary .... 515-271-1452. 177 H
mary.payne@dmu.edu
PAYNE, Molly .... 617-732-2218. 233 E
molly.payne@mcphs.edu
PAYNE, Natalie .... 215-965-4039. 424 D
npayne@moore.edu
PAYNE, O, J .... 641-648-6101. 179 I
orintheo.payne@iavalley.edu
PAYNE, Pat .... 617-349-8850. 226 D
ppayne@lesley.edu
PAYNE, Patricia .... 617-349-8841. 228 B
ppayne@lesley.edu
PAYNE, Ralph, C .... 304-256-0279. 528 D
rpayne@newriver.edu
PAYNE, Rich .... 928-523-7618... 16 C
rich.payne@nau.edu
PAYNE, Shari, L .... 412-397-6235. 431 I
payne@rmu.edu
PAYNE, Sherri .... 702-651-2678. 294 E
sherri.payne@csn.edu
PAYNE, Stephen, D .... 269-471-6534. 239 D
stephen@andrews.edu
PAYNE, Stephen, D .... 269-405-2837. 243 G
stephen@andrews.edu
PAYNE, Steven, W .... 772-462-7805. 106 P
spayne@irsc.edu
PAYNE, Sylvia, M .... 317-274-4417. 168 D
payne@iupui.edu
PAYNE, Tamara .... 205-853-1200..... 5 B
tlpayne@jeffstateonline.com
PAYNE, Tena .... 270-534-3342. 196 G
tena.payne@kctcs.edu
PAYNE, Terry .... 828-298-3325. 370 E
tpayne@warren-wilson.edu
PAYNE, Thomas, L .... 573-882-3846. 283 C
paynet@missouri.edu
PAYNE, Vernon .... 269-387-2136. 252 I
vernon.payne@wmich.edu
PAYNE, Wesley, A .... 573-840-9689. 282 K
wpayne@trcc.edu
PAYNE, William .... 218-726-7033. 264 D
wpayne@d.umn.edu
PAYNE-RILEY, Brenda .... 216-987-4624. 378 D
brenda.payne-riley@tri-c.edu
PAYNTER, Chris .... 704-330-6531. 359 C
chris.paynter@cpcc.edu
PAYNTER, Ronald .... 212-817-7650. 317 F
rpaynter@gc.cuny.edu

PAYTON, Alvin .... 229-333-2123. 134 K
alvin.payton@wiregrass.edu
PAYTON, Annie .... 256-372-4747.... 1 A
annie.payton@aamu.edu
PAYTON, Annie .... 478-825-6343. 124 H
paytona@fvsu.edu
PAYTON, Donald .... 407-708-2434. 113 E
paytond@seminolestate.edu
PAYTON, Paula .... 803-780-1023. 449 E
ppayton@voorhees.edu
PAYTON, Shannon .... 304-214-8917. 528 G
spayton@wvncc.edu
PAYTON, Tom .... 937-393-3431. 389 B
tpayton@sscc.edu
PAZ, Harold, L .... 717-531-8323. 426 A
hlp10@psu.edu
PAZ, Marvin .... 575-527-7694. 311 B
mpaz@nmsu.edu
PAZZANI, Michael, J .... 951-827-5535... 71 E
michael.pazzani@ucr.edu
PEACE, Derryle .... 903-886-5764. 483 E
derryle.peace@tamuc.edu
PEACH, Jennifer .... 415-380-1646... 45 H
jenniferpeach@ggbts.edu
PEACH, John .... 330-672-3111. 382 B
jpeach@kent.edu
PEACH, Kyle .... 618-262-8641. 147 C
peachk@iecc.edu
PEACHES, John .... 662-252-8000. 269 F
jpeaches@rustcollege.edu
PEACOCK, Ann .... 919-718-7542. 359 B
apeacock@cccc.edu
PEACOCK, Clyde .... 785-830-2753. 187 B
clyde.peacock@bie.edu
PEACOCK, Kenneth, E .... 828-262-2040. 367 A
peacockke@appstate.edu
PEACOCK, Ross .... 440-775-6927. 385 H
ross.peacock@oberlin.edu
PEACOCK, Sabrina .... 813-253-7995. 106 M
speacock4@hccfl.edu
PEACOCK, Steve .... 229-217-4234. 129 F
speacock@moultrietech.edu
PEACOCK, Steve .... 612-330-1583. 253 H
peacock@augsburg.edu
PEACOCK, Walter, H .... 229-333-5791. 134 B
wpeacock@valdosta.edu
PEACOCK-LANDRUM,
Linda, G .... 920-465-2163. 536 F
peacockl@uwgb.edu
PEAK, Douglas, C .... 817-515-3076. 482 B
doug.peak@tccd.edu
PEAK, JR., James, F .... 804-204-1230. 502 F
jpeak@btsr.edu
PEAK, Jamie .... 215-612-6600. 419 J
jpeak@chicareers.com
PEAK, Scott, S .... 414-229-5576. 537 A
speak@uwm.edu
PEAKE, Jaklin .... 503-493-6545. 402 J
jpeake@cu-portland.edu
PEAL, Regina, A .... 614-287-5343. 378 B
rpeal@cscc.edu
PEAL MORROW,
Rebecca .... 610-921-7641. 409 A
rmorrow@alb.edu
PEARCE, Arthur, B .... 229-333-5832. 134 B
apearce@valdosta.edu
PEARCE, Jared .... 641-673-2107. 183 H
pearcej@wmpenn.edu
PEARCE, Jeff .... 505-473-6470. 311 K
jeff.pearce@santafeuniversity.edu
PEARCE, Jennifer .... 614-823-1600. 387 K
jpearce@otterbein.edu
PEARCE, Katheryn, P .... 386-822-7459. 117 C
kpearce@stetson.edu
PEARCE, Kenneth, D .... 910-362-7423. 358 F
kpearce@cfcc.edu
PEARCE, Kim .... 612-977-5436. 254 C
kim.pearce@capella.edu
PEARCE, Laurence, W .... 803-777-8161. 447 G
lpearce@mailbox.sc.edu
PEARCE, Michael .... 813-974-1780. 116 C
mpearce@usf.edu
PEARCE, Nathaniel .... 704-334-6882. 357 K
npearce@nlts.edu
PEARCE, Richard, R .... 540-654-1246. 510 J
rpearce@umw.edu
PEARCE, Rick .... 309-268-8100. 146 B
rick.pearce@heartland.edu
PEARIGEN, Rob .... 601-974-1001. 267 I
rob.pearigen@millsaps.edu
PEARL, Cathleen .... 202-685-9082. 544 K
cathleen.pearl.ctr@ndu.edu
PEARL, Donald .... 240-567-5006. 216 F
donald.pearl@montgomerycollege.edu
PEARL, Melany .... 434-592-4020. 506 I
mapearl@liberty.edu
PEARLMUTTER,
Roberta, S .... 401-456-8043. 439 F
rpearlmutter@ric.edu
PEARON, Jill, R .... 315-267-2108. 344 C
pearonjr@potsdam.edu
PEARRING, Yu Yok .... 808-974-7501. 136 A
yuyok@hawaii.edu
PEARROW, Dorothy .... 409-772-8205. 493 C
dapearro@utmb.edu
PEARSALL, Donald .... 704-216-6080. 356 D
dpearsall@livingstone.edu
PEARSALL, Joel, K .... 208-467-8772. 139 A
jkpearsall@nnu.edu
PEARSALL, Kim .... 405-945-3250. 398 C
PEARSON, Aimee .... 716-829-7803. 323 D
pearsona@dyc.edu
PEARSON, Amelia .... 256-215-4261.... 2 G
apearson@cacc.edu
PEARSON, Andrew, L .... 540-828-5410. 502 J
apearson@bridgewater.edu
PEARSON, Ashton .... 662-915-7051. 270 B
ashton@olemiss.edu
PEARSON, Barry .... 914-251-6020. 344 D
barry.pearson@purchase.edu
PEARSON, Bob .... 580-477-7800. 401 J
bob.pearson@wosc.edu
PEARSON, Bryan, J .... 814-886-6424. 424 G
bpearson@mtaloy.edu
PEARSON, Craig .... 641-472-1186. 180 N
cpearson@mum.edu
PEARSON, David .... 760-768-5520... 35 D
dpearson@mail.sdsu.edu
PEARSON, David, L .... 515-574-1234. 179 D
pearson@iowacentral.edu
PEARSON, Denise .... 336-750-8932. 370 A
pearsond@wssu.edu
PEARSON, Doug .... 608-822-2401. 541 C
dpearson@swtc.edu
PEARSON, Doug, R .... 478-301-2685. 128 H
pearson_dr@mercer.edu
PEARSON, Elaine .... 713-221-8273. 489 D
pearsone@uhd.edu
PEARSON, Elizabeth, R .... 828-669-8012. 357 H
epearson@montreat.edu
PEARSON, Janice, L .... 559-323-2100... 63 B
jpearson@sjcl.edu
PEARSON, Juanitta .... 208-459-5307. 138 A
jpearson@collegeofidaho.edu
PEARSON, Judy, G .... 562-908-3415... 60 I
jgpearson@riohondo.edu
PEARSON, Karen, L .... 208-467-8663. 139 A
klpearson@nnu.edu
PEARSON, Lynn .... 626-815-6000... 29 H
lpearson@apu.edu
PEARSON, Matt .... 707-778-3974... 65 B
mpearson@santarosa.edu
PEARSON, Peggy .... 773-380-7041. 140 D
peggy.pearson@seabury.edu
PEARSON, Sarah, R .... 207-786-6247. 209 F
spearson@bates.edu
PEARSON, Sonya .... 480-461-7443... 15 A
sonya.pearson@mesacc.edu
PEARSON, Stacey .... 407-823-2811. 115 E
stacey.pearson@ucf.edu
PEARSON, Stacy .... 208-426-1200. 137 G
spearson@boisestate.edu
PEARSON, Steven, A .... 803-535-5434. 442 B
spearson@claflin.edu
PEARSON, Susan .... 219-785-5247. 172 A
spearson@pnc.edu
PEARSON, Thomas .... 732-571-3405. 303 C
pearson@monmouth.edu
PEARSON, Tracey .... 910-630-7122. 356 H
tpearson@methodist.edu
PEARSON, Walter, S .... 773-274-3000. 151 H
PEART, Sandra, J .... 804-289-6086. 510 L
speart@richmond.edu
PEASE, Rodney, W .... 413-796-2080. 238 A
rpease@wne.edu
PEASE, Susan .... 860-832-2605... 87 K
pease@ccsu.edu
PEASLEE, Deidra .... 763-433-1829. 257 P
deidra.peaslee@anokaramsey.edu
PEASTER, Carl, S .... 615-898-2424. 459 D
buddy.peaster@mtsu.edu
PEAT, Barbara .... 219-981-5645. 168 B
bpeat@iun.edu
PEAVEY, Marion, B .... 864-597-4200. 449 I
peaveymb@wofford.edu
PEAVY, Richard .... 863-784-7275. 113 G
peavyr@southflorida.edu
PEAVY, Terence .... 212-343-1234. 331 D
tpeavy@mcny.edu
PEAY, J. H. Binford .... 540-464-7311. 515 B
peayjb@vmi.edu
PEAY, Steven, A .... 262-646-6512. 535 B
speay@nashotah.edu
PECARD, Paulette .... 414-955-8235. 534 C
ppecard@mcw.edu
PECCHIA, John, P .... 845-575-3000. 330 D
john.pecchia@marist.edu
PECCOLO, JR.,
Charles (Butch), M .... 865-974-1763. 463 B
cpeccolo@tennessee.edu
PECEN, Reg, R .... 832-230-5540. 477 H
regpecen@northamerican.edu
PECENY, Mark .... 505-277-7381. 312 F
markpec@unm.edu
PECHA, David, M .... 580-327-8528. 396 N
dmpecha@nwosu.edu
PECILE, Nicola .... 661-824-2977... 55 I
PECINA, Greg .... 325-942-2021. 465 K
greg.pecina@angelo.edu
PECK, Adam .... 936-468-7249. 482 A
peckae@sfasu.edu
PECK, Cindy, J .... 217-443-8803. 143 G
cpeck@dacc.edu
PECK, Daniel, A .... 408-988-2200... 75 K
PECK, David .... 626-815-4503... 29 H
dpeck@apu.edu
PECK, Jeanie .... 651-641-8709. 255 B
peck@csp.edu
PECK, Jeffrey, M .... 646-312-3870. 316 J
Jeffrey.Peck@baruch.cuny.edu
PECK, Magda .... 414-229-3083. 537 A
mpeck@uwm.edu
PECK, Nan .... 563-876-3353. 177 I
npeck@dwci.edu
PECK, Robert .... 508-999-8539. 229 A
rpeck@umassd.edu
PECK, Ronald .... 717-361-1524. 415 H
peckr@etown.edu
PECK, Susan, M .... 607-871-2698. 313 E
pecksm@alfred.edu
PECK, Syndi .... 217-228-5432. 156 C
pecksy@quincy.edu
PECK, Teresa, M .... 570-208-5895. 419 P
tmpeck@kings.edu
PECKA, Kenneth, D .... 509-777-3292. 525 F
kpecka@whitworth.edu
PECKHAM, Karissa, L .... 203-576-4552... 91 G
kpeckham@bridgeport.edu
PECKITT, JR., Carl, S .... 610-799-1114. 421 I
cpeckitt@lccc.edu
PECKO, Joseph .... 708-237-5060. 155 B
jpecko@nc.edu
PECORONI, Deanna, L .... 314-434-2212. 275 D
PECSOK, Michael .... 808-455-0269. 137 A
mpecsok@hawaii.edu
PECTOL, James, B .... 423-585-6823. 462 A
james.pectol@ws.edu
PEDE, Michael .... 315-464-4329. 342 E
pedem@upstate.edu
PEDE, Mike .... 713-743-9551. 489 B
mlpede@uh.edu
PEDEN, Gary, S .... 315-470-6588. 345 B
gspeden@esf.edu
PEDERSEN, Daniel, T .... 320-308-2166. 261 B
dtpedersen@stcloudstate.edu
PEDERSEN, Eric, R .... 907-786-1266... 10 H
erpedersen@uaa.alaska.edu
PEDERSEN, Jennifer, L .... 308-635-6078. 293 E
pedersen@wncc.edu
PEDERSEN, Joel, D .... 402-472-1201. 292 G
jdpedersen@nebraska.edu
PEDERSEN, Mary, E .... 805-756-2246... 32 F
mdederse@calpoly.edu
PEDERSEN, Patricia, E .... 203-436-8518... 93 A
patty.pedersen@yale.edu
PEDERSEN, Phyllis .... 225-214-6966. 206 D
phyllis.pedersen@ololcollege.edu
PEDERSEN, Sarah .... 360-867-6647. 519 J
pederses@evergreen.edu
PEDERSON, Donald, O .... 479-575-5828... 23 I
dop@uark.edu
PEDERSON, E.J. (Jere) .... 979-436-9102. 484 B
president@tamhsc.edu
PEDERSON, Robert, A .... 207-778-7036. 212 D
pederson@maine.edu
PEDERSON, Steven, C .... 412-648-8230. 435 C
spederson@athletics.pitt.edu
PEDESCLEAUX, Desiree .... 404-270-5696. 132 E
dpedescl@spelman.edu
PEDIGO, Sue, H .... 615-230-3551. 461 G
sue.pedigo@volstate.edu
PEDNEAU, Judy .... 276-326-4461. 502 H
jpedneau@bluefield.edu
PEDRAZA, Jonathan, N .... 262-691-5308. 541 D
jpedraza2@wctc.edu
PEDRICK, Andrea .... 315-786-2236. 327 L
apedrick@sunyjefferson.edu
PEDRICK, James, A .... 319-385-6218. 179 K
jim.pedrick@iwc.edu
PEDRONE, Dino, J .... 607-729-1581. 322 F
dpedrone@davisny.edu
PEDUTO, Michelle, A .... 412-578-6157. 412 G
mapeduto@carlow.edu
PEE, Charles, M .... 803-934-3294. 445 F
cpee@morris.edu
PEEBLES, Carolyn .... 919-572-1625. 352 C
cpeebles@apexsot.edu
PEEBLES, Greg .... 321-674-7715. 104 H
peebles@fit.edu
PEEBLES, LaShondra .... 773-995-2215. 141 J
lpeebl20@csu.edu
PEEBLES, Lee .... 401-739-5000. 439 D
lpeebles@neit.edu
PEEBLES, Rex .... 432-685-4551. 476 G
rpeebles@midland.edu
PEEDIN, Pamela, L .... 603-646-1110. 296 G
pamela.l.peedin@dartmouth.edu
PEEK, Brian .... 706-245-7226. 124 D
bpeek@ec.edu
PEEK, John, M .... 304-462-4100. 529 G
john.peek@glenville.edu
PEEK, Katherine .... 909-652-6333... 37 M
kay.peek@chaffey.edu
PEEL, Bill .... 214-932-1112. 475 J
billpeel@letu.edu
PEEL, Henry .... 239-489-9011. 101 O
hpeel@edison.edu
PEEL, Michael, A .... 203-432-8362... 93 A
mikr.peel@yale.edu
PEELER, Chris Goff .... 704-461-6663. 352 G
chrisgoff@bac.edu
PEELER, Jody .... 740-695-9500. 374 H
jpeeler@belmontcollege.edu
PEELER, Mark, L .... 864-379-8745. 443 F
mlp@erskine.edu
PEELING, Rebecca .... 561-803-2024. 110 B
becky_peeling@pba.edu
PEEPLES, Junelyn .... 909-607-3884... 65 D
junelyn.peeples@scrippscollege.edu
PEEPLES, Terry, G .... 870-245-5169... 22 D
peeplest@obu.edu
PEEPLES, Tim .... 336-278-5613. 354 B
peeples@elon.edu
PEER, Ronda .... 307-754-6123. 543 G
Ronda.Peer@northwestcollege.edu
PEERY, Sharon .... 276-964-7244. 514 A
sharon.peery@sw.edu
PEET, Kara .... 617-262-5000. 223 F
kara.peet@the-bac.edu
PEEVEY, Robin .... 617-873-0274. 224 G
Robin.peevey@cambridgecollege.edu
PEFFALL, Marianne .... 610-436-2705. 430 A
mpeffall@wcupa.edu
PEFFER, Bruce .... 512-313-3000. 469 L
bruce.peffer@concordia.edu
PEFFER, Deb .... 313-593-5100. 251 D
dkpeffer@umich.edu
PEFFER, Tony .... 802-468-1203. 501 B
tony.peffer@castleton.edu
PEFFERS, Keith .... 219-785-5720. 172 A
kpeffers@pnc.edu
PEGAH, Mahmoud .... 941-359-7633. 111 O
mpegah@ringling.edu
PEGG, Steven, M .... 410-777-2651. 213 D
smpegg@aacc.edu
PEGGY, Gerard, S .... 219-989-2818. 171 N
psgerard@purduecal.edu
PEGHER, Paul, A .... 740-587-6267. 379 D
pegherp@denison.edu
PEGUERO, Hilary .... 316-295-4301. 186 H
hilaryp@friends.edu
PEGUES, Patricia .... 662-252-8000. 269 F
ppegues@rustcollege.edu
PEGUES, Patricia .... 662-252-2491. 269 F
ppegues@rustcollege.edu
PEHLMAN, Patricia, A .... 717-245-1545. 414 H
pehlman@dickinson.edu
PEHRSSON,
Dale-Elizabeth .... 989-774-6995. 240 N
pehrs1d@cmich.edu
PEIFER, Michelle .... 704-991-0393. 364 C
mpeifer7924@stanly.edu
PEIFFER, Cyndi .... 641-673-1040. 183 H
peifferc@wmpenn.edu
PEIFFER, Mark, J .... 515-271-1475. 177 H
mark.peiffer@dmu.edu
PEINOVICH, Paula .... 301-431-5401. 217 C
ppeinovich@nlc.edu
PEKARA, Gus .... 405-232-3382. 397 E
gpekara@occc.edu
PEKRUL, William, A .... 507-354-8221. 256 M
pekrulwa@mlc-wels.edu
PELAEZ, Indra .... 773-907-2474. 142 A
ipaolapelaez@ccc.edu
PELAEZ, Michelle .... 813-253-6251. 118 L
mpelaez@ut.edu
PELAK, Anne .... 570-408-4307. 437 F
anne.pelak@wilkes.edu
PELAK, Anne, C .... 914-654-5225. 320 H
apelak@cnr.edu
PELAZZA, Todd, A .... 203-254-4090... 89 I
tapelazza@fairfield.edu
PELC, Sharon .... 308-865-8523. 292 H
pelcs@unk.edu
PELESKY, Tim .... 301-784-5000. 213 B
tpelesky@allegany.edu
PELIO, JR., Joseph .... 516-299-4213. 329 C
joe.pelio@liu.edu
PELISSERO, John, P .... 312-915-7585. 151 H
jpeliss@luc.edu
PELKEY, Dave .... 425-235-2463. 522 F
dpelkey@rtc.edu
PELLEGRIN, Amy, E .... 304-367-4135. 529 F
Amy.Pellegrin@fairmontstate.edu

PELLEGRINI, Larry ... 570-674-6307. 424 A lpellegr@misericordia.edu
PELLEGRINO, Debra, A .. 570-941-6305. 436 A debra.pellegrino@scranton.edu
PELLEGRINO, Karen, A .. 203-254-4100... 89 I kpellegrino@fairfield.edu
PELLEGRINO, Thomas, C ... 203-254-4000... 89 I tpellegrino@fairfield.edu
PELLEGRINO, Vincent .... 218-935-0417. 265 E drvpellegrino@wetcc.edu
PELLERITO, Chris ... 989-386-6660. 247 B cpellerito@midmich.edu
PELLESCKI, Lori ... 610-558-5630. 424 I pellescl@neumann.edu
PELLETIER, David, J ... 573-629-3092. 274 J dpelletier@hlg.edu
PELLETIER, Jo-Ann, M ... 508-678-2811. 231 B jo-ann.pelletier@bristolcc.edu
PELLETIER, Kathe ... 612-977-5701. 254 C kathe.pelletier@capella.edu
PELLETIER, Kristan, M ... 518-629-7328. 326 G k.pelletier@hvcc.edu
PELLETT, Tracy ... 509-963-1404. 517 F tracy.pellett@cwu.edu
PELLICCIA, Michael, C ... 516-572-7538. 332 C michael.pelliccia@ncc.edu
PELLICCIOTTI, Joseph .... 219-980-6841. 168 B jpelli@iun.edu
PELLICCIOTTI, M. Beth ... 219-989-2239. 171 N pellicmb@purduecal.edu
PELLICO, Gary ... 317-921-4882. 169 L gpellico@ivytech.edu
PELLISH, Catherine ... 303-404-5022... 81 N catherine.pellish@frontrange.edu
PELLY, Michael ... 714-997-6982... 38 A pelly@chapman.edu
PELOQUIN, Andy ... 503-517-1815. 408 I apeloquin@westernseminary.edu
PELOQUIN-DODD, Mary, T ... 919-515-2143. 368 B mary_peloquin-dodd@ncsu.edu
PELOSO, Elizabeth, D ..... 215-746-0234. 435 B epeloso@upenn.edu
PELRINE, JR., John, P ... 773-298-3121. 158 E pelrine@sxu.edu
PELSMA, Lucy, C ... 207-859-1329. 211 H pelsmal@thomas.edu
PELTIER, Beverly ... 706-771-4023. 121 D bpeltier@augustatech.edu
PELTIER, Eileen ... 860-253-3032... 88 C epeltier@asnuntuck.edu
PELTIER, Linda, M ... 937-778-7802. 379 G lpeltier@edisonohio.edu
PELTIER, Matthew, S ... 423-652-4740. 455 I mspeltie@king.edu
PELTO, William, L ... 828-262-3021. 367 A peltowl@appstate.edu
PELTON, Jack ... 208-426-4203. 137 G jpelton@boisestate.edu
PELTON, M. Lee ... 617-824-8525. 226 A lee_pelton@emerson.edu
PELTON, Mark ... 478-445-2753. 125 A mark.pelton@gcsu.edu
PELTON, Woody ... 336-278-6700. 354 B wpelton@elon.edu
PELTSVERGER, Boris ... 229-931-2100. 126 D boris.peltsverger@gsw.edu
PELTZ, Mark ... 641-269-4940. 178 H peltzm@grinnell.edu
PELUSI, Mario, J ... 309-556-3061. 148 B mpelusi@iwu.edu
PELUSO, Constance ... 718-631-6297. 319 D cpeluso@qcc.cuny.edu
PELUSO, Tony ... 212-924-5900. 347 B apeluso@swedishinstitute.edu
PELUSO-VERDEND, Gary ... 918-270-6405. 398 I gary.peluso@ptstulsa.edu
PELY, Laszlo ... 410-617-2421. 216 A lpely@loyola.edu
PELZ, Beth ... 713-221-8575. 489 D pelzb@uhd.edu
PELZEL, Morris ... 812-749-1202. 171 K mpelzel@oak.edu
PEMBERTON, Barbara .... 870-245-5541... 22 D pembertonb@obu.edu
PEMBERTON, Cynthia ... 701-483-2330. 371 D cynthia.pemberton@dickinsonstate.edu
PEMBERTON, Cynthia, L 816-235-1868. 283 D pembertonc@umkc.edu
PEMBERTON, Dana, L .... 406-338-5441. 285 F danalou@bfcc.edu
PEMBERTON, Laurie ... 805-922-6966... 26 K laurie.pemberton@hancockcollege.edu
PEMBERTON, Loren ... 509-533-3503. 518 F loren.pemberton@spokanefalls.edu
PEMBERTON, Richard .... 573-897-5000. 276 E
PEMBERTON, Shelly ... 218-335-4202. 256 I shelly.pemberton@lltc.edu
PEMBROOK, Randall, G . 785-670-1649. 191 D randy.pembrook@washburn.edu
PEMSTEIN, Debra ... 845-758-7405. 314 D pemstein@bard.edu
PENA, Andrew, M ... 575-646-1694. 310 I ampena@nmsu.edu
PENA, Augusto, E ... 828-262-6252. 367 A penaae@appstate.edu
PENA, Damien ... 805-437-3218... 32 I damien.pena@csuci.edu
PENA, Denise ... 714-556-3610... 74 D denise.pena@vanguard.edu
PENA, Fred ... 956-364-4337. 485 H fred.pena@tstc.edu
PENA, Jesus ... 610-683-4700. 429 A pena@kutztown.edu
PENA, JR., Jose, A ... 956-721-5312. 475 F jpena@laredo.edu
PENA, Juanita ... 719-846-5537... 85 H juanita.pena@trinidadstate.edu
PENA, Maria ... 360-417-6340. 522 A mpena@pencol.edu
PENA, Michelle ... 305-220-4120. 111 E cemdir@ptcmatt.com
PENA, Nova ... 915-595-1935. 474 U
PENA, Phil ... 636-584-6701. 273 M pepena@eastcentral.edu
PENA, Sandra, V ... 956-326-2365. 483 B sandra@tamiu.edu
PENA, Stan ... 575-538-6470. 312 N stan.pena@wnmu.edu
PENA, Stephen ... 480-245-7971... 14 B stephen.pena@ibcs.edu
PENA, Vivian ... 757-497-4466. 510 B vpena@stratford.edu
PENA, William ... 608-243-6320. 540 C wpena@madisoncollege.edu
PENA-WARFIELD, Roseanna ... 508-362-2131. 231 D rpenawar@capecod.edu
PENCE, Bill ... 540-868-7061. 512 H bpence@lfcc.edu
PENCE, Heather ... 404-297-9522. 126 A penceh@gptc.edu
PENCE, Lorence, L ... 304-647-6295. 530 B lpence@osteo.wvsom.edu
PENCE, Nadine, S ... 765-361-6434. 175 B pencen@wabash.edu
PENCHI, Zulma ... 787-257-0000. 554 B zulmapenchi@hotmail.com
PENDAKUR, Sumun (Sumi) ... 909-607-3470... 46 H spendakur@hmc.edu
PENDERGAST, Katherine, N ... 617-373-2230. 235 F
PENDERGAST, Linda ... 309-672-5534. 152 I lpendergast@methodistcol.edu
PENDERGRAFT, Susan ... 336-386-3380. 364 D pendergrafts@surry.edu
PENDERGRASS, Brad ... 251-809-1521..... 5 A brad.pendergrass@jdcc.edu
PENDERGRASS, Martha . 919-843-5048. 368 D mjpender@email.unc.edu
PENDERGRASS, Todd .... 870-733-6880... 21 I dtpendergrass@midsouthcc.edu
PENDERGRASS, Toni ... 505-566-3209. 311 I pendergrasst@sancollege.edu
PENDERGRAST, Runan ... 859-246-6305. 194 L runan.pendergrast@kctcs.edu
PENDERS, Brooke ... 860-528-4111... 90 A bpenders@goodwin.edu
PENDHARKAR, Daya ... 813-253-7091. 106 M dpendharkar@hccfl.edu
PENDLETON, Brandon ... 312-553-5654. 141 N bpendleton2@ccc.edu
PENDLETON, Dennis, F .. 530 757 8663... 70 J dfpendleton@ucdavis.edu
PENDLETON, Edith ... 239-489-9213. 101 O ependleton@edison.edu
PENDLETON, Gail ... 510-981-2804... 59 A gpendleton@peralta.edu
PENDLETON, Janis, S .... 803-327-7402. 442 D jpendleton@clintonjuniorcollege.edu
PENDLETON, Kathy, J .... 502-852-6585. 200 D kathy.pendleton@louisville.edu
PENDLETON, Laurence ... 615-963-7923. 459 E laurence.pendleton@tnstate.edu
PENDLETON, Mitch ... 801-524-1948. 495 O mpendleton@ldsbc.edu
PENDLETON, Patrick ... 928-541-7777... 16 B
PENDLETON, Penny ... 479-788-7121... 24 A penny.pendleton@uafs.edu
PENDLETON, Sally ... 502-895-3411. 197 F spendleton@lpts.edu
PENDSE, Ravi ... 316-978-5053. 191 F ravi.pendse@wichita.edu
PENDSE, Ravindra ... 401-863-7250. 438 J ravi_pendse@brown.edu
PENFIELD, Gary, M ... 401-456-8123. 439 F gpenfield@ric.edu
PENGRA, Matt ... 407-679-0100. 106 D mpengra@fullsail.com
PENISTEN, Douglas ... 918-456-5511. 396 H penisten@nsuok.edu
PENKALA, Robert ... 586-445-7636. 246 A penkalar@macomb.edu
PENKE, Ann, K ... 920-565-1242. 533 R penkea@lakeland.edu
PENKOVA, Snejanka ... 787-764-0000. 555 B snejanka.penkova@upr.edu
PENLAND, Joni, M ... 502-410-6200. 194 B jpenland@galencollege.edu
PENLAND, Lynn, R ... 812-488-2360. 173 H lp22@evansville.edu
PENLAND, Nathan ... 417-328-1828. 282 C npenland@sbuniv.edu
PENLER, Karen ... 216-373-6364. 385 G kpenler@ndc.edu
PENLEY, Julie ... 915-831-7001. 472 B jpenley@epcc.edu
PENLEY, Larry ... 602-978-7200... 18 A larry.penley@thunderbird.edu
PENLEY, Laura ... 215-702-4307. 411 F lpenley@cairn.edu
PENN, Ann, E ... 919-966-3576. 368 D ann_penn@unc.edu
PENN, David ... 407-447-7300. 105 I dpenn@ftccollege.edu
PENN, Deborah ... 620-947-3121. 190 J deborahp@tabor.edu
PENN, Mark, A ... 801-878-1058. 295 E mpenn@roseman.edu
PENN, Ray ... 423-869-6312. 456 A rpenn@lmunet.edu
PENNA, Anthony ... 617-552-3475. 224 A anthony.penna@bc.edu
PENNA, Nancy ... 612-977-5522. 254 C nancy.penna@capella.edu
PENNACHIO, Michael .... 617-521-2190. 236 G michael.pennachio@simmons.edu
PENNARTZ, Kathy ... 940-397-4214. 476 H kathy.pennartz@mwsu.edu
PENNER, Julie ... 815-836-5667. 150 H pennerju@lewisu.edu
PENNETTI, Dianna ... 212-854-3362. 314 G dpennetti@barnard.edu
PENNEY, Jeff ... 574-239-8356. 166 N jpenney@hcc-nd.edu
PENNEY, R. William ... 386-822-7045. 117 C bpenney@stetson.edu
PENNIECOOK, Tricia, Y . 909-558-4578... 51 C tpenniecook@llu.edu
PENNINGS, Rhonda, R ... 712-324-5061. 181 G rpennings@nwicc.edu
PENNINGTON, David ... 740-420-5906. 385 L dpennington@ohiochristian.edu
PENNINGTON, Josianne, E ... 410-704-3255. 220 E jpennington@towson.edu
PENNINGTON, Karen, L . 973-655-4311. 303 D penningtonk@mail.montclair.edu
PENNINGTON, Kimberly 828-328-7473. 356 B kimberly.pennington@lr.edu
PENNINGTON, Laurie ..... 928-428-8231... 13 J laurie.pennington@eac.edu
PENNINGTON, Michael .. 910-521-6637. 369 B michael.pennington@uncp.edu
PENNINGTON, Ronald ... 636-922-8271. 280 J rpennington@stchas.edu
PENNINGTON, Sandra ... 801-375-5125. 496 G spennington@rmuohp.edu
PENNINGTON, Sherry, R ... 417-667-8181. 273 A spennington@cottey.edu
PENNINGTON, Thomas .. 479-964-0824... 20 E tpennington@atu.edu
PENNINGTON, Wayne .... 906-487-2005. 247 A wayne@mtu.edu
PENNINI, Susan, W ... 617-333-2165. 225 E spennini@curry.edu
PENNIPEDE, Barbara, S . 914-923-2699. 335 J bpennipede@pace.edu
PENNIPIECE, Deirdre ... 718-960-8675. 318 A deirdre.pettipiece@lehman.cuny.edu
PENNISON, Bret ... 504-865-2290. 205 H bmpennis@loyno.edu
PENNISTON, Mary Ann .. 660-541-5127. 279 I mpenn@nwmissouri.edu
PENNIX, James ... 540-831-5371. 508 C jpennix@radford.edu
PENNIX, James ... 540-831-5460. 508 C jpennix@radford.edu
PENNOCK, Margaret ... 605-367-7667. 452 C margaret.pennock@southeasttech.edu
PENNOYER, Douglas ... 562-903-4844... 29 L doug.pennoyer@biola.edu
PENNY, Helen ... 229-333-5366. 134 K helen.penny@wiregrass.edu
PENNY, Rick ... 440-525-7320. 382 M rpenny@lakelandcc.edu
PENNY, Robert ... 601-923-1600. 269 E bpenny@rts.edu
PENROD, Curtis ... 318-357-5960. 208 B penrodc@nsula.edu
PENROD, Donald ... 562-985-5091... 33 F dpenrod@csulb.edu
PENROSE, Betsy, S ... 315-786-2249. 327 L bpenrose@sunyjefferson.edu
PENROSE, John ... 513-875-3344. 376 H john.penrose@chatfield.edu
PENRY, Jason ... 870-972-3030... 19 N jpenry@astate.edu
PENRY, Jason ... 870-972-2060... 19 N jpenry@astate.edu
PENRY, Michael, A ... 919-866-5532. 364 G mapenry@waketech.edu
PENSE, Christine ... 610-861-5312. 425 D cpense@northampton.edu
PENSGARD, Sara, E ... 540-338-1776. 508 A library@phc.edu
PENSIS, Claude ... 602-639-7500... 13 S
PENSKAR, Donald ... 269-387-8804. 252 I donald.penskar@wmich.edu
PENSON, Amy, M ... 828-395-1296. 361 C apenson@isothermal.edu
PENYACK, Megan ... 781-595-6768. 228 C mpenyack@mariancourt.edu
PENZENSTADLER, SSND, Joan ... 414-256-1226. 535 A penzenj@mtmary.edu
PENZIUL, Carl ... 607-844-8222. 347 I penziuc@tc3.edu
PEOPLE, Yasha ... 732-247-5241. 303 E ypeople@nbts.edu
PEOPLES, Peg ... 845-758-7432. 314 D peoples@bard.edu
PEOPLES, Verjanis ... 225-771-2360. 206 J verjanis_peoples@subr.edu
PEPE, Joseph ... 239-513-1122. 106 O jpepe@hodges.edu
PEPICELLO, William ... 602-557-1081... 18 I bill.pepicello@phoenix.edu
PEPION, Kenneth ... 970-247-7334... 81 M pepion_k@fortlewis.edu
PEPITO, Bobby ... 714-542-8086... 29 N bpepito@kensington.edu
PEPITONE, Dianne ... 914-831-0367. 321 B dpepitone@cw.edu
PEPLINSKI, Michael ... 724-938-4950. 428 A peplinski@calu.edu
PEPLOW, Nena ... 309-677-3223. 140 I nena@bradley.edu
PEPPARD, Timothy ... 216-397-4444. 381 R tpeppard@jcu.edu
PEPPER, Jeff ... 715-852-1314. 539 J jpepper@cvtc.edu
PEPPERS, Larry, C ... 540-458-8602. 516 A pepperst@wlu.edu
PEPPIN, Patricia ... 480-461-7456... 15 A pat.peppin@mesacc.edu
PERAGALLO, Nilda, P .... 305-284-2107. 118 F nperagallo@miami.edu
PERALES, Jose ... 585-385-8067. 338 H jperales@sjfc.edu
PERANANAMGAM, Reetha ... 313-593-5390. 251 D reetha@umich.edu
PERANTONI, Ed ... 636-949-4705. 276 D aperantoni@lindenwood.edu
PERCHINSKY, Tessa ... 715-836-3887. 536 E perchita@uwec.edu
PERCIANTE, Linda, K ..... 303-963-3237... 79 C lperciante@ccu.edu
PERCIVAL, Laura ... 989-275-5000. 245 B laura.percival@kirtland.edu
PERCIVAL, Nicole ... 620-331-4100. 187 G npercival@indycc.edu
PERCUOCO, Robert, E .... 563-884-5460. 182 A robert.percuoco@palmer.edu
PERCUS, Allon ... 909-621-8080... 39 C henry.schellhorn@cgu.edu
PERCY, Steve ... 410-837-5359. 221 A spercy@ubalt.edu
PERDOMO, Jose, A ... 425-235-2352. 522 F jperdomo@rtc.edu
PERDUE, K. Alan ... 304-876-5009. 529 I aperdue@shepherd.edu
PERDUE, Mark ... 859-858-3511. 192 B mark.perdue@asbury.edu
PERDUE, Robin, A ... 843-383-8025. 442 F rperdue@coker.edu
PERDUE, Tina, K ... 740-376-4730. 383 E tina.perdue@marietta.edu
PERDUE, Wendy, C ... 804-289-1779. 510 L wperdue@richmond.edu
PEREBOOM, Maarten, L . 410-543-6450. 220 D mlpereboom@salisbury.edu
PERECHI, Reuben ... 904-470-8078. 102 A rperechi@ewc.edu
PERECMAN, Dov ... 845-434-5240. 352 B dperecman@fallsburgyeshiva.com

PEREGOY, Robert ... 406-275-4976. 288 C
bob_peregoy@skc.edu

PEREIRA, Freyja ... 707-527-4512... 65 B
fpereira@santarosa.edu

PEREIRA, Malin ... 704-687-7198. 368 E
mpereira@uncc.edu

PEREIRA, Mary Ellen ... 541-485-1780. 405 B
registrar@newhope.edu

PEREIRA, Sandra ... 508-849-3363. 222 B
spereira@annamaria.edu

PERERA, Curtis ... 360-752-8330. 517 B
cperera@btc.ctc.edu

PERERA-BRIDGES,
Sonali ... 310-434-3493... 65 A
perera_sonali@smc.edu

PERES, Phyllis ... 202-885-2125... 94 F
academicaffairs@american.edu

PERESS, Kenneth ... 906-635-2634. 245 G
kperess@lssu.edu

PERETZ, Marc ... 989-964-7013. 249 G
mhp@svsu.edu

PERETZ, Marc, H ... 989-964-4387. 249 G
mhp@svsu.edu

PEREY, James ... 928-649-6513... 19 H
james.perey@yc.edu

PEREYRA, Moises ... 212-694-1000. 315 E
mpereyra@boricuacollege.edu

PEREZ, Amy ... 610-225-5414. 415 G
aperez2@eastern.edu

PEREZ, Andrew ... 518-438-3111. 330 C
andyp@mariacollege.edu

PEREZ, Angel ... 909-621-8129... 59 G
angel_perez@pitzer.edu

PEREZ, Angeles ... 787-725-6500. 547 H
aperez@albizu.edu

PEREZ, Antonio ... 212-220-1234. 317 A
aperez@bmcc.cuny.edu

PEREZ, Awilda ... 787-766-1717. 552 J
um_aperez@suagm.edu

PEREZ, Carlos ... 787-754-8000. 553 E
cperez@pupr.edu

PEREZ, Carlos ... 787-622-8000. 553 E
cperez@pupr.edu

PEREZ, Carlos ... 956-364-4236. 485 H
charlie.perez@tstc.edu

PEREZ, Carlos, G ... 956-721-5109. 475 F
carlos.perez@laredo.edu

PEREZ, Carmen, I ... 787-279-1912. 550 B
cperez@bayamon.inter.edu

PEREZ, Cheryle ... 787-852-1430. 549 C
cperez@hccpr.edu

PEREZ, Daisy ... 787-898-6442. 551 A
daisy.perez@sg.inter.edu

PEREZ, Diana ... 805-922-6966... 26 K
dperez@hancockcollege.edu

PEREZ, Doris ... 787-891-0925. 549 K
dperez@aguadilla.inter.edu

PEREZ, Doris, U ... 671-735-5517. 546 C
doris.perez@guamcc.edu

PEREZ, Eduardo ... 407-447-7300. 105 I
eperez@ftccollege.edu

PEREZ, Enrique ... 714-480-7460... 60 F
perez_enrique@rsccd.edu

PEREZ, Ernesto ... 305-644-1171. 100 P
ernesto@dademedical.edu

PEREZ, Gay ... 434-243-3605. 511 B
bgd2j@virginia.edu

PEREZ, Glenda ... 787-746-1400. 549 B
gperez@huertas.edu

PEREZ, Heather, K ... 816-604-3007. 277 G
heatherk.perez@mcckc.edu

PEREZ, Ivelisse ... 787-834-9595. 553 B
iperez@uaa.edu

PEREZ, Jesus ... 718-951-5908. 317 C
jperez@brooklyn.cuny.edu

PEREZ, Joel ... 206-281-2043. 523 C

PEREZ, Joel ... 503-554-2305. 403 C
jperez@georgefox.edu

PEREZ, Jose ... 787-738-2161. 554 C
jose.perez@upr.edu

PEREZ, Jose ... 915-532-3737. 494 J
jperez@westerntech.edu

PEREZ, Joseph, L ... 860-444-8352. 545 G
Joseph.L.Perez@uscg.mil

PEREZ, Juan ... 406-275-4978. 288 C
juan_perez@skc.edu

PEREZ, L. Jeffrey ... 843-953-6965. 442 A
jeff.perez@citadel.edu

PEREZ, Lance, C ... 402-472-3751. 292 I
lperez1@unl.edu

PEREZ, Lawrence, P ... 671-735-5522. 546 C
lawrence.perez@guamcc.edu

PEREZ, Lydia ... 212-742-8770. 348 B
lydia.perez@touro.edu

PEREZ, Lynwood, C ... 407-366-9493. 269 E
lperez@rts.edu

PEREZ, Manuel ... 562-985-4151... 33 F
mperez@csulb.edu

PEREZ, Manuel ... 916-484-8925... 53 A
perezm@arc.losrios.edu

PEREZ, Margarita ... 251-380-3025..... 7 D
mperez@shc.edu

PEREZ, Maria ... 787-891-0925. 549 K
mperez@aguadilla.inter.edu

PEREZ, Maria del C ... 787-284-1912. 550 F
mcperezr@ponce.inter.edu

PEREZ, Mercedes ... 787-815-0000. 553 I
mercedes.perez@upr.edu

PEREZ, Michael, G ... 801-581-6510. 496 Q
mike.perez@fm.utah.edu

PEREZ, Michelle ... 717-871-8943. 429 D
michelle.perez@millersville.edu

PEREZ, Miralys ... 787-600-0979. 555 C
miralys.perez@upr.edu

PEREZ, Monica ... 864-644-5133. 446 I
mperez@sw.edu

PEREZ, Monte, E ... 818-364-7796... 52 A
perezme@lamission.edu

PEREZ, Myrna ... 787-786-3030. 547 F
mperez@ucb.edu.pr

PEREZ, Omar ... 787-740-1611. 553 C
omar.perez@uccaribe.edu

PEREZ, Orlando ... 512-444-8082. 485 B
admissions@thsu.edu

PEREZ, Oscar ... 305-821-3333. 105 A
operez@fnu.edu

PEREZ, Raymond ... 702-968-1975. 295 E
rperez@roseman.edu

PEREZ, Ricardo ... 818-240-1000... 45 G
perez@glendale.edu

PEREZ, Ron ... 760-744-1150... 58 D
rperez@palomar.edu

PEREZ, Rowena Ellen ... 671-735-5640. 546 C
rowenaellen.perez@guamcc.edu

PEREZ, Ruperto ... 404-894-2575. 125 D
ruperto.perez@vpss.gatech.edu

PEREZ, Scott, L ... 818-677-2901... 34 C
scott.perez@csun.edu

PEREZ, Sonny, P ... 671-735-2372. 546 E
sonnypz@uguam.uog.edu

PEREZ, Suleyma ... 773-442-5400. 154 H
s-perez6@neiu.edu

PEREZ, Tony ... 940-553-4403. 493 F
tperez@vernoncollege.edu

PEREZ, Wanda ... 787-878-5475. 549 L
wperez@arecibo.inter.edu

PEREZ, William ... 787-780-0070. 547 G
wperez@caribbean.edu

PEREZ, Yolanda ... 787-834-9595. 553 B
yperez@uaa.edu

PEREZ DEL VALLE,
Lourdes ... 787-863-2390. 550 C
lourdes.perez@fajardo.inter.edu

PEREZ-FRANCO, Mayte .. 619-260-2395... 73 I
mpf@sandiego.edu

PEREZ GARCIA, Cesar ... 208-732-6250. 138 B
cperez@csi.edu

PEREZ-LOPEZ, Myrna, E 787-763-6700. 549 A
meperez@se-pr.edu

PEREZ RODRIGUEZ,
Sandra, I ... 787-890-2681. 553 H
sandra.perez3@upr.edu

PEREZ-SILVA, Glaisma ... 860-906-5042... 88 D
gperez-silva@ccc.commnet.edu

PEREZ-TORO, Angeles ... 787-725-6500. 547 H
aperez@albizu.edu

PERFETTI, Anthony ... 516-323-3035. 331 J
aperfetti@molly.edu

PERFETTI, Heather ... 845-341-4768. 335 H
heather.perfetti@sunyorange.edu

PERFETTI, Lisa, R ... 509-527-5187. 525 E
perfetlr@whitman.edu

PERFETTI, Margi, L ... 301-387-3042. 214 I
margi.perfetti@garrettcollege.edu

PERGI, Brenan ... 740-283-6445. 379 N
bpergi@franciscan.edu

PERGL, Denise ... 254-526-1291. 468 G
denise.pergl@ctcd.edu

PERGOLA-RIVERA,
Maribelle ... 787-993-8951. 554 A
maribelle.pergola@upr.edu

PERGOLIS, Robert ... 718-940-5419. 339 B
rpergolis@sjcny.edu

PERGOLIZZI, Vanessa ... 860-913-2160... 90 A
vpergolizzi@goodwin.edu

PERI, Jonathan ... 610-358-4585. 424 I
perij@neumann.edu

PERILLO, Brian ... 212-998-6843. 334 D
bperillo@nyu.edu

PERILLO, Cheryl ... 312-980-9250. 148 D
cperillo@iadtchicago.edu

PERILLO, Patricia, A ... 540-231-6272. 515 C
pperillo@vt.edu

PERIN, Thomas ... 567-661-7880. 387 L
thomas_perin@owens.edu

PERINO, Donna, B ... 814-456-7504. 416 A
perinod@eriebc.edu

PERKINS, JR.,
Andrew, M ... 336-285-4551. 367 E
perkins@ncat.edu

PERKINS, Anika, M ... 662-329-7119. 268 E
aperkins@pa.muw.edu

PERKINS, Bethany ... 603-645-9611. 297 I
b.perkins@snhu.edu

PERKINS, Bruce ... 405-585-5120. 397 C
bruce.perkins@okbu.edu

PERKINS, Carolyn ... 717-262-2006. 437 H
cperkins@wilson.edu

PERKINS, Caron ... 432-552-2747. 493 D
perkins_c@utpb.edu

PERKINS, Charles ... 620-792-9245. 184 F
perkinsc@bartonccc.edu

PERKINS, Chris ... 770-531-6396. 128 B
cperkins@laniertech.edu

PERKINS, Claude, G ... 804-257-5835. 515 F
cgperkins@vuu.edu

PERKINS, Crasha ... 540-831-5765. 508 C
cperkins5@radford.edu

PERKINS, D. Clay ... 252-334-2004. 357 A
clay.perkins@macuniversity.edu

PERKINS, David, G ... 913-684-5621. 545 E

PERKINS, Don ... 913-469-8500. 187 J
dperkins@jccc.edu

PERKINS, OP, Ignatius .. 615-297-7545. 452 J
perkinsi@aquinascollege.edu

PERKINS, Jeri Parris ... 864-833-7000. 446 D
jpperkins@presby.edu

PERKINS, Jim ... 601-979-2024. 267 E
james.perkins@jsums.edu

PERKINS, Joseph, E ... 919-572-1689. 352 C
jperkins@apexsot.edu

PERKINS, Kathy ... 417-447-8114. 279 K

PERKINS, Keith ... 937-376-6640. 376 E
kperkins@centralstate.edu

PERKINS, Kenneth, B ... 434-395-2010. 506 J
perkinskb@longwood.edu

PERKINS, Leeann ... 937-328-6104. 377 A
perkinsl@clarkstate.edu

PERKINS, JR., Louis ... 202-238-2332... 95 G
louis.perkins@howard.edu

PERKINS, Lynn ... 815-921-4268. 157 A
g.perkins@rockvalleycollege.edu

PERKINS, Mary ... 847-214-7414. 144 F
mperkins@elgin.edu

PERKINS, Michele ... 561-297-3735. 114 L
mperkins@fau.edu

PERKINS, Michele, D ... 603-428-2222. 297 D
mperkins@nec.edu

PERKINS, Myrna, L ... 620-792-9270. 184 F
perkinsm@bartonccc.edu

PERKINS, Pamela, M ... 620-417-1011. 190 F
pam.perkins@sccc.edu

PERKINS, Patricia ... 304-645-6336. 530 B
pperkins@osteo.wvsom.edu

PERKINS, Peter ... 315-792-7273. 346 C
peter.perkins@sunyit.edu

PERKINS, Priscilla, L ... 413-782-1531. 238 A
pperkins@wne.edu

PERKINS, Robert, J ... 570-945-8276. 419 N
robert.perkins@keystone.edu

PERKINS, Russell ... 800-955-2527. 274 I
rperkins@grantham.edu

PERKINS, Sarah, F ... 650-738-4321... 64 D
perkinss@smccd.edu

PERKINS, Susan, K ... 732-906-2505. 303 B
sperkins@middlesexcc.edu

PERKINS, Tracey, G ... 603-526-3702. 295 I
tperkins@colby-sawyer.edu

PERKINS, Will ... 503-352-2120. 407 A
wperkins@pacificu.edu

PERKINS BROWN,
Jayne ... 912-478-5218. 126 C
jperkins@georgiasouthern.edu

PERKINSON, A. P ... 314-968-5964. 284 N
apperkinson@webster.edu

PERKINSON, James ... 757-822-5150. 514 C
jperkinson@tcc.edu

PERKINSON, Stephen ... 330-867-1996. 385 C

PERKNER, Stanislav ... 209-478-0800... 47 M
sperkner@humphreys.edu

PERKO, Janet, A ... 330-471-8340. 383 D
jperko@malone.edu

PERKOWSKI, C, L ... 718-259-2525. 315 C

PERKOWSKI, Henry ... 212-678-3016. 347 G
hp2125@tc.columbia.edu

PERL, Emily ... 410-337-6122. 215 A
eperl@goucher.edu

PERLICK, Nick ... 615-898-2502. 459 D
nick.perlick@mtsu.edu

PERLIN, Jeremy ... 513-487-3215. 325 G
jperlin@huc.edu

PERLMAN, Harvey ... 402-472-2116. 292 I
hperlman1@unl.edu

PERLMAN, Lynn ... 617-277-3915. 224 C
perlmanl@bgsp.edu

PERLMUTTER, David ... 806-742-3385. 487 D
david.perlmutter@ttu.edu

PERLOFF, Carey ... 415-439-2422... 27 M
cep@act-sf.org

PERLOW, Yaakov ... 718-438-2727. 351 O

PERLSTROM,
Christine, L ... 847-574-5208. 150 C
cperlstrom@lfgsm.edu

PERMAN, Jay, A ... 410-706-7002. 219 C
jperman@umaryland.edu

PERMENTER, Andrew, H 863-667-5078. 113 P
ahpermenter@seu.edu

PERNA, Michael ... 201-200-3542. 303 F
mperna@njcu.edu

PERNELL, Leroy ... 407-254-3268. 114 K
leroy.pernell@famu.edu

PERNICIARO, Richard .... 609-343-5670. 299 A
rpernici@atlantic.edu

PERNICK HUBER,
Maureen ... 716-827-2444. 348 G
huberm@trocaire.edu

PERNOT, Laurent ... 312-553-2500. 141 M
lpernot@ccc.edu

PERONE, Julie ... 610-436-2301. 430 A
jperone@wcupa.edu

PERONI-CALLAHAN,
Kathy ... 617-521-2150. 236 G
kathleen.peroni-callahan@simmons.edu

PEROO, Rama ... 620-441-5587. 186 A
peroo@cowley.edu

PEROZZI, Brett ... 801-626-6361. 497 D
brettperozzi@weber.edu

PERR, Yechiel, I ... 718-327-7600. 350 J
yfr1@verizon.net

PERRA, Thomas, J ... 860-768-4636... 92 D
perra@hartford.edu

PERREAULT, Melanie, L . 410-548-4085. 220 D
mlperreault@salisbury.edu

PERREN, Ray ... 770-531-6304. 128 B
rperren@laniertech.edu

PERRENOD, William, L .. 914-337-9300. 321 E
william.perrenod@concordia-ny.edu

PERRES, Irving ... 718-232-7800. 351 C

PERRET, Geraldine ... 973-618-3536. 300 A
gperret@caldwell.edu

PERRETTI, Richel ... 814-863-5538. 426 A
rap126@psu.edu

PERRI, Christine ... 619-216-6668... 68 B
cperri@swccd.edu

PERRI, Geraldine, M ... 626-914-8821... 38 K
gperri@citruscollege.edu

PERRI, Mary Lynn ... 440-646-8329. 392 D
mperri@ursuline.edu

PERRI, Michael ... 352-273-6214. 116 A
mperri@phhp.ufl.edu

PERRI, Ralph ... 361-593-2174. 484 A
ralph.perri@tamuk.edu

PERRIEN, Shane ... 402-941-6268. 290 K
perrien@midlandu.edu

PERRIN, Amy ... 847-214-7217. 144 F
aperrin@elgin.edu

PERRIN, Annette ... 585-266-0430. 324 A
aperrin@cci.edu

PERRIN, David, H ... 336-334-5494. 369 A
dhperrin@uncg.edu

PERRIN, Dawn ... 513-569-1706. 376 L
dawn.perrin@cincinnatistate.edu

PERRIN, L. Timothy ... 806-720-7125. 476 B
tim.perrin@lcu.edu

PERRIN, Nicholas ... 630-752-5227. 163 F
nicholas.perrin@wheaton.edu

PERRIN, Ralph ... 530-242-7730... 65 G
rperrin@shastacollege.edu

PERRINE, Mary, A ... 315-786-2485. 327 L
mperrine@sunyjefferson.edu

PERRINE, Paul ... 828-298-3325. 370 E
pperrine@warren-wilson.edu

PERRINE, Richard ... 603-897-8206. 297 F
rperrine@rivier.edu

PERRING, Sally, A ... 559-323-2100... 63 B
sperring@sjcl.edu

PERRITON, Caleb ... 307-755-2114. 544 B
cperriton@wyotechstaff.edu

PERRON, Evelyn, R ... 603-206-8121. 296 A
eperron@ccsnh.edu

PERRONE, Brenda ... 815-226-4010. 157 C
bperrone@rockford.edu

PERRONE, Dona, J ... 203-371-7890... 91 C
perroned@sacredheart.edu

PERRONE, Kim ... 518-631-9852. 348 K
perronek@uniongraduatecollege.edu

PERRONE, Mary ... 315-792-7333. 346 C
mary.perrone@sunyit.edu

PERROTT, Emma ... 716-888-3145. 316 C
perrotte@canisius.edu

PERROTTA, Steve ... 603-513-1341. 298 E
steve.perrotta@granite.edu

PERRSINGER, Angela ... 812-288-8878. 171 E
apersinger@mid-america.edu

PERRUCI,
Gamaliel (Gama) ... 740-376-4760. 383 E
gama.perruci@marietta.edu

PERRY, Andy ... 217-443-8777. 143 G
aperry@dacc.edu

PERRY, Anne ... 618-650-3972. 159 H
saperry@siue.edu

PERRY, Candace ... 404-756-4004. 121 A
cperry@atlm.edu
PERRY, Candace ... 218-322-2340. 258 I
candace.perry@itascacc.edu
PERRY, Carol, A ... 304-710-3141. 528 C
perry@mctc.edu
PERRY, Carolyn, J ... 573-592-5212. 285 B
carolyn.perry@westminster-mo.edu
PERRY, Christine, M ... 617-573-8470. 237 B
cperry@suffolk.edu
PERRY, Cynthia, R ... 757-594-7003. 503 M
cperry@cnu.edu
PERRY, David, L ... 850-644-1240. 115 C
dlperry@admin.fsu.edu
PERRY, Derrick ... 702-579-3530. 294 B
dperry@kaplan.edu
PERRY, Don ... 214-378-1732. 470 F
don.perry@dcccd.edu
PERRY, Douglas, E ... 815-939-5240. 155 H
dperry@olivet.edu
PERRY, Eddie, L ... 540-654-1025. 510 J
eperry@umw.edu
PERRY, Erma ... 334-687-3543. 3 N
eperry@wallace.edu
PERRY, Foster ... 256-824-6880. 8 F
Foster.Perry@uah.edu
PERRY, Frank, E ... 412-397-6233. 431 I
perry@rmu.edu
PERRY, George ... 304-260-4380. 527 N
gperry@blueridgectc.edu
PERRY, George ... 210-458-4450. 492 C
george.perry@utsa.edu
PERRY, Gretchen ... 845-758-7276. 314 D
gperry@bard.edu
PERRY, Gwendolyn ... 919-546-8564. 366 E
gperry@shawu.edu
PERRY, James ... 903-813-2277. 466 H
jperry@austincollege.edu
PERRY, Janet ... 970-207-4550. 83 B
JanetP@westondistancelearning.com
PERRY, Janet ... 970-207-4500. 86 G
JanetP@uscareerinstitute.edu
PERRY, Janet ... 405-682-1611. 397 E
jcperry@occc.edu
PERRY, Jason ... 801-581-8514. 496 Q
jason.perry@utah.edu
PERRY, Jeff ... 800-962-7682. 285 A
jperry@wma.edu
PERRY, Jerry ... 303-724-2133. 86 A
jerry.perry@ucdenver.edu
PERRY, Jessica, M ... 787-743-7979. 552 I
ut_jperry@suagm.edu
PERRY, Johanna, L ... 914-337-9300. 321 E
johanna.perry@concordia-ny.edu
PERRY, John ... 708-534-4518. 145 F
jperry@govst.edu
PERRY, John, F ... 864-503-5242. 448 H
jperry@uscupstate.edu
PERRY, Jonathan, C ... 479-575-5276. 23 I
jperry@uark.edu
PERRY, Judy ... 206-592-3349. 520 E
jperry@highline.edu
PERRY, Judy, A ... 432-837-8058. 487 B
jperry@sulross.edu
PERRY, Katherine ... 315-498-2602. 335 G
perryka@sunyocc.edu
PERRY, Keith ... 404-297-9522. 126 A
perryk@gptc.edu
PERRY, Kimberly ... 530-895-2484. 30 F
perryki@butte.edu
PERRY, Kristine ... 973-300-2772. 307 F
kperry@sussex.edu
PERRY, Laura ... 315-268-6760. 320 A
lperry@clarkson.edu
PERRY, Mansco ... 651-696-6735. 256 L
mperry@macalester.edu
PERRY, Maria ... 650-493-4430. 66 E
maria.perry@itp.edu
PERRY, Marilynn ... 732-571-3489. 303 C
mperry@monmouth.edu
PERRY, Mark ... 417-862-9533. 274 F
mperry@globaluniversity.edu
PERRY, Mark ... 559-734-9000. 63 D
president@sjvc.edu
PERRY, Marva ... 781-239-3151. 231 G
mperry@massbay.edu
PERRY, Mary Elaine ... 610-660-1045. 432 E
mperry01@sju.edu
PERRY, Maryann, B ... 508-565-1105. 237 A
mperry@stonehill.edu
PERRY, Melissa ... 386-312-4058. 112 C
melissaperry@sjrstate.edu
PERRY, Meredith ... 423-425-4431. 463 D
meredith-perry@utc.edu
PERRY, Michael ... 321-674-7127. 104 H
perrymj@fit.edu
PERRY, Michael ... 559-734-9000. 63 D
mikep@sjvc.edu
PERRY, Michael, J ... 315-386-7123. 345 F
perrymj@canton.edu
PERRY, Missy ... 864-941-8367. 446 C
perry.m@ptc.edu
PERRY, Nancy ... 410-386-8231. 214 A
nperry@carrollcc.edu
PERRY, Nauleen, A ... 302-857-1080. 93 G
nperry@dtcc.edu
PERRY, Pamela ... 708-456-0300. 161 A
pperry13@triton.edu
PERRY, Pat, B ... 252-246-1327. 365 C
pperry@wilsoncc.edu
PERRY, Paul ... 231-995-1114. 248 B
pperry@nmc.edu
PERRY, Renee ... 602-285-7433. 15 C
renee.perry@phoenixcollege.edu
PERRY, Robert, K ... 423-746-5209. 462 C
rkperry@twcnet.edu
PERRY, Roberta ... 610-526-2967. 432 B
rperry@rosemont.edu
PERRY, Robin ... 704-637-4384. 353 E
raperry@catawba.edu
PERRY, Rodger ... 704-669-4032. 359 D
perryr@clevelandcc.edu
PERRY, Roslyn ... 606-783-2571. 198 A
ro.perry@moreheadstate.edu
PERRY, Sam, J ... 773-508-8781. 151 H
sperry@luc.edu
PERRY, Scott ... 312-777-8664. 147 D
smperry@aii.edu
PERRY, Stephanie, D ... 276-328-0240. 511 C
sdh9y@uvawise.edu
PERRY, Steve ... 864-294-2458. 444 C
steve.perry@furman.edu
PERRY, Steven ... 201-684-7363. 305 A
sperry@ramapo.edu
PERRY, Steven ... 325-738-3341. 486 C
steven.perry@tstc.edu
PERRY, Steven, R ... 607-436-2513. 343 E
perrysr@oneonta.edu
PERRY, Stuart ... 320-363-5047. 263 P
sperry@csbsju.edu
PERRY, Stuart ... 320-363-5047. 254 J
sperry@csbsju.edu
PERRY, Sue, A ... 856-691-8600. 301 A
sperry@cccnj.edu
PERRY, Thomas, D ... 740-376-4408. 383 E
tom.perry@marietta.edu
PERRY, Tom ... 479-524-7122. 21 G
tperry@jbu.edu
PERRY, Walter ... 215-596-8890. 435 H
w.perry@usciences.edu
PERRY, William, L ... 217-581-2011. 144 E
wlperry@eiu.edu
PERRY-JOHNSON,
Arlethia ... 770-423-6350. 127 N
aperryjo@kennesaw.edu
PERRY-NAUSE, Sharon .. 419-448-3504. 389 J
perrynauses@tiffin.edu
PERRY-SPEARS, Megan . 218-723-6029. 254 K
mperryspears@css.edu
PERRYMAN, Larry ... 707-468-3069. 54 B
lperryman@mendocino.edu
PERRYMAN, Linda ... 864-225-7653. 444 A
lindaperryman@forrestcollege.edu
PERRYMAN, Nancy, S ... 309-655-4119. 158 C
nancy.s.perryman@osfhealthcare.org
PERRYMAN, Patricia ... 214-613-3770. 471 E
PERSAUD, Damindra ... 718-261-5800. 315 F
dpersaud@bramsonort.edu
PERSAUD, Roxanne ... 718-489-5379. 338 G
rpersaud@sfc.edu
PERSAVICH, Jon ... 415-808-1430. 46 I
jon_persavich@heald.edu
PERSHING, David, W ... 801-581-5701. 496 Q
david.pershing@utah.edu
PERSICHITTE, Kay, A ... 307-766-3145. 543 I
kpersi@uwyo.edu
PERSICO, Frank, G ... 202-319-5100. 94 G
persico@cua.edu
PERSICO, Patrice ... 570-208-5972. 419 P
patricepersico@kings.edu
PERSICO, Sebastian, T ... 212-817-7600. 317 F
spersico@gc.cuny.edu
PERSINGER, Bill ... 931-221-6309. 459 B
persingerb@apsu.edu
PERSKY, Ira ... 718-982-2240. 317 E
ira.persky@csi.cuny.edu
PERSON, Andy ... 914-330-1450. 330 J
aperson@mercy.edu
PERSON, Gretchen ... 615-322-2457. 463 G
religiouslife@vanderbilt.edu
PERSON, Mark ... 601-979-2021. 267 E
mark.s.person@jsums.edu
PERSON, Ruth, J ... 810-762-3322. 251 E
rjperson@umflint.edu
PERSON, Walter ... 202-686-0876. 97 C
walter.person@potomac.edu
PERSON, William ... 334-229-4276. 1 D
wperson@alasu.edu
PERSSON, Carol ... 413-572-5365. 230 F
cpersson@westfield.ma.edu
PERSSON, Katherine ... 281-312-1640. 476 A
katherine.persson@lonestar.edu
PERTL, Brian, G ... 920-832-6614. 533 S
brian.g.pertl@lawrence.edu
PERTTULA, Dave ... 262-551-5925. 532 D
dperttula@carthage.edu
PERUMAL, Santhi ... 415-561-6555. 60 C
PERUSO, Dominick, F ... 814-472-3005. 432 D
dperuso@francis.edu
PERUSSE, Charles, E ... 919-962-1000. 366 K
ceperusse@northcarolina.edu
PERVIER, Curt ... 432-685-4677. 476 G
cpervier@midland.edu
PERVINE, Robert ... 270-809-4274. 198 B
rpervine@murraystate.edu
PERYGA, Erica ... 203-596-8527. 90 I
eperyga@post.edu
PESARCHICK, Robert, A . 610-785-6204. 432 C
rpesarchick@scs.edu
PESCHL, Alan ... 262-524-7343. 532 C
apeschl@carrollu.edu
PESCINSKI, Robert ... 908-526-1200. 305 B
rpescinski@raritanval.edu
PESCOVITZ, Ora, H ... 734-647-9351. 251 C
opescovi@umich.edu
PESHEK, Mary ... 712-274-5274. 181 B
peshek@morningside.edu
PESKA, Don ... 817-735-2149. 490 E
Don.Peska@unthsc.edu
PESOLD, Dan ... 314-968-7130. 284 N
pesoldd@webster.edu
PESOTSKI, Chris ... 215-717-6170. 435 A
cpesotski@uarts.edu
PESSINK, Martin ... 903-983-8650. 475 E
mpessink@kilgore.edu
PESTA, Donna ... 518-255-5624. 344 E
Pestadh@cobleskill.edu
PESTA, John ... 570-408-4641. 437 F
john.pesta@wilkes.edu
PESTANA, John ... 508-565-1315. 237 A
jpestana@stonehill.edu
PESTELLO, Fred, P ... 315-445-4120. 328 F
president@lemoyne.edu
PESTRUE, Wendy ... 419-783-2463. 379 C
wpestrue@defiance.edu
PETAK, Katty ... 402-399-2411. 289 A
vpetak@csm.edu
PETCHER, Douglas ... 312-362-7595. 143 H
dpetcher@depaul.edu
PETE, Mary, C ... 907-543-4502. 10 I
mpete@alaska.edu
PETEET, Allison ... 903-923-2072. 471 J
apeteet@etbu.edu
PETELL, James ... 401-874-4807. 440 D
jkpetell@uri.edu
PETER, Beth, C ... 651-641-8795. 255 B
peter@csp.edu
PETER, David, M ... 812-888-4166. 174 F
dpeter@vinu.edu
PETER, Florence, L ... 692-625-3394. 546 F
flpeter@cmi.edu
PETER, Lori ... 660-263-3900. 272 A
lbp@cccb.edu
PETERKA, Cynthia, J ... 443-518-4809. 215 E
cpeterka@howardcc.edu
PETERMAN, Francine ... 973-655-5167. 303 D
petermanf@mail.montclair.edu
PETERS, Anna ... 212-659-3610. 328 E
apeters@tkc.edu
PETERS, Bob ... 360-736-9391. 517 G
bpeters@centralia.edu
PETERS, Brett ... 414-229-4126. 537 A
petersba@uwm.edu
PETERS, Brian, S ... 847-491-8420. 155 D
b-peters2@northwestern.edu
PETERS, C. Ellen ... 253-879-3104. 524 F
epeters@pugetsound.edu
PETERS, Chad ... 864-644-5325. 446 I
cpeters@swu.edu
PETERS, Cherise ... 334-229-6771. 1 D
cpeters@alasu.edu
PETERS, Clark ... 814-732-2921. 428 E
cpeters@edinboro.edu
PETERS, Craig ... 605-367-5462. 452 C
craig.peters@southeasttech.edu
PETERS, Cydney ... 713-718-8596. 473 C
cydney.peters@hccs.edu
PETERS, David ... 304-473-8540. 531 G
peters_d@wvwc.edu
PETERS, Dennis ... 610-799-1658. 421 I
PETERS, Doug, D ... 218-477-2306. 259 H
petersd@mnstate.edu
PETERS, Earic ... 323-953-4000. 51 G
peterseb@lacitycollege.edu
PETERS, Eva ... 909-621-8471. 59 G
eva_peters@pitzer.edu
PETERS, Fred, M ... 903-510-2627. 488 E
fpet@tjc.edu
PETERS, Hermina, P ... 202-274-6256. 97 A
hpeters@udc.edu
PETERS, J. Lee ... 860-768-4165. 92 D
lpeters@hartford.edu
PETERS, James ... 616-538-2330. 243 A
jpeters@gbcol.edu
PETERS, Jana ... 661-763-7809. 69 D
jpeters@taftcollege.edu
PETERS, Jerry ... 760-252-2411. 29 I
jpeters@barstow.edu
PETERS, Jessica ... 620-365-5116. 183 I
peters@allencc.edu
PETERS, John, E ... 270-824-8593. 196 A
john.peters@kctcs.edu
PETERS, Joseph, R ... 502-410-6200. 194 B
jpeters@galencollege.edu
PETERS, Joyce ... 662-685-4771. 266 C
jpeters@bmc.edu
PETERS, Kirk ... 860-255-3561. 89 G
kpeters@txcc.commnet.edu
PETERS, Larry ... 580-349-1560. 397 G
lpeters@opsu.edu
PETERS, Lee ... 617-262-5000. 223 F
lee.peters@the-bac.edu
PETERS, Leonard ... 203-432-3262. 93 A
leonard.peters@yale.edu
PETERS, Libby ... 606-436-5721. 195 C
libby.peters@kctcs.edu
PETERS, Marcia, J ... 404-471-6348. 119 I
mpeters@agnesscott.edu
PETERS, Margaret ... 505-428-1000. 311 J
margaret.peters@sfcc.edu
PETERS, RET., MaryAnn . 401-841-7004. 545 A
PETERS, MaryAnne ... 610-341-5834. 415 G
mpeters@eastern.edu
PETERS, Matthew ... 570-702-8914. 419 G
mpeters@johnson.edu
PETERS, Melissa ... 386-481-2580. 99 C
petersm@cookman.edu
PETERS, Michael, P ... 505-984-6098. 311 H
president@sjcsf.edu
PETERS, Michele ... 716-827-4333. 348 G
petersm@trocaire.edu
PETERS, Monica ... 936-633-5250. 465 J
mpeters@angelina.edu
PETERS, Pamela, J ... 607-746-4635. 345 G
peterspj@delhi.edu
PETERS, Randall ... 770-228-7365. 132 B
rpeters@sctech.edu
PETERS, Scott ... 573-897-5000. 276 E
PETERS, Sheila ... 615-329-8575. 454 F
speters@fisk.edu
PETERS, Sherry ... 610-902-8202. 411 E
sherry.a.peters@cabrini.edu
PETERS, Steve ... 316-295-5567. 186 H
steve_peters@friends.edu
PETERS, Sue ... 925-631-4842. 61 F
speters@stmarys-ca.edu
PETERS, Suzanne ... 413-545-0356. 228 F
sepeters@finaid.umass.edu
PETERS, Terry ... 515-244-4221. 175 C
peterst@aib.edu
PETERS, Thomas, A ... 417-836-4525. 278 E
tpeters@missouristate.edu
PETERS, Timothy, C ... 949-214-3363. 41 I
tim.peters@cui.edu
PETERS, Tom, D ... 308-398-7365. 288 I
tpeters@cccneb.edu
PETERS, Vincent ... 651-638-6124. 253 K
v-peters@bethel.edu
PETERS-NGUYEN, Diane 808-735-4772. 135 D
dpeters@chaminade.edu
PETERSDORFF, Joe ... 478-988-6800. 122 G
jpetersdorff@centralgatech.edu
PETERSEN, Aaron ... 517-437-7341. 243 I
aaron.petersen@hillsdale.edu
PETERSEN, Barbara ... 814-254-0471. 413 C
bpetersen@pa.gov
PETERSEN, Calvin ... 402-280-2796. 289 D
creighton@bkstr.com
PETERSEN, Dana ... 207-216-4454. 211 C
dpetersen@yccc.edu
PETERSEN, Donna ... 813-974-6603. 116 C
dpeters@hsc.usf.edu
PETERSEN, Dorene ... 503-244-0726. 401 M
dorenepetersen@achs.edu
PETERSEN, George ... 805-493-3419. 31 H
gjpeters@clunet.edu
PETERSEN, Glenn ... 507-457-5031. 262 A
gpetersen@winona.edu
PETERSEN, Karl ... 314-768-7800. 278 C
kpetersen@missouricollege.com
PETERSEN, Kristin ... 402-471-2505. 291 C
kpetersen@nscs.edu
PETERSEN, Linda ... 785-243-1435. 185 M
lpetersen@cloud.edu
PETERSEN, Lynne ... 928-757-0809. 15 L
lpetersen@mohave.edu
PETERSEN, Mark, A ... 336-758-6053. 370 D
map@wfu.edu
PETERSEN, Mark, T ... 540-378-5125. 509 B
petersen@roanoke.edu

PETERSEN, Marty ... 425-602-3027. 516 K
mpetersen@bastyr.edu
PETERSEN, Mary, S ... 206-296-2043. 523 E
marypete@seattleu.edu
PETERSEN, Page ... 507-433-0650. 260 I
ppeterse@riverland.edu
PETERSEN, Stephen ... 847-925-6255. 145 H
speterse@harpercollege.edu
PETERSEN, Stephen, H ... 901-678-5426. 460 B
shptrsen@memphis.edu
PETERSEN, Ted ... 815-802-8602. 149 C
tpetersen@kcc.edu
PETERSEN, Tina ... 916-577-2200... 76 J
tpetersen@jessup.edu
PETERSON, Al, L ... 661-824-2977... 55 I
PETERSON, Andrew ... 215-596-8877. 435 H
a.peterson@usciences.edu
PETERSON, Andrew, J ... 704-366-4853. 269 E
apeterson@rts.edu
PETERSON, Arlene ... 718-482-5088. 318 F
apeterson@lagcc.cuny.edu
PETERSON, Barbara ... 732-224-2643. 299 G
bpeterson@brookdalecc.edu
PETERSON, Bill ... 218-281-6510. 264 E
PETERSON, Bill ... 706-233-7469. 131 E
bpeterson@shorter.edu
PETERSON, Bruce, E ... 740-376-4736. 383 E
bruce.peterson@marietta.edu
PETERSON, Candace ... 503-280-8500. 402 J
cpeterson@cu-portland.edu
PETERSON, Carolyn ... 919-546-3750. 366 E
cpeterson@shawu.edu
PETERSON, JR., Charles 804-523-5821. 512 F
cpeterson@reynolds.edu
PETERSON, Charles, D ... 701-231-7456. 371 G
charles.peterson@ndsu.edu
PETERSON, Charles, I ... 773-244-5615. 154 G
cpeterson@northpark.edu
PETERSON, Chris ... 501-569-3167... 24 B
tlcampbell@ualr.edu
PETERSON, Chris ... 405-491-6333. 399 K
cpeterso@snu.edu
PETERSON, Christine ... 443-423-1467. 216 C
cpetersn@mica.edu
PETERSON, Cindy ... 913-971-3533. 188 H
cpeterso@mnu.edu
PETERSON, Cynthia ... 903-923-2257. 471 J
cpeterson@etbu.edu
PETERSON, Cynthia, L ... 706-778-8500. 130 E
cpeterson@piedmont.edu
PETERSON, Daniel, C ... 217-244-1206. 162 A
dcpeters@illinois.edu
PETERSON, David ... 260-481-6130. 168 C
petersod@ipfw.edu
PETERSON, David, F ... 608-743-4525. 539 I
dpeterson38@blackhawk.edu
PETERSON, Deborah, A .. 952-885-5412. 263 B
dpeterson@nwhealth.edu
PETERSON, Derek ... 605-688-4163. 452 B
derek.peterson@sdstate.edu
PETERSON, Dolores ... 610-372-4721. 431 D
dpeterson@racc.edu
PETERSON, Don ... 209-384-6182... 54 D
peterson.d@mccd.edu
PETERSON, Ericka, K ... 218-299-3250. 255 A
haug@cord.edu
PETERSON, Frances ... 606-759-7141. 196 B
frances.peterson@kctcs.edu
PETERSON, G. P. (Bud) . 404-894-5051. 125 D
president@gatech.edu
PETERSON, Gail ... 414-326-2303. 532 G
gpeterso@ccon.edu
PETERSON, Graham ... 870-862-8131... 23 D
gpeterson@southark.edu
PETERSON, Greg ... 562-938-4140... 51 D
gpeterson@lbcc.edu
PETERSON, Greg ... 507-457-2800. 262 A
gpeterson@winona.edu
PETERSON, Heather ... 609-343-5008. 299 A
hpeterso@atlantic.edu
PETERSON,
Jacqueline, D ... 508-793-2414. 225 B
jpeterso@holycross.edu
PETERSON, James ... 510-540-7747... 51 A
jamespeterson@lincolnuca.edu
PETERSON, James, R ... 509-527-4686. 524 H
PETERSON, Jill ... 916-278-6940... 34 D
jill.peteson@csus.edu
PETERSON, JoAnn ... 712-279-1633. 176 B
joann.peterson@briarcliff.edu
PETERSON, John, A ... 671-735-2170. 546 E
jpeterson@uguam.uog.edu
PETERSON, John, A ... 671-735-0219. 546 E
jpeterson@uguam.uog.edu
PETERSON, Joyce, C ... 218-722-4000. 255 E
joycep@dbumn.edu
PETERSON, Julie ... 773-702-0689. 161 B
juliep@uchicago.edu
PETERSON, Kate, M ... 541-737-0759. 406 A
kate.peterson@oregonstate.edu
PETERSON, Kent, A ... 414-277-7176. 534 G
peterson@msoe.edu
PETERSON, Kirk ... 937-484-1242. 392 C
kpeterson@urbana.edu
PETERSON, Klay ... 864-503-5254. 448 H
kpeterson@uscupstate.edu
PETERSON, Kurtis, M ... 860-882-1690... 91 E
PETERSON, Laura ... 940-397-4919. 476 H
laura.peterson@mwsu.edu
PETERSON, Laura, K ... 614-235-4136. 390 A
lpeterson@TLSohio.edu
PETERSON, Linda ... 305-899-3020... 98 O
lpeterson@barry.edu
PETERSON, Linda, C ... 865-694-6404. 461 D
lcpeterson@pstcc.edu
PETERSON, Linda, M ... 563-556-5110. 181 E
petersol@nicc.edu
PETERSON, Lori ... 406-447-5432. 285 G
lpeterson@carroll.edu
PETERSON, Lori ... 612-330-1637. 253 H
petersol@augsburg.edu
PETERSON, Maggie ... 406-496-4316. 287 F
mpeterson@mtech.edu
PETERSON, Marc ... 214-768-3417. 481 A
mpeterso@smu.edu
PETERSON, Margrette ... 510-869-6512... 61 I
mpeterson@samuelmerritt.edu
PETERSON, Marie ... 206-296-6241. 523 E
mpeters@seattleu.edu
PETERSON, Mark ... 651-450-3373. 258 H
mpeters@inverhills.edu
PETERSON, Mark ... 715-682-1332. 535 D
mpeterson@northland.edu
PETERSON, Michael ... 215-248-7141. 413 A
petersonm@chc.edu
PETERSON, Michael, E ... 260-422-5561. 167 B
mepterson@indianatech.edu
PETERSON, Michael, W .. 512-448-8788. 479 C
michaelp@stedwards.edu
PETERSON, Michele ... 970-247-7435... 81 M
peterson_m@fortlewis.edu
PETERSON, Michele ... 505-566-3363. 311 I
petersonm@sanjuancollege.edu
PETERSON, Michelle ... 507-285-7180. 261 A
michelle.peterson@rctc.edu
PETERSON, Nedra ... 818-767-0888... 76 K
nedra.peterson@woodbury.edu
PETERSON, Nicole ... 931-221-7979. 459 B
petersonn@apsu.edu
PETERSON, Norman ... 406-994-7150. 287 B
normp@montana.edu
PETERSON, Pamela ... 831-459-5380... 72 C
pgpeters@ucsc.edu
PETERSON, Pamela ... 561-912-2166. 103 C
ppeterson@evergladesuniversity.edu
PETERSON, Paul ... 218-683-8800. 260 D
paul.peterson@northlandcollege.edu
PETERSON, Penelope, L . 847-467-1190. 155 D
p-peterson@northwestern.edu
PETERSON, Phyllis, M ... 815-740-3848. 162 F
ppeterson@stfrancis.edu
PETERSON, Polly, J ... 701-252-3467. 373 D
ppeterso@jc.edu
PETERSON, Randolph, L 479-979-1431... 25 J
rpeterson@ozarks.edu
PETERSON, Rebecca ... 802-865-6425. 499 A
peterson@champlain.edu
PETERSON, Robert ... 801-840-4800. 495 K
rpeterson@cci.edu
PETERSON, Robert ... 435-722-6900. 496 M
bobp@ubatc.edu
PETERSON, Robert ... 216-987-2836. 378 D
robert.peterson@tri-c.edu
PETERSON, Rod ... 330-823-2683. 391 E
petersro@mountunion.edu
PETERSON, Roy ... 262-243-5700. 532 H
roy.peterson@cuw.edu
PETERSON, Samantha ... 918-335-6223. 398 F
speterson@okwu.edu
PETERSON, Sandy ... 608-785-9207. 541 E
petersons@westerntc.edu
PETERSON, Scott ... 740-392-6868. 384 K
scott.peterson@mvnu.edu
PETERSON, Stella ... 770-426-2930. 128 D
peterson@life.edu
PETERSON, Susan, K ... 785-532-6221. 188 A
skp@ksu.edu
PETERSON, Terry ... 312-942-7020. 157 G
PETERSON, Thomas ... 732-906-2512. 303 B
TPeterson@middlesexcc.edu
PETERSON, Tom ... 209-228-7964... 71 D
tpeterson@UCMerced.edu
PETERSON, Trayce ... 765-983-1501. 165 G
petertr@earlham.edu
PETERSON, Tyler ... 334-244-3266..... 2 A
tpeters7@aum.edu
PETERSON, Val, L ... 801-863-8424. 497 C
petersva@uvu.edu
PETERSON, Wendy ... 509-335-5586. 525 A
wendyp@wsu.edu
PETERSON,
Wilbur (Pete) ... 615-547-1275. 454 A
ppeterson@cumberland.edu
PETERSON-SENIUK,
Peggy ... 419-473-2700. 378 I
pseniuk@daviscollege.edu
PETERSON-VEATCH,
Ross ... 574-535-7504. 166 A
rosspv@goshen.edu
PETERSON-VEATCH,
Ross ... 574-535-7508. 166 A
rosspv@goshen.edu
PETERSSON, Arlette ... 561-912-1211. 103 C
apetersson@evergladesuniversity.edu
PETHE-COOK, Marlyn ... 813-253-6231. 118 L
mpethe@ut.edu
PETHICK, Michael ... 231-591-3900. 242 F
pethicj@ferris.edu
PETILLO, John, J ... 203-371-7900... 91 C
petilloj@sacredheart.edu
PETINAK, Craig ... 909-384-8978... 62 A
cpetinak@sbccd.cc.ca.us
PETIPRIN, Gary ... 502-272-8480. 192 E
gpetiprin@bellarmine.edu
PETIT, Emily ... 706-778-8500. 130 E
epetit@piedmont.edu
PETITT, Charles, W ... 336-725-8344. 365 F
petittc@piedmontu.edu
PETITTI, Mario ... 440-525-7328. 382 M
mpetitti@lakelandcc.edu
PETKASH, John ... 607-778-5011. 315 I
petkashjc@sunybroome.edu
PETKO, Karen ... 859-846-5390. 197 I
kpetko@midway.edu
PETLEY, Kathleen ... 518-629-4574. 326 G
k.petley@hvcc.edu
PETR, Carrie ... 402-826-8271. 289 E
carrie.petr@doane.edu
PETRAGNANI, Joseph, F 610-660-1528. 432 E
petragna@sju.edu
PETRAS, Donna ... 586-263-6266. 246 A
petrasd@macomb.edu
PETREE, Daniel ... 585-395-2623. 342 F
dpetree@brockport.edu
PETRELLA, Yvonne ... 315-312-2270. 344 A
yvonne.petrella@oswego.edu
PETRI, Basia ... 503-682-1862. 407 B
bpetri@pioneerpacific.edu
PETRI, Elizabeth ... 413-662-5219. 230 C
e.petri@mcla.edu
PETRI, OP, Thomas ... 202-495-3832... 96 C
dean@dhs.edu
PETRICCA, Joe ... 323-856-7721... 27 O
jpetricca@afi.com
PETRICHENKO,
Kathleen, J ... 410-822-5400. 214 C
kpetrichenko@chesapeake.edu
PETRICK, Joseph, E ... 802-287-8377. 499 D
petrickj@greenmtn.edu
PETRICK, Laurie ... 920-832-6525. 533 S
laurie.a.petrick@lawrence.edu
PETRIDIS, Heather ... 626-815-4570... 29 H
hpetridis@apu.edu
PETRIE, Mark, J ... 716-878-3640. 343 A
petriemj@buffalostate.edu
PETRIKAT, Douglas ... 714-547-9625... 30 J
dpetrikat@calcoast.edu
PETRILLO, Emilia, K ... 410-328-8404. 219 C
epetr001@umaryland.edu
PETRILLO, Tracee ... 781-239-5695. 222 D
tpetrillo@babson.edu
PETRILLOSE, Lindsay ... 607-735-1855. 323 H
lpetrillose@elmira.edu
PETRILLOSE, Michael ... 401-598-4621. 439 B
mpetrillose@jwu.edu
PETRITES, Cindy ... 414-229-4519. 537 A
petrites@uwm.edu
PETRIZZO, Louis, S ... 631-451-4235. 346 E
petrizl@sunysuffolk.edu
PETRO, Patrice, S ... 414-229-4523. 537 A
ppetro@uwm.edu
PETRO, Tony ... 239-687-5443... 98 J
tpetro@avemarialaw.edu
PETROCCIA, Anthony, M 315-568-3256. 333 C
apetrocc@nycc.edu
PETROCCO-NAPULI,
Kristina, L ... 315-568-3886. 333 C
kpetrocco@nycc.edu
PETROFF, Les ... 317-738-8108. 165 I
lpetroff@franklincollege.edu
PETROKA, Louise, A ... 203-285-2393... 88 E
lpetroka@gwcc.commnet.edu
PETROSIAN, Anahid ... 956-872-8336. 480 I
PETROSIAN, Anahid ... 956-872-6790. 480 I
anahid@southtexascollege.edu
PETROSINO, Linda ... 607-274-3265. 327 E
lpetrosino@ithaca.edu
PETROSKI, Paul, S ... 410-706-8338. 219 C
ppetrosk@umaryland.edu
PETROSKY, Joseph ... 586-498-4181. 246 A
petroskyj@macomb.edu
PETROV, John ... 240-684-5566. 219 F
human-resources@umuc.edu
PETROVICH, Tamberly ... 831-582-4137... 34 B
tpetrovich@csumb.edu
PETRUCCI, Michele ... 724-357-2295. 428 F
michelep@iup.edu
PETRUS, John ... 412-536-1033. 420 A
john.petrus@laroche.edu
PETRUS, Robin ... 607-778-5201. 315 I
petrusre@sunybroome.edu
PETRUSCH, Suzanne, M . 210-436-3995. 479 D
spetrusch@stmarytx.edu
PETRUSO, Karl ... 817-272-7215. 491 B
petruso@uta.edu
PETRUZZELLI,
Barbara, W ... 845-569-3601. 332 B
barbara.petruzzelli@msmc.edu
PETRY, Laura ... 312-332-0707. 160 J
PETRY, Ric ... 614-222-3227. 378 A
rpetry@ccad.edu
PETRYSHAK, Bruce ... 615-898-5570. 459 D
bruce.petryshak@mtsu.edu
PETRYSHYN, Laryssa ... 716-829-8119. 323 D
petryshl@dyc.edu
PETSCH, Verl, E ... 307-532-8248. 542 a
verl.petsch@ewc.wy.edu
PETSCHE, Carolyn ... 815-599-3577. 146 D
carolyn.petsche@highland.edu
PETSCHE, Daniel ... 660-944-2875. 272 H
daniel@conception.edu
PETTAZZONI, Jodi, E ... 336-334-5531. 369 A
jepettaz@uncg.edu
PETTEGREW, Larry ... 800-672-3060. 366 F
PETTERSON, Jennifer ... 573-592-4280. 285 D
jennie.petterson@williamwoods.edu
PETTIBONE, John, C ... 770-720-5939. 130 G
jcp@reinhardt.edu
PETTIFORD, Anthony ... 937-376-6223. 376 E
apettiford@centralstate.edu
PETTIGREW, Frank, E ... 419-289-5051. 374 C
fpettigr@ashland.edu
PETTIGREW, Jason ... 605-229-8350. 450 J
jason.pettigrew@presentation.edu
PETTINARI, Gayle ... 719-549-3329... 84 G
gayle.pettinari@pueblocc.edu
PETTINGER, Connie ... 708-209-3045. 143 E
constance.pettinger@cuchicago.edu
PETTINICO, JR.,
Nicholas ... 860-832-1766... 87 K
pettinico@ccsu.edu
PETTIS, Curtis ... 937-376-6349. 376 E
cpettis@centralstate.edu
PETTIS, Deloris ... 617-373-2226. 235 F
PETTIS, Stephanie ... 850-729-5362. 109 I
pettiss@nwfsc.edu
PETTIS, William ... 808-981-2790. 135 E
PETTIS-WALDEN,
Karen, M ... 804-523-5029. 512 F
kpettis-walden@reynolds.edu
PETTIT, Charlene, M ... 920-924-3112. 540 F
cpettit@morainepark.edu
PETTIT, Cyndi ... 214-333-5235. 470 D
cyndi@dbu.edu
PETTIT, Frederick ... 570-208-5881. 419 P
frederickpettit@kings.edu
PETTIT, Gretchen, A ... 636-584-6535. 273 M
gmpettet@eastcentral.edu
PETTIT, Jeanne ... 859-572-7544. 198 I
pettitje@nku.edu
PETTIT, Linda ... 517-264-7661. 250 B
lpettit@sienaheights.edu
PETTIT, Patricia, A ... 217-362-6488. 153 C
ppettit@millikin.edu
PETTIT, Paul, E ... 214-887-5102. 471 F
ppettit@dts.edu
PETTITT, Maureen ... 360-416-7919. 523 G
maureen.pettitt@skagit.edu
PETTUS, James ... 410-287-6060. 214 B
pett0916@cecil.edu
PETTY, Bradley ... 325-942-2191. 465 K
bradley.petty@angelo.edu
PETTY, Daniel, W ... 813-988-5131. 104 A
pettyd@floridacollege.edu
PETTY, Jamie ... 706-295-7733. 125 C
jpetty@highlands.edu
PETTY, JoBeth ... 601-968-8901. 266 A
JBpetty@belhaven.edu
PETTY, Jonathan ... 806-291-3588. 494 F
pettyj@wbu.edu
PETTY, Jovan ... 703-812-4757. 506 H
jpetty@leland.edu
PETTY, Leslie ... 734-462-4400. 250 A
lpetty@schoolcraft.edu
PETTY, Leslie ... 708-802-6213. 158 E
petty@sxu.edu
PETTY, Marcia, L ... 504-865-3030. 205 H
mlpetty@loyno.edu
PETTY, Mark ... 605-677-5434. 451 F
mark.petty@usd.edu
PETTY, Mikel, D ... 256-824-4368..... 8 F
mikel.petty@uah.edu

PETTY, Nina .... 817-515-5433. 482 B
nina.petty@tccd.edu
PETTY, Philip .... 802-728-1533. 501 F
ppetty@vtc.edu
PETTY, Rachel .... 202-274-5072... 97 A
rpetty@udc.edu
PETTY, Tanjula .... 334-229-4004..... 1 D
tpetty@alasu.edu
PETTY, Tricia, L .... 304-293-8500. 530 D
tricia.petty@mail.wvu.edu
PETTY, Yolanda .... 478-471-5364. 128 I
yolanda.petty@maconstate.edu
PETTY-WARD, Paula, J .. 931-540-2572. 460 E
ppettyward@columbiastate.edu
PETTYJOHN, Susan, H ... 828-262-2090. 367 A
pettyjohnsh@appstate.edu
PETULA, Eileen, E .... 610-328-8399. 433 I
epetula1@swarthmore.edu
PETZ, Dan .... 620-672-5641. 190 A
danp@prattcc.edu
PETZKE, Greg .... 704-378-1190. 355 K
gpetzke@jcsu.edu
PETZNICK, Michelle, L ... 641-422-4205. 181 D
petznmic@niacc.edu
PEUGH-WADE,
Martha, A .... 415-422-2444... 73 J
peugh@usfca.edu
PEWE, Richard, P .... 517-607-2518. 243 I
rich.pewe@hillsdale.edu
PEYER, Patrick .... 815-921-4103. 157 A
p.peyer@rockvalleycollege.edu
PEYSER, Roma .... 503-297-5544. 405 D
rpeyser@ocac.edu
PEYTON, Janice .... 936-270-7392. 476 A
janice.peyton@lonestar.edu
PEYTON, Marcia .... 706-754-7789. 129 G
mpeyton@northgatech.edu
PEZOLD, Frank .... 361-825-2349. 483 F
frank.pezold@tamucc.edu
PEZZAROSSI, Alba .... 773-481-8872. 142 F
apezzarossi@ccc.edu
PEZZELLE, Patrick .... 406-293-2721. 286 B
ppezzell@fvcc.edu
PEZZI, Eileen .... 315-464-7853. 342 E
pezzie@upstate.edu
PEZZOLI, Jean .... 808-984-3234. 137 B
pezzoli@hawaii.edu
PEZZUTO, John .... 808-933-2909. 136 A
pezzuto@hawaii.edu
PFAFF, Ardys .... 701-323-8065. 372 I
Ardyth.Pfaff@SanfordCollege.edu
PFANNENSTIEHL, Craig . 617-217-9050. 222 G
cfp@baystate.edu
PFEFER, Mark, T .... 913-234-0796. 185 L
mark.pfefer@cleveland.edu
PFEFFER, Carole .... 502-272-8184. 192 E
cpfeffer@bellarmine.edu
PFEFFER, Richard .... 732-224-2262. 299 G
rpfeffer@brookdalecc.edu
PFEFFER, Richard, J .... 732-224-2262. 299 G
rpfeffer@brookdalecc.edu
PFEIFER, Alan, D .... 815-288-5511. 158 K
pfeifer@svcc.edu
PFEIFER, Donald .... 413-236-2131. 231 A
dpfeifer@berkshirecc.edu
PFEIFER, Joseph .... 503-251-5775. 408 G
jpfeifer@uws.edu
PFEIFER, Tad .... 308-535-3684. 290 J
pfeifert@mpcc.edu
PFEIFFER, Francine .... 202-220-1336. 306 A
francine@rutgers.edu
PFEIFFER, Julie .... 540-362-6318. 505 G
jpfeiffer@hollins.edu
PFEIFFER, Kelley .... 636-922-8544. 280 J
kpfeiffer@stchas.edu
PFEIFFER, Patricia, D ..... 772-462-7301. 106 P
ppfeiffe@irsc.edu
PFEIFFER, Pattie .... 919-735-5151. 364 H
ppfeiffer@waynecc.edu
PFEIL, Robert .... 716-286-8689. 334 F
fpfeil@niagara.edu
PFLANZ, Mary .... 913-621-8764. 186 C
mpflanz@donnelly.edu
PFLEIGER, Kelly .... 215-368-5000. 410 F
kpfleiger@biblical.edu
PFLUG, Anna .... 425-889-5212. 521 G
anna.pflug@northwestu.edu
PFLUKE, Deanna .... 585-266-0430. 324 A
dpfluke@cci.edu
PFURSICH, Fred .... 562-907-4236... 76 I
fpfursich@whittier.edu
PFUTZENREUTER,
Richard, H .... 612-625-4517. 264 G
pfutz001@umn.edu
PHAIAH, Peter .... 218-281-8505. 264 E
phaiah@umn.edu
PHAKITTHONG,
Rachelle .... 715-675-3331. 541 A
phakitth@ntc.edu
PHALIN, Teri .... 715-365-4464. 540 G
tphalin@nicoletcollege.edu

PHAM, Hue .... 714-432-5764... 39 K
hpham@occ.cccd.edu
PHAM, Michael .... 206-934-4193. 522 J
michael.pham@seattlecolleges.edu
PHAM, Paul .... 219-866-6258. 172 E
paulphamsjc@saintjoe.edu
PHAM, Tom, C .... 617-984-1699. 235 I
tpham@quincycollege.edu
PHAN, Luyen .... 507-222-4451. 254 D
phan@carleton.edu
PHAN, Nga .... 619-684-8815... 56 C
nphan@newschoolarch.edu
PHARO, SCN, Diane .... 812-357-6598. 173 A
dpharo@saintmeinrad.edu
PHARR, Christine .... 402-399-2419. 289 A
msellers@csm.edu
PHARR, Dianne .... 254-442-5151. 468 I
dianne.pharr@cisco.edu
PHARR, Kathy, R .... 706-542-0054. 133 C
pharr@uga.edu
PHARR, Maria .... 252-493-7224. 362 G
mpharr@email.pittcc.edu
PHEASANT, Joel, C .... 814-641-5334. 419 H
pheasaj@juniata.edu
PHELAN, Carol .... 617-585-1139. 234 I
carol.phelan@necmusic.edu
PHELAN, Carol .... 516-877-3154. 313 A
phelan@adelphi.edu
PHELAN, Daniel, J .... 517-787-0800. 244 J
phelandanielj@jccmi.edu
PHELAN JOHNSON,
Marcia .... 860-297-2041... 91 F
marcia.johnson@trincoll.edu
PHELAN-NINH, Jennifer . 315-792-7500. 346 C
jennifer.phelan@sunyit.edu
PHELON, Elmer .... 212-237-8541. 318 D
ephelon@jjay.cuny.edu
PHELPS, Bill .... 870-245-5567... 22 D
phelpswr@obu.edu
PHELPS, Camille .... 580-745-2080. 399 J
cphelps@se.edu
PHELPS, Craig .... 660-626-2391. 271 A
cphelps@atsu.edu
PHELPS, Cynthia .... 212-960-5836. 351 M
cphelps@yu.edu
PHELPS, Dani, J .... 610-841-3333. 427 F
dphelps@psb.edu
PHELPS, Debbie .... 620-331-4100. 187 G
dphelps@indycc.edu
PHELPS, Dennis, L .... 504-282-4455. 206 A
dphelps@nobts.edu
PHELPS, Esther .... 330-337-6403. 373 F
depemp@raex.com
PHELPS, Gary, L .... 330-471-8127. 383 D
gphelps@malone.edu
PHELPS, Hilary .... 860-343-5856... 89 A
hphelps@mxcc.commnet.edu
PHELPS, Jean .... 718-262-2285. 319 F
phelps@york.cuny.edu
PHELPS, Joel .... 802-447-6306. 500 D
jphelps@svc.edu
PHELPS, Martha .... 270-824-8591. 196 A
martha.phelps@kctcs.edu
PHELPS, Sherri .... 870-245-5410... 22 D
phelpss@obu.edu
PHELPS, Susan, Q .... 336-734-7236. 360 E
sphelps@forsythtech.edu
PHELPS-ELLERKER,
Lena .... 863-784-7303. 113 G
lena.phelps@southflorida.edu
PHENICIE,
Christopher, N .... 864-488-4549. 444 L
cphenicie@limestone.edu
PHENIX, Amy .... 612-626-1616. 264 G
pheni001@umn.edu
PHHIPPS, Heidi .... 602-943-2311... 19 C
Heidi.Phipps@west.edu
PHILBECK, Daniel, L .... 864-587-4223. 447 B
philbed@smcsc.edu
PHILBERT, Martin, A .... 734-763-5454. 251 C
philbert@umich.edu
PHILBIN, Catherine .... 617-296-8300. 227 I
catherine_philbin@laboure.edu
PHILBIN, Kathleen .... 585-389-2451. 332 D
kphilbi8@naz.edu
PHILEMON, Suzanne, B . 704-233-8303. 370 G
ksbostic@wingate.edu
PHILIE, Lauren .... 802-635-1657. 501 D
lauren.philie@jsc.edu
PHILIPKOSKY,
Thomas, G .... 843-953-6907. 442 A
tom.philipkosky@citadel.edu
PHILIPP, Diane .... 517-437-7341. 243 I
diane.philipp@hillsdale.edu
PHILIPP, Shirin .... 617-349-9600. 228 B
philipp@lesley.edu
PHILIPPA, Laine, M .... 414-410-4187. 532 B
lmphilippa@stritch.edu
PHILIPPON, Roger .... 207-755-5357. 210 J
rphilippon@cmcc.edu

PHILIPS, JR., Billy, U .... 806-743-1388. 487 E
billy.philips@ttuhsc.edu
PHILLEY, Tim .... 918-495-6970. 398 H
tphilley@oru.edu
PHILLIP, Neal .... 718-289-5939. 317 B
neal.phillip@bcc.cuny.edu
PHILLIP, Thomas, G .... 262-243-5700. 532 H
thomas.phillip@cuw.edu
PHILLIPS, Adrian .... 313-496-2820. 252 B
aphilli1@wcccd.edu
PHILLIPS, Adrienne .... 662-252-8000. 269 F
aphillips@rustcollege.edu
PHILLIPS, Allison .... 336-838-6491. 365 B
allison.phillips@wilkescc.edu
PHILLIPS, Amanda .... 724-653-2195. 415 A
aphillips@dec.edu
PHILLIPS, Andrew, T .... 410-293-1583. 545 J
aphillip@usna.edu
PHILLIPS, Angela .... 614-234-5717. 384 J
aphillips-lowe@mccn.edu
PHILLIPS, Brad, C .... 607-733-7177. 323 F
bphillips@ebi-college.com
PHILLIPS, Brian .... 562-903-4897... 29 L
brian.phillips@biola.edu
PHILLIPS, Bridget .... 217-479-7031. 152 D
bridget.phillips@mac.edu
PHILLIPS, Calvin .... 605-626-2530. 451 I
Calvin.Phillips@northern.edu
PHILLIPS, Carme .... 205-970-9205..... 7 B
cphillips@sebc.edu
PHILLIPS, Carol .... 910-938-6343. 359 E
phillipsc@coastalcarolina.edu
PHILLIPS,
Christopher, G .... 410-706-2261. 219 C
cphillip@umaryland.edu
PHILLIPS, Cinda, K .... 812-749-1271. 171 K
cphillip@oak.edu
PHILLIPS, Cindy .... 417-477-8212. 279 K
phillipc@otc.edu
PHILLIPS, Clarenda, M .. 606-783-2434. 198 A
c.phillips@moreheadstate.edu
PHILLIPS, Clay .... 866-331-4153. 453 D
phillipsc@bethelu.edu
PHILLIPS, Dave .... 870-777-5722... 25 B
dave.phillips@uacch.edu
PHILLIPS, Dave .... 615-248-1683. 462 D
dphillips@trevecca.edu
PHILLIPS, David .... 410-516-8341. 215 H
dphillips@jhu.edu
PHILLIPS, Delsie .... 803-321-2033. 445 G
delsie.phillips@newberry.edu
PHILLIPS, Denise .... 972-721-5168. 488 F
dphilli@udallas.edu
PHILLIPS, Dianna .... 732-224-2265. 299 G
PHILLIPS, Douglas .... 585-275-3311. 349 C
dphillips@admin.rochester.edu
PHILLIPS, E. Clorisa .... 276-466-7910. 514 G
PHILLIPS, Earnest .... 702-895-2388. 294 I
earnest.phillips@unlv.edu
PHILLIPS, Edward .... 504-520-6787. 209 D
ephillips@xula.edu
PHILLIPS, Elaine, W .... 405-273-5331. 395 I
ephillips@familyoffaithcollege.edu
PHILLIPS, Eli, H .... 205-226-4600..... 2 C
ephillip@bsc.edu
PHILLIPS, Elizabeth, D ... 480-965-1224... 11 K
betty.phillips@asu.edu
PHILLIPS, Faith .... 740-366-9492. 376 A
phillips.495@osu.edu
PHILLIPS, Farley .... 252-451-8287. 362 D
farley@nashcc.edu
PHILLIPS, Gail, G .... 615-353-3703. 461 B
gail.phillips@nscc.edu
PHILLIPS, Gary, A .... 765-361-6224. 175 B
phillipg@wabash.edu
PHILLIPS, Gina .... 817-531-6548. 488 A
gphillips@txwes.edu
PHILLIPS, Glen .... 478-387-4731. 125 E
PHILLIPS, Heather .... 218-477-4363. 259 H
phillipshe@mnstate.edu
PHILLIPS, Jacqueline ...... 860-885-2309... 89 F
PHILLIPS, James, J .... 847-491-8880. 155 D
j-phillips@northwestern.edu
PHILLIPS, James, K .... 910-630-7149. 356 H
jphillips@methodist.edu
PHILLIPS, James, L .... 713-798-6598. 467 F
phillips@bcm.edu
PHILLIPS, Janet, E .... 540-224-6973. 506 G
jephillips@jchs.edu
PHILLIPS, Jay .... 785-864-5604. 190 L
jay.phillips@ku.edu
PHILLIPS, Jeffrey, J .... 404-880-8480. 122 J
jphillips@cau.edu
PHILLIPS, Jennifer .... 315-859-4243. 325 E
jlphillips@hamilton.edu
PHILLIPS, Jerrett .... 918-456-5511. 396 H
phillijd@nsuok.edu
PHILLIPS, Jo, C .... 870-759-4101... 25 K
jphillips@wbcoll.edu
PHILLIPS, John, A .... 619-260-4523... 73 I
jphillips@sandiego.edu

PHILLIPS, Joseph, M ...... 206-296-5700. 523 E
phillipsj@seattleu.edu
PHILLIPS, June .... 318-670-6365. 207 A
jphillips@susla.edu
PHILLIPS, Karen .... 413-775-1305. 231 E
phillips@gcc.mass.edu
PHILLIPS, Kathleen .... 304-205-6600. 527 O
kphillips@kvctc.edu
PHILLIPS, Kevin, J .... 203-932-7318... 92 E
kphillips@newhaven.edu
PHILLIPS, Kimberley, L .. 510-430-2096... 54 F
kphillips@mills.edu
PHILLIPS, Krystal .... 910-938-6234. 359 E
phillipsk@coastalcarolina.edu
PHILLIPS, Lanetta .... 256-331-5348..... 6 A
lanetta.phillips@nwscc.edu
PHILLIPS, Larry, M .... 936-639-1301. 465 J
phillips@angelina.edu
PHILLIPS, Linda .... 580-581-2238. 394 G
lindap@cameron.edu
PHILLIPS, Lynette .... 516-299-2461. 329 C
Lynette.Phillips@liu.edu
PHILLIPS, Margaret, R .... 304-293-2545. 530 D
margaret.phillips@mail.wvu.edu
PHILLIPS, Mari Anne ...... 417-667-8181. 273 A
mphillips@cottey.edu
PHILLIPS, Marie .... 413-265-2365. 225 C
phillipsmarie@elms.edu
PHILLIPS, Mary Lou .... 860-343-5751... 89 A
mphillips@mxcc.commnet.edu
PHILLIPS, Matthew .... 815-394-5003. 157 C
mphillips@rockford.edu
PHILLIPS, Maynard .... 918-343-7773. 399 C
mphillips@rsu.edu
PHILLIPS, Melissa, C ...... 828-733-5883. 361 H
mphillips@mayland.edu
PHILLIPS, Michael .... 815-921-4482. 157 A
m.phillips@rockvalleycollege.edu
PHILLIPS, Michael, C ...... 843-953-4942. 443 A
phillipsm@cofc.edu
PHILLIPS, Mike .... 309-796-5012. 140 E
phillipsm@bhc.edu
PHILLIPS, Mitsu .... 801-274-3280. 498 E
mitsu.phillips@wgu.edu
PHILLIPS, Monika .... 870-512-7703... 20 B
monika_phillips@asun.edu
PHILLIPS, Morgan, A ...... 910-642-7141. 364 A
Morgan.Phillips@sccnc.edu
PHILLIPS, Myra .... 804-524-5352. 515 D
mhphilli@vsu.edu
PHILLIPS, Nyambura, M 609-894-9311. 299 I
nphillip@bcc.edu
PHILLIPS, Pamela .... 920-498-5418. 541 B
pamela.phillips@nwtc.edu
PHILLIPS, Patricia .... 401-454-6134. 440 A
pphillip02@risd.edu
PHILLIPS, Patsy .... 505-428-5901. 309 J
pphillips@iaia.edu
PHILLIPS, Phil, E .... 310-506-7227... 58 H
phil.phillips@pepperdine.edu
PHILLIPS, Rachel .... 215-965-4025. 424 D
rphillips@moore.edu
PHILLIPS, Ralph, N .... 724-847-6766. 417 A
rphillip@geneva.edu
PHILLIPS, Raymond, B ... 207-859-4209. 209 J
Ray.Phillips@colby.edu
PHILLIPS, Rebecca, J ..... 724-847-6843. 417 A
rjphilli@geneva.edu
PHILLIPS, Richard, W .... 901-722-3220. 458 K
rphillips@sco.edu
PHILLIPS, Rita, M .... 515-294-0231. 175 H
rphillip@iastate.edu
PHILLIPS, Robert .... 304-243-2321. 531 H
phillips@wju.edu
PHILLIPS, Sandy .... 724-222-5330. 425 K
sphillips@penncommercial.edu
PHILLIPS, Shannon .... 843-863-7035. 441 H
sphillip@csuniv.edu
PHILLIPS, Sheri .... 417-865-2815. 274 B
phillipss@evangel.edu
PHILLIPS, Stephen, S ..... 443-412-2286. 215 C
sphillips@harford.edu
PHILLIPS, Steve .... 845-675-4741. 335 C
steve.phillips@nyack.edu
PHILLIPS, Sue .... 570-702-8916. 419 G
sphillips@johnson.edu
PHILLIPS, Susan, D .... 518-956-8030. 341 D
provost@albany.edu
PHILLIPS, Susanne, D .... 610-399-2217. 428 B
sphillips@cheyney.edu
PHILLIPS, Teddy .... 815-226-3387. 157 C
TPhillips@rockford.edu
PHILLIPS, Teri, P .... 253-535-7187. 521 I
phillitp@plu.edu
PHILLIPS, Terri .... 406-243-2665. 286 H
terri.phillips@umontana.edu
PHILLIPS, Thomas .... 303-797-5739... 78 F
thomas.phillips@arapahoe.edu
PHILLIPS, Timothy .... 563-333-6259. 182 B
PhillipsTimothy@sau.edu

PHILLIPS, Tina, A ... 610-499-1161. 437 E
taphillips@widener.edu
PHILLIPS, Tom ... 570-389-4775. 427 H
tphilli2@bloomu.edu
PHILLIPS, Valerie ... 619-596-2766... 26 I
valerie@advancedtraining.edu
PHILLIPS, Vickie ... 229-430-4766. 119 J
vickie.phillips@asurams.edu
PHILLIPS, Virginia ... 619-684-8869... 56 C
vphillips@newschoolarch.edu
PHILLIPS, Wendy, S ... 724-838-7399. 412 G
phillipsws@carlow.edu
PHILLIPS, William ... 401-232-6045. 438 K
wphillip@bryant.edu
PHILLIPS, Wilma, D ... 334-386-7274... 3 H
wphillips@faulkner.edu
PHILLIPS, Winfred, M ... 352-392-9122. 116 A
wphil@ufl.edu
PHILLIPS, Yancy ... 812-237-2100. 167 A
yancy.phillips@indstate.edu
PHILLIPS-HAUSER,
Robin ... 336-838-6122. 365 B
robin.phillips@wilkescc.edu
PHILLIPS-MADSON,
Robyn ... 509-452-5100. 521 J
PHILO, Denise, M ... 518-564-2100. 344 B
belldm@plattsburgh.edu
PHILPOTT, Cecil ... 252-331-4881. 359 F
caphilpott@albemarle.edu
PHILPOTT, Jeffrey, L ... 212-938-5500. 345 C
jphilpott@sunyopt.edu
PHILYAW, Michael ... 828-726-2303. 358 E
mphilyaw@cccti.edu
PHINAZEE, Karen, B ... 919-532-5663. 364 G
kbphinazee@waketech.edu
PHINNEY, D. Nathan ... 330-471-8194. 383 D
nphinney@malone.edu
PHINNEY, James ... 419-755-4720. 385 D
jphinney@ncstatecollege.edu
PHINNEY, Nancy, L ... 805-565-6055... 76 D
nphinney@westmont.edu
PHINNEY, Raymond, R ... 207-834-7562. 212 E
rphinney@maine.edu
PHIPPS, Adam ... 301-784-5000. 213 B
aphipps@allegany.edu
PHIPPS, Angela ... 606-368-6134. 191 J
angelaphipps@alc.edu
PHIPPS, Kim, S ... 717-796-5085. 423 L
kphipps@messiah.edu
PHIPPS, Kylene ... 406-874-6292. 286 E
phippsk@milescc.edu
PHIPPS, Sam ... 336-841-4545. 355 C
sphipps@highpoint.edu
PHIPPS, Sid ... 410-626-2545. 217 G
sid.phipps@sjca.edu
PHIPPS, Terry ... 972-825-4802. 481 F
tphipps@sagu.edu
PHIPPS-BOGER, Jayne ... 336-372-5061. 365 B
jayne.boger@wilkescc.edu
PHLEGAR, Charles, D ... 607-255-5142. 322 A
cdp25@cornell.edu
PHOENIX, Dru ... 505-471-5756. 312 D
admissions@swc.edu
PHUNG, Minh, N ... 202-885-3541... 94 F
mphung@american.edu
PIAGET, Nicole ... 207-780-4071. 212 H
npiaget@usm.maine.edu
PIANEZZOLA, Cristina ... 801-863-8204. 497 C
cristina.pianezzola@uvu.edu
PIANKA, Stephanie ... 212-998-2910. 334 D
stephanie.pianka@nyu.edu
PIANTA, Robert, C ... 434-243-5483. 511 B
rcp4p@virginia.edu
PIAR, Daniel ... 704-971-8500. 353 F
PIASKOWSKY, Robert ... 201-200-2067. 303 F
rpiaskowsky@njcu.edu
PIATT, Bill, A ... 417-268-6387. 271 I
bpiatt@gobbc.edu
PIATT, James, B ... 336-278-7440. 354 B
jpiatt@elon.edu
PIATT, Janet, M ... 423-775-7237. 453 E
piattja@bryan.edu
PIATT, Ronda ... 217-732-3155. 151 C
rpiatt@lincolncollege.edu
PIAZZA, Bradley ... 262-691-5594. 541 D
bpiazza@wctc.edu
PIAZZA, Chuck ... 916-564-1525. 390 C
chuck.piazza@myunion.edu
PIAZZA, Rachel ... 815-939-5331. 155 H
rpiazza@shet.follett.com
PIAZZA, Vincent ... 618-537-6500. 152 G
vppiazzo@mckendree.edu
PIBURN, Mike ... 816-322-0110. 271 O
admissions@calvary.edu
PIBURN, Mike ... 816-322-0110. 271 O
mike.piburn@calvary.edu
PICARD, Chris ... 801-957-4182. 498 B
chris.picard@slcc.edu
PICARD, Sharon, A ... 401-825-2150. 439 A
sapicard@ccri.edu
PICARDO, Alice ... 732-906-2509. 303 B
apicardo@middlesexcc.edu
PICCHI, Danielle ... 915-532-3737. 494 J
dpicchi@westerntech.edu
PICCININNI, James ... 713-525-2192. 490 L
jpicci@stthom.edu
PICCIRILLO, Tony ... 814-864-6666. 417 D
PICCOLI, Tracey ... 970-247-7464... 81 M
piccoli_t@fortlewis.edu
PICCOLO, Nicholas, A ... 989-463-7333. 239 B
piccolo@alma.edu
PICCOLO, JR., Stephen ... 914-594-4570. 334 A
stephen_piccolo@nymc.edu
PICCONE, James ... 856-691-8600. 301 A
jpiccone@cccnj.edu
PICCORELLI, Tom ... 440-775-8445. 385 H
tom.piccorelli@oberlin.edu
PICERNO, Nicholas, P ... 540-828-5761. 502 J
npicerno@bridgewater.edu
PICHA, Mike ... 847-317-7029. 160 M
mikep@tiu.edu
PICHA, Patti ... 907-474-7596... 10 I
plpicha@alaska.edu
PICHARDO, Jeanette ... 718-405-3255. 320 G
jeanette.pichardo@mountsaintvincent.edu
PICINICH, Susan ... 410-704-3288. 220 E
spicinich@towson.edu
PICK, Danial ... 831-242-5200. 544 F
PICKA, Chenek ... 757-490-1241. 501 G
cpicka@auto.edu
PICKARD, Larry ... 415-451-2803... 63 A
lpickard@sfts.edu
PICKEL, Wendy ... 816-501-4824. 280 I
wendy.pickel@rockhurst.edu
PICKELL, Barsha ... 706-233-7394. 131 E
bpickell@shorter.edu
PICKENS, Eva, K ... 713-313-4205. 485 F
pickensek@tsu.edu
PICKENS, Joe ... 386-312-4111. 112 C
joepickens@sjrstate.edu
PICKENS, Leo ... 410-295-6926. 217 G
leo.pickens@sjca.edu
PICKERELL, Jennifer, K ... 618-537-6805. 152 G
jkpickerell@mckendree.edu
PICKERILL, Ted, O ... 513-529-6225. 384 G
ted.pickerill@miamioh.edu
PICKERING, David ... 815-939-5240. 155 H
dpickrng@olivet.edu
PICKERING,
Jonathan, M ... 630-637-5253. 154 F
jmpickering@noctrl.edu
PICKERING, Robert, P ... 843-953-5096. 442 A
robert.pickering@citadel.edu
PICKETT, Brent ... 307-268-3563. 543 I
bpickett@uwyo.edu
PICKETT, Clyde ... 412-237-4436. 413 D
cpickett@ccac.edu
PICKETT, Kareen ... 863-638-7248. 119 C
kareen.pickett@warner.edu
PICKETT, Regina ... 281-283-2626. 489 C
pickett@uhcl.edu
PICKETT, Rich ... 619-594-8370... 35 D
rich.pickett@sdsu.edu
PICKETT, Todd ... 562-903-4754... 29 L
todd.pickett@biola.edu
PICKETT, Valerie ... 575-646-2422. 310 I
vpickett@nmsu.edu
PICKING, Margaret ... 501-760-4203... 22 A
mpicking@npcc.edu
PICKINS, Dave ... 903-593-8311. 485 A
dpickins@texascollege.edu
PICKLESIMER,
Donna, M ... 937-327-6309. 393 E
dpicklesimer@wittenberg.edu
PICKMAN, Jerry ... 816-271-5647. 279 A
pickman@missouriwestern.edu
PICKREN, Wade ... 607-274-3734. 327 E
wpickren@ithaca.edu
PICKRON, Carlton ... 413-572-5400. 230 F
cpickron@westfield.ma.edu
PICKUS, Keith ... 316-978-3600. 191 F
keith.pickus@wichita.edu
PICOLO MANZI,
Stephanie ... 401-254-3369. 440 B
smanzi@rwu.edu
PICONE, Deborah ... 212-686-9244. 313 G
PICONE, Gary ... 208-792-2863. 138 G
gapicone@lcsc.edu
PICONE, Joe Al ... 979-627-0286. 467 I
jpicone@blinn.edu
PICUS, Sharon, M ... 610-683-1353. 429 A
picus@kutztown.edu
PIDDINGTON, Josh, R ... 856-415-2270. 302 C
jpiddington@gccnj.edu
PIECHOTA, Thomas, C ... 702-895-4412. 294 I
thomas.piechota@unlv.edu
PIECORA, Annette ... 718-405-3212. 320 G
annette.piecora@mountsaintvincent.edu
PIECZYNSKI, William, C 508-213-2162. 235 E
william.pieczynski@nichols.edu
PIEDRAS, Alex, H ... 515-263-6017. 178 G
apiedras@grandview.edu
PIEKARA, Lita ... 570-208-5962. 419 P
litapiekara@kings.edu
PIEKUTOWSKI, Michelle 864-656-4286. 442 C
mtp@clemson.edu
PIELOCK, Stephen ... 413-545-5768. 228 F
pielock@oit.umass.edu
PIENKOWSKI, Cynthia ... 714-241-6240... 39 I
cpienkowski@coastline.edu
PIEPENBRINK,
Kenneth, M ... 317-788-3231. 173 I
kpiepenbrink@uindy.edu
PIEPENBURG,
Marianne, B ... 214-768-3410. 481 A
mpiepenb@smu.edu
PIEPER, John, A ... 314-367-8700. 281 C
john.pieper@stlcop.edu
PIEPER, Michael, C ... 608-785-9162. 541 E
pieperm@westerntc.edu
PIEPER, Sandi, J ... 515-574-1139. 179 D
pieper@iowacentral.edu
PIEPER-OLSON, Heather 320-363-5964. 254 J
hpeiperolso@csbsju.edu
PIER, David ... 916-608-6500... 53 C
PIER, Julie, H ... 605-677-5446. 451 F
julie.pier@usd.edu
PIERCE, Barb ... 800-962-7682. 285 A
bpierce@wma.edu
PIERCE, Bill ... 479-788-7188... 24 A
bill.pierce@uafs.edu
PIERCE, Bill ... 502-852-8372. 200 D
wmpier01@louisville.edu
PIERCE, Bob ... 601-266-6796. 270 E
bob.pierce@usm.edu
PIERCE, Bradley, W ... 860-632-3012... 90 C
admissions@holyapostles.edu
PIERCE, Brandon ... 316-295-5200. 186 H
piercb@friends.edu
PIERCE, Brynn ... 541-383-7402. 402 D
bpierce@cocc.edu
PIERCE, Carl, G ... 610-499-4555. 437 E
cgpierce@widener.edu
PIERCE, Carolyn ... 559-438-4222... 46 K
carolyn_pierce@heald.edu
PIERCE, Cleon ... 919-546-8244. 366 E
cpierce@shawu.edu
PIERCE, David ... 417-328-1512. 282 C
dpierce@sbuniv.edu
PIERCE, Deborah, L ... 815-753-1989. 154 I
dpierce@niu.edu
PIERCE, Donald, E ... 864-294-2024. 444 C
don.pierce@furman.edu
PIERCE, Donna, L ... 931-598-1880. 458 H
dopierce@sewanee.edu
PIERCE, JR., Earl, E ... 607-871-2159. 313 E
pierce@alfred.edu
PIERCE, JR., Earl, E ... 607-871-2406. 313 E
pierce@alfred.edu
PIERCE, Evan, F ... 716-286-8769. 334 F
epierce@niagara.edu
PIERCE, Frederic ... 607-753-2518. 343 B
fred.pierce@cortland.edu
PIERCE, Greg ... 601-266-5006. 270 E
greg.pierce@usm.edu
PIERCE, Heather ... 773-252-5308. 156 I
heather.pierce@resu.edu
PIERCE, James ... 254-968-9781. 483 A
jrpierce@tarleton.edu
PIERCE, Jason, A ... 828-689-1237. 356 F
jpierce@mhc.edu
PIERCE, Jerry, D ... 318-357-6588. 208 B
pierce@nsula.edu
PIERCE, Joan ... 608-785-9915. 541 E
piercej@westerntc.edu
PIERCE, John ... 828-251-6742. 368 C
jpierce@unca.edu
PIERCE, John, E ... 402-280-3084. 289 D
jpierce@creighton.edu
PIERCE, IV, John, Q ... 202-687-4020... 95 E
piercej@georgetown.edu
PIERCE, Jonathan ... 503-883-2490. 404 A
jdpierce@linfield.edu
PIERCE, June ... 724-946-7136. 437 B
piercejg@westminster.edu
PIERCE, Keith ... 803-641-2838. 448 A
keithp@usca.edu
PIERCE, Kellee ... 406-657-1166. 288 B
piercek@rocky.edu
PIERCE, Kenetta ... 803-786-3012. 443 B
PIERCE, Kenneth ... 210-458-4555. 492 C
kenneth.pierce@utsa.edu
PIERCE, LaRue ... 937-512-2291. 388 O
larue.pierce@sinclair.edu
PIERCE, Leighton ... 718-636-3633. 336 F
lpierce@pratt.edu
PIERCE, Linda ... 732-987-2287. 302 B
piercel@georgian.edu
PIERCE, Lois ... 314-516-6384. 283 E
piercel@umsl.edu
PIERCE, Lori, J ... 734-764-0151. 251 C
ljpierce@umich.edu
PIERCE, Malisa ... 918-270-6478. 398 I
malisa.pierce@ptstulsa.edu
PIERCE, Marianne ... 864-294-2269. 444 C
marianne.pierce@furman.edu
PIERCE, Marisa ... 915-831-2224. 472 B
mpierce6@epcc.edu
PIERCE, Marisa ... 425-640-1513. 519 D
marisa.pierce@edcc.edu
PIERCE, Mark ... 865-573-4517. 455 G
mpierce@johnsonU.edu
PIERCE, Melinda ... 918-647-1217. 394 I
mpierce@carlalbert.edu
PIERCE, Melody, C ... 336-334-7696. 367 E
mcpierce@ncat.edu
PIERCE, Michael ... 562-903-4777... 29 L
michael.pierce@biola.edu
PIERCE, Peg ... 248-204-3143. 245 I
mpierce@ltu.edu
PIERCE, Robert ... 334-291-4964... 2 H
robert.pierce@cv.edu
PIERCE, Sharon ... 443-518-4807. 215 E
spierce@howardcc.edu
PIERCE, Stacey ... 315-781-3824. 326 C
pierces@hws.edu
PIERCE, Susan, G ... 214-860-2042. 470 J
s.pierce@dcccd.edu
PIERCE, Tracy ... 904-632-5094. 105 E
tpierce@fscj.edu
PIERCEFIELD, John ... 517-321-0242. 243 F
jpiercefield@glcc.edu
PIERCY, Mitchell ... 417-626-1234. 279 J
mpiercy@occ.edu
PIERI, Sean ... 719-389-6741... 79 D
sean.pieri@coloradocollege.edu
PIERNER, Tracy ... 313-845-9607. 243 H
tpierner@hfcc.edu
PIERNIK, Thomas, E ... 818-677-2393... 34 C
tom.piernik@csun.edu
PIERPOINT, Paul, E ... 610-861-5580. 425 D
ppierpoint@northampton.edu
PIERPONT, Hugh, P ... 713-486-4151. 492 E
hugh.p.pierpont@uth.tmc.edu
PIERRE, Christophe ... 217-333-3077. 161 C
chppierre@uillinois.edu
PIERRE, Thelma, J ... 926-261-1401. 482 F
tjpierre@pvamu.edu
PIERRE, Vivica, D ... 617-228-2366. 231 C
vdpierre@bhcc.mass.edu
PIERRE-PIERRE, Karine ... 201-360-4159. 302 D
kpierre-pierre@hccc.edu
PIERSANTE, Joseph, G ... 734-763-3434. 251 C
piersant@umich.edu
PIERSOL, John ... 386-752-1822. 104 G
john.piersol@fgc.edu
PIERSON, Cathy ... 541-245-7912. 407 F
cpierson@roguecc.edu
PIERSON, Donald ... 978-934-2635. 229 B
Donald_Pierson@uml.edu
PIERSON, Gary ... 970-943-2049... 86 I
gpierson@western.edu
PIERSON, Karen ... 530-283-0202... 44 H
KPierson@frc.edu
PIERSON, Katricia ... 580-559-5486. 395 F
kpierson@ecok.edu
PIERSON, Kenn ... 562-463-3100... 60 I
kpierson@riohondo.edu
PIERSON, Tim, J ... 434-395-2039. 506 J
piersontj@longwood.edu
PIESCKI, Traci ... 845-675-5701. 335 C
traci.piescki@nyack.edu
PIESIK, Deanette ... 701-774-4246. 372 F
deanette.piesik@willistonstate.edu
PIETA, Sandy ... 660-248-6213. 272 B
spieta@centralmethodist.edu
PIETRO, Kimberly ... 607-753-2518. 343 B
kimberly.pietro@cortland.edu
PIETROK, Mark ... 503-768-7065. 403 K
pietrok@lclark.edu
PIETROPAOLI,
Stephen, R ... 202-685-3924. 544 K
Stephen.Pietropaoli@ndu.edu
PIETROWSKI, Michael ... 505-565-1082. 237 A
mpietrowski@stonehill.edu
PIETRUSZKIEWICZ,
Christopher ... 727-562-7809. 117 C
cmp@law.stetson.edu
PIETRYKOWSKI, Chet ... 406-791-5283. 288 E
cpietrykowski@ugf.edu
PIETRYKOWSKI,
Robert, J ... 954-262-7893. 109 K
rpietrykowski@nova.edu
PIETSCH, Amy ... 920-236-6139. 539 K
pietsch@fvtc.edu
PIETZ, Vicky ... 715-675-3331. 541 A
pietz@ntc.edu
PIFER, Ken ... 909-607-0809... 39 B
ken_pifer@cuc.claremont.edu
PIFER, Kenneth ... 503-370-6104. 408 J
kpifer@willamette.edu

PIFER, Richard ... 585-273-5830. 349 C
richard.pifer@rochester.edu

PIGATTI, Kimberly ... 708-596-2000. 159 C
kpigatti@ssc.edu

PIGG, Donna ... 251-460-6050... 9 E
dpigg@southalabama.edu

PIGGOTT, Patrick, L ... 209-478-0800... 47 M
ppiggott@humphreys.edu

PIGNATELLO, Robert ... 212-237-8500. 318 D
rpignatello@jjay.cuny.edu

PIGNATORE, Amy ... 928-317-6092... 11 L
amy.pignatore@azwestern.edu

PIGOTT, Kelly ... 325-671-2179. 472 O
kpigott@hsutx.edu

PIGUES, D. Keith ... 919-530-6100. 368 A
dpigues@nccu.edu

PIGZA, Jennifer ... 925-631-4755... 61 F
jpigza@stmarys-ca.edu

PIKE, Alan ... 336-334-4822. 360 G
adpike@gtcc.edu

PIKE, Dale ... 208-426-3289. 137 G
dalepike@boisestate.edu

PIKE, Gary ... 317-278-2282. 168 D
pikeg@iupui.edu

PIKE, John, E ... 603-862-1520. 298 C
john.pike@unh.edu

PIKE, Patricia ... 562-903-4713... 29 L
patricia.pike@biola.edu

PIKE, Susan ... 479-936-5145... 22 C
spike@nwacc.edu

PIKOR, Susan ... 413-542-8099. 221 G
spikor@amherst.edu

PIKOWSKY, Reta ... 404-894-4181. 125 D
reta.pikowsky@registrar.gatech.edu

PILACHOWSKI,
David, M ... 413-597-2502. 238 D
david.m.pilachowski@williams.edu

PILARZ, SJ, Scott, R ... 414-288-7223. 534 B
scott.pilarz@marquette.edu

PILAT, Tom ... 309-694-5367. 146 E
tpilat@icc.edu

PILCHICK, Mayer ... 718-232-7800. 351 C

PILCHICK, Yochanan ... 718-232-7800. 351 C

PILEWSKI, Tim, W ... 814-732-5555. 428 E
pilewski@edinboro.edu

PILGRIM, Andrea ... 864-644-5011. 446 I
apilgrim@swu.edu

PILGRIM, David ... 231-591-3946. 242 F
DavidPilgrim@ferris.edu

PILGRIM, Jacqueline ... 617-422-7401. 235 B
jpilgrim@nesl.edu

PILGRIM, Mark ... 717-477-1154. 429 E
mepilg@ship.edu

PILIECI, Kim ... 616-538-2330. 243 A
kpilieci@gbcol.edu

PILLAI, Bindu ... 631-370-3300. 340 F
BPillai@sbmelville.edu

PILLAR, James ... 732-571-3465. 303 C
jpillar@monmouth.edu

PILLARELLI, Tina ... 734-384-4229. 247 C
tpillarelli@monroeccc.edu

PILLARI, Vimala ... 404-880-8549. 122 J
vpillari@cau.edu

PILLAY, Gautam ... 610-436-3592. 430 A
gpillay@wcupa.edu

PILLON, Greg, S ... 615-460-6645. 453 C
greg.pillon@belmont.edu

PILLOW, Kirk, E ... 215-717-6388. 435 A
kpillow@uarts.edu

PILLSBURY-GUYOT,
Brooke ... 503-244-0726. 401 M
brookeguyot@achs.edu

PILOCZEWSKI,
Lawrence ... 262-554-2010. 534 D
mcomadmissions@aol.com

PILON, Maryann ... 845-569-3332. 332 B
maryannpilon@msmc.edu

PILSNER, Joseph ... 713-942-5049. 490 L
pilsnerj@stthom.edu

PILTZ, Anthony ... 406-657-1020. 288 B
piltza@rocky.edu

PIMENTEL, Elizabeth, W . 203-576-4110... 91 G
epimente@bridgeport.edu

PIMENTEL, German ... 787-840-8894. 555 A
german.pimentel@upr.edu

PIMENTEL, Kristin ... 805-546-3182... 42 C
kpimente@cuesta.edu

PIMENTEL, Robert ... 559-934-2793... 75 G
robertpimentel@whccd.edu

PINA, Bernard ... 575-527-7610. 311 B
bepina@nmsu.edu

PINA, Christine, M ... 860-768-2403... 92 D
cpina@hartford.edu

PINA, Elsa ... 915-351-8100. 465 I

PINA, Jason ... 508-531-1276. 229 D
jason.pina@bridgew.edu

PINA HOUDE,
Ana Maria ... 915-351-8100. 465 I

PINAR, Kemale ... 507-457-2394. 262 A
kpinar@winona.edu

PINCHBACK, Keith ... 501-882-8855... 19 M
gkpinchback@asub.edu

PINCHBACK, Rebekah ... 248-218-2096. 249 D
rpinchback@rc.edu

PINCHOT, III, Gifford ... 206-780-6203. 516 I
gifford.pinchot@bgi.edu

PINCKNEY, Jloundia ... 843-574-6120. 447 E
jloundia.pinckney@tridenttech.edu

PINDER, Elaine ... 202-462-2101... 96 A
pinder@iwp.edu

PINDER, Kymberly ... 505-277-2112. 312 F
kpinder@unm.edu

PINDER, Walt ... 912-427-5778. 120 B
wpinder@altamahatech.edu

PINE, Gary ... 626-815-5081... 29 H
gpine@apu.edu

PINE, Karey ... 585-475-6230. 337 L
ktprla@rit.edu

PINEDA, Carmen ... 617-348-6224. 237 E
carmen.pineda@urbancollege.edu

PINEDA, Gladys ... 212-423-2768. 325 H
gladys.pineda@helenefuld.edu

PINEDA, Marika ... 541-463-5824. 403 I
pinedam@lanecc.edu

PINEDO, Ciriaco ... 909-652-6160... 37 M
cid.pinedo@chaffey.edu

PINEIRO, Mildred ... 787-728-1515. 555 D
mpineiro@sagrado.edu

PINEIRO, Pedro ... 718-997-4446. 319 C
pedro.pineiro@qc.cuny.edu

PINEO, Sara ... 814-332-4392. 409 D
spineo@allegheny.edu

PINER, Brandy ... 803-981-7391. 449 J
bpiner@yorktech.edu

PINERES, Sheila, A ... 903-813-2226. 466 H

PINERO, Luis, A ... 608-263-2378. 536 D
lapinero@vc.wisc.edu

PINES, Darryll, J ... 301-405-3869. 219 B
pines@umd.edu

PINES, Shlomo ... 908-354-6057. 308 M

PINESCHI, David ... 916-348-4689... 43 F
dpineschi@epic.edu

PINET, Celine ... 831-646-4034... 54 I
cpinet@mpc.edu

PINI, John ... 781-891-2228. 223 C
jpini@bentley.edu

PINI, John, A ... 781-891-2228. 223 C
jpini@bentley.edu

PINIZZOTTO, Russell ... 617-989-4485. 237 G
pinizzottor@wit.edu

PINK, Bill ... 405-945-3240. 398 C

PINK, Kathleen ... 641-844-5739. 179 H
Kathy.Pink@iavalley.edu

PINK, Kathy ... 641-844-5539. 179 J
kathy.pink@iavalley.edu

PINK, Kevin ... 641-683-5105. 179 A
kevin.pink@indianhills.edu

PINK, Larry ... 619-388-7665... 62 F
lpink@sdccd.edu

PINK, Thomas, A ... 906-635-2315. 245 G
tpink@lssu.edu

PINKALL, Rita ... 620-672-5641. 190 A
ritap@prattcc.edu

PINKARD, Elfred, A ... 704-378-1000. 355 K
epinkard@jcsu.edu

PINKE, Taylor, A ... 813-258-7401. 118 L
tpinke@ut.edu

PINKELTON, Lawrence ... 773-995-2042. 141 J
lpinkelt@csu.edu

PINKERMAN, Loren, L ... 706-880-8234. 128 A
lpinkerman@lagrange.edu

PINKERTON, Mary ... 262-472-1712. 538 D
pinkertm@uww.edu

PINKHAM, JoEllen ... 585-389-2060. 332 D
jpinkha0@naz.edu

PINKHAM, Wesley, M ... 818-779-8413... 50 A
wpinkham@kingsuniversity.edu

PINKNEY, Adrell, L ... 504-286-5229. 206 K
apinkney@suno.edu

PINKNEY, Dwayne ... 919-962-1091. 368 D
dpinkney@email.unc.edu

PINKNEY-PASTRANA,
Jill ... 218-726-6537. 264 D
cehsp@d.umn.edu

PINKOWSKI, JR.,
Richard, J ... 716-926-8820. 326 B
rickp@hilbert.edu

PINKSTON, Glen, P ... 580-581-2225. 394 G
glenp@cameron.edu

PINKSTON, Paul ... 920-465-2373. 536 F
pinkstop@uwgb.edu

PINKSTON, Scott ... 870-368-7371... 22 E
spinkston@ozarka.edu

PINKSTON, Terri, B ... 405-325-3021. 401 B
terri@ou.edu

PINKSTON-MCKEE, Ria .. 773-291-6251. 142 D
rmckee@ccc.edu

PINN, Carolyn ... 518-381-1176. 340 G
taylorc@sunysccc.edu

PINNELL, Julie ... 402-826-8565. 289 E
julie.pinnell@doane.edu

PINNER, Ray ... 256-824-6350... 8 F
ray.pinner@uah.edu

PINNICK, Denise ... 812-749-1267. 171 K
dpinnick@oak.edu

PINNICK, Maureen ... 317-738-8028. 165 I
mpinnick@franklincollege.edu

PINO, Diana ... 713-718-5115. 473 C
diana.pino@hccs.edu

PINO, Lori ... 510-780-4500... 50 I
lpino@lifewest.edu

PINOCCI, Tina, M ... 856-256-4604. 305 E
pinocci@rowan.edu

PINOTTI, Gerald ... 708-209-3032. 143 E
jerry.pinotti@cuchicago.edu

PINS, Jacqueline, J ... 608-757-7772. 539 I
jpins@blackhawk.edu

PINSKY, Linda ... 973-278-5400. 299 D
lsp@BerkeleyCollege.edu

PINSON, J. Matthew ... 615-844-5248. 464 E
president@welch.edu

PINSON, Marcie ... 601-635-2111. 266 H
mpinson@eccc.edu

PINTAK, Lawrence, E ... 509-335-8535. 525 A
lpintak@wsu.edu

PINTER-LUCKE,
Claudia, L ... 909-869-3328... 32 G
clpinterluck@csupomona.edu

PINTO, John ... 712-274-5158. 181 B
pinto@morningside.edu

PINTO, Neville ... 502-852-6281. 200 D
ngpint01@louisville.edu

PINTO, Savio ... 773-291-6606. 142 D
spinto3@ccc.edu

PIOTRKOWSKI, Joann ... 440-646-8327. 392 D
jpiotrkowski@ursuline.edu

PIPER, Everett, G ... 918-335-6234. 398 F
epiper@okwu.edu

PIPER, Judy ... 336-334-4703. 369 A
jrpiper@uncg.edu

PIPER, Kathy ... 704-216-3492. 363 D
kathy.piper@rccc.edu

PIPER, Renee ... 985-448-4143. 208 A
renee.piper@nicholls.edu

PIPER, Richard ... 913-627-4126. 187 L
rpiper@kckcc.edu

PIPER, Terry ... 305-899-3649... 98 O
tpiper@barry.edu

PIPER, Wendy, L ... 740-368-3177. 387 J
wlpiper@owu.edu

PIPERATA, Diana ... 215-637-7700. 418 G
dpiperata@holyfamily.edu

PIPES, Dianne, L ... 210-431-4373. 479 D
dpipes@stmarytx.edu

PIPES, Elizabeth, M ... 617-726-8003. 234 B
epipes@mghihp.edu

PIPES, III, J. Kelly ... 336-838-6424. 365 B
kelly.pipes@wilkescc.edu

PIPINSKI, Ann, L ... 570-702-8901. 419 G
apipinski@johnson.edu

PIPITONE, Linda ... 314-889-1493. 274 E
lpipitone@fontbonne.edu

PIPKIN, Chad ... 573-518-2333. 278 A
cpipkin@mineralarea.edu

PIPKIN, Lisa, W ... 252-334-2020. 357 A
lisa.pipkin@macuniversity.edu

PIPPIN, Jeff ... 310-506-7500... 58 H
jeff.pippin@pepperdine.edu

PIPPIN, Jill ... 315-786-2238. 327 L
jpippin@sunyjefferson.edu

PIQUETTE, Diane ... 508-588-9100. 232 A

PIRELLI, Nicholas ... 617-541-5309. 232 G
npirelli@rcc.mass.edu

PIRES, Jennifer, P ... 302-857-1200... 93 G
jmosley1@dtcc.edu

PIRIUS, Landon ... 763-424-0712. 260 C
lpirius@nhcc.edu

PIRKLE, Bill ... 803-641-3395 448 A
billp@usca.edu

PIRKLE, Martha ... 706-880-8245. 128 A
mpirkle@lagrange.edu

PIRKUL, Hasan ... 972-883-6813. 491 E
hpirkul@utdallas.edu

PIRRI, Christine ... 518-381-1331. 340 G
pirricm@sunysccc.edu

PIRRMAN, Martin, E ... 706-880-8232. 128 A
mpirrman@lagrange.edu

PIRRONG, Cary ... 405-208-5463. 397 F
cpirrong@okcu.edu

PIRSCH, Lori ... 402-557-7467. 288 G
lori.pirsch@bellevue.edu

PIRSCHEL, C. Sue ... 419-434-5333. 391 D
pirschel@findlay.edu

PIRTLE, Gina ... 219-473-4379. 164 K
gpirtle@ccsj.edu

PIRTLE, Ron ... 601-968-8990. 266 A
rpirtle@belhaven.edu

PISA, Michael, C ... 315-312-3572. 344 A
michael.pisa@oswego.edu

PISANI, Carol ... 973-290-4364. 300 F
cpisani@cse.edu

PISANI, Carol ... 973-290-4491. 300 F
cpisani@cse.edu

PISANO, Donna ... 480-732-7125... 14 J
donna.pisano@cgc.edu

PISANO, Douglas, J ... 617-732-2874. 233 E
douglas.pisano@mcphs.edu

PISANO, Etta, D ... 843-792-2842. 445 B
pisanoe@musc.edu

PISANO, Lou ... 860-832-1760... 87 K
lpisano@ccsu.edu

PISANO, Rebecca, L ... 410-704-2451. 220 E
rpisano@towson.edu

PISCAL, Richard ... 610-989-1276. 436 D
rpiscal@vfmac.edu

PISCHKE, Kevin ... 916-577-2200... 76 J
kpischke@jessup.edu

PISCOPO, Carmine, R ... 401-865-2727. 439 E
cpiscopo@providence.edu

PISHKIN, Richard, J ... 617-228-2427. 231 C
rpishkin@bhcc.mass.edu

PISKADLO, Kevin ... 508-565-1306. 237 A
kpiskadlo@stonehill.edu

PISORS, Jesse ... 918-495-6588. 398 H
jpisors@oru.edu

PISTILLI, Fran ... 352-323-3680. 108 S
pistillf@lssc.edu

PISTILLO, Jason ... 602-383-8228... 18 E
jay@uat.edu

PISTORINO, Thomas, G . 781-768-7075. 236 A
t.pistorino@regiscollege.edu

PISZKER, James ... 814-824-2429. 423 J
jpiszker@mercyhurst.edu

PITARO, Teresa ... 781-239-4452. 222 D
tpitaro@babson.edu

PITCHER, Carole, D ... 302-295-1133... 94 E
carole.d.pitcher@wilmu.edu

PITCHER, Christopher, G 302-295-1152... 94 E
christopher.g.pitcher@wilmu.edu

PITCHER, Darren ... 509-533-3514. 518 F
darren.pitcher@spokanefalls.edu

PITCHER, Darrin ... 509-533-3514. 518 D
darrin.pitcher@spokanefalls.edu

PITCHER, John, K ... 856-691-8600. 301 A
jpitcher@cccnj.edu

PITCHER, Mark ... 918-293-5412. 398 B
mark.pitcher@okstate.edu

PITCHER, Paula, R ... 978-656-3281. 232 B
pitcherp@middlesex.mass.edu

PITCHER, Scott ... 641-585-8112. 183 D
pitchers@waldorf.edu

PITCHFORD, Jeffery, L ... 501-450-3185... 25 H
jeffp@uca.edu

PITCHFORD, Nicola ... 415-480-1880... 42 J
nicola.pitchford@dominican.edu

PITCHFORD, Steven, L ... 662-254-3327. 269 A
steven.pitchford@mvsu.edu

PITCOCK, Beth ... 559-323-2100... 63 B
bpitcock@sjcl.edu

PITEGOFF, Peter ... 207-780-4344. 212 H
pitegoff@usm.maine.edu

PITHIS, Nancy ... 617-236-8800. 226 F
npithis@fisher.edu

PITMAN, Bruce ... 716-645-2711. 341 F
cas-dean@buffalo.edu

PITMAN, Bruce, M ... 208-885-6757. 139 D
bpitman@uidaho.edu

PITMAN, Julia ... 716-614-6240. 334 E
jpitman@niagaracc.suny.edu

PITNEY, Pat ... 907-474-7907... 10 I
kppitney@alaska.edu

PITONZO, Beth ... 336-334-4822. 360 G
bjpitonzo@gtcc.edu

PITRE, Jude ... 318-876-2701. 202 J

PITRUZZELLO, Carl ... 203-932-7047... 92 E
cpitruzzello@newhaven.edu

PITSCHMANN, Louis, A . 205-348-7561... 8 D
lpitschm@bama.ua.edu

PITSIRI, Lisa ... 405-736-0315. 309 F
lpitsiri@rose.edu

PITT, Ronald, E ... 401-456-8003. 439 F
rpitt@ric.edu

PITTENGER, David ... 304-696-7263. 529 H
pittengerd@marshall.edu

PITTENGER, Mike ... 858-635-4475... 26 M
mpittenger@alliant.edu

PITTENGER, Susan, D ... 315-568-3069. 333 C
spittenger@nycc.edu

PITTER, Yeruchem ... 516-225-4700. 337 C

PITTMAN, Crystal ... 864-941-8328. 446 C
pittman.cg@ptc.edu

PITTMAN, Dale ... 626-585-7077... 58 F
depittman@pasadena.edu

PITTMAN, David ... 903-586-2518. 474 N
dpittman@jacksonville-college.edu

PITTMAN, Edward, L ... 845-437-5426. 349 G
edpittman@vassar.edu

PITTMAN, James ... 541-885-1800. 405 J
james.pittman@oit.edu

PITTMAN, Jane, D ... 540-665-3489. 509 E
jpittman@su.edu

PITTMAN, Julia .... 410-462-8380. 213 F
jpitman@bccc.edu
PITTMAN, Karan .... 229-732-5944. 120 D
karanpittman@andrewcollege.edu
PITTMAN, Kathy, L .... 985-549-2150. 208 C
kpittman@selu.edu
PITTMAN, L. Monique .... 269-471-3297. 239 D
pittman@andrews.edu
PITTMAN, Nancy Claire .. 918-610-8303. 398 I
PITTMAN, Patrick .... 910-362-7043. 358 F
ppittman@cfcc.edu
PITTMAN, Shannon .... 325-649-8052. 473 F
spittman@hputx.edu
PITTMAN, Stanley, G ...... 260-982-5270. 170 U
sgpittman@manchester.edu
PITTMAN, Stephanie, M . 262-554-2010. 534 D
pittmanmwc@aol.com
PITTMAN, Suzanne .... 478-445-6283. 125 A
suzanne.pittman@gcsu.edu
PITTMAN, Trevor .... 864-596-9752. 443 D
trevor.pittman@converse.edu
PITTMAN, Valerie, T .... 334-229-4475..... 1 D
vpittman@alasu.edu
PITTMAN, W. Randall ..... 205-726-2331..... 6 F
rpittman@samford.edu
PITTMAN, Wayne .... 205-726-2020..... 6 F
rwpittma@samford.edu
PITTS, Chuck .... 713-942-9505. 473 D
capitts@hgst.edu
PITTS, Eleanor .... 205-929-6389..... 5 D
epitts@lawsonstate.edu
PITTS, Gail, S .... 248-341-2151. 248 D
gspitts@oaklandcc.edu
PITTS, Gary .... 229-227-2414. 132 D
gpitts@southwestgatech.edu
PITTS, James, E .... 850-644-0538. 115 C
jpitts@admin.fsu.edu
PITTS, Karen, H .... 315-684-6068. 345 A
pittskh@morrisville.edu
PITTS, Mark .... 619-849-2548... 59 L
markpitts@pointloma.edu
PITTS, Mike .... 417-328-1412. 282 C
mpitts@sbuniv.edu
PITTS, Otis .... 828-328-7179. 356 B
otis.pitts@lr.edu
PITTS, Paul .... 618-650-2333. 159 H
ppitts@siue.edu
PITTS-TAYLOR, Victoria .. 212-817-8895. 317 F
womstu@gc.cuny.edu
PITZ, Megan .... 515-244-4221. 175 C
pitzm@aib.edu
PITZNER, Alex, C .... 717-901-5124. 418 E
apitzner@harrisburgu.edu
PIUMETTI FARLAND,
Lisa .... 310-338-7896... 53 E
lpiumett@lmu.edu
PIUROWSKI, Robert, C .. 607-746-4559. 345 G
piurowrc@delhi.edu
PIVARNIK, OP,
R. Gabriel .... 401-865-2245. 439 E
gpivarni@providence.edu
PIVERAL, Joyce .... 660-562-1671. 279 I
piveral@nwmissouri.edu
PIXLEY, Alan .... 479-788-7093... 24 A
alan.pixley@uafs.edu
PIXLEY, Susan .... 651-846-1471. 261 D
susan.pixley@saintpaul.edu
PIXLEY, Zaide, E .... 269-337-5755. 244 K
Zaide.Pixley@kzoo.edu
PIZAM, Abraham .... 407-903-8010. 115 E
abraham.pizam@ucf.edu
PIZANA, Kathleen .... 574-520-4878. 168 E
kpizana@iusb.edu
PIZER, Lori .... 518-292-7785. 338 C
inst_res@sage.edu
PIZIO, Jennifer .... 419-251-1710. 383 G
jennifer.pizio@mercycollege.edu
PIZIO, William .... 336-316-2418. 355 A
wipizio@guilford.edu
PIZZANO, Patti .... 704-461-6573. 352 G
pattipizzano@bac.edu
PIZZO, Lauren .... 276-944-6940. 504 H
lpizzo@ehc.edu
PIZZUTI, Anthony .... 704-971-8500. 353 F
PIZZUTI, Linda, J .... 309-677-3153. 140 I
lindap@bradley.edu
PIZZUTO, William, J .... 203-236-9818... 92 A
william.j.pizzuto@uconn.edu
PIZZUTO, William, J .... 860-626-6803... 92 A
william.j.pizzuto@uconn.edu
PJATAK, Jennifer .... 203-932-7082... 92 E
jpjatak@newhaven.edu
PLACCO, Christopher ...... 401-598-2900. 439 B
cplacco@jwu.edu
PLACE, Linna, F .... 816-235-6230. 283 D
placel@umkc.edu
PLACE, Nick, T .... 352-392-1761. 116 A
nplace@ufl.edu
PLACE, Ted, P .... 816-654-7286. 275 K
tplace@kcumb.edu
PLACERES, Sonia .... 787-738-2161. 554 C
sonia.placeres@upr.edu
PLACIDI, Kathleen .... 434-381-6596. 510 F
kplacidi@sbc.edu
PLACIDO, Rob .... 940-898-3980. 488 B
rplacido@twu.edu
PLAEHN, Kristin, H .... 253-535-7615. 521 I
plaehnkh@plu.edu
PLAGENS, Leslie, F .... 325-649-8705. 473 F
lplagens@hputx.edu
PLAGGEMEYER, Ted .... 775-674-7552. 294 H
tplaggemeyer@tmcc.edu
PLAISANCE, Beverly, S ... 225-768-1797. 206 D
beverly.plaisance@ololcollege.edu
PLAISANCE, Deshey .... 985-448-4191. 208 A
desley.plaisance@nicholls.edu
PLAKE, John .... 417-865-2815. 274 B
plakej@evangel.edu
PLANAS-RIVERA,
José, M .... 787-890-2681. 553 G
jose.planas@upra.edu
PLANAS RIVERA,
Jose, M .... 787-890-2681. 553 H
jose.planas@upr.edu
PLANCHOCK, Norann ...... 318-677-3100. 208 B
planchockn@nsula.edu
PLANEK, John .... 815-836-5937. 150 H
planekjo@lewisu.edu
PLANELL, Lilia .... 787-728-1515. 555 D
lplanell@sagrado.edu
PLANETA, Michael .... 815-740-3496. 162 F
mplaneta@stfrancis.edu
PLANK, Donna .... 254-295-4591. 490 B
dplank@umhb.edu
PLANT, Fred, W .... 219-464-5436. 174 E
fred.plant@valpo.edu
PLANT, Jonathan .... 361-593-2599. 484 A
jonathan.plant@tamuk.edu
PLANT, Maureen, C .... 301-443-5362. 217 B
mplant@msmary.edu
PLANTE, Dawn, M .... 440-525-7327. 382 M
dplante@lakelandcc.edu
PLANTE, Jacques .... 603-641-7380. 297 G
jplante@anselm.edu
PLANTE, John, J .... 412-396-4937. 415 F
plantej@duq.edu
PLANTEFABER, Lisa .... 413-572-5733. 230 F
lplantefaber@westfield.ma.edu
PLASSE, Robert .... 413-572-8131. 230 F
rplasse@westfield.ma.edu
PLASTOW, Ed .... 605-995-2689. 450 A
edplasto@dwu.edu
PLATA, Ernest, J .... 903-923-2476. 495 A
eplata@wileyc.edu
PLATE, William .... 561-297-3025. 114 L
wplate@fau.edu
PLATE, William .... 843-349-4066. 442 E
billplate@coastal.edu
PLATER, Michael .... 202-419-0400... 96 F
PLATER-ZYBERK,
Elizabeth, M .... 305-284-5000. 118 F
epz@miami.edu
PLATI, Heather .... 207-893-7898. 211 G
hplati@sjcme.edu
PLATOVSKY, Jonathan .... 718-268-4700. 337 F
PLATSOUCAS,
Christopher .... 757-683-3274. 507 N
cplatsoucas@odu.edu
PLATT, Jeffrey .... 716-829-7766. 323 D
plattjh@dyc.edu
PLATT, Mary .... 714-997-6607... 38 A
platt@chapman.edu
PLATT, Rich .... 240-895-4922. 218 A
rdplatt@smcm.edu
PLATT, Sharon .... 412-536-1120. 420 A
sharon.platt@laroche.edu
PLATT, Steve .... 541-278-5904. 402 C
splatt@bluecc.edu
PLATT, Steven .... 401-456-8554. 439 F
splatt@ric.edu
PLATT, Susan .... 215-780-1311. 433 A
splatt@salus.edu
PLATTEN, Peter, G .... 920-565-1043. 533 R
plattenpg@lakeland.edu
PLATUKUS, Graceann ..... 570-740-0355. 422 G
gplatukus@luzerne.edu
PLATZ, Matthew .... 808-974-7707. 136 A
mplatz@hawaii.edu
PLAW, Avery .... 508-999-8840. 229 A
aplaw@umassd.edu
PLAZA, Gloria .... 312-935-6625. 156 K
gplaza@robertmorris.edu
PLAZA, Laurie .... 610-526-6038. 417 H
lplaza@harcum.edu
PLAZA, Luis .... 212-749-2802. 330 A
lplaza@msmnyc.edu
PLEAS, Dorothy, J .... 630-637-5156. 154 F
djpleas@noctrl.edu
PLEAS-BAILEY, Dawn, E . 620-229-6336. 190 G
dawn.pleas-bailey@sckans.edu
PLEASANT, Kimberly ...... 216-987-5331. 378 D
kimberly.pleasant@tri-c.edu
PLEASANT, Klint .... 248-218-2058. 249 D
kpleasant@rc.edu
PLEASANT, Lori .... 850-973-9469. 109 H
pleasantl@nfcc.edu
PLEASANTS, David, J ..... 608-796-3913. 539 E
djpleasants@viterbo.edu
PLECENIK, Jeanne .... 352-588-8215. 112 D
jeanne.plecenik@saintleo.edu
PLEGER, Kimberly .... 253-680-7102. 516 L
kpleger@bates.ctc.edu
PLEGER, Tom .... 608-356-8351. 538 E
thomas.pleger@uwc.edu
PLEIS, Mitch .... 916-577-2200... 76 J
mpleis@jessup.edu
PLEMMONS, Donna .... 501-450-1351... 21 E
plemmons@hendrix.edu
PLEMMONS, Kim .... 704-403-1751. 352 J
kim.plemmons@carolinashealthcare.org
PLETCHER, Barbara .... 561-297-2145. 114 L
pletcher@fau.edu
PLETCHER, James .... 740-587-6469. 379 D
pletcher@denison.edu
PLETCHER, Jill, M .... 316-978-3435. 191 F
jill.pletcher@wichita.edu
PLETSCHER, Anthony, W 215-368-5000. 410 F
tpletscher@biblical.edu
PLEUSS, Carol, J .... 330-684-8928. 390 F
cjpleus@uakron.edu
PLEVER, Steve .... 828-251-6526. 368 C
splever@unca.edu
PLINER, Susan .... 315-781-3354. 326 C
pliner@hws.edu
PLINSKE, Kathleen, A ..... 407-582-4975. 118 M
kplinske@valenciacollege.edu
PLINSKI, Christie .... 503-491-7295. 404 E
christie.plinski@mhcc.edu
PLISKA, John .... 415-338-2037... 35 E
jpliska@sfsu.edu
PLISSEY, Bethany .... 802-635-1313. 501 D
bethany.plissey@jsc.edu
PLOEGER, SM, Bernard . 808-735-4741. 135 D
bploeger@chaminade.edu
PLONSKY, Christine, A .. 512-471-4780. 491 C
chris.plonsky@athletics.utexas.edu
PLOTKIN, David .... 503-699-6316. 404 C
dplotkin@marylhurst.edu
PLOTKIN, Helen, S .... 501-450-1225... 21 E
plotkin@hendrix.edu
PLOTKOWSKI, Paul .... 616-331-6260. 243 C
plotkowp@gvsu.edu
PLOTNER, Amy .... 315-312-3702. 344 A
amy.plotner@oswego.edu
PLOTNICK, Tamra .... 212-346-1244. 335 J
tplotnick@pace.edu
PLOTROWSKI, Cheryl ..... 317-789-8263. 165 E
cplotrowski@crossroads.edu
PLOTT, Richard, K .... 972-860-8325. 470 I
RichardPlott@dcccd.edu
PLOTTS, Debra .... 334-214-4866..... 2 H
debra.plotts@cv.edu
PLOTTS, Douglas, J .... 610-861-1560. 424 E
plottsd@moravian.edu
PLOTTS, John .... 972-721-5266. 488 F
jplotts@udallas.edu
PLOTTS, John, E .... 415-476-4148... 72 A
John.Plotts@ucsf.edu
PLOUF, Joe .... 425-602-3043. 516 K
PLOUFFE, Audrey .... 406-275-4969. 288 C
audrey_plouffe@skc.edu
PLOUFFE, Jeffrey .... 401-874-4198. 440 D
jeff@uri.edu
PLOURDE, Mike .... 937-512-2597. 388 O
mike.plourde@sinclair.edu
PLOWMAN, Donde .... 402-472-9500. 292 I
dplowman2@unl.edu
PLUCHUTA, Alexander .... 610-359-5057. 414 D
apluchut@dccc.edu
PLUEMER, Julie .... 608-822-2369. 541 C
jpluemer@swtc.edu
PLUHTA, Elizabeth, A ..... 206-934-5141. 523 A
elizabeth.pluhta@seattlecolleges.edu
PLUMB, Anne, M .... 901-572-2842. 453 B
anne.plumb@bchs.edu
PLUMB, Richard .... 310-338-2834... 53 E
rplumb@lmu.edu
PLUMLEE, Darrel .... 614-251-4548. 386 B
plumleed@ohiodominican.edu
PLUMLY, Wayne, L .... 229-245-3825. 134 B
lwplumly@valdosta.edu
PLUMMER, Dale, H .... 610-566-1776. 437 G
dplummer@williamson.edu
PLUMMER, Deborah, L .. 508-856-2179. 229 C
deborah.plummer@umassmed.edu
PLUMMER, Dianne .... 617-989-4036. 237 G
plummerd@wit.edu
PLUMMER, Donna, M .... 859-238-5308. 193 E
donna.plummer@centre.edu
PLUMMER, Eric .... 701-777-3491. 371 C
eric.plummer@und.edu
PLUMMER, James, D ..... 650-723-3938... 68 E
plummer@ee.stanford.edu
PLUMMER, James, D ..... 513-556-1299. 390 G
james.plummer@uc.edu
PLUMMER, Lisa .... 610-902-8549. 411 E
lisa.m.plummer@cabrini.edu
PLUMMER, Meredith ...... 760-366-5284... 42 B
mplummer@cmccd.edu
PLUMMER, Robert, M .... 423-439-4218. 459 C
plummerb@etsu.edu
PLUMMER, Troy, A .... 515-263-6050. 178 G
tplummer@grandview.edu
PLUMMER, Vince .... 701-671-2319. 372 E
vince.plummer@ndscs.edu
PLUNK, Kelly .... 870-584-4471... 24 F
kplunk@cccua.edu
PLUNKETT, Christine, A . 802-862-9616. 498 I
cplunkett@burlington.edu
PLUNKETT, Jackie .... 314-529-9398. 276 G
jplunkett@maryville.edu
PLUNKETT, James, C ..... 215-951-1500. 420 B
plunkett@lasalle.edu
PLUNKETT, Nancy .... 916-638-1616... 47 B
nancy_plunkett@heald.edu
PLUSCH, Kimberly .... 302-225-6256... 93 H
pluschk@gbc.edu
PLUTCHAK, Scott .... 205-934-5460..... 8 E
tscott@uab.edu
PLUTCHOK, Yisroel .... 718-438-5476. 350 H
PLUTE, David .... 307-754-6025. 543 G
David.Plute@northwestcollege.edu
PLUTINO-CALABRESE,
Stella .... 585-389-2465. 332 D
splutin2@naz.edu
PLYLER, Bill .... 704-216-3564. 363 D
bill.plyler@rccc.edu
PLYLER, Chris, P .... 803-777-7695. 447 G
plyler.chris@sc.edu
PLYMALE, Chad .... 585-567-9480. 326 F
chad.plymale@houghton.edu
PLYMPTON, Margaret, F 610-758-3178. 422 A
mfp3@lehigh.edu
POARCH, Mark .... 828-726-2214. 358 E
mpoarch@cccti.edu
POAT, Erica .... 618-634-3375. 158 M
ericap@shawneecc.edu
POATS, Lillian, B .... 713-313-7978. 485 F
poats_lb@tsu.edu
POBAT, Peter .... 718-368-5109. 318 E
ppobat@kbcc.cuny.edu
POBLENZ, Scott, B .... 978-468-7111. 227 A
spoblenz@gcts.edu
POBLETE, Juan .... 831-459-4792... 72 C
jpoblete@ucsc.edu
POCHARD, Brad .... 864-294-3406. 444 C
brad.pochard@furman.edu
POCHE, Paulette, M .... 985-549-5638. 208 C
ppoche@selu.edu
POCK, Arnyce .... 301-295-9945. 545 C
Arnyce.pock@usuhs.edu
PODANY, Jeremy .... 970-491-5709... 80 I
jeremy.podany@colostate.edu
PODELL, David .... 212-517-0520. 330 E
dpodell@mmm.edu
PODEMSKI, Richard, S .. 850-474-7713. 117 B
rpodemski@uwf.edu
PODESTÁ, Guido .... 608-262-9833. 536 D
gpodesta@wisc.edu
PODESZWA, Steve .... 860-434-5232... 90 F
spodeszwa@lymeacademy.edu
PODGORSKI, Richard, S 619-239-0391... 36 D
rpodgorski@cwsl.edu
PODIS, JoAnne .... 440-646-8107. 392 D
jpodis@ursuline.edu
PODOLSKY, Daniel, K .... 214-648-2508. 493 E
priscilla.alderman@utsouthwestern.edu
POE, D. Zizwe .... 484-365-7180. 422 D
dpoe@lincoln.edu
POE, JR., Donald .... 704-463-3041. 365 E
don.poe@fsmail.pfeiffer.edu
POE, Donnis .... 318-335-3944. 202 L
dpoe@ltc.edu
POE, Elmer .... 252-328-9066. 367 B
poee@ecu.edu
POE, Scott .... 304-424-8212. 530 E
scott.poe@wvup.edu
POEHLER, M, J .... 816-802-3393. 275 J
mpoehler@kcai.edu
POEHLERT, Edward .... 760-757-2121... 54 G
epoehlert@miracosta.edu
POEHLING, Andrea .... 608-265-4562. 536 D
apoehling@secfac.wisc.edu
POEHLS, Alice .... 202-885-2210... 94 F
apoehls@american.edu
POELKER, Scott .... 843-574-6197. 447 E
scott.poelker@tridenttech.edu
POELKING, Karen, L .... 216-373-5234. 385 G
kpoelking@ndc.edu
POELVOORDE, Tracy, L . 309-779-7708. 160 L
tracy.poelvoorde@trinitycollegeqc.edu

POERTNER, Gary .... 949-582-4840... 67 A
gpoertner@socccd.edu
POETTKER, Tricia .... 617-537-6843. 152 G
tapoettker@mckendree.edu
POETZL, Steven .... 541-485-1780. 405 B
stevepoetzl@newhope.edu
POFF, G. Elaine, N .... 954-262-7261. 109 K
poff@nova.edu
POGGENDORF,
Brenda, P .... 540-375-2270. 509 B
poggendorf@roanoke.edu
POGGENDORF,
Richard, J .... 540-375-2043. 509 B
rpoggendorf@roanoke.edu
POGUE, Frank, G .... 318-247-3811. 207 E
POGUE, Gregory .... 609-771-2201. 300 E
pogueg@tcnj.edu
POGUE, Gregory .... 609-771-3078. 300 E
pogueg@tcnj.edu
POGUE, Roslynn .... 318-342-5327. 208 E
pogue@ulm.edu
POHAS, Joanie .... 310-338-3068... 53 E
jpohas@lmu.edu
POHERO, Mary Jane ...... 973-596-3106. 303 G
mary.j.pohero@njit.edu
POHL, Charles, A .... 215-503-6988. 434 C
charles.pohl@jefferson.edu
POHL, Don .... 314-286-3653. 280 F
dpohl@ranken.edu
POHL, Henry, S .... 518-262-5919. 313 D
pohlh@mail.amc.edu
POHL, Laurie .... 617-353-9814. 224 D
lpohl@bu.edu
POHL, Sara .... 815-825-2086. 149 F
sarapohl@kishwaukeecollege.edu
POHLIG, Holly .... 407-646-2161. 111 Q
hpohlig@rollins.edu
POHLMAN, Nancy, A ..... 815-740-3496. 162 F
npohlman@stfrancis.edu
POIGER, Uta .... 617-373-5173. 235 F
POINDEXTER, Freddy, D 816-654-7910. 275 K
fpoindexter@kcumb.edu
POINDEXTER, Jeanne ..... 757-382-9900... 96 F
POINDEXTER-KERR,
Monica .... 410-276-0306. 218 D
mpoindexter@host.sdc.edu
POINTDEXTER,
Michael, C .... 916-558-2142... 53 D
poindem@scc.losrios.edu
POINTS, Dan .... 405-733-7359. 399 F
dpoints@rose.edu
POIRIER, J. Nicolas .... 315-568-3197. 333 C
npoirier@nycc.edu
POIRIER, Janet, L .... 603-641-7010. 297 G
jpoirier@anselm.edu
POIRIER, Mary, A .... 937-229-3333. 391 C
mpoirier1@udayton.edu
POIRRIER, Gail, P .... 337-482-6808. 208 D
poirrier@louisiana.edu
POISEL, Mark Allen .... 212-346-1200. 335 J
mpoisel@pace.edu
POITER, Emilia .... 410-532-5184. 217 E
epoiter@ndm.edu
POK, Shirley, M .... 209-667-3131... 35 B
smpok@csustan.edu
POKORA, Thomas .... 810-766-4103. 239 H
tom.pokora@baker.edu
POKORAK, Jeffrey .... 617-573-8000. 237 B
jpokorak@suffolk.edu
POKORNY, Anita, R .... 330-325-6476. 385 E
app@neomed.edu
POKORNY, Sarah .... 262-646-6506. 535 B
spokorny@nashotah.edu
POKOSH, Tricia .... 740-392-6868. 384 K
tricia.pokosh@mvnu.edu
POKOT, Elena .... 262-472-1001. 538 D
pokote@uww.edu
POKRAS, Martha .... 617-627-3389. 237 C
martha.pokras@tufts.edu
POL, Lou .... 402-554-2303. 293 A
lpol@unomaha.edu
POLAK, Benjamin .... 203-432-4444... 93 A
benjamin.polak@yale.edu
POLAND, D'Ann .... 361-698-2209. 471 G
dpoland@delmar.edu
POLAND, Jennifer .... 724-222-5330. 425 K
jpoland@penncommercial.edu
POLAND, Russell .... 615-327-6171. 456 E
rpoland@mmc.edu
POLANIECKI, Andrew ..... 574-239-8315. 166 N
apolaniecki@hcc-nd.edu
POLATAJKO, Mark, M .... 937-775-2002. 393 G
mark.polatajko@wright.edu
POLAZZI, Eileen, M .... 973-748-9000. 299 F
eileen_polazzi@bloomfield.edu
POLCYN, Laura, J .... 253-535-8225. 521 I
polcyn@plu.edu
POLCZYNSKI, Mimi .... 618-545-3363. 149 D
mpolczynski@kaskaskia.edu
POLD, Rein, A .... 814-393-2166. 428 C
rpold@clarion.edu

POLDING, John .... 973-720-2887. 308 I
poldingj@wpunj.edu
POLEMENI, Anthony .... 212-463-0400. 348 B
apolemeni@touro.edu
POLESHEK, Jeffrey, A ..... 941-359-7635. 111 O
jpoleshe@ringling.edu
POLETTI, Ed .... 215-972-2053. 426 Y
epoletti@pafa.edu
POLEY, Darren .... 610-519-6371. 436 F
POLICASTRO, Mike .... 422-472-7141. 460 D
mpolicastro@clevelandstatecc.edu
POLICH, Susan, M .... 540-985-4478. 506 G
SMPolich@jchs.edu
POLIN, Michael .... 941-782-5927. 420 E
mpolin@lecom.edu
POLINAK, Peter .... 315-781-3337. 326 C
polinak@hws.edu
POLING, Jana .... 503-255-0332. 404 F
jpoling@multnomah.edu
POLIRSTOK, Susan .... 908-737-3750. 302 F
polirsts@kean.edu
POLIS, Jennifer .... 516-299-5673. 329 D
jennifer.polis@liu.edu
POLISENO, Nick .... 212-226-7300. 336 G
nickpoliseno@pbcny.edu
POLISI, Joseph, W .... 212-799-5000. 328 B
POLITE-SOLOMON, Sue . 229-430-4658. 119 J
wendy.wilson@asurams.edu
POLIZZI, Dianne .... 617-243-2133. 227 K
dpolizzi@lasell.edu
POLK, Ali .... 831-476-9424... 44 K
marketing@fivebranches.edu
POLK, Alisa, L .... 540-636-2900. 503 L
finaid@christendom.edu
POLK, Coreylon .... 951-343-4374... 30 H
cpolk@calbaptist.edu
POLK, Fred .... 213-637-1360... 76 G
fpolk@westwood.edu
POLK, JD .... 515-271-1515. 177 H
james.polk@dmu.edu
POLK, Laura .... 301-934-7506. 214 D
laurap@csmd.edu
POLK, Molly .... 262-551-5702. 532 D
mpolk@carthage.edu
POLKABLA-BYERS, Joy .. 330-941-2242. 394 A
jlbyers@ysu.edu
POLKOWSKI, James, R .. 734-462-4400. 250 A
jpolkows@schoolcraft.edu
POLL, Michael .... 724-552-4372. 433 E
mpoll@setonhill.edu
POLLACK, Ann, M .... 310-794-0387... 71 C
apollack@resadmin.ucla.edu
POLLACK, Dianne .... 802-224-3000. 501 A
dianne.pollak@vsc.edu
POLLACK, Gary .... 509-335-4750. 525 A
gary.pollack@wsu.edu
POLLACK, Martha, E .... 734-764-9292. 251 C
pollackm@umich.edu
POLLACK, Meyer .... 323-731-2383... 57 I
pollack@psuca.edu
POLLACK, Pamela .... 718-951-3118. 317 C
pamela@brooklyn.cuny.edu
POLLACK, Sean .... 503-594-3002. 402 F
POLLAK, Georgia, B .... 212-960-5285. 351 M
gpollak@yu.edu
POLLARD, Al .... 254-299-8669. 476 D
apollard@mclennan.edu
POLLARD, III, Alton, B .. 202-806-0500... 95 G
abpollard@howard.edu
POLLARD, Charles .... 479-524-7200... 21 G
cpollard@jbu.edu
POLLARD, Cindy .... 503-517-1026. 408 H
cpollard@warnerpacific.edu
POLLARD, DeRionne, P .. 240-567-5264. 216 F
president@montgomerycollege.edu
POLLARD, Jamie, B .... 515-294-0123. 175 H
jbp@iastate.edu
POLLARD, Janet, L .... 361-593-2439. 484 A
janet.pollard@tamuk.edu
POLLARD, Leslie .... 256-726-7000..... 6 B
lpollard@oakwood.edu
POLLARD, Mary Lee .... 518-464-8500. 324 B
mpollard@excelsior.edu
POLLARD, Natalie, M ...... 609-896-5340. 305 D
pollardn@rider.edu
POLLARD, Pamela .... 914-606-6851. 350 F
pamela.pollard@sunywcc.edu
POLLARD, Prudence, L .. 256-726-7734..... 6 B
ppollard@oakwood.edu
POLLARD, Sherry .... 573-882-8420. 283 C
pollards@missouri.edu
POLLARD, Simcha .... 800-375-9878... 70 A
stephen.pollard@trident.edu
POLLARD, Thomas, D ..... 203-432-3565... 93 A
thomas.pollard@yale.edu
POLLARD-BURNS,
Cheryl .... 336-334-7946. 367 E
cdpollar@ncat.edu
POLLASTRINI, Laura ...... 847-233-7700. 155 B
lpollastrini@nc.edu

POLLENZ, Hal .... 212-678-8000. 328 A
hapollenz@jtsa.edu
POLLERT, Tim .... 708-596-2000. 159 C
tpollert@ssc.edu
POLLEY, Debra Lee .... 518-454-2066. 321 A
polleyd@strose.edu
POLLION, Sean .... 231-348-6621. 247 H
spollion@ncmich.edu
POLLITZ, John, H .... 715-836-3715. 536 E
pollitjh@uwec.edu
POLLMAN, Janeen .... 701-228-5458. 372 C
bookcell@dakotacollege.edu
POLLOCK, Charles, R ..... 413-782-1233. 238 A
cpollock@wne.edu
POLLOCK, Holly, L .... 606-783-2000. 198 A
h.pollock@moreheadstate.edu
POLLOCK, Jill .... 303-860-5600... 85 K
jill.pollock@cu.edu
POLLOCK, Judy .... 972-708-7547. 472 L
judy_pollock@gial.edu
POLLOCK, Kevin, A .... 810-989-5545. 249 H
kapollock@sc4.edu
POLLOCK, Shannon .... 770-975-4000. 122 I
POLMANTEER,
Kathryn, N .... 606-783-2040. 198 A
k.polmanteer@moreheadstate.edu
POLONSKY, Kenneth .... 773-702-9306. 161 B
polonsky@bsd.uchicago.edu
POLSBY, Daniel, D .... 703-993-8087. 505 C
polsby@gmu.edu
POLSDOFER, Duane .... 641-585-8121. 183 D
polsdofed@waldorf.edu
POLSKY, Andrew .... 212-772-5195. 318 C
apolsky@hunter.cuny.edu
POLSKY, John .... 212-686-9244. 313 G
POLSON, Mary, E .... 717-245-1835. 414 H
polsonm@dickinson.edu
POLSON, William Jerry .. 580-745-2212. 399 J
jpolson@se.edu
POLTERSDORF, Todd ..... 973-300-2253. 307 F
tpoltersdorf@sussex.edu
POLTORAK, Jeff .... 310-243-3787... 33 B
jpoltorak@csudh.edu
POLTORAK, Jeff .... 310-243-2182... 33 B
jpoltorak@csudh.edu
POLYCHRONIS, Paul, D . 660-543-4060. 283 A
ppolychr@ucmo.edu
POMAKOY, Keith .... 864-592-4634. 447 A
pomakoyk@sccsc.edu
POMALES, Reinaldo .... 787-758-2525. 554 F
reinaldo.pomales@upr.edu
POMBO, Rachel .... 518-292-1915. 338 C
pombor@sage.edu
POMERENK, Julia .... 509-335-5511. 525 A
pomerenk@wsu.edu
POMEROY, Jordana .... 225-389-7200. 204 O
jpomeroy@lsu.edu
POMFREY, Elaine .... 641-472-7000. 180 N
epomfrey@mum.edu
POMMERER, Ron .... 701-845-7700. 372 A
ron.pommerer@vcsu.edu
POMPER, Gwen, E .... 303-492-8223... 85 L
gwen.pomper@colorado.edu
POMPEY, JR., Robert ..... 336-334-7587. 367 E
rpompey@ncat.edu
POMPLUN, Joann .... 605-626-2283. 451 I
jpomplun@northern.edu
PONCE, Christy .... 915-831-6614. 472 B
cponce29@epcc.edu
PONCE DE LEON,
Monica .... 734-764-1315. 251 C
mpdl@umich.edu
PONCELET, Jolene .... 507-453-2722. 259 E
jponcelet@southeastmn.edu
PONCELET, Jolene .... 507-453-2662. 259 E
jponcelet@southeastmn.edu
POND, Eugene, W .... 214 887-5201. 471 F
epond@dts.edu
POND, Lallon .... 540-887-7274. 507 A
lpond@mbc.edu
PONDER, Anne .... 828-251-6500. 368 C
chanoffi@unca.edu
PONDER, Anthony .... 937-512-2918. 388 O
anthony.ponder@sinclair.edu
PONDER, Leslee .... 940-397-4350. 476 H
leslee.ponder@mwsu.edu
PONDER, Nathan .... 318-473-6591. 205 A
nponder@lsua.edu
PONESSE, Matthew .... 614-251-4500. 386 B
ponessem@ohiodominican.edu
PONKO, Bill .... 352-365-3502. 108 S
ponkow@lssc.edu
PONREMY, Sue .... 708-524-6965. 144 C
sponremy@dom.edu
PONS, Jose, L .... 787-844-8181. 555 A
jose.pons@upr.edu
PONSETTO, Jean .... 773-325-7503. 143 H
jlentipo@depaul.edu
PONSFORD, Barbara ...... 870-230-5377... 21 D
ponsfob@hsu.edu

PONTEP, Tanya .... 818-654-1721... 59 E
tpontep@pgi.edu
PONTI, Marilyn, K .... 509-527-5986. 525 E
pontimk@whitman.edu
PONTICELLI, Jan .... 530-741-6795... 77 M
jpontice@yccd.edu
PONTINEN, Jodi .... 218-749-7753. 259 B
j.pontinen@mr.mnscu.edu
PONTIUS, JR., John, M . 518-608-8384. 324 B
jpontius@excelsior.edu
PONTO, Patricia, A .... 269-337-7191. 244 K
Pat.Ponto@kzoo.edu
PONTON, Cynthia, L ...... 434-381-6136. 510 F
cponton@sbc.edu
PONTON, Dennis, K .... 716-878-5903. 343 A
pontondk@buffalostate.edu
PONTURO, Joseph .... 973-328-5500. 300 G
jponturo@ccm.edu
PONZI, Melody .... 315-364-3208. 350 E
mponzi@wells.edu
POOL, Deborah, A .... 845-938-6947. 545 I
8drm@usma.edu
POOL, Madonna .... 301-387-3743. 214 I
madonna.pool@garrettcollege.edu
POOL, Robert .... 585-567-9220. 326 F
robert.pool@houghton.edu
POOLE, Bill .... 817-272-3571. 491 B
bpoole@uta.edu
POOLE, Cary .... 817-531-4872. 488 A
cpoole@txwes.edu
POOLE, David .... 951-343-4409... 30 H
dpoole@calbaptist.edu
POOLE, Dorothy .... 408-924-1177... 36 A
dorothy.poole@sjsu.edu
POOLE, John .... 434-832-7615. 512 A
poolej@cvcc.vccs.edu
POOLE, Lana .... 573-875-7237. 272 G
llpoole@ccis.edu
POOLE, Mary Ellen .... 415-503-6251... 62 H
abeckett@sfcm.edu
POOLE, Myra .... 252-862-1267. 363 A
poolem@roanokechowan.edu
POOLE, Paula .... 717-560-8257. 421 A
ppoole@lbc.edu
POOLE, Penny .... 806-291-3414. 494 F
poolep@wbu.edu
POOLE, Philip .... 205-726-2823..... 6 F
ppoole@samford.edu
POOLE, Robert, S .... 615-327-6273. 456 E
rpoole@mmc.edu
POOLE, Russell .... 303-724-0425... 86 A
russell.poole@ucdenver.edu
POOLE, Scott .... 865-974-5267. 463 C
scott.poole@utk.edu
POOLE, Stan .... 870-245-5196... 22 D
pooles@obu.edu
POOLE, Thomas, G .... 814-865-2507. 426 A
tgp1@psu.edu
POOLE, Warren, E .... 252-335-3670. 367 C
wepoole@mail.ecsu.edu
POOLER, Traci, M .... 270-384-8100. 197 D
poolert@lindsey.edu
POOLER, III, Willis .... 270-384-8070. 197 D
poolerw@lindsey.edu
POOLEY, Allison .... 602-943-2311... 19 C
Allison.Pooley@West.edu
POOLMAN, Leslie, J ...... 717-245-1269. 414 H
poolman@dickinson.edu
POON, Christine, A .... 614-292-2666. 386 E
poon.36@osu.edu
POON, Percy .... 702-895-3017. 294 I
percy.poon@unlv.edu
POOR, H. Vincent .... 609-258-1816. 304 F
poor@princeton.edu
POOR, Joan .... 660-785-4105. 282 L
pjpoor@truman.edu
POORANDI, Masood ...... 386-481-2340... 99 C
poorandm@cookman.edu
POORE, Scott .... 276-944-6890. 504 H
pooresc@ehc.edu
POORE, Sharon .... 859-442-1175. 195 B
sharon.poore@kctcs.edu
POORMAN, Brad .... 325-793-4910. 476 E
bpoorman@mcm.edu
POORMAN, Julie .... 252-328-6373. 367 B
poormanj@ecu.edu
POORMAN, CSC,
Mark, L .... 503-943-7207. 408 F
poorman@up.edu
POOS, Lawrence, R .... 202-319-5115... 94 G
poos@cua.edu
POOVEY, Gena, E .... 864-488-4509. 444 L
gpoovey@limestone.edu
POOVEY, Sara .... 256-439-6833..... 3 M
sbrenizer@gadsdenstate.edu
POPA, Hope .... 312-662-4011. 139 F
hpopa@adler.edu
POPE, Alexis .... 931-372-3888. 460 A
apope@tntech.edu
POPE, Bonnie, G .... 336-734-7412. 360 E
bpope@forsythtech.edu

POPE, Christina .... 315-464-4582. 342 E
popec@upstate.edu
POPE, Darryl .... 847-543-2477. 143 A
dpope1@clcillinois.edu
POPE, Edward .... 843-953-8235. 443 A
popeeb@cofc.edu
POPE, Eric .... 248-204-2210. 245 I
epope@ltu.edu
POPE, Iris .... 760-872-2000... 42 E
buck@deepsprings.edu
POPE, Jasmine .... 479-619-2673... 22 C
jpope5@nwacc.edu
POPE, Jennifer .... 312-662-4142. 139 F
jpope@adler.edu
POPE, John .... 770-412-4034. 132 B
jpope@sctech.edu
POPE, Kiesha, L .... 804-523-5137. 512 F
kpope@reynolds.edu
POPE, Myron .... 405-974-5370. 400 K
mpope5@uco.edu
POPE, Sharon .... 570-372-4108. 433 H
popes@susqu.edu
POPE, Tom .... 606-589-3023. 196 F
tom.pope@kctcs.edu
POPE-DAVIS, Donald, B . 312-362-7599. 143 H
DPD@depaul.edu
POPE-DAVIS, Donald, B . 574-631-8052. 174 A
pope-davis.1@nd.edu
POPER, James .... 562-463-3441... 60 I
JPoper@riohondo.edu
POPHAM, Heidi .... 706-295-6598. 125 F
hpopham@gntc.edu
POPIELSKI, Kathy .... 716-827-4343. 348 G
popielskik@trocaire.edu
POPIELSKI, Tina .... 603-448-2445. 297 A
tpopielski@lebanoncollege.edu
POPIOLEK, Marcus .... 313-664-7665. 241 C
mpopiolek@collegeforcreativestudies.edu
POPKIN, Eric .... 719-389-6657... 79 D
epopkin@coloradocollege.edu
POPKO, John, P .... 206-296-6222. 523 E
jpopko@seattleu.edu
POPKO, Susan .... 408-554-6940... 64 M
spopko@scu.edu
POPLAWSKI, Lisa .... 509-359-4555. 519 C
lpoplawski@ewu.edu
POPLIN GOSETTI,
Penny .... 419-530-5402. 392 B
penny.poplin.gosetti@utoledo.edu
POPOLI, John, N .... 847-574-5210. 150 C
jpopoli@lfgsm.edu
POPOLOSKI, Tanya .... 603-623-0313. 297 E
tpopoloski@nhia.edu
POPOOLA, Joseph, K ..... 803-934-3290. 445 F
jpopoola@morris.edu
POPOVICH, Donna, B ..... 813-253-6237. 118 L
dpopovich@ut.edu
POPOVICH, Joseph .... 443-885-3372. 217 A
joseph.popovich@morgan.edu
POPOVICS, Alexander, J 518-629-7307. 326 G
a.popovics@hvcc.edu
POPP, Connie .... 414-382-6352. 531 I
connie.popp@alverno.edu
POPP, Jodi .... 920-686-6127. 536 A
jodi.popp@sl.edu
POPP, Melissa, D .... 636-584-6703. 273 M
garrism@eastcentral.edu
POPP, William, C .... 770-720-5568. 130 G
wcp@reinhardt.edu
POPPE, Jan, R .... 989-964-2058. 249 G
jrpoppe@svsu.edu
POPPE, Kenneth .... 860-832-1633... 87 K
poppe@ccsu.edu
POPPO, Kristin .... 617-873-0232. 224 G
Kristin.Poppo@cambridgecollege.edu
POPPRE, Beth .... 480-219-6026. 271 A
bpoppre@atsu.edu
PORAT, Moshe .... 215-204-1836. 433 K
moshe.porat@temple.edu
PORATH, Wiona .... 517-264-7613. 250 B
wporath@sienaheights.edu
PORCARELLO, Irene .... 713-718-7071. 473 C
irene.porcarello@hccs.edu
PORCH, Linda .... 215-965-4037. 424 D
lporch@moore.edu
PORCHE, Demetrius .... 504-568-4106. 205 C
dporch@lsuhsc.edu
PORCHE, JR., Francis .... 337-421-6916. 204 E
francis.porche@sowela.edu
PORCHER, Coleen .... 973-877-3498. 301 H
cporcher@essex.edu
PORETTE, Joanne .... 845-848-7813. 322 G
joanne.porette@dc.edu
PORFIDO, Nancy .... 609-343-5095. 299 A
porfido@atlantic.edu
PORNKITTICHOTCHAROEN,
Gib .... 617-541-5399. 232 G
gibp@rcc.mass.edu
PORTE, Meaghen .... 503-297-5544. 405 D
mporte@ocac.edu
PORTELA, Stanley .... 787-752-4540. 554 B
stanley.portela@upr.edu
PORTELA IRIGOYEN,
Celso, E .... 787-725-8120. 548 O
cportela@centro.eap.edu
PORTELLEZ, Humberto ... 207-834-8646. 212 E
humberto.portellez@maine.edu
PORTER, Aaron, K .... 423-775-7574. 453 E
aaron.porter@bryan.edu
PORTER, Adam .... 217-245-3010. 146 F
aporter@mail.ic.edu
PORTER, Andrea .... 806-651-2037. 484 D
aporter@wtamu.edu
PORTER, Andrew, C .... 215-898-7014. 435 B
andyp@gse.upenn.edu
PORTER, Ava, G .... 540-985-8531. 506 G
agporter@jchs.edu
PORTER, Barbara, A .... 540-831-5408. 508 C
bporter@radford.edu
PORTER, Barbara, A .... 202-994-3121... 95 D
porter@gwu.edu
PORTER, Bonisha .... 229-430-4741. 119 J
bonisha.porter@asurams.edu
PORTER, Brandi .... 540-365-4428. 504 L
bporter@ferrum.edu
PORTER, Brenda, I .... 607-871-2186. 313 E
porterbi@alfred.edu
PORTER, Charles .... 206-296-4490. 523 E
porterc@seattleu.edu
PORTER, Chong, U .... 916-734-9402... 70 J
chong.porter@ucdmc.ucdavis.edu
PORTER, Christine, M .... 540-654-1058. 510 J
cjporter@umw.edu
PORTER, Clifford .... 229-430-4660. 119 J
clifford.porter@asurams.edu
PORTER, Clifton .... 413-755-4026. 233 A
ceporter@stcc.edu
PORTER, Clyde .... 972-860-7760. 470 F
cporter@dcccd.edu
PORTER, Curtis, R .... 505-277-2611. 312 F
cporter@unm.edu
PORTER, Cyndi .... 916-631-8108... 32 C
PORTER, David .... 731-661-5343. 462 F
dporter@uu.edu
PORTER, David, S .... 401-874-2370. 440 D
david.porter@uri.edu
PORTER, DeeDee .... 619-388-3976... 62 D
dporter@sdccd.edu
PORTER, Diane .... 719-549-3303... 84 G
diane.porter@pueblocc.edu
PORTER, Fonda .... 919-497-3205. 356 E
fporter@louisburg.edu
PORTER, Frank .... 937-376-6649. 376 E
fporter@centralstate.edu
PORTER, Gerald .... 417-823-3415. 281 M
gporter@forest.edu
PORTER, Hugh .... 503-777-7573. 407 E
hugh.porter@reed.edu
PORTER,
J. Davidson (Dusty) ..... 410-225-2422. 216 C
dporter@mica.edu
PORTER, Jeff .... 276-656-0309. 513 D
jporter@patrickhenry.edu
PORTER, Jennifer .... 813-882-0100... 96 F
PORTER, Jennifer, C .... 617-735-9772. 226 B
porterj@emmanuel.edu
PORTER, John, B .... 570-961-4772. 423 B
porter@marywood.edu
PORTER, Jon, K .... 802-656-0123. 500 F
jon.porter@uvm.edu
PORTER, Joseph, B .... 518-608-8370. 324 B
jporter@excelsior.edu
PORTER, Katherine .... 360-438-4312. 522 G
kporter@stmartin.edu
PORTER, Kim .... 314-763-6013. 281 E
kporter54@stlcc.edu
PORTER, Lauren .... 512-476-2772. 466 J
admissions@austingrad.edu
PORTER, Lisa .... 207-947-4591. 209 G
bookstore@bealcollege.edu
PORTER, II, Louis .... 715-425-3528. 537 E
louis.porter@uwrf.edu
PORTER, Mario .... 210-341-1366. 477 L
mporter@ost.edu
PORTER, Mark, J .... 401-863-3870. 438 J
mark_porter@brown.edu
PORTER, Mary Kay .... 301-654-7267. 218 C
PORTER, Michael .... 651-962-4376. 265 C
mporter@stthomas.edu
PORTER, Monica .... 313-583-6445. 251 D
dmporte@umich.edu
PORTER, Narda .... 276-328-0116. 511 C
nnb3h@uvawise.edu
PORTER, Rebecca .... 701-858-3126. 371 F
rebecca.porter@minotstateu.edu
PORTER, Rebecca, E .... 317-274-0401. 168 D
rporter@iupui.edu
PORTER, Sara .... 859-858-3511. 192 B
sara.porter@asbury.edu
PORTER, Sharon .... 864-587-4272. 447 B
portersd@smcsc.edu
PORTER, Steve .... 620-665-3552. 187 F
porters@hutchcc.edu
PORTER, Susie .... 801-581-8094. 496 Q
s.porter@utah.edu
PORTER, Timothy .... 702-895-2058. 294 I
tim.porter@unlv.edu
PORTER, Tina .... 773-256-3000. 152 H
tporter@meadville.edu
PORTER, Tracy .... 863-297-3743. 110 H
tporter@polk.edu
PORTER, Vincent .... 210-829-2770. 490 A
porterv@uiwtx.edu
PORTER, Wilma, B .... 248-341-2182. 248 D
wbporter@oaklandcc.edu
PORTERFIELD, Daniel, R 717-291-3911. 416 J
daniel.porterfield@fandm.edu
PORTERFIELD, Kent .... 314-977-2226. 281 I
kporter6@slu.edu
PORTERFIELD, Kim .... 512-245-9645. 487 C
kp10@txstate.edu
PORTERFIELD, Robyn, J 540-831-6331. 508 C
rjporterf@radford.edu
PORTERVINT, Bernice .... 360-676-2772. 521 D
bportervint@nwic.edu
PORTIER, Bonnie .... 301-447-5288. 217 B
bportier@msmary.edu
PORTILLO, Carlos .... 323-343-3440... 34 A
carlos.portillo@cslanet.calstatela.edu
PORTILLO, Cesar .... 909-537-5138... 34 E
cportillo@csusb.edu
PORTIS-TURNER, Erica .. 334-285-5177..... 4 J
erica.turner@istc.edu
PORTLOCK, Jeremy .... 785-594-8415. 184 C
jeremy.portlock@bakerU.edu
PORTNEY, Leslie .... 617-726-8009. 234 B
lportney@mghihp.edu
PORTNOY, Robert, N ...... 402-472-7450. 292 I
rportnoy1@unl.edu
PORTO, Enrico, A .... 304-367-4111. 529 F
rick.porto@fairmontstate.edu
PORTUGAL, Alberto .... 941-487-4360. 115 D
portugal@ncf.edu
PORTWINE, Ronald, E .... 989-964-2064. 249 G
report@svsu.edu
PORTWOOD, Ryan .... 402-354-7848. 291 B
ryan.portwood@methodistcollege.edu
PORTZ, Margaret, A .... 610-758-5794. 422 A
mak5@lehigh.edu
POSAMENTIER, Alfred .... 914-674-7447. 330 J
aposamentier@mercy.edu
POSEJPAL, Gigi .... 312-369-7458. 143 D
gposejpal@colum.edu
POSER, Susan .... 402-472-2161. 292 I
sposer1@unl.edu
POSEY, James, T .... 843-953-5708. 443 A
poseyjt@cofc.edu
POSEY, Jeff .... 601-643-8411. 266 F
jeff.posey@colin.edu
POSEY, Kathy .... 617-928-4003. 234 E
kposey@mountida.edu
POSEY, Monica .... 513-569-1511. 376 L
monica.posey@cincinnatistate.edu
POSHARD, Glenn .... 618-536-3471. 159 F
poshard@siu.edu
POSHEK, Joe .... 714-432-5536... 39 K
jposhek@occ.cccd.edu
POSILLICO, Joseph, J .... 973-618-3500. 300 A
jposillico@caldwell.edu
POSING, Mary .... 815-802-8202. 149 C
mposing@kcc.edu
POSKANZER, JR.,
Steven, G .... 507-222-4305. 254 D
president@carleton.edu
POSLER, Brian .... 785-594-8312. 184 C
brian.posler@bakeru.edu
POSLUSNY, Matthew ...... 919-760-8514. 356 G
mposlusny@meredith.edu
POSMAN, Jerald .... 212-650-7401. 317 D
jposman@ccny.cuny.edu
POSNER, Kenneth .... 352-588-8992. 112 D
kenneth.posner@saintleo.edu
POSNER, Marc .... 714-484-7006... 56 E
mposner@cypresscollege.edu
POSNER, Mark .... 651-638-6383. 253 K
m-posner@bethel.edu
POSNER, Sylvia .... 212-824-2211. 325 G
sposner@huc.edu
POSS, Joe .... 509-313-6215. 520 A
poss@gonzaga.edu
POSSEHL, DeAnn, L .... 262-595-2454. 537 C
deann.possehl@uwp.edu
POST, Carole .... 212-431-2894. 333 I
Carole.Post@nyls.edu
POST, Christine .... 304-424-8358. 530 E
christine.post@wvup.edu
POST, Jack .... 215-717-6080. 435 A
jpost@uarts.edu
POST, Julie .... 770-962-7580. 127 D
jpost@gwinnetttech.edu
POST, Michael .... 301-447-5214. 217 B
post@msmary.edu
POST, Nichole .... 607-729-1581. 322 F
npost@davisny.edu
POST, Regina .... 937-327-6404. 393 E
rpost@wittenberg.edu
POST, Robert .... 610-361-5233. 424 I
postr@neumann.edu
POST, Robert, C .... 203-432-1660... 93 A
robert.post@yale.edu
POST, Scott .... 870-338-6474... 24 G
POST-LUNDQUIST, Beth 518-580-5750. 341 A
bpostlun@skidmore.edu
POSTEMA, Miles, J .... 231-591-3894. 242 F
postemam@ferris.edu
POSTER, Michael, C .... 563-333-6032. 182 B
PosterMichaelC@sau.edu
POSTLETHWAITE,
Martha .... 651-255-6156. 264 C
mpostlethwaite@unitedseminary.edu
POSTLEWAIT, Cheryl ...... 913-288-7230. 187 L
cpostlewait@kckcc.edu
POSTLEWATE, Rusty .... 410-455-3260. 219 D
rpost@umbc.edu
POSTMA, Jill .... 616-988-1000. 241 D
POSTMA, Kurt .... 616-538-2330. 243 A
kpostma@gbcol.edu
POSTMA, Laura .... 906-248-8420. 240 J
lpostma@bmcc.edu
POSTON, Fred .... 517-884-7004. 246 H
poston@msu.edu
POSTON, Fulton .... 386-481-2970... 99 C
postonf@cookman.edu
POSTON, Kyle .... 619-574-6909... 57 E
kposton@pacificcollege.edu
POSTON, Linda, K .... 845-675-4434. 335 C
linda.poston@nyack.edu
POSTON, Michael, J .... 336-316-2178. 355 A
mposton@guilford.edu
POSTON, Muriel .... 909-621-8217... 59 G
dean_faculty@pitzer.edu
POSTON, R. Stephen ...... 704-233-8194. 370 G
poston@wingate.edu
POSTUPACK,
Mary Frances .... 570-422-7966. 428 D
mpostupack@po-box.esu.edu
POTASH, David .... 773-481-8175. 142 F
dpotash@ccc.edu
POTEAT, Tisha, L .... 864-488-4618. 444 L
tthompson@limestone.edu
POTEET, Tanya, J .... 614-236-6408. 375 H
tpoteet@capital.edu
POTEETE-YOUNG,
Lanette .... 847-628-1097. 149 B
lpoteete-young@judsonu.edu
POTEMPA, John, S .... 708-656-8000. 153 H
john.potempa@morton.edu
POTEMPA, Kathleen, M .. 734-764-7185. 251 C
potempa@umich.edu
POTESTIO, DenaSue .... 620-341-5440. 186 D
dpotesti@emporia.edu
POTH, Jean, C .... 978-556-3624. 232 E
jpoth@necc.mass.edu
POTOCZAK, Mel .... 978-762-4000. 232 D
POTOKA, Lisa .... 913-758-6120. 191 B
Lisa.Potoka@stmary.edu
POTRAFKA, Mark .... 573-341-4209. 284 A
markp@mst.edu
POTTEIGER, Jeffrey .... 616-331-7207. 243 C
potteigj@gvsu.edu
POTTER, Adam .... 207-326-4771. 211 D
adam.potter@mma.edu
POTTER, Alan .... 800-672-3060. 366 F
POTTER, Barbara .... 618-252-5400. 159 E
barb.potter@sic.edu
POTTER, Cheryl, J .... 704-406-4269. 354 C
cpotter@gardner-webb.edu
POTTER, Cindy .... 817-531-4821. 488 A
cpotter@txwes.edu
POTTER, Douglas, E .... 704-847-5600. 366 J
dpotter@ses.edu
POTTER, III, Earl, H .... 320-308-2122. 261 B
president@stcloudstate.edu
POTTER, Gia .... 606-218-5211. 200 F
giapotter@upike.edu
POTTER, James .... 406-265-3727. 287 D
potterj@msun.edu
POTTER, Jay .... 704-330-4409. 359 C
jay.potter@cpcc.edu
POTTER, Jeff .... 405-878-5621. 399 G
jdpotter@stgregorys.edu
POTTER, Jennifer, M .... 609-896-5009. 305 D
jpotter@rider.edu
POTTER, John .... 617-827-5962. 228 G
john.potter@umb.edu
POTTER, John .... 847-628-2015. 149 B
jpotter@judsonu.edu
POTTER, John, M .... 937-766-7855. 375 K
potterj@cedarville.edu
POTTER, Kay, C .... 205-853-1200..... 5 B
kpotter@jeffstateonline.com
POTTER, Laura, L .... 615-353-3217. 461 B
laura.potter@nscc.edu

POTTER, Lawrence ... 601-979-7036. 267 E lawrence.t.potter@jsums.edu
POTTER, Mike ... 425-739-8387. 520 K mike.potter@lwtech.edu
POTTER, Quentin, J ... 440-365-5222. 383 B
POTTER, Rachel ... 540-887-7134. 507 A rpotter@mbc.edu
POTTER, Robert, A ... 401-254-3498. 440 B bobpotter@rwu.edu
POTTER, Sarah ... 802-865-5445. 499 A potter@champlain.edu
POTTER, Sarah ... 207-786-6120. 209 F spotter@bates.edu
POTTER, Scott ... 740-389-4636. 383 F potters@mtc.edu
POTTER, Shawn ... 504-247-1237. 207 C spotter@tulane.edu
POTTER, Stephen, L ... 336-841-9125. 355 C spotter@highpoint.edu
POTTER, Tammy ... 270-534-3278. 196 G tammy.potter@kctcs.edu
POTTER, Terri, L ... 603-535-2376. 298 G tpotter@plymouth.edu
POTTER, Theresa, M ... 540-365-4201. 504 L tpotter@ferrum.edu
POTTER, Thomas, L ... 207-255-1221. 212 F potter@maine.edu
POTTER, William ... 985-732-6640. 203 D
POTTER, William ... 231-591-2428. 242 F potterw@ferris.edu
POTTER, William ... 231-591-2428. 242 F william_potter@ferris.edu
POTTER, William, G ... 706-542-0621. 133 C wpotter@uga.edu
POTTERVELD, Riess ... 510-849-8223... 57 H rpotterveld@psr.edu
POTTERVELD, Riess ... 510-649-2410... 46 B president@gtu.edu
POTTICK, Kathleen, J ... 732-932-7520. 306 B pottick@ssw.rutgers.edu
POTTORFF, Frank ... 319-656-2447. 182 D
POTTORFF, JR., James, P ... 785-864-3276. 190 L jpottorff@ku.edu
POTTORFF, Linda ... 605-721-5228. 450 G lpottorff@national.edu
POTTS, Carla ... 413-755-4812. 233 A cjpotts@stcc.edu
POTTS, Colin ... 404-894-5551. 125 D colin.potts@cc.gatech.edu
POTTS, David, E ... 334-683-5102... 5 C dpotts@judson.edu
POTTS, Edward ... 215-871-6500. 430 D edpotts@com.edu
POTTS, Flo, E ... 918-595-7224. 400 E flo.potts@tulsacc.edu
POTTS, Glenn, T ... 715-425-3335. 537 E glenn.t.potts@uwrf.edu
POTTS, Joe, D ... 765-494-5361. 171 M jdpotts@purdue.edu
POTTS, Jonathan ... 412-397-5291. 431 I potts@rmu.edu
POTTS, Lawrence, C ... 507-933-7529. 255 I cpotts@gustavus.edu
POTTS, Marcia ... 828-726-2471. 358 E mpotts@cccti.edu
POTTS, Nacole ... 828-884-8249. 352 I pottsna@brevard.edu
POTTS, Steven ... 310-506-4000... 58 H steve.potts@pepperdine.edu
POTTS, Teresa ... 912-443-5730. 131 D tpotts@savannahtech.edu
POTTS-BELL, Martha ... 319-385-6488. 179 K martha.potts-bell@iwc.edu
POTVIN, David ... 601-968-5904. 266 A dpotvin@belhaven.edu
POTVIN, Martha ... 406-994-4371. 287 B mpotvin@montana.edu
POTVIN, Terrence ... 313-845-9760. 243 H tpotvin@hfcc.edu
POTVIN-GIORDANO, Claudine ... 518-629-7451. 326 G c.potvingiordano@hvcc.edu
POU, Patricia ... 618-931-0600. 160 A patricia.pou@swic.edu
POUDRIER-AARONSON, Lucinda ... 508-999-8145. 229 A laaronson@umassd.edu
POUGET, Nicole ... 307-855-2332. 542 Y npouget@cwc.edu
POULIN, Eric ... 413-775-1834. 231 E pouline@gcc.mass.edu
POULIOS, Nanette ... 248-689-8282. 251 I npoulios@walshcollege.edu
POULLARD, Jonathan ... 510-642-6770... 70 I poullard@berkeley.edu
POULTER, Patricia, S ... 770-423-6742. 127 N ppoulter@kennesaw.edu
POUND, Lee Eliff ... 417-625-9355. 278 D pound-l@mssu.edu
POUNDER, Diana, G ... 501-450-3175... 25 H dianap@uca.edu
POUNDS, Dennis, J ... 304-462-4125. 529 G dennis.pounds@glenville.edu
POURCIAU, Lester ... 225-771-2680. 206 J lester_pourciau@subr.edu
POURE, Charles ... 480-726-4140... 14 J charles.poure@cgc.edu
POUREETEZADI, Sasan ... 480-461-7840... 15 A sasan.poureetezadi@mesacc.edu
POURHAMIDI, Jaleh ... 702-968-1652. 295 E jpourhamidi@roseman.edu
POURIER, Marilyn ... 605-455-6045. 450 I mpourier@olc.edu
POURIET-DE LA CRUZ, Zacarias ... 787-480-2470. 548 G zpoueriet@sanjuancapital.com
POUSSON, Mark ... 314-719-3627. 274 E mpousson@fontbonne.edu
POVENTUD, Irem ... 787-841-2000. 552 B ipoventud@pucpr.edu
POVLACK, Maria ... 716-827-2418. 348 G povlackm@trocaire.edu
POWAZEK, Jack ... 310-825-7286... 71 C powazek@facnet.ucla.edu
POWAZEK, Jack, J ... 310-825-2411... 71 C powazek@ucla.edu
POWEL, Wayne ... 814-472-3004. 432 D wpowel@francis.edu
POWELL, Aaron ... 360-867-6238. 519 J powella@evergreen.edu
POWELL, April ... 559-453-2027... 45 D agp@fresno.edu
POWELL, Betty ... 713-221-8072. 489 D powellb@uhd.edu
POWELL, Brett ... 870-245-5410... 22 D powellb@obu.edu
POWELL, Carl ... 734-487-4591. 242 D crpowell@emich.edu
POWELL, Charles ... 203-432-7458... 93 A charles.powell@yale.edu
POWELL, Charmaine ... 502-447-1000. 199 E cpowell@spencerian.edu
POWELL, Cody, J ... 513-529-7070. 384 G powellcj@miamioh.edu
POWELL, Curtis, N ... 518-276-6359. 337 I powelc2@rpi.edu
POWELL, Danny ... 501-450-1265... 21 E powell@hendrix.edu
POWELL, Darrin ... 859-336-1746. 195 A darrin.powell@kctcs.edu
POWELL, Dave ... 269-964-6653. 252 I dave.powell@wmich.edu
POWELL, Deborah ... 301-447-5840. 217 B dpowell@msmary.edu
POWELL, Deborah, L ... 434-381-6179. 510 F dpowell@sbc.edu
POWELL, Debra ... 303-937-4200... 79 E dpowell@chu.edu
POWELL, Denise ... 912-538-3162. 132 A dpowell@southeasterntech.edu
POWELL, Edna ... 310-506-6464... 58 H edna.powell@pepperdine.edu
POWELL, Gregory, S ... 903-693-2022. 478 A gpowell@panola.edu
POWELL, Hiram ... 386-481-2956... 99 C powellh@cookman.edu
POWELL, James ... 318-798-6868. 201 D
POWELL, Jane ... 213-738-6836... 68 C jpowell@swlaw.edu
POWELL, Janel ... 760-750-4311... 35 A jpowell@csusm.edu
POWELL, Jason ... 540-365-4376. 504 L jpowell@ferrum.edu
POWELL, Jason, B ... 860-832-2398... 87 K powell@ccsu.edu
POWELL, Jennifer ... 601-477-5454. 267 F jennifer.powell@jcjc.edu
POWELL, Jill ... 704-355-8894. 353 D jill.powell@carolinashealthcare.org
POWELL, John ... 502-897-4617. 199 B jpowell@sbts.edu
POWELL, John ... 304-734-6689. 527 O jpowell@bridgemont.edu
POWELL, John ... 304-205-6607. 528 B jpowell@kvctc.edu
POWELL, JR., John, W ... 843-953-5200. 442 A john.powell@citadel.edu
POWELL, Karan, H ... 304-724-3700. 526 B kpowell@apus.edu
POWELL, Karen ... 650-378-7359... 64 C powellk@smccd.edu
POWELL, Katherine ... 706-236-1707. 121 G kpowell@berry.edu
POWELL, Kathleen, I ... 740-587-6521. 379 D powellk@denison.edu
POWELL, Kevin ... 804-524-5691. 515 D manager525@nebook.com
POWELL, Linda ... 503-883-2627. 404 A lpowell@linfield.edu
POWELL, Lyn ... 352-854-2322. 100 K powelll@cf.edu
POWELL, Mac ... 925-969-3302... 49 B mpowell@jfku.edu
POWELL, Marjorie, L ... 410-706-3950. 219 C mlpowell@af.umaryland.edu
POWELL, Nancy, L ... 606-679-8501. 196 D nancy.powell@kctcs.edu
POWELL, Necole ... 314-367-8700. 281 C necole.powell@stlcop.edu
POWELL, Nikki ... 620-672-5641. 190 A nikkip@prattcc.edu
POWELL, Patricia ... 334-222-6591... 5 E ppowell@lbwcc.edu
POWELL, Patsy ... 912-871-1603. 129 J ppowell@ogeecheetech.edu
POWELL, Patty, T ... 615-230-3441. 461 G patty.powell@volstate.edu
POWELL, Phillip ... 919-530-6392. 368 A ppowell@nccu.edu
POWELL, R. Tony, A ... 270-809-2664. 198 B rpowell@murraystate.edu
POWELL, Richard, S ... 904-620-2015. 116 B rsp@unf.edu
POWELL, Skeet ... 254-298-8692. 482 C skeetpowell@templejc.edu
POWELL, Stephanie, E ... 850-263-3261... 98 N sepowell@baptistcollege.edu
POWELL, Steve ... 254-442-5133. 468 I steve.powell@cisco.edu
POWELL, Sue ... 601-936-5555. 267 A cspowell@hindscc.edu
POWELL, Theresa, A ... 215-204-6556. 433 K theresa.powell@temple.edu
POWELL, Thomas, H ... 301-447-5600. 217 B powell@msmary.edu
POWELL, Timothy, M ... 559-455-5572... 30 I vpacademics@calchristiancollege.edu
POWELL, Todd ... 785-628-4233. 186 F tpowell@fhsu.edu
POWELL, Torence ... 916-691-7170... 53 B powellt@crc.losrios.edu
POWELL, Wayne ... 828-328-7334. 356 B powellw@lr.edu
POWELL, William, W ... 601-266-4964. 270 E william.powell@usm.edu
POWELL-COHEN, Sheila 305-626-3657. 104 J shelia.powellcohen@fmuniv.edu
POWER, Colleen ... 510-883-7153... 42 I cpower@dspt.edu
POWER, Suzanne ... 858-513-9240. 175 F Suzanne.power@ashford.edu
POWER-BARNES, Marie, R ... 609-984-4839. 308 A mpowerbarnes@tesc.edu
POWER ROBISON, Elizabeth ... 562-907-4219... 76 I eprobison@whittier.edu
POWERS, Amber ... 215-576-0800. 431 E apowers@rrc.edu
POWERS, Andrew ... 740-593-1911. 387 C powersa@ohio.edu
POWERS, Barbara ... 989-686-9032. 242 C bjpowers@delta.edu
POWERS, Christopher ... 513-745-5700. 391 A christopher.power@uc.edu
POWERS, Cindy ... 304-896-7382. 528 F cindy.powers@southernwv.edu
POWERS, Danielle ... 856-227-7200. 300 B dpowers@camdencc.edu
POWERS, David ... 206-296-5300. 523 E powersda@seattleu.edu
POWERS, Doug ... 570-372-4522. 433 H powers@susqu.edu
POWERS, Elizabeth, A ... 401-232-6085. 438 K bpowers@bryant.edu
POWERS, Frank ... 509-544-4419. 518 C fpowers@columbiabasin.edu
POWERS, Jason ... 617-558-1788. 235 C jpowers@nesa.edu
POWERS, John ... 650-926-0250... 68 E jfpowers@stanford.edu
POWERS, Jon, R ... 740-368-3082. 387 J jrpowers@owu.edu
POWERS, Joshua ... 812-237-8378. 167 A joshua.powers@indstate.edu
POWERS, Keri ... 508-531-1324. 229 D keri.powers@bridgew.edu
POWERS, Lisa, M ... 814-865-7517. 426 A lmr8@psu.edu
POWERS, Lynn ... 407-708-2138. 113 E powers@seminolestate.edu
POWERS, Mark, R ... 508-626-4545. 230 A mpowers@framingham.edu
POWERS, Patrick ... 407-646-2115. 111 Q ppowers@rollins.edu
POWERS, Peter, K ... 717-766-2511. 423 L ppowers@messiah.edu
POWERS, Phillippa ... 585-475-6938. 337 L pxpcrp@rit.edu
POWERS, Richard ... 512-313-3000. 469 L richard.powers@concordia.edu
POWERS, Samantha ... 360-475-7580. 521 H spowers@olympic.edu
POWERS, Sherry ... 859-858-3511. 192 B sherry.powers@asbury.edu
POWERS, Susan ... 802-865-5490. 499 A spowers@champlain.edu
POWERS, Suzanne ... 417-328-1689. 282 C spowers@sbuniv.edu
POWERS, Tammy ... 575-528-7069. 311 B welchta@nmsu.edu
POWERS, Tim ... 949-794-9090... 68 D tpowers@stanbridge.edu
POWERS, Tyrone ... 410-777-7496. 213 D tpowers@aacc.edu
POWERS, William ... 617-989-4407. 237 G powersw2@wit.edu
POWERS, William, B ... 312-987-1435. 148 L 6powers@jmls.edu
POWERS, JR., William, C ... 512-471-1232. 491 C president@po.utexas.edu
POWERS-LEE, Susan, G . 617-373-2842. 235 F
POWICKI, Mike ... 402-375-7520. 291 F mipowic1@wsc.edu
POWLESS, David ... 205-970-9225... 7 B dpowless@sebc.edu
POWLEY, Mary, R ... 585-385-8057. 338 H mpowley@sjfc.edu
POYNTER, Barry ... 859-622-5012. 193 P barry.poynter@eku.edu
POYTHRESS, James ... 540-857-6004. 514 E jpoythress@virginiawestern.edu
POYUZINA, Alex ... 858-279-4500... 49 K apoyuzina@kaplan.edu
POYUZINA, Alex ... 760-630-1555... 49 L apoyuzina@kaplan.edu
POZNANSKI, Brad, F ... 603-656-6023. 297 G bfpoznanski@anselm.edu
POZZI, Dave ... 626-568-8850... 50 E
PRABHU, Vilas, A ... 717-872-3596. 429 D vilas.prabhu@millersville.edu
PRACHER, Mark ... 310-287-4467... 52 F prachem@wlac.edu
PRADO, Lenore, M ... 305-628-6514. 112 F lprado@stu.edu
PRADO, Marivi ... 305-474-6880. 112 F mprado@stu.edu
PRAET, Diane, M ... 313-993-3313. 250 K praetdm@udmercy.edu
PRAETORIUS, Elizabeth .. 718-409-7204. 346 D lpraetorius@sunymaritime.edu
PRAETZEL, Gary, D ... 716-286-8270. 334 F gdp@niagara.edu
PRAKASH, Siva ... 813-974-0880. 116 C sprakash@admin.usf.edu
PRALL, J. Andrew ... 260-399-7700. 174 C jprall@sf.edu
PRANGE, Raphaella ... 217-424-6395. 153 C rpalmer@millikin.edu
PRANGER, Henriette, M . 860-727-6740... 90 A hpranger@goodwin.edu
PRASAD, Rashmi ... 907-786-4126... 10 H afrp2@uaa.alaska.edu
PRASAD, Vish ... 316-978-3400. 191 F vish.prasad@wichita.edu
PRASHER, Sarah ... 419-772-1943. 386 D s-prasher@onu.edu
PRASIFKA, Matthew ... 713-525-3512. 490 L prasifm@stthom.edu
PRASLOVA, Ludmilla ... 714-556-3610... 74 D lpraslova@vanguard.edu
PRASSE, David, P ... 773-508-7470. 151 H dprasse@luc.edu
PRASTACOS, Gregory ... 201-216-8366. 307 E gregory.prastacos@stevens.edu
PRATER, Margaret ... 731-286-3585. 460 F prater@nwtnworks.org
PRATER, Michael ... 574-520-4319. 168 E maprater@iusb.edu
PRATER, Steve ... 580-477-7894. 401 J steve.prater@wosc.edu
PRATER, Susan ... 405-974-2300. 400 K sprater4@uco.edu
PRATER, Todd ... 706-880-8924. 128 A tprater@lagrange.edu
PRATHER, Kerry, N ... 317-738-8121. 165 I kprather@franklincollege.edu
PRATHER, Sean ... 925-424-1690... 37 L sprather@laspositascollege.edu
PRATHER, Tammy ... 662-329-7131. 268 E tprather@registrar.muw.edu
PRATT, Andrew, L ... 816-415-7557. 285 C pratta@william.jewell.edu
PRATT, Anne ... 802-251-7607. 499 F apratt@marlboro.edu
PRATT, Barbara ... 908-835-2355. 308 G pratt@warren.edu
PRATT, Bernard ... 207-778-7009. 212 D ben.pratt@maine.edu

PRATT, Charles ... 201-200-2141. 303 F cpratt@njcu.edu
PRATT, Denise ... 402-941-6135. 290 K pratt@midlandu.edu
PRATT, Edward ... 225-771-4545. 206 J edward_pratt@subr.edu
PRATT, Edward, E ... 561-297-0567. 114 L epratt2@fau.edu
PRATT, Eric ... 601-925-7652. 268 A epratt@mc.edu
PRATT, G. Michael ... 513-529-6721. 384 G prattgm@miamioh.edu
PRATT, Harold, W ... 417-836-4252. 278 E wpratt@missouristate.edu
PRATT, James ... 812-749-1215. 171 K jpratt@oak.edu
PRATT, Janice ... 520-494-6602... 12 P janice.pratt@centralaz.edu
PRATT, Jonathan, R ... 763-417-8250. 254 E
PRATT, Judy ... 513-244-8674. 376 J Judy.Pratt@ccuniversity.edu
PRATT, Kris ... 812-749-1408. 171 K kpratt@oak.edu
PRATT, Linda ... 951-571-6267... 60 K linda.pratt@mvc.edu
PRATT, Lisa ... 218-726-8829. 264 D lpratt@d.umn.edu
PRATT, Michael ... 205-652-3565..... 9 F mpratt@uwa.edu
PRATT, Michael ... 252-985-5146. 365 D mpratt@ncwc.edu
PRATT, Robert, C ... 517-750-1200. 250 E bpratt@arbor.edu
PRATT, Sarah ... 213-740-8867... 74 A pratt@usc.edu
PRATT, JR., Theodore, W ... 360-650-3450. 525 C ted.pratt@cc.wwu.edu
PRATT-CLARKE, Menah .. 217-333-0885. 162 A menahpc@illinois.edu
PRATT-CLARKE, Menah .. 217-333-4238. 162 A menahpc@illinois.edu
PRATT-COOK, Patricia .... 218-723-6602. 254 K pprattcook@css.edu
PRATTE, John ... 870-972-3079... 19 N jpratte@astate.edu
PRATTELLA, Todd ... 914-674-7844. 330 J tprattella@mercy.edu
PRATTS, Luis, N ... 787-780-0070. 547 G lpratts@caribbean.edu
PRAY, G. Jon ... 414-288-7532. 534 B jon.pray@marquette.edu
PRAYOR, Sharon ... 773-291-6210. 142 D sprayor@ccc.edu
PREAS, Derek ... 903-468-3148. 483 E derek.preas@tamuc.edu
PREATHER, Gary ... 817-515-6742. 482 B gary.preather@tccd.edu
PREBLE, Edwin, G ... 575-624-8070. 310 H preble@nmmi.edu
PREBLE, Holly ... 909-621-8130... 59 G holly_preble@pitzer.edu
PREBLE, Mark ... 774-455-7537. 228 E mpreble@umassp.edu
PRECHTER, Patricia ... 504-398-2213. 206 C pprechter@olhcc.edu
PRECHTL, Gregory, D ..... 716-673-3101. 342 A gregory.prechtl@fredonia.edu
PRECISE, Leigh ... 816-483-9600. 190 D leighp@spst.edu
PRECZEWSKI, Stanley .... 678-407-5001. 125 B president@ggc.edu
PRECZEWSKI, Stanley .... 678-407-5231. 125 B spreczewski@ggc.edu
PREDIC, Beba ... 303-937-4202... 79 E bpredic@chu.edu
PREECE, Barbara ... 410-617-6811. 216 A bpreece@loyola.edu
PREECE, Barbara ... 410-617-6811. 217 E bpreece@ndm.edu
PREECE, Jennifer, J ... 301-405-2033. 219 B preece@umd.edu
PREGEANT, Gene, E ... 985-549-5888. 208 C gpregeant@selu.edu
PREGITZER, Kurt ... 208-885-6442. 139 D kpregitzer@uidaho.edu
PREHN, Kevin ... 858-279-4500... 49 K kprehn@kaplan.edu
PREISINGER, George, T . 248-370-2127. 248 J preising@oakland.edu
PREISSER, Grant ... 912-525-5000. 131 B gpreisse@scad.edu
PRELLWITZ, Andrew, R ... 920-748-8175. 535 J prellwitza@ripon.edu
PRELOCK, Patricia, A ..... 802-656-2216. 500 F patricia.prelock@uvm.edu
PRELOGER, Robert ... 605-274-4922. 449 K bob.preloger@augie.edu
PREMNATH, Devadasan, N ... 585-271-3657. 338 D dnprem@stbernards.edu
PREMO, Brenda ... 909-469-5385... 76 B bpremo@westernu.edu
PREMO, Greg, V ... 253-535-8787. 521 I premogv@plu.edu
PRENATT, Ann, B ... 314-935-7746. 284 L aprenatt@wustl.edu
PRENDERGAST, Debra, L ... 708-709-3689. 156 A dprendergast@prairiestate.edu
PRENDERGAST, Lyn ... 781-762-1211. 226 E drlyn@fine-ne.com
PRENDERGAST, Nancy ... 847-635-1661. 155 F nprender@oakton.edu
PRENDERGAST, Thomas, M ... 419-755-4712. 385 D tprendergast@ncstatecollege.edu
PRENGAMAN, Diane ... 410-225-2285. 216 C dprengam@mica.edu
PRENGAMAN, John, C ... 434-223-6161. 505 E jprengaman@hsc.edu
PRENOVOST, Jason ... 206-878-3710. 520 E jprenovost@highline.edu
PRENTICE, Ernest, D ... 402-559-6045. 292 J edprenti@unmc.edu
PRENTICE, Marilyn ... 847-214-7992. 144 F mprentice@elgin.edu
PRENTISS, Kay ... 508-849-3228. 222 B kprentiss@annamaria.edu
PREOCANIN, Shelley ... 812-866-7097. 166 C preocanins@hanover.edu
PREPEJCHAL, Mary ... 956-364-4042. 485 H mary.prepejchal@tstc.edu
PRESCOD-CAESAR, Pamela ... 610-328-8397. 433 I ppresco1@swarthmore.edu
PRESCOTT, Herman ... 202-274-5072... 97 A tprescott@udc.edu
PRESCOTT, Jay, B ... 515-263-2890. 178 G jprescott@grandview.edu
PRESCOTT, Loren, D ... 570-408-4000. 437 F loren.prescott@wilkes.edu
PRESCOTT, Patricia, M ... 516-671-0439. 350 C pprescot@webb.edu
PRESENT, Melissa ... 212-678-8820. 328 A mepresent@jtsa.edu
PRESENT, Wendy ... 716-338-1070. 327 J wendypresent@mail.sunyjcc.edu
PRESLEY, Brian ... 276-935-4349. 502 A bpresley@asl.edu
PRESLEY, Doretha ... 601-977-4461. 270 A dpresley@tougaloo.edu
PRESLEY, Leandrew ... 662-621-4207. 266 D lpresley@coahomacc.edu
PRESLEY, Shawn ... 740-427-5158. 382 J presleys@kenyon.edu
PRESNELL, Anita ... 910-576-6222. 362 C presnella@montgomery.edu
PRESNELL, Sam ... 828-766-1225. 361 H spresnell@mayland.edu
PRESS, Jim ... 231-995-1327. 248 B jpress@nmc.edu
PRESSER, Art ... 800-290-4226. 454 M apresser@hchs.edu
PRESSEY, Natalie ... 212-229-5660. 332 E presseyn@newschool.edu
PRESSIMONE, J. Michael ... 610-796-8259. 409 E mike.pressimone@alvernia.edu
PRESSLEY, Dan ... 706-754-7791. 129 G dpressley@northgatech.edu
PRESSLEY, Pamela ... 903-927-3202. 495 A ppressley@wileyc.edu
PRESSLEY, Paula ... 336-770-3331. 369 D pressleyp@uncsa.edu
PRESSLEY, Rebecca, D ... 864-833-8287. 446 D rpressley@presby.edu
PRESSMAN, Avraham ... 570-346-1747. 438 C
PRESSON, Mark, A ... 563-588-8000. 178 D mpresson@emmaus.edu
PRESSON, Paul ... 801-832-2424. 498 F pkpresson@westminstercollege.edu
PRESSWOOD, Kristy ... 386-506-3822. 101 G presswk@DaytonaState.edu
PRESSWOOD, Theresa ... 281-283-2015. 489 C presswood@uhcl.edu
PREST, Stacy ... 509-527-4294. 524 H stacy.prest@wwcc.edu
PRESTA, James ... 847-970-4869. 162 G jpresta@usml.edu
PRESTA, Silvana ... 847-735-5036. 150 B presta@lakeforest.edu
PRESTAMO, Anne ... 305-348-5726. 115 B anne.prestamo@fiu.edu
PRESTENBACH, Celeste .. 205-329-7926..... 3 B celeste.prestenbach@ecacolleges.com
PRESTFELDT, Carl, F ... 270-809-3472. 198 B cprestfeldt@murraystate.edu
PRESTI, Coral ... 203-857-7123... 89 D cpresti@norwalk.edu
PRESTIACOMO, Angela, M ... 518-381-1381. 340 G prestiam@sunysccc.edu
PRESTON, April ... 615-366-4404. 459 A april.preston@tbr.edu
PRESTON, Betty, E ... 419-755-4756. 385 D bpreston@ncstatecollege.edu
PRESTON, Daniel ... 503-883-2294. 404 A dpreston@linfield.edu
PRESTON, David ... 979-230-3256. 468 A david.preston@brazosport.edu
PRESTON, Elizabeth ... 413-572-5213. 230 F epreston@westfield.ma.edu
PRESTON, Harold, R ... 325-670-1497. 472 O hpreston@hsutx.edu
PRESTON, James ... 559-925-3146... 75 I jamespreston@whccd.edu
PRESTON, James ... 312-329-4140. 153 E james.preston@moody.edu
PRESTON, Jeffrey, H ... 912-279-5751. 123 B jpreston@ccga.edu
PRESTON, Joanne ... 508-678-2811. 231 B Joanne.Preston@bristolcc.edu
PRESTON, Joanne ... 305-809-3538. 104 I joanne.preston@fkcc.edu
PRESTON, Karen ... 770-426-2688. 128 D kpreston@life.edu
PRESTON, Kenneth, G .... 330-972-8254. 390 E kpreston@uakron.edu
PRESTON, Kenneth, G .... 330-972-7845. 390 E kpreston@uakron.edu
PRESTON, Laura, C ... 443-412-2438. 215 C lpreston@harford.edu
PRESTON, Robert ... 240-567-5327. 216 F robert.preston@montgomerycollege.edu
PRESTON, Thomas ... 302-857-7749... 93 C tpreston@desu.edu
PRESTON, Toni ... 937-708-5703. 393 A kpreston@wilberforce.edu
PRESTON, Travis ... 661-255-1050... 31 C tpreston@calarts.edu
PRESTWICH, Aaron ... 308-432-6231. 291 D aprestwich@csc.edu
PRESTWICH, Kimberly .... 208-732-6293. 138 B kprestwich@csi.edu
PRESTWICH, Roger ... 612-659-7293. 259 C roger.prestwich@metrostate.edu
PRETTI, Janet ... 541-469-5017. 407 H jpretti@socc.edu
PRETTO, Felix ... 212-594-4000. 347 H fpretto@tcicollege.edu
PRETTO, Ninah ... 973-748-9000. 299 F ninah_pretto@bloomfield.edu
PRETTY, Keith, A ... 989-837-4203. 248 C pretty@northwood.edu
PRETTYMAN, Ronald ... 812-237-4089. 167 A ron.prettyman@indstate.edu
PREUS, Camille ... 541-278-5950. 402 C cpreus@bluecc.edu
PREUSS, Timothy ... 949-214-3286... 41 I timothy.preuss@cui.edu
PREUSZ, Mike ... 864-644-5048. 446 I mpreusz@swu.edu
PREVAUX, Steven, D ... 813-974-1669. 116 C prevaux@usf.edu
PREVOST, Blair ... 903-923-2326. 471 J bprevost@etbu.edu
PREVOST, JR., Hugh, L . 423-425-4735. 463 D hugh-prevost@utc.edu
PREVOST, Suzanne, S ... 205-348-1040..... 8 D suzanne.prevost@ua.edu
PREWETT, Nick ... 573-882-6200. 283 C prewettn@missouri.edu
PREWITT, Michael ... 304-696-3765. 529 H prewitta@marshall.edu
PREWITT, Steve ... 615-966-5804. 456 B steve.prewitt@lipscomb.edu
PREZANT, Robert, S ... 973-655-5108. 303 D prezantr@mail.montclair.edu
PREZIOSO, Randy ... 202-651-5000... 95 C
PRIBBENOW, Dean ... 608-663-2200. 532 I DPribbenow@edgewood.edu
PRIBBENOW, Paul, C .... 612-330-1212. 253 H president@augsburg.edu
PRIBBLE, Ronald, L ... 320-222-5204. 260 H ronald.pribble@ridgewater.edu
PRIBULSKY, Christopher 814-262-3824. 427 C cpribulsky@pennhighlands.edu
PRIBUSH, Bonnie, L ... 317-738-8251. 165 I bpribush@franklincollege.edu
PRICCI, Erica ... 570-955-1461. 420 C pricci@lackawanna.edu
PRICE, Adrian ... 501-370-5383... 22 F aprice@philander.edu
PRICE, Adrienne ... 909-274-5417... 55 A aprice@mtsac.edu
PRICE, Alan Paul ... 262-335-5203. 538 E paul.price@uwc.edu
PRICE, Angie, C ... 423-775-7269. 453 E aprice6832@bryan.edu
PRICE, Barbara ... 912-478-5555. 126 C baprice@georgiasouthern.edu
PRICE, Bernard ... 212-594-4000. 347 H bprice@tcicollege.edu
PRICE, Bill ... 540-231-4000. 504 G
PRICE, Brenda, G ... 313-927-1829. 246 D bprice@marygrove.edu
PRICE, Bryan ... 540-458-8184. 516 A bprice@wlu.edu
PRICE, Byron ... 718-270-5110. 319 A bprice@mec.cuny.edu
PRICE, Cecil, D ... 336-758-5218. 370 D price@wfu.edu
PRICE, Chad, P ... 208-496-1260. 137 H pricec@byui.edu
PRICE, Cynthia, J ... 206-281-2179. 523 C cprice@spu.edu
PRICE, Danny ... 706-368-5644. 121 G dprice@berry.edu
PRICE, David, E ... 706-778-8500. 130 E dprice2@piedmont.edu
PRICE, Dawne ... 402-494-2311. 290 O dprice@thenicc.edu
PRICE, Donna ... 931-221-7907. 459 B priced@apsu.edu
PRICE, Fred ... 718-270-5190. 319 A fredprice@mec.cuny.edu
PRICE, Gary ... 541-259-5808. 404 B priceg@linnbenton.edu
PRICE, Gordon ... 541-383-7592. 402 D gprice@cocc.edu
PRICE, Greer ... 575-835-5752. 310 F bureau@gis.nmt.edu
PRICE, Greg ... 334-670-3507..... 7 H wgprice@troy.edu
PRICE, Irene, L ... 517-750-1200. 250 E iprice@arbor.edu
PRICE, James ... 706-771-4096. 121 D jprice@augustatech.edu
PRICE, James, B ... 610-436-3063. 430 A jprice@wcupa.edu
PRICE, Jason ... 806-457-4200. 472 G jprice@fpctx.edu
PRICE, Jennifer ... 518-262-5679. 313 D pricej@mail.amc.edu
PRICE, Jerry ... 714-997-6721... 38 A jprice@chapman.edu
PRICE, Jewel, A ... 818-240-1000... 45 G jprice@glendale.edu
PRICE, Jill ... 715-365-4531. 540 G jmrjenovich@nicoletcollege.edu
PRICE, Jo Ann ... 270-444-9676. 193 N jprice@daymarcollege.edu
PRICE, Karen ... 704-461-6731. 352 G KarenPrice@bac.edu
PRICE, Kayli ... 417-624-7070. 476 F kprice@messengercollege.edu
PRICE, Kendrick ... 252-493-7627. 362 G kprice@email.pittcc.edu
PRICE, Kevin, L ... 208-496-1705. 137 H priceke@byui.edu
PRICE, Leigh ... 912-478-5211. 126 C llprice@georgiasouthern.edu
PRICE, Linda, A ... 301-784-5000. 213 B lprice@allegany.edu
PRICE, Linda, L ... 812-877-8165. 172 C price@rose-hulman.edu
PRICE, Lisa ... 618-437-5321. 156 H price@rlc.edu
PRICE, Lori ... 214-379-5485. 478 D lprice@pqc.edu
PRICE, Marla ... 717-755-2300. 410 C maprice@aii.edu
PRICE, Megan ... 864-388-8019. 444 K mprice@lander.edu
PRICE, Mike ... 952-446-4141. 255 D pricem@crown.edu
PRICE, Nicole, G ... 617-973-1101. 237 B nprice@suffolk.edu
PRICE, Nikol ... 623-935-8087... 14 K nikol.price@estrellamountain.edu
PRICE, Robin ... 304-637-1243. 526 E pricer@dewv.edu
PRICE, Ron ... 757-221-3115. 503 N
PRICE, Ronald, N ... 708-216-9949. 151 H rprice@lumc.edu
PRICE, Sarah ... 270-686-4501. 196 C sarah.price@kctcs.edu
PRICE, Vincent ... 215-898-7227. 435 B provost@upenn.edu
PRICE, Virginia ... 717-334-6286. 422 E vprice@ltsg.edu
PRICE, Viviane ... 303-220-1200... 78 K viviane.price@cffp.edu
PRICE, W. Craig ... 504-282-4455. 206 A cprice@nobts.edu
PRICE, Walter ... 972-524-3341. 481 H
PRICE, Wendy ... 206-934-5216. 523 A wendy.price@seattlecolleges.edu
PRICE BLOUNT, Grady .. 903-886-5781. 483 E grady.blount@tamuc.edu

PRICE-PERRY, Cassandra, F ... 901-334-5821. 457 A
cfperry@memphisseminary.edu

PRICHARD, Marion, L ... 580-774-3249. 400 B
marion.prichard@swosu.edu

PRICHARD, Patricia, A ... 503-517-1806. 408 I
paprichard@westernseminary.edu

PRICKEN, Stephanie ... 610-660-1379. 432 E
spricken@sju.edu

PRICKETT, Juanita (Nita), M ... 785-539-3571. 188 F
nprickett@mccks.edu

PRIDA, Jonas ... 802-773-5900. 499 B
jonas.prida@csj.edu

PRIDAL, Cathryn ... 417-667-8181. 273 A
cpridal@cottey.edu

PRIDDY, Claire ... 212-355-1501. 316 H
cpriddy@christies.edu

PRIDDY, Michele ... 615-297-7545. 452 J
priddym@aquinascollege.edu

PRIDE, Marcy ... 434-592-7062. 506 I

PRIDE, Nicole ... 336-334-7654. 367 E
npride@ncat.edu

PRIDE, Nicole ... 336-256-0863. 367 E
npride@ncat.edu

PRIDEAUX, Debra, K ... 785-628-4430. 186 F
dprideau@fhsu.edu

PRIES, Lonnie ... 734-995-7343. 241 E
priesl@cuaa.edu

PRIES, Lynn, L ... 630-637-5104. 154 F
llpries@noctrl.edu

PRIEST, Barry ... 910-879-5579. 358 B
bpriest@bladencc.edu

PRIEST, Catherine ... 856-351-2624. 307 B
cpriest@salemcc.edu

PRIEST, Jeffrey, M ... 803-641-3269. 448 A
jeffp@usca.edu

PRIEST, Kevin ... 715-324-6900. 535 E
kevin.priest@ni.edu

PRIEST, Margaret ... 313-831-5200. 242 E
mpriest@etseminary.edu

PRIEST, Rebecca ... 330-494-6170. 389 F
rpriest@starkstate.edu

PRIETO, Adanid ... 787-766-1717. 552 J
a_prieto@suagm.edu

PRIETO, Beth ... 603-645-9724. 297 I
b.prieto@snhu.edu

PRIETO, Diana ... 970-491-5836... 80 I
diana.prieto@colostate.edu

PRIETO, Eduardo ... 386-226-6000. 102 B
eduardo.prieto@erau.edu

PRIGAL, Helena ... 212-431-2318. 333 I
hprigal@nyls.edu

PRIGG, Benson ... 256-726-7186... 6 B
bprigg@oakwood.edu

PRIGGE, Amy ... 419-772-3961. 386 D
a-prigge@onu.edu

PRIGGE, Bill ... 678-915-7232. 132 C
bprigge@spsu.edu

PRIGGIE, Richard, W ... 309-794-7213. 139 L
richardpriggie@augustana.edu

PRILLELTENSKY, Isaac ... 305-284-3505. 118 F
isaacp@miami.edu

PRIMAVERA, Louis, H ... 631-665-1600. 348 B
louis.primavera@touro.edu

PRIMIANO, Leonard ... 610-902-8330. 411 E
leonard.primiano@cabrini.edu

PRIMO, John ... 405-733-7356. 399 F
jprimo@rose.edu

PRIMOFF, Mark ... 845-758-7412. 314 D
primoff@bard.edu

PRIMOZICH, Tracy ... 800-287-8822. 164 C
primotr@bethanyseminary.edu

PRIMUS, Joanna ... 719-590-6708... 81 B
jprimus@coloradotech.edu

PRIMUS, Lester ... 860-906-5050... 88 D
lprimus@ccc.commnet.edu

PRINCE, Bobby, A ... 901-678-4376. 460 B
baprince@memphis.edu

PRINCE, James, E ... 269-337-7225. 244 K
James.Prince@kzoo.edu

PRINCE, Jeff ... 510-642-9494... 70 I
jprince@berkeley.edu

PRINCE, Joan, M ... 414-229-3101. 537 A
jprince@uwm.edu

PRINCE, Judith ... 864-552-4243. 448 H
jprince@uscupstate.edu

PRINCE, Ken ... 812-866-7051. 166 C
princek@hanover.edu

PRINCE, T. Greg ... 410-546-6938. 220 D
tgprince@salisbury.edu

PRINCINSKY, Julianne, T ... 810-766-4036. 239 H
julianne.princinsky@baker.edu

PRINDIVILLE, Barbara, A ... 262-691-5435. 541 D
bprindiville@wctc.edu

PRINGLE, Eboni ... 330-672-8700. 382 B
epringle@kent.edu

PRINGLE, Ernest ... 803-641-3345. 448 A
epringle@usca.edu

PRINGLE, Karen ... 541-888-7211. 407 H
karen.pringle@socc.edu

PRINGLE, Nancy, E ... 607-274-3836. 327 E
npringle@ithaca.edu

PRINGLE, Randy ... 903-923-2233. 471 J
rpringle@etbu.edu

PRINTUP, Roger, O ... 212-998-4251. 334 D
roger.printup@nyu.edu

PRIOLEAU, Darwin ... 585-395-5806. 342 F
dpriolea@brockport.edu

PRIOLEAU-TAYLOR, Erica ... 803-536-7061. 446 G
esprioleau@scsu.edu

PRIOLO, Bob ... 616-949-5300. 241 F
bob.priolo@cornerstone.edu

PRIOR, Roberta ... 203-285-2209... 88 E
rprior@gwcc.commnet.edu

PRISCO, Anne ... 201-559-6022. 302 A
priscoa@felician.edu

PRISELAC, Thomas ... 310-423-5711... 37 H

PRISLIN, Radmilla ... 619-594-2309... 35 D
rprislin@mail.sdsu.edu

PRITCHARD, Brett ... 256-215-4254... 2 G
bpritchard@cacc.edu

PRITCHARD, Gary ... 562-860-2451... 37 I
gpritchard@cerritos.edu

PRITCHARD, Lamar ... 713-743-1253. 489 B
flpritchard@uh.edu

PRITCHARD, Mandie ... 541-440-4600. 408 D
mandie.pritchard@umpqua.edu

PRITCHARD, Michael, H 301-846-2417. 214 H
mpritchard@frederick.edu

PRITCHARD, Rod ... 319-399-8605. 176 G
rpritcha@coe.edu

PRITCHARD, Sarah, M ... 847-491-7640. 155 D
spritchard@northwestern.edu

PRITCHETT, Alondrea, J . 334-229-4737... 1 D
apritchett@alasu.edu

PRITCHETT, Beth ... 304-327-4139. 529 D
bpritchett@bluefieldstate.edu

PRITCHETT, H. Franklin .. 678-839-6582. 133 I
fpritche@westga.edu

PRITCHETT, Merrill, R ... 410-837-6207. 221 A
mpritchett@ubalt.edu

PRITCHETT, Nikki ... 850-644-2003. 115 C
npritchett@admin.fsu.edu

PRITCHETT, Wendell, E .. 856-225-6095. 306 A
chancellor@camden.rutgers.edu

PRITCHETT, Wendell, E .. 856-225-6095. 306 C
chancellor@camden.rutgers.edu

PRITTS, Barry ... 304-473-8040. 531 G
pritts@wvwc.edu

PRITZ, Stephen, J ... 352-392-1374. 116 A
spritz@ufl.edu

PRITZKER, Barry ... 518-580-5654. 341 A
bpritzke@skidmore.edu

PRIVETT, James, E ... 803-938-3758. 448 F
jamesp@uscsumter.edu

PRIVETT, SJ, Stephen, A 415-422-6762... 73 J
privett@usfca.edu

PROBST, Laura, K ... 218-299-4642. 255 A
lprobst@cord.edu

PROBST, Mark, W ... 804-523-5790. 512 F
mprobst@reynolds.edu

PROBST, Robert ... 513-556-9808. 390 G
robert.probst@uc.edu

PROBSTFELD, Carol, F ... 941-752-5201. 114 I
probstc@scf.edu

PROCARIO-FOLEY, Carl . 914-633-2632. 327 C
cprocariofoley@iona.edu

PROCHELLO, Marc ... 602-383-8228... 18 E

PROCHNOW, Allen ... 734-995-7588. 241 E
procha@cuaa.edu

PROCHNOW, Allen, J ... 262-243-5700. 532 H
allen.prochnow@cuw.edu

PROCTER, Everett ... 949-794-9090... 68 D
eprocter@stanbridge.edu

PROCTER, Ken ... 478-445-4441. 125 A
ken.procter@gcsu.edu

PROCTER, Sharon ... 313-664-1487. 241 C
sprocter@collegeforcreativestudies.edu

PROCTOR, Avis ... 954-201-2202... 99 D
aproctor@broward.edu

PROCTOR, Catherine ... 732-247-5241. 303 E
cproctor@nbts.edu

PROCTOR, Jon ... 303-797-5092... 78 F
jon.proctor@arapahoe.edu

PROCTOR, Kelly ... 864-388-8398. 444 K
kproctor@lander.edu

PROCTOR, Kristen ... 508-854-7552. 232 F
kproctor@qcc.mass.edu

PROCTOR, Matt ... 417-626-1234. 279 J
pres@occ.edu

PROCTOR, Michael, A ... 520-626-5531... 18 F
mproctor@arizona.edu

PROCTOR, R. Leland ... 336-322-2163. 362 F
Lee.Proctor@piedmontcc.edu

PROCTOR, Teresa ... 270-247-8521. 197 H
tproctor@midcontinent.edu

PROCTOR, William, L ... 904-819-6210. 103 E
proctorw@flagler.edu

PROEFROCK, Steve ... 269-467-9945. 242 H
sproefrock@glenoaks.edu

PROENZA, Luis, M ... 330-972-7074. 390 E
proenza@uakron.edu

PROFETA, Glen ... 714-432-5861... 39 K
gprofeta@occ.cccd.edu

PROFETA, Patricia, C ... 772-462-7590. 106 P
pprofeta@irsc.edu

PROFETA, Philip, S ... 585-275-5811. 349 C
philip_profeta@urmc.rochester.edu

PROFFITT, Beth ... 717-291-3871. 416 J
beth.proffitt@fandm.edu

PROFFITT, David ... 757-352-4876. 508 G
jdowney@regent.edu

PROFFITT, Roger ... 620-227-9422. 186 B
rproffitt@dc3.edu

PROFFITT, Ron ... 276-739-2421. 514 D
rproffitt@vhcc.edu

PROFITT, Aaron ... 513-721-7944. 380 D
aprofitt@gbs.edu

PROFITT, Adam ... 513-721-7944. 380 D
adamprofitt@gbs.edu

PROGAR, Patrick, R ... 973-618-3212. 300 A
progar@caldwell.edu

PROHASKA, Thomas, R . 703-993-1918. 505 C
tprohask@gmu.edu

PROITE, Rosanne ... 512-245-2931. 487 C
rp45@txstate.edu

PROKOP, Paul ... 530-754-8568... 70 J
pjprokop@ucdavis.edu

PROKOVICH, Jeffrey, D .. 724-458-3846. 417 E
jdprokovich@gcc.edu

PROKUSKI, Meredith ... 863-680-4110. 105 D
mprokuski@flsouthern.edu

PROMADES, Frederick, C ... 401-341-2117. 440 C
promadef@salve.edu

PROPER, Amy ... 703-329-9100... 96 F

PROPST, Jennifer ... 828-448-6051. 365 A
jpropst@wpcc.edu

PROPST, Joan, L ... 304-457-6251. 526 A
propstjl@ab.edu

PROPST, Kent ... 660-248-6238. 272 B
kpropst@centralmethodist.edu

PROPST, Marlene ... 541-917-4784. 404 B
propstm@linnbenton.edu

PROPST, William, S ... 310-794-6027... 71 C
wpropst@finance.ucla.edu

PROSPER, Yamilette ... 787-891-0925. 549 K
yprosper@aguadilla.inter.edu

PROSSER, Deborah ... 678-717-3466. 133 D
deborah.prosser@ung.edu

PROSSER, Sarah ... 262-646-6501. 535 B
sprosser@nashotah.edu

PROSTANO, Laura ... 914-323-7124. 330 B
laura.prostano@mville.edu

PROTAS, Elizabeth, J ... 409-772-3001. 493 C
ejprotas@utmb.edu

PROTHERO, Charles, L .. 570-945-8015. 419 N
charlie.prothero@keystone.edu

PROTO, Bill ... 516-877-3680. 313 A
proto@adelphi.edu

PROTOPAPA, Joseph ... 386-822-7315. 117 C
jprotopa@stetson.edu

PROUDFIT, Ann ... 216-987-5892. 378 D
ann.proudfit@tri-c.edu

PROUDFOOT, Donald, W ... 903-510-2975. 488 E
dpro@tjc.edu

PROUDFOOT, Tony ... 765-285-1560. 164 B
tproudfoot@bsu.edu

PROUGH, Gene ... 850-718-2288... 99 N
proughg@chipola.edu

PROULX, David, R ... 717-291-3993. 416 J
dave.proulx@fandm.edu

PROULX, Dennis ... 802-468-1249. 501 B
dennis.proulx@castleton.edu

PROULX, Diane ... 402-399-2456. 289 A
dproulx@csm.edu

PROULX-CURRY, Pamela ... 207-974-4603. 210 K
pproulx-curry@emcc.edu

PROUSE, Margaret, R ... 302-857-1065... 93 G
mprouse@dtcc.edu

PROUT, Wilson ... 716-926-8910. 326 B
wprout@hilbert.edu

PROUTY, Steve ... 941-752-5205. 114 I
proutys@scf.edu

PROVAN, Amy ... 410-532-5379. 217 E
aprovan@ndm.edu

PROVENCHER, Susan ... 603-668-6660. 297 C

PROVENCIO-VASQUEZ, Elias ... 915-747-8217. 492 A
eprovenciovasquez@utep.edu

PROVENZA, Joseph, S ... 904-819-6359. 103 E
jprovenza@flagler.edu

PROVINCE, Anne ... 512-492-3051. 466 B
aprovince@aoma.edu

PROVINE, Rick, E ... 765-658-4435. 165 F
provine@depauw.edu

PROVOST, David, J ... 802-865-6400. 499 A
djprovost@champlain.edu

PRUCE, Dora ... 216-397-4565. 381 R
dpruce@jcu.edu

PRUCHNICKI, Jennifer ... 580-581-2209. 394 G
jpruchni@cameron.edu

PRUCNAL, James, R ... 256-549-8242... 3 M
jprucnal@gadsdenstate.edu

PRUDE, Regina ... 615-256-1463. 452 G
rprude@abcnash.edu

PRUDEN, Elizabeth ... 513-487-1232. 390 C
elizabeth.pruden@myunion.edu

PRUDHOMME, Harvey, J ... 503-370-6348. 408 J
hprudhom@willamette.edu

PRUE, Stephen ... 785-832-6644. 187 B
stephen.prue@bie.edu

PRUETT, Dena ... 318-869-5715. 201 H
dpruett@centenary.edu

PRUETT, Diana ... 662-243-2675. 266 I
dpruett@eastms.edu

PRUETT, Karen ... 910-521-6270. 369 B
karen.pruett@uncp.edu

PRUETT, Kristine ... 570-408-4676. 437 F
kristine.pruett@wilkes.edu

PRUETT, Robert, R ... 919-658-7760. 357 I
rpruett@moc.edu

PRUETT, Tim ... 740-245-7358. 392 A
tpruett@rio.edu

PRUITT, Aaron ... 541-684-7217. 405 C
aaronp@nwcu.edu

PRUITT, Chris ... 402-449-2917. 289 H
cpruitt@graceu.edu

PRUITT, Dennis, A ... 803-777-4172. 447 G
dpruitt@sc.edu

PRUITT, George, A ... 609-984-1105. 308 A
gpruitt@tesc.edu

PRUITT, Glenell ... 903-730-4890. 474 O
gpruitt@jarvis.edu

PRUITT, Jason ... 470-239-3103. 133 D
jason.pruitt@ung.edu

PRUITT, John ... 408-848-4732... 45 F
jpruitt@gavilan.edu

PRUITT, Karl ... 205-929-6348... 5 D
kpruitt@lawsonstate.edu

PRUITT, Leah, L ... 864-587-4225. 447 B
pruittl@smcsc.edu

PRUITT, Nancy ... 315-228-7220. 320 F
npruitt@colgate.edu

PRUITT, Samory, T ... 205-348-8376... 8 D
samory.pruitt@ua.edu

PRUITT, Steven ... 561-237-7834. 108 X
spruitt@lynn.edu

PRUNTY, Bonnie, S ... 607-274-3141. 327 E
bprunty@ithaca.edu

PRUNTY, Kathleen, A ... 909-869-3380... 32 G
kaprunty@csupomona.edu

PRUNTY, Rose ... 715-365-4481. 540 G
rprunty@nicoletcollege.edu

PRUS, Mark ... 607-753-2207. 343 B
mark.prus@cortland.edu

PRUSHA, Todd ... 319-398-5565. 180 J
tprusha@kirkwood.edu

PRUSKOWSKI, Nancy ... 215-968-8514. 411 B
pruskows@bucks.edu

PRUSS, Linda ... 513-244-4408. 377 G
linda_pruss@mail.msj.edu

PRUSSIN, Shari ... 212-217-4000. 324 C
shari_prussin@fitnyc.edu

PRY, George ... 412-809-5100. 430 H
pry.georgel@pti.edu

PRYCE-SHEEHAN, Linda 559-453-2038... 45 D
linda.pryce-sheehan@fresno.edu

PRYJMAK, Myron ... 718-409-7311. 346 D
mpryjmak@sunypurchase.edu

PRYLES, Kathyrn ... 508-588-9100. 232 A

PRYOR, Charles ... 212-752-1530. 328 G
charles.pryor@limcollege.edu

PRYOR, Douglas ... 305-809-3184. 104 I
douglas.pryor@fkcc.edu

PRYOR, Kim, A ... 336-342-4261. 363 C
pryork@rockinghamcc.edu

PRYOR, Raymond, G ... 570-208-5828. 419 P
rgpryor@kings.edu

PRYOR, Sara ... 812-855-1610. 167 F
spryor@indiana.edu

PRYSTOWSKY, Richard .. 517-483-1156. 245 H
prystowr@lcc.edu

PRZEKURAT, Paris ... 405-422-1442. 399 B
przekuratp@redlandscc.edu

PRZYBLYSKI, Jeannene .. 661-255-1050... 31 C
jeannene@calarts.edu

PRZYGOCKI, Ginny ... 989-686-9276. 242 C
vlprzygo@delta.edu

PRZYGODA, Melitha, R .. 203-576-4588... 91 G
mprzygod@bridgeport.edu

PRZYMUSINSKI, Lori, A 248-942-3334. 248 D

PRZYWARA, Richard, T .. 610-430-4156. 430 A
rprzywara@wcufoundation.org

PSAILA, Marisa ... 585-475-4932. 337 L
mxpdar@rit.edu

PSARRIS, Kleanthis .... 718-951-3170. 317 C
LPsarris@brooklyn.cuny.edu
PUCCI, Tom .... 724-938-4351. 428 A
pucci@calu.edu
PUCINE, Richard .... 315-792-5309. 331 I
rpucine@mvcc.edu
PUCKETT, Benjamin .... 727-726-1153. 100 E
benpuckett@clearwater.edu
PUCKETT, Christopher .... 303-315-6619... 86 A
chris.puckett@ucdenver.edu
PUCKETT, Jack .... 252-492-2061. 364 F
puckett@vgcc.edu
PUCKETT, Jackie, A .... 864-488-4585. 444 L
jpuckett@limestone.edu
PUCKETT, Jeff .... 608-363-2651. 531 M
puckettj@beloit.edu
PUCKETT, Wendy .... 270-247-8521. 197 H
wpuckett@midcontinent.edu
PUCKETT-BOLER, Laura . 864-503-5194. 448 H
lpuckett-boler@uscupstate.edu
PUDDESTER,
Frederick, W .... 413-597-4421. 238 D
frederick.w.puddester@williams.edu
PUETT, Debbie .... 828-395-1481. 361 C
dpuett@isothermal.edu
PUFFENBARGER, Jess ... 270-534-3504. 196 G
jess.puffenbarger@kctcs.edu
PUFFER, Anna, L .... 606-436-5721. 195 C
lois.puffer@kctcs.edu
PUFHAL, Joy .... 207-780-5512. 212 H
jpufhal@usm.maine.edu
PUGH, Alicina .... 601-979-1325. 267 E
alcinia.j.pugh@jsums.edu
PUGH, Benjamin, W .... 318-670-9302. 207 A
bpugh@susla.edu
PUGH, Daniel .... 479-575-5004... 23 I
djpugh@uark.edu
PUGH, David .... 912-525-5000. 131 B
dpugh@scad.edu
PUGH, Jason .... 601-928-6233. 268 C
jason.pugh@mgccc.edu
PUGH, John .... 907-796-6568... 11 A
john.pugh@uas.alaska.edu
PUGH, Maureen, N .... 570-372-4157. 433 H
pugh@susqu.edu
PUGH, Nathaniel .... 631-451-4129. 346 E
pughn@sunysuffolk.edu
PUGH, Paul, F .... 610-519-4200. 436 F
paul.pugh@villanova.edu
PUGH, Vicki .... 561-803-2012. 110 B
viki_pugh@pba.edu
PUGH, W. Russ .... 330-684-8916. 390 F
wrp@uakron.edu
PUGH-SEEMSTER, Nora . 405-682-7831. 397 E
npseemster@occc.edu
PUGLIESE, Beth .... 408-924-1116... 36 A
beth.pugliese@sjsu.edu
PUGLIESE, Mike, A .... 918-663-9000. 398 L
mikep@plattcollege.org
PUGLIESE, Stephen .... 610-647-4400. 418 I
spugliese@immaculata.edu
PUGLIESI, Karen, L .... 928-523-1580... 16 C
karen.pugliesi@nau.edu
PUGLISI, Michael, J .... 276-944-6662. 504 H
mpuglisi@ehc.edu
PUGNAIRE, Michele, P .. 508-856-4250. 229 C
michele.pugnaire@umassmed.edu
PUHALA, Kimberly .... 617-984-1727. 235 I
kpuhala@quincycollege.edu
PUHL, Diane .... 313-927-1443. 246 D
dpuhl@marygrove.edu
PUICH, Sam .... 801-302-2800. 496 B
sam.puich@neumont.edu
PUIG, Ivan, O .... 787-257-7373. 552 H
ivpuig@suagm.edu
PULAKOS, Joan .... 208-885-6716. 139 D
pulakos@uidaho.edu
PULEIO, Samuel, T .... 814-393-2280. 428 C
spuleio@clarion.edu
PULIAFICO, Venus .... 216-368-4530. 375 J
venus.puliafico@case.edu
PULIAFITO, Carmen, A ... 323-442-1900... 74 A
deanksom@usc.edu
PULICE, Jon .... 814-732-1763. 428 E
jpulice@edinboro.edu
PULIDO, Susie .... 602-286-8224... 14 L
susie.pulido@gwmail.maricopa.edu
PULLEN, Roderick, C ...... 340-693-1536. 555 E
rpullen@live.uvi.edu
PULLER, Beverly, J .... 219-785-5337. 172 A
bpuller@pnc.edu
PULLEY, Brett .... 757-727-5000. 505 F
brett.pulley@hamptonu.edu
PULLEY, Eric .... 618-985-3741. 148 J
ericpulley@jalc.edu
PULLEY, Kay .... 903-675-6376. 488 D
kpulley@tvcc.edu
PULLEY, Lawrence, B ..... 757-221-2891. 503 N
larry.pulley@mason.wm.edu
PULLIAM, DeWayne .... 615-794-4254. 457 Q
dpulliam@omorecollege.edu
PULLIAM, Jim .... 218-755-2220. 258 A
jpulliam@bemidjistate.edu
PULLIAM, Joni, L .... 315-792-3344. 349 F
jpulliam@utica.edu
PULLIN, Daniel .... 405-325-2070. 401 B
dpullin@ou.edu
PULLIN, Darlene .... 361-570-4850. 489 E
pullind@uhv.edu
PULLING, David .... 337-550-1390. 205 B
PULLINS, Tami, P .... 620-229-6247. 190 G
tami.pullins@sckans.edu
PULLIUM, Mark, H .... 406-243-6260. 286 H
mark.pullium@umontana.edu
PULLIZA, Carmen .... 787-743-7979. 552 I
cpulliza@suagm.edu
PULS, Charles .... 585-275-3226. 349 C
cpuls@finaid.rochester.edu
PULS, Kevin .... 815-967-7329. 157 B
kpuls@rockfordcareercollege.edu
PULSIPHER, Allan, G ..... 225-578-4400. 204 O
agpul@lsu.edu
PULTRO, Judith .... 239-985-3477. 101 O
jpultro@edison.edu
PULTZ, Stephen, F .... 619-260-4506... 73 I
spultz@sandiego.edu
PULVER, Shayne .... 615-226-3990. 455 N
spulver@lincolntech.com
PUMA, Lynn, M .... 716-878-5509. 343 A
pumalm@buffalostate.edu
PUMARIEGA, Madeline .. 305-237-7600. 109 D
mpumarie@mdc.edu
PUMERANTZ, Philip .... 909-469-5200... 76 B
ppumerantz@westernu.edu
PUMPHREY, Dennis .... 970-351-2245... 86 C
dennis.pumphrey@unco.edu
PUMPHREY, Reri .... 323-953-4000... 51 G
pumphrrn@lacitycollege.edu
PUMROY, B.J .... 304-876-5155. 529 I
bpumroy@shepherd.edu
PUNCH, Walter .... 617-989-4097. 237 G
punchw@wit.edu
PUNCHES, Jeffery .... 989-386-6654. 247 B
jpunches@midmich.edu
PUNCHES, Kathy, M .... 419-783-2590. 379 C
kpunches@defiance.edu
PUNCKE, Frederick, D .... 864-503-5500. 448 H
rpuncke@uscupstate.edu
PUNEKY, Warren .... 504-671-6100. 203 A
wpunek@dcc.edu
PUNSONI, Art .... 315-228-7474. 320 F
apunsoni@colgate.edu
PUNZALAN HALL,
Alizza .... 727-864-7979. 101 N
punzalat@eckerd.edu
PUOTINEN, John, V .... 215-248-7304. 422 F
jpuotinen@ltsp.edu
PUPEK, Christine .... 845-569-3346. 332 B
christine.pupek@msmc.edu
PUPLIS, Allan .... 269-467-9945. 242 H
apuplis@glenoaks.edu
PUPPALA, Kuldeep .... 207-602-2708. 213 A
kpuppala@une.edu
PURA, Robert, L .... 413-775-1410. 231 E
pura@gcc.mass.edu
PURATICH, Kate .... 253-589-5846. 518 B
kate.puratich@cptc.edu
PURCE, Thomas, J .... 610-436-3307. 430 A
tpurce@wcupa.edu
PURCE, Thomas, L .... 360-867-6100. 519 J
purcel@evergreen.edu
PURCELL, Anthony, B ..... 205-934-2297..... 8 E
bpurcell@uab.edu
PURCELL, Chris .... 405-325-4122. 401 B
regentspurcell@ou.edu
PURCELL, Francesca ...... 781-239-3111. 231 G
fpurcell@massbay.edu
PURCELL, Ladonna, M .... 606-783-2323. 198 A
l.purcell@moreheadstate.edu
PURCELL, Meredith .... 815-802-8512. 149 C
mpurcell@kcc.edu
PURCELL, Ruth .... 724-287-8711. 411 C
ruth.purcell@bc3.edu
PURCELL, Satch .... 949-794-9090... 68 D
spurcell@stanbridge.edu
PURCELL, Stacy, R .... 757-446-6002. 504 E
purcellsr@evms.edu
PURCELL, Susan, K .... 305-284-9830. 118 F
skpurcell@miami.edu
PURCELL, William .... 412-392-3481. 431 B
wpurcell@pointpark.edu
PURDIE, Jim .... 815-825-2086. 149 F
jim.purdue@kishwaukeecollege.edu
PURDOM, Kirk .... 859-233-8551. 199 I
kpurdom@transy.edu
PURDUE-LYNCH,
Barbara .... 201-355-1122. 302 A
lynchb@felician.edu
PURDY, G. Michael .... 212-854-1656. 321 D
gmp63@columbia.edu
PURDY, Paulette .... 713-221-2746. 489 D
purdyp@uhd.edu
PURDY, Ryan .... 308-535-3720. 290 J
purdyr@mpcc.edu
PURECE, Sarita .... 415-257-0137... 42 J
sarita.purece@dominican.edu
PURI, Anil .... 657-278-2592... 33 E
apuri@fullerton.edu
PURIFOY, Tangela .... 251-578-1313..... 6 D
tpurifoy@rstc.edu
PUROHIT, Yasmin, S ..... 412-397-5472. 431 I
purohit@rmu.edu
PURSER, Charles .... 252-335-0821. 359 F
charles_purser@albemarle.edu
PURSLEY, Linda .... 617-349-8563. 228 B
lpursley@lesley.edu
PURVIS, Donnie .... 817-598-6284. 494 G
dpurvis@wc.edu
PURVIS, Kathy .... 317-274-5924. 168 D
kpurvis@iupui.edu
PURVIS, Sharon .... 937-393-3431. 389 B
spurvis@sscc.edu
PURVIS-ROBERTS,
Kathleen .... 909-621-8736... 59 G
kpurvis@jsd.claremont.edu
PURWIN, Lori .... 908-737-4880. 302 F
lpurwin@kean.edu
PURYEAR, Margaret .... 303-352-3038... 81 D
margaret.puryear@cccs.edu
PUSECKER, Kathleen, L .. 302-831-8537... 94 B
klp@udel.edu
PUSEY, Stephen, M .... 615-248-1258. 462 D
spusey@trevecca.edu
PUSICH, Ruth .... 630-617-3080. 145 A
ruthp@elmhurst.edu
PUSKA, Douglas, P .... 978-762-4000. 232 D
dpuska@northshore.edu
PUSTAY, Pamela, S .... 330-471-8159. 383 D
ppustay@malone.edu
PUSZCZEWICZ, Thomas . 517-264-7192. 250 B
tpuszcze@sienaheights.edu
PUTMAN, Jeffrey .... 718-270-2187. 342 D
jeffrey.putman@downstate.edu
PUTMAN, Joe .... 920-686-6233. 536 A
Joe.Putman@sl.edu
PUTMAN, Stephen, J ...... 256-765-4178..... 9 C
jsputman@una.edu
PUTNAM, Diana .... 518-736-3622. 325 A
diana.putnam@fmcc.suny.edu
PUTNAM, Jessica, J .... 641-422-4103. 181 D
putnajes@niacc.edu
PUTNAM, Lisa .... 805-378-1448... 74 F
lputnam@vcccd.edu
PUTNAM, Mark .... 281-756-3500. 465 D
mputnam@alvincollege.edu
PUTNAM, Mark, L .... 641-628-5269. 176 E
president@central.edu
PUTNAM, Robin .... 701-328-2960. 371 B
robin.putnam@ndus.edu
PUTO, Christopher, P ..... 651-962-4201. 265 C
cpputo@stthomas.edu
PUTTHOFF, Stephen .... 303-373-2008... 85 C
sputthoff@rvu.edu
PUTZKE, Robert .... 406-994-3220. 287 B
rputzke@montana.edu
PUZAROWSKI, Alice ...... 814-866-8114. 420 E
apuzarowski@lecom.edu
PUZO, Madeline .... 213-821-5491... 74 A
puzo@usc.edu
PUZZIFERRO, Maria .... 303-753-6046... 85 B
mariap@rmcad.edu
PYDO, Todd .... 715-682-1682. 535 D
tpydo@northland.edu
PYE, Christopher .... 973-353-5679. 306 D
cpye@rutgers.edu
PYE-JUMPER, Sadie .... 803-327-7402. 442 D
spjumper@clintonjuniorcollege.edu
PYER, Terri .... 831-755-6706... 46 G
tpyer@hartnell.edu
PYFFEROEN, Michelle .... 507-285-7425. 261 A
michelle.pyfferoen@rctc.edu
PYFFEROEN, Michelle .... 507-280-3110. 261 A
michelle.pyfferoen@rctc.edu
PYKE, David, F .... 619-260-4886... 73 I
davidpyke@sandiego.edu
PYLE, Brenda .... 770-962-7580. 127 D
bpyle@gwinnetttech.edu
PYLE, James .... 949-582-4585... 67 C
jpyle@saddleback.edu
PYLE, Jeanne .... 903-566-7351. 492 D
jpyle@uttyler.edu
PYLE, Marsha, A .... 816-235-2010. 283 D
pylem@umkc.edu
PYLE, Patrick .... 213-738-6691... 68 C
generalcounsel@swlaw.edu
PYLE, Rowdy .... 816-604-6524. 277 D
rowdy.pyle@mcckc.edu
PYLE, Sally .... 701-777-2219. 371 C
sally.pyle@und.edu
PYLES, Gloria, D .... 803-536-8266. 446 G
gpyles@scsu.edu
PYLES, Jesse .... 207-948-9295. 211 I
jpyles@unity.edu
PYLES, Marvin, L .... 410-543-6035. 220 D
mlpyles@salisbury.edu
PYLES, Rebecca, A .... 423-439-6076. 459 C
pylesr@etsu.edu
PYLICAN, Rhonda .... 303-352-3037... 81 D
rhonda.pylican@cccs.edu
PYNES, Penelope, J .... 336-334-5404. 369 A
penelope_pynes@uncg.edu
PYO, Chang Sun .... 770-279-0507. 124 I
changsun.pyo@gmail.com
PYO, George, F .... 814-472-3014. 432 D
gpyo@francis.edu
PYRON, Susan .... 717-337-6542. 417 B
spyron@gettysburg.edu
PYTLESKI, Kurt .... 402-844-7272. 291 I
athleticdirector@northeast.edu
PYZER, Shanna .... 425-249-4777. 524 D
shanna.pyzer@tlc.edu

Q

QADER, Mirwais .... 608-246-6198. 540 C
mqader@madisoncollege.edu
QAISSAUNEE, Laura, V .. 732-224-2756. 299 G
lqaissaunee@brookdalecc.edu
QAYOUMI, Mohammed .. 408-924-1177... 36 A
sjsupres@sjsu.edu
QUACKENBUSH,
Kent, B .... 303-762-6923... 81 G
kent.quackenbush@denverseminary.edu
QUACKENBUSH, Robert . 509-359-2366. 519 C
rquackenbush@ewu.edu
QUADE, Stephanie .... 414-288-1412. 534 B
stephanie.quade@marquette.edu
QUAGLIANA, David .... 423-614-8415. 455 L
dquagliana@leeuniversity.edu
QUAGLIERI, Philip, L ..... 617-287-7700. 228 G
philip.quaglieri@umb.edu
QUAID, Randi .... 510-848-5232... 45 A
rquaid@fst.edu
QUAID-MALTAGLIATI,
Marian .... 805-922-6966... 26 K
marianqm@hancockcollege.edu
QUAKENBUSH, Win .... 910-893-1245. 352 K
quakenbush@campbell.edu
QUALIA, Linda, R .... 972-881-5779. 469 G
lqualia@collin.edu
QUALLS, Mike .... 479-979-1378... 25 J
mqualls@ozarks.edu
QUAM, Jean, K .... 612-626-5177. 264 G
jquam@umn.edu
QUAN, Gamward .... 909-447-2560... 39 E
gquan@cst.edu
QUAN, Jeff .... 972-860-7371. 470 I
JQuan@dcccd.edu
QUAN, Peter .... 323-343-2700... 34 A
pquan@cslanet.calstatela.edu
QUANBECK, Kirsten, K ... 949-824-5594... 71 B
quanbeck@uci.edu
QUARBERG, Brad, R ...... 608-785-8572. 536 G
bquarberg@uwlax.edu
QUARLES, Markel .... 870-972-3025... 19 N
mquarles@astate.edu
QUARLES, Robert .... 404-756-4010. 121 A
rquarles@atlm.edu
QUARTEY, Kojo .... 734-384-4166. 247 C
kquartey@monroeccc.edu
QUASNEY, Thomas, D ... 803-777-8261. 447 G
tquasney@fmc.sc.edu
QUAST, Debra .... 805-565-6182... 76 D
dquast@westmont.edu
QUATRANO, Ralph, S .... 314-935-6350. 284 L
rsq@wustl.edu
QUATTLEBAUM, James .. 903-675-6223. 488 D
jquattlebaum@tvcc.edu
QUATTLEBAUM, Mickey . 501-812-2212... 22 G
mquattlebaum@pulaskitech.edu
QUATTRO, Mike .... 734-432-5341. 246 B
mquattro@madonna.edu
QUATTROCCHI, John ..... 518-743-2394. 345 E
quattrocchij@sunyacc.edu
QUATTROCCHI, Nancy ... 978-934-4991. 229 B
nancy_quattrocchi@uml.edu
QUAY, Sara .... 978-232-2200. 226 C
squay@endicott.edu
QUAYE, Chandra .... 202-408-2400... 96 F
QUAYE, Sandra .... 603-899-4241. 296 H
quayes@franklinpierce.edu
QUBBAJ, Ala .... 956-665-7899. 492 B
qubbaj@utpa.edu
QUBEIN, Nido, R .... 336-841-9201. 355 C
nqubein@highpoint.edu
QUDDUS, Munir .... 936-261-9200. 482 F
muquddus@pvamu.edu
QUEEN, Harrell, W .... 706-245-7226. 124 D
hqueen@ec.edu
QUEEN, Michael .... 864-587-4222. 447 B
queenm@smcsc.edu
QUEEN, Scott .... 336-506-4278. 357 M
scott.queen@alamancecc.edu

QUEEN, Scott .... 636-949-4920. 276 D
squeen@lindenwood.edu
QUEEN-HUBERT, Jody ... 212-346-1950. 335 J
jqueenhubert@pace.edu
QUEENAN, Rosemary ..... 518-445-3394. 313 C
rquee@albanylaw.edu
QUEENAN, Theresa .... 410-651-6447. 219 E
tqueenan@umes.edu
QUEENER, Frank, R .... 585-785-1375. 324 D
queenefr@flcc.edu
QUEENER, Karen, D .... 865-539-7025. 461 D
kqueener@pstcc.edu
QUEENER, Sherry, F .... 317-274-1577. 168 D
queens@iupui.edu
QUEHL-ENGEL,
Catherine, M .... 319-895-4402. 177 A
cquehl-engel@cornellcollege.edu
QUEIROZ, Hermano .... 270-789-5202. 193 D
hsqueiroz@cambpellsville.edu
QUEJADA, JoAnna .... 951-639-5320... 55 B
jequejada@msjc.edu
QUERO-MENDEZ, Doris . 787-725-6500. 547 H
dquero@albizu.edu
QUERY, Lance .... 504-865-5131. 207 C
lquery@tulane.edu
QUESADA, Edmond .... 719-502-3352... 84 A
ed.quesada@ppcc.edu
QUESENBERRY,
Marcia, K .... 276-328-0254. 511 C
mkq4w@uvawise.edu
QUESENBERRY, Scot, R . 336-734-7317. 360 E
squesn@forsythtech.edu
QUEST, Karen .... 315-568-3060. 333 C
kquest@nycc.edu
QUEST, Richard .... 315-334-7701. 331 I
rquest@mvcc.edu
QUICK, Angela .... 865-981-8038. 456 D
angela.quick@maryvillecollege.edu
QUICK, Debbie .... 520-515-5412... 12 R
quickd@cochise.edu
QUICK, Donna .... 803-786-3612. 443 B
dquick@columbiasc.edu
QUICK, James, E .... 214-768-1115. 481 A
jquick@smu.edu
QUICK, Matthew, D .... 816-501-4127. 280 I
matt.quick@rockhurst.edu
QUICK, Michael, W .... 213-740-6670... 74 A
evp@usc.edu
QUICK, Semetta .... 803-268-2543. 446 B
quicksv@octech.edu
QUIGLEY, Brian .... 603-358-2438. 298 F
bquigley1@keene.edu
QUIGLEY, David .... 617-552-2393. 224 A
david.quigley@bc.edu
QUIGLEY, James, M ...... 252-451-8227. 362 D
jquigley@nashcc.edu
QUIGLEY, JR.,
Kenneth, K .... 617-333-2236. 225 E
kquigley@curry.edu
QUIGLEY, Lori .... 518-244-2496. 338 C
l.quigley@sage.edu
QUIGLEY, Peter .... 808-956-3869. 136 D
quigleyp@hawaii.edu
QUIGLEY, Susan .... 773-380-6785. 140 D
susan.quigley@seabury.edu
QUIGLEY, William, R ...... 304-293-6600. 530 D
william.quigley@mail.wvu.edu
QUIJANO, Xochil .... 303-797-5635... 78 F
xochil.quijano@arapahoe.edu
QUILES, Elisa .... 787-257-7373. 552 H
equiles@suagm.edu
QUILL, Robin .... 508-929-8013. 230 G
rquill@worcester.edu
QUILLEN, Carol, E .... 704-894-2201. 353 J
caquillen@davidson.edu
QUILLEN, David .... 630-466-7900. 162 J
dquillen@waubonsee.edu
QUILLIAN, Benjamin, F .. 562-951-4600... 32 E
bquillian@calstate.edu
QUIMBY, Kristyn .... 574-520-4154. 168 E
krirhawk@iusb.edu
QUIMBY, Linda .... 603-899-4059. 296 H
quimbyl@franklinpierce.edu
QUINCY, Barbara, I .... 724-946-7928. 437 B
quincybi@westminster.edu
QUINDT, Willie .... 308-635-6083. 293 E
wquindt@wncc.edu
QUINER, Michael, W ...... 509-527-4975. 525 E
quinerm@whitman.edu
QUINLAN, Brian .... 508-213-2112. 235 E
brian.quinlan@nichols.edu
QUINLAN, Carolyn .... 517-265-5161. 238 G
QUINLAN, Catherine ...... 213-821-2344... 74 A
cquinlan@usc.edu
QUINLAN, Jeremiah .... 203-432-9321... 93 A
jeremiah.quinlan@yale.edu
QUINLAN, Joseph .... 201-761-7302. 306 L
jquinlan@saintpeters.edu
QUINLAN, Maureen .... 619-684-8779... 56 C
mquinlan@newschoolarch.edu
QUINLAN BRAME, Julie 414-382-6371. 531 I
julie.quinlan@alverno.edu
QUINLEY, Melissa .... 828-398-7633. 357 N
mquinley@abtech.edu
QUINLIVAN, Gary .... 724-537-4597. 432 G
gary.quinlivan@email.stvincent.edu
QUINN, Aaron .... 740-245-7234. 392 A
aquinn@rio.edu
QUINN, Amanda .... 815-729-9020. 149 A
aquinn@jjc.edu
QUINN, Anthony .... 734-384-4279. 247 C
aquinn@monroeccc.edu
QUINN, Arthur .... 561-732-4424. 112 G
aquinn@svdp.edu
QUINN, Bill .... 281-487-1170. 484 H
bquinn@txchiro.edu
QUINN, Bonnie .... 781-768-7184. 236 A
bonnie.quinn@regiscollege.edu
QUINN, Bridget .... 212-787-5300. 313 F
info@amda.edu
QUINN, Brigid .... 402-878-2380. 290 D
bquinn@littlepriest.edu
QUINN, Catherine .... 215-248-7137. 413 A
quinnc@chc.edu
QUINN, Charles, C .... 512-223-8119. 466 I
cquinn@austincc.edu
QUINN, Christine, J .... 312-261-3315. 153 I
christine.quinn@nl.edu
QUINN, Edward, M .... 202-687-4134... 95 E
quinne@georgetown.edu
QUINN, Erin .... 802-443-5253. 499 H
quinn@middlebury.edu
QUINN, Evelyn .... 732-987-2314. 302 B
quinne@georgian.edu
QUINN, Floyd .... 512-444-8082. 485 B
fquinn@thsu.edu
QUINN, Frank .... 619-849-2338... 59 L
frankquinn@pointloma.edu
QUINN, Gianna .... 215-641-5554. 417 F
quinn.g@gmc.edu
QUINN, Gina .... 228-896-9727. 266 B
QUINN, Jack, F .... 716-851-1200. 323 I
jquinn@ecc.edu
QUINN, Joseph, F .... 617-552-3260. 224 A
joseph.f.quinn@bc.edu
QUINN, Joseph, G .... 718-817-3013. 324 G
jgquinn@fordham.edu
QUINN, Kathy .... 314-529-9476. 276 G
kquinn@maryville.edu
QUINN, Kevin .... 610-647-4400. 418 I
kquinn@immaculata.edu
QUINN, Kevin .... 920-403-3051. 535 L
kevin.quinn@snc.edu
QUINN, Kevin, C .... 315-443-8338. 347 C
kcquinn@syr.edu
QUINN, SJ, Kevin, P ..... 570-941-7500. 436 A
presidentquinn@scranton.edu
QUINN, Kimbra .... 806-894-9611. 480 H
kquinn@southplainscollege.edu
QUINN, Laurie, A .... 603-822-5417. 298 E
laurie.quinn@granite.edu
QUINN, Leslie .... 913-469-8500. 187 J
lquinn2@jccc.edu
QUINN, Linda .... 402-941-6280. 290 K
quinn@midlandu.edu
QUINN, Marisa, A .... 401-863-2453. 438 J
marisa_quinn@brown.edu
QUINN, Michael .... 206-296-5500. 523 E
quinnm@seattleu.edu
QUINN, Michael, G .... 585-292-2151. 332 A
mquinn@monroecc.edu
QUINN, Michael, J .... 434-947-8100. 508 D
mjquinn@randolphcollege.edu
QUINN, Michael, P .... 401-598-2945. 439 B
mquinn@jwu.edu
QUINN, Michelle .... 970-351-2773... 86 C
michelle.quinn@unco.edu
QUINN, Molly .... 319-226-2001. 175 D
molly.quinn@allencollege.edu
QUINN, Nicole .... 973-748-9000. 299 F
nicole_quinn@bloomfield.edu
QUINN, Penny .... 620-792-9303. 184 F
quinnp@bartonccc.edu
QUINN, Robert, E .... 563-588-7736. 180 L
bob.quinn@loras.edu
QUINN, Sarah, F .... 610-660-1230. 432 E
squinn@sju.edu
QUINN, Shaman .... 307-754-6232. 543 G
Shaman.Quinn@northwestcollege.edu
QUINN, Sharon .... 410-455-2540. 219 D
squinn@umbc.edu
QUINN, Stephen .... 973-618-3320. 300 A
squinn@caldwell.edu
QUINN, Susan .... 707-524-1598... 65 B
squinn@santarosa.edu
QUINN, Tania .... 914-654-5257. 320 H
tquinn@cnr.edu
QUINN, Teresa .... 845-437-5370. 349 G
QUINN, Thomas .... 989-275-5000. 245 B
tom.quinn@kirtland.edu
QUINN, Wade .... 252-493-7279. 362 G
wquinn@email.pittcc.edu
QUINN, William, P .... 302-356-6775 ... 94 E
william.p.quinn@wilmu.edu
QUINNAN, Timothy .... 619-594-5211... 35 D
tquinnan@mail.sdsu.edu
QUINNETT, Jim .... 325-793-4611. 476 E
jquinnett@mcm.edu
QUINONES, Carlos, A .... 787-753-0039. 551 D
QUINONES, Irma .... 787-758-2525. 554 F
irma.quinones1@upr.edu
QUINONES, Rosa .... 787-257-0000. 554 B
rosa.quinones1@upr.edu
QUINONEZ, Juliette .... 567-661-7234. 387 L
juliette_quinonez@owens.edu
QUINT, Doug .... 620-242-0586. 188 G
quintd@mcpherson.edu
QUINTAL, Jorge .... 336-334-5536. 369 A
j_quinta@uncg.edu
QUINTAL, Rollande .... 508-849-3340. 222 B
rquintal@annamaria.edu
QUINTANA, Elena .... 312-662-4021. 139 F
lkunard@adler.edu
QUINTANA, Javier .... 787-279-1912. 550 B
jquintana@bayamon.inter.edu
QUINTANA, Karla .... 505-428-1203. 311 J
karla.quintana@sfcc.edu
QUINTANA, Rosaura ...... 787-815-0000. 553 I
rosaura.quintana@upr.edu
QUINTANILLA, Hector ..... 817-531-4840. 488 A
hquintanilla@txwes.edu
QUINTANILLA, Kelly ...... 361-825-2659. 483 F
kelly.quintanilla@tamucc.edu
QUINTANS, Joel .... 817-272-2025. 491 B
quintas@uta.edu
QUINTERO-DEVLAEMINCK,
Monica .... 503-682-1862. 407 B
monicaqd@pioneerpacific.edu
QUINTERO-JIMENEZ,
Noel .... 787-725-6500. 547 H
nquintero@albizu.edu
QUINTONG, Joel, R .... 203-416-3417... 91 C
quintongj@sacredheart.edu
QUINTYNE, Renee .... 845-398-4207. 340 A
rquintyn@stac.edu
QUIREY, Debbie .... 405-744-2212. 396 M
dquirey@okstate.edu
QUIRK, Donna .... 312-915-8723. 151 H
dquirk@luc.edu
QUIRK, Joe .... 360-442-2207. 521 A
jquirk@lowercolumbia.edu
QUIRK-BAILEY, Sheila ... 847-925-6668. 145 H
squirk@harpercollege.edu
QUIROGA, Mercedes, A . 954-201-6511... 99 D
mquiroga@broward.edu
QUIROLGICO, Ray .... 314-977-7226. 281 I
rquirolg@slu.edu
QUIROS, Kristi .... 830-372-8060. 485 C
kquiros@tlu.edu
QUIROZ, Gloria .... 773-878-3606. 158 B
gquiroz@staugustine.edu
QUISENBERRY, Brian ..... 205-226-4670..... 2 C
bqusenberry@bsc.edu
QUISENBERRY, JR.,
Henry, L .... 334-347-2623..... 3 G
cquisenberry@escc.edu
QUISTGARD, Fred .... 207-216-4406. 211 C
fquistgard@yccc.edu
QUIÑONES, Angel .... 787-258-1501. 548 H
alquinones@columbiaco.edu
QUIÑONES, Zulma .... 787-264-1912. 551 A
aquino@sg.inter.edu
QURAISHI, Farrukh .... 813-253-7014. 106 M
fquraishi@hccfl.edu

R

RAAB, David .... 212-463-0400. 348 B
david.raab@touro.edu
RAAB, Jennifer, J .... 212-772-4242. 318 C
jennifer.raab@hunter.cuny.edu
RAAB, Keith .... 541-881-5828. 408 C
kraab@tvcc.cc
RAAB, Lettie, M .... 936-261-5900. 482 F
lmraab@pvamu.edu
RAAB, Maryrose .... 315-792-7215. 346 C
maryrose.raab@sunyit.edu
RAADA, Hank .... 602-639-7500... 13 S
RAATTAMA, Kristina .... 305-348-2103. 115 B
maija.raattama@fiu.edu
RABAGO, Cristine .... 650-543-3782... 54 C
crabago@menlo.edu
RABALAIS, Nicole .... 615-248-1237. 462 D
nrabalais@trevecca.edu
RABB, Harriet .... 212-327-8070. 338 A
harriet.rabb@rockefeller.edu
RABBITT, Kara, M .... 973-720-2180. 308 I
rabbittk@wpunj.edu
RABBITT, Rhonda, M ..... 608-796-3384. 539 E
rmrabbitt@viterbo.edu
RABELO, Virginia .... 305-821-3333. 105 A
vrabelo@fnu.edu
RABENOLD, Scott .... 865-974-9557. 463 C
srabenol@utk.edu
RABENSTEIN, Dallas ...... 951-827-5034... 71 E
dallas.rabenstein@ucr.edu
RABER, II, Donald, R ..... 864-833-8233. 446 D
draber@presby.edu
RABIDEAU, Melissa .... 314-837-6777. 280 K
mrabideau@slcconline.edu
RABIDEAU, Shelly, S ...... 317-940-8423. 164 J
srabideа@butler.edu
RABIL, Alison .... 919-684-3501. 354 A
alison.rabil@duke.edu
RABINEAU, Kevin .... 269-965-3931. 244 O
rabineauk@kellogg.edu
RABINOVICH, Oleg .... 718-818-6470. 339 H
RABINOVICH, Sheryl ...... 213-624-1200... 44 D
srabinovich@fidm.edu
RABINOWITCH, Janet .... 812-855-4773. 167 F
jrabinow@indiana.edu
RABINOWITZ, Celia, E .. 240-895-4267. 218 A
cerabinowitz@smcm.edu
RABINOWITZ, Eli .... 718-377-0777. 336 I
RABINOWITZ, Stuart ...... 516-463-6800. 326 D
president@hofstra.edu
RABINOWITZ, Vita .... 212-772-4150. 318 C
vita.rabinowitz@hunter.cuny.edu
RABITOY, Eric .... 626-914-8788... 38 K
erabitoy@citruscollege.edu
RABLE, Michelle, A .... 419-824-3816. 383 C
mrable@lourdes.edu
RABY, Domonic .... 601-877-6333. 265 G
sm8053@bncollege.com
RABY, Susan .... 315-312-2260. 344 A
susan.raby@oswego.edu
RABY-GENTRY, Tori .... 931-393-1617. 461 A
RACCANELLO, Paul .... 415-485-3223... 42 J
raccanello@dominican.edu
RACE, Debbie .... 828-251-6417. 368 C
drace@unca.edu
RACE, John .... 614-251-4303. 386 B
racej@ohiodominican.edu
RACE, Mary Jo .... 412-624-4200. 435 C
mar6@pitt.edu
RACETTE, Patrick .... 906-353-4600. 245 A
pracette@kbocc.org
RACHAL, Michael .... 504-865-2486. 205 H
rachal@loyno.edu
RACHAVONG, Darrelene . 972-883-6236. 491 E
dar@utdallas.edu
RACHFORD, Jennifer ...... 909-607-2201... 60 A
jennifer.rachford@pomona.edu
RACHITA, David, A .... 281-283-2568. 489 C
rachita@uhcl.edu
RACINA, Kris .... 907-474-2600... 10 I
khracina@alaska.edu
RACINE, Gail, M .... 508-767-7283. 222 C
gracine@assumption.edu
RACINE, Leo .... 508-678-2811. 231 B
leo.racine@bristolcc.edu
RACIOPPI, Jerry .... 402-461-2503. 288 I
jerryracioppi@cccneb.edu
RACKETT, Peter .... 516-773-5564. 545 H
rackettp@usmma.edu
RACKLEY, J. Mike .... 662-325-9311. 268 D
mike.rackley@msstate.edu
RACKLEY, Richard, W ..... 865-688-9422. 454 I
info@fountainheadcollege.com
RACKLEY, Steven, P .... 419-434-4651. 391 D
rackley@findlay.edu
RACKLIFFE, Jerry, J .... 404-413-3000. 126 E
jracklif@gsu.edu
RACY, Mike .... 660-543-4112. 283 A
mracy@ucmo.edu
RACZYNSKI, James, M .. 501-526-6600... 24 C
RaczynskiJamesM@uams.edu
RACZYNSKI, Patricia, A . 205-934-5121..... 8 D
trish@uab.edu
RADAKOVICH, Dan .... 864-656-1935. 442 C
danrad1@clemson.edu
RADANT, Tia .... 651-450-3397. 258 H
tradant@inverhills.edu
RADCLIFFE, Denise .... 651-730-5100. 255 H
dradcliffe@globeuniversity.edu
RADCLIFFE, Shelby .... 323-259-2961... 56 I
Radcliffe@oxy.edu
RADCLIFFE, Steve .... 513-244-4381. 377 G
steve_radcliffe@mail.msj.edu
RADDA, Hank .... 602-639-7500... 13 S
RADDATZ, Susan .... 651-423-8205. 258 D
susan.raddatz@dctc.edu
RADECKE, Mark Wm .... 570-372-4220. 433 H
radecke@susqu.edu
RADECKI, Pete .... 417-873-7899. 273 H
pradecki@drury.edu
RADEL, Marie .... 765-455-9468. 168 A
meradel@iuk.edu
RADEMACHER, Eric .... 513-556-3304. 390 G
eric.rademacher@uc.edu

RADER, Brian 503-399-8074. 402 E brian.rader@chemeketa.edu
RADER, Claude, K 410-951-3858. 220 B drader@coppin.edu
RADER, Rachel 931-372-3016. 460 A rrader@tntech.edu
RADER, Sherri 309-649-6255. 160 E sherri.rader@src.edu
RADFORD, Amy, J 901-843-3870. 458 E radford@rhodes.edu
RADFORD, Laurie 503-552-1617. 404 H lradford@ncnm.edu
RADFORD, Marilyn 270-384-8022. 197 D radfordm@lindsey.edu
RADFORD, Ron 256-395-2211 7 C rradford@suscc.edu
RADFORD-HILL, Sheila 563-387-1486. 180 M radfsh01@luther.edu
RADIONOFF, Kathleen, A 608-258-2309. 540 C kradionoff@madisoncollege.edu
RADISH, Ross 215-596-7573. 435 H r.radish@usciences.edu
RADKE, Cheryl 623-245-4600 18 D cradke@uticuti.edu
RADLIFF, Mary 518-255-5211. 344 E radliffmd@cobleskill.edu
RADLO, Dolores 508-373-9705. 223 A dolores.radlo@becker.edu
RADLOWSKI, Mark, E 315-792-5467. 331 I mradlowski@mvcc.edu
RADNEY, Ron 661-654-3271 32 H rradney@csub.edu
RADSON, Darrell, J 309-677-2255. 140 I radson@bradley.edu
RADT, Jennifer 513-732-8964. 391 B jennifer.radt@uc.edu
RADT, Jennifer 513-732-5327. 391 B jennifer.radt@uc.edu
RADTKE, Elizabeth, L 651-523-2201. 256 A bradtke@hamline.edu
RADULESCU, Eugen 713-348-6725. 479 A eugen@rice.edu
RADVANSKY, Sandy, M 740-284-5357. 379 N sradvansky@franciscan.edu
RADWAN, Ann, B 320-308-4287. 261 B abradwan@stcloudstate.edu
RADYCKI, Diane, C 610-861-1680. 424 E medjr01@moravian.edu
RAE, Lisa 802-258-3149. 500 C lisa.rae@worldlearning.org
RAE, Mike, E 570-326-3761. 427 B mrae@pct.edu
RAE, Nicol 406-994-5023. 287 B nicol.rae@montana.edu
RAEFORD, James, E 540-828-5408. 502 J jraeford@bridgewater.edu
RAFATTI, Colleen 863-784-7411. 113 G colleen.rafatti@southflorida.edu
RAFERT, J. Bruce 701-231-7131. 371 G bruce.rafert@ndsu.edu
RAFES, Richard 315-792-3738. 349 F rsrafes@utica.edu
RAFFAELLE, Ryne 585-475-2055. 337 L ryne.raffaelle@rit.edu
RAFFAELLI, Bethany, M 920-924-6431. 540 F braffaelli@morainepark.edu
RAFFENSPERGER, Thomas 413-572-5233. 230 F traffensperger@westfield.ma.edu
RAFFERTY, Bobbie 502-585-9911. 199 C brafferty@spalding.edu
RAFFONE, Monica 203-392-5200 88 A
RAFFTERY, Cher, A 651-641-8235. 255 B rafftery@csp.edu
RAFIEE, Farnoosh 606-326-2069. 194 J farnoosh.rafiee@kctcs.edu
RAFIEYMEHR, Ali 603-641-4107. 298 C ali.rafieymehr@unh.edu
RAFN, H. Jeffrey 920-498-5411. 541 B jeff.rafn@nwtc.edu
RAFOOL, Dawn, M 863-638-3818. 119 C dawn.rafool@warner.edu
RAFOTH, Mary Ann 412-397-6020. 431 I rafoth@rmu.edu
RAGAIN, Charles 281-649-3314. 473 B cragain@hbu.edu
RAGAN, Jody 515-961-1517. 182 E jody.ragan@simpson.edu
RAGAN, Kathleen, E 973-655-3450. 303 D ragank@mail.montclair.edu
RAGAN, Nola 605-698-3966. 451 D nragan@swc.tc
RAGAN, Ronald, E 336-841-9193. 355 C rragan@highpoint.edu
RAGAR, Mel 785-670-2312. 191 D mel.ragar@washburn.edu
RAGENOVICH, Cassie 509-527-2815. 524 I cassie.ragenovich@wallawalla.edu
RAGER, Keith 814-254-0591. 413 C rorager@pa.gov
RAGER, Mary Jo 352-365-3550. 108 S ragermj@lssc.edu
RAGIO, Patricia, L 513-244-4871. 377 G patricia_ragio@mail.msj.edu
RAGLAND, Heather 901-272-5126. 456 F hragland@mca.edu
RAGLAND, Janet 903-233-3815. 475 J janetragland@letu.edu
RAGLAND, Mary 276-935-4349. 502 A mragland@asl.edu
RAGLAND, Mary, A 276-964-7286. 514 A mary.ragland@sw.edu
RAGLAND, Matthew 334-244-3138 2 A mragland@aum.edu
RAGNO, John 718-489-5364. 338 G jragno@sfc.edu
RAGNO, Kerry 757-822-1530. 514 C kragno@tcc.edu
RAGOSTA, Linda 508-541-1898. 225 F lragosta@dean.edu
RAGSDALE, Chad 417-626-1234. 279 J ragsdale.chad@occ.edu
RAGSDALE, Jennifer 201-761-6062. 306 L jragsdale@saintpeters.edu
RAGSDALE, Jill 507-284-9024. 254 G jill.ragsdale@mayo.edu
RAGSDALE, Katherine, H 617-682-1520. 226 D kragsdale@eds.edu
RAGSDALE, Keisha 336-517-2220. 352 H kragsdale@bennett.edu
RAGSDALE, Lisa, B 704-233-8710. 370 G lisa.ragsdale@wingate.edu
RAGSDALE, Lyn 713-348-4824. 479 A lyn.ragsdale@rice.edu
RAGSDALE, JR., Roy Lee 704-233-8118. 370 G lragsdale@wingate.edu
RAHEIM, Salome 860-570-9141 92 A Salome.Raheim@uconn.edu
RAHM, Carmen 509-963-2925. 517 F rahmc@cwu.edu
RAHM, Clare 216-687-3673. 377 F c.rahm@csuohio.edu
RAHMAN, Malik 209-946-2011 73 A mrahman@pacific.edu
RAHMAN, Pervez 773-907-4452. 142 A prahman@ccc.edu
RAHMANI, Loretta 909-593-3511 72 E lrahmani@laverne.edu
RAHN, Daniel 501-686-5680 24 C drahn@uams.edu
RAHN, Diane 419-251-1726. 383 G diane.rahn@mercycollege.edu
RAHN, Jason, M 651-641-8706. 255 B rahn@csp.edu
RAHNAMAY-AZAR, Amir 412-268-6011. 412 H amirr@andrew.cmu.edu
RAHNI, David, N 212-346-1555. 335 J drahni@pace.edu
RAHNI, Michael 213-383-8999 26 H
RAHR, JR., Carl, H 607-587-3535. 345 D rahrch@alfredstate.edu
RAI, Sanjay 240-567-7711. 216 F sanjay.rai@montgomerycollege.edu
RAIBLEY, Jon 503-517-1899. 408 I jraibley@westernseminary.edu
RAICH, Mike 218-262-6702. 258 G michaelraich@hibbing.edu
RAICHE, Brian 651-730-5100. 255 H braiche@globeuniversity.edu
RAICHE, Carol 978-232-2068. 226 C craiche@endicott.edu
RAICHE, Cheryl 617-217-9224. 222 G craiche@baystate.edu
RAICHIK, Shimon 323-937-2079 77 F
RAIKES, Mark, H 574-372-5100. 166 B raikesmh@grace.edu
RAIKES-COLBERT, Deborah 845-575-3000. 330 D Deborah.Raikes-Colbert@marist.edu
RAILEY, III, Clayton 610-359-5230. 414 D crailey@dccc.edu
RAILEY, George 559-324-6475 68 H george.railey@scccd.edu
RAILEY, Kevin, J 716-878-5601. 343 A raileykj@buffalostate.edu
RAILEY III, Clayton, A 610-359-5359. 414 D crailey@dccc.edu
RAILSBACK, Brian 828-227-7383. 369 E brailsba@wcu.edu
RAILSBACK, Travis 205-348-4904 8 D trailsback@sa.ua.edu
RAIMER, Ben, G 409-747-2789. 493 C bgraimer@utmb.edu
RAIMO, James 845-569-3227. 332 B james.raimo@msmc.edu
RAINE, Meredith 713-500-3050. 492 E meredith.raine@uth.tmc.edu
RAINE, Michael 505-454-3405. 310 E mraine@nmhu.edu
RAINER, Don 205-652-3576 9 F drainer@uwa.edu
RAINES, C. Fay 256-824-6345 8 F fay.raines@uah.edu
RAINES, Deborah 703-284-1530. 507 B debbie.raines@marymount.edu
RAINES, Jess, N 740-374-8716. 392 I jraines@wscc.edu
RAINES, Patrick 615-460-6000. 453 C pat.raines@belmont.edu
RAINES, Scott 432-264-5190. 473 E sraines@howardcollege.edu
RAINES, Stephany 912-525-5000. 131 B sraines@scad.edu
RAINEY, Jack, T 973-618-3230. 300 A jrainey@caldwell.edu
RAINEY, Kelli 704-378-1098. 355 K krainey@jcsu.edu
RAINEY, Marshall 706-821-8320. 130 C mrainey@paine.edu
RAINFORD, William 202-319-5454 94 G rainford@cua.edu
RAINONE, John, J 540-863-2827. 512 B rrainone@dslcc.edu
RAINS, Ben 501-812-2268 22 G brains@pulaskitech.edu
RAINS, Debbie 361-582-2560. 493 H deborah.rains@victoriacollege.edu
RAINS, Thomas, J 414-410-4535. 532 B tjrains@stritch.edu
RAINVILLE, Lynn 434-295-7210. 510 F lrainville@sbc.edu
RAINWATER, Robert 276-466-7924. 514 G robertrainwater@vic.edu
RAIOLA, Jill 203-285-2007 88 E jraiola@gwcc.commnet.edu
RAIOLA, Lisa 401-254-3302. 440 B lraiola@rwu.edu
RAISANEN, Gregg 320-762-4618. 257 O greggr@alextech.edu
RAISIAN, John 650-723-1198 68 E raisian@hoover.stanford.edu
RAISL, Gary 858-646-3126 64 E graisl@sanfordburnham.org
RAISOVICH, Andy 304-367-4682. 529 F andy.raisovich@fairmontstate.edu
RAISOVICH, Andy 304-367-4131. 529 F Andy.Raisovich@fairmontstate.edu
RAISOVICH, Joanie 304-367-4131. 529 F Joanie.Raisovich@fairmontstate.edu
RAJA, Jay 704-687-5737. 368 E jraja@uncc.edu
RAJA, Tasleem 312-939-0111. 144 D tasleem@eastwest.edu
RAJA, Tasleem 312-939-0113. 144 D tasleem@eastwest.edu
RAJABALLEY, Michael 787-751-0160. 548 J mrajaballey@cmpr.pr.gov
RAJALA, Sarah 515-294-9988. 175 H rajala@iastate.edu
RAJAN, Paul, G 212-563-6647. 348 I p.rajan@uts.edu
RAJAN, Ravi 914-251-6750. 344 D ravi.rajan@purchase.edu
RAJPUROHIT, Vikas 817-515-1254. 482 B vikas.rajpurohit@tccd.edu
RAJPUT, Hussein 651-523-2204. 256 A hrajput01@hamline.edu
RAKER, Keith 336-249-8186. 360 A kdraker@davidsonccc.edu
RAKER, Russell 702-992-2356. 294 G russell.raker@nsc.edu
RAKERS, Jason, T 330-941-3035. 394 A jtrakers@ysu.edu
RAKES, Melissa 302-259-6040 93 E mrakes@dtcc.edu
RAKES, Thomas, A 731-881-7500. 463 E trakes@utm.edu
RAKES, Thomas, D 910-962-3174. 369 C rakest@uncw.edu
RAKESTRAW, Jennie 803-323-2151. 449 G rakestrawj@winthrop.edu
RAKIN, Aluka 692-625-3394. 546 F
RAKNESS, Christy 419-530-4229. 392 B
RAKOCZY, Dana 562-907-4974 76 I drakoczy@whittier.edu
RAKOFF, Jill 860-701-5131 90 G rakoff_j@mitchell.edu
RAKOFF, Steve 817-515-3584. 482 B steve.rakoff@tccd.edu
RALEIGH, Edith 734-432-5457. 246 B eraleigh@madonna.edu
RALEIGH, Mary-Jeanne 910-521-6306. 369 B mary-jeanne.raleigh@uncp.edu
RALEIGH, Scott 602-639-7500 13 S
RALEY, Karen, C 240-895-3219. 218 A kcraley@smcm.edu
RALEY, Leonard, R 301-445-1941. 219 A lraley@usmd.edu
RALL, John, P 270-809-3399. 198 B jrall@murraystate.edu
RALLO, Joseph 806-742-0012. 487 D joseph.rallo@ttu.edu
RALLS, Diana 209-228-4306 71 D DRalls@UCMerced.edu
RALLS, R. Scott 919-807-6950. 357 L ralls@nccommunitycolleges.edu
RALPH, Brian 704-337-2445. 365 G ralphb@queens.edu
RALPH, James 802-443-5000. 499 H
RALPH, Ken 719-389-6945 79 D ken.ralph@coloradocollege.edu
RALPH, Lynette 504-520-7304. 209 D Lralph@xula.edu
RALPH, Nicole, M 217-786-2342. 151 F nicole.ralph@llcc.edu
RALPH, Scott 317-955-6789. 170 V sralph@marian.edu
RALPH, Susan 229-248-2585. 121 E sralph@bainbridge.edu
RALSTON, Nancy, M 402-552-2557. 288 L ralston@clarksoncollege.edu
RALSTON, Pamela 805-546-3123 42 C pamela_ralston@cuesta.edu
RALSTON, Ramona, M 315-267-2154. 344 C ralstorm@potsdam.edu
RALSTON, Tracy 203-596-4564 90 I tralston@post.edu
RALSTON, Troy 804-727-6826. 131 H tralston@southuniversity.edu
RAM, Rosalind 808-675-3457. 135 C ramr@byuh.edu
RAMAGE, Emily 217-234-5404. 150 D eramagel@lakeland.cc.il.us
RAMAGE, Thomas, R 217-351-2231. 155 J ramage@parkland.edu
RAMAGOS, Caroline 601-477-4249. 267 F caroline.ramagos@jcjc.edu
RAMAKER, Dawn 641-585-8197. 183 D ramakerd@waldorf.edu
RAMAKER, Jason 641-585-8160. 183 D ramakerj@waldorf.edu
RAMAKRISHNAN, Jolly 610-399-2032. 428 B jramakrishnan@cheyney.edu
RAMALHO, Erika, A 814-871-5584. 416 K ramalho001@gannon.edu
RAMAN, Saravana 714-300-0300 67 F sraman@scitech.edu
RAMARUI, Robert 680-488-2471. 547 B roramarui@gmail.com
RAMASWAMI, Anand 609-894-9311. 299 I aramaswami@bcc.edu
RAMASWAMY, Nandini 317-940-9032. 164 J nramaswa@butler.edu
RAMASWAMY, Sunder 831-647-4102. 499 H ramaswam@middlebury.edu
RAMBISH, Medea 630-466-7900. 162 J mrambish@waubonsee.edu
RAMBO, Andrea 805-378-1407 74 F arambo@vcccd.edu
RAMBO, Tom 570-372-4136. 433 H rambo@susqu.edu
RAMCHAND, Latha 713-743-4604. 489 B ramchand@uh.edu
RAMDATH, Danielle, D 413-585-3017. 236 H gradstdy@smith.edu
RAMDATH, Danielle, D 413-585-3017. 236 H dramdath@smith.edu
RAMDATH, Sanjay 336-334-4822. 360 G shramdath@gtcc.edu
RAMER, Rod 509-434-5325. 518 F rod.ramer@ccs.spokane.edu
RAMER, Rod 509-434-5325. 518 D rramer@ccs.spokane.edu
RAMER, Rodney 509-434-5325. 518 E rod.ramer@ccs.spokane.edu
RAMES, Marysz 605-688-4493. 452 B marysz.rames@sdstate.edu
RAMESH, S, K 818-677-4501 34 C s.ramesh@csun.edu
RAMET, Carlos 989-964-4042. 249 G ramet@svsu.edu
RAMEY, Alfred 201-200-2039. 303 F aramey@njcu.edu
RAMEY, Diana, M 254-710-2005. 467 G diana_ramey@baylor.edu
RAMEY, Iris 336-517-1761. 352 H iris.ramey@bennett.edu
RAMEY, Jennifer 212-226-5500. 314 A jramey@aii.edu
RAMEY, Judith 206-543-1829. 524 G jramey@uw.edu
RAMEY, Kenneth, H 859-572-5125. 198 I ramey@nku.edu
RAMEY, Lane 816-501-4633. 280 I lane.ramey@rockhurst.edu
RAMEY, Rob 336-334-4822. 360 G grramey@gtcc.edu
RAMEY, Susan 814-641-0440. 415 C hcc@dbcollege.edu
RAMEY, Teresa 843-661-1182. 444 B tramey@fmarion.edu

RAMEZANE, Marsha .... 650-574-6161... 64 C
ramezane@smccd.edu
RAMEZANE, Marsha .... 650-574-6413... 64 C
ramezanem@smccd.edu
RAMI, Janet .... 225-771-2151. 206 J
janet_rami@subr.edu
RAMIAN, Michael .... 219-866-6176. 172 E
RAMICONE, Arthur, G .... 412-624-6576. 435 C
aramicone@cfo.pitt.edu
RAMIREZ, Aixa .... 787-815-0000. 553 I
aixa.ramirez@upr.edu
RAMIREZ, Alberto .... 301-624-2636. 214 H
aramirez@frederick.edu
RAMIREZ, Alfred .... 818-240-1000... 45 G
aramirez@glendale.edu
RAMIREZ, Arnold .... 979-230-3235. 468 A
arnold.ramirez@brazosport.edu
RAMIREZ, Arthur .... 831-459-2158... 72 C
apr@soe.ucsc.edu
RAMIREZ, Aurelio .... 617-879-7847. 230 B
aramirez@massart.edu
RAMIREZ, Cecilia .... 757-825-3525. 514 B
ramirezc@tncc.edu
RAMIREZ, Cliff .... 909-607-4124... 39 C
cliff.ramirez@cgu.edu
RAMIREZ, Daniel .... 956-872-6411. 480 I
dramirez@southtexascollege.edu
RAMIREZ, David .... 909-652-6630... 37 M
david.ramirez@chaffey.edu
RAMIREZ, David .... 610-328-8175. 433 I
dramire1@swarthmore.edu
RAMIREZ, Glenda .... 281-487-1170. 484 H
gramirez@txchiro.edu
RAMIREZ, Hiram .... 404-471-6639. 119 I
hramirez@agnesscott.edu
RAMIREZ, Ines, C .... 717-815-1786. 438 D
iramirez@ycp.edu
RAMIREZ, Irving .... 347-964-8600. 315 E
iramirez@boricuacollege.edu
RAMIREZ, Jason .... 262-551-5800. 532 D
jramirez@carthage.edu
RAMIREZ, Joe .... 818-364-7642... 52 A
ramirejs@lamission.edu
RAMIREZ, Jose .... 787-620-2040. 547 C
jramirez@aupr.edu
RAMIREZ, Jose, L .... 915-831-2634. 472 B
jramir20@epcc.edu
RAMIREZ, Juan .... 909-469-5622... 76 B
jramirez@westernu.edu
RAMIREZ, Kathy .... 406-447-5185. 285 G
kramirez@carroll.edu
RAMIREZ, Laura, M .... 323-265-8641... 51 F
ramirelm@elac.edu
RAMIREZ, Lisa .... 602-274-4300... 12 K
lramirez@brymanschool.edu
RAMIREZ, Loida, R .... 787-744-8519. 548 L
lramirez@ediccollege.edu
RAMIREZ, Maria Luisa ... 956-721-5394. 475 F
mlramirez@laredo.edu
RAMIREZ, Mary Anne .... 804-290-4231. 510 B
mramirez@stratford.edu
RAMIREZ, Mayra, I .... 787-723-4481. 548 A
mramirez@ceaprc.edu
RAMIREZ, Minita .... 956-326-2278. 483 B
minita@tamiu.edu
RAMIREZ, Octavio .... 256-726-7340..... 6 B
oramirez@oakwood.edu
RAMIREZ, Roberto .... 361-593-3312. 484 A
roberto.ramirez@tamuk.edu
RAMIREZ, Sam .... 361-825-5826. 483 F
samuel.ramirez@tamucc.edu
RAMIREZ, Sam .... 440-826-2908. 374 F
sramirez@bw.edu
RAMIREZ, Val .... 361-593-5500. 484 A
val.ramirez@tamuk.edu
RAMIREZ, Yvonne .... 718-430-2541. 351 M
yramire1@aecom.yu.edu
RAMIREZ- RIVERA,
Rafael .... 787-878-5475. 549 L
rramirez@arecibo.inter.edu
RAMIREZ-JASSO, Diana . 617-262-5000. 223 F
Diane.Ramirez-Jasso@the-bac.edu
RAMM, Jennifer .... 254-295-5527. 490 B
jramm@umhb.edu
RAMMING, Ron .... 918-463-2931. 395 D
rronald@connorsstate.edu
RAMON, Luciano .... 956-794-4002. 475 F
lramon@laredo.edu
RAMON, Maria .... 787-744-1060. 551 J
mramon@mechtech.edu
RAMON, Ralph .... 325-574-7625. 494 K
rramon@wtc.edu
RAMON, Scott .... 312-629-6100. 158 L
sramon@saic.edu
RAMONES, Eric .... 408-848-4753... 45 F
eramones@gavilan.edu
RAMOS, Ana-Maria .... 214-860-1416. 470 J
AMRamos@dcccd.edu
RAMOS, Anthony .... 210-805-1201. 490 A
aramos@uiwtx.edu
RAMOS, Antonio .... 787-284-1912. 550 F
aramos@ponce.inter.edu
RAMOS, Charlene .... 248-204-2334. 245 I
cramos@ltu.edu
RAMOS, Cynthia .... 602-285-7410... 15 C
cynthia.ramos@phoenixcollege.edu
RAMOS, Daisy .... 787-738-2161. 554 C
daisy.ramos@upr.edu
RAMOS, Derek .... 620-276-9559. 187 A
derek.ramos@gcccks.edu
RAMOS, Edith .... 787-878-6000. 549 D
eramos@icprjc.edu
RAMOS, Gladys .... 787-738-2161. 554 C
gladys.ramos@upr.edu
RAMOS, Irma .... 951-487-3156... 55 B
iramos@msjc.edu
RAMOS, Josue .... 787-878-5475. 549 L
jramos@arecibo.inter.edu
RAMOS, Julio .... 787-720-4476. 553 D
biblioteca@mizpa.edu
RAMOS, Maria .... 903-886-5091. 483 E
maria.ramos@tamuc.edu
RAMOS, Maria, A .... 787-863-2390. 550 C
maria.ramos@fajardo.inter.edu
RAMOS, Maribel .... 407-888-1111. 551 J
maribelramos@mechtech.edu
RAMOS, Nancy, L .... 401-254-3455. 440 B
nramos@rwu.edu
RAMOS, Patricia .... 310-434-3311... 65 A
ramos_patricia@smc.edu
RAMOS, Patricia .... 212-343-1234. 331 D
pramos@mcny.edu
RAMOS, Rebecca .... 401-865-2345. 439 E
rramos@providence.edu
RAMOS, Richard, O .... 515-961-1536. 182 E
rich.ramos@simpson.edu
RAMOS, Theresa .... 505-277-5251. 312 F
tramos@unm.edu
RAMOS, Wilberto .... 256-761-8757..... 7 F
wramos@talladega.edu
RAMOS, Yolanda .... 432-685-4733. 476 G
yramos@midland.edu
RAMOS FONTEN,
Maiella .... 787-878-9218. 553 I
maiella.ramos@upr.edu
RAMPAUL, Andre .... 212-757-1190. 313 H
arampaul@funeraleducation.org
RAMPERSAD, Dave .... 334-386-7105..... 3 H
drampersad@faulkner.edu
RAMPINO, Tatiana .... 203-576-5990... 91 D
trampino@stvincentscollege.edu
RAMPP, Carrie, E .... 570-577-1557. 411 A
carrie.rampp@bucknell.edu
RAMPY, Bill .... 512-245-6761. 487 C
wr15@txstate.edu
RAMS, Richard .... 714-484-7374... 56 E
rrams@cypresscollege.edu
RAMS, Richard .... 714-484-7355... 56 E
RAMSAMMY, Jillian .... 352-854-2322. 100 K
jillian.ramsammy@cf.edu
RAMSAMMY, Roger .... 703-257-6664. 513 C
rramsammy@nvcc.edu
RAMSARAN, Rollin .... 423-461-1522. 454 E
rramsaran@ecs.edu
RAMSAY, Darlene .... 573-341-4584. 284 A
ramsayd@mst.edu
RAMSAY, John, G .... 484-664-3134. 424 H
ramsay@muhlenberg.edu
RAMSAY, John R, C .... 434-223-7154. 505 E
jramsay@hsc.edu
RAMSBOTTOM,
Mary, M .... 317-940-9516. 164 J
mramsbot@butler.edu
RAMSDELL, Twyla .... 651-213-4180. 256 B
tramsdell@hazelden.edu
RAMSDEN-MEIER,
Joanna .... 319-226-2004. 175 D
Joanna.Ramsden-Meier@AllenCollege.edu
RAMSEY, Betty Jo .... 910-642-7141. 364 A
BettyJo.Ramsey@sccnc.edu
RAMSEY, David .... 813-253-6227. 118 L
dramsey@ut.edu
RAMSEY, Dawn .... 678-915-4287. 132 C
dramsey@spsu.edu
RAMSEY, Derrick .... 410-951-3748. 220 B
dramsey@coppin.edu
RAMSEY, Gerald .... 619-388-7810... 62 F
gramsey@sdccd.edu
RAMSEY, Heather .... 610-526-6004. 417 H
hramsey@harcum.edu
RAMSEY, Heather .... 215-567-7080. 410 A
hramsey@edmc.edu
RAMSEY, James, R .... 502-852-5417. 200 D
jrrams02@louisville.edu
RAMSEY, Jason .... 719-590-6766... 81 B
jramsey@coloradotech.edu
RAMSEY, Joel .... 620-223-2700. 186 G
joelr@fortscott.edu
RAMSEY, Julie .... 865-981-8246. 456 D
julie.ramsey@maryvillecollege.edu
RAMSEY, Julie, L .... 717-337-6921. 417 B
ramsey@gettysburg.edu
RAMSEY, Marleen .... 509-527-4289. 524 H
marleen.ramsey@wwcc.edu
RAMSEY, Marty .... 828-227-7335. 369 E
mramsey@wcu.edu
RAMSEY, Natasha .... 217-228-5432. 156 C
ramsera@quincy.edu
RAMSEY, Paul, G .... 206-543-7718. 524 G
pramsey@uw.edu
RAMSEY, Sandy .... 828-898-8748. 356 A
ramseys@lmc.edu
RAMSEY, Stacy .... 309-438-2343. 147 J
srramse@ilstu.edu
RAMSEY, Tom .... 425-249-4748. 524 D
tom.ramsey@tlc.edu
RAMSEY, Vickie .... 530-251-8852... 50 F
vramsey@lassencollege.edu
RAMSEY-HAMACHER,
Paige .... 352-588-8489. 112 D
paige.ramsey.hamacher@saintleo.edu
RAMSEYER, Chuck .... 479-936-5188... 22 C
cramseyer@nwacc.edu
RAMSEYER, Larry, E .... 989-686-9234. 242 C
leramsey@delta.edu
RAMSOWER, Reagan ...... 254-710-3554. 467 G
reagan_ramsower@baylor.edu
RANABARGAR, Kerry, D 620-431-2820. 189 D
kranabargar@neosho.edu
RANALDI, Diane .... 413-565-1000. 222 F
dranaldi@baypath.edu
RANALLI, Carlee, K .... 814-641-3103. 419 H
ranallc@juniata.edu
RANALLI, George .... 212-650-7118. 317 D
gr1@ccny.cuny.edu
RANALLI, Robert .... 518-464-8533. 324 B
rranalli@excelsior.edu
RANCOURT, Ann .... 603-358-2118. 298 F
arancour@keene.edu
RANCOURT, Chad .... 646-717-9765. 325 B
rancourt@gts.edu
RAND, Amy .... 417-455-5740. 273 E
AmyRand@crowder.edu
RAND, Jonathan .... 617-879-7263. 230 B
jrand@massart.edu
RAND, Kathryn .... 701-777-2104. 371 C
rand@law.und.edu
RAND, Steven .... 207-780-5107. 212 H
srand@usm.maine.edu
RAND, Valarie .... 312-280-3500. 147 D
vrand@aii.edu
RANDALL, Christina, E ... 517-750-1200. 250 E
crandall@arbor.edu
RANDALL, David .... 617-253-4861. 233 B
RANDALL, Greg .... 256-840-4166..... 6 I
grandall@snead.edu
RANDALL, Greg .... 509-682-6465. 525 B
grandall@wvc.edu
RANDALL, Jeremy, C ..... 202-238-2344... 95 G
jcrandall@howard.edu
RANDALL, John .... 949-214-3358... 41 I
john.randall@cui.edu
RANDALL, Kenneth, C .... 205-348-5117..... 8 D
kcrandal@law.ua.edu
RANDALL, Linda .... 808-689-2300. 136 C
linda3@hawaii.edu
RANDALL, Meridith .... 530-242-7500... 65 G
mrandall@shastacollege.edu
RANDALL, Mike .... 801-274-3280. 498 E
mike.randall@wgu.edu
RANDALL, Monica .... 410-951-3596. 220 B
mrandall@coppin.edu
RANDALL, Monica, E ..... 410-951-3845. 220 B
mrandall@coppin.edu
RANDALL, Robin .... 508-286-8232. 238 B
rrandall@wheatonma.edu
RANDALL, Stacey .... 630-466-7900. 162 J
srandall@waubonsee.edu
RANDALL, Taylor .... 801-587-3869. 496 Q
taylor.randall@utah.edu
RANDAZZA, Paula .... 603-897-8303. 297 F
prandazza@rivier.edu
RANDAZZO, Jennifer, L . 563-884-5888. 182 A
jennifer.randazzo@palmer.edu
RANDAZZO, Mary .... 248-204-2309. 245 I
mrandazzo@ltu.edu
RANDAZZO, Nino .... 312-935-4000. 156 K
nrandazzo@robertmorris.edu
RANDELS, George .... 209-946-2011... 73 A
grandels@pacific.edu
RANDERSON, Mike .... 573-875-7661. 272 G
dmranderson@ccis.edu
RANDHAWA, Sabah, U .. 541-737-2111. 406 A
osu.provost@oregonstate.edu
RANDLE, Benjamin .... 716-829-7836. 323 D
randleb@dyc.edu
RANDLE, John .... 231-591-2892. 242 F
randlej@ferris.edu
RANDLE, Jonathan .... 601-925-3849. 268 A
randle@mc.edu
RANDLE, William, M ...... 336-334-7979. 367 E
wrandle@ncat.edu
RANDLES,
Christopher, M .... 217-351-2513. 155 J
crandles@parkland.edu
RANDLES, Jill, A .... 559-323-2100... 63 B
jrandles@sjcl.edu
RANDO, Robert, A .... 937-775-3409. 393 G
robert.rando@wright.edu
RANDOLPH, A.J .... 817-735-2336. 490 E
A.J.Randolph@unthsc.edu
RANDOLPH, Devin, L ..... 803-535-5301. 442 B
devin.randolph@claflin.edu
RANDOLPH, Robert, M .. 617-258-5484. 233 B
RANDORF, Lori .... 330-672-5368. 382 B
lrandorf@kent.edu
RANDY GREEN,
Jonathan .... 937-327-6406. 393 E
jgreen@wittenberg.edu
RANE-SZOSTAK, Donna . 949-582-4324... 67 C
draneszostak@saddleback.edu
RANELLI, F. Edward .... 850-474-2348. 117 B
eranelli@uwf.edu
RANES, Rodney .... 618-395-7777. 147 B
ranesr@iecc.edu
RANES, Zachary, T .... 727-376-6911. 117 I
zranes@trinitycollege.edu
RANEY, Curt .... 240-895-4395. 218 A
ccraney@smcm.edu
RANEY, Jonna, G .... 405-585-5020. 397 C
jonna.raney@okbu.edu
RANEY, Kristen, A .... 715-833-6491. 539 J
kraney@cvtc.edu
RANFT, Kimberly .... 817-261-1594. 469 K
RANGE, Ronald .... 205-391-2644..... 6 H
rrange@sheltonstate.edu
RANGE, Shirley .... 850-599-3491. 114 K
shirley.range@famu.edu
RANGEL, Andrea .... 806-894-9611. 480 H
arangel@southplainscollege.edu
RANGUETTE, Renea, L ... 608-757-7700. 539 I
rranguette@blackhawk.edu
RANHEIM, John .... 314-434-4044. 273 C
john.ranheim@covenantseminary.edu
RANIERI, Ann, E .... 610-526-6084. 417 H
aranieri@harcum.edu
RANIERI, Steve .... 513-875-3344. 376 H
steve.ranieri@chatfield.edu
RANIERI, Tracey, M .... 607-436-2446. 343 E
ranieritm@oneonta.edu
RANJEL, Mary .... 210-924-4338. 467 E
mary.ranjel@bua.edu
RANK, Carin .... 413-559-5385. 227 B
RANK, Kathy .... 303-458-4922... 84 M
krank@regis.edu
RANK, Kim .... 937-778-7852. 379 G
krank@edisonohio.edu
RANK, Mark .... 717-815-1218. 438 D
mrank@ycp.edu
RANKIN, Arthur .... 318-473-6581. 205 A
arankin@lsua.edu
RANKIN, David, F .... 870-235-4001... 23 F
dfrankin@saumag.edu
RANKIN, Donna .... 479-968-0394... 20 E
drankin@atu.edu
RANKIN, James, M .... 479-575-5900... 23 I
rankinj@uark.edu
RANKIN, Jason, A .... 501-450-5015... 25 H
jrankin@uca.edu
RANKIN, Jeffrey, D .... 309-457-2314. 153 D
jeffr@monmouthcollege.edu
RANKIN, Joseph .... 313-577-2024. 252 G
jrankin@wayne.edu
RANKIN, Mary Ann .... 301-405-5252. 219 B
mrankin@umd.edu
RANKIN, Mona, G .... 516-876-3160. 343 D
rankinm@oldwestbury.edu
RANKIN, Stephanie, A .... 717-361-1569. 415 H
rankins@etown.edu
RANKIN, Stephen .... 214-768-4564. 481 A
rankins@smu.edu
RANKIN, Stephen .... 214-768-4502. 481 A
rankins@smu.edu
RANKIN, Walter .... 202-687-8700... 95 E
rankinw@georgetown.edu
RANKINE, Patrice .... 616-395-7748. 244 A
rankine@hope.edu
RANKINS, JR., Alfred .... 662-254-3425. 269 A
arankins@mvsu.edu
RANKIS, Ray .... 646-312-5046. 316 J
Ray.Rankis@baruch.cuny.edu
RANOLPH, Angela .... 252-536-7254. 361 A
arandolph339@halifaxcc.edu
RANSDELL, Gary, A .... 270-745-4346. 200 G
gary.ransdell@wku.edu
RANSDELL, Junell, A ...... 217-786-4506. 151 F
junell.ransdell@llcc.edu
RANSDELL, Lynda .... 406-994-4135. 287 B
lynda.ransdell@montana.edu
RANSOM, Kimberly .... 304-793-6820. 530 B
kransom@osteo.wvsom.edu

RANSOM, Lakeesha .... 419-530-6033. 392 B
lakeesha.ransom@utoledo.edu
RANSOM, Scott, B .... 817-735-2509. 490 E
Scott.Ransom@unthsc.edu
RANSOME, Sheri .... 706-291-5339. 131 E
sransome@shorter.edu
RANTA, Richard, R .... 901-678-2350. 460 B
rranta@memphis.edu
RANTZ, Kristen .... 406-791-5291. 288 E
krantz01@ugf.edu
RANTZ, Rick .... 805-735-3366... 26 K
rrantz@hancockcollege.edu
RAO, Julie, M .... 585-245-5553. 343 C
rao@geneseo.edu
RAO, Michael .... 804-828-1200. 511 F
president@vcu.edu
RAPACCIOLI, Donna .... 718-817-4100. 324 G
rapaccioli@fordham.edu
RAPAPORT, Ross, J .... 989-774-3381. 240 N
rapap1rj@cmich.edu
RAPAPPORT, Laury .... 408-260-0208... 44 J
mindbody@fivebranches.edu
RAPE, Bruce, M .... 217-443-8786. 143 G
brape@dacc.edu
RAPELYE, Janet, L .... 609-258-6150. 304 E
jrapelye@princeton.edu
RAPER, Bridgette .... 423-746-5332. 462 C
braper@twcnet.edu
RAPER, Neely .... 706-291-5337. 131 E
nraper@shorter.edu
RAPESS, Paul .... 516-299-2214. 329 D
paul.rapess@liu.edu
RAPOPORT, Nancy .... 702-895-5831. 294 I
nancy.rapoport@unlv.edu
RAPOSA, Donna .... 781-239-2500. 231 G
draposa@massbay.edu
RAPOSA, Kristina .... 781-292-2264. 226 G
kristina.raposa@olin.edu
RAPOZA, Mark, F .... 401-865-2064. 439 E
mrapoza@providence.edu
RAPP, Bill .... 208-467-8825. 139 A
brapp@nnu.edu
RAPP, Cynthia, K .... 620-417-1012. 190 F
cynthia.rapp@sccc.edu
RAPP, Gary .... 316-295-5838. 186 H
rappg@friends.edu
RAPP, John .... 713-798-4517. 467 F
jrapp@bcm.edu
RAPP, Karen .... 323-260-8108... 51 F
rappk@elac.edu
RAPP, Norman .... 615-329-8848. 454 F
nrapp@fisk.edu
RAPP, Peter .... 503-494-8744. 405 I
hutching@ohsu.edu
RAPP, Timothy .... 301-295-4231. 545 C
timothy.rapp@usuhs.edu
RAPP, Virginia .... 310-660-3773... 43 B
vrapp@elcamino.edu
RAPPLEY, Marsha, D ...... 517-353-1730. 246 H
rappley@msu.edu
RAPTOSH, Joseph .... 412-321-8383. 411 D
RARIG, Jenny, M .... 610-359-5148. 414 D
jrarig@dccc.edu
RARIG, Kris .... 757-825-2801. 514 B
rarigk@tncc.edu
RASBAND, James, R .... 801-422-6383. 495 D
james_rasband@byu.edu
RASBERRY, Charles, J .... 914-395-2522. 340 E
crasberry@sarahlawrence.edu
RASBERRY, Sandra .... 601-968-8703. 266 A
srasberry@belhaven.edu
RASCATI, Ralph, J .... 770-499-3550. 127 N
rrascati@kennesaw.edu
RASCH, Carla .... 785-670-1074. 191 D
carla.rasch@washburn.edu
RASCH, J. Lee .... 608-785-9210. 541 E
raschl@westerntc.edu
RASCON, Tricia .... 805-893-3443... 72 B
tricia.rascon@sa.ucsb.edu
RASHED, D. Omar .... 864-622-6031. 441 B
orashed@andersonuniversity.edu
RASHED, Jamal .... 513-244-4273. 377 G
jamal_rashed@mail.msj.edu
RASHID, Jerry, T .... 570-321-4137. 422 H
rashid@lycoming.edu
RASK, Brenda .... 970-339-6332... 78 C
brenda.rask@aims.edu
RASK, Brenda .... 303-718-5907... 78 C
brenda.rask@aims.edu
RASK, Kevin .... 719-389-6446... 79 D
kevin.rask@coloradocollege.edu
RASKIND, Wayne .... 313-577-2519. 252 G
raskind@wayne.edu
RASMUS, James .... 678-891-2546. 125 G
james.rasmus@gpc.edu
RASMUSSEN, Brock .... 612-874-3749. 257 B
brock_rasmussen@mcad.edu
RASMUSSEN, Bruce, D .. 402-280-2720. 289 D
bdrass@creighton.edu
RASMUSSEN, Carrie, M . 209-667-3201... 35 B
cmrasmussen@csustan.edu
RASMUSSEN, Cheryl ...... 785-442-6021. 187 E
crasmussen@highlandcc.edu
RASMUSSEN, Clyde .... 509-793-2053. 517 C
clyder@bigbend.edu
RASMUSSEN, Connie, A 308-432-6366. 291 D
crasmussen@csc.edu
RASMUSSEN, David, W .. 850-644-5488. 115 C
dwrasmussen@admin.fsu.edu
RASMUSSEN, George, A 361-593-3712. 484 A
allen.rasmussen@tamuk.edu
RASMUSSEN, Jack, L ..... 801-626-6273. 497 D
jrasmussen@weber.edu
RASMUSSEN, Karla, R .... 757-455-3290. 515 H
krasmussen@vwc.edu
RASMUSSEN, Linda .... 601-266-4050. 270 E
linda.rasmussen@usm.edu
RASMUSSEN, Lowell, C . 320-589-6100. 264 F
rasmuslc@morris.umn.edu
RASMUSSEN, Mabel .... 407-277-0311. 103 C
mrasmussen@evergladesuniversity.edu
RASMUSSEN, Phil .... 425-889-5271. 521 G
phil.rasmussen@northwestu.edu
RASMUSSEN, Rob .... 815-479-7599. 152 F
rrasmuss@mchenry.edu
RASMUSSEN, Robert, H . 225-578-2154. 204 N
rrasmus@lsu.edu
RASMUSSEN, Robert, K . 213-740-6473... 74 A
rrasmussen@law.usc.edu
RASMUSSEN, Scott .... 208-282-2507. 138 E
rasmscot@isu.edu
RASMUSSON, Beth .... 605-626-2655. 451 I
rasmussb@northern.edu
RASNAKE, Martha, L .... 276-964-7389. 514 A
martha.rasnake@sw.edu
RASNICK, Becky, D .... 501-450-5200... 25 H
rebekahr@uca.edu
RASNICK, Natalie .... 417-690-2209. 272 E
nrasnick@cofo.edu
RASNICK, JR.,
William, B .... 423-439-7900. 459 C
rasnick@etsu.edu
RASOR, Mark .... 918-540-6213. 396 G
mrasor@neo.edu
RASOR, Peter .... 502-231-5221. 197 E
prasor@myLBC.us
RASPILLER, Ted .... 804-594-1571. 512 G
traspiller@jtcc.edu
RASS, Heike .... 215-972-2031. 426 Y
HRass@pafa.org
RASSOUL, Hamid .... 321-674-7260. 104 H
rassoul@fit.edu
RAST, Lawrence, R .... 260-452-2101. 165 D
lawrence.rast@ctsfw.edu
RASZEWSKI, Thomas ...... 410-864-3621. 218 B
traszewski@stmarys.edu
RATCHFORD, Jerome ..... 770-423-6310. 127 N
jratchfo@kennesaw.edu
RATCLIFF, Chris .... 870-460-1058... 24 D
ratcliff@uamont.edu
RATCLIFF, Christine, L ... 662-252-8000. 269 F
cratcliff@rustcollege.edu
RATCLIFF, Lance .... 417-269-3402. 273 D
lance.ratcliff@coxcollege.edu
RATCLIFF, Lance .... 417-269-8272. 273 D
lance.ratcliff@coxcollege.edu
RATCLIFF, Terry, D .... 509-777-3499. 525 F
tratcliff@whitworth.edu
RATCLIFFE, Jackson .... 415-485-3225... 42 J
jratcliffe@dominican.edu
RATCLIFFE, R. Samuel ... 540-464-7560. 515 B
ratcliffers@vmi.edu
RATERS, Michael, P .... 765-361-6289. 175 B
ratersm@wabash.edu
RATH, Lorie .... 419-783-2307. 379 C
lrath@defiance.edu
RATH, Phillip, S .... 812-888-5101. 174 F
prath@vinu.edu
RATH, Thomas .... 941-637-5672. 101 O
trath@edison.edu
RATHBONE, Thomas, M 607-436-3224. 343 E
rathbotm@oneonta.edu
RATHBUN, Robert, D ...... 570-577-3914. 411 A
bob.rathbun@bucknell.edu
RATHE, Dean .... 303-914-6303... 84 I
dean.rathe@rrcc.edu
RATHEAL, Juli .... 432-552-2530. 493 D
ratheal_j@utpb.edu
RATHERT, Greg .... 763-433-1864. 257 P
gregory.rathert@anokaramsey.edu
RATHJE, James, A .... 507-354-8221. 256 M
rathjeja@mlc-wels.edu
RATHJEN, Arthur, H .... 920-424-1020. 537 B
rathjena@uwosh.edu
RATHKE, Debra .... 567-661-7247. 387 L
debra_rathke@owens.edu
RATHMELL, Daniel .... 607-729-1581. 322 F
danrathmell@davisny.edu
RATIGAN, Jim .... 702-895-2380. 294 I
james.ratigan@unlv.edu
RATLIFF, Gerald, L .... 315-267-2108. 344 C
ratlifgl@potsdam.edu
RATLIFF, Jill, C .... 606-783-2256. 198 A
ji.ratliff@moreheadstate.edu
RATLIFF, John .... 704-272-5325. 363 G
jratliff@spcc.edu
RATLIFF, Kelly, M .... 530-754-6170... 70 J
kmratliff@ucdavis.edu
RATLIFF, Kerry .... 606-368-6064. 191 J
kerryratliff@alc.edu
RATLIFF, Kevin .... 540-453-2264. 511 H
ratliffk@brcc.edu
RATLIFF, Nicolle .... 816-802-3421. 275 J
nratliff@kcai.edu
RATLIFF, Thomas .... 765-677-2116. 169 B
thomas.ratliff@indwes.edu
RATLIFF, Thomas, R .... 304-462-4112. 529 G
thomas.ratliff@glenville.edu
RATLIFF, Vickie .... 276-523-7467. 513 A
vratliff@me.vccs.edu
RATLIFFE, Celina .... 503-699-6315. 404 C
cratliffe@marylhurst.edu
RATLIFFE, Wally .... 800-962-7682. 285 A
physicalplantdirector@wma.edu
RATNER, Hilary, H .... 313-577-5600. 252 G
aa3411@wayne.edu
RATNER, Neil .... 845-352-3431. 351 J
shaareitorah@optonline.net
RATTIGAN, Paulette .... 401-232-6320. 438 K
prattiga@bryant.edu
RATTY, Michael .... 617-732-2130. 233 E
michael.ratty@mcphs.edu
RAUB, Tammara .... 315-792-3011. 349 F
tlraub@utica.edu
RAUBENHEIMER,
Dianne .... 919-760-8913. 356 G
raubenhe@meredith.edu
RAUCCIO, Chasta .... 706-385-1069. 130 F
chasta.rauccio@point.edu
RAUCH, Dena .... 319-398-5476. 180 J
dena.rauch@kirkwood.edu
RAUCH, Kenneth, E .... 260-422-5561. 167 B
kerauch@Indianatech.edu
RAUDENBUSH, Reid, C . 410-778-7855. 221 C
rraudenbush2@washcoll.edu
RAULT, Pamela, V .... 504-280-6222. 205 G
pkvrana@uno.edu
RAULUK, Ruth .... 412-392-3996. 431 B
rrauluk@pointpark.edu
RAUP, Glenn .... 303-369-5151... 84 E
glenn.raup@plattcolorado.edu
RAUP, Kristin, A .... 412-578-6534. 412 G
raupka@carlow.edu
RAUSCH, Todd .... 712-274-6400. 183 G
todd.rausch@witcc.edu
RAUSCHENBACH,
Timothy .... 317-573-8930. 527 G
trauschenbach@salemu.edu
RAUSCHER, Victor, E ..... 518-445-3294. 313 C
vraus@albanylaw.edu
RAUTZHAN, Peter .... 610-282-1100. 414 F
peter.rautzhan@desales.edu
RAVAIOLI, Charlotte .... 570-945-8175. 419 N
charlotte.ravaioli@keystone.edu
RAVE, Carole .... 360-676-2772. 521 D
crave@nwic.edu
RAVELLI, James, B .... 503-943-7540. 408 F
ravelli@up.edu
RAVENELLE, Robert, G ... 508-767-7325. 222 C
rravenel@assumption.edu
RAVER, C. Cybele .... 212-998-2274. 334 D
cybele.raver@nyu.edu
RAVERT, Patricia .... 801-422-1167. 495 D
patricia_ravert@byu.edu
RAVINDRAN,
Tharanee, M .... 256-824-6036..... 8 F
Tharanee.Ravindran@uah.edu
RAVISHANKER,
Ganesan .... 781-283-2095. 237 F
gravisha@wellesley.edu
RAWICZ, Diane .... 707-654-1039... 31 I
drawicz@csum.edu
RAWITCH, Robert .... 818-677-2130... 34 C
robert.rawitch@csun.edu
RAWJEE, Roopa .... 508-531-6171. 229 D
roopa.rawjee@bridgew.edu
RAWL, Carolyn, D .... 334-244-3934..... 2 A
crawl@aum.edu
RAWLEIGH, Camilla, B .. 717-264-4141. 437 H
camilla.rawleigh@wilson.edu
RAWLES, Scott .... 318-869-5106. 201 H
srawles@centenary.edu
RAWLEY, Albert .... 434-791-5654. 502 D
brawley@averett.edu
RAWLEY, Ben .... 901-381-3939. 464 C
benrawley@visible.edu
RAWLINGS, Becky .... 360-383-3404. 525 D
brawling@whatcom.ctc.edu
RAWLINGS, Gilbert .... 410-276-0306. 218 D
grawlings@host.sdc.edu
RAWLINGS, Kristiaan ..... 402-872-2246. 291 E
krawlings@peru.edu
RAWLINGS, Michelle ...... 859-233-8116. 199 I
registrar@transy.edu
RAWLINS, Brad .... 870-972-2468... 19 N
brawlins@astate.edu
RAWLINS, Jim .... 541-346-1000. 406 D
RAWLINS, V. Lane .... 940-565-2026. 490 C
president@unt.edu
RAWLINSON, Ina, R .... 919-735-5151. 364 H
irrawlinson@waynecc.edu
RAWLS, Casey .... 601-403-1197. 269 D
crawls@prcc.edu
RAWLS, Terry .... 510-261-8500... 58 G
terry.rawls@patten.edu
RAWSKI, Jim .... 706-379-3111. 134 L
jkrawski@yhc.edu
RAWSON, Ken .... 903-586-2518. 474 N
deanofstudents@jacksonville-college.edu
RAWSON, Shawn .... 269-782-1385. 250 C
srawson01@swmich.edu
RAXTER, Jen .... 508-999-8034. 229 A
jraxter@umassd.edu
RAY, Aisha .... 312-893-7137. 145 B
aray@erikson.edu
RAY, Anita .... 706-245-7226. 124 D
aray@ec.edu
RAY, Barry, D .... 864-231-2015. 441 B
bray@andersonuniversity.edu
RAY, Bernard .... 615-327-6078. 456 E
bray@mmc.edu
RAY, Brandon .... 360-442-2254. 521 A
bray@lowercolumbia.edu
RAY, Cara .... 678-717-3622. 133 D
cara.ray@ung.edu
RAY, JR., Charles, A ...... 504-816-8010. 206 A
cray@nobts.edu
RAY, Darby, K .... 207-786-8241. 209 F
dray3@bates.edu
RAY, David .... 502-410-6200. 194 B
dray@galencollege.edu
RAY, David .... 513-244-8182. 376 J
david.ray@ccuniversity.edu
RAY, David, H .... 405-325-6426. 401 B
dray@ou.edu
RAY, David, W .... 312-280-3500. 147 D
dray@aii.edu
RAY, Douglas .... 305-474-2445. 112 F
dray@stu.edu
RAY, Edward, J .... 541-737-4133. 406 A
pres.office@oregonstate.edu
RAY, Gary .... 940-898-3010. 488 B
gray@twu.edu
RAY, Janell .... 713-942-9505. 473 D
jray@hgst.edu
RAY, Jasmine .... 501-812-2241... 22 G
jray@pulaskitech.edu
RAY, Jeffrey .... 678-915-7234. 132 C
jray@spsu.edu
RAY, Jerry .... 912-583-3115. 122 B
jray@bpc.edu
RAY, Jess, D .... 309-438-8586. 147 J
jdray@ilstu.edu
RAY, Johnnie .... 865-974-9767. 463 B
jray@utfi.org
RAY, Judy, K .... 336-841-9201. 355 C
jray@highpoint.edu
RAY, Katerina, R .... 419-372-8575. 374 K
krray@bgsu.edu
RAY, Kathlin, D .... 775-784-6500. 294 J
kray@unr.edu
RAY, Keith .... 334-229-6810..... 1 D
kray@alasu.edu
RAY, Keith, H .... 217-732-3168. 151 B
pres@lincolnchristian.edu
RAY, Ken .... 813-253-7054. 106 M
kray6@hccfl.edu
RAY, Lee Ann .... 979-436-9105. 484 B
Ray@tamhsc.edu
RAY, Leigh, A .... 931-372-3320. 460 A
lray@tntech.edu
RAY, Lorena .... 918-872-7706. 400 A
lorena.ray@swcu.edu
RAY, Mandy .... 978-542-7253. 230 E
mandy.ray@salemstate.edu
RAY, Marsha, M .... 215-751-8042. 413 I
mray@ccp.edu
RAY, Meg .... 312-226-6294. 151 A
RAY, Monica .... 256-372-5555..... 1 A
monica.ray@aamu.edu
RAY, Nicholas, T .... 812-941-2411. 168 F
nicray@ius.edu
RAY, Phillip .... 979-458-6001. 482 E
pray@tamus.edu
RAY, JR., R. Richard ...... 616-395-7785. 244 A
ray@hope.edu
RAY, Rhonda .... 503-760-3131. 402 B
rhonda@birthingway.edu
RAY, Roxie, L .... 203-576-4292... 91 G
roxieray@bridgeport.edu
RAY, S. Alan .... 630-617-3100. 145 A
president@elmhurst.edu

RAY, Sally .... 270-659-6933. 200 G
sally.ray@wku.edu
RAY, Sarah .... 802-443-5794. 499 H
ray@middlebury.edu
RAY, Scott .... 903-923-2148. 471 J
sray@etbu.edu
RAY, Teresa .... 828-327-7000. 359 A
tray@cvcc.edu
RAY, William .... 503-352-2786. 407 A
raywb@pacificu.edu
RAYAPPAN, Mary .... 860-343-5791... 89 A
mrayappan@mxcc.commnet.edu
RAYBUCK, Diane, R ...... 330-972-6427. 390 E
drr9@uakron.edu
RAYBURN, Judy, M ...... 731-881-7020. 463 E
jrayburn@utm.edu
RAYBURN, Michael .... 229-226-1621. 132 F
mrayburn@thomasu.edu
RAYBURN, T. Monroe .... 202-319-5765... 94 G
rayburn@cua.edu
RAYCHOUDHURY,
Samir, S .... 803-705-4648. 441 C
raychoudhurys@benedict.edu
RAYER, Susan, S .... 859-233-8193. 199 I
careerdevelopment@transy.edu
RAYMOND, Alice .... 256-551-3148..... 4 I
alice.raymond@drakestate.edu
RAYMOND, Annette .... 973-748-9000. 299 F
annette_raymond@bloomfield.edu
RAYMOND, Bruce .... 719-549-2142... 80 K
bruce.raymond@colostate-pueblo.edu
RAYMOND, Chris .... 413-572-5243. 230 F
craymond@westfield.ma.edu
RAYMOND, SR.,
John, R .... 414-955-8225. 534 C
jraymond@mcw.edu
RAYMOND, Margaret ..... 608-262-1234. 536 D
mraymond2@wisc.edu
RAYMOND, Mary .... 909-621-8144... 60 A
mary.raymond@pomona.edu
RAYMOND, Monica .... 805-339-6370... 64 F
RAYMOND, Monica .... 805-339-6370... 64 J
RAYMOND, Monica .... 805-339-6370... 64 I
RAYMOND, Sarah .... 406-496-4384. 287 F
sraymond@mtech.edu
RAYMOND, Thomas .... 605-455-6012. 450 I
traymond@olc.edu
RAYMOND, Wendy, E .... 704-894-2204. 353 J
weraymond@davidson.edu
RAYMUNDO, Laurie .... 671-735-2184. 546 E
lraymundo@gmail.com
RAYNER, Jill .... 706-864-1688. 133 D
jill.prayner@ung.edu
RAYNOR, Bill .... 781-239-2665. 231 G
braynor@massbay.edu
RAYNOR, Candra .... 510-231-5000... 49 D
RAYOME, David .... 906-227-2947. 248 A
RAZO, Bridget .... 661-722-6300... 28 F
brazo@avc.edu
RAZZAGHI, Farzaneh ..... 956-665-2755. 492 B
farzaneh@utpa.edu
RE, Cosmo, J .... 646-448-4288. 444 A
johnre@forrestcollege.edu
RE, Doug .... 415-239-3759... 38 L
dre@ccsf.edu
RE, John .... 646-448-4288. 444 A
johnre@nyc.rr.com
REA, Allyson .... 434-961-6541. 513 F
area@pvcc.edu
REA, Ann, W .... 207-947-4591. 209 G
librarian@bealcollege.edu
REA, Gail .... 314-454-8848. 274 G
grea@bjc.org
REABACK, Roslyn .... 203-932-7263... 92 E
rreaback@newhaven.edu
READ, Allison .... 860-297-2013... 91 F
allison.read@trincoll.edu
READ, Deborah .... 805-756-1445... 32 F
dawread@calpoly.edu
READ, Kirk, D .... 207-786-6280. 209 F
kread@bates.edu
READ, Melissa, P .... 508-541-1652. 225 F
mread@dean.edu
READE, Christopher .... 617-912-9165. 224 B
creade@bostonconservatory.edu
READEY, Mary, L .... 614-292-0257. 386 E
readey.3@osu.edu
READING, Sarah .... 781-239-2782. 231 G
sreading@massbay.edu
READY, Deana .... 573-592-4236. 285 D
deana.ready@williamwoods.edu
READY, Robert .... 973-408-3327. 301 C
rready@drew.edu
REAGAN, Cheryl .... 518-562-4110. 320 B
cheryl.reagan@clinton.edu
REAGAN, J Michael, E ... 979-845-8058. 483 C
PoliceChief@tamu.edu
REAGAN, Kate, M .... 423-869-6389. 456 A
kate.reagan@lmunet.edu
REAGAN, Margy .... 202-884-9707... 96 G
reaganm@trinitydc.edu

REAGAN, Melinda .... 972-279-6511. 465 F
mreagan@amberton.edu
REAGINS-LILLY,
Soncia, R .... 512-471-5017. 491 C
soncia.r.lilly@austin.utexas.edu
REAGLE, Mike .... 859-622-3855. 193 P
mike.reagle@eku.edu
REAGLES, Patricia, J ...... 507-344-7306. 253 J
patti.reagles@blc.edu
REAL, Yannick .... 562-860-2451... 37 I
yreal@cerritos.edu
REALIVASQUEZ, Yvonne 432-837-8032. 487 B
yrealivasquez@sulross.edu
REAM, Daniel, L .... 804-862-6208. 508 H
dream@rbc.edu
REAM, Debbie .... 213-477-2505... 54 J
dream@msmc.la.edu
REAMY, Brian .... 301-295-9942. 545 C
brian.reamy@usuhs.edu
REAP, Mary .... 413-265-2293. 225 C
reapm@elms.edu
REARDON, Colleen .... 708-524-6643. 144 C
creardon@dom.edu
REARDON, Maureen .... 508-457-1313. 234 F
mreardon@ngs.edu
REARDON, Pat .... 256-824-2561...... 8 F
reardonp@uah.edu
REARDON, Penny .... 304-434-8000. 528 A
reardon@eastern.wvnet.edu
REARDON, Thomas, J .... 662-915-5056. 270 B
sparky@olemiss.edu
REARDON, Timothy .... 440-646-8312. 392 D
treardon@ursuline.edu
REARIC, Sue .... 619-644-7576... 46 C
sue.rearic@gcccd.edu
REAS, Rae-Ellen .... 425-640-1401. 519 D
raeellen.reas@edcc.edu
REASH, Brenda .... 252-222-6141. 358 G
reashb@carteret.edu
REASONER, Carroll .... 319-335-2841. 175 I
carroll-reasoner@uiowa.edu
REAUME, Vicki .... 734-487-2410. 242 D
vreaume@emich.edu
REAVES, Donald, J .... 336-750-2041. 370 A
chancellorsoffice@wssu.edu
REAVES, Ken .... 678-872-8512. 125 C
kreaves@highlands.edu
REAVES, Kenneth, M ...... 863-680-3007. 105 D
kreaves@flsouthern.edu
REAVES, Nicole .... 724-925-4212. 437 D
reavesn@wccc.edu
REAVIS, Bob .... 785-654-2416. 183 I
breavis@allencc.edu
REAVIS, Ralph .... 434-528-5276. 515 G
reavis@vul.edu
REBA, Kathleen .... 516-323-3952. 331 J
kreba@molloy.edu
REBECK, G. William .... 202-687-5974... 95 E
gwr2@georgetown.edu
REBER, Christopher, M .. 814-676-6591. 428 C
creber@clarion.edu
REBIK, Clint .... 707-826-6205... 35 C
clint@humboldt.edu
REBIMBUS, Michael .... 803-705-4357. 441 C
rebimbus@benedict.edu
REBORI, Christine .... 636-949-4477. 276 D
crebori@lindenwood.edu
REBRO, Jan .... 206-239-4500. 517 M
jrebro@cityu.edu
REBULL, Patrick .... 305-237-0564. 109 D
prebull@mdc.edu
RECA, Michael, F .... 609-896-5080. 305 D
reca@rider.edu
RECA ZIPP, Marcella ..... 815-479-7515. 152 F
mrecazipp@mchenry.edu
RECCHIA, Karen .... 318-678-6000. 202 I
krecchia@bpcc.edu
RECCHINTI, John .... 856-351-2622. 307 B
jreccinti@salemcc.edu
RECH, Tara .... 510-594-3670... 30 K
trech@cca.edu
RECHEIUNGEL, Winfred . 680-488-3036. 547 B
winfredr@palau.edu
RECHLIN, Mike .... 304-358-2000. 526 G
mike@future.edu
RECHTSCHAFFEN,
Joyce, A .... 202-220-1364. 304 E
jrechtsc@princeton.edu
RECINOS, Diane .... 973-278-5400. 314 K
dr@berkeleycollege.edu
RECINOS, Diane .... 973-278-5400. 299 D
dr@berkeleycollege.edu
RECK, Ronald, D .... 302-736-2571... 94 C
ron.reck@wesley.edu
RECKER, Edward, R .... 419-434-4791. 391 D
reckere1@findlay.edu
RECKER, OSB, Ralph ..... 503-845-3320. 404 D
ralph.recker@mtangel.edu
RECKER, Sandy, M .... 563-588-7362. 180 L
sandy.recker@loras.edu

RECKNER, Angela, T ...... 215-489-2203. 414 E
Angela.Reckner@delval.edu
RECKTENWALD, Kay ...... 561-297-0026. 114 L
kreckten@fau.edu
RECORD, Ann .... 731-668-7240. 464 F
ann.record@wtbc.edu
RECORD, Kim .... 336-334-5952. 369 A
ksrecord@uncg.edu
RECORD, Victoria .... 315-787-4005. 324 E
RECTOR, Billy, C .... 713-313-6898. 485 F
rectorbc@tsu.edu
RECTOR, Brenda .... 865-882-4526. 461 E
rectorbw@roanestate.edu
RECTOR, Dave .... 360-596-5305. 524 A
drector@spscc.edu
RECTOR, David .... 660-785-7607. 282 L
daverec@truman.edu
RECTOR, Dawn .... 480-858-9100... 17 P
d.rector@scnm.edu
RECTOR, Lallene, J .... 847-866-3904. 145 E
ljr@garrett.edu
RECTOR, Larry .... 865-573-4517. 455 G
lrector@johnsonU.edu
RECTOR, Patricia .... 918-465-1769. 395 G
prector@eosc.edu
RECTOR, Rob .... 417-447-4852. 279 K
rectorr@otc.edu
RECZNIK, Joel, S .... 740-284-5236. 379 N
jrecznik@franciscan.edu
RECZNIK, John .... 740-283-6497. 379 N
jlrecznik@franciscan.edu
RECZNIK, Mark, E .... 740-284-5845. 379 N
mrecznik@franciscan.edu
REDD, Annie .... 386-481-2520... 99 C
redda@cookman.edu
REDD, Cliff .... 713-743-4921. 489 B
rbredd@central.uh.edu
REDD, Randy .... 901-751-8453. 457 B
rredd@mabts.edu
REDD, Rea .... 724-852-3254. 437 A
rredd@waynesburg.edu
REDD, Scott .... 703-448-3393. 269 E
sredd@rts.edu
REDD, Theresa, M .... 202-806-0870... 95 G
tredd@howard.edu
REDDA, Kinfe, K .... 850-412-5102. 114 K
kinfe.redda@famu.edu
REDDAY, Darlene .... 605-698-3966. 451 D
dredday@swc.tc
REDDER, Kelly .... 585-475-7412. 337 L
karrar@rit.edu
REDDER, Vince .... 605-995-2631. 450 A
viredder@dwu.edu
REDDERSON, Jeff, P ...... 864-294-3262. 444 C
jeff.redderson@furman.edu
REDDI, Lakshmi .... 305-348-2455. 115 B
lakshmi.reddi@fiu.edu
REDDICK, Amanda .... 678-891-2545. 125 G
Amanda.Reddick@gpc.edu
REDDICK, Niles .... 229-391-4782. 119 H
nreddick@abac.edu
REDDING, Melanie .... 865-471-3229. 453 F
mredding@cn.edu
REDDING, Michael .... 312-996-8153. 161 D
reddingm@uic.edu
REDDING, Richard .... 714-628-2688... 38 A
redding@chapman.edu
REDDING, Russell .... 215-489-4190. 414 E
russell.redding@delval.edu
REDDING, Vic .... 775-784-4901. 294 D
vic_redding@nshe.nevada.edu
REDDINGTON, Kathleen . 575-527-7604. 311 B
kredding@nmsu.edu
REDDY, Chandra .... 615-963-7561. 459 E
creddy@tnstate.edu
REDDY, Indra, K .... 361-593-4271. 484 B
ireddy@pharmacy.tamhsc.edu
REDDY, Michael, S .... 205-934-4720...... 8 E
mreddy@uab.edu
REDDY, Narem .... 678-466-4100. 123 A
naremreddy@clayton.edu
REDDY, JR., Robert, A .. 440-775-8142. 385 H
rob.reddy@oberlin.edu
REDDY, Venkateshwar .... 719-255-3408... 85 M
vreddy@uccs.edu
REDEKER, Michael .... 314-505-7225. 272 J
redekerm@csl.edu
REDEKER, Wade .... 620-341-5264. 186 D
wredekeri@emporia.edu
REDELL, Rebecca .... 541-440-4600. 408 D
Rebecca.Redell@umpqua.edu
REDFERN, Mark, S .... 412-624-5749. 435 C
mredfern@pitt.edu
REDFERN, Mylan .... 432-552-2220. 493 D
redfern_m@utpb.edu
REDFERN, Paul, W .... 717-337-6829. 417 B
predfern@gettysburg.edu
REDFERN, Vance .... 575-538-6310. 312 N
redfernw@wnmu.edu
REDFIELD, David .... 916-484-8408... 53 A
redfied@arc.losrios.edu

REDHEAD, Catherine ...... 406-683-7450. 286 I
c_redhead@umwestern.edu
REDING, Cheryl .... 913-360-7384. 184 H
creding@benedictine.edu
REDING, Nichole .... 503-760-3131. 402 B
nichole@birthingway.edu
REDING, Terrence .... 585-345-6850. 325 C
tareding@genesee.edu
REDINGER, Matthew .... 406-657-2204. 287 C
mredinger@msubillings.edu
REDINGTON, Joseph ...... 570-674-6756. 424 A
jredingt@misericordia.edu
REDLER, Susan .... 212-431-2121. 333 I
sredler@nyls.edu
REDLICH, Philip, N .... 414-805-5726. 534 C
predlich@mcw.edu
REDLINGER,
Lawrence, J .... 972-883-6188. 491 E
redling@utdallas.edu
REDMAN, Barbara, K ...... 313-577-4070. 252 G
ae9080@wayne.edu
REDMAN, Donald, L .... 717-334-6286. 422 E
dredman@ltsg.edu
REDMAN, Margaret, D .... 909-593-3511... 72 E
mredman@laverne.edu
REDMAN, Robert, R .... 503-255-0332. 404 F
rredman@multnomah.edu
REDMAN, Thomas, J ...... 978-232-2005. 226 C
tredman@endicott.edu
REDMOND, Angie .... 641-844-5712. 179 J
angie.redmond@iavalley.edu
REDMOND, John .... 845-752-3000. 348 I
j.redmond@uts.edu
REDMOND, Katrina .... 845-848-4034. 322 G
katrina.redmond@dc.edu
REDMOND, Michael, J ... 303-458-4944... 84 M
mredmond@regis.edu
REDMOND, Minor (Will) 717-871-5344. 429 D
minor.redmond@millersville.edu
REDMOND, Thomas, E .. 202-274-5935... 97 A
tredmond@udc.edu
REDO, Keith .... 516-323-4853. 331 J
kredo@molloy.edu
REDONNETT, Rosa .... 207-973-3231. 212 A
rosar@maine.edu
REDTOMAHAWK, James 701-255-3285. 373 C
jredtomahawk@uttc.edu
REDWINE, Marian .... 405-491-6336. 399 K
maredwin@snu.edu
REDWINE, Mike .... 405-491-6335. 399 K
mredwine@snu.edu
REDWINE, William .... 606-783-2680. 198 A
b.redwine@moreheadstate.edu
REECE, Bryan .... 909-389-3202... 61 K
REECE, E. Albert .... 410-706-7410. 219 C
deanmed@som.umaryland.edu
REECE, Jeremy .... 870-733-6722... 21 I
jreece@midsouthcc.edu
REECE, Jonathan .... 910-962-3122. 369 C
reecej@uncw.edu
REECE, LArissa .... 914-594-4550. 334 A
larissa_reece@nymc.edu
REECE, Marilyn .... 256-228-6001..... 5 H
reecem@nacc.edu
REECE, Randall .... 770-975-4000. 122 I
REECE, Ronda .... 405-945-8631. 398 C
REECE, Sheila .... 903-785-7661. 478 B
sreece@parisjc.edu
REECE, Terry .... 805-546-3283... 42 C
treece@cuesta.edu
REECK-IRBY, Joanne ...... 612-330-1111. 253 H
reeck@augsburg.edu
REED, Alexis .... 304-876-5157. 529 I
apalladi@shepherd.edu
REED, Ann, M .... 304-462-4117. 529 G
ann.reed@glenville.edu
REED, Anne, E .... 207-941-7176. 211 F
reeda@nescom.edu
REED, Annie, G .... 818-947-2320... 52 E
reedag@lavc.edu
REED, Arlene .... 909-537-7369... 34 E
areed@csusb.edu
REED, Barrett .... 870-584-4471... 24 F
breed@cccua.edu
REED, Beverly .... 630-942-4218. 142 G
reedbe@cod.edu
REED, Beverly, S .... 301-322-0495. 217 F
reedbs@pgcc.edu
REED, Brian, V .... 802-656-0903. 500 F
brian.reed@uvm.edu
REED, Burton, J .... 402-554-2262. 293 A
breed@unomaha.edu
REED, Chad .... 540-831-5760. 508 C
creed4@radford.edu
REED, Charlene, K .... 330-672-2121. 382 B
creed2@kent.edu
REED, Christine .... 805-922-6966... 26 K
creed@hancockcollege.edu
REED, Christopher, S .... 603-526-3797. 295 I
chreed@colby-sawyer.edu

REED, Claudia ... 310-954-4371... 54 J creed@msmc.la.edu
REED, Cristina ... 810-762-9584. 244 Q creed@kettering.edu
REED, Dan ... 530-898-6451... 33 A dmreed@csuchico.edu
REED, Daniel ... 319-335-2132. 175 I daniel-reed@uiowa.edu
REED, Darcy ... 507-284-3796. 254 G darcy.reed@mayo.edu
REED, David, D ... 906-487-3043. 247 A ddreed@mtu.edu
REED, Dee ... 812-535-5212. 172 F dreed@smwc.edu
REED, Diane ... 757-594-7202. 503 M dreed@cnu.edu
REED, Donna ... 971-722-4497. 407 D donna.reed@pcc.edu
REED, Doug ... 870-245-5167... 22 D reedd@obu.edu
REED, Eloise ... 903-923-3222. 486 A eloise.reed@tstc.edu
REED, Francesca ... 703-284-5901. 507 B francesca.reed@marymount.edu
REED, Gary ... 214-645-0137. 493 E gary.reed@utsouthwestern.edu
REED, Harry ... 713-646-1852. 480 J hreed@stcl.edu
REED, Hazell ... 919-530-6893. 368 A hreed@nccu.edu
REED, Helen ... 970-351-2601... 86 C helen.reed@unco.edu
REED, James, D ... 806-651-2055. 484 D jreed@mail.wtamu.edu
REED, Jeff ... 515-292-9694. 175 E
REED, Jeffrey, G ... 920-923-8760. 534 A jreed@marianuniversity.edu
REED, Jerry ... 570-389-4040. 427 H jreed@bloomu.edu
REED, John ... 617-253-6700. 233 B
REED, John ... 425-249-4800. 524 D john.reed@tlc.edu
REED, Jonathan ... 909-593-3511... 72 E jreed@laverne.edu
REED, Karen, A ... 419-755-4538. 385 D kreed@ncstatecollege.edu
REED, Kate ... 847-317-4064. 160 M kreed@tiu.edu
REED, Kathy ... 310-338-4404... 53 E kathy.reed@lmu.edu
REED, Kathy, S ... 217-581-3227. 144 E ksreed@eiu.edu
REED, Kevin ... 310-206-1355... 71 C kreed@conet.ucla.edu
REED, Kimberly ... 270-745-2434. 200 G kim.reed@wku.edu
REED, Kristen ... 217-245-3054. 146 F kristen.reed@ic.edu
REED, LaTonya ... 870-574-4504... 23 G lreed@sautech.edu
REED, Lee ... 202-687-2435... 95 E athletics@georgetown.edu
REED, Leslie ... 410-209-6006. 213 F lreed@bccc.edu
REED, Linda ... 901-572-2640. 453 B linda.reed@bchs.edu
REED, Lori ... 507-457-5005. 262 A lreed@winona.edu
REED, Mamie ... 205-652-3447..... 9 F mlr@uwa.edu
REED, Mark, C ... 203-254-4030... 89 I mcreed@fairfield.edu
REED, Mark, C ... 203-254-4000... 89 I mcreed@fairfield.edu
REED, Mark, F ... 610-861-1360. 424 E mreed@moravian.edu
REED, Mark, H ... 603-650-1488. 296 G mark.h.reed@dartmouth.edu
REED, Mark, V ... 607-777-6112. 341 E mreed@binghamton.edu
REED, Maryanne ... 304-293-5746. 530 D maryanne.reed@mail.wvu.edu
REED, Matthew ... 413-552-2227. 231 F mreed@hcc.edu
REED, Meredith ... 504-398-2236. 206 C mreed@olhcc.edu
REED, Michael, E ... 413-597-4376. 238 D michael.e.reed@williams.edu
REED, Michelle ... 985-549-2241. 208 C mreed@selu.edu
REED, Mike ... 618-282-6682. 160 A mike.reed@swic.edu
REED, Mike ... 208-426-1296. 137 G mreed@boisestate.edu
REED, Nancy ... 901-572-2662. 453 B nancy.reed@bchs.edu
REED, Natalie, K ... 630-515-6185. 153 B nreedx@midwestern.edu
REED, Pamela ... 806-874-3571. 468 J pamela.reed@clarendoncollege.edu
REED, Rahim ... 530-752-2071... 70 J rreed@ucdavis.edu
REED, Robert ... 443-334-2240. 218 E rreed1951@stevenson.edu
REED, Robert, A ... 504-865-3735. 205 H rareed@loyno.edu
REED, Robert, A ... 412-578-6349. 412 G rareed@carlow.edu
REED, Rod ... 479-524-7134... 21 G rreed@jbu.edu
REED, Scott ... 541-737-2713. 406 A scott.reed@oregonstate.edu
REED, Sharon ... 614-251-4595. 386 B reeds@ohiodominican.edu
REED, Sheleah, D ... 936-261-2121. 482 F sdreed@pvamu.edu
REED, Shirley, A ... 956-872-8366. 480 I yolandao@southtexascollege.edu
REED, Stephanie ... 610-902-1061. 411 E stephanie.d.reed@cabrini.edu
REED, Stephen ... 715-425-3701. 537 E stephen.reed@uwrf.edu
REED, Steve, E ... 417-667-8181. 273 A sreed@cottey.edu
REED, Steven ... 615-460-6367. 453 C steven.reed@belmont.edu
REED, Sue ... 484-365-7929. 422 D sreed@lincoln.edu
REED, Sung-Ae ... 616-222-3000. 245 C sreed@kuyper.edu
REED, Sylvia, K ... 920-923-7152. 534 A sreed@marianuniversity.edu
REED, Teresa ... 218-228-5432. 156 C reedte@quincy.edu
REED, Teresa ... 217-228-5432. 156 C reedte@quincy.edu
REED, Terri Harris ... 202-994-1000... 95 D treed@gwu.edu
REED, Thomas ... 804-524-5045. 515 D tereed@vsu.edu
REED, Tita ... 440-775-6200. 385 H tita.reed@oberlin.edu
REED, Tom ... 251-575-8283..... 1 C treed@ascc.edu
REED, Tracy ... 989-775-4123. 249 F reed.tracy@sagchip.edu
REED, Van ... 337-550-1211. 205 B
REED, Victoria ... 270-831-9849. 195 D victoria.reed@kctcs.edu
REED, Wayne, E ... 404-413-9500. 126 F reedw@gsu.edu
REED, William, O ... 503-943-7191. 408 F reed@up.edu
REED, Willie, M ... 765-494-7608. 171 M wreed@purdue.edu
REED-SEGRETTI, Deborah ... 516-572-7214. 332 C deborah.segretti@ncc.edu
REEDER, Chanel ... 812-535-5143. 172 F creeder@smwc.edu
REEDER, David, C ... 301-447-5207. 217 B reeder@msmary.edu
REEDER, Lynne ... 910-962-3746. 369 C reederl@uncw.edu
REEDER, Pam ... 573-518-2204. 278 A preeder@mineralarea.edu
REEDER, Pamela, K ... 660-831-4123. 278 I reedere@moval.edu
REEDER, Philip, P ... 412-396-4877. 415 F reederp@duq.edu
REEDER, Rhonda ... 252-527-6223. 361 F rreeder@lenoircc.edu
REEDER, William, F ... 703-993-8624. 505 C wreeder@gmu.edu
REEDSTROM, Cynthia, P 651-631-5246. 263 A clreedstrom@nwc.edu
REEDUS, Janice ... 815-280-6640. 149 A jreedus@jjc.edu
REEDY, Melody ... 612-343-4491. 262 X melody.reedy@northcentral.edu
REEDY, William ... 802-224-3000. 501 A william.reedy@vsc.edu
REEDY-HINES, Charity ... 202-651-5750... 95 C charity.reedy.hines@gallaudet.edu
REEGER, Jennifer ... 724-830-1069. 433 E jreeger@setonhill.edu
REEHL, Kathryn ... 740-284-5240. 379 N kreehl@franciscan.edu
REEKS, Kevin, L ... 419-995-8081. 381 Q reeks.k@rhodesstate.edu
REEL, Stephanie ... 410-735-6700. 215 H sreel@jhu.edu
REELS, Evanglene ... 252-222-6237. 358 G reelse@carteret.edu
REEM, Marvin, P ... 864-242-5100. 441 D
REEP, Jeff ... 937-766-7868. 375 K reepj@cedarville.edu
REES, David, G ... 802-440-4337. 498 G rees@bennington.edu
REES, Margaret ... 702-895-3890. 294 I peg.rees@unlv.edu
REES, Pamela, D ... 515-263-6098. 178 G prees@grandview.edu
REES, Richard ... 203-285-2170... 88 E rrees@gwcc.commnet.edu
REESE, Aaron, J ... 706-507-8735. 123 D reese_aaron@columbusstate.edu
REESE, Anna ... 520-206-4550... 17 A anreese@pima.edu
REESE, Benjamin, D ... 919-684-8222. 354 A ben.reese@duke.edu
REESE, Brian ... 717-337-6240. 417 B breese@gettysburg.edu
REESE, Brian, P ... 864-833-8242. 446 D bpreese@presby.edu
REESE, Brian, T ... 816-654-7103. 275 K breese@kcumb.edu
REESE, Camille ... 704-878-3264. 362 B creese@mitchellcc.edu
REESE, Carole, A ... 610-861-1645. 424 E creese@moravian.edu
REESE, Carole, A ... 610-861-1555. 424 E creese@moravian.edu
REESE, Cynthia ... 510-981-2851... 59 A creese@peralta.edu
REESE, David ... 503-725-2655. 406 B dcreese@pdx.edu
REESE, Debra, C ... 302-831-2164... 94 B dcreese@udel.edu
REESE, Don ... 315-733-2300. 349 D dreese@uscny.edu
REESE, Kimberly ... 504-520-7575. 209 D kreese@xula.edu
REESE, Kimberly ... 336-750-3145. 370 A reesekf@wssu.edu
REESE, Michael ... 209-228-4430... 71 D mreese@UCMerced.edu
REESE, Mike ... 619-644-7163... 46 E mike.reese@gcccd.edu
REESE, Robert ... 574-936-8898. 163 K gene.reese@ancilla.edu
REESE, Robert ... 610-902-8554. 411 E robert.reese@cabrini.edu
REESE, Robert, B ... 252-334-2049. 357 A robert.reese@macuniversity.edu
REESE, Thomas, L ... 410-293-9320. 545 J treese@usna.edu
REESE, William ... 352-395-5523. 113 C bill.reese@sfcollege.edu
REESER, Michael, L ... 254-867-3128 485 G mike.reeser@systems.tstc.edu
REESER, Mike ... 254-867-4891. 486 B mike.reeser@systems.tstc.edu
REESOR, Lori ... 701-777-2724. 371 C lori.reesor@und.edu
REEVE, Gilmore ... 225-578-5513. 204 O tgreeve@lsu.edu
REEVE, Margi ... 310-665-6957... 57 C mreeve@otis.edu
REEVERS, Stephanie ... 931-221-7572. 459 B reeverss@apsu.edu
REEVES, Ann, S ... 615-898-5926. 459 D ann.reeves@mtsu.edu
REEVES, Brent, W ... 618-537-6938. 152 G breeves@mckendree.edu
REEVES, Brian ... 918-343-7538. 399 C breeves@rsu.edu
REEVES, Christina ... 732-987-2249. 302 B reevesc@georgian.edu
REEVES, Christopher ... 319-656-2447. 182 D
REEVES, Colleen ... 661-362-3146... 40 E colleen.reeves@canyons.edu
REEVES, Earl, J ... 660-831-4108. 278 I
REEVES, Gary, M ... 203-576-4804... 91 G greeves@bridgeport.edu
REEVES, Gary, W ... 601-984-6000. 270 C greeves@umc.edu
REEVES, Herbert ... 334-670-3203..... 7 H hreeves@troy.edu
REEVES, Jacqueline, A ... 203-576-4496... 91 G purchase@bridgeport.edu
REEVES, James ... 310-377-5501... 53 F jreeves@marymountcalifornia.edu
REEVES, Jason ... 606-546-1209. 200 A jreeves@unionky.edu
REEVES, Joey ... 912-478-8607. 126 C jreeves@georgiasouthern.edu
REEVES, Kay ... 325-674-2675. 464 H reevesk@acu.edu
REEVES, Kent ... 903-923-2226. 471 J klreeves@etbu.edu
REEVES, Linda ... 864-225-7653. 444 A lindareeves@forrestcollege.edu
REEVES, Lindsay ... 706-864-1625. 133 D lindsay.reeves@ung.edu
REEVES, Mamiko ... 989-837-4136. 248 C reevesm@northwood.edu
REEVES, Mark ... 678-839-5079. 133 I mreeves@westga.edu
REEVES, Mark ... 870-972-3400... 19 N mreeves@astate.edu
REEVES, Mark ... 715-836-2517. 536 E reevesmt@uwec.edu
REEVES, Mary ... 414-256-1202. 535 A reevesm@mtmary.edu
REEVES, Meg ... 541-737-2474. 406 A meg.reeves@oregonstate.edu
REEVES, Rick ... 303-914-6400... 84 I rick.reeves@rrcc.edu
REEVES, Rodney ... 417-328-1770. 282 C rreeves@sbuniv.edu
REEVES, Ronald ... 818-401-1022... 41 B rreeves@columbiacollege.edu
REEVES, Russ ... 866-323-0233... 60 E
REEVES, Sparky ... 229-931-2150. 131 G sreeves@southgatech.edu
REFINETTI, Roberto ... 803-584-3446. 448 D refinetti@sc.edu
REGA, Elizabeth ... 909-469-5460... 76 B erega@westernu.edu
REGALADO, Juan ... 909-593-3511... 72 E jregalado@laverne.edu
REGALADO, Sylvia ... 707-654-1299... 31 I sregalado@csum.edu
REGALADO RODRIGUEZ, Margery ... 831-479-6285... 30 G maregala@cabrillo.edu
REGALIA, Delphine ... 510-642-3881... 70 I dmregalia@berkeley.edu
REGAN, Anna ... 732-255-0400. 304 A aregan@ocean.edu
REGAN, Dan ... 802-635-1242. 501 D dan.regan@jsc.edu
REGAN, Joseph, P ... 312-341-2110. 157 D jregan@roosevelt.edu
REGAN, Kathleen ... 315-781-3700. 326 C regan@hws.edu
REGAN, Laurie ... 503-552-1507. 404 H lregan@ncnm.edu
REGAN, Richard, M ... 508-793-2582. 225 B rregan@holycross.edu
REGAN, Sara ... 617-266-1400. 223 D
REGAN, Sheila, A ... 910-272-3305. 363 B sregan@robeson.edu
REGAN, Teresa ... 425-889-5252. 521 G teresa.regan@northwestu.edu
REGE, Karen, M ... 610-359-5145. 414 D krege@dccc.edu
REGENCIO, Eugenia ... 973-596-3068. 303 G eugenia.regencio@njit.edu
REGER, Mark, A ... 864-488-8317. 444 L mreger@limestone.edu
REGER, Sheila ... 651-201-1841. 257 N sheila.reger@so.mnscu.edu
REGGIO, Nancy ... 408-453-9900... 47 H nreggio@henley-putnam.edu
REGIER, Jeanette ... 816-322-0110. 271 O jeanette.regier@calvary.edu
REGIER, Philip, R ... 480-965-2457... 11 K phil.regier@asu.edu
REGINO, Rolando ... 760-245-4271... 75 B Rolando.Regino@vvc.edu
REGIS, Chris, C ... 214-768-1178. 481 A cregis@smu.edu
REGIS, Humphrey, A ... 713-313-1983. 485 F regisha@tsu.edu
REGIST-TOMLINSON, Tara ... 212-431-2808. 333 I tara.regist-tomlinson@nyls.edu
REGISTER, Shilpa ... 617-732-2800. 233 E shilpa.register@mcphs.edu
REGISTER, Tammy ... 307-382-1606. 543 J tregiste@wwcc.wy.edu
REGJO, Kathryn ... 860-628-4751... 90 D kregjo@lincolncollegene.edu
REGNERUS, Arlene ... 312-935-6651. 156 K aregnerus@robertmorris.edu
REGNERY, Marcia ... 540-338-2700. 503 A mregnery@cdu.edu
REGO, Dan ... 860-727-6907... 90 A drego@goodwin.edu
REGUEIRO, Maria, C ... 305-821-3333. 105 A mregueiro@fnu.edu
REGULSKA, Joanna ... 732-932-1777. 306 A vpglobal@gaiacenters.rutgers.edu
REHAGEN, James, F ... 262-691-5055. 541 D jrehagen@wctc.edu
REHAK, Carrie ... 510-436-1081... 47 J rehak@hnu.edu
REHAK, Patricia ... 361-582-2533. 493 H patricia.rehak@victoriacollege.edu
REHBEIN, Edna ... 512-716-4422. 487 C er04@txstate.edu
REHBEIN, Matt ... 615-966-6043. 456 B matt.rehbein@lipscomb.edu
REHBERG, Kathy ... 850-718-2233... 99 N rehbergk@chipola.edu
REHG, SJ, William ... 314-977-3150. 281 I rehgsp@slu.edu
REHM, David, B ... 301-447-5218. 217 B rehm@msmary.edu

REHM, Julie, M .... 216-368-6070. 375 J
julie.rehm@case.edu
REHM, Matthew .... 740-362-3136. 383 H
mrehm@mtso.edu
REHM, Roger, E .... 989-774-1474. 240 N
rehm1re@cmich.edu
REHNELT, Sherry .... 715-425-3962. 537 E
0375mgr@fheg.follett.com
REICH, Anna Marie .... 478-289-2039. 124 C
areich@ega.edu
REICH, Jim .... 841-585-3639. 281 K
jreich@sbc-fenton.com
REICH, Lewis .... 901-722-3234. 458 K
lreich@sco.edu
REICH, Patricia .... 570-422-3595. 428 D
preich@po-box.esu.edu
REICH COSENTINO,
Randi .... 202-419-0400... 96 F
randi@strayer.edu
REICHARD, David .... 831-582-3952... 34 B
dreichard@csumb.edu
REICHARD, Joseph, F ..... 610-372-1722. 410 E
joe.reichard@berks.edu
REICHARD, Joshua .... 303-743-8158. 458 A
jreichard@ogs.edu
REICHEL, Mary, L .... 828-262-2188. 367 A
reichelml@appstate.edu
REICHENBERG, Gerard ... 410-209-6037. 213 F
jreichenberg@bccc.edu
REICHENBERGER,
Douglas, C .... 330-471-8320. 383 D
dreichenberger@malone.edu
REICHERT, Dan .... 269-473-2222. 239 D
REICHERT, Greg .... 608-785-8672. 536 G
greichert@uwlax.edu
REICHGELT, Han .... 678-915-5572. 132 C
hreichge@spsu.edu
REICHSTEIN, Lisa, M ..... 252-493-7339. 362 G
lreichst@email.pittcc.edu
REICIS, Sandra .... 716-896-0700. 350 A
reicis@villa.edu
REID, Anne, M .... 610-861-1353. 424 E
areid@moravian.edu
REID, OP, Barbara .... 773-371-5422. 141 D
breid@ctu.edu
REID, Bob .... 803-323-2143. 449 G
reidb@winthrop.edu
REID, Carol .... 615-844-5274. 464 E
creid@welch.edu
REID, Colette .... 843-746-5100... 96 F
REID, Dana .... 480-517-8235... 15 D
dana.reid@riosalado.edu
REID, Don, C .... 435-652-7515. 497 E
reid@dixie.edu
REID, Helen .... 972-932-4309. 488 D
reid@tvcc.edu
REID, Helen, C .... 417-836-4176. 278 E
helenreid@missouristate.edu
REID, Jacquelyn, C .... 812-941-2340. 168 F
jreid@ius.edu
REID, John .... 805-437-8444... 32 I
john.reid@csuci.edu
REID, Julia .... 503-760-3131. 402 B
julia@birthingway.edu
REID, Kandace .... 585-266-0430. 324 A
kreid@cci.edu
REID, Kathleen, A .... 413-782-1211. 238 A
kreid@wne.edu
REID, Kevin .... 478-757-2511. 128 I
kevin.reid@maconstate.edu
REID, Lenzy .... 706-355-5008. 120 J
lreid@athenstech.edu
REID, Mark .... 206-281-2624. 523 C
mreid@spu.edu
REID, Melissa .... 606-546-1610. 200 A
REID, Michael .... 406-243-4662. 286 H
michael.reid@umontana.edu
REID, Michael, B .... 352-294-1601. 116 A
michael.reid@ufl.edu
REID, Michelle .... 701-231-8887. 371 G
michelle.reid@ndsu.edu
REID, Pam .... 601-643-8442. 266 F
pam.reid@colin.edu
REID, Pamela, T .... 860-231-5221... 92 F
preid@usj.edu
REID, Patricia .... 216-987-4659. 378 D
patricia.reid@tri-c.edu
REID, Richard, H .... 337-475-5588. 207 G
rreid@mcneese.edu
REID, Shannon .... 603-230-3504. 295 J
sreid@ccsnh.edu
REID, Stanley, G .... 512-476-2772. 466 J
president@austingrad.edu
REID, JR., Thomas, G .... 412-731-8690. 431 G
treid@rpts.edu
REID, Tina, S .... 864-592-4683. 447 A
reidt@sccsc.edu
REID-CHASSIAKOS,
Linda .... 818-677-3689... 34 C
linda.reid.chassiakos@csun.edu
REID-HART, De Reese .... 773-602-5118. 142 B

REID-MARTINEZ,
Kathaleen .... 405-691-3800. 396 D
kreidmartinez@macu.edu
REIDELBACH, Marie, A .. 402-559-7087. 292 J
mreidelb@unmc.edu
REIDELL, Mary Frances .. 412-578-6174. 412 G
reidellmf@carlow.edu
REIDER, Melissa, R .... 315-445-4297. 328 F
reidermr@lemoyne.edu
REIDHEAD, Van, A .... 570-422-3539. 428 D
vreidhead@po-box.esu.edu
REIDY, Fran .... 352-588-8246. 112 D
fran.reidy@saintleo.edu
REIDY, Joseph, P .... 202-806-2550... 95 G
jreidy@howard.edu
REIDY, Robert, C .... 650-723-6324... 68 E
rcr@stanford.edu
REIDY, Stephanie .... 410-462-8245. 213 F
sreidy@bccc.edu
REIF, L. Rafael .... 617-253-0148. 233 B
president@mit.edu
REIF, Steven, J .... 248-246-2511. 248 D
sjreif@oaklandcc.edu
REIFEL, John .... 616-331-7100. 243 C
reifelj@gvsu.edu
REIFENHEISER, Paul ...... 845-434-5750. 347 A
preifenh@sullivan.suny.edu
REIFENRATH, Lisa .... 402-844-7269. 291 I
lisar@northeast.edu
REIFLER, Sylvia .... 617-217-9237. 222 G
sreifler@baystate.edu
REIGELMAN, Milton, M . 859-238-5287. 193 E
milton.reigelman@centre.edu
REIGHARD, Erica .... 814-262-6440. 427 C
ereighard@pennhighlands.edu
REIGHARD, Frank .... 281-338-8050. 493 C
treigha@utmb.edu
REIGHLEY, Twila .... 517-355-5040. 246 H
reighley@msu.edu
REIHER, William .... 692-625-8424. 546 F
REILENDER,
Catherine, L .... 859-846-5315. 197 I
creilender@midway.edu
REILLY, Elizabeth, H .... 330-972-7331. 390 E
reilly@uakron.edu
REILLY, John, H .... 518-956-8050. 341 D
jreilly@albany.edu
REILLY, Joseph, R .... 973-313-6233. 307 C
joseph.reilly@shu.edu
REILLY, Karen .... 301-624-2849. 214 H
kreilly@frederick.edu
REILLY, Karen .... 301-624-2862. 214 H
kreilly@frederick.edu
REILLY, Kathryn .... 570-945-9110. 419 N
kathryn.reilly@keystone.edu
REILLY, Kevin .... 540-365-4407. 504 L
kreilly@ferrum.edu
REILLY, Kevin, P .... 608-262-2321. 536 C
kreilly@uwsa.edu
REILLY, MaryBeth .... 718-982-2426. 317 E
marybeth.reilly@csi.cuny.edu
REILLY, Maureen .... 518-743-2306. 345 E
reillym@sunyacc.edu
REILLY, Michael .... 858-513-9240. 175 F
michael.reilly@ashford.edu
REILLY, Nora .... 540-831-7204. 508 C
nreilly@radford.edu
REILLY, Patricia .... 617-627-2000. 237 C
patricia.reilly@tufts.edu
REILLY, Seamus .... 217-353-2170. 155 J
sereilly@parkland.edu
REILLY-KELLY, Tracy ...... 360-992-2163. 518 A
tkelly@clark.edu
REILLY-MYKLEBUST,
Alice .... 715-425-9884. 537 E
alice.m.reilly-myklebust@uwrf.edu
REIMAN, Dennis, M .... 904-997-2940. 105 E
dennis.reiman@fscj.edu
REIMAN, Rick .... 912-260-4480. 131 F
rick.reiman@sgsc.edu
REIMANN, Jan .... 573-334-9181. 276 I
jan@metrobusinesscollege.edu
REIMANN, Rick .... 518-587-2100. 346 A
rick.reimann@esc.edu
REIMER, Carol .... 907-822-3201... 10 A
registrar@akbible.edu
REIMER, Jay .... 972-241-3371. 470 E
jreimer@dallas.edu
REIMER, Linda .... 212-229-5350. 332 E
reimerl@newschool.edu
REIMER, Martin .... 712-274-6400. 183 G
martin.reimer@witcc.edu
REIMER, Michael .... 201-360-4156. 302 D
mreimer@hccc.edu
REIMER, Robert .... 773-291-6740. 142 D
rreimer@ccc.edu
REIMONDO, Sue .... 859-985-3212. 192 F
sue_reimondo@berea.edu
REIN, Jennifer, L .... 785-827-5541. 188 C
jennifer.rein@kwu.edu

REIN, Kim .... 303-914-6260... 84 I
kim.rein@rrcc.edu
REIN, Laura .... 314-968-7152. 284 N
lrein@webster.edu
REINA, Juana .... 212-650-5426. 317 D
jreina@ccny.cuny.edu
REINARD, Gretchen, M .. 814-456-7504. 416 A
gretchen.reinard@eriebc.edu
REINCKE, Nancy .... 515-271-2161. 177 K
nancy.reincke@drake.edu
REINDL, Kay .... 209-478-0800... 47 M
kreindl@humphreys.edu
REINECK, Marilyn .... 708-209-3088. 143 E
marilyn.reineck@cuchicago.edu
REINEMUND, Steven ...... 336-758-5110. 370 D
steve@wfu.edu
REINER, Christian .... 435-586-7783. 497 A
christianreiner@suu.edu
REINERT, Duane .... 660-944-2852. 272 H
dreinert@conception.edu
REINESS, Gary .... 503-768-7513. 403 K
reiness@lclark.edu
REING, Linda .... 212-875-4605. 314 C
alumrel@bankstreet.edu
REINHARD, Herb .... 229-333-5462. 134 B
hreinhar@valdosta.edu
REINHARDT, Alan, J .... 508-213-2201. 235 E
alan.reinhardt@nichols.edu
REINHARDT, John, W ...... 402-472-1344. 292 J
jreinhardt@unmc.edu
REINHARDT, Sharon .... 209-384-6188... 54 D
reinhardt.s@mccd.edu
REINHART, Charles, W .. 812-888-4480. 174 F
creinhart@vinu.edu
REINHART, Kellee, C ...... 205-348-5938..... 8 C
kreinhar@uasystem.ua.edu
REINHART, Rose .... 419-995-8310. 381 Q
reinhart.r@rhodesstate.edu
REINHOLD, David .... 269-387-4564. 252 I
david.reinhold@wmich.edu
REINISCH, Lou .... 631-420-2198. 346 B
lou.reinisch@farmingdale.edu
REINISCH, Sheryl .... 503-493-6233. 402 J
sreinisch@cu-portland.edu
REINKE, Brenda .... 405-682-7510. 397 E
breinke@occc.edu
REINKE, Jane .... 763-424-0819. 260 C
jreinke@nhcc.edu
REINKING, Jackie .... 212-686-9244. 313 G
REINLAND, Jeffrey, E ..... 509-527-4312. 524 H
jeffrey.reinland@wwcc.edu
REINLIE, Carla .... 850-729-5357. 109 I
reinliec@nwfsc.edu
REINSCH FRIESE, Ellen . 937-775-2709. 393 G
ellen.friese@wright.edu
REINSCHMIDT, Sheryl .... 323-856-7698... 27 O
sreinschmidt@afi.com
REIS, Elizabeth .... 708-974-5283. 153 F
reis@morainevalley.edu
REIS, Paul .... 203-837-9805... 88 B
reisp@wcsu.edu
REIS, Raul .... 305-348-2000. 115 B
REIS, Sally .... 860-486-4037... 92 A
sally.reis@uconn.edu
REISBERG, Jeff .... 727-873-4552. 116 D
reisberg@mail.usf.edu
REISCHE, Jim .... 641-269-3400. 178 H
reischej@grinnell.edu
REISECK, Carol, J .... 708-209-3262. 143 E
carol.reiseck@cuchicago.edu
REISETTER, Mary .... 641-585-8681. 183 D
reisettem@waldorf.edu
REISETTER-HART, Judith 414-382-6431. 531 I
judith.reisetter@alverno.edu
REISH, Brenda, J .... 800-287-8822. 164 C
reishbr@bethanyseminary.edu
REISH, Joseph, G .... 269-387-5202. 252 I
joe.reish@wmich.edu
REISIG, Jerry .... 212-870-1213. 334 C
jreisig@nyts.edu
REISING, Gregory .... 410-704-2512. 220 E
greising@towson.edu
REISINGER, Amanda, B .. 740-588-1275. 394 C
amreisinger@zanestate.edu
REISINGER, Scot, H .... 319-368-6472. 181 C
sreisinger@mtmercy.edu
REISINGER, Tracy .... 503-699-6253. 404 C
treisinger@marylhurst.edu
REISKE, Matthew .... 573-882-6574. 283 C
reiskem@missouri.edu
REISMAN, Lonn .... 254-968-9178. 483 A
reisman@tarleton.edu
REISNER, Carrie .... 765-973-8404. 167 G
hellerc@iue.edu
REISS, Michael, A .... 718-377-0777. 336 I
REISS, Mitchell, B .... 410-778-7201. 221 C
mreiss2@washcoll.edu
REISS, Richard .... 201-692-7003. 301 J
reissr@fdu.edu
REISS, Yona .... 212-960-5347. 351 M
yreiss@yu.edu

REISSENWEBER,
Beth, W .... 630-844-5490. 140 A
breissen@aurora.edu
REISSER, Linda .... 971-722-5292. 407 D
lreisser@pcc.edu
REIST, David .... 785-442-6010. 187 E
dreist@highlandcc.edu
REITER, Genevieve .... 516-364-0808. 333 D
greiter@nycollege.edu
REITER, Laurie .... 800-567-2344. 532 E
lreiter@menominee.edu
REITER, Lisa .... 773-508-2200. 151 H
lreiter1@luc.edu
REITER, Sharon, L .... 909-869-3016... 32 G
slreiter@csupomona.edu
REITMAN, Bruce .... 617-627-3158. 237 C
bruce.reitman@tufts.edu
REITMAN, Tzipora .... 845-574-4595. 338 B
zreitman@sunyrockland.edu
REITNOUR, Brian .... 585-567-9622. 326 F
brian.reitnour@houghton.edu
REITTER, Kim .... 314-977-2828. 281 I
reitterk@slu.edu
REITZ, Barbara .... 610-683-4132. 429 A
reitz@kutztown.edu
REITZ, Chris .... 801-524-8109. 495 O
creitz@ldsbc.edu
REITZ, Tiffany .... 352-638-9707... 99 B
treitz@beaconcollege.edu
REKEMEYER, Robbin .... 319-895-4000. 177 A
rrekemeyer@cornellcollege.edu
REKOWSKI, Lois, T .... 740-264-5591. 379 F
lrekowski@egcc.edu
REL, Ricardo .... 575-646-5909. 310 I
rrel@nmsu.edu
RELAY, Lyn .... 718-368-5034. 318 E
lrelay@kbcc.cuny.edu
RELEFORD, Michele .... 336-750-2171. 370 A
relefordmi@wssu.edu
RELIHAN, Constance, C . 334-844-4900..... 1 G
relihco@auburn.edu
RELLINGER, Brian, A ...... 740-368-3131. 387 J
barellin@owu.edu
RELYEA, Steven, W .... 858-534-3390... 71 F
srelyea@ucsd.edu
REMBACZ, Mark .... 307-382-1646. 543 J
mrembacz@wwcc.wy.edu
REMBERT, Johnny .... 904-470-8277. 102 A
jlrembert@ewc.edu
REMCHO, Vince .... 541-737-8181. 406 A
vincent.remcho@oregonstate.edu
REMELTS, Glenn, A .... 616-526-6299. 240 L
remelt@calvin.edu
REMENDER, Kathleen, A 810-762-9794. 244 Q
kremende@kettering.edu
REMER, Rosalind .... 215-895-1203. 415 B
rosalind.remer@drexel.edu
REMIAS, Roberta .... 586-498-4170. 246 A
remiasr@macomb.edu
REMIERES-MORIN,
Pamela .... 207-755-5224. 210 J
premieres@cmcc.edu
REMILLARD, Theresa ...... 413-755-4336. 233 A
remillard@stcc.edu
REMINGTON, Debra .... 440-375-7040. 382 L
dremington@lec.edu
REMINGTON, Judith, V .. 847-491-8413. 155 D
j-remington@northwestern.edu
REMLEY, Daniel, C .... 570-577-1195. 411 A
dan.remley@bucknell.edu
REMLEY, Karen .... 757-446-7414. 504 E
remleyk@evms.edu
REMLIN, Brittany .... 813-935-5700. 111 N
brittanyremlin@remingtoncollege.edu
REMMENGA, Brad .... 219-785-5749. 172 A
bremmenga@pnc.edu
REMMENGA, Kurt .... 641-784-5190. 178 F
remmenga@graceland.edu
REMMERS, Dawn .... 817-272-0777. 491 B
dremmers@uta.edu
REMSBURG, Barbara ...... 801-587-0851. 496 Q
bremsburg@housing.utah.edu
REMSBURG,
Katherine, M .... 317-738-8135. 165 I
kremsburg@franklincollege.edu
REMSBURG, Robin, E ..... 336-334-5016. 369 A
reremsbu@uncg.edu
REMULLA, Regan .... 323-259-2970... 56 I
rremulla@oxy.edu
REN, Linda .... 510-592-9688... 56 G
linda@npu.edu
RENACIA,
Victorina M, Y .... 671-735-2978. 546 E
vrenacia@uguam.uog.edu
RENAGHAN, Dorothy .... 617-287-5450. 228 G
dorothy.renaghan@umb.edu
RENAGHAN, Maureen ..... 626-857-4147... 38 K
mestrada@citruscollege.edu
RENAUD, Angela .... 401-598-1400. 439 B
arenaud@jwu.edu

RENAUD, Robert, E .... 717-245-1072. 414 H
renaudr@dickinson.edu
RENAULT, Heather, M .... 518-783-2423. 340 J
hrenault@siena.edu
RENBARGER, Bridgette ... 402-399-2646. 289 A
brenbarger@csm.edu
RENBARGER,
Christopher .... 805-986-5826... 74 G
crenbarger@vcccd.edu
RENCIS, Joseph .... 931-372-3172. 460 A
jrencis@tntech.edu
RENDER, Philip .... 843-477-2171. 444 F
philip.render@hgtc.edu
RENDON, Michael .... 361-825-2414. 483 F
michael.rendon@tamucc.edu
RENDON, Mindy, P .... 785-670-1065. 191 D
mindy.rendon@washburn.edu
RENDON, Rudolph, L ..... 512-448-8445. 479 C
rudolphr@stedwards.edu
RENEAR, Allen, H .... 217-333-3280. 162 A
renear@illinois.edu
RENER, Christine .... 616-331-3498. 243 C
renerc@gvsu.edu
RENEW, Steve .... 760-773-2551... 40 F
srenew@collegeofthedesert.edu
RENEY, Richard .... 978-762-4000. 232 D
rreney@northshore.edu
RENFREW, Michelle .... 907-474-5337... 10 I
mmrenfrew@alaska.edu
RENFRO, Bryan .... 319-296-4427. 178 J
bryan.renfro@hawkeyecollege.edu
RENFRO, Chrissy .... 307-778-1310. 543 D
crenfro@lccc.wy.edu
RENFRO, Linda .... 541-245-7517. 407 F
lrenfro@roguecc.edu
RENFRO, Roy, E .... 903-463-8717. 472 M
renfror@grayson.edu
RENGIIL, Yoichi, K .... 671-735-2249. 546 E
yoichi@uguam.uog.edu
RENICK, James .... 601-979-2244. 267 E
james.c.renick@jsums.edu
RENICK, Timothy, M ...... 404-413-2580. 126 E
trenick@gsu.edu
RENIFF, William, M .... 440-826-2212. 374 F
breniff@bw.edu
RENK, Stephanie, H .... 508-856-6507. 229 C
stephanie.renk@umassmed.edu
RENKEMA, Teresa .... 616-222-3000. 245 C
trenkema@kuyper.edu
RENKEN, Tracy .... 202-884-9095... 96 G
renkent@trinitydc.edu
RENN, Joanne, M .... 757-455-3303. 515 H
jrenn@vwc.edu
RENNA, Matt .... 914-773-3813. 335 J
mrenna@pace.edu
RENNER, Cathy .... 812-488-2519. 173 H
cr4@evansville.edu
RENNER, Tom, L .... 616-395-7860. 244 A
trenner@hope.edu
RENNERT, Mordechai ..... 718-438-5476. 350 H
RENNIE, Christopher ...... 810-989-5642. 249 H
ccrennie@sc4.edu
RENNIE, Robert, J .... 904-997-2901. 105 E
rrennie@fscj.edu
RENNIGER, Phyllis, R .... 904-632-3327. 105 E
prenning@fscj.edu
RENNINGER, Laura .... 304-876-5461. 529 I
lrenning@shepherd.edu
RENNIX, Louise .... 843-525-8318. 447 C
lrennix@tcl.edu
RENO, Adam .... 301-846-2560. 214 H
areno@frederick.edu
RENO, Eric .... 210-486-5484. 464 I
ereno@alamo.edu
RENO-MUNRO, Jane .... 843-953-6378. 443 A
munroj@cofc.edu
RENOLA, Elaine .... 409-944-1387. 472 I
erenola@gc.edu
RENSBERGER, Jeffrey, L 713-646-1853. 480 J
jrensberger@stcl.edu
RENSHLER, Kevin .... 252-399-6630. 352 F
renshler@barton.edu
RENTENBACH, Amy .... 404-364-8303. 130 A
arentenbach@oglethorpe.edu
RENTHROPE, Jullin .... 504-286-5117. 206 K
jrenthrope@suno.edu
RENTMEESTER, Matt, G .. 920-433-6657. 531 L
matt.rentmeester@bellincollege.edu
RENTSCH, Janet, D .... 989-964-7120. 249 G
jrentsch@svsu.edu
RENTSCH, Kathleen .... 508-854-2712. 232 F
krentsch@qcc.mass.edu
RENTSCHLER, Gina .... 417-865-2815. 274 B
rentschlerg@evangel.edu
RENTTO, Jessica .... 619-594-6017... 35 D
jrentto@mail.sdsu.edu
RENTZ, Judy .... 916-577-2200... 76 J
jrentz@jessup.edu
RENTZ, Linda, T .... 517-586-3010. 241 A
lrentz@cleary.edu
RENTZ, Shirley, A .... 618-537-6533. 152 G
sarentz@mckendree.edu
RENVILLE, Allen .... 530-895-2239... 30 F
renvilleal@butte.edu
RENWICK, Michael, D .... 860-297-2055... 91 F
michael.renwick@trincoll.edu
RENY, Denise .... 207-741-5568. 211 A
dreny@smccme.edu
RENY, James .... 207-741-5888. 211 A
jreny@smccme.edu
RENZ, Amy Button .... 785-532-5050. 188 A
arenz@ksu.edu
RENZ, Christopher, M .... 510-883-2084... 42 I
crenz@dspt.edu
RENZI, April .... 814-262-3833. 427 C
arenzi@pennhighlands.edu
RENZI, Paul, F .... 540-458-8596. 516 A
prenzi@wlu.edu
RENZULLI, Virgil, N .... 480-965-4980... 11 K
renzulli@asu.edu
REOME, Darryl .... 860-343-5897... 89 A
dreome@mxcc.commnet.edu
REPAC, Richard, A .... 301-687-4331. 220 C
rrepac@frostburg.edu
REPENNING, Thomas ..... 301-934-7630. 214 D
tomr@csmd.edu
REPETSKI, Michael .... 330-941-1457. 394 A
michael.repetski@cis.ysu.edu
REPHANN, Lola .... 212-752-1530. 328 G
lola.rephann@limcollege.edu
REPMAN, Denise .... 504-671-5330. 203 A
drepma@dcc.edu
REPP, A. Drew .... 260-399-7700. 174 C
arepp@sf.edu
REPP, Lolita .... 316-684-5335. 190 G
lolita.repp@sckans.edu
REPP, Philip, C .... 765-285-1034. 164 B
prepp@bsu.edu
REPPERT, Angela .... 610-398-5300. 422 B
areppert@lincolntech.com
REPPERT, David .... 610-796-8463. 409 E
david.reppert@alvernia.edu
RERKO, Renee, L .... 651-603-6318. 255 B
rerko@csp.edu
RERRICK, Charlotte .... 212-757-1190. 313 H
crerrick@funeraleducation.org
RESEBURG, Rhoda .... 503-493-6509. 402 J
rreseburg@cu-portland.edu
RESENIC, Enid .... 800-438-6424. 428 F
enid@iup.edu
RESH-KAMP, Jamie .... 301-387-3742. 214 I
jamie.reshkamp@garrettcollege.edu
RESIDES, Diane, L .... 443-412-2142. 215 C
dresides@harford.edu
RESINGER, Rodney .... 573-518-2110. 278 A
rresinger@mineralarea.edu
RESNICK, Coleen .... 508-541-1655. 225 F
cresnick@dean.edu
RESNICK, Donald .... 212-229-5600. 332 E
resnickd@newschool.edu
RESSEL, Dawn .... 406-243-5661. 286 H
dawn.ressel@umontana.edu
RESSLER, Koreen .... 701-854-8001. 372 J
koreenr@sbci.edu
RESTINE, Nan .... 940-898-2202. 488 B
lrestine@twu.edu
RESTO, Wilfredo .... 787-738-2161. 554 C
wilfredo.resto@upr.edu
RESTO-OLIVO,
Josephine .... 787-620-2040. 547 C
jolivo@aupr.edu
RESTO TORRES, Juan .... 787-765-4210. 548 E
jresto@cempr.edu
RESTUCCIA, Katie .... 508-626-4575. 230 A
krestuccia1@framingham.edu
RETCHIN, Sheldon, M .... 804-828-9771. 511 F
retchin@mcvh-vcu.edu
RETELLE, Mary Louise .... 508-849-3242. 222 B
mretelle@annamaria.edu
RETHANS, Arno .... 530-898-6101... 33 A
arethans@csuchico.edu
RETIF, Earl .... 504-865-5731. 207 C
eretif@tulane.edu
RETKA, James .... 218-683-8643. 260 D
james.retka@northlandcollege.edu
RETTIG, James .... 410-293-6900. 545 J
rettig@usna.edu
RETTIG, Perry .... 706-776-0110. 130 E
prettig@piedmont.edu
RETTLER, Peter, J .... 262-335-5706. 540 F
prettler@morainepark.edu
RETZAK, Lynn .... 920-693-1282. 540 B
lynn.retzak@gotoltc.edu
REUBEN, Rachel .... 607-274-3830. 327 E
rreuben@ithaca.edu
REUSS, Cindy .... 231-777-0364. 247 G
cindy.reuss@muskegoncc.edu
REUSS, Patricia, B .... 406-657-2168. 287 C
preuss@msubillings.edu
REUSTLE, Maureen .... 732-255-0400. 304 A
mreustle@ocean.edu
REUTER, Sara .... 541-885-1628. 405 J
sara.reuter@oit.edu
REUTER, Sarah .... 860-768-5101... 92 D
reuter@hartford.edu
REUTER, William, D .... 716-851-1700. 323 I
reuter@ecc.edu
REUTTER, John .... 256-551-3119..... 4 I
john.reutter@drakestate.edu
REVELEY, III, W. Taylor . 757-221-1693. 503 N
taylor@wm.edu
REVELEY, IV, W. Taylor . 434-395-2001. 506 J
reveleywt@longwood.edu
REVELL, Leana .... 863-784-7120. 113 G
revelll@southflorida.edu
REVELS, Judith, A .... 910-272-3347. 363 B
jrevels@robeson.edu
REVELT, Joseph, E .... 717-871-2390. 429 D
joseph.revelt@millersville.edu
REVENAUGH, Ken .... 314-392-2356. 278 B
revenaug@mobap.edu
REVENIS, Anthony .... 301-295-3068. 545 C
anthony.revenis@usuhs.edu
REVILLA, Elva .... 517-483-1413. 245 H
revillae@lcc.edu
REX, Barbara .... 805-493-3175... 31 H
rex@clunet.edu
REX, Lisa Youngkin .... 610-330-5060. 420 D
rexl@lafayette.edu
REX-COOK, Beverly .... 419-995-8177. 381 Q
rexcook.b@rhodestate.edu
REXILIUS-TUTHILL,
Reiko .... 518-327-6319. 336 B
rtuthill@paulsmiths.edu
REXROAT, Dee, A .... 319-895-4241. 177 A
drexroat@cornellcollege.edu
REXRODE, Richard, R .... 660-263-3900. 272 A
rrr@cccb.edu
REY, Jennifer .... 307-855-2113. 542 Y
jrey@cwc.edu
REYER, Otto .... 909-469-5350... 76 B
oreyer@westernu.edu
REYES, Allen .... 408-934-4900... 47 A
allen_reyes@heald.edu
REYES, Antonia .... 787-758-2525. 554 F
antonia.reyes@upr.edu
REYES, April .... 805-966-3888... 30 A
areyes2@brooks.edu
REYES, Arturo .... 707-468-3071... 54 B
areyes@mendocino.edu
REYES, Carlos .... 916-484-8428... 53 A
reyesc@arc.losrios.edu
REYES, Edgardo .... 787-780-0070. 547 G
ereyes@caribbean.edu
REYES, George, R .... 512-223-8007. 466 I
rey@austincc.edu
REYES, Ginger .... 805-437-8521... 32 I
ginger.reyes@csuci.edu
REYES, Jennifer .... 201-447-7456. 299 C
jreyes@bergen.edu
REYES, Jimmy .... 319-398-5630. 180 J
jreyes@kirkwood.edu
REYES, Joseph .... 831-755-6950... 46 G
jreyes@hartnell.edu
REYES, Loui .... 575-646-5746. 310 I
louireye@nmsu.edu
REYES, Mario, S .... 208-885-7146. 139 D
mreyes@uidaho.edu
REYES, Monica, B .... 989-964-7489. 249 G
mbreyes@svsu.edu
REYES, Pedro .... 512-322-3789. 491 A
preyes@utsystem.edu
REYES, Ray .... 619-660-4206... 46 D
ray.reyes@gcccd.edu
REYES, Raymond .... 509-313-5604. 520 A
reyes@gu.gonzaga.edu
REYES, Robert, G .... 214-860-2090. 470 J
rreyes@dcccd.edu
REYES, Rosana .... 570-740-0336. 422 G
rreyes@luzerne.edu
REYES, Saul .... 863-297-5282. 110 H
sreyes@polk.edu
REYES-GIL, Yanira .... 787-751-1912. 551 B
yreyes@juris.inter.edu
REYES-ROSELLO,
Rosana .... 845-341-4537. 335 H
rosana.reyesrosello@sunyorange.edu
REYMANN, Linda .... 443-352-4203. 218 E
lreymann@stevenson.edu
REYNA, Cynthia .... 870-862-8131... 23 D
creyna@southark.edu
REYNA, Deirdre .... 956-721-5140. 475 F
dreyna@laredo.edu
REYNA, Dorotea .... 415-575-6135... 31 D
dreyna@ciis.edu
REYNA, Mario .... 956-872-6116. 480 I
reyna@southtexascollege.edu
REYNA, Oscar .... 361-825-5934. 483 F
oscar.reyna@tamucc.edu
REYNA, Tony .... 713-942-5920. 490 L
reynat@stthom.edu
REYNA, Yolanda .... 210-486-3333. 465 A
yreyna@alamo.edu
REYNARD, Betty .... 409-839-2048. 486 E
bjreynard@lit.edu
REYNDERS, John, C .... 712-274-5100. 181 B
reynders@morningside.edu
REYNOLDS, Angela .... 479-968-0396... 20 E
areynolds@atu.edu
REYNOLDS, Brad .... 706-865-2134. 133 B
breynolds@truett.edu
REYNOLDS, Carolyn, H .. 276-523-2400. 513 A
creynolds@me.vccs.edu
REYNOLDS, Colleen .... 309-268-8188. 146 B
colleen.reynolds@heartland.edu
REYNOLDS, Curtis .... 352-392-1336. 116 A
curtrey@ufl.edu
REYNOLDS, Cynthia .... 847-233-7700. 155 B
careynolds@nc.edu
REYNOLDS, Debra .... 860-738-6309... 89 C
dreynolds@nwcc.commnet.edu
REYNOLDS, Diane, L ...... 804-828-3430. 511 F
dlreynol@vcu.edu
REYNOLDS, Don .... 334-386-7240..... 3 H
dreynolds2@faulkner.edu
REYNOLDS, Eleanor, L .... 248-370-3364. 248 J
reynolds@oakland.edu
REYNOLDS, Elizabeth, P 304-293-4245. 530 D
liz.reynolds@mail.wvu.edu
REYNOLDS, Ellen .... 914-395-2329. 340 E
ereynolds@sarahlawrence.edu
REYNOLDS, Gail .... 740-374-8716. 392 I
greynolds@wscc.edu
REYNOLDS, Gary .... 719-255-3505... 85 M
greynold@uccs.edu
REYNOLDS, Glenn .... 757-826-1883. 502 G
REYNOLDS, Holly .... 770-718-5314. 122 A
hreynolds@brenau.edu
REYNOLDS, Jack .... 706-272-4456. 123 G
jreynolds@daltonstate.edu
REYNOLDS, James .... 708-456-0300. 161 A
jreyno11@triton.edu
REYNOLDS, James, M ... 937-382-6661. 393 B
jim_reynolds@wilmington.edu
REYNOLDS, Jami .... 301-387-3035. 214 I
jami.reynolds@garrettcollege.edu
REYNOLDS, Jeff .... 970-339-6484... 78 C
jeff.reynolds@aims.edu
REYNOLDS, John, C .... 626-815-3887... 29 H
jreynolds@apu.edu
REYNOLDS, John Mark .. 281-649-3232. 473 B
jmnreynolds@hbu.edu
REYNOLDS, Judith, L ..... 617-573-8302. 237 B
jreynolds@suffolk.edu
REYNOLDS, Karen .... 802-773-5900. 499 B
karen.reynolds@csj.edu
REYNOLDS, Kay .... 978-665-3140. 229 E
kay.reynolds@fitchburgstate.edu
REYNOLDS, Kevin .... 503-725-5087. 406 B
reynoldk@pdx.edu
REYNOLDS, Kevin, W ..... 330-941-2742. 394 A
kwreynolds@ysu.edu
REYNOLDS, Kimberly ..... 785-243-1435. 185 M
kreynolds@cloud.edu
REYNOLDS, Lana .... 405-382-9218. 399 I
l.reynolds@sscok.edu
REYNOLDS, Linda .... 859-572-5208. 198 I
reynoldsl@nku.edu
REYNOLDS, Liz .... 914-594-4229. 334 A
nymc@bkstr.com
REYNOLDS, Lois, G .... 865-694-6693. 461 D
lreynolds@pstcc.edu
REYNOLDS, Lynn .... 732-571-3477. 303 C
lreynold@monmouth.edu
REYNOLDS, Mark, A .... 410-706-7461. 219 C
mreynolds@umaryland.edu
REYNOLDS, Marlene .... 419-372-9824. 374 K
mreyno@bgsu.edu
REYNOLDS, Mary .... 630-753-9087. 155 B
mreynolds@nc.edu
REYNOLDS, Mary, M ...... 828-327-7000. 359 A
mreynolds@cvcc.edu
REYNOLDS, Michael .... 757-825-2898. 514 B
reynoldsm@tncc.edu
REYNOLDS, Michael, C .. 334-844-4367..... 1 G
reynom2@auburn.edu
REYNOLDS, Nancy, W .... 270-686-4244. 192 G
nancy.reynolds@brescia.edu
REYNOLDS, Norman .... 812-749-1272. 171 K
nreynolds@oak.edu
REYNOLDS, Patrick, D ... 315-859-4607. 325 E
preynold@hamilton.edu
REYNOLDS, Patsy .... 931-540-2573. 460 E
preynolds4@columbiastate.edu
REYNOLDS, Randall .... 615-460-6443. 453 C
randall.reynolds@belmont.edu
REYNOLDS, Robert .... 269-965-3931. 244 O
reynoldsr@kellogg.edu
REYNOLDS, Robin .... 408-554-4397... 64 M
rreynolds@scu.edu
REYNOLDS, Rodney .... 805-493-3658... 31 H
rreynol@callutheran.edu

REYNOLDS, Sean, B .... 847-491-7326. 155 D
sean.reynolds@northwestern.edu
REYNOLDS, Sharon, P ... 336-633-0234. 362 H
spreynolds@randolph.edu
REYNOLDS, Shawn .... 320-629-5161. 260 F
reynoldss@pinetech.edu
REYNOLDS,
Stephanie, C .... 315-792-5456. 331 I
sreynolds@mvcc.edu
REYNOLDS, JR., Steven 440-375-7350. 382 L
sreynolds@lec.edu
REYNOLDS, Thomas, E .. 303-458-4087... 84 M
treynold@regis.edu
REYNOLDS, Thomas, L .. 704-687-7248. 368 E
tlreynol@uncc.edu
REYNOLDS, Virginia .... 916-691-7359... 53 B
mcreyng@crc.losrios.edu
REYNOLDS, Wally .... 815-455-8547. 152 F
wreynold@mchenry.edu
REYNOLDS, William, F ... 973-596-3004. 303 G
william.reynolds@njit.edu
REYNOLDS, William, G .. 202-687-2461... 95 E
wgr2@georgetown.edu
REYNOLDS-CASPER,
ReGina .... 620-792-9362. 184 F
casperr@bartonccc.edu
REZAC, Barb .... 605-668-1292. 450 F
barbara.rezac@mtmc.edu
REZAI, Saeed .... 801-832-2527. 498 F
srezai@westminstercollege.edu
REZEL, Elizabeth .... 608-743-4450. 539 I
erezel@blackhawk.edu
REZENDES, George .... 401-598-2029. 439 B
george.rezendes@jwu.edu
REZNIK, Inna .... 516-572-7637. 332 C
inna.reznik@ncc.edu
RHAMES, Ronald .... 803-822-3261. 445 C
rhamesr@midlandstech.edu
RHEA, Allison .... 937-512-4515. 388 O
allison.rhea@sinclair.edu
RHEA, Jessica .... 239-590-7016. 115 A
jrhea@fgcu.edu
RHEA, Kristy, K .... 540-828-5433. 502 J
thouff@bridgewater.edu
RHEA, Mitchell .... 423-478-6231. 460 D
MRhea01@clevelandstatecc.edu
RHEA, Teresa, C .... 256-549-8230..... 3 M
trhea@gadsdenstate.edu
RHEAD, Lori .... 608-363-2630. 531 M
rheadl@beloit.edu
RHEAULT, Wendy .... 847-578-8805. 157 F
wendy.rheault@rosalindfranklin.edu
RHEAUME, Steve .... 603-535-2266. 298 G
srheaume@plymouth.edu
RHEE, Edmund .... 626-448-0023... 48 L
RHEIN, John .... 610-430-4163. 430 A
jrhein@wcupa.edu
RHEINSCHMIDT,
Richard, E .... 319-399-8643. 176 G
rrheinsc@coe.edu
RHEW, Steven, W .... 336-334-5806. 369 A
steve_rhew@uncg.edu
RHI-KLEINERT, Susan .... 310-233-4339... 51 H
rhiks@lahc.edu
RHI-KLEINERT, Susan .... 818-364-7778... 52 A
Rhiks@lamission.edu
RHIM, Choonhee, L .... 323-265-8625... 51 F
rhimcl@elac.edu
RHINE, Lisa, B .... 757-822-5201. 514 C
lrhine@tcc.edu
RHINE, Randy .... 308-432-6201. 291 D
rrhine@csc.edu
RHINE, Thomas, E .... 304-829-7633. 526 D
trhine@bethanywv.edu
RHINEHARDT, Kimrey .... 919-843-0381. 366 K
kwr@northcarolina.edu
RHINEHART, Marilyn ..... 913-469-8500. 187 J
marilynr@jccc.edu
RHINESMITH, Betsy .... 630-829-6018. 140 B
brhinesmith@ben.edu
RHOADES, Dianne .... 252-536-7239. 361 A
dbarnes-rhoades128@halifaxcc.edu
RHOADES, IV, Mack, B . 713-743-9370. 489 B
mrhoades@uh.edu
RHOADES, Margot .... 704-461-6733. 352 G
MargotRhodes@bac.edu
RHOADES, Samuel, T ..... 804-257-5811. 515 F
strhoades@vuu.edu
RHOADES, Valerie .... 719-346-9300... 83 E
valerie.rhoades@morgancc.edu
RHOADES WILLIAMS,
Castine .... 706-821-8311. 130 C
crhoadeswilliams@paine.edu
RHOADS, Bill .... 620-768-2909. 186 G
billr@fortscott.edu
RHOADS, George, G .... 732-235-9700. 306 B
rhoads@rutgers.edu
RHOADS, Judith, L .... 270-824-8562. 196 A
judithl.rhoads@kctcs.edu
RHOADS, Kay, M .... 803-934-3255. 445 F
krhoads@morris.edu

RHOADS, Linden .... 206-543-0905. 524 G
lrhoads@uw.edu
RHODA, Christopher .... 207-859-1124. 211 H
chris@thomas.edu
RHODA, Karen .... 508-999-8305. 229 A
krhoda@umassd.edu
RHODARMER, Melanie .. 828-251-6700. 368 C
mrhodarm@unca.edu
RHODE, Carolyn .... 336-506-4128. 357 M
carolyn.rhode@alamancecc.edu
RHODE, Charles, G .... 404-894-4114. 125 D
chuck.rhode@facilities.gatech.edu
RHODEN, Brenda .... 256-761-6204..... 7 F
brhoden@talladega.edu
RHODEN, Deborah .... 256-840-4137...... 6 I
drhoden@snead.edu
RHODEN, Joyce .... 334-727-8011..... 8 A
jrhoden@tuskegee.edu
RHODEN, Laura .... 336-744-0900. 353 A
laura@carolina.edu
RHODEN, Richard, R ...... 337-475-5887. 207 G
rrhoden@mcneese.edu
RHODES, Angela .... 405-789-6400. 399 K
arhodes@snu.edu
RHODES, Anthony, P ..... 212-592-2000. 340 H
arhodes@sva.edu
RHODES, Carla .... 706-880-8240. 128 A
crhodes@lagrange.edu
RHODES, Carol, C .... 302-739-4060... 93 D
crhodes1@dtcc.edu
RHODES, David .... 318-371-3035. 203 E
drhodes@ltc.edu
RHODES, David, J .... 251-578-1313..... 6 D
jrhodes@rstc.edu
RHODES, David, J .... 212-592-2000. 340 H
drhodes@sva.edu
RHODES, David, J .... 724-946-7105. 437 B
rhodesdj@westminster.edu
RHODES, Dawn, M .... 317-274-4511. 168 D
dawnrhod@iupui.edu
RHODES, Eileen .... 860-628-4751... 90 D
erhodes@lincolncollegene.edu
RHODES, Fred, W .... 502-272-8150. 192 E
frhodes@bellarmine.edu
RHODES, Gale .... 502-852-5727. 200 D
gale.rhodes@louisville.edu
RHODES, Gary, L .... 804-523-5200. 512 F
grhodes@reynolds.edu
RHODES, Gina .... 704-290-5899. 363 G
grhodes@spcc.edu
RHODES, Jack, W .... 843-953-3708. 442 A
jack.rhodes@citadel.edu
RHODES, Jeff .... 956-665-2209. 492 B
rhodesjh@utpa.edu
RHODES, John .... 410-225-2201. 216 C
jrhodes@mica.edu
RHODES, Kathleen, S ..... 256-824-6775..... 8 F
Kathleen.Rhodes@uah.edu
RHODES, Kathy .... 206-934-3796. 522 I
kathy.rhodes@seattlecolleges.edu
RHODES, Kay .... 806-742-5170. 487 D
kay.rhodes@ttu.edu
RHODES, Lawrence .... 212-799-5000. 328 B
RHODES, Lisa, D .... 404-270-5728. 132 E
lrhodes@spelman.edu
RHODES, Mark .... 678-839-5561. 133 I
mrhodes@westga.edu
RHODES, Marlene .... 314-644-9245. 281 E
mrhodes@stlcc.edu
RHODES, Michelle .... 616-331-3234. 243 C
rhodesmi@gvsu.edu
RHODES, Phil .... 281-649-3417. 473 B
prhodes@hbu.edu
RHODES, Randall .... 301-687-4212. 220 C
rrhodes@frostburg.edu
RHODES, Rebecca .... 509-533-7075. 518 D
rebecca.rhodes@scc.spokane.edu
RHODES, Rebecca .... 509-533-7075. 518 E
Rebecca.Rhodes@scc.spokane.edu
RHODES, Richard, M ...... 512-223-7598. 466 I
rrhodes@austincc.edu
RHODES, Robert .... 325-674-2024. 464 H
rlr12a@acu.edu
RHODES, Robert .... 575-492-2640. 310 G
rrhodes@nmjc.edu
RHODES, Ruth .... 312-788-1145. 162 H
rrhodes@vandercook.edu
RHODES, Simon .... 317-274-7211. 168 D
srhodes@iupui.edu
RHODES, Tara .... 570-702-8950. 419 G
trhodes@johnson.edu
RHODES, Vincent, A .... 757-446-7070. 504 E
rhodesva@evms.edu
RHOLES, Julia .... 662-915-7092. 270 B
jrholes@olemiss.edu
RHONE, Henry, G .... 804-828-1244. 511 F
hgrhone@vcu.edu
RHOTEN, Darrell .... 305-386-9900. 102 D
drhoten@cci.edu
RHOTON, James, M .... 843-863-7050. 441 H
jrhoton@csuniv.edu

RHOTON, Patrick .... 740-392-6868. 384 K
patrick.rhoton@mvnu.edu
RHUE, Monika .... 704-371-6741. 355 K
mrhue@jcsu.edu
RHYNE, Teresa, L .... 757-455-3345. 515 H
trhyne@vwc.edu
RHYS WIETECHA,
Raji, A .... 520-626-5502... 18 F
rhys@email.arizona.edu
RIAL, Scott .... 847-543-2652. 143 A
srial@clcillinois.edu
RIAS, Curtis .... 212-650-7073. 317 D
curtis@ccny.cuny.edu
RIBAKOW, Larry .... 410-484-7200. 217 D
RIBAR, Robert .... 304-829-7744. 526 D
rribar@bethanywv.edu
RIBAR, Tom .... 724-852-3302. 437 A
tribar@waynesburg.edu
RIBARICH, Marie .... 914-654-5320. 320 H
mribarich@cnr.edu
RIBERDY, Michelle .... 413-552-2547. 231 F
mriberdy@hcc.edu
RIBICH, Fred, D .... 319-352-8320. 183 E
fred.ribich@wartburg.edu
RIBORDY, J. Clark .... 785-242-5200. 189 I
clark.ribordy@ottawa.edu
RICARDI, Jennifer .... 916-638-1616... 47 B
jennifer_ricardi@heald.edu
RICASA, Arlie .... 619-482-6360... 68 B
aricasa@swccd.edu
RICATTO, Pascal, J .... 201-493-3572. 299 C
pjricatto@bergen.edu
RICCA, Beth .... 201-684-7455. 305 A
bricca@ramapo.edu
RICCARDI, JR.,
Louis, D .... 415-442-7224... 45 I
lriccardi@ggu.edu
RICCARDI, Richard .... 203-392-5232... 88 A
riccardir1@southernct.edu
RICCI, Jose, L .... 787-727-7727. 555 D
jricci@sagrado.edu
RICCI, Jose, L .... 787-728-1515. 555 D
jricci@sagrado.edu
RICCIARDI, Julie, E .... 919-508-2362. 370 F
jricciardi@peace.edu
RICCIO, JudyAnn .... 203-365-4899... 91 C
riccioj@sacredheart.edu
RICCIO, Richard, A .... 201-692-7050. 301 J
riccio@fdu.edu
RICE, Alaina, M .... 620-417-1061. 190 F
alaina.rice@sccc.edu
RICE, Ann .... 803-584-3446. 448 D
annerice@mailbox.sc.edu
RICE, Ann, M .... 916-734-0751... 70 J
ann.rice@ucdmc.ucdavis.edu
RICE, Camellia, N .... 910-362-7065. 358 F
crice@cfcc.edu
RICE, Charles, L .... 301-295-3013. 545 C
charles.rice@usuhs.edu
RICE, Cheryl .... 330-494-6170. 389 F
crice@starkstate.edu
RICE, Cheryl, A .... 678-836-6280. 133 I
crice@westga.edu
RICE, Cynthia, E .... 410-706-3171. 219 C
crice@umaryland.edu
RICE, Daniel, B .... 785-628-4260. 186 F
drice@fhsu.edu
RICE, David .... 239-513-1122. 106 O
drice@hodges.edu
RICE, Debi .... 253-752-2020. 519 K
financialaid@faithseminary.edu
RICE, Dennis .... 925-631-4794... 61 F
drice@stmarys-ca.edu
RICE, Edward .... 662-246-6442. 268 B
erice@msdelta.edu
RICE, Eric, L .... 253-752-2020. 519 K
deanofstudents@faithseminary.edu
RICE, Hannah .... 314-918-2519. 274 A
hrice@eden.edu
RICE, Heather .... 256-228-6001..... 5 H
riceh@nacc.edu
RICE, Howard, T .... 270-809-2535. 198 B
hrice@murraystate.edu
RICE, James .... 513-231-2223. 374 D
jrice@athenaeum.edu
RICE, James, P .... 570-577-3655. 411 A
james.rice@bucknell.edu
RICE, James, W .... 320-222-7474. 260 H
jim.rice@ridgewater.edu
RICE, John .... 775-753-2260. 294 F
john.rice@gbcnv.edu
RICE, Jonah .... 618-252-5400. 159 E
jonah.rice@sic.edu
RICE, Larry, D .... 918-343-7612. 399 C
lrice@rsu.edu
RICE, Leila .... 315-781-3700. 326 C
rice@hws.edu
RICE, Malcolm .... 256-824-6347..... 8 F
malcom.rice@uah.edu
RICE, Michele .... 814-262-6447. 427 C
mrice@pennhighlands.edu

RICE, Peggy .... 815-836-5350. 150 H
ricepe@lewisu.edu
RICE, Peter .... 201-684-7601. 305 A
price@ramapo.edu
RICE, Priscilla .... 215-968-8450. 411 B
ricep@bucks.edu
RICE, Rachel .... 207-768-9447. 212 G
rachel.rice@umpi.edu
RICE, Rachel .... 800-567-2344. 532 E
rrice@menominee.edu
RICE, Sabra, L .... 336-386-3276. 364 D
rices@surry.edu
RICE, Scott .... 217-333-0560. 162 A
serice@uillinois.edu
RICE, Sherwin .... 910-879-5646. 358 B
srice@bladencc.edu
RICE, Stephen .... 201-684-7407. 305 A
srice@ramapo.edu
RICE, Stephen, C .... 301-295-3896. 545 C
stephen.rice@usuhs.edu
RICE, Susan, I .... 336-633-0282. 362 H
sirice@randolph.edu
RICE, Tammy .... 949-582-4701... 67 C
trice@saddleback.edu
RICE, Teresa .... 337-269-0620. 201 B
theresar@bluecliffcollege.com
RICE, Timothy, S .... 304-367-4917. 529 F
Timothy.Rice@fairmontstate.edu
RICE, Tom, W .... 319-335-0256. 175 I
tom-rice@uiowa.edu
RICE AYALA, Maggie ..... 773-907-4041. 142 A
mrice19@ccc.edu
RICE-CLAYBORN, Kathy . 501-450-3134... 25 H
kathyc@uca.edu
RICE-EVANS, Marla, D ... 910-962-7055. 369 C
riceevansm@uncw.edu
RICH, Arthur .... 402-457-2681. 290 G
aarich@mccneb.edu
RICH, Jack, W .... 325-674-2013. 464 H
richj@acu.edu
RICH, John .... 215-571-4013. 415 B
john.armand.rich@drexel.edu
RICH, Kathy .... 781-280-3501. 232 B
richk@middlesex.mass.edu
RICH, Kim .... 860-412-7317... 89 E
krich@qvcc.commnet.edu
RICH, Laura .... 910-893-4364. 352 K
richl@campbell.edu
RICH, Martha .... 315-279-5368. 328 D
mrich@mail.keuka.edu
RICH, Scott .... 620-278-4213. 190 I
srich@sterling.edu
RICH, Scott .... 620-278-4294. 190 I
srich@sterling.edu
RICH, Steven .... 617-236-8800. 226 F
srich@fisher.edu
RICH, Steven, W .... 217-581-6616. 144 E
swrich@eiu.edu
RICH, Tammy .... 570-484-2128. 429 B
trich@lhup.edu
RICH, Timothy, A .... 651-631-5489. 263 A
tarich@nwc.edu
RICH-COATES, Robin ...... 757-789-1748. 512 D
rrich-coates@es.vccs.edu
RICHARD, David .... 407-646-2232. 111 Q
dcrichard@rollins.edu
RICHARD, Ellen .... 415-439-2309... 27 M
erichard@act-sf.org
RICHARD, Francis, D ..... 904-620-2700. 116 B
drichard@unf.edu
RICHARD, George .... 440-826-2325. 374 F
grichard@bw.edu
RICHARD, Mark .... 256-840-4110..... 6 I
mrichard@snead.edu
RICHARD, Mark .... 814-871-7763. 416 K
richard004@gannon.edu
RICHARD, Renee .... 216-987-4865. 378 D
renee.richard@tri-c.edu
RICHARD, Robert .... 337-482-6923. 208 D
bookstore@louisiana.edu
RICHARD, Roseann .... 707-654-1175... 31 I
rrichard@csum.edu
RICHARD, Ryan .... 318-255-7950. 207 F
ryan@latechalumni.org
RICHARD, Thomas .... 603-358-2326. 298 F
trichard@keene.edu
RICHARD, Thomas, J .... 207-768-2795. 210 M
trichard@nmcc.edu
RICHARD, Valerie .... 704-403-3507. 352 J
valerie.richard@carolinashealthcare.org
RICHARDELLO, Denise .... 413-662-5201. 230 C
denise.richardello@mcla.edu
RICHARDS, Anjana .... 650-738-7076... 64 D
richardsa@smccd.edu
RICHARDS, Calvin, R ...... 214-860-2232. 470 J
crichards@dcccd.edu
RICHARDS, Char .... 262-524-6891. 532 C
crichard@carrollu.edu
RICHARDS, Chris .... 715-346-3908. 538 A
crichards@uwsp.edu

RICHARDS, Connie, L .... 229-333-5699. 134 B
clrichards@valdosta.edu
RICHARDS, David .... 626-584-5458... 45 E
richards@fuller.edu
RICHARDS, David, J .... 517-321-0242. 243 F
drichards@glcc.edu
RICHARDS, Debbie .... 304-424-8201. 530 E
debbie.richards@wvup.edu
RICHARDS, Doug .... 573-651-5923. 282 B
drichards@semo.edu
RICHARDS, Elaine, A ...... 858-499-0202... 40 C
erichards@coleman.edu
RICHARDS, Faith .... 605-455-6029. 450 I
frichards@olc.edu
RICHARDS, Gwyn .... 812-855-2435. 167 F
grichar@indiana.edu
RICHARDS, Harry, J .... 603-862-3000. 298 C
harry.richards@unh.edu
RICHARDS, Heraldo .... 615-963-5160. 459 E
hrichards@tnstate.edu
RICHARDS, James, G ..... 302-831-8697... 94 B
jimr@udel.edu
RICHARDS, Josh .... 816-932-6748. 281 J
jmrichards@saintlukescollege.edu
RICHARDS, Katharine ..... 630-466-7900. 162 J
krichards@waubonsee.edu
RICHARDS, Kathi, S .... 937-778-7843. 379 G
krichards@edisonohio.edu
RICHARDS, Kathy, A ...... 906-227-1237. 248 A
kathrich@nmu.edu
RICHARDS, Kent .... 218-733-5969. 259 A
k.richards@lsc.edu
RICHARDS, Larry, J .... 801-524-8101. 495 O
lrichards@ldsbc.edu
RICHARDS, Laurence, D . 765-973-8320. 167 G
laudrich@iue.edu
RICHARDS, Lawrence ..... 610-399-2405. 428 B
police@cheyney.edu
RICHARDS, Lee, P .... 602-429-4946... 16 O
lrichards@ps.edu
RICHARDS, Leon .... 808-734-9565. 136 E
lr24@hawaii.edu
RICHARDS, Mark .... 510-642-5872... 70 I
Mark_Richards@berkeley.edu
RICHARDS, Marvin .... 216-987-4883. 378 D
marvin.richards@tri-c.edu
RICHARDS, Maryanne .... 508-830-5039. 230 D
mrichards@maritime.edu
RICHARDS, Matthew .... 207-741-5927. 211 A
mrichards@smccme.edu
RICHARDS, Melissa .... 414-847-3336. 534 F
melissarichards@miad.edu
RICHARDS, Michael, D .. 702-651-5600. 294 E
mike.richards@csn.edu
RICHARDS, Paul .... 801-524-8139. 495 O
PRichards@ldsbc.edu
RICHARDS, Randy .... 561-803-2543. 110 B
randy_richards@pba.edu
RICHARDS, Renae, L ...... 801-524-8144. 495 O
renae@ldsbc.edu
RICHARDS, Robin .... 650-306-3234... 64 B
richardsr@smccd.edu
RICHARDS, Roger, C ...... 850-263-3261... 98 N
rcrichards@baptistcollege.edu
RICHARDS, Sandra, K .... 850-263-3261... 98 N
skrichards@baptistcollege.edu
RICHARDS, Sandra, K .... 800-328-2660... 98 N
skrichards@baptistcollege.edu
RICHARDS, Scott .... 413-236-3015. 231 A
srichards@berkshirecc.edu
RICHARDS, Steve .... 320-762-4692. 257 O
stever@alextech.edu
RICHARDS, Susan .... 307-754-6243. 543 G
Susan.Richards@northwestcollege.edu
RICHARDS, Terry .... 513-745-2984. 393 H
richardst1@xavier.edu
RICHARDS, Thomas, F .... 573-882-3611. 283 B
richardstf@umsystem.edu
RICHARDS, Tracey .... 215-619-7330. 424 B
trichards@mc3.edu
RICHARDS, Valena, V ..... 340-693-1421. 555 E
vrichar@live.uvi.edu
RICHARDS, William .... 845-341-4701. 335 H
president@sunyorange.edu
RICHARDS SAMUEL,
Pamela .... 340-693-1003. 555 E
pamelac.richardssamuel@live.uvi.edu
RICHARDSON, Andrea ... 419-772-2028. 386 D
a-richardson@onu.edu
RICHARDSON, Becky ..... 229-391-2624. 129 F
brichardson@moultrietech.edu
RICHARDSON,
Bernard, L .... 202-806-7280... 95 G
brichardson@howard.edu
RICHARDSON, Beverly ... 501-370-5280... 22 F
bevrich@philander.edu
RICHARDSON,
Beverly, A .... 609-894-9311. 299 I
brichard@bcc.edu
RICHARDSON, Bonita, L 412-237-4413. 413 D
brichardson@ccac.edu
RICHARDSON, Brent ...... 847-628-2540. 149 B
brichardson@judsonu.edu
RICHARDSON, Bruce ..... 520-515-3602... 12 R
richardsonb@cochise.edu
RICHARDSON, Camille .. 252-940-6236. 358 A
camiller@beaufortccc.edu
RICHARDSON, Carol ...... 858-642-8460... 55 J
crichardson@nu.edu
RICHARDSON, Charles .. 859-371-9393. 192 D
crichardson@beckfield.edu
RICHARDSON,
Charles, J .... 518-381-1210. 340 G
richarcj@sunysccc.edu
RICHARDSON, Christine 315-655-7147. 316 E
cwrichardson@cazenovia.edu
RICHARDSON,
Christopher .... 540-261-4234. 509 K
christopher.richardson@svu.edu
RICHARDSON, Cinzia .... 973-720-2976. 308 I
richardsonc@wpunj.edu
RICHARDSON, Cliff .... 303-556-2413... 81 D
cliff.richardson@ccd.edu
RICHARDSON, D. Scott .. 616-331-2215. 243 C
richarsc@gvsu.edu
RICHARDSON, David ..... 509-527-2511. 524 I
david.richardson@wallawalla.edu
RICHARDSON, Donna .... 214-645-5485. 493 E
donna.richardson@utsouthwestern.edu
RICHARDSON, Emily ...... 386-822-7518. 117 C
ecrichar@stetson.edu
RICHARDSON, Gail .... 918-335-6285. 398 F
grichardson@okwu.edu
RICHARDSON,
George, H .... 607-587-3101. 345 D
richargh@alfredstate.edu
RICHARDSON, Greer ...... 215-951-1806. 420 B
richards@lasalle.edu
RICHARDSON, Greg, C .. 606-474-3250. 194 H
greg@kcu.edu
RICHARDSON, Guy, L .... 601-923-1650. 269 E
grichardson@rts.edu
RICHARDSON, Irene .... 513-244-4432. 377 G
irene_richardson@mail.msj.edu
RICHARDSON, James ..... 509-682-6400. 525 B
jrichardson@wvc.edu
RICHARDSON, James, A 225-578-6745. 204 O
parich@lsu.edu
RICHARDSON, Jennifer .. 518-454-2023. 321 A
richardj@strose.edu
RICHARDSON, Jennifer .. 802-447-6359. 500 D
jrichardsonl@svc.edu
RICHARDSON, John .... 706-771-4111. 121 D
jrichard@augustatech.edu
RICHARDSON, John .... 303-837-0825... 78 H
jrichardson@aii.edu
RICHARDSON, John, F .. 502-852-6293. 200 D
john.richardson@louisville.edu
RICHARDSON, CM,
John, T .... 312-362-8712. 143 H
jrichard@depaul.edu
RICHARDSON, Julie .... 413-559-5471. 227 B
admissions@hampshire.edu
RICHARDSON, Karry, D . 573-629-3016. 274 J
krichardson@hlg.edu
RICHARDSON,
Kathy Brittain .... 706-236-2216. 121 G
krichardson@berry.edu
RICHARDSON, Krista ..... 419-995-8312. 381 Q
richardson.k@rhodesstate.edu
RICHARDSON, Lilliard ... 317-274-2016. 168 D
lillrichr@iupui.edu
RICHARDSON, Linda, L . 518-783-2307. 340 J
richardson@siena.edu
RICHARDSON, Luns, C .. 803-934-3211. 445 F
lcrichardson@morris.edu
RICHARDSON, Lynne, D 540-654-1561. 510 J
lrichar2@umw.edu
RICHARDSON, Mark .... 503-494-8220. 405 I
somdeansoffice@ohsu.edu
RICHARDSON, Mary .... 229-430-3588. 120 A
mrichardson@albanytech.edu
RICHARDSON,
Mary Kate .... 425-235-2352. 522 F
mrichardson@rtc.edu
RICHARDSON, Meg .... 716-829-7808. 323 D
richardm@dyc.edu
RICHARDSON, Melanie .. 360-438-4367. 522 G
mrichardson@stmartin.edu
RICHARDSON, Michael .. 417-667-8181. 273 A
mrichardson@cottey.edu
RICHARDSON,
Michael, W .... 406-496-4213. 287 F
mrichardson@mtech.edu
RICHARDSON, Michele .. 802-860-2756. 499 A
richards@champlain.edu
RICHARDSON, Pamela ... 717-396-7833. 427 A
prichardson@pcad.edu
RICHARDSON, Ralph, C . 785-532-5660. 188 A
vetdean@ksu.edu
RICHARDSON, Rick .... 302-736-2461... 94 C
workcontrol@wesley.edu
RICHARDSON, Rick .... 254-968-9890. 483 A
rrichardson@tarleton.edu
RICHARDSON, Roger ..... 607-274-1623. 327 E
rrichard@ithaca.edu
RICHARDSON, Rusty ...... 615-547-4401. 454 A
rrichardson@cumberland.edu
RICHARDSON, Sarah ..... 402-280-2703. 289 D
sarahrichardson@creighton.edu
RICHARDSON, Saundra . 910-410-1722. 362 I
sarichardson@richmondcc.edu
RICHARDSON, Scott ...... 570-674-6247. 424 A
srichard@misericordia.edu
RICHARDSON,
Silvana, F .... 608-796-3687. 539 E
sfrichardson@viterbo.edu
RICHARDSON, Steven ..... 562-860-2451... 37 I
srichardson@cerritos.edu
RICHARDSON, Terry ...... 276-944-6231. 504 H
trichard@ehc.edu
RICHARDSON,
Thomas, C .... 662-329-7386. 268 E
trichardson@as.muw.edu
RICHARDSON,
Thomas, J .... 717-872-3162. 429 D
tom.richardson@millersville.edu
RICHARDSON, Tracey .... 831-755-6752... 46 G
trichardson@hartnell.edu
RICHARDSON, Tracy ...... 812-535-5154. 172 F
trichard@smwc.edu
RICHARDSON, Valerie .... 256-549-8228..... 3 M
vrichardson@gadsdenstate.edu
RICHARDSON, Virginia .. 304-327-4402. 529 D
jrichardson@bluefieldstate.edu
RICHARDSON, W. Mark . 510-204-0733... 38 J
RICHARDSON-BOUIE,
Deborale .... 216-987-0204. 378 D
deborale.richardson-bouie@tri-c.edu
RICHARTZ, Paul .... 973-300-2295. 307 F
prichartz@sussex.edu
RICHBERG, Melissa .... 419-824-3726. 383 C
mrichberg@lourdes.edu
RICHEMOND, Donna, L . 978-762-4000. 232 D
drichemo@northshore.edu
RICHERT, David, G .... 651-631-5376. 263 A
dgrichert@nwc.edu
RICHES, Jonathan, S ...... 610-292-9852. 431 F
jonathan.riches@reseminary.edu
RICHEY, Angie .... 909-599-5433... 50 J
arichey@lifepacific.edu
RICHEY, Anthony .... 334-244-3570..... 2 A
arichey@aum.edu
RICHEY, D. Michael .... 859-257-3912. 200 C
mrichey@uky.edu
RICHEY, James, H .... 321-433-7000. 101 M
richeyj@easternflorida.edu
RICHEY, Lance, B .... 260-399-7700. 174 C
lrichey@sf.edu
RICHEY, Lizabeth, R .... 580-327-8593. 396 N
lrrichey@nwosu.edu
RICHEY, Matt .... 507-786-3418. 264 B
richeym@stolaf.edu
RICHEY, Matthew .... 507-786-3418. 264 B
richeym@stolaf.edu
RICHEY, Melody, H .... 901-843-3730. 458 E
richey@rhodes.edu
RICHEY, P. Jerome .... 412-624-4747. 435 C
jrichey@pitt.edu
RICHEY, Patrick, E .... 716-888-2480. 316 C
richeyp@canisius.edu
RICHEY, Suzanne .... 423-636-7303. 462 E
srichey@tusculum.edu
RICHEY, Thomas .... 562-860-2451... 37 I
trichey@cerritos.edu
RICHEY, Warren, A .... 901-843-3845. 458 E
richeyw@rhodes.edu
RICHIE, Darren, A .... 303-963-3187... 79 C
drichie@ccu.edu
RICHIE, Patricia, V .... 561-868-3540. 110 C
richiep@palmbeachstate.edu
RICHIEZ, Anthony .... 305-273-4499. 100 H
anthony.richiez@cbt.edu
RICHMAN, Jack, M .... 919-962-5650. 368 D
jrichman@email.unc.edu
RICHMAN, John .... 701-671-2221. 372 E
john.richman@ndscs.edu
RICHMAN, Melissa, G .... 212-517-0562. 330 E
mrichman@mmm.edu
RICHMAN, Robert .... 561-297-3166. 114 L
rrichman@fau.edu
RICHMAN, Steve .... 660-359-3948. 279 H
srichman@mail.ncmissouri.edu
RICHMOND, Jayne, E ..... 401-874-5505. 440 D
richmond@uri.edu
RICHMOND, Jennifer ..... 412-304-0727. 416 F
jrichmond@cci.edu
RICHMOND, Jillian .... 619-849-2209... 59 L
jillianrichmondl@pointloma.edu
RICHMOND, Lisa, T .... 630-752-5101. 163 F
lisa.richmond@wheaton.edu
RICHMOND, Margaret .... 603-358-2276. 298 F
mrichmon@keene.edu
RICHMOND, Rollin, C .... 707-826-3311... 35 C
rollinr@humboldt.edu
RICHMOND, Steve .... 606-783-5236. 198 A
s.richmond@moreheadstate.edu
RICHMOND, Vicki .... 757-825-3810. 514 B
richmondvc@tncc.edu
RICHTER, Deborah .... 563-244-7030. 178 A
drichter@eicc.edu
RICHTER, Mark, H .... 260-422-5561. 167 B
mhrichter@indianatech.edu
RICHTER, Sara .... 580-349-1472. 397 G
saraj@opsu.edu
RICHTER, Sheila, W .... 814-824-2287. 423 J
srichter@mercyhurst.edu
RICHTER, Suzanna, L ..... 717-358-5843. 416 J
suzanna.richter@fandm.edu
RICHTER-NORGEL, Ellen 651-690-8730. 263 O
erichter-norgel@stkate.edu
RICHTERS, Stephen, P .... 318-342-1025. 208 E
richters@ulm.edu
RICHTMAN, Margaret ..... 507-457-1618. 264 A
mrichtma@smumn.edu
RICHWALSKY, Michael .. 216-397-3022. 381 R
mrichwalsky@jcu.edu
RICIOPPO, Eric .... 631-370-3300. 340 F
ericioppo@sbmelville.edu
RICK, Mary, A .... 517-750-1200. 250 E
mrick@arbor.edu
RICKARD, Chuck .... 610-526-6522. 410 J
crickard@brynmawr.edu
RICKARD, Emma Lee ..... 803-774-3354. 441 F
rickardel@cctech.edu
RICKARD, Jenny .... 253-879-3211. 524 F
jrickard@pugetsound.edu
RICKARD, Lawrence, R ... 414-288-7320. 534 B
larry.rickard@marquette.edu
RICKARD, Scott .... 406-657-1763. 287 C
srickard@msubillings.edu
RICKARD, Vickie .... 615-547-1247. 454 A
vrickard@cumberland.edu
RICKARD, Walter .... 518-828-4181. 321 C
walter.rickard@sunycgcc.edu
RICKARDS, Brenden .... 856-415-2297. 302 C
brickards@gccnj.edu
RICKARDS, Laura .... 732-255-0400. 304 A
lrickards@ocean.edu
RICKENBAKER, Michael . 478-445-4467. 125 A
michael.rickenbaker@gcsu.edu
RICKER, Curtis .... 912-478-0779. 126 C
cricker@georgiasouthern.edu
RICKER, Deborah, D .... 717-815-1510. 438 D
dricker@ycp.edu
RICKER, Don .... 419-227-3141. 391 F
dricker@unoh.edu
RICKERT, Gail Ann .... 717-337-6579. 417 B
grickert@gettysburg.edu
RICKETT, Melanie .... 540-863-2807. 512 B
mrickett@dslcc.edu
RICKETTS, Carole .... 325-793-3819. 476 E
cricketts@mcm.edu
RICKETTS, Lloyd .... 609-771-2186. 300 E
ricketts@tcnj.edu
RICKETTS, Mike .... 423-697-4433. 460 C
RICKETTS, Tracy .... 541-885-1118. 405 J
tracy.ricketts@oit.edu
RICKEY, Jeffrey .... 315-229-5226. 339 F
jrickey@stlawu.edu
RICKEY, Jeffrey .... 315-229-5286. 339 F
jrickey@stlawu.edu
RICKEY, Tiffani .... 602-386-4103... 11 G
tiffani.rickey@arizonachristian.edu
RICKFORD, Donald .... 202-274-5415... 97 A
donald.rickford@udc.edu
RICKLE, SJ, William .... 304-243-2385. 531 H
rickle@wju.edu
RICKNER, Donald .... 949-582-4968... 67 C
drickner@saddleback.edu
RICKS, Suzy .... 208-524-3000. 138 D
suzanne.ricks@my.eitc.edu
RICKS, Venus .... 717-867-6165. 421 H
ricks@lvc.edu
RICO, Antonio .... 915-779-8031. 494 C
ccctrain@aol.com
RICO, Camilla .... 360-417-6442. 522 A
crico@pencol.edu
RICO, Oscar .... 661-654-2394... 32 H
orico@csub.edu
RICO-GUTIERREZ,
Luis, C .... 515-294-7427. 175 H
lrico@iastate.edu
RICORDATI, Timothy .... 630-617-3089. 145 A
timothy.ricordati@elmhurst.edu
RIDD-YOUNG, Kristi ...... 866-680-2756. 496 A
president@midwifery.edu
RIDDELL, Jeffrey, R .... 206-726-5020. 518 G
jriddell@cornish.edu
RIDDELL, Richard .... 919-684-2641. 354 A
richard.riddell@duke.edu
RIDDER, Cece .... 503-725-4457. 406 B
ridder@pdx.edu

RIDDER, Kari 402-941-6523. 290 K
ridder@midlandu.edu
RIDDER, Steven, G 386-323-5025. 102 B
ridders@erau.edu
RIDDICK, Iman 773-602-5000. 142 B
RIDDICK, Vera, E 757-683-3689. 507 N
vriddick@odu.edu
RIDDLE, Catherine 518-262-3593. 313 D
riddlec@mail.amc.edu
RIDDLE, Christy 662-846-4336. 266 G
criddle@deltastate.edu
RIDDLE, Heather 612-330-1177. 253 H
riddle@augsburg.edu
RIDDLE, Joyce, E 304-462-4107. 529 G
joyce.riddle@glenville.edu
RIDDLE, Marianne 502-863-8020. 194 C
marianne_riddle@georgetowncollege.edu
RIDDLEMOSER, Roger 305-348-6849. 115 B
roger.riddlemoser@fiu.edu
RIDEAUX, Larry 817-515-4507. 482 B
larry.rideaux@tccd.edu
RIDEL, Robert 480-557-9112... 18 I
robert.ridel@phoenix.edu
RIDENOUR, Nancy, A 505-272-6284. 312 F
nridenour@salud.unm.edu
RIDENS, Sheryl, L 858-499-0202... 40 C
sridens@coleman.edu
RIDEOUT, Dane 845-938-2022. 545 I
8gc@usma.edu
RIDEOUT, Kathy 585-275-8902. 349 C
Kathy_Rideout@urmc.rochester.edu
RIDER, Elizabeth, A 717-361-1333. 415 H
riderea@etown.edu
RIDER, Jeff 870-759-4194... 25 K
jrider@wbcoll.edu
RIDER, Jonathan 703-812-4757. 506 H
jrider@leland.edu
RIDER, Robert 865-974-2201. 463 C
brider@utk.edu
RIDGE, Sean 865-573-4517. 455 G
sridge@johnsonU.edu
RIDGEDELL, Ken, W 985-549-2121. 208 C
kridgedell@selu.edu
RIDGEWAY, Duff 319-368-6468. 181 C
dridgeway@mtmercy.edu
RIDGEWAY, Gloria 229-317-6919. 124 A
gloria.ridgeway@darton.edu
RIDGWAY, Susan, M 989-837-4219. 248 C
ridgway@northwood.edu
RIDINGTON,
M. Thomas 610-341-4377. 415 G
tridingt@eastern.edu
RIDLEY, Carolyn, L 859-858-3511. 192 B
carolyn.ridley@asbury.edu
RIDLEY, Emmett, L 804-524-5068. 515 D
eridley@vsu.edu
RIDLEY, Scott 806-742-1988. 487 D
scott.ridley@ttu.edu
RIDLEY, JR., Wadell 610-660-1223. 432 E
wridley@sju.edu
RIDOUT, Thomas, M 563-562-3263. 181 E
ridoutt@nicc.edu
RIDPATH, Lisa, H 540-831-5760. 508 C
lridpath@radford.edu
RIECK, Ray 217-234-5224. 150 D
rrieck@lakeland.cc.il.us
RIEDEL, Eric 612-312-2393. 265 D
eric.riedel@waldenu.edu
RIEDEL, Eric, R 330-569-5240. 380 I
riedeler@hiram.edu
RIEDEL, Herbert, H 334-222-6591..... 5 E
hriedel@lbwcc.edu
RIEDEL CARNEY,
Elizabeth 651-690-6836. 263 O
eacarney@stkate.edu
RIEDER, Rick 816-802-3431. 275 J
rrieder@kcai.edu
RIEDER, JR., Robert, W 256-824-6633..... 8 F
riederr@uah.edu
RIEFKOHL, Jorge 787-780-0070. 547 G
jriefkohl@caribbean.edu
RIEGELNEGG, F. Dennis 219-866-6157. 172 E
fdr@saintjoe.edu
RIEGER, Mark 302-831-2501... 94 B
mrieger@udel.edu
RIEGLE, Stephanie, L 734-936-2254. 251 C
sbrugler@umich.edu
RIEHL, Gretchen, K 972-860-7140. 470 I
GRiehl@dcccd.edu
RIEHL, James 218-726-6397. 264 D
jpriel@d.umn.edu
RIEHL, Shelle 503-517-1814. 408 I
sriehl@westernseminary.edu
RIEHS, Steven 630-515-7702. 144 A
sriehs@devry.edu
RIEKEMAN, Guy, F 770-426-2601. 128 D
riekeman@life.edu
RIELLO, Heidi, A 413-662-5331. 230 C
heidi.riello@mcla.edu
RIEMAN, Jef 419-772-3100. 386 D
j-rieman@onu.edu

RIEPMA, Edward 949-794-9090... 68 D
criepma@stanbridge.edu
RIES, Barry 507-389-1242. 259 G
barry.ries@mnsu.edu
RIES, Cheryl 906-487-7317. 242 G
cheryl.ries@finlandia.edu
RIES, Heidi, R 937-255-3633. 544 C
heidi.ries@afit.edu
RIES, Kenneth 320-629-5195. 260 F
riesk@pinetech.edu
RIES, Thomas Karl 651-641-8211. 255 B
ries@csp.edu
RIESGO, Andrea 760-366-5285... 42 B
ariesgo@cmccd.edu
RIESSLAND, Larry 308-865-8524. 292 H
riesslandl@unk.edu
RIESTER, Jon 812-866-7021. 166 C
riester@hanover.edu
RIESTER, Leslie 971-722-8288. 407 D
lriester@pcc.edu
RIESTRA, Liza 787-841-2000. 552 B
liza_riestra@pucpr.edu
RIESTRA, Miguel, A 787-622-8000. 553 E
mriestra@pupr.edu
RIFFE, Cindy 918-335-6842. 398 F
criffe@okwu.edu
RIFFEE, William, H 352-273-6309. 116 A
riffee@cop.ufl.edu
RIFFEL, Beth 620-947-3121. 190 J
bethr@tabor.edu
RIFFEY, Candy 701-323-8623. 372 I
Candy.Riffey@SanfordCollege.edu
RIFKIN, Benjamin 609-771-2277. 300 E
rifkin@tcnj.edu
RIGALI, Mary 203-596-4504... 90 I
mrigali@post.edu
RIGBY, Heather 248-476-1122. 246 G
hrigby@mispp.edu
RIGBY, Ullin, K 804-257-5608. 515 F
ukrigby@vuu.edu
RIGEL, Bill 863-638-7243. 119 C
bill.rigel@warner.edu
RIGG, Jenny 307-778-4326. 543 D
jrigg@lccc.wy.edu
RIGGERT, Mark 402-557-7070. 288 G
bubookstore@fheg.follett.com
RIGGINS, David, W 828-689-1219. 356 F
driggins@mhc.edu
RIGGLE, Elise 419-755-4313. 385 D
riggle.17@osu.edu
RIGGLE, Steve, E 818-779-8040... 50 A
mclemens@kingsuniversity.edu
RIGGS, Allen 435-283-7125. 498 A
allen.riggs@snow.edu
RIGGS, Becky 870-862-8131... 23 D
briggs@southark.edu
RIGGS, Bonnie 423-697-4465. 460 C
RIGGS, Channing 612-624-6868. 264 G
riggs035@umn.edu
RIGGS, David 765-677-2808. 169 B
david.riggs@indwes.edu
RIGGS, Jesse, A 816-322-0110. 271 O
security@calvary.edu
RIGGS, Jesse, A 816-322-0110. 271 O
jesse.riggs@calvary.edu
RIGGS, Jim 417-455-5466. 273 E
jriggs@crowder.edu
RIGGS, Joyce 270-824-8581. 196 A
joyce.riggs@kctcs.edu
RIGGS, M. Peggy 516-299-4206. 329 C
peggy.riggs@liu.edu
RIGGS, Robert, F 214-887-5007. 471 F
rriggs@dts.edu
RIGGS, Robert, F 214-887-5003. 471 F
rriggs@dts.edu
RIGHI, Paul, A 617-228-3474. 231 C
prighi@bhcc.mass.edu
RIGNEY, Doug 205-934-5493..... 8 E
drigney@uab.edu
RIGNEY, Steve 505-348-3750. 450 G
srigney@national.edu
RIGSBEE, Craig 530-895-2476... 30 F
rigsbeecr@butte.edu
RIGSBEE, David 217-641-4533. 148 M
drigsbee@jwcc.edu
RIGSBY, Dave 503-370-6217. 408 J
drigsby@willamette.edu
RIGSBY, Ellen, M 309-467-6311. 145 C
eraid@eureka.edu
RIHA, James 618-235-2700. 160 A
james.riha@swic.edu
RIHACEK, Robin 708-210-5754. 159 C
rrihacek@ssc.edu
RIHL-LEWINSKY,
Elizabeth 215-572-2956. 409 H
rihll@arcadia.edu
RIIS, Janet 406-447-5423. 285 G
jriis@carroll.edu
RIKEL, Randy 903-223-3005. 484 C
randy.rikel@tamut.edu

RIKHOFF, Gregory, S 541-346-2402. 406 D
grikhoff@uoregon.edu
RILEY, Andrea 405-631-3399. 395 J
RILEY, Anthony, G 806-894-9611. 480 H
triley@southplainscollege.edu
RILEY, Bruce 608-785-8218. 536 G
briley@uwlax.edu
RILEY, Carla 320-589-6066. 264 F
rileycj@morris.umn.edu
RILEY, Christine 828-251-6500. 368 C
criley@unca.edu
RILEY, Doreen, K 216-397-4345. 381 R
driley@jcu.edu
RILEY, Edward 617-254-2610. 236 B
RILEY, Eileen 412-809-5100. 430 H
riley.eileen@pti.edu
RILEY, Elaine 254-526-1106. 468 G
elaine.riley@ctcd.edu
RILEY, Francis, D 617-495-1780. 227 C
francis_riley@harvard.edu
RILEY, OSA, George, F 610-519-7715. 436 F
george.riley@villanova.edu
RILEY, Jan 334-222-6591..... 5 E
lriley@lbwcc.edu
RILEY, Jeannette 508-999-8279. 229 A
j1riley@umassd.edu
RILEY, Karen 303-871-7874... 86 B
kriley@du.edu
RILEY, Ken 432-685-4569. 476 G
kriley@midland.edu
RILEY, Kimberly 816-604-4523. 277 H
kim.riley@mcckc.edu
RILEY, Marsha 406-247-3009. 287 C
marsha.riley@msubillings.edu
RILEY, Matt 406-243-5455. 286 H
matt.riley@umontana.edu
RILEY, P. Thomas 703-654-1040. 510 J
priley@umw.edu
RILEY, Patrick 440-684-6022. 392 D
priley@ursuline.edu
RILEY, Robert 781-768-7147. 236 A
robert.riley@regiscollege.edu
RILEY, Robert, A 717-867-6202. 421 H
riley@lvc.edu
RILEY, Robert, K 253-535-7119. 521 I
rileyrk@plu.edu
RILEY, Sabrina 402-486-2514. 292 E
sariley@ucollege.edu
RILEY, Sarah 900-652-6176... 37 M
sarah.riley@chaffey.edu
RILEY, Sarah 305-899-3051... 98 O
sriley@barry.edu
RILEY, Scott, T 218-285-2205. 260 G
scott.riley@rainyriver.edu
RILEY, Sharon, E 434-971-3301. 544 I
sharon.e.riley.mil@mail.mil
RILEY, Stacy 262-564-3108. 540 A
rileys@gtc.edu
RILEY, Susan 513-732-5324. 391 B
rileysu@email.uc.edu
RILEY, Teri 330-941-4628. 394 A
triley@ysu.edu
RILEY, Terisa 361-593-3612. 484 A
terisa.riley@tamuk.edu
RILEY, Terisa, C 361-593-3612. 484 A
terisa.riley@tamuk.edu
RILEY, Tisa, R 717-736-4150. 417 I
trriley@hacc.edu
RILEY, Vicki 304-214-8857. 528 G
vriley@wvncc.edu
RILEY HAUSER, Ellen 715-682-4591. 541 F
ellen.hauser@witc.edu
RILING, Dean 918-836-6886. 400 D
driling@mail.spartan.edu
RILLING, David, S 864-488-4573. 444 L
drilling@limestone.edu
RILLORTA, Rhoda 704-355-3243. 353 D
rhoda.rillorta@carolinashealthcare.org
RIMA, Kyle 801-832-2008. 498 F
krima@westminstercollege.edu
RIMAI, Monica 503-725-5878. 406 B
monica.rimai@pdx.edu
RIMAL, Sanjana 973-353-5940. 306 D
srimal@andromeda.rutgers.edu
RIMANDO-CHAREUNSAP,
Rosie 206-934-6763. 523 A
rosie.rimando-chareunsap@seattlecolleges.edu
RIMBY, Susan 570-484-2073. 429 B
ser1116@lhup.edu
RIMER, Barbara, K 919-966-3215. 368 D
brimer@unc.edu
RIMIRCH, Bruce 680-488-2471. 547 B
brucer@palau.edu
RIMMER, Jessica 405-691-3800. 396 D
jrimmer@macu.edu
RINALDI, Marylyn 858-784-8469... 65 E
mrinaldi@scripps.edu
RINARD, Pat 727-341-3064. 112 E
rinard.pat@spcollege.edu

RINAS, Craig 972-825-4612. 481 F
crinas@sagu.edu
RINAUDO, Brooke, H 318-797-5108. 205 F
brooke.rinaudo@lsus.edu
RINCK, Jared 816-604-6740. 277 D
jared.rinck@mcckc.edu
RINCON, Amilcar 787-279-1912. 550 B
arincon@bayamon.inter.edu
RINCON, Mary Beth 219-989-2251. 171 N
mbrincon@purduecal.edu
RINCONES, Liza 210-308-8584. 475 C
RINCONES-GÓMEZ,
Rigoberto 954-201-6500... 99 D
RINDE, Carla, M 610-409-3599. 436 B
crinde@ursinus.edu
RINDE, Pat, J 701-252-3467. 373 D
rinde@jc.edu
RINDERKNECHT,
Bethany 319-368-6467. 181 C
brinderknecht@mtmercy.edu
RINDO, Michael, J 715-836-4742. 536 E
rindomj@uwec.edu
RINE, Veronica 740-755-7600. 376 A
vrine@cotc.edu
RINEHART, James 334-670-3399..... 7 H
rinehart@troy.edu
RINEHART, Jenna 319-352-8220. 183 E
jenna.rinehart@wartburg.edu
RINEHART, Kenton, W 845-575-3000. 330 D
kent.rinehart@marist.edu
RINEHART, Richard, J 570-577-3213. 411 A
r.rinehart@bucknell.edu
RINEHART, Shelley 281-998-6150. 479 H
shelley.rinehart@sjcd.edu
RINEY, OSU, Judith, N 270-686-4288. 192 G
judith.riney@brescia.edu
RING, Jeff 503-491-7286. 404 E
jeff.ring@mhcc.edu
RING, Joshua 828-328-7927. 356 B
joshua.ring@lr.edu
RING, Neal 864-242-5100. 441 D
RING, Patricia 508-793-3459. 225 B
pring@holycross.edu
RING, Ray 212-817-7394. 317 F
rring@gc.cuny.edu
RINGA, Melanie 914-961-8313. 340 B
finance@svots.edu
RINGENBERG, Ron 574-296-6212. 163 J
rringenb@ambs.edu
RINGER-FISHER, Denise 412-338-4770. 419 M
dringer-fisher@kaplan.edu
RINGGER, Nick 907-822-3201... 10 A
nringger@akbible.edu
RINGKAMP, Patricia, M 570-577-3167. 411 A
pat.ringkamp@bucknell.edu
RINGLE, John 217-206-6190. 161 E
ringle.john@uis.edu
RINGLE, Martin, D 503-777-7254. 407 E
martin.ringle@reed.edu
RINGLE, Suzanne 602-286-8110... 14 L
suzanne.ringle@gwmail.maricopa.edu
RINGLER, Neil, H 315-470-6606. 345 B
neilringler@esf.edu
RINGO, Teresa, T 936-294-1061. 487 A
reg_tat@shsu.edu
RINGOLD, Debra 503-370-6440. 408 J
dringold@willamette.edu
RINGOLD, Gordon 831-459-4479... 72 C
ringold@ucsc.edu
RINGSTAD, Ann 907-474-5922... 10 I
atringstad@alaska.edu
RINGWOOD, Karen, K 203-597-9036... 91 G
klozada@bridgeport.edu
RINI, Anthony 617-373-4774. 235 F
RINI, Lisa 212-686-9040. 350 G
lrini@woodtobecoburn.edu
RINK, Darrel, C 479-788-7701... 24 A
chris.rink@uafs.edu
RINK, Susan 734-481-2310. 242 D
srink@emich.edu
RINKENBAUGH, Bill 316-322-3297. 185 D
brinkenb@butlercc.edu
RINKER, Jonathan, A 304-877-6428. 526 C
jon.rinker@abc.edu
RINKER, Linda 616-554-5183. 241 H
lrinker@davenport.edu
RINN, Martha 830-372-8110. 485 C
mrinn@tlu.edu
RINN, Susan 830-372-8001. 485 C
srinn@tlu.edu
RINNE, Henry 479-788-7431... 24 A
henry.rinne@uafs.edu
RINNE, Jason 660-831-4088. 278 I
rinnej@moval.edu
RINNERT, Jennifer 904-819-6376. 103 E
JRinnert@flagler.edu
RIO, Deborah 661-362-3298... 40 E
debbie.rio@canyons.edu
RIORDAN, Charles 302-831-4007... 94 B
riordan@udel.edu

RIORDAN, Christine 859-257-2911. 200 C
christine.riordan@uky.edu
RIORDAN, Jean 773-298-3135. 158 E
riordan@sxu.edu
RIORDAN, Jennifer 717-564-4112. 419 I
jriordan@kaplan.edu
RIORDAN, Kevin 708-596-2000. 159 C
kriordan@ssc.edu
RIORDAN, Marsha 641-673-1045. 183 H
riordanm@wmpenn.edu
RIORDAN, Phil 561-237-7749. 108 X
priordan@lynn.edu
RIORDAN, Rob 619-929-9748... 47 I
RIOS, Adlin 787-728-1545. 555 D
adlinrios@sagrado.edu
RIOS, Alfonso 323-357-6209... 51 F
riosa@elac.edu
RIOS, Charlene 509-793-2020. 517 C
charlener@bigbend.edu
RIOS, Ed 718-982-2460. 317 E
eduardo.rios@csi.cuny.edu
RIOS, Eddie 801-274-3280. 498 E
erios@wgu.edu
RIOS, Efrain 787-844-8181. 555 A
efrain.rios@upr.edu
RIOS, Elizabeth 305-273-4499. 100 H
elizabeth.rios@cbt.edu
RIOS, Esther, A 671-735-5544. 546 C
financialaid@guamcc.edu
RIOS, Francisca 956-665-2551. 492 B
frios@utpa.edu
RIOS, Francisco 360-650-3319. 525 C
francisco.rios@wwu.edu
RIOS, Irene 203-777-7100... 87 G
irios@albertus.edu
RIOS, Laura 787-279-1912. 550 B
lriosr@bayamon.inter.edu
RIOS, Lourdes 787-884-6000. 549 D
lrios@icprjc.edu
RIOS, Patricia 312-369-7465. 143 D
prios@colum.edu
RIOS, Thomas, R 262-472-1172. 538 D
riost@uww.edu
RIOS, William 787-738-2161. 554 C
william.rios3@upr.edu
RIOS, Zilka 787-798-4050. 553 C
zilka.rios@uccaribe.edu
RIOS-HUSAIN,
Silvia Patricia 704-922-6217. 360 F
husain.silvia@gaston.edu
RIOS-KRAVITZ, Rhonda 916-558-2254... 53 D
rioskrr@scc.losrios.edu
RIOTTO, Karen, M 585-395-5484. 342 F
kriotto@brockport.edu
RIOUX, Ronald 603-230-3502. 295 J
rrioux@ccsnh.edu
RIPEPI, Maria 412-536-1527. 420 A
maria.ripepi@laroche.edu
RIPICH, Danielle 207-602-2306. 213 A
dripich@une.edu
RIPLEY, Anneliese 406-683-7537. 286 I
a_ripley@umwestern.edu
RIPLEY, Dave 701-477-7862. 373 B
dripley@tm.edu
RIPLEY, Judith 207-795-5974. 209 I
ripleyj@cmhc.org
RIPLEY, Kate 907-450-8102... 10 G
klripley@alaska.edu
RIPLEY, Melissa 423-636-7300. 462 E
mripley@tusculum.edu
RIPLEY, Ronald, L 414-288-1656. 534 B
ronald.ripley@marquette.edu
RIPPEN, Kelly 308-345-8107. 290 J
rippenk@mpcc.edu
RIPPERDA, Jan 618-545-3041. 149 D
jripperda@kaskaskia.edu
RIPPEY, Sharon, T 315-859-4672. 325 E
srippey@hamilton.edu
RIPPINGER, Timothy 414-288-4771. 534 B
timothy.rippinger@marquette.edu
RIPPKE, Greg 419-473-2700. 378 I
grippke@daviscollege.edu
RIPPLE, David, W 313-577-2275. 252 G
bb2607@wayne.edu
RIPPLE, Scott, A 765-658-4555. 165 F
sripple@depauw.edu
RIPTON, Elizabeth, R 585-292-2243. 332 A
eripton@monroecc.edu
RISBUD, Subhash, H 530-752-6659... 70 J
shrisbud@ucdavis.edu
RISCHBIETER, Natalie 678-359-5073. 127 A
natalier@gordonstate.edu
RISELING, Susan 608-262-4527. 536 D
riseling@wisc.edu
RISNER, Sam 606-337-1457. 193 F
srisner@ccbbc.edu
RISSE, Duane 303-352-3356... 81 D
duane.risse@ccd.edu
RISSER, Barbara, G 585-785-1201. 324 D
risserbg@flcc.edu
RISSLER, Jennifer 415-749-4586... 62 G
jrissler@sfai.edu
RISSMEYER, Patricia 617-735-9722. 226 B
rissmeye@emmanuel.edu
RISTAINO, John 401-341-2159. 440 C
john.ristaino@salve.edu
RISTE, Brian 920-832-7694. 533 S
brian.riste@lawrence.edu
RISTINE, Jennifer 401-949-2820. 439 C
jristine@inteducators.org
RITACCO, Judith 508-531-1244. 229 D
judith.ritacco@bridgew.edu
RITACCO, Kevin 508-854-4200. 232 F
kritacco@qcc.mass.edu
RITCHEL, Laurie 409-880-8419. 486 F
laurie.ritchel@lamar.edu
RITCHEY, Fred, L 903-233-4210. 475 J
fredritchey@letu.edu
RITCHEY, Mary, K 706-886-6831. 133 A
mritchey@tfc.edu
RITCHEY, Nathan 814-732-2400. 428 E
RITCHEY, William, V 757-594-7047. 503 M
bill.ritchey@cnu.edu
RITCHIE, David 765-998-5397. 173 C
dvritchie@taylor.edu
RITCHIE, Derek 610-341-1955. 415 G
dritchie@eastern.edu
RITCHIE, Gloria 412-809-5100. 430 H
ritchie.gloria@pti.edu
RITCHIE, Jay 707-638-5802... 69 K
jay.ritchie@tu.edu
RITENBAUGH, Robert, C 334-844-4190..... 1 G
ritenrc@auburn.edu
RITER, Jayme, S 716-878-3041. 343 A
riterjs@buffalostate.edu
RITER, Steve 915-747-7890. 492 A
sriter@utep.edu
RITO, Edward 513-241-4338. 373 J
edward.rito@antonellicollege.edu
RITSCHDORFF, John 845-575-3000. 330 D
john.ritschdorff@marist.edu
RITTENBERG,
Stephen, A 212-854-2254. 321 D
sar3@columbia.edu
RITTENBERGER, Alexis 724-503-1001. 436 G
arittenberger@washjeff.edu
RITTER, Barbara 843-349-2640. 442 E
britter@coastal.edu
RITTER, Duane, J 706-542-2621. 133 C
dritter@uga.edu
RITTER, Eugene, W 336-322-2243. 362 F
Gene.Ritter@piedmontcc.edu
RITTER, Gretchen 607-255-4146. 322 A
gr72@cornell.edu
RITTER, Gretchen 512-232-3312. 491 C
ritterg@mail.utexas.edu
RITTER, Joe 618-374-5176. 156 B
joe.ritter@principia.edu
RITTER, Karen, R 336-633-0206. 362 H
krritter@randolph.edu
RITTER, Kathy 904-620-2730. 116 B
k.ritter@unf.edu
RITTER, Mark 864-503-5939. 448 H
mritter@uscupstate.edu
RITTER, Melvin 910-695-3811. 363 F
ritterm@sandhills.edu
RITTER, Michael 618-664-7122. 145 G
michael.ritter@greenville.edu
RITTER, Monica 412-365-1280. 412 K
mritter@chatham.edu
RITTER, Nancy 575-527-7650. 311 B
naritter@nmsu.edu
RITTERBROWN, Michael 818-240-1000... 45 G
michaelr@glendale.edu
RITTLE, Dennis 870-368-7371... 22 E
drittle@ozarka.edu
RITTLING, Mary, E 336-249-8186. 360 A
merittli@davidsonccc.edu
RITTS, Bonnie, B 585-785-1281. 324 D
rittsbb@flcc.edu
RITZ, Cathy 661-362-3639... 40 E
cathy.ritz@canyons.edu
RITZ, Robert, L 434-592-4800. 506 I
rlritz@liberty.edu
RITZ, Steven 831-459-2635... 72 C
sritz@scipp.ucsc.edu
RITZE, Nancy 718-289-5156. 317 B
nancy.ritze@bcc.cuny.edu
RITZMAN, Elizabeth 708-524-6520. 144 C
eritzman@dom.edu
RITZMAN, Richard 901-678-2832. 460 B
rritzman@memphis.edu
RIUTTA, Janice 262-564-3072. 540 A
riuttaj@gtc.edu
RIVALEAU, Susan, A 843-953-4973. 443 A
rivaleaus@cofc.edu
RIVARD, Timothy 781-239-2631. 231 G
trivard@massbay.edu
RIVAS, JC 310-527-7105... 43 K
RIVAS, Jess 626-396-2263... 28 P
jesus.rivas@artcenter.edu
RIVELAND, Bruce 360-475-7500. 521 H
briveland@olympic.edu
RIVERA, Al 520-383-8401... 18 B
arivera@tocc.cc.az.us
RIVERA, Alba 787-743-7979. 552 I
albrivera@suagm.edu
RIVERA, Angel 718-368-5026. 318 E
arivera@kbcc.cuny.edu
RIVERA, Angel, A 787-720-4476. 553 D
presidente@mizpa.edu
RIVERA, Arcilia 787-864-2222. 550 D
ariverag@inter.edu
RIVERA, Beatriz 787-751-0500. 555 B
beatriz.rivera6@upr.edu
RIVERA, Beatriz 787-250-1912. 550 E
brivera@metro.inter.edu
RIVERA, Carlos 973-877-4415. 301 H
crivera10@essex.edu
RIVERA, Carlos, E 787-725-8120. 548 O
planificacion@eap.edu
RIVERA, Carmen 787-250-1912. 550 E
crivera@metro.inter.edu
RIVERA, Carmen 773-878-3545. 158 B
crivera@staugustine.edu
RIVERA, Carmen, G 787-864-2222. 550 D
cgrivera@inter.edu
RIVERA, Carmen, J 787-743-7979. 552 I
ut_crivera@suagm.edu
RIVERA, Carmen, M 787-258-1501. 548 H
crivera@columbiaco.edu
RIVERA, Caroline 757-822-1191. 514 C
crivera@tcc.edu
RIVERA, Daliana 787-780-5134. 551 L
drivera@nuc.edu
RIVERA, Damaris 312-935-4144. 156 K
drivera@robertmorris.edu
RIVERA, Diana 787-284-1912. 550 F
drivera@ponce.inter.edu
RIVERA, Dianne 787-864-2222. 550 D
drivera@inter.edu
RIVERA, Edfel 787-738-2161. 554 C
edfel.rivera@upr.edu
RIVERA, Edith 212-817-7410. 317 F
erivera@gc.cuny.edu
RIVERA, Edwin 787-279-1912. 550 B
edrivera@bayamon.inter.edu
RIVERA, Eileen 787-864-2222. 550 D
eirivera@inter.edu
RIVERA, Elaine 956-665-5372. 492 B
erivera11@utpa.edu
RIVERA, Elias 718-782-2200. 315 E
erivera@boricuacollege.edu
RIVERA, Eric 619-594-5211... 35 D
erivera@mail.sdsu.edu
RIVERA, Eric 215-702-4241. 411 F
erivera@cairn.edu
RIVERA, Francisco 787-765-1915. 551 C
frivera@opto.inter.edu
RIVERA, Gerardo 787-841-0003. 550 F
grivera@ponce.inter.edu
RIVERA, Gilbert 505-454-3311. 310 E
vpacademicaffairs@nmhu.edu
RIVERA, Gilbert 973-655-4498. 303 D
riverag@mail.montclair.edu
RIVERA, Ivelisse 787-850-9303. 554 D
ivelisse.rivera4@upr.edu
RIVERA, Janely 312-935-2004. 156 K
jrivera@robertmorris.edu
RIVERA, Janet 787-264-1912. 551 A
janriver@sg.inter.edu
RIVERA, Janice 787-789-4251. 547 E
jrivera@atlanticcollege.edu
RIVERA, Jason 909-607-7283... 59 G
jason_rivera@pitzer.edu
RIVERA, Jesus, M 787-258-1501. 548 H
jrivera@columbiaco.edu
RIVERA, Johana 718-270-6016. 319 A
jrivera@mec.cuny.edu
RIVERA, Jorge, A 787-731-3915... 18 I
jorge.rivera@phoenix.edu
RIVERA, Jose, A 787-751-1912. 551 B
jrivera@juris.inter.edu
RIVERA, Jose, A 787-264-1912. 551 A
joseanibalrivera@sg.inter.edu
RIVERA, Jose, J 787-727-7033. 555 D
jjrivera@sagrado.edu
RIVERA, Joshua 718-518-4342. 318 B
jorivera@hostos.cuny.edu
RIVERA, Juan, C 787-841-2000. 552 B
capellania@pucpr.edu
RIVERA, Juan, L 787-620-2040. 547 C
jrivera@aupr.edu
RIVERA, Julio, C 262-551-5850. 532 D
julio@carthage.edu
RIVERA, Karen 787-257-7373. 552 H
karivera@suagm.edu
RIVERA, Karen, P 713-221-8402. 489 D
riverak@uhd.edu
RIVERA, Laura 832-813-6564. 476 A
laura.rivera@lonestar.edu
RIVERA, Lisette 787-250-1912. 550 E
lriverao@metro.inter.edu
RIVERA, Liza 347-964-8600. 315 E
lrivera@boricuacollege.edu
RIVERA, Luis 787-765-3560. 548 M
lrivera@edpuniversity.edu
RIVERA, Luis, R 773-947-6306. 152 E
lrivera@mccormick.edu
RIVERA, Marcelino 787-743-7979. 552 I
ut_mrivera@suagm.edu
RIVERA, Marcos 216-987-5378. 378 D
marcos.rivera@tri-c.edu
RIVERA, Margarita 787-765-4210. 548 E
mrivera@cempr.edu
RIVERA, Mari Lillian 787-763-6700. 549 A
registro@se-pr.edu
RIVERA,
Maria de los, M 787-753-6000. 549 D
mrivera@icprjc.edu
RIVERA,
Maria de Lourdes 787-751-1912. 551 B
mdlrivera@juris.inter.edu
RIVERA, Maria del C 787-857-3600. 550 A
mcrivera@br.inter.edu
RIVERA, Mary Ann 757-388-2900. 509 D
marivera@sentara.com
RIVERA, Maximina 908-737-6800. 302 F
mrivera@kean.edu
RIVERA, Mayra 787-765-3560. 548 M
mrivera@edpuniversity.edu
RIVERA, Michael 309-796-5049. 140 E
riveram@bhc.edu
RIVERA, Milagros 787-621-2835. 547 C
mrivera@aupr.edu
RIVERA, Milagros, M 787-786-3030. 547 F
mrivera@ucb.edu.pr
RIVERA, Mildred 787-798-3001. 553 C
mildred.rivera@uccaribe.edu
RIVERA, Nelson 215-248-6376. 422 F
nrivera@ltsp.edu
RIVERA, Nitza 787-758-2525. 554 F
nitza.rivera@upr.edu
RIVERA, Noemi 787-725-8120. 548 O
mrivera0044@eap.edu
RIVERA, Olga 787-753-6335. 549 D
orivera@icprjc.edu
RIVERA, Paul 787-752-4575. 554 B
paul.rivera1@upr.edu
RIVERA, Peter 325-942-2035. 465 K
RIVERA, Ramón 787-622-8000. 553 E
rrivera@pupr.edu
RIVERA, Rey 602-243-8115... 15 F
rey.rivera@southmountaincc.edu
RIVERA, Rosa, M 856-225-6836. 306 C
rosarive@camden.rutgers.edu
RIVERA, Rosita, A 787-764-0000. 555 B
rosa.rivera.rivera@upr.edu
RIVERA, Ruben, L 207-859-4127. 209 J
rlrivera@colby.edu
RIVERA, Schvalla 812-888-4204. 174 F
srivera@vinu.edu
RIVERA, Serafin 787-279-1912. 550 B
sriverat@bayamon.inter.edu
RIVERA, Sergio 210-486-3888. 465 A
srivera@alamo.edu
RIVERA, Sharon 787-890-2681. 553 H
sharon.rivera4@upr.edu
RIVERA, Teresita 787-882-2065. 553 A
admisiones@unitecpr.net
RIVERA, Victoria 806-743-4569. 487 E
victoria.rivera@ttuhsc.edu
RIVERA, Virna 787-786-3030. 547 F
virivera@ucb.edu.pr
RIVERA, Wayne 719-846-5592... 85 H
wayne.rivera@trinidadstate.edu
RIVERA, Yolanda 787-758-2525. 554 F
yolanda.rivera3@rcm.upr.edu
RIVERA ARROYO,
Basilio 787-250-0000. 553 G
basilio.rivera@upr.edu
RIVERA-ARROYO,
Basilio 787-250-0000. 553 G
basilio.rivera@upr.edu
RIVERA-DREYER, Ivette 860-512-3382... 88 G
irivera-dreyer@manchestercc.edu
RIVERA-FLORES, Victor 787-480-2391. 548 G
vrivera@sanjuancapital.com
RIVERA-LACEY, Star 619-388-3246... 62 D
srivera@sdccd.edu
RIVERA LOPEZ, Luis, R 787-890-2681. 553 H
luis.rivera86@upr.edu
RIVERA MORALES,
Lizbeth, J 787-832-6772. 554 E
asesorialegal@uprm.edu
RIVERA NEGRON,
Adrian, O 787-725-8120. 548 O
actividadesculturales@eap.edu
RIVERA SANTIAGO,
Blanca 787-744-1060. 551 J
brivera@mechtech.edu

RIVERA SANTOS, Jorge . 787-265-3878. 554 E
rector.uprm@upr.edu
RIVERO, Brenda .... 601-928-6380. 268 C
brenda.rivero@mgccc.edu
RIVERO, David, A .... 305-284-1650. 118 F
darivero@miami.edu
RIVERO, Estela .... 518-442-5800. 341 D
erivero@albany.edu
RIVERO, William, T .... 601-318-6122. 270 I
ovid@wmcarey.edu
RIVERO, Yaidany .... 305-474-6965. 112 F
yrivero@stu.edu
RIVERS, Andrew .... 202-806-2500... 95 G
andrew.rivers@howard.edu
RIVERS, John, D .... 330-471-8133. 383 D
jrivers@malone.edu
RIVERS, Melissa .... 704-216-6222. 356 D
mrivers@livingstone.edu
RIVERS, Nancy, A .... 434-982-2662. 511 B
nan9k@virginia.edu
RIVERS, Noshuo .... 804-290-4231. 510 B
nrivers@stratford.edu
RIVERS, Verna .... 340-693-1087. 555 E
vrivers@live.uvi.edu
RIVES, Dan .... 812-855-3027. 167 E
drives@indiana.edu
RIVES, Dan .... 812-855-2239. 167 F
drives@indiana.edu
RIVES, Joseph .... 309-762-8090. 162 K
j-rives@wiu.edu
RIVETT, Donna .... 772-462-7656. 106 P
drivett@irsc.edu
RIVIERA, Giselle .... 407-843-3984. 105 P
griviera@fortiscollege.edu
RIVIERA, Jasmine .... 407-628-5870. 102 K
jriviera@cci.edu
RIXEN, Mary .... 580-371-2371. 396 E
mrixen@mscok.edu
RIZA, Robert .... 254-659-7791. 473 A
rriza@hillcollege.edu
RIZK, Michelle .... 907-450-8200... 10 G
marizk@alaska.edu
RIZK, Michelle .... 907-450-8191... 10 G
marizk@alaska.edu
RIZOR, Brenda .... 419-995-8431. 381 Q
rizor.b@rhodesstate.edu
RIZVI, S. Abu .... 802-656-9102. 500 F
abu.rizvi@uvm.edu
RIZVI, Syed .... 714-628-4967... 60 H
rizvi_syed@sccollege.edu
RIZVI, Teresa, J .... 937-229-3241. 391 C
trizvi1@udayton.edu
RIZZA, James .... 508-767-7419. 222 C
j.rizza@assumption.edu
RIZZI, Gino .... 518-828-4181. 321 C
rizzi@sunycgcc.edu
RIZZO, Bryan .... 734-432-5604. 246 B
brizzo@madonna.edu
RIZZO, Frank .... 949-508-2317. 370 F
frank.rizzo@peaace.edu
RIZZO, Matt .... 802-831-1206. 500 H
mrizzo@vermontlaw.edu
RIZZO, Pete .... 402-844-7151. 291 I
pete@northeast.edu
RIZZUTO, Bob .... 303-914-6403... 84 I
bob.rizzuto@rrcc.edu
RIZZUTO, James, T .... 719-384-6821... 83 M
jim.rizzuto@ojc.edu
ROACH, Bill .... 864-587-4396. 447 B
roachb@smcsc.edu
ROACH, J. Terrance .... 301-405-4942. 219 B
troach@umd.edu
ROACH, Jack .... 843-661-8121. 443 G
jack.roach@fdtc.edu
ROACH, Kenneth .... 704-334-6882. 357 K
kroach@nlts.edu
ROACH, Virginia .... 212-875-4668. 314 C
vroach@bankstreet.edu
ROADES, Nicole .... 937-393-3431. 389 B
nroades@sscc.edu
ROADRUCK, Nancy, L .... 330-972-7425. 390 E
nancy5@uakron.edu
ROAN, Kimberly .... 763-576-4813. 257 Q
kroan@anokatech.edu
ROAN, Tina .... 440-684-6085. 392 D
troan@ursuline.edu
ROANE, Kevin .... 732-571-3452. 303 C
kroane@monmouth.edu
ROARK, Deborah .... 817-531-4498. 488 A
droark@txwes.edu
ROARK, Donna .... 606-487-3128. 195 C
donna.roark@kctcs.edu
ROARK, Harold .... 503-352-3060. 407 A
roark@pacificu.edu
ROARK, Ian .... 432-335-6685. 477 M
iroark@odessa.edu
ROARK, Jack .... 406-756-3872. 286 B
jroark@fvcc.edu
ROARK, John, A .... 270-809-3536. 198 B
jroark3@murraystate.edu

ROARK, Tony .... 208-426-2030. 137 G
troark@boisestate.edu
ROATCH, Gay .... 910-576-6222. 362 C
roatchg@montgomery.edu
ROB, Lowe .... 702-651-7912. 294 E
rob.lowe@csn.edu
ROBACK, Joseph, M ...... 570-941-4385. 436 A
joseph.roback@scranton.edu
ROBAIN LACAILLE,
Jemma .... 718-482-5077. 318 F
jlacaille@lagcc.cuny.edu
ROBB, Annette, D .... 937-255-6800. 544 C
annette.robb@afit.edu
ROBB, Daniel .... 215-751-8266. 413 I
drobb@ccp.edu
ROBB, James .... 517-371-5140. 250 G
robbj@cooley.edu
ROBB, Jim .... 870-743-3000... 22 B
jrobb@northark.edu
ROBB, Mercy .... 630-829-6095. 140 B
mrobb@ben.edu
ROBB, Sarah .... 620-431-2820. 189 D
srobb@neosho.edu
ROBB, Susan, E .... 804-827-0479. 511 F
sarobb@vcu.edu
ROBB SHIMKO, Molly ... 724-830-4620. 433 E
shimko@setonhill.edu
ROBBEN, Richard, W ..... 734-763-9333. 251 C
rrobben@umich.edu
ROBBERT, Sharon .... 708-239-4771. 160 K
sharon.robbert@trnty.edu
ROBBIE, Kimberly .... 510-659-6165... 57 A
krobbie@ohlone.edu
ROBBINS, Brad .... 910-695-3724. 363 F
robbinsb@sandhills.edu
ROBBINS, Canty .... 901-678-3855. 460 B
crobbns1@memphis.edu
ROBBINS, Charles .... 707-527-4498... 65 B
crobbins@santarosa.edu
ROBBINS, Dennis .... 626-815-3004... 29 H
drobbins@apu.edu
ROBBINS, Donna .... 252-398-6280. 353 H
robbid@chowan.edu
ROBBINS, Gayle, M .... 706-542-2273. 133 C
grobbins@uga.edu
ROBBINS, George .... 518-276-6216. 337 I
robbig@rpi.edu
ROBBINS, Ginger .... 601-925-3210. 268 A
grobbins@mc.edu
ROBBINS, Kelly .... 509-574-4775. 525 G
krobbins@yvcc.edu
ROBBINS, Kristine .... 614-823-1232. 387 K
krobbins@otterbein.edu
ROBBINS, Mark .... 260-399-7700. 174 C
mrobbins@sf.edu
ROBBINS, Nickey, L .... 870-508-6108... 20 A
nrobbins@asumh.edu
ROBBINS, Patricia, A ..... 903-923-3262. 486 A
parobbins@tstc.edu
ROBBINS, Paul .... 608-265-5296. 536 D
director@nelson.wisc.edu
ROBBINS, Richard, E ..... 260-399-7700. 174 C
rrobbins@sf.edu
ROBBINS, Robert .... 954-201-7554... 99 D
rrobbins@broward.edu
ROBBINS, Ruth .... 215-965-4038. 424 D
rrobbins@moore.edu
ROBBINS, Sandra .... 617-735-9715. 226 B
robbins@emmanuel.edu
ROBBINS, Scott, D .... 731-881-7775. 463 E
sdrobbins@utm.edu
ROBBINS, Shawna, L ..... 760-252-2411... 29 I
srobbins@barstow.edu
ROBBINS, Shelly .... 215-637-7700. 418 G
robbins@holyfamily.edu
ROBBINS, Stacey .... 773-291-6413. 142 D
ssrobbins@ccc.edu
ROBBINS, Thomas .... 802-224-3000. 501 A
thomas.robbins@vsc.edu
ROBBINS, Thomas, G .... 617-353-5533. 224 D
tqresq@bu.edu
ROBBINS, Thomas, J ..... 563-589-3507. 182 J
trobbins@dbq.edu
ROBBINS SMITH,
Patricia .... 562-860-2451... 37 I
probbinssmith@cerritos.edu
ROBECK, Judy .... 507-433-0511. 260 I
jrobeck@riverland.edu
ROBECK, Mike .... 850-201-8546. 117 D
robeckm@tcc.fl.edu
ROBEL, Lauren .... 812-855-5752. 167 E
provost@indiana.edu
ROBEL, Lauren .... 812-855-9011. 167 F
lrobel@indiana.edu
ROBELOTTO, Vince .... 706-379-3111. 134 L
vrobelotto@yhc.edu
ROBERDS, Lauren .... 314-644-9673. 281 D
lroberds@stlcc.edu
ROBERS, Pam .... 262-551-5778. 532 D
probers@carthage.edu

ROBERSON, Angela, M .. 309-677-1000. 140 I
nickie@bradley.edu
ROBERSON, Carrie .... 870-230-5518... 21 D
robersc@hsu.edu
ROBERSON, Dennis .... 312-567-3032. 147 F
robersond@itt.edu
ROBERSON, James, A .... 919-335-1020. 364 G
jaroberson@waketech.edu
ROBERSON, James, L .... 904-620-1360. 116 B
len.roberson@unf.edu
ROBERSON, Janet .... 434-791-5891. 502 D
roberson@averett.edu
ROBERSON, John .... 910-893-1200. 352 K
robersonj@campbell.edu
ROBERSON, Larry .... 912-443-5828. 131 D
lroberson@savannahtech.edu
ROBERSON, Mark, A ...... 951-552-8652... 30 H
maroberson@calbaptist.edu
ROBERSON, Marla .... 864-646-1753. 447 D
mrobers1@tctc.edu
ROBERSON, Miriam, C .. 904-819-6204. 103 E
robersonm@flagler.edu
ROBERSON, Richard, E .. 717-766-2511. 423 L
rroberso@messiah.edu
ROBERSON, Rita, G .... 304-236-7648. 528 F
rita.roberson@southernwv.edu
ROBERSON, Steve .... 336-334-5393. 369 A
shrobers@uncg.edu
ROBERSON, Valerie, R ... 617-541-5301. 232 G
vroberson@rcc.mass.edu
ROBERT, Bernadette .... 310-954-4099... 54 J
brobert@msmc.la.edu
ROBERT, Charlyn, A .... 508-213-2368. 235 E
charlie.robert@nichols.edu
ROBERT, Jean .... 908-852-1400. 300 D
robertj@centenarycollege.edu
ROBERTS, Aaron .... 402-643-7233. 289 B
aaron.roberts@cune.edu
ROBERTS, Al .... 434-949-1019. 513 H
al.roberts@southside.edu
ROBERTS, Alan, L .... 772-462-7235. 106 P
aroberts@irsc.edu
ROBERTS, Amanda .... 573-876-7101. 282 H
aroberts@stephens.edu
ROBERTS, Amanda, T ..... 919-866-5933. 364 G
atroberts@waketech.edu
ROBERTS, Amber .... 616-331-3266. 243 C
roberamb@gvsu.edu
ROBERTS, Amy .... 405-425-5910. 397 D
amy.roberts@oc.edu
ROBERTS, Antonia .... 803-793-5197. 443 E
robertsa@denmarktech.edu
ROBERTS, Ashley .... 626-568-8850... 50 E
ROBERTS, Barbara .... 360-676-2772. 521 D
broberts@nwic.edu
ROBERTS, Betsy .... 707-527-4811... 65 B
eroberts@santarosa.edu
ROBERTS, Betty .... 601-877-6151. 265 G
broberts@alcorn.edu
ROBERTS, Bianca .... 661-255-1050... 31 C
broberts@calarts.edu
ROBERTS, Bob, E .... 304-293-3136. 530 D
bob.roberts@mail.wvu.edu
ROBERTS, Brent .... 406-657-2320. 287 C
broberts@msubillings.edu
ROBERTS, Carolyn .... 313-927-1474. 246 D
croberts@marygrove.edu
ROBERTS, Charlie, W ..... 225-578-3814. 204 O
croberts@lsualumni.org
ROBERTS, Cheryl .... 503-399-6591. 402 E
cheryl.roberts@chemeketa.edu
ROBERTS, Cheryl, A .... 340-692-4192. 555 E
crobert@live.uvi.edu
ROBERTS, Christine, B ... 919-209-2116. 361 E
cbroberts@johnstoncc.edu
ROBERTS,
Christopher, B .... 334-844-2308..... 1 G
robercr@auburn.edu
ROBERTS, Colleen, T ..... 540-831-5500. 508 C
ctroberts@radford.edu
ROBERTS, Craig, W .... 573-651-2513. 282 B
croberts@semo.edu
ROBERTS, Creighton ...... 912-358-3004. 131 C
robertsc@savannahstate.edu
ROBERTS, Cynthia .... 219-785-5219. 172 A
croberts@pnc.edu
ROBERTS, Cynthia, A ..... 412-624-8076. 435 C
croberts@cfo.pitt.edu
ROBERTS, Daniel, M ...... 804-524-6709. 515 D
droberts@vsu.edu
ROBERTS, Dave .... 775-674-7616. 294 H
droberts@tmcc.edu
ROBERTS, David .... 860-465-5395... 87 L
robertsda@easternct.edu
ROBERTS, David, M .... 213-740-4577... 74 A
dave.roberts@usc.edu
ROBERTS, Dawn .... 515-244-4221. 175 C
robertsd@aib.edu
ROBERTS, Dennis .... 530-938-5313... 41 A
robertsd@siskiyous.edu

ROBERTS, Doug .... 707-527-1709... 65 B
droberts@santarosa.edu
ROBERTS, Dustin .... 870-584-4471... 24 F
droberts@cccua.edu
ROBERTS, Ed .... 432-264-5055. 473 E
eroberts@howardcollege.edu
ROBERTS, Ellen .... 706-507-8503. 123 D
roberts_ellen@columbusstate.edu
ROBERTS, Ernst, E .... 915-831-6517. 472 B
erobert9@epcc.edu
ROBERTS, III,
Francis (Tri), A .... 859-246-6556. 194 L
tri.roberts@kctcs.edu
ROBERTS, Franklin, D .... 207-778-7215. 212 D
froberts@maine.edu
ROBERTS, Gail .... 229-225-5206. 132 D
groberts@southwestgatech.edu
ROBERTS, Gail .... 419-448-2013. 380 G
groberts@heidelberg.edu
ROBERTS, Gary, A .... 501-450-3416... 25 H
garyr@uca.edu
ROBERTS, Gary, O .... 607-871-2715. 313 E
roberts@alfred.edu
ROBERTS, Gayla .... 903-675-6212. 488 D
groberts@tvcc.edu
ROBERTS, Glenda, V ...... 607-746-4545. 345 G
robertgv@delhi.edu
ROBERTS, Glenn .... 978-632-6600. 232 C
g_roberts@mwcc.mass.edu
ROBERTS, Gregory, W .... 434-982-3200. 511 B
groberts@Virginia.EDU
ROBERTS, Gregory, W .... 425-739-8251. 520 K
greg.roberts@lwtech.edu
ROBERTS, Heather .... 916-660-7900... 66 B
hroberts@sierracollege.edu
ROBERTS, Howard, V ..... 606-218-5019. 200 F
howardroberts@upike.edu
ROBERTS, James .... 843-863-8083. 441 H
jroberts@csuniv.edu
ROBERTS, James .... 570-674-6758. 424 A
jroberts@misericordia.edu
ROBERTS, James, S .... 919-684-3501. 354 A
james.roberts@duke.edu
ROBERTS, Janet .... 248-341-2020. 248 D
jerobert@oaklandcc.edu
ROBERTS, Jayne .... 850-718-2209... 99 N
robertsj@chipola.edu
ROBERTS, Jean .... 231-777-0519. 247 G
jean.roberts@muskegoncc.edu
ROBERTS, Jeanette, C .... 608-262-1414. 536 D
jroberts@pharmacy.wisc.edu
ROBERTS, Jeanne, M ..... 813-253-6203. 118 L
jroberts@ut.edu
ROBERTS, Jeffrey, T .... 765-494-1730. 171 M
jtrob@purdue.edu
ROBERTS, Jeri .... 207-948-9261. 211 I
jroberts@unity.edu
ROBERTS, Jim, O .... 910-893-1240. 352 K
roberts@campbell.edu
ROBERTS, Jimmy .... 254-298-8340. 482 C
jdr@templejc.edu
ROBERTS, John .... 903-593-8311. 485 A
jroberts@texascollege.edu
ROBERTS, John .... 713-743-2992. 489 B
jwroberts@central.uh.edu
ROBERTS, Jon .... 501-279-4257... 21 C
jroberts@harding.edu
ROBERTS, Jonathan ...... 912-344-2910. 120 G
jonathan.roberts@armstrong.edu
ROBERTS, Juanita .... 334-727-8894..... 8 A
jroberts@tuskegee.edu
ROBERTS, Karen .... 559-737-6257... 40 I
karenr@cos.edu
ROBERTS, Kay Lynn .... 580-745-2977. 399 J
kroberts@se.edu
ROBERTS, Kelley .... 706-867-3280. 133 D
kelley.roberts@ung.edu
ROBERTS, Kevin, J .... 325-674-2675. 464 H
robertsk@acu.edu
ROBERTS, Kevin, W .... 518-564-5022. 344 B
robertkw@plattsburgh.edu
ROBERTS, II,
Laurence, W .... 315-792-3340. 349 F
lroberts@utica.edu
ROBERTS, Leonard .... 973-748-9000. 299 F
leonard_roberts@bloomfield.edu
ROBERTS, Lila .... 678-466-4357. 123 A
lilaroberts@clayton.edu
ROBERTS, Linda .... 912-688-6026. 129 J
lroberts@ogeecheetech.edu
ROBERTS, Lisa .... 618-374-5068. 156 B
lisa.roberts@principia.edu
ROBERTS, Lonnie, V ...... 912-427-5800. 120 B
lroberts@altamahatech.edu
ROBERTS, Lonnie, V ...... 912-427-5816. 120 B
lroberts@altamahatech.edu
ROBERTS, Mark .... 276-466-7869. 514 G
markroberts@vic.edu
ROBERTS, Mark .... 740-284-5345. 379 N
mroberts@franciscan.edu

ROBERTS, Mark, A .... 407-823-2771. 115 E roberts@ucf.edu
ROBERTS, Mark, A .... 770-720-5504. 130 G mar@reinhardt.edu
ROBERTS, Mary .... 478-445-5384. 125 A mary.roberts@gcsu.edu
ROBERTS, Mary .... 831-582-3609... 34 B mroberts@csumb.edu
ROBERTS, Matthew .... 423-652-4811. 455 I mroberts@king.edu
ROBERTS, Melvin .... 856-227-7200. 300 B mroberts@camdencc.edu
ROBERTS, Michael .... 907-773-4462. 142 A mroberts39@ccc.edu
ROBERTS, Michael, H ...... 843-349-2282. 442 E mroberts@coastal.edu
ROBERTS, Michelle, A ..... 662-846-4000. 266 G mroberts@deltastate.edu
ROBERTS, Mike .... 319-398-7797. 180 J mrobert@kirkwood.edu
ROBERTS, Nancy .... 610-606-4640. 412 I nroberts@cedarcrest.edu
ROBERTS, Pamela .... 360-385-4948. 521 F pamelar@nwboatschool.org
ROBERTS, Patrick, S .... 330-569-5278. 380 I robertsps@hiram.edu
ROBERTS, Patty, J .... 318-869-5747. 201 H pjrobert@centenary.edu
ROBERTS, Paul .... 229-225-4098. 132 D proberts@southwestgatech.edu
ROBERTS, Paul .... 205-970-9221..... 7 B proberts@sebc.edu
ROBERTS, Paul .... 405-585-4526. 397 C paul.roberts@okbu.edu
ROBERTS, Paul, G .... 773-508-8901. 151 H prober2@luc.edu
ROBERTS, Pauline .... 225-923-2524. 201 A
ROBERTS, Perry .... 678-717-3851. 133 D perry.roberts@ung.edu
ROBERTS, Philip .... 508-531-1331. 229 D proberts@bridgew.edu
ROBERTS, Phyllis, A .... 276-964-7588. 514 A phyllis.roberts@sw.edu
ROBERTS, Rachel .... 617-585-1100. 234 I rachel.roberts@necmusic.edu
ROBERTS, Randal, R .... 503-517-1860. 408 I rroberts@westernseminary.edu
ROBERTS, Randall .... 606-886-3863. 194 K randall.roberts@kctcs.edu
ROBERTS, Randy .... 620-235-4878. 189 L rroberts@pittstate.edu
ROBERTS, Richard .... 201-684-7616. 305 A rroberts@ramapo.edu
ROBERTS, Rick .... 904-620-2955. 116 B rtrobert@unf.edu
ROBERTS, Rick .... 830-372-8030. 485 C rroberts@tlu.edu
ROBERTS, Rob .... 303-871-3792... 86 B rroberts@du.edu
ROBERTS, Robert, W .... 920-424-1415. 537 B robertw@uwosh.edu
ROBERTS, Robin .... 317-738-8759. 165 I rroberts@franklincollege.edu
ROBERTS, Robin .... 386-226-7004. 102 B roberr36@erau.edu
ROBERTS, Ruth .... 972-825-4656. 481 F rroberts@sagu.edu
ROBERTS, Sallyann .... 815-226-4083. 157 C sroberts@rockford.edu
ROBERTS, Sarah .... 405-491-6312. 399 K saroberts@snu.edu
ROBERTS, Scott .... 702-895-2816. 294 I scott.roberts@unlv.edu
ROBERTS, Shandel .... 415-433-9200... 65 C sroberts@saybrook.edu
ROBERTS, Shannon .... 215-248-7111. 413 A roberts@chc.edu
ROBERTS, Steve .... 817-531-4403. 488 A sroberts@txwes.edu
ROBERTS, Susan .... 262-564-3224. 540 A robertss@gtc.edu
ROBERTS, Terri, L .... 317-738-8119. 165 I troberts@franklincollege.edu
ROBERTS, Tracy .... 270-809-3759. 198 B troberts@murraystate.edu
ROBERTS, Vanice .... 706-368-6943. 121 G vroberts@berry.edu
ROBERTS, Vonnie, W ...... 405-466-2999. 395 N vwroberts@langston.edu
ROBERTS, Wayne .... 601-643-8351. 266 F wayne.roberts@colin.edu
ROBERTS, Wendy .... 256-551-5211..... 4 I wendy.roberts@drakestate.edu
ROBERTS, William .... 201-692-2629. 301 J william_roberts@fdu.edu
ROBERTS, William, C ...... 240-895-4387. 218 A wcroberts@smcm.edu
ROBERTS, William, R ...... 906-487-2622. 247 A wrrobert@mtu.edu
ROBERTS-BRYAN, Vanessa .... 325-793-4681. 476 E vroberts@mcm.edu
ROBERTS-CAMPS, Traci . 209-946-2343... 73 A trobertscamps@pacific.edu
ROBERTS-CORB, Carol ... 562-985-4187... 33 F crcorb@csulb.edu
ROBERTS-DEUTSCH, Marcia .... 808-845-9110. 136 G robertsd@hawaii.edu
ROBERTS KRIEGER, Robin .... 405-945-3228. 398 C
ROBERTSHAW, Amy .... 719-549-2199... 80 K amy.robertshaw@colostate-pueblo.edu
ROBERTSON, Alan .... 404-215-2675. 129 D arobertson@morehouse.edu
ROBERTSON, Alan, D ..... 708-709-3568. 156 A arobertson@prairiestate.edu
ROBERTSON, Ali .... 269-956-3931. 244 O robertsona@kellogg.edu
ROBERTSON, Beverly ..... 828-689-1244. 356 F brobertson@mhc.edu
ROBERTSON, Blake .... 501-337-5000... 20 J brobertson@coto.edu
ROBERTSON, Brooke ...... 706-821-8392. 130 C brobertson@paine.edu
ROBERTSON, Bruce .... 920-403-3181. 535 L bruce.robertson@snc.edu
ROBERTSON, Carole ...... 213-627-2580... 38 G
ROBERTSON, Christopher .... 205-929-1655..... 5 G admissions@miles.edu
ROBERTSON, Courtney .. 941-907-2262. 103 C crobertson@evergladesuniversity.edu
ROBERTSON, Craig, L .... 618-537-6856. 152 G clrobertson@mckendree.edu
ROBERTSON, Dalana ...... 615-322-5179. 463 G dalana.robertson@vanderbilt.edu
ROBERTSON, Debbie ...... 405-382-9248. 399 I d.robertson@sscok.edu
ROBERTSON, Debora ..... 712-279-1771. 176 B debora.robertson@briarcliff.edu
ROBERTSON, Diana .... 785-864-7224. 190 L drobertson@ku.edu
ROBERTSON, Don .... 507-537-6018. 261 F Don.Robertson@smsu.edu
ROBERTSON, Don, E ...... 270-809-6831. 198 B drobertson@murraystate.edu
ROBERTSON, Doug .... 504-456-3141. 201 C dougr@bluecliffcollege.com
ROBERTSON, Douglas .... 305-348-3681. 115 B douglas.robertson@fiu.edu
ROBERTSON, Gloria .... 269-660-8021. 249 C robertsong@millercollege.edu
ROBERTSON, Ian .... 608-262-3482. 536 D irobertson@wisc.edu
ROBERTSON, Ian .... 828-298-3325. 370 E irobert@warren-wilson.edu
ROBERTSON, J. D .... 435-652-7576. 497 E jrobertson@dixie.edu
ROBERTSON, James .... 361-698-1561. 471 G jrobert@delmar.edu
ROBERTSON, Jeff .... 479-968-0498... 20 E jrobertson@atu.edu
ROBERTSON, Jennifer .... 903-675-6215. 488 D jrobertson@tvcc.edu
ROBERTSON, Jill .... 303-273-3207... 80 E jill.robertson@is.mines.edu
ROBERTSON, Jim .... 845-574-4466. 338 B jrobert7@sunyrockland.edu
ROBERTSON, John .... 402-844-7011. 291 I johnr@northeast.edu
ROBERTSON, Jon, H .... 561-237-7701. 108 X jrobertson@lynn.edu
ROBERTSON, Joseph, E . 503-494-8252. 405 I president@ohsu.edu
ROBERTSON, Leonard, A .... 972-721-5236. 488 F lrobertson@udallas.edu
ROBERTSON, Martha, S . 785-827-5541. 188 C martha.robertson@kwu.edu
ROBERTSON, Mary .... 870-512-7812... 20 B mary_robertson@asun.edu
ROBERTSON, Michael, N .... 901-722-3226. 458 K mike.robertson@sco.edu
ROBERTSON, Patricia ..... 843-574-6057. 447 E patricia.robertson@tridenttech.edu
ROBERTSON, Paul .... 520-383-8401... 18 B probertson@tocc.cc.az.us
ROBERTSON, Randall, A 336-734-7334. 360 E rrobertson@forsythtech.edu
ROBERTSON, Richard, J 760-757-2121... 54 G drobertson@miracosta.edu
ROBERTSON, Russell ..... 847-578-3000. 157 F russell.robertson@rosalindfranklin.edu
ROBERTSON, Sandra, L . 501-569-3200... 24 B slrobertson@ualr.edu
ROBERTSON, Sharon, N 703-323-3198. 513 C srobertson@nvcc.edu
ROBERTSON, Stacey ...... 309-677-2380. 140 I smr@bradley.edu
ROBERTSON, Summer ... 704-406-3271. 354 C srobertson@gardner-webb.edu
ROBERTSON, Thomas, S .... 215-898-4715. 435 B robertson@wharton.upenn.edu
ROBERTSON, William, J 717-866-5775. 416 E wrobertson@evangelical.edu
ROBESON, Dan .... 518-292-8657. 338 C robesd@sage.edu
ROBEY, Kim .... 646-717-9703. 325 B robey@gts.edu
ROBICHAUD, Betin .... 508-213-2292. 235 E betin.robichaud@nichols.edu
ROBICHAUD, Karen .... 615-966-5602. 456 B karen.robichaud@lipscomb.edu
ROBICHAUX, Renee .... 337-550-1301. 205 B
ROBIE, Curt, D .... 413-572-5280. 230 F crobie@westfield.ma.edu
ROBILLARD, Jean, E ...... 319-335-8064. 175 I jean-robillard@uiowa.edu
ROBILLARD, Marc .... 617-353-2148. 224 D robillrd@bu.edu
ROBIN, Ron .... 212-998-5609. 334 D ron.robin@nyu.edu
ROBIN, Tracy .... 212-229-1671. 332 E robint@newschool.edu
ROBINETTE, Stephen, H . 417-836-4127. 278 E steverobinette@missouristate.edu
ROBINS, Linda .... 580-371-2371. 396 E lrobins@mscok.edu
ROBINS, Luke .... 360-417-6200. 522 A lrobins@pencol.edu
ROBINS, Madeleine .... 773-256-3000. 152 H mrobins@meadville.edu
ROBINS, Mary .... 650-543-3735... 54 C mrobins@menlo.edu
ROBINS, Michael .... 831-477-3521... 30 G mirobins@cabrillo.edu
ROBINSON, Al .... 229-732-5919. 120 D alrobinson@andrewcollege.edu
ROBINSON, Albert .... 410-951-3803. 220 B arobinson@coppin.edu
ROBINSON, Alfred, L ...... 573-681-6156. 276 C robinsona@lincolnu.edu
ROBINSON, Alteia, L ...... 202-231-3302. 544 L alteia.robinson@dodiis.mil
ROBINSON, Anafe .... 818-610-6515... 52 B robinsa@piercecollege.edu
ROBINSON, Andrea .... 507-222-5465. 254 D arobinson@carleton.edu
ROBINSON, Andrew .... 603-358-2108. 298 F arobinso@keene.edu
ROBINSON, Andrew, G .. 301-322-0007. 217 F robinsag1@pgcc.edu
ROBINSON, Angela .... 817-515-5242. 482 B angela.robinson@tccd.edu
ROBINSON, Asha .... 404-270-5681. 132 E arobin46@spelman.edu
ROBINSON, Ashley, N ... 936-261-9100. 482 F anrobinson@pvamu.edu
ROBINSON, Audrey .... 540-665-4928. 509 E arobinso2@su.edu
ROBINSON, Bev .... 208-459-5680. 138 A brobinson@collegeofidaho.edu
ROBINSON, Beverly .... 972-825-4798. 481 F brobinson@sagu.edu
ROBINSON, Boyd, E .... 352-723-5800. 116 A brobinson@dental.ufl.edu
ROBINSON, Carrie .... 318-670-9663. 207 A crobinson@susla.edu
ROBINSON, Cassandra, M .... 301-860-4000. 220 A crobinson@bowiestate.edu
ROBINSON, Chad .... 970-943-3123... 86 I crobinson@western.edu
ROBINSON, Charles .... 479-575-7955... 23 I cfrobins@uark.edu
ROBINSON, Charles, F .. 510-987-9800... 70 H charles.robinson@ucop.edu
ROBINSON, Chase, F ...... 212-817-7100. 317 F crobinson@gc.cuny.edu
ROBINSON, Cheryl .... 407-582-6883. 118 M crobinson@valenciacollege.edu
ROBINSON, Christine, M .... 414-410-4183. 532 B cmrobinson@stritch.edu
ROBINSON, Christopher, D .... 336-246-3900. 365 B chris.robinson@wilkescc.edu
ROBINSON, Daniel .... 909-469-5561... 76 B drobinson@westernu.edu
ROBINSON, David .... 262-551-5900. 532 D drobinson@carthage.edu
ROBINSON, David .... 405-945-3241. 398 C
ROBINSON, David, W ...... 503-494-4460. 405 I provost@ohsu.edu
ROBINSON, Deborah ...... 540-831-6716. 508 C drobinson7@radford.edu
ROBINSON, Deborah, M 330-588-2586. 383 D drobinson@malone.edu
ROBINSON, Deborah, P . 850-201-6109. 117 D robindeb@tcc.fl.edu
ROBINSON, Debra A, G . 573-341-6154. 284 A debrar@mst.edu
ROBINSON, OSB, Denis 812-357-6522. 173 A drobinson@saintmeinrad.edu
ROBINSON, Denise .... 859-572-5347. 198 I robinson@nku.edu
ROBINSON, Dindy .... 817-257-5019. 484 I d.robinson@tcu.edu
ROBINSON, Dorothy, K .. 203-432-4949... 93 A dorothy.robinson@yale.edu
ROBINSON, Duan .... 731-426-7525. 455 J drobinson@lanecollege.edu
ROBINSON, Edward .... 202-686-0876... 97 C library@potomac.edu
ROBINSON, Edward, G .. 608-757-7713. 539 I erobinson@blackhawk.edu
ROBINSON, Elaine .... 816-483-9600. 190 D elaine.robinson@spst.edu
ROBINSON, Elwood .... 617-873-0607. 224 G Elwood.Robinson@cambridgecollege.edu
ROBINSON, Eric .... 414-258-4810. 535 A robinsoe@mtmary.edu
ROBINSON, Gail, D .... 901-334-5826. 457 A grobinson@memphisseminary.edu
ROBINSON, Gary .... 859-336-5082. 198 J grobinson@sccky.edu
ROBINSON, Gary .... 607-431-4420. 325 F robinsong@hartwick.edu
ROBINSON, Gina .... 910-755-7343. 358 D robinsong@brunswickcc.edu
ROBINSON, Gregory .... 407-823-5348. 115 E greg.robinson@ucf.edu
ROBINSON, Gregory .... 847-214-7226. 144 F grobinson@elgin.edu
ROBINSON, Helana .... 662-329-7409. 268 E hrobinson@oe.muw.edu
ROBINSON, Irene, M .... 281-756-3501. 465 D irobinson@alvincollege.edu
ROBINSON, Janice, S .... 212-678-3732. 347 G jsr167@tc.columbia.edu
ROBINSON, Jeannette .... 973-877-3084. 301 H robinson@essex.edu
ROBINSON, Jeffrey .... 256-372-8211..... 1 A jeffrey.robinson1@aamu.edu
ROBINSON, Jill .... 714-556-3610... 74 D jill.robinson@vanguard.edu
ROBINSON, Jo-Ann .... 937-708-5772. 393 A jrobinson@wilberforce.edu
ROBINSON, Joanne, P ... 856-225-2776. 306 C jprobins@camden.rutgers.edu
ROBINSON, Julie .... 214-658-8800. 494 E jrobinson@wadecollege.edu
ROBINSON, K. C .... 864-294-2164. 444 C kc.robinson@furman.edu
ROBINSON, Kalani .... 912-650-6223. 131 H karobinson@southuniversity.edu
ROBINSON, Karen .... 415-380-1616... 45 H karenrobinson@ggbts.edu
ROBINSON, Kasi .... 404-681-6500. 129 D krobinson@morehouse.edu
ROBINSON, Kelley .... 518-244-2201. 338 C robink3@sage.edu
ROBINSON, Kenneth, I ... 714-808-4830... 56 D krobinson@nocccd.edu
ROBINSON, Kent .... 502-213-2118. 195 F kent.robinson@kctcs.edu
ROBINSON, Kevin .... 559-734-9000... 63 D kevinr@sjvc.edu
ROBINSON, Kevin, W ...... 610-660-1357. 432 E krobinso@sju.edu
ROBINSON, LaNita .... 218-733-7616. 259 A l.robinson@lsc.edu
ROBINSON, Larry .... 973-761-9655. 307 C larry.robinson@shu.edu
ROBINSON, Larry .... 850-599-3225. 114 K larry.robinson@famu.edu
ROBINSON, Larry .... 701-845-7217. 372 A larry.robinson@vcsu.edu
ROBINSON, Larry, J .... 701-845-7217. 372 A larry.robinson@vcsu.edu
ROBINSON, Lorene, K ... 302-857-6050... 93 C lrobinso@desu.edu
ROBINSON, Lorne, T ...... 651-696-6358. 256 L robinson@macalester.edu
ROBINSON, Louester ...... 843-722-5556. 447 E lou.robinson@tridenttech.edu
ROBINSON, Lynne, P ...... 301-447-5296. 217 B lrobinso@msmary.edu
ROBINSON, Margaret, A 620-229-6232. 190 G margaret.robinson@sckans.edu
ROBINSON, Maria .... 979-458-6330. 482 E MRobinson@tamus.edu
ROBINSON, Marjorie ...... 951-785-2167... 50 B mrobinso@lasierra.edu
ROBINSON, Mary .... 716-896-0700. 350 A robinsonm@villa.edu

ROBINSON, Mary Kate ... 713-623-2040. 466 G mkrobinson@aii.edu
ROBINSON, Michael ... 901-435-1433. 455 M michael_robinson@loc.edu
ROBINSON, Michael ... 405-744-6528. 397 H michael.robinson@okstate.edu
ROBINSON, Michele' ... 847-925-6221. 145 H mrobinso@harpercollege.edu
ROBINSON, Mick ... 406-444-6570. 286 G mirobinson@montana.edu
ROBINSON, Mike ... 205-226-4935... 2 C mrobinso@bsc.edu
ROBINSON, Mitch ... 931-221-7883. 459 B robinsonm@apsu.edu
ROBINSON, Monica ... 251-578-1313... 6 D mrobinson@rstc.edu
ROBINSON, Morris ... 318-678-6005. 202 I mrobinson@bpcc.edu
ROBINSON, Myra ... 703-729-8800... 96 F
ROBINSON, Neal ... 802-654-2512. 500 B nrobinson@smcvt.edu
ROBINSON, Nell ... 334-244-3424... 2 A nrobins3@aum.edu
ROBINSON, Norm ... 615-248-1296. 462 D nrobinson@trevecca.edu
ROBINSON, Oscar ... 937-769-1823. 373 I orobinson@antioch.edu
ROBINSON, Pam ... 405-585-4100. 397 C pam.robinson@okbu.edu
ROBINSON, Patricia ... 661-362-3992... 40 E patty.robinson@canyons.edu
ROBINSON, Patricia ... 920-993-5133. 539 K robinsop@fvtc.edu
ROBINSON, Paul, A ... 734-647-3502. 251 C probins@umich.edu
ROBINSON, Perry, H ... 740-587-6624. 379 D robinson@denison.edu
ROBINSON, Peter, J ... 585-275-4036. 349 C Peter_Robinson@URMC.Rochester.edu
ROBINSON, Rachael, L .. 678-839-6614. 133 I rrobinso@westga.edu
ROBINSON, Rachel ... 660-831-4176. 278 I robinsonr@moval.edu
ROBINSON, Ralph ... 302-857-7381... 93 C rrobinson@desu.edu
ROBINSON, Regina ... 318-670-9617. 207 A rrobinson@susla.edu
ROBINSON, Robbie ... 225-342-6950. 207 D Robbie.Robinson@la.gov
ROBINSON, Robert ... 678-717-3654. 133 D robert.robinson@ung.edu
ROBINSON, Robert ... 909-621-8136... 60 A robert.robinson@pomona.edu
ROBINSON, Robert ... 802-654-2524. 500 B rrobinson@smcvt.edu
ROBINSON, Robert, L ... 717-815-1553. 438 D rrobinso@ycp.edu
ROBINSON, Ronald, R ... 864-597-4051. 449 I robinsonrr1@wofford.edu
ROBINSON, Roy ... 253-879-3653. 524 F rrobinson@pugetsound.edu
ROBINSON, Sam ... 706-737-1672. 126 B srobinson@gru.edu
ROBINSON, Sandra, L ... 407-823-5529. 115 E sandra.robinson@ucf.edu
ROBINSON, Sandy ... 216-987-4867. 378 D sandy.robinson@tri-c.edu
ROBINSON, Scott ... 901-320-9740. 463 J srobinson@victory.edu
ROBINSON, Shana ... 323-822-9700... 69 J shana.robinson@touro.edu
ROBINSON, Sharon ... 704-233-8249. 370 G s.robinson@wingate.edu
ROBINSON, Sharon ... 580-745-2364. 399 J srobinson@se.edu
ROBINSON, Shawn ... 813-253-7755. 106 M srobinson37@hccfl.edu
ROBINSON, Sid ... 909-537-5007... 34 E sidr@csusb.edu
ROBINSON, Stephanie, R ... 559-442-4600... 68 I stephanie.robinson@fresnocitycollege.edu
ROBINSON, Steve ... 810-762-0317. 247 F steve.robinson@mcc.edu
ROBINSON, Steve, E ... 304-293-0169. 530 D steve.robinsonr@mail.wvu.edu
ROBINSON, Sunnie ... 860-444-8508. 545 G Sunnie.Robinson@uscg.mil
ROBINSON, Tammy, R ... 530-251-8839... 50 F trobinson@lassencollege.edu
ROBINSON, Theotis ... 865-974-0518. 463 B trobins4@tennessee.edu
ROBINSON, Timothy ... 904-620-2657. 116 B trobinso@unf.edu
ROBINSON, Tom ... 308-635-6182. 293 E robinson@wncc.edu
ROBINSON, Tony ... 828-669-8012. 357 H trobinson@montreat.edu
ROBINSON, Tray ... 530-898-4764... 33 A trobinson@csuchico.edu
ROBINSON, Vickie, S ... 919-658-7757. 357 I vrobinson@moc.edu
ROBINSON, Wade ... 316-978-3021. 191 F wade.robinson@wichita.edu
ROBINSON, Wade, A ... 316-978-3021. 191 F wade.robinson@wichita.edu
ROBINSON, Walter, A ... 530-752-2971... 70 J uadirector@ucdavis.edu
ROBINSON, Warren ... 803-705-4662. 441 C robinson@benedict.edu
ROBINSON, Wayne ... 718-260-4900. 319 B wrobinson@citytech.cuny.edu
ROBINSON, Wayne ... 718-473-8960. 319 B wrobinson@citytech.cuny.edu
ROBINSON, Wayne ... 307-855-2104. 542 Y wrobinson@cwc.edu
ROBINSON, Wayne, G ... 919-718-7214. 359 B wrobinson@cccc.edu
ROBINSON, Wendi ... 614-947-6768. 380 A wendi.robinson@franklin.edu
ROBINSON, Wendy ... 212-616-7250. 325 H wendy.robinson@helenefuld.edu
ROBINSON, Wendy ... 212-616-7299. 325 H wendy.robinson@helenefuld.edu
ROBINSON, Wendy ... 515-964-6222. 177 B wsrobinson@dmacc.edu
ROBINSON, William ... 410-621-2355. 219 E wrobinson3@umes.edu
ROBINSON-ARMSTRONG, Abbie ... 310-338-7598... 53 E arobinso@lmu.edu
ROBINSON-GARDNER, Dorris, R ... 601-979-2455. 267 E dorris.r.gardner@jsums.edu
ROBINSON KLOOS, Jennifer ... 651-690-8831. 263 O jrkloos@stkate.edu
ROBINSON-LEWIS, Denise ... 973-720-2885. 308 I lewisd@wpunj.edu
ROBINSON-PAUL, Ann .. 701-231-8325. 371 G anne.robinson-paul@ndsu.edu
ROBINSON PIPPINS, Shirley ... 901-320-9710. 463 J spippins@victory.edu
ROBIS, Joanne ... 414-326-1797. 532 G jrobis@ccon.edu
ROBISON, Dan ... 312-280-3500. 147 D drobison@aii.edu
ROBISON, Daniel, J ... 304-293-2395. 530 D djrobison@mail.wvu.edu
ROBISON, Eileen ... 206-934-4700. 522 I eileen.robison@seattlecolleges.edu
ROBISON, Lori ... 419-267-1342. 385 F lrobison@northweststate.edu
ROBISON, Margaret ... 910-362-7101. 358 F mrobison@cfcc.edu
ROBISON, Mike ... 559-438-4222... 46 K mike_robison@heald.edu
ROBISON, Mike ... 662-562-3438. 269 C jmrobison@northwestms.edu
ROBISON, Richard ... 707-654-1093... 31 I rrobison@csum.edu
ROBISON, Timothy ... 617-349-8747. 228 B trobison@lesley.edu
ROBITAILLE, Marilyn ... 254-968-9632. 483 A robitaille@tarleton.edu
ROBLEDO, Richard ... 563-589-0219. 183 F helpdesk@wartburgseminary.edu
ROBLES, Elizabeth ... 213-477-2769... 54 J erobles@msmc.la.edu
ROBLES, Laura ... 310-243-3756... 33 B lrobles@csudh.edu
ROBLES, María, V ... 787-600-1070. 555 C maria.robles4@upr.edu
ROBLES, Pedro ... 787-786-3030. 547 F probles@ucb.edu.pr
ROBLES, Ray ... 787-864-2222. 550 D rayroble@inter.edu
ROBLES, Ruben ... 909-748-8289... 73 H ruben_robles@redlands.edu
ROBNETT, Regi ... 207-221-4102. 213 A rrobnett@une.edu
ROBOLE, Donna ... 715-425-3502. 537 E donna.robole@uwrf.edu
ROBOMAN, Lourdes ... 691-350-2296. 546 B comfsmyap@comfsm.fm
ROBOTHAM, Donald ... 212-817-7540. 317 F drobotham@gc.cuny.edu
ROBOTHAM, Rich ... 630-620-2129. 155 A rrobotham@seminary.edu
ROBOTHAM, Tena ... 847-628-2002. 149 B trobotham@judsonu.edu
ROBUCK, Chris ... 503-594-3090. 402 F chrisr@clackamas.edu
ROBUSTELLI, Carlo ... 309-556-3058. 148 B crobuste@iwu.edu
ROBY, Mary ... 704-406-4293. 354 C mroby@gardner-webb.edu
ROBY, Peter, P ... 617-373-2672. 235 F
ROCA, Carmen ... 305-592-1223. 547 H croca@albizu.edu
ROCA, Joan ... 507-389-5953. 259 G joan.roca@mnsu.edu
ROCAP, Donna ... 845-431-8066. 323 C rocap@sunydutchess.edu
ROCCHETTI, Lisa ... 310-453-8300... 43 D lisa@emperors.edu
ROCCIA, Miriam, I ... 314-516-5291. 283 E roccia@umsl.edu
ROCCO, Anne, L ... 718-990-2007. 339 A roccoa@stjohns.edu
ROCCO, Brian ... 212-774-4801. 330 E brocco@mmm.edu
ROCCO, Danette ... 412-281-2600. 433 B drocco@western-school.com
ROCCO, Denine, M ... 330-972-2672. 390 E drocco@uakron.edu
ROCCO, Karen, S ... 412-362-8500. 430 G pims5808@aol.com
ROCHA, Collette, G ... 323-343-3075... 34 A crocha@cslanet.calstate.edu
ROCHA, Daniel ... 210-486-3200. 465 A drocha@alamo.edu
ROCHA, Mark, W ... 626-585-7201... 58 F mwrocha@pasadena.edu
ROCHAT, Angela ... 970-247-7695... 81 M rochat_a@fortlewis.edu
ROCHE, Amarilis ... 787-848-1589. 551 O aroche@popac.edu
ROCHE, Daniel ... 973-655-4158. 303 D roched@mail.montclair.edu
ROCHE, Denise, A ... 716-829-7673. 323 D roche@dyc.edu
ROCHE, Isabel ... 802-440-4406. 498 G iroche@bennington.edu
ROCHE, Jack ... 617-236-8800. 226 F jroche@fisher.edu
ROCHE, James ... 413-545-6330. 228 F jroche@provost.umass.edu
ROCHE, Jason ... 313-993-1092. 250 K rochejj@udmercy.edu
ROCHE, Mary Beth ... 570-504-1589. 420 C rochem@lackawanna.edu
ROCHE, Stephen, H ... 407-303-8016... 97 H stephen.roche@adu.edu
ROCHEFORT, Mary ... 218-723-6505. 254 K mrochefo@css.edu
ROCHEFORT, Steven, C . 336-322-2215. 362 F Steve.Rochefort@piedmontcc.edu
ROCHELEAU, James ... 916-485-3276. 390 C james.rocheleau@myunion.edu
ROCHELEAU, Richard ... 310-338-6534... 53 E rrochele@lmu.edu
ROCHFORD, Rosemary ... 315-464-5468. 342 E rochforr@upstate.edu
ROCHLITZ, Mendel ... 718-853-8500. 348 A
ROCHON, Gilbert, L ... 334-727-8501... 8 A rochon@tuskegee.edu
ROCHON, Ronald, S ... 812-465-1617. 174 D rochon@usi.edu
ROCHON, Sandra ... 978-762-4000. 232 D srochon@northshore.edu
ROCHON, Thomas, R ... 607-274-3111. 327 E president@ithaca.edu
ROCK, Arlene, M ... 413-782-1538. 238 A arock@wne.edu
ROCK, David ... 662-915-7063. 270 B rock@olemiss.edu
ROCK, David ... 727-784-0003... 99 J drock@cfi.edu
ROCK, Harry ... 413-748-3914. 236 I hrock@springfieldcollege.edu
ROCK, Jennifer ... 215-489-2917. 414 E Jennifer.Rock@delval.edu
ROCK, John ... 305-348-0570. 115 B John.Rock@fiu.edu
ROCK, John ... 504-568 8448. 205 C jrock@lsuhsc.edu
ROCK, Megan ... 203-396-8086... 91 C rockm@sacredheart.edu
ROCK, Rachel ... 724-337-1000. 412 E rrock@careerta.edu
ROCK, Thomas ... 212-678-3083. 347 G tpr4@tc.columbia.edu
ROCKAFELLOW, Mollie .. 815-740-3363. 162 F mrockafellow@stfrancis.edu
ROCKECHARLIE, Barbara 704-372-0266. 355 M brockecharlie@kingscollegecharlotte.edu
ROCKETT, Beth Ann ... 612-343 4741. 262 X barocket@northcentral.edu
ROCKETT, Jeri, M ... 651-962-6780. 265 C gmrockett@stthomas.edu
ROCKETT, Kathryn, S ... 516-299-2523. 329 C kathryn.rockett@liu.edu
ROCKETT, Sandra ... 731-286-3238. 460 F rockett@dscc.edu
ROCKEY, Marci ... 217-786-2320. 151 F marci.rockey@llcc.edu
ROCKEY, Robin ... 570-484-2544. 429 B rrockey@lhup.edu
ROCKEY, Tim ... 210-486-0926. 465 C trockey@alamo.edu
ROCKHILL, Linda ... 718-779-1430. 336 D info@plazacollege.edu
ROCKHILL, Wendy ... 206-934-6921. 522 J wendy.rockhill@seattlecolleges.edu
ROCKHOLD, Robin ... 601-984-2810. 270 C rrockhold@umc.edu
ROCKLAND-MILLER, Harry, S ... 413-545-2337. 228 F rockmill@uhs.umass.edu
ROCKLIN, Thomas, R ... 319-335-3557. 175 I thomas-rocklin@uiowa.edu
ROCKMAN, Adam ... 718-997-5500. 319 C adam.rockman@qc.cuny.edu
ROCKS, JR., Thomas, E . 412-338-4770. 419 M trocks@kaplan.edu
ROCKWELL, Susan ... 408-924-6047... 36 A susan.rockwell@sjsu.edu
ROCKWELL-HOPKINS, Melissa ... 713-743-8750. 489 B mrockwel@central.uh.edu
ROCQUE, Jenna ... 207-795-2270. 209 I rocqueje@cmhc.org
ROCQUE, Marc ... 215-527-2961. 409 H rocquem@arcadia.edu
RODARTE, Susana ... 915-831-2018. 472 B srodart7@epcc.edu
RODAS, Mary ... 516-364-0808. 333 D rodas@nycollege.edu
RODDEN, Greg, A ... 863-638-7215. 119 C greg.rodden@warner.edu
RODDINI, Martin ... 516-572-7331. 332 C martin.roddini@ncc.edu
RODDY, Lowell ... 931-221-7213. 459 B roddyl@apsu.edu
RODDY, Shirley ... 405-691-3800. 396 D sroddy@macu.edu
RODE, Joe ... 817-515-7741. 482 B joe.rode@tccd.edu
RODECKER, Daniel ... 518-580-5860. 341 A drodecke@skidmore.edu
RODERICK, Daniel ... 617-253-1392. 233 B
RODERICK, Gerald, K ... 410-778-7810. 221 C jroderick2@washcoll.edu
RODESILER, Carrie ... 386-752-1822. 104 G carrie.rodesiler@fgc.edu
RODGER, Doug ... 712-324-5061. 181 G drodger@nwicc.edu
RODGERS, Ardie ... 405-733-7434. 399 F arodgers@rose.edu
RODGERS, Beverly ... 218-335-4262. 256 I beverly.rodgers@lltc.edu
RODGERS, JR., Bob ... 404-233-3949. 458 F brodgers@richmont.edu
RODGERS, Christie ... 636-949-4697. 276 D crodgers@lindenwood.edu
RODGERS, Christopher .. 718-817-4755. 324 G chrodgers@fordham.edu
RODGERS, Denise ... 973-972-3645. 306 A denise.rutgers@rutgers.edu
RODGERS, Harold ... 574-807-7751. 164 D rodgerh@bethelcollege.edu
RODGERS, Kenneth, G ... 919-530-5079. 368 A krodgers@nccu.edu
RODGERS, Larry ... 541-737-4582. 406 A larry.rodgers@oregonstate.edu
RODGERS, Laurie, A ... 314-719-3661. 274 E lrodgers@fontbonne.edu
RODGERS, Mark, E ... 570-340-6001. 423 B mrodgers@marywood.edu
RODGERS, Mary, P ... 662-246-6263. 268 B mrodgers@msdelta.edu
RODGERS, Mike ... 270-686-4481. 196 C mike.rodgers@kctcs.edu
RODGERS, Mike ... 214-818-1369. 470 A mrodgers@criswell.edu
RODGERS, Norma, L ... 918-595-7868. 400 E norma.rodgers@tulsacc.edu
RODGERS, Ronald, F ... 603-862-0960. 298 B ron.rodgers@usnh.edu
RODGERS, Ronald, F ... 603-862-0960. 298 C ron.rodgers@usnh.edu
RODGERS, Ruby ... 270-534-3184. 196 G ruby.rodgers@kctcs.edu
RODGERS, Ruth ... 317-955-6321. 170 V rrodgers@marian.edu
RODGERS, Sinead ... 516-364-0808. 333 D srodgers@nycollege.edu
RODGERS, Teresa, P ... 334-670-3221... 7 H trodgers@troy.edu
RODGERS, Terreta ... 404-225-4604. 121 B trodgers@atlantatech.edu
RODGERS, Thomas, C ... 585-385-8184. 338 H trodgers@sjfc.edu
RODGERS, Victor ... 671-735-5640. 546 C victor.rodgers@guamcc.edu
RODIER, Elizabeth, A ... 302-259-6085... 93 E brodier@dtcc.edu
RODIN, Merrill ... 213-477-2861... 54 J mrodin@msmc.la.edu

RODKIN, Carolyn .... 510-848-5232... 45 A
crodkin@fst.edu
RODKIN, Dan .... 352-395-4171. 113 C
dan.rodkin@sfcollege.edu
RODLER, Trina .... 323-856-7699... 27 O
trodler@afi.com
RODNE, Anne .... 561-912-2166. 103 C
arodne@evergladesuniversity.edu
RODNEY, Mae, L .... 336-750-2440. 370 A
rodneyml@wssu.edu
RODNING, Janet, M .... 770-720-5954. 130 G
jmr@reinhardt.edu
RODOCKER, Jason, L ..... 540-458-8753. 516 A
jrodocker@wlu.edu
RODOLF, Denise .... 405-974-2490. 400 K
dsmith111@uco.edu
RODOLF, Mark .... 405-974-3611. 400 K
mrodolf@uco.edu
RODRICK-SCHNAATH,
Heidi .... 215-248-6312. 422 F
hrodrick-schnaath@ltsp.edu
RODRIGUE, Kelly, J .... 985-448-4154. 208 A
kelly.rodrigue@nicholls.edu
RODRIGUE, Morris .... 530-242-7525... 65 G
mrodrigue@shastacollege.edu
RODRIGUES, Debra .... 561-912-1211. 103 C
dveloso@evergladesuniversity.edu
RODRIGUES, Leon .... 651-638-6810. 253 K
l-rodrigues@bethel.edu
RODRIGUEZ, Abel .... 787-834-9595. 553 B
arodriguez@uaa.edu
RODRIGUEZ, Abiezer ..... 787-834-9595. 553 B
abrodriguez@uaa.edu
RODRIGUEZ, Adrian .... 817-515-1007. 482 B
adrian.rodiguez@tccd.edu
RODRIGUEZ, Aida, E ...... 787-852-1430. 549 C
arodriguez@hccpr.edu
RODRIGUEZ, Alfred .... 210-999-7206. 488 C
alfred.rodriguez@trinity.edu
RODRIGUEZ, Alma .... 805-289-6360... 74 H
arodriguez@vcccd.edu
RODRIGUEZ, Andy .... 970-248-1337... 79 F
arodrigu@coloradomesa.edu
RODRIGUEZ, Angel .... 787-834-9595. 553 B
anrodriguez@uaa.edu
RODRIGUEZ, Anita .... 402-449-2821. 289 H
arodriguez@graceu.edu
RODRIGUEZ, Aristalia .... 212-772-4804. 318 C
aristalia.rodriguez@hunter.cuny.edu
RODRIGUEZ, Arlene .... 413-755-4218. 233 A
arodriguez@stcc.edu
RODRIGUEZ, Armando ... 787-279-1912. 550 B
arodriguez@bayamon.inter.edu
RODRIGUEZ, Armando ... 787-841-2000. 552 B
armando_rodriguez@pucpr.edu
RODRIGUEZ, Barbara ..... 305-821-3333. 105 A
bjrodriguez@fnu.edu
RODRIGUEZ, Barbara, J . 305-821-3333. 105 A
bjrodriguez@fnu.edu
RODRIGUEZ, Carlos .... 787-765-4210. 548 E
crodriguez@cempr.edu
RODRIGUEZ, Carmen ..... 787-878-5475. 549 L
clrodri@arecibo.inter.edu
RODRIGUEZ, Carmen, J . 787-480-2416. 548 G
crodriguez03@sanjuancapital.com
RODRIGUEZ, Claribel ..... 787-621-2835. 547 C
crodriguez@aupr.edu
RODRIGUEZ, Claribette .. 787-257-7373. 552 H
clrodriguez@suagm.edu
RODRIGUEZ, Daisy .... 787-766-1717. 552 J
drodriguez@mail.suagm.edu
RODRIGUEZ, Daniel, B .. 312-503-3460. 155 D
daniel.rodriguez@law.northwestern.edu
RODRIGUEZ, Daron .... 312-279-3997... 28 M
darodriguez@argosy.edu
RODRIGUEZ, Diana .... 925-424-1405... 37 L
drodriguez@laspositascollege.edu
RODRIGUEZ, Diana .... 787-852-1430. 549 C
drodriguez@hccpr.edu
RODRIGUEZ, Donna .... 361-572-6480. 493 H
donna.rodriguez@victoriacollege.edu
RODRIGUEZ, Duffy .... 505-277-2626. 312 F
dorodriguez20@unm.edu
RODRIGUEZ, Ed .... 816-802-3436. 275 J
erodriguez@kcai.edu
RODRIGUEZ, Edgar .... 787-841-2000. 552 B
edrodrios@pucpr.edu
RODRIGUEZ, Edgar, D .... 787-257-7373. 552 H
ue_erodrigue@suagm.edu
RODRIGUEZ, Edwin .... 787-744-1060. 551 J
erodriguez@mechtech.edu
RODRIGUEZ, Elisamuel .. 787-720-4476. 553 D
decanatofinanzas@mizpa.edu
RODRIGUEZ, Elizabeth ... 573-882-8279. 283 B
rodriguezea@umsystem.edu
RODRIGUEZ, Francisco .. 787-250-8581. 555 B
arquitecto.pr@gmail.com
RODRIGUEZ, Francisco .. 760-757-2121... 54 G
frodriguez@miracosta.edu
RODRIGUEZ, Freddy .... 903-593-8311. 485 A
frodriguez@texascollege.edu
RODRIGUEZ, JR.,
Gerardo .... 956-872-3746. 480 I
gerry@southtexascollege.edu
RODRIGUEZ, Glorimar ... 787-780-5134. 551 L
glrodriguez@nuc.edu
RODRIGUEZ, Havidan .... 956-665-2011. 492 B
havidan@utpa.edu
RODRIGUEZ, Heather ...... 210-805-1242. 490 A
hrodrig1@uiwtx.edu
RODRIGUEZ, Irma, I ...... 787-841-2000. 552 B
irodriguez@pucpr.edu
RODRIGUEZ, Israel .... 787-780-0070. 547 G
irodriguez@caribbean.edu
RODRIGUEZ, Jalibeth ..... 787-841-2000. 552 B
jalibeth_rodriguez@pucpr.edu
RODRIGUEZ, John .... 505-473-6659. 311 K
john.rodriguez@santafeuniversity.edu
RODRIGUEZ, Jorge .... 787-257-7373. 552 H
ac_jrodrigue@suagm.edu
RODRIGUEZ, Jorge .... 303-282-3422... 85 D
RODRIGUEZ, Jorge, L .... 718-990-1485. 339 A
rodriguj@stjohns.edu
RODRIGUEZ, Jose .... 305-237-2339. 109 D
jrodri28@mdc.edu
RODRIGUEZ, Jose .... 787-279-1912. 550 B
jarodriguez@bayamon.inter.edu
RODRIGUEZ, Jose .... 787-815-0000. 553 I
jose.rodriguez8@upr.edu
RODRIGUEZ, Jose, J ...... 787-815-0000. 553 I
jose.rodriguez158@upr.edu
RODRIGUEZ, Jose Ginel 787-798-6904. 553 C
jose.ginel@uccaribe.edu
RODRIGUEZ, Jose Ginel 787-269-4510. 553 C
jose.ginel@uccaribe.edu
RODRIGUEZ, Josefina .... 787-257-0000. 554 B
josefina.rodriguez@upr.edu
RODRIGUEZ, Juanita ..... 787-754-2744. 555 B
juana.rodriguez4@upr.edu
RODRIGUEZ, Judith .... 212-226-7300. 336 G
judithrodriguez@pbcny.edu
RODRIGUEZ, Julia .... 787-738-2161. 554 C
julia.rodriguez5@upr.edu
RODRIGUEZ, Julio .... 787-766-1717. 552 J
um_jurodrigu@suagm.edu
RODRIGUEZ, Katrina ...... 970-351-2796... 86 C
katrina.rodriguez@unco.edu
RODRIGUEZ, Leslie .... 847-233-7700. 155 B
lrodriguez@nc.edu
RODRIGUEZ, Liliana ...... 610-328-8000. 433 I
lrodrig3@swarthmore.edu
RODRIGUEZ, Lisa .... 909-593-3511... 72 E
lrodriguez@laverne.edu
RODRIGUEZ, Lynda .... 305-348-0286. 115 B
lynda.romaguera@fiu.edu
RODRIGUEZ, Maria .... 305-223-4561. 112 B
rodriguez@sjvcs.edu
RODRIGUEZ,
Maria-Judith .... 413-542-2372. 221 G
hr@amherst.edu
RODRIGUEZ, Mary, J ..... 419-755-4767. 385 D
mrodriguez@ncstatecollege.edu
RODRIGUEZ, Mary Ann . 310-243-3750... 33 B
marodriguez@csudh.edu
RODRIGUEZ, Mayra .... 787-743-7979. 552 I
ut_mrodriguez@suagm.edu
RODRIGUEZ, Melba .... 773-442-4200. 154 H
m-rodriguez44@neiu.edu
RODRIGUEZ, Meredith .... 386-481-2991... 99 C
rodriguezm@cookman.edu
RODRIGUEZ, Miguel .... 939-292-8915. 555 C
miguel.rodriguez10@upr.edu
RODRIGUEZ, Milagros ... 787-765-1915. 551 C
mrodrigo@inter.edu
RODRIGUEZ, Moises ...... 210-924-4338. 467 E
moises.rodriguez@bua.edu
RODRIGUEZ, Narce .... 971-722-7249. 407 D
nrodrigu@pcc.edu
RODRIGUEZ, Nilda .... 787-284-1912. 550 F
nilrodri@ponce.inter.edu
RODRIGUEZ, Nilda .... 914-422-4213. 335 J
nrodriguez@pace.edu
RODRIGUEZ, Nilda, E .... 787-852-1430. 549 C
nrodriguez@hccpr.edu
RODRIGUEZ, Norma .... 562-860-2451... 37 I
nrodriguez@cerritos.edu
RODRIGUEZ, Obed .... 787-834-9595. 553 B
obedr@uaa.edu
RODRIGUEZ, Olga .... 305-821-3333. 105 A
ordriguez@fnu.edu
RODRIGUEZ, Oscar .... 910-592-8084. 363 E
orodriguez@sampsoncc.edu
RODRIGUEZ, Raquel .... 559-934-2218... 75 H
raquelrodriguez@whccd.edu
RODRIGUEZ, Raul .... 714-480-7450... 60 F
rodriguez_raul@rsccd.edu
RODRIGUEZ, Raymond ... 630-560-6312. 148 K
rrodriguez@hancocku.edu
RODRIGUEZ, Reuban, B 804-828-8940. 511 F
rbrodriguez@vcu.edu
RODRIGUEZ, Ricardo, S 972-860-7241. 470 I
RicardoRodriguez@dcccd.edu
RODRIGUEZ, Ronald ...... 504-762-3021. 203 A
rrodri@dcc.edu
RODRIGUEZ, Rosa .... 860-832-1652... 87 K
rosa.rodriguez@ccsu.edu
RODRIGUEZ, Rosa .... 787-621-2835. 547 C
rrodriguez@aupr.edu
RODRIGUEZ, Rosalie, M 814-641-3125. 419 H
rodrigr@juniata.edu
RODRIGUEZ, Seph .... 626-529-8469... 57 G
srodriguez@pacificoaks.edu
RODRIGUEZ, Shari, M ... 574-284-4581. 172 G
srodriguez@saintmarys.edu
RODRIGUEZ, Sherri .... 818-947-2726... 52 E
rodrigsa@lavc.edu
RODRIGUEZ, Silvio .... 305-237-7445. 109 D
srodrig2@mdc.edu
RODRIGUEZ, Sonya, F ... 575-624-8066. 310 H
sonya@nmmi.edu
RODRIGUEZ, Stephanie . 310-660-3601... 43 B
srodriguez@elcamino.edu
RODRIGUEZ, Steven ...... 949-214-3003... 41 I
steven.rodriguez@cui.edu
RODRIGUEZ, Sylvia .... 925-424-1000... 37 L
RODRIGUEZ, Sylvia, L ... 305-474-6871. 112 F
srodriguez@stu.edu
RODRIGUEZ, Teresita .... 310-434-4774... 65 A
rodriguez_teresita@smc.edu
RODRIGUEZ, Vanessa .... 305-273-4499. 100 H
vanessa.rodriguez@cbt.edu
RODRIGUEZ, Velia .... 559-737-3775... 40 I
veliar@cos.edu
RODRIGUEZ, Victor .... 361-593-5781. 484 A
tamukcso@tamuk.edu
RODRIGUEZ, Vince .... 714-241-6195... 39 I
vrodriguez@coastline.edu
RODRIGUEZ, Vincent ..... 210-283-5096. 490 A
vincent@uiwtx.edu
RODRIGUEZ, Wanda ...... 787-257-0000. 554 B
wanda.rodriguez@upr.edu
RODRIGUEZ, Widilia ...... 787-815-0000. 553 I
widilia.rodriguez@upr.edu
RODRIGUEZ, Zulyn .... 787-764-0000. 555 B
zulyn.rodriguez@upr.edu
RODRIGUEZ-CANCEL,
Jaime, L .... 787-723-4481. 548 A
jarodriguez@ceaprc.edu
RODRIGUEZ-CHARDAVOYNE,
Esther .... 718-518-4308. 318 B
erodriguez@hostos.cuny.edu
RODRIGUEZ DE ARZOLA,
Olga .... 787-840-2575. 552 A
RODRIGUEZ-DORESTANT,
Simone .... 718-804-8805. 319 A
simone@mec.cuny.edu
RODRIGUEZ-GARCIA,
Ileana .... 787-725-6500. 547 H
irodriguez@sju.albizu.edu
RODRIGUEZ-GUILLEN,
Linda .... 956-364-4427. 485 H
lindarodriguez-guillen@tstc.edu
RODRIGUEZ-LOPEZ,
Miguel, A .... 787-723-4481. 548 A
centro@ceaprc.edu
RODRIGUEZ-ORENGO,
Jose .... 787-758-2525. 554 F
jose.rodriguez139@upr.edu
RODRIGUEZ-PAZ, Maria 787-620-2040. 547 C
mrodriguez_paz@aupr.edu
RODRIGUEZ PEREZ,
Carmen, A .... 787-890-2681. 553 H
carmen.rodriguez22@upr.edu
RODRIGUEZ-QUINONES,
Jose .... 787-725-6500. 547 H
jrodriguezq@albizu.edu
RODRIQUEZ, Jason .... 503-883-2574. 404 A
jrodriqu@linfield.edu
RODRIQUEZ, Mike .... 505-984-6058. 311 H
RODRIQUEZ, Nicky, M .. 219-942-1459. 165 C
nrodriquez@ccr.edu
RODRIQUEZ, Sylvia .... 925-424-1542... 37 L
srodriquez@laspositascollege.edu
RODRÍGUEZ, Glenda ...... 787-765-3560. 548 M
glenda@edpuniversity.edu
RODRÍGUEZ, Ibis .... 787-766-1717. 552 J
ibrodriguez@suagm.edu
RODRÍGUEZ, Israel .... 787-743-7979. 552 I
ut_irodriguez@suagm.edu
RODRÍGUEZ, Luis .... 787-850-9305. 554 D
luis.rodriguez39@upr.edu
RODRÍGUEZ, Wanda, L .. 787-850-9328. 554 D
wanda.rodriguez5@upr.edu
RODRÍGUEZ-CRESPO,
José .... 787-758-2525. 553 G
jose.rodriguez2139@upr.edu
RODRÍGUEZ-RIVERA,
Rafael, E .... 787-751-1600. 551 B
rrodriguez@juris.inter.edu
RODRÍGUEZ-VÁZQUEZ,
José .... 787-815-0000. 553 G
jose.rodriguez151@upra.edu
RODSKI, Pete .... 502-213-7227. 195 F
peter.rodski@kctcs.edu
ROE, Aaron .... 309-649-6230. 160 E
aaron.roe@src.edu
ROE, Dean .... 734-995-7309. 241 E
roed@cuaa.edu
ROE, Herb .... 605-221-3134. 450 C
hroe@kilian.edu
ROE, Michael .... 845-341-4205. 335 H
michael.roe@sunyorange.edu
ROE, Michael .... 845-431-8018. 323 C
michael.roe@sunydutchess.edu
ROE, Micheal, D .... 206-281-2252. 523 C
mroe@spu.edu
ROE, Robert .... 989-774-3933. 240 N
ROE, Robert .... 989-463-7326. 239 B
roe@alma.edu
ROEBUCK, David .... 573-875-8700. 272 G
ROEBUCK, Randy .... 316-677-9535. 191 E
rroebuck@watc.edu
ROECKER, Pamela .... 617-735-9985. 226 B
roeckerp@emmanuel.edu
ROECKLE, Charles, A ..... 512-471-1232. 491 C
car@po.texas.edu
ROEDEL, Glenn .... 215-780-1296. 433 A
groedel@salus.edu
ROEDER, Lynn, M .... 252-328-9297. 367 B
roederl@ecu.edu
ROEHL, Bob .... 206-546-4514. 523 F
broehl@shoreline.edu
ROELFS, Melinda, A .... 620-235-4226. 189 L
maroelfs@pittstate.edu
ROELFS, Pamela, J .... 860-486-4240... 92 A
pamela.roelfs@uconn.edu
ROELFSEMA, Cheryl, E ... 815-224-0419. 148 A
cheryl_roelfsema@ivcc.edu
ROELKE, Scott .... 651-423-8297. 258 D
scott.roelke@dctc.edu
ROELLKE, Christopher .... 845-437-5600. 349 G
chroellke@vassar.edu
ROELOFS, Lyle, D .... 859-985-3522. 192 F
roelofsl@berea.edu
ROERIG, Sandra, C .... 318-675-5000. 205 D
sroeri@lsuhsc.edu
ROESSLER, Billy .... 940-668-7731. 477 I
broessler@nctc.edu
ROETHEMEYER,
Robert, V .... 260-452-2146. 165 D
robert.roethemeyer@ctsfw.edu
ROETHER, Diane .... 940-668-4283. 477 I
droether@nctc.edu
ROETHLER, Don .... 701-224-5485. 372 B
donald.roethler@bismarckstate.edu
ROETTGER, Linda .... 219-464-5958. 174 E
linda.roettger@valpo.edu
ROETZEL, Mary .... 617-369-4292. 236 F
mroetzel@mfa.org
ROEWER, Anita .... 815-455-8737. 152 F
aroewer@mchenry.edu
ROFF, Lucinda, L .... 205-348-3924..... 8 D
lroff@sw.ua.edu
ROGALSKY, Amy .... 405-974-5376. 400 K
arogalsky@uco.edu
ROGAN, Doreen .... 207-216-4320. 211 C
drogan@yccc.edu
ROGAN, Edie, H .... 757-823-9159. 507 M
elrogan@nsu.edu
ROGAN, Fred, R .... 205-726-2837..... 6 F
cfrogan@samford.edu
ROGAN, Margaret .... 617-824-8590. 226 A
margaret_rogan@emerson.edu
ROGAN, Mary, T .... 718-960-8559. 318 A
mary.rogan@lehman.cuny.edu
ROGAN, Patricia, M .... 317-274-6862. 168 D
progan@iupui.edu
ROGAN, William, D .... 615-230-3595. 461 G
william.rogan@volstate.edu
ROGELSTAD, Todd .... 701-845-7209. 372 A
todd.rogelstad@vcsu.edu
ROGENTINE, Linda .... 218-723-6022. 254 K
lrogenti@css.edu
ROGER-GORDON,
A. Patrick .... 212-346-1295. 335 J
arogergordon@pace.edu
ROGERS, Adam .... 212-592-2000. 340 H
arogers@sva.edu
ROGERS, Andria .... 970-339-6518... 78 C
andria.rogers@aims.edu
ROGERS, Angela, K .... 561-237-7297. 108 X
arogers@lynn.edu
ROGERS, Beth .... 513-244-8134. 376 J
beth.rogers@ccuniversity.edu
ROGERS, Brian .... 503-494-8362. 405 I
cdrcadmin@ohsu.edu
ROGERS, Brian, D .... 907-474-7112... 10 I
uaf.chancellor@alaska.edu
ROGERS, Cheryl, L .... 903-510-3217. 488 E
crog@tjc.edu
ROGERS, Christopher ..... 610-647-4400. 418 I
crogers@immaculata.edu

ROGERS, Cindy, A .... 972-860-8186. 470 H
car3810@dcccd.edu
ROGERS, Craig, L .... 270-789-5057. 193 D
crogers@campbellsville.edu
ROGERS, Dana .... 409-882-3372. 486 G
dana.rogers@lsco.edu
ROGERS, Dana, N .... 409-882-3397. 486 G
dana.rogers@lsco.edu
ROGERS, David, E .... 315-684-6054. 345 A
rogersde@morrisville.edu
ROGERS, Deborah .... 215-641-6506. 424 B
drogers@mc3.edu
ROGERS, Donna .... 252-789-0290. 361 G
drogers@martincc.edu
ROGERS, Dwayne .... 318-487-7216. 202 F
dwayne.rogers@lacollege.edu
ROGERS, Elizabeth .... 931-372-3317. 460 A
erogers@tntech.edu
ROGERS, Elizabeth, A ..... 336-278-6350. 354 B
rogers@elon.edu
ROGERS, Fred, A .... 507-222-5411. 254 D
frogers@carleton.edu
ROGERS, Frederick .... 803-508-7272. 440 G
rogersf@atc.edu
ROGERS, Gail .... 423-746-5202. 462 C
grogers@twcnet.edu
ROGERS, Glen .... 414-382-6269. 531 I
glen.rogers@alverno.edu
ROGERS, Greg .... 412-392-3924. 431 B
grogers@pointpark.edu
ROGERS, Greg .... 623-845-4526... 14 M
greg.rogers@gcmail.maricopa.edu
ROGERS, Harry, C .... 215-898-7091. 435 B
rogers@pobox.upenn.edu
ROGERS, Helen .... 808-933-3132. 136 A
hrogers@hawaii.edu
ROGERS, Hudson .... 239-590-7329. 115 A
hrogers@fgcu.edu
ROGERS, J. Orion .... 540-831-5958. 508 C
jorogers@radford.edu
ROGERS, Jack, T .... 541-737-3010. 406 A
jack.rogers@oregonstate.edu
ROGERS, James .... 212-327-8506. 338 A
jrogers@mail.rockefeller.edu
ROGERS, James .... 212-517-0435. 330 E
jrogers@mmm.edu
ROGERS, Janet .... 765-998-5330. 173 C
jnrogers@taylor.edu
ROGERS, Janet .... 614-287-2727. 378 B
jrogers@cscc.edu
ROGERS, Jason .... 615-460-6441. 453 C
jason.rogers@belmont.edu
ROGERS, Jeanette .... 205-853-1200..... 5 B
jrogers@jeffstateonline.com
ROGERS, Jeffrey .... 704-406-4724. 354 C
jrogers3@gardner-webb.edu
ROGERS, Jenica, P .... 315-267-2482. 344 C
rogersjp@potsdam.edu
ROGERS, Jesse, W .... 940-397-4211. 476 H
jesse.rogers@mwsu.edu
ROGERS, Jessica .... 941-487-4900. 115 D
ncalum@ncf.edu
ROGERS, Jevita .... 719-255-3460... 85 M
jrogers3@uccs.edu
ROGERS, Johnell .... 803-934-3256. 445 F
jrogers@morris.edu
ROGERS, Jolayne .... 816-322-0110. 271 O
jolayne.rogers@calvary.edu
ROGERS, Jolene, R .... 712-362-0431. 179 E
jrogers@iowalakes.edu
ROGERS, Jolynn .... 509-359-2383. 519 C
jrogers@ewu.edu
ROGERS, Joseph .... 320-363-5230. 263 P
jrogers@csbsju.edu
ROGERS, Joseph, T .... 610-527-0200. 432 B
jtrogers@rosemont.edu
ROGERS, Judith .... 340-692-4132. 555 E
jrogers@live.uvi.edu
ROGERS, Judy, R .... 417-667-8181. 273 A
jrogers@cottey.edu
ROGERS, Justin .... 716-926-8785. 326 B
jrogers@hilbert.edu
ROGERS, Kathleen, R ..... 617-521-2276. 236 G
kathleen.rogers@simmons.edu
ROGERS, Katrina .... 805-898-2924... 44 I
krogers@fielding.edu
ROGERS, Keri .... 832-813-6597. 476 A
keri.rogers@lonestar.edu
ROGERS, Kiri .... 267-502-4890. 410 I
kiri.rogers@brynathyn.edu
ROGERS, Lalita .... 903-927-3304. 495 A
lestes@wileyc.edu
ROGERS, Leslie, D .... 252-493-7322. 362 G
lrogers@email.pittcc.edu
ROGERS, Lisa, C .... 615-898-5345. 459 D
lisa.rogers@mtsu.edu
ROGERS, Mary .... 619-388-6591... 62 C
mrogers@sdccd.edu
ROGERS, Michael .... 229-430-4014. 119 J
michael.rogers@asurams.edu

ROGERS, Michael .... 202-274-5986... 97 A
michael.rogers@udc.edu
ROGERS, Michael, B ...... 607-735-1891. 323 H
mrogers@elmira.edu
ROGERS, Michael, C ...... 202-274-5314... 97 A
michael.roger1@udc.edu
ROGERS, Michael, C ...... 202-274-5314... 97 A
michael.rogers1@udc.edu
ROGERS, Michael, F ...... 843-953-7696. 442 A
mike.rogers@citadel.edu
ROGERS, Mike .... 209-946-2569... 73 A
mrogers@pacific.edu
ROGERS, Nancy, B .... 812-237-7900. 167 A
nancy.rogers@indstate.edu
ROGERS, Patricia .... 507-457-5010. 262 A
progers@winona.edu
ROGERS, Patricia, A .... 781-891-2622. 223 C
progers@bentley.edu
ROGERS, Phil .... 208-459-5282. 138 A
progers@collegeofidaho.edu
ROGERS, Phyllis .... 864-592-4816. 447 A
rogersp@sccsc.edu
ROGERS, Phyllis .... 254-295-4501. 490 B
progers@umhb.edu
ROGERS, Ralph, V .... 219-989-2446. 171 N
rvrogers@purduecal.edu
ROGERS, Randy .... 317-921-4737. 169 L
rrogers@ivytech.edu
ROGERS, Randy .... 660-626-2395. 271 A
rrogers@atsu.edu
ROGERS, Randy .... 336-386-3466. 364 D
rogersr@surry.edu
ROGERS, Ray .... 407-646-2195. 111 Q
rrogers@rollins.edu
ROGERS, Richard, L .... 313-664-7474. 241 C
rrogers@collegeforcreativestudies.edu
ROGERS, Richard, R .... 909-593-3511... 72 E
rrogers2@laverne.edu
ROGERS, Rita .... 252-862-1232. 363 A
rogersri@roanokechowan.edu
ROGERS, Rob .... 352-638-9762... 99 B
rrogers@beaconcollege.edu
ROGERS, Rodney, K .... 419-372-2915. 374 K
rrogers@bgsu.edu
ROGERS, Russell .... 201-216-5688. 307 E
rrogers@stevens.edu
ROGERS, Sandra .... 801-422-1801. 495 D
sandra_rogers@byu.edu
ROGERS, Scott .... 828-726-2488. 358 E
srogers@cccti.edu
ROGERS, Scott .... 509-542-4834. 518 C
srogers@columbiabasin.edu
ROGERS, Scott, S .... 330-385-1070. 387 I
srogers@ovct.edu
ROGERS, Shannon .... 479-394-7622... 23 B
srogers@rmcc.edu
ROGERS, Sharon .... 609-894-9311. 299 I
srogers@bcc.edu
ROGERS, Stephanie .... 318-678-6000. 202 I
srogers@bpcc.edu
ROGERS, Stephen, K .... 405-744-8052. 397 H
steve.rogers@okstate.edu
ROGERS, Susan .... 972-883-4325. 491 E
susan.rogers@utdallas.edu
ROGERS, Tamara, E .... 617-496-3069. 227 C
tamara_rogers@harvard.edu
ROGERS, Tammy .... 706-880-8344. 128 A
trogers@lagrange.edu
ROGERS, Tamy .... 214-333-5158. 470 D
tamy@dbu.edu
ROGERS, Tanya .... 909-382-4041... 61 J
trogers@sbccd.cc.ca.us
ROGERS, Thomas .... 502-213-7310. 195 F
thomas.rogers@kctcs.edu
ROGERS, Tim .... 503-399-7506. 402 E
tim.rogers@chemeketa.edu
ROGERS, Tracy .... 719-587-7990... 78 B
tracy_rogers@adams.edu
ROGERS, W. Timothy ..... 865-974-6593. 463 C
timrogers@utk.edu
ROGERS-ADKINSON,
Diana .... 573-651-2408. 282 B
drogersadkinson@semo.edu
ROGERSON, Andrew ...... 707-664-2028... 36 B
andrew.rogerson@sonoma.edu
ROGERSON, Joanie .... 360-736-9391. 517 G
jrogerson@centralia.edu
ROGG, Cathie .... 616-698-7111. 241 H
crogg@davenport.edu
ROGGE, Ann .... 302-736-2445... 94 C
roggean@wesley.edu
ROGOFF, Mai-Lan, A ..... 508-856-5652. 229 C
mai-lan.rogoff@umassmed.edu
ROGOW, Robert .... 859-622-1409. 193 P
robert.rogow@eku.edu
ROGSTAD, Mark .... 509-574-4671. 525 G
mrogstad@yvcc.edu
ROHAN, James, P .... 920-465-2075. 536 F
rohanj@uwgb.edu
ROHANNA, Susan .... 610-902-8206. 411 E
susan.rohanna@cabrini.edu

ROHDE, Leslie .... 612-861-7554. 253 C
leslie@alfredadler.edu
ROHDE, Scott, W .... 608-785-8711. 536 G
srohde@uwlax.edu
ROHDER, Kelly .... 815-280-2915. 149 A
krohder@jjc.edu
ROHLEDER, Ann .... 812-357-6610. 173 A
arohleder@saintmeinrad.edu
ROHLEDER, John .... 651-779-3496. 258 C
john.rohleder@century.edu
ROHLER, James .... 740-362-3380. 383 H
jrohler@mtso.edu
ROHLFS, Jen .... 206-934-6794. 523 A
jen.rohlfs@seattlecolleges.edu
ROHLFS, Steven .... 301-447-5295. 217 B
rohlfs@msmary.edu
ROHLOF, Jason .... 612-624-9022. 264 G
rohloff@umn.edu
ROHM, Robert, K .... 937-766-7603. 375 K
rohmr@cedarville.edu
ROHNER, Christy .... 270-686-4243. 192 G
christy.rohner@brescia.edu
ROHNER, Tom .... 630-889-6661. 154 E
trohner@nuhs.edu
ROHR, Ann .... 970-207-4500... 86 G
AnnR@uscareerinstitute.edu
ROHR, Ann .... 970-207-4550... 83 B
AnnR@westondistancelearning.com
ROHRBACH, Anne, L ...... 814-865-5471. 426 A
alr3@psu.edu
ROHRBACH, Daniel, W .. 937-255-6565. 544 C
daniel.rohrbach@afit.edu
ROHRBACK, Jane, T .... 248-204-3160. 245 I
jrohrback@ltu.edu
ROHRBAUGH, Suzanne .. 252-335-0821. 359 F
suzanne_rohrbaugh@albemarle.edu
ROHRER, Douglas .... 270-901-3490. 200 G
douglas.rohrer@wku.edu
ROHRER, Katherine .... 609-258-7800. 304 E
krohrer@princeton.edu
ROHRER, Mary .... 507-457-2602. 262 A
mrohrer@winona.edu
ROHRS, Dawn, M .... 816-654-7012. 275 K
drohrs@kcumb.edu
ROIDT, Joseph, M .... 304-637-1277. 526 E
roidtj@dewv.edu
ROJAS, Annabelle .... 305-237-7617. 109 D
arojas6@mdc.edu
ROJAS, Carmen, I .... 787-743-4041. 548 H
crojas@columbiaco.edu
ROJAS, Isaias .... 787-744-1060. 551 J
isaiasrojas@mechtech.edu
ROJAS, Jason .... 860-297-4166... 91 F
jason.rojas@trincoll.edu
ROJAS, Lydia .... 787-744-1060. 551 J
lrojas@mechtech.edu
ROJAS, Rodney .... 213-613-2200... 67 E
rodney_rojas@sciarc.edu
ROJAS ALVAREZ LOPEREN,
Clara .... 713-221-8179. 489 D
rojasc@uhd.edu
ROJO, Richard .... 209-946-2311... 73 A
rrojo@pacific.edu
ROKAS, Tracy .... 615-460-5405. 453 C
tracy.rokas@belmont.edu
ROKOS, Jean, M .... 231-995-1248. 248 B
jrokos@nmc.edu
ROKOS, Nicole .... 561-297-3880. 114 L
nrokos@fau.edu
ROKOWSKY, Eli .... 845-425-1370. 335 F
ROKOWSKY, Israel .... 845-425-1370. 335 F
ROKSANDIC, Stevo .... 614-234-1644. 384 J
sroksandic@mchs.com
ROKUSEK, Jim .... 605-367-6109. 452 C
jim.rokusek@southeasttech.edu
ROLAND, Cheryl .... 269-387-8412. 252 I
cheryl.roland@wmich.edu
ROLAND, Christy .... 515-244-4221. 175 C
rolandc@aib.edu
ROLAND, David, E .... 706-233-7329. 131 E
droland@shorter.edu
ROLAND, Harriet, A .... 803-533-3790. 446 G
rolandha@scsu.edu
ROLAND, Kirc, J .... 360-442-2471. 521 A
kroland@lowercolumbia.edu
ROLAND, Meg .... 503-699-3336. 404 C
mroland@marylhurst.edu
ROLAND, Troy .... 909-396-6090... 31 F
ROLD, Gary, F .... 630-617-3078. 145 A
garyr@elmhurst.edu
ROLDAN, Marggi .... 864-578-8770. 446 F
mroldan@sherman.edu
ROLEN, Scott .... 541-917-4420. 404 B
rolens@linnbenton.edu
ROLEY, V. Vance .... 808-956-8377. 136 B
vroley@hawaii.edu
ROLFE, Cynthia .... 405-974-2688. 400 K
crolfe@uco.edu
ROLFE, Rial, D .... 806-743-2905. 487 E
rial.rolfe@ttuhsc.edu

ROLFES, Katherine .... 337-521-8906. 203 I
krolfes@southlouisiana.edu
ROLFS, Trevor .... 620-792-9378. 184 F
rolfst@bartoncc.edu
ROLFSON, Eric, F .... 207-581-1151. 212 B
eric.rolfson@maine.edu
ROLHEISER, Ronald .... 210-341-1366. 477 L
rrolheiser@ost.edu
ROLL, Debbie .... 907-564-8220... 10 C
droll@alaskapacific.edu
ROLLANS, Mary Ann ...... 479-968-0234... 20 E
mrollans@atu.edu
ROLLE, Kevin, A .... 256-372-5230..... 1 A
kevin.rolle@aamu.edu
ROLLENE, Jerry .... 479-524-7212... 21 G
jrollene@jbu.edu
ROLLER, Laura .... 612-330-1720. 253 H
roller@augsburg.edu
ROLLER, Steven, A .... 617-228-2394. 231 C
sroller@bhcc.mass.edu
ROLLESTON, George ...... 440-826-2081. 374 F
grollest@bw.edu
ROLLEY, LuAnn, K .... 802-656-7892. 500 F
luann.rolley@uvm.edu
ROLLINGS, Dave .... 775-445-4223. 295 A
david.rollings@wnc.edu
ROLLINS, Andrea .... 619-594-5201... 35 D
arollins@mail.sdsu.edu
ROLLINS, Cheryl .... 443-885-4429. 217 A
cheryl.rollins@morgan.edu
ROLLINS, Pam .... 334-420-4253..... 7 G
prollins@trenholmstate.edu
ROLLINS, Stephen, J ...... 907-786-1825... 10 H
srollins@uaa.alaska.edu
ROLLINS, Steve .... 309-672-4946. 152 I
srollin@methodistcol.edu
ROLLISON, Jeffrey, D ..... 610-647-4400. 418 I
jrollison@immaculata.edu
ROLLMAN, Catherine, A . 804-752-7270. 508 E
crollman@rmc.edu
ROLLO, Ann .... 315-364-3235. 350 E
arollo@wells.edu
ROLLO, J. Michael .... 239-590-7910. 115 A
jmrollo@fgcu.edu
ROLLOCK, Alysa, C .... 765-494-5830. 171 M
acrollock@purdue.edu
ROLLS, Dickie .... 620-252-7575. 185 O
dickier@coffeyville.edu
ROLON, Reynaldo .... 787-279-1912. 550 B
rrolon@bayamon.inter.edu
ROLPH, Chris .... 865-573-4517. 455 G
crolph@johnsonU.edu
ROM, Cristine .... 216-421-7440. 377 C
crom@cia.edu
ROM, Kjetil .... 541-881-5746. 408 C
krom@tvcc.cc
ROMA, Lawrence, J .... 607-777-2224. 341 E
lroma@binghamton.edu
ROMAGNI, Joanne .... 312-362-5460. 143 H
jromagni@depaul.edu
ROMAGNOLI, Janice .... 615-655-7274. 316 E
jaromagnoli@cazenovia.edu
ROMAIN, Pete .... 212-517-0414. 330 E
promain@mmm.edu
ROMALI, Reagan, F .... 773-907-4450. 142 A
rromali@ccc.edu
ROMAN, Albert, J .... 619-482-6328... 68 B
aroman@swccd.edu
ROMAN, Catalin .... 505-277-5521. 312 F
gcroman@unm.edu
ROMAN, Cathy .... 717-291-4197. 416 J
cathy.roman@fandm.edu
ROMAN, Cynthia .... 248-942-3300. 248 D
caroman@oaklandcc.edu
ROMAN, Ivan, F .... 787-882-2065. 553 A
director_ejecutivo@unitecpr.net
ROMAN, Juan, E .... 787-841-2000. 552 D
jroman@pucpr.edu
ROMAN, Kristen .... 312-850-7186. 142 C
1118mgr@theg.follett.com
ROMAN, Marcia .... 407-708-4722. 113 E
romanm@seminolestate.edu
ROMAN, Maria .... 559-791-2364... 49 P
mroman@portervillecollege.edu
ROMAN, Nilsa, M .... 787-891-0925. 549 K
nroman@aguadilla.inter.edu
ROMAN, Paul .... 724-838-4215. 433 E
roman@setonhill.edu
ROMAN, Vladimir .... 787-763-6425. 549 J
vroman@inter.edu
ROMAN-VARGAS,
Madeline .... 773-489-8910. 142 F
mroman-vargas@ccc.edu
ROMANDINI, Russ .... 513-618-1930. 376 K
rromandini@ccms.edu
ROMANELLO, Mary .... 202-884-9000... 96 G
romanellom@trinitydc.edu
ROMANO, C. Renee .... 217-333-1300. 162 A
romano3@illinois.edu
ROMANO, Carol, A .... 301-295-1180. 545 C
carol.romano@usuhs.edu

ROMANO, Christopher ... 201-684-7309. 305 A
cromano@ramapo.edu
ROMANO, Daniel, A .... 309-298-2517. 162 K
da-romano@wiu.edu
ROMANO, Fred, D .... 630-515-6388. 153 B
froman@midwestern.edu
ROMANO, Joan .... 401-254-3510. 440 B
jromano@rwu.edu
ROMANO, Joseph .... 718-420-4599. 350 B
joe.romano@wagner.edu
ROMANO, Joyce, C .... 407-582-3401. 118 M
jromano@valenciacollege.edu
ROMANO, Judith, J .... 864-294-3470. 444 C
judith.romano@furman.edu
ROMANO, Michael .... 623-245-4600... 18 D
mromano@uti.edu
ROMANO, Nicole .... 302-356-6846... 94 E
nicole.romano@wilmu.edu
ROMANO, Pam .... 910-272-3531. 363 B
promano@robeson.edu
ROMANO, Sandra .... 340-693-1238. 555 E
sromano@live.uvi.edu
ROMANO, Susan, M .... 585-785-1277. 324 D
romanosm@flcc.edu
ROMANO, Wendy .... 215-871-6300. 430 D
wendyr@pcom.edu
ROMANTIC, Thomas, W . 607-255-8574. 322 A
twr2@cornell.edu
ROMBOUTS, Stephen, R 814-472-3009. 432 D
srombouts@francis.edu
ROME, Alan, K .... 440-943-7600. 388 J
cpl@dioceseofcleveland.org
ROME, Dennis .... 262-595-2364. 537 C
dennis.rome@uwp.edu
ROME, JoAnne .... 413-552-2183. 231 F
jrome@hcc.edu
ROME, Kevin .... 573-681-5042. 276 C
romek@lincolnu.edu
ROMELDA, Simmons ..... 478-825-6219. 124 H
simmonsr@fvsu.edu
ROMEO, Lynn .... 732-571-7518. 303 C
lromeo@monmouth.edu
ROMEO, Monica .... 716-286-8536. 334 F
mromeo@niagara.edu
ROMER, Christine, E ...... 636-922-8362. 280 J
cromer@stchas.edu
ROMER, Terence .... 419-530-7804. 392 B
terence.romer@utoledo.edu
ROMERO, Aldemaro .... 618-650-5047. 159 H
aromero@siue.edu
ROMERO, Angel .... 787-765-1915. 551 C
aromero@opto.inter.edu
ROMERO, Bianca .... 909-593-3511... 72 E
bromero@laverne.edu
ROMERO, Carlos .... 505-277-4186. 312 F
crom@unm.edu
ROMERO, Carol .... 305-821-3333. 105 A
cromero@fnu.edu
ROMERO, Christina .... 714-564-6091... 60 G
romero_christina@sac.edu
ROMERO, David .... 575-624-8250. 310 H
romero@nmmi.edu
ROMERO, Georg .... 831-479-5771... 30 G
geromero@cabrillo.edu
ROMERO, Herminio .... 787-622-8000. 553 E
hromero@pupr.edu
ROMERO, Narda .... 914-674-7841. 330 J
nromero@mercy.edu
ROMERO, Peter .... 505-473-6328. 311 K
peter.romero@santafeuniversity.edu
ROMERO, Reyna .... 713-221-8460. 489 D
Romeror@uhd.edu
ROMERO, Sally .... 970-943-2150... 86 I
sromero@western.edu
ROMERO, Van, D .... 575-835-5646. 310 F
vromero@nmt.edu
ROMERO, Victoria .... 909-621-8149... 65 D
victoria.romero@scrippscollege.edu
ROMERO-LEGGOTT,
Valerie .... 505-272-2728. 312 F
vromero@salud.unm.edu
ROMESBURG,
Rosemarie .... 304-367-4284. 528 E
Rosemarie.Romesburg@pierpont.edu
ROMICH, Barbara .... 704-669-4163. 359 D
romich@clevelandcc.edu
ROMIG, Kenneth, J .... 724-946-7141. 437 B
romigkj@westminster.edu
ROMIG, Thomas, J .... 785-670-1662. 191 D
thomas.romig@washburn.edu
ROMINE, Connie .... 740-593-4300. 387 C
romine@ohio.edu
ROMINGER, Anna .... 219-980-6636. 168 B
arominge@iun.edu
ROMKEMA, Priscilla .... 605-642-6341. 451 G
priscilla.romkema@bhsu.edu
ROMO, Ricardo .... 210-458-4101. 492 C
president@utsa.edu
ROMO, Wayne .... 210-436-3538. 479 D
wromo@stmarytx.edu
ROMZEK, Barbara .... 202-885-6234... 94 F
romzek@american.edu
RONCA, Paul, L .... 804-523-5239. 512 F
pronca@reynolds.edu
RONCAL, Roy .... 815-226-4107. 157 C
rroncal@rockford.edu
RONCOLATO, David .... 814-332-5318. 409 D
david.roncolato@allegheny.edu
RONDÓN, Milagros .... 787-863-2390. 550 C
milagros.rondon@fajardo.inter.edu
RONDA, René, S .... 787-743-7979. 552 I
rsronda@suagm.edu
RONDINELLI, Diane .... 904-826-0084. 118 I
drondinelli@usa.edu
RONEVICH, Nancy, S ..... 740-284-5232. 379 N
nronevich@franciscan.edu
RONEY, Kristen .... 678-717-3419. 133 D
kristen.roney@ung.edu
RONEY, LaKesha .... 804-524-5845. 515 D
lroney@vsu.edu
RONEY, Linda, M .... 214-333-5334. 470 D
linda@dbu.edu
RONIS, Sheila, R .... 248-689-8282. 251 I
sronis@walshcollege.edu
RONKIN, Bruce, E .... 617-373-2170. 235 F
RONKOSKI, Bob .... 636-922-8604. 280 J
rronkoski@stchas.edu
RONNAU, John .... 956-665-2292. 492 B
ronnaujp@utpa.edu
RONNING, Greg .... 830-372-8160. 485 C
gronning@tlu.edu
RONNING, Teresa .... 518-743-2261. 345 E
ronningt@sunyacc.edu
RONNING LINDGREN,
Rachel .... 805-493-3690... 31 H
rronning@clunet.edu
RONVEAUX, Gail .... 951-343-4246... 30 H
gronveaux@calbaptist.edu
ROOB, Sharon, L .... 920-565-1327. 533 R
roobsl@lakeland.edu
ROOCK, Mark .... 314-529-9673. 276 G
mroock@maryville.edu
ROOD, Denine .... 262-691-5157. 541 D
drood@wctc.edu
ROOD, Kathleen, C .... 617-262-5000. 223 F
kathy.rood@the-bac.edu
ROODE, Dana, F .... 949-824-5173... 71 B
dana.roode@uci.edu
ROOF, Karin .... 843-953-7526. 443 A
roofk@cofc.edu
ROOFNER, Perry, F .... 412-397-5256. 431 I
roofner@rmu.edu
ROOK, Steve .... 479-394-7622... 23 B
srook@rmcc.edu
ROOKARD, Crystal .... 803-822-3251. 445 C
rookardc@midlandstech.edu
ROOKE, Michael .... 860-255-3615... 89 G
mrooke@txcc.commnet.edu
ROOKER, Allison .... 601-974-1102. 267 I
rookeab@millsaps.edu
ROOKER, Darrin .... 315-568-3063. 333 C
drooker@nycc.edu
ROOKER, Suzanne .... 580-477-7944. 401 J
suzanne.rooker@wosc.edu
ROOKS, Dana, C .... 713-743-9795. 489 B
drooks@uh.edu
ROOKS, Pamela, A .... 843-661-1526. 444 B
prooks@fmarion.edu
ROOKS, Stephanie .... 770-962-7580. 127 D
srooks@gwinnetttech.edu
ROOKSTOOL, Carol .... 213-624-1200... 44 D
crookstool@fidm.edu
ROOMSBURG, Jim .... 870-862-8131... 23 D
jroomsburg@southark.edu
ROONEY, Charles, J .... 201-559-6082. 302 A
rooneyc@felician.edu
ROONEY, Gail .... 217-333-0820. 162 A
grooney@illinois.edu
ROONEY, Gerard, J .... 585-385-8068. 338 H
grooney@sjfc.edu
ROONEY, L. David .... 845-257-3260. 342 B
rooneyd@lan.newpaltz.edu
ROONEY, Maryjane, S .... 570-941-7909. 436 A
maryjane.rooney@scranton.edu
ROONEY, Paula, M .... 508-541-1658. 225 F
prooney@dean.edu
ROONEY, Peter, J .... 413-542-2321. 221 G
prooney@amherst.edu
ROONEY, Peter, K .... 559-323-2100... 63 B
prooney@sjcl.edu
ROONEY, Thomas .... 651-690-6043. 263 O
tomrooney@stkate.edu
ROOP, Elizabeth .... 203-332-5060... 88 F
eroop@hcc.commnet.edu
ROOPNARINE, Darshini . 315-445-4661. 328 F
roopnatd@lemoyne.edu
ROORBACH, Karen .... 765-677-2975. 169 B
karen.roorbach@indwes.edu
ROOS, David .... 435-652-7704. 497 E
roos@dixie.edu
ROOS, Matthew, R .... 561-237-7433. 108 X
mroos@lynn.edu
ROOSA, Alexandra .... 310-506-6850... 58 H
alexandra.roosa@pepperdine.edu
ROOSA, Kathryn .... 281-998-6150. 479 H
kathryn.roosa@sjcd.edu
ROOSA, Mark, S .... 310-506-4252... 58 H
mark.roosa@pepperdine.edu
ROOSE, Robert .... 989-358-7200. 239 C
rooser@alpenacc.edu
ROOSMA, Eric .... 616-222-3000. 245 C
eroosma@kuyper.edu
ROOT, Carl .... 208-885-0298. 139 D
croot@uidaho.edu
ROOT, Clyde .... 574-807-7219. 164 D
rootc@bethelcollege.edu
ROOT, David .... 913-288-7215. 187 L
droot@kckcc.edu
ROOT, David .... 606-539-4406. 200 B
david.root@ucumberlands.edu
ROOT, Debra .... 607-587-3266. 345 D
rootda@alfredstate.edu
ROOT, Jeanne, V .... 802-287-8201. 499 D
rootj@greenmtn.edu
ROOT, Jeff .... 870-245-4186... 22 D
rootj@obu.edu
ROOT, Larry .... 409-944-1208. 472 I
lroot@gc.edu
ROOT, Linda, C .... 412-578-6258. 412 G
rootlc@carlow.edu
ROOT, Lisa .... 530-898-6897... 33 A
lmroot@csuchico.edu
ROOT, Miriam .... 530-741-6726... 77 M
mroot@yccd.edu
ROOT, Patricia, G .... 610-341-5923. 415 G
proot@eastern.edu
ROOT, Tom .... 505-277-4130. 312 F
troot@unm.edu
ROOZEN, David, A .... 860-509-9546... 90 B
roozen@hartsem.edu
ROPER, Carolyn .... 219-785-5686. 172 A
croper@pnc.edu
ROPER, Craig .... 618-545-3000. 149 D
croper@kaskaskia.edu
ROPER, David .... 843-349-6532. 442 E
droper@coastal.edu
ROPER, Kevin, F .... 901-678-5561. 460 B
kfroper@memphis.edu
ROPER, Larry, D .... 541-737-3626. 406 A
larry.roper@oregonstate.edu
ROPER, William, L .... 919-966-4161. 368 D
william_roper@med.unc.edu
ROQUE, Aurea .... 787-744-1060. 551 J
aroque@mechtech.edu
ROQUEMORE, Glenn, R . 949-451-5210... 67 B
groquemore@ivc.edu
RORER, John .... 215-895-2860. 415 B
john.a.rorer@drexel.edu
RORIE, Jan, W .... 870-612-2016... 25 A
jan.rorie@uaccb.edu
RORK, Jeannette .... 336-721-2618. 366 D
jeannette.rork@salem.edu
ROSA, Angel, R .... 787-738-2161. 554 C
actividades@upr.edu
ROSA, Benigno .... 787-728-1515. 555 D
bennyrosa@sagrado.edu
ROSA, Bob .... 574-296-6227. 163 J
brosa@ambs.edu
ROSA, Carmen, J .... 787-780-0070. 547 G
crosa@caribbean.edu
ROSA, Felipe .... 787-766-1717. 552 J
ferosa@suagm.edu
ROSA, Jerry .... 718-518-6768. 318 B
jrosa@hostos.cuny.edu
ROSA, John, W .... 843-953-5012. 442 A
john.rosa@citadel.edu
ROSA, Maria .... 787-850-9320. 554 D
maria.rosa5@upr.edu
ROSA, Marta .... 617-879-2314. 238 C
mrosa@wheelock.edu
ROSA, Ramonita .... 787-891-0925. 549 K
rrosa@aguadilla.inter.edu
ROSA, Sandra .... 787-279-1912. 550 B
srosa@bayamon.inter.edu
ROSA, Vicky .... 270-745-3830. 200 G
vicky.rosa@wku.edu
ROSA VELEZ, Mariam, L 787-265-3879. 554 E
prensa@uprm.edu
ROSACCO, Claire .... 216-987-4804. 378 D
claire.rosacco@tri-c.edu
ROSADO, Alexis .... 787-882-2065. 553 A
controller@unitecpr.net
ROSADO, Carmen .... 787-766-1717. 552 J
um_crosado@suagm.edu
ROSADO, David .... 660-263-3900. 272 A
drosado@cccb.edu
ROSADO, Izander .... 787-250-1912. 550 E
irosado@metro.inter.edu
ROSADO, Maria .... 787-279-1912. 550 B
mrosado@bayamon.inter.edu
ROSADO, Martin .... 787-884-6000. 549 D
mrosado@icprjc.edu
ROSADO, Nilda, I .... 787-257-7373. 552 H
ue_nrosado@suagm.edu
ROSADO, Reinaldo .... 787-284-1912. 550 F
rrosado@ponce.inter.edu
ROSADO, Robert .... 787-815-0000. 553 I
robert.rosado@upr.edu
ROSADO, Samuel .... 787-264-1912. 551 A
samuel_rosado_nazario@intersg.edu
ROSADO, Silvia .... 787-279-1912. 550 B
srosado@bayamon.inter.edu
ROSAKIS, Ares, J .... 626-395-4100... 31 E
rosakis@caltech.edu
ROSALES, Elvia, H .... 512-471-3391. 491 C
bd.elvia@austin.utexas.edu
ROSALES, John .... 773-291-6776. 142 D
jrosales57@ccc.edu
ROSANDICH, Thomas, J 251-626-3303..... 8 B
tjrosand@ussa.edu
ROSANDICH, Thomas, P 251-626-3303..... 8 B
president@ussa.edu
ROSANIA, Nick .... 641-472-1180. 180 N
nrosania@mum.edu
ROSANIA, Sandra .... 641-472-1180. 180 N
srosania@mum.edu
ROSARIO, Aida .... 787-764-0000. 555 B
aida.rosario1@upr.edu
ROSARIO, Antonio, J ..... 787-857-3600. 550 A
arosario@br.inter.edu
ROSARIO, Enrique .... 787-780-0070. 547 G
rel.publicas@caribbean.edu
ROSARIO, Lisanette .... 718-518-4311. 318 B
lrosario@hostos.cuny.edu
ROSARIO, Mirna .... 787-250-1912. 550 E
ROSARIO, Rocio .... 787-744-1060. 551 J
rrosario@mechtech.edu
ROSARIO, Victoria .... 916-568-3150... 52 K
rosariv@losrios.edu
ROSARIO, Vilma .... 305-821-3333. 105 A
vrosario@fnu.edu
ROSARIO, Yvette .... 718-960-8723. 318 A
yvette.rosario@lehman.cuny.edu
ROSARIO-MORALES,
Carmen, D .... 787-725-8120. 548 O
crosario@eap.edu
ROSARIO-ROSARIO,
Yolanda .... 787-725-6500. 547 H
yrosario@sju.albizu.edu
ROSAS, Alisha .... 909-593-3511... 72 E
arosas@laverne.edu
ROSAS, Luis, M .... 310-233-4028... 51 H
rosaslm@lahc.edu
ROSAS, Olivia .... 909-537-7577... 34 E
orosas@csusb.edu
ROSATI, David, M .... 508-849-3420. 222 B
drosati@annamaria.edu
ROSATI, Ron .... 308-367-5200. 293 B
rosati@unl.edu
ROSATO, Jennifer .... 815-753-1380. 154 I
jrosato@niu.edu
ROSATO, Mike .... 325-649-8203. 473 F
mrosato@hputx.edu
ROSBURY-HENNE,
Marcia .... 413-552-2850. 231 F
mrosburyhenne@hcc.edu
ROSCOE, Heather, S .... 617-521-2721. 236 G
heather.roscoe@simmons.edu
ROSDAIL, Lisa .... 803-938-3794. 448 F
lrosdai@uscsumter.edu
ROSDIL, Amy .... 303-404-5541... 81 N
amy.rosdil@frontrange.edu
ROSE, Alisha, D .... 901-678-2230. 460 B
arose3@memphis.edu
ROSE, Bonnie .... 716-286-8360. 334 F
brose@niagara.edu
ROSE, Brian .... 304-829-7292. 526 D
brose@bethanywv.edu
ROSE, Brian, T .... 607-777-4788. 341 E
brose@binghamton.edu
ROSE, Carey .... 254-298-8326. 482 C
carey.rose@templejc.edu
ROSE, Dan .... 706-507-8740. 123 D
rose_dan@columbusstate.edu
ROSE, Dana .... 718-862-7910. 329 M
dana.rose@manhattan.edu
ROSE, David, C .... 301-687-4457. 220 C
drose@frostburg.edu
ROSE, Deatrea .... 620-235-6556. 189 L
drose@pittstate.edu
ROSE, Don .... 620-665-3597. 877 F
rosed@hutchcc.edu
ROSE, Douglas, N .... 608-263-3046. 536 D
drose@fpm.wisc.edu
ROSE, E. Wayne .... 301-860-3957. 220 A
cio@bowiestate.edu
ROSE, Howard, A .... 713-525-6980. 490 L
horo@stthom.edu
ROSE, Jane .... 941-359-4200. 117 A
ROSE, Jean .... 845-687-5049. 348 H
rosej@sunyulster.edu

ROSE, Jeff .... 302-454-3944... 93 F
jrose8@dtcc.edu
ROSE, John .... 212-772-4242. 318 C
john.rose@hunter.cuny.edu
ROSE, John, S .... 602-944-3335... 11 D
jrose@aicag.edu
ROSE, Judy, W .... 704-687-6245. 368 E
jwrose@uncc.edu
ROSE, Kathleen, A .... 408-848-4760... 45 F
krose@gavilan.edu
ROSE, Ken, G .... 580-774-3790. 400 B
ken.rose@swosu.edu
ROSE, Kevin .... 903-434-8223. 477 J
krose@ntcc.edu
ROSE, Kristen .... 610-989-1301. 436 D
krose@vfmac.edu
ROSE, Kyle .... 402-375-7230. 291 F
kyrose1@wsc.edu
ROSE, Lawrence, D .... 909-537-3703... 34 E
lrose@csusb.edu
ROSE, Linda .... 714-564-6082... 60 G
rose_linda@sac.edu
ROSE, Lisa .... 310-434-4402... 65 A
rose_lisa@smc.edu
ROSE, Louise .... 978-681-0800. 233 C
lrose@mslaw.edu
ROSE, Margie .... 303-369-5151... 84 E
margie.rose@plattcolorado.edu
ROSE, Maria, C .... 304-367-4151. 529 F
Maria.Rose@fairmontstate.edu
ROSE, Melissa .... 315-792-7210. 346 C
melissa.rose@sunyit.edu
ROSE, Melissa .... 315-859-4413. 325 E
marose@hamilton.edu
ROSE, Melody .... 503-725-5707. 405 G
melody_rose@ous.edu
ROSE, Michael, J .... 215-898-5828. 435 B
mjrose@pobox.upenn.edu
ROSE, Mike .... 785-825-9505. 188 C
pastor@kwu.edu
ROSE, Patricia, L .... 215-898-3208. 435 B
prose@upenn.edu
ROSE, Rachel .... 276-376-4035. 511 C
rlb7q@uvawise.edu
ROSE, Rebecca .... 304-829-7221. 526 D
rrose@bethanywv.edu
ROSE, Sarah .... 602-274-4300... 12 K
srose@brymanschool.edu
ROSE, Sarah .... 423-585-6752. 462 A
sarah.rose@ws.edu
ROSE, Sharon .... 252-398-1229. 353 H
rosesh@chowan.edu
ROSE, Steve .... 509-527-2402. 524 I
steve.rose@wallawalla.edu
ROSE, Steven .... 973-684-5900. 304 B
srose@pccc.edu
ROSE, Susan .... 713-525-6957. 490 L
roses@stthom.edu
ROSE, Todd, S .... 703-993-5012. 505 C
trose2@gmu.edu
ROSE, Vanessa, R .... 202-994-0816... 95 D
vrose@gwu.edu
ROSE, Wanda, F .... 701-323-6271. 372 I
Wanda.Rose@SanfordCollege.edu
ROSEBERRY, Lynn .... 614-236-6782. 375 H
lroseber@capital.edu
ROSEBOOM, Julie .... 607-436-2503. 343 E
roseboj@oneonta.edu
ROSEBORO, Clevell, S ... 919-516-4606. 366 C
csroseboro@st-aug.edu
ROSEBORO-BARNES,
Edwina .... 803-981-7162. 449 J
eroseboro@yorktech.edu
ROSEBORO II,
Clevell, S .... 404-365 7370. 122 D
croseboro@lincoln.edu
ROSEBROUGH, Tom .... 731-661-5373. 462 F
trosebro@uu.edu
ROSEDALE, Jeff .... 914-323-5277. 330 B
jeff.rosedale@mville.edu
ROSELLI, Claudia .... 708-974-5357. 153 F
roselli@morainevalley.edu
ROSELLO, Tania .... 818-767-0888... 76 K
Tania.Rosello@woodbury.edu
ROSEMAN, Nancy, A ...... 717-245-1322. 414 H
roseman@dickinson.edu
ROSEMEYER, Abbie .... 561-803-2180. 110 B
abbie_rosemeyer@pba.edu
ROSEN, Abbey, E .... 920-923-7645. 534 A
aerosen95@marianuniversity.edu
ROSEN, Barry .... 212-220-1238. 317 A
brosen@bmcc.cuny.edu
ROSEN, C. Martin .... 812-941-2262. 168 F
crosen@ius.edu
ROSEN, David .... 616-451-2787. 242 F
DavidRosen@ferris.edu
ROSEN, Janet, S .... 218-723-6072. 254 K
jrosen@css.edu
ROSEN, Jeffrey .... 212-650-5967. 317 D
jrosen@ccny.cuny.edu
ROSEN, Jonathan, M ...... 518-262-5686. 313 D
rosenj@mail.amc.edu
ROSEN, Sara .... 785-864-4904. 190 L
rosen@ku.edu
ROSEN SINGLETON,
Suzanne .... 202-448-7213... 95 C
suzanne.singleton@gallaudet.edu
ROSENBALM, Whitney ... 972-238-6023. 471 C
wrosenbalm@dcccd.edu
ROSENBAUM, Carol .... 212-463-0400. 348 B
carolr@touro.edu
ROSENBAUM, David, R .. 864-941-8377. 446 C
rosenbaum.d@ptc.edu
ROSENBAUM, Irving ...... 954-262-1507. 109 K
irv@nova.edu
ROSENBAUM,
Thomas, F .... 773-702-8810. 161 B
provost@uchicago.edu
ROSENBERG, Alannah .... 949-582-4854... 67 C
aorrison@saddleback.edu
ROSENBERG, Brian, C ... 651-696-6207. 256 L
rosenbergb@macalester.edu
ROSENBERG, Chaim ...... 718-854-2290. 315 B
ROSENBERG, Eric .... 973-720-2303. 308 I
rosenbergel@wpunj.edu
ROSENBERG, John .... 801-422-2779. 495 D
john_rosenberg@byu.edu
ROSENBERG, Kris .... 503-251-2821. 408 G
krosenberg@uws.edu
ROSENBERG, Lea .... 414-258-4810. 535 A
rosenbel@mtmary.edu
ROSENBERG, Mark .... 305-348-2111. 115 B
mark.rosenberg@fiu.edu
ROSENBERG, Michael .... 845-257-2800. 342 B
rosenbem@newpaltz.edu
ROSENBERG, Naomi ...... 617-636-2143. 237 C
naomi.rosenberg@tufts.edu
ROSENBERG,
Richard, M .... 717-337-6396. 417 B
rrosenbe@gettysburg.edu
ROSENBERG, Samuel ..... 201-684-7624. 305 A
sjrosenb@ramapo.edu
ROSENBERG, Samuel ..... 312-341-3697. 157 D
srosenbe@roosevelt.edu
ROSENBERG, Sol .... 718-854-2290. 315 B
sr@bhsy.org
ROSENBERGER,
Benjamin .... 610-372-4721. 431 D
brosenberger@racc.edu
ROSENBERGER, Jeanne . 408-554-4583... 64 M
jrosenberger@scu.edu
ROSENBERGER,
Steven, H .... 614-823-1150. 387 K
srosenberger@otterbein.edu
ROSENBLATT, Jim .... 601-925-7104. 268 A
jim.rosenblatt@mc.edu
ROSENBLOOM, Stuart .... 312-461-0600. 139 H
srosenbloom@aaart.edu
ROSENBLUM, Donald ..... 954-262-8402. 109 K
donr@nova.edu
ROSENBLUM, Yosef .... 718-854-2290. 315 B
ROSENBOOM, David .... 661-255-1050... 31 C
drosenbo@calarts.edu
ROSENBURG, Ross .... 312-752-2262. 149 F
ross.rosenburg@kendall.edu
ROSENDAHL, Matt .... 218-726-8130. 264 D
lib@d.umn.edu
ROSENFELD, Lynn, R ..... 661-255-1050... 31 C
lynn@calarts.edu
ROSENFELD, Renee .... 215-637-7700. 418 G
rlrosenfeld@holyfamily.edu
ROSENFELD, Sholom ..... 718-774-5050. 347 F
ROSENFELDT, Mary .... 513-745-3022. 393 H
rosenfeldt@xavier.edu
ROSENGART, Sharon ..... 973-720-3019. 308 I
rosengarts@wpunj.edu
ROSENGARTEN, Elaine ... 419-559-2393. 389 I
erosengarten@terra.edu
ROSENGARTEN, Jayne ... 212-237-8624. 318 D
jrosengarten@jjay.cuny.edu
ROSENGARTEN, Jeffrey .. 212-960-5239. 351 M
rosengar@yu.edu
ROSENGARTEN, Lewis ... 607-753-4808. 343 B
lewis.rosengarten@cortland.edu
ROSENHECK, Sari .... 845-434-5750. 347 A
sarir@sullivan.suny.edu
ROSENHEIN, Jon .... 212-799-5000. 328 B
ROSENKRANS, Jane .... 949-582-4340... 67 C
jrosenkrans@saddleback.edu
ROSENKRANTZ, Laurie .. 817-531-4420. 488 A
lerosenkrantz@txwes.edu
ROSENRAUCH, Yair .... 718-259-5300. 315 F
yrosen@bramsonort.edu
ROSENSAFT, Jean, B ..... 212-824-2209. 325 G
jrosensaft@huc.edu
ROSENSTEIN, Arthur ...... 858-566-1200... 42 G
arthur@disd.edu
ROSENSTEIN, Gloria ...... 858-566-1200... 42 G
gloria@disd.edu
ROSENSTEIN, Ilena .... 860-768-4418... 92 D
rosenstei@hartford.edu
ROSENSTEIN, Ilene .... 213-740-7711... 74 A
irosenst@usc.edu
ROSENSTEIN, Paul .... 617-559-8600. 227 D
prosenstein@hebrewcollege.edu
ROSENSTOCK, Larry .... 619-398-4902... 47 I
ROSENSTONE, Steven, J 651-201-1696. 257 N
steven.rosenstone@so.mnscu.edu
ROSENTHAL, Amy .... 817-202-6211. 481 E
arosenthal@swau.edu
ROSENTHAL, Cheryl .... 617-824-8595. 226 A
cheryl_rosenthal@emerson.edu
ROSENTHAL, Elizabeth ... 773-907-6833. 142 A
erosenthal@ccc.edu
ROSENTHAL, Eric .... 847-925-6677. 145 H
erosenth@harpercollege.edu
ROSENTHAL, Jeffrey, E .. 315-255-1743. 316 D
rosenthal@cayuga-cc.edu
ROSENTHAL, Ken .... 818-677-2561... 34 C
ken.rosenthal@csun.edu
ROSENTHAL, Rachel .... 916-608-6500... 53 C
ROSENTHAL, Rich .... 704-330-6316. 359 C
rich.rosenthal@cpcc.edu
ROSENWALD, Nancy ...... 803-321-5229. 445 G
nancy.rosenwald@newberry.edu
ROSETH, Lisa .... 218-723-6016. 254 K
lroseth@css.edu
ROSEVEAR, Scott, G ...... 570-577-3647. 411 A
scott.rosevear@bucknell.edu
ROSEVEARE, Mark .... 864-592-4763. 447 A
rosevearem@sccsc.edu
ROSIENE, Tracy .... 860-885-2603... 89 F
trosiene@trcc.commnet.edu
ROSINE, Greg, J .... 269-387-2072. 252 I
greg.rosine@wmich.edu
ROSKOWSKI, Ed .... 520-515-3688... 12 R
roskoe@cochise.edu
ROSKOWSKI, Pamela ..... 415-476-5455... 72 A
proskowski@police.ucsf.edu
ROSKY, Bruce .... 818-610-6543... 52 B
roskybr@piercecollege.edu
ROSMAN, Andrew .... 516-299-3017. 329 D
andrew.rosman@liu.edu
ROSMUS, Julie .... 802-773-5900. 499 B
julie.rosmus@csj.edu
ROSNER-LENGELE,
Julie, A .... 215-572-2815. 409 H
rosner@arcadia.edu
ROSNIK, Peter .... 413-775-1441. 231 E
rosnick@gcc.mass.edu
ROSOFF, Nancy .... 215-572-2921. 409 H
rosoffn@arcadia.edu
ROSONET, Kay .... 228-497-7629. 268 C
kay.rosonet@mgccc.edu
ROSOVSKY, Leah .... 617-495-4193. 227 C
leah_rosovsky@harvard.edu
ROSOWSKY, David, V .... 802-656-1417. 500 F
david.rosowsky@uvm.edu
ROSPOND, Raylene .... 515-271-2982. 177 K
raylene.rospond@drake.edu
ROSS, Anthony .... 610-917-1418. 436 C
amross@vfcc.edu
ROSS, Anthony, J .... 651-641-8815. 255 B
ross@csp.edu
ROSS, Anthony, R .... 323-343-3100... 34 A
tross@cslanet.calstatela.edu
ROSS, Arthur, J .... 304-293-6607. 530 D
ajross@hsc.wvu.edu
ROSS, Beverly .... 334-420-4332..... 7 G
bross@trenholmstate.edu
ROSS, Brian .... 217-333-1350. 162 A
bross@illinois.edu
ROSS, Carla .... 510-869-6618... 61 I
cross@samuelmerritt.edu
ROSS, Carmin, E .... 217-875-7200. 156 J
cross@richland.edu
ROSS, Cheryl, A .... 212-854-2268. 321 D
cheryl.ross@columbia.edu
ROSS, Christine, C .... 434-223-6056. 505 E
cross@hsc.edu
ROSS, Christopher .... 206-239-4500. 517 M
c.ross@cityu.edu
ROSS, Corey .... 903-233-4460. 475 J
CoreyRoss@letu.edu
ROSS, David .... 501-279-4930... 21 C
dross@harding.edu
ROSS, David .... 270-247-8521. 197 H
dross@midcontinent.edu
ROSS, David, A .... 972-708-7340. 472 L
david_ross@gial.edu
ROSS, Deanna .... 208-459-5222. 138 A
dross@collegeofidaho.edu
ROSS, Donald, E .... 302-793-1101... 94 A
ROSS, Donald, E .... 561-237-7782. 108 X
dross@lynn.edu
ROSS, Duffy .... 301-447-5366. 217 B
ross@msmary.edu
ROSS, Dustin .... 319-895-4445. 177 A
dross@cornellcollege.edu
ROSS, Elizabeth .... 617-735-9701. 226 B
ross@emmanuel.edu
ROSS, Elizabeth .... 212-229-8947. 332 E
rosse@newschool.edu
ROSS, Eric .... 660-263-4110. 279 B
ericr@macc.edu
ROSS, JR., Ervin .... 386-481-2561... 99 C
rosse@cookman.edu
ROSS, Frank, E .... 773-442-4600. 154 H
f-ross@neiu.edu
ROSS, Gary .... 706-233-7326. 131 E
gross@shorter.edu
ROSS, Gary, L .... 315-228-7401. 320 F
gross@colgate.edu
ROSS, George, E .... 989-774-3131. 240 N
president@cmich.edu
ROSS, Gerald .... 410-225-2399. 216 C
gross@mica.edu
ROSS, James .... 434-961-5203. 513 F
jross@pvcc.edu
ROSS, James, A .... 734-384-4259. 247 C
jross@monroeccc.edu
ROSS, Jason .... 864-977-7026. 445 H
jason.ross@ngu.edu
ROSS, Jennifer, A .... 260-422-5561. 167 B
jaross@indianatech.edu
ROSS, Jeremy, B .... 423-439-4242. 459 C
rossjb@etsu.edu
ROSS, Jerrold .... 718-990-1305. 339 A
rossj@stjohns.edu
ROSS, JoAnn, L .... 304-766-4361. 530 C
jross15@wvstateu.edu
ROSS, Joe .... 570-504-9686. 413 B
ROSS, John, A .... 785-628-4431. 186 F
jross@fhsu.edu
ROSS, Julie, S .... 617-627-3360. 237 C
j.ross@tufts.edu
ROSS, Karen .... 734-432-5529. 246 B
kross@madonna.edu
ROSS, Kathleen .... 650-574-6532... 64 C
rossk@smccd.edu
ROSS, Keith .... 314-392-2301. 278 B
rossk@mobap.edu
ROSS, Ken .... 863-297-1096. 110 H
kross@polk.edu
ROSS, Kevin, M .... 561-237-7823. 108 X
kross@lynn.edu
ROSS, Laura .... 407-708-2058. 113 E
rossl@seminolestate.edu
ROSS, Lauren .... 937-512-2164. 388 O
lauren.ross@sinclair.edu
ROSS, Leigh, A .... 601-984-2620. 270 C
laross@umc.edu
ROSS, Lucy .... 763-576-4797. 257 Q
lross@anokatech.edu
ROSS, Meg .... 662-562-3204. 269 C
mross@northwestms.edu
ROSS, Michael, D .... 614-885-5585. 388 C
mross@pcj.edu
ROSS, Mindy .... 845-341-4541. 335 H
mindy.ross@sunyorange.edu
ROSS, Nancy, J .... 207-795-7596. 209 I
rossnj@cmhc.org
ROSS, Pam .... 706-385-1487. 130 F
pam.ross@point.edu
ROSS, Pam .... 864-231-2032. 441 B
pross@andersonuniversity.edu
ROSS, Patricia, A .... 801-585-7832. 496 Q
p.ross@utah.edu
ROSS, Patricia, A .... 937-778-7887. 379 G
pross@edisonohio.edu
ROSS, Paul .... 307-382-1696. 543 J
pross@wwcc.wy.edu
ROSS, III, Phillip .... 410-704-4053. 220 E
pross@towson.edu
ROSS, Ramsey .... 850-729-5229. 109 I
ramseyr@nwfsc.edu
ROSS, Rebecca .... 610-436-2501. 430 A
rross2@wcupa.edu
ROSS, Richard, S .... 860-297-2258... 91 F
richard.ross@trincoll.edu
ROSS, Rick .... 360-417-6533. 522 A
rross@pencol.edu
ROSS, Robert .... 787-738-2161. 554 C
robert.ross@upr.edu
ROSS, Ronald .... 973-877-3078. 301 H
ross@essex.edu
ROSS, Ryan .... 303-556-3926... 81 D
ryan.ross@ccd.edu
ROSS, Sadie .... 518-587-2100. 346 A
sadie.ross@esc.edu
ROSS, Sal .... 210-690-9000. 472 N
sross@hallmarkcollege.edu
ROSS, Sandy .... 406-243-2572. 286 H
sandy.ross@umontana.edu
ROSS, Scott .... 770-504-7595. 132 B
sross@sctech.edu
ROSS, Scott, T .... 304-877-6428. 526 C
admissions@abc.edu
ROSS, Sonia .... 210-690-9000. 472 N
sross@hallmarkcollege.edu
ROSS, Sonseeahray .... 937-708-5745. 393 A
sross@wilberforce.edu

ROSS, Stephen .... 541-552-6258. 406 C
rossS@sou.edu
ROSS, Stephen, C .... 724-847-6541. 417 A
scross@geneva.edu
ROSS, Thomas, W .... 919-962-4622. 366 K
tomross@northcarolina.edu
ROSS, Todd .... 626-815-6000... 29 H
tross@apu.edu
ROSS, Toni .... 901-321-3297. 453 H
tross@cbu.edu
ROSS, Tricia .... 212-799-5000. 328 B
ROSS, Vikki, F .... 210-562-6200. 493 A
rossv@uthscsa.edu
ROSS-GARCIA, Tracy ...... 210-486-2851. 465 B
tross20@alamo.edu
ROSS-JONES, Marvel, E . 716-884-9120. 315 K
merossjones@bryantstratton.edu
ROSS-LEE, Barbara .... 516-686-3996. 333 H
brosslee@nyit.edu
ROSSBACHER, Lisa, A ... 678-915-7230. 132 C
rossbach@spsu.edu
ROSSELLI, Robert .... 509-542-4688. 518 C
rrosselli@columbiabasin.edu
ROSSER, Sue, V .... 415-338-1141... 35 E
srosser@sfsu.edu
ROSSER, Ulrike .... 614-825-6255. 373 G
urosser@aiam.edu
ROSSER, William .... 805-493-3553... 31 H
rosser@clunet.edu
ROSSETTI, Elspeth .... 408-554-4861... 64 M
erossetti@scu.edu
ROSSETTI, Erin, S .... 802-626-6417. 501 E
erin.rossetti@lyndonstate.edu
ROSSI, Jason .... 773-697-2215. 144 B
jrossi@devry.edu
ROSSI, Joanne .... 650-508-3613... 56 H
jrossi@ndnu.edu
ROSSI, John .... 315-312-5555. 344 A
john.rossi@oswego.edu
ROSSI, John, J .... 626-256-4673... 39 A
jrossi@coh.org
ROSSI, Ralph .... 518-433-8277. 341 C
ralph.rossi@suny.edu
ROSSI, Richard .... 650-508-3585... 56 H
rrossi@ndnu.edu
ROSSI, Richard, E .... 402-280-2775. 289 D
rrossi@creighton.edu
ROSSI, Vincent .... 413-565-1000. 222 F
vrossi@baypath.edu
ROSSI-LE, Laura .... 978-232-2055. 226 C
lrossile@endicott.edu
ROSSINI, Tania .... 718-390-3187. 350 B
trossini@wagner.edu
ROSSITER, Andrew .... 808-923-9741. 136 B
andrewro@hawaii.edu
ROSSITER, Brian .... 888-897-3222... 50 G
brossiter@sf.chefs.edu
ROSSMAN, Marty .... 630-637-5601. 154 F
mprossman@noctrl.edu
ROSSMAN, Randy, S ...... 517-750-1200. 250 E
rrossman@arbor.edu
ROSSMAN, Rodger .... 252-335-0821. 359 F
rodger_rossman@albemarle.edu
ROSSMANN, Kathleen .... 205-226-4660...... 2 C
krossman@bsc.edu
ROSSMEIER, Joseph, G .. 301-322-0987. 217 F
jrossmeier@pgcc.edu
ROSSMILLER, Lindsay .... 406-657-1051. 288 B
lindsay.rosmiller@rocky.edu
ROSSO, Corey .... 703-892-5100... 96 F
ROSSON, Barry .... 561-297-0268. 114 L
rosson@fau.edu
ROSSON, Barry, T .... 561-297-1211. 114 L
rosson@fau.edu
ROSSON, Michael .... 718-368-5144. 318 E
mrosson@kbcc.cuny.edu
ROST, Gregory, S .... 215-898-7221. 435 B
gregrost@upenn.edu
ROST, Hong .... 715-232-2132. 538 B
rosth@uwstout.edu
ROSTAD, Jerry .... 701-777-6354. 371 B
jerry.rostad@ndus.edu
ROSTAD, Staney .... 612-330-1515. 253 H
rostads@augsburg.edu
ROSTAR, Jimmy .... 252-328-1275. 367 B
rostarj@ecu.edu
ROSZKOWSKI,
Michael, J .... 215-951-1428. 420 B
roszkows@lasalle.edu
ROT, Jeffrey .... 904-826-0084. 118 I
jrot@usa.edu
ROTELLI, Ronda .... 832-813-6285. 476 A
ronda.rotelli@lonestar.edu
ROTENBERG, Mark, B .... 410-516-8128. 215 H
mrotenb1@jhu.edu
ROTER, Petra .... 920-424-4000. 537 B
roterp@uwosh.edu
ROTGER, Mariolga .... 787-850-9324. 554 D
mariolga.rotger@upr.edu
ROTH, Andrew, P .... 216-373-5238. 385 G
aroth@ndc.edu
ROTH, Andrew, W .... 330-972-7340. 390 E
aroth1@uakron.edu
ROTH, Annette .... 763-488-2426. 258 F
annette.roth@hennepintech.edu
ROTH, Brenda .... 503-375-7010. 403 A
broth@corban.edu
ROTH, Brenda, F .... 202-685-3789. 544 K
RothB@ndu.edu
ROTH, Carol, A .... 814-393-2572. 428 C
croth@clarion.edu
ROTH, Darlene .... 610-921-7503. 409 A
droth@alb.edu
ROTH, Don, F .... 530-754-5000... 70 J
droth@ucdavis.edu
ROTH, Frank, A .... 610-758-3572. 422 A
far4@lehigh.edu
ROTH, Gregg .... 518-736-3622. 325 A
gregg.roth@fmcc.suny.edu
ROTH, Henry .... 650-508-3721... 56 H
hroth@ndnu.edu
ROTH, Jason .... 702-968-1633. 295 E
jroth@roseman.edu
ROTH, Jodi .... 610-436-3379. 430 A
jroth@wcupa.edu
ROTH, John .... 916-789-8600... 47 C
john_roth@heald.edu
ROTH, John, C .... 718-940-5616. 339 B
jroth@sjcny.edu
ROTH, Karen .... 541-383-7412. 402 D
kroth1@cocc.edu
ROTH, Lamar .... 620-327-8236. 187 D
lamarr@hesston.edu
ROTH, Laurie .... 610-861-1510. 424 E
melmr01@moravian.edu
ROTH, Linda .... 301-696-3919. 215 D
roth@hood.edu
ROTH, Marjorie .... 585-389-2686. 332 D
mroth1@naz.edu
ROTH, Martha, T .... 773-702-6229. 161 B
mroth@uchicago.edu
ROTH, Michael, L .... 509-313-4204. 520 A
roth@athletics.gonzaga.edu
ROTH, Michael, S .... 860-685-3500... 92 H
mroth@wesleyan.edu
ROTH, OSB, Neal, G ...... 360-491-4440. 522 G
theabbot@stmartin.edu
ROTH, Patty .... 231-995-1363. 248 B
proth@nmc.edu
ROTH, Paul, B .... 505-272-5849. 312 F
proth@salud.unm.edu
ROTH, Rebecca .... 706-880-8088. 128 A
rroth@lagrange.edu
ROTH, Sterling .... 404-413-1310. 126 E
roths@gsu.edu
ROTH, Susan .... 919-684-1964. 354 A
susan.roth@duke.edu
ROTH, Tara, E .... 406-756-3912. 286 B
troth@fvcc.edu
ROTH, Ted .... 217-479-7027. 152 D
ted.roth@mac.edu
ROTH, Teresa .... 937-778-7983. 379 G
troth@edisonohio.edu
ROTH, JR., Toby .... 989-774-3871. 240 N
rothj1t@cmich.edu
ROTH, Tonya .... 715-394-8264. 538 C
troth1@uwsuper.edu
ROTHAMER, Russ .... 928-226-4224... 13 B
russ.rothamer@coconino.edu
ROTHBERG, Heidi .... 413-528-7201. 222 E
registrar@simons-rock.edu
ROTHBERG, Jacob .... 914-736-1500. 335 E
ROTHBERG, Jayme, S .... 727-816-3284. 110 E
rothbej@phcc.edu
ROTHENBERG, James .... 617-495-1000. 227 C
ROTHENBUHLER, Eric .... 314-246-7615. 284 N
erothenbuhler@webster.edu
ROTHENHOEFER,
Lynn, S .... 610-527-0200. 432 B
lrothenhoefer@rosemont.edu
ROTHERMEL, Carolyn .... 740-362-3336. 383 H
crothermel@mtso.edu
ROTHGEB, Helen .... 714-241-6150... 39 I
hrothgeb@coastline.edu
ROTHGERBER, Hank, J .. 502-272-8045. 192 E
hrothgerber@bellarmine.edu
ROTHMAN, Paul .... 410-955-3180. 215 H
prothma1@jhmi.edu
ROTHMAN, Paul, D .... 410-955-3180. 215 H
prothma1@jhmi.edu
ROTHMAN, Rory .... 607-274-3374. 327 E
rrothman@ithaca.edu
ROTHMEIER, Rosemarie . 903-813-2247. 466 H
rrothmeier@austincollege.edu
ROTHMEYER, Michelle .... 815-921-4267. 157 A
m.rothmeyer@rockvalleycollege.edu
ROTHSCHILD, Dovid, N . 516-225-4700. 337 C
rdnr@mlb.edu
ROTHSCHILD,
Martha, D .... 410-777-2701. 213 D
mdrothschild@aacc.edu
ROTHSCHILD, Vivian, M 414-847-3239. 534 F
vivianrothschild@miad.edu
ROTHWELL, Krista .... 302-622-8000... 93 B
ROTMAN, David, L .... 937-766-7905. 375 K
rotmand@cedarville.edu
ROTMAN, Reesa .... 310-824-1586... 26 B
registrar@ajrca.org
ROTOLO, Rene, M .... 718-960-8226. 318 A
rene.rotolo@lehman.cuny.edu
ROTONDO, Denise .... 919-760-8487. 356 G
rotondo@meredith.edu
ROTROFF, Kristi .... 419-267-1271. 385 F
krotroff@northweststate.edu
ROTT, Cynthia .... 701-231-7458. 371 G
cynthia.rott@ndsu.edu
ROTTA, James .... 810-766-4056. 239 H
james.rotta@baker.edu
ROTTENBERG, Aaron ...... 718-854-2290. 315 B
rabbirottenberg@bhsy.org
ROTTER, Bruce, E .... 618-474-7120. 159 H
brotter@siue.edu
ROTTINGHAUS, Steve .... 785-594-8330. 184 C
steve.rottinghaus@bakeru.edu
ROTTWEILER, J, D .... 520-515-5401... 12 R
jdr@cochise.edu
ROTUNDO, Kim, M .... 906-227-2322. 248 A
krotundo@nmu.edu
ROTUNDO, Michael, R .... 906-227-2327. 248 A
mrotundo@nmu.edu
ROTUNNO, Nancy .... 312-935-6929. 156 K
nrotunno@robertmorris.edu
ROTZ, Ben .... 918-335-6279. 398 F
brotz@okwu.edu
ROUBIDEAUX, Jennifer .. 602-944-3335... 11 D
jroubideaux@aicag.edu
ROUBIDEAUX,
Vincent, R .... 602-944-3335... 11 D
vroubideaux@aicag.edu
ROUBIQUE, Jason, S ..... 318-342-5171. 208 E
roubique@ulm.edu
ROUGEAU, Vincent, D .... 617-552-4315. 224 A
vincent.rougeau@bc.edu
ROUGHTON, Dean .... 252-335-0821. 359 F
dean_roughton@albemarle.edu
ROUGHTON, Keith .... 912-478-0747. 126 C
kroughton@georgiasouthern.edu
ROULIER, Stephen .... 413-748-3717. 236 I
sroulier@springfieldcollege.edu
ROULIS, Eleni .... 651-962-6033. 265 C
eroulis@stthomas.edu
ROUNCE, Laura, L .... 312-949-7040. 146 G
lrounce@ico.edu
ROUND, Sara .... 816-415-5984. 285 C
rounds@william.jewell.edu
ROUNDS, Claude .... 518-276-6601. 337 I
roundc@rpi.edu
ROUNDS, Dayle, G .... 609-497-7991. 304 D
dayle.rounds@ptsem.edu
ROUNDS, Tyra .... 313-993-1046. 250 K
roundstc@udmercy.edu
ROUNDTREE, Gwen, D .... 914-606-6581. 350 F
gwen.roundtree@sunywcc.edu
ROUNDTREE, Hazel, G ... 937-775-3207. 393 G
hazel.roundtree@wright.edu
ROUNDTREE, Leslie, A .. 773-995-3987. 141 J
lroundtr@csu.edu
ROUNSVILLE, Lynn .... 315-470-7481. 322 C
lynnrounsville@crouse.org
ROUNTREE, Cynthia .... 718-997-5888. 319 C
cynthia.rountree@qc.cuny.edu
ROUNTREE, Jeffrey, W ... 540-654-2060. 510 J
jrountre@umw.edu
ROUNTREE, Kathleen ...... 510-885-3161... 33 C
kathleen.rountree@csueastbay.edu
ROUNTREE, Linda .... 503-493-6248. 402 J
lrountree@cu-portland.edu
ROUNTREE, Mike .... 478-289-2093. 124 C
rountree@ega.edu
ROURK, Darcy .... 360-992-2325. 518 A
drourk@clark.edu
ROURKE, Carol, M .... 315-267-2128. 344 C
rourkecm@potsdam.edu
ROUS, Philip .... 410-455-2598. 219 D
rous@umbc.edu
ROUSE, Barbi .... 714-556-3610... 74 D
brouse@vanguard.edu
ROUSE, Cecilia .... 609-258-4800. 304 E
rouse@princeton.edu
ROUSE, Kevin .... 828-327-7000. 359 A
Krouse@cvcc.edu
ROUSE, Lawrence, L .... 910-296-2414. 361 D
lrouse@jamessprunt.edu
ROUSE, Leo, E .... 202-806-0440... 95 G
lrouse@howard.edu
ROUSE, Taryn .... 402-486-2505. 292 E
tarouse@ucollege.edu
ROUSEY, Doris .... 972-860-4750. 470 G
drousey@dcccd.edu
ROUSH, Clark, A .... 402-363-5610. 293 I
croush@york.edu
ROUSH, John, A .... 859-238-5220. 193 E
john.roush@centre.edu
ROUSH, JR .... 937-393-3431. 389 B
ROUSH, Keith .... 570-484-2384. 429 B
kroush@lhup.edu
ROUSH, Linda .... 717-872-3820. 429 D
Linda.Roush@millersville.edu
ROUSH, Margaret, A .... 260-359-4097. 166 O
mroush@huntington.edu
ROUSH, Rebecca .... 910-695-3715. 363 F
roushr@sandhills.edu
ROUSH, Troy, E .... 606-474-3272. 194 H
troush@kcu.edu
ROUSMANIERE, David ... 704-687-7418. 368 E
drousman@uncc.edu
ROUSSEAU, David .... 518-442-5256. 341 D
drousseau@albany.edu
ROUSSEAU, Joseph .... 989-964-4195. 249 G
jgrousse@svsu.edu
ROUSSEAU, Karen, S ..... 413-205-3503. 221 F
karen.rousseau@aic.edu
ROUSSELL, Jeroid .... 503-699-6305. 404 C
jroussell@marylhurst.edu
ROUTBORT, Julia, C ...... 518-580-5555. 341 A
jroutbor@skidmore.edu
ROUTE, Annie .... 907-786-1221... 10 H
anair@uaa.alaska.edu
ROUTH, Larry, R .... 402-472-8103. 292 I
lrouth1@unl.edu
ROUTHIER, Nicholette .... 707-668-5663... 42 F
ROUX, Sue .... 704-355-6676. 353 D
sue.roux@carolinascollege.edu
ROVARIS, Jill .... 408-554-4501... 64 M
jrovaris@scu.edu
ROVEDA, Elizabeth .... 570-408-5000. 437 F
elizabeth.roveda@wilkes.edu
ROVIG, Nicole .... 517-355-8700. 246 H
rovig@msu.edu
ROVINSKY, Michele .... 215-895-1403. 415 B
mrovinsky@drexel.edu
ROWAN, John Paul .... 912-525-5000. 131 B
jprowan@scad.edu
ROWAN, Mary Ann .... 312-922-1884. 152 C
mrowan@maccormac.edu
ROWAN, Robert, M .... 410-706-8200. 219 C
rrowan@af.umaryland.edu
ROWDEN, Diana .... 479-788-7676... 24 A
diana.rowden@uafs.edu
ROWE, Al .... 319-398-7611. 180 J
arowe@kirkwood.edu
ROWE, Amy, W .... 814-866-8111. 420 E
arowe@lecom.edu
ROWE, B. David .... 318-869-5101. 201 H
president@centenary.edu
ROWE, Barbara, L .... 540-458-8454. 516 A
browe@wlu.edu
ROWE, Bob .... 252-398-6273. 353 H
roweb@chowan.edu
ROWE, Christine .... 914-337-9300. 321 E
christine.rowe@concordia-ny.edu
ROWE, Cindy .... 503-842-8222. 408 B
rowe@tillamookbay.cc
ROWE, Elizabeth, C .... 973-353-5112. 306 D
erowe@newark.rutgers.edu
ROWE, Jodi .... 217-854-3231. 140 G
jodi.rowe@blackburn.edu
ROWE, Kristin .... 212-986-4343. 314 K
kkr@berkeleycollege.edu
ROWE, Marshall, K .... 706-419-1649. 123 F
rowe@covenant.edu
ROWE, Mary .... 414-382-6047. 531 I
mary.rowe@alverno.edu
ROWE, Rebecca .... 319-385-6204. 179 K
rrowe@iwc.edu
ROWE, Theresa, M .... 248-370-4326. 248 J
rowe@oakland.edu
ROWE, Tom .... 641-472-1144. 180 N
trowe@mum.edu
ROWELL, Amy .... 251-275-8256..... 1 C
arowell@ascc.edu
ROWELL, Gid .... 678-466-4477. 123 A
gidrowell@clayton.edu
ROWELL, Reda .... 678-466-4474. 123 A
redarowell@clayton.edu
ROWELL, Sam, S .... 423-354-2582. 461 C
ssrowell@northeaststate.edu
ROWEN, Cate .... 413-585-3021. 236 H
crowen@smith.edu
ROWEN, Randall, C .... 803-777-4151. 447 G
rowen-randall@sc.edu
ROWETT-JAMES,
Kelly, A .... 336-334-5946. 369 A
karowett@uncg.edu
ROWH, Mark, C .... 540-674-3617. 513 B
mrowh@nr.edu
ROWH, Mark, E .... 806-354-6070. 465 E
merowh@actx.edu
ROWLAND, Alma, Z .... 276-739-2436. 514 D
arowland@vhcc.edu
ROWLAND, Bryan, K ...... 434-395-2030. 506 J
rowlandbk@longwood.edu

ROWLAND, David, L ...... 219-464-5313. 174 E
david.rowland@valpo.edu
ROWLAND, Gloria, T ...... 919-516-4206. 366 C
growland@st-aug.edu
ROWLAND, Linda .... 706-864-1358. 133 D
linda.rowland@ung.edu
ROWLAND, Randy .... 913-360-7372. 184 H
rrowland@benedictine.edu
ROWLAND, Rita, K ...... 626-584-5484... 45 E
rrowland@fuller.edu
ROWLAND, IV, Roy ...... 863-667-5081. 113 P
rrowland@seu.edu
ROWLAND, Sherri .... 478-471-2031. 128 I
sherri.rowland@maconstate.edu
ROWLAND, Susie .... 434-239-5222. 507 F
susie.rowland@miller-motte.edu
ROWLAND, Wayne .... 812-749-1288. 171 K
wrowland@oak.edu
ROWLANDS, Steve .... 325-674-2626. 464 H
rowlandss@acu.edu
ROWLES, Brian .... 863-638-7667. 119 C
brian.rowles@warner.edu
ROWLETT, Carol .... 540-857-7277. 514 E
crowlett@virginiawestern.edu
ROWLETT, Sharron .... 603-888-1311. 297 F
srowlett@rivier.edu
ROWLEY, Becky .... 575-769-4001. 309 F
becky.rowley@clovis.edu
ROWLEY, Bob .... 405-425-5109. 397 D
bob.rowley@oc.edu
ROWLEY, Charles, J ...... 951-827-7310... 71 E
charles.rowley@ucr.edu
ROWLEY, Jill .... 409-880-8450. 486 F
jill.rowley@lamar.edu
ROWLEY, Kathleen .... 909-387-1648... 62 A
krowley@sbccd.cc.ca.us
ROWLEY, Lisa .... 503-352-7252. 407 A
lisajrowley@pacificu.edu
ROWLEY, Richard .... 951-639-5420... 55 B
rrowley@msjc.edu
ROY, Alisa .... 704-922-6202. 360 F
roy.alisa@gaston.edu
ROY, Ashok .... 907-450-8028... 10 G
akroy@alaska.edu
ROY, James, C .... 904-276-6783. 112 C
jimroy@sjrstate.edu
ROY, Jocelyn .... 859-371-9393. 192 D
jroy@beckfield.edu
ROY, II, Joe, E .... 303-492-7311... 85 L
joe.roy@colorado.edu
ROY, Judy, K .... 260-422-5561. 167 B
jkroy@indianatech.edu
ROY, Justin, G .... 919-508-2206. 370 F
justin.roy@peace.edu
ROY, Lara .... 612-874-3778. 257 B
lara_roy@mcad.edu
ROY, Leonard .... 860-628-4751... 90 D
lroy@lincolncollegene.edu
ROY, Marc .... 410-337-6044. 215 A
marc.roy@goucher.edu
ROY, Mary Ellen .... 217-245-3000. 146 F
maryellen.roy@ic.edu
ROY, Melissa .... 845-574-4758. 338 B
mroy@sunyrockland.edu
ROY, Michael, D .... 802-443-5595. 499 H
mdroy@middlebury.edu
ROY, Omaira .... 617-928-4074. 234 E
Oroy@mountida.edu
ROY, Pallabi .... 410-337-6062. 215 A
pallabi.roy@goucher.edu
ROY, Paul .... 650-493-4430... 66 E
paul.roy@sofia.edu
ROY, Rani, R .... 718-862-7755. 329 M
rani.roy@manhattan.edu
ROY, Rina .... 916-404-8108... 53 A
royr@arc.losrios.edu
ROY, Tracey .... 218-322-2409. 258 I
tracey.roy@itascacc.edu
ROY, Tracey .... 218-322-2409. 258 G
troy@itascacc.edu
ROY, Tracey .... 218-322-2409. 259 B
troy@itascacc.edu
ROY, Tracey .... 218-322-2409. 261 G
t.roy@itascacc.edu
ROYAL, Angela .... 636-949-4983. 276 D
aroyal@lindenwood.edu
ROYAL, Christina .... 651-450-3618. 258 H
croyal@inverhills.edu
ROYAL, JR., Frank .... 615-327-5935. 456 E
froyal@mmc.edu
ROYAL, Rebecca .... 908-709-7089. 308 B
rebecca.royal@ucc.edu
ROYAL, Robert .... 540-338-2700. 503 A
rroyal@cdu.edu
ROYALL, Ann .... 617-262-5000. 223 F
ann.royall@the-bac.edu
ROYBAL, Walter .... 719-587-8281... 78 B
wsroybal@adams.edu
ROYCE, Kathy .... 530-339-3610... 65 G
kroyce@shastacollege.edu
ROYCE, Lee, G .... 601-925-3200. 268 A
lroyce@mc.edu
ROYCE, Rosa .... 909-274-4234... 55 A
rroyce@mtsac.edu
ROYE, Shauna .... 202-495-3837... 96 C
sroye@dhs.edu
ROYER, Drew .... 603-623-0313. 297 E
droyer@nhia.edu
ROYER, Joseph, M .... 765-641-4000. 163 L
jmroyer@anderson.edu
ROYER, Roma .... 602-429-4947... 16 O
rroyer@ps.edu
ROYOS, Andre .... 915-779-8031. 494 C
aroyos@computercareercenter.com
ROYS, Cindy .... 631-730-2028. 315 G
croys@bcl.edu
ROYSTER, Jacqueline, J . 404-894-1728. 125 D
jacqueline.royster@iac.gatech.edu
ROYSTER, James, T .... 419-866-0261. 389 H
jtroyster@stautzenberger.com
ROYSTER, Robynne .... 415-703-9532... 30 K
rroyster@cca.edu
ROYSTON, Mimi .... 413-205-3448. 221 F
mimi.royston@aic.edu
ROYSTON, Rosemary, R . 706-379-3111. 134 L
rosemary@yhc.edu
ROYUK, Brent .... 402-643-7304. 289 B
brent.royuk@cune.edu
ROZ, Mugur .... 617-964-1100. 222 A
mroz@ants.edu
ROZ, Mugur .... 617-850-1545. 227 E
mroz@hchc.edu
ROZADA, Mayra .... 787-891-0925. 549 K
mrozada@aguadilla.inter.edu
ROZAK, Edward .... 508-830-5030. 230 D
erozak@maritime.edu
ROZANSKI, Kathy .... 856-256-5400. 305 E
rozanski@rowan.edu
ROZANSKI, Mordechai ... 609-896-5001. 305 D
mrozanski@rider.edu
ROZEBOOM, Dave .... 325-671-2263. 472 O
Dave.Rozeboom@hsutx.edu
ROZEK, Charles, E .... 216-368-4390. 375 J
cer2@case.edu
ROZELL, Laura .... 518-327-6291. 336 B
lrozell@paulsmiths.edu
ROZELL, Liz .... 661-395-4231... 49 N
ROZELL, Mark .... 703-993-4108. 505 C
mrozell@gmu.edu
ROZEMA, Burton, J .... 708-239-4760. 160 K
burt.rozema@trnty.edu
ROZEMBAJGIER, John ... 614-885-5585. 388 C
jrozembajgier@pcj.edu
ROZEWSKI, Mark .... 812-464-1849. 174 D
mrozewski@usi.edu
ROZIER, Dekhasta, B .... 919-516-4022. 366 C
dbrozier@st-aug.edu
ROZIN, Miriam .... 503-399-8486. 402 E
miriam.rozin@chemeketa.edu
ROZIN, Vladmir .... 212-463-0400. 348 B
vladmirr@touro.edu
ROZNER, Frances .... 714-992-7832... 67 D
frozner@scco.edu
ROZOWSKI, Casey .... 612-343-4430. 262 X
cmrozows@northcentral.edu
RUANO, Norman .... 773-878-3894. 158 B
nruano@iwe.staugustine.edu
RUBACK, Ginger .... 954-492-5353. 100 A
gruback@citycollege.edu
RUBACK, Sally, A .... 920-929-2126. 540 F
sruback@morainepark.edu
RUBBELKE, Thomas, J ... 651-641-8700. 255 B
rubbelke@csp.edu
RUBECK, Dustin, D .... 972-241-3371. 470 E
drubeck@dallas.edu
RUBEL, Carol .... 617-587-5650. 234 H
rubelc@neco.edu
RUBEL, Robert, J .... 401-841-2200. 545 A
RUBEL, Tom .... 641-683-5252. 179 A
tom.rubel@indianhills.edu
RUBEMEYER, Susan .... 636-922-8360. 280 J
srubemeyer@stchas.edu
RUBENSTEIN, David .... 856-256-4222. 305 E
rubenstein@rowan.edu
RUBENSTEIN, David .... 202-687-1972... 95 E
dr94@georgetown.edu
RUBENSTEIN, Greg .... 660-626-2391. 271 A
RUBENZAHL, Ira, H .... 413-755-4906. 233 A
irubenzahl@stcc.edu
RUBERO, Maria, D .... 787-250-1912. 550 E
mdrubero@metro.inter.edu
RUBES, Larry .... 804-706-5041. 512 G
lrubes@jtcc.edu
RUBIN, JD, Gary, J .... 805-591-6220... 42 C
grubin@cuesta.edu
RUBIN, Gary, N .... 410-704-2358. 220 E
grubin@towson.edu
RUBIN, James .... 602-787-6546... 15 B
james.rubin@paradisevalley.edu
RUBIN, Joshua .... 718-436-2122. 347 E
RUBIN, Lisa .... 770-426-2725. 128 D
lrubin@life.edu
RUBIN, Marge .... 920-720-6811. 539 K
rubin@fvtc.edu
RUBIN, Mark, E .... 804-828-1235. 511 F
merubin@vcu.edu
RUBIN, Moshe .... 516-239-9002. 340 I
RUBIN, Rachel .... 860-486-2337... 92 A
rachel.rubin@uconn.edu
RUBIN, Steve .... 719-219-9636... 79 B
steverubindvm@att.net
RUBINO, Cynthia .... 212-986-4343. 314 K
cnr@berkeleycollege.edu
RUBINO, David .... 814-824-2241. 423 J
drubino@mercyhurst.edu
RUBINO, John .... 207-941-7109. 210 B
rubinoj@husson.edu
RUBINO, Joseph .... 410-293-1549. 545 J
rubino@usna.edu
RUBINO, Karen, M .... 401-456-8849. 439 F
krubino@ric.edu
RUBINO, Michael, H .... 508-767-7156. 222 C
rubino@assumption.edu
RUBINSTEIN, Mark .... 603-862-2053. 298 C
mark.rubinstein@unh.edu
RUBIO, Olga, D .... 956-721-5296. 475 F
drubio@laredo.edu
RUBIO, Paty .... 518-580-5705. 341 A
prubio@skidmore.edu
RUBLE, Celeste .... 507-433-0666. 260 I
celeste.ruble@riverland.edu
RUBLE, Joel .... 559-925-3127... 75 I
joelruble@whccd.edu
RUBLE, Justin .... 304-260-4380. 527 N
jruble@blueridgectc.edu
RUBLE, Michelle .... 301-934-4711. 214 D
micheller@csmd.edu
RUBLE, Robert, W .... 607-735-1802. 323 H
rruble@elmira.edu
RUBRITZ, Gerald .... 814-886-6460. 424 G
grubritz@mtaloy.edu
RUBY, Carl, A .... 937-766-7871. 375 K
rubyc@cedarville.edu
RUCABADO, Angel .... 787-993-8958. 554 A
angel.rucabado@upr.edu
RUCCIUS, Frederick, E ... 215-955-8733. 434 C
frederick.ruccius@jefferson.edu
RUCH, Douglas .... 678-891-3269. 125 G
douglas.ruch@gpc.edu
RUCH, J. Chuck .... 309-677-3100. 140 I
cruch@bradley.edu
RUCH, Lisa .... 815-965-7314. 157 B
lruch@rockfordcareercollege.edu
RUCHALA, Patsy, L .... 775-784-6841. 294 J
pruchala@unr.edu
RUCKER, Cedric, B .... 540-654-1655. 510 J
crucker@umw.edu
RUCKER, Lugene .... 662-254-3591. 269 A
lrucker@mvsu.edu
RUCKER, Marty, K .... 423-585-6983. 462 A
marty.rucker@ws.edu
RUCKER, Paul .... 206-685-9223. 524 G
uwalumni@uw.edu
RUCKER, Richard .... 937-433-3410. 379 J
rrucker@edaff.com
RUCKER, Robert, E .... 662-685-4771. 266 C
erucker@bmc.edu
RUCKER, Robin .... 937-376-6692. 376 E
rrucker@centralstate.edu
RUCKER, Sherri, B .... 615-329-8555. 454 F
srucker@fisk.edu
RUCKER-FRANKLIN,
Yvonne .... 870-633-4480... 21 A
yrucker@eacc.edu
RUCKER-SHAMU,
Marian .... 301-860-3849. 220 A
mshamu@bowiestate.edu
RUDA, Ryan .... 620-276-9597. 187 A
ryan.ruda@gcccks.edu
RUDASILL, Susann .... 850-644-1571. 115 C
srudasill@fsu.edu
RUDATSIKIRA,
Emmanuel .... 269-471-6648. 239 D
rudatsikira@andrews.edu
RUDAWITZ, Linda .... 503-517-1397. 408 H
lrudawitz@warnerpacific.edu
RUDAWSKY, Donald, J .. 954-262-5392. 109 K
rudawsky@nova.edu
RUDD, M. David .... 901-678-3643. 460 B
mdrudd@memphis.edu
RUDD, Martin .... 920-832-2610. 538 E
martin.rudd@uwc.edu
RUDD WEITZEL, Jann ... 636-949-4846. 276 D
jweitzel@lindenwood.edu
RUDDELL, Larry .... 281-579-9977. 266 A
lruddell@belhaven.edu
RUDDEN, David .... 847-214-7925. 144 F
drudden@elgin.edu
RUDE, John .... 323-267-3724... 51 F
rudejc@elac.edu
RUDEAU, William .... 609-771-2187. 300 E
rudeau@tcnj.edu
RUDECOFF, Christine, A 315-684-6055. 345 A
rudecoc@morrisville.edu
RUDEN, Lynne .... 989-275-5000. 245 B
lynne.ruden@kirtland.edu
RUDENGA, Elizabeth .... 708-239-4739. 160 K
liz.rudenga@trnty.edu
RUDGERS, Lisa, M .... 734-763-3526. 251 C
rudgers@umich.edu
RUDIE, Scott, H .... 414-410-4593. 532 B
shrudie@stritch.edu
RUDIGER, Brenda .... 906-487-2400. 247 A
brudiger@mtu.edu
RUDIGER, Jennifer .... 715-232-1151. 538 B
rudigerj@uwstout.edu
RUDIN, Mark .... 208-426-5732. 137 G
markrudin@boisestate.edu
RUDISILL, Frank .... 864-503-5511. 448 H
frudisill@uscupstate.edu
RUDLEY, John, M .... 713-313-7044. 485 F
rudleyjm@tsu.edu
RUDNEY, Gwen .... 320-589-6411. 264 F
rudneygl@morris.umn.edu
RUDNICK, Joseph .... 310-825-1042... 71 C
jrudnick@college.ucla.edu
RUDNICKI, Rosemary .... 512-448-8540. 479 C
rosemars@stedwards.edu
RUDNIK, Jeffrey, A .... 270-686-4324. 192 G
jeffrey.rudnik@brescia.edu
RUDNITSKI, Rose .... 201-559-3551. 302 A
rudnitskir@felician.edu
RUDNYTZKY, Leo .... 215-951-1204. 420 B
rudnytzkyl@lasalle.edu
RUDOLPH, Margaret .... 419-448-2111. 380 G
mrudolph@heidelberg.edu
RUDOLPH, Marva .... 865-974-2498. 463 C
mrudolp1@utk.edu
RUDOLPH, Mary Kay .... 707-524-1516... 65 B
mrudolph@santarosa.edu
RUDOLPH, Meloni .... 303-556-8164... 81 D
meloni.rudolph@ccd.edu
RUE, Penny .... 336-758-5943. 370 D
rue@wfu.edu
RUEB, Shirley .... 316-942-4291. 189 E
ruebs@newmanu.edu
RUEBEL, James, S .... 765-285-1024. 164 B
jruebel@bsu.edu
RUEBNER, Ralph .... 312-987-2384. 148 L
ruebner@jmls.edu
RUEFLE, Colleen .... 412-536-1069. 420 A
colleen.ruefle@laroche.edu
RUEGER, Nancy .... 718-409-5985. 346 D
nrueger@sunymaritime.edu
RUEGER, William .... 718-409-7323. 346 D
wrueger@sunymaritime.edu
RUEGG, Texas .... 903-813-2371. 466 H
truegg@austincollege.edu
RUELL, John .... 435-283-7250. 498 A
john.ruell@snow.edu
RUELLE, Joan .... 336-278-6572. 354 B
jruelle@elon.edu
RUESCH, Sherry .... 435-652-7551. 497 E
ruesch@dixie.edu
RUESCHMANN, Eva .... 413-559-5378. 227 B
erueschmann@hampshire.edu
RUETER, Kenneth, J .... 870-307-7326... 21 H
ken.rueter@lyon.edu
RUETTEN, Amy .... 417-667-8181. 273 A
aruetten@cottey.edu
RUFENER, Patrick, S .... 330-684-8906. 390 F
psr8@uakron.edu
RUFF, Corey .... 325-674-2665. 464 H
clr06a@acu.edu
RUFF, Joy, C .... 305-237-2090. 109 D
jruff@mdc.edu
RUFF, Margaret .... 903-785-7661. 478 B
mruff@parisjc.edu
RUFF, Rosemary, H .... 479-575-3845... 23 I
rruff@uark.edu
RUFFER, Carla .... 901-272-5160. 456 F
cruffer@mca.edu
RUFFIN, Beverly, W .... 713-313-1376. 485 F
ruffinbw@tsu.edu
RUFFIN, Cynthia .... 919-572-1625. 352 C
cruffin@apexsot.edu
RUFFIN, Finee .... 601-477-4082. 267 F
finee.ruffin@jcjc.edu
RUFFIN, Juretta .... 919-572-1625. 352 C
registrar@apexsot.edu
RUFFIN, Kimberly, N .... 312-341-2281. 157 D
kruffin@roosevelt.edu
RUFFIN, Shanda .... 803-780-1360. 449 E
sruffin@voorhees.edu
RUFFING, Rebecca .... 315-866-0300. 326 A
ruffingrj@herkimer.edu
RUFFINO, John, J .... 703-323-3023. 513 C
jruffino@nvcc.edu
RUFFOLO, Linda, L .... 260-481-6659. 168 C
ruffolo@ipfw.edu

RUFFRAGE, Jo 315-792-7172. 346 C
ruffraj@sunyit.edu
RUFFULO, Anna 773-834-2571. 160 I
RUFINO, Paul 856-415-2173. 302 C
prufino@gccnj.edu
RUFO, Joseph 315-470-6622. 345 B
jlrufo@esf.edu
RUFTY, Rebeca, C 919-515-1989. 368 B
rcrufty@ncsu.edu
RUGG, Marilyn 315-228-7288. 320 F
mrugg@colgate.edu
RUGG, William 918-444-2060. 396 H
rugg@nsuok.edu
RUGGIERI, David 407-447-7300. 105 I
druggieri@ftccollege.edu
RUGGIERO, Bruno 985-448-4262. 208 A
bruno.ruggiero@nicholls.edu
RUGGLES, Jennifer 216-368-1723. 375 J
jor15@case.edu
RUHL, Chris 317-921-4474. 169 K
cruhl@ivytech.edu
RUHLAND, Sheila 920-929-2127. 540 F
sruhland@morainepark.edu
RUIBAL, Pilar 787-751-0160. 548 J
pruibal@cmpr.pr.gov
RUIZ, Alberto 361-593-2837. 484 A
alberto.ruiz@tamuk.edu
RUIZ, Alfredo 269-471-6979. 239 D
jaruiz@andrews.edu
RUIZ, Andrew 806-894-9611. 480 H
aruiz@southplainscollege.edu
RUIZ, Carol 973-748-9000. 299 F
carol_ruiz@bloomfield.edu
RUIZ, Deborah 831-646-3097... 54 I
druiz@mpc.edu
RUIZ, Eddy, A 208-885-7716. 139 D
Ruiz@uidaho.edu
RUIZ, Encarnacion 209-228-4240... 71 D
ERuiz@UCMerced.edu
RUIZ, Eric, A 815-740-5037. 162 F
eruiz@stfrancis.edu
RUIZ, Israel 617-253-4495. 233 B
RUIZ, Joaquin 520-621-4090... 18 F
jruiz@email.arizona.edu
RUIZ, OP, John Martin 202-495-3821... 96 C
jruiz@dhs.edu
RUIZ, Jose 787-863-2390. 550 C
jose.ruiz@fajardo.inter.edu
RUIZ, Kathleen 310-377-5501... 53 F
kruiz@marymountcalifornia.edu
RUIZ, Kris 936-294-3492. 487 A
kjk001@shsu.edu
RUIZ, Lucy 559-638-3641... 69 A
lucy.ruiz@reedleycollege.edu
RUIZ, Luis, A 787-766-1717. 552 J
um_lruiz@suagm.edu
RUIZ, Luis, E 787-250-1912. 550 E
leruiz@metro.inter.edu
RUIZ, Mayra 787-832-6000. 549 D
mruiz@icprjc.edu
RUIZ, Miguel 713-221-8564. 489 D
ruizm@uhd.edu
RUIZ, Rafael 787-257-0000. 554 B
rafael.ruiz@upr.edu
RUIZ, Roseanna 909-537-7651... 34 E
rruiz@csusb.edu
RUIZ, Sacha, M 787-891-0925. 549 K
sruiz@aguadilla.inter.edu
RUIZ-HUSTON, Ines 209-946-2132... 73 A
iruiz@pacific.edu
RUIZMATTEI, Enid 719-389-6699... 79 D
enid.ruizmattei@coloradocollege.edu
RUKSNAITIS, Diane 978-632-6600. 232 C
d_ruksnaitis@mwcc.mass.edu
RULAND, Judith 989-964-4145. 249 G
jruland@svsu.edu
RULAND, Michael 432-552-2764. 493 D
ruland_m@utpb.edu
RULE, Anne 314-977-2495. 281 I
ruleam@slu.edu
RULE, David 425-564-2301. 517 A
dave.rule@bellevuecollege.edu
RULE, Scott 770-975-4000. 122 I
RULEY, Patricia, T 540-464-7637. 515 B
ruleypt@vmi.edu
RULLMAN, Loren, J 734-763-1291. 251 C
lrullman@umich.edu
RULNICK, Adrienne, A 202-994-6435... 95 D
arulnick@gwu.edu
RULOFSON, Eric 530-251-8878... 50 F
erulofson@lassencollege.edu
RULOFSON, Eric 541-885-1600. 405 J
eric.rulofson@oit.edu
RUMBERGER, Jana 415-351-3507... 62 G
jrumberger@sfai.edu
RUMER, Richard 215-204-5144. 433 K
richard.rumer@temple.edu
RUMERY, Joyce, V 207-581-1655. 212 B
rumery@maine.edu
RUMIANO, Sara 530-898-5134... 33 A
srumiano@csuchico.edu
RUMKER, Becky 912-260-4287. 131 F
becky.rumker@sgsc.edu
RUMLER, Robin 517-265-5161. 238 G
rrumler@adrian.edu
RUMMAGE, Spencer 704-216-3738. 363 D
spencer.rummage@rccc.edu
RUMMEL, Richard 401-454-6374. 440 A
rrummel@risd.edu
RUMMEL, Tina 903-675-6282. 488 D
trummel@tvcc.edu
RUMP, Rebecca 319-208-5065. 182 G
brump@scciowa.edu
RUMSEY, Greg 423-236-2733. 458 J
rumsey@southern.edu
RUNBERG, Bruce, L 919-962-7248. 368 D
bruce_runberg@unc.edu
RUND, James, A 480-965-2200... 11 K
james.rund@asu.edu
RUNDELL, Jay, A 740-362-3121. 383 H
jrundell@mtso.edu
RUNDELL, Judy 318-473-6474. 205 A
jrundell@lsua.edu
RUNDQUIST, Suellen 763-424-0950. 260 C
srundquist@nhcc.edu
RUNESTAD, Eric 507-537-6220. 261 F
Eric.Runestad@smsu.edu
RUNEY, Mim, L 401-598-1000. 439 B
mruney@jwu.edu
RUNG, Paul 718-405-3722. 320 G
paul.rung@mountsaintvincent.edu
RUNGE, Alan 512-313-3000. 469 L
alan.runge@concordia.edu
RUNGE, Carol, E 315-255-1743. 316 D
runge@cayuga-cc.edu
RUNGE, Mark, S 620-341-5331. 186 D
mrunge@emporia.edu
RUNGE, Steve 501-450-3126... 25 H
srunge@uca.edu
RUNGE, Thomas, G 765-361-6371. 175 B
runget@wabash.edu
RUNHOLT, Steve 828-771-9092. 370 E
srunholt@warren-wilson.edu
RUNIEWICZ, Michael 314-935-8976. 284 L
michael_runiewicz@wustl.edu
RUNION, Garth, E 434-592-3003. 506 I
gerunion2@liberty.edu
RUNION, Kevin, L 812-237-8101. 167 A
kevin.runion@indstate.edu
RUNION, Robert 304-929-5026. 528 D
rrunion@newriver.edu
RUNIS, Alice 303-765-3174... 82 E
arunis@iliff.edu
RUNKLE, Dan 563-589-3599. 182 J
drunkle@dbq.edu
RUNKSMEIER, Lori 603-428-2238. 297 D
lrunksmei@nec.edu
RUNNELS, Charles, B 310-506-4443... 58 H
charles.runnels@pepperdine.edu
RUNNELS, Marti, R 806-291-1086. 494 F
runnels@wbu.edu
RUNNING, Patrick 320-762-4483. 257 O
patrickr@alextech.edu
RUNYAN, Andy 937-766-3840. 375 K
arunyan@cedarville.edu
RUNYON, David 717-901-5137. 418 E
drunyon@harrisburgu.edu
RUNYON, Jean, M 410-777-1249. 213 D
jmrunyon@aacc.edu
RUNYON, Tim 417-626-1234. 279 J
runyon.tim@occ.edu
RUOCCO, Ann Michele 413-559-5411. 227 B
RUOFF, Pamela, J 215-871-6154. 430 D
pamr@pcom.edu
RUOKONEN, Mary 212-353-4113. 321 F
ruokon@cooper.edu
RUPE, Becky 901-272-5145. 456 F
brupe@mca.edu
RUPE, Jackie 602-548-1955... 14 G
RUPE, Jolene, K 785-539-3571. 188 F
jrupe@mccks.edu
RUPE, Manuel, R 989-774-3971. 240 N
rupe1mr@cmich.edu
RUPERT, Kimberly 517-750-1200. 250 E
krupert@arbor.edu
RUPERT, Terry, A 937-382-6661. 393 B
terry_rupert@wilmington.edu
RUPIPER, Russ 402-557-7291. 288 G
russ.rupiper@bellevue.edu
RUPP, Barbara, A 573-882-7744. 283 C
ruppb@missouri.edu
RUPP, Sharon, L 864-429-8728. 448 G
ruppsl@mailbox.sc.edu
RUPP, Sheila, R 810-762-9585. 244 Q
srupp@kettering.edu
RUPPEL, Stephen, A 208-769-3377. 138 I
saruppel@nic.edu
RUPPERSBURG, Hugh 706-542-5806. 133 C
hruppers@uga.edu
RUPPERT, Becky, L 301-784-5000. 213 B
rruppert@allegany.edu
RUPPERT, Ronald 972-438-6932. 478 C
rrupert@parkercc.edu
RUPSCH, Christina 757-822-1889. 514 C
crupsch@tcc.edu
RURKA, Jessica 410-225-2573. 216 C
jrurka@mica.edu
RURSCH, Keri 309-794-7721. 139 L
kerirursch@augustana.edu
RUSCH, Kathleen, M 414-464-9777. 539 G
kathleenrusch@sbcglobal.net
RUSCHER, Monica 859-344-4045. 199 H
ruschem@thomasmore.edu
RUSCHIVAL, Michael 303-292-0015... 81 F
m.ruschival@denverschoolofnursing.edu
RUSCHMAN, Doug 513-745-3185. 393 H
ruschman@xavier.edu
RUSCIO, Kenneth, P 540-458-8700. 516 A
president@wlu.edu
RUSE, Elaine 330-941-3505. 394 A
eruse@ysu.edu
RUSE, Michael 843-349-2548. 442 E
mruse@coastal.edu
RUSH, Amber 870-368-2008... 22 E
arush@ozarka.edu
RUSH, Catherine, I 973-655-5299. 303 D
rushc@mail.montclair.edu
RUSH, Cherlyn, L 215-951-1948. 420 B
rush@lasalle.edu
RUSH, Deanna 601-635-2111. 266 H
drush@eccc.edu
RUSH, Dennis 845-569-3492. 332 B
dennis.rush@msmc.edu
RUSH, JR., James 706-721-1626. 126 B
jrush@gru.edu
RUSH, James, C 409-880-8354. 486 F
james.rush@lamar.edu
RUSH, Janet 402-363-5661. 293 I
jgrush@york.edu
RUSH, Jim 864-225-7653. 444 A
jimrush@forrestcollege.edu
RUSH, John 662-325-7000. 268 D
jpr2@msstate.edu
RUSH, John, H 563-588-8000. 178 D
jrush@emmaus.edu
RUSH, John, P 662-325-9306. 268 D
rush@devalumni.msstate.edu
RUSH, Keith 225-769-8820. 204 M
RUSH, Mary, A 423-585-2687. 462 A
mary.rush@ws.edu
RUSH, Maureen 215-898-7515. 435 B
mrush@publicsafety.upenn.edu
RUSH, Nate 217-854-3231. 140 G
nrush@blackburn.edu
RUSH, Patrick 708-596-2000. 159 C
prush@ssc.edu
RUSH, Richard, R 805-437-8410... 32 I
richard.rush@csuci.edu
RUSH, Rosalee 570-389-4043. 427 H
rrush@bloomu.edu
RUSH, S. Bryan 864-379-8701. 443 F
rush@erskine.edu
RUSH, Tanya 443-885-3527. 217 A
tanya.rush@morgan.edu
RUSHER, Bryan 501-374-5576... 19 J
bryan.rusher@arkansasbaptist.edu
RUSHFORTH, Brenda 909-621-8175... 60 A
brenda.rushforth@pomona.edu
RUSHFORTH, Samuel 801-863-8981. 497 C
sam.rushforth@uvu.edu
RUSHING, Beth 240-895-4389. 218 A
brushing@smcm.edu
RUSHING, Cheri 618-437-5321. 156 H
rushing@rlc.edu
RUSHING, Douglas, R 816-654-7252. 275 K
drushing@kcumb.edu
RUSHING,
James Kenneth 904-264-2172. 111 P
krushing@iwsfla.org
RUSHING, Linda 870-364-6414... 24 D
rushingl@uamont.edu
RUSHING, Mark 910-592-8081. 363 E
mrushing@sampsoncc.edu
RUSHING, Wanda 601-923-1699. 269 E
wrushing@rts.edu
RUSHMER, Bernadette 570-674-8028. 424 A
brushmer@misericordia.edu
RUSHNAWITZ, P 248-968-3360. 253 A
RUSHTON, Jeffery, A 502-852-6171. 200 D
jeff.rushton@louisville.edu
RUSILOSKI, Benjamin 215-489-2911. 414 E
Benjamin.Rusiloski@delval.edu
RUSINEK, Ken 207-985-7976. 210 G
kenrusinek@landingschool.edu
RUSNAK NOON, Anna 570-504-9695. 413 B
RUSS, Daniel 978-867-4062. 226 H
dan.russ@gordon.edu
RUSS, Larry 201-216-5379. 307 E
lruss@stevens.edu
RUSSE, Sarah, R 630-844-4620. 140 A
srusse@aurora.edu
RUSSEK, Lori 361-593-4191. 484 A
lori.russek@tamuk.edu
RUSSEL, William, B 609-258-3035. 304 E
graddean@princeton.edu
RUSSELL, Agnes, M 616-222-3000. 245 C
arussell@kuyper.edu
RUSSELL, Ann 910-879-5526. 358 B
arussell@bladencc.edu
RUSSELL, Anne Marie, T 207-786-8211. 209 F
arussell@bates.edu
RUSSELL, Audrey, L 574-372-5100. 166 B
Audrey.Russell@grace.edu
RUSSELL, Barbara 716-338-1210. 327 J
barbararussell@mail.sunyjcc.edu
RUSSELL, Brent 803-778-6689. 441 F
russellrd@cctech.edu
RUSSELL, Chris, A 641-844-5716. 179 J
chris.russell@iavalley.edu
RUSSELL, Constance 404-225-4502. 121 B
crowan@atlantatech.edu
RUSSELL, Danny 740-362-3322. 383 H
drussell@mtso.edu
RUSSELL, David, W 214-648-2695. 493 E
david.russell@utsouthwestern.edu
RUSSELL, Denise 614-236-6196. 375 H
drussell@capital.edu
RUSSELL, Dororthy 561-297-3266. 114 L
druss@fau.edu
RUSSELL, Dorothy 561-297-3266. 114 L
drussell@fau.edu
RUSSELL, Elizabeth 314-246-8298. 284 N
russelmb@webster.edu
RUSSELL, Freda, R 414-410-4000. 532 B
frrussell@stritch.edu
RUSSELL, Gary, T 941-752-5200. 114 I
russelg@scf.edu
RUSSELL, Irma 406-243-4311. 286 H
irma.russell@umontana.edu
RUSSELL, James, H 903-823-3198. 482 D
jameshenry.russell@texarkanacollege.edu
RUSSELL, Jeff, D 276-739-2491. 514 D
jrussell@vhcc.edu
RUSSELL, Jeffery 419-289-5212. 374 C
jrussell@ashland.edu
RUSSELL, Jeffrey 608-262-5823. 536 D
jrussell@dcs.wisc.edu
RUSSELL, Jennie 314-921-9290. 284 D
jrussell@ugst.edu
RUSSELL, Jeri, L 307-686-0254. 543 F
jrussell@sheridan.edu
RUSSELL, Jessica 510-594-3764... 30 K
jrussell@cca.edu
RUSSELL, Jill, F 413-748-3241. 236 I
jrussell@springfieldcollege.edu
RUSSELL, Jill, T 717-867-6076. 421 H
russell@lvc.edu
RUSSELL, Joanna, S 503-223-5100. 408 A
RUSSELL, Joanne 914-606-6712. 350 F
Joanne.Russell@sunywcc.edu
RUSSELL, John, P 402-559-5343. 292 J
jrussel@unmc.edu
RUSSELL, Joyce, W 336-342-4261. 363 C
russellj@rockinghamcc.edu
RUSSELL, Juanita 601-877-6191. 265 G
juanita@alcorn.edu
RUSSELL, Judith 352-273-2505. 116 A
jcrussell@ufl.edu
RUSSELL, Julia, H 802-656-4063. 500 F
julia.russell@uvm.edu
RUSSELL, Kathleen, M 914-367-8208. 339 E
Kathleen.Russell@archny.org
RUSSELL, Kelly 620-227-9510. 186 B
krussell@dc3.edu
RUSSELL, Kendra 478-752-4278. 125 A
kendra.russell@gcsu.edu
RUSSELL, Kevin 601-968-8746. 266 A
krussell@belhaven.edu
RUSSELL, Kimberly 307-532-8251. 542 a
kimberly.russell@ewc.wy.edu
RUSSELL, Kimberly, A 903-510-2382. 488 E
krus@tjc.edu
RUSSELL, Leah, R 540-375-2210. 509 B
russell@roanoke.edu
RUSSELL, Lisa 541-684-4644. 407 B
lrussell@pioneerpacific.edu
RUSSELL, Malcolm 402-486-2501. 292 E
marussel@ucollege.edu
RUSSELL, Marilyn 785-749-8470. 187 B
mrussell@haskell.edu
RUSSELL, Mary Jane 802-654-2494. 500 B
mrussell@smcvt.edu
RUSSELL, Michael 785-827-5541. 188 C
mike.russell@kwu.edu
RUSSELL, Michael 912-478-5234. 126 C
mjrussel@georgiasouthern.edu
RUSSELL, Mindy 620-223-2700. 186 G
mindyr@fortscott.edu
RUSSELL, Nancy 816-604-1326. 277 C
nancy.russell@mcckc.edu
RUSSELL, Patrick, J 414-425-8300. 535 K
prussell@shst.edu

RUSSELL, Robert ... 650-433-3820 ... 58 B r.russell@paloaltou.edu
RUSSELL, Robert ... 605-626-7770. 451 I Robert.Russell@northern.edu
RUSSELL, Ronda ... 406-994-5541. 287 B rrussell@montana.edu
RUSSELL, Ruby ... 205-853-1200 ... 5 B rrussell@jeffstateonline.com
RUSSELL, Samuel, J ... 660-944-2810. 272 H samuel@conception.edu
RUSSELL, Scott ... 978-232-2113. 226 C srussell@endicott.edu
RUSSELL, Starla ... 605-394-4034. 452 E starla.russell@wdt.edu
RUSSELL, Stephanie, J ... 414-288-1881. 534 B stephanie.russell@marquette.edu
RUSSELL, Susan ... 254-659-7631. 473 A srussell@hillcollege.edu
RUSSELL, Tammy ... 269-467-9945. 242 H trussell@glenoaks.edu
RUSSELL, Terry ... 636-949-4980. 276 D trussell@lindenwood.edu
RUSSELL, Thad ... 620-227-9325. 186 B trussell@dc3.edu
RUSSELL, Thomas ... 312-369-7940. 143 D trussell@colum.edu
RUSSELL, Tracy, E ... 570-577-1375. 411 A tracy.russell@bucknell.edu
RUSSELL, William ... 860-632-3050 ... 90 C busoffice@holyapostles.edu
RUSSELL O'GRADY, Marijo ... 212-346-1306. 335 J mogrady@pace.edu
RUSSO, Cecelia, M ... 718-990-6667. 339 A russoc@stjohns.edu
RUSSO, Kim ... 661-255-1050 ... 31 C krusso@calarts.edu
RUSSO, Lisa ... 213-613-2200 ... 67 E lisarusso@sciarc.edu
RUSSO, Richard ... 510-642-2700 ... 70 I russo@berkeley.edu
RUSSO, Robert ... 215-699-5700. 421 E rrusso@LSB.edu
RUSSO, Robert, C ... 203-254-4288 ... 89 I rcrusso@fairfield.edu
RUSSO, Ted ... 973-655-3219. 303 D russot@mail.montclair.edu
RUSSOM, Kenneth, S ... 904-819-6230. 103 E krussom@flagler.edu
RUSSOM, Vaughn, N ... 715-394-8327. 538 C vrussom@uwsuper.edu
RUSSOMANNO, David, J ... 317-274-0802. 168 D drussoma@iupui.edu
RUSSOS, Milton, A ... 904-632-3123. 105 E mrussos@fscj.edu
RUSSOW, Craig ... 414-443-8544. 539 F craig.russow@wlc.edu
RUSSOW, Rodd ... 928-541-7777 ... 16 B rrussow@ncu.edu
RUST, Kathleen ... 630-617-3419. 145 A kathyrst@elmhurst.edu
RUST, Mark, M ... 410-857-2503. 216 E mrust@mcdaniel.edu
RUST, Melissa ... 501-686-2532 ... 23 H mrust@uasys.edu
RUSTOWICZ, Mary Louis ... 716-896-0700. 350 A rustowim@villa.edu
RUTBERG, Barbara ... 617-824-8275. 226 A barbara_rutberg@emerson.edu
RUTENBECK, Jeffrey ... 202-885-2019 ... 94 F jeff@american.edu
RUTER, Josh ... 702-651-3162. 294 F josh.ruter@csn.edu
RUTH, David, A ... 215-895-2501. 415 B ruthda@drexel.edu
RUTH, Rick ... 717-477-1835. 429 E reruth@ship.edu
RUTHENBECK, Julie, J ... 325-942-2255. 465 K julie.ruthenbeck@angelo.edu
RUTHER, Aisha ... 312-850-7176. 142 C aruther@ccc.edu
RUTHERFOORD, Becky ... 678-915-7400. 132 C brutherf@spsu.edu
RUTHERFORD, Ann, O ... 406-874-6196. 286 E rutherforda@milescc.edu
RUTHERFORD, Ben ... 740-374-8716. 392 I brutherford@wscc.edu
RUTHERFORD, Cynthia ... 215-572-4091. 409 H rutherfc@arcadia.edu
RUTHERFORD, Gina ... 850-973-9414. 109 H rutherfordg@nfcc.edu
RUTHERFORD, Greg, F ... 803-327-8050. 449 J grutherford@yorktech.edu
RUTHERFORD, Joan, M ... 419-251-1301. 383 G joan.rutherford@mercycollege.edu
RUTHERFORD, John, D ... 214-648-0400. 493 E john.rutherford@utsouthwestern.edu
RUTHERFORD, Karen, W ... 803-705-4671. 441 C rutherk@benedict.edu
RUTHERFORD, Kimberly 504-278-6421. 203 F krutherford@nunez.edu
RUTHERFORD, Laurie, G ... 713-500-2101. 492 E laurie.g.rutherford@uth.tmc.edu
RUTHERFORD, Lisa, H ... 413-542-5645. 221 G lrutherford@amherst.edu
RUTHERFORD, Marcella, M ... 954-262-1963. 109 K rmarcell@nova.edu
RUTHERFORD, Marylyn ... 973-877-3408. 301 H rutherford@essex.edu
RUTHERFORD, Paul ... 304-327-4403. 529 D prutherford@bluefieldstate.edu
RUTHERMAN, Kathy ... 270-852-3142. 197 B krutherman@kwc.edu
RUTIGLIANO, Serafina ... 212-772-4451. 318 C serafina.rutigliano@hunter.cuny.edu
RUTKOWSKI, Edmund ... 718-636-3784. 336 F ekow@pratt.edu
RUTKOWSKI, Sandra ... 419-824-3762. 383 C srutkowski@lourdes.edu
RUTLEDGE, Brian ... 601-984-1010. 270 C brutledge@umc.edu
RUTLEDGE, Catherine ... 484-365-8087. 422 D crutledge@lincoln.edu
RUTLEDGE, James ... 662-846-4021. 266 G jrutledge@deltastate.edu
RUTLEDGE, Janet ... 410-455-1781. 219 D jrutledge@umbc.edu
RUTLEDGE, Melissa, B ... 540-378-5120. 509 B rutledge@roanoke.edu
RUTLEDGE, Susan ... 314-392-2355. 278 B rutledges@mobap.edu
RUTLEDGE, Todd ... 417-269-3873. 273 D trutle@coxcollege.edu
RUTT, Charles, D ... 660-543-4370. 283 A rutt@ucmo.edu
RUTT, Jack, H ... 540-432-4478. 504 D ruttj@emu.edu
RUTT, Richard ... 503-352-7377. 407 A ruttra@pacificu.edu
RUTTEN, Erich ... 651-962-6561. 265 C erutten@stthomas.edu
RUUD, William, N ... 319-273-2566. 176 A bill.ruud@uni.edu
RUXTON, Brooke ... 815-753-1206. 154 I bruxton@niu.edu
RUYLE, Dianna ... 217-854-3231. 140 G druyl@blackburn.edu
RUYS, Jasmine ... 661-362-3466 ... 40 E jasmine.ruys@canyons.edu
RUZICH, Steve ... 708-596-2000. 159 C sruzich@ssc.edu
RUZICKA, James ... 402-461-7337. 289 I jruzicka@hastings.edu
RYALL, Patrick ... 503-768-7294. 403 K ryall@lclark.edu
RYALS, Reginald ... 540-423-9055. 512 E rryals@germanna.edu
RYAN, Aaron ... 304-876-5527. 529 I aryan@shepherd.edu
RYAN, Andrew ... 718-862-8000. 329 M andrew.ryan@manhattan.edu
RYAN, Angela ... 480-994-9244 ... 17 Q angelar@swiha.edu
RYAN, Barry, T ... 949-783-4800 ... 75 E barry.ryan@westcoastuniversity.edu
RYAN, Bruce ... 607-844-8222. 347 I ryanb@tc3.edu
RYAN, Bryan, K ... 919-866-5146. 364 G bkryan@waketech.edu
RYAN, Carol ... 859-572-5152. 198 I ryanc@nku.edu
RYAN, Caroll ... 714-882-7800 ... 32 D cryan@calsouthern.edu
RYAN, Catherine ... 413-572-5218. 230 F cryan@westfield.ma.edu
RYAN, Christopher ... 508-830-5003. 230 D cryan@maritime.edu
RYAN, Curtis, W ... 801-832-2148. 498 F cryan@westminstercollege.edu
RYAN, Dan ... 800-962-7682. 285 A dryan@wma.edu
RYAN, Dennis ... 757-340-2121. 503 I registrarcvab@centura.edu
RYAN, Duane ... 575-562-2112. 309 H duane.ryan@enmu.edu
RYAN, Elaine ... 202-314-3300 ... 95 F
RYAN, Gail, L ... 313-577-6595. 252 G gailryan@wayne.edu
RYAN, Greg ... 714-992-7092 ... 56 F gryan@fullcoll.edu
RYAN, Heather ... 970-786-6407 ... 10 H hdryan@uaa.alaska.edu
RYAN, Helen, G ... 502-272-8426. 192 E hryan@bellarmine.edu
RYAN, James ... 617-262-5000. 223 F James.Ryan@the-bac.edu
RYAN, James ... 734-462-4400. 250 A jryan@schoolcraft.edu
RYAN, James, G ... 336-217-5128. 367 E jgryan@ncat.edu
RYAN, Jenny ... 801-832-2502. 498 F sjryan@westminstercollege.edu
RYAN, Jerry ... 318-345-9262. 203 C jryan@ladelta.edu
RYAN, CSC, John ... 570-208-5899. 419 P jjryan@kings.edu
RYAN, John, F ... 802-656-4418. 500 F jfryan@uvm.edu
RYAN, Judith, S ... 207-581-1581. 212 B judyryan@maine.edu
RYAN, Kapono ... 808-735-4797. 135 D kryan@chaminade.edu
RYAN, Karen ... 386-822-7515. 117 C kryan@stetson.edu
RYAN, Kathleen ... 508-541-1515. 225 F kryan@dean.edu
RYAN, Kathleen ... 617-732-5042. 233 E Kathleen.Ryan@mcphs.edu
RYAN, Kent ... 386-246-4801. 101 G ryank@DaytonaState.edu
RYAN, Kevin ... 305-428-5700. 109 E kryan@aii.edu
RYAN, Kyle ... 781-899-5500. 223 E kryan@blessedjohnxxiii.edu
RYAN, Larry ... 505-277-2847. 312 F larry@unm.edu
RYAN, Lawrence ... 310-577-3000 ... 77 G lryan@yosan.edu
RYAN, Linda, S ... 515-271-2147. 177 K linda.ryan@drake.edu
RYAN, Lori ... 602-331-7500 ... 12 A lryan@aii.edu
RYAN, Loyd ... 501-450-1348 ... 21 E ryan@hendrix.edu
RYAN, Mark, R ... 573-882-0314. 283 C ryanmr@missouri.edu
RYAN, Mary, A ... 651-962-6133. 265 C maryan@stthomas.edu
RYAN, Mary, L ... 501-686-6730 ... 24 C ryanmaryl@uams.edu
RYAN, Melissa ... 904-725-0525. 100 L mryan@concorde.edu
RYAN, SSJ, Meriliyn ... 215-753-3623. 413 A ryanm@chc.edu
RYAN, Michael ... 617-585-1187. 234 I michael.ryan@necmusic.edu
RYAN, Molly ... 661-255-1050 ... 31 C mryan@calarts.edu
RYAN, Pat ... 503-842-8222. 408 B ryan@tillamookbay.cc
RYAN, Patricia ... 540-674-3613. 513 B pryan@nr.edu
RYAN, Peter ... 662-325-3742. 268 D ryan@cvm.msstate.edu
RYAN, Philip ... 508-362-2131. 231 D pryan@capecod.edu
RYAN, Philip, B ... 508-831-5200. 238 F pbryan@wpi.edu
RYAN, Robert ... 800-782-2422 ... 32 B rryan851@earthlink.net
RYAN, Robin ... 858-795-5244 ... 64 E rryan@sanfordburnham.org
RYAN, Ron ... 954-262-8856. 109 K ronr@nova.edu
RYAN, Rosaleen ... 831-646-4035 ... 54 I rryan@mpc.edu
RYAN, Scott ... 817-272-3181. 491 B sdryan@uta.edu
RYAN, Sean, J ... 502-272-8376. 192 E sryan@bellarmine.edu
RYAN, Sharon ... 213-624-1200 ... 44 D sryan@fidm.edu
RYAN, Spencer ... 405-878-5177. 399 G shryan@stgregorys.edu
RYAN, Susan ... 386-822-7181. 117 C sryan@stetson.edu
RYAN, Suzanne ... 812-856-5572. 167 F sryan@indiana.edu
RYAN, Tiffiney ... 618-634-3242. 158 M tiffineyr@shawneecc.edu
RYAN, Tim ... 574-520-4261. 168 E timryan@iusb.edu
RYAN, Tim ... 845-452-9600. 322 D t_ryan@culinary.edu
RYAN, Timothy, M ... 207-725-3247. 209 H tryan@bowdoin.edu
RYAN, Valerie ... 858-642-8513 ... 55 J vryan@nu.edu
RYAN, Vicky ... 419-473-2700. 378 I vryan@daviscollege.edu
RYAN BULONE, Mary ... 419-473-2700. 378 I mryan@daviscollege.edu
RYAN-HOFFMAN, Maureen ... 732-987-2218. 302 B ryan-hoffman@georgian.edu
RYANT, Marion ... 229-430-4609. 119 J marion.ryant@asurams.edu
RYCHLEC, Tim ... 713-313-1810. 485 F rychlect@tsu.edu
RYCHLY, Carol ... 706-737-1422. 126 B crychly@gru.edu
RYCZKOWSKI, Sandy ... 920-498-6829. 541 B sandra.ryczkowski@nwtc.edu
RYCZYWOT, Marie ... 901-320-9700. 463 J mryczywot@victory.edu
RYDEN, Tod ... 325-235-7366. 486 C tod.ryden@tstc.edu
RYDER, Ellen ... 508-793-2419. 225 B eryder@holycross.edu
RYDER, Laura ... 717-755-2300. 410 C lryder@aii.edu
RYDER-FOX, Jennifer ... 530-898-5844 ... 33 A jrfox@csuchico.edu
RYDL, Chareny, L ... 979-845-3158. 483 C chareny@tamu.edu
RYE, Colleen ... 906-635-2626. 245 G crye@lssu.edu
RYE, Tara ... 402-449-2849. 289 H trye@graceu.edu
RYEA, Alan, E ... 802-656-2010. 500 F alan.ryea@uvm.edu
RYERSON, James ... 703-284-5926. 507 B james.ryerson@marymount.edu
RYKEN, Philip, G ... 630-752-5002. 163 F philip.ryken@wheaton.edu
RYLE, Jerry ... 203-371-7840 ... 91 C rylef@sacredheart.edu
RYLES, Ruby ... 718-368-5000. 318 E rryles@kbcc.cuny.edu
RYMAN, Denny, G ... 318-342-1622. 208 E ryman@ulm.edu
RYNNE, Jeanne ... 360-867-6115. 519 J rynnej@evergreen.edu
RYON, Diane ... 704-372-0266. 355 M dryon@kingscollegecharlotte.edu
RYSLINGE, Birgitte ... 971-722-7267. 407 D birgitte.ryslinge@pcc.edu
RYSTROM, Andrea ... 651-779-3953. 258 C andrea.rystrom@century.edu
RYTHER, Richard, H ... 585-292-2122. 332 A rryther@monroecc.edu
RZONCA, Chet ... 319-335-2527. 175 I chet-rzonca@uiowa.edu
RZONCA, Chet, S ... 319-335-2527. 175 I chet-rzonca@uiowa.edu
RZONCA, Stephen ... 910-892-3178. 355 B srzonca@heritagebiblecollege.edu
RÍOS ORLANDI, Ethel ... 787-764-0000. 553 G ethel.rios1@uprrp.edu

S

SÁEZ-HERNÁNDEZ, Samuel ... 787-993-8896. 554 A samuel.saez@upr.edu
SÁNCHEZ, Melba, G ... 787-743-7979. 552 I msanchez@suagm.edu
SÁNCHEZ PINTOR, Linda ... 787-725-8120. 548 O lsanchez0053@eap.edu
S.A. LEON GUERRERO, Ann ... 671-735-2862. 546 E annsalg@uguam.uog.edu
S.A. LEON GUERRERO, Ann ... 671-735-2941. 546 E annsalg@uguam.uog.edu
SAACKE, David ... 540-458-8400. 516 A dsaacke@wlu.edu
SAADL, Christine ... 610-796-8356. 409 E christine.saadl@alvernia.edu
SAAED, Jan ... 801-832-2232. 498 F jsaaed@westminstercollege.edu
SAARIAHO, Ginger, K ... 617-552-9168. 224 A ginger.saariaho@bc.edu
SAATKAMP, JR., Herman, J ... 609-652-4521. 305 C president@stockton.edu
SAAVEDRA, Adrianna ... 520-494-5287 ... 12 P adriana.saavedra@centralaz.edu
SAAVEDRA, Marc ... 505-277-1670. 312 F msaav@unm.edu
SAAVEDRA, Michael ... 505-454-3053. 310 E
SAAVEDRA, Rebecca ... 409-772-2909. 493 C rsaavedr@utmb.edu
SABATH BEIT-HALACHMI, Rachel ... 513-221-1875. 325 G rsabath@huc.edu
SABATINE, Stephanie ... 906-635-6664. 245 G ssabatine@lssu.edu
SABATINI, JR., John, A ... 410-843-8278. 265 D john.sabatini@laureate.net
SABATINO, Charles, A ... 330-941-3589. 394 A casabatino@ysu.edu
SABATINO, Patricia ... 718-678-8817. 330 J psabatino@mercy.edu

SABATKA, Hauli 402-461-7433. 289 I hsabatka@hastings.edu
SABATTINI, Mark 904-680-7621. 103 Q msabattini@fcsl.edu
SABATTIS, Robert, G 973-642-4586. 303 G robert.g.sabattis@njit.edu
SABBAR, Carol 262-551-5950. 532 D csabbar@carthage.edu
SABBATINI, Robert 423-869-6849. 456 A robert.sabbatini@lmunet.edu
SABELLA, Marc 530-541-4660... 50 D sabella@ltcc.edu
SABEY, Brenda 435-652-7841. 497 E sabey@dixie.edu
SABIN, Christopher, P 910-938-6321. 359 E sabinc@coastalcarolina.edu
SABIN, Laurie 567-661-7282. 387 L laurie_sabin@owens.edu
SABIN, Melody 864-578-8770. 446 F msabin@sherman.edu
SABINE, Neil 765-973-8389. 167 G nsabine@iue.edu
SABINO, Lyn 330-363-4227. 374 E lsabino@aultman.com
SABINSON, Allen 215-895-1621. 415 B allen.c.sabinson@drexel.edu
SABIT, Farhad 510-659-6146... 57 A fsabit@ohlone.edu
SABITSANA, Andrea 312-915-8722. 151 H asabits@luc.edu
SABLAN, Becky 670-234-5498. 547 A beckys@nmcnet.edu
SABLAN, Karen, M 671-735-5581. 546 C karen.sablan@guamcc.edu
SABLAN-ZEBEDY, Ellia 207-834-7805. 212 E ellia.sablanzebedy@maine.edu
SABLE, Marjorie 573-882-0914. 283 C SableM@missouri.edu
SABLE, Ray 229-333-5875. 134 B rasable@valdosta.edu
SABLO, Kahan 814-732-2313. 428 E ksablo@edinboro.edu
SABO, Arlene 518-564-2022. 344 B sabocaa@plattsburgh.edu
SABO, Rebekah 412-338-4770. 419 M rsabo@kaplan.edu
SABO, Sylvia 814-254-0569. 413 C ssabo@pa.gov
SABOE, Mike 843-820-5090. 447 E mike.saboe@tridenttech.edu
SABOLD, Steven 412-346-2122. 430 F ssabold@pia.edu
SABOLO, Martin 217-479-7130. 152 D martin.sabolo@mac.edu
SABOTA, Fred 727-864-8895. 101 N sabotafr@eckerd.edu
SABOU, Michelle, L 864-977-7004. 445 H michelle.sabou@ngu.edu
SABOUNI, Ikhlas 936-261-9800. 482 F isabouni@pvamu.edu
SACCENTI, Thomas, M 740-376-4611. 383 E tom.saccenti@marietta.edu
SACCENTI, Tom 864-294-2111. 444 C tom.saccenti@furman.edu
SACCO, Albert 806-742-3451. 487 D al.sacco-jr@ttu.edu
SACCO, Denise 904-680-7706. 103 Q dsacco@fcsl.edu
SACCO, John 617-296-8300. 227 I john_sacco@laboure.edu
SACCOCCIO, Louis, J 401-874-4486. 440 D ljslaw@uri.edu
SACHER, Lesley 850-644-8869. 115 C lsacher@admin.fsu.edu
SACHNOFF, Neil 732-906-2601. 303 B nsachnoff@middlesexcc.edu
SACHS, Steven, G 703-323-3387. 513 C ssachs@nvcc.edu
SACK, Bob 616-222-1421. 241 F bob.sack@cornerstone.edu
SACK, Chuck 610-558-5627. 424 I sackc@neumann.edu
SACKETT, Mike 562-947-8755... 67 H mikesackett@scuhs.edu
SACKMAN, Dwayne 309-438-5451. 147 J dsackma@ilstu.edu
SACKS, Arlene 305-653-6713. 390 C arlene.sacks@myunion.edu
SACOPULOS, Melony, A 812-237-4141. 167 A melony.sacopulos@indstate.edu
SACZAWA, Eric 508-373-9454. 223 A eric.saczawa@becker.edu
SADAN, Avishai 213-740-3124... 74 A dentdean@usc.edu
SADAO, Amy 215-573-9973. 435 B asadao@ica.upenn.org
SADD, Tracy 717-361-1260. 415 H saddt@etown.edu
SADDIGH, Farah 310-233-4501... 51 H saddigf@lahc.edu
SADDLEMIRE, Melissa, A 570-961-4733. 423 B saddlemire@marywood.edu
SADDLER, Sterling 309-298-1690. 162 K s-saddler2@wiu.edu
SADDORIS-TRAUGHBER, Janiece, L 217-424-6253. 153 C jtraughber@millikin.edu
SADEGHIPOUR, Keya 215-204-5285. 433 K keya.sadeghipour@temple.edu
SADLEK, Gregory, M 216-687-3660. 377 F g.sadlek@csuohio.edu
SADLEK, Lance, A 563-333-6252. 182 B SadlekLanceA@sau.edu
SADLER, David, L 925-969-3372... 49 B dsadler@jfku.edu
SADLER, Martin 404-687-4512. 123 C sadlerm@ctsnet.edu
SADLER, Paul, L 806-291-1163. 494 F sadlerp@wbu.edu
SADLER, Tommy 731-661-5218. 462 F tsadler@uu.edu
SADOWSKI, Sherri 717-262-2006. 437 H sherri.sadowski@wilson.edu
SADWICK, Rick, F 585-262-1695. 332 A rsadwick@monroecc.edu
SAECHAO, Jenny 559-438-4222... 46 K jenny_saechao@heald.edu
SAEED, Najam 651-846-1324. 261 D najam.saeed@saintpaul.edu
SAENZ, Kelly 281-992-3413. 479 H kelly.saenz@sjcd.edu
SAENZ, Miguel 320-308-5272. 261 B msaenz@stcloudstate.edu
SAENZ, Rogelio 210-458-2715. 492 C rogelio.saenz@utsa.edu
SAETRE, David 715-682-1253. 535 D dsaetre@northland.edu
SAEVIG, Daniel, J 419-530-4008. 392 B daniel.saevig@utoledo.edu
SAEZ, Jose 503-228-6528. 402 A jsaez@aii.edu
SAFADY, Randa, S 512-499-4777. 491 A rsafady@utsystem.edu
SAFARZADEH, Mohammad 714-533-3946... 36 C msafar@calums.edu
SAFFORD, Mary, C 828-448-3539. 365 A msafford@wpcc.edu
SAFINICK, Nancy 310-506-4136... 58 H nancy.safinick@pepperdine.edu
SAFLEY, Ellen 972-883-2916. 491 E safley@utdallas.edu
SAFLEY, Mallory 770-531-6330. 128 B msafley@laniertech.edu
SAFLEY, Michael, W 910-630-7157. 356 H msafley@methodist.edu
SAFRAN, Robert, L 717-764-9550. 413 J rsafran@csb.edu
SAFRAN, Robert, L 717-764-9550. 414 A rsafran@csb.edu
SAFRANSKI, Scott 314-977-3833. 281 I safranski@slu.edu
SAFYER, Andrew 516-877-4354. 313 A asafyer@adelphi.edu
SAGARDIA OLIVERAS, Paula 787-863-2390. 550 C paula.sagardia@fajardo.inter.edu
SAGE, James 715-346-4446. 538 A jsage@uwsp.edu
SAGE, James, L 330-972-6542. 390 E jsage@uakron.edu
SAGE, Roger 952-356-3602. 450 G rsage@national.edu
SAGE, William, M 512-232-7806. 491 C bsage@law.utexas.edu
SAGENDORF, Brian 208-282-2517. 138 E sagebria@isu.edu
SAGER, Brian 815-921-4053. 157 A b.sager@rockvalleycollege.edu
SAGER, Scott 615-966-5156. 456 B scott.sager@lipscomb.edu
SAGER GENTRY, Jennifer 804-819-4961. 511 G jgentry@vccs.edu
SAGERS, Keith 404-297-9522. 126 A sagersr@gptc.edu
SAGESTER, Fred 606-539-4059. 200 B fred.sagester@ucumberlands.edu
SAGGIO, Joseph, J 602-944-3335... 11 D jsaggio@aicag.edu
SAGHAFI, Shirin 703-330-8400... 96 F shirin.saghafi@strayer.edu
SAGO, Anthony 815-599-3437. 146 D anthony.sago@highland.edu
SAGUIL, Aaron 301-295-3383. 545 C
SAH, Cynthia 312-987-1407. 148 L 6sah@jmls.edu
SAHLHOFF, Kathleen, A 715-836-3373. 536 E sahlhoka@uwec.edu
SAHLI, Daniel 330-941-3700. 394 A desahli@ysu.edu
SAHNI, Ashish 831-459-4380... 72 C ashish@ucsc.edu
SAHS, Scott 507-281-7787. 261 A scott.sahn@rctc.edu
SAIEH, Jerry 718-260-3226. 336 E jsaieh@poly.edu
SAIFF, Edward 201-684-7723. 305 A esaiff@ramapo.edu
SAIKI, Linda 808-689-2500. 136 C saiki@hawaii.edu
SAIKIA, Paul 717-815-1245. 438 D psaikia@ycp.edu
SAIN, Becky 704-669-4093. 359 D sain@clevelandcc.edu
SAIN, Nathan 479-979-1331... 25 J nsain@ozarks.edu
ST. AMAND, Gerard, A 859-572-5129. 198 I stamand@nku.edu
ST. ANDRE, Joe 318-678-6000. 202 I st@bpcc.edu
ST. ANGELO, Paul 317-916-7826. 169 L pstangelo@ivytech.edu
ST. ANTOINE, Tom 561-803-2279. 110 B tom_stantoine@pba.edu
ST. CLAIR, Ann, F 406-496-4284. 287 F astclair@mtech.edu
ST. CLAIR, Becky 269-471-3348. 239 D pr@andrews.edu
ST. CLAIR, Don, E 818-767-0888... 76 K don.stclair@woodbury.edu
ST. CLAIR, Karen 307-674-6446. 543 F kstclair@sheridan.edu
ST. COLUMBIA, Rhonda 870-338-6474... 24 G
ST. CROIX, Jerome, S 585-292-2278. 332 A jstcroix@monroecc.edu
ST. DENNIS, Grady, I 507-933-7661. 255 I stdennis@gustavus.edu
ST. JAMES, Tim 860-253-3087... 88 C tstjames@asnuntuck.edu
ST. JEAN, Robert 603-899-4022. 296 H stjean@franklinpierce.edu
ST. JOHN, Caron 256-824-6736..... 8 F caron.stjohn@uah.edu
ST. JOHN, Cynthia 920-686-6350. 536 A Cynthia.St.John@sl.edu
ST. JOHN, Meredith 617-558-1788. 235 C mstjohn@nesa.edu
ST. JOHN, Ronald 718-262-5114. 319 F stjohn@york.cuny.edu
ST. LOUIS, Daniel, C 828-327-7000. 359 A dstlouis@cvcc.edu
ST. LOUIS, Mark 941-487-4877. 115 D mstlouis@ncf.edu
ST. LOUIS, Moise 802-654-2663. 500 B mstlouis@smcvt.edu
ST. MARKS, Wanda 406-395-4313. 288 D wstmarks@stonecild.edu
ST. MAURO, Anne 609-258-3403. 304 E stmauro@princeton.edu
ST. MICHEL, Peter 207-621-3119. 212 C stmichel@maine.edu
ST. ONER, Indira 954-783-7339. 102 M istoner@cci.edu
ST. ONGE, Susan 321-674-6400. 104 H sstonge@fit.edu
ST. OURS, Paulette 207-602-2400. 213 A pstours@une.edu
ST. PETER, Heidi 802-654-2674. 500 B hstpeter2@smcvt.edu
ST. PIERRE, Traci 207-780-4771. 212 H stspierre@usm.maine.edu
ST. PIERRE-SLEBODA, Cheryl 617-928-4516. 234 E csleboda@mountida.edu
ST. PREUX, Morisset 617-427-0060. 232 G mpreux@rcc.mass.edu
ST. ROMAIN, Claudette, L 973-642-8290. 307 D claudette.stromain@shu.edu
SAINTJONES, Jerome 256-372-5654..... 1 A jerome.saintjones@aamu.edu
SAINTVIL, Yamiley 718-409-7220. 346 D ysaintvil@sunymaritime.edu
SAIRS, Reuben 740-857-1311. 388 I rsairs@rosedale.edu
SAJDAK, Jeff 616-957-6016. 240 M jsajdak@calvinseminary.edu
SAJKO, Brian 928-350-2109... 17 K brian.sajko@prescott.edu
SAJKO, Helena 860-768-7834... 92 D sajko@hartford.edu
SAKAGUCHI, Gary 559-638-3641... 69 A gary.sakaguchi@reedleycollege.edu
SAKAI, Eric 802-828-2800. 501 C sakaie@ccv.edu
SAKAI, Eric 425-739-8100. 520 K eric.sakai@lwtech.edu
SAKAI, Hiro 949-480-4008... 66 F sakai@soka.edu
SAKAI, Marcia 808-974-7750. 136 A marcias@hawaii.edu
SAKAKI, Judy, K 510-987-0158... 70 H judy.sakaki@ucop.edu
SAKAMOTO, Clyde 808-984-3636. 137 B clydes@hawaii.edu
SAKARYA, Mustafa 914-674-7258. 330 J msakarya@mercy.edu
SAKO, Wanda 808-983-4109. 135 G wsako@tokai.edu
SAKRY, Janice 218-726-6593. 264 D jsakry@d.umn.edu
SAKS, Deborah 916-558-2582... 53 D SaksD@scc.losrios.edu
SAKS, Greg 657-278-7030... 33 E gsaks@fullerton.edu
SALA, Anca 810-766-4111. 239 H anca.sala@baker.edu
SALADIN, Lisa 843-792-3328. 445 B saladinl@musc.edu
SALAHUDDIN, Mecca 210-486-2897. 465 B msalahuddin1@alamo.edu
SALAMY, James 315-866-0300. 326 A salamyjr@herkimer.edu
SALANI, Chris 906-487-7378. 242 G chris.salani@finlandia.edu
SALARI, Gholamereza 717-394-6211. 413 J rsalari@csb.edu
SALAS, Charles, G 860-685-2002... 92 H csalas@wesleyan.edu
SALAS-BELTRAN, Rocio 714-533-1495... 66 H rsbeltran@southbaylo.edu
SALATINO, Michael 630-829-6667. 140 B msalatino@ben.edu
SALAVITABAR, Hadi 518-454-5160. 321 A salavith@strose.edu
SALAY, Lawrence 203-285-2046... 88 E lsalay@gwcc.commnet.edu
SALAZ, Eduardo 925-631-4212... 61 F els3@stmarys-ca.edu
SALAZ, Mark 520-494-5250... 12 P mark.salaz@centralaz.edu
SALAZAR, David 562-985-4131... 33 F salazar@csulb.edu
SALAZAR, Ed 928-541-7777... 16 B esalazar@ncu.edu
SALAZAR, Marilu 361-593-2861. 484 A marilu.salazar@tamuk.edu
SALAZAR, Michael 562-860-2451... 37 I msalazar@cerritos.edu
SALAZAR, Norma 956-364-4557. 485 H norma.salazar@tstc.edu
SALAZAR-VALENTINE, Marcia 419-372-8185. 374 K marcias@bgsu.edu
SALAZAR-VALENTINE, Marcia 419-372-8183. 374 K marcias@bgsu.edu
SALAZAR-VALENTINE, Marcia 419-372-8185. 374 K marcias@bgsu.edu
SALBU, Steven, C 404-894-2600. 125 D steven.salbu@scheller.gatech.edu
SALCIDO, Kevin, J 480-965-6608... 11 K kevin.j.salcido@asu.edu
SALDANA-TALLEY, Jane 707-778-3931... 65 B lsaldana-talley@santarosa.edu
SALDIVAR, Julie 304-766-3156. 530 C jsaldivar@wvstateu.edu
SALE, Gene 561-803-2352. 110 B gene_sale@pba.edu
SALE, Rachel 573-681-5442. 276 C saler@lincolnu.edu
SALEH, Bahaa 407-882-3326. 115 E besaleh@creol.ucf.edu
SALEH, Donald, A 315-443-5559. 347 C dasaleh@syr.edu
SALEM, Susan 310-954-4112... 54 J ssalem@msmc.la.edu
SALEM, Susan 801-957-4447. 498 B susan.salem@slcc.edu
SALEMME, Brenda 716-488-3023. 327 I brendasalemme@jamestownbusinesscollege.edu
SALEMME, Kevin 978-837-5377. 234 A kevin.salemme@merrimack.edu
SALERNO, Dena 570-372-4302. 433 H salerno@susqu.edu
SALES, Cathy 405-422-1262. 399 B salesc@redlandscc.edu
SALES, Vince 916-278-7043... 34 D vsales@csus.edu
SALESTROM, Charles 308-535-3781. 290 J salestromc@mpcc.edu
SALGUERO, Jossie 787-766-1912. 549 J jsalguer@inter.edu
SALIBA, Joseph, E 937-229-2245. 391 C jsaliba1@udayton.edu
SALIBA, Tony, E 937-229-2306. 391 C TSaliba1@udayton.edu

SALIBA, Yvette, C ... 407-303-6413... 97 H
yvette.saliba@adu.edu
SALICHS, Eduardo ... 787-765-1915. 551 C
esalichs@inter.edu
SALII, Uroi, N ... 680-488-2471. 547 B
usalii@palau.edu
SALIM, Ellis, P ... 810-766-4276. 239 G
ellis.salim@baker.edu
SALIMAN, Todd ... 303-860-5600... 85 K
todd.saliman@cu.edu
SALIMBENE, Franklyn, P 781-891-2462. 223 C
fsalimbene@bentley.edu
SALINAS, Alberto ... 956-721-5357. 475 F
albert.salinas@laredo.edu
SALINAS, Antonio ... 575-439-3601. 310 J
antsalin@nmsu.edu
SALINAS, Felix ... 210-486-4788. 464 J
fsalinas26@alamo.edu
SALINAS, Jessica ... 956-665-3361. 492 B
lopezj@utpa.edu
SALINAS, Lelia ... 956-872-7209. 480 I
lelias1@southtexascollege.edu
SALINAS, Sallie ... 714-241-4901... 39 I
ssalinas@coastline.edu
SALINAS, Stacy ... 845-848-7818. 322 G
stacy.salinas@dc.edu
SALINE, Terrie ... 309-341-7436. 150 A
tsaline@knox.edu
SALINGER, Mary, G ... 610-799-1165. 421 I
msalinger@lccc.edu
SALINGER, Sharon, V ... 949-824-7761... 71 B
sharon.salinger@uci.edu
SALISBURY, Mark ... 309-794-7504. 139 L
marksalisbury@augustana.edu
SALISBURY, Mark ... 651-962-4425. 265 C
SALKIN, Patricia ... 631-761-7100. 348 B
patricia.salkin@touro.edu
SALLAN, Veena ... 270-686-4639. 196 C
veena.sallan@kctcs.edu
SALLEE, David, L ... 816-415-5026. 285 C
salleed@william.jewell.edu
SALLEE, L. James ... 219-785-5667. 172 A
jsallee@pnc.edu
SALLEH-BARONE,
Normah ... 708-974-5209. 153 F
salleh-barone@morainevalley.edu
SALLER, Richard, P ... 650-723-9784... 68 E
rsaller@stanford.edu
SALLEY, JR., DeWitt ... 864-656-3978. 442 C
witt@clemson.edu
SALLEY, Dug ... 610-282-1100. 414 F
dug.salley@desales.edu
SALLIN, Dennis ... 573-897-5000. 276 E
SALLY, Dana ... 828-227-7307. 369 E
dsally@wcu.edu
SALMEIER, Michael ... 909-599-5433... 50 J
msalmeier@lifepacific.edu
SALMERI, Patrice ... 612-330-1166. 253 H
salmeri@augsburg.edu
SALMI, SJ, Richard, P ... 251-380-3866..... 7 D
raslmi@shc.edu
SALMO, Jim ... 618-453-7174. 159 G
jims@foundation.siu.edu
SALMON, Edward, L ... 262-646-6508. 535 B
esalmon@nashotah.edu
SALMON, Mark ... 334-670-3342..... 7 H
msalmon@troy.edu
SALMON, Sheri ... 205-226-4692..... 2 C
ssalmon@bsc.edu
SALOMANSON, Kristen .. 231-591-3801. 242 F
kristen_salomonson@ferris.edu
SALOME, Joann ... 575-835-5206. 310 F
jsalome@admin.nmt.edu
SALOMON, Carol ... 212-353-4187. 321 F
salomo@cooper.edu
SALOMON, Mattisyahu ... 732-367-1060. 299 E
SALOMON, Rachel ... 629-625-5979. 546 F
rsalomon@cmi.edu
SALOMON-FERNÁNDEZ,
Yves ... 781-239-3159. 231 G
ysalomonfernandez@massbay.edu
SALOMONE, Joseph, J ... 215-895-4948. 415 B
salomojj@drexel.edu
SALOMONSON, Kristen .. 231-591-3801. 242 F
Kristen_Salomonson@ferris.edu
SALONEN, Neil Albert ... 203-576-4665... 91 G
nas@bridgeport.edu
SALONER, Garth ... 650-723-1940... 68 E
saloner@stanford.edu
SALOUN, Pamela ... 414-256-1207. 535 A
salounp@mtmary.edu
SALOVEY, Peter ... 203-432-2550... 93 A
peter.salovey@yale.edu
SALOWITZ, Stewart, I ... 309-556-3206. 148 B
salowitz@iwu.edu
SALOWITZ, Susan ... 860-343-5724... 89 A
ssalowitz@mxcc.commnet.edu
SALSBURY, Lysa ... 208-885-9358. 139 D
lsalsbur@uidaho.edu

SALTALAMACHIA,
Joseph ... 207-948-9205. 211 I
jsalty@unity.edu
SALTER, Anne ... 404-364-8514. 130 A
asalter@oglethorpe.edu
SALTER, James ... 415-457-4440... 42 J
SALTER, Phyllis ... 937-512-3700. 388 O
phyllis.salter@sinclair.edu
SALTER, Sid ... 662-325-7454. 268 D
ss51@msstate.edu
SALTER-SMITH,
Cassandra, L ... 716-839-8237. 322 E
csalters@daemen.edu
SALTIEL, Henry ... 718-482-6120. 318 F
hsaltiel@lagcc.cuny.edu
SALTON, Susan ... 607-431-4465. 325 F
saltons@hartwick.edu
SALTONSTALL,
Thomas, L ... 617-228-3311. 231 C
tlsaltonstall@bhcc.mass.edu
SALTZMAN, Robert ... 516-463-4134. 326 D
robert.saltzman@hofstra.edu
SALVA, William, M ... 914-337-9300. 321 E
william.salva@concordia-ny.edu
SALVADOR, Daniel ... 319-656-2447. 182 D
SALVAGE, Lynn ... 718-818-6470. 339 H
SALVAGGIO, Brian ... 508-531-1276. 229 D
SALVAIL, Leslie, H ... 410-777-2709. 213 D
lhsalvail@aacc.edu
SALVATO, Alfred ... 215-503-7570. 434 C
alfred.salvato@jefferson.edu
SALVATO, Scott ... 516-323-3225. 331 J
ssalvato@molloy.edu
SALVATORE, Loretta ... 318-869-5013. 201 H
lsalvatore@centenary.edu
SALVESEN, Guy ... 858-646-3114... 64 E
gsalvesen@sanfordburnham.org
SALVIDIO, Nanci ... 413-572-8123. 230 F
nsalvidio@westfield.ma.edu
SALVO, Robyn ... 732-571-3470. 303 C
rsalvo@monmouth.edu
SALVUCCI, James ... 443-334-2215. 218 E
jsalvucci@stevenson.edu
SALYERS, Catherine, A ... 219-866-6187. 172 E
cathys@saintjoe.edu
SALZMAN, Christine ... 201-714-2198. 302 D
csalzman@hccc.edu
SALZMANN, Nick ... 847-628-2492. 149 B
nsalzmann@judsonu.edu
SAM, David ... 847-214-7374. 144 F
dsam@elgin.edu
SAM, David, A ... 540-423-9039. 512 E
dsam@germanna.edu
SAM, Mary ... 218-855-8159. 258 B
msam@clcmn.edu
SAMA, Eduardo ... 305-553-6065. 103 L
esama@careercollege.edu
SAMAHA, Ahmed ... 803-641-3411. 448 A
ahmeds@usca.edu
SAMALOT-RIVERA, OP,
Yamil, A ... 787-786-4508. 548 K
ysamalot@cedoc.edu
SAMAN, Sarmad ... 508-678-2811. 231 B
sarmad.saman@bristolcc.edu
SAMANGO, Melissa ... 610-526-6196. 417 H
msamango@harcum.edu
SAMANIEGO, Sue ... 719-384-6821... 83 M
sue.samaniego@ojc.edu
SAMANT, Ajay ... 904-620-2590. 116 B
ajay.samant@unf.edu
SAMANTA, Shivajl ... 434-961-5229. 513 F
ssamanta@pvcc.edu
SAMARKOS, Christy ... 619-594-4609... 35 D
csamarko@mail.sdsu.edu
SAMBERG, Carol ... 212-875-4680. 314 C
csamberg@bankstreet.edu
SAMBERG, Wendy ... 203-285-2108... 88 E
wsamberg@gwcc.commnet.edu
SAMDAHL, JR.,
Donald, H ... 540-464-7228. 515 B
samdahldh@vmi.edu
SAMDPERIL, Debra ... 617-369-3116. 236 F
dsamdperil@smfa.edu
SAMEK, Linda ... 503-554-2871. 403 C
lsamek@georgefox.edu
SAMEK, Tom ... 503-375-7031. 403 A
tsamek@corban.edu
SAMENFINK, William, H 978-232-2402. 226 C
bsamenfi@endicott.edu
SAMET, Jan ... 301-696-3934. 215 D
jsamet@hood.edu
SAMHAN, Tisha, L ... 318-795-4215. 205 F
tisha.samhan@lsus.edu
SAMHAT, Nayef, H ... 864-597-4010. 449 I
president@wofford.edu
SAMIA, Cris ... 425-564-2973. 517 A
cris.samia@bellevuecollege.edu
SAMIIAN, Vida ... 559-278-3056... 33 D
vida_samiian@csufresno.edu
SAMITORE, Wendy ... 509-527-4300. 524 H
wendy.samitore@wwcc.edu

SAMMAKIA, Bahgat ... 607-777-4818. 341 E
bahgat@binghamton.edu
SAMMARCO, Ed ... 800-955-2527. 274 I
esammarco@grantham.edu
SAMMARCO, Erica, C ... 716-888-2100. 316 C
sammarce@canisius.edu
SAMMARTINO, Hallie, G 718-990-2781. 339 A
sammarth@stjohns.edu
SAMMIS, Robert ... 626-914-8550... 38 K
rsammis@citruscollege.edu
SAMMONS, Gregory, S .. 607-587-3911. 345 D
sammongs@alfredstate.edu
SAMMONS, Gregory, S .. 607-587-3992. 345 D
sammongs@alfredstate.edu
SAMMONS, Kenneth, R .. 509-313-6951. 520 A
ksammons@plant.gonzaga.edu
SAMMONS, Morgan ... 415-955-2066... 26 L
msammons@alliant.edu
SAMOLEWICZ, Mark ... 201-216-5218. 307 E
msamolew@stevens.edu
SAMOLEWSKI,
Patrick, C ... 989-964-4221. 249 G
pcs@svsu.edu
SAMORA, Tracy ... 719-549-2850... 80 K
tracy.samora@colostate-pueblo.edu
SAMP, Mike ... 307-766-5188. 543 I
bowhntr@uwyo.edu
SAMPERTON, Amy ... 910-678-8236. 360 D
samperta@faytechcc.edu
SAMPH, Thomas ... 203-596-4652... 90 I
tsamph@post.edu
SAMPITE, Chris ... 318-869-5018. 201 H
csampite@centenary.edu
SAMPLE, Bradford, W ... 423-775-7232. 453 E
bradford.sample@bryan.edu
SAMPLE, Mark ... 704-991-0247. 364 C
jsample7479@stanly.edu
SAMPLE, Michael ... 812-855-0850. 167 E
mmsample@indiana.edu
SAMPLE, Mike ... 812-855-0850. 167 F
mmsample@indiana.edu
SAMPLE, Rick, A ... 301-369-2800. 213 G
rsample@capitol-college.edu
SAMPLE, Steven, B ... 213-740-5400... 74 A
SAMPLER, Jason ... 337-550-1302. 205 B
jsampler@lsue.edu
SAMPLES, Donald, A ... 423-439-7457. 459 C
samplesd@etsu.edu
SAMPLES, Jim ... 562-903-4751... 29 L
jim.samples@biola.edu
SAMPLES, Robert, D ... 314-516-5665. 283 E
bob@umsl.edu
SAMPLEY, Curtis ... 334-387-3877..... 1 E
curtissampley@amridgeuniversity.edu
SAMPSON, Allison ... 213-621-2200... 40 B
SAMPSON, Betty, J ... 509-865-8600. 520 D
sampson_b@heritage.edu
SAMPSON, Christina ... 304-829-7401. 526 D
csampson@bethanywv.edu
SAMPSON, Christopher .. 920-465-2527. 536 F
sampsonc@uwgb.edu
SAMPSON, Connie, B ... 404-413-3230. 126 E
csampson@gsu.edu
SAMPSON, David, G ... 518-381-1370. 340 G
sampsodg@sunysccc.edu
SAMPSON, Diana ... 206-546-4512. 523 F
dsampson@shoreline.edu
SAMPSON, Mark ... 412-731-6000. 431 G
msampson@rpts.edu
SAMPSON, Marsha ... 406-657-2085. 287 C
msampson@msubillings.edu
SAMPSON, Michael ... 928-523-2611... 16 C
michael.sampson@nau.edu
SAMPSON, Robert ... 401-841-1323. 545 A
SAMPSON, Sharon ... 412-731-8690. 431 G
bookstore@rpts.edu
SAMPSON, Sharon ... 412-731-8690. 431 G
ssampson@rpts.edu
SAMPSON, Sonya ... 207-755-5246. 210 J
ssampson@cmcc.edu
SAMPSON, Therese ... 609-343-5116. 299 A
sampson@atlantic.edu
SAMPSON, Zora, J ... 608-342-1688. 537 D
sampsonz@uwplatt.edu
SAMRA, Rajinder ... 925-424-1027... 37 L
rsamra@laspositascollege.edu
SAMS, Aaron ... 412-731-8690. 431 G
asams@rpts.edu
SAMS, Catherine, T ... 864-656-4233. 442 C
willsam@clemson.edu
SAMS, Susan ... 714-997-6829... 38 A
sams@chapman.edu
SAMS, Timothy, E ... 518-276-6201. 337 I
samst@rpi.edu
SAMSA, Heather ... 706-886-6831. 133 A
hsamsa@tfc.edu
SAMSON, Keri ... 563-589-3775. 182 J
ksamson@dbq.edu
SAMSON, Kim, M ... 218-477-2133. 259 H
samson@mnstate.edu

SAMUEL, Bryan ... 423-425-5670. 463 D
bryan-samuel@utc.edu
SAMUEL, Ginny ... 973-408-3258. 301 C
vsamuel@drew.edu
SAMUEL, Jacinta ... 692-625-6724. 546 F
jsamuel@cmi.edu
SAMUEL LOFTUS,
Barbara ... 570-674-6195. 424 A
bloftus@misericordia.edu
SAMUELS, A. Dexter ... 615-963-5646. 459 E
asamuels01@tnstate.edu
SAMUELS, Darlette, C ... 731-426-7595. 455 J
dsamuels@lanecollege.edu
SAMUELS, Deby, K ... 615-966-7133. 456 B
deby.samuels@lipscomb.edu
SAMUELS, Diana ... 410-276-0306. 218 D
dsamuels@host.sdc.edu
SAMUELS, Elena ... 212-220-8061. 317 A
esamuels@bmcc.cuny.edu
SAMUELS, Milton ... 617-427-0060. 232 G
msamuels@rcc.mass.edu
SAMUELS, Rick ... 217-732-3155. 151 C
rsamuels@lincolncollege.edu
SAMUELS, Robert ... 401-874-2288. 440 D
rsamuels@mail.uri.edu
SAMUELS, Sandra ... 973-353-5231. 306 D
szsamuls@newark.rutgers.edu
SAMUELS, Scott ... 248-218-2057. 249 D
ssamuels@rc.edu
SAMUELS-JONES,
Michelle ... 910-678-1009. 360 D
SAMUELSON, Cecil, O ... 801-422-2521. 495 D
cecil_samuelson@byu.edu
SAMUELSON, Erik ... 425-249-4759. 524 D
erik.samuelson@tlc.edu
SAMUELSON, Pamela ... 570-372-4272. 433 H
samuelson@susqu.edu
SAMUELSON, Scott ... 847-317-4194. 160 M
ssamuels@tiu.edu
SAMUL, Margaret ... 203-582-8431... 91 A
margaret.samul@quinnipiac.edu
SAN FRANCISCO,
Michael ... 806-742-3904. 487 D
michael.sanfrancisco@ttu.edu
SAN JOSE, Rodney ... 386-822-6690. 117 C
rsanjose@stetson.edu
SAN NICOLAS, Heidi, E . 671-735-2481. 546 E
heidisan@ite.net
SAN NICOLAS, Jennifer . 760-384-6221... 49 O
jsannico@cerrocoso.edu
SANAGUSTIN, Mary ... 760-744-1150... 58 D
msanagustin@palomar.edu
SANAI, Fardin ... 518-956-8062. 341 D
fsanai@albany.edu
SANANES, Amram ... 718-339-1090. 351 G
amramsananes@mikdashmelech.org
SANANES, Josh ... 718-339-1090. 351 G
rjsananes@mikdashmelech.org
SANBERG, Paul ... 813-974-3154. 116 C
psanberg@usf.edu
SANBORN, Brett ... 303-220-1200... 78 K
brett.sanborn@cffp.edu
SANBORN, Karen ... 734-432-5843. 246 B
ksanborn@madonna.edu
SANBORN, Merlene ... 207-974-4871. 210 K
msanborn@emcc.edu
SANCHEZ, Angel ... 559-278-3906... 33 D
aansanchez@csufresno.edu
SANCHEZ, Ann ... 914-961-8313. 340 B
aks@svots.edu
SANCHEZ, Anna ... 505-224-4687. 309 E
asanchez420@cnm.edu
SANCHEZ, Bonifacio ... 692-625-3394. 546 F
pecatflo@yahoo.com
SANCHEZ, Cheryl ... 719-336-1516... 82 R
cheryl.sanchez@lamarcc.edu
SANCHEZ, Cheryl, L ... 830-591-7202. 481 C
clsanchez547@swtjc.edu
SANCHEZ, Diane ... 210-829-5866. 490 A
castaned@uiwtx.edu
SANCHEZ, Domingo ... 505-747-2143. 311 E
domingo_sanchez@nnmc.edu
SANCHEZ, Dwight, B ... 404-880-8043. 122 J
dsanchez@cau.edu
SANCHEZ, Elda, E ... 361-593-3805. 484 A
elda.sanchez@tamuk.edu
SANCHEZ, Frank ... 646-664-8759. 316 I
frank.sanchez@cuny.edu
SANCHEZ, Gregory ... 619-388-3354... 62 D
gsanchez@sdccd.edu
SANCHEZ, Hector Ruben 787-751-1912. 551 B
hrsanchez@juris.inter.edu
SANCHEZ, Ines ... 787-850-9348. 554 D
ines.sanchez@upr.edu
SANCHEZ, John ... 210-434-6711. 477 N
jdsanchez@lake.ollusa.edu
SANCHEZ, Jorge, R ... 714-241-6338... 39 I
jsanchez@coastline.edu
SANCHEZ, Jose ... 787-878-5475. 549 L
jsanchez@arecibo.inter.edu

SANCHEZ, Joseph .... 817-735-2522. 490 E
Joseph.Sanchez@unthsc.edu
SANCHEZ, Juan, M .... 512-471-2877. 491 C
jsanchez@austin.utexas.edu
SANCHEZ, Judy .... 623-845-3481... 14 M
judy.sanchez@gcmail.maricopa.edu
SANCHEZ, Leopoldo, A .. 314-863-2772. 272 J
sanchezl@csl.edu
SANCHEZ, Librada .... 973-720-2586. 308 I
sanchezl@wpunj.edu
SANCHEZ, Lisa .... 323-343-3694... 34 A
lsanchez@cslanet.calstate.edu
SANCHEZ, Luis .... 520-494-5266... 12 P
luis.sanchez@centralaz.edu
SANCHEZ, Luiz, P .... 805-922-6966... 26 K
lsanchez@hancockcollege.edu
SANCHEZ, Margaret .... 415-239-3000... 38 L
msanchez@ccsf.edu
SANCHEZ, Mark .... 831-755-6711... 46 G
msanchez@hartnell.edu
SANCHEZ, Mark .... 559-442-8226... 68 I
mark.sanchez@fresnocitycollege.edu
SANCHEZ, Matthew .... 978-665-3454. 229 E
msanche2@fitchburgstate.edu
SANCHEZ, Nicolas .... 928-855-7812... 15 L
nsanchez@mohave.edu
SANCHEZ, Omar .... 305-821-3333. 105 A
omarsnc@fnu.edu
SANCHEZ, Pete .... 901-381-3939. 464 C
pete@visible.edu
SANCHEZ, Ramiro .... 805-289-6464... 74 H
rsanchez@vcccd.edu
SANCHEZ, Rebecca .... 951-343-4236... 30 H
rsanchez@calbaptist.edu
SANCHEZ, Roxanne .... 210-434-6711. 477 N
rlsanchez@lake.ollusa.edu
SANCHEZ, Samuel .... 787-751-1912. 551 B
ssanchez@juris.inter.edu
SANCHEZ, Sandra .... 310-233-4041... 51 H
sanches@lahc.edu
SANCHEZ, Steven .... 314-977-2611. 281 I
ssanche6@slu.edu
SANCHEZ, Willie .... 402-363-5620. 293 I
willie.sanchez@york.edu
SANCHEZ, Xiomara .... 787-743-4041. 548 H
xsanchez@columbiaco.edu
SANCILIO, Leonard .... 585-245-5706. 343 C
sancilio@geneseo.edu
SANCOMB, Danny .... 304-243-2365. 531 H
athletics@wju.edu
SANDBERG, Curtis .... 859-985-3208. 192 F
curtis_sandberg@berea.edu
SANDBERG, Gary .... 614-236-7737. 375 H
gsandberg@capital.edu
SANDBERG, Peter .... 507-786-3611. 264 B
sandberg@stolaf.edu
SANDBOTHE, Lindsay ...... 312-461-0600. 139 H
lsandbothe@aaart.edu
SANDBOTHE, Robin .... 913-667-5700. 185 J
rsandbothe@cbts.edu
SANDBULTE, Deb .... 712-707-7224. 181 H
debfs@nwciowa.edu
SANDE, Jeff, A .... 218-755-3988. 258 A
jsande@bemidjistate.edu
SANDE, Nora .... 503-552-1531. 404 H
nsande@ncnm.edu
SANDEEN, Beverly, A ...... 916-568-3075... 52 K
sandeen@losrios.edu
SANDEEN, Cathy .... 310-825-5551... 71 C
csandeen@unex.ucla.edu
SANDEL, Robert, H .... 540-857-7311. 514 E
rsandel@virginiawestern.edu
SANDELL, Julie .... 617-358-5846. 224 D
jsandell@bu.edu
SANDELL, Stanley, C .... 310-233-4181... 51 H
sandelsc@lahc.edu
SANDER, Dennis, M .... 620-417-1018. 190 F
dennis.sander@sccc.edu
SANDER, Jean, E .... 405-744-6651. 397 H
jean.sander@okstate.edu
SANDER, Richard, L .... 423-439-4343. 459 C
sander@etsu.edu
SANDERLIN,
September, C .... 757-683-4324. 507 N
ssanderl@odu.edu
SANDERS, Alphonso .... 662-254-3484. 269 A
asanders@mvsu.edu
SANDERS, Angela .... 501-370-5259... 22 F
asanders@philander.edu
SANDERS, Art .... 515-271-3172. 177 K
arthur.sanders@drake.edu
SANDERS, Barbara .... 509-777-4303. 525 F
bsanders@whitworth.edu
SANDERS, Beth .... 808-322-4850. 136 F
sanders@hawaii.edu
SANDERS, Blanche .... 601-877-6350. 265 G
blanche@alcorn.edu
SANDERS, Brian .... 209-575-6701... 77 J
sandersb@mjc.edu
SANDERS, Chris .... 314-744-5345. 278 B
sanders@mobap.edu
SANDERS, Clifton .... 801-957-5180. 498 B
clifton.sanders@slcc.edu
SANDERS, Deborah, L ..... 903-923-3239. 486 A
deborah.sanders@tstc.edu
SANDERS, Diana .... 918-293-5222. 398 B
diana.sanders@okstate.edu
SANDERS, Emily, J .... 608-246-6073. 540 C
ejsanders@madisoncollege.edu
SANDERS, Frances .... 913-621-8716. 186 C
sanders@donnelly.edu
SANDERS, George, E ...... 904-646-2205. 105 E
gsanders@fscj.edu
SANDERS, Gwendolyn .... 252-335-3226. 367 C
gsanders@mail.ecsu.edu
SANDERS, J. Michael ..... 806-742-2120. 487 D
mike.sanders@ttu.edu
SANDERS, JC .... 405-224-3140. 401 E
jsanders@usao.edu
SANDERS, Jerry, R .... 651-696-6700. 256 L
sanders@macalester.edu
SANDERS, Jill .... 503-552-1994. 404 H
jsanders@ncnm.edu
SANDERS, Jo-Ann .... 419-448-2288. 380 G
jsanders@heidelberg.edu
SANDERS, Jocelyn .... 423-425-4515. 463 D
jocelyn-sanders@utc.edu
SANDERS, Joe .... 432-552-2620. 493 D
sanders_j@utpb.edu
SANDERS, Joe .... 432-552-2740. 493 D
sanders_j@utpb.edu
SANDERS, John .... 740-753-6449. 380 K
sandersjohn@hocking.edu
SANDERS, John .... 336-316-2134. 355 A
sandersja@guilford.edu
SANDERS, John, J .... 843-792-3811. 445 B
sanderjj@musc.edu
SANDERS, Joseph, R ...... 856-225-6286. 306 C
joe.sanders@camden.rutgers.edu
SANDERS, Judy .... 501-977-2016... 25 C
sanders@uaccm.edu
SANDERS, Karen .... 386-506-3050. 101 G
sanderk@DaytonaState.edu
SANDERS, Karen, A .... 217-786-2784. 151 F
karen.sanders@llcc.edu
SANDERS, Kimberly .... 713-525-3889. 490 L
sanderk1@stthom.edu
SANDERS, Lakisia .... 478-825-6363. 124 H
sandersl@fvsu.edu
SANDERS, Laura .... 315-364-3221. 350 E
lsanders@wells.edu
SANDERS, Laurie .... 515-244-4221. 175 C
lauries@aib.edu
SANDERS, Lee .... 870-574-4455... 23 G
lsanders@sautech.edu
SANDERS, Leon .... 318-274-6401. 207 E
sandersl@gram.edu
SANDERS, Liz .... 312-362-5289. 143 H
lsander3@depaul.edu
SANDERS, Marcy .... 817-272-2101. 491 B
sanders@uta.edu
SANDERS, Michael .... 863-638-7239. 119 C
michael.sanders@warner.edu
SANDERS, Nancy, A .... 815-395-5100. 158 A
nancysanders@sacn.edu
SANDERS, Nena, F .... 205-726-2861..... 6 F
nfsander@samford.edu
SANDERS, Paula .... 713-348-4002. 479 A
sanders@rice.edu
SANDERS, Philip .... 609-984-4099. 308 A
psanders@tesc.edu
SANDERS, Robert .... 662-254-3478. 269 A
rlsanders@mvsu.edu
SANDERS, Robert .... 334-241-5477..... 7 H
rsanders@troy.edu
SANDERS, Ron .... 254-867-4834. 486 B
ron.sanders@tstc.edu
SANDERS, Sal .... 330-941-3091. 394 A
sasanders@ysu.edu
SANDERS, Sally .... 816-271-4287. 279 A
sanders@missouriwestern.edu
SANDERS, Sandra .... 816-584-6816. 280 C
sandra.sanders@park.edu
SANDERS, Sue, E .... 817-515-4573. 482 B
sue.sanders@tccd.edu
SANDERS, RSM,
Susan, M .... 773-298-3981. 158 E
sanders@sxu.edu
SANDERS, Tiffany .... 256-395-2211..... 7 C
tsanders@suscc.edu
SANDERS, Timothy, J ..... 765-494-6838. 171 M
sanderstj@purdue.edu
SANDERS, Tom .... 330-337-6403. 373 F
college@awc.edu
SANDERS, Tommy .... 903-923-2076. 471 J
tsanders@etbu.edu
SANDERS, Tricia .... 218-281-8326. 264 E
sand0803@umn.edu
SANDERS, W, C .... 507-389-7299. 261 E
wc.sanders@southcentral.edu
SANDERS,
Wm Gerard (Gerry), Y .. 210-458-4313. 492 C
gerry.sanders@utsa.edu
SANDERS-KELLEY, Kelly 731-352-4000. 453 D
kelleyk@bethelu.edu
SANDERS-MCMURTRY,
Kijua .... 404-471-6064. 119 I
ksandersmcmurtry@agnesscott.edu
SANDERSON, Carla, D ... 731-661-5355. 462 F
csanders@uu.edu
SANDERSON,
Francie, W .... 919-866-5944. 364 G
fwsanderson@waketech.edu
SANDERSON, Karri .... 402-465-2411. 291 G
ksanders@nebrwesleyan.edu
SANDERSON, Larry .... 575-492-2787. 310 G
lsanderson@nmjc.edu
SANDFORD, Art .... 805-289-6587... 74 H
asandford@vcccd.edu
SANDGREN, Eric .... 501-569-3333... 24 B
exsandgren@ualr.edu
SANDIDGE, Steven .... 817-598-6421. 494 G
ssandidge@wc.edu
SANDIDGE, Will .... 434-832-7641. 512 A
sandidgew@cvcc.vccs.edu
SANDIFER, Betty .... 843-792-0552. 445 B
sandifbw@musc.edu
SANDIFER, Joyce .... 504-520-5230. 209 D
jsandife@xula.edu
SANDIFER, William, A .... 803-584-3446. 448 D
sandifea@mailbox.sc.edu
SANDLER, Chaya .... 312-752-2584. 149 E
chaya.sandler@kendall.edu
SANDLIN, Rebecca .... 540-375-2400. 509 B
sandlin@roanoke.edu
SANDMAN, Elizabeth ...... 740-774-6300. 378 J
esandman@daymarcollege.edu
SANDMAN, Joseph, G .... 740-376-4711. 383 E
jgs001@marietta.edu
SANDMANN, Warren .... 973-720-2122. 308 I
sandmannw@wpunj.edu
SANDMANN, Warren .... 507-389-1333. 259 G
warren.sandmann@mnsu.edu
SANDNESS, Debra .... 701-224-5524. 372 B
debra.sandness@bismarckstate.edu
SANDONE, Dawn .... 217-424-3593. 153 C
dsandone@millikin.edu
SANDOVAL, Derek, M .... 830-703-1555. 481 C
mdsandoval@swtjc.edu
SANDOVAL, Greg .... 951-571-6120... 60 K
greg.sandoval@mvc.edu
SANDOVAL, James, W ... 951-827-4641... 71 E
james.sandoval@ucr.edu
SANDOVAL, Nikki .... 480-557-2314... 18 I
nikki.sandoval@phoenix.edu
SANDOVAL, Victor, A ..... 801-878-1401. 295 E
vsandoval@roseman.edu
SANDQUIST, Rick, A ...... 515-574-1347. 179 D
sandquist@iowacentral.edu
SANDROCK, Teresa, L .... 904-620-2903. 116 B
teresa.sandrock@unf.edu
SANDS, Bryan, A .... 714-879-3901... 47 K
basands@hiu.edu
SANDS, Charles .... 951-343-4619... 30 H
csands@calbaptist.edu
SANDS, Deanna .... 206-296-5696. 523 E
sandsd@seattleu.edu
SANDS, Harlan, M .... 205-975-9934..... 8 E
hsands@uab.edu
SANDS, Timothy, D .... 765-494-9709. 171 M
tsands@purdue.edu
SANDS-VANKERK,
Linda .... 630-942-2621. 142 G
sands-vankerkl@cod.edu
SANDSTROM, Kent .... 701-231-9588. 371 G
kent.sandstrom@ndsu.edu
SANDSTROM, Lynne .... 707-826-4031... 35 C
les37@humboldt.edu
SANDT, Jennifer, A .... 410-334-2911. 221 D
jsandt@worwic.edu
SANDU, Terri, B .... 440-365-5222. 383 B
SANDUM TUNE, Rachel . 937-327-7411. 393 E
rtune@wittenberg.edu
SANDUSKY, Brian .... 989-837-4459. 248 C
sandusky@northwood.edu
SANDWEISS, Daniel, H .. 207-581-3217. 212 B
daniel@maine.edu
SANDY, Michael, B .... 717-780-3277. 417 I
mbsandy@hacc.edu
SANDY, Paula .... 716-614-6220. 334 E
psandy@niagaracc.suny.edu
SANER, Eileen .... 574-296-6233. 163 J
esaner@ambs.edu
SANFILIPPO, Rick .... 610-526-4600. 417 H
rsanfilippo@harcum.edu
SANFILIPPO, Sarah .... 802-447-6311. 500 D
ssanfilippo@svc.edu
SANFORD, Debra .... 301-624-2583. 214 H
dsanford@frederick.edu
SANFORD, Delacy .... 904-470-8290. 102 A
dsanford@ewc.edu
SANFORD, Janell .... 757-826-1883. 502 G
SANFORD, Jennifer .... 707-826-3236... 35 C
jls7003@humboldt.edu
SANFORD, Matthew .... 607-431-4460. 325 F
sanfordm@hartwick.edu
SANFORD, Susan, H ...... 315-470-6604. 345 B
shsanfor@esf.edu
SANGER, Bryna .... 212-229-8947. 332 E
sanger@newschool.edu
SANGER, Laurel, T .... 585-292-3398. 332 A
lsanger@monroecc.edu
SANGER, Patrick .... 281-756-3663. 465 D
psanger@alvincollege.edu
SANGHVI, Kamlesh .... 847-543-2974. 143 A
ksanghvi@clcillinois.edu
SANGREY-BILLY, Cory .... 406-395-4313. 288 D
csangrey@stonechild.edu
SANIDAD, Daniel .... 408-855-5139... 75 K
daniel.sanidad@wvmccd.cc.ca.us
SANJANA, Espi .... 415-351-3550... 62 G
esanjana@sfai.edu
SANKEY, Dean, A .... 715-232-2258. 538 B
sankeyd@uwstout.edu
SANKO, Jerry .... 620-672-5641. 190 A
jerrys@prattcc.edu
SANKS GUIDRY,
Beverly .... 909-469-5341... 76 B
bguidry@westernu.edu
SANNS, Aaron, D .... 208-496-1610. 137 H
sannsa@byui.edu
SANO, Michael .... 415-282-7600... 27 L
michaelsano@actcm.edu
SANSEVERE, Susanne ..... 201-360-4284. 302 D
ssansevere@hccc.edu
SANSEVIRO, Michael, L . 770-423-6310. 127 N
msansevi@kennesaw.edu
SANSING, Joyce .... 706-355-5018. 120 J
jsansing@athenstech.edu
SANSING, Lucille .... 510-215-0277... 28 M
lsansing@argosy.edu
SANSING, Perry .... 662-329-7104. 268 E
psansing@pres.muw.edu
SANSOLA, Steve .... 845-575-3000. 330 D
steve.sansola@marist.edu
SANSOM, Mel .... 501-279-4485... 21 C
msansom@harding.edu
SANSON, Calvin .... 352-638-9729... 99 B
csanson@beaconcollege.edu
SANSON, Jerry .... 318-473-6470. 205 A
jsanson@lsua.edu
SANSONE, Joseph .... 201-360-4006. 302 D
jsansone@hccc.edu
SANSONE, Linda .... 716-827-2496. 348 G
sansonel@trocaire.edu
SANT, Anne, M .... 508-565-1343. 237 A
asant@stonehill.edu
SANTANA, Arleen .... 787-264-1912. 551 A
arleen-santana@sg.inter.edu
SANTANA, Giovanny .... 718-855-3661. 327 B
SANTANA, Pedro .... 609-652-4601. 305 C
pedro.santana@stockton.edu
SANTANA, Yara .... 312-427-2737. 148 L
6santanay@jmls.edu
SANTANA-BRAVO,
Maydel .... 305-348-1555. 115 B
santanam@fiu.edu
SANTEE, Wendi .... 913-758-6120. 191 B
wendi.santee@stmary.edu
SANTELL, Candice .... 937-769-1343. 373 H
csantell@antioch.edu
SANTELL, Ross .... 859-442-4146. 195 B
ross.santell@kctcs.edu
SANTIAGO, Alfonso .... 787-841-2000. 552 B
alfonso.santiago@pucpr.edu
SANTIAGO, Alma, L .... 787-841-2000. 552 B
alsantiago@pucpr.edu
SANTIAGO, Cástula .... 787-850-0000. 554 D
castula.santiago@upr.edu
SANTIAGO, Cariluz .... 787-841-2000. 552 B
cariluz_santiago@pucpr.edu
SANTIAGO, Carol .... 787-620-2040. 547 C
csantiago@aupr.edu
SANTIAGO, Dalia .... 787-882-2065. 553 A
orientacion@unitecpr.net
SANTIAGO, Edny .... 787-864-2222. 550 D
edsantiago@inter.edu
SANTIAGO, Elias .... 787-765-1915. 551 C
esantiago@opto.inter.edu
SANTIAGO, JR., George 516-918-3601. 315 G
gsantiago@bcl.edu
SANTIAGO, Jaime .... 787-250-1912. 550 E
jaimesantiago@metro.inter.edu
SANTIAGO, Judith .... 212-343-1234. 331 D
jsantiago@mcny.edu
SANTIAGO, Kenneth .... 773-489-8989. 142 F
ksantiago6@ccc.edu
SANTIAGO, Lori .... 918-857-3711... 18 I
lori.santiago@phoenix.edu
SANTIAGO, Lori .... 918-851-3711... 18 I
lori.santiago@phoenix.edu

SANTIAGO, Luis, R .... 787-738-2161. 554 C
luis.galarza30@upr.edu
SANTIAGO, Marilia .... 787-664-0466. 555 C
marilia.santiago1@upr.edu
SANTIAGO, Marya, Z ...... 787-844-2318. 555 A
marya.santiago@upr.edu
SANTIAGO, Miguel .... 787-600-6297. 555 C
miguel.santiago16@upr.edu
SANTIAGO, Milton .... 413-572-8241. 230 F
santiagom@westfield.ma.edu
SANTIAGO, Rafael .... 787-780-0070. 547 G
rsantiago@caribbean.edu
SANTIAGO, Ruben .... 787-815-0000. 553 I
ruben.santiago@upr.edu
SANTIAGO, Soriel .... 787-815-0000. 553 I
soriel.santiago@upr.edu
SANTIAGO, Victor .... 787-857-3600. 550 A
vsantiago@br.inter.edu
SANTIAGO, Yinaira .... 787-260-5665. 550 F
yinsant@ponce.inter.edu
SANTIAGO ANADON,
Héctor .... 787-265-3850. 554 E
hector.santiago15@upr.edu
SANTIAGO-CANET,
Jaime, L .... 787-841-2000. 552 B
jstgocan@pucpr.edu
SANTIAGO GABRIELINI,
Wilma .... 787-265-3862. 554 E
wilma.santiago1@upr.edu
SANTIAGO ROSADO,
Lydia, E .... 787-863-2390. 550 C
lydia.santiago@fajardo.inter.edu
SANTIAGO-TORO,
Clarissa .... 787-723-4481. 548 A
centro@ceaprc.edu
SANTIAGO VELAZQUEZ,
U. Birilo .... 787-890-2681. 553 H
birilo.santiago@upr.edu
SANTILLI, Nick .... 216-373-5310. 385 G
nsantilli@ndc.edu
SANTILLI, Patricia .... 508-286-3857. 238 B
psantill@wheatonma.edu
SANTINI, Cathy .... 925-969-3584... 49 B
csantini@jfku.edu
SANTIROCCO,
Matthew, S .... 212-998-2197. 334 D
matthew.santirocco@nyu.edu
SANTIVASCI, Joseph ...... 610-436-3085. 430 A
jsantivasci@wcupa.edu
SANTIZO, Roberto .... 847-628-2532. 149 B
rsantizo@judsonu.edu
SANTOMAURO,
Kristine, M .... 302-225-6233... 93 H
santomk@gbc.edu
SANTORA, Anthony .... 908-737-6000. 302 F
afs@kean.edu
SANTORE, JR., Chuck ... 724-439-4900. 421 F
csantore@laurel.edu
SANTORO, C. James ...... 402-449-2910. 289 H
jsantoro@graceu.edu
SANTOS, Adele Naude .... 617-253-4403. 233 B
SANTOS, Allison .... 312-280-3500. 147 D
asantos@aii.edu
SANTOS, Ana, L .... 973-642-8392. 307 D
ana.santos@shu.edu
SANTOS, Carlo .... 408-288-3761... 63 N
carlo.santos@sjeccd.org
SANTOS, Carmen, K .... 671-735-5548. 546 C
carmen.kweksantos@guamcc.edu
SANTOS, Carol .... 508-999-8388. 229 A
csantos1@umassd.edu
SANTOS, Catherine .... 315-312-2500. 344 A
catherine.santos@oswego.edu
SANTOS, Claudio .... 787-844-8621. 555 A
claudio.santos@upr.edu
SANTOS, Cynthia .... 713-221-8136. 489 D
santosc@uhd.edu
SANTOS, Denny .... 914-251-6320. 344 D
denny.santos@purchase.edu
SANTOS, Helena .... 617-243-2127. 227 K
hsantos@lasell.edu
SANTOS, Leslie .... 209-228-2977... 71 D
LSantos@UCMerced.edu
SANTOS, Mae .... 323-343-3555... 34 A
msantos@cslanet.calstatela.edu
SANTOS, Maria del, C .... 787-743-7979. 552 I
ut_masantos@suagm.edu
SANTOS, Maricarmen ..... 787-743-7979. 552 I
m_santos@suagm.edu
SANTOS, Maritza .... 787-878-5475. 549 L
msantos@arecibo.inter.edu
SANTOS, Matthew .... 610-683-4113. 429 A
santos@kutztown.edu
SANTOS, Paul .... 704-330-6689. 359 C
paul.santos@cpcc.edu
SANTOS, Ramon .... 305-223-4561. 112 B
santos@sjvcs.edu
SANTOS, Rick .... 559-442-8222... 68 I
rick.santos@fresnocitycollege.edu
SANTOS, Robert .... 212-650-8830. 317 D
rdsantos@ccny.cuny.edu

SANTOS, Samuel .... 415-239-3762... 38 L
ssantos@ccsf.edu
SANTOS, Sandra .... 787-758-2525. 554 F
sandra.santos@upr.edu
SANTOS, Victor .... 508-362-2131. 231 D
vsantos@capecod.edu
SANTOS DE BARONA,
Maryann .... 765-494-2336. 171 M
msdb@purdue.edu
SANTOS-GEORGE,
Arlene .... 847-543-2310. 143 A
asgeorge@clcillinois.edu
SANTOS-PEREZ,
Kennia, I .... 787-480-2405. 548 G
kisantos@sanjuancapital.com
SANTOSTEFANO,
Donald .... 717-867-6341. 421 H
facilities-services@lvc.edu
SANTOTOMAS, Dennis ... 671-735-5554. 546 C
dennis.santotomas@guamcc.edu
SANTUCCI, Wayne .... 212-517-0544. 330 E
wsantucci@mmm.edu
SANYAL, Rajib, N .... 765-285-8192. 164 B
rnsanyal@bsu.edu
SANYAL, Sabyasachi ...... 972-721-5156. 488 F
ssanyal@udallas.edu
SAO, Ry-Yon .... 206-239-4500. 517 M
rgsao@cityu.edu
SAPARILAS, John, W ..... 919-866-5450. 364 G
jwsaparilas@waketech.edu
SAPATA, Tony .... 708-237-5050. 155 B
tsapata@nc.edu
SAPERSTEIN, Shari .... 954-262-7201. 109 K
ssaperst@nova.edu
SAPERSTONE,
Barbara, L .... 703-323-3222. 513 C
bsaperstone@nvcc.edu
SAPHIRE, Diane, G .... 210-999-8483. 488 C
dsaphire@trinity.edu
SAPIENZA, Matthew .... 646-746-4275. 316 I
matthew.sapienza@mail.cuny.edu
SAPIENZA, Michael, C .... 423-775-7224. 453 E
misapienza@bryan.edu
SAPIRO, Virginia .... 617-353-2401. 224 D
vsapiro@bu.edu
SAPP, Aimee .... 573-592-4391. 285 D
asapp@williamwoods.edu
SAPP, Buddy .... 912-871-1634. 129 J
bsapp@ogeecheetech.edu
SAPP, David .... 203-254-4000... 89 I
dsapp@fairfield.edu
SAPP, Fred .... 910-672-1204. 367 D
fsapp@uncfsu.edu
SAPP, Geneva .... 509-865-8631. 520 D
sapp_g@heritage.edu
SAPP, Judy .... 606-877-1421. 196 D
judy.sapp@kctcs.edu
SAPP, Marge .... 843-525-8276. 447 C
msapp@tcl.edu
SAPP, Mary, M .... 305-284-3856. 118 F
msapp@miami.edu
SAPP, Sarah .... 662-562-3274. 269 C
ssapp@northwestms.edu
SAPPENFIELD, Elizabeth . 317-738-8075. 165 I
esappenfield@franklincollege.edu
SAPPENFIELD,
George, O .... 336-386-3280. 364 D
sappeng@surry.edu
SAPPINGTON, Eric .... 660-831-4168. 278 I
sappingtone@moval.edu
SAPPINGTON, Lee Ann .. 970-339-6223... 78 C
leeann.sappington@aims.edu
SAPYTA, Lynn .... 630-942-2219. 142 G
sapytal@cod.edu
SARA, Ligaya .... 680-488-2471. 547 B
ligayas@palau.edu
SARA, Tejnder .... 334-727-8704..... 8 A
tsara@tuskegee.edu
SARAC, Isa .... 703-591-7042. 515 A
isarac@viu.edu
SARACENO, William .... 509-542-4408. 518 C
bsaraceno@columbiabasin.edu
SARAJIAN, Charles .... 973-655-7480. 303 D
sarajianc@mail.montclair.edu
SARANTAKOS, Paul .... 217-351-2385. 155 J
psarantakos@parkland.edu
SARAT, Austin, D .... 413-542-2308. 221 G
adsarat@amherst.edu
SARBER, John .... 765-455-9505. 168 A
jrsarber@iuk.edu
SARBER, Sarah .... 765-455-9204. 168 A
shawkins@iuk.edu
SARGE, Billy .... 859-344-3402. 199 H
billy.sarge@thomasmore.edu
SARGEANT, Kari .... 815-802-8256. 149 C
ksargeant@kcc.edu
SARGENT, Anneila, I .... 626-395-6100... 31 E
afs@caltech.edu
SARGENT, Frank, A .... 401-598-4463. 439 B
fsargent@jwu.edu

SARGENT, Gary .... 254-295-4242. 490 B
gsargent@umhb.edu
SARGENT, Jeffrey .... 708-456-0300. 161 A
jsargent@triton.edu
SARGENT, Joe, E .... 423-585-6836. 462 A
joe.sargent@ws.edu
SARGENT, Judy, L .... 701-777-4251. 371 C
judy.sargent@und.edu
SARGENT, Linda .... 618-842-3711. 146 I
sargentl@iecc.edu
SARGENT, Madeline .... 215-568-9215. 423 M
msargent@phmc.org
SARGENT, Mark, L .... 805-565-6007... 76 D
msargent@westmont.edu
SARGENT, Peter, E .... 314-968-7006. 284 N
sargenpe@webster.edu
SARGENT, Sheri .... 507-389-2015. 259 G
sheri.sargent@mnsu.edu
SARIAN, Richard .... 216-421-7432. 377 C
rsarian@cia.edu
SARIKAS, Bridget .... 202-806-2411... 95 G
bridget.sarikas@howard.edu
SARIN, Sanjiv .... 336-334-7920. 367 E
sarin@ncat.edu
SARIN, Sanjiv .... 336-285-2371. 367 E
sarin@ncat.edu
SARK, Donna, L .... 260-422-5561. 167 B
dlsark@indianatech.edu
SARKAR, Amin .... 256-372-5092..... 1 A
amin.sarkar@aamu.edu
SARKAR, Ratna .... 713-348-4293. 479 A
rgs1@rice.edu
SARLES, Harry .... 913-684-3097. 545 E
harry.sarles@us.army.mil
SARMA, Sanjay .... 617-715-4532. 233 B
SARMIENTO, Reine .... 718-482-5414. 318 F
rsarmiento@lagcc.cuny.edu
SARNA, Ruth .... 785-594-8409. 184 C
ruth.sarna@bakeru.edu
SARNOVSKY, Joseph ...... 407-708-2430. 113 E
sarnovsj@seminolestate.edu
SARRAFIAN, Armen .... 312-553-5911. 141 N
asarrafian@ccc.edu
SARRATORE, Steve, T .... 260-481-6536. 168 C
sarrator@ipfw.edu
SARRATORI, Peter .... 315-781-3647. 326 C
sarratori@hws.edu
SARRETT, David, C .... 804-828-7235. 511 F
dcsarrett@vcu.edu
SARRUBBO, Joseph, M . 407-582-2586. 118 M
jsarrubbo@valenciacollege.edu
SARSAR, Saliba .... 732-571-4474. 303 C
sarsar@monmouth.edu
SARTARELLI, Jose, V ..... 304-293-7800. 530 D
jose.sartarelli@mail.wvu.edu
SARTIN, Mici .... 405-691-3800. 396 D
msartin@macu.edu
SARTINI, Chad .... 540-857-8922. 514 E
csartini@virginiawestern.edu
SARTOR, Curtis .... 847-628-1017. 149 B
csartor@judsonu.edu
SARTORI, Lillian .... 212-229-5300. 332 E
sartoril@newschool.edu
SARVELA, Paul .... 618-536-3465. 159 F
psarvela@siu.edu
SARVEY, Sharon .... 252-399-6401. 352 F
sisarvey@barton.edu
SARVIS, Randall, F .... 937-382-6661. 393 B
randy_sarvis@wilmington.edu
SASAKI, Charles .... 808-734-9517. 136 E
sasakich@hawaii.edu
SASS, Michael .... 518-694-7367. 313 B
michael.sass@acphs.edu
SASS, Sharon, A .... 561-868-3147. 110 C
sasss@palmbeachstate.edu
SASS, Terricita, E .... 757-823-8679. 507 M
tesass@nsu.edu
SASSAMAN, Margo, J .... 717-872-3312. 429 D
margo.sassaman@millersville.edu
SASSE, Benjamin, E .... 402-941-6000. 290 K
president@midlandu.edu
SASSER, Jackson, N .... 352-395-5164. 113 C
j.sasser@sfcollege.edu
SASSER, Jennifer .... 503-675-3964. 404 C
jsasser@marylhurst.edu
SASSER, Susan, M .... 919-735-5151. 364 H
msm@waynecc.edu
SASSMAN, Jen, L .... 319-352-8262. 183 E
jennifer.sassman@wartburg.edu
SASSO, Gary, M .... 610-758-3221. 422 A
gms208@lehigh.edu
SASSSER, Craig-Ellis ...... 662-720-7411. 269 B
cesasser@nemcc.edu
SASTRY, S. Shankar .... 510-642-5771... 70 I
sastry@coe.berkeley.edu
SATCHWELL, Carol .... 315-655-7144. 316 E
csatchwell@cazenovia.edu
SATELE, Arleen .... 619-660-4654... 46 D
arleen.satele@gcccd.edu
SATEY, Linda, S .... 828-448-3531. 365 A
lsatey@wpcc.edu

SATHER, Steven, M .... 609-258-6479. 304 E
sather@princeton.edu
SATKOWIAK, Ann, E ...... 865-539-7153. 461 D
asatkowiak@pstcc.edu
SATKOWSKI, John .... 313-845-9636. 243 H
jssatkowski@hfcc.edu
SATKOWSKI, John .... 567-661-7233. 387 L
john_satkowski@owens.edu
SATO, Heidi .... 714-816-0366... 70 A
heidi.sato@trident.edu
SATO, Kay .... 516-299-2584. 329 D
kay.sato@liu.edu
SATO, Sara .... 808-544-0238. 135 F
ssato@hpu.edu
SATO, Tami, A .... 714-449-7447... 67 D
tsato@scco.edu
SATRIANA, Dan .... 970-351-2399... 86 C
dan.satriana@unco.edu
SATTAR, Mo .... 413-565-1000. 222 F
msattar@baypath.edu
SATTERFIELD, Billy .... 281-283-2480. 489 C
satterfield@uhcl.edu
SATTERFIELD, Derick ...... 336-342-4261. 363 C
satterfieldd@rockinghamcc.edu
SATTERFIELD, Jay .... 731-989-6058. 454 J
jsatterfield@fhu.edu
SATTERLEE, David .... 717-801-3244. 417 I
dsatterl@hacc.edu
SATTERLEE, Kevin .... 208-426-1203. 137 G
ksatterl@boisestate.edu
SATTERLEE, Richard .... 718-862-7352. 329 M
richard.satterlee@manhattan.edu
SATTERLY, Amy .... 812-749-1392. 171 K
asatterly@oak.edu
SATTERLY, Eric .... 502-272-8098. 192 E
esatterly@bellarmine.edu
SATTERTHWAITE,
Shad, B .... 405-325-3546. 401 B
shad@ou.edu
SATTERWHITE, Robin ...... 806-743-3223. 487 E
robin.satterwhite@ttuhsc.edu
SATTLER, Brian .... 409-880-8396. 486 F
brian.sattler@lamar.edu
SATTLER, Joan, L .... 309-677-3180. 140 I
jls@bradley.edu
SATZ, Michael .... 208-885-6792. 139 D
msatz@uidaho.edu
SAUBERT, IV, Carl, W ... 636-227-2100. 276 F
carl.saubert@logan.edu
SAUCEDA, Marshall .... 310-338-5808... 53 E
msauceda@lmu.edu
SAUCEDO, Veronica .... 312-935-4536. 156 K
vsaucedo@robertmorris.edu
SAUCHUK, Stacey .... 610-989-1203. 436 D
ssauchuk@vfmac.edu
SAUCIER, Ruth, M .... 360-475-7250. 521 H
rsaucier@olympic.edu
SAUCIER, Todd .... 207-581-1138. 212 B
todd.saucier@umit.maine.edu
SAUDER, Vinita, R .... 423-236-2580. 458 J
sauder@southern.edu
SAUDERS, Charlette, R ... 574-372-5100. 166 B
saudercr@grace.edu
SAUER, Alan, R .... 860-297-2043... 91 F
alan.sauer@trincoll.edu
SAUER, James .... 610-341-5957. 425 I
jsauer@eastern.edu
SAUER, James, L .... 610-341-5957. 415 G
jsauer@eastern.edu
SAUER, Jenni .... 610-647-4400. 418 I
jsauer@immaculata.edu
SAUER, Marty, R .... 630-637-5801. 154 F
mrsauer@noctrl.edu
SAUER, Mike .... 702-895-1073. 294 I
sauer@unlv.edu
SAUER, Peter .... 340-693-1102. 555 E
psauer@live.uvi.edu
SAUERBREI, Aaron .... 319-277-2490. 178 J
aaron.sauerbrei@hawkeyecollege.edu
SAUERESSIG, Sarah .... 785-320-4559. 188 E
sarahsaueressig@matc.net
SAUERS, Darlene .... 724-838-4210. 433 E
sauers@setonhill.edu
SAUERS, Diane .... 256-233-8260..... 1 F
diane.sauers@athens.edu
SAUERWEIN, David, A ... 603-526-3758. 295 I
dsauerwein@colby-sawyer.edu
SAUK, John, J .... 502-852-5295. 200 D
john.sauk@louisville.edu
SAUL, Amy .... 610-861-1509. 424 E
awsaul@moravian.edu
SAUL, J. Beau .... 607-844-8222. 347 I
saulj@TC3.edu
SAUL, Tamika .... 504-286-5279. 206 K
tsaul@suno.edu
SAULE, Mara, R .... 802-656-2020. 500 F
mara.saule@uvm.edu
SAULNIER, Richard .... 212-237-8118. 318 D
rsaulnier@jjay.cuny.edu
SAULS, Con .... 276-466-7935. 514 G
consauls@vic.edu

SAULS, Jina, M 276-935-4349. 502 A
jsauls@asl.edu
SAULS, Steve 305-348-3505. 115 B
steve.sauls@fiu.edu
SAULSBERRY, Keith 334-556-2470. 3 N
ksaulsberry@wallace.edu
SAUM, Rob 386-506-3484. 101 G
saumr@DaytonaState.edu
SAUNDERS, Benjie 540-831-7109. 508 C
bookstor@radford.edu
SAUNDERS, Brian 310-544-6487. 61 H
brian.saunders@usw.salvationarmy.org
SAUNDERS, C. Tom 912-279-5757. 123 B
tsaunders@ccga.edu
SAUNDERS, Gary 336-506-4152. 357 M
gary.saunders@alamancecc.edu
SAUNDERS, Gayle, M 217-875-7200. 156 J
gsaunder@richland.edu
SAUNDERS, Gerry 207-948-9282. 211 I
gsaunders@unity.edu
SAUNDERS, Greer 804-819-4906. 511 G
gsaunders@vccs.edu
SAUNDERS, James 650-508-3502. 56 H
safety@ndnu.edu
SAUNDERS, Joseph 304-766-3353. 530 C
saundejs@wvstateu.edu
SAUNDERS, Julie 713-646-1815. 480 J
jsaunders@stcl.edu
SAUNDERS, Kari 314-744-5301. 278 B
saundersk@mobap.edu
SAUNDERS, Kathy 716-614-6201. 334 E
saundersk@niagaracc.suny.edu
SAUNDERS, Keith 319-335-0553. 175 I
keith-saunders@uiowa.edu
SAUNDERS, Kenneth, K 516-572-7205. 332 C
kenneth.saunders@ncc.edu
SAUNDERS, Kevin 831-582-3397. 34 B
kesaunders@csumb.edu
SAUNDERS, Laura 912-871-1600. 129 J
lsaunders@ogeecheetech.edu
SAUNDERS, Laverna, M 412-396-6136. 415 F
lsaunders@duq.edu
SAUNDERS, Lenore 323-953-4000. 51 G
saundele@lacitycollege.edu
SAUNDERS, Mark 405-878-5402. 399 G
msaunders@stgregorys.edu
SAUNDERS, Martha 850-474-3135. 117 B
msaunders@uwf.edu
SAUNDERS, Mary, M 434-395-2063. 506 J
saundersmm@longwood.edu
SAUNDERS, MaryAnne 505-277-4032. 312 F
masaunders@unm.edu
SAUNDERS, Melinda, D 304-896-7364. 528 F
melinda.saunders@southernwv.edu
SAUNDERS, Robert 334-983-6556. 7 H
rsaunders@troy.edu
SAUNDERS, Scott, D 716-673-3171. 342 A
scott.saunders@fredonia.edu
SAUNDERS, Sharon 850-599-3413. 114 K
sharon.saunders@famu.edu
SAUNDERS, Sharon 434-947-8114. 508 D
ssaunders@randolphcollege.edu
SAUNDERS, Sharon, E 281-649-3206. 473 B
ssaunders@hbu.edu
SAUNDERS, Tanya, R 607-274-3063. 327 E
tsaunders@ithaca.edu
SAUNDERS, William, T 713-313-7846. 485 F
saunders_wt@tsu.edu
SAUNDERS-FIELDS,
Christine, V 718-270-7657. 342 D
christine.saunders-fields@downstate.edu
SAUNDERS-KEURJIAN,
J.C 310-434-4144. 65 A
keurjian_jc@smc.edu
SAUNDERS-WHITE,
Debra 919-530-6104. 368 A
debra.saunders-white@nccu.edu
SAURENNANN, Denise 215-951-2985. 420 B
saurennann@lasalle.edu
SAUTER, David, M 513-529-8781. 384 G
sauterdm@miamioh.edu
SAUTER, Marcia, K 260-399-7700. 174 C
msauter@sf.edu
SAUVE, Stephanie, L 585-340-9588. 320 E
ssauve@crcds.edu
SAVAGE, Deana 432-685-4515. 476 G
docsavage@midland.edu
SAVAGE, Donna 254-968-9246. 483 A
dsavage@tarleton.edu
SAVAGE, Frederick 410-516-8128. 215 H
fsavage@jhu.edu
SAVAGE, Jeffery 575-624-8050. 310 H
savage@nmmi.edu
SAVAGE, Jennie, R 207-768-9551. 212 G
jennie.savage@umpi.edu
SAVAGE, Joe 251-442-7551. 9 A
jsavage@umobile.edu
SAVAGE, Monique, J 517-265-5161. 238 G
msavage@adrian.edu
SAVAGE, Pam 314-744-5331. 278 B
savagep@mobap.edu
SAVAGE, Randy 575-492-2132. 312 M
rsavage@usw.edu
SAVAGE, Robert, S 318-473-6492. 205 A
rsavage@lsua.edu
SAVAGE, Sheryl 508-588-9100. 232 A
SAVAGE, Suzanne 757-233-8736. 515 H
ssavage@vwc.edu
SAVAGIAN, John 414-382-6358. 531 I
john.savagian@alverno.edu
SAVANI, Nimisha 214-648-7144. 493 E
nimisha.savani@utsouthwestern.edu
SAVAS, Steven 781-768-7201. 236 A
steven.savas@regiscollege.edu
SAVERANCE, R. Kyle 843-383-8017. 442 F
ksaverance@coker.edu
SAVIANESO, Michael 201-684-7402. 305 A
msaviane@ramapo.edu
SAVIDGE, Lawrence 843-574-6051. 447 E
lawrence.savidge@tridenttech.edu
SAVILLE, Roy, E 540-831-7812. 508 C
rsaville@radford.edu
SAVIN, Laura 651-846-1469. 261 D
laura.savin@saintpaul.edu
SAVINO, Jeffrey, L 814-641-3301. 419 H
savinoj@juniata.edu
SAVINO, Julie 203-371-7984. 91 C
savinoj@sacredheart.edu
SAVIOR, Valerie 323-259-2623. 56 I
vsavior@oxy.edu
SAVISKI, Mitchell 413-236-3031. 231 A
msaviski@berkshirecc.edu
SAVOCA, Marianna 631-632-6810. 342 C
marianna.savoca@stonybrook.edu
SAVOIE, E. Joseph 337-482-6203. 208 D
president@louisiana.edu
SAVOIE, James 215-717-6394. 435 A
jsavoie@uarts.edu
SAVOIE, Leslie, L 321-674-7362. 104 H
lsavoie@fit.edu
SAVOIE, Michael, P 229-249-4894. 134 B
mpsavoie@valdosta.edu
SAVOIT, Taina, J 337-475-5065. 207 G
tsavoit@mcneese.edu
SAVORY, Paul, A 402-354-7258. 291 B
paul.savory@methodistcollege.edu
SAVUKINAS, Robert 831-242-5828. 544 F
SAWASKY, Joseph 313-577-2095. 252 G
dx0297@wayne.edu
SAWATZKY, Rachel, R 540-432-4133. 504 D
rachel.sawatzky@emu.edu
SAWAY, Sabine 206-239-4500. 517 M
ssaway@cityu.edu
SAWICKI, Jerzy 216-687-3630. 377 F
j.sawicki@csuohio.edu
SAWTELLE, Jimmy 225-308-4420. 202 G
jsawtelle@lctcs.edu
SAWYER, Cary, A 757-455-3310. 515 H
casawyer@vwc.edu
SAWYER, Charles, E 952-888-4777. 263 B
csawyer@nwhealth.edu
SAWYER, Dana, L 302-857-1400. 93 G
dsawyer1@dtcc.edu
SAWYER, Darrell, R 605-394-2667. 452 A
darrell.sawyer@sdsmt.edu
SAWYER, Diane 410-295-5545. 217 G
diane.sawyer@sjca.edu
SAWYER, James 586-445-7196. 246 A
sawyerj@macomb.edu
SAWYER, Janis 501-760-4215. 22 A
jsawyer@npcc.edu
SAWYER, Jenny, L 502-852-4957. 200 D
jsawyer@louisville.edu
SAWYER, John 208-882-1566. 138 H
johnsawyer@nsa.edu
SAWYER, John, E 302-831-2021. 94 B
sawyerj@udel.edu
SAWYER, Jonathan, C 202-319-5619. 94 G
sawyerj@cua.edu
SAWYER, Julie 918-444-3083. 396 H
sawjerjk@nsuok.edu
SAWYER, Kate 912-650-6231. 131 H
kasawyer@southuniversity.edu
SAWYER, Katherine 847-214-7143. 144 F
ksawyer@elgin.edu
SAWYER, Maconica 251-575-8265. 1 C
msawyer@ascc.edu
SAWYER, Michael 307-268-2492. 542 X
msawyer@caspercollege.edu
SAWYER, Rebecca 410-532-5308. 217 E
rsawyer@ndm.edu
SAWYER, Rick 781-736-3600. 224 F
sawyer@brandeis.edu
SAWYER, Sara 603-230-3503. 295 J
ssawyer@ccsnh.edu
SAWYER, Stephen 207-786-6223. 209 F
ssawyer@bates.edu
SAWYER, Terrence, M 410-617-5161. 216 A
tsawyer@loyola.edu
SAWYER, Thomas 812-941-2287. 168 F
sawyer@ius.edu
SAWYER, Wm. Gregory 805-437-8546. 32 I
greg.sawyer@csuci.edu
SAWYERS, Dorret 305-348-2436. 115 B
Dorret.Sawyers@fiu.edu
SAWZAK, Vicki 805-546-3171. 42 C
vsawzak@cuesta.edu
SAX, Christina 717-477-1348. 429 E
csax@ship.edu
SAX, Lisa 518-587-2100. 346 A
lisa.sax@esc.edu
SAXBY, William, R 303-963-3124. 79 C
wsaxby@ccu.edu
SAXENA, Ashok 479-575-3054. 23 I
asaxena@uark.edu
SAXENA, Pradeep 585-594-6430. 337 K
saxenap@roberts.edu
SAXENIAN, AnnaLee 510-642-9980. 70 I
anno@ischool.berkeley.edu
SAXON, Jackie 512-404-4869. 467 A
jsaxon@austinseminary.edu
SAXTON, Jane 425-602-3024. 516 K
jsaxton@bastyr.edu
SAXTON, Tresa, M 336-334-3134. 369 A
tmsaxton@uncg.edu
SAY, Elizabeth, A 818-677-3301. 34 C
elizabeth.say@csun.edu
SAY, Linda 330-337-6403. 373 F
business@awc.edu
SAYEGH, Jean, J 716-376-7509. 327 J
johnsayegh@mail.sunyjcc.edu
SAYERS, Kevin, W 614-236-6943. 375 H
ksayers@capital.edu
SAYERS, Kimberly, J 330-287-0100. 386 F
sayers.1@osu.edu
SAYLER, David, A 513-529-7286. 384 G
saylerda@miamioh.edu
SAYLES, Bridget, M 540-674-3605. 513 B
bsayles@nr.edu
SAYLES, Thomas 213-740-5371. 74 A
sayles@usc.edu
SAYRE, Carmen 503-228-6528. 402 A
csayre@aii.edu
SAYRE, Patrice, M 515-281-6421. 175 G
psayre@iastate.edu
SAYRE, Richard 309-457-2190. 153 D
rsayre@monmouthcollege.edu
SAYRE, William 505-424-2364. 309 J
bsayre@iaia.edu
SAYRES, Byron, A 304-457-6225. 526 A
sayresba@ab.edu
SBALBI, Anthony 413-552-2550. 231 F
asbalbi@hcc.edu
SBRAGIA, Alberta, M 412-624-2137. 435 C
sbragia@pitt.edu
SBREGA, John, J 508-678-2811. 231 B
john.sbrega@bristolcc.edu
SCACCIA, Jeff 479-979-1310. 25 J
jscaccia@ozarks.edu
SCADUTO, Dana, E 717-245-1013. 414 H
scadutod@dickinson.edu
SCADUTO, George, C 904-256-7024. 107 Q
gscadut@ju.edu
SCAFFIDI CLARKE,
Nancy 845-569-3254. 332 B
nancy.scaffidi@msmc.edu
SCAGGS, Randy 870-743-3000. 22 B
rscaggs@northark.edu
SCAGGS, Susan 228-896-2519. 268 C
susan.scaggs@mgccc.edu
SCAGLIONE, Kathy, L 515-271-1460. 177 H
kathleen.scaglione@dmu.edu
SCALA, Kristen 413-236-3065. 231 A
kscale@berkshirecc.edu
SCALA, Natalie 440-375-7530. 382 L
nscala@lec.edu
SCALABRINI, Joanna 914-361-6221. 323 A
SCALDINI, Richard 215-635-7300. 417 C
rscaldini@gratz.edu
SCALES, Alton, D 303-360-4775. 81 C
Alton.Scales@CCAurora.edu
SCALES, Andy 334-291-4960. 2 H
andy.scales@cv.edu
SCALES, Michael 215-204-7184. 433 K
michael.scales@temple.edu
SCALES, Michael, G 845-675-4777. 335 C
president@nyack.edu
SCALES, Suzanne 928-213-6060. 13 E
suzanne.scales@collegeamerica.edu
SCALESSI, Lisa 708-456-0300. 161 A
lscaless@triton.edu
SCALI, Justin 706-776-0104. 130 E
jscali@piedmont.edu
SCALLEY, Elizabeth 787-766-1912. 549 J
escalley@inter.edu
SCALZO-MCNEIL, Anne 508-588-9100. 232 A
SCAMMELL, Richard, E 518-276-6281. 337 I
scammr@rpi.edu
SCANDURA, Teresa, A 305-284-4154. 118 F
scandura@miami.edu
SCANLAN, Melissa 802-831-1066. 500 H
mscanlan@vermontlaw.edu
SCANLAN, Therese, A 773-252-5301. 156 I
therese.scanlan@resu.edu
SCANLON, Angie 317-921-4962. 169 L
ascanlon1@ivytech.edu
SCANLON, Jennifer 207-725-3578. 209 H
jscanlon@bowdoin.edu
SCANLON, Tom 617-732-2775. 233 E
tom.scanlon@mcphs.edu
SCANNELL, Janet 507-222-4077. 254 D
jscannell@carleton.edu
SCANTLING,
Edgar (Ed), L 308-865-8502. 292 H
scantlinge@unk.edu
SCARANO, John 216-397-4717. 381 R
jscarano@jcu.edu
SCARANO, Martin 603-862-2013. 298 C
marty.scarano@unh.edu
SCARANO, Michael 641-585-8163. 183 D
michael.scarano@waldorf.edu
SCARBERRY, Randy 606-218-5208. 200 F
randalscarberry@upike.edu
SCARBORO, Cristofer 570-208-5900. 419 P
cristoferscarboro@kings.edu
SCARBORO, Donna 202-994-6360. 95 D
scarboro@gwu.edu
SCARBORO, Kim 850-973-1613. 109 H
scarborok@nfcc.edu
SCARBORO, Lynne, B 310-338-5236. 53 E
lscarbor@lmu.edu
SCARBOROUGH,
Donald, A 336-841-9135. 355 C
dscarbor@highpoint.edu
SCARBOROUGH,
Scott, L 419-530-2739. 392 B
scott.scarborough@utoledo.edu
SCARBROUGH,
Jeremiah 757-340-2121. 503 I
directorcvab@centura.edu
SCARCELLE, Ed 212-229-5598. 332 E
scarcele@newschool.edu
SCARDINO, Janell 402-375-7553. 291 F
jascard1@wsc.edu
SCARINGE, John 562-902-3330. 67 H
johnscaringe@scuhs.edu
SCARLATOS, Pete 561-297-0466. 114 L
scarlatos@fau.edu
SCARPELLI, Geoff 817-735-5030. 490 E
Geoffrey.Scarpelli@unthsc.edu
SCARPINO, John 407-708-2148. 113 E
scarpinj@seminolestate.edu
SCARTELLI, Joseph, P 540-831-5265. 508 C
jscartel@radford.edu
SCATES, LouAnn, P 704-406-4263. 354 C
lscates@gardner-webb.edu
SCATLIFFE-WALLACE,
Kathleen 847-543-2998. 143 A
per286@clcillinois.edu
SCAVONE, Victoria, R 248-689-8282. 251 I
vscavone@walshcollege.edu
SCAVUZZO, Connie, M 312-949-7079. 146 G
cscavuzzo@ico.edu
SCERE, Rubie, J 318-670-9473. 207 A
rscere@susla.edu
SCHAAD, Dean 419-755-4855. 385 D
dschaad@ncstatecollege.edu
SCHAAF, Shannon 952-446-4177. 255 D
schaafs@crown.edu
SCHAAKE, Vicki 518-587-2100. 346 A
vicki.schaake@esc.edu
SCHAAL, Barbara, A 314-935-6820. 284 L
schaal@wustl.edu
SCHAAL, Mary 928-344-7772. 11 L
mary.schaal@azwestern.edu
SCHAAL, Michael, L 810-762-9733. 244 Q
mschaal@kettering.edu
SCHAB, Diana 541-888-7312. 407 H
dschab@socc.edu
SCHABERG, David 310-825-4856. 71 C
dschaberg@college.ucla.edu
SCHABERT, Daniel 215-646-7300. 417 F
schabert.d@gmc.edu
SCHACHT, Linda 615-966-6155. 456 B
linda.schacht@lipscomb.edu
SCHACHT, Otto, B 806-291-1022. 494 F
schachto@wbu.edu
SCHACHTER, Crystal 845-341-4070. 335 H
crystal.schachter@sunyorange.edu
SCHACHTER, Ronald 508-213-2219. 235 E
ronald.schachter@nichols.edu
SCHACHTER, Ruth 215-567-7080. 410 A
rschachter@edmc.edu
SCHACHTER, Shmuel 410-484-7200. 217 D
finaid@nirc.edu
SCHACHTSIEK, David 319-208-5053. 182 G
dschachtsiek@scciowa.edu
SCHACKMUTH, Kurt 815-836-5810. 150 H
schackku@lewisu.edu
SCHACTLER, Linda 509-963-1221. 517 F
schactler@cwu.edu
SCHADE, Carrie 773-298-3123. 158 E
schade@sxu.edu

SCHADEMAN, Emily .... 215-248-3648. 413 A
schademane@chc.edu
SCHADING, Douglas ...... 212-938-5880. 345 C
dschading@sunyopt.edu
SCHAECHTER, Alexander 718-854-8791. 329 K
mh@thejnet.com
SCHAEFER, Francine, Z .. 716-375-2102. 338 E
fschaefe@sbu.edu
SCHAEFER, Jane .... 262-595-2208. 537 C
schaefer@uwp.edu
SCHAEFER, Joe, P .... 703-247-2500... 96 F
SCHAEFER, Joseph .... 914-674-7473. 330 J
jschaefer@mercy.edu
SCHAEFER, K. C .... 540-458-8216. 516 A
schaeferk@wlu.edu
SCHAEFER, Karen, D ...... 575-646-2731. 310 I
kschaefe@nmsu.edu
SCHAEFER, Karla .... 641-585-8159. 183 D
schaeferk@waldorf.edu
SCHAEFER, Kelly, A .... 847-491-2323. 155 D
kelly.schaefer@northwestern.edu
SCHAEFER, Lynne .... 410-455-2939. 219 D
lschaefer@umbc.edu
SCHAEFER, Maryann ...... 312-629-6118. 158 L
mschaefer@saic.edu
SCHAEFER, Rhonda .... 505-566-3087. 311 I
schaeferr@sanjuancollege.edu
SCHAEFER, Ronald, P .... 618-650-3785. 159 H
rschaef@siue.edu
SCHAEFER, Sharon, P .... 813-253-6250. 118 L
sschaefer@ut.edu
SCHAEFER, Thomas, G ... 412-536-1198. 420 A
thomas.schaefer@laroche.edu
SCHAEFER, Verdell .... 909-558-4509... 51 C
vschaefer@llu.edu
SCHAEFFER, Kathi .... 617-984-1676. 235 I
kschaeffer@quincycollege.edu
SCHAEFFER, Lisa .... 910-521-6175. 369 B
lisa.schaeffer@uncp.edu
SCHAEFFER, Scot .... 563-387-1287. 180 M
schasc01@luther.edu
SCHAEFFER, William ...... 310-665-6940... 57 C
wschaeffer@otis.edu
SCHAEFFLER, Jan .... 203-332-5220... 88 F
jschaeffler@hcc.commnet.edu
SCHAEL, John, M .... 314-935-5288. 284 L
schael@wustl.edu
SCHAFER, Jay .... 413-545-0284. 228 F
jschafer@library.umass.edu
SCHAFER, Michael .... 419-772-2190. 386 D
m-schafer@onu.edu
SCHAFER, Stephen, A ..... 610-330-5136. 420 D
schafers@lafayette.edu
SCHAFER, William .... 404-385-8772. 125 D
william.schafer@vpss.gatech.edu
SCHAFF, Justine .... 607-274-3177. 327 E
jschaff@ithaca.edu
SCHAFFER, Andy .... 812-206-8382. 168 F
schaffer@purdue.edu
SCHAFFER, Connie .... 567-661-7737. 387 L
connie_schaffer@owens.edu
SCHAFFER, Frederick, P . 646-664-9210. 316 I
frederick.schaffer@cuny.edu
SCHAFFER, James, P ..... 610-330-5000. 420 D
schaffej@lafayette.edu
SCHAFFER, Joe .... 307-778-1102. 543 D
jschaffer@lccc.wy.edu
SCHAFFER, Kerry .... 812-877-8172. 172 C
schaffer@rose-hulman.edu
SCHAFFER, Lois, A .... 717-358-2975. 417 I
laschaff@hacc.edu
SCHAFFER, Lonnie .... 757-825-2952. 514 B
schafferl@tncc.edu
SCHAFFER, Mindy, M .... 410-822-5400. 214 C
mschaffer@chesapeake.edu
SCHAFFER, Sandy .... 931-393-1536. 461 A
sschaffer@mscc.edu
SCHAFFHAUSER,
Anthony .... 218-736-1528. 259 F
anthony.schaffhauserl@minnesota.edu
SCHAFFNER, Ashley .... 502-895-3411. 197 F
aschaffner@lpts.edu
SCHAFFNER, Barbara, H . 614-823-1735. 387 K
bschaffner@otterbein.edu
SCHAFFNER, Bradley ...... 507-222-4267. 254 D
bschaffner@carleton.edu
SCHAFRICK, James, A .... 203-773-8507... 87 G
jschafrick@albertus.edu
SCHALK, Lawrence, E .... 269-471-3484. 239 D
schalk@andrews.edu
SCHALL, Jeffrey .... 603-752-1113. 296 E
jschall@ccsnh.edu
SCHALL, Lawrence, M .... 404-364-8320. 130 A
lschall@oglethorpe.edu
SCHALLENKAMP, Kay ...... 605-642-6111. 451 G
kay.schallenkamp@bhsu.edu
SCHALLER, Rhonda .... 718-636-3506. 336 F
rshal20@pratt.edu
SCHALLOCK, Heather ..... 715-365-4518. 540 G
hschallock@nicoletcollege.edu
SCHALO, Pamela, A .... 530-226-4702... 66 D
pschalo@simpsonu.edu
SCHAMANN, Matthew .... 716-926-8925. 326 B
mschamann@hilbert.edu
SCHAMP, Rosemary .... 856-374-4941. 300 B
rschamp@camdencc.edu
SCHANCK, Donald, S ...... 401-863-9570. 438 J
donald_schanck@brown.edu
SCHANDORFF, M. Gene 208-467-8665. 139 A
meschandorff@nnu.edu
SCHANTZ, Janet, D .... 317-738-8009. 165 I
jschantz@franklincollege.edu
SCHANTZ, Mark .... 205-226-4650...... 2 C
mschantz@bsc.edu
SCHANTZ, Peter, K .... 740-368-3404. 387 J
pkschant@owu.edu
SCHANZ, Jeff .... 518-276-6205. 337 I
schanj@rpi.edu
SCHAPER, Nikki .... 760-757-2121... 54 G
nschaper@miracosta.edu
SCHAPER, Sue .... 208-459-5837. 138 A
sschaper@collegeofidaho.edu
SCHAPERKOTTER,
Nancy .... 715-422-5526. 540 D
nancy.schaperkotter@mstc.edu
SCHAPIRA, Ruth .... 215-635-7300. 417 C
rschapira@gratz.edu
SCHAPIRO, Chaim .... 973-455-9031. 304 G
chaimschap@aol.com
SCHAPIRO, Mendel .... 323-937-3763... 77 F
SCHAPIRO, Morton, O ... 847-491-7456. 155 D
nu-president@northwestern.edu
SCHAPIRO, Robert .... 404-712-8815. 124 E
rschapi@emory.edu
SCHAPP, Rebecca, M ..... 408-554-4528... 64 M
rschapp@scu.edu
SCHAPPE, David .... 971-236-9231. 405 A
SCHAPPERT, David, G .... 570-961-4764. 423 B
dschappert@marywood.edu
SCHARER, Gregory .... 937-775-2620. 393 G
greg.scharer@wright.edu
SCHARER, Lloyd, S .... 517-321-0242. 243 F
lscharer@glcc.edu
SCHARFENBERGER,
James .... 315-312-3214. 344 A
james.scharfenberger@oswego.edu
SCHARLE, Joyce .... 215-646-7300. 417 F
scharle.j@gmc.edu
SCHARLEMANN,
Linette, M .... 507-354-8221. 256 M
scharllm@mlc-wels.edu
SCHARMAN, Janet, S ..... 801-422-2387. 495 D
Jan_Scharman@byu.edu
SCHARMER, Judy .... 575-624-8076. 310 H
scharmer@nmmi.edu
SCHARN, Theresa .... 605-394-4034. 452 E
theresa.scharn@wdt.edu
SCHARPER, Alice .... 805-965-0581... 64 L
scharper@sbcc.edu
SCHARRÓN, Edna, M ..... 787-250-0000. 553 G
edna.scharron@upr.edu
SCHARTMAN, Laura, A ... 248-370-2387. 248 J
schartma@oakland.edu
SCHASS, Monty .... 701-255-3285. 373 C
mschass@uttc.edu
SCHATTMAN, Lisa .... 858-566-1200... 42 G
lschattman@disd.edu
SCHATZ, Erica .... 252-940-6425. 358 A
ericas@beaufortccc.edu
SCHATZ, Julianne .... 336-272-7102. 354 E
julies@greensboro.edu
SCHATZEL, Kim .... 734-487-3200. 242 D
kschatze@emich.edu
SCHAUB, J. Michael .... 202-687-3493... 95 E
jms46@georgetown.edu
SCHAUB, Linda .... 517-750-1200. 250 E
lindas@arbor.edu
SCHAUB, Mark .... 616-331-3898. 243 C
schaubm@gvsu.edu
SCHAUB, Scott, A .... 308-635-6793. 293 E
schaubs@wncc.edu
SCHAUBHUT, Diana .... 504-398-2100. 206 C
dschaubhut@olhcc.edu
SCHAUBROECK, Tom .... 309-794-7616. 139 L
tomschaubroeck@augustana.edu
SCHAUER, Ariane .... 310-377-5501... 53 F
aschauer@marymountcalifornia.edu
SCHAUER, Rhonda .... 701-224-2497. 371 B
rhonda.schauer@ndus.edu
SCHAUFELBERGER,
John .... 206-685-4440. 524 G
jesbcon@u.washington.edu
SCHAUMANN, Neils .... 619-239-0391... 36 D
nschaumann@cwsl.edu
SCHAUS, Deborah .... 256-233-8136..... 1 F
deborah.schaus@athens.edu
SCHAUS, Jim .... 740-593-0982. 387 C
schaus@ohio.edu
SCHEARS, Ben .... 620-441-5245. 186 A
schears@cowley.edu
SCHEBLER, Meg .... 563-242-4023. 175 F
meg.schebler@ashford.edu
SCHECHTER, Aaron, M ... 718-377-0777. 336 I
SCHECHTER, Mendel ...... 718-377-0777. 336 I
SCHECHTER, Steven .... 718-951-5391. 317 C
sschechter@brooklyn.cuny.edu
SCHECK, Stephen .... 503-838-8271. 406 E
schecks@wou.edu
SCHEDIN, Karen .... 603-897-8516. 297 F
kschedin@rivier.edu
SCHEERER, Jerry .... 361-825-5785. 483 F
jerry.scheerer@tamucc.edu
SCHEERER, Teresa .... 215-785-0111. 426 X
SCHEETT, Rod .... 701-355-8181. 373 E
scheett@umary.edu
SCHEETZ, Anita, A .... 406-768-6341. 286 C
ascheetz@fpcc.edu
SCHEETZ, Charles .... 570-662-4854. 429 C
cscheetz@mansfield.edu
SCHEFF, Deborah, M ...... 314-977-2802. 281 I
scheff@slu.edu
SCHEFFEL, Kent .... 618-468-5000. 150 G
kscheffe@lc.edu
SCHEFFKE, Joan .... 435-797-7191. 497 B
joan.scheffke@usu.edu
SCHEFFLER, Jonathan, C 310-243-2139... 33 B
jscheffler@csudh.edu
SCHEFFLER, Keith .... 281-425-6498. 475 I
kscheffl@lee.edu
SCHEHR, Terra .... 410-617-2271. 216 A
tschehr@loyola.edu
SCHEIB, Roger .... 620-417-1240. 190 F
roger.scheib@sccc.edu
SCHEIBMEIR, Monica, S 785-670-1526. 191 D
monica.scheibmeir@washburn.edu
SCHEIDT, Doug .... 585-395-2651. 342 F
dscheidt@brockport.edu
SCHEINBERG, Mark, E ... 860-727-6757... 90 A
mscheinberg@goodwin.edu
SCHEINER, Steve .... 660-596-7208. 282 G
sscheiner@sfccmo.edu
SCHEINMAN, Steven, J .. 570-504-7000. 413 B
SCHELCHER, Cindy .... 408-741-2165... 75 L
cindy.schelcher@westvalley.edu
SCHELCHER, Cindy .... 408-741-2165... 75 L
cindy.schelcher@wvm.edu
SCHELCHER, Cynthia ...... 408-741-2165... 75 J
cindy_schelcher@wvm.edu
SCHELIN, Kelly, R .... 336-322-2107. 362 F
Kelly.Schelin@piedmontcc.edu
SCHELL, Christopher .... 608-246-6384. 540 C
chschell@madisoncollege.edu
SCHELL, Courtney .... 307-755-2122. 544 B
cschell@wyotechstaff.edu
SCHELL, John .... 407-823-5711. 115 E
rick.schell@ucf.edu
SCHELL, Karen .... 518-292-1719. 338 C
schelk@sage.edu
SCHELL, Michael, J .... 541-885-1452. 405 J
michael.schell@oit.edu
SCHELLACK, Emil, F .... 913-971-3299. 188 H
cpolice@mnu.edu
SCHELLENBERGER, Kim . 573-876-7172. 282 H
kschellenberger@stephens.edu
SCHELLENBERGER,
Lauren .... 573-288-6429. 273 F
lschellenberger@culver.edu
SCHELLER, William, L .... 814-871-7912. 416 K
scheller002@gannon.edu
SCHEMENT, Jorge, R ...... 732-932-7500. 306 A
jr.schement@rutgers.edu
SCHEMPER, Lugene, L .... 616-526-6121. 240 M
lschempe@calvin.edu
SCHENA, Donna .... 240-567-3085. 216 F
donna.schena@montgomerycollege.edu
SCHENCK, Ken .... 765 677 2258. 169 B
ken.schenck@indwes.edu
SCHENCK, Robert, B .... 252-335-0821. 359 F
rschenck@albemarle.edu
SCHENEWERK, Randal ... 573-875-7256. 272 G
raschenewerk@ccis.edu
SCHENK, Evelyn .... 989-275-5000. 245 B
evelyn.schenk@kirtland.edu
SCHENK, Glenn .... 310-287-4275... 52 F
schenkga@wlac.edu
SCHENK, Kimberely .... 925-969-2036... 41 L
schenk@dvc.edu
SCHENK, Matthew, R ...... 757-446-6043. 504 E
schenkmr@evms.edu
SCHENK, Rebecca, J ...... 716-878-4312. 343 A
schenkrj@buffalostate.edu
SCHENK, Stacy, L .... 814-886-6357. 424 G
sschenk@mtaloy.edu
SCHENKEL, Beverly, S .... 660-562-1149. 279 I
bevs@nwmissouri.edu
SCHENKER, Beth .... 312-922-9012. 160 D
bschenker@spertus.edu
SCHENKER, Marc .... 530-754-8942... 70 J
mbschenker@ucdavis.edu
SCHEPEL, Bill .... 708-239-4805. 160 K
bill.schepel@trnty.edu
SCHEPENS, Bennett .... 845-675-4543. 335 C
bennett.schepens@nyack.edu
SCHEPENS, Dona, P .... 845-675-4618. 335 C
dona.schepens@nyack.edu
SCHEPLER, Richard, A .... 630-617-3456. 145 A
dscheplr@elmhurst.edu
SCHEPP, Robina, C .... 212-346-1281. 335 J
rschepp@pace.edu
SCHEPPARD, Carol, A .... 540-828-5608. 502 J
cscheppa@bridgewater.edu
SCHER, Anne .... 510-869-6130... 61 I
ascher@samuelmerritt.edu
SCHERBERGER, Tom ...... 727-873-4456. 116 D
tscherberger@usfsp.edu
SCHERER, Melanie .... 847-543-2627. 143 A
mscherer@clcillinois.edu
SCHERER, Robert .... 972-721-5000. 488 F
SCHERER, Tim .... 989-275-5000. 245 B
tim.scherer@kirtland.edu
SCHERGER, Celinda .... 419-448-3313. 389 J
schergercm@tiffin.edu
SCHERLING, Sarah .... 303-524-5198... 79 C
sscherling@ccu.edu
SCHERMERHORN,
Donald .... 251-343-8200..... 6 E
donald.schermerhorn@remingtoncollege.edu
SCHERMERHORN,
Robert .... 574-239-8335. 166 N
rschermerhorn@hcc-nd.edu
SCHERR, Albert .... 603-513-5144. 298 D
albert.scherr@law.unh.edu
SCHERRENS,
Maurice, W .... 803-321-5102. 445 G
mscherrens@newberry.edu
SCHERSTEN, Mark .... 517-264-7667. 250 B
mschersten@sienaheights.edu
SCHERTZ, Mary, H .... 574-296-6218. 163 J
mschertz@ambs.edu
SCHERTZ, Ronald, L ...... 401-825-2179. 439 A
rschertz@ccri.edu
SCHERWITZ, Shelli .... 325-235-7425. 486 C
shelli.scherwitz@tstc.edu
SCHERZER, Erin .... 973-642-8242. 307 D
erin.scherzer@shu.edu
SCHETTLER, Martha, A ... 330-569-5205. 380 I
shettlerma@hiram.edu
SCHEUBER, Arthur, F ..... 414-288-1463. 534 B
arthur.scheuber@marquette.edu
SCHEUERMANN, Angela 336-838-6558. 365 B
angela.scheuermann@wilkescc.edu
SCHEUERMANN, Laurie . 530-749-3851... 77 M
lscheuer@yccd.edu
SCHEUERMANN,
Michael .... 215-895-0244. 415 B
mes27@drexel.edu
SCHEUERMANN,
Thomas, A .... 541-737-4771. 406 A
tom.scheuermann@oregonstate.edu
SCHEULEN, Kathy .... 573-897-5000. 276 E
SCHEWE, Sharon, R .... 651-641-8228. 255 B
schewe@csp.edu
SCHEXNAYDER, Ken ...... 239-590-1083. 115 A
kschexnayder@fgcu.edu
SCHEXNIDER-FIELDS,
Ingenue, S .... 504-520-6209. 209 D
itschexn@xula.edu
SCHEYETTE, Anna, M ..... 803-777-7886. 447 G
anna.scheyette@sc.edu
SCHIAVELLI, Mel, D ...... 703-323-4291. 513 C
mschiavelli@nvcc.edu
SCHIAVO, Antoinette ...... 215-637-7700. 418 G
schiavo@holyfamily.edu
SCHIAVONI, Robert .... 603-646-9758. 297 I
r.schiavoni@snuh.edu
SCHIAZZA, Douglas, J .... 413-597-3696. 238 D
douglas.schiazza@williams.edu
SCHICK, Beth Ann .... 814-871-7659. 416 K
shick001@gannon.edu
SCHICK, Marilyn .... 815-455-8591. 152 F
mschick@mchenry.edu
SCHICK, Marvin .... 732-985-6533. 304 F
SCHICK, Wendell .... 419-227-3141. 391 F
wschick@unoh.edu
SCHICKLING, William ..... 716-614-5931. 334 E
bschickling@niagaracc.suny.edu
SCHIDLOW, Daniel .... 215-895-2000. 415 B
daniel.schidlow@drexelmed.edu
SCHIEBER, Amy, K .... 660-944-2847. 272 H
aschieber@conception.edu
SCHIEBER, Craig .... 206-239-4500. 517 M
cschieber@cityu.edu
SCHIEBER, Gary, W .... 816-604-1320. 277 C
gary.schieber@mcckc.edu
SCHIEBER, Jeanette .... 660-944-2839. 272 H
jschieber@conception.edu
SCHIEBER, Ryan .... 925-288-5800... 46 J
ryan_schieber@heald.edu
SCHIEFEN, Kathleen .... 585-345-6975. 325 C
kmschiefen@genesee.edu

SCHIELE, Ann, E 614-234-5032. 384 J aschiele@mccn.edu
SCHIELE, Evelyn, R 847-543-2622. 143 A eschiele@clcillinois.edu
SCHIELE, Jerome, H 301-860-3705. 220 A jschiele@bowiestate.edu
SCHIERBEEK, Hannah 616-222-3000. 245 C hschierbeek@kuyper.edu
SCHIFF, Ed 561-297-3080. 114 L schiff@fau.edu
SCHIFF, Sidney 845-356-1980. 336 J
SCHIFFER, Peter, E 217-333-0034. 162 A pschiffe@illinois.edu
SCHIFFGENS, Hope 412-536-1266. 420 A hope.schiffgens@laroche.edu
SCHIFFNER, Carli 509-682-6605. 525 B cschiffner@wvc.edu
SCHIFILLITI, Roy 617-879-2419. 238 C rschifilliti@wheelock.edu
SCHIFINO, Charlie 401-874-2611. 440 D schifino@uri.edu
SCHILBERG, Ruth, E 972-708-7379. 472 L dean-students@gial.edu
SCHILDT, Brenda 785-749-8445. 187 B bschildt@haskell.edu
SCHILL, Michael, C 530-226-4179... 66 D mschill@simpsonu.edu
SCHILL, Michael, H 773-702-9495. 161 B mschill@uchicago.edu
SCHILLER, Elizabeth, N 207-859-4622. 209 J enschill@colby.edu
SCHILLER, Teri 845-352-3431. 351 J shaareitorah@optonline.net
SCHILLING, Denise 909-469-5294... 76 B dschilling@westernu.edu
SCHILLING, Eileen 732-255-0400. 304 A eschilling@ocean.edu
SCHILLING, Jennifer 503-682-1862. 407 B jschilling@pioneerpacific.edu
SCHILLING, JoAnna 562-860-2451... 37 I jschilling@cerritos.edu
SCHILLING, Mary, E 757-221-3228. 503 N meschi@wm.edu
SCHILLING, Michael 530-898-6212... 33 A mlschilling@csuchico.edu
SCHILLING, Peter 781-595-6768. 228 C pschilling@mariancourt.edu
SCHILLO, Stephen 716-673-3109. 342 A stephen.schillo@fredonia.edu
SCHILT, Louis, J 480-212-1704... 17 N
SCHILZ, Nancy 402-465-2237. 291 G nschilz@nebrwesleyan.edu
SCHILZ, Thomas 619-388-7500... 62 F tschilz@sdccd.edu
SCHIMELFINIG, Marianne 610-660-3140. 432 E mschimel@sju.edu
SCHIMER, Maria, R 330-325-6357. 385 E maria@neomed.edu
SCHIMETZ, Colette 701-228-5444. 372 C colette.schimetz@dakotacollege.edu
SCHIMPF, Martin 208-426-1202. 137 G mschimpf@boisestate.edu
SCHINABECK, Karen, M 434-395-2077. 506 J schinabeckkm@longwood.edu
SCHINDLER, Christian 443-627-7331. 265 D Christian.Schindler@waldenu.edu
SCHINDLER, Kerry 254-965-8875. 478 H kschindler@rangercollege.edu
SCHINDLER, Lindsay 417-328-1806. 282 C lschindler@sbuniv.edu
SCHION, Donna 409-984-6101. 486 H donna.schion@lamarpa.edu
SCHIPPER, Chris 505-566-3449. 311 I schipperc@sanjuancollege.edu
SCHIPPOREIT, Kim 308-865-8527. 292 H schipporeitk@unk.edu
SCHIRALLI, Charlie 315-792-7340. 346 C charles.schiralli@sunyit.edu
SCHIRER-SUTER, Myron 978-867-4419. 226 H myron.schirer-suter@gordon.edu
SCHIRMER, Barbara 419-783-2402. 379 C
SCHIRMER-SMITH, Sally, J 413-565-1000. 222 F salsmith@baypath.edu
SCHISSLER, John 330-490-7263. 392 H jschissler@walsh.edu
SCHISSLER, Kathy 303-914-6214... 84 I kathy.schissler@rrcc.edu
SCHIZER, David, M 212-854-2675. 321 D dschiz@law.columbia.edu
SCHLABACH, June 603-535-2338. 298 G jlschlabach@plymouth.edu
SCHLACHTER, Stephany, S 815-836-5639. 150 H schlacst@lewisu.edu
SCHLACK, Marilyn, J 269-488-4200. 244 L mschlack@kvcc.edu
SCHLAF, John 309-341-7255. 150 A jschlaf@knox.edu
SCHLAG, Kevin 808-675-3653. 135 C kevin@byuh.edu
SCHLAGER, Bernard 510-849-8225... 57 H bschlager@psr.edu
SCHLAK, Tim 712-707-7238. 181 H tim.schlak@nwciowa.edu
SCHLAPP, Andrew 316-978-3001. 191 F andy.schlapp@witchita.edu
SCHLATHER, Mary Margaret 540-338-2700. 503 A srschlather@cdu.edu
SCHLECHTE, Dawn 217-234-5210. 150 D dschlechte@lakeland.cc.il.us
SCHLECT, Brenda 208-882-1566. 138 H bschlect@nsa.edu
SCHLEGEL, Alice 509-542-4823. 518 C aschlegel@columbiabasin.edu
SCHLEGEL, Len 518-262-9331. 313 D schlegell@mail.amc.edu
SCHLEICH, David, J 503-552-1702. 404 H president@ncnm.edu
SCHLEICH, Tamatha 309-649-6632. 160 E tamatha.schleich@src.edu
SCHLEICHER, Julie 781-239-3053. 231 G jschleicher@massbay.edu
SCHLEICHER, Rolf 818-710-4142... 52 B schleir@piercecollege.edu
SCHLEIFER, H. William 603-897-8630. 297 F bschleifer@rivier.edu
SCHLEIFFER, Richard 214-698-0461. 470 J ecc5100@dcccd.edu
SCHLENBECKER, Darlene 847-925-6008. 145 H dschlenb@harpercollege.edu
SCHLENKER, Steven 215-702-4340. 411 F sschlenker@cairn.edu
SCHLEPPENBACH, Barbara 217-228-5432. 156 C bschlepp@quincy.edu
SCHLESINGER, Kenneth 718-960-8000. 318 A kenneth.schlesinger@lehman.cuny.edu
SCHLESINGER, Patrick 510-642-2866... 70 I pschlesinger@berkeley.edu
SCHLESSINGER, Shirley 601-815-5235. 270 C sschlessinger@umc.edu
SCHLEY, Alisa, S 715-833-6266. 539 J ahoepner1@cvtc.edu
SCHLICHT, Terri 913-469-8500. 187 J tschlich@jccc.edu
SCHLICHTING, Linda, G 804-257-5727. 515 F lgschlichting@vuu.edu
SCHLICKMANN, Paul 860-832-3038... 87 K paulschlickmann@ccsu.edu
SCHLIMGEN, Matt 317-931-2382. 165 B mschlimgen@cts.edu
SCHLIMPERT, Charles, E 503-280-8509. 402 J cschlimpert@cu-portland.edu
SCHLINGMANN, Dirk 864-503-5663. 448 H dschlingmann@uscupstate.edu
SCHLISSEL, Mark, S 401-863-2706. 438 J mark_schlissel@brown.edu
SCHLOER, Wolfgang 217-333-6104. 162 A wfschlor@illinois.edu
SCHLOSSER, David 507-222-4150. 254 D dschloss@carleton.edu
SCHLOSSER-BACON, Angela 616-632-2860. 239 E schloang@aquinas.edu
SCHLOSSMAN, Paul 818-240-1000... 45 G pschloss@glendale.edu
SCHLOTTER, Pat 303-457-2757... 81 L
SCHLOTTERHAUSEN, Lisa 651-779-3934. 258 C lisa.schlotterhausen@century.edu
SCHLUETER, Carol, J 504-865-5722. 207 C cjs@tulane.edu
SCHLUETER, Lita 978-468-7111. 227 A litas@gcts.edu
SCHLUGE, Daniel 317-738-8026. 165 I dschluge@franklincollege.edu
SCHLUTT, Fred 907-474-7246... 10 I efschluttjr@alaska.edu
SCHMAEF, Robert 800-290-4226. 454 M rschmaef@hchs.edu
SCHMAILZL, Randy 402-457-2415. 290 G rschmailzl@mccneb.edu
SCHMAL, Daniel 414-443-8875. 539 F dan.schmal@wlc.edu
SCHMALENBERG, Kate 218-793-2401. 260 D kate.schmalenberg@northlandcollege.edu
SCHMALL, Steve 507-285-7214. 261 A steve.schmall@rctc.edu
SCHMALTZ, John 860-768-7987... 92 D schmaltz@hartford.edu
SCHMALTZ, Kim 503-682-1862. 407 B kschmaltz@pioneerpacific.edu
SCHMELCZER, Moshe 773-463-7738. 160 H mschmelczer@aol.com
SCHMELKIN, Liora, P 516-463-5408. 326 D liora.p.schmelkin@hofstra.edu
SCHMELZ, Kimberly, G 608-342-1024. 537 D schmelzk@uwplatt.edu
SCHMEUSSER, Meghan, R 302-356-6809... 94 E meghan.r.schmeusser@wilmu.edu
SCHMID, Gary 414-443-8821. 539 F gary.schmid@wlc.edu
SCHMID, Karen, L 219-785-5750. 172 A kschmid@pnc.edu
SCHMID, Mark, A 312-595-1006. 161 B mschmid@inv.uchicago.edu
SCHMID, Patti, A 856-691-8600. 301 A paschmid@cccnj.edu
SCHMIDLI, Troy 517-265-5161. 238 G
SCHMIDT, Adeny 951-785-2210... 50 B aschmidt@lasierra.edu
SCHMIDT, Amy 608-785-9139. 541 E schmidta@westerntc.edu
SCHMIDT, Betsy 317-738-8054. 165 I bschmidt@franklincollege.edu
SCHMIDT, Brian 503-375-7199. 403 A bschmidt@corban.edu
SCHMIDT, Carol 419-995-8218. 381 Q schmidt.c@rhodesstate.edu
SCHMIDT, Chris 515-244-4221. 175 C schmidtc@aib.edu
SCHMIDT, Chris, R 419-995-8342. 381 Q schmidt.cr@rhodesstate.edu
SCHMIDT, Christina 585-271-3657. 338 D admissions@stbernards.edu
SCHMIDT, Christopher 270-384-8136. 197 D schmidtc@lindsey.edu
SCHMIDT, Chuck 509-542-4747. 518 C cschmidt@columbiabasin.edu
SCHMIDT, Clayton, F 334-387-3877..... 1 E claytonschmidt@amridgeuniversity.edu
SCHMIDT, Curt 612-659-6902. 259 D curt.schmidt@minneapolis.edu
SCHMIDT, Dan 701-224-5735. 372 B daniel.j.schmidt@bismarckstate.edu
SCHMIDT, Danielle 515-244-4221. 175 C schmidtd@aib.edu
SCHMIDT, David, E 785-628-4487. 186 F dschmidt@fhsu.edu
SCHMIDT, David, O 701-777-4151. 371 C david.schmidt@research.und.edu
SCHMIDT, Denise 973-328-5245. 300 G dschmidt@ccm.edu
SCHMIDT, Douglas 845-574-4572. 338 B dschmidt@sunyrockland.edu
SCHMIDT, Ed 785-670-1010. 191 D
SCHMIDT, Eric, R 608-796-3017. 539 E erschmidt@viterbo.edu
SCHMIDT, Gary 732-255-0400. 304 A gschmidt@ocean.edu
SCHMIDT, Gene 989-386-6604. 247 B gschmidt@midmich.edu
SCHMIDT, Harry, R 847-259-1840. 141 L hschmidt@christianlifecollege.edu
SCHMIDT, James, C 715-836-2327. 536 E jschmidt@uwec.edu
SCHMIDT, James, W 312-996-2695. 161 D jschmidt@uic.edu
SCHMIDT, Jaqueline, L 620-341-5223. 186 D jschmidt@emporia.edu
SCHMIDT, Jaqueline, L 620-341-5221. 186 D jschmidt@emporia.edu
SCHMIDT, Jeffrey 410-704-3414. 220 E jschmidt@towson.edu
SCHMIDT, John 334-670-3201..... 7 H jschmidt@troy.edu
SCHMIDT, Jolene 515-271-3957. 177 K jolene.schmidt@drake.edu
SCHMIDT, Jona, M 605-256-5857. 451 H jona.schmidt@dsu.edu
SCHMIDT, Julie 402-826-8200. 289 E julie.schmidt@doane.edu
SCHMIDT, Karen 309-556-3172. 148 B kschmidt@iwu.edu
SCHMIDT, Keith, E 712-749-2230. 176 D schmidt@bvu.edu
SCHMIDT, London 910-755-8393. 358 D schmidtl@brunswickcc.edu
SCHMIDT, Martin, A 617-253-7817. 233 B
SCHMIDT, Mellis 505-747-2213. 311 E mschmidt@nnmc.edu
SCHMIDT, Michael, E 402-554-2336. 293 A mschmidt@unomaha.edu
SCHMIDT, Patricia 631-656-2176. 324 F patricia.schmidt@ftc.edu
SCHMIDT, Patty 309-649-6272. 160 E patty.schmidt@src.edu
SCHMIDT, Phil 801-274-3280. 498 E pschmidt@wgu.edu
SCHMIDT, Rachel 216-687-5594. 377 F r.m.schmidt@csuohio.edu
SCHMIDT, Rachelle, M 651-846-1348. 261 D rachelle.schmidt@saintpaul.edu
SCHMIDT, Scott, J 821-821-3333. 105 A sschmidt@fnu.edu
SCHMIDT, Shana 715-833-6410. 539 J sschmidt42@cvtc.edu
SCHMIDT, Soren 906-487-7239. 242 G soren.schmidt@finlandia.edu
SCHMIDT, Susan 712-324-5061. 181 G sschmidt@nwicc.edu
SCHMIDT, Tabitha 816-802-3445. 275 J tschmidt@kcai.edu
SCHMIDT, Wayne 765-677-2245. 169 B wayne.schmidt@indwes.edu
SCHMIDT-NORRIS, Jenae 607-778-5001. 315 I norrisjs@sunybroome.edu
SCHMIEDEL, Mary, E 202-687-3911... 95 E schmiedm@georgetown.edu
SCHMIEDL, Bruce 630-942-2972. 142 G schmiedlb@cod.edu
SCHMIEDL, Joe 808-544-1105. 135 F jschmiedl@hpu.edu
SCHMIEG, Rose, A 540-665-5534. 509 E rschmieg@su.edu
SCHMIEL, Paul 727-726-1153. 100 E paulschmiel@clearwater.edu
SCHMIESING, David, A 740-284-6513. 379 N dschmiesing@franciscan.edu
SCHMILL, Stuart 617-258-5514. 233 B
SCHMISEK, Brian 312-915-7400. 151 H bschmisek@luc.edu
SCHMIT, Clayton, J 803-461-3211. 445 A clayton.schmit@lr.edu
SCHMIT, Matt 563-441-4125. 178 C
SCHMIT, Michele 920-498-7106. 541 B michele.schmit@nwtc.edu
SCHMIT, Shelly, M 641-422-4211. 181 D schmishe@niacc.edu
SCHMITT, Barbara, L 570-348-6225. 423 B schmitt@marywood.edu
SCHMITT, Karen 815-825-2086. 149 F Karen.schmitt@kishwaukeecollege.edu
SCHMITT, Karen, R 907-786-6494... 10 H apkrs@uaa.alaska.edu
SCHMITT, Linda 908-821-9701. 304 C lschmitt@pillar.edu
SCHMITT, Mark 315-464-4538. 342 E schmittm@upstate.edu
SCHMITT, Patrick 408-741-2011... 75 J patrick.schmitt@wvm.edu
SCHMITT, Storm 563-425-5857. 183 B schmitts@uiu.edu
SCHMITTLEIN, David, C 617-253-2804. 233 B
SCHMITTMANN, Beate 515-294-3220. 175 H schmittb@iastate.edu
SCHMITZ, Cody 612-343-4410. 262 X cschmitz@northcentral.edu
SCHMITZ, Diane 503-399-6031. 402 E diane.schmitz@chemeketa.edu
SCHMITZ, Donna 701-252-3467. 373 D dschmitz@jc.edu
SCHMITZ, Nancy, A 248-370-3352. 248 J schmitz@oakland.edu
SCHMITZ, Stevie 406-657-1134. 288 B schmitzs@rocky.edu
SCHMOKE, Kurt, L 202-806-2650... 95 G kurt.schmoke@howard.edu
SCHMOLL, Beverly, J 419-530-5451. 392 B beverly.schmoll@utoledo.edu
SCHMOLL, Robert 724-589-2102. 434 B rschmoll@thiel.edu
SCHMOOCK, Allen 208-792-2215. 138 G atschmoock@lcsc.edu
SCHMOTTER, James, W 203-837-8300... 88 B schmotterj@wcsu.edu
SCHMOTZER, Jacquelyn 330-363-1283. 374 E schmotzer@aultman.com
SCHMOTZER, Mark 516-299-3547. 329 C mark.schmotzer@liu.edu
SCHMUCKER, Angie 248-364-6129. 248 J schmucke@oakland.edu
SCHMUTTE, Gregory, T 413-205-3364. 221 F gregory.schmutte@aic.edu
SCHMUTTE, Jerry 402-461-7331. 289 I jschmutte@hastings.edu
SCHMUTZ, Betsy 314-968-6960. 284 N schmutz@webster.edu
SCHNABEL, Bobby 812-856-1079. 167 F schnabel@indiana.edu
SCHNABL, JC 413-545-5542. 228 F schnabl@admin.umass.edu
SCHNACKENBERG, Scott 212-678-3706. 347 G sps19@tc.columbia.edu
SCHNAIDMAN, Yaakov 570-346-1747. 438 C
SCHNALL, David, J 212-340-7705. 351 M dschnall@yu.edu
SCHNAPP, Derek 217-206-7823. 161 E schnapp.derek@uis.edu
SCHNARR, Carmin, A 812-888-4332. 174 F cschnarr@vinu.edu
SCHNEBERGER, Scott 618-374-5155. 156 B scott.schneberger@principia.edu

SCHNECK, Ken ... 802-258-9238. 499 F kschneck@marlboro.edu
SCHNEID, Thomas ... 210-292-6258. 545 C thomas.schneid@us.af.mil
SCHNEIDER, Ali ... 814-871-7490. 416 K schneider@gannon.edu
SCHNEIDER, Amye ... 620-792-9302. 184 F schneidera@bartonccc.edu
SCHNEIDER, Audrey ... 215-204-4607. 433 K audrey.schneider@temple.edu
SCHNEIDER, Brandt, L ... 806-743-2700. 487 E brandt.schneider@ttuhsc.edu
SCHNEIDER, Carrie ... 651-423-8244. 258 D carrie.schneider@dctc.edu
SCHNEIDER, Chad ... 740-389-4636. 383 F schneiderc@mtc.edu
SCHNEIDER, Colleen ... 316-448-5400. 450 G cschneider@national.edu
SCHNEIDER, Debbie ... 314-531-7925. 281 I bksustlouis@bncollege.com
SCHNEIDER, Edward, D . 530-226-4156... 66 D eschneider@simpsonu.edu
SCHNEIDER, Greg ... 913-288-7155. 187 L gschneid@kckcc.edu
SCHNEIDER, Helen ... 410-617-2995. 216 A hschneider@loyola.edu
SCHNEIDER, Howard ... 631-632-6265. 342 C howard.schneider@stonybrook.edu
SCHNEIDER, Jed, S ... 315-445-4500. 328 F schneij@lemoyne.edu
SCHNEIDER, Jeffrey, A ... 814-332-3355. 409 D jschneider@allegheny.edu
SCHNEIDER, Joan ... 660-562-1250. 279 I jschneider@nwmissouri.edu
SCHNEIDER, Joanne ... 315-228-7362. 320 F jschneider@colgate.edu
SCHNEIDER, Jon ... 610-372-1722. 410 E jon.schneider@berks.edu
SCHNEIDER, Judy ... 704-922-6226. 360 F schneider.judy@gaston.edu
SCHNEIDER, Julia ... 816-271-4369. 279 A schneide@missouriwestern.edu
SCHNEIDER, Karen ... 510-436-1160... 47 J schneider@hnu.edu
SCHNEIDER, Kenneth, J . 507-266-7095. 254 F schneider.kenneth@mayo.edu
SCHNEIDER, Marc ... 770-426-2700. 128 D marcs@life.edu
SCHNEIDER, Mark ... 641-269-3018. 178 H schneidm@grinnell.edu
SCHNEIDER, Mary Ann .. 216-381-1680. 385 G mschneider@ndc.edu
SCHNEIDER, Michael, P . 620-242-0405. 188 G schneidm@mcpherson.edu
SCHNEIDER, Pamela ... 732-987-2234. 302 B schneiderp@georgian.edu
SCHNEIDER, Richard, W 802-485-2065. 500 A pres@norwich.edu
SCHNEIDER, Scott ... 417-255-7258. 278 F scottshcneider@missouristate.edu
SCHNEIDER, Scott ... 563-588-6354. 176 F scott.schneider@clarke.edu
SCHNEIDER, Scott ... 239-280-2525... 98 K scott.schneider@avemaria.edu
SCHNEIDER, Steve ... 402-872-2393. 291 E sschneider@peru.edu
SCHNEIDER, Tammi ... 909-607-3217... 39 C tammi.schneider@cgu.edu
SCHNEIDER, Tina ... 419-995-8326. 381 Q tschneider@lima.ohio-state.edu
SCHNEIDER, Todd ... 970-542-3218... 83 E todd.schneider@morgancc.edu
SCHNEIDER, Tom ... 727-864-8409. 101 N schneite@eckerd.edu
SCHNEIDER, Wayne, R ... 785-827-5541. 188 C kwaynes@kwu.edu
SCHNEIDER BINGHAM, Stacy Lee ... 845-437-5285. 349 G stbingham@vassar.edu
SCHNEIDERMAN, Davis . 847-735-5282. 150 B dschneid@lakeforest.edu
SCHNEIDERMAN, Edward, S ... 718-933-6700. 331 K eschneid@monroecollege.edu
SCHNEIKART-LUEBBE, Christine ... 316-978-3149. 191 F christine.luebbe@wichita.edu
SCHNEITER, R. Wane ... 540-464-7212. 515 B schneiterrw@vmi.edu
SCHNELL, Ann, B ... 585-785-1532. 324 D schnelab@flcc.edu
SCHNELL, Carolyn, A ... 701-231-7189. 371 G carolyn.schnell@ndsu.edu
SCHNELL, Tamara ... 217-786-2353. 151 F tammy.schnell@llcc.edu
SCHNELLER, Barbara ... 610-436-2513. 430 A bschneller@wcupa.edu
SCHNELLER, Beverly ... 410-837-6205. 221 A bscneller@ubalt.edu
SCHNEPF, Chester, H ... 203-285-2151... 88 E cschnepf@gwcc.commnet.edu
SCHNETZLER, Greta ... 415-476-5003... 72 A gschnetzler@legal.ucsf.edu
SCHNIERLE, Caryn ... 312-567-5240. 147 F cschnier@iit.edu
SCHNITKEY, Dawn, I ... 517-750-1200. 250 E danderso@arbor.edu
SCHNITZER, Carol, N ... 518-580-5849. 341 A cschnitz@skidmore.edu
SCHNOOR, Barry ... 540-665-4543. 509 E bschnoor@su.edu
SCHNOOR, Chuck ... 520-494-5303... 12 P chuck.schnoor@centralaz.edu
SCHNOOR, Neal, H ... 308-865-8208. 292 H schnoorn@unk.edu
SCHNUPP, Chris ... 718-357-0500. 339 G cschnupp@edaff.com
SCHNUR, Fred ... 212-678-8008. 328 A frschnur@jtsa.edu
SCHOCHET, Ezra, B ... 323-937-3763... 77 F eschochet@yoec.edu
SCHODOWSKI, Francis .. 717-872-3820. 429 D francis.schodowski@millersville.edu
SCHOEFFLER, Susan ... 775-445-3249. 295 A susan.schoeffler@wnc.edu
SCHOELER, Mary ... 608-757-7769. 539 I mschoeler@blackhawk.edu
SCHOELLES, SSJ, Patricia, A ... 585-271-3657. 338 D pschoelles@stbernards.edu
SCHOEN, David ... 716-286-8001. 334 F schoen@niagara.edu
SCHOEN, Linda ... 614-251-4715. 386 B schoenl@ohiodominican.edu
SCHOEN, Susan ... 516-364-0808. 333 D sschoen@nycollege.edu
SCHOENBACHLER, Denise ... 815-753-1755. 154 I denises@niu.edu
SCHOENBERG, Lynn ... 386-822-7139. 117 C lschoenb@stetson.edu
SCHOENECKE, Marvin ... 417-690-2204. 272 E schoenecke@cofo.edu
SCHOENECKER, Craig, V ... 651-201-1864. 257 N craig.schoenecker@so.mnscu.edu
SCHOENECKER, Mark ... 719-587-7696... 78 B mwschoen@adams.edu
SCHOENEERGER, Susan . 860-509-9519... 90 B sschoeneerger@hartsem.edu
SCHOENEFELD, Dale, A . 918-631-2881. 401 F schoend@utulsa.edu
SCHOENER, Lois ... 607-735-1890. 323 H lschoener@elmira.edu
SCHOENFELD, Diane ... 617-573-8454. 237 B dschoenf@suffolk.edu
SCHOENFELD, Michael ... 802-443-3180. 499 H schoenfe@middlebury.edu
SCHOENFELD, Michael, J ... 919-681-3788. 354 A michael.schoenfeld@duke.edu
SCHOENFELDER, Louis .. 605-995-2191. 450 A loschoen@dwu.edu
SCHOENGOOD, Matthew, G ... 212-817-7400. 317 F mschoengood@gc.cuny.edu
SCHOENHERR, Holly ... 320-308-3203. 261 B hjschoenherr@stcloudstate.edu
SCHOENLE, JR., Gerald, W ... 716-645-2230. 341 F gws3@buffalo.edu
SCHOENWETTER, Beth ... 414-256-0169. 535 A schoenwb@mtmary.edu
SCHOENWILL, Chad ... 719-389-6941... 79 D cschoenwill@coloradocollege.edu
SCHOEPHOERSTER, Richard, T ... 915-747-6444. 492 A schoephoerster@utep.edu
SCHOFFMAN, Garth, D ... 330-684-8938. 390 F gds@uakron.edu
SCHOFIELD, Anna, M ... 614-222-3274. 378 A aschofield@ccad.edu
SCHOFIELD, Audrey ... 561-803-2145. 110 B audrey_schofield@pba.edu
SCHOFIELD, John ... 410-293-1521. 545 J pao@usna.edu
SCHOFIELD, Krystal, R ... 813-253-6239. 118 L kschofield@ut.edu
SCHOFIELD, Sherri ... 906-248-8424. 240 J sschofield@bmcc.edu
SCHOFIELD, Wil ... 559-244-5920... 68 H wil.schofield@scccd.edu
SCHOH, Eric ... 507-457-5210. 262 A eschoh@winona.edu
SCHOKKER, Andrea ... 218-726-7103. 264 D aschokke@d.umn.edu
SCHOKNECHT, Pat ... 407-646-2700. 111 Q pschoknecht@rollins.edu
SCHOL, Kristin ... 202-885-8675... 97 D kschol@wesleyseminary.edu
SCHOLBE, Karen ... 314-529-9392. 276 G kscholbe@maryville.edu
SCHOLES, J. Scott, A ... 208-732-6221. 138 B sscholes@csi.edu
SCHOLL, Bill ... 765-285-5131. 164 B wgscholl@bsu.edu
SCHOLL, Heather ... 847-214-7177. 144 F hscholl@elgin.edu
SCHOLL-FIEDLER, Anne . 443-394-9257. 218 E ascholl-fiedler@stevenson.edu
SCHOLLA, James ... 320-308-5028. 261 C jscholla@sctcc.edu
SCHOLLES, Holly ... 503-760-3131. 402 B holly@birthingway.edu
SCHOLLMEIER, John ... 507-457-1436. 264 A jschollm@smumn.edu
SCHOLTE, Hugh ... 509-793-2291. 517 C
SCHOLTEN, Brian ... 607-274-3075. 327 E bscholten@ithaca.edu
SCHOLZ, Ben ... 201-761-7109. 306 L bscholz@saintpeters.edu
SCHOLZ, Daniel, J ... 414-410-4010. 532 B djscholz@stritch.edu
SCHOLZ, Greg ... 603-428-2470. 297 D gscholz@nec.edu
SCHOLZ, Joan, M ... 262-243-5700. 532 H joan.scholz@cuw.edu
SCHOLZ, John, K ... 608-263-2303. 536 D jkscholz@ls.wisc.edu
SCHOLZE, Roberta ... 217-351-2383. 155 J rscholze@parkland.edu
SCHONBERGER, Beth ... 215-635-7300. 417 C bschonberger@gratz.edu
SCHONE, Jeffrey, L ... 507-354-8221. 256 M schonejl@mlc-wels.edu
SCHONFELD, Leah, S ... 843-953-6922. 442 A leah.schonfeld@citadel.edu
SCHONGALLA-BOWMAN, Nancy, L ... 609-497-7890. 304 D nancy.schongalla@ptsem.edu
SCHOOF, Aaron, D ... 773-244-5564. 154 G aschoof@northpark.edu
SCHOOK, Lawrence ... 217-265-5440. 161 C schook@uillinois.edu
SCHOOLCRAFT, Tracy, A 717-477-1148. 429 E tascho@ship.edu
SCHOOLFIELD, David ... 417-269-8423. 273 D david.schoolfield@coxcollege.edu
SCHOOLMASTER, Andrew ... 817-257-7160. 484 I a.schoolmaster@tcu.edu
SCHOOLNIK, Rita, W ... 860-628-4751... 90 D rschoolnik@lincolncollegene.edu
SCHOON, Kristin, M ... 651-641-8839. 255 B schoon@csp.edu
SCHOON, Perry ... 309-438-2453. 147 J pschoon@ilstu.edu
SCHOONARD, Eric ... 423-236-2290. 458 J erics@southern.edu
SCHOONMAKER, Linda ... 253-589-5555. 518 B linda.schoonmaker@cptc.edu
SCHOONMAKER, Nancy . 616-222-1415. 241 F nancy.schoonmaker@cornerstone.edu
SCHOONMAKER, Stephen ... 501-337-5000... 20 J sschoonmaker@coto.edu
SCHOONOVER, Sandra ... 406-243-2611. 286 H sandra.schoonover@umontana.edu
SCHOONVELD, Tim ... 616-395-7698. 244 A schoonveld@hope.edu
SCHOOP, Michael ... 216-987-4045. 378 D michael.schoop@tri-c.edu
SCHOOR, Alan ... 212-463-0400. 348 B alan.schoor@touro.edu
SCHOOS, Ketwana ... 724-503-1001. 436 G kschoos@washjeff.edu
SCHOPP, Mary, C ... 414-847-3215. 534 F maryschopp@miad.edu
SCHOPP, Mary, E ... 312-942-5959. 157 G me_schopp@rush.edu
SCHORE, Robin ... 609-586-4800. 302 G schorer@mccc.edu
SCHORIN, Gerald, A ... 914-395-2218. 340 E gschorin@sarahlawrence.edu
SCHORNACK, Julie, A ... 714-449-7418... 67 D jschornack@scco.edu
SCHORNACK, Kent, A ... 515-263-2986. 178 G kschornack@grandview.edu
SCHORR, Timothy, B ... 608-796-3774. 539 E tbschorr@viterbo.edu
SCHORSKE, Nanda ... 415-883-2211... 40 G nanda.schorske@marin.edu
SCHOTT, Brett, T ... 314-367-8700. 281 C brett.schott@stlcop.edu
SCHOTT, Charles ... 212-998-1398. 334 D charles.schott@nyu.edu
SCHOTT, Linda, K ... 207-768-9525. 212 G linda.schott@umpi.edu
SCHOTTLAENDER, Brian E, C ... 858-534-3060... 71 F becs@ucsd.edu
SCHOU, Larry ... 605-677-5481. 451 F larry.schou@usd.edu
SCHOUWE, Cecilia ... 657-278-3128... 33 E cschowe@fullerton.edu
SCHOVANEC, Lawrence .. 806-742-2184. 487 D lawrence.schovanec@ttu.edu
SCHOWE, Dorothy, A ... 636-584-6507. 273 M schoweda@eastcentral.edu
SCHRADER, Cheryl, B ... 573-341-4116. 284 A schrader@mst.edu
SCHRADER, Ed, L ... 770-534-6110. 122 A eschrader@brenau.edu
SCHRADER, Kathleen ... 805-289-6430... 74 H kschrader@vcccd.edu
SCHRADER, Marcus ... 317-789-8240. 165 E mschrader@crossroads.edu
SCHRADER, Thomas ... 630-942-3890. 142 G schrader@cod.edu
SCHRAG, Betty ... 574-535-7501. 166 A bettyls@goshen.edu
SCHRAG, Dale ... 316-284-5356. 184 J dschrag@bethelks.edu
SCHRAGE, Charles ... 217-206-7395. 161 E schrage.charles@uis.edu
SCHRAGE, Doug ... 907-474-7681... 10 I drschrage@alaska.edu
SCHRAGE, Jim ... 661-362-3222... 40 E jim.schrage@canyons.edu
SCHRAGE, Nancy ... 712-325-3413. 179 L nschrage@iwcc.edu
SCHRAM, Kandis ... 865-981-8290. 456 D kandis.schram@maryvillecollege.edu
SCHRAMM, Christine, M 937-229-2229. 391 C cschramm1@udayton.edu
SCHRAMM, Dorothy ... 315-279-5862. 328 D dschramm@mail.keuka.edu
SCHRAMM, Peter, W ... 419-289-5414. 374 C pschramm@ashland.edu
SCHRAMMEL, Debra, S .. 215-670-9270. 425 J dsschrammel@peirce.edu
SCHRAMSKI, Holley, W .. 706-542-2802. 133 C hscrams@uga.edu
SCHRANZ, Michael ... 719-632-8116... 82 K mschranz@intelliteccollege.edu
SCHRANZ, William ... 402-643-7246. 289 B bill.schranz@cune.edu
SCHRECK, Christopher, J ... 614-885-5585. 388 C cschreck@pcj.edu
SCHRECK, Jayne, A ... 309-457-2129. 153 D jayne@monmouthcollege.edu
SCHRECK, Peter ... 484-384-2973. 425 I pshreck@eastern.edu
SCHREFFLER, Paul ... 304-367-4920. 528 E Paul.Schreffler@pierpont.edu
SCHREIBER, Carl, W ... 540-338-1776. 508 A
SCHREIBER, Jim ... 785-628-4279. 186 F jschreib@fhsu.edu
SCHREIBER, Meredith ... 503-399-2535. 402 E meredith.schreiber@chemeketa.edu
SCHREIBMAN, Andi ... 925-424-1585... 37 L aschreibman@laspositascollege.edu
SCHREIBMAN, Marla, H . 718-951-5065. 317 C marlag@brooklyn.cuny.edu
SCHREIER, Chad ... 406-657-1746. 287 C chad.schreier@msubillings.edu
SCHREIN OSF, Shannon 419-824-3819. 383 C sschrein@lourdes.edu
SCHREINER, Bruce ... 801-524-8162. 495 O Bruceas@ldsbc.edu
SCHREINER, Rebecca ... 618-537-6514. 152 G rlschreiner@mckendree.edu
SCHREINER, Scott ... 701-777-2681. 371 C scott.schreiner@und.edu
SCHREINER, Steven ... 609-771-2529. 300 E schreine@tcnj.edu
SCHREMMER, Johnna, M ... 620-235-4761. 189 L jschremm@pittstate.edu
SCHRIEFER, John ... 304-647-6205. 530 B jschriefer@osteo.wvsom.edu
SCHRIER, Hugh ... 301-387-3098. 214 I hugh.schrier@garrettcollege.edu
SCHRINER, Brian ... 305-348-3181. 115 B Brian.Schriner@fiu.edu
SCHROAT, David ... 313-593-5430. 251 D dschroat@umich.edu
SCHROCK, Lynford ... 740-857-1311. 388 I lschrock@rosedale.edu
SCHROCK, Missy, K ... 574-296-6223. 163 J mkschrock@ambs.edu
SCHRODER, Arlie ... 405-422-1287. 399 B schrodera@redlandscc.edu
SCHRODER, Michael ... 760-750-8727... 35 A mschrode@csusm.edu
SCHROEDER, Alisha ... 406-265-4191. 287 D alisha.schroeder@msun.edu
SCHROEDER, Betzi ... 973-803-5000. 304 C bschroeder@pillar.edu
SCHROEDER, Brock ... 740-392-6868. 384 K brock.schroeder@mvnu.edu
SCHROEDER, David, E ... 973-803-5000. 304 C dschroeder@pillar.edu

SCHROEDER, Debbie ...... 308-865-8950. 292 H
schroederd@unk.edu
SCHROEDER, Debra .... 218-723-6595. 254 K
dschroed@css.edu
SCHROEDER, Dennis, J .. 818-364-7650... 52 A
Schroedj@lamission.edu
SCHROEDER,
Douglas, R .... 651-631-5160. 263 A
drschroeder@nwc.edu
SCHROEDER, Francie ..... 512-863-1454. 481 I
schroedf@southwestern.edu
SCHROEDER, Fritz .... 410-516-6328. 215 H
fschroed@jhu.edu
SCHROEDER, Henning .... 612-625-2809. 264 G
schro601@umn.edu
SCHROEDER, Jennifer .... 785-243-1435. 185 M
jschroeder@cloud.edu
SCHROEDER, Lisa .... 409-880-2137. 486 E
lwschroeder@lit.edu
SCHROEDER, Michael .... 912-358-3202. 131 C
schroedm@savannahstate.edu
SCHROEDER, Patricia ..... 414-382-6284. 531 I
patricia.schroeder@alverno.edu
SCHROEDER, Paul .... 309-677-3845. 140 I
pschroeder@bradley.edu
SCHROEDER, Petra .... 608-262-1044. 536 D
pschroeder@wisc.edu
SCHROEDER, Philip .... 719-587-7306... 78 B
philip_schroeder@adams.edu
SCHROEDER, Phillip .... 320-308-5580. 261 C
pschroeder@sctcc.edu
SCHROEDER, Randall ..... 651-690-6650. 263 O
SCHROEDER, Ross .... 979-830-4118. 467 I
ross.schroeder@blinn.edu
SCHROEDER, Sally .... 515-964-6291. 177 B
ssschroeder@dmacc.edu
SCHROEDER, Sandra .... 620-343-4600. 186 E
sschroeder@fhtc.edu
SCHROEDER, Stephanie . 320-629-5126. 260 F
schroeders@pinetech.edu
SCHROEDER,
Stephen, C .... 727-816-3403. 110 E
schroes@phcc.edu
SCHROEDER, Steven ...... 414-443-8601. 539 F
steve.schroeder@wlc.edu
SCHROEDER, Tracy .... 617-353-2780. 224 D
tas@bu.edu
SCHROEDER-BIEK, Julie 574-284-4333. 172 G
jsbiek@saintmarys.edu
SCHROEDER-GREEN,
Suzanna .... 440-646-8178. 392 D
sschroeder@ursuline.edu
SCHROER, Tara .... 785-460-5487. 185 P
tara.schroer@colbycc.edu
SCHROER, Timothy .... 507-786-3615. 264 B
schroert@stolaf.edu
SCHROM, Patricia .... 701-671-2430. 372 E
patricia.schrom@ndscs.edu
SCHROTH, Katie .... 715-346-3930. 538 A
kschroth@uwsp.edu
SCHROYER, Carol .... 301-696-3411. 215 D
schroyerl@hood.edu
SCHRUM, Jake, B .... 276-944-6107. 504 H
jschrum@ehc.edu
SCHRUM, Lynn .... 304-293-5704. 530 D
lynn.Schrum@mail.wvu.edu
SCHUBERT, Donna .... 334-670-5830..... 7 H
schubert@troy.edu
SCHUBERT, Marianne, A 336-758-5273. 370 D
schubem@wfu.edu
SCHUBERT, Phil .... 325-674-2412. 464 H
schubert@acu.edu
SCHUBERT, Susan .... 410-837-4866. 221 A
sschubert@ubalt.edu
SCHUCH, Debra .... 717-299-7408. 434 A
schuch@stevenscollege.edu
SCHUCHARD, Bruce, G .. 314-505-7103. 272 J
schuchardb@csl.edu
SCHUCHARDT, Bob .... 605-229-8406. 450 J
bob.schuchardt@presentation.edu
SCHUCHARDT, Maureen 605-229-8426. 450 J
maureen.schuchardt@presentation.edu
SCHUCHERT, Michael ..... 703-284-3810. 507 B
michael.schuchert@marymount.edu
SCHUCK, Emily, G .... 740-374-8716. 392 I
eschuck@wscc.edu
SCHUCKEL, Harry .... 410-837-4743. 221 A
hschuckel@ubalt.edu
SCHUELE, Karen .... 216-397-4391. 381 R
kschuele@jcu.edu
SCHUELKE, Mark .... 231-591-2606. 242 F
schuelkm@ferris.edu
SCHUELKE, Nicholle .... 605-331-6765. 452 D
nicholle.schuelke@usiouxfalls.edu
SCHUELLER, Kenneth ...... 660-543-4721. 283 A
schueller@ucmo.edu
SCHUENAMAN,
Bruce, R .... 361-593-3528. 484 A
brs@tamuk.edu
SCHUEREN, Monika .... 516-686-7615. 333 H
mschuere@nyit.edu
SCHUERMER, David, A ... 270-824-8633. 196 A
david.schuermer@kctcs.edu
SCHUESSLER, George ..... 212-678-3302. 347 G
gs56@tc.columbia.edu
SCHUETZ, Bill .... 541-463-3355. 403 I
schuetzb@lanecc.edu
SCHUETZ, Gina .... 618-545-3099. 149 D
gschuetz@kaskaskia.edu
SCHUETZ, Ronald, L ...... 317-738-8160. 165 I
rschuetz@franklincollege.edu
SCHUETZ, Steven, M ...... 218-299-3004. 255 A
sschuetz@cord.edu
SCHUH, Mary Paula .... 859-572-5122. 198 I
schuh@nku.edu
SCHUHLE-WILLIAMS,
Karen .... 585-395-8000. 342 F
kschuhle@brockport.edu
SCHUILING, Kerri, D ...... 248-370-4081. 248 J
schuilin@oakland.edu
SCHULER, Carol, M .... 304-637-1338. 526 E
schulerc@dewv.edu
SCHULER, Jill .... 502-447-1000. 199 E
jschuler@spencerian.edu
SCHULER, Stephanie ...... 304-647-6347. 530 B
sschuler@osteo.wvsom.edu
SCHULL, Gail .... 208-732-6232. 138 B
gschull@csi.edu
SCHULL,
Stephanie Grace .... 480-860-2700... 13 Q
sschull@taliesin.edu
SCHULMAN, Avrohom .... 908-354-6057. 308 M
SCHULMAN, Jane .... 718-482-5302. 318 F
janes@lagcc.cuny.edu
SCHULMAN, Mark .... 415-433-9200... 65 C
mschulman@saybrook.edu
SCHULMAN, Paul .... 315-792-7435. 346 C
paul.schulman@sunyit.edu
SCHULMAN, Sharon .... 609-626-3541. 305 C
sharon.schulman@stockton.edu
SCHULT, Richard .... 310-377-5501... 53 F
mschult@marymountcalifornia.edu
SCHULTE, David .... 314-529-9329. 276 G
dschulte@maryville.edu
SCHULTE, Gerald .... 218-683-8557. 260 D
gerald.schulte@northlandcollege.edu
SCHULTE, Mary .... 618-468-3300. 150 G
mschulte@lc.edu
SCHULTE, Nancy .... 540-665-4530. 509 E
nschulte@su.edu
SCHULTE, Priscilla .... 907-228-4548... 11 A
priscilla.schulte@uas.alaska.edu
SCHULTE, R. Gregg .... 706-886-6831. 133 A
gschulte@tfc.edu
SCHULTE, Tim .... 660-831-4148. 278 I
schultet@moval.edu
SCHULTE, Vickie .... 618-437-5321. 156 H
schultev@rlc.edu
SCHULTE-SHOBERG,
Kim .... 715-232-1285. 538 B
schulteshobergk@uwstout.edu
SCHULTES, Brian .... 563-588-8167. 176 F
brian.schultes@clarke.edu
SCHULTHEIS, Luke, D .... 804-827-2064. 511 F
ldschultheis@vcu.edu
SCHULTHEIS, Stephen .... 914-632-5400. 331 K
sschultheis@monroecollege.edu
SCHULTINGKEMPER,
Kathy .... 910-323-5614. 353 B
registrar@ccbs.edu
SCHULTZ, Amber .... 814-732-1373. 428 E
aschultz@edinboro.edu
SCHULTZ, Barb .... 563-425-5283. 183 B
schultzb@uiu.edu
SCHULTZ, Barry .... 901-572-2500. 453 B
barry.schultz@bchs.edu
SCHULTZ, Bruce .... 907-786-6108... 10 H
anbrs@uaa.alaska.edu
SCHULTZ, Christina .... 435-652-7542. 497 E
schultz@dixie.edu
SCHULTZ, Jackie .... 406-377-9406. 286 A
Schultz@dawson.edu
SCHULTZ, Joseph, P .... 607-777-2187. 341 E
jschultz@binghamton.edu
SCHULTZ, Kelly .... 814-868-9900. 416 C
schultzk@erieit.edu
SCHULTZ, Kevin, J .... 989-964-4049. 249 G
kschultz@svsu.edu
SCHULTZ, Lisa .... 210-805-3596. 490 A
lisas@uiwtx.edu
SCHULTZ, Michael, J ...... 618-650-4628. 159 H
mschult@siue.edu
SCHULTZ, Robert .... 845-434-5750. 347 A
rschultz@sullivan.suny.edu
SCHULTZ, Roger, D .... 434-592-4030. 506 I
rschultz@liberty.edu
SCHULTZ, Roger, W .... 951-487-3002... 55 B
rschultz@msjc.edu
SCHULTZ, Russ .... 409-880-8137. 486 F
russ.schultz@lamar.edu
SCHULTZ, Steven .... 559-791-2218... 49 P
sschultz@portervillecollege.edu
SCHULTZ, Travis .... 701-323-5390. 372 I
Travis.Schulz@SanfordHealth.org
SCHULTZ, William, A ...... 414-955-4780. 534 C
wschultz@mcw.edu
SCHULZ, Christa .... 360-416-7974. 523 G
christa.schulz@skagit.edu
SCHULZ, Chuck .... 309-341-7205. 150 A
cschulz@knox.edu
SCHULZ, Karyn .... 410-837-4775. 221 A
kschulz@ubalt.edu
SCHULZ, Kathy, L .... 201-216-5667. 307 E
kathy.schulz@stevens.edu
SCHULZ, Kirk, H .... 785-532-6221. 188 A
kirks@ksu.edu
SCHULZ, Leslie .... 928-523-4331... 16 C
leslie.schulz@nau.edu
SCHULZ, Michael .... 406-683-7492. 286 I
m_schulz@umwestern.edu
SCHULZ, Paul, A .... 914-337-9300. 321 E
paul.schulz@concordia-ny.edu
SCHULZ, Robert .... 619-594-5901... 35 D
rschulz@mail.sdsu.edu
SCHULZ, Scott .... 623-845-3876... 14 M
scott.schulz@gcmail.maricopa.edu
SCHULZ, Scott .... 218-726-7171. 264 D
sschulz1@d.umn.edu
SCHULZ, Scott .... 360-486-8860. 522 G
sschulz@stmartin.edu
SCHULZ, Steve .... 712-792-8308. 177 B
sdschulz@dmacc.edu
SCHULZE, Christine, L ... 218-299-4544. 255 A
schulze@cord.edu
SCHULZE, Edee .... 651-638-6300. 253 K
e-schulze@bethel.edu
SCHULZE, Lori, A .... 920-748-8108. 535 J
schulzel@ripon.edu
SCHULZE, Lori, A .... 920-748-8310. 535 J
schulzel@ripon.edu
SCHULZE, Louann, T ...... 817-515-1280. 482 B
louann.schulze@tccd.edu
SCHULZKE, Mario .... 406-243-2323. 286 H
mario.schulzke@umontana.edu
SCHUM, Jennifer .... 919-530-6658. 368 A
jschum@nccu.edu
SCHUMACHER, Betty, A . 701-845-7412. 372 A
betty.schumacher@vcsu.edu
SCHUMACHER, Bryan, J 605-394-2215. 452 A
bryan.schumacher@sdsmt.edu
SCHUMACHER,
Charlotte .... 806-291-3549. 494 F
schumacherc@wbu.edu
SCHUMACHER, Gail .... 847-233-7700. 155 B
gschumacher@nc.edu
SCHUMACHER, Jane .... 803-641-3328. 448 A
janes@usca.edu
SCHUMACHER, Janette ... 484-664-3180. 424 H
schumach@muhlenberg.edu
SCHUMACHER,
Lawrence .... 847-233-7700. 155 B
lschumacher@nc.edu
SCHUMACHER, Lillian .... 419-448-3053. 389 J
schumacherlb@tiffin.edu
SCHUMACHER,
Mary Jeanne .... 812-357-6501. 173 A
mschumacher@saintmeinrad.edu
SCHUMACHER, Ron .... 419-448-3584. 389 J
schumacherrm@tiffin.edu
SCHUMACHER, Scott .... 979-830-4172. 467 I
scott.schumacher@blinn.edu
SCHUMACHER-BRIGHT,
Erin .... 503-943-7125. 408 F
bright@up.edu
SCHUMAKER, Ashley ..... 304-766-3000. 530 C
SCHUMAKER, Ashley, L . 304-558-0699. 529 C
schumaker@hepc.wvnet.edu
SCHUMAKER, Jennifer .... 910-755-7359. 358 D
schumakerj@brunswickcc.edu
SCHUMAKER, Terry, W .. 641-422-4222. 181 D
schumter@niacc.edu
SCHUMAN, Alan, M .... 410-386-8495. 214 A
aschuman@carrollcc.edu
SCHUMAN, Shmuel .... 847-982-2500. 146 C
schuman@htc.edu
SCHUMANN, James .... 651-523-2100. 256 A
jschumann01@hamline.edu
SCHUMANN, Kenneth ...... 503-352-2180. 407 A
schumank@pacificu.edu
SCHUMANN, Patricia, J . 304-766-3020. 530 C
pschumann@wvstateu.edu
SCHUMANN, Renae .... 281-649-3300. 473 B
rschumann@hbu.edu
SCHUMANN, Sherry .... 972-548-6803. 469 G
sschumann@collin.edu
SCHUMER, Jason .... 314-792-6120. 275 L
schumer@kenrick.edu
SCHUNK, Jill .... 812-855-5646. 167 F
jschunk@iu.edu
SCHUPACK, Sara .... 773-481-8434. 142 F
schupack1@ccc.edu
SCHUR, Jill .... 773-508-7392. 151 H
jschur@luc.edu
SCHURE, Matthew .... 215-871-6800. 430 D
mschure@pcom.edu
SCHURMAN, Jane .... 610-957-5700. 414 D
jschurman@dccc.edu
SCHURMAN, Susan, J .... 732-932-6965. 306 B
schurman@dceo.rutgers.edu
SCHURMAN, Susan, J .... 732-932-6965. 306 B
sschurman@dceo.rutgers.edu
SCHURMANN, Linda .... 605-886-6777. 450 F
lschurmann@mtmc.edu
SCHURR, Jill .... 903-813-2340. 466 H
jschurr@austincollege.edu
SCHUSTER, Alice-Ann .... 845-451-1262. 322 D
a_schust@culinary.edu
SCHUSTER, Barbara, L ... 706-369-5911. 133 C
bschust@uga.edu
SCHUSTER, Danny .... 516-295-5700. 351 N
SCHUSTER, Julian, Z ...... 314-968-8242. 284 N
julianschuster31@webster.edu
SCHUSTER, Leslie .... 401-456-9723. 439 F
lschuster@ric.edu
SCHUSTER, Marilyn, R ... 413-585-3000. 236 H
mschuste@smith.edu
SCHUSTER, Sheldon, M . 909-607-0108... 39 F
sheldon_schuster@kgi.edu
SCHUSTER, Stacy .... 609-771-3214. 300 E
schuster@tcnj.edu
SCHUSTER-MATLOCK,
Tracy .... 563-333-6049. 182 B
SchusterTracy@sau.edu
SCHUTH, Kristen .... 585-345-6898. 325 C
keschuth@genesee.edu
SCHUTT, Stephen, D .... 847-735-5100. 150 B
presiden@lakeforest.edu
SCHUTTA, Katharine .... 312-629-6821. 158 L
kschutta@saic.edu
SCHUTTE, Janet, L .... 260-422-5561. 167 B
jlschutte@indianatech.edu
SCHUTTE, Thomas, F ..... 718-636-3647. 336 F
tschutte@pratt.edu
SCHUTTINGA, Bethany .... 712-722-6075. 177 J
bethany.schuttinga@dordt.edu
SCHUTZ, Christine .... 208-459-5524. 138 A
cschutz@collegeofidaho.edu
SCHUTZ, Greg .... 615-366-3933. 459 A
greg.schutz@tbr.edu
SCHUTZLER, Lyndon ...... 831-646-4221... 54 I
lschutzler@mpc.edu
SCHUYLER, Lori, G .... 804-289-8781. 510 L
lschuyle@richmond.edu
SCHWAB, Carrie, L .... 215-248-6309. 422 F
cschwab@ltsp.edu
SCHWAB, Duane .... 701-662-1534. 372 D
duane.schwab@lrsc.edu
SCHWAB, Etta .... 503-654-8000. 407 B
eschwab@pioneerpacific.edu
SCHWAB, Kenneth, L ..... 615-868-6503. 457 D
kschwab@mtsa.edu
SCHWAB, Linda .... 615-383-4848. 464 D
lschwab@watkins.edu
SCHWAB, Martin, J .... 215-248-7311. 422 F
mschwab@ltsp.edu
SCHWAB, Mary, S .... 540-828-5487. 502 J
mschwab@bridgewater.edu
SCHWAB, Nancy .... 916-660-7900... 66 B
nschwab@sierracollege.edu
SCHWAB, Stewart, J .... 607-255-3527. 322 A
sjs15@cornell.edu
SCHWABACH, Katie .... 315-866-0300. 326 A
schwabaka@herkimer.edu
SCHWABE, Jean, D .... 478-289-2464. 124 C
jdschwabe@ega.edu
SCHWABROW,
Lynsey, A .... 414-410-4005. 532 B
laschwabrow@stritch.edu
SCHWAGER, Kathleen ..... 860-255-3571... 89 G
kschwager@txcc.commnet.edu
SCHWAIG, Kathy, S .... 770-423-6425. 127 N
kschwaig@kennesaw.edu
SCHWAIGER, Patsy .... 513-244-4371. 377 G
patsy_schwaiger@mail.msj.edu
SCHWALBACH, Eileen ..... 414-256-1207. 535 A
schwale@mtmary.edu
SCHWAM, Michael .... 561-547-6130. 103 L
mschwam@careercollege.edu
SCHWANER, Terry .... 315-792-5376. 331 I
tschwaner@mvcc.edu
SCHWANKE, Deborah ..... 785-460-5411. 185 P
debbie.schwanke@colbycc.edu
SCHWANKE, Shellie .... 309-467-6316. 145 C
sschwanke@eureka.edu
SCHWARTZ, Alycia .... 570-961-7845. 420 C
schwartza@lackawanna.edu
SCHWARTZ, Anna .... 207-775-3052. 210 H
aschwartz@meca.edu
SCHWARTZ, Celeste, M . 215-641-6492. 424 B
cschwartz@mc3.edu
SCHWARTZ, Corene .... 909-652-6242... 37 M
cory.schwartz@chaffey.edu
SCHWARTZ, David .... 845-783-9901. 349 E
vtamds@gmail.com

SCHWARTZ, David, J ..... 248-370-3465. 248 J
schwart3@oakland.edu
SCHWARTZ, Diane .... 908-737-3340. 302 F
dischwar@kean.edu
SCHWARTZ, Doreen .... 847-635-1632. 155 F
doreen@oakton.edu
SCHWARTZ, Eric .... 612-625-0669. 264 G
eschwart@umn.edu
SCHWARTZ, Ernest .... 718-384-5460. 351 H
SCHWARTZ, Gary .... 718-960-6093. 318 A
gary.schwartz@lehman.cuny.edu
SCHWARTZ, Hayim .... 718-268-4700. 337 F
SCHWARTZ, Janis .... 973-720-2175. 308 I
schwartzj@wpunj.edu
SCHWARTZ, Jennifer ...... 317-955-6056. 170 V
jschwartz@marian.edu
SCHWARTZ, Jessica .... 715-833-6256. 539 J
jschwartz31@cvtc.edu
SCHWARTZ, Joel, D .... 757-221-2460. 503 N
jxschw@wm.edu
SCHWARTZ, Joshua .... 215-619-7419. 424 B
jschwart1@mc3.edu
SCHWARTZ, Judy, A .... 972-860-7184. 470 I
JudySchwartz@dcccd.edu
SCHWARTZ, Kenneth ...... 504-865-5389. 207 C
kschwartz@tulane.edu
SCHWARTZ, Lance, W .... 507-344-7427. 253 J
schwartz@blc.edu
SCHWARTZ, Mary, L ...... 301-295-3013. 545 C
mary.schwartz.ctr@usuhs.edu
SCHWARTZ, Mary Beth .. 803-327-8042. 449 J
mbschwartz@yorktech.edu
SCHWARTZ, Matthew, J . 812-888-5832. 174 F
mschwartz@vinu.edu
SCHWARTZ, Micheal, H . 501-324-9434... 24 B
mhschwartz@ualr.edu
SCHWARTZ, Patti .... 412-392-3959. 431 B
pschwartz@pointpark.edu
SCHWARTZ, Regina, L ... 330-684-8786. 390 F
reginas@uakron.edu
SCHWARTZ, Robert .... 206-296-5831. 523 E
schwartr@seattleu.edu
SCHWARTZ, Robert, W ... 573-882-2011. 283 B
rschwartz@umsystem.edu
SCHWARTZ, Sandor .... 718-963-1212. 328 C
kyrs@thejnet.com
SCHWARTZ, Shari, P ...... 404-413-2273. 126 E
spiotrowski@gsu.edu
SCHWARTZ, Shuly .... 212-678-8826. 328 A
shschwartz@jtsa.edu
SCHWARTZ, Steven .... 212-938-5712. 345 C
sschwartz@sunyopt.edu
SCHWARTZ, Steven, J .... 970-247-7196... 81 M
schwartz_s@fortlewis.edu
SCHWARTZ, Teri .... 310-825-7891... 71 C
tschwartz@tft.ucla.edu
SCHWARTZ, Terry .... 719-255-4047... 85 M
tschwart@uccs.edu
SCHWARTZMAN,
Michael .... 215-596-8855. 435 H
m.schwartman@usciences.edu
SCHWARZ, Felipe .... 978-837-5459. 234 A
schwarzf@merrimack.edu
SCHWARZ, May, L .... 614-235-4136. 390 A
mschwarz@TLSohio.edu
SCHWARZ, Steven .... 718-997-5903. 319 C
steven.schwarz@qc.cuny.edu
SCHWARZ, Thomas .... 386-822-7405. 117 C
tschwarz@stetson.edu
SCHWARZ, Thomas, J .... 914-251-6010. 344 D
thomas.schwarz@purchase.edu
SCHWARZMILLER, Paul . 412-237-3001. 413 D
pschwarzmiller@ccac.edu
SCHWARZMILLER, Paul . 412-237-3034. 413 D
pschwarzmiller@ccac.edu
SCHWEBEL, Lisa .... 718-951-4114. 317 C
lisas@brooklyn.cuny.edu
SCHWEDER, Wendy .... 803-641-3689. 448 A
wendys@usca.edu
SCHWEHN, Mark, R .... 219-464-5310. 174 E
mark.schwehn@valpo.edu
SCHWEIGER, Theresa ..... 941-756-0690. 420 E
tschweiger@lecom.edu
SCHWEIGERT, Rich .... 303-534-6290... 80 H
rich.schweigert@colostate.edu
SCHWEITZER, Carrie ...... 972-860-4848. 470 G
cschweitzer@dcccd.edu
SCHWEITZER, Cathie ...... 413-748-3333. 236 I
cschweitzer@springfieldcollege.edu
SCHWEITZER, Connie, J. 989-964-4160. 249 G
schw@svsu.edu
SCHWEITZER, Glenna, L 734-763-9954. 251 C
glenna@umich.edu
SCHWEITZER, Laura .... 518-631-9841. 348 K
schweitzerl@uniongraduatecollege.edu
SCHWEITZER, Mike .... 210-999-8409. 488 C
mschweit@trinity.edu
SCHWEITZER, Steven, J . 800-287-8822. 164 C
schwest@bethanyseminary.edu
SCHWENK, Terry .... 978-232-2066. 226 C
terrys@endicott.edu
SCHWENK, Thomas, L .... 775-784-6001. 294 J
tschwenk@medicine.nevada.edu
SCHWENN, John, O .... 706-272-4438. 123 G
jschwenn@daltonstate.edu
SCHWERDTFEGER,
Patrick .... 951-487-3420... 55 B
pschwerdtfeger@msjc.edu
SCHWERTNER, Melanie .. 325-574-6503. 494 K
mschwertner@wtc.edu
SCHWIEBERT, Ryan .... 828-339-4600. 364 B
ryans@southwesterncc.edu
SCHWIETERMAN, Jerry .. 219-473-4239. 164 K
jschwieterman@ccsj.edu
SCHWIETZ, Michele .... 970-351-2161... 86 C
michele.schwietz@unco.edu
SCHWINER, Mary .... 920-923-8937. 534 A
mschwiner@marianuniversity.edu
SCHWINKE, Victoria .... 573-897-5000. 276 E
SCIAME, Joseph, A .... 718-990-1941. 339 A
sciamej@stjohns.edu
SCIAME-GIESECKE,
Susan .... 765-455-9221. 168 A
sgieseck@iuk.edu
SCIANNA, Dominic .... 718-990-6185. 339 A
sciannad@stjohns.edu
SCIGLITANO, JR.,
Anthony, C .... 973-275-5847. 307 C
anthony.sciglitano@shu.edu
SCIOLA, Michael .... 315-228-7380. 320 F
msciola@colgate.edu
SCIOLA, Michael, A .... 860-685-3377... 92 H
msciola@wesleyan.edu
SCIOTTO, Page, C .... 401-598-2145. 439 B
psciotto@jwu.edu
SCIPIO, Julius .... 478-825-6330. 124 H
scipioj@fvsu.edu
SCIPIO, Julius, E .... 804-257-5606. 515 F
jescipio@vuu.edu
SCIPLE, Judith, A .... 302-739-4068... 93 D
sciple@dtcc.edu
SCIPLE, Melinda .... 662-476-5040. 266 I
msciple@eastms.edu
SCISM, Bruce .... 615-230-3555. 461 G
bruce.scism@volstate.edu
SCISM, Bruce, R .... 434-797-8400. 512 C
bscism@dcc.vccs.edu
SCISM, Darby, C .... 812-237-5000. 167 A
darby.scism@indstate.edu
SCIUTO, Jim .... 925-631-8043... 61 F
jsciuto@stmarys-ca.edu
SCLAFANI, Michael .... 718-399-4211. 336 F
msclafan@pratt.edu
SCLAFANI, Sandra .... 212-875-4675. 314 C
ssclafani@bankstreet.edu
SCOBEE, Georgia .... 225-216-8608. 202 H
scobeeg@mybrcc.edu
SCOBEY, David .... 212-229-5613. 332 E
scobeyd@newschool.edu
SCOBY, Jerry, L .... 231-591-2164. 242 F
scobyj@ferris.edu
SCOFIELD, Elizabeth, A .. 215-951-1040. 420 B
scofield@lasalle.edu
SCOFIELD, Jeff .... 808-974-7324. 136 A
jscofiel@hawaii.edu
SCOGGINS, Amy .... 229-227-2687. 132 D
ascoggins@southwestgatech.edu
SCOGGINS, M, W .... 303-273-3280... 80 E
presoffice@mines.edu
SCOGIN, James .... 903-223-3003. 484 C
james.scogin@tamut.edu
SCOGIN, James .... 903-223-3110. 484 C
james.scogin@tamut.edu
SCOLFORO, David .... 610-917-3952. 436 C
dmscolforo@vfcc.edu
SCOLFORO, Karen .... 800-759-2727. 412 J
SCOMA, Sam .... 309-796-5650. 140 E
scomas@bhc.edu
SCOPA, Pat .... 606-589-3042. 196 F
pat.scopa@kctcs.edu
SCOPAS, Constantine ...... 212-686-9244. 313 G
SCOPELLITI, Theresa ...... 570-961-7840. 420 C
scopellitit@lackawanna.edu
SCORDINO, Anthony .... 914-606-6521. 350 F
anthony.scordino@sunywcc.edu
SCORSE, Bill .... 417-873-7200. 273 H
bscorse@drury.edu
SCORZELLO, Joseph .... 617-254-2610. 236 B
SCOTKA, Mary, F .... 210-434-6711. 477 N
mscotka@lake.ollusa.edu
SCOTT, A. Nicole .... 260-422-5561. 167 B
anscott@indianatech.edu
SCOTT, Adrian .... 205-247-8145..... 7 E
ascott@stillman.edu
SCOTT, Adrienne .... 717-564-4112. 419 I
ascott@kaplan.edu
SCOTT, Amy .... 309-677-2814. 140 I
alscott@bradley.edu
SCOTT, Angela .... 305-899-3666... 98 O
ascott@barry.edu
SCOTT, Anita .... 937-708-5798. 393 A
ascott@wilberforce.edu
SCOTT, Anne .... 940-898-2586. 488 B
ascott2@twu.edu
SCOTT, Annie .... 860-343-5767... 89 A
ascott@mxcc.commnet.edu
SCOTT, Bette, J .... 405-325-1974. 401 B
bscott@ou.edu
SCOTT, Billy .... 662-254-3319. 269 A
bscott@mvsu.edu
SCOTT, Bob .... 580-349-1597. 397 G
bobs@opsu.edu
SCOTT, Candice .... 830-792-7318. 480 F
cscott@schreiner.edu
SCOTT, Catherine, R .... 509-533-3567. 518 D
cscott@ccs.spokane.edu
SCOTT, Cathy .... 509-533-7082. 518 E
cathy.scott@scc.spokane.edu
SCOTT, Charles .... 309-438-8851. 147 J
cascott@ilstu.edu
SCOTT, Charles .... 423-425-4463. 463 D
Charles-Scott@utc.edu
SCOTT, Cheryl .... 971-722-7555. 407 D
cscott@pcc.edu
SCOTT, Christopher, D .... 815-772-7218. 153 G
cdscott@morrisontech.edu
SCOTT, Clifford .... 617-266-2030. 234 H
scottc@neco.edu
SCOTT, Connie, L .... 314-434-2212. 275 D
SCOTT, Constance, E ...... 260-422-5561. 167 B
cescott@indianatech.edu
SCOTT, Dave .... 970-245-8101... 82 K
dscott@intelliteccollege.edu
SCOTT, Dave .... 360-416-7751. 523 G
dave.scott@skagit.edu
SCOTT, David .... 410-651-7933. 219 E
dlscott@umes.edu
SCOTT, David, L .... 850-474-2587. 117 B
dscott@uwf.edu
SCOTT, Dawn, M .... 262-524-7297. 532 C
dscott@carrollu.edu
SCOTT, Deborah, C .... 508-831-6075. 238 F
dscott@wpi.edu
SCOTT, Delbert .... 913-722-0272. 187 K
SCOTT, Deloria .... 270-707-3823. 195 E
deloria.scott@kctcs.edu
SCOTT, Donna .... 512-404-4807. 467 A
dscott@austinseminary.edu
SCOTT, Dwayne .... 901-333-5025. 461 F
dscott@southwest.tn.edu
SCOTT, Eileen .... 856-256-4139. 305 E
scotte@rowan.edu
SCOTT, Elijah .... 706-295-6318. 125 C
escott@highlands.edu
SCOTT, Frances .... 312-893-7100. 145 B
fscott@erikson.edu
SCOTT, Fred .... 979-230-3213. 468 A
fred.scott@brazosport.edu
SCOTT, Gayanne .... 719-255-3388... 85 M
gscott@uccs.edu
SCOTT, Gaye Lynn .... 512-223-3770. 466 I
gls@austincc.edu
SCOTT, George .... 386-752-1822. 104 G
george.scott@fgc.edu
SCOTT, Greg .... 616-222-3000. 245 C
gscott@kuyper.edu
SCOTT, Heidi .... 618-468-5110. 150 G
hscott@lc.edu
SCOTT, Henrietta .... 803-774-3339. 441 F
scotth@cctech.edu
SCOTT, James .... 305-899-3950... 98 O
jscott@barry.edu
SCOTT, James .... 602-978-7784... 18 A
james.scott@thunderbird.edu
SCOTT, James .... 307-766-6226. 543 I
jscott@uwyo.edu
SCOTT, James, C .... 940-565-2791. 490 C
james.scott@unt.edu
SCOTT, James, K .... 573-882-6008. 283 C
scottj@missouri.edu
SCOTT, Janice, L .... 727-816-3424. 110 E
cessnaj@phcc.edu
SCOTT, Jeffrey .... 740-392-6868. 384 K
jeffrey.scott@mvnu.edu
SCOTT, Jeffrey, F .... 212-854-6639. 321 D
jscott@columbia.edu
SCOTT, Jillian .... 212-355-1501. 316 H
jscott@christies.edu
SCOTT, Jo Ann .... 662-252-8000. 269 F
jscott2@rustcollege.edu
SCOTT, Joseph .... 937-878-7985. 544 C
scottjoseph@aafes.com
SCOTT, Kathleen .... 805-289-6468... 74 H
kscott@vcccd.edu
SCOTT, Kathleen, E .... 937-255-3636. 544 C
kathleen.scott@afit.edu
SCOTT, Kathleen, J .... 410-543-6070. 220 D
kjscott@salisbury.edu
SCOTT, Kenneth .... 518-458-5359. 321 A
scottk@strose.edu
SCOTT, Lana .... 580-477-7719. 401 J
lana.scott@wosc.edu
SCOTT, Laura .... 707-864-7000... 66 G
laura.scott@solano.edu
SCOTT, Linda .... 706-776-0116. 130 E
lscott@piedmont.edu
SCOTT, Linda .... 804-524-5304. 515 D
lscott@vsu.edu
SCOTT, Lisa, L .... 585-785-1454. 324 D
scottll@flcc.edu
SCOTT, Lisa, M .... 570-372-4415. 433 H
scottl@susqu.edu
SCOTT, Lloyd, M .... 828-262-2120. 367 A
scottlm@appstate.edu
SCOTT, Louis, B .... 404-413-2400. 126 E
lscott01@gsu.edu
SCOTT, Louise .... 563-425-5214. 183 B
scottl@uiu.edu
SCOTT, Marcia .... 805-546-3119... 42 C
mscott@cuesta.edu
SCOTT, CSA, Marie .... 920-923-7624. 534 A
mscott@marianuniversity.edu
SCOTT, Mark .... 412-809-5100. 430 H
scott.mark@pti.edu
SCOTT, Mark .... 731-989-6002. 454 J
mscott@fhu.edu
SCOTT, Mark, J .... 901-321-4126. 453 H
mscott5@cbu.edu
SCOTT, Martha Lou .... 254-710-1761. 467 G
martha_lou_scott@baylor.edu
SCOTT, Mary .... 617-984-1768. 235 I
mscott@quincycollege.edu
SCOTT, Mary, K .... 949-214-3201... 41 I
mary.scott@cui.edu
SCOTT, Megan .... 309-341-7948. 150 A
mscott@knox.edu
SCOTT, Melissa .... 800-962-7682. 285 A
mscott@wma.edu
SCOTT, Michael .... 540-863-2850. 512 B
mscott@dslcc.edu
SCOTT, Michael, H .... 817-257-7858. 484 I
m.scott@tcu.edu
SCOTT, Michael, R .... 540-863-2850. 512 B
mscott@dslcc.edu
SCOTT, Michelle, T .... 240-567-5276. 216 F
michelle.scott@montgomerycollege.edu
SCOTT, Monica, R .... 843-953-5579. 443 A
scottmr@cofc.edu
SCOTT, Neil .... 334-386-7200..... 3 H
nscott@faulkner.edu
SCOTT, Patricia, A .... 410-706-7347. 219 C
pscott@umaryland.edu
SCOTT, Patty .... 541-888-7401. 407 H
pscott@socc.edu
SCOTT, Phyllis .... 305-899-3900... 98 O
pscott@barry.edu
SCOTT, Rebecca .... 707-256-7438... 55 F
rscott@napavalley.edu
SCOTT, Renay .... 567-661-7005. 387 L
renay_scott@owens.edu
SCOTT, Rhonda, J .... 423-236-2932. 458 J
rjscott@southern.edu
SCOTT, Richard .... 269-965-3931. 244 O
scottr@kellogg.edu
SCOTT, Richard .... 801-957-3263. 498 B
richard.scott@slcc.edu
SCOTT, Richard .... 801-957-3334. 498 B
richard.scott@slcc.edu
SCOTT, Richard, I .... 501-450-3198... 25 H
ricks@uca.edu
SCOTT, Richard, L .... 269-471-3284. 239 D
scott@andrews.edu
SCOTT, Richard, M .... 352-365-3525. 108 S
scottr@lssc.edu
SCOTT, Rob .... 770-426-2603. 128 D
rob.scott@life.edu
SCOTT, Robert, A .... 516-877-3838. 313 A
ras@adelphi.edu
SCOTT, Robert, F .... 785-628-5866. 186 F
rfscott@fhsu.edu
SCOTT, Ronald, B .... 513-529-0143. 384 G
scottrb@miamioh.edu
SCOTT, Ruth, A .... 724-287-8711. 411 C
ruth.scott@bc3.edu
SCOTT, Sally .... 703-654-1266. 510 J
sscott2@umw.edu
SCOTT, Sean .... 901-272-5139. 456 F
sscott@mca.edu
SCOTT, Sharion .... 516-323-4110. 331 J
sscott@molloy.edu
SCOTT, Sharon .... 802-635-1208. 501 D
sharon.scott@jsc.edu
SCOTT, Sharron, R .... 802-635-1208. 501 D
sharron.scott@jsc.edu
SCOTT, Sherrill, B .... 731-426-7522. 455 J
sbscott@lanecollege.edu
SCOTT, Stanley, V .... 325-235-7438. 486 C
stanley.scott@tstc.edu
SCOTT, Stephen, C .... 919-866-5141. 364 G
scscott@waketech.edu
SCOTT, Steven, A .... 620-235-4100. 189 L
sascott@pittstate.edu

SCOTT, Susan .... 740-366-9513. 376 A
scott.37@osu.edu
SCOTT, Tawana .... 864-877-1598. 445 H
tawana.scott@ngu.edu
SCOTT, Teresa, M .... 209-575-6530... 77 H
scottt@yosemite.edu
SCOTT, Thomas, R .... 864-656-7551. 442 C
trscott@clemson.edu
SCOTT, Todd .... 323-953-4000... 51 G
scottj@lacitycollege.edu
SCOTT, Vann .... 256-840-4188..... 6 I
vscott@snead.edu
SCOTT, Wayne .... 731-989-6790. 454 J
wscott@fhu.edu
SCOTT, Will .... 727-725-2688. 102 I
WScott@cci.edu
SCOTT, Will .... 727-725-2688. 102 I
wscott@cci.edu
SCOTT, William, J .... 260-399-7700. 174 C
bscott@sf.edu
SCOTT, Winston .... 321-674-8470. 104 H
wscott@fit.edu
SCOTT-JOHNSON,
Pamela .... 443-885-3509. 217 A
pamela.scottjohnson@morgan.edu
SCOTT-KINNEY,
Wanda, A .... 803-705-4680. 441 C
scottkinney@benedict.edu
SCOTT PAYNE, Moira ..... 206-726-5181. 518 G
SCOTT-SCURRY, Darlene 434-924-3200. 511 B
ds7sb@virginia.edu
SCOTT-SKILLMAN,
Thelma .... 415-239-3003... 38 L
tscott-skillman@ccsf.edu
SCOTT-SMITH,
Christine, K .... 671-735-2332. 546 E
csctsmith@uguam.uog.edu
SCOTT SOUFAS, Teresa . 215-204-7747. 433 K
teresa.scott.soufas@temple.edu
SCOTT SOUFAS, Teresa . 215-204-7747. 433 K
SCOTT-TRAMMELL,
Suzanne .... 205-934-4470..... 8 E
sstrammell@uab.edu
SCOTTI, Frank .... 714-879-3901... 47 K
fscotti@hiu.edu
SCOTTO, TOR, Dominic . 740-283-6276. 379 N
dscotto@franciscan.edu
SCOUBES, Jim .... 530-283-0202... 44 H
jscoubes@frc.edu
SCOUFOS, Lucretia .... 580-745-2278. 399 J
lscoufos@se.edu
SCOUTEN, Margaret, A ... 434-381-6109. 510 F
jyf@sbc.edu
SCOVELL, Gail, A .... 212-772-4220. 318 C
gail.scovell@hunter.cuny.edu
SCOVENS, Tarsha .... 215-751-8164. 413 I
tscovens@ccp.edu
SCOZZARI, Ron .... 704-216-7115. 363 D
ron.scozzari@rccc.edu
SCRAGG, Raymond .... 216-421-7312. 377 C
rscragg@cia.edu
SCRANAGE, Kimberly ..... 304-876-5009. 529 I
kscranag@shepherd.edu
SCRANTON, Alec .... 319-335-5672. 175 I
SCRAPER, Cassie .... 812-749-1225. 171 K
cscraper@oak.edu
SCREEN, Tommy .... 504-864-7082. 205 H
tscreen@loyno.edu
SCREMENTI, Lori .... 708-239-4842. 160 K
lori.scrementi@trnty.edu
SCREWS, Jacqueline, B .. 334-556-2485..... 3 N
jscrews@wallace.edu
SCRIBBICK, Michelle ...... 570-622-7622. 423 G
michele.scribbick@mccann.edu
SCRIBNER, Andrea .... 518-736-3622. 325 A
andrea.scribner@fmcc.suny.edu
SCRIMGEOUR, Andrew ... 973-408-3322. 301 C
ascrimge@drew.edu
SCRIMSHAW, Susan, C .. 518-244-2214. 338 C
scrims@sage.edu
SCROGGINS, Anita .... 205-970-9213..... 7 B
ascroggins@sebc.edu
SCROGGINS, Melinda .... 559-455-5580... 30 I
financialaid@calchristiancollege.edu
SCROGGINS, Pennie, R .. 229-732-5928. 120 D
penniescroggins@andrewcollege.edu
SCROGGINS, Susan .... 219-464-6395. 174 E
susan.scroggins@valpo.edu
SCROGGINS, Wayne .... 704-461-6717. 352 G
waynescroggins@bac.edu
SCROGGINS, William, T . 909-274-4250... 55 A
bscroggins@mtsac.edu
SCROGGS, Catherine, C . 573-882-6776. 283 C
scroggsc@missouri.edu
SCROGGS, Lori, E .... 815-224-0406. 148 A
lori_scroggs@ivcc.edu
SCRUGGS, Granville .... 901-322-0120. 452 F
SCRUGGS, Jeffrey .... 478-988-6852. 122 G
jscruggs@centralgatech.edu
SCUDDER, Mary, C .... 260-422-5561. 167 B
mcscudder@indianatech.edu
SCUDDER, Paul .... 941-487-4392. 115 D
scudder@ncf.edu
SCUDELLARI-PRESTO,
Marilyn .... 508-999-9130. 229 A
mscudellaripresto@umassd.edu
SCUKANEC, Gail .... 715-836-3671. 536 E
scukangp@uwec.edu
SCULCO, SC, Lois .... 724-838-4200. 433 E
sculco@setonhill.edu
SCULLEY, Patrick .... 210-292-3272. 545 C
patrick.sculley@usuhs.edu
SCULLY, Diana, H .... 804-828-4041. 511 F
dscully@vcu.edu
SCULLY, JR., Frank, E ... 215-646-7300. 417 F
scully.f@gmc.edu
SCULLY, Joseph, F .... 856-256-4127. 305 E
scullyj@rowan.edu
SCURRY, Frank, P .... 336-315-8660. 353 C
fscurry@carolinagrad.edu
SCURTI, Adam .... 740-283-6526. 379 N
ascurti@franciscan.edu
SCUTELLA, Clifford, M ... 585-345-6832. 325 C
cmscutella@genesee.edu
SCUTTI, Diane .... 610-902-8415. 411 E
diane.m.scutti@cabrini.edu
SEA, Karen .... 209-954-5151... 63 C
SEABERG, Doug .... 570-372-4408. 433 H
seaberg@susqu.edu
SEABERRY, Ben .... 619-482-6336... 68 B
bseaberry@swccd.edu
SEABOY, Donna .... 701-854-8013. 372 J
donnas@sbci.edu
SEABROOK, Gloria .... 803-535-5574. 442 B
gseabrook@claflin.edu
SEABROOKS, Joe .... 816-604-4205. 277 H
joe.seabrooks@mcckc.edu
SEACOTT, Damon, M ...... 517-750-1200. 250 E
dseacott@arbor.edu
SEACRIST, Ronald .... 806-742-3931. 487 D
ronald.seacrist@ttu.edu
SEADLER, Alan, W .... 412-396-5168. 415 F
seadlera@duq.edu
SEAGA, Andrew .... 305-237-7581. 109 D
aseaga@mdc.edu
SEAGER, Carol .... 785-864-9525. 190 L
cseager@ku.edu
SEAGO, Brenda .... 706-721-2856. 126 B
bseago@gru.edu
SEAGRAVES, Ronda .... 318-869-5087. 201 H
rseagraves@centenary.edu
SEAL, John .... 510-649-2462... 46 B
jseal@gtu.edu
SEAL, Robert .... 973-720-2104. 308 I
sealr@wpunj.edu
SEAL, Robert, A .... 773-508-2657. 151 H
rseal@luc.edu
SEAL, Sherry .... 706-754-7730. 129 G
sseal@northgatech.edu
SEAL, Timothy .... 901-751-8453. 457 B
tseal@mabts.edu
SEALE, Danette .... 865-471-3248. 453 F
dseale@cn.edu
SEALE, Francis Marie ..... 510-883-2068... 42 I
sfmseale@dspt.edu
SEALE, Lisa .... 928-317-6438... 11 L
lisa.seale@azwestern.edu
SEALE, Lisa .... 608-263-7217. 538 E
lisa.seale@uwc.edu
SEALINE, Alma .... 217-333-0610. 162 A
asealine@illinois.edu
SEALS, Jennifer .... 605-394-4034. 452 E
jennifer.seals@wdt.edu
SEALS, Lisa .... 760-355-6257... 48 A
lisa.seals@imperial.edu
SEALS, Logan .... 800-962-7682. 285 A
lseals@wma.edu
SEALS, Victoria .... 770-962-7580. 127 D
vseals@gwinnetttech.edu
SEALY, Spence .... 706-507-8955. 123 D
sealy_spence@columbusstate.edu
SEAMAN, Chuck .... 615-248-1240. 462 D
cseaman@trevecca.edu
SEAMAN, Cynthia .... 610-372-4721. 431 D
cseaman@racc.edu
SEAMAN, Daniel, B .... 315-229-5601. 339 F
dseaman@stlawu.edu
SEAMAN, Diane .... 937-328-6014. 377 A
seamand@clarkstate.edu
SEAMAN, Gerald, E .... 920-748-8109. 535 J
seamang@ripon.edu
SEAMAN, James .... 215-895-6012. 415 B
jks35@drexel.edu
SEAMAN, Jennifer .... 415-503-6230... 62 H
jseaman@sfcm.edu
SEAMAN, Sally .... 860-434-5232... 90 F
sseaman@lymeacademy.edu
SEAMAN, Sara .... 501-760-4101... 22 A
sseaman@npcc.edu
SEAMAN, Scott, H .... 740-593-2705. 387 C
seaman@ohio.edu
SEAMANS, Nancy, H ...... 404-413-2700. 126 E
nseamans@gsu.edu
SEAMEN, Erica .... 417-864-7220. 274 D
eseamen@cci.edu
SEAMS, Jennifer .... 304-645-6383. 530 B
jseams@osteo.wvsom.edu
SEANE, Oupa .... 904-620-2475. 116 B
oseane@unf.edu
SEARCH, Sally .... 850-201-8490. 117 D
searchs@tcc.fl.edu
SEARCY, Douglas, N .... 540-654-1062. 510 J
dsearcy@umw.edu
SEARCY, Lee Ann .... 660-359-3948. 279 H
lsearcy@mail.ncmissouri.edu
SEARCY, Scott .... 641-585-8133. 183 D
searcys@waldorf.edu
SEARCY, Tim .... 912-583-3142. 122 B
tsearcy@bpc.edu
SEARCY, Tony, V .... 336-386-3246. 364 D
searcyt@surry.edu
SEARFOSS, Alexis .... 727-873-4519. 116 D
asearfoss@usfsp.edu
SEARING, Linda .... 585-389-2870. 332 D
lsearin9@naz.edu
SEARLE, Natalie .... 802-786-5148. 501 C
natalie.searle@ccv.edu
SEARS, Andrew .... 617-282-9798. 272 D
andrew@techmission.org
SEARS, Andrew, L .... 585-475-4786. 337 L
alsics@rit.edu
SEARS, Connie .... 562-938-4155... 51 D
csears@lbcc.edu
SEARS, David .... 240-567-7492. 216 F
david.sears@montgomerycollege.edu
SEARS, Douglas .... 617-358-4608. 224 D
dsears@bu.edu
SEARS, James, R .... 313-577-4301. 252 G
aa0830@wayne.edu
SEARS, John .... 303-220-1200... 78 K
john.sears@cffp.edu
SEARS, Laura .... 402-826-6773. 289 E
laura.sears@doane.edu
SEARS, Paul .... 419-434-4439. 391 D
sears@findlay.edu
SEARS, Richard .... 678-839-5353. 133 I
rsears@westga.edu
SEARS, Robert, E .... 864-644-5064. 446 I
rsears@swu.edu
SEARS, Steve, R .... 956-326-2480. 483 B
steve.sears@tamiu.edu
SEARS, Steven, A .... 401-865-2425. 439 E
ssears@providence.edu
SEARS, Tad .... 218-723-6017. 254 K
tsears@css.edu
SEARSON, Robert .... 216-987-3943. 378 D
robert.searson@tri-c.edu
SEATON, Ann .... 845-758-6822. 314 D
aseaton@bard.edu
SEATON, Steven .... 405-691-3800. 396 D
sseaton@macu.edu
SEATON, William, J .... 609-984-1120. 308 A
bseaton@tesc.edu
SEAVER, Catherine .... 860-512-2623... 88 G
cseaver@manchestercc.edu
SEAVER, Kent .... 972-273-3430. 471 B
kseaver@dcccd.edu
SEAVERS, Norm .... 954-201-7813... 99 D
nseavers@broward.edu
SEAWORTH, Timothy .... 701-355-8150. 373 E
seaworth@umary.edu
SEAY, Gary .... 718-270-5031. 319 A
garys@mec.cuny.edu
SEBALD, Austin .... 606-546-1602. 200 A
asebald@unionky.edu
SEBASTIAN, David, L ..... 765-641-4032. 163 L
dlsebastian@anderson.edu
SEBASTIAN, Denise .... 573-518-2249. 278 A
denise@mineralarea.edu
SEBASTIAN, Donald, H ... 973-596-2963. 303 G
sebastian@njit.edu
SEBASTIAN, J. Jayakiran 215-248-6306. 422 F
Jsebastian@ltsp.edu
SEBASTIAN, Juliann .... 402-559-4000. 292 J
julie.sebastian@unmc.edu
SEBASTIAN, Pam .... 660-831-4142. 278 I
sebastianp@moval.edu
SEBASTIAN-FRUEHAUF,
Tracie .... 724-503-1001. 436 G
tfruehauf@washjeff.edu
SEBASTIANI, Richard ..... 713-221-8225. 489 D
sebastianir@uhd.edu
SEBOLT, George, W .... 412-291-6210. 410 B
gsebolt@aii.edu
SEBOLT, Kevin, G .... 740-284-5192. 379 N
ksebolt@franciscan.edu
SEBOLT, Lara .... 412-291-6315. 410 B
lsebolt@aii.edu
SEBRANEK, Lori, A .... 608-243-4185. 540 C
lsebranek@madisoncollege.edu
SECHLER, Elizabeth .... 304-876-5172. 529 I
esechler@shepherd.edu
SECHLER, Elizabeth, S .... 540-464-7345. 515 B
sechleres@vmi.edu
SECHLER, Mary Jo .... 620-431-2820. 189 D
msechler@neosho.edu
SECHREST, Thomas, L .... 512-637-1954. 479 C
thomasls@stedwards.edu
SECHRIST, Ann .... 770-972-7580. 127 D
asechrist@gwinnetttech.edu
SECHRIST, Paul, W .... 405-682-7503. 397 E
psechrist@occc.edu
SECHRIST, Shana .... 503-725-8310. 406 B
shana.sechrist@pdx.edu
SECKA, Lamine .... 619-594-7903... 35 D
lsecka@mail.sdsu.edu
SECKER, Eric .... 847-628-2084. 149 B
webmaster@judsonu.edu
SECKMAN, Colleen .... 740-695-9500. 374 H
cseckman@belmontcollege.edu
SECORD, Anne-Marie ..... 858-541-7913... 55 J
asecord@nu.edu
SECRIST, Tammi .... 304-336-8281. 530 A
tsecrist@westliberty.edu
SECTOR, Stuart, A .... 937-328-3857. 377 A
secttors@clarkstate.edu
SEDA, Eric .... 718-357-0500. 339 G
eseda@edaff.com
SEDANO, George .... 510-594-5033... 30 K
gsedano@cca.edu
SEDDIKI, Mohamed .... 973-877-3080. 301 H
seddiki@essex.edu
SEDER, Diana .... 909-607-7785... 39 D
diana.seder@cmc.edu
SEDILLO, Eileen .... 505-454-3430. 310 E
sedillo_e@nmhu.edu
SEDILLO, Robert .... 928-226-4283... 13 B
bobby.sedillo@coconino.edu
SEDLACEK, Bernard .... 402-457-2529. 290 G
bsedlacek@mccneb.edu
SEDLACEK, Beverly .... 402-354-7249. 291 B
bev.sedlacek@methodistcollege.edu
SEDLAK, John .... 570-740-0234. 422 G
jsedlak@luzerne.edu
SEDORE, Christopher, M 315-443-5324. 347 C
cmsedore@syr.edu
SEDUTTO, Dawn .... 603-668-2211. 297 I
d.sedutto@snhu.edu
SEDWICK, Susan, W ...... 512-471-6424. 491 C
sedwick@austin.utexas.edu
SEE, David .... 501-337-5000... 20 J
dsee@coto.edu
SEE, Jonathan .... 310-506-6256... 58 H
Jonathan.See@pepperdine.edu
SEE, Leslie .... 304-260-4380. 527 N
lsee@blueridgectc.edu
SEEBER, Terry .... 740-374-8716. 392 I
tseeber@wscc.edu
SEEBERGER, Debra .... 410-704-2360. 220 E
dseeberger@towson.edu
SEEBO, Elane .... 806-291-3417. 494 F
seeboe@wbu.edu
SEEDHOUSE, Julie .... 406-657-1008. 288 B
julie.seedhouse@rocky.edu
SEEGER, Daniel .... 828-298-3325. 370 E
dseeger@warren-wilson.edu
SEEGER, Matthew .... 313-577-5342. 252 G
aa4331@wayne.edu
SEEGMILLER, Jesse .... 540-261-2746. 509 K
jesse.seegmiller@svu.edu
SEEHERMAN, Elisa .... 215-717-6075. 435 A
careerservices@uarts.edu
SEEK, Linda .... 301-846-2457. 214 H
lseek@frederick.edu
SEEKINS, Travis, P .... 325-670-1589. 472 O
seekins@hsutx.edu
SEEKLANDER, Marlene ... 605-882-5284. 450 D
seeklanm@lakeareatech.edu
SEEL, Max .... 906-487-2440. 247 A
seel@mtu.edu
SEELEY, Michael .... 321-674-8422. 104 H
mseeley@fit.edu
SEELEY, Natalie .... 801-957-4041. 498 B
natalie.seeley@slcc.edu
SEELY, Bruce, E .... 906-487-2156. 247 A
bseely@mtu.edu
SEEM, Mark, D .... 212-242-2255. 348 F
mark.seem@tsca.edu
SEEM, Susan .... 585-395-2504. 342 F
sseem@brockport.edu
SEEMAN, Steve, C .... 563-588-8000. 178 D
financialaid@emmaus.edu
SEEMANN, Jeffrey .... 860-486-3619... 92 A
jeff.seemann@uconn.edu
SEEMAYER, Jackson .... 573-288-6375. 273 F
jseemayer@culver.edu
SEESE, Christine .... 410-225-2222. 216 C
cseese@mica.edu
SEEVERS, JR., Gary .... 417-862-9533. 274 F
president@globaluniversity.edu
SEEVERS, Scott .... 402-643-7233. 289 B
scott.seevers@cune.edu

SEFCIK, Jeff .... 325-942-2333. 465 K
jeff.sefcik@angelo.edu
SEFFERS, Tracy .... 304-876-5463. 529 I
tseffers@shepherd.edu
SEFFINGER, Michael ...... 909-469-5423... 76 B
mseffinger@westernu.edu
SEFTON, Cindy .... 513-569-1699. 376 L
cindy.sefton@cincinnatistate.edu
SEGAL, Gordon .... 691-320-2481. 546 B
gsegal@comfsm.fm
SEGAR, Robert, B .... 530-752-2172... 70 J
rbsegar@ucdavis.edu
SEGAR, Thomas .... 304-876-5214. 529 I
tsegar@shepherd.edu
SEGAR-JOHNSON,
Emily .... 218-723-7013. 254 K
ejohns11@css.edu
SEGARRA, Carlos .... 787-264-1912. 551 A
carlos-segarra@sg.inter.edu
SEGARRA, Jose .... 787-878-5475. 549 L
jsegarra@arecibo.inter.edu
SEGARS, Glenda .... 662-862-8383. 267 C
grsegars@iccms.edu
SEGAT, Susana .... 617-879-7073. 230 B
ssegat@massart.edu
SEGAWA, Mike .... 253-879-2837. 524 F
msegawa@pugetsound.edu
SEGAY, Gary .... 928-724-6956... 13 H
gsegay@dinecollege.edu
SEGERSON, Joan .... 401-739-5000. 439 D
jsegerson@neit.edu
SEGGELKE, Linda .... 217-732-3168. 151 B
lseggelke@lincolnchristian.edu
SEGGERMAN, Richard .... 319-352-8521. 183 E
richard.seggerman@wartburg.edu
SEGGERMAN,
Richard, W .... 319-352-8276. 183 E
richard.seggerman@wartburg.edu
SEGOVIA, Ricardo .... 708-456-0300. 161 A
rsegovia@triton.edu
SEGRAN, Sam .... 806-742-5151. 487 D
sam.segran@ttu.edu
SEGROVES, Dawn, M ..... 214-860-2064. 470 J
dsegroves@dcccd.edu
SEGUEL, Jaime .... 787-265-3822. 554 E
decano.ingenieria@upr.edu
SEGUINN, Nancy .... 989-358-7212. 239 C
seguinn@alpenacc.edu
SEGURA, Steve .... 916-570-5011... 53 A
seguras@arc.losrios.edu
SEHEULT, Erin .... 909-558-4508... 51 C
eseheult@llu.edu
SEHGAL, Varun .... 718-518-6641. 318 B
vsehgal@hostos.cuny.edu
SEHL, JR., Patrick .... 316-295-5488. 186 H
sehl@friends.edu
SEHLOFF, John, M .... 507-344-7342. 253 J
john@blc.edu
SEIBEL, Kathleen .... 619-239-0391... 36 D
kseibel@cwsl.edu
SEIBENHAR, Neil .... 315-279-5428. 328 D
nseiben@mail.keuka.edu
SEIBERT, Jon .... 620-431-2820. 189 D
jseibert@neosho.edu
SEIBERT, Rhonda, K .... 563-562-3263. 181 E
seibertr@nicc.edu
SEIBERT, Susan .... 618-650-3708. 159 H
sseiber@siue.edu
SEIBLE, Frieder .... 858-534-6237... 71 F
fseible@ucsd.edu
SEIBOLD, Kathy .... 208-459-5882. 138 A
kseibold@collegeofidaho.edu
SEIBOLD, Kathy .... 716-896-0700. 350 A
seiboldke@villa.edu
SEIBRING, Scott .... 309-556-3096. 148 B
iwufaid@iwu.edu
SEIBRING, Steve, D .... 309-556-3135. 148 B
sseibrin@iwu.edu
SEICHRIST, Pipa .... 305-538-3193. 109 C
henry@miamiadschool.com
SEIDEL, Andrew, B .... 214-887-5252. 471 F
aseidel@dts.edu
SEIDEL, Ethan, A .... 410-857-2200. 216 E
eseidel@mcdaniel.edu
SEIDELMAN, James, E .... 801-832-2581. 498 F
cseidelman@westminstercollege.edu
SEIDEMAN, Nancy .... 404-727-0640. 124 E
nancy.seideman@emory.edu
SEIDEMANN, Jonathan ... 410-484-7200. 217 D
SEIDEN, Dena .... 813-879-6000. 103 B
dseiden@cci.edu
SEIDEN, Peggy .... 610-328-8489. 433 I
pseiden1@swarthmore.edu
SEIDENSTICKER,
Duane, P .... 414-847-3274. 534 F
duaneseidensticker@miad.edu
SEIDL, Daniel, J .... 920-498-5712. 541 B
daniel.seidl@nwtc.edu
SEIDLER, Nick .... 414-277-6922. 534 G
seidler@msoe.edu

SEIDMAN, Stephen, B .... 512-245-2119. 407 C
ss76@txstate.edu
SEIF, Gershon .... 874-982-2500. 146 C
seif@htc.edu
SEIFERT, Alice .... 914-923-2616. 335 J
aseifert@pace.edu
SEIGART, Denise .... 443-334-2821. 218 E
dseigart@stevenson.edu
SEIGEL, Denise .... 516-299-3392. 329 D
denise.seigel@liu.edu
SEIJO, Haydee .... 787-764-0000. 555 B
hseijo@degi.uprrp.edu
SEILER, David .... 512-863-1908. 481 I
seilerd@southwestern.edu
SEILER, Susan .... 414-256-1230. 535 A
mktg@mtmary.edu
SEILER, Tom .... 614-947-6103. 380 A
tom.seiler@franklin.edu
SEINFELD, Lynn .... 847-635-2186. 155 F
lynns@oakton.edu
SEIPEL, Joseph, H .... 804-828-2787. 511 F
jseipel@vcu.edu
SEIPP, Dale .... 503-517-1024. 408 H
dseipp@warnerpacific.edu
SEITZ, Carl .... 586-498-4066. 246 A
seitzc@macomb.edu
SEITZ, Kathy .... 828-726-2269. 358 E
kseitz@cccti.edu
SEITZ, Rebecca .... 573-592-4222. 285 D
rebecca.seitz@williamwoods.edu
SEITZER, Joan, M .... 410-827-5808. 214 C
jseitzer@chesapeake.edu
SEIVERS, Lana, C .... 615-898-2874. 459 D
lana.seivers@mtsu.edu
SEIWERT, Lisa .... 773-896-2400. 141 K
SEIXAS, Karyn .... 626-395-6161... 31 E
karyn@caltech.edu
SEJDINAJ, John, A .... 574-631-4130. 174 A
sejdinaj.1@nd.edu
SEK, Mary, S .... 610-861-1567. 424 E
memss01@moravian.edu
SEKELSKY, Mary Jo, S ... 810-762-3434. 251 E
maryjoss@umflint.edu
SEKUL, Michelle .... 601-928-6205. 268 C
michelle.sekul@mgccc.edu
SEKULICH, Brad .... 704-687-7747. 368 E
sekulich@uncc.edu
SELANDER, Ralph .... 843-349-5296. 444 F
ralph.selander@hgtc.edu
SELBE, James, H .... 240-684-2303. 219 F
jselbe@umuc.edu
SELBERT, Daphne .... 435-652-7711. 497 E
selbert@dixie.edu
SELBY, David, K .... 317-788-3386. 173 I
selbyd@uindy.edu
SELBY, Holly .... 410-337-6184. 215 A
holly.selby@goucher.edu
SELBY, Rosemary .... 478-553-2055. 129 H
rselby@oftc.edu
SELBY, Steve .... 714-992-7081... 56 F
sselby@fullcoll.edu
SELBY, Tammy .... 310-506-6500... 58 H
Tammy.Selby@pepperdine.edu
SELBY, Terri, P .... 802-654-2462. 500 B
tselby@smcvt.edu
SELDEN, Pete .... 870-733-6722... 21 I
pjselden@midsouthcc.edu
SELDERS, Ronald, J .... 304-637-1268. 526 E
seldersr@dewv.edu
SELF, George .... 520-515-5385... 12 R
selfg@cochise.edu
SELF, Michael .... 305-237-7445. 109 D
mself@mdc.edu
SELF, Michael .... 615-329-8697. 454 F
mself@fisk.edu
SELF, Sheila .... 918-456-5511. 396 H
selfsj@nsuok.edu
SELF-DAVIS, LeAnn .... 731-989-6931. 454 J
ldavis@fhu.edu
SELGO, Tim .... 616-331-8800. 243 C
selgot@gvsu.edu
SELIG, C. Wood .... 757-683-3369. 507 N
wselig@odu.edu
SELIGMAN, Joel .... 585-275-8356. 349 C
seligman@rochester.edu
SELIGMAN, Richard, P ... 626-395-6073... 31 E
richard.seligman@caltech.edu
SELIGMANN, Wendy .... 828-298-3325. 370 E
wseligmann@warren-wilson.edu
SELIGSOHN, Andrew, J .. 856-225-6754. 306 C
ajs@camden.rutgers.edu
SELIMO, Tony .... 973-300-2229. 307 F
tselimo@sussex.edu
SELINSKY, Brian .... 703-993-2446. 505 C
bselins2@gmu.edu
SELKIRK, Sara, E .... 816-654-7214. 275 K
sselkirk@kcumb.edu
SELL, JR., Edgar, S .... 410-857-2711. 216 E
esell@mcdaniel.edu
SELL, Justin .... 605-688-5625. 452 B
justin.sell@sdstate.edu

SELL, Randall, L .... 402-554-3408. 293 A
rsell@unomaha.edu
SELL, Sean .... 619-298-1829... 68 A
ssell@ssu.edu
SELLARS, John .... 641-784-5111. 178 F
jsellars@graceland.edu
SELLARS, Telly .... 502-213-2181. 195 F
telly.sellars@kctcs.edu
SELLECK, Mike .... 806-720-7775. 476 B
michael.selleck@lcu.edu
SELLEN, Mary, K .... 757-594-7130. 503 M
mary.sellen@cnu.edu
SELLERS, Calvin .... 662-915-7234. 270 B
csellers@olemiss.edu
SELLERS, JR.,
Cleveland, L .... 803-780-1019. 449 E
csellers@voorhees.edu
SELLERS, Cynthia, D ...... 334-727-4746..... 8 A
sellersc@mytu.tuskegee.edu
SELLERS, Emma .... 828-328-7288. 356 B
emma.sellers@lr.edu
SELLERS, James, E .... 216-368-5872. 375 J
jes3@case.edu
SELLERS, Jennifer .... 802-287-8072. 499 D
sellersj@greenmtn.edu
SELLERS, Martin .... 423-869-6815. 456 A
martin.sellers@lmunet.edu
SELLERS, Patrick, J .... 704-894-2078. 353 J
pasellers@davidson.edu
SELLERS, Patti .... 602-429-4931... 16 O
psellers@ps.edu
SELLERS, Randy .... 806-720-7161. 476 B
randy.sellers@lcu.edu
SELLERS, Terrie, O .... 912-408-3024. 131 D
tsellers@savannahtech.edu
SELLERS, Timothy .... 315-279-5685. 328 D
tsellers@keuka.edu
SELLERS, Tyler .... 903-923-2325. 471 J
tsellers@etbu.edu
SELLHEIM, Linda .... 619-684-8800... 56 C
lsellheim@newschoolarch.edu
SELLICK, Megan .... 570-208-5900. 419 P
megansellick@kings.edu
SELLMANN, James, D ...... 671-735-2805. 546 E
jsellman@uguam.uog.edu
SELLNAU, Ron .... 507-453-2738. 259 E
rsellnau@southeastmn.edu
SELLNER, Hildegard .... 907-796-6226... 11 A
hildegard.sellner@uas.alaska.edu
SELLS, Ben .... 765-998-5389. 173 C
bnsells@taylor.edu
SELLS, Debra, K .... 615-898-5342. 459 D
debra.sells@mtsu.edu
SELLS, Tamatha .... 864-941-8363. 446 C
sells.t@ptc.edu
SELLS, Vicki, G .... 931-598-3220. 458 H
vsells@sewanee.edu
SELMAN, Brenda, V .... 573-884-9153. 283 C
selmanb@missouri.edu
SELMER, Paula .... 518-244-2093. 338 C
selmep@sage.edu
SELMO, Barbara, J .... 781-239-6147. 222 D
bselmo@babson.edu
SELMON, John .... 231-777-0265. 247 G
john.selmon@muskegoncc.edu
SELMON, Michael, L .... 989-463-7176. 239 B
selmon@alma.edu
SELSOR, Melinda, K .... 636-481-3329. 275 I
mselsor@jeffco.edu
SELTZ, Paul .... 651-641-8225. 255 B
seltz@csp.edu
SELTZER, Robert .... 561-297-4747. 114 L
seltzerr@fau.edu
SELVIN, Molly .... 213-738-6624... 68 C
interdisciplinary@swlaw.edu
SELZER, Mary .... 828-339-4000. 364 B
marys@southwesterncc.edu
SELZER, Michael, M .... 605-394-2436. 452 A
michael.selzer@sdsmt.edu
SEMAH, Charles .... 732-431-1600. 307 G
SEMANIK, Janet .... 217-786-2217. 151 F
janet.semanik@llcc.edu
SEMANIK, Joyce .... 949-582-4342... 67 C
jsemanik@saddleback.edu
SEMENCHUCK, Amy .... 815-967-7326. 157 B
asemenchuck@rockfordcareercollege.edu
SEMENOFF, Michael .... 310-377-5501... 53 F
msemenoff@marymountcalifornia.edu
SEMENTA, Deborah .... 617-951-2350. 234 G
deborah.sementa@necb.edu
SEMENZA, Michael, L .... 401-341-2465. 440 C
semenzam@salve.edu
SEMIEN, Karen, L .... 443-412-2345. 215 C
ksemien@harford.edu
SEMMEL, Abraham .... 718-268-4700. 337 F
SEMMEL, Ralph .... 443-778-6278. 215 H
ralph.semmel@jhuapl.edu
SEMMEL, Stacey .... 561-297-2748. 114 L
ssemmel@fau.edu
SEMMES, Laurel .... 386-752-1822. 104 G
laurel.semmes@fgc.edu

SEMMES, Paul .... 931-372-3118. 460 A
psemmes@tntech.edu
SEMPLE, John .... 708-596-2000. 159 C
jsemple@ssc.edu
SEMRAU, Marv .... 701-858-3000. 371 F
marv.semrau@minotstateu.edu
SEMTNER, Anita .... 405-878-5295. 399 G
amsemtner@stgregorys.edu
SEMTNER, Pat .... 706-419-1138. 123 F
pat.semtner@covenant.edu
SEN, Arup .... 716-829-7658. 323 D
sena@dyc.edu
SENA, Anthony .... 505-747-2291. 311 E
asena@nnmc.edu
SENA, Donato .... 505-454-3369. 310 E
dfsena@nmhu.edu
SENA, Kathleen .... 505-747-2115. 311 E
SENCER, Stephen, D .... 404-727-2016. 124 E
steve.sencer@emory.edu
SENDALL, Patricia .... 978-837-5322. 234 A
sendallp@merrimack.edu
SENECA, Eric .... 225-768-0804. 206 D
eric.seneca@ololcollege.edu
SENEGAL, Pamela .... 919-718-7254. 359 B
psenegal@cccc.edu
SENEQUE, Guy .... 516-877-3650. 313 A
seneque@adelphi.edu
SENFT, James .... 847-543-2975. 143 A
jsenft@clcillinois.edu
SENG, Chris .... 970-491-4860... 80 I
christopher.seng@colostate.edu
SENG, Victoria, S .... 731-881-7855. 463 E
vseng@utm.edu
SENGENBERGER,
Jennifer .... 719-502-3198... 84 A
jennifer.sengenberger@ppcc.edu
SENGER, Susan .... 651-846-1490. 261 D
susan.senger@saintpaul.edu
SENGUPTA, Shivaji .... 212-694-1000. 315 E
ssengupta@boricuacollege.edu
SENICH, Greg .... 303-986-2320... 80 D
greg@csha.net
SENIOR, Ann Marie .... 609-984-1151. 308 A
amsenior@tesc.edu
SENIOR, Sandra .... 212-616-7271. 325 H
sandra.senior@helenefuld.edu
SENIOR, Timothy, C .... 610-785-6200. 432 C
rectorscs@adphila.org
SENKBEIL, Peter .... 949-214-3202... 41 I
peter.senkbeil@cui.edu
SENKER, Richard .... 813-253-7017. 106 M
rsenker@hccfl.edu
SENKFOR, Sherrie .... 618-650-2190. 159 H
ssenkfo@siue.edu
SENKO, John .... 313-927-1519. 246 D
jsenko@marygrove.edu
SENN, Gary .... 803-641-3558. 448 A
garys@usca.edu
SENNETT, Peter .... 413-775-1312. 231 E
sennettp@gcc.mass.edu
SENNYEY, Pongracz .... 512-448-8470. 479 C
pongracz@stedwards.edu
SENSENIG, Victor, J .... 518-255-5408. 344 E
sensenvj@cobleskill.edu
SENSER, Randie .... 212-247-3434. 329 L
rsenser@mandl.edu
SENSI, Patricia .... 732-224-2232. 299 G
psensi@brookdalecc.edu
SENTE, Marjory .... 928-350-4509... 17 K
msente@prescott.edu
SENTER, Jerry .... 662-862-8016. 267 C
tjsenter@iccms.edu
SENTER, Timothy, C .... 662-862-8460. 267 C
tcsenter@iccms.edu
SEO, Hoon .... 213-487-0110... 42 K
drubook@hotmail.com
SEO, Kyoo, W .... 636-327-4645. 277 K
wdciso@midwest.edu
SEO, Un Kyo .... 213-487-0110... 42 K
info@dula.edu
SEPA, Lisa .... 808-984-3577. 137 B
sepa@hawaii.edu
SEPANIC, Michael, J .... 856-225-6026. 306 C
msepanic@camden.rutgers.edu
SEPE, Matt .... 781-280-3523. 232 B
sepem@middlesex.mass.edu
SEPICH, Kim, W .... 336-249-8186. 360 A
kwsepich@davidsoncc.edu
SEPION, Daniel .... 605-394-2348. 452 A
daniel.sepion@sdsmt.edu
SEPKO, Cathy .... 864-977-7068. 445 H
cathy.sepko@ngu.edu
SEPPELT, Troy .... 970-248-1536... 79 F
tseppelt@coloradomesa.edu
SEPPER, Dennis, G .... 253-535-7467. 521 I
sepperdg@plu.edu
SEPPY, Donna .... 692-625-3394. 546 F
SEPT, Megann .... 415-351-3509... 62 G
msept@sfai.edu
SEPÚLVEDA, Carmen .... 787-850-9383. 554 D
carmen.sepulveda1@upr.edu

SEQUEIRA, Gerald .... 626-914-8517... 38 K
gsequeira@citruscollege.edu
SERAFIN, Renata .... 210-486-4689. 464 J
rserafin@alamo.edu
SERAFINO, Candice, J ... 413-545-6253. 228 F
serafino@acad.umass.edu
SERAICHICK, Laura .... 603-358-2526. 298 F
lseraich@keene.edu
SERAPHIN, Micheal, K ... 503-370-6055. 408 J
mseraphi@willamette.edu
SERBALIK, James .... 518-783-2314. 340 J
serbalik@siena.edu
SERBALIK, Sandy .... 518-783-2596. 340 J
sserbalik@siena.edu
SERBAN, Andreea .... 714-438-4698... 39 H
aserban@mail.cccd.edu
SERBEIN, John, G .... 909-748-8142... 73 H
john_serbein@redlands.edu
SERBER, Michael .... 214-648-9569. 493 E
michael.serber@utsouthwestern.edu
SERDYUK, Yana, V .... 708-209-3053. 143 E
yana.serdyuk@cuchicago.edu
SERGI, Joseph .... 603-645-9650. 297 I
j.sergi@snhu.edu
SERIANNI, Catherine, E .. 716-286-8571. 334 F
cs@niagara.edu
SERIO, Vincent .... 208-426-1459. 137 G
vinceserio@boisestate.edu
SERJOIE, Ara .... 510-885-4602... 33 C
ara.serjoie@csueastbay.edu
SERMERSHEIM,
Katherine .... 618-453-2461. 159 G
sermersh@siu.edu
SERMONS, Debra .... 913-667-5700. 185 J
dsermons@cbts.edu
SERMONS, Penny .... 252-940-6243. 358 A
pennys@beaufortccc.edu
SERNA, Frank .... 619-849-2783... 59 L
frankserna@pointloma.edu
SERNA, Ricky .... 505-747-2116. 311 E
raserna@nnmc.edu
SERNAU, Scott .... 574-520-4429. 168 E
ssernau@iusb.edu
SEROTA COTE, Pamela .. 540-375-2299. 509 B
cote@roanoke.edu
SEROTKIN, Patricia .... 814-472-3222. 432 D
pserotkin@francis.edu
SEROTKIN, Rita, S .... 336-316-2211. 355 A
sserotkinrs@guilford.edu
SEROTKIN, Rita, S .... 336-316-2211. 355 A
serotkinrs@guilford.edu
SEROVICH, Julianne .... 813-974-7196. 116 C
jserovich@usf.edu
SERPLISS, Ron .... 563-244-7021. 178 A
rserpliss@eicc.edu
SERR, Jim .... 815-280-6641. 149 A
jim.serr@jjc.edu
SERR, Roger, L .... 717-477-1308. 429 E
rlserr@ship.edu
SERRA, N. Maria .... 856-225-6005. 306 C
nmserra@camden.rutgers.edu
SERRA, Neddie .... 973-748-9000. 299 F
neddie_serra@bloomfield.edu
SERRANO, Aixa .... 787-857-3600. 550 A
aserrano@br.inter.edu
SERRANO, Carlos .... 212-772-4475. 318 C
cs171@hunter.cuny.edu
SERRANO, Gladys .... 787-743-4041. 548 H
gserrano@columbiaco.edu
SERRANO, Iris .... 787-743-7979. 552 I
ut_iserrano@suagm.edu
SERRANO, Luz, D .... 787-780-0070. 547 G
lserrano@caribbean.edu
SERRANO, Melba .... 787-890-2681. 553 H
melba.serrano@upr.edu
SERRANO, Rebecca .... 859-846-6052. 197 I
rserrano@midway.edu
SERRANO, Sandra, V ...... 661-336-5104... 49 M
sserrano@kccd.edu
SERRANO, Zaida .... 787-890-2681. 553 H
zaida.serrano@upr.edu
SERRATA, William .... 915-831-6511. 472 B
wserrata@epcc.edu
SERRAULT, Susan .... 608-663-3367. 532 I
sserrault@edgewood.edu
SERRAVILLO, JR., Lee .... 518-442-3080. 341 D
lserravillo@albany.edu
SERRETT, Marc .... 605-688-4128. 452 B
marc.serrett@sdstate.edu
SERVANTES, Lourdes ...... 956-665-2243. 492 B
servantesl@utpa.edu
SERVIDIO, Denise .... 718-990-6247. 339 A
stjohns@bkstr.com
SERWATKA, Thomas, S .. 904-620-2500. 116 B
tserwatk@unf.edu
SESSINK, Lanette .... 740-392-6868. 384 K
lanette.sessink@mvnu.edu
SESSION, Willie, M .... 386-481-2100... 99 C
sessionm@cookman.edu
SESSIONS, Lisa, H .... 828-448-3126. 365 A
lsessions@wpcc.edu
SESSIONS, Robin .... 251-809-1591..... 5 A
robin.sessions@jdcc.edu
SESSLER, April, L .... 806-371-5321. 465 E
alsessler@actx.edu
SESSLER, Jeff .... 909-621-8057... 65 D
jeff.sessler@scrippscollege.edu
SESSOMS, Denise, L .... 252-246-1290. 365 C
dsessoms@wilsoncc.edu
SESSOMS, F. Clayton ..... 252-328-9317. 367 B
sessomsf@ecu.edu
SESSUMS, Cassandra ..... 601-925-3464. 268 A
sessums@mc.edu
SESTAK, Barbara .... 503-725-3340. 406 B
sestakb@pdx.edu
SESTAK, Brandi .... 402-465-7579. 291 G
bsestak@nebrwesleyan.edu
SETCHELL, Cara .... 765-658-4154. 165 F
carasetchell@depauw.edu
SETCHELL, Steven, J .... 765-658-4215. 165 F
ssetchell@depauw.edu
SETH, Phil .... 503-883-2500. 404 A
phils@linfield.edu
SETHARES, Greg .... 508-678-2811. 231 B
greg.sethares@bristolcc.edu
SETHI, Kerry .... 610-625-7847. 424 E
sethi@moravian.edu
SETHI, S.J .... 956-665-2383. 492 B
sjsethi@utpa.edu
SETHNA, Bishar, M .... 409-882-3312. 486 G
bishar.sethna@lsco.edu
SETMEYER, Adam .... 317-955-6131. 170 V
asetmeyer@marian.edu
SETON-SCHUR, Matthew 518-327-6490. 336 B
msetonschur@paulsmiths.edu
SETSER, Henry, R .... 660-543-4730. 283 A
setser@ucmo.edu
SETTER, Paul, W .... 972-708-7321. 472 L
accounting@gial.edu
SETTERGREN, Jennifer .... 616-957-6675. 240 M
jsetterg@calvinseminary.edu
SETTLE, Karen .... 214-768-3211. 481 A
ksettle@smu.edu
SETTOON, Paula .... 918-595-7728. 400 E
paula.settoon@tulsacc.edu
SETTOON, Randy, P .... 985-549-2258. 208 C
rsettoon@selu.edu
SETZER, Kristen .... 704-406-4491. 354 C
ksetzer@gardner-webb.edu
SETZER, Pat .... 619-660-4674... 46 D
pat.setzer@gcccd.edu
SETZER, Patrick, K .... 828-262-3002. 367 A
setzerpk@appstate.edu
SETZER, Tim, W .... 409-944-1365. 472 I
tsetzer@gc.edu
SEUBERT, Jack .... 305-809-3195. 104 I
jack.seubert@fkcc.edu
SEUFERLING, Dale .... 785-832-7400. 190 L
dseuferling@kuendowment.org
SEUMANUTAFA, Loligi ... 684-699-9155. 546 A
l.siaki@amsamoa.edu
SEUNARINE, Patricia ...... 973-408-3246. 301 C
pseunarine@drew.edu
SEVER, Dennis .... 432-685-4690. 476 G
dsever@midland.edu
SEVERA, Anne Agosto .... 219-989-2977. 171 N
severas@purduecal.edu
SEVERANCE, Dana, A ...... 301-687-4121. 220 C
dseverance@frostburg.edu
SEVERANCE, Mary Ellen . 508-793-7478. 225 A
meseverance@clarku.edu
SEVERINO, Dan .... 215-596-8793. 435 H
d.severino@usciences.edu
SEVERNS, Mel .... 740-392-6868. 384 K
mel.severns@mvnu.edu
SEVERS, Doug .... 541-737-2241. 406 A
financial.aid@oregonstate.edu
SEVERSON, Christopher . 715-675-3331. 541 A
seversonc@ntc.edu
SEVERSON, Karen, J ...... 402-844-7273. 291 I
karens@northeast.edu
SEVERSON, Mark, W ...... 716-878-6434. 343 A
seversmw@buffalostate.edu
SEVERSON, Rick .... 503-552-1543. 404 H
rseverson@ncnm.edu
SEVERSON, Sheila .... 608-796-3001. 539 E
smseverson@viterbo.edu
SEVERSON, Stacy .... 612-436-7524. 257 J
sseverson@msbcollege.edu
SEVERY, Lisa, E .... 303-492-4104... 85 L
lisa.severy@colorado.edu
SEVICK, Leona .... 301-447-5333. 217 B
sevick@msmary.edu
SEVIER, Karen .... 603-752-1060. 296 E
ksevier@ccsnh.edu
SEVIER, Owen .... 405-691-3800. 396 D
osevier@macu.edu
SEVIG, Todd, D .... 734-764-8312. 251 C
tdsevig@umich.edu
SEVILLA, Henry .... 787-780-0070. 547 G
hsevilla@caribbean.edu
SEVIM, Hasan .... 618-650-2861. 159 H
hsevim@siue.edu
SEWARD, David .... 415-565-4710... 71 A
sewardd@uchastings.edu
SEWARD, David .... 815-280-2701. 149 A
dseward@jjc.edu
SEWARD, Karen .... 518-629-7356. 326 G
k.seward@hvcc.edu
SEWARD, Stephen .... 860-231-5503... 92 F
sseward@usj.edu
SEWARD, II, William ..... 704-463-3066. 365 E
bill.seward@fsmail.pfeiffer.edu
SEWART, John, J .... 650-574-6196... 64 C
sewart@smccd.edu
SEWELL, Ann, C .... 817-257-5070. 484 I
a.sewell@tcu.edu
SEWELL, Daniel, R .... 415-433-9200... 65 C
dsewell@saybrook.edu
SEWELL, Devona .... 352-854-2322. 100 K
sewelld@cf.edu
SEWELL, Gary .... 423-236-2700. 458 J
garysewell@southern.edu
SEWELL, Jason .... 423-472-7141. 460 D
jsewell@clevelandstatecc.edu
SEWELL, Keli .... 864-977-7733. 445 H
keli.sewell@ngu.edu
SEWELL, Kenneth .... 504-280-6836. 205 G
ksweell@uno.edu
SEWELL, Lisa .... 610-519-4646. 436 F
lisa.sewell@villanova.edu
SEWELL, Robert .... 760-245-4271... 75 B
Robert.Sewell@vvc.edu
SEWELL, Teresa .... 432-552-2600. 493 D
sewell_t@utpb.edu
SEWELL, Thomas, R .... 423-585-2644. 462 A
thomas.sewell@ws.edu
SEWELL, Zennabelle .... 212-261-1682. 333 H
zsewell@nyit.edu
SEXSON, Marla .... 620-229-6364. 190 G
marla.sexson@sckans.edu
SEXTER, Jay .... 646-981-4500. 348 B
jsexter@touro.edu
SEXTON, Brad .... 773-481-8752. 142 F
bsexton3@ccc.edu
SEXTON, Clarence .... 865-938-8186. 453 J
SEXTON, Edwin, A .... 208-496-1137. 137 H
sextone@byui.edu
SEXTON, Eric, L .... 316-978-3250. 191 F
eric.sexton@goshockers.com
SEXTON, Gary .... 330-941-1778. 394 A
sexton@wysu.org
SEXTON, Glenna, W .... 970-247-7331... 81 M
sexton_g@fortlewis.edu
SEXTON, John .... 212-998-2345. 334 D
john.sexton@nyu.edu
SEXTON, Michele, D .... 620-235-4187. 189 L
msexton@pittstate.edu
SEXTON, Mike, B .... 408-554-4700... 64 M
mbsexton@scu.edu
SEXTON, Robert, M .... 215-572-3816. 437 C
bsexton@wts.edu
SEXTON, Steve .... 615-248-7792. 462 D
ssexton@trevecca.edu
SEXTON, Susan .... 651-690-6565. 263 O
swsexton@stkate.edu
SEXTON, Susan, K .... 937-229-4333. 391 C
ssexton1@udayton.edu
SEXTON-JOHNSON,
Sara .... 509-533-8486. 518 D
ssexton-johnson@ccs.spokane.edu
SEYBOLD, Marc, P .... 516-876-3379. 343 D
seyboldm@oldwestbury.edu
SEYDEL, Tim .... 541-962-3740. 405 H
tseydel@eou.edu
SEYERLE, Amy .... 626-529-8007... 57 G
aseyerle@pacificoaks.edu
SEYLE, David, C .... 229-732-5928. 120 D
davidseyle@andrewcollege.edu
SEYMAN, Elaine .... 503-222-3225. 403 B
eseyman@cci.edu
SEYMOUR, Cheryl .... 518-562-4125. 320 B
cheryl.stein@clinton.edu
SEYMOUR, Dennis .... 815-939-5302. 155 H
dseymour@olivet.edu
SEYMOUR, Dorothy .... 406-683-7010. 286 I
d_seymour@umwestern.edu
SEYMOUR, Jodi, L .... 641-784-5112. 178 F
seymour@graceland.edu
SEYMOUR, Michael .... 218-726-7101. 264 D
vcfo@d.umn.edu
SEYMOUR, Richard, R .... 252-335-0821. 359 F
rseymour@albemarle.edu
SEYMOUR, Teresa .... 318-473-6424. 205 A
tseymour@lsua.edu
SEYMOUR, William .... 731-425-8825. 460 G
wseymour@jscc.edu
SEYMOUR-ROUTE,
Paulette .... 508-856-5758. 229 C
Paulette.SeymourRoute@umassmed.edu
S.F. VAN DE PUTTE,
André .... 215-972-2047. 426 Y
avandeputte@pafa.edu
SFEIR, Raymond .... 714-997-6551... 38 A
SFRAGA, Mike .... 907-474-6533... 10 I
msfraga@alaska.edu
SGANGA, Fred .... 631-444-8606. 342 C
fred.sganga@stonybrook.edu
SGRO, Michael .... 607-753-2517. 343 B
michael.sgro@cortland.edu
SHAABAN-MAGANA,
Elle .... 205-348-5040..... 8 D
lshaaban@sa.ua.edu
SHAAK, Melissa, J .... 781-239-4398. 222 D
shaak@babson.edu
SHABAHANG, Homa ...... 909-593-3511... 72 E
hshabahang@laverne.edu
SHABAZZ, Amilcar .... 413-545-5703. 228 F
shabazz@afroam.umass.edu
SHABAZZ, Roxie .... 910-672-1784. 367 D
rshabazz@uncfsu.edu
SHABLIA, Nataliia .... 215-572-2887. 409 H
shablian@arcadia.edu
SHABLIN, Steven, J .... 248-370-3470. 248 J
shablin@oakland.edu
SHABLOSKI, Regan .... 814-866-6641. 420 E
rshabloski@lecom.edu
SHACHTER, Amy, M .... 408-554-7041... 64 M
ashachter@scu.edu
SHACKELFORD, Carol .... 601-635-2111. 266 H
cshackelford@eccc.edu
SHACKELFORD, Harper .. 910-678-8413. 360 D
shackelh@faytechcc.edu
SHACKELFORD, Judy ..... 217-544-6464. 158 D
SHACKELFORD,
Michelle .... 918-540-6188. 396 G
mshackelford@neo.edu
SHACKELFORD, Peter, J 517-750-1200. 250 E
pshackel@arbor.edu
SHACKLEFORD, Keith .... 949-451-5407... 67 B
kshackleford@ivc.edu
SHACKLEFORD, Michael 804-524-5350. 515 D
mshackle@vsu.edu
SHACKLEFORD, JR.,
Robert, S .... 336-633-0287. 362 H
rsshackleford@randolph.edu
SHACKLETON, Larry .... 434-592-3007. 506 I
lshackleton@liberty.edu
SHADARAM, Mehdi .... 210-458-5526. 492 C
mehdi.shadaram@utsa.edu
SHADDY, Deborah .... 913-758-6143. 191 B
shaddy15@stmary.edu
SHADDY, Robert .... 718-997-3760. 319 C
robert.shaddy@qc.cuny.edu
SHADE-DAVISON,
Stephanie .... 580-745-2267. 399 J
sdavison@se.edu
SHADER, Gail .... 518-828-4181. 321 C
gail.shader@sunycgcc.edu
SHADICK, Richard .... 212-346-1526. 335 J
rshadick@pace.edu
SHADKO, Jacqueline .... 248-942-3300. 248 D
jashadko@oaklandcc.edu
SHADLE, Joseph .... 513-745-3567. 393 H
shadle@xavier.edu
SHADLEY-HUTTON,
Tammy .... 937-382-6661. 393 B
tammy_shadley@wilmington.edu
SHADOIAN, Holly, L .... 401-456-8884. 439 F
hshadoian@ric.edu
SHAFER, Glenn, R .... 973-353-1604. 306 D
gshafer@business.rutgers.edu
SHAFER, Jack, L .... 610-499-4454. 437 E
jlshafer@widener.edu
SHAFER, Jesse .... 215-951-5626. 430 E
shaferj@philau.edu
SHAFER, John, R .... 317-738-8080. 165 I
jshafer@franklincollege.edu
SHAFER, Kathrynne, G ... 717-691-6003. 423 L
kshafer@messiah.edu
SHAFER, Lisa .... 610-328-8009. 433 I
lshafer1@swarthmore.edu
SHAFER, Pamela .... 832-559-4217. 476 A
pamela.n.shafer@lonestar.edu
SHAFER, Stephanie, C .... 540-432-4118. 504 D
stephanie.shafer@emu.edu
SHAFER, Trish .... 610-660-3101. 432 E
tshafer@sju.edu
SHAFFER, Alan, D .... 740-392-6868. 384 K
alan.shaffer@mvnu.edu
SHAFFER, Barbara .... 315-312-3557. 344 A
barbara.shaffer@oswego.edu
SHAFFER, Brian, W .... 901-843-3976. 458 E
shaffer@rhodes.edu
SHAFFER, Cathy .... 509-533-8037. 518 E
cathy.shaffer@scc.spokane.edu
SHAFFER, Chris .... 334-983-6556..... 7 H
shafferc@troy.edu
SHAFFER, Chris .... 503-494-6057. 405 I
library@ohsu.edu

SHAFFER, Christopher .... 740-351-3207. 388 N
cshaffer@shawnee.edu
SHAFFER, Germaine .... 606-487-3409. 195 C
germaine.shaffer@kctcs.edu
SHAFFER, Janette .... 802-828-0124. 501 C
janette.shaffer@ccv.edu
SHAFFER, Jason, S .... 704-894-2188. 353 J
jashaffer@davidson.edu
SHAFFER, Kelli .... 254-968-9050. 483 A
shaffer@tarleton.edu
SHAFFER, Michael .... 706-721-4413. 126 B
wshaffer@gru.edu
SHAFFER, Patti .... 724-357-2621. 428 F
pshaffer@iup.edu
SHAFFER, Ruth, E .... 309-692-4092. 152 J
rshaffer@midstate.edu
SHAFFER, Tammy .... 812-877-8003. 172 C
shaffer@rose-hulman.edu
SHAFFER, Wade .... 806-651-2931. 484 D
wshaffer@mail.wtamu.edu
SHAFFER, Wendy .... 978-556-3858. 232 E
wshaffer@necc.mass.edu
SHAFFER FRYLING,
Michelle .... 724-357-2302. 428 F
mfryling@iup.edu
SHAFFER LILIENTHAL,
Robin .... 641-844-5730. 179 J
robin.lilienthal@iavalley.edu
SHAFFER LILIENTHAL,
Robin .... 641-844-5730. 179 H
robin.lilienthal@iavalley.edu
SHAFKOWITZ,
Marshall, J .... 312-944-0882. 150 F
SHAFQAT, Sahar .... 240-895-4910. 218 A
sshafqat@smcm.edu
SHAFT, Scott, E .... 315-255-1743. 316 D
shafts@cayuga-cc.edu
SHAGER, Dorian .... 765-658-4270. 165 F
dshager@depauw.edu
SHAH, Bindiya .... 434-528-5276. 515 G
bshah@vul.edu
SHAH, Kashif .... 708-974-5348. 153 F
shah@morainevalley.edu
SHAH-GORDON, Ruta .... 718-390-3423. 350 B
rshahgor@wagner.edu
SHAHAN, J. Michael ..... 409-882-3314. 486 G
mike.shahan@lsco.edu
SHAHEEN, Lisa .... 212-229-8930. 332 E
shaheenl@newschool.edu
SHAHIN, Hamdi .... 201-559-6076. 302 A
shahinh@felician.edu
SHAHMIRZA, Bijan .... 510-580-6742... 77 C
bijan.shshmirza@cci.edu
SHAHRABI, Kamal .... 631-420-2115. 346 B
kamal.shahrabi@farmingdale.edu
SHAHROKHI, Hossein .... 713-221-8542. 489 D
shahrokhi@uhd.edu
SHAIKH, Usama .... 516-876-3323. 343 D
shaikhu@oldwestbury.edu
SHAIN, Sue .... 978-556-3710. 232 E
sshain@necc.mass.edu
SHAIN, Yeruchim .... 732-431-1600. 307 G
SHAINDLIN, Andrew ...... 412-268-6286. 412 H
shaindlin@andrew.cmu.edu
SHAINK, Dick .... 810-762-0453. 247 F
dick.shaink@mcc.edu
SHAKE, Miranda .... 217-554-6846. 150 E
mshake@lakeviewcol.edu
SHAKER, Lucy, G .... 773-244-5526. 154 G
lshaker@northpark.edu
SHAKER, Melanie .... 312-553-2500. 141 M
mshaker@ccc.edu
SHAKIR, Salah .... 859-846-6248. 197 I
sshakir@midway.edu
SHAKLEE, Ronald .... 330-941-4740. 394 A
rshaklee@ysu.edu
SHALALA, Donna, E .... 305-284-5155. 118 F
dshalala@miami.edu
SHALAMOV, Marina .... 718-261-5800. 315 F
mshalamov@bramsonort.edu
SHALLA, Annie .... 970-521-6702... 83 L
annie.shalla@njc.edu
SHALLBERG,
Mary Ann, H .... 281-283-2004. 489 C
shallberg@uhcl.edu
SHALLCROSS, Dorothy ... 303-797-5647... 78 F
dorothy.shallcross@arapahoe.edu
SHALLO, Michael, J .... 914-594-4574. 334 A
michael_shallo@nymc.edu
SHALVA, Sara .... 617-559-8610. 227 D
sshalva@hebrewcollege.edu
SHAMAH, Irwin .... 347-394-1036. 315 A
SHAMASH, Yacov .... 631-632-8380. 342 C
yacov.shamash@stonybrook.edu
SHAMBACH, Teresa .... 330-369-3200. 390 B
tbcmail@tbc-trumbullbusiness.com
SHAMBAUGH, Jeannine . 330-363-5420. 374 E
jshambaugh@aultman.com
SHAMIM, Jina .... 415-476-8850... 72 A
jinashamim@ucsf.edu
SHAMPENY, Renelle .... 518-587-2100. 346 A
renelle.shampeny@esc.edu
SHAMPINE, Memorie, L . 315-386-7042. 345 F
shampinem@canton.edu
SHAMS, Arian .... 714-300-0300... 67 F
ashams@scitech.edu
SHAMS, Nazila .... 714-300-0300... 67 F
nshams@scitech.edu
SHAMS, Parviz .... 714-300-0300... 67 F
pshams@scitech.edu
SHANAFELT, Rebecca ..... 727-816-3288. 110 E
shanafr@phcc.edu
SHANAHAN, Jenny .... 508-531-2764. 229 D
jenny.shanahan@bridgew.edu
SHANAHAN, Judy .... 636-949-4900. 276 D
jshanahan@lindenwood.edu
SHANAHAN, Megan .... 906-353-4600. 245 A
megan@kbocc.org
SHANAHAN, Thomas ..... 919-962-0533. 366 K
tcshanahan@northcarolina.edu
SHANBLATT, Stephanie .. 215-968-8222. 411 B
stephanie.shanblatt@bucks.edu
SHANDLEY, Thomas, C .. 704-894-2225. 353 J
toshandley@davidson.edu
SHANE, J. Michael .... 716-372-2155. 338 E
jmshane@eznet.net
SHANE, Mike .... 215-637-7700. 418 G
SHANER, Carl, L .... 570-326-3761. 427 B
cshaner@pct.edu
SHANGLE, Max, S .... 312-939-4975. 146 A
SHANGRAW, Rick .... 480-965-7393... 11 K
rick.shangraw@asu.edu
SHANK, Barbara, W .... 651-962-5801. 265 C
bwshank@stthomas.edu
SHANK, Harold .... 304-865-6003. 527 F
harold.shank@ovu.edu
SHANK, Larry .... 740-826-6109. 384 L
lshank@muskingum.edu
SHANK, Leanne, M .... 540-458-8940. 516 A
lshank@wlu.edu
SHANK, Matthew, D .... 703-284-1598. 507 B
matthew.shank@marymount.edu
SHANK, Scott .... 434-381-6202. 510 F
sshank@sbc.edu
SHANK, Sherri .... 704-233-8025. 370 G
s.shank@wingate.edu
SHANK, Theresa, M .... 240-500-2000. 215 B
tmshank@hagerstowncc.edu
SHANKAR, Jille .... 509-793-2031. 517 C
jilles@bigbend.edu
SHANKEL, James, V .... 412-578-6351. 412 G
jvshankel@carlow.edu
SHANKEL, James, V .... 724-741-1028. 412 G
shankeljv@carlow.edu
SHANKLE, Nancy .... 325-674-2402. 464 H
shanklen@acu.edu
SHANKLIN, Bart .... 309-298-1544. 162 K
b-shanklin@wiu.edu
SHANKLIN, Carol .... 785-532-7927. 188 A
shanklin@ksu.edu
SHANKLIN, Iris .... 404-756-4916. 121 A
ishanklin@atlm.edu
SHANKMAN,
Kimberly, C .... 913-360-7413. 184 H
kshankman@benedictine.edu
SHANKS, Carol .... 314-918-2501. 274 A
cshanks@eden.edu
SHANKS, Martha .... 828-398-7112. 357 N
mshanks@abtech.edu
SHANKWEILER, Jean ..... 310-660-3350... 43 B
jshankweiler@elcamino.edu
SHANLEY, OP, Brian, J . 401-865-2153. 439 E
bshanley@providence.edu
SHANLEY, Deborah, A .... 718-951-5214. 317 C
dshanley@brooklyn.cuny.edu
SHANLEY, Mark, G .... 540-831-5433. 508 C
mshanley@radford.edu
SHANLEY, Michael, V ..... 978-665-3178. 229 E
mshanley@fitchburgstate.edu
SHANMUGARATNAM,
Carol .... 781-283-2308. 237 F
cshanmug@wellesley.edu
SHANNON, Beth .... 301-431-5413. 217 C
bshannon@nlc.edu
SHANNON, Cheryl .... 203-285-2321... 88 E
cshannon@gwcc.commnet.edu
SHANNON, Daniel .... 773-702-1731. 161 B
dshannon@uchicago.edu
SHANNON, David .... 405-585-5249. 397 C
david.shannon@okbu.edu
SHANNON, Denise .... 313-496-2744. 252 B
dshanno1@wcccd.edu
SHANNON, Henry, D ...... 909-652-6100... 37 M
henry.shannon@chaffey.edu
SHANNON, Jeff .... 479-575-2702... 23 I
jshannon@uark.edu
SHANNON, Joe .... 903-693-2028. 478 A
jshannon@panola.edu
SHANNON, John .... 260-665-4224. 173 E
shannonj@trine.edu
SHANNON, John, T .... 973-655-4214. 303 D
shannonj@mail.montclair.edu
SHANNON, Kelly .... 312-915-6159. 151 H
kshann2@luc.edu
SHANNON, Linda, A ...... 718-990-6578. 339 A
shannonl@stjohns.edu
SHANNON, Mike .... 513-244-8620. 376 J
mike.shannon@ccuniversity.edu
SHANNON, Mike .... 956-872-3535. 480 I
mshannon@southtexascollege.edu
SHANNON, Pat .... 208-426-1125. 137 G
pshannon@boisestate.edu
SHANNON, Scott, S .... 315-470-6537. 345 B
sshannon@esf.edu
SHANNON, Susan, K ...... 717-766-2511. 423 L
sshannon@messiah.edu
SHANNON, Vanessa .... 617-228-2102. 231 C
vshannon@bhcc.mass.edu
SHANNON-CLOUSE,
Monica .... 606-546-1215. 200 A
mshannon@unionky.edu
SHANTZ, Dale .... 989-275-5000. 245 B
dale.shantz@kirkland.edu
SHAO, Alan, T .... 843-953-6651. 443 A
shaoa@cofc.edu
SHAPARD, Christy .... 912-650-5675. 131 H
cshapard@southuniversity.edu
SHAPE, Ronald .... 605-721-5220. 450 G
rshape@national.edu
SHAPIRO, Adam .... 760-750-4195... 35 A
ashapiro@csusm.edu
SHAPIRO, Alex .... 505-424-2309. 309 J
ashapiro@iaia.edu
SHAPIRO, Claire, R .... 901-843-3750. 458 E
shapiro@rhodes.edu
SHAPIRO, Helen .... 831-459-5852... 72 C
hshapiro@ucsc.edu
SHAPIRO, Herbert .... 561-297-2146. 114 L
hshapir3@fau.edu
SHAPIRO, Jeff .... 973-877-3142. 301 H
shapiro@essex.edu
SHAPIRO, Joe .... 619-594-5822... 35 D
jshapiro@mail.sdsu.edu
SHAPIRO, Joel .... 802-287-8298. 499 D
shapiroj@greenmtn.edu
SHAPIRO, Jon, A .... 920-924-3363. 540 F
jshapiro@morainepark.edu
SHAPIRO, Joseph, I .... 304-691-1700. 529 H
shapiroj@marshall.edu
SHAPIRO, Larry, J .... 314-362-6827. 284 L
shapirol@wustl.edu
SHAPIRO, Philip .... 781-239-5698. 222 D
pshapiro@babson.edu
SHAPIRO, Sandra .... 216-791-5000. 377 E
sxs131@case.edu
SHAPIRO, Tracie .... 502-863-8149. 194 C
tracie_shapiro@georgetowncollege.edu
SHAPIRO, Yonason .... 718-941-8000. 331 C
SHAPLEIGH, Shari .... 607-844-8222. 347 I
shaples@tc3.edu
SHAPOVAL, Sandy .... 918-270-6459. 398 I
sandy.shapoval@ptstulsa.edu
SHARAR, Bill .... 510-659-6524... 57 A
wsharar@ohlone.edu
SHARBAUGH, Catherine . 610-896-1089. 418 F
csharbau@haverford.edu
SHARBAUGH, Sheila, M 302-356-3917... 94 E
sheila.m.sharbaugh@wilmu.edu
SHARBAUGH, Tim .... 724-357-3011. 428 F
timshar@iup.edu
SHARDLOW, Mark .... 607-871-2144. 313 E
shardlow@alfred.edu
SHARDON, Taylor .... 843-953-5012. 442 A
tskardon@citadel.edu
SHARER, C. Gregory ...... 607-753-4721. 343 B
greg.sharer@cortland.edu
SHARER, Jack .... 502-895-3411. 197 F
jsharer@lpts.edu
SHARFMAN, Glenn, R .... 260-982-5051. 170 U
grsharfman@manchester.edu
SHARIAT, Vahid .... 714-816-0366... 70 A
vahid.shariat@trident.edu
SHARIF, Yasmin .... 740-245-7215. 392 A
ysharif@rio.edu
SHARIF, Zaki .... 740-245-7407. 392 A
zsharif@rio.edu
SHARIK, Terry .... 906-487-2454. 247 A
SHARKEY, Eric .... 888-384-0849... 27 E
esharkey@allied.edu
SHARKEY, Melissa .... 641-628-5180. 176 E
sharkeym@central.edu
SHARKEY, Neil .... 814-865-6332. 426 A
nas9@psu.edu
SHARKEY, Thomas, W .... 419-530-5426. 392 B
thomas.sharkey@utoledo.edu
SHARKIN, Bruce .... 610-683-4072. 429 A
sharkin@kutztown.edu
SHARMA, Anand, D .... 787-265-3809. 554 E
egraduados.uprm@upr.edu
SHARMA, Madhav, P ...... 570-389-4973. 427 H
msharma@bloomu.edu
SHARMA, Nimala .... 714-816-0366... 70 A
nimala.sharma@trident.edu
SHARMA, Pradeep .... 401-454-6283. 440 A
psharma@risd.edu
SHARMA, Sanjay .... 802-656-3175. 500 F
sanjay.sharma@uvm.edu
SHARMA, Sunny .... 561-391-1148. 101 J
ssharma@dmac.edu
SHARMAN, William, R ... 609-497-7750. 304 D
seminary.relations@ptsem.edu
SHARON, Daniel .... 914-632-5400. 331 K
dsharon@monroecollege.edu
SHARP, Andrew .... 601-477-4025. 267 F
andrew.sharp@jcjc.edu
SHARP, Bobby, H .... 828-262-4090. 367 A
sharpbh@appstate.edu
SHARP, David .... 870-245-5181... 22 D
sharpd@obu.edu
SHARP, Debbie .... 940-668-4213. 477 I
dsharp@nctc.edu
SHARP, Jane .... 443-518-4794. 215 E
jsharp@howardcc.edu
SHARP, Jennifer .... 630-743-0699. 163 C
jsharp@westwood.edu
SHARP, Joe .... 561-803-2102. 110 B
joe_sharp@pba.edu
SHARP, John .... 979-458-6000. 482 E
chancellor@tamus.edu
SHARP, John, M .... 304-877-6428. 526 C
john.sharp@abc.edu
SHARP, Jordon .... 435-652-7513. 497 E
jsharp@dixie.edu
SHARP, Kelvin, W .... 806-894-9611. 480 H
ksharp@southplainscollege.edu
SHARP, Linda .... 573-876-7277. 282 H
lsharp@stephens.edu
SHARP, Melody, F .... 540-224-4694. 506 G
mfsharp@jchs.edu
SHARP, Monica, A .... 405-325-3337. 401 B
msharp@ou.edu
SHARP, Nick .... 417-690-2224. 272 E
sharp@cofo.edu
SHARP, Randy .... 808-675-3400. 135 C
sharpr@byuh.edu
SHARP, Sandra .... 203-576-5612... 91 D
sandra.sharp@stvincentscollege.edu
SHARP, Shayna .... 208-524-3000. 138 D
shayna.sharp@my.eitc.edu
SHARP, Stacy, M .... 859-846-5347. 197 I
smsharp@midway.edu
SHARP, Suzanne .... 573-876-7207. 282 H
ssharp@stephens.edu
SHARP, Valerie .... 417-865-2815. 274 B
sharpv@evangel.edu
SHARPE, Allan .... 915-532-3737. 494 J
asharpe@westerntech.edu
SHARPE, Amory .... 415-439-2350... 27 M
asharpe@act-sf.org
SHARPE, Aubrey, D .... 903-510-2900. 488 E
asha@tjc.edu
SHARPE, Clarence .... 218-723-6044. 254 K
csharpe@css.edu
SHARPE, Dolores .... 810-762-0501. 247 F
dolores.sharpe@mcc.edu
SHARPE, Jessica, G .... 336-272-7102. 354 E
jessica.sharpe@greensboro.edu
SHARPE, Jon .... 916-568-3058... 52 K
sharpej@losrios.edu
SHARPE, Karen .... 508-929-8786. 230 G
Karen.Sharpe@worcester.edu
SHARPE, Martha, S .... 757-683-4046. 507 N
msharpe@odu.edu
SHARPE, Paul .... 219-981-4218. 168 B
pwsharpe@iun.edu
SHARPE, Shane .... 205-348-5506..... 8 D
ssharpe@ua.edu
SHARPHORN, Dan .... 512-499-4563. 491 A
dsharphorn@utsystem.edu
SHARPLES, Russell .... 704-463-3401. 365 E
russ.sharples@fsmail.pfeiffer.edu
SHARPS, Alonia, C .... 301-322-0170. 217 F
asharps@pgcc.edu
SHARRAR, Jack .... 415-439-2412... 27 M
jsharrar@act-sf.org
SHARROCK, Christopher 215-717-6121. 435 A
csharrock@uarts.edu
SHATTUCK, Larry .... 410-532-5551. 217 E
lshattuck@ndm.edu
SHATTUCK, R. Cooper ... 205-348-8345..... 8 C
cshattuck@uasystem.ua.edu
SHATTUCK, Wendy .... 626-396-2403... 28 P
wendy.shattuck@artcenter.edu
SHAUGHNESSY, Anne .... 617-824-8525. 226 A
anne_shaughnessy@emerson.edu
SHAUGHNESSY, Joseph . 781-768-7133. 236 A
joseph.shaughnessy@regiscollege.edu
SHAUGHNESSY, Joseph . 254-659-7821. 473 A
jxs@hillcollege.edu
SHAUGHNESSY, Josette . 915-831-6330. 472 B
jshaugh2@epcc.edu

SHAUGHNESSY, Michael .... 724-503-1001. 436 G mshaughnessy@washjeff.edu
SHAUL, Lesa .... 205-652-3460.... 9 F lcc@uwa.edu
SHAUNAK, Raj .... 662-243-1911. 266 I rshaunak@eastms.edu
SHAUNAK, Sudershan .... 760-757-2121... 54 G sshaunak@miracosta.edu
SHAUT, William .... 607-753-2211. 343 B william.shaut@cortland.edu
SHAVER, Debra, D .... 413-585-2523. 236 H dshaver@smith.edu
SHAVER, Joan, L .... 520-626-6154... 18 F jshaver@nursing.arizona.edu
SHAVER, Joseph .... 304-326-1481. 527 G jshaver@salemu.edu
SHAVER, Judson, R .... 212-517-0560. 330 E jshaver@mmm.edu
SHAVKIN, April .... 770-394-8300. 120 H ashavkin@aii.edu
SHAW, Anne, C .... 910-938-6322. 359 E shawa@coastalcarolina.edu
SHAW, Barbara, L .... 209-946-2424... 73 A bshaw@pacific.edu
SHAW, Becky .... 413-585-4940. 236 H rshaw@smith.edu
SHAW, Brad .... 618-664-7021. 145 G brad.shaw@greenville.edu
SHAW, Brian, R .... 202-231-8698. 544 L brian.shaw@dodiis.mil
SHAW, Chester .... 708-974-5360. 153 F schawc6@morainevalley.edu
SHAW, Chip .... 806-743-1500. 487 E chip.shaw@ttuhsc.edu
SHAW, Christi .... 325-236-8292. 486 C christi.shaw@tstc.edu
SHAW, Dameon, A .... 601-877-2470. 265 G dashaw@alcorn.edu
SHAW, Darlene, L .... 843-792-2228. 445 B shawd@musc.edu
SHAW, David .... 662-325-3570. 268 D dshaw@research.msstate.edu
SHAW, David .... 979-230-3234. 468 A david.shaw@brazosport.edu
SHAW, Debora .... 812-855-3261. 167 F shawd@indiana.edu
SHAW, Deborah, L .... 334-844-1134..... 1 G shawdeb@auburn.edu
SHAW, Howard .... 256-726-7312..... 6 B hshaw@oakwood.edu
SHAW, James, A .... 606-783-2599. 198 A j.shaw@moreheadstate.edu
SHAW, Jen, D .... 352-392-1261. 116 A jends@dso.ufl.edu
SHAW, Jerone .... 662-621-4085. 266 D jshaw@coahomacc.edu
SHAW, Karen .... 765-455-9216. 168 A kgallati@iuk.edu
SHAW, Karen .... 828-232-5109. 368 C kshaw@unca.edu
SHAW, Kathleen .... 804-828-6683. 511 F kshaw5@vcu.edu
SHAW, Katie, R .... 407-303-5548... 97 H katie.shaw@adu.edu
SHAW, Ken .... 850-644-2103. 115 C kshaw@pc.fsu.edu
SHAW, Kevin .... 909-469-5401... 76 B kshaw@westernu.edu
SHAW, Linda .... 480-732-7307... 14 J linda.shaw@cgc.edu
SHAW, Lori .... 620-331-2480. 187 G lshaw@indycc.edu
SHAW, Marc .... 646-664-3013. 316 I marc.shaw@cuny.edu
SHAW, Mary, V .... 815-740-3403. 162 F mshaw@stfrancis.edu
SHAW, Nancy .... 802-224-3000. 501 A nancy.shaw@vsc.edu
SHAW, Penelope .... 707-826-3942... 35 C pjs25@humboldt.edu
SHAW, Richard .... 806-291-1162. 494 F shawr@wbu.edu
SHAW, Rick .... 661-722-6300... 28 F rshaw@avc.edu
SHAW, Robert, A .... 801-832-2474. 498 F rshaw@westminstercollege.edu
SHAW, Robert, S .... 570-348-6245. 423 B rsshaw@marywood.edu
SHAW, Ron .... 304-829-7349. 526 D rshaw@bethanywv.edu
SHAW, Russell .... 601-857-3961. 267 A RDShaw@hindscc.edu
SHAW, Stephen .... 937-769-1881. 373 I sshaw@antioch.edu
SHAW, Teresa .... 909-602-2505... 60 A teresa.shaw@pomona.edu
SHAW, Tom .... 269-965-3931. 244 O tshaw@kellogg.edu
SHAW, Tom, A .... 312-329-4261. 153 E tshaw@moody.edu
SHAW, Wade, H .... 478-301-2459. 128 H shaw_wh@mercer.edu
SHAW-BURNETT, Margaret, A .... 716-878-5907. 343 A shawma@buffalostate.edu
SHAW HORTON, Sheilah .... 410-617-2842. 216 A sshorton@loyola.edu
SHAWANOKASIC, Norman .... 800-567-2344. 532 E nshawanokasic@menominee.edu
SHAWN, Donna, S .... 913-627-4171. 187 L dshawn@kckcc.edu
SHAWNEY, Lisa, L .... 603-513-1335. 298 E lisa.shawney@granite.edu
SHAWVER, Jeffrey .... 304-647-6325. 530 B jshawver@osteo.wvsom.edu
SHAWVER, Rebecca .... 979-230-3313. 468 A rebecca.shawver@brazosport.edu
SHAWVER, William, G .... 513-529-9203. 384 G shawvewg@miamioh.edu
SHAY, Carla, E .... 231-843-5942. 252 H ceshay@westshore.edu
SHAY, Kristine, M .... 585-245-5571. 343 C shay@geneseo.edu
SHAY, Pamela .... 614-947-6135. 380 A pamela.shay@franklin.edu
SHAY, Robert .... 573-882-2606. 283 C shayr@missouri.edu
SHCHEGOL, Alex .... 718-522-9073. 314 B ashchegol@asa.edu
SHEA, Catherine .... 303-492-7896... 85 L catherine.shea@colorado.edu
SHEA, Christine, M .... 603-862-3290. 298 C christine.shea@unh.edu
SHEA, Donald, A .... 904-620-2500. 116 B d.shea.138994@unf.edu
SHEA, Donna .... 617-353-5124. 224 D dshea@bu.edu
SHEA, James, P .... 701-355-8100. 373 E president@umary.edu
SHEA, Jane .... 508-854-4358. 232 F jshea@qcc.mass.edu
SHEA, Kevin, J .... 617-552-3250. 224 A k.shea@bc.edu
SHEA, Kim .... 203-285-2013... 88 E kshea@gwcc.commnet.edu
SHEA, Lori, L .... 906-786-5802. 240 K sheal@baycollege.edu
SHEA, Rich, J .... 814-886-6474. 424 G rshea@mtaloy.edu
SHEA, Timothy, P .... 978-542-6517. 230 E tshea@salemstate.edu
SHEA-BYRNES, Pamela, G .... 718-990-6479. 339 A sheabyrp@stjohns.edu
SHEAFF, Shannon .... 928-757-0817... 15 L ssheaff@mohave.edu
SHEAFFER, Andrea .... 510-649-2465... 46 B asheaffer@gtu.edu
SHEAFFER, Ellen .... 301-387-3003. 214 I ellen.sheaffer@garrettcollege.edu
SHEAFFER, Karen, M .... 570-321-4311. 422 H sheaffer@lycoming.edu
SHEAHAN, John .... 217-351-2555. 155 J JSheahan@parkland.edu
SHEAHAN, Mary .... 479-394-7622... 23 B msheahan@rmcc.edu
SHEALEY, Monika .... 856-256-4751. 305 E shealey@rowan.edu
SHEAN, Andrew .... 858-513-9240. 175 F andrew.shean@ashford.edu
SHEAR, Kris .... 707-524-1579... 65 B kshear@santarosa.edu
SHEAR, Skip .... 660-944-2853. 272 H sshear@conception.edu
SHEARD, Reed .... 805-565-7171... 76 D rsheard@westmont.edu
SHEARED, Vanessa .... 916-278-6639... 34 D vsheared@saclink.csus.edu
SHEARER, Nancy, B .... 607-587-3959. 345 D shearenb@alfredstate.edu
SHEARER, Richard .... 320-308-2244. 261 B rsshearer@stcloudstate.edu
SHEARER-CREMEAN, Christine .... 406-265-3768. 287 D c.shearercremean@msun.edu
SHEARIN, Lisa .... 252-246-1310. 365 C lshearin@wilsoncc.edu
SHEARIN, Wally, M .... 336-506-4279. 357 M wally.shearin@alamancecc.edu
SHEARN, Robert .... 859-344-3683. 199 H shearnr@thomasmore.edu
SHEARON, Randall .... 919-735-5151. 364 H shearon@waynecc.edu
SHEARRILL, Charmagne . 661-255-1050... 31 C hrdirector@calarts.edu
SHEASGREEN, William ... 607-274-3306. 327 E wsheasgreen@ithacalondon.co.uk
SHECKELLS, Sara .... 617-730-7072. 235 D sara.sheckells@newbury.edu
SHECTERLE, Ross, A .... 414-425-8300. 535 K rector@shst.edu
SHEDD, Jean, E .... 847-491-8546. 155 D j-shedd@northwestern.edu
SHEDD, Sally .... 757-455-3283. 515 H sshedd@vwc.edu
SHEDRICK, Karen, R .... 601-877-6111. 265 G karen@alcorn.edu
SHEDRON, Brandon .... 314-264-1802. 293 D brandon.shedron@vatterott-college.edu
SHEDRON, Brandon .... 314-264-1802. 162 I brandon.shedron@vatterott-college.edu
SHEEHAN, Diep .... 781-768-7078. 236 A diep.sheehan@regiscollege.edu
SHEEHAN, Eugene .... 970-351-2817... 86 C eugene.sheehan@unco.edu
SHEEHAN, Heather .... 701-224-5465. 372 B heather.sheehan@bismarckstate.edu
SHEEHAN, James, P .... 413-545-1581. 228 F sheehan@admin.umass.edu
SHEEHAN, Kristin .... 518-445-3361. 313 C kshee@albanylaw.edu
SHEEHAN, Maria, C .... 775-673-7025. 294 H msheehan@tmcc.edu
SHEEHAN, Martha .... 617-349-8267. 228 B msheeha4@lesley.edu
SHEEHAN, Phil .... 360-992-2118. 518 A psheehan@clark.edu
SHEEHAN, Rhonda .... 518-631-9835. 348 K sheehanr@uniongraduatecollege.edu
SHEEHAN, Robert, J .... 410-546-4127. 220 D rjsheehan@salisbury.edu
SHEEHAN, Tim .... 801-957-2001. 498 B tim.sheehan@slcc.edu
SHEEHAN, Timothy .... 651-213-4166. 256 B tsheehan@hazelden.edu
SHEEHAN, JR., William, F .... 573-592-5327. 285 B bill.sheehan@westminster-mo.edu
SHEEHEY, John, D .... 802-654-2571. 500 B jsheehey@smcvt.edu
SHEEHY, Colette .... 434-924-3349. 511 B cc@virginia.edu
SHEEHY, Harry .... 603-646-2465. 296 G harry.sheehy@dartmouth.edu
SHEEHY, Maureen, H ..... 978-656-3105. 232 B sheehym@middlesex.mass.edu
SHEEKS, Gina .... 706-507-8730. 123 D sheeks_gina@columbusstate.edu
SHEELEY, Robert, G .... 203-392-6050... 88 A sheeleyr1@southernct.edu
SHEERAN, Robert, M .... 513-745-3151. 393 H sheeran@xavier.edu
SHEERER, Marilyn .... 252-328-5419. 367 B sheererm@ecu.edu
SHEETS, Christine .... 740-593-4094. 387 C sheetsch@ohio.edu
SHEETS, Helene .... 419-824-3965. 383 C hsheets@lourdes.edu
SHEETS, Julie .... 573-518-2206. 278 A jsheets@mineralarea.edu
SHEETS, Sarah .... 304-326-1243. 527 G ssheets@salemu.edu
SHEFF, Kimberly .... 207-948-9224. 211 I ksheff@unity.edu
SHEFFER, Ilene .... 574-520-4344. 168 E isheffer@iusb.edu
SHEFFER, Mary .... 603-513-5175. 298 D mary.sheffer@law.unh.edu
SHEFFIELD, Ann, D .... 814-332-2357. 409 D ann.sheffield@allegheny.edu
SHEFFIELD, Linda .... 434-736-2002. 513 H linda.sheffield@southside.edu
SHEFFIELD, Ric, S .... 740-427-5117. 382 J sheffier@kenyon.edu
SHEFFIELD, Roy, S .... 828-884-8312. 352 I scotts@brevard.edu
SHEFFLETTE, Nancy, A ... 501-882-4581... 19 M nashefflette@asub.edu
SHEFTIC, Alissa .... 269-927-6749. 245 D asheftic@lakemichigancollege.edu
SHEGAN, Christine .... 570-662-4900. 429 C cshegan@mansfield.edu
SHEH, Chi .... 626-571-8811... 74 B chisheh@uwest.edu
SHEHEANE, Dene .... 404-894-1238. 125 D dene.sheheane@dev.gatech.edu
SHEHEE, Amy .... 859-985-3002. 192 F sheheea@berea.edu
SHEIBLEY, Thomas, J .... 610-660-1030. 432 E tsheible@sju.edu
SHEID, Christopher .... 307-382-1661. 543 J csheid@wwcc.wy.edu
SHEIN, David .... 845-758-7454. 314 D shein@bard.edu
SHEKLETON, James, F .... 605-773-3455. 451 E jim.shekleton@sdbor.edu
SHELB, Jane .... 937-775-5515. 393 G jane.schelb@wright.edu
SHELBY, Jane .... 907-786-4708... 10 H njshelby@uaa.alaska.edu
SHELBY, Liz .... 541-552-7672. 406 C shelbyl@sou.edu
SHELDON, Frederick, H .. 225-578-2887. 204 O fsheld@lsu.edu
SHELDON, Jane .... 308-865-8427. 292 H sheldonj@unk.edu
SHELDON, Marianne .... 510-430-3221... 54 F mshel@mills.edu
SHELDON, Michael .... 207-221-4591. 213 A msheldon@une.edu
SHELDON, Todd .... 402-363-5601. 293 I tlsheldon@york.edu
SHELEY, Joseph, F .... 209-667-3201... 35 B president@csustan.edu
SHELL, Cathy .... 828-898-8740. 356 A shell@lmc.edu
SHELL, Larry .... 405-744-5370. 397 H larry.shell@okstate.edu
SHELL, Martin .... 650-723-4186... 68 E mshell@stanford.edu
SHELLBERG, David .... 208-562-3000. 138 C
SHELLEDY, David .... 312-942-7120. 157 G david_shelledy@rush.edu
SHELLEY, Chris .... 815-288-5511. 158 K shellec@svcc.edu
SHELLEY, Daniel .... 585-475-6736. 337 L drsadm@rit.edu
SHELLEY, Ena, M .... 317-940-9752. 164 J eshelley@butler.edu
SHELLEY, Jeff .... 205-929-3416..... 5 D jshelley@lawsonstate.edu
SHELLEY, MargE .... 913-469-8500. 187 J mshelley@jccc.edu
SHELLEY, Michael .... 773-256-0721. 152 B mshelley@lstc.edu
SHELLEY, Stephen .... 940-397-4110. 476 H stephen.shelley@mwsu.edu
SHELLY, Anne .... 315-498-2237. 335 G shellya@sunyocc.edu
SHELLY, Heather .... 715-682-1254. 535 D hshelly@northland.edu
SHELLY, Peggy .... 215-780-1284. 433 A pshelly@salus.edu
SHELLY, Thomas, R .... 248-218-2011. 249 D rshelly@rc.edu
SHELMAN, Gary .... 210-486-3920. 465 A jshelman@alamo.edu
SHELNUT, Lindsey .... 662-241-7494. 268 E lshelnut@sa.muw.edu
SHELOW, Stephen, G .... 814-865-1864. 426 A sps8@psu.edu
SHELPMAN, JR., David . 561-912-1211. 103 C dshelpman@evergladesuniversity.edu
SHELTON, Alice .... 317-955-6022. 170 V ashelton@marian.edu
SHELTON, Amy .... 202-885-8657... 97 D ashelton@wesleyseminary.edu
SHELTON, Amy .... 615-794-4254. 457 Q ashelton@omorecollege.edu
SHELTON, Charlita .... 877-442-0505... 86 F charlita.shelton@rockies.edu
SHELTON, Christie .... 256-782-5276..... 4 K cshelton@jsu.edu
SHELTON, Donna .... 276-523-7478. 513 A dshelton@me.vccs.edu
SHELTON, Elisabeth .... 304-293-1784. 530 D eshelton@hsc.wvu.edu
SHELTON, Garry, M .... 540-857-7282. 514 E mshelton@virginiawestern.edu
SHELTON, Iverna .... 404-527-4520. 122 E ishelton@carver.edu
SHELTON, Janice .... 540-674-3611. 513 B jshelton@nr.edu
SHELTON, Joyce, A .... 847-317-7172. 160 M
SHELTON, M. Dwight ..... 540-231-8775. 515 C mdsjr@vt.edu
SHELTON, Maggie .... 270-901-1112. 196 E maggie.shelton@kctcs.edu
SHELTON, Myles .... 409-944-1200. 472 I mshelton@gc.edu
SHELTON, Nancy, B .... 434-395-2129. 506 J sheltonnb@longwood.edu
SHELTON, Robby, C .... 931-363-9890. 456 C rshelton@martinmethodist.edu
SHELTON, Sharron .... 940-552-6291. 493 F sshelton@vernoncollege.edu
SHELTON, Stacia .... 602-978-7200... 18 A stacia.shelton@thunderbird.edu
SHELTON, Tasha .... 847-491-3024. 155 D t-shelton@northwestern.edu
SHELTON, Terri, L .... 336-256-0426. 369 A shelton@uncg.edu
SHELTON, Treva .... 812-866-7056. 166 C shelton@hanover.edu
SHELTON, Vickie .... 806-371-5017. 465 E vlshelton@actx.edu
SHELTON, W. Brian .... 706-886-6831. 133 A bshelton@tfc.edu
SHELTON-CLARK, Anne . 662-621-4220. 266 D ashelton-clark@coahomacc.edu

SHEMMER, Rosalie .... 914-323-5484. 330 B
rosalie.shemmer@mville.edu
SHEMTOV, Kasriel .... 248-414-6900. 246 F
rabbi@theshul.net
SHEMWELL, Bridget .... 870-762-3174... 19 K
bshemwell@smail.anc.edu
SHEMWELL, James .... 870-762-3191... 19 K
jshemwell@smail.anc.edu
SHEMWELL, Latasha .... 270-926-4040. 193 M
lshemwell@daymarcollege.edu
SHEN, Shiji .... 908-737-3470. 302 F
sshen@kean.edu
SHEN, Sunny .... 516-739-1545. 333 F
academic_dean@nyctcm.edu
SHENDY, Joellen .... 240-684-2201. 219 F
student-services@umuc.edu
SHENETTE, John .... 413-585-2400. 236 H
jshenett@smith.edu
SHENK, Sara, W .... 574-295-3726. 163 J
swshenk@ambs.edu
SHENNAN, Andrew .... 781-283-3583. 237 F
ashennan@wellesley.edu
SHENNUM, Barry .... 602-944-3335... 11 D
bshennum@aicag.edu
SHENOSKY, Joseph, T ... 610-785-6520. 432 C
jshenosky@scs.edu
SHENOY, Kallya .... 661-654-2155... 32 H
kshenoy@csub.edu
SHENOY, Kallya .... 661-654-2115... 32 H
kshenoy@csub.edu
SHENOY, Kallya .... 661-654-3425... 32 H
kshenoy@csub.edu
SHENTON, Helen .... 617-495-3650. 227 C
helen_shenton@harvard.edu
SHEPARD, Bruce .... 360-650-3480. 525 C
president@wwu.edu
SHEPARD, Charles .... 859-858-3511. 192 B
charlie.shepard@asbury.edu
SHEPARD, Dave .... 757-221-2255. 503 N
dbshep@wm.edu
SHEPARD, James, P .... 334-844-1007..... 1 G
jps0028@auburn.edu
SHEPARD, Joseph .... 575-538-6238. 312 N
shepardj@wnmu.edu
SHEPARD, Kathy, J .... 717-728-2261. 412 J
kathyshepard@centralpenn.edu
SHEPARD, Lorrie .... 303-492-6937... 85 L
lorrie.shepard@colorado.edu
SHEPARD, Nancy .... 530-938-5331... 41 A
shepard@siskiyous.edu
SHEPARD, Richard, K ..... 303-855-6014... 82 C
rshepard@heritage-education.com
SHEPARD, Robert, S ...... 919-684-3363. 354 A
robert.shepard@duke.edu
SHEPARD, Robin .... 209-381-6470... 54 D
shepard.r@mccd.edu
SHEPARD-SMITH,
Andrew .... 931-221-7881. 459 B
shepardsmitha@apsu.edu
SHEPARDSON,
Andrew, J .... 781-891-2161. 223 C
ashepardson@bentley.edu
SHEPARDSON,
J. Andrew .... 781-891-2161. 223 C
ashepardson@bentley.edu
SHEPARDSON,
Timothy, M .... 715-738-3852. 539 J
tshepardson@cvtc.edu
SHEPELSKY, Ernie .... 718-429-6600. 349 H
ernie.shepelsky@vaughn.edu
SHEPHARD, Debra .... 605-882-5284. 450 D
shephard@lakeareatech.edu
SHEPHERD, Candace, H . 334-271-1670..... 6 C
cshepherd@princeinstitute.edu
SHEPHERD, Chad .... 314-367-8700. 281 C
chad.shepherd@stlcop.edu
SHEPHERD, Gay .... 931-372-3234. 460 A
gshepherd@tntech.edu
SHEPHERD, Gregory, J ... 305-284-3420. 118 F
shepherd@miami.edu
SHEPHERD, Janet .... 563-425-5788. 183 B
shepherdj@uiu.edu
SHEPHERD, Jennifer .... 260-982-5222. 170 U
jkshepherd@manchester.edu
SHEPHERD, Joseph, E ... 626-395-5802... 31 E
joseph.e.shepherd@caltech.edu
SHEPHERD, Judy .... 434-949-1049. 513 H
judy.shepherd@southside.edu
SHEPHERD, Karen .... 510-261-8500... 58 G
karen.shepherd@patten.edu
SHEPHERD, Karla, M ...... 410-837-4760. 221 A
kshepherd@ubalt.edu
SHEPHERD, Lewis .... 870-230-5081... 21 D
shephel@hsu.edu
SHEPHERD, Margaret, A 206-543-7604. 524 G
mshep@uw.edu
SHEPHERD, Nancy .... 505-566-3264. 311 I
shepherdn@sanjuancollege.edu
SHEPHERD, Paul .... 715-425-4444. 537 E
paul.shepherd@uwrf.edu
SHEPHERD, Roger .... 334-387-3877..... 1 E
rogershepherd@amridgeuniversity.edu
SHEPHERD, Tamara, A ... 703-370-6600. 508 B
SHEPHERD-GREGG,
Debbie .... 740-392-6868. 384 K
dshepher@mvnu.edu
SHEPLER, Kent .... 608-663-2000. 533 T
kshepler@mediainstitute.edu
SHEPPARD, Elizabeth ..... 478-387-4882. 125 E
SHEPPARD, Ellen .... 704-355-5316. 353 D
ellen.sheppard@carolinascollege.edu
SHEPPARD, Eric, J .... 757-727-6970. 505 F
eric.sheppard@hamptonu.edu
SHEPPARD, James, A ..... 620-229-6227. 190 G
james.sheppard@sckans.edu
SHEPPARD, Kirsten .... 865-273-8991. 456 D
kirsten.sheppard@maryvillecollege.edu
SHEPPARD, Lyle .... 910-630-7225. 356 H
lsheppard@methodist.edu
SHEPPARD, Matt .... 218-299-6519. 259 F
matt.sheppard@minnesota.edu
SHEPPARD, Nancy .... 412-809-5100. 430 H
sheppard.nancy@pti.edu
SHEPPARD, Phillip .... 508-588-9100. 232 A
SHEPPARD, Rebecca ...... 856-691-8600. 301 A
bsheppard@cccnj.edu
SHEPPARD, Tina, F .... 573-341-4218. 284 A
tinas@mst.edu
SHEPPARD, Vicki .... 336-917-5090. 366 D
vicki.sheppard@salem.edu
SHEPPERSON, Dale .... 317-632-5553. 170 T
dshepperson@lincolntech.com
SHEPROW, Lauren .... 631-632-4896. 342 C
lauren.sheprow@stonybrook.edu
SHEPTAK, Dale .... 440-375-7368. 382 L
dsheptak@lec.edu
SHER, Ephraim, Y .... 845-434-5240. 352 B
esher@fallsburgyeshiva.com
SHERADIN, Pamela .... 315-364-3221. 350 E
psheridan@wells.edu
SHERAN, Yvette .... 305-237-8965. 109 D
ysheran@mdc.edu
SHERBURNE, Mark .... 570-484-2135. 429 B
mcs6313@lhup.edu
SHEREMAN, Sandra .... 562-985-5537... 33 F
ssherem@csulb.edu
SHEREN, Deborah .... 216-373-5347. 385 G
dsheren@ndc.edu
SHERER, Michael .... 574-535-7406. 166 A
msherer@goshen.edu
SHERF, Tom .... 215-702-4848. 411 F
tsherf@cairn.edu
SHERIDAN, Catherine ..... 614-222-3205. 378 A
csheridan@ccad.edu
SHERIDAN, Chris .... 216-368-2774. 375 J
chris.sheridan@case.edu
SHERIDAN, Eileen .... 617-730-7010. 235 D
eileen.sheridan@newbury.edu
SHERIDAN, John .... 620-341-5208. 186 D
jsherida@emporia.edu
SHERIDAN, Nora .... 978-556-3616. 232 E
nsheridan@necc.mass.edu
SHERIDAN, Pamela .... 610-436-3383. 430 A
psheridan@wcupa.edu
SHERIDAN, TOR, Sean .. 740-283-6216. 379 N
ssheridan@franciscan.edu
SHERIDAN, Terence .... 334-387-3877..... 1 E
terencesheridan@amridgeuniversity.edu
SHERIFF-TAYLOR,
Patricia .... 601-979-2127. 267 E
patricia.sherriff-taylor@jsums.edu
SHERLIN, Joe, H .... 423-439-4210. 459 C
sherlin@etsu.edu
SHERLOCK, Jean .... 818-733-2600... 56 B
SHERLOCK, Julia, B .... 989-774-3068. 240 N
julia.b.sherlock@cmich.edu
SHERMAN, Ann .... 617-243-2216. 227 K
asherman@lasell.edu
SHERMAN, Ann, M .... 906-227-2330. 248 A
asherman@nmu.edu
SHERMAN, Catherine ...... 813-879-6000. 103 B
csherman@cci.edu
SHERMAN, Catherine ...... 724-503-1001. 436 G
csherman@washjeff.edu
SHERMAN, Curt .... 402-643-7369. 289 B
curt.sherman@cune.edu
SHERMAN, Daniel .... 713-500-3270. 492 E
Daniel.Sherman@uth.tmc.edu
SHERMAN, Debra .... 985-732-6640. 203 D
SHERMAN, Douglas, H .. 401-739-5000. 439 D
dsherman@neit.edu
SHERMAN, Gary .... 240-895-2000. 218 A
SHERMAN, George .... 718-631-6273. 319 D
gsherman@qcc.cuny.edu
SHERMAN, George, M ... 978-232-2009. 226 C
gsherman@endicott.edu
SHERMAN, Glen .... 973-720-2761. 308 I
shermang@wpunj.edu
SHERMAN, Hugh .... 740-593-2000. 387 C
shermanh@ohio.edu
SHERMAN, III, James .... 605-856-5880. 451 B
james.sherman@sintegleska.edu
SHERMAN, Jennifer .... 719-549-3322... 84 G
jennifer.sherman@pueblocc.edu
SHERMAN, Jill .... 502-456-6509. 199 F
jsherman@sctd.edu
SHERMAN, Julee .... 660-248-6203. 272 B
jsherman@centralmethodist.edu
SHERMAN, Kathleen, A .. 970-491-6614... 80 I
kathleen.sherman@colostate.edu
SHERMAN, Kristen .... 617-670-4419. 226 F
ksherman01@fisher.edu
SHERMAN, Marilyn .... 213-613-2200... 67 E
marilyn_sherman@sciarc.edu
SHERMAN, Michael .... 773-252-5135. 156 I
michael.sherman@resu.edu
SHERMAN, Mike .... 330-972-7593. 390 E
provost@uakron.edu
SHERMAN, Robert, A ...... 631-656-2117. 324 F
robert.sherman@ftc.edu
SHERMAN, Roger, H ...... 631-656-2189. 324 F
roger.sherman@ftc.edu
SHERMAN, Ross .... 903-566-7218. 492 D
rsherman@uttyler.edu
SHERMAN, Ruby .... 240-567-1720. 216 F
ruby.sherman@montgomerycollege.edu
SHERMAN, Ruth, D .... 617-333-2364. 225 E
rsherman@curry.edu
SHERMAN, Sharon .... 609-896-5120. 305 D
sherman@rider.edu
SHERMAN, Todd .... 907-474-7231... 10 I
tlsherman@alaska.edu
SHERMANN, Janice .... 507-457-2570. 262 A
jsherman@winona.edu
SHERRELL, Jeff .... 205-226-4939..... 2 C
jsherrel@bsc.edu
SHERRER, Margaret .... 662-254-3335. 269 A
margaret.sherrer@mvsu.edu
SHERRICK, Rebecca, L ... 630-844-5476. 140 A
sherrick@aurora.edu
SHERRILL, Audrey .... 704-922-6223. 360 F
sherrill.audrey@gaston.edu
SHERRILL, Christy .... 501-812-2214... 22 G
csherrill@pulaskitech.edu
SHERRILL, Jan-Mitchell . 412-392-8026. 431 B
jsherrill@pointpark.edu
SHERRILL, Linda, G .... 517-750-1200. 250 E
lsherrill@arbor.edu
SHERROD, Vicki .... 478-289-2105. 124 C
vsherrod@ega.edu
SHERRON, Catherine ...... 859-344-3387. 199 H
catherine.sherron@thomasmore.edu
SHERRY, J.P .... 916-568-3042... 52 K
sherryj@losrios.edu
SHERRY, Michael .... 716-652-8900. 316 G
msherry@cks.edu
SHERRY, William .... 773-508-7551. 151 H
wsherry@luc.edu
SHERSTAD, Brian, P ...... 616-538-2330. 243 A
bsherstad@gbcol.edu
SHERWEN, Laurie .... 215-596-8501. 435 H
l.sherwen@usciences.edu
SHERWIN, Paul .... 415-338-1541... 35 E
psherwin@sfsu.edu
SHERWOOD, David, G ... 262-646-6534. 535 B
dsherwood@nashotah.edu
SHERWOOD, Dennis ...... 262-564-3218. 540 A
sherwoodd@gtc.edu
SHERWOOD, Emily .... 574-807-7023. 164 D
emily.sherwood@bethelcollege.edu
SHERWOOD, James .... 631-451-4330. 346 F
sherwoj@sunysuffolk.edu
SHERWOOD, Kenneth .... 805-986-5804... 74 G
ksherwood@vcccd.edu
SHERWOOD, Marlan, D . 814-332-2983. 409 D
marian.sherwood@allegheny.edu
SHERWOOD, Mary .... 361-825-2621. 483 F
mary.sherwood@tamucc.edu
SHERWOOD,
Mary Frances .... 337-421-6926. 204 E
mary.sherwood@sowela.edu
SHERWOOD, Regina ...... 617-521-2082. 236 G
regina.sherwood@simmons.edu
SHERWOOD, Sue .... 410-296-5350. 218 I
SHERWOOD, Susan .... 404-237-7573. 121 F
ssherwood@bauder.edu
SHERWOOD COOPER,
Kristi .... 713-798-7552. 467 F
kgc@bcm.edu
SHETH, Sujata .... 909-607-0434... 39 C
SHETLER, Clay, E .... 574-535-7351. 166 A
clayes@goshen.edu
SHETTEL, Kristi .... 406-265-3536. 287 D
kristi.shettel@msun.edu
SHETTY, Devdas .... 202-274-5027... 97 A
dshetty@udc.edu
SHEUCRAFT, Derrek, G .. 615-353-3272. 461 B
derrek.sheucraft@nscc.edu
SHEVACH, Shirley .... 718-518-6650. 318 B
sshevach@hostos.cuny.edu
SHEVYAKOVA, Marina ..... 415-955-2005... 26 L
mshevyakova@alliant.edu
SHEW, Rick .... 828-726-2704. 358 E
rshew@cccti.edu
SHEWMAKER, Jennifer ... 325-674-2381. 464 H
jws02b@acu.edu
SHEWMAKER, Julie .... 317-931-2313. 165 B
jshewmaker@cts.edu
SHEWMAKER, Stephen ... 325-674-2710. 464 H
sbs02a@acu.edu
SHIA, Mary .... 781-239-3123. 231 G
mshia@massbay.edu
SHIAO, Jerry .... 408-435-8989... 66 C
jshiao@svuca.edu
SHIBATA, Martin, C .... 805-756-2501... 32 F
mshibata@calpoly.edu
SHIBAZAKI, Kozue .... 210-567-2648. 493 A
shibazaki@uthscsa.edu
SHIBER, Cheryl .... 908-709-7511. 308 B
cheryl.shiber@ucc.edu
SHIBLEY, Deborah .... 254-526-1347. 468 G
deborah.shibley@ctcd.edu
SHIBLEY, Lisa, R .... 717-871-2390. 429 D
lisa.shibley@millersville.edu
SHIBLEY, Robert .... 716-829-3981. 341 F
rshibley@buffalo.edu
SHIBUYA, Hisatake .... 323-462-1384... 55 E
SHICK, Richard, A .... 716-888-2160. 316 C
shick@canisius.edu
SHICKLE, SR.,
Richard, C .... 540-665-4533. 509 E
rshickle@su.edu
SHIDELER, Janet, L .... 518-783-2320. 340 J
jshideler@siena.edu
SHIDELER, Lorri, P .... 814-641-3605. 419 H
shidell@juniata.edu
SHIDELER, Margo .... 318-869-5073. 201 H
mshideler@centenary.edu
SHIDEMANTLE, Ronald .. 580-548-2327. 396 M
ronald.shidemantle@noc.edu
SHIEH, Charles .... 863-638-2975. 119 D
shiehc@webber.edu
SHIELDS, Brenda .... 610-399-2080. 428 B
bshields@cheyney.edu
SHIELDS, Carolyn, M ..... 313-577-1625. 252 G
es7731@wayne.edu
SHIELDS, Chris .... 248-218-2114. 249 D
cshields@rc.edu
SHIELDS, Daniel .... 860-231-5223... 92 F
dshields@usj.edu
SHIELDS, David .... 248-689-8282. 251 I
david.shields@walshcollege.edu
SHIELDS, JR., David, P . 256-765-4223..... 9 C
dpshields@una.edu
SHIELDS, Deanna, J ...... 304-367-4775. 529 F
deanna.shields@fairmontstate.edu
SHIELDS, Dennis, J .... 608-342-1234. 537 D
shieldsd@uwplatt.edu
SHIELDS, Edith .... 352-854-2322. 100 K
shieldse@cf.edu
SHIELDS, Francis .... 860-439-2570... 89 H
fjshi@conncoll.edu
SHIELDS, George, C .... 570-577-3292. 411 A
george.shields@bucknell.edu
SHIELDS, Greg .... 803-935-4294. 131 H
gshields@southuniversity.edu
SHIELDS, Jerri .... 575-392-5018. 310 G
jshields@nmjc.edu
SHIELDS, Jonathan .... 402-486-2897. 292 E
joshield@ucollege.edu
SHIELDS, Joseph .... 740-593-0371. 387 C
shieldj1@ohio.edu
SHIELDS, Lauren .... 410-386-8442. 214 A
lshields@carrollcc.edu
SHIELDS, Loretta .... 330-672-2038. 382 B
lshields@kent.edu
SHIELDS, Melany .... 716-896-0700. 350 A
shieldsm@villa.edu
SHIELDS, Peter, C .... 781-736-4520. 224 F
pshields@brandeis.edu
SHIELDS, Portia, H .... 615-963-7401. 459 E
president@tnstate.edu
SHIELDS, Ronald .... 936-294-2771. 487 A
SHIELDS, Sally .... 309-649-6250. 160 E
sally.shields@src.edu
SHIELDS, Theodosia, T .. 919-530-5233. 368 A
tshields@nccu.edu
SHIELDS, Todd .... 479-575-5900... 23 I
tshild@uark.edu
SHIELDS, Todd, G .... 479-575-4804... 23 I
tshild@uark.edu
SHIELDS, Vickie .... 509-359-6081. 519 C
vshields@ewu.edu
SHIELL, Steve .... 907-834-1622... 11 B
sshiell@pwscc.edu
SHIELS, Michael .... 262-691-7823. 541 D
mshiels@wctc.edu
SHIER, Pat .... 907-786-4754... 10 H
SHIFFERT, John .... 678-466-4460. 123 A
johnshiffert@clayton.edu

SHIFFLER, Ronald .... 704-337-2234. 365 G
shifflerr@queens.edu
SHIFFLETT, Lee, A .... 540-568-7926. 506 F
shiffla@jmu.edu
SHIFFLETT, Pamela, D .... 540-423-9039. 512 E
pshifflett@germanna.edu
SHIFFMAN, Paul .... 518-464-8803. 324 B
pshiffman@excelsior.edu
SHIFFRAR, Margaret, M . 973-353-5834. 306 D
mag@psychology.rutgers.edu
SHIGEHARA, Deborah .... 808-934-2516. 136 F
deborahs@hawaii.edu
SHIGEMOTO, Steven ...... 808-845-9166. 136 G
ssigemo@hawaii.edu
SHIGEOKA, Claire .... 808-974-7449. 136 A
shigeoka@hawaii.edu
SHILK, Peggy .... 814-371-2090. 434 F
pshilk@triangle-tech.edu
SHILL, Deb .... 641-269-3230. 178 H
shilldeb@grinnell.edu
SHILLER, Barry .... 408-924-1141... 36 A
barry.shiller@sjsu.edu
SHILLET, Gary .... 212-592-2000. 340 H
gshillet@sva.edu
SHILS, Nancy .... 215-895-1106. 435 H
n.shils@usciences.edu
SHIM, Soyeon .... 608-262-4847. 536 D
sshim7@wisc.edu
SHIMABUKURO, Julie .... 314-935-4893. 284 L
jshimabukuro@wustl.edu
SHIMADA, Gerald .... 510-723-6744... 37 K
gshimada@chabotcollege.edu
SHIMAZAKI, Leslie .... 619-388-2873... 62 E
lshimaza@sdccd.edu
SHIMEK, Dennis, W .... 209-667-3351... 35 B
dshimek@csustan.edu
SHIMEK, Gary, S .... 414-277-7181. 534 G
shimek@msoe.edu
SHIMIZU, Jeffery .... 310-434-4317... 65 A
shimizu_jeffery@smc.edu
SHIMIZU, Stacey .... 309-556-3190. 148 B
abroad@iwu.edu
SHIMMEL, Kurt .... 724-738-2008. 429 F
kurt.shimmel@sru.edu
SHIMOKAWA, Brandon .. 808-245-8230. 136 H
shimokaw@hawaii.edu
SHIMP, Sandra .... 941-752-5434. 114 I
shimps@scf.edu
SHIN, David, H .... 714-527-0691... 43 H
info@evangelia.edu
SHIN, Jason .... 714-533-3946... 36 C
jshin@calums.edu
SHIN, Jason .... 714-533-1495... 66 H
jshin@southbaylo.edu
SHINBERGER, Darcie, R . 309-298-1993. 162 K
dr-shinberger@wiu.edu
SHINDE, Prashant .... 773-995-2019. 141 J
pshinde@csu.edu
SHINDLER, Kenda E, G .. 573-592-4216. 285 D
kshindle@williamwoods.edu
SHINE, Deanna .... 614-251-4645. 386 B
shined@ohiodominican.edu
SHINER, Mark .... 315-228-7680. 320 F
mshiner@colgate.edu
SHINEW, Dawn .... 419-372-7364. 374 K
dshinew@bgsu.edu
SHINGLE, Barbara .... 814-472-3170. 432 D
bshingle@francis.edu
SHINGLE, Betty .... 724-222-5330. 425 K
bshingle@penncommercial.edu
SHINGLETON, Jay .... 252-493-7777. 362 G
SHINN, David .... 217-641-4514. 148 M
dshinn@jwcc.edu
SHINTAKU, Rich .... 530-752-8787... 70 J
rshintaku@ucdavis.edu
SHINVILLE, Padriac .... 309-268-8000. 146 B
padriac.shinville@heartland.edu
SHIPES, Bertie .... 912-427-5800. 120 B
bshipes@altamahatech.edu
SHIPLEY, Aletha .... 614-287-2640. 378 B
ashipley@cscc.edu
SHIPLEY, David .... 205-726-2064..... 6 F
dsshiple@samford.edu
SHIPLEY, John, R .... 305-284-6297. 118 F
jshipley@miami.edu
SHIPLEY, Robert .... 918-631-3092. 401 F
robert-shipley@utulsa.edu
SHIPLEY, Suzanne .... 304-876-5107. 529 I
sshipley@shepherd.edu
SHIPMAN, Doug .... 618-395-7777. 147 B
shipmand@iecc.edu
SHIPMAN, Jean, P .... 801-581-8771. 496 Q
jean.shipman@utah.edu
SHIPMAN, Richard .... 517-353-5940. 246 H
shipmanr@msu.edu
SHIPP, Daniel .... 402-554-2779. 293 A
dshipp@unomaha.edu
SHIPP, Judith .... 217-206-7122. 161 E
shipp.judy@uis.edu
SHIPP, Kevin .... 325-235-7337. 486 C
kevin.shipp@tstc.edu
SHIPP, Melvin, D .... 614-292-3246. 386 E
shipp.25@osu.edu
SHIPP, Steve .... 940-397-4539. 476 H
steve.shipp@mwsu.edu
SHIPP, Tina .... 251-981-3771..... 2 I
tina.shipp@columbiasouthern.edu
SHIPPEE, Ellen .... 603-535-2255. 298 G
eshippee@plymouth.edu
SHIPPER, Jody .... 213-740-5086... 74 A
jshipper@usc.edu
SHIPPS, Mark, H .... 740-368-3310. 387 J
mhshipps@owu.edu
SHIPWAY, Ann, M .... 304-260-4380. 527 N
ashipway@blueridgectc.edu
SHIRACHI, Susan .... 808-933-0816. 136 A
shirachi@hawaii.edu
SHIRAH, Hank .... 850-484-2500. 110 G
hshirah@pensacolastate.edu
SHIRAI, Calvin .... 808-245-8333. 136 H
shiraic@hawaii.edu
SHIRAZI, Rhonda .... 251-380-2255..... 7 D
rshirazi@shc.edu
SHIREMAN, Kimberly ...... 336-342-4261. 363 C
shiremank@rockinghamcc.edu
SHIREY, Benton .... 859-622-3311. 193 P
benton.shirey@eku.edu
SHIREY, III, Bo .... 740-446-4367. 380 C
bshirey@gallipoliscareercollege.edu
SHIREY, Brian, D .... 302-739-4064... 93 D
bshirey@dtcc.edu
SHIREY, Jeanette .... 740-446-4367. 380 C
finaid@gallipoliscareercollege.edu
SHIREY, Jonathan .... 940-397-4324. 476 H
jonathan.shirey@mwsu.edu
SHIREY, JR., Robert, L .. 740-446-4367. 380 C
gcc@gallipoliscareercollege.edu
SHIRING, Jennifer .... 724-852-3332. 437 A
jshiring@waynesburg.edu
SHIRK, Jan, M .... 785-827-5541. 188 C
jan@kwu.edu
SHIRLEY, Dana, R .... 816-501-2410. 271 H
dana.shirley@avila.edu
SHIRLEY, Dustin .... 425-889-5206. 521 G
dustin.shirley@northwestu.edu
SHIRLEY, John .... 607-753-7668. 343 B
john.shirley@cortland.edu
SHIRLEY, Kelly .... 704-355-4275. 353 D
kelly.shirley@carolinashealthcare.org
SHIRLEY, Natalie .... 405-947-3200. 398 C
SHIRLEY, Phil, E .... 806-874-4800. 468 J
phil.shirley@clarendoncollege.edu
SHIRLEY, Robert .... 334-387-3877..... 1 E
robertshirley@amridgeuniversity.edu
SHIRLEY, Steven, W .... 701-845-7102. 372 A
steven.shirley@vcsu.edu
SHIRLEY, JR.,
Thomas, R .... 215-951-2720. 430 E
shirleyt@philau.edu
SHIRLEY, Vikki .... 850-245-0466. 114 J
vikki.shirley@flbog.edu
SHIRTZ, Michael .... 419-559-2147. 389 I
mshirtz@terra.edu
SHISHOFF, John, W .... 937-778-7878. 379 G
jshishoff@edisonohio.edu
SHISIDO, Jack, L .... 831-656-2192. 544 M
jlshishi@nps.edu
SHISLER, Kirk, L .... 540-432-4203. 504 D
kirk.shisler@emu.edu
SHISLER-RAPP,
Susan, M .... 610-359-5040. 414 D
srapp@dccc.edu
SHIVEL, Gail .... 305-595-9500... 97 G
dean@amcollege.edu
SHIVELY, Brett .... 714-816-0366... 70 A
brett.shively@trident.edu
SHIVELY, Bruce, L .... 775-784-6516. 294 J
shively@unr.edu
SHIVELY, C. Randall .... 618-437-5321. 156 H
shively@rlc.edu
SHIVELY, Debby, L .... 520-621-7151... 18 F
dshively@email.arizona.edu
SHIVELY, Marnie .... 209-588-5105... 77 I
shively@yosemite.edu
SHIVER, Michael .... 770-229-3044. 132 B
mshiver@sctech.edu
SHIVERS, Sandra .... 914-594-3723. 334 A
sandra_shivers@nymc.edu
SHKOP, Esther .... 773-973-0241. 146 C
shkop@htc.edu
SHLAFER, David .... 352-395-5230. 113 C
david.shlafer@sfcollege.edu
SHLESINGER, Ned .... 610-785-6202. 432 C
nshlesinger@scs.edu
SHMIDMAN, Michael, A 212-463-0400. 348 B
michaels@touro.edu
SHNEYDER, Mikhail .... 801-689-2160. 496 C
SHNIDMAN, Avrohom ..... 410-484-7200. 217 D
SHOAF, Victoria, L .... 718-990-6800. 339 A
shoafv@stjohns.edu
SHOCK, Stephanie .... 701-662-1655. 372 D
stephanie.shock@lrsc.edu
SHOCKEY, James, W ...... 520-626-2422... 18 F
jshockey@email.arizona.edu
SHOCKEY, Julie .... 563-387-1865. 180 M
shocju01@luther.edu
SHOCKEY, Sherri, L .... 260-982-5237. 170 U
slshockey@manchester.edu
SHOCKEY, Stacy .... 712-325-3282. 179 L
sshockey@iwcc.edu
SHOCKLEY, Darlas .... 641-683-5174. 179 A
darlas.shockley@indianhills.edu
SHOCKLEY, David, R ...... 336-386-3213. 364 D
shockleyd@surry.edu
SHOCKLEY, Erica .... 607-274-3222. 327 E
eshockley@ithaca.edu
SHOCKLEY, Robin, L .... 614-234-5213. 384 J
rshockley@mccn.edu
SHOCKLEY-ZALABAK,
Pam .... 719-255-3436... 85 M
chancellor@uccs.edu
SHOCKNEY, Bethany ...... 256-306-2839..... 2 F
bclem@calhoun.edu
SHOEMAKE, James, M ... 214-388-5466. 471 D
difs@dallasinstitute.edu
SHOEMAKE, Kellie .... 910-695-3714. 363 F
shoemakek@sandhills.edu
SHOEMAKE, Monte .... 417-626-1234. 279 J
shoemake.monte@occ.edu
SHOEMAKER, Ben .... 614-823-1534. 387 K
bshoemaker@otterbein.edu
SHOEMAKER, Carol .... 417-328-1531. 282 C
cshoemaker@sbuniv.edu
SHOEMAKER, Chris .... 276-326-4212. 502 H
cshoemaker@bluefield.edu
SHOEMAKER, Cindy .... 717-262-2006. 437 H
cshoemaker@wilson.edu
SHOEMAKER, Norm .... 619-849-2784... 59 L
normshoemaker@pointloma.edu
SHOEMAKER,
Patricia, B .... 540-831-6374. 508 C
pshoemak@radford.edu
SHOEMAKER, Peter .... 202-319-5220... 94 G
shoemaker@cua.edu
SHOEMAKER, Polly .... 803-754-4100. 443 C
SHOEMAKER, Scott .... 619-849-2565... 59 L
scottshoemaker@pointloma.edu
SHOEMAKER, Troy .... 850-478-8496. 110 F
SHOEN, Eric .... 607-431-4432. 325 F
shoene@hartwick.edu
SHOENBERGER, George . 301-985-7873. 219 F
cfo@umuc.edu
SHOENER, Gary .... 570-504-7949. 420 C
shoenerg@lackawanna.edu
SHOENER, Pattie .... 504-282-4455. 206 A
pshoener@nobts.edu
SHOESMITH, Meighan ...... 425-558-0299. 519 B
smeighan@digipen.edu
SHOGE, Ruth, C .... 410-778-7292. 221 C
rshoge2@washcoll.edu
SHOGER, Diane, L .... 585-262-1504. 332 A
dshoger@monroecc.edu
SHOJAI, Siamack .... 860-832-3228... 87 K
shojaisia@ccsu.edu
SHOLLENBERGER,
Kevin .... 410-516-8382. 215 H
ksholle1@jhu.edu
SHOLOCK, Adale .... 610-436-2122. 430 A
asholock@wcupa.edu
SHOLTEN, Bryan .... 303-963-3398... 79 C
bsholten@ccu.edu
SHOMAKER, Darrell, K ... 540-985-8362. 506 G
dkshomaker@jchs.edu
SHOMAKER, Kelli .... 979-830-4459. 467 I
kelli.shomaker@blinn.edu
SHOMO, Thomas, H .... 434-223-6262. 505 E
tshomo@hsc.edu
SHOMOUR, Karlisa .... 505-346-2346. 312 E
karlisa.shomour@bie.edu
SHONBRUN, Anne .... 718-270-4551. 342 D
anne.shonbrun@downstate.edu
SHONK, Brian .... 870-612-2003... 25 A
brian.shonk@uaccb.edu
SHONROCK, Michael ...... 620-341-5551. 186 D
shonroc@emporia.edu
SHONTZ, Gary, B .... 319-273-3576. 176 A
gary.shontz@uni.edu
SHONTZ, Susan, F .... 814-641-3304. 419 H
shontzs@juniata.edu
SHOOK, Douglas .... 213-740-4623... 74 A
shook@esd.usc.edu
SHOOK, Mark .... 706-880-8976. 128 A
mshook@lagrange.edu
SHOOT, Madge .... 217-234-5375. 150 D
mbailey1292@lakeland.cc.il.us
SHOPE, Mary Ann .... 501-812-2251... 22 G
mashope@pulaskitech.edu
SHOPE, Ronald, J .... 402-449-2872. 289 H
rshope@graceu.edu
SHOPSHIRE, Sandra .... 208-282-2997. 138 E
shopsand@isu.edu
SHOR, Eric, M .... 304-457-6276. 526 A
shorem@ab.edu
SHOR, Mark .... 212-463-0400. 348 B
mshor@touro.edu
SHOR, Stuart, B .... 212-817-7604. 317 F
sshor@gc.cuny.edu
SHORB, Deanna .... 641-269-4981. 178 H
shorb@grinnell.edu
SHORB, Stephen .... 402-554-2640. 293 A
sshorb@unomaha.edu
SHORE, Cecilia, M .... 513-529-9266. 384 G
shorec@miamioh.edu
SHORE, Cliff .... 703-993-2580. 505 C
cshore@gmu.edu
SHORE, Daniel .... 617-496-2650. 227 C
dan_shore@harvard.edu
SHORE, Elliott .... 610-526-5270. 410 J
eshore@brynmawr.edu
SHORE, Jim .... 412-521-6200. 432 A
jim.shore@rosedaletech.org
SHORE, Michael, J .... 815-599-3491. 146 D
mike.shore@highland.edu
SHORE, Muriel .... 201-559-6030. 302 A
shorem@felician.edu
SHORE, Sara .... 612-798-3757. 257 J
sshore@msbcollege.edu
SHORES, Dennis .... 610-647-4400. 418 I
dshores@immaculata.edu
SHORES, Jonathan .... 828-669-8012. 357 H
jeshores@montreat.edu
SHORES, Robin, H .... 610-690-6879. 433 I
rshores1@swarthmore.edu
SHORETTE, Charles .... 601-877-6115. 265 G
shorette@alcorn.edu
SHOREY, David .... 978-468-7111. 227 A
shorey@gcts.edu
SHOREY, Denise .... 717-815-1353. 438 D
dshorey@ycp.edu
SHORT, Al .... 303-722-5724... 83 A
ashort@lincolntech.com
SHORT, Anthony, E .... 419-372-7019. 374 K
ashort@bgsu.edu
SHORT, Aric .... 979-845-2217. 483 C
SHORT, Brent .... 352-588-8258. 112 D
brent.short@saintleo.edu
SHORT, David .... 276-328-0196. 511 C
dps4v@uvawise.edu
SHORT, JR., David .... 409-880-8060. 486 F
david.short@lamar.edu
SHORT, Donna .... 828-652-0631. 362 A
donnas@mcdowelltech.edu
SHORT, Donna .... 828-652-0631. 362 A
donnasho@mcdowelltech.edu
SHORT, Emily .... 615-230-3447. 461 G
emily.short@volstate.edu
SHORT, Evelyn .... 360-417-6381. 522 A
eshort@pencol.edu
SHORT, Frank .... 585-395-2350. 342 F
fshort@brockport.edu
SHORT, Genia .... 719-384-6890... 83 M
genia.short@ojc.edu
SHORT, Joel, D .... 574-535-7784. 166 A
joelds@goshen.edu
SHORT, John .... 610-921-7500. 409 A
jshort@alb.edu
SHORT, John .... 920-929-3602. 538 E
john.short@uwc.edu
SHORT, Kyla .... 918-343-7865. 399 C
kshort@rsu.edu
SHORT, Laura, M .... 740-392-6868. 384 K
laura.short@mvnu.edu
SHORT, Mary Ann .... 937-769-1860. 373 I
mshort2@antioch.edu
SHORT, Paula .... 713-743-5227. 489 B
pmshort@uh.edu
SHORT, Paula .... 713-743-5227. 489 A
pmshort@uh.edu
SHORT, Rick .... 281-283-3300. 489 C
short@uhcl.edu
SHORT, Rosanna .... 623-935-8941... 14 K
rosanna.short@estrellamountain.edu
SHORT, Royce, B .... 864-242-5100. 441 D
SHORT, Trey .... 309-556-3017. 148 B
tshort@iwu.edu
SHORT, William .... 407-646-2619. 111 Q
wshort@rollins.edu
SHORT, OFM, William ... 510-848-5232... 45 A
wshort@fst.edu
SHORT-THOMPSON,
Cady .... 513-745-5660. 391 A
shortcw@ucmail.uc.edu
SHORTBULL, Thomas ..... 605-455-6011. 450 I
tshortbull@olc.edu
SHORTBULL, Thomas, H 605-455-6022. 450 I
tshortb@olc.edu
SHORTELL, Stephen, M .. 510-642-2082... 70 I
shortell@berkeley.edu
SHORTER, Dwayne, R ..... 512-505-3024. 473 G
drshorter@htu.edu
SHORTER, Paula .... 816-501-4115. 280 I
paula.shorter@rockhurst.edu
SHORTER, William, H ..... 540-831-5794. 508 C
wshorter@radford.edu

SHORTER-GOODEN, Kumea .... 301-405-6810. 219 B kshorter@umd.edu
SHORTY, Ursula .... 225-771-2790. 206 J ursula_shorty@subr.edu
SHOSTACK, Pauline .... 315-498-2708. 335 G
SHOTT, Brandy .... 704-233-8028. 370 G b.shott@wingate.edu
SHOTT, Diane, T .... 276-326-4201. 502 H dshott@bluefield.edu
SHOTWELL SMITH, Mary .... 706-233-7278. 131 E msmith@shorter.edu
SHOUDY, Peter, D .... 610-499-1036. 437 E pdshoudy@widener.edu
SHOULDIS, Martha, K .... 203-576-5277... 91 D mshouldis@stvincentscollege.edu
SHOUN, Stan .... 314-286-4801. 280 F sshoun@ranken.edu
SHOUP, John .... 951-343-4205... 30 H jshoup@calbaptist.edu
SHOURESHI, Rahmat ..... 516-686-7630. 333 H rshoures@nyit.edu
SHOVAN, Lisa .... 518-562-4130. 320 B lisa.shovan@clinton.edu
SHOVLAIN, Raymond, J . 563-333-6233. 182 B ShovlainRaymondJ@sau.edu
SHOWALTER, Marc, K .... 662-915-3784. 270 B mshowalt@olemiss.edu
SHOWALTER, Martha ..... 734-973-3722. 252 A showalter@wccnet.edu
SHOWALTER, Matthew ... 740-857-1311. 388 I mshowalter@rosedale.edu
SHOWALTER, Rodney, J 540-338-1776. 508 A ie@phc.edu
SHOWALTER, Stephanie . 215-836-2222. 409 G finaid@antonelli.edu
SHOWELL, JR., Charles . 937-376-6441. 376 E cshowell@centralstate.edu
SHOWELL, Jeffrey, A ...... 419-372-8603. 374 K jashowe@bgsu.edu
SHOWERS, Anita .... 434-961-6574. 513 F ashowers@pvcc.edu
SHOWERS, Bill .... 412-809-5100. 430 H showers.william@pti.edu
SHOWERS, Nancy, C ...... 248-232-4731. 248 D ncshower@oaklandcc.edu
SHOWERS, Shane .... 315-568-3125. 333 C sshowers@nycc.edu
SHOWS, Alicia .... 601-276-3706. 269 H showsa@smcc.edu
SHOWS, Deidre .... 601-318-6583. 270 I dede.shows@wmcarey.edu
SHOWS, John .... 228-897-4373. 268 C john.shows1@mgcc.edu
SHOWS-PEREZ, Cindy .... 337-482-6497. 208 D cperez@louisiana.edu
SHPER, Paul .... 802-322-1656. 499 C paul.shper@goddard.edu
SHRADER, Rachel .... 817-923-8459. 469 F rachel.shrader@fishermore.edu
SHREFFLER, Christine .... 314-344-4440. 277 J cshreff@aol.com
SHREVE, Penny .... 760-252-2411... 29 I pshreve@barstow.edu
SHREVE, Teresa .... 205-348-7625..... 8 D tshreve@bama.ua.edu
SHREVES, Michael .... 252-493-7289. 362 G mshreves@email.pittcc.edu
SHRIER, Douglas, M ...... 540-868-7199. 512 H dshrier@lfcc.edu
SHRIMPTON, Nikki .... 315-472-5730. 346 A nikki.shrimpton@esc.edu
SHRINER, Kevin, N .... 239-304-7819... 98 K kevin.shriner@avemaria.edu
SHRINER, Michael, B ..... 409-772-3501. 493 C mshriner@utmb.edu
SHRIVER, Michael .... 970-542-3174... 83 E michael.shriver@morgancc.edu
SHRODE, Scott .... 715-682-1373. 535 D sshrode@northland.edu
SHROFF, Meghana .... 612-874-3796. 257 B mshroff@mcad.edu
SHROKA, Julie .... 847-543-2847. 143 A julieshroka@clcillinois.edu
SHROM-RHOADS, Kirstin .... 717-872-6840. 429 D kirstin.shrom-roads@millersville.edu
SHROPSHIRE, Douglas .. 508-531-1281. 229 D dshropshire@bridgew.edu
SHROPSHIRE, Martin, W .... 336-386-3453. 364 D shropsm@surry.edu
SHROPSHIRE, Pamela .... 215-717-6381. 435 A pshropshire@uarts.edu
SHROYER, Margaret (Peg) .... 320-308-5030. 261 C pshroyer@sctcc.edu
SHRUBB, Richard .... 507-372-3491. 260 A richard.shrubb@mnwest.edu
SHRYACK, Jessica .... 612-659-6527. 259 D jessica.shryack@minneapolis.edu
SHUBERT, David .... 316-942-4291. 189 E shubertd@newmanu.edu
SHUBERT, Lisa, A .... 507-344-7324. 253 J lshubert@blc.edu
SHUBSDA, Adam .... 908-737-4840. 302 F ashubsda@kean.edu
SHUCHAT, Rena .... 937-512-2919. 388 O rena.shuchat@sinclair.edu
SHUCK, Richard .... 765-658-4020. 165 F dickshuck@depauw.edu
SHUE, Mindy .... 970-824-1151... 80 B mindy.shue@cncc.edu
SHUFFELTON, George .... 507-222-4300. 254 D gshuffel@carleton.edu
SHUFORD, Bettina .... 919-966-4045. 368 D bcshufor@email.unc.edu
SHUFORD, Eddie .... 828-652-0652. 362 A eddieshuford@mcdowelltech.edu
SHUGART, Sanford, C ..... 407-582-3250. 118 M sshugart@valenciacollege.edu
SHUHY, Taryn .... 212-226-7300. 336 G tshuhy@pbcny.edu
SHULER, Peggy .... 803-321-5117. 445 G peggy.shuler@newberry.edu
SHULKEN, Mary, C .... 252-328-6481. 367 B schulkenma@ecu.edu
SHULL, Roger .... 806-894-9611. 480 H rshull@southplainscollege.edu
SHULL, Roxanna .... 260-459-4600. 169 C rshull@ibcfortwayne.edu
SHULMAN, Brian .... 973-275-2168. 307 C brian.shulman@shu.edu
SHULMAN, Hedy .... 212-463-0400. 348 B hedy.shulman@touro.edu
SHULMAN, Jacob .... 732-367-1060. 299 E yshulman@bmg.edu
SHULNAK, Jody .... 360-992-2447. 518 A jshulnak@clark.edu
SHULTES, Kenneth, E ..... 717-245-1272. 414 H shultes@dickinson.edu
SHULTIS, Terri .... 415-442-7079... 45 I tshultis@ggu.edu
SHULTS, Joel .... 719-587-7901... 78 B jshults@adams.edu
SHULTZ, Cathleen, M ..... 501-279-4475... 21 C shultz@harding.edu
SHULTZ, Christopher ...... 949-824-5337... 71 B chris.shultz@uci.edu
SHULTZ, Eric .... 605-882-5284. 450 D eric.schultz@lakeareatech.edu
SHULTZ, John .... 913-758-6308. 191 B John.Shultz@stmary.edu
SHULTZ, John, C .... 419-289-5160. 374 C jshultz@ashland.edu
SHULTZ, Kari .... 423-236-2484. 458 J kshultz@southern.edu
SHULTZ, Walter, J .... 570-326-3761. 427 B wshultz@pct.edu
SHUMAKE, Connie, C .... 502-852-3551. 200 D ccshum01@louisville.edu
SHUMAKER, Deb .... 989-275-5000. 245 B deb.shumaker@kirtland.edu
SHUMAKER, Nancy .... 507-285-7461. 261 A nancy.shumaker@rctc.edu
SHUMAKER, Steve, A ..... 570-586-2400. 410 D sshumaker@bbc.edu
SHUMAN, Jenny .... 478-296-6117. 129 I jshuman@oftc.edu
SHUMAN, Kelli, R .... 605-394-1203. 452 A kelli.shuman@sdsmt.edu
SHUMAN, Michaeline, M .... 814-332-2381. 409 D michaeline.shuman@allegheny.edu
SHUMAN, Ruth .... 617-243-2140. 227 K rshuman@lasell.edu
SHUMAN, Shari, A .... 904-620-2002. 116 B sshuman@unf.edu
SHUMAN, Victoria .... 304-793-6898. 530 B vshuman@osteo.wvsom.edu
SHUMANTE, Walter .... 903-927-3249. 495 A wshumate@wileyc.edu
SHUMATE, Connie .... 304-384-5366. 529 E cshumate@concord.edu
SHUMPERT, Glenn .... 803-641-3444. 448 A glenns@usca.edu
SHUMWAY, Nicolas .... 713-348-4810. 479 A shumway@rice.edu
SHUNKWILER, Susan ..... 313-845-9731. 243 H stshunkwiler@hfcc.edu
SHUPALA, Christine .... 361-825-2643. 483 F christine.shupala@tamucc.edu
SHUPE, Gary .... 217-641-4505. 148 M gshupe@jwcc.edu
SHUPE, John .... 845-257-3335. 342 B shupej@newpaltz.edu
SHUPENUS, Sarah .... 217-424-6350. 153 C sshupenus@millikin.edu
SHUPENUS, Sarah .... 217-424-6340. 153 C sshupenus@millikin.edu
SHUPP, Edward, K .... 610-758-4200. 422 A eks0@lehigh.edu
SHUPP, Michael, D .... 515-263-6136. 178 G mshupp@grandview.edu
SHUPPY, Brian, L .... 801-626-6114. 497 D bshuppy@weber.edu
SHUR, Barry .... 303-724-2910... 86 A barry.shur@ucdenver.edu
SHURAN, Melanie .... 847-578-3403. 157 F melanie.shuran@rosalindfranklin.edu
SHURES, Aaron, G .... 217-206-6003. 161 E shures.aaron@uis.edu
SHURTZ, Mary Ann .... 703-539-6890. 510 B mshurtz@stratford.edu
SHURTZ, Richard .... 703-539-6890. 510 B rshurtz@stratford.edu
SHUSTER, Arthur .... 828-298-3325. 370 E ashuster@warren-wilson.edu
SHUSTER, Patricia .... 603-641-7150. 297 G pshuster@anselm.edu
SHUTE, Marcus, W .... 404-880-6990. 122 J mwshute@cau.edu
SHUTE, William .... 202-955-9091. 491 A wshute@utsystem.edu
SHUTKIN, William .... 415-561-6555... 60 C
SHUTLER, Troy .... 419-755-4896. 385 D tshutler@ncstatecollege.edu
SHUTT, Barbara, C .... 207-859-5415. 209 J bcshutt@colby.edu
SHUTT, Gary .... 405-744-4800. 397 H gary.shutt@okstate.edu
SHUTTER, Jamie, L .... 512-475-8445. 491 C j.shutter@uhs.utexas.edu
SHYDIAN, Joanne .... 760-750-4954... 35 A jshydian@csusm.edu
SIAHMAKOUN, Azad .... 812-877-8400. 172 C azad.siahmakoun@rose-hulman.edu
SIAMPOS, Christa .... 314-421-0949. 282 I financialaid@siba.edu
SIAMUNDELE, Andre ...... 315-364-3215. 350 E asiamundele@wells.edu
SIAS, Mary, E .... 502-597-6260. 197 A mary.sias@kysu.edu
SIBAL, Thomas .... 574-936-8898. 163 K tom.sibal@ancilla.edu
SIBENALLER, Jim .... 773-508-7665. 151 H jsibena@luc.edu
SIBENALLER-WOODALL, Beth .... 712-324-5061. 181 G beths@nwicc.edu
SIBERT, Kimberley .... 740-366-9233. 376 A ksibert@cotc.edu
SIBERT, Sonja .... 775-753-2181. 294 F sonja.sibert@gbcnv.edu
SIBLEY, Debra, H .... 504-568-6107. 205 C dsible@lsuhsc.edu
SICARD, OP, Kenneth, R .... 401-865-2055. 439 E ksicard@providence.edu
SICARD, Rex, E .... 785-243-1435. 185 M rsicard@cloud.edu
SICHTERMAN, David .... 313-927-1391. 246 D dsichterman@marygrove.edu
SICIENSKY, Emily .... 931-540-2704. 460 E esiciensky@columbiastate.edu
SICILIANO, Julie .... 413-782-1553. 238 A jsicilia@wne.edu
SICILIANO, Stephen, N .. 231-995-1373. 248 B ssiciliano@nmc.edu
SICK, Volker .... 734-763-1290. 251 C vsick@umich.edu
SICKBERT, Alan, A .... 651-523-2421. 256 A asickbert01@hamline.edu
SICKLES, Susan .... 513-772-9888. 386 C susan.sickles@omw.edu
SICONOLFI, Steven .... 815-226-4065. 157 C Ssiconolfi@rockford.edu
SIDBURY, Carmen .... 404-270-5705. 132 E csidbury@spelman.edu
SIDDARAJU, Raj .... 309-649-6387. 160 E raj.siddaraju@src.edu
SIDDENS, Nancy .... 217-732-3168. 151 B nsiddens@lincolnchristian.edu
SIDDIQI, Melanie .... 909-652-6780... 37 M melanie.siddiqi@chaffey.edu
SIDDIQI, Muhammad ...... 708-656-8000. 153 H muhammad.siddiqi@morton.edu
SIDDIQUI, Murtuza .... 651-793-1910. 259 C murtuza.siddiqui@metrostate.edu
SIDEBOTTOM, Daniel ...... 607-753-2501. 343 B daniel.sidebottom@cortland.edu
SIDEBOTTOM, Sara, L .... 859-572-5588. 198 I sidebottoms@nku.edu
SIDERAKIS, John .... 212-650-7226. 317 D jsiderakis@ccny.cuny.edu
SIDERAS, John, F .... 216-368-4340. 375 J john.sideras@case.edu
SIDERS, Angie .... 765-455-9515. 168 A asiders@iuk.edu
SIDERS, Janet .... 229-931-2000. 126 D janet.siders@gsw.edu
SIDES, Diane, O .... 573-651-2256. 282 B dosides@semo.edu
SIDES, Karen .... 210-486-2339. 465 B ksides@alamo.edu
SIDHU, Elda .... 702-895-5185. 294 I elda.sidhu@unlv.edu
SIDIO, Jerome .... 401-874-5488. 440 D jerrysidio@uri.edu
SIDLE, Meg .... 606-218-5290. 200 F margaretsidle@upike.edu
SIDNEY, Cheri .... 773-995-3534. 141 J csidney@csu.edu
SIDOCK, Andrew .... 217-479-7066. 152 D andrew.sidock@mac.edu
SIDOR, Stanley, M .... 704-290-5252. 363 G ssidor@spcc.edu
SIDOTI, Dennis .... 860-412-7351... 89 E dsidoti@qvcc.commnet.edu
SIDWELL, Scott, A .... 415-422-2923... 73 J sasidwell@usfca.edu
SIDY, Victor .... 480-860-2700... 13 Q vsidy@earthlink.net
SIEBENECK, Paula, J ...... 419-995-8458. 381 Q siebeneck.p@rhodesstate.edu
SIEBENMORGEN, Tom .... 501-450-1333... 21 E
SIEBENS, Libby .... 509-682-6436. 525 B lsiebens@wvc.edu
SIEBER, Frederick, C ...... 610-519-7730. 436 F frederick.sieber@villanova.edu
SIEBER, Yvonne .... 620-327-8112. 187 D yvonnes@hesston.edu
SIEBERT, David, J .... 847-735-5040. 150 B siebert@lakeforest.edu
SIEBERT, Laurie .... 248-689-8282. 251 I lsiebert@walshcollege.edu
SIEBERT, Mary Anne .... 501-450-1372... 21 E siebert@hendrix.edu
SIEBERT, Scotti .... 417-873-7434. 273 H ssiebert@drury.edu
SIECKE, Elizabeth .... 201-684-7318. 305 A esiecke@ramapo.edu
SIEDOW, James, N .... 919-681-6438. 354 A jim.siedow@duke.edu
SIEDZIK, Richard .... 401-232-6505. 438 K rsiedzik@bryant.edu
SIEFERT, Ruth .... 507-285-7472. 261 A ruth.siefert@rctc.edu
SIEFERT, Tom .... 773-291-6412. 142 D tsiefert@ccc.edu
SIEFFERMAN, Larry, D ... 706-213-2139. 120 J lsiefferman@athenstech.edu
SIEGEL, Christine .... 203-254-4000... 89 I csiegel@fairfield.edu
SIEGEL, Donald, S .... 518-442-4910. 341 D dsiegel@albany.edu
SIEGEL, Fred .... 909-621-8965... 39 C fred.siegel@cgu.edu
SIEGEL, James .... 845-574-4729. 338 B jsiegel3@sunyrockland.edu
SIEGEL, Larry .... 978-934-2107. 229 B larry_siegel@uml.edu
SIEGEL, Lawrence, J .... 212-430-4204. 351 M lsiegel@aecom.yu.edu
SIEGEL, Peter .... 213-740-7197... 74 A
SIEGEL, Peter, M .... 530-752-4998... 70 J pmsiegel@ucdavis.edu
SIEGER, Eric .... 507-222-4183. 254 D esieger@carleton.edu
SIEGERT, Gerald, A .... 513-556-5006. 390 G gerald.siegert@uc.edu
SIEGERT, Kara, O .... 410-543-6023. 220 D kosiegert@salisbury.edu
SIEGFRIED, Jessica .... 435-283-7169. 498 A jessica.siegfried@snow.edu
SIEGFRIED, Kathy .... 610-861-5460. 425 D ksiegfried@northampton.edu
SIEGGREEN, Stephanie ... 989-964-7028. 249 G smsieggr@svsu.edu
SIEGMANN, Starla, C ...... 414-443-8862. 539 F starla.siegmann@wlc.edu
SIEKER, Tina .... 636-922-8314. 280 J tsieker@stchas.edu
SIEMERING, John .... 920-498-5488. 541 B john.siemering@nwtc.edu
SIEMERS, Barbara .... 830-792-7368. 480 F jbsiemers@schreiner.edu
SIEMINSKI, Daniel, W ..... 814-865-6574. 426 A dws8@psu.edu
SIEMINSKI, Randy, B ...... 315-386-7335. 345 F sieminski@canton.edu
SIEMSEN, Deanna .... 719-336-6646... 82 R deanna.siemsen@lamarcc.edu
SIENER, Estelle, M .... 716-888-2450. 316 C siener@canisius.edu
SIERRA CONCEPCION, Yadexy .... 787-744-1060. 551 J ysierra@mechtech.edu
SIEVERS, Alex .... 812-888-5421. 174 F asievers@vinu.edu
SIEVERS, Debbie .... 708-974-5330. 153 F sievers@morainevalley.edu

SIFFERLEN, Ned, J .... 937-512-2510. 388 O
ned.sifferlen@sinclair.edu
SIFFRING, Ed .... 402-643-7230. 289 B
ed.siffring@cune.edu
SIFUENTES, Alma .... 831-459-3755... 72 C
alma@ucsc.edu
SIFUENTES, Lucas .... 301-628-5604. 217 C
lsifuentes@nlc.edu
SIFUENTES, Miguel .... 915-747-5544. 492 A
msifuentes@utep.edu
SIGAUKE, Erica .... 417-667-8181. 273 A
esigauke@cottey.edu
SIGGERS, Julian, F .... 215-898-4052. 435 B
siggers@upenn.edu
SIGGERS, Lauretta .... 617-873-0170. 224 G
lauretta.siggers@cambridgecollege.edu
SIGGINS, Jack, A .... 202-994-6455... 95 D
siggins@gwu.edu
SIGISMOND, William, D 585-292-3220. 332 A
wsigismond@monroecc.edu
SIGLER, Jeffrey .... 718-270-4979. 319 A
jeffrey@mec.cuny.edu
SIGLER, Julius, A .... 434-544-8232. 506 K
sigler.ja@lynchburg.edu
SIGLER, Katie .... 405-491-6365. 399 K
ksigler@snu.edu
SIGLER, Todd, D .... 618-453-3771. 159 G
todds@dps.siu.edu
SIGLER, Wayne .... 703-993-2391. 505 C
wsigler@gmu.edu
SIGMON, Judy .... 336-917-5471. 366 D
judy.sigmon@salem.edu
SIGMON, Patty .... 540-365-4449. 504 L
psigmon@ferrum.edu
SIGNOR, Mary .... 212-998-2352. 334 D
mary.signor@nyu.edu
SIGNORELLO, John .... 973-761-9615. 307 C
john.signorello@shu.edu
SIGNORELLO, Rose .... 713-525-3162. 490 L
signorr@stthom.edu
SIGUAW, Judy .... 252-328-1098. 367 B
siguawj@ecu.edu
SIGUENZA, Rafael .... 509-527-2683. 524 I
rosa.jimenez@wallawalla.edu
SIGWORTH, Steve .... 713-798-4951. 467 F
sigworth@bcm.edu
SIHOTA HE'BERT,
Gurdeep .... 559-324-6481... 68 H
gurdeep.sihota@sccd.edu
SIKES, Janine .... 352-846-3903. 116 A
jysikes@ufl.edu
SIKES, Pamela, J .... 619-260-4595... 73 I
psikes@sandiego.edu
SIKES, Steddon, L .... 402-363-5668. 293 I
slsikes@york.edu
SIKORA, Patty .... 253-833-9111. 520 C
psikora@greenriver.edu
SIKORA, Zdzislaw .... 603-623-0310. 297 E
zdzislawsikora@nhia.edu
SIKORSKI, Henry .... 631-420-2142. 346 B
henry.sikorski@farmingdale.edu
SIKORSKY, LC, Charles . 703-416-1441. 505 I
csikorsky@ipsciences.edu
SILAFAU, Emey .... 684-699-9155. 546 A
e.silafau@amsamoa.edu
SILAK, Cathy .... 503-955-1001. 402 J
csilak@cu-portland.edu
SILANDER, Liisa .... 401-454-6349. 440 A
lsilande@risd.edu
SILANSKIS, Theresa .... 410-837-6838. 221 A
tsilanskis@ubalt.edu
SILBER, Daniel, K .... 573-288-6325. 273 F
dsilber@culver.edu
SILBER, Irene .... 612-977-4132. 254 C
irene.silber@capella.edu
SILBER, Jeffrey, A .... 607-255-2016. 322 A
jas9@cornell.edu
SILBERBERGER, Cindy ... 760-757-2121... 54 G
csilberberger@miracosta.edu
SILBERLING, Rosanne .... 818-299-5500... 75 E
rsilberling@westcoastuniversity.edu
SILBERMAN, Gerald, L ... 610-683-4106. 429 A
silberma@kutztown.edu
SILBERQUIT, Paul .... 203-285-2368... 88 E
psilberquit@gwcc.commnet.edu
SILBERSTEIN, Dara, J ..... 607-777-2815. 341 E
lael@binghamton.edu
SILBERT, Alan .... 706-864-1942. 133 D
alan.sibert@ung.edu
SILBURSTEIN, Jeffrey ..... 212-659-9091. 327 A
SILCOX, Greg .... 602-787-6622... 15 B
greg.silcox@paradisevalley.edu
SILER, Ginni .... 706-802-5136. 125 C
gsiler@highlands.edu
SILER, Linda, K .... 616-538-2330. 243 A
lsiler@gbcol.edu
SILES, Marcelo, E .... 757-683-4419. 507 N
msiles@odu.edu
SILICIANO, John, A .... 607-255-3062. 322 A
jas83@cornell.edu
SILK, Eleana .... 914-961-8313. 340 B
es@svots.edu
SILK, Elizabeth .... 708-524-6481. 144 C
esilk@dom.edu
SILK, Mary, L .... 692-625-4410. 546 F
mlsilk@hotmail.com
SILKWORTH, Sabina ...... 410-209-6017. 213 F
ssilkworth@bccc.edu
SILLCOX, James .... 718-260-3148. 336 E
jsillcox@poly.edu
SILLEN, Andrew .... 718-951-5074. 317 C
asillen@brooklyn.cuny.edu
SILLIMAN, Robert .... 502-213-4294. 195 F
bob.silliman@kctcs.edu
SILLIMAN, Steve .... 509-313-3522. 520 A
silliman@gonzaga.edu
SILLS, CreSaundra .... 410-617-2232. 216 A
csills@loyola.edu
SILMAN, Linda, C .... 314-516-5406. 283 E
lindas@umsl.edu
SILMAN, Shawn .... 281-998-6150. 479 G
shawn.silman@sjcd.edu
SILTANEN, Susan .... 601-266-4373. 270 E
susan.siltanen@usm.edu
SILVA, Adelina .... 210-485-0153. 464 I
asilva@alamo.edu
SILVA, Alan .... 651-690-6500. 263 O
ajsilva@stkate.edu
SILVA, Alyson .... 954-262-5258. 109 K
asilva@nova.edu
SILVA, Dashia .... 718-261-5800. 315 F
dsilva@bramsonort.edu
SILVA, Denise .... 615-871-2260... 96 F
SILVA, Efrain .... 760-355-6249... 48 A
efrain.silva@imperial.edu
SILVA, Hilda .... 956-882-5133. 491 D
hilda.silva@utb.edu
SILVA, Jack .... 401-454-6480. 440 A
jsilva@risd.edu
SILVA, Jessica, L .... 401-456-8047. 439 F
jsilva@ric.edu
SILVA, Karen, L .... 510-723-6641... 37 K
ksilva@chabotcollege.edu
SILVA, Liz .... 956-364-4311. 485 H
liz.silva@tstc.edu
SILVA, Lourdes .... 704-463-3062. 365 E
lourdes.silva@fsmail.pfeiffer.edu
SILVA, Maritza .... 401-949-2820. 439 C
msilva@inteducators.org
SILVA, Mariza .... 312-922-1884. 152 C
msilva@maccormac.edu
SILVA, Maureen, C .... 240-895-4282. 218 A
mcsilva@smcm.edu
SILVA, Tammy, A .... 508-999-8486. 229 A
tsilva@umassd.edu
SILVAGNI, Anthony .... 954-262-1407. 109 K
silvagni@nova.edu
SILVANO, Brian .... 949-794-9090... 68 D
bsilvano@stanbridge.edu
SILVER, Bret .... 212-854-7651. 314 G
bsilver@barnard.edu
SILVER, Charles .... 480-423-6299... 15 E
charles.silver@scottsdalecc.edu
SILVER, Christopher .... 352-392-4836. 116 A
silver2@dcp.ufl.edu
SILVER, Edward .... 313-593-5090. 251 D
easilver@umich.edu
SILVER, Frank, D .... 828-659-7810. 362 A
franksil@mcdowelltech.edu
SILVER, Jonas .... 336-770-1408. 369 D
silverj@uncsa.edu
SILVER, Mariko .... 802-440-4300. 498 G
msilver@bennington.edu
SILVER, Norman, E .... 617-266-1400. 223 D
SILVER, Paul .... 802-635-1347. 501 D
paul.silver@jsc.edu
SILVER, Paula .... 610-499-4352. 437 E
psilver@widener.edu
SILVER, Rhonda .... 828-652-0630. 362 A
rhonda@mcdowelltech.edu
SILVER, Steve .... 541-684-7235. 405 C
ssilver@nwcu.edu
SILVER, Tammy .... 702-651-5639. 294 E
tammy.silver@csn.edu
SILVER, William .... 707-664-2220... 36 B
silverw@sonoma.edu
SILVERBLATT,
Pamela, S .... 646-664-2977. 316 I
pamela.silverblatt@cuny.edu
SILVERI, Annmarie .... 313-993-1170. 250 K
silveran@udmercy.edu
SILVERI, Donald, V .... 716-839-8346. 322 E
dsilveri@daemen.edu
SILVERIA, John .... 617-573-8320. 237 B
jsilveria@suffolk.edu
SILVERMAN, Edward .... 212-650-6480. 317 D
esilverman@ccny.cuny.edu
SILVERMAN, Stanley, B . 330-972-6372. 390 E
stanley@uakron.edu
SILVERS, Cathy .... 859-344-3538. 199 H
cathy.silvers@thomasmore.edu
SILVERS, Liz .... 828-766-1273. 361 H
lsilvers@mayland.edu
SILVERSTEIN, Lee .... 813-889-3427. 107 C
lsilverstein@academy.edu
SILVERSTEIN, Melinda ... 831-479-6338... 30 G
mesilver@cabrillo.edu
SILVERTHORN, Mike ...... 989-463-7327. 239 B
silverthorn@alma.edu
SILVESTER, John .... 402-461-7477. 289 I
jsilvester@hastings.edu
SILVESTER, Maria .... 215-635-7300. 417 C
msilvester@gratz.edu
SILVESTRI, Mary Ann ..... 508-541-1602. 225 F
msilvestri@dean.edu
SILVESTRI, Sandro .... 313-845-9878. 243 H
sandro@hfcc.edu
SILVESTRINI, Maria .... 787-284-1912. 550 F
msilvest@ponce.inter.edu
SILVESTRO, Michael .... 973-684-6107. 304 B
msilvestro@pccc.edu
SILVEY, Dan .... 518-743-2335. 345 E
silveyd@sunyacc.edu
SILVEY, Greg .... 660-831-4183. 278 I
silveyg@moval.edu
SILVEY, Kelle .... 573-592-5195. 285 B
kelle.silvey@westminster-mo.edu
SILVIO, Carl, A .... 585-266-0430. 324 A
csilvio@cci.edu
SILVYN, Jeffrey .... 520-206-4678... 17 A
jsilvyn@pima.edu
SILY, Michel .... 305-899-3781... 98 O
msily@barry.edu
SIMALA, Jay .... 847-317-6507. 160 M
jsimala@tiu.edu
SIMAMA, Jabari .... 404-297-9522. 126 A
simamaj@gptc.edu
SIMAR, Gina, A .... 409-882-3311. 486 G
gina.simar@lsco.edu
SIMAS, Andrew .... 415-351-3537... 62 G
asimas@sfai.edu
SIMBERG, Ken .... 218-262-7241. 258 G
kennethsimberg@hibbing.edu
SIMCOX, Mary Grace ..... 717-544-4787. 421 C
mrsimcox@lancastergeneralcollege.edu
SIMEK, Vicki .... 856-691-8600. 301 A
vsimek@cccnj.edu
SIMER, Lauren .... 864-250-8484. 444 E
lauren.simer@gvltec.edu
SIMERAL, RET., Robert .. 831-656-3276. 544 M
rlsimera@nps.edu
SIMERSON, Gordon .... 203-932-7290... 92 E
gsimerson@newhaven.edu
SIMES, Sharon .... 206-934-3615. 522 I
sharon.simes@seattlecolleges.edu
SIMFUKWE, David .... 904-470-8176. 102 A
dsimfukwe@ewc.edu
SIMHAI, Toofawn .... 701-662-1511. 372 D
toofawn.simhai@lrsc.edu
SIMIC, Laura .... 208-426-2051. 137 G
laurasimic@boisestate.edu
SIMIEN, Kali .... 704-355-1547. 353 D
kali.simien@carolinashealthcare.org
SIMILI, Sal .... 208-467-8365. 139 A
ssimili@nnu.edu
SIMINOE, Judith, P .... 320-308-2122. 261 B
jpsiminoe@stcloudstate.edu
SIMIO, Frank .... 718-817-4975. 324 G
simio@fordham.edu
SIMION, Karen .... 691-320-2480. 546 B
ksimion@comfsm.fm
SIMKIN, Breanne .... 904-256-7243. 107 Q
bsimkin@ju.edu
SIMKINS, Will .... 646-557-4709. 318 D
wsimpkins@jjay.cuny.edu
SIMMA, April .... 812-535-5225. 172 F
asimma@smwc.edu
SIMMELINK, Scott, K ..... 712-707-7170. 181 H
scotts@nwciowa.edu
SIMMERS, Susan .... 970-351-2109... 86 C
susan.simmers@unco.edu
SIMMONDS, Marilyn ...... 208-459-5561. 138 A
msimmonds@collegeofidaho.edu
SIMMONS, Alan, D .... 513-875-3344. 376 H
alan.simmons@chatfield.edu
SIMMONS, Alicia .... 256-782-8145..... 4 K
asimmons@jsu.edu
SIMMONS, Annette .... 704-403-3517. 352 J
annette.simmons@carolinashealthcare.org
SIMMONS, Bette, M .... 973-328-5171. 300 G
bsimmons@ccm.edu
SIMMONS, Blair .... 510-869-1592... 61 I
bsimmons@samuelmerritt.edu
SIMMONS, Charles, W .... 410-276-0306. 218 D
csimmons@host.sdc.edu
SIMMONS, Charlotte .... 405-974-2481. 400 K
SIMMONS, Chuck .... 845-758-7878. 314 D
simmons@bard.edu
SIMMONS, D. Glenn ...... 602-279-1011. 494 F
simmonsg@wbu.edu
SIMMONS, Dale, H .... 630-844-4220. 140 A
dsimmons@aurora.edu
SIMMONS, David .... 770-975-4000. 122 I
SIMMONS, Doreen .... 408-733-1878... 72 D
doreen.simmons@uewm.edu
SIMMONS, Eddie .... 843-574-6268. 447 E
eddie.simmons@tridenttech.edu
SIMMONS, Edna .... 410-951-3384. 220 B
esimmons@coppin.edu
SIMMONS, Elaine, R ...... 620-792-9214. 184 F
simmonse@bartonccc.edu
SIMMONS, Elizabeth, H .. 517-353-6486. 246 H
esimmons@msu.edu
SIMMONS, Gail .... 914-323-5262. 330 B
gail.simmons@mville.edu
SIMMONS, Gerald .... 606-337-1164. 193 F
gp.simmons@ccbbc.edu
SIMMONS, Gregory .... 410-455-1452. 219 D
gsimmons@umbc.edu
SIMMONS, Guy .... 972-238-6263. 471 C
gsimmons@dcccd.edu
SIMMONS, Hezekiah, N .. 585-292-3320. 332 A
hsimmons@monroecc.edu
SIMMONS, Howard, L .... 410-276-0306. 218 D
hsimmons@host.sdc.edu
SIMMONS, Jacqueline .... 812-855-9730. 167 F
simmonja@iu.edu
SIMMONS,
Jacqueline, A .... 812-855-9739. 167 E
simmonja@iu.edu
SIMMONS, Jay, K .... 515-961-1566. 182 E
jay.simmons@simpson.edu
SIMMONS, Jennifer, A ... 662-915-7226. 270 B
jasimmon@olemiss.edu
SIMMONS, Jeremy .... 415-351-3510... 62 G
jsimmons@sfai.edu
SIMMONS, Kathy .... 405-466-3228. 395 N
ksimmons@langston.edu
SIMMONS, Kitty .... 951-785-2397... 50 B
ksimmons@lasierra.edu
SIMMONS, Laura, L .... 309-655-3450. 158 C
laura.l.simmons@osfhealthcare.org
SIMMONS, Lysa .... 315-498-2228. 335 G
simmonsl@sunyocc.edu
SIMMONS, Michael .... 724-738-3333. 429 F
michael.simmons@sru.edu
SIMMONS, Pat .... 478-471-2717. 128 I
pat.simmons@maconstate.edu
SIMMONS, Patricia .... 270-824-1795. 196 A
patricia.simmons@kctcs.edu
SIMMONS, Patricia .... 507-284-7817. 254 F
simmons.patricia@mayo.edu
SIMMONS, Paul, M .... 651-962-6706. 265 C
pmsimmons@stthomas.edu
SIMMONS, Regina Ray ... 404-756-4047. 121 A
rsimmons@atlm.edu
SIMMONS, Richard, E .... 864-488-8344. 444 L
rsimmons@limestone.edu
SIMMONS, Rick .... 318-257-2912. 207 F
simmons@latech.edu
SIMMONS, Robert, A ...... 816-235-1368. 283 D
simmonsr@umkc.edu
SIMMONS, Rosemary, E . 618-453-5371. 159 G
rsimmons@siu.edu
SIMMONS, Roy .... 304-205-6600. 527 O
rsimmons@kvctc.edu
SIMMONS, Roy .... 304-205-6708. 528 B
rsimmons@kvctc.edu
SIMMONS, Sam .... 866-931-4300. 280 H
SIMMONS, Sheila .... 912-583-3184. 122 B
ssimmons@bpc.edu
SIMMONS, Solon .... 703-993-1300. 505 C
ssimmon5@gmu.edu
SIMMONS, Steve .... 251-460-6132..... 9 E
ssimmons@southalabama.edu
SIMMONS, Steven .... 803-508-7270. 440 G
simmonss@atc.edu
SIMMONS, Tacuma .... 410-276-0306. 218 D
tsimmons@host.sdc.edu
SIMMONS, Teisha .... 907-474-5441... 10 I
tmsimmons@alaska.edu
SIMMONS, Thomas .... 419-772-2450. 386 D
t-simmons@onu.edu
SIMMONS, Timothy, J .... 414-288-5048. 534 B
tim.simmons@marquette.edu
SIMMONS, Todd .... 480-517-8137... 15 D
todd.simmons@riosalado.edu
SIMMONS, Victoria .... 209-575-6507... 77 H
simmonsv@yosemite.edu
SIMMONS-JOHNSON,
Deborah .... 713-718-7332. 473 C
deborah.johnson@hccs.edu
SIMMONS-WALSTON,
Valerie .... 770-531-3110. 122 A
vsimmons-walston@brenau.edu
SIMMS, Carl .... 559-442-8255... 68 H
carl.simms@scccd.edu
SIMMS, Marcie .... 740-351-3549. 388 N
msimms@shawnee.edu
SIMMS, Michele .... 713-942-5918. 490 L
simmsm@stthom.edu
SIMMS, Pat .... 501-337-5000... 20 J
pats@coto.edu

SIMMS, Rebecca .... 859-246-6761. 194 L
rebecca.simms@kctcs.edu
SIMMS, Ruth .... 859-246-6433. 194 L
ruth.simms@kctcs.edu
SIMON, Barbara, J .... 563-588-7103. 180 L
barb.simon@loras.edu
SIMON, Bashe .... 212-463-0400. 348 B
simonb@touro.edu
SIMON, Carol .... 916-348-4689... 43 F
csimon@epic.edu
SIMON, Caroline, J .... 509-777-3755. 525 F
csimon@whitworth.edu
SIMON, Dale .... 319-887-3614. 180 J
dale.simon@kirkwood.edu
SIMON, Darica .... 225-216-8171. 202 H
simond@mybrcc.edu
SIMON, Donald, E .... 718-933-6700. 331 K
dsimon@monroecollege.edu
SIMON, Ellis .... 212-650-5310. 317 D
esimon@ccny.cuny.edu
SIMON, Jan .... 217-351-3818. 155 J
jsimon@parkland.edu
SIMON, Janet .... 406-657-2278. 287 C
jsimon@msubillings.edu
SIMON, Jason, F .... 940-565-2085. 490 C
jason.simon@unt.edu
SIMON, Jill, K .... 651-641-8211. 255 B
simon@csp.edu
SIMON, John, D .... 434-924-0311. 511 B
jds2ts@virginia.edu
SIMON, Kathryn, C .... 859-233-8124. 199 I
ksimon@transy.edu
SIMON, Lou Anna, K ..... 517-355-6560. 246 H
laksimon@msu.edu
SIMON, Marlene .... 310-954-4135... 54 J
msimon@msmc.la.edu
SIMON, Michelle, S .... 914-422-4407. 335 J
msimon@pace.edu
SIMON, Mike .... 406-377-9408. 286 A
msimon@dawson.edu
SIMON, Patricia .... 602-274-4300... 12 K
psimon@brymanschool.edu
SIMON, Paul, M .... 203-837-8494... 88 B
simonp@wcsu.edu
SIMON, Robert .... 724-357-2217. 428 F
rjsimon@iup.edu
SIMON, Scott .... 419-824-3743. 383 C
ssimon@lourdes.edu
SIMON, Tina, L .... 419-372-2700. 374 K
tsimon@bgsu.edu
SIMON, Toby .... 401-232-6855. 438 K
tsimon@bryant.edu
SIMONDS, Kurt .... 971-722-5573. 407 D
kurt.simonds@pcc.edu
SIMONDS, Linda, A .... 413-565-1000. 222 F
lsimonds@baypath.edu
SIMONDS, Sprague .... 203-837-8691... 88 B
simonds@wcsu.edu
SIMONE, Carmen, M ...... 719-846-5541... 85 H
carmen.simone@trinidadstate.edu
SIMONE, John .... 609-586-4800. 302 G
simonej@mccc.edu
SIMONE, Lucian .... 203-285-2223... 88 E
lsimone@gwcc.commnet.edu
SIMONE, Nick .... 516-323-4810. 331 J
nsimone@molloy.edu
SIMONE, Tony .... 360-538-4154. 520 B
tsimone@ghc.edu
SIMONEAU,
Christopher (Chris), J .. 239-590-1067. 115 A
csimoneau@fgcu.edu
SIMONEAU, Matt .... 651-450-3568. 258 H
msimone@inverhills.edu
SIMONEAUX, Mike .... 912-583-2241. 122 B
msimoneaux@bpc.edu
SIMONEAUX, Wendy ...... 225-578-8878. 204 N
wendys@lsu.edu
SIMONELLI, Ray .... 937-769-1845. 373 I
rsimonelli@antioch.edu
SIMONETTI, Salvatore, J 585-245-5651. 343 C
simonetti@geneseo.edu
SIMONI, Mary .... 518-276-3315. 337 I
simonm@rpi.edu
SIMONIAN, Yasmen .... 801-626-7117. 497 D
ysimonian@weber.edu
SIMONS, Earl, G .... 718-262-3795. 319 F
esimons@york.cuny.edu
SIMONS, Ernest, L .... 828-694-1881. 358 C
e_simons@blueridge.edu
SIMONS, Horace .... 614-837-4088. 392 E
simonsh@valorcollege.com
SIMONS, Jill .... 870-972-3574... 19 N
jsimons@astate.edu
SIMONS, Ken .... 314-434-2212. 275 D
ksimons@hickeycollege.edu
SIMONS, Kenneth, B ...... 414-955-8279. 534 C
SIMONS, Kenneth, B ...... 414-955-4577. 534 C
ksimons@mcw.edu
SIMONS, Michael, A ...... 718-990-6601. 339 A
simonsm@stjohns.edu
SIMONS, Robert, E .... 336-322-2128. 362 F
Robert.Simons@piedmontcc.edu
SIMONS, Sherri, J .... 308-432-6355. 291 D
ssimons@csc.edu
SIMONS, Shino .... 626-812-3053... 29 H
ssimons@apu.edu
SIMONSON, Brian .... 406-265-3525. 287 D
brian.simonson@msun.edu
SIMOTAS, Monica .... 718-405-3290. 320 G
monica.simotas@mountsaintvincent.edu
SIMPER, Craig, J .... 435-797-1156. 497 B
craig.simper@usu.edu
SIMPKINS, Alice, M .... 706-396-8111. 130 C
asimpkins@paine.edu
SIMPKINS, Pamela, P .... 540-831-5419. 508 C
ppsimpkin@radford.edu
SIMPSON, Amanda .... 973-803-5000. 304 C
asimpson@pillar.edu
SIMPSON, Amanda .... 940-898-3456. 488 B
asimpson1@twu.edu
SIMPSON, Andrea .... 336-386-3263. 364 D
simpsoaj@surry.edu
SIMPSON, Andrew, L ..... 651-631-5239. 263 A
alsimpson@nwc.edu
SIMPSON, Angela .... 606-589-3025. 196 F
angela.simpson@kctcs.edu
SIMPSON, Anita .... 580-628-6237. 396 M
anita.simpson@noc.edu
SIMPSON, Atticus, J .... 828-448-3120. 365 A
asimpson@wpcc.edu
SIMPSON, Brandy .... 701-228-5613. 372 C
brandy.simpson@dakotacollege.edu
SIMPSON, Brendt .... 315-228-6208. 320 F
bsimpson@colgate.edu
SIMPSON, Carol .... 757-683-3079. 507 N
csimpson@odu.edu
SIMPSON, Caroline .... 304-724-3700. 526 B
csimpson@apus.edu
SIMPSON, Cindy .... 708-209-3156. 143 E
cindy.simpson@cuchicago.edu
SIMPSON, Colleen .... 952-358-8146. 260 B
colleen.simpson@normandale.edu
SIMPSON, Connie .... 303-797-5601... 78 F
connie.simpson@arapahoe.edu
SIMPSON, Cynthia .... 281-649-3240. 473 B
csimpson@hbu.edu
SIMPSON, Cynthia, F ..... 718-990-6333. 339 A
simpsoc1@stjohns.edu
SIMPSON, Dennis .... 303-986-2320... 80 D
dennis@csha.net
SIMPSON, Donald, E ...... 417-836-5514. 278 E
donsimpson@missouristate.edu
SIMPSON, Gina .... 303-986-2320... 80 D
gina@csha.net
SIMPSON, JR.,
Grant, W .... 512-448-8651. 479 C
grants@stedwards.edu
SIMPSON, Gregory .... 309-438-5669. 147 J
gsimpso@ilstu.edu
SIMPSON, Jack .... 423-461-8955. 457 H
jasimpson@milligan.edu
SIMPSON, Jacklyn, A ..... 704-687-7501. 368 E
jasimpso@uncc.edu
SIMPSON, III, James, D 904-632-5049. 105 E
jsimpson@fscj.edu
SIMPSON, James, E .... 434-395-2093. 506 J
simpsonje@longwood.edu
SIMPSON, Jane .... 678-839-5306. 133 I
jsimpson@westga.edu
SIMPSON, Jennifer .... 229-225-5072. 132 D
jsimpson@southwestgatech.edu
SIMPSON, John, A .... 512-505-3019. 473 G
jasimpson@htu.edu
SIMPSON, Juliene .... 973-290-4207. 300 F
jsimpson@cse.edu
SIMPSON, Kurt .... 815-599-3501. 146 D
kurt.simpson@highland.edu
SIMPSON, Larry .... 662-562-3219. 269 C
jlsimpson@northwestms.edu
SIMPSON, Lawrence, J ... 617-266-1400. 223 D
SIMPSON, Mallory, M .... 313-593-5130. 251 D
mallorys@umich.edu
SIMPSON, Mark .... 801-626-6047. 497 D
marksimpson1@weber.edu
SIMPSON, Matthew .... 252-335-3532. 367 C
mdsimpson@mail.escu.edu
SIMPSON, Megan .... 706-368-7739. 125 C
msimpson@highlands.edu
SIMPSON, Micah .... 205-970-9243..... 7 B
msimpson@sebc.edu
SIMPSON, Michael, E ..... 518-564-2155. 344 B
simpsome@plattsburgh.edu
SIMPSON, Michael, J ..... 415-338-2218... 35 E
msimpson@sfsu.edu
SIMPSON, Nancy, P .... 864-231-2029. 441 B
nsimpson@andersonuniversity.edu
SIMPSON, Patricia .... 605-642-6551. 451 G
patricia.simpson@bhsu.edu
SIMPSON, Philip .... 321-433-5078. 101 M
simpsonp@easternflorida.edu
SIMPSON, Phyllis .... 225-768-1713. 206 D
psimpson@ololcollege.edu
SIMPSON, Ralph .... 484-365-7528. 422 D
rsimpson@lincoln.edu
SIMPSON, Rebecca .... 502-852-6397. 200 D
becky.simpson@louisville.edu
SIMPSON, Renee, K .... 407-582-1511. 118 M
rsimpson@valenciacollege.edu
SIMPSON, Richard .... 614-236-6383. 375 H
rsimpson@law.capital.edu
SIMPSON, Robert .... 248-222-1503. 241 F
robert.simpson@cornerstone.edu
SIMPSON, Robert .... 731-661-5219. 462 F
rsimpson@uu.edu
SIMPSON, Robert, G .... 714-484-7308... 56 E
rsimpson@cypresscollege.edu
SIMPSON, Robert, L .... 810-762-7949. 244 Q
rsimpson@kettering.edu
SIMPSON, Stacey .... 541-278-5933. 402 C
ssimpson@bluecc.edu
SIMPSON, Susan .... 217-786-9629. 151 F
susan.simpson@llcc.edu
SIMPSON, Suzanne .... 662-846-4051. 266 G
ssimpson@deltastate.edu
SIMPSON, Teresa .... 409-880-8879. 486 F
teresa.simpson@lamar.edu
SIMPSON, Thomas, W ... 864-429-7732. 448 G
twsimpso@mailbox.sc.edu
SIMPSON, Todd .... 402-872-2304. 291 E
tsimpson@peru.edu
SIMPSON, Tony .... 909-537-5166... 34 E
tsimpson@csusb.edu
SIMPSON, Traci .... 305-899-3150... 98 O
tsimpson@barry.edu
SIMPSON-LOGG,
Anastasia .... 707-468-3102... 54 B
asimpson@mendocino.edu
SIMS, Bradford (Brad) .... 812-237-3166. 167 A
bradford.sims@indstate.edu
SIMS, Charles, E .... 206-934-4136. 522 H
charles.sims@seattlecolleges.edu
SIMS, Dacien .... 650-433-3848... 58 B
dsims@paloaltou.edu
SIMS, Dale .... 615-366-3921. 459 A
dale.sims@tbr.edu
SIMS, Dale .... 214-333-5249. 470 D
dale@dbu.edu
SIMS, Damon .... 814-865-0909. 426 A
drs37@psu.edu
SIMS, David .... 478-471-2780. 128 I
david.sims@maconstate.edu
SIMS, Dora .... 281-756-3524. 465 D
dsims@alvincollege.edu
SIMS, Frank .... 641-673-1703. 183 H
simsf@wmpenn.edu
SIMS, Gayle .... 919-536-7250. 360 B
simso@durhamtech.edu
SIMS, George, E .... 251-380-2262..... 7 D
gsims@shc.edu
SIMS, Glenn .... 910-410-1684. 362 I
glenns@richmondcc.edu
SIMS, Jack .... 814-871-7464. 416 K
sims003@gannon.edu
SIMS, Jane .... 402-354-7073. 291 B
jane.sims@methodistcollege.edu
SIMS, Jeanette .... 704-687-5827. 368 E
aoster@uncc.edu
SIMS, Kathy, L .... 310-206-7774... 71 C
ksims@career.ucla.edu
SIMS, Lesley .... 510-436-1405... 47 J
sims@hnu.edu
SIMS, Leslie .... 304-424-8221. 530 E
leslie.sims@wvup.edu
SIMS, Marcella .... 251-405-7133..... 2 D
msims@bishop.edu
SIMS, Mary, J .... 831-656-3658. 544 M
mjsims@nps.edu
SIMS, Mary, L .... 803-536-8198. 446 G
msims@scsu.edu
SIMS, Myra .... 276-944-6236. 504 H
msims@ehc.edu
SIMS, Patricia .... 256-551-1717..... 4 I
patricia.sims@drakestate.edu
SIMS, Sonja, M .... 312-939-0111. 144 D
SIMS, Sue .... 803-508-7341. 440 G
simss@atc.edu
SIMS, Sue, A .... 803-938-3729. 448 F
sues@uscsumter.edu
SIMS, Suzanne .... 256-216-3314..... 1 F
suzanne.sims@athens.edu
SIMS-TUCKER,
Bernita, M .... 410-651-3553. 219 E
bsimstucker@umes.edu
SIMSHEUSER, Carrie, L .. 816-654-7072. 275 K
csimsheuser@kcumb.edu
SIMSON, Earl, L .... 401-456-8106. 439 F
esimson@ric.edu
SIMSON, Gary, J .... 478-301-2602. 128 H
simson_g@mercer.edu
SINCAVAGE, Joseph .... 610-436-3535. 430 A
jsincavage@wcupa.edu
SINCLAIR, Alex .... 212-678-8030. 328 A
sinclair@jtsa.edu
SINCLAIR, Joyce .... 512-313-3000. 469 L
joyce.sinclair@concordia.edu
SINCLAIR, Kelli .... 630-466-7900. 162 J
ksinclair@waubonsee.edu
SINCLAIR, Nancy .... 270-384-8001. 197 D
sinclairn@lindsey.edu
SINCLAIR, Rick .... 509-467-1727. 520 F
rsinclai@interface.edu
SINCLAIR, Tori .... 816-802-3379. 275 J
tsinclair@kcai.edu
SINDER, Janet .... 718-780-7975. 315 H
janet.sinder@brooklaw.edu
SINDLE, Patricia .... 870-574-4492... 23 G
psindle@sautech.edu
SINDLINGER, Susan ...... 312-369-7984. 143 D
ssindlinger@colum.edu
SINDT, Christopher .... 925-631-4088... 61 F
csindt@stmarys-ca.edu
SINDT, Christopher .... 925-631-4309... 61 F
csindt@stmarys-ca.edu
SINE, Josh .... 435-652-7591. 497 E
jsine@dixie.edu
SINEWAY, Carla .... 989-775-4123. 249 F
sineway.carla@sagchip.edu
SINEX, Nancy .... 765-983-1600. 165 G
nancys@earlham.edu
SINGEL, David .... 406-994-4371. 287 B
dsingel@montana.edu
SINGELL, Larry .... 812-856-7700. 167 F
lsingell@indiana.edu
SINGER, David .... 518-445-3211. 313 C
dsing@albanylaw.edu
SINGER, Ethan, A .... 619-594-5166... 35 D
singer@mail.sdsu.edu
SINGER, Judith .... 617-495-1961. 227 C
judith_singer@harvard.edu
SINGER, Lynn, T .... 216-368-4389. 375 J
lts5@case.edu
SINGER, Marc .... 609-984-1130. 308 A
msinger@tesc.edu
SINGER, Mark .... 201-684-7550. 305 A
msinger@ramapo.edu
SINGER, Mark .... 914-493-1909. 334 A
mark_singer@nymc.edu
SINGER, Nancy .... 801-957-4186. 498 B
nancy.singer@slcc.edu
SINGER, Terry, L .... 502-852-6402. 200 D
terry.singer@louisville.edu
SINGER, Timothy .... 315-498-2485. 335 G
singert@sunyocc.edu
SINGER, Walter .... 215-884-8942. 438 A
cfo@woninstitute.edu
SINGER, Yossi .... 718-268-4700. 337 F
SINGH, Amit .... 216-987-5556. 378 D
amit.singh@tri-c.edu
SINGH, Avena .... 541-888-1583. 407 H
asingh@socc.edu
SINGH, Gangaram .... 619-594-5259... 35 D
gsingh@mail.sdsu.edu
SINGH, Hamwant (Neil) .. 718-429-6600. 349 H
neil.singh@vaughn.edu
SINGH, Holly .... 219-464-5333. 174 E
holly.singh@valpo.edu
SINGH, Inder .... 845-451-1361. 322 D
i_singh@culinary.edu
SINGH, Kanwal .... 914-395-2303. 340 E
ksingh@slc.edu
SINGH, Nancy .... 559-251-5025... 30 I
library@calchristiancollege.edu
SINGH, Sarjit .... 920-748-8169. 535 J
singhs@ripon.edu
SINGH, Shailindar .... 315-267-2335. 344 C
singhs@potsdam.edu
SINGH, Surya, P .... 918-877-8151. 395 N
ssingh@langston.edu
SINGH, Tanuja .... 210-436-3706. 479 D
tsingh@stmarytx.edu
SINGH, Vijai, P .... 412-624-4555. 435 C
singh@pitt.edu
SINGH CHAUHAN,
Indrajeet .... 212-423-2769. 325 H
indrajeet.singh@helenefuld.edu
SINGH MOONILALL,
Seeta .... 561-912-1211. 103 C
seetas@evergladesuniversity.edu
SINGHAL, Meena .... 562-938-3903... 51 D
msinghal@lbcc.edu
SINGLETARY, Chip .... 850-201-8544. 117 D
singlech@tcc.fl.edu
SINGLETARY, James, M . 740-392-6868. 384 K
jim.singletary@mvnu.edu
SINGLETARY, Michael .... 360-383-3035. 525 D
msingletary@whatcom.ctc.edu
SINGLETARY, Shelia .... 985-732-6640. 203 D
SINGLETON,
Alma (Nickie) .... 904-680-7601. 103 Q
nsingleton@fcsl.edu
SINGLETON, Brian .... 313-496-2778. 252 B
bsingle1@wcccd.edu

SINGLETON, Derrick 859-985-3130. 192 F
singletonp@berea.edu
SINGLETON, Gena, L 713-646-1778. 480 J
gsingleton@stcl.edu
SINGLETON, Gregory 931-221-7005. 459 B
singletong@apsu.edu
SINGLETON, H. Wells 954-262-8731. 109 K
singlew@nova.edu
SINGLETON, J. Ron 864-488-8274. 444 L
rsingleton@limestone.edu
SINGLETON, Janet 404-880-8286. 122 J
jsingleton@cau.edu
SINGLETON, John, L 817-257-7871. 484 I
j.singleton@tcu.edu
SINGLETON, Loy 205-348-4786... 8 D
loy.singleton@ua.edu
SINGLETON, Robin 870-762-3161... 19 K
rsingleton@smail.anc.edu
SINGLETON, Shawn, T 859-233-8154. 199 I
ssingleton@transy.edu
SINGLETON, Stanley 317-917-3249. 171 A
ssingleton@martin.edu
SINGLETON-WALKER,
Catherine 662-254-3365. 269 A
cswalker@mvsu.edu
SINGLETON-YOUNG,
Patricia 843-349-2304. 442 E
psyoung@coastal.edu
SINHA, Monica 510-592-9688... 56 G
monica@npu.edu
SINIARD, Michelle 478-218-3330. 122 F
msiniard@centralgatech.edu
SINIARD, Michelle 478-988-6840. 122 G
msiniard@centralgatech.edu
SINIARI, Jayne 215-728-4700. 425 G
Jayne.siniari@jevs.org
SINIGAGLIA, Frank 845-434-5750. 347 A
fsinigaglia@sunysullivan.edu
SINK, Joyce, A 540-375-2201. 509 B
sink@roanoke.edu
SINK, Susanna, C 724-357-2205. 428 F
scsink@iup.edu
SINK, Tom 567-661-7221. 387 L
thomas_sink@owens.edu
SINKOW, Alexis 610-558-5625. 424 I
sinkowa@neumann.edu
SINN, Brad 320-363-5211. 254 J
bsinn@csbsju.edu
SINNAMON, Walt 864-644-5221. 446 I
wsinnamon@swu.edu
SINNOTT, Anneliese 313-831-5200. 242 E
asinnott@etseminary.edu
SINNOTT, Cindy Ann 636-573-9300. 278 G
csinnott@motech.edu
SINSABAUGH, Emily, F 716-375-2334. 338 E
esinsaba@sbu.edu
SINTEF, Paul, R 512-448-8773. 479 C
paulrs@stedwards.edu
SINUTKO, John 805-378-1454... 74 F
jsinutko@vcccd.edu
SIPE, Brian 912-279-5819. 123 B
bsipe@ccga.edu
SIPE, Deborah 503-399-6045. 402 E
deborah.sipe@chemeketa.edu
SIPE, Rebecca 734-487-0341. 242 D
rsipe@emich.edu
SIPES, Jennifer, L 217-581-3221. 144 E
jlsipes@eiu.edu
SIPES, Shannon, M 812-877-8529. 172 C
sipes@rose-hulman.edu
SIPHER, Justin 315-229-5319. 339 F
jsipher@stlawu.edu
SIPLE, Samuel, D 724-589-2842. 434 B
ssiple@thiel.edu
SIPP, Richard, G 419-372-3230. 374 K
rsipp@bgsu.edu
SIPPEL, Len 215-572-2943. 409 H
sippell@arcadia.edu
SIPPIN, Ana, M 305-348-2421. 115 B
sippina@fiu.edu
SIRACH, Gina 618-252-5400. 159 E
gina.sirach@sic.edu
SIRANGELO-ELBADAWY,
Catherine 201-360-4261. 302 D
csirangelo@hccc.edu
SIRBAUGH, William, A 540-868-7093. 512 H
bsirbaugh@lfsbdc.org
SIRBU, Jerald, B 303-369-5151... 84 E
jbs@plattcolorado.edu
SIRENO, Peter, J 229-317-6705. 124 A
peter.sireno@darton.edu
SIRIANNI, Frank 212-636-6265. 324 G
sirianni@fordham.edu
SIRIANNI, John, F 515-961-1620. 182 E
john.sirianni@simpson.edu
SIRIMANGKALA,
Pawena 305-899-3453... 98 O
psirimangkala@barry.edu
SIRJU-JOHNSON,
Nicole 607-777-4472. 341 E
njohnson@binghamton.edu

SIRMON, John 850-973-9495. 109 H
sirmonj@nfcc.edu
SIRNEY, Marie 626-966-4576... 27 P
mariesirney@agu.edu
SIRRINE, Erica 863-638-7678. 119 C
erica.sirrine@warner.edu
SISCO, Rodney, K 630-752-5028. 163 F
rodney.sisco@wheaton.edu
SISCO, Teri 951-487-3110... 55 B
tsisco@msjc.edu
SISCOE, Denita 417-836-5526. 278 E
SISE, Jack, R 518-783-2315. 340 J
jsise@siena.edu
SISK, Beth 402-399-2415. 289 A
bsisk@csm.edu
SISK, Kathy 706-864-1840. 133 D
kathy.sisk@ung.edu
SISK, Ronald, D 605-336-6588. 451 C
rsisk@sfseminary.edu
SISKAR, John, F 716-878-3787. 343 A
siskarjf@buffalostate.edu
SISNEROS, Caroline 818-386-5642... 59 E
csisneros@pgi.edu
SISNEROS, Kathy 970-491-6384... 80 I
kathy.sisneros@colostate.edu
SISNEROS, Patrick 425-388-9026. 519 I
psisnero@everettcc.edu
SISNEY, David 816-483-9600. 190 D
david.sisney@spst.edu
SISOIAN, Katherine 210-436-3331. 479 D
ksisoian@stmarytx.edu
SISON, Christine, B 671-735-1121. 546 C
christine.sison@guamcc.edu
SISSION, Amanda 843-863-7991. 441 H
asission@csuniv.edu
SISSON, Cindy, N 574-372-5100. 166 B
sissoncn@grace.edu
SISSON, Jeanne, M 518-580-5664. 341 A
jsisson@skidmore.edu
SISSON, Karen 909-621-8132... 60 A
karen.sisson@pomona.edu
SISSON, Laura 205-226-4861... 2 C
lsisson@bsc.edu
SISSON, Linda, G 248-370-3266. 248 J
lgsisson@oakland.edu
SISSON, Paul, D 318-797-5234. 205 F
paul.sisson@lsus.edu
SISSON, Paul, D 318-797-5374. 205 F
paul.sisson@lsus.edu
SISSON, Philip, J 978-322-8488. 232 B
sissonp@middlesex.mass.edu
SISSON, Russell 606-546-1321. 200 A
rsisson@unionky.edu
SISTARE, Janet 704-991-0189. 364 C
jsistare6776@stanly.edu
SISTARENIK, Daniel 845-257-3250. 342 B
sistared@newpaltz.edu
SITARSKI, Karen 856-415-2110. 302 C
ksitarski@gccnj.edu
SITES, John 954-776-4456. 108 C
jsites@keiseruniversity.edu
SITHARAMAN, Sri 706-507-8963. 123 D
sri@columbusstate.edu
SITORIUS, Patty 402-461-7799. 289 I
psitorius@hastings.edu
SITTEMA, Carol, B 904-264-2172. 111 P
mlopez@iwsfla.org
SITTERLY, Carol 413-205-3260. 221 F
carol.sitterly@aic.edu
SITTON, Michael, R 315-267-2415. 344 C
sittonmr@potsdam.edu
SIU, Lily 217-875-7200. 156 J
lsiu@richland.edu
SIVAKUMARAN,
Thillainatarajan 870-972-3057... 19 N
tsivakumaran@astate.edu
SIVERIO, Carlos 516-299-3922. 329 C
carlos.siverio@liu.edu
SIVERT, Shayla 760-744-1150... 58 D
ssivert@palomar.edu
SIVILLO, Jeremy 814-866-8143. 420 E
jsivillo@lecom.edu
SIVILLS, Catherine, M 270-809-4894. 198 B
csivills@murraystate.edu
SIX, Margaret, J 304-336-8030. 530 A
sixmj@westliberty.edu
SIXTA, Jeff 913-288-7613. 187 L
jsixta@kckcc.edu
SIZEMORE, Amanda 636-922-8388. 280 J
asizemoer@stchas.edu
SIZEMORE, Carolyn, G 304-256-0262. 528 D
csizemore@newriver.edu
SIZEMORE, Debra 219-866-6149. 172 E
debbie@saintjoe.edu
SIZEMORE, Dorethea 434-736-2051. 513 H
dorethea.sizemore@southside.edu
SIZER, E. Maggie 703-892-5100... 96 F
SIZER, Judith, R 781-736-3011. 224 F
sizer@brandeis.edu
SJOGREN, Roxie, L 785-227-3380. 184 I
sjogrenr@bethanylb.edu

SJOQUIST, Corey 608-785-8939. 536 G
csjoquist@uwlax.edu
SJUE, Jessie 575-624-7151. 309 I
jessie.sjue@roswell.enmu.edu
SJUTS, Joseph, H 816-501-3700. 271 H
joe.sjuts@avila.edu
SKACH, Peter 773-298-3548. 158 E
skach@sxu.edu
SKADBERG, Ingrid 508-854-7545. 232 F
iskadberg@qcc.mass.edu
SKAFF, Leslie 828-328-7142. 356 B
leslie.skaff@lr.edu
SKAFTADOTTIR, Margret 727-864-8363. 101 N
skaftami@eckerd.edu
SKAGGS, Brandon 405-585-5250. 397 C
brandon.skaggs@okbu.edu
SKAGGS, Derek, S 417-625-9378. 278 D
skaggs-d@mssu.edu
SKAGGS, Steve 513-244-8456. 376 J
steve.skaggs@ccuniversity.edu
SKALAK, Thomas, C 434-924-0270. 511 B
tcs4z@virginia.edu
SKALLERUD, Ron 715-365-4644. 540 G
rskallerud@nicoletcollege.edu
SKALUBA, Nicole 312-935-6710. 156 K
nskaluba@robertrmorris.edu
SKAMRA, Brian 920-748-8174. 535 J
skamrab@ripon.edu
SKANDERA TROMBLEY,
Laura 909-621-8198... 59 G
president@pitzer.edu
SKANTZ, Ingrid 423-236-2833. 458 J
ilskantz@southern.edu
SKARI, Lisa 206-878-3710. 520 E
lskari@highline.edu
SKARR, Kimberly 312-752-2286. 149 E
Kimberly.Skarr@kendall.edu
SKARSTEN, Fawn 810-762-3327. 251 E
skarsten@umflint.edu
SKARUPPA, Cindy 503-725-9854. 406 B
skaruppa@pdx.edu
SKATES, Kathy 229-430-3524. 120 A
kskates@albanytech.edu
SKAUG, Ben 415-380-1498... 45 H
benskaug@ggbts.edu
SKEENS, Randy 304-896-7366. 528 F
randy.skeens@southernwv.edu
SKELLON, Hilary 720-890-8922... 82 I
director@itea.edu
SKELLY, Dawn 612-659-6222. 259 D
dawn.skelly@minneapolis.edu
SKELLY, Theresa 978-921-4242. 234 C
theresa.skelly@montserrat.edu
SKELTON, Lonnie 714-867-5009... 66 J
SKELTON, Sara 563-441-2462. 180 E
scampie@kucampus.edu
SKENE, Kathy 801-524-8118. 495 O
KSkene@ldsbc.edu
SKERRETT, Kathleen, R 804-289-8128. 510 L
kskerrett@richmond.edu
SKEVAKIS, Anthony 201-761-7364. 306 L
askevakis@saintpeters.edu
SKIDMORE, Charlene 515-271-2999. 177 K
charlene.skidmore@drake.edu
SKIDMORE, Daniel, L 315-445-4759. 328 F
skidmodl@lemoyne.edu
SKIDMORE, Heather 304-424-8210. 530 E
heather.skidmore@wvup.edu
SKIDMORE, James, L 304-558-0265. 529 C
skidmore@wvctcs.org
SKIDMORE, James, L 304-558-0265. 527 M
skidmore@wvctcs.org
SKIDMORE, Ron 301-387-3024. 214 I
ron.skidmore@garrettcollege.edu
SKIDMORE, Shirley 503-699-6302. 404 C
sskidmore@marylhurst.edu
SKIDMORE, Sue 423-461-8729. 457 H
shskidmore@milligan.edu
SKILES, Adam, L 260-359-4130. 166 O
askiles@huntington.edu
SKILL, Thomas, D 937-229-3511. 391 C
tskill1@udayton.edu
SKILLE, Steve 714-895-8117... 39 J
sskille@gwc.cccd.edu
SKILLINGS, Laura 269-782-1312. 250 C
lskillings@swmich.edu
SKILLINGS, Yvonne 404-270-5003. 132 E
yskillings@spelman.edu
SKINDER, Michelle, M 630-637-5754. 154 F
mmskinder@noctrl.edu
SKINKLE, Lee 601-968-5942. 266 A
lskinkle@belhaven.edu
SKINNER, Bruce 573-651-2274. 282 B
bskinner@semo.edu
SKINNER, Catherine 609-343-5102. 299 A
cskinner@atlantic.edu
SKINNER, Dana 978-934-2310. 229 B
dana_skinner@uml.edu
SKINNER, David 847-317-7051. 160 M
davids@tiu.edu

SKINNER, Dean 479-248-7236... 21 B
dskinner@ecollege.edu
SKINNER, Deb 641-784-5108. 178 F
dskinner@graceland.edu
SKINNER, Denese 806-651-2050. 484 D
dskinner@wtamu.edu
SKINNER, Katherine 615-460-6407. 453 C
kathryn.skinner@belmont.edu
SKINNER, Patricia, A 704-922-6475. 360 F
skinner.pat@gaston.edu
SKINNER, Randall 928-428-8252... 13 J
randall.skinner@eac.edu
SKINNER, Rick 580-774-3788. 400 B
rick.skinner@swosu.edu
SKINNER, Robert 304-473-8557. 531 G
skinner_b@wvwc.edu
SKINNER, Sally 208-459-5770. 138 A
sskinner@collegeofidaho.edu
SKINNER, Thom 215-368-5000. 410 F
tskinner@biblical.edu
SKINNER, Wendy 508-999-8570. 229 A
wskinner@umassd.edu
SKINNER, William, F 920-993-6025. 533 S
william.f.skinner@lawrence.edu
SKIPP, Steven, I 904-819-6258. 103 E
sskipp@flagler.edu
SKIPPER, Bob 270-745-4295. 200 G
bob.skipper@wku.edu
SKIPPER, Curt 601-635-2111. 266 H
cskipper@eccc.edu
SKIPPER, Eric 706-310-6219. 133 D
eric.skipper@ung.edu
SKIPPER, Eric 678-717-3698. 133 D
eric.skipper@ung.edu
SKIPPER, Wray 229-931-2354. 131 G
wskipper@southgatech.edu
SKIPWORTH, Stanley, T 909-593-3511... 72 E
sskipworth@laverne.edu
SKIVIAT, David, M 740-283-6223. 379 N
dskiviat@franciscan.edu
SKLAR, David 914-347-3910. 350 F
David.Sklar@sunywcc.edu
SKLAR, Jay 314-434-4044. 273 C
jay.sklar@covenantseminary.edu
SKLBA, Stephanie 262-564-2662. 540 A
sklba@gtc.edu
SKLEDER, Anne 610-902-8301. 411 E
anne.skleder@cabrini.edu
SKOGEN, Larry, C 701-224-5430. 371 B
larry.skogen@bismarckstate.edu
SKOGEN, Larry, C 701-224-5431. 372 B
larry.skogen@bismarckstate.edu
SKOGLUND,
Elizabeth, A 410-543-6161. 220 D
easkoglund@salisbury.edu
SKOLNIK, Richard, J 315-312-3168. 344 A
richard.skolnik@oswego.edu
SKONER, Peter, R 814-472-3085. 432 D
pskoner@francis.edu
SKOPITZ, Ronald, J 678-915-4962. 132 C
rskopitz@spsu.edu
SKORACZEWSKI, Paul 715-682-1841. 535 D
pskoraczewski@northland.edu
SKORTON, David, J 607-255-5201. 322 A
president@cornell.edu
SKORTZ, Brian 270-686-6416. 192 G
brian.skortz@brescia.edu
SKOUGSTAD, Becky 303-753-6046... 85 B
bskougstad@rmcad.edu
SKOWYRA, Jamie 508-213-2131. 235 E
jamie.skowyra@nichols.edu
SKRADE, Mark 417-823-3450. 281 M
mskrade@forest.edu
SKRESLET, Stanley 804-355-0671. 510 G
sskreslet@upsem.edu
SKRHA, Pattie 440-826-8011. 374 F
pskrha@bw.edu
SKRODZKI, Edmund 410-516-4600. 215 H
eskrodzki@jhu.edu
SKUCE, Anne, M 812-941-2212. 168 F
askuce@ius.edu
SKUDZINSKAS, Al 610-399-2000. 428 B
askudzinskas@cheyney.edu
SKUL, Jeanne 864-503-5960. 448 H
jskul@uscupstate.edu
SKURJA, Michael 801-375-5125. 496 G
mskurja@rmuohp.edu
SLAATS, Jacqueline 847-735-5285. 150 B
slaats@lakeforest.edu
SLABACH, Frederick, G 817-531-4401. 488 A
fslabach@txwes.edu
SLABAUGH, Katie 765-285-1545. 164 B
kslabaugh@bsu.edu
SLABODEN, Carolyn 781-283-2216. 237 F
cslaboden@wellesley.edu
SLABODEN, Scott, A 860-439-5328... 89 H
scott.slaboden@conncoll.edu
SLACK, Craig 301-314-7164. 219 B
cslack@umd.edu
SLACK, David 785-227-3380. 184 I
slackd@bethanylb.edu

SLACK, Gregory, C .... 315-268-6475. 320 A
gslack@clarkson.edu
SLACK, Karen .... 320-762-4463. 257 O
karens@alextech.edu
SLACK, Robert .... 626-914-8581... 38 K
rslack@citruscollege.edu
SLADE, Brenda .... 212-854-2091. 314 G
bslade@barnard.edu
SLADE, Patricia .... 973-877-3209. 301 H
slade@essex.edu
SLADE, Priscilla .... 601-979-1781. 267 E
priscilla.d.slade@jsums.edu
SLAFF, Sara .... 410-576-7847. 218 A
SLAFKOSKY, Mary, V ..... 260-422-5561. 167 B
mvslafkosky@indianatech.edu
SLAGELL, Jeff .... 662-846-4440. 266 G
jslagell@deltastate.edu
SLAICH, Lucy .... 410-704-2050. 220 E
lslaich@towson.edu
SLANGER, William, D ..... 701-231-7418. 371 G
william.slanger@ndsu.edu
SLANGER, Zvi Dov .... 410-486-0006. 213 E
SLANN, Martin .... 903-566-7368. 492 D
mslann@uttyler.edu
SLATER, Bernata .... 650-949-7364... 44 N
barkershirley@foothill.edu
SLATER, Glenn .... 215-785-0111. 426 X
SLATER, Jamie, B .... 336-750-8036. 370 A
slaterjb@wssu.edu
SLATER, Jane Ann .... 210-434-6711. 477 N
jslater@lake.ollusa.edu
SLATER, Janet .... 217-333-2350. 162 A
slaterj@illinois.edu
SLATER, Joe .... 215-893-5272. 414 B
joe.slater@curtis.edu
SLATER, Peter .... 212-594-4000. 347 H
pslater@tcicollege.edu
SLATER, Troy .... 231-348-6610. 247 H
tslater@ncmich.edu
SLATER-DUFFY, Carrie ... 715-682-1482. 535 D
cslaterduffy@northland.edu
SLATON, Christa, D .... 575-646-3500. 310 I
cslaton@nmsu.edu
SLATON, Gwendolyn .... 973-877-3233. 301 H
slaton@essex.edu
SLATON, Hugh .... 229-931-2302. 126 D
hugh.slaton@gsw.edu
SLATON, Nathanial .... 270-534-3244. 196 G
nathanial.slaton@kctcs.edu
SLATTERY, Kathryn .... 815-836-5275. 150 H
slatteka@lewisu.edu
SLATTERY, Kimberly .... 610-436-0043. 430 A
kslattery@wcupa.edu
SLATTERY, SCC,
Mary Catherine .... 973-543-6528. 298 I
academicdean@acs350.org
SLATTERY, Suzanne .... 978-837-5446. 234 A
slatterys@merrimack.edu
SLAUGHTER, Arnie .... 859-572-5538. 198 I
slaughtera@nku.edu
SLAUGHTER, Beverly, J .. 321-433-7060. 101 M
slaughterb@easternflorida.edu
SLAUGHTER, Clinton ...... 530-895-2366... 30 F
slaughtercl@butte.edu
SLAUGHTER, Craig, A .... 765-658-4030. 165 F
craigslaughter@depauw.edu
SLAUGHTER, Dane, S ..... 864-622-6001. 441 B
dslaughter@andersonuniversity.edu
SLAUGHTER, Gayle, R .... 713-798-6644. 467 F
gayles@bcm.edu
SLAUGHTER, Jacqueline 512-245-2273. 487 C
js47@txstate.edu
SLAUGHTER, Jane .... 505-277-2611. 312 F
mjane@unm.edu
SLAUGHTER, John .... 254-647-3234. 478 H
jslaughter@rangercollege.edu
SLAUGHTER, Keith .... 404-614-6378. 127 I
kslaughter@itc.edu
SLAUGHTER, Michael ..... 361-354-2559. 468 K
slaughter@coastalbend.edu
SLAUGHTER, Millicent ... 956-721-5746. 475 F
mslaughter@laredo.edu
SLAUGHTER, Sabra, C ... 843-792-2228. 445 B
slaughsc@musc.edu
SLAUGHTER, Shirley ...... 510-981-2840... 59 A
sslaughter@peralta.edu
SLAVENS, Joe, C .... 530-226-4108... 66 D
jslavens@simpsonu.edu
SLAVIK, Kenneth .... 215-871-6527. 430 D
kennethsl@pcom.edu
SLAVIN, Dennis .... 646-660-6504. 316 J
Dennis.Slavin@baruch.cuny.edu
SLAVIN, Joan, L .... 714-850-4800... 69 E
slavin@taftu.edu
SLAVIN, Kevin, B .... 914-606-6733. 350 F
kevin.slavin@sunywcc.edu
SLAVIN, Lisa .... 617-879-2260. 238 C
lslavin@wheelock.edu
SLAVIN, Patricia .... 775-673-7812. 294 H
pslavin@tmcc.edu

SLAVITT, Lesley .... 312-341-2351. 157 D
lslavitt@roosevelt.edu
SLAWSON, Linda .... 903-785-7661. 478 B
lslawson@parisjc.edu
SLAWSON, Mark .... 617-873-0106. 224 G
Mark.Slawson@cambridgecollege.edu
SLAWTER, Laura .... 336-917-5312. 366 D
laura.slawter@salem.edu
SLAYDEN, John, L .... 417-268-6042. 271 I
jslayden@gobbc.edu
SLAYMAKER, Valerie ...... 651-213-4746. 256 B
vslaymaker@hazelden.edu
SLAYTON, Deborah, L .... 217-420-6774. 153 C
dslayton@millikin.edu
SLAYTON, William, J ...... 260-399-7700. 174 C
wslayton@sf.edu
SLED, Jill .... 503-682-1862. 407 B
jsled@pioneerpacific.edu
SLEDGE, Donald .... 205-929-6442..... 5 D
dsledge@lawsonstate.edu
SLEDGE, Janet .... 386-506-3899. 101 G
sledgej@DaytonaState.edu
SLEEMAN, Geoffrey .... 313-664-7480. 241 C
gsleeman@collegeforcreativestudies.edu
SLEEVI, Timothy .... 269-948-9500. 244 O
sleevit@kellogg.edu
SLEIGH-LAYMAN, Staci . 509-963-2205. 517 F
staci@cwu.edu
SLEIGHT, Garth .... 406-874-6212. 286 E
sleightg@milescc.edu
SLEJKO, Christa .... 972-273-3010. 471 B
cslejko@dcccd.edu
SLENSKI, Amanda .... 989-463-7299. 239 B
slenskiar@alma.edu
SLENSKI, Brian .... 517-321-0242. 243 F
bslenski@glcc.edu
SLEPITZA, Ron .... 816-501-3750. 271 H
ron.slepitza@avila.edu
SLESNICK, Daniel, T .... 512-471-4363. 491 C
slesnick@austin.utexas.edu
SLETTEDAHL, Gene, A .... 507-354-8221. 256 M
slettega@mlc-wels.edu
SLEVA, Michael .... 616-451-3511. 241 H
msleva@davenport.edu
SLEVIN, Kathleen, F .... 757-221-2601. 503 N
keslev@wm.edu
SLIGH, Gary .... 352-323-3670. 108 S
slighg@lssc.edu
SLIGO, Sarah .... 413-545-5479. 228 F
sligo@admin.umass.edu
SLIKE, Robert .... 808-543-8019. 135 F
rslike@hpu.edu
SLIMAN, David .... 601-266-6633. 270 E
david.sliman@usm.edu
SLIMAN, George, S .... 412-578-8826. 412 G
slimangs@carlow.edu
SLIND, Steve .... 715-836-4643. 536 E
slindsd@uwec.edu
SLINGER, Ron .... 303-914-6417... 84 I
ron.slinger@rrcc.edu
SLINKARD, Tiffany .... 417-455-5636. 273 E
TiffanySlinkard@crowder.edu
SLINKER, Bryan, K .... 509-335-9515. 525 A
slinker@vetmed.wsu.edu
SLISZ, John, P .... 716-851-1851. 323 I
slisz@ecc.edu
SLIZEWSKI, James .... 215-489-2220. 414 E
james.slizewski@delval.edu
SLOAN, Barbara .... 312-752-2122. 149 E
SLOAN, Barbara .... 850-201-8680. 117 D
sloanb@tcc.fl.edu
SLOAN, Barry .... 310-287-4278... 52 F
sloanba@wlac.edu
SLOAN, Candice, Y .... 864-587-4282. 447 B
sloanc@smcsc.edu
SLOAN, Damon, N .... 815-740-3398. 162 F
dsloan@stfrancis.edu
SLOAN, LaMonica .... 336-750-3240. 370 A
singletonls@wssu.edu
SLOAN, Lee .... 361-698-1259. 471 G
lsloan@delmar.edu
SLOAN, Michael .... 309-694-5512. 146 E
msloan@icc.edu
SLOAN, Robert, B .... 281-649-3450. 473 B
rsloan@hbu.edu
SLOAN, Susan .... 503-253-3443. 405 E
ssloan@ocom.edu
SLOAN, Susan .... 315-364-3264. 350 E
ssloan@wells.edu
SLOANE, Tomecca .... 919-760-8633. 356 G
sloaneto@meredith.edu
SLOAS, Ike .... 901-843-3880. 458 E
SLOBERT, Yantee .... 585-385-8423. 338 H
yslobert@sjfc.edu
SLOCUM, Cameron, W ... 409-772-3448. 493 C
cwslocum@utmb.edu
SLOCUM, Jeff .... 315-655-7290. 316 E
jslocum@cazenovia.edu
SLOCUM, Stacy, S .... 585-385-8388. 338 H
sslocum@sjfc.edu

SLOCUMB, Douglas .... 423-478-7036. 458 B
dslocumb@ptseminary.edu
SLOKA, Sandra, L .... 815-740-5026. 162 F
ssloka@stfrancis.edu
SLOMBIA, Sonia .... 937-376-6574. 376 E
sslombia@centralstate.edu
SLOMOVITS, Mendel ...... 732-414-2834. 308 K
SLOMOVITS, Yosef .... 732-367-1060. 299 E
SLON, Dennis .... 310-338-5127... 53 E
dslon@lmu.edu
SLONE, Jason .... 419-448-5851. 389 J
slonej@tiffin.edu
SLONE, Tammy, L .... 937-766-7987. 375 K
slonet@cedarville.edu
SLOSS, Robert, E .... 401-232-6046. 438 K
rsloss@bryant.edu
SLOTKIN, Jacquelyn, H .. 619-239-0391... 36 D
jslotkin@cwsl.edu
SLOTTOW, Timothy, P .... 734-764-7272. 251 C
tslottow@umich.edu
SLOUGH, Rebecca .... 574-296-6228. 163 J
rslough@ambs.edu
SLOVAK, Jeffrey .... 708-534-4981. 145 F
jslovak@govst.edu
SLOWENSKY, Joseph ..... 714-744-7882... 38 A
slowensky@chapman.edu
SLUDER, Patrick .... 770-394-8300. 120 H
psluder@aii.edu
SLUDER, Richard, D .... 660-543-4811. 283 A
sluder@ucmo.edu
SLUDER, Robin .... 423-478-7727. 458 B
rsluder@ptseminary.edu
SLUIS, Kimberly .... 630-637-5152. 154 F
kasluis@noctrl.edu
SLUSARCZYK, Richard ... 212-226-7300. 336 G
rslusar@pbcny.edu
SLUSHER, Jennifer, J ..... 540-985-8502. 506 G
jjslusher@jchs.edu
SLUSHER, Max .... 609-894-9311. 299 I
gslusher@bcc.edu
SLUSSER, Karen, L .... 570-389-4055. 427 H
kslusse2@bloomu.edu
SLUTSKY, Madeleine ...... 630-353-9027. 144 A
mslutsky@devry.edu
SLY, Doug .... 509-793-2003. 517 C
dougs@bigbend.edu
SMAIL, John .... 704-687-5630. 368 E
jsmail@uncc.edu
SMALES, Sandra .... 617-984-1723. 235 I
ssmales@quincycollege.edu
SMALL, Brenda, L .... 423-585-6772. 462 A
brenda.small@ws.edu
SMALL, Brent .... 575-562-2194. 309 H
brent.small@enmu.edu
SMALL, Cindy .... 406-265-3787. 287 D
csmall@msun.edu
SMALL, Daniel, E .... 202-994-6620... 95 D
dsmall@gwu.edu
SMALL, Daphne .... 650-949-7389... 44 N
smalldaphne@foothill.edu
SMALL, Darlene .... 843-383-8039. 442 F
dsmall@coker.edu
SMALL, David .... 406-638-3110. 286 D
smalld@lbhc.edu
SMALL, Gillian .... 646-664-8906. 316 I
gillian.small@cuny.edu
SMALL, Hank .... 843-863-7080. 441 H
hsmall@csuniv.edu
SMALL, Jacquelyn .... 863-667-5157. 113 P
jrsmall@seu.edu
SMALL, Joe, A .... 509-526-6432. 524 H
joe.small@wwcc.edu
SMALL, John, J .... 630-637-5701. 154 F
jjsmall@noctrl.edu
SMALL, Jonathan, A .... 317-940-9249. 164 J
jasmall@butler.edu
SMALL, Josh .... 803-648-6851. 448 A
SMALL, Mario .... 773-702-8798. 161 B
mariosmall@uchicago.edu
SMALL, Natissia .... 314-516-5128. 283 E
smalln@umsl.edu
SMALL, Topeka .... 870-733-6722... 21 I
tsmall@midsouthcc.edu
SMALLEN, David, L .... 315-859-4169. 325 E
dsmallen@hamilton.edu
SMALLEY, David .... 217-732-3155. 151 C
dsmalley@lincolncollege.edu
SMALLEY, Michelle .... 414-258-4810. 535 A
smalleym@mtmary.edu
SMALLEY, Reid .... 585-345-6999. 325 C
rjsmalley@genesee.edu
SMALLEY, Robin .... 727-864-7756. 101 N
smallerm@eckerd.edu
SMALLS, Eppechal, T .... 937-708-5710. 393 A
esmalls@wilberforce.edu
SMALLS, Gerald .... 803-705-4694. 441 C
smallsg@benedict.edu
SMALLS, Mary, L .... 803-536-8638. 446 G
smallsml@scsu.edu
SMALLWOOD, Pamela ...... 417-865-2815. 274 B
smallwoodp@evangel.edu

SMALLWOOD, Will .... 405-878-2703. 397 C
will.smallwood@okbu.edu
SMARRELLI, JR., John .. 901-321-3250. 453 H
jsmarrel@cbu.edu
SMARRITO, Fiona .... 845-758-7245. 314 D
smarrito@bard.edu
SMART, III, Clifton, M ... 417-836-8500. 278 E
president@missouristate.edu
SMART, Denise, T .... 512-245-2311. 487 C
ds37@txstate.edu
SMART, James, G .... 305-284-4505. 118 F
jsmart@miami.edu
SMART, Lucille .... 315-781-3449. 326 C
smart@hws.edu
SMART, Robert .... 616-331-2281. 243 C
smartr@gvsu.edu
SMART, Scott .... 575-562-2611. 309 H
scott.smart@enmu.edu
SMART, Stephanie .... 845-434-5750. 347 A
ssmart@sunysullivan.edu
SMART, William .... 615-297-7545. 452 J
smartb@aquinascollege.edu
SMARZIK, Linda, S .... 512-223-9214. 466 I
lsmarzik@austincc.edu
SMATRESK, Neal .... 702-895-3201. 294 I
president@unlv.edu
SMAY, Kevin .... 412-237-3094. 413 D
ksmay@ccac.edu
SMEATON, John, W .... 610-758-3890. 422 A
jws2@lehigh.edu
SMEDINGHOFF, Susan .. 708-456-0300. 161 A
ssmeding@triton.edu
SMEDLEY, Patricia .... 615-460-6403. 453 C
patricia.smedley@belmont.edu
SMEDLEY, Susan .... 361-354-2399. 468 K
smedleys@coastalbend.edu
SMEE, Greg .... 816-331-5700. 280 D
gsmee@pcitraining.edu
SMEE, Sheryl .... 619-849-2509... 59 L
sherylsmee@pointloma.edu
SMEED, Shane .... 913-266-8620. 189 I
shane.smeed@ottawa.edu
SMELSER, Dick .... 865-694-6565. 461 D
rwsmelser@pstcc.edu
SMELTZ, Emily .... 724-357-5555. 428 F
Emily.Smeltz@iup.edu
SMELTZER, Brian, K .... 717-815-1293. 438 D
bksmeltzer@ycp.edu
SMELTZER, Deirdre .... 540-432-4141. 504 D
deirdre.smeltzer@emu.edu
SMELTZER, Jill, M .... 276-944-6923. 504 H
jsmeltzer@ehc.edu
SMELTZER, Paul .... 336-725-8344. 365 F
smeltzer@piedmontu.edu
SMETANKA, John .... 724-805-2227. 432 G
john.smetanka@email.stvincent.edu
SMIALEK, William .... 903-730-4890. 474 O
william.smialek@jarvis.edu
SMICK-ATTISANO,
Regina, A .... 603-862-1025. 298 C
regina.smick-attisano@unh.edu
SMID, Terry .... 563-425-5359. 183 B
smidt@uiu.edu
SMIELL, John, R .... 202-885-2840... 94 F
jsmiell@american.edu
SMILEY, Brad .... 903-675-6218. 488 D
bsmiley@tvcc.edu
SMILEY, Ellen .... 318-274-3228. 207 E
smileye@gram.edu
SMILEY, Joseph .... 727-712-5851. 112 E
smiley.joseph@spcollege.edu
SMILEY, Scott .... 432-552-2605. 493 D
smiley_s@utpb.edu
SMIRNOFF, Joel .... 216-791-5000. 377 E
avt6@case.edu
SMIT, Cori .... 318-342-5329. 208 E
scroggins@ulm.edu
SMITH, Adam, A .... 330-972-7856. 390 E
aas56@uakron.edu
SMITH, Adrienne .... 413-755-4561. 233 A
asmith@stcc.edu
SMITH, Adrienne .... 252-399-6331. 352 F
adsmith2@barton.edu
SMITH, Alan .... 714-997-6652... 38 A
smith@chapman.edu
SMITH, Alastair .... 415-338-1759.... 35 E
aksmith@sfsu.edu
SMITH, Alex G, H .... 570-372-4109. 433 H
smithal@susqu.edu
SMITH, Alexa .... 870-612-2165.... 25 A
alexa.smith@uaccb.edu
SMITH, Alice .... 417-255-7230. 278 F
masmith@missouristate.edu
SMITH, Allison .... 360-475-7100. 521 H
asmith@olympic.edu
SMITH, Amy .... 912-478-5391. 126 C
amysmith@georgiasouthern.edu
SMITH, Amy, E .... 716-926-8877. 326 B
asmith@hilbert.edu
SMITH, Amy, J .... 815-224-0540. 148 A
amy_smith@ivcc.edu

SMITH, Amy, L 269-337-7156. 244 K
Amy.Smith@kzoo.edu
SMITH, Andrea 503-552-1692. 404 H
acsmith@ncnm.edu
SMITH, Andrew, D 803-461-3277. 445 A
andy.smith@lr.edu
SMITH, Andy 512-475-6608. 491 C
andy.smith@universityunions.utexas.edu
SMITH, Angela 720-890-8922... 82 I
finance@itea.edu
SMITH, Angi 706-379-3111. 134 L
adsmith@yhc.edu
SMITH, Ann 334-229-4406..... 1 D
annsmith@alasu.edu
SMITH, Ann, T 859-238-5459. 193 E
ann.smith@centre.edu
SMITH, Annabelle 254-526-1205. 468 G
annabelle.smith@ctcd.edu
SMITH, Anson 203-332-5229... 88 F
asmith@hcc.commnet.edu
SMITH, April 731-410-6730. 455 J
asmith@lanecollege.edu
SMITH, Argile 318-487-7897. 202 F
argile.smith@lacollege.edu
SMITH, Art 870-236-6901... 20 K
artsmith@crc.edu
SMITH, Ashley 260-359-4171. 166 O
asmith@huntington.edu
SMITH, Ashley 252-493-7229. 362 G
adsmith@email.pittcc.edu
SMITH, Audrey 215-780-1364. 433 A
audrey@salus.edu
SMITH, Audrey, Y 413-585-4900. 236 H
aysmith@smith.edu
SMITH, Barbara 205-366-8816..... 7 E
bsmith@stillman.edu
SMITH, Barbara 404-756-4098. 121 A
bsmith@atlm.edu
SMITH, Barry, C 570-586-2400. 410 D
bsmith@bbc.edu
SMITH, Barry, V 731-989-6009. 454 J
bvsmith@fhu.edu
SMITH, Bea, W 864-503-5235. 448 H
bwsmith@uscupstate.edu
SMITH, Benjamin, J 620-431-2820. 189 D
bsmith@neosho.edu
SMITH, Benny, R 828-398-7482. 357 N
brsmith@abtech.edu
SMITH, Beth 910-576-6222. 362 C
smithb@montgomery.edu
SMITH, Beth 870-972-2586... 19 N
smitty@astate.edu
SMITH, Betsy, R 251-626-3303..... 8 B
bsmith2@ussa.edu
SMITH, Betty 610-917-1426. 436 C
blsmith@vfcc.edu
SMITH, Betty, J 910-678-8250. 360 D
smithbj@faytechcc.edu
SMITH, Bettye Parker 601-977-7737. 270 A
bpsmith@tougaloo.edu
SMITH, Beverly, H 405-466-3204. 395 N
bhsmith@langston.edu
SMITH, Bill 401-232-6078. 438 K
bsmith8@bryant.edu
SMITH, Bill 213-763-3612... 52 D
smithb@lattc.edu
SMITH, Billy, R 731-989-6623. 454 J
bsmith@fhu.edu
SMITH, Blair 480-557-1241... 18 I
blair.smith@phoenix.edu
SMITH, Bob 904-819-6332. 103 E
BSmith@flagler.edu
SMITH, Bobby 731-424-3520. 460 G
bsmith@jscc.edu
SMITH, Bobby 254-442-5111. 468 I
bobby.smith@cisco.edu
SMITH, Brad 719-384-6869... 83 M
brad.smith@ojc.edu
SMITH, Brad 206-264-9100. 516 J
brads@bgu.edu
SMITH, Brad, D 937-766-7872. 375 K
smthb@cedarville.edu
SMITH, Bradley, A 610-921-7529. 409 A
bsmith@alb.edu
SMITH, Bradley, D 574-807-7232. 164 D
smithb@bethelcollege.edu
SMITH, Brenda 601-643-8318. 266 F
brenda.smith@colin.edu
SMITH, Brenda, A 585-292-2365. 332 A
bsmith2@monroecc.edu
SMITH, Brenda, C 785-227-3380. 184 I
bsmith@bethanylb.edu
SMITH, Brian 517-321-0242. 243 F
bsmith@glcc.edu
SMITH, Brian, D 260-399-7700. 174 C
bsmith@sf.edu
SMITH, Brian, K 401-454-6207. 440 A
bsmith@risd.edu
SMITH, Brian, L 334-833-4575..... 4 D
bsmith@huntingdon.edu
SMITH, Brien, N 812-237-2000. 167 A
brien.smith@indstate.edu
SMITH, Britt 432-264-5040. 473 E
bsmith@howardcollege.edu
SMITH, Bruce 503-777-7527. 407 E
smithb@reed.edu
SMITH, Bruce 217-244-8446. 162 A
smithb@law.uiuc.edu
SMITH, Bruce 701-777-2791. 371 C
bsmith@aero.und.edu
SMITH, Bryan 270-706-8616. 195 A
bryan.smith@kctcs.edu
SMITH, Bryan 757-789-1727. 512 D
bsmith@es.vccs.edu
SMITH, Bryan 757-789-1732. 512 D
bsmith@es.vccs.edu
SMITH, Byron 315-312-3642. 344 A
byron.smith@oswego.edu
SMITH, Calvin 314-968-7138. 284 N
smithca@webster.edu
SMITH, Candace, E 202-994-3566... 95 D
cesmith@gwu.edu
SMITH, Carl 760-245-4271... 75 B
Carl.Smith@vvc.edu
SMITH, Carol 719-587-7820... 78 B
carolsmith@adams.edu
SMITH, Carol 970-247-7265... 81 M
smith_c@fortlewis.edu
SMITH, Carol 973-278-5400. 299 D
crs@berkeleycollege.edu
SMITH, Carol 973-405-2111. 314 K
crs@berkeleycollege.edu
SMITH, Carol, L 765-658-4580. 165 F
clsmith@depauw.edu
SMITH, Carola 805-965-0581... 64 L
smithc@sbcc.edu
SMITH, Carolyn 305-273-4499. 100 H
carolyn@cbt.edu
SMITH, Carolyn 307-766-2376. 543 I
csmith@uwyo.edu
SMITH, Carolyn, A 304-697-7550. 526 H
csmith@huntingtonjuniorcollege.edu
SMITH, Carolyn, S 414-288-7184. 534 B
carolyn.s.smith@marquette.edu
SMITH, Carter 502-410-6200. 194 B
csmith1@galencollege.edu
SMITH, Catherine, E 585-292-2341. 332 A
ksmith@monroecc.edu
SMITH, Cathy, A 801-524-8106. 495 O
csmith@ldsbc.edu
SMITH, Caye 619-849-2313... 59 L
cayesmith@pointloma.edu
SMITH, Charlene 513-241-4338. 373 J
charlene.smith@antonellicollege.edu
SMITH, Charles 912-525-5000. 131 B
csmith@scad.edu
SMITH, Charles 816-414-3700. 277 L
csmith@mbts.edu
SMITH, Charly 316-942-4291. 189 E
smithc@newmanu.edu
SMITH, Charmian 516-572-7376. 332 C
charmian.smith@ncc.edu
SMITH, Chris 620-241-0723. 185 K
chris.smith@centralchristian.edu
SMITH, Chris 303-986-2320... 80 D
chris@csha.net
SMITH, Christine 678-466-5406. 123 A
christinesmith@clayton.edu
SMITH, Christine, J 630-617-3150. 145 A
chriss@elmhurst.edu
SMITH, Christy, c 859-846-5485. 197 I
ccsmith@midway.edu
SMITH, Chuck 956-364-4200. 485 H
chuck.smith@tstc.edu
SMITH, Cindy 432-264-5034. 473 E
csmith@howardcollege.edu
SMITH, Claire 210-999-8401. 488 C
csmith9@trinity.edu
SMITH, Claire, L 410-777-7383. 213 D
clsmith@aacc.edu
SMITH, Clarence, E 662-252-8000. 269 F
csmith@rustcollege.edu
SMITH, Clarence, L 910-362-7176. 358 F
csmith@cfcc.edu
SMITH, Claude 937-433-3410. 379 J
csmith@edaff.com
SMITH, Cliff 913-627-4122. 187 L
clsmith@kckcc.edu
SMITH, Cliff, L 864-379-8802. 443 F
smith@erskine.edu
SMITH, Colleen 972-758-3880. 469 G
csmith@collin.edu
SMITH, Connie 706-295-6972. 125 F
csmith@gntc.edu
SMITH, Corey 662-246-6405. 268 B
csmith@msdelta.edu
SMITH, Craig 406-768-5555. 286 C
csmith@fpcc.edu
SMITH, Curtis 325-674-6300. 464 H
ccs05j@acu.edu
SMITH, Cynthia 301-687-4328. 220 C
colsmith@frostburg.edu
SMITH, Cynthia 412-281-2600. 433 B
csmith@western-school.com
SMITH, Dale, T 914-831-0311. 321 B
dsmith@cw.edu
SMITH, Dalton 903-983-8259. 475 E
dsmith@kilgore.edu
SMITH, Dan 662-562-3305. 269 C
dsmith@northwestms.edu
SMITH, Dan, K 806-651-2133. 484 D
dsmith@mail.wtamu.edu
SMITH, Dana 760-944-4449... 54 G
dsmith@miracosta.edu
SMITH, Dana 865-981-8199. 456 D
dana.smith@maryvillecollege.edu
SMITH, Daniel 864-242-5100. 441 D
SMITH, Daniel 562-860-2451... 37 I
dsmith@cerritos.edu
SMITH, Daniel 802-224-3000. 501 A
dan.smith@vsc.edu
SMITH, Daniel, C 812-855-6679. 167 F
dansmith@indiana.edu
SMITH, Daniel, J 706-355-5085. 120 J
dsmith@athenstech.edu
SMITH, Daniel, R 828-448-6036. 365 A
dsmith@wpcc.edu
SMITH, Darlene 410-837-4955. 221 A
dsmith@ubalt.edu
SMITH, Daryl 864-592-4600. 447 A
smithd@sccsc.edu
SMITH, Daryl 716-829-7623. 323 D
smithd@dyc.edu
SMITH, David 585-567-9321. 326 F
david.smith@houghton.edu
SMITH, David 518-743-2313. 345 E
smithd@sunyacc.edu
SMITH, David 970-824-3258... 80 B
david.smith@cncc.edu
SMITH, David 626-584-5448... 45 E
dwsmith@fuller.edu
SMITH, David 270-247-8521. 197 H
dsmith@midcontinent.edu
SMITH, David 912-358-3118. 131 C
smithd@savannahstate.edu
SMITH, David, B 518-783-2431. 340 J
dsmith@siena.edu
SMITH, David, R 315-464-4513. 342 E
smith@upstate.edu
SMITH, Dayle, M 315-268-2300. 320 A
dayle.smith@clarkson.edu
SMITH, DeAnna, M 205-665-6012..... 9 B
dsmith23@montevallo.edu
SMITH, Deborah 409-212-5724. 467 C
SMITH, Debra 919-658-7776. 357 I
dsmith@moc.edu
SMITH, Debra 252-536-7213. 361 A
dsmith600@halifaxcc.edu
SMITH, Debra, M 330-665-1084. 386 A
debbie@ocm.edu
SMITH, DeLancey 314-539-5141. 281 D
dsmith852@stlcc.edu
SMITH, Delois 256-824-4600..... 8 F
delois.smith@uah.edu
SMITH, Denise 567-661-7250. 387 L
denise_smith4@owens.edu
SMITH, Denise, M 603-862-3396. 298 C
denise.smith@unh.edu
SMITH, Derek 215-489-2476. 414 E
Derek.Smith@delval.edu
SMITH, Devin 402-643-7328. 289 B
devin.smith@cune.edu
SMITH, Devon 918-335-7331. 398 F
dsmith@okwu.edu
SMITH, Diane, K 513-562-6260. 373 K
dksmith@artacademy.edu
SMITH, Dianne 510-204-0718... 38 J
dsmith@cdsp.edu
SMITH, Don 229-931-2731. 131 G
dsmith@southgatech.edu
SMITH, Donald 907-786-1389... 10 G
donald.smith@alaska.edu
SMITH, Donald 270-745-6256. 200 G
donald.smith@wku.edu
SMITH, Donald 863-667-5805. 113 P
dsmith@seu.edu
SMITH, Donald 216-987-5020. 378 D
donald.smith@tri-c.edu
SMITH, Donald, E 716-286-8348. 334 F
des@niagara.edu
SMITH, Donald, E 848-445-1750. 306 A
don.smith@rutgers.edu
SMITH, Donald, R 318-342-1050. 208 E
dosmith@ulm.edu
SMITH, Donna 601-925-3313. 268 A
dsmith@mc.edu
SMITH, Donna 610-861-1384. 424 E
medgs01@moravian.edu
SMITH, Dorothy 504-816-4527. 201 K
dsmith@dillard.edu
SMITH, Dorothy 213-763-5507... 52 D
smithd@lattc.edu
SMITH, Dorsey 334-244-3232..... 2 A
dsmith@aum.edu
SMITH, Douglas 408-270-6426... 63 N
douglas.smith@sjeccd.org
SMITH, Douglas, F 610-796-8393. 409 E
doug.smith@alvernia.edu
SMITH, Douglas, J 508-565-1341. 237 A
dsmith@stonehill.edu
SMITH, Drew 870-230-5265... 21 D
smithc@hsu.edu
SMITH, Dustin 479-788-7591... 24 A
dustin.smith@uafs.edu
SMITH, Dwayne 813-974-2267. 116 C
mdsmith8@usf.edu
SMITH, Dwayne 314-340-3511. 275 A
smithd@hssu.edu
SMITH, Dwight, L 973-328-5090. 300 G
dsmith@ccm.edu
SMITH, III, Earl 713-743-1899. 489 B
esmith@uh.edu
SMITH, Ed 601-477-4029. 267 F
edd.smith@jcjc.edu
SMITH, Ed 615-771-7821. 464 G
ed.smith@williamsoncc.edu
SMITH, Edith 229-732-5974. 120 D
edithsmith@andrewcollege.edu
SMITH, Edmond, C 276-964-7338. 514 A
ed.smith@sw.edu
SMITH, Edward, L 501-569-3400... 24 B
elsmith@ualr.edu
SMITH, Elizabeth 925-631-4278... 61 F
jes5@stmarys-ca.edu
SMITH, Elmer, R 770-216-2960. 127 F
ers@ict-ils.edu
SMITH, Ephraim, P 562-951-4710... 32 E
esmith@calstate.edu
SMITH, Eric 210-690-9000. 472 N
esmith@hallmarkcollege.edu
SMITH, Eric 315-464-5763. 342 E
smither@upstate.edu
SMITH, Eric, J 570-577-1097. 411 A
eric.smith@bucknell.edu
SMITH, Eric, L 906-227-1314. 248 A
esmith@nmu.edu
SMITH, Erik 207-255-1327. 212 F
erik.smith@maine.edu
SMITH, Erin, T 724-946-7330. 437 B
smithet@westminster.edu
SMITH, Eva 425-640-1171. 519 D
esmith@edcc.edu
SMITH, Felicia 770-593-2257. 127 B
gjcfs@gupton-jones.edu
SMITH, Frank 760-245-4271... 75 B
Frank.Smith@vvc.edu
SMITH, Fred, R 740-376-4791. 383 E
fred.smith@marietta.edu
SMITH, Frederick 201-200-3474. 303 F
fsmith@njcu.edu
SMITH, Frederick, M 517-264-7876. 250 B
fsmith@sienaheights.edu
SMITH, Fritz 562-907-4951... 76 I
fritz@whittier.edu
SMITH, G. Ben 704-637-4111. 353 E
gbsmith@catawba.edu
SMITH, G. Richard, H 501-526-4533... 24 C
SmithGRichard@uams.edu
SMITH, Gary 315-279-5352. 328 D
gsmith@mail.keuka.edu
SMITH, Gary 817-515-6400. 482 B
gary.smithr@tccd.edu
SMITH, Gary 435-283-7301. 498 A
gary.smith@snow.edu
SMITH, Gary, R 701-231-7494. 371 G
gary.smith@ndsu.edu
SMITH, Geary 815-455-8788. 152 F
gsmith@mchenry.edu
SMITH, Gene 919-735-5151. 364 H
gsmith@waynecc.edu
SMITH, Gene 614-292-7572. 386 E
smith.5407@osu.edu
SMITH, George 207-879-8955. 210 C
SMITH, George 617-349-8886. 228 B
ggsmith@lesley.edu
SMITH, George 425-640-1668. 519 D
gsmith@edcc.edu
SMITH, Gerald 817-461-8741. 466 D
gsmith@arlingtonbaptistcollege.edu
SMITH, Gladys 313-927-1259. 246 D
gsmith8938@marygrove.edu
SMITH, Glenn, C 503-280-8512. 402 J
glsmith@cu-portland.edu
SMITH, Glenn, R 610-526-7935. 410 J
gsmith@brynmawr.edu
SMITH, Gloria 337-521-8922. 203 I
gsmith@southlouisiana.edu
SMITH, Grady 601-276-3704. 269 H
gsmith@smcc.edu
SMITH, Greg, H 573-341-6995. 284 A
gsmith@mst.edu

SMITH, Greg, P .... 308-398-7300. 288 I gpsmith@cccneb.edu
SMITH, Gregory .... 662-720-7449. 269 B gsmith@nemcc.edu
SMITH, Gregory .... 225-578-8491. 205 E
SMITH, Gregory .... 714-449-7456... 67 D gsmith@scco.edu
SMITH, Gregory, L .... 920-465-2343. 536 F smithg@uwgb.edu
SMITH, Gretna .... 757-822-1708. 514 C gsmith@tcc.edu
SMITH, Harlan .... 216-687-3910. 377 F
SMITH, Heather, C .... 508-531-1295. 229 D h2smith@bridgew.edu
SMITH, Herbert, C .... 410-857-2413. 216 E hsmith@mcdaniel.edu
SMITH, Hilary .... 212-355-1501. 316 H hsmith@christies.edu
SMITH, Holly .... 253-964-6408. 522 C hsmith@pierce.ctc.edu
SMITH, Howard, W .... 620-235-4518. 189 L smith@pittstate.edu
SMITH, Ian .... 765-983-1215. 165 G smithia@earlham.edu
SMITH, Idelia .... 413-552-2228. 231 F ismith@hcc.edu
SMITH, Ileana, M .... 302-259-6020... 93 E ismith@dtcc.edu
SMITH, J, R .... 630-752-5061. 163 F jr.smith@wheaton.edu
SMITH, J. Fitz .... 937-327-7076. 393 E jfsmith@wittenberg.edu
SMITH, J. Malcolm .... 401-341-2206. 440 C malcolm.smith@salve.edu
SMITH, Jace .... 541-463-5561. 403 I smithj@lanecc.edu
SMITH, Jackie .... 256-233-8172..... 1 F jackie.smith@athens.edu
SMITH, Jacqueline .... 334-876-9242..... 4 A jacqueline.smith@wccs.edu
SMITH, Jacqueline .... 713-221-8541. 489 D smithja@uhd.edu
SMITH, Jade .... 310-338-8753... 53 E jsmith@lmu.edu
SMITH, James .... 740-654-6711. 387 C smithj27@ohio.edu
SMITH, James .... 718-489-5306. 338 G jsmith@sfc.edu
SMITH, James .... 334-241-5436..... 7 H jesmith@troy.edu
SMITH, James .... 909-384-8600... 62 A jsmith@sbccd.cc.ca.us
SMITH, James .... 802-879-2337. 501 F jsmith@vtc.edu
SMITH, James, H .... 575-492-2159. 312 M jsmith@usw.edu
SMITH, James, M .... 605-626-2521. 451 I James.Smith@northern.edu
SMITH, Jane .... 304-384-5241. 529 E smithjw@concord.edu
SMITH, Jane, L .... 630-942-2481. 142 G smithja@cod.edu
SMITH, Janet .... 423-869-6287. 456 A janet.smith@lmunet.edu
SMITH, Janet .... 601-643-8383. 266 F janet.smith@colin.edu
SMITH, Janet, F .... 931-540-2510. 460 E janet.smith@columbiastate.edu
SMITH, Janet, M .... 724-946-7143. 437 B smithjm@westminster.edu
SMITH, Jared .... 404-215-2666. 129 D jjsmith@morehouse.edu
SMITH, Jarret, L .... 540-828-5469. 502 J jlsmith@bridgewater.edu
SMITH, Jason .... 425-388-9142. 519 I
SMITH, Jason .... 415-503-6281... 62 H jsmith@sfcm.edu
SMITH, Jason .... 312-567-7112. 147 F jsmith31@iit.edu
SMITH, Jason .... 214-333-5443. 470 D jasons@dbu.edu
SMITH, Jean .... 718-780-0638. 315 H jean.smith@brooklaw.edu
SMITH, Jean, L .... 610-989-1438. 436 D jsmith@vfmac.edu
SMITH, Jeanne .... 304-734-6617. 527 O jsmith@bridgemont.edu
SMITH, Jeannean .... 903-813-2431. 466 H jsmith@austincollege.edu
SMITH, Jeannie .... 901-678-2261. 460 B jesmith@memphis.edu
SMITH, Jeff .... 585-395-2385. 342 F jsmith@brockport.edu
SMITH, Jeff .... 806-720-7482. 476 B jeff.smith@lcu.edu
SMITH, Jeff .... 941-487-4353. 115 D jsmith@ncf.edu
SMITH, Jeffrey .... 919-546-8238. 366 E jeffrey.smith@shawu.edu
SMITH, Jenna .... 716-896-0700. 350 A
SMITH, Jennifer .... 307-674-6446. 543 F jsmith@sheridan.edu
SMITH, Jennifer, B .... 270-745-6824. 200 G Jennifer.breiwa.smith@wku.edu
SMITH, Jennifer, J .... 714-556-3610... 74 D jennifer.j.smith@vanguard.edu
SMITH, Jenny .... 828-328-7252. 356 B jenny.smith@lr.edu
SMITH, Jeremy .... 601-276-3720. 269 H jsmith@smcc.edu
SMITH, Jeremy .... 716-829-7551. 323 D smithj@dyc.edu
SMITH, Jerry .... 229-217-4210. 129 F jsmith@moultrietech.edu
SMITH, Jerry .... 928-344-7535... 11 L jerry.smith@azwestern.edu
SMITH, Jesse .... 661-255-1050... 31 C jsmith@calarts.edu
SMITH, Jesse, R .... 601-477-4100. 267 F jesse.smith@jcjc.edu
SMITH, Jessie, C .... 615-329-8731. 454 F jcsmith@fisk.edu
SMITH, Jill, A .... 818-677-2118... 34 C jill.smith@csun.edu
SMITH, Jim .... 918-293-5234. 398 B jim.smith10@okstate.edu
SMITH, Jimmie .... 727-784-0003... 99 J jsmith@cfi.edu
SMITH, Jimmy, L .... 601-877-6170. 265 G jsmith@alcorn.edu
SMITH, Jo .... 615-353-3303. 461 B jo.smith@nscc.edu
SMITH, Joan .... 303-914-6410... 84 I joan.smith@rrcc.edu
SMITH, Joan, E .... 209-575-6508... 77 H smithj@yosemite.edu
SMITH, JoAnn .... 610-917-1456. 436 C jlsmith@vfcc.edu
SMITH, Joanne, H .... 512-245-2152. 487 C js14@txstate.edu
SMITH, Joe .... 509-313-6801. 520 A smithj@gonzaga.edu
SMITH, Joe, L .... 321-433-7018. 101 M smithj@easternflorida.edu
SMITH, Joel .... 518-255-5731. 344 E smithjm@cobleskill.edu
SMITH, Joel .... 308-432-6345. 291 D jsmith@csc.edu
SMITH, Joel, M .... 607-746-4600. 345 G smithjm@delhi.edu
SMITH, John .... 251-460-6111..... 9 E johns@southalabama.edu
SMITH, John .... 251-460-6171..... 9 E johns@southalabama.edu
SMITH, John .... 515-271-2969. 177 K john.smith@drake.edu
SMITH, John .... 919-530-7423. 368 A jsmith@nccu.edu
SMITH, John, W .... 401-454-6501. 440 A jsmith@risd.edu
SMITH, Johnny .... 828-395-1435. 361 C jsmith@isothermal.edu
SMITH, Joianne .... 847-635-1739. 155 F joismith@oakton.edu
SMITH, Jonathan, E .... 216-397-4605. 381 R jsmith@jcu.edu
SMITH, Joseph, E .... 423-439-4317. 459 C smithje@etsu.edu
SMITH, Joseph, T .... 410-706-7302. 219 C jtsmith@af.umaryland.edu
SMITH, Josephine .... 412-809-5100. 430 H smith.josephine@pti.edu
SMITH, Joy, S .... 864-656-0471. 442 C joy@clemson.edu
SMITH, Joy, S .... 864-833-8275. 446 D jssmith@presby.edu
SMITH, Joyya .... 912-478-8746. 126 C joyyasmith@georgiasouthern.edu
SMITH, Judy .... 814-824-3650. 423 J jsmith@mercyhurst.edu
SMITH, June .... 402-481-3967. 288 H june.smith@bryanhealthcollege.edu
SMITH, June .... 325-942-2169. 465 K june.smith@angelo.edu
SMITH, Justin .... 910-642-7141. 364 A Justin.Smith@sccnc.edu
SMITH, Justin .... 580-477-7915. 401 J justin.smith@newmoodle.wosc.edu
SMITH, Kara .... 337-475-5148. 207 G ksmith2@mcneese.edu
SMITH, Karen .... 815-455-8781. 152 F ksmith@mchenry.edu
SMITH, Karen, J .... 251-981-3771..... 2 I karen.smith@columbiasouthern.edu
SMITH, Karen, J .... 914-831-0343. 321 B ksmith@cw.edu
SMITH, Katherine .... 702-968-2010. 295 E ksmith@roseman.edu
SMITH, Kathleen, E .... 562-902-3367... 67 H kathleensmith@scuhs.edu
SMITH, Kathleen, M .... 502-852-5419. 200 D kathleen@louisville.edu
SMITH, Kathryn .... 503-517-7462. 407 E smithk@reed.edu
SMITH, Kathy .... 614-234-2230. 384 J ksmith@mccn.edu
SMITH, Kathy .... 614-292-2991. 386 E
SMITH, Kathy, S .... 336-888-6391. 355 C ksmith@highpoint.edu
SMITH, Katie, J .... 651-631-5222. 263 A kjsmith@nwc.edu
SMITH, Katrina .... 806-291-3540. 494 F smithk@wbu.edu
SMITH, Kay, H .... 843-953-7402. 443 A smithkh@cofc.edu
SMITH, Keith .... 973-328-5400. 300 G ksmith@ccm.edu
SMITH, Keith .... 252-451-8264. 362 D ksmith@nashcc.edu
SMITH, Kelly .... 907-564-8289... 10 C kelsmith@alaskapacific.edu
SMITH, Kelly, A .... 804-523-5449. 512 F ksmith@reynolds.edu
SMITH, Kendra .... 425-235-2356. 522 F ksmith@rtc.edu
SMITH, Kenneth .... 508-929-8121. 230 G Kenneth.Smith@worcester.edu
SMITH, Kenneth, A .... 724-847-6610. 417 A kasmith@geneva.edu
SMITH, JR., Kent, J .... 405-466-3201. 395 N president@langston.edu
SMITH, Kevin, B .... 409-880-8400. 486 F kevin.smith@lamar.edu
SMITH, Kevin, J .... 773-508-7605. 151 H ksmit23@luc.edu
SMITH, Khrystal .... 864-503-5125. 448 H ksmith@uscupstate.edu
SMITH, Kimberley .... 352-854-2322. 100 K smithk@cf.edu
SMITH, Kimberly .... 423-697-3370. 460 C
SMITH, Kris .... 808-544-0840. 135 F ksmith@hpu.edu
SMITH, Kris, M .... 703-993-8841. 505 C ksmitr@gmu.edu
SMITH, Krista .... 229-928-1331. 126 D krista.smith@gsw.edu
SMITH, Kristen .... 516-686-7751. 333 H mksmith@nyit.edu
SMITH, Krystal, D .... 304-462-4101. 529 G krystal.smith@glenville.edu
SMITH, Kyle .... 325-235-7415. 486 C kyle.smith@tstc.edu
SMITH, Kyle .... 979-230-3489. 468 A kyle.smith@brazosport.edu
SMITH, Lane, M .... 205-726-2905..... 6 F
SMITH, Larry .... 310-954-4018... 54 J lsmith@msmc.la.edu
SMITH, LaTisha, T .... 314-340-3662. 275 A smithl@hssu.edu
SMITH, Laura .... 502-213-2136. 195 F laura.smith@kctcs.edu
SMITH, Laura, L .... 361-570-4801. 489 E smithl@uhv.edu
SMITH, Laurel, A .... 812-888-4176. 174 F lasmith@vinu.edu
SMITH, Laurens, H .... 435-797-2373. 497 B lhsmith@cc.usu.edu
SMITH, Lawrence .... 516-463-7202. 326 D lawrence.smith@hofstra.edu
SMITH, Leanne .... 901-572-2444. 453 B leanne.smith@bchs.edu
SMITH, Lee .... 928-541-7777... 16 B lsmith@ncu.edu
SMITH, Lee .... 205-934-2384..... 8 E lmsmith@uab.edu
SMITH, Lee, C .... 662-254-3721. 269 A lcsmith@mvsu.edu
SMITH, Leila .... 606-436-5721. 195 C leila.smith@kctcs.edu
SMITH, Les .... 801-375-5125. 496 G lsmith@rmuohp.edu
SMITH, Leslie .... 601-643-8340. 266 F leslie.smith@colin.edu
SMITH, Leslie .... 804-333-6781. 513 G lsmith@rappahannock.edu
SMITH, Leslie, M .... 812-888-4501. 174 F lmsmith@vinu.edu
SMITH, Lewis .... 312-503-0501. 155 D ljsmith@northwestern.edu
SMITH, Linda .... 340-692-4023. 555 E lsmith@live.uvi.edu
SMITH, Linda, P .... 856-351-2644. 307 B lsmith@salemcc.edu
SMITH, Lisa .... 352-854-2322. 100 K smithl@cf.edu
SMITH, Lisa .... 931-363-9805. 456 C lsmith@martinmethodist.edu
SMITH, Lois .... 704-991-0249. 364 C
SMITH, Lorraine .... 716-375-7873. 338 E lsmith@sbu.edu
SMITH, LuAnn .... 801-863-8472. 497 C smithlu@uvu.edu
SMITH, Lura .... 978-656-3110. 232 B smithlm@middlesex.mass.edu
SMITH, Lynn .... 727-726-1153. 100 E lynnsmith@clearwater.edu
SMITH, Lynn .... 606-546-1206. 200 A tlsmith@unionky.edu
SMITH, M. Scott .... 859-257-4772. 200 C mssmith@uky.edu
SMITH, Mable, H .... 702-968-2075. 295 E msmith@roseman.edu
SMITH, MacKenzie .... 530-752-2110... 70 J macsmith@ucdavis.edu
SMITH, Madeleine .... 317-738-8051. 165 I msmith3@franklincollege.edu
SMITH, Malia .... 808-543-8068. 135 F msmith@hpu.edu
SMITH, Malinda .... 607-274-3222. 327 E mbsmith@ithaca.edu
SMITH, Marcie .... 334-844-5588..... 1 G smithmc@auburn.edu
SMITH, Marcus .... 575-769-4014. 309 F marcus.smith@clovis.edu
SMITH, Margaret .... 607-778-5180. 315 I smithma@sunybroome.edu
SMITH, Margaret, D .... 931-540-2517. 460 E margaret.smith@columbiastate.edu
SMITH, Marian .... 270-384-7351. 197 D smithm@lindsey.edu
SMITH, Marian .... 410-225-2237. 216 C mariansmith@mica.edu
SMITH, Marianne .... 626-914-8701... 38 K msmith@citruscollege.edu
SMITH, Marianne .... 610-896-1298. 418 F msmith@haverford.edu
SMITH, Maribel .... 305-628-6704. 112 F maribel.smith@stu.edu
SMITH, Marie .... 916-484-8211... 53 A smithm@arc.losrios.edu
SMITH, Marilyn .... 303-914-6301... 84 I marilyn.smith@rrcc.edu
SMITH, Marilyn .... 763-433-1306. 257 P marilyn.smith@anokaramsey.edu
SMITH, Mark .... 607-871-2494. 313 E msmith@alfred.edu
SMITH, Mark .... 518-276-6266. 337 I smithm@rpi.edu
SMITH, Mark .... 615-327-6336. 456 E msmith@mmc.edu
SMITH, Mark, A .... 254-298-8344. 482 C mark.a.smith@templejc.edu
SMITH, Mark, A .... 740-477-7713. 385 L mark.smith@ohiochristian.edu
SMITH, Mark, J .... 765-494-2604. 171 M mjts@purdue.edu
SMITH, Mark, W .... 314-935-6489. 284 L msmith@wustl.edu
SMITH, Marla .... 605-995-7157. 450 E marla.smith@mitchelltech.edu
SMITH, Marlaine .... 561-297-3207. 114 L msmit230@fau.edu
SMITH, Marsha .... 319-656-2447. 182 D
SMITH, Martha, J .... 260-359-4040. 166 O msmith@huntington.edu
SMITH, Martha, J .... 757-352-4070. 508 G martsmi@regent.edu
SMITH, Martha, L .... 601-403-1269. 269 D mbyrd@prcc.edu
SMITH, Martin, W .... 309-556-3710. 148 B mwsmith@iwu.edu
SMITH, Marvin .... 563-288-6162. 178 B msmith@eicc.edu
SMITH, Mary, A .... 713-500-9236. 492 E mary.a.smith@uth.tmc.edu
SMITH, Mary, C .... 478-289-2165. 124 C mcsmith@ega.edu
SMITH, Mary, J .... 701-323-6271. 372 I Mary.J.Smith@SanfordCollege.edu
SMITH, Matt .... 931-372-3124. 460 A mrsmith@tntech.edu
SMITH, Matthew .... 717-815-6579. 438 D cmsmith@ycp.edu
SMITH, Matthew, J .... 269-399-7700. 174 C msmith@sf.edu
SMITH, Matthew, J .... 253-535-7545. 521 I smithmf@plu.edu
SMITH, Maureen, A .... 617-296-8300. 227 I maureen_smith@laboure.edu
SMITH, Melissa .... 415-439-2413... 27 M mysmith@act-sf.org
SMITH, Micah .... 731-989-6005. 454 J msmith@fhu.edu
SMITH, Michael .... 513-585-0361. 376 I michael.smith@thechristcollege.edu
SMITH, Michael .... 850-599-3868. 114 K michael.smith@famu.edu
SMITH, Michael .... 770-426-1193. 128 D michael.smith@life.edu
SMITH, Michael .... 660-543-4523. 283 A msmith@ucmo.edu

SMITH, Michael ... 806-720-7521. 476 B michael.smith@lcu.edu
SMITH, Michael, A ... 434-223-6219. 505 E msmith@hsc.edu
SMITH, Michael, D ... 617-495-1566. 227 C mike_smith@harvard.edu
SMITH, Michael, J ... 401-874-4977. 440 D msmith@foundation.uri.edu
SMITH, Michael, J ... 419-824-3723. 383 C msmith@lourdes.edu
SMITH, Michael, R ... 919-966-4107. 368 D msmith@sog.unc.edu
SMITH, Michael, R ... 915-747-5000. 492 A msmith4@utep.edu
SMITH, Michael, W ... 202-687-4798... 95 E smithm4@georgetown.edu
SMITH, Mike ... 903-586-2518. 474 N msmith@jacksonville-college.edu
SMITH, Mike ... 803-584-3446. 448 D pmsmith@mailbox.sc.edu
SMITH, Misty ... 918-343-7707. 399 C msmith@rsu.edu
SMITH, Molly, E ... 360-438-4310. 522 G msmith@stmartin.edu
SMITH, Molly Keene ... 859-336-5082. 198 J mollysmith@sccky.edu
SMITH, Morgan ... 603-428-2477. 297 D msmith@nec.edu
SMITH, Morgan ... 252-222-6240. 358 G smithm@carteret.edu
SMITH, Myra, D ... 413-755-4414. 233 A msmith@stcc.edu
SMITH, JR., Myron, J ... 423-636-7320. 462 E jsmith@tusculum.edu
SMITH, Nan, L ... 610-359-7355. 414 D nsmith@dccc.edu
SMITH, Nancy ... 325-793-4667. 476 E smith.nancy@mcm.edu
SMITH, Nancy ... 719-255-4411... 85 M nsmith2@uccs.edu
SMITH, Nancy, L ... 607-746-4665. 345 G smithnl@delhi.edu
SMITH, Naomi ... 760-921-5453... 58 C naomi.smith@paloverde.edu
SMITH, Nichloas, A ... 508-767-7416. 222 C na.smith@assumption.edu
SMITH, Nicola ... 425-640-1554. 519 D nsmith@edcc.edu
SMITH, Noreen ... 212-343-1234. 331 D nsmith@mcny.edu
SMITH, Norma ... 972-599-3159. 469 G nsmith@collin.edu
SMITH, Norma, M ... 207-768-2788. 210 M nsmith@nmcc.edu
SMITH, Norman ... 727-864-7676. 101 N smithnr@eckerd.edu
SMITH, Norman ... 256-228-6001..... 5 H smithn@nacc.edu
SMITH, Norman, R ... 631-244-3200. 323 B president@dowling.edu
SMITH, Ole, M ... 801-422-5500. 495 D ole_smith@byu.edu
SMITH, Paige ... 936-294-3981. 487 A paigesmith@shsu.edu
SMITH, Pam ... 303-937-4225... 79 E psmith@chu.edu
SMITH, Pam ... 727-341-3080. 112 E smith.pam@spcollege.edu
SMITH, Pamela ... 518-694-7268. 313 B pamela.smith@acphs.edu
SMITH, Pamela, A ... 918-631-2329. 401 F pamela-smith@utulsa.edu
SMITH, Pamela, J ... 215-368-5000. 410 F psmith@biblical.edu
SMITH, Pat, A ... 559-323-2100... 63 B psmith@sjcl.edu
SMITH, Patricia ... 909-537-5040... 34 E psmith@csusb.edu
SMITH, Patricia ... 931-372-3331. 460 A plsmith@tntech.edu
SMITH, Patricia, A ... 516-876-3092. 343 D smithp@oldwestbury.edu
SMITH, Paul, M ... 616-392-8555. 252 J pauls@westernsem.edu
SMITH, Paula ... 270-789-5211. 193 D pjsmith@campbellsville.edu
SMITH, Peggy ... 843-349-5269. 444 F peggy.smith@hgtc.edu
SMITH, Peggy ... 340-693-1446. 555 E psmith@live.uvi.edu
SMITH, Penny, L ... 814-871-7748. 416 K smith006@gannon.edu
SMITH, Peter, L ... 563-589-3668. 182 J plsmith@dbq.edu
SMITH, Peyton ... 608-262-8214. 536 D plsmith@bascom.wisc.edu
SMITH, Philip, A ... 678-891-2445. 125 G philip.smith@gpc.edu
SMITH, Pierre ... 312-935-4232. 148 C psmith@icsw.edu
SMITH, Quentin, R ... 806-356-4000. 487 E quentin.smith@ttuhsc.edu
SMITH, Rachel, E ... 814-865-7641. 426 A rem4@psu.edu
SMITH, Rae Marie ... 336-334-4822. 360 G rmsmith@gtcc.edu
SMITH, Raechell ... 816-802-3574. 275 J raechell@earthlink.net
SMITH, Randall, R ... 626-584-5363... 45 E rsmith@fuller.edu
SMITH, Randy ... 912-427-5829. 120 B rsmith@altamahatech.edu
SMITH, Randy ... 920-498-5505. 541 B randall.smith@nwtc.edu
SMITH, Randy, L ... 405-585-5810. 397 C randy.smith@okbu.edu
SMITH, Rashad ... 270-852-3126. 197 B rsmith@kwc.edu
SMITH, Rebecca, F ... 614-823-1400. 387 K rsmith@otterbein.edu
SMITH, Regina ... 310-660-3444... 43 B rsmith@elcamino.edu
SMITH, Regina ... 310-660-3670... 43 B rsmith@elcamino.edu
SMITH, Regina ... 212-757-1190. 313 H rtsmith@funeraleducation.org
SMITH, Rene ... 843-349-7835. 444 F rene.smith@hgtc.edu
SMITH, Richard ... 770-394-8300. 120 H rsmith@aii.edu
SMITH, Richard ... 770-787-8530. 126 A smithr@gptc.edu
SMITH, Richard ... 701-788-4697. 371 E Richard.E.Smith@mayvillestate.edu
SMITH, Richard, A ... 540-375-2203. 509 B rsmith@roanoke.edu
SMITH, Richard, J ... 314-935-4843. 284 L rjsmith@wustl.edu
SMITH, Richard, L ... 512-223-7792. 466 I rlsmith@austincc.edu
SMITH, Richard, S ... 718-409-7350. 346 D rsmith@sunymaritime.edu
SMITH, Rick ... 715-682-1597. 535 D rsmith@northland.edu
SMITH, Rick, H ... 910-695-3716. 363 F smithr@sandhills.edu
SMITH, Rilda ... 405-585-5260. 397 C rilda.smith@okbu.edu
SMITH, Robert ... 806-720-7111. 476 B robert.smith@lcu.edu
SMITH, Robert ... 612-728-5100. 264 A rsmith@smunm.edu
SMITH, Robert ... 601-979-2260. 267 E robert.m.smith@jsums.edu
SMITH, Robert ... 305-626-3168. 104 J Robert.Smith@fmuniv.edu
SMITH, Robert ... 205-929-6470..... 5 D rsmith@lawsonstate.edu
SMITH, Robert ... 617-824-8555. 226 A bob_smith@emerson.edu
SMITH, III, Robert ... 409-740-4403. 483 C rsmith101839@tamu.edu
SMITH, Robert, E ... 301-687-4489. 220 C rsmith@frostburg.edu
SMITH, Robert, R ... 520-621-7777... 18 F rrsmith@u.arizona.edu
SMITH, Robert, T ... 717-872-3407. 429 D robert.smith@millersville.edu
SMITH, Robert, W ... 208-282-7954. 139 D smithbob@uidaho.edu
SMITH, Robert, W ... 252-334-2018. 357 A bob.smith@macuniversity.edu
SMITH, Robet ... 859-985-3330. 192 F smithro@berea.edu
SMITH, Robin, R ... 517-750-1200. 250 E rsmith@arbor.edu
SMITH, Robin Ann ... 401-825-2096. 439 A rasmith@ccri.edu
SMITH, Roger ... 719-389-6897... 79 D roger.smith@coloradocollege.edu
SMITH, Roland, B ... 713-348-5688. 479 A rbsmith@rice.edu
SMITH, Roland, K ... 512-463-1887. 486 D roland.smith@tsus.edu
SMITH, Ron ... 408-741-2126... 75 J ron_smith@wvm.edu
SMITH, Ron ... 208-885-7090. 139 D smithr@uidaho.edu
SMITH, Ronette ... 515-244-4221. 175 C smithr@aib.edu
SMITH, Rosemary ... 920-424-3089. 537 B smithr@uwosh.edu
SMITH, Roslyn ... 845-341-4905. 335 H roz.smith@sunyorange.edu
SMITH, Rueben ... 626-585-7277... 58 F rcsmith@pasadena.edu
SMITH, Russell ... 402-554-2367. 293 A rsmith@unomaha.edu
SMITH, Ruth ... 757-825-2807. 514 B smithru@tncc.edu
SMITH, Ryan ... 256-726-7398..... 6 B
SMITH, Ryan ... 916-649-8168... 49 I rsmith@kaplan.edu
SMITH, Ryan, M ... 814-886-6373. 424 G rsmith@mtaloy.edu
SMITH, Sam ... 415-503-6265... 62 H ssmith@sfcm.edu
SMITH, Sam ... 615-966-6056. 456 B sam.smith@lipscomb.edu
SMITH, Sam, E ... 601-984-1065. 270 C sesmith@umc.edu
SMITH, Sandra, B ... 540-674-3600. 513 B ssmith@nr.edu
SMITH, Sandy ... 760-366-5296... 42 B ssmith@cmccd.edu
SMITH, Sara, E ... 918-270-6451. 398 I sara.smith@ptstulsa.edu
SMITH, Scott ... 706-865-2134. 133 B ssmith@truett.edu
SMITH, Scott, A ... 803-786-3672. 443 B scsmith@columbiasc.edu
SMITH, Scott, F ... 305-899-3085... 98 O sfsmith@barry.edu
SMITH, Scott, R ... 251-460-7093..... 9 E srsmith@southalabama.edu
SMITH, Sean ... 805-565-6061... 76 D sesmith@westmont.edu
SMITH, Sharon ... 205-726-2247..... 6 F ssmith12@samford.edu
SMITH, Sharon ... 202-495-3830... 96 C secretary@dhs.edu
SMITH, Sharon ... 609-984-1180. 308 A registrar@tesc.edu
SMITH, Sharon, E ... 616-632-2902. 239 E smithsha@aquinas.edu
SMITH, Sharon, P ... 828-652-0697. 362 A sharons@mcdowelltech.edu
SMITH, SharonAnn ... 618-374-5199. 156 B sharonann.smith@principia.edu
SMITH, Shawn ... 217-732-3168. 151 B ssmith@lincolnchristian.edu
SMITH, Sheila ... 615-329-8710. 454 F shsmith@fisk.edu
SMITH, Shelley ... 256-840-4128..... 6 I ssmith@snead.edu
SMITH, Shirley ... 714-484-7455... 56 E ssmith@cypresscollege.edu
SMITH, Solomon, S ... 405-466-3275. 395 N sssmith@langston.edu
SMITH, Stacie ... 904-680-7724. 103 Q ssmith@fcsl.edu
SMITH, Stan ... 702-895-3197. 294 I stan.smith@unlv.edu
SMITH, Stanley, B ... 864-656-2171. 442 C sbsmith@clemson.edu
SMITH, Stephanie ... 606-546-1259. 200 A sasmith@unionky.edu
SMITH, Stephanie ... 312-362-7552. 143 H ssmit185@depaul.edu
SMITH, Stephanie ... 770-962-7580. 127 D ssmith@gwinnetttech.edu
SMITH, Stephanie ... 304-696-2599. 529 H smiths@marshall.edu
SMITH, Stephanie, M ... 800-782-2422... 32 B smsmith@mail.cnuas.edu
SMITH, Stephanie, S ... 302-739-6819... 93 D ssmith@dtcc.edu
SMITH, Stephen ... 206-546-4694. 523 F spsmith@shoreline.edu
SMITH, Stephen, C ... 415-338-3879... 35 E scsmith@sfsu.edu
SMITH, Stephen, E ... 918-465-1723. 395 G ssmith@eosc.edu
SMITH, Stephen, P ... 215-951-1153. 420 B smiths@lasalle.edu
SMITH, Steve ... 951-343-4360... 30 H ssmith@calbaptist.edu
SMITH, Steve ... 716-829-7600. 323 D smith@dyc.edu
SMITH, Steve ... 910-410-1850. 362 I ssmith@richmondcc.edu
SMITH, Steve ... 256-765-4233..... 9 C wssmith@una.edu
SMITH, Steve ... 970-521-6657... 83 L steve.smith@njc.edu
SMITH, Steve ... 915-831-6472. 472 B ssmith54@epcc.edu
SMITH, Steve ... 865-974-4127. 463 C
SMITH, Steve ... 512-837-2665. 475 G jbrooks@tca.edu
SMITH, Steve ... 505-323-9282. 494 F smiths@wbu.edu
SMITH, Steve ... 802-586-7711. 500 E ssmith@sterlingcollege.edu
SMITH, Steve, A ... 801-422-6291. 495 D steve_smith@byu.edu
SMITH, Steven ... 707-826-3256... 35 C ss7006@humboldt.edu
SMITH, Steven ... 601-979-6944. 267 E steven.smith@jsums.edu
SMITH, Steven ... 715-344-3063. 540 D steve.smith@mstc.edu
SMITH, Steven ... 410-455-1511. 219 D smithst@umbc.edu
SMITH, Steven ... 601-977-4462. 270 A ssmith@tougaloo.edu
SMITH, Steven ... 817-923-1921. 481 G swsmith@swbts.edu
SMITH, Steven, F ... 989-774-7328. 240 N smith1sf@cmich.edu
SMITH, Steven, J ... 413-565-1000. 222 F ssmith@baypath.edu
SMITH, Steven, N ... 262-243-5700. 532 H steve.smith@cuw.edu
SMITH, Stuart ... 501-812-2256... 22 G ssmith@pulaskitech.edu
SMITH, Stuart, A ... 859-858-3511. 192 B stuart.smith@asbury.edu
SMITH, Sue ... 916-361-1660... 36 H ssmith@carrington.edu
SMITH, Susan ... 858-534-3583... 71 F susmith@ucsd.edu
SMITH, Susan, M ... 305-628-6661. 112 F ssmith@stu.edu
SMITH, Susanne ... 614-947-6160. 380 A suzanne.smith@franklin.edu
SMITH, Suzanne ... 413-755-4221. 233 A smsmith@stcc.edu
SMITH, Sybil ... 425-352-8133. 517 E ssmith@cascadia.edu
SMITH, Sylvia, A ... 706-880-8229. 128 A ssmith@lagrange.edu
SMITH, Tamalea ... 908-709-7093. 308 B tsmith@ucc.edu
SMITH, Teresa ... 850-201-8590. 117 D smithte@tcc.fl.edu
SMITH, Teresa ... 843-953-5660. 443 A smitht@cofc.edu
SMITH, Teresa, C ... 217-245-3002. 146 F tcsmith@ic.edu
SMITH, Teresa, L ... 714-879-3901... 47 K tlsmith@hiu.edu
SMITH, Teresa, L ... 504-278-6491. 203 F tsmith@nunez.edu
SMITH, Terri ... 661-763-7700... 69 D tsmith@taftcollege.edu
SMITH, Terri ... 336-249-8186. 360 A tlsmith@davidsonccc.edu
SMITH, Terry ... 713-646-1708. 480 J tsmith@stcl.edu
SMITH, Terry, B ... 573-875-7500. 272 G tsmith@ccis.edu
SMITH, Terry, L ... 814-732-2400. 428 E tlsmith@edinboro.edu
SMITH, Terry, S ... 512-505-3004. 473 G tssmith@htu.edu
SMITH, Theresa ... 515-643-6732. 181 A tsmith@mercydesmoines.org
SMITH, Therese, A ... 989-328-1284. 247 D terrys@montcalm.edu
SMITH, Thomas ... 314-392-2264. 278 B smitht@mobap.edu
SMITH, Thomas ... 970-351-2838... 86 C thomas.smith@unco.edu
SMITH, Thomas, J ... 616-234-3951. 243 B tsmith@grcc.edu
SMITH, Thomas, M ... 225-578-4843. 204 O tmsmith@lsu.edu
SMITH, Thomas, P ... 570-941-7620. 436 A thomas.smith@scranton.edu
SMITH, Thomas, W ... 610-519-4651. 436 F thomas.w.smith@villanova.edu
SMITH, Tierra ... 813-253-7160. 106 M tsmith175@hccfl.edu
SMITH, Tiffany ... 770-426-2780. 128 D tiffany.smith@life.edu
SMITH, Tilmon ... 202-806-2940... 95 G tilmon.smith@howard.edu
SMITH, Tim ... 773-838-7526. 142 E tsmith2@ccc.edu
SMITH, Timothy ... 731-661-5201. 462 F tsmith@uu.edu
SMITH, Todd ... 801-818-8900. 496 F todd.smith@provocollege.edu
SMITH, Tom ... 479-575-3208... 23 I tecsmith@uark.edu
SMITH, Tomesa ... 256-352-8233..... 9 G tomesa.smith@wallacestate.edu
SMITH, Tommy ... 504-671-5608. 203 A tsmith@dcc.edu
SMITH, Tracy ... 617-912-9193. 224 B tsmith@bostonconservatory.edu
SMITH, Tracy ... 601-403-1332. 269 D tsmith@prcc.edu
SMITH, Tracy ... 336-334-7631. 367 E tellmore@ncat.edu
SMITH, Tracy, D ... 501-882-8806... 19 M tdsmith@asub.edu
SMITH, Travis ... 315-386-7300. 345 F smitht@canton.edu
SMITH, Trent ... 620-276-9510. 187 A trent.smith@gcccks.edu

SMITH, Treva .... 706-864-1902. 133 D
treva.smith@ung.edu
SMITH, Tyre .... 816-412-7702. 450 G
tsmith@national.edu
SMITH, Valerie .... 609-258-3040. 304 E
SMITH, Valerie, T .... 617-228-2032. 231 C
vtsmith@bhcc.mass.edu
SMITH, Vergina .... 501-337-5000... 20 J
vsmith@coto.edu
SMITH, Vicki .... 301-784-5000. 213 B
vsmith@allegany.edu
SMITH, Vicki .... 315-536-5666. 328 D
vlsmith@mail.keuka.edu
SMITH, Vicky .... 319-363-8213. 181 C
vsmith@mtmercy.edu
SMITH, Vicky .... 815-455-8725. 152 F
vsmith@mchenry.edu
SMITH, Victoria .... 315-279-5255. 328 D
vsmith@mail.keuka.edu
SMITH, W. Stuart .... 843-792-4000. 445 B
smithstu@musc.edu
SMITH, Walter .... 301-846-2674. 214 H
wsmith@frederick.edu
SMITH, Walter, L .... 765-641-4156. 163 L
wlsmith@anderson.edu
SMITH, Wendall .... 610-896-1000. 418 F
w1smith@haverford.edu
SMITH, Wendy, B .... 724-847-6104. 417 A
wbsmith@geneva.edu
SMITH, Wendy, M .... 307-674-6446. 543 F
wsmith@sheridan.edu
SMITH, Whitman .... 662-915-7226. 270 B
whitman@olemiss.edu
SMITH, William, C .... 508-767-7157. 222 C
wc.smith@assumption.edu
SMITH, William, G .... 252-335-3225. 367 C
wgsmith@mail.ecsu.edu
SMITH, William, S .... 508-531-1100. 229 D
w1smith@bridgew.edu
SMITH, Willie .... 337-521-8896. 203 I
willie.smith@southlouisiana.edu
SMITH, Zach .... 951-827-5611... 71 E
zach.smith@ucr.edu
SMITH-BATES, Jacqui, S 206-281-2488. 523 C
jacquisb@spu.edu
SMITH-BRUSH, Lynn ..... 972-273-3464. 471 B
lsmith@dcccd.edu
SMITH-BUTLER, Lisa ...... 843-377-2144. 441 G
lsbutler@charlestonlaw.edu
SMITH-CAMPBELL,
Vesta .... 517-338-3042. 241 A
vscampbell@cleary.edu
SMITH-CLAY, Deborah ... 859-371-9393. 192 D
dsmithclay@beckfield.edu
SMITH-COX, Cathy .... 276-964-7340. 514 A
cathy.smith-cox@sw.edu
SMITH-EGGERT, Megan . 312-935-4141. 156 K
msmith@robertmorris.edu
SMITH-HOWELL, Deb ...... 402-554-3378. 293 A
dsmith-howell@unomaha.edu
SMITH-HUPP, Karen .... 301-934-7701. 214 D
karens@csmd.edu
SMITH-IRONS, Nancy ..... 312-935-3030. 156 K
nsmithirons@robertmorris.edu
SMITH-KIAWU, Rena .... 718-997-5100. 319 C
rena.smithkiawu@qc.cuny.edu
SMITH-MCQUEENIE,
Lisa .... 617-521-2120. 236 G
lisa.smithmcqueenie@simmons.edu
SMITH MORGAN, Terry . 334-683-5100..... 5 C
tmorgan1@judson.edu
SMITH-MURPHY,
Victoria .... 773-995-3521. 141 J
vsmith34@csu.edu
SMITH-PATTERSON,
Trina .... 817-515-7059. 482 B
trina.patterson@tccd.edu
SMITH QUIST, Bonnie ... 614-947-6068. 380 A
bonnie.quist@frankli.edu
SMITH-ROBINSON,
Marilyn .... 404-225-4612. 121 B
msmithro@atlantatech.edu
SMITH-SEBASTO,
Nicholas .... 908-737-3613. 302 F
nsmithse@kean.edu
SMITH-SIMMONS,
Margie .... 317-274-5434. 168 D
smithsim@iu.edu
SMITH-WARD, Lori, A .... 606-474-3121. 194 H
lsmithward@kcu.edu
SMITH-WORTHINGTON,
Darlene .... 252-493-7429. 362 G
dsmith@email.pittcc.edu
SMITHER, Robert .... 407-646-2280. 111 Q
rsmither@rollins.edu
SMITHEY, Van .... 386-752-1822. 104 G
van.smithey@fgc.edu
SMITHSON, Amanda ...... 281-756-3500. 465 D
asmithson@alvincollege.edu
SMITHSON, John, W ...... 610-660-1216. 432 E
smithson@sju.edu
SMITHSON, V. Scott ...... 219-785-5356. 172 A
ssmithson@pnc.edu
SMITLEY, Debra, K .... 309-438-2373. 147 J
dsmitle@ilstu.edu
SMITS, Karen .... 920-498-5615. 541 B
karen.smits@nwtc.edu
SMITS, Karen, J .... 920-498-5615. 541 B
karen.smits@nwtc.edu
SMITS, Peter, N .... 559-278-6050... 33 D
peter_smits@csufresno.edu
SMITS, Sally, A .... 414-425-8300. 535 K
ssmits@shst.edu
SMOCK, Cathy .... 979-458-7177. 482 E
cathy-smock@tamus.edu
SMOKOWSKI, Peter .... 617-358-7000. 224 D
psmokows@bu.edu
SMOLKO, Rita, M .... 330-287-1296. 386 F
smolko.3@osu.edu
SMOLOVA, Alona .... 757-823-8214. 507 M
asmolova@nsu.edu
SMOLSKI, Lisa .... 401-456-2809. 439 F
lsmolski@ric.edu
SMOOT, Kathy .... 606-487-3088. 195 C
Kathy.Smoot@kctcs.edu
SMOOT, Lori .... 410-334-2898. 221 D
lsmoot@worwic.edu
SMOROL, Bobbie, H .... 315-792-3128. 349 F
bsmorol@utica.edu
SMOTHERA, Roderick, L 512-505-3070. 473 G
rlsmothers@htu.edu
SMOTHERS, Traci .... 504-762-3004. 203 A
tsmoth@dcc.edu
SMRHA, Judith .... 785-594-8337. 184 C
judy.smrha@bakeru.edu
SMUCKER, Amy .... 330-966-5456. 389 F
asmucker@starkstate.edu
SMULSON, Erik .... 202-687-8496... 95 E
ems62@georgetown.edu
SMUNT, Timothy, L .... 414-229-6256. 537 A
tsmunt@uwm.edu
SMURDON, Melissa, J ... 317-940-8200. 164 J
msmurdon@butler.edu
SMUTZ, Wayne, D .... 814-863-6726. 426 A
wds4@psu.edu
SMYER, Michael, A .... 570-577-1561. 411 A
smyer@bucknell.edu
SMYLE, Faye .... 707-256-7156... 55 F
fsmyle@napavalley.edu
SMYRE, Russell .... 704-216-6130. 356 D
rsmyre@livingstone.edu
SMYRE HINES, Beverly .. 706-771-4156. 121 D
bsmyre@augustatech.edu
SMYRL, Kevin, A .... 404-364-8333. 130 A
ksmyrl@oglethorpe.edu
SMYRSKI, Rose, M .... 608-342-1282. 537 D
smyrskir@uwplatt.edu
SMYTH, Conor .... 608-266-2991. 539 H
conor.smyth@wtcsystem.edu
SMYTH, Curt .... 207-602-2562. 213 A
csmyth@une.edu
SMYTH, Nancy, J .... 716-645-1267. 341 F
sw-dean@buffalo.edu
SMYTH, Sheila .... 585-271-3657. 338 D
ssmyth@stbernards.edu
SMYTH-MCGAHA,
Bonnie .... 501-882-8826... 19 M
bmsmyth@asub.edu
SMYTHE, Jennifer .... 503-352-2770. 407 A
smythej@pacificu.edu
SNAPP, Diana .... 207-326-2243. 211 D
diana.snapp@mma.edu
SNAPP, John .... 325-670-1507. 472 O
John.Snapp@hsutx.edu
SNARE, Charles .... 308-432-6203. 291 D
csnare@csc.edu
SNAVELY, Deanne .... 724-357-2609. 428 F
Deanne.Snavely@iup.edu
SNAZA, DeeAnn .... 507-389-1111. 259 G
deeann.snaza@mnsu.edu
SNEAD, III, L. Rucker .... 434-223-6106. 505 E
rsnead@hsc.edu
SNEDDEN, Kelly .... 316-942-4291. 189 E
sneddenk@newmanu.edu
SNEDDON, Jay, N .... 208-732-6247. 138 B
jsneddon@csi.edu
SNEED, Bronwyn, C .... 870-235-4023... 23 F
bcsneed@saumag.edu
SNEED, Carlos .... 651-523-2423. 256 A
csneed@hamline.edu
SNEED, Janice .... 318-670-9471. 207 A
jsneed@susla.edu
SNEED, Mike .... 501-812-2238... 22 G
msneed@pulaskitech.edu
SNEED-JACOBS,
Mychell .... 610-869-5113. 414 D
msneedjacobs@dccc.edu
SNEERINGER, Megan ..... 215-641-6535. 424 B
msneerin@mc3.edu
SNELL, Carolyn, R .... 803-535-5338. 442 B
csnell@claflin.edu
SNELL, Kim .... 937-298-3399. 382 K
kim.snell@kc.edu
SNELL, Laurence, I .... 904-632-3294. 105 E
lsnell@fscj.edu
SNELL, Tiffany .... 225-308-4401. 202 G
tsnell@lctcs.edu
SNELLGROVE,
Michael, R .... 256-824-2560..... 8 F
michael.snellgrove@uah.edu
SNELLING, John .... 602-787-6840... 15 B
john.snelling@paradisevalley.edu
SNELSON, Pamela .... 717-291-3843. 416 J
pam.snelson@fandm.edu
SNIDER, Ann .... 614-253-3537. 386 B
snidera@ohiodominican.edu
SNIDER, Blake .... 864-656-4097. 442 C
sniderb@clemson.edu
SNIDER, Darlene .... 509-527-3689. 524 H
darlene.snider@wwcc.edu
SNIDER, Dean, C .... 509-527-5288. 525 E
sniderdc@whitman.edu
SNIDER, Donnie .... 325-674-2946. 464 H
donnie.snider@acu.edu
SNIDER, Dwayne .... 254-968-9103. 483 A
snider@tarleton.edu
SNIDER, Glen .... 928-428-8217... 13 J
glen.snider@eac.edu
SNIDER, Katharine, J ...... 717-291-3989. 416 J
kate.snider@fandm.edu
SNIDER, Lisa .... 318-371-3035. 203 E
lsnider@ltc.edu
SNIDER, Lora .... 859-622-2246. 193 P
lora.snider@eku.edu
SNIDER, Neil .... 205-652-3614..... 9 F
nsnider@uwa.edu
SNIDER, Theresa .... 540-338-2700. 503 A
tsnider@cdu.edu
SNIP, Bob .... 502-897-4703. 199 B
besnip@sbts.edu
SNIPES, Lloyd .... 803-327-7402. 442 D
SNITKER, Connie .... 319-363-8213. 181 C
csnitker@mtmercy.edu
SNODDY, Catherine, E ... 304-697-7550. 526 H
csnoddy@huntingtonjuniorcollege.edu
SNODGRASS, Burnie, L .. 417-836-4040. 278 E
bsnodgrass@missouristate.edu
SNODGRASS, Gregory .... 512-245-2208. 487 C
gs03@txstate.edu
SNODGRASS, Madelyn ... 512-472-4133. 480 G
madelyn.snodgrass@ssw.edu
SNODGRASS, Mark, T .... 815-740-3432. 162 F
msnodgrass@stfrancis.edu
SNODGRASS, Rosemary . 256-765-7111..... 4 B
rsnodgrass@hcu.edu
SNODGRASS, Wendell ... 509-452-5100. 521 J
SNOE, Terri .... 412-392-4207. 431 B
tsnoe@pointpark.edu
SNOOK, Dawn .... 704-637-4416. 353 E
dsnook@catawba.edu
SNOREK, Karen .... 507-332-5890. 261 E
karen.snorek@southcentral.edu
SNOVER, Lydia, S .... 617-253-5838. 233 B
SNOW, Barbara .... 607-962-9223. 322 B
snow@corning-cc.edu
SNOW, Cathy, C .... 478-757-5173. 134 G
csnow@wesleyancollege.edu
SNOW, Darian .... 608-757-7706. 539 I
dsnow@blackhawk.edu
SNOW, Kathryn .... 815-288-5511. 158 K
snowk@svcc.edu
SNOW, Kathryn .... 434-961-5275. 513 F
ksnow@pvcc.edu
SNOW, Laura .... 816-483-9600. 190 D
laura.snow@spst.edu
SNOW, Marie .... 904-470-8124. 102 A
marie.snow@ewc.edu
SNOW, Natalie .... 610-683-4153. 429 A
snow@kutztown.edu
SNOW, Nicholas .... 973-761-9018. 307 C
nicholas.snow@shu.edu
SNOW-FLAMER, Keith ...... 707-476-4177... 40 H
keith-snowflamer@redwoods.edu
SNOW FLESHER, LeAnn 510-841-1905... 27 H
lflesher@absw.edu
SNOWDEN, Bradley, C ... 540-665-5455. 509 E
bsnowden@su.edu
SNOWDEN, Kent .... 334-241-9783..... 7 H
kesnowden@troy.edu
SNOWDEN, Michael, T ... 337-475-5426. 207 G
msnowden@mcneese.edu
SNOWDEN, Monique, L . 805-898-4154... 44 I
msnowden@fielding.edu
SNOWDEN, Scott .... 908-737-5170. 302 F
snowdens@kean.edu
SNUFFIN, Gary .... 901-722-3260. 458 K
gsnuffin@sco.edu
SNUGGS, Kristi, L .... 252-823-5166. 360 C
snuggsk@edgecombe.edu
SNYDER, Alan, J .... 610-758-6964. 422 A
ajs410@lehigh.edu
SNYDER, Alan, R .... 301-687-4242. 220 C
arsnyder@frostburg.edu
SNYDER, Andrea .... 717-545-4747. 419 O
SNYDER, Angie, P .... 479-248-7236... 21 B
angie@ecollege.edu
SNYDER, Arthur, E .... 260-422-5561. 167 B
aesnyder@indianatech.edu
SNYDER, Barbara, H .... 801-581-7793. 496 Q
bsnyder@sa.utah.edu
SNYDER, Barbara, R .... 216-368-4344. 375 J
barbara.snyder@case.edu
SNYDER, C. Vernon .... 419-530-4249. 392 B
vernon.snyder@utoledo.edu
SNYDER, Chris .... 724-830-1895. 433 E
csnyder@setonhill.edu
SNYDER, Christopher ..... 662-325-2522. 268 D
cas741@msstate.edu
SNYDER, Cindy, L .... 540-654-2062. 510 J
csnyder@umw.edu
SNYDER, Darla .... 217-641-4205. 148 M
dsnyder@jwcc.edu
SNYDER, David .... 415-485-9506... 40 G
david.snyder@marin.edu
SNYDER, David, W .... 717-545-4747. 419 O
SNYDER, Dee Dee .... 330-287-1223. 386 F
snyder.426@osu.edu
SNYDER, Diane, E .... 210-485-0010. 464 I
dsnyder12@alamo.edu
SNYDER, Dianne, O .... 704-403-1521. 352 J
dianne.snyder@carolinashealthcare.org
SNYDER, Donald .... 702-895-3308. 294 I
donald.snyder@unlv.edu
SNYDER, Donald, W .... 610-799-1121. 421 I
dsnyder@lccc.edu
SNYDER, Edward, A .... 203-432-6035... 93 A
edward.snyder@yale.edu
SNYDER, Gerry .... 505-473-6292. 311 K
gerry.snyder@santafeuniversity.edu
SNYDER, Grant, S .... 610-359-5060. 414 D
gsnyder@dccc.edu
SNYDER, Gregory, J .... 810-762-3488. 251 E
gsnyders@umflint.edu
SNYDER, Jacqueline .... 413-565-1000. 222 F
jsnyder@baypath.edu
SNYDER, Jan .... 262-524-1211. 532 C
jsnyder@carrollu.edu
SNYDER, Jan, E .... 712-324-5061. 181 G
jsnyder@nwicc.edu
SNYDER, Jason .... 205-970-9235..... 7 B
jsnyder@sebc.edu
SNYDER, Jeff, B .... 651-631-5142. 263 A
jbsnyder@nwc.edu
SNYDER, Jenefer .... 757-822-2430. 514 C
jsnyder@tcc.edu
SNYDER, Jim .... 859-336-5082. 198 J
jsnyder@sccky.edu
SNYDER, John, F .... 724-738-2028. 429 F
john.snyder@sru.edu
SNYDER, Jon, D .... 212-875-4466. 314 C
jsnyder@bankstreet.edu
SNYDER, Joshua .... 513-244-8442. 376 J
joshua.snyder@ccuniversity.edu
SNYDER, Julie, A .... 419-372-9623. 374 K
jmaiuri@bgsu.edu
SNYDER, Katherine .... 301-687-4105. 220 C
ksnyder@frostburg.edu
SNYDER, Keith .... 423-236-2929. 458 J
kasnyder@southern.edu
SNYDER, Kenneth .... 517-629-0213. 239 A
ksnyder@albion.edu
SNYDER, Ky, L .... 619-260-2930... 73 I
kysnyder@sandiego.edu
SNYDER, Lesley, A .... 704-687-8693. 368 E
lasnyder@uncc.edu
SNYDER, Linda .... 617-627-3334. 237 C
linda.snyder@tufts.edu
SNYDER, Lisa .... 864-977-7669. 445 H
lisa.snyder@ngu.edu
SNYDER, Lisa, M .... 260-356-4070. 166 O
lsnyder@huntington.edu
SNYDER, Lorraine, G ...... 312-915-6411. 151 H
lsnyde2@luc.edu
SNYDER, Marcella .... 304-336-8345. 530 A
msnyder@westliberty.edu
SNYDER, Marian, L .... 610-799-1734. 421 I
msnyder@lccc.edu
SNYDER, Mary .... 719-255-4119... 85 M
mary.snyder@uccs.edu
SNYDER, Matthew .... 315-792-5331. 331 I
msnyder2@mvcc.edu
SNYDER, Paul .... 239-590-7050. 115 A
psnyder@fgcu.edu
SNYDER, Randolph .... 614-947-6024. 380 A
randy.snyder@franklin.edu
SNYDER, Reonna .... 515-244-4221. 175 C
snyderr@aib.edu
SNYDER, Rob, A .... 724-287-8711. 411 C
rob.snyder@bc3.edu
SNYDER, Robert, A .... 707-826-3722... 35 C
ras1@humboldt.edu

SNYDER, Robert, J .... 610-282-1100. 414 F
robert.snyder@desales.edu
SNYDER, Sandra .... 503-552-1514. 404 H
ssnyder@ncnm.edu
SNYDER, Sheri .... 580-628-6208. 396 M
sheri.snyder@noc.edu
SNYDER, Stephen, E ...... 229-931-2037. 126 D
stephen.snyder@gsw.edu
SNYDER, Steven, C .... 540-636-2900. 503 L
ssnyder@christendom.edu
SNYDER, Susan, M .... 716-829-3316. 341 F
student-health@buffalo.edu
SNYDER, Terry .... 610-896-1272. 418 F
tsnyder@haverford.edu
SNYDER, Thomas, J .... 317-921-4265. 169 K
tsnyder@ivytech.edu
SNYDER, Tim .... 414-443-8798. 539 F
tim.snyder@wlc.edu
SNYDER, Timothy, L ...... 410-617-2495. 216 A
tlsnyder@loyola.edu
SNYDER, Walter, W .... 816-654-7122. 275 K
wsnyder@kcumb.edu
SOARDS, Kathy .... 419-267-1314. 385 F
ksoards@northweststate.edu
SOBANET, Jennifer .... 303-404-5560... 81 N
jennifer.sobanet@frontrange.edu
SOBEK, Christine, J .... 630-466-7900. 162 J
csobek@waubonsee.edu
SOBH, Tarek, M .... 203-576-4111... 91 G
sobh@bridgeport.edu
SOBIERALSKI, Joe .... 803-641-3399. 448 A
joes@usca.edu
SOBIESUO, Andrew, M .. 843-953-5537. 443 A
sobiesuoa@cofc.edu
SOBISCH, Andreas .... 216-397-4183. 381 R
sobisch@jcu.edu
SOBKY-SHAFFER, Yvette 310-665-6819... 57 C
ysobky@otis.edu
SOBLEY, Susan .... 662-329-7210. 268 E
ssobley@comptroller.muw.edu
SOBOLEWSKI, Rich .... 662-329-7119. 268 E
rsobolewski@pa.muw.edu
SOBOLIK, Kristin .... 937-775-2225. 393 G
kristin.sobolik@wright.edu
SOBOTTA, Sharon .... 925-631-4193... 61 F
ssobotta@stmarys-ca.edu
SOCASH, Thomas .... 212-431-2825. 333 I
tsocash@nyls.edu
SOCCI, Patrick, J .... 516-463-5676. 326 D
patrick.socci@hofstra.edu
SOCHA, Maureen .... 413-755-4460. 233 A
mesocha@stcc.edu
SODEN, Richard .... 212-938-4030. 345 C
rsoden@sunyopt.edu
SODERBERG, Lynn .... 707-826-5555... 35 C
lls47@humboldt.edu
SODERQUIST, Rich .... 815-802-8173. 149 C
rsoderquist@kcc.edu
SOEFFING, William .... 605-331-6759. 452 D
william.soeffing@usiouxfalls.edu
SOEFFKER-CULICERTO,
Heike, I .... 304-929-6731. 528 D
hsoeffker@newriver.edu
SOENEN, Laurie, A .... 843-953-3418. 443 A
soenenl@cofc.edu
SOFFA, Kari .... 661-362-5417... 40 E
Kari.soffa@canyons.edu
SOFISH, Marion .... 408-283-7500... 36 A
marion.sofish@sjsu.edu
SOFO, Dianna .... 973-290-4478. 300 F
dsofo@cse.edu
SOFRANKO, Greg .... 724-938-4274. 428 A
sofranko@calu.edu
SOFTLEIGH, George .... 718-270-6095. 319 A
george@mec.cuny.edu
SOHAN, Donna .... 860-412-7261... 89 E
dsohan@qvcc.commnet.edu
SOHL, Amanda .... 614-236-6574. 375 H
asohl@capital.edu
SOHN, Christopher .... 937-766-2789. 375 K
chrissohn@cedarville.edu
SOHN, David, Y .... 703-941-2020. 505 H
SOHN, Eugene .... 718-518-4284. 318 B
esohn@hostos.cuny.edu
SOHOLT, Pam, B .... 701-788-4823. 371 E
Pam.Soholt@mayvillestate.edu
SOIFER, Aviam .... 808-956-6363. 136 B
soifer@hawaii.edu
SOIFER, B, T .... 626-395-4241... 31 E
pmachair@caltech.edu
SOIFER, Yitzchok .... 845-362-3053. 314 H
yitzchoks@bytsem.org
SOIFFER, Stephen .... 718-260-5400. 319 B
ssoiffer@citytech.cuny.edu
SOIKA, Brian .... 713-348-4726. 479 A
brian.soika@rice.edu
SOILEAU, M, J .... 407-823-5538. 115 E
mj@ucf.edu
SOJA, Walter .... 502-456-6504. 199 G
wsoja@sullivan.edu
SOJKA, Gregory, S .... 513-732-5209. 391 B
sojkagy@email.uc.edu
SOJO, Norma, I .... 787-265-3810. 554 E
library@uprm.edu
SOKANY, Stephen, G ...... 330-672-2222. 382 B
ssokany@kent.edu
SOKENU, Julius .... 805-378-1572... 74 F
jsokenu@vcccd.edu
SOKOL, Bryan .... 314-977-2041. 281 I
bsokol1@slu.edu
SOKOL, Karen, A .... 973-642-8738. 307 D
karen.sokol@shu.edu
SOKOL, Moshe, Z .... 718-820-4800. 348 B
sokolm@touro.edu
SOKOLOSKI, Matthew ...... 334-386-7914..... 3 H
msokoloski@faulkner.edu
SOKOLS, Patricia, L .... 864-488-8255. 444 L
psokols@limestone.edu
SOKOLSKY, Pierre, V ...... 801-581-6958. 496 Q
ps@physics.utah.edu
SOLA, Peter, L .... 651-631-5349. 263 A
plsola@nwc.edu
SOLAN, George .... 252-399-6399. 352 F
gsolan@barton.edu
SOLAND, Linda .... 602-285-7748... 15 C
linda.soland@phoenixcollege.edu
SOLANDER, Sondra, K .... 620-431-2820. 189 D
ssolander@neosho.edu
SOLANO, Laura .... 719-549-3221... 84 G
Laura.Solano@pueblocc.edu
SOLARI, Joe, P .... 317-788-3425. 173 I
jsolari@uindy.edu
SOLBACH, Robin .... 732-987-2681. 302 B
solbach@georgian.edu
SOLBERG, Eric, J .... 563-588-7969. 180 L
eric.solberg@loras.edu
SOLBERG, Larry .... 715-425-3774. 537 E
larry.c.solberg@uwrf.edu
SOLBERG, Lori .... 605-995-2805. 450 A
losolber@dwu.edu
SOLBERG, Susan, R .... 708-709-3758. 156 A
ssolberg@prairiestate.edu
SOLBRIG, Ronald .... 208-282-2330. 138 E
solbrona@isu.edu
SOLCHER, Iris .... 210-832-2110. 490 A
isolcher@uiwtx.edu
SOLDWISCH, Sandie .... 773-252-5345. 156 I
sandie.soldwisch@resu.edu
SOLEIM, Heather, M .... 218-477-4060. 259 H
heather.soleim@mnstate.edu
SOLEMSAAS, Rachel .... 775-673-7013. 294 H
rsolemsaas@tmcc.edu
SOLERNOU, Sheila .... 203-285-2393... 88 E
ssolernou@gwcc.commnet.edu
SOLES, Jason .... 903-923-2011. 471 J
jsoles@etbu.edu
SOLHEIM, Derek, N .... 319-352-8330. 183 E
derek.solheim@wartburg.edu
SOLHEIM, Joan, C .... 704-847-5600. 366 J
jsolheim@ses.edu
SOLIMON, Ron .... 505-424-5701. 309 J
rsolimon@iaia.edu
SOLINGA, Elaine, F .... 860-439-2058... 89 H
efsol@conncoll.edu
SOLIS, Enrique .... 512-223-7612. 466 I
enrique.solis@austincc.edu
SOLIS, JR., Federico ...... 956-764-5866. 475 F
fsolis@laredo.edu
SOLIS, Rafael .... 787-758-2525. 554 F
rafael.solis@upr.edu
SOLIS, Ricardo .... 713-718-8173. 473 C
ricardo.solis@hccs.edu
SOLIS, Robert .... 774-455-7711. 228 E
rsolis@umassp.edu
SOLIS, Vincent, R .... 956-764-5950. 475 F
vincent.solis@laredo.edu
SOLITRO, Patricia, A ...... 508-854-4203. 232 F
psolitro@qcc.mass.edu
SOLIZ, Sandra .... 713-525-3103. 490 L
solizs@stthom.edu
SOLL, Andrew .... 978-542-6120. 230 E
asoll@salemstate.edu
SOLLARS, David .... 785-670-2045. 191 D
david.sollars@washburn.edu
SOLLENBERGER,
Donna, K .... 409-772-6116. 493 C
dksoll@utmb.edu
SOLLER, Dan .... 301-447-7407. 217 B
soller@msmary.edu
SOLLER, Kerry .... 614-251-4718. 386 B
sollerk@ohiodominican.edu
SOLLEY, Anna .... 602-285-7433... 15 C
anna.solley@phoenixcollege.edu
SOLLOSI, Nancy, B .... 336-334-4822. 360 G
nbsollosi@gtcc.edu
SOLMS, Daniel .... 765-677-2138. 169 B
daniel.solms@indwes.edu
SOLNICK, Steven, L .... 828-298-3325. 370 E
president@warren-wilson.edu
SOLODUCHA, Kathy, J ... 816-501-4250. 280 I
kathy.soloducha@rockhurst.edu
SOLOMON, Brenda .... 310-303-7293... 53 F
bsolomom@marymountcalifornia.edu
SOLOMON, Daniel, L ...... 919-515-7277. 368 B
solomon@ncsu.edu
SOLOMON, Debbie .... 425-235-2352. 522 F
dsolomon@rtc.edu
SOLOMON, Ian, H .... 773-702-9781. 161 B
iansolomon@uchicago.edu
SOLOMON, Ira .... 504-865-5422. 207 C
isolomon@tulane.edu
SOLOMON, Jeffrey, S ..... 508-831-5288. 238 F
solomon@wpi.edu
SOLOMON, Jeremy .... 781-239-3122. 231 G
jsolomon@massbay.edu
SOLOMON, Jill .... 617-277-3915. 224 C
jsolomon@bgsp.edu
SOLOMON, Mendel .... 973-267-9404. 304 G
rabbisolo@aol.com
SOLOMON, Rayman, L .... 856-225-6191. 306 C
raysol@camlaw.rutgers.edu
SOLOMON, Robert .... 912-754-2879. 131 D
rsolomon@savannahtech.edu
SOLOMON, Samuel, B ... 617-373-2597. 235 F
SOLOMON, Shoshana .... 973-267-9404. 304 G
rca069@aol.com
SOLOMON, Sigrid, B ..... 937-382-6661. 393 B
sigrid_solomon@wilmington.edu
SOLOMON, Stephanie .... 803-754-4100. 443 C
SOLOMON, William, G .... 478-301-2771. 128 H
solomon_wg@mercer.edu
SOLOMONS, Mary, L ...... 518-580-5619. 341 A
msolomon@skidmore.edu
SOLOMONSON, Heidi .... 651-213-4126. 256 B
SOLOMONT, Alan .... 617-628-5000. 237 C
alan.solomont@tufts.edu
SOLORZANO, Fernando . 562-985-4101... 33 F
fsolorza@csulb.edu
SOLORZANO-THOMPSON,
Nohemy .... 801-832-2822. 498 F
nst@westminstercollege.edu
SOLSKI, Ed .... 661-824-2977... 55 I
SOLT, Karen .... 630-942-2292. 142 G
soltka@cod.edu
SOLT, Michael .... 562-985-5306... 33 F
msolt@csulb.edu
SOLTAN, Joanna .... 617-369-3655. 236 F
jsoltan@smfa.edu
SOLTANOVICH, Dorit ..... 818-774-0550... 43 M
SOLTIS, Corinne .... 907-796-6255... 11 A
corinne.soltic@uas.alaska.edu
SOLTIS, Kay, W .... 253-535-8725. 521 I
soltiskw@plu.edu
SOLTMAN, Mary .... 360-596-5364. 524 A
msoltman@spscc.edu
SOLTZ, David, L .... 570-389-4526. 427 H
dsoltz@bloomu.edu
SOLVASON, Nanette .... 650-940-7730... 44 N
solvasonnanette@foothill.edu
SOLVERSON, Natalie ...... 608-785-8006. 536 G
nsolverson@uwlax.edu
SOM, Andrew .... 415-338-3145... 35 E
asom@sfsu.edu
SOMAN, Rajiv, S .... 513-732-5212. 391 B
somanrs@ucmail.uc.edu
SOMAN, Sherril .... 616-331-3327. 243 C
somans@gvsu.edu
SOMERA, R. Ray, D .... 671-735-5528. 546 C
reneray.somera@guamcc.edu
SOMERO, Marty .... 970-351-2502... 86 C
marty.somero@unco.edu
SOMERS, Christine .... 570-674-6314. 424 A
csomers@misericordia.edu
SOMERS, Cindy .... 303-797-5972... 78 F
cindy.somers@arapahoe.edu
SOMERS, Kevin .... 870-743-3000... 22 B
ksomers@northark.edu
SOMERS, Michael .... 508-531-1255. 229 D
msomers@bridgew.edu
SOMERS, Micki .... 870-743-3000... 22 B
msomers@northark.edu
SOMERS, Robert, J .... 410-455-2695. 219 D
somers@umbc.edu
SOMERS, Vickie, L .... 336-278-5584. 354 B
somersv@elon.edu
SOMERSON, Rosanne .... 401-277-4945. 440 A
rsomerso@risd.edu
SOMERVELL, Ronald ...... 703-284-6941. 507 B
ronald.somervell@marymount.edu
SOMERVILLE, Charles .... 304-696-2424. 529 H
somervil@marshall.edu
SOMERVILLE, Dionne, D 570-389-4062. 427 H
dsomervi@bloomu.edu
SOMERVILLE, Jerry .... 707-256-7155... 55 F
jsomerville@napavalley.edu
SOMERVILLE, Mary .... 303-556-4587... 86 A
mary.somerville@ucdenver.edu
SOMERVILLE, Tim .... 951-719-2994... 60 D
doc@golfcollege.edu
SOMICH, Michael, L .... 919-613-7611. 354 A
msomich@duke.edu
SOMMA, Ann Marie .... 518-327-6201. 336 B
asomma@paulsmiths.edu
SOMMA, Lauren .... 951-781-2727... 61 C
lsomma@sagecollege.edu
SOMMA, Victor .... 508-425-1216. 232 F
vsomma@qcc.mass.edu
SOMMER, John .... 201-360-4042. 302 D
jsommer@hccc.edu
SOMMER, Maralyn .... 870-230-5134... 21 D
sommerm@hsu.edu
SOMMER, Sally, W .... 419-358-3317. 374 J
sommers@bluffton.edu
SOMMER, Toni .... 805-546-3120... 42 C
tsommer@cuesta.edu
SOMMERFELD, Curtis .... 541-956-7238. 407 F
curt@roguecc.edu
SOMMERFELD, Curtis .... 541-956-7016. 407 F
curt@roguecc.edu
SOMMERFELDT,
Scott, D .... 801-422-2674. 495 D
scott_sommerfeldt@byu.edu
SOMMERS, Bill .... 970-945-8691... 79 G
SOMMERS, Janet, B .... 651-631-5201. 263 A
jbsommers@nwc.edu
SOMMERS, Mary .... 308-865-8520. 292 H
sommersm@unk.edu
SOMMERS, Mary, C .... 713-942-5048. 490 L
sommers@stthom.edu
SOMMERS, Megan .... 252-940-6327. 358 A
megans@beaufortccc.edu
SOMMERS, Rhoda, C ..... 330-471-8538. 383 D
rsommers@malone.edu
SOMMERS, Robert, E ..... 260-359-4014. 166 O
rsommers@huntington.edu
SOMMERS, William, E .... 717-477-1231. 429 E
wesommers@ship.edu
SOMPOLSKI, Robert .... 847-635-1690. 155 F
somplski@oakton.edu
SOMVICHIAN, Kamol ...... 323-731-2383... 57 I
ksomvichian@psuca.edu
SON, Dong Won .... 636-327-4645. 277 K
son@midwest.edu
SON, Rachel .... 714-533-1495... 66 H
rachel@southbaylo.edu
SONDER, Henk, E .... 401-456-9577. 439 F
hsonder@ric.edu
SONDEY, Joann .... 914-831-0288. 321 B
jsondey@cw.edu
SONDEY, Stephen .... 201-684-7496. 305 A
ssondey@ramapo.edu
SONENBERG, Dave .... 402-437-2619. 292 C
dsonenbe@southeast.edu
SONES, Rodney .... 740-477-7786. 385 L
rsones@ohiochristian.edu
SONG, A. Li .... 516-364-0808. 333 D
asong@nycollege.edu
SONG, Bok, H .... 636-327-4645. 277 K
dbo@midwest.edu
SONG, Connie .... 513-231-2223. 374 D
csong@athenaeum.edu
SONG, HeeSook .... 770-279-0507. 124 I
joysong@gcuniv.edu
SONG, Jae, M .... 636-327-4645. 277 K
vpson@midwest.edu
SONG, Jae, P .... 636-327-4645. 277 K
jp@midwest.edu
SONG, James .... 636-327-4645. 277 K
president@midwest.edu
SONG, John, M .... 213-385-2322... 77 A
president@wmu.edu
SONG, Sarah .... 657-278-2304... 33 E
ssong@fullerton.edu
SONG,
Shin-Min (Simon) .... 330-672-9780. 382 B
ssong3@kent.edu
SONGER, Gerald .... 501-337-5000... 20 J
gsonger@coto.edu
SONGSTER, Nora .... 707-546-4000... 43 E
nsongster@empirecollege.com
SONGSTER, Roger .... 402-941-6128. 290 K
songster@midlandu.edu
SONI, Bharat .... 931-372-3374. 460 A
bsoni@tntech.edu
SONI, Jaya, K .... 512-505-3019. 473 G
jksoni@htu.edu
SONI, P. Sarita .... 812-855-3931. 167 F
sonip@indiana.edu
SONI, Varun .... 213-740-6110... 74 A
vasoni@usc.edu
SONJA, Daniels .... 310-243-3784... 33 B
sdaniels@csudh.edu
SONNEMA, Roy .... 719-549-2865... 80 K
roy.sonnema@colostate-pueblo.edu
SONNENBERG, Jeff .... 602-557-1740... 18 I
jeff.sonnenberg@phoenix.edu
SONNENBERG, Judith .... 512-863-1252. 481 I
sonnenbj@southwestern.edu
SONNENBERGER, David 630-829-6538. 140 B
dsonnenberger@ben.edu
SONNENBLICK, Carol .... 718-552-1170. 319 B
csonnenblick@citytech.cuny.edu

SONNENSTEIN, Mark ..... 718-933-6700. 331 K
ssonnenstein@monroecollege.edu
SONNENSTRAHL, Samuel .... 202-651-5060... 95 C
samuel.sonnenstrahl@gallaudet.edu
SONNENTAG, Rachel ...... 414-258-4810. 535 A
sonnentr@mtmary.edu
SONNER, Mary .... 423-636-7345. 462 E
msonner@tusculum.edu
SONNLEITNER, Thomas, G .... 920-424-3030. 537 B
sonnleit@uwosh.edu
SONNTAG, Dave .... 509-313-6192. 520 A
sonntagd@gonzaga.edu
SONNTAG, Gabriela .... 909-748-8096... 73 H
gabriela_sonntag@redlands.edu
SONNTAG, Michael, E .... 207-768-9520. 212 G
michael.sonntag@umpi.edu
SONODA, Kazuhiro .... 509-865-8581. 520 D
sonoda_k@heritage.edu
SONQUIST, Eric, J .... 805-893-8585... 72 B
eric.sonquist@ia.ucsb.edu
SONSTEBY, Jill .... 651-638-6254. 253 K
jks44888@bethel.edu
SONTAG, Michael .... 513-244-4766. 377 G
michael_sontag@mail.msj.edu
SOOHOO, Liane .... 206-239-2222. 516 H
lsoohoo@aii.edu
SOONS, Peter, D .... 802-654-2374. 500 B
psoons@smcvt.edu
SOOS, Lori .... 716-286-8390. 334 F
lsoos@niagara.edu
SOPCHAK, Elaine .... 802-224-3001. 501 A
elaine.sopchak@vsc.edu
SOPCICH, Joe .... 913-469-8500. 187 J
jsopcich@jccc.edu
SOPCZYK, Debbie .... 518-464-8728. 324 B
dsopczyk@excelsior.edu
SOPER, Elaine .... 304-647-6260. 530 B
esoper@osteo.wvsom.edu
SOPER, Sarah .... 765-973-8231. 167 G
saeaton@iue.edu
SOPKO, Bryn .... 503-943-7331. 408 F
sopko@up.edu
SORA, Gail .... 603-623-0313. 297 E
gsora@nhia.edu
SORACI, Ross .... 617-739-1700. 235 A
rsoraci@aii.edu
SORBER, Jerad .... 360-596-5240. 524 A
jsorber@spscc.edu
SORBER, Ken .... 801-274-3280. 498 E
ksorber@wgu.edu
SORBER, Todd .... 973-684-5656. 304 B
tsorber@pccc.edu
SORCE, Tanya .... 973-290-4465. 300 F
tsorce@cse.edu
SORCINELLI, Mary Deane .... 413-545-1225. 228 F
msorcinelli@acad.umass.edu
SORDELET, Teresa, A ..... 260-399-7700. 174 C
tsordelet@sf.edu
SORELLE, Patrick .... 920-465-2323. 536 F
sorellep@uwgb.edu
SOREM, JR., James, R .. 918-631-2288. 401 F
james-sorem@utulsa.edu
SORENSEN, Carl, K .... 804-289-8166. 510 L
csorense@richmond.edu
SORENSEN, Charles, W . 715-232-2441. 538 B
sorensenc@uwstout.edu
SORENSEN, Dennis .... 815-802-8360. 149 C
dsorensen@kcc.edu
SORENSEN, Gary .... 928-428-8247... 13 J
gary.sorensen@eac.edu
SORENSEN, Niles, F .... 704-687-7201. 368 E
nfsorens@uncc.edu
SORENSEN, Robin .... 704-378-1048. 355 K
rsorensen@jcsu.edu
SORENSEN, Sarah .... 801-524-8149. 495 O
ssorenson@ldsbc.edu
SORENSEN, Zak .... 616-538-2330. 243 A
zsorensen@gbcol.edu
SORENSON, Amanda ...... 573-288-6420. 273 F
asorenson@culver.edu
SORENSON, Jennifer ...... 612-332-3361. 253 G
jsorenson@aii.edu
SORENSON, Nancy .... 651-523-2103. 256 A
nsorenson01@hamline.edu
SORENSON, Sally .... 541-383-7216. 402 D
ssorenson@cocc.edu
SORENSON, Shad .... 801-863-7072. 497 C
shad.sorenson@uvu.edu
SOREY, Kellie .... 757-822-1065. 514 C
ksorey@tcc.edu
SORG, Charlotte .... 419-267-1317. 385 F
csorg@northweststate.edu
SORIA, Deborah .... 559-925-3316... 75 I
deborahsoria@whccd.edu
SORIA, Laura .... 773-777-4220. 155 B
lsoria@nc.edu
SORIANO, Brenda .... 212-962-0002. 333 B
bsoriano@nyci.edu
SORIERO, Julie .... 617-253-4499. 233 B
SORK, Victoria .... 310-825-7755... 71 C
vlsork@ucla.edu
SOROKES, Lawrence .... 716-375-2304. 338 E
lsorokes@sbu.edu
SORRELL, Carson .... 315-792-7456. 346 C
sorrelc@sunyit.edu
SORRELL, Clyde, H .... 240-567-5271. 216 F
rocky.sorrell@montgomerycollege.edu
SORRELL, Garry .... 660-596-7301. 282 G
gsorrell@sfccmo.edu
SORRELL, Michael, J ...... 214-379-5550. 478 D
president@pqc.edu
SORRELLS, Glenn .... 972-279-6511. 465 F
gsorrells@amberton.edu
SORRELS, Paul .... 830-279-3013. 487 B
psorrels@sulross.edu
SORRENTINO, Angelo .... 610-409-3359. 436 B
asorrentino@ursinus.edu
SORRENTINO, Donna Marie .... 603-862-2930. 298 C
dms@unh.edu
SORRENTINO, Sebastian 860-768-4034... 92 D
sorrentin@hartford.edu
SORRENTO, Anthony ...... 973-300-2769. 307 F
asorrento@sussex.edu
SORROW, Russ, L .... 770-484-1204. 128 E
rsorrow@lru.edu
SORTOR, Janet, M .... 207-741-5504. 211 A
jsortor@smccme.edu
SORTOR, Marci, J .... 507-786-3004. 264 B
sortor@stolaf.edu
SORVAAG, Scott .... 507-457-6612. 264 A
ssorvaag@smumn.edu
SOSA, Dona .... 212-343-1234. 331 D
dsosa@mcny.edu
SOSA, Horacio .... 856-256-4129. 305 E
sosa@rowan.edu
SOSA, Velma Leticia .... 787-761-0640. 553 F
biblioteca@cbp.edu
SOSA, Victor .... 603-862-2001. 298 C
victor.sosa@unh.edu
SOSA-HEGARTY, Dina, M .... 972-860-7205. 470 I
DinaSosa-Hegarty@dcccd.edu
SOSCIA, Peter .... 845-341-4180. 335 H
peter.soscia@sunyorange.edu
SOSNOWSKI, Scott .... 815-455-8720. 152 F
ssosnowski@mchenry.edu
SOSSEN, Nina .... 413-545-4741. 228 F
nsossen@admin.umass.edu
SOTHERDEN, James, J ... 717-691-6012. 423 L
jsotherd@messiah.edu
SOTHERLAND, Paul, R ... 269-337-7012. 244 K
Paul.Sotherland@kzoo.edu
SOTHMANN, Mark, S ..... 843-792-3031. 445 B
sothmann@musc.edu
SOTHMANN, Mark, S ..... 512-499-4201. 445 B
sothmann@musc.edu
SOTIROS, James .... 707-638-5460... 69 K
james.sotiros@tu.edu
SOTO, Amilcar .... 787-878-5475. 549 L
asoto@arecibo.inter.edu
SOTO, Arlene .... 541-756-6445. 407 H
asoto@socc.edu
SOTO, Bobby .... 214-333-5360. 470 D
bobby@dbu.edu
SOTO, Carlos .... 813-253-7860. 106 M
csoto@hccfl.edu
SOTO, Cecilia .... 602-243-8125... 15 F
cecilia.soto@southmountaincc.edu
SOTO, Edgar .... 520-206-3260... 17 A
esoto@pima.edu
SOTO, Emilia .... 787-269-4510. 553 C
emilia.soto@uccaribe.edu
SOTO, Emilia .... 787-740-6631. 553 C
emilia.soto@uccaribe.edu
SOTO, Jose .... 402-323-3412. 292 C
jsoto@southeast.edu
SOTO, Limaris .... 787-725-8120. 548 O
lisotoa@eap.edu
SOTO, Luis, A .... 787-864-2222. 550 D
luissoto@inter.edu
SOTO, Monica .... 305-899-3057... 98 O
msoto@barry.edu
SOTO, Nelson .... 513-861-6400. 390 C
nelson.soto@myunion.edu
SOTO-LÓPEZ, Heriberto . 787-751-1912. 551 B
herisoto@juris.inter.edu
SOTTER, Trudy .... 724-964-8811. 425 A
tsotterfa@aol.com
SOTTILE, Christian .... 912-525-5000. 131 B
SOUBA, JR., Wiley, W ... 603-650-1200. 296 G
wiley.w.souba.jr@dartmouth.edu
SOUCIER, JoEllen .... 713-718-8891. 473 C
joellen.soucier@hccs.edu
SOUCY, Erin .... 207-834-7830. 212 E
esoucy@maine.edu
SOUCY, Ken, R .... 937-229-2641. 391 C
ksoucy1@udayton.edu
SOUCY, Matthew, R .... 906-786-5802. 240 K
soucym@baycollege.edu
SOUHRADA, Rick .... 209-384-6135... 54 D
souhrada.r@mccd.edu
SOULES, Robert, C .... 518-388-6176. 348 J
soulesr@union.edu
SOULLIERE, Robert, H .... 260-399-7700. 174 C
rsoulliere@sf.edu
SOURBEER, Dan .... 760-744-1150... 58 D
dsourbeer@palomar.edu
SOUSA, David .... 207-454-1000. 211 B
SOUSA, Jalynne .... 707-638-5824... 69 K
jalynne.sousa@tu.edu
SOUSA, Jennifer .... 573-288-6343. 273 F
jsousa@culver.edu
SOUSA, Marsha .... 907-796-6518... 11 A
marsha.sousa@uas.alaska.edu
SOUSA, Marsha .... 907-796-6531... 11 A
mcsousa@uas.alaska.edu
SOUSA, Sheryl, A .... 781-736-3630. 224 F
sousa@brandeis.edu
SOUSA-PEOPLES, Kim ... 336-334-5231. 369 A
ksp@uncg.edu
SOUTER, Sharon .... 254-295-4667. 490 B
ssouter@umhb.edu
SOUTH, Anne .... 410-225-2516. 216 C
asouth@mica.edu
SOUTH, Gregory .... 530-938-5375... 41 A
gsouth@siskiyous.edu
SOUTH, James, D .... 580-774-3771. 400 B
james.south@swosu.edu
SOUTH, III, John, T .... 912-650-6200. 131 H
jsouthiii@southuniversity.edu
SOUTH, Nick .... 828-398-2513. 366 G
nsouth@southcollegenc.edu
SOUTH, Shannon .... 970-564-6212... 84 G
Shannon.South@pueblocc.edu
SOUTH, Stephen, A .... 828-398-2500. 366 G
ssouth@southcollegetn.edu
SOUTH, Stephen, A .... 865-251-1800. 458 I
ssouth@southcollegetn.edu
SOUTHALL, Ann .... 870-862-8131... 23 D
asouthall@southark.edu
SOUTHARD, Anne .... 850-729-6040. 109 I
southara@nwfsc.edu
SOUTHARD, Doug .... 603-228-1355. 296 H
SOUTHARD, Sonya .... 270-686-4526. 196 C
sonya.southard@kctcs.edu
SOUTHERLAND, Johnnie .... 919-530-5321. 368 A
jsoutherland@nccu.edu
SOUTHERN, Debbie .... 309-341-7225. 150 A
dsouther@knox.edu
SOUTHERN, Lori .... 254-299-8686. 476 D
lsouthern@mclennan.edu
SOUTHWELL, Michael .... 570-422-2871. 428 D
msouthwell@po-box.esu.edu
SOUTHWOOD, Lori .... 859-572-6383. 198 I
southwoodl1@nku.edu
SOUTHWORTH, Linda .... 978-934-2373. 229 B
Linda_Southworth@uml.edu
SOUTULLO, Stephen, C .. 832-842-4681. 489 B
scsoutullo@uh.edu
SOUVAINE, Diane .... 617-636-3536. 237 C
diane.souvaine@tufts.edu
SOUZA, Diana .... 231-348-6837. 247 H
dsouza@ncmich.edu
SOUZA, Nicole, L .... 212-346-1232. 335 J
nsouza@pace.edu
SOVA, Devin, A .... 336-318-7820. 362 H
dasova@randolph.edu
SOVINE, Kim .... 304-205-6676. 528 B
ksovine@kvctc.edu
SOWELL, Debra .... 918-495-6703. 398 H
dsowell@oru.edu
SOWELL, Frank .... 662-254-3531. 269 A
frank.u.sowell@mvsu.edu
SOWELL, John, T .... 404-995-8484. 269 E
jsowell@rts.edu
SOWELL, Kathy .... 615-230-3476. 461 G
kathy.sowell@volstate.edu
SOWELL, Madison, U ...... 540-261-4083. 509 K
madison.sowell@svu.edu
SOWELL, Richard, L .... 770-423-6565. 127 N
rsowell@kennesaw.edu
SOWER, Michelle .... 530-541-4660... 50 D
sower@ltcc.edu
SOWERS, Donna, S .... 301-846-2466. 214 H
dsowers@frederick.edu
SOWERS, Karen .... 865-974-3176. 463 C
kmsowers@utk.edu
SOWINSKI, Tomasz .... 212-472-1500. 334 B
tsowinski@nysid.edu
SOYARS, Tim .... 214-860-8587. 471 A
tsoyars@dcccd.edu
SOYOMBO, Richard .... 650-738-7099... 64 D
soyombor@smccd.edu
SOYRING, Mary .... 218-879-0811. 258 E
msoyring@fdltcc.edu
SOZZO, Anthony, M .... 914-594-4491. 334 A
tony_sozzo@nymc.edu
SPACH, Robert, C .... 704-894-2420. 353 J
rospach@davidson.edu
SPADARO, Joseph .... 610-896-1045. 418 F
jspadaro@haverford.edu
SPADE, Douglas, R .... 713-798-7391. 467 F
dspade@bcm.edu
SPADEMAN, Robert .... 216-687-7284. 377 F
r.spademan@csuohio.edu
SPAETH, Jason .... 320-629-5100. 260 F
spaethj@pinetech.edu
SPAETH, Nick, A .... 950-565-1007. 533 R
spaethna@lakeland.edu
SPAETH, Paul, J .... 716-375-2327. 338 E
pspaeth@sbu.edu
SPAETH-BAUM, Barbara . 701-671-2483. 372 E
barbara.baum@ndscs.edu
SPAGNA, Michael, E ...... 818-677-2590... 34 C
michael.spagna@csun.edu
SPAGNOLO, Jean Paul ... 260-399-7700. 174 C
jspagnolo@sf.edu
SPAHN, Tim .... 512-444-8082. 485 B
faid@thsu.edu
SPAHR, Steven .... 301-687-4112. 220 C
sspahr@frostburg.edu
SPAID, Darla .... 814-732-1364. 428 E
dspaid@edinboro.edu
SPAIGHT, Lynn .... 828-251-6501. 368 C
lspaight@unca.edu
SPAIN, Ashley .... 309-692-4092. 152 J
arspain@midstate.edu
SPAIN, Diara .... 415-257-1343... 42 J
diara.spain@dominican.edu
SPAIN, James .... 573-882-5995. 283 C
SpainJ@missouri.edu
SPAIN, Judy .... 859-622-1842. 193 P
judy.spain@eku.edu
SPAIN, William, R .... 401-841-3499. 545 A
SPAK, Gale, T .... 973-596-8540. 303 G
gale.spak@njit.edu
SPAKE, Deborah, F .... 330-672-6317. 382 B
dspake@kent.edu
SPAKE, Ellen .... 816-501-4597. 280 I
ellen.spake@rockhurst.edu
SPALDING, Carol .... 704-216-3450. 363 D
carol.spalding@rccc.edu
SPALDING, David .... 515-294-4111. 175 H
SPALDING, Jane .... 206-296-6118. 523 E
spalding@seattleu.edu
SPALDING, Kristina .... 626-914-8597... 38 K
kspaulding@citruscollege.edu
SPALDING, Richard, E ... 413-597-2483. 238 D
richard.e.spalding@williams.edu
SPALDING, Wendy .... 513-244-8492. 376 J
wendy.spalding@ccuniversity.edu
SPALLA, Tara .... 614-234-5950. 384 J
tspalla@mccn.edu
SPALTER, Mendel .... 323-937-3763... 77 F
mspalter@yoec.edu
SPALTER, Sholom .... 973-267-9404. 304 G
shspalter1@aol.com
SPANCAKE, Richard .... 229-391-4890. 119 H
rspancake@abac.edu
SPANG, David, I .... 609-894-9311. 299 I
dspang@bcc.edu
SPANGENBERG, Eric .... 509-335-3596. 525 A
ers@wsu.edu
SPANGENBERG, Laurie .. 906-786-5802. 240 K
laurie.spangenberg@baycollege.edu
SPANGLER, Dena .... 704-406-4255. 354 C
dspangler@gardner-webb.edu
SPANGLER, John, R .... 717-334-6286. 422 E
jspangler@ltsg.edu
SPANGLER, Lee .... 406-994-4399. 287 B
spangler@montana.edu
SPANGLER, Michael .... 702-651-4959. 294 E
michael.spangler@csn.edu
SPANGLER, Stephanie .... 203-432-4446... 93 A
stephanie.spangler@yale.edu
SPANGLER, Todd .... 315-655-7121. 316 E
tspangler@cazenovia.edu
SPANIOL, Lee .... 217-234-5263. 150 D
lspaniol@lakeland.cc.il.us
SPANJER, Pat .... 509-359-6358. 519 C
pspanjer@ewu.edu
SPANN, B. Steven .... 615-327-3927. 455 F
spann@guptoncollege.edu
SPANN, Chante .... 312-427-2737. 148 L
cspann@jmls.edu
SPANN-PACK, Robin ...... 601-979-2015. 267 E
robin.m.spann-pack@jsums.edu
SPANNER, Benjamin, J .. 312-332-0707. 160 J
SPANO, David, B .... 704-687-0311. 368 E
dspano@uncc.edu
SPAR, Debora, L .... 212-854-2021. 314 G
dspar@barnard.edu
SPARANGES, Judith, M .. 508-849-3345. 222 B
jsparanges@annamaria.edu
SPARGEN, Dan .... 402-399-2600. 289 A
dspargen@csm.edu
SPARKES, Mike .... 281-425-6327. 475 I
msparkes@lee.edu

SPARKMAN, Calvin .... 951-343-4356... 30 H
csparkman@calbaptist.edu
SPARKMAN, Margo .... 606-368-6039. 191 J
margosparkman@alc.edu
SPARKMAN, Susan .... 205-652-3587..... 9 F
sgt@uwa.edu
SPARKS, Brad .... 618-235-2700. 160 A
bradley.sparks@swic.edu
SPARKS, Cheryl, T .... 432-264-5030. 473 E
csparks@howardcollege.edu
SPARKS, Doug .... 602-285-7254... 15 C
douglas.sparks@phoenixcollege.edu
SPARKS, George, E .... 540-568-7073. 506 F
sparksge@jmu.edu
SPARKS, Jay .... 706-565-3669. 123 D
sparks_jay@columbusstate.edu
SPARKS, Jon .... 405-789-7661. 400 A
jon.sparks@swcu.edu
SPARKS, Kenton .... 610-341-5929. 415 G
ksparks@eastern.edu
SPARKS, Larry, D .... 662-915-7200. 270 B
lsparks@olemiss.edu
SPARKS, Mark .... 410-455-2872. 219 D
SPARKS, Matt .... 606-783-2822. 198 A
m.sparks@moreheadstate.edu
SPARKS, Melanie .... 505-277-7464. 312 F
msparks@unm.edu
SPARKS, Sonny .... 662-472-2312. 267 B
ssparks@holmescc.edu
SPARKS, Steve .... 252-222-6087. 358 G
sparkss@carteret.edu
SPARKS, Tiffany .... 402-494-2311. 290 O
tsparks@thenicc.edu
SPARKS, William, O .... 505-272-5849. 312 F
WSparks@salud.unm.edu
SPARR, Cynthia .... 630-466-7900. 162 J
csparr@waubonsee.edu
SPARROW, Meghan .... 304-357-4741. 527 H
meghansparrow@ucwv.edu
SPARROW, Rebecca, M . 607-255-2723. 322 A
rms18@cornell.edu
SPARROW, Suzanne .... 610-409-3600. 436 B
ssparrow@ursinus.edu
SPARY, Wayne .... 402-826-8228. 289 E
wayne.spary@doane.edu
SPATAFORE, Marisa .... 408-864-8672... 44 M
spataforemarisa@deanza.edu
SPATARO, Charles .... 270-706-8476. 195 A
charles.spataro@kctcs.edu
SPATARO, Keith .... 650-543-3853... 54 C
kspataro@menlo.edu
SPATARO-WILSON,
Jennifer, A .... 540-665-5412. 509 E
jspataro@su.edu
SPATES, Gerald .... 336-334-7800. 367 E
gspates@ncat.edu
SPATH, Christine .... 303-784-8637... 82 Q
cspath@jiu.edu
SPATZ, Dan .... 541-506-6110. 402 H
dspatz@cgcc.cc.or.us
SPATZ, Ronald .... 907-786-1086... 10 H
afrms1@uaa.alaska.edu
SPAULDING, Angela .... 806-651-2730. 484 D
aspaulding@mail.wtamu.edu
SPAULDING, David, L .... 931-598-1325. 458 H
dspauldi@sewnee.edu
SPAULDING, II,
Henry, W .... 740-392-6868. 384 K
hspauldi@mvnu.edu
SPAULDING, Thad .... 303-556-3591... 81 D
thad.spaulding@ccd.edu
SPAULDING, Tonia .... 912-583-3222. 122 B
tspaulding@bpc.edu
SPAUR, Rita .... 209-228-7865... 71 D
RSpaur@UCMerced.edu
SPAVENTA, Jon .... 805-893-3702... 72 B
jon.spaventa@parec.ucsb.edu
SPAVENTA, Marilynn ...... 805-965-0581... 64 L
spaventa@sbcc.edu
SPAYD, Alexandra .... 717-361-1123. 415 H
spaydal@etown.edu
SPAYER, Roger .... 847-925-6360. 145 H
rspayer@harpercollege.edu
SPAZIANI, Gina .... 978-656-3145. 232 B
spazianig@middlesex.mass.edu
SPEAKE, Dianne .... 850-644-6846. 115 C
dspeake@nursing.fsu.edu
SPEAKER, Cindy .... 315-364-3474. 350 E
cspeaker@wells.edu
SPEAKMAN, Thomas, W 989-774-1840. 240 N
speak1tw@cmich.edu
SPEAKS, Michael, A .... 315-443-2255. 347 C
SPEAKS, Tiffany .... 202-885-3651... 94 F
tspeaks@american.edu
SPEAR, Diana .... 618-262-8641. 147 C
speard@iecc.edu
SPEAR, Margaret, E .... 814-865-6555. 426 A
mes10@psu.edu
SPEAR, Robert .... 208-885-0243. 139 D
rspear@uidaho.edu
SPEARING, Mike .... 205-348-5490..... 8 D
mspearing@uasystem.ua.edu
SPEARMAN, Tim .... 619-961-4221... 69 I
tspearman@tjsl.edu
SPEARS, Barbara, A .... 334-420-4479..... 7 G
bspears@trenholmstate.edu
SPEARS, Gary Lee .... 662-562-3227. 269 C
glspears@northwestms.edu
SPEARS, Jacqueline, A ... 409-882-3018. 486 G
jackie.spears@lsco.edu
SPEARS, James, W .... 304-462-4125. 529 G
james.spears@glenville.edu
SPEARS, Lanny .... 859-858-2298. 192 A
SPEARS, Linda, C .... 615-963-5281. 459 E
lspears@tnstate.edu
SPEARS, Marty .... 501-279-4789... 21 C
mspears@harding.edu
SPEARS, SR., Peter, J .... 334-727-8421..... 8 A
SPEARS, Ron .... 806-894-9611. 480 H
rspears@southplainscollege.edu
SPEARS, Ronald .... 806-894-9611. 480 H
rspears@southplainscollege.edu
SPEARS, Sylvia .... 617-824-8500. 226 A
sylvia_spears@emerson.edu
SPEARS, Tim .... 802-443-5391. 499 H
spears@middlebury.edu
SPEARS-BOYD, Amy .... 931-540-2764. 460 E
aspears@columbiastate.edu
SPEAS, Philip, E .... 606-693-5000. 196 H
pspeas@kmbc.edu
SPEAS, Wanda .... 606-693-5000. 196 H
wspeas@kmbc.edu
SPECHLER, Julie .... 954-262-5348. 109 K
julies@nova.edu
SPECHT, Alice, W .... 325-670-1229. 472 O
aspecht@hsutx.edu
SPECHT, Mark, A .... 610-566-1776. 437 G
mspecht@williamson.edu
SPECK, Anne .... 484-664-3165. 424 H
aspeck@muhlenberg.edu
SPECK, Christie .... 707-864-7000... 66 G
christie.speck@solano.edu
SPECK, Nancy .... 585-275-5348. 349 C
nans@mail.rochester.edu
SPECTOR, Carol .... 617-824-8586. 226 A
carol_spector@emerson.edu
SPECTOR, Franklin .... 314-935-6525. 284 L
FSpector@WUSTL.EDU
SPECTOR, Harvey .... 212-678-3042. 347 G
spector@tc.edu
SPECTOR, Magaly .... 972-883-4566. 491 E
magaly.spector@utdallas.edu
SPECTOR, Phillip .... 410-516-8068. 215 H
pspecto1@jhu.edu
SPEDDEN, Nanette .... 973-290-4245. 300 F
nspedden@cse.edu
SPEECE, Brian .... 559-244-5917... 68 H
brian.speece@scccd.edu
SPEED, Bonnie .... 404-727-6289. 124 E
baspeed@emory.edu
SPEED, Coleen .... 318-274-3338. 207 E
speedc@gram.edu
SPEEDIE, Marilyn, K .... 612-624-1900. 264 G
speed001@umn.edu
SPEER, Brian .... 717-264-4141. 437 H
brian.speer@wilson.edu
SPEER, Brian .... 704-406-4269. 354 C
bspeer@gardner-webb.edu
SPEER, Julie .... 716-614-6251. 334 E
speer@niagaracc.suny.edu
SPEER, William .... 702-895-3375. 294 I
william.speer@unlv.edu
SPEHN, Steven .... 507-222-4271. 254 D
sspehn@carleton.edu
SPEIDEL, Daniel .... 603-897-8576. 297 F
dspeidel@rivier.edu
SPEIDEL, William .... 714-357-5661. 428 F
William.Speidel@iup.edu
SPEIGHT, Virginia .... 419-530-7262. 392 B
virginia.speight@utoledo.edu
SPEIR, Mary .... 540-828-5706. 502 J
mspeir@bridgewater.edu
SPEISER, Lynn .... 419-267-1312. 385 F
lspeiser@northweststate.edu
SPELL, Donald, R .... 252-493-7211. 362 G
dspell@email.pittcc.edu
SPELLACY, Karen, M ...... 315-386-7202. 345 F
spellacy@canton.edu
SPELLMAN, Joseph .... 203-932-7134... 92 E
jspellman@newhaven.edu
SPELLMAN, Mary .... 909-621-8114... 39 D
mary.spellman@cmc.edu
SPELLMAN, Peter .... 617-266-1400. 223 D
SPELLS, Doretha, J .... 757-727-5213. 505 F
doretha.spells@hamptonu.edu
SPELLS, Kaschia .... 252-246-1214. 365 C
kspells@wilsoncc.edu
SPELMAN, Amy .... 309-298-1914. 162 K
ae-spelman@wiu.edu
SPENCE, Bob, C .... 254-710-3731. 467 G
bob_spence@baylor.edu
SPENCE, Colleen .... 617-427-0060. 232 G
cspenc@rcc.mass.edu
SPENCE, Curtis .... 718-260-3502. 336 E
cspence@poly.edu
SPENCE, Lisa .... 812-237-8439. 167 A
lisa.spence@indstate.edu
SPENCE, Mary .... 716-829-7736. 323 D
spencem@dyc.edu
SPENCE, Stan .... 817-461-8741. 466 D
sspence@arlingtonbaptistcollege.edu
SPENCE, Thom .... 504-865-2573. 205 H
tgspence@loyno.edu
SPENCE, Weymouth .... 301-891-4128. 221 B
wspence@wau.edu
SPENCER, A. Clayton ...... 207-786-6100. 209 F
cspencer@bates.edu
SPENCER, Andrea, M ...... 914-773-3870. 335 J
aspencer@pace.edu
SPENCER, Carol .... 508-999-8705. 229 A
cspencer@umassd.edu
SPENCER, Catherine .... 212-636-6522. 324 G
caspencer@fordham.edu
SPENCER, Dan .... 254-298-8619. 482 C
dan.spencer@templejc.edu
SPENCER, Deborah .... 860-231-5390... 92 F
dspencer@usj.edu
SPENCER, Delmy .... 530-749-5002... 77 M
dspencer@yccd.edu
SPENCER, Denise .... 802-447-4631. 500 D
dspencer@svc.edu
SPENCER, Dorothy, A ..... 252-744-2212. 367 B
spencerdo@ecu.edu
SPENCER, Elizabeth, A .... 530-226-4602... 66 D
bspencer@simpsonu.edu
SPENCER, Erin .... 254-298-8590. 482 C
erin.spencer@templejc.edu
SPENCER, Estelle, H .... 413-205-3461. 221 F
estelle.spencer@aic.edu
SPENCER, James, D .... 570-321-4126. 422 H
spencer@lycoming.edu
SPENCER, Janie, M .... 608-785-8495. 536 G
jspencer@uwlax.edu
SPENCER, Jed .... 801-626-6586. 497 D
jedspencer@weber.edu
SPENCER, Jeremy .... 508-626-4500. 230 A
jspencer1@framingham.edu
SPENCER, John .... 617-735-9780. 226 B
spencerj@emmanuel.edu
SPENCER, John, D .... 817-515-4591. 482 B
john.spencer@tccd.edu
SPENCER, Judith .... 662-325-3713. 268 D
jspencer@hrm.msstate.edu
SPENCER, Keith, J .... 417-667-8181. 273 A
kspencer@cottey.edu
SPENCER, Krystal, F .... 812-888-4587. 174 F
kspencer@vinu.edu
SPENCER, Lisa .... 575-769-4115. 309 F
lisa.spencer@clovis.edu
SPENCER, Mary .... 414-277-4517. 534 G
spencer@msoe.edu
SPENCER, Meleah .... 417-873-7444. 273 H
mspencer02@drury.edu
SPENCER, Pamela .... 513-875-3344. 376 H
pam.spencer@chatfield.edu
SPENCER, Ray .... 217-351-2376. 155 J
rcspencer@parkland.edu
SPENCER, Richard .... 618-235-2700. 160 A
richard.spencer@swic.edu
SPENCER, Rick, E .... 630-637-5209. 154 F
respencer@noctrl.edu
SPENCER, Robert .... 206-296-5822. 523 E
bspencer@seattleu.edu
SPENCER, Roger, W .... 276-739-2407. 514 D
rspencer@vhcc.edu
SPENCER, Ruth .... 845-437-6820. 349 G
ruspencer@vassar.edu
SPENCER, Sandra, L .... 217-353-2637. 155 J
sspencer@parkland.edu
SPENCER, Scott .... 703-284-1520. 507 B
scott.spencer@marymount.edu
SPENCER, Shannon .... 419-372-6389. 374 K
spensha@bgsu.edu
SPENCER, Terri .... 602-331-7500... 12 A
tspencer@aii.edu
SPENCER, Theodore, L .... 734-647-0102. 251 C
tsz@umich.edu
SPENCER, Tiffany .... 618-453-2903. 159 G
spencer@siu.edu
SPENCER, Yvette .... 205-226-7720..... 2 C
yspencer@bsc.edu
SPENGEMAN, Erin .... 804-204-1218. 502 F
registrar@btsr.edu
SPENGLER, Gregory, C .. 410-706-1264. 219 C
gspengle@umaryland.edu
SPENNER, Anne .... 816-235-1576. 283 D
spennerae@umkc.edu
SPERAZZA, Alex .... 570-408-4465. 437 F
alexander.sperazza@wilkes.edu
SPERBER, Greg .... 562-947-8755... 67 H
gregsperber@scuhs.edu
SPERGER, Herb .... 610-785-6264. 432 C
hsperger@scs.edu
SPERLING, Michael .... 845-451-4616. 322 D
m_sperli@culinary.edu
SPERLING, Susan, S ...... 510-723-6641... 37 K
ssperling@chabotcollege.edu
SPERLING, William .... 206-546-4788. 523 F
wsperling@shoreline.edu
SPEROS, Michael .... 916-278-4239... 34 D
msperos@csus.edu
SPEROS, Michael .... 916-278-6655... 34 D
msperos@saclink.csus.edu
SPERRING, Tiffany .... 614-222-6183. 378 A
tsperring@ccad.edu
SPERRY, Sarah .... 412-396-5894. 415 F
sperrys@duq.edu
SPETKA, Rosemary, V ..... 315-792-5495. 331 I
rspetka@mvcc.edu
SPEWOCK, Kelly .... 412-291-6244. 410 B
kspewock@aii.edu
SPEWOCK, Kelly J, K ..... 412-291-6244. 410 B
kspewock@aii.edu
SPEZIA, Robert .... 313-883-8576. 249 E
spezia.robert@shms.edu
SPEZIALE, Michael .... 570-408-4679. 437 F
michael.speziale@wilkes.edu
SPEZZACATENA, Maricel 305-273-4499. 100 H
maricel@cbt.edu
SPICCIA, Michael .... 219-473-4234. 164 K
mspiccia@ccsj.edu
SPICER, Donald, Z .... 301-445-2729. 219 A
dspicer@usmd.edu
SPICER, Erin .... 850-484-1706. 110 G
espicer@pensacolastate.edu
SPICER, Jacqueline .... 810-766-4273. 239 G
jacqueline.spicer@baker.edu
SPICER, Julie .... 515-244-4221. 175 C
spicerj@aib.edu
SPICER, Kim, A .... 479-979-1320... 25 J
kaspicer@ozarks.edu
SPICER, Michael .... 909-621-8142... 60 A
michael.spicer@pomona.edu
SPICER, Thomas .... 303-273-3368... 80 E
tspicer@mines.edu
SPICER, Tom .... 970-248-1503... 79 F
tspicer@coloradomesa.edu
SPICKLER, Angela .... 717-396-7833. 427 A
aspickler@pcad.edu
SPIEGEL, Allen, M .... 212-430-2801. 351 M
spiegel@aecom.yu.edu
SPIEGEL, Allen, M .... 212-960-3179. 351 M
aspiegel@aecom.yu.edu
SPIEGEL, Benjamin .... 732-367-1060. 299 E
SPIEGEL, John .... 516-572-7118. 332 C
john.spiegel@ncc.edu
SPIEGEL, Mary, K .... 205-348-8666..... 8 D
mary.spiegel@ua.edu
SPIEGEL, Sara .... 312-777-8616. 147 D
sspiegel@aii.edu
SPIEGELMAN, Kathy .... 617-373-2226. 235 F
SPIELMAKER, Shallan ..... 616-451-3511. 241 H
SPIELMANN, Dan .... 920-465-2067. 536 F
spielmad@uwgb.edu
SPIELVOGEL, Jennifer ..... 216-987-4767. 378 D
jennifer.spielvogel@tri-c.edu
SPIERS, Cynthia, E .... 419-995-8439. 381 Q
spiers.c@rhodesstate.edu
SPIERS, Jessica .... 419-227-3141. 391 F
jspiers@unoh.edu
SPIERS, William .... 850-201-8399. 117 D
spiersw@tcc.fl.edu
SPIES, Brent .... 314-889-4564. 274 E
bspies@fontbonne.edu
SPIES, Carolyn, I .... 973-748-9000. 299 F
carolyn_spies@bloomfield.edu
SPIES, Gail .... 563-288-6004. 178 B
gspies@eicc.edu
SPIESMAN, John .... 440-375-7426. 382 L
jspiesman@lec.edu
SPIEZIO, Kim .... 239-513-1122. 106 O
kspiezio@hodges.edu
SPIGELMYER, Francie, P 724-287-8711. 411 C
frances.spigelmyer@bc3.edu
SPIGELMYER, Kathleen .. 215-248-7025. 413 A
spigelmyerk@chc.edu
SPIKER, Jackie .... 757-569-6708. 513 E
jspiker@pdc.edu
SPIKER, William, J .... 440-826-3623. 374 F
wspiker@bw.edu
SPIKEREIT, Damien .... 417-626-1234. 279 J
spikereit.damien@occ.edu
SPILDE, Mary .... 541-463-5200. 403 I
spildem@lanecc.edu
SPILKER, Christopher ..... 313-883-8651. 249 E
spilker.christopher@shms.edu
SPILLANE, Judith .... 575-769-4967. 309 F
judith.spillane@clovis.edu
SPILLER, James .... 585-395-2525. 342 F
jspiller@brockport.edu
SPILLER, Judith .... 603-862-2165. 298 C
judy.spiller@unh.edu

SPILLETT, Margaret, D .... 315-255-1743. 316 D
margaret.spillett@cayuga-cc.edu
SPILLMAN, Tom .... 951-487-3945... 55 B
tspillma@msjc.edu
SPILLUM, Carol .... 605-274-4090. 449 K
carol.spillum@augie.edu
SPILMAN, Todd .... 505-473-6295. 311 K
todd.spilman@laureate.net
SPILOVOY, Tanya .... 701-328-4102. 371 B
tanya.spilovoy@ndus.edu
SPINA, Anthony .... 716-829-7648. 323 D
spinaaw@dyc.edu
SPINA, Eric, F .... 315-443-2494. 347 C
efspina@syr.edu
SPINA, Matthew, R .... 609-497-7870. 304 D
admissions@ptsem.edu
SPINARD, John .... 410-951-3577. 220 B
jspinard@coppin.edu
SPINATO, Donna .... 903-886-5860. 483 E
donna.spinato@tamuc.edu
SPINAZZA, Terri .... 208-426-2168. 137 G
tspinazz@boisestate.edu
SPINDEL, Donna .... 304-696-2818. 529 H
spindel@marshall.edu
SPINDLE, Blair .... 405-491-6608. 399 K
bspindle@snu.edu
SPINDLE, William .... 907-786-4620... 10 H
anwhs@uaa.alaska.edu
SPINDLER, Deborah .... 858-635-4700... 26 M
dspindler@alliant.edu
SPINELLI, Paul .... 727-341-3070. 112 E
spinelli.paul@spcollege.edu
SPINELLI, JR., Stephen . 215-951-2727. 430 E
spinellis@philau.edu
SPINELLI-SEXTER, Eva ... 212-463-0400. 348 B
espinelli@touro.edu
SPINHIRNE,
Raymond, J .... 512-448-8662. 479 C
rays@stedwards.edu
SPINILLO, Anthony .... 570-340-6057. 423 B
spinillo@marywood.edu
SPINK, Nancy .... 907-450-8153... 10 G
nkspink@alaska.edu
SPINKS, Henry .... 478-825-6400. 124 H
spinksh@fvsu.edu
SPINKS, Robert .... 337-475-5711. 207 G
rspinks@mcneese.edu
SPINOSA, Tony .... 202-685-3946. 544 K
spinosat@ndu.edu
SPINRAD, Rick .... 541-737-3467. 406 A
rick.spinrad@oregonstate.edu
SPIRES, Chris .... 803-641-3463. 448 A
chriss@usca.edu
SPIRES, Tracy, M .... 864-379-8773. 443 F
tspires@erskine.edu
SPIRIDON, Charles, P .... 203-837-8663... 88 B
spiridonc@wcsu.edu
SPIRO, Elaine .... 215-489-2346. 414 E
Elaine.Spiro@delval.edu
SPIRO, Mark .... 413-559-5528. 227 B
mkstr@hampshire.edu
SPISAK, Art, L .... 319-335-1681. 175 I
art-spisak@uiowa.edu
SPITTAL, David, J .... 913-971-3392. 188 H
president@mnu.edu
SPITTAL, Ryan .... 815-939-5452. 155 H
rspittal@olivet.edu
SPITZ, Catherine .... 309-556-3120. 148 B
cspitz@iwu.edu
SPITZ, Cody .... 575-562-2178. 309 H
cody.spitz@enmu.edu
SPITZER, Linda .... 301-295-3357. 545 C
linda.spitzer@usuhs.edu
SPITZER, Michael .... 516-876-4062. 346 A
michael.spitzer@esc.edu
SPIVAK, Howard .... 718-951-5342. 317 C
howards@brooklyn.cuny.edu
SPIVAK, Michael .... 641-472-7000. 180 N
mspivak@mum.edu
SPIVEY, Margaret, C .... 240-500-2000. 215 B
mcspivey@hagerstowncc.edu
SPIVEY, Randy .... 615-966-2503. 456 B
randy.spivey@lipscomb.edu
SPIVEY, Sheila, D .... 904-620-2528. 116 B
sspivey@unf.edu
SPIVEY, Sheryl .... 404-215-2638. 129 D
sspivey@morehouse.edu
SPIWAK, Doug .... 847-925-6969. 145 H
dspiwak@harpercollege.edu
SPIZZIRRO, Diane .... 914-654-5568. 320 H
dspizzirro@cnr.edu
SPIZZIRRI, Erica .... 609-984-1588. 308 A
espizzirri@tesc.edu
SPOALES, Gary .... 304-724-3700. 526 B
gspoales@apus.edu
SPOERRI, Tamara, D .... 207-725-3837. 209 H
tspoerri@bowdoin.edu
SPOFFORD, Kathy .... 657-278-2800... 33 E
kspofford@fullerton.edu
SPOHN, Debborah .... 661-395-4211... 49 N
dspohn@bakersfieldcollege.edu
SPOHR, Jean .... 513-562-8752. 373 K
business@artacademy.edu
SPOHR, Robert .... 989-328-1241. 247 D
robs@montcalm.edu
SPOLJORIC, Diane .... 219-785-5476. 172 A
dspoljoric@pnc.edu
SPOLTORE, Janet, D .... 860-439-2692... 89 H
janet.spoltore@conncoll.edu
SPONG, Mark, W .... 972-883-2974. 491 E
mspong@utdallas.edu
SPONG, Melinda .... 859-572-1464. 198 I
spongm1@nku.edu
SPONHOLZ, Karin .... 650-508-3714... 56 H
ksponholz@ndnu.edu
SPONSELLER, Eric .... 401-254-3192. 440 B
esponsellers@rwu.edu
SPOONER, David .... 518-276-6890. 337 I
spoond@rpi.edu
SPOONER, James .... 229-243-6456. 121 E
james.spooner@bainbridge.edu
SPOONER, Natalie, M ...... 315-786-2268. 327 L
nspooner@sunyjefferson.edu
SPOOR, Darlene .... 415-239-3014... 38 L
dspoor@ccsf.edu
SPOOR, Suzanne, J .... 410-777-2448. 213 D
sjspoor@aacc.edu
SPOR, Arvid .... 626-914-8534... 38 K
aspor@citruscollege.edu
SPORE, MaryBeth .... 724-537-4567. 432 G
marybeth.spore@email.stvincent.edu
SPORE, Robert, B .... 540-464-7322. 515 B
sporerb@vmi.edu
SPORES, Jon .... 360-383-3440. 525 D
jspores@whatcom.ctc.edu
SPORS, Jonathon, L .... 217-443-8577. 143 G
jspors@dacc.edu
SPORTES, Christine .... 202-319-5050... 94 G
sportes@cua.edu
SPORTSMAN, Joseph, S 513-244-4389. 377 G
scott_sportsman@mail.msj.edu
SPOSILI, Michael .... 518-580-5610. 341 A
msposili@skidmore.edu
SPOTO, Mary .... 352-588-8463. 112 D
mary.spoto@saintleo.edu
SPRADLEY, Minou .... 619-388-3520... 62 D
mspradl@sdccd.edu
SPRADLEY, Paul .... 517-264-7175. 250 B
pspradley@sienaheights.edu
SPRADLIN, Michael, R ... 901-751-8453. 457 B
mspradlin@mabts.edu
SPRADLING, Carol .... 304-357-4747. 527 H
carolspradling@ucwv.edu
SPRADLING, Jane .... 337-550-1216. 205 B
SPRADLING, John .... 903-785-7661. 478 B
jspradling@parisjc.edu
SPRADLING, Steve .... 330-494-6170. 389 F
sspradling@starkstate.edu
SPRAGGINS, Timothy ..... 334-244-3220..... 2 A
tspraggins@aum.edu
SPRAGUE, Brinton .... 425-739-8165. 520 K
brinton.sprague@lwtech.edu
SPRAGUE, Carol .... 413-545-0698. 228 F
sprague@research.umass.edu
SPRAGUE, Jennifer .... 505-984-6041. 311 H
jsprague@sjcsf.edu
SPRAGUE, Jon, E .... 419-772-2276. 386 D
j-sprague@onu.edu
SPRAGUE, Karen, U .... 541-346-1246. 406 D
kus@uoregon.edu
SPRAGUE, Kendra .... 360-442-2121. 521 A
ksprague@lowercolumbia.edu
SPRAGUE, Robert, L .... 310-287-4398... 52 F
spragurl@wlac.edu
SPRAGUE, Todd .... 360-867-6042. 519 J
spraguet@evergreen.edu
SPRAGUE, Viola .... 810-762-9668. 244 Q
vsprague@kettering.edu
SPRAKE, Timothy .... 206-239-4500. 517 M
tsprake@cityu.edu
SPRAKER, Matt .... 615-248-1245. 462 D
mspraker@trevecca.edu
SPRANGERS, Lynn .... 414-256-4810. 535 A
sprangel@mtmary.edu
SPRANZA, John .... 706-295-6363. 125 C
jspranza@highlands.edu
SPRATLIN, Jim .... 334-386-7265..... 3 H
jspratlin@faulkner.edu
SPRATLIN, Steve .... 256-395-2211..... 7 C
sspratlin@suscc.edu
SPRATT, Bruce, R .... 404-413-3071. 126 E
bspratt@gsu.edu
SPRATT, Sharon .... 270-706-8478. 195 A
sharon.spratt@kctcs.edu
SPRAW, Deanna .... 419-434-4589. 391 D
spraw@findlay.edu
SPREHE, Tara .... 503-594-3370. 402 F
taras@clackamas.edu
SPRENGEL, Archie .... 573-651-2217. 282 B
awsprengel@semo.edu
SPRENGER, Cathy, J ...... 717-477-1381. 429 E
cjspre@ship.edu
SPRICK, David, W .... 715-836-2222. 536 E
sprickdw@uwec.edu
SPRIGGS, Barry, L .... 610-799-1634. 421 I
bspriggs@lccc.edu
SPRIGGS, Edward, J .... 858-534-3475... 71 F
espriggs@ucsd.edu
SPRIGGS, Janet .... 704-219-7165. 363 D
janet.spriggs@rccc.edu
SPRING, Corinne .... 201-559-3515. 302 A
springc@felician.edu
SPRING, SCC, Joseph .... 973-543-6528. 298 I
president@acs350.org
SPRING, Ted .... 910-362-7555. 358 F
tspring@cfcc.edu
SPRINGALL, Robert, G ... 570-577-1446. 411 A
r.springall@bucknell.edu
SPRINGER, Colleen .... 641-844-5523. 179 H
colleen.springer@iavalley.edu
SPRINGER, Colleen .... 641-844-7106. 179 J
colleen.springer@iavalley.edu
SPRINGER, D. Bruce ...... 410-777-2346. 213 D
bdspringer@aacc.edu
SPRINGER, Gail, L .... 407-888-8689. 104 B
gspringer@fcim.edu
SPRINGER, Laureen .... 405-491-6325. 399 K
springer@snu.edu
SPRINGER, Mark .... 320-308-3093. 261 B
mspringer@stcloudstate.edu
SPRINGER, Patrick .... 951-487-3590... 55 B
pspringer@msjc.edu
SPRINGER, Robert, I .... 336-278-6644. 354 B
springer@elon.edu
SPRINGER, Tracy .... 765-455-9356. 168 A
tracylb@iuk.edu
SPRINGER-BALDWIN,
Nancy .... 512-472-4133. 480 G
nancy.springer-baldwin@ssw.edu
SPRINGHORN, Polly .... 415-749-4504... 62 G
pspringhorn@sfai.edu
SPRINGS, Andre .... 704-216-6012. 356 D
asprings@livingstone.edu
SPRINKEL, Beth .... 916-608-6500... 53 C
SPRINKLE, Dean, E .... 336-838-6128. 365 B
dean.sprinkle@wilkescc.edu
SPRINKLE, Stephen, D ... 619-260-4655... 73 I
sdsprinkle@sandiego.edu
SPRITZ, Ken .... 617-731-7623. 235 H
kspritz@pmc.edu
SPROLE, JoLynn, F .... 817-515-4563. 482 B
jolynn.sprole@tccd.edu
SPROLES, Karyn, Z .... 740-376-4741. 383 E
karyn.sproles@marietta.edu
SPROULS, David .... 212-452-4191. 334 B
dsprouls@nysid.edu
SPROUSE, Clay .... 706-721-5632. 126 B
csprouse@gru.edu
SPROUSE, Judy .... 434-381-6323. 510 F
jsprouse@sbc.edu
SPROUSE, Keith .... 435-722-6900. 496 M
keiths@ubatc.edu
SPROUSE, Marlene .... 641-683-5104. 179 A
marlene.sprouse@indianhills.edu
SPROWL, Don .... 765-677-1002. 169 B
don.sprowl@indwes.edu
SPRUIELL, Clemit, W ..... 205-652-3533..... 9 F
cspruiell@uwa.edu
SPRUIELL, Vicki, P .... 205-652-3627..... 9 F
vspruiell@uwa.edu
SPRUILL, Crhistina .... 806-291-3406. 494 F
spruillc@wbu.edu
SPRUILL, Juliet, A .... 304-457-6317. 526 A
spruillj@ab.edu
SPRUILL, Rose .... 210-486-2420. 465 B
rspruill1@alamo.edu
SPRUILL, Wayne .... 615-844-5078 464 F
wspruill@welch.edu
SPRUNG, Meghan .... 314-340-3305. 275 A
sprungm@hssu.edu
SPRUNGER, Philip, W .... 570-321-4038. 422 H
sprunger@lycoming.edu
SPRUNT GRUMBLES,
Julia .... 919-962-0329. 368 D
Julia.Grumbles@unc.edu
SPRY, Larry .... 816-322-0110. 271 O
larry.spry@calvary.edu
SPRY, Susan .... 570-740-0407. 422 G
sspry@luzerne.edu
SPUCHES, Charles, M .... 315-470-6817. 345 B
cspuches@esf.edu
SPUCK, Dennis, W .... 281-283-3500. 489 C
spuck@uhcl.edu
SPURGEON-HARRIS,
Bobbie .... 405-691-3800. 396 D
bspurgeon-harris@macu.edu
SPURLING, John .... 818-779-8259... 50 A
jspurling@kingsuniversity.edu
SPURLOCK, Chad .... 918-293-4622. 398 B
chad.spurlock@okstate.edu
SPURLOCK, Jennifer .... 513-562-8771. 373 K
jspurlock@artacademy.edu
SPURLOCK, Rhonda .... 918-343-7612. 399 C
rspurlock@rsu.edu
SPURLOCK-EVANS,
Karla .... 860-297-4234... 91 F
karla.spurlockevans@trincoll.edu
SPURRIER, Robert, L ...... 405-744-6799. 397 H
robert.spurrier@okstate.edu
SPYBEY, Joseph .... 614-222-3246. 378 A
jspybey@ccad.edu
SQUARE, Marilyn, C ...... 713-313-7859. 485 F
squaremc@tsu.edu
SQUIER, Ragan, A .... 315-470-6681. 345 B
rasquier@esf.edu
SQUIER, Steven .... 815-825-2086. 149 F
steven.squier@kishwaukeecollege.edu
SQUILLACE, Paul .... 303-404-5109... 81 N
paul.squillace@frontrange.edu
SQUIRE, Frances .... 559-934-2134... 75 G
francessquire@whccd.edu
SQUIRE, Michael, E .... 630-637-5559. 154 F
mesquire@noctrl.edu
SQUIRE, Roland .... 435-797-8380. 497 B
roland.squire@usu.edu
SQUIRES, Nancy .... 631-632-6976. 342 C
nancy.squires@stonybrook.edu
SQUIRES, Nicole .... 218-235-2171. 261 G
n.squires@vcc.edu
SQUIRES, R. Duwane ..... 304-473-8311. 531 G
squires@wvwc.edu
SQUIRES, Roy .... 727-726-1153. 100 E
roysquires@clearwater.edu
SQUIRES, Thomas .... 315-792-5445. 331 I
tsquires@mvcc.edu
SQUIRES, Toni .... 651-641-8232. 255 B
squires@csp.edu
SQUIREWELL, Robert ..... 803-705-4698. 441 C
squirewellr@benedict.edu
SREBRO, Michele, M ...... 570-702-8953. 419 G
msrebro@johnson.edu
SREENIVASAN, Katepalli 718-260-3500. 336 E
krs3@nyu.edu
SREENIVASAN, Katepalli 718-260-3166. 336 E
krs3@nyu.edu
SREENIVASAN,
Katepalli, R .... 212-992-7914. 334 D
katepalli.sreenivasan@nyu.edu
SRIHARI, Hari .... 607-777-2871. 341 E
srihari@binghamton.edu
SRIKANTH, Rajini .... 617-287-5520. 228 G
rajini.srikanth@umb.edu
SRINIVASAN, Ganesan ... 707-527-4880... 65 B
gsrinivasan@santarosa.edu
SROF, Brenda, S .... 574-535-7375. 166 A
brendajs@goshen.edu
STAAB, Eric, P .... 269-337-7172. 244 K
Eric.Staab@kzoo.edu
STAATS, Mark .... 602-350-6525. 400 J
mstaats@twsweld.com
STABB, Kristin .... 626-873-2144... 55 C
STABEN, Charles, A .... 605-677-6497. 451 F
chuck.staben@usd.edu
STABER, Karl, D .... 678-915-6841. 132 C
kstaber@spsu.edu
STABILE, Randy .... 617-349-8388. 228 B
rstabile@lesley.edu
STABILE, Steve .... 212-229-3500. 332 E
stabiles@newschool.edu
STABOLEPSZY, Judy, S .. 570-577-2405. 411 A
judy.stabolepszy@bucknell.edu
STACE, Peter, A .... 718-817-3200. 324 G
stace@fordham.edu
STACEY, Heather, J .... 606-474-3186. 194 H
hstacy@kcu.edu
STACEY, John .... 910-695-3822. 363 F
stacyj@sandhills.edu
STACEY, Robert .... 206-221-3491. 524 G
bstacey@u.washington.edu
STACEY, Robert, D .... 281-649-3630. 473 B
rstacey@hbu.edu
STACEY, Simon .... 410-455-2164. 219 D
spstacey@umbc.edu
STACEY-CLEMONS, June 253-589-5546. 518 B
june.stacey-clemons@cptc.edu
STACHACZ, John .... 570-408-4254. 437 F
john.stachaz@wilkes.edu
STACHOWIAK, Kris .... 610-359-5310. 414 D
kstachowiak@dccc.edu
STACHOWSKI,
Mary Albertine .... 716-896-0700. 350 A
smalbertine@villa.edu
STACHURA, Hubert .... 212-752-1530. 328 G
hubert.stachura@limcollege.edu
STACK, Barbara, J .... 920-832-6546. 533 S
barbara.j.stack@lawrence.edu
STACK, Bob .... 205-665-6512..... 9 B
bstack@montevallo.edu
STACK, Dana .... 619-388-7579... 62 F
dandras@sdccd.edu
STACK, Dennis .... 585-567-9220. 326 F
dennis.stack@houghton.edu

STACK, OSA, John, P .... 610-519-4550. 436 F
john.stack@villanova.edu
STACK, Lisa .... 617-984-1663. 235 I
lstack@quincycollege.edu
STACK, Lynne .... 508-286-8251. 238 B
lstack@wheatoncollege.edu
STACK, Patrick .... 314-968-6921. 284 N
stackpa@webster.edu
STACK, Richard .... 617-353-9344. 224 D
rmstack@bu.edu
STACK, Shane .... 304-336-8365. 530 A
sstack@westliberty.edu
STACKHOUSE TAETZCH,
Cindra .... 630-752-5049. 163 F
cindra.taetzsch@wheaton.edu
STACKPOLE, Ronnie .. 813-988-5131. 104 A
businessoffice@floridacollege.edu
STACKPOOLE, Kenneth ... 321-674-8971. 104 H
kenstackpoole@fit.edu
STACKPOOLE, Roger, W 315-445-4174. 328 F
stackprw@lemoyne.edu
STACKS, Pamela .... 408-924-2427... 36 A
pamela.stacks@jupiter.sjsu.edu
STACY, Jeanne .... 225-216-8591. 202 H
stacyj@mybrcc.edu
STACY, Karin .... 847-214-7957. 144 F
kstacy@elgin.edu
STACY, Mark, W .... 585-395-5149. 342 F
mstacy@brockport.edu
STACY, Roger .... 580-371-2371. 396 E
rstacy@mscok.edu
STADDEN, Mary .... 717-396-7833. 427 A
mstadden@pcad.edu
STADING, Gary, L .... 713-221-2775. 489 D
stadingg@uhd.edu
STADLER, Albert (Al) ...... 417-625-9807. 278 D
stadler-a@mssu.edu
STADLER, Holly .... 312-853-4780. 157 D
hstadler@roosevelt.edu
STADLER, Ueli .... 503-777-7287. 407 E
ueli.stadler@reed.edu
STAFFEL, Peter, L .... 304-336-8193. 530 A
staffelp@westliberty.edu
STAFFIER, Carol .... 781-239-2703. 231 G
cstaffier@massbay.edu
STAFFORD, Alan .... 325-670-1486. 472 O
stafford@hsutx.edu
STAFFORD, Ben .... 409-984-6390. 486 H
staffordbk@lamarpa.edu
STAFFORD, Ben .... 409-984-6354. 486 H
staffordbk@lamarpa.edu
STAFFORD, Charles, A ... 845-938-3419. 545 I
8sgs@usma.edu
STAFFORD, Ingrid, S ..... 847-491-7350. 155 D
i-stafford@northwestern.edu
STAFFORD, Jake .... 510-849-8239... 46 B
jstafford@psr.edu
STAFFORD, James .... 254-295-4607. 490 B
jstafford@umhb.edu
STAFFORD, Joanne .... 405-733-7373. 399 F
jmcmillen@rose.edu
STAFFORD, Kathryn .... 734-477-8581. 252 A
stafford@wccnet.edu
STAFFORD, Kenneth .... 785-532-6520. 188 A
kens@ksu.edu
STAFFORD, Kyle .... 580-745-2236. 399 J
kstafford@se.edu
STAFFORD, Laura .... 419-372-2079. 374 K
llstaff@bgsu.edu
STAFFORD, Mary .... 503-251-5707. 408 G
mstafford@uws.edu
STAFFORD, Michael .... 281-290-5276. 476 A
michael.d.stafford@lonestar.edu
STAFFORD, Pam .... 606-759-7141. 196 B
pam.stafford@kctcs.edu
STAFFORD, Tomas, L ..... 608-263-6105. 536 C
tstafford@uwsa.edu
STAGER, Helen, H .... 570-941-4330. 436 A
helen.stager@scranton.edu
STAGER, Karl .... 281-756-3594. 465 D
kstager@alvincollege.edu
STAGGERS, Leroy .... 803-934-3274. 445 F
lstaggers@morris.edu
STAGNARO, Leta .... 510-659-6220... 57 A
lstagnaro@ohlone.edu
STAGNI, Joshua, C .... 260-399-7700. 174 C
jstagni@sf.edu
STAHL, Frank .... 620-672-5641. 190 A
franks@prattcc.edu
STAHL, Jann .... 508-999-8181. 229 A
jstahl@umassd.edu
STAHL, Jason .... 989-686-9559. 242 C
jfstahl@delta.edu
STAHL, Kim .... 252-335-3203. 367 C
krstahl@mail.ecsu.edu
STAHL, Norman, S .... 808-933-3115. 136 A
nstahl@hawaii.edu
STAHL, Ritarose .... 920-686-6134. 536 A
Ritarose.Stahl@sl.edu
STAHL, Sharon .... 314-935-5040. 284 L
sstahl@wustl.edu
STAHL, Stephen, D .... 440-826-2379. 374 F
sstahl@bw.edu
STAHL, Timothy, W .... 724-925-4073. 437 D
stahlt@wccc.edu
STAHLE, Noel .... 641-673-1010. 183 H
stahlen@wmpenn.edu
STAHLEY, Joseph .... 201-216-8228. 307 E
jstahley@stevens.edu
STAHLY, Dannielle, N ..... 530-226-4608... 66 D
dstahly@simpsonu.edu
STAIANO-COICO, Lisa .... 212-650-7285. 317 D
president@ccny.cuny.edu
STAINE, Kristin .... 617-217-9228. 222 G
kstaine@baystate.edu
STAIR, David, L .... 417-865-2815. 274 B
staird@evangel.edu
STAIRS, Donna .... 724-653-2216. 415 A
dstairs@dec.edu
STAKENAS, James, M .... 413-662-5245. 230 C
j.stakenas@mcla.edu
STAKER, Julie .... 319-399-8500. 176 G
jstaker@coe.edu
STAKES, Robert, L .... 915-747-5683. 492 A
rlstakes@utep.edu
STALCUP, Susie .... 615-322-6673. 463 G
susie.stalcup@vanderbilt.edu
STALDER, Michele .... 907-455-2850... 10 I
mestalder@alaska.edu
STALEY, Betty .... 916-961-8727... 61 B
STALEY, Marc .... 419-772-2462. 386 D
m-staley@onu.edu
STALEY, Michael .... 407-708-2390. 113 E
staleym@seminolestate.edu
STALEY, Priscilla, A .... 214-860-2037. 470 J
pstaley@dcccd.edu
STALEY, Sally .... 216-368-4306. 375 J
sjs29@case.edu
STALKER, Michael .... 901-320-9730. 463 J
mstalker@victory.edu
STALLARD, Gary .... 936-633-5344. 465 J
gstallard@angelina.edu
STALLARD, Michael .... 570-586-2400. 410 D
mstallard@bbc.edu
STALLER, Arlene, D .... 713-500-3268. 492 E
arlene.d.staller@uth.tmc.edu
STALLINGS, Tamya .... 870-512-7822... 20 B
tamya_stallings@asun.edu
STALLINGS,
Virginia (Lyn) .... 202-885-3724... 94 F
vstalli@american.edu
STALLMAN, Jeanne .... 541-552-6221. 406 C
stallman@sou.edu
STALLMAN, Scott, R .... 217-287-7081. 151 F
scott.stallman@llcc.edu
STALNAKER, Lynn .... 307-772-4245. 543 D
lstalnak@lccc.wy.edu
STALTER, Anita, K .... 574-535-7503. 166 A
dean@goshen.edu
STALTER, Catherine .... 217-351-2290. 155 J
cstalter@parkland.edu
STALVEY, John .... 907-786-1706... 10 H
jstalvey@uaa.alaska.edu
STAM, Theodore, R .... 207-798-4282. 209 H
tstam@bowdoin.edu
STAMM, Timothy .... 504-671-5482. 203 A
tstamm@dcc.edu
STAMMEL, Andrew .... 607-436-2830. 343 E
andrew.stammel@oneonta.edu
STAMP, Diane, L .... 540-568-6495. 506 F
stampdl@jmu.edu
STAMP, Robert, L .... 203-392-6900... 88 A
stampr1@southernct.edu
STAMPER, Andrea, L .... 606-474-3212. 194 H
astamper@kcu.edu
STAMPER, Richard, E ..... 812-877-8956. 172 C
richard.stamper@rose-hulman.edu
STAMPS, Clara, R .... 601-877-6130. 265 G
cstamps@alcorn.edu
STAMPS,
Delores Bolden .... 601-977-7871. 270 A
dbstamps@tougaloo.edu
STANAITIS, Judi .... 610-558-5544. 424 I
stanaitj@neumann.edu
STANBACK STROUD,
Regina .... 650-738-4110... 64 D
stroudr@smccd.edu
STANCEL, George, M .... 713-500-9880. 492 E
george.m.stancel@uth.tmc.edu
STANCIL, Darlene .... 864-644-5111. 446 I
dstancil@swu.edu
STANCIL, Jay .... 606-546-1292. 200 A
jstancil@unionky.edu
STANCIU, Hope .... 330-490-7142. 392 H
hstanciu@walsh.edu
STANDAHL, Jerry, J .... 757-569-6719. 513 E
jstandahl@pdc.edu
STANDEN, Jeffrey .... 859-572-6406. 198 I
standenj1@nku.edu
STANDERFER, Mary .... 479-394-7622... 23 B
mstanderfer@rmcc.edu
STANDERFER, Steve .... 661-722-6300... 28 F
sstanderfer@avc.edu
STANDIFIRD, Stephen .... 812-488-2856. 173 H
ss500@evansville.edu
STANDISH, Leanna .... 425-602-3000. 516 K
ljs@bastyr.edu
STANDLEA, Donna .... 909-607-3305... 39 C
donna.standlea@cgu.edu
STANDLEY, Susan .... 309-794-7207. 139 L
suestandley@augustana.edu
STANDRIDGE, Joe .... 254-968-9065. 483 A
jstandr@tarleton.edu
STANEK, Karla, E .... 608-785-8515. 536 G
kstanek@uwlax.edu
STANFIELD, Lori, J .... 785-539-3571. 188 F
ljstanfield@mccks.edu
STANFIELD, Margot, J .... 509-313-5995. 520 A
stanfield@gu.gonzaga.edu
STANFIELD, Vicki .... 409-933-8213. 469 E
vstanfield@com.edu
STANFIELD,
Vincent (Shelby) .... 512-475-7510. 491 C
s.stanfield@austin.utexas.edu
STANFILL, Sandy .... 731-968-5722. 460 G
sstanfill@jscc.edu
STANFORD, Jeanne .... 805-893-4411... 72 B
stanford-j@sa.ucsb.edu
STANFORD, Linda .... 907-852-3333... 10 F
linda.stanford@ilisagvik.edu
STANFORD, Linda, O ..... 517-355-5767. 246 H
stanford@msu.edu
STANFORD, Roger, J ...... 715-858-1857. 539 J
rstanford@cvtc.edu
STANFORD, Steve .... 601-925-3205. 268 A
stanford@mc.edu
STANFORD, Virgil .... 760-252-2411... 29 I
vstanford@barstow.edu
STANFORD, Yvonne .... 662-621-4287. 266 D
ystanford@coahomacc.edu
STANG, Michael .... 815-753-6102. 154 I
mstang@niu.edu
STANGE, Carl .... 507-457-5100. 262 A
cstange@winona.edu
STANGE, Pat .... 402-460-2152. 288 I
pstange@cccneb.edu
STANGE, Randy .... 620-665-3594. 187 F
stanger@hutchcc.edu
STANGE, Von .... 319-335-3000. 175 I
von-stange@uiowa.edu
STANGER, Christina .... 410-455-2122. 219 D
stanger@umbc.edu
STANGER, Winn .... 801-626-6876. 497 D
wstanger@weber.edu
STANGLE, James, R .... 563-333-6060. 182 B
StangleJamesR@sau.edu
STANGLIN, Gerald, M .... 903-983-8104. 475 E
gstanglin@kilgore.edu
STANGO, Linda .... 203-575-8016... 89 B
lstango@nvcc.commnet.edu
STANICH, Chris .... 832-842-0545. 489 A
cstanich@uh.edu
STANICH, Chris, M .... 832-842-0545. 489 B
cstanich@central.uh.edu
STANICIC, Rob .... 281-998-6150. 479 E
rob.stanicic@sjcd.edu
STANIEWICZ, Theodore .. 215-489-2228. 414 E
Theodore.Staniewicz@delval.edu
STANKEY, Lindy, J .... 651-631-5344. 263 A
ljstankey@nwc.edu
STANKEY, Michael .... 940-898-3350. 488 B
mstankey1@twu.edu
STANKIEWICZ, Donna .... 973-684-5218. 304 B
dstankiewicz@pccc.edu
STANKOVICH, Joseph .... 518-580-5719. 341 A
jstankovich@skidmore.edu
STANKOWSKI, Lisa .... 231-843-5802. 252 H
lmstankowski@westshore.edu
STANLEY, Allen, D .... 501-569-8474... 24 B
adstanley@ualr.edu
STANLEY, Brian .... 478-471-2864. 128 I
brian.stanley@maconstate.edu
STANLEY, Carol .... 706-355-5019. 120 J
cstanley@athenstech.edu
STANLEY, Carol A, J .... 434-924-4122. 511 B
cas4b@virginia.edu
STANLEY, Cheryl .... 413-572-5713. 230 F
cstanley@westfield.ma.edu
STANLEY, Christine .... 979-458-2905. 483 C
cstanley@tamu.edu
STANLEY, Cole .... 405-974-2590. 400 K
cstanley2@uco.edu
STANLEY, David .... 724-838-4270. 433 E
stanley@setonhill.edu
STANLEY, Deborah .... 301-860-3543. 220 A
dstanley@bowiestate.edu
STANLEY, Deborah, F .... 315-312-2211. 344 A
deborah.stanley@oswego.edu
STANLEY, Donna, G .... 276-523-7493. 513 A
dstanley@me.vccs.edu
STANLEY, Graydon .... 208-769-7863. 138 I
gastanley@nic.edu
STANLEY, Harold, W .... 214-768-3454. 481 A
hstanley@smu.edu
STANLEY, Jack .... 806-457-4200. 472 G
jstanley@fpctx.edu
STANLEY, Jason .... 251-343-8200..... 6 E
jason.stanley@remingtoncollege.edu
STANLEY, Jay .... 910-879-5503. 358 B
jstanley@bladencc.edu
STANLEY, Jennifer .... 401-254-3123. 440 B
jstanley@rwu.edu
STANLEY, Jeremiah .... 904-596-2333. 117 H
jstanley@tbc.edu
STANLEY, John .... 812-488-2238. 173 H
js405@evansville.edu
STANLEY, Mark .... 805-966-3888... 30 A
mstanley@brooks.edu
STANLEY, Mark .... 712-325-3375. 179 L
mstanley@iwcc.edu
STANLEY, N, J .... 570-321-4131. 422 H
stanley@lycoming.edu
STANLEY, Robert .... 630-829-6625. 140 B
rstanley@ben.edu
STANLEY, Ryan .... 706-355-5114. 120 J
rstanley@athenstech.edu
STANLEY, Samuel, L .... 631-632-6265. 342 C
samuel.stanley@stonybrook.edu
STANLEY, Scott, A .... 603-513-1334. 298 E
scott.stanley@granite.edu
STANLEY, Tuesday, L ..... 816-604-1253. 277 C
tuesday.stanley@mcckc.edu
STANLEY, Valarie, J .... 203-432-0849... 93 A
valarie.stanley@yale.edu
STANLEY-MCAULAY,
Deborah .... 203-436-4072... 93 A
deborah.stanley-mcaulay@yale.edu
STANO, Diana .... 440-646-8101. 392 D
dstano@ursuline.edu
STANOWSKI, Gary .... 573-875-7353. 272 G
gstanowski@ccis.edu
STANSBERRY, Jason ...... 970-207-4500... 86 G
JasonS@uscareerinstitute.edu
STANSBERRY, Terri .... 423-585-6813. 462 A
terri.stansberry@ws.edu
STANSBURY, Calvin .... 252-536-6381. 361 A
cstansbury797@halifaxcc.edu
STANSBURY, Donald, M 757-683-3446. 507 N
dstansbe@odu.edu
STANSBURY, Todd .... 407-823-2261. 115 F
tstansbury@athletics.ucf.edu
STANSLOSKI, Donald ..... 419-434-5327. 391 D
stansloski@findlay.edu
STANTON, Amanda .... 806-291-3414. 494 F
stanton@wbu.edu
STANTON, Danielle .... 603-668-2211. 297 I
d.stanton@snhu.edu
STANTON, Lisa .... 541-956-7024. 407 F
lstanton@roguecc.edu
STANTON, Marian .... 410-276-0306. 218 D
mstanton@host.sdc.edu
STANTON, Mark .... 626-812-3087... 29 H
mstanton@apu.edu
STANTON, Maureen, L ... 530-752-2072... 70 J
mlstanton@ucdavis.edu
STANTON, Michael, J ..... 508-213-2285. 235 E
michael.stanton@nichols.edu
STANTON, Paul .... 617-627-4239. 237 C
paul.stanton@tufts.edu
STANTON, Paul, E .... 413-565-1000. 222 F
pstanton@baypath.edu
STANTON, Tim .... 715-833-6217. 539 J
tstanton@cvtc.edu
STANTON, Timothy, R .... 508-767-7205. 222 C
tr.stanton@assumption.edu
STANTON, William .... 954-262-0225. 109 K
wstanton@moafl.org
STAPLES, Mark .... 617-989-4592. 237 G
staplesm@wit.edu
STAPLES, William, A .... 281-283-2004. 489 C
president@uhcl.edu
STAPLETON, Gregg .... 864-646-1796. 447 D
gstaplet@tctc.edu
STAPLETON, Kemp .... 419-267-1308. 385 F
kstapleton@northweststate.edu
STAPLETON, Marilyn .... 518-243-4471. 314 J
stapletonm@ellismedicine.org
STAPLETON, Michael, F . 706-867-2781. 133 D
michael.stapleton@ung.edu
STAPLETON, Scot .... 205-552-1217..... 3 B
scot.stapleton@ecacolleges.com
STAPLETON, Susan .... 269-387-8212. 252 I
susan.stapleton@wmich.edu
STARACE, Melissa .... 610-861-4589. 425 D
mstarace@northampton.edu
STARASTA, Mike .... 217-732-3155. 151 C
mstarasta@lincolncollege.edu
STARBIRD, S. Andrew .... 408-554-4523... 64 M
sstarbird@scu.edu
STARCEVICH, Joe .... 641-856-2224. 179 A
joe.starcevich@indianhills.edu
STARCEVICH, Mick .... 319-398-5501. 180 J
mstarce@kirkwood.edu

STARCHER, Kevin, M ..... 304-637-1410. 526 E
starcherk@dewv.edu
STARCK, Aaron .... 619-216-6617... 68 B
astarck@swccd.edu
STARCK, Brenda .... 602-286-8060... 14 L
brenda.starck@gwmail.maricopa.edu
STARCK, Brenda .... 602-285-7503... 15 C
brenda.starck@phoenixcollege.edu
STARCK, Patricia, L .... 713-500-2001. 492 E
patricia.l.starck@uth.tmc.edu
STARCZEWSKI, Kirk .... 518-587-2100. 346 A
kirk.starczewski@esc.edu
STAREK, Renee .... 724-838-4276. 433 E
rstarek@setonhill.edu
STARER, Paul .... 650-949-7227... 44 N
starerpaul@foothill.edu
STARGARDTER,
Steven, A .... 619-477-6310... 70 D
sstargardter@usuniveristy.edu
STARGEL, Denton, L .... 201-761-7425. 306 L
dstargel@saintpeters.edu
STARICH, Gale, H .... 770-718-5304. 122 A
gstarich@brenau.edu
STARK, Anne, M .... 906-227-1052. 248 A
astark@nmu.edu
STARK, Brent .... 614-508-7221. 381 E
bstark@hondros.edu
STARK, Debra .... 201-684-7221. 305 A
dstark@ramapo.edu
STARK, Gary .... 623-245-4600... 18 D
gstark@uti.edu
STARK, Inger .... 510-464-3224... 59 C
istark@peralta.edu
STARK, Jared, A .... 402-363-5635. 293 I
jastark@york.edu
STARK, John, D .... 307-766-6242. 543 I
jdstark@uwyo.edu
STARK, Louis, W .... 216-368-2020. 375 J
lou.stark@case.edu
STARK, Michael, M .... 608-246-6737. 540 C
mmstark@madisoncollege.edu
STARK, Paul .... 419-448-2066. 380 G
pstark@heidelberg.edu
STARK, SJ, Paul .... 314-977-7065. 281 I
pstarksj@slu.edu
STARK, Ronald, B .... 678-891-2515. 125 G
ron.stark@gpc.edu
STARK, Scott .... 909-384-8958... 62 A
sstark@sbccd.cc.ca.us
STARK, Wayne, F .... 434-381-6151. 510 F
wstark@sbc.edu
STARK LANE, Nicole ...... 661-255-1050... 31 C
nstark@calarts.edu
STARKE, Christhina .... 800-962-7682. 285 A
cstarke@wma.edu
STARKE, Sandra .... 607-777-2728. 341 E
sstarke@binghamton.edu
STARKE, Sandra .... 607-777-6226. 341 E
sstarke@binghamton.edu
STARKE, William .... 724-266-3838. 434 J
wstarke@tsm.edu
STARKENBURG,
Rebekah, L .... 708-239-4597. 160 K
becky.starkenburg@trnty.edu
STARKEY, Amanda, M ..... 618-235-2700. 160 A
amanda.starkey@swic.edu
STARKEY, Jeremy .... 304-424-8379. 530 E
jeremy.starkey@wvup.edu
STARKEY, Paul, L .... 570-326-3761. 427 B
pls1@pct.edu
STARKEY, Stan, R .... 865-882-4565. 461 E
starkeys@roanestate.edu
STARKEY, Terry .... 870-574-4421... 23 G
tstarkey@sautech.edu
STARKEY-WOODS, Lisa . 607-431-4000. 325 F
STARKMAN, Kenneth, J . 608-243-4440. 540 C
kstarkman@madisoncollege.edu
STARKOVICH, Steven, P 253-535-7126. 521 I
starkosp@plu.edu
STARKS, Ivy .... 256-726-7484..... 6 B
starks@oakwood.edu
STARKS, Jacqueline, M .. 610-660-1081. 432 E
jstarks@sju.edu
STARKS, Marilyn .... 662-621-4154. 266 D
mstarks@coahomacc.edu
STARKS, Sam, B .... 215-898-6993. 435 B
sstarks@upenn.edu
STARKSON, Mary Jo, H . 507-344-7310. 253 J
maryjo.starkson@blc.edu
STARLEY, Monica .... 478-445-4444. 125 A
monica.starley@gcsu.edu
STARLING, Buddy .... 334-670-3243..... 7 H
bstar@troy.edu
STARLING, Sharron .... 206-726-5018. 518 G
sstarling@cornish.edu
STARLING, William, J ...... 910-592-8081. 363 E
bstarlin@sampsoncc.edu
STARNER, Wendy, S .... 717-766-2511. 423 L
wstarner@messiah.edu
STARNES, Richard .... 828-227-7646. 369 E
starnes@wcu.edu

STARNES, Scott .... 434-592-4191. 506 I
sastarnes@liberty.edu
STARNES, Shane .... 704-461-6200. 352 G
shanestarnes@bac.edu
STAROS, James, V .... 413-545-6223. 228 F
jstaros@provost.umass.edu
STARR, Bettie, C .... 270-384-8030. 197 D
starrb@lindsey.edu
STARR, Brian .... 806-720-7405. 476 B
brian.starr@lcu.edu
STARR, Clara .... 415-241-2249... 38 L
cstarr@ccsf.edu
STARR, Dolores .... 904-256-7016. 107 Q
dstarr@ju.edu
STARR, J. Barton .... 561-803-2250. 110 B
barton_starr@pba.edu
STARR, Jeannine .... 914-251-6014. 344 D
jeannine.starr@purchase.edu
STARR, Kenneth, W .... 254-710-3555. 467 G
ken_starr@baylor.edu
STARR, Peter .... 202-885-2446... 94 F
pstarr@american.edu
STARR, Valorie .... 817-598-6252. 494 G
vstarr@wc.edu
STARR FIEDLER,
Heather .... 412-392-3409. 431 B
hstarr@pointpark.edu
STARRATT, Christopher .. 305-899-4757... 98 O
cstarratt@barry.edu
STARRATT, Joseph .... 509-335-4558. 525 A
jstarratt@wsu.edu
STARRETT, David .... 573-986-7477. 282 B
dstarrett@semo.edu
STARSICK, Josh .... 724-852-3425. 437 A
jstarsic@waynesburg.edu
STARTUP, Kenneth, M .... 870-759-4128... 25 K
kstartup@wbcoll.edu
STASA, Joan .... 419-530-2814. 392 B
joan.stasa@utoledo.edu
STASAK, Eric .... 541-880-2234. 403 H
STASCHAK, John, J .... 716-250-7500. 315 J
jjstaschak@bryantstratton.edu
STASHER, Jesse .... 702-968-2004. 295 E
jstasher@roseman.edu
STASIAK, Joan, C .... 773-508-3143. 151 H
jstasia@luc.edu
STASOLLA, Debbie .... 609-896-5228. 305 D
dstasolla@rider.edu
STASSEN, Anne, K .... 215-972-2039. 426 Y
astassen@pafa.edu
STASSEN, Jodi .... 218-793-2539. 260 D
jodistassen@northlandcollege.edu
STASSEN, Martha, L .... 413-545-5146. 228 F
mstassen@acad.umass.edu
STASSIS, Bassel .... 973-684-6500. 304 B
bstassis@pccc.edu
STATE, Timothy .... 847-735-6022. 150 B
state@lakeforest.edu
STATEN, Carmela .... 662-246-6256. 268 B
cstaten@msdelta.edu
STATEN, Michael .... 270-384-8106. 197 D
statenm@lindsey.edu
STATEN, Shannon, D ...... 502-852-6636. 200 D
sdstat01@louisville.edu
STATES, Hollyce .... 508-588-9100. 232 A
STATMORE, Kelly .... 203-910-7258... 90 I
kstatmore@post.edu
STATMORE, Michael .... 203-591-5056... 90 I
mstatmore@post.edu
STATON, Ann .... 940-898-3326. 488 B
astaton@twu.edu
STATON, Trina, J .... 551-574-1312. 179 D
staton@iowacentral.edu
STATON, Wendell .... 478-445-6341. 125 A
wendell.staton@gcsu.edu
STATTON, Christine .... 559-730-3734... 40 I
christines@cos.edu
STATZELL, Donna, S .... 952-995-1447. 258 F
dstatzell@hennepintech.edu
STAUB, Susan .... 814-393-2337. 428 C
sstaub@clarion.edu
STAUBER, Melissa .... 414-410-4057. 532 B
mstauber@stritch.edu
STAUDERMAN, Elizabeth 203-432-1345... 93 A
elizabeth.stauderman@yale.edu
STAUDINGER, Scott, J .... 701-355-8096. 373 E
sjstaudinger@umary.edu
STAUDT, Denise .... 210-829-2761. 490 A
staudt@uiwtx.edu
STAUDT, Loretta .... 202-319-5744... 94 G
staudt@cua.edu
STAUFFENBERG, Serol ... 307-855-2272. 542 Y
serol@cwc.edu
STAUFFER, Denise .... 314-918-2620. 274 A
dstauffer@eden.edu
STAUFFER, Donald .... 757-455-3401. 515 H
dstauffer@vwc.edu
STAUFFER, George, B ..... 848-932-5224. 306 B
stauffer@masongross.rutgers.edu
STAUFFER, Gregory .... 801-321-7104. 496 P
gstaufferr@ushe.edu

STAUFFER, Larry .... 208-885-6470. 139 D
stauffer@uidaho.edu
STAUFFER, Lynn .... 707-664-2171... 36 B
lynn.stauffer@sonoma.edu
STAUFFER, Patricia .... 978-478-3400. 235 G
pstauffer@northpoint.edu
STAUFFER, II, Ronald, E 570-577-3305. 411 A
ron.stauffer@bucknell.edu
STAUNTON, Annette .... 419-448-3410. 389 J
astaunto@tiffin.edu
STAUSS, Michelle .... 973-618-3555. 300 A
mstauss@caldwell.edu
STAUTZ, Shay, D .... 520-621-3108... 18 F
stautzs@email.arizona.edu
STAVENGA, Mink .... 619-482-6442... 68 B
mstavenga@swccd.edu
STAVER, Mathew, D .... 434-592-5300. 506 I
mstaver@liberty.edu
STAVITSKY, Alan .... 775-784-6656. 294 J
ags@unr.edu
STAVRIDIS, James .... 617-628-5000. 237 C
james.stavridis@tufts.edu
ST.CHARLES, Kenneth .... 504-520-7575. 209 D
kstcharl@xula.edu
STEADMAN, Charles .... 972-721-5305. 488 F
cstead@udallas.edu
STEADMAN, Jacqui .... 423-461-8686. 457 H
jrsteadman@milligan.edu
STEADMAN, Jacqui, R .... 423-461-8686. 454 E
JRSteadman@milligan.edu
STEADMAN, Jessica .... 937-695-0307. 389 B
jsteadman@sscc.edu
STEADMAN, John .... 251-460-6140..... 9 E
jsteadman@southalabama.edu
STEADMAN, Mimi, H ..... 716-839-8567. 322 E
msteadma@daemen.edu
STEADMAN, Sheryl .... 801-832-2168. 498 F
ssteadman@westminstercollege.edu
STEADMAN, II,
William, A .... 914-594-4607. 334 A
gus_steadman@nymc.edu
STEAGALL, Jeffrey .... 801-626-6063. 497 D
jeffsteagall@weber.edu
STEANE, Joanne, E .... 307-766-2130. 543 I
jesteane@uwyo.edu
STEARNEY, Michael .... 920-465-2236. 536 F
stearnem@uwgb.edu
STEARNS, Gail .... 714-628-7289... 38 A
stearns@chapman.edu
STEARNS, Jill .... 209-575-6067... 77 J
stearnsj@mjc.edu
STEARNS, Joan .... 352-873-5808. 100 K
stearnsj@cf.edu
STEARNS, Keith .... 559-934-2234... 75 G
keithstearns@whccd.edu
STEARNS, Marc .... 215-503-0155. 434 C
marc.stearns@jefferson.edu
STEARNS, Mary, F .... 513-732-5278. 391 B
mary.stearns@uc.edu
STEARNS, Peter, N .... 703-993-8776. 505 C
pstearns@gmu.edu
STEARNS, Roger .... 956-665-2727. 492 B
stearns@utpa.edu
STEARNS, Sandra .... 262-691-5368. 541 D
sstearns@wctc.edu
STEARNS, Susan, M .... 515-263-2955. 178 G
sstearns@grandview.edu
STEARNS, Thaine .... 707-664-2146... 36 B
stearnst@sonoma.edu
STEARNS MOORE, Kai ... 714-808-4831... 56 D
kstearns@nocccd.edu
STEARNS-SIMS,
Elizabeth .... 406-447-6903. 287 A
STEBACK, Thomas, G ..... 410-857-2205. 216 E
tsteback@mcdaniel.edu
STEBBINS, Barbara .... 207-228-8598. 212 H
stebbins@usm.maine.edu
STEBBINS, Carla .... 515-271-1497. 177 H
carla.stebbins@dmu.edu
STEBBINS, Gerald .... 304-829-7640. 526 D
gstebbins@bethanywv.edu
STEBBINS, Tim .... 202-462-2101... 96 A
tstebbins@iwp.edu
STEBBINS, Todd, H .... 608-246-6976. 540 C
stebbins@madisoncollege.edu
STEC, Gina .... 413-236-2110. 231 A
gstec@berkshirecc.edu
STEC, Paul, T .... 518-783-2314. 340 J
pstec@siena.edu
STECKER, Ann Page .... 603-526-3644. 295 I
astecker@colby-sawyer.edu
STECKMANN, Chris .... 217-732-3155. 151 C
csteckmann@lincolncollege.edu
STEDMAN, Mary .... 631-420-2171. 346 B
mary.stedman@farmingdale.edu
STEED, Caleb .... 325-670-1252. 472 O
csteed@hsutx.edu
STEED, Martha .... 903-233-3803. 475 J
MarthaSteed@letu.edu
STEED, Melody .... 785-227-3380. 184 I
steedm@bethanylb.edu

STEEDLEY, Dwight .... 251-442-2314..... 9 A
dsteedley@umobile.edu
STEEDLEY, Lorrie .... 863-638-7202. 119 C
lorrie.steedley@warner.edu
STEEGE, David .... 262-551-5847. 532 D
steege@carthage.edu
STEEGE, Judi .... 417-667-8181. 273 A
jsteege@cottey.edu
STEEHLER, Jack, K .... 540-375-2540. 509 B
jsteehler@roanoke.edu
STEEL, Ann, E .... 717-866-5775. 416 E
asteel@evangelical.edu
STEEL, Diane, M .... 559-323-2100... 63 B
dsteel@sjcl.edu
STEEL, John .... 620-654-2416. 183 I
jsteel@allencc.edu
STEEL, Virginia .... 310-825-1201... 71 C
vsteel@library.ucla.edu
STEEL, Virginia .... 831-459-2076... 72 C
vsteel@ucsc.edu
STEELE, Anne, C .... 740-826-8115. 384 L
asteele@muskingum.edu
STEELE, Athornia .... 954-262-6100. 109 K
asteele@nova.edu
STEELE, Cherie .... 253-589-6010. 518 B
cherie.steele@cptc.edu
STEELE, Cheryl, L .... 434-381-6134. 510 F
csteele@sbc.edu
STEELE, Claude .... 650-725-9090... 68 E
STEELE, Clint .... 253-566-5207. 524 C
csteele@tacomacc.edu
STEELE, Clover .... 212-247-3434. 329 L
csteele@mandl.edu
STEELE, David .... 863-297-1000. 110 H
dsteele@polk.edu
STEELE, David .... 408-924-3400... 36 A
david.m.steele@sjsu.edu
STEELE, Diane .... 913-758-6102. 191 B
Kathryn.Mustain@stmary.edu
STEELE, Donna .... 731-989-6001. 454 J
dsteele@fhu.edu
STEELE, E. Springs .... 610-660-1879. 432 E
ssteele@sju.edu
STEELE, Emily .... 859-371-9393. 192 D
esteele@beckfield.edu
STEELE, Jessica .... 207-948-9293. 211 I
jsteele@unity.edu
STEELE, Joanne .... 914-633-2691. 327 C
jsteele@iona.edu
STEELE, Karen, B .... 718-631-6604. 319 D
ksteele@qcc.cuny.edu
STEELE, Kemper .... 434-961-6585. 513 F
ksteele@pvcc.edu
STEELE, Kevin, L .... 913-971-3278. 188 H
klsteele@mnu.edu
STEELE, Larry, W .... 540-283-6647. 501 H
lsteele@national-college.edu
STEELE, Laura, L .... 714-879-3901... 47 K
llsteele@hiu.edu
STEELE, Leslie .... 615-547-1268. 454 A
lsteele@cumberland.edu
STEELE, Lia .... 501-370-5286... 22 F
lstelle@philander.edu
STEELE, Linda, M .... 614-947-6583. 380 A
linda.steele@franklin.edu
STEELE, Michael .... 308-535-3723. 290 J
steelem@mpcc.edu
STEELE, Misty .... 405-224-3140. 401 E
msteele@usao.edu
STEELE, Mitzi, B .... 540-375-2249. 509 B
steele@roanoke.edu
STEELE, Patricia, A .... 301-405-9127. 219 B
pasteele@umd.edu
STEELE, Patrick, W .... 701-788-4794. 371 E
Patrick.Steele@mayvillestate.edu
STEELE, Renee .... 910-521-6533. 369 B
renee.steele@uncp.edu
STEELE, Richard .... 404-894-2803. 125 D
rich.steele@gatech.edu
STEELE, Sarah .... 203-582-8905... 91 A
sarah.steele@quinnipiac.edu
STEELE, Scott .... 859-985-3416. 192 F
steeles@berea.edu
STEELE, Steven .... 970-223-2669... 82 F
ssteele@ibmc.edu
STEELE, Todd .... 312-332-0707. 160 J
todd.stelle@tfa.edu
STEELE, Todd, J .... 810-762-9502. 244 Q
tsteele@kettering.edu
STEELE, Valerie .... 212-217-4530. 324 C
valerie_steele@fitnyc.edu
STEELE-MIDDLETON,
Amanda .... 919-760-8424. 356 G
registrar@meredith.edu
STEELE OLIDGE, Trina ... 404-752-5223. 129 E
tolidge@msm.edu
STEELY, Jeffrey .... 254-710-2464. 467 G
jeff_steely@baylor.edu
STEELY, Wayne .... 860-231-5257... 92 F
wsteely@usj.edu

STEEN, Clayton .... 301-860-4363. 220 A
csteen@bowiestate.edu
STEEN, Franklin .... 212-463-0400. 348 B
franklin.steen@touro.edu
STEEN, James .... 281-649-3208. 473 B
jsteen@hbu.edu
STEEN, Kenneth, L .... 540-654-1159. 510 J
ksteen@umw.edu
STEEN, Sara Jayne .... 603-535-2210. 298 G
sjsteen@plymouth.edu
STEEN, Susan .... 256-824-2843..... 8 F
susan.steen@uah.edu
STEENHOEK, David .... 515-643-6680. 181 A
dsteenhoek@mercydesmoines.org
STEENIS, Paul, R .... 309-341-7145. 150 A
psteenis@knox.edu
STEENKEN, Betsy .... 304-327-4176. 529 D
bsteenken@bluefieldstate.edu
STEENSON, Greg .... 651-690-8825. 263 O
gpsteenson@stkate.edu
STEENWYK, Thomas, L .. 616-526-6549. 240 L
steeto@calvin.edu
STEERE-SALAZAR,
Carrie .... 415-502-8296... 72 A
carrie.steere-salazar@ucsf.edu
STEEVES, Myron, R .... 714-836-7500. 160 M
msteeves@tiu.edu
STEFANCO, Carolyn, J .... 404-471-6361. 119 I
cstefanco@agnesscott.edu
STEFANI COMERFORD,
Sandra .... 650-574-6337... 64 C
comerford@smccd.edu
STEFANICK, Susan, A ..... 609-896-5065. 305 D
stefanic@rider.edu
STEFANOWICZ, Michael . 860-512-2663... 88 G
mstefanowicz@manchestercc.edu
STEFANSKI, Kimberly .... 303-404-5481... 81 N
kimberly.stefanski@frontrange.edu
STEFANSKY, Chaim .... 718-259-2525. 315 C
STEFANUCA, Pamela ...... 410-225-2506. 216 C
pstefanuca@mica.edu
STEFFAN, Dee .... 802-654-0505. 501 C
steffand@ccv.edu
STEFFEE, David, J .... 616-632-2895. 239 E
steffdav@aquinas.edu
STEFFEN, Lloyd, H .... 610-758-3877. 422 A
lhs1@lehigh.edu
STEFFEN, Rebecca .... 269-927-8861. 245 D
steffen@lakemichigancollege.edu
STEFFEN, Susan, S .... 630-617-3172. 145 A
susanss@elmhurst.edu
STEFFEN, Wayne .... 559-453-2215... 45 D
wsteffen@fresno.edu
STEFFENS, Kate .... 410-245-2198. 265 D
kate.steffens@waldenu.edu
STEFFENS, Kathy .... 217-732-3155. 151 C
ksteffens@lincolncollege.edu
STEFFES, Gary .... 660-263-4110. 279 B
garys@macc.edu
STEFFES, Jeanne, S .... 413-782-1282. 238 A
jsteffes@wne.edu
STEFFES, Thomas .... 765-983-1366. 165 G
steffto@earlham.edu
STEGALL, Corre, A .... 318-255-7950. 207 F
corre@latechalumni.org
STEGER, Alicia .... 516-572-9634. 332 C
alicia.steger@ncc.edu
STEGER, Charles, W .... 540-231-6231. 515 C
president@vt.edu
STEGMAN, Lindsay .... 765-658-4668. 165 F
lindsaystegman@depauw.edu
STEGMAN, Stephen, J .... 518-629-7158. 326 G
s.stegman@hvcc.edu
STEGMEIER, Randy .... 360-650-3555. 525 C
randy.stegmeier@wwu.edu
STEHLE, Allen .... 207-947-4591. 209 G
astehle@bealcollege.edu
STEHLE, Allen, T .... 207-947-4591. 209 G
astehle@bealcollege.edu
STEHNEY, Ann .... 301-628-5625. 217 C
astehney@nlc.edu
STEHOUWER, Kristin ...... 989-837-4224. 248 C
stehouwer@northwood.edu
STEIBE-PASALICH,
Susan .... 574-631-7336. 174 A
steibe-pasalich.1@nd.edu
STEIDEL, Michael .... 412-268-2082. 412 H
ms44@andrew.cmu.edu
STEIDL, Douglas .... 330-672-2917. 382 B
dsteidl@kent.edu
STEIL, Lora .... 563-387-1134. 180 M
steilo02@luther.edu
STEIN, Beki .... 610-796-8202. 409 E
beki.stein@alvernia.edu
STEIN, Bob .... 207-621-3447. 212 C
rstein@maine.edu
STEIN, Carla .... 303-678-3755... 81 N
carla.stein@frontrange.edu
STEIN, Cliff .... 503-517-1878. 408 I
cstein@westernseminary.edu
STEIN, Dov .... 248-414-6900. 246 F
dstein@mji.edu
STEIN, Jeff .... 336-278-7304. 354 B
jstein@elon.edu
STEIN, Jennifer .... 415-551-9313... 30 K
jstein@cca.edu
STEIN, Jerrold .... 631-632-7320. 342 C
jerrold.stein@stonybrook.edu
STEIN, John .... 914-594-4696. 334 A
john_stein@nymc.edu
STEIN, John .... 404-894-6367. 125 D
john.stein@vpss.gatech.edu
STEIN, Karen P, Z .... 585-785-1298. 324 D
steinkp@flcc.edu
STEIN, Kathy .... 432-837-8770. 487 B
kstein@sulross.edu
STEIN, Linda .... 610-917-1416. 436 C
llstein@vfcc.edu
STEIN, Lisa .... 308-432-6263. 291 D
lstein@csc.edu
STEIN, Maria, K .... 617-373-2430. 235 F
STEIN, Mark, A .... 507-354-8221. 256 M
steinma@mlc-wels.edu
STEIN, Mary, T .... 248-370-3045. 248 J
stein@oakland.edu
STEIN, Melanie .... 860-297-5244... 91 F
melanie.stein@trincoll.edu
STEIN, N .... 732-364-1220. 299 B
STEIN, Scott .... 802-447-6349. 500 D
sstein@svc.edu
STEIN, Sonya .... 907-786-1517... 10 H
sefisher@uaa.alaska.edu
STEIN, Sue .... 503-352-7285. 407 A
steins@pacificu.edu
STEIN, Tom .... 423-636-7300. 462 E
STEIN-SMITH, Kathy .... 201-692-2653. 301 J
stein@fdu.edu
STEIN-WEBBER, Brian .... 510-559-2711... 57 F
bsteinwebber@plts.edu
STEINACKER, Kathy .... 815-939-5359. 155 H
ksteinac@olivet.edu
STEINBACK, Robin .... 951-571-6350... 60 K
robin.steinback@mvc.edu
STEINBERG, Aaron .... 718-868-2300. 314 I
STEINBERG, Bettie .... 516-562-1159. 323 E
bsteinbe@lij.edu
STEINBERG, Bryan, E .... 302-356-6858... 94 E
bryan.e.steinberg@wilmu.edu
STEINBERG, Don .... 802-258-3357. 500 C
donald.steinberg@worldlearning.org
STEINBERG, James, B .... 315-443-5450. 347 C
jbstein@syr.edu
STEINBERG, Joseph .... 973-642-8746. 307 D
joseph.steinberg@shu.edu
STEINBERG, Kurt .... 617-879-7269. 230 B
ksteinberg@massart.edu
STEINBERG, Laura, J .... 315-443-4341. 347 C
ljs@syr.edu
STEINBERG, Leslie, R ..... 213-738-6731... 68 C
publicaffairs@swlaw.edu
STEINBERG, Stacey .... 414-847-3255. 534 F
staceysteinberg@miad.edu
STEINBOCK, Daniel .... 419-530-5099. 392 B
daniel.steinbock@utoledo.edu
STEINBOCK, Valerie .... 928-541-7777... 16 B
vsteinbock@ncu.edu
STEINER, Ann .... 717-291-3986. 416 J
ann.steiner@fandm.edu
STEINER, David .... 440-646-8302. 392 D
dsteiner@ursuline.edu
STEINER, David .... 212-772-4000. 318 C
david.steiner@hunter.cuny.edu
STEINER, Fred .... 313-845-9621. 243 H
fred@hfcc.edu
STEINER, Frederick, R .... 512-471-1922. 491 C
fsteiner@austin.utexas.edu
STEINER, Glen, D .... 708-209-3328. 143 E
glen.steiner@cuchicago.edu
STEINER, Gregory, G ...... 276-944-6763. 504 H
gsteiner@ehc.edu
STEINER, James, D .... 563-589-3210. 182 J
jsteiner@dbq.edu
STEINER, Joseph, F .... 307-766-6556. 543 I
jspharmd@uwyo.edu
STEINER, Karl, V .... 410-455-5827. 219 D
STEINER, Kat .... 937-484-1282. 392 C
ksteiner@urbana.edu
STEINER, Mark .... 731-989-6099. 454 J
msteiner@fhu.edu
STEINER, Michael .... 330-287-7504. 386 F
steiner.255@osu.edu
STEINER, Rita, L .... 410-617-2504. 216 A
rsteiner@loyola.edu
STEINER, Terry .... 406-657-1078. 288 B
steinert@rocky.edu
STEINER-LANG, Kathy .... 314-935-5910. 284 L
ksteiner@wustl.edu
STEINERT, Brandon .... 620-792-9307. 184 F
steinertb@bartonccc.edu
STEINFELD, Peter, K .... 712-749-2205. 176 D
steinfeld@bvu.edu
STEINFELD, Trudy, G ..... 212-998-4735. 334 D
trudy.steinfeld@nyu.edu
STEINHAGEN, Robert ..... 206-316-2458. 516 J
roberts@bgu.edu
STEINHOFF, Cynthia, K .. 410-777-2483. 213 D
cksteinhoff@aacc.edu
STEINKAMP, Janet .... 320-308-5933. 261 C
jsteinkamp@sctcc.edu
STEINKE, Deana, B .... 304-877-6428. 526 C
financialaid@abc.edu
STEINKE, Robin, J .... 717-334-6286. 422 E
rsteinke@ltsg.edu
STEINKEOWAY,
Louise, A .... 407-851-2525. 102 K
lsteinke@cci.edu
STEINKIRCHNER,
Linda, M .... 585-385-5242. 338 H
lsteinkirchner@sjfc.edu
STEINMAN, Alan .... 616-331-3749. 243 C
steinmaa@gvsu.edu
STEINMETZ, JR.,
Edward, J .... 570-941-4289. 436 A
edward.steinmetz@scranton.edu
STEINMETZ, Joseph, E ... 614-292-5881. 386 E
steinmetz.53@osu.edu
STEINMETZ, Michael .... 859-253-3637. 194 A
michael.steinmetz@frontier.edu
STEINMETZ, Paul .... 203-837-9805... 88 B
steinmetzp@wcsu.edu
STEINMETZ, Paul, M ...... 203-837-9805... 88 B
steinmetzp@wcsu.edu
STEINMETZ, Rob, R .... 717-736-4140. 417 I
rrsteinm@hacc.edu
STEINNERD, Sarah .... 573-651-2588. 282 B
ssteinnerd@semo.edu
STEINOUR, David .... 703-726-3602... 95 D
steinour@gwu.edu
STEINRUCK, Jessica, M . 202-231-3344. 544 L
jessica.steinruck@dodiis.mil
STEINWEDEL, Cheryl ...... 419-227-3141. 391 F
csteinwedel@unoh.edu
STEISKAL, Mokie .... 614-287-2572. 378 B
msteiska@cscc.edu
STEITZ, John, A .... 740-284-5177. 379 N
jsteitz@franciscan.edu
STEJSKAL, Patricia .... 815-479-7530. 152 F
pstejskal@mchenry.edu
STEKETEE, Gail .... 617-353-3760. 224 D
steketee@bu.edu
STELLA, Hilde, V .... 787-284-1912. 550 F
hstella@ponce.inter.edu
STELLA, Mark .... 304-384-5356. 529 E
markstella@hotmail.com
STELLA, Steven .... 518-454-5139. 321 A
stellas@strose.edu
STELTER, Caroline, W ..... 804-758-6728. 513 G
cstelter@rappahannock.edu
STELZER, Stuart, P .... 479-979-1381... 25 J
sstelzer@ozarks.edu
STEM, Elaine .... 252-492-2061. 364 F
stem@vgcc.edu
STEMBRIDGE, Allen, F ... 269-471-3622. 239 D
stem@andrews.edu
STEMBRIDGE,
Catherine, L .... 847-491-3246. 155 D
c-stembridge@northwestern.edu
STEMEN, Derek .... 419-358-3661. 374 J
stemend@bluffton.edu
STEMKOSKI, Stephen ..... 315-859-4301. 325 E
sstemkos@hamilton.edu
STEMMER, John, K .... 502-272-8140. 192 E
jstemmer@bellarmine.edu
STEMPER, Diane, L .... 614-292-3600. 386 E
stemper.1@osu.edu
STEMPLE, Fred .... 757-822-7415. 514 C
fstemple@tcc.edu
STEN, Andrea .... 503-493-6529. 402 J
asten@cu-portland.edu
STENBECK, Amber, L ...... 919-508-2037. 370 F
astenbeck@peace.edu
STENBERG, Richard, W .. 937-327-7460. 393 E
rstenberg@wittenberg.edu
STENBERG, Steve .... 503-517-1238. 408 H
sstenberg@warnerpacific.edu
STENCIL, Debra .... 715-675-3331. 541 A
stencil@ntc.edu
STENDARDI,
Deborah, M .... 585-475-5040. 337 L
dmsgrl@rit.edu
STENDER, Julie .... 435-652-7703. 497 E
stender@dixie.edu
STENEHJEM, Keith, A ..... 701-788-4755. 371 E
Keith.Stenehjem@mayvillestate.edu
STENGEL, Mark .... 805-546-3159... 42 C
mark_stengel@cuesta.edu
STENGER, JR.,
Harvey, G .... 607-777-2131. 341 E
president@binghamton.edu
STENGER, Karen .... 440-826-2726. 374 F
kstenger@bw.edu
STENHOUSE, Andrew ...... 714-556-3610... 74 D
andrew.stenhouse@vanguard.edu
STENKO, Michael .... 860-465-4509... 87 L
stenkom@easternct.edu
STENNES-SPIDAHL,
Naomi, R .... 608-796-3481. 539 E
nrstennesspidahl@viterbo.edu
STENNETT, Debbie .... 806-291-3500. 494 F
stennettd@wbu.edu
STENNETTE, Jan .... 434-544-8381. 506 K
stennette@lynchburg.edu
STENSON, Charlene .... 701-845-7105. 372 A
c.stenson@vcsu.edu
STENSON, Charlene .... 701-845-7105. 372 A
charlene.stenson@vcsu.edu
STENSON, Linnea .... 612-659-6103. 259 D
linnea.stenson@minneapolis.edu
STENTIFORD, Deanna ..... 352-854-2322. 100 K
stentifd@cf.edu
STEORTS, Ken .... 901-381-3939. 464 C
ken@visible.edu
STEPANOVICH, Michael . 661-395-4840... 49 N
mstepano@bakersfieldcollge.edu
STEPHAN, Andrew .... 330-494-6170. 389 F
astephan@starkstate.edu
STEPHAN, Arline .... 215-641-6534. 424 B
astephen@mc3.edu
STEPHAN, Lisa, M .... 920-565-1255. 533 R
stephanlm@lakeland.edu
STEPHAN, Sharon, R .... 402-472-7554. 292 G
sstephan@nebraska.edu
STEPHAN, W. Karl .... 989-837-4211. 248 C
stephan@northwood.edu
STEPHAN, William, B ...... 812-855-0850. 167 E
wstephan@indiana.edu
STEPHAN, William, B ..... 317-231-2114. 167 F
wstephan@indiana.edu
STEPHAN HAINS,
Theresa, R .... 716-878-6711. 343 A
stephatr@buffalostate.edu
STEPHEN, Carolyn .... 530-895-2311... 30 F
stephenca@butte.edu
STEPHEN, Cathleen .... 610-607-6205. 431 D
cstephen@racc.edu
STEPHEN BURT,
M. Rachel .... 317-940-9867. 164 J
rstephen@butler.edu
STEPHEN-SELBY,
Heather .... 509-533-7311. 518 E
heather.stephen-selby@scc.spokane.edu
STEPHENOFF, Gail, C .... 614-292-5648. 386 E
stephenoff.1@osu.edu
STEPHENS, Amy, M .... 503-255-0332. 404 F
astephens@multnomah.edu
STEPHENS, Arthur .... 828-227-7203. 369 E
stephena@wcu.edu
STEPHENS, Cathy .... 217-641-4515. 148 M
cstephens@jwcc.edu
STEPHENS, Charlene .... 302-736-2505... 94 C
stephech@wesley.edu
STEPHENS, Christina ...... 207-326-2441. 211 D
christina.stephens@mma.edu
STEPHENS, Crystal .... 661-726-1911... 70 G
crystal.stephens@uav.edu
STEPHENS, David .... 877-442-0505... 86 F
david.stephens@rockies.edu
STEPHENS, David, J .... 931-363-9865. 456 C
dstephens@martinmethodist.edu
STEPHENS, Denise .... 805-893-3256... 72 B
dstephensr@library.ucsb.edu
STEPHENS, Diane, S .... 818-677-5929... 34 C
diane.stephens@csun.edu
STEPHENS, Edward .... 417-455-5596. 273 E
EdwardStephens@crowder.edu
STEPHENS, Elisa .... 415-274-2200... 26 C
STEPHENS, Fred, W .... 407-303-5752... 97 H
fred.stephens@adu.edu
STEPHENS, Janice .... 256-378-2003..... 2 G
jstephens@cacc.edu
STEPHENS, Jay .... 541-552-8557. 406 C
stephenj1@sou.edu
STEPHENS, Jerry, W .... 205-934-6360..... 8 E
jerryws@uab.edu
STEPHENS, Josh .... 806-720-7502. 476 B
josh.stephens@lcu.edu
STEPHENS, Kevin, N ...... 309-655-2291. 158 C
kevin.n.stephens@osfhealthcare.org
STEPHENS, Lisa .... 760-379-5001... 49 O
lisa.stephens@cerrocoso.edu
STEPHENS, Mark .... 931-372-3224. 460 A
mstephens@tntech.edu
STEPHENS, Mark, R .... 701-355-8123. 373 E
STEPHENS, Mary .... 213-624-1200... 44 D
mstephens@fidm.edu
STEPHENS, Mary, E .... 562-985-1658... 33 F
mestephe@csulb.edu
STEPHENS, Mary Ann ..... 330-672-2121. 382 B
mstephen@kent.edu
STEPHENS, Michael .... 323-259-2651... 56 I
mstephens@oxy.edu

STEPHENS, Ralph ... 361-593-3814. 484 A
ralph.stephens@tamuk.edu
STEPHENS, Rick ... 607-871-2137. 313 E
stephens@alfred.edu
STEPHENS, Robert, E ... 816-654-7533. 275 K
rstephens@kcumb.edu
STEPHENS, Robin ... 501-212-6608... 20 I
rstephens@cbc.edu
STEPHENS, Rusty ... 252-246-1223. 365 C
rstephens@wilsoncc.edu
STEPHENS, Sandra, S ... 901-722-3220. 458 K
sandra@sco.edu
STEPHENS, Scott ... 205-665-6663... 9 B
stephens@montevallo.edu
STEPHENS, Sharon ... 215-968-8468. 411 B
stephens@bucks.edu
STEPHENS, Sonya ... 812-855-8783. 167 F
sonsteph@indiana.edu
STEPHENS, Sonya ... 413-538-2372. 234 D
stephens@mtholyoke.edu
STEPHENS, Toni ... 972-883-2693. 491 E
tmesser@utdallas.edu
STEPHENS, Valerie ... 865-471-4727. 453 F
vstephens@cn.edu
STEPHENS, Vincent, L ... 570-577-1095. 411 A
vincent.stephens@bucknell.edu
STEPHENS, Virginia, L ... 203-396-8302... 91 C
stephensv@sacredheart.edu
STEPHENS, Zena, A ... 936-261-1387. 482 F
zastephens@pvamu.edu
STEPHENSON, Alan, H ... 828-694-1821. 358 C
ah_stephenson@blueridge.edu
STEPHENSON, Cathy ... 828-694-1807. 358 C
ck_stephenson@blueridge.edu
STEPHENSON, Devin ... 573-840-9698. 282 K
dstephenson@trcc.edu
STEPHENSON, Diane ... 903-593-8311. 485 A
dstephenson@texascollege.edu
STEPHENSON, Diane ... 217-732-3155. 151 C
dstephenson@lincolncollege.edu
STEPHENSON, E. Frank .. 252-398-6278. 353 H
stephf@chowan.edu
STEPHENSON, Jeffrey ... 916-484-8376... 53 A
stephej@arc.losrios.edu
STEPHENSON, Laura ... 785-670-1561. 191 D
laura.stephenson@washburn.edu
STEPHENSON,
Melissa, K ... 603-924-2481. 297 D
mstephenson@nec.edu
STEPHENSON,
Norman, J ... 308-635-6121. 293 E
stephens@wncc.edu
STEPHENSON, Rod ... 206-878-3710. 520 E
rstephenson@highline.edu
STEPHENSON, Susan ... 307-532-8325. 542 a
susan.stephenson@ewc.wy.edu
STEPHENSON, Susan, E . 850-474-2487. 117 B
sstephenson@uwf.edu
STEPHENSON, Thomas .. 610-328-8319. 433 I
tstephe1@swarthmore.edu
STEPHERSON, Kenneth ... 814-824-2273. 423 J
kstepherson@mercyhurst.edu
STEPHNEY, Jessie ... 601-877-6471. 265 G
jstephney@alcorn.edu
STEPLIGHT-JOHNSON,
Stephanie ... 973-877-3496. 301 H
ssteplig@essex.edu
STEPNIAK, Michael, J ... 540-665-4600. 509 E
mstepnia@su.edu
STEPP, James, D ... 207-768-9560. 212 G
james.stepp@umpi.edu
STEPP, Jim ... 606-368-6454. 191 J
jamesstepp@alc.edu
STEPP, Joe, A ... 606-368-6027. 191 J
jocstepp@alc.edu
STEPP, Perry ... 972-241-3371. 470 E
pstepp@dallas.edu
STEPPE, Stephen ... 412-536-1275. 420 A
stephen.steppe@laroche.edu
STEPTOE, David ... 478-289-2049. 124 C
dsteptoe@ega.edu
STERK, Claire, E ... 404-727-6055. 124 E
claire.sterk@emory.edu
STERK, Jim ... 619-594-6357... 35 D
adsdsu@mail.sdsu.edu
STERKOWITZ, Robert ... 708-974-5250. 153 F
sterkowitz@morainevalley.edu
STERLING, Alan ... 972-721-5347. 488 F
asterling@udallas.edu
STERLING, Althea ... 718-951-5916. 317 C
asterling@brooklyn.cuny.edu
STERLING, Christa ... 860-832-2277... 87 K
csterling@ccsu.edu
STERLING, Gregory, E ... 203-432-5304... 93 A
gregory.sterling@yale.edu
STERLING, Marcia ... 505-566-3588. 311 I
sterlingm@sanjuancollege.edu
STERLING, Michael ... 770-426-2979. 128 D
mike.sterling@life.edu
STERLING, Monique ... 610-992-1700... 96 F
STERLING, Shauna ... 479-619-3136... 22 C
ssterling1@nwacc.edu
STERLING, Ted ... 216-381-1680. 385 G
tsterling@ndc.edu
STERLING, Walter, J ... 505-984-6070. 311 H
dean@sjcsf.edu
STERN, Dana ... 419-473-2700. 378 I
dstern@daviscolleg.edu
STERN, David ... 813-258-7360. 118 L
provost@ut.edu
STERN, Deborah ... 215-576-0800. 431 E
dstern@rrc.edu
STERN, Dennis ... 802-831-1155. 500 H
dstern@vermontlaw.edu
STERN, Donna ... 203-371-7929... 91 C
sternd@sacredheart.edu
STERN, Gail ... 413-205-3549. 221 F
gail.stern@aic.edu
STERN, Hal, S ... 949-824-7405... 71 B
icsdean@uci.edu
STERN, Holly, C ... 973-596-6379. 303 G
holly.stern@njit.edu
STERN, Jonathan, S ... 765-361-6152. 175 B
sternj@wabash.edu
STERN, Joshua ... 215-572-2934. 409 H
sternj@arcadia.edu
STERN, Joyce ... 641-269-3702. 178 H
sternjm@grinnell.edu
STERN, Kevin, D ... 214-887-5111. 471 F
kstern@dts.edu
STERN, Robert A, M ... 203-432-2279... 93 A
robert.stern@yale.edu
STERN, Shannyn ... 928-541-7777... 16 B
sstern@ncu.edu
STERN, Sharon ... 254-710-1010. 467 G
sharon_stern@baylor.edu
STERN, Steve ... 608-263-1841. 536 D
sjstern@wisc.edu
STERN, Susan ... 262-695-3451. 541 D
sstern1@wctc.edu
STERN LANIAK, Lorna ... 215-572-2145. 409 H
sternl@arcadia.edu
STERNBERG, Robert ... 307-766-4121. 543 I
robert.sternberg@uwyo.edu
STERNER, Sheri ... 714-432-5081... 39 K
ssterner@occ.cccd.edu
STERNS, Teresa, G ... 304-462-4110. 529 G
teresa.sterns@glenville.edu
STERRETT, Joseph, D ... 610-758-4320. 422 A
jds7@lehigh.edu
STERRETT, Myra ... 352-395-5150. 113 C
myra.sterrett@sfcollege.edu
STETLER, P. Daniel ... 772-546-5534. 106 N
danstetler@hsbc.edu
STETLER, Paul ... 772-546-5534. 106 N
paulstetler@hsbc.edu
STETTER, Mark ... 970-491-7051... 80 I
mark.stetter@colostate.edu
STEURBAUT, Margo ... 213-740-2561... 74 A
steurbau@usc.edu
STEVANUS, Linda ... 301-387-3011. 214 I
linda.stevanus@garrettcollege.edu
STEVENS, Adrian ... 909-607-8684... 59 G
adrian_stevens@pitzer.edu
STEVENS, Alison ... 206-934-4547. 522 I
alison.stevens@seattlecolleges.edu
STEVENS, Andrea, N ... 662-329-7431. 268 E
astevens@dev.muw.edu
STEVENS, Andrew ... 303-914-6201... 84 I
andrew.stevens@rrcc.edu
STEVENS, Anne, A ... 704-461-6718. 352 G
annestevens@bac.edu
STEVENS, Annie ... 802-656-3380. 500 F
annie.stevens@uvm.edu
STEVENS, Arshele ... 312-553-2500. 141 M
astevens11@ccc.edu
STEVENS, Audrey ... 937-484-1319. 392 C
astevens@urbana.edu
STEVENS, Bren ... 304-357-4911. 527 H
brenstevens@ucwv.edu
STEVENS, Brenda, D ... 330-471-8328. 383 D
bstevens@malone.edu
STEVENS, Carol ... 845-431-8974. 323 C
cstevens@sunydutchess.edu
STEVENS, Cathleen, M ... 585-389-2001. 332 D
csteven9@naz.edu
STEVENS, Cheryl, L ... 270-745-4448. 200 G
cheryl.stevens@wku.edu
STEVENS, Darryl ... 406-771-4321. 287 E
darryl.stevens@gfcmsu.edu
STEVENS, Debbie ... 641-673-2173. 183 H
stevensd@wmpenn.edu
STEVENS, Dennis, G ... 434-223-6112. 505 E
dstevens@hsc.edu
STEVENS, Doug ... 715-232-2488. 538 B
stevensd@uwstout.edu
STEVENS, Elizabeth ... 651-690-8600. 263 O
ejstevens@stkate.edu
STEVENS, Gladstone, H .. 650-289-3344... 61 G
gladstone.stevens@stpatricksseminary.org
STEVENS, Greg ... 509-434-5037. 518 E
greg.stevens@ccs.spokane.edu
STEVENS, Greg ... 509-434-5037. 518 F
greg.stevens@ccs.spokane.edu
STEVENS, Greg, L ... 509-434-5037. 518 D
gstevens@ccs.spokane.edu
STEVENS, Ian ... 704-216-7138. 363 D
ian.stevens@rccc.edu
STEVENS, Irene, E ... 317-940-9470. 164 J
istevens@butler.edu
STEVENS, Jim ... 651-290-6328. 265 F
jim.stevens@wmitchell.edu
STEVENS, John, V ... 540-665-4925. 509 E
jstevens@su.edu
STEVENS, Karl P, B ... 740-427-5223. 382 J
stevensk@kenyon.edu
STEVENS, Kasey ... 937-327-7800. 393 E
kstevens@wittenberg.edu
STEVENS, Ken ... 312-279-3804... 28 M
kcstevens@argosy.edu
STEVENS, Mark ... 818-677-4069... 34 C
mark.stevens@csun.edu
STEVENS, Mark, W ... 920-206-2314. 533 U
mstevens@mbbc.edu
STEVENS, Marty ... 717-334-6286. 422 E
mstevens@ltsg.edu
STEVENS, RSM,
Maryanne ... 402-399-2435. 289 A
mstevens@csm.edu
STEVENS, Matt ... 561-803-2200. 110 B
national@pba.edu
STEVENS, Michael ... 616-222-1430. 241 F
michael.stevens@cornerstone.edu
STEVENS, Michele ... 806-457-4200. 472 G
mstevens@fpctx.edu
STEVENS, Moira ... 207-775-3052. 210 H
mstevens@meca.edu
STEVENS, Nick ... 906-487-7231. 242 G
nick.stevens@finlandia.edu
STEVENS, Phil ... 207-775-3052. 210 H
pstevens@meca.edu
STEVENS, Randy ... 909-558-4558... 51 C
rstevens@llu.edu
STEVENS, Robert ... 203-932-7435... 92 E
rstevens@newhaven.edu
STEVENS, Roger, K ... 847-259-1840. 141 L
rstevens@christianlifecollege.edu
STEVENS, Roxanne ... 503-682-3903. 407 B
rstevens@pioneerpacific.edu
STEVENS, Ruth ... 609-258-8108. 304 E
stevens@princeton.edu
STEVENS, Sheri, R ... 207-621-3110. 212 C
sheri@maine.edu
STEVENS, Timothy, S ... 847-491-7256. 155 D
tstevens@northwestern.edu
STEVENS, Turney ... 615-966-7657. 456 B
turney.stevens@lipscomb.edu
STEVENS, Wayne ... 570-586-2400. 410 D
wstevens@bbc.edu
STEVENS-RICHMAN,
Jana ... 718-260-3164. 336 E
jrichman@poly.edu
STEVENS-TAYLOR,
Calley ... 610-372-4721. 431 D
cstevenstaylor@racc.edu
STEVENSON, Adalynn, J . 660-543-4195. 283 A
stevenson@ucmo.edu
STEVENSON, Bill ... 479-524-7119... 21 G
wstevens@jbu.edu
STEVENSON, Deirdra, M 405-466-3216. 395 N
dmstevenson@langston.edu
STEVENSON, Duncan ... 253-964-6612. 522 C
dstevenson@pierce.ctc.edu
STEVENSON, Elizabeth ... 508-830-6683. 230 D
estevenson@maritime.edu
STEVENSON,
Gwendolyn, A ... 937-778-7949. 379 G
gstevenson@edisonohio.edu
STEVENSON, James, E ... 904-632-3191. 105 E
james.stevenson@fscj.edu
STEVENSON, Jeffry, J ... 850-872-3805. 106 H
jstevenson@gulfcoast.edu
STEVENSON, John ... 954-545-4500. 113 F
STEVENSON, John, A ... 303-492-2890... 85 L
john.stevenson@colorado.edu
STEVENSON, Karen, L ... 615-353-3430. 461 B
karen.stevenson@nscc.edu
STEVENSON, Laura ... 904-819-6205. 103 E
lstevenson@flagler.edu
STEVENSON, Leslie, W ... 804-289-8141. 510 L
lsteven2@richmond.edu
STEVENSON, Mark ... 724-266-3838. 434 J
mstevenson@tsm.edu
STEVENSON, Martha ... 570-674-6224. 424 A
mstevens@misericordia.edu
STEVENSON, Martha, A .. 205-226-4648... 2 C
mstevens@bsc.edu
STEVENSON, Melissa ... 270-707-3811. 195 E
melissa.stevenson@kctcs.edu
STEVENSON, Michael ... 207-780-4485. 212 H
mstevenson@usm.maine.edu
STEVENSON, Michael ... 406-994-2513. 287 B
michael@montana.edu
STEVENSON, Michael ... 406-994-2053. 287 B
michael@montana.edu
STEVENSON, Paula ... 954-545-4500. 113 F
library@sfbc.edu
STEVENSON, Roberta ... 973-748-9000. 299 F
STEVENSON, Rosalie ... 864-941-8529. 446 C
stevenson.r@ptc.edu
STEVENSON, Sarah ... 718-405-3723. 320 G
sarah.stevenson@mountsaintvincent.edu
STEVENSON, Susan, G ... 334-683-2303... 5 F
sstevenson@marionmilitary.edu
STEVENSON, Tara ... 904-826-8508. 103 E
tstevenson@flagler.edu
STEVENSON, Terree, L ... 740-368-3151. 387 J
tlsteven@owu.edu
STEVENSON, JR.,
Tommy ... 662-325-2493. 268 D
tstevenson@pres.msstate.edu
STEVENSON, Ty, S ... 313-577-2300. 252 G
ty.stevenson@wayne.edu
STEVENSON, Valerie, O .. 904-620-2920. 116 B
vstevens@unf.edu
STEVENSON MARSHALL,
Brenda ... 509-313-3569. 520 A
stevenson-marshall@gonzaga.edu
STEVENSON-RATLIFF,
Peggy ... 803-535-5233. 442 B
pratliff@claflin.edu
STEVER, Matthew ... 518-694-7221. 313 B
matthew.stever@acphs.edu
STEVERSON, Les ... 228-897-7137. 270 I
les.steverson@wmcarey.edu
STEVICK, David ... 585-567-9607. 326 F
david.stevick@houghton.edu
STEVICK, Thomas ... 734-481-2303. 242 D
tstevick@emich.edu
STEWARD, Agnes ... 253-840-8403. 522 C
asteward@pierce.ctc.edu
STEWARD, Deborah ... 315-781-3500. 326 C
stewart@hws.edu
STEWARD, Derrick ... 803-793-5147. 443 E
stewardd@denmarktech.edu
STEWARD, Donald ... 937-376-6425. 376 E
dsteward@centralstate.edu
STEWARD, Gary ... 405-974-5528. 400 K
gsteward@uco.edu
STEWARD, Irene ... 217-709-0926. 150 E
isteward@lakeviewcol.edu
STEWARD, Jerry ... 405-682-7879. 397 E
jsteward@occc.edu
STEWARD, Kent, L ... 785-628-4206. 186 F
ksteward@fhsu.edu
STEWARD, Kyle ... 662-325-3221. 268 D
ksteward@pres.msstate.edu
STEWARD, JR., Sterling . 912-358-3449. 131 C
ssuathletics@savannahstate.edu
STEWARD-BRIDGES,
Stephanie ... 574-284-4721. 172 G
sbridges@saintmarys.edu
STEWART, Andrea ... 870-575-8053... 24 E
stewarta@uapb.edu
STEWART, Avis ... 765-983-1393. 165 G
aviss@earlham.edu
STEWART, Barbara ... 937-769-1863. 373 I
bstewart@antioch.edu
STEWART, Barbara, A ... 408-554-4396... 64 M
bstewart@scu.edu
STEWART, Barbara, E ... 608-785-5092. 536 G
bstewart@uwlax.edu
STEWART, Beth ... 828-398-7650. 357 N
bethstewart@abtech.edu
STEWART, Betsy ... 610-526-5632. 410 J
estewart@brynmawr.edu
STEWART, Betty ... 940-397-4226. 476 H
betty.stewart@mwsu.edu
STEWART, Billy, W ... 601-635-6200. 266 H
bstewart@eccc.edu
STEWART, Brad, J ... 240-567-1312. 216 F
brad.stewart@montgomerycollege.edu
STEWART, Brent, A ... 843-953-1618. 442 A
brent.stewart@citadel.edu
STEWART, Bryan ... 817-515-1011. 482 B
bryan.stewart@tccd.edu
STEWART, Carolyn, G ... 803-327-8014. 449 J
cstewart@yorktech.edu
STEWART, Carrie ... 310-665-6981... 57 C
cstewart@otis.edu
STEWART, Colin ... 309-556-3850. 148 B
cstewar1@iwu.edu
STEWART, Colin ... 540-338-1776. 508 A
STEWART, Concetta ... 914-674-7500. 330 J
cstewart@mercy.edu
STEWART, Connie ... 989-328-1249. 247 D
connies@montcalm.edu
STEWART, Constance ... 410-572-5640. 218 D
cstewart@host.sdc.edu
STEWART, Craig ... 812-855-4240. 167 F
stewart@iu.edu

STEWART, Dan .... 512-499-4616. 491 A
dstewart@utsystem.edu
STEWART, Daniel, P .... 904-818-6238. 103 E
stewartd@flagler.edu
STEWART, Dave .... 303-753-6046... 85 B
dstewart@rmcad.edu
STEWART, David .... 304-865-6089. 527 F
david.stewart@ovu.edu
STEWART, David, C .... 304-293-5811. 530 D
david.stewart@mail.wvu.edu
STEWART, David, R .... 651-638-6225. 253 K
d-stewart@bethel.edu
STEWART, Dawn .... 614-823-3529. 387 K
dstewart@otterbein.edu
STEWART, Dean .... 920-498-6995. 541 B
dean.stewart@nwtc.edu
STEWART, Deborah .... 802-885-8370. 501 C
stewartd@ccv.edu
STEWART, DeShaunta ..... 773-907-4044. 142 A
dstewart75@ccc.edu
STEWART, Diane .... 661-362-3503... 40 E
diane.stewart@canyons.edu
STEWART, Donette .... 864-503-5280. 448 H
dstewart@uscupstate.edu
STEWART, Donna, H .... 630-942-3978. 142 G
stewartdo@cod.edu
STEWART, Dorothy .... 313-993-1028. 250 K
stewardm@udmercy.edu
STEWART, Doug .... 970-945-8691... 79 G
STEWART, Douglas, J ..... 585-385-8427. 338 H
dstewart@sjfc.edu
STEWART, Elizabeth, J .... 585-292-2536. 332 A
estewart@monroecc.edu
STEWART, Emily .... 765-983-1393. 165 G
stewaem@earlham.edu
STEWART, Gloria .... 740-376-4458. 383 E
gloria.stewart@marietta.edu
STEWART, Gloria .... 830-792-7265. 480 F
gpstewart@schreiner.edu
STEWART, Graham, G ..... 479-575-2801... 23 I
stewartg@uark.edu
STEWART, Henry .... 334-670-3266..... 7 H
hstewart@troy.edu
STEWART, Jacqueline ..... 606-368-6059. 191 J
jacquelinestewart@alc.edu
STEWART, James .... 410-951-2639. 220 B
jstewart@coppin.edu
STEWART, James .... 731-352-4093. 453 D
stewartj@bethelu.edu
STEWART, James .... 503-517-1898. 408 I
jstewart@westernseminary.edu
STEWART, Janeen, K .... 319-352-8331. 183 E
janeen.stewart@wartburg.edu
STEWART, Janie .... 810-766-4209. 239 H
janie.stewart@baker.edu
STEWART, Jeanine .... 410-857-2248. 216 E
jstewart@mcdaniel.edu
STEWART, Jeb .... 540-231-2134. 515 C
jebs@vt.edu
STEWART, Jeffrey .... 239-433-9119. 101 O
jstewart10@edison.edu
STEWART, Jellema .... 716-673-3398. 342 A
jellema.stewart@fredonia.edu
STEWART, Jennifer .... 314-968-7105. 284 N
violett@webster.edu
STEWART, Jerry, D .... 515-294-6762. 175 H
jdstewa@iastate.edu
STEWART, Jo Moore .... 404-270-5061. 132 E
jstewart@spelman.edu
STEWART, Joan, H .... 315-859-4105. 325 E
jstewart@hamilton.edu
STEWART, John, R .... 563-589-3642. 182 J
jstewart@dbq.edu
STEWART, III, John, W .. 205-665-6001..... 9 B
presidentsoffice@montevallo.edu
STEWART, Juarine .... 256-372-5750..... 1 A
juarine.stewart@aamu.edu
STEWART, Karen .... 630-466-7900. 162 J
kstewart@waubonsee.edu
STEWART, Kate .... 850-201-6200. 117 D
stewartk@tcc.fl.edu
STEWART, Larry .... 248-218-2023. 249 D
lstewart@rc.edu
STEWART, Lea, P .... 848-445-4088. 306 B
lstewart@rci.rutgers.edu
STEWART, Leah .... 859-572-6437. 198 I
stewartl1@nku.edu
STEWART, Lisa .... 850-599-3730. 114 K
lisa.stewart@famu.edu
STEWART, Lori .... 601-979-4224. 267 E
lori.j.stewart@jsums.edu
STEWART, Makena .... 704-290-5840. 363 G
mstewart@spcc.edu
STEWART, Mark .... 718-270-2740. 342 D
mark.stewart@downstate.edu
STEWART, Michael .... 229-248-2560. 121 E
michael.stewart@bainbridge.edu
STEWART, Michael .... 478-471-2710. 128 I
michael.stewart@maconstate.edu
STEWART, Michael, S ..... 706-245-7226. 124 D
mstewart@ec.edu
STEWART, Patty, H .... 318-678-6004. 202 I
pstewart@bpcc.edu
STEWART, Pinkey .... 312-935-6017. 156 K
pstewart@robertmorris.edu
STEWART, R. Wayne .... 580-349-1408. 397 G
rwstewart@opsu.edu
STEWART, Renee .... 615-366-4416. 459 A
renee.stewart@tbr.edu
STEWART, Rob .... 806-742-2184. 487 D
rob.stewart@ttu.edu
STEWART, Robert .... 251-380-3030..... 7 D
rstewart@shc.edu
STEWART, Robert .... 617-552-2671. 224 A
bobstewart@theq.follett.com
STEWART, Robert .... 864-596-9223. 443 D
bobby.stewart@converse.edu
STEWART, Rod, S .... 517-750-1200. 250 E
rods@admin.arbor.edu
STEWART, Scott .... 616-222-1446. 241 F
scott.stewart@cornerstone.edu
STEWART, Sharon .... 859-323-1100. 200 C
srstew01@uky.edu
STEWART, Shawn .... 919-530-6367. 368 A
sstewart@nccu.edu
STEWART, Sheilynda ...... 580-559-5668. 395 F
sstewart@ecok.edu
STEWART, Sonja .... 931-221-7342. 459 B
stewarts@apsu.edu
STEWART, Spencer .... 229-248-2504. 121 E
sstewart@bainbridge.edu
STEWART, Spencer .... 702-992-2040. 294 G
spencer.stewart@nsc.edu
STEWART, Stephanie .... 773-508-7716. 151 H
sstewa2@luc.edu
STEWART, Stephanie, M . 920-433-6639. 531 L
stephanie.stewart@bellincollege.edu
STEWART, Susan .... 909-652-6591... 37 M
susan.stewart@chaffey.edu
STEWART, Tammy .... 512-313-3000. 469 L
tammy.stewart@concordia.edu
STEWART, Terri .... 607-274-3758. 327 E
tastewart@ithaca.edu
STEWART, Theresia .... 270-706-8504. 195 A
theresia.stewart@kctcs.edu
STEWART, Todd, I .... 937-255-2321. 544 C
todd.stewart@afit.edu
STEWART, Todd, M .... 270-745-5276. 200 G
todd.stewart@wku.edu
STEWART, Tommie, T ..... 334-229-4232..... 1 D
tstewart@alasu.edu
STEWART, Tommy .... 901-761-9494. 453 I
tstewart@concorde.edu
STEWART, Tracy .... 907-564-8261... 10 C
tstewart@alaskapacific.edu
STEWART, Tracy .... 717-545-4747. 419 O
STEWART, Tracy, R .... 757-352-4146. 508 G
tstewart@regent.edu
STEWART, Trevor .... 530-895-2421... 30 F
stewarttr@butte.edu
STEWART, Vicki, L .... 717-815-1287. 438 D
vstewart@ycp.edu
STEWART, Wendy .... 760-757-2121... 54 G
wstewart@miracosta.edu
STEWART, William, M ...... 518-464-8593. 324 B
wstewart@excelsior.edu
STEWART ALEXANDER,
Mary .... 203-837-8839... 88 B
alexanderm@wcsu.edu
STEWART-GAMBINO,
Hannah, W .... 610-330-5080. 420 D
stewarth@lafayette.edu
STEWART-JAMES, Joy ..... 916-278-6461... 34 D
jsjames@csus.edu
STEWART-LOVELL,
Valerie, M .... 718-951-5538. 317 C
vstewart@brooklyn.cuny.edu
STIBER, Greg, F .... 954-262-5381. 109 K
stiber@nova.edu
STICE, Nic .... 479-248-7236... 21 B
nicstice@ecollege.edu
STICH, Joan .... 320-762-4401. 257 O
joans@alextech.edu
STICH, Lisa .... 231-843-5923. 252 H
ekstich@westshore.edu
STICHNOTE, Lynn .... 573-341-4075. 284 A
lks@mst.edu
STICK, Jim .... 515-964-6429. 177 B
jwstick@dmacc.edu
STICKA, Stephen .... 925-969-3337... 49 B
ssticka@jfku.edu
STICKEL, Marianne .... 415-458-3722... 42 J
mstickel@dominican.edu
STICKELMAIER, Laurie .... 608-363-2250. 531 M
stickelmaierll@beloit.edu
STICKLEY, Ronald, G ...... 540-665-4530. 509 E
rstickle3@su.edu
STIEFEL, Debra .... 815-288-5511. 158 K
stiefed@svcc.edu
STIEFEL, Joseph P, D ..... 630-889-6604. 154 E
jstiefel@nuhs.edu
STIEFEL, Sheryl .... 425-602-3008. 516 K
sstiefel@bastyr.edu
STIEFFEL, Deborah .... 313-993-1496. 250 K
deborah.stieffel@udmercy.edu
STIELOW, Fred .... 304-724-3700. 526 B
fstielow@apus.edu
STIENBARGER,
Mary Ann .... 765-983-1346. 165 G
stienma@earlham.edu
STIFEL, David .... 860-412-7363... 89 E
dstifel@qvcc.commnet.edu
STIFF, Cindra, K .... 270-852-3113. 197 B
cindrast@kwc.edu
STIFFIN, Rose Mary .... 305-626-3697. 104 J
Rose.Stiffin@fmuniv.edu
STIFFLER, Daniel, J .... 314-367-8700. 281 C
daniel.stiffler@stlcop.edu
STIFFLER, Gregory, S ..... 989-837-4154. 248 C
stiffler@northwood.edu
STIFFLER, Jamee .... 919-718-7526. 359 B
jstiffler@cccc.edu
STIFTER, Michael, J .... 715-425-3827. 537 E
michael.j.stifter@uwrf.edu
STIGER, Barry, R .... 570-326-3761. 427 B
bstiger@pct.edu
STIGER, Kathleen .... 323-241-5338... 52 C
stigerk@lasc.edu
STIGLITZ, Eloise .... 510-430-3178... 54 F
estiglitz@mills.edu
STILES, Bill .... 610-796-8273. 409 E
bill.stiles@alvernia.edu
STILES, Chip .... 978-837-5357. 234 A
stilesc@merrimack.edu
STILES, Elizabeth .... 610-902-8420. 411 E
elizabeth.g.stiles@cabrini.edu
STILES, Marsha .... 610-861-1369. 424 E
mlstiles@moravian.edu
STILES, Michael, D .... 712-279-3149. 182 C
stilesmd@stlukescollege.edu
STILES, Randall .... 641-269-4000. 178 H
STILL, Guy, M .... 856-225-2900. 306 C
guystill@camden.rutgers.edu
STILL, Jill .... 936-468-5406. 482 A
jstill@sfasu.edu
STILL, Kathy .... 276-376-0130. 511 C
kls72d@uvawise.edu
STILL, Kennie, M .... 864-242-5100. 441 D
STILL SMOKING,
Dorothy .... 406-338-5411. 285 F
drstillsmoking@bfcc.edu
STILLE, Brand, R .... 864-597-4130. 449 I
stillebr@wofford.edu
STILLE, Robyn, L .... 906-227-2661. 248 A
rstille@nmu.edu
STILLE, Suzette .... 843-953-8148. 443 A
stilles@cofc.edu
STILLERMAN, Harry .... 704-878-4321. 362 B
hstillerman@mitchellcc.edu
STILLEY, Dana .... 845-574-4224. 338 B
dstilley@sunyrockland.edu
STILLMAN, Brian, C .... 208-467-8460. 139 A
bcstillman@nnu.edu
STILLMAN, Bruce .... 516-367-8497. 320 D
stillman@cshl.edu
STILLMAN, John, P .... 801-581-3655. 496 Q
john.stillman@hsc.utah.edu
STILLWAGGON, James .. 914-633-2697. 327 C
jstillwaggon@iona.edu
STILWELL, Martha .... 269-965-3931. 244 O
stilwellm@kellogg.edu
STILWELL, Rebecca .... 615-794-4254. 457 Q
STIMAC, Robin .... 816-604-3071. 277 G
robin.stimac@mcckc.edu
STIMELING, Kurt .... 603-897-8215. 297 F
kstimeling@rivier.edu
STIMELING, Kurt .... 603-897-8247. 297 F
kstimeling@rivier.edu
STIMPERT, Larry .... 765-658-4359. 165 F
larrystimpert@depauw.edu
STIMPLE, Janet .... 216-687-3831. 377 F
j.stimple@csuohio.edu
STINCHCOMB, Jan .... 410-225-2289. 216 C
jstinchc@mica.edu
STINE, Karen .... 334-244-3678..... 2 A
kstine@aum.edu
STINE, Terry, E .... 208-376-7731. 137 F
terrys@boisebible.edu
STINEBECK, David .... 570-662-4877. 429 C
dstinebe@mansfield.edu
STINEMETZ, Charles, L .. 740-368-3101. 387 J
clstinem@owu.edu
STINER, Margaret .... 440-826-8061. 374 F
mstiner@bw.edu
STINES, Marsha .... 828-627-4529. 361 B
mstines@haywood.edu
STINESPRING,
James, M .... 304-457-6243. 526 A
stinespringjm@ab.edu
STINNER, Erin .... 308-635-6081. 293 E
stinnere@wncc.edu
STINNER, Jerry .... 818-677-2004... 34 C
jerry.stinner@csun.edu
STINNETT, Gary, W .... 704-687-0644. 368 E
gwstinne@uncc.edu
STINNETTE, Anne .... 671-734-1812. 546 D
astinnette@piu.edu
STINSON, Barbara, J ...... 715-425-3141. 537 E
barbara.stinson@uwrf.edu
STINSON, Barry .... 516-877-3486. 313 A
bstinson@adelphi.edu
STINSON, Becky .... 573-592-4237. 285 D
bstinson@williamwoods.edu
STINSON, Charlie .... 256-761-6301..... 7 F
cstinson@talladega.edu
STINSON, Claire .... 931-372-3311. 460 A
cstinson@tntech.edu
STINSON, Greg .... 219-464-5212. 174 E
greg.stinson@valpo.edu
STINSON, Laura .... 760-630-1555... 49 L
lastinson@kaplan.edu
STINSON, Lori .... 208-792-2213. 138 G
lstinson@lcsc.edu
STINSON, Mark .... 636-573-9300. 278 G
mstinson@motech.edu
STINSON, Matt .... 330-823-7803. 391 E
stinsomp@mountunion.edu
STINSON, Pamela .... 580-628-6210. 396 M
pamela.stinson@no.edu
STINSON, Randy .... 502-897-4897. 199 B
rstinson@sbts.edu
STINSON, Willette .... 937-708-5629. 393 A
wstinson@wilberforce.edu
STIPCAK, Sondra, L .... 570-321-4322. 422 H
stipcak@lycoming.edu
STIREWALT, Jesse .... 218-879-0708. 258 E
housing@fdltcc.edu
STIRLING, Diane, S .... 704-894-2462. 353 J
distirling@davidson.edu
STIRLING, James, S .... 301-405-3372. 219 B
jstirlin@umd.edu
STIRLING, Joan, R .... 870-368-2007... 22 E
jstirling@ozarka.edu
STIRLING, Wynn, C .... 801-422-4465. 495 D
wynn_stirling@byu.edu
STIRTON, E. Rob .... 313-993-1588. 250 K
stirtoer@udmercy.edu
STIRTON, Rob .... 734-462-4400. 250 A
rstirton@schoolcraft.edu
STIRTZ, Michele, D .... 402-552-2543. 288 L
stirtz@clarksoncollege.edu
STISO, Joseph .... 978-632-6600. 232 C
j_stiso@mwcc.mass.edu
STITES, Dorothy, D .... 785-749-8456. 187 B
dstites@haskell.edu
STITH, Kay, K .... 405-878-5434. 399 G
kkstith@stgregorys.edu
STITH, Kevin, U .... 740-368-3398. 387 J
kustith@owu.edu
STITHEM, Diana .... 928-757-0881... 15 L
dstithem@mohave.edu
STITT, Teresa .... 989-686-9422. 242 C
tfstitt@delta.edu
STITTS, Doria, K .... 336-750-2345. 370 A
stittsd@wssu.edu
STITZINGER, Jim .... 502-897-4721. 199 B
jstitziner@sbts.edu
STIVERS, Mary Elizabeth 515-263-2805. 178 G
mestivers@grandview.edu
STOB, Jeffrey, A .... 616-526-6280. 240 L
stobje@calvin.edu
STOB, Michael .... 616-526-7114. 240 L
stob@calvin.edu
STOBER, Dan .... 650-723-7162... 68 E
dan.stober@stanford.edu
STOBNICKE, Michelle .... 505-428-1659. 311 J
michelle.stobnicke@sfcc.edu
STOBO, John, D .... 510-987-9071... 70 H
john.stobo@ucop.edu
STOCK, Jack, P .... 810-762-7873. 244 Q
jstock@kettering.edu
STOCK, Kenneth .... 708-656-8000. 153 H
kenneth.stock@morton.edu
STOCK, Laura, D .... 573-651-2021. 282 B
lstock@semo.edu
STOCK, Lawrence, E .... 724-287-8711. 411 C
larry.stock@bc3.edu
STOCK, Lisa, A .... 630-942-2351. 142 G
stockl@cod.edu
STOCK, Renee .... 304-829-7572. 526 D
rstock@bethanywv.edu
STOCK, Susan .... 312-341-3548. 157 D
sstock@roosevelt.edu
STOCK, Tom .... 320-363-2629. 263 P
tstock@csbsju.edu
STOCK KUPPERMAN,
Gretel, L .... 608-796-3272. 539 E
glstock@viterbo.edu
STOCKE, Mike .... 253-964-6534. 522 C
mstocke@pierce.ctc.edu
STOCKER, Jane Ellen ...... 708-596-2000. 159 C
jstocker@ssc.edu

STOCKER, Morgan, A ..... 717-337-6304. 417 B
mstocker@gettysburg.edu
STOCKERT, Patricia, A .... 309-655-4124. 158 C
patricia.a.stockert@osfhealthcare.org
STOCKS, Janet .... 202-884-9380... 96 G
stocksj@trinitydc.edu
STOCKS, Morris, H .... 662-915-5315. 270 B
mhstocks@olemiss.edu
STOCKSLADER, Jon Jay . 716-286-8189. 334 F
js@niagara.edu
STOCKSTILL, Stephanie .. 281-756-3531. 465 D
sstockstill@alvincollege.edu
STOCKTON, Carl, A .... 281-283-3000. 489 C
stockton@uhcl.edu
STOCKTON, Chris .... 314-773-0083. 271 K
STOCKTON, Hans .... 713-525-3530. 490 L
stockton@stthom.edu
STOCKTON, Nancy .... 812-855-5711. 167 F
stocktnj@indiana.edu
STOCKTON, Thomas, B .. 336-841-4592. 355 C
tstockto@highpoint.edu
STOCKTON, Ty .... 307-778-1170. 543 D
tstockto@lccc.wy.edu
STOCKWELL, Dave .... 614-222-3216. 378 A
dstockwell@ccad.edu
STODDARD, Eric .... 928-541-7777... 16 B
estoddard@ncu.edu
STODDARD, Reed, J .... 208-496-9370. 137 H
stoddardr@byui.edu
STODDART, Scott, F .... 212-217-4320. 324 C
scott_stoddart@fitnyc.edu
STODDART, Sue, A .... 920-923-7177. 534 A
sstoddart@marianuniversity.edu
STOECKLEIN, Amanda ..... 660-596-7379. 282 G
astoecklein@sfccmo.edu
STOECKLIN, Dennis, J .... 503-280-8503. 402 J
dstoecklin@cu-portland.edu
STOEFFEL, Virginia .... 845-431-8908. 323 C
virginia.stoeffel@sunydutchess.edu
STOEHR, Gary .... 716-829-7796. 323 D
stoehrg@dyc.edu
STOELTING, Diane .... 716-286-8064. 334 F
ds@niagara.edu
STOFAN, James .... 504-865-5901. 207 C
jstofan@tulane.edu
STOFFLE, Carla, J .... 520-621-6432... 18 F
stofflec@u.library.arizona.edu
STOFFT, Lori .... 928-314-9595... 11 L
lorraine.stofft@azwestern.edu
STOGNER, Becky .... 806-651-2311. 484 D
bstogner@mail.wtamu.edu
STOICESCU, Dan .... 410-287-6060. 214 B
dstoicescu@cecil.edu
STOJEVICH, Jean .... 218-733-5908. 259 A
j.stojevich@lsc.edu
STOJKOVIC, Stan .... 414-229-4400. 537 A
stojkovi@uwm.edu
STOKAN, Matthew .... 724-852-3227. 437 A
mstokan@waynesburg.edu
STOKELY, Madlyn .... 212-772-4847. 318 C
madlyn.stokely@hunter.cuny.edu
STOKELY, Sarah .... 717-477-1395. 429 E
sestokely@ship.edu
STOKER, Susan .... 254-968-9120. 483 A
stoker@tarleton.edu
STOKES, Douglas .... 803-535-1393. 446 B
stokesd@octech.edu
STOKES, Garnett, S .... 850-644-1765. 115 C
gstokes@fsu.edu
STOKES, Ginger, C .... 386-312-4074. 112 C
gingerstokes@sjrstate.edu
STOKES, Isaac .... 510-567-6174... 69 C
istokes@sum.edu
STOKES, Judi .... 845-431-8405. 323 C
judi.stokes@sunydutchess.edu
STOKES, Kenneth, M ...... 803-535-5176. 442 B
kstokes@claflin.edu
STOKES, Larry .... 912-358-4190. 131 C
stokesl@savannahstate.edu
STOKES, Leroy .... 336-334-4822. 360 G
lstokes@gtcc.edu
STOKES, Madeline .... 251-405-4457..... 2 D
mstokes@bishop.edu
STOKES, Mark .... 423-636-7316. 462 E
STOKES, Maureen, O ...... 760-252-2411... 29 I
mstokes@barstow.edu
STOKES, Michael .... 423-478-6218. 460 D
mstokes@clevelandstatecc.edu
STOKES, Mickey, E .... 662-476-5068. 266 I
mstokes@eastms.edu
STOKES, Robert, D .... 610-519-4311. 436 F
robert.stokes@villanova.edu
STOKES, Scott, M .... 712-362-7913. 179 E
sstokes@iowalakes.edu
STOKES, Timothy .... 360-596-5206. 524 A
tstokes@spscc.edu
STOKES-WILSON, Linda . 708-596-2000. 159 C
lwilson@ssc.edu
STOLL, James, G .... 978-542-6401. 230 E
jstoll@salemstate.edu
STOLL, Laura, K .... 573-341-6292. 284 A
lstoll@mst.edu
STOLL, Nancy, C .... 617-573-8239. 237 B
nstoll@suffolk.edu
STOLL, Sherideen, S .... 419-372-8262. 374 K
sstoll@bgsu.edu
STOLL, William, S .... 314-935-7574. 284 L
stoll@wustl.edu
STOLLER, Andrea .... 713-718-8598. 473 C
andrea.stoller@hccs.edu
STOLLER, Brett .... 309-649-6211. 160 E
brett.stoller@src.edu
STOLLERY, Chris .... 206-726-5052. 518 G
cstollery@cornish.edu
STOLLSTEIMER, Terry ..... 248-370-2160. 248 J
stollste@oakland.edu
STOLPER, Edward, M ..... 626-395-6336... 31 E
ems@caltech.edu
STOLPER, Edward, M ..... 626-395-6504... 31 E
ems@caltech.edu
STOLPER, Lauren, B .... 626-395-6361... 31 E
lstolper@caltech.edu
STOLT, Wilbur .... 701-777-2617. 371 C
wilbur.stolt@und.edu
STOLTE, Scott .... 702-968-5944. 295 E
sstolte@roseman.edu
STOLTZ, Jacklyn, C .... 860-701-5040... 90 G
stoltz_j@mitchell.edu
STOLTZ, Marlene .... 406-756-3846. 286 B
mstoltz@fvcc.edu
STOLTZ-LOIKE, Marion .. 212-287-3510. 348 B
mstoltz-loike@touro.edu
STOLWORTHY, Charity ... 970-675-3203... 80 B
charity.stolworthy@cncc.edu
STOLZ, Rebecca .... 323-259-2691... 56 I
rstolz@oxy.edu
STOLZER, Donna .... 908-526-1200. 305 B
dstolzer@raritanval.edu
STOMBER, Richard .... 973-720-2277. 308 I
stomberr@wpunj.edu
STOMPER, Jeffrey, A .... 847-543-2531. 143 A
stomper@clcillinois.edu
STONE, Adam .... 212-484-1303. 318 D
astone@jjay.cuny.edu
STONE, Amy, E .... 803-777-3106. 447 G
astone@sc.edu
STONE, Barbara .... 312-235-3507. 159 A
b.stone@shimer.edu
STONE, Carolyn .... 561-803-2567. 110 B
carolyn_stone@pba.edu
STONE, David .... 815-753-9282. 154 I
dastone@niu.edu
STONE, David, M .... 212-854-9962. 321 D
dms2148@columbia.edu
STONE, Denise .... 503-255-0332. 404 F
dstone@multnomah.edu
STONE, Eddie .... 931-393-1593. 461 A
estone@mscc.edu
STONE, Emily .... 925-969-2113... 41 L
estone@dvc.edu
STONE, Gaylund, K .... 262-243-5700. 532 H
gaylund.stone@cuw.edu
STONE, Glenice .... 662-720-7237. 269 B
gwstone@nemcc.edu
STONE, James .... 325-670-1258. 472 O
jstone@hsutx.edu
STONE, Jan .... 602-749-5181. 189 I
jan.stone@ottawa.edu
STONE, Janice .... 806-720-7270. 476 B
janice.stone@lcu.edu
STONE, Jenna .... 315-268-3790. 320 A
jestone@clarkson.edu
STONE, John .... 661-362-2271... 53 G
jstone@masters.edu
STONE, John .... 262-472-1006. 538 D
stonej@uww.edu
STONE, Kai .... 303-477-7240... 82 C
kais@heritage-education.com
STONE, Karen, J .... 904-620-2828. 116 B
kstone@unf.edu
STONE, Karin .... 216-791-5000. 377 E
kls160@case.edu
STONE, Katie .... 503-223-2245. 403 J
kstone@portland.chefs.edu
STONE, Keith, H .... 530-221-4275... 65 F
pkstone@shasta.edu
STONE, Kelly .... 801-622-1573. 496 I
kelly.stone@stevenhenager.edu
STONE, Ken .... 773-896-2400. 141 K
kstone@ctschicago.edu
STONE, Kim .... 612-330-1173. 253 H
stonek@augsburg.edu
STONE, Lauren .... 443-627-7103. 265 D
lauren.stone@laureate.net
STONE, Linda .... 520-322-6330... 13 T
STONE, Marion .... 816-235-5758. 283 D
stonema@umkc.edu
STONE, Mark .... 979-458-6440. 482 E
MStone@tamus.edu
STONE, Melissa .... 302-831-8189... 94 B
mstone@udel.edu
STONE, Michael, C .... 512-448-8605. 479 C
mikecs@stedwards.edu
STONE, Paul .... 817-599-8324. 494 G
stone@wc.edu
STONE, Polly .... 601-923-1630. 269 E
pstone@rts.edu
STONE, Ralinda .... 817-598-6276. 494 G
rstone@wc.edu
STONE, Sandra .... 706-272-4420. 123 G
sstone@daltonstate.edu
STONE, Scott .... 410-225-2398. 216 C
sstone@mica.edu
STONE, Shelly, T .... 336-694-8042. 362 F
Shelly.Stone@piedmontcc.edu
STONE, Sue .... 229-226-1621. 132 F
sstone@thomasu.edu
STONE, Susan .... 859-253-3637. 194 A
sstone@frontier.edu
STONE, Ty .... 937-512-3107. 388 O
ty.stone@sinclair.edu
STONE, Tyanne, S .... 205-652-3852..... 9 F
tstone@uwa.edu
STONECIPHER,
Amanda, G .... 812-941-2674. 168 F
agstonec@ius.edu
STONECIPHER,
Charla, K .... 812-941-2200. 168 F
ckstonec@ius.edu
STONEKING, Carole, B .. 336-841-9168. 355 C
stoneki@highpoint.edu
STONEMAN, Marcia, L ... 828-694-1804. 358 C
marcias@blueridge.edu
STONER, Gayla .... 618-453-4033. 159 G
gstoner@siu.edu
STONER, Jennifer, E .... 708-709-3949. 156 A
jstoner@prairiestate.edu
STONER, Keith .... 419-755-4810. 385 D
kstoner@ncstatecollege.edu
STONER, Ken .... 865-974-2571. 463 C
kstoner@utk.edu
STONER, Melinda .... 402-354-7230. 291 B
melinda.stoner@methodistcollege.edu
STONESIFER, Cyndi .... 815-921-4158. 157 A
c.stonesifer@rockvalleycollege.edu
ST ONGE, Stephen .... 802-862-9616. 498 I
sstonge@burlington.edu
STOOKS, George, F .... 585-245-5663. 343 C
stooks@geneseo.edu
STOOKSBERRY, Robert .. 210-436-3301. 479 D
tstooksberry@stmarytx.edu
STOOPS, Angela, D .... 240-500-2000. 215 B
adstoops@hagerstowncc.edu
STOOPS, Melinda, K .... 508-626-4596. 230 A
mstoops@framingham.edu
STOOPS, T.J .... 219-980-6832. 168 B
tkstoops@iun.edu
STOOS, Barbara .... 419-251-1702. 383 G
barbara.stoos@mercycollege.edu
STOPAK, Erin .... 712-325-3204. 179 L
estopak@iwcc.edu
STOPPENBRINK, Ken ..... 559-934-2160... 75 G
kenstoppenbrink@whccd.edu
STOPPENBRINK,
Norman, V .... 818-779-8271... 50 A
nstoppenbrink@kingsuniversity.edu
STOPPER, Suzanne, T ..... 570-326-3761. 427 B
sstoppe2@pct.edu
STOPPS, Charles .... 708-366-3288. 144 C
cstoops@dom.edu
STORCK, Christine, M .... 410-777-2219. 213 D
cmstorck@aacc.edu
STORCK, Dennis .... 850-872-3842. 106 H
dstorck@gulfcoast.edu
STORCK, Eileen .... 772-462-7361. 106 P
estorck@irsc.edu
STORER, Gail .... 614-222-3225. 378 A
gstorer@ccad.edu
STORES, Chaun .... 724-503-1001. 436 G
cstores@washjeff.edu
STOREY, Amy .... 315-279-5235. 328 D
astorey@mail.keuka.edu
STOREY, Bruce .... 309-796-5129. 140 E
storeyb@bhc.edu
STOREY, G. Paul .... 909-869-2951... 32 G
gpstorey@csupomona.edu
STOREY, Karen .... 906-635-2418. 245 G
kstorey@lssu.edu
STOREY, Linn .... 706-649-1935. 123 E
lstorey@columbustech.edu
STOREY, Richard, D .... 406-683-7151. 286 I
r_storey@umwestern.edu
STOREY GROVES,
Margaret .... 802-443-5196. 499 H
mgroves@middlebury.edu
STORFA, Kristin .... 503-352-2883. 407 A
kstorfa@pacificu.edu
STORIE, Cheryl .... 240-582-2682. 219 F
financial-affairs@umuc.edu
STORIE, Leslie .... 606-759-7141. 196 B
leslie.mccord@kctcs.edu
STORIE, Monique, C .... 671-735-2162. 546 E
mstorie@uguam.uog.edu
STORIN, Matthew, V .... 574-631-6798. 174 A
storin.2@nd.edu
STORK, Gilbert, H .... 805-546-3118... 42 C
gstork@cuesta.edu
STORLAZZI, Caesar, T ... 203-432-0371... 93 A
caesar.storlazzi@yale.edu
STORM, Kathleen, H .... 509-777-4535. 525 F
kstorm@whitworth.edu
STORMER, P. Ronald ..... 573-288-6485. 273 F
rstormer@culver.edu
STORMS, Joyce, A .... 616-538-2330. 243 A
jstorms@gbcol.edu
STORMS, Melanie .... 410-843-6390. 265 D
Melanie.Storms@waldenu.edu
STORMS, Melanie .... 410-843-6390. 265 D
melanie.storms@waldenu.edu
STORR, Robert .... 203-432-2606... 93 A
robert.storr@yale.edu
STORRS, Debbie .... 701-777-2749. 371 C
debbie.storrs@und.edu
STORRS, Regina, M .... 313-593-5020. 251 D
rstorrs@umich.edu
STORTI, John .... 781-736-8686. 224 F
jstorti@brandeis.edu
STORY, Debra, D .... 518-629-4507. 326 G
d.story@hvcc.edu
STORY, Ed .... 606-759-7141. 196 B
ed.story@kctcs.edu
STORY, JR., John, H ..... 315-733-4764. 349 D
jstory@uscny.edu
STORY, Lisa, L .... 712-324-5061. 181 G
lstory@nwicc.edu
STORY, Megan .... 757-457-8101. 502 C
megan.story@atlanticuniv.edu
STORY, Nancy .... 303-556-3801... 81 D
nancy.story@ccd.edu
STORY-HUFFMAN, Ru .... 229-931-2259. 126 D
ru.story-huffman@gsw.edu
STOSBERG, Tobey .... 816-276-4740. 280 G
tobey.stosberg@researchcollege.edu
STOSKOPF, Janna, M ..... 701-231-6537. 371 G
janna.stoskopf@ndsu.edu
STOSZ, Sandra, L .... 860-444-8285. 545 G
Sandra.L.Stosz@uscg.mil
STOTHART, Natalie .... 413-565-1000. 222 F
nstothart@baypath.edu
STOTLER, Doug .... 636-481-3386. 275 I
dstotler@jeffco.edu
STOTO, Robert .... 609-896-5140. 305 D
stoto@rider.edu
STOTT, Andrew, M .... 716-645-5001. 341 F
vpue@buffalo.edu
STOTTLEMEYER,
Rebecca .... 304-876-5287. 529 I
bstottle@shepherd.edu
STOTTS, Bob .... 270-789-5017. 193 D
restotts@campbellsville.edu
STOTTS, Keith .... 304-865-6005. 527 F
keith.stotts@ovu.edu
STOTTS, Melissa .... 701-662-1538. 372 D
melissa.stotts@lrsc.edu
STOUDMIRE, Cynthia ..... 516-572-7124. 332 C
cynthia.stoudmire@ncc.edu
STOUFFER, Wendy, D .... 479-575-2711... 23 I
wstouff@uark.edu
STOUT, Brandon .... 402-878-2380. 290 D
bstout@littlepriest.edu
STOUT, Chris .... 248-689-8282. 251 I
cstout@walshcollege.edu
STOUT, David, L .... 515-964-0601. 178 E
stoutd@faith.edu
STOUT, Karen, A .... 215-641-6500. 424 B
kstout@mc3.edu
STOUT, Rebecca, Y .... 404-413-1500. 126 F
rebeccastout@gsu.edu
STOUTENBOROUGH,
Donna .... 540-986-1800. 198 E
dstoutenborough@national-college.edu
STOVALL, Alfred, J .... 662-252-8000. 269 F
ajstovall@rustcollege.edu
STOVALL, Bill .... 201-684-7506. 305 A
bstovall@ramapo.edu
STOVALL, George, A .... 434-924-6431. 511 B
gas5a@virginia.edu
STOVALL, Jerry .... 229-931-2562. 131 G
jstovall@southgatech.edu
STOVALL, Randall, H ...... 352-518-1301. 110 E
stovalr@phcc.edu
STOVALL, Terri .... 817-923-1921. 481 G
tstovall@swbts.edu
STOVALL, Tina .... 217-234-5250. 150 D
tstovall@lakeland.cc.il.us
STOVALL, Tyler .... 510-642-5640... 70 I
tstovall@berkeley.edu
STOVALL, Vincent .... 703-284-1612. 507 B
vincent.stovall@marymount.edu
STOVER, Cheryln .... 425-602-3093. 516 K
cstover@bastyr.edu
STOVER, Dennis, L .... 941-359-4200. 117 A

STOVER, Kathleen, J ...... 847-214-7374. 144 F
kstover@elgin.edu
STOVER, Kathy, J ...... 402-844-7268. 291 I
kathy@northeast.edu
STOVER, Keith ...... 507-389-7207. 261 E
keith.stover@southcentral.edu
STOVER, Lois ...... 703-284-1620. 507 B
lois.stover@marymount.edu
STOVER, Mark ...... 818-677-2271... 34 C
mark.stover@csun.edu
STOVER, Mary ...... 207-255-1223. 212 F
mstover@maine.edu
STOVER, Pam ...... 717-846-5000. 438 E
STOVER, Paul, A ...... 714-449-7461... 67 D
pstover@scco.edu
STOVER, Ronalda, S ...... 803-778-6688. 441 F
stoverrs@cctech.edu
STOVER, Teri ...... 903-223-3088. 484 C
teri.stover@tamut.edu
STOVERINK, Al ...... 870-972-2066... 19 N
astoverink@astate.edu
STOWASSER, Melissa ...... 843-574-6111. 447 E
melissa.stowasser@tridenttech.edu
STOWE, Lentz ...... 252-940-6306. 358 A
Lentzs@beaufortccc.edu
STOWE, Ron, M ...... 336-316-2907. 355 A
stowerm@guilford.edu
STOWE, Susan ...... 412-392-3931. 431 B
sstowe@pointpark.edu
STOWELL, Dale ...... 541-917-4214. 404 B
stowelld@linnbenton.edu
STOWELL, Joseph, M ...... 616-222-1428. 241 F
joe.stowell@cornerstone.edu
STOWELL, Mike ...... 616-538-2330. 243 A
mstowell@gbcol.edu
STOWERS, Deborah ...... 256-824-6686..... 8 F
debbie.stowers@uah.edu
STOWERS, Marian ...... 269-337-7192. 244 K
Marian.Stowers@kzoo.edu
STOWERS, Rebecca ...... 937-766-7872. 375 K
stowersr@cedarville.edu
STOWIK, Stanley ...... 401-232-6240. 438 K
STOWMAN, Heidi ...... 503-581-8600. 403 A
hstowman@corban.edu
STRACHER, Janet ...... 478-289-2109. 124 C
jstrach@ega.edu
STRADA, Richard ...... 732-255-0400. 304 A
rstrada@ocean.edu
STRADA, Samuel, J ...... 251-460-7189..... 9 E
sstrada@southalabama.edu
STRADER, Bob, A ...... 325-674-2932. 464 H
straderb@acu.edu
STRADER, Scott, C ...... 727-864-8248. 101 N
stradesc@eckerd.edu
STRADLEY, Bill ...... 931-526-3660. 454 G
STRADLEY, Christina ...... 254-968-9007. 483 A
stradley@tarleton.edu
STRAFFE, Judith ...... 215-568-9215. 423 M
jstraffe@phmc.org
STRAIN, David, M ...... 479-979-1349... 25 J
dstrain@ozarks.edu
STRAIT, LuAnn ...... 605-882-5284. 450 D
straitl@lakeareatech.edu
STRAIT, Tia ...... 417-625-9328. 278 D
strait-t@mssu.edu
STRAIT, Willie ...... 301-423-3600... 96 F
willie.strait@strayer.edu
STRAITS, Jeffrey ...... 202-885-8684... 97 D
jstraits@wesleyseminary.edu
STRAKA, Richard ...... 507-389-6621. 259 G
richard.straka@mnsu.edu
STRAKA, Ronald ...... 952-446-4127. 255 D
strakar@crown.edu
STRAMPEL, William, D ... 517-355-9616. 246 H
strampe3@msu.edu
STRAND, Naomi, M ...... 785-227-3311. 184 I
strandn@bethanylb.edu
STRANDBERG, Kevin ...... 309-556-3134. 148 B
strandbe@iwu.edu
STRANEY, Donald, O ...... 808-974-7444. 136 A
dstraney@hawaii.edu
STRANG, Bryce ...... 503-943-8009. 408 F
strang@up.edu
STRANG, Fred, F ...... 423-652-4708. 455 I
ffstrang@king.edu
STRANG, Steven ...... 314-246-8025. 284 N
stevenstrang87@webster.edu
STRANGE, Alan ...... 219-864-2400. 171 F
astrange@midamerica.edu
STRANGE, Thomas ...... 423-585-2668. 462 A
thomas.strange@ws.edu
STRANIAK, Kimberly ...... 330-369-3200. 390 B
tbcmail@tbc-trumbullbusiness.com
STRANO, Diana ...... 603-897-8211. 297 F
dstrano@rivier.edu
STRANO, Kimberly ...... 845-257-3215. 342 B
lavoiek@newpaltz.edu
STRASENBURGH,
David, R ...... 585-395-2385. 342 F
dstrasen@brockport.edu
STRASS, Troy ...... 503-352-2882. 407 A
troy.strass@pacificu.edu
STRASSER, Nora ...... 316-295-5818. 186 H
strasser@friends.edu
STRATFORD, Denis, G ...... 617-724-6340. 234 B
dgstratford@mghihp.edu
STRATFORD-YOUNCE,
Carolyn ...... 410-225-2263. 216 C
cstratford@mica.edu
STRATING, Linda ...... 202-462-2101... 96 A
STRATMAN, Allan, M ...... 217-333-2500. 162 A
stratmn@illinois.edu
STRATMAN, Debbie ...... 931-553-0071. 457 F
debbie.stratman@miller-motte.com
STRATMAN, Jason, L ...... 308-635-6740. 293 E
stratman@wncc.edu
STRATMAN, Victoria, D .. 626-395-5940... 31 E
victoria.stratman@caltech.edu
STRATMANN,
Charles, M ...... 904-632-3299. 105 E
cstratma@fscj.edu
STRATTON, Andrew, B ...... 270-247-8521. 197 H
astratton@midcontinent.edu
STRATTON, James ...... 208-524-3000. 138 D
james.stratton@my.eitc.edu
STRATTON, Jonathan ...... 772-546-5534. 106 N
jonstratton@hsbc.edu
STRATTON, Michael ...... 518-454-5456. 321 A
strattom@mail.strose.edu
STRATTON, Nathan ...... 952-995-1406. 258 F
nathan.stratton@hennepintech.edu
STRAUB, Bernie ...... 843-574-6994. 447 E
bernie.straub@tridenttech.edu
STRAUB, Dahnja ...... 707-546-4000... 43 E
dstraub@empirecollege.com
STRAUB, Jeff ...... 763-417-8250. 254 E
STRAUB, Steve ...... 920-735-5717. 539 K
straub@fvtc.edu
STRAUCH, Pierre ...... 203-287-3018... 90 H
paier.admin@snet.net
STRAUCHLER, Orin ...... 845-569-3547. 332 B
orin.strauchler@msmc.edu
STRAUGHAN, Rusty ...... 573-518-2361. 278 A
rstraugh@mineralarea.edu
STRAUGHN, Greg ...... 325-674-2850. 464 H
gbs00a@acu.edu
STRAUS, Julie ...... 573-288-6314. 273 F
jstraus@culver.edu
STRAUS, Susan ...... 301-934-7567. 214 D
susans@csmd.edu
STRAUSBAUGH, Greg ...... 541-684-7357. 405 C
gstrausbaugh@nwcu.edu
STRAUSBAUGH, Lisa ...... 440-375-7379. 382 L
lstrausbaugh@lec.edu
STRAUSBAUGH,
William, G ...... 717-796-5375. 423 L
strausba@messiah.edu
STRAUSE, Sandra ...... 610-607-6210. 431 D
sstrause@racc.edu
STRAUSS, Daniel ...... 727-394-6217. 154 E
dstrauss@nuhs.edu
STRAUSS, David, J ...... 313-577-1010. 252 G
ak3096@wayne.edu
STRAUSS, Douglas ...... 608-785-9235. 541 E
straussd@westerntc.edu
STRAUSS, Jason ...... 510-841-9230... 77 B
jstrauss@wi.edu
STRAUSS, Jerome, F ...... 804-828-9788. 511 F
jfstrauss@vcu.edu
STRAUSS, Jon, C ...... 914-323-5230. 330 B
jon.strauss@mville.edu
STRAUSS, Kate ...... 714-772-3330... 28 C
admissions@anaheim.edu
STRAUSS, Ronald ...... 919-962-4510. 368 D
ron_strauss@unc.edu
STRAUT COLLARD,
Susan ...... 718-940-5689. 339 B
sstrautcollard@sjcny.edu
STRAUTZ-SPRINGBORN,
Shelly ...... 989-328-1243. 247 D
shellys@montcalm.edu
STRAVERS, Meredith ...... 269-965-3931. 244 O
straversm@kellogg.edu
STRAWBRIDGE, Richard 603-623-0313. 297 E
rickstrawbridge@nhia.edu
STRAWDERMAN,
Andrea, A ...... 252-334-2073. 357 A
andrea.strawderman@macuniversity.edu
STRAWLEY, George ...... 252-473-2264. 359 F
gstrawley@albemarle.edu
STRAWN, Roxanna ...... 920-686-6150. 536 A
Roxanna.Strawn@sl.edu
STRAWN, Scott ...... 405-491-6306. 399 K
sstrawn@snu.edu
STRAWSER, Jerry ...... 979-845-4711. 483 C
jstrawser@tamu.edu
STRAWSER, Joyce, A ...... 973-761-9225. 307 C
joyce.strawser@shu.edu
STRAYER, Colleen ...... 419-530-2516. 392 B
colleen.strayer@utoledo.edu
STRAYER, James, E ...... 308-398-7355. 288 I
jstrayer@cccneb.edu
STRAZDAS, Peter, J ...... 269-387-8584. 252 I
peter.strazdas@wmich.edu
STREBE, Chet, A ...... 715-675-3331. 541 A
strebe@ntc.edu
STRECKENBEIN, Mark .... 609-343-5127. 299 A
strecken@atlantic.edu
STRECKER, Deborah ...... 610-896-1129. 418 F
dstrecke@haverford.edu
STRECKER, William ...... 636-922-8607. 280 J
wstrecker@stchas.edu
STREET, Aaron, J ...... 870-235-5011... 23 F
ajstreet@saumag.edu
STREET, Helen ...... 662-252-8000. 269 F
hstreet@rustcollege.edu
STREET, Kathleen, A ...... 909-869-2572... 32 G
kastreet@csupomona.edu
STREET, Kenneth ...... 936-639-1301. 465 J
kstreet@angelina.edu
STREET, Margaret, F ...... 573-629-3006. 274 J
mstreet@hlg.edu
STREET, Scott, V ...... 617-266-1400. 223 D
STREET, Sheila ...... 336-506-4186. 357 M
sheila.street@alamancecc.edu
STREETER, Carrie ...... 979-230-3215. 468 A
carrie.streeter@brazosport.edu
STREETER, Holly ...... 319-425-5340. 183 B
streeterh@uiu.edu
STREETER, Karen ...... 901-755-9399. 224 G
karen.streeter@cambridgecollege.edu
STREETER, Lucy ...... 808-739-4686. 135 D
lstreete@chaminade.edu
STREETER, Montrose ...... 315-781-3900. 326 C
streeter@hws.edu
STREETMAN, Craig ...... 423-652-4158. 455 I
wcstreetman@king.edu
STREFF, Frederick, M ...... 540-674-3637. 513 B
fstreff@nr.edu
STREGE, Ron ...... 715-346-3574. 538 A
rstrege@uwsp.edu
STREHLE, Susan ...... 607-777-2070. 341 E
sstrehle@binghamton.edu
STREHLOW, Betty, J ...... 320-222-5203. 260 H
betty.strehlow@ridgewater.edu
STREICH, Jodi ...... 201-216-8724. 307 E
jstreich@stevens.edu
STREID, David ...... 641-472-1130. 180 N
dstreid@mum.edu
STREIFFER, Rick ...... 205-348-1288..... 8 D
rhstreiffer@cchs.ua.edu
STREIM, Nancy ...... 212-678-7407. 347 G
streim@tc.edu
STREIT, Linda, A ...... 678-547-6799. 128 H
streit_la@mercer.edu
STRETCHER, Gary, D ...... 409-984-6209. 486 H
gary.stretcher@lamarpa.edu
STREUBERT, Helen ...... 973-290-4474. 300 F
hjstreubert@cse.edu
STREUFERT, Billie ...... 605-331-6648. 452 D
billie.streufert@usiouxfalls.edu
STREY, Charles ...... 641-628-5621. 176 E
streyc@central.edu
STREY, Mary, M ...... 641-628-5188. 176 E
streym@central.edu
STRICHERZ, Shanda, L ... 605-336-6588. 451 C
shandas@sfseminary.edu
STRICKER, Edward, M .... 412-624-6880. 435 C
edstrick@pitt.edu
STRICKER, Terri ...... 816-322-0110. 271 O
terri.stricker@calvary.edu
STRICKLAND, Brian ...... 251-580-2214..... 4 L
bstrickland@faulknerstate.edu
STRICKLAND, Brooke ...... 334-556-2418..... 3 N
bstrickland@wallace.edu
STRICKLAND, Carol ...... 620-341-5660. 186 D
cstrickl@emporia.edu
STRICKLAND,
Carolyn, R ...... 570-326-3761. 427 B
cstrickl@pct.edu
STRICKLAND, Charles .... 252-862-1256. 363 A
stricklandc@roanokechowan.edu
STRICKLAND, Claire, I ... 207-581-1593. 212 B
cpratt@maine.edu
STRICKLAND,
Earnestine, J ...... 512-505-3082. 473 G
eestrickland@htu.edu
STRICKLAND, JR.,
Elliott ...... 570-326-3761. 427 B
estrickl@pct.edu
STRICKLAND, Fatisha ...... 215-567-7080. 410 A
fstrickland@aii.edu
STRICKLAND, Gary ...... 912-279-5835. 123 B
gstrickland@ccga.edu
STRICKLAND, Gary, E ...... 605-336-6588. 451 C
gstrickland@sfseminary.edu
STRICKLAND,
Haywood, L ...... 903-927-3200. 495 A
hstrickland@wileyc.edu
STRICKLAND, Jason ...... 910-642-7141. 364 A
Jason.Strickland@sccnc.edu
STRICKLAND, Joy ...... 303-963-3012... 79 C
jstrickland@ccu.edu
STRICKLAND, Ken ...... 229-217-4188. 129 F
kstrickland@moultrietech.edu
STRICKLAND, Ken ...... 617-879-7365. 230 B
kstrickland@massart.edu
STRICKLAND, Kristine .... 504-762-3188. 203 A
kstric@dcc.edu
STRICKLAND, Les ...... 480-423-6510... 15 E
les.strickland@scottsdalecc.edu
STRICKLAND, Liz, F ...... 870-575-8471... 24 E
stricklandl@uapb.edu
STRICKLAND, Mark ...... 727-341-3408. 112 E
strickland.mark@spcollege.edu
STRICKLAND,
Michael, D ...... 615-460-6420. 453 C
mike.strickland@belmont.edu
STRICKLAND, Michele ...... 478-553-2097. 129 H
mstrickland@oftc.edu
STRICKLAND, Ora ...... 304-348-0231. 115 B
ora.strickland@fiu.edu.edu
STRICKLAND, Randy ...... 502-585-7101. 199 C
rstrickland@spalding.edu
STRICKLAND, Samuel .... 919-532-5705. 364 G
sstrickland@waketech.edu
STRICKLAND,
Sandra, W ...... 252-335-0821. 359 F
sstrickland@albemarle.edu
STRICKLAND, Sherry ...... 254-559-7707. 486 C
sherry.strickland@tstc.edu
STRICKLAND, Sidney ...... 215-327-8084. 338 A
strickland@rockefeller.edu
STRICKLAND, Timothy ... 252-493-7330. 362 G
stricklandj@thomasmore.edu
STRICKLAND, Tina ...... 229-217-4141. 129 F
tstrickland@moultrietech.edu
STRICKLAND, Tonya ...... 229-248-2515. 121 E
tstrickland@bainbridge.edu
STRICKLAND, Valerie ...... 770-962-7580. 127 D
vstrickland@gwinnetttech.edu
STRICKLAND, Wayne, G . 503-255-0332. 404 F
udub@multnomah.edu
STRICKLER, Andy ...... 336-316-2220. 355 A
stricklerak@guilford.edu
STRICKLER, Tammy ...... 505-224-4325. 309 E
tammys@cnm.edu
STRICKLIN, Jan ...... 503-352-2890. 407 A
jstricklin@pacificu.edu
STRICKLIN, Linda ...... 208-792-2439. 138 G
lsstricklin@lcsc.edu
STRICKLIN, Scott ...... 662-325-8082. 268 D
sas24@msstate.edu
STRICKLING, Judy ...... 859-344-3513. 199 H
strickj@thomasmore.edu
STRIEF, Kristi, L ...... 563-556-5110. 181 E
striefk@nicc.edu
STRIEGEL WEISSMAN,
Ruth ...... 860-685-2010... 92 H
rweissman@wesleyan.edu
STRIKWERDA, Carl, J .... 717-361-1193. 415 H
strikwerdac@etown.edu
STRIMKOVSKY, Lauri ...... 215-248-7168. 413 A
strimkovsky@chc.edu
STRIMPLE, Karen ...... 620-252-7555. 185 O
karens@coffeyville.edu
STRINGER, Calandra ...... 850-201-6036. 117 D
stringec@tcc.fl.edu
STRINGER, Christopher .. 609-984-1110. 308 A
cstringer@tesc.edu
STRINGER, Cindy ...... 254-647-3120. 478 H
cstringer@rangercollege.edu
STRINGER, Eddy ...... 850-201-9856. 117 D
stringee@tcc.fl.edu
STRINGER, Janet ...... 650-306-3291... 64 B
stringerj@smccd.net
STRINGER, Martin ...... 714-628-4816... 60 H
stringer_martin@sccollege.edu
STRINGER, Sarah ...... 334-727-8254..... 8 A
ssstringer@tuskegee.edu
STRINGER, Tommy ...... 903-875-7380. 477 G
tommy.stringer@navarrocollege.edu
STRINGFELLOW, Alan .... 405-682-7522. 397 E
astringfellow@occc.edu
STRINGFELLOW,
Catherine ...... 256-395-2211..... 7 C
cstringfellow@suscc.edu
STRINGFELLOW, Eric ...... 601-979-2272. 267 E
eric.d.stringfellow@jsums.edu
STRIPE PORTILLO,
Jennifer ...... 213-627-2580... 38 G
STRIPLING, William, R ... 870-972-2048... 19 N
ricks@astate.edu
STRITIKUS, Tom ...... 206-543-2100. 524 G
tstrit@uw.edu
STRMISKA, Kenneth, D .. 920-565-1478. 533 R
strmiskakd@lakeland.edu
STROBECK, Carol ...... 973-290-4418. 300 F
cstrobeck@cse.edu
STROBEL, Corbin ...... 620-665-3537. 187 F
strobelc@hutchcc.edu
STROBEL, Nathan ...... 414-443-8825. 539 F
nathan.strobel@wlc.edu

STROBLE, Elizabeth, J .... 314-968-6996. 284 N
stroble@webster.edu
STROCKBINE, Richard .... 972-721-5207. 488 F
dick@udallas.edu
STRODEMIER, Tammy .... 360-736-9391. 517 G
tstrodmeier@centralla.edu
STROEH, Mark .... 713-692-0077. 470 B
STROH, Julie .... 765-285-1080. 164 B
jstroh@bsu.edu
STROHECKER, Carol .... 336-354-7358. 369 D
cs@centerfordesigninnovation.org
STROHM, Bobbie, A .... 858-499-0202... 40 C
bstrohm@coleman.edu
STROHM, Shelly .... 203-332-5179... 88 F
sstrohm@hcc.commnet.edu
STROHMETZ, David .... 732-263-5212. 303 C
dstrohme@monmouth.edu
STROHMEYER, George ... 814-871-7436. 416 K
strohmeyer@gannon.edu
STROJNY, Duane .... 517-371-5140. 250 G
strojnyd@cooley.edu
STROKER, Robert .... 215-204-8301. 433 K
robert.stroker@temple.edu
STROLLO, Ronald, A ...... 330-941-2385. 394 A
rastrollo@ysu.edu
STROLLO HOLBROOK,
Toni .... 407-646-2355. 111 Q
tsholbrook@rollins.edu
STROM, Donald .... 314-935-5514. 284 L
don_strom@wustl.edu
STROM, Laura, A .... 618-650-3330. 159 H
lstrom@siue.edu
STROM, Siri, J .... 509-865-8613. 520 D
strom_s@heritage.edu
STROM, Steven .... 845-451-1552. 322 D
s_strom@culinary.edu
STROMAN, Gerry, G .... 765-455-9316. 168 A
gstroman@iuk.edu
STROMAN, Jay .... 706-379-3111. 134 L
jtstroman@yhc.edu
STROMAN, Kozman .... 305-430-1168. 104 J
kozman.stroman@fmuniv.edu
STROMBERG, Lori, S ..... 308-635-6703. 293 E
stromber@wncc.edu
STROMIRE, Kim .... 303-464-2340... 84 K
STROMMEN, Kim .... 215-204-7000. 433 K
strommen@temple.edu
STROMPF, Richard .... 203-596-4588... 90 I
rstrompf@post.edu
STROMQUIST, Eric .... 888-624-2433. 407 B
estromquist@pioneerpacific.edu
STRONACH, Bruce .... 215-204-7000. 433 K
bruce.stronach@temple.edu
STRONACH, Jeanne .... 619-594-8712... 35 D
jstronac@mail.sdsu.edu
STRONG, Charles, T .... 318-371-3035. 203 E
cstrong@ltc.edu
STRONG, Charmaine, R .. 724-838-4242. 433 E
strong@setonhill.edu
STRONG, Chuck .... 662-562-3494. 269 C
cwstrong@northwestms.edu
STRONG, Douglas, M ..... 206-281-2473. 523 C
dstrong@spu.edu
STRONG, James, T .... 209-667-3203... 35 B
jtstrong@csustan.edu
STRONG, Jennifer .... 843-355-4111. 449 F
strongj@wiltech.edu
STRONG, Karen .... 702-895-4074. 294 I
karen.strong@unlv.edu
STRONG, Kira .... 641-673-1014. 183 H
strongk@wmpenn.edu
STRONG, III, L. Thomas 504-282-4455. 206 A
tstrong@nobts.edu
STRONG, Mike .... 909-389-3383... 61 K
mstrong@craftonhills.edu
STRONG, R. Kirk .... 801-422-5000. 495 D
ksstrong@byu.edu
STRONG, Shawn .... 218-755-3732. 258 A
sdstrong@bemidjistate.edu
STRONG, Shirley .... 415-575-6171... 31 D
sstrong@ciis.edu
STROTHER, Jennielle ...... 512-472-4133. 480 G
jstrother@ssw.edu
STROTHER, Jennifer .... 425-564-4250. 517 A
jennifer.strother@bellevuecollege.edu
STROTHER, William .... 318-670-6472. 207 A
wstrother@susla.edu
STROUD, Clarke .... 405-325-3161. 401 B
cstroud@ou.edu
STROUD, Cynthia .... 904-680-7799. 103 Q
cstroud@fcsl.edu
STROUD, George .... 610-902-8417. 411 E
george.stroud@cabrini.edu
STROUD, Jonathan .... 765-983-1600. 165 G
stroujo@earlham.edu
STROUD, Nancy .... 478-471-2728. 128 I
nancy.stroud@maconstate.edu
STROUD, Ron .... 915-831-2614. 472 B
jstroud2@epcc.edu
STROUD, Tina .... 712-279-5428. 176 B
tina.stroud@briarcliff.edu
STROUP-BENHAM,
Christine .... 303-315-2835... 86 A
christine.stroup-benham@ucdenver.edu
STROUSE, Nancy .... 702-895-2811. 294 I
nancy.strouse@unlv.edu
STROUSE, Robert, K .... 714-850-4800... 87 E
Strouse@TaftU.edu
STROUSE, Robert, K .... 714-850-4800... 69 E
strouse@taftu.edu
STROUTH, Crystal .... 507-372-3451. 260 A
crystal.strouth@mnwest.edu
STROUTS, Paul .... 404-894-1822. 125 D
paul.strouts@gatech.edu
STRUBEL, Eric .... 215-574-9600. 418 H
estrubel@hussianart.edu
STRUBEL, John .... 843-863-8044. 441 H
jstrubel@csuniv.edu
STRUBLE, Robert .... 716-896-0700. 350 A
restruble@villa.edu
STRUBLER, David .... 802-865-5725. 499 A
strubler@champlain.edu
STRUBY, Hazel .... 478-757-3430. 122 F
hstruby@centralgatech.edu
STRUBY, Shannon .... 402-354-7104. 291 B
shannon.struby@methodistcollege.edu
STRUCHTEMEYER,
Derek, L .... 770-720-5549. 130 G
dls1@reinhardt.edu
STRUCK, Kathy .... 605-367-4625. 452 C
kathryn.struck@southeasttech.edu
STRUCKMEYER,
Jacqueline .... 931-221-7466. 459 B
struckmeyerj@apsu.edu
STRUDWICK, Daniel .... 217-228-5432. 156 C
strudda@quincy.edu
STRUEBEL, Phil, J .... 716-884-9120. 315 K
pjstruebel@bryantstratton.edu
STRULOEFF, Mark .... 503-699-6252. 404 C
mstruloeff@marylhurst.edu
STRUNK, Jeffrey .... 859-572-6448. 198 I
strunk@nku.edu
STRUNK, Mary, C .... 518-783-2314. 340 J
strunk@siena.edu
STRUPP, Kindra .... 812-464-1902. 174 D
ksstrupp@usi.edu
STRUPPA, Daniele, C ..... 714-997-6826... 38 A
struppa@chapman.edu
STRYBOS, John .... 210-485-0701. 464 I
jstrybos@alamo.edu
STRYKER, H. Ford .... 814-865-4402. 426 A
hfs2@psu.edu
STRYKER, Joann .... 570-422-3211. 428 D
jstryker@po-box.esu.edu
STRYKER, Joanne .... 401-454-6177. 440 A
jstryker@risd.edu
STRYKER, Marcy .... 518-608-8287. 324 B
mstryker@excelsior.edu
STRYKER, Marcy .... 518-464-8527. 324 B
mstryker@excelsior.edu
STRYSICK, Michael, P .... 859-238-5710. 193 E
michael.strysick@centre.edu
STUARD, Avis .... 504-520-7583. 209 D
astuard@xula.edu
STUART, Alesia, K .... 251-578-1313..... 6 D
akstuart@rstc.edu
STUART, Ann .... 940-898-3201. 488 B
astuart@twu.edu
STUART, Carol, M .... 252-334-2010. 357 A
carol.stuart@macuniversity.edu
STUART, Cledis, D .... 870-235-4046... 23 F
cdstuart@sauniag.edu
STUART, Dana, S .... 765-641-4114. 163 L
dsstuart@anderson.edu
STUART, D'Anne .... 575-646-2431. 310 I
dstuart@nmsu.edu
STUART, Forrest, M .... 864-294-2204. 444 C
forrest.stuart@furman.edu
STUART, Gail, W .... 843-792-3941. 445 B
stuartg@musc.edu
STUART, Jay, L .... 630-829-6431. 140 B
jstuart@ben.edu
STUART, Kathryn .... 440-775-8540. 385 H
kathryn.stuart@oberlin.edu
STUART, Lofton, K .... 865-974-2508. 463 B
jstuart@tennessee.edu
STUART, Maggie .... 360-442-2531. 521 A
mstuart@lowercolumbia.edu
STUART, Martha Wynne . 434-924-3728. 511 B
mws4s@virginia.edu
STUART, Nancy, M .... 860-768-5135... 92 D
nstuart@hartford.edu
STUART, Roberta, P .... 413-559-5724. 227 B
STUART, Susan .... 913-288-7265. 187 L
sstuart@kckcc.edu
STUART, T. Ramon .... 304-766-3022. 530 C
stuarttr@wvstateu.edu
STUBAUS, Karen, R .... 848-932-4889. 306 A
diversity@rutgers.edu
STUBAUS, Karen, R .... 848-932-4889. 306 A
stubaus@oldqueens.rutgers.edu
STUBBE, Alethea, F .... 712-324-5061. 181 G
aletheas@nwicc.edu
STUBBEMAN, Nancy ...... 513-569-1501. 376 L
nancy.stubbeman@cincinnatistate.edu
STUBBLEFIELD, Claire .... 580-745-3090. 399 J
cstubblefield@se.edu
STUBBLEFIELD, Jay .... 912-650-6234. 131 H
rstubblefield@southuniversity.edu
STUBBLEFIELD, Michael 225-771-3890. 206 J
michael_stubblefield@subr.edu
STUBBS, Brent .... 912-443-5352. 131 D
bstubbs@savannahtech.edu
STUBBS, Gail .... 617-287-5500. 228 G
gail.stubbs@umb.edu
STUBBS, Michelle .... 912-486-7865. 129 J
mstubbs@ogeecheetech.edu
STUBBS, Robert .... 303-492-8631... 85 L
robert.stubbsd@colorado.edu
STUBBS, Sidney, J .... 334-833-4236..... 4 D
provost@huntingdon.edu
STUBBS, OSB, Simon .... 985-892-1800. 206 H
brsimon@sjasc.edu
STUBER, Heidi .... 206-934-3706. 522 I
heidi.stuber@seattlecolleges.edu
STUCHELL, Tina .... 330-823-8584. 391 E
stuchetm@mountunion.edu
STUCK, Helen .... 315-568-3133. 333 C
hstuck@nycc.edu
STUCK, Shelly .... 315-568-3111. 333 C
sstuck@nycc.edu
STUCKEY, Dennis .... 612-330-1713. 253 H
stuckey@augsburg.edu
STUCKEY, Jon, C .... 717-766-2511. 423 L
jstuckey@messiah.edu
STUCKEY, Julie .... 210-434-6711. 477 N
jstuckey@lake.ollusa.edu
STUCKEY, Larry .... 816-802-3437. 275 J
lstuckey@kcai.edu
STUCKEY, Mike .... 816-501-2414. 271 H
mike.stuckey@avila.edu
STUCKEY, Sheila .... 502-597-6852. 197 A
sheila.stuckey@kysu.edu
STUCKEY, Thomas, L ...... 419-267-1310. 385 F
tstuckey@northweststate.edu
STUCKEY, Vicki .... 618-395-7777. 147 B
stuckeyv@iecc.edu
STUCKLY, JR., Elton, E .. 254-867-4824. 485 G
elton.stuckly@tstc.edu
STUCKLY, JR., Elton, E .. 254-867-4800. 486 B
elton.stuckly@tstc.edu
STUCKY, Duane .... 618-536-3475. 159 F
dustucky@siu.edu
STUCKY, Gail .... 316-284-5363. 184 J
gstucky@bethelks.edu
STUCKY, Kent, D .... 260-665-4311. 173 E
stuckyk@trine.edu
STUDDARD, Phil .... 256-352-8060..... 9 G
phil.studdard@wallacestate.edu
STUDDERT, Thomas .... 817-257-7855. 484 I
thomas.studdert@tcu.edu
STUDDS, Susan, M .... 202-231-3322. 544 L
susan.studds@dodiis.mil
STUDEBAKER, Brian .... 574-239-8407. 166 N
bstudebaker@hcc-nd.edu
STUDENC, Bill .... 828-227-7122. 369 E
bstudenc@wcu.edu
STUDER, Mary Ann .... 419-783-2553. 379 C
mstuder@defiance.edu
STUDER, Nancy .... 219-866-6150. 172 E
nancys@saintjoe.edu
STUDHAM, Scott .... 612-625-8855. 264 G
studham@umn.edu
STUDWELL, II,
Raymond, W .... 540-828-5660. 502 J
cstudwel@bridgewater.edu
STUDWELL, Roberta .... 239-687-5501... 98 J
rstudwell@avemarialaw.edu
STUEBER, Ross .... 734-995-7393. 241 E
stuebr@cuaa.edu
STUEBER, Ross .... 262-243-5700. 532 H
ross.stueber@cuw.edu
STUGELMAYER,
Lesley, A .... 608-796-3808. 539 E
lastugelmayer@viterbo.edu
STUGELMEYER, Dennis .. 788-227-3380. 184 I
stugelmeyerdd@bethanylb.edu
STUHL, Mordechai .... 718-236-1171. 337 B
STUHLER, Eric .... 636-949-4617. 276 D
estuhler@lindenwood.edu
STUHR, Eloise, D .... 713-743-8165. 489 B
edstuhr@central.uh.edu
STUHR, Eloise, D .... 713-743-8165. 489 A
edstuhr@central.uh.edu
STUHR, Patricia, L .... 715-389-6538. 538 E
patricia.stuhr@uwc.edu
STUIFBERGEN, Alexa, M 512-471-4100. 491 C
astuifbergen@mail.utexas.edu
STUKANE, Edward .... 201-216-3472. 307 E
estukane@stevens.edu
STULL, David .... 415-503-6230... 62 H
jseaman@sfcm.edu
STULL, Robert, W .... 915-747-5347. 492 A
rstull@utep.edu
STULTS, Karen .... 410-225-2438. 216 C
kstults@mica.edu
STULTZ, James, L .... 304-336-8029. 530 A
jstultz@westliberty.edu
STUMB, Paul .... 615-547-1210. 454 A
pstumb@cumberland.edu
STUMBO, Christine .... 606-368-6125. 191 J
christinestumbo@alc.edu
STUMBRIS, Steven, V ..... 570-577-3791. 411 A
steven.stumbris@bucknell.edu
STUMO, Karl, A .... 253-535-7151. 521 I
stumo@plu.edu
STUMP, Colleen .... 301-687-3171. 220 C
cstump@frostburg.edu
STUMP, Linda, J .... 352-392-5445. 116 A
lstump@ufl.edu
STUMP, Ron, W .... 303-735-2382... 85 L
stump@colorado.edu
STUMP, Shelley .... 503-253-3443. 405 E
sstump@ocom.edu
STUMP, Tom .... 406-994-2661. 287 B
stump@montana.edu
STUMPF, Fran .... 573-897-5000. 276 E
STUMPF, Michelle .... 814-262-6436. 427 C
mstumpf@pennhighlands.edu
STUPAK, Elayne .... 740-695-9500. 374 H
estupak@belmontcollege.edu
STUPAR, Eric, H .... 202-231-2767. 544 L
eric.stupar@dodiis.mil
STUPPLE, Paul .... 845-752-3000. 348 I
p.stupple@uts.edu
STUPPY, Charles .... 216-397-4976. 381 R
cstuppy@jcu.edu
STURCH, Patty, J .... 740-264-5591. 379 F
psturch@egcc.edu
STURCH, Patty Jo .... 740-264-5591. 379 F
psturch@egcc.edu
STURDEVANT, Nancee .... 605-367-7464. 452 C
nancee.sturdevant@southeasttech.edu
STURDEVANT, Peggy ..... 641-784-5125. 178 F
peggys@graceland.edu
STURDEVANT, Ruthie ..... 573-681-5178. 276 C
sturdevr@lincolnu.edu
STURDIVANT, Alvin .... 206-296-6066. 523 E
sturdial@seattleu.edu
STURDIVANT, Brian, C ... 410-706-1678. 219 C
bsturdivant@umaryland.edu
STURDIVANT, Jauquinda 305-626-3641. 104 J
Jauquinda.Sturdivant@fmuniv.edu
STURDIVANT, Toni .... 678-422-4100... 96 F
toni.sturdivant@strayer.edu
STURDON, Andrew .... 614-837-4088. 392 E
STURDY, Ryan .... 785-460-5548. 185 P
ryan.sturdy@colbycc.edu
STURE, Linda .... 907-563-7575... 10 B
STURE, Stein .... 303-492-5537... 85 L
stein.sture@colorado.edu
STURGEON, Kathy, R ..... 217-443-8805. 143 G
ksturgeon@dacc.edu
STURGEON, Kimberley ... 843-574-6195. 447 E
kim.sturgeon@tridenttech.edu
STURGEON, Paul .... 270-706-8639. 195 A
paul.sturgeon@kctcs.edu
STURGEON, Stacy .... 435-797-1266. 497 B
stacy.sturgeon@usu.edu
STURGEON, Timothy, A . 502-272-8131. 192 E
tsturgeon@bellarmine.edu
STURGILL, Stephen .... 606-573-3228. 196 F
stephen.sturgill@kctcs.edu
STURGIS, Leah .... 803-323-2189. 449 G
sturgisl@winthrop.edu
STURGIS, Maureen .... 603-899-4000. 296 H
STURGIS, Paul .... 573-592-1116. 285 D
paul.sturgis@williamwoods.edu
STURGIS, Thomas, C ..... 601-877-6138. 265 G
tsturgis@alcorn.edu
STURM, James, P .... 716-926-8935. 326 B
jsturm@hilbert.edu
STURM, Joel .... 212-410-8047. 333 E
jsturm@nycpm.edu
STURM, Joey .... 337-482-6449. 208 D
joey.sturm@louisiana.edu
STURM, Neal, M .... 973-443-8689. 301 J
sturm@fdu.edu
STURM-SMITH, Melissa . 515-271-2835. 177 K
melissa.sturm-smith@drake.edu
STURRUP, Daniel, H .... 207-581-4707. 212 B
dsturrup@maine.edu
STURRUS, Teresa .... 231-777-0251. 247 G
teresa.sturrus@muskegoncc.edu
STURTZ, Alan, J .... 860-913-2034... 90 A
asturtz@goodwin.edu
STURZENBECKER, Diane 716-488-3021. 327 I
financialaid@jamestownbusinesscollege.
edu
STUTES, Ann, B .... 806-291-1066. 494 F
stutesa@wbu.edu
STUTEVILLE, Rebekkah ... 816-559-5634. 280 C
rebekkah.stuteville@park.edu

STUTTS, Rosie .... 805-289-6313... 74 H
rstutts@vcccd.edu
STUTZ, Trevor .... 937-778-7969. 379 G
tstutz@edisonohio.edu
STUTZMAN, Dallas .... 620-327-8110. 187 D
dallass@hesston.edu
STUTZMAN, Timothy ...... 540-432-4197. 504 D
timothy.stutzman@emu.edu
STYER, Bryan .... 312-939-4975. 146 A
bstyer@harrington.edu
STYLES, Elise .... 864-977-7018. 445 H
elise.styles@ngu.edu
STYLES, Kathleen .... 410-462-8365. 213 F
kstyles@bccc.edu
STYRON, Kelli .... 254-968-9141. 483 A
styron@tarleton.edu
STYRON, Ken .... 251-981-3771..... 2 I
ken.styron@columbiasouthern.edu
SU, Nancy .... 212-217-3640. 324 C
nancy_su@fitnyc.edu
SU, Renjeng .... 503-725-8393. 406 B
renjengs@pdx.edu
SU, Susan .... 516-739-1545. 333 F
records@nyctcm.edu
SUAREZ, Angelica .... 619-482-6315... 68 B
asuarez@swccd.edu
SUAREZ, Anthony .... 602-386-4122... 11 G
anthony.suarez@arizonachristian.edu
SUAREZ, Carmen, A .... 208-885-4285. 139 D
csuarez@uidaho.edu
SUAREZ, Jeri, L .... 540-362-6000. 505 G
jsuarez@hollins.edu
SUAREZ, Michelle .... 618-453-5855. 159 G
msuarez@siu.edu
SUAREZ-ESPINAL,
Cynthia .... 718-289-5914. 317 B
cynthia.suarez-espinal@bcc.cuny.edu
SUAREZ-HERRERO,
Ismael .... 787-863-2390. 550 C
ismael.suarez@fajardo.inter.edu
SUAREZ-OROZCO,
Marcelo, M .... 310-825-8308... 71 C
mms-o@gseis.ucla.edu
SUBBASWAMY,
Kumble, R .... 413-545-2211. 228 F
chancellor@umass.edu
SUBBIONDO, Joseph, L 415-575-6105... 31 D
jsubbiondo@ciis.edu
SUBER, Jennifer .... 601-477-4040. 267 F
jennifer.suber@jcjc.edu
SUBLETT, Roger, H .... 513-861-6400. 390 C
roger.sublett@myunion.edu
SUBLETTE, Gaylah .... 660-626-2860. 271 A
gsublette@atsu.edu
SUBOCZ, Sue .... 301-934-7846. 214 D
ssubocz@csmd.edu
SUBOTNICK, Stuart .... 718-625-2200. 315 H
SUBRAMANI, Suresh ..... 858-534-2230... 71 F
evc@ucsd.edu
SUBRAMANIAN, Ashok .. 712-749-2422. 176 D
subramaniana@bvu.edu
SUBRAMANIAN, Chitra .. 314-644-9167. 281 E
csubramanian@stlcc.edu
SUBRAMANIAN,
Sandhya .... 440-775-8401. 385 H
sandhya.subramanian@oberlin.edu
SUCH, Colette .... 209-588-5505... 77 I
suchc@yosemite.edu
SUCHAN, Richard .... 716-847-8371. 316 G
rsuchan@buffalodiocese.org
SUCHANIC, Angela, C .... 302-356-6924... 94 E
angela.c.suchanic@wilmu.edu
SUCHAR, Charles, S .... 773-325-7305. 143 H
csuchar@depaul.edu
SUCHON, Donnetta .... 281-425-6400. 475 I
dsuchon@lee.edu
SUCHORSKI, Joan, M .... 352-395-5200. 113 C
joan.suchorski@sfcollege.edu
SUDAK, Sarah .... 615-898-5342. 459 D
sarah.sudak@mtsu.edu
SUDDICK, Lori .... 920-498-5401. 541 B
lori.suddick@nwtc.edu
SUDDITH, Judith, J .... 540-843-0722. 512 H
jsuddith@lfcc.edu
SUDEIKIS, Barbara .... 269-965-3931. 244 O
sudeikisb@kellogg.edu
SUDERMAN, Bonnie .... 661-395-4610... 49 N
bsuderma@bakersfieldcollege.edu
SUDHAKAR, Rama .... 203-254-4000... 89 I
rsudhakar@fairfield.edu
SUDHAKAR, Samuel .... 909-537-5100... 34 E
ssudhakar@csusb.edu
SUDHAKAR, Samuel ...... 309-341-5297. 141 A
ssudhakar@sandburg.edu
SUDKAMP, Thomas, A .... 937-775-2097. 393 G
thomas.sudkamp@wright.edu
SUDLER, Kimberly, R ..... 302-857-7036... 93 C
krsudler@desu.edu
SUDOL, Mary .... 845-434-5750. 347 A
msudol@sullivan.suny.edu
SUEOKA, Mike .... 415-808-3000... 47 E
mike_sueoka@heald.edu
SUESS, Jack, J .... 410-455-2582. 219 D
jack@umbc.edu
SUESS, Michael .... 661-654-6324... 32 H
msuess@csub.edu
SUESSER, John, P .... 724-346-2073. 411 C
john.suesser@bc3.edu
SUFFEL, Charles .... 201-216-8031. 307 E
csuffel@stevens.edu
SUGARMAN, Roger, P ... 859-257-7989. 200 C
rpsuga0@uky.edu
SUGDEN, Mark, A .... 208-732-6849. 138 B
msugden@csi.edu
SUGG, Donald .... 870-743-3000... 22 B
dsugg@northark.edu
SUGG, Joe .... 408-551-1606... 64 M
jsugg@scu.edu
SUGGS, Benny .... 919-515-3375. 368 B
benny_suggs@ncsu.edu
SUGGS, Leah .... 706-821-8322. 130 C
lsuggs@paine.edu
SUGGS, Philana .... 205-929-6383..... 5 D
psuggs@lawsonstate.edu
SUGGS, Sheena .... 252-862-1316. 363 A
suggss@roanokechowan.edu
SUGIMOTO, Lara .... 808-845-9190. 136 G
larahs@hawaii.edu
SUH, Duckin .... 262-554-2010. 534 D
duckin_suh@yahoo.com
SUHAJDA, Kathleen .... 312-935-6446. 156 K
ksuhajda@robertmorris.edu
SUHAYDA, Rosemarie .... 312-942-6204. 157 G
rosemarie_suhayda@rush.edu
SUHLER, Mitzi .... 620-278-4226. 190 I
msuhler@sterling.edu
SUHR, Theodore, G .... 402-323-3414. 292 C
tsuhr@southeast.edu
SUIB, Steven, L .... 860-486-4623... 92 A
steven.suib@uconn.edu
SUIT, Teresa .... 256-233-8167..... 1 F
teresa.suit@athens.edu
SUITE, Denzil .... 206-543-0128. 524 G
SUJECKI, Gailmarie .... 516-671-2277. 350 C
gsujecki@webb.edu
SUJITPARAPITAYA,
Sutee .... 408-924-1516... 36 A
sutee.sujitparapitaya@sjsu.edu
SUK, Jeannine, D .... 716-880-2339. 330 F
jeannine.e.suk@medaille.edu
SUKHATME, Uday .... 212-346-1956. 335 J
provost@pace.edu
SUKKIL YOON, Mark ..... 323-643-0301... 27 N
SULAIMAN-HARA,
Sadika .... 773-508-3335. 151 H
ssulaimanhara@luc.edu
SULESKI, Andrew .... 530-895-2353... 30 F
suleskian@butte.edu
SULFRIDGE, Jay .... 606-337-1103. 193 F
jsulfridge@ccbbc.edu
SULLENBERGER,
A. Gale .... 918-631-3184. 401 F
gale-sullenberger@utulsa.edu
SULLINS, Dori .... 815-455-8559. 152 F
dsullens@mchenry.edu
SULLINS, Richard, W ...... 919-335-1200. 364 G
rwsullins@waketech.edu
SULLINS, W. Robert .... 813-974-4051. 116 C
rsullins@usf.edu
SULLIVAN, A, R .... 502-451-0815. 199 F
ars@sullivan.edu
SULLIVAN, A, R .... 502-451-0815. 199 G
ars@sullivan.edu
SULLIVAN, Adelfa .... 702-992-2110. 294 G
adelfa.sullivan@nsc.edu
SULLIVAN, Allison .... 864-503-5341. 448 H
asullivan@uscupstate.edu
SULLIVAN, Amy .... 803-323-2141. 449 G
sullivana@winthrop.edu
SULLIVAN, Anne, R .... 212-854-4038. 321 D
asullivan@columbia.edu
SULLIVAN, Becky .... 972-438-6932. 478 C
bsullivn@parkercc.edu
SULLIVAN,
Bobby (BJ), A .... 817-515-4206. 482 B
bobby.sullivan@tccd.edu
SULLIVAN, Brendan .... 508-565-1667. 237 A
bjsullivan@stonehill.edu
SULLIVAN, Brian .... 513-558-1559. 391 B
brian.sullivan@uc.edu
SULLIVAN, Brigitte .... 410-225-2209. 216 C
bsullivan01@mica.edu
SULLIVAN, Bryce .... 615-460-6437. 453 C
bryce.sullivan@belmont.edu
SULLIVAN, Charles .... 973-642-8870. 307 D
charles.sullivan@shu.edu
SULLIVAN, Cheryl .... 231-995-1147. 248 B
csullivan@nmc.edu
SULLIVAN, Cheryl .... 559-489-2232... 68 I
cheryl.sullivan@fresnocitycollege.edu
SULLIVAN,
Christopher, B .... 585-385-8001. 338 H
csullivan@sjfc.edu
SULLIVAN, Claudia .... 541-956-7176. 407 F
csullivan@roguecc.edu
SULLIVAN, Colin .... 401-341-2268. 440 C
colin.sullivan@salve.edu
SULLIVAN, Crystal, C ..... 937-229-3369. 391 C
csulllivan1@udayton.edu
SULLIVAN, Dan .... 919-658-7748. 357 I
dsullivan@moc.edu
SULLIVAN, David .... 772-462-2505. 106 P
dsulliva@irsc.edu
SULLIVAN, Durelle .... 360-736-9391. 517 G
dsullivan@centralia.edu
SULLIVAN, E. Thomas .... 802-656-7878. 500 F
thomas.sullivan@uvm.edu
SULLIVAN, Edward .... 657-278-8325... 33 E
esullivan@fullerton.edu
SULLIVAN, Eileen, G ..... 630-617-3050. 145 A
esullivan@elmhurst.edu
SULLIVAN, Elizabeth .... 201-761-7106. 306 L
esullivan2@saintpeters.edu
SULLIVAN, Erin .... 540-831-5226. 508 C
esullivan12@radford.edu
SULLIVAN, George, J ..... 610-359-4151. 414 D
gsulliva@dccc.edu
SULLIVAN, Glenda, F ..... 423-425-4553. 463 D
glenda-sullivan@utc.edu
SULLIVAN, Glenn, D ...... 502-451-0815. 199 F
gds@sullivan.edu
SULLIVAN, Glenn, D ...... 502-451-0815. 199 G
gds@sullivan.edu
SULLIVAN, Jack .... 973-328-5252. 300 G
jsullivan@ccm.edu
SULLIVAN, Jay .... 252-940-6203. 358 A
jsullivan@beaufortccc.edu
SULLIVAN, Jeff .... 715-874-4608. 539 J
jsullivan25@cvtc.edu
SULLIVAN, Jem .... 202-495-3820... 96 C
jrsullivan@dhs.edu
SULLIVAN, Joan, D .... 781-768-7212. 236 A
joan.sullivan@regiscollege.edu
SULLIVAN, John .... 727-864-8331. 101 N
sullivjf@eckerd.edu
SULLIVAN, John, L .... 508-586-1572. 229 C
john.sullivan@umassmed.edu
SULLIVAN, John, M .... 508-286-3484. 238 B
jsulliva@wheatonma.edu
SULLIVAN, John, M .... 513-562-8743. 373 K
president@artacademy.edu
SULLIVAN, Joseph .... 805-965-0581... 64 L
sullivanj@sbcc.edu
SULLIVAN, Kathleen .... 207-893-7705. 211 G
ksullivan@sjcme.edu
SULLIVAN, Kathleen .... 845-848-7804. 322 G
kathleen.sullivan@dc.edu
SULLIVAN, Kathleen, A ... 412-536-1819. 420 A
kathleen.sullivan@laroche.edu
SULLIVAN, Kenneth, A ... 775-445-4246. 295 A
ken.sullivan@wnc.edu
SULLIVAN, Kristie .... 910-695-3907. 363 F
sullivank@sandhills.edu
SULLIVAN, Kristin .... 817-272-2761. 491 B
knsull@uta.edu
SULLIVAN, Kristopher, T 401-232-6707. 438 K
ktsulliv@bryant.edu
SULLIVAN, Laura .... 715-682-4591. 541 F
laura.sullivan@witc.edu
SULLIVAN, Lawrence ...... 212-237-8364. 318 D
lsullivan@jjay.cuny.edu
SULLIVAN, Leah .... 440-646-8126. 392 D
lsullivan@ursuline.edu
SULLIVAN, Leo, V .... 617-552-3335. 224 A
leo.sullivan@bc.edu
SULLIVAN, Leslie .... 269-749-7638. 249 A
lsullivan@olivetcollege.edu
SULLIVAN, Liam .... 207-775-5037. 210 H
lsullivan@meca.edu
SULLIVAN, Linda .... 310-434-3427... 65 A
sullivan_linda@smc.edu
SULLIVAN, Lori .... 617-735-9825. 226 B
sullivlo@emmanuel.edu
SULLIVAN, Lynette .... 419-334-8400. 389 I
lsullivan@terra.edu
SULLIVAN, Lynn .... 352-395-5514. 113 C
lynn.sullivan@sfcollege.edu
SULLIVAN, M .... 401-874-5339. 440 D
mcsullivan@uri.edu
SULLIVAN, Maggie .... 401-456-8216. 439 F
msullivan@ric.edu
SULLIVAN, Maria .... 508-565-1402. 237 A
msullivan7@stonehill.edu
SULLIVAN, Marie .... 603-897-8246. 297 F
mariesullivan@rivier.edu
SULLIVAN, Mark .... 937-327-6181. 393 E
msullivan@wittenberg.edu
SULLIVAN, Mark .... 614-825-6255. 373 G
msullivan@aiam.edu
SULLIVAN, Martha .... 508-793-2276. 225 B
sullivan@holycross.edu
SULLIVAN, Mary .... 570-740-0429. 422 G
msullivan@luzerne.edu
SULLIVAN, Melanie .... 508-531-1411. 229 D
melanie.sullivan@bridgew.edu
SULLIVAN, Melanie, P .... 502-272-8477. 192 E
msullivan@bellarmine.edu
SULLIVAN, Michael .... 413-265-2494. 225 C
sullivanm@elms.edu
SULLIVAN, Monty .... 504-762-3000. 203 A
SULLIVAN, Myron .... 605-642-6297. 451 G
myron.sullivan@bhsu.edu
SULLIVAN, Nancy .... 781-292-2304. 226 G
nancy.sullivan@olin.edu
SULLIVAN, Nancy .... 508-588-9100. 232 A
SULLIVAN, Patricia .... 402-354-7024. 291 B
pat.sullivan@methodistcollege.edu
SULLIVAN, Patrick .... 610-499-4202. 437 E
ptsullivan@widener.edu
SULLIVAN, JR.,
Richard, F .... 617-333-2302. 225 E
rsulliva@curry.edu
SULLIVAN, Richard, J .... 574-239-8401. 166 N
rsullivan@hcc-nd.edu
SULLIVAN, Robert, S ..... 858-822-0830... 71 F
rssullivan@ucsd.edu
SULLIVAN, Roger, B .... 607-436-2513. 343 E
sullivrb@oneonta.edu
SULLIVAN, Ruth, D .... 401-825-2488. 439 A
rsullivan@ccri.edu
SULLIVAN, Samuel .... 706-821-8312. 130 C
ssullivan@paine.edu
SULLIVAN, Samuel .... 706-821-8132. 130 C
ssullivan@paine.edu
SULLIVAN, Sarah .... 213-613-2200... 67 E
sarah_sullivan@sciarc.edu
SULLIVAN, Scott .... 817-257-7601. 484 I
s.sullivan@tcu.edu
SULLIVAN, Sean .... 708-456-0300. 161 A
ssulliva@triton.edu
SULLIVAN, Sean .... 508-793-7160. 225 A
ssullivan@clarku.edu
SULLIVAN, Sean, P .... 716-645-2287. 341 F
sps@buffalo.edu
SULLIVAN, Shawn, P ..... 715-675-3331. 541 A
sullivan@ntc.edu
SULLIVAN, Skip .... 678-664-0530. 134 H
skip.sullivan@westgatech.edu
SULLIVAN, Slade .... 325-674-2485. 464 H
sullivans@acu.edu
SULLIVAN, Stephanie ..... 770-426-2632. 128 D
stephanie.sullivan@life.edu
SULLIVAN, Susan .... 812-749-1223. 171 K
ssullivan@oak.edu
SULLIVAN, Suzanne .... 601-968-8746. 266 A
ssullivan@belhaven.edu
SULLIVAN, Teresa, A ...... 434-924-3337. 511 B
tas6n@virginia.edu
SULLIVAN, Thomas .... 660-944-2860. 272 H
thomas@conception.edu
SULLIVAN, Thomas .... 617-243-2059. 227 K
tpsullivan@lasell.edu
SULLIVAN, Thomas, B .... 512-448-8727. 479 C
toms@stedwards.edu
SULLIVAN, Thomas, P ... 517-586-3012. 241 A
tsullivan@cleary.edu
SULLIVAN, Timothy, J .... 508-929-8073. 230 G
tsullivan@worcester.edu
SULLIVAN, Toyette .... 410-386-8429. 214 A
tsullivan@carrollcc.edu
SULLIVAN, Tracy .... 708-235-2179. 145 F
tsullivan@govst.edu
SULLIVAN, Wayne .... 662-862-8101. 267 C
jwsullivan@iccms.edu
SULLIVAN, Wayne .... 505-277-2383. 312 F
sullivan@unm.edu
SULLIVAN, Wayne .... 315-792-3201. 349 F
wasullivan@utica.edu
SULLIVAN ALIOTO,
Kathleen .... 415-239-3816... 38 L
ksalioto@ccsf.edu
SULLIVAN-CROWLEY,
Lianne, C .... 609-258-2430. 304 E
lsulliva@princeton.edu
SULLIVAN-TRAINOR,
Deborah .... 651-638-6804. 253 K
suldeb@bethel.edu
SULLIVAN-WILLIAMS,
Lizziel .... 856-256-4226. 305 E
sullivan@rowan.edu
SULLIVANT, Stan .... 870-338-6474... 24 G
SULLO, Fred .... 914-654-5555. 320 H
fsullo@cnr.edu
SULTAN, Sonia .... 612-436-7520. 257 J
ssultan@msbcollege.edu
SULTAN, Sonia .... 651-730-5100. 255 H
ssultan@globeuniversity.edu
SULZBACH, J. Bonnie .... 443-412-2119. 215 C
bsulzbach@harford.edu
SUMADI, Mohammad ..... 813-882-0100... 96 F
SUMAJIT, Rosemary .... 808-845-9143. 136 G
rosea@hawaii.edu

SUMAS, Keith, P .... 404-413-0783. 126 E
ksumas1@gsu.edu
SUMEREL, Marie, B .... 919-760-8341. 356 G
sumerelm@meredith.edu
SUMICHRAST, Robert, T 540-231-6152. 515 C
rsumichr@vt.edu
SUMMA, Louise, J .... 860-892-5734... 89 F
lsumma@trcc.commnet.edu
SUMMA-WOLFE, Cathy .. 415-485-9528... 40 G
cathy.summawolfe@marin.edu
SUMMARY, Sherry .... 618-985-3741. 148 J
sherrysummary@jalc.edu
SUMME, Shawn .... 239-280-1531... 98 K
shawn.summe@avemaria.edu
SUMMER, Gail .... 540-365-4208. 504 L
gsummer@ferrum.edu
SUMMER, Gail .... 540-365-4206. 504 L
gsummer@ferrum.edu
SUMMER, Rebekah .... 320-762-4612. 257 O
rebekahs@alextech.edu
SUMMERFIELD, Liane .... 703-284-6478. 507 B
liane.summerfield@marymount.edu
SUMMERLIN, Chris .... 478-471-2317. 128 I
chris.summerlin@maconstate.edu
SUMMERLIN,
Christopher, A .... 606-783-2060. 198 A
c.summerlin@moreheadstate.edu
SUMMERLIN, Timothy .... 830-792-7345. 480 F
tsummerlin@schreiner.edu
SUMMERS, Amanda .... 281-425-6533. 475 I
asummers@lee.edu
SUMMERS, Carol .... 425-640-1559. 519 D
carol.summers@edcc.edu
SUMMERS, Chris .... 404-364-8355. 130 A
csummers@oglethorpe.edu
SUMMERS, Cindy .... 312-362-5653. 143 H
csummers@depaul.edu
SUMMERS, Diane .... 713-226-5519. 489 D
summersd@uhd.edu
SUMMERS, Edward .... 518-388-6101. 348 J
summerse@union.edu
SUMMERS, Eric, J .... 985-549-3850. 208 C
esummers@selu.edu
SUMMERS, Greg .... 715-346-4686. 538 A
gsummers@uwsp.edu
SUMMERS, Janie, K .... 314-286-3665. 280 F
jksummers@ranken.edu
SUMMERS, Jean .... 816-932-6751. 281 J
jsummers@saintlukescollege.edu
SUMMERS, Jerry .... 903-923-2084. 471 J
jsummers@etbu.edu
SUMMERS, LeRoy .... 336-517-2116. 352 H
lsummers@bennett.edu
SUMMERS, Lori .... 201-200-3489. 303 F
lsummers@njcu.edu
SUMMERS, Matthew, A .. 304-637-1373. 526 E
summersm@dewv.edu
SUMMERS, Michael .... 706-821-8293. 130 C
msummers@paine.edu
SUMMERS, Michael .... 757-822-7122. 514 C
msummers@tcc.edu
SUMMERS, Micheal .... 806-291-1165. 494 F
summersm@wbu.edu
SUMMERS, Nathan .... 937-294-0592. 388 M
nathan@saa.edu
SUMMERS, Robert .... 870-512-7710... 20 B
robert_summers@asun.edu
SUMMERS, Tiffany .... 615-966-1791. 456 B
tiffany.summers@lipscomb.edu
SUMMERS, Tony, E .... 972-238-6202. 471 C
tesummers@dcccd.edu
SUMMERS, Wally .... 229-931-2040. 131 G
wsummers@southgatech.edu
SUMMERSELL, Charley ... 518-587-2100. 346 A
charley.summersell@esc.edu
SUMMERVILLE, Jamie .... 270-247-8521. 197 H
jsummerville@midcontinent.edu
SUMMERVILLE, Rachele . 541-888-7259. 407 H
rsummerville@socc.edu
SUMMINS, Lisa .... 908-835-2322. 308 G
lsummins@warren.edu
SUMNER, Connie .... 229-468-2033. 134 K
Connie.sumner@wiregrass.edu
SUMNER, Henry, A .... 610-558-5513. 424 I
hsumner@neumann.edu
SUMNER, James .... 503-370-6021. 408 J
jsumner@willamette.edu
SUMNER, Karen .... 602-386-4148... 11 G
karen.sumner@arizonachristian.edu
SUMNER, Shelia .... 218-879-0715. 258 E
ssumner@fdltcc.edu
SUMNER, Wesley .... 321-674-6218. 104 H
wsumner@fit.edu
SUN, Yanling .... 973-655-4091. 303 D
suny@mail.montclair.edu
SUNAHARA, Wayne .... 808-845-9272. 136 G
waynens@hawaii.edu
SUNATA, Cem .... 805-756-6016... 32 F
csunata@calpoly.edu
SUNBURY, Mary Ann ..... 704-463-3203. 365 E
maryann.sunbury@fsmail.pfeiffer.edu
SUND, Andrew, C .... 773-878-7502. 158 B
asund@staugustine.edu
SUND, Reyna .... 619-849-2983... 59 L
reynasund@pointloma.edu
SUNDBERG, Lori, H .... 847-735-5030. 150 B
lsundberg@lakeforest.edu
SUNDBERG, Lori, L .... 309-341-5214. 141 A
lsundberg@sandburg.edu
SUNDBORG, SJ,
Stephen, V .... 206-296-1891. 523 E
sundborg@seattleu.edu
SUNDBY, Oliver .... 307-532-8304. 542 a
oliver.sundby@ewc.wy.edu
SUNDEEN, Joseph, T ..... 626-529-8234... 57 G
tsundeen@pacificoaks.edu
SUNDERMAN, Rick .... 614-947-6605. 380 A
rick.sunderman@franklin.edu
SUNDERMANN, Brigitte . 970-255-2600... 79 F
bsunderm@coloradomesa.edu
SUNDGREN, Donald, E .. 434-982-5834. 511 B
des5j@virginia.edu
SUNDQUIST, Mike .... 209-575-6081... 77 J
sundquistm@yosemite.cc.ca.us
SUNDSEDT, Casey .... 847-628-1561. 149 B
csundsedt@judsonu.edu
SUNDSMO, Alecia, D ...... 717-245-1485. 414 H
sundsmoa@dickinson.edu
SUNDSTEDT, Bernard ..... 815-226-3371. 157 C
bsunstedt@rockford.edu
SUNDSTROM, Sandra ..... 507-786-3357. 264 B
sundstro@stolaf.edu
SUNDY, Carolyn .... 606-589-3052. 196 F
carolyn.sundy@kctcs.edu
SUNG, Mankyung .... 562-926-1023... 60 B
psung@ptsa.edu
SUNG CHOI, Jason .... 323-643-0301... 27 N
SUNI, Ellen, Y .... 816-235-1007. 283 D
sunie@umkc.edu
SUNIGA, Nova .... 808-847-9860. 136 G
nsuniga@hawaii.edu
SUNLEAF, Arthur, W ...... 563-588-7137. 180 L
arthur.sunleaf@loras.edu
SUNNUCKS, Carol .... 602-978-7541... 18 A
carol.sunnucks@thunderbird.edu
SUNQUIST, Scott, W ...... 626-584-5265... 45 E
sunquist@fuller.edu
SUNSER, James .... 585-345-6812. 325 C
jmsunser@genesee.edu
SUNSHINE, Eugene, S ... 847-491-5534. 155 D
e-sunshine@northwestern.edu
SUNSHINE, Lisbet .... 415-338-1120... 35 E
lisbet@sfsu.edu
SUNSHINE, Phyllis .... 410-337-6046. 215 A
psunshine@goucher.edu
SUOREZ, Paula .... 760-384-6298... 49 O
pasouroez@cerrocoso.edu
SUPERNAW, Robert, B .... 704-233-8015. 370 G
supernaw@wingate.edu
SUPINSKI, Jessica .... 425-235-2352. 522 F
jsupinski@rtc.edu
SUPOWITZ, Paul, A .... 412-624-2901. 435 C
psupowit@pitt.edu
SUPPLEE, JR., Jack .... 859-257-8288. 200 C
supplee@uky.edu
SUPPLEE, Janice .... 937-766-8319. 375 K
suppleej@cedarville.edu
SUPPLER, Robin .... 954-262-4349. 109 K
rsupler@nova.edu
SUPURGECI, Jonna .... 605-668-1515. 450 F
jsupurgeci@mtmc.edu
SURATY-CLARKE,
Mercedes .... 713-743-1185. 489 B
msclarke@uh.edu
SURBAUGH, Joyce .... 304-734-6603. 527 O
jsurbaugh@bridgemont.edu
SURBECK, III,
Carlton, E .... 410-337-6100. 215 A
csurbeck@goucher.edu
SURBROOK, Will .... 619-388-6589... 62 C
wsurbroo@sdccd.edu
SURESH, Subra .... 412-268-2201. 412 H
suresh@andrew.cmu.edu
SURETHING, Nicole, A ... 540-654-1053. 510 J
nsurethi@umw.edu
SURGALA, David, J .... 570-577-3811. 411 A
dsurgala@bucknell.edu
SURGEONER, James ...... 610-607-6236. 431 D
jsurgeoner@racc.edu
SURH, Tina, H .... 212-998-2371. 334 D
tina.surh@nyu.edu
SURIEL, Wanda .... 781-768-7061. 236 A
wanda.suriel@regiscollege.edu
SUROWIEC, Barbara .... 203-332-5049... 88 F
bsurowiec@hcc.commnet.edu
SURPRENANT, Neil .... 518-327-6313. 336 B
nsurprenant@paulsmiths.edu
SURRELL, Matt .... 662-472-2312. 267 B
msurrell@holmescc.edu
SURRETT, Caron .... 828-884-8261. 352 I
caron@brevard.edu
SURRIDGE, Jack, F .... 773-244-5676. 154 G
jsurridge@northpark.edu
SURRIDGE, Margot .... 847-578-8594. 157 F
margot.surridge@rosalindfranklin.edu
SURRIDGE, Mary, M ...... 773-244-5710. 154 G
msurridge@northpark.edu
SURRRUSCO, Anet .... 203-576-5675... 91 D
asurrusco@stvincentscollege.edu
SUSANKA, Thomas, J .... 805-525-4417... 69 H
tsusanka@thomasaquinas.edu
SUSHINSKY, David, M ... 240-895-4282. 218 A
dmsushinksy@smcm.edu
SUSICK, Timothy .... 724-938-4056. 428 A
susick@calu.edu
SUSKI, Katharine, J .... 618-453-2987. 159 G
ksuski@siu.edu
SUSMAN, Catherine, D ... 541-346-1255. 406 D
susman@uoregon.edu
SUSMAN, Jeffrey, L .... 330-325-6254. 385 E
jsusman@neomed.edu
SUSMANN, Phillip .... 802-485-2213. 500 A
susmann@norwich.edu
SUSS, Stuart .... 718-368-5109. 318 E
president@kbcc.cuny.edu
SUSS, Stuart .... 718-368-5661. 318 E
ssuss@kbcc.cuny.edu
SUSSENBACH, Michelle . 618-664-7025. 145 G
michelle.sussenbach@greenville.edu
SUSSKIND, Gary .... 718-953-5889. 347 F
SUSSMAN, Nan, M .... 718-982-2315. 317 E
nan.sussman@csi.cuny.edu
SUSSWEIN, Gary, J .... 512-471-4945. 491 C
susswein@austin.utexas.edu
SUSTICH, Andrew .... 870-972-2025... 19 N
sustich@astate.edu
SUTER, Cindy .... 419-448-2090. 380 G
csuter@heidelberg.edu
SUTER, Rebecca .... 304-232-0361. 527 L
rsuter@wvbc.edu
SUTER, Vicki .... 503-699-6339. 404 C
vsuter@marylhurst.edu
SUTERA, Paul, J .... 914-637-2710. 327 C
psutera@iona.edu
SUTHERLAND, David ...... 218-879-0816. 258 E
dsutherland@fdltcc.edu
SUTHERLAND, David ...... 501-450-1254... 21 E
sutherlandd@hendrix.edu
SUTHERLAND, Duncan ... 802-831-1359. 500 H
dsutherland@vermontlaw.edu
SUTHERLAND, Gloria ..... 479-575-4140... 23 I
gsuther@uark.edu
SUTHERLAND, Jim .... 678-839-6410. 133 I
sutherla@westga.edu
SUTHERLAND, John .... 252-328-6249. 367 B
sutherlandj@ecu.edu
SUTHERLAND, Richard ... 989-358-7368. 239 C
sutherlr@alpenacc.edu
SUTHERLAND, Ronald .... 765-998-5118. 173 C
rnsutherl@taylor.edu
SUTHERLAND, Sarah, R . 931-598-5241. 458 H
ssutherl@sewanee.edu
SUTHERLAND, Timothy .. 219-980-6946. 168 B
sutherla@iun.edu
SUTHERLAND, Tricia ...... 712-274-6400. 183 G
tricia.sutherland@witcc.edu
SUTHERLIN, Julia .... 765-658-4154. 165 F
juliasutherlin@depauw.edu
SUTINEN, Paul .... 503-699-6242. 404 C
psutinen@marylhurst.edu
SUTKOWSKI, Ernest, H .. 914-831-0343. 321 B
SUTKUS, Janel .... 412-268-8729. 412 H
jsutkus@cmu.edu
SUTLIFF, Michael .... 714-432-0202... 39 K
msutliff@occ.cccd.edu
SUTLIFF, Michael .... 714-432-5638... 39 K
msutliff@occ.cccd.edu
SUTPHEN, Debra .... 916-660-7502... 66 B
dsutphen@sierracollege.edu
SUTPHIN, Mamie, M .... 336-734-7520. 360 E
msutphin@forsythtech.edu
SUTTER, Frankie, K .... 910-592-8081. 363 E
fsutter@sampsoncc.edu
SUTTER, Thaddeus .... 309-556-3059. 148 B
tsutter@iwu.edu
SUTTERFIELD, Joellen .... 408-934-4900... 47 A
joellen_sutterfield@heald.edu
SUTTERFIELD, Shirley .... 251-442-2414..... 9 A
ssutterfield@umobile.edu
SUTTHOFF, Maggi .... 425-235-2352. 522 F
msutthoff@rtc.edu
SUTTLE, J. Lloyd .... 203-432-4453... 93 A
j.suttle@yale.edu
SUTTON, Ann .... 706-776-0100. 130 E
asutton@piedmont.edu
SUTTON, Barbara .... 773-298-3504. 158 E
sutton@sxu.edu
SUTTON, Barbara, B .... 252-335-3224. 367 C
bbsutton@mail.ecsu.edu
SUTTON, Brooke .... 620-278-4209. 190 I
bsutton@sterling.edu
SUTTON, Cynthia .... 314-392-2291. 278 B
sutttonc@mobap.edu
SUTTON, Deborah .... 252-527-6223. 361 F
dsutton@lenoircc.edu
SUTTON, Deborah, S ...... 252-527-6223. 361 F
dsutton@lenoircc.edu
SUTTON, Ellen .... 630-942-2659. 142 G
suttone@cod.edu
SUTTON, Janice .... 903-675-6229. 488 D
jsutton@tvcc.edu
SUTTON, John .... 812-749-1542. 171 K
jsutton@oak.edu
SUTTON, Judith .... 304-485-5487. 527 C
jsutton@msc.edu
SUTTON, Kay .... 309-690-6886. 146 E
ksutton@icc.edu
SUTTON, Kenneth, W ..... 410-778-7269. 221 C
ksutton2@washcoll.edu
SUTTON, Linda .... 913-288-7652. 187 L
lsutton@kckcc.edu
SUTTON, Lynn .... 336-758-5480. 370 D
suttonls@wfu.edu
SUTTON, Michael .... 909-607-3562... 39 D
mike.sutton@cms.claremont.edu
SUTTON, Nancy .... 217-351-2402. 155 J
nsutton@parkland.edu
SUTTON, R. Anderson .... 808-956-8922. 136 B
SUTTON, Robert, E .... 509-452-5100. 521 J
SUTTON, Stephanie .... 440-365-5222. 383 B
SUTTON, Steve .... 660-562-1248. 279 I
alumni@nwmissouri.edu
SUTTON, Whitney .... 970-248-1078... 79 F
wsutton@coloradomesa.edu
SUTTON, William .... 423-425-2256. 463 D
William-sutton@utc.edu
SUTTON-HAYWOOD,
Marilyn .... 919-546-8330. 366 E
mhaywood@shawu.edu
SUTTON-JACKSON,
Vicky, L .... 803-934-3168. 445 F
vsutton-jackson@morris.edu
SUTTON-SMITH, Leslie .. 646-312-1190. 316 J
Leslie.Sutton-Smith@baruch.cuny.edu
SUTZKO, Christopher ..... 570-208-5874. 419 P
christophersutzko@kings.edu
SUVAK, Daniel, S .... 330-490-7183. 392 H
dsuvak@walsh.edu
SUYAMA, Barbara .... 262-695-7842. 541 D
bsuyama@wctc.edu
SUZO, Michael .... 419-783-2361. 379 C
msuzo@defiance.edu
SUZOR, Michael, J .... 413-755-4044. 233 A
msuzor@stcc.edu
SUZOW, Bo .... 213-738-6762... 68 C
mis@swlaw.edu
SUZUKI, Hayato .... 973-618-3419. 300 A
hsuzuki@caldwell.edu
SUZUKI, Joyce .... 707-664-4470... 36 B
joyce.suzuki@sonoma.edu
SUZUKI, Takeo .... 479-788-7166... 24 A
takeo.suzuki@uafs.edu
SVAJDA, Deborah .... 254-298-8609. 482 C
debbie.svajda@templejc.edu
SVALDI, David, P .... 719-587-7341... 78 B
dpsvaldi@adams.edu
SVANDA, Gary .... 402-559-4432. 292 J
gsvanda@unmc.edu
SVATOS, Liz, A .... 402-552-3038. 288 L
svatos@clarksoncollege.edu
SVEC, Andrew .... 218-281-8438. 264 E
asvec@umn.edu
SVEI, Yehuda .... 215-477-1000. 433 J
talmudicalyeshiva@yahoo.com
SVENDSEN, Carol .... 303-721-1313... 83 D
svendsec@msudenver.edu
SVENSSON, Craig, K ...... 765-494-1368. 171 M
svensson@purdue.edu
SVENSSON, Nancy .... 510-841-1905... 27 H
nsvensson@absw.edu
SVETE, Lee, J .... 574-631-5200. 174 A
svete.1@nd.edu
SVOBODA, Angela, M ...... 512-448-8622. 479 C
asvoboda@stedwards.edu
SWAFFORD, Denise .... 239-489-9358. 101 O
jswafford@edison.edu
SWAFFORD, Jeanna, C .. 731-881-7629. 463 E
jswafford@utm.edu
SWAGER, Sarah, L .... 509-963-1515. 517 F
swagers@cwu.edu
SWAGERS, Christin .... 918-781-7281. 394 D
swagersc@bacone.edu
SWAGGER, Russell .... 701-255-3285. 373 C
rswagger@uttc.edu
SWAHN, Monica, H .... 404-413-3505. 126 E
mswahn@gsu.edu
SWAID, Samar .... 501-370-5334... 22 F
sswaid@philander.edu
SWAIM, Kevin, C .... 765-361-6252. 175 B
swaimk@wabash.edu
SWAIN, Carole .... 925-631-4695... 61 F
cswain@stmarys-ca.edu

SWAIN, Corliss ... 507-786-3277. 264 B
swain@stolaf.edu
SWAIN, Cristal ... 970-351-1142... 86 C
cristal.wain@unco.edu
SWAIN, Emily ... 330-823-2674. 391 E
swainej@mountunion.edu
SWAIN, Emily, L ... 304-367-4015. 529 F
Emily.Swain@fairmontstate.edu
SWAIN, Heather, C ... 517-355-2262. 246 H
heather.swain@cabs.msu.edu
SWAIN, Jackie ... 406-275-4755. 288 C
jackie_swain@skc.edu
SWAIN, Jeffrey ... 305-626-3663. 104 J
Jeffrey.Swain@fmuniv.edu
SWAIN, Laurie ... 757-789-1797. 512 D
lswain@es.vccs.edu
SWAIN, Richard ... 610-436-2747. 430 A
rswain@wcupa.edu
SWAIN, Rodney ... 414-229-5895. 537 A
rswain@uwm.edu
SWAIN, Ronald, L ... 512-863-1940. 481 I
swainr@southwestern.edu
SWAIN, Stuart, G ... 207-255-1224. 212 F
sswain@maine.edu
SWALGA, Dan ... 412-392-3911. 431 B
dswalga@pointpark.edu
SWALLOW, John, R ... 931-598-1101. 458 H
jrswallo@sewanee.edu
SWALWELL, Joe ... 405-682-1611. 397 E
jswalwell@occc.edu
SWAN, Beth Ann ... 215-503-8057. 434 C
BethAnn.Swan@jefferson.edu
SWAN, Bobi ... 503-493-6526. 402 J
bswan@cu-portland.edu
SWAN, Deba ... 254-526-1237. 468 G
deborah.swan@ctcd.edu
SWAN, III, George, W ... 313-496-2344. 252 B
gswan1@wcccd.edu
SWAN, Kirsten ... 207-778-7347. 212 D
kswan@maine.edu
SWAN, S. Tomeka ... 410-287-6060. 214 B
tswan@cecil.edu
SWAN, Steve ... 360-650-3482. 525 C
steve.swan@wwu.edu
SWAN, Terry, W ... 270-384-8148. 197 D
swant@lindsey.edu
SWAN, William ... 718-636-3518. 336 F
wswan@pratt.edu
SWANAGAN, Diana ... 706-233-7301. 131 E
dswanagan@shorter.edu
SWANBERG, Jeff ... 815-967-7321. 157 B
jswanberg@rockfordcareercollege.edu
SWANEY, Alica ... 864-225-7653. 444 A
alicaswaney@forrestcollege.edu
SWANGER, Dustin ... 518-736-3622. 325 A
dustin.swanger@fmcc.suny.edu
SWANGER, Rachel ... 310-393-0411... 58 E
rswanger@rand.org
SWANGER, Stefanie ... 478-757-5218. 134 G
sswanger@wesleyancollege.edu
SWANGER, Stefanie ... 478-757-5257. 134 G
sswanger@wesleyancollege.edu
SWANGER, Thomas ... 760-750-4813... 35 A
tswanger@csusm.edu
SWANK, Dennis, W ... 570-577-3363. 411 A
dennis.swank@bucknell.edu
SWANK, Jamie, R ... 724-450-4045. 417 E
jrswank@gcc.edu
SWANN, John ... 315-792-7113. 346 C
swannj@sunyit.edu
SWANN, Patricia ... 315-792-3060. 349 F
SWANN, Ruth ... 850-599-3370. 114 K
ruth.swann@famu.edu
SWANNACK, Patricia ... 732-571-3546. 303 C
pswannac@monmouth.edu
SWANQUIST, Leah ... 847-635-1780. 155 F
lswanqui@oakton.edu
SWANSON, Alison ... 515-961-1696. 182 E
alison.swanson@simpson.edu
SWANSON, Barry, K ... 785-864-5978. 190 L
bswanson@ku.edu
SWANSON, Brenda ... 781-762-1211. 226 E
SWANSON, Brian, R ... 909-869-2261... 32 G
bswanson@csupomona.edu
SWANSON, Chad ... 912-588-2521. 120 B
cswanson@altamahatech.edu
SWANSON, Chris ... 541-683-5141. 403 D
cswanson@gutenberg.edu
SWANSON, Darren ... 320-363-5810. 254 J
dswanson@csbsju.edu
SWANSON, Eleanor ... 732-571-7529. 303 C
eswanson@monmouth.edu
SWANSON, Gary, L ... 724-946-7188. 437 B
gswanson@westminster.edu
SWANSON, Greg ... 262-472-6703. 538 D
swansong@uww.edu
SWANSON, Gregory ... 704-461-5073. 352 G
GregSwanson@bac.edu
SWANSON, Guy ... 816-501-4862. 280 I
guy.swanson@rockhurst.edu
SWANSON, Hope ... 802-224-3000. 501 A
hope.swanson@vsc.edu
SWANSON, James, E ... 574-372-5700. 166 B
swansoje@grace.edu
SWANSON, Jeanne ... 760-795-6840... 54 G
jswanson@miracosta.edu
SWANSON, Jim, M ... 719-389-6651... 79 D
jswanson@coloradocollege.edu
SWANSON, JR., Joe ... 404-752-1542. 129 E
jswanson@msm.edu
SWANSON, Kathrine ... 215-641-6510. 424 B
kswanson@mc3.edu
SWANSON, Kristen, M ... 919-966-3731. 368 D
kswanson@unc.edu
SWANSON, Lou ... 970-491-2785... 80 I
louis.swanson@colostate.edu
SWANSON, Margaret, A . 309-694-8584. 146 E
mswanson@icc.edu
SWANSON, Richard ... 510-261-8500... 58 G
richard.swanson@patten.edu
SWANSON, Rick ... 478-274-7871. 129 I
rswanson@oftc.edu
SWANSON, Robert ... 419-448-2125. 380 G
rswanso1@heidelberg.edu
SWANSON, Robert, P ... 716-286-8538. 334 F
rps@niagara.edu
SWANSON, Ronald ... 770-407-1001... 28 M
raswanson@argosy.edu
SWANSON, Steven ... 415-575-6178... 31 D
sswanson@ciis.edu
SWANSON-MADDEN,
Pamela ... 618-395-7777. 146 H
swansonp@iecc.edu
SWANSON-ORR, Tamara 503-845-3549. 404 D
tamara.swanson@mtangel.edu
SWANSTROM, Eugene ... 847-317-8038. 160 M
gswanstr@tiu.edu
SWANT, Steven ... 404-894-4615. 125 D
steve.swant@carnegie.gatech.edu
SWANTON, Deborah ... 978-232-2430. 226 C
dswanton@endicott.edu
SWANZEY, Thomas ... 201-692-2749. 301 J
thomas_swanzey@fdu.edu
SWARBRICK,
John "Jack", B ... 574-631-7546. 174 A
swarbrick.1@nd.edu
SWARNES, Neal, R ... 417-667-8181. 273 A
nswarnes@cottey.edu
SWARR, Amy ... 630-617-5370. 145 A
amys@elmhurst.edu
SWARTHOUT, Jeanne ... 928-524-7420... 16 E
jeanne.swarthout@npc.edu
SWARTWOOD, Ron ... 719-549-3026... 84 G
ron.swartwood@pueblocc.edu
SWARTWOOD, Ronald ... 719-502-2061... 84 A
ronald.swartwood@ppcc.edu
SWARTWOUT, Donna, L 978-837-5503. 234 A
donna.swartwout@merrimack.edu
SWARTZ, David, L ... 202-885-2612... 94 F
dswartz@american.edu
SWARTZ, Mark ... 212-410-8457. 333 E
mswartz@nycpm.edu
SWARTZ, Mary, K ... 757-683-3623. 507 N
mswartz@odu.edu
SWARTZBAUGH, Keith ... 956-380-8140. 479 B
kswartzbaugh@riogrande.edu
SWARTZENDRUBER,
Loren, E ... 540-432-4100. 504 D
lorens@emu.edu
SWARTZENTRUBER,
Dale, E ... 740-368-3811. 387 J
deswartz@owu.edu
SWARTZLANDER,
Barbara ... 207-602-2363. 213 A
bswartzlander@une.edu
SWARTZWELDER,
Roger, L ... 205-329-7903... 3 B
roger.swartzwelder@ecacolleges.com
SWATCHICK, Abby ... 610-568-1474. 409 E
abby.swatchick@alvernia.edu
SWEANY, Lisa ... 912-344-2730. 120 G
lisa.sweany@armstrong.edu
SWEARENGIN, Paul ... 412-237-3050. 413 D
pswearengin@ccac.edu
SWEARER, Randy ... 215-951-2705. 430 E
swearerr@philau.edu
SWEARINGEN, Jodie ... 651-423-8216. 258 D
jodie.swearingen@dctc.edu
SWEARINGIN, Bubba ... 940-325-2591. 494 G
bswearingin@wc.edu
SWEAT, Carl ... 757-925-6342. 513 E
csweat@pdc.edu
SWEATMAN, Robert, A ... 217-245-3289. 146 F
rsweatma@ic.edu
SWEEDLER, Alan, R ... 619-594-1354... 35 D
asweedler@sciences.sdsu.edu
SWEEK, Cristina ... 541-278-5753. 402 C
csweek@bluecc.edu
SWEELEY, Rebecca ... 209-228-4667... 71 D
RSweeley@UCMerced.edu
SWEEN, Barbara ... 859-572-5650. 198 I
sweenb@nku.edu
SWEENER, Kathleen ... 518-629-7320. 326 G
k.sweener@hvcc.edu
SWEENEY, Beth ... 859-572-6371. 198 I
sweeneyb@nku.edu
SWEENEY, Christina, C ... 302-857-1072... 93 G
csweeney@dtcc.edu
SWEENEY, Donnie ... 256-331-5438... 6 A
dsweeney@nwscc.edu
SWEENEY, Jeff ... 503-699-6269. 404 C
jsweeney@marylhurst.edu
SWEENEY, John, M ... 401-865-2281. 439 E
john.sweeney@providence.edu
SWEENEY, Katherine ... 706-737-1632. 126 B
ksweeney@gru.edu
SWEENEY, Kathleen, J ... 978-656-3046. 232 B
sweeneyk@middlesex.mass.edu
SWEENEY, Laurie Beth ... 614-222-3268. 378 A
lsweeney@ccad.edu
SWEENEY, Marc ... 937-766-7480. 375 K
msweeney@cedarville.edu
SWEENEY, Michael ... 510-883-2083... 42 I
msweeney@dspt.edu
SWEENEY, Michael, E ... 513-231-2223. 374 D
msweeney@athenaeum.edu
SWEENEY, Michael, F ... 530-754-6295... 70 J
mfsweeney@ucdavis.edu
SWEENEY, Michael, L ... 423-461-1510. 454 E
msweeney@ecs.edu
SWEENEY, Richard, T ... 973-596-3208. 303 G
richard.sweeney@njit.edu
SWEENEY, Rick ... 978-867-4036. 226 H
rick.sweeney@gordon.edu
SWEENEY, Robert, D ... 434-924-1008. 511 B
rds2j@virginia.edu
SWEENEY, Robert, J ... 937-775-3346. 393 G
robert.sweeney@wright.edu
SWEENEY, Timothy ... 252-335-0821. 359 F
timothy_sweeney@albemarle.edu
SWEENEY, Victoria ... 630-889-6572. 154 E
vsweeney@nuhs.edu
SWEENEY, Vince ... 608-265-2822. 536 D
vsweeney@wisc.edu
SWEENEY, Yvette ... 816-604-4114. 277 H
SWEENEY, Yvette, M ... 636-922-8238. 280 J
ysweeney@stchas.edu
SWEET, Brett ... 615-343-6735. 463 G
brett.sweet@vanderbilt.edu
SWEET, Chris ... 503-699-6268. 404 C
csweet@marylhurst.edu
SWEET, Cyndi ... 865-981-8095. 456 D
cyndi.sweet@maryvillecollege.edu
SWEET, Darryl ... 415-565-4604... 71 A
sweetd@uchastings.edu
SWEET, David ... 972-721-5288. 488 F
dsweet@udallas.edu
SWEET, David, M ... 315-279-5249. 328 D
dsweet@mail.keuka.edu
SWEET, Don ... 252-328-9103. 367 B
sweetd@ecu.edu
SWEET, Doris Ann ... 508-767-7272. 222 C
dasweet@assumption.edu
SWEET, Fred ... 616-222-1329. 241 F
fred.sweet@cornerstone.edu
SWEET, Jodie, L ... 574-239-8374. 166 N
jsweet@hcc-nd.edu
SWEET, Lu ... 307-382-1639. 543 J
lsweet@wwcc.wy.edu
SWEET, Stephanie ... 631-244-3047. 323 B
sweets@dowling.edu
SWEET, Stephen ... 802-258-3361. 500 C
stephen.sweet@sit.edu
SWEET, Stephen, A ... 919-658-7493. 357 I
ssweet@moc.edu
SWEET, Tracy ... 802-224-3000. 501 A
tracy.sweet@vsc.edu
SWEETANA, Michael ... 610-282-1100. 414 F
michael.sweetana@desales.edu
SWEETEN, Lacy ... 573-592-1658. 285 D
lacey.sweeten@williamwoods.edu
SWEETENBURG-LEE,
Penni ... 804-257-5656. 515 F
pbsweetenburg@vuu.edu
SWEETING, Don, W ... 407-366-9493. 269 E
dsweeting@rts.edu
SWEETMAN, Tim ... 816-414-3700. 277 L
tsweetman@mbts.edu
SWEEZEY, Gail, M ... 717-337-6100. 417 B
gsweezey@gettysburg.edu
SWEGAN, Gary, D ... 419-372-7799. 374 K
gswegan@bgsu.edu
SWEIGARD, Richard, J ... 901-678-2171. 460 B
rjswgard@memphis.edu
SWEITZER, JR.,
Frank, X ... 716-839-8222. 322 E
fsweitze@daemen.edu
SWEITZER, Frederick ... 860-768-4504... 92 D
sweitzer@hartford.edu
SWEITZER-RILEY,
Beth, E ... 260-982-5052. 170 U
besweitzer-riley@manchester.edu
SWEIZER, Jim ... 703-330-5398. 526 B
jsweizer@apus.edu
SWENDER, Herbert ... 620-276-9602. 187 A
herbert.swender@gcccks.edu
SWENGLER, Eleni ... 410-386-8157. 214 A
eswengler@carrollcc.edu
SWENSON, Andrew ... 402-643-7220. 289 B
andrew.swenson@cune.edu
SWENSON, Beth, I ... 701-788-4750. 371 E
Beth.Swenson@mayvillestate.edu
SWENSON, Cherie ... 262-524-7240. 532 C
cswenson@carrollu.edu
SWENSON, Craig, D ... 312-899-9900... 28 M
cswenson@argosy.edu
SWENSON, Jeffrey, F ... 612-330-1241. 253 H
swensonj@augsburg.edu
SWENSON, Jenni ... 218-733-7600. 259 A
jswenson@lsc.edu
SWENSON, Michael ... 608-785-9892. 541 E
swensonm@westerntc.edu
SWENSON, III,
Ralph, M ... 802-656-2699. 500 F
ralph.swenson@uvm.edu
SWENSON, Randy, L ... 630-889-6544. 154 E
rswenson@nuhs.edu
SWENSON, Tammy ... 423-697-4418. 460 C
SWENSON, Terry ... 909-558-8348... 51 C
tswenson@llu.edu
SWENSON, Tim ... 502-456-6506. 199 G
tswenson@sullivan.edu
SWENTON, Gina, D ... 860-628-4751... 90 D
gswenton@lincolncollegene.edu
SWERBINSKY, Megan ... 216-791-5000. 377 E
megan.swerbinsky@case.edu
SWETICH, Mary ... 775-289-3589. 294 F
mary.swetich@gbcnv.edu
SWETS, Paul ... 325-942-2024. 465 K
paul.swets@angelo.edu
SWETT, Denise ... 650-949-7524... 44 N
swettdenise@foothill.edu
SWICEGOOD, Claudia ... 704-216-3551. 363 D
claudia.swicegood@rccc.edu
SWICK, Dean ... 901-722-3202. 458 K
dswick@sco.edu
SWICKARD, Allison ... 719-502-2666... 84 A
allison.swickard@ppcc.edu
SWIECINSKI, Deborah, L 757-683-3127. 507 N
dswiecin@odu.edu
SWIFT, Rick ... 803-754-4100. 443 C
SWIFT, Sheila ... 318-670-9646. 207 A
sswift@susla.edu
SWIFT, Vikki ... 208-792-2269. 138 G
vswift@lcsc.edu
SWIFT, William ... 978-632-6600. 232 C
w_swift@mwcc.mass.edu
SWIGART, Scott, A ... 585-385-8430. 338 H
sswigart@sjfc.edu
SWIHART, Karin ... 620-278-4213. 190 I
kswihart@sterling.edu
SWINDAL, James ... 412-396-6388. 415 F
swindalj@duq.edu
SWINDALL, Linda ... 727-864-8217. 101 N
swindal@eckerd.edu
SWINDELL, Hal ... 252-940-6444. 358 A
HalGS@beaufortccc.edu
SWINDLE, Jackquline ... 713-718-5206. 473 C
jackquline.swindle@hccs.edu
SWINDLE, Richard, V ... 678-547-6456. 128 H
swindle_rv@mercer.edu
SWINDOLL, George ... 843-349-5238. 444 F
george.swindoll@hgtc.edu
SWINEY, John ... 509-963-3130. 517 F
swineyj@cwu.edu
SWINEY, Karen ... 910-521-6222. 369 B
karen.swiney@uncp.edu
SWINEY, R. Preston ... 910-521-6228. 369 B
preston.swiney@uncp.edu
SWINFORD, Bill ... 859-257-1705. 200 C
wswin2@uky.edu
SWINFORD, Jessica, L ... 260-399-7700. 174 C
SWINGLE, Mary ... 320-251-5600. 263 F
mary.swingle@rasmussen.edu
SWINK, Doug ... 816-235-1213. 283 D
swinkd@umkc.edu
SWINNEY, Victoria ... 405-208-5071. 397 F
vswinney@okcu.edu
SWINSON, Phyllis ... 570-422-2820. 428 D
pswinson@po-box.esu.edu
SWINT, Lisa ... 937-708-5532. 393 A
Lswint@wilberforce.edu
SWINTON, David, H ... 803-705-4681. 441 C
swintond@benedict.edu
SWINTON, Jan ... 818-240-1000... 45 G
jswinton@glendale.edu
SWINTON, Kelly ... 515-244-4221. 175 C
swintonk@aib.edu
SWISHER, Gary ... 614-251-4734. 386 B
swisherg@ohiodominican.edu

SWISHER, Susan ... 773-298-3070. 158 E
swisher@sxu.edu
SWISHER, Wayne ... 701-777-3232. 371 C
wayne.swisher@und.edu
SWISHER, William, K ... 859-344-3600. 199 H
bill.swisher@thomasmore.edu
SWISS, Jane, M ... 260-399-7700. 174 C
jswiss@sf.edu
SWITZER, Aimee ... 304-776-6290. 526 F
aswitzer@cci.edu
SWITZER, Devon ... 718-409-7260. 346 D
dswitzer@sunymaritime.edu
SWITZER, Ray ... 864-592-4770. 447 A
switzerr@sccsc.edu
SWITZER, Robin, A ... 603-862-0927. 298 B
robin.switzer@usnh.edu
SWITZER, Teri ... 719-255-3115... 85 M
tswitzer@uccs.edu
SWOMLEY, Brian ... 610-917-3939. 436 C
blswomley@vfcc.edu
SWOPE, Cindi ... 740-588-1221. 394 C
cswope@zanestate.edu
SWOPE, Geri ... 509-279-6215. 518 E
geri.swope@scc.spokane.edu
SWOPE, Suzanne ... 314-889-1478. 274 E
sswope@fontbonne.edu
SWORDS, Jason ... 229-317-6449. 124 A
jason.swords@darton.edu
SYATA, Diana ... 870-777-5722... 25 B
diana.syata@uacch.edu
SYBROWSKY, Paul, K ... 540-261-8430. 509 K
paul.sybrowsky@svu.edu
SYDNOR, Kim ... 443-885-4012. 217 A
kim.sydnor@morgan.edu
SYDOW, Debbie, L ... 804-862-6221. 508 H
dsydow@rbc.edu
SYGIELSKI, John, J ... 717-736-4100. 417 I
ski@hacc.edu
SYKES, David ... 860-343-5704... 89 A
dsykes@mxcc.commnet.edu
SYKES, Eric ... 617-824-8268. 226 A
eric_sykes@emerson.edu
SYKES, Reginald ... 251-575-8223... 1 C
rlsykes@ascc.edu
SYKORA, Sarah ... 781-239-6278. 222 D
ssykora@babson.edu
SYKORA, Terrance ... 563-876-3353. 177 I
SYKTICH, Jackie, D ... 814-371-6920. 415 C
mainc@dbcollege.edu
SYLER-JONES, Tracy ... 817-257-7811. 484 I
t.syler-jones@tcu.edu
SYLVESTER, Barbara ... 732-750-1800. 299 D
bms@Berkeleycollege.edu
SYLVESTER, Barbara, N .. 903-813-2457. 466 H
bsylvester@austincollege.edu
SYLVESTER, Danielle ... 954-201-7395... 99 D
dsylves1@broward.edu
SYLVESTER, Douglas ... 480-965-6188... 11 K
douglas.sylvester@asu.edu
SYLVESTER, James ... 860-444-2683. 545 G
jsylvester@cgaalumni.org
SYLVESTER, Lori ... 918-495-7708. 398 H
lsylvester@oru.edu
SYLVESTER-CAESAR,
Jemma ... 713-221-8006. 489 D
caesarj@uhd.edu
SYLWESTER, Donald ... 402-643-7446. 289 B
don.sylwester@cune.edu
SYMANCYK, Daniel, F ... 410-777-2587. 213 D
dfsymancyk@aacc.edu
SYMANK, Kathryn, B ... 979-862-4572. 483 C
k-symank@tamu.edu
SYMONS, Gretchen, A ... 814-332-2159. 409 D
gretchen.symons@allegheny.edu
SYMS, Deirdre ... 586-445-7062. 246 A
symsd@macomb.edu
SYNDER, Brittany ... 305-809-3233. 104 I
brittany.snyder@fkcc.edu
SYNDER, Jake ... 978-921-4242. 234 C
jake.synder@montserrat.edu
SYNDER, Jane ... 617-277-3915. 224 C
synderj@bgsp.edu
SYNDER, Tamara ... 352-638-9764... 99 B
tsnyder@beaconcollege.edu
SYNER, Alicia ... 304-734-6610. 527 O
asyner@bridgemont.edu
SYNODI, George, S ... 203-832-7273... 92 E
gsynodi@newhaven.edu
SYTSMA, Mark ... 503-725-2213. 406 B
sytsmam@pdx.edu
SYVERTSON, Debra ... 701-228-5454. 372 C
deb.syvertson@dakotacollege.edu
SYVERUD, Kent, D ... 314-935-6420. 284 L
kdsyverud@wustl.edu
SZABO, Janie ... 812-877-8882. 172 C
janie.szabo@rose-hulman.edu
SZABO, Julia ... 419-358-3245. 374 J
szaboj@bluffton.edu
SZABO, Mihaela, A ... 304-336-8270. 530 A
mszabo@westliberty.edu
SZAFRAN, Zvi ... 678-915-7238. 132 C
zszafran@spsu.edu
SZAKAS, Joe, S ... 207-621-3198. 212 C
szakas@maine.edu
SZALANKIEWICZ, Linda . 413-552-2155. 231 F
lszalankiewicz@hcc.edu
SZANI, Phyllis ... 201-200-3350. 303 F
pszani@njcu.edu
SZANTO, Edit ... 208-732-6863. 138 B
eszanto@csi.edu
SZAREK, Michael ... 201-559-6047. 302 A
szarekm@felician.edu
SZARLETA, Ellen ... 219-980-6698. 168 B
eszarlet@iun.edu
SZASZ-PALMER, Suzy ... 434-395-2431. 506 J
palmerss@longwood.edu
SZATMARY, David, P ... 206-685-6306. 524 G
dszatmar@uw.edu
SZEJKO, Thomas ... 724-503-1001. 436 G
tszejko@washjeff.edu
SZEKERES, Shirley ... 585-389-2773. 332 D
sszeker3@naz.edu
SZELEST, Bruce ... 518-437-4928. 341 D
bszelest@albany.edu
SZELISTOWSKI, Warren . 410-532-5110. 217 E
wszelistowski@ndm.edu
SZENTMIKLOSI,
Jillian, M ... 407-582-4142. 118 M
jszentmiklosi@valenciacollege.edu
SZEP, Chris Ann ... 410-287-8327. 214 B
caszep@cecil.edu
SZERI, Andrew, J ... 510-642-5472... 70 I
graddean@berkeley.edu
SZESZYCKI, Donald, J ... 319-335-3565. 175 I
donald-szeszycki@uiowa.edu
SZKODZINSKI,
Michael, W ... 920-832-7348. 533 S
michael.w.szkodzinski@lawrence.edu
SZOPINSKI, Leonard ... 918-343-7818. 399 C
lszopinski@rsu.edu
SZPYRKA, Susan ... 719-255-3678... 85 M
sszpyrka@uccs.edu
SZTAINBERG,
Marcelo, O ... 773-442-6012. 154 H
m-sztainberg@neiu.edu
SZUCH, Paul ... 409-880-8185. 486 E
pjszuch@lit.edu
SZUDY, Lois, F ... 614-823-1414. 387 K
lszudy@otterbein.edu
SZUR, Katalin ... 212-237-8041. 318 D
kszur@jjay.cuny.edu
SZYMANSKI, David, M ... 513-556-7001. 390 G
david.szymanski@uc.edu
SZYMANSKI, Edna, M ... 218-477-2243. 259 H
szymanski@mnstate.edu
SZYMONIAK, Steve ... 956-364-4826. 485 H
steve.szymoniak@stc.edu

T

TA, Minh-Hoa ... 415-561-1850... 38 L
mta@ccsf.edu
TA, Minh-Hoa ... 415-239-3363... 38 L
mhta@ccsf.edu
TABACHNICK, Sharon, E 901-722-3237. 458 K
stabachnick@sco.edu
TABACK, Peter ... 212-229-5667. 332 E
tabackp@newschool.edu
TABARELLA-REED,
Cheryl ... 319-363-8213. 181 C
credd@mtmercy.edu
TABB, Myrtis ... 662-846-4023. 266 G
mtabb@deltastate.edu
TABB, Winston, G ... 410-516-8330. 215 H
wtabb@jhu.edu
TABBACK, George ... 201-684-6842. 305 A
gtabback@ramapo.edu
TABER, Michael, S ... 240-895-4900. 218 A
mstaber@smcm.edu
TABER, Ralph ... 717-291-4390. 416 J
ralph.taber@fandm.edu
TABER, Robert, L ... 919-684-3628. 354 A
taber002@mc.duke.edu
TABERNER, Ian ... 617-262-5000. 223 F
ian.taberner@the-bac.edu
TABERSKI, Carol, J ... 231-995-1058. 248 B
ctaberski@nmc.edu
TABERSKI, Michael ... 301-447-5848. 217 B
taberski@msmary.edu
TABLE, Charles ... 631-632-7035. 342 C
charles.taber@stonybrook.edu
TABOADA, Luz, E ... 915-831-7796. 472 B
ltaboad2@epcc.edu
TABOL, Tim ... 614-234-2682. 384 J
ttabol@mccn.edu
TABOR, Geoff ... 413-236-1610. 231 A
gtabor@berkshirecc.edu
TABOR, Pamela ... 615-687-6896. 452 G
registrar@abcnash.edu
TABOR, Robert ... 715-346-2606. 538 A
btabor@uwsp.edu
TABOR, William ... 803-327-7402. 442 D
wtabor@clintonjuniorcollege.edu
TABRON, Judith, L ... 516-463-6316. 326 D
judith.t.tabron@hofstra.edu
TACCONE, Al ... 760-757-2121... 54 G
ataccone@miracosta.edu
TACHA, Deanell ... 310-506-4611... 58 H
deanelle.tacha@pepperdine.edu
TACK, Eric ... 404-364-8340. 130 A
etack@oglethorpe.edu
TACKE, Diane, L ... 563-387-1507. 180 M
tackedia@luther.edu
TACKE, Kristi ... 605-668-1526. 450 F
kristi.tacke@mtmc.edu
TACKE, Paula ... 605-668-1545. 450 F
paula.tacke@mtmc.edu
TACKET, Karen ... 805-546-3100... 42 C
ktacket@cuesta.edu
TACKETT, Larry ... 304-510-8760. 528 G
ltackett@wvncc.edu
TADAMY, Everett, L ... 412-268-1018. 412 H
et19@andrew.cmu.edu
TADAO, Tzuchie ... 680-488-2471. 547 B
tzuchiet@gmail.com
TADDEO, Justine ... 718-405-3376. 320 G
justine.taddeo@mountsaintvincent.edu
TADDIE, Daniel, L ... 479-979-1431... 25 J
dtaddie@ozarks.edu
TADEO, Joseph ... 352-588-8244. 112 D
joseph.tadeo@saintleo.edu
TADEPALLI, Raghu ... 336-278-6000. 354 B
rtadepalli@elon.edu
TADLOCK, Katherine ... 740-597-2577. 387 C
tadlockk@ohio.edu
TADLOCK, Martin ... 218-755-2015. 258 A
mtadlock@bemidjistate.edu
TADLOCK, Patty ... 601-925-3200. 268 A
tadlock@mc.edu
TADLOCK, Steve ... 619-216-6631... 68 B
stadlock@swccd.edu
TAETZSCH, Blixy, K ... 607-844-8222. 347 I
taetzsb@tc3.edu
TAFARO, John, P ... 513-875-3344. 376 H
john.tafaro@chatfield.edu
TAFAWA, Weusi, A ... 617-228-2115. 231 C
wtafawa@bhcc.mass.edu
TAFOYA, Christina ... 619-644-7158... 46 E
christina.tafoya@gcccd.edu
TAFOYA, Yvette ... 562-860-2451... 37 I
ytafoya@cerritos.edu
TAGGART, Bruce, M ... 610-758-3025. 422 A
bmt2@lehigh.edu
TAGGART, James ... 205-247-8927... 7 E
jtaggart@stillman.edu
TAGGART, James, R ... 801-627-8306. 496 D
taggartj@owatc.edu
TAGGART, Julie ... 614-222-4025. 378 A
jtaggart@ccad.edu
TAGGART, Kathleen, J ... 402-280-2360. 289 D
ktaggart@creighton.edu
TAGGART, Thomas ... 904-256-1234. 103 Q
ttaggart@fcsl.edu
TAGLIARENI, James ... 910-272-3560. 363 B
jtagliareni@robeson.edu
TAGLIATELA, Gayle, S ... 203-932-7455... 92 E
gtagliatela@newhaven.edu
TAGYE, Jim ... 515-643-6678. 181 A
jtagye@mercydesmoines.org
TAHA, Dianne ... 516-726-5837. 545 H
tahad@usmma.edu
TAHERI, Reza ... 818-299-5500... 75 E
rTaheri@westcoastuniversity.edu
TAHTINEN, Dale, R ... 906-487-2318. 247 A
drtahtin@mtu.edu
TAIT, Lanc, H ... 830-792-7462. 480 F
ltait@schreiner.edu
TAIT, Melissa ... 847-214-7365. 144 F
mtait@elgin.edu
TAIT, Raymond ... 314-977-4817. 281 I
taitrc@slu.edu
TAKACS, Audrey ... 586-445-7314. 246 A
takacsa@macomb.edu
TAKAHASHI, Esme ... 805-482-2755... 61 E
registrar-sjs@stjohnsem.edu
TAKAHASHI, Jack ... 414-257-2939. 534 E
TAKAHASHI, Tomoko ... 949-480-4047... 66 F
ttakahashi@soka.edu
TAKAMURA, Jeanette, C 212-851-2288. 321 D
jct8@columbia.edu
TAKASH, Joe ... 312-935-5129. 156 K
jtakash@robertmorris.edu
TAKEDA, Hiroki ... 505-438-8884. 312 A
hiroki@acupuncturecollege.edu
TAKEDA, Kenneth, B ... 310-287-4368... 52 F
takedakb@wlac.edu
TAKEDA-TINKER, Becky . 720-279-0159... 80 J
TAKEMOTO, Mary Ann ... 562-985-5587... 33 F
maryann.takemoto@csulb.edu
TAKES, Deb ... 610-902-8200. 411 E
pres@cabrini.edu
TAKES, Faith, A ... 518-786-0855. 331 E
faith.takes@mildred-elley.edu
TAKIGUCHI, Amy ... 808-735-4707. 135 D
ahigashi@chaminade.edu
TAKIGUCHI, Mark ... 503-821-8960. 406 F
mtakiguchi@pnca.edu
TAKSAR, Stephen ... 603-535-2550. 298 G
sjtaksar@plymouth.edu
TALABER, Matthew ... 845-938-3415. 545 I
Matthew.Talaber@usma.edu
TALAVERA, Karla ... 661-255-1050... 31 C
talavera@calarts.edu
TALBOOM, Scott ... 928-226-4374... 13 B
scott.talboom@coconino.edu
TALBOT, A. Scott ... 435-652-7601. 497 E
talbot@dixie.edu
TALBOT, Ann ... 312-915-8902. 151 H
atalbot@luc.edu
TALBOT, Laura ... 956-872-5051. 480 I
ltalbot@southtexascollege.edu
TALBOT, Laura ... 610-328-8358. 433 I
ltalbot1@swarthmore.edu
TALBOT, Miranda ... 626-568-8850... 50 E
TALBOT, William ... 212-594-4000. 347 H
btalbot@tcicollege.edu
TALBOTT, Jeffrey ... 909-748-8888... 73 H
jeffrey_talbott@redlands.edu
TALBOTT, John, E ... 805-893-2622... 72 B
john.talbott@ap.ucsb.edu
TALBOTT, Richard ... 251-380-2785... 9 E
rtalbott@southalabama.edu
TALBOTT, Robert ... 650-543-3714... 54 C
rtalbott@menlo.edu
TALBOTT, Sherry ... 540-828-5369. 502 J
stalbott@bridgewater.edu
TALDO, Tom ... 785-242-5200. 189 I
tom.taldo@ottawa.edu
TALENTINO, Andrea ... 802-485-2410. 500 A
atalenti@norwich.edu
TALENTINO, Karen, A ... 802-654-2216. 500 B
ktalentino@smcvt.edu
TALERICO, Katie ... 412-291-6247. 410 B
ktalerico@aii.edu
TALESH, Rameen, A ... 949-824-5590... 71 B
rtalesh@uci.edu
TALIAFERRO, Kevin ... 813-827-0103. 544 L
kevin.c.taliaferro@centcom.mil
TALIENTO, Tamela, K ... 931-431-9700. 457 O
ttaliento@nci.edu
TALKEN, Rebecca, G ... 816-654-7702. 275 K
btalken@kcumb.edu
TALL, Gregory ... 312-935-6706. 156 K
gtall@robertmorris.edu
TALLANT, Pat, L ... 903-434-8102. 477 J
ptallant@ntcc.edu
TALLANT, Steven, H ... 361-593-3209. 484 A
steven.tallant@tamuk.edu
TALLARICO, Sean, M ... 240-895-4911. 218 A
smtallarico@smcm.edu
TALLARIDA, Ronald, J ... 856-256-5413. 305 E
tallarida@rowan.edu
TALLENT, Edward ... 617-333-2935. 225 E
etallent0811@curry.edu
TALLENT, Judy ... 606-679-8501. 196 D
judy.tallent@kctcs.edu
TALLERICO, Betty, L ... 724-458-3790. 417 E
bltallerico@gcc.edu
TALLEY, Brent ... 870-777-5722... 25 B
brent.talley@uacch.edu
TALLEY, Chestley ... 903-730-4890. 474 O
chestley.talley@jarvis.edu
TALLEY, Willis ... 816-322-0110. 271 O
willis.talley@calvary.edu
TALLMAN, Doug ... 402-486-2534. 292 E
dotallma@ucollege.edu
TALLMAN, Jonathan ... 276-466-7959. 514 G
jtallman@vic.edu
TALLON, William ... 920-424-1444. 537 B
tallon@uwosh.edu
TALMADGE, Rosemary ... 718-482-5059. 318 F
rtalmadge@lagcc.cuny.edu
TALMO, Richard ... 760-744-1150... 58 D
rtalmo@palomar.edu
TALUSAN, Liza ... 508-565-1323. 237 A
ltalusan@stonehill.edu
TAM, Stanley ... 607-871-2300. 313 E
tam@alfred.edu
TAMADA, Michael, D ... 323-259-2966... 56 I
tamada@oxy.edu
TAMADA, Mike ... 503-788-6613. 407 E
tamadam@reed.edu
TAMANAHA, David ... 808-984-3253. 137 B
davidt@hawaii.edu
TAMASCO, Mary ... 973-353-5541. 306 D
tamasc@newark.rutgers.edu
TAMAYO, Carlo ... 956-882-8295. 491 D
carlo.tamayo@utb.edu
TAMAYO, Carlo ... 956-882-3814. 491 D
carlo.tamayo@utb.edu
TAMAYO, Daniel ... 559-934-2432... 75 H
danieltamayo@whccd.edu

TAMBE, Jayanti .... 626-529-8033... 57 G
jtambe@pacificoaks.edu
TAMBOUE, Helene .... 803-705-4573. 441 C
tamboueh@benedict.edu
TAMEO, John .... 401-254-3859. 440 B
jtameo@rwu.edu
TAMERIUS, Travis .... 573-592-4241. 285 D
travis.tamerius@williamwoods.edu
TAMMARO, Susan .... 781-768-7390. 236 A
susan.tammaro@regiscollege.edu
TAMMES, Eric .... 312-341-6960. 157 D
etammes@roosevelt.edu
TAMMEUS, Lisen .... 816-235-5613. 283 D
tammeusli@umkc.edu
TAMMONE, William .... 309-694-8584. 146 E
william.tammone@icc.edu
TAMTE-HORAN,
Deborah .... 484-664-3190. 424 H
tamte-horan@muhlenberg.edu
TAMZARIAN, Hrayr .... 413-585-4944. 236 H
htamzari@smith.edu
TAN, Finian .... 909-396-6090... 31 F
TAN, Lay Tuan .... 657-278-5845... 33 E
lttan@fullerton.edu
TAN, Lin-Ying .... 512-444-8082. 485 B
ltan@thsu.edu
TAN, Nestor .... 310-233-4053... 51 H
tanng@lahc.edu
TAN, Norbert, N .... 805-289-6160... 74 H
ntan@vcccd.edu
TAN, Sharon, M .... 651-255-6108. 264 C
stan@unitedseminary.edu
TAN, Teng-Kee .... 816-235-2204. 283 D
tant@umkc.edu
TANAKA, Elizabeth .... 254-295-4949. 490 B
etanaka@umhb.edu
TANAKA, Jason, K .... 808-974-7348. 136 A
jasonkt@hawaii.edu
TANAKA, Kenneth .... 408-741-2092... 75 J
kenneth.tanaka@wvm.edu
TANAKA, Kenneth .... 408-855-5438... 75 K
kenneth.tanaka@wvm.edu
TANAKA, Paul, N .... 515-294-5352. 175 H
ptanaka@iastate.edu
TANAKA, Winona, M .... 918-631-3054. 401 F
winona-tanaka@utulsa.edu
TANAKA, Yasuo .... 510-666-8248... 26 F
ytanaka@aimc.edu
TANAKEYOWMA, Lilia ..... 714-564-6971... 60 G
tanakeyowma_lilia@sac.edu
TANASESCU, Mihaela ...... 858-513-9240. 175 F
mihaela.tanasescu@ashford.edu
TANBARA, Sabrina .... 212-799-5000. 328 B
TANCK, Buddy Jo .... 913-294-4178. 186 G
buddyt@fortscott.edu
TANDE, Korinne .... 402-471-2505. 291 C
ktande@nscs.edu
TANDIA, Mary .... 410-337-3355. 215 A
mary.tandia@goucher.edu
TANEJA, Amit .... 315-859-4582. 325 E
ataneja@hamilton.edu
TANG, Meiling .... 707-638-5880... 69 K
meiling.tang@tu.edu
TANG, Philip .... 410-516-6087. 215 H
ptang@jhu.edu
TANIGAWA, Shane .... 415-380-1388... 45 H
shanetanigawa@ggbts.edu
TANJI, Lorelei, A .... 949-824-5212... 71 B
ltanji@uci.edu
TANKERSLEY, Melondy .. 330-672-2220. 382 B
mtankers@kent.edu
TANKING, Tony .... 913-360-7485. 184 H
ttanking@benedictine.edu
TANKLEFSKY, Paul .... 617-573-8483. 237 B
ptanklef@suffolk.edu
TANKSLEY, Wallace .... 614-222-6165. 378 A
wtanksley@ccad.edu
TANNEHILL, Darcy, B ...... 412-397-6301. 431 I
tannehilld@rmu.edu
TANNEHILL, Steven .... 661-362-9375... 40 E
steven.tannehill@canyons.edu
TANNENBAUM, Ilene ...... 718-951-5580. 317 C
ilenet@brooklyn.cuny.edu
TANNENBAUM, Michael 607-431-4405. 325 F
tannenbaumm@hartwick.edu
TANNER, Audrey .... 661-255-1050... 31 C
atanner@calarts.edu
TANNER, Beth, L .... 732-247-5241. 303 E
btanner@nbts.edu
TANNER, Caroline .... 760-750-4040... 35 A
ctanner@csusm.edu
TANNER, Cindy .... 912-287-5829. 130 B
ctanner@okefenokeetech.edu
TANNER, Cynthia, A .... 248-341-2133. 248 D
catanner@oaklandcc.edu
TANNER, David .... 617-732-2908. 233 E
David.Tanner@mcphs.edu
TANNER, Douglas, R .... 229-333-5935. 134 B
dtanner@valdosta.edu
TANNER, Elizabeth .... 210-486-3933. 465 A
etanner@alamo.edu
TANNER, Greg .... 912-260-4217. 131 F
greg.tanner@sgc.edu
TANNER, Jamie .... 912-260-4377. 131 F
jamie.tanner@sgsc.edu
TANNER, Kim .... 765-983-1631. 165 G
tanneki@earlham.edu
TANNER, Mary .... 423-425-4249. 463 D
mary-tanner@utc.edu
TANNER, Michael .... 601-643-8302. 266 F
michael.tanner@colin.edu
TANNER, Norma, J .... 251-460-6141..... 9 E
ntanner@southalabama.edu
TANNER, Pamela .... 262-472-5227. 538 D
tannerp@uww.edu
TANNER, Paula .... 254-295-8671. 490 B
ptanner@umhb.edu
TANNER, Ray .... 803-777-0116. 447 G
rtanner@mailbox.sc.edu
TANNER, Starla, H .... 919-530-5402. 368 A
starla.tanner@nccu.edu
TANNER, Tara .... 406-791-5294. 288 E
ttanner01@ugf.edu
TANNIRU, Mohan, R .... 248-370-3286. 248 J
tanniru@oakland.edu
TANON, Alma .... 408-270-6432... 63 O
alma.tanon@evc.edu
TANOUYE, Allyson, M .... 808-956-7927. 136 B
atanouye@hawaii.edu
TANSEY, Barbara .... 252-940-6201. 358 A
barbarat@beaufortccc.edu
TANSLEY, Robert .... 203-596-4502... 90 I
btansley@post.edu
TANTILLO, Richard, C ..... 315-859-4412. 325 E
rtantill@hamilton.edu
TANTSITS, SCC,
Gerardine .... 973-543-6528. 298 I
deanregistrar@acs350.org
TANZER, Ken .... 415-703-9592... 30 K
ktanzer@cca.edu
TANZER, Kim .... 434-924-7019. 511 B
kmt8t@Virginia.EDU
TAPEDO, Burgess .... 785-830-2774. 187 B
btapedo@bie.edu
TAPHORN, Rick .... 423-775-7411. 453 E
rtaphorn6113@bryan.edu
TAPIA, Damaris .... 773-442-4205. 154 H
d-tapia1@neiu.edu
TAPIA, Erren .... 219-473-4257. 164 K
etapia@ccsj.edu
TAPIA URZUA, Andres .. 412-291-6423. 410 B
atapia-urzua@aii.edu
TAPLEY, Robyn .... 321-674-8050. 104 H
rtapley@fit.edu
TAPLIN, Cheryl .... 716-645-2450. 341 F
ctaplin@buffalo.edu
TAPP, Paul .... 903-923-2042. 471 J
ptapp@etbu.edu
TAPP, Rita .... 903-785-7661. 478 B
rtapp@parisjc.edu
TAPPAN, Charlene .... 860-512-2912... 88 G
ctappan@manchestercc.edu
TAPPER, Janet .... 503-251-5757. 408 G
jtapper@uws.edu
TAPSCOTT, Michael, R ... 202-994-1463... 95 D
tapscott@gwu.edu
TARANTELLI, Thomas, L 518-276-6234. 337 I
tarant@rpi.edu
TARANTO, John, A .... 816-501-3630. 271 H
john.taranto@avila.edu
TARASCHI, Theodore .... 215-955-3900. 434 C
Theodore.Taraschi@jefferson.edu
TARBELL, Levi .... 641-673-1024. 183 H
tarbelll@wmpenn.edu
TARBELL, Mary .... 413-755-4855. 233 A
Tarbell@stcc.edu
TARBETT, Matthew .... 740-695-9500. 374 H
mtarbett@belmontcollege.edu
TARBOX, James .... 619-594-4379... 35 D
jtarbox@mail.sdsu.edu
TARBOX, Norm .... 801-626-6003. 497 D
ntarbox@weber.edu
TARBOX, Sandra .... 717-477-1131. 429 E
sltarbox@ship.edu
TARBY, Jay .... 216-397-1703. 381 R
tarby@jcu.edu
TARCA, Fred, E .... 203-582-3429... 91 A
fred.tarca@quinnipiac.edu
TARDIF, Mark .... 207-948-9292. 211 I
mtardif@unity.edu
TARENCE, Elaine, P .... 334-387-3877..... 1 E
elainetarence@amridgeuniversity.edu
TARGETT, Nancy, M .... 302-831-2841... 94 B
ntargett@udel.edu
TARGONSKI, Conrad, A . 608-796-3804. 539 E
catargonski@viterbo.edu
TARGONSKI, Dave .... 704-461-6735. 352 G
davetargonski@bac.edu
TARMAN, Christopher ..... 619-644-7000... 46 E
christopher.tarman@gcccd.edu
TARNOWSKI, Jeffrey .... 678-891-2520. 125 G
Jeffrey.Tarnowski@gpc.edu
TARNOWSKI, Susan .... 612-332-3361. 253 G
starnowski@aii.edu
TARO, Thomas .... 680-488-2746. 547 B
tarothomas@yahoo.com
TAROLA, Robert .... 202-806-2411... 95 G
robert.tarola@howard.edu
TARPEY, Andrea .... 413-755-4847. 233 A
tarpey@stcc.edu
TARPEY, Gerard .... 914-923-2804. 335 J
gtarpey@pace.edu
TARPLEE, Marc .... 803-327-8017. 449 J
mtarplee@yorktech.edu
TARPLEY, Sue .... 706-236-2292. 121 G
starpley@berry.edu
TARQUINO, Beth, A .... 716-250-7500. 315 J
batarquino@bryantstratton.edu
TARR, Barbara, L .... 818-779-8240... 50 A
btarr@kingsuniversity.edu
TARR, Steven .... 610-526-1425. 409 F
steve.tarr@theamericancollege.edu
TARRANT, David, S .... 208-467-8520. 139 A
dtarrant@nnu.edu
TARRANT, Kaneesha .... 562-938-4268... 51 D
ktarrant@lbcc.edu
TARRER, Jerry .... 414-229-3262. 537 A
jtarrer@uwm.edu
TARSIA, Robert .... 805-893-4080... 72 B
robert.tarsia@audit.ucsb.edu
TARSKI, Anne .... 830-591-7294. 481 C
ahtarski@swtjc.edu
TART, Judy .... 202-884-9704... 96 G
tartj@trinitydc.edu
TART, Judye .... 910-592-8081. 363 E
jtart@sampsoncc.edu
TART, Kathryn .... 361-570-4376. 489 E
tartk@uhv.edu
TART, Marla, L .... 919-866-5901. 364 G
mltart@waketech.edu
TARTAGLIA, Joseph, F ... 973-596-5279. 303 G
tartaglia@njit.edu
TARTOF, Linda, M .... 773-702-3212. 161 B
ltartof@uchicago.edu
TARTT, Tom .... 205-652-5467..... 9 F
ttartt@uwa.edu
TARVER, Jerome, S .... 301-736-3631. 216 B
jerome.tarver@msbbcs.edu
TARVER, Micheal .... 479-968-0274... 20 E
mtarver@atu.edu
TARVER, Stephanie, B .... 337-562-4249. 207 G
starver@mcneese.edu
TARVER, III, Walter, L .... 609-652-4804. 305 C
walter.tarver@stockton.edu
TARVER-ROSS,
Cassandra .... 256-372-5835..... 1 A
cassandra.ross@aamu.edu
TARVIN, Patricia .... 412-809-5100. 430 H
tarvin.pat@pti.edu
TASHIMA, Jaye .... 760-245-4271... 75 B
Jaye.Tashima@vvc.edu
TASHMAN, Jodi, L .... 215-699-5700. 421 E
jtashman@LSB.edu
TASKER, Janet .... 770-479-9538. 130 G
jkt@reinhardt.edu
TASSIN, Shannon .... 318-487-7151. 202 F
shannon.tassin@lacollege.edu
TASSON, Dana .... 503-725-4429. 406 B
tassond@pdx.edu
TASSONI, John, P .... 513-529-7135. 384 G
tassonjp@miamioh.edu
TAST, Maryellen .... 307-778-1146. 543 D
mtast@lccc.wy.edu
TASTAD, Renee .... 303-404-5332... 81 N
renee.tastad@frontrange.edu
TATARKA, Donna .... 973-290-4700. 300 F
dtatarka@cse.edu
TATE, Allen .... 717-391-7285. 434 A
tate@stevenscollege.edu
TATE, Amy, L .... 414-229-3844. 537 A
lensing@uwm.edu
TATE, Andrew .... 417-823-3454. 281 M
atate@forest.edu
TATE, David .... 307-382-1882. 543 J
dtate@wwcc.wy.edu
TATE, Don .... 864-587-4227. 447 B
tated@smcsc.edu
TATE, Helen .... 229-931-2019. 126 D
helen.tate@gsw.edu
TATE, Kelly .... 336-506-4135. 357 M
kelly.tate@alamancecc.edu
TATE, Louella, H .... 512-223-0045. 466 I
ltate@austincc.edu
TATE, Mike .... 254-968-9107. 483 A
tate@tarleton.edu
TATE, Nancy, A .... 785-670-1648. 191 D
nancy.tate@washburn.edu
TATE, Randall .... 870-972-2056... 19 N
rtate@astate.edu
TATE, Robert, H .... 863-680-4347. 105 D
rtate@flsouthern.edu
TATE, Susan, E .... 614-236-6813. 375 H
state@capital.edu
TATE, Thomas, L .... 334-683-2321..... 5 F
ttate@marionmilitary.edu
TATE, Verlanda .... 205-929-1440..... 5 G
vtate@miles.edu
TATGE, Kellie .... 320-762-4489. 257 O
kelliet@alextech.edu
TATHAM, Sarah .... 828-835-4233. 364 E
sctatham@tricountycc.edu
TATLOCK, Mark .... 661-362-2220... 53 G
mtatlock@masters.edu
TATLOCK, Mark .... 661-362-2222... 53 G
mtatlock@masters.edu
TATNALL, Amber .... 207-216-4392. 211 C
atatnall@yccc.edu
TATRO, Clayton .... 620-223-2700. 186 G
claytont@fortscott.edu
TATRO, Donna, E .... 609-258-2845. 304 E
tatro@princeton.edu
TATRO, Fred .... 617-364-3510. 223 G
ftatro@boston.edu
TATUM, Alfred .... 312-996-5641. 161 D
atatum1@uic.edu
TATUM, Ashley .... 940-668-7323. 477 I
atatum@nctc.edu
TATUM, Beverly Daniel ... 404-270-5001. 132 E
presidentsoffice@spelman.edu
TATUM, C. Ray .... 478-301-2653. 128 H
tatum_cr@mercer.edu
TATUM, Judy, B .... 313-577-9753. 252 G
jtatum@wayne.edu
TATUM, Lance .... 334-670-3617..... 7 H
ltatum@troy.edu
TATUM, Tanya .... 850-599-3777. 114 K
tanya.tatum@famu.edu
TATUM, Terry .... 361-825-2693. 483 F
terry.tatum@tamucc.edu
TATUM, Veronda .... 870-862-8131... 23 D
vtatum@southark.edu
TAUB, Carol .... 503-253-3443. 405 E
ctaub@ocom.edu
TAUBER, Hendy .... 323-937-3763... 77 F
htauber@yoec.edu
TAUBMAN, Mark, B .... 585-275-0017. 349 C
Mark_Taubman@URMC.Rochester.edu
TAUER, Ritamarie .... 281-649-3702. 473 B
rtauer@hbu.edu
TAUPIER, Andrea, S .... 413-748-3609. 236 I
ataupier@springfieldcollege.edu
TAURIELLO, Claire .... 301-447-5202. 217 B
tauriello@msmary.edu
TAUSSIG, Martha .... 870-512-7824... 20 B
martha_taussig@asun.edu
TAUSZ, Jerrad .... 816-204-2109... 18 I
jerrad.tausz@phoenix.edu
TAUZIN, Kristie, R .... 985-448-4509. 208 A
kristie.tauzin@nicholls.edu
TAVADA, Dwight, L .... 810-762-9825. 244 Q
dtavada@kettering.edu
TAVAKOLI, Assad .... 910-672-1527. 367 D
atavakoli@uncfsu.edu
TAVAKOLI, Roozbeh .... 716-829-7515. 323 D
tavakoli@dyc.edu
TAVAKOLI, Sue .... 623-935-8020... 14 K
sue.tavakoli@estrellamountain.edu
TAVARES, Shirley, A .... 787-725-8120. 548 O
investigacion@eap.edu
TAVAREZ, Luis, A .... 856-256-4276. 305 E
tavarez@rowan.edu
TAVELLI, Nancy, J .... 509-527-5297. 525 E
tavelln@whitman.edu
TAVES, Michael, E .... 607-274-3061. 327 E
taves@ithaca.edu
TAVES, Michael, E .... 607-274-3867. 327 E
taves@ithaca.edu
TAYAG, Cindy .... 510-780-4500... 50 I
ctayag@lifewest.edu
TAYAR, Adina .... 610-892-1511. 427 E
atayar@pit.edu
TAYEBI, Kandi .... 936-294-1971. 487 A
kanditayebi@shsu.edu
TAYEH, Raja .... 402-826-6776. 289 E
raja.tayeh@doane.edu
TAYLOE, John .... 252-398-1232. 353 H
tayloj@chowan.edu
TAYLOR, Alicia .... 256-306-2621..... 2 F
ataylor@calhoun.edu
TAYLOR, Amy .... 410-704-4931. 220 E
altaylor@towson.edu
TAYLOR, Andrea .... 562-985-5197... 33 F
ataylor@csulb.edu
TAYLOR, Angela .... 757-388-2900. 509 D
astaylor@sentara.com
TAYLOR, Angie .... 859-442-1162. 195 B
angie.taylor@kctcs.edu
TAYLOR, Anna .... 770-233-5560. 132 B
ataylor@sctech.edu
TAYLOR, Anne Marie .... 925-969-3491... 49 B
amtaylor@jfku.edu
TAYLOR, Barbara .... 540-423-9032. 512 E
btaylor@germanna.edu

TAYLOR, Barry .... 716-645-6136. 341 F barrytay@buffalo.edu

TAYLOR, Beck, A .... 509-777-3200. 525 F btaylor@whitworth.edu

TAYLOR, Bill .... 408-741-2642... 75 L bill.taylor@westvalley.edu

TAYLOR, Bill .... 641-782-1406. 182 I taylor@swcciowa.edu

TAYLOR, Blair .... 276-326-4282. 502 H btaylor@bluefield.edu

TAYLOR, Bradley .... 910-879-5661. 358 B btaylor@bladencc.edu

TAYLOR, Brandi .... 615-687-6907. 452 G btaylor@abcnash.edu

TAYLOR, Brandon .... 334-683-2350..... 5 F btaylor@marionmilitary.edu

TAYLOR, Brandy .... 912-871-1616. 129 J btaylor@ogeecheetech.edu

TAYLOR, Brian .... 808-956-6182. 136 B taylorb@hawaii.edu

TAYLOR, Carol, A .... 417-865-2815. 274 B taylorc@evangel.edu

TAYLOR, Cathy .... 615-460-6916. 453 C cathy.taylor@belmont.edu

TAYLOR, Charles .... 256-331-5462..... 6 A taylor@nwscc.edu

TAYLOR, Charles .... 417-873-7391. 273 H ctaylor@drury.edu

TAYLOR, Charles .... 330-325-6461. 385 E ctaylor@neomed.edu

TAYLOR, Chelsa .... 276-739-2423. 514 D ctaylor@vhcc.edu

TAYLOR, Cherilyn, Y .... 803-536-7245. 446 G ctaylor@scsu.edu

TAYLOR, Chris .... 801-863-8484. 497 C taylorch@uvu.edu

TAYLOR, Craig .... 541-463-5364. 403 I taylorc@lanecc.edu

TAYLOR, Craig, B .... 503-554-2911. 403 C ctaylor@georgefox.edu

TAYLOR, Curtis, J .... 712-722-6006. 177 J curtis.taylor@dordt.edu

TAYLOR, Cynthia, S .... 972-860-7191. 470 I CynthiaSTaylor@dcccd.edu

TAYLOR, Cyrus, C .... 216-368-4437. 375 J casdean@case.edu

TAYLOR, Danny .... 615-966-7650. 456 B danny.taylor@lipscomb.edu

TAYLOR, Darrell .... 304-896-7432. 528 F darrell.taylor@southernwv.edu

TAYLOR, David .... 276-326-4206. 502 H dtaylor@bluefield.edu

TAYLOR, David .... 276-326-4257. 502 H dtaylor@bluefield.edu

TAYLOR, David, A .... 718-289-5598. 317 B david.taylor@bcc.cuny.edu

TAYLOR, David, E .... 202-885-2121... 94 F taylor@american.edu

TAYLOR, David, M .... 205-652-3531..... 9 F dmt@uwa.edu

TAYLOR, Deb, A .... 864-622-6063. 441 B dtaylor@andersonuniversity.edu

TAYLOR, Debora, W .... 512-448-8450. 479 C deboraw@stedwards.edu

TAYLOR, Deborah .... 562-777-4069... 29 L deborah.taylor@biola.edu

TAYLOR, Deborah, A .... 603-526-3760. 295 I dtaylor@colby-sawyer.edu

TAYLOR, Deborah, D .... 336-734-7178. 360 E ddtaylor@forsythtech.edu

TAYLOR, Delores, T .... 804-827-8730. 511 F dttaylor@vcu.edu

TAYLOR, Dennis .... 318-869-5360. 201 H dtaylor@centenary.edu

TAYLOR, Dennis, D .... 740-392-6868. 384 K denny.taylor@mvnu.edu

TAYLOR, Dickerson, E .... 706-233-7240. 131 E dtaylor@shorter.edu

TAYLOR, Dinny, S .... 413-597-3072. 238 D dinny.s.taylor@williams.edu

TAYLOR, Don .... 415-338-3326... 35 E dtaylor@sfsu.edu

TAYLOR, Don .... 949-582-4541... 67 C dtaylor@saddleback.edu

TAYLOR, Donald .... 630-829-6240. 140 B dtaylor@ben.edu

TAYLOR, Donald, R .... 870-307-7203... 21 H donald.taylor@lyon.edu

TAYLOR, Donald, R .... 870-307-7230... 21 H donald.taylor@lyon.edu

TAYLOR, Doug .... 404-687-4568. 123 C taylord@ctsnet.edu

TAYLOR, Douglas Anne .. 337-373-0011. 204 D douglas.taylor@solacc.edu

TAYLOR, Ed .... 206-616-7175. 524 G edtaylor@uw.edu

TAYLOR, Edward .... 608-663-2333. 532 I EdTaylor@edgewood.edu

TAYLOR, Ella .... 503-838-8757. 406 E taylore@wou.edu

TAYLOR, Ellen .... 540-831-5771. 508 C eltaylor@radford.edu

TAYLOR, Francis, H .... 334-833-4556..... 4 D ftaylor@huntingdon.edu

TAYLOR, G. Christine .... 765-494-6969. 171 M taylorgc@purdue.edu

TAYLOR, Gary .... 406-243-6131. 286 H gary.taylor@umontana.edu

TAYLOR, Gary .... 865-251-1800. 458 I gtaylor@southcollegetn.edu

TAYLOR, Gene, F .... 701-231-5614. 371 G gene.taylor@ndsu.edu

TAYLOR, Geraldine, S .... 781-891-2222. 223 C gtaylor@bentley.edu

TAYLOR, Gia .... 480-423-6300... 15 E gia.taylor@scottsdalecc.edu

TAYLOR, Greg .... 307-755-2135. 544 B gtaylor@wyotechstaff.edu

TAYLOR, Gregory .... 559-244-5909... 68 H gregory.taylor@scccd.edu

TAYLOR, Gregory .... 314-719-3609. 274 E gtaylor@fontbonne.edu

TAYLOR, Gregory .... 914-251-6831. 344 D gregory.taylor@purchase.edu

TAYLOR, Gwen .... 706-771-4180. 121 D gtaylor@augustatech.edu

TAYLOR, Henry, W .... 404-880-6186. 122 J hwtaylor@cau.edu

TAYLOR, Howard, E .... 330-471-8235. 383 D htaylor@malone.edu

TAYLOR, Hunter .... 252-536-7228. 361 A htaylor397@halifaxcc.edu

TAYLOR, Ian, L .... 718-270-3171. 342 D itaylor@downstate.edu

TAYLOR, Jackie .... 731-661-5302. 462 F jtaylor@uu.edu

TAYLOR, Jacqueline .... 609-771-3032. 300 E taylorj@tcnj.edu

TAYLOR, Jaime .... 931-221-7971. 459 B taylorjr@apsu.edu

TAYLOR, James .... 502-456-6504. 199 G jtaylor@sullivan.edu

TAYLOR, James .... 801-626-6055. 497 D jamestaylor8@weber.edu

TAYLOR, James, H .... 606-539-4201. 200 B presoff@ucumberlands.edu

TAYLOR, Jan .... 304-558-4128. 529 C jan.taylor@wvresearch.org

TAYLOR, Janice .... 617-521-2360. 236 G janice.taylor@simmons.edu

TAYLOR, Janie .... 817-461-8741. 466 D jhall@arlingtonbaptistcollege.edu

TAYLOR, Jasmine, P .... 601-984-1340. 270 C jptaylor@umc.edu

TAYLOR, Jason .... 609-586-4800. 302 G taylorj@mccc.edu

TAYLOR, Jeffrey, D .... 315-268-6477. 320 A jdtaylor@clarkson.edu

TAYLOR, Jeffrey, S .... 814-871-7213. 416 K taylor030@gannon.edu

TAYLOR, Jennifer .... 805-565-6085... 76 D jmtaylor@westmont.edu

TAYLOR, Jim .... 253-964-6589. 522 C jtaylor@pierce.ctc.edu

TAYLOR, Joe .... 970-248-1020... 79 F jtaylor@coloradomesa.edu

TAYLOR, John, M .... 315-255-1743. 316 D john.taylor@cayuga-cc.edu

TAYLOR, Joseph, P .... 276-944-6124. 504 H jptaylor@ehc.edu

TAYLOR, Joseph, R .... 801-581-3325. 496 Q jtaylor@utah.edu

TAYLOR, Joyce .... 501-812-2221... 22 G jtaylor@pulaskitech.edu

TAYLOR, Judy .... 404-297-9522. 126 A taylorj@gptc.edu

TAYLOR, June .... 602-386-4104... 11 G june.taylor@arizonachristian.edu

TAYLOR, K.D .... 801-863-8949. 497 C taylorkd@uvu.edu

TAYLOR, Karen .... 585-785-1684. 324 D taylorkd@flcc.edu

TAYLOR, Katherine, A .... 217-245-3035. 146 F kataylor@ic.edu

TAYLOR, Kathy .... 870-230-5103... 21 D taylork@hsu.edu

TAYLOR, Kathy, J .... 603-526-3766. 295 I ktaylor@colby-sawyer.edu

TAYLOR, Keith .... 814-871-7609. 416 K ktaylor@gannon.edu

TAYLOR, Kelley, G .... 334-844-4794..... 1 G taylokg@auburn.edu

TAYLOR, Kenneth .... 870-230-5214... 21 D taylork@hsu.edu

TAYLOR, Kent .... 575-624-8235. 310 H kent@nmmi.edu

TAYLOR, Kenya, S .... 308-865-8843. 292 H taylorks@unk.edu

TAYLOR, Kerri .... 217-732-3155. 151 C ktaylor@lincolncollege.edu

TAYLOR, Kevin .... 864-242-5100. 441 D

TAYLOR, Kristen .... 509-257-2539. 524 I kristen.taylor@wallawalla.edu

TAYLOR, Kristi .... 817-531-4403. 488 A ktaylor@txwes.edu

TAYLOR, Kyle .... 706-419-1516. 123 F kyle.taylor@covenant.edu

TAYLOR, Ladd .... 601-928-6224. 268 C ladd.taylor@mgccc.edu

TAYLOR, Lance .... 904-620-2820. 116 B ltaylor@unf.edu

TAYLOR, LaTonya .... 630-752-5015. 163 F media.relations@wheaton.edu

TAYLOR, Lauren, M .... 205-726-2956..... 6 F lmtaylor@samford.edu

TAYLOR, Leah, A .... 304-929-6701. 528 D ltaylor@newriver.edu

TAYLOR, Lealon .... 405-682-7591. 397 E ltaylor@occc.edu

TAYLOR, Lee .... 334-387-3877..... 1 E leetaylor@amridgeuniversity.edu

TAYLOR, Leslie .... 740-362-3126. 383 H ltaylor@mtso.edu

TAYLOR, Leslie .... 406-994-4570. 287 B lesliet@montana.edu

TAYLOR, Leslie, W .... 501-686-8998... 24 C TaylorLeslieW@uams.edu

TAYLOR, Linda .... 270-686-4595. 196 C linda.taylor@kctcs.edu

TAYLOR, Linda .... 800-567-2344. 532 E ltaylor@menominee.edu

TAYLOR, Linda .... 610-499-1039. 437 E lmtaylor@widener.edu

TAYLOR, Loralyn .... 518-327-6231. 336 B ltaylor@paulsmiths.edu

TAYLOR, Loren, R .... 217-333-1478. 161 C lrtaylor@uillinois.edu

TAYLOR, Lori .... 740-245-7204. 392 A ltaylor@rio.edu

TAYLOR, Marcie, J .... 765-641-4495. 163 L mjtaylor@anderson.edu

TAYLOR, Margaret .... 870-575-8733... 24 E taylorm@uapb.edu

TAYLOR, Margaret, G .... 540-674-3603. 513 B ptaylor@nr.edu

TAYLOR, Marianne .... 508-678-2811. 231 B marianne.taylor@bristolcc.edu

TAYLOR, Marilyn .... 520-621-3876... 18 F taylorm@email.arizona.edu

TAYLOR, Marilyn, J .... 215-898-3425. 435 B mjtaylor@design.upenn.edu

TAYLOR, Mark .... 740-420-5919. 385 L mtaylor@ohiochristian.edu

TAYLOR, Mark .... 562-938-4206... 51 D mtaylor@lbcc.edu

TAYLOR, Mark .... 601-477-4030. 267 F mark.taylor@jcjc.edu

TAYLOR, Maurice .... 443-885-4075. 217 A maurice.taylor@morgan.edu

TAYLOR, Melanie .... 562-903-4800... 29 L melanie.taylor@biola.edu

TAYLOR, Melody .... 843-574-6225. 447 E melody.taylor@tridenttech.edu

TAYLOR, Mervin, V .... 340-693-1560. 555 E mtaylor2@live.uvi.edu

TAYLOR, Mia .... 617-348-6220. 237 E taylor@urbancollege.edu

TAYLOR, Michael .... 617-348-6390. 237 E michael.taylor@urbancollege.edu

TAYLOR, Michael .... 253-589-6085. 518 B michael.taylor@cptc.edu

TAYLOR, Michael, A .... 812-877-8145. 172 C michael.a.taylor@rose-hulman.edu

TAYLOR, Michele .... 610-841-3333. 427 F mtaylor@psb.edu

TAYLOR, Michelle .... 918-495-6581. 398 H mtaylor@oru.edu

TAYLOR, Michelle, O .... 801-863-6158. 497 C taylormo@uvu.edu

TAYLOR, Missy .... 703-897-1972. 510 B mtaylor@stratford.edu

TAYLOR, Monica, M .... 302-831-7138... 94 B mmtaylor@udel.edu

TAYLOR, Nancy, K .... 716-375-2317. 338 E nktaylor@sbu.edu

TAYLOR, Orlando .... 213-627-2580... 38 G

TAYLOR, Pam .... 618-664-6513. 145 G pam.taylor@greenville.edu

TAYLOR, Pat .... 417-328-1500. 282 C ptaylor@sbuniv.edu

TAYLOR, Patricia .... 734-677-5003. 252 A ptaylor@wccnet.edu

TAYLOR, Patty, L .... 920-565-1298. 533 R taylorpl@lakeland.edu

TAYLOR, OSB, Paul .... 724-805-2527. 432 G paut.taylor@email.stvincent.edu

TAYLOR, Phillip .... 518-327-6272. 336 B ptaylor@paulsmiths.edu

TAYLOR, Quinton .... 225-922-2391. 202 G qtaylor@lctcs.edu

TAYLOR, R .... 503-399-6566. 402 E r.taylor@chemeketa.edu

TAYLOR, Rad, W .... 518-783-2573. 340 J rtaylor@siena.edu

TAYLOR, Reade .... 336-334-5200. 369 A reade_taylor@uncg.edu

TAYLOR, Rich .... 405-325-7370. 401 B rich.taylor@ou.edu

TAYLOR, Richard .... 814-393-2361. 428 C rtaylor@clarion.edu

TAYLOR, Richard, A .... 214-887-5316. 471 F rtaylor@dts.edu

TAYLOR, Rickie .... 417-447-4802. 279 K taylorrd@otc.edu

TAYLOR, Robbin, M .... 270-745-5858. 200 G robbin.taylor@wku.edu

TAYLOR, Robert .... 850-561-2644. 114 K robert.taylor@famu.edu

TAYLOR, Robert .... 712-722-6077. 177 J robert.taylor@dordt.edu

TAYLOR, Rod .... 509-533-8122. 518 E rod.taylor@scc.spokane.edu

TAYLOR, Ron .... 209-384-6101... 54 D ron.taylor@mccd.edu

TAYLOR, Rose .... 434-381-6140. 510 F rtlewis@sbc.edu

TAYLOR, Russell .... 828-898-8770. 356 A taylorrg@lmc.edu

TAYLOR, Sandi .... 909-748-8428... 73 H sandi_taylor@redlands.edu

TAYLOR, Sharon .... 562-985-4162... 33 F staylor@csulb.edu

TAYLOR, Sharon .... 360-438-4370. 522 G staylor@stmartin.edu

TAYLOR, Sharon .... 412-924-1350. 431 A staylor@pts.edu

TAYLOR, Sherri .... 641-673-1048. 183 H taylors@wmpenn.edu

TAYLOR, Sherri .... 229-732-5950. 120 D sherritaylor@andrewcollege.edu

TAYLOR, Sherry .... 417-447-8801. 279 K taylorst@otc.edu

TAYLOR, Sheryl, S .... 712-722-6047. 177 J sheryl.taylor@dordt.edu

TAYLOR, Spence .... 864-455-7992. 448 E staylor@ghs.org

TAYLOR, Stacey .... 617-732-2790. 233 E stacey.taylor@mcphs.edu

TAYLOR, Stan .... 214-648-7518. 493 E stan.taylor@utsouthwestern.edu

TAYLOR, Stephanie .... 423-614-8600. 455 L staylor@leeuniversity.edu

TAYLOR, Stephanie .... 317-921-4473. 169 L staylor@ivytech.edu

TAYLOR, Stephanie .... 704-637-4470. 353 E sataylor@catawba.edu

TAYLOR, Stephanie .... 412-291-6200. 410 B staylor@aii.edu

TAYLOR, Steve .... 662-325-0939. 268 D steve.taylor@msstate.edu

TAYLOR, Steve, M .... 308-432-6210. 291 D staylor@csc.edu

TAYLOR, Steve, P .... 262-243-5700. 532 H steve.taylor@cuw.edu

TAYLOR, Steven .... 734-995-7439. 241 E steve.taylor@cuw.edu

TAYLOR, Steven, T .... 303-963-3138... 79 C staylor@ccu.edu

TAYLOR, Sue .... 972-883-4694. 491 E setaylor@utdallas.edu

TAYLOR, Suzanne .... 806-742-2121. 487 D suzanne.taylor@ttu.edu

TAYLOR, T. A .... 214-638-0484. 475 D tataylor@kdstudio.com

TAYLOR, Tammy .... 903-927-3300. 495 A ttaylor@wileyc.edu

TAYLOR, Tamra .... 801-524-8140. 495 O ttaylor@ldsbc.edu

TAYLOR, Thomas .... 978-934-3933. 229 B thomas_taylor@uml.edu

TAYLOR, Thomas .... 205-391-2617..... 6 H ttaylor@sheltonstate.edu

TAYLOR, Thomas, T .... 937-327-7012. 393 E ttaylor@wittenberg.edu

TAYLOR, Tim .... 618-842-3711. 146 I taylort@iecc.edu

TAYLOR, Timothy .... 803-376-5766. 441 A

TAYLOR, Tom .... 765-285-1444. 164 B taylor@bsu.edu

TAYLOR, Toni .... 334-808-6305..... 7 H tltaylor@troy.edu

TAYLOR, Tracy .... 605-668-1518. 450 F tracy.taylor@mtmc.edu

TAYLOR, Tyra .... 217-786-4509. 151 F tyra.taylor@llcc.edu

TAYLOR, Valerie, A .... 570-941-6344. 436 A valerie.taylor@scranton.edu

TAYLOR, Verna .... 337-269-0620. 201 B vernat@bluecliffcollege.com

TAYLOR, Vernon .... 540-442-0395... 55 J vtaylor@nu.edu

TAYLOR, Vicki .... 870-230-5148... 21 D taylorv@hsu.edu

TAYLOR, Virginia 585-345-6886. 325 C vmtaylor@genesee.edu

TAYLOR, Virginia, L 330-569-5214. 380 I TaylorVL@hiram.edu

TAYLOR, Vorley 740-366-9443. 376 A taylor.1051@osu.edu

TAYLOR, JR., Walter, F . 614-235-4136. 390 A wtaylor@TLSohio.edu

TAYLOR, William, F 804-706-5016. 512 G ftaylor@jtcc.edu

TAYLOR, William, R 626-395-3727... 31 E bill.taylor@cco.caltech.edu

TAYLOR, Yolanda, D 918-631-2327. 401 F yolanda-taylor@utulsa.edu

TAYLOR-ALLEYNE, Dian . 215-572-2932. 409 H taylor-alleyne@arcadia.edu

TAYLOR-ARCHER, Mordean 502-852-6153. 200 D motayl01@louisville.edu

TAYLOR-BURCH, Linda, J 856-225-6039. 306 C ltburch@camden.rutgers.edu

TAYLOR-COLBERT, Alice 864-427-9409. 448 G

TAYLOR-DUPREE, Lesa .. 318-678-6000. 202 I ltaylordupre@bpcc.edu

TAYLOR-RODRIGUEZ, Amanda 404-297-9522. 126 A taylora@gptc.edu

TAYLOR-SAWYER, Sandra 575-769-4138. 309 F sandra.sawyer@clovis.edu

TAYLOR-WEBB, Traki 301-860-3230. 220 A ttaylorwebb@bowiestate.edu

TCHEOU, Pang 717-872-3350. 429 D fathertcheou@gmail.com

TEACHMAN, Debra 575-439-3622. 310 J teachman@nmsu.edu

TEAGUE, Barbara 606-546-4151. 200 A bteague@unionky.edu

TEAGUE, Brad 501-450-3150... 25 H bteague@uca.edu

TEAGUE, Clay 478-757-3544. 122 F cteague@centralgatech.edu

TEAGUE, Dion 253-680-7023. 516 L dteague@bates.ctc.edu

TEAGUE, Donna, O 812-488-2212. 173 H dt52@evansville.edu

TEAGUE, Ellen 703-812-4757. 506 H eteague@leland.edu

TEAGUE, Norwood 612-625-0775. 264 G norwood@umn.edu

TEAGUE, Pam 501-205-8923... 20 I pteague@cbc.edu

TEAGUE, Peggy, S 919-735-5151. 364 H psteague@waynecc.edu

TEAGUE, Peter, W 717-560-8278. 421 A pteague@lbc.edu

TEAGUE, Rebecca 951-487-3072... 55 B rteague@msjc.edu

TEAGUE, Sharyn, J 910-221-2224. 354 D

TEAGUE, Tracie 805-969-3626... 57 K tteague@pacifica.edu

TEAGUE, Willard 417-862-9533. 274 F wteague@globaluniversity.edu

TEAHEN, Rebecca, M 231-995-1855. 248 B rteahen@nmc.edu

TEAHEN, Roberta 231-591-3532. 242 F teahenr@ferris.edu

TEAL, Holly 970-248-1898... 79 F hteal@coloradomesa.edu

TEAL, Lysa 860-486-2434... 92 A lysa.teal@uconn.edu

TEAL, P, J 919-515-2191. 368 B pj_teal@ncsu.edu

TEAL, Rick 864-592-4618. 447 A tealr@sccsc.edu

TEAL, Rita, J 803-516-4586. 446 G rfjteal@scsu.edu

TEAT, Jonathan 214-333-5128. 470 D jonathan@dbu.edu

TEATER, Kristian 314-792-6384. 275 L teater@kenrick.edu

TEBBE, Robert 618-235-2700. 160 A robert.tebbe@swic.edu

TEBOUL, Jean-Claude .... 773-325-7647. 143 H jteboul@depaul.edu

TECLE, Barbara 310-665-6946... 57 C btecle@otis.edu

TEDESCHI, Lisa, F 603-526-3451. 295 I ltedeschi@colby-sawyer.edu

TEDESCO, Joanne 573-875-7207. 272 G jtedesco@ccis.edu

TEDESCO, Joseph, W 713-743-4207. 489 B jtedesco@uh.edu

TEDESCO, Lisa, A 404-727-2669. 124 E lisa.tedesco@emory.edu

TEDESCO, Nicole 585-594-6140. 337 K tedesco_nicole@roberts.edu

TEDJESKE, David 610-519-6979. 436 F david.tedjeske@villanova.edu

TEDUITS, Doug 713-222-5366. 489 D teduitsd@uhd.edu

TEED, Debbie 360-596-5451. 524 A dteed@spscc.edu

TEEHAN, Dyan 617-928-4780. 234 E dteehan@mountida.edu

TEEHAN, Kathleen 617-287-6020. 228 G kathleen.teehan@umb.edu

TEEL, Eunice 231-348-6615. 247 H eteel@ncmich.edu

TEEL, Katrin 207-947-4591. 209 G kteel@bealcollege.edu

TEEL, Maria 662-685-4771. 266 C mteel@bmc.edu

TEEL, Nancy, A 617-427-0060. 232 G nteel@rcc.mass.edu

TEEPLE, Cynthia 714-547-9625... 30 J cteeple@calcoast.edu

TEERINK, Susan, M 414-288-1583. 534 B susan.teerink@marquette.edu

TEETER, Deborah, J 785-864-4412. 190 L irdjt@ku.edu

TEETS, Andrew 814-871-5856. 416 K teets001@gannon.edu

TEETSEL, Craig, M 260-399-7700. 174 C cteetsel@sf.edu

TEGART, Doris, A 502-272-8208. 192 E dtegart@bellarmine.edu

TEGEGNE, Yahana 630-560-6242. 148 K ytegegne@hancocku.edu

TEGERSTRAND, Julene, M 208-467-8338. 139 A jtegerstrand@nnu.edu

TEICHERT, Scott 801-626-7670. 497 D ScottTeichert@weber.edu

TEICHMAN, Carl, F 309-556-3429. 148 B cteich@iwu.edu

TEICHMAN, Shlomo 516-225-4700. 337 C teichman@mlb.edu

TEICHMILLER, Cheryl, A 920-923-7618. 534 A cteichmiller@marianuniversity.edu

TEIG, Kathy 563-588-6385. 176 F kathy.teig@clarke.edu

TEIG, Trisha 801-832-2235. 498 F tteig@westminstercollege.edu

TEIS, Lawrence, B 512-245-2114. 487 C lt10@txstate.edu

TEITELBAUM, Aharon 845-783-0994. 349 E

TEITELBAUM, Jeremy 860-486-2713... 92 A Jeremy.Teitelbaum@uconn.edu

TEITELBAUM, Kenneth 910-962-7671. 369 C teitelbaumk@uncw.edu

TEITLBAUM, Zalman 718-963-9770. 349 B ed@utsny.edu

TEJADA, Adan 925-631-4052... 61 F at11@stmarys-ca.edu

TEJADA, Lavinia 803-376-5700. 441 A ltejada@allenuniversity.edu

TEJADA, Mirta 201-360-4651. 302 D mtejada@hccc.edu

TEJES, Pam 256-824-5135..... 8 F pam.tejes@uah.edu

TEKELY, Angela 610-647-4400. 418 I atekely@immaculata.edu

TEKIPPE, Stephanie, S 319-352-8628. 183 E stephanie.tekippe@wartburg.edu

TEKLEGIORGIS, Kidesti .. 610-558-5615. 424 I teklegik@neumann.edu

TELBERG, Tamara 845-758-6822. 314 D telberg@bard.edu

TELFER, Richard, J 262-472-1918. 538 D telferr@uww.edu

TELFORD, Rebecca, P 937-778-7809. 379 G btelford@edisonohio.edu

TELL, Barbara 310-954-4348... 54 J btell@msmc.la.edu

TELLEEN, Jane, A 651-523-2202. 256 A jtelleen@hamline.edu

TELLEI, Patrick, U 680-488-1669. 547 B tellei@palau.edu

TELLER, Ryan 402-486-2538. 292 E ryteller@ucollege.edu

TELLES-IRVIN, Patricia ... 847-491-5360. 155 D tellesirvin@northwestern.edu

TELLEZ, J. Carlos 574-372-5100. 166 B tellezjc@grace.edu

TELLEZ, Laura 915-831-6359. 472 B ltellez8@epcc.edu

TELLI, Suzette 615-297-7545. 452 J tellis@aquinascollege.edu

TELLO, Steven 978-934-4240. 229 B Steven_Tello@uml.edu

TEMAAT, Beverly 620-227-9119. 186 B bgtemaat@dc3.edu

TEMKIN, Aron 802-485-2624. 500 A atemkin@norwich.edu

TEMPEL, Eugene, R 317-274-4200. 168 D etempel@indiana.edu

TEMPEL, Gene 812-855-4613. 167 E etempel@indiana.edu

TEMPERA, Jeffrey, L 631-451-4506. 346 E temperj@sunysuffolk.edu

TEMPLE, Austin 318-357-6699. 208 B temple@nsula.edu

TEMPLE, Glena, G 608-796-3393. 539 E ggtemple@viterbo.edu

TEMPLE, Jack 334-387-3877..... 1 E jacktemple@amridgeuniversity.edu

TEMPLE, Jim 661-362-3535... 40 E james.temple@canyons.edu

TEMPLE, Lori 702-895-3628. 294 I lorit@unlv.edu

TEMPLE, Melanie 252-538-4319. 361 A mtemple295@halifaxcc.edu

TEMPLE, Tisha 512-863-1857. 481 I woodyj@southwestern.edu

TEMPLE, Vickie 318-678-6025. 202 I vtemple@bpcc.edu

TEMPLER, Lisa 409-933-8262. 469 E ltempler@com.edu

TEMPLETON, Cary 707-468-3043... 54 B ctempleton@mendocino.edu

TEMPLETON, Debra, R ... 540-831-6030. 508 C drtemplet@radford.edu

TEMPLETON, Etheldra 215-871-6486. 430 D etheldrat@pcom.edu

TEMPLETON, Heidi 660-785-4016. 282 L heidi@truman.edu

TEMPLETON, Leslie 501-450-1320... 21 E templeton@hendrix.edu

TEMPLETON, Linda, B .... 219-980-6767. 168 B litemple@iun.edu

TEMPLETON, Rosalyn 406-265-3726. 287 D rosalyn.templeton@msun.edu

TEMPLETON, William 907-786-4005... 10 H anwgt@uaa.alaska.edu

TEMPLETON-CORNELL, Vicki, L 315-267-2190. 344 C templevl@postdam.edu

TEMPLIN, Carl, R 435-586-5401. 497 A templin@suu.edu

TEMPLIN, JR., Robert, G 703-323-3101. 513 C rtemplin@nvcc.edu

TEMTE, Andrew 603-668-6660. 297 C

TEMTE, Anne, T 218-683-8610. 260 D anne.temte@northlandcollege.edu

TENA, Lydia 915-831-8818. 472 B lpere121@epcc.edu

TENCHER, Donald, E 401-456-8007. 439 F dtencher@ric.edu

TENCZAR, JR., Robert, C 773-298-3326. 158 E tenczar@sxu.edu

TENDALL, Michael, W 309-794-7357. 139 L michaeltendall@augustana.edu

TENDALL, Stephen 563-333-6423. 182 B TendallStephen@sau.edu

TENENBAUM, Elchonon . 707-638-5507... 69 K rabbi@tu.edu

TENGERES, Laura, N 954-308-2224... 98 G ltengeres@aii.edu

TENGLIN, Ingrid, K 773-244-5601. 154 G itenglin@northpark.edu

TENIENTE-MATSON, Cynthia 559-278-2083... 33 D cmatson@csufresno.edu

TENNANT, Otto 270-789-5034. 193 D otennant@campbellsville.edu

TENNENT, Lee 864-646-1777. 447 D ltennent@tctc.edu

TENNENT, Timothy, C .... 859-858-2202. 192 A

TENNER, Jack 713-743-5671. 489 B jdtenner@central.uh.edu

TENNEY, David 713-348-8036. 479 A dtenney@rice.edu

TENNEY, Peter 509-532-8888. 517 D ptenney@carrington.edu

TENNEY, Randall 304-473-8099. 531 G tenney_r@wvwc.edu

TENNILL, William 217-245-3338. 146 F bill.tennill@ic.edu

TENNY, Elissa 312-899-5100. 158 L etenny@saic.edu

TENNYSON, Pat 423-869-6286. 456 A ptennyson@lmunet.edu

TENO, Babette 562-902-3327... 67 H babetteteno@scuhs.edu

TENSEN, Jan 973-300-2153. 307 F jtensen@sussex.edu

TENSUAN, Theresa 610-896-1268. 418 F ttensuan@haverford.edu

TENUTA, Bob 815-455-8585. 152 F btenuta@mchenry.edu

TENUTA, Robert 312-322-1733. 160 D rtenuta@spertus.edu

TEPATTI, Eileen, G 217-786-2885. 151 F eileen.tepatti@llcc.edu

TEPE, Chabha 563-884-5442. 182 A chabha.tepe@palmer.edu

TERAGAWACHI, Lori 808-984-3406. 137 B loritera@hawaii.edu

TERAVEST, Daniel, J 707-259-6041... 55 F dteravest@napavalley.edu

TERCHEK, Daniel 212-472-1500. 334 B dterchek@nysid.edu

TEREBESSY, Hilarie 312-942-7100. 157 G hilarie_terebessy@rush.edu

TERENZIO, Marion 973-748-9000. 299 F marion_terenzio@bloomfield.edu

TERESA, Daniel 831-755-6840... 46 G dteresa@hartnell.edu

TERESI, Mark 847-566-6401. 162 G mteresi@usml.edu

TERHAAR, Jody, L 320-363-5601. 254 J jterhaar@csbsju.edu

TERHORST, Dan 760-480-8474... 76 C dterhorst@wscal.edu

TERHUNE, James, S 207-859-4780. 209 J jterhune@colby.edu

TERKLA, Dawn, G 617-627-3274. 237 C dawn.terkla@tufts.edu

TERMOTT, Kenneth 732-247-5241. 303 E ktermott@nbts.edu

TERNES, Roger 715-425-3246. 537 E roger.ternes@uwrf.edu

TERP, Douglas, C 207-859-4770. 209 J dcterp@colby.edu

TERP, Jeff 317-921-4225. 169 K jterp@ivytech.edu

TERPACK, Sallie, A 814-732-1024. 428 E terpack@edinboro.edu

TERPENNING, Marlene, K 740-284-5179. 379 N mterpenning@franciscan.edu

TERPSTRA, Joylita 423-478-7707. 458 B jterpstra@ptseminary.edu

TERRASO, Megan 404-471-6171. 119 I mterraso@agnesscott.edu

TERRELL, Beth 812-535-5172. 172 F bterrell@smwc.edu

TERRELL, Bill 915-532-3737. 494 J bterrell@westerntech.edu

TERRELL, Billie, P 815-740-3399. 162 F bterrell@stfrancis.edu

TERRELL, Charles 304-434-8001. 528 A cterrell@eastern.wvnet.edu

TERRELL, Gaither, M 336-316-2143. 355 A gterrell@guilford.edu

TERRELL, Jan (Denny) .... 717-477-1375. 429 E dterrell@ship.edu

TERRELL, Janice 704-355-4305. 353 D janice.terrell@carolinascollege.edu

TERRELL, Mark 814-866-6641. 420 E mterrell@lecom.edu

TERRELL, Patricia 208-282-2315. 138 E terrpatr@isu.edu

TERRELL, Sherri, I 915-747-5302. 492 A siterrell@utep.edu

TERRELL, Tracy 509-963-3001. 517 F terrell@cwu.edu

TERRELL-BAMIRO, Caryl 480-732-7134... 14 J caryl.terrell-bamiro@cgc.edu

TERRELL-POWELL, Yvonne, L 206-546-4509. 523 F yterrell@shoreline.edu

TERRELL-POWELL, Yvonne, L 206-546-6910. 523 F yterrell@shoreline.edu

TERRIO, Dan, M 509-527-4981. 525 E terrio@whitman.edu

TERRIO, Paul, L 612-330-1049. 253 H terriop@augsburg.edu

TERRONEZ, Randy 515-244-4221. 175 C terronezr@aib.edu

TERRY, Alicia 760-757-2121... 54 G aterry@miracosta.edu

TERRY, Brooks 904-680-7700. 103 Q bterry@fcsl.edu

TERRY, Brooks 904-680-7730. 103 Q bterry@fcsl.edu

TERRY, Bryan, J 973-655-4153. 303 D terryb@mail.montclair.edu

TERRY, Carol, S 401-454-6278. 440 A cterry@risd.edu

TERRY, Chihoko 910-410-1821. 362 I ckterry@richmondcc.edu

TERRY, Denise 574-372-5100. 166 B Denise.Terry@grace.edu

TERRY, Edward 828-726-2202. 358 E eterry@cccti.edu

TERRY, Heidi 816-654-7152. 275 K hterry@kcumb.edu

TERRY, Heidi 330-325-6479. 385 E hterry@neomed.edu

TERRY, James, E 304-696-2486. 529 H terry@marshall.edu

TERRY, Jan, M 217-245-1097. 151 F jan.terry@llcc.edu

TERRY, John 605-394-4800. 450 G jterry@national.edu

TERRY, Justyn ... 724-266-3838. 434 J
jterry@tsm.edu
TERRY, Laura, C ... 423-439-4210. 459 C
terryl@etsu.edu
TERRY, Martin, L ... 419-434-4521. 391 D
terry@findlay.edu
TERRY, Missy, D ... 503-554-2101. 403 C
terrym@georgefox.edu
TERRY, Neil, W ... 806-651-2530. 484 D
nterry@mail.wtamu.edu
TERRY, Penelope ... 718-951-5924. 317 C
pterry@brooklyn.cuny.edu
TERRY, Rondale ... 510-567-6174... 69 C
rterry@sum.edu
TERRY, Sara Beth ... 334-833-4062... 4 D
sbterry@huntingdon.edu
TERRY, Scott ... 304-357-4363. 527 H
scottterry@ucwv.edu
TERRY, Stephen, B ... 843-383-8035. 442 F
sterry@coker.edu
TERRY, Steven ... 804-330-0111. 503 G
careercrim@centura.edu
TERRY, Susan ... 206-543-0535. 524 G
nahe@uw.edu
TERRY, Terri ... 205-348-0609... 8 D
teri.terry@ua.edu
TERRY, Tina ... 606-886-3863. 194 K
tterry0025@kctcs.edu
TERRY, Troy, M ... 864-294-2213. 444 C
troy.terry@furman.edu
TERVALA, Debra ... 410-528-7602. 265 D
debra.tervala@waldenu.edu
TERWILLIGER, Linda ... 845-451-1342. 322 D
l_terwil@culinary.edu
TESAR, Dan ... 714-992-7040... 56 F
dtesar@fullcoll.edu
TESAR, Daniel ... 714-992-7048... 56 F
dtesar@fullcoll.edu
TESFAGIORGIS,
Gebre, H ... 515-294-1181. 175 H
gebretes@iastate.edu
TESFAMARIAM, Biniam ... 574-520-4104. 168 E
biktesfa@iusb.edu
TESH, J. Michael ... 210-567-2590. 493 A
tesh@uthscsa.edu
TESH, Vernon, L ... 979-436-9112. 484 B
tesh@medicine.tamhsc.edu
TESKE, Paul ... 303-315-2805... 86 A
paul.teske@ucdenver.edu
TESKE, Yolanda ... 252-334-2012. 357 A
yolanda.teske@macuniversity.edu
TESKEY, Michael ... 503-777-7593. 407 E
michael.teskey@reed.edu
TESORIERE, Joseph, P ... 518-564-4601. 344 B
tesorijp@plattsburgh.edu
TESS, Dan, E ... 570-484-2238. 429 B
dtess@lhup.edu
TESS, Paul, A ... 507-354-8221. 256 M
tesspa@mlc-wels.edu
TESSIER, Michael, A ... 812-488-2956. 173 H
mt28@evansville.edu
TESSIER, Nanci ... 804-287-6425. 510 L
ntessier@richmond.edu
TESSIER-LAVIGNE, Marc 212-327-8080. 338 A
marctl@rockefeller.edu
TESSMANN, Cary, A ... 262-691-5214. 541 D
ctessmann@wctc.edu
TESTA, Henry ... 315-866-0300. 326 A
testahp@herkimer.edu
TESTA, Noelle ... 785-242-5200. 189 I
noelle.testa@ottawa.edu
TESTA, Phil ... 607-778-5575. 315 I
testapf@sunybroome.edu
TESTANI, Joseph, A ... 804-827-0408. 511 F
jatestani@vcu.edu
TESTI, Andrea ... 541-881-5761. 408 C
atesti@tvcc.cc
TESTY, Kellye, Y ... 206-543-2586. 524 G
lawdean@uw.edu
TETEN, Dixie ... 402-872-2226. 291 E
dteten@peru.edu
TETI, Polly ... 215-242-7777. 413 A
tetip@chc.edu
TETRAULT, Martha, R ... 413-597-2681. 238 D
martha.r.tetrault@williams.edu
TETREAU, Jerry, C ... 480-245-7944... 14 B
jerry.tetreau@ibcs.edu
TETREAULT, Jules ... 603-899-4178. 296 H
tetreaj@franklinpierce.edu
TETTEH, Edem ... 706-821-8259. 130 C
etetteh@paine.edu
TETZLAFF-BELHASEN,
Chris, M ... 361-698-1308. 471 G
chris@delmar.edu
TETZLOFF, Jason ... 320-308-5377. 261 C
jtetzloff@sctcc.edu
TETZLOFF, Lisa ... 920-465-2200. 536 F
tetzlofl@uwgb.edu
TEUFEL, Kyla ... 513-745-5650. 391 A
kyla.teufel@uc.edu
TEUFEL, Pamela ... 215-503-7015. 434 C
pamela.teufel@jeffersonhospital.org
TEURNER, Mary ... 660-596-7249. 282 G
mteurner@sfccmo.edu
TEVEPAUGH, Dawn ... 336-334-4822. 360 G
adtevepaugh@gtcc.edu
TEVIS, Glenna, J ... 712-274-5269. 181 B
tevis@morningside.edu
TEW, Glade ... 808-675-3470. 135 C
tewg@byuh.edu
TEW, JR., John ... 816-584-6410. 280 C
john.tew@park.edu
TEW, Mark ... 325-649-8002. 473 F
mtew@hputx.edu
TEW, Rebecca ... 706-568-2039. 123 D
tew_rebecca@columbusstate.edu
TEWS, Anne ... 269-927-8117. 245 D
tews@lakemichigancollege.edu
TEXIDOR, Migdalia ... 787-250-1912. 550 E
mtexidor@metro.inter.edu
TEYMOURTASH,
Janet, L ... 415-422-5898... 73 J
janet@usfca.edu
THACKER, Allison ... 713-348-4818. 479 A
invest@rice.edu
THACKER, Karen, S ... 610-796-8306. 409 E
karen.thacker@alvernia.edu
THACKER, Linda ... 314-529-6573. 276 G
lthacker@maryville.edu
THACKSTON, Russell, C . 619-260-5998... 73 I
rthackston@sandiego.edu
THADEN, Mark ... 540-654-2160. 510 J
mthad2zw@umw.edu
THAI, Khi ... 954-762-5650. 114 L
thai@fau.edu
THAMES, Brenda ... 209-575-6060... 77 J
thamesb@mjc.edu
THAMES, James, H ... 214-887-5013. 471 F
jthames@dts.edu
THAMES, Jamie ... 478-757-4024. 134 G
jthames@wesleyancollege.edu
THAMES, Kathleen, A ... 337-482-6397. 208 D
kat@louisiana.edu
THANNICKAL, Steve ... 918-495-6620. 398 H
sthannical@oru.edu
THAO, Maisee ... 805-898-2927... 44 I
mthao@fielding.edu
THARP, Brent ... 912-478-5444. 126 C
btharp@georgiasouthern.edu
THARP, Carla ... 201-761-7360. 306 L
ctharp@saintpeters.edu
THARP, Karen ... 931-598-1270. 458 H
kmtharp@sewanee.edu
THARPE, Barbara ... 615-327-6827. 456 E
btharpe@mmc.edu
THARPE, Debbie ... 864-941-8319. 446 C
tharpe.d@ptc.edu
THARRINGTON, Sally ... 434-949-1061. 513 H
sally.tharrington@southside.edu
THATCHER, Debra ... 518-255-5111. 344 E
thatchdh@cobleskill.edu
THATCHER, Derek ... 740-366-9453. 376 A
dthatche@cotc.edu
THATCHER, Janese, V ... 620-417-1014. 190 F
janese.thatcher@sccc.edu
THATCHER, Patricia ... 215-951-2730. 430 E
thatcherp@philau.edu
THATCHER, Paula ... 503-352-1556. 407 A
thatchep@pacificu.edu
THATCHER, Tom ... 513-244-8172. 376 J
tom.thatcher@ccuniversity.edu
THAXTON, Deron ... 318-473-6574. 205 A
dthaxton@lsua.edu
THAXTON, Gail ... 706-754-7701. 129 G
gthaxton@northgatech.edu
THAXTON, Janlyn ... 325-670-1264. 472 O
jthaxton@hsutx.edu
THAYER, OP, Gerard ... 202-495-3834... 96 C
gthayer@dhs.edu
THAYER, Janelle, R ... 509-777-4216. 525 F
jthayer@whitworth.edu
THAYER, Mary Ann ... 810-766-2057. 239 H
maryann.thayer@baker.edu
THAYER, Scott ... 304-829-7138. 526 D
sthayer@bethanywv.edu
THAYER, Scott, W ... 626-585-7798... 58 F
swthayer@pasadena.edu
THAYER, Tammy ... 608-246-6451. 540 C
tthayer2@madisoncollege.edu
THAYNE, Lewis, E ... 717-867-6211. 421 H
thayne@lvc.edu
THE, James ... 817-202-6719. 481 E
jthe@swau.edu
THEEUWES, Jim ... 251-580-2154... 4 L
jtheeuwes@faulknerstate.edu
THEIMER, Donna ... 970-824-1111... 80 B
donna.theimer@cncc.edu
THEIS, Ann ... 567-661-7270. 387 L
ann_theis@owens.edu
THEIS, Lori, C ... 318-257-2238. 207 F
ltheis@latech.edu
THEISEN, Darlene, A ... 814-871-7609. 416 K
theisen001@gannon.edu
THEISEN, Jason ... 320-308-6012. 261 C
jtheisen@sctcc.edu
THEISING, Andrew ... 618-482-6912. 159 H
atheisi@siue.edu
THEISS, Tom ... 217-773-4441. 150 D
tom.theiss@doc.illinois.gov
THELANDER, Laura ... 651-641-3216. 256 J
lthelander001@luthersem.edu
THELEN, Cindy ... 715-675-3331. 541 A
Thelen@ntc.edu
THELLMAN, Wendy ... 678-717-3845. 133 D
wendy.thellman@ung.edu
THEOBALD, Brent ... 714-556-3610... 74 D
brent.theobald@vanguard.edu
THEOBALD, Michael, J ... 816-501-4061. 280 I
mike.theobald@rockhurst.edu
THEOBALD, Neil, D ... 215-204-7405. 433 K
president@temple.edu
THEOBALD, Paul ... 712-749-2277. 176 D
theobaldp@bvu.edu
THEODORE, Rennelle ... 570-586-2400. 410 D
rTheodore@bbc.edu
THEODORE, Steve ... 254-295-4500. 490 B
stheodore@umhb.edu
THEODOROPOULOS,
Christine ... 805-756-1414... 32 F
ctheodor@calpoly.edu
THEODOSIOU,
Constantine ... 718-862-7948. 329 M
constantine.theodosiou@manhattan.edu
THEODOULOU, Stella, Z 818-677-3317... 34 C
stella.theodoulou@csun.edu
THEOKAS, Mary ... 864-503-5392. 448 H
mtheokas@uscupstate.edu
THEONUGRAHA, Felix ... 847-317-4061. 160 M
ftheonu@tiu.edu
THEORET, Julie ... 802-635-1333. 501 D
julie.theoret@jsc.edu
THERIAULT, Monique ... 206-726-5013. 518 G
mtheriault@cornish.edu
THERIOT, Lisa, M ... 214-860-2247. 470 J
ltheriot@dcccd.edu
THERMER, Clifford ... 860-913-2058... 90 A
cthermer@goodwin.edu
THEROUX, Robert, R ... 401-739-5000. 439 D
rtheroux@neit.edu
THERRIEN, Michael ... 603-271-6484. 296 C
mtherrien@ccsnh.edu
THESENVITZ,
Michael, D ... 918-631-2583. 401 F
michael-thesenvitz@utulsa.edu
THESING-RITTER, Jodi ... 715-836-2325. 536 E
thesinjm@uwec.edu
THEULE, Ryan ... 661-362-5930... 40 E
ryan.theule@canyons.edu
THEULEN, Michael ... 413-782-1377. 238 A
mtheulen@wne.edu
THIBEAULT, Alan ... 207-602-2253. 213 A
athibeault@une.edu
THIBEAULT, Dennis ... 617-333-2158. 225 E
dthibeau@curry.edu
THIBEAULT, Nancy ... 937-512-2926. 388 O
nancy.thibeault@sinclair.edu
THIBEDEAU, Dawn ... 414-277-7126. 534 G
thibedeau@msoe.edu
THIBODEAU, John ... 262-564-3050. 540 A
thibodeauj@gtc.edu
THIBODEAU, Wayne, J ... 248-370-4240. 248 J
thibodea@oakland.edu
THIBODEAUX, Amy ... 337-421-6902. 204 E
amy.thibodeaux@sowela.edu
THIBODEAUX, Chad ... 337-475-5524. 207 G
cthibodeaux@mcneese.edu
THIBOUTOT, Paul ... 507-222-4190. 254 D
pthibout@carleton.edu
THIE, Susan ... 605-331-6592. 452 D
susan.thie@usiouxfalls.edu
THIEBAUX, Brian ... 760-921-5501... 58 C
bthiebaux@paloverde.edu
THIEHOFF, Jack, O ... 972-860-8365. 470 I
JThiehoff@dcccd.edu
THIEL, Chuck ... 810-762-5003. 247 F
chuck.thiel@mcc.edu
THIEL, OSF, Janet ... 610-358-4219. 424 I
thielj@neumann.edu
THIEL, John, E ... 203-254-4000... 89 I
jthiel@fairfield.edu
THIELE, Dianna ... 206-878-3710. 520 E
dthiele@highline.edu
THIELE, Dwain, L ... 214-648-8711. 493 E
dwain.thiele@utsouthwestern.edu
THIELE, Nicholas ... 573-276-4577. 282 B
njthiele@semo.edu
THIELEMANN, Heather ... 936-294-1345. 487 A
thielemann@shsu.edu
THIEMANN, James, A ... 410-778-7710. 221 C
dthiemann2@washcoll.edu
THIEME, Sacha ... 773-325-8335. 143 H
sthieme@depaul.edu
THIEMENS, Mark, H ... 858-534-6882... 71 F
mthiemens@ucsd.edu
THIERFELDER,
William, K ... 704-461-6726. 352 G
billthierfelder@bac.edu
THIERSTEIN, Joel ... 502-597-6442. 197 A
joel.thierstein@kysu.edu
THIES, Jeannie ... 636-949-4689. 276 D
jthies@lindenwood.edu
THIESEN, Lynn ... 707-476-4187... 40 H
lynn-thiesen@redwoods.edu
THIESFELDT, Steven, R ... 507-354-8221. 256 M
thiesfsr@mlc-wels.edu
THIESSEN, Ron ... 727-816-3236. 110 E
thiessr@phcc.edu
THIGPEN, Paula, M ... 410-864-3605. 218 B
pthigpen@stmarys.edu
THILL, Robert ... 212-353-4348. 321 F
thill@cooper.edu
THILLMAN, Peter ... 920-693-1119. 540 B
peter.thillman@gotoltc.edu
THIMMEL, Lori ... 973-642-8711. 307 D
lori.thimmel@shu.edu
THIMMESCH, Timothy ... 616-331-3845. 243 C
thimmest@gvsu.edu
THIRSK, William, T ... 845-575-3000. 330 D
william.thirsk@marist.edu
THISS, Patrick ... 619-660-4505... 46 D
patrick.thiss@gcccd.edu
THISS, Ramona, H ... 540-985-9828. 506 G
rhthiss@jchs.edu
THISSEN, Sally, L ... 863-680-4127. 105 D
sthissen@flsouthern.edu
THISTLE, Dawn, M ... 508-767-7095. 222 C
dthistle@assumption.edu
THISTLETHWAITE, Polly . 212-817-7060. 317 F
pthistlethwaite@gc.cuny.edu
THOBABEN, James ... 859-858-2369. 192 A
THODE, Arnold ... 563-441-4131. 178 C
athode@eicc.edu
THOM, Greg ... 612-977-5470. 254 C
greg.thom@capella.edu
THOM, Michelle ... 952-358-8271. 260 B
michelle.thom@normandale.edu
THOMAN, Richard, C ... 651-628-3411. 263 A
rcthoman@nwc.edu
THOMANDER, Corbin ... 808-675-3565. 135 C
thomandc@byuh.edu
THOMAS, Adam ... 334-214-4880... 2 H
adam.thomas@cv.edu
THOMAS, Alexander ... 607-436-2520. 343 E
thomasa@oneonta.edu
THOMAS, Alvetta, P ... 404-225-4601. 121 B
athomas@atlantatech.edu
THOMAS, Alvina ... 318-345-9145. 203 C
athomas@ladelta.edu
THOMAS, Amanda ... 410-617-5590. 216 A
athomas@loyola.edu
THOMAS, Anisa ... 941-907-2262. 103 C
anithomas@evergladesuniversity.edu
THOMAS, Anita ... 410-837-4533. 221 A
athomas@ubalt.edu
THOMAS, Anne, C ... 317-788-3543. 173 I
athomas@uindy.edu
THOMAS, Auden ... 518-580-5590. 341 A
athomas@skidmore.edu
THOMAS, B. Elaine ... 413-559-5482. 227 B
THOMAS, Barbara ... 903-785-7661. 478 B
bthomas@parisjc.edu
THOMAS, Barbara, J ... 415-422-6352... 73 J
thomasb@admin.usfca.edu
THOMAS, Barry ... 443-394-3377... 96 F
barry.thomas@strayer.edu
THOMAS, Becky ... 949-451-5484... 67 B
bthomas@ivc.edu
THOMAS, Bethel ... 615-460-6434. 453 C
bethel.thomas@belmont.edu
THOMAS, Bonnie, L ... 240-629-7992. 214 H
bthomas@frederick.edu
THOMAS, Brenda, R ... 501-569-3245... 24 B
brthomas2@ualr.edu
THOMAS, Brice ... 937-529-2201. 390 D
bthomas@united.edu
THOMAS, Bridgett ... 217-732-3155. 151 C
bthomas@lincolncollege.edu
THOMAS, Carl ... 541-885-1151. 405 J
carl.thomas@oit.edu
THOMAS, Carlos ... 225-771-6247. 206 J
carlos_thomas@subr.edu
THOMAS, Carol ... 626-914-8592... 38 K
cthomas@citruscollege.edu
THOMAS, Carol ... 614-287-2780. 378 B
cthomas13@cscc.edu
THOMAS, Carol ... 614-508-7233. 381 E
cthomas@hondros.edu
THOMAS, Carolyn ... 401-874-5250. 440 D
cfthomas@uri.edu
THOMAS, Carolyn, D ... 504-520-7364. 209 D
cthomas@xula.edu
THOMAS, Carrie ... 603-526-3686. 295 I
cathomas@colby-sawyer.edu

THOMAS, JR.,
Charles, E .... 404-527-7711. 127 I
cthomas@itc.edu
THOMAS, Cheryl .... 484-365-7441. 422 D
cthomas@lincoln.edu
THOMAS, Christiana, J ... 504-280-6021. 205 G
cjthoma2@uno.edu
THOMAS, Christine .... 916-691-7333... 53 B
thomasc@crc.losrios.edu
THOMAS, Christine, C .... 334-229-4327..... 1 D
ccthomas@alasu.edu
THOMAS, Christine, L .... 715-346-4617. 538 A
cthomas@uwsp.edu
THOMAS, Claudine, R .... 215-965-4061. 424 D
cthomas@moore.edu
THOMAS, Clay .... 620-278-4240. 190 I
cthomas@sterling.edu
THOMAS, Clyde, G .... 503-554-2013. 403 C
cthomas@georgefox.edu
THOMAS, Corlisse .... 646-312-4574. 316 J
Corlisse.Thomas@baruch.cuny.edu
THOMAS, Dana, L .... 907-450-8018... 10 G
dlthomas@alaska.edu
THOMAS, Daphne, J .... 901-435-1539. 455 M
daphne_thomas@loc.edu
THOMAS, David .... 509-527-2194. 524 I
dave.thomas@wallawalla.edu
THOMAS, David, A .... 202-687-3883... 95 E
dat42@georgetown.edu
THOMAS, David, E .... 215-751-8000. 413 I
dthomas@ccp.edu
THOMAS, Deborah .... 502-776-1443. 199 A
THOMAS, Deborah .... 402-559-5245. 292 J
thomasd@unmc.edu
THOMAS, Dene Kay .... 970-247-7100... 81 M
thomas_d@fortlewis.edu
THOMAS, Denee .... 361-570-4149. 489 E
thomasd@uhv.edu
THOMAS, Denitä .... 601-635-2111. 266 H
dthomas@eccc.edu
THOMAS, Deon .... 618-468-6200. 150 G
delthomas@lc.edu
THOMAS, Dianne .... 269-749-6638. 249 A
dthomas@olivetcollege.edu
THOMAS, Domani .... 718-368-5696. 318 E
dthomas@kbcc.cuny.edu
THOMAS, Donna .... 301-369-2800. 213 G
dgthomas@capitol-college.edu
THOMAS, Dorian .... 773-291-6384. 142 D
dthomas236@ccc.edu
THOMAS, Dorothy .... 608-758-6900. 539 I
THOMAS, Doug .... 978-665-4095. 229 E
dthoma27@fitchburgstate.edu
THOMAS, Downing .... 319-335-0370. 175 I
downing-thomas@uiowa.edu
THOMAS, Eddie, B .... 205-366-8848..... 7 E
ebthomas@stillman.edu
THOMAS, Fitzroy .... 301-891-4115. 221 B
fthomas@wau.edu
THOMAS, Flecia .... 815-479-7620. 152 F
fthomas@mchenry.edu
THOMAS, Fredel .... 605-995-2902. 450 A
frthomas@dwu.edu
THOMAS, Gregory, A ...... 708-709-3501. 156 A
gthomas@prairiestate.edu
THOMAS, Helen .... 912-538-3126. 132 A
hthomas@southeasterntech.edu
THOMAS, Huw, F .... 617-636-6636. 237 C
huw.thomas@tufts.edu
THOMAS, SR., Ira .... 504-286-5432. 206 K
ithomas@suno.edu
THOMAS, J. Matthew ..... 770-534-6174. 122 A
mthomas@brenau.edu
THOMAS, Jack .... 309-298-1824. 162 K
j-thomas2@wiu.edu
THOMAS, James .... 269-387-8785. 252 I
jim.thomas@wmich.edu
THOMAS, James .... 910-296-1974. 361 D
jthomas@jamessprunt.edu
THOMAS, Janell, D .... 701-323-6270. 372 I
Janell.Thomas@SanfordCollege.edu
THOMAS, Janette, B .... 607-587-4122. 345 D
thomasj@alfredstate.edu
THOMAS, Jeremy .... 936-633-5213. 465 J
jthomas@angelina.edu
THOMAS, Jerry, P .... 614-236-6900. 375 H
jthomas@capital.edu
THOMAS, Jerry, R .... 940-565-2231. 490 C
jerry.thomas@unt.edu
THOMAS, Joan .... 413-755-4817. 233 A
jthomas@stcc.edu
THOMAS, Joan .... 715-232-1181. 538 B
thomasj@uwstout.edu
THOMAS, Joe .... 541-888-7399. 407 H
jthomas@socc.edu
THOMAS, Joe, R .... 318-257-2769. 207 F
jthomas@latech.edu
THOMAS, John .... 312-939-0111. 144 D
john@eastwest.edu
THOMAS, John .... 951-785-2064... 50 B
jthomas@lasierra.edu
THOMAS, JR., John .... 918-270-6455. 398 I
john.thomas@ptstulsa.edu
THOMAS, John, L .... 863-680-6215. 105 D
jthomas@flsouthern.edu
THOMAS, Joseph .... 803-536-7033. 446 G
jthomas@scsu.edu
THOMAS, Joseph, M ...... 610-921-7556. 409 A
jthomas@alb.edu
THOMAS, Julia, M .... 585-385-8015. 338 H
jthomas@sjfc.edu
THOMAS, K. B .... 318-487-7389. 202 F
kb.thomas@lacollege.edu
THOMAS, Kanet .... 310-506-4264... 58 H
kanet.thomas@pepperdine.edu
THOMAS, Karen .... 229-430-3525. 120 A
kthomas@albanytech.edu
THOMAS, Karla .... 773-298-3937. 158 E
kthomas@sxu.edu
THOMAS, Kathryn, S ...... 706-355-5116. 120 J
kthomas@athenstech.edu
THOMAS, Katie .... 207-859-1295. 211 H
bookstore@thomas.edu
THOMAS, Kay .... 601-484-8689. 267 G
kthomas@meridiancc.edu
THOMAS, Kay, M .... 252-398-6226. 353 H
thomak@chowan.edu
THOMAS, Keith .... 979-830-4151. 467 I
keith.thomas@blinn.edu
THOMAS, Kenneth, C ...... 972-438-6932. 478 C
kthomas@parkercc.edu
THOMAS, Lauree .... 409-772-1442. 493 C
lauthoma@utmb.edu
THOMAS, Laurita, E .... 734-647-5574. 251 C
laurita@umich.edu
THOMAS, Letrell .... 912-871-1624. 129 J
lthomas@ogeecheetech.edu
THOMAS, Linda .... 309-772-2177. 141 A
lthomas@sadnburg.edu
THOMAS, Linda .... 340-693-1324. 555 E
lthomas2@live.uvi.edu
THOMAS, Lisa .... 651-905-3490. 254 B
lthomas@browncollege.edu
THOMAS, Marcia, M .... 913-234-0809. 185 L
marcia.thomas@cleveland.edu
THOMAS, Marcia, R .... 312-460-0600. 139 H
mthomas@aaart.edu
THOMAS, Maria .... 601-977-7769. 270 A
mthomas@tougaloo.edu
THOMAS, Marjorie .... 757-221-2510. 503 N
mthomas@wm.edu
THOMAS, Marjorie, S ..... 843-953-5522. 443 A
thomasmm@cofc.edu
THOMAS, Mark .... 863-638-2345. 119 C
mark.thomas@warner.edu
THOMAS, Mary Beth .... 617-735-9766. 226 B
thomasmb@emmanuel.edu
THOMAS, Matthew, D ...... 507-933-7510. 255 I
mthomas@gustavus.edu
THOMAS, Maurice .... 856-351-2697. 307 B
mthomas@salemcc.edu
THOMAS, Maxcie .... 870-575-8101... 24 E
thomasm@uapb.edu
THOMAS, May .... 540-362-6519. 505 G
mthomas@hollins.edu
THOMAS, Melaney, A ...... 308-635-6063. 293 E
mthomas@wncc.edu
THOMAS, Melissa .... 503-554-2214. 403 C
mthomas@georgefox.edu
THOMAS, Michael .... 601-979-3060. 267 E
michael.thomas@jsums.edu
THOMAS, Michael .... 989-837-4140. 248 C
thomam@northwood.edu
THOMAS, Michael .... 706-880-8217. 128 A
mthomas@lagrange.edu
THOMAS, Michael .... 618-985-3741. 146 H
thomasm@iecc.edu
THOMAS, Michael, A .... 706-880-8911. 128 A
mathomas@lagrange.edu
THOMAS, Michael, J .... 217-333-3631. 162 A
mthomas@illinois.edu
THOMAS, Michelle .... 765-973-2602. 165 G
thomami1@earlham.edu
THOMAS, Mike, R .... 618-235-2700. 160 A
michael.thomas@swic.edu
THOMAS, Nancy .... 248-204-3203. 245 I
nthomas@ltu.edu
THOMAS, Nathan .... 309-677-3140. 140 I
nthomas@bradley.edu
THOMAS, Ned .... 713-348-4009. 479 A
elt@rice.edu
THOMAS, Nichole .... 828-689-1103. 356 F
nthomas@mhc.edu
THOMAS, Nishanth .... 973-803-5000. 304 C
nthomas@pillar.edu
THOMAS, Pam .... 630-889-6661. 154 E
pthomas@nuhs.edu
THOMAS, Patricia, A ...... 202-274-6314... 97 A
pthomas@udc.edu
THOMAS, Paul .... 443-627-7322. 265 D
paul.thomas@waldenu.edu
THOMAS, Paul .... 901-333-5760. 461 F
pthomas@southwest.tn.edu
THOMAS, Paulette .... 407-277-0311. 103 C
pathomas@evergladesuniversity.edu
THOMAS, Pauline .... 870-575-8970... 24 E
thomas@uapb.edu
THOMAS, Peter .... 419-530-4235. 392 B
peter.thomas@utoledo.edu
THOMAS, Peter, A .... 508-831-6074. 238 F
pthomas@wpi.edu
THOMAS, Phil .... 608-822-2721. 541 C
pthomas@swtc.edu
THOMAS,
Randi Malcolm .... 513-529-4151. 384 G
randi.thomas@miamioh.edu
THOMAS, Renard .... 661-362-3327... 40 E
renard.thomas@canyons.edu
THOMAS, Rhonda .... 662-329-7138. 268 E
rthomas@acadsupp.muw.edu
THOMAS, Rikki .... 757-727-5250. 505 F
rikki.thomas@hamptonu.edu
THOMAS, Ronald, C .... 718-262-2332. 319 F
rthomas@york.cuny.edu
THOMAS, Ronald, R .... 253-879-3201. 524 F
president@pugetsound.edu
THOMAS, Rosemary, M .. 301-687-4161. 220 C
rhomas@frostburg.edu
THOMAS, Ryan .... 801-626-7931. 497 D
ryanthomas2@weber.edu
THOMAS, Sam .... 662-915-7690. 270 B
sethomas@olemiss.edu
THOMAS, Samantha .... 214-768-3603. 481 A
thomassa@smu.edu
THOMAS, Sandra .... 760-252-2411... 29 I
sthomas@barstow.edu
THOMAS, Scott .... 909-621-8075... 39 C
scott.thomas@cgu.edu
THOMAS, Stacey .... 765-455-9391. 168 A
stathoma@iuk.edu
THOMAS, Stephen, W ...... 252-328-4400. 367 B
thomass@ecu.edu
THOMAS, Steve .... 432-685-4521. 476 G
steve@midland.edu
THOMAS, Stuart .... 970-339-6232... 78 C
stuart.thomas@aims.edu
THOMAS, Susan, L .... 618-650-3674. 159 H
suthoma@siue.edu
THOMAS, Suzanne, W .... 330-471-8239. 383 D
sthomas@malone.edu
THOMAS, Tammi, L .... 301-860-3506. 220 A
tthomas@bowiestate.edu
THOMAS, Teresa, W .... 615-898-2600. 459 D
teresa.thomas@mtsu.edu
THOMAS, Terri .... 607-436-3388. 343 E
terri.thomas@oneonta.edu
THOMAS, Todd .... 423-652-6045. 455 I
tthomas@king.edu
THOMAS, Todd, S .... 518-464-8526. 324 B
tthomas@excelsior.edu
THOMAS, Tracey .... 609-894-9311. 299 I
tthomas@bcc.edu
THOMAS, Tracy .... 205-226-4902..... 2 C
tthomas@bsc.edu
THOMAS, Tyrone .... 843-355-4152. 449 F
thomast@wiltech.edu
THOMAS, Valerie, A .... 410-455-3142. 219 D
valerie.thomas@umbc.edu
THOMAS, Verian .... 850-599-3505. 114 K
verian.thomas@famu.edu
THOMAS, W, E .... 252-335-3292. 367 C
wethomas@mail.ecsu.edu
THOMAS, Wanda .... 330-675-8821. 382 B
wthomas4@kent.edu
THOMAS, Wilbert, L .... 757-727-5356. 505 F
bill.thomas@hamptonu.edu
THOMAS, William, A .... 713-313-6816. 485 F
thomaswa@tsu.edu
THOMAS, Willie, G .... 302-259-6050... 93 E
wthomas6@dtcc.edu
THOMAS, Yvette .... 317-738-8100. 165 I
ythomas@franklincollege.edu
THOMAS FRATICELLI,
Cynthia .... 787-265-3883. 554 E
cynthia.thomas@upr.edu
THOMAS-GLOVER,
Linda .... 757-789-1775. 512 D
lglover@es.vccs.edu
THOMAS-GOLDEN,
Tammalyn, M .... 919-516-4533. 366 C
tgolden@st-aug.edu
THOMAS-LARUE, Kim .... 865-694-6681. 461 D
kthomas@pstcc.edu
THOMAS-MOBLEY,
Linda .... 619-684-8843... 56 C
lthomas@newschoolarch.edu
THOMAS-PARROTT,
Sharon .... 630-353-3832. 144 A
stparrott@devry.edu
THOMAS-SMITH,
E. Joahanne .... 936-261-2175. 482 F
ejthomas-smith@pvamu.edu
THOMAS TROUPE,
Jennifer .... 978-921-4242. 234 C
jennifer.troupe@montserrat.edu
THOMAS-WILLIAMS,
Regina .... 912-443-5708. 131 D
rthomas@savannahtech.edu
THOMASI, SR.,
Edward, J .... 203-773-8506... 87 G
ethomasi@albertus.edu
THOMASON, Brian .... 310-506-7269... 58 H
brian.thomason@pepperdine.edu
THOMASON, Chris .... 870-777-5722... 25 B
Chris.Thomason@uacch.edu
THOMASON, Don, A ...... 513-244-8162. 376 J
don.thomason@ccuniversity.edu
THOMASON, Mary .... 870-574-4719... 23 G
mthomaso@sautech.edu
THOMASON, Scotty .... 530-938-5220... 41 A
sthomason1@siskiyous.edu
THOMASSON, Kim .... 859-253-0621. 198 E
kthomasson@national-college.edu
THOMASSON, Susan ...... 704-355-3921. 353 D
susan.thomasson@carolinas.org
THOMES, Christopher, P 850-747-3250. 106 H
cthomes@gulfcoast.edu
THOMEY, Bane .... 262-564-3096. 540 A
thomeyb@gtc.edu
THOMLINSON, Gene ...... 417-865-2815. 274 B
thomlinsong@evangel.edu
THOMPSOM, Cathy .... 423-614-8200. 455 L
cthompson@leeuniversity.edu
THOMPSON, Adelia, P ... 757-594-8759. 503 M
adelia.thompson@cnu.edu
THOMPSON, Al .... 715-346-2481. 538 A
al.thompson@uwsp.edu
THOMPSON, Alan .... 406-447-6941. 287 A
thompsona@umhelena.edu
THOMPSON, Allison, L .. 318-342-6917. 208 E
althompson@ulm.edu
THOMPSON, Alton .... 302-857-6100... 93 C
athompson@desu.edu
THOMPSON, Amber .... 719-336-1592... 82 R
amber.thompson@lamarcc.edu
THOMPSON, Amber .... 828-395-1443. 361 C
athompson@isothermal.edu
THOMPSON, Amy .... 229-732-5938. 120 D
amythompson@andrewcollege.edu
THOMPSON, Amy .... 620-278-4228. 190 I
athompson@sterling.edu
THOMPSON, Amy .... 315-568-3129. 333 C
athompson@nycc.edu
THOMPSON, Amy .... 718-940-5713. 339 B
althompson@sjcny.edu
THOMPSON, Andrew ...... 605-455-6076. 450 I
athompson@olc.edu
THOMPSON, Andy .... 319-656-2447. 182 D
THOMPSON, Ann .... 270-706-8444. 195 A
ann.thompson@kctcs.edu
THOMPSON, Ann .... 734-487-0250. 242 D
athomp51@emich.edu
THOMPSON, Annette ...... 210-283-5091. 490 A
athompson@uiwtx.edu
THOMPSON, April .... 607-777-2804. 341 E
athompso@binghamton.edu
THOMPSON, Barbara ...... 334-556-2629..... 3 N
bthompson@wallace.edu
THOMPSON, Barbara, A . 260-359-4049. 166 O
bthompson@huntington.edu
THOMPSON, Beth .... 903-434-8106. 477 J
bthompson@ntcc.edu
THOMPSON, Bill, T .... 919-735-5151. 364 H
billt@waynecc.edu
THOMPSON, Bob .... 405-912-9453. 395 K
bthompson@hc.edu
THOMPSON, Bradley ...... 901-751-8453. 457 B
bthompson@mabts.edu
THOMPSON, Brenda .... 512-863-1290. 481 I
THOMPSON, Brenda, L .. 812-888-4125. 174 F
bthompson@vinu.edu
THOMPSON, Brenda, S .. 304-293-3837. 530 D
brenda.thompson@mail.wvu.edu
THOMPSON, Brian, L ..... 904-819-6249. 103 E
bthompson@flagler.edu
THOMPSON, Carey .... 901-843-3000. 458 E
THOMPSON, Carlene, M 317-274-7617. 168 D
hra@iupui.edu
THOMPSON, Carlyle .... 718-270-4987. 319 A
carlyle@mec.cuny.edu
THOMPSON, Carmela ..... 716-878-5519. 343 A
thompsc@buffalostate.edu
THOMPSON, Carrie .... 615-966-5250. 456 B
carrie.thompson@lipscomb.edu
THOMPSON, Cesarina .... 413-205-3056. 221 F
cesarina.thompson@aic.edu
THOMPSON, Chad .... 412-995-7643. 131 H
cthompson@southuniversity.edu
THOMPSON, Charles, G . 413-542-2221. 221 G
cgthompson@amherst.edu
THOMPSON, Charles, S . 423-652-4742. 455 I
csthomps@king.edu

THOMPSON, Chavon ...... 803-508-7247. 440 G
thompsonc4@atc.edu
THOMPSON, Cheryl .... 402-559-2792. 292 J
cbthompson@unmc.edu
THOMPSON,
Christopher, J .... 651-962-5771. 265 C
cjthompson@stthomas.edu
THOMPSON, Claudette ... 305-386-9900. 102 D
cthompson@cci.edu
THOMPSON, Cole, P ...... 970-207-4500... 86 G
THOMPSON, Corinne, B 802-656-7898. 500 F
corinne.thompson@uvm.edu
THOMPSON, Craig .... 646-888-6639. 329 J
thompsonc@mskcc.org
THOMPSON, Cynthia ...... 217-206-6665. 161 E
thompson.cynthia@uis.edu
THOMPSON, D. D .... 423-442-2001. 454 L
thompson@hiwassee.edu
THOMPSON, Daniel, J ... 651-290-6362. 265 F
dan.thompson@wmitchell.edu
THOMPSON, Darlene ...... 334-214-4807..... 2 H
darlene.thompson@cv.edu
THOMPSON, Dave .... 714-546-7600... 39 I
dthompson@coastline.edu
THOMPSON, David .... 304-424-8303. 530 E
dave.thompson@wvup.edu
THOMPSON, Dawn .... 503-777-7500. 407 E
dthomp@reed.edu
THOMPSON, Dawn, M ... 302-831-3266... 94 B
dawnt@udel.edu
THOMPSON, Deanna ...... 815-802-8552. 149 C
dthompson@kcc.edu
THOMPSON, Debbi, N ... 864-597-4208. 449 I
thompsondn@wofford.edu
THOMPSON, Deborah, J 864-833-8278. 446 D
dthompson@presby.edu
THOMPSON, Deborah, L 269-337-7318. 244 K
Debbie.Roberts@kzoo.edu
THOMPSON, Debra .... 480-731-8510... 14 I
debra.thompson@domail.maricopa.edu
THOMPSON, Delores ...... 575-492-2519. 310 G
dthompson@nmjc.edu
THOMPSON, Dennis, F .. 580-774-3764. 400 B
dennis.thompson@swosu.edu
THOMPSON, Desiree ...... 207-454-1020. 211 B
dthompson@wccc.me.edu
THOMPSON, Diane .... 518-587-2100. 346 A
diane.thompson@esc.edu
THOMPSON, Dick .... 207-973-3224. 212 A
dick.thompson@maine.edu
THOMPSON, Donovan ..... 718-289-5796. 317 B
donovan.thompson@bcc.cuny.edu
THOMPSON, E. Maria .... 607-436-2517. 343 E
thompsem@oneonta.edu
THOMPSON, Edward, J .. 516-323-4602. 331 J
ethompson@molloy.edu
THOMPSON, Eichelle ..... 414-256-1210. 535 A
thompsoe@mtmary.edu
THOMPSON, Eileen .... 617-879-2413. 238 C
ethompson@wheelock.edu
THOMPSON, Emily .... 816-604-3022. 277 G
emily.thompson@mcckc.edu
THOMPSON, Eric .... 970-223-2669... 82 F
ethompson@ibmc.edu
THOMPSON, Eric .... 617-369-3486. 236 F
ethompson@smfa.edu
THOMPSON, Fannie, G .. 301-736-3631. 216 B
fannie.thompson@msbbcs.edu
THOMPSON, Gary .... 701-845-7197. 372 A
gary.thompson@vcsu.edu
THOMPSON, Gary, B ...... 518-783-2550. 340 J
thompson@siena.edu
THOMPSON, III,
George, R .... 803-938-3839. 448 F
bobt@uscsumter.edu
THOMPSON, Greg .... 843-349-5247. 444 F
greg.thompson@hgtc.edu
THOMPSON, Greg .... 513-861-6400. 390 C
greg.thompson@myunion.edu
THOMPSON, Gregory ...... 850-644-5260. 115 C
gwthompson@fsu.edu
THOMPSON, III,
H. Lawrence .... 724-266-3838. 434 J
lthompson@tsm.edu
THOMPSON, Haley .... 580-477-2000. 401 J
haley.thompson@wosc.edu
THOMPSON, Helen .... 330-287-1231. 386 F
thompson.959@osu.edu
THOMPSON, Herbert ...... 386-481-2661... 99 C
thompsoh@cookman.edu
THOMPSON, Howard .... 563-425-5307. 183 B
thompsonh@uiu.edu
THOMPSON, J. Michael . 209-228-4482... 71 D
jthompson@UCMerced.edu
THOMPSON, Jack .... 479-619-4140... 22 C
jthompson19@nwacc.edu
THOMPSON, James .... 301-736-3631. 216 B
james.thompson@msbbcs.edu
THOMPSON, James, E ... 573-882-4378. 283 C
thompsonje@missouri.edu
THOMPSON, James, P ... 865-974-7262. 463 C
jthompson@utk.edu
THOMPSON, Jamie .... 210-999-7547. 488 C
Jamie.Thompson@trinity.edu
THOMPSON, Jane, W ...... 412-624-6576. 435 C
jthompson@cfo.pitt.edu
THOMPSON, Janet .... 908-526-1200. 305 B
jthompso@raritanval.edu
THOMPSON, Jean-Noel .. 334-386-7300...... 3 H
jthompson@faulkner.edu
THOMPSON, Jeanne, E .. 715-394-8598. 538 C
jthomp51@uwsuper.edu
THOMPSON, Jeff, S .... 256-824-2605...... 8 F
jeff.thompson@uah.edu
THOMPSON, Jeffrey, M .. 909-537-5315... 34 E
jthompso@csusb.edu
THOMPSON, Jeffrey, M .. 909-537-5058... 34 E
jthompso@csusb.edu
THOMPSON, Jeffrey, S ... 775-784-4591. 294 J
thompson@physics.unr.edu
THOMPSON, Jennifer ..... 815-921-4272. 157 A
j.thompson@rockvalleycollege.edu
THOMPSON, Jennifer ..... 605-677-5339. 451 F
jennifer.thompson@usd.edu
THOMPSON, Jeremiah ... 847-628-2016. 149 B
jeremiah.thompson@judsonu.edu
THOMPSON, Jeremy ...... 617-349-8598. 228 B
jthomp18@lesley.edu
THOMPSON, Jerry .... 252-536-7265. 361 A
gthompson605@halifaxcc.edu
THOMPSON, Jerry, L ..... 501-882-4523... 19 M
jthompson@asub.edu
THOMPSON, Jesse, M ... 617-228-2208. 231 C
jthompson@bhcc.mass.edu
THOMPSON, Jill, E .... 336-841-9044. 355 C
jthompso@highpoint.edu
THOMPSON, Jim .... 585-275-2158. 349 C
jathompson@admin.rochester.edu
THOMPSON, Joan .... 781-595-6768. 228 C
jthompson@mariancourt.edu
THOMPSON, Joan .... 478-218-3298. 122 F
jthompson@centralgatech.edu
THOMPSON, Joanna .... 304-327-4050. 529 D
jthompson@bluefieldstate.edu
THOMPSON, Joe, H .... 563-387-1575. 180 M
thompsjo@luther.edu
THOMPSON, John .... 562-938-4102... 51 D
jthompson@lbcc.edu
THOMPSON, John .... 252-985-5218. 365 D
jthompson@ncwc.edu
THOMPSON, John .... 817-257-7860. 484 I
j.thompson@tcu.edu
THOMPSON, Jonathan ... 270-706-8456. 195 A
jonathan.thompson@kctcs.edu
THOMPSON, Julie, G ..... 828-694-1752. 358 C
juliet@blueridge.edu
THOMPSON, Karen, S .... 252-328-6212. 367 B
thompsonkar@ecu.edu
THOMPSON, Karla, K ..... 575-234-9265. 311 A
kthompso@nmsu.edu
THOMPSON, Kathy .... 641-628-5186. 176 E
thompsonk@central.edu
THOMPSON, Kelly, M ..... 252-399-6314. 352 F
kthompson@barton.edu
THOMPSON, Kelsel .... 214-379-5532. 478 D
kthompson@pqc.edu
THOMPSON, Kenira .... 787-840-2575. 552 A
THOMPSON, Kevin, A .... 270-384-8400. 197 D
thompsonk@lindsey.edu
THOMPSON, Kevin, J ..... 701-483-2004. 371 D
thompson@dsufamily.com
THOMPSON, Kim .... 206-546-6910. 523 F
kthompson@shoreline.edu
THOMPSON, Kirsten .... 617-951-2350. 234 G
kirsten.thompson@necb.edu
THOMPSON, Kristy .... 801-818-8900. 496 F
kristyt@provocollege.edu
THOMPSON, LaDarius .... 302-736-2458... 94 C
ladarius.thompson@wesley.edu
THOMPSON, Larry, R ..... 941-359-7601. 111 O
lthompson@ringling.edu
THOMPSON, Laurie, L ... 214-648-2626. 493 E
laurie.thompson@utsouthwestern.edu
THOMPSON, Lenora, H .. 757-683-4401. 507 N
lthompso@odu.edu
THOMPSON, Leroy .... 918-360-9694. 394 D
thompsol@bacone.edu
THOMPSON, Lisa .... 425-640-1148. 519 D
lthompson@edcc.edu
THOMPSON, Lonnie .... 386-506-3824. 101 G
thompsl@DaytonaState.edu
THOMPSON, Lynda .... 508-588-9100. 232 A
THOMPSON, Lynda, N ..... 540-863-2837. 512 B
lthompson@dslcc.edu
THOMPSON, Lynn .... 386-481-2216... 99 C
thompsol@cookman.edu
THOMPSON, Marcy .... 847-214-7486. 144 F
mthompson@elgin.edu
THOMPSON, Mark .... 641-683-5306. 179 A
mark.thompson@indianhills.edu
THOMPSON, Mark .... 732-906-4252. 303 B
MThompson@middlesexcc.edu
THOMPSON, Mark .... 315-228-7385. 320 F
mdthompson@colgate.edu
THOMPSON, Mark, A ...... 203-582-8914... 91 A
mark.thompson@quinnipiac.edu
THOMPSON, Matt .... 641-782-1413. 182 I
thompson@swcciowa.edu
THOMPSON, Matt .... 641-683-5185. 179 A
matt.thompson@indianhills.edu
THOMPSON, Matt .... 641-782-1413. 182 I
thompson@swcciowa.edu
THOMPSON, Matthew, R 785-827-5541. 188 C
matt.thompson@kwu.edu
THOMPSON, Maxine .... 315-464-5234. 342 E
thompsms@upstate.edu
THOMPSON, Maynard ..... 812-855-2074. 167 F
thompson@indiana.edu
THOMPSON, Michael ...... 309-556-3760. 148 B
mthomps4@iwu.edu
THOMPSON, Michael ...... 404-687-4530. 123 C
thompsonm@ctsnet.edu
THOMPSON, Michael ...... 850-599-3301. 114 K
michael.thompson@famu.edu
THOMPSON, Michael ...... 601-484-8700. 267 G
mthompso@meridiancc.edu
THOMPSON, Michele ...... 804-290-4231. 510 B
mthompson@stratford.edu
THOMPSON, Michelle ..... 386-481-2769... 99 C
thompsonmi@cookman.edu
THOMPSON, Nancy .... 620-343-4600. 186 E
nthompson@fhtc.edu
THOMPSON, Nancy, R .... 315-859-4020. 325 E
nthompso@hamilton.edu
THOMPSON, Naomi .... 401-874-7077. 440 D
Naomi@mail.uri.edu
THOMPSON, Natalie .... 607-778-5477. 315 I
thompsonm@sunybroome.edu
THOMPSON, Nina .... 503-760-3131. 402 B
nina@birthingway.edu
THOMPSON, Pat .... 972-825-4670. 481 F
pthompson@sagu.edu
THOMPSON, Patricia, A . 607-735-1730. 323 H
pthompson@elmira.edu
THOMPSON, Paul .... 443-885-3300. 217 A
paul.thompson@morgan.edu
THOMPSON, Paula, C ..... 757-823-2291. 507 M
pcthompson@nsu.edu
THOMPSON, Phyllis .... 803-705-4720. 441 C
thompsonp@benedict.edu
THOMPSON, Phyllis, A .. 423-439-4125. 459 C
thompsop@etsu.edu
THOMPSON, Priscilla, C 301-322-0462. 217 F
thompspc@pgcc.edu
THOMPSON, Rebecca ..... 808-245-8384. 136 H
ret@hawaii.edu
THOMPSON, Richard, H . 914-654-5421. 320 H
rthompson@cnr.edu
THOMPSON, Richard, P . 989-964-4166. 249 G
thompson@svsu.edu
THOMPSON, Robert .... 920-206-2377. 533 U
rthompson@mbbc.edu
THOMPSON, Robert, J ... 301-295-3013. 545 C
robert.thompson@usuhs.edu
THOMPSON, Robin .... 909-607-3822... 59 G
robin_thompson@pitzer.edu
THOMPSON, Roger, J .... 541-346-2542. 406 D
rjt@uoregon.edu
THOMPSON, Ronald, C .. 864-294-2092. 444 C
ron.thompson@furman.edu
THOMPSON, Ronda .... 573-897-5000. 276 E
THOMPSON, Ronelle ...... 605-274-4921. 449 K
ronelle.thompson@augie.edu
THOMPSON, Sabrina ...... 404-656-2202. 134 A
sabrina.thompson@usg.edu
THOMPSON, Samantha .. 651-855-6302. 450 G
sthompson@national.edu
THOMPSON, Sara, M ..... 202-319-5256... 94 G
thompson@cua.edu
THOMPSON, Sarah .... 303-724-1679... 86 A
sarah.thompson@ucdenver.edu
THOMPSON, Scott .... 530-242-7512... 65 G
sthompson@shastacollege.edu
THOMPSON, Seth .... 607-844-8222. 347 I
thompss@tc3.edu
THOMPSON, Sharling ..... 803-705-4721. 441 C
thompsons@benedict.edu
THOMPSON, Sharon .... 215-751-8450. 413 I
sthompson@ccp.edu
THOMPSON, Sharon .... 910-755-7474. 358 D
thompsons@brunswickcc.edu
THOMPSON, Sheila .... 517-586-3013. 241 A
sthompson@cleary.edu
THOMPSON, Sheila .... 303-556-3022... 83 D
sthomp83@msudenver.edu
THOMPSON, Stuart .... 509-963-1004. 517 F
Thompsst@cwu.edu
THOMPSON, Susan .... 843-349-7818. 444 F
susan.thompson@hgtc.edu
THOMPSON, Susie .... 812-535-5220. 172 F
sthompson@smwc.edu
THOMPSON, Suzanne .... 301-369-2800. 213 G
sthompson@capitol-college.edu
THOMPSON, Teresa .... 912-478-1863. 126 C
thompson@georgiasouthern.edu
THOMPSON, Teresa .... 520-621-4608... 18 F
tlthompson@email.arizona.edu
THOMPSON, Teresa .... 734-432-5465. 246 B
tthompson@madonna.edu
THOMPSON, Teri .... 859-985-3524. 192 F
thompsonte@berea.edu
THOMPSON, Terri .... 443-627-7533. 265 D
terri.thompson@laureate.net
THOMPSON, Terry, E ..... 509-527-5777. 525 E
thompste@whitman.edu
THOMPSON, Thomas .... 928-428-8376... 13 J
thomas.thompson@eac.edu
THOMPSON, Tola .... 850-599-3225. 114 K
tola.thompson@famu.edu
THOMPSON, Traci .... 719-219-9636... 79 B
THOMPSON, Travis .... 501-279-4464... 21 C
thompson@harding.edu
THOMPSON, Troy, J .... 336-841-9404. 355 C
tthompso@highpoint.edu
THOMPSON, Venesia ...... 415-405-4061... 35 E
venesia@sfsu.edu
THOMPSON, Vinton .... 212-343-1234. 331 D
vthompson@mcny.edu
THOMPSON, Virginia ...... 918-781-7275. 394 D
thompsonv@bacone.edu
THOMPSON, Walter .... 603-880-8308. 298 A
jthompson@thomasmorecollege.edu
THOMPSON, William .... 856-374-4931. 300 B
wthompson@camdencc.edu
THOMPSON, William .... 859-572-5768. 198 I
thompsonw4@nku.edu
THOMPSON, William, R . 717-299-7793. 434 A
thompson@stevenscollege.edu
THOMPSON, Zoe .... 804-330-0111. 503 G
directorcrim@centura.edu
THOMPSON-BRADSHAW,
Adriane .... 419-772-2433. 386 D
a-thompson@onu.edu
THOMPSON BROWN,
Kim .... 912-478-5224. 126 C
kthompson@georgiasouthern.edu
THOMPSON-SELLERS,
Ingrid .... 678-891-2773. 125 G
ingrid.thompson-sellers@gpc.edu
THOMPSON SMITH,
Amy .... 814-838-7673. 416 G
athompson@fortisinstitute.edu
THOMPSON-STACY,
Cheryl .... 540-868-7101. 512 H
cstacy@lfcc.edu
THOMPSON-TWEEDY,
Sara .... 845-434-5750. 347 A
stweedy@sullivan.suny.edu
THOMPSON-WELLS,
Amy, C .... 270-384-8065. 197 D
thompsoa@lindsey.edu
THOMS, Jacqueline .... 410-626-2513. 217 G
jacqueline.thoms@sjca.edu
THOMSEN, Cristina, M ... 817-202-6732. 481 E
thomsenc@swau.edu
THOMSEN, Marilyn .... 951-785-2000... 50 B
mthomsen@lasierra.edu
THOMSEN, Pamela .... 218-855-8129. 258 B
pthoms@clcmn.edu
THOMSEN, Sandy .... 818-364-7750... 52 A
thomsens@lamission.edu
THOMSON, David, T .... 870-230-5129... 21 D
thomsond@hsu.edu
THOMSON, Gregg .... 925-631-4754... 61 F
get1@stmarys-ca.edu
THOMSON, J, M .... 216-987-3944. 378 D
j.michael.thomson@tri-c.edu
THOMSON, Kendra .... 405-491-6312. 399 K
kthomson@snu.edu
THOMSON, Lisa .... 407-646-2010. 111 Q
lthomson@rollins.edu
THOMSON, Margaret .... 859-442-1172. 195 B
margaret.thomson@kctcs.edu
THOMSON, Thomas, J ... 864-488-4500. 444 L
tthomson@limestone.edu
THOR, James, A .... 716-878-4312. 343 A
thorja@buffalostate.edu
THOR, Linda, M .... 650-949-6100... 44 L
thorlinda@fhda.edu
THOR, Nadine, L .... 810-762-7904. 244 Q
nthor@kettering.edu
THOR, Veronica .... 620-624-1951. 190 F
veronica.thor@sccc.edu
THORDARSON, Karen ..... 310-377-5501... 53 F
kthodarson@marymountcalifornia.edu
THORESON, Jay, H .... 218-299-3020. 255 A
career@cord.edu
THORIN, Suzanne, E ...... 315-443-2573. 347 C
sethorin@syr.edu
THORIUS, James, D .... 515-961-1532. 182 E
jim.thorius@simpson.edu

THORN, Andre 907-786-4080... 10 H
eathorn@uaa.alaska.edu
THORN, George 908-737-5050. 302 F
gthorn@kean.edu
THORN, Lawrence, B 318-342-5170. 208 E
thorn@ulm.edu
THORN, Robert 724-938-4432. 428 A
thorn@calu.edu
THORN, Sharon 610-399-2550. 428 B
sthorn@cheyney.edu
THORN, Trevor 936-294-1584. 487 A
trevor@shsu.edu
THORNBRUGH, Jean 918-610-8888. 399 G
jtthornbrugh@stgregorys.edu
THORNBURG, Gregory, W 843-349-2037. 442 E
gthornbu@coastal.edu
THORNBURG, L. Steve 704-669-4004. 359 D
thornburg@clevelandcc.edu
THORNBURG, Marlon 620-252-7550. 185 O
marlont@coffeyville.edu
THORNBURRY, Gregory, A 212-659-7207. 328 E
gthornburry@tkc.edu
THORNBURY, Gregory 731-661-5082. 462 F
gthornbu@uu.edu
THORNBURY, Kimberly 731-661-5090. 462 F
kthornbu@uu.edu
THORNDIKE, Sara 314-514-3103. 156 B
sara.thorndike@principia.edu
THORNDYKE, Luanne 508-856-3844. 229 C
luanne.thorndyke@umassmed.edu
THORNE, Bradford, E 617-745-3894. 225 G
bradford.e.thorne@enc.edu
THORNE, Debbie 512-245-7966. 487 C
dm29@txstate.edu
THORNE, Debbie, M 512-245-2322. 487 C
dm29@txstate.edu
THORNE, Debbie, M 512-245-1217. 487 C
dm29@txstate.edu
THORNE, Geneva 202-687-5440... 95 E
thorneg@georgetown.edu
THORNELL, John 256-765-4258.... 9 C
jthornell@una.edu
THORNELL, Susan 617-735-9824. 226 B
thornsu@emmanuel.edu
THORNGREN, Jill 605-688-6181. 452 B
jill.thorngren@sdstate.edu
THORNHILL, Brenda 903-983-8204. 475 E
bthornhill@kilgore.edu
THORNHILL, Mike, D 828-689-1298. 356 F
mthornhill@mhc.edu
THORNHILL, Paula 318-342-1032. 208 E
thornhill@ulm.edu
THORNHILL-HUDSON, Valerie 617-879-2211. 238 C
vhudson@wheelock.edu
THORNLEY, Mary 843-574-6241. 447 E
mary.thornley@tridenttech.edu
THORNQUIST, Cynthia, J 406-447-4389. 285 G
cthornqu@carroll.edu
THORNS, Mamie, T 989-964-4397. 249 G
mtthorns@svsu.edu
THORNSBERRY, Thelmarie 606-368-6041. 191 J
thelmariethornsberry@alc.edu
THORNTHWAITE, Kevin 205-665-6351..... 9 B
kthornthwaite@montevallo.edu
THORNTON, Amy 608-785-9262. 541 E
thorntona@westerntc.edu
THORNTON, Barry 660-263-3900. 272 A
bthornton@cccb.edu
THORNTON, Billy 601-925-3373. 268 A
bthornto@mc.edu
THORNTON, Brian 334-229-6994..... 1 D
bthornton@alasu.edu
THORNTON, Brittany 620-331-4100. 187 G
bthornton@indycc.edu
THORNTON, Bryan, C 406-243-1234. 286 H
bthornton@umtbookstore.com
THORNTON, Danielle 407-628-5870. 102 K
dthornton@cci.edu
THORNTON, Dee 904-743-1122. 107 T
dthornto@jones.edu
THORNTON, Donna 848-932-7061. 306 A
dthornton@alumni.rutgers.edu
THORNTON, Evan 256-216-3310..... 1 F
evan.thornton@athens.edu
THORNTON, George 610-526-6049. 417 H
gthornton@harcum.edu
THORNTON, Glenda 216-687-2475. 377 F
g.thornton@csuohio.edu
THORNTON, Hannah 512-492-3017. 466 B
hthornton@aoma.edu
THORNTON, James 937-484-1297. 392 C
jthornton@urbana.edu
THORNTON, Jessica 985-448-7920. 203 B
jessica.thornton@fletcher.edu
THORNTON, Julie 507-222-4075. 254 D
jthornto@carleton.edu
THORNTON, Linda 507-222-4171. 254 D
lthornto@carleton.edu
THORNTON, Lynn, L 806-371-5044. 465 E
llthornton@actx.edu
THORNTON, Matha 434-947-8119. 508 D
mthornton@randolphcollege.edu
THORNTON, Melanie 912-284-2565. 130 B
mthornton@okefenokeetech.edu
THORNTON, Mona 803-705-4594. 441 C
thorntonm@benedict.edu
THORNTON, Paul 239-425-3274. 115 A
pthornton@fgcu.edu
THORNTON, Tracey 270-247-8521. 197 H
tthornton@midcontinent.edu
THORNTON, Willie 973-443-8929. 301 J
wthornton@fdu.edu
THORNTON, Yevette 941-487-4417. 115 D
ythornton@ncf.edu
THORNTON, Zoe 641-844-5706. 179 J
zoe.thornton@iavalley.edu
THOROUGHMAN, David 740-351-3888. 388 N
dthoroughman@shawnee.edu
THORP, Herbert Holden 314-935-3000. 284 L
thorp@wustl.edu
THORP, Stephen, M 575-624-8442. 310 H
thorp@nmmi.edu
THORPE, Abigail 718-933-6700. 331 K
athorpe@monroecollege.edu
THORPE, Alayne 269-471-6581. 239 D
alayne@andrews.edu
THORPE, Alayne, D 269-471-6581. 243 G
alayne@andrews.edu
THORPE, Charles, E 315-268-4430. 320 A
cthorpe@clarkson.edu
THORPE, Melissa 610-358-4588. 424 I
thorpem@neumann.edu
THORPE, Queenston 404-225-4420. 121 B
qthorpe@atlantatech.edu
THORPE, Sima 509-313-6856. 520 A
thorpe@gu.gonzaga.edu
THORPE, Stephen, W 610-499-4117. 437 E
swthorpe@mail.widener.edu
THORSETT, Stephen 503-370-6209. 408 J
president@willamette.edu
THORSNES, Brian 541-737-3102. 406 A
brian.thorsnes@oregonstate.edu
THORSNESS, Brian, K 541-737-3102. 406 A
brian.thorsness@oregonstate.edu
THORSON, Carola 218-281-6510. 264 E
THORSON, Phil 320-308-5396. 261 B
pthorson@stcloudstate.edu
THORSTAD, Todd, M 320-222-5572. 260 H
todd.thorstad@ridgewater.edu
THORSTENSON, Deb 605-626-2530. 451 I
deb.thorstenson@northern.edu
THORSTENSON, Deb 605-626-2371. 451 I
deb.thorstenson@northern.edu
THORTON, Mike 325-574-6572. 494 K
mthornton@wtc.edu
THORUD, Jeffrey 972-385-1446. 474 T
THOTA, Vykuntapathi 804-524-5024. 515 D
vthota@vsu.edu
THRANE, Linda 713-348-6281. 479 A
thrane@rice.edu
THRASHER, Barbara, S 434-947-8143. 508 D
bthrasher@randolphcollege.edu
THRASHER, James, T 724-458-2200. 417 E
jtthrasher@gcc.edu
THRASHER, Jordan, S 770-720-5634. 130 G
jst@reinhardt.edu
THREINEN, Noni 562-902-3322... 67 H
nonithreinen@scuhs.edu
THRIFT, Jerry, L 910-755-7381. 358 D
thriftj@brunswickcc.edu
THRO, William, E 859-257-2936. 200 C
william.thro@uky.edu
THROCKMORTON, Julie 724-503-1001. 436 G
jthrockmorton@washjeff.edu
THROGMORTON, Daniel 916-563-3206... 52 K
throgmd@losrios.edu
THRONEBERRY, Angela 575-646-2431. 310 I
athroneb@nmsu.edu
THRONEBURG, Dennis 217-234-5296. 150 D
dthroneb@lakeland.cc.il.us
THROOP, Elizabeth, A 608-342-1491. 537 D
throope@uwplatt.edu
THROOP, William, M 802-287-8214. 499 D
throopw@greenmtn.edu
THROWER, Merinda 706-385-1106. 130 F
merinda.thrower@point.edu
THROWER, Minda 816-501-4057. 280 I
minda.thrower@rockhurst.edu
THROWER, Raymond, H 507-933-8809. 255 I
rthrower@gustavus.edu
THRUMAN, Michelle 815-588-3575. 146 D
michelle.thruman@highland.edu
THRUSH, Claudia 570-389-4012. 427 H
cthrush@bloomu.edu
THUHA, Permy, K 601-877-6118. 265 G
pthuha@alcorn.edu
THULIN, Andrew 805-756-2161... 32 F
athulin@calpoly.edu
THUM, Dennis, L 605-331-6777. 452 D
dennis.thum@usiouxfalls.edu
THUM, Scott, W 260-422-5561. 167 B
swthum@indianatech.edu
THUMMA, Scott 860-509-9571... 90 B
sthumma@hartsem.edu
THURBER, John, P 609-984-1155. 308 A
jthurber@tesc.edu
THURLER, Kimberly, M 617-627-3175. 237 C
kim.thurler@tufts.edu
THURLOW, III, George 805-893-4799... 72 B
george.thurlow@ia.ucsb.edu
THURLOW, Hugh 303-753-6046... 85 B
hthurlow@rmcad.edu
THURLOW-COLLEN, Mary 740-587-6775. 379 D
collen@denison.edu
THURMAN, Clifton, Q 432-837-8036. 487 B
qthurman@sulross.edu
THURMAN, Constance 309-341-5251. 141 A
cthurman@sandburg.edu
THURMAN, Jackie 937-708-5611. 393 A
jthurman@wilberforce.edu
THURMAN, Kerri, L 217-443-8850. 143 G
kthurman@dacc.edu
THURMAN, Lynne, F 580-774-3267. 400 B
lynne.thurman@swosu.edu
THURMAN, Mike 270-831-9790. 195 D
mike.thurman@kctcs.edu
THURMAN, Todd, A 580-774-3068. 400 B
todd.thurman@swosu.edu
THURMOND, Wade 636-651-1600. 281 K
wthurmond@sbc-fenton.com
THURSTON, Amy 610-917-1444. 436 C
acthurston@vfcc.edu
THURSTON, Cathryn, Q 202-231-4011. 544 L
cathryn.thurston@dodiis.mil
THURSTON, Katie, S 256-824-6042..... 8 F
katie.thurston@uah.edu
THURSTON, Maureen 720-279-8992... 82 D
mthurston@csl.org
THURY, Spencer 641-673-1088. 183 H
thurys@wmpenn.edu
THWEATT, Herbert 684-699-4834. 546 A
h.thweatt@amsamoa.edu
THYEN, Gary, L 651-962-6107. 265 C
glthyen@stthomas.edu
THYREEN, Timothy, R 724-852-7777. 437 A
thyreen@waynesburg.edu
TIAGA, Sally 760-776-7441... 40 F
stiaga@collegeofthedesert.edu
TIBBETTS, John 518-629-4552. 326 G
j.tibbetts@hvcc.edu
TIBBS, Lori, A 540-674-3615. 513 B
lnunn@nr.edu
TICE, Gene, E 270-684-9797. 200 G
gene.tice@wku.edu
TICE, Jared 252-399-6372. 352 F
jtice@barton.edu
TICHENOR, Kristin, R 508-831-6720. 238 F
tichenor@wpi.edu
TICK, Michael 859-257-1707. 200 C
michael.tick@uky.edu
TIDWELL, Daniel 206-876-6100. 523 D
dtidwell@theseattleschool.edu
TIDWELL, Jerry 731-661-5496. 462 F
tidwell@uu.edu
TIDWELL, Michael 734-487-4140. 242 D
mtidwell@emich.edu
TIEDE, David, L 563-387-1001. 180 M
president@luther.edu
TIEDEMAN, Angie 303-340-7524... 81 C
Angela.Tiedeman@ccaurora.edu
TIEDEMANN, Andrew 617-824-8540. 226 A
andrew_tiedemann@emerson.edu
TIEDT, Penny 608-785-6501. 536 G
ptiedt@uwlax.edu
TIEFENTHALER, Jill 719-389-6748... 79 D
president@coloradocollege.edu
TIEMANN, Kathleen 978-837-5000. 234 A
tiemannk@merrimack.edu
TIEMEIER, Thomas, L 563-884-5653. 182 A
tom.tiemeier@palmer.edu
TIEMEIER, Tracy 310-338-6234... 53 E
ttiemeier@lmu.edu
TIEN, Anita 617-552-0753. 224 A
anita.tien@bc.edu
TIEN, James, M 305-284-6035. 118 F
jmtien@miami.edu
TIENOU, Tite 847-317-8086. 160 M
tedsdean@tiu.edu
TIERCE, Joan 662-472-2312. 267 B
jtierce@holmescc.edu
TIERNAN, Bernadette 973-720-2463. 308 I
tiernanb@wpunj.edu
TIERNEY, Deborah, J 515-961-1699. 182 E
deb.tierney@simpson.edu
TIERNEY, JoAnn 413-662-5421. 230 C
j.tierney@mcla.edu
TIERNEY, Kathleen 610-526-5364. 410 J
ktierney01@brynmawr.edu
TIERNEY, Margaret, A 718-390-4447. 339 A
tierneym@stjohns.edu
TIERNO, Mark, J 315-655-7116. 316 E
mtierno@cazenovia.edu
TIERNO, Scott 603-668-2211. 297 I
s.tierno@snhu.edu
TIETJE, Brian 805-756-1757... 32 F
btietje@calpoly.edu
TIETJEN, Rick 845-451-1380. 322 D
r_tietje@culinary.edu
TIETZ, Leah Jo 406-444-6570. 286 G
ltietz@montana.edu
TIFFANY, David, M 716-673-3321. 342 A
david.tiffany@fredonia.edu
TIFFANY, Janice 641-784-5120. 178 F
tiffany@graceland.edu
TIFFIN, Doug 972-708-7338. 472 L
gial_dean-academic@gial.edu
TIFFIN, Phyllis 817-598-6246. 494 G
ptiffin@wc.edu
TIFFNEY, Bruce, H 805-893-3827... 72 B
bruce.tiffney@ccs.ucsb.edu
TIFONE, Jay 215-895-3120. 435 H
j.tifone@usciences.edu
TIGHE, Jan 831-656-2511. 544 M
jtighe@nps.edu
TIGHE, Peter 718-262-2351. 319 F
ptighe@york.cuny.edu
TIGNOR, Buddy 828-627-4576. 361 B
mtignor@haywood.edu
TIGUE, John, W 740-374-8716. 392 I
jtigue@wscc.edu
TIJERINA, Vanessa, J 765-641-4114. 163 L
vjtijerina@anderson.edu
TIKALSKY, Paul, J 405-744-5140. 397 H
paul.tikalsky@okstate.edu
TILDEN, Kevin 949-214-3127... 41 I
kevin.tilden@cui.edu
TILDEN, Marsha, A 740-368-3163. 387 J
matilden@owu.edu
TILFORD, Joseph 336-770-3232. 369 D
tilford@uncsa.edu
TILGHMAN, Patricia, E 410-651-6449. 219 E
petilghman@umes.edu
TILL, Brian 513-745-3528. 393 H
tillb@xavier.edu
TILL, Ellen, P 850-474-2080. 117 B
etill@uwf.edu
TILL, Kimberly, B 214-887-5061. 471 F
ktill@dts.edu
TILL, Stacey 636-227-2100. 276 F
stacey.till@logan.edu
TILLAR, JR., Thomas, C 540-231-6285. 515 C
ttillar@vt.edu
TILLARD, Bill 386-506-4433. 101 G
tillarw@DaytonaState.edu
TILLBERG, Rebecca 310-287-4361... 52 F
tillberw@wlac.edu
TILLER, Matt 615-966-6190. 456 B
matt.tiller@lipscomb.edu
TILLERY, Carmen 812-237-3888. 167 A
carmen.tillery@indstate.edu
TILLERY, Mariann, W 336-841-9286. 355 C
mtillery@highpoint.edu
TILLETT, Guy 605-394-4976. 450 G
gtillett@national.edu
TILLETT, Kerry 609-771-3139. 300 E
thompsok@tcnj.edu
TILLEY, Genoria 225-216-8292. 202 H
tilleyg@mybrcc.edu
TILLEY, Jeff 979-830-4129. 467 I
jeff.tilley@blinn.edu
TILLEY, Neil 828-689-1306. 356 F
ntilley@mhc.edu
TILLINGHAST, David 508-531-6140. 229 D
dtillinghast@bridgew.edu
TILLIPMAN, David, A 310-338-7880... 53 E
david.tillipman@lmu.edu
TILLMAN, Henry 225-771-5497. 206 I
henry_tillman@sus.edu
TILLMAN, John, P 209-667-3646... 35 B
jtillman1@csustan.edu
TILLMAN, Keith 815-280-2385. 149 A
ktillman@jjc.edu
TILLMAN, Rosalyn, P 865-329-3101. 461 D
rtillman@pstcc.edu
TILLMAN, JR., Walter, T 225-771-4680. 206 I
walter_tillman@subr.edu
TILLOTSON, Jeanette 607-778-5195. 315 I
tillotsonjo@sunybroome.edu
TILMA, Lisa 316-295-5525. 186 H
lisa_tilma@friends.edu
TILSON, E. Vincent 704-233-8115. 370 G
tilson@wingate.edu
TILSON, Heather, L 520-206-4886... 17 A
htilson@pima.edu
TILSON, Linda 864-656-4542. 442 C
nilson@clemson.edu

TILSTRA, Luanne .... 812-877-8741. 172 C
tilstra@rose-hulman.edu
TILTON, Brent .... 715-232-2346. 538 B
tiltonb@uwstout.edu
TILTON, James .... 401-863-2721. 438 J
james_tilton@brown.edu
TILTON, Roger, L .... 803-754-4100. 443 C
TIMBERLAKE, Gregory ... 419-755-4740. 385 D
gtimberlake@ncstatecollege.edu
TIMKO, Michael, A .... 724-503-1001. 436 G
mtimko@washjeff.edu
TIMLIN, Laynee, H .... 757-455-2137. 515 H
etimlin@vwc.edu
TIMMANN, David .... 610-436-2984. 430 A
dtimmann@wcupa.edu
TIMMER, Amy .... 517-371-5140. 250 G
timmera@cooley.edu
TIMMER, JR., James ...... 616-526-6037. 240 L
jrt3@calvin.edu
TIMMERMAN, David, M . 309-457-2325. 153 D
dtimmerman@monmouthcollege.edu
TIMMERMANS, Steven ... 708-239-4791. 160 K
steven.timmermans@trnty.edu
TIMMINS, Alan, P .... 503-943-7507. 408 F
timmins@up.edu
TIMMONS, Christopher .. 670-234-5498. 547 A
christophert@nmcnet.edu
TIMMONS, George .... 518-464-8830. 324 B
gtimmons@excelsior.edu
TIMMONS, Joseph, F ..... 918-631-2710. 401 F
joseph-timmons@utulsa.edu
TIMMONS, Lora .... 815-685-6779. 156 K
ltimmons@robertmorris.edu
TIMMONS, Susan, G ...... 864-941-8307. 446 C
timmons.s@ptc.edu
TIMMONS, Tim .... 708-239-4787. 160 K
tim.timmons@trnty.edu
TIMMS, Lindsay .... 478-757-5233. 134 G
ltimms@wesleyancollege.edu
TIMPANO, Anne .... 540-654-1013. 510 J
atimpano@umw.edu
TIMPSON, Brigham, J .... 312-341-2322. 157 D
btimpson@roosevelt.edu
TIMS, Deana .... 870-512-7811... 20 B
deana_tims@asun.edu
TIMS, Ray, L .... 919-532-5523. 364 G
rltims@waketech.edu
TINAJERO, Josefina, V ... 915-747-5572. 492 A
tinajero@utep.edu
TINANT, Jason .... 605-455-6001. 450 I
jtinant@olc.edu
TINCHER-JOHNSON,
Elaine .... 262-595-2230. 537 C
johnsone@uwp.edu
TINDALL, Amanda .... 502-212-2255. 195 F
amanda.tindall@kctcs.edu
TINDALL, David, W .... 206-281-2982. 523 C
dtindall@spu.edu
TINDALL, Michelle .... 804-706-5228. 512 G
mtindall@jtcc.edu
TINDELL, Tyrone .... 703-729-8800... 96 F
TINERELLA, Vincent .... 501-977-2033... 25 C
tinerella@uaccm.edu
TING, John .... 978-934-2215. 229 B
John_Ting@uml.edu
TINGELSTAD, Erik .... 425-352-8162. 517 E
etingelstad@cascadia.edu
TINGEY, Jeff .... 208-282-4064. 138 E
tingjeff@isu.edu
TINGEY, Kent, M .... 208-282-3198. 138 E
tingkent@isu.edu
TINGLE, Caroline, D .... 386-312-4270. 112 C
carolinetingle@sjrstate.edu
TINGLEFF, Brian, P .... 515-643-6663. 181 A
btingleff@mercydesmoines.org
TINGLEY, Paula .... 207-992-4913. 210 B
tingleyp@husson.edu
TINGSON-GATUZ,
Connie .... 734-432-5883. 246 B
ctingson-gatuz@madonna.edu
TINKER, Nancy .... 860-465-5348... 87 L
tinkern@easternct.edu
TINKEY, Danya .... 412-536-1029. 420 A
dayna.tinkey@laroche.edu
TINKEY, Jim .... 412-536-1011. 420 A
jim.tinkey@laroche.edu
TINKHAM, Brenda, S ..... 252-398-6304. 353 H
tinkhb@chowan.edu
TINLING, Walter .... 301-295-6013. 545 C
walter.tinling@usuhs.edu
TINSLEY, Harold .... 410-337-6170. 215 A
htinsley@goucher.edu
TINSLEY, Vanessa .... 919-508-2048. 370 F
vtinsley@peace.edu
TINTERA, Judi, E .... 321-674-6303. 104 H
jtintera@fit.edu
TIO, Adrian .... 508-999-9295. 229 A
atio@umassd.edu
TIPMORE, Barbara .... 270-686-4530. 196 C
barbara.tipmore@kctcs.edu

TIPMORE, David .... 334-302-1013..... 5 F
dtipmore@marionmilitary.edu
TIPPENS, Darryl .... 310-506-4261... 58 H
darryl.tippens@pepperdine.edu
TIPPETT, Bryan .... 623-935-8030... 14 K
bryan.tippett@estrellamountain.edu
TIPPIN, Peggy .... 270-444-9676. 193 N
ptippin@daymarcolleg.edu
TIPPING, Sarah .... 913-266-8619. 189 I
sarah.tipping@ottawa.edu
TIPPINS, Kira .... 559-442-4600... 68 I
kira.tippins@fresnocitycollege.edu
TIPPS, Donna, F .... 256-765-4231..... 9 C
dftipps@una.edu
TIPPS, Jane .... 615-898-2670. 459 D
jane.tipps@mtsu.edu
TIPS, Jean .... 817-735-5031. 490 E
Jean.Tips@unthsc.edu
TIPTON, Alzada .... 630-617-3063. 145 A
tiptona@elmhurst.edu
TIPTON, David, K .... 859-985-3728. 192 F
tiptond@berea.edu
TIPTON, Joellen, N .... 936-294-1810. 487 A
joellen@shsu.edu
TIPTON, Ryan .... 575-492-2137. 312 M
rtipton@usw.edu
TIPTON-ROGERS, Donna 828-835-4204. 364 E
dtipton@tricounty.edu
TIRADO, Betty, M .... 607-436-2081. 343 E
tiradoem@oneonta.edu
TIRADO, Deborah .... 803-738-7601. 445 C
tiradod@midlandstech.edu
TIRONE, Shannon .... 330-941-3732. 394 A
stirone@ysu.edu
TIRPAK, Anne, M .... 773-371-5417. 141 D
atirpak@ctu.edu
TIRRELL, Matthew .... 773-834-2001. 161 B
mtirrell@uchicago.edu
TISDALE, Bradley .... 601-923-1600. 269 E
btisdale@rts.edu
TISDALE, Christy .... 207-786-6199. 209 F
ctisdale@bates.edu
TISDALE, Henry, N .... 803-535-5412. 442 B
tisdale@claflin.edu
TISDALE, James .... 843-208-8050. 448 B
jtisdale@mailbox.sc.edu
TISDALE, Travis .... 276-656-0311. 513 D
ttisdale@patrickhenry.edu
TISDALE, Verlie, A .... 803-535-5433. 442 B
vtisdale@claflin.edu
TISNADO, Carmen .... 717-291-3985. 416 J
carmen.tisnado@fandm.edu
TITLER, R. Barry .... 301-447-5357. 217 B
titler@msmary.edu
TITSWORTH, Scott .... 740-593-4828. 387 C
titswort@ohio.edu
TITSWORTH, Tobie .... 918-343-7579. 399 C
ttitsworth@rsu.edu
TITTLE, Matthew, D .... 801-524-8146. 495 O
mtittle@ldsbc.edu
TITUS, Charlie .... 617-287-7895. 228 G
charlie.titus@umb.edu
TITUS, Elizabeth .... 575-646-1508. 310 I
etitus@nmsu.edu
TITUS, Garrett .... 701-627-4738. 371 A
gtitus@fbcc.bia.edu
TITUS, Iyana .... 212-220-1236. 317 A
ititus@bmcc.cuny.edu
TITUS, Lisa .... 609-497-7756. 304 D
lisa.titus@ptsem.edu
TITUS, Sherry .... 760-744-1150... 58 D
stitus@palomar.edu
TITUS, Steven, E .... 319-385-6204. 179 K
stitus@iwc.edu
TITUS, Varkey, K .... 478-471-2724. 128 I
varkey.titus@maconstate.edu
TITUS, Winston .... 701-349-5774. 373 A
wtitus@trinitybiblecollege.edu
TITZER, Mark .... 312-362-8053. 143 H
mtitzer@depaul.edu
TIVEY, Margaret, K .... 508-289-3362. 238 E
mktivey@whoi.edu
TIWARI, Suresh .... 651-779-3493. 258 C
suresh.tiwari@century.edu
TIYAMBE ZELEZA, Paul . 203-582-8200... 91 A
TIZOL, Iris .... 787-258-1502. 548 H
itizol@columbiaco.edu
TJADEN, Scott .... 651-846-2882... 28 M
stjaden@argosy.edu
TJEERDSMA, Nel .... 660-562-1212. 279 I
ntjeerdsma@nwmissouri.edu
TKACH, Christopher .... 832-813-6824. 476 A
chris.tkach@lonestar.edu
TO, Dai, L .... 925-631-4362... 61 F
dlt4@stmarys-ca.edu
TO, Karen .... 719-389-6144... 79 D
kto@coloradocollege.edu
TOBAKOS, Leslie .... 248-645-3360. 241 G
ltobakos@cranbrook.edu
TOBEK, Alexandra, C .... 626-395-6594... 31 E
atobeck@caltech.edu

TOBEN, Bradley J, B .... 254-710-1911. 467 G
brad_toben@baylor.edu
TOBIA, Rajia, C .... 210-567-2400. 493 A
tobia@uthscsa.edu
TOBIAS, Barbara .... 330-325-6726. 385 E
btobias@neomed.edu
TOBIAS-JOHNSON,
Jaynn .... 708-239-4759. 160 K
jaynn.tobias-johnson@trnty.edu
TOBIN, Christopher .... 843-953-3694. 443 A
tobinc@cofc.edu
TOBIN, Doreen .... 570-422-3463. 428 D
dtobin@po-box.esu.edu
TOBIN, Elizabeth, H .... 217-245-3010. 146 F
etobin@ic.edu
TOBIN, Gabrielle .... 516-299-3641. 329 C
Gabrielle.Tobin@liu.edu
TOBIN, Gerry, A .... 814-824-2468. 423 J
gtobin@mercyhurst.edu
TOBIN, John, M .... 617-373-7666. 235 F
TOBIN, Kimberly .... 413-572-8030. 230 F
ktobin@westfield.ma.edu
TOBIN, Mary Ann .... 708-456-0300. 161 A
mtobin@triton.edu
TOBIN, JR., Walt .... 803-535-1202. 446 B
tobinw@octech.edu
TOBIN, William, M .... 765-658-4156. 165 F
wtobin@depauw.edu
TOBROCKE, Toby .... 518-587-2100. 346 A
toby.tobrocke@esc.edu
TOBUREN, Amy .... 608-262-0925. 536 D
atoburen@wisc.edu
TOBY, Deanne .... 270-809-4049. 198 B
dtoby@murraystate.edu
TODA, Frank .... 541-506-6103. 402 H
ftoda@cgcc.cc.or.us
TODARO, Carla .... 423-585-6956. 462 A
carla.todaro@ws.edu
TODARO, Julie, B .... 512-223-3071. 466 I
jtodaro@austincc.edu
TODD, Barbara, J .... 303-492-2459... 85 L
barbara.todd@colorado.edu
TODD, JR., Billy, R .... 214-887-5351. 471 F
btodd@dts.edu
TODD, Carl .... 413-552-2261. 231 F
ctodd@hcc.edu
TODD, Christine .... 212-799-5000. 328 B
TODD, Christine .... 440-934-3101. 385 K
ctodd@ohiobusinesscollege.edu
TODD, Christopher .... 670-234-5498. 547 A
christophert@nmcnet.edu
TODD, Darrylinn .... 312-850-7048. 142 C
dtodd4@ccc.edu
TODD, Dwayne .... 614-222-4015. 378 A
dtodd@ccad.edu
TODD, Jason, L .... 417-268-6139. 271 I
jtodd@gobbc.edu
TODD, Jimmie, L .... 806-291-1045. 494 F
toddj@wbu.edu
TODD, Jon .... 212-592-2000. 340 H
jtodd@sva.edu
TODD, Keith .... 503-777-7510. 407 E
ktodd@reed.edu
TODD, Lisa .... 937-766-4125. 375 K
toddl@cedarville.edu
TODD, Marissa .... 573-442-2211. 282 H
mtodd@stephens.edu
TODD, Patricia, A .... 315-386-7333. 345 F
toddpa@canton.edu
TODD, Sarah, E .... 315-379-3975. 345 F
todds@canton.edu
TODD, Sharon, O .... 850-872-3891. 106 H
stodd@gulfcoast.edu
TODD, Timothy, S .... 270-809-4181. 198 B
ttodd@murraystate.edu
TODESCHI, Kevin .... 757-631-8101. 502 C
ktodeschi@atlanticuniv.edu
TODHUNTER, Jody .... 903-886-5072. 483 E
jody.todhunter@tamuc.edu
TODINI, Vivian .... 212-237-8628. 318 D
vtodini@jjay.cuny.edu
TODISH, Marian .... 616-632-2959. 239 E
todismar@aquinas.edu
TODMAN, Lynn .... 312-662-4011. 139 F
ltodman@adler.edu
TODO, Howard .... 808-956-8903. 135 L
htodo@hawaii.edu
TODOKI, Gayle .... 808-947-4788. 137 E
g.todoki@wmi.edu
TODT, David .... 641-472-7000. 180 N
dtodt@mum.edu
TODT, David .... 740-351-3472. 388 N
dtodt@shawnee.edu
TOEBBEN, Martha, A .... 636-922-8243. 280 J
mtoebben@stchas.edu
TOENISKOETTER,
Richard .... 812-464-1899. 174 D
rtoeniskoe@usi.edu
TOEPPER, Lorin, K .... 608-243-5415. 540 C
ltoepper@madisoncollege.edu

TOERING, Rose .... 605-221-3211. 450 C
rtoering@kilian.edu
TOEWS, Brian, G .... 215-702-4227. 411 F
provost@cairn.edu
TOGLIA, Joan .... 914-674-7813. 330 J
jtoglia@mercy.edu
TOHLE, Paul .... 816-584-6229. 280 C
paul.tohle@park.edu
TOKAR, Stephen, A .... 317-788-4905. 173 I
tokarsa@uindy.edu
TOKARSKY, Andra, M ..... 412-578-8897. 412 G
tokarskyam@carlow.edu
TOKPAH, Christopher ..... 610-359-5106. 414 D
TOLA, Mary, A .... 301-687-4309. 220 C
mtola@frostburg.edu
TOLAND, Claude, W .... 954-308-2101... 98 G
ctoland@aii.edu
TOLAND, Jane .... 617-262-5000. 223 F
Jane.Toland@the-bac.edu
TOLANO-LEVEQUE,
Maryann .... 909-274-4525... 55 A
mtolano@mtsac.edu
TOLBERT, Arnold, J .... 305-623-1440. 104 J
arnold.tolbert@fmuniv.edu
TOLBERT, Dawn, C .... 706-233-7215. 131 E
dtolbert@shorter.edu
TOLBERT, Herb .... 530-226-4773... 66 D
htolbert@simpsonu.edu
TOLBERT, Michael .... 848-932-4371. 306 B
mtolbert@rci.rutgers.edu
TOLBERT, Stephanie, B .. 919-497-3233. 356 E
stolbert@louisburg.edu
TOLCHER, Edward, A ...... 989-774-1441. 240 N
tolch1e@cmich.edu
TOLEDO, Angelica .... 323-267-3746... 51 F
toledoa@elac.edu
TOLEDO, Diana .... 360-596-5206. 524 A
dtoledo@spscc.edu
TOLEDO, Rich .... 209-946-2211... 73 A
rtoledo@pacific.edu
TOLER, Terry .... 405-491-6314. 399 K
ttoler@snu.edu
TOLER, Trinita .... 281-283-2180. 489 C
toler@uhcl.edu
TOLER, Whiting .... 252-940-6334. 358 A
wtoler@beaufortccc.edu
TOLFA, Jill .... 415-749-4530... 62 G
jtolfa@sfai.edu
TOLIA, Sam .... 708-456-0300. 161 A
stolia@triton.edu
TOLIVER, Felicia .... 270-706-8438. 195 A
felicia.toliver@kctcs.edu
TOLIVER, Sherry .... 210-486-2212. 465 B
stoliver@alamo.edu
TOLIVER-ROBERTS,
Rita, J .... 215-670-9265. 425 J
rjtoliver@peirce.edu
TOLL, David, J .... 215-895-4982. 415 B
dtoll@drexel.edu
TOLL, Ronald, B .... 239-590-7035. 115 A
rtoll@fgcu.edu
TOLL, William .... 765-998-4931. 173 C
btoll@cse.taylor.edu
TOLLE, Melissa .... 937-512-2259. 388 O
melissa.tolle@sinclair.edu
TOLLEFSON, Allen .... 530-752-5418... 70 J
jatollefson@ucdavis.edu
TOLLEFSON, Deborah ..... 336-334-5702. 369 A
deborah_tollefson@uncc.edu
TOLLEFSON, Leah .... 218-879-0813. 258 E
leah@fdltcc.edu
TOLLESON, Jennifer .... 312-935-4244. 148 C
jtolleson@icsw.edu
TOLLESON, Joanne, P .... 770-781-6950. 128 B
jtolleso@laniertech.edu
TOLLEY, April .... 540-863-2808. 512 B
atolley@dslcc.edu
TOLLEY, Laura .... 713-646-1799. 480 J
ltolley@stcl.edu
TOLLEY, Robin .... 215-785-0111. 426 X
TOLLEY, Warren, D .... 406-756-3841. 286 B
wtolley@fvcc.edu
TOLLISON, Scott .... 662-329-7152. 268 E
stollison@bu.muw.edu
TOLLIVER, Joseph .... 315-229-5311. 339 F
jtolliver@stlawu.edu
TOLLIVER, Ona .... 903-565-5645. 492 D
otolliver@uttyler.edu
TOLMASOFF, Bill, W ...... 714-449-7823... 67 D
btolmasoff@scco.edu
TOLSMA, Robert .... 303-315-3701... 86 A
robert.tolsma@ucdenver.edu
TOLSON, Chris .... 270-789-5013. 193 D
cytolson@campbellsville.edu
TOLSON, Janice .... 252-823-5166. 360 C
tolsonj@edgecombe.edu
TOLSON, Renae .... 850-201-6074. 117 D
tolsonr@tcc.fl.edu
TOLSON, Stephanie .... 636-922-8512. 280 J
stolson@stchas.edu

TOMA, Abe 808-544-0209. 135 F atoma@hpu.edu
TOMAN, Janelle 605-773-3455. 451 E janelle.toman@sdbor.edu
TOMAN, Sherry 562-908-2500... 43 J stoman@cci.edu
TOMANEK, Debra, J 520-621-7380... 18 F dtomanek@email.arizona.edu
TOMANEK, Jody 308-535-3724. 290 J tomanekj@mpcc.edu
TOMANENG, Rowena 408-864-8510... 44 M tomanengrowena@deanza.edu
TOMAS, Don 828-339-4242. 364 B d_tomas@southwesterncc.edu
TOMASIK, Paula, J 304-336-8340. 530 A ptomasik@westliberty.edu
TOMASZKIEWICZ, Ed 636-481-3501. 275 I etomaszk@jeffco.edu
TOMASZKIEWICZ, Teri 630-844-5511. 140 A ttomaszk@aurora.edu
TOMBA, Fran 216-987-2333. 378 D frances.tomba@tri-c.edu
TOMBARGE, Chuck 612-625-8510. 264 G tombarge@umn.edu
TOMBARGE, John 540-458-8134. 516 A tombargej@wlu.edu
TOMBERLIN, Lisa 229-468-2078. 134 K lisa.tomberlin@wiregrass.edu
TOMBLIN, Joanne, J 304-896-7439. 528 F joanne.tomblin@southernwv.edu
TOMBLIN, John, S 316-978-6427. 191 F john.tomblin@wichita.edu
TOMBLIN-BYRD, Terri, L 304-710-3141. 528 C tomblin@mctc.edu
TOMCZAK, Patricia 217-228-5432. 156 C tomczpa@quincy.edu
TOMCZYK, Christie, L 304-243-2304. 531 H ctomczyk@wju.edu
TOMEI, Lawrence, A 412-397-6229. 431 I tomei@rmu.edu
TOMEK, Deb 402-552-3395. 288 L tomekdeb@clarksoncollege.edu
TOMENENDAL, Robert 757-479-3706. 503 C rtomenendal@baptistseminary.edu
TOMESCU, Cosmin 212-592-2000. 340 H ctomescu@sva.edu
TOMETSKO, Jim 814-824-2279. 423 J jtometsko@mercyhurst.edu
TOMHAVE, Brad 253-879-3529. 524 F btomhave@pugetsound.edu
TOMHAVE, Brian 909-599-5433... 50 J btomhave@lifepacific.edu
TOMKINS, Patrick 757-825-2799. 514 B tomkinsp@tncc.edu
TOMKO, Amy, A 330-823-2674. 391 E tomkoaa@mountunion.edu
TOMKO, Andrew 201-447-7184. 299 C atomko@bergen.edu
TOMLIN, George 253-879-3522. 524 F tomlin@pugetsound.edu
TOMLIN, Kathy, H 540-464-7323. 515 B tomlinkh@vmi.edu
TOMLIN, Michael 719-587-7161... 78 B miketomlin@adams.edu
TOMLIN, Ross 541-888-7417. 407 H ross.tomlin@socc.edu
TOMLIN, Scott 801-774-9900. 498 D stomlin@vistacollege.edu
TOMLIN, Sharynn 325-942-2083. 465 K sharynn.tomlin@angelo.edu
TOMLINSON, Ann, W 310-233-4051... 51 H tomlinaw@lahc.edu
TOMLINSON, Bill 518-580-5177. 341 A wtomlins@skidmore.edu
TOMLINSON, Elise 907-796-6300... 11 A elise.tomlinson@uas.alaska.edu
TOMLINSON, Jan 740-364-9510. 376 A jtomlins@cotc.edu
TOMLINSON, Jessica, J 207-775-5098. 210 H jtomlinson@meca.edu
TOMLINSON, John, A 662-325-1008. 268 D jtomlinson@pres.msstate.edu
TOMLINSON, Karen 706-864-1948. 133 D karen.tomlinson@ung.edu
TOMLINSON, Meghan 641-844-5767. 179 J meghan.tomlinson@iavalley.edu
TOMLINSON, Norma, J 419-383-3407. 392 B norma.tomlinson@utoledo.edu
TOMLINSON, Rob 573-840-9649. 282 K rtomlinson@trcc.edu
TOMLINSON, Sasheka 352-365-3526. 108 S tomlins@lssc.edu
TOMLINSON, Tim 865-938-8186. 453 J
TOMLINSON, Virginia, R 770-720-5551. 130 G vrt@reinhardt.edu
TOMMASINO, Joseph 631-665-1600. 348 B tpaphd@aol.com
TOMMEY, Dale 870-574-4512... 23 G dtommey@sautech.edu
TOMPKINS, Anthony "Tony" 913-288-7150. 187 L atompkins@kckcc.edu
TOMPKINS, OSB, John-Mary 724-805-2771. 432 H johnmary.tompkins@email.stvincent.edu
TOMPKINS, Michael 845-758-7523. 314 D tompkins@bard.edu
TOMPKINS, Paige, L 678-547-6187. 128 H tompkins_pl@mercer.edu
TOMPKINS, Perry 417-328-1488. 282 C ptompkins@sbuniv.edu
TOMPKINS, Philip 520-494-5341... 12 P philip.tompkins@centralaz.edu
TOMPKINS, Ricky 479-619-3107... 22 C rtompkins1@nwacc.edu
TOMPKINS, Sandra 303-360-4738... 81 C sandra.tompkins@ccaurora.edu
TOMPKINS, JR., Wendell 912-478-2586. 126 C wtompkins@georgiasouthern.edu
TOMPOS, Betty 717-391-6947. 434 A tomposb@stevenscollege.edu
TOMS, Lisa, C 870-235-4300... 23 F lctoms@saumag.edu
TOMSIC, Margie 651-846-1316. 261 D margie.tomsic@saintpaul.edu
TONCHE, JR., Carlos 845-569-3249. 332 B carlos.tonche@msmc.edu
TONCIC, JR., Andrew, A 724-458-2170. 417 E aatoncic@gcc.edu
TONE, Nicole 503-222-3225. 403 B ntone@cci.edu
TONELLI, David, L 209-667-3610... 35 B dtonelli@csustan.edu
TONELLI, Laura 978-921-4242. 234 C laura.tonelli@montserrat.edu
TONER, James, D 207-778-7494. 212 D james.d.toner@maine.edu
TONETTI, Richard 508-999-8001. 229 A rtonetti@umassd.edu
TONEY, Charles, G 706-542-9167. 133 C ctoney@uga.edu
TONEY, Eileen 269-782-1301. 250 C etoney01@swmich.edu
TONEY, Glenn 706-245-7226. 124 D gtoney@ec.edu
TONEY, Jeffrey 908-737-7030. 302 F jetoney@kean.edu
TONEY, Patricia, A 508-854-4425. 232 F ptoney@qcc.mass.edu
TONEY, Rosie 225-216-8311. 202 H toneyr@mybrcc.edu
TONG, Diep 704-330-6859. 359 C diep.tong@cpcc.edu
TONG, Vincent, P 203-285-2415... 88 E vtong@gwcc.commnet.edu
TONI, Keith 508-678-2811. 231 B keith.toni@bristolcc.edu
TONIONI, Renee 630-466-7900. 162 J rtonioni@waubonsee.edu
TONJES, Janet 402-643-7290. 289 B janet.tonjes@cune.edu
TONN, Sheri, J 253-535-7121. 521 I tonnsj@plu.edu
TONN BOOKER, Paulette, L 507-344-7840. 253 J ptbooker@blc.edu
TONNESON, Julie, A 612-625-4517. 264 G tonne001@umn.edu
TONONO, Hiroko 949-480-4116... 66 F htonono@soka.edu
TONREY, Donna, A 215-991-3726. 420 B tonrey@lasalle.edu
TONSING, Cecilia 415-451-2822... 63 A ctonsing@sfts.edu
TOOEY, Mary, J 410-706-2693. 219 C mjtooey@hshsl.umaryland.edu
TOOHEY, Katherine, M 413-205-3352. 221 F tina.toohey@aic.edu
TOOKE-RAWLINS, Dixie 540-231-4000. 504 G
TOOLE, Genesis 602-285-7230... 15 C genesis.toole@phoenixcollege.edu
TOOLE, Lisa 570-702-8903. 419 G ltoole@johnson.edu
TOOLE, Raymond, L 610-359-5330. 414 D rtoole@dccc.edu
TOOLIN, Cynthia 860-632-3033... 90 C registrar@holyapostles.edu
TOOMBS, Jean 216-791-5000. 377 E jst4@case.edu
TOOMER, Victoria, E 856-225-6140. 306 C vikki.toomer@camden.rutgers.edu
TOOMEY, Elaine 617-323-6662. 233 D elaine_toomey@mspp.edu
TOOMEY, Kimberly 732-224-2268. 299 G ktoomey@brookdalecc.edu
TOOMEY, Marcia, D 978-232-2060. 226 C mtoomey@endicott.edu
TOOMEY, Richard 408-554-4966... 64 M rtoomey@scu.edu
TOOMEY, Richard, J 812-237-2510. 167 A richard.toomey@indstate.edu
TOON, Rhonda 678-359-5124. 127 A rhondat@gordonstate.edu
TOONE, Danette 785-243-1435. 185 M dtoone@cloud.edu
TOOR, Mark 304-558-2104. 529 C mtoor@hepc.wvnet.edu
TOOTOONCHI, Ahmad 301-687-4019. 220 C tootoonchi@frostburg.edu
TOPHAM, Susan 619-388-2896... 62 E stopham@sdccd.edu
TOPLIFF, Don 806-651-2585. 484 D dtopliff@mail.wtamu.edu
TOPLIFF, Michael, L 575-835-5735. 310 F mtopliff@nmt.edu
TOPOLSKI, Virginia 201-559-6055. 302 A topolskiv@felician.edu
TOPOREK, Bob 847-317-6400. 160 M btopore@tiu.edu
TOPP, Joelle 517-371-5140. 250 G toppj@cooley.edu
TOPPE, Michele 503-725-4422. 406 B toppem@pdx.edu
TOPPER, David 717-477-1124. 429 E datopp@ship.edu
TOPPER, Janet 610-341-5955. 415 G jtopper@eastern.edu
TOPPER, Maria, L 301-447-5211. 217 B mtopper@msmary.edu
TOPPING, Ann, V 585-262-1676. 332 A atopping@monroecc.edu
TOPPING, Scott 269-782-1249. 250 C stopping@swmich.edu
TOPPING, Thomas, E 585-785-1209. 324 D toppinte@flcc.edu
TOPPING, W. Frank 205-929-1448..... 5 G wftopping@miles.edu
TOPPLE, Dianne 518-828-4181. 321 C dianne.topple@sunycgcc.edu
TOPSHE, Joyce 860-685-3757... 92 H jtopshe@wesleyan.edu
TOPUZ, John, C 832-230-5350. 477 H john@northamerican.edu
TORABI, Mohammed 812-855-4808. 167 F torabi@indiana.edu
TORAN, Peter 410-837-5582. 221 A ptoran@ubalt.edu
TORBERT, Edgar, C 404-413-2574. 126 E etorbert@gsu.edu
TORBORG, Kate 843-208-8115. 448 B ktorgorg@uscb.edu
TORCHIA, Richard 215-572-2131. 409 H torchia@arcadia.edu
TORCZON, Virginia 757-221-3460. 503 N vjtorc@wm.edu
TORDENTI, Laura 860-832-1605... 87 K tordentilau@ccsu.edu
TORELLO, Tom 978-542-2591. 230 E ttorello@salemstate.edu
TORES, Evelyn 787-264-1912. 551 A evetores@sg.inter.edu
TORGERSEN, Arlene 360-538-4066. 520 B atorgers@ghc.edu
TORGERSON, Adam 503-370-6274. 408 J atorgers@willamette.edu
TORGERSON, Don 402-494-2311. 290 O dtorgerson@thenicc.edu
TORGERSON, Jane 817-257-7940. 484 I j.torgerson@tcu.edu
TORGERSON, Roberta 218-879-0803. 258 E roberta@fdltcc.edu
TORGERSON, Tad 701-483-2531. 371 D tad.torgerson@dickinsonstate.edu
TORGESEN, Stafford 410-857-2714. 216 E
TORICK, Marc 717-396-7833. 427 A mtorick@pcad.edu
TORINO, Frank 212-659-7200. 328 E ftorino@tkc.edu
TORNAMBE, Matthew, J 716-375-7673. 338 E mtornamb@sbu.edu
TORNO, Keith 616-222-3000. 245 C ITDirector@kuyper.edu
TORNQUIST, Kristi 605-688-5106. 452 B kristi.tornquist@sdstate.edu
TORNQUIST, Wade 734-487-0354. 242 D wtornquis@emich.edu
TORO, César 787-763-3120. 551 J ctoro@mechtech.edu
TORO, Elba 787-878-5475. 549 L etoro@arecibo.inter.edu
TORO, Zulma, R 501-569-3204... 24 B zrtoro@ualr.edu
TORO-ZAPATA, Rogelio 787-264-1912. 551 A rtoro@sg.inter.edu
TOROK, Michael 209-588-5143... 77 I torokm@yosemite.edu
TOROSYAN, Roben 508-531-2435. 229 D roben.torosyan@bridgew.edu
TORPEY, Graham 641-472-7000. 180 N gtorpey@mum.edu
TORPEY GARGANTA, Kathleen 508-678-2811. 231 B kathy.garganta@bristolcc.edu
TORRANCE, Peggy, L 218-299-3339. 255 A torrance@cord.edu
TORRE, Patrick 203-932-7224... 92 E ptorre@newhaven.edu
TORRE, Timothy 856-256-4105. 305 E torre@rowan.edu
TORRECILHA, Ramon, S 310-243-3307... 33 B rtorrecilha@csudh.edu
TORRENCE, Gary, G 314-367-8700. 281 C gary.torrence@stlcop.edu
TORRENCE, Michael 615-230-3350. 461 G michael.torrence@volstate.edu
TORRENS, Michael 435-797-0220. 497 B michael.torrens@usu.edu
TORRENS-BURTON, Jonathan 507-284-3627. 254 G
TORRES, Ana, D 787-834-9595. 553 B atorres@uaa.edu
TORRES, Angélica 787-850-0000. 554 D angelica.torres3@upr.edu
TORRES, Angela 787-751-1912. 551 B atorres@juris.inter.edu
TORRES, Antoinette 215-895-0253. 415 B at59@drexel.edu
TORRES, Aurelio 956-364-4222. 485 H aurelio.torres@tstc.edu
TORRES, Betania 863-667-5463. 113 P btorres@seu.edu
TORRES, Cari 415-485-9378... 40 G cari.torres@marin.edu
TORRES, Carmen 787-864-2222. 550 D cjtorres@inter.edu
TORRES, Carmen 787-892-4300. 551 A cdtorres@sg.inter.edu
TORRES, Carmen 702-579-3531. 294 B ctorres2@kaplan.edu
TORRES, Carmen, Z 787-841-2000. 552 B cl_torres@pucpr.edu
TORRES, Cathy 305-809-3250. 104 I cathy.torres@fkcc.edu
TORRES, Cynthia 773-602-5000. 142 B
TORRES, Darlin 787-250-1912. 550 E djtorres@metro.inter.edu
TORRES, David 951-222-8000... 60 J david.torres@rccd.edu
TORRES, Eliseo, S 505-277-0952. 312 F cheo@unm.edu
TORRES, Elsie, M 787-258-1501. 548 H etorres@columbiaco.edu
TORRES, Ernle, M 803-536-7011. 446 G etorres@scsu.edu
TORRES, Evelyn 787-882-2065. 553 A directora_planificacion@unitecpr.net
TORRES, Francisco 608-663-2000. 533 T ftorres@mediainstitute.edu
TORRES, Frank 623-845-3904... 14 M frank.torres@gcmail.maricopa.edu
TORRES, Gaile 406-395-4313. 288 D gtorres@stonechild.edu
TORRES, Gema, C 787-279-1912. 550 B gtorres@bayamon.inter.edu
TORRES, Greg 325-574-7640. 494 K gtorres@wtc.edu
TORRES, Henry 870-972-3033... 19 N htorres@astate.edu
TORRES, Jorge, A 787-257-7373. 552 H jotorres@suagm.edu
TORRES, Juan, C 817-515-3055. 482 B juan.torres@tccd.edu
TORRES, Julio 954-499-9815. 144 A jtorres@devry.edu
TORRES, Lourdes 718-518-4151. 318 B ltorres@hostos.cuny.edu
TORRES, Luis 303-556-3040... 83 D torresl@msudenver.edu
TORRES, Luis, D 787-276-0226. 554 B luis.torres31@upr.edu
TORRES, Luz 718-862-7313. 329 M luz.torres@manhattan.edu
TORRES, Maribel 787-884-6000. 549 D mtorres@icprjc.edu
TORRES, Marlon 718-262-2916. 319 F mtorres@york.cuny.edu
TORRES, Mary 713-221-8611. 489 D torresm@uhd.edu
TORRES, Michael 516-323-4834. 331 J mtorres@molly.edu
TORRES, Miguel 787-664-0352. 555 C miguel.torres10@upr.edu
TORRES, Miriam 215-489-2267. 414 E Miriam.Torres@delval.edu
TORRES, Monica 574-527-7520. 311 B mtorres@nmsu.edu
TORRES, Nancy 562-985-4031... 33 F nancy.torres@csulb.edu
TORRES, Nitza, J 787-864-2222. 550 D njtorres@inter.edu

TORRES, Norma 787-265-3811. 554 F admisiones@uprm.edu

TORRES, Omar 661-362-3135... 40 E omar.torres@canyons.edu

TORRES, Patricia 240-629-7905. 214 H ptorres@frederick.edu

TORRES, Rhonda 817-598-6212. 494 G rtorres@wc.edu

TORRES, Roberto 312-922-1884. 152 C rtorres@maccormac.edu

TORRES, Roberto 787-832-4040. 554 E ossoa@uprm.edu

TORRES, Rosa 303-986-2320... 80 D rosa@csha.net

TORRES, Rosalie, S 818-364-7612... 52 A torresr@lamission.edu

TORRES, Rosie 787-832-4040. 554 E servmed@uprm.edu

TORRES, Sonia 520-322-6330... 13 T

TORRES, Sulynet 787-753-6000. 549 D storres@icprjc.edu

TORRES, Vanessa 210-486-0881. 465 C vtorres120@alamo.edu

TORRES, Vasti 813-974-0349. 116 C vtorres@usf.edu

TORRES, Viviana 787-884-6000. 549 D vtorres@icprjc.edu

TORRES, Wilmarie 787-743-4041. 548 H wtorres@columbiaco.edu

TORRES, Yolanda 787-766-1717. 552 J yotorres@suagm.edu

TORRES DUGGAN, Nancy 626-396-2210... 28 P nancy.torresduggan@artcenter.edu

TORRES-LUGO, Irmannette 787-738-2161. 554 C irmannette.torres@upr.edu

TORRES-PETERS, Christina 209-384-6000... 54 D christina.torres-peters@mccd.edu

TORRES-PETRILLI, Diana 212-678-8011. 328 A dipetrilli@jtsa.edu

TORRES-SÁNCHEZ, Jorge, L 787-993-8965. 554 A jorge.torres17@upr.edu

TORRES-TORRES, Luis, D 787-257-0000. 553 G luis.torres31@upr.edu

TORRESCANO, Moises 210-829-3928. 490 A moisest@uiwtx.edu

TORRESDAL, Pamela, C 563-387-1375. 180 M torrespa@luther.edu

TORRIJAS, Christopher 574-239-8390. 166 N ctorrijas@hcc-nd.edu

TORRUELLA-LAWTON, Alfredo 787-993-8863. 554 A alfredo.torruella@upr.edu

TORRY, Phyllis 901-435-1555. 455 M phyllis_torry@loc.edu

TORTAROLO, John 760-744-1150... 58 D jtortarolo@palomar.edu

TORTI, Frank 860-679-2594... 92 A frank.torti@uchc.edu

TORTI, Sylvia 801-581-7339. 496 Q sylvia.torti@utah.edu

TORTURELLI, Joseph 201-360-4693. 302 D jtorturelli@hccc.edu

TOSCANO, James, P 757-822-1015. 514 C jtoscano@tcc.edu

TOSCH, Robert 509-963-1011. 517 F ToschR@cwu.edu

TOSCHKOFF, Marisa, L 989-837-4337. 248 C toschkof@northwood.edu

TOSO, Mary 605-274-5530. 449 K mary.toso@augie.edu

TOSTEN, Lori 717-262-2017. 437 H ltosten@wilson.edu

TOSTEN, Rod 717-337-6601. 417 B rtosten@gettysburg.edu

TOSTENSON, Wendi 229-217-4142. 129 F wtostenson@moultrietech.edu

TOSTI-LANE, Dave 206-726-5136. 518 G dtostilane@cornish.edu

TOSTON, Margaret, Y 731-881-7710. 463 E mtoston@utm.edu

TOTH, Joseph 609-652-4895. 305 C joseph.toth@stockton.edu

TOTINO, Nancy 718-405-3252. 320 G nancy.totino@mountsaintvincent.edu

TOTINO, Robert 617-989-4325. 237 G totinor@wit.edu

TOTTEN, Herman, L 940-565-2445. 490 C totten@unt.edu

TOTTEN, Julie 402-554-2322. 293 A jtotten@unomaha.edu

TOTTEN, Willette 870-575-4713... 24 E tottenw@uapb.edu

TOTTERMAN, Henrik 617-746-1990. 227 F henrik.totterman@hult.edu

TOTTY, Angela 573-840-9668. 282 K atotty@trcc.edu

TOU, Phillip 510-763-7787... 26 D ktou@acchs.edu

TOUCHETTE, Lindsey 239-590-1016. 115 A ltouchet@fgcu.edu

TOUGAS, Tim 320-762-4402. 257 O timt@alextech.edu

TOUHY, Jack 773-298-3540. 158 E jtouhy@sxu.edu

TOULIATOS-MILES, Diane, H 314-516-5904. 283 E touliatosd@umsl.edu

TOUMA, Elizabeth 415-503-6261... 62 H eat@sfcm.edu

TOUMA, Michael 727-726-1153. 100 E michaeltouma@clearwater.edu

TOUPS, David, L 561-732-4424. 112 G dtoups@svdp.edu

TOURE, Kathleen 252-862-1329. 363 A ktoure@roanokechowan.edu

TOUSSAINT, Edward 651-290-6394. 265 F edward.toussaint@wmitchell.edu

TOUSSAINT, Jess 630-466-7900. 162 J jtoussaint@waubonsee.edu

TOUTAIN, Henry, P 740-427-5137. 382 J toutainh@kenyon.edu

TOUTGES, Greg, A 218-477-2131. 259 H toutges@mnstate.edu

TOUZEAU, Karen, E 573-882-4256. 283 C touzeauk@missouri.edu

TOUZEAU, Leigh, A 865-539-7013. 461 D latouzeau@pstcc.edu

TOVAR, Cindy 312-788-1122. 162 H ctovar@vandercook.edu

TOVAR, Rina 386-822-7773. 117 C rtovar@stetson.edu

TOVARES, Carlos 951-487-3410... 55 B ctovares@msjc.edu

TOVES, Louise, M 671-735-2995. 546 E lmtoves@uguam.uog.edu

TOWAL, Patricia 340-692-4187. 555 E ptowal@live.uvi.edu

TOWERS, Joel 212-229-8950. 332 E towersj@newschool.edu

TOWEY, James 239-280-2511... 98 K jim.towey@avemaria.edu

TOWLE, David, C 319-273-2676. 176 A david.towle@uni.edu

TOWLE, Roger, K 724-458-3355. 417 E rktowle@gcc.edu

TOWLE, Thomas 603-271-6484. 296 C ttowle@ccsnh.edu

TOWNE, Becky, L 713-942-9505. 473 D btowne@hgst.edu

TOWNER, Mark 978-232-2255. 226 C mtowner@endicott.edu

TOWNER, Valmadge, T 662-621-4130. 266 D

TOWNLEY, Rod 704-216-3850. 363 D rod.townley@rccc.edu

TOWNS, Elmer 434-592-4140. 506 I eltowns@liberty.edu

TOWNS, Elmer, L 434-582-2169. 506 I eltowns@liberty.edu

TOWNS, Gail 732-987-2266. 302 B towsg@georgian.edu

TOWNSEND, Bill 601-925-3257. 268 A btownsen@mc.edu

TOWNSEND, Candace, V 337-475-5635. 207 G ctownsend@mcneese.edu

TOWNSEND, Elizabeth, R 336-322-2102. 362 F Elizabeth.Townsend@piedmontcc.edu

TOWNSEND, George 913-667-5700. 185 J gtownsend@cbts.edu

TOWNSEND, Heidi 360-475-7160. 521 H htownsend@olympic.edu

TOWNSEND, James, R 574-535-7368. 166 A james.townsend@goshen.edu

TOWNSEND, Janis 972-721-4142. 488 F jtownsend@udallas.edu

TOWNSEND, Joshua, W 410-334-2958. 221 D jtownsend@worwic.edu

TOWNSEND, Joyce 636-949-4971. 276 D jtownsend@lindenwood.edu

TOWNSEND, Karen 617-879-7065. 230 B ktownsend@massart.edu

TOWNSEND, Lani 323-668-7555... 27 I

TOWNSEND, Pam 256-331-5233..... 6 A townsend@nwscc.edu

TOWNSEND, Ralph 507-457-5017. 262 A rtownsend@winona.edu

TOWNSEND, Rosa 434-736-2045. 513 H rosa.townsend@southside.edu

TOWNSEND-GAMBLE, Jennifer 803-533-3750. 446 G jgamble2@scsu.edu

TOWNSHEND, John, R 301-405-1691. 219 B jtownshe@umd.edu

TOWNSLEY, Debra, M 919-508-2220. 370 F officeofthepresident@peace.edu

TOWNSLEY, R. Mike 260-422-5561. 167 B rmtownsley@indianatech.edu

TOWSLEY, Scott 507-574-4929. 525 G stowsley@yvcc.edu

TOY, Charles 517-371-5140. 250 G toyc@cooley.edu

TOY, Matthew 615-248-1380. 462 D mtoy@trevecca.edu

TOY, Sharon, S 405-744-5984. 397 H sharon.toy@okstate.edu

TOY, Tasha 706-368-6985. 121 G ttoy@berry.edu

TOYAMA, Gordon, K 503-370-6265. 408 J gtoyama@willamette.edu

TOYE-HALE, Bernadette 270-686-4506. 196 C bernie.hale@kctcs.edu

TOZER, Rich 928-314-9565... 11 L rich.tozer@azwestern.edu

TRAAS, Michael 270-926-4040. 193 M mtraas@daymarcollege.edu

TRACEY, SC, Kathleen 718-405-3775. 320 G kathleen.tracey@mountsaintvincent.edu

TRACEY, Kevin, J 516-562-3467. 323 E

TRACEY, Patrick 401-739-5000. 439 D ptracey@neit.edu

TRACHIAN, Barkev 336-725-8344. 365 F trachianb@piedmontu.edu

TRACHIER, Steven 817-531-4874. 488 A strachier@txwes.edu

TRACHTA, Yvonne 361-593-4338. 484 A yvonne.trachta@tamuk.edu

TRACHTE, Kent, C 570-321-4101. 422 H trachte@lycoming.edu

TRACHTE, Kent, C 717-291-4000. 416 J kent.trachte@fandm.edu

TRACIA, Michele 617-582-4498. 235 A mtracia@aii.edu

TRACY, Carla, B 309-794-7266. 139 L carlatracy@augustana.edu

TRACY, David 508-588-9100. 232 A

TRACY, II, Edward 313-993-1554. 250 K tracyeg@udmercy.edu

TRACY, Emily 315-733-2300. 349 D etracy@uscny.edu

TRACY, Geofrey, L 419-372-8262. 374 K gtracy@bgsu.edu

TRACY, Gloria 941-752-5323. 114 I tracyg@scf.edu

TRACY, Heidi, L 614-823-1400. 387 K htracy@otterbein.edu

TRACY, James, W 859-257-5294. 200 C jtracy@uky.edu

TRACY, Jerry, W 818-767-0888... 76 K jerry.tracy@woodbury.edu

TRACY, Kim 773-442-4190. 154 H k-tracy@neiu.edu

TRACY, Morgan, A 859-858-3511. 192 B morgan.tracy@asbury.edu

TRACY, Rhonda 304-424-8242. 530 E rhonda.tracy@wvup.edu

TRACY, Roy 505-786-4111. 310 D rtracy@navajotech.edu

TRACY, Sandra, G 901-843-3800. 458 E tracy@rhodes.edu

TRACY, Tim 859-257-5290. 200 C tim.tracy@uky.edu

TRACZYK, Joyce 763-433-1243. 257 P joyce.traczyk@anokaramsey.edu

TRADO, Donna 828-327-7000. 359 A dtrado@cvcc.edu

TRAFFIE, Tim 651-523-2015. 256 A ttraffie@hamline.edu

TRAFFORD, Beth 501-812-2232... 22 G btrafford@pulaskitech.edu

TRAGESER, Susan 540-831-6297. 508 C strageser@radford.edu

TRAGNI, Carolyn 845-451-1615. 322 D c_tragni@culinary.edu

TRAIGER, Jeff 816-235-5660. 283 D traigerj@umkc.edu

TRAINA, Joyce 201-327-8877. 301 G jtraina@eastwick.edu

TRAINA, Samuel 209-228-2857... 71 D STraina@UCMerced.edu

TRAINER, James, F 610-519-7578. 436 F james.trainer@villanova.edu

TRAINER, Jason 218-793-2437. 260 D jason.trainer@northlandcollege.edu

TRAINER, Jill 916-278-4655... 34 D jill.trainer@csus.edu

TRAINER, Karin 609-258-3170. 304 E ktrainer@princeton.edu

TRAINO, Joe 928-226-4285... 13 B joe.traino@coconino.edu

TRAINOR, Judith, L 508-831-5423. 238 F jtrainor@wpi.edu

TRAINOR, Timothy 845-938-2000. 545 I 8dean@usma.edu

TRAINOR, Tom 651-638-6259. 253 K t-trainor@bethel.edu

TRAISTER, Jerry 607-729-1581. 322 F jtraister@davisny.edu

TRAKINAT, Mary Beth 309-268-8172. 146 B marybeth.trakinat@heartland.edu

TRAMDACK, Philip, J 724-738-2630. 429 F philip.tramdack@sru.edu

TRAME, Michael 217-351-2433. 155 J mtrame@parkland.edu

TRAMEL, Caitlin 212-353-4139. 321 F ctramel@cooper.edu

TRAMELLI, Marianne 212-678-3148. 347 G mt772@tc.columbia.edu

TRAMMEL, Sheila 318-257-2235. 207 F strammel@latech.edu

TRAMMELL, C. David 859-858-3511. 192 B david.trammell@asbury.edu

TRAMMELL, Genie 918-293-5210. 398 B genie.trammell@okstate.edu

TRAMMELL, Phil 940-898-3863. 488 B ptrammell@twu.edu

TRAMMELL, Webster, B 732-224-2282. 299 G wtrammell@brookdalecc.edu

TRAMONTANO, William, A 718-951-5864. 317 C tramontano@brooklyn.cuny.edu

TRAMONTE, Mark 541-552-7246. 406 C tramontem@sou.edu

TRAMONTE, Michael 713-500-3158. 492 E michael.tramonte@uth.tmc.edu

TRAMPF, Judith, M 262-472-4672. 538 D trampfj@uww.edu

TRAMUTA, Daniel, M 716-673-3181. 342 A daniel.tramuta@fredonia.edu

TRAMUTA, Daniel, M 716-673-3253. 342 A daniel.tramuta@fredonia.edu

TRAN, Christy 415-371-0002... 57 B

TRAN, Deborah 415-565-4740... 71 A trand@uchastings.edu

TRAN, My Linh 773-907-4770. 142 A mtran@ccc.edu

TRAN, Nathanael 415-371-0002... 57 B

TRAN, Vu 310-825-3101... 71 C vtran@saonet.ucla.edu

TRANEL, Mark 314-516-5273. 283 E mtranel@umsl.edu

TRANG, Thuy 408-855-5081... 75 K thuy.trang@wvm.edu

TRANQUADA, Jim 323-259-2990... 56 I jtranqua@oxy.edu

TRANSUE, Mary 678-717-3410. 133 D mary.transue@ung.edu

TRANSUE, Pamela 253-566-5100. 524 C ptransue@tacomacc.edu

TRANT, John, M 956-665-2404. 492 B trantjm@utpa.edu

TRANT, Meg 617-217-9018. 222 G mtrant@baystate.edu

TRANT, Rachel 508-626-4523. 230 A rtrant@framingham.edu

TRAPANICK, Benjamin, J 508-626-4505. 230 A btrapanick@framingham.edu

TRAPASSO, Kristen, P 315-445-4265. 328 F trapaskp@lemoyne.edu

TRAPP, Daniel 313-883-8540. 249 E trapp.daniel@shms.edu

TRAPP, Erin 303-556-5126... 83 D etrapp@msudenver.edu

TRAPP, Harry 301-369-2800. 213 G htrapp@capitol-college.edu

TRAPP, Lori 734-973-3529. 252 A lori@wccnet.edu

TRAQUAIR, Brianna 651-641-8866. 255 B traquair@csp.edu

TRAQUINA, Perry 781-736-2000. 224 F traquina@brandeis.edu

TRASK, III, Tallman 919-684-6600. 354 A t3@duke.edu

TRASVINA, John, D 415-422-6304... 73 J jdtrasvina@usfca.edu

TRAUB, Gilbert 718-409-7385. 346 D gtraub@sunymaritime.edu

TRAUBE, Eve 212-410-8006. 333 E etraube@nycpm.edu

TRAUPMAN-CARR, Carol 610-861-1348. 424 E caroltcarr@moravian.edu

TRAUTH, Denise, M 512-245-2121. 487 C president@txstate.edu

TRAUTMAN, Stewart 352-854-2322. 100 K trautmas@cf.edu

TRAUTMANN, Roger 503-255-0332. 404 F rtrautmann@multnomah.edu

TRAVENICK, Ron 510-659-6107... 57 A rtravenick@ohlone.edu

TRAVER, Virginia 239-687-5343... 98 J vtraver@avemarialaw.edu

TRAVER, William 518-458-5337. 321 A traverw@strose.edu

TRAVERS, Michael, E ..... 919-761-2127. 366 I
mtravers@sebts.edu
TRAVERS, Nan ..... 518-587-2100. 346 A
nan.travers@esc.edu
TRAVERSI, Diane ..... 707-527-4508... 65 B
dtraversi@santarosa.edu
TRAVERSO, Celeste ..... 787-620-2040. 547 C
ctraverso@aupr.edu
TRAVERSO, Susan ..... 717-361-1416. 415 H
traversos@etown.edu
TRAVIS, Annie ..... 662-252-8094. 269 F
atravis@rustcollege.edu
TRAVIS, Antonio ..... 404-756-4023. 121 A
atravis@atlm.edu
TRAVIS, Artie, L ..... 301-860-3391. 220 A
atravis@bowiestate.edu
TRAVIS, Brantly, D ..... 270-809-2155. 198 B
btravis@murraystate.edu
TRAVIS, Cathy ..... 808-974-7326. 136 A
zenz@hawaii.edu
TRAVIS, Deborah, J ..... 916-691-7321... 53 B
travisd@crc.losrios.edu
TRAVIS, Delite ..... 714-997-6681... 38 A
dtravis@chapman.edu
TRAVIS, Douglas, B ..... 512-472-4133. 480 G
doug.travis@ssw.edu
TRAVIS, Frederick ..... 641-472-7000. 180 N
ftravis@mum.edu
TRAVIS, Heather ..... 515-961-1579. 182 E
heather.travis@simpson.edu
TRAVIS, Jeremy ..... 212-237-8600. 318 D
jtravis@jjay.cuny.edu
TRAVIS, Kay ..... 270-534-3084. 196 G
kay.travis@kctcs.edu
TRAVIS, Patricia, J ..... 914-594-4575. 334 A
pat_travis@nymc.edu
TRAVIS, Scott ..... 616-395-7251. 244 A
remenschneider@hope.edu
TRAVIS, Shawn ..... 985-448-7941. 203 B
shawn.travis@fletcher.edu
TRAVIS, William ..... 757-258-6531. 514 B
travisw@tncc.edu
TRAVIS, William ..... 757-253-4297. 514 B
travisw@tncc.edu
TRAVISANO,
Jacqueline, A ..... 954-262-7555. 109 K
jtravisano@nova.edu
TRAWEEK, Vicki ..... 817-598-6218. 494 G
vtraweek@wc.edu
TRAWICK, Rebecca ..... 909-652-6493... 37 M
rebecca.trawick@chaffey.edu
TRAWICK, Thomas ..... 404-880-8812. 122 J
ttrawick@cau.edu
TRAXLER, Matt ..... 651-450-3885. 258 H
mtraxle@inverhills.edu
TRAXLER, Pete ..... 907-796-6139... 11 A
pete.traxler@uas.alaska.edu
TRAYLOR, Delores ..... 256-761-6246..... 7 F
ddtraylor@talladega.edu
TRAYLOR, Judy, G ..... 903-434-8242. 477 J
jtraylor@ntcc.edu
TRAYNHAM, Earle, C ..... 904-620-2700. 116 B
traynham@unf.edu
TRAYNOR, Kathy ..... 715-682-1227. 535 D
ktraynor@northland.edu
TRAYNUM, Elise ..... 415-565-4715... 71 A
traynume@uchastings.edu
TRAYSTMAN, Richard ..... 303-724-8155... 86 A
richard.traystman@ucdenver.edu
TREACLE, James ..... 330-494-6170. 389 F
jtreacle@starkstate.edu
TREACY, SJ, Jack, R ..... 408-554-4372... 64 M
jtreacy@scu.edu
TREADAWAY, Glenda, J ..... 828-262-6311. 367 A
treadawaygj@appstate.edu
TREADWELL, Andrew ..... 772-462-4804. 106 P
atreadwe@irsc.edu
TREADWELL, Jane, B ..... 217-206-6597. 161 E
treadwell.jane@uis.edu
TREADWELL, IV,
Lawrence ..... 305-474-6860. 112 F
ltreadwell@stu.edu
TREADWELL, Melinda ..... 603-358-2105. 298 F
mtreadwe@keene.edu
TREAKLE-MOORE,
Evelyn ..... 202-806-7540... 95 G
etreakle-moore@howard.edu
TREANOR, William, M ..... 202-662-9031... 95 E
wtreanor@georgetown.edu
TREAT, Bruce, J ..... 585-785-1216. 324 D
treatbj@flcc.edu
TREAT, Tod ..... 253-566-5022. 524 C
ttreat@tacomacc.edu
TREBAR, Robert ..... 440-375-7115. 382 L
rtrebar@lec.edu
TREBER, Karen, A ..... 301-687-4102. 220 C
ktreber@frostburg.edu
TREBOW, Elizabeth ..... 818-654-1707... 59 E
etrebow@pgi.edu
TRECARTIN, Ralph, R ..... 585-395-2119. 342 F
rtrecart@brockport.edu
TRECKER, Stan ..... 617-585-6651. 228 B
strecker@lesley.edu
TREDUP, Fred ..... 702-895-3201. 294 I
fred.tredup@unlv.edu
TREECE, Brian ..... 419-434-4570. 391 D
treeceb@findlay.edu
TREECE, T. Gerald ..... 713-646-1776. 480 J
gtreece@stcl.edu
TREFF, Shaya ..... 732-370-3360. 308 L
TREFF, Yisroel Meir ..... 732-370-3360. 308 L
TREFFILETTI, Elaine ..... 914-674-7540. 330 J
etreffiletti@mercy.edu
TREFNEY, Marcie ..... 508-457-1313. 234 F
mtrefney@ngs.edu
TREFT, Paul ..... 712-274-5221. 181 B
treft@morningside.edu
TREICHEL, Jeff, D ..... 512-232-5114. 491 C
jeff.treichel@austin.utexas.edu
TREIZENBERG,
Steven, J ..... 616-234-5708. 251 G
TRELA, D, J ..... 810-762-3234. 251 E
djtrela@umflint.edu
TRELISKY, Nina ..... 973-720-2305. 308 I
treliskyn@wpunj.edu
TRELLA, Joseph ..... 610-282-1100. 414 F
joseph.trella@desales.edu
TRELOW, Cheryl, D ..... 660-543-4255. 283 A
trelow@ucmo.edu
TRELSTAD-PORTER,
James ..... 612-330-1686. 253 H
porter@augsburg.edu
TREMBLAY,
Christopher, W ..... 269-387-4336. 252 I
christopher.tremblay@wmich.edu
TREMBLAY, Pamela ..... 706-880-8313. 128 A
ptremblay@lagrange.edu
TREMBLAY, Rocky ..... 203-285-2185... 88 E
rtremblay@gwcc.commnet.edu
TREMBLE, Gayle ..... 912-443-5724. 131 D
gtremble@savannahtech.edu
TREMBLEY, Michael ..... 336-309-5814. 131 H
mtrembley@southuniversity.edu
TREMPE, James, P ..... 419-530-2844. 392 B
James.Trempe@utoledo.edu
TRENDE, Richard ..... 715-425-3133. 537 E
richard.trende@uwrf.edu
TRENDT, Diana, J ..... 608-342-1183. 537 D
trendtd@uwplatt.edu
TRENIS, Neva, S ..... 540-654-1688. 510 J
ntrenis@umw.edu
TRENKLE, Lizza ..... 254-659-7823. 473 A
ltrenkle@hillcollege.edu
TRENOWITH, Arthur ..... 617-369-3230. 236 F
atrenowith@mfa.org
TRENSCH, Kit ..... 678-915-7307. 132 C
ktrensch@spsu.edu
TRENT, Coe Ann ..... 336-342-4261. 363 C
trentc@rockinghamcc.edu
TRENT, Sean ..... 276-466-7912. 514 G
seantrent@vic.edu
TREPAL, Michael, J ..... 212-410-8067. 333 E
mtrepal@nycpm.edu
TREPKOWSKI, Patti ..... 616-234-4226. 243 B
ptrepkow@grcc.edu
TREPKOWSKI, Ronald, E ..... 989-964-4285. 249 G
ret@svsu.edu
TRESER-OSGOOD,
Nancy, J ..... 909-621-8110... 60 A
nancy.treser-osgood@pomona.edu
TRESOLINI, Carol ..... 919-962-3907. 368 D
carol_tresolini@unc.edu
TRESS, Samuel, D ..... 410-837-5529. 221 A
stress@ubalt.edu
TRESSEL, James, P ..... 330-972-5524. 390 E
jtressel@uakron.edu
TRESSLER, Dan ..... 575-538-6000. 312 N
tresslerd@wumu.edu
TREUER, Anton ..... 218-755-2590. 258 A
atreuer@bemidjistate.edu
TREUTHART, Jean, M ..... 717-801-3211. 417 I
jmtreuth@hacc.edu
TREVAN, Timothy, J ..... 818-677-2160... 34 C
timothy.j.trevan@csun.edu
TREVATHAN, Ed ..... 314-977-8188. 281 I
etravath@slu.edu
TREVATHAN, Michael, R ..... 318-342-5242. 208 E
trevathan@ulm.edu
TREVETHICK, Nancy ..... 617-824-8515. 226 A
nancy_trevethick@emerson.edu
TREVINIO, Jesus ..... 605-677-5011. 451 F
jesus.trevinio@usd.edu
TREVINO, Crispin ..... 361-593-4036. 484 A
crispin.trevino@tamuk.edu
TREVINO, JR., Esteban ..... 956-721-5140. 475 F
stevet@laredo.edu
TREVINO, Mary, T ..... 956-326-2275. 483 B
maryt@tamiu.edu
TREVINO, Melba ..... 956-872-3113. 480 I
melbat@southtexascollege.edu
TREVINO, Miguel, A ..... 956-326-2283. 483 B
mtrevino@tamiu.edu
TREVINO, Monica ..... 405-224-3140. 401 E
mtrevino@usao.edu
TREVINO, Nicole, G ..... 512-428-1037. 479 C
nicoleg@stedwards.edu
TREVINO, Rick ..... 805-289-6155... 74 H
rtrevino@vcccd.edu
TREVINO BAUER,
Blanca ..... 956-882-7081. 491 D
blanca.bauer@utb.edu
TREVIS, Michael ..... 310-660-3101... 43 B
mtrevis@elcamino.edu
TREVISAN, Maurizio ..... 212-650-6638. 317 D
provost@ccny.cuny.edu
TREVISAN, Maurizio ..... 212-650-5275. 317 D
mtrevisan@ccny.cuny.edu
TREVISAN, Michael ..... 509-335-4853. 525 A
trevisan@wsu.edu
TREVISAN, Sandi ..... 619-388-7752... 62 F
strevisa@sdccd.edu
TREVIZO, Melissa ..... 281-487-1170. 484 H
mtrevizo@txchiro.edu
TREVOR, Tyler ..... 406-444-0311. 286 G
ttrevor@montana.edu
TREWERN, Jay, S ..... 978-468-7111. 227 A
TREWYN, Ronald, W ..... 785-532-6195. 188 A
trewyn@ksu.edu
TREXLER, Grant ..... 805-756-1141... 32 F
gtrexler@calpoly.edu
TREXLER, William, H ..... 814-886-6421. 424 G
wtrexler@mtaloy.edu
TRIANTAFILOU,
Nicholas, C ..... 617-850-1280. 227 E
pres_office@hchc.edu
TRIBBEY, Ann ..... 804-330-0111. 503 G
directoredcrim@centura.edu
TRIBBLE, Judy ..... 812-535-5255. 172 F
jtribble@smwc.edu
TRIBLE, JR., Paul, S ..... 757-594-7001. 503 M
ptrible@cnu.edu
TRIBLEY, Walter ..... 831-646-4060... 54 I
wtribley@mpc.edu
TRICARICO, Kerri, J ..... 212-998-2913. 334 D
kerri.tricarico@nyu.edu
TRICE, Gwinetta, L ..... 229-430-4739. 119 J
gwinetta.trice@asurams.edu
TRICE, John, P ..... 336-272-7102. 354 E
john.trice@greensboro.edu
TRICE, Matt ..... 229-430-6618. 120 A
mtrice@albanytech.edu
TRICE, Sarah ..... 803-822-3321. 445 C
trices@midlandstech.edu
TRICHE, Casie ..... 985-448-4077. 208 A
casie.triche@nicholls.edu
TRICHE, III, Charles, W ..... 337-482-6396. 208 D
ctriche@louisiana.edu
TRICKEY, JR.,
Rafe Edward ..... 692-625-3994. 546 F
TRICOLI, Robin, J ..... 423-442-2001. 454 L
president@hiwassee.edu
TRIDENTE, Teresa ..... 201-216-5176. 307 E
ttrident@stevens.edu
TRIER, Vicki ..... 509-533-8090. 518 E
vicki.trier@scc.spokane.edu
TRIERWEILER,
Charles, S ..... 205-329-7907..... 3 B
chuck.trierweiler@ecacolleges.com
TRIETLEY, JR.,
Richard, C ..... 716-375-2513. 338 E
rtrietley@sbu.edu
TRIEZENBERG, Glenn, E ..... 616-526-6485. 240 L
gtriezen@calvin.edu
TRIGALO, Ophir ..... 312-567-3290. 147 F
trigalo@iit.edu
TRIGG, Debra ..... 510-659-7376... 57 A
dtrigg@ohlone.edu
TRILLER, Mark, V ..... 608-757-7701. 539 I
mtriller@blackhawk.edu
TRILLI, Victor ..... 316-942-4291. 189 E
trilliv@newmanu.edu
TRIMBLE, Ferris, E ..... 323-241-5467... 52 C
trimblfe@lasc.edu
TRIMBLE, Joe ..... 615-966-5672. 456 B
joe.trimble@lipscomb.edu
TRIMBLE, Karen ..... 530-749-3804... 77 K
ktrimble@yccd.edu
TRIMBLE, LaDonna ..... 661-722-6300... 28 F
ltrimble@avc.edu
TRIMBLE, Lisa ..... 307-778-1603. 543 D
lisatrimble@lcccfoundation.edu
TRIMBLE, Logan ..... 860-486-5249... 92 A
logan.trimble@uconn.edu
TRIMBLE, Marshall ..... 480-423-6314... 15 E
marshall.trimble@scottsdalecc.edu
TRIMBLE, Michael, D ..... 203-365-7557... 91 C
trimblem@sacredheart.edu
TRIMBOLI, James ..... 716-614-6202. 334 E
trimboli@niagaracc.suny.edu
TRINCHESE, Rebecca ..... 724-738-4340. 429 F
rebecca.trinchese@sru.edu
TRINIDAD, Vanessa ..... 787-884-6000. 549 D
vtrinidad@icprjc.edu
TRINIDAD, Ysabel ..... 805-437-8877... 32 I
ysabel.trinidad@csuci.edu
TRINKLEIN, Andrea ..... 404-727-4144. 124 E
ajtrink@emory.edu
TRIOLO, Peter, T ..... 713-486-4012. 492 E
Peter.T.Triolo@uth.tmc.edu
TRIONFI, Thomas, P ..... 989-774-3166. 240 N
trion1tp@cmich.edu
TRIPATHI, Satish, K ..... 716-645-2901. 341 F
president@buffalo.edu
TRIPLET, Jeff ..... 971-722-4406. 407 D
jtriplet@pcc.edu
TRIPLETT, Anastasia ..... 540-868-7133. 512 H
atriplett@lfcc.edu
TRIPLETT, Beth ..... 563-588-6468. 176 F
beth.triplett@clarke.edu
TRIPLETT, Clark ..... 314-392-2221. 278 B
triplett@mobap.edu
TRIPLETT, Jill ..... 404-270-5677. 132 E
jtriple1@spelman.edu
TRIPLETT, Lynn ..... 781-768-7315. 236 A
lynn.triplett@regiscollege.edu
TRIPLETT, Neal ..... 919-668-9995. 354 A
neal.triplett@duke.edu
TRIPLETT, Teresa ..... 910-642-7141. 364 A
Teresa.Triplett@sccnc.edu
TRIPLETT III, Charles ..... 503-725-5717. 405 G
charles_triplett@ous.edu
TRIPLITT, Tom, A ..... 864-294-3464. 444 C
tom.triplitt@furman.edu
TRIPODI, Michael ..... 908-737-7020. 302 F
mtripodi@kean.edu
TRIPOVICH, Maria ..... 409-944-1303. 472 I
mtripovi@gc.edu
TRIPP, Harry, E ..... 814-393-2351. 428 C
htripp@clarion.edu
TRIPP, Susan ..... 315-866-0300. 326 A
trippsk@herkimer.edu
TRIPP, Susan ..... 870-612-2133... 25 A
susan.tripp@uaccb.edu
TRIPPETT, William ..... 608-263-7727. 538 E
william.trippett@uwc.edu
TRIPURANENI,
Vinaya, L ..... 909-593-3511... 72 E
vtripuraneni@laverne.edu
TRISH, Maggie ..... 573-341-4011. 284 A
trishm@mst.edu
TRITAK, Ann ..... 201-761-6272. 306 L
atritak@saintpeters.edu
TRITLE, Madonna ..... 219-785-5244. 172 A
mtritle@pnc.edu
TRIVEDI, Tushar ..... 201-761-6264. 306 L
ttrivedi@saintpeters.edu
TRIVUNOVICH, Nick ..... 813-974-4903. 116 C
ntrivuno@usf.edu
TRIZZINO-PECOR, June ..... 212-965-8340. 313 A
trizzino@adelphi.edu
TRNCAK, Stephen ..... 281-998-6348. 479 E
stephen.trncak@sjcd.edu
TROASTLE, Greta, J ..... 304-637-1331. 526 E
troastleg@dewv.edu
TROCHIM, Shawn ..... 254-299-8811. 476 D
strochim@mclennan.edu
TROCHUCK, Mike ..... 708-239-4836. 160 K
mike.trochuck@trnty.edu
TROELSTRA, Kate ..... 678-466-4300. 123 A
katetroelstra@clayton.edu
TROHA, James, A ..... 814-641-3101. 419 H
trohaj@juniata.edu
TROIANO, Peter, F ..... 203-392-5556... 88 A
troianop2@southernct.edu
TROILO, David ..... 212-938-5658. 345 C
dtroilo@sunyopt.edu
TROISI, Kenneth ..... 678-603-0981. 132 B
ktroisi@sctech.edu
TROJAN, John ..... 908-526-1200. 305 B
jtrojan@raritanval.edu
TROLLINGER,
Richard, W ..... 859-238-5209. 193 E
richard.trollinger@centre.edu
TROMBELLA, Jerry ..... 201-559-6185. 302 A
trombellaj@felician.edu
TROMBETTA, Marcy ..... 814-393-2111. 428 C
mrupp@clarion.edu
TROMBLEY, Jane, E ..... 212-817-7179. 317 F
jtrombley@gc.cuny.edu
TROMBLEY OAKES,
Martha ..... 802-728-1732. 501 F
moakes@vtc.edu
TRONGALE, Nicholas ..... 630-889-6599. 154 E
ntrongale@nuhs.edu
TRONGALE, Nicholas, A ..... 630-889-6603. 154 E
ntrongale@nuhs.edu
TRONTO, Stacie ..... 252-328-9025. 367 B
trontos@ecu.edu
TROPP, Judybeth ..... 619-961-4319... 69 I
jtropp@tjsl.edu
TROST, Patricia, G ..... 708-709-3637. 156 A
ptrost@prairiestate.edu
TROSVIG, Kelli ..... 206-616-0114. 524 G
kelli@uw.edu

TROTT CLARK, Beth .... 717-796-5066. 423 L
bclark@messiah.edu
TROTTA, Neil .... 617-236-8867. 226 F
ntrotta@fisher.edu
TROTTER, Cheryl .... 704-461-6714. 352 G
cheryltrotter@bac.edu
TROTTER, David .... 913-360-7655. 184 H
dtrotter@benedictine.edu
TROTTER, Johnny .... 706-295-6974. 125 F
jtrotter@gntc.edu
TROTTER, Steve .... 360-867-6185. 519 J
trotters@evergreen.edu
TROTTIER, Sheila .... 701-477-7862. 373 B
strottier@tm.edu
TROTTY, Willie, F .... 936-261-3500. 482 F
wftrotty@pvamu.edu
TROTTY, Willie, F .... 936-261-1550. 482 F
wftrotty@pvamu.edu
TROUP, James .... 203-575-8220... 89 B
jtroup@nvcc.commnet.edu
TROUP, Pat .... 251-981-3771..... 2 I
pat.troup@columbiasouthern.edu
TROUPE, Bonnie, L .... 508-565-1069. 237 A
btroupe@stonehill.edu
TROUSDELL, Roy .... 218-748-2413. 259 B
r.trousdell@mr.mnscu.edu
TROUT, Curtis, C .... 309-556-3195. 148 B
ctrout@iwu.edu
TROUT, Darice .... 847-925-6070. 145 H
dtrout@harpercollege.edu
TROUT, Margaret .... 503-370-6971. 408 J
mtrout@willamette.edu
TROUTMAN, Dara, L ...... 402-472-7143. 292 G
dtroutman@nebraska.edu
TROUTMAN, Donald .... 570-321-4064. 422 H
troutman@lycoming.edu
TROUTMAN, Marcus .... 312-922-1884. 152 C
mtroutman@maccormac.edu
TROUTMAN, Nakia .... 918-879-8400. 450 G
ntroutman@national.edu
TROUTT, Amy .... 618-545-3048.. 149 D
atroutt@kaskaskia.edu
TROUTT, William, E .... 901-843-3730. 458 E
trouttw@rhodes.edu
TROVALL, Carl .... 512-313-3000. 469 L
carl.trovall@concordia.edu
TROVER, Clay .... 706-721-4854. 126 B
ctrover@gru.edu
TROW, Kirk .... 515-244-4221. 175 C
trowk@aib.edu
TROWBRIDGE,
Christian, A .... 302-295-1151... 94 E
christian.a.trowbridge@wilmu.edu
TROWBRIDGE, Cory, D .. 316-322-0110. 271 O
cory.trowbridge@calvary.edu
TROWBRIDGE, Larry ...... 217-479-7079. 152 D
larry.trowbridge@mac.edu
TROXEL, Steve .... 620-365-5116. 183 I
troxel@allencc.edu
TROXELL, Regina .... 513-263-1444. 376 I
regina.troxell@thechristhospital.com
TROXLER, Debra, J .... 302-571-5380... 93 F
dtroxler@dtcc.edu
TROY, Randy, D .... 260-399-7700. 174 C
rtroy@sf.edu
TROY, Robert, C .... 718-960-7825. 318 A
robert.troy@lehman.cuny.edu
TROY, Shawn .... 989-386-6658. 247 B
stroy@midmich.edu
TROYER, Carol, A .... 717-334-6286. 422 E
ctroyer@ltsg.edu
TROYER, Cindy .... 903-566-7461. 492 D
ctroyer@uttyler.edu
TROYER, Mark, J .... 859-858-3511. 192 B
mark.troyer@asbury.edu
TRUBE, Julie .... 248 370-3915. 248 J
dichtel@oakland.edu
TRUCKENMILLER, Greg .. 518-736-3622. 325 A
gtrucken@fmcc.suny.edu
TRUDEAU, Dave .... 252-492-2061. 364 F
trudeaud@vgcc.edu
TRUDEAU, Mary, L .... 701-788-4754. 371 E
mary.trudeau@mayvillestate.edu
TRUDEAU, Sara, L .... 202-526-3799... 96 D
TRUDEAU, Scott .... 248-204-3850. 245 I
strudeau@ltu.edu
TRUDEAU, Skip .... 765-998-5368. 173 C
sktrudeau@taylor.edu
TRUDEL, Jeannie .... 864-644-5486. 446 I
jtrudel@swu.edu
TRUDELL, Kyle .... 573-288-6450. 273 F
ktrudell@culver.edu
TRUE, Don .... 803-508-7491. 440 G
trued@atc.edu
TRUE, Douglas, K .... 319-335-3552. 175 I
douglas-true@uiowa.edu
TRUE, Elizabeth .... 207-326-2251. 211 D
elizabeth.true@mma.edu
TRUEBLOOD-GAMBLE,
Marjorie .... 541-552-6459. 406 C
truebloom@sou.edu

TRUEMAN, Amy .... 607-844-8222. 347 I
truemaa@TC3.edu
TRUESDALE, Karen .... 678-891-2542. 125 G
karen.truesdale@gpc.edu
TRUESDELL, Cheryl, B ... 260-481-6506. 168 C
truesdel@ipfw.edu
TRUESDELL, Joanne .... 503-594-3000. 402 F
joannet@clackamas.edu
TRUESDELL, Nancy, D .... 920-832-6596. 533 S
nancy.d.truesdell@lawrence.edu
TRUETT, William, M .... 704-272-5363. 363 G
wtruett@spcc.edu
TRUFANT, Nicole .... 207-602-2157. 213 A
ntrufant@une.edu
TRUILLO, Lawrence, T .... 607-778-5207. 315 I
truillolt@sunybroome.edu
TRUITT, Bettie .... 309-796-5048. 140 E
Truittb@bhc.edu
TRUITT, Jennifer .... 217-228-5432. 156 C
truitje@quincy.edu
TRUITT, Terry, C .... 765-641-4354. 163 L
tctruitt@anderson.edu
TRUJILLO, Daniel, A .... 718-990-6774. 339 A
trujilld@stjohns.edu
TRUJILLO, Fidel, J .... 505-454-3020. 310 E
fidel@nmhu.edu
TRUJILLO, George .... 301-985-7283. 219 F
gtrujillo@umuc.edu
TRUJILLO, Henrietta .... 505-747-2134. 311 E
henri@nnmc.edu
TRUJILLO, Tamara .... 707-638-5317... 69 K
tamara.trujillo@tu.edu
TRULL, Gregory .... 503-588-2722. 403 A
gtrull@corban.edu
TRULOVE, Milyon .... 651-523-2207. 256 A
mtrulove01@hamline.edu
TRUMAN, Grace, H .... 561-868-3122. 110 C
trumang@palmbeachstate.edu
TRUMAN, Kevin, Z .... 816-235-2399. 283 D
trumank@umkc.edu
TRUMBLE, Elaine .... 207-893-7804. 211 G
etrumble@sjcme.edu
TRUMBOWER, Jeffrey, A 802-654-2492. 500 B
jtrumbower@smcvt.edu
TRUMBULL, William, N .. 843-953-7416. 442 A
wtrumbul@citadel.edu
TRUMPICK, Susan, A ..... 518-743-2248. 345 E
trumpics@sunyacc.edu
TRUMPOWER, Peter .... 330-494-6170. 389 F
ptrumpower@starkstate.edu
TRUMPS, Thomas, H ...... 540-464-7313. 515 B
trumpsth@vmi.edu
TRUNZO, Christina .... 713-646-1793. 480 J
ctrunzo@stcl.edu
TRUONG, Chris .... 714-564-6043... 60 G
truong_chris@sac.edu
TRUPP, Kim, L .... 334-844-4580..... 1 G
truppki@auburn.edu
TRUSCH, Robert .... 413-755-4039. 233 A
rbtrusch@stcc.edu
TRUSCHKE, Michael, E ... 310-506-4392... 58 H
michael.truschke@pepperdine.edu
TRUSHEIM, Dale, W .... 410-778-7709. 221 C
dtrusheim2@washcoll.edu
TRUSS, B. Donta .... 478-827-7594. 124 H
trussd@fvsu.edu
TRUSSELL, Jay .... 828-884-8340. 352 I
trussellj@brevard.edu
TRUSTY, Denise .... 606-886-3863. 194 K
denise.trusty@kctcs.edu
TRUSTY, LeRoy, A .... 443-412-2145. 215 C
letrusty@harford.edu
TRUSZ, Robert, J .... 740-351-3610. 388 N
btrusz@shawnee.edu
TRUTNA, Kevin .... 530-283-0202... 44 H
ktrutna@frc.edu
TRUXILLO, Betty, D .... 225-923-2524. 201 A
director@brsc.edu
TRYON, Sandy .... 515-964-6408. 177 B
sbtryon@dmacc.edu
TRZASKA, Ken, J .... 906-932-4231. 242 I
kent@gogebic.edu
TRZEBIATOWSKI, Brian . 773-481-8287. 142 F
btrzebiatowski@ccc.edu
TRZECIAK, Jeffrey, G ...... 314-935-5415. 284 L
Jeffrey.Trzeciak@wustl.edu
TRZEPACZ, Angie .... 270-809-6861. 198 B
atrzepacz@murraystate.edu
TSAFFARAS, Peter, H ..... 617-984-1776. 235 I
ptsaffaras@quincycollege.edu
TSAI, Chih-Yang .... 845-257-2930. 342 B
tsaic@newpaltz.edu
TSAI, Frank .... 510-849-8200... 57 H
ftsia@psr.edu
TSAI, Patty .... 866-323-0233... 60 E
TSANG, Chui, L .... 310-434-4200... 65 A
tsang_chui@smc.edu
TSANG, Edmund .... 269-276-3249. 252 I
edmund.tsang@wmich.edu
TSARK, Gregory .... 321-674-7584. 104 H
gtsark@fit.edu

TSATSOULIS, Costas ...... 940-565-4300. 490 C
costas.tsatsoulis@unt.edu
TSCHABRUN, Susan .... 657-278-2714... 33 E
stschabrun@fullerton.edu
TSCHERTER, Andrea, G .. 812-888-5794. 174 F
atscherter@vinu.edu
TSCHETTER, Wesley, G ... 605-688-4920. 452 B
wesley.tschetter@sdstate.edu
TSCHUY, Eric .... 503-491-7469. 404 E
eric.tschuy@mhcc.edu
TSEGAI, Adiam .... 716-884-9120. 315 K
aktsegai@bryantstratton.edu
TSEGAYE, Teferi .... 502-597-6310. 197 A
teferi.tsegaye@kysu.edu
TSO, Jay .... 212-757-1190. 313 H
jtso@funeraleducation.org
TSOUMAS, Linda, J .... 508-373-5709. 233 E
linda.tsoumas@mcphs.edu
TSUCHIYAMA, Ray .... 808-984-3471. 137 B
ray.tsuchiyama@uhfoundation.org
TSUEI-STRAUSE, Angela . 704-337-2374. 365 G
TSUQUIASHI-DADDESIO,
Eva .... 724-738-4863. 429 F
eva.tsuquiashi@sru.edu
TSUTSUI, William, M ...... 214-768-3212. 481 A
btsutsui@smu.edu
TUBB, Joe .... 806-894-9611. 480 H
jtubb@southplainscollege.edu
TUBBS, Jeffrey, L .... 704-406-4427. 354 C
jtubbs@gardner-webb.edu
TUBBS, Richard, E .... 941-351-4742. 111 O
rtubbs@ringling.edu
TUBBS, Teresa .... 910-272-3662. 363 B
ttubbs@robeson.edu
TUBBS, Trenton .... 417-864-7220. 274 D
ttubbs@cci.edu
TUBMAN, Jonathan, G ... 202-885-3753... 94 F
jtubman@american.edu
TUBMAN, Lynn .... 215-248-7046. 413 A
tubmanl@chc.edu
TUCCI, Barbara .... 505-428-1264. 311 J
barbara.tucci@sfcc.edu
TUCCI, Karen, L .... 740-264-5591. 379 F
ktucci@egcc.edu
TUCCI, Paul .... 518-587-2100. 346 A
paul.tucci@esc.edu
TUCHMAN, Richard, J .... 203-932-7268... 92 E
rtuchman@newhaven.edu
TUCK, Amy .... 662-325-3221. 268 D
at25@msstate.edu
TUCK, Inez .... 336-334-7751. 367 E
ituck@ncat.edu
TUCK, Martin .... 740-774-7200. 387 C
tuck@ohio.edu
TUCKER, Anne .... 509-434-5108. 518 E
anne.tucker@ccs.spokane.edu
TUCKER, Anne .... 509-434-5109. 518 F
anne.tucker@ccs.spokane.edu
TUCKER, Anne, M .... 509-434-5109. 518 D
atucker@ccs.spokane.edu
TUCKER, Anthony .... 706-419-1663. 123 F
anthony.tucker@covenant.edu
TUCKER, Archie .... 256-372-8344..... 1 A
archie.tucker@aamu.edu
TUCKER, Arlene, C .... 337-550-1288. 205 B
TUCKER, Barbara .... 608-822-2456. 541 C
btucker@swtc.edu
TUCKER, Bill .... 601-276-3726. 269 H
wtucker@smcc.edu
TUCKER, Brandon .... 734-677-5087. 252 A
brtucker@wccnet.edu
TUCKER, Carol, M .... 713-221-8269. 489 D
tuckerca@uhd.edu
TUCKER, Cecelia, T .... 757-683-5210. 507 N
ctucker@odu.edu
TUCKER, Cheryl .... 707-476-4293... 40 H
cheryl-tucker@redwoods.edu
TUCKER, David, C .... 812-888-4266. 174 F
dtucker@vinu.edu
TUCKER, Dawn .... 919-718-7437. 359 B
dmtucker@cccc.edu
TUCKER, Diane, P .... 617-358-6887. 224 D
dtucker@bu.edu
TUCKER, Donald, L .... 330-471-8119. 383 D
dtucker@malone.edu
TUCKER, Eileen .... 610-660-1346. 432 E
tucker@sju.edu
TUCKER, Ella .... 334-229-4156..... 1 D
etucker@alasu.edu
TUCKER, G.L .... 218-846-3765. 259 F
gl.tucker@minnesota.edu
TUCKER, Geraldine .... 512-223-7572. 466 I
gtucker@austincc.edu
TUCKER, Gretchen .... 276-944-6491. 504 H
gtucker@ehc.edu
TUCKER, Herman, V .... 254-299-8660. 476 D
htucker@mclennan.edu
TUCKER, Irene .... 775-445-4234. 295 A
irene.tucker@wnc.edu
TUCKER, Jameel .... 610-526-6092. 417 H
jtucker@harcum.edu

TUCKER, James .... 518-327-6286. 336 B
jtucker@paulsmiths.edu
TUCKER, James, R .... 215-895-2800. 415 B
jrt55@drexel.edu
TUCKER, Jim .... 785-749-8460. 187 B
jtucker@haskell.edu
TUCKER, John, D .... 619-298-1829... 68 A
jtucker@ssu.edu
TUCKER, Joy .... 252-492-2061. 364 F
tuckerj@vgcc.edu
TUCKER, Karen .... 630-752-5060. 163 F
karen.tucker@wheaton.edu
TUCKER, Karin, T .... 323-856-7609... 27 O
ktucker@afi.com
TUCKER, Keith .... 210-829-3125. 490 A
tucker@uiwtx.edu
TUCKER, Ken .... 205-652-3471..... 9 F
ktucker@uwa.edu
TUCKER, Kim .... 970-675-3335... 80 B
kim.tucker@cncc.edu
TUCKER, Mark .... 336-386-3217. 364 D
tuckerm@surry.edu
TUCKER, Mary, E .... 520-621-9438... 18 F
mtucker@email.arizona.edu
TUCKER, Michael, A .... 765-641-4295. 163 L
matucker@anderson.edu
TUCKER, Murl .... 714-547-9625... 30 J
mtucker@calcoast.edu
TUCKER, NaDene .... 252-246-1425. 365 C
ntucker@wilsoncc.edu
TUCKER, Nate .... 423-473-1190. 455 L
ntucker@leeuniversity.edu
TUCKER, Ned .... 402-826-8601. 289 E
ned.tucker@doane.edu
TUCKER, Patrick .... 860-832-1786... 87 K
ptucker@ccsu.edu
TUCKER, Raymond, A ..... 785-827-5541. 188 C
rtucker@kwu.edu
TUCKER, Raymond, T ..... 304-367-4861. 529 F
Raymond.Tucker@fairmontstate.edu
TUCKER, Robert .... 325-670-1427. 472 O
Robert.Tucker@hsutx.edu
TUCKER, Robert .... 325-649-8600. 473 F
rtucker@hputx.edu
TUCKER, Sandra .... 318-670-9641. 207 A
stucker@susla.edu
TUCKER, Seth .... 315-498-2123. 335 G
tuckers@sunyocc.edu
TUCKER, Sharon "Nyota" 229-430-2799. 119 J
nyota.tucker@asurams.edu
TUCKER, Sheryl .... 405-744-6368. 397 H
sheryl.tucker@okstate.edu
TUCKER, Stacey .... 423-614-8637. 455 L
stucker@leeuniversity.edu
TUCKER, Stacy .... 913-288-7239. 187 L
stucker@kckcc.edu
TUCKER, Terry, W .... 607-587-3621. 345 D
tuckertw@alfredstate.edu
TUCKER, Tommy .... 870-307-7324... 21 H
thomas.tucker@lyon.edu
TUCKER, W. Steven .... 205-348-8396..... 8 D
uadps01@bama.ua.edu
TUCKER-LOEWE,
Cheryle, L .... 618-650-3701. 159 H
chtucke@siue.edu
TUCKER-MCCLOUD,
Janice .... 740-826-8134. 384 L
jtucker@muskingum.edu
TUDELA, Virginia, C .... 671-735-5590. 546 C
virginia.tudela@guamcc.edu
TUDOR, Donna, K .... 615-248 7703. 462 D
dtudor@trevecca.edu
TUDOR, Gail .... 207-941-7039. 210 B
tudorg@husson.edu
TUDOR, Lisa .... 239-489-9350. 101 O
ltudor@edison.edu
TUDRYN, Jonathan .... 413-755-4420. 233 A
jtudryn@stcc.edu
TUEDIO, James, A .... 209-667-3531... 35 B
tuedio@csustan.edu
TUEL, Alexander .... 301-387-3028. 214 I
alexander.tuel@garrettcollege.edu
TUFANO, Joseph, J .... 718-990-5800. 339 A
tufanoj@stjohns.edu
TUFAU-AFRIYIE,
Michelle .... 508-854-7568. 232 F
mtufau@qcc.mass.edu
TUFEL, Peter .... 212-686-9244. 313 G
TUGGLE, Joseph .... 601-477-5406. 267 F
joseph.tuggle@jcjc.edu
TUIA, Jennifer .... 360-596-5369. 524 A
jtuia@spscc.edu
TUITASI, Michael .... 310-434-4389... 65 A
tuitasi_michael@smc.edu
TUITASI, Sifagatogo .... 684-699-9155. 546 A
s.tuitasi@amsamoa.edu
TUITE, Jayme .... 724-222-5330. 425 K
jtuite@penncommercial.edu
TUITE, Kathleen .... 973-618-3534. 300 A
ktuite@caldwell.edu

TUITT, Frank 303-871-2591 86 B ftuitt@du.edu
TULAFONO, Grace 684-699-9155 546 A g.tulafono@amsamoa.edu
TULAK, William, H 985-448-7902 203 B william.tulak@fletcher.edu
TULEYA-PAYNE, Helena 717-872-3379 429 D helena.tuleya-payne@millersville.edu
TULL, Ashley 254-968-9080 483 A tull@tarleton.edu
TULLER, RN, Jodi 413-528-7253 222 E jtuller@simons-rock.edu
TULLIO, Ann 718-631-6215 319 D atullio@qcc.cuny.edu
TULLOCH, Helen (Meg) 202-685-3948 544 K tullochh@ndu.edu
TULLY, Greg, J 815-772-7218 153 G jprombo@morrisontech.edu
TULLY, Patricia 860-685-2887 92 H ptully@wesleyan.edu
TULLY-DARTEZ, Stephanie 870-862-8131 23 D stully-dartez@southark.edu
TUMA, Alicia 305-220-4120 111 E phadir@ptcmatt.com
TUMBLIN, Tom 859-858-2301 192 A
TUMELTY, Susanne, M 718-960-1190 318 A susanne.tumelty@lehman.cuny.edu
TUMEO, Mark, A 904-620-1350 116 B m.tumeo@unf.edu
TUMEO, Michael, D 214-768-2808 481 A mtumeo@smu.edu
TUMER, Lisa, L 540-568-7820 506 F tumerll@jmu.edu
TUMEY, Terrance, J 530-752-4557 70 J athleticsdirector@ucdavis.edu
TUMMINO, Pauline 718-990-6106 339 A tumminop@stjohns.edu
TUMMOLO, Paul 212-353-4100 321 F pault@cooper.edu
TUNCAP, Michael 253-833-9111 520 C mtuncap@greenriver.edu
TUNE, Kathie 434-791-7106 502 D ktune@averett.edu
TUNG, Lisa 617-879-7335 230 B ltung@massart.edu
TUNG, Yuming 315-470-6861 345 B ytung@esf.edu
TUNGSETH, Margaret 641-628-5276 176 E tungsethm@central.edu
TUNSIL, Debberin 386-752-1822 104 G debbie.tunsil@fgc.edu
TUNSTALL, Denise, S 804-523-5029 512 F dtunstall@reynolds.edu
TUNSTILL, Hilda 931-393-1573 461 A htunstill@mscc.edu
TUNSTILL, Jerry 931-393-1688 461 A jtunstill@mscc.edu
TUNUGUNTLA, Rama 318-274-3234 207 E tunuguntla@gram.edu
TUOHEY, Christina 413-781-7822 233 A cctuohey@stcc.edu
TUOMEY, Lianne, M 802-656-2027 500 F lianne.tuomey@uvm.edu
TUPALA, Kay 920-498-5482 541 B kay.tupala@nwtc.edu
TURAK, Ronald, A 716-338-1065 327 J ronturak@mail.sunyjcc.edu
TURANO, Rosemary 617-964-1100 222 A rturano@ants.edu
TURANSKY, June, S 302-857-1126 93 G june.turansky@dtcc.edu
TURBEVILLE, Donna 910-642-7141 364 A Donna.Turbeville@sccnc.edu
TURBEVILLE, John 315-470-6660 345 B jturbev@esf.edu
TURBIDE, Gerard 607-274-3124 327 E gturbide@ithaca.edu
TURCO, John, H 603-650-1423 296 G john.h.turco@dartmouth.edu
TURCOTT, Scott 617-745-3000 225 G scott.turcott@enc.edu
TURCOTTE, Jim 601-925-3809 268 A turcotte@mc.edu
TURCOTTE, Louis, H 812-877-8192 172 C louis.turcotte@rose-hulman.edu
TUREK, John, G 714-879-3901 47 K jgturek@hiu.edu
TUREK, Joseph 434-544-8417 506 K turek@lynchburg.edu
TURELL, Susan 607-436-2125 343 E susan.turell@onenta.edu
TUREN, Christopher 310-965-0888 76 H
TURGEON, Paul 714-556-3610 74 D paul.turgeon@vanguard.edu
TURGEON, Pennie 508-421-3813 225 A pturgeon@clarku.edu
TURICO, Michael 602-538-9396 11 C
TURK, David, F 845-675-4422 335 C david.turk@nyack.edu
TURK, Laura 540-831-5827 508 C lturk@radford.edu
TURK, Mike 334-833-4322 4 D mturk@huntingdon.edu
TURKKAN, Jaylan 415-405-3995 35 E jturkkan@sfsu.edu
TURKOWSKI, Addie 320-308-2151 261 B aturkowski@stcloudstate.edu
TURKS, Stacie 209-946-2225 73 A sturks@pacific.edu
TURLETES, Christopher 907-786-1110 10 H ancmt2@uaa.alaska.edu
TURLEY, Alicestyne 859-985-3783 192 F turlleya@berea.edu
TURLEY, Cricket 620-276-9574 187 A cricket.turley@gcccks.edu
TURLEY, Jason, J 740-376-4600 383 E jason.turley@marietta.edu
TURLEY-AMES, Kandi 208-282-3204 138 E turlkand@isu.edu
TURLINGTON, Lisa 910-592-8081 363 E lturlington@sampsoncc.edu
TURMAN, Paul 605-773-3455 451 E paul.turman@sdbor.edu
TURMON, Janie 864-225-7653 444 A janieturmon@forrestcollege.edu
TURNAU, Michelle 651-255-6117 264 C mturnau@unitedseminary.edu
TURNBLOM, Sarah, E 530-226-4127 66 D sturnblom@simpsonu.edu
TURNBO, Doreen, B 302-295-1192 94 E doreen.b.turnbo@wilmu.edu
TURNBOUGH, Dale 205-934-9518 8 E dalet@uab.edu
TURNER, A. Kay 870-575-8735 24 E turnera@uapb.edu
TURNER, Aimee, L 607-255-3581 322 A aimee.turner@cornell.edu
TURNER, Amanda 708-456-0300 161 A aturner1@triton.edu
TURNER, B, P 334-387-3877 1 E businessoffice@amridgeuniversity.edu
TURNER, Barbara, J 870-759-4112 25 K bturner@wbcoll.edu
TURNER, Barry 912-688-6958 129 J bturner@ogeecheetech.edu
TURNER, Beth 315-781-3315 326 C turner@hws.edu
TURNER, Brad 315-279-5604 328 D bturner@mail.keuka.edu
TURNER, Brenda 334-386-7501 3 H bturner@faulkner.edu
TURNER, Brent 407-646-2624 111 Q bturner@rollins.edu
TURNER, Carolyn 870-946-3506 24 G
TURNER, Carolyn 513-861-6400 390 C carolyn.turner@myunion.edu
TURNER, Catherine, P 540-224-4644 506 G cpturner@jchs.edu
TURNER, Christine 503-699-3381 404 C cturner@marylhurst.edu
TURNER, Colt 817-461-8741 466 D cturner@arlingtonbaptistcollege.edu
TURNER, Craig 270-852-3104 197 B cturner@kwc.edu
TURNER, Curtis 719-336-1519 82 R curtis.turner@lamarcc.edu
TURNER, Darron 817-257-5566 484 I d.turner@tcu.edu
TURNER, Debra 304-384-5338 529 E turner@concord.edu
TURNER, Donna, A 252-246-1240 365 C daturner@wilsoncc.edu
TURNER, Eddie, C 806-291-3615 494 F turnere@wbu.edu
TURNER, Eric 870-759-4220 25 K eturner@wbcoll.edu
TURNER, Fran 205-391-2663 6 H ftruner@sheltonstate.edu
TURNER, Franklin, R 714-539-6561 68 F
TURNER, Gary 615-844-5276 464 E gturner@welch.edu
TURNER, J. C 507-433-0627 260 I j.c.turner@riverland.edu
TURNER, J. Leigh 979-845-7725 483 C jl-turner@tamu.edu
TURNER, James 607-844-8222 347 I turnerj@TC3.edu
TURNER, James 601-318-6610 270 I jturner@wmcarey.edu
TURNER, James, C 434-924-2670 511 B jct4w@virginia.edu
TURNER, Jana 901-572-2455 453 B jana.turner@bchs.edu
TURNER, Janet 503-943-7311 408 F Turnerj@up.edu
TURNER, Jeff 615-248-1223 462 D jturner@trevecca.edu
TURNER, Jere 603-206-8165 296 A jturner@ccsnh.edu
TURNER, Jim 419-755-4735 385 D jturner@ncstatecollege.edu
TURNER, Joe 239-513-1122 106 O jturner@hodges.edu
TURNER, John, T 910-695-3704 363 F turnerj@sandhills.edu
TURNER, Joseph, T 252-473-5936 359 F joseph_turner@albemarle.edu
TURNER, June 760-921-5558 58 C june.turner@paloverde.edu
TURNER, Kara 443-885-3350 217 A kara.turner@morgan.edu
TURNER, Kathy 321-674-8839 104 H kturner@fit.edu
TURNER, Keith 218-879-0805 258 E kturner@fdltcc.edu
TURNER, Larry 704-355-7577 353 D larry.turner@carolinashealthcare.org
TURNER, Lathan, E 252-328-6495 367 B turnerla@ecu.edu
TURNER, Lauren 978-934-1804 229 B Lauren_Turner@uml.edu
TURNER, Laurie, L 253-535-7361 521 I turnerll@plu.edu
TURNER, Leslie 561-803-2473 110 B leslie_turner@pba.edu
TURNER, Linda 707-962-2662 40 H linda-turner@redwoods.edu
TURNER, Lois "Casey" 215-895-6711 415 B lat59@drexel.edu
TURNER, Lori 507-457-1709 264 A lturner@smumn.edu
TURNER, Louise 406-586-3585 286 F louise.turner@montanabiblecollege.edu
TURNER, Marcia 239-513-1122 106 O mturner@hodges.edu
TURNER, Marietta 217-351-2505 155 J mturner@parkland.edu
TURNER, Mary 916-558-2226 53 D turnerm@scc.losrios.edu
TURNER, Matt 304-696-6713 529 H turner6@marshall.edu
TURNER, Michael 218-723-6387 254 K mturner@css.edu
TURNER, Michael, C 334-387-3877 1 E mcturner@amridgeuniversity.edu
TURNER, Michelle 214-368-3680 475 K
TURNER, Mitzi 270-247-8521 197 H mturner@midcontinent.edu
TURNER, Nancy, L 608-342-1789 537 D turnern@uwplatt.edu
TURNER, Patricia, A 310-206-3961 71 C pturner@college.ucla.edu
TURNER, Paul 859-246-6717 194 L paul.turner@kctcs.edu
TURNER, Paul, S 561-237-7245 108 X pturner@lynn.edu
TURNER, Peter 315-268-6544 320 A pturner@clarkson.edu
TURNER, R. Gerald 214-768-3300 481 A mjj@smu.edu
TURNER, Rachel 305-626-3605 104 J ra.turner@fmuniv.edu
TURNER, Raphael 757-822-2181 514 C raturner@tcc.edu
TURNER, Rebecca, B 812-941-2243 168 F rebeturn@ius.edu
TURNER, Rebecca, E 256-782-5485 4 K bturner@jsu.edu
TURNER, Rebecca, O 256-782-5540 4 K rturner@jsu.edu
TURNER, Richard 417-447-8202 279 K turnerr@otc.edu
TURNER, Robert 662-846-4744 266 G rturner@deltastate.edu
TURNER, Robert 910-296-2416 361 D rturner@jamessprunt.edu
TURNER, Sally, J 716-673-3424 342 A sally.turner@fredonia.edu
TURNER, Sandra 212-242-5499 348 F sandra.turner@tsca.edu
TURNER, Sarah 304-384-5348 529 E slturner@concord.edu
TURNER, Scott 208-282-3470 138 E turnscot@isu.edu
TURNER, Sharisse 850-201-8582 117 D turners@tcc.fl.edu
TURNER, Sharon, P 859-323-1881 200 C sharon.turner@uky.edu
TURNER, Shawna, C 270-745-6463 200 G shawna.turner@wku.edu
TURNER, Stephen, R 219-785-5401 172 A sturner@pnc.edu
TURNER, Steve 918-456-5511 396 H turner@nsuok.edu
TURNER, Sue, Z 912-443-5485 131 D sturner@savannahtech.edu
TURNER, Susan 203-932-7478 92 E sturner@newhaven.edu
TURNER, Tara 410-951-3812 220 B tturner@coppin.edu
TURNER, Terrance, A 903-233-4441 475 J terryturner@letu.edu
TURNER, Terry, J 505-277-5115 312 F terryjturner@unm.edu
TURNER, Thomas, H 540-375-2311 509 B turner@roanoke.edu
TURNER, Vickie 662-243-1940 266 I vturner@eastms.edu
TURNER, Walter 404-627-2681 121 H walter.turner@beulah.org
TURNER, Zoa Ann 972-524-3341 481 H
TURNER-SAMPLE, Margaret 480-517-4556 15 D margaret.turner-sample@riosalado.edu
TURNER-WATTS, Sheryl 864-503-5490 448 H sturner-watts@uscupstate.edu
TURNEY, Judy 815-772-7218 153 G jturney@morrisontech.edu
TURNEY, Keith 303-273-3333 80 E keith.turney@is.mines.edu
TURNIS, Jane 719-389-6138 79 D jturnis@coloradocollege.edu
TURNOCK, Madeline 503-493-8550 402 J mturnock@cu-portland.edu
TURNQUIST, David, C 303-724-1100 86 A david.turnquist@ucdenver.edu
TURNQUIST, James 906-487-2313 247 A jaturnqu@mtu.edu
TURNQUIST, Sandra 906-487-7240 242 G sandra.turnquist@finlandia.edu
TURNS, Estevanny 410-225-2363 216 C eturns@mica.edu
TURPEN, James 402-559-4388 292 J jterpen@unmc.edu
TURPIN, Barbara 848-932-3625 306 B turpin@rutgers.edu
TURPIN, Craig 502-213-2110 195 F craig.turpin@kctcs.edu
TURPIN, Jennifer, E 415-422-6136 73 J turpinj@usfca.edu
TURPIN, John, C 336-841-9000 355 C jturpin@highpoint.edu
TURPIN, Kay 828-227-7239 369 E turpin@wcu.edu
TURPIN, Linda 513-585-2619 376 I linda.turpin@thechristhospital.com
TURRENTINE, Cathryn 603-358-2117 298 F cturrentine@keene.edu
TURRIETTA, Anthony 915-747-6127 492 A aturrietta@utep.edu
TURTELTAUB, Rhea 310-794-5567 71 C rheat@support.ucla.edu
TURZAI, Eric, C 717-361-1157 415 H turzaiec@etown.edu
TURZANSKI, Edward, A 215-951-1391 420 B turzansk@lasalle.edu
TUSACK, Donna 619-594-7500 35 D donna.tusack@sdsu.edu
TUSCHAK, Mark 830-792-7215 480 F mctuschak@schreiner.edu
TUSCHMAN, Keli 620-331-4100 187 G ktuschman@indycc.edu
TUSKI, Donald 207-775-5098 210 H dtuski@meca.edu
TUTEN, Jane 803-641-3460 448 A janet@usca.edu
TUTHILL, George, F 603-535-2286 298 G gftuthilli@plymouth.edu
TUTSOCK, Robert, J 989-964-4082 249 G tutsock@svsu.edu
TUTT, Larry 270-831-9783 195 D larry.tutt@kctcs.edu
TUTTER, Catherine 617-369-3602 236 F ctutter@smfa.edu
TUTTLE, David, M 210-999-8843 488 C dtuttle@trinity.edu
TUTTLE, Gail 315-792-3016 349 F gtuttle@utica.edu
TUTTLE, Gail, C 336-841-9120 355 C gtuttle@highpoint.edu
TUTTLE, Heather 517-327-6253 336 B htuttle@paulsmiths.edu
TUTTLE, Isaac 573-442-2211 282 H ituttle@stephens.edu
TUTTLE, James 253-589-5533 518 B jim.tuttle@cptc.edu
TUTTLE, Nick 580-349-1353 397 G nick.tuttle@opsu.edu
TUTTLE, Ronald 914-968-6200 339 E ronald.tuttle@archny.org
TUTTLE, Stephen 212-217-4030 324 C
TUXHORN, Rick 620-242-0468 188 G tuxhornr@mcpherson.edu
TVARKUNAS, Michael 662-476-5059 266 I mtvar@eastms.edu
TVRDY, Peggy 402-826-8260 289 E peggy.tvrdy@doane.edu
TWADDELL, Gerald, E 859-344-3307 199 H gerald.twaddell@thomasmore.edu
TWARDOCK, Rob 847-543-2499 143 A eng491@clcillinois.edu

TWEED, Emily, J .... 952-888-4777. 263 B
etweed@nwhealth.edu
TWEED, James .... 617-243-2225. 227 K
jtweed@lasell.edu
TWEEDELL, Cynthia .... 270-247-8521. 197 H
ctweedell@midcontinent.edu
TWEEDIE, Frank .... 401-598-2503. 439 B
ftweedie@jwu.edu
TWIGG, Sharon .... 802-635-1351. 501 D
sharon.twigg@jsc.edu
TWILL, Sarah .... 937-775-3162. 393 G
sarah.twill@wright.edu
TWILLEY, Shirley .... 918-463-6358. 395 D
shirley.twilley@connorsstate.edu
TWIST, Tony .... 317-299-0333. 173 D
TWITTY, Brian .... 951-487-3103... 55 B
btwitty@msjc.edu
TWO BULLS, Wayne .... 406-768-6312. 286 C
wtwobulls@fpcc.edu
TWOMBLY, Meredith ...... 413-559-5890. 227 B
TWYMAN, Edward .... 262-595-2039. 537 C
twyman@uwp.edu
TYBURSKI, Marcelle ...... 315-228-7431. 320 F
mtyburski@colgate.edu
TYBURSKI, Robert, L ...... 315-228-7445. 320 F
rtyburski@colgate.edu
TYDINGS, Flora, W .... 706-355-5110. 120 J
ftydings@athenstech.edu
TYKOCINSKI, Mark, L .... 215-955-1628. 434 C
mark.tykocinski@jefferson.edu
TYKSINSKI, Deborah ...... 315-792-7151. 346 C
deborah.tyksinski@sunyit.edu
TYKWINSKI, Joseph .... 701-845-7332. 372 A
joe.tykwinski@vcsu.edu
TYLER, Alan .... 360-438-4495. 522 G
atyler@stmartin.edu
TYLER, Barry .... 210-924-4338. 467 E
barry.tyler@bua.edu
TYLER, Carol .... 304-829-7567. 526 D
ctyler@bethanywv.edu
TYLER, Greg .... 251-626-3303..... 8 B
gtyler@ussa.edu
TYLER, Gwendolyn, J ..... 609-896-5058. 305 D
tyler@rider.edu
TYLER, Harold .... 310-660-3504... 43 B
htyler@elcamino.edu
TYLER, Jaimee .... 517-578-7100. 236 E
jtyler@sbboston.com
TYLER, Jeanie .... 619-388-3924... 62 D
jtyler@sdccd.edu
TYLER, Julie .... 901-320-9700. 463 J
juliet@victory.edu
TYLER, Karlene, M .... 620-242-0441. 188 G
tylerk@mcpherson.edu
TYLER, Ken, D .... 540-654-1876. 510 J
ktyler2@umw.edu
TYLER, Kimberly .... 312-850-7013. 142 C
Kimkwooley-tyler@ccc.edu
TYLER, Lauren .... 903-510-2611. 488 E
ltyl@tjc.edu
TYLER, Melvin, C .... 816-235-1141. 283 D
tylerm@umkc.edu
TYLER, Nathan .... 256-306-2817..... 2 F
ntyler@calhoun.edu
TYLER, Ralph .... 203-332-5081... 88 F
rtyler@hcc.commnet.edu
TYLER, Rhonda .... 575-492-2116. 312 M
rtyler@usw.edu
TYLER, Rico .... 773-325-4680. 143 H
rtyler@depaul.edu
TYLER, Victoria .... 914-455-3515. 330 J
vtyler@mercy.edu
TYLER, Wanda .... 203-932-7427... 92 E
wtyler@newhaven.edu
TYMANN, Daniel .... 978 867-4260. 226 H
dan.tymann@gordon.edu
TYMAS-JONES,
Raymond .... 801-581-3887. 496 Q
r.tymasjones@finearts.utah.edu
TYMKOW, Tony, A .... 708-534-4108. 145 F
ttymkow@govst.edu
TYMOCZKO, Michelle ..... 303-477-7240... 82 C
michellet@heritage-education.com
TYMUS, Peter .... 516-299-3370. 329 C
peter.tymus@liu.edu
TYNAN, Craig .... 518-694-7201. 313 B
craig.tynan@acphs.edu
TYNDALL, Brad .... 970-945-8691... 79 G
TYNER, Dennis .... 785-242-5200. 189 I
dennis.tyner@ottawa.edu
TYNER, JR., Gary .... 214-638-0484. 475 D
tynerjr1@yahoo.com
TYNER, Jennifer .... 707-965-6311... 57 J
jtyner@puc.edu
TYNER, Kathy .... 619-482-6337... 68 B
ktyner@swccd.edu
TYNER, Kathy .... 214-638-0484. 475 D
ktyner@kdstudio.com
TYNER, Lee .... 662-915-7792. 270 B
ltyner@olemiss.edu
TYNES, Craig .... 601-403-1155. 269 D
ctynes@prcc.edu
TYNES, James .... 212-220-1377. 317 A
jtynes@bmcc.cuny.edu
TYNES, Sheryl, R .... 210-999-8201. 488 C
stynes@trinity.edu
TYNON, Kathy .... 402-872-2365. 291 E
ktynon@peru.edu
TYO, Keith, D .... 518-564-3930. 344 B
tyokd@plattsburgh.edu
TYPOLT, Jeanie .... 406-586-3585. 286 F
jeanie.typolt@montanabiblecollege.edu
TYPOLT, Ty .... 406-586-3585. 286 F
typoltj@hotmail.com
TYRE, Yulanda .... 334-244-3430..... 2 A
ytyre@aum.edu
TYREE, John, K .... 432-837-8228. 487 B
jtyree@sulross.edu
TYREE, Jonathan .... 434-947-8112. 508 D
jtyree@randolphcollege.edu
TYREE, Tracy .... 203-392-5550... 88 A
tyreet1@southernct.edu
TYRELL, Steve, J .... 518-891-2915. 335 A
president@nccc.edu
TYRRELL, Elizabeth .... 408-270-6453... 63 O
elizabeth.tyrrell@evc.edu
TYRRELL, Wil .... 914-323-7178. 330 B
wil.tyrrell@mville.edu
TYSON, April .... 901-572-2446. 453 B
april.tyson@bchs.edu
TYSON, John .... 248-218-2000. 249 D
jtyson@rc.edu
TYSON, Linda .... 252-399-6330. 352 F
ltyson@barton.edu
TYSON, Thomas, N .... 410-334-2913. 221 D
ttyson@worwic.edu
TYSON, William, R .... 919-893-9101. 359 B
btyson@cccc.edu
TYSZLER, Ira .... 212-463-0400. 348 B
tysz@touro.edu
TYUS, Bing .... 863-297-1004. 110 H
btyus@polk.edu
TZENG, Julia .... 415-371-0002... 57 B
TZENG, Walker .... 415-371-0002... 57 B
TZIMBAL, Tootie .... 831-479-5730... 30 G
totzimba@cabrillo.edu

U

UBAGO, Maria .... 323-343-2586... 34 A
mubago@cslanet.calstatela.edu
UBAMADU, Ben .... 423-697-3254. 460 C
UBARRI-DE LEÓN,
Lydia .... 787-993-8858. 554 A
lydia.ubarri@upr.edu
UBELL, Robert, N .... 718-260-3407. 336 E
rubell@poly.edu
UCCI, Anthony .... 508-678-2811. 231 B
anthony.ucci@bristolcc.edu
UCCI, Martha .... 508-565-1033. 237 A
mucci@stonehill.edu
UCHIN, Robert, A .... 954-262-7311. 109 K
ruchin@nova.edu
UDA, Jon .... 208-426-1304. 137 G
jonuda@boisestate.edu
UDALL, David .... 928-428-8295... 13 J
david.udall@eac.edu
UDD, Kris, J .... 402-449-2811. 289 H
registrar@graceu.edu
UDDIN, Rita .... 718-260-5610. 319 B
ruddin@citytech.cuny.edu
UDE, Wayne .... 360-331-0307. 521 E
UDEH, Igwe, E .... 504-286-5331. 206 K
iudeh@suno.edu
UDELHOFEN, Angela, M .. 608-342-1125. 537 D
rulea@uwplatt.edu
UDEN, Michael .... 262-243-5700. 532 H
michael.uden@cuw.edu
UDEOGALANYA,
Anthony .... 718-270-6213. 319 A
anthonyu@mec.cuny.edu
UDIS-KESSLER, Amanda 719-227-8177... 79 D
audiskessler@coloradocollege.edu
UDKOW, David .... 516-686-7902. 333 H
dudkow@nyit.edu
UDOH, Emmanuel .... 502-456-6504. 199 G
eudoh@sullivan.edu
UDOM, Udoh .... 615-871-2260... 96 F
UDOVIC, Edward, R .... 312-362-8042. 143 H
eudovic@depaul.edu
UDOVIC, CM, Edward, R 312-362-8042. 143 H
eudovic@depaul.edu
UDPA, Satish, S .... 517-355-5014. 246 H
udpa@adminsv.msu.edu
UDUMA, Letitia .... 313-943-4058. 252 B
UECKER, Grant .... 605-995-7138. 450 E
grant.uecker@mitchelltech.edu
UEDA, Rikklyn, S .... 619-239-0391... 36 D
rueda@cwsl.edu
UEHARA, Edwina .... 206-685-2480. 524 G
eddi@uw.edu
UEKI, Omdasu, T .... 680-488-2471. 547 B
oueki@palau.edu
UERLING, Laura, J .... 508-565-1378. 237 A
luerling@stonehill.edu
UFERT FAIRLESS,
Nancy, J .... 618-650-3187. 159 H
nufert@siue.edu
UFFORD, Brian, K .... 207-778-7334. 212 D
brian.ufford@maine.edu
UFFORD, Lori .... 541-506-6025. 402 H
lufford@cgcc.cc.or.us
UFOMATA, Titilayo .... 315-781-3304. 326 C
ufomata@hws.edu
UGALDE, Aileen, M .... 305-284-2700. 118 F
augalde@miami.edu
UGLIANO, Don .... 352-854-2322. 100 K
uglianod@cf.edu
UGLUM, Abby .... 540-831-6667. 508 C
aeeckhart@radford.edu
UGORJI, Lauren, D .... 609-258-5732. 304 E
lauren@princeton.edu
UGRAS, Joseph, Y .... 215-951-5124. 420 B
ugras@lasalle.edu
UHAL, Len .... 563-876-3353. 177 I
svdalum@aol.com
UHAZY, Les .... 661-722-6300... 28 F
luhazy@avc.edu
UHDE, Alicia .... 701-224-5764. 372 B
alicia.uhde@bismarckstate.edu
UHER, Bill .... 505-277-5598. 312 F
wuher@salud.unm.edu
UHLIG, Ronald .... 858-642-8439... 55 J
ruhlig@nu.edu
UHLINGER, Eleanor, S ... 831-656-2342. 544 M
euhlinger@nps.edu
UHLIR, James .... 715-232-2188. 538 B
uhlirj@uwstout.edu
UITTO, Denise .... 330-684-8788. 390 F
duitto@uakron.edu
UJLAKI, Stephen, G .... 310-338-5800... 53 E
stephen.ujlaki@lmu.edu
UKACHUKWU, Victoria .. 973-618-3595. 300 A
vukachukwu@caldwell.edu
UKPOLO, Victor .... 504-286-5311. 206 K
vukpolo@suno.edu
ULASZEK, David .... 312-567-3366. 147 F
dulaszek@iit.edu
ULATE, David, D .... 650-738-7069... 64 D
ulated@smccd.edu
ULBRICH, Casandra .... 586-445-7244. 246 A
ulbrichc@macomb.edu
ULBRICHT, Alexandra, K 330-569-5182. 380 I
Ulbrichtak@hiram.edu
ULBRIGHT, Heather .... 503-375-7035. 403 A
hulbright@corban.edu
ULCH, Christine .... 609-894-9311. 299 I
hulch@bcc.edu
ULIBARRI, Debbie .... 719-846-5533... 85 H
debbie.ulibarri@trinidadstate.edu
ULIBARRI, Katherine ...... 505-224-4413. 309 E
kulibarri8@cnm.edu
ULLMAN,
Christopher, C .... 847-259-1840. 141 L
cullman@christianlifecollege.edu
ULLMAN, David, F .... 973-596-2915. 303 G
david.ullman@njit.edu
ULLMAN, Julie .... 414-382-6053. 531 I
julie.ullman@alverno.edu
ULLMANN, Brian .... 301-314-6650. 219 B
ullmann@umd.edu
ULLOA, Alicia .... 361-354-2245. 468 K
ulloaa@coastalbend.edu
ULLOM, Craig, E .... 740-368-3135. 387 J
ceullom@owu.edu
ULMAN, Ed .... 253-680-7713. 516 L
eulman@bates.ctc.edu
ULMEN, Dan .... 406-265-3755. 287 D
dulman@msun.edu
ULMER, Deborah .... 804-622-8700. 512 G
dulmer@jtcc.edu
ULMER, Laverne .... 601-477-4022. 267 F
laverne.ulmer@jcjc.edu
ULMSCHNEIDER,
John, E .... 804-828-1105. 511 F
jeulmsch@vcu.edu
ULRICH, Dennis .... 513-569-1414. 376 L
dennis.ulrich@cincinnatistate.edu
ULRICH, Gail, L .... 814-641-3194. 419 H
ulrichg@juniata.edu
ULRICH, James .... 312-235-3523. 159 A
j.ulrich@shimer.edu
ULRICH, Jana .... 704-991-0328. 364 C
ulrich7442@stanly.edu
ULRICH, Karl .... 406-683-7115. 286 I
k_ulrich@umwestern.edu
ULRICH, Paul .... 262-551-2112. 532 D
pulrich@carthage.edu
ULRICH, Rae .... 312-499-4219. 158 L
rulrich@saic.edu
ULRICH, Sigrid .... 718-270-1995. 342 D
sigrid.ulrich@downstate.edu
ULRICH, Tina, J .... 231-995-1063. 248 B
tulrich@nmc.edu
ULRICH, Trey, P .... 215-951-1671. 420 B
ulrich@lasalle.edu
ULSETH, Julie, A .... 810-762-9844. 244 Q
julseth@kettering.edu
ULSHAFER, Kevin, L .... 478-757-5125. 134 G
kulshafer@wesleyancollege.edu
ULZ, Mary Ann .... 847-566-6401. 162 G
mulz@usml.edu
UMANSKY, Lauri .... 870-972-3973... 19 N
lumansky@astate.edu
UMBAUGH, Rob .... 970-339-6237... 78 C
rob.umbaugh@aims.edu
UMBERGER, Stanley, F .. 540-375-2293. 509 B
umberger@roanoke.edu
UMBLE, Diane .... 717-872-3024. 429 D
diane.umble@millersville.edu
UMEHIRA, Ron .... 808-455-0321. 137 A
umehira@hawaii.edu
UMFRESS, Jason .... 843-383-8036. 442 F
jumfress@coker.edu
UMHOEFER, Gary, A ...... 920-403-3210. 535 L
gary.umhoefer@snc.edu
UMMER, Christopher, T . 802-626-6477. 501 E
christopher.ummer@lyndonstate.edu
UMSTATTD, Rustin .... 816-414-3700. 277 L
rumstattd@mbts.edu
UNBEHAGEN, Leonard ... 504-278-6438. 203 F
lunbehagen@nunez.edu
UNDEM, Obert .... 406-657-1142. 288 B
undemo@rocky.edu
UNDERBAKKE, Rick .... 509-682-6705. 525 B
runderbakke@wvc.edu
UNDERCOFFER, Anita .... 909-652-6032... 37 M
anita.undercoffer@chaffey.edu
UNDERDUE MURPH,
Yvette .... 218-477-2171. 259 H
yvette.underduemurph@mnstate.edu
UNDERWOOD, Alex .... 312-850-7125. 142 C
aunderwood3@ccc.edu
UNDERWOOD, Allen ...... 419-893-1986. 380 G
aunderwo@heidelberg.edu
UNDERWOOD, Anita ...... 845-675-4476. 335 C
anita.underwood@nyack.edu
UNDERWOOD, Ann .... 806-651-2121. 484 D
aunderwood@wtamu.edu
UNDERWOOD, Anthony . 304-424-8209. 530 E
anthony.underwood@wvup.edu
UNDERWOOD, Chloris .. 954-486-7728. 118 E
UNDERWOOD, Craig ..... 610-861-1500. 424 E
cunderwood@moravian.edu
UNDERWOOD, David ..... 479-964-0540... 20 E
dunderwood@atu.edu
UNDERWOOD, Dawn ..... 812-237-3088. 167 A
dawn.underwood@indstate.edu
UNDERWOOD, Elizabeth 479-788-7008... 24 A
elizabeth.underwood@uafs.edu
UNDERWOOD, Glenda ... 617-587-5662. 234 H
underwoodg@neco.edu
UNDERWOOD,
James, C .... 618-545-3010. 149 D
junderwood@kaskaskia.edu
UNDERWOOD, Julie, K .. 608-262-1763. 536 D
junderwood@wisc.edu
UNDERWOOD, Kathy, A 702-895-0283. 294 I
kathyunderwood@unlv.edu
UNDERWOOD, Ken .... 865-573-4517. 455 G
kunderwood@johnsonU.edu
UNDERWOOD, Lori, J .... 757-594-8828. 503 M
underwoo@cnu.edu
UNDERWOOD, Mark ...... 830-591-7286. 481 C
meunderwood@swtjc.edu
UNDERWOOD, Michelle 229-931-2627. 126 D
michelle.underwood@gsw.edu
UNDERWOOD, Michelle 503-255-0332. 404 F
munderwood@multnomah.edu
UNDERWOOD, Richard .. 615-248-1213. 462 D
runderwood@trevecca.edu
UNDERWOOD,
Robert, A .... 671-735-2990. 546 E
raunderwood@uguam.uog.edu
UNDERWOOD, Ruth .... 478-289-2134. 124 C
runderwood@ega.edu
UNDERWOOD,
Timothy, J .... 304-462-4114. 529 G
timothy.underwood@glenville.edu
UNDERWOOD, Von, E ... 580-581-2491. 394 G
vonu@cameron.edu
UNDERWOOD,
William, D .... 478-301-2500. 128 H
underwood_wd@mercer.edu
UNEBASAMI, Michael, T 808-956-6280. 136 D
mune@hawaii.edu
UNELL, Murry .... 303-797-5901... 78 F
murry.unell@arapahoe.edu
UNFERTH, Vickie, L .... 608-796-3841. 539 E
vlunferth@viterbo.edu
UNGAR, Jacob .... 845-362-3053. 314 H
jacobu@bytsem.org
UNGAR, Samuel, D .... 718-384-5460. 351 H

UNGAR, Sanford, J ... 410-337-6040. 215 A sungar@goucher.edu
UNGAR, Shaya ... 732-370-3360. 308 L
UNGARO, John ... 843-574-6891. 447 E john.ungaro@tridenttech.edu
UNGER, Karen ... 845-758-7490. 314 D kunger@bard.edu
UNGER, Maggie ... 952-446-4323. 255 D ungerm@crown.edu
UNGER, Sue ... 630-889-6565. 154 E sunger@nuhs.edu
UNIS, Corry, D ... 607-871-2115. 313 E unis@alfred.edu
UNKE, James, M ... 507-354-8221. 256 M unkejm@mlc-wels.edu
UNNI, V, K ... 401-232-6227. 438 K vunni@bryant.edu
UNNIKRISHNAN, Raman ... 657-278-3362... 33 E runnikrishnan@fullerton.edu
UNO, Ashley ... 770-394-8300. 120 H auno@aii.edu
UNRUH, David ... 310-825-1083... 71 C dunruh@summer.ucla.edu
UNRUH, Nancy ... 620-276-9571. 187 A nancy.unruh@gcccks.edu
UNSWORTH, John ... 781-736-4540. 224 F unsworth@brandeis.edu
UNTERREINER, Coleen ... 406-756-3962. 286 B cunterre@fvcc.edu
UNVER, Amira ... 973-290-4233. 300 F aunver@cse.edu
UPCHURCH, Jason ... 845-434-5750. 347 A jupchurch@sunysullivan.edu
UPCHURCH, Jim ... 815-928-5429. 155 H jupchurch@olivet.edu
UPCHURCH, Sharon, K .. 573-288-6478. 273 F supchurch@culver.edu
UPHAM, Daren ... 858-642-7201... 55 J dupham@nu.edu
UPHAM, Steadman ... 918-631-3244. 401 F steadman-upham@utulsa.edu
UPNEJA, Arun ... 617-353-3261. 224 D aupneja@bu.edu
UPPALA, Guru ... 951-785-3531... 50 B guppala@lasierra.edu
UPSHAW, Jane ... 843-208-8242. 448 B jupshaw@uscb.edu
UPTON, Brian ... 417-865-2815. 274 B uptonb@evangel.edu
UPTON, John ... 706-295-6606. 125 C jupton@highlands.edu
UPTON, John ... 910-362-7027. 358 F jupton@cfcc.edu
UPTON, Stacy ... 662-246-6452. 268 B supton@msdelta.edu
URAN, Mike, T ... 320-308-2116. 261 B mturan@stcloudstate.edu
URASKI, Thomas, S ... 815-740-3200. 162 F turaski@stfrancis.edu
URBAITIS, Carol, S ... 585-785-1212. 324 D urbaitcs@flcc.edu
URBAN, David, J ... 615-898-2764. 459 D david.urban@mtsu.edu
URBAN, Kathleen ... 307-778-1157. 543 D kurban@lccc.wy.edu
URBAN, Kenneth, E ... 715-365-4416. 540 G kurban@nicoletcollege.edu
URBAN, Kristi ... 979-830-4141. 467 I kristi.urban@blinn.edu
URBAN, Laura ... 859-442-1181. 195 B laura.urban@kctcs.edu
URBAN, Lynn ... 970-247-2929... 84 G Lynn.Urban@pueblocc.edu
URBAN, Ralph ... 860-486-4241... 92 A ralph.urban@uconn.edu
URBAN, Rhonda, P ... 309-692-4092. 152 J rpurban@midstate.edu
URBAN, Susan ... 305-809-3236. 104 I susan.urban@fkcc.edu
URBANCZYK, Aaron ... 615-297-7545. 452 J urbanczyka@aquinascollege.edu
URBANEK, Andrew ... 315-866-0300. 326 A urbanekar@herkimer.edu
URBANEK, Lauren ... 617-585-1113. 234 I lauren.urbanek@necmusic.edu
URBANIAK, David ... 989-686-9083. 242 C drubani@delta.edu
URBANICK, John ... 231-591-2138. 242 F urbanicj@ferris.edu
URBANO, George ... 863-297-1086. 110 H gurbano@polk.edu
URBANSKI, Thomas ... 815-280-2269. 149 A turbansk@jjc.edu
URBANSKI, Tom ... 218-879-0820. 258 E urbanski@fdltcc.edu
URBINE, Shawn ... 724-938-4444. 428 A urbine@calu.edu
URBONYA, Tim ... 608-263-9676. 538 E tim.urbonya@uwex.uwc.edu
URCIAGA, Jennifer ... 651-213-4175. 256 B graduateschool@hazelden.edu
URCIUOLI, Jannette ... 718-631-6370. 319 D jurciuoli@qcc.cuny.edu
URDAN, Joely, B ... 414-229-4278. 537 A jurdan@uwm.edu
UREN, Mary ... 608-822-2310. 541 C muren@swtc.edu
URETZ, Alan ... 773-975-1295. 534 D dragongi@comcast.net
UREY, Denise ... 724-589-2007. 434 B durey@thiel.edu
URIAGEREKA, Juan ... 301-405-4252. 219 B juan@umd.edu
URIBE-JENNINGS, Marcela ... 508-929-8543. 230 G muribejennings@worcester.edu
URICK, Cynthia ... 610-796-8428. 409 E cynthia.urick@alvernia.edu
URISH, Jonathan, E ... 608-363-2663. 531 M urishj@beloit.edu
URNER-JONES, Katharine ... 617-243-2223. 227 K kurnerjones@lasell.edu
URQUIDEZ, Kasandra, K 520-621-3705... 18 F kurquidez@arizona.edu
URRABAZO, Gloria ... 210-434-6711. 477 N gaurrabazo@lake.ollusa.edu
URREA, Edda ... 956-364-4522. 485 H edda.urrea@tstc.edu
URSO, David ... 540-453-2376. 511 H ursod@brcc.edu
URSUY, Andrea, L ... 989-686-9222. 242 C alnadols@delta.edu
URTECHO, Robert ... 559-730-3942... 40 I robertur@cos.edu
URTZ, Anastasia ... 315-498-2692. 335 G urtza@sunyocc.edu
URTZ, Mike ... 607-753-4953. 343 B mike.urtz@cortland.edu
USATCH, Jeri ... 518-255-5227. 344 E usatchj@cobleskill.edu
USCHER, Nancy, J ... 206-726-5000. 518 G nuscher@cornish.edu
USINGER, Peter ... 863-297-1009. 110 H pusinger@polk.edu
USOFF, Catherine ... 508-793-7670. 225 A cusoff@clarku.edu
USRY, Lori ... 706-771-4010. 121 D lusry@augustatech.edu
USSERY, Janyth ... 325-734-3600. 486 C janyth.ussery@tstc.edu
UTASH, Sheree ... 316-677-9536. 191 E sutash@watc.edu
UTHOFF, Jay, L ... 563-387-1012. 180 M uthoffja@luther.edu
UTLEY, Shawn ... 229-333-1294. 134 K shawn.utley@wiregrass.edu
UTSMAN, Michael ... 704-463-1360. 365 E
UTTERBACK, Jim, W ... 405-382-9200. 399 I j.utterback@sscok.edu
UTTICH, Richard ... 312-341-3640. 157 D ruttich@roosevelt.edu
UTZINGER, J. Michael ... 434-223-6118. 505 E jutzinger@hsc.edu
UVA, Mariflor ... 978-762-4000. 232 D muva@northshore.edu
UWAKWEH, Benjamin, O ... 336-334-7567. 367 E bouwakweh@ncat.edu
UYEHARA, Alan, M ... 409-944-1285. 472 I auyehara@gc.edu
UYEHARA, Penny ... 808-455-0272. 137 A pennys@hawaii.edu
UYENO, Russell ... 808-845-9158. 136 G ruyeno@hawaii.edu
UZMAN, Akif ... 713-221-8015. 489 D uzmana@uhd.edu
UZNANSKI, Laurel ... 360-867-6361. 519 J uznanski@evergreen.edu
UZORUO, Petra ... 409-984-6151. 486 H petra.uzoruo@lamarpa.edu
UZZELL, Yolanda ... 714-628-7201... 38 A uzzell@chapman.edu

V

VÉLEZ, Maritza ... 787-264-1912. 551 A maritza-velez@sg.inter.edu
VÉLEZ, Martha, L ... 787-250-0000. 553 G martha.velez@upr.edu
VÉLEZ RIVERA, Marcos . 787-725-8120. 548 O mvelez@eap.edu
VÁZQUEZ, Pedro ... 787-850-9361. 554 D pedro.vazquez6@upr.edu
VÁZQUEZ-ESPEJO, Nelson ... 787-993-8957. 554 A nelson.vazquez1@upr.edu
VÁZQUEZ-MARTÍNEZ, Ernesto ... 787-622-8000. 553 E evazquezjr@pupr.edu
VABRE, Bert ... 201-761-7834. 306 L bvabre@saintpeters.edu
VACARR, Barbara ... 802-322-1600. 499 C barbara.vacarr@goddard.edu
VACCA, Sheryl, S ... 510-987-9090... 70 H sheryl.vacca@ucop.edu
VACCARI, Peter, I ... 914-968-6200. 339 E sjsr@archny.org
VACCARO, Anne ... 718-862-7409. 329 M anne.vaccaro@manhattan.edu
VACCARO, Paul ... 781-768-7354. 236 A paul.vaccaro@regiscollege.edu
VACCARO, Thomas ... 845-451-1618. 322 D t_vaccar@culinary.edu
VACCHIANO, Joanna ... 215-646-7300. 417 F vacchiano.j@gmc.edu
VACHON, Nicole ... 207-941-7176. 211 F vachonn@nescom.edu
VACHON, Robert ... 603-645-9613. 297 I r.vachon@snh.edu
VACIK, Stephen, M ... 785-460-5400. 185 P steve.vacik@colbycc.edu
VADEN, David ... 716-250-7500. 315 J dvaden@bryantstratton.edu
VADEN-GOAD, Linda ... 508-626-4582. 230 A lvadengoad@framingham.edu
VADER, Patricia ... 909-469-5318... 76 B pvader@westernu.edu
VADGAMA, Jadutt ... 323-563-9397... 38 B jayvadgama@cdrewu.edu
VAGLIENTI, Kendra ... 972-860-4555. 470 G kvaglienti@dcccd.edu
VAHEY, Terry ... 408-924-7808... 36 A terry.vahey@sjsu.edu
VAHLBUSCH, Jefford, B . 715-836-3621. 536 E vahlbujb@uwec.edu
VAHLE, Kirby, L ... 214-648-2400. 493 E kirby.vahle@utsouthwestern.edu
VAHSEN, Steven, S ... 410-293-1568. 545 J vahsen@usna.edu
VAIDYA, Ashish ... 323-343-3800... 34 A avaidya@calstatela.edu
VAIL, Mita, K ... 757-455-3217. 515 H mvail@vwc.edu
VAILAS, Arthur, C ... 208-282-3440. 138 E vailarth@isu.edu
VAILLANCOURT, Allison, M ... 520-621-1684... 18 F vaillana@email.arizona.edu
VAIRO, Carl, A ... 610-565-1095. 437 G cvairo@williamson.edu
VAITHYLINGAM, Mugunth ... 702-651-5900. 294 E mugunth.vaithylingam@csn.edu
VAKALIS, Marianne ... 973-278-5400. 299 D mpv@berkeleycollege.edu
VAKALIS, Marianne ... 973-278-5400. 314 K mpv@berkeleycollege.edu
VAKAMUDI, Ramesh ... 404-413-0721. 126 E fmdrkv@gsu.edu
VAKAS, Dean ... 816-584-6570. 280 C dean.vakas@park.edu
VAKIL, David ... 951-571-6162... 60 K david.vakil@mvc.edu
VAKNIN, Lauren ... 619-660-4295... 46 D lauren.vaknin@gcccd.edu
VALADEZ, James ... 909-748-8791... 73 H james_valadez@redlands.edu
VALADEZ, Martin ... 509-542-4430. 518 C mvaladez@columbiabasin.edu
VALASEK, Katherine ... 973-642-8747. 307 D katherine.valasek@shu.edu
VALBUENA, Ruben ... 561-912-1211. 103 C rvalbuena@evergladesuniversity.edu
VALCKE, Cathy ... 765-455-9226. 168 A chightow@iuk.edu
VALCOURT, George ... 813-491-6125. 153 I george.valcourt@nl.edu
VALDES, Jose, L ... 305-821-3333. 105 A jvaldes@fnu.edu
VALDES, Mario ... 262-243-5700. 532 H mario.valdes@cuw.edu
VALDEZ, Al ... 951-785-2115... 50 B avaldez@lasierra.edu
VALDEZ, Alex ... 956-665-7021. 492 B alexv@utpa.edu
VALDEZ, Anna ... 707-527-4529... 65 B avaldez@santarosa.edu
VALDEZ, Benjamin ... 303-837-0825... 78 H valdezb@aii.edu
VALDEZ, Cristobal, O ... 937-778-7801. 379 G cvaldez@edisonohio.edu
VALDEZ, Jude ... 210-458-2401. 492 C jude.valdez@utsa.edu
VALDIVIA, Nicolas ... 562-985-8391... 33 F nvaldiv2@csulb.edu
VALDIVIESO, Luigi ... 305-821-3333. 105 A lvaldivieso@fnu.edu
VALE, SSJ, Carol Jean ... 215-248-7021. 413 A cvale@chc.edu
VALE, Darla ... 513-244-4295. 377 G darla_vale@mail.msj.edu
VALE, Louise ... 303-492-7523... 85 L louise.vale@colorado.edu
VALEK, Alan ... 216-791-5000. 377 E ajv2@case.edu
VALEK, Millicent, M ... 979-230-3200. 468 A millicent.valek@brazosport.edu
VALENCIA, Karen ... 214-860-3687. 471 A kvalencia@dcccd.edu
VALENCIA, Marilyn, F ... 216-397-4268. 381 R mvalencia@jcu.edu
VALENCIA, Steven, J ... 580-327-8478. 396 N sjvalencia@nwosu.edu
VALENCIA, Susan ... 510-869-8628... 61 I svalencia@samuelmerritt.edu
VALENCIA-DAYE, Carmelita, E ... 203-285-2172... 88 E cvalencia-daye@gwcc.commnet.edu
VALENTE, Aurelio ... 708-235-7594. 145 F avalente@govst.edu
VALENTE, Bianca ... 610-359-5292. 414 D bvalente@dccc.edu
VALENTE, Elizabeth ... 510-869-6243... 61 I evalente@samuelmerritt.edu
VALENTE, Jason ... 517-787-0800. 244 J valentejasonh@jccmi.edu
VALENTE, Mario ... 760-757-2121... 54 G mvalente@miracosta.edu
VALENTE, Melinda ... 818-386-5652... 59 E mvalente@pgi.edu
VALENTE, Richard ... 312-777-8656. 147 D rvalente@aii.edu
VALENTI, Joseph ... 845-569-3216. 332 B jospeh.valenti@msmc.edu
VALENTIN, Allison ... 773-697-2089. 144 B avalentin@devry.edu
VALENTIN, Annette ... 787-786-3030. 547 F anvalentin@ucb.edu.pr
VALENTIN, Cruz Belinda 787-764-0000. 555 B cruz.valentin1@upr.edu
VALENTIN, Julio ... 407-708-2281. 113 E valentij@seminolestate.edu
VALENTIN, Luz, C ... 787-786-3030. 547 F lvalentin@ucb.edu.pr
VALENTINE, Bobby ... 203-396-8444... 91 C valentiner@sacredheart.edu
VALENTINE, Bryan ... 505-984-6096. 311 H bvalentine@sjcsf.edu
VALENTINE, Carey, G ... 248-204-3800. 245 I campfac@ltu.edu
VALENTINE, David ... 617-928-4710. 234 E dvalentine@mountida.edu
VALENTINE, Jared ... 503-517-1008. 408 H jvalentine@warnerpacific.edu
VALENTINE, Leanne ... 712-749-2164. 176 D valentinel@bvu.edu
VALENTINE, Maureen ... 724-503-1001. 436 G mvalentine@washjeff.edu
VALENTINE, Peggy ... 336-750-2570. 370 A valentinepe@wssu.edu
VALENTINE, Richard, D .. 573-288-6323. 273 F rvalentine@culver.edu
VALENTINE, Sidney ... 803-327-8017. 449 J svalentine@yorktech.edu
VALENTINI, James, J ... 212-854-2443. 321 D jjv1@columbia.edu
VALENTINO, Teresa ... 828-652-0657. 362 A teresavalentino@mcdowelltech.edu
VALENTO, Bernard ... 304-473-8510. 531 G valento@wvwc.edu
VALENZA, John, A ... 713-486-4021. 492 E john.a.valenza@uth.tmc.edu
VALENZUELA, Cesario, E ... 432-837-8076. 487 B cesariov@sulross.edu
VALENZUELA, Eileen ... 925-439-2181... 42 A evalenzuela@losmedanos.edu
VALENZUELA, Ernesto ... 520-494-5459... 12 P ernesto.valenzuela@centralaz.edu
VALERA, Luis ... 702-895-2389. 294 I luis.valera@unlv.edu
VALERA, Marc ... 718-817-3842. 324 G valera@fordham.edu
VALERIANO, Oscar ... 323-265-8779... 51 F valerio@elac.edu
VALERIANO, Zaira ... 432-685-4534. 476 G zaira@midland.edu
VALERIO, Brett ... 414-443-8785. 539 F brett.valerio@wlc.edu
VALERO, Hernando ... 787-844-8181. 555 A hernando.valero@upr.edu
VALERY, Suzanne ... 805-922-6966... 26 K svalery@hancockcollege.edu
VALINES, Francisco ... 305-348-2347. 115 B valinesf@fiu.edu
VALINTIS, Michelle ... 503-253-3443. 405 E mvalintis@ocom.edu
VALINTIS, Michelle ... 503-777-7705. 407 E mvalintis@reed.edu

VALK, Dana 323-259-2602 56 I dvalk@oxy.edu
VALLADARES, Paola 512-444-8082 485 B administrator@thsu.edu
VALLANCE, Brenda, J 512-448-8550 479 C brendac@stedwards.edu
VALLANDINGHAM, Richard 309-796-5047 140 E vallandinghamd@bhc.edu
VALLAR, Larry 304-243-2359 531 H lvallar@wju.edu
VALLE, Laura 909-748-8335 73 H laura_valle@redlands.edu
VALLE, Sondra, E 518-629-7622 326 G s.valle@hvcc.edu
VALLEJO, Isabel 408-273-2695 55 H ivallejo@nhu.edu
VALLEJO, Maria, M 561-868-3400 110 C vallejom@palmbeachstate.edu
VALLEJO, Matthew 858-513-9240 175 F matthew.vallejo@ashford.edu
VALLES, Arleen 575-835-5162 310 F avalles@admin.nmt.edu
VALLEY, Timothy 414-277-7150 534 G valley@msoe.edu
VALLOZZI, Jason 412-359-1000 434 I jvallozzi@triangle-tech.edu
VALOSKY, Kenneth, G 610-519-4530 436 F ken.valosky@villanova.edu
VALSAMIS, Ariadne 617-873-0178 224 G Ariadne.Valsamis@cambridgecollege.edu
VALSARAJ, Kalliat, T 225-578-7696 204 O valsaraj@lsu.edu
VALTOS, Jennifer 770-426-2762 128 D jvaltos@life.edu
VALUCKAS, Christine, A 410-287-1027 214 B cvaluckas@cecil.edu
VAMVAKIDES, Judite 203-396-8272 91 C vamvakidesj@sacredheart.edu
VAN AKEN, Troy, D 724-589-2100 434 B tvanaken@thiel.edu
VAN ALLEN, George, H 615-353-3236 461 B george.vanallen@nscc.edu
VAN ALLEN, Terry 810-766-6842 251 E terryva@umflint.edu
VAN ALSBURG, Teresa, D 304-457-6320 526 A
VAN ARNAM, Sherrie 718-940-5754 339 B svanarnam@sjcny.edu
VAN ARSDEL, James, D 520-621-0079 18 F vanarsdel@life.arizona.edu
VAN AUKEN, James 757-457-8101 502 C james.vanauken@atlanticuniv.edu
VAN AUKEN, Sharon 518-327-6242 336 B svanauken100@paulsmiths.edu
VAN BAAREN, Valerie, L 973-655-5225 303 D vanbaarenv@mail.montclair.edu
VAN BERGEN, Mildred 516-876-4076 346 A mildred.vanbergen@esc.edu
VAN BERKOM, Debbie 701-224-5431 372 B debbie.vanberkom@bismarckstate.edu
VAN BLAIR, Katherine 515-263-6037 178 G kvanblair@grandview.edu
VAN BLARCOM, Ronald 949-214-3135 41 I ron.vanblarcom@cui.edu
VAN BROEKHOVEN, Rollin 704-243-0737 458 A rvanbroekhoven@futurelead.org
VAN BRUNT, Troy, G 956-721-5326 475 F troyvb@laredo.edu
VAN BUREN, Mary 386-226-6525 102 B vanburem@erau.edu
VAN BUSKIRK, Christina, P 717-245-1640 414 H vanbuski@dickinson.edu
VAN CANNEYT, Donna, S 901-678-2810 460 B dvncnnyt@memphis.edu
VAN CLEAVE, Martha 503-883-2308 404 A mvcleave@linfield.edu
VAN CLEAVE, Martha 503-883-2449 404 A mvcleave@linfield.edu
VAN CLEAVE, Rachel 415-442-6601 45 I rvancleave@ggu.edu
VAN CLEAVE, Robb 541-506-6150 402 H rvancleave@cgcc.cc.or.us
VAN CLEAVE, Samuel, J 480-423-6003 15 E samuel.vancleave@scottsdalecc.edu
VAN CLEAVE, William 504-865-5767 207 C wvanclea@tulane.edu
VAN CLEEF, Robert 978-867-4610 226 H robert.vancleef@gordon.edu
VAN CLEEF, Sarah, E 903-510-2033 488 E svan@tjc.edu
VAN DAM, Dale 530-642-5644 53 C
VAN DE CAR, Katharyn 702-651-4516 294 E kathy.vandecar@csn.edu
VAN DE LOO, John 715-365-4553 540 G vandeloo@nicoletcollege.edu
VAN DE MOORTELL, Raymond 617-254-2610 236 B
VAN DE PUTTE, Andre 312-629-6100 158 L avande2@saic.edu
VAN DEKKER, Angela 718-817-3800 324 G avandekker@fordham.edu
VAN DEN ABBEELE, Georges 949-824-5133 71 B gvandena@uci.edu
VAN DEN BERG, Rex 805-922-6966 26 K rvandenberg@hancockcollege.edu
VAN DEN HEEVER, Nicolaas 949-783-4800 75 E nvandenheever@westcoastuniversity.edu
VAN DEN HEUVEL, Nicole 713-348-4055 479 A nvdh@rice.edu
VAN DEN HUL, Richard, D 360-650-3182 525 C rich.vandenhul@wwu.edu
VAN DENEND, Michael, J 616-526-6142 240 L vanden@calvin.edu
VAN DER BURG, Anna 860-685-2810 92 H avanderburg@wesleyan.edu
VAN DER GIESSEN, Hans 203-576-4668 91 G hvdg@bridgeport.edu
VAN DER KAAY, Christopher 863-784-7413 113 G christopher.vanderKaay@southflorida.edu
VAN DER KAAY, Christopher 863-784-7413 113 G Christopher.vanderKaay@southflorida.edu
VAN DER KARR, Carol 607-753-2206 343 B carol.vanderkarr@cortland.edu
VAN DER KLEY, Jan 269-387-2365 252 I jan.vanderkley@wmich.edu
VAN DER LEEUW, Sander 480-965-6214 11 K vanderle@asu.edu
VAN DER MEID, J. Scott 781-736-3483 224 F svanderm@brandeis.edu
VAN DER MERWE, Derek 931-221-7903 459 B vandermerwed@apsu.edu
VAN DER POL, Willem 657-278-2065 33 E wvanderpol@fullerton.edu
VAN DER SCHYF, Cornelis 208-282-2490 138 E vandcorn@isu.edu
VAN DER VEER, Mary Caroline 518-587-2100 346 A marycaroline.powers@esc.edu
VAN DER WALL, Melissa 201-684-7540 305 A mvanderw@ramapo.edu
VAN DERVEER, Rachael, E 724-847-6596 417 A revander@geneva.edu
VAN DEVEN, Randy 903-468-8181 483 E randy.vandeven@tamuc.edu
VAN DINE, Kathryn, L 563-588-8000 178 D registrar@emmaus.edu
VAN DONSELAAR, Brian 712-722-6299 177 J brian.vandonselaar@dordt.edu
VAN DUSEN, Michael 561-912-2166 103 C mvandusen@evergladesuniversity.edu
VAN DUSER, Kathy 773-371-5450 141 D admissions@ctu.edu
VAN DUYNE, Patrick 815-280-6696 149 A pvanduyn@jjc.edu
VAN DUZER, Jeffrey, B 206-281-2508 523 C vandj@spu.edu
VAN DYK, Leanne 616-392-8555 252 J leanne.vandyk@westernsem.edu
VAN DYKE, James 920-923-8083 534 A jvandyke@marianuniversity.edu
VAN DYKE, Jon 217-234-5378 150 D jvandyke@lakeland.cc.il.us
VAN DYKE, Karin 906-487-7361 242 G karin.vandyke@finlandia.edu
VAN DYKE, Patricia 716-829-7802 323 D vandykep@dyc.edu
VAN DYKEN, Douglas 616-395-7810 244 A vandyken@hope.edu
VAN ECK, Thomas, A 616-526-8553 240 L tveck@calvin.edu
VAN ESS, Jami 928-226-4209 13 B jami.vaness@coconino.edu
VAN-ESS, Michelle 212-217-4132 324 C michelle_vaness@fitnyc.edu
VAN ESSEN, Quentin 712-722-6080 177 J quentin.vanessen@dordt.edu
VAN FOSSEN, Dell Jean 951-785-2088 50 B dvanfoss@lasierra.edu
VAN FOSSEN, Drew 920-403-4427 535 L drew.vanfossen@snc.edu
VAN GALEN, Dean, A 715-425-3201 537 E dean.vangalen@uwrf.edu
VAN GIESON, Christine, N 805-893-3641 72 B christine.vangieson@sa.ucsb.edu
VAN GILDER, Holly 330-490-7144 392 H hvangilder@walsh.edu
VAN GINHOVEN, Lee, H 269-927-8611 245 D vanginhoven@lakemichigancollege.edu
VAN GORDON, Beth 219-980-7202 168 B vgordon@iun.edu
VAN GORDON, Elizabeth 574-520-4463 168 E vgordon@iusb.edu
VAN GRONINGEN, Willis 708-239-4880 160 K bill.vangroningen@trnty.edu
VAN GRUENSVEN, Sheryl 920-465-2326 536 F vangrues@uwgb.edu
VAN GUNDY, Douglas 304-473-8243 531 G vangundy@wvwc.edu
VAN HAMERSVELD, Pete 310-243-3825 33 B pvanhamersveld@csudh.edu
VAN HARPEN, Robin, L 414-229-4461 537 A rvanharp@uwm.edu
VAN HEMERT, John, L 540-674-3660 513 B jvanhemert@nr.edu
VAN HOLLAND, Phyllis, L 360-417-6291 522 A pvanholland@pencol.edu
VAN HOOK, Dianne, G 661-362-3400 40 E dianne.vanhook@canyons.edu
VAN HOOK, Jayson 423-614-8695 455 L jvanhook@leeuniversity.edu
VAN HORN, Brian, W 270-809-4159 198 B bvanhorn@murraystate.edu
VAN HORN, Donald, L 304-696-6433 529 H vanhorn@marshall.edu
VAN HORN, Drew 828-328-7108 356 B drew.vanhorn@lr.edu
VAN HORN, Fredrick 478-387-4778 125 E fvanhorn@gmc.cc.ga.us
VAN HORN, Guy 843-863-7102 441 H gvanhorn@csuniv.edu
VAN HORN, Keith, F 419-267-1303 385 F kvanhorn@northweststate.edu
VAN HORN, Stu 916-608-6500 53 C
VAN HORN, Stuart 559-934-2180 75 G
VAN HORN, Wayne 601-925-3297 268 A wvanhorn@mc.edu
VAN HOUT, Vicky 920-735-5731 539 K
VAN HOUTEN, Michael 517-629-0567 239 A mvanhouten@albion.edu
VAN KERCKVOORDE, Colette 413-528-7232 222 E colette@simons-rock.edu
VAN KEUREN, Karen, A 585-785-1206 324 D vankeuka@flcc.edu
VAN KIRK, Shannon 541-278-5916 402 C svankirk@bluecc.edu
VAN KLEY, Eric 641-628-5310 176 E vankleye@central.edu
VAN KLEY, Sandy 712-707-7145 181 H svankley@nwciowa.edu
VAN KOOY, Samantha 856-415-2276 302 C svankooy@gccnj.edu
VAN LANINGHAM, Kathy, M 479-575-5910 23 I kvl@uark.edu
VAN LEIDEN, Melissa 785-594-8306 184 C melissa.vanleiden@bakeru.edu
VAN LOO, Scott, D 419-289-5088 374 C svanloo@ashland.edu
VAN MARTER, Dianne 313-831-5200 242 E dvanmarter@etseminary.edu
VAN NATTA, Gretchen 312-341-2479 157 D gvannatta@roosevelt.edu
VAN NESS, Forrest, L 314-516-6680 283 E vannessf@umsl.edu
VAN NIEKERK, Andre 818-767-0888 76 K andre.vanniekerk@woodbury.edu
VAN NORMAN, Karen 973-761-9076 307 C karen.vannorman@shu.edu
VAN OMMEREN, Ryan 805-493-3211 31 H rvommere@clunet.edu
VAN OORT, Harlan 712-707-7190 181 H hvanoort@nwciowa.edu
VAN ORMAN, Kit 315-364-3317 350 E kit@wells.edu
VAN ORMAN, Sarah, A 608-262-1885 536 D svanorman@uhs.wisc.edu
VAN ORSDEL, Lee 616-331-2621 243 C vanorsdl@gvsu.edu
VAN RIPER, Lisa 804-289-8778 510 L lvanripe@richmond.edu
VAN SCHARREL, Mark, H 773-256-0676 152 B mvanscha@lstc.edu
VAN SCHYNDEL, C. Richard 208-467-8445 139 A crvanschyndel@nnu.edu
VAN SICKLE, Frederick, M 212-851-7929 321 D fmv2001@columbia.edu
VAN SICKLE, Lee 773-298-3410 158 E vansickle@sxu.edu
VAN SLYCK, Abigail, A 860-439-2731 89 H abigail.van-slyck@conncoll.edu
VAN SLYKE, Craig 928-523-7941 16 C craig.vanslyke@nau.edu
VAN SOELEN, Timothy 712-722-6228 177 J timothy.vansoelen@dcrdt.edu
VAN SOMEREN, Charles 202-462-2101 96 A vansomeren@iwp.edu
VAN STEAMBURG, Ingrid 802-728-1513 501 F ivansteamburg@vtc.edu
VAN STRATEN, Amy 920-831-4355 539 K vanstrat@fvtc.edu
VAN TASSEL, Kristin 785-227-3380 184 I vantasselk@bethanylb.edu
VAN THUYNE, Michael, E 215-637-7700 418 G mvanthuyne@holyfamily.edu
VAN TIL, Seth, J 724-458-3887 417 E sjvantil@gcc.edu
VAN TRAN, Lac 312-942-3400 157 G lac_tran@rush.edu
VAN TUYL, Jonah 928-350-4406 17 K jvantuyl@prescott.edu
VAN UUM, Elizabeth 314-516-5774 283 E vanuum@umsl.edu
VAN VACTOR, Myra 425-564-2255 517 A myra.vanvactor@bellevuecollege.edu
VAN VALEN, Gretchen 607-274-3846 327 E gvanvalen@ithaca.edu
VAN VLECK, Thomas 660-626-2138 271 A tvanvleck@atsu.edu
VAN VOLKENBURGH, Linda, C 513-861-6400 390 C linda.van@myunion.edu
VAN VOORHIS, Sue, N 612-625-8098 264 G vanvo002@umn.edu
VAN WAGNER, Molly 715-425-3195 537 E molly.van-wagner@uwrf.edu
VAN WAGNER, Thomas 202-231-4193 544 L thomas.vanwagner@dodiis.mil
VAN WAGONER, Randall, J 315-792-5333 331 I rvanwagoner@mvcc.edu
VAN WEELDEN, Kathy 603-428-2235 297 D kvanweelden@nec.edu
VAN WIE, Lisa 518-629-8143 326 G l.vanwie@hvcc.edu
VAN WINGERDEN, Thomas, J 616-526-6378 240 L tjv6@calvin.edu
VAN WINKLE, Robynne 541-440-4600 408 D robynne.vanwinkle@umpqua.edu
VAN WYK, Natalie 610-361-5418 424 I vanwykn@neumann.edu
VAN WYK, Sharon 304-724-3700 526 B svanwyk@apus.edu
VAN ZANDT, David 212-229-5656 332 E vanzandt@newschool.edu
VAN ZANDT, Patricia, R 423-439-4337 459 C vanzandt@etsu.edu
VAN ZINDEREN, Gary 701-252-3467 373 D gvanzind@jc.edu
VAN ZYL, Henry 609-292-4000 308 A phvanzyl@tesc.edu
VANACKER, Jason 414-443-8944 539 F jason.vanacker@wlc.edu
VANARSDALL, Cathy 765-361-6421 175 B vanarsdc@wabash.edu
VANASSE, Dennis 508-849-3372 222 B dvanasse@annamaria.edu
VANAUSDLE, Steven, L 509-527-4274 524 H steven.vanausdle@wwcc.edu
VANBERGEIJK, Ernst 631-348-3117 333 H evanberg@nyit.edu
VANBILLIARD, Jason 215-702-4548 411 F jvanbilliard@cairn.edu
VANBROCKLIN, Michael 903-233-4332 475 J mikevanbrocklin@letu.edu
VANCE, Carl 503-768-7801 403 K cvance@lclark.edu
VANCE, Elaine 202-651-5288 95 C janet.vance@gallaudet.edu
VANCE, Gary 843-863-7665 441 H gvance@csuniv.edu
VANCE, Gina, M 724-946-7110 437 B vancegm@westminster.edu
VANCE, Maria 707-965-7000 57 J mvance@puc.edu
VANCE, Mickey 601-635-6208 266 H mvance@eccc.edu
VANCE, Richard, N 765-658-4233 165 F richardvance@depauw.edu

VANCE, Robert 414-577-2658. 153 I rvance@nl.edu
VANCE, Sheilah 610-399-2430. 428 B svance@cheyney.edu
VANCE, Susan 423-636-7331. 462 E svance@tusculum.edu
VANCE, W.C 419-289-4142. 374 C wvance@ashland.edu
VANCKO, Candace, S 607-746-4090. 345 G vanckocs@delhi.edu
VANCLEAVE, Donna 804-819-4695. 511 G dvancleave@vccs.edu
VANCOTT, Mary Grooms 707-826-3146. 35 C vancott@humboldt.edu
VANDALL, Christopher, P 608-258-2448. 540 C cvandall@madisoncollege.edu
VANDE YACHT, Dan 715-425-3342. 537 E daniel.vandeyacht@uwrf.edu
VANDE ZANDE, Carleen 920-424-3190. 537 B vandezac@uwosh.edu
VANDEGRIFT, OP, Raymond 202-495-3856. 96 C rvandegrift@dhs.edu
VANDELL, Deborah, L 949-824-8026. 71 B dvandell@uci.edu
VANDEMAN, Nancy 740-753-7009. 380 K vandemann@hocking.edu
VANDEN BOOM, Leonard, A 414-277-7154. 534 G vandenbo@msoe.edu
VANDENAKKER, John 313-883-8750. 249 E vandenakker.john@shms.edu
VANDENAVOND, Steve 920-465-2641. 536 F vandenas@uwgb.edu
VANDENBOSCH, Kathryn 608-262-4930. 536 D kvandenbosch@cals.wisc.edu
VANDER FEEN, Aimee 605-331-6602. 452 D aimee.vanderfeen@usiouxfalls.edu
VANDER HOEK, Nancy 605-229-8545. 450 J nancy.vanderhoek@presentation.edu
VANDER HOOVEN, James 520-383-8401. 18 B
VANDER HORN, Alexis, A 563-884-5102. 182 A alexis.vanderhorn@palmer.edu
VANDER PLOEG, Sally 616-526-7112. 240 L svploeg@calvin.edu
VANDER PLOEG, Scott 270-824-8684. 196 A scott.vanderploeg@kctcs.edu
VANDER SANDEN, Karen 651-290-7526. 265 F karen.vandersanden@wmitchell.edu
VANDER STELT, Rachel 616-988-1000. 241 D
VANDER STOEP, Scott, D 616-395-7903. 244 A vanderstoep@hope.edu
VANDER VEER, Lisa 815-939-5256. 155 H lvanderv@olivet.edu
VANDER WEELE, Dennis 845-368-7200. 340 C dennis.vanderweele@use.salvationarmy.org
VANDER WERF, Dave 712-722-6020. 177 J dave.vanderwerff@dordt.edu
VANDER ZWAAG, Lora 712-274-6400. 183 G lora.vanderzwaag@witcc.edu
VANDERBILL, Liz 320-222-6090. 260 H liz.vanderbill@ridgewater.edu
VANDERBILT, Robin 937-298-3399. 382 K robin.vanderbilt@kc.edu
VANDERBILT, William 616-395-7850. 244 A vanderbilt@hope.edu
VANDERBOUT, Jennifer, L 660-543-8000. 283 A vanderbout@ucmo.edu
VANDERBURG, Judy, J 503-838-8490. 406 E vanderj@wou.edu
VANDERBURGH, Paul, M 937-229-2390. 391 C PVanderburgh1@udayton.edu
VANDERFORD, Brenda 304-766-5107. 530 C bvanderf@wvstateu.edu
VANDERHART, Mark 219-864-2400. 171 F mvanderhart@midamerica.edu
VANDERHILL, Dan 517-750-1200. 250 E danv@arbor.edu
VANDERHILL, Steven, T 214-528-8600. 478 I
VANDERHOFF, Jessica 860-906-5021. 88 D jvanderhoff@ccc.commnet.edu
VANDERHOOF, Karen 973-328-5012. 300 G kvanderhoof@ccm.edu
VANDERLAND, Helen 804-819-4951. 511 G hvanderland@vccs.edu
VANDERLICK, T. Kyle 203-432-4220. 93 A kyle.vanderlick@yale.edu
VANDERMAAS-PEELER, Maureen 336-278-6453. 354 B vanderma@elon.edu
VANDERMEER, Mary 616-222-3000. 245 C mvandermeer@kuyper.edu
VANDERPOL, Diane 801-832-2013. 498 F dvanderpol@westminstercollege.edu
VANDERPOOL, Janet 660-359-3948. 279 H jvanderpool@mail.ncmissouri.edu
VANDERPOOL, Molly 765-973-8415. 167 G moberry@iue.edu
VANDERPUYE, Archibald, W 512-505-6444. 473 G awvanderpuye@htu.edu
VANDERSLICE, Ronna, J 580-581-2250. 394 G rvanderslice@cameron.edu
VANDERSPOEL, James 906-932-4231. 242 I jimv@gogebic.edu
VANDERSTAAY, Steven, L 360-650-3004. 525 C steven.vanderstaay@wwu.edu
VANDERSTEL, David 317-917-3388. 171 A dvanderstel@martin.edu
VANDERVEEN, Kathleen 616-331-2662. 243 C vandervk@gvsu.edu
VANDERVEEN, R. Pete, L 323-442-1369. 74 A phardean@usc.edu
VANDERVELDEN, Michael 208-459-5851. 138 A mvandervelden@collegeofidaho.edu
VANDERVOORT, Patricia, A 361-582-2587. 493 H patricia.vandervoort@victoriacollege.edu
VANDERVORT, Michael, W 512-471-7117. 491 C mike.vandervort@austin.utexas.edu
VANDERWEL, David 616-395-7777. 244 A vanderwel@hope.edu
VANDERWORP, Erin 517-265-5161. 238 G evanderworp@adrian.edu
VANDERWOUDE, Chris 703-658-4304. 503 L coachvw@christendom.edu
VANDERWOUDE, Katrina 619-644-7104. 46 E katrina.vanderwoude@gcccd.edu
VANDERWYST, Roxann, S 715-233-5358. 539 J rvanderwyst@cvtc.edu
VANDERZEE, Lenore 315-386-7109. 345 F vanderzeel@canton.edu
VANDERZWAAG, George 585-275-4301. 349 C george.vanderzwaag@rochester.edu
VANDESSEL, Larry 603-862-2099. 298 C larry.vandessel@unh.edu
VANDEVANDER, David, R 540-828-5316. 502 J dvandeva@bridgewater.edu
VANDEVER, Jennifer 618-650-5234. 159 H jvandev@siue.edu
VANDEVILLE, Denise 906-487-7379. 242 G denise.vandeville@finlandia.edu
VANDREHLE, Michael 507-537-6257. 261 F Michael.Vandrehel@smsu.edu
VANDUSEN, Lee 281-998-1170. 484 H lvandusen@txchiro.edu
VANDYKE, Jacki 262-691-5266. 541 D jvandyke@wctc.edu
VANDYKE, Rhonda, L 276-964-7388. 514 A rhonda.vandyke@sw.edu
VANDYKE COLBY, Rhonda 540-665-4862. 509 E rcolby@su.edu
VANECEK, Frank 802-485-2725. 500 A vanecek@norwich.edu
VANEERDEN, Kathy, S 262-335-5757. 540 F kvaneerden@morainepark.edu
VANEGAS, Jorge 979-845-1221. 483 C jvanegas@tamu.edu
VANEK, Susan 574-284-4594. 172 G svanek@saintmarys.edu
VANFLEET, Rita 402-552-3516. 288 L vanfleetrita@clarksoncollege.edu
VANG, Mai 715-346-2002. 538 A mavang@uwsp.edu
VANG, Pakou 651-773-1741. 258 C pakou.vang@century.edu
VANGALDER, Jeanette 970-351-2341. 86 C jeanette.vangalder@unco.edu
VANGARELLI, Kim 570-226-4625. 420 C vangarellik@lackawanna.edu
VANGEMERT, Edward 608-262-2600. 536 D evangemert@library.wisc.edu
VANGSGARD, Mark, D 651-962-6095. 265 C mdvangsgard@stthomas.edu
VANHECKE, JoNes, R 507-933-7526. 255 I jvanheck@gustavus.edu
VANHEE, Tonya 970-943-2493. 86 I tvanhee@western.edu
VANHOOK, John 405-682-7857. 397 E john.t.vanhook@occc.edu
VANHOORELBEKE, Jack 989-964-4109. 249 G jvh@svsu.edu
VANKERCKHOVE, Iris 718-409-5514. 346 D ivankerckhove@sunymaritime.edu
VANKEUREN, James, P 419-289-5377. 374 C jvankeu1@ashland.edu
VANKO, David 410-704-2121. 220 E dvanko@towson.edu
VANLANDINGHAM, Brenda 662-246-6301. 268 B bvanlandingham@msdelta.edu
VANLANDINGHAM, Liz 303-360-4769. 81 C liz.vanlandingham@ccaurora.edu
VANLONDEN, April 800-287-8822. 164 C vanloap@earlham.edu
VANLONDEN, April 765-983-1816. 165 G vonloap@earlham.edu
VANLONE, Jeffrey 315-781-3000. 326 C vanlone@hws.edu
VANMETER, Terry 270-789-5031. 193 D twvanmeter@campbellsville.edu
VANN, Allen 305-348-2465. 115 B Allen.Vann@fiu.edu
VANN, Wendy 252-862-1234. 363 A vannw@roanokechowan.edu
VANNESS, Kathryn, A 540-375-2257. 509 B vanness@roanoke.edu
VANNEY, Greg 701-845-7227. 372 A greg.vanney@vcsu.edu
VANNEY, Pete 715-365-4419. 540 G pvanney@nicoletcollege.edu
VANNIMAN, Dawn 810-762-0045. 247 F dawn.vanniman@mcc.edu
VANNOY, Roger 423-869-6285. 456 A athletics@lmunet.edu
VANOVER, Chance 405-425-5086. 397 D chance.vanover@oc.edu
VANOVER, Kathryn 918-540-6388. 396 G kathryn.vanover@neo.edu
VANRHEENEN, Mark 248-218-2049. 249 D mvanrheenen@rc.edu
VANSCOY, Irma, J 803-777-6728. 447 G ivanscoy@mailbox.sc.edu
VANSELL, Kimberly, J 660-543-4123. 283 A kvansell@ucmo.edu
VANSICKLE, Cissy 301-387-3083. 214 I cissy.vansickle@garrettcollege.edu
VANSTEEN, John 631-656-3187. 324 F john.vansteen@ftc.edu
VANSTRYDONCK, Gerald, E 585-340-9640. 320 E gvanstrydonck@crcds.edu
VANSWEDEN, James, A 269-337-7291. 244 K James.VanSweden@kzoo.edu
VANTASSEL, Sherri 740-264-5591. 379 F svantassel@egcc.edu
VANTILBURG, Mark, W 330-941-3518. 394 A mwvantilburg@ysu.edu
VANTOORN, Kay 817-531-4414. 488 A kvantoorn@txwes.edu
VANTYLE, Peter, R 315-568-3146. 333 C pvantyle@nycc.edu
VANVOORST, James, R 607-777-2157. 341 E vanvoors@binghamton.edu
VANWALBECK, Patti 269-387-2365. 252 I patti.vanwalbeck@wmich.edu
VARAHRAMYAN, Kody 317-274-1020. 168 D kvarahra@iupui.edu
VARBLE, Susan 504-762-3031. 203 A svarbl@dcc.edu
VARDAMAN, Lee 334-808-6319. 7 H vardaman@troy.edu
VAREBROOK, Cathy 414-277-4523. 534 G varebrook@msoe.edu
VARELA, Lorell 787-834-9595. 553 B lovarela@uaa.edu
VARGA, Alane, P 315-792-3100. 349 F avarga@utica.edu
VARGAS, Alicia 510-559-2736. 57 F avargas@plts.edu
VARGAS, Anna 503-297-5544. 405 D avargas@ocac.edu
VARGAS, Elizabeth 787-728-1515. 555 D evargas@sagrado.edu
VARGAS, Hector 787-279-1912. 550 B hvargas@bayamon.inter.edu
VARGAS, Ileana 787-765-1915. 551 C ivargas@inter.edu
VARGAS, Jose 787-738-2161. 554 C jose.vargas12@upr.edu
VARGAS, Jose 714-628-5941. 60 H vargas_jose@sccollege.edu
VARGAS, Jose 760-744-1150. 58 D jvargas@palomar.edu
VARGAS, Karla 210-434-6711. 477 N kvargas@lake.ollusa.edu
VARGAS, Lizzette 787-753-6335. 549 D lvargas@icpruc.edu
VARGAS, Magda 787-841-2000. 552 B mivargas@pucpr.edu
VARGAS, Manuel 336-750-2370. 370 A vargasma@wssu.edu
VARGAS, Mark, A 773-298-3350. 158 E vargas@sxu.edu
VARGAS, Phillip 210-434-6711. 477 N pvargas@lake.ollusa.edu
VARGAS, Wanda 787-891-0925. 549 K wvargas@aguadilla.inter.edu
VARGAS, Yanina 413-552-2231. 231 F yvargas@hcc.edu
VARGAS-ABURTO, Carlos 610-683-4212. 429 A cvargas@kutztown.edu
VARGO, Anthony 412-359-1000. 434 I avargo@triangle-tech.edu
VARHOLAK, Mark 203-582-8613. 91 A mark.varholak@quinnipiac.edu
VARHUS, Sara 585-389-2011. 332 D svarhus0@naz.edu
VARI, April 215-489-2413. 414 E April.Vari@delval.edu
VARIAN, Heather, A 904-620-2112. 116 B heather.varian@unf.edu
VARKONYI, Istvan, L 215-204-3177. 433 K istvan.varkonyi@temple.edu
VARLOTTA, Lori 916-278-6060. 34 D varlotta@csus.edu
VARMA, Mrinal Mugdh 281-283-3020. 489 C varma@uhcl.edu
VARN, James, S 603-862-3290. 298 C jim.varn@unh.edu
VARNAU, Chris 317-931-2316. 165 B cvarnau@cts.edu
VARNELL, Jonathan, P 336-316-2153. 355 A jvarnell@guilford.edu
VARNELL, Michael 281-458-4050. 479 G michael.varnell@sjcd.edu
VARNER, Donna, A 757-594-8816. 503 M dvarner@cnu.edu
VARNER, Jenny, M 336-249-8186. 360 A jmvarner@davidsonccc.edu
VARNER, Katy 502-213-7303. 195 F katy.varner@kctcs.edu
VARNER, Mary, C 610-526-1302. 409 F mary.varner@theamericancollege.edu
VARNER, Stu 501-279-4331. 21 C svarner@harding.edu
VARNET, Harvey 843-208-8203. 448 B varnet@uscb.edu
VARNET, Harvey 843-208-8025. 448 B varnet@uscb.edu
VARNEY, Janice 269-639-8442. 245 D varney@lakemichigancollege.edu
VARNEY, Ruth 804-594-1559. 512 G rvarney@jtcc.edu
VARNSON, Stacie 701-483-2999. 371 D stacie.varnson@dickinsonstate.edu
VARNUM, Linda, J 603-526-3738. 295 I lindav@colby-sawyer.edu
VARRIENTOS, Joe 620-672-5641. 190 A joev@prattcc.edu
VARSA, Barbara 301-314-7735. 219 B bvarsa@umd.edu
VARSALONA, Jack, P 302-356-6818. 94 E donna.m.quinn@wilmu.edu
VARSALONA, Jacque, R 302-295-1168. 94 E jacqueline.r.varsalona@wilmu.edu
VARSEK, Tamara, B 814-393-2240. 428 C tvarsek@clarion.edu
VARSHNEY, Sanjay 916-278-6011. 34 D varshney@csus.edu
VARTABEDIAN, Robert, A 816-271-4237. 279 A president@missouriwestern.edu
VARTANIAN, Heather 414-326-2333. 532 G heather.vartanian@ccon.edu
VARVILLE, Paul 956-872-2330. 480 I pbvarvil@southtexascollege.edu
VARVIS, Stephen 559-453-2031. 45 D slvarvis@fresno.edu
VARWIG, Jana 410-704-2270. 220 E jvarwig@towson.edu
VASARHELYI, Marina 914-323-5139. 330 B marina.vasarhelyi@mville.edu
VASCONCELLOS, Tina 510-986-6992. 59 C tvasconcellos@peralta.edu
VASCURA, Jacquelyn, L 740-826-8084. 384 L jkent@muskingum.edu
VASILAS, Darcy 828-898-8785. 356 A vasilas@lmc.edu
VASILOPOULOS, Helena 312-752-2104. 149 E helena.vasilopoulos@kendall.edu
VASKELIS, Frank, M 650-358-6720. 64 A vaskelis@smccd.edu
VASQUEZ, Albert 310-434-4302. 65 A vasquez_albert@smc.edu
VASQUEZ, Andrew 830-372-8017. 485 C avasquez@tlu.edu
VASQUEZ, Beatriz, J 530-251-8836. 50 F bvasquez@lassencollege.edu
VASQUEZ, Graciela 562-860-2451. 37 I gvasquez@cerritos.edu

VASQUEZ, James .... 718-260-5244. 319 B
jvazquez@citytech.cuny.edu
VASQUEZ, Jeffrey .... 206-934-3643. 522 I
jeffrey.vasquez@seattlecolleges.edu
VASQUEZ, Lisa, R .... 972-758-3894. 469 G
lvasquez@collin.edu
VASQUEZ, Patricia .... 617-745-3851. 225 G
patty.vasquez@enc.edu
VASQUEZ, Sandy .... 915-747-7873. 492 A
svasquez@utep.edu
VASQUEZ, Sharon .... 860-768-4505... 92 D
svasquez@hartford.edu
VASQUEZ DE VELASCO, Guillermo, P .... 765-285-5863. 164 B
guillermo@bsu.edu
VASQUEZ-HUERTA, Jessika .... 310-665-6898... 57 C
otisaid@otis.edu
VASS, Robert .... 203-576-4228... 91 G
rvass@bridgeport.edu
VASSAR, David, K .... 713-348-4043. 479 A
dvassar@rice.edu
VASSAR, John, S .... 318-797-5326. 205 F
john.s.vassar@lsus.edu
VASSAR, Pam .... 913-469-8500. 187 J
pvassar@jccc.edu
VASTINE-NORMAN, Paula .... 817-515-6456. 482 B
paula.vastinenorman@tccd.edu
VATANDOOST, Nossi ..... 615-514-2787. 457 P
nossi@nossi.edu
VATISTAS, Vatistas .... 262-551-6001. 532 D
vvatistas@carthage.edu
VAUBEL, Thomas, M ...... 920-748-8117. 535 J
vaubelt@ripon.edu
VAUGHAN, Anna .... 504-398-2165. 206 C
avaughan@olhcc.edu
VAUGHAN, Bruce, F ...... 757-455-3309. 515 H
bvaughan@vwc.edu
VAUGHAN, Cheryl .... 804-763-6300... 96 F
cheryl.vaughan@strayer.edu
VAUGHAN, Chris .... 309-794-7292. 139 L
chrisvaughan@augustana.edu
VAUGHAN, Dixie, L ...... 740-374-8716. 392 I
dvaughan@wscc.edu
VAUGHAN, Greg .... 562-903-4752... 29 L
greg.vaughan@biola.edu
VAUGHAN, Icer .... 316-942-4291. 189 E
vaughani@newmanu.edu
VAUGHAN, Jesse .... 804-524-5877. 515 D
jvaughan@vsu.edu
VAUGHAN, Joseph .... 909-621-8613... 46 H
joseph_vaughan@hmc.edu
VAUGHAN, II, Juan, E ... 252-862-1375. 363 A
vaughanje@roanokechowan.edu
VAUGHAN, Karen .... 908-526-1200. 305 B
kvaughan@raritanval.edu
VAUGHAN, Larry, F ...... 615-547-1222. 454 A
lvaughan@cumberland.edu
VAUGHAN, Leslie .... 617-989-4510. 237 G
vaughanl@wit.edu
VAUGHAN, Linda .... 602-496-2404... 11 K
linda.vaughan@asu.edu
VAUGHAN, Michael, B ... 801-626-6006. 497 D
mvaughan@weber.edu
VAUGHAN, JR., Robert, A .... 678-466-4100. 123 A
robertvaughan@clayton.edu
VAUGHAN, Sally, J ...... 585-385-8196. 338 H
svaughan@sjfc.edu
VAUGHAN-COOKE, Melanie .... 502-213-2183. 195 F
melanie.vaughan-cooke@kctcs.edu
VAUGHN, Andy .... 714-816-0366... 70 A
andrew.vaughn@trident.edu
VAUGHN, Arthur .... 678-915-3282. 132 C
avaughn@spsu.edu
VAUGHN, Cathy .... 541-440-4600. 408 D
cathy.vaughn@umpqua.edu
VAUGHN, Deborah .... 843-953-5674. 443 A
vaughnd@cofc.edu
VAUGHN, Deborah, S .... 662-915-1687. 270 B
dvaughn@olemiss.edu
VAUGHN, Denise .... 919-278-2673. 366 E
dvaughn@shawu.edu
VAUGHN, Edward, L ...... 601-877-6227. 265 G
elvaughn@alcorn.edu
VAUGHN, Jason .... 417-328-1714. 282 C
jvaughn@sbuniv.edu
VAUGHN, Jennifer .... 270-852-3118. 197 B
jvaughn@kwc.edu
VAUGHN, John .... 919-681-9355. 354 A
JAV14@duke.edu
VAUGHN, Joseph .... 660-543-4621. 283 A
vaughn@ucmo.edu
VAUGHN, Joyce .... 870-575-8969... 24 E
vaughnj@uapb.edu
VAUGHN, Katherine .... 870-743-3000... 22 B
kvaughn@northark.edu
VAUGHN, Kellie .... 270-789-5001. 193 D
kpvaughn@campbellsville.edu
VAUGHN, Lori .... 413-565-1000. 222 F
lvaughn@baypath.edu
VAUGHN, Lyn .... 404-527-4520. 122 E
VAUGHN, Michele .... 847-543-2153. 143 A
mvaughn@clcillinois.edu
VAUGHN, Patti .... 617-262-5000. 223 F
Patti.Vaughn@the-bac.edu
VAUGHN, Ray .... 256-824-6100..... 8 F
ray.vaughn@uah.edu
VAUGHN, Robert .... 323-856-7661... 27 O
rvaughn@afi.com
VAUGHN, Robert .... 610-372-4721. 431 D
rvaughn@racc.edu
VAUGHN, Ronald, L ...... 813-253-6201. 118 L
president@ut.edu
VAUGHN, Sandra .... 662-252-8000. 269 F
svaughn@rustcollege.edu
VAUGHN, Suzanne, A .... 661-395-4301... 49 N
svaughn@bakersfieldcollege.edu
VAUGHN, Troy .... 817-515-5034. 482 B
troy.vaughn@tccd.edu
VAUGHN, Woodrow .... 256-726-7306..... 6 B
wvaughn@oakwood.edu
VAUGHT, Wayne .... 816-235-2815. 283 D
vaughtw@umkc.edu
VAUPEL, Chris .... 516-877-3258. 313 A
cpvaupel@adelphi.edu
VAVASOUR, JoEllen, L ... 914-654-5541. 320 H
jvavasour@cnr.edu
VAVOLIZZA, Ann .... 845-848-4001. 322 G
ann.vavolizza@dc.edu
VAVRICKA, Janda .... 414-277-2234. 534 G
vavricka@msoe.edu
VAWTER, Cheryl, D .... 509-777-4518. 525 F
cvawter@whitworth.edu
VAYDA, Melissa, M .... 717-728-2248. 412 J
melissavayda@centralpenn.edu
VAYDA, Michael, E .... 479-575-2034... 23 I
mvayda@uark.edu
VAZ, Maria, J .... 248-204-2400. 245 I
provost@ltu.edu
VAZQUEZ, Airlyn .... 787-882-2065. 553 A
biblioteca@unitecpr.net
VAZQUEZ, Carmen .... 718-289-5151. 317 B
carmen.vazquez@bcc.cuny.edu
VAZQUEZ, Carmen, M ... 619-260-4588... 73 I
carmenvazquez@sandiego.edu
VAZQUEZ, David .... 239-590-1123. 115 A
dvazquez@fgcu.edu
VAZQUEZ, Drianfel .... 787-844-8991. 555 A
drianfel.vazquez@upr.edu
VAZQUEZ, Frank .... 888-384-0849... 27 E
fvazquez@allied.edu
VAZQUEZ, Heber .... 787-834-9595. 553 B
heberv@uaa.edu
VAZQUEZ, Jaime .... 787-780-0070. 547 G
jvazquez@caribbean.edu
VAZQUEZ, Juan, A .... 714-628-4930... 60 H
vazquez_juan@sccollege.edu
VAZQUEZ, Magda .... 787-878-5475. 549 L
mavazquez@arecibo.inter.edu
VAZQUEZ, Maria .... 787-864-2222. 550 D
mavazrom@inter.edu
VAZQUEZ, Maria .... 787-725-8120. 548 O
mvazquez0060@eap.edu
VAZQUEZ, Marie .... 402-457-2430. 290 G
mvazquez@mccneb.edu
VAZQUEZ, Obed .... 925-969-2423... 41 L
ovazquez@dvc.edu
VAZQUEZ, Ramon .... 787-840-2955. 547 G
rvazquez@ponce.caribbean.edu
VAZQUEZ, Regina .... 631-420-2369. 346 B
regina.vasquez@farmingdale.edu
VAZQUEZ, Silvio .... 805-565-6200... 76 D
svazquez@westmont.edu
VAZQUEZ, Vilmaris .... 787-878-5475. 549 L
vvazquez@arecibo.inter.edu
VAZQUEZ-BARQUET, Ernesto .... 787-754-8000. 553 E
evazquez@pupr.edu
VAZQUEZ MEDINA, Edwin .... 787-890-2681. 553 H
edwin.vazquez7@upr.edu
VAZQUEZ-SKILLINGS, Rebecca, D .... 614-823-1354. 387 K
rvazquez-skillings@otterbein.edu
VEACH, Grace .... 863-667-5061. 113 P
gveach@seu.edu
VEACH, Leslie .... 252-985-5369. 365 D
lveach@ncwc.edu
VEAL, Sharon .... 478-553-2056. 129 H
sveal@oftc.edu
VEAZEY, Barbara .... 270-534-3082. 196 G
barbara.veazey@kctcs.edu
VEAZEY, David, A .... 253-535-8145. 521 I
veazeyda@plu.edu
VECCHIO, John .... 716-827-4344. 348 G
vecchioj@trocaire.edu
VECCHIO, Maria .... 201-559-6017. 302 A
vecchiom@felician.edu
VECCHIO, Paul .... 607-871-2193. 313 E
vecchio@alfred.edu
VECCHIONE, Tom .... 336-278-6538. 354 B
tvecchione@elon.edu
VECHINI, Jose, A .... 787-864-2222. 550 D
javechi@inter.edu
VEDDER, Lori .... 810-762-3444. 251 E
lvedder@umflint.edu
VEDIA, Roxanne .... 956-721-5437. 475 F
rvedia@laredo.edu
VEDRO, Angela, M .... 724-480-3440. 413 H
angela.vedro@ccbc.edu
VEDVICK, Kathryn, A ...... 206-934-6415. 523 A
kathy.vedvick@seattlecolleges.edu
VEECH, Guthrie .... 314-837-6777. 280 K
gveech@slcconline.edu
VEEDER, Samantha .... 585-389-2310. 332 D
sveeder0@naz.edu
VEEN, Leslie .... 415-451-2834... 63 A
lveen@sfts.edu
VEENEMAN, Larry .... 877-751-5783. 141 F
VEENSTRA, Derick, A .... 301-369-2800. 213 G
rveenstra@capitol-college.edu
VEENSTRA, Dianne, M ... 301-369-2800. 213 G
dveenstra@capitol-college.edu
VEENSTRA, Myron .... 701-777-2127. 371 C
myron.veenstra@und.edu
VEENSTRA, Tim .... 517-586-3014. 241 A
tveenstra@cleary.edu
VEESER, Margaret, I .... 901-321-3324. 453 H
pveeser@cbu.edu
VEGA, Aixa .... 787-834-9595. 553 B
avega@uaa.edu
VEGA, Annette .... 787-878-5475. 549 L
avega@arecibo.inter.edu
VEGA, Barbara .... 432-837-8810. 487 B
bvega@sulross.edu
VEGA, Erlinda .... 787-264-1912. 551 A
yaremi@sg.inter.edu
VEGA, Esther, Z .... 787-850-9303. 554 D
esther.vega@upr.edu
VEGA, Eva .... 787-746-1400. 549 B
evega@huertas.edu
VEGA, Evelyn .... 787-250-1912. 550 E
evega@metro.inter.edu
VEGA, Francesca .... 818-677-2123... 34 C
francesca.vega@csun.edu
VEGA, Fredrick .... 787-250-1912. 550 E
fredrickvega@metro.inter.edu
VEGA, Javier .... 212-592-2000. 340 H
jvega@sva.edu
VEGA, Juan .... 787-844-8181. 555 A
juan.vegavega@upr.edu
VEGA, Manfredo .... 787-620-2040. 547 C
mvega@aupr.edu
VEGA, Zaida .... 787-766-1717. 552 J
um_zvega@suagm.edu
VEGA, Zaida .... 787-766-1717. 552 J
zvega@suagm.edu
VEGA-GONZALEZ, Melvin .... 787-480-2406. 548 G
melvega@sanjuancapital.com
VEHR, Gregory, J .... 513-556-3028. 390 G
greg.vehr@uc.edu
VEHRKENS, Kenneth, T .. 201-692-2671. 301 J
vehrkens@fdu.edu
VEILLEUX, Jennifer .... 413-577-2956. 228 F
veilleux@admin.umass.edu
VEILLEUX, John .... 817-531-4269. 488 A
jveilleux@txwes.edu
VEIT, Kenneth, J .... 215-871-6770. 430 D
kenv@pcom.edu
VEIT, TC .... 405-878-5152. 399 G
tcviet@stgregorys.edu
VEITCH, Jonathan .... 323-259-2691... 56 I
VEITH, Gene, E .... 540-338-1776. 508 A
provost@phc.edu
VEJSICKY, Janet .... 740-826-8139. 384 L
janv@muskingum.edu
VELA, Alicia, L .... 512-448-8515. 479 C
aliciav@stedwards.edu
VELA, JR., Cesar, E ...... 956-721-5370. 475 F
cvela@laredo.edu
VELA, Eddie .... 530-898-6171... 33 A
evela@csuchico.edu
VELA, Robert, H .... 210-486-0953. 465 C
rvela63@alamo.edu
VELA, SM, Rudy .... 210-431-8094. 479 D
rvela3@stmarytx.edu
VELARDE, Mark .... 602-286-8327... 14 L
mark.velarde@gwmail.maricopa.edu
VELASCO, Steven, C ...... 805-893-2434... 72 B
steve.velasco@bap.ucsb.edu
VELASQUEZ, Lorrie .... 719-846-5534... 85 H
lorrie.velasquez@trinidadstate.edu
VELASQUEZ, Melissa ..... 575-581-4145. 311 E
mvelasqu@nnmc.edu
VELASQUEZ, Tom .... 661-654-2211... 32 H
tvelasquez2@csub.edu
VELAUTHAPILLAI, Ravi .. 910-362-7074. 358 F
rvelauthapillai@cfcc.edu
VELAZQUEZ, Acmin .... 787-844-8181. 555 A
acmin.velazquez@upr.edu
VELAZQUEZ, Acmin .... 787-844-2750. 555 A
acmin.velazquez@upr.edu
VELAZQUEZ, Carmen, G 787-253-7373. 552 H
ue_evelazquez@suagm.edu
VELAZQUEZ, Ginger .... 217-333-9634. 162 A
gmayol@uillinois.edu
VELAZQUEZ, Isander .... 787-753-6335. 549 D
ivelazquez@icprjc.edu
VELAZQUEZ, Zoraida ...... 787-841-2000. 552 B
zvelazquez@pucpr.edu
VELDERMAN, Joe .... 708-239-4837. 160 K
joe.velderman@trnty.edu
VELEK, Thomas .... 662-241-6850. 268 E
tvelek@as.muw.edu
VELEZ, Alice .... 732-987-2201. 302 B
veleza@georgian.edu
VELEZ, Angel .... 787-250-1912. 550 E
avelez@metro.inter.edu
VELEZ, Ashley .... 787-841-2000. 552 B
avelez@pucpr.edu
VELEZ, Carlos .... 310-243-3639... 33 B
cvelez@csudh.edu
VELEZ, Ginny .... 787-840-8108. 555 A
ginny.velez@upr.edu
VELEZ, María, C .... 787-753-6000. 549 D
mvelez@icprjc.edu
VELEZ, Miguel, A .... 787-257-0000. 554 B
miguel.velez4@upr.edu
VELEZ, Roland .... 718-518-4406. 318 B
rvelez@hostos.cuny.edu
VELEZ, Rosa .... 787-758-2525. 554 F
rosa.velez2@upr.edu
VELEZ, Sarah, M .... 716-878-4631. 343 A
yacklysm@buffalostate.edu
VELEZ, Vivian .... 787-664-0331. 555 C
vivan.velez1@upr.edu
VELEZ, Wanda .... 845-675-4792. 335 C
wanda.velez@nyack.edu
VELEZ AROCHO, Jorge, I .... 787-841-2000. 552 B
jivelezarocho@pucpr.edu
VELEZ LUCE, Melissa ..... 773-244-5273. 154 G
mvelezluce@northpark.edu
VELEZ-YELIN, Johanna ... 856-256-5440. 305 E
velez-yelin@rowan.edu
VELGUTH, Peter .... 989-386-6622. 247 B
pvelguth@midmich.edu
VELI, Ravil .... 802-485-2170. 500 A
rveli1@norwich.edu
VELIKY, Dawn .... 252-536-7227. 361 A
rveliky004@halifaxcc.edu
VELKOFF, Townsend ..... 570-321-4258. 422 H
velkoff@lycoming.edu
VELLACCIO, Frank .... 508-793-3010. 225 B
fvellacc@holycross.edu
VELO, Jason .... 209-946-2233... 73 A
jvelo@pacific.edu
VELORIA, Ruth .... 602-557-1544... 18 I
ruth.veloria@phoenix.edu
VELTRI, Sandra .... 303-404-5497... 81 N
sandy.veltri@frontrange.edu
VELTRI, Valerie, L .... 412-531-4433. 414 C
info@deantech.edu
VELVEL, Lawrence, R ...... 978-681-0800. 233 C
velvel@mslaw.edu
VENABLE, James, E .... 901-722-3260. 458 K
jvenable@sco.edu
VENABLE, Margaret .... 678-359-5018. 127 A
mvenable@gordonstate.edu
VENABLE, Marion, F .... 336-386-3269. 364 D
venablem@surry.edu
VENDITTI, Ferdinand .... 518-262-5376. 313 D
venditf@mail.amc.edu
VENDITTI, Leona .... 515-289-9200. 179 C
lvenditti@inste.edu
VENDITTI, Nicholas .... 515-289-9200. 179 C
nvenditti@inste.edu
VENEGAS, Valerie, A ...... 714-895-5117... 39 J
vvenegas@gwc.cccd.edu
VENEKLASE, Dave .... 616-732-1095. 241 H
dveneklase@davenport.edu
VENEMA, Cornelius .... 219-864-2400. 171 F
cvenema@midamerica.edu
VENEMA, Kathryn .... 419-448-2028. 380 G
kvenema@heidelberg.edu
VENIE, Evan .... 312-567-3202. 147 F
venie@iit.edu
VENKAT, Rama .... 702-895-1094. 294 I
rama.venkat@unlv.edu
VENKER, Teri, H .... 608-263-5061. 538 E
teri.venker@uwex.uwc.edu
VENN, Martha, L .... 478-471-2730. 128 I
martha.venn@maconstate.edu
VENNEMAN, Martin .... 918-456-5511. 396 H
venneman@nsuok.edu
VENNER, Thomas .... 734-487-4344. 242 D
tom.venner@emich.edu
VENNERI, Richard .... 773-298-3946. 158 E
venneri@sxu.edu

VENSON, Alvin ... 202-274-6361 ... 97 A
avenson@udc.edu
VENSON, John ... 510-869-8726 ... 61 I
jvenson@samuelmerritt.edu
VENTA, Henry ... 409-880-8603. 486 F
henry.venta@lamar.edu
VENTANTONIO, James ... 908-526-1200. 305 B
jamesventantonio@raritanval.edu
VENTERS, III, Golden, T 415-422-2824 ... 73 J
ventersg@usfca.edu
VENTERS, Monoka ... 850-245-0466. 114 J
monoka.venters@flbog.edu
VENTIMIGLIA, Laura ... 978-762-4000. 232 D
lventimi@northshore.edu
VENTIMIGLIA, Thomas ... 516-796-5923. 333 C
tventimig@nycc.edu
VENTO, Robert, D ... 318-257-2176. 207 F
bvento@latech.edu
VENTO-CIFELLI, Lauren .. 732-571-3456. 303 C
lvento@monmouth.edu
VENTOLINI, Gary ... 432-335-5113. 487 E
gary.ventolini@ttuhsc.edu
VENTURA, Frank, J ... 330-569-5974. 380 I
venturafj@hiram.edu
VENTURA, Jamey ... 802-635-1285. 501 D
jamey.ventura@jsc.edu
VENTURA, Nilo ... 650-543-3717 ... 54 C
nventura@menlo.edu
VENTURA, Paul ... 503-534-4008. 404 C
pventura@marylhurst.edu
VENTURELLA,
Gordon, D ... 217-732-3168. 151 B
gdventurella@lincolnchristian.edu
VENTURINI, Vincent ... 662-254-3800. 269 A
vincent@mvsu.edu
VENUGOPAL, Junias, V . 312-329-4113. 153 E
junias.venugopal@moody.edu
VENUGOPALAN,
Devarajan ... 414-229-5561. 537 A
dv@uwm.edu
VENUTI, Andrea ... 315-498-2183. 335 G
venutia@sunyocc.edu
VENUTI, John, A ... 804-828-1210. 511 F
javenuti@vcu.edu
VER BERKMOES, John ... 616-945-5300. 241 F
john.verberkmoes@cornerstone.edu
VERA, Fonda, L ... 972-238-6992. 471 C
fondav@dcccd.edu
VERA, Hernan ... 787-841-2000. 552 B
hvera@pucpr.edu
VERA-MORALES, Sheila . 787-480-2363. 548 G
shvera@sanjuancapital.com
VERACKA, Peter, G ... 614-885-5585. 388 C
pveracka@pcj.edu
VERANO, Jeoffrey ... 808-735-4831. 135 D
jverano@chaminade.edu
VERAY, Jaime ... 787-725-6500. 547 H
jveray@albizu.edu
VERAY, Jaime ... 787-725-6500. 547 H
jveray@sju.albizu.edu
VERAY, Jaime ... 787-725-6500. 547 H
jveray@albizu.edu
VERCAUTEREN, Tammy .. 303-404-5243 ... 81 N
tammy.vercauteren@frontrange.edu
VERDELL, Tommy ... 662-254-3580. 269 A
tverdell@mvsu.edu
VERDERBER, Carl ... 845-752-3000. 348 I
carlv@uts.edu
VERDEROSA, Patricia, K . 717-337-6225. 417 B
pverdero@gettysburg.edu
VERDI, Ed ... 212-229-5323. 332 E
verdie@newschool.edu
VERDICCHIO, James ... 718-289-5923. 317 B
james.verdicchio@bcc.cuny.edu
VERDILE, Vincent, P ... 518-262-6008. 313 D
verdilv@mail.amc.edu
VERDOW, Tom ... 315-733-2300. 349 D
tverdow@uscny.edu
VERDUCE, Cynthia, P ... 260-422-5561. 167 B
cpverduce@indianatech.edu
VERDUGO, Jason ... 651-523-2035. 256 A
jverdugo@hamline.edu
VERDUGO, Paula, E ... 909-593-3511 ... 72 E
pverdugo@laverne.edu
VERDUZCO, Oscar ... 509-865-8500. 520 D
verduzco_o@heritage.edu
VEREBELY, James, S ... 402-557-7200. 288 G
jim.verebely@bellevue.edu
VEREEN, Karen ... 478-289-2271. 132 A
kvereen@southeasterntech.edu
VEREEN, Richard ... 678-359-5104. 127 A
richard_v@gordonstate.edu
VEREM, Jas ... 201-443-8936. 301 J
jasmin31_verem@fdu.edu
VERES, III, John, G ... 334-244-3602 ... 2 A
jveres@aum.edu
VERES, Karen ... 610-861-5344. 425 D
kveres@northampton.edu
VERES, Richard ... 413-748-3136. 236 I
rveres@springfieldcollege.edu
VERES, Wayne ... 760-750-4775 ... 35 A
veres@csusm.edu
VERGARE, Michael, J ... 215-955-5431. 434 C
michael.vergare@jefferson.edu
VERHOFF, Monica ... 419-448-2202. 380 G
mverhoff@heidelberg.edu
VERITY, Melena ... 423-636-7376. 462 E
mverity@tusculum.edu
VERKENNES, Joseph ... 734-384-4207. 247 C
jverkennes@monroeccc.edu
VERKEST, Diane ... 928-523-6144 ... 16 C
diane.verkest@nau.edu
VERLANIC, Amy ... 406-496-4289. 287 F
averlanic@mtech.edu
VERMA, Dinesh ... 201-216-8025. 307 E
dverma@stevens.edu
VERMEER ELLIOTT,
Julie ... 712-707-7200. 181 H
julie.elliott@nwciowa.edu
VERMEULEN, Lori, A ... 610-436-3521. 430 A
lvermeulen@wcupa.edu
VERMEYCHUK, Janice ... 609-771-2483. 300 E
vermeyj@tcnj.edu
VERMILLION, Laurel ... 701-854-8033. 372 J
laurelv@sbci.edu
VERMILLION, Mary ... 360-383-3312. 525 D
mvermillion@whatcom.ctc.edu
VERMILYEA, Doug ... 541-684-7269. 405 C
dvermilyea@nwcu.edu
VERNOLD, Eric ... 315-866-0300. 326 A
vernoldem@herkimer.edu
VERNON, Janelle ... 765-677-2710. 169 B
VERNON, Randy ... 606-539-4540. 200 B
randy.vernon@ucumberlands.edu
VERNONE, Alex ... 501-450-1258 ... 21 E
vernon@hendrix.edu
VERNOOY, Andrew ... 806-742-3136. 487 D
andrew.vernooy@ttu.edu
VERNOOY, Jeffrey, A ... 937-775-5680. 393 G
jeffrey.vernooy@wright.edu
VERONEAU, Diane ... 607-274-7983. 327 E
dveroneau@ithaca.edu
VERRECCHIA, Paul, V ... 843-953-4980. 443 A
verrecchiap@cofc.edu
VERRET, Reynold ... 912-358-4190. 131 C
vpaa@savannahstate.edu
VERRILL, Tom ... 423-236-2816. 458 J
tverrill@southern.edu
VERRY, Erin ... 314-529-9336. 276 G
everry@maryville.edu
VERSCHUYL, Molly ... 425-739-8223. 520 K
molly.verschuyl@lwtech.edu
VERSEMAN, Gina ... 734-995-7468. 241 E
verseg@cuaa.edu
VERTA, Larissa, M ... 610-799-1877. 421 I
lverta@lccc.edu
VERTIN, Diane ... 651-846-1363. 261 D
diane.vertin@saintpaul.edu
VERTREES, Gloria, J ... 314-367-8700. 281 C
gloria.vertrees@stlcop.edu
VERTREES, Richard, W ... 217-786-2253. 151 F
richard.vertrees@llcc.edu
VERYSER, Joseph, C ... 248-204-2818. 245 I
jveryser@ltu.edu
VERZOSA, Jay ... 610-527-0200. 432 B
jay.verzosa@rosemont.edu
VERZYL, Scott ... 803-777-7700. 447 G
verzyl@mailbox.sc.edu
VESCI, Diane ... 603-623-0313. 297 E
dianevesci@nhia.edu
VESCIO, Donald ... 508-929-8157. 230 G
dvescio@worcester.edu
VESCOGNI, Emily, B ... 815-224-0462. 148 A
emily_vescogni@ivcc.edu
VESELIK, William, A ... 276-223-4835. 514 F
bveselik@wcc.vccs.edu
VESPASIAN, Bill ... 828-835-4211. 364 E
bvespasian@tricountycc.edu
VESS, Deborah ... 718-982-2558. 317 E
deborah.vess@csi.cuny.edu
VEST, Ann ... 502-456-6509. 199 F
annvest@sullivan.edu
VEST, Ann ... 502-456-6509. 199 G
avest@sullivan.edu
VEST, Eric ... 479-619-4345 ... 22 C
evest@nwacc.edu
VEST, Mark, H ... 928-532-6141 ... 16 E
mark.vest@npc.edu
VESTAL, Allan ... 515-271-3985. 177 K
allan.vestal@drake.edu
VESTAL, Jon ... 870-307-7208 ... 21 H
jonathan.vestal@lyon.edu
VESTAL, Teresa ... 620-331-4100. 187 G
tvestal@indycc.edu
VESTER, Jonathan ... 252-451-8364. 362 D
jvester@nashcc.edu
VESTRAND, Joan ... 734-372-4900. 250 G
vestranj@cooley.edu
VETETO, Steve ... 303-779-6431 ... 45 H
stephenveteto@ggbts.edu
VETRANO, Dawn ... 718-779-1430. 336 D
dvetrano@plazacollege.edu
VETTER, Brandon ... 605-995-2919. 450 A
brvetter@dwu.edu
VETTER, Chris ... 503-375-7017. 403 A
cvetter@corban.edu
VETTER, Gregory, A ... 701-355-8005. 373 E
gavetter@umary.edu
VETTER, Kay ... 502-585-9911. 199 C
kvetter@spalding.edu
VETTER, Ron ... 910-962-3224. 369 C
vetterr@uncw.edu
VETTICKAL, Jay ... 219-942-1459. 165 C
jvettickal@ccr.edu
VEUM, David ... 218-739-3375. 256 K
dveum@lbs.edu
VIADA, Marta ... 787-164-1912. 551 A
marta_viada@intersg.edu
VIALA, Linda ... 212-686-9244. 313 G
VIAR, David ... 818-240-1000 ... 45 G
dviar@glendale.edu
VIAU, Bill, J ... 330-972-6402. 390 E
viau@uakron.edu
VIAUD, Cindy ... 713-525-2160. 490 L
viaudc@stthom.edu
VIBBERT, Candiss ... 765-494-7929. 171 M
vibbert@purdue.edu
VIBERT, Mary ... 202-885-8663 ... 97 D
mvibert@wesleyseminary.edu
VIBOCH, Paul ... 304-263-6262. 527 B
pviboch@martinsburginstitute.edu
VICARS, Jim ... 276-523-7491. 513 A
jvicars@me.vccs.edu
VICE, Janna ... 859-622-8812. 193 P
janna.vice@eku.edu
VICE, Tiffany ... 614-837-4088. 392 E
vicet@valorcollege.com
VICENTE, Jose ... 305-237-1152. 109 D
jvicente@mdc.edu
VICHCALES, Kevin ... 210-829-2759. 490 A
vichcales@uiwtx.edu
VICKERMAN, Pat ... 309-677-3159. 140 I
pvickerman@bradley.edu
VICKERS, Cheryl, C ... 256-549-8376 ... 3 M
ccephus-vickers@gadsdenstate.edu
VICKERS, Jacqueline ... 912-260-4324. 131 F
jacqueline.vickers@sgsc.edu
VICKERS, Karen ... 563-244-7027. 178 A
kvickers@eicc.edu
VICKERS, Kelly, G ... 706-886-6831. 133 A
registrar@tfc.edu
VICKERS, Kimberly ... 404-471-6325. 119 I
kvickers@agnesscott.edu
VICKERS, Lelia ... 704-216-6195. 356 D
lvickers@livingstone.edu
VICKERS, Neil, W ... 512-223-1078. 466 I
nvickers@austincc.edu
VICKERS, Robbie ... 770-531-6425. 128 B
rvickers@laniertech.edu
VICKERS-KOCH, Mary ... 704-330-4656. 359 C
mary.vickers-koch@cpcc.edu
VICKERY, Ann Marie ... 215-637-7700. 418 G
avickery@holyfamily.edu
VICKERY, Deborah ... 801-832-2284. 498 F
dvickery@westminstercollege.edu
VICKNAIR, Allison, D ... 225-675-8270. 203 G
adauzat@rpcc.edu
VICKSTROM, Russell, E .. 508-929-8022. 230 G
rvickstrom@worcester.edu
VICTOR, Jan ... 847-317-7121. 160 M
jvictor@tiu.edu
VICTOR, Michael, T ... 440-375-7000. 382 L
mvictor@lec.edu
VICTORIN-VANGERUD,
Nancy, M ... 651-523-2878. 256 A
nvictorinvangerud01@hamline.edu
VICTORINE, Jon ... 978-934-5060. 229 B
Jon_Victorine@uml.edu
VICTORY, Darrell, D ... 785-827-5541. 188 C
victory@kwu.edu
VICTORY, Gregory, J ... 401-454-6619. 440 A
risdcareers@risd.edu
VIDA, Peter ... 201-360-4111. 302 D
pvida@hccc.edu
VIDAL, Floridalia ... 787-786-3030. 547 F
fvidal@ucb.edu.pr
VIDAL, Lili, C ... 818-677-2085 ... 34 C
lili.vidal@csun.edu
VIDAL, Terry ... 914-337-9300. 321 E
theresa.vidal@concordia-ny.edu
VIDAL, Yajahira ... 787-751-1912. 551 B
yvidal@juris.inter.edu
VIDAL-KENDALL, Olive .. 706-649-1442. 123 E
ovidal-kendall@columbustech.edu
VIDINHA, Phyllis ... 808-245-8213. 136 H
pvidinha@hawaii.edu
VIDOVIC, Lou ... 314-652-0300. 281 B
VIDRINE, Christopher ... 504-568-5976. 205 C
cvidri@lsuhsc.edu
VIEBROCK, Stan ... 816-654-7216. 275 K
sviebrock@kcumb.edu
VIECK, Jana, L ... 812-888-5090. 174 F
jvieck@vinu.edu
VIEIRA, Elvira ... 973-877-1912. 301 H
vieira@essex.edu
VIEIRA, Margarida ... 508-531-2877. 229 D
mvieira@bridgew.edu
VIEIRA, Michael ... 508-678-2811. 231 B
michael.vieira@bristolcc.edu
VIEIRA, Robert ... 503-494-7878. 405 I
acad@ohsu.edu
VIEIRA, Stanley ... 508-849-3447. 222 B
svieira@annamaria.edu
VIEIRA, Stephen, A ... 401-825-2004. 439 A
savieira@ccri.edu
VIELE, Dan ... 314-529-9671. 276 G
dan.viele@maryville.edu
VIEN, Michele ... 518-694-7216. 313 B
michele.vien@acphs.edu
VIENCEK, Jenifer ... 708-237-5060. 155 B
jviencek@nc.edu
VIENNA, Michael, P ... 410-548-3503. 220 D
mpvienna@salisbury.edu
VIENNE, Charlie ... 936-294-1840. 487 A
cvienne@shsu.edu
VIERA, Lisandra ... 787-740-1611. 553 C
lisandra.viera@uccaribe.edu
VIERA, Michelle ... 615-963-5880. 459 E
mviera@tnstate.edu
VIERECK, Shannon ... 605-668-1467. 450 F
shannon.viereck@mtmc.edu
VIERS, Christopher ... 812-855-4418. 167 F
cviers@indiana.edu
VIERTEL, Cynthia, S ... 920-748-8312. 535 J
viertelc@ripon.edu
VIERUS, Glen ... 979-830-4181. 467 I
gvierus@blinn.edu
VIERZBA, Shawn ... 320-363-2144. 263 P
svierzba@csbsjhu.edu
VIETMEIER, Barbara ... 847-617-6698. 160 M
bvietmei@tiu.edu
VIETOR, Sandi ... 605-274-4127. 449 K
sandi.vietor@augie.edu
VIETS, Hermann ... 414-277-7101. 534 G
viets@msoe.edu
VIEW, John, E ... 315-470-6670. 345 B
jeview@esf.edu
VIEWEG, Bruce, W ... 218-299-4737. 255 A
bvieweg@cord.edu
VIGEANT, Paul ... 508-999-9143. 229 A
pvigeant@umassd.edu
VIGESAA, Linda ... 503-491-6928. 404 E
linda.vigesaa@mhcc.edu
VIGGIANO, Thomas, R ... 507-284-3268. 254 G
viggiano.thomas@mayo.edu
VIGIL, Georgette ... 928-523-3757 ... 16 C
georgette.vigil@nau.edu
VIGIL, James ... 304-876-5219. 529 I
jvigil@shepherd.edu
VIGIL, Renee ... 719-587-7526 ... 78 B
reneevigil@adams.edu
VIGIL-GARCIA, Nickie ... 575-624-8035. 310 H
vigil-garcia@nmmi.edu
VIGNA, Natan ... 951-785-2100 ... 50 B
nvigna@lasierra.edu
VIGNERON, David ... 978-232-2376. 226 C
dvignero@endicott.edu
VIGNES, Beau ... 251-981-3771 ... 2 I
beau.vignes@columbiasouthern.edu
VIGO, Luisa ... 787-764-0000. 555 B
egcti.upr@upr.edu
VIHOS, Lisa, B ... 920-565-1295. 533 R
vihosl@lakeland.edu
VIJITHA-KUMARA,
Kanaka ... 309-467-6434. 145 C
kumara@eureka.edu
VIKANDER, David ... 507-537-6281. 261 F
David.Vikander@smsu.edu
VILA, Dendy ... 787-765-3560. 548 M
dmvila@edpuniversity.edu
VILA CRUZ, Geraldo, G . 608-246-6442. 540 C
gvilacruz@madisoncollege.edu
VILABOY, Teresa ... 619-388-7485 ... 62 F
tvilaboy@sdccd.edu
VILE, John, R ... 615-898-2152. 459 D
john.vile@mtsu.edu
VILEGI-PETERS,
Deborah ... 570-740-0232. 422 G
dvilegi@luzerne.edu
VILELLE, Luke ... 540-362-6592. 505 G
lvilelle@hollins.edu
VILES, Vickery ... 541-383-7258. 402 D
vviles@cocc.edu
VILIC, Boris ... 609-896-5033. 305 D
bvilic@rider.edu
VILKINA, Galina ... 212-616-7270. 325 H
galina.vilkina@helenefuld.edu
VILLA, Christopher, M ... 559-442-4600 ... 68 I
chris.villa@fresnocitycollege.edu
VILLA, Cindy ... 915-747-5113. 492 A
cvilla@utep.edu

VILLA, William .... 808-739-4695. 135 D
william.villa@chaminade.edu
VILLAIZAN, Sonia .... 787-878-5475. 549 L
svillaiz@arecibo.inter.edu
VILLALOBOS, Bobbi .... 310-233-4021... 51 H
villalb@lahc.edu
VILLALPANDO, Octavio .. 801-581-7569. 496 Q
octavio.villalpando@utah.edu
VILLAMIL, Juanita .... 787-758-2525. 554 F
juanita.villamil1@upr.edu
VILLAMIL, Margarita, E .. 787-844-8959. 555 A
margarita.villamil@upr.edu
VILLAMIL, Olga .... 787-250-1912. 550 E
ovillamil@metro.inter.edu
VILLAMIL-TORRES,
Margarita, E .... 787-844-8181. 553 G
margarita.villamil@upr.edu
VILLANI, Christine .... 718-260-3360. 336 E
cvillani@poly.edu
VILLANTI, Athony .... 315-792-3053. 349 F
avillanti@utica.edu
VILLANUEVA, Brianna .... 617-364-3510. 223 G
bvillanueva@boston.edu
VILLANUEVA, Christina .. 210-431-6789. 479 D
cvillanueva@stmarytx.edu
VILLANUEVA, Daniel, G . 818-364-7772... 52 A
villand@lamission.edu
VILLANUEVA,
Donna Mae .... 818-719-6444... 52 B
villandm@piercecollege.edu
VILLANUEVA, Gil .... 804-289-8640. 510 L
gvillanu@richmond.edu
VILLANUEVA, Lynda .... 979-230-3422. 468 A
lynda.villanueva@brazosport.edu
VILLANUEVA, Sumaya .... 212-484-1346. 318 D
svillanueva@jjay.cuny.edu
VILLANUEVA, Teresa ...... 830-569-4222. 468 K
terry@coastalbend.edu
VILLANUEVE, Lauren ...... 215-717-6000. 435 A
lvillanueve@uarts.edu
VILLAR, Abby .... 843-661-8351. 443 G
abby.villar@fdtc.edu
VILLAR, Dianne .... 610-527-0200. 432 B
dvillar@rosemont.edu
VILLAR, Jeremy .... 323-953-4000... 51 G
villarjv@lacitycollege.edu
VILLAREAL, Henry .... 650-574-6590... 64 C
henry.villareal@smccd.edu
VILLARREAL, Abe .... 575-538-6336. 312 N
news@wnmu.edu
VILLARREAL, Elisabeth ... 210-829-2736. 490 A
villaret@uiwtx.edu
VILLARREAL, Graciela, B 832-822-3441. 467 F
gbv@bcm.edu
VILLARREAL, James .... 210-436-3714. 479 D
jvillarreal12@stmarytx.edu
VILLARREAL, Oscar .... 956-665-2770. 492 B
oscar@utpa.edu
VILLARREAL, Rick .... 940-565-2662. 490 C
rickv@unt.edu
VILLARUAL, Elizabeth ..... 210-486-3713. 465 A
eaguilar-villarr@alamo.edu
VILLAS, Christine .... 312-893-7114. 145 B
cvillas@erikson.edu
VILLATORO, Gustavo ...... 617-682-1565. 226 D
gvillato@eds.edu
VILLAVICENCIO, Libby ... 740-753-6088. 380 K
villavicenciol@hocking.edu
VILLEDA, Fernando .... 312-935-4812. 156 K
fvilleda@robertmorris.edu
VILLEGAS, Kevin, J .... 717-766-2511. 423 L
kvillega@messiah.edu
VILLEGAS-VIDAL, Ludi ... 818-364-7643... 52 A
villegl@lamission.edu
VILLELLA, Theresa .... 814-732-1297. 428 C
tvillella@edinboro.edu
VILLENEUVE, Martha ...... 603-897-8260. 297 F
mvilleneuve@rivier.edu
VILLERS, Koreen .... 304-457-6455. 526 A
villerskr@ab.edu
VILLINES, Trish .... 870-743-3000... 22 B
tvillines@northark.edu
VILLOLDO, Sergio .... 787-754-8000. 553 E
svilloldo@pupr.edu
VINCENT, Alisha .... 605-995-2937. 450 A
alvincen@dwu.edu
VINCENT, Andrew .... 502-897-4785. 199 B
avincent@sbts.edu
VINCENT, Danny .... 740-826-8155. 384 L
dvincent@muskingum.edu
VINCENT, Endas .... 225-771-3670. 206 J
endas_vincent@subr.edu
VINCENT, Endas .... 225-771-3670. 206 I
endas_vincent@sus.edu
VINCENT, Eugenia .... 951-571-6384... 60 K
eugenia.vincent@mvc.edu
VINCENT, Gregory, J .... 512-471-3212. 491 C
gvincent@mail.utexas.edu
VINCENT, Herb .... 225-578-3861. 204 O
vincent@lsu.edu
VINCENT, Michael .... 928-523-5011... 16 C
michael.vincent@nau.edu
VINCENT, Michael .... 314-505-7257. 272 J
vincentm@csl.edu
VINCENT, Nelson, C .... 513-556-2323. 390 G
nelson.vincent@uc.edu
VINCENT, Rebecca .... 478-289-2361. 124 C
rvincent@ega.edu
VINCENT, Sara .... 860-512-2909... 88 G
svincent@manchestercc.edu
VINCENT, Stephanie .... 617-739-1700. 235 A
svincent@aii.edu
VINCENT, William, B ...... 215-572-3802. 437 C
bvincent@wts.edu
VINCENT, William, K ...... 951-639-5201... 55 B
bvincent@msjc.edu
VINCZE, John .... 203-285-2310... 88 E
jvincze@gwcc.commnet.edu
VINES, Erin, E .... 661-722-6300... 28 F
evines@avc.edu
VINES, Robert .... 239-590-7044. 115 A
rvines@fgcu.edu
VINEYARD, Ed .... 580-548-2207. 396 M
edwin.vineyard@noc.edu
VINEYARD, George .... 618-536-2384. 159 G
gmv1@siu.edu
VINEYARD, John, P .... 931-598-1890. 458 H
jpvineya@sewanee.edu
VINEYARD, Judy .... 618-985-3741. 148 J
judyvineyard@jalc.edu
VINIAR, Barbara, A .... 410-827-5802. 214 C
bviniar@chesapeake.edu
VINING, Isaac .... 404-225-4750. 121 B
ivining@atlantatech.edu
VINK, Cher .... 715-468-2815. 541 F
cher.vink@witc.edu
VINOVRSKI, Bernie .... 559-278-2061... 33 D
bernard_vinovrski@csufresno.edu
VINSKI, Jerome .... 908-526-1200. 305 B
jvinski@raritanval.edu
VINSON, Brandon .... 212-752-1530. 328 G
brandon.vinson@limcollege.edu
VINSON, Larry, J .... 402-552-6108. 288 L
vinson@clarksoncollege.edu
VINSON, Richard .... 336-721-2619. 366 D
richard.vinson@salem.edu
VINSON, Valerie .... 404-880-8773. 122 J
vvinson@cau.edu
VINSON, Wendy .... 706-245-7226. 124 D
wvinson@ec.edu
VINT, Patricia .... 734-432-5595. 246 B
pvint@madonna.edu
VINZANT, Douglas .... 601-266-5005. 270 E
douglas.vinzant@usm.edu
VINZANT, Jeffrey, P .... 334-244-3576..... 2 A
jvinzant@aum.edu
VIOLA, Joe .... 541-383-7776. 402 D
jviola@cocc.edu
VIOLANTE, Marc, N .... 847-543-2580. 143 A
mviolante@clcillinois.edu
VIOLET, Cynthia .... 215-965-4028. 424 D
cviolet@moore.edu
VIOLETTE, Elizabeth .... 207-834-7607. 212 E
elizabeth.r.violette@maine.edu
VIOLETTE, Mike .... 706-771-4037. 121 D
mviolette@augustatech.edu
VIOLLT, Kathleen .... 312-935-4155. 156 K
kviollt@robertmorris.edu
VIOLLT, Michael, P .... 312-935-6600. 156 K
mviollt@robertmorris.edu
VIOTTI, Karen .... 901-321-3254. 453 H
kviotti@cbu.edu
VIRASAWMI, Errol .... 516-364-0808. 333 D
errol@nycollege.edu
VIRELLO, Mark .... 617-296-8300. 227 I
mark_virello@laboure.edu
VIRES, Charles .... 731-989-6171. 454 J
cvires@fhu.edu
VIRES, Tina, E .... 864-488-8245. 444 L
tvires@limestone.edu
VIRGIN, Richard, P .... 402-280-1773. 289 D
richardvirgin@creighton.edu
VIRGINT, Jacqueline .... 505-428-1409. 311 J
jacqueline.virgint@sfcc.edu
VIRK, Sunny .... 718-960-8261. 318 A
sunny.virk@lehman.cuny.edu
VIRKLER, Lyndon .... 802-225-3258. 499 I
lyndon.virkler@neci.edu
VIRTS, Paul, H .... 651-631-5096. 263 A
phvirts@nwc.edu
VISCHER, Robert .... 651-962-4838. 265 C
VISCI, Chip .... 805-756-7008... 32 F
vcisci@calpoly.edu
VISCOME, Susan .... 315-312-2378. 344 A
susan.viscome@oswego.edu
VISCONAGE,
Elizabeth, L .... 410-864-4261. 218 B
bvisconage@stmarys.edu
VISCUSI, Raymond .... 610-359-5070. 414 D
rviscusi@dccc.edu
VISEL, OSB, Jeana .... 812-357-6721. 173 A
jvisel@saintmeinrad.edu
VISENTIN, Peter .... 203-837-8680... 88 B
visentinp@wcsu.edu
VISHWANATHA,
Jamboor, K .... 817-735-2560. 490 E
Jamboor.Vishwanatha@unthsc.edu
VISKER, Thomas, L .... 574-807-7259. 164 D
viskert@bethelcollege.edu
VISKOZKI, Lynette .... 318-869-5137. 201 H
lviskozki@centenary.edu
VISOT, Cynthia, S .... 813-974-1678. 116 C
cvisot@usf.edu
VISSCHER, Caitlin .... 508-373-9527. 223 A
caitlin.visscher@becker.edu
VISTOCCO, Valerie .... 315-781-3309. 326 C
vistocco@hws.edu
VISUANO, Denise .... 503-838-8349. 406 E
visuanod@wou.edu
VITA, Claudine .... 610-526-6012. 417 H
cvita@harcum.edu
VITA, Paul .... 314-977-2500. 281 I
vitap@slu.edu
VITAGLIANO, James, V .. 617-726-3136. 234 B
jvitagliano@mghihp.edu
VITALE, Bob .... 319-385-6270. 179 K
bob.vitale@iwc.edu
VITALE, Eve .... 810-762-9525. 244 Q
evitale@kettering.edu
VITALE, Fran .... 480-423-6133... 15 E
fran.vitale@scottsdalecc.edu
VITALE, Frank .... 410-888-9048. 216 D
fvitale@muih.edu
VITALE, Joseph .... 973-328-5060. 300 G
jvitale@ccm.edu
VITALE, Joseph .... 330-672-2901. 382 B
jvitale1@kent.edu
VITALE, Lori .... 816-995-2806. 280 G
lori.vitale@researchcollege.edu
VITALE, Tim .... 435-797-1351. 497 B
tim.vitale@usu.edu
VITALI, John .... 215-596-8862. 435 H
j.vitali@usciences.edu
VITALOS, Mark .... 610-606-4642. 412 I
mavitalo@cedarcrest.edu
VITANGELI, Kory, M .... 317-788-3485. 173 I
kvitangeli@uindy.edu
VITATOE, David, A .... 216-397-1984. 381 R
dvitatoe@jcu.edu
VITATOE, Steven, P .... 216-397-4277. 381 R
svitatoe@jcu.edu
VITELLI, Chris .... 209-588-5142... 77 I
vitellic@yosemite.edu
VITELLI, Chris .... 209-588-5107... 77 I
vitellic@yosemite.edu
VITELLI, Mary .... 407-628-6303. 111 Q
mvitelli@rollins.edu
VITELLI, Michele .... 215-646-7300. 417 F
vitelli.m@gmc.edu
VITO, Melissa .... 520-621-0963... 18 F
mmvito@email.arizona.edu
VITOLA, Anthony .... 203-332-5034... 88 F
avitola@hcc.commnet.edu
VITTER, Jeffrey, S .... 785-864-4904. 190 L
jsv@ku.edu
VITTES, Elliot .... 407-823-2373. 115 E
elliot@ucf.edu
VITTETOE, Stanley .... 727-791-2475. 112 E
vittetoe.stan@spcollege.edu
VITTITOE, Sheryl, S .... 772-462-4705. 106 P
svittitoe@irsc.edu
VITTO, Cindy .... 856-256-3553. 305 E
vitto@rowan.edu
VITTONE, Jason .... 573-592-4387. 285 D
jason.vittone@williamwoods.edu
VITUCCI, Tom .... 954-262-7304. 109 K
tomv@nova.edu
VIVEIROS, Derek .... 508-678-2811. 231 B
derek.viveiros@bristolcc.edu
VIVERETTE, Maggie, J .... 229-333-5463. 134 B
mviveret@valdosta.edu
VIVERITO, Diane .... 708-974-5334. 153 F
viverito@morainevalley.edu
VIVIAN, Daniel .... 716-645-4540. 341 F
dtvivian@buffalo.edu
VIVIANI, Jeanne .... 941-487-4649. 115 D
jviviani@ncf.edu
VIVIANO, Paul .... 619-543-6654... 71 F
pviviano@ucsd.edu
VIVILECCHIA, Joe .... 603-623-0313. 297 E
jvivilecchia@nhia.edu
VIVONA, Joseph, F .... 301-445-1923. 219 A
jvivona@usmd.edu
VIVONI, Johanna .... 787-257-7373. 552 H
jovivoni@suagm.edu
VIZCARRONDO, Roberto 787-750-4405. 554 B
roberto.vizcarrondo@upr.edu
VIZZINI, Anthony .... 316-978-3010. 191 F
tony.vizzini@wichita.edu
VIZZINI, Gail .... 631-451-4236. 346 E
vizzig@sunysuffolk.edu
VLACH, Erin .... 614-222-4000. 378 A
evlach@ccad.edu
VLAHAKIS, Stacy .... 312-752-2232. 149 E
stacy.vlahakis@kendall.edu
VLAHAKIS, Valerie .... 217-641-4561. 148 M
vlahakis@jwcc.edu
VLAHOS, Christopher, J . 216-368-6280. 375 J
christopher.vlahos@case.edu
VLAHOV, David .... 415-476-1805... 72 A
david.vlahov@nursing.ucsf.edu
VLIET, Rodney, M .... 562-903-4834... 29 L
rod.vliet@biola.edu
VO, Thoa Hoang .... 972-860-4604. 470 G
tVo@dcccd.edu
VOELKER, Joseph .... 860-768-4103... 92 D
voelker@hartford.edu
VOELZ, Zach, r .... 920-565-1287. 533 R
voelzZR@lakeland.edu
VOELZKE, Max .... 692-625-4035. 546 F
mvoelzke@cmi.edu
VOETTERL, Robin .... 315-866-0300. 326 A
VOGAN, Jessica .... 970-943-2891... 86 I
jvogan@western.edu
VOGEL, Allan .... 605-626-2544. 451 I
vogel@northern.edu
VOGEL, Christine .... 773-947-6316. 152 E
cvogel@mccormick.edu
VOGEL, Joanne .... 407-646-2194. 111 Q
jvogel@rollins.edu
VOGEL, Kim .... 541-684-4644. 407 B
kvogel@pioneerpacific.edu
VOGEL, Kristin, D .... 920-403-3290. 535 L
kristin.vogel@snc.edu
VOGEL, Petra .... 802-586-7711. 500 E
pvogel@sterlingcollege.edu
VOGEL, Rich .... 352-588-8361. 112 D
rich.vogel@saintleo.edu
VOGEL, Richard .... 631-420-2189. 346 B
richard.vogel@farmingdale.edu
VOGEL, Richard .... 601-318-6762. 270 I
dvogel@wmcarey.edu
VOGEL, Robert .... 412-536-1032. 420 A
bob.vogel@laroche.edu
VOGEL, Terri .... 660-562-1151. 279 I
tvogel@nwmissouri.edu
VOGELE, William .... 617-731-7114. 235 H
vogelewi@pmc.edu
VOGELGESANG, Bruce .... 314-539-5245. 281 D
bvogelgesang@stlcc.edu
VOGELMANN,
Thomas, C .... 802-656-0137. 500 F
thomas.vogelmann@uvm.edu
VOGELSANG, Amy .... 510-204-0734... 38 J
avogelsang@cdsp.edu
VOGELZANG HOOGSTRA,
Shirley .... 616-526-6453. 240 L
shoogstr@calvin.edu
VOGEN, Shawn .... 708-216-5642. 151 H
svogen@lumc.edu
VOGHEL-OCHS, Sydney . 203-575-8297... 89 B
svoghel-ochs@nvcc.commnet.edu
VOGL, Joseph, A .... 989-964-4051. 249 G
javogl@svsu.edu
VOGT, Gail .... 619-574-6909... 57 E
gvogt@pacificcollege.edu
VOGT, Mark, A .... 502-410-6200. 194 B
mvogt@galencollege.edu
VOGT, Marlene .... 815-479-7559. 152 F
mvogt@mchenry.edu
VOGT, Randy .... 559-244-5940... 68 H
randy.vogt@scccd.edu
VOGT, Tracy .... 734-384-4230. 247 C
tvogt@monroeccc.edu
VOHRA, Promod .... 815-753-2256. 154 I
pvohra@niu.edu
VOIGT, Darry .... 307-268-2596. 542 X
dvoigt@caspercollege.edu
VOIGT, Francis .... 802-225-3207. 499 I
francis.voigt@neci.edu
VOIGTS, Adam, J .... 515-263-2821. 178 G
avoigts@grandview.edu
VOIGTS, Sheryl .... 859-858-3511. 192 B
sheryl.voigts@asbury.edu
VOISIN, Anthony, A .... 989-774-3346. 240 N
voisi1a@cmich.edu
VOISINE, Scott, A .... 207-834-8644. 212 E
voisine@maine.edu
VOKES, Bill .... 724-838-4282. 433 E
vokes@setonhill.edu
VOLAK, Renee .... 973-408-3637. 301 C
finaid@drew.edu
VOLAND, Gerard .... 810-762-3177. 251 E
gvoland@umflint.edu
VOLANT, Adam, C .... 540-464-7221. 515 B
volantac@vmiaa.org
VOLDEN, Lora .... 907-786-6190... 10 H
llvolden@uaa.alaska.edu
VOLES, Lorraine, A .... 202-994-8810... 95 D
lvoles@gwu.edu
VOLETY, Aswani .... 239-590-7156. 115 A
avolety@fgcu.edu

VOLIBER, Delores .... 501-244-5124... 19 J
delores.voliber@arkansasbaptist.edu
VOLK, Mark .... 570-961-7850. 420 C
volkm@lackawanna.edu
VOLK, Michael, S .... 616-554-5695. 241 H
mvolk@davenport.edu
VOLKER, Janice .... 402-872-2228. 291 E
jvolker@peru.edu
VOLKER, Jeanette .... 402-437-2554. 292 C
jvolker@southeast.edu
VOLKERS, Erica .... 505-224-3699. 309 E
evolkers@cnm.edu
VOLKERT, Jo .... 415-338-2032... 35 E
jvolkert@sfsu.edu
VOLKERT, Jo .... 415-338-7264... 35 E
jvolkert@sfsu.edu
VOLL, William .... 914-923-2772. 335 J
wvoll@pace.edu
VOLLENDORF, Lisa .... 408-924-4300... 36 A
lisa.vollendorf@sjsu.edu
VOLLER, Julie .... 602-285-7558... 15 C
julie.voller@phoenixcollege.edu
VOLLMER, Raymond .... 443-885-3144. 217 A
raymond.vollmer@morgan.edu
VOLLMERT, Brian .... 815-753-5791. 154 I
bvollmert@niu.edu
VOLLRATH, David, A ...... 574-520-4260. 168 E
vollrath@iusb.edu
VOLNICK, Stacy .... 561-297-0143. 114 L
svolnick@fau.edu
VOLPE, Ronald, J .... 301-696-3855. 215 D
volpe@hood.edu
VOLPE-CASALINO,
Kimberly .... 516-299-2621. 329 C
Kimberly.Volpe-Casalino@liu.edu
VOLPI, Kirsten .... 303-273-3240... 80 E
kvolpi@mines.edu
VOLPI, Robert, P .... 413-597-2121. 238 D
robert.p.volpi@williams.edu
VOLTAS, Catherine .... 401-454-6629. 440 A
cvoltas@risd.edu
VOLTURO, Tom .... 918-343-7861. 399 C
tvolturo@rsu.edu
VOLTZ, Deborah, L .... 205-934-8320.... 8 E
voltz@uab.edu
VOLTZ, Larry, E .... 202-274-6195... 97 A
lvoltz@udc.edu
VOMACHKA, Archie, J ... 215-572-2199. 409 H
vomachka@arcadia.edu
VON ARX, SJ,
Jeffrey, P .... 203-254-4000... 89 I
president@fairfield.edu
VON BEHREN, Linda ..... 217-234-5211. 150 D
lvonbehr@lakeland.cc.il.us
VON DAUM THOLL,
Susan .... 617-264-7659. 226 B
tholl@emmanuel.edu
VON DER MEHDEN,
Kass .... 707-546-4000... 43 E
kvondermehden@empirecollege.com
VON EBERS, Marie .... 708-524-6950. 144 C
vonebers@dom.edu
VON EYE, Rochelle .... 605-995-2625. 450 A
rovoneye@dwu.edu
VON HOLZEN, Roger ..... 660-562-1134. 279 I
rvonholzen@nwmissouri.edu
VON MUNKWITZ-SMITH,
Jeffrey .... 617-353-8353. 224 D
jvon@bu.edu
VON PFAHL, Stephen .... 231-843-5985. 252 H
smvonpfahl@westshore.edu
VON SCHLIEDER, Lynn .. 202-546-4734. 523 F
lvonschl@shoreline.edu
VON TRAPP, Jane .... 203-837-8419... 88 B
vontrappj@wcsu.edu
VON WALD, Greg .... 605-995-3062. 450 E
Greg.Vonwald@mitchelltech.edu
VONDER HEIDE, Dan .... 773-508-6093. 151 H
dvonder@luc.edu
VONHAHMANN,
Jennifer .... 315-568-3270. 333 C
jvonhahmann@nycc.edu
VONHANDORF, Teri .... 859-442-4173. 195 B
teri.vonhandorf@kctcs.edu
VONVILLE, Gerry .... 304-384-5266. 529 E
lgvonville@concord.edu
VOOGT, Donna .... 818-240-1000... 45 G
dvoogt@glendale.edu
VOORHEES, Bill .... 918-293-5394. 398 B
bill.voorhees@okstate.edu
VOORHEES, Herschel ..... 940-565-4911. 490 C
herschel.voorhees@unt.edu
VOORHEES, Lorraine, I ... 714-449-7445... 67 D
lvoorhees@scco.edu
VOORHEES, Rhondie ...... 406-243-5225. 286 H
rhondie.voorhees@umontana.edu
VOOS, Angela .... 641-269-3000. 178 H
voos@grinnell.edu
VOOS, Gerard .... 828-232-5040. 368 C
gvoos@unca.edu

VOPATEK, Christina .... 218-855-8027. 258 B
cvopatek@clcmn.edu
VORDERBRUEGGE,
Darren .... 808-544-0223. 135 F
dvord@hpu.edu
VORMWALD, Sean .... 315-498-2847. 335 G
vormwals@sunyocc.edu
VOROUS, Teresa .... 863-297-1089. 110 H
tvorous@polk.edu
VORP, Donald, M .... 609-497-7935. 304 D
don.vorp@ptsem.edu
VORP, Laurie, A .... 716-338-1090. 327 J
laurievorp@mail.sunyjcc.edu
VORSAS, Joe .... 903-566-7294. 492 D
jvorsas@uttyler.edu
VORTHERMS, Kristie ...... 605-367-6115. 452 C
kristie.vortherms@southeasttech.edu
VOS, Dale, R .... 810-989-5671. 249 H
dvos@sc4.edu
VOS, Lois .... 503-255-0332. 404 F
lvos@multnomah.edu
VOSATKA, Carol .... 518-255-5380. 344 E
vosatc@cobleskill.edu
VOSBURGH, Grant .... 931-363-9815. 456 C
gvosburgh@martinmethodist.edu
VOSBURGH, Paula .... 617-296-8300. 227 I
paula_vosburgh@laboure.edu
VOSE, Annette .... 412-304-0722. 416 F
avose@cci.edu
VOSEVICH, Mary .... 505-277-6644. 312 F
mvosevic@unm.edu
VOSKUIL, Dave .... 512-863-1202. 481 I
voskuild@southwestern.edu
VOSPER, Susan .... 206-398-4317. 523 E
vospers@seattleu.edu
VOSS, Brian, D .... 301-405-7700. 219 B
bdvoss@umd.edu
VOSS, Ingrid .... 559-251-4215... 30 I
izv@fpu.edu
VOSS, Karen .... 641-269-3500. 178 H
voss@grinnell.edu
VOSS, Lori .... 507-223-7252. 260 A
lori.voss@mnwest.edu
VOSS, Todd, S .... 864-644-5011. 446 I
tvoss@swu.edu
VOSS, Trish .... 406-390-0084. 194 A
trish.voss@frontier.edu
VOTAW, Floyd .... 503-375-7016. 403 A
fvotaw@corban.edu
VOTH, Deanna .... 651-385-6314. 259 E
dvoth@southeastmn.edu
VOTRUBA, Jason .... 719-255-4665... 85 M
jvotruba@uccs.edu
VOTRUBA, Nell .... 402-844-7051. 291 I
nell@northeast.edu
VOTTERO, Timothy, J ..... 605-394-2347. 452 A
tim.vottero@sdsmt.edu
VOURNELIS, April, J ...... 203-576-4914... 91 G
vourneli@bridgeport.edu
VOUTE MACDONALD,
Kathleen .... 718-990-6435. 339 A
macdonak@stjohns.edu
VOVES, Mary .... 509-359-4210. 519 C
mvoves@ewu.edu
VOVES, Renee .... 319-352-8491. 183 E
renee.voves@wartburg.edu
VOWELS, Kelly, J .... 913-360-7418. 184 H
kvowels@benedictine.edu
VOWELS, Robert .... 313-993-1700. 250 K
robert.vowels@udmercy.edu
VOWINKEL, Paul .... 407-628-5870. 102 K
pvowinkel@cci.edu
VOX, Donald .... 914-337-9300. 321 E
donald.vos@concordia-ny.edu
VOYER, Pamela, B .... 716-878-3725. 343 A
voyerpb@buffalostate.edu
VOYLES, Brad .... 706-419-1107. 123 F
voyles@covenant.edu
VOYTEK, Robert .... 928-226-4208... 13 B
bob.voytek@coconino.edu
VOYTOVICH, Steven, A .. 570-561-1818. 432 F
svoytovich@gmail.com
VOZZOLA, Elizabeth .... 860-231-5545... 92 F
evozzola@usj.edu
VRIESMAN, Douglas .... 616-538-2330. 243 A
dvriesman@gbcol.edu
VRIEZE, Scott .... 715-246-6561. 541 F
scott.vrieze@witc.edu
VROMAN, Mona, O .... 315-267-2120. 344 C
vromanmo@potsdam.edu
VU, Nancy .... 619-961-4325... 69 I
nancyv@tjsl.edu
VU, Tommy .... 425-564-2250. 517 A
tommy.vu@bellevuecollege.edu
VUCHINICH, Donna .... 808-956-3711. 135 L
donna.vuchinich@uhf.hawaii.edu
VUGTEVEEN, Troy .... 909-335-8863... 41 C
tvugteveen@cccollege.edu
VUJNOVICH, Denise, T .. 608-785-9190. 541 E
vujnovichd@westerntc.edu

VUKIC, Kelsey .... 626-529-8453... 57 G
kvukic@pacificoaks.edu
VUKICH, John .... 719-549-3334... 84 G
John.Vukich@pueblocc.edu
VUKODER, Scott .... 717-755-2300. 410 C
svukoder@aii.edu
VUKSTA, Rebecca .... 864-294-2448. 444 C
rebecca.vuksta@furman.edu
VULAJ, Julie .... 248-204-2313. 245 I
jvulaj@ltu.edu
VULLO, Russell .... 478-301-2902. 128 H
vullo_ra@mercer.edu
VULLO, Stephanie .... 646-312-3320. 316 J
Stephanie.Vullo@baruch.cuny.edu
VULOVICH, Daisy .... 941-363-7200. 114 I
vulovid@scf.edu
VULPIS, Marieelena .... 516-918-3675. 315 G
mvulpis@bcl.edu
VUMBACO, Thomas .... 518-587-2100. 346 A
thomas.vumbaco@esc.edu
VUONO, Vincent .... 610-989-1232. 436 D
vvuono@vfmac.edu
VUORI, Kristiina .... 858-646-3100... 64 E
kvuori@sanburnham.org
VURDIEN, Rajen .... 714-992-7001... 56 F
rvurdien@fullcoll.edu
VYE, Christopher .... 651-962-4666. 265 C
cvye@stthomas.edu
VYSKOCIL, Cindy .... 562-938-4095... 51 D
cvyskocil@lbcc.edu
VYSKOCIL, Michelle .... 989-275-5000. 245 B
michelle.vyskocil@kirtland.edu

W

WABLER, Timothy, J ...... 937-229-2165. 391 C
TWabler1@udayton.edu
WACHHOLZ, Patricia .... 912-344-2502. 120 G
patricia.wachholz@armstrong.edu
WACHOWSKI, Robert ..... 773-325-7762. 143 H
bwachows@depaul.edu
WACHS, Joy, E .... 423-439-7881. 459 C
wachs@etsu.edu
WACHSMUTH, Wayne, R 847-259-1840. 141 L
wwachsmuth@christianlifecollege.edu
WACHTEL, Elizabeth .... 859-622-8835. 193 P
elizabeth.wachtel@eku.edu
WACHTEL, Jeffrey, H ...... 650-725-0589... 68 E
jwachtel@stanford.edu
WACHTEL, Lynn, A .... 401-456-8520. 439 F
lwachtel@ric.edu
WACHTEL, Theodore .... 610-807-9221. 418 J
WACHTER, Renee .... 715-394-8221. 538 C
rwachter@uwsuper.edu
WACHTERHAUSER,
Brice, R .... 610-660-1207. 432 E
bwachter@sju.edu
WACK, Mary, F .... 509-335-8044. 525 A
mwack@wsu.edu
WACKER, Cary, E .... 903-813-2042. 466 H
cwacker@austincollege.edu
WACKER, Robbyn .... 970-351-2305... 86 C
robbyn.wacker@unco.edu
WADA-MCKEE, Nancy .... 323-343-6076... 34 A
nwadamckee@calstatela.edu
WADDELL, Barbara .... 419-372-5312. 374 K
bwaddel@bgsu.edu
WADDELL, Edwin, B .... 336-734-7326. 360 E
ewaddell@forsythtech.edu
WADDELL, Greg .... 901-375-4400. 457 C
gregwaddell@midsouthcc.org
WADDELL, Jenetta .... 662-685-4771. 266 C
jwaddell@bmc.edu
WADDELL, Josh .... 405-208-4913. 397 F
jwaddell@okcu.edu
WADDELL, Sandy .... 816-501-4689. 280 I
sandy.waddell@rockhurst.edu
WADDEN, Douglas, J ..... 206-543-6616. 524 G
djwad@uw.edu
WADDINGTON, Cheryl .... 402-375-7403. 291 F
chwaddi1@wsc.edu
WADDLE, Chris .... 308-398-7325. 288 I
cwaddle@cccneb.edu
WADDLE, Tonya .... 252-492-2061. 364 F
waddlet@vgcc.edu
WADDY, Jeff .... 708-596-2000. 159 C
jwaddy@ssc.edu
WADE, Alton .... 901-321-4102. 453 H
awade2@cbu.edu
WADE, Andrea .... 607-778-5014. 315 I
wadeac@sunybroome.edu
WADE, Connie, H .... 678-359-5053. 127 A
connie_w@gordonstate.edu
WADE, Courtney .... 413-597-4139. 238 D
courtney.wade@williams.edu
WADE, Damon, R .... 252-335-3063. 367 C
drwade@mail.ecsu.edu
WADE, David .... 606-337-1148. 193 F
dwade@ccbbc.edu
WADE, Douglas .... 661-654-2251... 32 H
dwade3@csub.edu

WADE, H. Keith .... 863-638-2975. 119 D
wadehk@webber.edu
WADE, James, E .... 256-782-5649..... 4 K
jwade@jsu.edu
WADE, Jennifer, G .... 901-843-3850. 458 E
goodloe@rhodes.edu
WADE, John .... 859-622-1405. 193 P
john.wade@eku.edu
WADE, John .... 847-635-2602. 155 F
jwade@oakton.edu
WADE, John, M .... 423-461-1540. 454 E
jwade@ecs.edu
WADE, Katharine .... 352-854-2322. 100 K
wadek@cf.edu
WADE, Keith .... 706-865-2134. 133 B
kwade@truett.edu
WADE, Lara .... 813-974-9060. 116 C
larawade@usf.edu
WADE, Marcia .... 310-434-4010... 65 A
wade_marcia@smc.edu
WADE, Margaret .... 432-685-4615. 476 G
mwade@midland.edu
WADE, Mark .... 215-572-2986. 409 H
wade@arcadia.edu
WADE, Melanie .... 570-408-4400. 437 F
melanie.mickelson@wilkes.edu
WADE, Melissa .... 954-969-9771. 104 F
melissaw@steinerleisure.com
WADE, Noreen .... 516-572-3559. 332 C
noreen.wade@ncc.edu
WADE, Robin .... 678-915-7515. 132 C
rwade@spsu.edu
WADE, Scott .... 406-683-7402. 286 I
s_wade@umwestern.edu
WADE, Scott .... 509-963-2160. 517 F
wades@cwu.edu
WADE, Susan .... 785-594-8382. 184 C
susan.wade@bakeru.edu
WADE, Virginia .... 310-377-5501... 53 F
vwade@marymountcalifornia.edu
WADE ATTEBERRY,
Mary .... 317-788-3310. 173 I
matteberry@uindy.edu
WADHVANI, Rashmi ...... 212-472-1500. 334 B
rwadhvani@nysid.edu
WADIAN, Becky .... 563-425-5270. 183 B
wadianb@uiu.edu
WADKINS, Jesse, E .... 479-248-7236... 21 B
jwadkins@ecollege.edu
WADSWORTH, Michael .. 517-629-0224. 239 A
mwadsworth@albion.edu
WAECHTER, Julie .... 719-587-7165... 78 B
jmwaecht@adams.edu
WAELCHLI, Paul .... 319-895-4000. 177 A
pwaelchli@cornellcollege.edu
WAFA, Marwan, A .... 812-372-8266. 168 D
mawafa@iupuc.edu
WAGEMAN, Magxina ...... 773-481-8830. 142 F
mwageman@ccc.edu
WAGEMESTER, Doug ...... 319-398-4909. 180 J
dwageme@kirkwood.edu
WAGENER, Mark .... 973-278-5400. 314 K
maw@berkeleycollege.edu
WAGENER, Pam .... 815-825-2086. 149 F
pam.wagener@kishwaukeecollege.edu
WAGENER, William, C .... 304-336-8177. 530 A
wagenerw@westliberty.edu
WAGER, Lisa .... 212-217-4700. 324 C
lisa_wager@fitnyc.edu
WAGES, Charlene .... 843-661-1146. 444 B
cwages@fmarion.edu
WAGES, Sam .... 210-805-5836. 490 A
wages@uiwtx.edu
WAGGONER, Bill .... 970-339-6290... 78 C
bill.waggoner@aims.edu
WAGGONER, David .... 410-837-6877. 221 A
dwaggoner@ubalt.edu
WAGGONER, Earl .... 714-256-1311... 45 H
earlwaggoner@ggbts.edu
WAGGONER, Jon .... 334-844-4000..... 1 G
WAGGONER, Julia .... 715-682-1302. 535 D
jwaggoner@northland.edu
WAGGONER, R. Greg ..... 970-943-2079... 86 I
gwaggoner@western.edu
WAGGONER, Reneau ...... 502-213-2620. 195 F
reneau.waggoner@kctcs.edu
WAGGONER, Todd .... 417-862-9533. 274 F
twaggoner@globaluniversity.edu
WAGGONER, Wes, K .... 214-768-4115. 481 A
wwaggoner@smu.edu
WAGNER, Alex .... 617-236-8879. 226 F
awagner@fisher.edu
WAGNER, Anne Marie .... 513-244-4810. 377 G
anne_marie_wagner@mail.msj.edu
WAGNER, Anthony, E ..... 706-721-2901. 126 B
awagner@gru.edu
WAGNER, Ashley .... 619-684-8825... 56 C
awagner@newschoolarch.edu
WAGNER, Claire, M .... 513-529-7592. 384 G
wagnercm@miamioh.edu

WAGNER, Clark .... 920-498-6859. 541 B clark.wagner@nwtc.edu

WAGNER, Colette .... 718-951-5637. 317 C cwagner@brooklyn.cuny.edu

WAGNER, Cori .... 217-479-7141. 152 D cori.wagner@mac.edu

WAGNER, Danielle .... 610-558-5502. 424 I wagnerd@neumann.edu

WAGNER, Dave .... 740-389-4636. 383 F wagnerd@mtc.edu

WAGNER, Dave .... 615-966-5683. 456 B dave.wagner@lipscomb.edu

WAGNER, Donald, I .... 901-678-4265. 460 B diwagner@memphis.edu

WAGNER, Hudlin .... 507-222-4248. 254 D hwagner@carleton.edu

WAGNER, James, M ...... 214-648-2168. 493 E james.wagner@utsouthwestern.edu

WAGNER, James, W ...... 404-727-6013. 124 E james.wagner@emory.edu

WAGNER, Jane .... 617-682-1511. 226 D jwagner@eds.edu

WAGNER, Janel .... 605-229-8427. 450 J janel.wagner@presentation.edu

WAGNER, Janet, M .... 609-652-4534. 305 C janet.wagner@stockton.edu

WAGNER, Jean .... 503-491-6113. 404 E jean.wagner@mhcc.edu

WAGNER, Jeanne, A ...... 717-901-5117. 418 E JWagner@HarrisburgU.edu

WAGNER, JoAnn .... 937-529-2201. 390 D jwagner@united.edu

WAGNER, Jodi .... 509-527-2772. 524 I jodi.wagner@wallawalla.edu

WAGNER, John .... 402-486-2500. 292 E jowagner@ucollege.edu

WAGNER, Joseph .... 413-592-3189. 225 C wagnerj@elms.edu

WAGNER, Karen .... 212-799-5000. 328 B

WAGNER, Ken .... 808-675-3760. 135 C wagnerk@byuh.edu

WAGNER, Kevin, J .... 740-826-6129. 384 L kevinw@muskingum.edu

WAGNER, Kimberly .... 260-481-6103. 168 C wagnerk@ipfw.edu

WAGNER, Lana .... 325-649-8076. 473 F lwagner@hputx.edu

WAGNER, Laura .... 219-866-6116. 172 E lwagner@saintjoe.edu

WAGNER, Linda, L .... 814-871-7423. 416 K wagner001@gannon.edu

WAGNER, Lynn .... 252-246-1293. 365 C lwagner@wilsoncc.edu

WAGNER, Marci, K .... 724-450-4089. 417 E mkwagner@gcc.edu

WAGNER, Marilyn, D ...... 940-565-3487. 490 C mwagner@unt.edu

WAGNER, Mary .... 803-777-7700. 447 G mary.wagner@sc.edu

WAGNER, Michael, F ..... 603-646-2349. 296 G michael.f.wagner@dartmouth.edu

WAGNER, Nancy .... 907-377-4398. 494 F wagnern@wbu.edu

WAGNER, Nancy, B .... 860-832-2050... 87 K wagnernab@ccsu.edu

WAGNER, Owen, W .... 724-946-7335. 437 B owagner@westminster.edu

WAGNER, Patrick .... 920-403-3017. 535 L pat.wagner@snc.edu

WAGNER, Rich .... 612-374-5800. 255 F rwagner@dunwoody.edu

WAGNER, Richard, A ...... 413-796-2306. 238 A rwagner@wne.edu

WAGNER, Richard, T ...... 240-895-3421. 218 A rtwagner@smcm.edu

WAGNER, Robin .... 717-337-7000. 417 B rowagner@gettysburg.edu

WAGNER, Roger .... 760-366-5289... 42 B rwagner@cmccd.edu

WAGNER, Sandra .... 620-672-5641. 190 A pamd@prattcc.edu

WAGNER, Steve .... 218-733-5934. 259 A s.wagner@lsc.edu

WAGNER, Susan .... 520-795-0787... 11 J registrar@asaom.edu

WAGNER, Tammy .... 540-868-7182. 512 H twagner@lfcc.edu

WAGNER, Teresa, J .... 315-464-4252. 342 E wagnert@upstate.edu

WAGNER, Tina .... 651-690-8890. 263 O tmwagner@stkate.edu

WAGNER, Tracy, A .... 941-359-7511. 111 O twagner@ringling.edu

WAGNER, Tricia .... 417-269-8316. 273 D twagner@coxcollege.edu

WAGNER, Virginia .... 414-382-6115. 531 I virginia.wagner@alverno.edu

WAGNER-FOSSEN, Dena 406-771-4312. 287 E dfossen@gfcmsu.edu

WAGNER-LIND, Wendy .. 954-308-2620... 98 G wwagner@aii.edu

WAGNITZ, Jeff .... 206-878-3710. 520 E jwagnitz@highline.edu

WAGNON, Bill .... 205-652-3579..... 9 F bwagnon@uwa.edu

WAGONER, Dale .... 510-723-6626... 37 K dwagoner@chabotcollege.edu

WAGONER, Jessica .... 657-278-2570... 33 E jwagoner@fullerton.edu

WAGONER, Zandra, L .... 909-593-3511... 72 E zwagoner@laverne.edu

WAGSTAFF, Grayson ...... 202-319-5417... 94 G wagstaff@cua.edu

WAGSTAFF, John .... 310-660-3262... 43 B jwagstaff@elcamino.edu

WAGSTAFF, Robert .... 617-951-2350. 234 G robert.wagstaff@necb.edu

WAGUESPACK, Cathy ...... 504-398-2111. 206 C cwaguespack@olhcc.edu

WAGUESPACK, F. Poche .... 251-981-3771..... 2 I poche@columbiasouthern.edu

WAHL, Chris .... 201-360-4030. 302 D cwahl@hccc.edu

WAHL, David .... 925-439-2181... 42 A dwahl@losmedanos.edu

WAHL, Doug, J .... 715-232-2501. 538 B wahld@uwstout.edu

WAHL, John .... 435-722-6900. 496 M john@ubatc.edu

WAHL, Lynette .... 651-523-3000. 256 A lwahl@hamline.edu

WAHL, Robert .... 860-255-3472... 89 G rwahl@txcc.commnet.edu

WAHLBERG, David, C .... 218-477-2175. 259 H david.wahlberg@mnstate.edu

WAHLERS, Mark, E .... 503-280-8578. 402 J mwahlers@cu-portland.edu

WAHLERT, Christine, A .. 816-654-7285. 275 K cwahlert@kcumb.edu

WAHLFELDT, Tracy, D .... 217-443-8772. 143 G twahlfeldt@dacc.edu

WAHLSTROM, David, A .. 617-989-4552. 237 G wahlstromd@wit.edu

WAHR, David .... 567-661-7401. 387 L david_wahr@owens.edu

WAHR, Linda .... 312-329-2213. 153 E lwahr@moody.edu

WAID, Monica, K .... 941-359-7511. 111 O mwaid@ringling.edu

WAID, Patti, W .... 209-228-4483... 71 D pwaid@UCMerced.edu

WAIDE, Rory .... 405-425-5162. 397 D rory.waide@oc.edu

WAINDLE, Kaylene .... 207-741-5571. 211 A kwaindle@smccme.edu

WAINES, Bridgette .... 904-680-7780. 103 Q bwaines@fcsl.edu

WAINWRIGHT, Lisa .... 312-629-1236. 158 L lwainwright@saic.edu

WAINWRIGHT, William, S .... 985-732-6640. 203 D

WAIS, Marc, L .... 212-998-4401. 334 D marc.wais@nyu.edu

WAIT, Mark .... 615-322-7660. 463 G mark.wait@vanderbilt.edu

WAITE, Boyd, A .... 410-293-1582. 545 J waite@usna.edu

WAITE, Dan .... 949-214-3472... 41 I dan.waite@cui.edu

WAITE, David .... 541-885-1075. 405 J david.waite@oit.edu

WAITE, George .... 616-234-3818. 243 B gwaite@grcc.edu

WAITE, Joann .... 509-313-5870. 520 A waite@gonzaga.edu

WAITE, Kristi .... 952-806-3900. 263 E

WAITE, Michelle .... 402-472-2116. 292 I mwaite1@unl.edu

WAITE, William .... 973-300-2100. 307 F wwaite@sussex.edu

WAITE, Zauyah .... 412-365-2794. 412 K zwaite@chatham.edu

WAITE-FRANZEN, Ellen, J .... 603-646-2643. 296 G ellen.waite-franzen@dartmouth.edu

WAITERS, Destinee .... 713-718-7514. 473 C destinee.waiters@hccs.edu

WAITERS, Ernest .... 301-860-4040. 220 A ewaiters@bowiestate.edu

WAITES, Alan .... 785-460-5402. 185 P alan.waites@colbycc.edu

WAITES, Cheryl, E .... 313-577-4401. 252 G dv7029@wayne.edu

WAITS, Lisa .... 707-638-5270... 69 K lisa.waits@tu.edu

WAITZ, Ian, A .... 617-253-0218. 233 B

WAJDA, Phillip, J .... 518-388-8394. 348 J wajdap@union.edu

WAJERT, Susan, C .... 309-779-7710. 160 L susan.wajert@trinitycollegeqc.edu

WAKE, Sue .... 606-539-4201. 200 B sue.wake@ucumberlands.edu

WAKEFIELD, Jill .... 206-934-3872. 522 H jill.wakefield@seattlecolleges.edu

WAKEFIELD, Larry .... 229-430-4609. 119 J larry.wakefield@asurams.edu

WAKEFIELD, Sandra .... 563-441-2454. 180 E swakefield@kucampus.edu

WAKELEE, Dan .... 805-437-8542... 32 I dan.wakelee@csuci.edu

WAKELING, William, M . 617-373-5001. 235 F

WAKEMAN, Joe .... 740-753-6098. 380 K wakemanj@hocking.edu

WAKEMAN, Wendy .... 626-584-5423... 45 E wwakeman@fuller.edu

WAKSDAHL, Robert, B ... 715-394-8017. 538 C rwaksdah@uwsuper.edu

WALBERT, Janet, E .... 215-572-2088. 409 H walbertj@arcadia.edu

WALBERT, Mark .... 309-438-7306. 147 J mswalber@ilstu.edu

WALBERT, Tim .... 501-812-2366... 22 G twalbert@pulaskitech.edu

WALBORN, Ronald .... 845-770-5716. 335 C ronald.walborn@nyack.edu

WALBORN, Wanda, F ..... 845-675-4457. 335 C wanda.walborn@nyack.edu

WALCERZ, Douglas .... 973-877-3483. 301 H dwalcerz@essex.edu

WALCHESKI, Michael ..... 651-603-6184. 255 B walcheski@csp.edu

WALCHTER, James .... 727-341-4772. 112 E jwalchter@spcollege.edu

WALCK, Barbara .... 716-614-5902. 334 E bwalck@niagaracc.suny.edu

WALCK, Brad .... 405-382-9231. 399 I b.walck@sscok.edu

WALCROFT, Marie, B ..... 215-699-5700. 421 E mwalcroft@LSB.edu

WALCZAK, David .... 954-308-2370... 98 G dwalczak@aii.edu

WALD, Cara .... 651-638-6400. 253 K c-wald@bethel.edu

WALD, Frederica, N .... 212-346-1200. 335 J fwald@pace.edu

WALD, Jonathan, D .... 941-355-9080. 101 L jwald@ewcollege.org

WALDECK, Steve .... 661-362-2767... 53 G swaldeck@masters.edu

WALDEN, Dan .... 323-953-4000... 51 G waldendw@lacitycollege.edu

WALDEN, Valerie .... 361-570-4815. 489 E waldenv@uhv.edu

WALDMANN, Robert, G . 718-429-6600. 349 H robert.waldmann@vaughn.edu

WALDNER, Joanne, L ..... 978-232-2013. 226 C jwaldner@endicott.edu

WALDNER, Louann .... 559-737-4838... 40 I louannw@cos.edu

WALDO-JOHNSON, Leandre .... 802-728-1527. 501 F lwaldo@vtc.edu

WALDON, James .... 215-895-1116. 435 H j.waldon@usciences.edu

WALDREP, Dwain .... 205-970-9231..... 7 B dwaldrep@sebc.edu

WALDRON, Cathy .... 561-586-0121. 106 I

WALDRON, David, E ...... 512-448-8453. 479 C dwaldron@stedwards.edu

WALDRON, Gregory, T ... 860-439-2408... 89 H gregory.waldron@conncoll.edu

WALDRON, Janet, E .... 207-581-1554. 212 B jwaldron@maine.edu

WALDRON, Kathleen ...... 973-720-2222. 308 I waldronk@wpunj.edu

WALDRON, Sara .... 973-408-3390. 301 C swaldron@drew.edu

WALDRON, Steve .... 800-955-2527. 274 I

WALDROP, Heath .... 870-862-8131... 23 D hwaldrop@southark.edu

WALDROP, Nadine .... 602-944-3335... 11 D nwaldrop@aicag.net

WALDROP, Tony, G .... 407-823-2303. 115 E twaldrop@ucf.edu

WALDROUP, Linda, L .... 812-888-4333. 174 F lwaldroup@vinu.edu

WALDRUP, Bobby, E ...... 904-620-2700. 116 B bwaldrup@unf.edu

WALDRUP, J. Charles .... 336-334-7592. 367 E cwaldrup@ncat.edu

WALDSTEIN, Edith, J ..... 319-352-8272. 183 E edith.waldstein@wartburg.edu

WALDSTEIN, Steve .... 712-324-5061. 181 G swaldstein@nwicc.edu

WALDVOGEL, Marlene .... 517-264-7190. 250 B mwaldvogel@sienaheights.edu

WALDVOGEL, Todd, S ... 817-257-7955. 484 I todd.waldvogel@tcu.edu

WALE, Rebecca .... 503-883-2602. 404 A rwale@linfield.edu

WALEK, Chuck .... 972-708-7574. 472 L chuck_walek@gial.edu

WALENGA, Gail, A .... 513-529-7506. 384 G walengga@miamioh.edu

WALENTA, Michael .... 616-331-6737. 243 C walentam@gvsu.edu

WALERIUS, Kenneth .... 419-434-4601. 391 D walerius@findlay.edu

WALESBY, Anthony, J .... 734-763-0325. 251 C walesby@umich.edu

WALFORD, Ron .... 502-213-5101. 195 F ronald.walford@kctcs.edu

WALHOUT, Matthew .... 616-526-6566. 240 L mwalhout@calvin.edu

WALK, Kerry .... 310-665-6979... 57 C kwalk@otis.edu

WALKE, Lindsey .... 843-863-8047. 441 H lwalke@csuniv.edu

WALKER, Adam .... 262-243-5700. 532 H adam.walker@cuw.edu

WALKER, Albert .... 314-340-3380. 275 A walkera@hssu.edu

WALKER, Alonzo, P .... 414-955-8656. 534 C awalker@mcw.edu

WALKER, Amanda .... 360-867-6343. 519 J walkera@evergreen.edu

WALKER, Anne, E .... 713-348-8025. 479 A anne.e.walker@rice.edu

WALKER, Anthony, H ..... 757-823-2199. 507 M ahwalker@nsu.edu

WALKER, Barbara .... 713-798-3437. 467 F blw@bcm.edu

WALKER, Bernard .... 516-364-0808. 333 D bwalker@nycollege.edu

WALKER, Beth .... 313-664-7641. 241 C bwalker@collegeforcreativestudies.edu

WALKER, Bev .... 419-755-4786. 385 D bwalker@ncstatecollege.edu

WALKER, Brenda .... 803-376-5727. 441 A bwalker@allenuniversity.edu

WALKER, Brenda .... 256-824-6971..... 8 F brenda.walker@uah.edu

WALKER, Bruce, R .... 304-558-0695. 529 C walkerb@hepc.wvnet.edu

WALKER, Carol .... 352-273-4000. 116 A cjw@ufl.edu

WALKER, Carol .... 352-588-8308. 112 D carol.walker@saintleo.edu

WALKER, Charlene .... 859-246-6438. 194 L charlene.walker@kctcs.edu

WALKER, Charles .... 870-512-7874... 20 B charles_walker@asun.edu

WALKER, Cherilee .... 913-288-7134. 187 L cwalker@kckcc.edu

WALKER, Cheryl .... 410-888-9048. 216 D cwalker@muih.edu

WALKER, Cheryl .... 713-677-7440. 484 B cwalker@ibt.tamhsc.edu

WALKER, Christopher ..... 405-224-3140. 401 E cwalker@usao.edu

WALKER, Cindy .... 334-386-7305..... 3 H cwalker@faulkner.edu

WALKER, Dalbert, N .... 772-546-5534. 106 N dalbertwalker@hsbc.edu

WALKER, David, S .... 717-796-5237. 423 L dwalker@messiah.edu

WALKER, Dawn .... 718-270-6901. 319 A dwalker@mec.cuny.edu

WALKER, Debbie .... 803-822-3269. 445 C walkerd@midlandstech.edu

WALKER, Debi .... 510-649-2400... 46 B dwalker@gtu.edu

WALKER, Deborah .... 510-849-8290... 57 H dwalker@psr.edu

WALKER, Deborah .... 845-675-4430. 335 C deborah.walker@nyack.edu

WALKER, Donna .... 972-238-6880. 471 C dwalker1@dcccd.edu

WALKER, Douglas .... 845-675-4595. 335 C douglas.walker@nyack.edu

WALKER, Dwayne .... 215-489-2372. 414 E Dwayne.Walker@delval.edu

WALKER, Eddie .... 318-869-5116. 201 H ewalker@centenary.edu

WALKER, Elaine .... 909-447-2510... 39 E ewalker@cst.edu

WALKER, Ellen, L .... 330-569-5250. 380 I walkerel@hiram.edu

WALKER, Eunice, E .... 870-235-5113... 23 F eewalker@saumag.edu

WALKER, Gail, D .... 208-467-8844. 139 A gwalker@nnu.edu

WALKER, Garth .... 802-225-3306. 499 I garth.walker@neci.edu

WALKER, Gerry .... 816-584-6256. 280 C gerry.walker@park.edu

WALKER, Glenda .... 956-326-2574. 483 B

WALKER, Graham .... 540-338-1776. 508 A president@phc.edu

WALKER, Gwendolyn, M 716-839-8244. 322 E gwalker@daemen.edu

WALKER, H. Fred .... 585-475-5955. 337 L
hfwast@rit.edu
WALKER, Ivan .... 910-672-1811. 367 D
iwalker@uncfsu.edu
WALKER, Jack .... 865-882-4567. 461 E
walkerjd@roanestate.edu
WALKER, Janice, B .... 513-745-3101. 393 H
walkerj@xavier.edu
WALKER, Jeannie .... 714-744-7078... 38 A
walker@chapman.edu
WALKER, Jeff, W .... 404-413-1521. 126 E
jeffwalker@gsu.edu
WALKER, Jefferson .... 256-322-3103..... 7 F
jwalker@talladega.edu
WALKER, Jen, C .... 859-622-1303. 193 P
jen.walker@eku.edu
WALKER, Jeremy .... 847-851-5468... 81 B
jwalker@coloradotech.edu
WALKER, Jewell .... 870-575-7099... 24 E
walkerj@uapb.edu
WALKER, Jim .... 806-894-9611. 480 H
jwalker@southplainscollege.edu
WALKER, Joe .... 828-227-7441. 369 E
jwalker@wcu.edu
WALKER, John .... 949-794-9090... 68 D
jwalker@stanbridge.edu
WALKER, John .... 575-528-7220. 311 B
jwalker@nmsu.edu
WALKER, Joshua .... 805-581-1233... 43 G
WALKER, Josie .... 985-549-5920. 208 C
jwalker@selu.edu
WALKER, Judith, D .... 402-559-6409. 292 J
jdwalker@unmc.edu
WALKER, Judy .... 734-929-9092. 241 A
jwalker@cleary.edu
WALKER, Karen .... 573-651-2253. 282 B
kmwalker@semo.edu
WALKER, Kate .... 651-696-6562. 256 L
kwalker@macalester.edu
WALKER, Katherine .... 941-752-5320. 114 I
walkerk@scf.edu
WALKER, Ken .... 859-256-3100. 194 I
ken.walker@kctcs.edu
WALKER, Kenneth .... 205-652-3665..... 9 F
kwalker@uwa.edu
WALKER, Kimberly, G .... 314-935-6976. 284 L
kimberly.walker@wustl.edu
WALKER, Kristin .... 972-937-7612. 477 G
kristin.walker@navarrocollege.edu
WALKER, Kyle .... 817-923-1921. 481 G
admissions@swbts.edu
WALKER, L. David .... 864-833-8310. 446 D
dwalker@presby.edu
WALKER, Larry .... 831-646-4290... 54 I
lwalker@mpc.edu
WALKER, Larry .... 405-585-5130. 397 C
larry.walker@okbu.edu
WALKER, Larry .... 425-388-9328. 519 I
lwalker@everettcc.edu
WALKER, Larry, A .... 405-585-5130. 397 C
larry.walker@okbu.edu
WALKER, Larry, S .... 540-375-2258. 509 B
lwalker@roanoke.edu
WALKER, LaShante .... 615-687-6891. 452 G
lwalker@abcnash.edu
WALKER, Lloyd .... 256-372-5783..... 1 A
lloyd.walker@aamu.edu
WALKER, Lori .... 405-682-7568. 397 E
lwalker@occc.edu
WALKER, Lori .... 201-355-1308. 302 A
lori.walker@felician.edu
WALKER, Lucy .... 845-257-3227. 342 B
walkerl@newpaltz.edu
WALKER, Lynn .... 660-263-4110. 279 B
lynnw@macc.edu
WALKER, Mark .... 972-825-4739. 481 F
mwalker@sagu.edu
WALKER, Mary .... 910-521-6695. 369 B
mary.walker@uncp.edu
WALKER, Mary Beth .... 404-413-0093. 126 E
mbwalker@gsu.edu
WALKER, Meagan .... 425-352-8491. 517 E
mwalker@cascadia.edu
WALKER, Mel .... 570-586-2400. 410 D
mwalker@bbc.edu
WALKER, Melveta .... 575-562-2624. 309 H
melveta.walker@enmu.edu
WALKER, Michael, A ...... 910-962-3117. 369 C
walkerm@uncw.edu
WALKER, Michael, D ...... 972-860-7156. 470 I
MWalker@dcccd.edu
WALKER, Michelle .... 804-355-0671. 510 G
mwalker@upsem.edu
WALKER, Michelle, K ..... 563-884-5866. 182 A
michelle.walker@palmer.edu
WALKER, Mike .... 617-541-5373. 232 G
mwalker@rcc.mass.edu
WALKER, Mindy .... 816-501-4047. 280 I
mindy.walker@rockhurst.edu
WALKER, Mitch .... 910-576-6222. 362 C
walkerm@montgomery.edu
WALKER, Monte .... 704-406-2361. 354 C
mkwalker@gardner-webb.edu
WALKER, Nancy .... 413-236-2151. 231 A
nwalker@berkshirecc.edu
WALKER, Nate .... 918-463-2931. 395 D
nate.walker@connorsstate.edu
WALKER, Norm .... 212-875-4400. 314 C
nwalker@bankstreet.edu
WALKER, Pamela, B .... 901-320-9770. 463 J
pwalker@victory.edu
WALKER, Pamela, D .... 916-484-8461... 53 A
walkerp@arc.losrios.edu
WALKER, Patricia .... 212-678-3133. 347 G
pwalker@tc.edu
WALKER, Patricia .... 731-286-3331. 460 F
walker@dscc.edu
WALKER, Patricia, W ...... 203-396-8024... 91 C
walkerp@sacredheart.edu
WALKER, JR., Ralph, R . 813-988-5131. 104 A
pubrel@floridacollege.edu
WALKER, Richard .... 618-650-2536. 159 H
rwalker@siue.edu
WALKER, Richard .... 713-743-5390. 489 A
rwalker2@central.uh.edu
WALKER, Richard .... 713-743-5390. 489 B
rwalker2@central.uh.edu
WALKER, Robert .... 843-574-6788. 447 E
bob.walker@tridenttech.edu
WALKER, Robert .... 601-862-8223. 267 C
rdwalker@iccms.edu
WALKER, Robert, D .... 402-280-2731. 289 D
rwalker@creighton.edu
WALKER, Robert, L .... 979-845-8181. 483 C
rwalker@tamu.edu
WALKER, Ronald .... 609-896-5786. 305 D
walker@rider.edu
WALKER, Sally, J .... 517-629-0226. 239 A
swalker@albion.edu
WALKER, Sandra .... 318-342-1040. 208 E
nwalker@ulm.edu
WALKER, Sandra, L .... 817-515-6692. 482 B
sandra.walker@tccd.edu
WALKER, Sharon .... 618-634-3235. 158 M
sharonw@shawneecc.edu
WALKER, Stephanie .... 718-951-5342. 317 C
swalker@brooklyn.cuny.edu
WALKER, Stephanie .... 615-547-1387. 454 A
swalker@cumberland.edu
WALKER, Stephen, J .... 914-654-5508. 320 H
stwalker@cnr.edu
WALKER, Steve .... 928-776-2063... 19 H
steve.walker@yc.edu
WALKER, Susan .... 541-888-7298. 407 H
swalker@socc.edu
WALKER, Teresa .... 256-840-4211..... 6 I
twalker@snead.edu
WALKER, Teresa .... 212-650-5920. 317 D
twalker@ccny.cuny.edu
WALKER, Teri .... 254-659-7818. 473 A
twalker@hillcollege.edu
WALKER, Teri, F .... 405-585-5102. 397 C
teri.walker@okbu.edu
WALKER, Thomas .... 212-410-8020. 333 E
twalker@nycpm.edu
WALKER, JR., Thomas .. 314-644-9009. 281 E
twalker122@stlcc.edu
WALKER, Tim .... 618-252-5400. 159 E
tim.walker@sic.edu
WALKER, Tracy .... 773-380-6852. 163 D
twalker@westwood.edu
WALKER, Vernell, E .... 210-486-0920. 465 C
vwalker@alamo.edu
WALKER, Virginia .... 918-610-8303. 398 I
virginia.walker@ptstulsa.edu
WALKER, Wendy .... 626-584-5204... 45 E
wswalker@fuller.edu
WALKER, William "Billy" 202-885-3129... 94 F
walker@american.edu
WALKER, William .... 910-630-7152. 356 H
wwalker@methodist.edu
WALKER, Willis .... 330-672-2982. 382 B
wwalker@kent.edu
WALKER, Wm Thomas ... 314-516-5915. 283 E
walkertom@umsl.edu
WALKER, Yvonne, S .... 540-365-4276. 504 L
ywalker@ferrum.edu
WALKER-ANDREWS,
Arlene .... 406-243-4689. 286 H
arlene.walker-andrews@umontana.edu
WALKER DE FELIX,
Judith .... 314-516-5920. 283 E
walkerfelix@umsl.edu
WALKER FRANKLIN,
Angela, L .... 515-271-1400. 177 H
WALKER-FREEBURG,
Karen .... 630-620-2103. 155 A
kwalkerfreeburg@seminary.edu
WALKER-FREEBURG,
Karen .... 630-620-2179. 155 A
kwalkerfreeburg@faculty.seminary.edu
WALKER-GRIFFEA,
Beverly .... 240-567-4344. 216 F
beverly.walker-griffea@
montgomerycollege.edu
WALKER-JOHNSON,
Geneva .... 718-262-2981. 319 F
gwalkerjohnson@york.cuny.edu
WALKOWIAK,
Rebecca, A .... 219-464-5430. 174 E
becky.walkowiak@valpo.edu
WALKUP, Kraig .... 212-346-1368. 335 J
studyabroad@pace.edu
WALKUP, Ross .... 580-745-2148. 399 J
rwalkup@se.edu
WALL, Amanda .... 907-474-7552... 10 I
aiwall@alaska.edu
WALL, Barbara, E .... 610-519-5431. 436 F
barbara.wall@villanova.edu
WALL, Becky .... 704-991-0176. 364 C
rwall8535@stanly.edu
WALL, Bruce .... 717-815-1500. 438 D
bwall@ycp.edu
WALL, Charles .... 508-588-9100. 232 A
WALL, Charles, B .... 931-221-7588. 459 B
wallc@apsu.edu
WALL, Claudia, E .... 804-257-5814. 515 F
cewall@vuu.edu
WALL, David, H .... 609-497-7820. 304 D
registrar@ptsem.edu
WALL, Gregory .... 334-683-2333..... 5 F
gwall@marionmilitary.edu
WALL, Jody, Y .... 770-534-6110. 122 A
jwall@brenau.edu
WALL, John .... 615-383-3230. 452 J
wallj1@dominicancampus.org
WALL, Karen, J .... 310-243-3750... 33 B
kjwall@csudh.edu
WALL, Kay .... 864-656-3026. 442 C
kwall@clemson.edu
WALL, Mike .... 636-949-4880. 276 D
mwall@lindenwood.edu
WALL, Richard, A .... 716-888-2120. 316 C
wall@canisius.edu
WALL, Robert .... 870-575-7187... 24 E
wallr@uapb.edu
WALL, Seth, P .... 603-314-1705. 233 E
seth.wall@mcphs.edu
WALL, Thomas .... 617-552-4470. 224 A
thomas.wall.2@bc.edu
WALL, Yvette .... 718-270-4894. 319 A
ywall@mec.cuny.edu
WALL JONES, Monica ... 601-979-3704. 267 E
monica.w.jones@jsums.edu
WALLACE, Amy .... 805-437-8911... 32 I
amy.wallace@csuci.edu
WALLACE, Bentley .... 501-907-6670... 22 G
bwallace@pulaskitech.edu
WALLACE, Beth .... 413-236-1662. 231 A
bwallace@berkshirecc.edu
WALLACE, Beth, D .... 864-597-4370. 449 I
wallacebd@wofford.edu
WALLACE, Brent .... 940-668-7731. 477 I
bwallace@nctc.edu
WALLACE, Brian .... 210-349-4173. 477 L
bwallace@ost.edu
WALLACE, Bryan .... 303-784-8016... 82 Q
bwallace@jiu.edu
WALLACE, Cathie, L .... 561-297-3516. 114 L
cwallace@fau.edu
WALLACE, Christina .... 718-780-0305. 315 H
christina.wallace@brooklaw.edu
WALLACE, Christine .... 616-451-3511. 241 H
cwallace21@davenport.edu
WALLACE, Cindy .... 704-406-2361. 354 C
cwallace@gardner-webb.edu
WALLACE, Cindy, A .... 828-262-2060. 367 A
wallaceca@appstate.edu
WALLACE, Craig .... 626-815-3223... 29 H
cwallace@apu.edu
WALLACE, Dave .... 912-583-3262. 122 B
dewallace@bpc.edu
WALLACE, Dave .... 972-800-4616... 69 C
dwallace@sum.edu
WALLACE, David .... 562-985-5381... 33 F
david.wallace@csulb.edu
WALLACE, David .... 573-882-6601. 283 C
wallaced@missouri.edu
WALLACE, Debbie .... 870-543-5996... 23 E
dwallace@seark.edu
WALLACE, Deborah .... 818-677-2305... 34 C
deborah.wallace@csun.edu
WALLACE, Debra, S .... 919-866-5920. 364 G
dswallace@waketech.edu
WALLACE, Denise .... 504-816-4546. 201 K
dwallace@dillard.edu
WALLACE, Don .... 912-583-3172. 122 B
dwallace@bpc.edu
WALLACE, Don .... 509-527-2147. 524 I
don.wallace@wallawalla.edu
WALLACE, Donald .... 760-921-5499... 58 C
donald.wallace@paloverde.edu
WALLACE, Donald .... 760-921-5469... 58 C
WALLACE, Donald .... 916-691-7252... 53 B
wallacd@crc.losrios.edu
WALLACE, JR., Glenn, E 912-525-5000. 131 B
gwallace@scad.edu
WALLACE, Greg .... 641-269-3800. 178 H
wallace@grinnell.edu
WALLACE, Harvey, A ...... 906-227-2400. 248 A
hwallace@nmu.edu
WALLACE, JR., James ... 219-980-6601. 168 B
jamewall@iun.edu
WALLACE, James, A .... 405-466-3462. 395 N
jawallace@langston.edu
WALLACE, Jamey .... 206-834-4100. 516 K
jwallace@bastyr.edu
WALLACE, Jeff .... 765-998-5395. 173 C
jfwallace@taylor.edu
WALLACE, Jerry, M .... 910-893-1205. 352 K
wallace@campbell.edu
WALLACE, Joel .... 817-202-6714. 481 E
WALLACE, Jon, R .... 626-812-3075... 29 H
jwallace@apu.edu
WALLACE, Joyce .... 214-333-5229. 470 D
joycew@dbu.edu
WALLACE, Julia, E .... 920-465-2334. 536 F
wallacej@uwgb.edu
WALLACE, Kim .... 303-404-5671... 81 N
kim.wallace@frontrange.edu
WALLACE, Kim .... 303-404-5316... 82 R
kim.wallace@frontrange.edu
WALLACE, Larry .... 423-746-5329. 462 C
lwallace@twcnet.edu
WALLACE, Laura, J .... 434-592-7330. 506 I
jwallac@liberty.edu
WALLACE, Leigh .... 229-217-4143. 129 F
lwallace@moultrietech.edu
WALLACE, Linda .... 765-455-9288. 168 A
lwallace@iuk.edu
WALLACE, Linda .... 240-895-4289. 218 A
llwallace@smcm.edu
WALLACE, Lynn, H .... 215-702-4337. 411 F
lwallace@cairn.edu
WALLACE, Marcus, L ...... 580-327-8418. 396 N
mlwallace@nwosu.edu
WALLACE, Mary Beth ...... 941-359-4200. 117 A
WALLACE, Michael .... 804-524-5598. 515 D
mwallace@vsu.edu
WALLACE, Michelle .... 479-986-6683... 22 C
mwallace1@nwacc.edu
WALLACE, Mike, J .... 408-554-4981... 64 M
mjwallace@scu.edu
WALLACE, Paul, N .... 724-946-7306. 437 B
wallace@westminster.edu
WALLACE, Paula .... 912-525-5000. 131 B
pwallace@scad.edu
WALLACE, Paula, J .... 434-947-8126. 508 D
pwallace@randolphcollege.edu
WALLACE, Randy .... 512-499-4527. 491 A
rwallace@utsystem.edu
WALLACE, Ray .... 479-788-7030... 24 A
ray.wallace@uafs.edu
WALLACE, Renee, L .... 512-232-3320. 491 C
rlwallace@austin.utexas.edu
WALLACE, Steve .... 704-688-4214. 269 E
swallace@rts.edu
WALLACE, Susan .... 312-893-7120. 145 B
jpromer@erikson.edu
WALLACE, Tami .... 615-230-3573. 461 G
tami.wallace@volstate.edu
WALLACE, Teresa .... 307-268-2621. 542 X
twallace@caspercollege.edu
WALLACE, Terry .... 501-370-5359... 22 F
twallace@philander.edu
WALLACE, Thomas .... 661-654-2161... 32 H
twallace4@csub.edu
WALLACE, Tiffany .... 662-254-3440. 269 A
trwallace@mvsu.edu
WALLACE, Tim .... 864-587-4237. 447 B
wallacet@smcsc.edu
WALLACE, Tom .... 615-898-2271. 459 D
tom.wallace@mtsu.edu
WALLACK, Lawrence .... 503-725-4043. 406 B
wallackl@pdx.edu
WALLANDER, Marcia, M 412-578-8772. 412 G
mmwallander@carlow.edu
WALLEN, Esther .... 773-252-5133. 156 I
esther.wallen@resu.edu
WALLENDAL, Deborah ..... 262-691-5240. 541 D
dwallendal@wctc.edu
WALLENFELSZ, Nicole ... 843-863-8054. 441 H
WALLER, Cynthia, G .... 615-353-3645. 461 B
cynthia.waller@nscc.edu
WALLER, Frank .... 301-860-3813. 220 A
fwaller@bowiestate.edu
WALLER, J. Michael .... 202-462-2101... 96 A
waller@iwp.edu
WALLER, J.J .... 912-525-5000. 131 B
jwaller@scad.edu
WALLER, Janet .... 256-824-6282..... 8 F
janet.waller@uah.edu

WALLER, Jennifer .... 662-645-3555. 266 G
jwaller@deltastate.edu
WALLER, Karen .... 325-235-7341. 486 C
karen.waller@tstc.edu
WALLER, Lorie .... 919-735-5151. 364 H
loriew@waynecc.edu
WALLER, Peter .... 970-945-8691... 79 G
WALLER, Steve .... 610-372-4721. 431 D
swaller@racc.edu
WALLER, Steven .... 402-472-2201. 292 I
swaller1@unl.edu
WALLERSTEIN,
Mitchel, B .... 646-312-3310. 316 J
president@baruch.cuny.edu
WALLESER, Diane, K ...... 608-246-6550. 540 C
dwalleser@madisoncollege.edu
WALLETT, Robert .... 410-617-2195. 216 A
rmwallett@loyola.edu
WALLEY, Anna-Jean .... 559-455-5566... 30 I
cccbusiness@hotmail.com
WALLEY, Jennifer .... 559-251-4215... 30 I
jwalley@calchristiancollege.edu
WALLEY, Jim .... 601-477-4173. 267 F
jim.walley@jcjc.edu
WALLEY, Trent .... 559-455-5571... 30 I
admissions@calchristiancollege.edu
WALLEY, Wendell, L .... 559-455-5560... 30 I
wwalley@calchristiancollege.edu
WALLIEN, Dayle, L .... 308-635-6551. 293 E
walliend@wncc.edu
WALLIN, Celeste .... 212-616-7273. 325 H
celeste.wallin@helenefuld.edu
WALLING, Brenda .... 580-559-5350. 395 F
bwalling@ecok.edu
WALLING, Stella .... 603-899-4147. 296 H
stella@franklinpierce.edu
WALLINGFORD,
JoAnne, L .... 207-768-9432. 212 G
joanne.wallingford@umpi.edu
WALLIS, Madeline .... 978-762-4000. 232 D
mwallis@northshore.edu
WALLIS, Matthew .... 817-257-5808. 484 I
matthew.wallis@tcu.edu
WALLIS, Sherry .... 660-263-3900. 272 A
publicrelations@cccb.edu
WALLIS, W. Jeff .... 718-933-6760. 331 K
jwallis@monroecollege.edu
WALLMAN, Marc .... 701-231-8640. 371 G
marc.wallman@ndsu.edu
WALLNER, Steve .... 262-595-2451. 537 C
steve.wallner@uwp.edu
WALLRAPP, Gary, G .... 617-984-1662. 235 I
gwallrapp@quincycollege.edu
WALLS, Elizabeth, M ...... 402-465-2337. 291 G
ewalls@nebrwesleyan.edu
WALLS, George, H .... 301-369-2800. 213 G
ghwalls@capitol-college.edu
WALLS, Kelly .... 276-326-4232. 502 H
kwalls@bluefield.edu
WALLY, William .... 680-488-6223. 547 B
willyw@palau.edu
WALN, Ursula .... 402-872-2341. 291 E
uwaln@peru.edu
WALPOLE, Tommy, A ..... 318-342-5419. 208 E
walpole@ulm.edu
WALRATH, Ron .... 803-461-3237. 445 A
ronald.walrath@lr.edu
WALSH, Ann .... 516-299-3874. 329 D
ann.walsh@liu.edu
WALSH, Brendan .... 845-451-1616. 322 D
b_walsh@culinary.edu
WALSH, Clifton .... 915-747-6636. 492 A
cwalsh@utep.edu
WALSH, CSSP, Daniel .... 412-396-4827. 415 F
walshd@duq.edu
WALSH, Debra .... 715-852-1353. 539 J
dwalsh7@cvtc.edu
WALSH, Denise .... 559-438-4222... 46 K
denise_walsh@heald.edu
WALSH, Erin .... 718-405-3345. 320 G
erin.walsh@mountsaintvincent.edu
WALSH, James, A .... 904-276-6839. 112 C
tonywalsh@sjrstate.edu
WALSH, Jeff .... 813-226-4901. 112 D
jeffrey.walsh@saintleo.edu
WALSH, Jodi .... 508-849-3266. 222 B
jwalsh@annamaria.edu
WALSH, John .... 978-632-6600. 232 C
j_walsh@mwcc.mass.edu
WALSH, John .... 775-682-7190. 294 J
walshj@unr.edu
WALSH, John, T .... 909-748-8368... 73 H
john_walsh@redlands.edu
WALSH, Joseph, T .... 847-491-3485. 155 D
vp-research@northwestern.edu
WALSH, Kathleen .... 312-261-3828. 153 I
kathleen.walsh@nl.edu
WALSH, Kimberly, A ...... 563-588-7417. 180 L
kimberly.walsh@loras.edu
WALSH, Lenore, J .... 516-876-4974. 343 D
walshle@oldwestbury.edu
WALSH, Lindy .... 802-862-9616. 498 I
lwalsh@burlington.edu
WALSH, Margaret .... 614-251-4605. 386 B
walshm@ohiodominican.edu
WALSH, Margurete .... 215-951-1013. 420 B
walshm@lasalle.edu
WALSH, Mark .... 813-974-2660. 116 C
mwalsh@usf.edu
WALSH, Mary, T .... 504-314-2537. 207 C
mary@tulane.edu
WALSH, Mary Lee .... 434-961-6540. 513 F
mwalsh@pvcc.edu
WALSH, Melissa .... 215-965-4042. 424 D
mwalsh@moore.edu
WALSH, Michael .... 414-297-6246. 540 E
walshm@matc.edu
WALSH, Michael, D .... 540-568-5681. 506 F
walshmd@jmu.edu
WALSH, Michele, M .... 781-891-2070. 223 C
mwalsh1@bentley.edu
WALSH, Patricia, J .... 417-255-7904. 278 F
pwalsh@missouristate.edu
WALSH, Peter, J .... 512-448-8441. 479 C
peterjw@stedwards.edu
WALSH, Philip .... 207-786-6240. 209 F
pwalsh@bates.edu
WALSH, Richard .... 541-552-6258. 406 C
walshr@sou.edu
WALSH, Rosalie, K .... 406-447-5440. 285 G
rwalsh@carroll.edu
WALSH, Susan .... 541-552-6114. 406 C
walsh@sou.edu
WALSH, Susan .... 209-384-6082... 54 D
walsh.s@mccd.edu
WALSH, Tammy, S .... 941-359-7505. 111 O
twalsh@ringling.edu
WALSH, Thomas, J .... 315-443-2881. 347 C
twalsh@syr.edu
WALSH, Timothy .... 919-684-5055. 354 A
tim.walsh@duke.edu
WALSH, Timothy, J .... 716-878-4201. 343 A
walshtj@buffalostate.edu
WALSH, Timothy, L .... 662-915-7375. 270 B
tim@olemiss.edu
WALSH, Tracy .... 732-255-0400. 304 A
twalsh@ocean.edu
WALSHOK, Mary, L .... 858-534-3411... 71 F
mwalshok@ucsd.edu
WALSKI, Don .... 507-457-5555. 262 A
dwalski@winona.edu
WALSTEAD, Brenda .... 360-992-2474. 518 A
bwalstead@clark.edu
WALSTRUM, John, W ...... 253-589-5500. 518 B
john.walstrum@cptc.edu
WALTER, Alexis .... 386-481-2668... 99 C
waltera@cookman.edu
WALTER, Almar .... 419-434-6967. 391 D
waltera@findlay.edu
WALTER, B. Kaye .... 201-447-7237. 299 C
president@bergen.edu
WALTER, Blake .... 630-620-2115. 155 A
bwalter@seminary.edu
WALTER, George, J .... 215-951-1024. 420 B
walter@lasalle.edu
WALTER, Jim .... 706-355-5120. 120 J
jwalter@athenstech.edu
WALTER, John, M .... 661-362-2239... 53 G
jwalter@masters.edu
WALTER, Kelly .... 617-353-2300. 224 D
kwalter@bu.edu
WALTER, Kristy .... 617-243-2147. 227 K
kwalter@lasell.edu
WALTER, Lisa, A .... 715-232-2266. 538 B
walterl@uwstout.edu
WALTER, Robyn, C .... 636-584-6617. 273 M
walterr@eastcentral.edu
WALTER, Ruth .... 412-809-5100. 430 H
walter.ruth@pti.edu
WALTER, Shulem .... 718-855-4092. 337 D
WALTER, Susan .... 530-541-4660... 50 D
walter@ltcc.edu
WALTER, Tom .... 706-864-1818. 133 D
tom.walter@ung.edu
WALTER, Willis .... 386-481-2087... 99 C
walterw@cookman.edu
WALTER-MACK, Kathy .... 816-604-1587. 277 C
kathy.walter-mack@mcckc.edu
WALTER-SCHUMACHER,
Joan .... 414-382-6064. 531 I
joan.walter@alverno.edu
WALTERREIT, Jay .... 989-358-7215. 239 C
walterrj@alpenacc.edu
WALTERS, Alice .... 845-569-3259. 332 B
alice.walters@msmc.edu
WALTERS, Carmen .... 228-497-7700. 268 C
carmen.walters@mgccc.edu
WALTERS, Charity .... 406-683-7471. 286 I
c_walterst@umwestern.edu
WALTERS, Dale .... 423-236-2860. 458 J
dwalters@southern.edu
WALTERS, Dave .... 270-789-5007. 193 D
dlwalters@campbellsville.edu
WALTERS, Gary, D .... 609-258-3535. 304 E
walters@princeton.edu
WALTERS, Greg .... 208-885-3478. 139 D
gregwalters@uidaho.edu
WALTERS, Irene, A .... 260-481-6104. 168 C
walters@ipfw.edu
WALTERS, Isaac .... 267-256-0200... 96 F
WALTERS, Jennifer, L ...... 413-585-2797. 236 H
jwalters@smith.edu
WALTERS, Jim .... 951-343-4323... 30 H
jmwalters@calbaptist.edu
WALTERS, Joanna .... 785-242-5200. 189 I
joanna.walters@ottawa.edu
WALTERS, Joe .... 303-963-3376... 79 C
jwalters@ccu.edu
WALTERS, Judy, E .... 925-485-5207... 37 J
jwalters@clpccd.org
WALTERS, June .... 870-762-3102... 19 K
jwalters@smail.anc.edu
WALTERS, Kenneth .... 412-268-1151. 412 H
walters1@andrew.cmu.edu
WALTERS, Kent, L .... 904-264-2172. 111 P
kwalters@iws.edu
WALTERS, Leigh Anne .... 973-290-4219. 300 F
lwalters@cse.edu
WALTERS, Linda .... 570-740-0462. 422 G
lwalters@luzerne.edu
WALTERS, Maria .... 602-942-4141... 13 N
mwalters@cci.edu
WALTERS, Mark .... 608-262-3666. 536 D
mwalters@ohr.wisc.edu
WALTERS, Meridee .... 505-428-1232. 311 J
meridee.walters@sfcc.edu
WALTERS, Michael .... 309-341-5290. 141 A
mwalters@sandburg.edu
WALTERS, Paula .... 423-236-2657. 458 J
pkwalters@southern.edu
WALTERS, Richard, P ..... 423-775-6597. 458 A
WALTERS, Ricki .... 507-433-0534. 260 I
rwalters@riverland.edu
WALTERS, Robby .... 828-395-1602. 361 C
rwalters@isothermal.edu
WALTERS, Robert .... 310-665-6916... 57 C
rwalters@otis.edu
WALTERS, Robert .... 540-231-6077. 515 C
rwalters@vt.edu
WALTERS, Roland .... 540-365-4267. 504 L
rwalters@ferrum.edu
WALTERS, Tamyra .... 269-749-7197. 249 A
twalters@olivetcollege.edu
WALTERS, Tigh .... 512-472-2472. 480 G
tigh.walters@ssw.edu
WALTERS, Timothy, L ...... 509-359-2777. 519 C
twalters@ewu.edu
WALTERS, Tyler .... 540-231-5595. 515 C
tyler.walters@vt.edu
WALTERS, William "Bill" 202-885-2023... 94 F
walters@american.edu
WALTERS, William .... 650-543-3827... 54 C
wwalters@menlo.edu
WALTERS, William, D ...... 336-334-5824. 369 A
bill_walters@uncg.edu
WALTERSCHEID, Dianne 940-668-4274. 477 I
dwalterscheid@nctc.edu
WALTHER, Barb .... 734-995-7499. 241 E
walthb@cuaa.edu
WALTHER-THOMAS,
Christine, S .... 804-828-3382. 511 F
cswalthertho@vcu.edu
WALTHERS, Bruce .... 970-204-8100... 81 N
bruce.walthers@frontrange.edu
WALTHERS, Kevin, G .... 805-922-6966... 26 K
kevin.walthers@hancockcollege.edu
WALTON, Anita, B .... 919-530-7517. 368 A
awalton@nccu.edu
WALTON, Clayton .... 973-353-5934. 306 D
cwalton@andromeda.rutgers.edu
WALTON, Connie .... 318-247-3811. 207 E
WALTON, Dean .... 617-236-8800. 226 F
dwalton@fisher.edu
WALTON, Ed .... 417-328-1622. 282 C
ewalton@sbuniv.edu
WALTON, Edward .... 513-487-1261. 390 C
ed.walton@myunion.edu
WALTON, Edward, I .... 803-777-7000. 447 G
ed.walton@sc.edu
WALTON, Elaine, L .... 262-551-5702. 532 D
ewalton@carthage.edu
WALTON, F. Carl .... 484-365-7222. 422 D
fwalton@lincoln.edu
WALTON, Hermecender .. 803-508-7280. 440 G
waltonh@atc.edu
WALTON, James, M .... 360-736-9391. 517 G
jwalton@centralia.edu
WALTON, James, W .... 972-708-7340. 472 L
jim_walton@gial.edu
WALTON, Jason, L .... 561-237-7787. 108 X
jwalton@lynn.edu
WALTON, Jeffrey, T .... 518-327-6236. 336 B
jwalton@paulsmiths.edu
WALTON, Jinx, P .... 412-624-6100. 435 C
jpw@pitt.edu
WALTON, Karen .... 610-282-1100. 414 F
karen.walton@desales.edu
WALTON, Kathy, S .... 310-287-4396... 52 F
waltonks@wlac.edu
WALTON, Lars .... 562-951-4700... 32 E
lwalton@calstate.edu
WALTON, Lindsay .... 910-755-7330. 358 D
waltonl@brunswickcc.edu
WALTON, Mary .... 252-222-6179. 358 G
waltonm@carteret.edu
WALTON, Patrick .... 530-251-8823... 50 F
pwalton@lassencollege.edu
WALTON, Robert .... 909-621-8026... 39 B
rwalton@cuc.claremont.edu
WALTON, Robert .... 845-437-5500. 349 G
rowalton@vassar.edu
WALTON, Robin .... 609-777-5654. 308 A
rwalton@tesc.edu
WALTON, Sheila .... 425-739-8314. 520 K
sheila.walton@lwtech.edu
WALTON, Susan .... 701-777-2038. 371 C
susan.walton@und.edu
WALTON, Trudy, J .... 323-241-5279... 52 C
waltontj@lasc.edu
WALTZ, John .... 304-473-8510. 531 G
waltz@wvwc.edu
WALTZ, JR., Thomas, A 717-872-3282. 429 D
thomas.waltz@millersville.edu
WALWORTH, Maurice ...... 906-635-2211. 245 G
mwalworth@lssu.edu
WALYUCHOW, Ashley .... 361-570-4343. 489 E
walyuchowa@uhv.edu
WALZ, John .... 859-257-1687. 200 C
john.walz@uky.edu
WALZEL, JR., Robert, L . 785-864-3421. 190 L
robert.walzel@ku.edu
WAMBAUGH, Genie, M . 859-344-3684. 199 H
genie.wambaugh@thomasmore.edu
WAMBSGANS, Cynthia ... 408-254-6900... 55 H
cwabmsgans@nhu.edu
WAMBUGU-COBB,
Angela .... 718-482-5028. 318 F
awcobb@lagcc.cuny.edu
WAMPLER, Fredrick, H ... 215-898-5859. 435 B
fhoopes@upenn.edu
WAMPLER, Jim .... 423-236-2782. 458 J
jwampler@southern.edu
WAMSLEY, Allan, A .... 636-481-3342. 275 I
awamsley@jeffco.edu
WAMSLEY, Michelle, E ... 804-287-6615. 510 L
mwamsley@richmond.edu
WAND, David .... 423-775-6596. 458 A
dwand@ogs.edu
WANG, Alvin .... 407-823-3449. 115 E
alvin.wang@ucf.edu
WANG, Amy .... 323-343-3170... 34 A
awang@cslanet.calstatela.edu
WANG, Ching-Hua .... 415-482-1888... 42 J
ching-hua.wang@dominican.edu
WANG, David .... 212-226-7300. 336 G
dwang@pbcny.edu
WANG, Hao .... 518-320-1212. 341 C
hao.wang@suny.edu
WANG, Jason .... 818-677-2325... 34 C
jason.wang@csun.edu
WANG, Jenny .... 860-906-5106... 88 D
jwang@ccc.commnet.edu
WANG, Jianping .... 732-255-0400. 304 A
jwang@ocean.edu
WANG, Jin .... 801-832-2601. 498 F
jwang@westminstercollege.edu
WANG, Jing .... 916-278-6566... 34 D
jwang@csus.edu
WANG, JuAn .... 618-536-6682. 159 G
awang@siu.edu
WANG, Lan .... 731-426-7654. 455 J
lwang@lanecollege.edu
WANG, Lei .... 850-201-9775. 117 D
wangl@tcc.fl.edu
WANG, Linda .... 906-227-2670. 248 A
lwang@nmu.edu
WANG, Minghui .... 609-431-4997. 325 F
wangm@hartwick.edu
WANG, Nan .... 408-260-0208... 44 J
doctoral@fivebranches.edu
WANG, Ray .... 909-869-3088... 32 G
jwang@csupomona.edu
WANG, Sara .... 415-355-1601... 27 L
sarawang@actcm.edu
WANG, Tracy .... 310-577-3000... 77 G
swang@yosan.edu
WANG, Willis, G .... 617-353-2000. 224 D
wgwang@bu.edu
WANG, Xiaoping .... 423-354-2552. 461 C
xpwang@northeaststate.edu
WANG, Xinying .... 501-450-1226... 21 E
wang@hendrix.edu

WANG, Xuemao .... 513-556-1515. 390 G xuemao.wang@uc.edu
WANG, Ying Qiu .... 408-733-1878... 72 D yingwang@uewm.edu
WANG, Yumin .... 203-576-4395... 91 G yuminw@bridgeport.edu
WANG, Yungzeng .... 951-827-4237... 71 E yunzeng.wang@ucr.edu
WANKE, Tom, S .... 414-277-7191. 534 G wanke@msoe.edu
WANKEL, Laura, A .... 617-373-4384. 235 F
WANLESS, Terry .... 916-278-6348... 34 D twanless@csus.edu
WANN, Maribeth, K .... 601-974-1002. 267 I wannmk@millsaps.edu
WANOUS, Mike .... 605-274-4712. 449 K mike.wanous@augie.edu
WANSER, Pam .... 425-640-1884. 519 D pam.wanser@edcc.edu
WANSICK, Janet .... 918-302-3617. 395 G jwansick@eosc.edu
WANSICK, Janet .... 918-465-2361. 395 G jwansick@eosc.edu
WANTZ, David, W .... 317-788-3297. 173 I wantz@uindy.edu
WANTZ, Steven .... 410-386-8154. 214 A swantz@carrollcc.edu
WANZA, Mary .... 410-951-3400. 220 B mwanza@coppin.edu
WAPLE, Jeffrey .... 859-572-5147. 198 I waplej1@nku.edu
WAPPES, Loran .... 218-879-0839. 258 E loran@fdltcc.edu
WARCH, David, P .... 651-696-6475. 256 L dwarch@macalester.edu
WARD, Alan .... 812-877-8265. 172 C alan.ward@rose-hulman.edu
WARD, Annette, P .... 740-245-7431. 392 A award@rio.edu
WARD, Audrey .... 336-517-1502. 352 H award@bennett.edu
WARD, Avery, W .... 443-412-2361. 215 C award@harford.edu
WARD, Barry .... 310-377-5501... 53 F bward@marymountcalifornia.edu
WARD, Beth, I .... 413-559-5838. 227 B bward@hampshire.edu
WARD, Bill .... 520-206-2610... 17 A wward@pima.edu
WARD, Bill .... 843-863-7514. 441 H wward@csuniv.edu
WARD, C. Allen .... 270-809-6184. 198 B cward@murraystate.edu
WARD, Candace .... 207-974-4625. 210 K cward@emcc.edu
WARD, Carolyn .... 828-898-8754. 356 A ward@lmc.edu
WARD, Carolyn, A .... 804-758-6737. 513 G cward@rappahannock.edu
WARD, Chris .... 303-361-7361... 81 C chris.ward@ccaurora.edu
WARD, Cynthia, L .... 212-647-7800. 346 A cynthia.ward@esc.edu
WARD, Dane .... 309-438-7215. 147 J dmward@ilstu.edu
WARD, Darryl .... 575-624-7172. 309 I darryl.ward@roswell.enmu.edu
WARD, David .... 912-344-2565. 120 G david.ward@armstrong.edu
WARD, David, A .... 435-586-7981. 497 A ward@suu.edu
WARD, Debra .... 562-860-2451... 37 I dsward@cerritos.edu
WARD, Denise .... 651-696-6385. 256 L ward@macalester.edu
WARD, Denise .... 718-281-5643. 319 D dward@qcc.cuny.edu
WARD, Diane .... 865-882-4513. 461 E wardd@roanestate.edu
WARD, Diane, M .... 216-397-4272. 381 R ward@jcu.edu
WARD, Doris .... 803-780-1069. 449 E dward@voorhees.edu
WARD, Elizabeth .... 914-594-4846. 334 A elizabeth_ward@nymc.edu
WARD, Faith, W .... 334-670-3318..... 7 H alumdev@troy.edu
WARD, Gary, L .... 573-882-2661. 283 C wardga@missouri.edu
WARD, Gayle .... 312-942-2819. 157 G Gayle_Ward@rush.edu
WARD, Hazel .... 512-223-5015. 466 I hazelw@austincc.edu
WARD, IV, James .... 207-581-2201. 212 B jsward@maine.edu
WARD, James, W .... 713-313-7741. 485 F ward_jw@tsu.edu
WARD, Janet .... 575-835-5443. 310 F jward@admin.nmt.edu
WARD, Janet, L .... 206-281-2701. 523 C jward@spu.edu
WARD, Jenifer .... 206-315-5801. 518 G jward@cornish.edu
WARD, Jerome, V .... 520-515-5313... 12 R wardj@cochise.edu
WARD, John .... 626-584-5460... 45 E johnward@fuller.edu
WARD, Joseph, P .... 219-785-5571. 172 A jward@pnc.edu
WARD, Keith, C .... 253-879-3700. 524 F kward@pugetsound.edu
WARD, Laurie .... 215-489-4939. 414 E Laurie.Ward@delval.edu
WARD, Leah .... 712-279-1682. 176 B leah.ward@briarcliff.edu
WARD, Lynne .... 801-321-7157. 496 P lward@utahsbr.edu
WARD, Marcus, D .... 601-877-6296. 265 G mdward@alcorn.edu
WARD, Mark .... 563-589-3202. 182 J mward@dbq.edu
WARD, Mary .... 218-755-2010. 258 A mward@bemidjistate.edu
WARD, Mary .... 505-454-5301. 309 L mward@luna.edu
WARD, Matthew .... 716-839-8424. 322 E mward@daemen.edu
WARD, Matthew .... 805-493-3135... 31 H mward@clunet.edu
WARD, Michael .... 314-362-9155. 274 G mward@bjc.org
WARD, Michael, S .... 334-833-4463..... 4 D mward@huntingdon.edu
WARD, Michelle .... 937-769-1351. 373 H mward2@antioch.edu
WARD, Mike .... 270-686-9572. 192 G mike.ward@brescia.edu
WARD, Nathan .... 570-208-5900. 419 P nathanward@kings.edu
WARD, Nayamka .... 718-818-6470. 339 H
WARD, Pam .... 580-371-2371. 396 E pward@mscok.edu
WARD, Paul, J .... 214-768-3233. 481 A paulw@smu.edu
WARD, Perry, W .... 205-929-6300..... 5 D pward@lawsonstate.edu
WARD, Peter, J .... 203-396-8223... 91 C wardp@sacredheart.edu
WARD, Randall .... 815-753-1303. 154 I rward1@niu.edu
WARD, Randall .... 617-364-3510. 223 G rward@boston.edu
WARD, Robert, A .... 585-385-8310. 338 H bward@sjfc.edu
WARD, Roger, J .... 410-706-1850. 219 C rward005@umaryland.edu
WARD, Ryan .... 406-586-3585. 286 F ryan.ward@montanabiblecollege.edu
WARD, Sarah, E .... 304-457-6213. 526 A wardse@ab.edu
WARD, Scott .... 231-845-6211. 252 H scward@westshore.edu
WARD, Stephen, P .... 704-687-7225. 368 E Stephen.Ward@uncc.edu
WARD, Steve .... 360-736-9391. 517 G sward@centralia.edu
WARD, Steve .... 605-677-5307. 451 F steve.ward@usd.edu
WARD, Susie .... 402-354-7063. 291 B susie.ward@methodistcollege.edu
WARD, Tamica .... 415-685-4428... 56 A tward@new.edu
WARD, Thomas, J .... 203-576-4966... 91 G ward@bridgeport.edu
WARD, Thomas, J .... 516-877-3131. 313 A tward@adelphi.edu
WARD, Tim .... 718-862-7307. 329 M tim.ward@manhattan.edu
WARD, Timothy, J .... 601-974-1405. 267 I wardtj@millsaps.edu
WARD, Tony .... 334-727-8364..... 8 A tward@tuskegee.edu
WARD, Tracy .... 951-343-4552... 30 H tward@calbaptist.edu
WARD, Vicki .... 409-880-8931. 486 F vicki.ward@lamar.edu
WARD, Zachary, A .... 304-457-6256. 526 A wardza@ab.edu
WARD-ROOF, Jeanine ..... 850-644-2428. 115 C jwardroof@admin.fsu.edu
WARDALL, Scott .... 909-218-3253... 27 J
WARDE, Robin, T .... 401-232-6253. 438 K rwarde@bryant.edu
WARDELL, Mark .... 940-565-3946. 490 C mark.wardell@unt.edu
WARDELL-GHIRARDUZZI, Mary, J .... 415-422-2821... 73 J mjwardell@usfca.edu
WARDEN, Bill .... 903-923-2296. 471 J bwarden@etbu.edu
WARDEN, Jean .... 301-891-4110. 221 B jwarden@wau.edu
WARDEN, Margo .... 802-635-1260. 501 D margo.warden@jsc.edu
WARDEN, Michael, L ...... 404-894-0870. 125 D michael.warden@gatech.edu
WARDINSKY, Ken .... 406-771-4331. 287 E kenwar@gfcmsu.edu
WARDLAW, Theodore, J 512-404-4824. 467 A twardlaw@austinseminary.edu
WARDLEY, Lloyd .... 914-337-9300. 321 E lloyd.wardley@concordia-ny.edu
WARDLOW, Jack .... 806-894-9611. 480 H jwardlow@southplainscollege.edu
WARDLOW, Rebecca .... 858-513-9240. 175 F rebecca.wardlow@ashford.edu
WARDWELL, Ruth, S ...... 509-527-5768. 525 E wardwers@whitman.edu
WARE, A. Charles .... 317-789-8247. 165 E president@crossroads.edu
WARE, Amy .... 901-321-3331. 453 H aware1@cbu.edu
WARE, Ben, R .... 315-443-1899. 347 C brware@syr.edu
WARE, Bob .... 870-222-5360... 24 D wareb@uamont.edu
WARE, Helen, B .... 337-475-5126. 207 G hware@mcneese.edu
WARE, Larry .... 304-647-6220. 530 B lware@osteo.wvsom.edu
WARE, Sonya .... 937-708-5488. 393 A sware@wilberforce.edu
WARE, Steven, J .... 218-751-8670. 263 C stevenware@oakhills.edu
WARE, Thomas .... 662-476-5087. 266 I tware@eastms.edu
WARF, Larry .... 606-589-3026. 196 F larry.warf@kctcs.edu
WARFIELD, Aimee, S ...... 518-381-1207. 340 G warfieas@sunysccc.edu
WARFIELD, Martha, B .... 269-387-6313. 252 I martha.warfield@wmich.edu
WARFORD, Jill .... 620-223-2700. 186 G jillw@fortscott.edu
WARFORD, Pam .... 281-425-6361. 475 I pwarford@lee.edu
WARGO, Edward .... 570-961-7923. 420 C wargoe@lackawanna.edu
WARGO, Lisa .... 318-678-6000. 202 I lwargo@bpcc.edu
WARGO, Melissa .... 828-227-7100. 369 E wargo@wcu.edu
WARK, Maureen .... 978-921-4242. 234 C maureen.wark@montserrat.edu
WARKENTIN, Don .... 559-925-3217... 75 I donwarkentin@whccd.edu
WARMACK, Dwaun, J ...... 386-481-2165... 99 C warmackd@cookman.edu
WARMACK, Dwaun, J ...... 386-481-2494... 99 C warmackd@cookman.edu
WARMANN, Cheryl .... 847-635-1719. 155 F cwarmann@oakton.edu
WARMKE, Joseph, E .... 740-587-6204. 379 D warmke@denison.edu
WARMOTH, Kristin .... 701-858-3822. 371 F kris.warmoth@minotstateu.edu
WARNE, Janie .... 573-334-9181. 276 I janie@metrobusinesscollege.edu
WARNER, Amy, C .... 317-274-7400. 168 D awarner@iupui.edu
WARNER, Charles .... 610-436-2117. 430 A cwarner@wcupa.edu
WARNER, Charles .... 740-351-3468. 388 N cwarner@shawnee.edu
WARNER, Connie .... 810-766-4107. 239 H connie.warner@baker.edu
WARNER, David .... 240-500-2000. 215 B cdwarner@hagerstowncc.edu
WARNER, Donald, D .... 406-874-6201. 286 E warnerd@milescc.edu
WARNER, Isiah, M .... 225-578-7230. 204 O iwarner@lsu.edu
WARNER, JR., J. Curtis . 617-266-1400. 223 D
WARNER, Jack, R .... 605-773-3455. 451 E jack.warner@sdbor.edu
WARNER, Janice .... 732-987-2662. 302 B warnerj@georgian.edu
WARNER, Jessica .... 302-736-2444... 94 C jessica.warner@wesley.edu
WARNER, Joanne .... 503-943-7211. 408 F warnerj@up.edu
WARNER, John .... 214-645-5476. 493 E john.warner@utsouthwestern.edu
WARNER, Karen, R .... 330-471-8120. 383 D kwarner@malone.edu
WARNER, Kee .... 719-255-3203... 85 M kwarner@uccs.edu
WARNER, LeeAnn .... 901-272-5113. 456 F lwarner@mca.edu
WARNER, Mark .... 507-538-0554. 254 F warner.mark@mayo.edu
WARNER, Mark, J .... 540-568-3685. 506 F warnermj@jmu.edu
WARNER, Mark, S .... 319-335-3127. 175 I mark-warner@uiowa.edu
WARNER, Martin, O .... 610-328-8299. 433 I mwarner1@swarthmore.edu
WARNER, Nicholas .... 909-621-8117... 39 D nicholas.warner@cmc.edu
WARNER, Rebecca .... 541-737-0732. 406 A rwarner@oregonstate.edu
WARNER, Sandra .... 913-469-8500. 187 J swarner@jccc.edu
WARNER, Sean .... 404-880-8980. 122 J swarner@cau.edu
WARNER, Steve .... 863-638-2918. 119 D warnerss@webber.edu
WARNER, Susan .... 516-686-7647. 333 H swarner@nyit.edu
WARNER, Thomas, R ..... 504-278-6468. 203 F twarner@nunez.edu
WARNER, Timothy, R ..... 650-723-4567... 68 E trw@stanford.edu
WARNICK, Mark .... 870-236-6901... 20 K mwarnick@crc.edu
WARNKE, Kelly .... 419-448-2517. 380 G kwarnke@heidelberg.edu
WARNOCK, Brenda .... 928-317-6470... 11 L brenda.warnock@azwestern.edu
WARNOCK, Michael .... 573-882-4329. 283 C warnockm@missouri.edu
WARPNESS, Wm. Guy .... 307-755-2120. 544 B gwarpness@wyotechstaff.edu
WARREN, Barbara .... 478-471-2714. 128 I barbara.warren@maconstate.edu
WARREN, Beverly .... 619-594-2569... 35 D bwarren@mail.sdsu.edu
WARREN, Beverly, J .... 804-828-1345. 511 F bjwarren@vcu.edu
WARREN, Carolyn .... 662-562-3205. 269 C cwarren@northwestms.edu
WARREN, Charlotte, J .... 217-786-2273. 151 F charlotte.warren@llcc.edu
WARREN, Cheryl .... 925-424-1156... 37 L cwarren@laspositascollege.edu
WARREN, Chris .... 601-643-8306. 266 F chris.warren@colin.edu
WARREN, Cleve, E .... 904-632-3218. 105 E clwarren@fscj.edu
WARREN, David .... 717-464-7050. 421 B
WARREN, Debbie .... 703-284-1619. 507 B debbie.warren@marymount.edu
WARREN, Diana .... 812-535-5284. 172 F dwarren@smwc.edu
WARREN, Doris, C .... 281-649-3013. 473 B dcwarren@hbu.edu
WARREN, Earl .... 256-782-5306..... 4 K ewarren@jsu.edu
WARREN, Elisabeth, B ... 940-565-2892. 490 C warren@unt.edu
WARREN, Greg .... 918-465-1756. 395 G gwarren@eosc.edu
WARREN, James .... 212-410-8063. 333 E jwarren@nycpm.edu
WARREN, Jason, D .... 270-707-3801. 195 E jason.warren@kctcs.edu
WARREN, Joan, D .... 212-779-5000. 328 B
WARREN, John .... 616-222-1433. 241 F john.warren@cornerstone.edu
WARREN, John, S .... 850-474-2022. 117 B jwarren@uwf.edu
WARREN, Leslie, A .... 906-227-2117. 248 A
WARREN, M.A .... 256-726-7357..... 6 B
WARREN, Marta .... 906-635-2697. 245 G mwarren1@lssu.edu
WARREN, Nicholas .... 781-736-4414. 224 F nwarren@brandeis.edu
WARREN, Pamela .... 920-923-7614. 534 A pwarren@marianuniversity.edu
WARREN, Patricia .... 503-338-2306. 402 G pwarren@clatsopcc.edu
WARREN, Robert, D .... 408-554-4300... 64 M rwarren@scu.edu
WARREN, Roscoe .... 305-626-3741. 104 J rwarren@fmuniv.edu
WARREN, Ruth .... 252-335-0821. 359 F rwarren@albemarle.edu
WARREN, Sara .... 410-225-2264. 216 C swarren@mica.edu
WARREN, Shannon .... 304-645-6382. 530 B swarren@osteo.wvsom.edu
WARREN, Steven, F .... 785-864-7298. 190 L sfwarren@ku.edu
WARREN, Sydney .... 270-686-6415. 192 G sydney.warren@brescia.edu
WARREN, Thad .... 402-643-7476. 289 B Thad.Warren@cune.edu
WARREN, Todd .... 251-380-3095..... 7 D twarren@shc.edu
WARREN, V'Ella .... 206-543-8765. 524 G vwarren@uw.edu
WARREN, Wade .... 318-487-7436. 202 F wade.warren@lacollege.edu

WARREN, William, J ...... 801-581-6773. 496 Q
william.warren@utah.edu
WARREN-MARLATT,
Rebeccah .... 909-389-3355... 61 K
rmarla@craftonhills.edu
WARRENER, Mary .... 845-341-4007. 335 H
mary.warrener@sunyorange.edu
WARRENS, Shelline .... 803-376-5930. 441 A
swarrens@allenuniversity.edu
WARRIAX, Morgan .... 910-521-6829. 369 B
morgan.warriax@uncp.edu
WARRICK, JR.,
Douglas, R .... 803-641-3406. 448 A
randyw@usca.edu
WARRINGTON, Adam ..... 802-654-0505. 501 C
adam.warrington@ccv.edu
WARRINGTON, Richard . 800-567-2344. 532 E
richwarrington@menominee.edu
WARRINGTON, Scott, C 909-869-6989... 32 G
scwarrington@csupomona.edu
WARRINGTON, Traci ...... 401-341-2477. 440 C
traci.warrington@salve.edu
WARSHAWER, Elizabeth . 215-717-3171. 414 B
elizabeth.warshawer@curtis.edu
WARSHEL, Chad .... 315-568-3297. 333 C
cwarshel@nycc.edu
WARTHAN, Nathan .... 503-375-7006. 403 A
nwarthan@corban.edu
WARTHMAN, Susan .... 401-739-5000. 439 D
swarthman@neit.edu
WARTMAN, Jed, W .... 207-859-4280. 209 J
jwartman@colby.edu
WARTZOK, Douglas .... 305-348-2151. 115 B
wartzok@fiu.edu
WARWICK, Ann .... 212-938-5600. 345 C
awarwick@sunyopt.edu
WARWICK, James .... 323-463-2500... 69 G
WARWICK, John, J .... 618-453-4321. 159 G
warwicke@siu.edu
WARZECKA, Greg .... 916-484-8403... 53 A
warzeckg@arc.losrios.edu
WASAN, Darsh, T .... 312-567-3001. 147 F
wasan@iit.edu
WASDEN, Mitch .... 573-884-8738. 283 B
wasdenm@health.missouri.edu
WASESCHA, Anna .... 860-343-5703... 89 A
awasescha@mxcc.commnet.edu
WASHAM, Jim .... 870-972-3035... 19 N
jwasham@astate.edu
WASHAM, Ronnie .... 606-337-1722. 193 F
rwasham@ccbbc.edu
WASHBURN, Curtis .... 808-739-4627. 135 D
cwashbur@chaminade.edu
WASHBURN, Dava .... 903-271-5862. 478 H
dwashburn@rangercollege.edu
WASHBURN, Lois, M ..... 904-470-8266. 102 A
lois.washburn@ewc.edu
WASHBURN, Terri .... 248-689-8282. 251 I
twashburn@walshcollege.edu
WASHBURNE, Cynthia ... 860-512-3353... 88 G
cwashburne@manchestercc.edu
WASHINGTON,
A. Eugene .... 310-825-5687... 71 C
ewashington@mednet.ucla.edu
WASHINGTON, Al .... 314-264-1000. 284 G
alfred.washington@vatterott.edu
WASHINGTON, Andre .... 859-442-4176. 195 B
andre.washington@kctcs.edu
WASHINGTON, Aubrey .. 340-692-4151. 555 E
awashin@live.uvi.edu
WASHINGTON,
August, J .... 615-343-9750. 463 G
august.j.washington@vanderbilt.edu
WASHINGTON, Cheryl ... 334-874-5700..... 3 A
cwashington@ccal.edu
WASHINGTON,
Christopher, L .... 614-947-6129. 380 A
christopher.washington@franklin.edu
WASHINGTON, Crystal .. 773-838-7535. 142 E
cwashington59@ccc.edu
WASHINGTON, Dana ..... 815-802-8962. 149 C
dwashington@kcc.edu
WASHINGTON,
Dennis, C .... 804-342-5203. 515 F
dcwashington@vuu.edu
WASHINGTON,
DeSandra .... 910-678-0037. 360 D
washingd@faytechcc.edu
WASHINGTON, Earlie ..... 269-387-2638. 252 I
earlie.washington@wmich.edu
WASHINGTON, Eric .... 718-960-8181. 318 A
eric.washington@lehman.cuny.edu
WASHINGTON, Erin .... 864-587-4208. 447 B
washingtone@smcsc.edu
WASHINGTON, Fred, E .. 936-261-2140. 482 F
fewashington@pvamu.edu
WASHINGTON, Gregory . 847-851-5309. 139 I
WASHINGTON, Gregory . 949-824-6002... 71 B
gregory.washington@uci.edu
WASHINGTON, Harold ... 816-483-9600. 190 D
haroldw@spst.edu

WASHINGTON, Harry ..... 484-365-8064. 422 D
hwashington@lincoln.edu
WASHINGTON, Ingrid .... 859-442-1148. 195 B
ingrid.washington@kctcs.edu
WASHINGTON, J. Leon . 610-758-3100. 422 A
jnw207@lehigh.edu
WASHINGTON,
James Bernard .... 252-536-7220. 361 A
jwashington660@halifaxcc.edu
WASHINGTON, Jennifer . 860-515-3820... 87 I
jwashington@charteroak.edu
WASHINGTON, Jewel ..... 505-277-1555. 312 F
unmvphr@unm.edu
WASHINGTON, Joann .... 773-291-6313. 142 D
jwashington@ccc.edu
WASHINGTON, Kaye ...... 318-670-9450. 207 A
kwashington@susla.edu
WASHINGTON, Kelvin .... 803-533-3736. 446 G
kwashington@scsu.edu
WASHINGTON,
Kheysia, H .... 318-670-9417. 207 A
kwashington@susla.edu
WASHINGTON,
L. Marshall .... 304-929-5472. 528 D
lmwashington@newriver.edu
WASHINGTON, Leila ...... 410-951-3660. 220 B
lwashington@coppin.edu
WASHINGTON, Mary ..... 229-317-6761. 124 A
mary.washington@darton.edu
WASHINGTON, Maurice . 404-653-7857. 129 D
mwashington@morehouse.edu
WASHINGTON, Michael . 901-435-1601. 455 M
michael_washington@loc.edu
WASHINGTON, Tanisha . 602-331-7500... 12 A
tawashington@aii.edu
WASHINGTON, Ted, M .. 615-353-3228. 461 B
ted.washington@nscc.edu
WASHINGTON,
William, O .... 847-317-7091. 160 M
wwashington@tiu.edu
WASHINGTON, Willie .... 803-705-4734. 441 C
washingtonw@benedict.edu
WASHINGTON-LACEY,
Bonita .... 765-983-1515. 165 G
washibo@earlham.edu
WASHINGTON-WOODS,
Paula .... 870-235-4145... 23 F
pwwoods@saumag.edu
WASHKEVICH, Stephen .. 978-632-6600. 232 C
s_washkevich@mwcc.mass.edu
WASHKO, Chris .... 907-834-1631... 11 B
cwashko@pwscc.edu
WASHKO, Mary Jo .... 804-523-5345. 512 F
mwashko@reynolds.edu
WASIELEWSKI, Laura ..... 603-656-6051. 297 G
lwasielewski@anselm.edu
WASIK, David, G .... 330-972-7926. 390 E
wasik@uakron.edu
WASILENKO, William, J . 757-446-8480. 504 E
wasilewj@evms.edu
WASIOLEK, Sue .... 919-684-6313. 354 A
dean.sue@duke.edu
WASKIE, Kenneth, G .... 607-777-2184. 341 E
kwaskie@binghamton.edu
WASKOSKY, Julia .... 815-802-8510. 149 C
jwaskosky@kcc.edu
WASLEY, Patrick .... 415-338-3068... 35 E
pwasley@sfsu.edu
WASMER, Jody .... 708-344-4700. 151 E
WASSBERG, Catherine .... 651-523-2616. 256 A
cwassberg01@hamline.edu
WASSENAAR, Dave .... 714-484-7345... 56 E
dwassenaar@cypresscollege.edu
WASSERMAN, Ahron ...... 303-629-8200... 87 F
WASSERMAN, Ed .... 510-642-3383... 70 I
ed.wasserman@berkeley.edu
WASSERMAN, Harriet ..... 206-934-4344. 522 J
harriet.wasserman@seattlecolleges.edu
WASSERMAN, Joy .... 847-328-1124. 325 G
jwasserman@huc.edu
WASSERMAN, Melissa ... 215-574-9600. 418 H
mwasserman@hussianart.edu
WASSERMAN, Scott .... 775-784-4901. 294 D
scott_wasserman@nshe.nevada.edu
WASSON, Dale .... 817-272-5401. 491 B
wasson@uta.edu
WASSON, Leslie .... 928-532-6148... 16 E
leslie.wasson@npc.edu
WASSON, Tanlee, T .... 812-941-2293. 168 F
tawasson@ius.edu
WASSON, Thomas .... 601-857-3367. 267 A
thwasson@hindscc.edu
WASSUM, Keith, N .... 704-687-5747. 368 E
knwassum@uncc.edu
WASTLER, Cyndi, L .... 703-339-2516... 96 F
clw@strayer.edu
WASTVEDT, Ross .... 515-263-6036. 178 G
rwastvedt@grandview.edu
WASUKANIS, John, T ..... 561-868-3480. 110 C
wasukanj@palmbeachstate.edu

WATANABE, Mie .... 808-956-6423. 135 L
mie@hawaii.edu
WATERBURY, Sarah, P .. 212-998-6961. 334 D
sarah.waterbury@nyu.edu
WATERFIELD, James, R . 757-683-4631. 507 N
rwater@odu.edu
WATERMAN,
Christopher .... 310-206-6469... 71 C
cwater@arts.ucla.edu
WATERS, Barry, D .... 989-774-7493. 240 N
water1b@cmich.edu
WATERS, Christine .... 810-424-5294. 251 E
cwaters@umflint.edu
WATERS, Christopher, C 336-278-5055. 354 B
cwaters@elon.edu
WATERS, Gary .... 706-236-2251. 121 G
gwaters@berry.edu
WATERS, Gloria .... 617-353-2704. 224 D
gwaters@bu.edu
WATERS, Gloriana .... 646-664-3254. 316 I
gloriana.waters@cuny.edu
WATERS, Gregory, L .... 973-655-7374. 303 D
watersg@mail.montclair.edu
WATERS, Jeff .... 417-328-1632. 282 C
jwaters@sbuniv.edu
WATERS, Jennifer .... 312-369-7831. 143 D
jwaters@colum.edu
WATERS, Jennifer .... 410-293-1586. 545 J
jwaters@usna.edu
WATERS, Joan .... 334-291-4951..... 2 H
joan.waters@cv.edu
WATERS, John, B .... 512-472-4133. 480 G
john.waters@ssw.edu
WATERS, Lynne, T .... 808-956-8109. 135 L
lynnew@hawaii.edu
WATERS, Marlo .... 707-965-6676... 57 J
mwaters@puc.edu
WATERS, Melissa .... 770-426-2901. 128 D
melissa.waters@life.edu
WATERS, Michelle .... 252-335-0821. 359 F
michelle_waters@albemarle.edu
WATERS, Myra .... 410-837-5159. 221 A
mwaters@ubalt.edu
WATERS, Patrick .... 734-432-5839. 246 B
pwaters@madonna.edu
WATERS, Ron .... 707-476-4331... 40 H
ron-waters@redwoods.edu
WATERS, Roy, S .... 318-257-2893. 207 F
roy@latech.edu
WATERS, Sarah .... 419-372-2011. 374 K
waterss@bgsu.edu
WATERS, Shari .... 714-997-6726... 38 A
swaters@chapman.edu
WATERS, Taylor .... 410-626-2512. 217 G
taylor.waters@sjca.edu
WATFORD, John .... 229-931-2004. 131 G
jwatford@southgatech.edu
WATFORD, Lettie .... 229-931-2145. 126 D
lettie.watford@gsw.edu
WATHEN, Cory .... 916-691-7418... 53 B
wathenc@crc.losrios.edu
WATJEN, Russ (Lynn) ...... 415-403-1235... 65 C
lwatjen@saybrook.edu
WATKIN, Anna Maria, S 217-351-2596. 155 J
amwatkin@parkland.edu
WATKIN, Steve .... 661-654-3277... 32 H
swatkin@csub.edu
WATKINS, Alison, L .... 941-359-6111. 111 O
awatkins@ringling.edu
WATKINS, Brenda, F ...... 864-488-4473. 444 L
bwatkins@limestone.edu
WATKINS, Bryan .... 773-244-5770. 154 G
bjwatkins@northpark.edu
WATKINS, Dan .... 215-612-6600. 419 J
dwatkins@chicareers.com
WATKINS, Daniel .... 601-979-2433. 267 E
daniel.watkins@jsums.edu
WATKINS, Dorla .... 816-584-6231. 280 C
dorla.watkins@park.edu
WATKINS, Elizabeth .... 415-502-7786... 72 A
Graduate.Dean@ucsf.edu
WATKINS, Faye .... 757-727-5371. 505 F
faye.watkins@hamptonu.edu
WATKINS, Frank .... 772-462-7475. 106 P
fwatkins@irsc.edu
WATKINS, Jennifer .... 918-463-2931. 395 D
jennifer.watkins@connorsstate.edu
WATKINS, Joe .... 619-849-2650... 59 L
jwatkins@pointloma.edu
WATKINS, John .... 724-938-1569. 428 A
watkins@calu.edu
WATKINS, Judi .... 707-967-2911... 55 F
jwatkins@napavalley.edu
WATKINS, Kristin .... 971-722-4696. 407 D
kwatkins@pcc.edu
WATKINS, Laurie .... 307-382-1647. 543 J
lwatkins@wwcc.wy.edu
WATKINS, Lee .... 610-896-1023. 418 F
lwatkins@haverford.edu
WATKINS, Marie .... 585-389-2304. 332 D
mwatkin2@naz.edu

WATKINS, Marilyn .... 765-973-8211. 167 G
mwatkins@iue.edu
WATKINS, Mark .... 620-421-6700. 188 D
markw@labette.edu
WATKINS, Nancy .... 704-355-5043. 353 D
nancy.watkins@carolinashealthcare.org
WATKINS, Pat, E .... 727-864-8854. 101 N
watkinpe@eckerd.edu
WATKINS, Rebecca, R .... 828-398-7151. 357 N
bwatkins@abtech.edu
WATKINS, Ruth .... 801-581-5057. 496 Q
ruth.watkins@utah.edu
WATKINS, Susan, J .... 617-745-3855. 225 G
susan.j.watkins@enc.edu
WATKINS, Tammy, K ..... 302-739-4623... 93 D
tkellywa@dtcc.edu
WATKINS, Tracy .... 903-233-4356. 475 J
tracywatkins@letu.edu
WATKINS, Wayne, H ..... 330-972-8124. 390 E
wwatkins@uakron.edu
WATKINS, William .... 818-677-2391... 34 C
william.watkins@csun.edu
WATKINS-WENDELL,
Katie .... 330-972-6764. 390 E
kwatkin@uakron.edu
WATMAN, Mark .... 603-428-2383. 297 D
mwatman@nec.edu
WATMAN, Mark .... 603-428-2908. 297 D
mwatman@nec.edu
WATNICK, Beryl .... 305-653-7141. 390 C
beryl.watnick@munion.edu
WATRING, Jack, W .... 573-882-3518. 283 C
watringj@missouri.edu
WATROUS, Robert .... 610-683-1320. 429 A
watrous@kutztown.edu
WATSKY, Mitchell .... 706-721-3278. 126 B
mwatsky@gru.edu
WATSON, Andrew .... 870-759-4118... 25 K
awatson@wbcoll.edu
WATSON, Angela .... 270-831-9671. 195 D
angie.watson@kctcs.edu
WATSON, Angela .... 907-277-1000... 10 D
contact@chartercollege.edu
WATSON, Aretha .... 732-906-4243. 303 B
awatson@middlesexcc.edu
WATSON, Benjamin, O ... 803-780-1039. 449 E
bowatson@voorhees.edu
WATSON, Beverly .... 540-535-3592. 509 E
brecny@su.edu
WATSON, Billy .... 864-977-7123. 445 H
jw.watson@ngu.edu
WATSON, Bret .... 408-864-8857... 44 M
watsonbret@deanza.edu
WATSON, Christopher .... 847-491-4100. 155 D
christopher-watson@northwestern.edu
WATSON, Craig, T .... 404-727-6115. 124 E
craig.watson@emory.edu
WATSON, Dana .... 254-526-1733. 468 G
dana.watson@ctcd.edu
WATSON, Daryl .... 301-736-3631. 216 B
daryl.watson@msbbcs.edu
WATSON, David .... 937-529-2201. 390 D
dwatson@united.edu
WATSON, David .... 803-778-7882. 441 F
watsonds@cctech.edu
WATSON, Doug .... 402-941-6519. 290 K
watson@midlandu.edu
WATSON, Dwight, C .... 319-273-2717. 176 A
dwight.watson@uni.edu
WATSON, Ellen .... 718-270-1176. 342 D
ewatson@downstate.edu
WATSON, Ellen .... 901-678-8324. 460 B
eiwatson@memphis.edu
WATSON, Ernest .... 602-274-4300... 12 K
ewatson@brymanschool.edu
WATSON, Ernest .... 219-866-6128. 172 E
ernestw@saintjoe.edu
WATSON, George, H .... 302-831-2793... 94 B
ghw@udel.edu
WATSON, James, D .... 516-367-8311. 320 D
WATSON, James, W .... 304-336-8200. 530 A
watsonjw@westliberty.edu
WATSON, Jeff .... 903-729-0256. 488 D
jwatson@tvcc.edu
WATSON, Jennifer .... 618-453-6689. 159 G
jlwatson@siu.edu
WATSON, Jill .... 562-903-4808... 29 L
jill.watson@biola.edu
WATSON, John .... 479-968-0319... 20 E
jwwatson@atu.edu
WATSON, John .... 972-273-3353. 471 B
jwatson@dcccd.edu
WATSON, Johnnie, B ..... 901-435-1676. 455 M
johnnie_watson@loc.edu
WATSON, Jonelle .... 701-858-3577. 371 F
jonelle.watson@minotstateu.edu
WATSON, Joseph .... 518-828-4181. 321 C
watson@sunycgcc.edu
WATSON, Justin .... 574-239-8367. 166 N
jwatson@hcc-nd.edu

WATSON, Karan, L .... 979-845-4016. 483 C provost@tamu.edu
WATSON, Kathryn, J ...... 727-864-7673. 101 N watsonkj@eckerd.edu
WATSON, Keith .... 509-452-5100. 521 J
WATSON, Kimberly .... 314-529-9505. 276 G kwatson@maryville.edu
WATSON, Kimberly .... 419-251-1852. 383 G kimberly.watson@mercycollege.edu
WATSON, Kirk .... 309-854-1810. 140 E watsonk@bhc.edu
WATSON, Lemuel .... 803-777-3828. 447 G watsonlw@mailbox.sc.edu
WATSON, Lisa .... 406-874-6181. 286 E watsonl@milescc.edu
WATSON, Loree .... 281-649-3221. 473 B lwatson@hbu.edu
WATSON, Lori .... 313-664-7431. 241 C lwatson@collegeforcreativestudies.edu
WATSON, Lynda .... 903-434-8204. 477 J lwatson@ntcc.edu
WATSON, Malcolm, W ... 781-736-3249. 224 F watson@brandeis.edu
WATSON, Marc .... 513-745-8318. 391 A marc.watson@uc.edu
WATSON, Marsha .... 312-261-3048. 153 I marsha.watson@nl.edu
WATSON, Marva .... 907-786-1800... 10 H anmw@uaa.alaska.edu
WATSON, Mary .... 205-853-1200..... 5 B mwatson@jeffstateonline.com
WATSON, Mary .... 509-682-6614. 525 B mwatson@wvc.edu
WATSON, Mary, P .... 304-367-4399. 529 F Trish.Watson@fairmontstate.edu
WATSON, Melissa .... 870-512-7805... 20 B melissa_watson@asun.edu
WATSON, Michael, E ...... 989-964-7310. 249 G mewatson@svsu.edu
WATSON, Michael, W .... 920-424-2184. 537 B watson@uwosh.edu
WATSON, Nana .... 614-947-6093. 380 A nana.watson@franklin.edu
WATSON, Nancy .... 712-279-5416. 176 B nancy.watson@briarcliff.edu
WATSON, Pamela, G ...... 409-772-1510. 493 C pgwatson@utmb.edu
WATSON, Patricia .... 401-863-9573. 438 J patricia_watson@brown.edu
WATSON, Paul .... 715-346-4771. 538 A pwatson@uwsp.edu
WATSON, Peggy .... 817-257-7125. 484 I p.watson@tcu.edu
WATSON, Phil .... 816-235-5776. 283 D watsonp@umkc.edu
WATSON, Phyllis .... 850-599-3474. 114 K phyllis.watson@famu.edu
WATSON, Rebecca .... 205-934-3555..... 8 E bwatson@uab.edu
WATSON, Renee' .... 502-597-6346. 197 A renee.watson@kysu.edu
WATSON, Rick .... 607-274-3958. 327 E rwatson@ithaca.edu
WATSON, Robert .... 419-448-3278. 389 J rwatson@tiffin.edu
WATSON, Robert .... 724-738-2003. 429 F robert.watson@sru.edu
WATSON, Robert .... 215-702-4318. 411 F rwatson@cairn.edu
WATSON, Robin .... 615-963-7451. 459 E rwatson@tnstate.edu
WATSON, Ronald, P .... 248-370-3486. 248 J rwatson@oakland.edu
WATSON, III, Samuel, E 940-397-4746. 476 H samuel.watson@mwsu.edu
WATSON, Sandra, E .... 404-752-1723. 129 E watson@msm.edu
WATSON, Steve .... 716-375-2282. 338 E stwatson@sbu.edu
WATSON, Susan, M .... 870-759-4188... 25 K swatson@wbcoll.edu
WATSON, Tammi .... 406-657-2044. 287 C tammi.watson@msubillings.edu
WATSON, Tim .... 618-936-2064. 150 D timothy.w.watson@doc.illinois.gov
WATSON, Tim .... 903-233-3116. 475 J TimWatson@letu.edu
WATSON, Wayne, D .... 773-995-2400. 141 J president@csu.edu
WATSON, William .... 650-738-7035... 64 D watsonw@smccd.edu
WATSON, William .... 213-740-5376... 74 A wwatson@usc.edu
WATSON, Wyatt .... 479-964-3213... 20 E wwatson@atu.edu
WATSON-HALL, Sherrell 908-737-3220. 302 F swatson@kean.edu
WATSON-MAURO, Sharon .... 215-568-4515. 424 D library@moore.edu
WATSON MOLINE, Susan .... 585-475-5498. 337 L swmdar@rit.edu
WATSTEIN, Sarah .... 910-962-3271. 369 C watsteins@uncw.edu
WATT, Andy .... 612-977-5310. 254 C andy.watt@capella.edu
WATT, Charles, K .... 864-656-3178. 442 C wattc@clemson.edu
WATT, JR., George, P .... 843-953-4369. 443 A wattgp@cofc.edu
WATT, Robert .... 671-734-1812. 546 D rwatt@piu.edu
WATTERS, Christina .... 706-290-2167. 121 G cwatters@berry.edu
WATTERS, James, H .... 585-475-2378. 337 L jhwbgt@rit.edu
WATTERS, Steve .... 502-897-4000. 199 B sowatters@sbts.edu
WATTERSON, Renva .... 706-295-6329. 125 C rwatters@highlands.edu
WATTS, Amy .... 731-286-3358. 460 F watts@dscc.edu
WATTS, Ann, B .... 336-593-2483. 360 E awatts@forsythtech.edu
WATTS, Anne .... 559-442-4600... 68 I anne.watts@fresnocitycollege.edu
WATTS, Bruce .... 312-567-3253. 147 F bwatts1@iit.edu
WATTS, Connie .... 606-487-3184. 195 C connie.watts@kctcs.edu
WATTS, Denise .... 432-552-3110. 493 D watts_de@utpb.edu
WATTS, Gary .... 701-252-3467. 373 D watts@jc.edu
WATTS, Gordon .... 501-760-4202... 22 A gwatts@npcc.edu
WATTS, Jason .... 256-840-4118..... 6 I jwatts@snead.edu
WATTS, John .... 615-794-4254. 457 Q jwatts@omorecollege.edu
WATTS, Jonathan, C .... 308-865-8525. 292 H wattsjc@unk.edu
WATTS, Katherine, K .... 336-917-5563. 366 D watts@salem.edu
WATTS, Kathy .... 559-934-2393... 75 G kathywatts@whccd.edu
WATTS, Kimberly .... 830-372-6060. 485 C kwatts@tlu.edu
WATTS, Laurie, S .... 504-816-8180. 206 A lawatts@nobts.edu
WATTS, Lynwood .... 803-938-3724. 448 F lynwood@uscsumter.edu
WATTS, Parris, R .... 641-784-5115. 178 F pwatts@graceland.edu
WATTS, Ray .... 909-748-8358... 73 H ray_watts@redlands.edu
WATTS, Ray, L .... 205-934-4636..... 8 E rlwatts@uab.edu
WATTS, Rhonda .... 252-335-0821. 359 F rhonda_watts@albemarle.edu
WATTS, Robert, E .... 678-891-2700. 125 G rob.watts@gpc.edu
WATTS, Ronald, R .... 440-775-8460. 385 H ron.watts@oberlin.edu
WATTS, Ruby, W .... 803-705-4738. 441 C watts@benedict.edu
WATTS, Rufus, C .... 803-705-4739. 441 C wattsrw@benedict.edu
WATTS, Sharon, A .... 732-247-5241. 303 E swatts@nbts.edu
WATTS, Sherry .... 304-434-8000. 528 A swatts@eastern.wvnet.edu
WATTS, W. David .... 432-552-2100. 493 D watts_d@utpb.edu
WATTS, Whitney .... 843-383-8360. 442 F wwatts@coker.edu
WATTS-MARTINEZ, Evanda .... 804-862-6263. 508 H ewatts@rbc.edu
WATZIN, Mary .... 919-515-2883. 368 B mary_watzin@ncsu.edu
WATZKE, John .... 503-943-7135. 408 F watzke@up.edu
WAUGH, Derek .... 706-272-2046. 123 G dwaugh@daltonstate.edu
WAUGH, Edith .... 316-322-3227. 185 D ewaugh@butlercc.edu
WAUGH, Kaye, N .... 828-398-7113. 357 N kwaugh@abtech.edu
WAUGH, Linda .... 513-244-8451. 376 J linda.waugh@ccuniversity.edu
WAUGH, Scott .... 310-825-2052... 71 C evc@conet.ucla.edu
WAUKAU-WILBER, Juanita .... 800-567-2344. 532 E jwaukau@menominee.edu
WAUKECHON, Chad .... 800-567-2344. 532 E cwaukechon@menominee.edu
WAVLE, Dana, C .... 812-941-2202. 168 F dwavle@ius.edu
WAVLE, Elizabeth, M ...... 607-735-1865. 323 H ewavle@elmira.edu
WAWRZUSIN, Andrea, C .... 828-262-2050. 367 A wawrzusinac@appstate.edu
WAXLER, Lawrence .... 207-780-4413. 212 H larryw@usm.maine.edu
WAY, Joshua .... 845-675-4416. 335 C joshua.way@nyack.edu
WAY, Kimera .... 715-836-5180. 536 E waykk@uwec.edu
WAY, Philip .... 724-738-2170. 429 F philip.way@sru.edu
WAY, Philip (PJ) .... 815-394-5047. 157 C pjway@rockford.edu
WAY, Sara, A .... 305-684-6030. 345 A waysa@morrisville.edu
WAY BOLT, Mary .... 410-287-6060. 214 B mbolt@cecil.edu
WAYE, Holly Anne .... 315-568-3055. 333 C hwaye@nycc.edu
WAYE, Kathy .... 315-279-5602. 328 D kwaye@mail.keuka.edu
WAYLAND, Jane, P .... 501-569-3000... 24 B jpwayland@ualr.edu
WAYLAND, Marilina, L .... 787-250-1912. 550 E mwayland@metro.inter.edu
WAYLAND, Marty .... 859-985-3199. 192 F waylandm@berea.edu
WAYMAN-GORDON, Ellen .... 201-200-3026. 303 F ewaymangordo@njcu.edu
WAYMIRE, Rachel .... 501-205-8873... 20 I rwaymire@cbc.edu
WAYNE, Don .... 858-534-1571... 71 F dwayne@ucsd.edu
WAYNE, Jerry, A .... 812-941-2417. 168 F jerwayne@ius.edu
WAYNE, William .... 315-568-3025. 333 C bwayne@nycc.edu
WAYNE, William .... 405-325-4611. 401 B wwayne@ou.edu
WCISLO, Frank .... 615-322-4948. 463 G frank.wcislo@vanderbilt.edu
WEAKLEY, Jerry .... 785-594-8332. 184 C jerry.weakley@bakeru.edu
WEARDA, Lisa .... 805-546-3119... 42 C lisa_wearda@cuesta.edu
WEARDEN, Stanley, T .... 330-672-2950. 382 B swearden@kent.edu
WEARIN, Jody .... 541-684-4644. 407 B jwearin@pioneerpacific.edu
WEAS, John .... 585-475-5539. 337 L john.weas@rit.edu
WEASENFORTH, Donald . 972-881-5794. 469 G dweasenforth@collin.edu
WEAST, Phil .... 828-339-4431. 364 B pweast@southwesterncc.edu
WEAST, Wade .... 336-770-3251. 369 D weastw@uncsa.edu
WEATHERALL, Maureen . 310-338-2833... 53 E maureen.weatherall@lmu.edu
WEATHERBY, Beth .... 507-537-6246. 261 F Beth.Weatherby@smsu.edu
WEATHERFORD, Dani .... 765-658-4540. 165 F daniweatherford@depauw.edu
WEATHERINGTON, Elsie, S .... 804-524-5040. 515 D estephens@vsu.edu
WEATHERLY, Elizabeth ... 912-279-5704. 123 B eweatherly@ccga.edu
WEATHERLY, Joanie .... 503-338-2480. 402 G jweatherly@clatsopcc.edu
WEATHERLY, Phyllis, N . 678-915-7391. 132 C pweather@spsu.edu
WEATHERMAN, Donald, V .... 870-307-7201... 21 H president@lyon.edu
WEATHERMAN, Tammy . 559-934-2117... 75 G tammyweatherman@whccd.edu
WEATHERS, Diane .... 718-289-5770. 317 B diane.weathers@bcc.cuny.edu
WEATHERS, Madonna .... 606-783-2070. 198 A m.weathers@moreheadstate.edu
WEATHERS, Melonie ...... 336-386-3207. 364 D weathersms@surry.edu
WEATHERSBEE, Byron .... 254-295-4150. 490 B bweathersbee@umhb.edu
WEATHERSBY, Aaron ..... 818-778-5705... 52 E weatheae@lavc.edu
WEATHERSPOON, David 847-543-2138. 143 A dweatherspoon@clcillinois.edu
WEATHERSPOON, David 317-738-8141. 165 I dweatherspoon@franklincollege.edu
WEATHERWAX, Allan ..... 518-783-5089. 340 J aweatherwax@siena.edu
WEAVER, Andrew, M ...... 256-824-6241..... 8 F andrew.weaver@uah.edu
WEAVER, Angela .... 618-468-5300. 150 G aweaver@lc.edu
WEAVER, Bradley, K .... 765-361-6308. 175 B weaverb@wabash.edu
WEAVER, Candace .... 601-477-4075. 267 F candace.weaver@jcjc.edu
WEAVER, Carolyn .... 515-271-1426. 177 H carolyn.weaver@dmu.edu
WEAVER, III, Elton .... 901-435-1205. 455 M
WEAVER, Gina .... 585-345-6808. 325 C gmweaver@genesee.edu
WEAVER, Gregory .... 713-920-1120. 127 F gweaver@ict-ils.edu
WEAVER, H. Danny .... 816-654-7102. 275 K hweaver@kcumb.edu
WEAVER, Harrison .... 415-380-1376... 45 H harryweaver@ggbts.edu
WEAVER, James .... 540-231-3977. 515 C weaverj@vt.edu
WEAVER, John .... 325-674-2387. 464 H jbw11a@acu.edu
WEAVER, JR., Joseph, B .... 405-744-2690. 397 H joe.weaver@okstate.edu
WEAVER, Julie .... 231-439-6306. 247 H jweaver@ncmich.edu
WEAVER, Karyn .... 870-733-6722... 21 I kweaver@midsouthcc.edu
WEAVER, Kenneth .... 620-341-5367. 186 D kweaver@emporia.edu
WEAVER, Laura .... 219-785-5742. 172 A lweaver@pnc.edu
WEAVER, Linza, M .... 757-569-6735. 513 E lweaver@pdc.edu
WEAVER, Melanie .... 419-772-2272. 386 D m-weaver@onu.edu
WEAVER, Neal .... 806-651-2070. 484 D nweaver@mail.wtamu.edu
WEAVER, Neal .... 806-651-2070. 484 D nweaver@wtamu.edu
WEAVER, Sam .... 501-370-5348... 22 F sweaver@philander.edu
WEAVER, Sandie .... 562-903-4760... 29 L sandie.weaver@biola.edu
WEAVER, Sean .... 505-545-3380. 310 E slweaver@nmhu.edu
WEAVER, Shannon .... 972-273-3390. 471 B sweaver@dcccd.edu
WEAVER, Susan, F .... 724-653-2211. 415 A sweaver@dec.edu
WEAVER, Tammy .... 479-968-0272... 20 E trhodes@atu.edu
WEAVER, Terri, E .... 312-996-7808. 161 D teweaver@uic.edu
WEAVER, Theresa .... 906-635-2733. 245 G tweaver@lssu.edu
WEAVER, Vicki .... 660-359-3948. 279 H vweaver@mail.ncmissouri.edu
WEAVER, Vickie, L .... 609-896-5029. 305 D weaver@rider.edu
WEAVER, Wendy .... 414-443-3608. 535 A weaverw@mtmary.edu
WEAVER, William, H .... 478-757-2549. 128 I bill.weaver@maconstate.edu
WEAVER-GRIGGS, Linda 803-327-8024. 449 J lwgriggs@yorktech.edu
WEAVER HART, Ann .... 520-621-5511... 18 F president@email.arizona.edu
WEAVIL, Vicki .... 336-770-3266. 369 D weavilv@uncsa.edu
WEBB, Anda, L .... 434-924-0999. 511 B al6b@virginia.edu
WEBB, Arla, J .... 443-518-4690. 215 E awebb@howardcc.edu
WEBB, Barbara .... 989-686-9228. 242 C brwebb@delta.edu
WEBB, Brandon .... 979-209-7285. 467 I brandon.webb@blinn.edu
WEBB, Brent, W .... 801-422-6201. 495 D webb@byu.edu
WEBB, Brian .... 336-386-3530. 364 D webbb@surry.edu
WEBB, Burton, J .... 208-467-8539. 139 A bwebb@nnu.edu
WEBB, Carol .... 281-487-1170. 484 H cwebb@txchiro.edu
WEBB, Carolyn, S .... 318-670-9314. 207 A cwebb@susla.edu
WEBB, Charlie .... 806-720-7156. 476 B charlie.webb@lcu.edu
WEBB, Cheryl, A .... 803-327-7402. 442 D cwebb@clintonjuniorcollege.edu
WEBB, Corinne, M .... 313-577-1090. 252 G cwebb@wayne.edu
WEBB, Dan .... 423-425-4729. 463 D dan-webb@utc.edu
WEBB, Dann .... 478-988-6800. 122 G dwebb@centralgatech.edu
WEBB, Dann .... 478-218-3321. 122 F dwebb@centralgatech.edu
WEBB, David .... 775-831-1314. 295 F dwebb@sierranevada.edu

WEBB, Dixie .... 931-221-6346. 459 B
webbd@apsu.edu
WEBB, Donna .... 229-391-5001. 119 H
dwebb@abac.edu
WEBB, Donnetta .... 916-558-2408... 53 D
webbd@scc.losrios.edu
WEBB, Duncan .... 312-461-0600. 139 H
dwebb@aaart.edu
WEBB, Elnora, T .... 510-464-3236... 59 C
ewebb@peralta.edu
WEBB, Eric, C .... 484-365-7451. 422 D
ewebb@lincoln.edu
WEBB, II, Ernest, R .... 915-831-5051. 472 B
WEBB, Greg .... 270-444-9676. 193 N
gwebb@daymarcollege.edu
WEBB, Gwendolyn .... 919-546-8223. 366 E
gwebb@shawu.edu
WEBB, James, D .... 806-651-1240. 484 D
jwebb@mail.wtamu.edu
WEBB, Jay, K .... 434-544-8218. 506 K
webb@lynchburg.edu
WEBB, Jeanie .... 405-733-7374. 399 F
jwebb@rose.edu
WEBB, Jeanie .... 405-733-7300. 399 F
jwebb@rose.edu
WEBB, Joe, B .... 626-584-5491... 45 E
jwebb@fuller.edu
WEBB, Joshua, M .... 989-964-4359. 249 G
jmwebb@svsu.edu
WEBB, Karen .... 805-756-2661... 32 F
kwebb@calpoly.edu
WEBB, Karen Schuster ... 415-955-2050... 26 L
kwebb@alliant.edu
WEBB, Kathleen, M .... 937-229-4263. 391 C
kwebb1@udayton.edu
WEBB, Kathryn, J .... 404-527-5785. 127 I
kwebb@itc.edu
WEBB, Kathy .... 606-546-1616. 200 A
kwebb@unionky.edu
WEBB, Kathy .... 334-727-8510..... 8 A
kwebb@mytu.tuskegee.edu
WEBB, Keith .... 404-270-5279. 132 E
kwebb5@spelman.edu
WEBB, Ken .... 619-680-4430... 31 A
ken.webb@cc-sd.edu
WEBB, Kenneth .... 903-785-7661. 478 B
kwebb@parisjc.edu
WEBB, Kristine, W .... 904-620-2769. 116 B
kwebb@unf.edu
WEBB, Kyle .... 901-843-3760. 458 E
webb@rhodes.edu
WEBB, Lee .... 870-512-7849... 20 B
lee_webb@asun.edu
WEBB, Lindsie, B .... 330-684-8941. 390 F
llamb@uakron.edu
WEBB, Lynda .... 432-685-6884. 476 G
lwebb@midland.edu
WEBB, Mark, F .... 931-598-1284. 458 H
mwebb@sewanee.edu
WEBB, Melessia, D .... 423-354-5106. 461 C
mdwebb@northeaststate.edu
WEBB, Michael .... 815-921-2151. 157 A
m.webb@rockvalleycollege.edu
WEBB, Michelle .... 207-453-5020. 210 L
mwebb@kvcc.me.edu
WEBB, Mona .... 904-743-1122. 107 T
mwebb@jones.edu
WEBB, R. Brian .... 254-710-8797. 467 G
brian_webb@baylor.edu
WEBB, Randall, J .... 318-357-6441. 208 B
webb@nsula.edu
WEBB, Randy .... 870-733-6750... 21 I
rwebb@midsouthcc.edu
WEBB, Reggie .... 863-669-2305. 110 H
rwebb@polk.edu
WEBB, Reggie .... 540-828-8014. 502 J
rwebb@bridgewater.edu
WEBB, Reginald .... 863-669-2305. 110 H
rwebb@polk.edu
WEBB, Richard, E .... 610-896-1290. 418 F
rwebb@haverford.edu
WEBB, Robert, L .... 781-891-2283. 223 C
rwebb@bentley.edu
WEBB, Sandy .... 641-782-1422. 182 I
webb@swcciowa.edu
WEBB, Terrance, S .... 608-246-6270. 540 C
tswebb@madisoncollege.edu
WEBB, Terry .... 607-777-4787. 341 E
twebb@binghamton.edu
WEBB, Truly .... 651-793-1272. 259 C
truly.webb@metrostate.edu
WEBB, Vicki .... 870-307-7227... 21 H
vicki.webb@lyon.edu
WEBB, Vincent .... 936-294-1632. 487 A
vjw002@shsu.edu
WEBB, Walter, W .... 815-939-5333. 155 H
wwebb@olivet.edu
WEBB, JR., William, C .. 810-762-3324. 251 E
bwebb@umflint.edu
WEBB SHARPE, Lisa ...... 517-483-1106. 245 H
sharpel@lcc.edu
WEBBER, Chris .... 618-395-7777. 147 B
webberc@iecc.edu
WEBBER, Eleanor .... 802-635-1309. 501 D
eleanor.webber@jsc.edu
WEBBER, Henry, S .... 314-935-7877. 284 L
hwebber@wustl.edu
WEBBER, Karen .... 303-458-3561... 84 M
kwebber@regis.edu
WEBBER, Karen, B .... 303-458-3561... 84 M
kwebber@regis.edu
WEBBER, Ken, P .... 641-422-4275. 181 D
webbeken@niacc.edu
WEBBER, Leah .... 617-928-4513. 234 E
lwebber@mountida.edu
WEBBER, Louise .... 909-621-8265... 39 C
louise.webber@cgu.edu
WEBBER, Mike .... 415-422-2508... 73 J
webberm@usfca.edu
WEBBER, Tracy, E .... 828-766-1251. 361 H
twebber@mayland.edu
WEBBER, Wendi .... 617-364-3510. 223 G
wwebber@boston.edu
WEBBER-COLBERT,
Wilma, F .... 662-915-7735. 270 B
wcolbert@olemiss.edu
WEBER, A. Scott .... 716-645-6029. 341 F
sweber@buffalo.edu
WEBER, Allison .... 920-693-1631. 540 B
allison.weber@gotoltc.edu
WEBER, Brad .... 620-252-7076. 185 O
bradw@coffeyville.edu
WEBER, Brian .... 570-945-8130. 419 N
brian.weber@keystone.edu
WEBER, Bruce, W .... 302-831-1211... 94 B
bweber@udel.edu
WEBER, Charlotte .... 304-696-4812. 529 H
cweber@rcbi.org
WEBER, Cheryl .... 617-585-1157. 234 I
cheryl.weber@necmusic.edu
WEBER, Chris .... 231-995-1039. 248 B
cweber@nmc.edu
WEBER, Daniel, R .... 773-442-4000. 154 H
d-weber3@neiu.edu
WEBER, Dave .... 507-285-7217. 261 A
dave.weber@rctc.edu
WEBER, Dave, N .... 507-285-7217. 261 A
dave.weber@rctc.edu
WEBER, Dawn .... 419-289-4142. 374 C
dweber1@ashland.edu
WEBER, Deborah .... 718-260-3251. 336 E
dweber@poly.edu
WEBER, Donna, J .... 715-836-3871. 536 E
weberdj@uwec.edu
WEBER, Eric .... 801-957-4136. 498 B
eric.weber@slcc.edu
WEBER, Girard, W .... 847-543-2201. 143 A
jweber@clcillinois.edu
WEBER, Heidi .... 413-236-2116. 231 A
hweber@berkshirecc.edu
WEBER, J. Christopher ... 570-577-1795. 411 A
weber@bucknell.edu
WEBER, Jacqueline, J .... 573-592-5307. 285 B
jackie.weber@westminster-mo.edu
WEBER, Janet .... 419-473-2700. 378 I
jweber@daviscollege.edu
WEBER, Jeff .... 414-443-8819. 539 F
jeff.weber@wlc.edu
WEBER, Joan .... 509-574-4984. 525 G
jweber@yvcc.edu
WEBER, Jodi .... 903-434-8114. 477 J
jweber@ntcc.edu
WEBER, Joe .... 931-221-7618. 459 B
weberj@apsu.edu
WEBER, Joe .... 440-375-7000. 382 L
jweber@lec.edu
WEBER, John .... 219-785-5368. 172 A
jweber@pnc.edu
WEBER, Jolanta, A .... 509-313-6504. 520 A
weberj@gonzaga.edu
WEBER, Joseph, F .... 979-845-4728. 483 C
vpsa@tamu.edu
WEBER, Julie .... 575-646-3202. 310 I
jeweber@nmsu.edu
WEBER, Keith, A .... 513-244-4350. 377 G
keith_weber@mail.msj.edu
WEBER, Kevin .... 502-585-9911. 199 C
kweber@spalding.edu
WEBER, Laurie .... 701-858-3375. 371 F
laurie.weber@minotstateu.edu
WEBER, Lou Anne .... 864-503-5197. 448 H
lweber@uscupstate.edu
WEBER, Margaret .... 740-284-5244. 379 N
mweber@franciscan.edu
WEBER, Margaret, J .... 310-568-5615... 58 H
margaret.weber@pepperdine.edu
WEBER, Mark .... 920-498-5663. 541 B
mark.weber@nwtc.edu
WEBER, Marsha, L .... 218-477-2076. 259 H
marsha.weber@mnstate.edu
WEBER, Mary .... 831-646-4048... 54 I
mweber@mpc.edu
WEBER, Melissa .... 320-589-6414. 264 F
weberm@morris.umn.edu
WEBER, Melissa, A .... 570-577-1201. 411 A
melissa.weber@bucknell.edu
WEBER, Merlin, D .... 530-226-4501... 66 D
mweber@simpsonu.edu
WEBER, Nancy .... 843-525-8226. 447 C
nweber@tcl.edu
WEBER, Peter, M .... 401-863-7799. 438 J
peter_weber@brown.edu
WEBER, Phil .... 740-857-1311. 388 I
pweber@rosedale.edu
WEBER, Randy .... 719-502-3563... 84 A
randy.weber@ppcc.edu
WEBER, OP, Sharon, R .. 517-264-7102. 250 B
srweber@sienaheights.edu
WEBER, Stephen .... 405-224-3140. 401 E
sweber@usao.edu
WEBER, Susan .... 212-501-3050. 314 D
weber@bgc.bard.edu
WEBER, Susan .... 847-628-2465. 149 B
sweber@judsonu.edu
WEBER, Teresa .... 914-323-5304. 330 B
teresa.weber@mville.edu
WEBER, Wayne, C .... 608-342-1547. 537 D
weberwa@uwplatt.edu
WEBER, William, V .... 217-581-2921. 144 E
wvweber@eiu.edu
WEBLEY, Radha .... 707-826-4502... 35 C
rw76@humboldt.edu
WEBSTER, Aaron .... 337-475-5243. 207 G
awebster@mcneese.edu
WEBSTER, Alex .... 206-239-4500. 517 M
alexwebster@cityu.edu
WEBSTER, Darci .... 816-802-3448. 275 J
dwebster@kcai.edu
WEBSTER, Ian .... 410-617-2292. 216 A
iawebster@loyola.edu
WEBSTER, Jeremy .... 740-593-2723. 387 C
webstej1@ohio.edu
WEBSTER, Jerome .... 419-559-2326. 389 I
jwebster@terra.edu
WEBSTER, John, W .... 951-785-2041... 50 B
jwebster@lasierra.edu
WEBSTER, Keith .... 412-268-2447. 412 H
kwebster@andrew.cmu.edu
WEBSTER, Lynn .... 208-459-5325. 138 A
lwebster@collegeofidaho.edu
WEBSTER, Mary, L .... 626-395-6304... 31 E
mwebster@caltech.edu
WEBSTER, Matthew, H ... 859-344-3306. 199 H
matthew.webster@thomasmore.edu
WEBSTER, Michael .... 610-361-2222. 424 I
websterm@neumann.edu
WEBSTER, Michael, N ..... 410-857-2202. 216 E
mwebster@mcdaniel.edu
WEBSTER, Ondes .... 865-471-3352. 453 F
owebster@cn.edu
WEBSTER, Reede .... 612-659-6501. 259 D
reede.webster@minneapolis.edu
WEBSTER, Richard, C ...... 410-334-2896. 221 D
rwebster@worwic.edu
WEBSTER, Robert, O ...... 518-437-4550. 341 D
rwebster@albany.edu
WEBSTER, Scott .... 508-999-8202. 229 A
swebster@umassd.edu
WEBSTER, Tom .... 903-923-2157. 471 J
twebster@etbu.edu
WEBSTER, Valerie .... 229-293-6135. 131 F
valerie.webster@sgsc.edu
WEBSTER, Wayne, P .... 920-748-8351. 535 J
websterw@ripon.edu
WEBSTER, William, C ..... 646-717-9708. 325 B
webster@gts.edu
WECHSLER, Barton, J ..... 573-882-3304. 283 C
wechslerb@missouri.edu
WECKMAN, Judith .... 859-985-3791. 192 F
judith_weckman@berea.edu
WEDDELL, Leslie .... 719-389-6038... 79 D
leslie.weddell@coloradocollege.edu
WEDDERBURN, Anette .... 301-860-3939. 220 A
awedderburn@bowiestate.edu
WEDDINGTON, Hank .... 828-328-7035. 356 B
hank.weddington@lr.edu
WEDDLE-WEST,
Karen, D .... 901-678-2531. 460 B
kweddle@memphis.edu
WEDEL, Allen .... 316-284-5242. 184 J
awedel@bethelks.edu
WEDERSKI, Brooks .... 785-460-5542. 185 P
brooks.wederski@colbycc.edu
WEDGE, Luann .... 616-234-4170. 243 B
lwedge@grcc.edu
WEDIG, Tyler .... 319-895-4378. 177 A
twedig@cornellcollege.edu
WEDINCAMP, Jimmy .... 478-289-2166. 124 C
wedincamp@ega.edu
WEDLER, Andrea .... 518-445-2388. 313 C
awedl@albanylaw.edu
WEDLER-JOHNSON,
Darlene .... 941-408-1404. 114 I
wedlerd@scf.edu
WEDLOCK, Monica .... 404-687-4516. 123 C
wedlockm@ctsnet.edu
WEDMAN, John .... 573-882-4546. 283 C
wedmanj@missouri.edu
WEE, Liang, C .... 563-562-3263. 181 E
weel@portal.nicc.edu
WEEAKS, Cindy .... 325-942-2043. 465 K
cindy.weeaks@angelo.edu
WEECH, Darwin .... 928-428-8473... 13 J
darwin.weech@eac.edu
WEED, Anne, K .... 315-279-5202. 328 D
aweed@mail.keuka.edu
WEED, Kenneth .... 918-495-6004. 398 H
kweed@oru.edu
WEEDE, Thomas, D .... 317-940-8408. 164 J
tweede@butler.edu
WEEDEN, Jared .... 315-781-3700. 326 C
weeden@hws.edu
WEEDMAN, Gary, E .... 865-573-4517. 455 G
gweedman@johnsonU.edu
WEEKES, Eric, B .... 386-226-6499. 102 B
eric.weekes@erau.edu
WEEKLEY, Matt .... 402-375-7318. 291 F
maweekl1@wsc.edu
WEEKS, David .... 626-969-3434... 29 H
dweeks@apu.edu
WEEKS, Donald .... 603-752-1113. 296 E
dweeks@ccsnh.edu
WEEKS, Donna .... 601-968-5922. 266 A
dweeks@belhaven.edu
WEEKS, Larry, D .... 904-819-6350. 103 E
lweeks@flagler.edu
WEEKS, Patricia .... 609-652-4826. 305 C
patty.weeks@stockton.edu
WEEMS, Heather .... 320-308-3102. 261 B
hlweems@stcloudstate.edu
WEEMS, Howard .... 256-726-7035..... 6 B
hweems@oakwood.edu
WEEMS, Jeff .... 918-465-1750. 395 G
jweems@eosc.edu
WEEMS, Linda .... 575-562-2147. 309 H
linda.weems@enmu.edu
WEEMS, Lorne .... 201-684-7543. 305 A
lweems@ramapo.edu
WEEMS, Renita .... 615-256-1463. 452 G
abcofficeacademicaffairs@gmail.com
WEEMS, Rick .... 541-552-6554. 406 C
weemsr@sou.edu
WEEMS, Sherryl, D .... 901-320-9767. 463 J
sweems@victory.edu
WEEMS, William, A .... 713-500-5224. 492 E
william.a.weems@uth.tmc.edu
WEERASURIYA, Yasith ..... 949-794-9090... 68 D
yasithw@stanbridge.edu
WEERHEIM, Revalee .... 307-755-2150. 544 B
rweerheim@wyotechstaff.edu
WEERS, Terry .... 830-372-8009. 485 C
tweers@tlu.edu
WEESE, JR., Narvel, G ... 304-293-2545. 530 D
narvel.weese@mail.wvu.edu
WEETER, Mark .... 918-335-6803. 398 F
mweeter@okwu.edu
WEFFER, Rafaela .... 312-362-6477. 143 H
rweffer@depaul.edu
WEGENER, David .... 414-256-1248. 535 A
wegenerd@mtmary.edu
WEGER, Brandon .... 618-544-8657. 146 H
wegerb@iecc.edu
WEGLARZ, Joseph, R ...... 845-575-3000. 330 D
joseph.weglarz@marist.edu
WEGLEIN, Jessica .... 410-225-2503. 216 C
jweglein@mica.edu
WEGMAN, Barbara, A ...... 260-452-2153. 165 D
barb.wegman@ctsfw.edu
WEGMAN, Patie .... 707-527-4906... 65 B
pwegman@santarosa.edu
WEGNER, Janis .... 320-629-5123. 260 F
wegnerj@pinetech.edu
WEGNER, Paige .... 715-833-6245. 539 J
pwegner3@cvtc.edu
WEHLBURG, Catherine ... 817-257-7156. 484 I
c.wehlburg@tcu.edu
WEHLE, Arlean .... 504-398-2181. 206 C
awehle@olhcc.edu
WEHMEIER, Teresa .... 620-417-1603. 190 F
teresa.wehmeier@sccc.edu
WEHNER, STD,
James, A .... 504-866-7426. 206 B
rector@nds.edu
WEHRBEIN, Nancy .... 402-465-2488. 291 G
nwehrbei@nebrwesleyan.edu
WEHRENBERG, Fritz .... 515-961-1684. 182 E
fritz.wehrenberg@simpson.edu
WEHRLEY, James, B .... 336-841-4560. 355 C
jwehrley@highpoint.edu
WEHRLI, Brenda .... 248-364-6103. 248 J
wehrli@oakland.edu

WEHRLI, Dana .... 636-949-4806. 276 D
dwehrli@lindenwood.edu
WEHRUNG, Melodye ...... 717-477-1161. 429 E
mwwehr@ship.edu
WEHUNT, Nikki .... 770-720-5897. 130 G
hnw@reinhardt.edu
WEI, Belle .... 530-898-6101... 33 A
bellewei@csuchico.edu
WEI, Cheng-I .... 301-405-2072. 219 B
wei@umd.edu
WEI, Timothy .... 402-472-3181. 292 I
twei3@unl.edu
WEIAND, Steven .... 847-578-8349. 157 F
steven.weiand@rosalindfranklin.edu
WEIBLE, Frederick .... 717-846-5000. 438 E
WEIBLE, JR., Raymond .. 814-262-3816. 427 C
rweible@pennhighlands.edu
WEICH, Ronald .... 410-837-5518. 221 A
rweich@ubalt.edu
WEICHOLD, Mark, H ...... 979-845-2217. 483 C
mark.weichold@qatar.tamu.edu
WEIDA, Michael .... 845-431-8054. 323 C
weida@sunydutchess.edu
WEIDEMANN, Craig, D .. 814-865-7581. 426 A
cdw12@psu.edu
WEIDEMANN, Gregory ... 860-486-2917... 92 A
Gregory.Weidemann@uconn.edu
WEIDENSAUL,
Rebecca, L .... 215-895-2501. 415 B
rebecca@drexel.edu
WEIDER, Susan .... 425-602-3014. 516 K
sweider@bastyr.edu
WEIDLEY, Tom .... 703-784-2105. 544 J
WEIDNER, Donald .... 850-644-3071. 115 C
dweidner@law.fsu.edu
WEIDNER, Karen, K .... 402-844-7330. 291 I
karenkw@northeast.edu
WEIDNER, Laura, E .... 410-777-2371. 213 D
leweidner@aacc.edu
WEIDNER, Ted .... 402-472-3131. 292 I
tweidner2@unl.edu
WEIER, Gary, M .... 864-242-5100. 441 D
WEIGAND, Donald .... 914-606-6709. 350 F
Donald.Weigand@sunywcc.edu
WEIGAND, Mark, T .... 317-788-3350. 173 I
weigand@uindy.edu
WEIGEL, Elmer .... 701-224-5515. 372 B
elmer.weigel@bismarckstate.edu
WEIGHILL, Rita .... 816-584-6211. 280 C
rita.weighill@park.edu
WEIGHT, Shelly .... 406-874-6192. 286 E
weights@milescc.edu
WEIGMAN, Brice, M ...... 585-245-5606. 343 C
weigman@geneseo.edu
WEIKEL, Karen, A .... 717-245-1315. 414 H
weikelk@dickinson.edu
WEIKLE, Roger, D .... 803-323-2186. 449 G
weikler@winthrop.edu
WEIL, Carola .... 202-885-5990... 94 F
weil@american.edu
WEIL, Gordon .... 610-861-1349. 424 E
gweil@moravian.edu
WEILAND, Bruce .... 920-735-5678. 539 K
weilandb@fvtc.edu
WEILAND-ZALEZNAK,
Carla .... 914-251-6046. 344 D
carla.weiland@purchase.edu
WEILER, Joan .... 828-652-0651. 362 A
jweiler@mcdowelltech.edu
WEILER, Peter, B .... 301-405-4683. 219 B
pweiler@umd.edu
WEILER, Robert .... 301-369-2800. 213 G
rweiler@capitol-college.edu
WEILERT, Deborah .... 620-417-1121. 190 F
deb.weilert@sccc.edu
WEILL, Donald, A .... 414-229-4129. 537 A
xdw@uwm.edu
WEILMINSTER, Deidre .... 301-846-2610. 214 H
dweilminster@frederick.edu
WEIMAR, Caroline .... 404-364-8865. 130 A
cweimar@oglethorpe.edu
WEIMER, Brett .... 417-865-2815. 274 B
weimerb@evangel.edu
WEIMER, Doug .... 225-578-6774. 204 O
dweimer@outreach.lsu.edu
WEIMER, Ferne, L .... 972-708-7416. 472 L
ferne_weimer@gial.edu
WEIMER, Jean .... 414-847-3272. 534 F
jeanweimer@miad.edu
WEIMER, Nancy, L .... 574-372-5100. 166 B
nlweimer@grace.edu
WEIMER, Theresa .... 718-390-3122. 350 B
tweimer@wagner.edu
WEIMER, Tresa .... 304-293-5242. 530 D
kaye.widney@mail.wvu.edu
WEIN, Mitchell, L .... 610-330-5133. 420 D
weinm@lafayette.edu
WEINACKER, Emily .... 480-461-7211... 15 A
emily.weinacker@mesacc.edu
WEINAUR, Ellen .... 601-266-4319. 270 E
ellen.weinaur@usm.edu
WEINBACH, Donald, J ... 203-582-8908... 91 A
donald.weinbach@quinnipiac.edu
WEINBAUM, Marvin .... 415-369-5260... 45 I
mweinbaum@ggu.edu
WEINBERG, Adam, S ..... 740-587-6281. 379 D
weinberga@denison.edu
WEINBERG, Ben .... 213-624-1200... 44 D
bweinberg@fidm.edu
WEINBERG, Jerry .... 305-474-6886. 112 F
jweinberg@stu.edu
WEINBERG, Jerry, B .... 618-650-3010. 159 H
jweinbe@siue.edu
WEINBERG, Julie .... 415-749-4512... 62 G
jweinberg@sfai.edu
WEINBERG, Karen .... 713-500-9873. 492 E
Karen.Weinberg@uth.tmc.edu
WEINBERG, Rivka .... 323-822-9700... 69 J
rivka.weinberg@touro.edu
WEINBERG-KINSEY,
David, W .... 414-410-4261. 532 B
dwweinberg-kins@stritch.edu
WEINBERGER, Meyer ..... 718-236-1171. 337 B
WEINBERGER, Steve ...... 860-493-0252... 87 J
weinbergers@ct.edu
WEINER, Alfred, B .... 740-593-1616. 387 C
weiner@ohio.edu
WEINER, Brad .... 787-765-9695. 555 B
brad@hpcf.upr.edu
WEINER, Daniel .... 860-486-3152... 92 A
dan.weiner@uconn.edu
WEINER, Fred .... 202-448-7134... 95 C
fred.weiner@gallaudet.edu
WEINER, Gail .... 516-299-2505. 329 C
gail.weiner@liu.edu
WEINER, Howard, D .... 216-421-7314. 377 C
hweiner@cia.edu
WEINER, Linda .... 919-807-7100. 357 L
weinerl@nccommunitycolleges.edu
WEINER, Marc .... 212-247-3434. 329 L
mweiner@mandl.edu
WEINER, Marjorie .... 203-285-2132... 88 E
mweiner@gwcc.commnet.edu
WEINER, Melvyn, P .... 212-247-3434. 329 L
WEINER, Stephen, F .... 202-651-5085... 95 C
stephen.weiner@gallaudet.edu
WEINER, Steven .... 650-543-3927... 54 C
steven.weiner@menlo.edu
WEINER, Stuart .... 212-247-3434. 329 L
WEINER, Terry .... 518-244-2301. 338 C
weinet@sage.edu
WEINER, Wendy .... 702-651-5860. 294 E
wendy.weiner@csn.edu
WEINERT, Daniel, J .... 563-884-5761. 182 A
dan.weinert@palmer.edu
WEINERT, Sara, S .... 620-229-6343. 190 G
sara.weinert@sckans.edu
WEINGARD, Alice .... 330-337-6403. 373 F
library@awc.edu
WEINGARDT, Alice .... 970-521-6751... 83 L
alice.weingardt@njc.edu
WEINGART, Brian .... 304-558-4618. 529 C
bweingart@hepc.wvnet.edu
WEINGARTNER, Mary ..... 708-216-3209. 151 H
mweingartner@lumc.edu
WEINHOLD, Tammy, A .. 636-584-6577. 273 M
weinhota@eastcentral.edu
WEININGER, David .... 419-448-2216. 380 G
dweining@heidelberg.edu
WEININGER, Juli .... 419-448-2293. 380 G
jweining@heidelberg.edu
WEINKAUF, Richard .... 743-462-4400. 250 A
rweinkau@schoolcraft.edu
WEINKFAUF, Donald, H . 651-962-5762. 265 C
wein6756@stthomas.edu
WEINKOPF, Christopher . 805-525-4417... 69 H
cweinkopf@thomasaquinas.edu
WEINMAN, Geoffrey .... 201-443-8750. 301 J
weinman@fdu.edu
WEINMAN, Kevin, C .... 413-542-2325. 221 G
kweinman@amherst.edu
WEINMAN, Todd, N .... 802-656-3340. 500 F
todd.weinman@uvm.edu
WEINREICH,
Christine, M .... 901-722-3311. 458 K
cweinreich@sco.edu
WEINS, Sean, A .... 918-595-7906. 400 E
sean.weins@tulsacc.edu
WEINS, W. Jesse .... 605-995-2686. 450 A
jeweins@dwu.edu
WEINSHALL, Iris .... 646-664-2605. 316 I
iris.weinshall@cuny.edu
WEINSTEIN, Heather .... 802-828-2800. 501 C
heather.weinstein@ccv.edu
WEINSTEIN, Kimberly ..... 718-818-6470. 339 H
WEINSTEIN, Mark .... 937-766-8800. 375 K
mweinstein@cedarville.edu
WEINSTEIN, Sheryl, M .... 973-596-3436. 303 G
sheryl.m.weinstein@njit.edu
WEINSTEIN, Steve .... 856-256-5106. 305 E
weinstein@rowan.edu
WEINSTEIN, Susan, L .... 650-724-3658... 68 E
susan.weinstein@stanford.edu
WEINTRAUB, Jane .... 919-537-3236. 368 D
jane_weintraub@dentistry.unc.edu
WEINTRAUB, Seth .... 213-621-2200... 40 B
WEINTRAUB, Susan .... 603-641-7600. 297 G
sweintraub@anselm.edu
WEINTRAUB, Yitzchok .... 732-985-6533. 304 F
WEINTROP, Joseph .... 646-312-3092. 316 J
Joseph.Weintrop@baruch.cuny.edu
WEIR, Ashley, M .... 304-462-4128. 529 G
ashley.weir@glenville.edu
WEIR, Dennis .... 434-961-5447. 513 F
dweir@pvcc.edu
WEIR, George .... 361-593-2831. 484 A
george.weir@tamuk.edu
WEIR, Karissa, L .... 704-406-4732. 354 C
kweir@gardner-webb.edu
WEIR, Robert .... 303-860-5600... 85 K
bob.weir@cu.edu
WEIR, Roseanne, N .... 315-786-2408. 327 L
rweir@sunyjefferson.edu
WEIR, Walter, G .... 402-472-2862. 292 G
wweir@nebraska.edu
WEIS, Bob, M .... 863-638-2920. 119 D
weisrm@webber.edu
WEIS, Dallas .... 509-527-2608. 524 I
dallas.weis@wallawalla.edu
WEIS, Ed .... 914-674-7632. 330 J
eweis@mercy.edu
WEIS, John, A .... 717-245-1503. 414 H
weisj@dickinson.edu
WEIS, Mary Kay .... 216-987-3014. 378 D
mary-kay.weis@tri-c.edu
WEIS, Richard .... 859-280-1256. 197 C
rweis@lextheo.edu
WEIS, Robert, M .... 217-854-3231. 140 G
rweis@blackburn.edu
WEIS, Thomas .... 414-425-8300. 535 K
tweis@shst.edu
WEIS, Tim .... 217-228-5432. 156 C
weisti@quincy.edu
WEISBERG, Moshe .... 973-267-9404. 304 G
WEISBORD, Beryl .... 410-484-7200. 217 D
WEISBROD, Angela .... 507-457-1493. 264 A
aweisbro@smumn.edu
WEISEN, Jan, G .... 617-745-3705. 225 G
jan.weisen@enc.edu
WEISEN, Sheryl .... 317-745-3703. 225 G
sheryl.weisen@enc.edu
WEISENBERG, Myles, E . 781-736-4005. 224 F
weisen@brandeis.edu
WEISENBERGER,
Susan, D .... 620-431-2820. 189 D
sweisenberger@neosho.edu
WEISENBURGER, Earl .... 605-626-2529. 451 I
weisenbe@northern.edu
WEISENBURGER, Leigh . 207-786-6000. 209 F
lweisenb@bates.edu
WEISENBURGER, Perk ... 231-591-2863. 242 F
weisenj1@ferris.edu
WEISENHOLZ, Stephen .. 718-260-3285. 336 E
sweisenh@poly.edu
WEISENSTEIN, Greg, R .. 610-436-2471. 430 A
gweisenstein@wcupa.edu
WEISER, Bridget, R .... 785-827-5541. 188 C
bridget@kwu.edu
WEISER, Irwin, H .... 765-494-3661. 171 M
iweiser@purdue.edu
WEISER, Kent, L .... 620-341-5350. 186 D
kweiser@emporia.edu
WEISER, Philip, J .... 303-492-3084... 85 L
phil.weiser@colorado.edu
WEISER, Sharon .... 660-831-4146. 278 I
weisers@moval.edu
WEISGERBER,
James (Chip) .... 937-484-1369. 392 C
cweisgerber@urbana.edu
WEISHAR, Peter .... 850-644-5244. 115 C
pweishar@fsu.edu
WEISLER, Steven, E .... 415-458-3759... 42 J
steven.weisler@dominican.edu
WEISMAN, Iris .... 937-769-1890. 373 H
iweisman@antioch.edu
WEISMAN, Sarah .... 607-962-9385. 322 B
sweismal@corning-cc.edu
WEISNER, Andrew .... 828-328-7248. 356 B
andrew.weisner@lr.edu
WEISPFENNING,
John, G .... 714-432-5015... 39 K
jweispfenning@occ.cccd.edu
WEISS, Carin, S .... 206-934-4101. 522 H
carin.weiss@seattlecolleges.edu
WEISS, Charles, S .... 508-793-2735. 225 B
cweiss@holycross.edu
WEISS, Daniel, H .... 610-896-1021. 418 F
dweiss@haverford.edu
WEISS, David .... 210-567-3709. 493 A
weissd@uthscsa.edu
WEISS, Dennis .... 609-652-4548. 305 C
dennis.weiss@stockton.edu
WEISS, H .... 732-364-1220. 299 B
WEISS, Ira, R .... 919-515-5560. 368 B
ira_weiss@ncsu.edu
WEISS, Jack, M .... 225-578-8491. 205 E
WEISS, Janet, A .... 734-764-4401. 251 C
janetw@umich.edu
WEISS, Jeffery, I .... 718-990-6357. 339 A
weissj@stjohns.edu
WEISS, Johanna .... 804-594-1500. 512 G
jweiss@jtcc.edu
WEISS, Karen .... 618-252-5400. 159 E
karen.weiss@sic.edu
WEISS, Kay .... 909-384-8535... 62 A
kweiss@sbccd.cc.ca.us
WEISS, Mark .... 541-917-4780. 404 B
weissm@linnbenton.edu
WEISS, Mark, D .... 503-838-8888. 406 E
weissm@wou.edu
WEISS, Michelle .... 860-412-7353... 89 E
mweiss@qvcc.commnet.edu
WEISS, Nicolas .... 303-245-4664... 83 F
nweiss@naropa.edu
WEISS, Paul .... 510-987-0522... 70 H
paul.weiss@ucop.edu
WEISS, Rod, P .... 858-499-0202... 40 C
rweiss@coleman.edu
WEISS, Roy, E .... 773-702-0344. 161 B
rweiss@medicine.bsd.uchicago.edu
WEISS, Stephanie .... 612-330-1476. 253 H
weisss@augsburg.edu
WEISSENBURGER,
David .... 254-968-9123. 483 A
weissenburger@tarleton.edu
WEISSENBURGER,
Jackie .... 715-232-2421. 538 B
weissenburgerj@uwstout.edu
WEISSENFLUH, Anji .... 541-962-3236. 405 H
aweissen@eou.edu
WEISSINGER, Ellen .... 402-472-3751. 292 I
eweissinger1@unl.edu
WEISSMAN, Julie .... 314-246-4256. 284 N
julieweissman22@webster.edu
WEISSMAN, Neil, B .... 717-245-1321. 414 H
weissmne@dickinson.edu
WEISZ, David .... 773-256-0784. 152 B
dweisz@lstc.edu
WEITER, Stephen .... 315-470-6715. 345 B
spweiter@esf.edu
WEITZ, Anna, D .... 610-607-6210. 431 D
aweitz@racc.edu
WEITZ, Eric .... 212-650-8166. 317 D
eweitz@ccny.cuny.edu
WEITZER, Joseph .... 262-695-7824. 541 D
jweitzer@wctc.edu
WEITZMAN, Lauren .... 801-581-6826. 496 Q
lweitzman@sa.utah.edu
WEIZER, Paul .... 978-665-3272. 229 E
pweizer@fitchburgstate.edu
WELAGE, Lynda, S .... 505-272-3241. 312 F
LSWelage@salude.unm.edu
WELBORN, Ruth, B .... 512-245-3300. 487 C
rw01@txstate.edu
WELBOURNE, Claudia .... 315-279-6868. 328 D
cwelbour@mail.keuka.edu
WELBURN, Janice .... 414-288-7214. 534 B
janice.welburn@marquette.edu
WELBURN, Marsha .... 617-928-4599. 234 E
mwelburn@mountida.edu
WELBURN, William .... 414-288-8028. 534 B
william.welburn@marquette.edu
WELCH, Alexis .... 252-527-6223. 361 F
awelch@lenoircc.edu
WELCH, Ba-Shen .... 205-929-1445..... 5 G
bwelch@miles.edu
WELCH, C. Brigid .... 209-946-2949... 73 A
bwelch@pacific.edu
WELCH, Charles, L .... 501-660-1000... 19 L
president@asusystem.edu
WELCH, Dan .... 814-866-8151. 420 E
dwelch@lecom.edu
WELCH, Denise .... 903-693-1121. 478 A
dwelch@panola.edu
WELCH, Dirk .... 940-397-4972. 476 H
dirk.welch@mwsu.edu
WELCH, Edwin .... 765-998-5523. 173 C
edwelch@taylor.edu
WELCH, Edwin, H .... 304-357-4713. 527 H
edwinwelch@ucwv.edu
WELCH, Eric .... 901-321-3419. 453 H
ewelch@cbu.edu
WELCH, Felicia .... 602-978-7412... 18 A
felicia.welch@thunderbird.edu
WELCH, Frances, C .... 943-953-5613. 443 A
welchf@cofc.edu
WELCH, George .... 619-684-8826... 56 C
gwelch@newschoolarch.edu
WELCH, Jennifer, C .... 315-464-4570. 342 E
welchj@upstate.edu
WELCH, Jim .... 843-383-8098. 442 F
jwelch@coker.edu

WELCH, Joe Ben ... 225-675-8270. 203 G jbwelch@rpcc.edu
WELCH, John ... 412-924-1401. 431 A jwelch@pts.edu
WELCH, Julia ... 707-638-5425... 69 K julia.perhac@tu.edu
WELCH, Kathleen ... 831-479-5076... 30 G kawelch@cabrillo.edu
WELCH, Kathy ... 407-691-1098. 111 Q kjwelch@rollins.edu
WELCH, Lena ... 615-248-1393. 462 D lwelch@trevecca.edu
WELCH, Leo ... 970-351-2515... 86 C leo.welch@unco.edu
WELCH, Lynne ... 908-709-7167. 308 B welch@ucc.edu
WELCH, Marjorie ... 641-673-1328. 183 H welchmar@wmpenn.edu
WELCH, Mark ... 202-885-3287... 94 F mark@american.edu
WELCH, Marshall ... 925-631-8135... 61 F mjw6@stmarys-ca.edu
WELCH, Mary Ellen ... 540-665-5436. 509 E shenandoah@bkstr.com
WELCH, Michael ... 847-578-3238. 157 F michael.welch@rosalindfranklin.edu
WELCH, Nick ... 740-588-1224. 394 C nwelch@zanestate.edu
WELCH, Olga, M ... 412-396-1360. 415 F welcho@duq.edu
WELCH, Patricia ... 443-885-3385. 217 A pwelch@morgan.edu
WELCH, Paul ... 858-635-4709... 26 M pwelch@alliant.edu
WELCH, Paul ... 508-626-4640. 230 A pwelch@framingham.edu
WELCH, Regina ... 804-627-5300. 502 I
WELCH, Renee ... 970-351-2127... 86 C renee.welch@unco.edu
WELCH, Ronald, W ... 843-953-6588. 442 A rwelch1@citadel.edu
WELCH, Sally ... 313-927-1319. 246 D swelch@marygrove.edu
WELCH, Sandra, T ... 210-458-4706. 492 C sandra.welch@utsa.edu
WELCH, Sarah ... 617-726-2947. 234 B
WELCH, Sharon ... 773-256-3000. 152 H swelch@meadville.edu
WELCH, Sherri, L ... 856-691-8600. 301 A swelch@cccnj.edu
WELCH, Susan ... 814-865-7691. 426 A sxw11@psu.edu
WELCH, Susan, T ... 518-564-5062. 344 B welchst@plattsburgh.edu
WELCH, Terry ... 828-227-7100. 369 E welcht@wcu.edu
WELCH, Val ... 208-376-7731. 137 F vwelch@boisebible.edu
WELCH, Vince ... 706-245-7226. 124 D vwelch@ec.edu
WELD, Jeff ... 802-468-1241. 501 B jeff.weld@castleton.edu
WELDEN, David ... 770-962-7580. 127 D dwelden@gwinnetttech.edu
WELDEN, Jonathan ... 901-272-5121. 456 F jweldon@mca.edu
WELDEN, Soraya ... 601-484-8628. 267 G swelden@meridiancc.edu
WELDON, James ... 803-780-1119. 449 E jweldon@voorhees.edu
WELDON, Leslie ... 406-657-2188. 287 C leslie.weldon@msubillings.edu
WELDON, Leslie ... 618-634-3337. 158 M lesliew@shawneecc.edu
WELDON, Rich ... 803-508-7382. 440 G weldonr@atc.edu
WELDON, S, L ... 765-494-4185. 171 M weldons@purdue.edu
WELDON, Stephanie, J ... 603-206-8111. 296 A sjweldon@ccsnh.edu
WELDY, Eric ... 815-753-1573. 154 I eweldy@niu.edu
WELGE, Vicky, L ... 217-443-8702. 143 G voliver@dacc.edu
WELKER, Dan ... 928-428-8300... 13 J dan.welker@eac.edu
WELKER, Joan, C ... 570-484-2181. 429 B jwelker@lhup.edu
WELKER, Josh ... 217-641-4110. 148 M jwelker@jwcc.edu
WELKER, Kristen ... 605-668-1577. 450 F kristen.welker@mtmc.edu
WELKEY, Sharon ... 210-832-2115. 490 A welkey@uiwtx.edu
WELLBORN, Linda ... 417-865-2815. 274 B wellbornl@evangel.edu
WELLER, Eddie ... 281-484-1900. 479 E eddie.weller@sjcd.edu
WELLER, Lisa ... 610-225-5007. 415 G lweller2@eastern.edu
WELLER, Steve ... 972-438-6932. 478 C sweller@parkercc.edu
WELLER, Vicki ... 410-617-2201. 216 A vweller@loyola.edu
WELLER-DENGEL, Pamela ... 507-389-6061. 259 G pamela.weller-dengel@mnsu.edu
WELLHAM, Ann ... 301-387-3045. 214 I ann.wellham@garrettcollege.edu
WELLHAUSEN, Chad ... 712-542-5117. 179 L cwellhausen@iwcc.edu
WELLINGTON, Eric, R ... 610-359-5127. 414 D ewellington@dccc.edu
WELLINGTON-BAKER, Kristi ... 509-527-4263. 524 H kristi.wellington-baker@wwcc.edu
WELLMAN, Barbara ... 217-228-5432. 156 C wellmba@quincy.edu
WELLMAN, Chris ... 941-752-5443. 114 I wellmac@scf.edu
WELLMAN, Debra ... 407-646-2175. 111 Q dwellman@rollins.edu
WELLMAN, Ronald, D ... 336-758-5616. 370 D wellmanr@wfu.edu
WELLS, Barbara ... 901-333-4259. 461 F bwells@southwest.tn.edu
WELLS, Barbara ... 865-981-8278. 456 D barbara.wells@maryvillecollege.edu
WELLS, Beth ... 503-845-3243. 404 D beth.wells@mtangel.edu
WELLS, Bill ... 912-478-2622. 126 C wwells@georgiasouthern.edu
WELLS, Billy ... 706-864-1630. 133 D billy.wells@ung.edu
WELLS, Bonnie ... 860-439-5001... 89 H bonnie.wells@conncoll.edu
WELLS, Brad ... 510-885-3803... 33 C brad.wells@csueastbay.edu
WELLS, Brian ... 731-286-3207. 460 F wells@dscc.edu
WELLS, Brian, J ... 502-776-1443. 199 A
WELLS, C. Gene ... 812-488-2664. 173 H gw5@evansville.edu
WELLS, Carole ... 610-683-4212. 429 A wells@kutztown.edu
WELLS, Cathy ... 253-833-9111. 520 C cwells@greenriver.edu
WELLS, Christina ... 217-479-7030. 152 D christina.wells@mac.edu
WELLS, Christopher, J ... 765-658-4226. 165 F christopherwells@depauw.edu
WELLS, Dan ... 812-877-8205. 172 C dan.wells@rose-hulman.edu
WELLS, Dan ... 713-743-2619. 489 B dwells2@uh.edu
WELLS, David, A ... 817-515-5250. 482 B david.wells@tccd.edu
WELLS, Debra ... 724-335-5336. 425 F dwells@oaa.edu
WELLS, Douglas ... 605-394-1763. 452 A douglas.wells@sdsmt.edu
WELLS, Elaine ... 212-938-5690. 345 C ewells@sunyopt.edu
WELLS, Gail, W ... 859-572-5788. 198 I wells@nku.edu
WELLS, JR., Henry, D ... 919-572-1625. 352 C hdwells@apexsot.edu
WELLS, Johann ... 334-291-4954... 2 H johann.wells@cv.edu
WELLS, John, M ... 252-335-0821. 359 F jmwells@albemarle.edu
WELLS, John, T ... 804-684-7103. 503 N wells@vims.edu
WELLS, John, W ... 828-689-1250. 356 F jwells@mhc.edu
WELLS, Jovita ... 202-274-6260... 97 A jwells@udc.edu
WELLS, Keith, P ... 303-762-6963... 81 G keith.wells@denverseminary.edu
WELLS, Lisa ... 540-887-7330. 507 A lwells@mbc.edu
WELLS, Nancy, L ... 716-645-4666. 341 F nwells@buffalo.edu
WELLS, Nick ... 785-460-4684. 185 P nick.wells@colbycc.edu
WELLS, Peter ... 508-767-7350. 222 C pd.wells@assumption.edu
WELLS, R. Hal ... 612-874-3634. 257 B hal_wells@mcad.edu
WELLS, Rebecca ... 270-831-9682. 195 D rebecca.wells@kctcs.edu
WELLS, Regina, A ... 302-454-3941... 93 F rwells@dtcc.edu
WELLS, Richard, H ... 920-424-0200. 537 B wellsr@uwosh.edu
WELLS, JR., Robert, J ... 864-656-0244. 442 C rjwells@clemson.edu
WELLS, Sherry ... 913-758-6123. 191 B wellss@stmary.edu
WELLS, Sherry ... 409-880-8968. 486 F sherry.wells@lamar.edu
WELLS, Teri ... 304-896-7443. 528 F teri.wells@southernwv.edu
WELLS, Twyla, C ... 919-209-2119. 361 E tcwells@johnstoncc.edu
WELLS, Virginia, D ... 757-221-4386. 503 N vdwell@wm.edu
WELLS, Warren ... 660-785-4121. 282 L wwells@truman.edu
WELLS, William, C ... 419-995-8213. 381 Q wells.w@rhodesstate.edu
WELLS, William, T ... 336-758-5154. 370 D wellswt@wfu.edu
WELLS-BOOTH, Shawna ... 352-638-9733... 99 B swellsbooth@beaconcollege.edu
WELMERS, Laura ... 312-752-2504. 149 E laura.welmers@kendall.edu
WELP, Cindy ... 712-274-5114. 181 B welp@morningside.edu
WELSCH, Cheryl ... 845-434-5750. 347 A cwelsch@sullivan.suny.edu
WELSCH, Colleen ... 269-782-1204. 250 C cwelsch@swmich.edu
WELSCH, Gabriel ... 814-641-3131. 419 H welschg@juniata.edu
WELSH, Beth ... 706-737-1796. 126 B bwelsh@gru.edu
WELSH, Connie ... 406-444-0614. 286 G cwelsh@montana.edu
WELSH, David ... 860-255-3513... 89 G dwelsh@txcc.commnet.edu
WELSH, Deb ... 615-383-3230. 452 J welshd@aquinascollege.edu
WELSH, Eleanor ... 410-827-5847. 214 C ewelsh@chesapeake.edu
WELSH, James, C ... 202-687-4554... 95 E welshj@georgetown.edu
WELSH, Jennifer, R ... 860-701-6114... 90 G welsh_j@mitchell.edu
WELSH, Johnelle ... 254-526-1298. 468 G johnelle.welsh@ctcd.edu
WELSH, Marcia, G ... 570-422-3546. 428 D mwelsh@po-box.esu.edu
WELSH, Patrick, J ... 610-785-6265. 432 C pwelsh@scs.edu
WELSH, Robert ... 626-815-6000... 29 H rwelsh@apu.edu
WELSH, Sarah ... 617-264-7756. 226 B swelsh@emmanuel.edu
WELSH, Suzanne, P ... 610-328-8316. 433 I swelsh1@swarthmore.edu
WELSH, Tasha, D ... 636-481-3157. 275 I twelsh@jeffco.edu
WELSH, Tracy ... 605-688-4121. 452 B tracy.welsh@sdstate.edu
WELSH, William, J ... 570-941-6300. 436 A william.welsh@scranton.edu
WELTER, Brian ... 847-566-6401. 162 G bwelter@usml.edu
WELTER, Gwen ... 715-634-4790. 533 Q gwelter@lco.edu
WELTER, Linda Allaire ... 617-879-2233. 238 C lwelter@wheelock.edu
WELTER, Stephanie ... 785-827-5541. 188 C stephanie.welter@kwu.edu
WELTER, Stephen ... 619-594-2978... 35 D swelter@mail.sdsu.edu
WELTON, Ronald, J ... 516-876-3135. 343 D weltonr@oldwestbury.edu
WELZ, Linda ... 626-914-8811... 38 K lwelz@citruscollege.edu
WEN, H. Joseph ... 310-243-3745... 33 B jwen@csudh.edu
WEN, Hui-Men ... 941-487-4601. 115 D hwen@ncf.edu
WENBERG, Carrie ... 314-889-1403. 274 E cwenberg@fontbonne.edu
WENCK, Lisa, M ... 607-436-2518. 343 E wenckIm@oneonta.edu
WENDALL, Alan, B ... 215-951-1916. 420 B wendall@lasalle.edu
WENDEL, O.T ... 480-219-6011. 271 A twendel@atsu.edu
WENDEL, Shirley, A ... 913-288-7626. 187 L swendel@kckcc.edu
WENDEROTH, Christine ... 773-753-0735. 152 E cwendero@lstc.edu
WENDEROTH, Christine ... 773-256-0735. 152 B cwenderoth@jkmlibrary.org
WENDLER, David, O ... 507-354-8221. 256 M wendledo@mlc-wels.edu
WENDOVER, Wendy ... 303-963-3268... 79 C wwendover@ccu.edu
WENDT, Dean ... 805-756-1508... 32 F dwendt@calpoly.edu
WENDT, Donna ... 706-771-4146. 121 D dwendt@augustatech.edu
WENDT, Hunter ... 586-498-4090. 246 A wendth@macomb.edu
WENDT, Tim ... 217-353-3673. 155 J twendt@parkland.edu
WENDZEL, Anita ... 941-907-2262. 103 C awendzel@evergladesuniversity.edu
WENER, Kara ... 507-457-6632. 264 A kwener@smumn.edu
WENGER, Andrea, S ... 540-432-4208. 504 D wengeras@emu.edu
WENNER, Annamaria ... 617-989-4410. 237 G wennera@wit.edu
WENNERGREN, Mindy ... 801-832-2186. 498 F mwennergren@westminstercollege.edu
WENNERSTROM, Zandy ... 303-762-6887... 81 G zandy.wennerstrom@denverseminary.edu
WENRICK, Jason ... 707-664-3155... 36 B jason.wenrick@sonoma.edu
WENSEL, Tara ... 208-459-5016. 138 A twensel@collegeofidaho.edu
WENSLEY, Roy ... 925-631-4409... 61 F rwensley@stmarys-ca.edu
WENSOWITCH, Andrea ... 419-448-2261. 380 G awensowi@heidelberg.edu
WENTHE, Andrew ... 563-425-5348. 183 B wenthea@uiu.edu
WENTHE, Andrew ... 563-425-5260. 183 B wenthea@uiu.edu
WENTLAND, Briana ... 320-363-5512. 254 J bwentland@csbsju.edu
WENTWORTH, Craig, R ... 229-225-5069. 132 D cwentworth@southwestgatech.edu
WENTWORTH, Jackie ... 605-995-2151. 450 A jawentwo@dwu.edu
WENTWORTH, Kristen ... 207-326-2280. 211 D kristen.wentworth@mma.edu
WENTWORTH, Monica ... 615-966-6296. 456 B monica.wentworth@lipscomb.edu
WENTWORTH, Renae ... 864-242-5100. 441 D
WENTZ, James ... 601-984-1010. 270 C jwentz@umc.edu
WENTZLAFF, Maribeth ... 605-668-1392. 450 F mwentzlaff@mtmc.edu
WENYIKA, Reggies ... 405-789-7661. 400 A reggies.wenyika@swcu.edu
WENZ, Donald, A ... 718-951-5511. 317 C donald@brooklyn.cuny.edu
WENZEL, Claudia ... 216-397-4248. 381 R cwenzel@jcu.edu
WENZEL, Loren, A ... 304-336-8152. 530 A lwenzel@westliberty.edu
WENZLER, John ... 510-885-3664... 33 C john.wenzler@csueastbay.edu
WEPNER, Shelley ... 914-323-5192. 330 B shelley.wepner@mville.edu
WERA, Chris ... 303-871-7785... 86 B cjwera@du.edu
WERBEL DASHEFSKY, Linda ... 718-489-5370. 338 G lwerbel@sfc.edu
WERBER, Frank ... 646-312-1112. 316 J Frank.Werber@baruch.cuny.edu
WERDANN, Frank ... 607-431-4340. 325 F werdannf@hartwick.edu
WERLE, Kathy ... 949-451-5565... 67 B kwerle@ivc.edu
WERLE, Kathy ... 949-582-4795... 67 C kwerle@saddleback.edu
WERLING, Karen, J ... 229-931-2902. 131 G kwerling@southgatech.edu
WERMAN, Steve ... 970-248-1881... 79 F swerman@coloradomesa.edu
WERMUTH, Thomas, S ... 845-575-3000. 330 D thomas.wermuth@marist.edu
WERNE, Stanley, J ... 812-888-4361. 174 F swerne@vinu.edu
WERNER, Elizabether ... 727-726-1153. 100 E elizabethwerner@clearwater.edu
WERNER, Kathleen ... 301-369-2800. 213 G kwerner@capitol-college.edu
WERNER, Paul, F ... 316-978-3030. 191 F paul.werner@wichita.edu
WERNER, Shraga ... 718-941-8000. 331 C
WERNTZ, Kevin ... 912-443-3015. 131 D kwerntz@savannahtech.edu
WEROSH, Keith ... 334-271-1670... 6 C kwerosh@princeinstitute.edu
WERT, Joseph, L ... 812-941-2391. 168 F jwert@ius.edu
WERTHEIMER, Howard ... 404-385-7604. 125 D howard.wertheimer@spaceplan.gatech.edu
WERTHMANN, David ... 314-256-8806. 271 F werthmann@ai.edu
WERTIME, Richard, A ... 215-572-2963. 409 H wertime@arcadia.edu
WERTMAN, Devin ... 406-477-6215. 285 H dwertman@cdkc.edu
WERTMAN, William ... 406-477-6215. 285 H bwertman@cdkc.edu
WERTS, Shelley ... 323-242-5536... 52 C wertss@lasc.edu
WERTSCH, James, V ... 314-935-9015. 284 L jwertsch@wustl.edu
WESELEY, Laura ... 239-687-5351... 98 J lweseley@avemarialaw.edu

WESENER-MICHAEL, Kelley .... 815-753-6103. 154 I kwesener@niu.edu
WESLEY, Derek, M .... 607-587-3930. 345 D wesleydm@alfredstate.edu
WESLEY, III, Homer, A .. 719-255-3582... 85 M hwesley@uccs.edu
WESLEY, Jeanne .... 540-891-3095. 512 E jwesley@germanna.edu
WESLEY, Jill .... 585-395-5415. 342 F jwesley@brockport.edu
WESLEY, Kevin, P .... 585-276-3575. 349 C kwesley@alumni.rochester.edu
WESLEY, Olan, L .... 334-229-4317..... 1 D owesley@alasu.edu
WESLEY, Vinetta .... 256-306-2828..... 2 F vlw@calhoun.edu
WESLEY FORD, Charles . 937-376-6431. 376 E cford@centralstate.edu
WESLOW, Suzanne .... 414-229-4463. 537 A sweslow@uwm.edu
WESNER, Katrin .... 910-962-4126. 369 C wesnerk@uncw.edu
WESNER, Samantha .... 610-921-7531. 409 A swesner@alb.edu
WESOLEK, Christina .... 718-405-3334. 320 G christina.wesolek@mountsaintvincent.edu
WESOLOWSKI, Mitch ..... 434-947-8114. 508 D mwesolowski@randolphcollege.edu
WESS, Linda .... 814-536-5168. 412 C lwess@crbc.net
WESSE, David .... 318-473-6408. 205 A dwesse@lsua.edu
WESSEL, Kirk .... 602-749-5108. 189 I kirk.wessel@ottawa.edu
WESSEL, Walter, G .... 217-424-6217. 153 C wwessell@millikin.edu
WESSELLS, Christopher, W .... 619-260-6886... 73 I chris@sandiego.edu
WESSELS, Gus .... 979-532-6505. 494 L gusw@wcjc.edu
WESSMAN, Kathleen .... 240-567-7971. 216 F kathleen.wessman@montgomerycollege.edu
WESSON, Garlen, D .... 410-651-8371. 219 E gdwesson@umes.edu
WEST, Aaron .... 850-484-1477. 110 G awest@pensacolastate.edu
WEST, Allen .... 903-693-1171. 478 A awest@panola.edu
WEST, Amy .... 731-425-2621. 460 G awest12@jscc.edu
WEST, Andrew .... 512-472-4133. 480 G andrew.west@ssw.edu
WEST, Anita .... 909-748-8048... 73 H anita_west@redlands.edu
WEST, Caroline, S .... 310-206-8264... 71 C cwest@ponet.ucla.edu
WEST, Cathy .... 361-698-1265. 471 G cwest@delmar.edu
WEST, Charlene, C .... 919-536-7235. 360 B westc@durhamtech.edu
WEST, Cheryl .... 508-270-4108. 231 G cwest@massbay.edu
WEST, David .... 318-357-6466. 208 B west@nsula.edu
WEST, David .... 575-624-8014. 310 H West@nmmi.edu
WEST, David, L .... 901-722-3210. 458 K dwest@sco.edu
WEST, Denise .... 630-829-6027. 140 B dwest@ben.edu
WEST, Detra, E .... 330-569-5237. 380 I westde@hiram.edu
WEST, Donald .... 919-466-1154... 96 F donald.west@strayer.edu
WEST, George, E .... 714-879-3901... 47 K gewest@hiu.edu
WEST, Greg .... 262-691-5417. 541 D gwest@wctc.edu
WEST, Greg .... 757-455-3400. 515 H gwest@vwc.edu
WEST, Holly .... 845-938-3334. 545 I Holly.West@usma.edu
WEST, J. Cameron .... 334-833-4409..... 4 D camwest@huntingdon.edu
WEST, James, L .... 662-325-2202. 268 D jwest@sarc.msstate.edu
WEST, Janice .... 912-478-5164. 126 C jwest@georgiasouthern.edu
WEST, Jeff .... 206-934-5449. 522 J jeff.west@seattlecolleges.edu
WEST, Jeffrey, J .... 801-581-7520. 496 Q jeff.west@admin.utah.edu
WEST, Jennifer .... 575-758-8914. 310 C info@midwiferycollege.org
WEST, John, R .... 903-813-2536. 466 H jwest@austincollege.edu
WEST, Karen, P .... 702-774-2500. 294 I karen.west@unlv.edu
WEST, Karla .... 208-426-1459. 137 G kwest@boisestate.edu
WEST, Kevin .... 419-530-4053. 392 B kevin.west@utoledo.edu
WEST, Kim .... 770-423-6414. 127 N kwest26@kennesaw.edu
WEST, Kristie .... 916-691-7199... 53 B westk@crc.losrios.edu
WEST, Lance .... 304-696-6440. 529 H west24@marshall.edu
WEST, Linda, J .... 304-697-7550. 526 H lwest@huntingtonjuniorcollege.edu
WEST, Lisa .... 304-865-6228. 527 F lisa.west@ovu.edu
WEST, Mark, D .... 734-764-0514. 251 C markwest@umich.edu
WEST, Mary .... 513-244-4935. 377 G mary_west@mail.msj.edu
WEST, Michael .... 262-551-6300. 532 D mwest@carthage.edu
WEST, Michael, D .... 518-580-5810. 341 A mwest@skidmore.edu
WEST, Mickey .... 615-329-8680. 454 F mwest@fisk.edu
WEST, Mike .... 817-272-5988. 491 B mpwest@uta.edu
WEST, Monica .... 301-445-1937. 219 A mwest@usmd.edu
WEST, Pat .... 843-349-2009. 442 E patw@coastal.edu
WEST, Peter, C .... 954-308-2204... 98 G pwest@aii.edu
WEST, Rosemary, W .... 702-651-7690. 294 E rosemary.west@csn.edu
WEST, Sally .... 618-524-4001. 158 M sallyw@shawneecc.edu
WEST, Stephanie .... 606-886-3863. 194 K stephanie.west@kctcs.edu
WEST, Susan, H .... 615-460-5602. 453 C susan.west@belmont.edu
WEST, Thomas, H .... 740-392-6868. 384 K twest@mvnu.edu
WEST, Tom .... 954-262-4994. 109 K twest@nova.edu
WEST, Tom .... 323-856-7680... 27 O twest@afi.com
WEST, Vicki .... 806-742-2166. 487 D vicki.west@ttu.edu
WEST-DAVIS, Angela .... 518-381-1279. 340 G westaa@sunysccc.edu
WEST ENGELKEMEYER, Susan .... 508-213-2215. 235 E president@nichols.edu
WEST FIGUEREDO, Ann 610-896-4279. 418 F afiguero@haverford.edu
WESTACOTT, Vicky .... 607-871-2269. 313 E fcobb@alfred.edu
WESTARY, Kenneth .... 443-840-3213. 214 E kwestary@ccbcmd.edu
WESTAWAY, Shawn .... 248-218-2064. 249 D swestaway@rc.edu
WESTBROOK, Denise, Z . 302-356-6915... 94 E denise.z.westbrook@wilmu.edu
WESTBROOK, Diane .... 716-884-9120. 315 K dwestbrook@bryantstratton.edu
WESTBROOK, Gail, L ..... 304-462-4109. 529 G gail.westbrook@glenville.edu
WESTBROOK, Marianne . 575-492-2165. 312 M mwestbrook@usw.edu
WESTBROOK, Steve .... 936-468-2701. 482 A swestbrook@sfasu.edu
WESTBROOK, Velma, S . 985-448-4687. 208 A sue.westbrook@nicholls.edu
WESTBROOKS, Lance .... 615-361-7555. 454 D lwestbrooks@daymarinstitute.edu
WESTBY, Kim .... 562-860-2451... 37 I westby@cerritos.edu
WESTCOTT, James .... 605-367-5675. 452 C james.westcott@southeasttech.edu
WESTCOTT, Kathy, M ..... 814-641-3121. 419 H westcott@juniata.edu
WESTCOTT, III, S. Wickes .... 864-656-0161. 442 C westc@clemson.edu
WESTCOTT, Theresa, C ... 212-353-4150. 321 F westcott@cooper.edu
WESTENBROEK, Steve ..... 402-399-2465. 289 A swestenbroek@csm.edu
WESTENDORF, Nichole .. 785-227-3380. 184 I westendorfn@bethanylb.edu
WESTENDORF, Thomas, J .... 937-229-4141. 391 C twestendorf1@udayton.edu
WESTER, Beth .... 256-551-5219..... 4 I beth.wester@drakestate.edu
WESTER, Ken .... 479-968-0218... 20 E kwester@atu.edu
WESTERFIELD, Barbara, M .... 601-984-1080. 270 C bwesterfield@umc.edu
WESTERFIELD, MaryAnn 856-691-8600. 301 A mwesterfield@cccnj.edu
WESTERFIELD, Michael, W .... 573-592-4383. 285 D michael.westerfield@williamwoods.edu
WESTERGAARD, Patricia 806-874-3571. 468 J patricia.westergaard@clarendoncollege.edu
WESTERMAN, Al .... 931-221-7883. 459 B westermana@apsu.edu
WESTERMAN, III, W. Scott .... 517-355-8314. 246 H wsw@msu.edu
WESTERMEYER, Lawrence, W .... 314-516-4010. 283 E larry_westermeyer@umsl.edu
WESTERMEYER, Susan, M .... 317-940-9135. 164 J swesterm@butler.edu
WESTERN, Linda Jean .... 801-274-3280. 498 E lwestern@wgu.edu
WESTERVELT, Robert, K . 503-554-2136. 403 C rwestervelt@georgefox.edu
WESTERVELT, Wayne ..... 315-655-7377. 316 E wawestervelt@cazenovia.edu
WESTFALL, Andrew .... 410-337-6500. 215 A andrew.westfall@goucher.edu
WESTFALL, Michael .... 509-359-7099. 519 C mwestfall@ewu.edu
WESTFALL, Sarah, B .... 269-337-7209. 244 K Sarah.Westfall@kzoo.edu
WESTGARD, Joyce .... 360-438-4333. 522 G jwestgard@stmartin.edu
WESTHOFF, James .... 207-992-4909. 210 B westhoffj@husson.edu
WESTLAKE, Christopher, J .... 850-872-3844. 106 H cwestlake@gulfcoast.edu
WESTLAKE, Rachel .... 925-969-2689... 41 L rwestlak@dvc.edu
WESTLEY, Elizabeth, K .... 757-594-7345. 503 M elizabeth.westley@cnu.edu
WESTLEY, Lindsey .... 708-456-0300. 161 A lwestley@triton.edu
WESTLUND, Julie, A ...... 218-726-7985. 264 D jwestlun@d.umn.edu
WESTMAN, Craig, E .... 915-747-5093. 492 A cewestman@utep.edu
WESTMAN, Dennis .... 580-371-2371. 396 E dwestman@mscok.edu
WESTMAN, Hans .... 412-291-6409. 410 B hwestman@aii.edu
WESTMORELAND, T. Andrew .... 205-726-2727..... 6 F tawestmo@samford.edu
WESTON, JR., Donald, E .... 609-258-3407. 304 E donw@princeton.edu
WESTON, John, H .... 507-284-2073. 254 F weston.john@mayo.edu
WESTOVER, Kristin .... 276-656-0315. 513 D kwestover@patrickhenry.edu
WESTPHAL, Arthur, P ..... 507-344-7375. 253 J awest@blc.edu
WESTPHAL, Donald, M .. 507-344-7320. 253 J dwestpha@blc.edu
WESTPHAL, Kenneth, C .. 507-933-7499. 255 I kwestpha@gustavus.edu
WESTPHAL, Kristianne, R .... 507-933-7495. 255 I kristi@gustavus.edu
WESTPHAL, Lee .... 402-557-5235. 288 G lee.westphal@bellevue.edu
WESTPHAL, Lorraine, M . 757-594-7608. 503 M lwestpha@cnu.edu
WESTPHAL, Matt .... 918-540-6249. 396 G mwestphal@neo.edu
WESTPHAL, Stephen, A .. 231-995-1130. 248 B swestphal@nmc.edu
WESTPHAL-BENEFIEL, Melissa, C .... 219-785-5274. 172 A mwestpha@pnc.edu
WESTRA, Jeff .... 608-249-6611. 533 I careers@msn.herzing.edu
WESTRA, Kayla .... 507-372-3435. 260 A kayla.westra@mnwest.edu
WESTRICK, Karyn, J .... 419-434-4758. 391 D westrick@findlay.edu
WESTWATER, Julia .... 508-289-3379. 238 E jwestwater@whoi.edu
WETHERBEE-METCALF, Pamela .... 410-617-2330. 216 A pwetherbeemetcalf@loyola.edu
WETHERELL, Bill .... 386-506-3813. 101 G wetherb@DaytonaState.edu
WETHERELL, Dale, R ...... 401-825-2109. 439 A drwetherell@ccri.edu
WETHERILL, G. Richard . 580-559-5455. 395 F rwethrll@ecok.edu
WETHERILL, Jeffrey .... 315-781-3390. 326 C wetherill@hws.edu
WETHERILL, Jeffrey .... 315-781-3000. 326 C wetherill@hws.edu
WETHERINGTON, Lee .... 252-527-6223. 361 F lwetherington@lenoircc.edu
WETMORE, David .... 620-227-9201. 186 B dwetmore@dc3.edu
WETMORE, Dawn .... 567-661-7338. 387 L dawn_wetmore@owens.edu
WETSELL, Linda, S .... 814-332-4790. 409 D linda.wetsell@allegheny.edu
WETSIT, Larry .... 406-768-6311. 286 C lwetsit@fpcc.edu
WETSTEIN, Kenneth, A ... 419-783-2587. 379 C kwetstein@defiance.edu
WETSTEIN, Matt .... 209-954-5047... 63 C mwetstein@deltacollege.edu
WETTER, Kevin .... 808-356-5261. 135 F kvetter@hpu.edu
WETTICK, Elizabeth .... 412-383-1805. 435 C wettickes@upmc.edu
WETZEL, Barbara .... 716-896-0700. 350 A wetzel@villa.edu
WETZEL, Derrick .... 610-282-1100. 414 F derrick.wetzel@desales.edu
WETZEL, Mary, E .... 717-728-2260. 412 J marywetzel@centralpenn.edu
WETZEL, Mike .... 717-358-4759. 416 J mike.wetzel@fandm.edu
WETZEL, Robert .... 215-637-7700. 418 G rwetzel@holyfamily.edu
WETZEL, Shelby .... 307-754-6110. 543 G Shelby.Wetzel@northwestcollege.edu
WETZEL, Suzanne, M ..... 734-384-4206. 247 C swetzel@monroeccc.edu
WETZEL HARDER, Wendy .... 949-480-4081... 66 F wwharder@soka.edu
WETZSTEIN, James .... 219-464-5096. 174 E james.wetzstein@valpo.edu
WEXLER, Arthur .... 609-343-4905. 299 A wexler@atlantic.edu
WEXLER, Joan, G .... 718-780-7900. 315 H joan.wexler@brooklaw.edu
WEXLER, Jon .... 201-692-7304. 301 J jwexler@fdu.edu
WEXLER, Judie .... 415-575-6104... 31 D jwexler@ciis.edu
WEY, Lora .... 309-438-2592. 147 J lwey@ilstu.edu
WEYAND, Joel .... 402-826-8242. 289 E joel.weyand@doane.edu
WEYERS, Lori, A .... 715-675-3331. 541 A weyers@ntc.edu
WEYGAND, Robert, A ..... 401-874-4312. 440 D bobw@uri.edu
WEYGANT, Susan .... 914-923-2397. 335 J sweygant@pace.edu
WEYHENMEYER, James, A .... 404-413-3516. 126 E jweyhenmeyer@gsu.edu
WEYL, Ronnie .... 908-526-1200. 305 B rweyl@raritanval.edu
WEZNER, Kelley, C .... 270-809-3340. 198 B kwezner@murraystate.edu
WHALEN, David .... 517-607-2321. 243 I david.whalen@hillsdale.edu
WHALEN, David .... 845-451-1406. 322 D d_whalen@culinary.edu
WHALEN, Eileen .... 206-744-3036. 524 G whalene@uw.edu
WHALEN, Jeff .... 209-588-5126... 77 I whalenj@yosemite.edu
WHALEN, Lynn .... 217-786-2219. 151 F lynn.whalen@llcc.edu
WHALEN, Michael .... 419-251-1824. 383 G michael.whalen@mercycollege.edu
WHALEN, Patricia .... 814-824-3070. 423 J pwhalen@mercyhurst.edu
WHALEN, Scott, M .... 315-255-1743. 316 D scott.whalen@cayuga-cc.edu
WHALEN, Shawn .... 415-338-1948... 35 E swhalen@sfsu.edu
WHALEN, Thomas .... 212-229-5456. 332 E whalent@newschool.edu
WHALEN, Timothy, F ..... 724-805-2592. 432 H timothy.whalen@stvincent.edu
WHALEY, Chris .... 865-882-4501. 461 E whaleycl@roanestate.edu
WHALEY, David .... 803-705-4742. 441 C whaleyd@benedict.edu
WHALEY, David .... 270-809-6849. 198 B dwhaley2@murraystate.edu
WHALEY, David, J .... 802-485-2300. 500 A davew@norwich.edu
WHALEY, Frances, A ...... 815-224-0387. 148 A frances_whaley@ivcc.edu
WHALEY, John .... 912-525-5000. 131 B jwhaley@scad.edu
WHALEY, Lindsay, J .... 603-646-4091. 296 G lindsay.j.whaley@dartmouth.edu

WHALEY, Melanie, A ...... 814-871-7470. 416 K
whaley003@gannon.edu
WHALEY, Michael .... 636-949-4561. 276 D
mwhaley@lindenwood.edu
WHALEY, Michael .... 636-949-4561. 276 D
WHALEY, Michael, J .... 860-685-3160... 92 H
mwhaley@wesleyan.edu
WHALEY, Mitchell, H ..... 765-285-5818. 164 B
mwhaley@bsu.edu
WHALEY, Sheree .... 530-242-7667... 65 G
swhaley@shastacollege.edu
WHALEY, Stephanie .... 912-344-2658. 120 G
stephanie.whaley@armstrong.edu
WHALEY, Tammey, E ..... 864-503-5210. 448 H
twhaley@uscupstate.edu
WHALEY, Vanessa .... 617-228-2346. 231 C
vwhaley@bhcc.mass.edu
WHANG, Kyu-Jung .... 607-255-4394. 322 A
kw253@cornell.edu
WHARTON, Barbara, I .... 614-823-1576. 387 K
bwharton@otterbein.edu
WHARTON, Beverly, A ... 712-279-5400. 176 B
beverly.wharton@briarcliff.edu
WHARTON, Bill .... 636-227-2100. 276 F
bill.wharton@logan.edu
WHARTON, Kristin .... 704-233-8366. 370 G
kwharton@wingate.edu
WHARTON, Martha, L .... 410-617-2988. 216 A
mwharton1@loyola.edu
WHARTON, Randy .... 567-661-7457. 387 L
william_wharton@owens.edu
WHATELY, Lorrie .... 253-752-2020. 519 K
admissions@faithseminary.edu
WHATLEY, John .... 209-473-5200... 47 F
john_whatley@heald.edu
WHATLEY, Melissa .... 657-278-2380... 33 E
mkwhatley@fullerton.edu
WHATLEY, Sherri .... 903-566-7247. 492 D
swhatley@uttyler.edu
WHEAT, Adriane, M .... 205-802-1200..... 3 C
adriane.wheat@vc.edu
WHEAT, Casie .... 650-949-7200... 44 N
wheatcasie@fhda.edu
WHEAT, Gary .... 417-626-1234. 279 J
gwheat@occ.edu
WHEAT, Zach .... 434-243-2096. 511 B
zjw6b@virginia.edu
WHEATLEY, Diane .... 757-789-1754. 512 D
dwheatley@es.vccs.edu
WHEATLEY, Jennifer .... 541-956-7291. 407 F
jwheatley@roguecc.edu
WHEATLEY, Michelle, M 509-313-4238. 520 A
wheatleym@gonzaga.edu
WHEATLY, Michele, G .... 304-293-5701. 530 D
michele.wheatly@mail.wvu.edu
WHEATLY, Stephen .... 805-493-3828... 31 H
wheatly@clunet.edu
WHEATON, David, M ..... 651-696-6211. 256 L
wheaton@macalester.edu
WHEATON, Janilee, B .... 216-687-2277. 377 F
j.wheaton@csuohio.edu
WHEATON, Jawuan .... 757-873-4235. 510 B
jwheaton@stratford.edu
WHEATON, Tom .... 605-642-6446. 451 G
tom.wheaton@bhsu.edu
WHEELAN, Elliot .... 804-524-5090. 515 D
ewheelan@vsu.edu
WHEELAND, Craig .... 610-519-4520. 436 F
craig.wheeland@villanova.edu
WHEELDON, Tim, T .... 515-263-6152. 178 G
twheeldon@grandview.edu
WHEELER, Amber .... 603-882-6923. 296 B
awheeler@ccsnh.edu
WHEELER, Brad .... 812-855-4717. 167 F
bwheeler@indiana.edu
WHEELER, Brad, C .... 812-855-3478. 167 E
bwheeler@indiana.edu
WHEELER, Cassandra, L 956-326-4473. 483 B
cwheeler@tamiu.edu
WHEELER, Cecilia, B ...... 919-528-4737. 364 F
wheelerc@vgcc.edu
WHEELER, Darrell, P ...... 312-915-7024. 151 H
dwheeler@luc.edu
WHEELER, Erin .... 518-631-9850. 348 K
wheelere@uniongraduatecollege.edu
WHEELER, Frank, E .... 402-363-5646. 293 I
fwheeler@york.edu
WHEELER, Gary .... 269-467-9945. 242 H
gwheeler@glenoaks.edu
WHEELER, Gregory .... 510-231-5000... 49 D
WHEELER, H. William .... 434-592-3003. 506 I
hwwheeler@liberty.edu
WHEELER, Ike .... 870-512-7865... 20 B
ike_wheeler@asun.edu
WHEELER, Jeff .... 803-754-4100. 443 C
WHEELER, Jessica .... 213-613-2200... 67 E
jessica_wheeler@sciarc.edu
WHEELER, John, D .... 216-368-5555. 375 J
john.wheeler@case.edu
WHEELER, John, J .... 843-953-5871. 442 A

WHEELER, Karen, J .... 501-569-3204... 24 B
kjwheeler@ualr.edu
WHEELER, Laurie .... 707-965-7200... 57 J
lwheeler@puc.edu
WHEELER, Linda .... 706-272-4547. 123 G
lwheeler@daltonstate.edu
WHEELER, Lisa .... 318-678-6000. 202 I
lwheeler@bpcc.edu
WHEELER, Lisa .... 952-358-8286. 260 B
lisa.wheeler@normandale.edu
WHEELER, Margi .... 630-353-8730. 141 G
mwheeler@chamberlain.edu
WHEELER, Mark .... 208-426-1140. 137 G
mwheeler@boisestate.edu
WHEELER, Mark .... 714-564-6319... 60 G
wheeler_mark@sac.edu
WHEELER, Mary .... 254-526-1200. 468 G
mary.wheeler@ctcd.edu
WHEELER, Mary Anne .... 850-973-1605. 109 H
wheelerm@nfcc.edu
WHEELER, Michelle .... 907-564-8210... 10 C
mwheeler@alaskapacific.edu
WHEELER, Michelle .... 248-476-1122. 246 G
mwheeler@mispp.edu
WHEELER, Nolan .... 360-442-2201. 521 A
nwheeler@lowercolumbia.edu
WHEELER, Pamela .... 503-413-7165. 404 A
pwheele@linfield.edu
WHEELER, Susan .... 309-694-8855. 146 E
swheeler@icc.edu
WHEELER, Susan, L .... 540-568-3727. 506 F
wheel2sl@jmu.edu
WHEELER, Terry .... 561-803-2500. 110 B
terry_wheeler@pba.edu
WHEELER, Thomas .... 816-604-5240. 277 E
thomas.wheeler@mcckc.edu
WHEELER, Tim .... 425-739-8252. 520 K
tim.wheeler@lwtech.edu
WHEELER, Walter .... 252-789-0259. 361 G
wwheeler@martincc.edu
WHEELER-DUNNER,
Aundrea .... 251-405-7100..... 2 D
awheeler@bishop.edu
WHEELESS, Kent .... 252-399-6338. 352 F
kwheeles@barton.edu
WHEELING, Barbara .... 406-657-1651. 287 C
barbara.wheeling@msubillings.edu
WHEELIS, Tina .... 870-368-2008... 22 E
twheelis@ozarka.edu
WHEELOCK, Pam .... 612-624-3557. 264 G
wheelock@umn.edu
WHEELOCK, William ...... 330-941-3165. 394 A
wwheelock@ysu.edu
WHEELUS, Angie .... 678-872-8012. 125 C
awheelus@highlands.edu
WHEELWRIGHT,
Steven, C .... 808-675-3700. 135 C
wheelwrights@byuh.edu
WHELAN, Ann .... 212-229-5656. 332 E
whelan2@newschool.edu
WHELAN, JR.,
Donald, J .... 817-257-7785. 484 I
d.whelan@tcu.edu
WHELAN, Janet .... 410-837-4779. 221 A
jwhelan@ubalt.edu
WHELAN, John .... 254-710-8562. 467 G
John_Whelan@baylor.edu
WHELAN, Matthew .... 631-632-6857. 342 C
matthew.whelan@stonybrook.edu
WHELAN, Michaele .... 617-824-8570. 226 A
michaele_whelan@emerson.edu
WHELAN, Robert .... 718-289-5162. 317 B
robert.whelan@bcc.cuny.edu
WHELIHAN, Tom .... 218-846-3778. 259 F
tom.whelihan@minnesota.edu
WHERRY, Cassandra, J .. 641-269-3424. 178 H
wherry@grinnell.edu
WHIDDON, Tifini .... 936-633-4555. 465 J
twhiddon@angelina.edu
WHIFFEN, Sarah, E .... 585-785-1284. 324 D
whiffes@flcc.edu
WHILLOCK, David .... 817-257-5918. 484 I
d.whillock@tcu.edu
WHIPKEY, Brady .... 304-424-8200. 530 E
brady.whipkey@wvup.edu
WHIPPLE, Ashlee .... 319-385-6375. 179 K
ashlee.whipple@iwc.edu
WHIPPLE, P. Michael ..... 504-861-5543. 205 H
pmwhipple@loyno.edu
WHIPPLE, Richard Dick .. 830-591-7326. 481 C
rbwhipple@swtjc.edu
WHIPPY, Helen .... 808-735-4825. 135 D
helen.whippy@chaminade.edu
WHISENAND, Gary, D .... 509-777-4313. 525 F
gwhisenand@whitworth.edu
WHISENANT, Mary Alice 540-365-4235. 504 L
mwhisenant@ferrum.edu
WHISENHUNT, Denise ... 619-388-3464... 62 D
dwhisenh@sdccd.edu
WHISENNAND, Jack .... 405-382-9950. 399 I
j.whisennand@sscok.edu

WHISLER, Janice .... 219-785-5283. 172 A
jwhlsler@pnc.edu
WHISLER, Ruth .... 928-344-7505... 11 L
ruth.whisler@azwestern.edu
WHISLER, Ryan .... 740-477-7721. 385 L
rwhisler@ohiochristian.edu
WHISMAN, Kathryn, E .... 520-621-3324... 18 F
kwhisman@email.arizona.edu
WHISMAN, Linda, A .... 213-738-6729... 68 C
library@swlaw.edu
WHISNANT, David, M .... 864-597-4294. 449 I
whistnantdm@wofford.edu
WHISNANT, John .... 504-278-6479. 203 F
jwhisnant@nunez.edu
WHISNANT, Rebecca, S . 937-229-3421. 391 C
RWhisnant1@udayton.edu
WHITACRE, Aaron .... 540-868-7073. 512 H
lwhitacre@lfcc.edu
WHITACRE, Caroline ...... 614-292-1582. 386 E
whitacre.3@osu.edu
WHITACRE, Norma .... 360-475-7360. 521 H
nwhitacre@olympic.edu
WHITAKER, A. Dale .... 765-494-0615. 171 M
dwhittake@purdue.edu
WHITAKER, Adrienne ..... 804-524-1062. 515 D
awhitaker@vsu.edu
WHITAKER, Cindy .... 505-254-7575... 17 R
cwhitaker@suva.edu
WHITAKER, Dan .... 603-448-2445. 297 A
dwhitaker@lebanoncollege.edu
WHITAKER, Debbie .... 951-222-8434... 61 A
debbie.whitaker@rccd.edu
WHITAKER, Evans, P ..... 864-231-2100. 441 B
ewhitaker@andersonuniversity.edu
WHITAKER, Gwen, D ...... 336-734-7471. 360 E
gwhitaker@forsythtech.edu
WHITAKER, Helene, M ... 610-861-5460. 425 D
hwhitaker@northampton.edu
WHITAKER, Janice .... 972-825-4759. 481 F
jwhitaker@sagu.edu
WHITAKER, Jason .... 859-233-8289. 199 I
jwhitaker@transy.edu
WHITAKER, Keila .... 405-945-3252. 398 C
WHITAKER, Keisha .... 407-843-3984. 105 P
kwhitaker@fortiscollege.edu
WHITAKER, Michelle ...... 910-672-1958. 367 D
mwhitaker@uncfsu.edu
WHITAKER, Rob .... 912-478-5491. 126 C
rwhitaker@georgiasouthern.edu
WHITAKER, Scott .... 505-428-1268. 311 J
scott.whitaker@sfcc.edu
WHITAKER, Shari .... 315-655-7332. 316 E
sswhitaker@cazenovia.edu
WHITAKER, Whit .... 706-236-2227. 121 G
awhitaker@berry.edu
WHITAKER, Xavier .... 903-923-2319. 471 J
xwhitaker@etbu.edu
WHITAKER-LEA, Laura ... 828-689-1212. 356 F
lwhitaker-lea@mhc.edu
WHITCOMB, Connie, F .. 716-375-2351. 338 E
cwhitcomb@sbu.edu
WHITCOMB, Cynthia ...... 860-231-5387... 92 F
cwhitcomb@usj.edu
WHITCOMB, Debi .... 205-726-2885..... 6 F
drwhitco@samford.edu
WHITCOMB, Michael, E . 860-685-5340... 92 H
mwhitcomb@wesleyan.edu
WHITE, A. Jay .... 812-941-2362. 168 F
jwhite04@ius.edu
WHITE, Aaron .... 901-272-5136. 456 F
finaid@mca.edu
WHITE, Alisa .... 903-566-7104. 492 D
awhite@uttyler.edu
WHITE, Alison Boord ..... 302-225-6343... 93 H
whitea@gbc.edu
WHITE, Andrew, W .... 207-786-6491. 209 F
awhite@bates.edu
WHITE, Ann, H .... 812-465-1173. 174 D
AWhite@usi.edu
WHITE, Anne .... 253-964-6623. 522 C
awhite@pierce.ctc.edu
WHITE, Anthony .... 410-225-2311. 216 C
awhite03@mica.edu
WHITE, Barbara .... 720-872-5608... 79 C
bwhite@ccu.edu
WHITE, Barbara, A .... 208-496-7010. 137 H
whiteb@byui.edu
WHITE, Barbara, L .... 972-860-8348. 470 I
BWhite@dcccd.edu
WHITE, Belva .... 404-727-2584. 124 E
belva.white@ctrl.emory.edu
WHITE, Bradley .... 615-963-5817. 459 E
bwhite2@tnstate.edu
WHITE, Brenda .... 770-975-4000. 122 I
WHITE, Brian .... 503-768-7307. 403 K
bdwhite@lclark.edu
WHITE, Byron .... 216-687-3577. 377 F
byron.white@csuohio.edu
WHITE, Byron .... 216-523-7292. 377 F
byron.white@csuohio.edu

WHITE, Caleb .... 608-822-2446. 541 C
cwhite@swtc.edu
WHITE, Carolee .... 315-228-7422. 320 F
cwhite@colgate.edu
WHITE, Carolee .... 315-228-7488. 320 F
cwhite@colgate.edu
WHITE, Catherine, D ..... 256-765-4291..... 9 C
cdwhite1@una.edu
WHITE, Charles, B .... 210-999-7345. 488 C
cwhite@trinity.edu
WHITE, Charlie .... 276-223-4848. 514 F
cwhite@wcc.vccs.edu
WHITE, Christopher .... 312-567-3734. 147 F
whitec@iit.edu
WHITE, Courtney .... 864-646-1484. 447 D
cwhite12@tctc.edu
WHITE, Craig .... 217-424-6344. 153 C
ccwhite@millikin.edu
WHITE, Curtis .... 419-289-5777. 374 C
cwhite@ashland.edu
WHITE, Cynthia, L .... 972-758-3871. 469 G
clwhite@collin.edu
WHITE, Daniel .... 907-474-6222... 10 I
dmwhite@alaska.edu
WHITE, Danny .... 716-645-3454. 341 F
ub-athleticdirector@buffalo.edu
WHITE, Darren .... 817-531-5808. 488 A
dwhite@txwes.edu
WHITE, David .... 334-448-5112..... 7 H
whited@troy.edu
WHITE, David .... 252-328-1552. 367 B
whited@ecu.edu
WHITE, David .... 304-424-8225. 530 E
david.white@wvup.edu
WHITE, David .... 336-887-3000. 355 N
dwhite@laureluniversity.edu
WHITE, David, B .... 828-398-7175. 357 N
dwhite@abtech.edu
WHITE, Deborah .... 810-762-3200. 251 E
debwhite@umflint.edu
WHITE, Deborah .... 978-934-2173. 229 B
Deborah_White@uml.edu
WHITE, Deborah .... 330-972-8259. 390 E
dwhite1@uakron.edu
WHITE, Dewayne .... 212-678-3315. 347 G
white@exchange.tc.columbia.edu
WHITE, Diane .... 703-284-1610. 507 B
diane.white@marymount.edu
WHITE, Diane, M .... 707-864-7000... 66 G
diane.white@solano.edu
WHITE, Don .... 910-642-7141. 364 A
Don.White@sccnc.edu
WHITE, Donald, T .... 540-464-7251. 515 B
whitedt@vmi.edu
WHITE, Donna .... 304-829-7622. 526 D
dwhite@bethanywv.edu
WHITE, Douglas .... 856-691-8600. 301 A
dwhite@cccnj.edu
WHITE, Dwayne .... 601-877-6500. 265 G
dwhite1@alcorn.edu
WHITE, Eddie .... 615-248-1242. 462 D
ewhite@trevecca.edu
WHITE, Erin .... 910-672-1128. 367 D
ewhite@uncfsu.edu
WHITE, Ernie .... 919-735-5151. 364 H
ewhite@waynecc.edu
WHITE, Evelyn, M .... 256-761-6216..... 7 F
ewhite@talladega.edu
WHITE, Gary .... 215-953-5999... 96 F
gary.white@strayer.edu
WHITE, Gary .... 615-226-3990. 455 N
gwhite@nadcedu.com
WHITE, Gary, R .... 805-893-2182... 72 B
gary.white@sa.ucsb.edu
WHITE, Hayne .... 704-272-5259. 363 G
hwhite@spcc.edu
WHITE, Heather, B .... 352-392-1601. 116 A
heatherwhite@crc.ufl.edu
WHITE, Ian, K .... 973-618-3236. 300 A
iwhite@caldwell.edu
WHITE, Jackie .... 478-757-3400. 122 F
jwhite@centralgatech.edu
WHITE, Jacqueline, M .... 401-865-2811. 439 E
jwhite@providence.edu
WHITE, James .... 509-313-6568. 520 A
whitej@gonzaga.edu
WHITE, James, M .... 410-651-8440. 219 E
jmwhite@umes.edu
WHITE, Jerre .... 714-556-3610... 74 D
jwhite@vanguard.edu
WHITE, Jerry, L .... 517-750-1200. 250 E
jwhite@arbor.edu
WHITE, Jessie .... 254-659-7841. 473 A
jwhite@hillcollege.edu
WHITE, Jim .... 231-995-1939. 248 B
jwhite@nmc.edu
WHITE, Joan .... 928-226-4217... 13 B
joan.white@coconino.edu
WHITE, Joel .... 541-917-4840. 404 B
whitej@linnbenton.edu

WHITE, John .... 503-352-7355. 407 A
whiteja@pacificu.edu
WHITE, John .... 404-687-4522. 123 C
whitej@ctsnet.edu
WHITE, John, A .... 413-748-3408. 236 I
jawhite@springfieldcollege.edu
WHITE, John, E .... 609-497-7880. 304 D
john.white@ptsem.edu
WHITE, John, V .... 702-895-3301. 294 I
john.white@unlv.edu
WHITE, Jonathan .... 956-380-8194. 479 B
jwhite@riogrande.edu
WHITE, Jonathan, S .... 973-290-4720. 300 F
jwhite@cse.edu
WHITE, Judi .... 918-647-1474. 394 I
jpwhite@carlalbert.edu
WHITE, Julie, A .... 315-255-1743. 316 D
julie.white@cayuga-cc.edu
WHITE, Julie, R .... 315-464-4816. 342 E
whitejul@upstate.edu
WHITE, Justin .... 870-584-4471... 24 F
jwhite@cccua.edu
WHITE, Karen .... 207-453-5117. 210 L
kwhite@kvcc.me.edu
WHITE, Karen, K .... 727-341-4656. 112 E
white.karenkaufman@spcollege.edu
WHITE, Karen, L .... 574-520-4477. 168 E
kwhite@iusb.edu
WHITE, Kelly, L .... 361-698-1641. 471 G
kwhite@delmar.edu
WHITE, Kenneth, L .... 435-797-2201. 497 B
ken.white@usu.edu
WHITE, Kevin .... 919-684-2431. 354 A
kwhite@duaa.duke.edu
WHITE, Kristie, L .... 804-342-3565. 515 F
klwhite@vuu.edu
WHITE, Kyle .... 918-335-6289. 398 F
kwhite@okwu.edu
WHITE, Laura .... 276-326-4294. 502 H
lwhite@bluefield.edu
WHITE, Lauri .... 309-341-5461. 141 A
lwhite@sandburg.edu
WHITE, Laurie .... 386-506-4499. 101 G
whitela@DaytonaState.edu
WHITE, Lawrence .... 302-831-7361... 94 B
lawwhite@udel.edu
WHITE, Linda .... 901-435-1316. 455 M
linda_white@loc.edu
WHITE, Lisa .... 417-626-1234. 279 J
white.lisa@occ.edu
WHITE, Lori, S .... 214-768-2821. 481 A
lswhite@smu.edu
WHITE, Lynn .... 812-888-4241. 174 F
lwhite@vinu.edu
WHITE, M. Chrisopher ... 252-398-6221. 353 H
whitec@chowan.edu
WHITE, Margaret, A .... 630-637-5454. 154 F
mawhite@noctrl.edu
WHITE, Marsha, S .... 770-720-5512. 130 G
msw@reinhardt.edu
WHITE, JR.,
Marshall Sonny .... 803-738-7600. 445 C
whites@midlandstech.edu
WHITE, Mary Jo .... 206-934-5378. 523 A
maryjo.white@seattlecolleges.edu
WHITE, Maureen .... 860-701-5047... 90 G
white_m@mitchell.edu
WHITE, Michael .... 559-638-3641... 69 A
michael.white@reedleycollege.edu
WHITE, Michael .... 612-343-4434. 262 X
mwhite@northcentral.edu
WHITE, Michael, L .... 319-399-8643. 176 G
mwhite@coe.edu
WHITE, Michele, M .... 540-568-6281. 506 F
whitemm@jmu.edu
WHITE, Michelle .... 918-647-1399. 394 I
mwhite@carlalbert.edu
WHITE, Monica, J .... 716-673-3271. 342 A
monica.white@fredonia.edu
WHITE, Nicole .... 615-687-6904. 452 G
nwhite@abcnash.edu
WHITE, Norman .... 863-638-7264. 119 C
norman.white@warner.edu
WHITE, O. Ivan .... 903-927-3384. 495 A
oiwhite@wileyc.edu
WHITE, Olivia, G .... 301-696-3573. 215 D
owhite@hood.edu
WHITE, P. Phillip .... 518-629-7149. 326 G
p.white@hvcc.edu
WHITE, Pamela .... 515-294-5380. 175 H
pjwhite@iastate.edu
WHITE, Pamela .... 413-755-4452. 233 A
pjwhite@stcc.edu
WHITE, Patricia .... 305-284-2394. 118 F
pwhite@miami.edu
WHITE, Patrick, E .... 217-424-6208. 153 C
pwhite@millikin.edu
WHITE, Patty .... 406-447-4454. 285 G
pwhite@carroll.edu
WHITE, Perry, D .... 316-284-5241. 184 J
pwhite@bethelks.edu

WHITE, Randy .... 260-665-4171. 173 E
whiter@trine.edu
WHITE, Ray .... 334-241-9538..... 7 H
grwhite@troy.edu
WHITE, Ray .... 425-564-2446. 517 A
ray.white@bellevuecollege.edu
WHITE, Rebecca .... 229-209-5145. 120 D
rebeccawhite@andrewcollege.edu
WHITE, Rebecca, H .... 706-542-7140. 133 C
rhwhite@uga.edu
WHITE, Renee .... 617-521-2079. 236 G
renee.white@simmons.edu
WHITE, Rex .... 713-221-8505. 489 D
whiter@uhd.edu
WHITE, Rhonda .... 336-517-2183. 352 H
rjwhite@bennett.edu
WHITE, Richard, D .... 225-578-5297. 204 O
rwhit12@lsu.edu
WHITE, Richard E, T .... 206-726-5127. 518 G
retwhite@cornish.edu
WHITE, Robert .... 870-574-4463... 23 G
rwhite@sautech.edu
WHITE, Robert, L .... 937-327-7411. 393 E
rwhite@wittenberg.edu
WHITE, Roger .... 504-865-2427. 205 H
rwhite@loyno.edu
WHITE, Ronald, J .... 605-394-2493. 452 A
ronald.white@sdsmt.edu
WHITE, Samantha .... 573-875-7352. 272 G
sjwhite@ccis.edu
WHITE, Sammis, B .... 414-227-3203. 537 A
sbwhite@uwm.edu
WHITE, Samuel, L .... 601-877-6142. 265 G
slwhite@alcorn.edu
WHITE, Samuel, L .... 601-877-6388. 265 G
slwhite@alcorn.edu
WHITE, Shae .... 254-442-5127. 468 I
shae.white@cisco.edu
WHITE, Sharon .... 203-251-8406... 92 A
sharon.white@uconn.edu
WHITE, Shelley .... 828-398-7937. 357 N
swhite@abtech.edu
WHITE, Stephanie, M .... 804-257-5745. 515 F
swhite@vuu.edu
WHITE, Stephen .... 718-862-7548. 329 M
stephen.white@manhattan.edu
WHITE, Stephen, E .... 401-254-3681. 440 B
swhite@rwu.edu
WHITE, Stephen, F .... 615-898-5454. 459 D
stephen.white@mtsu.edu
WHITE, Steven .... 316-978-3782. 191 F
steven.white@wichita.edu
WHITE, Sue .... 602-274-4300... 12 K
swhite@brymanschool.edu
WHITE, Susan, E .... 912-583-3169. 122 B
swhite@bpc.edu
WHITE, Susan, K .... 913-627-4125. 187 L
swhite@kckcc.edu
WHITE, Tamisia .... 212-870-1229. 334 C
finaid@nyts.edu
WHITE, Tammy, S .... 205-652-3651..... 9 F
thw@uwa.edu
WHITE, Terry, A .... 615-460-6617. 453 C
terry.white@belmont.edu
WHITE, Thelma .... 270-706-8409. 195 A
thelma.white@kctcs.edu
WHITE, Theodore .... 816-235-1330. 283 D
whitetc@umkc.edu
WHITE, Timothy, L .... 352-846-0850. 116 A
tlwhite@ufl.edu
WHITE, Timothy, P .... 562-951-4700... 32 E
twhite@calstate.edu
WHITE, Tracy .... 715-234-8176. 538 E
tracy.white@uwc.edu
WHITE, W. Scott .... 704-406-4259. 354 C
swhite@gardner-webb.edu
WHITE, Wayman .... 252-335-0821. 359 F
waywhite@albemarle.edu
WHITE, Wendy, S .... 215-746-5240. 435 B
wendy.white@ogc.upenn.edu
WHITE, William, A .... 407-582-1185. 118 M
bwhite@valenciacollege.edu
WHITE CASTENADA,
April .... 626-395-8167... 31 E
april@caltech.edu
WHITE-DANIELS, Sheila . 410-462-8043. 213 F
swhite-daniels@bccc.edu
WHITE SIMMONS,
Renita .... 718-951-5137. 317 C
rwsimmons@brooklyn.cuny.edu
WHITECAVAGE, Michele 714-449-7404... 67 D
mwhitecavage@scco.edu
WHITED, Frances, P .... 330-287-1216. 386 F
whited.16@osu.edu
WHITED, Jimmy .... 276-944-6240. 504 H
jwhited@ehc.edu
WHITEFIELD, Philip, D ... 573-341-7887. 284 A
pwhite@mst.edu
WHITEFORD, Aaron .... 503-768-7944. 403 K
ahw@lclark.edu

WHITEHAIR, Bruce .... 814-332-2451. 409 D
bwhitehair@allegheny.edu
WHITEHEAD, Carolyn .... 303-492-5366... 85 L
carolyn.whitehead@cufund.org
WHITEHEAD, Doug .... 435-652-7500. 497 E
dkw@dixie.edu
WHITEHEAD, George .... 435-652-7906. 497 E
whiteheg@dixie.edu
WHITEHEAD, Gwen .... 409-882-3933. 486 G
gwen.whitehead@lsco.edu
WHITEHEAD, Heidi, M ... 812-888-4313. 174 F
hwhitehead@vinu.edu
WHITEHEAD, Joe .... 601-266-4884. 270 E
joe.whitehead@usm.edu
WHITEHEAD, JR.,
Joe, B .... 336-334-7965. 367 E
jbwhiteh@ncat.edu
WHITEHEAD, Johnny .... 713-348-6000. 479 A
johnny.whitehead@rice.edu
WHITEHEAD, Joyce, E ... 630-889-6610. 154 E
jwhitehead@nuhs.edu
WHITEHEAD, Kimberly ... 304-766-3147. 530 C
WHITEHEAD, Richard, G 540-261-4347. 509 K
richard.whitehead@svu.edu
WHITEHEAD, Sharon, F . 606-679-8501. 196 D
sharon.whitehead@kctcs.edu
WHITEHEAD, Susan .... 617-984-1721. 235 I
swhitehead@quincycollege.edu
WHITEHEAD, Teresa .... 575-769-4066. 309 F
teresa.whitehead@clovis.edu
WHITEHEAD, Wesley .... 229-248-2560. 121 E
wesley.whitehead@bainbridge.edu
WHITEHOUSE, Deborah . 859-622-1523. 193 P
deborah.whitehouse@eku.edu
WHITEHOUSE, Donna .... 434-381-6479. 510 F
dwhitehouse@sbc.edu
WHITEHURST, Alan .... 540-261-4318. 509 K
alan.whitehurst@svu.edu
WHITEHURST, Alan .... 540-261-4318. 509 K
alalan.whitehurst@svu.edu
WHITEHURST-MCLEAN,
Makitta .... 252-335-3355. 367 C
mmmclean@mail.ecsu.edu
WHITELAW, Lydia .... 610-896-1177. 418 F
lwhitela@haverford.edu
WHITELEY, Herbert, E .... 217-333-2760. 162 A
hwhiteley@illinois.edu
WHITELEY, Janell .... 360-475-7504. 521 H
jwhiteley@olympic.edu
WHITELY, Patricia, A .... 305-284-4922. 118 F
pwhitely@miami.edu
WHITEMAN, Betty .... 386-822-8869. 117 C
bwhiteman@stetson.edu
WHITEMAN, Charles, H . 814-863-0448. 426 A
chw17@psu.edu
WHITEMAN, Ray .... 574-807-7139. 164 D
ray.whiteman@bethelcollege.edu
WHITEMORE, Alan, T .... 617-989-4307. 237 G
whitemorea@wit.edu
WHITESIDE, Christopher 559-442-4600... 68 I
christopher.whiteside@fresnocitycollege.edu
WHITESIDE, Harold, D ... 615-898-2900. 459 D
harold.whiteside@mtsu.edu
WHITEY, Jeff .... 541-888-7634. 407 H
jwhitey@socc.edu
WHITFIELD, Aleczander .. 704-378-3501. 355 K
awhitfield@jcsu.edu
WHITFIELD, Gary .... 209-588-5112... 77 I
whitfieldg@yosemite.edu
WHITFIELD, Jacques .... 530-741-6976... 77 K
jwhitfie@yccd.edu
WHITFIELD, Keith .... 919-660-0330. 354 A
keith.whitfield@duke.edu
WHITFIELD, Rick, N .... 910-962-3383. 369 C
whitfieldr@uncw.edu
WHITFIELD, Walter, V .... 252-789-0232. 361 G
wwhitfield@martincc.edu
WHITFILL, Jill .... 731-352-4083. 453 D
whitfillj@bethelu.edu
WHITFORD, Betty Lou .... 334-844-4448..... 1 G
blw0017@auburn.edu
WHITFORD, Daryl .... 808-675-3211. 135 C
whitford@byuh.edu
WHITFORD, Jewel, L .... 406-395-4313. 288 D
jewelwhitford@hotmail.com
WHITHAM, John, H .... 610-526-1308. 409 F
john.whitham@theamericancollege.edu
WHITHAUS, Becky .... 573-897-5000. 276 E
WHITING, Alison .... 808-675-3552. 135 C
whitinga@byuh.edu
WHITING, Mary .... 870-460-1026... 24 D
whitingm@uamont.edu
WHITING, Sarah, M .... 713-348-4044. 479 A
sarah.whiting@rice.edu
WHITING, Scott .... 334-874-5700..... 3 A
swhiting@ccal.edu
WHITING, Shari, K .... 315-859-4313. 325 E
swhiting@hamilton.edu
WHITING, Svea .... 970-943-7057... 86 I
swhiting@western.edu

WHITIS, Andrew .... 419-434-4767. 391 D
whitis@findlay.edu
WHITIS, Matt .... 815-939-5350. 155 H
mwhitis@olivet.edu
WHITIS, Sarah .... 530-842-1245... 41 A
swhitis@siskiyous.edu
WHITLATCH, Frank .... 707-826-5101... 35 C
frank@humboldt.edu
WHITLATCH, Michael, D 712-749-2172. 176 D
whitlatch@bvu.edu
WHITLEDGE, Terry .... 907-474-7229... 10 I
terry@ims.uaf.edu
WHITLEY, Darrell, S .... 252-985-5105. 365 D
dwhitley@ncwc.edu
WHITLEY, Freddy .... 252-823-5166. 360 C
whitleyf@edgecombe.edu
WHITLEY, Norman .... 504-280-7120. 205 G
nwhitley@uno.edu
WHITLEY, Rebecca .... 575-492-2112. 312 M
rwhitley@usw.edu
WHITLING, Jacqueline ... 570-484-3045. 429 B
jwhitlin@lhup.edu
WHITLOCK, David, W .... 405-585-5801. 397 C
david.whitlock@okbu.edu
WHITLOCK, John, L .... 727-816-3325. 110 E
whitloj@phcc.edu
WHITLOCK, Luder .... 954-771-0376. 108 Q
WHITLOCK, Marshall .... 414-475-4846. 183 B
whitlockm@uiu.edu
WHITLOCK, Roger .... 601-635-2111. 266 H
rwhitlock@eccc.edu
WHITLOCK, Sharon, K ... 765-494-9708. 171 M
whitlock@purdue.edu
WHITLOCK, Stephen .... 678-839-6426. 133 I
swhitlock@westga.edu
WHITLOCK, Tonya .... 678-664-0532. 134 H
tonya.whitlock@westgatech.edu
WHITLOCK, Veronica .... 212-472-1500. 334 B
vwhitlock@nysid.edu
WHITMAN, Carl, E .... 209-667-3343... 35 B
cwhitman@csustan.edu
WHITMAN, Christina .... 734-764-0747. 251 C
cwhitman@umich.edu
WHITMAN, David .... 651-604-4118. 257 A
WHITMAN, Deirdre .... 914-674-7316. 330 J
dwhitman@mercy.edu
WHITMAN, Joshua .... 608-785-8616. 536 G
jwhitman@uwlax.edu
WHITMAN, Melissa .... 252-527-6223. 361 F
mwhitman@lenoircc.edu
WHITMAN, Rebecca, R .. 616-234-4010. 243 B
rwhitman@grcc.edu
WHITMAN, William, D ... 989-386-6696. 247 B
wwhitman@midmich.edu
WHITMER, Ann .... 517-629-0440. 239 A
awhitmer@albion.edu
WHITMIRE, Teresa .... 479-619-4175... 22 C
twhitmire@nwacc.edu
WHITMIRE, Thomas .... 215-884-8942. 438 A
registrar@woninstitute.edu
WHITMORE, Joe .... 256-782-5777..... 4 K
whitmore@jsu.edu
WHITMORE, Karen .... 973-328-5671. 300 G
kwhitmore@ccm.edu
WHITMORE,
Kimberly, N .... 515-574-1138. 179 D
whitmore@iowacentral.edu
WHITMORE, Michele .... 802-635-1452. 501 D
michele.whitmore@jsc.edu
WHITMORE-HANSEN,
Anne .... 518-564-2090. 344 B
hansenaw@plattsburgh.edu
WHITNEY, Candice .... 408-848-4754... 45 F
cwhitney@gavilan.edu
WHITNEY, Gleaves .... 616-331-2770. 243 C
whitneyg@gvsu.edu
WHITNEY, Glenda .... 573-897-5000. 276 E
WHITNEY, Heidi .... 802-468-6072. 501 B
heidi.whitney@castleton.edu
WHITNEY, Jarrid .... 626-395-6341... 31 E
WHITNEY, Joan, G .... 610-519-4050. 436 F
joan.whitney@villanova.edu
WHITNEY, Karen, M .... 814-393-2220. 428 C
president@clarion.edu
WHITNEY, Patricia, C .... 207-859-5002. 209 J
pcwhitne@colby.edu
WHITNEY, Patrick, F .... 312-595-4900. 147 F
whitney@id.iit.edu
WHITNEY, Paul .... 401-874-5224. 440 D
pwhitney@uri.edu
WHITNEY, Phyllis .... 319-385-6206. 179 K
phyllis.whitney@iwc.edu
WHITNEY, Richard .... 641-269-3300. 178 H
whitney@grinnell.edu
WHITSON, Brian .... 757-221-7876. 503 N
bwwhit@wm.edu
WHITSON, Janet .... 512-313-3000. 469 L
janet.whitson@concordia.edu
WHITSON, Tony .... 901-435-1733. 455 M
tony_whitson@loc.edu

WHITT, Cynthia, L .... 423-869-6394. 456 A
cindy.whitt@lmunet.edu
WHITT, David, T .... 205-726-2386..... 6 F
dtwhitt@samford.edu
WHITT, Edith, L .... 828-689-1151. 356 F
ewhitt@mhc.edu
WHITT, Elizabeth .... 314-977-3951. 281 I
ewhitt@slu.edu
WHITT, Marc .... 859-622-2301. 193 P
marc.whitt@eku.edu
WHITT, Susan .... 910-521-6212. 369 B
susan.whitt@uncp.edu
WHITTAKER, Robert .... 718-960-7806. 318 A
robert.whittaker@lehman.cuny.edu
WHITTAKER, Robert, E ... 802-626-6427. 501 E
robert.whittaker@lyndonstate.edu
WHITTAKER-DAVIS,
Sharon .... 205-366-8838..... 7 E
swhittaker@stillman.edu
WHITTEMORE, Nancy ...... 661-255-1050... 31 C
nwhittem@calarts.edu
WHITTEN, James .... 207-844-2103. 211 A
jwhitten@smccme.edu
WHITTEN, Mandy .... 864-503-5420. 448 H
mwhitten@uscupstaet.edu
WHITTEN, Pamela .... 517-355-3410. 246 H
pwhitten@msu.edu
WHITTEN, Patrice .... 850-484-1714. 110 G
pwhitten@pensacolastate.edu
WHITTEN,
Virgina "Ginni" .... 281-425-6302. 475 I
vwhitten@lee.edu
WHITTENBURG, Nashia . 912-344-2514. 120 G
nashia.whittenburg@armstrong.edu
WHITTENBURG, Scott ..... 406-243-6670. 286 H
scott.whittenburg@umontana.edu
WHITTENTON, Kathy ...... 870-307-7505... 21 H
kathy.whittenton@lyon.edu
WHITTEY, Chris .... 216-421-7455. 377 C
cwhittey@cia.edu
WHITTINGHAM,
Michelle .... 831-459-1453... 72 C
michelle@ucsc.edu
WHITTINGHAM, Rachel . 501-205-8876... 20 I
rwhittingham@cbc.edu
WHITTINGTON,
Christine, A .... 336-272-7102. 354 E
cwhittington@greensboro.edu
WHITTINGTON, Connie .. 318-869-5101. 201 H
cwhitt@centenary.edu
WHITTINGTON, Donna ... 225-675-8270. 203 G
dwhittington@rpcc.edu
WHITTINGTON,
Elizabeth .... 713-623-2040. 466 G
ewhittington@aii.edu
WHITTINGTON,
Gerald, O .... 336-278-5434. 354 B
whitting@elon.edu
WHITTINGTON,
Kimberly .... 281-425-6457. 475 I
kwhittin@lee.edu
WHITTINGTON, Lee .... 828-766-1196. 361 H
lwhittington@mayland.edu
WHITTINGTON, Marcia .. 608-663-6713. 532 I
mwhittington@edgewood.edu
WHITTINGTON, Ray .... 312-362-6781. 143 H
rwhittin@depaul.edu
WHITTLESEY, Valerie, D . 770-423-6023. 127 N
vwhittle@kennesaw.edu
WHITTUM, Terry, E .... 904-256-7099. 107 Q
twhittu@ju.edu
WHITWELL, Jeff .... 615-898-2700. 459 D
jeff.whitwell@mtsu.edu
WHITWORTH, Bruce .... 559-278-2795... 33 D
bwhitwor@csufresno.edu
WHITWORTH, Ling, Y ..... 434-395-2319. 506 J
whitworthly@longwood.edu
WHORLEY, Frank .... 410-951-2600. 220 B
fwhorley@coppin.edu
WHORTON, Susan .... 864-656-6256. 442 C
whorton@clemson.edu
WHTYE, William .... 262-564-3228. 540 A
whytew@gtc.edu
WHYNOTT, Anne .... 262-564-2758. 540 A
whynotta@gtc.edu
WHYTE, Novia, P .... 516-463-6928. 326 D
novia.p.whyte@hofstra.edu
WHYTE, William .... 262-564-3228. 540 A
whytew@gtc.edu
WIBBENMEYER, Kana .... 773-508-3489. 151 H
kwibben@luc.edu
WIBLE, Doug .... 949-214-3029... 41 I
doug.wible@cui.edu
WICHERN, Adam .... 718-405-3776. 320 G
adam.wichern@mountsaintvincent.edu
WICHERT, Jerome, L ...... 580-774-3786. 400 B
jerome.wichert@swosu.edu
WICHROSKI, Pamela, J .. 207-786-6207. 209 F
pwichros@bates.edu
WICHSER, John .... 301-696-3545. 215 D
wichser@hood.edu

WICK, Martha .... 641-683-5231. 179 A
martha.wick@indianhills.edu
WICK, Michael, R .... 715-836-2033. 536 E
wickmr@uwec.edu
WICKEHAM, Daniel .... 414-955-8826. 534 C
dwickeha@mcw.edu
WICKER, Jeff .... 803-321-5676. 445 G
jeffrey.wicker@newberry.edu
WICKER-MCCREE,
Ingrid, L .... 919-530-7057. 368 A
iwicker@nccu.edu
WICKERT, Jonathan, A ... 515-294-0070. 175 H
wickert@iastate.edu
WICKES, David .... 203-576-4278... 91 G
dwickes@bridgeport.edu
WICKHAM, Larry .... 575-461-4413. 309 M
larryw@mesalands.edu
WICKIZER, Della, H .... 434-395-2074. 506 J
wickizerdh@longwood.edu
WICKLAND, Mary .... 409-984-6115. 486 H
mary.wickland@lamarpa.edu
WICKLESS, Megan .... 402-552-6119. 288 L
wicklessmegan@clarksoncollege.edu
WICKLIFFE, Cari, S .... 314-977-2350. 281 I
wicklics@slu.edu
WICKLUND, Greg, A ...... 817-202-6743. 481 E
wicklund@swau.edu
WICKLUND, Joe .... 218-723-6479. 254 K
jwicklun@css.edu
WICKS, Donna .... 810-762-7853. 244 Q
dwicks@kettering.edu
WICKS, Michelle, D .... 304-205-6705. 528 B
mwicks@kvctc.edu
WICKSTROM, Sherry ...... 763-576-4874. 257 Q
swickstrom@anokatech.edu
WIDDERS, Pat .... 479-788-7390... 24 A
pat.widders@uafs.edu
WIDEMAN, Gene .... 918-595-7262. 400 E
gene.wideman@tulsacc.edu
WIDENHOFER,
Stephen, B .... 217-424-6300. 153 C
swidenhofer@millikin.edu
WIDGER, Mari Jo .... 308-345-8106. 290 J
widgerm@mpcc.edu
WIDING, II, Robert, E ... 216-368-1156. 375 J
WIDMER, Robert, D .... 309-268-8100. 146 B
rob.widmer@heartland.edu
WIDMER, Robet, D .... 309-268-8100. 146 B
rob.widmer@heartland.edu
WIDNER, Bobby .... 229-430-2837. 120 A
bwidner@albanytech.edu
WIDNER, Kenneth .... 662-329-7021. 268 E
kwidner@audit.muw.edu
WIDNEY, Kaye .... 304-367-4303. 529 F
kwidney@fairmontstate.edu
WIEBE, Harold, D .... 740-368-3656. 387 J
hdwiebe@owu.edu
WIEBE, Henry, A .... 573-341-4579. 284 A
wiebe@mst.edu
WIECHMAN, Jeffery, P .... 507-354-8221. 256 M
wiechmjp@mlc-wels.edu
WIECHOWSKI, Linda ...... 248-689-8282. 251 I
lwiechow@walshcollege.edu
WIECKI, Lisa .... 864-388-8035. 444 K
lwiecki@lander.edu
WIECKOWSKI, Ellen, G .. 412-397-6901. 431 I
wieckowski@rmu.edu
WIED, Christine .... 979-830-4224. 467 I
cwied@blinn.edu
WIEDENHOEFT, Jason .... 773-907-4830. 142 A
jwiedenhoeft@ccc.edu
WIEDERSPAHN, Keri ...... 603-924-7256. 297 E
keri@sharonarts.org
WIEDOW, Gale .... 605-256-5177. 451 H
gale.wiedow@dsu.edu
WIEDOWER, CSC,
Veronique .... 574-284-4886. 172 G
vwiedowe@saintmarys.edu
WIEGAND, Mark .... 502-272-8368. 192 E
mwiegand@bellarmine.edu
WIEGAND, Stephanie ..... 425-640-1423. 519 D
stephanie.wiegand@edcc.edu
WIEGANDT, Scott, P ...... 502-272-8496. 192 E
swiegandt@bellarmine.edu
WIEGEL, Lisa .... 563-288-6003. 178 B
lwiegel@eicc.edu
WIEGENSTEIN, Steve, C . 573-875-8700. 272 G
scwiegenstein@ccis.edu
WIEGERT, Tim .... 517-750-1200. 250 E
twiegert@arbor.edu
WIEGMANN, Dawn, R .... 319-352-8437. 183 E
dawn.wiegmann@wartburg.edu
WIEL, Susan, K .... 740-368-3376. 387 J
skwiel@owu.edu
WIELAND, John .... 502-213-3653. 195 F
john.wieland@kctcs.edu
WIELEBINSKI, Daria .... 570-422-3282. 428 D
dwielebinski@po-box.esu.edu
WIELENGA, Jay .... 712-707-7111. 181 H
jayw@nwciowa.edu

WIELHORSKI, Karen .... 281-283-3930. 489 C
wielhorski@uhcl.edu
WIELINSKI, Peter .... 218-631-7810. 259 F
peter.wielinski@minnesota.edu
WIELK, Larry, J .... 203-371-7916... 91 C
wielkl@sacredheart.edu
WIEMERS, Eugene, L ..... 207-786-6261. 209 F
ewiemers@bates.edu
WIEMEYER, Steve, R ...... 402-449-2820. 289 H
swiemeyer@graceu.edu
WIENCEK, John, M .... 813-974-3780. 116 C
jwiencek@eng.usf.edu
WIENER, Evelyn .... 215-746-0803. 435 B
wiener@upenn.edu
WIENER, Madeleine .... 858-635-4428... 26 M
mwiener@alliant.edu
WIENER, Stuart, A .... 702-968-2008. 295 E
swiener@roseman.edu
WIENER, William, R .... 336-334-5375. 369 A
wrwiener@uncg.edu
WIENS, Ann .... 312-499-4214. 158 L
awiens@saic.edu
WIENS, Chris .... 620-242-0436. 188 G
wiensc@mcpherson.edu
WIER, Judyth .... 417-667-8181. 273 A
jwier@cottey.edu
WIERDA, Bruce .... 231-777-0657. 247 G
bruce.wierda@muskegoncc.edu
WIERDA, Kire .... 989-328-1268. 247 D
kire.wierda@montcalm.edu
WIERGACZ, Nora .... 219-464-5335. 174 E
nora.wiergacz@valpo.edu
WIERNICKI, Peter .... 617-243-2322. 227 K
pwiernicki@lasell.edu
WIERS, Alison .... 336-334-4822. 360 G
ajwiers@gtcc.edu
WIERTEL, Anthony .... 716-926-8818. 326 B
twiertel@hilbert.edu
WIERZBICKI, Andrzej ..... 251-460-6280..... 9 E
awierzbicki@southalabama.edu
WIESCAMP, Cheryl .... 970-247-7364... 81 M
wiescamp_c@fortlewis.edu
WIESCHOWSKI, Marilyn . 269-467-9945. 242 H
mwieschowski@glenoaks.edu
WIESE, Barry .... 281-487-1170. 484 H
bwiese@txchiro.edu
WIESE, Karen .... 641-269-4939. 178 H
wiese@grinnell.edu
WIESE, Vicki .... 605-995-3023. 450 E
vicki.wiese@mitchelltech.edu
WIESEHAN, Terry .... 765-973-8221. 167 G
twieseha@iue.edu
WIESEMANN, Lois .... 801-957-4255. 498 B
lois.wiesemann@slcc.edu
WIESEN, Elizabeth .... 207-893-6630. 211 G
lwiesen@sjcme.edu
WIESENBERG, Mark .... 801-863-8740. 497 C
mwiesenberg@uvu.edu
WIESENBURG, Denis .... 601-266-5116. 270 E
denis.wiesenburg@usm.edu
WIESENTHAL, Steve .... 773-834-3529. 161 B
swiesenthal@uchicago.edu
WIESNER, Bob .... 803-641-3522. 448 A
bobw@usca.edu
WIESNER, Don .... 316-942-4291. 189 E
wiesnerd@newmanu.edu
WIETZ, Ophelia .... 305-220-4120. 111 E
libdir@ptcmatt.com
WIEWEL, Wim .... 503-725-4411. 406 B
president@pdx.edu
WIGAND, Debra .... 920-686-6121. 536 A
Debra.Wigand@sl.edu
WIGENT, Rodney .... 215-596-7545. 435 H
r.wigent@usciences.edu
WIGFALL, Arthur .... 212-463-0400. 348 B
arthur.wigfall@touro.edu
WIGGINS, Amy .... 252-862-1225. 363 A
wigginsa@roanokechowan.edu
WIGGINS, Amy, F .... 252-862-1200. 363 A
wigginsa@roanokechowan.edu
WIGGINS, Annette .... 715-634-4790. 533 Q
awiggins@lco.edu
WIGGINS, Charles .... 828-395-1306. 361 C
cpwiggins@isothermal.edu
WIGGINS, David .... 405-789-7661. 400 A
david.wiggins@swcu.edu
WIGGINS, David, J .... 952-446-4112. 255 D
wigginsj@crown.edu
WIGGINS, Devon .... 903-510-2385. 488 E
dwig@tjc.edu
WIGGINS, Glenn .... 617-989-4470. 237 G
wigginsg@wit.edu
WIGGINS, Jack .... 409-839-2014. 486 E
jowiggins@lit.edu
WIGGINS, Jana .... 229-217-4139. 129 F
jwiggins@moultrietech.edu
WIGGINS, Jill .... 417-873-6980. 273 H
jillwiggins@drury.edu
WIGGINS, Kristy .... 207-985-7976. 210 G
kristywiggins@landingschool.edu

WIGGINS, Lavaugn .... 334-874-5700..... 3 A
lwiggins@ccal.edu
WIGGINS, Michael .... 870-743-3000... 22 B
mwiggins@northark.edu
WIGGINS, Nimmi .... 859-257-6547. 200 C
nwiggin@uky.edu
WIGGINS, Rob .... 503-517-1876. 408 I
rwiggins@westernseminary.edu
WIGGINS, Sandra .... 541-684-4644. 407 B
swiggins@pioneerpacific.edu
WIGGINS, Shelia .... 252-527-6223. 361 F
swiggins@lenoircc.edu
WIGGINS, Timothy .... 630-515-3136. 144 A
twiggins@devry.edu
WIGGINS, Urban .... 225-771-4150. 206 J
urban_wiggins@subr.edu
WIGGINTON, Van .... 281-542-2050. 479 F
van.wigginton@sjcd.edu
WIGHT, Charles, A .... 801-626-6001. 497 D
cwight@weber.edu
WIGHT, Laura .... 406-771-4318. 287 E
laura.wight@gfcmsu.edu
WIGHT, Randall .... 870-245-5107... 22 D
wight@obu.edu
WIGHTMAN, Beth, A ...... 818-677-2969... 34 C
beth.wightman@csun.edu
WIGHTMAN, Todd .... 208-524-3000. 138 D
todd.wightman@my.eitc.edu
WIGINTON, Chad .... 580-477-7918. 401 J
chad.wiginton@wosc.edu
WIGINTON, Melissa .... 512-404-4862. 467 A
mwiginton@austinseminary.edu
WIGLEY, Mark, A .... 212-854-3473. 321 D
maw152@columbia.edu
WIGNALL, Eric .... 574-936-8898. 163 K
eric.wignall@ancilla.edu
WIGNALL, Scott .... 309-467-6302. 145 C
swignall@eureka.edu
WIGNER, Dee .... 620-276-9577. 187 A
dee.wigner@gcccks.edu
WIGNES, David, R .... 608-785-9140. 541 E
wignesd@westerntc.edu
WIGREN, Katrina .... 912-650-5678. 131 H
kwigren@southuniversity.edu
WIHBEY, Jean .... 561-207-5400. 110 C
wihbeyj@palmbeachstate.edu
WIILKINSON, Joann, F .. 314-516-5301. 283 E
wilkinsonj@umsl.edu
WIKE, Lauren, C .... 910-630-7167. 356 H
lwike@methodist.edu
WIKE, Wayne, D .... 704-233-8319. 370 G
wike@wingate.edu
WILBANKS, Cynthia, H .. 734-763-5554. 251 C
wilbanks@umich.edu
WILBANKS, Jennifer ...... 660-596-7229. 282 G
jwilbanks@sfccmo.edu
WILBANKS, Jennifer ...... 803-276-9000. 446 C
wilbanks.j@ptc.edu
WILBANKS, Laura .... 734-484-1322. 242 D
laura.wilbanks@emich.edu
WILBECK, Tom .... 713-623-2040. 466 G
twilbeck@aii.edu
WILBER, Renita .... 800-567-2344. 532 E
rwilber@menominee.edu
WILBON, Matisa .... 502-272-8172. 192 E
mwilbon@bellarmine.edu
WILBORN, Colin .... 254-295-8642. 490 B
cwilborn@umhb.edu
WILBOUR, Jim .... 407-673-7406. 108 W
jwilbour@lincolntech.com
WILBRATTE, Barry .... 713-525-2100. 490 L
wilbratt@stthom.edu
WILBUR, Janice .... 508-849-3406. 222 B
jwilbur@annamaria.edu
WILBUR, Kathleen, M .... 989-774-7161. 240 N
wilbu1km@cmich.edu
WILBUR, Peter .... 401-254-3365. 440 B
pwilbur@rwu.edu
WILBUR, Roy .... 215-965-4068. 424 D
rwilbur@moore.edu
WILBURN, Brenda, K ..... 606-783-2024. 198 A
b.wilburn@moreheadstate.edu
WILBURN, Eric .... 903-923-2099. 471 J
ewilburn@etbu.edu
WILBURN, Howard, L ..... 336-725-8344. 365 F
piedmontu@piedmontu.edu
WILBURN, James, R ...... 310-506-7490... 58 H
james.wilburn@pepperdine.edu
WILBURN, Jim .... 410-287-1017. 214 B
jwilburn@cecil.edu
WILBURN, Sherryl, E ..... 601-974-1200. 267 I
wilbuse@millsaps.edu
WILCH, Peter, J .... 415-422-6423... 73 J
pwilch@usfca.edu
WILCOCKSON, Mark .... 773-442-5100. 154 H
m-wilcockson@neiu.edu
WILCOTS, Barbara .... 303-871-2706... 86 B
bwilcots@du.edu
WILCOX, Anthony .... 978-665-3482. 229 E
awilcox@fitchburgstate.edu

WILCOX, Bonnie ... 843-383-8010. 442 F
bwilcox@coker.edu
WILCOX, David, O ... 501-686-6840... 24 C
WilcoxDavidO@uams.edu
WILCOX, Dean ... 336-770-3243. 369 D
wilcoxd@uncsa.edu
WILCOX, Denise ... 909-469-5393... 76 B
dwilcox@westernu.edu
WILCOX, Denise ... 918-781-7215. 394 D
wilcoxd@bacone.edu
WILCOX, Erin ... 425-739-8385. 520 K
erin.wilcox@lwtech.edu
WILCOX, Eva ... 585-266-0430. 324 A
ewilcox@cci.edu
WILCOX, Heather ... 303-797-5674... 78 F
heather.wilcox@arapahoe.edu
WILCOX, Jerry ... 203-837-8242... 88 B
wilcoxj@wcsu.edu
WILCOX, Kathleen, J ... 937-328-6060. 377 A
wilcoxk@clarkstate.edu
WILCOX, Kevin ... 518-956-8120. 341 D
kwilcox@albany.edu
WILCOX, Kim ... 970-351-2496... 86 C
kim.wilcox@unco.edu
WILCOX, Ralph ... 813-974-5543. 116 C
rcwilcox@usf.edu
WILCOX, Randy ... 229-226-1621. 132 F
rwilcox@thomasu.edu
WILCOX, Robbin ... 419-267-1460. 385 F
rwilcox@northweststate.edu
WILCOX, Robert, M ... 803-777-6112. 447 G
wilcox.robert@sc.edu
WILCOX, Sharon ... 414-382-6127. 531 I
sharon.wilcox@alverno.edu
WILCOX, Stan ... 850-644-2525. 115 C
WILCOXON, Sharisue ... 712-279-1628. 176 B
sharisue.wilcoxon@briarcliff.edu
WILCOXSON,
Douglas, A ... 859-858-3511. 192 B
doug.wilcoxson@asbury.edu
WILCOXSON, Elizabeth .. 314-644-9274. 281 E
ewilcoxson@stlcc.edu
WILCZENSKI, Felicia ... 617-287-7592. 228 G
felicia.wilczenski@umb.edu
WILD, Bradford ... 617-989-4361. 237 G
wildb@wit.edu
WILD, Larry ... 847-628-2036. 149 B
lwild@judsonu.edu
WILD, Linda ... 402-557-7154. 288 G
linda.wild@bellevue.edu
WILD, Lorie ... 206-281-2608. 523 C
wildl@spu.edu
WILD, Lynn, A ... 585-475-6543. 337 L
lynn.wild@rit.edu
WILD, Terry, D ... 727-726-1153. 100 E
terrywild@clearwater.edu
WILDA, Christine ... 774-455-7549. 228 E
cwilda@umassp.edu
WILDECK, Steven, C ... 608-265-3040. 538 E
steven.wildeck@uwc.edu
WILDENBORG, Paul, J ... 507-457-1442. 264 A
pwildenb@smumn.edu
WILDENTHAL,
B. Hobson ... 972-883-2271. 491 E
wildenbh@utdallas.edu
WILDER, Aliza ... 860-486-4038... 92 A
aliza.wilder@uconn.edu
WILDER, Carmen, C ... 704-216-6009. 356 D
cwilder@livingstone.edu
WILDER, Dana ... 860-486-6527... 92 A
dana.wilder@uconn.edu
WILDER, Diane ... 610-896-1209. 418 F
dwilder@haverford.edu
WILDER, Jennifer, A ... 919-530-6342. 368 A
jwilder@nccu.edu
WILDER, Jim ... 419-434-4220. 393 D
jwilder@winebrenner.edu
WILDER, John ... 229-931-2068. 131 G
jwilder@southgatech.edu
WILDER, Judy ... 207-755-5250. 210 J
jwilder@cmcc.edu
WILDER, Martin, A ... 540-654-1301. 510 J
mwilder@umw.edu
WILDER, Michael ... 630-752-5818. 163 F
michael.wilder@wheaton.edu
WILDER, Paul, J ... 812-888-5131. 174 F
pwilder@vinu.edu
WILDER, Richard, D ... 352-392-1271. 116 A
rwilder@ufl.edu
WILDER, Stanley, J ... 704-687-3110. 368 E
swilder2@uncc.edu
WILDER, Sterly ... 919-684-2782. 354 A
sterly.wilder@daa.duke.edu
WILDER, Vernon ... 903-823-3252. 482 D
vernon.wilder@texarkanacollege.edu
WILDER, W. Mark ... 662-915-5317. 270 B
acwilder@olemiss.edu
WILDER-BYRD, Ellen, M 803-323-2236. 449 G
wilderbyrde@winthrop.edu
WILDERMUTH, Amy ... 801-581-8763. 496 Q
amy.wildermuth@utah.edu
WILDES, David ... 850-201-8177. 117 D
wildesd@tcc.fl.edu
WILDES, SJ, Kevin, W ... 504-865-3847. 205 H
wildesk@loyno.edu
WILDING, Michael ... 661-362-3498... 40 E
michael.wilding@canyons.edu
WILDING-FARRELL,
Jody ... 281-649-3070. 473 B
jwilding@hbu.edu
WILDNER-BASSETT,
Mary, E ... 520-621-9294... 18 F
wildnerb@email.arizona.edu
WILES, David, A ... 606-679-8501. 196 D
david.wiles@kctcs.edu
WILES, Jan ... 618-842-3711. 146 I
wilesj@iecc.edu
WILES, Mari, E ... 252-398-6268. 353 H
wilesm@chowan.edu
WILES, Michael ... 952-888-4777. 263 B
mwiles@nwhealth.edu
WILES, Rhonda ... 301-784-5000. 213 B
rwiles@allegany.edu
WILEVSKI, Jason ... 563-441-2485. 180 E
jwilevski@kucampus.edu
WILEY, Byron, A ... 864-656-3553. 442 C
bwiley@clemson.edu
WILEY, Esther ... 909-607-9228... 39 C
esther.wiley@cgu.edu
WILEY, Fran, K ... 864-941-8351. 446 C
wiley.f@ptc.edu
WILEY, Janet ... 717-867-6220. 421 H
wiley@lvc.edu
WILEY, Joe ... 731-989-6001. 454 J
jwiley@fhu.edu
WILEY, Karen ... 815-825-2086. 149 F
karen.wiley@kishwaukeecollege.edu
WILEY, Karen ... 903-923-2018. 471 J
kwiley@etbu.edu
WILEY, Louise ... 903-983-8242. 475 E
lwiley@kilgore.edu
WILEY, LuSharon ... 850-474-2161. 117 B
lwiley@uwf.edu
WILEY, Paul, G ... 931-598-1731. 458 H
pwiley@sewanee.edu
WILEY, Stacey ... 585-245-5721. 343 C
wileys@geneseo.edu
WILEY-HARRIS,
Courtney ... 212-870-1253. 331 C
cwiley@nyts.edu
WILF, Carol ... 870-762-3121... 19 K
cwilf@smail.anc.edu
WILFAHRT, Dannette, C . 651-631-5190. 263 A
dcwilfahrt@nwc.edu
WILFALK, Lena, L ... 727-864-8258. 101 N
wilfalll@eckerd.edu
WILFINGER, Pam ... 309-694-5215. 146 E
pwilfinger@icc.edu
WILFONG, Earl ... 309-457-2300. 153 D
ewilfong@monmouthcollege.edu
WILGENBUSCH, Sandy .. 563-876-3353. 177 I
wilgenbu@dwci.edu
WILHELM, George, E ... 305-899-3336... 98 O
gwilhelm@barry.edu
WILHELM, Jane ... 608-663-2203. 532 I
jwilhelm@edgewood.edu
WILHELM, John, L ... 402-280-2762. 289 D
johnwilhelm@creighton.edu
WILHELM, Laura ... 773-256-0741. 152 B
lwilhelm@lstc.edu
WILHELM, Leonard ... 734-432-5380. 246 B
lwilhelm@madonna.edu
WILHELM, Robert, W ... 704-687-8428. 368 E
rgwilhel@uncc.edu
WILHELM-NELSON,
Kristina ... 215-248-7182. 413 A
wilhelmk@chc.edu
WILHELMI, Lisa ... 254-299-8640. 476 D
lwilhelmi@mclennan.edu
WILHELMSON, Paul ... 608-796-3040. 539 E
pjwilhelmson@viterbo.edu
WILHITE, David ... 502-863-8016. 194 C
david_wilhite@georgetowncollege.edu
WILHITE, Dennis ... 570-586-2400. 410 D
dwilhite@bbc.edu
WILHITE, Jana, S ... 386-312-4190. 112 C
janawilhite@sjrstate.edu
WILHITE, Saige ... 318-869-5115. 201 H
awilhite@centenary.edu
WILHITE, Stephen, C ... 610-499-4105. 437 E
scwilhite@widener.edu
WILHOIT, Cathy ... 314-837-6777. 280 K
cwilhoit@slcconline.edu
WILHOUR, Reo ... 217-351-2558. 155 J
rwilhour@parkland.edu
WILHOYTE, David ... 503-654-8000. 407 B
dwilhoyte@pioneerpacific.edu
WILINSKI, Grant ... 609-343-4937. 299 A
wilinski@atlantic.edu
WILJANEN, Lynn, M ... 410-334-2893. 221 D
lwiljanen@worwic.edu
WILK, Thomas ... 586-445-7135. 246 A
wilkt@macomb.edu
WILKE, Dennis, F ... 412-521-6200. 432 A
dennis.wilke@rosedaletech.org
WILKE, Ekkehard, T ... 312-939-0111. 144 D
wil3t@eastwest.edu
WILKE, Janet, S ... 308-865-8595. 292 H
wilkej@unk.edu
WILKE, Stephen, K ... 620-229-6277. 190 G
steve.wilke@sckans.edu
WILKEN, Danielle, S ... 860-727-6780... 90 A
dwilken@goodwin.edu
WILKERSON, Aimee, J ... 270-824-8696. 196 A
aimee.wilkerson@kctcs.edu
WILKERSON, Ame ... 912-260-4407. 131 F
ame.wilkerson@sgsc.edu
WILKERSON, Charles ... 931-372-3634. 460 A
cwilkerson@tntech.edu
WILKERSON, Jeffrey ... 563-387-1005. 180 M
wilkerje@luther.edu
WILKERSON, Karen, D ... 816-235-2757. 283 D
wilkersonkd@umkc.edu
WILKERSON, Kristi ... 304-473-8509. 531 G
wilkerson@wvwc.edu
WILKERSON, Lindsey, S 318-342-1530. 208 E
lwilkerson@ulm.edu
WILKERSON, Lois ... 714-241-6160... 39 I
lwilkerson@coastline.edu
WILKERSON, Mathew, C 540-654-1048. 510 J
mwilkers@umw.edu
WILKERSON, Mindy ... 847-317-8001. 160 M
mwilkers@tiu.edu
WILKERSON, Patsy ... 912-427-5839. 120 B
pwilkerson@altamahatech.edu
WILKERSON, Phil ... 870-236-6901... 20 K
pwilkerson@crc.edu
WILKERSON, Sharon, A . 979-436-0111. 484 B
wilkerson@tamhsc.edu
WILKERSON, Tanya ... 443-885-3170. 217 A
tanya.wilkerson@morgan.edu
WILKERSON, Terry ... 618-437-5321. 156 H
wilkersont@rlc.edu
WILKERSON, Zeda ... 870-368-2028... 22 E
zwilkerson@ozarka.edu
WILKES, Barrie, J ... 989-774-3331. 240 N
wilke1bj@cmich.edu
WILKES, Chris ... 503-352-1479. 407 A
wilkes@pacificu.edu
WILKES, Jeremy ... 901-572-2670. 453 B
jeremy.wilkes@bchs.edu
WILKES, Pamela ... 650-949-7609... 44 N
wilkespam@fhda.edu
WILKES, Steve ... 262-741-8522. 540 A
wilkess@gtc.edu
WILKEY, Jill, J ... 701-231-8466. 371 G
jill.wilkey@ndsu.edu
WILKIE, Marilyn, L ... 212-517-0453. 330 E
mwilkie@mmm.edu
WILKIE, William ... 360-475-7835. 521 H
wwilkie@olympic.edu
WILKIN, John ... 419-448-2227. 380 G
jwilkin@heidelberg.edu
WILKIN, John, P ... 217-333-0790. 162 A
jpwilkin@illinois.edu
WILKIN, Lori ... 732-906-2574. 303 B
lwilkin@middlesexcc.edu
WILKIN, Noel, E ... 662-915-1071. 270 B
nwilkin@olemiss.edu
WILKINS, Brian, J ... 716-839-8395. 322 E
bwilkins@daemen.edu
WILKINS, Deborah, T ... 270-745-5398. 200 G
deborah.wilkins@wku.edu
WILKINS, Harry, T ... 304-724-3700. 526 B
hwilkins@apus.edu
WILKINS, Mardell ... 775-753-2265. 294 F
mardell.wilkins@gbcnv.edu
WILKINS, Patricia, A ... 512-505-3081. 473 G
pawilkins@htu.edu
WILKINS, Pyeper, L ... 214-560-2234. 470 J
pwilkins@dcccd.edu
WILKINS, Stan ... 318-678-6000. 202 I
swilkins@bpcc.edu
WILKINSON, Cathryn ... 630-942-2425. 142 G
wilkin@cod.edu
WILKINSON,
Christine, K ... 480-965-7782... 11 K
c.wilkinson@asu.edu
WILKINSON, James ... 662-254-3554. 269 A
jgwilkinson@mvsu.edu
WILKINSON, Jay ... 515-961-1288. 182 E
jay.wilkinson@simpson.edu
WILKINSON, Julie ... 941-782-5678. 420 E
jwilkinson@lecom.edu
WILKINSON, Karen ... 304-776-6290. 526 F
kwilkinson@cci.edu
WILKINSON, Kevin ... 305-949-9500. 102 E
kwilkinson@cci.edu
WILKINSON, Lonnie ... 225-771-3015. 206 J
lonnie_wilkinson@subr.edu
WILKINSON, Lyndy, D ... 806-335-4352. 465 E
lwilkinson@actx.edu
WILKINSON, Mike ... 817-923-1921. 481 G
mwilkinson@swbts.edu
WILKINSON, Mike ... 405-691-3800. 396 D
mwilkinson@macu.edu
WILKINSON, Missy ... 309-649-6305. 160 E
missy.wilkinson@src.edu
WILKINSON, Patrick, J ... 920-424-2147. 537 B
wilkinso@uwosh.edu
WILKINSON, Robert ... 260-481-6375. 168 C
wilkinrb@ipfw.edu
WILKINSON, Timothy, J 509-777-4585. 525 F
twilkinson@whitworth.edu
WILKINSON, W. David ... 601-974-1172. 267 I
wilkiwd@millsaps.edu
WILKINSON, William, J . 215-204-4775. 433 K
william.wilkinson@temple.edu
WILKOSKI, Donna, M ... 215-698-8203. 411 B
wilkoski@bucks.edu
WILKS, Barbara ... 704-378-1042. 355 K
bwilks@jcsu.edu
WILKS, David ... 302-736-2508... 94 C
WILKS, Karrin, E ... 718-270-4900. 319 A
WILKS, Preston ... 509-793-2194. 517 C
prestonw@bigbend.edu
WILKS, Ronald, W ... 317-788-3517. 173 I
wilks@uindy.edu
WILL, Kris ... 303-986-2320... 80 D
kris@csha.net
WILL, Lee ... 480-245-7937... 14 B
lee.will@ibcs.edu
WILLAMON, Nancy, R ... 217-351-2533. 155 J
nwillamon@parkland.edu
WILLAMS, Mike ... 501-279-4312... 21 C
mwilliams@harding.edu
WILLAN, Dawn, E ... 843-953-5997. 443 A
willande@cofc.edu
WILLAN, William ... 740-593-2551. 387 C
willanw@ohio.edu
WILLARD, Jessica ... 803-786-3856. 443 B
jwillard@columbiasc.edu
WILLARD, Joseph ... 215-991-3586. 420 B
willard@lasalle.edu
WILLARD, Judith, A ... 716-286-8418. 334 F
jaw@niagara.edu
WILLARD, Paul, S ... 727-376-6911. 117 I
paul.willard@trinitycollege.edu
WILLBORG, Erik ... 406-657-1110. 288 B
erik.willborg@rocky.edu
WILLCOX, Abby ... 239-489-9059. 101 O
awillcox@edison.edu
WILLCOX, Jan, M ... 540-231-4000. 504 G
WILLCOX, Wayne ... 912-344-2689. 120 G
wayne.willcox@armstrong.edu
WILLE, Diane, E ... 812-941-2300. 168 F
dwille@ius.edu
WILLEKENS, Rene, G ... 623-935-8069... 14 K
rene.willekens@estrellamountain.edu
WILLEMSEN, David ... 417-865-2815. 274 B
willemsend@evangel.edu
WILLENBORG, Andy, B .. 563-589-0217. 183 F
awillenborg@wartburgseminary.edu
WILLENSKY, Violet, J ... 908-526-1200. 305 B
vwillens@raritanval.edu
WILLER, Anthony ... 701-483-2215. 371 D
Anthony.Willer@dickinsonstate.edu
WILLERTH, Dale ... 630-466-7900. 162 J
dwillerth@waubonsee.edu
WILLETT, Dana ... 931-221-7779. 459 B
willettd@apsu.edu
WILLETT, Terrence ... 831-477-5656... 30 G
terrence@cabrillo.edu
WILLETTS, Jeffrey, G ... 703-812-4757. 506 H
jwilletts@leland.edu
WILLEY, Sharon ... 408-924-5900... 36 A
sharon.willey@sjsu.edu
WILLEY, Sue, C ... 317-788-3412. 173 I
swilley@uindy.edu
WILLFAHRT, Connie ... 715-422-5525. 540 D
connie.willfahrt@mstc.edu
WILLGING, Gregory, A ... 563-556-5110. 181 E
willging@nicc.edu
WILLGING, Pete ... 815-599-3421. 146 D
pete.willging@highland.edu
WILLI, John ... 215-335-0800. 422 C
jwilli@lincolntech.com
WILLIAM, Karen ... 502-456-6509. 199 F
kwilliam@sctd.edu
WILLIAMS, Alex ... 402-363-5689. 293 I
aawilliams@york.edu
WILLIAMS, Alfred ... 860-412-7212... 89 E
awilliams@qvcc.commnet.edu
WILLIAMS, Alfred ... 508-588-9100. 232 A
WILLIAMS, Alison ... 603-623-0310. 297 E
alisonwilliams@nhia.edu
WILLIAMS, Alison ... 440-775-5363. 385 H
Alison.Williams@oberlin.edu
WILLIAMS, Allison ... 617-277-3915. 224 C
awilliams@bgsp.edu
WILLIAMS, Alvin ... 973-877-3243. 301 H
williams@essex.edu

WILLIAMS, Amanda .... 913-288-7218. 187 L
awilliams@kckcc.edu
WILLIAMS, Amy, H .... 704-637-4414. 353 E
ahwillia@catawba.edu
WILLIAMS, Angela .... 803-738-7691. 445 C
williamsa@midlandstech.edu
WILLIAMS, Annette .... 540-453-2332. 511 H
williamsa@brcc.edu
WILLIAMS, Annie .... 719-549-2116... 80 K
annie.williams@colostate-pueblo.edu
WILLIAMS, Anthony .... 312-980-9255. 148 D
awilliams@iadtchicago.edu
WILLIAMS, Anthony .... 212-343-1234. 331 D
awilliams@mcny.edu
WILLIAMS, Anthony, T ... 325-674-5288. 464 H
williamsa@acu.edu
WILLIAMS, Antonio .... 410-706-7032. 219 C
awilliams@police.umaryland.edu
WILLIAMS, Arley .... 307-766-4839. 543 I
awill44@uwyo.edu
WILLIAMS, Audrey .... 352-365-3510. 108 S
williama@lssc.edu
WILLIAMS, Audrey .... 865-694-6545. 461 D
ajwilliams@pstcc.edu
WILLIAMS, Barry .... 570-208-5932. 419 P
barrywilliams@kings.edu
WILLIAMS, Benecia .... 573-681-5271. 276 C
williamb@lincolnu.edu
WILLIAMS, Benecia, R ... 573-681-5096. 276 C
williamb@lincolnu.edu
WILLIAMS, Bert .... 478-387-4782. 125 E
WILLIAMS, Betty, B .... 843-383-8055. 442 F
bwilliams@coker.edu
WILLIAMS, BJ .... 907-834-1649... 11 B
bjwilliams@pwscc.edu
WILLIAMS, Bobby .... 936-294-4205. 487 A
ath_brw@shsu.edu
WILLIAMS, Brad .... 954-262-7282. 109 K
bradwill@nova.edu
WILLIAMS, Brad .... 405-945-3204. 398 C
WILLIAMS, Bradley, E ..... 530-226-4172... 66 D
bwilliams@simpsonu.edu
WILLIAMS, Brandy .... 662-329-7293. 268 E
bwilliams@dev.muw.edu
WILLIAMS, Brenda, K ..... 256-372-5254..... 1 A
brenda.williams@aamu.edu
WILLIAMS, Brian, G .... 216-397-4296. 381 R
bwilliams@jcu.edu
WILLIAMS, Brockton ...... 615-343-4411. 463 G
brock.williams@vanderbilt.edu
WILLIAMS, Byron, C ...... 225-771-4680. 206 I
byronc_williams@sus.edu
WILLIAMS, Calvin .... 607-962-9233. 322 B
williams@corning-cc.edu
WILLIAMS, Calvin, H ...... 717-815-1226. 438 D
cwilliam@ycp.edu
WILLIAMS, Carl, M .... 610-399-2297. 428 B
cwilliams@cheyney.edu
WILLIAMS, Carla .... 601-877-6188. 265 G
cwilliams@alcorn.edu
WILLIAMS, Carly .... 580-327-8545. 396 N
cjwilliams@nwosu.edu
WILLIAMS, Carmen .... 701-777-4358. 371 C
carmen.williams@und.edu
WILLIAMS, Carol .... 804-763-6711... 96 F
ctw@strayer.edu
WILLIAMS, Carol .... 804-527-7087... 96 F
WILLIAMS, Carol, J .... 860-465-5250... 87 L
williamsc@easternet.edu
WILLIAMS, Carolyn .... 903-983-8277. 475 E
cwilliams@kilgore.edu
WILLIAMS, Carolyn, J .... 936-261-5122. 482 F
cjwilliams@pvamu.edu
WILLIAMS, Catherine, M 541-737-2494. 406 A
catherine.williams@oregonstate.edu
WILLIAMS, Catherine, R . 607-778-5182. 315 I
williamscr@sunybroome.edu
WILLIAMS, Cathy .... 315-781-3696. 326 C
cwilliams@hws.edu
WILLIAMS, Cathy .... 417-865-2815. 274 B
williamsc@evangel.edu
WILLIAMS, Celeastia ...... 818-767-0888... 76 K
celeastia.williams@woodbury.edu
WILLIAMS, Chad .... 602-331-7500... 12 A
cwilliams@aii.edu
WILLIAMS, Chad .... 336-633-0183. 362 H
gcwilliams@randolph.edu
WILLIAMS, Charles .... 630-829-6025. 140 B
cwilliams@ben.edu
WILLIAMS, Charles, B .... 662-476-5016. 266 I
cwilliams@eastms.edu
WILLIAMS, Charles, F .... 704-637-4550. 353 E
cwilliam@catawba.edu
WILLIAMS, Charlie .... 908-737-3330. 302 F
chwillia@kean.edu
WILLIAMS, Charlotte ...... 828-328-7214. 356 B
charlotte.williams@lr.edu
WILLIAMS, Chris .... 864-644-5303. 446 I
cwilliams@swu.edu
WILLIAMS, Chris, C .... 417-268-6026. 271 I
cwilliams@gobbc.edu
WILLIAMS, Chris, J .... 765-641-4235. 163 I
cjwilliams@anderson.edu
WILLIAMS, Christine .... 906-786-5802. 240 K
williamc@baycollege.edu
WILLIAMS, Christopher .. 507-288-4563. 255 C
cwilliams@crossroadscollege.edu
WILLIAMS, Christopher .. 516-299-3834. 329 C
christopher.williams@liu.edu
WILLIAMS, Christy .... 828-232-5116. 368 C
cwilliam@unca.edu
WILLIAMS, Chuck, R ...... 317-940-8491. 164 J
crwillia@butler.edu
WILLIAMS, Clara, A .... 615-687-6895. 452 G
cawilliams@abcnash.edu
WILLIAMS, Clark .... 620-441-5233. 186 A
williamsc@cowley.edu
WILLIAMS, Clark .... 541-278-5796. 402 C
clwilliams@bluecc.edu
WILLIAMS, Clifford, S .... 860-515-3760... 87 I
cwilliams@charteroak.edu
WILLIAMS, Connie .... 513-556-6998. 390 G
connie.williams@uc.edu
WILLIAMS, Connie .... 803-793-5129. 443 E
williamsco@denmarktech.edu
WILLIAMS, Connie .... 509-963-2956. 517 F
CWilliamC@cwu.edu
WILLIAMS, Corey .... 708-456-0300. 161 A
cwillia1@triton.edu
WILLIAMS, Corrie .... 734-929-9104. 241 A
cwilliams@cleary.edu
WILLIAMS, Crystal .... 503-517-7888. 407 E
williamsc@reed.edu
WILLIAMS, Crystal, G .... 919-516-4362. 366 C
cgwilliams@st-aug.edu
WILLIAMS, Cynthia .... 662-621-4126. 266 D
cwilliams@coahomacc.edu
WILLIAMS, D. Newell ..... 817-257-7231. 468 B
n.williams@tcu.edu
WILLIAMS, Damien .... 501-370-5551... 22 F
dwilliams@philander.edu
WILLIAMS, Dan .... 501-279-4449... 21 C
bible@harding.edu
WILLIAMS, Dan .... 352-846-3903. 116 A
danwill@ufl.edu
WILLIAMS, Dan .... 940-397-4239. 476 H
dan.williams@mwsu.edu
WILLIAMS, Dan .... 215-368-5000. 410 F
dwilliams@biblical.edu
WILLIAMS, III,
Daniel, A .... 202-806-6763... 95 G
dwilliams@howard.edu
WILLIAMS, Daniel, R ...... 724-847-6590. 417 A
drwillia@geneva.edu
WILLIAMS, Darlene .... 318-357-6100. 208 B
darlene@nsula.edu
WILLIAMS, Darlene .... 510-261-8500... 58 G
Darlene.Williams@patten.edu
WILLIAMS, Darrell, W .... 479-979-1208... 25 J
dwwillia@ozarks.edu
WILLIAMS, David .... 859-622-2966. 193 P
david.williams@eku.edu
WILLIAMS, David .... 270-247-8521. 197 H
dwilliams@midcontinent.edu
WILLIAMS, David .... 916-608-6500... 53 C
WILLIAMS, David .... 615-343-1107. 463 G
david.williams@vanderbilt.edu
WILLIAMS, David, B .... 614-292-6446. 386 E
WILLIAMS, David, S .... 706-542-3240. 133 C
dwilliam@uga.edu
WILLIAMS, Dawn .... 504-816-4914. 201 K
dwilliams@dillard.edu
WILLIAMS, Debra, J .... 724-925-4200. 437 D
williamsd@wccc.edu
WILLIAMS, Denise .... 937-708-5685. 393 A
dwilliams@wilberforce.edu
WILLIAMS, Denise .... 586-445-7897. 246 A
williamsdl@macomb.edu
WILLIAMS, Dennis .... 405-789-6400. 399 K
dwilliam@snu.edu
WILLIAMS, DeWayne ...... 706-233-7357. 131 E
dwilliams@shorter.edu
WILLIAMS, Diann, W ...... 870-543-5929... 23 E
dwilliams@seark.edu
WILLIAMS, Donald, E ..... 407-303-5671... 97 H
don.williams@adu.edu
WILLIAMS, Donald, J ..... 540-231-5991. 515 C
dowilli3@vt.edu
WILLIAMS, Donald, S .... 906-487-2538. 247 A
dswillia@mtu.edu
WILLIAMS, Donna, M .... 610-799-1107. 421 I
dwilliams@lccc.edu
WILLIAMS, Dorothy .... 404-756-4016. 121 A
dwilliams@atlm.edu
WILLIAMS, Drew, H .... 214-887-5211. 471 F
dwilliams@dts.edu
WILLIAMS, E. Keith .... 404-756-4003. 121 A
kwilliams@atlm.edu
WILLIAMS, Edward .... 336-506-4178. 357 M
edward.williams@alamancecc.edu
WILLIAMS, Eirian .... 650-433-3847... 58 B
ewilliams@paloaltou.edu
WILLIAMS, Elizabeth ...... 803-778-7873. 441 F
williamsel@cctech.edu
WILLIAMS, Elizabeth, N . 240-895-4467. 218 A
enwilliams@smcm.edu
WILLIAMS, Eric .... 616-234-3720. 243 B
ewilliam@grcc.edu
WILLIAMS, Erik, W .... 540-857-8914. 514 E
ewilliams@virginiawestern.edu
WILLIAMS, Erika, T .... 817-515-3049. 482 B
erika.williams@tccd.edu
WILLIAMS, Eunice .... 315-498-2565. 335 G
williame@sunyocc.edu
WILLIAMS, F. Clark .... 615-343-3808. 463 G
f.clark.williams@vanderbilt.edu
WILLIAMS, Falecia, D .... 407-582-1235. 118 M
fawilliams@valenciacollege.edu
WILLIAMS, Fathia .... 985-448-7955. 203 B
fathia.williams@fletcher.edu
WILLIAMS, Felica .... 304-327-4212. 529 D
fblanks@bluefieldstate.edu
WILLIAMS, Frances .... 716-851-1198. 323 I
williams@ecc.edu
WILLIAMS, Frank .... 716-839-8225. 322 E
fwilliam@daemen.edu
WILLIAMS, Frank .... 580-559-5256. 395 F
fwilliams@ecok.edu
WILLIAMS, Frank, G .... 217-245-3003. 146 F
fwilliam@ic.edu
WILLIAMS, Fred .... 714-808-4746... 56 D
fwilliams@nocccd.edu
WILLIAMS, JR., Freddie 334-229-4291..... 1 D
fwilliams@alasu.edu
WILLIAMS, Gail .... 239-513-1122. 106 O
gwilliams@hodges.edu
WILLIAMS, Gail, C .... 757-446-5869. 504 E
williamsgc@evms.edu
WILLIAMS, Gary .... 740-374-8716. 392 I
gwilliams@wscc.edu
WILLIAMS, Gary .... 262-551-5800. 532 D
gwilliams@carthage.edu
WILLIAMS, Gary .... 956-384-2866. 479 B
gwilliams@riogrande.edu
WILLIAMS, George .... 615-327-6815. 456 E
gwilliams@mmc.edu
WILLIAMS, George, D .... 919-516-4236. 366 C
gdwilliams@st-aug.edu
WILLIAMS, Georgia, E .... 252-398-6439. 353 H
willig@chowan.edu
WILLIAMS, Gerald .... 256-761-6128..... 7 F
gwilliams@talladega.edu
WILLIAMS, Gerhild, S .... 314-935-5106. 284 L
gerhildwilliams@wustl.edu
WILLIAMS, Gerry .... 303-333-4224... 78 I
WILLIAMS, Glorya, E ...... 229-430-4654. 119 J
glorya.williams@asurams.edu
WILLIAMS, Gregory, D ... 432-335-6410. 477 M
gwilliams@odessa.edu
WILLIAMS, Gregory, G ... 713-313-1962. 485 F
williamsg@tsu.edu
WILLIAMS, H. James ..... 615-329-8555. 454 F
president@fisk.edu
WILLIAMS, Harry, L .... 302-857-6001... 93 C
hwilliams@desu.edu
WILLIAMS, Heidi .... 724-938-5700. 428 A
williams_h@calu.edu
WILLIAMS, Hila .... 937-708-5252. 393 A
hwilliams@wilberforce.edu
WILLIAMS, Ingrid .... 707-654-1135... 31 I
iwilliams@csum.edu
WILLIAMS, Irma .... 201-761-6052. 306 L
iwilliams@saintpeters.edu
WILLIAMS, Isaac .... 903-593-8311. 485 A
iwilliams@texascollege.edu
WILLIAMS, Jack .... 615-844-5290. 464 E
jack@welch.edu
WILLIAMS, Jacqueline .... 718-951-5352. 317 C
williams@brooklyn.cuny.edu
WILLIAMS,
Jacqueline, A .... 662-254-3347. 269 A
jwill@mvsu.edu
WILLIAMS,
Jacqueline, H .... 410-951-6481. 220 B
jwilliams@coppin.edu
WILLIAMS, Jaha .... 713-221-8184. 489 D
williamsjah@uhd.edu
WILLIAMS, James .... 417-865-2815. 274 B
williamsj@evangel.edu
WILLIAMS, James .... 303-871-2203... 86 B
james.herbert@du.edu
WILLIAMS, James .... 215-871-6115. 430 D
jimw@pcom.edu
WILLIAMS, James .... 414-297-6492. 540 E
williaje@matc.edu
WILLIAMS, James, C ...... 317-738-8213. 165 I
jwilliams@franklincollege.edu
WILLIAMS, James, E ...... 620-341-5267. 186 D
jwilliam@emporia.edu
WILLIAMS, James, F ...... 303-492-7511... 85 L
james.williams@colorado.edu
WILLIAMS, JR.,
James, L .... 540-464-7119. 515 B
williamsjl@vmi.edu
WILLIAMS, James, V ...... 904-256-7025. 107 Q
jwillia3@ju.edu
WILLIAMS, Jan .... 410-617-2928. 216 A
jwilliams@loyola.edu
WILLIAMS, Jane .... 401-456-8013. 439 F
jwilliams@ric.edu
WILLIAMS, Jane Ann ..... 501-450-3445... 25 H
WILLIAMS, Janelle, D .... 817-202-6510. 481 E
janellew@swau.edu
WILLIAMS, Janet .... 601-318-6147. 270 I
jwilliams@wmcarey.edu
WILLIAMS, Jeff .... 806-742-2566. 487 D
jeff.williams@ttu.edu
WILLIAMS, Jefferson, D . 217-443-8871. 143 G
jeff@dacc.edu
WILLIAMS, Jennifer .... 813-253-7027. 106 M
jwilliams301@hccfl.edu
WILLIAMS, Jennifer, L ... 800-287-8822. 164 C
willije1@bethanyseminary.edu
WILLIAMS, Jermaine, F .. 773-442-4600. 154 H
j-williams26@neiu.edu
WILLIAMS, Jerome .... 401-254-3536. 440 B
jwilliams@rwu.edu
WILLIAMS, Jessica .... 712-324-5061. 181 G
jwilliams@nwicc.edu
WILLIAMS, Joan .... 319-208-5049. 182 G
jwilliams@scciowa.edu
WILLIAMS, Joan .... 336-370-8639. 352 H
jwilliams@bennett.edu
WILLIAMS, Joan, J .... 256-765-6341..... 9 C
jjwilliams@una.edu
WILLIAMS, Joan, P .... 716-827-4341. 348 G
williamsjo@trocaire.edu
WILLIAMS, Joanne .... 269-749-6630. 249 A
jwilliams@olivetcollege.edu
WILLIAMS, John .... 607-587-4611. 345 D
williajc@alfredstate.edu
WILLIAMS, John .... 212-817-7460. 317 F
jwilliams3@gc.cuny.edu
WILLIAMS, John .... 504-280-6954. 205 G
john.a.williams@uno.edu
WILLIAMS, John, A .... 334-727-8011..... 8 A
williamsj@mytu.tuskegee.edu
WILLIAMS, John, D .... 903-813-2220. 466 H
jwilliams@austincollege.edu
WILLIAMS, John, F .... 718-270-2611. 342 D
john.williams@downstate.edu
WILLIAMS, John, N .... 317-274-5403. 168 D
jnwill01@iupui.edu
WILLIAMS, Jonathan ...... 404-756-8919. 129 E
jowilliams@msm.edu
WILLIAMS, Joni .... 404-225-4602. 121 B
jwilliam@atlantatech.edu
WILLIAMS, Joseph .... 206-281-2087. 523 C
josephwi@spu.edu
WILLIAMS, Joseph .... 918-456-5511. 396 H
willi142@nsuok.edu
WILLIAMS, Joslyn .... 310-577-3000... 77 G
admissions@yosan.edu
WILLIAMS, Joyce .... 626-815-4702... 29 H
jwilliams@apu.edu
WILLIAMS, Judy .... 207-948-9165. 211 I
jwilliams@unity.edu
WILLIAMS, Judy, G .... 501-569-3194... 24 B
jwilliams1@ualr.edu
WILLIAMS, Julia .... 303-477-7240... 82 C
juliaw@heritage-education.com
WILLIAMS, Julia, M .... 812-877-8186. 172 C
julia.williams@rose-hulman.edu
WILLIAMS, Julie .... 989-463-7176. 239 B
williamsjm@alma.edu
WILLIAMS, Julie, E .... 603-862-1997. 298 C
julie.williams@unh.edu
WILLIAMS, Julie, R .... 712-362-7912. 179 E
jrwilliams@iowalakes.edu
WILLIAMS, Justin .... 254-968-9002. 483 A
jwwilliams@tarleton.edu
WILLIAMS, Karla, R .... 718-289-5809. 317 B
karla.williams@bcc.cuny.edu
WILLIAMS, Kate .... 770-229-3155. 132 B
kewilliams@sctech.edu
WILLIAMS, Kathleen .... 603-358-2101. 298 F
kwilliams7@keene.edu
WILLIAMS, Kathleen, L .. 717-337-6616. 417 B
kawillia@gettysburg.edu
WILLIAMS, Kathy .... 406-496-4266. 287 F
kwilliams@mtech.edu
WILLIAMS, Katraya .... 318-670-6415. 207 A
kwilliams@susla.edu
WILLIAMS, Kehven .... 618-468-6300. 150 G
kwilliams@lc.edu
WILLIAMS, Keith, P .... 802-656-2045. 500 F
keith.williams@uvm.edu
WILLIAMS, Kelley .... 316-295-5864. 186 H
kwilliams@friends.edu
WILLIAMS, Kelly .... 610-409-3698. 436 B
kwilliams@ursinus.edu

WILLIAMS, Kent 316-322-3103. 185 D
kwilliams@butlercc.edu
WILLIAMS, Kevin 518-956-8030. 341 D
graduate@albany.edu
WILLIAMS, Kimberly 708-239-4528. 160 K
kim.williams@trnty.edu
WILLIAMS, Kris 270-831-9626. 195 D
kris.williams@kctcs.edu
WILLIAMS, Kristi 304-205-6623. 528 B
kwilliams@kvctc.edu
WILLIAMS, Kristin 202-994-5136... 95 D
ksw@gwu.edu
WILLIAMS, Kristin 757-455-3115. 515 H
krwilliams@vwc.edu
WILLIAMS, Kyle 405-945-9152. 398 C
WILLIAMS, Kyra 503-842-8222. 408 B
williams@tillamookbay.cc
WILLIAMS, Larion 404-756-4666. 121 A
lwilliams@atlm.edu
WILLIAMS, Larry 318-473-6540. 205 A
lwilliams@lsua.edu
WILLIAMS, Larry 316-942-4291. 189 E
williamsl@newmanu.edu
WILLIAMS, Larry, N 870-512-7851... 20 B
larry_williams@asun.edu
WILLIAMS, LaTosha 406-791-5224. 288 E
lwilliams01@ugf.edu
WILLIAMS, Laura, M 217-443-8878. 143 G
lwms@dacc.edu
WILLIAMS, Laureen 320-629-5114. 260 F
williamsl@pinetech.edu
WILLIAMS, Lawrence 414-288-4739. 534 B
lawrence.williams@marquette.edu
WILLIAMS, Lawrence, R 210-458-5191. 492 C
lawrence.williams@utsa.edu
WILLIAMS, Lee 903-823-3358. 482 D
lee.williams@texarkanacollege.edu
WILLIAMS, Lee, B 508-286-8218. 238 B
williams_lee@wheatonma.edu
WILLIAMS, Leslie, K 319-273-2332. 176 A
leslie.williams@uni.edu
WILLIAMS, Linda 916-660-7311... 66 B
lwilliams@sierracollege.edu
WILLIAMS, Linda, C 540-985-8481. 506 G
lcwilliams@jchs.edu
WILLIAMS, Linda, M 510-642-7516... 70 I
lwilliams@berkeley.edu
WILLIAMS, Lisa 858-653-6740... 49 C
WILLIAMS, Lisa 419-448-3444. 389 J
lwilliam@tiffin.edu
WILLIAMS, Lisa 419-559-2395. 389 I
lwilliams01@terra.edu
WILLIAMS, Lisa 615-383-4848. 464 D
lwilliams@watkins.edu
WILLIAMS, Lisa, L 325-793-3821. 476 E
lwilliams@mcm.edu
WILLIAMS, Lloyd 919-719-5061. 366 E
llwilliams@shawu.edu
WILLIAMS, Lois, H 704-637-4402. 353 E
lhwillia@catawba.edu
WILLIAMS, Lonnie, R 870-972-3355... 19 N
lonniew@astate.edu
WILLIAMS, Loretta 870-248-4000... 20 G
loretta@blackrivertech.edu
WILLIAMS, Lucille, W 803-934-3258. 445 F
lwilliams@morris.edu
WILLIAMS, Luther, S 334-727-8164..... 8 A
lswilliams@mytu.tuskegee.edu
WILLIAMS, Lyn 610-606-4666. 412 I
lcwillia@cedarcrest.edu
WILLIAMS, Lynn 803-641-3352. 448 A
lynnw@usca.edu
WILLIAMS, Lynne, M 715-394-8213. 538 C
lwilli29@uwsuper.edu
WILLIAMS, Lyrae 719-389-6699... 79 D
lyrae.williams@coloradocollege.edu
WILLIAMS, Mandy 303-963-3365... 79 C
aewilliams@ccu.edu
WILLIAMS, Marcellette 617-287-7050. 228 E
mwilliams@umassp.edu
WILLIAMS, Marchetta, L 803-938-3721. 448 F
mlwillia@uscsumter.edu
WILLIAMS, Margaret 313-577-4501. 252 G
eh4292@wayne.edu
WILLIAMS, Mark 616-526-6293. 240 L
wilm@calvin.edu
WILLIAMS, Mark 661-763-7871... 69 D
WILLIAMS, Martha 601-484-8614. 267 G
mwilliam@meridiancc.edu
WILLIAMS, Martha, W 407-582-8090. 118 M
mwilliams@valenciacollege.edu
WILLIAMS, Martita 919-536-7217. 360 B
williamsm@durhamtech.edu
WILLIAMS, Mary 425-739-8269. 520 K
mary.williams@lwtech.edu
WILLIAMS, Mary, B 814-641-3353. 419 H
williabe@juniata.edu
WILLIAMS, Max, E 423-585-6861. 462 A
max.williams@ws.edu
WILLIAMS, Melba 703-330-8400... 96 F
WILLIAMS, Melisa, L 716-880-2448. 330 F
melisa.l.williams@medaille.edu
WILLIAMS, Melva 504-520-7449. 209 D
mewillia@xula.edu
WILLIAMS, Melvenia 803-535-5412. 442 B
mwilliams@claflin.edu
WILLIAMS, Melvin 386-481-2900... 99 C
wiliamsm@cookman.edu
WILLIAMS, Melvin, G 202-994-7818... 95 D
vadm1@gwu.edu
WILLIAMS, Michael 609-984-1130. 308 A
mwilliams@tesc.edu
WILLIAMS, Michael 252-638-7260. 359 G
williamsm@cravencc.edu
WILLIAMS, Michael, C 205-329-7870..... 3 B
mike.williams@ecacolleges.com
WILLIAMS, Michelle 570-961-7833. 420 C
williamsm@lackawanna.edu
WILLIAMS, Michelle, L 314-286-4863. 280 F
mlwilliams@ranken.edu
WILLIAMS, Monette 252-335-3400. 367 C
mdwilliams2@mail.escu.edu
WILLIAMS, Monica 313-993-1028. 250 K
leonarmj@udmercy.edu
WILLIAMS, Monica 815-967-7306. 157 B
mwilliams@rockfordcareercollege.edu
WILLIAMS, Murray 404-225-4545. 121 B
mwilliams@atlantatech.edu
WILLIAMS, Myles 803-778-6643. 441 F
williamsmh@cctech.edu
WILLIAMS, Nancy 515-244-4221. 175 C
nancyw@aib.edu
WILLIAMS, Nancy 314-529-9471. 276 G
nwilliams@maryville.edu
WILLIAMS, Natalie 303-650-5050... 87 B
WILLIAMS, Natalie 801-840-4800. 495 K
nwilliams@cci.edu
WILLIAMS, Nate 254-295-4696. 490 B
nwilliams@umhb.edu
WILLIAMS, Nathaniel 803-705-4730. 441 C
williams@benedict.edu
WILLIAMS, Nicola 305-222-2812. 103 L
nwilliams@careercollege.edu
WILLIAMS, Nicole 508-999-9208. 229 A
nwilliams2@umassd.edu
WILLIAMS, Nicole 816-584-6803. 280 C
nicole.williams@park.edu
WILLIAMS, Nicole 910-755-7391. 358 D
williamsn@brunswickcc.edu
WILLIAMS, Nikisha 212-752-1530. 328 G
nikisha.williams@limcollege.edu
WILLIAMS, Noel 606-759-7141. 196 B
noel.williams@kctcs.edu
WILLIAMS, Owen 218-281-8395. 264 E
owilliam@umn.edu
WILLIAMS, Parham 865-545-5313. 456 A
parham.williams@lmunet.edu
WILLIAMS, Patricia, A 515-263-2912. 178 G
pwilliams@grandview.edu
WILLIAMS, Patricia, R 585-292-3026. 332 A
pwilliams@monroecc.edu
WILLIAMS, Patrick, S 713-221-8982. 489 D
williamsp@uhd.edu
WILLIAMS, Paul 760-245-4271... 75 B
Paul.Williams@vvc.edu
WILLIAMS, Paul 804-330-0111. 503 G
p.williams@centura.edu
WILLIAMS, Peter, E 317-955-6054. 170 V
pewilliams@marian.edu
WILLIAMS, Petrina 814-824-2369. 423 J
pwilliams@mercyhurst.edu
WILLIAMS, Philip, C 337-475-5556. 207 G
pwilliams@mcneese.edu
WILLIAMS, Philip, M 315-733-2300. 349 D
pwilliams@uscny.edu
WILLIAMS, Phillip, L 706-542-0939. 133 C
pwilliam@uga.edu
WILLIAMS, R. Owen 859-233-8111. 199 I
rowilliams@transy.edu
WILLIAMS, Rachel 256-726-8406..... 6 B
rwilliams@oakwood.edu
WILLIAMS, Ramona, A 423-439-4219. 459 C
ramona@etsu.edu
WILLIAMS, Randy 252-985-5228. 365 D
rwilliams@ncwc.edu
WILLIAMS, Ray 631-632-8950. 342 C
ray.williams@stonybrook.edu
WILLIAMS, Rayanne 619-594-1686... 35 D
william7@mail.sdsu.edu
WILLIAMS, Renee, M 610-527-0200. 432 B
renee.williams@rosemont.edu
WILLIAMS,
Richard "Biff" 812-237-2309. 167 A
provost@indstate.edu
WILLIAMS, Richard 229-430-4754. 119 J
richard.williams@asurams.edu
WILLIAMS, Richard 312-915-7290. 151 H
rwilli8@luc.edu
WILLIAMS, Richard 724-532-5084. 432 G
richard.williams@stvincent.edu
WILLIAMS, Rick 870-743-3000... 22 B
rickw@northark.edu
WILLIAMS, Rick, E 909-558-4510... 51 C
rwilliams@llu.edu
WILLIAMS, Ritchie 662-720-7299. 269 B
rwilliams@nemcc.edu
WILLIAMS, Robert 310-825-8011... 71 C
bwilliams@asucla.ucla.edu
WILLIAMS, Robert, F 757-446-5099. 504 E
williarf@evms.edu
WILLIAMS, Roger 603-623-0313. 297 E
rwilliams@nhia.edu
WILLIAMS, Roger, L 814-865-6516. 426 A
rlw1@psu.edu
WILLIAMS, Ron 478-471-2490. 128 I
ron.williams@maconstate.edu
WILLIAMS, Ron 915-747-7390. 492 A
rwilliams@utep.edu
WILLIAMS, Ronald 309-298-1066. 162 K
rc-williams@wiu.edu
WILLIAMS, Ronda, L 304-462-4114. 529 G
ronda.williams@glenville.edu
WILLIAMS, Ronnie, D 501-450-3416... 25 H
ronniew@uca.edu
WILLIAMS, Rosemary 718-270-5104. 319 A
rosemary@mec.cuny.edu
WILLIAMS, Russ 706-721-9311. 126 B
rwilliam@gru.edu
WILLIAMS, Ryan 845-569-3105. 332 B
ryan.williams@msmc.edu
WILLIAMS, Samuel 610-896-1032. 418 F
sawillia@haverford.edu
WILLIAMS, Sanchia 954-492-5353. 100 A
swilliams@citycollege.edu
WILLIAMS, Sandra 912-427-5818. 120 B
swilliams@altamahatech.edu
WILLIAMS, Sara 570-702-8912. 419 G
swilliams@johnson.edu
WILLIAMS, Sara 402-399-2467. 289 A
swilliams@csm.edu
WILLIAMS, Saundra 919-807-7100. 357 L
swilliams@nccommunitycolleges.edu
WILLIAMS, Scott 570-662-4913. 429 C
Scott.Williams@mansfield.edu
WILLIAMS, Scott 718-990-3284. 339 A
williams@stjohns.edu
WILLIAMS, Scott 270-686-4503. 196 C
scott.williams@kctcs.edu
WILLIAMS, Scott, K 315-733-2300. 349 D
swilliams@uscny.edu
WILLIAMS, Scott, T 706-542-3375. 133 C
scottw@uga.edu
WILLIAMS, Selase, W 617-349-8518. 228 B
williams@lesley.edu
WILLIAMS, Shakeena 413-565-1783. 222 F
swilliams@baypath.edu
WILLIAMS, Shanae 951-639-5240... 55 B
swilliams@msjc.edu
WILLIAMS, Shane 601-484-8620. 267 G
swilliam@meridiancc.edu
WILLIAMS, Shaun 817-515-5154. 482 B
shaun.williams@tccd.edu
WILLIAMS, Shawn, A 423-585-6849. 462 A
shawn.williams@ws.edu
WILLIAMS, Shelitha, W 585-292-3010. 332 A
sdickerson@monroecc.edu
WILLIAMS, Sheree 502-213-2156. 195 F
sheree.williams@kctcs.edu
WILLIAMS, Shirley, J 610-796-8340. 409 E
shirley.williams@alvernia.edu
WILLIAMS, Stacie 803-641-3321. 448 A
staciew@usca.edu
WILLIAMS, Stelfanie 252-492-2061. 364 F
swilliams@vgcc.edu
WILLIAMS, Stephen 270-247-8521. 197 H
swilliams@midcontinent.edu
WILLIAMS, Stephen 414-277-7114. 534 G
williams@msoe.edu
WILLIAMS, Stephen, R 419-755-4811. 385 D
swilliam@ncstatecollege.edu
WILLIAMS, Steve 479-788-7807... 24 A
steve.williams@uafs.edu
WILLIAMS, Steve 256-840-4174..... 6 I
swilliams@snead.edu
WILLIAMS, Steve 903-693-2023. 478 A
swilliams@panola.edu
WILLIAMS, Sue 360-992-2619. 518 A
swilliams@clark.edu
WILLIAMS, Susan 304-255-0793. 529 E
swilliams@concord.edu
WILLIAMS, Susan 828-448-3178. 365 A
swilliams@wpcc.edu
WILLIAMS, Susan, D 828-694-1824. 358 C
susanw@blueridge.edu
WILLIAMS, Susan, D 203-576-4651... 91 G
swilliams@bridgeport.edu
WILLIAMS, Suzanne 336-917-5588. 366 D
suzanne.williams@salem.edu
WILLIAMS, T. H. Lee 405-325-6670. 401 B
lwilliams@ou.edu
WILLIAMS, Tamara 704-330-4119. 359 C
tamara.williams@cpcc.edu
WILLIAMS, Tamara, R 253-531-7203. 521 I
williatr@plu.edu
WILLIAMS, Tara, A 336-633-0279. 362 H
tawil@randolph.edu
WILLIAMS, Tasha 312-850-7120. 142 C
tholmes@ccc.edu
WILLIAMS, Teresa 815-599-3445. 146 D
teresa.williams@highland.edu
WILLIAMS, Teresa 615-966-7076. 456 B
teresa.williams@lipscomb.edu
WILLIAMS, Teresa, G 704-233-8210. 370 G
tgwilliams@wingate.edu
WILLIAMS, Terri, B 724-847-6892. 417 A
twilliam@geneva.edu
WILLIAMS, Terria, C 803-535-5720. 442 B
twilliams@claflin.edu
WILLIAMS, Terry 601-484-8615. 267 G
twilliam@meridiancc.edu
WILLIAMS, Theodore, D 304-829-7465. 526 D
twilliams@bethanywv.edu
WILLIAMS, Theresa 718-270-5010. 319 A
twilliams@mec.cuny.edu
WILLIAMS, Thomas 877-751-5783. 141 F
WILLIAMS, Tiffany, S 816-235-5599. 283 D
williamsti@umkc.edu
WILLIAMS, Tim 502-895-3411. 197 F
twilliams@lpts.edu
WILLIAMS, Todd 901-320-9700. 463 J
twilliams@victory.edu
WILLIAMS, Todd, J 215-702-4861. 411 F
president@cairn.edu
WILLIAMS, Tom 318-678-6000. 202 I
twilliams@bpcc.edu
WILLIAMS, Toni, J 803-983-3722. 448 F
toniw@uscsumter.edu
WILLIAMS, Tonjua, L 727-341-3344. 112 E
williams.tonjua@spcollege.edu
WILLIAMS, Traci, N 423-746-5213. 462 C
twilliams@twcnet.edu
WILLIAMS, Tracy 651-523-2651. 256 A
twilliams05@hamline.edu
WILLIAMS, Tracy 801-524-1923. 495 O
williamstl@ldsbc.edu
WILLIAMS, Treby 609-258-7097. 304 E
trebyw@princeton.edu
WILLIAMS, Trudy 412-392-8085. 431 B
twilliams@pointpark.edu
WILLIAMS, Trysta 785-320-4565. 188 E
trystawilliams@matc.net
WILLIAMS, Tyler, R 208-496-1331. 137 H
williamst@byui.edu
WILLIAMS, Valerie 229-430-3867. 120 A
vwilliams@albanytech.edu
WILLIAMS, Valerie, A 305-626-3622. 104 J
vwilliam@fmuniv.edu
WILLIAMS, Vaughn, A 770-423-6284. 127 N
vwilliam@kennesaw.edu
WILLIAMS, Velma, J 804-828-1347. 511 F
vjwillia@vcu.edu
WILLIAMS, Vicki 501-492-0570... 19 J
vicki.williams@arkansasbaptist.edu
WILLIAMS, Vicki 662-846-4011. 266 G
vwilliams@deltastate.edu
WILLIAMS, Vickie 334-214-4803..... 2 H
vickie.williams@cv.edu
WILLIAMS, Victoria 870-972-2054... 19 N
vrwilliams@astate.edu
WILLIAMS, Victoria 610-796-5511. 409 E
victoria.williams@alvernia.edu
WILLIAMS, Walter 205-929-6317..... 5 D
wwilliams@lawsonstate.edu
WILLIAMS, Wanda, K 713-500-3864. 492 E
wanda.k.williams@uth.tmc.edu
WILLIAMS, William, T 303-458-4122... 84 M
wwilliam@regis.edu
WILLIAMS, Willie 478-825-6473. 124 H
williamsw@fvsu.edu
WILLIAMS, Wright 847-543-2210. 143 A
wwilliams@clcillinois.edu
WILLIAMS, Yolanda 407-708-2069. 113 E
williamy@seminolestate.edu
WILLIAMS, Yolanda 813-879-6000. 103 B
ywilliams@cci.edu
WILLIAMS, Zena 773-380-6850. 163 D
zwilliams@westwood.edu
WILLIAMS-BETHEA,
Melanie 212-678-3702. 347 G
mwilliams@tc.edu
WILLIAMS-GAUDIOSO,
Amy 610-359-5341. 414 D
awilliam@dccc.edu
WILLIAMS-GOLDSTEIN,
Brittany 201-684-7609. 305 A
bwillia1@ramapo.edu
WILLIAMS-HARMON,
Arlitha 559-791-2374... 49 P
arlitha.williams@portervillecollege.edu

WILLIAMS-KIRKSEY, Shirley .... 404-880-6774. 122 J skirksey@cau.edu
WILLIAMS KNIGHT, Emily .... 312-752-2104. 149 E helena.vasilopoulos@kendall.edu
WILLIAMS LOSTON, Adena .... 210-486-2900. 465 B aloston@alamo.edu
WILLIAMS LOSTON, Adena .... 210-486-2900. 464 I aloston@alamo.edu
WILLIAMS-PEREZ, Kendra .... 319-226-2040. 175 D Kendra.Williams-Perez@AllenCollege.edu
WILLIAMS RUSHIN, Palisa .... 859-246-6522. 194 L palisa.rushin@kctcs.edu
WILLIAMSON, Angela ..... 417-690-2208. 272 E awilliamson@cofo.edu
WILLIAMSON, Bob .... 360-992-2123. 518 A bwilliamson@clark.edu
WILLIAMSON, Carla .... 919-658-7749. 357 I cwilliamson@moc.edu
WILLIAMSON, Carol .... 641-628-7667. 176 E williamsonc@central.edu
WILLIAMSON, Celia .... 940-565-4961. 490 C celia@unt.edu
WILLIAMSON, Colin, W . 570-326-3761. 427 B cwilliam@pct.edu
WILLIAMSON, Dean .... 936-261-2188. 482 F cdwilliamson@pvamu.edu
WILLIAMSON, Debbie .... 843-863-7050. 441 H dwilliam@csuniv.edu
WILLIAMSON, Donna ..... 717-544-4786. 421 C dfwillia@lancastergeneralcollege.edu
WILLIAMSON, Fernanda . 612-977-5458. 254 C fernanda.williamson@capella.edu
WILLIAMSON, George .... 619-849-2610... 59 L georgewilliamson@pointloma.edu
WILLIAMSON, Gerald ..... 706-886-6831. 133 A jerryw@tfc.edu
WILLIAMSON, Handy ..... 573-882-9061. 283 C williamsonha@missouri.edu
WILLIAMSON, Harold, A 573-882-5606. 283 B williamsonh@health.missouri.edu
WILLIAMSON, JR., Harold, A .... 573-882-5606. 283 C williamsonh@health.missouri.edu
WILLIAMSON, Heather ... 254-442-5001. 468 I heather.williamson@cisco.edu
WILLIAMSON, James ..... 561-304-3466. 454 G
WILLIAMSON, James, E . 706-542-5813. 133 C jwilliamson@police.uga.edu
WILLIAMSON, James, R 858-784-8469... 65 E gradprgm@scripps.edu
WILLIAMSON, Jane, K .... 901-334-5812. 457 A jwilliamson@memphisseminary.edu
WILLIAMSON, Jeff .... 507-372-3408. 260 A jeff.williamson@mnwest.edu
WILLIAMSON, Joann ...... 803-641-3668. 448 A joannw@usca.edu
WILLIAMSON, Joshua .... 276-591-5699. 509 J
WILLIAMSON, Katherine 252-492-2061. 364 F williamsonk@vgcc.edu
WILLIAMSON, Kathleen .. 757-683-4564. 507 N kcwillia@odu.edu
WILLIAMSON, Kathy ...... 252-246-1263. 365 C kwilliamson@wilsoncc.edu
WILLIAMSON, Keith .... 940-397-4231. 476 H keith.williamson@mwsu.edu
WILLIAMSON, Keith, M . 804-524-5285. 515 D kwilliamson@vsu.edu
WILLIAMSON, Kimberly . 252-493-7217. 362 G kwilliamson@email.pittcc.edu
WILLIAMSON, Kimberly . 773-481-8106. 142 F kwilliamson13@ccc.edu
WILLIAMSON, Laurel ..... 281-998-6182. 479 E laurel.williamson@sjcd.edu
WILLIAMSON, Laurel ..... 281-484-1900. 479 H laurel.williamson@sjcd.edu
WILLIAMSON, Laurel ..... 281-458-4050. 479 G
WILLIAMSON, Laurel ..... 281-476-1501. 479 F laurel.williamson@sjcd.edu
WILLIAMSON, Lisa .... 715-682-1678. 535 D lwilliamson@northland.edu
WILLIAMSON, Marty ...... 661-654-2111... 32 H mwilliamson@csub.edu
WILLIAMSON, Michael ... 843-383-8300. 442 F mwilliamson@coker.edu
WILLIAMSON, Nancy ..... 301-985-7080. 219 F legal-affairs@umuc.edu
WILLIAMSON, Nancy ..... 516-572-7406. 332 C nancy.williamson@ncc.edu
WILLIAMSON, Pamela .... 757-823-2037. 507 M pwilliamson@nsu.edu
WILLIAMSON, Patricia, A .... 815-224-0440. 148 A patty_williamson@ivcc.edu
WILLIAMSON, Rhea .... 707-826-4189... 35 C Rhea.Williamson@humboldt.edu
WILLIAMSON, Sean .... 706-245-7226. 124 D swilliamson@ec.edu
WILLIAMSON, Shane ..... 636-949-4728. 276 D swilliamson@lindenwood.edu
WILLIAMSON, Sharon .... 806-742-4250. 487 D sharon.williamson@ttu.edu
WILLIAMSON, Stan .... 205-652-3652..... 9 F swilliamson@uwa.edu
WILLIAMSON, Sue .... 206-878-3710. 520 E swilliamson@highline.edu
WILLIAMSON, Sue .... 306-416-7679. 523 G sue.williamson@skagit.edu
WILLIAMSON, Tom .... 651-450-3680. 258 H twillia@inverhills.edu
WILLIAMSON, Tommy .... 336-721-2824. 366 D tommy.williamson@salem.edu
WILLIAR, Marc, G .... 904-819-6220. 103 E mwilliar@flagler.edu
WILLIARD, Stacey .... 724-266-3838. 434 J swilliard@tsm.edu
WILLIE, John .... 318-487-7194. 202 F john.willie@lacollege.edu
WILLIFORD, A. Michael . 740-593-1059. 387 C willifor@ohio.edu
WILLIFORD, Andrea, G .. 478-757-5170. 134 G awilliford@wesleyancollege.edu
WILLIFORD, Darryl .... 301-860-4186. 220 A dwilliford@bowiestate.edu
WILLIFORD, David .... 615-844-5205. 464 E dwilliford@welch.edu
WILLIFORD, Don .... 325-670-1491. 472 O willifrd@hsutx.edu
WILLIFORD, Joey .... 662-720-7564. 269 B jewilliford@nemcc.edu
WILLIFORD, Lynn, E ...... 919-962-1339. 368 D lynn_williford@unc.edu
WILLIFORD, Pamela, K .. 325-670-1347. 472 O pwillifo@hsutx.edu
WILLIHNGANZ, Shirley, C .... 502-852-6153. 200 D scwill01@louisville.edu
WILLINGER, Katie .... 920-693-1247. 540 B katie.willinger@gotoltc.edu
WILLINGHAM, Bobbi Jo 575-234-9208. 311 A willingh@nmsu.edu
WILLINGHAM, Paul .... 281-283-2222. 489 C willingham@uhcl.edu
WILLINGHAM, Ralph ..... 817-598-6248. 494 G rwillingham@wc.edu
WILLINGHAM-HINTON, Shelley, M .... 919-516-4190. 366 C swhinton@st-aug.edu
WILLIS, Amy .... 229-391-5014. 119 H apwillis@abac.edu
WILLIS, Bob .... 334-983-6556..... 7 H rwillis@troy.edu
WILLIS, Brandon .... 904-596-2476. 117 H bwillis@tbc.edu
WILLIS, Brian .... 828-398-7929. 357 N bwillis@abtech.edu
WILLIS, Chris .... 540-831-6849. 508 C cwillis5@radford.edu
WILLIS, Christine .... 617-369-3581. 236 F cwillis@smfa.edu
WILLIS, Christopher .... 412-536-1194. 420 A christopher.willis@laroche.edu
WILLIS, Cliff, K .... 814-332-2860. 409 D cliff.willis@allegheny.edu
WILLIS, Connie .... 510-464-3232... 59 C cwillis@peralta.edu
WILLIS, Connie .... 510-723-6618... 37 K cwillis@chabotcollege.edu
WILLIS, Darley .... 716-851-1118. 323 I willis@ecc.edu
WILLIS, Dave .... 541-463-5566. 403 I willisd@lanecc.edu
WILLIS, Doug .... 318-257-3267. 207 F doug@latech.edu
WILLIS, Douglas .... 972-377-1793. 469 G dwillis@collin.edu
WILLIS, Edward, M .... 757-823-8141. 507 M emwillis@nsu.edu
WILLIS, Eric, R .... 319-352-8470. 183 E rick.willis@wartburg.edu
WILLIS, Gerry .... 401-341-2200. 440 C willisg@salve.edu
WILLIS, Harvey .... 973-328-5232. 300 G hwillis@ccm.edu
WILLIS, James, A .... 585-395-2129. 342 F jwillis@brockport.edu
WILLIS, Jason .... 859-572-5746. 198 I willisj2@nku.edu
WILLIS, Jeff .... 270-384-8097. 197 D willisj@lindsey.edu
WILLIS, Joy .... 601-857-3224. 267 A Joy.Willis@hindscc.edu
WILLIS, Kathy .... 618-468-5700. 150 G kwillis@lc.edu
WILLIS, Kim .... 309-677-4118. 140 I goblue@bradley.edu
WILLIS, Kimberley, D ..... 585-292-2197. 332 A kwillis@monroecc.edu
WILLIS, Lesia .... 718-522-9073. 314 B lwillis@asa.edu
WILLIS, Lisa .... 312-850-7066. 142 C lwillis04@ccc.edu
WILLIS, Lori, A .... 541-383-7572. 402 D lwillis@cocc.edu
WILLIS, Matesina .... 684-699-9155. 546 A m.willis@amsamoa.edu
WILLIS, Michaela .... 402-872-2221. 291 E mwillis@peru.edu
WILLIS, Paul .... 229-391-5052. 119 H pwillis@abac.edu
WILLIS, Quantrell .... 217-424-6395. 153 C qwillis@millikin.edu
WILLIS, Sharon .... 301-295-3578. 545 C sharon.willis@usuhs.edu
WILLIS, Steven .... 336-517-2302. 352 H swillis@bennett.edu
WILLIS, Tamie, L .... 405-425-5320. 397 D tamie.willis@oc.edu
WILLIS, Wanda, J .... 904-470-8251. 102 A wanda.willi098@ewc.edu
WILLISON, Brian .... 608-249-6611. 533 I bwillison@msn.herzing.edu
WILLITS, Lynn .... 314-529-9333. 276 G lwillits@maryville.edu
WILLITS, Mary Lou .... 802-287-8316. 499 D willitsml@greenmtn.edu
WILLKIE, Dan .... 619-388-7527... 62 F dwillkie@sdccd.edu
WILLMANN, Ellie .... 207-326-2232. 211 D ellie.willmann@mma.edu
WILLMARTH, Ephraim .... 315-858-0945. 326 E ejwillmarth@hts.edu
WILLMON, Nixon .... 256-228-6001..... 5 H willmonn@nacc.edu
WILLMORE, Sharman ..... 513-732-5296. 391 B sharman.willmore@uc.edu
WILLMSCHEN, Montica .. 307-766-2671. 543 I mwillmsc@uwyo.edu
WILLOME, Donna .... 585-389-2501. 332 D dwillom0@naz.edu
WILLOQUET-MARICONDI, Paula .... 802-651-5924. 499 A pwilloquetmaricondi@champlain.edu
WILLOUGHBY, Dan .... 714-992-7036... 56 F dwilloughby@fullcoll.edu
WILLOUGHBY, Gordon, C .... 724-287-8711. 411 C gordon.willoughby@bc3.edu
WILLOUGHBY, Karen, P 412-536-1201. 420 A karen.willoughby@laroche.edu
WILLOUGHBY, Thomas . 303-871-3383... 86 B twilloug@du.edu
WILLRICH, Penny, L .... 602-682-6833... 16 N pwillrich@phoenixlaw.edu
WILLS, Deleen .... 503-375-7003. 403 A dwills@corban.edu
WILLS, Deri .... 803-641-3787. 448 A deriw@usca.edu
WILLS, G. Benjamin .... 702-968-1611. 295 E bwills@roseman.edu
WILLS, Greg .... 502-897-4112. 199 B gwills@sbts.edu
WILLS, Joe .... 530-898-4143... 33 A jwills@csuchico.edu
WILLS, Mike .... 417-836-7635. 278 E mikewills@missouristate.edu
WILLS, Mike .... 573-592-1191. 285 D mike.wills@williamwoods.edu
WILLS, Penelope .... 928-776-2022... 19 H penny.wills@yc.edu
WILLS, Scott, D .... 419-772-2705. 386 D s-wills@onu.edu
WILLS, Tim .... 618-437-5321. 156 H wills@rlc.edu
WILLS, Yvonne .... 636-922-8315. 280 J ywills@stchas.edu
WILLSON, Robert, W ...... 692-625-3031. 546 F rwwillson@cmi.edu
WILLY, Randy .... 630-560-6314. 148 K rwilly@hancocku.edu
WILMER, Elizabeth .... 540-857-7313. 514 E ewilmer@virginiawestern.edu
WILMER, Wesley .... 402-449-2945. 289 H wwilmer232@graceu.edu
WILMES, Gerald .... 660-562-1350. 279 I gwilmes@nwmissouri.edu
WILMES, Teresa .... 301-784-5000. 213 B twilmes@allegany.edu
WILMESHERR, Jon .... 828-766-1360. 361 H jwilmesherr@mayland.edu
WILMOTH, Dirk, E .... 276-944-6814. 504 H dwilmoth@ehc.edu
WILMOTH, Jamie .... 865-882-4270. 461 E wilmoth@roanestate.edu
WILMOTH, Karen, L .... 304-637-1374. 526 E wilmothk@dewv.edu
WILMOTH, Margaret, C .. 404-413-1082. 126 E mwilmoth@gsu.edu
WILMOTH, Wendy .... 620-223-2700. 186 G wendyw@fortscott.edu
WILMOUTH, Robert .... 406-657-1015. 288 B bob.wilmouth@rocky.edu
WILMOWSKY, Joseph .... 718-774-3430. 316 F
WILMS, Amy .... 909-793-2121... 73 H amy_wilms@redlands.edu
WILSEY, Mary, M .... 585-785-1360. 324 D wilseym@flcc.edu
WILSKE, Don .... 517-483-1765. 245 H wilsked@lcc.edu
WILSON, Alan, G .... 660-263-3900. 272 A awilson@cccb.edu
WILSON, Ally .... 828-298-3325. 370 E awilson@warren-wilson.edu
WILSON, Andrew, G .... 412-578-2095. 412 G wilsonag@carlow.edu
WILSON, Angela .... 618-252-5400. 159 E angela.wilson@sic.edu
WILSON, Angulus .... 559-453-2000... 45 D angulus.wilson@fresno.edu
WILSON, Anne .... 213-738-6845... 68 C awilson@swlaw.edu
WILSON, Annette .... 972-860-4689. 470 G arwlson@dcccd.edu
WILSON, Anthony .... 727-726-1153. 100 E anthonywilson@clearwater.edu
WILSON, Arthur, L .... 260-359-4031. 166 O alwilson@huntington.edu
WILSON, Barbara .... 217-333-6677. 162 A bjwilson@illinois.edu
WILSON, Barbara .... 770-534-6203. 122 A bwilson@brenau.edu
WILSON, Barbara .... 719-389-6791... 79 D bwilson@coloradocollege.edu
WILSON, Barbara, A .... 262-243-5700. 532 H barbara.wilson@cuw.edu
WILSON, Barbara-Jan ..... 860-685-2547... 92 H bjwilson@wesleyan.edu
WILSON, Becky .... 806-742-3681. 487 D becky.wilson@ttu.edu
WILSON, Belyn .... 831-443-1700... 47 D belyn_wilson@heald.edu
WILSON, Bob .... 714-556-3610... 74 D bwilson@vanguard.edu
WILSON, Bradley .... 724-738-2379. 429 F bradley.wilson@sru.edu
WILSON, Bruce .... 904-680-7720. 103 Q bwilson@fcsl.edu
WILSON, Bryan, W .... 828-652-0635. 362 A bryanwi@mcdowelltech.edu
WILSON, Carla .... 415-355-1601... 27 L carlawilson@actcm.edu
WILSON, Carlton, E .... 919-530-6794. 368 A cwilson@nccu.edu
WILSON, Carmen .... 608-758-6565. 538 E carmen.wilson@uwc.edu
WILSON, Carol, J .... 815-740-3840. 162 F cwilson@stfrancis.edu
WILSON, Carolyn .... 615-966-5837. 456 B carolyn.wilson@lipscomb.edu
WILSON, Catherine .... 707-527-4763... 65 B cwilson@santarosa.edu
WILSON, Cathy .... 616-234-3971. 243 B cwilson@grcc.edu
WILSON, Cecil, B .... 304-293-2021. 530 D cbwilson@mail.wvu.edu
WILSON, Charlene .... 909-558-4040... 51 C cwilson@llu.edu
WILSON, Charles .... 913-288-7674. 187 L drchuck@kckcc.edu
WILSON, Charles .... 704-922-6428. 360 F wilson.charles@gaston.edu
WILSON, JR., Charles, E .... 757-683-3925. 507 N cwilson@odu.edu
WILSON, Charles (Gary) 731-881-7340. 463 E cwilson@utm.edu
WILSON, Charleston, D .. 262-646-6517. 535 B cwilson@nashotah.edu
WILSON, Cheryl, L .... 817-257-7834. 484 I c.l.wilson@tcu.edu
WILSON, Chris .... 518-454-5436. 321 A wilsonc@strose.edu
WILSON, Chris .... 701-231-7215. 371 G chris.wilson@ndsu.edu
WILSON, Christina .... 325-793-4607. 476 E wilson.christina@mcm.edu
WILSON, Christine .... 785-243-1435. 185 M cwilson@cloud.edu
WILSON, Chuck, A .... 301-314-8249. 219 B chuckw@umd.edu
WILSON, Cleveland .... 803-535-1419. 446 B wilsonc@octech.edu
WILSON, Clive .... 937-298-3399. 382 K clive.wilson@kc.edu
WILSON, Cynthia .... 251-928-8133..... 9 E cwilson@southalabama.edu

WILSON, Cynthia, A .... 847-866-3936. 145 E
cynthia.wilson@garrett.edu
WILSON, Cynthia, L .... 713-348-5048. 479 A
clwilson@rice.edu
WILSON, Daniel .... 703-416-1441. 505 I
dwilson@ipsciences.edu
WILSON, Daniel .... 252-940-6233. 358 A
DanielW@beaufortccc.edu
WILSON, Daniel, B .... 740-826-8164. 384 L
dwilson@muskingum.edu
WILSON, Darin .... 678-407-5000. 125 B
WILSON, Dave .... 509-467-1727. 520 F
dwilson@interface.edu
WILSON, David .... 443-885-3200. 217 A
david.wilson@morgan.edu
WILSON, David .... 432-837-0107. 487 B
dwilson@sulross.edu
WILSON, David, C .... 314-968-7488. 284 N
wilson@webster.edu
WILSON, David, E .... 215-895-6038. 415 B
david.e.wilson@drexel.edu
WILSON, David, P .... 814-472-3211. 432 D
dwilson@francis.edu
WILSON, Deborah .... 509-574-6872. 525 G
dwilson@yvcc.edu
WILSON, Debra, J .... 906-248-8442. 240 J
dwilson@bmcc.edu
WILSON, Debra, J .... 208-732-6245. 138 B
dwilson@csi.edu
WILSON, Delwin, C .... 207-725-3706. 209 H
dwilson@bowdoin.edu
WILSON, Denise .... 704-290-5247. 363 G
d-wilson@spcc.edu
WILSON, Derek, J .... 303-273-3986... 80 E
dwilson@mines.edu
WILSON, JR.,
Donald, D .... 770-720-5953. 130 G
ddw@reinhardt.edu
WILSON, Donna .... 570-484-2576. 429 B
dwilson@lhup.edu
WILSON, Doug .... 251-442-2406..... 9 A
dwilson@umobile.edu
WILSON, Douglas .... 205-726-4266..... 6 F
dwilson@samford.edu
WILSON, Dwayne .... 731-989-6094. 454 J
dwilson@fhu.edu
WILSON, D'Andre, H ...... 757-873-3100... 96 F
WILSON, Elaine .... 606-679-8501. 196 D
elaine.wilson@kctcs.edu
WILSON, Elizabeth .... 912-344-3248. 120 G
elizabeth.wilson@armstrong.edu
WILSON, Elizabeth .... 229-931-2090. 126 D
liz.wilson@gsw.edu
WILSON, Elizabeth, K ..... 404-471-6000. 119 I
ewilson@agnesscott.edu
WILSON, III, Ernest, J ... 213-740-9891... 74 A
ernestw@usc.edu
WILSON, Evelyn .... 978-542-7321. 230 E
evelyn.wilson@salemstate.edu
WILSON, Floarine .... 502-597-6271. 197 A
floarine.wilson@kysu.edu
WILSON, Fran .... 817-274-4284. 467 H
WILSON, Gary .... 816-604-4125. 277 H
gary.wilson@mcckc.edu
WILSON, Gena .... 423-472-7141. 460 D
GWilson01@clevelandstatecc.edu
WILSON, Glen .... 303-464-2300... 84 K
gwilson@redstone.edu
WILSON, Gordon, N .... 801-581-3079. 496 Q
gordon.wilson@aux.utah.edu
WILSON, Hamsa .... 602-942-4141... 13 N
hwilson@cci.edu
WILSON, Hart .... 541-552-8283. 406 C
wilsonh@sou.edu
WILSON, Heather .... 605-394-2256. 452 A
heather.wilson@sdsmt.edu
WILSON, Howard .... 712-722-6007. 177 J
howard.wilson@dordt.edu
WILSON, Huie, G .... 850-263-3261... 98 N
hgwilson@baptistcollege.edu
WILSON, Ian .... 801-863-8951. 497 C
ian.wilson@uvu.edu
WILSON, J. David .... 270-809-2310. 198 B
david.wilson@murraystate.edu
WILSON, Jacqueline .... 334-683-2309..... 5 F
jwilson@marionmilitary.edu
WILSON, James .... 336-316-2132. 355 A
jwilson@guilford.edu
WILSON, JR., James, D 302-295-1194... 94 E
jim.d.wilson@wilmu.edu
WILSON, JR., James, J . 936-261-2175. 482 F
jjwilson@pvamu.edu
WILSON, JR., James, J . 936-261-5256. 482 F
jjwilson@pvamu.edu
WILSON, James, R .... 740-826-8113. 384 L
jrwilson@muskingum.edu
WILSON, Jan .... 316-295-5824. 186 H
jan_wilson@friends.edu
WILSON, Jeff .... 615-966-7617. 456 B
jeff.wilson@lipscomb.edu
WILSON, Jennifer .... 858-635-4526... 26 M
jwilson@alliant.edu
WILSON, Jerre, W .... 703-784-6917. 544 J
jerre.wilson@usmc.mil
WILSON, Jerry .... 719-255-3594... 85 M
jwilson@uccs.edu
WILSON, Jim .... 641-844-5550. 179 H
jim.wilson@iavalley.edu
WILSON, Joan, B .... 323-731-2383... 57 I
jbwilson@psuca.edu
WILSON, Jocelyn, M ...... 516-671-2213. 350 C
jwilson@webb.edu
WILSON, JoEllen, B .... 770-720-5545. 130 G
jew@reinhardt.edu
WILSON, John .... 706-867-2844. 133 D
john.wilson@ung.edu
WILSON, John .... 928-757-0860... 15 L
jwilson@mohave.edu
WILSON, John .... 413-748-3249. 236 I
jwilson@springfieldcollege.edu
WILSON, John .... 212-217-4200. 324 C
john_wilsonn@fitnyc.edu
WILSON, John, R .... 804-355-0671. 510 G
jwilson@upsem.edu
WILSON, JR., John, S ... 404-215-2645. 129 D
WILSON, Jonathan .... 501-205-8889... 20 I
jwilson@cbc.edu
WILSON, Josh .... 706-272-2473. 123 G
jwilson@daltonstate.edu
WILSON, Judge .... 859-985-3131. 192 F
judge_wilson@berea.edu
WILSON, Julie .... 307-778-1218. 543 D
jwilson@lccc.wy.edu
WILSON, Kathi .... 865-981-8211. 456 D
kathy.wilson@maryvillecollege.edu
WILSON, Kathryn .... 585-395-2137. 342 F
kwilson@brockport.edu
WILSON, Kathy .... 864-578-8770. 446 F
kwilson@sherman.edu
WILSON, Kathy, A .... 863-638-2930. 119 D
wilsonka@webber.edu
WILSON, Keisha .... 704-330-1455. 355 K
kwilson@jcsu.edu
WILSON, Keith .... 618-453-7313. 159 G
kbwilson@siu.edu
WILSON, Kelly .... 417-625-9363. 278 D
wilson-k@mssu.edu
WILSON, Kelly .... 740-264-5591. 379 F
kwilson@egcc.edu
WILSON, Kenny .... 636-481-3356. 275 I
kwilso20@jeffco.edu
WILSON, Kevin .... 570-945-8376. 419 N
kevin.wilson@keystone.edu
WILSON, Kevin, H .... 304-637-1337. 526 E
wilsonk@dewv.edu
WILSON, Kim, L .... 402-472-9212. 292 I
kwilson4@unl.edu
WILSON, Kimberly .... 317-299-6001. 170 R
WILSON, Kimberly, P ...... 859-257-4751. 200 C
kimberly.wilson@uky.edu
WILSON, Kristin .... 270-707-3711. 195 E
kristin.wilson@kctcs.edu
WILSON, Kyla .... 773-907-4443. 142 A
kwilson@ccc.edu
WILSON, Kym .... 202-806-1277... 95 G
ka_wilson@howard.edu
WILSON, Larry, L .... 972-860-7613. 470 I
LarryWilson@dcccd.edu
WILSON, Laura .... 619-684-8781... 56 C
lwilson@newschoolarch.edu
WILSON, Laura, J .... 410-778-7849. 221 C
lwilson3@washcoll.edu
WILSON, Laura, L .... 650-723-9633... 68 E
laura.wilson@stanford.edu
WILSON, Leana .... 228-896-2500. 268 C
leana.wilson@mgccc.edu
WILSON, Leon, C .... 334-229-5176..... 1 D
lwilson@alasu.edu
WILSON, Linda .... 336-334-7880. 367 E
wilsonl@ncat.edu
WILSON, Lisa .... 888-897-3222... 50 G
lwilson@sf.chefs.edu
WILSON, Lisa .... 770-531-2558. 128 B
lwilson@laniertech.edu
WILSON, Lisa .... 505-566-3217. 311 I
wilsonl@sanjuancollege.edu
WILSON, Lizabeth, A ...... 206-543-1760. 524 G
betsyw@uw.edu
WILSON, Lonny, L .... 641-673-1118. 183 H
wilsonl@wmpenn.edu
WILSON, Lori, J .... 570-577-3334. 411 A
lwilson@bucknell.edu
WILSON, Lorraine .... 707-524-1506... 65 B
lwilson@santarosa.edu
WILSON, Louise, B .... 315-255-1743. 316 D
wilsonl@cayuga-cc.edu
WILSON, Lucy, P .... 478-301-2460. 128 H
wilson_l@mercer.edu
WILSON, Lynn .... 715-836-5521. 536 E
wilsonly@uwec.edu
WILSON, M. Roy .... 313-577-2230. 252 G
mrw@wayne.edu
WILSON, Maleta .... 504-865-3262. 205 H
mawilson@loyno.edu
WILSON, Marcus .... 806-743-6443. 487 E
marcus.wilson@ttuhsc.edu
WILSON, Mardell .... 309-438-7018. 147 J
mawilso@ilstu.edu
WILSON, Margaret .... 660-626-2354. 271 A
mwilson@atsu.edu
WILSON, Mark .... 605-718-2401. 452 E
mark.wilson@wdt.edu
WILSON, Mark .... 423-472-7141. 460 D
mwilson@clevelandstatecc.edu
WILSON, Mark .... 931-372-3961. 460 A
mwilson@tntech.edu
WILSON, Mark .... 215-887-5511. 437 C
mwilson@wts.edu
WILSON, Martha .... 207-221-4985. 213 A
mwilson13@une.edu
WILSON, Mary .... 931-598-1381. 458 H
mewilson@sewanee.edu
WILSON, Matthew .... 734-462-4400. 250 A
mwilson@schoolcraft.edu
WILSON, Meltida .... 337-373-0172. 203 I
meltida.wilson@southlouisiana.edu
WILSON, Michael, D ...... 714-556-3610... 74 D
mdwilson@vanguard.edu
WILSON, Michael, P .... 610-861-1365. 424 E
wilson@moravian.edu
WILSON, Michelle .... 870-633-4480... 21 A
rwilson@eacc.edu
WILSON, Natalie, L .... 412-578-6171. 412 G
wilsonnl@carlow.edu
WILSON, Neyle .... 843-349-5201. 444 F
neyle.wilson@hgtc.edu
WILSON, Pam .... 940-898-3503. 488 B
pwilson@twu.edu
WILSON, Pamala, P .... 270-831-9649. 195 D
pamala.wilson@kctcs.edu
WILSON, Pamela, M .... 803-376-5701. 441 A
pwilson@allenuniversity.edu
WILSON, Patricia .... 205-366-8151..... 7 E
mpwilson@stillman.edu
WILSON, Patricia .... 302-831-2078... 94 B
wilsonp@udel.edu
WILSON, Patrick .... 615-366-3917. 459 A
patrick.wilson@tbr.edu
WILSON, Peggy, M .... 865-694-6403. 461 D
pwilson@pstcc.edu
WILSON, Perry, T .... 843-661-1486. 444 B
WILSON, Phillip .... 479-394-7622... 23 B
pwilson@rmcc.edu
WILSON, Randi .... 314-889-1410. 274 E
rwilson@fontbonne.edu
WILSON, Richard, F .... 309-556-3151. 148 B
president@iwu.edu
WILSON, Rickie, W .... 270-901-1004. 196 E
rickw.wilson@kctcs.edu
WILSON, Roger .... 425-889-5336. 521 G
roger.wilson@northwestu.edu
WILSON, Rosemary .... 734-973-3724. 252 A
wilbur@wccnet.edu
WILSON, Rowena, C .... 757-823-8668. 507 M
rgwilson@nsu.edu
WILSON, S. Dale .... 864-941-8331. 446 C
wilson.d@ptc.edu
WILSON, Sharon .... 847-214-7485. 144 F
swilson@elgin.edu
WILSON, Shawn .... 785-784-5225. 183 B
wilsons@uiu.edu
WILSON, Shawn .... 989-964-7090. 249 G
swilson@svsu.edu
WILSON, Sherry .... 828-726-2306. 358 E
swilson@cccti.edu
WILSON, Sherwood, G ... 540-231-4416. 515 C
sgwilson@vt.edu
WILSON, Shirley .... 213-624-1200... 44 D
swilson@fidm.edu
WILSON, Sonali, B .... 216-687-3543. 377 F
s.b.wilson@csuohio.edu
WILSON, Stacey .... 704-403-1639. 352 J
stacey.wilson@carolinashealthcare.org
WILSON, Stephan, M ...... 405-744-9805. 397 H
stephan.m.wilson@okstate.edu
WILSON, Stephanie .... 540-828-5749. 502 J
swilson@bridgewater.edu
WILSON, Stephanie .... 724-589-2027. 434 B
swilson@thiel.edu
WILSON, Susan .... 219-785-5236. 172 A
swilson@pnc.edu
WILSON, Susan .... 952-446-4120. 255 D
wilsons@crown.edu
WILSON, Susan, A .... 802-322-1641. 499 C
susan.wilson@goddard.edu
WILSON, Susanne .... 270-831-9804. 195 D
susanne.wilson@kctcs.edu
WILSON, Susie .... 304-326-1358. 527 G
swilson@salemu.edu
WILSON, Suzanne .... 617-585-1100. 234 I
suzanne.wilson@necmusic.edu
WILSON, Ted, H .... 270-707-3865. 195 E
ted.wilson@kctcs.edu
WILSON, Thalia .... 901-333-5112. 461 F
WILSON, Tiffany .... 803-778-6668. 441 F
wilsontd@cctech.edu
WILSON, Timothy, B ...... 805-565-6038... 76 D
twilson@westmont.edu
WILSON, Tommy .... 706-649-1894. 123 E
twilson@columbustech.edu
WILSON, Tracy .... 601-928-6230. 268 C
tracy.wilson@mgccc.edu
WILSON, Tressey, D .... 936-361-1700. 482 F
tdwilson@pvamu.edu
WILSON, Valerie .... 870-574-4514... 23 G
vwilson@sautech.edu
WILSON, Valvia .... 601-977-7844. 270 A
vwilson@tougaloo.edu
WILSON, Vicki .... 859-246-6316. 194 L
vicki.wilson@kctcs.edu
WILSON, Vicki .... 724-852-3375. 437 A
vwilson@waynesburg.edu
WILSON, Victor, K .... 843-953-5522. 443 A
wilsonv@cofc.edu
WILSON, Victor, K .... 706-542-3564. 133 C
wilsonv@uga.edu
WILSON, W. Bruce .... 909-869-3065... 32 G
wbwilson@csupomona.edu
WILSON, Warren .... 605-642-6930. 451 G
warren.wilson@bhsu.edu
WILSON, Wendy .... 229-317-6925. 124 A
wendy.wilson@darton.edu
WILSON, William .... 423-354-2541. 461 C
wrwilson@northeaststate.edu
WILSON, William .... 715-682-1865. 535 D
bwilson@northland.edu
WILSON, William, M ...... 918-495-6175. 398 H
president@oru.edu
WILSON, William, P .... 207-859-4692. 209 J
wpwilson@colby.edu
WILSON, Yolanda, S .... 336-734-7251. 360 E
ywilson@forsythtech.edu
WILSON, Yvette .... 212-280-1396. 349 A
ywilson@uts.columbia.edu
WILSON, Zaphon .... 919-516-4280. 366 C
zrwilson@st-aug.edu
WILSON-BARKER,
Sharon .... 207-992-1934. 210 B
wilsonbarkers@husson.edu
WILSON-FENNELL,
Nicole .... 734-462-4400. 250 A
nwilson@schoolcraft.edu
WILSON-OYELARAN,
Eileen, B .... 269-337-7220. 244 K
wilsonoy@kzoo.edu
WILSON-PARKER,
Sharnita, L .... 252-335-3747. 367 C
slwilson@mail.ecsu.edu
WILSON-PORTER, Cyndi 210-829-2706. 490 A
porter@uiwtx.edu
WILSON-STALLINGS,
Samaria .... 617-682-1508. 226 D
swilson@eds.edu
WILSON-TAYLOR,
Sharon .... 312-369-7221. 143 D
swilson-taylor@colum.edu
WILT, Jason .... 269-783-2159. 250 C
jwilt@swmich.edu
WILT, Jeff .... 816-604-6704. 277 D
jeff.wilt@mcckc.edu
WILT, Larry, M .... 410-455-2356. 219 D
wilt@umbc.edu
WILT, Richard, W .... 610-799-1186. 421 I
rwilt@lccc.edu
WILTBANK, J. Kelley ...... 207-973-3229. 212 A
university.counsel@maine.edu
WILTENBURG, Robert, E 314-935-4806. 284 L
rewilten@wustl.edu
WILTENMUTH, III,
John, P .... 540-654-1047. 510 J
jwiltenm@umw.edu
WILTGEN, JR., Jim .... 501-450-1222... 21 E
wiltgen@hendrix.edu
WILTON, Courtney .... 503-594-3010. 402 F
courtneyw@clackamas.edu
WILTON, John .... 510-642-3100... 70 I
vcaf@berkeley.edu
WILTSCHEK, Walt .... 260-982-5243. 170 U
wjwiltschek@manchester.edu
WILTSE, Mary Alane .... 518-828-4181. 321 C
wiltse@sunycgcc.edu
WILTZIUS, Pierre .... 805-893-5024... 72 B
mlpsdean@ltsc.ucsb.edu
WIMBERLEY,
Bernadette, H .... 302-225-6312... 93 H
wimberlb@gbc.edu
WIMBERLY, Edward, P ... 404-527-7702. 127 I
epwimberly@itc.edu
WIMBISH, Jennifer, L .... 972-860-8251. 470 H
jwimbish@dcccd.edu
WIMBUSH, James .... 812-855-2739. 167 F
jwimbush@indiana.edu

WIMER, Valinda .... 386-822-8850. 117 C
vwimer@stetson.edu
WIMES, Edward, D .... 402-472-7161. 292 G
ewimes@nebraska.edu
WIMS, Daniel, K .... 256-372-5275..... 1 A
daniel.wims@aamu.edu
WIMS, Lois, A .... 401-825-2124. 439 A
lawims@ccri.edu
WIN, Judith .... 413-528-7350. 222 E
jwin@simons-rock.edu
WIN, U. Ba .... 413-528-7392. 222 E
bawin@simons-rock.edu
WINANT, Richard, M ...... 718-270-7411. 342 D
rwinant@downstate.edu
WINBORNE, Malverne .... 734-487-2086. 242 D
mwinborne@emich.edu
WINCH, Eric, D .... 973-642-8289. 307 D
eric.winch@shu.edu
WINCHELL, Barbara .... 845-569-3298. 332 B
barbara.winchell@msmc.edu
WINCHESTER, Andrea .... 731-425-2644. 460 G
awinchester@jscc.edu
WINCHESTER,
Elizabeth, A .... 314-977-2354. 281 I
wincheea@slu.edu
WINCHESTER, Gina, S ... 270-809-5086. 198 B
gwinchester@murraystate.edu
WINCHESTER, Paul .... 316-295-5836. 186 H
winchp@friends.edu
WINCHESTER, Samuel .... 800-672-3060. 366 F
WINCHESTER, Sara .... 732-255-0400. 304 A
swinchester@ocean.edu
WINCKELMAN, Stephen . 952-358-8597. 260 B
stephen.winckelman@normandale.edu
WIND, Joseph, E .... 859-572-5916. 198 I
wind@nku.edu
WINDBERG, Becky .... 262-551-2153. 532 D
rwindberg@carthage.edu
WINDER, Katie .... 541-917-4547. 404 B
winderk@linnbenton.edu
WINDERL, James .... 845-434-5750. 347 A
jwinderl@sullivan.suny.edu
WINDERS, Tim .... 806-894-9611. 480 H
twinders@southplainscollege.edu
WINDHAM, Ana, M .... 210-999-7306. 488 C
awindham@trinity.edu
WINDHAM, Don .... 772-462-7357. 106 P
dwindham@irsc.edu
WINDHAM, Greg .... 662-720-7210. 269 B
gwindham@nemcc.edu
WINDHAM, Jameka .... 216-373-5287. 385 G
jwindham@ndc.edu
WINDHAM, James, R ...... 662-915-7448. 270 B
jwindham@olemiss.edu
WINDHAM, John .... 731-661-5006. 462 F
jwindham@uu.edu
WINDHOLZ, Kevin .... 405-208-5600. 397 F
kwindholz@okcu.edu
WINDISCH, Ray .... 614-825-6255. 373 G
rwindisch@aiam.edu
WINDLE, Frank, H .... 215-871-6750. 430 D
frankwi@pcom.edu
WINDLE, Lawrence, B ..... 956-380-8100. 479 B
lwindle@riogrande.edu
WINDLE, Ruth, M .... 956-380-8183. 479 B
psecretary@riogrande.edu
WINDROW, Vincent .... 615-898-5812. 459 D
vincent.windrow@mtsu.edu
WINDSOR, Lang .... 281-756-3639. 465 D
lwindsor@alvincollege.edu
WINDY BOY, Helen .... 406-395-4313. 288 D
hwindyboy@stonechild.edu
WINE, Stony .... 252-527-6223. 361 F
swine@lenoircc.edu
WINE IMBLER, Toni ...... 918-270-6412. 398 I
toni.imbler@ptstulsa.edu
WINEBARGER,
Conley, F .... 336-734-7182. 360 E
cwinebarger@forsythtech.edu
WINEBRAKE, James, J ... 585-475-2447. 337 L
jjwgpt@rit.edu
WINEGAR, Lucien, T ...... 610-409-3720. 436 B
twinegar@ursinus.edu
WINEGARD, Kathryn ...... 660-248-6208. 272 B
kwinegar@centralmethodist.edu
WINEGARDEN, Alan, D .. 651-641-8258. 255 B
winegarden@csp.edu
WINEGARDEN, Daniel, J 641-422-4191. 181 D
winegdan@niacc.edu
WINER, Toby, R .... 212-346-1200. 335 J
twiner@pace.edu
WINES, Ed .... 952-358-8159. 260 B
ed.wines@normandale.edu
WINFIELD, Robert, A ...... 734-763-6880. 251 C
rwinf@umich.edu
WINFIELD-THOMAS,
Evelyn .... 269-387-6316. 252 I
evelyn.winfield@wmich.edu
WINFORD, Judith .... 662-846-4807. 266 G
jwinford@deltastate.edu

WINFREE, Natalie .... 910-576-6222. 362 C
winfreen@montgomery.edu
WINFREE, Terri, L .... 708-709-3638. 156 A
twinfree@prairiestate.edu
WINFREY, Heather .... 425-235-2415. 522 F
hwinfrey@rtc.edu
WINFREY, Steve .... 606-759-7141. 196 B
steve.winfrey@kctcs.edu
WINFREY GRIFFIN,
Polly .... 609-258-6191. 304 E
polly@princeton.edu
WING, Derek .... 425-602-3107. 516 K
media@bastyr.edu
WING, Edward .... 401-863-3330. 438 J
edward_wing_md@brown.edu
WINGARD, Alan, B .... 706-233-7248. 131 E
awingard@shorter.edu
WINGARD, Larry, R .... 724-847-6733. 417 A
lwingard@geneva.edu
WINGATE, Margaret .... 850-201-8366. 117 D
wingatem@tcc.fl.edu
WINGATE, Susan, F .... 903-923-3231. 486 A
susan.wingate@tstc.edu
WINGE, Jennifer, D .... 330-263-2116. 377 H
jwinge@wooster.edu
WINGE, Joseph .... 330-263-2317. 377 H
joewinge@wooster.edu
WINGER, Nancy .... 785-242-5200. 189 I
nancy.wingert@ottawa.edu
WINGER, Philip, E .... 570-372-4135. 433 H
winger@susqu.edu
WINGER, Philip, G .... 716-375-2622. 338 E
pwinger@sbu.edu
WINGET, Paul .... 515-244-4221. 175 C
wingetp@aib.edu
WINGFIELD, Albert, B .... 260-452-2106. 165 D
al.wingfield@ctsfw.edu
WINGFIELD, Rob .... 706-272-4436. 123 G
WINGFIELD, Tim .... 865-573-4517. 455 G
twingfield@johnsonU.edu
WINGLER, Mike .... 336-838-6178. 365 B
michael.wingler@wilkescc.edu
WINGO, Heidi .... 916-649-8168... 49 I
hwingo@kaplan.edu
WINGS, Arron .... 319-398-5403. 180 J
arron.wings@kirkwood.edu
WINIECKI, Jayna .... 501-337-5000... 20 J
jwiniecki@coto.edu
WININGS, Kathy .... 212-563-6647. 348 I
academics@uts.edu
WINISTORFER, Paul, M . 540-231-5481. 515 C
pwinisto@vt.edu
WINKELBAUER, Brian .... 303-273-3140... 80 E
bwinkelb@mines.edu
WINKELFOOS, Natalie .... 440-775-6463. 385 H
Natalie.Winkelfoos@oberlin.edu
WINKELMAN, Bryce .... 360-596-5333. 524 A
bwinkelman@spscc.edu
WINKELMANN, John, F . 608-363-2350. 531 M
winkelj@beloit.edu
WINKLEMAN, Mark .... 512-651-4750. 450 G
mwinkleman@national.edu
WINKLER, Carol, J .... 314-286-3651. 280 F
cjwinkler@ranken.edu
WINKLER, Chris .... 512-313-3000. 469 L
chris.winkler@concordia.edu
WINKLER, Janet .... 678-466-5050. 123 A
janetwinkler@clayton.edu
WINKLER, Linda .... 570-408-4600. 437 F
WINKLER, Nick .... 262-551-5800. 532 D
nwinkler@carthage.edu
WINKLEY, Robert .... 617-585-1280. 234 I
robert.winkley@necmusic.edu
WINN, Emmett .... 334-844-5771..... 1 G
winnjoh@auburn.edu
WINN, James .... 603-645-9700. 297 I
j.winn@snhu.edu
WINN, Lori .... 870-972-3454... 19 N
lwinn@astate.edu
WINN, Regina .... 318-670-9411. 207 A
rwinn@susla.edu
WINN-RATLIFF,
Maria, L .... 308-635-6189. 293 E
winnm@wncc.edu
WINNEY, Maureen .... 518-587-2100. 346 A
maureen.winney@esc.edu
WINNIFORD, Janet .... 801-626-6008. 497 D
jwinniford@weber.edu
WINNINGHAM, Laura .... 909-389-3323... 61 K
lwinningham@craftonhills.edu
WINOGRAD,
Katharine, W .... 505-224-4412. 309 E
winograd@cnm.edu
WINQUIST, Melissa .... 480-858-9100... 17 P
m.winquist@scnm.edu
WINSHIP, Nancy, K .... 781-736-4002. 224 F
winship@brandeis.edu
WINSLOW, Bridgette ...... 517-264-3981. 238 G
bwinslow@adrian.edu
WINSLOW, Christopher .. 775-674-7500. 294 H
cwinslow@tmcc.edu

WINSLOW, Kathy .... 252-985-5134. 365 D
kwinslow@ncwc.edu
WINSLOW, Mark .... 405-789-6400. 399 K
mwinslow@snu.edu
WINSLOW, Nadine, J ..... 775-673-7025. 294 H
nwinslow@tmcc.edu
WINSLOW, Pamela .... 973-720-2843. 308 I
winslowp@wpunj.edu
WINSLOW, Valerie .... 908-737-7100. 302 F
vwinslow@kean.edu
WINSLOW-SCHABER,
Deborah, J .... 716-888-2240. 316 C
winslowd@canisius.edu
WINSOR, Susan, A .... 803-508-7240. 440 G
winsors@atc.edu
WINSTEL, Susan, M .... 412-578-6330. 412 G
winstelsm@carlow.edu
WINSTON, Bruce, E .... 757-352-4306. 508 G
brucwin@regent.edu
WINSTON, David .... 870-512-7829... 20 B
david_winston@asun.edu
WINSTON, Eric .... 312-369-7418. 143 D
ewinston@colum.edu
WINSTON, Kathleen .... 951-639-5560... 55 B
kwinston@msjc.edu
WINSTON, Mark .... 330-972-7495. 390 E
WINSTON, JR.,
Matthew, M .... 706-542-0054. 133 C
mwinston@uga.edu
WINSTON, Robert, P ...... 717-245-1363. 414 H
winston@dickinson.edu
WINSTON, Robin .... 678-891-3417. 125 G
robin.winston@gpc.edu
WINSTON, Van Buren .... 212-217-3400. 324 C
vanburen_winston@fitnyc.edu
WINSTON-MUIR, Jeanni 301-846-2489. 214 H
jwinston-muir@frederick.edu
WINTEMUTE, Kelly .... 512-463-3280. 486 D
kelly.wylie@tsus.edu
WINTEMUTE, Mike .... 512-463-4862. 486 D
mike.wintemute@tsus.edu
WINTER, Barbara, J .... 620-235-4152. 189 L
bwinter@pittstate.edu
WINTER, Karla, R .... 563-562-3263. 181 E
winterk@nicc.edu
WINTER, Stacey, O .... 701-231-8954. 371 G
stacey.winter@ndsu.edu
WINTER, Tara .... 518-255-5418. 344 E
wintertl@cobleskill.edu
WINTER, Tara, L .... 607-746-4536. 345 G
wintertl@delhi.edu
WINTER, Walt .... 850-484-1903. 110 G
wwinter@pensacolastate.edu
WINTER, JR.,
William, F .... 618-650-5380. 159 H
wwinter@siue.edu
WINTERBAUER,
Nancy, S .... 848-932-7832. 306 A
winterbauer@oldqueens.rutgers.edu
WINTEREGG, Steven ...... 937-766-3235. 375 K
winteregg@cedarville.edu
WINTERER, James, C ..... 651-962-6404. 265 C
jcwinterer@stthomas.edu
WINTERFIELD,
Catherine .... 973-300-2119. 307 F
cwinterfield@sussex.edu
WINTERHALTER, Teresa . 912-344-3135. 120 G
teresa.winterhalter@armstrong.edu
WINTERLING,
Stephen, A .... 727-816-3340. 110 E
winters@phcc.edu
WINTERMEYER,
Stephen, F .... 317-274-8214. 168 D
swinter@iupui.edu
WINTERS, Amy .... 845-687-5124. 348 H
wintersa@sunyulster.edu
WINTERS, Chet .... 610-372-4721. 431 D
cwinters@racc.edu
WINTERS, Curt, D .... 215-702-4206. 411 F
cwinters@cairn.edu
WINTERS, Hyla .... 702-651-4554. 294 E
hyla.winters@csn.edu
WINTERS, James, W ...... 630-617-6447. 145 A
jwinters@elmhurst.edu
WINTERS, Jill .... 414-961-3897. 535 A
jwinters@ccon.edu
WINTERS, Jill, M .... 414-326-2301. 532 G
jwinters@ccon.edu
WINTERS, John .... 508-531-2717. 229 D
jwinters@bridgew.edu
WINTERS, Margaret, E .... 313-577-2200. 252 G
provost@wayne.edu
WINTERS-DUNN, Teresa 413-265-2210. 225 C
wintersdunnt@elms.edu
WINTERS-PALACIO, CM 312-850-7247. 142 C
cwinterspalacio@ccc.edu
WINTERSTEEN, Wendy ... 515-294-2518. 175 H
wwinters@iastate.edu
WINTERWOOD, Fawn ..... 614-947-6235. 380 A
fawn.winterwood@franklin.edu

WINWARD, Cindy .... 866-680-2756. 496 A
office@midwifery.edu
WINWARD, Cindy .... 801-918-6548. 496 A
office@midwifery.edu
WIORKOWSKI, John ...... 972-883-2274. 491 E
wiorkow@utdallas.edu
WIPPERMAN, Gary, L .... 319-352-8353. 183 E
gary.wipperman@wartburg.edu
WIPPMAN, David .... 612-625-4841. 264 G
dwippman@umn.edu
WIRT, Gary, L .... 302-225-6260... 93 H
wirtgl@gbc.edu
WIRT, Susan .... 706-507-8463. 123 D
wirt_susan@columbusstate.edu
WIRTH, Carolyn .... 516-561-0050. 316 B
WIRTH, Karen .... 612-874-3665. 257 B
kwirth@mcad.edu
WIRTH, Michael .... 865-974-3031. 463 C
mwirth@utk.edu
WIRTH, Ross .... 614-947-6128. 380 A
ross.wirth@franklin.edu
WIRTH, Sandy .... 860-913-2063... 90 A
swirth@goodwin.edu
WIRTHLIN, Gayle .... 319-656-2447. 182 D
WIRTHLIN, James .... 319-656-2447. 182 D
WIRTZ, James, J .... 831-656-3781. 544 M
jwirtz@nps.edu
WIRTZ, Kelly, J .... 515-574-2823. 179 D
wirtz@iowacentral.edu
WISBEY, Randal, R .... 951-785-2020... 50 B
rwisbey@lasierra.edu
WISCHNOWSKI,
Michael .... 585-385-7316. 338 H
mwischnowski@sjfc.edu
WISE, Adam, K .... 617-353-5282. 224 D
awise@bu.edu
WISE, Ashley .... 724-852-7625. 437 A
awise@waynesburg.edu
WISE, Eliezer .... 215-635-7300. 417 C
ewise@gratz.edu
WISE, Janet .... 505-428-1217. 311 J
janet.wise@sfcc.edu
WISE, Jessica .... 740-333-5115. 389 B
jwise@sscc.edu
WISE, Jody .... 626-914-8656... 38 K
jwise@citruscollege.edu
WISE, John .... 585-567-9456. 326 F
john.wise@houghton.edu
WISE, L. Anthony .... 865-694-6616. 461 D
lawise@pstcc.edu
WISE, Maria .... 480-732-7274... 14 J
maria.wise@cgc.edu
WISE, Mary, B .... 336-278-6642. 354 B
wisemary@elon.edu
WISE, Mary, K .... 402-457-2250. 290 G
mwise@mccneb.edu
WISE, Phyllis .... 217-333-6290. 161 C
pmwise@illinois.edu
WISE, Phyllis, M .... 217-333-6290. 162 A
pmwise@illinois.edu
WISE, Sandra .... 615-525-2832... 28 M
slwise@argosy.edu
WISE, Steve .... 304-818-2009. 528 D
swise@newriver.edu
WISE, Teresa .... 205-348-5256..... 8 D
teresa.wise@ua.edu
WISE, Tim .... 601-974-1243. 267 I
wiseta@millsaps.edu
WISE, Timothy .... 352-873-5828. 100 K
wiset@cf.edu
WISEL, Lee Marie .... 301-891-4222. 221 B
lwisel@wau.edu
WISEMAN, Ana Maria .... 864-597-4510. 449 I
wisemana@wofford.edu
WISEMAN, Bob .... 859-257-5929. 200 C
robert.wiseman@uky.edu
WISEMAN, Chris .... 504-861-5499. 205 H
cwiseman@loyno.edu
WISEMAN, Christine, M . 773-298-3309. 158 E
president@sxu.edu
WISEMAN, Donna .... 301-405-2336. 219 B
dlwise@umd.edu
WISEMAN, James, V ...... 262-524-7221. 532 C
jwiseman@carrollu.edu
WISEMAN, Tina .... 573-288-6307. 273 F
twiseman@culver.edu
WISEMAN, Tom .... 702-579-3548. 294 B
twiseman@kaplan.edu
WISER, Bob, H .... 801-524-8107. 495 O
bwiser@ldsbc.edu
WISER, Elizabeth, A .... 802-656-3370. 500 F
elizabeth.wiser@uvm.edu
WISER, Hayes .... 843-525-8333. 447 C
hwiser@tcl.edu
WISHING, III, Lee, S ..... 724-458-3332. 417 E
lswishing@gcc.edu
WISHON, Angela .... 214-648-0455. 493 E
angela.wishon@utsouthwestern.edu
WISHON, Gordon, D .... 480-965-9334... 11 K
gordon.wishon@asu.edu

WISHON, Phillip, M .... 540-568-6572. 506 F
wishonpm@jmu.edu
WISLOCK, Robert .... 570-389-4529. 427 H
rwislock@bloomu.edu
WISNER, Arthur, S .... 410-857-2218. 216 E
awisner@mcdaniel.edu
WISNER, David .... 716-896-0700. 350 A
dmwisner@villa.edu
WISNER, Jay .... 802-485-2075. 500 A
jwisner@norwich.edu
WISNER, Marie .... 651-638-6543. 253 K
m-wisner@bethel.edu
WISNER, Paul .... 714-892-7711... 39 J
pwisner@gwc.cccd.edu
WISNESKI, Thomas, E ... 610-566-1776. 437 G
twisneski@williamson.edu
WISNEWSKI, Michael ..... 401-341-2275. 440 C
michael.wisnewski@salve.edu
WISNIEWSKA, Sophia ..... 727-873-4466. 116 C
wiesniewska@mail.usf.edu
WISNIEWSKA,
Sophia, T .... 727-873-4151. 116 D
wisniewska@usfsp.edu
WISNIEWSKI, Michael .... 215-951-1070. 420 B
wisniews@lasalle.edu
WISNIOWICZ, Lisa .... 630-844-6852. 140 A
lwisni@aurora.edu
WISOFSKY, Tami .... 979-230-3308. 468 A
tami.wisofsky@brazosport.edu
WISSINGER, Kristin .... 724-222-5330. 425 K
kwissinger@penncommercial.edu
WISSMILLER, Andrew ..... 310-206-6771... 71 C
awissmiller@ais.ucla.edu
WISSMILLER, Becky .... 563-425-5248. 183 B
wissmillerb@uiu.edu
WISSMILLER, Kia .... 713-525-3117. 490 L
kritick@stthom.edu
WISSWELL, Keith, R .... 858-499-0202... 40 C
kwisswell@coleman.edu
WISTRCILL, Tom .... 330-972-7080. 390 E
krex@uakron.edu
WISTROM, Carl, H .... 773-244-4961. 154 G
cwistrom@northpark.edu
WISWALL, Derry .... 660-248-6296. 272 B
dwiswall@centralmethodist.edu
WISWALL, Irv .... 503-883-2575. 404 A
irvw@linfield.edu
WITCHER, Pamela, M ..... 508-531-1295. 229 D
pamela.witcher@bridgew.edu
WITCHNER, Anne .... 412-268-4886. 412 H
awow@andrew.cmu.edu
WITH, Elizabeth .... 940-565-4909. 490 C
elizabeth.with@unt.edu
WITHEM, Ron .... 402-472-7132. 292 G
rwithem@nebraska.edu
WITHERELL, Meghan ...... 530-938-5500... 41 A
witherellm@siskiyous.edu
WITHERELL, Michael, S . 805-893-8270... 72 B
witherell@research.ucsb.edu
WITHERELL, Paula .... 716-926-8792. 326 B
witherell@hilbert.edu
WITHERELL, Paula, A ...... 716-878-4101. 343 A
witherpa@buffalostate.edu
WITHERITE, Richard, L ... 606-337-1015. 193 F
rwitherite@ccbbc.edu
WITHEROW, Laurie, B .... 615-898-2111. 459 D
laurie.witherow@mtsu.edu
WITHEROW, Melissa .... 434-381-6131. 510 F
mwitherow@sbc.edu
WITHERS, Allen, B .... 304-929-5011. 528 D
awithers@newriver.edu
WITHERS, Ben .... 859-257-8450. 200 C
bwithers@uky.edu
WITHERS, Dale .... 707-965-7150... 57 J
dwithers@puc.edu
WITHERS, Gail .... 620-672-5641. 190 A
gailw@prattcc.edu
WITHERS, Gary .... 503-493-6207. 402 J
gwithers@cu-portland.edu
WITHERS, Stacie .... 816-995-2832. 280 G
stacie.withers@researchcollege.edu
WITHERSPOON,
Alanna, S .... 312-850-7031. 142 C
awitherspoon5@ccc.edu
WITHERSPOON,
Everette, L .... 336-750-2131. 370 A
witherspoone@wssu.edu
WITHERSPOON, Karen ... 212-650-6400. 317 D
kwitherspoon@ccny.cuny.edu
WITHERSPOON, Patricia 915-747-7018. 492 A
withersp@utep.edu
WITHERSPOON, Tonya .. 316-978-7751. 191 F
tonya.witherspoon@wichita.edu
WITHROW, Amy, S .... 717-221-1303. 417 I
aswithro@hacc.edu
WITKOVSKY, Lowell, D .. 814-641-3360. 419 H
witkovl@juniata.edu
WITKOWSKI, Barbara ..... 609-894-9311. 299 I
bwitkows@bcc.edu
WITMER, Kenneth, D ...... 610-436-2321. 430 A
kwitmer@wcupa.edu
WITMER, Timothy, Z ...... 215-572-3831. 437 C
twitmer@wts.edu
WITRAK, Marty .... 218-723-6021. 254 K
mwitrak@css.edu
WITRYK, Ted .... 269-337-7391. 244 K
Ted.Witryk@kzoo.edu
WITSCHEN, Peter, J .... 954-262-8832. 109 K
witschen@nova.edu
WITSON, Mike .... 740-588-1237. 394 C
mwitson@zanestate.edu
WITT, JR., Al .... 704-334-6882. 357 K
awitt@nlts.edu
WITT, Allen .... 813-259-6151. 106 M
awitt3@hccfl.edu
WITT, Anne .... 704-334-6882. 357 K
abwitt@nlts.edu
WITT, Betsy, A .... 864-488-8288. 444 L
bwitt@limestone.edu
WITT, Don .... 859-257-3458. 200 C
dwitt@uky.edu
WITT, Jack .... 567-661-7314. 387 L
fjwitt@owens.edu
WITT, Karen .... 202-639-1763... 95 B
kwitt@corcoran.org
WITT, Marie, D .... 215-898-1199. 435 B
witt@upenn.edu
WITT, Robert, E .... 205-348-9731..... 8 C
witt@uasystem.ua.edu
WITT, Sherra .... 423-472-7141. 460 D
switt@clevelandatatecc.edu
WITT, Tiffanie .... 270-824-8575. 196 A
tiffanie.witt@kctcs.edu
WITTE, Bob .... 417-626-1234. 279 J
witte.bob@occ.edu
WITTE, Dennis, E .... 708-209-3205. 143 E
dennis.witte@cuchicago.edu
WITTE, John .... 616-526-6547. 240 L
jwitte@calvin.edu
WITTE, Lois, J .... 417-667-8181. 273 A
lwitte@cottey.edu
WITTE, Peter, T .... 816-235-2731. 283 D
wittep@umkc.edu
WITTE, Sarah .... 541-962-3594. 405 H
switte@eou.edu
WITTENBERG, Diane ...... 626-396-2326... 28 P
diane.wittenberg@artcenter.edu
WITTENBORG, Karin ...... 434-924-3026. 511 B
kw7g@virginia.edu
WITTENMYER, Kathryn ... 415-503-6223... 62 H
klw@sfcm.edu
WITTER, Kevin, G .... 540-857-7341. 514 E
kwitter@virginiawestern.edu
WITTHOFT, Andrea .... 618-437-5321. 156 H
witthoft@rlc.edu
WITTIG, William .... 313-993-1532. 250 K
wittigw@udmercy.edu
WITTLER, Michele, A ...... 920-748-8119. 535 J
wittlerm@ripon.edu
WITTMAN, William .... 301-295-3185. 545 C
william.wittman@usuhs.edu
WITTMER, Michael .... 636-227-2100. 276 F
michael.wittmer@logan.edu
WITTNER, Charity .... 251-442-2507..... 9 A
cwittner@umobile.edu
WITTNER, Derek .... 212-353-4136. 321 F
dwittner@cooper.edu
WITTROCK, David, A ...... 701-231-7033. 371 G
david.wittrock@ndsu.edu
WITTROCK, Monica .... 920-403-3146. 535 L
monica.wittrock@snc.edu
WITTY, Janeen .... 803-705-4761. 441 C
wittyj@benedict.edu
WITZEL, Stephanie .... 707-668-5663... 42 F
WITZIGREUTER,
Danielle, L .... 260-422-5561. 167 B
dlwitzigreuter@indianatech.edu
WITZKE, Steve .... 989-686-9145. 242 C
smwitzke@delta.edu
WIXON, Tom .... 559-934-2132... 75 G
tomwixon@whccd.edu
WIXSOM, Richard .... 413-236-3003. 231 A
rwixsom@berkshirecc.edu
WIXSON, Karen .... 336-334-3403. 369 A
kkwixson@uncg.edu
WNUK, Beth .... 414-443-3631. 535 A
wnukb@mtmary.edu
WOBBE, Michelle .... 314-918-2599. 274 A
mwobbe@eden.edu
WOBBY, Lauren .... 802-485-2040. 500 A
lwobby@norwich.edu
WOBIG, Jayne .... 507-457-1438. 264 A
jwobig@smumn.edu
WOBSCHALL, Rachel, A . 651-962-6992. 265 C
rawobschall@stthomas.edu
WODKA, Chris .... 520-494-5230... 12 P
chris.wodka@centralaz.edu
WOEBKENBERG, Eric ..... 610-499-4090. 437 E
eewoebkenberg@widener.edu
WOELL, John .... 517-629-0222. 239 A
jwoell@albion.edu
WOERDEHOFF,
Valorie, A .... 563-588-7565. 180 L
woerdehoff.valorie@loras.edu
WOERHEIDE, Walter, J .. 610-526-1398. 409 F
walt.woerheide@theamericancollege.edu
WOEST, James .... 714-879-3901... 47 K
jwoest@hiu.edu
WOESTE, Lori .... 319-398-5516. 180 J
lwoeste@kirkwood.edu
WOFFORD, Rufus .... 843-863-7194. 441 H
jwofford@csuniv.edu
WOGAN, Maureen .... 773-298-3010. 158 E
wogan@sxu.edu
WOHL, David .... 803-323-2323. 449 G
wohld@winthrop.edu
WOHL, James .... 860-486-5143... 92 A
jim.wohl@uconn.edu
WOHLER, Tina .... 620-278-4218. 190 I
twohler@sterling.edu
WOHLERS, Anton .... 580-581-6775. 394 G
awohlers@cameron.edu
WOHLERS, William, R .... 423-236-2814. 458 J
wohlers@southern.edu
WOHLERT, Amy .... 505-277-1092. 312 F
awohlert@unm.edu
WOHLFORD, Mary Pat ... 641-673-1001. 183 H
Wohlfordm@wmpenn.edu
WOHLGEMUTH,
Darin, B .... 515-294-5842. 175 H
darinw@iastate.edu
WOHLMAN, Jason, L ...... 530-752-9793... 70 J
jlwohlman@ucdavis.edu
WOHLPART, Jim .... 239-590-1094. 115 A
wohlpart@fgcu.edu
WOIKE, David .... 734-487-0076. 242 D
dwoike@emich.edu
WOITOWITZ, Chris .... 417-455-5712. 273 E
cwoitowitz@crowder.edu
WOJAK, Angie .... 212-592-2000. 340 H
awojak@sva.edu
WOJCICKI, Edward .... 217-206-7795. 161 E
wojcicki.edward@uis.edu
WOJCIECHOWSKA,
Bogusia .... 617-228-2025. 231 C
bwojciechowska@bhcc.mass.edu
WOJCIECHOWSKI, Keli .. 708-524-6827. 144 C
kallen@dom.edu
WOJCIECHOWSKI,
William, A .... 620-672-2700. 190 A
williamw@prattcc.edu
WOJCIK, Alketa .... 760-757-2121... 54 G
awojcik@miracosta.edu
WOJCIK, Frank .... 603-358-2736. 298 F
fwojcik@keene.edu
WOJKE, Katie .... 360-491-4700. 522 G
kwojke@stmartin.edu
WOJNOWSKI, Mark, E ... 716-286-9718. 334 F
mew@niagara.edu
WOJTAS, Susan, A .... 508-849-3298. 222 B
swojtas@annamaria.edu
WOLANIN, Monique .... 860-412-7328... 89 E
mwolanin@qvcc.commnet.edu
WOLANSKYJ,
Alexandra, A .... 507-284-3627. 254 G
wolanskyj.alexandra@mayo.edu
WOLAVER, Rob .... 254-867-3366. 486 B
rob.wolaver@tstc.edu
WOLBERT, Jodi .... 603-513-1302. 298 E
jodi.wolbert@granite.edu
WOLCH, Jennifer .... 510-642-0831... 70 I
wolch@berkeley.edu
WOLCOWITZ, Jeffrey ...... 216-368-2928. 375 J
jeffrey.wolcowitz@case.edu
WOLD, Donald, C .... 630-844-5610. 140 A
dwold@aurora.edu
WOLD, Mark, C .... 608-363-2359. 531 M
woldm@beloit.edu
WOLD, Paul, G .... 507-344-7346. 253 J
pwold@blc.edu
WOLD-MCCORMICK,
Kristi, D .... 701-231-7981. 371 G
kristi.wold-mccormick@ndsu.edu
WOLEVER, Jack .... 805-893-4581... 72 B
jack.wolever@dcs.ucsb.edu
WOLF, Alan .... 212-353-4286. 321 F
awolf.physics@gmail.com
WOLF, Andrea .... 617-521-2488. 236 G
andrea.wolf@simmons.edu
WOLF, Andreas .... 650-574-6461... 64 C
wolf@smccd.edu
WOLF, George .... 517-264-7177. 250 B
gwolf@sienaheights.edu
WOLF, Greg .... 508-856-4296. 229 C
greg.wolf@umassmed.edu
WOLF, Howard, E .... 650-724-5992... 68 E
howardwolf@stanford.edu
WOLF, Jay, D .... 812-888-4172. 174 F
jwolf@vinu.edu
WOLF, Jeffery, M .... 812-488-2183. 173 H
jw268@evansville.edu
WOLF, Jennifer, J .... 812-941-2676. 168 F
jejwolf@ius.edu
WOLF, Jonathon .... 814-536-5168. 412 C
jwolf@crbc.net
WOLF, Kelly, B .... 541-346-3165. 406 D
kbwolf@uoregon.edu
WOLF, Kenneth .... 973-720-2432. 308 I
wolfk@wpunj.edu
WOLF, Kurt .... 941-359-7534. 111 O
kwolf@ringling.edu
WOLF, Laurie .... 515-964-6437. 177 B
lawolf@dmacc.edu
WOLF, Nick .... 619-849-2384... 59 L
nickwolf@pointloma.edu
WOLF, Paul, J .... 937-255-0452. 544 C
paul.wolf@afit.edu
WOLF, Rachel, B .... 972-860-7358. 470 I
RWolf@dcccd.edu
WOLF, Rebecca, E .... 501-882-8867... 19 M
rewolf@asub.edu
WOLF, Robert .... 813-253-7144. 106 M
rwolf@hccfl.edu
WOLF, Robert .... 718-409-2258. 346 D
rwolf@sunymaritime.edu
WOLF JOHNSON,
Cynthia .... 704-687-7226. 368 E
cwolfjo@uncc.edu
WOLFE, Agata .... 201-216-8162. 307 E
awolfe@stevens.edu
WOLFE, Andrew .... 315-792-7234. 346 C
andrew.wolfe@sunyit.edu
WOLFE, Ben .... 509-533-8861. 518 E
ben.wolfe@scc.spokane.edu
WOLFE, Bill .... 318-797-5279. 205 F
bill.wolfe@lsus.edu
WOLFE, Connie .... 336-386-3220. 364 D
wolfec@surry.edu
WOLFE, David .... 732-255-0400. 304 A
dwolfe@ocean.edu
WOLFE, Debbie .... 336-386-3401. 364 D
wolfed@surry.edu
WOLFE, Elizabeth .... 304-696-6007. 529 H
mccormi8@marshall.edu
WOLFE, Gregory .... 508-565-1357. 237 A
gwolfe@stonehill.edu
WOLFE, JR., James .... 812-941-2330. 168 F
jaewolfe@ius.edu
WOLFE, James, F .... 540-231-4000. 504 G
WOLFE, Joel .... 205-970-9208..... 7 B
jwolfe@sebc.edu
WOLFE, Johanna .... 713-221-8909. 489 D
wolfej@uhd.edu
WOLFE, John, S .... 812-877-8590. 172 C
john.s.wolfe@rose-hulman.edu
WOLFE, Jonathan .... 409-880-7633. 486 E
jcwolfe@lit.edu
WOLFE, Karl .... 507-288-2886. 253 H
wolfek@augsburg.edu
WOLFE, Katherine, J .... 402-465-2312. 291 G
kjw@nebrwesleyan.edu
WOLFE, Ken .... 727-864-8835. 101 N
wolfefk@eckerd.edu
WOLFE, Lisa, C .... 636-481-3161. 275 I
lwolfe@jeffco.edu
WOLFE, NJ .... 212-217-4370. 324 C
nj_wolfe@fitnyc.edu
WOLFE, Peggy, L .... 337-475-5820. 207 G
pwolfe@mcneese.edu
WOLFE, Thomas, V .... 303-765-3102... 82 E
tvwolfe@iliff.edu
WOLFE, Thomas, V .... 315-443-4263. 347 C
tvwolfe@syr.edu
WOLFE, Timothy, M .... 573-882-2011. 283 B
umpresident@umsystem.edu
WOLFE, Tina .... 618-533-4111. 149 D
twolfe@kaskaskia.edu
WOLFE, Todd .... 818-677-3700... 34 C
todd.wolfe@csun.edu
WOLFE, Vicki .... 205-970-9245..... 7 B
vwolfe@sebc.edu
WOLFE-LEE, Chyerl .... 360-650-3774. 525 C
chyerl.wolfe-lee@wwu.edu
WOLFE-STEPRO,
Charlene .... 603-206-8072. 296 A
cwolfe@ccsnh.edu
WOLFENDEN, Robert, W 610-758-3430. 422 A
rww3@lehigh.edu
WOLFER, Diane, G .... 859-371-9393. 192 D
dwolfer@beckfield.edu
WOLFERT, Kelly .... 920-693-1171. 540 B
ltc.bookstore@gotoltc.edu
WOLFF, David .... 605-642-6504. 451 G
WOLFF, Dawn .... 813-880-8017. 107 C
dwolff@academy.edu
WOLFF, Holly, D .... 563-425-5221. 183 B
wolffh@uiu.edu
WOLFF, Michael, A .... 314-977-2774. 281 I
mwolff3@slu.edu
WOLFF, Peg, A .... 308-635-6064. 293 E
pwolff@wncc.edu

WOLFF, Susan .... 815-939-5203. 155 H
swolff@olivet.edu
WOLFF, Susan, J .... 406-771-4305. 287 E
susan.wolff@gfcmsu.edu
WOLFF, Timothy .... 775-784-4666. 294 J
tawolff@unr.edu
WOLFGANG, Tamara, L . 540-338-1776. 508 A
registrar@phc.edu
WOLFORD, Gail .... 859-985-3150. 192 F
gail_wolford@berea.edu
WOLFORD, Norman, R ... 239-513-1135. 119 E
WOLFSON, Amy .... 508-793-2541. 225 B
awolfson@holycross.edu
WOLFSON, Bob, E .... 619-594-6304... 35 D
bwolfson@foundation.sdsu.edu
WOLFSON, Hannah .... 205-226-4922..... 2 C
hwolfson@bsc.edu
WOLFSON, Michael .... 617-262-5000. 223 F
Michael.Wolfson@the-bac.edu
WOLFSON, Philip, G ...... 562-988-2278... 28 B
pwolfson@auhs.edu
WOLIN, Richard, R .... 231-995-2003. 248 B
rwolin@nmc.edu
WOLINSKY, Lawrence, E 214-828-8300. 484 B
wolinsky@bcd.tamhsc.edu
WOLK, David, S .... 802-468-1201. 501 B
dave.wolk@castleton.edu
WOLK, Ira .... 516-561-0050. 316 B
WOLKING, Daryl .... 540-338-1776. 508 A
WOLLENBURG, Doug ...... 912-525-5000. 131 B
dwollenbu@scad.edu
WOLLENS, Jack .... 360-383-3016. 525 D
jwollens@whatcom.ctc.edu
WOLLER, Eric, K .... 507-344-7790. 253 J
ewoller@blc.edu
WOLLMAN, Julie, E .... 814-732-2711. 428 E
WOLLMAN, Rick .... 712-274-5320. 181 B
wollman@morningside.edu
WOLLMERING, Jerry ...... 660-785-4235. 282 L
jerryw@truman.edu
WOLMAN, Tara .... 413-552-2495. 231 F
twolman@hcc.edu
WOLMARK, Adrienne ..... 503-552-1605. 404 H
awolmark@ncnm.edu
WOLMARK, Mordechai ... 845-352-3431. 351 J
mwolmark@optonline.net
WOLPERN, Kevin .... 952-888-4777. 263 B
kwolpern@nwhealth.edu
WOLPERT, Ann, J .... 617-253-5297. 233 B
WOLPERT, David .... 330-823-2286. 391 E
wolperds@mountunion.edu
WOLPIN, Aryeh .... 718-232-7800. 351 C
WOLPIN, Chaim .... 718-232-7800. 351 C
WOLPIN, Ken .... 908-737-3290. 302 F
wolpin@kean.edu
WOLSZCZAK, Jennifer .... 219-785-5299. 172 A
jwolszczak@pnc.edu
WOLSZON, Linda .... 817-257-7863. 484 I
l.wolszon@tcu.edu
WOLTEN, Lori .... 515-574-1156. 179 D
wolten@iowacentral.edu
WOLTMANN, Tanya, L ... 312-341-2006. 157 D
twoltmann@roosevelt.edu
WOLZ, Jay .... 573-651-2930. 282 B
jwolz@semo.edu
WOMACK, Donna .... 318-678-6000. 202 I
dwomack@bpcc.edu
WOMACK, Joseph .... 541-684-7241. 405 C
jwomack@nwcu.edu
WOMACK, Veronica .... 478-445-1382. 125 A
veronica.womack@gcsu.edu
WOMACK, Wayne .... 479-788-7407... 24 A
wayne.womack@uafs.edu
WOMACK, William .... 918-495-7088. 398 H
wwomack@oru.edu
WOMBLE, Haley .... 314-837-6777. 280 K
hwomble@slcconline.edu
WOMBLE, Jeff .... 910-672-1474. 367 D
jwomble@uncfsu.edu
WOMBLE, Lynn, Z .... 903-813-2891. 466 H
lwomble@austincollege.edu
WOMBLE, Michael .... 314-837-6777. 280 K
mwomble@slcconline.edu
WOMBLE, Ron .... 620-235-4124. 189 L
kwomble@pittstate.edu
WOMELSDUFF, Gary, E .. 206-281-2678. 523 C
womelg@spu.edu
WON, Cha Hi .... 714-527-0691... 43 H
WONDERS, Christopher . 717-477-1251. 429 E
cawonders@ship.edu
WONDRA, Ellen .... 773-380-7040. 140 D
ellen.wondra@seabury.edu
WONG, David, W .... 216-397-1510. 381 R
dwong@jcu.edu
WONG, Erwin .... 212-220-8322. 317 A
ewong@bmcc.cuny.edu
WONG, Gene .... 978-232-2311. 226 C
gwong@endicott.edu
WONG, Jane .... 415-476-8434... 72 A
jane.wong@ucsf.edu
WONG, Jeannie .... 916-278-2067... 34 D
WONG, Julie .... 727-873-4882. 116 D
juliewong@mail.usf.edu
WONG, Kathy .... 828-227-7218. 369 E
wong@wcu.edu
WONG, Lam .... 216-987-4265. 378 D
lam.wong@tri-c.edu
WONG, Leslie, E .... 415-338-1381... 35 E
president@sfsu.edu
WONG, Michael .... 808-455-0491. 137 A
mckwong@hawaii.edu
WONG, Nancy, C .... 323-265-8820... 51 F
wongnc@elac.edu
WONG, Paul .... 619-594-5456... 35 D
pwong@sdsu.edu
WONG, Richard .... 804-355-0671. 510 G
rwong@upsem.edu
WONG, Sandra .... 719-389-6682... 79 D
swong@coloradocollege.edu
WONG, Walter .... 510-643-1640... 70 I
oua2wong@berkeley.edu
WONG-NICKERSON,
Agnes .... 415-338-2582... 35 E
agnesw@sfsu.edu
WONGSAROJ, Ben .... 305-623-4100. 104 J
ben.wongsaroj@fmuniv.edu
WOO, Deborah .... 201-200-3003. 303 F
dwoo@njcu.edu
WOO, Don .... 708-239-4861. 160 K
don.woo@trnty.edu
WOO, Ho, K .... 714-517-1945... 29 K
librarian@buc.edu
WOO, Melissa, Z .... 541-346-1702. 406 D
mwoo@uoregon.edu
WOO, Meredith, J .... 434-924-4611. 511 B
mjw8q@virginia.edu
WOO, Michael .... 909-869-2661... 32 G
WOO, Tommy Lee .... 650-723-2300... 68 E
WOOD, Alda .... 678-915-3931. 132 C
awood@spsu.edu
WOOD, Amy .... 828-328-7728. 356 B
amy.wood@lr.edu
WOOD, Amy, B .... 615-963-5772. 459 E
awood@tnstate.edu
WOOD, Andy .... 662-472-2312. 267 B
awood@holmescc.edu
WOOD, Barbara .... 702-968-2055. 295 E
bwood@roseman.edu
WOOD, Bob, G .... 410-548-5391. 220 D
bgwood@salisbury.edu
WOOD, Bonnie .... 985-867-2237. 206 H
rouquette@sjasc.edu
WOOD, Bret .... 405-733-7413. 399 F
bwood@rose.edu
WOOD, Casey .... 570-662-4078. 429 C
cmwood@mansfield.edu
WOOD, Cathy, R .... 202-319-5606... 94 G
woodcr@cua.edu
WOOD, Charlene .... 828-479-9256. 364 E
cwood@tricountycc.edu
WOOD, Charles .... 850-201-6428. 117 D
woodc@tcc.fl.edu
WOOD, Chris .... 302-736-2316... 94 C
chriswood@wesley.edu
WOOD, Chris .... 903-923-2062. 471 J
cwood@etbu.edu
WOOD, Cliff, L .... 845-574-4214. 338 B
cwood@sunyrockland.edu
WOOD, Danielle, L .... 479-575-4019... 23 I
dlw11@uark.edu
WOOD, Darrow .... 718-260-5497. 319 B
dwood@citytech.cuny.edu
WOOD, David .... 713-973-3000. 144 A
dwood4@devry.edu
WOOD, David .... 210-486-0063. 465 C
dwood30@alamo.edu
WOOD, David, H .... 906-227-2112. 248 A
dwood@nmu.edu
WOOD, David, S .... 864-597-4020. 449 I
woodds@wofford.edu
WOOD, Debra .... 704-216-6079. 356 D
dwood@livingstone.edu
WOOD, Donald .... 432-335-6340. 477 M
dwood@odessa.edu
WOOD, Donna, G .... 918-595-7841. 400 E
donna.wood@tulsacc.edu
WOOD, Douglas .... 207-602-2807. 213 A
dwood@une.edu
WOOD, Douglas .... 207-602-2340. 213 A
dwood@une.edu
WOOD, Douglas, M .... 717-766-2511. 423 L
dwood@messiah.edu
WOOD, Elizabeth, B .... 609-258-3354. 304 E
lizwood@princeton.edu
WOOD, Erin .... 701-662-1598. 372 D
erin.wood@lrsc.edu
WOOD, Evelyn .... 606-487-3141. 195 C
evelyn.wood@kctcs.edu
WOOD, Faye .... 843-863-7502. 441 H
fwood@csuniv.edu
WOOD, Frank .... 305-809-3287. 104 I
frank.wood@fkcc.edu
WOOD, Fred .... 218-281-8343. 264 E
fewood@crk.umn.edu
WOOD, Fred .... 423-478-6229. 460 D
fwood@clevelandstatecc.edu
WOOD, Gail .... 607-753-2221. 343 B
gail.wood@cortland.edu
WOOD, Gary, M .... 262-595-2430. 537 C
gary.wood@uwp.edu
WOOD, Gaye .... 704-991-0221. 364 C
gwood7693@stanly.edu
WOOD, Gayle, E .... 865-539-7160. 461 D
gwood@pstcc.edu
WOOD, Jack .... 989-686-9822. 242 C
jackwood@delta.edu
WOOD, Jan .... 251-442-2456..... 9 A
jwood@umobile.edu
WOOD, Jane, M .... 724-946-7123. 437 B
woodjm@westminster.edu
WOOD, Janice, R .... 707-965-6315... 57 J
jwood@puc.edu
WOOD, Jason .... 479-394-7622... 23 B
jwood@rmcc.edu
WOOD, Jason .... 307-855-2111. 542 Y
jswood@cwc.edu
WOOD, Jeff .... 509-574-4691. 525 G
jwood@yvcc.edu
WOOD, Jeffrey, A .... 309-438-7602. 147 J
jwood@ilstu.edu
WOOD, Jocelyn .... 215-222-4200. 431 H
jmwood@walnuthillcollege.edu
WOOD, John .... 307-855-2162. 542 Y
jwood@cwc.edu
WOOD, John .... 303-762-6901... 81 G
john.wood@denverseminary.edu
WOOD, John .... 314-286-4855. 280 F
jewood@ranken.edu
WOOD, Joseph, S .... 410-837-5244. 221 A
jwood@ubalt.edu
WOOD, Joyce .... 765-998-5117. 173 C
jywood@taylor.edu
WOOD, Julia, H .... 865-694-6530. 461 D
jwood@pstcc.edu
WOOD, Karen .... 503-370-6213. 408 J
kwood@willamette.edu
WOOD, Kathryn .... 909-748-8069... 73 H
kathryn_wood@redlands.edu
WOOD, Kathryn .... 671-735-2658. 546 E
kwood@uguam.uog.edu
WOOD, Kelley .... 325-670-1251. 472 O
kwood@hsutx.edu
WOOD, Kim .... 865-251-1800. 458 I
kwood@southcollegetn.edu
WOOD, Kris .... 270-706-8412. 195 A
kris.wood@kctcs.edu
WOOD, Kurt, W .... 563-884-5127. 182 A
kurt.wood@palmer.edu
WOOD, Larry, E .... 931-598-1374. 458 H
lwood@sewanee.edu
WOOD, Laura .... 903-923-8207. 478 A
lwood@panola.edu
WOOD, Laura .... 617-627-3345. 237 C
laura.wood@tufts.edu
WOOD, Lisa .... 202-319-6794... 94 G
woodlm@cua.edu
WOOD, Lynn .... 617-873-0154. 224 G
Lynn.Wood@cambridgecollege.edu
WOOD, Mark .... 909-621-8146... 60 A
mark.wood@pomona.edu
WOOD, Mark, U .... 530-226-4603... 66 D
mwood@simpsonu.edu
WOOD, Martin .... 719-255-3438... 85 M
mwood@uccs.edu
WOOD, Matt .... 603-271-6484. 296 C
mwood@ccsnh.edu
WOOD, Merrillene, E ...... 308-635-6133. 293 E
woodm234@wncc.edu
WOOD, Michael .... 952-446-4100. 255 D
woodm@crown.edu
WOOD, Michael .... 609-652-4294. 305 C
michael.wood@stockton.edu
WOOD, Michael .... 570-408-4300. 437 F
michael.wood@wilkes.edu
WOOD, Michael, T .... 301-369-2800. 213 G
president@capitol-college.edu
WOOD, Murray .... 661-362-3433... 40 E
murray.wood@canyons.edu
WOOD, Pamela, R .... 919-658-7753. 357 I
pwood@moc.edu
WOOD, Phoebe .... 773-481-8525. 142 F
pwood3@ccc.edu
WOOD, Richard, C .... 806-743-2205. 487 E
richard.wood@ttuhsc.edu
WOOD, Richard, J .... 251-460-7021..... 9 E
rwood@southalabama.edu
WOOD, Rick .... 559-297-4500... 48 C
WOOD, Robert .... 904-620-4200. 116 B
robert.wood@unf.edu
WOOD, Robert .... 610-989-1257. 436 D
rwood@vfmac.edu
WOOD, Robert, A .... 740-368-3945. 387 J
rawood@owu.edu
WOOD, Robert, H .... 315-268-6474. 320 A
rwood@clarkson.edu
WOOD, Robert, S .... 901-334-5830. 457 A
rswood@memphisseminary.edu
WOOD, Scott .... 701-231-7411. 371 G
scott.wood@ndsu.edu
WOOD, Shelia .... 504-286-5368. 206 K
swood@suno.edu
WOOD, Sherri, L .... 573-882-0683. 283 C
woods@missouri.edu
WOOD, Steve .... 828-835-4254. 364 E
swood@tricountycc.edu
WOOD, Susan .... 804-819-4972. 511 G
swood@vccs.edu
WOOD, Tiffany .... 706-385-1019. 130 F
tiffany.wood@point.edu
WOOD, Tim .... 616-331-2240. 243 C
woodt@gvsu.edu
WOOD, Tom .... 615-966-6174. 456 B
tom.wood@lipscombs.edu
WOOD, Vicky .... 740-389-4636. 383 F
woodv@mtc.edu
WOOD, Wayne .... 508-678-2811. 231 B
wayne.wood@bristolcc.edu
WOOD, Wende .... 843-377-2156. 441 G
wwood@charlestonlaw.edu
WOOD, William, W .... 610-921-7749. 409 A
wwood@alb.edu
WOOD, Wm. Michael ..... 989-686-9216. 242 C
williamwood@delta.edu
WOOD, Yolanda .... 716-829-7602. 323 D
woodyo@dyc.edu
WOOD-GAINES, Kirk ...... 509-313-5996. 520 A
wood-gaines@gonzaga.edu
WOODALL, Allegra .... 410-532-5395. 217 E
awoodall@ndm.edu
WOODALL, Andy .... 540-665-4581. 509 E
awoodall@su.edu
WOODALL, Betty, C .... 919-209-2019. 361 E
bcwoodall@johnstoncc.edu
WOODALL, Stephen .... 404-756-4635. 121 A
swoodall@atlm.edu
WOODALL, Stephen .... 812-464-1845. 174 D
sgwoodall@usi.edu
WOODARD, Brandyn ...... 641-628-5134. 176 E
woodardb@central.edu
WOODARD, Brandyn ...... 320-363-5455. 254 J
WOODARD, Greg .... 206-239-2275. 516 H
gwoodard@aii.edu
WOODARD, Joanne, G ... 919-515-4559. 368 B
joanne_woodard@ncsu.edu
WOODARD, Johnnie, D . 704-499-9200... 96 F
WOODARD, Kimberly ..... 334-727-8076..... 8 A
kwoodard@tuskegee.edu
WOODARD, Lance, L ..... 615-353-3367. 461 B
lance.woodard@nscc.edu
WOODARD, Laura, J ...... 318-342-5447. 208 E
woodard@ulm.edu
WOODARD, Linda .... 216-987-3427. 378 D
linda.woodard@tri-c.edu
WOODARD, Timothy, E .. 919-658-7793. 357 I
twoodard@moc.edu
WOODBERRY, Peter, N .. 401-825-2147. 439 A
pwoodberry@ccri.edu
WOODBROOKS,
Catherine, M .... 508-767-7325. 222 C
cwoodbroo@assumption.edu
WOODBURN, Don, A ..... 620-227-9378. 186 B
donwoodburn@dc3.edu
WOODBURN, Steve, M .. 303-963-3233... 79 C
swoodburn@ccu.edu
WOODBURN, Steven ...... 252-335-0821. 359 F
steven_woodburn@albemarle.edu
WOODCOCK, Jonathan ... 603-623-0313. 297 E
jwoodcock@nhia.edu
WOODCOCK, Tony .... 617-585-1200. 234 I
tony.woodcock@necmusic.edu
WOODDELL, Kathleen .... 540-338-2700. 503 A
kwooddell@cdu.edu
WOODEN, Mark .... 602-639-7500... 13 S
WOODEN, Ontario, S ..... 919-530-5235. 368 A
owooden@nccu.edu
WOODERSON, Linda ...... 417-328-1715. 282 C
lwooderson@sbuniv.edu
WOODESHICK, Alisha .... 859-371-9393. 192 D
awoodeshick@beckfield.edu
WOODFAULK, Ashley .... 773-947-6276. 152 E
WOODFIELD, Richard .... 419-995-8222. 381 Q
woodfield.r@rhodesstate.edu
WOODFORD, Steve .... 865-251-1800. 458 I
swoodford@southcollegetn.edu
WOODHAM, Margo .... 478-471-2800. 128 I
margo.woodham@maconstate.edu
WOODHOUSE,
Bryan, M .... 608-246-6337. 540 C
woodhouse@madisoncollege.edu
WOODHOUSE, Francine . 702-651-5600. 294 E
francine.woodhouse@csn.edu
WOODHOUSE, Michelle . 757-822-7242. 514 C
mwoodhouse@tcc.edu

WOODLAND, Calvin .... 202-274-6203... 97 A
calvin.woodland@udc.edu
WOODLE, Tom .... 843-349-2357. 442 E
twoodle@coastal.edu
WOODLEE, Stephanie, A 325-674-2412. 464 H
stephanie.woodlee@acu.edu
WOODLEY, Charlie .... 706-396-8145. 130 C
cwoodley@paine.edu
WOODLEY, Michael, P ... 701-252-3467. 373 D
woodley@jc.edu
WOODLEY, Sandra, K .... 225-342-6950. 207 D
ulspresident@la.gov
WOODLEY, Xeturah .... 303-360-4729... 81 C
Xeturah.Woodley@CCAurora.edu
WOODMANSEE,
Holly, M .... 206-546-6955. 523 F
hwoodmansee@shoreline.edu
WOODMANSEE, Ken ...... 901-843-3874. 458 E
woodmanseek@rhodes.edu
WOODRICK, Rebecca ..... 601-266-6618. 270 E
rebecca.woodrick@usm.edu
WOODROW, Adam .... 413-782-1583. 238 A
awoodrow@wne.edu
WOODRUFF, Aaron .... 309-438-8631. 147 J
apwoodr@ilstu.edu
WOODRUFF, Kenneth, A 843-953-6859. 442 A
ken.woodruff@citadel.edu
WOODRUFF, Kevin .... 423-493-4250. 462 B
cierpke@prodigy.net
WOODRUFF, Kristin .... 785-442-6016. 187 E
kwoodruff@highlandcc.edu
WOODRUFF, Martha ...... 903-983-8287. 475 E
mwoodruff@kilgore.edu
WOODRUFF, Robert .... 937-512-4529. 388 O
robert.woodruff@sinclair.edu
WOODRUFF, Steven, W . 336-342-4261. 363 C
woodruffs@rockinghamcc.edu
WOODRUFF, Tina .... 215-871-6870. 430 D
tinawo@pcom.edu
WOODS, Amy, K .... 845-575-3000. 330 D
amy.k.coppola@marist.edu
WOODS, JR., Arnold, A . 641-269-3250. 178 H
woods@grinnell.edu
WOODS, Benjamin, E ..... 575-646-1727. 310 I
bwoods@nmsu.edu
WOODS, Billy .... 336-838-6496. 365 B
billy.woods@wilkescc.edu
WOODS, Brandy .... 618-634-3417. 158 M
brandyw@shawneecc.edu
WOODS, Brett .... 828-227-7124. 369 E
bwoods@wcu.edu
WOODS, Carolyn .... 717-264-4141. 437 H
carolyn.woods@wilson.edu
WOODS, Colleen .... 617-236-8800. 226 F
cwoods@fisher.edu
WOODS, Dannie .... 601-925-3830. 268 A
drwoods@mc.edu
WOODS, Debra .... 714-449-7434... 67 D
danderson@scco.edu
WOODS, Debra, D .... 724-925-4083. 437 D
woodsde@wccc.edu
WOODS, Gilda, Q .... 540-365-4290. 504 L
gwoods@ferrum.edu
WOODS, James, M .... 630-515-6173. 153 B
jwoods@midwestern.edu
WOODS, Jami .... 336-386-3266. 364 D
woodsj@surry.edu
WOODS, John, J .... 601-857-3387. 267 A
jjwoods@hindscc.edu
WOODS, Kimberly, J ...... 830-792-7282. 480 F
kjwoods@schreiner.edu
WOODS, Kristin, J .... 804-289-8026. 510 L
kwoods@richmond.edu
WOODS, Kristy, F .... 202-865-7470... 95 G
kristy.woods@howard.edu
WOODS, Larry .... 484-365-7211. 422 D
lwoods@lincoln.edu
WOODS, Linda .... 619-388-7434... 62 F
lwoods@sdccd.edu
WOODS, Marilyn, J .... 956-882-7147. 491 D
marilyn.woods@utb.edu
WOODS, Mary .... 830-792-7375. 480 F
zmwoods@schreiner.edu
WOODS, Mary Lou .... 909-621-8000... 60 A
marylou.woods@pomona.edu
WOODS, Maura, A .... 718-990-1985. 339 A
woodsm@stjohns.edu
WOODS, Mike .... 405-744-2474. 397 H
mike.woods@okstate.edu
WOODS, Pamela .... 304-214-8911. 528 G
pwoods@wvncc.edu
WOODS, Patrick .... 312-341-6360. 157 D
pwoods@roosevelt.edu
WOODS, Phillip .... 423-478-7993. 458 B
pwoods@ptseminary.edu
WOODS, R. Dean .... 864-231-2068. 441 B
dwoods@andersonuniversity.edu
WOODS, Rebekah .... 517-787-0800. 244 J
woodsrebekahs@jccmi.edu
WOODS, Richard, G .... 765-361-6188. 175 B
woodsr@wabash.edu
WOODS, Rick .... 508-213-2111. 235 E
rick.woods@nichols.edu
WOODS, Roderick .... 803-327-7402. 442 D
rwoods@clintonjuniorcollege.edu
WOODS, Sandra .... 541-737-5232. 406 A
sandra.woods@oregonstate.edu
WOODS, Scott .... 731-425-2638. 460 G
swoods@jscc.edu
WOODS, Sharmon .... 520-325-0123... 17 R
WOODS, Susan .... 781-280-3200. 232 B
woodss@middlesex.mass.edu
WOODS, Suzy .... 760-921-5410... 58 C
swoods@paloverde.edu
WOODS, Timothy .... 559-489-2352... 68 I
tim.woods@fresnocitycollege.edu
WOODS, Tracie, J .... 225-771-4680. 206 I
tracie_woods@sus.edu
WOODS, Tracy .... 478-289-2035. 124 C
twoods@ega.edu
WOODSIDE,
Christina, S .... 704-847-5600. 366 J
cwoodside@ses.edu
WOODSON, Corliss, B ... 804-523-5877. 512 F
cwoodson@reynolds.edu
WOODSON, Heather .... 704-922-6310. 360 F
woodson.heather@gaston.edu
WOODSON, Lenee .... 973-290-4227. 300 F
lwoodson@cse.edu
WOODSON, Lovisa .... 215-635-7300. 417 C
lwoodson@gratz.edu
WOODSON, Terrance, S . 214-887-5371. 471 F
twoodson@dts.edu
WOODSON, William .... 651-962-4226. 265 C
wwoodson@stthomas.edu
WOODSON, William .... 317-917-3323. 171 A
wwoodson@martin.edu
WOODSON,
William Randy .... 919-515-2191. 368 B
randy_woodson@ncsu.edu
WOODWARD, Angus ...... 225-768-1704. 206 D
angus.woodward@ololcollege.edu
WOODWARD, Beth .... 503-534-4023. 404 C
bwoodward@marylhurst.edu
WOODWARD, Bill .... 434-791-7103. 502 D
woodward@averett.edu
WOODWARD,
Gregory, S .... 262-551-5858. 532 D
president@carthage.edu
WOODWARD, John .... 253-879-3375. 524 F
woodward@pugetsound.edu
WOODWARD, Jonathan . 228-497-7627. 268 C
jonathan.woodward@mgccc.edu
WOODWARD, LouAnn ... 601-984-1010. 270 C
lawoodward@umc.edu
WOODWARD, Paul, J .... 207-893-6644. 211 G
pwoodward@sjcme.edu
WOODWARD, Scott .... 206-543-2212. 524 G
huskyad@uw.edu
WOODWARD, Scott .... 210-341-1366. 477 L
rsw@ost.edu
WOODWARD, Travis ...... 432-552-2806. 493 D
woodward_t@utpb.edu
WOODWARD, Wade .... 864-596-9072. 443 D
wade.woodward@converse.edu
WOODWORTH, Jody .... 402-552-3373. 288 L
woodworth@clarksoncollege.edu
WOODWORTH, Judith ..... 215-965-4059. 424 D
jwoodworth@moore.edu
WOODWORTH, Stephen . 706-886-6831. 133 A
swoodworth@tfc.edu
WOODWORTH-NEY,
Laura .... 208-282-2171. 138 E
woodlaur@isu.edu
WOODY, Craig .... 303-871-3588... 86 B
cwoody@du.edu
WOODY, Jaime .... 512-863-1624. 481 I
woodyj@southwestern.edu
WOODY, Jeannine, H ...... 336-249-8186. 360 A
jwoody@davidsonccc.edu
WOODY, Keith .... 425-602-3045. 516 K
kwoody@bastyr.edu
WOOLARD, Doug .... 813-974-2125. 116 C
dwoolard@admin.usf.edu
WOOLARD, Emily .... 252-940-6204. 358 A
EmilyW@beaufortccc.edu
WOOLARD, Larry .... 217-732-3168. 151 B
lwoolard@lincolnchristian.edu
WOOLARD, Nyla .... 309-796-5501. 140 E
woolardn@bhc.edu
WOOLARD, Rebecca, P .. 252-789-0224. 361 G
rwoolard@martincc.edu
WOOLBERT, Stephanie ... 617-277-3915. 224 C
WOOLDRIDGE,
Deborah, G .... 419-372-7851. 374 K
dgwoold@bgsu.edu
WOOLDRIDGE, Heath .... 870-612-2039... 25 A
heath.wooldridge@uaccb.edu
WOOLDRIDGE, Peter ..... 919-536-7200. 360 B
wooldridgep@durhamtech.edu
WOOLEVER, James .... 650-543-3757... 54 C
jwoolever@menlo.edu
WOOLEVER, Kristin, R ... 928-350-4100... 17 K
kwoolever@prescott.edu
WOOLEY, Travis .... 407-303-9440... 97 H
travis.wooley@adu.edu
WOOLF, Sarah .... 617-731-7080. 235 H
woolfsar@pmc.edu
WOOLFOLK, Alan .... 904-819-6248. 103 E
awoolfolk@flagler.edu
WOOLFORD, Ann .... 540-891-3051. 512 E
awoolford@germanna.edu
WOOLIVER, Matt .... 918-293-4888. 398 B
matt.wooliver@okstate.edu
WOOLLARD, Lynne .... 304-424-8263. 530 E
Lynne.Woollard@wvup.edu
WOOLLEN, Liz .... 405-325-2864. 401 B
lwoolen@ou.edu
WOOLLEY, Peter .... 973-443-8084. 301 J
woolley@fdu.edu
WOOLLEY, Rose, M .... 412-578-6274. 412 G
rmwoolley@carlow.edu
WOOLLEY, Susan, O ...... 610-861-1332. 424 E
mesow01@moravian.edu
WOOLLISCROFT,
James, O .... 734-764-8175. 251 C
woolli@umich.edu
WOOLMAN, Janet, R ...... 337-475-5125. 207 G
jwoolman@mcneese.edu
WOOLPERT, Steve .... 925-631-4145... 61 F
woolpert@stmarys-ca.edu
WOOLRIDGE, Cindy, B .. 910-938-6145. 359 E
burkhartc@coastalcarolina.edu
WOOLSEY, Andrew .... 949-480-4112... 66 F
awoolsey@soka.edu
WOOLSEY, Clint .... 812-749-1440. 171 K
WOOLSEY, Roger, W ...... 603-646-2215. 296 G
roger.w.woolsey@dartmouth.edu
WOOLSON, Mary, D .... 717-291-4270. 416 J
mary.woolson@fandm.edu
WOOLSTENHULME,
David, R .... 435-722-6900. 496 M
davew@ubatc.edu
WOOLVERTON, Rick ...... 912-583-3204. 122 B
rwoolverton@bpc.edu
WOOSLEY, Wendy .... 417-864-7220. 274 D
wwoosley@cci.edu
WOOST, Michael, G .... 440-943-7600. 388 J
mgwoost@yahoo.com
WOOSTER, Ginger .... 979-230-3210. 468 A
ginger.wooster@brazosport.edu
WOOSTER, Phyllis, L ..... 973-655-4212. 303 D
woosterp@mail.montclair.edu
WOOSTER, Timothy, T ... 617-745-3707. 225 G
timothy.t.wooster@enc.edu
WOOSTER, Timothy, T ... 617-745-3732. 225 G
timothy.t.wooster@enc.edu
WOOTEN, Bradley .... 847-635-1912. 155 F
bwooten@oakton.edu
WOOTEN, Chris .... 903-730-4890. 474 O
CWooten@jarvis.edu
WOOTEN, Cornelius .... 724-357-2202. 428 F
Cornelius.Wooten@iup.edu
WOOTEN, Dean, A .... 757-352-4062. 508 G
deanwoo@regent.edu
WOOTEN, Dolores .... 662-560-1105. 269 C
dbwooten@northwestms.edu
WOOTEN, Jennifer, L ..... 912-583-3208. 122 B
jwooten@bpc.edu
WOOTEN, Judy .... 843-349-5212. 444 F
judy.wooten@hgtc.edu
WOOTEN, Maria .... 901-751-8453. 457 B
mwooten@mabts.edu
WOOTEN, Pam .... 662-562-3349. 269 C
pwooten@northwestms.edu
WOOTEN, Randall .... 903-923-3201. 485 G
randall.wooten@marshall.tstc.edu
WOOTEN, Randall, E ...... 903-935-1010. 486 A
randall.wooten@tstc.edu
WOOTEN, Rodney .... 304-865-6113. 527 F
rodney.wooten@ovu.edu
WOOTEN, Sheila .... 973-748-9000. 299 F
sheila_wooten@bloomfield.edu
WOOTEN, Susan, B .... 864-231-2151. 441 B
swooten@andersonuniversity.edu
WOOTTEN, Ida Lee .... 434-924-1321. 511 B
ilw2t@virginia.edu
WOOTTON, Katie .... 304-424-8203. 530 E
katie.wootton@wvup.edu
WOOTTON, Tim .... 562-938-4072... 51 D
twootton@lbcc.edu
WORD, John .... 559-791-2254... 49 P
jword@portervillecollege.edu
WORDELL, Kathleen, A ... 508-678-2811. 231 B
kathleen.wordell@bristolcc.edu
WORDEN, Jeannie, M ..... 715-675-3331. 541 A
worden@ntc.edu
WORDEN, Michael .... 845-341-4901. 335 H
michael.worden@sunyorange.edu
WORDEN, Randy .... 559-453-2246... 45 D
randy.worden@fresno.edu
WORDEN, Richard, B ..... 315-568-3095. 333 C
rworden@nycc.edu
WORDEN, Sylvia .... 714-432-5026... 39 K
sworden@occ.cccd.edu
WORK, Christine .... 845-341-4763. 335 H
christine.work@sunyorange.edu
WORK, Denise .... 402-552-2796. 288 L
workdenise@clarksoncollege.edu
WORKMAN, Andrew .... 401-254-3030. 440 B
aworkman@rwu.edu
WORKMAN, Christine .... 410-857-2267. 216 E
cworkman@mcdaniel.edu
WORKMAN, Greg .... 336-887-3000. 355 N
gworkman@laureluniversity.edu
WORKMAN, Harry .... 704-971-8500. 353 F
WORKMAN, Nikki .... 740-389-4636. 383 F
workman@mtc.edu
WORKU, Adu .... 707-965-6242... 57 J
aworku@puc.edu
WORLAND, Brooke, A .... 317-738-8167. 165 I
bworland@franklincollege.edu
WORLEY, Brian .... 909-621-8112... 39 D
brian.worley@cmc.edu
WORLEY, Charles .... 903-693-2044. 478 A
cworley@panola.edu
WORLEY, David .... 303-765-3107... 82 E
dworley@iliff.edu
WORLEY, Jewell, B .... 276-376-1004. 511 C
ljw4k@uvawise.edu
WORLEY, Louise .... 717-815-1446. 438 D
lworley@ycp.edu
WORLEY, Mark .... 972-241-3371. 470 E
mworley@dallas.edu
WORLEY, Paul .... 828-835-9564. 364 E
pworley@tricountycc.edu
WORLEY, Tim .... 561-803-2002. 110 B
tim_worley@pba.edu
WORM, Lori, M .... 920-424-3033. 537 B
worm@uwosh.edu
WORMACK, Janet .... 240-567-1744. 216 F
janet.wormack@montgomerycollege.edu
WORMAN, Ernie .... 803-947-2052. 445 G
ernie.worman@newberry.edu
WORMLEY, David, N ...... 814-865-7537. 426 A
dnw2@psu.edu
WORMLEY, Nicholas ...... 203-582-3719... 91 A
nicholas.wormley@quinnipiac.edu
WORMLEY, Wayne .... 215-751-6122. 413 I
wwormley@ccp.edu
WORMSER, Jennifer .... 949-376-6000... 50 C
jwormser@lagunacollege.edu
WORNALL, Robyn .... 707-256-7192... 55 F
rwornall@napavalley.edu
WORRALL, Jay .... 610-796-8371. 409 E
jay.worrall@alvernia.edu
WORRELL, Cortney .... 718-409-7477. 346 D
cworrell@sunymaritime.edu
WORSHAM, Earl .... 610-361-5323. 424 I
worshame@neumann.edu
WORSLEY, Christina .... 925-969-2747... 41 L
cworsley@dvc.edu
WORSTER, Kate .... 715-346-3827. 538 A
kworster@uwsp.edu
WORSTER, Kathy .... 803-321-3353. 445 G
kathy.worster@newberry.edu
WORTH, Ben .... 859-246-6353. 194 L
ben.worth@kctcs.edu
WORTH, Donald .... 575-492-2741. 310 G
dworth@nmjc.edu
WORTHAM, Dan .... 901-321-3256. 453 H
dwortham@cbu.edu
WORTHAM, Donald .... 651-403-8638. 254 K
dwortham@css.edu
WORTHAM, Trudy .... 361-570-4110. 489 E
worthamt@uhv.edu
WORTHEN, Kevin .... 585-389-2880. 332 D
kworthe6@naz.edu
WORTHEN, Kevin, J .... 801-422-2640. 495 D
kevin_worthen@byu.edu
WORTHEN, Shannon ...... 479-248-7236... 21 B
sworthen@ecollege.edu
WORTHERLY,
Churchill, B .... 443-885-4022. 217 A
churchill.wortherly@morgan.edu
WORTHINGTON, Jill ...... 405-422-1464. 399 B
worthingtonj@redlandscc.edu
WORTHINGTON, Joni .... 919-962-4929. 366 K
worthj@northcarolina.edu
WORTHINGTON,
Melissa .... 920-924-6326. 540 F
mworthington@morainepark.edu
WORTHY, Mark .... 225-752-4233. 202 C
mworthy@iticollege.edu
WOSSUM, Doris, F .... 931-363-9895. 456 C
dwossum@martinmethodist.edu
WOTEN, Elizabeth .... 708-209-3528. 143 E
lizz.woten@cuchicago.edu
WOUDENBERG, Bob .... 315-866-0300. 326 A
woudenbra@herkimer.edu
WOUGHTER, Kathy .... 607-871-2132. 313 E
woughter@alfred.edu
WOULFE, Rebecca .... 303-797-5822... 78 F
rebecca.woulfe@arapahoe.edu

WOZENCRAFT, Theresa .. 337-482-6599. 208 D
taw2679@louisiana.edu
WOZNIAK, Andrew .... 630-889-6878. 154 E
awozniak@nuhs.edu
WOZNIAK, Thomas, P ... 413-782-1317. 238 A
twozniak@wne.edu
WRAITH, Jon, M .... 603-862-2468. 298 C
jon.wraith@unh.edu
WRASMAN, PHJC,
Carleen .... 574-936-8898. 163 K
carleen.wrasman@ancilla.edu
WRAY, Chuck .... 704-922-6432. 360 F
wray.chuck@gaston.edu
WRAY, Jesse, B .... 804-862-6460. 508 H
jwray@rbc.edu
WRAY, John .... 330-325-6728. 385 E
jwray@neomed.edu
WRAY, Kyle .... 405-744-4366. 397 H
kyle.wray@okstate.edu
WRAY, Lois .... 804-862-6206. 508 H
lwray@rbc.edu
WRAY, Roger .... 434-949-1040. 513 H
roger.wray@southside.edu
WRAY, Theresa .... 818-386-5679... 59 E
twray@pgi.edu
WRAY, Virginia, F .... 870-307-7202... 21 H
virginia.wray@lyon.edu
WRAY, Warren, K .... 573-341-4138. 284 A
wkwray@mst.edu
WREN, Brent, M .... 256-824-6681..... 8 F
brent.wren@uah.edu
WREN, Emily, C .... 317-274-4553. 168 D
ewren@iupui.edu
WREN, Jan .... 606-539-4328. 200 B
jan.wren@ucumberlands.edu
WREN, Lanell, E .... 530-221-4275... 65 F
lwren@shasta.edu
WREN, Richard .... 312-553-5641. 141 N
rwren@ccc.edu
WRENN, Christy .... 318-869-5059. 201 H
cwrenn@centenary.edu
WRENN, Donna, C .... 508-793-3391. 225 B
dwrenn@holycross.edu
WRIGHT, Adam .... 214-333-5597. 470 D
adam@dbu.edu
WRIGHT, Alexis, S .... 212-875-4422. 314 C
awright@bankstreet.edu
WRIGHT, Allison .... 212-247-3434. 329 L
awright@mandl.edu
WRIGHT, Andrew .... 417-836-5518. 278 E
andrewwright@missouristate.edu
WRIGHT, Angelina .... 325-942-2017. 465 K
angie.wright@angelo.edu
WRIGHT, Angie .... 478-757-5192. 134 G
awright@wesleyancollege.edu
WRIGHT, Anita .... 559-934-2144... 75 G
anitawright@whccd.edu
WRIGHT, Ann .... 515-244-4221. 175 C
wrighta@aib.edu
WRIGHT, Barbara .... 304-357-4813. 527 H
barbarawright@ucwv.edu
WRIGHT, Barbara .... 918-293-4952. 398 B
barbara.wright@okstate.edu
WRIGHT, Barbara .... 803-778-6695. 441 F
wrightb@cctech.edu
WRIGHT, Beth .... 817-272-3291. 491 B
b.wright@uta.edu
WRIGHT, Bonnie, M .... 864-488-8318. 444 L
bwright@limestone.edu
WRIGHT, Brant .... 248-689-8282. 251 I
bwright@walshcollege.edu
WRIGHT, Brian .... 952-446-4133. 255 D
wrightb@crown.edu
WRIGHT, Bruce, A .... 520-247-4645... 18 F
wrightb@email.arizona.edu
WRIGHT, Carl .... 719-549-2313... 80 K
carl.wright@colostate-pueblo.edu
WRIGHT, Cathleen .... 830-372-8078. 485 C
cwright@tlu.edu
WRIGHT, Cathy .... 770-254-7280. 133 I
cwright@westga.edu
WRIGHT, Cathy .... 334-420-4252..... 7 G
cwright@trenholmstate.edu
WRIGHT, Cathy .... 502-213-7273. 195 F
catherine.wright@kctcs.edu
WRIGHT, Charles, W .... 803-938-3867. 448 F
wrightcw@uscsumter.edu
WRIGHT, Chatt, G .... 808-544-0202. 135 F
cwright@hpu.edu
WRIGHT, Cheryl .... 208-562-3000. 138 C
WRIGHT, Christine .... 617-217-9066. 222 G
cwright@baystate.edu
WRIGHT, Claudia .... 830-758-5006. 487 B
crwright@sulross.edu
WRIGHT, Colleen .... 269-965-3931. 244 O
wrightc@kellogg.edu
WRIGHT, Constance .... 864-977-7064. 445 H
constance.wright@ngu.edu
WRIGHT, Cory .... 718-270-4842. 319 A
cwright@mec.cuny.edu
WRIGHT, Craig, J .... 516-572-7121. 332 C
craig.wright@ncc.edu
WRIGHT, Curtis .... 718-390-3423. 350 B
curtis.wright@wagner.edu
WRIGHT, Dale, F .... 585-567-9321. 326 F
dale.wright@houghton.edu
WRIGHT, Daniel, W .... 973-803-5000. 304 C
dwright@pillar.edu
WRIGHT, David .... 505-566-3837. 311 I
wrightd@sanjuancollege.edu
WRIGHT, David .... 336-386-3252. 364 D
wrightd@surry.edu
WRIGHT, David .... 765-677-3061. 169 B
david.wright@indwes.edu
WRIGHT, David .... 316-978-7157. 191 F
david.wright@wichita.edu
WRIGHT, David, A .... 610-738-0536. 430 A
dwright@wcupa.edu
WRIGHT, David, W .... 717-337-6400. 417 B
dwright@gettysburg.edu
WRIGHT, Deborah, G ..... 757-825-3527. 514 B
wrightd@tncc.edu
WRIGHT, Debra .... 951-785-2011... 50 B
dwright@lasierra.edu
WRIGHT, Denis .... 239-489-9087. 101 O
dwright8@edison.edu
WRIGHT, Don .... 559-651-2500... 63 D
donw@sjvc.edu
WRIGHT, Donna .... 270-789-5010. 193 D
dwright@campbellsville.edu
WRIGHT, Earl .... 731-881-7733. 463 E
ewright@utm.edu
WRIGHT, Edwin, R .... 610-499-4281. 437 E
erwright@widener.edu
WRIGHT, Erin, D .... 606-783-9555. 198 A
e.wright@moreheadstate.edu
WRIGHT, Francine .... 617-745-3723. 225 G
fran.c.wright@enc.edu
WRIGHT, Gary .... 404-215-2636. 129 D
gwright@morehouse.edu
WRIGHT, Gayla .... 509-359-6874. 519 C
gwright@ewu.edu
WRIGHT, Gayla .... 509-359-6824. 519 C
gwright@ewu.edu
WRIGHT, George .... 949-214-3379... 41 I
george.wright@cui.edu
WRIGHT, George, C .... 936-261-2111. 482 F
gcwright@pvamu.edu
WRIGHT, Gregory, R .... 610-292-9852. 431 F
greg.wright@reseminary.edu
WRIGHT, Irvin .... 570-389-4492. 427 H
iwright@bloomu.edu
WRIGHT, JR., James, A 864-231-2061. 441 B
jwright@andersonuniversity.edu
WRIGHT, Jared .... 801-524-8197. 495 O
JWright@ldsbc.edu
WRIGHT, Jason .... 315-568-3268. 333 C
jwright@nycc.edu
WRIGHT, Jeff .... 360-650-6400. 525 C
jeff.wright@wwu.edu
WRIGHT, Jeffrey .... 802-287-8395. 499 D
jwright@greenmtn.edu
WRIGHT, Jeffrey .... 207-326-2215. 211 D
jeff.wright@mma.edu
WRIGHT, Jeffrey, E .... 765-641-4544. 163 L
jewright@anderson.edu
WRIGHT, Jerry .... 517-265-5161. 238 G
WRIGHT, Jill .... 309-694-5361. 146 E
jwright@icc.edu
WRIGHT, Jimmy .... 606-886-3863. 194 K
jimmy.wright@kctcs.edu
WRIGHT, Joann .... 708-974-5358. 153 F
wright@morainevalley.edu
WRIGHT, John .... 845-569-3592. 332 B
john.wright@msmc.edu
WRIGHT, John, E .... 304-336-8180. 530 A
jewright@westliberty.edu
WRIGHT, Jonas .... 415-503-6297... 62 H
jwright@sfcm.edu
WRIGHT, Julie .... 573-288-6640. 273 F
jwright@culver.edu
WRIGHT, Karen, F .... 270-384-7313. 197 D
wrightk@lindsey.edu
WRIGHT, Karen, M .... 606-679-8501. 196 D
karen.wright@kctcs.edu
WRIGHT, Karl, S .... 803-535-5417. 442 B
kawright@claflin.edu
WRIGHT, Kay .... 979-230-3377. 468 A
kay.wright@brazosport.edu
WRIGHT, Kristin .... 417-626-1234. 279 J
wright.kristin@occ.edu
WRIGHT, Kristine, A .... 612-626-0302. 264 G
wrigh084@umn.edu
WRIGHT, LeAnne .... 903-223-3078. 484 C
leanne.wright@tamut.edu
WRIGHT, Leroy .... 231-591-2686. 242 F
wrightl@ferris.edu
WRIGHT, Logan, S .... 816-483-9600. 190 D
lswright@spst.edu
WRIGHT, Lori .... 216-791-5000. 377 E
lxw21@case.edu
WRIGHT, Lynn, C .... 304-724-3700. 526 B
lwright@apus.edu
WRIGHT, Matt .... 706-419-1557. 123 F
matt.wright@covenant.edu
WRIGHT, May, F .... 270-824-8649. 196 A
may.wright@kctcs.edu
WRIGHT, Michael .... 229-931-2351. 131 G
mwright@southgatech.edu
WRIGHT, Michael, D .... 660-543-4272. 283 A
mwright@ucmo.edu
WRIGHT, Michael, G .... 313-577-8155. 252 G
dx2558@wayne.edu
WRIGHT, Milton .... 773-838-7606. 142 E
mwright@ccc.edu
WRIGHT, Nathan .... 218-322-2323. 258 I
nathan.wright@itascacc.edu
WRIGHT, Norman .... 801-863-8239. 497 C
norman.wright@uvu.edu
WRIGHT, Nova .... 540-863-2868. 512 B
nwright@dslcc.edu
WRIGHT, Paul .... 610-902-8562. 411 E
paul.r.wright@cabrini.edu
WRIGHT, Peter .... 603-513-5163. 298 D
peter.wright@law.unh.edu
WRIGHT, Peter .... 920-206-2395. 533 U
peter.wright@mbbc.edu
WRIGHT, Phil .... 503-584-7261. 402 E
phil.wright@chemeketa.edu
WRIGHT, Raymond, M ... 401-874-2186. 440 D
wrightr@egr.uri.edu
WRIGHT, Renee .... 814-838-7673. 416 G
rwright@fortisinstitute.edu
WRIGHT, Rick, L .... 785-539-3571. 188 F
rwright@mccks.edu
WRIGHT, Robert, F .... 413-597-2303. 238 D
robert.f.wright@williams.edu
WRIGHT, Robin .... 859-441-4500. 195 B
robin.wright@kctcs.edu
WRIGHT, Rodner .... 850-599-3276. 114 K
rodner.wright@famu.edu
WRIGHT, Rodner, B .... 850-599-3244. 114 K
rodner.wright@famu.edu
WRIGHT, Sannie, M .... 803-754-3950. 449 H
swright@wlbc.edu
WRIGHT, Sean .... 205-726-4591..... 6 F
swright@samford.edu
WRIGHT, Shelly, A .... 845-257-3291. 342 B
wrights@newpaltz.edu
WRIGHT, Sheri .... 760-757-2121... 54 G
swright@miracosta.edu
WRIGHT, Sherry .... 870-230-5352... 21 D
wrights@hsu.edu
WRIGHT, Sonia .... 530-938-5373... 41 A
swright5@siskiyous.edu
WRIGHT, Stephanie .... 336-334-4822. 360 G
swweeks@gtcc.edu
WRIGHT, Stephen .... 928-523-6533... 16 C
stephen.wright@nau.edu
WRIGHT, Susan .... 860-509-9520... 90 B
swright@hartsem.edu
WRIGHT, Susan, F .... 716-878-4301. 343 A
orrsf@buffalostate.edu
WRIGHT, Terri .... 443-334-2653. 218 E
twright2@stevenson.edu
WRIGHT, Terry .... 501-450-3293... 25 H
twright@uca.edu
WRIGHT, Thomas .... 423-473-2750. 460 D
twright@clevelandstatecc.edu
WRIGHT, Tim .... 307-268-2706. 542 X
twright@caspercollege.edu
WRIGHT, Timothy, S .... 863-680-4297. 105 D
twright@flsouthern.edu
WRIGHT, Travis .... 318-487-7601. 202 F
travis.wright@lacollege.edu
WRIGHT, Voncille, T .... 512-223-3128. 466 I
vwright@austincc.edu
WRIGHT, Webster .... 845-938-3808. 545 I
Webster.Wright@usma.edu
WRIGHT, William, A .... 805-565-7262... 76 D
wright@westmont.edu
WRIGHT-DUBOSE,
Alexis .... 843-355-4165. 449 F
wrighta@wiltech.edu
WRIGHT-HENDERSON,
Jacquita, L .... 302-657-5112... 93 F
jwright@dtcc.edu
WRIGHT-HOWARD,
Debra .... 619-388-3513... 62 D
dewright@sdccd.edu
WRIGHT-MOORE, Karyn 516-686-7958. 333 H
kwrightm@nyit.edu
WRIGHT-SANDERS,
Barbara .... 775-673-7123. 294 H
bsanders@tmcc.edu
WRIGHT-SWADEL,
William .... 919-660-1050. 354 A
william.wright-swadel@duke.edu
WRIGHTANDERSON,
Nikisha .... 309-694-5581. 146 E
nwrightanderson@icc.edu
WRIGHTEN, Karen .... 843-899-8049. 447 E
karen.wrighten@tridenttech.edu
WRIGHTMAN, Diane ...... 775-727-2017. 294 F
diane.wrightman@gbcnv.edu
WRIGHTON, Mark .... 217-206-6523. 161 E
WRIGHTON, Mark, S ..... 314-935-5100. 284 L
wrighton@wustl.edu
WRIGHTSON,
Madeleine, V .... 610-526-6008. 417 H
mwrightson@harcum.edu
WRIGLEY, Dawn .... 518-828-4181. 321 C
wrigley@sunycgcc.edu
WRIGLEY, Steve .... 404-962-3240. 134 A
steve.wrigley@usg.edu
WRIGLEY, Telaina .... 931-221-6353. 459 B
wrigleyt@apsu.edu
WRIGLEY, Vicki, A .... 217-362-6485. 153 C
vwrigley@millikin.edu
WRINGER, Monica .... 269-471-6321. 239 D
wringerm@andrews.edu
WRINN, Stephen .... 859-257-8432. 200 C
smwrin2@uky.edu
WRISTON, Welton .... 423-478-7250. 458 B
wwriston@ptseminary.edu
WROBBEL, Karen .... 847-317-7178. 160 M
kwrobbel@tiu.edu
WROBEL, Deborah, R ..... 443-412-2240. 215 C
dwrobel@harford.edu
WROBLEWSKI, Carol ..... 317-940-9904. 164 J
cwroble1@butler.edu
WROBLEWSKI, Kathleen 413-565-1000. 222 F
kwroblew@baypath.edu
WRUCK, Craig .... 707-826-5101... 35 C
craig.wruck@humboldt.edu
WU, Adam .... 909-593-3511... 72 E
awu@laverne.edu
WU, Bill .... 510-592-9688... 56 G
wjw@npu.edu
WU, Diana .... 510-642-4181... 70 I
dwu@unex.berkeley.edu
WU, Felix .... 518-442-3535. 341 D
fwu@albany.edu
WU, Frank, H .... 415-565-4700... 71 A
wuf@uchastings.edu
WU, Hannah .... 808-974-7306. 136 A
hannahwu@hawaii.edu
WU, Helen .... 262-554-3278. 534 D
helen_wu@yahoo.com
WU, Hong .... 804-523-5324. 512 F
hwu@reynolds.edu
WU, Jin .... 516-364-0808. 333 D
jwu@nycollege.edu
WU, John .... 640-466-7900. 162 J
jwu@waubonsee.edu
WU, Jonathan .... 626-289-9004... 26 J
WU, Qianzhi .... 512-454-1188. 466 B
WU, S. David .... 610-758-5308. 422 A
sdw1@lehigh.edu
WU, Shao-Wei .... 845-848-7822. 322 G
shao-wei.wu@dc.edu
WU, Sonia .... 941-487-5000. 115 D
swu@ncf.edu
WU, Yenbo .... 415-338-1293... 35 E
ywu@sfsu.edu
WUBAH, Daniel .... 540-458-8418. 516 A
dwubah@wlu.edu
WUBBEN, Kris .... 608-822-2706. 541 C
kwubben@swtc.edu
WUCHENICH,
Christopher, L .... 803-777-8400. 447 G
clw@mailbox.sc.edu
WUENSCHEL, Carol, M .. 301-696-3556. 215 D
wuenschel@hood.edu
WUERTZ, John, A .... 319-352-8318. 183 E
john.wuertz@wartburg.edu
WUERZEBERGER, Ken ... 913-758-6307. 191 B
Wuerzeberger53@stmary.edu
WUEST, Beth, E .... 512-245-8113. 487 C
bw09@txstate.edu
WUEST, Kelly .... 702-651-5928. 294 E
kelly.wuest@csn.edu
WUESTENBERG, Pam, J . 512-245-7952. 487 C
pw05@txstate.edu
WULF, Lincoln .... 719-502-3178... 84 A
lincoln.wulf@ppcc.edu
WULFEMEYER, Lori .... 619-961-4315... 69 I
loriw@tjsl.edu
WULFERT, Edelgard .... 518-442-4654. 341 D
ewulfert@albany.edu
WULFF, Deborah .... 805-546-3122... 42 C
deborah_wulff@cuesta.edu
WULFF, Debra .... 908-835-2309. 308 G
dwulff@warren.edu
WULFF, Susan .... 816-501-3767. 271 H
susan.wulff@avila.edu
WUNDERLICH, Dustin .... 208-459-5820. 138 A
dwunderlich@collegeofidaho.edu
WUNDERLICH, Kathryn .. 607-844-8222. 347 I
wunderk@tc3.edu
WUNDERLICH, Mark, E .. 518-388-8031. 348 J
wunderlm@union.edu

WUNDERLICH, Tom .... 757-683-4388. 507 N
twunderl@odu.edu
WUNDERLICH,
Warren, P .... 507-933-7507. 255 I
wwunderl@gustavus.edu
WUNDERLY, Nancy .... 610-683-4060. 429 A
wunderly@kutztown.edu
WUNKER, Charles .... 863-638-2916. 119 D
wunkerc@webber.edu
WUORI, Misti, L .... 701-788-4631. 371 E
Misti.Wuori@mayvillestate.edu
WURM, Sharon .... 775-673-7074. 294 H
swurm@tmcc.edu
WURMFELD, Claire .... 321-674-8057. 104 H
cwurmfeld@fit.edu
WURMFELD, Claire .... 802-447-6342. 500 D
cwurmfeld@svc.edu
WURST, Karin, A .... 517-355-4597. 246 H
wurst@msu.edu
WURSTER, Paul, E .... 585-292-2814. 332 A
pwurster@monroecc.edu
WURTZ, Joseph .... 913-360-7500. 184 H
jwurtz@benedictine.edu
WURTZ, Keith .... 909-389-3206... 61 K
kwurtz@craftonhills.edu
WURTZEL, Barbara .... 413-755-4816. 233 A
bwurtzel@stcc.edu
WURTZEL, Julie, A .... 563-562-3263. 181 E
wurtzelj@nicc.edu
WURZER, Christine .... 916-608-6500... 53 C
WUST, Rachel, L .... 260-359-4200. 166 O
rwust@huntington.edu
WUSTMAN, Brent .... 803-641-3293. 448 A
wustman-brent@aramark.com
WUTHO, Rita .... 301-860-4170. 220 A
rwutoh@bowiestate.edu
WUTHRICH, Philip .... 979-532-6305. 494 L
philipw@wcjc.edu
WUTOH, Anthony .... 202-806-6530... 95 G
awutoh@howard.edu
WYAND, Diane, A .... 518-564-2130. 344 B
wyandda@plattsburgh.edu
WYANDOTTE,
Annette, M .... 812-941-2208. 168 F
awyandot@ius.edu
WYATT, Alicia .... 325-793-4748. 476 E
awyatt@mcm.edu
WYATT, Ben .... 859-280-1246. 197 C
bwyatt@lexthco.edu
WYATT, Bruce .... 503-883-2217. 404 A
bwyatt@linfield.edu
WYATT, Carl, V .... 512-245-9650. 487 C
cw23@txstate.edu
WYATT, Clarence, R .... 859-238-5243. 193 E
clarence.wyatt@centre.edu
WYATT, Harry .... 740-593-2911. 387 C
wyatth@ohio.edu
WYATT, Jan .... 603-668-6660. 297 C
WYATT, Jimmy .... 865-471-7164. 453 F
jwyatt@cn.edu
WYATT, Joy, D .... 440-826-2180. 374 F
jwyatt@bw.edu
WYATT, Linda, L .... 913-288-7243. 187 L
lwyatt@kckcc.edu
WYATT, Lisa .... 707-664-2153... 36 B
lisa.wyatt@sonoma.edu
WYATT, Mark, A .... 951-343-4474... 30 H
mwyatt@calbaptist.edu
WYATT, Molly .... 252-985-5194. 365 D
mwyatt@ncwc.edu
WYATT, Robert, L .... 843-383-8010. 442 F
rwyatt@coker.edu
WYATT, Scott, L .... 435-283-7010. 498 A
scott.wyatt@snow.edu
WYATT, Shay .... 801-832-2344. 498 F
swyatt@westminstercollege.edu
WYATT, Steve .... 859-218-2247. 200 C
steve.wyatt@uky.edu
WYATT, Terri .... 804-257-5726. 515 F
vuu@bkstr.com
WYATT, Tracey, L .... 402-363-5675. 293 I
tlwyatt@york.edu
WYBLE, Shannon .... 410-778-7200. 221 C
swyble2@washcoll.edu
WYBORNY, Jeff .... 206-726-5024. 518 G
jwyborny@cornish.edu
WYBOURNE, Martin, N .. 603-646-2404. 296 G
martin.n.wybourne@dartmouth.edu
WYCHE, Sandy .... 972-860-4282. 470 G
swyche@dcccd.edu
WYCKOFF, Blaine, M ..... 330-325-6191. 385 E
bwyckoff@neomed.edu
WYCKOFF, Charles .... 951-571-6341... 61 A
WYCKOFF, Harold .... 910-678-8287. 360 D
wyckoffh@faytechcc.edu
WYCKOFF, Steven .... 718-960-8720. 318 A
steven.wyckoff@lehman.cuny.edu
WYCOFF, Jennifer .... 205-929-1456..... 5 G
jwycoff@miles.edu
WYCOFF, Joseph .... 914-633-2373. 327 C
jwycoff@iona.edu
WYCOFF-HORN, Marcie . 608-785-8127. 536 G
mwycoff-horn@uwlax.edu
WYDEN, Leon .... 419-448-3272. 389 J
wydenl@tiffin.edu
WYDER, Bruce .... 330-494-6170. 389 F
bwyder@starkstate.edu
WYKE, Rebecca .... 207-973-3350. 212 A
wyke@maine.edu
WYKERT, Todd .... 307-268-2555. 542 X
twykert@caspercollege.edu
WYKES, Paul .... 508-793-7385. 225 A
pwykes@clarku.edu
WYKOFF, Dan .... 706-410-1129. 123 F
dan.wykoff@covenant.edu
WYKOFF, Randolph, F ... 423-439-4243. 459 C
wykoff@etsu.edu
WYKOFF, Tom .... 330-684-8910. 390 F
twykoff@uakron.edu
WYLD, Jean, A .... 413-748-3959. 236 I
jwyld@springfieldcollege.edu
WYLIE, Brian .... 978-232-2440. 226 C
bwylie@endicott.edu
WYLIE, Michael .... 513-569-1492. 376 L
michael.wylie@cincinnatistate.edu
WYLIE, Richard, E .... 978-232-2001. 226 C
rwylie@endicott.edu
WYLIE, Rick .... 770-454-9270... 96 F
WYMAN, J. Vernon .... 401-874-2501. 440 D
jvern@uri.edu
WYMER, Greg .... 605-688-4482. 452 B
greg.wymer@sdstate.edu
WYNBERRY, Travis .... 909-621-8077... 39 C
travis.wynberry@cgu.edu
WYND, Christine .... 440-646-8166. 392 D
cwynd@ursuline.edu
WYNDER, Bernard .... 301-687-3132. 220 C
bwynder@frostburg.edu
WYNDER, Robin .... 301-687-4050. 220 C
rwynder@frostburg.edu
WYNEGAR, Robert .... 775-445-4431. 295 A
robert.wynegar@wnc.edu
WYNES, David, L .... 404-727-3889. 124 E
david.wynes@emory.edu
WYNES, Tim .... 651-423-8213. 258 D
tim.wyes@dctc.edu
WYNES, Timothy .... 651-450-3641. 258 H
twynes@inverhills.edu
WYNKOOP, Karen .... 360-992-2288. 518 A
kwynkoop@clark.edu
WYNN, Amanda .... 757-352-4148. 508 G
amanwyn@regent.edu
WYNN, Bobby, C .... 910-672-1232. 367 D
bwynn@uncfsu.edu
WYNN, G. Richard .... 610-896-1223. 418 F
grwynn@haverford.edu
WYNN, Keren .... 229-333-2103. 134 K
keren.wynn@wiregrass.edu
WYNN, Sandra .... 304-327-4213. 529 D
swynn@bluefieldstate.edu
WYNN, Steve .... 617-746-1990. 227 F
steve.wynn@hult.edu
WYNNE, Debbie .... 760-252-2411... 29 I
dwynne@barstow.edu
WYNNE, Jane .... 406-377-9449. 286 A
wynnej@dawson.edu
WYNNE, Joe .... 713-221-2799. 489 D
wynnejo@uhd.edu
WYNNE, Joshua .... 701-777-2516. 371 C
joshua.wynne@med.und.edu
WYNNE, Joshua .... 701-777-2514. 371 C
joshua.wynne@med.und.edu
WYNTER, Cadence .... 949-582-4958... 67 C
cwynter@saddleback.edu
WYONT, Kimberly .... 704-922-6482. 360 F
wyont.kimberly@gaston.edu
WYPISZYNSKI, Gregory . 920-424-0007. 537 B
wypiszyn@uwosh.edu
WYRICK, Chris .... 479-575-6800... 23 I
cwyrick1@uark.edu
WYRICK, Kathleen .... 907-564-8265... 10 C
kwyrick@alaskapacific.edu
WYSE, Joe .... 530-242-7510... 65 G
jwyse@shastacollege.edu
WYSOCKI, Joseph, T ...... 815-740-3415. 162 F
jwysocki@stfrancis.edu
WYSOCKI, Karen, L .... 630-515-6321. 153 B
bwysoc@midwestern.edu
WYSOCKI, Sherida .... 517-371-5140. 250 G
wysockis@cooley.edu
WYSOGLAD, Anne .... 773-481-8660. 142 F
awysoglad@ccc.edu
WYSONG, James .... 813-253-7236. 106 M
rwysong@hccfl.edu
WYTCHERLEY, Gary .... 562-903-4722... 29 L
gary.wytcherley@biola.edu

X

XAVIER, Bob .... 617-912-9148. 224 B
bxavier@bostonconservatory.edu
XIE, Jin Hua .... 262-554-2010. 534 D
drj-xie@yahoo.com
XIE, Philip, F .... 419-372-7595. 374 K
pxie@bgsu.edu
XIMENEZ, David .... 817-515-5354. 482 B
david.ximenez@tccd.edu
XIMINES, Sheryl, H .... 919-516-4343. 366 C
sximines@st-aug.edu
XING, Jun .... 323-343-3830... 34 A
jun.xing2@calstatela.edu
XIONG, Joua .... 414-326-2334. 532 G
joua.xiong@ccon.edu
XIPPOLITOS, Lee .... 631-444-3549. 342 C
lee.xippolitos@stonybrook.edu
XIRINACHS, Susan .... 207-947-4591. 209 G
sxirinachs@bealcollege.edu
XISTRIS, Angela .... 352-335-2332... 97 E
XU, Charlie .... 908-737-3220. 302 F
cxu@kean.edu
XU, Shuli .... 508-373-5640. 233 E
shuli.xu@mcphs.edu
XU, Wenying .... 412-365-1157. 412 K
wxu@chatham.edu

Y

YACAVONE, Mark .... 607-753-4711. 343 B
mark.yacavone@cortland.edu
YACKEE, Grace, B .... 734-384-4221. 247 C
gyackee@monroeccc.edu
YADEGAR, Mahvash .... 310-662-2101... 55 J
myadegar@nu.edu
YAEGER, Evelyn .... 810-762-9782. 244 Q
eyaeger@kettering.edu
YAEGER, John, W .... 202-685-0080. 544 K
yaegerj@ndu.edu
YAEGER, Lisa .... 802-828-2800. 501 C
Lisa.Yaeger@ccv.edu
YAGER, David .... 831-459-4940... 72 C
yager@ucsc.edu
YAGER, Michael .... 301-937-8448. 218 H
YAGIL, Oren .... 402-471-2505. 291 C
oyagil@nscs.edu
YAGNITINSKY, Roman ... 800-955-2527. 274 I
ryagnitinsky@grantham.edu
YAHNG, Charles .... 314-529-9312. 276 G
cyahng@maryville.edu
YAHNKE, Eric .... 503-838-8459. 406 E
yahnkee@wou.edu
YAHR, Scott .... 907-822-3201... 10 A
YAHYAZADEH, Bizhan ... 802-485-2145. 500 A
bizhan@norwich.edu
YAKLICH, Richard .... 305-430-1167. 104 J
richard.yaklich@fmuniv.edu
YAKOVLEV, Ilya .... 262-595-2010. 537 C
yakovlev@uwp.edu
YAKOWICZ, William .... 201-612-5253. 299 C
wyakowicz@bergen.edu
YAKSHE, Patti, L .... 412-281-2600. 433 B
pyakeshe@western-school.com
YALE, Amanda, A .... 724-738-2011. 429 F
amanda.yale@sru.edu
YALE, Janet .... 402-557-7095. 288 G
janet.yale@bellevue.edu
YALOWITZ, Daniel .... 802-258-3178. 500 C
daniel.yalowitz@sit.edu
YAM, Marylou .... 201-761-6020. 306 L
myam@saintpeters.edu
YAM, Tony .... 516-739-1545. 333 F
admis2@nyctcm.edu
YAMADA, Frank, M .... 773-947-6301. 152 E
fyamada@mccormick.edu
YAMAGATA-NOJI,
Audrey .... 909-274-4505... 55 A
ayamagat@mtsac.edu
YAMAGUCHI,
James (Kimo) .... 808-689-2535. 136 C
jyamaguc@hawaii.edu
YAMAKAWA, Lynn .... 310-233-4387... 51 H
yamakalm@lahc.edu
YAMAMOTO, Catherine .. 402-472-7749. 292 I
cyamamoto1@unl.edu
YAMAMOTO, Cindy .... 808-984-3288. 137 B
cindy@hawaii.edu
YAMAMOTO, June, Y ..... 909-389-3216... 61 K
jyamamoto@craftonhills.edu
YAMAMOTO, Louise .... 808-734-9513. 136 E
yamamotl@hawaii.edu
YAMAMOTO, Roy .... 808-675-3406. 135 C
roy.yamamoto@byuh.edu
YAMAMURA, Whitney .... 916-691-7326... 53 B
yamamuw@crc.losrios.edu
YAMANE, Noreen .... 808-934-2504. 136 F
noreeny@hawaii.edu
YAMAUCHI, Kent .... 626-585-7995... 58 F
ktyamauchi@pasadena.edu
YAMBA, A. Zachary .... 973-877-3022. 301 H
yamba@essex.edu
YAMBA, Mohamed .... 724-938-4240. 428 A
yamba@calu.edu
YAMEEN, Deanna .... 508-588-9100. 232 A
YAMILKOSKI, Vince, J ... 770-534-6134. 122 A
vyamilkoski@brenau.edu
YAMIN, Isabel .... 787-728-1515. 555 D
iyamin@sagrado.edu
YAN, Raymond .... 425-558-0299. 519 B
ryan@digipen.edu
YAN, Ruth .... 319-226-2080. 175 D
Ruth.Yan@AllenCollege.edu
YANCEY, Deborah .... 540-857-6004. 514 E
dyancey@virginiawestern.edu
YANCEY, Gary .... 850-729-5364. 109 I
yanceyg@nwfsc.edu
YANCEY, Jennifer, L .... 361-582-2519. 493 H
jennifer.yancey@victoriacollege.edu
YANCEY, John, E .... 904-620-2624. 116 B
jyancey@unf.edu
YANCEY, Laurica .... 252-398-6454. 353 H
yancel@chowan.edu
YANCHAK, Frank .... 614-947-6723. 380 A
frank.yanchak@franklin.edu
YANCHICK, Victor, A ...... 804-828-3006. 511 F
vyanchick@vcu.edu
YANCKELLO, Robert ...... 407-823-2711. 115 E
bob.yanckello@ucf.edu
YANCY, Chad .... 205-929-3497..... 5 D
cyancy@lawsonstate.edu
YANCY, Ginny .... 770-962-7580. 127 D
gyancy@gwinnetttech.edu
YANDA, Wayne .... 619-482-6414... 68 B
wyanda@swccd.edu
YANEZ, Mercedes .... 310-233-4127... 51 H
yanezm@lahc.edu
YANG, Alice .... 831-459-2328... 72 C
ayang@ucsc.edu
YANG, Henry, T .... 805-893-2231... 72 B
henry.yang@chancellor.ucsb.edu
YANG, Hong .... 401-232-6885. 438 K
hyang@bryant.edu
YANG, Honggang .... 954-262-3048. 109 K
yang@nova.edu
YANG, Kuan .... 510-780-4500... 50 I
kyang@lifewest.edu
YANG, Neng .... 503-838-8590. 406 E
yangn@wou.edu
YANG, Nicole .... 920-693-1120. 540 B
nicole.yang@gotoltc.edu
YANG, Olivia .... 509-335-5571. 525 A
olivia.yang@wsu.edu
YANG, Steve .... 651-450-3330. 258 H
syang@inverhills.edu
YANG, Xiaoyun .... 336-770-1457. 369 D
yangx@uncsa.edu
YANG, Xuemei .... 785-460-5418. 185 P
xuemei.yang@colbycc.edu
YANISH, Paula .... 970-339-6537... 78 C
paula.yanish@aims.edu
YANKELEWITZ, Yoel ...... 718-846-1940. 351 I
yyankelewitz@gmail.com
YANKELITIS, Wendy .... 570-348-6201. 423 B
yankelitis@marywood.edu
YANKEY, Terry, L .... 606-474-3222. 194 H
tly@kcu.edu
YANNA, Dan .... 304-876-5236. 529 I
dyanna@shepherd.edu
YANNICK, Lisa .... 610-436-3075. 430 A
lyannick@wcupa.edu
YANNIELLO, Michael, C 516-876-3146. 343 D
yanniellom@oldwestbury.edu
YANNUZZI, Raymond .... 856-227-7200. 300 B
ryannuzzi@camdencc.edu
YANTIS, Rachel .... 847-317-8103. 160 M
ryantis@tiu.edu
YAO, Chunmei .... 607-436-3592. 343 E
chunmao.yao@oneonta.edu
YAO, Min .... 858-534-3396... 71 F
myao@ucsd.edu
YAO, Sheng .... 610-399-2219. 428 B
syao@cheyney.edu
YAQUB, Samia .... 530-895-2547... 30 F
yaqubsa@butte.edu
YAQUINTA, Donald .... 304-243-2044. 531 H
dony@wju.edu
YARBERRY, Cindy .... 406-447-6952. 287 A
yarberryc@umhelena.edu
YARBROUGH, David ...... 337-482-1015. 208 D
yarbrough@louisiana.edu
YARBROUGH, David ...... 707-546-4000... 43 E
dyarbrough@empirecollege.com
YARBROUGH, Howard ... 423-697-4785. 460 C
YARBROUGH, J. Keith ... 432-552-2415. 493 D
yarbrough_k@utpb.edu
YARBROUGH, John .... 706-865-2134. 133 B
jyarbrough@truett.edu
YARBROUGH, Kenny ...... 615-230-3443. 461 G
kenny.yarbrough@volstate.edu
YARBROUGH, Keva .... 770-650-3000... 96 F
YARBROUGH, Laura .... 870-762-3105... 19 K
lyarbrough@smail.anc.edu
YARBROUGH, Laura, L .. 336-249-8186. 360 A
llyarbro@davidsoncc.edu

YARBROUGH, Mark, M .. 214-887-5011. 471 F
myarbrough@dts.edu
YARBROUGH, Nancy, J . 731-881-7800. 463 E
nyarbrough@utm.edu
YARBROUGH, Scott ...... 843-863-7563. 441 H
syarbrou@csuniv.edu
YARDLEY, Katherine, W . 207-778-7153. 212 D
kyardley@maine.edu
YARDLEY, Owen .... 402-472-8809. 292 I
oyardley2@unl.edu
YARKIN, Cherisa .... 206-934-6903. 522 J
cherisa.yarkin@seattlecolleges.edu
YARLOTT, JR., David ..... 406-638-3107. 286 D
davidyarlott@lbhc.edu
YARNELL, Thomas, V ..... 614-823-1502. 387 K
tyarnell@otterbein.edu
YARRISH, Julie .... 310-434-3762... 65 A
yarrish_julie@smc.edu
YARSIAH, James .... 803-780-1264. 449 E
jyarsiah@voorhees.edu
YARWORTH, Joseph ...... 610-921-6758. 409 A
jyarworth@alb.edu
YASBIN, Ronald .... 314-516-5504. 283 E
yasbinr@umsl.edu
YASECKO, Susan .... 847-543-2218. 143 A
syasecko@clcillinois.edu
YASINSAC, Alec .... 251-460-6390..... 9 E
yasinsac@southalabama.edu
YASINSKI, W. Arnold ..... 503-370-6728. 408 J
ayasinski@willamette.edu
YASMAN, Shannon .... 805-493-3838... 31 H
yasman@clunet.edu
YASUDA, Cathy .... 541-881-5585. 408 C
cyasuda@tvcc.cc
YASUHARA, June .... 808-739-4603. 135 D
jyasuhar@chaminade.edu
YATES, Brian .... 434-592-4108. 506 I
bcyates@liberty.edu
YATES, Dorothy, C .... 307-766-5320. 543 I
dyates4@uwyo.edu
YATES, Frances .... 765-973-8470. 167 G
fyates@iue.edu
YATES, Jacob .... 606-337-4524. 193 F
registrar@ccbbc.edu
YATES, James .... 918-647-1230. 394 I
jyates@carlalbert.edu
YATES, JK .... 231-591-2898. 242 F
yatesj@ferris.edu
YATES, Kristin .... 402-472-5242. 292 G
kyates@nebraska.edu
YATES, Mark .... 903-923-2339. 471 J
myates@etbu.edu
YATES, Marvin, L .... 985-549-5250. 208 C
myates@selu.edu
YATES, Marylynn .... 951-827-3101... 71 E
marylynn.yates@ucr.edu
YATES, Sandra .... 202-274-7050... 97 A
syates@udc.edu
YATES, Susan .... 559-442-4600... 68 I
susan.yates@fresnocitycollege.edu
YATES, Vivian, M .... 216-987-4000. 378 D
YATIM, Fouad .... 617-570-4855. 237 B
fyatim@suffolk.edu
YATOOMA, Chris .... 916-660-7600... 66 B
cyatooma@sierracollege.edu
YATS, Kirk, M .... 989-774-3674. 240 N
yats1km@cmich.edu
YAU, Lishan .... 864-294-3609. 444 C
lishan.yau@furman.edu
YAU, Tow, Y .... 513-556-0648. 390 G
tow.yau@uc.edu
YAU, Yeeka .... 919-658-7708. 357 I
yyau@moc.edu
YAUN, John .... 304-696-3152. 529 H
yaun@marshall.edu
YAUNEY, Alan, J .... 518-381-1256. 340 G
yauneyaj@sunysccc.edu
YAW, Edward, J .... 973-328-5031. 300 G
eyaw@ccm.edu
YAW, Steve .... 574-807-7388. 164 D
yaws@bethelcollege.edu
YAZDANI, Linda .... 303-914-6536... 84 I
linda.yazdani@rrcc.edu
YAZDI, Aliakbar, R .... 205-853-1200..... 5 B
ayazdi@jeffstateonline.com
YBANEZ, Elsa .... 210-436-3725. 479 D
eybanez@stmarytx.edu
YBARRA, Nancy .... 925-439-2181... 42 A
nybarra@losmedanos.edu
YBARRA, Tomas .... 509-574-4640. 525 G
tybarra@yvcc.edu
YE, Eugene .... 630-942-3821. 142 G
yee8@cod.edu
YE, Michael, H .... 240-895-4696. 218 A
mhye@smcm.edu
YEAGER, Carolyn .... 717-245-1686. 414 H
yeager@dickinson.edu
YEAGER, David .... 812-866-7075. 166 C
yeagerd@hanover.edu
YEAGER, David .... 979-830-4454. 467 I
david.yeager@blinn.edu
YEAGER, Ed .... 480-732-7177... 14 J
ed.yeager@cgc.edu
YEAGER, Michelle .... 314-652-0300. 281 B
myeager@slchcmail.com
YEAGER, Phyllis .... 859-442-1150. 195 B
phyllis.yeager@kctcs.edu
YEAGER, Robert, E .... 812-749-1210. 171 K
ryeager@oak.edu
YEAGLEY, JR., William .. 989-774-3081. 240 N
yeagl1b@cmich.edu
YEAKEL, Lois, M .... 610-799-1961. 421 I
lyeakel@lccc.edu
YEAKLEY, Randy .... 325-649-8804. 473 F
ryeakley@hputx.edu
YEAP, Soon Beng .... 303-964-6358... 84 M
syeap@regis.edu
YEAROUT, Teresa, A ...... 276-964-7266. 514 A
teresa.yearout@sw.edu
YEARWOOD, George, A . 919-508-2035. 370 F
ryearwood@peace.edu
YEARWOOD, Jody .... 478-387-4233. 125 E
YEATER, Michael .... 409-882-3342. 486 G
mike.yeater@lsco.edu
YEATTS, Debra .... 910-630-7385. 356 H
dyeatts@methodist.edu
YEATTS, Dewey .... 240-567-7356. 216 F
dewey.yeatts@montgomerycollege.edu
YEAZEL, Bill .... 913-288-7690. 187 L
yeazel@kckcc.edu
YEBEI, Philemon .... 765-455-9291. 168 A
YEBOAH, Yaw .... 850-410-6258. 115 C
yyeboah@eng.fsu.edu
YEBOAH, Yaw, D .... 850-410-6161. 114 K
dean@eng.fsu.edu
YECK, Laura .... 254-647-3237. 478 H
lyeck@rangercollege.edu
YEE, Atom .... 408-554-4455... 64 M
ayee@scu.edu
YEE, David .... 415-239-3669... 38 L
dyee@ccsf.edu
YEE, Diane .... 212-229-5900. 332 E
yeed@newschool.edu
YEE, Elena, T .... 401-865-1525. 439 E
eyee@providence.edu
YEE, Robert .... 617-989-4938. 237 G
yeer@wit.edu
YEE, Sandra, G .... 313-577-4059. 252 G
aj0533@wayne.edu
YEH, Frank .... 662-252-8000. 269 F
fyeh@rustcollege.edu
YEH, Li-An .... 919-530-7001. 368 A
lyeh@nccu.edu
YEHL, Robert, F .... 870-230-5014... 21 D
yehlb@hsu.edu
YEHUDAH, Shoshana ...... 212-463-0400. 348 B
shulys@touro.edu
YEISER, Jimmie .... 870-460-1033... 24 D
yeiserj@uamont.edu
YEISER, Linda .... 870-460-1120... 24 D
yeiser@uamont.edu
YEKOVICH, Robert .... 713-348-4837. 479 A
yekovr@rice.edu
YELKUR, Rama .... 989-964-4064. 249 G
ryelkur@svsu.edu
YELLE, Dave .... 413-565-1000. 222 F
dyelle@baypath.edu
YELLE, Richard, W .... 203-576-4222... 91 G
ryelle@bridgeport.edu
YELLEN, David, N .... 312-915-7838. 151 H
dyellen@luc.edu
YELNOSKY, Robert, E ...... 814-641-3707. 419 H
yelnosr@juniata.edu
YELVINGTON, Philip, R .. 901-321-3396. 453 H
pyelving@cbu.edu
YELVINGTON, Sherry ...... 901-272-5125. 456 F
syelvington@mca.edu
YEN, Charlie .... 310-434-3002... 65 A
yen_charlie@smc.edu
YEN, David .... 607-436-3458. 343 E
YEN, Flora, B .... 916-568-3132... 52 K
yenf@losrios.edu
YEN, Jion .... 815-838-5640. 150 H
yenji@lewisu.edu
YEN, Johanna, C .... 954-763-9840... 98 I
atom@atom.edu
YEN, S.C. Max .... 260-481-6839. 168 C
yens@ipfw.edu
YENA, John, A .... 401-598-1100. 439 B
jyena@jwu.edu
YENCHA, Matthew .... 610-606-4666. 412 I
myencha@cedarcrest.edu
YENCHA, Tom .... 304-424-8309. 530 E
tom.yencha@wvup.edu
YENSON, Evelyn .... 206-934-3227. 522 H
evelyn.yenson@seattlecolleges.edu
YENTES, Matt .... 863-638-2963. 119 D
yentesms@webber.edu
YEO, Frances .... 850-484-1795. 110 G
fyeo@pensacolastate.edu
YEO, Frederick, L .... 920-424-3322. 537 B
yeof@uwosh.edu
YEOM, Kyong, S .... 636-327-4645. 277 K
finance@midwest.edu
YEOM, Kyong, S .... 636-327-4645. 277 K
iss@midwest.edu
YEOMANS, Jennifer .... 603-888-1311. 297 F
jyeomans@rivier.edu
YEONOPOLUS, Jim .... 254-526-1781. 468 G
jim.yeonopolus@ctcd.edu
YEP, Katie .... 651-846-1372. 261 D
katie.yep@saintpaul.edu
YEPES, Maria, E .... 323-265-8957... 51 F
yepesme@elac.edu
YEPES, Maria Elena .... 323-265-8957... 51 F
yepesme@elac.edu
YERGEN, Norman .... 951-785-2307... 50 B
nyergen@lasierra.edu
YERGER, Mark, E .... 570-577-1795. 411 A
mark.yerger@bucknell.edu
YERIAN, Diane .... 540-568-8090. 506 F
yeriandg@jmu.edu
YERICH, Nicolette .... 660-248-6255. 272 B
nyerich@centralmethodist.edu
YERK, Melanie .... 239-939-4766. 114 F
myerk@swfc.edu
YESALONIA, SJ, Dennis 773-274-3000. 151 H
YESTRAMSKI, Joanne ..... 978-934-2206. 229 B
Joanne_Yestramski@uml.edu
YETMAN, Barbara, H ...... 215-968-8045. 411 B
yetmanb@bucks.edu
YETMAR, Theresa .... 785-594-8316. 184 C
theresa.yetmar@bakeru.edu
YEVIN, G. Bernard .... 336-734-7224. 360 E
gyevin@forsythtech.edu
YEW, Phillip .... 213-487-0110... 42 K
chinese@dula.edu
YIANOUKOS, Steven, J .. 315-268-6622. 320 A
stevey@clarkson.edu
YIGZAW, Erika .... 503-244-0726. 401 M
erikayigzaw@achs.edu
YIH, T. C .... 239-590-7021. 115 A
tcyih@fgcu.edu
YILIBUW, Dolores .... 859-280-1224. 197 C
dyilibuw@lextheo.edu
YIN, Carol .... 706-880-8339. 128 A
cyin@lagrange.edu
YIN, Kong .... 713-221-8975. 489 D
YinK@uhd.edu
YING, Amber .... 317-829-9384. 163 I
YING, Robin L, P .... 757-822-1970. 514 C
rying@tcc.edu
YINGLING, Julie, R .... 419-434-4550. 391 D
yinglingj@findlay.edu
YINGLING, Kevin, W .... 304-696-3170. 529 H
yingling@marshall.edu
YIRKA, Carl, A .... 802-831-1443. 500 H
cyirka@vermontlaw.edu
YLINEN, Jeff .... 612-374-5800. 255 F
jylinen@dunwoody.edu
YOACHIM, Maureen .... 610-740-3725. 412 I
bookstore@cedarcrest.edu
YOAKUM, Cole .... 248-218-2042. 249 D
YOAKUM, Katrina, M ...... 785-864-3261. 190 L
kyoakum@ku.edu
YOANNONE, Carol .... 412-237-4421. 413 D
cyoannone@ccac.edu
YOCHUM, Denise .... 253-964-6776. 522 C
dyochum@pierce.ctc.edu
YOCHUM, Gilbert, R .... 757-683-3521. 507 N
gyochum@odu.edu
YOCKEY, Glenn .... 830-372-8040. 485 C
gyockey@tlu.edu
YOCOM, Jim .... 574-520-4806. 168 E
jyocom@iusb.edu
YOCUM, Amanda .... 330-325-6758. 385 E
ayocum1@neomed.edu
YOCUM, Carrie, A .... 574-372-5100. 166 B
yocumca@grace.edu
YODER, Anita, R .... 574-535-7114. 166 A
anitay@goshen.edu
YODER, Brad, L .... 260-422-5561. 167 B
blyoder@indianatech.edu
YODER, Brent .... 620-327-8231. 187 D
brenty@hesston.edu
YODER, Dan .... 541-440-4600. 408 D
dan.yoder@umpqua.edu
YODER, Donna, K .... 814-886-6368. 424 G
dyoder@mtaloy.edu
YODER, Ernest, L .... 989-774-7570. 240 N
yoder1el@cmich.edu
YODER, James, A .... 508-289-2252. 238 E
jyoder@whoi.edu
YODER, Julie .... 301-387-3101. 214 I
julie.yoder@garrettcollege.edu
YODER, Mari .... 419-267-1268. 385 F
myoder@northweststate.edu
YODER, Mindy, J .... 260-399-7700. 174 C
myoder@sf.edu
YODER, Norris .... 828-328-7145. 356 B
norris.yoder@lr.edu
YODER, Robert, E .... 574-535-7244. 166 A
robertey@goshen.edu
YODER, Twila, K .... 540-432-4100. 504 D
yodertk@emu.edu
YOHANNES, Edna .... 323-563-5985... 38 B
ednayohannes@cdrewu.edu
YOHANNES, Paulos .... 678-891-2876. 125 G
paulos.yohannes@gpc.edu
YOHE, Michael, E .... 864-231-2073. 441 B
myohe@andersonuniversity.edu
YOHE, Roger .... 480-461-7151... 15 A
roger.yohe@mesacc.edu
YOHN, Richard, V .... 303-963-3485... 79 C
ryohn@ccu.edu
YOHNK, Dean .... 262-595-2188. 537 C
yohnk@uwp.edu
YOHO, Robert .... 515-271-1464. 177 H
robert.yoho@dmu.edu
YOHO, Steven, K .... 912-650-6215. 131 H
syoho@southuniversity.edu
YOIA, Dominic .... 203-582-5224... 91 A
dominic.yoia@quinnipiac.edu
YOK, Larry .... 206-878-3710. 520 E
lyok@highline.edu
YOKLIC, Deborah .... 520-206-4650... 17 A
dyoklic@pima.edu
YOKOTOBI, Fusako .... 760-245-4271... 75 B
Fusako.Yokotobi@vvc.edu
YOKOYAMA, Janis, K .... 213-738-6714... 68 C
deansoffice@swlaw.edu
YOLITZ, Brian, D .... 651-201-1777. 257 N
brian.yolitz@so.mnscu.edu
YONAN, Glen .... 530-251-8815... 50 F
gyonan@lassencollege.edu
YONAN, Jonathan .... 610-225-5704. 415 G
jyonan@eastern.edu
YONEMITSU, Lori .... 206-546-4552. 523 F
lyonemitsu@shoreline.edu
YONG, Henry, C .... 408-270-6471... 63 O
henry.yong@evc.edu
YONG, Yan Yan .... 540-834-1048. 512 E
yyong@germanna.edu
YONGUE, Marelle .... 337-482-6826. 208 D
darlene@louisiana.edu
YONKERS, Molly, L .... 507-933-7588. 255 I
myunkers@gustavus.edu
YONUTAS, Dave .... 352-395-5379. 113 C
dave.yonutas@sfcollege.edu
YOOK, JungMo .... 714-525-0088... 46 A
gmu@gm.edu
YOON, Michelle .... 562-926-1023... 60 B
mhyoon@ptsa.edu
YOPP, Jan .... 919-966-4364. 368 D
jan_yopp@unc.edu
YORDAN, Carlos .... 973-408-3365. 301 C
cyordan@drew.edu
YORK, Allison .... 319-398-4998. 180 J
ayork@kirkwood.edu
YORK, Barry .... 412-731-8690. 431 G
byork@rpts.edu
YORK, Brenda .... 406-994-2824. 287 B
byork@montana.edu
YORK, Corey .... 914-251-6080. 344 D
corey.york@purchase.edu
YORK, David .... 512-492-3032. 466 B
dyork@aoma.edu
YORK, Stan .... 912-681-5667. 129 J
syork@ogeecheetech.edu
YORK-LANGSTON,
Aaron .... 903-875-7328. 477 G
aaron.york@navarrocollege.edu
YORK-LEMELIN, Lisa ..... 207-453-5128. 210 L
lyork@kvcc.me.edu
YORKER, Beatrice .... 323-343-4600... 34 A
byorker@calstatela.edu
YORKIN, Sheila .... 801-832-2685. 498 F
syorkin@westminstercollege.edu
YORKIS, Kathleen .... 617-287-5666. 228 G
kathleen.yorkis@umb.edu
YORTSOS, Yannis, C .... 213-740-0617... 74 A
yortsos@usc.edu
YOSHIDA, James .... 808-934-2508. 136 F
jamesyos@hawaii.edu
YOSHIKAWA, Naoto .... 808-983-4105. 135 G
yoshinao@tokai.edu
YOSHIMURA, Marlys ..... 408-453-9900... 47 H
myoshimura@henley-putnam.edu
YOSHIMURA, Nancy ...... 949-480-4045... 66 F
nyoshimura@soka.edu
YOSHINA, Eileen .... 360-596-5383. 524 A
eyoshina@spscc.edu
YOSHINO, Lori .... 909-621-8856... 59 G
lori_yoshino@pitzer.edu
YOST, Deborah .... 215-951-5008. 420 B
yost@lasalle.edu
YOST, Robert, A .... 704-334-6882. 357 K
ryost@nlts.edu
YOUATT, June, P .... 517-355-1524. 246 H
youatt@msu.edu
YOUGH, Kelly .... 845-569-3184. 332 B
kelly.yough@msmc.edu
YOUHOUSE, John .... 610-558-5518. 424 I
youhousej@neumann.edu

YOUKEY, Jerry, R .... 864-455-7880. 447 G
youkey@mailbox.sc.edu
YOUKEY, Jerry, R .... 864-455-7992. 448 E
jyoukeymd@ghs.org
YOUMANS, Art .... 201-761-7403. 306 L
ayoumans@saintpeters.edu
YOUNG, Aaron .... 505-984-6140. 311 H
aaron.young@sjcsf.edu
YOUNG, Al .... 205-929-3424..... 5 D
ayoung@lawsonstate.edu
YOUNG, Alissa .... 270-707-3717. 195 E
alissa.young@kctcs.edu
YOUNG, Allene .... 510-981-2908... 59 A
ayoung@peralta.edu
YOUNG, Amanda .... 864-644-5558. 446 I
ayoung@swu.edu
YOUNG, Amber .... 256-824-6604..... 8 F
Amber.Young@uah.edu
YOUNG, Andrea .... 213-613-2200... 67 E
andrea_young@sciarc.edu
YOUNG, Andrew .... 812-888-4323. 174 F
ayoung@vinu.edu
YOUNG, Ann, S .... 859-238-5480. 193 E
ann.young@centre.edu
YOUNG, Barbara .... 662-562-3202. 269 C
ba_young@northwestms.edu
YOUNG, Benjamin .... 317-916-7918. 169 K
byoung@ivytech.edu
YOUNG, Beth .... 815-825-2086. 149 F
beth.young@kishwaukeecollege.edu
YOUNG, Betty .... 478-553-2090. 129 H
byoung@oftc.edu
YOUNG, Betty, K .... 713-718-7628. 473 C
betty.young@hccs.edu
YOUNG, Bradford .... 732-255-0400. 304 A
byoung@ocean.edu
YOUNG, Bradley, J .... 310-233-4066... 51 H
youngbj@lahc.edu
YOUNG, Brandon .... 217-540-3512. 150 D
byoung17159@lakeland.cc.il.us
YOUNG, Brian, A .... 402-280-2121. 289 D
bay@creighton.edu
YOUNG, Caryn .... 770-423-6333. 127 N
cyoung48@kennesaw.edu
YOUNG, Cathy .... 617-912-9139. 224 B
cyoung@bostonconservatory.edu
YOUNG, Charlotte .... 321-674-7400. 104 H
cyoung@fit.edu
YOUNG, Cheryl, D .... 513-529-8600. 384 G
youngcd@miamioh.edu
YOUNG, Christina .... 603-899-1131. 296 H
youngca@franklinpierce.edu
YOUNG, Christopher ...... 219-980-6804. 168 B
cjy@iun.edu
YOUNG, Colletta .... 541-956-7296. 407 F
cyoung@roguecc.edu
YOUNG, Connie .... 217-709-0931. 150 E
cyoung@lakeviewcol.edu
YOUNG, Corey, D .... 601-877-4063. 265 G
cyoung1@alcorn.edu
YOUNG, Dale .... 478-445-5497. 125 A
dale.young@gcsu.edu
YOUNG, Dana .... 541-881-5580. 408 C
dyoung@tvcc.cc
YOUNG, Danielle .... 440-775-8692. 385 H
danielle.young@oberlin.edu
YOUNG, Darlene, P .... 812-941-2306. 168 F
dyoung01@ius.edu
YOUNG, David, L .... 434-582-2071. 506 I
dlyoung@liberty.edu
YOUNG, Deborah .... 606-589-3323. 196 F
deborah.young@kctcs.edu
YOUNG, Deborah .... 718-270-6059. 319 A
young@mec.cuny.edu
YOUNG, Denise .... 706-867-3281. 133 D
denise.young@ung.edu
YOUNG, Dennis .... 513-244-4727. 377 G
dennis_young@mail.msj.edu
YOUNG, Djuana .... 832-842-9058. 489 B
dyoun2@central.uh.edu
YOUNG, Donald, B .... 808-956-7703. 136 B
young@hawaii.edu
YOUNG, Donald, R .... 336-744-0900. 353 A
don@carolina.edu
YOUNG, Donna .... 480-423-6300... 15 E
donna.young@scottsdalecc.edu
YOUNG, Doug .... 937-484-1308. 392 C
dyoung@urbana.edu
YOUNG, Edward .... 704-337-2464. 365 G
younge@queens.edu
YOUNG, Eldon .... 714-484-7177... 56 E
eyoung@cypresscollege.edu
YOUNG, Elizabeth .... 262-551-2145. 532 D
eyoung@carthage.edu
YOUNG, Evelyn .... 661-654-2241... 32 H
eyoung3@csub.edu
YOUNG, F. Rick .... 662-476-8442. 266 I
ryoung@eastms.edu
YOUNG, Frank .... 718-420-4494. 350 B
frank.young@wagner.edu

YOUNG, Garland .... 423-461-8720. 457 H
rgyoung@milligan.edu
YOUNG, Gene .... 936-294-1477. 487 A
young@shsu.edu
YOUNG, Gerald .... 507-222-4057. 254 D
gyoung@carleton.edu
YOUNG, Gwyn .... 601-643-8318. 266 F
gwyn.young@colin.edu
YOUNG, Heather, M .... 916-734-4745... 70 J
heather.young@ucdmc.ucdavis.edu
YOUNG, Hester .... 843-863-8020. 441 H
hyoung@csuniv.edu
YOUNG, J.R .... 412-536-1100. 420 A
JR.young@laroche.edu
YOUNG, Jackie .... 502-585-7130. 199 C
jyoung04@spalding.edu
YOUNG, James .... 708-656-8000. 153 H
james.young@morton.edu
YOUNG, James, B .... 847-491-8542. 155 D
jbyoung@northwestern.edu
YOUNG, Janet .... 209-228-4419... 71 D
JYoung@UCMerced.edu
YOUNG, Jay .... 614-251-4715. 386 B
youngj@ohiodominican.edu
YOUNG, Jeff .... 931-372-3311. 460 A
jyoung@tntech.edu
YOUNG, Joanna .... 603-862-3530. 298 C
joanna.young@unh.edu
YOUNG, Joanna, C .... 603-862-3530. 298 C
joanna.young@unh.edu
YOUNG, John .... 973-328-5026. 300 G
jyoung@ccm.edu
YOUNG, John .... 315-781-3748. 326 C
jyoung@hws.edu
YOUNG, John .... 937-327-7800. 393 E
jyoung@wittenberg.edu
YOUNG, John .... 303-360-4707... 81 C
john.young@ccaurora.edu
YOUNG, John, O .... 203-392-6275... 88 A
youngj1@southernct.edu
YOUNG, John, O .... 248-370-2946. 248 J
joyoung@oakland.edu
YOUNG, John, W .... 770-720-5522. 130 G
jyw@reinhardt.edu
YOUNG, Johnny .... 757-683-6702. 507 N
jwyoung@odu.edu
YOUNG, Jon .... 910-672-1460. 367 D
jyoung@uncfsu.edu
YOUNG, Jordan, M .... 802-862-9616. 498 I
jyoung@burlington.edu
YOUNG, Joseph .... 619-388-7672... 62 F
jyoung@sdccd.edu
YOUNG, Josie .... 818-654-1732... 59 E
jyoung@pgi.edu
YOUNG, Julian, M .... 843-661-1228. 444 B
jyoung@fmarion.edu
YOUNG, K. Richard .... 801-422-3695. 495 D
Richard_Young@byu.edu
YOUNG, JR., Karl, J ...... 985-380-2957. 203 H
karlyoung@scl.edu
YOUNG, Katie .... 501-683-7302... 24 B
kcyoung@ualr.edu
YOUNG, Kay .... 817-598-6303. 494 G
kyoung@wc.edu
YOUNG, Kay, F .... 508-213-2114. 235 E
kay.young@nichols.edu
YOUNG, Ken .... 516-323-4501. 331 J
kyoung@molloy.edu
YOUNG, Keri .... 618-453-2391. 159 G
keri.young@siu.edu
YOUNG, Kerry, A .... 315-786-2279. 327 L
kyoung@sunyjefferson.edu
YOUNG, Kimberly .... 760-252-2411... 29 I
kyoung@barstow.edu
YOUNG, Kirk .... 801-863-8806. 497 C
kirk.young@uvu.edu
YOUNG, Kristen .... 702-895-0143. 294 I
kristen.young@unlv.edu
YOUNG, Kristine .... 775-881-7509. 295 F
kyoung@sierranevada.edu
YOUNG, Kristine, M .... 217-351-2542. 155 J
kyoung@parkland.edu
YOUNG, Laura .... 501-450-3126... 25 H
lyoung@uca.edu
YOUNG, Laura, R .... 336-334-4374. 369 A
lryoung2@uncg.edu
YOUNG, Lavern .... 312-949-7430. 146 G
lyoung@ico.edu
YOUNG, Lee, D .... 804-257-5713. 515 F
ldyoung@vuu.edu
YOUNG, Lenna .... 864-250-8185. 444 E
lenna.young@gvltec.edu
YOUNG, Lester, C .... 909-869-2204... 32 G
lcyoung@csupomona.edu
YOUNG, Linda, C .... 334-556-2234..... 3 N
lyoung@wallace.edu
YOUNG, Linda, K .... 715-836-5287. 536 E
younglk@uwec.edu
YOUNG, Linda, K .... 512-223-7889. 466 I
lyoung@austincc.edu

YOUNG, Linda, L .... 440-826-2127. 374 F
lyoung@bw.edu
YOUNG, Lisa .... 718-270-5000. 319 A
lisa@mec.cuny.edu
YOUNG, Lloyd, Y .... 313-577-1574. 252 G
eg1264@wayne.edu
YOUNG, Luria .... 225-771-2290. 206 J
luria_young@subr.edu
YOUNG, Margaret .... 505-454-3522. 310 E
young_m@nmhu.edu
YOUNG, Marie .... 814-472-3022. 432 D
myoung@francis.edu
YOUNG, Mark, S .... 303-762-6902... 81 G
president@denverseminary.edu
YOUNG, Mary, L .... 603-513-1307. 298 E
mary.young@granite.edu
YOUNG, MaryAnne .... 413-538-2756. 234 D
mayoung@mtholyoke.edu
YOUNG, Meghan .... 301-369-2800. 213 G
myoung@capitol-college.edu
YOUNG, Micah .... 312-850-7161. 142 C
myoung93@ccc.edu
YOUNG, Michael .... 508-531-1295. 229 D
myoung@bridgew.edu
YOUNG, Michael .... 212-674-2600... 56 B
YOUNG, Michael, D .... 805-893-3651... 72 B
michael.young@sa.ucsb.edu
YOUNG, Michael, E .... 270-809-6831. 198 B
myoung@murraystate.edu
YOUNG, Michael, K .... 206-543-5010. 524 G
president@uw.edu
YOUNG, Michael, W .... 212-327-8000. 338 A
michael.young@rockefeller.edu
YOUNG, Michaela, J .... 315-386-7204. 345 F
youngm@canton.edu
YOUNG, Michelle, L .... 315-268-4465. 320 A
myoung@clarkson.edu
YOUNG, Miles .... 903-434-8146. 477 J
mgyoung@ntcc.edu
YOUNG, Misty .... 573-681-5580. 276 C
youngm@lincolnu.edu
YOUNG, Nancy .... 410-455-2393. 219 D
nyoung@umbc.edu
YOUNG, Nancy .... 620-242-0427. 188 G
youngn@mcpherson.edu
YOUNG, Nancy, N .... 336-750-8764. 370 A
youngnn@wssu.edu
YOUNG, Nate .... 602-331-7500... 12 A
nlyoung@aii.edu
YOUNG, Nicole .... 731-989-6768. 454 J
nyoung@fhu.edu
YOUNG, Norman .... 860-768-7819... 92 D
young@hartford.edu
YOUNG, Patricia .... 707-864-7124... 66 G
patricia.young@solano.edu
YOUNG, Patricia .... 925-969-4229... 41 L
tyoung@dvc.edu
YOUNG, Paul, J .... 740-588-1225. 394 C
pyoung@zanestate.edu
YOUNG, Paul, R .... 307-674-6446. 543 F
pyoung@sheridan.edu
YOUNG, Peter, C .... 240-684-5268. 219 F
cio@umuc.edu
YOUNG, Randy .... 660-359-3948. 279 H
ryoung@mail.ncmissouri.edu
YOUNG, Raymond .... 609-984-1141. 308 A
ryoung@tesc.edu
YOUNG, Rena .... 270-707-3732. 195 E
rena.young@kctcs.edu
YOUNG, Rhett .... 740-283-6441. 379 N
ryoung@franciscan.edu
YOUNG, Richard .... 207-581-1700. 212 B
ryoung@maine.edu
YOUNG, Robert .... 501-370-5365... 22 F
ryoung@philander.edu
YOUNG, Robert .... 423-236-2805. 458 J
ryoung@southern.edu
YOUNG, Robert .... 540-234-9261. 511 H
youngb@brcc.edu
YOUNG, Robert, B .... 440-365-5222. 383 B
YOUNG, Robert, J .... 214-378-1703. 470 F
ryoung@dcccd.edu
YOUNG, Robin .... 425-235-2352. 522 F
Robin.Young@rtc.edu
YOUNG, Ronald .... 269-782-1272. 250 C
hyoung@swmich.edu
YOUNG, Rosemary .... 513-732-5232. 391 B
rosemary.young@uc.edu
YOUNG, Sean, B .... 262-243-5700. 532 H
sean.young@cuw.edu
YOUNG, Shauna .... 562-907-4986... 76 I
syoung2@whittier.edu
YOUNG, Sheridan .... 580-581-2408. 394 G
YOUNG, Sheryl .... 828-766-1350. 361 H
syoung@mayland.edu
YOUNG, Stephen, W .... 513-732-5318. 391 B
steve.young@uc.edu
YOUNG, Steve .... 828-694-1891. 358 C
sd_young@blueridge.edu
YOUNG, Steve .... 850-718-2203... 99 N
youngs@chipola.edu

YOUNG, Steve .... 602-386-4115... 11 G
steve.young@arizonachristian.edu
YOUNG, Tammy .... 479-394-7622... 23 B
tyoung@rmcc.edu
YOUNG, Tasheka .... 718-368-5597. 318 E
tyoung@kbcc.cuny.edu
YOUNG, Tellis, S .... 260-399-7700. 174 C
tyoung@sf.edu
YOUNG, Terry .... 325-793-4683. 476 E
tyoung@mcm.edu
YOUNG, Thomas, W ...... 507-933-7551. 255 I
tyoung3@gustavus.edu
YOUNG, Tim .... 714-556-3610... 74 D
tyoung@vanguard.edu
YOUNG, Tommy .... 903-923-2137. 471 J
tyoung@etbu.edu
YOUNG, Tyrone .... 410-651-6411. 219 E
tyoung@umes.edu
YOUNG, Virginia, E .... 804-752-7256. 508 E
vyoung@rmc.edu
YOUNG, Von .... 217-351-2884. 155 J
vyoung@parkland.edu
YOUNG, W. Dale .... 304-724-3700. 526 B
dyoung@apus.edu
YOUNG, Wes .... 740-446-4367. 380 C
director@gallipoliscareercollege.edu
YOUNG, William, R .... 512-223-7069. 466 I
pyoung@austincc.edu
YOUNG SANDERS,
Candy .... 302-857-6030... 93 C
csanders@desu.edu
YOUNG SWITZER, Jo ..... 260-982-5050. 170 U
jyswitzer@manchester.edu
YOUNG WON, Duk .... 323-643-0301... 27 N
YOUNG-YASSINE,
Debra, L .... 610-526-6118. 417 H
elaharcum@harcum.edu
YOUNGBEAR-TIBBETS,
Holly .... 800-567-2344. 532 E
hyoungbear@menominee.edu
YOUNGBLOOD, Amy ..... 281-649-3413. 473 B
ayoungblood@hbu.edu
YOUNGBLOOD, Betty, J . 248-370-3500. 248 J
youngblo@oakland.edu
YOUNGBLOOD, Cecil .... 608-363-2237. 531 M
youngblc@beloit.edu
YOUNGBLOOD, Dan ...... 317-278-7631. 168 D
dyoungbl@iupui.edu
YOUNGBLOOD, Joseph . 607-777-4351. 308 A
jyoungblood@tesc.edu
YOUNGBLOOD, Kerry, L 252-222-6140. 358 G
youngbloodk@carteret.edu
YOUNGBLOOD, Merna .. 618-842-3711. 146 I
youngbloodm@iecc.edu
YOUNGBLOOD, Pamela . 979-532-6542. 494 L
pamy@wcjc.edu
YOUNGBLOOD, Randy ... 205-226-4700..... 2 C
ryoungbl@bsc.edu
YOUNGBLOOD, Rick ...... 601-477-4014. 267 F
rick.youngblood@jcjc.edu
YOUNGE, Jeffrey, W .... 507-344-7328. 253 J
jyounge@blc.edu
YOUNGER, Allan .... 336-725-4746. 360 E
ayounger@forsythtech.edu
YOUNGER, Jamie .... 859-442-1719. 195 B
jamie.younger@kctcs.edu
YOUNGERS, Jane, A ...... 210-567-2333. 493 A
youngers@uthscsa.edu
YOUNGLOVE, Theodore . 909-652-6402... 37 M
ted.younglove@chaffey.edu
YOUNGQUIST, Jim, L .... 501-569-8476... 24 B
jlyoungquist@ualr.edu
YOUNGQUIST, Joan .... 360-416-7675. 523 G
joan.youngquist@skagit.edu
YOUNGREN, Malcolm .... 212-982-3456... 57 E
myoungren@pacificcollege.edu
YOUNGS, Joel .... 309-764-2213. 140 E
youngsj@bhc.edu
YOUNGS, JR.,
Thomas, E .... 412-624-8785. 435 C
tyoungs@cfo.pitt.edu
YOUNKIN, Michelle .... 402-486-2529. 292 E
miyounki@ucollege.edu
YOUNT, Diana .... 617-964-1100. 222 A
dyount@ants.edu
YOUNT, Rebecca, H ...... 401-333-7159. 439 A
ryount@ccri.edu
YOUNT-PETTINGILL,
Sara .... 502-272-8401. 192 E
syount@bellarmine.edu
YOUSE, Lauren .... 573-629-3122. 274 J
Lauren.Youse@hlg.edu
YOUVICH, Rudy .... 567-661-7974. 387 L
rudy_youvich@owens.edu
YOVANOVICH, Michele .. 239-590-7900. 115 A
myovanov@fgcu.edu
YOW, Deborah .... 919-515-2109. 368 B
d_yow@ncsu.edu
YOWELL, Lee, P .... 706-886-6831. 133 A
lyowell@tfc.edu

YOWELL, Susan, K 308-635-6104. 293 E yowells@wncc.edu
YOXALL, Andrea, G 620-417-1125. 190 F andrea.yoxall@sccc.edu
YOXALL, Daniel 210-434-6711. 477 N dyoxall@lake.ollusa.edu
YSAIS, David 213-763-7063... 52 D dpysais@lattc.edu
YSEBAERT, Emily 920-498-5612. 541 B emily.ysebaert@nwtc.edu
YSURSA, JR., Bernie, J . 618-235-2700. 160 A bernard.ysursa@swic.edu
YU, Alexander 330-471-8303. 383 D ayu@malone.edu
YU, Bin 401-456-8160. 439 F byu@ric.edu
YU, David 414-229-2937. 537 A yu@uwm.edu
YU, Dennis 510-592-9688... 56 G wub@npu.edu
YU, Diane 212-998-2340. 334 D diane.yu@nyu.edu
YU, John 707-864-7110... 66 G john.yu@solano.edu
YU, Lei 713-313-7282. 485 F yu_lx@tsu.edu
YU, Maya 505-438-8884. 312 A maya@acupuncturecollege.edu
YU, Roger 516-686-7700. 333 H ryu@nyit.edu
YUAN, Qing 301-387-3043. 214 I qing.yuan@garrettcollege.edu
YUASA, Miyoko 808-946-3773. 135 B
YUCHA, Carolyn 702-895-4070. 294 I carolyn.yucha@unlv.edu
YUDIN, Lee, S 671-735-2002. 546 E lyudin@uguam.uog.edu
YUDT, Angela, L 312-355-2412. 161 D ayudt@uic.edu
YUEN, Dan 212-924-5900. 347 B
YUEN, Karen 212-217-3650. 324 C karen_yuen@fitnyc.edu
YUHNKE, Laurie 215-951-2543. 430 E yuhnkel@philau.edu
YULFO, Monserrate 787-891-0925. 549 K myulfo@aguadilla.inter.edu
YUNDEM, Mustafa 918-781-7312. 394 D yundemm@bacone.edu
YUNEK, Brent, W 949-824-6362... 71 B bwyunek@uci.edu
YUNES, Trini 956-882-8205. 491 D Trini.Yunes@utb.edu
YUNG, Josephine 360-438-4375. 522 G jyung@stmartin.edu
YUNGBLUT, Michelle 972-438-6932. 478 C myungblut@parkercc.edu
YUNKAI, Chen 910-672-1957. 367 D ychen@uncfsu.edu
YUNKER, Kristin, L 585-343-0055. 325 C klyunker@genesee.edu
YURA, Catherine, A 304-293-2547. 530 D cathy.yura@mail.wvu.edu
YURACHEK, Hunter, R 843-349-2813. 442 E hunter@coastal.edu
YURAN, Mark, A 218-477-2066. 259 H mark.yuran@mnstate.edu
YUST, Rob 417-625-9395. 278 D yust-r@mssu.edu
YUSUFOV, Daniil 303-937-4572... 79 E dyusufov@chu.edu
YUTUC, Lloyd 301-891-4477. 221 B ylloyd@wau.edu
YZZI, Nicholas, Y 215-368-7538. 412 A nyzzi@cbs.edu

Z

ZABEL, Darcy 316-295-5436. 186 H dzabel@friends.edu
ZABEL, Randy 405-491-6609. 399 K rzabel@snu.edu
ZABOJNIK, Linda, S 972-860-7370. 470 I LindaZabojnik@dcccd.edu
ZABORAC, Tom 309-647-7030. 150 D tom.zaborac@doc.illinois.gov
ZABOROWSKI, Barbara .. 814-262-6425. 427 C bzabor@pennhighlands.edu
ZABOROWSKI, Joseph, J 402-280-2100. 289 D josephzaborowski@creighton.edu
ZABOSKI, Gerald, C 570-941-6668. 436 A gerald.zaboski@scranton.edu
ZABRISKIE, Mark 541-737-5774. 406 A mark.zabriskie@oregonstate.edu
ZACARIAS, Celina 805-437-8920... 32 I celina.zacarias@csuci.edu
ZACHAREK, John 315-498-2512. 335 G zacharej@sunyocc.edu
ZACHARIAH, Sajit 216-687-4625. 377 F sajit.zachariah@csuohio.edu
ZACHARIAS, Holly 252-399-6366. 352 F hzacharias@barton.edu
ZACHARIAS, Larry 972-883-2232. 491 E larry.zacharias@utdallas.edu
ZACHARY, Samuel 859-572-5495. 198 I zachary@nku.edu
ZACHMEYER, Dru 805-756-6473... 32 F dzachmey@calpoly.edu
ZACHOCKI, Peter 312-567-5983. 147 F pzachock@iit.edu
ZACK, Gary, L 314-719-8017. 274 E gzack@fontbonne.edu
ZACKER, John 301-314-7775. 219 B jzacker@umd.edu
ZACOVIC, Anne 206-934-5661. 522 I anne.zacovic@seattlecolleges.edu
ZACOVIC, Mark, J 619-660-4221... 46 D mark.zacovic@gcccd.edu
ZAFFUTO, George, T 412-536-1115. 420 A george.zaffuto@laroche.edu
ZAGALO-MELO, Paulo ... 406-243-0211. 286 H paulo.zagalo-melo@umontana.edu
ZAGNONI, Paul, L 480-314-2102... 17 O paul@sdi.edu
ZAGO, Susan 603-513-5129. 298 D susan.zago@law.unh.edu
ZAGORA, Marilyn, A 716-338-1020. 327 J marilynzagora@mail.sunyjcc.edu
ZAHED, Fereshtah 803-705-4771. 441 C zahedf@benedict.edu
ZAHEER, Srilata, A 612-624-7876. 264 G szaheer@umn.edu
ZAHLER, Noel 516-299-2396. 329 D noel.zahler@liu.edu
ZAHN, Jeffrey, A 920-403-3071. 535 L jeffrey.zahn@snc.edu
ZAHN, JoAnn 503-338-2422. 402 G jzahn@clatsopcc.edu
ZAHN, Karla 920-693-1172. 540 B karla.zahn@gotoltc.edu
ZAHN, Patricia 314-516-5267. 283 E zahnp@umsl.edu
ZAHZAM, Nancy, L 718-780-7915. 315 H nancy.zahzam@brooklaw.edu
ZAIDI, Syed, S 570-422-3077. 428 D zaidi@po-box.esu.edu
ZAIDMAN, Ron 831-476-9424... 44 K president@fivebranches.edu
ZAIDMAN, Ron 408-260-0208... 44 J president@fivebranches.edu
ZAIMES, Leon 617-559-8783. 227 D lzaimes@hebrewcollege.edu
ZAIS, Diana, P 781-239-4382. 222 D prescottzais@babson.edu
ZAISER, Greg 336-278-3566. 354 B zaiser@elon.edu
ZAJAC, SND, Brendon ... 440-943-7600. 388 J bzajac@dioceseofcleveland.org
ZAJAC, Carol, S 718-357-0500. 339 G czajac@edaff.com
ZAJACESKOWSKI, John . 518-244-2253. 338 C zajacj@sage.edu
ZAJCHOWSKI, Ann 860-727-6757... 90 A azajchowski@goodwin.edu
ZAK, Diane, S 605-677-5671. 451 F diane.zak@usd.edu
ZAKAHI, Walter 507-389-5465. 259 G walter.zakahi@mnsu.edu
ZAKARIA, Roland 619-574-6909... 57 E rzakaria@pacificcollege.edu
ZAKARIN, Joann 619-596-2766... 26 I jo@advancedtraining.edu
ZAKEL, Lori 937-512-2881. 388 O lori.zakel@sinclair.edu
ZAKERY, Fatemeh 314-256-8163. 275 A zakeryf@hssu.edu
ZAKOWSKI, Paul 630-942-2895. 142 G zakows@cod.edu
ZALACCA, James, A 315-267-2314. 344 C zalaccja@potsdam.edu
ZALAPI, Diane 248-476-1122. 246 G dzalapi@mispp.edu
ZALDIVAR, Edward 305-821-3333. 105 A ezaldivar@fnu.edu
ZALETEL, Cora 719-549-2576... 80 K cora.zaletel@colostate-pueblo.edu
ZALIMAS, Robert 803-934-3181. 445 F rzalimas@morris.edu
ZALOT, Marcella, K 207-859-4904. 209 J mkzalot@colby.edu
ZAMBARDI, Victor, A 248-370-3112. 248 J zambardi@oakland.edu
ZAMBELLA, BethAnn 740-587-6215. 379 D zambellab@denison.edu
ZAMBELLI, William, W 914-337-9300. 321 E william.zambelli@concordia-ny.edu
ZAMBITO, Angela, R 304-336-8490. 530 A azambito@westliberty.edu
ZAMBLE, Anthony 773-244-5568. 154 G azamble@northpark.edu
ZAMBONINO, Maria 773-878-3813. 158 B mzambonino@staugustine.edu
ZAMBRANA, Maritza 787-279-1912. 550 B mzambrana@bayamon.inter.edu
ZAMBRANO, Gabe 918-587-6789. 400 J gzambrano@twsweld.com
ZAMBRANO, Thomas 732-987-2613. 302 B zambrano@georgian.edu
ZAMBRINI, Dante 330-480-0726. 379 F dzambrini@egcc.edu
ZAMORA, Felix, A 214-860-8700. 471 A fzamora@dcccd.edu
ZAMORA, Juan, M 305-628-6593. 112 F jzamora@stu.edu
ZAMORA, Teri 956-364-4400. 485 H teri.zamora@tstc.edu
ZAMORA-AGUILAR, Beatrice 619-482-6379... 68 B bzamora@swccd.edu
ZAMPANO, Gary, S 570-941-4273. 436 A gary.zampano@scranton.edu
ZAMSKY, Robert 941-487-4225. 115 D rzamsky@ncf.edu
ZAMUDIO, Cynthia 210-486-4601. 464 J czamudio1@alamo.edu
ZANCHELLI, Denise 845-451-1458. 322 D d_zanche@culinary.edu
ZANDBERGEN, Dianne, V 616-222-3000. 245 C dzandbergen@kuyper.edu
ZANDER, Kirk 406-756-3806. 286 B kzander@fvcc.edu
ZANDERS, Ann 225-216-8723. 202 H zandersa@mybrcc.edu
ZANDERS, Joan, A 703-323-3199. 513 C jzanders@nvcc.edu
ZANDI, Nader 205-853-1200..... 5 B nzandi@jeffstateonline.com
ZANDSTRA, Laura, J 207-741-5501. 211 A lzandstra@smccme.edu
ZANE, Cynthia, A 716-926-8923. 326 B czane@hilbert.edu
ZANE, Gary 207-948-9241. 211 I gzane@unity.edu
ZANELLA-LITKE, Joanne 508-999-8772. 229 A joanne.zanellalitke@umassd.edu
ZANETTI, Erika, P 713-348-2939. 479 A epz@rice.edu
ZANETTI, Mary, L 508-856-6009. 229 C Mary.Zanetti@umassmed.edu
ZANG, Connie 740-366-9246. 376 A czang@cotc.edu
ZANG, Paul 810-766-4112. 239 H paul.zang@baker.edu
ZANGER, Kate 563-588-6313. 176 F kate.zanger@clarke.edu
ZANGHI, Palma 716-896-0700. 350 A zanghi@villa.edu
ZANGHI, Palma, M 716-896-0700. 350 A zanghi@villa.edu
ZANIC, Van, G 724-847-6105. 417 A vgzanic@geneva.edu
ZANIOS, Jamie, T 641-422-4162. 181 D zaniojam@niacc.edu
ZANJANI, Mellissia 732-987-2244. 302 B zanjanim@georgian.edu
ZANK, Gary 256-824-6575..... 8 F gary.zank@uah.edu
ZANKICH, Mark, A 310-233-4171... 51 H zankicma@lahc.edu
ZANKO, Michael 973-655-5457. 303 D zankom@mail.montclair.edu
ZANSITIS, Richard, A 713-348-5237. 479 A zansitis@rice.edu
ZANT, Don 662-325-2231. 268 D dzant@budgetplan.msstate.edu
ZANTINGH, Ryan 708-239-4872. 160 K ryan.zantingh@trnty.edu
ZAPALSKA, Alina, M 860-444-8334. 545 G alina.m.zapalska@uscg.mil
ZAPATA, Fred 210-999-7401. 488 C fred.zapata@trinity.edu
ZAPATA, Grace 210-486-2269. 465 B zapata@alamo.edu
ZAPATA, Hector 225-578-2766. 204 O hozapat@lsu.edu
ZAPATA, Jesse, T 210-458-2700. 492 C jesse.zapata@utsa.edu
ZAPATA, Rafael, A 401-865-2878. 439 E rzapata@providence.edu
ZAPATA, Sergio 915-351-8100. 465 I
ZAPOLSKI, Mike 309-794-7223. 139 L mikezapolski@augustana.edu
ZAPPALA, Henry, W 617-824-8281. 226 A hank_zappala@emerson.edu
ZAPPALORTI, Robert, E .. 203-287-3028... 90 H paier.admin@snet.net
ZAPPAS, Barbara 831-582-3908... 34 B bzappas@csumb.edu
ZAPPE, Christopher 717-337-6820. 417 B czappe@gettysburg.edu
ZAPPI, Mark, E 337-482-6685. 208 D zappi@louisiana.edu
ZAPPIA, Charles 619-388-2801... 62 E czappia@sdccd.edu
ZAPPIA, Gerard 585-389-2570. 332 D gzappia4@naz.edu
ZAPPONE, Michael 412-291-6248. 410 B mzappone@aii.edu
ZAPROROZHETZ, Laurene, E 937-255-5894. 544 C laurene.zaporozhetz@afit.edu
ZARAGOZA, Federico 210-485-0015. 464 I fzaragoza@alamo.edu
ZARCHI, Shloime 718-434-0784. 316 F
ZAREMBA, Terah 269-965-3931. 244 O zarembat@kellogg.edu
ZARET, David 812-855-5021. 167 E zaret@iu.edu
ZARET, David 812-855-5021. 167 F zaret@indiana.edu
ZAREVA, John 503-255-0332. 404 F jzareva@multnomah.edu
ZARIAROW, Esmail 954-783-7339. 102 M ezariarow@cci.edu
ZARING, Gayle 618-544-8657. 147 A zaringg@iecc.edu
ZARKOWSKI, Pamela 313-993-1585. 250 K zarkowp1@udmercy.edu
ZARLING, Mark, G 507-354-8221. 256 M zarlinmg@mlc-wels.edu
ZARR, Joel 719-549-3062... 84 G joel.zarr@pueblocc.edu
ZARRAS, Ginny 313-593-5666. 251 D gzarras@umich.edu
ZARRILLO, Deirdre 518-292-1704. 338 C zarrid@sage.edu
ZARRINNAM, Ali, R 608-246-6446. 540 C azarrinnam@madisoncollege.edu
ZARTERN, Ken 432-335-6606. 477 M kzartner@odessa.edu
ZASTE, Kathe 701-477-7862. 373 B kzaste@tm.edu
ZASTOUPIL, Brenda 701-224-2541. 371 B brenda.zastoupil@ndus.edu
ZATAR, Wael 304-696-6043. 529 H zatar@marshall.edu
ZAUFT, Richard 617-824-8912. 226 A richard_zauft@emerson.edu
ZAUHAR, Frances, M 570-348-6233. 423 B zauhar@marywood.edu
ZAVADA, Michael, S 973-761-9022. 307 C michael.zavada@shu.edu
ZAVADA, Paul 262-551-2158. 532 D pzavada@carthage.edu
ZAVADA, Robert 570-674-8018. 424 A rzavada@misericordia.edu
ZAVALA, Joseph 858-642-8024... 55 J jzavala@nu.edu
ZAVALA, Tracy 559-438-4222... 46 K tracy_zavala@heald.edu
ZAVALA-COLÓN, Maria de los Angeles ... 787-993-8877. 554 A maria.zavala1@upr.edu
ZAVALA-QUIÑONES, Javier 787-993-8854. 554 A javier.zavala@upr.edu
ZAVARICH, Joyce 610-519-4080. 436 F joyce.zavarich@villanova.edu
ZAWACKI, Rosemary 810-766-4028. 239 H rosemary.zawacki@baker.edu
ZAWACKI, Rosemary 810-766-4028. 239 G rosemary.zawacki@baker.edu
ZAWALICH, Barbara 508-849-3401. 222 B bzawalich@annamaria.edu
ZAWIA, Nasser, H 401-874-5909. 440 D nzawia@uri.edu
ZAWISTOWSKI, Lee 845-569-3229. 332 B lee.zawistowski@msmc.edu
ZAWODNY, Laurel, E 419-372-2211. 374 K lzawodn@bgsu.edu
ZAYAITZ, Anne, E 610-683-4305. 429 A zayaitz@kutztown.edu
ZAYAS, Brendaliz 787-258-1501. 548 H bzayas@columbiaco.edu
ZAYAS, Luis, H 512-471-1937. 491 C lzayas@austin.utexas.edu
ZAYAS, Maria 787-758-2525. 554 F mariadelosa.zayas3@upr.edu
ZAYAS, Myriam 787-841-2000. 552 B mzayas@pucpr.edu
ZAYAS, Niza 787-786-3030. 547 F nzayas@ucb.edu.pr
ZAYAS-HERNÁNDEZ, Haydee, M 787-480-2379. 548 G hzayas@sanjuancapital.com
ZAYAS-HERNANDEZ, Haydee, M 787-480-2406. 548 G hzayas@sanjuancapital.com
ZAZUETA, Fedro, S 352-392-0365. 116 A fsz@ufl.edu

ZAZZALI, Robert .... 856-256-4110. 305 E
zazzali@rowan.edu
ZBIKOWSKI, Lawrence ... 773-702-8500. 161 B
larry@uchicago.edu
ZBOCK, Jason .... 607-778-5024. 315 I
zbockjp@sunybroome.edu
ZDANCEWICZ, Heather ... 703-370-6600. 508 B
ZDZIARSKI, II,
Eugene, L .... 540-375-2592. 509 B
zdziarski@roanoke.edu
ZEALAND, Matthew, J .... 434-582-2000. 506 I
mjzealan@liberty.edu
ZEBEDIS, Frank, J .... 803-323-3333. 449 G
zebedisf@winthrop.edu
ZEBROWSKI, Michael, J 414-288-7172. 534 B
michael.zebrowski@marquette.edu
ZECCA, Frank .... 956-665-5078. 492 B
zecca@utpa.edu
ZECCA, Marie .... 267-341-3650. 418 G
mzecca@holyfamily.edu
ZECH, Susan .... 212-686-9244. 313 G
ZECKOVICH, Kim .... 906-932-4231. 242 I
kimz@gogebic.edu
ZEEK, Raymond .... 203-285-2210... 88 E
rzeek@gwcc.commnet.edu
ZEFF, Ira, A .... 402-465-2360. 291 G
izeff@nebrwesleyan.edu
ZEFF, Jane .... 973-720-2379. 308 I
zeffj@wpunj.edu
ZEGARSKI, Len .... 619-684-8788... 56 C
lzegarski@newschoolarch.edu
ZEGER, Brian .... 212-799-5000. 328 B
ZEGER, Scott, L .... 410-516-8770. 215 H
scott.zeger@jhu.edu
ZEGLEN, Marie .... 352-392-0456. 116 A
zeglenm@ufl.edu
ZEHEL, Renee, G .... 570-961-4715. 423 B
rzehel@marywood.edu
ZEHR, David .... 603-535-2235. 298 G
zehr@plymouth.edu
ZEHREN, Carolyn, F ...... 218-477-2085. 259 H
zehren@mnstate.edu
ZEICH, Heidi, E .... 202-319-5615... 94 G
zeich@cua.edu
ZEIDENSTEIN, Darrow .... 713-348-6090. 479 A
darrowz@rice.edu
ZEIGER, Britt .... 641-472-1126. 180 N
housing@mum.edu
ZEIGLER, Michael .... 803-535-5340. 442 B
mike.zeigler@claflin.edu
ZEIGLER, Michael, C ...... 717-867-6060. 421 H
zeigler@lvc.edu
ZEIGLER, Robert .... 210-486-0961. 464 I
rzeigler@alamo.edu
ZEIGLER, Robert, E .... 210-486-0959. 465 C
rzeigler@alamo.edu
ZEIGLER, Sara .... 859-622-2222. 193 P
sara.zeigler@eku.edu
ZEILBERGER, Yeruchom . 203-325-4351... 87 H
ZEILE, Carol .... 989-463-7227. 239 B
zeile@alma.edu
ZEILENGA, Jeffrey .... 573-882-5397. 283 C
zeilingaj@missouri.edu
ZEILMAN, JR., Charles .. 318-473-6486. 205 A
czeilman@lsua.edu
ZEIMET, Dan, L .... 563-333-6202. 182 B
ZeimetDanielL@sau.edu
ZEIRD, Susan .... 706-233-7466. 131 E
szeird@shorter.edu
ZEIS, TOR, Gabriel .... 814-472-3001. 432 D
gzeis@francis.edu
ZEISER, Richard, A .... 860-768-4181... 92 D
zeiser@hartford.edu
ZEISS, P. Anthony .... 704-330-6566. 359 C
tony.zeiss@cpcc.edu
ZEISS, Timothy .... 732-224-2887. 299 G
tzeiss@brookdalecc.edu
ZEITHAML, Carl, P .... 434-924-3176. 511 B
cpz6n@virginia.edu
ZEITLOW, Terry, A .... 574-807-7120. 164 D
terry.zeitlow@bethelcollege.edu
ZELECHOWSKI, Deborah 773-697-2200. 144 B
dzelechowski@devry.edu
ZELENAK, Angeline .... 248-204-2216. 245 I
azelenak@ltu.edu
ZELENAK, Christine .... 609-896-5395. 305 D
czelenak@rider.edu
ZELENSKI, Paul .... 517-371-5140. 250 G
zelensp@cooley.edu
ZELENZ, Margot .... 218-723-6460. 254 K
mzelenz@css.edu
ZELESKY, Jason .... 508-793-7423. 225 A
jzelesky@clarku.edu
ZELESNIK, Kelly .... 440-365-5222. 383 B
ZELEZNY, Lynnette .... 559-278-0333... 33 D
lynnette@csufresno.edu
ZELEZNY, Lynnette .... 559-278-2636... 33 D
lynnette@csufresno.edu
ZELICK, Stacia, A .... 973-353-1734. 306 D
stacia.zelick@rutgers.edu
ZELINSKI, Bob .... 352-854-2322. 100 K
zelinskb@cf.edu
ZELLER, John, H .... 215-898-5169. 435 B
jzeller@upenn.edu
ZELLER, Lisa, L .... 303-963-3210... 79 C
lzeller@ccu.edu
ZELLERS, Andrew .... 270-831-9627. 195 D
andrew.zellers@kctcs.edu
ZELLERS, Jeff, W .... 740-826-8139. 384 L
jzellers@muskingum.edu
ZELLMER, Aaron .... 952-562-4200. 450 G
azellmer@national.edu
ZELLMER, Jill, A .... 617-627-3298. 237 C
jill.zellmer@tufts.edu
ZELLNER, Alan .... 570-662-4071. 429 C
ezellner@mansfield.edu
ZELTWANGER, Todd ...... 574-936-8898. 163 K
todd.zeltwanger@ancilla.edu
ZEMAN, Janet .... 845-569-3159. 332 B
janet.zeman@msmc.edu
ZEMAN, Mary .... 860-509-9502... 90 B
mzeman@hartsem.edu
ZEMAN, Mary Beth .... 973-720-2971. 308 I
zemanm@wpunj.edu
ZEMAN, Scott, C .... 305-474-6805. 112 F
szeman@stu.edu
ZEMBAR, Mary Jo .... 937-327-7921. 393 E
mzembar@wittenberg.edu
ZEMBRODT, Belle .... 859-572-5634. 198 I
zembrodt@nku.edu
ZEMKE, Mary Ann .... 541-885-1105. 405 J
maryann.zemke@oit.edu
ZENCHECK, Jack .... 718-430-8889. 351 M
zencheck@yu.edu
ZENELIS, John, G .... 703-993-2223. 505 C
jzenelis@gmu.edu
ZENG, Zheng .... 512-454-1188. 466 B
info@aoma.edu
ZENGER, Sheahon .... 785-864-3143. 190 L
kuathletics@ku.edu
ZENNER, Art .... 405-733-7343. 399 F
azenner@rose.edu
ZENO, Mark .... 419-448-2058. 380 G
mzeno@heidelberg.edu
ZENSEN, Sanford .... 423-775-7255. 453 E
zensensa@bryan.edu
ZENTMEYER, James, R .. 248-370-3570. 248 J
zentmeye@oakland.edu
ZENTNER, Aeron .... 530-251-6181... 50 F
azentner@lassencollege.edu
ZENZ, David, M .... 517-437-7341. 243 I
david.zenz@hillsdale.edu
ZEONE, Alicia .... 217-479-7059. 152 D
alicia.zeone@mac.edu
ZEPEDA, Andrea .... 918-335-6833. 398 F
azepeda@okwu.edu
ZEPH, Lucille, A .... 207-581-3113. 212 B
lzeph@maine.edu
ZEPPOS, Nicholas .... 615-322-1813. 463 G
nick.zeppos@vanderbilt.edu
ZERA, Richard .... 978-934-2654. 229 B
Richard_Zera@uml.edu
ZERA, Richard .... 517-629-0960. 239 A
rzera@alpha.albion.edu
ZERAH, Carol .... 516-299-3952. 329 D
Carol.Zerah@liu.edu
ZERANGUE, Greg .... 337-482-6378. 208 D
gregz@louisiana.edu
ZERBE, Jack .... 336-316-2351. 355 A
jzerbe@guilford.edu
ZERBE, Linda .... 610-282-1100. 414 F
linda.zerbe@desales.edu
ZERBIAN, Lindsey .... 815-802-8628. 149 C
lzerbian@kcc.edu
ZERBONIA, Liza .... 563-355-3500. 180 E
lzerbonia@kucampus.edu
ZERGER, Sandra .... 620-327-8207. 187 D
sandraz@hesston.edu
ZERHUSEN KRUER,
Karen .... 859-572-5126. 198 I
zerhusenkk1@nku.edu
ZERMENO, Christina ...... 714-997-6517... 38 A
curiel@chapman.edu
ZERNICKE, Ronald, F ..... 734-764-5210. 251 C
zernicke@umich.edu
ZERTUCHE, Bernie .... 210-486-4879. 464 J
zertuche@alamo.edu
ZERZAN, Phil .... 503-725-4782. 406 B
pzerzan@pdx.edu
ZETARSKI, Jennifer .... 802-225-3230. 499 I
jennifer.zetarski@neci.edu
ZETTERGREN, David, G .. 901-678-2121. 460 B
dzttrgrn@memphis.edu
ZETTLER, Chuck, H .... 561-868-3242. 110 C
zettlerc@palmbeachstate.edu
ZEWE, Beth .... 814-732-1420. 428 E
zewe@edinboro.edu
ZEWE, Judith, L .... 303-556-5031... 83 D
jzewe@msudenver.edu
ZHAI, Lijuan .... 559-489-2224... 68 I
lijuan.zhai@fresnocitycollege.edu
ZHAI, Meihua .... 706-452-3183. 133 C
mzhai@uga.edu
ZHAN, Lin .... 901-678-2020. 460 B
lzhan@memphis.edu
ZHANG, Biao .... 605-677-6836. 451 F
biao.zhang@usd.edu
ZHANG, Cheryl .... 212-226-7300. 336 G
czhang@pbcny.edu
ZHANG, Chunsheng ...... 256-765-4898..... 9 C
czhang@una.edu
ZHANG, Chuqian .... 516-686-3786. 333 H
czhang03@nyit.edu
ZHANG, James .... 828-227-2159. 369 E
zhang@wcu.edu
ZHANG, Jane .... 510-763-7787... 26 D
jane@acchs.edu
ZHANG, Jiajie, W .... 713-500-3922. 492 E
jiajie.zhang@uth.tmc.edu
ZHANG, Ming .... 360-650-4454. 525 C
ming.zhang@wwu.edu
ZHANG, Minghua .... 631-632-8781. 342 C
minghua.zhang@stonybrook.edu
ZHANG, Robert .... 412-365-1292. 412 K
rzhang@chatham.edu
ZHANG, Sha Li .... 406-243-6800. 286 H
shali.zhang@umontana.edu
ZHANG, Shouhong .... 605-688-6312. 452 B
shouhong.zhang@sdstate.edu
ZHANG, Tong-Ai .... 361-570-4323. 489 E
zhangt@uhv.edu
ZHANG, Xiao, Y .... 716-673-4806. 342 A
xiao.zhang@fredonia.edu
ZHAO, Jielu .... 831-242-5801. 544 F
jielu.zhao.civ@mail.mil
ZHAO, Joanna .... 408-260-0208... 44 J
dean@fivebranches.edu
ZHAO, Joanna .... 832-476-8211... 44 K
dean@fivebranches.edu
ZHAO, Joanna .... 831-476-9424... 44 K
dean@fivebranches.edu
ZHAO, Lianna .... 949-451-5238... 67 B
lzhao@ivc.edu
ZHAO, Yiping .... 516-739-1545. 333 F
clinicmanager@nyctcm.edu
ZHENG, John .... 662-254-3452. 269 A
zheng@mvsu.edu
ZHONG, Baisong .... 713-780-9777. 465 G
info@acaom.edu
ZHOU, Chenn .... 219-989-2665. 171 N
czhou@purduecal.edu
ZHOU, Claire .... 914-337-9300. 321 E
claire.zhou@concordia-ny.edu
ZHOU, Kai .... 518-782-6888. 340 J
kzhou@siena.edu
ZHOU, Tiannan .... 770-426-2712. 128 D
tiannan.zhou@life.edu
ZHOU, Wei .... 619-660-4226... 46 D
wei.zhou@gcccd.edu
ZHOU, Wei .... 760-366-5273... 42 B
wzhou@cmccd.edu
ZHOU, Wei .... 301-985-7705. 219 F
institutional-planning@umuc.edu
ZHU, Jianping .... 216-687-3595. 377 F
j.zhu94@csuohio.edu
ZHU, Jie .... 843-953-6670. 443 A
zhuj2@cofc.edu
ZHUANG, Miao .... 361-593-4480. 484 A
miao.zhuang@tamuk.edu
ZIADY, Eric .... 302-831-4006... 94 B
eziady@udel.edu
ZIAJKA, Alan, L .... 415-422-2846... 73 J
ziajka@usfca.edu
ZIAVRAS, Sotirios, G ...... 973-596-3462. 303 G
sotirios.g.ziavras@njit.edu
ZIBELL, Tammy .... 509-533-8135. 518 E
tammy.zibell@scc.spokane.edu
ZIBLUK, Patricia, M ...... 203-392-6800... 88 A
ziblukp1@southernct.edu
ZICCARDI, C. Anthony ... 973-313-6053. 307 C
anthony.ziccardi@shu.edu
ZICHER, Marie-Ange ...... 708-456-0300. 161 A
mzicher@triton.edu
ZICOLELLO, Vincent .... 201-360-4351. 302 D
vzicolello@hccc.edu
ZIEBARTH, Timothy, J .... 574-372-5100. 166 B
ziebartj@grace.edu
ZIEGLER, Chris .... 734-432-5662. 246 B
cziegler@madonna.edu
ZIEGLER, Daniel .... 740-857-1311. 388 I
dziegler@rosedale.edu
ZIEGLER, Dennis .... 701-228-5451. 372 C
dennis.ziegler@dakotacollege.edu
ZIEGLER, Erich .... 402-721-5480. 290 K
ziegler@midlandu.edu
ZIEGLER, Jan .... 870-248-4000... 20 G
janz@blackrivertech.edu
ZIEGLER, John, H .... 412-396-1090. 415 F
ziegler@duq.edu
ZIEGLER, Patricia .... 212-472-1500. 334 B
pziegler@nysid.edu
ZIEL, Michelle .... 208-524-3000. 138 D
michelle.ziel@my.eitc.edu
ZIEL, Michelle, P .... 208-524-3000. 138 D
michelle.ziel@my.eitc.edu
ZIELINSKI, James, S ...... 608-363-2176. 531 M
zielinsk@beloit.edu
ZIELINSKI, Walter .... 353-638-9704... 99 B
wzielinski@beaconcollege.edu
ZIEMBA, David .... 508-362-2131. 231 D
dziemba@capecod.edu
ZIEMIANSKI, Michael .... 812-357-6501. 173 A
mziemianski@saintmeinrad.edu
ZIENCIK, Catherine .... 919-497-3306. 356 E
cziencik@louisburg.edu
ZIENIEWICZ, Stephen, P 206-598-6364. 524 G
stephenz@uw.edu
ZIENTARSKI,
Nicholas, A .... 914-367-8216. 339 E
nzientarski@dunwoodie.org
ZIENTEK, Rita, M .... 716-878-4698. 343 A
zienterm@buffalostate.edu
ZIER, Joni, I .... 423-236-2895. 458 J
jzier@southern.edu
ZIESEMER, Marty .... 503-375-7005. 403 A
mziesemer@corban.edu
ZIKOPOULOS, Marianthi 718-399-4256. 336 F
mzikopou@pratt.edu
ZILLGES, Ginger .... 757-352-4494. 508 G
gingzil@regent.edu
ZILLMER, Eric, A .... 215-895-1977. 415 B
zillmer@drexel.edu
ZIMA, Bonita .... 920-498-5753. 541 B
bonita.zima@nwtc.edu
ZIMIC, Deborah, L .... 410-843-6995. 265 D
deborah.zimic@laureate.net
ZIMLICH, Robert, L .... 502-272-8263. 192 E
bzimlich@bellarmine.edu
ZIMMER, Brandi .... 785-738-9056. 189 F
bzimmer@ncktc.edu
ZIMMER, Joseph .... 716-375-2394. 338 E
jezimmer@sbu.edu
ZIMMER, Keri .... 712-325-3285. 179 L
kzimmer@iwcc.edu
ZIMMER, Robert, J .... 773-702-8001. 161 B
president@uchicago.edu
ZIMMER, Scott .... 858-635-4553... 26 M
szimmer@alliant.edu
ZIMMER, Tim .... 618-262-8641. 147 C
zimmert@iecc.edu
ZIMMERLEE, Karla, J ...... 530-898-5201... 33 A
kzimmerlee@csuchico.edu
ZIMMERMAN, Barri .... 410-543-6165. 220 D
ebzimmerman@salisbury.edu
ZIMMERMAN, Christine . 315-229-5394. 339 F
christinezimmerman@stlawu.edu
ZIMMERMAN, Debbie .... 706-776-0108. 130 E
dzimmerman@piedmont.edu
ZIMMERMAN, Eileen, P . 207-753-6970. 209 F
ezimmerm@bates.edu
ZIMMERMAN, Ellen .... 508-626-4582. 230 A
ezimmerman@framingham.edu
ZIMMERMAN, Gail .... 603-358-2842. 298 F
gzimmerman@keene.edu
ZIMMERMAN, Heidi .... 615-898-2025. 459 D
heidi.zimmerman@mtsu.edu
ZIMMERMAN, Jean .... 269-467-9945. 242 H
jzimmerman@glenoaks.edu
ZIMMERMAN, Jeffrey, A 260-422-5561. 167 B
jazimmerman@indianatech.edu
ZIMMERMAN, Jeremy .... 951-343-5023... 30 H
jzimmerman@calbaptist.edu
ZIMMERMAN, Jill .... 661-722-6300... 28 F
jzimmerman@avc.edu
ZIMMERMAN, Joanna .... 281-922-3455. 479 F
joanna.zimmerman@sjcd.edu
ZIMMERMAN, Joanna .... 281-922-3455. 479 G
joanna.zimmerman@sjcd.edu
ZIMMERMAN, Joe .... 316-295-5700. 186 H
zimmerj@friends.edu
ZIMMERMAN, John, A ... 916-339-1500... 55 D
jzimmerman@mticollege.edu
ZIMMERMAN, John, E .... 724-503-1001. 436 G
jzimmerman@washjeff.edu
ZIMMERMAN, Judith, D 860-727-6714... 90 A
jzimmerman@goodwin.edu
ZIMMERMAN, Julia .... 850-644-5211. 115 C
jazimmerman@fsu.edu
ZIMMERMAN, Lynn .... 404-712-1238. 124 E
lynn.zimmerman@emory.edu
ZIMMERMAN, Michael .... 586-445-7159. 246 A
zimmermanm@macomb.edu
ZIMMERMAN, Michael ... 575-646-3411. 310 I
mzimmerm@nmsu.edu
ZIMMERMAN, Michael ... 360-867-6400. 519 J
mz@evergreen.edu
ZIMMERMAN, Midge .... 757-455-3230. 515 H
mlzimmerman@vwc.edu
ZIMMERMAN, Morgan ... 501-977-2085... 25 C
zimmerman@uaccm.edu
ZIMMERMAN, Nancy ...... 704-637-4307. 353 E
nzimmera@catawba.edu

ZIMMERMAN, Robert, E 479-575-3301... 23 I
bobz@uark.edu
ZIMMERMAN, Sari .... 415-565-4619... 71 A
zimmerma@uchastings.edu
ZIMMERMAN, Stephanie 217-875-7200. 156 J
szimmerman@richland.edu
ZIMMERMAN, Thomas, P .... 260-452-2152. 165 D
thomas.zimmerman@ctsfw.edu
ZIMMERMAN, Timothy .. 606-679-8501. 196 D
timothy.zimmerman@kctcs.edu
ZIMMERMAN, Zvi .... 847-982-2500. 146 C
zimmerman@htc.edu
ZIMMERMANN, Christian .... 301-934-7513. 214 D
czimmermann@csmd.edu
ZIMMERMANN, Gilbert .. 956-326-2890. 483 B
ZIMMERMANN, Joanna . 281-998-6150. 479 H
joanna.zimmermann@sjcd.edu
ZIMMERMANN, Susan ... 518-255-5523. 344 E
zimmersj@cobleskill.edu
ZIMMERS, Jennifer, J ..... 208-732-6277. 138 B
jzimmers@csi.edu
ZIMPHER, Nancy, L .... 518-320-1355. 341 C
chancellor@suny.edu
ZINDER, Dave .... 740-351-3398. 388 N
dzinder@shawnee.edu
ZINDT, Gina .... 309-341-7200. 150 A
gzindt@knox.edu
ZINGA, Patricia .... 708-456-0300. 161 A
pzinga@triton.edu
ZINGARO, Louise, S ...... 434-381-6316. 510 F
lzingaro@sbc.edu
ZINGG, Paul, J .... 530-898-5201... 33 A
pzingg@csuchico.edu
ZINGSHEIM, Shairon ..... 510-659-6201... 57 A
szingsheim@ohlone.edu
ZINK, Abbey .... 361-593-2717. 484 A
abbey.zink@tamuk.edu
ZINK, Diane .... 315-568-3065. 333 C
dzink@nycc.edu
ZINK, Ellen, L .... 615-353-3224. 461 B
ellen.zink@nscc.edu
ZINK, Glenda .... 330-494-6170. 389 F
gzink@starkstate.edu
ZINK, Larry, W .... 502-852-7072. 200 D
lwzink01@louisville.edu
ZINK, Paul .... 618-537-6981. 152 G
pwzink@mckendree.edu
ZINKAN, Rob .... 765-973-8444. 167 G
rzinkan@iue.edu
ZINKEN, Pamela .... 763-576-4801. 257 Q
pzinken@anokatech.edu
ZINN, Annalisa .... 203-582-3395... 91 A
annalisa.zinn@quinnipiac.edu
ZINN, David .... 540-362-6435. 505 G
coachzinn@gmail.com
ZINNAR-SHAVIT, Efrat ... 617-731-7163. 235 H
ezinnarshavit@pmc.edu
ZINNERMAN-BETHEA, Darlene .... 803-705-4733. 441 C
bethead@benedict.edu
ZINNI, Amanda .... 440-375-7150. 382 L
azinni@lec.edu
ZINS, Rosemary, S .... 718-281-5144. 319 D
rzins@qcc.cuny.edu
ZINSMEISTER, Robin ...... 252-335-0821. 359 F
robin_zinsmeister@albemarle.edu
ZIOLA, Anne .... 402-826-6795. 289 E
anne.ziola@doane.edu
ZIONTS, Paul .... 773-325-7740. 143 H
pzionts@depaul.edu
ZIPF, Marianne, C .... 718-779-1430. 336 D
mzipf@plazacollege.edu
ZIPKIN, Susan .... 617-552-8917. 224 A
susan.zipkin@bc.edu
ZIPP, Doug .... 540-665-4566. 509 E
dzipp@su.edu
ZIPPERLEN, Marlene ...... 254-295-4573. 490 B
mzipperlen@umhb.edu
ZIRBES, Darla .... 520-206-2111... 17 A
dzirbes@pima.edu
ZIRBLIS, Ellalou .... 802-485-2631. 500 A
ellalou@norwich.edu
ZIRKIN, Barbara .... 443-352-4039. 218 E
bzirkin@stevenson.edu
ZIRKLE, Kenneth .... 814-725-7080. 423 J
kzirkle@mercyhurst.edu
ZIRPOLI, Tom .... 410-857-3352. 216 E
tzirpoli@mcdaniel.edu
ZISOOK, Joshua .... 847-982-2500. 146 C
jzissok@htc.edu
ZITELLI, Joanne .... 310-243-3737... 33 B
jzitelli@csudh.edu
ZITO, Joseph .... 508-767-7505. 222 C
jzito@assumption.edu
ZITTEL, Kimberly .... 716-829-7816. 323 D
zittelk@dyc.edu
ZITZNER, Linda .... 510-430-2024... 54 F
lzitzner@mills.edu
ZITZOW, Larry, L .... 701-777-4137. 371 C
larry.zitzow@und.edu
ZIX, Theresa .... 626-396-2477... 28 P
theresa.zix@artcenter.edu
ZLATA, William .... 212-772-4482. 318 C
bill.zlata@hunter.cuny.edu
ZLATANOV, Milla .... 408-541-0100... 40 A
mzlatanov@cogswell.edu
ZLATEVA, Tanya .... 617-353-3010. 224 D
zlateva@bu.edu
ZLATIC, Steve .... 815-836-5550. 150 H
zlaticst@lewisu.edu
ZLOCK, Molly .... 973-642-8707. 307 D
molly.marmion@shu.edu
ZLOMEK, Nancy, S .... 315-684-6078. 345 A
zlomekns@morrisville.edu
ZLOTOCHA, Seth, J .... 414-229-3045. 537 A
zlotocha@uwm.edu
ZMIJEWSKI, Christine .... 916-649-2400... 30 C
ZOBEL, Keith .... 703-257-5515. 502 E
directoramm@aviationmaintenance.edu
ZOBRIST, Vicki .... 402-399-2391. 289 A
vzobrist@csm.edu
ZOCH, Brandon .... 252-398-6464. 353 H
zochbr@chowan.edu
ZOELLER, Marisa .... 502-272-8335. 192 E
mzoeller@bellarmine.edu
ZOELLNER, Mark .... 605-229-8585. 450 J
mark.zoellner@presentation.edu
ZOINO, Mia .... 508-531-2102. 229 D
menright@bridgew.edu
ZOLA, Carol .... 724-838-4212. 433 E
zola@setonhill.edu
ZOLA, Gary .... 513-221-7444. 325 G
gzola@huc.edu
ZOLA, Stuart, M .... 404-727-7707. 124 E
szola@rmy.emory.edu
ZOLDESSY, Margo .... 516-671-0379. 350 C
mzoldessy@webb.edu
ZOLFO, Elana .... 631-244-3434. 323 B
zolfoe@dowling.edu
ZOLLARS, Scott, M .... 620-421-6700. 188 D
scottz@labette.edu
ZOLLER, Karen .... 216-373-5267. 385 G
kzoller@ndc.edu
ZOLLINGER, Richard ...... 704-330-6730. 359 C
richard.zollinger@cpcc.edu
ZOLOTH, Stephen .... 617-373-4644. 235 F
ZONDLO, Tim .... 763-433-1427. 257 P
tim.zondlo@anokaramsey.edu
ZONER, Kathy, R .... 607-255-8945. 322 A
krz1@cornell.edu
ZOOK, Kevin .... 215-637-7700. 418 G
Zook@holyfamily.edu
ZOOK, Letha .... 304-357-4875. 527 H
lethazook@ucwv.edu
ZOOK, Rosemarie, E ...... 248-689-8282. 251 I
rzook@walshcollege.edu
ZORIC, Joseph .... 740-284-5801. 379 N
jzoric@franciscan.edu
ZORN, David, C .... 303-837-0825... 78 H
zornd@aii.edu
ZORN, Diane .... 941-955-8862. 111 O
dzorn@ringling.edu
ZORN, Jenny .... 909-537-5024... 34 E
jzorn@csusb.edu
ZORN, Linda .... 530-879-9069... 30 F
zornli@butte.edu
ZORN, Robert, L .... 724-946-7055. 437 B
zornrl@westminster.edu
ZOROMSKI, Lorraine ...... 715-675-3331. 541 A
zoromski@ntc.edu
ZOU, Bingzeng .... 415-282-7600... 27 L
bingzou@actem.edu
ZOU, Lily .... 516-739-1545. 333 F
controller@nyctcm.edu
ZOUMADAKIS, Bill .... 801-957-4042. 498 B
bill.zoumadakis@slcc.edu
ZOZAYA, Pat .... 702-651-5078. 294 E
pat.zozaya@csn.edu
ZRALY, Sharon .... 845-452-1614. 322 D
s_zraly@culinary.edu
ZRIMSEK, Becky .... 507-222-4160. 254 D
rzrimsek@carleton.edu
ZUBER, Maria, T .... 617-253-3206. 233 B
ZUBERBUELER, OP, Mary Anne .... 615-297-7545. 452 J
srmanne@aquinascollege.edu
ZUBIATE, Jyl .... 309-467-6322. 145 C
jzubiate@eureka.edu
ZUBIZARRETA, John ...... 803-786-3014. 443 B
jzubizarreta@columbiasc.edu
ZUCALLA, Fred, P .... 315-733-2300. 349 D
fzucalla@uscny.edu
ZUCCARELLI, Anthony, J 909-558-4528... 51 C
azuccarelli@llu.edu
ZUCCARELLO, Patricia .... 708-709-2947. 156 A
pzuccarello@prairiestate.edu
ZUCCHERI, Nicole .... 215-335-0800. 422 C
nzuccheri@lincolntech.com
ZUCCHETTO, Vincent ...... 718-960-8242. 318 A
vincent.zucchetto@lehman.cuny.edu
ZUCCOLA, Jen .... 612-874-3626. 257 B
jzuccola@mcad.edu
ZUCCONI, Michael, J ..... 540-432-4211. 504 D
michael.zucconi@emu.edu
ZUCKER, Avraham .... 718-382-8702. 351 B
ZUCKER, Nicole, M .... 215-572-2103. 409 H
zuckern@arcadia.edu
ZUCKERMAN, Mary Ellen .... 607-274-3341. 327 E
mzuckerman@ithaca.edu
ZUCKERMAN-AVILES, Stephanie, B .... 716-878-5811. 343 A
zuckersb@buffalostate.edu
ZUDEKOFF, Rosanne ...... 203-773-8502... 87 G
zudekoff@albertus.edu
ZUEHLKE, Karen, A .... 920-924-6320. 540 F
zkuehlke@morainepark.edu
ZUELKE, Bill .... 503-534-4073. 404 C
bzuelke@marylhurst.edu
ZUERCHER, Makenzie .... 559-445-5565... 30 I
registrar@calchristiancollege.edu
ZUG, Mary Ann .... 515-271-1440. 177 H
maryann.zug@dmu.edu
ZUHLKE, James .... 610-436-3316. 430 A
jzuhlke@wcupa.edu
ZUICHES, Carol .... 773-702-8604. 161 B
czuiches@uchicago.edu
ZUIDEMA, Leah .... 712-722-6328. 177 J
leah.zuidema@dordt.edu
ZUILL, Karen .... 607-431-4303. 325 F
zuillk@hartwick.edu
ZUKER, Fred .... 281-487-1170. 484 H
fzuker@txchiro.edu
ZUKOR, Tevya .... 412-648-7930. 435 C
tez5@pitt.edu
ZUKOSKI, Charles, F ..... 716-645-2992. 341 F
provost@buffalo.edu
ZULUAGA, Hoober .... 516-918-3679. 315 G
hzuluaga@bcl.edu
ZUMBACH, Deborah, J ... 319-335-3815. 175 I
deborah-zumbach@uiowa.edu
ZUMBRUN, Christina ..... 260-665-4242. 173 E
zumbrunc@trine.edu
ZUMWALT, Debra, L ...... 650-723-6397... 68 E
zumwalt@stanford.edu
ZUNIGA, Donna, P .... 936-291-0447. 475 I
dzuniga@lee.edu
ZUNIGA, Leo .... 210-485-0035. 464 I
lzuniga@alamo.edu
ZUPAN, Mark .... 585-275-3316. 349 C
mark.zupan@simon.rochester.edu
ZUPANCICH, Patti .... 218-235-2166. 261 G
p.zupancich@vcc.edu
ZURAW, Peter .... 781-283-2474. 237 F
pzuraw@wellesley.edu
ZURAWSKA, Izabela .... 708-456-0300. 161 A
izurawsk@triton.edu
ZURAWSKI, Ray .... 920-403-3964. 535 L
ray.zurawski@snc.edu
ZURAWSKY, Walter .... 718-260-3725. 336 E
zurawsky@poly.edu
ZURCHER, Bradley, A ..... 317-788-3228. 173 I
zurcherb@uindy.edu
ZUREK, Ronald, M .... 775-784-4031. 294 J
zurek@unr.edu
ZUROMSKI, Steven .... 508-531-2396. 229 D
steven.zuromski@bridgew.edu
ZURZOLO, Debbie .... 575-769-4030. 309 F
debbie.zurzolo@clovis.edu
ZUSCHIN, Andrea, P ...... 540-365-4456. 504 L
azuschin@ferrum.edu
ZUZACK, Judith, A .... 724-287-8711. 411 C
judith.zuzack@bc3.edu
ZUZEVICH, Theresa .... 661-362-3644... 40 E
theresa.zuzevich@canyons.edu
ZUZOLO, Renee .... 330-652-9919. 379 I
reneezuzolo@eticollege.edu
ZVACEK, Susan, M .... 785-864-2600. 190 L
szvacek@ku.edu
ZVARITCH, Jeanne .... 330-337-6403. 373 F
college@awc.edu
ZVOSEC, Almut .... 216-421-7447. 377 C
azvosec@cia.edu
ZWEIG, Yitzchak .... 305-534-7050. 117 E
yzweig@talmudicu.edu
ZWEIG, Yochanan .... 305-534-7050. 117 E
rosh@talmudicu.edu
ZWICKEY, Heather .... 503-552-1742. 404 H
hzwickey@ncnm.edu
ZWIER, Robert .... 585-594-6659. 337 K
zwier_robert@roberts.edu
ZWIREN, Martin .... 718-960-1117. 318 A
martin.zwiren@lehman.cuny.edu
ZWISLER, Stasia .... 847-574-5222. 150 C
szwisler@lfgsm.edu
ZYLSTRA, Art .... 206-264-9100. 516 J
artz@bgu.edu
ZYLSTRA, Brian .... 641-628-5641. 176 E
zylstrab@central.edu
ZYLSTRA, James .... 608-266-1739. 539 H
james.zylstra@wtcsystem.edu

Accreditation Index of Institutions by Regional, National, Professional and Specialized Agencies

Degree levels are shown by the following symbols: (C) diploma/certificate; (A) associate; (B) baccalaureate; (M) master's; (S) beyond master's but less than doctorate; (FP) first professional; (D) doctorate.

AA: Commission on Accreditation of Allied Health Education Programs: anesthesiologist assistant (M)

University of Colorado DenverlAnschutz Medical Campus ... CO ... 86
Nova Southeastern University ... FL ... 109
Emory University ... GA .. 124
South University ... GA .. 131
University of Missouri - Kansas City ... MO .. 283
Case Western Reserve University ... OH .. 375

AAB: Aviation Accreditation Board International: aviation (A,B,M)

Auburn University ... AL ... 1
Arizona State University ... AZ ... 11
Embry-Riddle Aeronautical University ... FL ... 102
Florida Institute of Technology ... FL ... 104
Jacksonville University ... FL ... 107
Southern Illinois University Carbondale ... IL ... 159
Purdue University Main Campus ... IN ... 171
University of Dubuque ... IA ... 182
Louisiana Tech University ... LA ... 207
University of Louisiana at Monroe ... LA ... 208
North Shore Community College ... MA .. 232
Western Michigan University ... MI ... 252
St. Cloud State University ... MN .. 261
Saint Louis University ... MO .. 281
University of Central Missouri ... MO .. 283
Rocky Mountain College ... MT .. 288
University of Nebraska at Omaha ... NE .. 293
Daniel Webster College ... NH .. 296
Mercer County Community College ... NJ ... 302
University of North Dakota Main Campus . ND .. 371
Kent State University Main Campus ... OH .. 382
Oklahoma State University ... OK .. 397
Southeastern Oklahoma State University . OK .. 399
University of Oklahoma Norman Campus . OK .. 401
Inter American University of Puerto Rico Bayamon Campus ... PR ... 550
South Dakota State University ... SD ... 452
Middle Tennessee State University ... TN ... 459
Westminster College ... UT ... 498

AAFCS: American Association of Family and Consumer Sciences: family and consumer science (B)

Alabama Agricultural and Mechanical University ... AL ... 1
Jacksonville State University ... AL ... 4
University of Alabama, The ... AL ... 8
University of Montevallo ... AL ... 9
University of Arkansas at Pine Bluff ... AR ... 24
University of Arkansas Main Campus ... AR ... 23
California State University-Long Beach ... CA ... 33
California State University-Northridge ... CA ... 34
San Francisco State University ... CA ... 35
Florida State University ... FL ... 115
Fort Valley State University ... GA ... 124
University of Georgia ... GA .. 133
Eastern Illinois University ... IL ... 144
Illinois State University ... IL ... 147
Ball State University ... IN ... 164
Indiana State University ... IN ... 167
Eastern Kentucky University ... KY ... 193
University of Kentucky ... KY ... 200
Louisiana State University and Agricultural and Mechanical College ... LA ... 204
Louisiana Tech University ... LA ... 207
McNeese State University ... LA ... 207
Nicholls State University ... LA ... 208
Northwestern State University ... LA ... 208
Southeastern Louisiana University ... LA ... 208
Southern University and A&M College ... LA ... 206
Alcorn State University ... MS ... 265
Delta State University ... MS ... 266
Mississippi State University ... MS ... 268
University of Southern Mississippi ... MS ... 270
University of Central Missouri ... MO ... 283
City University of New York Queens College ... NY ... 319
State University of New York College at Oneonta ... NY ... 343
Appalachian State University ... NC ... 367
East Carolina University ... NC ... 367
North Carolina Agricultural and Technical State University ... NC ... 367
Ohio University Main Campus ... OH ... 387
University of Akron, Main Campus, The ... OH ... 390
Youngstown State University ... OH .. 394
South Carolina State University ... SC ... 446
South Dakota State University ... SD ... 452
Carson-Newman University ... TN ... 453
Middle Tennessee State University ... TN ... 459
Tennessee State University ... TN ... 459
Tennessee Technological University ... TN ... 460
University of Tennessee at Martin ... TN ... 463
Baylor University ... TX ... 467
Stephen F. Austin State University ... TX ... 482
Texas Tech University ... TX ... 487
University of Houston ... TX ... 489

ABHES: Accrediting Bureau of Health Education Schools: allied health (C, A,B)

Fortis College ... AL ... 3
Arizona College ... AZ ... 11
Pima Medical Institute-Tucson ... AZ ... 17
American Career College-Los Angeles ... CA ... 27
American Career College-Ontario ... CA ... 27
Angeles College ... CA ... 28
Casa Loma College-Van Nuys ... CA ... 37
CNI College ... CA ... 39
Gurnick Academy of Medical Arts ... CA ... 46
National Career College ... CA ... 55
Valley College of Medical Careers ... CA ... 74
Heritage College ... CO ... 82
IntelliTec Medical Institute ... CO ... 82
Pima Medical Institute ... CO ... 84
Allied Health Institute ... FL ... 97
American Medical Academy ... FL ... 97
Azure College ... FL ... 98
Cambridge Institute of Allied Health & Technology ... FL ... 99
Central Florida Institute ... FL ... 99
Dade Medical College ... FL ... 100
Heritage Institute-Fort Myers ... FL ... 106
Heritage Institute-Jacksonville ... FL ... 106
Lincoln Tech Fern Park Orlando Campus FL ... 108
Orlando Medical Institute ... FL ... 110
Ultimate Medical Academy-Clearwater ... FL ... 118
ATA College ... KY ... 192
Fortis College ... LA ... 202
Anthem College ... MO .. 271
Midwest Institute ... MO .. 277
Midwest Institute-Earth City ... MO .. 277
Saint Louis College of Health Careers-South Taylor ... MO .. 281
Universal College of Healing Arts ... NE ... 292
Northwest Career College ... NV ... 295
Mandl School ... NY ... 329
St. Paul's School of Nursing ... NY ... 339
Saint Paul's School of Nursing-Staten Island ... NY ... 339
Fortis College ... OH ... 379
Professional Skills Institute ... OH ... 388
Heritage College ... OK ... 395
National College of Technical Instruction-College of Emergency Services ... OR ... 405
Baptist Health System School of Health Professions ... TX ... 467
College of Health Care Professions, The . TX ... 469
Concorde Career Institute ... TX ... 469
Dallas Nursing Institute ... TX ... 471
Southwest University at El Paso ... TX ... 481
Nightingale College ... UT ... 496
Centra College of Nursing ... VA ... 503
Riverside School of Health Careers ... VA ... 509
Southside Regional Medical Center Professional Schools ... VA ... 509
Standard Healthcare Services College of Nursing ... VA ... 510
Milwaukee Career College ... WI ... 534

ACAE: Accreditation Commission for Audiology Education: audiology (D)

Nova Southeastern University ... FL ... 109
Central Michigan University ... MI ... 240
Washington University in St. Louis ... MO .. 284
University of North Carolina at Chapel Hill NC .. 368

ACBSP: Accreditation Council for Business Schools and Programs: business administration, management, accounting and related business fields (A,B,M,D)

Alabama State University ... AL ... 1
Athens State University ... AL ... 1
Bishop State Community College ... AL ... 2
Calhoun Community College ... AL ... 2
Gadsden State Community College ... AL ... 3
Jefferson State Community College ... AL ... 5
Lawson State Community College ... AL ... 5
Oakwood University ... AL ... 6
Troy University ... AL ... 7
University of Mobile ... AL ... 9
University of North Alabama ... AL ... 9
University of West Alabama, The ... AL ... 9
Wallace State Community College - Hanceville ... AL ... 9
Grand Canyon University ... AZ ... 13
Northcentral University ... AZ ... 16
Northern Arizona University ... AZ ... 16
University of Phoenix ... AZ ... 18
Cossatot Community College of the University of Arkansas ... AR ... 24
Harding University Main Campus ... AR ... 21
John Brown University ... AR ... 21
North Arkansas College ... AR ... 22
Philander Smith College ... AR ... 22
Phillips Community College of the University of Arkansas ... AR ... 24
Biola University ... CA ... 29
California Baptist University ... CA ... 30
Notre Dame de Namur University ... CA ... 56
Point Loma Nazarene University ... CA ... 59
Skyline College ... CA ... 64
Woodbury University ... CA ... 76
Post University ... CT ... 90
Three Rivers Community College ... CT ... 89
Tunxis Community College ... CT ... 89
University of Bridgeport ... CT ... 91
Delaware Technical Community College, Owens Campus ... DE ... 93
Delaware Technical Community College, Stanton-Wilmington Campus ... DE ... 93
Delaware Technical Community College, Terry Campus ... DE ... 93
Goldey-Beacom College ... DE ... 93
Gallaudet University ... DC ... 95
Strayer University ... DC ... 96
University of the District of Columbia ... DC ... 97
Embry-Riddle Aeronautical University ... FL ... 102
Florida Agricultural and Mechanical University ... FL ... 114
Florida Memorial University ... FL ... 104
Florida State College at Jacksonville ... FL ... 105
Albany State University ... GA .. 119
Athens Technical College ... GA .. 120
Atlanta Metropolitan State College ... GA .. 121
Brenau University ... GA .. 122
LaGrange College ... GA .. 128
Paine College ... GA .. 130
Piedmont College ... GA .. 130
Southern Polytechnic State University ... GA .. 132
University of North Georgia ... GA .. 133
West Georgia Technical College ... GA .. 134
Northwest Nazarene University ... ID ... 139
American InterContinental University ... IL ... 139
Chicago State University ... IL ... 141
City Colleges of Chicago Harold Washington College ... IL ... 141
City Colleges of Chicago Wilbur Wright College ... IL ... 142
Dominican University ... IL ... 144
Governors State University ... IL ... 145
Harper College ... IL ... 145
Joliet Junior College ... IL ... 149
Lewis University ... IL ... 150
Millikin University ... IL ... 153
Northwestern College ... IL ... 155
Roosevelt University ... IL ... 157
Saint Xavier University ... IL ... 158
Trinity Christian College ... IL ... 160
University of St. Francis ... IL ... 162
Anderson University ... IN ... 163
Indiana University East ... IN ... 167
Ivy Tech Community College-Central Indiana ... IN ... 169
Purdue University North Central Campus . IN ... 172
Trine University ... IN ... 173
University of Indianapolis ... IN ... 173
University of Saint Francis ... IN ... 174
Vincennes University ... IN ... 174
Des Moines Area Community College ... IA ... 177
Kaplan University ... IA ... 180
Kirkwood Community College ... IA ... 180
St. Ambrose University ... IA ... 182
Baker University ... KS ... 184
Butler Community College ... KS ... 185
Hutchinson Community College and Area Vocational School ... KS ... 187
Johnson County Community College ... KS ... 187
Kansas City Kansas Community College . KS ... 187
Neosho County Community College ... KS ... 189
Pratt Community College ... KS ... 190
Seward County Community College/Area Technical School ... KS ... 190
Kentucky State University ... KY ... 197
West Kentucky Community and Technical College ... KY ... 196
Baton Rouge Community College ... LA ... 202
Delgado Community College ... LA ... 203
Louisiana College ... LA ... 202
Xavier University of Louisiana ... LA ... 209
Kennebec Valley Community College ... ME .. 210
Northern Maine Community College ... ME .. 210
University of New England ... ME .. 213
Baltimore City Community College ... MD .. 213
Bowie State University ... MD .. 220
College of Southern Maryland ... MD .. 214
Community College of Baltimore County, The ... MD .. 214
Hood College ... MD .. 215
Ferris State University ... MI ... 242
Jackson College ... MI ... 244
Kettering University ... MI ... 244
Lawrence Technological University ... MI ... 245
Mott Community College ... MI ... 247
Walsh College of Accountancy and Business Administration ... MI ... 251
Concordia University, St. Paul ... MN .. 255
Hennepin Technical College ... MN .. 258
Inver Hills Community College ... MN .. 258
Normandale Community College ... MN .. 260
North Hennepin Community College ... MN .. 260
Riverland Community College ... MN .. 260
Saint Paul College-A Community & Technical College ... MN .. 261
Walden University ... MN .. 265
Alcorn State University ... MS .. 265
Delta State University ... MS .. 266
Jones County Junior College ... MS .. 267
Mississippi College ... MS .. 268
Mississippi University for Women ... MS .. 268
Mississippi Valley State University ... MS .. 269
Drury University ... MO .. 273
Fontbonne University ... MO .. 274
Harris-Stowe State University ... MO .. 275
#Lincoln University ... MO .. 276
Lindenwood University ... MO .. 276
Maryville University of Saint Louis ... MO .. 276
Missouri Southern State University ... MO .. 278
Northwest Missouri State University ... MO .. 279
Park University ... MO .. 280
Southwest Baptist University ... MO .. 282
Three Rivers Community College ... MO .. 282
Webster University ... MO .. 284
Chadron State College ... NE ... 291
Metropolitan Community College ... NE ... 290
Nebraska Wesleyan University ... NE ... 291
Southeast Community College ... NE ... 292
College of Southern Nevada ... NV ... 294
Great Bay Community College ... NH .. 295
Manchester Community College ... NH .. 296
NHTI-Concord's Community College ... NH .. 296
Plymouth State University ... NH .. 298
River Valley Community College ... NH .. 296
Southern New Hampshire University ... NH .. 297
Caldwell College ... NJ ... 300
County College of Morris ... NJ ... 300
Georgian Court University ... NJ ... 302
New Jersey City University ... NJ ... 303
Central New Mexico Community College . NM .. 309
Eastern New Mexico University Main Campus ... NM .. 309
New Mexico Highlands University ... NM .. 310
New Mexico State University Dona Ana Community College ... NM .. 311

Northern New Mexico College NM 311
San Juan College NM 311
Western New Mexico University NM 312
City University of New York Bronx Community College NY 317
City University of New York Medgar Evers College NY 319
City University of New York Queensborough Community College NY 319
College of Mount Saint Vincent NY 320
College of Saint Rose, The NY 321
LIM College NY 328
Metropolitan College of New York NY 331
Orange County Community College NY 335
State University of New York College of Agriculture and Technology at Morrisville NY 345
Sullivan County Community College NY 347
Wagner College NY 350
Campbell University NC 352
Gardner-Webb University NC 354
Gaston College NC 360
Greensboro College NC 354
Lenoir-Rhyne University NC 356
Methodist University NC 356
Mount Olive College NC 357
North Carolina Central University NC 368
Queens University of Charlotte NC 365
Wingate University NC 370
Ashland University OH 374
Capital University OH 375
Cedarville University OH 375
Columbus State Community College OH 378
Hocking College OH 380
James A. Rhodes State College OH 381
Malone University OH 383
Mount Vernon Nazarene University OH 384
North Central State College OH 385
Northwest State Community College OH 385
Ohio Dominican University OH 386
Owens Community College OH 387
Sinclair Community College OH 388
Stark State College OH 389
Tiffin University OH 389
University of Akron, Main Campus, The OH 390
University of Northwestern Ohio OH 391
Cameron University OK 394
Carl Albert State College OK 394
East Central University OK 395
Langston University OK 395
Northeastern State University OK 396
Northern Oklahoma College OK 396
Northwestern Oklahoma State University OK 396
Oklahoma Baptist University OK 397
Oklahoma Christian University OK 397
Oklahoma City Community College OK 397
Oklahoma City University OK 397
Oral Roberts University OK 398
Southern Nazarene University OK 399
University of Central Oklahoma OK 400
George Fox University OR 403
Southern Oregon University OR 406
Alvernia University PA 409
Arcadia University PA 409
Bucks County Community College PA 411
Butler County Community College PA 411
Cedar Crest College PA 412
DeSales University PA 414
Edinboro University of Pennsylvania PA 428
Elizabethtown College PA 415
Gannon University PA 416
Geneva College PA 417
Harrisburg Area Community College PA 417
Holy Family University PA 418
Immaculata University PA 418
La Roche College PA 420
Lebanon Valley College PA 421
Lehigh Carbon Community College PA 421
Lock Haven University PA 429
Luzerne County Community College PA 422
Manor College PA 423
Marywood University PA 423
Messiah College PA 423
Millersville University of Pennsylvania PA 429
Neumann University PA 424
Northampton Community College PA 425
Peirce College PA 425
Pennsylvania College of Technology PA 427
Saint Vincent College PA 432
Slippery Rock University of Pennsylvania PA 429
Wilkes University PA 437
York College of Pennsylvania PA 438
Universidad del Este PR 552
University of Puerto Rico-Aguadilla PR 553
University of Puerto Rico at Arecibo PR 553
University of Puerto Rico at Bayamon PR 554
University of Puerto Rico at Cayey PR 554
University of Puerto Rico at Ponce PR 555
University of Puerto Rico at Utuado PR 555
University of Puerto Rico-Carolina PR 554
University of Puerto Rico-Humacao PR 554
University of Puerto Rico-Rio Piedras Campus PR 555
Community College of Rhode Island RI 439
Aiken Technical College SC 440
Anderson University SC 441
Benedict College SC 441
Claflin University SC 442
Denmark Technical College SC 443
Florence - Darlington Technical College SC 443
Greenville Technical College SC 444
Horry-Georgetown Technical College SC 444
Midlands Technical College SC 445
Morris College SC 445
Orangeburg-Calhoun Technical College SC 446
Spartanburg Community College SC 447
Technical College of the Lowcountry SC 447
Tri-County Technical College SC 447
Trident Technical College SC 447
Voorhees College SC 449
Williamsburg Technical College SC 449
York Technical College SC 449
Dakota State University SD 451
Chattanooga State Community College TN 460
Cleveland State Community College TN 460
Columbia State Community College TN 460
Cumberland University TN 454
Dyersburg State Community College TN 460
Freed-Hardeman University TN 454
Jackson State Community College TN 460
Lee University TN 455
Lincoln Memorial University TN 456
Lipscomb University TN 456
Motlow State Community College TN 461
Nashville State Community College TN 461
Northeast State Community College TN 461
Pellissippi State Community College TN 461
Roane State Community College TN 461
Southwest Tennessee Community College TN 461
Volunteer State Community College TN 461
Walters State Community College TN 462
Angelo State University TX 465
Austin Community College District TX 466
Dallas Baptist University TX 470
Hardin-Simmons University TX 472
Houston Baptist University TX 473
Huston-Tillotson University TX 473
Jarvis Christian College TX 474
Our Lady of the Lake University TX 477
South Texas College TX 480
Tarleton State University TX 483
Texas A & M University - Central Texas TX 483
#Texas A & M University - Kingsville TX 484
Texas Lutheran University TX 485
Texas Wesleyan University TX 488
Texas Woman's University TX 488
University of the Incarnate Word TX 490
Wiley College TX 495
Salt Lake Community College UT 498
Snow College UT 498
Southern Utah University UT 497
Westminster College UT 498
Norwich University VT 500
Lynchburg College VA 506
Marymount University VA 507
Regent University VA 508
Roanoke College VA 509
Virginia Union University VA 515
Virginia Western Community College VA 514
Northwest University WA 521
Walla Walla University WA 524
American Public University System WV 526
Bluefield State College WV 529
Fairmont State University WV 529
Mountwest Community and Technical College WV 528
West Virginia State University WV 530
West Virginia University at Parkersburg WV 530
Wheeling Jesuit University WV 531
Cardinal Stritch University WI 532
Edgewood College WI 532
Viterbo University WI 539
Casper College WY 542

ACCSC: Accrediting Commission of Career Schools and Colleges: occupational, trade, and technical education (C,A,B,M)

Remington College, Mobile Campus AL 6
Alaska Career College AK 10
CollegeAmerica-Flagstaff AZ 13
Kaplan College AZ 14
Le Cordon Bleu College of Culinary Arts in Scottsdale AZ 14
Refrigeration School, The AZ 17
Universal Technical Institute AZ 18
Bryan College CA 30
Bryman College-LA Wilshire CA 30
California College San Diego CA 31
Concorde Career College CA 41
Everest College-Anaheim CA 43
Everest College-City of Industry CA 43
Everest College-Gardena CA 43
Everest College-Reseda CA 43
Ex'pression College for Digital Arts CA 44
Fremont College CA 45
Institute of Technology CA 48
Interior Designers Institute CA 48
Kaplan College CA 49
Le Cordon Bleu College of Culinary Arts CA 50
Los Angeles Film School CA 52
Mount Sierra College CA 55
Pacific College CA 57
Pacific College of Oriental Medicine CA 57
Platt College CA 59
Southern California Institute of Technology CA 67
Stanbridge College CA 68
Unitek College CA 70
West Coast Ultrasound Institute CA 75
WyoTech-Fremont CA 77
WyoTech-Long Beach CA 77
Bel-Rea Institute of Animal Technology CO 78
CollegeAmerica Denver CO 78
Colorado School of Healing Arts CO 80
Colorado School of Trades CO 80
Concorde Career College CO 81
Denver School of Nursing CO 81
IntelliTec College CO 82
Lincoln College of Technology CO 83
Platt College CO 84
Paier College of Art CT 90
Acupuncture & Massage College FL 97
Aviator College of Aeronautical Science & Technology FL 98
Centura College FL 99
Concorde Career Institute FL 100
Daytona College FL 101
Florida College of Natural Health FL 104
Fortis College FL 105
Full Sail University FL 106
Health Career Institute FL 106
Institute of Technical Arts FL 107
Meridian College FL 109
Remington College-Tampa Campus FL 111
Southeastern College FL 113
WyoTech FL 119
American Academy of Art IL 139
Coyne College IL 143
Lincoln College of Technology IL 151
Rockford Career College IL 157
Vatterott College-Quincy IL 162
Kaplan College IN 170
Lincoln College of Technology IN 170
Hamilton Technical College IA 178
Vatterott College-Des Moines IA 183
Wichita Technical Institute KS 191
Baton Rouge School of Computers LA 201
Blue Cliff College LA 201
Delta College of Arts & Technology LA 201
ITI Technical College LA 202
Landing School, The ME 210
New England School of Communications ME 211
Lincoln College of Technology MD 215
TESST College of Technology MD 218
Compass College of Cinematic Arts MI 241
MIAT College of Technology MI 246
Institute of Production and Recording MN 256
Blue Cliff College MS 266
Concorde Career College MO 272
Missouri Tech MO 278
Vatterott College-NorthPark MO 284
Creative Center NE 289
Myotherapy Institute NE 290
Vatterott College-Omaha NE 293
Career College of Northern Nevada NV 293
Kaplan College NV 294
St. Joseph School of Nursing NH 297
Eastern International College NJ 301
Business Informatics Center, Inc. NY 316
Island Drafting and Technical Institute NY 327
Swedish Institute--College of Health Sciences NY 347
American Institute of Alternative Medicine OH 373
Antonelli College OH 373
Art Institute of Cincinnati, The OH 374
ETI Technical College of Niles OH 379
Fortis College OH 379
International College of Broadcasting OH 381
Kaplan Career Institute OH 381
Kaplan College OH 382
Ohio College of Massotherapy OH 386
Ohio Technical College OH 387
Remington College Cleveland Campus OH 388
School of Advertising Art OH 388
Virginia Marti College of Art & Design OH 392
Platt College OK 398
Spartan College of Aeronautics and Technology OK 400
Tulsa Welding School OK 400
Concorde Career College OR 402
Antonelli Institute of Art and Photography PA 409
Berks Technical Institute PA 410
Bidwell Training Center PA 410
Career Training Academy PA 412
Commonwealth Technical Institute at the Hiram G. Andrews Center PA 413
Dean Institute of Technology PA 414
Erie Institute of Technology PA 416
Fortis Institute PA 416
Great Lakes Institute of Technology PA 417
Hussian School of Art PA 418
JNA Institute of Culinary Arts PA 419
Johnson College PA 419
Kaplan Career Institute PA 419
Kaplan Career Institute/Broomall Campus PA 419
Keystone Technical Institute PA 419
Lincoln Technical Institute PA 422
Metropolitan Career Center Computer Technology Institute PA 423
New Castle School of Trades PA 425
Oakbridge Academy of Arts PA 425
Orleans Technical Institute PA 425
Pennco Tech PA 426
Pennsylvania School of Business PA 427
Pittsburgh Institute of Aeronautics PA 430
#Prism Career Institute-Upper Darby Campus PA 431
Restaurant School at Walnut Hill College, The PA 431
Rosedale Technical Institute PA 432
Triangle Tech, Dubois PA 434
Triangle Tech, Erie PA 434
Triangle Tech, Greensburg PA 434
Triangle Tech, Pittsburgh PA 434
Vet Tech Institute PA 436
Williamson Free School of Mechanical Trades PA 437
YTI Career Institute PA 438
YTI Career Institute-Capital Region PA 438
Atenas College PR 547
Centro de Estudios Multidisciplinarios PR 548
Colegio de Cinematografia, Artes y Television PR 548
Ponce Paramedical College PR 551
Universal Technology College of Puerto Rico PR 553
Chattanooga College TN 453
Fountainhead College of Technology TN 454
Lincoln College of Technology Nashville TN 455
Nossi College of Art TN 457
O'More College of Design TN 457
SAE Institute of Technology Nashville TN 458
Concorde Career Institute TX 469
Culinary Institute LeNotre TX 470
Hallmark College of Technology TX 472
Kaplan College TX 474
Kaplan College TX 475
Lincoln College of Technology TX 475
Remington College TX 478
Southwest Institute of Technology TX 481
Western Technical College TX 494
Independence University UT 495
Stevens-Henager College UT 496
Utah College of Dental Hygiene at Careers Unlimited, The UT 496
Vista College UT 498
New England Culinary Institute VT 499
Advanced Technology Institute VA 501
Aviation Institute of Maintenance VA 502
Centura College VA 503
Skyline College VA 509
DigiPen Institute of Technology WA 519
Northwest College of Art & Design (NCAD) WA 521
Northwest School of Wooden Boatbuilding WA 521
Perry Technical Institute WA 522
Everest Institute WV 526
Madison Media Institute-College of Media Arts WI 533
WyoTech WY 544

ACFEI: American Culinary Federation, Inc.: culinary arts and culinary management (C,A,B)

Bishop State Community College AL 2
James H. Faulkner State Community College AL 4
Jefferson State Community College AL 5
Trenholm State Technical College AL 7
Virginia College AL 3
Wallace State Community College - Hanceville AL 9
Art Institute of Phoenix, The AZ 12
Le Cordon Bleu College of Culinary Arts in Scottsdale AZ 14
Scottsdale Community College AZ 15
Pulaski Technical College AR 22
City College of San Francisco CA 38
Columbia College CA 77
Diablo Valley College CA 41
Institute of Technology CA 48
Le Cordon Bleu College of Culinary Arts CA 50
Le Cordon Bleu College of Culinary Arts in Los Angeles CA 50
Los Angeles Trade-Technical College CA 52
Orange Coast College CA 39
San Joaquin Delta College CA 63
Santa Barbara City College CA 64
Art Institute of Colorado, The CO 78
Pikes Peak Community College CO 84
Pueblo Community College CO 84

Manchester Community College ... CT ... 88
Delaware Technical Community College, Stanton-Wilmington Campus ... DE ... 93
Delaware Technical Community College, Terry Campus ... DE ... 93
Art Institute of Fort Lauderdale, The ... FL ... 98
Florida State College at Jacksonville ... FL ... 105
Gulf Coast State College ... FL ... 106
Hillsborough Community College ... FL ... 106
Lincoln College of Technology ... FL ... 108
Pensacola State College ... FL ... 110
Art Institute of Atlanta, The ... GA ... 120
Atlanta Technical College ... GA ... 121
Chattahoochee Technical College ... GA ... 122
College of Coastal Georgia ... GA ... 123
Gwinnett Technical College ... GA ... 127
North Georgia Technical College ... GA ... 129
Savannah Technical College ... GA ... 131
Kapiolani Community College ... HI ... 136
University of Hawaii Hawaii Community College ... HI ... 136
University of Hawaii Kauai Community College ... HI ... 136
University of Hawaii Leeward Community College ... HI ... 137
University of Hawaii Maui College ... HI ... 137
Boise State University ... ID ... 137
Idaho State University ... ID ... 138
College of DuPage ... IL ... 142
Illinois Institute of Art, The ... IL ... 147
Joliet Junior College ... IL ... 149
Kendall College ... IL ... 149
Le Cordon Bleu College of Culinary Arts in Chicago ... IL ... 150
Southwestern Illinois College ... IL ... 160
Harrison College - Indianapolis Downtown Campus ... IN ... 166
Ivy Tech Community College-Central Indiana ... IN ... 169
Des Moines Area Community College ... IA ... 177
Indian Hills Community College ... IA ... 179
Iowa Western Community College ... IA ... 179
Kirkwood Community College ... IA ... 180
Johnson County Community College ... KS ... 187
Jefferson Community and Technical College ... KY ... 195
Southcentral Kentucky Community and Technical College ... KY ... 196
Sullivan University ... KY ... 199
West Kentucky Community and Technical College ... KY ... 196
Bossier Parish Community College ... LA ... 202
Delgado Community College ... LA ... 203
Louisiana Culinary Institute ... LA ... 204
South Louisiana Community College Ardoin Campus ... LA ... 203
Southern Maine Community College ... ME ... 211
Anne Arundel Community College ... MD ... 213
Wor-Wic Community College ... MD ... 221
Holyoke Community College ... MA ... 231
Salter College ... MA ... 236
Grand Rapids Community College ... MI ... 243
Henry Ford Community College ... MI ... 243
Macomb Community College ... MI ... 246
Northwestern Michigan College ... MI ... 248
Oakland Community College ... MI ... 248
Schoolcraft College ... MI ... 250
Washtenaw Community College ... MI ... 252
Art Institutes International Minnesota, The. MN ... 253
Hennepin Technical College ... MN ... 258
Saint Paul College-A Community & Technical College ... MN ... 261
East Central College ... MO ... 273
Hickey College ... MO ... 275
Ozarks Technical Community College ... MO ... 279
Saint Louis Community College at Forest Park ... MO ... 281
Metropolitan Community College ... NE ... 290
Southeast Community College ... NE ... 292
College of Southern Nevada ... NV ... 294
Truckee Meadows Community College ... NV ... 294
Southern New Hampshire University ... NH ... 297
Atlantic Cape Community College ... NJ ... 299
Hudson County Community College ... NJ ... 302
Central New Mexico Community College . NM ... 309
Navajo Technical College ... NM ... 310
Monroe College ... NY ... 331
Niagara County Community College ... NY ... 334
Paul Smith's College ... NY ... 336
Schenectady County Community College . NY ... 340
State University of New York College of Agriculture and Technology at Coble skill ... NY ... 344
State University of New York College of Technology at Delhi ... NY ... 345
Alamance Community College ... NC ... 357
Asheville - Buncombe Technical Community College ... NC ... 357
Central Piedmont Community College ... NC ... 359
Guilford Technical Community College ... NC ... 360
Lenoir Community College ... NC ... 361
Wake Technical Community College ... NC ... 364
Cincinnati State Technical and Community College ... OH ... 376
Columbus State Community College ... OH ... 378
Cuyahoga Community College ... OH ... 378
Hocking College ... OH ... 380
Sinclair Community College ... OH ... 388
Zane State College ... OH ... 394
Platt College ... OK ... 398
Lane Community College ... OR ... 403
Le Cordon Bleu College of Culinary Arts in Portland ... OR ... 403
Southwestern Oregon Community College OR ... 407
Art Institute of Philadelphia ... PA ... 410
Art Institute of Pittsburgh ... PA ... 410
Harrisburg Area Community College ... PA ... 417
Indiana University of Pennsylvania ... PA ... 428
Pennsylvania College of Technology ... PA ... 427
Westmoreland County Community College ... PA ... 437
YTI Career Institute ... PA ... 438
Universidad del Este ... PR ... 552
Greenville Technical College ... SC ... 444
Horry-Georgetown Technical College ... SC ... 444
Spartanburg Community College ... SC ... 447
Trident Technical College ... SC ... 447
Nashville State Community College ... TN ... 461
Walters State Community College ... TN ... 462
Art Institute of Houston, The ... TX ... 466
Austin Community College District ... TX ... 466
Collin County Community College District TX ... 469
Culinary Institute LeNotre ... TX ... 470
Del Mar College ... TX ... 471
El Centro College ... TX ... 470
Lamar University ... TX ... 486
Le Cordon Bleu College of Culinary Arts in Austin ... TX ... 475
St. Philip's College ... TX ... 465
San Jacinto College North ... TX ... 479
Tarrant County College District ... TX ... 482
Salt Lake Community College ... UT ... 498
Dabney S. Lancaster Community College VA ... 512
ECPI College of Technology ... VA ... 504
J. Sargeant Reynolds Community College VA ... 512
Stratford University ... VA ... 510
Tidewater Community College ... VA ... 514
Art Institute of Seattle, The ... WA ... 516
Bellingham Technical College ... WA ... 517
Lake Washington Institute of Technology . WA ... 520
Olympic College ... WA ... 521
Renton Technical College ... WA ... 522
Seattle Central Community College ... WA ... 522
Skagit Valley College ... WA ... 523
South Puget Sound Community College .. WA ... 524
Spokane Community College ... WA ... 518
Walla Walla University ... WA ... 524
Pierpont Community & Technical College WV ... 528
University of Charleston ... WV ... 527
West Virginia Northern Community College ... WV ... 528
Blackhawk Technical College ... WI ... 539
Fox Valley Technical College ... WI ... 539
Madison Area Technical College ... WI ... 540
Milwaukee Area Technical College ... WI ... 540
Waukesha County Technical College ... WI ... 541

ACICS: Accrediting Council for Independent Colleges and Schools: business and business related programs (C,A,B,M)

Prince Institute - Southeast ... AL ... 6
Virginia College ... AL ... 3
Charter College ... AK ... 10
Anthem College ... AZ ... 11
Art Institute of Phoenix, The ... AZ ... 12
Brookline College ... AZ ... 12
Bryman School, The ... AZ ... 12
Carrington College - Phoenix ... AZ ... 12
Le Cordon Bleu College of Culinary Arts in Scottsdale ... AZ ... 14
Academy of Couture Art ... CA ... 26
American University of Health Sciences ... CA ... 28
Bergin University of Canine Studies ... CA ... 29
Bristol University ... CA ... 29
Brooks Institute ... CA ... 30
Bryan College ... CA ... 30
California International Business University ... CA ... 31
California Miramar University ... CA ... 32
California University of Management and Sciences ... CA ... 36
Cambridge Junior College ... CA ... 36
Charter College-Canyon Country ... CA ... 38
Coleman University ... CA ... 40
Design Institute of San Diego ... CA ... 42
Empire College School of Business ... CA ... 43
Everest College-San Bernardino ... CA ... 43
Kaplan College ... CA ... 49
Le Cordon Bleu College of Culinary Arts .. CA ... 50
Le Cordon Bleu College of Culinary Arts in Los Angeles ... CA ... 50
Lincoln University ... CA ... 51
NewSchool of Architecture and Design ... CA ... 56
Northwestern Polytechnic University ... CA ... 56
Pacific States University ... CA ... 57
Professional Golfers Career College ... CA ... 60
Sage College ... CA ... 61
Santa Barbara Business College ... CA ... 64
Silicon Valley University ... CA ... 66
South Coast College ... CA ... 66
Southern States University ... CA ... 68
University of Antelope Valley ... CA ... 70
Westwood College - Los Angeles Campus CA ... 76
Westwood College-South Bay ... CA ... 76
Colorado Heights University ... CO ... 79
Everest College ... CO ... 81
Institute of Business and Medical Careers. CO ... 82
Prince Institute-Rocky Mountains ... CO ... 84
Redstone College ... CO ... 84
Remington College-Colorado Springs ... CO ... 85
Westwood College-Denver North ... CO ... 87
Sanford-Brown College-Farmington ... CT ... 91
Radians College ... DC ... 96
Art Institute of Fort Lauderdale, The ... FL ... 98
City College ... FL ... 99
City College ... FL ... 100
College of Business and Technology ... FL ... 100
Digital Media Arts College ... FL ... 101
Everest Institute ... FL ... 102
Everest University-Largo ... FL ... 102
Everest University-North Orlando Campus FL ... 102
Everest University-Pompano Beach Campus ... FL ... 102
Everest University-Tampa Campus ... FL ... 103
Florida Career College ... FL ... 103
Florida Technical College ... FL ... 105
Fortis College ... FL ... 105
International Academy of Design and Technology ... FL ... 107
Jones College ... FL ... 107
Jose Maria Vargas University ... FL ... 107
Key College ... FL ... 108
Lincoln College of Technology ... FL ... 108
Millennia Atlantic University ... FL ... 109
Professional Training Center ... FL ... 111
San Ignacio College ... FL ... 112
Sanford-Brown Institute ... FL ... 112
Schiller International University ... FL ... 113
Southern Technical College ... FL ... 114
Southwest Florida College ... FL ... 114
Unilatina International College ... FL ... 118
University of Southernmost Florida ... FL ... 118
Gwinnett College ... GA ... 127
SAE Institute Atlanta ... GA ... 130
Sanford-Brown College ... GA ... 131
Carrington College - Boise ... ID ... 137
Ambria College of Nursing ... IL ... 139
International Academy of Design and Technology ... IL ... 148
SOLEX College ... IL ... 159
Taylor Business Institute ... IL ... 160
Tribeca Flashpoint Media Arts Academy .. IL ... 160
Westwood College-DuPage ... IL ... 163
Westwood College-O'Hare Airport ... IL ... 163
College of Court Reporting, Inc. ... IN ... 165
Harrison College - Indianapolis Downtown Campus ... IN ... 166
International Business College ... IN ... 169
ITT Technical Institute ... IN ... 169
Kaplan College ... IN ... 170
MedTech College ... IN ... 171
National College ... IN ... 171
Radiological Technologies University-VT .. IN ... 172
Bryan University ... KS ... 185
Pinnacle Career Institute ... KS ... 189
Wright Career College ... KS ... 191
Beckfield College ... KY ... 192
Daymar College-Owensboro ... KY ... 193
Daymar College-Paducah ... KY ... 193
National College ... KY ... 198
Spencerian College ... KY ... 199
Sullivan College of Technology and Design ... KY ... 199
Career Technical College ... LA ... 201
Delta School of Business & Technology, DBA Delta Tech ... LA ... 201
Beal College ... ME ... 209
TESST College of Technology ... MD ... 218
Salter College ... MA ... 236
Sanford-Brown College of Boston, Inc. ... MA ... 236
Michigan Jewish Institute ... MI ... 246
Academy College ... MN ... 253
Art Institutes International Minnesota, The. MN ... 253
Brown College ... MN ... 254
Duluth Business University, Inc. ... MN ... 255
Globe University ... MN ... 255
Minneapolis Business College ... MN ... 257
Minnesota School of Business ... MN ... 257
Bryan University ... MO ... 271
Everest College ... MO ... 274
Hickey College ... MO ... 275
Metro Business College ... MO ... 276
Missouri College ... MO ... 278
Pinnacle Career Institute ... MO ... 280
Sanford-Brown College ... MO ... 281
Stevens Institute of Business & Arts ... MO ... 282
Texas County Technical College ... MO ... 282
Everest College ... NV ... 293
Kaplan College ... NV ... 294
Lebanon College ... NH ... 297
Eastwick College ... NJ ... 301
Art Institute of New York City, The ... NY ... 314
Elmira Business Institute ... NY ... 323
Everest Institute ... NY ... 324
Long Island Business Institute ... NY ... 329
Mildred Elley ... NY ... 331
Professional Business College ... NY ... 336
SBI Campus-An Affiliate of Sanford-Brown NY ... 340
King's College ... NC ... 355
Living Arts College @ School of Communication Arts ... NC ... 356
South College-Asheville ... NC ... 366
Bradford School ... OH ... 375
Daymar College-Chillicothe ... OH ... 378
Gallipolis Career College ... OH ... 380
Hondros College ... OH ... 381
Kaplan Career Institute ... OH ... 381
Ohio Business College, Lorain Branch ... OH ... 385
Ohio Valley College of Technology ... OH ... 387
Stautzenberger College ... OH ... 389
Trumbull Business College ... OH ... 390
Community Care College ... OK ... 395
Everest College ... OR ... 403
Le Cordon Bleu College of Culinary Arts in Portland ... OR ... 403
Pioneer Pacific College ... OR ... 407
Sumner College ... OR ... 408
Art Institute of York - Pennsylvania, The .. PA ... 410
Berks Technical Institute ... PA ... 410
Bradford School ... PA ... 410
Cambria-Rowe Business College ... PA ... 412
Consolidated School of Business ... PA ... 413
Consolidated School of Business ... PA ... 414
Douglas Education Center ... PA ... 415
DuBois Business College ... PA ... 415
Erie Business Center, Main ... PA ... 416
Everest Institute ... PA ... 416
Fortis Institute ... PA ... 416
Kaplan Career Institute ... PA ... 419
Kaplan Career Institute/Broomall Campus PA ... 419
Kaplan Career Institute - ICM Campus ... PA ... 419
Lansdale School of Business ... PA ... 421
Laurel Business Institute ... PA ... 421
Laurel Technical Institute ... PA ... 421
McCann School of Business & Technology ... PA ... 423
Newport Business Institute ... PA ... 425
Pace Institute ... PA ... 425
Penn Commercial Business/Technical School ... PA ... 425
Sanford-Brown Institute-Pittsburgh ... PA ... 433
South Hills School of Business and Technology ... PA ... 433
Yorktowne Business Institute ... PA ... 438
Atlantic University College ... PR ... 547
EDIC College ... PR ... 548
Humacao Community College ... PR ... 549
Instituto de Banca y Comercio ... PR ... 549
John Dewey College ... PR ... 551
National University College ... PR ... 551
Forrest College ... SC ... 444
Daymar Institute ... TN ... 454
Kaplan Career Institute ... TN ... 455
Miller-Motte Technical College ... TN ... 457
National College of Business and Technology ... TN ... 457
West Tennessee Business College ... TN ... 464
Anamarc College ... TX ... 465
Career Point College ... TX ... 468
Court Reporting Institute of Dallas ... TX ... 469
International Business College ... TX ... 474
Kaplan College ... TX ... 474
Kaplan College ... TX ... 475
Le Cordon Bleu College of Culinary Arts in Austin ... TX ... 475
Lighthouse College ... TX ... 475
North American College ... TX ... 477
Sanford-Brown College ... TX ... 480
Texas Health and Science University ... TX ... 485
Texas School of Business ... TX ... 485
Vet Tech Institute of Houston ... TX ... 493
Broadview University ... UT ... 495
Eagle Gate College ... UT ... 495
Everest College ... UT ... 495
Neumont University ... UT ... 496
Provo College ... UT ... 496
American National University ... VA ... 501
Bon Secours Memorial College of Nursing VA ... 502
Everest College ... VA ... 504
Fortis College ... VA ... 505
Global Health College ... VA ... 505
iGlobal University ... VA ... 505
Miller-Motte Technical College ... VA ... 507
Sanford-Brown College-Tysons Corner ... VA ... 509
Sentara College of Health Sciences ... VA ... 509
Stratford University ... VA ... 510
Virginia International University ... VA ... 515
Bainbridge Graduate Institute ... WA ... 516
Carrington College - Spokane ... WA ... 517
Everest College ... WA ... 519
ITT Technical Institute ... WA ... 520
Mountain State College ... WV ... 527
Valley College - Beckley Campus ... WV ... 527

Valley College - Martinsburg Campus ... WV .. 527
West Virginia Business College ... WV .. 527
West Virginia Junior College ... WV .. 531

ACUP: Accreditation Commission for Acupuncture and Oriental Medicine: acupuncture (C,M,D)

Arizona School of Acupuncture and Oriental Medicine ... AZ ... 11
Han University of Traditional Medicine ... AZ ... 13
Phoenix Institute of Herbal Medicine and Acupuncture ... AZ ... 16
Academy of Chinese Culture and Health Sciences ... CA ... 26
Acupuncture and Integrative Medicine College-Berkeley ... CA ... 26
@Alhambra Medical University ... CA ... 26
American College of Traditional Chinese Medicine ... CA ... 27
Dongguk University ... CA ... 42
Emperor's College of Traditional Oriental Medicine ... CA ... 43
Five Branches University, Graduate School of Traditional Chinese Medicine . CA ... 44
Pacific College of Oriental Medicine ... CA ... 57
South Baylo University ... CA ... 66
Southern California University of Health Sciences ... CA ... 67
Southern California University School of Oriental Medicine and Acupuncture ... CA ... 67
@Stanton University ... CA ... 68
University of East-West Medicine ... CA ... 72
Yo San University of Traditional Chinese Medicine ... CA ... 77
Colorado School of Traditional Chinese Medicine ... CO ... 80
Institute of Taoist Education and Acupuncture ... CO ... 82
University of Bridgeport ... CT ... 91
Academy for Five Element Acupuncture ... FL ... 97
Acupuncture & Massage College ... FL ... 97
Atlantic Institute of Oriental Medicine ... FL ... 98
Dragon Rises College of Oriental Medicine ... FL ... 101
East West College of Natural Medicine ... FL ... 101
Florida College of Integrative Medicine ... FL ... 104
Hawaii College of Oriental Medicine ... HI ... 135
Institute of Clinical Acupuncture and Oriental Medicine ... HI ... 135
World Medicine Institute ... HI ... 137
National University of Health Sciences ... IL ... 154
Maryland University of Integrative Health . MD .. 216
New England School of Acupuncture ... MA .. 235
American Academy of Acupuncture and Oriental Medicine ... MN .. 253
Northwestern Health Sciences University . MN .. 263
Southwest Acupuncture College ... NM .. 312
New York Chiropractic College ... NY ... 333
New York College of Health Professions .. NY ... 333
New York College of Traditional Chinese Medicine ... NY ... 333
Tri-State College of Acupuncture ... NY ... 348
Daoist Traditions College of Chinese Medical Arts ... NC ... 353
American Institute of Alternative Medicine OH .. 373
National College of Natural Medicine ... OR .. 404
Oregon College of Oriental Medicine ... OR .. 405
Won Institute of Graduate Studies ... PA ... 438
American College of Acupuncture and Oriental Medicine ... TX ... 465
AOMA Graduate School of Integrative Medicine ... TX ... 466
Texas Health and Science University ... TX ... 485
Bastyr University ... WA .. 516
Seattle Institute of Oriental Medicine ... WA .. 523
Midwest College of Oriental Medicine ... WI ... 534

ADNUR: Accreditation Commission for Education in Nursing: nursing (A)

Alabama Southern Community College ... AL ... 1
Bevill State Community College ... AL ... 2
Bishop State Community College ... AL ... 2
Calhoun Community College ... AL ... 2
Central Alabama Community College ... AL ... 2
Chattahoochee Valley Community College AL ... 2
Gadsden State Community College ... AL ... 3
George C. Wallace Community College - Dothan ... AL ... 3
George Corley Wallace State Community College - Selma ... AL ... 4
James H. Faulkner State Community College ... AL ... 4
Jefferson Davis Community College ... AL ... 5
Jefferson State Community College ... AL ... 5
Lawson State Community College ... AL ... 5
Lurleen B. Wallace Community College ... AL ... 5
Northeast Alabama Community College ... AL ... 5
Northwest - Shoals Community College ... AL ... 6
Shelton State Community College ... AL ... 6
Snead State Community College ... AL ... 6
Southern Union State Community College AL ... 7
Troy University ... AL ... 7
University of Mobile ... AL ... 9
University of West Alabama, The ... AL ... 9
Wallace State Community College - Hanceville ... AL ... 9
University of Alaska Anchorage ... AK ... 10
Arizona Western College ... AZ ... 11
Carrington College - Phoenix ... AZ ... 12
Central Arizona College ... AZ ... 12
Chandler-Gilbert Community College ... AZ ... 14
Cochise College ... AZ ... 12
Estrella Mountain Community College ... AZ ... 14
Gateway Community College ... AZ ... 14
Glendale Community College ... AZ ... 14
Mesa Community College ... AZ ... 15
Mohave Community College ... AZ ... 15
Northland Pioneer College ... AZ ... 16
Paradise Valley Community College ... AZ ... 15
Phoenix College ... AZ ... 15
Pima Community College ... AZ ... 17
Scottsdale Community College ... AZ ... 15
Yavapai College ... AZ ... 19
Arkansas Northeastern College ... AR ... 19
Arkansas State University-Jonesboro ... AR ... 19
East Arkansas Community College ... AR ... 21
National Park Community College ... AR ... 22
North Arkansas College ... AR ... 22
Phillips Community College of the University of Arkansas ... AR ... 24
Southeast Arkansas College ... AR ... 23
Southern Arkansas University ... AR ... 23
University of Arkansas at Fort Smith ... AR ... 24
University of Arkansas at Little Rock ... AR ... 24
University of Arkansas Community College at Batesville ... AR ... 25
Cerritos College ... CA ... 37
Chaffey College ... CA ... 37
College of Marin ... CA ... 40
College of the Canyons ... CA ... 40
Cypress College ... CA ... 56
El Camino College ... CA ... 43
Evergreen Valley College ... CA ... 63
Golden West College ... CA ... 39
Grossmont College ... CA ... 46
Long Beach City College ... CA ... 51
Los Angeles Harbor College ... CA ... 51
Los Angeles Pierce College ... CA ... 52
Los Angeles Valley College ... CA ... 52
Monterey Peninsula College ... CA ... 54
Moorpark College ... CA ... 74
Ohlone College ... CA ... 57
Pacific Union College ... CA ... 57
Palomar College ... CA ... 58
Riverside City College ... CA ... 61
Saddleback College ... CA ... 67
San Bernardino Valley College ... CA ... 62
San Diego City College ... CA ... 62
San Joaquin Delta College ... CA ... 63
Santa Ana College ... CA ... 60
Santa Barbara City College ... CA ... 64
Santa Monica College ... CA ... 65
Southwestern College ... CA ... 68
Ventura College ... CA ... 74
Aims Community College ... CO ... 78
Arapahoe Community College ... CO ... 78
Colorado Mesa University ... CO ... 79
Colorado Mountain College ... CO ... 79
Colorado Northwestern Community College ... CO ... 80
Denver School of Nursing ... CO ... 81
Front Range Community College ... CO ... 81
Lamar Community College ... CO ... 82
Morgan Community College ... CO ... 83
Northeastern Junior College ... CO ... 83
Otero Junior College ... CO ... 83
Pikes Peak Community College ... CO ... 84
Pueblo Community College ... CO ... 84
Capital Community College ... CT ... 88
Gateway Community College ... CT ... 88
Goodwin College ... CT ... 90
Naugatuck Valley Community College ... CT ... 89
Northwestern Connecticut Community-Technical College ... CT ... 89
Norwalk Community College ... CT ... 89
St. Vincent's College ... CT ... 91
Three Rivers Community College ... CT ... 89
Delaware Technical Community College, Owens Campus ... DE ... 93
Delaware Technical Community College, Stanton-Wilmington Campus ... DE ... 93
Delaware Technical Community College, Terry Campus ... DE ... 93
University of the District of Columbia ... DC ... 97
Adventist University of Health Sciences ... FL ... 97
Broward College ... FL ... 99
College of Central Florida ... FL ... 100
Daytona State College ... FL ... 101
Edison State College ... FL ... 101
Florida Gateway College ... FL ... 104
Florida State College at Jacksonville ... FL ... 105
Gulf Coast State College ... FL ... 106
Hillsborough Community College ... FL ... 106
Indian River State College ... FL ... 106
Keiser University ... FL ... 108
Lake-Sumter State College ... FL ... 108
Miami Dade College ... FL ... 109
Palm Beach State College ... FL ... 110
Pasco-Hernando Community College ... FL ... 110
Pensacola State College ... FL ... 110
Polk State College ... FL ... 110
St. Johns River State College ... FL ... 112
St. Petersburg College ... FL ... 112
Santa Fe College ... FL ... 113
Seminole State College of Florida ... FL ... 113
South Florida State College ... FL ... 113
State College of Florida, Manatee-Sarasota ... FL ... 114
Tallahassee Community College ... FL ... 117
Valencia College ... FL ... 118
Abraham Baldwin Agricultural College ... GA .. 119
Athens Technical College ... GA .. 120
Bainbridge College ... GA .. 121
College of Coastal Georgia ... GA .. 123
Columbus Technical College ... GA .. 123
Dalton State College ... GA .. 123
Darton State College ... GA .. 124
Georgia Highlands College ... GA .. 125
Georgia Northwestern Technical College . GA .. 125
Georgia Perimeter College ... GA .. 125
Gordon State College ... GA .. 127
Gwinnett Technical College ... GA .. 127
Middle Georgia State College ... GA .. 128
South Georgia State College ... GA .. 131
Southwest Georgia Technical College ... GA .. 132
University of North Georgia ... GA .. 133
West Georgia Technical College ... GA .. 134
Kapiolani Community College ... HI ... 136
University of Hawaii Hawaii Community College ... HI ... 136
University of Hawaii Kauai Community College ... HI ... 136
University of Hawaii Maui College ... HI ... 137
Brigham Young University-Idaho ... ID ... 137
College of Southern Idaho ... ID ... 138
College of Western Idaho ... ID ... 138
Idaho State University ... ID ... 138
North Idaho College ... ID ... 138
Black Hawk College ... IL ... 140
Carl Sandburg College ... IL ... 141
City Colleges of Chicago Harry S Truman College ... IL ... 142
City Colleges of Chicago Richard J. Daley College ... IL ... 142
College of DuPage ... IL ... 142
College of Lake County ... IL ... 143
Elgin Community College ... IL ... 144
Harper College ... IL ... 145
Heartland Community College ... IL ... 146
Illinois Central College ... IL ... 146
Illinois Eastern Community Colleges Frontier Community College ... IL ... 146
Illinois Eastern Community Colleges Lincoln Trail College ... IL ... 147
Illinois Eastern Community Colleges Olney Central College ... IL ... 147
Illinois Eastern Community Colleges Wabash Valley College ... IL ... 147
Illinois Valley Community College ... IL ... 148
Joliet Junior College ... IL ... 149
Kaskaskia College ... IL ... 149
Lake Land College ... IL ... 150
Lewis and Clark Community College ... IL ... 150
Lincoln Land Community College ... IL ... 151
Morton College ... IL ... 153
Oakton Community College ... IL ... 155
Parkland College ... IL ... 155
Prairie State College ... IL ... 156
Richland Community College ... IL ... 156
Robert Morris University ... IL ... 156
South Suburban College of Cook County . IL ... 159
Southwestern Illinois College ... IL ... 160
Trinity College of Nursing & Health Sciences ... IL ... 160
Triton College ... IL ... 161
Bethel College ... IN ... 164
Ivy Tech Community College-Central Indiana ... IN ... 169
University of Indianapolis ... IN ... 173
University of Saint Francis ... IN ... 174
Vincennes University ... IN ... 174
Des Moines Area Community College ... IA ... 177
Mercy College of Health Sciences ... IA ... 181
North Iowa Area Community College ... IA ... 181
St. Luke's College ... IA ... 182
Barton County Community College ... KS ... 184
Butler Community College ... KS ... 185
Cloud County Community College ... KS ... 185
Colby Community College ... KS ... 185
Dodge City Community College ... KS ... 186
Fort Scott Community College ... KS ... 186
Garden City Community College ... KS ... 187
Hesston College ... KS ... 187
Hutchinson Community College and Area Vocational School ... KS ... 187
Johnson County Community College ... KS ... 187
Kansas City Kansas Community College . KS ... 187
Labette Community College ... KS ... 188
Manhattan Area Technical College ... KS ... 188
Neosho County Community College ... KS ... 189
North Central Kansas Technical College .. KS ... 189
Pratt Community College ... KS ... 190
Seward County Community College/Area Technical School ... KS ... 190
Ashland Community and Technical College ... KY ... 194
Bluegrass Community and Technical College ... KY ... 194
Eastern Kentucky University ... KY ... 193
Elizabethtown Community and Technical College ... KY ... 195
Henderson Community College ... KY ... 195
Hopkinsville Community College ... KY ... 195
Jefferson Community and Technical College ... KY ... 195
Kentucky State University ... KY ... 197
Madisonville Community College ... KY ... 196
Midway College ... KY ... 197
Morehead State University ... KY ... 198
St. Catharine College ... KY ... 198
Somerset Community College ... KY ... 196
Southeast Kentucky Community and Technical College ... KY ... 196
West Kentucky Community and Technical College ... KY ... 196
Western Kentucky University ... KY ... 200
Baton Rouge Community College ... LA ... 202
Bossier Parish Community College ... LA ... 202
Delgado Community College ... LA ... 203
Louisiana Delta Community College ... LA ... 203
Louisiana State University at Alexandria .. LA ... 205
Louisiana State University at Eunice ... LA ... 205
Louisiana Tech University ... LA ... 207
McNeese State University ... LA ... 207
Northwestern State University ... LA ... 208
Our Lady of the Lake College ... LA ... 206
Southern University at Shreveport-Louisiana ... LA ... 207
Central Maine Community College ... ME .. 210
Central Maine Medical Center College of Nursing and Health Professions ... ME .. 209
Eastern Maine Community College ... ME .. 210
Kennebec Valley Community College ... ME .. 210
Northern Maine Community College ... ME .. 210
Southern Maine Community College ... ME .. 211
University of Maine at Augusta ... ME .. 212
University of New England ... ME .. 213
Allegany College of Maryland ... MD .. 213
Anne Arundel Community College ... MD .. 213
Baltimore City Community College ... MD .. 213
Cecil College ... MD .. 214
Chesapeake College ... MD .. 214
College of Southern Maryland ... MD .. 214
Community College of Baltimore County, The ... MD .. 214
Frederick Community College ... MD .. 214
Hagerstown Community College ... MD .. 215
Harford Community College ... MD .. 215
Howard Community College ... MD .. 215
Montgomery College ... MD .. 216
Prince George's Community College ... MD .. 217
Bay State College ... MA .. 222
Becker College-Worcester ... MA .. 223
Berkshire Community College ... MA .. 231
Bristol Community College ... MA .. 231
Bunker Hill Community College ... MA .. 231
Cape Cod Community College ... MA .. 231
Greenfield Community College ... MA .. 231
Holyoke Community College ... MA .. 231
Laboure College ... MA .. 227
Massachusetts Bay Community College ... MA .. 231
Massasoit Community College ... MA .. 232
Middlesex Community College ... MA .. 232
Mount Wachusett Community College ... MA .. 232
North Shore Community College ... MA .. 232
Northern Essex Community College ... MA .. 232
Quincy College ... MA .. 235
Quinsigamond Community College ... MA .. 232
Regis College ... MA .. 236
Roxbury Community College ... MA .. 232
Springfield Technical Community College MA .. 233
Bay Noc Community College ... MI ... 240
Delta College ... MI ... 242
Grand Rapids Community College ... MI ... 243
Henry Ford Community College ... MI ... 243
Lake Michigan College ... MI ... 245
Lansing Community College ... MI ... 245
Macomb Community College ... MI ... 246
Monroe County Community College ... MI ... 247
Mott Community College ... MI ... 247
Muskegon Community College ... MI ... 247
Oakland Community College ... MI ... 248
St. Clair County Community College ... MI ... 249
Schoolcraft College ... MI ... 250
Washtenaw Community College ... MI ... 252
Anoka-Ramsey Community College ... MN .. 257
Century College ... MN .. 258
Hibbing Community College, A Technical and Community College ... MN .. 258
Inver Hills Community College ... MN .. 258
Lake Superior College ... MN .. 259
Minneapolis Community and Technical College ... MN .. 259

Minnesota West Community and Technical College .... MN .. 260
Normandale Community College .... MN .. 260
North Hennepin Community College .... MN .. 260
Northland Community and Technical College .... MN .. 260
Ridgewater College .... MN .. 260
Riverland Community College .... MN .. 260
Rochester Community and Technical College .... MN .. 261
St. Catherine University .... MN .. 263
Alcorn State University .... MS .. 265
Copiah-Lincoln Community College .... MS .. 266
East Central Community College .... MS .. 266
East Mississippi Community College .... MS .. 266
Hinds Community College .... MS .. 267
Holmes Community College .... MS .. 267
Itawamba Community College .... MS .. 267
Jones County Junior College .... MS .. 267
Meridian Community College .... MS .. 267
Mississippi Delta Community College .... MS .. 268
Mississippi Gulf Coast Community College .... MS .. 268
Mississippi University for Women .... MS .. 268
Northeast Mississippi Community College MS .. 269
Northwest Mississippi Community College MS .. 269
Pearl River Community College .... MS .. 269
Southwest Mississippi Community College MS .. 269
Cox College .... MO .. 273
Hannibal-La Grange University .... MO .. 274
Lincoln University .... MO .. 276
Metropolitan Community College - Penn Valley .... MO .. 277
Missouri State University .... MO .. 278
Ozarks Technical Community College .... MO .. 279
Park University .... MO .. 280
St. Charles Community College .... MO .. 280
Saint Louis Community College at Forest Park .... MO .. 281
Southeast Missouri Hospital College of Nursing and Health Sciences .... MO .. 282
Southwest Baptist University .... MO .. 282
Three Rivers Community College .... MO .. 282
Miles Community College .... MT .. 286
Montana State University - Northern .... MT .. 287
Montana Tech of The University of Montana .... MT .. 287
Salish Kootenai College .... MT .. 288
University of Montana - Helena College of Technology, The .... MT .. 287
Central Community College .... NE ... 288
College of Saint Mary .... NE ... 289
Metropolitan Community College .... NE ... 290
Mid-Plains Community College .... NE ... 290
Northeast Community College .... NE ... 291
Southeast Community College .... NE ... 292
College of Southern Nevada .... NV ... 294
Great Basin College .... NV ... 294
Truckee Meadows Community College .... NV ... 294
Western Nevada College .... NV ... 295
Great Bay Community College .... NH .. 295
Manchester Community College .... NH .. 296
Nashua Community College .... NH .. 296
NHTI-Concord's Community College .... NH .. 296
River Valley Community College .... NH .. 296
Rivier University .... NH .. 297
St. Joseph School of Nursing .... NH .. 297
Atlantic Cape Community College .... NJ ... 299
Bergen Community College .... NJ ... 299
Brookdale Community College .... NJ ... 299
Burlington County College .... NJ ... 299
County College of Morris .... NJ ... 300
Cumberland County College .... NJ ... 301
Essex County College .... NJ ... 301
Gloucester County College .... NJ ... 302
Mercer County Community College .... NJ ... 302
Middlesex County College .... NJ ... 303
Ocean County College .... NJ ... 304
Passaic County Community College .... NJ ... 304
Raritan Valley Community College .... NJ ... 305
Salem Community College .... NJ ... 307
Warren County Community College .... NJ ... 308
Central New Mexico Community College . NM .. 309
Clovis Community College .... NM .. 309
Eastern New Mexico University-Roswell ... NM .. 309
Luna Community College .... NM .. 309
New Mexico Junior College .... NM .. 310
New Mexico State University at Alamogordo .... NM .. 310
New Mexico State University at Carlsbad . NM .. 311
San Juan College .... NM .. 311
Santa Fe Community College .... NM .. 311
Western New Mexico University .... NM .. 312
Alfred State College .... NY ... 345
Belanger School of Nursing, The .... NY ... 314
Broome Community College .... NY ... 315
Cayuga Community College .... NY ... 316
City University of New York Borough of Manhattan Community College .... NY ... 317
City University of New York Bronx Community College .... NY ... 317
City University of New York College of Staten Island .... NY ... 317
City University of New York Medgar Evers College .... NY ... 319
City University of New York Queensborough Community College .... NY ... 319
Clinton Community College .... NY ... 320
Cochran School of Nursing .... NY ... 320
Columbia-Greene Community College .... NY ... 321
Corning Community College .... NY ... 322
Crouse Hospital College of Nursing .... NY ... 322
Dorothea Hopfer School of Nursing at Mount Vernon Hospital .... NY ... 323
Dutchess Community College .... NY ... 323
Erie Community College City Campus .... NY ... 323
Excelsior College .... NY ... 324
Finger Lakes Community College .... NY ... 324
Finger Lakes Health College of Nursing ... NY ... 324
Genesee Community College .... NY ... 325
Helene Fuld College of Nursing .... NY ... 325
Hudson Valley Community College .... NY ... 326
Jamestown Community College .... NY ... 327
Jefferson Community College .... NY ... 327
La Guardia Community College/City University of New York .... NY ... 318
Maria College of Albany .... NY ... 330
Mohawk Valley Community College .... NY ... 331
Monroe Community College .... NY ... 332
Nassau Community College .... NY ... 332
New York City College of Technology/City University of New York .... NY ... 319
Niagara County Community College .... NY ... 334
Onondaga Community College .... NY ... 335
Orange County Community College .... NY ... 335
Phillips Beth Israel School of Nursing .... NY ... 336
Rockland Community College .... NY ... 338
St. Elizabeth College of Nursing .... NY ... 338
Saint Joseph's College, New York .... NY ... 339
State University of New York College of Agriculture and Technology at Morrisville .... NY ... 345
State University of New York College of Technology at Delhi .... NY ... 345
Suffolk County Community College Ammerman Campus .... NY ... 346
SUNY Adirondack .... NY ... 345
SUNY Canton-College of Technology .... NY ... 345
Tompkins Cortland Community College .... NY ... 347
Trocaire College .... NY ... 348
Ulster County Community College .... NY ... 348
Cabarrus College of Health Sciences .... NC .. 352
Cape Fear Community College .... NC .. 358
Carolinas College of Health Sciences .... NC .. 353
Carteret Community College .... NC .. 358
Catawba Valley Community College .... NC .. 359
College of the Albemarle .... NC .. 359
Davidson County Community College .... NC .. 360
Durham Technical Community College .... NC .. 360
Fayetteville Technical Community College NC .. 360
Gardner-Webb University .... NC .. 354
Gaston College .... NC .. 360
Mitchell Community College .... NC .. 362
Pitt Community College .... NC .. 362
Queens University of Charlotte .... NC .. 365
Randolph Community College .... NC .. 362
Rowan-Cabarrus Community College .... NC .. 363
Sampson Community College .... NC .. 363
Wayne Community College .... NC .. 364
Western Piedmont Community College .... NC .. 365
Aultman College of Nursing and Health Sciences .... OH .. 374
Central Ohio Technical College .... OH .. 376
Christ College of Nursing and Health Sciences, The .... OH .. 376
Cincinnati State Technical and Community College .... OH .. 376
Clark State Community College .... OH .. 377
Columbus State Community College .... OH .. 378
Cuyahoga Community College .... OH .. 378
Edison State Community College .... OH .. 379
Fortis College .... OH .. 379
Good Samaritan College of Nursing and Health Science .... OH .. 380
Hocking College .... OH .. 380
James A. Rhodes State College .... OH .. 381
Kettering College .... OH .. 382
Lakeland Community College .... OH .. 382
Lorain County Community College .... OH .. 383
Marion Technical College .... OH .. 383
Mercy College of Ohio .... OH .. 383
North Central State College .... OH .. 385
Northwest State Community College .... OH .. 385
Ohio University Main Campus .... OH .. 387
Owens Community College .... OH .. 387
Shawnee State University .... OH .. 388
Sinclair Community College .... OH .. 388
Southern State Community College .... OH .. 389
Stark State College .... OH .. 389
Terra State Community College .... OH .. 389
University of Cincinnati-Blue Ash College . OH .. 391
University of Rio Grande .... OH .. 392
Carl Albert State College .... OK .. 394
Connors State College .... OK .. 395
Eastern Oklahoma State College .... OK .. 395
Murray State College .... OK .. 396
Northeastern Oklahoma Agricultural and Mechanical College .... OK .. 396
Northern Oklahoma College .... OK .. 396
Oklahoma City Community College .... OK .. 397
Oklahoma State University Institute of Technology-Okmulgee .... OK .. 398
Oklahoma State University - Oklahoma City .... OK .. 398
Redlands Community College .... OK .. 399
Rogers State University .... OK .. 399
Rose State College .... OK .. 399
Seminole State College .... OK .. 399
Tulsa Community College .... OK .. 400
Western Oklahoma State College .... OK .. 401
Chemeketa Community College .... OR .. 402
Portland Community College .... OR .. 407
Treasure Valley Community College .... OR .. 408
Umpqua Community College .... OR .. 408
Bucks County Community College .... PA ... 411
Butler County Community College .... PA ... 411
Community College of Allegheny County . PA ... 413
Community College of Beaver County .... PA ... 413
Community College of Philadelphia .... PA ... 413
Delaware County Community College .... PA ... 414
Gwynedd-Mercy University .... PA ... 417
Harcum College .... PA ... 417
Harrisburg Area Community College .... PA ... 417
La Roche College .... PA ... 420
Lancaster General College of Nursing and Health Sciences .... PA ... 421
Lehigh Carbon Community College .... PA ... 421
Lock Haven University .... PA ... 429
Luzerne County Community College .... PA ... 422
Mercyhurst University .... PA ... 423
Montgomery County Community College . PA ... 424
Mount Aloysius College .... PA ... 424
Northampton Community College .... PA ... 425
Penn State University Park .... PA ... 426
Pennsylvania College of Technology .... PA ... 427
Reading Area Community College .... PA ... 431
Westmoreland County Community College .... PA ... 437
Colegio Universitario de San Juan .... PR ... 548
Inter American University of Puerto Rico Metropolitan Campus .... PR ... 550
Universidad Metropolitana .... PR ... 552
University of Puerto Rico at Arecibo .... PR ... 553
University of Puerto Rico-Humacao .... PR ... 554
Community College of Rhode Island .... RI ... 439
New England Institute of Technology .... RI ... 439
Aiken Technical College .... SC ... 440
Central Carolina Technical College .... SC ... 441
Florence - Darlington Technical College ... SC ... 443
Greenville Technical College .... SC ... 444
Horry-Georgetown Technical College .... SC ... 444
Midlands Technical College .... SC ... 445
Orangeburg-Calhoun Technical College ... SC ... 446
Piedmont Technical College .... SC ... 446
Spartanburg Community College .... SC ... 447
Technical College of the Lowcountry .... SC ... 447
Tri-County Technical College .... SC ... 447
Trident Technical College .... SC ... 447
York Technical College .... SC ... 449
Dakota Wesleyan University .... SD ... 450
Presentation College .... SD ... 450
University of South Dakota, The .... SD ... 451
Aquinas College .... TN ... 452
Chattanooga State Community College .... TN ... 460
Cleveland State Community College .... TN ... 460
Columbia State Community College .... TN ... 460
Dyersburg State Community College .... TN ... 460
Jackson State Community College .... TN ... 460
Lincoln Memorial University .... TN ... 456
Motlow State Community College .... TN ... 461
Nashville State Community College .... TN ... 461
Northeast State Community College .... TN ... 461
Pellissippi State Community College .... TN ... 461
Roane State Community College .... TN ... 461
Southern Adventist University .... TN ... 458
Southwest Tennessee Community College .... TN ... 461
Tennessee State University .... TN ... 459
Walters State Community College .... TN ... 462
Alvin Community College .... TX ... 465
Amarillo College .... TX ... 465
Angelo State University .... TX ... 465
Austin Community College District .... TX ... 466
Baptist Health System School of Health Professions .... TX ... 467
Blinn College .... TX ... 467
Brookhaven College .... TX ... 470
Central Texas College .... TX ... 468
College of the Mainland .... TX ... 469
Collin County Community College District TX ... 469
Del Mar College .... TX ... 471
El Centro College .... TX ... 470
El Paso Community College .... TX ... 472
Galveston College .... TX ... 472
Grayson College .... TX ... 472
Howard College .... TX ... 473
Kilgore College .... TX ... 475
Lamar University .... TX ... 486
Laredo Community College .... TX ... 475
Lee College .... TX ... 475
Lone Star College System .... TX ... 476
McLennan Community College .... TX ... 476
Navarro College .... TX ... 477
North Central Texas College .... TX ... 477
Odessa College .... TX ... 477
Panola College .... TX ... 478
Paris Junior College .... TX ... 478
San Antonio College .... TX ... 465
San Jacinto College Central .... TX ... 479
San Jacinto College South .... TX ... 479
South Plains College .... TX ... 480
Tarrant County College District .... TX ... 482
Temple College .... TX ... 482
Texarkana College .... TX ... 482
Trinity Valley Community College .... TX ... 488
University of Texas at Brownsville and Texas Southmost College, The .... TX ... 491
Victoria College .... TX ... 493
Weatherford College .... TX ... 494
Dixie State College of Utah .... UT ... 497
Provo College .... UT ... 496
Salt Lake Community College .... UT ... 498
Stevens-Henager College .... UT ... 496
Utah Valley University .... UT ... 497
Weber State University .... UT ... 497
Castleton State College .... VT ... 501
Vermont Technical College .... VT ... 501
University of the Virgin Islands .... VI ... 555
Blue Ridge Community College .... VA ... 511
Dabney S. Lancaster Community College VA ... 512
Germanna Community College .... VA ... 512
J. Sargeant Reynolds Community College VA ... 512
John Tyler Community College .... VA ... 512
Mountain Empire Community College .... VA ... 513
Norfolk State University .... VA ... 507
Northern Virginia Community College .... VA ... 513
Patrick Henry Community College .... VA ... 513
Piedmont Virginia Community College .... VA ... 513
Southside Regional Medical Center Professional Schools .... VA ... 509
Southwest Virginia Community College .... VA ... 514
Thomas Nelson Community College .... VA ... 514
Tidewater Community College .... VA ... 514
Virginia Highlands Community College .... VA ... 514
Wytheville Community College .... VA ... 514
Bellevue College .... WA .. 517
Big Bend Community College .... WA .. 517
Clark College .... WA .. 518
Columbia Basin College .... WA .. 518
Everett Community College .... WA .. 519
Grays Harbor College .... WA .. 520
Highline Community College .... WA .. 520
Lower Columbia College .... WA .. 521
North Seattle Community College .... WA .. 522
Olympic College .... WA .. 521
Peninsula College .... WA .. 522
Pierce College District .... WA .. 522
Seattle Central Community College .... WA .. 522
Shoreline Community College .... WA .. 523
Skagit Valley College .... WA .. 523
Spokane Community College .... WA .. 518
Tacoma Community College .... WA .. 524
Walla Walla Community College .... WA .. 524
Wenatchee Valley College .... WA .. 525
Whatcom Community College .... WA .. 525
Yakima Valley Community College .... WA .. 525
Blue Ridge Community and Technical College .... WV .. 527
Bluefield State College .... WV .. 529
Davis & Elkins College .... WV .. 526
Fairmont State University .... WV .. 529
Kanawha Valley Community & Technical College .... WV .. 528
Marshall University .... WV .. 529
Southern West Virginia Community and Technical College .... WV .. 528
West Virginia Northern Community College .... WV .. 528
West Virginia University at Parkersburg ... WV .. 530
Blackhawk Technical College .... WI ... 539
Cardinal Stritch University .... WI ... 532
Chippewa Valley Technical College .... WI ... 539
College of Menominee Nation .... WI ... 532
Fox Valley Technical College .... WI ... 539
Gateway Technical College .... WI ... 540
Herzing University .... WI ... 533
Lakeshore Technical College .... WI ... 540
Madison Area Technical College .... WI ... 540
Mid-State Technical College .... WI ... 540
Milwaukee Area Technical College .... WI ... 540
Moraine Park Technical College .... WI ... 540
Nicolet Area Technical College .... WI ... 540
Northcentral Technical College .... WI ... 541
Northeast Wisconsin Technical College .... WI ... 541
Southwest Wisconsin Technical College .. WI ... 541
Waukesha County Technical College .... WI ... 541
Western Technical College .... WI ... 541
Wisconsin Indianhead Technical College . WI ... 541
Casper College .... WY .. 542
Central Wyoming College .... WY .. 542
Laramie County Community College .... WY .. 543
Northern Wyoming Community College District .... WY .. 543
Northwest College .... WY .. 543

ANEST: Council on Accreditation of Nurse Anesthesia Educational Programs: nurse anesthesia (C,M,D)

Samford University ... AL ... 6
University of Alabama at Birmingham ... AL ... 8
Arkansas State University-Jonesboro ... AR ... 19
California State University-Fullerton ... CA ... 33
Loma Linda University ... CA ... 51
National University ... CA ... 55
Samuel Merritt University ... CA ... 61
University of Southern California ... CA ... 74
Central Connecticut State University ... CT ... 87
Fairfield University ... CT ... 89
Georgetown University ... DC ... 95
Adventist University of Health Sciences ... FL ... 97
Barry University ... FL ... 98
Bay Medical Center ... FL ... 99
Florida Gulf Coast University ... FL ... 115
Florida International University ... FL ... 115
University of Miami ... FL ... 118
University of North Florida ... FL ... 116
University of South Florida ... FL ... 116
Wolford College ... FL ... 119
Georgia Regents University ... GA ... 126
DePaul University ... IL ... 143
Millikin University ... IL ... 153
Rosalind Franklin University of Medicine & Science ... IL ... 157
Rush University ... IL ... 157
Southern Illinois University Edwardsville ... IL ... 159
University of Iowa ... IA ... 175
Newman University ... KS ... 189
Murray State University ... KY ... 198
Louisiana State University Health Sciences Center-New Orleans ... LA ... 205
Our Lady of the Lake College ... LA ... 206
University of New England ... ME ... 213
Uniformed Services University of the Health Sciences ... MD ... 545
University of Maryland Baltimore ... MD ... 219
Boston College ... MA ... 224
Northeastern University ... MA ... 235
Michigan State University ... MI ... 246
Oakland University ... MI ... 248
University of Detroit Mercy ... MI ... 250
University of Michigan-Flint ... MI ... 251
Wayne State University ... MI ... 252
Saint Mary's University of Minnesota ... MN ... 264
University of Minnesota-Twin Cities ... MN ... 264
University of Southern Mississippi ... MS ... 270
Goldfarb School of Nursing at Barnes-Jewish College ... MO ... 274
Missouri State University ... MO ... 278
University of Missouri - Kansas City ... MO ... 283
Webster University ... MO ... 284
Bryan College of Health Sciences ... NE ... 288
Clarkson College ... NE ... 288
Rutgers the State University of New Jersey Newark Campus ... NJ ... 306
Albany Medical College ... NY ... 313
Columbia University in the City of New York ... NY ... 321
State University of New York Health Science Center at Brooklyn ... NY ... 342
University at Buffalo-SUNY ... NY ... 341
Duke University ... NC ... 354
East Carolina University ... NC ... 367
University of North Carolina at Charlotte ... NC ... 368
University of North Carolina at Greensboro ... NC ... 369
Wake Forest University ... NC ... 370
Western Carolina University ... NC ... 369
University of North Dakota Main Campus ... ND ... 371
Case Western Reserve University ... OH ... 375
Lourdes University ... OH ... 383
Otterbein University ... OH ... 387
University of Akron, Main Campus, The ... OH ... 390
University of Cincinnati Main Campus ... OH ... 390
Youngstown State University ... OH ... 394
Oregon Health & Science University ... OR ... 405
Bloomsburg University of Pennsylvania ... PA ... 427
Drexel University ... PA ... 415
Gannon University ... PA ... 416
La Roche College ... PA ... 420
La Salle University ... PA ... 420
Saint Joseph's University ... PA ... 432
Saint Vincent College ... PA ... 432
Thomas Jefferson University ... PA ... 434
University of Pennsylvania ... PA ... 435
University of Pittsburgh ... PA ... 435
University of Scranton, The ... PA ... 436
Villanova University ... PA ... 436
York College of Pennsylvania ... PA ... 438
Inter American University of Puerto Rico Arecibo Campus ... PR ... 549
University of Puerto Rico-Medical Sciences Campus ... PR ... 554
Medical University of South Carolina ... SC ... 445
University of South Carolina Columbia ... SC ... 447
Mount Marty College ... SD ... 450
Lincoln Memorial University ... TN ... 456
Middle Tennessee School of Anesthesia ... TN ... 457
Union University ... TN ... 462
University of Tennessee at Chattanooga ... TN ... 463
University of Tennessee, Knoxville ... TN ... 463
Baylor College of Medicine ... TX ... 467
Texas Christian University ... TX ... 484
Texas Wesleyan University ... TX ... 488
University of Texas Health Science Center at Houston (UTHealth), The ... TX ... 492
Westminster College ... UT ... 498
Old Dominion University ... VA ... 507
Virginia Commonwealth University ... VA ... 511
Gonzaga University ... WA ... 520
Marshall University ... WV ... 529
University of Wisconsin-La Crosse ... WI ... 536

ARCPA: Accreditation Review Commission on Education for the Physician Assistant: physician assisting programs (C,A,B,M)

University of Alabama at Birmingham ... AL ... 8
University of South Alabama ... AL ... 9
#Northern Arizona University ... AZ ... 16
Harding University Main Campus ... AR ... 21
#University of Arkansas for Medical Sciences ... AR ... 24
Loma Linda University ... CA ... 51
#Riverside City College ... CA ... 61
Samuel Merritt University ... CA ... 61
#San Joaquin Valley College, Inc. - Visalia ... CA ... 63
Stanford University ... CA ... 68
Touro University California ... CA ... 69
University of California-Davis ... CA ... 70
University of Southern California ... CA ... 74
Western University of Health Sciences ... CA ... 76
Red Rocks Community College ... CO ... 84
University of Colorado DenverIAnschutz Medical Campus ... CO ... 86
Quinnipiac University ... CT ... 91
#University of Bridgeport ... CT ... 91
Yale University ... CT ... 93
George Washington University ... DC ... 95
#Howard University ... DC ... 95
Barry University ... FL ... 98
Keiser University ... FL ... 108
Miami Dade College ... FL ... 109
Nova Southeastern University ... FL ... 109
University of Florida ... FL ... 116
Emory University ... GA ... 124
Georgia Regents University ... GA ... 126
Mercer University ... GA ... 128
South University ... GA ... 131
Idaho State University ... ID ... 138
#City Colleges of Chicago Malcolm X College ... IL ... 142
Midwestern University ... IL ... 153
Northwestern University ... IL ... 155
Rosalind Franklin University of Medicine & Science ... IL ... 157
#Rush University ... IL ... 157
Southern Illinois University Carbondale ... IL ... 159
Butler University ... IN ... 164
#Indiana State University ... IN ... 167
#Indiana University-Purdue University Indianapolis ... IN ... 168
University of Saint Francis ... IN ... 174
Des Moines University ... IA ... 177
University of Iowa ... IA ... 175
Wichita State University ... KS ... 191
University of Kentucky ... KY ... 200
University of the Cumberlands ... KY ... 200
#Louisiana State University Health Sciences Center-New Orleans ... LA ... 205
Louisiana State University in Shreveport ... LA ... 205
#Our Lady of the Lake College ... LA ... 206
University of New England ... ME ... 213
Anne Arundel Community College ... MD ... 213
Towson University ... MD ... 220
University of Maryland Eastern Shore ... MD ... 219
#Bay Path College ... MA ... 222
MCPHS University ... MA ... 233
Northeastern University ... MA ... 235
Springfield College ... MA ... 236
#Tufts University ... MA ... 237
Central Michigan University ... MI ... 240
Grand Valley State University ... MI ... 243
University of Detroit Mercy ... MI ... 250
Wayne State University ... MI ... 252
Western Michigan University ... MI ... 252
Augsburg College ... MN ... 253
#Bethel University ... MN ... 253
#St. Catherine University ... MN ... 263
#Mississippi College ... MS ... 268
Missouri State University ... MO ... 278
Saint Louis University ... MO ... 281
Rocky Mountain College ... MT ... 288
Union College ... NE ... 292
University of Nebraska Medical Center ... NE ... 292
Franklin Pierce University ... NH ... 296
Seton Hall University ... NJ ... 307
#University of New Mexico Main Campus ... NM ... 312
Albany Medical College ... NY ... 313
City University of New York The City College ... NY ... 317
City University of New York York College ... NY ... 319
#Clarkson University ... NY ... 320
Daemen College ... NY ... 322
D'Youville College ... NY ... 323
Hofstra University ... NY ... 326
Le Moyne College ... NY ... 328
Mercy College ... NY ... 330
New York Institute of Technology ... NY ... 333
Pace University ... NY ... 335
Rochester Institute of Technology ... NY ... 337
St. John's University ... NY ... 339
State University of New York at Stony Brook ... NY ... 342
State University of New York Health Science Center at Brooklyn ... NY ... 342
State University of New York Upstate Medical University ... NY ... 342
Touro College ... NY ... 348
Wagner College ... NY ... 350
#Campbell University ... NC ... 352
Duke University ... NC ... 354
East Carolina University ... NC ... 367
#Elon University ... NC ... 354
Methodist University ... NC ... 356
Wake Forest University ... NC ... 370
Wingate University ... NC ... 370
University of North Dakota Main Campus ... ND ... 371
#Baldwin Wallace University ... OH ... 374
Cleveland State University ... OH ... 377
Cuyahoga Community College ... OH ... 378
Kettering College ... OH ... 382
Marietta College ... OH ... 383
#Ohio Dominican University ... OH ... 386
University of Findlay, The ... OH ... 391
University of Mount Union ... OH ... 391
University of Toledo ... OH ... 392
Oregon Health & Science University ... OR ... 405
Pacific University ... OR ... 407
Arcadia University ... PA ... 409
#Chatham University ... PA ... 412
DeSales University ... PA ... 414
Drexel University ... PA ... 415
Duquesne University ... PA ... 415
Gannon University ... PA ... 416
King's College ... PA ... 419
Lock Haven University ... PA ... 429
Marywood University ... PA ... 423
#Misericordia University ... PA ... 424
Pennsylvania College of Technology ... PA ... 427
Philadelphia College of Osteopathic Medicine ... PA ... 430
Philadelphia University ... PA ... 430
Saint Francis University ... PA ... 432
Salus University ... PA ... 433
Seton Hill University ... PA ... 433
University of Pittsburgh ... PA ... 435
#University of the Sciences in Philadelphia ... PA ... 435
Medical University of South Carolina ... SC ... 445
University of South Dakota, The ... SD ... 451
#Bethel University ... TN ... 453
#Christian Brothers University ... TN ... 453
Lincoln Memorial University ... TN ... 456
South College ... TN ... 458
Trevecca Nazarene University ... TN ... 462
Baylor College of Medicine ... TX ... 467
Texas Tech University ... TX ... 487
University of North Texas Health Science Center at Fort Worth ... TX ... 490
University of Texas Health Science Center at San Antonio ... TX ... 493
University of Texas Medical Branch, The ... TX ... 493
University of Texas - Pan American ... TX ... 492
University of Texas Southwestern Medical Center ... TX ... 493
University of Utah, The ... UT ... 496
Eastern Virginia Medical School ... VA ... 504
James Madison University ... VA ... 506
Jefferson College of Health Sciences ... VA ... 506
Shenandoah University ... VA ... 509
University of Washington ... WA ... 524
#Alderson Broaddus University ... WV ... 526
#University of Charleston ... WV ... 527
#West Liberty University ... WV ... 530
#Carroll University ... WI ... 532
#Concordia University Wisconsin ... WI ... 532
Marquette University ... WI ... 534
University of Wisconsin-La Crosse ... WI ... 536
University of Wisconsin-Madison ... WI ... 536

ART: National Association of Schools of Art and Design: art and design (C,A,B,M,D)

Alabama State University ... AL ... 1
Auburn University ... AL ... 1
Jacksonville State University ... AL ... 4
University of Alabama at Birmingham ... AL ... 8
University of Alabama in Huntsville ... AL ... 8
University of Alabama, The ... AL ... 8
University of Montevallo ... AL ... 9
University of North Alabama ... AL ... 9
University of Alaska Anchorage ... AK ... 10
Arizona State University ... AZ ... 11
University of Arizona ... AZ ... 18
Arkansas State University-Jonesboro ... AR ... 19
University of Arkansas at Little Rock ... AR ... 24
University of Arkansas at Pine Bluff ... AR ... 24
University of Central Arkansas ... AR ... 25
Academy of Art University ... CA ... 26
American Film Institute Conservatory ... CA ... 27
Art Center College of Design ... CA ... 28
Azusa Pacific University ... CA ... 29
Biola University ... CA ... 29
California College of the Arts ... CA ... 30
California Institute of the Arts ... CA ... 31
California Polytechnic State University-San Luis Obispo ... CA ... 32
California State Polytechnic University-Pomona ... CA ... 32
California State University-Chico ... CA ... 33
California State University-Fullerton ... CA ... 33
California State University-Long Beach ... CA ... 33
California State University-Los Angeles ... CA ... 34
California State University-Northridge ... CA ... 34
California State University-Sacramento ... CA ... 34
California State University-San Bernardino ... CA ... 34
California State University-Stanislaus ... CA ... 35
Columbia College Hollywood ... CA ... 41
Fashion Institute of Design and Merchandising-Los Angeles ... CA ... 44
Humboldt State University ... CA ... 35
Laguna College of Art & Design ... CA ... 50
Loyola Marymount University ... CA ... 53
New York Film Academy, Los Angeles ... CA ... 56
Otis College of Art and Design ... CA ... 57
San Diego State University ... CA ... 35
San Francisco Art Institute ... CA ... 62
San Francisco State University ... CA ... 35
San Jose State University ... CA ... 36
Sonoma State University ... CA ... 36
University of the Pacific ... CA ... 73
Woodbury University ... CA ... 76
Metropolitan State University of Denver ... CO ... 83
Rocky Mountain College of Art & Design ... CO ... 85
University of Denver ... CO ... 86
University of Northern Colorado ... CO ... 86
Lyme Academy College of Fine Arts ... CT ... 90
University of Bridgeport ... CT ... 91
University of Connecticut ... CT ... 92
University of Hartford ... CT ... 92
Delaware College of Art and Design ... DE ... 93
Corcoran College of Art and Design ... DC ... 95
Howard University ... DC ... 95
Florida International University ... FL ... 115
Florida State University ... FL ... 115
Miami Dade College ... FL ... 109
Ringling College of Art and Design ... FL ... 111
University of Florida ... FL ... 116
University of South Florida ... FL ... 116
Columbus State University ... GA ... 123
Georgia Institute of Technology ... GA ... 125
Georgia Regents University ... GA ... 126
Georgia Southern University ... GA ... 126
Georgia State University ... GA ... 126
Kennesaw State University ... GA ... 127
University of Georgia ... GA ... 133
University of West Georgia ... GA ... 133
Valdosta State University ... GA ... 134
Boise State University ... ID ... 137
University of Idaho ... ID ... 139
Bradley University ... IL ... 140
College of DuPage ... IL ... 142
Eastern Illinois University ... IL ... 144
Illinois State University ... IL ... 147
Northeastern Illinois University ... IL ... 154
Northern Illinois University ... IL ... 154
School of the Art Institute of Chicago ... IL ... 158
Southern Illinois University Carbondale ... IL ... 159
University of Illinois at Chicago ... IL ... 161
University of Illinois at Urbana-Champaign ... IL ... 162
Western Illinois University ... IL ... 162
Ball State University ... IN ... 164
Indiana State University ... IN ... 167
Indiana University Bloomington ... IN ... 167
Indiana University-Purdue University Indianapolis ... IN ... 168
Purdue University Main Campus ... IN ... 171
Saint Mary's College ... IN ... 172
University of Indianapolis ... IN ... 173
University of Notre Dame ... IN ... 174
University of Saint Francis ... IN ... 174
University of Southern Indiana ... IN ... 174
Vincennes University ... IN ... 174
Drake University ... IA ... 177
Iowa State University ... IA ... 175
Emporia State University ... KS ... 186
Kansas State University ... KS ... 188
University of Kansas Main Campus ... KS ... 190
Washburn University ... KS ... 191
Wichita State University ... KS ... 191
Murray State University ... KY ... 198
University of Kentucky ... KY ... 200
Western Kentucky University ... KY ... 200
Louisiana State University and Agricultural and Mechanical College ... LA ... 204
Louisiana Tech University ... LA ... 207

McNeese State University ... LA ... 207
Nicholls State University ... LA ... 208
Northwestern State University ... LA ... 208
Southeastern Louisiana University ... LA ... 208
Southern University and A&M College ... LA ... 206
University of Louisiana at Lafayette ... LA ... 208
University of New Orleans ... LA ... 205
Maine College of Art ... ME .. 210
University of Maine ... ME .. 212
University of Southern Maine ... ME .. 212
Maryland Institute College of Art ... MD .. 216
Bridgewater State University ... MA .. 229
Endicott College ... MA .. 226
Lesley University ... MA .. 228
Massachusetts College of Art and Design MA .. 230
Montserrat College of Art ... MA .. 234
Mount Ida College ... MA .. 234
Salem State University ... MA .. 230
School of the Museum of Fine Arts-Boston ... MA .. 236
Suffolk University ... MA .. 237
University of Massachusetts Dartmouth ... MA .. 229
University of Massachusetts Lowell ... MA .. 229
Wentworth Institute of Technology ... MA .. 237
Central Michigan University ... MI 240
College for Creative Studies ... MI 241
Cranbrook Academy of Art ... MI 241
Ferris State University ... MI 242
Grand Rapids Community College ... MI 243
Grand Valley State University ... MI 243
Hope College ... MI 244
Lawrence Technological University ... MI 245
Siena Heights University ... MI 250
University of Michigan-Ann Arbor ... MI 251
Western Michigan University ... MI 252
Minneapolis College of Art Design ... MN .. 257
Minnesota State University Moorhead ... MN .. 259
Minnesota State University, Mankato ... MN .. 259
Normandale Community College ... MN .. 260
St. Cloud State University ... MN .. 261
Belhaven University ... MS .. 266
Delta State University ... MS .. 266
Jackson State University ... MS .. 267
Mississippi State University ... MS .. 268
Mississippi University for Women ... MS .. 268
Mississippi Valley State University ... MS .. 269
University of Mississippi ... MS .. 270
University of Southern Mississippi ... MS .. 270
Kansas City Art Institute ... MO .. 275
Maryville University of Saint Louis ... MO .. 276
Saint Louis University ... MO .. 281
University of Central Missouri ... MO .. 283
Washington University in St. Louis ... MO .. 284
Montana State University ... MT .. 287
Montana State University - Billings ... MT .. 287
University of Montana - Missoula, The ... MT .. 286
University of Nebraska at Omaha ... NE .. 293
University of Nebraska - Lincoln ... NE .. 292
Wayne State College ... NE .. 291
University of Nevada, Las Vegas ... NV .. 294
New Hampshire Institute of Art ... NH .. 297
Plymouth State University ... NH .. 298
Kean University ... NJ ... 302
Montclair State University ... NJ ... 303
New Jersey City University ... NJ ... 303
Rowan University ... NJ ... 305
William Paterson University of New Jersey ... NJ ... 308
Institute of American Indian Arts ... NM .. 309
Alfred University ... NY ... 313
College of Saint Rose, The ... NY ... 321
Cooper Union ... NY ... 321
Fashion Institute of Technology ... NY ... 324
Hartwick College ... NY ... 325
New School, The ... NY ... 332
New York Academy of Art ... NY ... 333
New York School of Interior Design ... NY ... 334
Pratt Institute ... NY ... 336
Purchase College, State University of New York ... NY ... 344
Roberts Wesleyan College ... NY ... 337
Rochester Institute of Technology ... NY ... 337
Sage Colleges, The ... NY ... 338
St. John's University ... NY ... 339
School of Visual Arts ... NY ... 340
Skidmore College ... NY ... 341
Sotheby's Institute of Art ... NY ... 341
State University of New York at New Paltz NY ... 342
State University of New York College at Buffalo ... NY ... 343
State University of New York College at Oswego ... NY ... 344
Syracuse University Main Campus ... NY ... 347
Appalachian State University ... NC .. 367
East Carolina University ... NC .. 367
North Carolina State University ... NC .. 368
University of North Carolina at Pembroke NC .. 369
Western Carolina University ... NC .. 369
North Dakota State University Main Campus ... ND .. 371
University of North Dakota Main Campus . ND .. 371
Art Academy of Cincinnati ... OH .. 373
Bowling Green State University ... OH .. 374
Central State University ... OH .. 376
Cleveland Institute of Art ... OH .. 377
Columbus College of Art & Design ... OH .. 378
Kent State University Main Campus ... OH .. 382
Lorain County Community College ... OH .. 383
Miami University ... OH .. 384
Ohio State University Main Campus, The . OH .. 386
Sinclair Community College ... OH .. 388
University of Akron, Main Campus, The ... OH .. 390
University of Cincinnati-Blue Ash College . OH .. 391
University of Cincinnati Main Campus ... OH .. 390
University of Dayton ... OH .. 391
University of Toledo ... OH .. 392
Youngstown State University ... OH .. 394
Oregon College of Art and Craft ... OR .. 405
Pacific Northwest College of Art ... OR .. 406
University of Oregon ... OR .. 406
Arcadia University ... PA ... 409
Bloomsburg University of Pennsylvania ... PA ... 427
Bucks County Community College ... PA ... 411
California University of Pennsylvania ... PA ... 428
Clarion University of Pennsylvania ... PA ... 428
Drexel University ... PA ... 415
Edinboro University of Pennsylvania ... PA ... 428
Indiana University of Pennsylvania ... PA ... 428
Kutztown University of Pennsylvania ... PA ... 429
La Roche College ... PA ... 420
Marywood University ... PA ... 423
Messiah College ... PA ... 423
Millersville University of Pennsylvania ... PA ... 429
Moore College of Art and Design ... PA ... 424
Penn State University Park ... PA ... 426
Pennsylvania Academy of the Fine Arts ... PA ... 426
Pennsylvania College of Art & Design ... PA ... 427
Philadelphia University ... PA ... 430
Slippery Rock University of Pennsylvania . PA ... 429
Temple University ... PA ... 433
University of the Arts, The ... PA ... 435
West Chester University of Pennsylvania . PA ... 430
Escuela de Artes Plasticas de Puerto Rico ... PR ... 548
Rhode Island College ... RI 439
Rhode Island School of Design ... RI 440
Salve Regina University ... RI 440
Anderson University ... SC ... 441
Benedict College ... SC ... 441
Clemson University ... SC ... 442
Coastal Carolina University ... SC ... 442
Columbia College ... SC ... 443
Converse College ... SC ... 443
Francis Marion University ... SC ... 444
Lander University ... SC ... 444
South Carolina State University ... SC ... 446
University of South Carolina Columbia ... SC ... 447
University of South Carolina Upstate ... SC ... 448
Winthrop University ... SC ... 449
University of South Dakota, The ... SD ... 451
Austin Peay State University ... TN ... 459
Belmont University ... TN ... 453
Carson-Newman University ... TN ... 453
East Tennessee State University ... TN ... 459
Memphis College of Art ... TN ... 456
Middle Tennessee State University ... TN ... 459
Tennessee State University ... TN ... 459
Tennessee Technological University ... TN ... 460
Union University ... TN ... 462
University of Memphis, The ... TN ... 460
University of Tennessee at Chattanooga .. TN ... 463
University of Tennessee, Knoxville ... TN ... 463
Watkins College of Art, Design & Film ... TN ... 464
Brookhaven College ... TX ... 470
Del Mar College ... TX ... 471
Midwestern State University ... TX ... 476
Southern Methodist University ... TX ... 481
Stephen F. Austin State University ... TX ... 482
Texas A & M University - Commerce ... TX ... 483
Texas Christian University ... TX ... 484
Texas Tech University ... TX ... 487
University of North Texas ... TX ... 490
University of Texas at Arlington, The ... TX ... 491
University of Texas at Austin ... TX ... 491
University of Texas at San Antonio ... TX ... 492
University of Texas of the Permian Basin . TX ... 493
Brigham Young University ... UT ... 495
Southern Utah University ... UT ... 497
Weber State University ... UT ... 497
George Mason University ... VA ... 505
James Madison University ... VA ... 506
Old Dominion University ... VA ... 507
Virginia Commonwealth University ... VA ... 511
Virginia Polytechnic Institute and State University ... VA ... 515
Virginia State University ... VA ... 515
Cornish College of the Arts ... WA ... 518
Western Washington University ... WA ... 525
West Virginia University ... WV ... 530
Milwaukee Institute of Art & Design ... WI ... 534
University of Wisconsin-Madison ... WI ... 536
University of Wisconsin-Stevens Point ... WI ... 538
University of Wisconsin-Stout ... WI ... 538
University of Wisconsin-Whitewater ... WI ... 538
Casper College ... WY ... 542

AUD: American Speech-Language-Hearing Association: audiology (D)

#Auburn University ... AL ... 1
University of South Alabama ... AL ... 9
Arizona State University ... AZ ... 11
University of Arizona ... AZ ... 18
University of Arkansas at Little Rock ... AR ... 24
San Diego State University ... CA ... 35
University of California-San Diego ... CA ... 71
University of Colorado Boulder ... CO ... 85
University of Northern Colorado ... CO ... 86
University of Connecticut ... CT ... 92
Gallaudet University ... DC ... 95
Nova Southeastern University ... FL ... 109
University of Florida ... FL ... 116
University of South Florida ... FL ... 116
Idaho State University ... ID ... 138
Illinois State University ... IL ... 147
Northern Illinois University ... IL ... 154
Northwestern University ... IL ... 155
Rush University ... IL ... 157
University of Illinois at Urbana-Champaign IL ... 162
Ball State University ... IN ... 164
Indiana University Bloomington ... IN ... 167
Purdue University Main Campus ... IN ... 171
University of Iowa ... IA ... 175
University of Kansas Main Campus ... KS ... 190
Wichita State University ... KS ... 191
University of Louisville ... KY ... 200
Louisiana State University Health Sciences Center-New Orleans ... LA ... 205
Louisiana Tech University ... LA ... 207
Towson University ... MD ... 220
University of Maryland College Park ... MD .. 219
Northeastern University ... MA ... 235
University of Massachusetts ... MA ... 228
Central Michigan University ... MI ... 240
Wayne State University ... MI ... 252
Western Michigan University ... MI ... 252
University of Minnesota-Twin Cities ... MN ... 264
University of Southern Mississippi ... MS ... 270
Missouri State University ... MO ... 278
Washington University in St. Louis ... MO ... 284
University of Nebraska - Lincoln ... NE ... 292
Montclair State University ... NJ ... 303
Richard Stockton College of New Jersey, The ... NJ ... 305
Adelphi University ... NY ... 313
City University of New York Brooklyn College ... NY ... 317
City University of New York Hunter College ... NY ... 318
Hofstra University ... NY ... 326
St. John's University ... NY ... 339
Syracuse University Main Campus ... NY ... 347
University at Buffalo-SUNY ... NY ... 341
East Carolina University ... NC ... 367
University of North Carolina at Chapel Hill NC .. 368
Kent State University Main Campus ... OH ... 382
Ohio State University Main Campus, The . OH ... 386
Ohio University Main Campus ... OH ... 387
University of Akron, Main Campus, The ... OH ... 390
University of Cincinnati Main Campus ... OH ... 390
@Pacific University ... OR ... 407
Bloomsburg University of Pennsylvania ... PA ... 427
Salus University ... PA ... 433
University of Pittsburgh ... PA ... 435
University of Puerto Rico-Medical Sciences Campus ... PR ... 554
University of South Dakota, The ... SD ... 451
East Tennessee State University ... TN ... 459
University of Memphis, The ... TN ... 460
University of Tennessee, Knoxville ... TN ... 463
Vanderbilt University ... TN ... 463
Lamar University ... TX ... 486
Texas Tech University Health Sciences Center ... TX ... 487
University of North Texas ... TX ... 490
University of Texas at Austin ... TX ... 491
University of Texas at Dallas, The ... TX ... 491
University of Utah, The ... UT ... 496
Utah State University ... UT ... 497
James Madison University ... VA ... 506
University of Washington ... WA ... 524
West Virginia University ... WV ... 530
University of Wisconsin-Madison ... WI ... 536
University of Wisconsin-Stevens Point ... WI ... 538

BBT: Commission on Accreditation of Allied Health Education Programs: blood bank technology (C,M)

Rush University ... IL ... 157
Johns Hopkins University ... MD ... 215
University of Cincinnati Main Campus ... OH ... 390
University of Texas Health Science Center at San Antonio ... TX ... 493
University of Texas Medical Branch, The . TX ... 493

BI: Association for Biblical Higher Education: bible college education (C, A,B,M,FP,D)

Heritage Christian University ... AL ... 4
Huntsville Bible College ... AL ... 4
Selma University ... AL ... 6
Southeastern Bible College ... AL ... 7
Alaska Bible College ... AK ... 10
Ecclesia College ... AR ... 21
@American Evangelical University ... CA ... 27
Bethesda University of California ... CA ... 29
@Eternity Bible College ... CA ... 43
Grace Mission University ... CA ... 46
Hope International University ... CA ... 47
#Horizon University ... CA ... 47
International Reformed University and Seminary ... CA ... 48
King's University, The ... CA ... 50
Life Pacific College ... CA ... 50
@Methodist Theological Seminary in America ... CA ... 54
Olivet University ... CA ... 57
Presbyterian Theological Seminary in America ... CA ... 60
SUM Bible College and Theological Seminary ... CA ... 69
William Jessup University ... CA ... 76
World Mission University ... CA ... 77
Nazarene Bible College ... CO ... 83
Hobe Sound Bible College ... FL ... 106
Robert E. Webber Institute for Worship Studies, The ... FL ... 111
South Florida Bible College ... FL ... 113
Trinity College of Florida ... FL ... 117
Beulah Heights University ... GA .. 121
Carver College ... GA .. 122
Toccoa Falls College ... GA .. 133
Boise Bible College ... ID ... 137
Lincoln Christian University ... IL ... 151
Moody Bible Institute ... IL ... 153
Crossroads Bible College ... IN ... 165
Emmaus Bible College ... IA ... 178
Faith Baptist Bible College and Seminary IA ... 178
Barclay College ... KS ... 184
@Kansas City College and Bible School ... KS ... 187
Manhattan Christian College ... KS ... 188
Clear Creek Baptist Bible College ... KY ... 193
Kentucky Mountain Bible College ... KY ... 196
Louisville Bible College ... KY ... 197
@Simmons College of Kentucky ... KY ... 199
@New England Bible College ... ME ... 211
Northpoint Bible College ... MA .. 235
Grace Bible College ... MI ... 243
Great Lakes Christian College ... MI ... 243
Kuyper College ... MI ... 245
@Bethany College of Missions ... MN ... 253
Crossroads College ... MN ... 255
Oak Hills Christian College ... MN ... 263
Southeastern Baptist College ... MS ... 269
Baptist Bible College ... MO ... 271
@Brookes Bible Institute ... MO ... 271
Calvary Bible College and Theological Seminary ... MO ... 271
Central Christian College of the Bible ... MO ... 272
@Heartland Christian College ... MO ... 275
Midwest University ... MO ... 277
Ozark Christian College ... MO ... 279
Saint Louis Christian College ... MO ... 280
Montana Bible College ... MT ... 286
Grace University ... NE ... 289
Nebraska Christian College ... NE ... 290
Pillar College ... NJ ... 304
Davis College ... NY ... 322
Carolina Christian College ... NC ... 353
Carolina College of Biblical Studies ... NC ... 353
Grace College of Divinity ... NC ... 354
Laurel University ... NC ... 355
@Native American Bible College ... NC ... 357
#Trinity Bible College ... ND ... 373
Allegheny Wesleyan College ... OH ... 373
Cincinnati Christian University ... OH ... 376
God's Bible School and College ... OH ... 380
Ohio Christian University ... OH ... 385
Rosedale Bible College ... OH ... 388
Tri-State Bible College ... OH ... 389
@Valor Christian College ... OH ... 392
Family of Faith College ... OK ... 395
Multnomah University ... OR ... 404
New Hope Christian College ... OR ... 405
Baptist Bible College and Seminary ... PA ... 410
Cairn University ... PA ... 411
Lancaster Bible College ... PA ... 421
Universidad Pentecostal Mizpa ... PR ... 553
Universidad Teologica Del Caribe ... PR ... 553
Columbia International University ... SC ... 443
#W.L. Bonner College ... SC ... 449
@All Saints Bible College ... TN ... 452
American Baptist College ... TN ... 452
Johnson University ... TN ... 455
@Mid-South Christian College ... TN ... 457
Welch College ... TN ... 464
Williamson Christian College ... TN ... 464

Arlington Baptist College TX ... 466
Baptist University of the Americas TX ... 467
B.H. Carroll Theological Institute TX ... 467
College of Biblical Studies-Houston TX ... 468
Dallas Christian College TX ... 470
Rio Grande Bible Institute TX ... 479
Bethel College VA ... 502
Washington Baptist University VA ... 516
Appalachian Bible College WV .. 526

BUS: AACSB-The Association to Advance Collegiate Schools of Business: business and management (B,M,D)

Auburn University AL ... 1
Auburn University at Montgomery AL ... 2
Jacksonville State University AL ... 4
Samford University AL ... 6
Tuskegee University AL ... 8
University of Alabama at Birmingham AL ... 8
University of Alabama in Huntsville AL ... 8
University of Alabama, The AL ... 8
University of Montevallo AL ... 9
University of South Alabama AL ... 9
University of Alaska Anchorage AK ... 10
University of Alaska Fairbanks AK ... 10
Arizona State University AZ ... 11
Northern Arizona University AZ ... 16
Thunderbird School of Global Management AZ ... 18
University of Arizona AZ ... 18
Arkansas State University-Jonesboro AR ... 19
Arkansas Tech University AR ... 20
Henderson State University AR ... 21
Ouachita Baptist University AR ... 22
Southern Arkansas University AR ... 23
University of Arkansas at Fort Smith AR ... 24
University of Arkansas at Little Rock AR ... 24
University of Arkansas Main Campus AR ... 23
University of Central Arkansas AR ... 25
California Polytechnic State University-San Luis Obispo CA ... 32
California State Polytechnic University-Pomona CA ... 32
California State University-Bakersfield CA ... 32
California State University-Chico CA ... 33
California State University-East Bay CA ... 33
California State University-Fresno CA ... 33
California State University-Fullerton CA ... 33
California State University-Long Beach CA ... 33
California State University-Los Angeles CA ... 34
California State University-Northridge CA ... 34
California State University-Sacramento CA ... 34
California State University-San Bernardino CA ... 34
California State University-Stanislaus CA ... 35
Chapman University CA ... 38
Claremont Graduate University CA ... 39
Loyola Marymount University CA ... 53
Naval Postgraduate School CA ... 544
Pepperdine University CA ... 58
San Diego State University CA ... 35
San Francisco State University CA ... 35
San Jose State University CA ... 36
Santa Clara University CA ... 64
Sonoma State University CA ... 36
Stanford University CA ... 68
University of California-Berkeley CA ... 70
University of California-Davis CA ... 70
University of California-Irvine CA ... 71
University of California-Los Angeles CA ... 71
University of California-Riverside CA ... 71
University of California-San Diego CA ... 71
University of San Diego CA ... 73
University of San Francisco CA ... 73
University of Southern California CA ... 74
University of the Pacific CA ... 73
Colorado State University CO ... 80
Colorado State University-Pueblo CO ... 80
Fort Lewis College CO ... 81
United States Air Force Academy CO .. 545
University of Colorado Boulder CO ... 85
University of Colorado Colorado Springs CO ... 85
University of Colorado Denver|Anschutz Medical Campus CO ... 86
University of Denver CO ... 86
University of Northern Colorado CO ... 86
Fairfield University CT ... 89
Quinnipiac University CT ... 91
Sacred Heart University CT ... 91
United States Coast Guard Academy CT ... 545
University of Connecticut CT ... 92
University of Hartford CT ... 92
Yale University CT ... 93
Delaware State University DE ... 93
University of Delaware DE ... 94
American University DC ... 94
George Washington University DC ... 95
Georgetown University DC ... 95
Howard University DC ... 95
Barry University FL ... 98
Florida Atlantic University FL ... 114
Florida Gulf Coast University FL ... 115
Florida International University FL ... 115
Florida Southern College FL ... 105
Florida State University FL ... 115
Jacksonville University FL ... 107
Rollins College FL ... 111
Stetson University FL ... 117
University of Central Florida FL ... 115
University of Florida FL ... 116
University of Miami FL ... 118
University of North Florida FL ... 116
University of South Florida FL ... 116
University of South Florida St. Petersburg FL ... 116
University of Tampa FL ... 118
University of West Florida FL ... 117
Berry College GA .. 121
Clark Atlanta University GA .. 122
Clayton State University GA .. 123
Columbus State University GA .. 123
Dalton State College GA .. 123
Emory University GA .. 124
Georgia College & State University GA .. 125
Georgia Institute of Technology GA .. 125
Georgia Regents University GA .. 126
Georgia Southern University GA .. 126
Georgia Southwestern State University GA .. 126
Georgia State University GA .. 126
Kennesaw State University GA .. 127
Mercer University GA .. 128
Morehouse College GA .. 129
Savannah State University GA .. 131
University of Georgia GA .. 133
University of North Georgia GA .. 133
University of West Georgia GA .. 133
Valdosta State University GA .. 134
University of Hawaii at Hilo HI ... 136
University of Hawaii at Manoa HI ... 136
Boise State University ID ... 137
Idaho State University ID ... 138
University of Idaho ID ... 139
Bradley University IL ... 140
DePaul University IL ... 143
Eastern Illinois University IL ... 144
Illinois Institute of Technology IL ... 147
Illinois State University IL ... 147
Loyola University Chicago IL ... 151
Northern Illinois University IL ... 154
Northwestern University IL ... 155
Southern Illinois University Carbondale IL ... 159
Southern Illinois University Edwardsville IL ... 159
University of Chicago IL ... 161
University of Illinois at Chicago IL ... 161
University of Illinois at Springfield IL ... 161
University of Illinois at Urbana-Champaign IL ... 162
Western Illinois University IL ... 162
Ball State University IN ... 164
Butler University IN ... 164
Indiana State University IN ... 167
Indiana University Bloomington IN ... 167
Indiana University Kokomo IN ... 168
Indiana University Northwest IN ... 168
Indiana University-Purdue University Fort Wayne IN ... 168
Indiana University South Bend IN ... 168
Indiana University Southeast IN ... 168
Purdue University Main Campus IN ... 171
University of Evansville IN ... 173
University of Notre Dame IN ... 174
University of Southern Indiana IN ... 174
Valparaiso University IN ... 174
Drake University IA ... 177
Iowa State University IA ... 175
University of Iowa IA ... 175
University of Northern Iowa IA ... 176
Emporia State University KS ... 186
Kansas State University KS ... 188
Pittsburg State University KS ... 189
University of Kansas Main Campus KS ... 190
Washburn University KS ... 191
Wichita State University KS ... 191
Bellarmine University KY ... 192
Eastern Kentucky University KY ... 193
Morehead State University KY ... 198
Murray State University KY ... 198
Northern Kentucky University KY ... 198
University of Kentucky KY ... 200
University of Louisville KY ... 200
Western Kentucky University KY ... 200
Grambling State University LA ... 207
Louisiana State University and Agricultural and Mechanical College LA ... 204
Louisiana State University in Shreveport LA ... 205
Louisiana Tech University LA ... 207
Loyola University New Orleans LA ... 205
McNeese State University LA ... 207
Nicholls State University LA ... 208
Northwestern State University LA ... 208
Southeastern Louisiana University LA ... 208
Southern University and A&M College LA ... 206
Southern University at New Orleans LA ... 206
Tulane University LA ... 207
University of Louisiana at Lafayette LA ... 208
University of Louisiana at Monroe LA ... 208
University of New Orleans LA ... 205
University of Maine ME .. 212
University of Southern Maine ME .. 212
Frostburg State University MD .. 220
Loyola University Maryland MD .. 216
Morgan State University MD .. 217
Salisbury University MD .. 220
Towson University MD .. 220
University of Baltimore MD .. 221
University of Maryland College Park MD .. 219
University of Maryland Eastern Shore MD .. 219
Babson College MA .. 222
Bentley University MA .. 223
Boston College MA .. 224
Boston University MA .. 224
Brandeis University MA .. 224
Clark University MA .. 225
Harvard University MA .. 227
Massachusetts Institute of Technology MA .. 233
Northeastern University MA .. 235
Simmons College MA .. 236
Stonehill College MA .. 237
Suffolk University MA .. 237
University of Massachusetts MA .. 228
University of Massachusetts Boston MA .. 228
University of Massachusetts Dartmouth MA .. 229
University of Massachusetts Lowell MA .. 229
Western New England University MA .. 238
Worcester Polytechnic Institute MA .. 238
Central Michigan University MI ... 240
Eastern Michigan University MI ... 242
Grand Valley State University MI ... 243
Michigan State University MI ... 246
Michigan Technological University MI ... 247
Northern Michigan University MI ... 248
Oakland University MI ... 248
Saginaw Valley State University MI ... 249
University of Detroit Mercy MI ... 250
University of Michigan-Ann Arbor MI ... 251
University of Michigan-Dearborn MI ... 251
University of Michigan-Flint MI ... 251
Wayne State University MI ... 252
Western Michigan University MI ... 252
Minnesota State University Moorhead MN .. 259
Minnesota State University, Mankato MN .. 259
St. Cloud State University MN .. 261
University of Minnesota Duluth MN .. 264
University of Minnesota-Twin Cities MN .. 264
University of Saint Thomas MN .. 265
Winona State University MN .. 262
Jackson State University MS .. 267
Millsaps College MS .. 267
Mississippi State University MS .. 268
University of Mississippi MS .. 270
University of Southern Mississippi MS .. 270
Drury University MO .. 273
Missouri State University MO .. 278
Missouri University of Science & Technology MO .. 284
Missouri Western State University MO .. 279
Rockhurst University MO .. 280
Saint Louis University MO .. 281
Southeast Missouri State University MO .. 282
Truman State University MO .. 282
University of Central Missouri MO .. 283
University of Missouri - Columbia MO .. 283
University of Missouri - Kansas City MO .. 283
University of Missouri - Saint Louis MO .. 283
Washington University in St. Louis MO .. 284
Montana State University MT .. 287
Montana State University - Billings MT .. 287
University of Montana - Missoula, The MT .. 286
Creighton University NE ... 289
University of Nebraska at Kearney NE ... 292
University of Nebraska at Omaha NE ... 293
University of Nebraska - Lincoln NE ... 292
University of Nevada, Las Vegas NV ... 294
University of Nevada, Reno NV ... 294
Dartmouth College NH ... 296
University of New Hampshire NH ... 298
College of New Jersey, The NJ ... 300
Fairleigh Dickinson University NJ ... 301
Monmouth University NJ ... 303
Montclair State University NJ ... 303
New Jersey Institute of Technology NJ ... 303
Ramapo College of New Jersey NJ ... 305
Rider University NJ ... 305
Rowan University NJ ... 305
Rutgers the State University of New Jersey Camden Campus NJ ... 306
Rutgers the State University of New Jersey Newark Campus NJ ... 306
Seton Hall University NJ ... 307
William Paterson University of New Jersey NJ ... 308
New Mexico State University Main Campus NM .. 310
University of New Mexico Main Campus NM .. 312
Adelphi University NY ... 313
Alfred University NY ... 313
Baruch College/City University of New York NY ... 316
Canisius College NY ... 316
Clarkson University NY ... 320
Columbia University in the City of New York NY ... 321
Cornell University NY ... 322
Fordham University NY ... 324
Hofstra University NY ... 326
Iona College NY ... 327
Ithaca College NY ... 327
Le Moyne College NY ... 328
Long Island University - Post Campus NY ... 329
Manhattan College NY ... 329
Marist College NY ... 330
New York University NY ... 334
Niagara University NY ... 334
Pace University NY ... 335
Rensselaer Polytechnic Institute NY ... 337
Rochester Institute of Technology NY ... 337
St. Bonaventure University NY ... 338
St. John Fisher College NY ... 338
St. John's University NY ... 339
Siena College NY ... 340
State University of New York at Binghamton NY ... 341
State University of New York at New Paltz NY ... 342
State University of New York College at Geneseo NY ... 343
State University of New York College at Oneonta NY ... 343
State University of New York College at Oswego NY ... 344
State University of New York College at Plattsburgh NY ... 344
State University of New York Institute of Technology at Utica-Rome NY ... 346
State University of New York, The College at Brockport NY ... 342
Syracuse University Main Campus NY ... 347
Union Graduate College NY ... 348
University at Albany, SUNY NY ... 341
University at Buffalo-SUNY NY ... 341
University of Rochester NY ... 349
Yeshiva University NY ... 351
Appalachian State University NC .. 367
Duke University NC .. 354
East Carolina University NC .. 367
Elizabeth City State University NC .. 367
Elon University NC .. 354
Fayetteville State University NC .. 367
Meredith College NC .. 356
North Carolina Agricultural and Technical State University NC .. 367
North Carolina Central University NC .. 368
North Carolina State University NC .. 368
Queens University of Charlotte NC .. 365
University of North Carolina at Asheville NC .. 368
University of North Carolina at Chapel Hill NC .. 368
University of North Carolina at Charlotte NC .. 368
University of North Carolina at Greensboro NC .. 369
University of North Carolina at Pembroke NC .. 369
University of North Carolina Wilmington NC .. 369
Wake Forest University NC .. 370
Western Carolina University NC .. 369
Winston-Salem State University NC .. 370
North Dakota State University Main Campus ND .. 371
University of North Dakota Main Campus ND .. 371
Bowling Green State University OH .. 374
Case Western Reserve University OH .. 375
Cleveland State University OH .. 377
John Carroll University OH .. 381
Kent State University Main Campus OH .. 382
Miami University OH .. 384
Ohio Northern University OH .. 386
Ohio State University Main Campus, The OH .. 386
Ohio University Main Campus OH .. 387
University of Akron, Main Campus, The OH .. 390
University of Cincinnati Main Campus OH .. 390
University of Dayton OH .. 391
University of Toledo OH .. 392
Wright State University Main Campus OH .. 393
Xavier University OH .. 393
Youngstown State University OH .. 394
Oklahoma State University OK .. 397
Southeastern Oklahoma State University OK .. 399
University of Oklahoma Norman Campus OK .. 401
University of Tulsa OK .. 401
Oregon State University OR .. 406
Portland State University OR .. 406
University of Oregon OR .. 406
University of Portland OR .. 408
Willamette University OR .. 408
Bloomsburg University of Pennsylvania PA ... 427
Carnegie Mellon University PA ... 412
Clarion University of Pennsylvania PA ... 428
Drexel University PA ... 415
Duquesne University PA ... 415
Indiana University of Pennsylvania PA ... 428
King's College PA ... 419
La Salle University PA ... 420
Lehigh University PA ... 422
Penn State University Park PA ... 426
Robert Morris University PA ... 431
Saint Joseph's University PA ... 432
Shippensburg University of Pennsylvania PA ... 429
Susquehanna University PA ... 433
Temple University PA ... 433

University of Pennsylvania ... PA ... 435
University of Pittsburgh ... PA ... 435
University of Scranton, The ... PA ... 436
Villanova University ... PA ... 436
West Chester University of Pennsylvania . PA ... 430
Widener University ... PA ... 437
Universidad Del Turabo ... PR ... 552
Bryant University ... RI ... 438
Providence College ... RI ... 439
Roger Williams University ... RI ... 440
University of Rhode Island ... RI ... 440
Citadel, The Military College of South Carolina, The ... SC ... 442
Clemson University ... SC ... 442
Coastal Carolina University ... SC ... 442
College of Charleston ... SC ... 443
Francis Marion University ... SC ... 444
Lander University ... SC ... 444
South Carolina State University ... SC ... 446
University of South Carolina Aiken ... SC ... 448
University of South Carolina Columbia ... SC ... 447
University of South Carolina Upstate ... SC ... 448
Winthrop University ... SC ... 449
University of South Dakota, The ... SD ... 451
Belmont University ... TN ... 453
East Tennessee State University ... TN ... 459
Middle Tennessee State University ... TN ... 459
Tennessee State University ... TN ... 459
Tennessee Technological University ... TN ... 460
Union University ... TN ... 462
University of Memphis, The ... TN ... 460
University of Tennessee at Chattanooga .. TN ... 463
University of Tennessee at Martin ... TN ... 463
University of Tennessee, Knoxville ... TN ... 463
Vanderbilt University ... TN ... 463
Abilene Christian University ... TX ... 464
Baylor University ... TX ... 467
Lamar University ... TX ... 486
Midwestern State University ... TX ... 476
Prairie View A & M University ... TX ... 482
Rice University ... TX ... 479
St. Mary's University ... TX ... 479
Sam Houston State University ... TX ... 487
Southern Methodist University ... TX ... 481
Stephen F. Austin State University ... TX ... 482
Texas A & M International University ... TX ... 483
Texas A & M University ... TX ... 483
Texas A & M University - Commerce ... TX ... 483
Texas A & M University - Corpus Christi .. TX ... 483
Texas Christian University ... TX ... 484
Texas Southern University ... TX ... 485
Texas State University-San Marcos ... TX ... 487
Texas Tech University ... TX ... 487
Trinity University ... TX ... 488
University of Dallas ... TX ... 488
University of Houston ... TX ... 489
University of Houston - Clear Lake ... TX ... 489
University of Houston - Downtown ... TX ... 489
University of Houston - Victoria ... TX ... 489
University of North Texas ... TX ... 490
University of St. Thomas ... TX ... 490
University of Texas at Arlington, The ... TX ... 491
University of Texas at Austin ... TX ... 491
University of Texas at Brownsville and Texas Southmost College, The ... TX ... 491
University of Texas at Dallas, The ... TX ... 491
University of Texas at El Paso ... TX ... 492
University of Texas at San Antonio ... TX ... 492
University of Texas at Tyler ... TX ... 492
University of Texas of the Permian Basin . TX ... 493
University of Texas - Pan American ... TX ... 492
West Texas A & M University ... TX ... 484
Brigham Young University ... UT ... 495
Southern Utah University ... UT ... 497
University of Utah, The ... UT ... 496
Utah State University ... UT ... 497
Utah Valley University ... UT ... 497
Weber State University ... UT ... 497
University of Vermont ... VT ... 500
Christopher Newport University ... VA ... 503
College of William & Mary ... VA ... 503
George Mason University ... VA ... 505
James Madison University ... VA ... 506
Longwood University ... VA ... 506
Norfolk State University ... VA ... 507
Old Dominion University ... VA ... 507
Radford University ... VA ... 508
Shenandoah University ... VA ... 509
University of Richmond ... VA ... 510
University of Virginia ... VA ... 511
Virginia Commonwealth University ... VA ... 511
Virginia Military Institute ... VA ... 515
Virginia Polytechnic Institute and State University ... VA ... 515
Virginia State University ... VA ... 515
Washington and Lee University ... VA ... 516
Central Washington University ... WA ... 517
Eastern Washington University ... WA ... 519
Gonzaga University ... WA ... 520
Pacific Lutheran University ... WA .. 521
Seattle Pacific University ... WA .. 523
Seattle University ... WA .. 523
University of Washington ... WA .. 524
Washington State University ... WA .. 525
Western Washington University ... WA .. 525
Marshall University ... WV .. 529
West Virginia University ... WV .. 530
Marquette University ... WI ... 534
University of Wisconsin-Eau Claire ... WI ... 536
University of Wisconsin-La Crosse ... WI ... 536
University of Wisconsin-Madison ... WI ... 536
University of Wisconsin-Milwaukee ... WI ... 537
University of Wisconsin-Oshkosh ... WI ... 537
University of Wisconsin-Parkside ... WI ... 537
University of Wisconsin-River Falls ... WI ... 537
University of Wisconsin-Whitewater ... WI ... 538
University of Wyoming ... WY .. 543

BUSA: AACSB-The Association to Advance Collegiate Schools of Business: accounting (B,M,D)

Auburn University ... AL ... 1
Auburn University at Montgomery ... AL ... 2
University of Alabama at Birmingham ... AL ... 8
University of Alabama, The ... AL ... 8
University of South Alabama ... AL ... 9
University of Alaska Fairbanks ... AK ... 10
Arizona State University ... AZ ... 11
University of Arizona ... AZ ... 18
University of Arkansas Main Campus ... AR ... 23
California State University-Fullerton ... CA ... 33
San Diego State University ... CA ... 35
Santa Clara University ... CA ... 64
University of San Diego ... CA ... 73
University of Southern California ... CA ... 74
University of Colorado DenverlAnschutz Medical Campus ... CO ... 86
University of Denver ... CO ... 86
University of Northern Colorado ... CO ... 86
University of Connecticut ... CT ... 92
University of Delaware ... DE ... 94
George Washington University ... DC ... 95
Howard University ... DC ... 95
Florida International University ... FL ... 115
Florida State University ... FL ... 115
Stetson University ... FL ... 117
University of Central Florida ... FL ... 115
University of Florida ... FL ... 116
University of Miami ... FL ... 118
University of North Florida ... FL ... 116
University of South Florida ... FL ... 116
University of South Florida St. Petersburg FL ... 116
Georgia Southern University ... GA .. 126
Georgia State University ... GA .. 126
Kennesaw State University ... GA .. 127
University of Georgia ... GA .. 133
University of West Georgia ... GA .. 133
Boise State University ... ID ... 137
Idaho State University ... ID ... 138
University of Idaho ... ID ... 139
Bradley University ... IL ... 140
DePaul University ... IL ... 143
Eastern Illinois University ... IL ... 144
Illinois State University ... IL ... 147
Loyola University Chicago ... IL ... 151
Northern Illinois University ... IL ... 154
Southern Illinois University Carbondale ... IL ... 159
Southern Illinois University Edwardsville ... IL ... 159
University of Illinois at Chicago ... IL ... 161
University of Illinois at Urbana-Champaign IL ... 162
Western Illinois University ... IL ... 162
Ball State University ... IN ... 164
Indiana University Bloomington ... IN ... 167
University of Notre Dame ... IN ... 174
University of Southern Indiana ... IN ... 174
Drake University ... IA ... 177
Iowa State University ... IA ... 175
University of Iowa ... IA ... 175
Kansas State University ... KS ... 188
University of Kansas Main Campus ... KS ... 190
Wichita State University ... KS ... 191
University of Kentucky ... KY ... 200
University of Louisville ... KY ... 200
Western Kentucky University ... KY ... 200
Louisiana Tech University ... LA ... 207
Nicholls State University ... LA ... 208
Southeastern Louisiana University ... LA ... 208
University of Louisiana at Lafayette ... LA ... 208
University of Louisiana at Monroe ... LA ... 208
University of New Orleans ... LA ... 205
Loyola University Maryland ... MD .. 216
Morgan State University ... MD .. 217
Towson University ... MD .. 220
Bentley University ... MA .. 223
Suffolk University ... MA .. 237
University of Massachusetts ... MA .. 228
Central Michigan University ... MI ... 240
Grand Valley State University ... MI ... 243
Michigan State University ... MI ... 246
Oakland University ... MI ... 248
Western Michigan University ... MI ... 252
Mississippi State University ... MS .. 268
University of Mississippi ... MS .. 270
University of Southern Mississippi ... MS .. 270
Missouri State University ... MO .. 278
Truman State University ... MO .. 282
University of Central Missouri ... MO .. 283
University of Missouri - Columbia ... MO .. 283
University of Missouri - Saint Louis ... MO .. 283
University of Montana - Missoula, The ... MT .. 286
Creighton University ... NE .. 289
University of Nebraska at Omaha ... NE .. 293
University of Nebraska - Lincoln ... NE .. 292
University of Nevada, Las Vegas ... NV .. 294
University of Nevada, Reno ... NV .. 294
Rider University ... NJ .. 305
Seton Hall University ... NJ .. 307
New Mexico State University Main Campus ... NM .. 310
University of New Mexico Main Campus .. NM .. 312
Baruch College/City University of New York ... NY ... 316
Hofstra University ... NY .. 326
Pace University ... NY .. 335
St. John's University ... NY .. 339
University at Albany, SUNY ... NY ... 341
University at Buffalo-SUNY ... NY ... 341
North Carolina Agricultural and Technical State University ... NC .. 367
North Carolina State University ... NC .. 368
University of North Carolina at Charlotte .. NC .. 368
University of North Carolina at Greensboro ... NC .. 369
Wake Forest University ... NC .. 370
Bowling Green State University ... OH .. 374
Case Western Reserve University ... OH .. 375
Cleveland State University ... OH .. 377
John Carroll University ... OH .. 381
Kent State University Main Campus ... OH .. 382
Miami University ... OH .. 384
Ohio State University Main Campus, The . OH .. 386
Ohio University Main Campus ... OH .. 387
University of Akron, Main Campus, The ... OH .. 390
University of Dayton ... OH .. 391
Wright State University Main Campus ... OH .. 393
Oklahoma State University ... OK .. 397
University of Oklahoma Norman Campus . OK .. 401
Oregon State University ... OR .. 406
Portland State University ... OR .. 406
University of Oregon ... OR .. 406
Lehigh University ... PA .. 422
Saint Joseph's University ... PA .. 432
Villanova University ... PA .. 436
University of Rhode Island ... RI .. 440
Clemson University ... SC .. 442
College of Charleston ... SC .. 443
University of South Carolina Columbia ... SC .. 447
Belmont University ... TN .. 453
East Tennessee State University ... TN .. 459
Middle Tennessee State University ... TN .. 459
Tennessee Technological University ... TN .. 460
University of Memphis, The ... TN .. 460
University of Tennessee at Chattanooga .. TN .. 463
University of Tennessee, Knoxville ... TN .. 463
Baylor University ... TX .. 467
Texas A & M University ... TX .. 483
Texas A & M University - Corpus Christi .. TX .. 483
Texas Christian University ... TX .. 484
Texas State University-San Marcos ... TX .. 487
Texas Tech University ... TX .. 487
University of Houston ... TX .. 489
University of Houston - Clear Lake ... TX .. 489
University of North Texas ... TX .. 490
University of Texas at Arlington, The ... TX .. 491
University of Texas at Austin ... TX .. 491
University of Texas at Dallas, The ... TX .. 491
University of Texas at El Paso ... TX .. 492
University of Texas at San Antonio ... TX .. 492
Brigham Young University ... UT .. 495
University of Utah, The ... UT .. 496
Utah State University ... UT .. 497
Weber State University ... UT .. 497
College of William & Mary ... VA .. 503
George Mason University ... VA .. 505
James Madison University ... VA .. 506
Old Dominion University ... VA .. 507
University of Richmond ... VA .. 510
University of Virginia ... VA .. 511
Virginia Commonwealth University ... VA .. 511
Virginia Polytechnic Institute and State University ... VA .. 515
Gonzaga University ... WA .. 520
University of Washington ... WA .. 524
Washington State University ... WA .. 525
Marshall University ... WV .. 529
West Virginia University ... WV .. 530
Marquette University ... WI .. 534
University of Wisconsin-Madison ... WI .. 536

CA: National Accrediting Agency for Clinical Laboratory Sciences: clinical assistant (C)

Springfield Technical Community College MA .. 233
Northern Michigan University ... MI .. 248
Clackamas Community College ... OR .. 402
Community College of Allegheny County . PA .. 413
Edmonds Community College ... WA .. 519

CACREP: Council for Accreditation of Counseling & Related Educational Programs: addiction counseling, career counseling, marriage, couple and family counseling, mental health counseling, school counseling, student affairs and college counseling (M) and counselor education and supervision (D)

Alabama State University ... AL ... 1
Auburn University ... AL ... 1
Auburn University at Montgomery ... AL ... 2
Jacksonville State University ... AL ... 4
Troy University ... AL ... 7
University of Alabama at Birmingham ... AL ... 8
University of Alabama, The ... AL ... 8
University of Montevallo ... AL ... 9
University of North Alabama ... AL ... 9
Arizona State University ... AZ ... 11
Northern Arizona University ... AZ ... 16
University of Phoenix ... AZ ... 18
Arkansas State University-Jonesboro ... AR ... 19
Henderson State University ... AR ... 21
University of Arkansas Main Campus ... AR ... 23
California State University-Fresno ... CA ... 33
California State University-Fullerton ... CA ... 33
California State University-Los Angeles ... CA ... 34
California State University-Northridge ... CA ... 34
California State University-Sacramento ... CA ... 34
San Francisco State University ... CA ... 35
Sonoma State University ... CA ... 36
University of San Diego ... CA ... 73
Adams State University ... CO ... 78
Colorado Christian University ... CO ... 79
Colorado State University ... CO ... 80
Denver Seminary ... CO ... 81
Regis University ... CO ... 84
University of Colorado Colorado Springs .. CO ... 85
University of Colorado DenverlAnschutz Medical Campus ... CO ... 86
University of Northern Colorado ... CO ... 86
Central Connecticut State University ... CT ... 87
Fairfield University ... CT ... 89
Southern Connecticut State University ... CT ... 88
University of Connecticut ... CT ... 92
University of Saint Joseph ... CT ... 92
Western Connecticut State University ... CT ... 88
Wilmington University ... DE ... 94
Gallaudet University ... DC ... 95
George Washington University ... DC ... 95
University of the District of Columbia ... DC ... 97
Barry University ... FL ... 98
Florida Atlantic University ... FL ... 114
Florida Gulf Coast University ... FL ... 115
Florida International University ... FL ... 115
Florida State University ... FL ... 115
Rollins College ... FL ... 111
Stetson University ... FL ... 117
University of Central Florida ... FL ... 115
University of Florida ... FL ... 116
University of North Florida ... FL ... 116
University of South Florida ... FL ... 116
Clark Atlanta University ... GA .. 122
Columbus State University ... GA .. 123
Fort Valley State University ... GA .. 124
Georgia Regents University ... GA .. 126
Georgia Southern University ... GA .. 126
Georgia State University ... GA .. 126
Mercer University ... GA .. 128
University of Georgia ... GA .. 133
University of North Georgia ... GA .. 133
University of West Georgia ... GA .. 133
Valdosta State University ... GA .. 134
Boise State University ... ID ... 137
Idaho State University ... ID ... 138
Northwest Nazarene University ... ID ... 139
Bradley University ... IL ... 140
Chicago State University ... IL ... 141
Concordia University Chicago ... IL ... 143
Eastern Illinois University ... IL ... 144
Governors State University ... IL ... 145
National-Louis University ... IL ... 153
Northeastern Illinois University ... IL ... 154
Northern Illinois University ... IL ... 154
Roosevelt University ... IL ... 157
Southern Illinois University Carbondale ... IL ... 159
University of Illinois at Springfield ... IL ... 161
Western Illinois University ... IL ... 162
Ball State University ... IN ... 164
Butler University ... IN ... 164
Grace College and Seminary ... IN ... 166
Indiana State University ... IN ... 167
Indiana University Bloomington ... IN ... 167
Indiana University South Bend ... IN ... 168
Indiana Wesleyan University ... IN ... 169
Purdue University Calumet ... IN ... 171
Purdue University Main Campus ... IN ... 171
Valparaiso University ... IN ... 174
University of Iowa ... IA ... 175
University of Northern Iowa ... IA ... 176

Emporia State University ... KS ... 186
Kansas State University ... KS ... 188
MidAmerica Nazarene University ... KS ... 188
Pittsburg State University ... KS ... 189
Eastern Kentucky University ... KY ... 193
Lindsey Wilson College ... KY ... 197
Northern Kentucky University ... KY ... 198
University of Louisville ... KY ... 200
Western Kentucky University ... KY ... 200
Louisiana State University and Agricultural and Mechanical College ... LA ... 204
Louisiana Tech University ... LA ... 207
Loyola University New Orleans ... LA ... 205
Our Lady of Holy Cross College ... LA ... 206
Southeastern Louisiana University ... LA ... 208
Southern University and A&M College ... LA ... 206
University of Louisiana at Monroe ... LA ... 208
University of New Orleans ... LA ... 205
University of Southern Maine ... ME ... 212
Johns Hopkins University ... MD ... 215
Loyola University Maryland ... MD ... 216
University of Maryland College Park ... MD ... 219
Bridgewater State University ... MA ... 229
Andrews University ... MI ... 239
Eastern Michigan University ... MI ... 242
Oakland University ... MI ... 248
University of Detroit Mercy ... MI ... 250
Wayne State University ... MI ... 252
Western Michigan University ... MI ... 252
Capella University ... MN ... 254
Minnesota State University Moorhead ... MN ... 259
Minnesota State University, Mankato ... MN ... 259
St. Cloud State University ... MN ... 261
Walden University ... MN ... 265
Winona State University ... MN ... 262
Delta State University ... MS ... 266
Jackson State University ... MS ... 267
Mississippi College ... MS ... 268
Mississippi State University ... MS ... 268
University of Mississippi ... MS ... 270
Southeast Missouri State University ... MO ... 282
University of Central Missouri ... MO ... 283
University of Missouri - Saint Louis ... MO ... 283
Montana State University ... MT ... 287
University of Montana - Missoula, The ... MT ... 286
University of Nebraska at Kearney ... NE ... 292
University of Nebraska at Omaha ... NE ... 293
University of Nevada, Las Vegas ... NV ... 294
University of Nevada, Reno ... NV ... 294
Plymouth State University ... NH ... 298
Caldwell College ... NJ ... 300
College of New Jersey, The ... NJ ... 300
Fairleigh Dickinson University ... NJ ... 301
Kean University ... NJ ... 302
Monmouth University ... NJ ... 303
Montclair State University ... NJ ... 303
Rider University ... NJ ... 305
Rowan University ... NJ ... 305
Rutgers the State University of New Jersey New Brunswick Campus ... NJ ... 306
William Paterson University of New Jersey ... NJ ... 308
New Mexico State University Main Campus ... NM ... 310
University of New Mexico Main Campus ... NM ... 312
Canisius College ... NY ... 316
City University of New York Brooklyn College ... NY ... 317
City University of New York Herbert H. Lehman College ... NY ... 318
City University of New York Hunter College ... NY ... 318
Long Island University - Post Campus ... NY ... 329
St. Bonaventure University ... NY ... 338
St. John Fisher College ... NY ... 338
St. John's University ... NY ... 339
State University of New York College at Plattsburgh ... NY ... 344
State University of New York, The College at Brockport ... NY ... 342
Syracuse University Main Campus ... NY ... 347
University of Rochester ... NY ... 349
Appalachian State University ... NC ... 367
Gardner-Webb University ... NC ... 354
North Carolina Agricultural and Technical State University ... NC ... 367
North Carolina Central University ... NC ... 368
North Carolina State University ... NC ... 368
University of North Carolina at Chapel Hill ... NC ... 368
University of North Carolina at Charlotte ... NC ... 368
University of North Carolina at Greensboro ... NC ... 369
University of North Carolina at Pembroke ... NC ... 369
Wake Forest University ... NC ... 370
Western Carolina University ... NC ... 369
North Dakota State University Main Campus ... ND ... 371
Ashland University ... OH ... 374
Bowling Green State University ... OH ... 374
Cleveland State University ... OH ... 377
Heidelberg University ... OH ... 380
John Carroll University ... OH ... 381
Kent State University Main Campus ... OH ... 382
Malone University ... OH ... 383
Ohio University Main Campus ... OH ... 387
University of Akron, Main Campus, The ... OH ... 390
University of Cincinnati Main Campus ... OH ... 390
University of Dayton ... OH ... 391
University of Toledo ... OH ... 392
Walsh University ... OH ... 392
Wright State University Main Campus ... OH ... 393
Xavier University ... OH ... 393
Youngstown State University ... OH ... 394
Oklahoma State University ... OK ... 397
George Fox University ... OR ... 403
Lewis and Clark College ... OR ... 403
Oregon State University ... OR ... 406
Portland State University ... OR ... 406
Southern Oregon University ... OR ... 406
California University of Pennsylvania ... PA ... 428
Duquesne University ... PA ... 415
Edinboro University of Pennsylvania ... PA ... 428
Gannon University ... PA ... 416
Geneva College ... PA ... 417
Indiana University of Pennsylvania ... PA ... 428
Marywood University ... PA ... 423
Messiah College ... PA ... 423
Neumann University ... PA ... 424
Penn State University Park ... PA ... 426
Shippensburg University of Pennsylvania ... PA ... 429
Slippery Rock University of Pennsylvania ... PA ... 429
University of Scranton, The ... PA ... 436
Waynesburg University ... PA ... 437
West Chester University of Pennsylvania ... PA ... 430
Citadel, The Military College of South Carolina, The ... SC ... 442
Clemson University ... SC ... 442
South Carolina State University ... SC ... 446
University of South Carolina Columbia ... SC ... 447
Winthrop University ... SC ... 449
South Dakota State University ... SD ... 452
University of South Dakota, The ... SD ... 451
East Tennessee State University ... TN ... 459
Lincoln Memorial University ... TN ... 456
Middle Tennessee State University ... TN ... 459
University of Memphis, The ... TN ... 460
University of Tennessee at Chattanooga ... TN ... 463
University of Tennessee, Knoxville ... TN ... 463
Vanderbilt University ... TN ... 463
St. Mary's University ... TX ... 479
Sam Houston State University ... TX ... 487
Stephen F. Austin State University ... TX ... 482
Texas A & M University - Commerce ... TX ... 483
Texas A & M University - Corpus Christi ... TX ... 483
Texas State University-San Marcos ... TX ... 487
Texas Tech University ... TX ... 487
Texas Woman's University ... TX ... 488
University of Houston - Victoria ... TX ... 489
University of Mary Hardin-Baylor ... TX ... 490
University of North Texas ... TX ... 490
University of Texas at Brownsville and Texas Southmost College, The ... TX ... 491
University of Texas at San Antonio ... TX ... 492
University of Vermont ... VT ... 500
College of William & Mary ... VA ... 503
Eastern Mennonite University ... VA ... 504
James Madison University ... VA ... 506
Lynchburg College ... VA ... 506
Marymount University ... VA ... 507
Old Dominion University ... VA ... 507
Radford University ... VA ... 508
Regent University ... VA ... 508
University of Virginia ... VA ... 511
Virginia Commonwealth University ... VA ... 511
Virginia Polytechnic Institute and State University ... VA ... 515
Central Washington University ... WA ... 517
Eastern Washington University ... WA ... 519
Gonzaga University ... WA ... 520
Seattle University ... WA ... 523
Western Washington University ... WA ... 525
West Virginia University ... WV ... 530
University of Wisconsin-Oshkosh ... WI ... 537
University of Wisconsin-Stout ... WI ... 538
University of Wisconsin-Whitewater ... WI ... 538
University of Wyoming ... WY ... 543

CAHIIM: Commission on Accreditation for Health Informatics and Information Management Education: health information management and health informatics (A,B,M)

Alabama State University ... AL ... 1
Bishop State Community College ... AL ... 2
University of Alabama at Birmingham ... AL ... 8
Wallace State Community College - Hanceville ... AL ... 9
University of Alaska Southeast ... AK ... 11
Central Arizona College ... AZ ... 12
Phoenix College ... AZ ... 15
Arkansas Tech University ... AR ... 20
National Park Community College ... AR ... 22
University of Arkansas for Medical Sciences ... AR ... 24
Charles R. Drew University of Medicine & Science ... CA ... 38
City College of San Francisco ... CA ... 38
Claremont Graduate University ... CA ... 39
Cosumnes River College ... CA ... 53
Cypress College ... CA ... 56
East Los Angeles College ... CA ... 51
Fresno City College ... CA ... 68
Kaplan College ... CA ... 49
Loma Linda University ... CA ... 51
San Diego Mesa College ... CA ... 62
Santa Barbara City College ... CA ... 64
Lincoln College of New England ... CT ... 90
Broward College ... FL ... 99
College of Central Florida ... FL ... 100
Daytona State College ... FL ... 101
Edison State College ... FL ... 101
Florida Agricultural and Mechanical University ... FL ... 114
Florida State College at Jacksonville ... FL ... 105
Hodges University ... FL ... 106
Indian River State College ... FL ... 106
Keiser University ... FL ... 108
Lake-Sumter State College ... FL ... 108
Miami Dade College ... FL ... 109
Palm Beach State College ... FL ... 110
Pensacola State College ... FL ... 110
Polk State College ... FL ... 110
St. Johns River State College ... FL ... 112
St. Petersburg College ... FL ... 112
Santa Fe College ... FL ... 113
Seminole State College of Florida ... FL ... 113
University of Central Florida ... FL ... 115
Athens Technical College ... GA ... 120
Atlanta Technical College ... GA ... 121
Columbus Technical College ... GA ... 123
Darton State College ... GA ... 124
Georgia Northwestern Technical College ... GA ... 125
Georgia Regents University ... GA ... 126
Middle Georgia State College ... GA ... 128
Ogeechee Technical College ... GA ... 129
Southern Crescent Technical College ... GA ... 132
Wiregrass Georgia Technical College ... GA ... 134
Boise State University ... ID ... 137
Idaho State University ... ID ... 138
Chicago State University ... IL ... 141
College of DuPage ... IL ... 142
College of Lake County ... IL ... 143
Danville Area Community College ... IL ... 143
DeVry University - Chicago Campus ... IL ... 144
Harper College ... IL ... 145
Illinois State University ... IL ... 147
John A. Logan College ... IL ... 148
Joliet Junior College ... IL ... 149
Kaskaskia College ... IL ... 149
Midstate College ... IL ... 152
Moraine Valley Community College ... IL ... 153
Northwestern College ... IL ... 155
Oakton Community College ... IL ... 155
Rend Lake College ... IL ... 156
Resurrection University ... IL ... 156
Shawnee Community College ... IL ... 158
Southwestern Illinois College ... IL ... 160
University of Illinois at Chicago ... IL ... 161
Indiana University Northwest ... IN ... 168
Indiana University-Purdue University Indianapolis ... IN ... 168
ITT Technical Institute ... IN ... 169
Ivy Tech Community College-Central Indiana ... IN ... 169
National College ... IN ... 171
Vincennes University ... IN ... 174
Indian Hills Community College ... IA ... 179
Kaplan University ... IA ... 180
Kirkwood Community College ... IA ... 180
Northeast Iowa Community College ... IA ... 181
Northwest Iowa Community College ... IA ... 181
Scott Community College ... IA ... 178
Hutchinson Community College and Area Vocational School ... KS ... 187
Neosho County Community College ... KS ... 189
Washburn University ... KS ... 191
Eastern Kentucky University ... KY ... 193
Jefferson Community and Technical College ... KY ... 195
Western Kentucky University ... KY ... 200
Delgado Community College ... LA ... 203
Louisiana Tech University ... LA ... 207
Southern University at New Orleans ... LA ... 206
Southern University at Shreveport-Louisiana ... LA ... 207
University of Louisiana at Lafayette ... LA ... 208
Beal College ... ME ... 209
Kennebec Valley Community College ... ME ... 210
Anne Arundel Community College ... MD ... 213
Baltimore City Community College ... MD ... 213
Community College of Baltimore County, The ... MD ... 214
Coppin State University ... MD ... 220
Montgomery College ... MD ... 216
Prince George's Community College ... MD ... 217
University of Maryland University College ... MD ... 219
Bristol Community College ... MA ... 231
Fisher College ... MA ... 226
Laboure College ... MA ... 227
Baker College of Flint ... MI ... 239
Davenport University ... MI ... 241
Ferris State University ... MI ... 242
Macomb Community College ... MI ... 246
Mid Michigan Community College ... MI ... 247
Schoolcraft College ... MI ... 250
Southwestern Michigan College ... MI ... 250
Anoka Technical College ... MN ... 257
College of Saint Scholastica, The ... MN ... 254
Minnesota State Community and Technical College ... MN ... 259
Rasmussen College - St. Cloud ... MN ... 263
Ridgewater College ... MN ... 260
Rochester Community and Technical College ... MN ... 261
St. Catherine University ... MN ... 263
Saint Cloud Technical and Community College ... MN ... 261
Saint Paul College-A Community & Technical College ... MN ... 261
Hinds Community College ... MS ... 267
Itawamba Community College ... MS ... 267
Meridian Community College ... MS ... 267
Southwest Mississippi Community College ... MS ... 269
University of Mississippi Medical Center ... MS ... 270
Metropolitan Community College - Penn Valley ... MO ... 277
Missouri Western State University ... MO ... 279
Ozarks Technical Community College ... MO ... 279
St. Charles Community College ... MO ... 280
Saint Louis Community College at Forest Park ... MO ... 281
Saint Louis University ... MO ... 281
Stephens College ... MO ... 282
Great Falls College Montana State University ... MT ... 287
Central Community College ... NE ... 288
Clarkson College ... NE ... 288
Western Nebraska Community College ... NE ... 293
College of Southern Nevada ... NV ... 294
Kaplan College ... NV ... 294
Brookdale Community College ... NJ ... 299
Burlington County College ... NJ ... 299
Camden County College ... NJ ... 300
Passaic County Community College ... NJ ... 304
Raritan Valley Community College ... NJ ... 305
Central New Mexico Community College ... NM ... 309
San Juan College ... NM ... 311
Alfred State College ... NY ... 345
Broome Community College ... NY ... 315
City University of New York Borough of Manhattan Community College ... NY ... 317
Long Island University - Post Campus ... NY ... 329
Mohawk Valley Community College ... NY ... 331
Monroe Community College ... NY ... 332
Onondaga Community College ... NY ... 335
State University of New York Institute of Technology at Utica-Rome ... NY ... 346
Trocaire College ... NY ... 348
Brunswick Community College ... NC ... 358
Catawba Valley Community College ... NC ... 359
Central Piedmont Community College ... NC ... 359
Davidson County Community College ... NC ... 360
Durham Technical Community College ... NC ... 360
East Carolina University ... NC ... 367
Edgecombe Community College ... NC ... 360
McDowell Technical Community College ... NC ... 362
Pitt Community College ... NC ... 362
Southwestern Community College ... NC ... 364
Western Carolina University ... NC ... 369
North Dakota State College of Science ... ND ... 372
United Tribes Technical College ... ND ... 373
Cincinnati State Technical and Community College ... OH ... 376
Columbus State Community College ... OH ... 378
Cuyahoga Community College ... OH ... 378
Eastern Gateway Community College - Jefferson County Campus ... OH ... 379
Hocking College ... OH ... 380
Lakeland Community College ... OH ... 382
Marion Technical College ... OH ... 383
Mercy College of Ohio ... OH ... 383
Ohio State University Main Campus, The ... OH ... 386
Owens Community College ... OH ... 387
Sinclair Community College ... OH ... 388
Stark State College ... OH ... 389
Terra State Community College ... OH ... 389
University of Cincinnati Main Campus ... OH ... 390
University of Toledo ... OH ... 392
Zane State College ... OH ... 394
Rose State College ... OK ... 399
Southwestern Oklahoma State University ... OK ... 400
Tulsa Community College ... OK ... 400
Central Oregon Community College ... OR ... 402
Oregon Health & Science University ... OR ... 405
Portland Community College ... OR ... 407
Community College of Allegheny County ... PA ... 413
Gwynedd-Mercy University ... PA ... 417
Lehigh Carbon Community College ... PA ... 421
Peirce College ... PA ... 425
Pennsylvania College of Technology ... PA ... 427
South Hills School of Business and Technology ... PA ... 433
Temple University ... PA ... 433
University of Pittsburgh ... PA ... 435

Huertas Junior College ... PR ... 549
University of Puerto Rico-Medical Sciences Campus ... PR ... 554
Florence - Darlington Technical College ... SC ... 443
Greenville Technical College ... SC ... 444
Midlands Technical College ... SC ... 445
University of South Carolina Upstate ... SC ... 448
Dakota State University ... SD ... 451
National American University ... SD ... 450
Chattanooga State Community College ... TN ... 460
Dyersburg State Community College ... TN ... 460
Roane State Community College ... TN ... 461
Tennessee State University ... TN ... 459
Volunteer State Community College ... TN ... 461
Walters State Community College ... TN ... 462
Austin Community College District ... TX ... 466
College of the Mainland ... TX ... 469
Collin County Community College District ... TX ... 469
Del Mar College ... TX ... 471
El Paso Community College ... TX ... 472
Houston Community College ... TX ... 473
Howard College ... TX ... 473
Kaplan College ... TX ... 475
Lamar Institute of Technology ... TX ... 486
Lee College ... TX ... 475
Lone Star College System ... TX ... 476
McLennan Community College ... TX ... 476
Midland College ... TX ... 476
Panola College ... TX ... 478
St. Philip's College ... TX ... 465
San Jacinto College North ... TX ... 479
South Plains College ... TX ... 480
South Texas College ... TX ... 480
Tarrant County College District ... TX ... 482
Texas Southern University ... TX ... 485
Texas State Technical College Harlingen . TX ... 485
Texas State Technical College West Texas ... TX ... 486
Texas State University-San Marcos ... TX ... 487
Tyler Junior College ... TX ... 488
Vernon College ... TX ... 493
Wharton County Junior College ... TX ... 494
Weber State University ... UT ... 497
Western Governors University ... UT ... 498
Northern Virginia Community College ... VA ... 513
Tidewater Community College ... VA ... 514
Shoreline Community College ... WA .. 523
Spokane Community College ... WA .. 518
Tacoma Community College ... WA .. 524
University of Washington ... WA .. 524
Marshall University ... WV .. 529
Mountwest Community and Technical College ... WV .. 528
Pierpont Community & Technical College WV .. 528
West Virginia Northern Community College ... WV .. 528
Chippewa Valley Technical College ... WI ... 539
Gateway Technical College ... WI ... 540
Mid-State Technical College ... WI ... 540
Moraine Park Technical College ... WI ... 540
Northeast Wisconsin Technical College ... WI ... 541
Waukesha County Technical College ... WI ... 541
Western Technical College ... WI ... 541

CEA: Commission on English Language Program Accreditation: english language (C)

University of Alabama, The ... AL ... 8
University of Arizona ... AZ ... 18
Arkansas State University-Jonesboro ... AR ... 19
California State University-Long Beach ... CA ... 33
Diablo Valley College ... CA ... 41
San Jose State University ... CA ... 36
University of California-Irvine ... CA ... 71
University of California-San Diego ... CA ... 71
University of Southern California ... CA ... 74
University of Colorado Boulder ... CO ... 85
University of Denver ... CO ... 86
University of Northern Colorado ... CO ... 86
Sacred Heart University ... CT ... 91
University of Connecticut ... CT ... 92
University of Delaware ... DE ... 94
Georgetown University ... DC ... 95
University of Central Florida ... FL ... 115
University of Florida ... FL ... 116
University of Miami ... FL ... 118
University of South Florida ... FL ... 116
Valencia College ... FL ... 118
Georgia State University ... GA ... 126
University of Hawaii at Hilo ... HI ... 136
University of Hawaii at Manoa ... HI ... 136
University of Hawaii Hawaii Community College ... HI ... 136
University of Idaho ... ID ... 139
Harper College ... IL ... 145
Southern Illinois University Carbondale ... IL ... 159
University of Illinois at Chicago ... IL ... 161
Western Illinois University ... IL ... 162
Ball State University ... IN ... 164
Indiana University Bloomington ... IN ... 167
Taylor University ... IN ... 173
University of Iowa ... IA ... 175
University of Northern Iowa ... IA ... 176

Kansas State University ... KS ... 188
University of Kansas Main Campus ... KS ... 190
University of Maryland College Park ... MD .. 219
Boston University ... MA .. 224
Michigan State University ... MI ... 246
University of Michigan-Flint ... MI ... 251
Western Michigan University ... MI ... 252
Missouri State University ... MO .. 278
University of Central Missouri ... MO .. 283
College of Southern Nevada ... NV ... 294
Rutgers the State University of New Jersey New Brunswick Campus ... NJ ... 306
University at Buffalo-SUNY ... NY ... 341
Xavier University ... OH .. 393
University of Oregon ... OR .. 406
Drexel University ... PA ... 415
Duquesne University ... PA ... 415
Penn State University Park ... PA ... 426
University of Pennsylvania ... PA ... 435
University of Pittsburgh ... PA ... 435
Wilkes University ... PA ... 437
University of South Carolina Columbia ... SC ... 447
Lone Star College System ... TX ... 476
Texas A & M University ... TX ... 483
University of Houston ... TX ... 489
University of North Texas ... TX ... 490
University of Texas at Arlington, The ... TX ... 491
University of Utah, The ... UT ... 496
Utah State University ... UT ... 497
Utah Valley University ... UT ... 497
Weber State University ... UT ... 497
Saint Michael's College ... VT ... 500
George Mason University ... VA ... 505
Virginia Polytechnic Institute and State University ... VA ... 515
Eastern Washington University ... WA .. 519
Gonzaga University ... WA .. 520
University of Washington ... WA .. 524
Washington State University ... WA .. 525
University of Wisconsin-Milwaukee ... WI ... 537

CGTECH: National Accrediting Agency for Clinical Laboratory Sciences: cytogenetic technologist (B)

University of Connecticut ... CT ... 92
Kennesaw State University ... GA .. 127
Northern Michigan University ... MI ... 248
University of Texas M.D. Anderson Cancer Center, The ... TX ... 493

CHIRO: Council on Chiropractic Education: chiropractic education (FP,D)

Life Chiropractic College West ... CA ... 50
Southern California University of Health Sciences ... CA ... 67
University of Bridgeport ... CT ... 91
Life University ... GA .. 128
National University of Health Sciences ... IL ... 154
Palmer College of Chiropractic ... IA ... 182
Cleveland University - Kansas City ... KS ... 185
Northwestern Health Sciences University . MN .. 263
Logan College of Chiropractic ... MO .. 276
D'Youville College ... NY ... 323
New York Chiropractic College ... NY ... 333
University of Western States ... OR .. 408
Sherman College of Chiropractic ... SC ... 446
Parker University ... TX ... 478
Texas Chiropractic College ... TX ... 484

CIDA: Council for Interior Design Accreditation: interior design (B,M)

Auburn University ... AL ... 1
Samford University ... AL ... 6
University of Alabama, The ... AL ... 8
Virginia College ... AL ... 3
Arizona State University ... AZ ... 11
Art Institute of Phoenix, The ... AZ ... 12
Southwest University of Visual Arts ... AZ ... 17
Harding University Main Campus ... AR ... 21
University of Arkansas Main Campus ... AR ... 23
#University of Central Arkansas ... AR ... 25
Academy of Art University ... CA ... 26
California College of the Arts ... CA ... 30
California State Polytechnic University-Pomona ... CA ... 32
California State University-Fresno ... CA ... 33
California State University-Northridge ... CA ... 34
California State University-Sacramento ... CA ... 34
Design Institute of San Diego ... CA ... 42
Interior Designers Institute ... CA ... 48
San Diego State University ... CA ... 35
Woodbury University ... CA ... 76
Art Institute of Colorado, The ... CO ... 78
Colorado State University ... CO ... 80
Rocky Mountain College of Art & Design . CO ... 85
George Washington University ... DC ... 95
#Art Institute of Fort Lauderdale, The ... FL ... 98
Florida International University ... FL ... 115
Florida State University ... FL ... 115

International Academy of Design and Technology ... FL ... 107
Miami International University of Art & Design ... FL ... 109
Ringling College of Art and Design ... FL ... 111
University of Florida ... FL ... 116
Art Institute of Atlanta, The ... GA .. 120
Brenau University ... GA .. 122
Georgia Southern University ... GA .. 126
Savannah College of Art and Design ... GA .. 131
University of Georgia ... GA .. 133
Chaminade University of Honolulu ... HI ... 135
Brigham Young University-Idaho ... ID ... 137
University of Idaho ... ID ... 139
Columbia College Chicago ... IL ... 143
Harrington College of Design ... IL ... 146
Illinois Institute of Art, The ... IL ... 147
Illinois State University ... IL ... 147
Southern Illinois University Carbondale ... IL ... 159
Ball State University ... IN ... 164
Indiana State University ... IN ... 167
Indiana University Bloomington ... IN ... 167
Indiana University-Purdue University Indianapolis ... IN ... 168
Purdue University Main Campus ... IN ... 171
Iowa State University ... IA ... 175
Kansas State University ... KS ... 188
University of Kentucky ... KY ... 200
University of Louisville ... KY ... 200
Louisiana State University and Agricultural and Mechanical College ... LA ... 204
Louisiana Tech University ... LA ... 207
University of Louisiana at Lafayette ... LA ... 208
Boston Architectural College ... MA ... 223
Endicott College ... MA ... 226
Mount Ida College ... MA ... 234
Suffolk University ... MA ... 237
Wentworth Institute of Technology ... MA ... 237
Central Michigan University ... MI ... 240
College for Creative Studies ... MI ... 241
Eastern Michigan University ... MI ... 242
Ferris State University ... MI ... 242
Lawrence Technological University ... MI ... 245
Michigan State University ... MI ... 246
Western Michigan University ... MI ... 252
Dunwoody College of Technology ... MN ... 255
University of Minnesota-Twin Cities ... MN ... 264
Mississippi College ... MS ... 268
Mississippi State University ... MS ... 268
University of Southern Mississippi ... MS ... 270
Maryville University of Saint Louis ... MO ... 276
University of Missouri - Columbia ... MO ... 283
University of Nebraska at Kearney ... NE ... 292
University of Nebraska - Lincoln ... NE ... 292
University of Nevada, Las Vegas ... NV ... 294
Kean University ... NJ ... 302
Cornell University ... NY ... 322
Fashion Institute of Technology ... NY ... 324
New York Institute of Technology ... NY ... 333
New York School of Interior Design ... NY ... 334
Pratt Institute ... NY ... 336
Rochester Institute of Technology ... NY ... 337
School of Visual Arts ... NY ... 340
State University of New York College at Buffalo ... NY ... 343
Syracuse University Main Campus ... NY ... 347
Villa Maria College of Buffalo ... NY ... 350
Appalachian State University ... NC ... 367
East Carolina University ... NC ... 367
High Point University ... NC ... 355
Meredith College ... NC ... 356
University of North Carolina at Greensboro ... NC ... 369
Western Carolina University ... NC ... 369
North Dakota State University Main Campus ... ND ... 371
Columbus College of Art & Design ... OH ... 378
Kent State University Main Campus ... OH ... 382
Miami University ... OH ... 384
Ohio State University Main Campus, The . OH ... 386
Ohio University Main Campus ... OH ... 387
University of Akron, Main Campus, The ... OH ... 390
University of Cincinnati Main Campus ... OH ... 390
Oklahoma Christian University ... OK ... 397
Oklahoma State University ... OK ... 397
University of Central Oklahoma ... OK ... 400
University of Oklahoma Norman Campus . OK ... 401
Art Institute of Portland, The ... OR ... 402
Marylhurst University ... OR ... 404
University of Oregon ... OR ... 406
Art Institute of Philadelphia ... PA ... 410
Art Institute of Pittsburgh ... PA ... 410
Chatham University ... PA ... 412
Drexel University ... PA ... 415
La Roche College ... PA ... 420
Moore College of Art and Design ... PA ... 424
Philadelphia University ... PA ... 430
Converse College ... SC ... 443
Winthrop University ... SC ... 449
South Dakota State University ... SD ... 452
Middle Tennessee State University ... TN ... 459
O'More College of Design ... TN ... 457
University of Memphis, The ... TN ... 460
University of Tennessee at Chattanooga .. TN ... 463

University of Tennessee, Knoxville ... TN ... 463
Watkins College of Art, Design & Film ... TN ... 464
Abilene Christian University ... TX ... 464
Art Institute of Houston, The ... TX ... 466
Baylor University ... TX ... 467
Sam Houston State University ... TX ... 487
Stephen F. Austin State University ... TX ... 482
Texas Christian University ... TX ... 484
Texas State University-San Marcos ... TX ... 487
Texas Tech University ... TX ... 487
University of North Texas ... TX ... 490
University of Texas at Arlington, The ... TX ... 491
University of Texas at Austin ... TX ... 491
University of Texas at San Antonio ... TX ... 492
University of the Incarnate Word ... TX ... 490
Utah State University ... UT ... 497
Weber State University ... UT ... 497
James Madison University ... VA ... 506
Marymount University ... VA ... 507
Radford University ... VA ... 508
Virginia Commonwealth University ... VA ... 511
Virginia Polytechnic Institute and State University ... VA ... 515
Art Institute of Seattle, The ... WA ... 516
Bellevue College ... WA ... 517
Washington State University ... WA .. 525
Mount Mary University ... WI ... 535
University of Wisconsin-Madison ... WI ... 536
University of Wisconsin-Stevens Point ... WI ... 538
University of Wisconsin-Stout ... WI ... 538

CLPSY: American Psychological Association: clinical psychology (D)

Auburn University ... AL ... 1
University of Alabama at Birmingham ... AL ... 8
University of Alabama, The ... AL ... 8
University of Alaska Anchorage ... AK ... 10
University of Alaska Fairbanks ... AK ... 10
Arizona State University ... AZ ... 11
University of Arizona ... AZ ... 18
University of Arkansas Main Campus ... AR ... 23
Alliant International University-San Diego . CA ... 26
Argosy University, Orange County ... CA ... 28
Azusa Pacific University ... CA ... 29
Biola University ... CA ... 29
Fielding Graduate University ... CA ... 44
Fuller Theological Seminary ... CA ... 45
#John F. Kennedy University ... CA ... 49
Loma Linda University ... CA ... 51
Palo Alto University ... CA ... 58
Pepperdine University ... CA ... 58
San Diego State University ... CA ... 35
University of California-Berkeley ... CA ... 70
University of California-Los Angeles ... CA ... 71
University of California-San Diego ... CA ... 71
University of LaVerne ... CA ... 72
University of Southern California ... CA ... 74
Wright Institute, The ... CA ... 77
University of Colorado Boulder ... CO ... 85
University of Colorado Colorado Springs .. CO ... 85
University of Denver ... CO ... 86
University of Connecticut ... CT ... 92
University of Hartford ... CT ... 92
Yale University ... CT ... 93
University of Delaware ... DE ... 94
American University ... DC ... 94
Catholic University of America, The ... DC ... 94
Gallaudet University ... DC ... 95
George Washington University ... DC ... 95
Howard University ... DC ... 95
Florida Institute of Technology ... FL ... 104
Florida State University ... FL ... 115
Nova Southeastern University ... FL ... 109
University of Central Florida ... FL ... 115
University of Florida ... FL ... 116
University of Miami ... FL ... 118
University of South Florida ... FL ... 116
Emory University ... GA ... 124
Georgia State University ... GA ... 126
University of Georgia ... GA ... 133
University of Hawaii at Manoa ... HI ... 136
Idaho State University ... ID ... 138
Adler School of Professional Psychology . IL ... 139
DePaul University ... IL ... 143
Illinois Institute of Technology ... IL ... 147
Loyola University Chicago ... IL ... 151
Northern Illinois University ... IL ... 154
Northwestern University ... IL ... 155
Roosevelt University ... IL ... 157
Rosalind Franklin University of Medicine & Science ... IL ... 157
Southern Illinois University Carbondale ... IL ... 159
University of Illinois at Chicago ... IL ... 161
University of Illinois at Urbana-Champaign IL ... 162
Wheaton College ... IL ... 163
Indiana State University ... IN ... 167
Indiana University Bloomington ... IN ... 167
Indiana University-Purdue University Indianapolis ... IN ... 168
Purdue University Main Campus ... IN ... 171
University of Indianapolis ... IN ... 173
University of Iowa ... IA ... 175
University of Kansas Main Campus ... KS ... 190

- Wichita State University ... KS ... 191
- Spalding University ... KY ... 199
- University of Kentucky ... KY ... 200
- University of Louisville ... KY ... 200
- Louisiana State University and Agricultural and Mechanical College ... LA ... 204
- University of Maine ... ME ... 212
- Loyola University Maryland ... MD ... 216
- Uniformed Services University of the Health Sciences ... MD ... 545
- University of Maryland Baltimore County ... MD ... 219
- University of Maryland College Park ... MD ... 219
- Boston University ... MA ... 224
- Clark University ... MA ... 225
- Harvard University ... MA ... 227
- Massachusetts School of Professional Psychology ... MA ... 233
- Suffolk University ... MA ... 237
- University of Massachusetts ... MA ... 228
- University of Massachusetts Boston ... MA ... 228
- Central Michigan University ... MI ... 240
- Eastern Michigan University ... MI ... 242
- Michigan State University ... MI ... 246
- University of Detroit Mercy ... MI ... 250
- University of Michigan-Ann Arbor ... MI ... 251
- Wayne State University ... MI ... 252
- Western Michigan University ... MI ... 252
- University of Minnesota-Twin Cities ... MN ... 264
- Jackson State University ... MS ... 267
- University of Mississippi ... MS ... 270
- University of Southern Mississippi ... MS ... 270
- Saint Louis University ... MO ... 281
- #School of Professional Psychology at Forest Institute, The ... MO ... 281
- University of Missouri - Columbia ... MO ... 283
- University of Missouri - Kansas City ... MO ... 283
- University of Missouri - Saint Louis ... MO ... 283
- Washington University in St. Louis ... MO ... 284
- University of Montana - Missoula, The ... MT ... 286
- University of Nebraska - Lincoln ... NE ... 292
- University of Nevada, Las Vegas ... NV ... 294
- University of Nevada, Reno ... NV ... 294
- Fairleigh Dickinson University ... NJ ... 301
- Rutgers the State University of New Jersey New Brunswick Campus ... NJ ... 306
- University of New Mexico Main Campus ... NM ... 312
- Adelphi University ... NY ... 313
- City University of New York The City College ... NY ... 317
- Fordham University ... NY ... 324
- Hofstra University ... NY ... 326
- Long Island University - Post Campus ... NY ... 329
- New School, The ... NY ... 332
- St. John's University ... NY ... 339
- State University of New York at Binghamton ... NY ... 341
- State University of New York at Stony Brook ... NY ... 342
- Syracuse University Main Campus ... NY ... 347
- Teachers College, Columbia University ... NY ... 347
- University at Albany, SUNY ... NY ... 341
- University at Buffalo-SUNY ... NY ... 341
- University of Rochester ... NY ... 349
- Yeshiva University ... NY ... 351
- Duke University ... NC ... 354
- East Carolina University ... NC ... 367
- University of North Carolina at Chapel Hill ... NC ... 368
- University of North Carolina at Charlotte ... NC ... 368
- University of North Carolina at Greensboro ... NC ... 369
- University of North Dakota Main Campus ... ND ... 371
- Bowling Green State University ... OH ... 374
- Case Western Reserve University ... OH ... 375
- Kent State University Main Campus ... OH ... 382
- Miami University ... OH ... 384
- Ohio State University Main Campus, The ... OH ... 386
- Ohio University Main Campus ... OH ... 387
- University of Cincinnati Main Campus ... OH ... 390
- University of Toledo ... OH ... 392
- Wright State University Main Campus ... OH ... 393
- Xavier University ... OH ... 393
- Oklahoma State University ... OK ... 397
- University of Tulsa ... OK ... 401
- George Fox University ... OR ... 403
- Pacific University ... OR ... 407
- University of Oregon ... OR ... 406
- Chestnut Hill College ... PA ... 413
- Drexel University ... PA ... 415
- Duquesne University ... PA ... 415
- Immaculata University ... PA ... 418
- Indiana University of Pennsylvania ... PA ... 428
- La Salle University ... PA ... 420
- Marywood University ... PA ... 423
- Penn State University Park ... PA ... 426
- Philadelphia College of Osteopathic Medicine ... PA ... 430
- Temple University ... PA ... 433
- University of Pittsburgh ... PA ... 435
- Widener University ... PA ... 437
- Carlos Albizu University ... PR ... 547
- Ponce School of Medicine & Health Sciences ... PR ... 552
- University of Rhode Island ... RI ... 440
- University of South Carolina Columbia ... SC ... 447
- University of South Dakota, The ... SD ... 451
- East Tennessee State University ... TN ... 459
- University of Memphis, The ... TN ... 460
- University of Tennessee, Knoxville ... TN ... 463
- Vanderbilt University ... TN ... 463
- Baylor University ... TX ... 467
- Sam Houston State University ... TX ... 487
- Southern Methodist University ... TX ... 481
- Texas A & M University ... TX ... 483
- Texas Tech University ... TX ... 487
- University of Houston ... TX ... 489
- University of North Texas ... TX ... 490
- University of Texas at Austin ... TX ... 491
- University of Texas Southwestern Medical Center ... TX ... 493
- Brigham Young University ... UT ... 495
- University of Utah, The ... UT ... 496
- University of Vermont ... VT ... 500
- Eastern Virginia Medical School ... VA ... 504
- George Mason University ... VA ... 505
- Norfolk State University ... VA ... 507
- Old Dominion University ... VA ... 507
- Regent University ... VA ... 508
- University of Virginia ... VA ... 511
- Virginia Commonwealth University ... VA ... 511
- Virginia Polytechnic Institute and State University ... VA ... 515
- Seattle Pacific University ... WA ... 523
- University of Washington ... WA ... 524
- Washington State University ... WA ... 525
- Marshall University ... WV ... 529
- West Virginia University ... WV ... 530
- Marquette University ... WI ... 534
- University of Wisconsin-Madison ... WI ... 536
- University of Wisconsin-Milwaukee ... WI ... 537
- Wisconsin School of Professional Psychology ... WI ... 539
- University of Wyoming ... WY ... 543

CNCE: Accrediting Council for Continuing Education and Training: continuing education (C,A)

- Southwest Institute of Healing Arts ... AZ ... 17
- CBD College ... CA ... 37
- Los Angeles ORT College ... CA ... 52
- United Education Institute ... CA ... 70
- Zarem/Golde ORT Technical Institute ... IL ... 163
- National Institute of Massotherapy ... OH ... 385
- Mech-Tech College ... PR ... 551
- Interface College ... WA ... 520

COARC: Commission on Accreditation for Respiratory Care: respiratory care (A,B,M)

- George C. Wallace Community College - Dothan ... AL ... 3
- #Shelton State Community College ... AL ... 6
- University of Alabama at Birmingham ... AL ... 8
- University of South Alabama ... AL ... 9
- Virginia College ... AL ... 3
- Wallace State Community College - Hanceville ... AL ... 9
- Gateway Community College ... AZ ... 14
- Kaplan College ... AZ ... 14
- Pima Community College ... AZ ... 17
- Pima Medical Institute-Tucson ... AZ ... 17
- Arkansas State University-Mountain Home ... AR ... 20
- Black River Technical College ... AR ... 20
- #Mid-South Community College ... AR ... 21
- #National Park Community College ... AR ... 22
- NorthWest Arkansas Community College ... AR ... 22
- Pulaski Technical College ... AR ... 22
- South Arkansas Community College ... AR ... 23
- Southeast Arkansas College ... AR ... 23
- University of Arkansas Community College at Hope ... AR ... 25
- University of Arkansas for Medical Sciences ... AR ... 24
- American Career College-Ontario ... CA ... 27
- American River College ... CA ... 53
- Antelope Valley College ... CA ... 28
- Butte College ... CA ... 30
- California College San Diego ... CA ... 31
- Concorde Career College ... CA ... 41
- Crafton Hills College ... CA ... 61
- East Los Angeles College ... CA ... 51
- El Camino College ... CA ... 43
- Foothill College ... CA ... 44
- Fresno City College ... CA ... 68
- Grossmont College ... CA ... 46
- #Hartnell College ... CA ... 46
- Kaplan College ... CA ... 49
- Loma Linda University ... CA ... 51
- Los Angeles Valley College ... CA ... 52
- Modesto Junior College ... CA ... 77
- Mt. San Antonio College ... CA ... 55
- Napa Valley College ... CA ... 55
- Ohlone College ... CA ... 57
- Orange Coast College ... CA ... 39
- Platt College ... CA ... 59
- San Joaquin Valley College, Inc. - Visalia ... CA ... 63
- Skyline College ... CA ... 64
- Victor Valley College ... CA ... 75
- Concorde Career College ... CO ... 81
- Pueblo Community College ... CO ... 84
- Goodwin College ... CT ... 90
- Manchester Community College ... CT ... 88
- Naugatuck Valley Community College ... CT ... 89
- Norwalk Community College ... CT ... 89
- University of Hartford ... CT ... 92
- Delaware Technical Community College, Owens Campus ... DE ... 93
- Delaware Technical Community College, Stanton-Wilmington Campus ... DE ... 93
- University of the District of Columbia ... DC ... 97
- Broward College ... FL ... 99
- Concorde Career Institute ... FL ... 100
- Daytona State College ... FL ... 101
- Edison State College ... FL ... 101
- Florida Agricultural and Mechanical University ... FL ... 114
- Florida National University Hialeah Campus ... FL ... 105
- Florida State College at Jacksonville ... FL ... 105
- Gulf Coast State College ... FL ... 106
- Hillsborough Community College ... FL ... 106
- Indian River State College ... FL ... 106
- Keiser University ... FL ... 108
- Miami Dade College ... FL ... 109
- Palm Beach State College ... FL ... 110
- Polk State College ... FL ... 110
- St. Johns River State College ... FL ... 112
- St. Petersburg College ... FL ... 112
- Seminole State College of Florida ... FL ... 113
- Tallahassee Community College ... FL ... 117
- Valencia College ... FL ... 118
- Armstrong Atlantic State University ... GA ... 120
- Augusta Technical College ... GA ... 121
- Central Georgia Technical College ... GA ... 122
- Columbus Technical College ... GA ... 123
- Dalton State College ... GA ... 123
- Darton State College ... GA ... 124
- Georgia Northwestern Technical College ... GA ... 125
- Georgia Regents University ... GA ... 126
- Georgia State University ... GA ... 126
- Gwinnett Technical College ... GA ... 127
- Oconee Fall Line Technical College-South Campus ... GA ... 129
- Okefenokee Technical College ... GA ... 130
- Southern Crescent Technical College ... GA ... 132
- Southwest Georgia Technical College ... GA ... 132
- Kapiolani Community College ... HI ... 136
- Boise State University ... ID ... 137
- Idaho State University ... ID ... 138
- City Colleges of Chicago Malcolm X College ... IL ... 142
- College of DuPage ... IL ... 142
- Illinois Central College ... IL ... 146
- Kankakee Community College ... IL ... 149
- Kaskaskia College ... IL ... 149
- Lincoln Land Community College ... IL ... 151
- Moraine Valley Community College ... IL ... 153
- Parkland College ... IL ... 155
- Rock Valley College ... IL ... 157
- Rush University ... IL ... 157
- St. Augustine College ... IL ... 158
- Southwestern Illinois College ... IL ... 160
- Trinity College of Nursing & Health Sciences ... IL ... 160
- Ivy Tech Community College-Central Indiana ... IN ... 169
- University of Southern Indiana ... IN ... 174
- Des Moines Area Community College ... IA ... 177
- Hawkeye Community College ... IA ... 178
- Kirkwood Community College ... IA ... 180
- Northeast Iowa Community College ... IA ... 181
- St. Luke's College ... IA ... 182
- Southeastern Community College ... IA ... 182
- #Hutchinson Community College and Area Vocational School ... KS ... 187
- Johnson County Community College ... KS ... 187
- Kansas City Kansas Community College ... KS ... 187
- Labette Community College ... KS ... 188
- Newman University ... KS ... 189
- Northwest Kansas Technical College ... KS ... 189
- Seward County Community College/Area Technical School ... KS ... 190
- Washburn University ... KS ... 191
- Bellarmine University ... KY ... 192
- Big Sandy Community and Technical College ... KY ... 194
- Bluegrass Community and Technical College ... KY ... 194
- Elizabethtown Community and Technical College ... KY ... 195
- Jefferson Community and Technical College ... KY ... 195
- Madisonville Community College ... KY ... 196
- Northern Kentucky University ... KY ... 198
- Somerset Community College ... KY ... 196
- Southcentral Kentucky Community and Technical College ... KY ... 196
- Southeast Kentucky Community and Technical College ... KY ... 196
- #Spencerian College ... KY ... 199
- West Kentucky Community and Technical College ... KY ... 196
- Bossier Parish Community College ... LA ... 202
- Delgado Community College ... LA ... 203
- L.E. Fletcher Technical Community College ... LA ... 203
- #Louisiana State University at Eunice ... LA ... 205
- Louisiana State University Health Sciences Center at Shreveport ... LA ... 205
- Louisiana State University Health Sciences Center-New Orleans ... LA ... 205
- Our Lady of the Lake College ... LA ... 206
- Southern University at Shreveport-Louisiana ... LA ... 207
- Kennebec Valley Community College ... ME ... 210
- Southern Maine Community College ... ME ... 211
- Allegany College of Maryland ... MD ... 213
- Baltimore City Community College ... MD ... 213
- Community College of Baltimore County, The ... MD ... 214
- Frederick Community College ... MD ... 214
- Prince George's Community College ... MD ... 217
- Salisbury University ... MD ... 220
- Washington Adventist University ... MD ... 221
- Berkshire Community College ... MA ... 231
- #Bunker Hill Community College ... MA ... 231
- Massasoit Community College ... MA ... 232
- North Shore Community College ... MA ... 232
- Northern Essex Community College ... MA ... 232
- Quinsigamond Community College ... MA ... 232
- Springfield Technical Community College ... MA ... 233
- Delta College ... MI ... 242
- Ferris State University ... MI ... 242
- Henry Ford Community College ... MI ... 243
- Jackson College ... MI ... 244
- Kalamazoo Valley Community College ... MI ... 244
- Macomb Community College ... MI ... 246
- Monroe County Community College ... MI ... 247
- Mott Community College ... MI ... 247
- Muskegon Community College ... MI ... 247
- Northern Michigan University ... MI ... 248
- Oakland Community College ... MI ... 248
- Lake Superior College ... MN ... 259
- Northland Community and Technical College ... MN ... 260
- St. Catherine University ... MN ... 263
- Saint Paul College-A Community & Technical College ... MN ... 261
- University of Minnesota-Twin Cities ... MN ... 264
- #Coahoma Community College ... MS ... 266
- Copiah-Lincoln Community College ... MS ... 266
- Hinds Community College ... MS ... 267
- Itawamba Community College ... MS ... 267
- Meridian Community College ... MS ... 267
- Northeast Mississippi Community College ... MS ... 269
- Northwest Mississippi Community College ... MS ... 269
- Pearl River Community College ... MS ... 269
- Concorde Career College ... MO ... 272
- #Jefferson College ... MO ... 275
- Missouri Southern State University ... MO ... 278
- #Missouri State University - West Plains ... MO ... 278
- Ozarks Technical Community College ... MO ... 279
- Saint Louis Community College at Forest Park ... MO ... 281
- Sanford-Brown College ... MO ... 281
- University of Missouri - Columbia ... MO ... 283
- Great Falls College Montana State University ... MT ... 287
- University of Montana - Missoula, The ... MT ... 286
- Metropolitan Community College ... NE ... 290
- Midland University ... NE ... 290
- Nebraska Methodist College ... NE ... 291
- Southeast Community College ... NE ... 292
- University of Nebraska at Kearney ... NE ... 292
- College of Southern Nevada ... NV ... 294
- River Valley Community College ... NH ... 296
- Bergen Community College ... NJ ... 299
- Brookdale Community College ... NJ ... 299
- County College of Morris ... NJ ... 300
- Central New Mexico Community College ... NM ... 309
- Eastern New Mexico University-Roswell ... NM ... 309
- New Mexico State University Dona Ana Community College ... NM ... 311
- #San Juan College ... NM ... 311
- Santa Fe Community College ... NM ... 311
- City University of New York Borough of Manhattan Community College ... NY ... 317
- Genesee Community College ... NY ... 325
- Hudson Valley Community College ... NY ... 326
- #Mandl School ... NY ... 329
- Mohawk Valley Community College ... NY ... 331
- Molloy College ... NY ... 331
- Nassau Community College ... NY ... 332
- Onondaga Community College ... NY ... 335
- State University of New York at Stony Brook ... NY ... 342
- State University of New York Upstate Medical University ... NY ... 342
- Sullivan County Community College ... NY ... 347
- Westchester Community College ... NY ... 350
- Carteret Community College ... NC ... 358
- Catawba Valley Community College ... NC ... 359
- Central Piedmont Community College ... NC ... 359
- Durham Technical Community College ... NC ... 360

Edgecombe Community College ... NC .. 360
Fayetteville Technical Community College NC .. 360
Forsyth Technical Community College ... NC .. 360
Pitt Community College ... NC .. 362
Robeson Community College ... NC .. 363
Rockingham Community College ... NC .. 363
Sandhills Community College ... NC .. 363
Southwestern Community College ... NC .. 364
Stanly Community College ... NC .. 364
Wilkes Community College ... NC .. 365
North Dakota State University Main Campus ... ND .. 371
University of Mary ... ND .. 373
Cincinnati State Technical and Community College ... OH .. 376
Columbus State Community College ... OH .. 378
Cuyahoga Community College ... OH .. 378
Eastern Gateway Community College - Jefferson County Campus ... OH .. 379
James A. Rhodes State College ... OH .. 381
Kettering College ... OH .. 382
Lakeland Community College ... OH .. 382
North Central State College ... OH .. 385
Ohio State University Main Campus, The . OH .. 386
Shawnee State University ... OH .. 388
Sinclair Community College ... OH .. 388
Stark State College ... OH .. 389
University of Akron, Main Campus, The ... OH .. 390
University of Cincinnati-Clermont College . OH .. 391
University of Rio Grande ... OH .. 392
University of Toledo ... OH .. 392
Washington State Community College ... OH .. 392
Youngstown State University ... OH .. 394
Northern Oklahoma College ... OK .. 396
Rose State College ... OK .. 399
Tulsa Community College ... OK .. 400
Concorde Career College ... OR .. 402
Lane Community College ... OR .. 403
Mt. Hood Community College ... OR .. 404
Oregon Institute of Technology ... OR .. 405
Community College of Allegheny County . PA ... 413
Community College of Philadelphia ... PA ... 413
Delaware County Community College ... PA ... 414
Gannon University ... PA ... 416
Gwynedd-Mercy University ... PA ... 417
Harrisburg Area Community College ... PA ... 417
Indiana University of Pennsylvania ... PA ... 428
Kaplan Career Institute ... PA ... 419
Lancaster General College of Nursing and Health Sciences ... PA ... 421
Laurel Business Institute ... PA ... 421
Laurel Technical Institute ... PA ... 421
Luzerne County Community College ... PA ... 422
Mansfield University of Pennsylvania ... PA ... 429
Millersville University of Pennsylvania ... PA ... 429
Reading Area Community College ... PA ... 431
West Chester University of Pennsylvania . PA ... 430
York College of Pennsylvania ... PA ... 438
#YTI Career Institute ... PA ... 438
#YTI Career Institute-Capital Region ... PA ... 438
Community College of Rhode Island ... RI ... 439
#New England Institute of Technology ... RI ... 439
Florence - Darlington Technical College ... SC ... 443
Greenville Technical College ... SC ... 444
Midlands Technical College ... SC ... 445
Orangeburg-Calhoun Technical College ... SC ... 446
Piedmont Technical College ... SC ... 446
Spartanburg Community College ... SC ... 447
Trident Technical College ... SC ... 447
Dakota State University ... SD ... 451
Baptist College of Health Sciences ... TN ... 453
Chattanooga State Community College ... TN ... 460
Columbia State Community College ... TN ... 460
Concorde Career College ... TN ... 453
East Tennessee State University ... TN ... 459
Jackson State Community College ... TN ... 460
Miller-Motte Technical College ... TN ... 457
Roane State Community College ... TN ... 461
Tennessee State University ... TN ... 459
Volunteer State Community College ... TN ... 461
Walters State Community College ... TN ... 462
Alvin Community College ... TX ... 465
Amarillo College ... TX ... 465
Angelina College ... TX ... 465
Cisco College ... TX ... 468
Collin County Community College District TX ... 469
Del Mar College ... TX ... 471
El Centro College ... TX ... 470
El Paso Community College ... TX ... 472
Houston Community College ... TX ... 473
Howard College ... TX ... 473
Lamar Institute of Technology ... TX ... 486
Lone Star College System ... TX ... 476
McLennan Community College ... TX ... 476
Midland College ... TX ... 476
Midwestern State University ... TX ... 476
St. Philip's College ... TX ... 465
San Jacinto College Central ... TX ... 479
South Plains College ... TX ... 480
South Texas College ... TX ... 480
Tarrant County College District ... TX ... 482
Temple College ... TX ... 482
Texas Southern University ... TX ... 485
Texas State University-San Marcos ... TX ... 487
Tyler Junior College ... TX ... 488
University of Texas at Brownsville and Texas Southmost College, The ... TX ... 491
University of Texas Health Science Center at San Antonio ... TX ... 493
University of Texas Medical Branch, The . TX ... 493
Victoria College ... TX ... 493
Weatherford College ... TX ... 494
Dixie State College of Utah ... UT ... 497
Independence University ... UT ... 495
Weber State University ... UT ... 497
Vermont Technical College ... VT ... 501
Central Virginia Community College ... VA ... 512
J. Sargeant Reynolds Community College VA ... 512
Jefferson College of Health Sciences ... VA ... 506
Mountain Empire Community College ... VA ... 513
Northern Virginia Community College ... VA ... 513
Shenandoah University ... VA ... 509
Tidewater Community College ... VA ... 514
Highline Community College ... WA .. 520
Seattle Central Community College ... WA .. 522
Spokane Community College ... WA .. 518
Tacoma Community College ... WA .. 524
Bridgemont Community and Technical College ... WV .. 527
Marshall University ... WV .. 529
#Pierpont Community & Technical College WV .. 528
Southern West Virginia Community and Technical College ... WV .. 528
West Virginia Northern Community College ... WV .. 528
Wheeling Jesuit University ... WV .. 531
Chippewa Valley Technical College ... WI ... 539
Madison Area Technical College ... WI ... 540
Mid-State Technical College ... WI ... 540
Milwaukee Area Technical College ... WI ... 540
Moraine Park Technical College ... WI ... 540
Northeast Wisconsin Technical College ... WI ... 541
Western Technical College ... WI ... 541
Casper College ... WY .. 542

COARCP: Commission on Accreditation for Respiratory Care: polysomnography (C)

Valencia College ... FL ... 118
Southern Crescent Technical College ... GA .. 132
Ivy Tech Community College-Central Indiana ... IN ... 169
State University of New York at Stony Brook ... NY ... 342
Youngstown State University ... OH .. 394
Gannon University ... PA ... 416
Texas State University-San Marcos ... TX ... 487

COE: Council on Occupational Education: occupational, trade, and technical education (C,A)

J.F. Ingram State Technical College ... AL ... 4
Reid State Technical College ... AL ... 6
Trenholm State Technical College ... AL ... 7
National Park Community College ... AR ... 22
Advanced College ... CA ... 26
Advanced Computing Institute ... CA ... 26
Advanced Training Associates ... CA ... 26
Ashdown College of Health Sciences ... CA ... 29
East San Gabriel Valley Regional Occupational Program and Technical Center ... CA ... 43
Los Angeles Pacific College ... CA ... 52
Mayfield College ... CA ... 54
Colorado Academy of Veterinary Technology ... CO ... 79
Academy for Nursing and Health Occupations ... FL ... 97
Fortis College ... FL ... 105
Miami Ad School ... FL ... 109
Praxis Institute, The ... FL ... 111
Saber College ... FL ... 112
Brown College of Court Reporting ... GA .. 122
#Interactive College of Technology ... GA .. 127
Lanier Technical College ... GA .. 128
Medtech College ... GA .. 128
Moultrie Technical College ... GA .. 129
Oconee Fall Line Technical College-North Campus ... GA .. 129
Oconee Fall Line Technical College-South Campus ... GA .. 129
Ogeechee Technical College ... GA .. 129
South Georgia Technical College ... GA .. 131
Morrison Institute of Technology ... IL ... 153
Galen College of Nursing ... KY ... 194
Cameron College ... LA ... 201
Career Technical College ... LA ... 201
Central Louisiana Technical College Avoyelles Campus ... LA ... 202
Central Louisiana Technical College Huey P. Long Campus ... LA ... 202
Central Louisiana Technical College Oakdale Campus ... LA ... 202
Central Louisiana Technical Community College ... LA ... 202
L.E. Fletcher Technical Community College ... LA ... 203
Louisiana Culinary Institute ... LA ... 204
Northshore Technical Community College LA ... 203
Northwest Louisiana Technical College Northwest Campus ... LA ... 203
South Central Louisiana Technical College Young Memorial Campus ... LA ... 203
South Louisiana Community College Ardoin Campus ... LA ... 203
South Louisiana Community College Charles B Coreil Campus ... LA ... 204
South Louisiana Community College Gulf Area Campus ... LA ... 204
South Louisiana Community College Teche Area Campus ... LA ... 204
South Louisiana Community College T.H. Harris Campus ... LA ... 204
Sowela Technical Community College ... LA ... 204
Lancaster County Career and Technology Center ... PA ... 421
Concorde Career College ... TN ... 453
Fortis Institute ... TN ... 454
Kaplan Career Institute ... TN ... 455
North Central Institute ... TN ... 457
Center for Advanced Legal Studies ... TX ... 468
Kaplan College ... TX ... 474
Kaplan College ... TX ... 475
Quest College ... TX ... 478
Vista College ... TX ... 494
Ogden-Weber Applied Technology College ... UT ... 496
Uintah Basin Applied Technology College UT ... 496
Career Training Solutions ... VA ... 502
Chester Career College ... VA ... 503
Columbia College ... VA ... 504
Medtech College ... VA ... 507
Southeast Culinary and Hospitality College ... VA ... 509

COMTA: Commission on Massage Therapy Accreditation: massage therapy, bodywork, aesthetics/ esthetics and skin care (C,A)

International Professional School of Bodywork ... CA ... 48
Academy of Natural Therapy ... CO ... 78
Florida College of Natural Health ... FL ... 104
Elgin Community College ... IL ... 144
Kishwaukee College ... IL ... 149
Moraine Valley Community College ... IL ... 153
National University of Health Sciences ... IL ... 154
SOLEX College ... IL ... 159
Allegany College of Maryland ... MD .. 213
Community College of Baltimore County, The ... MD .. 214
Bristol Community College ... MA .. 231
Lansing Community College ... MI ... 245
Northwestern Health Sciences University . MN .. 263
University of Western States ... OR .. 408
Community College of Rhode Island ... RI ... 439
Technical College of the Lowcountry ... SC ... 447
Roane State Community College ... TN ... 461
Parker University ... TX ... 478

CONST: American Council for Construction Education: construction education (A,B)

Auburn University ... AL ... 1
Jefferson State Community College ... AL ... 5
University of Alaska Anchorage ... AK ... 10
Arizona State University ... AZ ... 11
Northern Arizona University ... AZ ... 16
John Brown University ... AR ... 21
University of Arkansas at Little Rock ... AR ... 24
California Polytechnic State University-San Luis Obispo ... CA ... 32
California State University-Chico ... CA ... 33
California State University-Fresno ... CA ... 33
California State University-Long Beach ... CA ... 33
California State University-Northridge ... CA ... 34
California State University-Sacramento ... CA ... 34
Colorado State University ... CO ... 80
Central Connecticut State University ... CT ... 87
Florida International University ... FL ... 115
Santa Fe College ... FL ... 113
University of Florida ... FL ... 116
University of North Florida ... FL ... 116
Georgia Institute of Technology ... GA ... 125
Georgia Southern University ... GA .. 126
Southern Polytechnic State University ... GA .. 132
Boise State University ... ID ... 137
Bradley University ... IL ... 140
College of DuPage ... IL ... 142
Illinois State University ... IL ... 147
John A. Logan College ... IL ... 148
Southern Illinois University Edwardsville ... IL ... 159
Ball State University ... IN ... 164
Indiana State University ... IN ... 167
Purdue University Main Campus ... IN ... 171
Kansas State University ... KS ... 188
Eastern Kentucky University ... KY ... 193
Northern Kentucky University ... KY ... 198
Western Kentucky University ... KY ... 200
Louisiana State University and Agricultural and Mechanical College ... LA ... 204
University of Louisiana at Monroe ... LA ... 208
University of Maryland Eastern Shore ... MD .. 219
Wentworth Institute of Technology ... MA .. 237
Eastern Michigan University ... MI ... 242
Ferris State University ... MI ... 242
Michigan State University ... MI ... 246
Michigan Technological University ... MI ... 247
Minnesota State University Moorhead ... MN .. 259
Minnesota State University, Mankato ... MN .. 259
University of Southern Mississippi ... MS .. 270
Missouri State University ... MO .. 278
State Fair Community College ... MO .. 282
University of Central Missouri ... MO .. 283
University of Nebraska - Lincoln ... NE ... 292
University of Nevada, Las Vegas ... NV ... 294
Central New Mexico Community College . NM .. 309
University of New Mexico Main Campus .. NM .. 312
Alfred State College ... NY ... 345
State University of New York College of Technology at Delhi ... NY ... 345
East Carolina University ... NC .. 367
North Carolina Agricultural and Technical State University ... NC .. 367
Western Carolina University ... NC .. 369
North Dakota State University Main Campus ... ND .. 371
Bowling Green State University ... OH .. 374
Cincinnati State Technical and Community College ... OH .. 376
Columbus State Community College ... OH .. 378
University of Cincinnati Main Campus ... OH .. 390
University of Oklahoma Norman Campus . OK .. 401
Oregon State University ... OR .. 406
Drexel University ... PA ... 415
Pennsylvania College of Technology ... PA ... 427
Roger Williams University ... RI ... 440
Clemson University ... SC ... 442
South Dakota State University ... SD ... 452
North Lake College ... TX ... 471
Texas A & M University ... TX ... 483
Texas State University-San Marcos ... TX ... 487
University of Houston ... TX ... 489
Brigham Young University ... UT ... 495
Weber State University ... UT ... 497
Virginia Polytechnic Institute and State University ... VA ... 515
Central Washington University ... WA .. 517
Edmonds Community College ... WA .. 519
University of Washington ... WA .. 524
Washington State University ... WA .. 525
Milwaukee School of Engineering ... WI ... 534
University of Wisconsin-Stout ... WI ... 538

COPSY: American Psychological Association: counseling psychology (D)

Auburn University ... AL ... 1
Arizona State University ... AZ ... 11
Colorado State University ... CO ... 80
University of Denver ... CO ... 86
University of Northern Colorado ... CO ... 86
#Howard University ... DC ... 95
University of Florida ... FL ... 116
University of Miami ... FL ... 118
Georgia State University ... GA .. 126
University of Georgia ... GA .. 133
Loyola University Chicago ... IL ... 151
Southern Illinois University Carbondale ... IL ... 159
University of Illinois at Urbana-Champaign IL ... 162
Ball State University ... IN ... 164
Indiana State University ... IN ... 167
Indiana University Bloomington ... IN ... 167
Purdue University Main Campus ... IN ... 171
Iowa State University ... IA ... 175
University of Iowa ... IA ... 175
University of Kansas Main Campus ... KS ... 190
University of Kentucky ... KY ... 200
University of Louisville ... KY ... 200
Louisiana Tech University ... LA ... 207
University of Maryland College Park ... MD .. 219
Boston College ... MA .. 224
Western Michigan University ... MI ... 252
University of Minnesota-Twin Cities ... MN .. 264
University of Saint Thomas ... MN .. 265
University of Southern Mississippi ... MS .. 270
University of Missouri - Columbia ... MO .. 283
University of Missouri - Kansas City ... MO .. 283
University of Nebraska - Lincoln ... NE ... 292
Seton Hall University ... NJ ... 307
New Mexico State University Main Campus ... NM .. 310
Fordham University ... NY ... 324
New York University ... NY ... 334
Teachers College, Columbia University ... NY ... 347
University at Albany, SUNY ... NY ... 341
University of North Dakota Main Campus . ND ... 371
Cleveland State University ... OH .. 377
University of Akron, Main Campus, The ... OH .. 390
Oklahoma State University ... OK .. 397

University of Oklahoma Norman Campus ... OK ... 401
University of Oregon ... OR ... 406
Carlow University ... PA ... 412
Lehigh University ... PA ... 422
Penn State University Park ... PA ... 426
Tennessee State University ... TN ... 459
University of Memphis, The ... TN ... 460
University of Tennessee, Knoxville ... TN ... 463
Our Lady of the Lake University ... TX ... 477
Texas A & M University ... TX ... 483
Texas Tech University ... TX ... 487
Texas Woman's University ... TX ... 488
University of Houston ... TX ... 489
University of North Texas ... TX ... 490
University of Texas at Austin ... TX ... 491
Brigham Young University ... UT ... 495
University of Utah, The ... UT ... 496
Radford University ... VA ... 508
Virginia Commonwealth University ... VA ... 511
Washington State University ... WA ... 525
West Virginia University ... WV ... 530
Marquette University ... WI ... 534
University of Wisconsin-Madison ... WI ... 536
University of Wisconsin-Milwaukee ... WI ... 537

CORE: Council of Rehabilitation Education: rehabilitation counseling and rehabilitation services (B,M)

Alabama Agricultural and Mechanical University ... AL ... 1
Alabama State University ... AL ... 1
Auburn University ... AL ... 1
Troy University ... AL ... 7
University of Alabama, The ... AL ... 8
University of Arizona ... AZ ... 18
Arkansas State University-Jonesboro ... AR ... 19
Arkansas Tech University ... AR ... 20
University of Arkansas at Little Rock ... AR ... 24
University of Arkansas Main Campus ... AR ... 23
California State University-Fresno ... CA ... 33
California State University-Los Angeles ... CA ... 34
California State University-Sacramento ... CA ... 34
California State University-San Bernardino CA ... 34
San Diego State University ... CA ... 35
San Francisco State University ... CA ... 35
University of Northern Colorado ... CO ... 86
Central Connecticut State University ... CT ... 87
George Washington University ... DC ... 95
Florida Atlantic University ... FL ... 114
Florida State University ... FL ... 115
University of South Florida ... FL ... 116
Fort Valley State University ... GA ... 124
Georgia State University ... GA ... 126
Thomas University ... GA ... 132
University of Hawaii at Manoa ... HI ... 136
University of Idaho ... ID ... 139
Illinois Institute of Technology ... IL ... 147
Northeastern Illinois University ... IL ... 154
Northern Illinois University ... IL ... 154
Southern Illinois University Carbondale ... IL ... 159
Ball State University ... IN ... 164
Drake University ... IA ... 177
University of Iowa ... IA ... 175
Emporia State University ... KS ... 186
University of Kentucky ... KY ... 200
Louisiana State University Health Sciences Center-New Orleans ... LA ... 205
Southern University and A&M College ... LA ... 206
University of Southern Maine ... ME ... 212
Coppin State University ... MD ... 220
University of Maryland Eastern Shore ... MD ... 219
Assumption College ... MA ... 222
Springfield College ... MA ... 236
University of Massachusetts Boston ... MA ... 228
Michigan State University ... MI ... 246
Wayne State University ... MI ... 252
Western Michigan University ... MI ... 252
Minnesota State University, Mankato ... MN ... 259
St. Cloud State University ... MN ... 261
Jackson State University ... MS ... 267
Mississippi State University ... MS ... 268
Maryville University of Saint Louis ... MO ... 276
Montana State University - Billings ... MT ... 287
New Mexico Highlands University ... NM ... 310
City University of New York Hunter College ... NY ... 318
Hofstra University ... NY ... 326
University at Buffalo-SUNY ... NY ... 341
East Carolina University ... NC ... 367
North Carolina Agricultural and Technical State University ... NC ... 367
University of North Carolina at Chapel Hill NC ... 368
Winston-Salem State University ... NC ... 370
Kent State University Main Campus ... OH ... 382
Ohio University Main Campus ... OH ... 387
Wilberforce University ... OH ... 393
Wright State University Main Campus ... OH ... 393
East Central University ... OK ... 395
Langston University ... OK ... 395
Portland State University ... OR ... 406
Western Oregon University ... OR ... 406
Clarion University of Pennsylvania ... PA ... 428
Edinboro University of Pennsylvania ... PA ... 428
Penn State University Park ... PA ... 426
University of Pittsburgh ... PA ... 435
University of Scranton, The ... PA ... 436
Bayamon Central University ... PR ... 547
Pontifical Catholic University of Puerto Rico, The ... PR ... 552
University of Puerto Rico-Rio Piedras Campus ... PR ... 555
Salve Regina University ... RI ... 440
South Carolina State University ... SC ... 446
University of South Carolina Columbia ... SC ... 447
University of Memphis, The ... TN ... 460
University of Tennessee, Knoxville ... TN ... 463
Stephen F. Austin State University ... TX ... 482
Texas Tech University Health Sciences Center ... TX ... 487
University of North Texas ... TX ... 490
University of Texas at Austin ... TX ... 491
University of Texas - Pan American ... TX ... 492
University of Texas Southwestern Medical Center ... TX ... 493
Utah State University ... UT ... 497
Virginia Commonwealth University ... VA ... 511
Western Washington University ... WA ... 525
West Virginia University ... WV ... 530
University of Wisconsin-Madison ... WI ... 536
University of Wisconsin-Stout ... WI ... 538

CS: ABET, Inc.: computer science (B)

Alabama Agricultural and Mechanical University ... AL ... 1
Auburn University ... AL ... 1
Jacksonville State University ... AL ... 4
University of Alabama at Birmingham ... AL ... 8
University of Alabama in Huntsville ... AL ... 8
University of Alabama, The ... AL ... 8
University of North Alabama ... AL ... 9
University of South Alabama ... AL ... 9
University of Alaska Fairbanks ... AK ... 10
Arizona State University ... AZ ... 11
Northern Arizona University ... AZ ... 16
Arkansas Tech University ... AR ... 20
University of Arkansas at Little Rock ... AR ... 24
University of Arkansas Main Campus ... AR ... 23
University of Central Arkansas ... AR ... 25
California Polytechnic State University-San Luis Obispo ... CA ... 32
California State Polytechnic University-Pomona ... CA ... 32
California State University-Chico ... CA ... 33
California State University-Dominguez Hills ... CA ... 33
California State University-Fullerton ... CA ... 33
California State University-Long Beach ... CA ... 33
California State University-Los Angeles ... CA ... 34
California State University-Northridge ... CA ... 34
California State University-Sacramento ... CA ... 34
California State University-San Bernardino CA ... 34
San Francisco State University ... CA ... 35
San Jose State University ... CA ... 36
Santa Clara University ... CA ... 64
University of California-Berkeley ... CA ... 70
University of California-Davis ... CA ... 70
University of California-Irvine ... CA ... 71
University of California-Los Angeles ... CA ... 71
University of California-Riverside ... CA ... 71
University of California-Santa Barbara ... CA ... 72
University of Southern California ... CA ... 74
University of the Pacific ... CA ... 73
Metropolitan State University of Denver ... CO ... 83
Regis University ... CO ... 84
United States Air Force Academy ... CO ... 545
University of Colorado Boulder ... CO ... 85
University of Colorado Colorado Springs ... CO ... 85
University of Colorado DenverlAnschutz Medical Campus ... CO ... 86
Central Connecticut State University ... CT ... 87
Quinnipiac University ... CT ... 91
Southern Connecticut State University ... CT ... 88
University of Connecticut ... CT ... 92
University of New Haven ... CT ... 92
George Washington University ... DC ... 95
Howard University ... DC ... 95
University of the District of Columbia ... DC ... 97
Florida Agricultural and Mechanical University ... FL ... 114
Florida Atlantic University ... FL ... 114
Florida Institute of Technology ... FL ... 104
Florida International University ... FL ... 115
Florida Memorial University ... FL ... 104
Florida State University ... FL ... 115
University of Central Florida ... FL ... 115
University of North Florida ... FL ... 116
University of South Florida ... FL ... 116
Armstrong Atlantic State University ... GA ... 120
Georgia Institute of Technology ... GA ... 125
Georgia Southern University ... GA ... 126
Kennesaw State University ... GA ... 127
Mercer University ... GA ... 128
Middle Georgia State College ... GA ... 128
Southern Polytechnic State University ... GA ... 132
University of West Georgia ... GA ... 133
Boise State University ... ID ... 137
Idaho State University ... ID ... 138
University of Idaho ... ID ... 139
Illinois Institute of Technology ... IL ... 147
Illinois State University ... IL ... 147
Southern Illinois University Carbondale ... IL ... 159
Southern Illinois University Edwardsville ... IL ... 159
University of Illinois at Chicago ... IL ... 161
University of Illinois at Urbana-Champaign IL ... 162
Indiana University-Purdue University Fort Wayne ... IN ... 168
Indiana University-Purdue University Indianapolis ... IN ... 168
Purdue University Calumet ... IN ... 171
Purdue University Main Campus ... IN ... 171
Rose-Hulman Institute of Technology ... IN ... 172
University of Evansville ... IN ... 173
University of Notre Dame ... IN ... 174
Iowa State University ... IA ... 175
Kansas State University ... KS ... 188
University of Kansas Main Campus ... KS ... 190
Eastern Kentucky University ... KY ... 193
University of Kentucky ... KY ... 200
University of Louisville ... KY ... 200
Grambling State University ... LA ... 207
Louisiana State University and Agricultural and Mechanical College ... LA ... 204
Louisiana State University in Shreveport ... LA ... 205
Louisiana Tech University ... LA ... 207
McNeese State University ... LA ... 207
Southeastern Louisiana University ... LA ... 208
Southern University and A&M College ... LA ... 206
University of Louisiana at Lafayette ... LA ... 208
University of Louisiana at Monroe ... LA ... 208
University of New Orleans ... LA ... 205
University of Maine ... ME ... 212
University of Southern Maine ... ME ... 212
Johns Hopkins University ... MD ... 215
Loyola University Maryland ... MD ... 216
Towson University ... MD ... 220
United States Naval Academy ... MD ... 545
University of Maryland Baltimore County ... MD ... 219
Fitchburg State University ... MA ... 229
Massachusetts Institute of Technology ... MA ... 233
Northeastern University ... MA ... 235
Salem State University ... MA ... 230
Tufts University ... MA ... 237
University of Massachusetts Boston ... MA ... 228
University of Massachusetts Dartmouth ... MA ... 229
Wentworth Institute of Technology ... MA ... 237
Westfield State University ... MA ... 230
Worcester Polytechnic Institute ... MA ... 238
Calvin College ... MI ... 240
Grand Valley State University ... MI ... 243
Kettering University ... MI ... 244
Michigan State University ... MI ... 246
Oakland University ... MI ... 248
University of Michigan-Ann Arbor ... MI ... 251
University of Michigan-Dearborn ... MI ... 251
Western Michigan University ... MI ... 252
Capella University ... MN ... 254
St. Cloud State University ... MN ... 261
University of Minnesota Duluth ... MN ... 264
Jackson State University ... MS ... 267
Mississippi State University ... MS ... 268
Mississippi Valley State University ... MS ... 269
University of Mississippi ... MS ... 270
University of Southern Mississippi ... MS ... 270
Missouri State University ... MO ... 278
Missouri University of Science & Technology ... MO ... 284
Southeast Missouri State University ... MO ... 282
University of Missouri - Columbia ... MO ... 283
University of Missouri - Kansas City ... MO ... 283
Montana State University ... MT ... 287
Montana Tech of The University of Montana ... MT ... 287
University of Montana - Missoula, The ... MT ... 286
University of Nebraska at Omaha ... NE ... 293
University of Nebraska - Lincoln ... NE ... 292
University of Nevada, Las Vegas ... NV ... 294
University of Nevada, Reno ... NV ... 294
University of New Hampshire ... NH ... 298
College of New Jersey, The ... NJ ... 300
Fairleigh Dickinson University ... NJ ... 301
Montclair State University ... NJ ... 303
New Jersey Institute of Technology ... NJ ... 303
Rowan University ... NJ ... 305
Stevens Institute of Technology ... NJ ... 307
William Paterson University of New Jersey ... NJ ... 308
New Mexico Institute of Mining and Technology ... NM ... 310
University of New Mexico Main Campus ... NM ... 312
City University of New York College of Staten Island ... NY ... 317
City University of New York The City College ... NY ... 317
Iona College ... NY ... 327
Pace University ... NY ... 335
Rochester Institute of Technology ... NY ... 337
State University of New York at Binghamton ... NY ... 341
State University of New York at Stony Brook ... NY ... 342
State University of New York, The College at Brockport ... NY ... 342
Syracuse University Main Campus ... NY ... 347
United States Military Academy ... NY ... 545
Appalachian State University ... NC ... 367
Fayetteville State University ... NC ... 367
North Carolina Agricultural and Technical State University ... NC ... 367
North Carolina State University ... NC ... 368
University of North Carolina at Greensboro ... NC ... 369
University of North Carolina Wilmington ... NC ... 369
Winston-Salem State University ... NC ... 370
University of North Dakota Main Campus ... ND ... 371
Case Western Reserve University ... OH ... 375
Cedarville University ... OH ... 375
Miami University ... OH ... 384
Ohio Northern University ... OH ... 386
Ohio State University Main Campus, The ... OH ... 386
Ohio University Main Campus ... OH ... 387
University of Cincinnati Main Campus ... OH ... 390
University of Toledo ... OH ... 392
Wright State University Main Campus ... OH ... 393
Oklahoma State University Institute of Technology-Okmulgee ... OK ... 398
University of Central Oklahoma ... OK ... 400
University of Oklahoma Norman Campus ... OK ... 401
University of Tulsa ... OK ... 401
Oregon State University ... OR ... 406
Portland State University ... OR ... 406
University of Portland ... OR ... 408
Bloomsburg University of Pennsylvania ... PA ... 427
Bucknell University ... PA ... 411
California University of Pennsylvania ... PA ... 428
Drexel University ... PA ... 415
East Stroudsburg University of Pennsylvania ... PA ... 428
Edinboro University of Pennsylvania ... PA ... 428
Gannon University ... PA ... 416
Indiana University of Pennsylvania ... PA ... 428
Lafayette College ... PA ... 420
Lehigh University ... PA ... 422
Millersville University of Pennsylvania ... PA ... 429
Robert Morris University ... PA ... 431
Shippensburg University of Pennsylvania ... PA ... 429
Slippery Rock University of Pennsylvania ... PA ... 429
University of Pennsylvania ... PA ... 435
University of Scranton, The ... PA ... 436
Villanova University ... PA ... 436
West Chester University of Pennsylvania ... PA ... 430
York College of Pennsylvania ... PA ... 438
University of Puerto Rico at Arecibo ... PR ... 553
University of Puerto Rico-Rio Piedras Campus ... PR ... 555
Citadel, The Military College of South Carolina, The ... SC ... 442
Clemson University ... SC ... 442
Coastal Carolina University ... SC ... 442
College of Charleston ... SC ... 443
South Carolina State University ... SC ... 446
University of South Carolina Columbia ... SC ... 447
University of South Carolina Upstate ... SC ... 448
Winthrop University ... SC ... 449
South Dakota School of Mines and Technology ... SD ... 452
South Dakota State University ... SD ... 452
East Tennessee State University ... TN ... 459
Middle Tennessee State University ... TN ... 459
Southern Adventist University ... TN ... 458
Tennessee State University ... TN ... 459
Tennessee Technological University ... TN ... 460
University of Memphis, The ... TN ... 460
University of Tennessee at Chattanooga ... TN ... 463
University of Tennessee, Knoxville ... TN ... 463
Baylor University ... TX ... 467
Lamar University ... TX ... 486
Prairie View A & M University ... TX ... 482
Sam Houston State University ... TX ... 487
Southern Methodist University ... TX ... 481
Stephen F. Austin State University ... TX ... 482
Texas A & M University ... TX ... 483
Texas A & M University - Corpus Christi ... TX ... 483
Texas Christian University ... TX ... 484
Texas State University-San Marcos ... TX ... 487
University of Houston ... TX ... 489
University of Houston - Clear Lake ... TX ... 489
University of North Texas ... TX ... 490
University of Texas at Arlington, The ... TX ... 491
University of Texas at Brownsville and Texas Southmost College, The ... TX ... 491
University of Texas at Dallas, The ... TX ... 491
University of Texas at El Paso ... TX ... 492
University of Texas - Pan American ... TX ... 492
Brigham Young University ... UT ... 495
Southern Utah University ... UT ... 497
Utah State University ... UT ... 497
Utah Valley University ... UT ... 497
George Mason University ... VA ... 505
Hampton University ... VA ... 505
James Madison University ... VA ... 506
Norfolk State University ... VA ... 507
Radford University ... VA ... 508
University of Virginia ... VA ... 511

Institution	State	Page
University of Virginia's College at Wise, The	VA	511
Virginia Commonwealth University	VA	511
Virginia Military Institute	VA	515
Virginia Polytechnic Institute and State University	VA	515
Virginia State University	VA	515
Eastern Washington University	WA	519
Pacific Lutheran University	WA	521
Washington State University	WA	525
Western Washington University	WA	525
West Virginia University	WV	530
University of Wisconsin-Eau Claire	WI	536
University of Wisconsin-Milwaukee	WI	537
University of Wisconsin-Oshkosh	WI	537
University of Wyoming	WY	543

CVT: Commission on Accreditation of Allied Health Education Programs: cardiovascular technology (C,A,B)

Institution	State	Page
Grossmont College	CA	46
Orange Coast College	CA	39
Central Florida Institute	FL	99
Edison State College	FL	101
Polk State College	FL	110
Sanford-Brown Institute	FL	112
Santa Fe College	FL	113
Valencia College	FL	118
Augusta Technical College	GA	121
Darton State College	GA	124
Sanford-Brown College	GA	131
Spencerian College	KY	199
Louisiana State University Health Sciences Center-New Orleans	LA	205
Howard Community College	MD	215
Sanford-Brown College of Boston, Inc.	MA	236
Grand Valley State University	MI	243
Northland Community and Technical College	MN	260
Saint Cloud Technical and Community College	MN	261
Bryan College of Health Sciences	NE	288
Molloy College	NY	331
Central Piedmont Community College	NC	359
Mercy College of Ohio	OH	383
Geneva College	PA	417
Gwynedd-Mercy University	PA	417
Harrisburg Area Community College	PA	417
Lancaster General College of Nursing and Health Sciences	PA	421
Piedmont Technical College	SC	446
Southeast Technical Institute	SD	452
Northeast State Community College	TN	461
El Centro College	TX	470
Sanford-Brown College	TX	480
Sentara College of Health Sciences	VA	509
Spokane Community College	WA	518
Milwaukee Area Technical College	WI	540

CYTO: Commission on Accreditation of Allied Health Education Programs: cytotechnology (C,B,M)

Institution	State	Page
University of Alabama at Birmingham	AL	8
University of Arkansas for Medical Sciences	AR	24
Loma Linda University	CA	51
University of California-Los Angeles	CA	71
Indiana University-Purdue University Indianapolis	IN	168
University of Mississippi Medical Center	MS	270
Saint Louis University	MO	281
University of Nebraska Medical Center	NE	292
Albany College of Pharmacy and Health Sciences	NY	313
Central Piedmont Community College	NC	359
University of North Dakota Main Campus	ND	371
Thomas Jefferson University	PA	434
University of Puerto Rico-Medical Sciences Campus	PR	554
University of Rhode Island	RI	440
University of Texas M.D. Anderson Cancer Center, The	TX	493
University of Utah, The	UT	496
Old Dominion University	VA	507
Marshall University	WV	529
University of Wisconsin-Madison	WI	536
University of Wisconsin-Milwaukee	WI	537

DA: American Dental Association: dental assisting (C,A)

Institution	State	Page
Calhoun Community College	AL	2
Fortis College	AL	3
James H. Faulkner State Community College	AL	4
Lawson State Community College	AL	5
Trenholm State Technical College	AL	7
Wallace State Community College - Hanceville	AL	9
University of Alaska Anchorage	AK	10
Phoenix College	AZ	15
Pima Community College	AZ	17
Rio Salado College	AZ	15
Arkansas Northeastern College	AR	19
Pulaski Technical College	AR	22
Cerritos College	CA	37
Chaffey College	CA	37
Citrus College	CA	38
City College of San Francisco	CA	38
College of Alameda	CA	59
College of Marin	CA	40
College of San Mateo	CA	64
College of the Redwoods Community College District	CA	40
Contra Costa College	CA	41
Cypress College	CA	56
Diablo Valley College	CA	41
Foothill College	CA	44
Heald College, Concord	CA	46
Heald College, Hayward	CA	46
Heald College, Stockton	CA	47
Moreno Valley College	CA	60
Orange Coast College	CA	39
Palomar College	CA	58
Pasadena City College	CA	58
Sacramento City College	CA	53
San Diego Mesa College	CA	62
San Jose City College	CA	63
Santa Rosa Junior College	CA	65
Front Range Community College	CO	81
IntelliTec Medical Institute	CO	82
Pikes Peak Community College	CO	84
Pueblo Community College	CO	84
Lincoln College of New England	CT	90
Tunxis Community College	CT	89
Broward College	FL	99
College of Central Florida	FL	100
Daytona State College	FL	101
Eastern Florida State College	FL	101
Florida State College at Jacksonville	FL	105
Gulf Coast State College	FL	106
Hillsborough Community College	FL	106
Indian River State College	FL	106
Lincoln Tech Fern Park Orlando Campus	FL	108
Northwest Florida State College	FL	109
Palm Beach State College	FL	110
Santa Fe College	FL	113
South Florida State College	FL	113
Tallahassee Community College	FL	117
Albany Technical College	GA	120
Athens Technical College	GA	120
Atlanta Technical College	GA	121
Augusta Technical College	GA	121
Columbus Technical College	GA	123
Georgia Northwestern Technical College	GA	125
Gwinnett Technical College	GA	127
Lanier Technical College	GA	128
Ogeechee Technical College	GA	129
Savannah Technical College	GA	131
Southern Crescent Technical College	GA	132
Wiregrass Georgia Technical College	GA	134
University of Hawaii Maui College	HI	137
Carrington College - Boise	ID	137
College of Western Idaho	ID	138
Elgin Community College	IL	144
Illinois Valley Community College	IL	148
John A. Logan College	IL	148
Kaskaskia College	IL	149
Lewis and Clark Community College	IL	150
Indiana University Northwest	IN	168
Indiana University-Purdue University Fort Wayne	IN	168
Indiana University-Purdue University Indianapolis	IN	168
Kaplan College	IN	170
University of Southern Indiana	IN	174
Des Moines Area Community College	IA	177
Hawkeye Community College	IA	178
Indian Hills Community College	IA	179
Iowa Western Community College	IA	179
Kirkwood Community College	IA	180
Marshalltown Community College	IA	179
Northeast Iowa Community College	IA	181
Scott Community College	IA	178
Vatterott College-Des Moines	IA	183
Western Iowa Tech Community College	IA	183
Flint Hills Technical College	KS	186
Labette Community College	KS	188
Salina Area Technical College	KS	190
Wichita Area Technical College	KS	191
Bluegrass Community and Technical College	KY	194
West Kentucky Community and Technical College	KY	196
University of Maine at Augusta	ME	212
Hagerstown Community College	MD	215
Massasoit Community College	MA	232
Middlesex Community College	MA	232
Mount Wachusett Community College	MA	232
Northern Essex Community College	MA	232
Quinsigamond Community College	MA	232
Salter College	MA	236
Springfield Technical Community College	MA	233
Delta College	MI	242
Grand Rapids Community College	MI	243
Lake Michigan College	MI	245
Mott Community College	MI	247
Northwestern Michigan College	MI	248
Washtenaw Community College	MI	252
Wayne County Community College District	MI	252
Central Lakes College	MN	258
Century College	MN	258
Dakota County Technical College	MN	258
Hennepin Technical College	MN	258
Hibbing Community College, A Technical and Community College	MN	258
Minneapolis Community and Technical College	MN	259
Minnesota State Community and Technical College	MN	259
Minnesota West Community and Technical College	MN	260
Northwest Technical College	MN	260
Rochester Community and Technical College	MN	261
Saint Cloud Technical and Community College	MN	261
South Central College	MN	261
Hinds Community College	MS	267
Meridian Community College	MS	267
Pearl River Community College	MS	269
Metropolitan Community College - Penn Valley	MO	277
Missouri College	MO	278
Ozarks Technical Community College	MO	279
Saint Louis Community College at Forest Park	MO	281
Great Falls College Montana State University	MT	287
Salish Kootenai College	MT	288
Central Community College	NE	288
Metropolitan Community College	NE	290
Mid-Plains Community College	NE	290
Southeast Community College	NE	292
Vatterott College-Omaha	NE	293
College of Southern Nevada	NV	294
Truckee Meadows Community College	NV	294
NHTI-Concord's Community College	NH	296
Camden County College	NJ	300
Central New Mexico Community College	NM	309
Luna Community College	NM	309
New Mexico State University Dona Ana Community College	NM	311
Santa Fe Community College	NM	311
Monroe Community College	NY	332
University at Buffalo-SUNY	NY	341
Alamance Community College	NC	357
Asheville - Buncombe Technical Community College	NC	357
Cape Fear Community College	NC	358
Central Carolina Community College	NC	359
Central Piedmont Community College	NC	359
Coastal Carolina Community College	NC	359
Fayetteville Technical Community College	NC	360
Forsyth Technical Community College	NC	360
Guilford Technical Community College	NC	360
Martin Community College	NC	361
Montgomery Community College	NC	362
Rowan-Cabarrus Community College	NC	363
University of North Carolina at Chapel Hill	NC	368
Wake Technical Community College	NC	364
Wayne Community College	NC	364
Western Piedmont Community College	NC	365
Wilkes Community College	NC	365
North Dakota State College of Science	ND	372
Eastern Gateway Community College - Jefferson County Campus	OH	379
Fortis College	OH	379
Rose State College	OK	399
Blue Mountain Community College	OR	402
Central Oregon Community College	OR	402
Chemeketa Community College	OR	402
Lane Community College	OR	403
Linn-Benton Community College	OR	404
Portland Community College	OR	407
Bradford School	PA	410
Harcum College	PA	417
Harrisburg Area Community College	PA	417
Luzerne County Community College	PA	422
Manor College	PA	423
Westmoreland County Community College	PA	437
University of Puerto Rico-Medical Sciences Campus	PR	554
Community College of Rhode Island	RI	439
Aiken Technical College	SC	440
Florence - Darlington Technical College	SC	443
Greenville Technical College	SC	444
Horry-Georgetown Technical College	SC	444
Midlands Technical College	SC	445
Spartanburg Community College	SC	447
Tri-County Technical College	SC	447
Trident Technical College	SC	447
York Technical College	SC	449
Lake Area Technical Institute	SD	450
Chattanooga State Community College	TN	460
Concorde Career College	TN	453
Kaplan Career Institute	TN	455
Northeast State Community College	TN	461
Volunteer State Community College	TN	461
Del Mar College	TX	471
El Paso Community College	TX	472
Grayson College	TX	472
Houston Community College	TX	473
San Antonio College	TX	465
Texas State Technical College Waco	TX	486
Ogden-Weber Applied Technology College	UT	496
Germanna Community College	VA	512
J. Sargeant Reynolds Community College	VA	512
Northern Virginia Community College	VA	513
Bates Technical College	WA	516
Bellingham Technical College	WA	517
Clover Park Technical College	WA	518
Lake Washington Institute of Technology	WA	520
Renton Technical College	WA	522
South Puget Sound Community College	WA	524
Spokane Community College	WA	518
Blackhawk Technical College	WI	539
Fox Valley Technical College	WI	539
Gateway Technical College	WI	540
Northeast Wisconsin Technical College	WI	541
Western Technical College	WI	541

DANCE: National Association of Schools of Dance: dance (C,A,B,M,D)

Institution	State	Page
University of Alabama, The	AL	8
University of Arizona	AZ	18
California Institute of the Arts	CA	31
California State University-Fullerton	CA	33
California State University-Long Beach	CA	33
Chapman University	CA	38
Loyola Marymount University	CA	53
San Jose State University	CA	36
University of California-Santa Barbara	CA	72
University of Hartford	CT	92
Florida State University	FL	115
Jacksonville University	FL	107
Miami Dade College	FL	109
University of Florida	FL	116
Brenau University	GA	122
University of Georgia	GA	133
University of Illinois at Urbana-Champaign	IL	162
Ball State University	IN	164
Butler University	IN	164
University of Iowa	IA	175
Wichita State University	KS	191
Western Kentucky University	KY	200
Towson University	MD	220
University of Maryland Baltimore County	MD	219
Hope College	MI	244
Oakland University	MI	248
University of Michigan-Ann Arbor	MI	251
Wayne State University	MI	252
Western Michigan University	MI	252
St. Olaf College	MN	264
University of Minnesota-Twin Cities	MN	264
Belhaven University	MS	266
University of Southern Mississippi	MS	270
University of Missouri - Kansas City	MO	283
University of Nebraska - Lincoln	NE	292
Montclair State University	NJ	303
Rutgers the State University of New Jersey New Brunswick Campus	NJ	306
University of New Mexico Main Campus	NM	312
Barnard College	NY	314
Fordham University	NY	324
State University of New York, The College at Brockport	NY	342
University of North Carolina at Greensboro	NC	369
Kent State University Main Campus	OH	382
Ohio State University Main Campus, The	OH	386
Ohio University Main Campus	OH	387
University of Akron, Main Campus, The	OH	390
University of Cincinnati Main Campus	OH	390
Mercyhurst University	PA	423
Point Park University	PA	431
Slippery Rock University of Pennsylvania	PA	429
Temple University	PA	433
Columbia College	SC	443
Winthrop University	SC	449
Southern Methodist University	TX	481
Texas Christian University	TX	484
Texas Woman's University	TX	488
University of Texas at Austin	TX	491
Brigham Young University	UT	495
Southern Utah University	UT	497
University of Utah, The	UT	496
James Madison University	VA	506
Virginia Commonwealth University	VA	511
University of Wisconsin-Milwaukee	WI	537
University of Wisconsin-Stevens Point	WI	538

DENT: American Dental Association: dentistry (FP,D)

Institution	State	Page
University of Alabama at Birmingham	AL	8
Loma Linda University	CA	51
University of California-Los Angeles	CA	71
University of California-San Francisco	CA	72
University of Southern California	CA	74
University of the Pacific	CA	73

Western University of Health Sciences	CA	76
United States Air Force Academy	CO	545
University of Colorado DenverlAnschutz Medical Campus	CO	86
Howard University	DC	95
Jacksonville University	FL	107
Nova Southeastern University	FL	109
University of Florida	FL	116
University of Miami	FL	118
Emory University	GA	124
Georgia Regents University	GA	126
Idaho State University	ID	138
Loyola University Chicago	IL	151
Midwestern University	IL	153
Southern Illinois University Edwardsville	IL	159
University of Illinois at Chicago	IL	161
Indiana University-Purdue University Indianapolis	IN	168
University of Iowa	IA	175
Wichita State University	KS	191
University of Kentucky	KY	200
University of Louisville	KY	200
Louisiana State University Health Sciences Center at Shreveport	LA	205
Louisiana State University Health Sciences Center-New Orleans	LA	205
University of New England	ME	213
University of Maryland Baltimore	MD	219
Harvard University	MA	227
Tufts University	MA	237
University of Detroit Mercy	MI	250
University of Michigan-Ann Arbor	MI	251
University of Minnesota-Twin Cities	MN	264
University of Mississippi Medical Center	MS	270
Saint Louis University	MO	281
University of Missouri - Kansas City	MO	283
Creighton University	NE	289
University of Nebraska Medical Center	NE	292
Roseman University of Health Sciences	NV	295
University of Nevada, Las Vegas	NV	294
University of New Mexico Main Campus	NM	312
Columbia University in the City of New York	NY	321
Icahn School of Medicine at Mount Sinai	NY	327
New York Medical College	NY	334
New York University	NY	334
State University of New York at Stony Brook	NY	342
State University of New York Upstate Medical University	NY	342
University at Buffalo-SUNY	NY	341
University of Rochester	NY	349
Yeshiva University	NY	351
East Carolina University	NC	367
University of North Carolina at Chapel Hill	NC	368
Wake Forest University	NC	370
Case Western Reserve University	OH	375
Ohio State University Main Campus, The	OH	386
University of Cincinnati Main Campus	OH	390
University of Toledo	OH	392
Oregon Health & Science University	OR	405
Drexel University	PA	415
Lake Erie College of Osteopathic Medicine	PA	420
Seton Hill University	PA	433
Temple University	PA	433
Thomas Jefferson University	PA	434
University of Pennsylvania	PA	435
University of Pittsburgh	PA	435
University of Puerto Rico-Medical Sciences Campus	PR	554
Medical University of South Carolina	SC	445
Meharry Medical College	TN	456
University of Tennessee, Knoxville	TN	463
Vanderbilt University	TN	463
University of Texas Health Science Center at Houston (UTHealth), The	TX	492
University of Texas Health Science Center at San Antonio	TX	493
University of Texas M.D. Anderson Cancer Center, The	TX	493
University of Texas Medical Branch, The	TX	493
University of Utah, The	UT	496
University of Virginia	VA	511
Virginia Commonwealth University	VA	511
University of Washington	WA	524
West Virginia University	WV	530
Marquette University	WI	534
Medical College of Wisconsin	WI	534

DETC: Distance Education and Training Council: home study schools (A,B,M,D)

Columbia Southern University	AL	2
Acacia University	AZ	11
Brighton College	AZ	12
Dunlap-Stone University	AZ	13
Harrison Middleton University	AZ	14
National Paralegal College	AZ	16
Paralegal Institute, The	AZ	16
Penn Foster College	AZ	16
Sessions College for Professional Design	AZ	17
Sonoran Desert Institute	AZ	17
Abraham Lincoln University	CA	26
Allied American University	CA	27
American Graduate University	CA	27
Anaheim University	CA	28
Apollos University	CA	28
APT College	CA	28
California Coast University	CA	30
California Intercontinental University	CA	31
California Miramar University	CA	32
California National University for Advanced Studies	CA	32
California Southern University	CA	32
Grace Communion Seminary	CA	45
Henley-Putnam University	CA	47
New Charter University	CA	56
Southwestern Law School	CA	68
Taft Law School	CA	69
University of Philosophical Research	CA	73
American Sentinel University	CO	78
Aspen University	CO	78
Holmes Institute of Consciousness Studies	CO	82
McKinley College	CO	83
U.S. Career Institute	CO	86
William Howard Taft University	CO	87
University of St. Augustine for Health Sciences	FL	118
Ashworth College	GA	120
Babel University Professional School of Translation	HI	135
John Hancock University	IL	148
Antioch School of Church Planting and Leadership Development	IA	175
Inste Bible College	IA	179
Shiloh University	IA	182
Southwest University	LA	207
Griggs University	MI	243
American College of Technology	MO	271
City Vision College	MO	272
Global University	MO	274
Grantham University	MO	274
Rockbridge Seminary	MO	280
Cleveland Institute of Electronics	OH	377
Lakewood College	OH	383
American College of Healthcare Sciences	OR	401
Huntington College of Health Sciences	TN	454
Atlantic University	VA	502
Catholic Distance University, The	VA	503
University of Fairfax	VA	510
University of Management & Technology	VA	510
World College	VA	516
Northwest Institute of Literary Arts	WA	521
Martinsburg College	WV	527

DH: American Dental Association: dental hygiene (C,A,B,M)

Wallace State Community College - Hanceville	AL	9
University of Alaska Anchorage	AK	10
University of Alaska Fairbanks	AK	10
Mesa Community College	AZ	15
Mohave Community College	AZ	15
Northern Arizona University	AZ	16
Phoenix College	AZ	15
Pima Community College	AZ	17
Rio Salado College	AZ	15
University of Arkansas at Fort Smith	AR	24
University of Arkansas for Medical Sciences	AR	24
Cabrillo College	CA	30
Carrington College California - Sacramento	CA	36
Cerritos College	CA	37
Chabot College	CA	37
Concorde Career College	CA	41
Cypress College	CA	56
Diablo Valley College	CA	41
Foothill College	CA	44
Fresno City College	CA	68
Loma Linda University	CA	51
Moreno Valley College	CA	60
Oxnard College	CA	74
Pasadena City College	CA	58
Sacramento City College	CA	53
San Joaquin Valley College, Inc. - Visalia	CA	63
Santa Rosa Junior College	CA	65
Shasta College	CA	65
Southwestern College	CA	68
Taft College	CA	69
University of Southern California	CA	74
University of the Pacific	CA	73
West Coast University	CA	75
West Los Angeles College	CA	52
Colorado Northwestern Community College	CO	80
Community College of Denver	CO	81
Concorde Career College	CO	81
Pueblo Community College	CO	84
Lincoln College of New England	CT	90
Tunxis Community College	CT	89
University of Bridgeport	CT	91
University of New Haven	CT	92
Delaware Technical Community College, Stanton-Wilmington Campus	DE	93
Howard University	DC	95
Broward College	FL	99
Daytona State College	FL	101
Eastern Florida State College	FL	101
Edison State College	FL	101
Florida State College at Jacksonville	FL	105
Gulf Coast State College	FL	106
Hillsborough Community College	FL	106
Indian River State College	FL	106
Miami Dade College	FL	109
Palm Beach State College	FL	110
Pasco-Hernando Community College	FL	110
Pensacola State College	FL	110
St. Petersburg College	FL	112
Sanford-Brown Institute	FL	112
Santa Fe College	FL	113
South Florida State College	FL	113
State College of Florida, Manatee-Sarasota	FL	114
Tallahassee Community College	FL	117
Valencia College	FL	118
Athens Technical College	GA	120
Atlanta Technical College	GA	121
Central Georgia Technical College	GA	122
Clayton State University	GA	123
Columbus Technical College	GA	123
Darton State College	GA	124
Georgia Highlands College	GA	125
Georgia Perimeter College	GA	125
Georgia Regents University	GA	126
Lanier Technical College	GA	128
Savannah Technical College	GA	131
Southeastern Technical College	GA	132
West Georgia Technical College	GA	134
Wiregrass Georgia Technical College	GA	134
University of Hawaii at Manoa	HI	136
University of Hawaii Maui College	HI	137
Carrington College - Boise	ID	137
College of Southern Idaho	ID	138
Idaho State University	ID	138
Carl Sandburg College	IL	141
City Colleges of Chicago Kennedy-King College	IL	142
College of DuPage	IL	142
College of Lake County	IL	143
Harper College	IL	145
Illinois Central College	IL	146
John A. Logan College	IL	148
Lake Land College	IL	150
Lewis and Clark Community College	IL	150
Parkland College	IL	155
Prairie State College	IL	156
Rock Valley College	IL	157
Southern Illinois University Carbondale	IL	159
Indiana University Northwest	IN	168
Indiana University-Purdue University Fort Wayne	IN	168
Indiana University-Purdue University Indianapolis	IN	168
Indiana University South Bend	IN	168
University of Southern Indiana	IN	174
Des Moines Area Community College	IA	177
Hawkeye Community College	IA	178
Iowa Central Community College	IA	179
Iowa Western Community College	IA	179
Kirkwood Community College	IA	180
Flint Hills Technical College	KS	186
Johnson County Community College	KS	187
Manhattan Area Technical College	KS	188
Wichita State University	KS	191
Big Sandy Community and Technical College	KY	194
Bluegrass Community and Technical College	KY	194
Henderson Community College	KY	195
University of Louisville	KY	200
Western Kentucky University	KY	200
Louisiana State University Health Sciences Center-New Orleans	LA	205
Southern University at Shreveport-Louisiana	LA	207
University of Louisiana at Monroe	LA	208
University of Maine at Augusta	ME	212
University of New England	ME	213
Allegany College of Maryland	MD	213
Baltimore City Community College	MD	213
Community College of Baltimore County, The	MD	214
University of Maryland Baltimore	MD	219
Bristol Community College	MA	231
Cape Cod Community College	MA	231
MCPHS University	MA	233
Middlesex Community College	MA	232
Mount Ida College	MA	234
Mount Wachusett Community College	MA	232
Quinsigamond Community College	MA	232
Springfield Technical Community College	MA	233
Delta College	MI	242
Ferris State University	MI	242
Grand Rapids Community College	MI	243
Kalamazoo Valley Community College	MI	244
Kellogg Community College	MI	244
Lansing Community College	MI	245
Mott Community College	MI	247
Oakland Community College	MI	248
University of Detroit Mercy	MI	250
University of Michigan-Ann Arbor	MI	251
Wayne County Community College District	MI	252
Century College	MN	258
Lake Superior College	MN	259
Minnesota State University Moorhead	MN	259
Minnesota State University, Mankato	MN	259
Normandale Community College	MN	260
Rochester Community and Technical College	MN	261
Saint Cloud Technical and Community College	MN	261
University of Minnesota-Twin Cities	MN	264
Meridian Community College	MS	267
Mississippi Delta Community College	MS	268
Northeast Mississippi Community College	MS	269
Pearl River Community College	MS	269
University of Mississippi Medical Center	MS	270
Concorde Career College	MO	272
Missouri College	MO	278
Missouri Southern State University	MO	278
North Central Missouri College	MO	279
Ozarks Technical Community College	MO	279
Saint Louis Community College at Forest Park	MO	281
State Fair Community College	MO	282
University of Missouri - Kansas City	MO	283
Great Falls College Montana State University	MT	287
Central Community College	NE	288
University of Nebraska Medical Center	NE	292
College of Southern Nevada	NV	294
Truckee Meadows Community College	NV	294
NHTI-Concord's Community College	NH	296
Bergen Community College	NJ	299
Burlington County College	NJ	299
Camden County College	NJ	300
Eastern International College	NJ	301
Middlesex County College	NJ	303
Eastern New Mexico University-Roswell	NM	309
New Mexico State University Dona Ana Community College	NM	311
San Juan College	NM	311
University of New Mexico Main Campus	NM	312
Briarcliffe College	NY	315
Broome Community College	NY	315
Farmingdale State College	NY	346
Hostos Community College-City University of New York	NY	318
Hudson Valley Community College	NY	326
Monroe Community College	NY	332
New York City College of Technology/City University of New York	NY	319
New York University	NY	334
Orange County Community College	NY	335
SUNY Canton-College of Technology	NY	345
Asheville - Buncombe Technical Community College	NC	357
Cape Fear Community College	NC	358
Catawba Valley Community College	NC	359
Central Carolina Community College	NC	359
Central Piedmont Community College	NC	359
Coastal Carolina Community College	NC	359
Fayetteville Technical Community College	NC	360
Forsyth Technical Community College	NC	360
Guilford Technical Community College	NC	360
Halifax Community College	NC	361
University of North Carolina at Chapel Hill	NC	368
Wake Technical Community College	NC	364
Wayne Community College	NC	364
North Dakota State College of Science	ND	372
Columbus State Community College	OH	378
Cuyahoga Community College	OH	378
James A. Rhodes State College	OH	381
Lakeland Community College	OH	382
Lorain County Community College	OH	383
Ohio State University Main Campus, The	OH	386
Owens Community College	OH	387
Shawnee State University	OH	388
Sinclair Community College	OH	388
Stark State College	OH	389
University of Cincinnati-Blue Ash College	OH	391
Youngstown State University	OH	394
Rose State College	OK	399
Tulsa Community College	OK	400
Lane Community College	OR	403
Mt. Hood Community College	OR	404
Oregon Institute of Technology	OR	405
Pacific University	OR	407
Portland Community College	OR	407
Community College of Philadelphia	PA	413
Fortis Institute	PA	416
Harcum College	PA	417
Harrisburg Area Community College	PA	417
Luzerne County Community College	PA	422
Manor College	PA	423
Montgomery County Community College	PA	424
Northampton Community College	PA	425
Pennsylvania College of Technology	PA	427
University of Pittsburgh	PA	435

Westmoreland County Community College .... PA ... 437
Community College of Rhode Island .... RI ... 439
Florence - Darlington Technical College ... SC ... 443
Greenville Technical College .... SC ... 444
Horry-Georgetown Technical College .... SC ... 444
Midlands Technical College .... SC ... 445
Trident Technical College .... SC ... 447
York Technical College .... SC ... 449
University of South Dakota, The .... SD ... 451
Chattanooga State Community College .... TN ... 460
Concorde Career College .... TN ... 453
East Tennessee State University .... TN ... 459
Hiwassee College .... TN ... 454
Roane State Community College .... TN ... 461
Tennessee State University .... TN ... 459
Amarillo College .... TX ... 465
Austin Community College District .... TX ... 466
Blinn College .... TX ... 467
Coastal Bend College .... TX ... 468
Collin County Community College District .... TX ... 469
Del Mar College .... TX ... 471
El Paso Community College .... TX ... 472
Houston Community College .... TX ... 473
Howard College .... TX ... 473
Lamar Institute of Technology .... TX ... 486
Lone Star College System .... TX ... 476
Midwestern State University .... TX ... 476
Northeast Texas Community College .... TX ... 477
Sanford-Brown College .... TX ... 480
Tarrant County College District .... TX ... 482
Temple College .... TX ... 482
Texas State Technical College Harlingen .... TX ... 485
Texas Woman's University .... TX ... 488
Tyler Junior College .... TX ... 488
University of Texas Health Science Center at Houston (UTHealth), The .... TX ... 492
Wharton County Junior College .... TX ... 494
Dixie State College of Utah .... UT ... 497
Salt Lake Community College .... UT ... 498
Utah College of Dental Hygiene at Careers Unlimited, The .... UT ... 496
Utah Valley University .... UT ... 497
Weber State University .... UT ... 497
Vermont Technical College .... VT ... 501
Northern Virginia Community College .... VA ... 513
Old Dominion University .... VA ... 507
Thomas Nelson Community College .... VA ... 514
Virginia Commonwealth University .... VA ... 511
Virginia Western Community College .... VA ... 514
Wytheville Community College .... VA ... 514
Bellingham Technical College .... WA ... 517
Clark College .... WA .. 518
Columbia Basin College .... WA .. 518
Eastern Washington University .... WA .. 519
Lake Washington Institute of Technology .... WA .. 520
Pierce College District .... WA .. 522
Seattle Central Community College .... WA .. 522
Shoreline Community College .... WA .. 523
Yakima Valley Community College .... WA .. 525
Bridgemont Community and Technical College .... WV .. 527
Southern West Virginia Community and Technical College .... WV .. 528
West Liberty University .... WV .. 530
West Virginia University .... WV .. 530
Chippewa Valley Technical College .... WI ... 539
Fox Valley Technical College .... WI ... 539
Madison Area Technical College .... WI ... 540
Milwaukee Area Technical College .... WI ... 540
Nicolet Area Technical College .... WI ... 540
Northcentral Technical College .... WI ... 541
Northeast Wisconsin Technical College .... WI ... 541
Waukesha County Technical College .... WI ... 541
Laramie County Community College .... WY .. 543
Northern Wyoming Community College District .... WY .. 543

DIETC: Academy of Nutrition and Dietetics: coordinated dietetics programs (B,M)

University of Alabama, The .... AL 8
@Arkansas State University-Jonesboro .... AR 19
California State University-Los Angeles .... CA 34
Loma Linda University .... CA 51
Colorado State University .... CO 80
University of Connecticut .... CT 92
Howard University .... DC 95
Florida International University .... FL ... 115
Georgia State University .... GA .. 126
University of Idaho .... ID ... 139
Dominican University .... IL 144
University of Illinois at Chicago .... IL 161
Indiana State University .... IN 167
Purdue University Main Campus .... IN 171
Kansas State University .... KS ... 188
University of Kentucky .... KY ... 200
Johns Hopkins University .... MD .. 215
Framingham State University .... MA .. 230
Eastern Michigan University .... MI ... 242
Wayne State University .... MI ... 252
University of Minnesota-Twin Cities .... MN .. 264
Delta State University .... MS .. 266
@University of Mississippi .... MS .. 270
University of Missouri - Columbia .... MO .. 283
D'Youville College .... NY ... 323
State University of New York College at Buffalo .... NY ... 343
University of North Carolina at Chapel Hill .... NC .. 368
North Dakota State University Main Campus .... ND .. 371
University of North Dakota Main Campus .... ND .. 371
Ohio State University Main Campus, The .... OH .. 386
University of Akron, Main Campus, The .... OH .. 390
University of Cincinnati Main Campus .... OH .. 390
Youngstown State University .... OH .. 394
La Salle University .... PA ... 420
Marywood University .... PA ... 423
Seton Hill University .... PA ... 433
University of Pittsburgh .... PA ... 435
Universidad Del Turabo .... PR ... 552
Texas Christian University .... TX ... 484
University of Texas at Austin .... TX ... 491
@University of Texas Health Science Center at San Antonio .... TX ... 493
University of Texas - Pan American .... TX ... 492
University of Texas Southwestern Medical Center .... TX ... 493
University of Utah, The .... UT ... 496
Utah State University .... UT ... 497
University of Vermont .... VT ... 500
University of Washington .... WA .. 524
Washington State University .... WA .. 525
Mount Mary University .... WI ... 535
Viterbo University .... WI ... 539

DIETD: Academy of Nutrition and Dietetics: didactic dietetics programs (B,M)

Alabama Agricultural and Mechanical University .... AL 1
Auburn University .... AL 1
Jacksonville State University .... AL 4
Oakwood University .... AL 6
Samford University .... AL 6
Tuskegee University .... AL 8
University of Alabama, The .... AL 8
University of Montevallo .... AL 9
@University of Alaska Anchorage .... AK 10
Arizona State University .... AZ 11
University of Arizona .... AZ 18
Harding University Main Campus .... AR 21
Henderson State University .... AR 21
Ouachita Baptist University .... AR 22
@University of Arkansas at Pine Bluff .... AR 24
University of Arkansas Main Campus .... AR 23
University of Central Arkansas .... AR 25
California Polytechnic State University-San Luis Obispo .... CA 32
California State Polytechnic University-Pomona .... CA 32
California State University-Chico .... CA 33
California State University-Fresno .... CA 33
California State University-Long Beach .... CA 33
California State University-Los Angeles .... CA 34
California State University-Northridge .... CA 34
California State University-Sacramento .... CA 34
California State University-San Bernardino .... CA 34
Pepperdine University .... CA 58
Point Loma Nazarene University .... CA 59
San Diego State University .... CA 35
San Francisco State University .... CA 35
San Jose State University .... CA 36
University of California-Berkeley .... CA 70
University of California-Davis .... CA 70
Colorado State University .... CO 80
Metropolitan State University of Denver .... CO 83
University of Colorado Colorado Springs .... CO 85
University of Northern Colorado .... CO 86
University of Connecticut .... CT 92
University of New Haven .... CT 92
University of Saint Joseph .... CT 92
#Delaware State University .... DE 93
University of Delaware .... DE 94
University of the District of Columbia .... DC 97
Florida International University .... FL ... 115
Florida State University .... FL ... 115
University of Florida .... FL ... 116
University of North Florida .... FL ... 116
Georgia Southern University .... GA .. 126
Georgia State University .... GA .. 126
Life University .... GA .. 128
University of Georgia .... GA .. 133
University of Hawaii at Manoa .... HI ... 136
Idaho State University .... ID ... 138
Benedictine University .... IL 140
Bradley University .... IL 140
Dominican University .... IL 144
Eastern Illinois University .... IL 144
Illinois State University .... IL 147
Northern Illinois University .... IL 154
Olivet Nazarene University .... IL 155
Southern Illinois University Carbondale .... IL 159
University of Illinois at Chicago .... IL 161
University of Illinois at Urbana-Champaign .... IL 162
Western Illinois University .... IL 162
Ball State University .... IN 164
Indiana University Bloomington .... IN 167
Purdue University Main Campus .... IN 171
@University of Southern Indiana .... IN 174
Iowa State University .... IA 175
Kansas State University .... KS ... 188
Eastern Kentucky University .... KY ... 193
Murray State University .... KY ... 198
University of Kentucky .... KY ... 200
Western Kentucky University .... KY ... 200
Louisiana State University and Agricultural and Mechanical College .... LA ... 204
Louisiana Tech University .... LA ... 207
McNeese State University .... LA ... 207
Nicholls State University .... LA ... 208
Southern University and A&M College .... LA ... 206
University of Louisiana at Lafayette .... LA ... 208
University of Maine .... ME ... 212
Morgan State University .... MD .. 217
University of Maryland College Park .... MD .. 219
University of Maryland Eastern Shore .... MD .. 219
Boston University .... MA .. 224
Framingham State University .... MA .. 230
Simmons College .... MA .. 236
University of Massachusetts .... MA .. 228
Andrews University .... MI ... 239
Central Michigan University .... MI ... 240
Madonna University .... MI ... 246
Michigan State University .... MI ... 246
University of Michigan-Ann Arbor .... MI ... 251
Western Michigan University .... MI ... 252
College of Saint Benedict .... MN .. 254
Concordia College .... MN .. 255
Minnesota State University, Mankato .... MN .. 259
St. Catherine University .... MN .. 263
Saint John's University .... MN .. 263
University of Minnesota-Twin Cities .... MN .. 264
#Alcorn State University .... MS .. 265
Mississippi State University .... MS .. 268
University of Mississippi .... MS .. 270
University of Southern Mississippi .... MS .. 270
College of the Ozarks .... MO .. 272
Fontbonne University .... MO .. 274
Missouri State University .... MO .. 278
Northwest Missouri State University .... MO .. 279
Saint Louis University .... MO .. 281
Southeast Missouri State University .... MO .. 282
University of Central Missouri .... MO .. 283
Montana State University .... MT .. 287
University of Nebraska - Lincoln .... NE ... 292
University of Nevada, Las Vegas .... NV ... 294
University of Nevada, Reno .... NV ... 294
Keene State College .... NH .. 298
University of New Hampshire .... NH .. 298
College of Saint Elizabeth .... NJ ... 300
Montclair State University .... NJ ... 303
Rutgers the State University of New Jersey New Brunswick Campus .... NJ ... 306
New Mexico State University Main Campus .... NM .. 310
University of New Mexico Main Campus .... NM .. 312
City University of New York Brooklyn College .... NY ... 317
City University of New York Herbert H. Lehman College .... NY ... 318
City University of New York Hunter College .... NY ... 318
City University of New York Queens College .... NY ... 319
Cornell University .... NY ... 322
Long Island University - Post Campus .... NY ... 329
New York University .... NY ... 334
Rochester Institute of Technology .... NY ... 337
Sage Colleges, The .... NY ... 338
State University of New York College at Buffalo .... NY ... 343
State University of New York College at Oneonta .... NY ... 343
State University of New York College at Plattsburgh .... NY ... 344
Syracuse University Main Campus .... NY ... 347
Appalachian State University .... NC .. 367
East Carolina University .... NC .. 367
Meredith College .... NC .. 356
North Carolina Agricultural and Technical State University .... NC .. 367
North Carolina Central University .... NC .. 368
University of North Carolina at Greensboro .... NC .. 369
Western Carolina University .... NC .. 369
North Dakota State University Main Campus .... ND ... 371
@Ashland University .... OH .. 374
Bluffton University .... OH .. 374
Bowling Green State University .... OH .. 374
Case Western Reserve University .... OH .. 375
Kent State University Main Campus .... OH .. 382
Miami University .... OH .. 384
Ohio State University Main Campus, The .... OH .. 386
Ohio University Main Campus .... OH .. 387
University of Akron, Main Campus, The .... OH .. 390
University of Cincinnati Main Campus .... OH .. 390
University of Dayton .... OH .. 391
Youngstown State University .... OH .. 394
Northeastern State University .... OK .. 396
Oklahoma State University .... OK .. 397
University of Central Oklahoma .... OK .. 400
Oregon State University .... OR .. 406
Cedar Crest College .... PA ... 412
Drexel University .... PA ... 415
Immaculata University .... PA ... 418
Indiana University of Pennsylvania .... PA ... 428
La Salle University .... PA ... 420
Mansfield University of Pennsylvania .... PA ... 429
Marywood University .... PA ... 423
Messiah College .... PA ... 423
Penn State University Park .... PA ... 426
University of Pittsburgh .... PA ... 435
West Chester University of Pennsylvania .... PA ... 430
University of Puerto Rico-Rio Piedras Campus .... PR ... 555
Johnson & Wales University .... RI ... 439
University of Rhode Island .... RI ... 440
Clemson University .... SC ... 442
South Carolina State University .... SC ... 446
Winthrop University .... SC ... 449
South Dakota State University .... SD ... 452
Carson-Newman University .... TN ... 453
East Tennessee State University .... TN ... 459
Lipscomb University .... TN ... 456
Middle Tennessee State University .... TN ... 459
Tennessee State University .... TN ... 459
Tennessee Technological University .... TN ... 460
University of Memphis, The .... TN ... 460
University of Tennessee at Chattanooga .... TN ... 463
University of Tennessee at Martin .... TN ... 463
University of Tennessee, Knoxville .... TN ... 463
Abilene Christian University .... TX ... 464
Baylor University .... TX ... 467
Lamar University .... TX ... 486
Prairie View A & M University .... TX ... 482
Sam Houston State University .... TX ... 487
Stephen F. Austin State University .... TX ... 482
Texas A & M University .... TX ... 483
Texas A & M University - Kingsville .... TX ... 484
Texas Christian University .... TX ... 484
Texas Southern University .... TX ... 485
Texas State University-San Marcos .... TX ... 487
Texas Tech University .... TX ... 487
Texas Woman's University .... TX ... 488
University of Houston .... TX ... 489
University of Texas at Austin .... TX ... 491
University of the Incarnate Word .... TX ... 490
Brigham Young University .... UT ... 495
Utah State University .... UT ... 497
University of Vermont .... VT ... 500
James Madison University .... VA ... 506
Norfolk State University .... VA ... 507
Radford University .... VA ... 508
Virginia Polytechnic Institute and State University .... VA ... 515
Virginia State University .... VA ... 515
Bastyr University .... WA .. 516
Central Washington University .... WA .. 517
Seattle Pacific University .... WA .. 523
Marshall University .... WV ... 529
West Virginia University .... WV ... 530
University of Wisconsin-Green Bay .... WI ... 536
University of Wisconsin-Madison .... WI ... 536
University of Wisconsin-Stevens Point .... WI ... 538
University of Wisconsin-Stout .... WI ... 538
University of Wyoming .... WY .. 543

DIETI: Academy of Nutrition and Dietetics: dietetic post-baccalaureate internships

Oakwood University .... AL 6
University of Alabama at Birmingham .... AL 8
University of Alaska Anchorage .... AK 10
Arizona State University .... AZ 11
University of Arizona .... AZ 18
University of Arkansas for Medical Sciences .... AR 24
University of Central Arkansas .... AR 25
California Polytechnic State University-San Luis Obispo .... CA 32
California State Polytechnic University-Pomona .... CA 32
California State University-Chico .... CA 33
California State University-Fresno .... CA 33
California State University-Long Beach .... CA 33
California State University-Northridge .... CA 34
California State University-Sacramento .... CA 34
San Francisco State University .... CA 35
San Jose State University .... CA 36
University of California-Davis .... CA 70
@University of California-San Diego .... CA 71
University of California-San Francisco .... CA 72
University of Southern California .... CA 74
University of Northern Colorado .... CO 86
University of Connecticut .... CT 92
University of Saint Joseph .... CT 92
University of Delaware .... DE 94
Florida State University .... FL ... 115
University of Florida .... FL ... 116
University of North Florida .... FL ... 116
@Georgia Southern University .... GA .. 126

Life University ... GA .. 128
University of Georgia ... GA .. 133
Idaho State University ... ID 138
Benedictine University ... IL 140
@Bradley University ... IL 140
Eastern Illinois University ... IL 144
Illinois State University ... IL 147
Loyola University Chicago ... IL 151
Northern Illinois University ... IL 154
Rush University ... IL 157
Southern Illinois University Carbondale ... IL 159
University of Illinois at Urbana-Champaign IL 162
Ball State University ... IN 164
Indiana University-Purdue University Indianapolis ... IN 168
Iowa State University ... IA 175
University of Iowa ... IA 175
Eastern Kentucky University ... KY ... 193
Murray State University ... KY ... 198
University of Kentucky ... KY ... 200
@Western Kentucky University ... KY ... 200
Louisiana Tech University ... LA ... 207
McNeese State University ... LA ... 207
Southern University and A&M College ... LA ... 206
Tulane University ... LA ... 207
University of Louisiana at Lafayette ... LA ... 208
University of Maine ... ME .. 212
University of Maryland Baltimore ... MD .. 219
University of Maryland College Park ... MD .. 219
University of Maryland Eastern Shore ... MD .. 219
Boston University ... MA .. 224
Simmons College ... MA .. 236
Tufts University ... MA .. 237
University of Massachusetts ... MA .. 228
Andrews University ... MI 239
Central Michigan University ... MI 240
Michigan State University ... MI 246
University of Michigan-Ann Arbor ... MI 251
Western Michigan University ... MI 252
Concordia College ... MN .. 255
University of Minnesota-Twin Cities ... MN .. 264
Mississippi State University ... MS .. 268
University of Southern Mississippi ... MS .. 270
Cox College ... MO .. 273
@Missouri State University ... MO .. 278
Saint Louis University ... MO .. 281
Southeast Missouri State University ... MO .. 282
@Montana State University ... MT .. 287
University of Nebraska - Lincoln ... NE .. 292
University of Nebraska Medical Center ... NE .. 292
University of Nevada, Las Vegas ... NV .. 294
University of Nevada, Reno ... NV .. 294
Keene State College ... NH .. 298
University of New Hampshire ... NH .. 298
College of Saint Elizabeth ... NJ .. 300
Montclair State University ... NJ .. 303
@New Mexico State University Main Campus ... NM .. 310
University of New Mexico Main Campus .. NM .. 312
City University of New York Brooklyn College ... NY ... 317
City University of New York Herbert H. Lehman College ... NY ... 318
City University of New York Hunter College ... NY ... 318
City University of New York Queens College ... NY ... 319
Cornell University ... NY ... 322
Long Island University - Post Campus ... NY ... 329
New York University ... NY ... 334
Sage Colleges, The ... NY ... 338
State University of New York at Stony Brook ... NY ... 342
State University of New York College at Oneonta ... NY ... 343
Syracuse University Main Campus ... NY ... 347
Teachers College, Columbia University ... NY ... 347
University at Buffalo-SUNY ... NY ... 341
Appalachian State University ... NC .. 367
East Carolina University ... NC .. 367
@Lenoir-Rhyne University ... NC .. 356
Meredith College ... NC .. 356
North Carolina Central University ... NC .. 368
University of North Carolina at Greensboro ... NC .. 369
Western Carolina University ... NC .. 369
Bowling Green State University ... OH .. 374
Case Western Reserve University ... OH .. 375
Kent State University Main Campus ... OH .. 382
Ohio State University Main Campus, The . OH .. 386
Oklahoma State University ... OK .. 397
University of Central Oklahoma ... OK .. 400
Oregon Health & Science University ... OR .. 405
Oregon State University ... OR .. 406
@Cedar Crest College ... PA .. 412
Immaculata University ... PA .. 418
Indiana University of Pennsylvania ... PA .. 428
Marywood University ... PA .. 423
Penn State University Park ... PA .. 426
University of Puerto Rico-Medical Sciences Campus ... PR .. 554
University of Rhode Island ... RI 440
Medical University of South Carolina ... SC ... 445
Winthrop University ... SC ... 449
University of South Dakota, The ... SD ... 451
East Tennessee State University ... TN ... 459
Lipscomb University ... TN ... 456
University of Memphis, The ... TN ... 460
#University of Tennessee at Martin ... TN ... 463
University of Tennessee, Knoxville ... TN ... 463
Vanderbilt University ... TN ... 463
Baylor College of Medicine ... TX ... 467
Lamar University ... TX ... 486
Prairie View A & M University ... TX ... 482
Sam Houston State University ... TX ... 487
Stephen F. Austin State University ... TX ... 482
Texas A & M University ... TX ... 483
Texas A & M University - Kingsville ... TX ... 484
Texas State University-San Marcos ... TX ... 487
Texas Tech University ... TX ... 487
Texas Woman's University ... TX ... 488
University of Houston ... TX ... 489
University of Texas Health Science Center at Houston (UTHealth), The ... TX ... 492
@University of Texas Medical Branch, The . TX ... 493
University of the Incarnate Word ... TX ... 490
Brigham Young University ... UT ... 495
Utah State University ... UT ... 497
University of Virginia ... VA ... 511
Virginia Commonwealth University ... VA ... 511
Virginia Polytechnic Institute and State University ... VA ... 515
Virginia State University ... VA ... 515
Bastyr University ... WA .. 516
Central Washington University ... WA .. 517
Marshall University ... WV .. 529
West Virginia University ... WV .. 530
Mount Mary University ... WI ... 535
University of Wisconsin-Green Bay ... WI ... 536
University of Wisconsin-Stout ... WI ... 538
Viterbo University ... WI ... 539

DIETT: Academy of Nutrition and Dietetics: dietetic technician (A)

Central Arizona College ... AZ 12
Chandler-Gilbert Community College ... AZ 14
Paradise Valley Community College ... AZ 15
Black River Technical College ... AR 20
Los Angeles City College ... CA 51
Merritt College ... CA 59
Orange Coast College ... CA 39
Santa Rosa Junior College ... CA 65
Gateway Community College ... CT 88
Lincoln College of New England ... CT 90
Florida State College at Jacksonville ... FL ... 105
Hillsborough Community College ... FL ... 106
Harper College ... IL 145
Delgado Community College ... LA ... 203
Southern Maine Community College ... ME .. 211
Laboure College ... MA .. 227
Normandale Community College ... MN .. 260
@Great Falls College Montana State University ... MT .. 287
Southeast Community College ... NE .. 292
Truckee Meadows Community College ... NV .. 294
University of New Hampshire ... NH .. 298
Camden County College ... NJ ... 300
Middlesex County College ... NJ ... 303
La Guardia Community College/City University of New York ... NY ... 318
State University of New York College of Agriculture and Technology at Morrisville ... NY ... 345
@Trocaire College ... NY ... 348
Westchester Community College ... NY ... 350
Gaston College ... NC .. 360
Cincinnati State Technical and Community College ... OH .. 376
Columbus State Community College ... OH .. 378
Cuyahoga Community College ... OH .. 378
Owens Community College ... OH .. 387
Sinclair Community College ... OH .. 388
@Stark State College ... OH .. 389
Youngstown State University ... OH .. 394
@Oklahoma State University - Oklahoma City ... OK .. 398
Community College of Allegheny County . PA ... 413
Southwest Tennessee Community College ... TN ... 461
Tarrant County College District ... TX ... 482
Milwaukee Area Technical College ... WI ... 540

DMOLS: National Accrediting Agency for Clinical Laboratory Sciences: diagnostic molecular scientist (C,B,M)

University of Connecticut ... CT 92
Michigan State University ... MI ... 246
Northern Michigan University ... MI ... 248
State University of New York Upstate Medical University ... NY ... 342
University of North Carolina at Chapel Hill NC .. 368
Texas Tech University Health Sciences Center ... TX ... 487
University of Texas M.D. Anderson Cancer Center, The ... TX ... 493

DMS: Commission on Accreditation of Allied Health Education Programs: diagnostic medical sonography (C,A, B,M)

Lurleen B. Wallace Community College ... AL 5
Trenholm State Technical College ... AL 7
Virginia College ... AL 3
Wallace State Community College - Hanceville ... AL 9
Central Arizona College ... AZ 12
Gateway Community College ... AZ 14
Arkansas State University-Jonesboro ... AR 19
University of Arkansas at Fort Smith ... AR 24
University of Arkansas for Medical Sciences ... AR 24
Cypress College ... CA 56
Foothill College ... CA 44
Kaiser Permanente School of Allied Health Sciences ... CA 49
Loma Linda University ... CA 51
Orange Coast College ... CA 39
Platt College ... CA 59
Santa Barbara City College ... CA 64
University of California-San Diego ... CA 71
University of Colorado Denver/Anschutz Medical Campus ... CO 86
Delaware Technical Community College, Owens Campus ... DE 93
Delaware Technical Community College, Stanton-Wilmington Campus ... DE 93
George Washington University ... DC 95
Adventist University of Health Sciences ... FL 97
Broward College ... FL 99
Cambridge Institute of Allied Health & Technology ... FL 99
#Central Florida Institute ... FL 99
Dade Medical College ... FL ... 100
Hillsborough Community College ... FL ... 100
Keiser University ... FL ... 108
Miami Dade College ... FL ... 109
Nova Southeastern University ... FL ... 109
Palm Beach State College ... FL ... 110
Polk State College ... FL ... 110
Santa Fe College ... FL ... 113
Valencia College ... FL ... 118
Athens Technical College ... GA .. 120
Columbus Technical College ... GA .. 123
Georgia Northwestern Technical College . GA .. 125
Ogeechee Technical College ... GA .. 129
Sanford-Brown College ... GA .. 131
Boise State University ... ID 137
College of DuPage ... IL 142
Harper College ... IL 145
John A. Logan College ... IL 148
Rush University ... IL 157
Southern Illinois University Carbondale ... IL 159
Triton College ... IL 161
St. Anthony School of Echocardiography . IN 172
University of Southern Indiana ... IN 174
Mercy College of Health Sciences ... IA 181
University of Iowa ... IA 175
Labette Community College ... KS 188
Washburn University ... KS 191
Hazard Community and Technical College KY ... 195
Jefferson Community and Technical College ... KY ... 195
Morehead State University ... KY ... 198
St. Catharine College ... KY ... 198
Southcentral Kentucky Community and Technical College ... KY ... 196
West Kentucky Community and Technical College ... KY ... 196
Delgado Community College ... LA ... 203
Louisiana State University at Eunice ... LA ... 205
Kennebec Valley Community College ... ME .. 210
Johns Hopkins University ... MD .. 215
Montgomery College ... MD .. 216
University of Maryland Baltimore County .. MD .. 219
Bunker Hill Community College ... MA .. 231
Middlesex Community College ... MA .. 232
Springfield Technical Community College MA .. 233
Delta College ... MI ... 242
Ferris State University ... MI ... 242
Grand Valley State University ... MI ... 243
Jackson College ... MI ... 244
Lansing Community College ... MI ... 245
Madonna University ... MI ... 246
Oakland Community College ... MI ... 248
St. Catherine University ... MN .. 263
Saint Cloud Technical and Community College ... MN .. 261
Hinds Community College ... MS .. 267
Cox College ... MO .. 273
Saint Louis Community College at Forest Park ... MO .. 281
Sanford-Brown College ... MO .. 281
University of Missouri - Columbia ... MO .. 283
Bryan College of Health Sciences ... NE ... 288
Nebraska Methodist College ... NE ... 291
University of Nebraska Medical Center ... NE ... 292
College of Southern Nevada ... NV ... 294
NHTI-Concord's Community College ... NH .. 296
Bergen Community College ... NJ ... 299
Burlington County College ... NJ ... 299
Gloucester County College ... NJ ... 302
Central New Mexico Community College . NM .. 309
New Mexico State University Dona Ana Community College ... NM .. 311
Hudson Valley Community College ... NY .. 326
Rochester Institute of Technology ... NY ... 337
State University of New York Health Science Center at Brooklyn ... NY ... 342
Asheville - Buncombe Technical Community College ... NC ... 357
Caldwell Community College and Technical Institute ... NC ... 358
Cape Fear Community College ... NC ... 358
Forsyth Technical Community College ... NC ... 360
Johnston Community College ... NC ... 361
#Pitt Community College ... NC ... 362
South Piedmont Community College ... NC ... 363
Southwestern Community College ... NC ... 364
Central Ohio Technical College ... OH .. 376
Cincinnati State Technical and Community College ... OH .. 376
Cuyahoga Community College ... OH .. 378
Kettering College ... OH .. 382
Lorain County Community College ... OH .. 383
Owens Community College ... OH .. 387
University of Rio Grande ... OH .. 392
Oklahoma State University - Oklahoma City ... OK .. 398
Community College of Allegheny County . PA ... 413
Great Lakes Institute of Technology ... PA ... 417
Harrisburg Area Community College ... PA ... 417
Lackawanna College ... PA ... 420
Lancaster General College of Nursing and Health Sciences ... PA ... 421
Misericordia University ... PA ... 424
Mount Aloysius College ... PA ... 424
Northampton Community College ... PA ... 425
Sanford-Brown Institute-Pittsburgh ... PA ... 433
South Hills School of Business and Technology ... PA ... 433
Thomas Jefferson University ... PA ... 434
Westmoreland County Community College ... PA ... 437
Community College of Rhode Island ... RI ... 439
Greenville Technical College ... SC ... 444
Horry-Georgetown Technical College ... SC ... 444
Southeast Technical Institute ... SD ... 452
Baptist College of Health Sciences ... TN ... 453
Chattanooga State Community College ... TN ... 460
Vanderbilt University ... TN ... 463
Volunteer State Community College ... TN ... 461
Alvin Community College ... TX ... 465
Angelina College ... TX ... 465
Austin Community College District ... TX ... 466
Del Mar College ... TX ... 471
El Centro College ... TX ... 470
El Paso Community College ... TX ... 472
Houston Community College ... TX ... 473
Lamar Institute of Technology ... TX ... 486
Lone Star College System ... TX ... 476
Midland College ... TX ... 476
Sanford-Brown College ... TX ... 480
Temple College ... TX ... 482
Tyler Junior College ... TX ... 488
University of Texas at Brownsville and Texas Southmost College, The ... TX ... 491
Weatherford College ... TX ... 494
Northern Virginia Community College ... VA ... 513
Southside Regional Medical Center Professional Schools ... VA ... 509
Tidewater Community College ... VA ... 514
Bellevue College ... WA .. 517
Seattle University ... WA .. 523
Spokane Community College ... WA .. 518
Tacoma Community College ... WA .. 524
West Virginia University ... WV .. 530
Blackhawk Technical College ... WI ... 539
Chippewa Valley Technical College ... WI ... 539
Northeast Wisconsin Technical College ... WI ... 541
University of Wisconsin-Madison ... WI ... 536
University of Wisconsin-Milwaukee ... WI ... 537
Laramie County Community College ... WY .. 543

DNUR: Accreditation Commission for Education in Nursing: nursing (C)

Centra College of Nursing ... VA ... 503
Riverside School of Health Careers ... VA ... 509
Southside Regional Medical Center Professional Schools ... VA ... 509

DT: American Dental Association: dental laboratory technology (C,A)

Pima Community College ... AZ 17
Los Angeles City College ... CA 51
Pasadena City College ... CA 58
Indian River State College ... FL ... 106
Atlanta Technical College ... GA .. 121
Indiana University-Purdue University Fort Wayne ... IN 168
Kirkwood Community College ... IA 180

Bluegrass Community and Technical College KY 194
Louisiana State University Health Sciences Center-New Orleans LA 205
Middlesex Community College MA 232
New York City College of Technology/City University of New York NY 319
Durham Technical Community College NC 360
Portland Community College OR 407
San Antonio College TX 465
J. Sargeant Reynolds Community College VA 512
Bates Technical College WA 516

EH: New England Association of Schools and Colleges, Commission on Institutions of Higher Education

Albertus Magnus College CT 87
Asnuntuck Community College CT 88
Capital Community College CT 88
Central Connecticut State University CT 87
Charter Oak State College CT 87
Connecticut College CT 89
Eastern Connecticut State University CT 87
Fairfield University CT 89
Gateway Community College CT 88
Goodwin College CT 90
Hartford Seminary CT 90
Holy Apostles College and Seminary CT 90
Housatonic Community College CT 88
Lincoln College of New England CT 90
Lyme Academy College of Fine Arts CT 90
Manchester Community College CT 88
Middlesex Community College CT 89
Mitchell College CT 90
Naugatuck Valley Community College CT 89
Northwestern Connecticut Community-Technical College CT 89
Norwalk Community College CT 89
Post University CT 90
Quinebaug Valley Community College CT 89
Quinnipiac University CT 91
Sacred Heart University CT 91
St. Vincent's College CT 91
Southern Connecticut State University CT 88
Three Rivers Community College CT 89
Trinity College CT 91
Tunxis Community College CT 89
United States Coast Guard Academy CT 545
University of Bridgeport CT 91
University of Connecticut CT 92
University of Hartford CT 92
University of New Haven CT 92
University of Saint Joseph CT 92
Wesleyan University CT 92
Western Connecticut State University CT 88
Yale University CT 93
Bangor Theological Seminary ME 209
Bates College ME 209
Bowdoin College ME 209
Central Maine Community College ME 210
Central Maine Medical Center College of Nursing and Health Professions ME 209
Colby College ME 209
College of the Atlantic ME 210
Eastern Maine Community College ME 210
Husson University ME 210
@Institute for Doctoral Studies in the Visual Arts ME 210
Kennebec Valley Community College ME 210
Maine College of Art ME 210
Maine Maritime Academy ME 211
Northern Maine Community College ME 210
Saint Joseph's College of Maine ME 211
Southern Maine Community College ME 211
Thomas College ME 211
Unity College ME 211
University of Maine ME 212
University of Maine at Augusta ME 212
University of Maine at Farmington ME 212
University of Maine at Fort Kent ME 212
University of Maine at Machias ME 212
University of Maine at Presque Isle ME 212
University of New England ME 213
University of Southern Maine ME 212
Washington County Community College ME 211
York County Community College ME 211
American International College MA 221
Amherst College MA 221
Andover Newton Theological School MA 222
Anna Maria College MA 222
Assumption College MA 222
Babson College MA 222
Bard College at Simon's Rock MA 222
Bay Path College MA 222
Bay State College MA 222
Becker College-Worcester MA 223
Benjamin Franklin Institute of Technology MA 223
Bentley University MA 223
Berklee College of Music MA 223
Berkshire Community College MA 231
Boston Architectural College MA 223
Boston College MA 224
Boston Conservatory, The MA 224
Boston Graduate School of Psychoanalysis MA 224
Boston University MA 224
Brandeis University MA 224
Bridgewater State University MA 229
Bristol Community College MA 231
Bunker Hill Community College MA 231
Cambridge College MA 224
Cape Cod Community College MA 231
Clark University MA 225
College of Our Lady of the Elms MA 225
College of the Holy Cross MA 225
Conway School of Landscape Design MA 225
Curry College MA 225
Dean College MA 225
Eastern Nazarene College MA 225
Emerson College MA 226
Emmanuel College MA 226
Endicott College MA 226
Fisher College MA 226
Fitchburg State University MA 229
Framingham State University MA 230
Franklin W. Olin College of Engineering MA 226
Gordon College MA 226
Gordon-Conwell Theological Seminary MA 227
Greenfield Community College MA 231
Hampshire College MA 227
Harvard University MA 227
Hebrew College MA 227
Hellenic College-Holy Cross Greek Orthodox School of Theology MA 227
Holyoke Community College MA 231
Hult International Business School MA 227
Laboure College MA 227
Lasell College MA 227
Lesley University MA 228
Marian Court College MA 228
Massachusetts Bay Community College MA 231
Massachusetts College of Art and Design MA 230
Massachusetts College of Liberal Arts MA 230
Massachusetts Institute of Technology MA 233
Massachusetts Maritime Academy MA 230
Massachusetts School of Law at Andover MA 233
Massachusetts School of Professional Psychology MA 233
Massasoit Community College MA 232
MCPHS University MA 233
Merrimack College MA 234
MGH Institute of Health Professions MA 234
Middlesex Community College MA 232
Montserrat College of Art MA 234
Mount Holyoke College MA 234
Mount Ida College MA 234
Mount Wachusett Community College MA 232
National Graduate School of Quality Systems Management, The MA 234
New England College of Business and Finance MA 234
New England College of Optometry, The MA 234
New England Conservatory of Music MA 234
New England Institute of Art, The MA 235
Newbury College MA 235
Nichols College MA 235
North Shore Community College MA 232
Northeastern University MA 235
Northern Essex Community College MA 232
#Pine Manor College MA 235
Quincy College MA 235
Quinsigamond Community College MA 232
Regis College MA 236
Roxbury Community College MA 232
Saint John's Seminary MA 236
Salem State University MA 230
Simmons College MA 236
Smith College MA 236
Springfield College MA 236
Springfield Technical Community College MA 233
Stonehill College MA 237
Suffolk University MA 237
Tufts University MA 237
University of Massachusetts MA 228
University of Massachusetts Boston MA 228
University of Massachusetts Dartmouth MA 229
University of Massachusetts Lowell MA 229
University of Massachusetts Medical School MA 229
#Urban College of Boston MA 237
Wellesley College MA 237
Wentworth Institute of Technology MA 237
Western New England University MA 238
Westfield State University MA 230
Wheaton College MA 238
Wheelock College MA 238
Williams College MA 238
Woods Hole Oceanographic Institution MA 238
Worcester Polytechnic Institute MA 238
Worcester State University MA 230
Colby-Sawyer College NH 295
Daniel Webster College NH 296
Dartmouth College NH 296
Franklin Pierce University NH 296
Granite State College NH 298
Great Bay Community College NH 295
Keene State College NH 298
Lakes Region Community College NH 295
Manchester Community College NH 296
Mount Washington College NH 297
Nashua Community College NH 296
New England College NH 297
New Hampshire Institute of Art NH 297
NHTI-Concord's Community College NH 296
Plymouth State University NH 298
River Valley Community College NH 296
Rivier University NH 297
Saint Anselm College NH 297
Southern New Hampshire University NH 297
Thomas More College of Liberal Arts, The NH 298
University of New Hampshire NH 298
University of New Hampshire School of Law NH 298
White Mountains Community College NH 296
Brown University RI 438
Bryant University RI 438
Community College of Rhode Island RI 439
Johnson & Wales University RI 439
Mater Ecclesiae College RI 439
Naval War College RI 545
New England Institute of Technology RI 439
Providence College RI 439
Rhode Island College RI 439
Rhode Island School of Design RI 440
Roger Williams University RI 440
Salve Regina University RI 440
University of Rhode Island RI 440
Bennington College VT 498
Burlington College VT 498
Castleton State College VT 501
Champlain College VT 499
College of St. Joseph VT 499
Community College of Vermont VT 501
Goddard College VT 499
Green Mountain College VT 499
Johnson State College VT 501
Landmark College VT 499
Lyndon State College VT 501
Marlboro College VT 499
Middlebury College VT 499
Norwich University VT 500
Saint Michael's College VT 500
SIT VT 500
Southern Vermont College VT 500
Sterling College VT 500
University of Vermont VT 500
Vermont College of Fine Arts VT 500
Vermont Law School VT 500
Vermont Technical College VT 501

EMT: Commission on Accreditation of Allied Health Education Programs: emergency medical technician-paramedic (C,A,B)

Bevill State Community College AL 2
Calhoun Community College AL 2
Gadsden State Community College AL 3
George C. Wallace Community College - Dothan AL 3
James H. Faulkner State Community College AL 4
Jefferson State Community College AL 5
Lurleen B. Wallace Community College AL 5
Northeast Alabama Community College AL 5
Northwest - Shoals Community College AL 6
Southern Union State Community College AL 7
Trenholm State Technical College AL 7
University of South Alabama AL 9
Wallace State Community College - Hanceville AL 9
University of Alaska Fairbanks AK 10
Cochise College AZ 12
Glendale Community College AZ 14
Mohave Community College AZ 15
Pima Community College AZ 17
Yavapai College AZ 19
Arkansas Northeastern College AR 19
Arkansas State University-Beebe AR 19
Arkansas State University-Mountain Home AR 20
Arkansas Tech University AR 20
Black River Technical College AR 20
East Arkansas Community College AR 21
National Park Community College AR 22
North Arkansas College AR 22
NorthWest Arkansas Community College AR 22
South Arkansas Community College AR 23
Southeast Arkansas College AR 23
University of Arkansas at Monticello AR 24
University of Arkansas Community College at Batesville AR 25
University of Arkansas Community College at Hope AR 25
University of Arkansas for Medical Sciences AR 24
American River College CA 53
Bakersfield College CA 49
Butte College CA 30
California State University-Sacramento CA 34
City College of San Francisco CA 38
College of the Redwoods Community College District CA 40
Crafton Hills College CA 61
Cuesta College CA 42
Foothill College CA 44
Fresno City College CA 68
Imperial Valley College CA 48
Moreno Valley College CA 60
Mt. San Antonio College CA 55
Napa Valley College CA 55
Palomar College CA 58
Point Loma Nazarene University CA 59
Saddleback College CA 67
Santa Rosa Junior College CA 65
Southwestern College CA 68
University of Antelope Valley CA 70
University of California-Los Angeles CA 71
Ventura College CA 74
Victor Valley College CA 75
Aims Community College CO 78
Arapahoe Community College CO 78
Colorado Mesa University CO 79
Colorado Mountain College CO 79
Community College of Aurora CO 81
Pikes Peak Community College CO 84
Pueblo Community College CO 84
Capital Community College CT 88
Delaware Technical Community College, Terry Campus DE 93
Broward College FL 99
City College FL 99
City College FL 100
College of Central Florida FL 100
Daytona State College FL 101
Eastern Florida State College FL 101
Edison State College FL 101
Florida Gateway College FL 104
Florida State College at Jacksonville FL 105
Gulf Coast State College FL 106
Hillsborough Community College FL 106
Indian River State College FL 106
Miami Dade College FL 109
Palm Beach State College FL 110
Pasco-Hernando Community College FL 110
Pensacola State College FL 110
Polk State College FL 110
St. Petersburg College FL 112
Santa Fe College FL 113
Seminole State College of Florida FL 113
Tallahassee Community College FL 117
Valencia College FL 118
Atlanta Technical College GA 121
Darton State College GA 124
Georgia Northwestern Technical College GA 125
Georgia Piedmont Technical College GA 126
Gwinnett Technical College GA 127
Lanier Technical College GA 128
Southeastern Technical College GA 132
Brigham Young University-Idaho ID 137
College of Southern Idaho ID 138
Idaho State University ID 138
Black Hawk College IL 140
City Colleges of Chicago Malcolm X College IL 142
Illinois Central College IL 146
Loyola University Chicago IL 151
Indiana University-Purdue University Indianapolis IN 168
Vincennes University IN 174
Clinton Community College IA 178
Indian Hills Community College IA 179
Kirkwood Community College IA 180
Mercy College of Health Sciences IA 181
Muscatine Community College IA 178
Scott Community College IA 178
Southeastern Community College IA 182
University of Iowa IA 175
Western Iowa Tech Community College IA 183
Barton County Community College KS 184
Coffeyville Community College KS 185
Cowley County Community College KS 186
Garden City Community College KS 187
Hutchinson Community College and Area Vocational School KS 187
Johnson County Community College KS 187
Kansas City Kansas Community College KS 187
Eastern Kentucky University KY 193
Bossier Parish Community College LA 202
Delgado Community College LA 203
Louisiana State University and Agricultural and Mechanical College LA 204
South Louisiana Community College LA 203
Northern Maine Community College ME 210
Southern Maine Community College ME 211
Anne Arundel Community College MD 213
Cecil College MD 214
Community College of Baltimore County, The MD 214
Garrett College MD 214
Hagerstown Community College MD 215
Howard Community College MD 215
Prince George's Community College MD 217
University of Maryland Baltimore County MD 219
Kalamazoo Valley Community College MI 244

Lansing Community College ... MI ... 245
Century College ... MN ... 258
Inver Hills Community College ... MN ... 258
Mesabi Range Community & Technical College ... MN ... 259
Northland Community and Technical College ... MN ... 260
Ridgewater College ... MN ... 260
Rochester Community and Technical College ... MN ... 261
Saint Cloud Technical and Community College ... MN ... 261
South Central College ... MN ... 261
East Central Community College ... MS ... 266
East Mississippi Community College ... MS ... 266
Hinds Community College ... MS ... 267
Holmes Community College ... MS ... 267
Itawamba Community College ... MS ... 267
Jones County Junior College ... MS ... 267
Mississippi Gulf Coast Community College ... MS ... 268
Northwest Mississippi Community College ... MS ... 269
Crowder College ... MO ... 273
Ozarks Technical Community College ... MO ... 279
Sanford-Brown College ... MO ... 281
Flathead Valley Community College ... MT ... 286
Great Falls College Montana State University ... MT ... 287
Montana State University - Billings ... MT ... 287
Central Community College ... NE ... 288
Creighton University ... NE ... 289
Metropolitan Community College ... NE ... 290
Mid-Plains Community College ... NE ... 290
Northeast Community College ... NE ... 291
College of Southern Nevada ... NV ... 294
NHTI-Concord's Community College ... NH ... 296
Hudson County Community College ... NJ ... 302
Ocean County College ... NJ ... 304
Central New Mexico Community College ... NM ... 309
Eastern New Mexico University-Roswell ... NM ... 309
New Mexico State University Dona Ana Community College ... NM ... 311
University of New Mexico Main Campus ... NM ... 312
City University of New York Borough of Manhattan Community College ... NY ... 317
Dutchess Community College ... NY ... 323
Herkimer County Community College ... NY ... 326
Hudson Valley Community College ... NY ... 326
Monroe Community College ... NY ... 332
St. John's University ... NY ... 339
State University of New York College of Agriculture and Technology at Coble skill ... NY ... 344
Blue Ridge Community College ... NC ... 358
Catawba Valley Community College ... NC ... 359
Piedmont Community College ... NC ... 362
Southwestern Community College ... NC ... 364
Western Carolina University ... NC ... 369
Bismarck State College ... ND ... 372
North Dakota State College of Science ... ND ... 372
Columbus State Community College ... OH ... 378
Fortis College ... OH ... 379
Lorain County Community College ... OH ... 383
Owens Community College ... OH ... 387
University of Cincinnati-Blue Ash College ... OH ... 391
Youngstown State University ... OH ... 394
Oklahoma City Community College ... OK ... 397
Rogers State University ... OK ... 399
Central Oregon Community College ... OR ... 402
Chemeketa Community College ... OR ... 402
Lane Community College ... OR ... 403
National College of Technical Instruction-College of Emergency Services ... OR ... 405
Oregon Health & Science University ... OR ... 405
Portland Community College ... OR ... 407
Southwestern Oregon Community College ... OR ... 407
Community College of Allegheny County ... PA ... 413
Fortis Institute ... PA ... 416
Harrisburg Area Community College ... PA ... 417
Lancaster General College of Nursing and Health Sciences ... PA ... 421
Pennsylvania College of Technology ... PA ... 427
University of Pittsburgh ... PA ... 435
Greenville Technical College ... SC ... 444
Horry-Georgetown Technical College ... SC ... 444
Trident Technical College ... SC ... 447
Lake Area Technical Institute ... SD ... 450
Chattanooga State Community College ... TN ... 460
Columbia State Community College ... TN ... 460
Jackson State Community College ... TN ... 460
Northeast State Community College ... TN ... 461
Roane State Community College ... TN ... 461
Southwest Tennessee Community College ... TN ... 461
Tennessee Technological University ... TN ... 460
Volunteer State Community College ... TN ... 461
Walters State Community College ... TN ... 462
Amarillo College ... TX ... 465
Austin Community College District ... TX ... 466
Blinn College ... TX ... 467
Brazosport College ... TX ... 468
Brookhaven College ... TX ... 470
Central Texas College ... TX ... 468
College of the Mainland ... TX ... 469
Collin County Community College District ... TX ... 469
Galveston College ... TX ... 472
Grayson College ... TX ... 472
Houston Community College ... TX ... 473
Howard College ... TX ... 473
Lone Star College System ... TX ... 476
Midland College ... TX ... 476
Navarro College ... TX ... 477
North Central Texas College ... TX ... 477
Panola College ... TX ... 478
Paris Junior College ... TX ... 478
San Antonio College ... TX ... 465
San Jacinto College Central ... TX ... 479
San Jacinto College North ... TX ... 479
South Plains College ... TX ... 480
Tarrant County College District ... TX ... 482
Temple College ... TX ... 482
Texas State Technical College West Texas ... TX ... 486
Trinity Valley Community College ... TX ... 488
Tyler Junior College ... TX ... 488
University of Texas Health Science Center at San Antonio ... TX ... 493
University of Texas Southwestern Medical Center ... TX ... 493
Weatherford College ... TX ... 494
#Wharton County Junior College ... TX ... 494
Dixie State College of Utah ... UT ... 497
University of Utah, The ... UT ... 496
Utah Valley University ... UT ... 497
Weber State University ... UT ... 497
American National University ... VA ... 501
Central Virginia Community College ... VA ... 512
J. Sargeant Reynolds Community College ... VA ... 512
Jefferson College of Health Sciences ... VA ... 506
Northern Virginia Community College ... VA ... 513
Piedmont Virginia Community College ... VA ... 513
Southside Virginia Community College ... VA ... 513
Southwest Virginia Community College ... VA ... 514
Tidewater Community College ... VA ... 514
Virginia Commonwealth University ... VA ... 511
Central Washington University ... WA ... 517
Columbia Basin College ... WA ... 518
Tacoma Community College ... WA ... 524
University of Washington ... WA ... 524
Blue Ridge Community and Technical College ... WV ... 527
New River Community and Technical College ... WV ... 528
Lakeshore Technical College ... WI ... 540
Northcentral Technical College ... WI ... 541
Northeast Wisconsin Technical College ... WI ... 541
Waukesha County Technical College ... WI ... 541
Casper College ... WY ... 542
Laramie County Community College ... WY ... 543

ENG: ABET, Inc.: engineering (B,M)

Alabama Agricultural and Mechanical University ... AL ... 1
Auburn University ... AL ... 1
Tuskegee University ... AL ... 8
University of Alabama at Birmingham ... AL ... 8
University of Alabama in Huntsville ... AL ... 8
University of Alabama, The ... AL ... 8
University of South Alabama ... AL ... 9
University of Alaska Anchorage ... AK ... 10
University of Alaska Fairbanks ... AK ... 10
Arizona State University ... AZ ... 11
Northern Arizona University ... AZ ... 16
University of Arizona ... AZ ... 18
Arkansas State University-Jonesboro ... AR ... 19
Arkansas Tech University ... AR ... 20
Harding University Main Campus ... AR ... 21
John Brown University ... AR ... 21
University of Arkansas at Little Rock ... AR ... 24
University of Arkansas Main Campus ... AR ... 23
California Baptist University ... CA ... 30
California Institute of Technology ... CA ... 31
California Maritime Academy ... CA ... 31
California Polytechnic State University-San Luis Obispo ... CA ... 32
California State Polytechnic University-Pomona ... CA ... 32
California State University-Chico ... CA ... 33
California State University-East Bay ... CA ... 33
California State University-Fresno ... CA ... 33
California State University-Fullerton ... CA ... 33
California State University-Long Beach ... CA ... 33
California State University-Los Angeles ... CA ... 34
California State University-Northridge ... CA ... 34
California State University-Sacramento ... CA ... 34
Harvey Mudd College ... CA ... 46
Humboldt State University ... CA ... 35
Loyola Marymount University ... CA ... 53
National Test Pilot School ... CA ... 55
Naval Postgraduate School ... CA ... 544
San Diego State University ... CA ... 35
San Francisco State University ... CA ... 35
San Jose State University ... CA ... 36
Santa Clara University ... CA ... 64
Stanford University ... CA ... 68
University of California-Berkeley ... CA ... 70
University of California-Davis ... CA ... 70
University of California-Irvine ... CA ... 71
University of California-Los Angeles ... CA ... 71
University of California-Riverside ... CA ... 71
University of California-San Diego ... CA ... 71
University of California-Santa Barbara ... CA ... 72
University of California-Santa Cruz ... CA ... 72
University of San Diego ... CA ... 73
University of Southern California ... CA ... 74
University of the Pacific ... CA ... 73
Colorado School of Mines ... CO ... 80
Colorado State University ... CO ... 80
Colorado State University-Pueblo ... CO ... 80
Colorado Technical University ... CO ... 81
Fort Lewis College ... CO ... 81
United States Air Force Academy ... CO ... 545
University of Colorado Boulder ... CO ... 85
University of Colorado Colorado Springs ... CO ... 85
University of Colorado DenverlAnschutz Medical Campus ... CO ... 86
University of Denver ... CO ... 86
Central Connecticut State University ... CT ... 87
Fairfield University ... CT ... 89
Trinity College ... CT ... 91
United States Coast Guard Academy ... CT ... 545
University of Bridgeport ... CT ... 91
University of Connecticut ... CT ... 92
University of Hartford ... CT ... 92
University of New Haven ... CT ... 92
Yale University ... CT ... 93
University of Delaware ... DE ... 94
Catholic University of America, The ... DC ... 94
George Washington University ... DC ... 95
Howard University ... DC ... 95
University of the District of Columbia ... DC ... 97
Embry-Riddle Aeronautical University ... FL ... 102
Florida Agricultural and Mechanical University ... FL ... 114
Florida Atlantic University ... FL ... 114
Florida Gulf Coast University ... FL ... 115
Florida Institute of Technology ... FL ... 104
Florida International University ... FL ... 115
Florida State University ... FL ... 115
University of Central Florida ... FL ... 115
University of Florida ... FL ... 116
University of Miami ... FL ... 118
University of North Florida ... FL ... 116
University of South Florida ... FL ... 116
University of West Florida ... FL ... 117
Georgia Institute of Technology ... GA ... 125
Mercer University ... GA ... 128
Southern Polytechnic State University ... GA ... 132
University of Georgia ... GA ... 133
University of Hawaii at Manoa ... HI ... 136
Boise State University ... ID ... 137
Brigham Young University-Idaho ... ID ... 137
Idaho State University ... ID ... 138
University of Idaho ... ID ... 139
Bradley University ... IL ... 140
Illinois Institute of Technology ... IL ... 147
Northern Illinois University ... IL ... 154
Northwestern University ... IL ... 155
Olivet Nazarene University ... IL ... 155
Southern Illinois University Carbondale ... IL ... 159
Southern Illinois University Edwardsville ... IL ... 159
University of Illinois at Chicago ... IL ... 161
University of Illinois at Urbana-Champaign ... IL ... 162
Western Illinois University ... IL ... 162
Indiana Tech ... IN ... 167
Indiana University-Purdue University Fort Wayne ... IN ... 168
Indiana University-Purdue University Indianapolis ... IN ... 168
Purdue University Calumet ... IN ... 171
Purdue University Main Campus ... IN ... 171
Rose-Hulman Institute of Technology ... IN ... 172
Taylor University ... IN ... 173
Trine University ... IN ... 173
University of Evansville ... IN ... 173
University of Notre Dame ... IN ... 174
University of Southern Indiana ... IN ... 174
Valparaiso University ... IN ... 174
Dordt College ... IA ... 177
Iowa State University ... IA ... 175
St. Ambrose University ... IA ... 182
University of Iowa ... IA ... 175
Kansas State University ... KS ... 188
University of Kansas Main Campus ... KS ... 190
Wichita State University ... KS ... 191
Murray State University ... KY ... 198
University of Kentucky ... KY ... 200
University of Louisville ... KY ... 200
Western Kentucky University ... KY ... 200
Louisiana State University and Agricultural and Mechanical College ... LA ... 204
Louisiana Tech University ... LA ... 207
McNeese State University ... LA ... 207
Southern University and A&M College ... LA ... 206
Tulane University ... LA ... 207
University of Louisiana at Lafayette ... LA ... 208
University of New Orleans ... LA ... 205
Maine Maritime Academy ... ME ... 211
University of Maine ... ME ... 212
University of Southern Maine ... ME ... 212
Capitol College ... MD ... 213
Johns Hopkins University ... MD ... 215
Loyola University Maryland ... MD ... 216
Morgan State University ... MD ... 217
United States Naval Academy ... MD ... 545
University of Maryland Baltimore County ... MD ... 219
University of Maryland College Park ... MD ... 219
Boston University ... MA ... 224
Franklin W. Olin College of Engineering ... MA ... 226
Harvard University ... MA ... 227
Massachusetts Institute of Technology ... MA ... 233
Merrimack College ... MA ... 234
Northeastern University ... MA ... 235
Smith College ... MA ... 236
Suffolk University ... MA ... 237
Tufts University ... MA ... 237
University of Massachusetts ... MA ... 228
University of Massachusetts Dartmouth ... MA ... 229
University of Massachusetts Lowell ... MA ... 229
Wentworth Institute of Technology ... MA ... 237
Western New England University ... MA ... 238
Worcester Polytechnic Institute ... MA ... 238
Andrews University ... MI ... 239
Baker College of Flint ... MI ... 239
Calvin College ... MI ... 240
Central Michigan University ... MI ... 240
Ferris State University ... MI ... 242
Grand Valley State University ... MI ... 243
Hope College ... MI ... 244
Kettering University ... MI ... 244
Lake Superior State University ... MI ... 245
Lawrence Technological University ... MI ... 245
Michigan State University ... MI ... 246
Michigan Technological University ... MI ... 247
Oakland University ... MI ... 248
Saginaw Valley State University ... MI ... 249
University of Detroit Mercy ... MI ... 250
University of Michigan-Ann Arbor ... MI ... 251
University of Michigan-Dearborn ... MI ... 251
Wayne State University ... MI ... 252
Western Michigan University ... MI ... 252
Minnesota State University, Mankato ... MN ... 259
St. Cloud State University ... MN ... 261
University of Minnesota Duluth ... MN ... 264
University of Minnesota-Twin Cities ... MN ... 264
University of Saint Thomas ... MN ... 265
Winona State University ... MN ... 262
Jackson State University ... MS ... 267
Mississippi State University ... MS ... 268
University of Mississippi ... MS ... 270
Missouri University of Science & Technology ... MO ... 284
Saint Louis University ... MO ... 281
Southeast Missouri State University ... MO ... 282
University of Missouri - Columbia ... MO ... 283
University of Missouri - Kansas City ... MO ... 283
University of Missouri - Saint Louis ... MO ... 283
Washington University in St. Louis ... MO ... 284
Carroll College ... MT ... 285
Montana State University ... MT ... 287
Montana Tech of The University of Montana ... MT ... 287
University of Nebraska - Lincoln ... NE ... 292
University of Nevada, Las Vegas ... NV ... 294
University of Nevada, Reno ... NV ... 294
Daniel Webster College ... NH ... 296
Dartmouth College ... NH ... 296
University of New Hampshire ... NH ... 298
College of New Jersey, The ... NJ ... 300
Fairleigh Dickinson University ... NJ ... 301
Monmouth University ... NJ ... 303
New Jersey Institute of Technology ... NJ ... 303
Princeton University ... NJ ... 304
Rowan University ... NJ ... 305
Rutgers the State University of New Jersey New Brunswick Campus ... NJ ... 306
Stevens Institute of Technology ... NJ ... 307
New Mexico Institute of Mining and Technology ... NM ... 310
New Mexico State University Main Campus ... NM ... 310
University of New Mexico Main Campus ... NM ... 312
Alfred University ... NY ... 313
City University of New York College of Staten Island ... NY ... 317
City University of New York The City College ... NY ... 317
Clarkson University ... NY ... 320
Columbia University in the City of New York ... NY ... 321
Cooper Union ... NY ... 321
Cornell University ... NY ... 322
Hofstra University ... NY ... 326
Manhattan College ... NY ... 329
New York Institute of Technology ... NY ... 333
Polytechnic Institute of New York University ... NY ... 336
Rensselaer Polytechnic Institute ... NY ... 337
Rochester Institute of Technology ... NY ... 337
State University of New York at Binghamton ... NY ... 341
State University of New York at New Paltz ... NY ... 342
State University of New York at Stony Brook ... NY ... 342

State University of New York College of Environmental Science and Forestry ... NY ... 345
State University of New York Maritime College ... NY ... 346
Syracuse University Main Campus ... NY ... 347
Union College ... NY ... 348
United States Merchant Marine Academy ... NY ... 545
United States Military Academy ... NY ... 545
University at Buffalo-SUNY ... NY ... 341
University of Rochester ... NY ... 349
Webb Institute ... NY ... 350
Duke University ... NC ... 354
East Carolina University ... NC ... 367
North Carolina Agricultural and Technical State University ... NC ... 367
North Carolina State University ... NC ... 368
University of North Carolina at Asheville ... NC ... 368
University of North Carolina at Charlotte ... NC ... 368
Western Carolina University ... NC ... 369
North Dakota State University Main Campus ... ND ... 371
University of North Dakota Main Campus ... ND ... 371
Air Force Institute of Technology ... OH ... 544
Case Western Reserve University ... OH ... 375
Cedarville University ... OH ... 375
Central State University ... OH ... 376
Cleveland State University ... OH ... 377
Marietta College ... OH ... 383
Miami University ... OH ... 384
Muskingum University ... OH ... 384
Ohio Northern University ... OH ... 386
Ohio State University Main Campus, The ... OH ... 386
Ohio University Main Campus ... OH ... 387
University of Akron, Main Campus, The ... OH ... 390
University of Cincinnati Main Campus ... OH ... 390
University of Dayton ... OH ... 391
University of Toledo ... OH ... 392
Wright State University Main Campus ... OH ... 393
Youngstown State University ... OH ... 394
Oklahoma Christian University ... OK ... 397
Oklahoma State University ... OK ... 397
Oral Roberts University ... OK ... 398
University of Central Oklahoma ... OK ... 400
University of Oklahoma Norman Campus ... OK ... 401
University of Tulsa ... OK ... 401
George Fox University ... OR ... 403
Oregon Institute of Technology ... OR ... 405
Oregon State University ... OR ... 406
Portland State University ... OR ... 406
University of Portland ... OR ... 408
Bucknell University ... PA ... 411
Carnegie Mellon University ... PA ... 412
Drexel University ... PA ... 415
Elizabethtown College ... PA ... 415
Gannon University ... PA ... 416
Geneva College ... PA ... 417
Grove City College ... PA ... 417
Lafayette College ... PA ... 420
Lehigh University ... PA ... 422
Messiah College ... PA ... 423
Penn State University Park ... PA ... 426
Philadelphia University ... PA ... 430
Robert Morris University ... PA ... 431
Swarthmore College ... PA ... 433
Temple University ... PA ... 433
University of Pennsylvania ... PA ... 435
University of Pittsburgh ... PA ... 435
University of Scranton, The ... PA ... 436
Villanova University ... PA ... 436
Widener University ... PA ... 437
Wilkes University ... PA ... 437
York College of Pennsylvania ... PA ... 438
Inter American University of Puerto Rico Bayamon Campus ... PR ... 550
Universidad Del Turabo ... PR ... 552
Universidad Politecnica De Puerto Rico ... PR ... 553
University of Puerto Rico-Mayaguez Campus ... PR ... 554
Brown University ... RI ... 438
Roger Williams University ... RI ... 440
University of Rhode Island ... RI ... 440
Citadel, The Military College of South Carolina, The ... SC ... 442
Clemson University ... SC ... 442
South Carolina State University ... SC ... 446
University of South Carolina Columbia ... SC ... 447
South Dakota School of Mines and Technology ... SD ... 452
South Dakota State University ... SD ... 452
Christian Brothers University ... TN ... 453
Lipscomb University ... TN ... 456
Tennessee State University ... TN ... 459
Tennessee Technological University ... TN ... 460
Union University ... TN ... 462
University of Memphis, The ... TN ... 460
University of Tennessee at Chattanooga ... TN ... 463
University of Tennessee at Martin ... TN ... 463
University of Tennessee, Knoxville ... TN ... 463
Vanderbilt University ... TN ... 463
Baylor University ... TX ... 467
Lamar University ... TX ... 486
LeTourneau University ... TX ... 475
Midwestern State University ... TX ... 476
Prairie View A & M University ... TX ... 482
Rice University ... TX ... 479
St. Mary's University ... TX ... 479
Southern Methodist University ... TX ... 481
Tarleton State University ... TX ... 483
Texas A & M University ... TX ... 483
Texas A & M University - Commerce ... TX ... 483
Texas A & M University - Kingsville ... TX ... 484
Texas Christian University ... TX ... 484
Texas State University-San Marcos ... TX ... 487
Texas Tech University ... TX ... 487
Trinity University ... TX ... 488
University of Houston ... TX ... 489
University of Houston - Clear Lake ... TX ... 489
University of North Texas ... TX ... 490
University of Texas at Arlington, The ... TX ... 491
University of Texas at Austin ... TX ... 491
University of Texas at Brownsville and Texas Southmost College, The ... TX ... 491
University of Texas at Dallas, The ... TX ... 491
University of Texas at El Paso ... TX ... 492
University of Texas at San Antonio ... TX ... 492
University of Texas at Tyler ... TX ... 492
University of Texas of the Permian Basin ... TX ... 493
University of Texas - Pan American ... TX ... 492
West Texas A & M University ... TX ... 484
Brigham Young University ... UT ... 495
Southern Utah University ... UT ... 497
University of Utah, The ... UT ... 496
Utah State University ... UT ... 497
Norwich University ... VT ... 500
University of Vermont ... VT ... 500
Christopher Newport University ... VA ... 503
George Mason University ... VA ... 505
Hampton University ... VA ... 505
Liberty University ... VA ... 506
Norfolk State University ... VA ... 507
Old Dominion University ... VA ... 507
Sweet Briar College ... VA ... 510
University of Virginia ... VA ... 511
University of Virginia's College at Wise, The ... VA ... 511
Virginia Commonwealth University ... VA ... 511
Virginia Military Institute ... VA ... 515
Virginia Polytechnic Institute and State University ... VA ... 515
Virginia State University ... VA ... 515
Eastern Washington University ... WA ... 519
Gonzaga University ... WA ... 520
Pacific Lutheran University ... WA ... 521
Saint Martin's University ... WA ... 522
Seattle Pacific University ... WA ... 523
Seattle University ... WA ... 523
University of Washington ... WA ... 524
Walla Walla University ... WA ... 524
Washington State University ... WA ... 525
Marshall University ... WV ... 529
West Virginia University ... WV ... 530
Marquette University ... WI ... 534
Milwaukee School of Engineering ... WI ... 534
University of Wisconsin-Madison ... WI ... 536
University of Wisconsin-Milwaukee ... WI ... 537
University of Wisconsin-Platteville ... WI ... 537
University of Wisconsin-Stevens Point ... WI ... 538
University of Wisconsin-Stout ... WI ... 538
University of Wyoming ... WY ... 543

ENGR: ABET, Inc.: applied science (A, B,M)

Troy University ... AL ... 7
University of North Alabama ... AL ... 9
University of Alaska Anchorage ... AK ... 10
University of California-Los Angeles ... CA ... 71
Colorado State University ... CO ... 80
Trinidad State Junior College ... CO ... 85
University of Florida ... FL ... 116
University of South Florida ... FL ... 116
Southern Polytechnic State University ... GA ... 132
Idaho State University ... ID ... 138
University of Illinois at Chicago ... IL ... 161
Purdue University Main Campus ... IN ... 171
University of Iowa ... IA ... 175
Murray State University ... KY ... 198
Nicholls State University ... LA ... 208
Southeastern Louisiana University ... LA ... 208
Tulane University ... LA ... 207
Johns Hopkins University ... MD ... 215
Uniformed Services University of the Health Sciences ... MD ... 545
University of Massachusetts Lowell ... MA ... 229
Oakland University ... MI ... 248
University of Michigan-Ann Arbor ... MI ... 251
Wayne State University ... MI ... 252
St. Cloud State University ... MN ... 261
University of Minnesota-Twin Cities ... MN ... 264
University of Central Missouri ... MO ... 283
Montana Tech of The University of Montana ... MT ... 287
University of Nevada, Las Vegas ... NV ... 294
City University of New York Hunter College ... NY ... 318
Rochester Institute of Technology ... NY ... 337
University of Akron, Main Campus, The ... OH ... 390
University of Cincinnati Main Campus ... OH ... 390
University of Findlay, The ... OH ... 391
University of Toledo ... OH ... 392
Oregon Institute of Technology ... OR ... 405
Oregon State University ... OR ... 406
Indiana University of Pennsylvania ... PA ... 428
Millersville University of Pennsylvania ... PA ... 429
Universidad Politecnica De Puerto Rico ... PR ... 553
Clemson University ... SC ... 442
Chattanooga State Community College ... TN ... 460
East Tennessee State University ... TN ... 459
Texas A & M University - Corpus Christi ... TX ... 483
University of Houston - Clear Lake ... TX ... 489
University of Texas Health Science Center at Houston (UTHealth), The ... TX ... 492
University of Utah, The ... UT ... 496
Utah State University ... UT ... 497
James Madison University ... VA ... 506
Fairmont State University ... WV ... 529
Marshall University ... WV ... 529
West Virginia University ... WV ... 530

ENGT: ABET, Inc.: engineering technology (A,B)

Alabama Agricultural and Mechanical University ... AL ... 1
Arizona State University ... AZ ... 11
University of Arkansas at Little Rock ... AR ... 24
California Maritime Academy ... CA ... 31
California State Polytechnic University-Pomona ... CA ... 32
Colorado State University-Pueblo ... CO ... 80
Metropolitan State University of Denver ... CO ... 83
Central Connecticut State University ... CT ... 87
Naugatuck Valley Community College ... CT ... 89
Three Rivers Community College ... CT ... 89
University of Hartford ... CT ... 92
Delaware Technical Community College, Owens Campus ... DE ... 93
Delaware Technical Community College, Stanton-Wilmington Campus ... DE ... 93
University of Delaware ... DE ... 94
Florida Agricultural and Mechanical University ... FL ... 114
Augusta Technical College ... GA ... 121
Fort Valley State University ... GA ... 124
Georgia Piedmont Technical College ... GA ... 126
Georgia Southern University ... GA ... 126
Savannah State University ... GA ... 131
Savannah Technical College ... GA ... 131
Southern Polytechnic State University ... GA ... 132
Idaho State University ... ID ... 138
Bradley University ... IL ... 140
DeVry University - Chicago Campus ... IL ... 144
Morrison Institute of Technology ... IL ... 153
Northern Illinois University ... IL ... 154
Southern Illinois University Carbondale ... IL ... 159
Ball State University ... IN ... 164
Indiana State University ... IN ... 167
Indiana University-Purdue University Fort Wayne ... IN ... 168
Indiana University-Purdue University Indianapolis ... IN ... 168
Purdue University Calumet ... IN ... 171
Purdue University Main Campus ... IN ... 171
Purdue University North Central Campus ... IN ... 172
University of Northern Iowa ... IA ... 176
Butler Community College ... KS ... 185
Pittsburg State University ... KS ... 189
Murray State University ... KY ... 198
Northern Kentucky University ... KY ... 198
Delgado Community College ... LA ... 203
Grambling State University ... LA ... 207
Louisiana Tech University ... LA ... 207
McNeese State University ... LA ... 207
Northwestern State University ... LA ... 208
Southern University and A&M College ... LA ... 206
Central Maine Community College ... ME ... 210
Maine Maritime Academy ... ME ... 211
University of Maine ... ME ... 212
Capitol College ... MD ... 213
Northeastern University ... MA ... 235
Springfield Technical Community College ... MA ... 233
University of Massachusetts Lowell ... MA ... 229
Wentworth Institute of Technology ... MA ... 237
Baker College of Flint ... MI ... 239
Eastern Michigan University ... MI ... 242
Ferris State University ... MI ... 242
Lake Superior State University ... MI ... 245
Michigan Technological University ... MI ... 247
Northern Michigan University ... MI ... 248
Wayne State University ... MI ... 252
Western Michigan University ... MI ... 252
Minnesota State University, Mankato ... MN ... 259
University of Southern Mississippi ... MS ... 270
Linn State Technical College ... MO ... 276
Missouri Southern State University ... MO ... 278
Missouri Western State University ... MO ... 279
Southeast Missouri State University ... MO ... 282
Montana State University ... MT ... 287
Montana State University - Northern ... MT ... 287
College of Southern Nevada ... NV ... 294
Nashua Community College ... NH ... 296
NHTI-Concord's Community College ... NH ... 296
University of New Hampshire ... NH ... 298
Burlington County College ... NJ ... 299
County College of Morris ... NJ ... 300
Essex County College ... NJ ... 301
Fairleigh Dickinson University ... NJ ... 301
Middlesex County College ... NJ ... 303
New Jersey Institute of Technology ... NJ ... 303
Passaic County Community College ... NJ ... 304
Thomas Edison State College ... NJ ... 308
New Mexico State University Main Campus ... NM ... 310
Alfred State College ... NY ... 345
Broome Community College ... NY ... 315
City University of New York Bronx Community College ... NY ... 317
City University of New York College of Staten Island ... NY ... 317
City University of New York Queensborough Community College ... NY ... 319
Excelsior College ... NY ... 324
Farmingdale State College ... NY ... 346
Hudson Valley Community College ... NY ... 326
Mohawk Valley Community College ... NY ... 331
Monroe Community College ... NY ... 332
Nassau Community College ... NY ... 332
New York City College of Technology/City University of New York ... NY ... 319
New York Institute of Technology ... NY ... 333
Onondaga Community College ... NY ... 335
Paul Smith's College ... NY ... 336
Rochester Institute of Technology ... NY ... 337
State University of New York College at Buffalo ... NY ... 343
State University of New York College of Agriculture and Technology at Morrisville ... NY ... 345
State University of New York College of Environmental Science and Forestry ... NY ... 345
State University of New York Institute of Technology at Utica-Rome ... NY ... 346
SUNY Canton-College of Technology ... NY ... 345
Technical Career Institutes ... NY ... 347
Vaughn College of Aeronautics and Technology ... NY ... 349
Central Piedmont Community College ... NC ... 359
Forsyth Technical Community College ... NC ... 360
Gaston College ... NC ... 360
University of North Carolina at Charlotte ... NC ... 368
Western Carolina University ... NC ... 369
Bismarck State College ... ND ... 372
Cincinnati State Technical and Community College ... OH ... 376
Cleveland State University ... OH ... 377
Columbus State Community College ... OH ... 378
Cuyahoga Community College ... OH ... 378
James A. Rhodes State College ... OH ... 381
Lakeland Community College ... OH ... 382
Lorain County Community College ... OH ... 383
Miami University ... OH ... 384
Sinclair Community College ... OH ... 388
Stark State College ... OH ... 389
University of Akron, Main Campus, The ... OH ... 390
University of Cincinnati Main Campus ... OH ... 390
University of Dayton ... OH ... 391
University of Toledo ... OH ... 392
Youngstown State University ... OH ... 394
Zane State College ... OH ... 394
Oklahoma State University ... OK ... 397
Southwestern Oklahoma State University ... OK ... 400
Oregon Institute of Technology ... OR ... 405
Bloomsburg University of Pennsylvania ... PA ... 427
California University of Pennsylvania ... PA ... 428
Drexel University ... PA ... 415
Pennsylvania College of Technology ... PA ... 427
Point Park University ... PA ... 431
Temple University ... PA ... 433
University of Puerto Rico at Arecibo ... PR ... 553
University of Puerto Rico at Bayamon ... PR ... 554
University of Puerto Rico-Humacao ... PR ... 554
New England Institute of Technology ... RI ... 439
Denmark Technical College ... SC ... 443
Greenville Technical College ... SC ... 444
Horry-Georgetown Technical College ... SC ... 444
Midlands Technical College ... SC ... 445
Orangeburg-Calhoun Technical College ... SC ... 446
Piedmont Technical College ... SC ... 446
South Carolina State University ... SC ... 446
Spartanburg Community College ... SC ... 447
University of South Carolina Upstate ... SC ... 448
York Technical College ... SC ... 449
South Dakota State University ... SD ... 452
Austin Peay State University ... TN ... 459
Belmont University ... TN ... 453
Chattanooga State Community College ... TN ... 460
East Tennessee State University ... TN ... 459
Middle Tennessee State University ... TN ... 459
Southwest Tennessee Community College ... TN ... 461
University of Memphis, The ... TN ... 460
Houston Community College ... TX ... 473
LeTourneau University ... TX ... 475
Prairie View A & M University ... TX ... 482
Texas A & M University ... TX ... 483
Texas A & M University - Corpus Christi ... TX ... 483

Texas Southern University ... TX ... 485
Texas Tech University ... TX ... 487
University of Houston ... TX ... 489
University of Houston - Downtown ... TX ... 489
University of North Texas ... TX ... 490
Brigham Young University ... UT ... 495
Weber State University ... UT ... 497
Vermont Technical College ... VT ... 501
Old Dominion University ... VA ... 507
Virginia State University ... VA ... 515
Central Washington University ... WA .. 517
Eastern Washington University ... WA .. 519
Western Washington University ... WA .. 525
Bluefield State College ... WV .. 529
Bridgemont Community and Technical College ... WV .. 527
Fairmont State University ... WV .. 529
Milwaukee School of Engineering ... WI ... 534
Northeast Wisconsin Technical College ... WI ... 541
Waukesha County Technical College ... WI ... 541

EXSC: Commission on Accreditation of Allied Health Education Programs: exercise science (C,B,M)

Metropolitan State University of Denver ... CO 83
Central Connecticut State University ... CT 87
Southern Connecticut State University ... CT 88
Georgia State University ... GA .. 126
Indiana Wesleyan University ... IN 169
University of Indianapolis ... IN 173
Murray State University ... KY ... 198
University of Louisville ... KY ... 200
University of Louisiana at Monroe ... LA ... 208
University of Southern Maine ... ME .. 212
Salisbury University ... MD .. 220
Lasell College ... MA .. 227
Springfield College ... MA .. 236
Westfield State University ... MA .. 230
St. Catherine University ... MN .. 263
Missouri Baptist University ... MO .. 278
University of North Carolina at Charlotte .. NC .. 368
North Dakota State University Main Campus ... ND .. 371
University of Mary ... ND .. 373
Bowling Green State University ... OH .. 374
Kent State University Main Campus ... OH .. 382
Ohio Northern University ... OH .. 386
University of Central Oklahoma ... OK .. 400
Bloomsburg University of Pennsylvania ... PA ... 427
East Stroudsburg University of Pennsylvania ... PA ... 428
Eastern University ... PA ... 415
Indiana University of Pennsylvania ... PA ... 428
Slippery Rock University of Pennsylvania . PA ... 429
West Chester University of Pennsylvania . PA ... 430
South Dakota State University ... SD ... 452
Middle Tennessee State University ... TN ... 459
Lyndon State College ... VT ... 501
Liberty University ... VA ... 506
Longwood University ... VA ... 506
Lynchburg College ... VA ... 506
Old Dominion University ... VA ... 507
University of Wisconsin-Oshkosh ... WI ... 537

FEPAC: American Academy of Forensic Sciences: forensic science (B,M)

University of Alabama at Birmingham ... AL 8
California State University-Los Angeles ... CA 34
University of California-Davis ... CA 70
Metropolitan State University of Denver ... CO 83
University of New Haven ... CT 92
George Washington University ... DC 95
Florida International University ... FL ... 115
Albany State University ... GA .. 119
Loyola University Chicago ... IL 151
University of Illinois at Chicago ... IL 161
Indiana University-Purdue University Indianapolis ... IN 168
Eastern Kentucky University ... KY ... 193
Towson University ... MD .. 220
Boston University ... MA .. 224
Michigan State University ... MI ... 246
University of Mississippi ... MS .. 270
Nebraska Wesleyan University ... NE ... 291
University at Albany, SUNY ... NY ... 341
Ohio University Main Campus ... OH .. 387
Arcadia University ... PA ... 409
Cedar Crest College ... PA ... 412
Duquesne University ... PA ... 415
Penn State University Park ... PA ... 426
Sam Houston State University ... TX ... 487
Texas A & M University ... TX ... 483
University of North Texas ... TX ... 490
University of North Texas Health Science Center at Fort Worth ... TX ... 490
Virginia Commonwealth University ... VA ... 511
Marshall University ... WV .. 529
West Virginia University ... WV .. 530

FOR: Society of American Foresters: forestry (B,M)

Alabama Agricultural and Mechanical University ... AL 1
Auburn University ... AL 1
University of Alaska Fairbanks ... AK 10
Northern Arizona University ... AZ 16
University of Arkansas at Monticello ... AR 24
California Polytechnic State University-San Luis Obispo ... CA 32
Humboldt State University ... CA 35
University of California-Berkeley ... CA 70
Colorado State University ... CO 80
Yale University ... CT 93
University of Florida ... FL ... 116
University of Georgia ... GA .. 133
University of Idaho ... ID ... 139
Southern Illinois University Carbondale ... IL 159
University of Illinois at Urbana-Champaign IL 162
Purdue University Main Campus ... IN 171
Iowa State University ... IA 175
University of Kentucky ... KY ... 200
Louisiana State University and Agricultural and Mechanical College ... LA ... 204
Louisiana Tech University ... LA ... 207
University of Maine ... ME .. 212
University of Massachusetts ... MA .. 228
Michigan State University ... MI ... 246
Michigan Technological University ... MI ... 247
University of Minnesota-Twin Cities ... MN .. 264
Mississippi State University ... MS .. 268
University of Missouri - Columbia ... MO .. 283
University of Montana - Missoula, The ... MT .. 286
University of New Hampshire ... NH .. 298
Paul Smith's College ... NY ... 336
State University of New York College of Environmental Science and Forestry ... NY ... 345
Duke University ... NC .. 354
North Carolina State University ... NC .. 368
Ohio State University Main Campus, The . OH .. 386
Oklahoma State University ... OK .. 397
Oregon State University ... OR .. 406
Penn State University Park ... PA ... 426
Clemson University ... SC ... 442
University of Tennessee, Knoxville ... TN ... 463
Stephen F. Austin State University ... TX ... 482
Texas A & M University ... TX ... 483
Utah State University ... UT ... 497
Virginia Polytechnic Institute and State University ... VA ... 515
University of Washington ... WA .. 524
West Virginia University ... WV .. 530
University of Wisconsin-Madison ... WI ... 536
University of Wisconsin-Stevens Point ... WI ... 538

FUSER: American Board of Funeral Service Education: funeral service education (C,A,B)

Bishop State Community College ... AL 2
Jefferson State Community College ... AL 5
Mesa Community College ... AZ 15
#University of Arkansas Community College at Hope ... AR 25
American River College ... CA 53
Cypress College ... CA 56
Arapahoe Community College ... CO 78
Lincoln College of New England ... CT 90
#University of the District of Columbia ... DC 97
Florida State College at Jacksonville ... FL ... 105
Miami Dade College ... FL ... 109
St. Petersburg College ... FL ... 112
Gupton Jones College of Funeral Service GA .. 127
Ogeechee Technical College ... GA .. 129
Carl Sandburg College ... IL 141
City Colleges of Chicago Malcolm X College ... IL 142
Southern Illinois University Carbondale ... IL 159
Worsham College of Mortuary Science ... IL 163
Ivy Tech Community College-Central Indiana ... IN 169
Mid-America College of Funeral Service .. IN 171
Vincennes University ... IN 174
Des Moines Area Community College ... IA 177
Kansas City Kansas Community College . KS ... 187
Delgado Community College ... LA ... 203
Community College of Baltimore County, The ... MD .. 214
FINE Mortuary College ... MA .. 226
Mount Ida College ... MA .. 234
Wayne State University ... MI ... 252
University of Minnesota-Twin Cities ... MN .. 264
East Mississippi Community College ... MS .. 266
Holmes Community College ... MS .. 267
Mississippi Gulf Coast Community College ... MS .. 268
#Northwest Mississippi Community College MS .. 269
Mercer County Community College ... NJ ... 302
American Academy McAllister Institute of Funeral Service ... NY ... 313
Hudson Valley Community College ... NY ... 326
Nassau Community College ... NY ... 332
SUNY Canton-College of Technology ... NY ... 345
Fayetteville Technical Community College NC .. 360
Cincinnati College of Mortuary Science ... OH .. 376
University of Central Oklahoma ... OK .. 400
Mt. Hood Community College ... OR .. 404
Northampton Community College ... PA ... 425
Pittsburgh Institute of Mortuary Science ... PA ... 430
Piedmont Technical College ... SC ... 446
John A. Gupton College ... TN ... 455
Amarillo College ... TX ... 465
Commonwealth Institute of Funeral Service ... TX ... 469
Dallas Institute of Funeral Service ... TX ... 471
San Antonio College ... TX ... 465
Salt Lake Community College ... UT ... 498
John Tyler Community College ... VA ... 512
Tidewater Community College ... VA ... 514
Lake Washington Institute of Technology . WA ... 520
Milwaukee Area Technical College ... WI ... 540

HSA: Commission on Accreditation of Healthcare Management Education: healthcare management (B,M)

University of Alabama at Birmingham ... AL 8
University of Arkansas for Medical Sciences ... AR 24
California State University-Long Beach ... CA 33
San Diego State University ... CA 35
University of California-Los Angeles ... CA 71
University of Southern California ... CA 74
University of Colorado DenverlAnschutz Medical Campus ... CO 86
George Washington University ... DC 95
Georgetown University ... DC 95
Florida International University ... FL ... 115
University of Central Florida ... FL ... 115
University of Florida ... FL ... 116
University of Miami ... FL ... 118
University of North Florida ... FL ... 116
University of South Florida ... FL ... 116
Armstrong Atlantic State University ... GA .. 120
Georgia State University ... GA .. 126
Governors State University ... IL 145
Rush University ... IL 157
University of Illinois at Chicago ... IL 161
Indiana University-Purdue University Indianapolis ... IN 168
University of Iowa ... IA 175
University of Kansas Main Campus ... KS ... 190
University of Kentucky ... KY ... 200
Tulane University ... LA ... 207
University of Southern Maine ... ME .. 212
Johns Hopkins University ... MD .. 215
Boston University ... MA .. 224
Simmons College ... MA .. 236
University of Michigan-Ann Arbor ... MI 251
University of Minnesota-Twin Cities ... MN .. 264
University of Saint Thomas ... MN .. 265
Saint Louis University ... MO .. 281
University of Missouri - Columbia ... MO .. 283
Baruch College/City University of New York ... NY ... 316
Columbia University in the City of New York ... NY ... 321
Cornell University ... NY ... 322
New York University ... NY ... 334
Union Graduate College ... NY ... 348
University of North Carolina at Chapel Hill NC .. 368
University of North Carolina at Charlotte .. NC .. 368
Ohio State University Main Campus, The . OH .. 386
Xavier University ... OH .. 393
Portland State University ... OR .. 406
Penn State University Park ... PA ... 426
Temple University ... PA ... 433
University of Pittsburgh ... PA ... 435
University of Scranton, The ... PA ... 436
Widener University ... PA ... 437
University of Puerto Rico-Medical Sciences Campus ... PR ... 554
Medical University of South Carolina ... SC ... 445
University of South Carolina Columbia ... SC ... 447
University of Memphis, The ... TN ... 460
Baylor University ... TX ... 467
Texas A & M University ... TX ... 483
Texas State University-San Marcos ... TX ... 487
Texas Tech University ... TX ... 487
Texas Woman's University ... TX ... 488
Trinity University ... TX ... 488
University of the Incarnate Word ... TX ... 490
University of Utah, The ... UT ... 496
Weber State University ... UT ... 497
George Mason University ... VA ... 505
Marymount University ... VA ... 507
Virginia Commonwealth University ... VA ... 511
University of Washington ... WA .. 524
Washington State University ... WA .. 525

HT: National Accrediting Agency for Clinical Laboratory Sciences: histologic technology (C,A,B)

Phoenix College ... AZ 15
Mt. San Antonio College ... CA 55
Goodwin College ... CT 90
Delaware Technical Community College, Stanton-Wilmington Campus ... DE 93
Barry University ... FL 98
Florida State College at Jacksonville ... FL ... 105
Miami Dade College ... FL ... 109
Darton State College ... GA .. 124
Elgin Community College ... IL 144
Indiana University-Purdue University Indianapolis ... IN 168
Harford Community College ... MD .. 215
Lansing Community College ... MI ... 245
North Hennepin Community College ... MN .. 260
State University of New York College of Agriculture and Technology at Coble skill ... NY ... 344
Davidson County Community College ... NC .. 360
University of North Dakota Main Campus . ND .. 371
Lakeland Community College ... OH .. 382
Youngstown State University ... OH .. 394
Drexel University ... PA ... 415
Harcum College ... PA ... 417
University of Pittsburgh ... PA ... 435
Community College of Rhode Island ... RI ... 439
Medical University of South Carolina ... SC ... 445
Houston Community College ... TX ... 473
St. Philip's College ... TX ... 465
Tarleton State University ... TX ... 483
University of Texas Health Science Center at San Antonio ... TX ... 493
University of Texas M.D. Anderson Cancer Center, The ... TX ... 493
Clover Park Technical College ... WA .. 518
West Virginia University ... WV .. 530

IACBE: International Assembly for Collegiate Business Education: business programs in institutions that grant bachelor/graduate degrees (A,B, M,D)

Stillman College ... AL 7
John Brown University ... AR 21
University of the Ozarks ... AR 25
Azusa Pacific University ... CA 29
California Maritime Academy ... CA 31
John F. Kennedy University ... CA 49
National University ... CA 55
Pacific Union College ... CA 57
Albertus Magnus College ... CT 87
Goldey-Beacom College ... DE 93
Wilmington University ... DE 94
Edward Waters College ... FL ... 102
Hodges University ... FL ... 106
Lynn University ... FL ... 108
Nova Southeastern University ... FL ... 109
Palm Beach Atlantic University ... FL ... 110
Saint Leo University ... FL ... 112
Southeastern University ... FL ... 113
Webber International University ... FL ... 119
Thomas University ... GA .. 132
University of Guam ... GU .. 546
Chaminade University of Honolulu ... HI ... 135
Lewis-Clark State College ... ID ... 138
Lincoln College ... IL 151
McKendree University ... IL 152
National-Louis University ... IL 153
North Park University ... IL 154
Robert Morris University ... IL 156
Rockford University ... IL 157
Bethel College ... IN 164
Grace College and Seminary ... IN 166
Marian University ... IN 170
Oakland City University ... IN 171
Purdue University Calumet ... IN 171
Saint Joseph's College ... IN 172
Ashford University ... IA 175
Maharishi University of Management ... IA 180
Northwestern College ... IA 181
University of Saint Mary ... KS ... 191
Campbellsville University ... KY ... 193
Kentucky Wesleyan College ... KY ... 197
Lindsey Wilson College ... KY ... 197
Spalding University ... KY ... 199
Sullivan University ... KY ... 199
Our Lady of Holy Cross College ... LA ... 206
Husson University ... ME .. 210
University of Maine at Fort Kent ... ME .. 212
Capitol College ... MD .. 213
Mount St. Mary's University ... MD .. 217
University of Maryland College Park ... MD .. 219
American International College ... MA .. 221
College of Our Lady of the Elms ... MA .. 225
Fitchburg State University ... MA .. 229
Nichols College ... MA .. 235
Springfield College ... MA .. 236
Wentworth Institute of Technology ... MA .. 237
Andrews University ... MI ... 239
Baker College of Flint ... MI ... 239
Davenport University ... MI ... 241
Lawrence Technological University ... MI ... 245
Walsh College of Accountancy and Business Administration ... MI 251
Bemidji State University ... MN .. 258

Saint Mary's University of Minnesota ... MN .. 264
Belhaven University ... MS .. 266
Avila University ... MO .. 271
Culver-Stockton College ... MO .. 273
Harris-Stowe State University ... MO .. 275
Stephens College ... MO .. 282
University of Montana Western, The ... MT .. 286
Bellevue University ... NE .. 288
Clarkson College ... NE .. 288
College of Saint Mary ... NE .. 289
Concordia University ... NE .. 289
Wayne State College ... NE .. 291
Roseman University of Health Sciences ... NV .. 295
Centenary College ... NJ .. 300
Felician College ... NJ .. 302
Cazenovia College ... NY .. 316
Daemen College ... NY .. 322
Dominican College of Blauvelt ... NY .. 322
Dowling College ... NY .. 323
D'Youville College ... NY .. 323
Excelsior College ... NY .. 324
Keuka College ... NY .. 328
Manhattanville College ... NY .. 330
Medaille College ... NY .. 330
Mount Saint Mary College ... NY .. 332
Nazareth College of Rochester ... NY .. 332
Roberts Wesleyan College ... NY .. 337
St. Thomas Aquinas College ... NY .. 340
State University of New York College at Potsdam ... NY .. 344
State University of New York Empire State College ... NY .. 346
Vaughn College of Aeronautics and Technology ... NY .. 349
Montreat College ... NC .. 357
Dickinson State University ... ND .. 371
Minot State University ... ND .. 371
University of Jamestown ... ND .. 373
University of Mary ... ND .. 373
Defiance College, The ... OH .. 379
Franklin University ... OH .. 380
Lake Erie College ... OH .. 382
Lourdes University ... OH .. 383
University of Rio Grande ... OH .. 392
Urbana University ... OH .. 392
Ursuline College ... OH .. 392
Bacone College ... OK .. 394
Oklahoma Wesleyan University ... OK .. 398
Southwestern Oklahoma State University ... OK .. 400
Eastern Oregon University ... OR .. 405
Marylhurst University ... OR .. 404
Northwest Christian University ... OR .. 405
Oregon Institute of Technology ... OR .. 405
Cairn University ... PA .. 411
Gwynedd-Mercy University ... PA .. 417
Mercyhurst University ... PA .. 423
Misericordia University ... PA .. 424
Point Park University ... PA .. 431
Saint Francis University ... PA .. 432
Seton Hill University ... PA .. 433
Universidad Politecnica De Puerto Rico ... PR .. 553
Salve Regina University ... RI .. 440
Charleston Southern University ... SC .. 441
National American University ... SD .. 450
Presentation College ... SD .. 450
University of Sioux Falls ... SD .. 452
Bryan College ... TN .. 453
Southern Adventist University ... TN .. 458
Concordia University Texas ... TX .. 469
Howard Payne University ... TX .. 473
LeTourneau University ... TX .. 475
Southwestern Adventist University ... TX .. 481
Hampton University ... VA .. 505
Davis & Elkins College ... WV .. 526
Ohio Valley University ... WV .. 527
Shepherd University ... WV .. 529
West Liberty University ... WV .. 530
Concordia University Wisconsin ... WI .. 532
Marian University ... WI .. 534

IFSAC: International Fire Service Accreditation Congress Degree Assembly: fire and emergency related degree (A,B)

Yavapai College ... AZ .. 19
NorthWest Arkansas Community College ... AR .. 22
Aims Community College ... CO .. 78
Southern Illinois University Carbondale ... IL .. 159
Johnson County Community College ... KS .. 187
Ashland Community and Technical College ... KY .. 194
Bluegrass Community and Technical College ... KY .. 194
Eastern Kentucky University ... KY .. 193
Elizabethtown Community and Technical College ... KY .. 195
Gateway Community and Technical College ... KY .. 195
Hazard Community and Technical College ... KY .. 195
Jefferson Community and Technical College ... KY .. 195
Madisonville Community College ... KY .. 196
Maysville Community and Technical College ... KY .. 196
Owensboro Community and Technical College ... KY .. 196
Somerset Community College ... KY .. 196
Southcentral Kentucky Community and Technical College ... KY .. 196
West Kentucky Community and Technical College ... KY .. 196
Lake Superior State University ... MI .. 245
Lansing Community College ... MI .. 245
Hennepin Technical College ... MN .. 258
Ozarks Technical Community College ... MO .. 279
New Mexico State University Dona Ana Community College ... NM .. 311
Cincinnati State Technical and Community College ... OH .. 376
Lakeland Community College ... OH .. 382
University of Akron, Main Campus, The ... OH .. 390
Chemeketa Community College ... OR .. 402
Holy Family University ... PA .. 418
Montgomery County Community College ... PA .. 424
Blinn College ... TX .. 467
Weatherford College ... TX .. 494
Utah Valley University ... UT .. 497
South Puget Sound Community College ... WA .. 524

IPSY: American Psychological Association: pre-doctoral internships in professional psychology

University of Alabama at Birmingham ... AL .. 8
Arizona State University ... AZ .. 11
University of Arizona ... AZ .. 18
University of Arkansas for Medical Sciences ... AR .. 24
California State University-Long Beach ... CA .. 33
California State University-Northridge ... CA .. 34
Loma Linda University ... CA .. 51
San Jose State University ... CA .. 36
Stanford University ... CA .. 68
University of California-Berkeley ... CA .. 70
University of California-Davis ... CA .. 70
University of California-Irvine ... CA .. 71
University of California-Los Angeles ... CA .. 71
University of California-San Diego ... CA .. 71
University of California-San Francisco ... CA .. 72
University of California-Santa Barbara ... CA .. 72
University of California-Santa Cruz ... CA .. 72
University of San Diego ... CA .. 73
University of Southern California ... CA .. 74
University of the Pacific ... CA .. 73
Colorado State University ... CO .. 80
University of Colorado Boulder ... CO .. 85
University of Colorado DenverlAnschutz Medical Campus ... CO .. 86
University of Denver ... CO .. 86
Yale University ... CT .. 93
University of Delaware ... DE .. 94
American University ... DC .. 94
Catholic University of America, The ... DC .. 94
Howard University ... DC .. 95
Florida International University ... FL .. 115
Florida State University ... FL .. 115
Nova Southeastern University ... FL .. 109
University of Central Florida ... FL .. 115
University of Florida ... FL .. 116
University of Miami ... FL .. 118
University of South Florida ... FL .. 116
Emory University ... GA .. 124
Georgia Institute of Technology ... GA .. 125
Georgia Regents University ... GA .. 126
Georgia State University ... GA .. 126
University of Hawaii at Manoa ... HI .. 136
University of Idaho ... ID .. 139
Adler School of Professional Psychology ... IL .. 139
Illinois State University ... IL .. 147
Northern Illinois University ... IL .. 154
Northwestern University ... IL .. 155
Rush University ... IL .. 157
Southern Illinois University Carbondale ... IL .. 159
University of Chicago ... IL .. 161
University of Illinois at Chicago ... IL .. 161
University of Illinois at Urbana-Champaign ... IL .. 162
Ball State University ... IN .. 164
Butler University ... IN .. 164
Indiana University Bloomington ... IN .. 167
Indiana University-Purdue University Indianapolis ... IN .. 168
Purdue University Main Campus ... IN .. 171
University of Notre Dame ... IN .. 174
Iowa State University ... IA .. 175
University of Iowa ... IA .. 175
Kansas State University ... KS .. 188
University of Kansas Main Campus ... KS .. 190
Wichita State University ... KS .. 191
University of Louisville ... KY .. 200
Louisiana State University and Agricultural and Mechanical College ... LA .. 204
Louisiana State University Health Sciences Center-New Orleans ... LA .. 205
Tulane University ... LA .. 207
University of Maine ... ME .. 212
Johns Hopkins University ... MD .. 215
Towson University ... MD .. 220
University of Maryland Baltimore ... MD .. 219
University of Maryland College Park ... MD .. 219
Boston University ... MA .. 224
Harvard University ... MA .. 227
Massachusetts School of Professional Psychology ... MA .. 233
Suffolk University ... MA .. 237
Tufts University ... MA .. 237
University of Massachusetts ... MA .. 228
University of Massachusetts Medical School ... MA .. 229
Grand Valley State University ... MI .. 243
Michigan State University ... MI .. 246
University of Michigan-Ann Arbor ... MI .. 251
Western Michigan University ... MI .. 252
University of Minnesota-Twin Cities ... MN .. 264
University of Saint Thomas ... MN .. 265
University of Mississippi Medical Center ... MS .. 270
School of Professional Psychology at Forest Institute, The ... MO .. 281
University of Missouri - Columbia ... MO .. 283
University of Missouri - Kansas City ... MO .. 283
University of Missouri - Saint Louis ... MO .. 283
Montana State University ... MT .. 287
University of Nebraska - Lincoln ... NE .. 292
Dartmouth College ... NH .. 296
University of New Hampshire ... NH .. 298
University of New Mexico Main Campus ... NM .. 312
Albany Medical College ... NY .. 313
Columbia University in the City of New York ... NY .. 321
Icahn School of Medicine at Mount Sinai ... NY .. 327
New York University ... NY .. 334
Pace University ... NY .. 335
State University of New York at Stony Brook ... NY .. 342
State University of New York Upstate Medical University ... NY .. 342
University at Albany, SUNY ... NY .. 341
University at Buffalo-SUNY ... NY .. 341
University of Rochester ... NY .. 349
Yeshiva University ... NY .. 351
Appalachian State University ... NC .. 367
Duke University ... NC .. 354
University of North Carolina at Chapel Hill ... NC .. 368
University of North Carolina at Charlotte ... NC .. 368
University of North Dakota Main Campus ... ND .. 371
Bowling Green State University ... OH .. 374
Miami University ... OH .. 384
Northeast Ohio Medical University ... OH .. 385
Ohio State University Main Campus, The ... OH .. 386
University of Akron, Main Campus, The ... OH .. 390
Wright State University Main Campus ... OH .. 393
Oregon Health & Science University ... OR .. 405
Oregon State University ... OR .. 406
Pacific University ... OR .. 407
University of Oregon ... OR .. 406
Penn State University Park ... PA .. 426
Temple University ... PA .. 433
University of Pennsylvania ... PA .. 435
University of Pittsburgh ... PA .. 435
Widener University ... PA .. 437
Brown University ... RI .. 438
Clemson University ... SC .. 442
Medical University of South Carolina ... SC .. 445
University of South Carolina Columbia ... SC .. 447
University of Memphis, The ... TN .. 460
University of Tennessee, Knoxville ... TN .. 463
Vanderbilt University ... TN .. 463
Baylor College of Medicine ... TX .. 467
Texas A & M University ... TX .. 483
Texas State University-San Marcos ... TX .. 487
Texas Tech University ... TX .. 487
Texas Woman's University ... TX .. 488
University of Houston ... TX .. 489
University of Texas at Austin ... TX .. 491
University of Texas at Dallas, The ... TX .. 491
University of Texas Health Science Center at San Antonio ... TX .. 493
University of Texas Southwestern Medical Center ... TX .. 493
Brigham Young University ... UT .. 495
University of Utah, The ... UT .. 496
Utah State University ... UT .. 497
University of Vermont ... VT .. 500
College of William & Mary ... VA .. 503
Eastern Virginia Medical School ... VA .. 504
George Mason University ... VA .. 505
James Madison University ... VA .. 506
University of Virginia ... VA .. 511
Virginia Commonwealth University ... VA .. 511
Virginia Polytechnic Institute and State University ... VA .. 515
Central Washington University ... WA .. 517
University of Washington ... WA .. 524
Washington State University ... WA .. 525
West Virginia University ... WV .. 530
University of Wisconsin-Madison ... WI .. 536

JOUR: Accrediting Council on Education for Journalism and Mass Communications: journalism and mass communications (B,M)

#Auburn University ... AL .. 1
Jacksonville State University ... AL .. 4
University of Alabama, The ... AL .. 8
University of Alaska Anchorage ... AK .. 10
University of Alaska Fairbanks ... AK .. 10
Arizona State University ... AZ .. 11
University of Arizona ... AZ .. 18
Arkansas State University-Jonesboro ... AR .. 19
University of Arkansas Main Campus ... AR .. 23
California State University-Chico ... CA .. 33
California State University-Fullerton ... CA .. 33
California State University-Northridge ... CA .. 34
San Diego State University ... CA .. 35
San Francisco State University ... CA .. 35
San Jose State University ... CA .. 36
University of California-Berkeley ... CA .. 70
University of Southern California ... CA .. 74
Colorado State University ... CO .. 80
University of Colorado Boulder ... CO .. 85
University of Connecticut ... CT .. 92
American University ... DC .. 94
Howard University ... DC .. 95
Florida Agricultural and Mechanical University ... FL .. 114
Florida International University ... FL .. 115
University of Florida ... FL .. 116
University of South Florida St. Petersburg ... FL .. 116
Savannah State University ... GA .. 131
University of Georgia ... GA .. 133
Eastern Illinois University ... IL .. 144
Northwestern University ... IL .. 155
Southern Illinois University Carbondale ... IL .. 159
Southern Illinois University Edwardsville ... IL .. 159
University of Illinois at Urbana-Champaign ... IL .. 162
Ball State University ... IN .. 164
Indiana University Bloomington ... IN .. 167
University of Southern Indiana ... IN .. 174
Drake University ... IA .. 177
Iowa State University ... IA .. 175
University of Iowa ... IA .. 175
Kansas State University ... KS .. 188
University of Kansas Main Campus ... KS .. 190
Murray State University ... KY .. 198
University of Kentucky ... KY .. 200
Western Kentucky University ... KY .. 200
Grambling State University ... LA .. 207
Louisiana State University and Agricultural and Mechanical College ... LA .. 204
Nicholls State University ... LA .. 208
#Southern University and A&M College ... LA .. 206
University of Louisiana at Lafayette ... LA .. 208
University of Maryland College Park ... MD .. 219
Central Michigan University ... MI .. 240
Michigan State University ... MI .. 246
St. Cloud State University ... MN .. 261
University of Minnesota-Twin Cities ... MN .. 264
Jackson State University ... MS .. 267
University of Mississippi ... MS .. 270
University of Southern Mississippi ... MS .. 270
Southeast Missouri State University ... MO .. 282
University of Missouri - Columbia ... MO .. 283
University of Montana - Missoula, The ... MT .. 286
University of Nebraska - Lincoln ... NE .. 292
University of Nevada, Reno ... NV .. 294
University of New Mexico Main Campus ... NM .. 312
Columbia University in the City of New York ... NY .. 321
Hofstra University ... NY .. 326
Iona College ... NY .. 327
New York University ... NY .. 334
State University of New York College at Buffalo ... NY .. 343
Syracuse University Main Campus ... NY .. 347
Elon University ... NC .. 354
North Carolina Agricultural and Technical State University ... NC .. 367
University of North Carolina at Chapel Hill ... NC .. 368
Bowling Green State University ... OH .. 374
Kent State University Main Campus ... OH .. 382
Ohio University Main Campus ... OH .. 387
Oklahoma State University ... OK .. 397
University of Oklahoma Norman Campus ... OK .. 401
University of Oregon ... OR .. 406
Penn State University Park ... PA .. 426
Shippensburg University of Pennsylvania ... PA .. 429
Temple University ... PA .. 433
University of Puerto Rico at Arecibo ... PR .. 553
University of Puerto Rico-Rio Piedras Campus ... PR .. 555
University of South Carolina Columbia ... SC .. 447
Winthrop University ... SC .. 449
South Dakota State University ... SD .. 452
University of South Dakota, The ... SD .. 451
Middle Tennessee State University ... TN .. 459
University of Memphis, The ... TN .. 460
University of Tennessee at Chattanooga ... TN .. 463
University of Tennessee at Martin ... TN .. 463
University of Tennessee, Knoxville ... TN .. 463

#Abilene Christian University ... TX ... 464
Baylor University ... TX ... 467
Texas Christian University ... TX ... 484
Texas State University-San Marcos ... TX ... 487
University of North Texas ... TX ... 490
University of Texas at Austin ... TX ... 491
Brigham Young University ... UT ... 495
Hampton University ... VA ... 505
Norfolk State University ... VA ... 507
Virginia Commonwealth University ... VA ... 511
Washington and Lee University ... VA ... 516
University of Washington ... WA .. 524
Marshall University ... WV .. 529
West Virginia University ... WV .. 530
Marquette University ... WI ... 534
University of Wisconsin-Eau Claire ... WI ... 536
University of Wisconsin-Oshkosh ... WI ... 537

KIN: Commission on Accreditation of Allied Health Education Programs: kinesiotherapy (B)

California State University-Long Beach ... CA ... 33
University of Southern Mississippi ... MS .. 270
Shaw University ... NC .. 366
Norfolk State University ... VA ... 507

LAW: American Bar Association: law (FP,D)

Faulkner University ... AL ... 3
Samford University ... AL ... 6
University of Alabama, The ... AL ... 8
Arizona State University ... AZ ... 11
Phoenix School of Law ... AZ ... 16
University of Arizona ... AZ ... 18
University of Arkansas at Little Rock ... AR ... 24
University of Arkansas Main Campus ... AR ... 23
California Western School of Law ... CA ... 36
Chapman University ... CA ... 38
Golden Gate University ... CA ... 45
Loyola Marymount University ... CA ... 53
Pepperdine University ... CA ... 58
Santa Clara University ... CA ... 64
Southwestern Law School ... CA ... 68
Stanford University ... CA ... 68
Thomas Jefferson School of Law ... CA ... 69
University of California-Berkeley ... CA ... 70
University of California-Davis ... CA ... 70
University of California-Hastings College of the Law ... CA ... 71
#University of California-Irvine ... CA ... 71
University of California-Los Angeles ... CA ... 71
#University of LaVerne ... CA ... 72
University of San Diego ... CA ... 73
University of San Francisco ... CA ... 73
University of Southern California ... CA ... 74
University of the Pacific ... CA ... 73
Whittier College ... CA ... 76
University of Colorado Boulder ... CO ... 85
University of Denver ... CO ... 86
Quinnipiac University ... CT ... 91
University of Connecticut ... CT ... 92
Yale University ... CT ... 93
American University ... DC ... 94
Catholic University of America, The ... DC ... 94
George Washington University ... DC ... 95
Georgetown University ... DC ... 95
Howard University ... DC ... 95
University of the District of Columbia ... DC ... 97
Ave Maria School of Law ... FL ... 98
Barry University ... FL ... 98
Florida Agricultural and Mechanical University ... FL ... 114
Florida Coastal School of Law ... FL ... 103
Florida International University ... FL ... 115
Florida State University ... FL ... 116
Nova Southeastern University ... FL ... 109
St. Thomas University ... FL ... 112
Stetson University ... FL ... 117
University of Florida ... FL ... 116
University of Miami ... FL ... 118
Atlanta's John Marshall Law School ... GA .. 121
Emory University ... GA .. 124
Georgia State University ... GA .. 126
Mercer University ... GA .. 128
University of Georgia ... GA .. 133
University of Hawaii at Manoa ... HI ... 136
University of Idaho ... ID ... 139
DePaul University ... IL ... 143
Illinois Institute of Technology ... IL ... 147
John Marshall Law School ... IL ... 148
Loyola University Chicago ... IL ... 151
Northern Illinois University ... IL ... 154
Northwestern University ... IL ... 155
Southern Illinois University Carbondale ... IL ... 159
University of Chicago ... IL ... 161
University of Illinois at Urbana-Champaign ... IL ... 162
Indiana University Bloomington ... IN ... 167
Indiana University-Purdue University Indianapolis ... IN ... 168
University of Notre Dame ... IN ... 174
Valparaiso University ... IN ... 174
Drake University ... IA ... 177
University of Iowa ... IA ... 175
University of Kansas Main Campus ... KS ... 190
Washburn University ... KS ... 191
Northern Kentucky University ... KY ... 198
University of Kentucky ... KY ... 200
University of Louisville ... KY ... 200
Louisiana State University Paul M. Hebert Law Center ... LA ... 205
Loyola University New Orleans ... LA ... 205
Southern University and A&M College ... LA ... 206
Tulane University ... LA ... 207
University of Southern Maine ... ME .. 212
University of Baltimore ... MD .. 221
University of Maryland Baltimore ... MD .. 219
Boston College ... MA .. 224
Boston University ... MA .. 224
Harvard University ... MA .. 227
New England Law | Boston ... MA .. 235
Northeastern University ... MA .. 235
Suffolk University ... MA .. 237
#University of Massachusetts Dartmouth ... MA .. 229
Western New England University ... MA .. 238
Michigan State University ... MI ... 246
Thomas M. Cooley Law School ... MI ... 250
University of Detroit Mercy ... MI ... 250
University of Michigan-Ann Arbor ... MI ... 251
Wayne State University ... MI ... 252
Hamline University ... MN .. 256
University of Minnesota-Twin Cities ... MN .. 264
University of Saint Thomas ... MN .. 265
William Mitchell College of Law ... MN .. 265
Mississippi College ... MS .. 268
University of Mississippi ... MS .. 270
Saint Louis University ... MO .. 281
University of Missouri - Columbia ... MO .. 283
University of Missouri - Kansas City ... MO .. 283
Washington University in St. Louis ... MO .. 284
University of Montana - Missoula, The ... MT .. 286
Creighton University ... NE ... 289
University of Nebraska - Lincoln ... NE ... 292
University of Nevada, Las Vegas ... NV ... 294
University of New Hampshire School of Law ... NH ... 298
Rutgers the State University of New Jersey Camden Campus ... NJ ... 306
Rutgers the State University of New Jersey Newark Campus ... NJ ... 306
Seton Hall University ... NJ ... 307
Seton Hall University School of Law ... NJ ... 307
University of New Mexico Main Campus .. NM .. 312
Albany Law School ... NY ... 313
Brooklyn Law School ... NY ... 315
City University of New York Queens College ... NY ... 319
Columbia University in the City of New York ... NY ... 321
Cornell University ... NY ... 322
Fordham University ... NY ... 324
Hofstra University ... NY ... 326
New York Law School ... NY ... 333
New York University ... NY ... 334
Pace University ... NY ... 335
St. John's University ... NY ... 339
Syracuse University Main Campus ... NY ... 347
Touro College ... NY ... 348
University at Buffalo-SUNY ... NY ... 341
Yeshiva University ... NY ... 351
Campbell University ... NC .. 352
Charlotte School of Law ... NC .. 353
Duke University ... NC .. 354
Elon University ... NC .. 354
North Carolina Central University ... NC .. 368
University of North Carolina at Chapel Hill NC .. 368
Wake Forest University ... NC .. 370
University of North Dakota Main Campus . ND .. 371
Capital University ... OH .. 375
Case Western Reserve University ... OH .. 375
Cleveland State University ... OH .. 377
Ohio Northern University ... OH .. 386
Ohio State University Main Campus, The . OH .. 386
University of Akron, Main Campus, The ... OH .. 390
University of Cincinnati Main Campus ... OH .. 390
University of Dayton ... OH .. 391
University of Toledo ... OH .. 392
Oklahoma City University ... OK .. 397
University of Oklahoma Norman Campus . OK .. 401
University of Tulsa ... OK .. 401
Lewis and Clark College ... OR .. 403
University of Oregon ... OR .. 406
Willamette University ... OR .. 408
Drexel University ... PA ... 415
Duquesne University ... PA ... 415
Temple University ... PA ... 433
University of Pennsylvania ... PA ... 435
University of Pittsburgh ... PA ... 435
Villanova University ... PA ... 436
Widener University ... PA ... 437
Inter American University of Puerto Rico School of Law ... PR ... 551
Pontifical Catholic University of Puerto Rico, The ... PR ... 552
University of Puerto Rico-Rio Piedras Campus ... PR ... 555
Roger Williams University ... RI ... 440
Charleston School of Law ... SC ... 441
University of South Carolina Columbia ... SC ... 447
University of South Dakota, The ... SD ... 451
#Belmont University ... TN ... 453
University of Memphis, The ... TN ... 460
University of Tennessee, Knoxville ... TN ... 463
Vanderbilt University ... TN ... 463
Baylor University ... TX ... 467
St. Mary's University ... TX ... 479
South Texas College of Law ... TX ... 480
Southern Methodist University ... TX ... 481
Texas A & M University ... TX ... 483
Texas Southern University ... TX ... 485
Texas Tech University ... TX ... 487
University of Houston ... TX ... 489
University of Texas at Austin ... TX ... 491
Brigham Young University ... UT ... 495
University of Utah, The ... UT ... 496
Vermont Law School ... VT ... 500
Appalachian School of Law ... VA ... 502
College of William & Mary ... VA ... 503
George Mason University ... VA ... 505
Judge Advocate General's Legal Center & School, The ... VA ... 544
Liberty University ... VA ... 506
Regent University ... VA ... 508
University of Richmond ... VA ... 510
University of Virginia ... VA ... 511
Washington and Lee University ... VA ... 516
Gonzaga University ... WA .. 520
Seattle University ... WA .. 523
University of Washington ... WA .. 524
West Virginia University ... WV .. 530
Marquette University ... WI ... 534
University of Wisconsin-Madison ... WI ... 536
University of Wyoming ... WY .. 543

LIB: American Library Association: librarianship (M)

University of Alabama, The ... AL ... 8
University of Arizona ... AZ ... 18
San Jose State University ... CA ... 36
University of California-Los Angeles ... CA ... 71
University of Denver ... CO ... 86
#Southern Connecticut State University ... CT ... 88
Catholic University of America, The ... DC ... 94
Florida State University ... FL ... 115
University of South Florida ... FL ... 116
#Valdosta State University ... GA .. 134
University of Hawaii at Manoa ... HI ... 136
Dominican University ... IL ... 144
University of Illinois at Urbana-Champaign IL ... 162
Indiana University Bloomington ... IN ... 167
University of Iowa ... IA ... 175
Emporia State University ... KS ... 186
University of Kentucky ... KY ... 200
Louisiana State University and Agricultural and Mechanical College ... LA ... 204
University of Maryland College Park ... MD .. 219
Simmons College ... MA .. 236
University of Michigan-Ann Arbor ... MI ... 251
Wayne State University ... MI ... 252
St. Catherine University ... MN .. 263
University of Southern Mississippi ... MS .. 270
#University of Missouri - Columbia ... MO .. 283
Rutgers the State University of New Jersey New Brunswick Campus ... NJ ... 306
#City University of New York Queens College ... NY ... 319
#Long Island University - Post Campus ... NY ... 329
Pratt Institute ... NY ... 336
St. John's University ... NY ... 339
Syracuse University Main Campus ... NY ... 347
University at Albany, SUNY ... NY ... 341
#University at Buffalo-SUNY ... NY ... 341
North Carolina Central University ... NC ... 368
University of North Carolina at Chapel Hill NC .. 368
University of North Carolina at Greensboro ... NC .. 369
Kent State University Main Campus ... OH .. 382
University of Oklahoma Norman Campus . OK .. 401
Clarion University of Pennsylvania ... PA ... 428
Drexel University ... PA ... 415
University of Pittsburgh ... PA ... 435
University of Puerto Rico-Rio Piedras Campus ... PR ... 555
University of Rhode Island ... RI ... 440
University of South Carolina Columbia ... SC ... 447
University of Tennessee, Knoxville ... TN ... 463
Texas Woman's University ... TX ... 488
University of North Texas ... TX ... 490
University of Texas at Austin ... TX ... 491
University of Washington ... WA .. 524
University of Wisconsin-Madison ... WI ... 536
University of Wisconsin-Milwaukee ... WI ... 537

LSAR: American Society of Landscape Architects: landscape architecture (B,M)

Auburn University ... AL ... 1
Arizona State University ... AZ ... 11
University of Arizona ... AZ ... 18
University of Arkansas Main Campus ... AR ... 23
California Polytechnic State University-San Luis Obispo ... CA ... 32
California State Polytechnic University-Pomona ... CA ... 32
University of California-Berkeley ... CA ... 70
University of California-Davis ... CA ... 70
University of Southern California ... CA ... 74
Colorado State University ... CO ... 80
University of Colorado DenverlAnschutz Medical Campus ... CO ... 86
University of Connecticut ... CT ... 92
Florida International University ... FL ... 115
University of Florida ... FL ... 116
University of Georgia ... GA .. 133
University of Idaho ... ID ... 139
Illinois Institute of Technology ... IL ... 147
University of Illinois at Urbana-Champaign IL ... 162
Ball State University ... IN ... 164
Purdue University Main Campus ... IN ... 171
Iowa State University ... IA ... 175
Kansas State University ... KS ... 188
University of Kentucky ... KY ... 200
Louisiana State University and Agricultural and Mechanical College ... LA ... 204
Morgan State University ... MD .. 217
University of Maryland College Park ... MD .. 219
Boston Architectural College ... MA .. 223
Harvard University ... MA .. 227
University of Massachusetts ... MA .. 228
Michigan State University ... MI ... 246
University of Michigan-Ann Arbor ... MI ... 251
University of Minnesota-Twin Cities ... MN .. 264
Mississippi State University ... MS .. 268
University of Nebraska - Lincoln ... NE ... 292
University of Nevada, Las Vegas ... NV ... 294
Rutgers the State University of New Jersey New Brunswick Campus ... NJ ... 306
University of New Mexico Main Campus .. NM .. 312
City University of New York The City College ... NY ... 317
Cornell University ... NY ... 322
State University of New York College of Environmental Science and Forestry ... NY ... 345
North Carolina Agricultural and Technical State University ... NC ... 367
North Carolina State University ... NC .. 368
#North Dakota State University Main Campus ... ND ... 371
Ohio State University Main Campus, The . OH .. 386
Oklahoma State University ... OK .. 397
University of Oklahoma Norman Campus . OK .. 401
University of Oregon ... OR ... 406
Chatham University ... PA ... 412
Penn State University Park ... PA ... 426
Philadelphia University ... PA ... 430
Temple University ... PA ... 433
University of Pennsylvania ... PA ... 435
Universidad Politecnica De Puerto Rico ... PR ... 553
Rhode Island School of Design ... RI ... 440
University of Rhode Island ... RI ... 440
Clemson University ... SC ... 442
University of Tennessee, Knoxville ... TN ... 463
Texas A & M University ... TX ... 483
Texas Tech University ... TX ... 487
University of Texas at Arlington, The ... TX ... 491
University of Texas at Austin ... TX ... 491
Utah State University ... UT ... 497
University of Virginia ... VA ... 511
Virginia Polytechnic Institute and State University ... VA ... 515
University of Washington ... WA .. 524
Washington State University ... WA .. 525
West Virginia University ... WV .. 530
University of Wisconsin-Madison ... WI ... 536

M: Middle States Commission on Higher Education

Delaware College of Art and Design ... DE ... 93
Delaware State University ... DE ... 93
Delaware Technical Community College, Owens Campus ... DE ... 93
Delaware Technical Community College, Stanton-Wilmington Campus ... DE ... 93
Delaware Technical Community College, Terry Campus ... DE ... 93
Goldey-Beacom College ... DE ... 93
@Irish American University ... DE ... 94
University of Delaware ... DE ... 94
Wesley College ... DE ... 94
Wilmington University ... DE ... 94
American University ... DC ... 94
Catholic University of America, The ... DC ... 94
Corcoran College of Art and Design ... DC ... 95
Gallaudet University ... DC ... 95
George Washington University ... DC ... 95
Georgetown University ... DC ... 95
@Graduate School USA ... DC ... 95
Howard University ... DC ... 95
Institute of World Politics, The ... DC ... 96
National Defense University ... DC .. 544
National Intelligence University ... DC .. 544

Pontifical Faculty of the Immaculate Conception at the Dominican House of S tudies ... DC 96
Pontifical John Paul II Institute for Studies on Marriage and Family ... DC 96
Strayer University ... DC 96
Trinity Washington University ... DC 96
University of the District of Columbia ... DC 97
University of the Potomac ... DC 97
Wesley Theological Seminary ... DC 97
Allegany College of Maryland ... MD .. 213
Anne Arundel Community College ... MD .. 213
Baltimore City Community College ... MD .. 213
Bowie State University ... MD .. 220
Capitol College ... MD .. 213
Carroll Community College ... MD .. 214
Cecil College ... MD .. 214
Chesapeake College ... MD .. 214
College of Southern Maryland ... MD .. 214
Community College of Baltimore County, The ... MD .. 214
Coppin State University ... MD .. 220
Frederick Community College ... MD .. 214
Frostburg State University ... MD .. 220
Garrett College ... MD .. 214
Goucher College ... MD .. 215
Hagerstown Community College ... MD .. 215
Harford Community College ... MD .. 215
Hood College ... MD .. 215
Howard Community College ... MD .. 215
Johns Hopkins University ... MD .. 215
Loyola University Maryland ... MD .. 216
Maryland Institute College of Art ... MD .. 216
Maryland University of Integrative Health . MD .. 216
McDaniel College ... MD .. 216
Montgomery College ... MD .. 216
Morgan State University ... MD .. 217
Mount St. Mary's University ... MD .. 217
National Labor College ... MD .. 217
Notre Dame of Maryland University ... MD .. 217
Prince George's Community College ... MD .. 217
St. John's College ... MD .. 217
St. Mary's College of Maryland ... MD .. 218
Saint Mary's Seminary and University ... MD .. 218
Salisbury University ... MD .. 220
@SANS Technology Institute, The ... MD .. 218
Sojourner-Douglass College ... MD .. 218
Stevenson University ... MD .. 218
Towson University ... MD .. 220
Uniformed Services University of the Health Sciences ... MD .. 545
United States Naval Academy ... MD .. 545
University of Baltimore ... MD .. 221
University of Maryland Baltimore ... MD .. 219
University of Maryland Baltimore County .. MD .. 219
University of Maryland College Park ... MD .. 219
University of Maryland Eastern Shore ... MD .. 219
University of Maryland University College MD .. 219
Washington Adventist University ... MD .. 221
Washington College ... MD .. 221
Wor-Wic Community College ... MD .. 221
Assumption College for Sisters ... NJ ... 298
Atlantic Cape Community College ... NJ ... 299
Bergen Community College ... NJ ... 299
Berkeley College ... NJ ... 299
Bloomfield College ... NJ ... 299
Brookdale Community College ... NJ ... 299
Burlington County College ... NJ ... 299
Caldwell College ... NJ ... 300
Camden County College ... NJ ... 300
Centenary College ... NJ ... 300
College of New Jersey, The ... NJ ... 300
College of Saint Elizabeth ... NJ ... 300
County College of Morris ... NJ ... 300
Cumberland County College ... NJ ... 301
Drew University ... NJ ... 301
Essex County College ... NJ ... 301
Fairleigh Dickinson University ... NJ ... 301
Felician College ... NJ ... 302
Georgian Court University ... NJ ... 302
Gloucester County College ... NJ ... 302
Hudson County Community College ... NJ ... 302
Kean University ... NJ ... 302
Mercer County Community College ... NJ ... 302
Middlesex County College ... NJ ... 303
Monmouth University ... NJ ... 303
Montclair State University ... NJ ... 303
New Jersey City University ... NJ ... 303
New Jersey Institute of Technology ... NJ ... 303
Ocean County College ... NJ ... 304
Passaic County Community College ... NJ ... 304
Pillar College ... NJ ... 304
Princeton Theological Seminary ... NJ ... 304
Princeton University ... NJ ... 304
Ramapo College of New Jersey ... NJ ... 305
Raritan Valley Community College ... NJ ... 305
Richard Stockton College of New Jersey, The ... NJ ... 305
Rider University ... NJ ... 305
Rowan University ... NJ ... 305
&Rutgers the State University of New Jersey Camden Campus ... NJ ... 306
Rutgers the State University of New Jersey New Brunswick Campus ... NJ ... 306
&Rutgers the State University of New Jersey Newark Campus ... NJ ... 306
Saint Peter's University ... NJ ... 306
Salem Community College ... NJ ... 307
Seton Hall University ... NJ ... 307
&Seton Hall University School of Law ... NJ ... 307
Stevens Institute of Technology ... NJ ... 307
Sussex County Community College ... NJ ... 307
Thomas Edison State College ... NJ ... 308
Union County College ... NJ ... 308
Warren County Community College ... NJ ... 308
William Paterson University of New Jersey ... NJ ... 308
Adelphi University ... NY ... 313
Albany College of Pharmacy and Health Sciences ... NY ... 313
Albany Medical College ... NY ... 313
Alfred State College ... NY ... 345
Alfred University ... NY ... 313
American Academy of Dramatic Arts ... NY ... 313
ASA Institute of Business & Computer Technology ... NY ... 314
Bank Street College of Education ... NY ... 314
Bard College ... NY ... 314
Barnard College ... NY ... 314
Baruch College/City University of New York ... NY ... 316
Berkeley College ... NY ... 314
Boricua College ... NY ... 315
Briarcliffe College ... NY ... 315
Broome Community College ... NY ... 315
Bryant & Stratton College ... NY ... 315
Canisius College ... NY ... 316
Cayuga Community College ... NY ... 316
Cazenovia College ... NY ... 316
Christ the King Seminary ... NY ... 316
City University of New York Borough of Manhattan Community College ... NY ... 317
City University of New York Bronx Community College ... NY ... 317
City University of New York Brooklyn College ... NY ... 317
City University of New York College of Staten Island ... NY ... 317
City University of New York Graduate Center ... NY ... 317
City University of New York Herbert H. Lehman College ... NY ... 318
City University of New York Hunter College ... NY ... 318
City University of New York John Jay College of Criminal Justice ... NY ... 318
City University of New York Kingsborough Community College ... NY ... 318
City University of New York Medgar Evers College ... NY ... 319
City University of New York Queens College ... NY ... 319
City University of New York Queensborough Community College ... NY ... 319
City University of New York The City College ... NY ... 317
City University of New York York College NY ... 319
Clarkson University ... NY ... 320
Clinton Community College ... NY ... 320
Colgate University ... NY ... 320
College of Mount Saint Vincent ... NY ... 320
College of New Rochelle, The ... NY ... 320
College of Saint Rose, The ... NY ... 321
College of Westchester, The ... NY ... 321
Columbia-Greene Community College ... NY ... 321
Columbia University in the City of New York ... NY ... 321
Concordia College ... NY ... 321
Cooper Union ... NY ... 321
Cornell University ... NY ... 322
Corning Community College ... NY ... 322
Culinary Institute of America ... NY ... 322
Daemen College ... NY ... 322
Davis College ... NY ... 322
Dominican College of Blauvelt ... NY ... 322
Dowling College ... NY ... 323
Dutchess Community College ... NY ... 323
D'Youville College ... NY ... 323
Elmira College ... NY ... 323
Erie Community College City Campus ... NY ... 323
Excelsior College ... NY ... 324
Farmingdale State College ... NY ... 346
Fashion Institute of Technology ... NY ... 324
Finger Lakes Community College ... NY ... 324
Five Towns College ... NY ... 324
Fordham University ... NY ... 324
Fulton-Montgomery Community College ... NY ... 325
Genesee Community College ... NY ... 325
Hamilton College ... NY ... 325
Hartwick College ... NY ... 325
Hebrew Union College-Jewish Institute of Religion ... NY ... 325
Helene Fuld College of Nursing ... NY ... 325
Herkimer County Community College ... NY ... 326
Hilbert College ... NY ... 326
Hobart and William Smith Colleges ... NY ... 326
Hofstra University ... NY ... 326
Hostos Community College-City University of New York ... NY ... 318
Houghton College ... NY ... 326
Hudson Valley Community College ... NY ... 326
Icahn School of Medicine at Mount Sinai . NY ... 327
Iona College ... NY ... 327
Ithaca College ... NY ... 327
Jamestown Business College ... NY ... 327
Jamestown Community College ... NY ... 327
Jefferson Community College ... NY ... 327
Jewish Theological Seminary of America . NY ... 328
Juilliard School, The ... NY ... 328
Keuka College ... NY ... 328
King's College, The ... NY ... 328
La Guardia Community College/City University of New York ... NY ... 318
Le Moyne College ... NY ... 328
LIM College ... NY ... 328
Long Island University - Post Campus ... NY ... 329
Manhattan College ... NY ... 329
Manhattan School of Music ... NY ... 330
Manhattanville College ... NY ... 330
Maria College of Albany ... NY ... 330
Marist College ... NY ... 330
Marymount Manhattan College ... NY ... 330
Medaille College ... NY ... 330
Mercy College ... NY ... 330
Metropolitan College of New York ... NY ... 331
Mohawk Valley Community College ... NY ... 331
Molloy College ... NY ... 331
Monroe College ... NY ... 331
Monroe Community College ... NY ... 332
Mount Saint Mary College ... NY ... 332
Nassau Community College ... NY ... 332
Nazareth College of Rochester ... NY ... 332
New School, The ... NY ... 332
New York Chiropractic College ... NY ... 333
New York City College of Technology/City University of New York ... NY ... 319
New York Institute of Technology ... NY ... 333
New York Medical College ... NY ... 334
@New York School of Interior Design ... NY ... 334
New York University ... NY ... 334
Niagara County Community College ... NY ... 334
Niagara University ... NY ... 334
North Country Community College ... NY ... 335
Northeastern Seminary ... NY ... 335
Nyack College ... NY ... 335
Onondaga Community College ... NY ... 335
Orange County Community College ... NY ... 335
Pace University ... NY ... 335
Paul Smith's College ... NY ... 336
Plaza College ... NY ... 336
Polytechnic Institute of New York University ... NY ... 336
Pratt Institute ... NY ... 336
Purchase College, State University of New York ... NY ... 344
Relay Graduate School of Education ... NY ... 337
Rensselaer Polytechnic Institute ... NY ... 337
Roberts Wesleyan College ... NY ... 337
Rochester Institute of Technology ... NY ... 337
Rockland Community College ... NY ... 338
Sage Colleges, The ... NY ... 338
St. Bonaventure University ... NY ... 338
St. Elizabeth College of Nursing ... NY ... 338
St. Francis College ... NY ... 338
St. John Fisher College ... NY ... 338
St. John's University ... NY ... 339
St. Joseph's College of Nursing ... NY ... 339
Saint Joseph's College, New York ... NY ... 339
Saint Joseph's Seminary ... NY ... 339
St. Lawrence University ... NY ... 339
St. Thomas Aquinas College ... NY ... 340
Sarah Lawrence College ... NY ... 340
Schenectady County Community College . NY ... 340
School of Visual Arts ... NY ... 340
Siena College ... NY ... 340
Skidmore College ... NY ... 341
State University of New York at Binghamton ... NY ... 341
State University of New York at Fredonia . NY ... 342
State University of New York at New Paltz NY ... 342
State University of New York at Stony Brook ... NY ... 342
State University of New York College at Buffalo ... NY ... 343
State University of New York College at Cortland ... NY ... 343
State University of New York College at Geneseo ... NY ... 343
State University of New York College at Old Westbury ... NY ... 343
State University of New York College at Oneonta ... NY ... 343
State University of New York College at Oswego ... NY ... 344
State University of New York College at Plattsburgh ... NY ... 344
State University of New York College at Potsdam ... NY ... 344
State University of New York College of Agriculture and Technology at Coble skill ... NY ... 344
State University of New York College of Agriculture and Technology at Morri sville ... NY ... 345
State University of New York College of Environmental Science and Forestry ... NY ... 345
State University of New York College of Optometry ... NY ... 345
State University of New York College of Technology at Delhi ... NY ... 345
State University of New York Empire State College ... NY ... 346
State University of New York Health Science Center at Brooklyn ... NY ... 342
State University of New York Institute of Technology at Utica-Rome ... NY ... 346
State University of New York Maritime College ... NY ... 346
State University of New York Upstate Medical University ... NY ... 342
State University of New York, The College at Brockport ... NY ... 342
Suffolk County Community College Ammerman Campus ... NY ... 346
Sullivan County Community College ... NY ... 347
SUNY Adirondack ... NY ... 345
SUNY Canton-College of Technology ... NY ... 345
Syracuse University Main Campus ... NY ... 347
Teachers College, Columbia University ... NY ... 347
Technical Career Institutes ... NY ... 347
Tompkins Cortland Community College ... NY ... 347
Touro College ... NY ... 348
Trocaire College ... NY ... 348
Ulster County Community College ... NY ... 348
Unification Theological Seminary ... NY ... 348
Union College ... NY ... 348
Union Graduate College ... NY ... 348
Union Theological Seminary ... NY ... 349
United States Merchant Marine Academy NY ... 545
United States Military Academy ... NY ... 545
University at Albany, SUNY ... NY ... 341
University at Buffalo-SUNY ... NY ... 341
University of Rochester ... NY ... 349
Utica College ... NY ... 349
Vassar College ... NY ... 349
Vaughn College of Aeronautics and Technology ... NY ... 349
Villa Maria College of Buffalo ... NY ... 350
Wagner College ... NY ... 350
Webb Institute ... NY ... 350
Wells College ... NY ... 350
Westchester Community College ... NY ... 350
Yeshiva University ... NY ... 351
Albright College ... PA ... 409
Allegheny College ... PA ... 409
Alvernia University ... PA ... 409
American College, The ... PA ... 409
Arcadia University ... PA ... 409
Art Institute of Philadelphia ... PA ... 410
Art Institute of Pittsburgh ... PA ... 410
Baptist Bible College and Seminary ... PA ... 410
Biblical Theological Seminary ... PA ... 410
Bloomsburg University of Pennsylvania ... PA ... 427
Bryn Athyn College of the New Church ... PA ... 410
Bryn Mawr College ... PA ... 410
Bucknell University ... PA ... 411
Bucks County Community College ... PA ... 411
Butler County Community College ... PA ... 411
Cabrini College ... PA ... 411
Cairn University ... PA ... 411
California University of Pennsylvania ... PA ... 428
Calvary Baptist Theological Seminary ... PA ... 412
Carlow University ... PA ... 412
Carnegie Mellon University ... PA ... 412
Cedar Crest College ... PA ... 412
Central Penn College ... PA ... 412
Chatham University ... PA ... 412
Chestnut Hill College ... PA ... 413
Cheyney University of Pennsylvania ... PA ... 428
Clarion University of Pennsylvania ... PA ... 428
@Commonwealth Medical College, The ... PA ... 413
Community College of Allegheny County . PA ... 413
Community College of Beaver County ... PA ... 413
Community College of Philadelphia ... PA ... 413
Curtis Institute of Music ... PA ... 414
Delaware County Community College ... PA ... 414
Delaware Valley College ... PA ... 414
DeSales University ... PA ... 414
Dickinson College ... PA ... 414
Drexel University ... PA ... 415
Duquesne University ... PA ... 415
East Stroudsburg University of Pennsylvania ... PA ... 428
Eastern University ... PA ... 415
Edinboro University of Pennsylvania ... PA ... 428
Elizabethtown College ... PA ... 415
Evangelical Theological Seminary ... PA ... 416
Franklin & Marshall College ... PA ... 416
Gannon University ... PA ... 416
Geneva College ... PA ... 417
Gettysburg College ... PA ... 417
Gratz College ... PA ... 417
Grove City College ... PA ... 417
Gwynedd-Mercy University ... PA ... 417
Harcum College ... PA ... 417

Harrisburg Area Community College ... PA ... 417
Harrisburg University of Science and Technology ... PA ... 418
Haverford College ... PA ... 418
Holy Family University ... PA ... 418
Immaculata University ... PA ... 418
Indiana University of Pennsylvania ... PA ... 428
International Institute for Restorative Practices ... PA ... 418
Juniata College ... PA ... 419
Keystone College ... PA ... 419
King's College ... PA ... 419
Kutztown University of Pennsylvania ... PA ... 429
La Roche College ... PA ... 420
La Salle University ... PA ... 420
Lackawanna College ... PA ... 420
Lafayette College ... PA ... 420
Lake Erie College of Osteopathic Medicine ... PA ... 420
Lancaster Bible College ... PA ... 421
Lancaster General College of Nursing and Health Sciences ... PA ... 421
Lancaster Theological Seminary ... PA ... 421
Lebanon Valley College ... PA ... 421
Lehigh Carbon Community College ... PA ... 421
Lehigh University ... PA ... 422
Lincoln University ... PA ... 422
Lock Haven University ... PA ... 429
Lutheran Theological Seminary at Gettysburg ... PA ... 422
Lutheran Theological Seminary at Philadelphia ... PA ... 422
Luzerne County Community College ... PA ... 422
Lycoming College ... PA ... 422
Manor College ... PA ... 423
Mansfield University of Pennsylvania ... PA ... 429
Marywood University ... PA ... 423
Mercyhurst University ... PA ... 423
Messiah College ... PA ... 423
Millersville University of Pennsylvania ... PA ... 429
Misericordia University ... PA ... 424
Montgomery County Community College ... PA ... 424
Moore College of Art and Design ... PA ... 424
Moravian College ... PA ... 424
Mount Aloysius College ... PA ... 424
Muhlenberg College ... PA ... 424
Neumann University ... PA ... 424
Northampton Community College ... PA ... 425
Peirce College ... PA ... 425
Penn State University Park ... PA ... 426
Pennsylvania Academy of the Fine Arts ... PA ... 426
Pennsylvania College of Art & Design ... PA ... 427
Pennsylvania College of Technology ... PA ... 427
Pennsylvania Highlands Community College ... PA ... 427
Pennsylvania Institute of Technology ... PA ... 427
Philadelphia College of Osteopathic Medicine ... PA ... 430
Philadelphia University ... PA ... 430
Pittsburgh Technical Institute ... PA ... 430
Pittsburgh Theological Seminary ... PA ... 431
Point Park University ... PA ... 431
Reading Area Community College ... PA ... 431
Reconstructionist Rabbinical College ... PA ... 431
Robert Morris University ... PA ... 431
Rosemont College ... PA ... 432
Saint Charles Borromeo Seminary ... PA ... 432
Saint Francis University ... PA ... 432
Saint Joseph's University ... PA ... 432
Saint Vincent College ... PA ... 432
Salus University ... PA ... 433
Seton Hill University ... PA ... 433
Shippensburg University of Pennsylvania ... PA ... 429
Slippery Rock University of Pennsylvania ... PA ... 429
Susquehanna University ... PA ... 433
Swarthmore College ... PA ... 433
Temple University ... PA ... 433
Thaddeus Stevens College of Technology ... PA ... 434
Thiel College ... PA ... 434
Thomas Jefferson University ... PA ... 434
United States Army War College ... PA ... 545
University of Pennsylvania ... PA ... 435
University of Pittsburgh ... PA ... 435
University of Scranton, The ... PA ... 436
University of the Arts, The ... PA ... 435
University of the Sciences in Philadelphia ... PA ... 435
Ursinus College ... PA ... 436
Valley Forge Christian College ... PA ... 436
Valley Forge Military College ... PA ... 436
Villanova University ... PA ... 436
Washington & Jefferson College ... PA ... 436
Waynesburg University ... PA ... 437
West Chester University of Pennsylvania ... PA ... 430
Westminster College ... PA ... 437
Westminster Theological Seminary ... PA ... 437
Westmoreland County Community College ... PA ... 437
Widener University ... PA ... 437
Wilkes University ... PA ... 437
Wilson College ... PA ... 437
Won Institute of Graduate Studies ... PA ... 438
York College of Pennsylvania ... PA ... 438
American University of Puerto Rico ... PR ... 547
Bayamon Central University ... PR ... 547
Caribbean University ... PR ... 547
Carlos Albizu University ... PR ... 547
Center for Advanced Studies On Puerto Rico and the Caribbean ... PR ... 548
Colegio Universitario de San Juan ... PR ... 548
Columbia Centro Universitario ... PR ... 548
Conservatory of Music of Puerto Rico ... PR ... 548
EDP University of Puerto Rico ... PR ... 548
Escuela de Artes Plasticas de Puerto Rico ... PR ... 548
Evangelical Seminary of Puerto Rico ... PR ... 549
Huertas Junior College ... PR ... 549
ICPR Junior College ... PR ... 549
Inter American University of Puerto Rico Aguadilla Campus ... PR ... 549
Inter American University of Puerto Rico Arecibo Campus ... PR ... 549
Inter American University of Puerto Rico Barranquitas Campus ... PR ... 550
Inter American University of Puerto Rico Bayamon Campus ... PR ... 550
Inter American University of Puerto Rico Fajardo Campus ... PR ... 550
Inter American University of Puerto Rico Guayama Campus ... PR ... 550
Inter American University of Puerto Rico Metropolitan Campus ... PR ... 550
Inter American University of Puerto Rico Ponce Campus ... PR ... 550
Inter American University of Puerto Rico San German Campus ... PR ... 551
Inter American University of Puerto Rico School of Law ... PR ... 551
Inter American University of Puerto Rico School of Optometry ... PR ... 551
National University College ... PR ... 551
Ponce School of Medicine & Health Sciences ... PR ... 552
Pontifical Catholic University of Puerto Rico, The ... PR ... 552
San Juan Bautista School of Medicine ... PR ... 552
Universidad Adventista de las Antillas ... PR ... 553
Universidad Central Del Caribe ... PR ... 553
Universidad del Este ... PR ... 552
Universidad Del Turabo ... PR ... 552
Universidad Metropolitana ... PR ... 552
Universidad Politecnica De Puerto Rico ... PR ... 553
University of Puerto Rico-Aguadilla ... PR ... 553
University of Puerto Rico at Arecibo ... PR ... 553
University of Puerto Rico at Bayamon ... PR ... 554
University of Puerto Rico at Cayey ... PR ... 554
University of Puerto Rico at Ponce ... PR ... 555
University of Puerto Rico at Utuado ... PR ... 555
University of Puerto Rico-Carolina ... PR ... 554
University of Puerto Rico-Humacao ... PR ... 554
University of Puerto Rico-Mayaguez Campus ... PR ... 554
University of Puerto Rico-Medical Sciences Campus ... PR ... 554
University of Puerto Rico-Rio Piedras Campus ... PR ... 555
University of the Sacred Heart ... PR ... 555
University of the Virgin Islands ... VI ... 555

MAAB: Accrediting Bureau of Health Education Schools: medical assisting (C,A)

Bryman School, The ... AZ ... 12
Carrington College - Phoenix ... AZ ... 12
Penn Foster College ... AZ ... 16
Phoenix College ... AZ ... 15
Everest College-City of Industry ... CA ... 43
Kaplan College ... CA ... 49
WyoTech-Long Beach ... CA ... 77
Goodwin College ... CT ... 90
Everest Institute ... FL ... 102
Everest University-Pompano Beach Campus ... FL ... 102
Florida Technical College ... FL ... 105
Keiser University ... FL ... 108
Southeastern College ... FL ... 113
Southwest Florida College ... FL ... 114
Carrington College - Boise ... ID ... 137
Coyne College ... IL ... 143
Fox College ... IL ... 145
Vatterott College-Des Moines ... IA ... 183
Bay State College ... MA ... 222
Globe University ... MN ... 255
Minnesota School of Business ... MN ... 257
Rasmussen College - St. Cloud ... MN ... 263
Vatterott College-Omaha ... NE ... 293
Everest College ... NV ... 293
Kaplan College ... NV ... 294
Community Care College ... OK ... 395
Fortis Institute ... PA ... 416
South Hills School of Business and Technology ... PA ... 433
Vista College ... TX ... 494
Broadview University ... UT ... 495
ECPI College of Technology ... VA ... 504
Skyline College ... VA ... 509
Carrington College - Spokane ... WA ... 517
Herzing University ... WI ... 533

MAC: Commission on Accreditation of Allied Health Education Programs: medical assisting (C,A)

George C. Wallace Community College - Dothan ... AL ... 3
Trenholm State Technical College ... AL ... 7
Wallace State Community College - Hanceville ... AL ... 9
University of Alaska Anchorage ... AK ... 10
University of Alaska Fairbanks ... AK ... 10
Central Arizona College ... AZ ... 12
Pima Community College ... AZ ... 17
Arkansas Tech University ... AR ... 20
Cabrillo College ... CA ... 30
Carrington College California - Sacramento ... CA ... 36
Chabot College ... CA ... 37
City College of San Francisco ... CA ... 38
Cosumnes River College ... CA ... 53
East San Gabriel Valley Regional Occupational Program and Technical Center ... CA ... 43
Everest College-Anaheim ... CA ... 43
Everest College-Gardena ... CA ... 43
Everest College-San Bernardino ... CA ... 43
Heald College, Concord ... CA ... 46
Heald College, Fresno ... CA ... 46
Heald College, Hayward ... CA ... 46
Heald College, Milpitas ... CA ... 47
Heald College, Rancho Cordova ... CA ... 47
Heald College, Roseville ... CA ... 47
Heald College, Salinas ... CA ... 47
Heald College, San Francisco ... CA ... 47
Heald College, Stockton ... CA ... 47
Modesto Junior College ... CA ... 77
Orange Coast College ... CA ... 39
Pasadena City College ... CA ... 58
Everest College ... CO ... 81
Front Range Community College ... CO ... 81
Red Rocks Community College ... CO ... 84
Capital Community College ... CT ... 88
Goodwin College ... CT ... 90
Lincoln College of New England ... CT ... 90
Northwestern Connecticut Community-Technical College ... CT ... 89
Norwalk Community College ... CT ... 89
Quinebaug Valley Community College ... CT ... 89
St. Vincent's College ... CT ... 91
Delaware Technical Community College, Stanton-Wilmington Campus ... DE ... 93
Broward College ... FL ... 99
Daytona State College ... FL ... 101
Everest University-Largo ... FL ... 102
Everest University-North Orlando Campus ... FL ... 102
Everest University-Tampa Campus ... FL ... 103
Fortis College ... FL ... 105
Hodges University ... FL ... 106
Indian River State College ... FL ... 106
Palm Beach State College ... FL ... 110
Pensacola State College ... FL ... 110
Albany Technical College ... GA ... 120
Atlanta Technical College ... GA ... 121
Augusta Technical College ... GA ... 121
Chattahoochee Technical College ... GA ... 122
Columbus Technical College ... GA ... 123
Dalton State College ... GA ... 123
Georgia Northwestern Technical College ... GA ... 125
Georgia Piedmont Technical College ... GA ... 126
Gwinnett Technical College ... GA ... 127
Lanier Technical College ... GA ... 128
Moultrie Technical College ... GA ... 129
North Georgia Technical College ... GA ... 129
Oconee Fall Line Technical College-South Campus ... GA ... 129
Ogeechee Technical College ... GA ... 129
Okefenokee Technical College ... GA ... 130
Savannah Technical College ... GA ... 131
South University ... GA ... 131
Southeastern Technical College ... GA ... 132
Southern Crescent Technical College ... GA ... 132
Southwest Georgia Technical College ... GA ... 132
West Georgia Technical College ... GA ... 134
Guam Community College ... GU ... 546
Kapiolani Community College ... HI ... 136
Brigham Young University-Idaho ... ID ... 137
College of Southern Idaho ... ID ... 138
Eastern Idaho Technical College ... ID ... 138
Idaho State University ... ID ... 138
Lewis-Clark State College ... ID ... 138
North Idaho College ... ID ... 138
College of DuPage ... IL ... 142
College of Lake County ... IL ... 143
Harper College ... IL ... 145
Highland Community College ... IL ... 146
Illinois Central College ... IL ... 146
Midstate College ... IL ... 152
Moraine Valley Community College ... IL ... 153
Northwestern College ... IL ... 155
Robert Morris University ... IL ... 156
Rockford Career College ... IL ... 157
South Suburban College of Cook County ... IL ... 159
Southwestern Illinois College ... IL ... 160
Waubonsee Community College ... IL ... 162
Harrison College - Indianapolis Downtown Campus ... IN ... 166
International Business College ... IN ... 169
Ivy Tech Community College-Central Indiana ... IN ... 169
#MedTech College ... IN ... 171
National College ... IN ... 171
Des Moines Area Community College ... IA ... 177
Ellsworth Community College ... IA ... 179
Iowa Central Community College ... IA ... 179
Iowa Lakes Community College ... IA ... 179
Iowa Western Community College ... IA ... 179
Kaplan University ... IA ... 180
Kirkwood Community College ... IA ... 180
Mercy College of Health Sciences ... IA ... 181
North Iowa Area Community College ... IA ... 181
Southeastern Community College ... IA ... 182
Western Iowa Tech Community College ... IA ... 183
Coffeyville Community College ... KS ... 185
Northwest Kansas Technical College ... KS ... 189
Wichita Area Technical College ... KS ... 191
Bluegrass Community and Technical College ... KY ... 194
Henderson Community College ... KY ... 195
Jefferson Community and Technical College ... KY ... 195
Maysville Community and Technical College ... KY ... 196
National College ... KY ... 198
Spencerian College ... KY ... 199
Sullivan University ... KY ... 199
Bossier Parish Community College ... LA ... 202
Career Technical College ... LA ... 201
Beal College ... ME ... 209
Eastern Maine Community College ... ME ... 210
Kennebec Valley Community College ... ME ... 210
Northern Maine Community College ... ME ... 210
Washington County Community College ... ME ... 211
Allegany College of Maryland ... MD ... 213
Anne Arundel Community College ... MD ... 213
Cecil College ... MD ... 214
Harford Community College ... MD ... 215
Bristol Community College ... MA ... 231
Cape Cod Community College ... MA ... 231
Massasoit Community College ... MA ... 232
Middlesex Community College ... MA ... 232
Mount Wachusett Community College ... MA ... 232
North Shore Community College ... MA ... 232
Northern Essex Community College ... MA ... 232
Quinsigamond Community College ... MA ... 232
Salter College ... MA ... 236
Springfield Technical Community College ... MA ... 233
Alpena Community College ... MI ... 239
Baker College of Flint ... MI ... 239
Davenport University ... MI ... 241
Finlandia University ... MI ... 242
Glen Oaks Community College ... MI ... 242
Grand Rapids Community College ... MI ... 243
Henry Ford Community College ... MI ... 243
Jackson College ... MI ... 244
Kalamazoo Valley Community College ... MI ... 244
Macomb Community College ... MI ... 246
Mid Michigan Community College ... MI ... 247
Montcalm Community College ... MI ... 247
Oakland Community College ... MI ... 248
Schoolcraft College ... MI ... 250
Academy College ... MN ... 253
Anoka Technical College ... MN ... 257
Central Lakes College ... MN ... 258
Century College ... MN ... 258
Dakota County Technical College ... MN ... 258
Duluth Business University, Inc. ... MN ... 255
Hennepin Technical College ... MN ... 258
Lake Superior College ... MN ... 259
Minneapolis Business College ... MN ... 257
Minnesota West Community and Technical College ... MN ... 260
Ridgewater College ... MN ... 260
South Central College ... MN ... 261
Hinds Community College ... MS ... 267
Northeast Mississippi Community College ... MS ... 269
Everest College ... MO ... 274
Flathead Valley Community College ... MT ... 286
Great Falls College Montana State University ... MT ... 287
Central Community College ... NE ... 288
Metropolitan Community College ... NE ... 290
Nebraska Methodist College ... NE ... 291
Southeast Community College ... NE ... 292
College of Southern Nevada ... NV ... 294
Manchester Community College ... NH ... 296
Mount Washington College ... NH ... 297
River Valley Community College ... NH ... 296
White Mountains Community College ... NH ... 296
Bergen Community College ... NJ ... 299
Raritan Valley Community College ... NJ ... 305
Sussex County Community College ... NJ ... 307
Warren County Community College ... NJ ... 308
Eastern New Mexico University-Roswell ... NM ... 309
Santa Fe Community College ... NM ... 311
ASA Institute of Business & Computer Technology ... NY ... 314
Broome Community College ... NY ... 315

Institution	State	Page
Bryant & Stratton College	NY	315
Elmira Business Institute	NY	323
#Everest Institute	NY	324
Niagara County Community College	NY	334
Plaza College	NY	336
Trocaire College	NY	348
Wood Tobé-Coburn School	NY	350
Alamance Community College	NC	357
Asheville - Buncombe Technical Community College	NC	357
Cabarrus College of Health Sciences	NC	352
Carteret Community College	NC	358
Central Carolina Community College	NC	359
Central Piedmont Community College	NC	359
College of the Albemarle	NC	359
Craven Community College	NC	359
Davidson County Community College	NC	360
Durham Technical Community College	NC	360
Edgecombe Community College	NC	360
Forsyth Technical Community College	NC	360
Gaston College	NC	360
Guilford Technical Community College	NC	360
Haywood Community College	NC	361
James Sprunt Community College	NC	361
Johnston Community College	NC	361
King's College	NC	355
Lenoir Community College	NC	361
Living Arts College @ School of Communication Arts	NC	356
Martin Community College	NC	361
Mayland Community College	NC	361
Mitchell Community College	NC	362
Montgomery Community College	NC	362
Nash Community College	NC	362
Pamlico Community College	NC	362
Piedmont Community College	NC	362
Pitt Community College	NC	362
Richmond Community College	NC	362
South College-Asheville	NC	366
South Piedmont Community College	NC	363
Southwestern Community College	NC	364
Stanly Community College	NC	364
Surry Community College	NC	364
Tri-County Community College	NC	364
Vance-Granville Community College	NC	364
Wake Technical Community College	NC	364
Wayne Community College	NC	364
Western Piedmont Community College	NC	365
Wilkes Community College	NC	365
Belmont College	OH	374
Bradford School	OH	375
Cincinnati State Technical and Community College	OH	376
Clark State Community College	OH	377
Columbus State Community College	OH	378
Cuyahoga Community College	OH	378
Davis College	OH	378
Eastern Gateway Community College - Jefferson County Campus	OH	379
Edison State Community College	OH	379
Fortis College	OH	379
Hocking College	OH	380
James A. Rhodes State College	OH	381
Kaplan College	OH	382
Lakeland Community College	OH	382
Lorain County Community College	OH	383
Marion Technical College	OH	383
Northwest State Community College	OH	385
Ohio Business College, Lorain Branch	OH	385
Ohio Valley College of Technology	OH	387
Owens Community College	OH	387
Sinclair Community College	OH	388
Southern State Community College	OH	389
Stark State College	OH	389
Stautzenberger College	OH	389
University of Akron, Main Campus, The	OH	390
University of Cincinnati-Blue Ash College	OH	391
University of Cincinnati-Clermont College	OH	391
University of Northwestern Ohio	OH	391
Youngstown State University	OH	394
Zane State College	OH	394
Tulsa Community College	OK	400
Central Oregon Community College	OR	402
Clackamas Community College	OR	402
Columbia Gorge Community College	OR	402
Concorde Career College	OR	402
#Everest College	OR	403
Lane Community College	OR	403
Linn-Benton Community College	OR	404
Portland Community College	OR	407
Berks Technical Institute	PA	410
Bradford School	PA	410
Butler County Community College	PA	411
Central Penn College	PA	412
Community College of Allegheny County	PA	413
Community College of Philadelphia	PA	413
Delaware County Community College	PA	414
Everest Institute	PA	416
Fortis Institute	PA	416
Harrisburg Area Community College	PA	417
Kaplan Career Institute	PA	419
Kaplan Career Institute - ICM Campus	PA	419
Lehigh Carbon Community College	PA	421
McCann School of Business & Technology	PA	423
Montgomery County Community College	PA	424
Mount Aloysius College	PA	424
Penn Commercial Business/Technical School	PA	425
Pittsburgh Technical Institute	PA	430
Westmoreland County Community College	PA	437
YTI Career Institute	PA	438
YTI Career Institute-Capital Region	PA	438
Aiken Technical College	SC	440
Central Carolina Technical College	SC	441
Forrest College	SC	444
Greenville Technical College	SC	444
Midlands Technical College	SC	445
Orangeburg-Calhoun Technical College	SC	446
Piedmont Technical College	SC	446
Spartanburg Community College	SC	447
Tri-County Technical College	SC	447
Trident Technical College	SC	447
Lake Area Technical Institute	SD	450
Mitchell Technical Institute	SD	450
National American University	SD	450
Presentation College	SD	450
Chattanooga State Community College	TN	460
Cleveland State Community College	TN	460
Miller-Motte Technical College	TN	457
National College of Business and Technology	TN	457
South College	TN	458
Cisco College	TX	468
College of the Mainland	TX	469
El Centro College	TX	470
El Paso Community College	TX	472
Hallmark College of Technology	TX	472
Houston Community College	TX	473
Kaplan College	TX	474
Kaplan College	TX	475
Lone Star College System	TX	476
Northeast Texas Community College	TX	477
Richland College	TX	471
San Antonio College	TX	465
San Jacinto College North	TX	479
Texas School of Business	TX	485
Texas State Technical College Harlingen	TX	485
Vista College	TX	494
Everest College	UT	495
LDS Business College	UT	495
Ogden-Weber Applied Technology College	UT	496
Salt Lake Community College	UT	498
Stevens-Henager College	UT	496
American National University	VA	501
Miller-Motte Technical College	VA	507
Clark College	WA	518
Clover Park Technical College	WA	518
Columbia Basin College	WA	518
Everest College	WA	519
Everett Community College	WA	519
Highline Community College	WA	520
Lake Washington Institute of Technology	WA	520
Lower Columbia College	WA	521
North Seattle Community College	WA	522
Olympic College	WA	521
Renton Technical College	WA	522
Skagit Valley College	WA	523
South Puget Sound Community College	WA	524
Spokane Community College	WA	518
Walla Walla Community College	WA	524
Wenatchee Valley College	WA	525
Whatcom Community College	WA	525
Yakima Valley Community College	WA	525
Huntington Junior College	WV	526
Mountwest Community and Technical College	WV	528
West Virginia Northern Community College	WV	528
Blackhawk Technical College	WI	539
Chippewa Valley Technical College	WI	539
Concordia University Wisconsin	WI	532
Fox Valley Technical College	WI	539
Gateway Technical College	WI	540
Lac Courte Oreilles Ojibwa Community College	WI	533
Madison Area Technical College	WI	540
Mid-State Technical College	WI	540
Milwaukee Area Technical College	WI	540
Moraine Park Technical College	WI	540
Nicolet Area Technical College	WI	540
Northcentral Technical College	WI	541
Northeast Wisconsin Technical College	WI	541
Southwest Wisconsin Technical College	WI	541
Waukesha County Technical College	WI	541
Western Technical College	WI	541
Wisconsin Indianhead Technical College	WI	541

MACTE: Montessori Accreditation Council for Teacher Education: Montessori teacher education (C)

Institution	State	Page
South Mountain Community College	AZ	15
Saint Mary's College of California	CA	61
Barry University	FL	98
Kennesaw State University	GA	127
Chaminade University of Honolulu	HI	135
Indiana University South Bend	IN	168
St. Catherine University	MN	263
Xavier University	OH	393
Oklahoma City University	OK	397
Chestnut Hill College	PA	413
Lander University	SC	444
Belmont University	TN	453

MEAC: Midwifery Education Accreditation Council: midwifery education (C,A,B,M,D)

Institution	State	Page
National College of Midwifery	NM	310
Birthingway College of Midwifery	OR	402
Midwives College of Utah	UT	496
Bastyr University	WA	516

MED: Liaison Committee on Medical Education: medicine (FP,D)

Institution	State	Page
University of Alabama at Birmingham	AL	8
University of South Alabama	AL	9
University of Arizona	AZ	18
University of Arkansas for Medical Sciences	AR	24
Loma Linda University	CA	51
Stanford University	CA	68
University of California-Davis	CA	70
University of California-Irvine	CA	71
University of California-Los Angeles	CA	71
#University of California-Riverside	CA	71
University of California-San Diego	CA	71
University of California-San Francisco	CA	72
University of Southern California	CA	74
University of Colorado Denver|Anschutz Medical Campus	CO	86
#Quinnipiac University	CT	91
Yale University	CT	93
George Washington University	DC	95
Georgetown University	DC	95
Howard University	DC	95
#Florida Atlantic University	FL	114
Florida International University	FL	115
Florida State University	FL	115
University of Central Florida	FL	115
University of Florida	FL	116
University of Miami	FL	118
University of South Florida	FL	116
Emory University	GA	124
Georgia Regents University	GA	126
Mercer University	GA	128
Morehouse School of Medicine	GA	129
University of Hawaii at Manoa	HI	136
Loyola University Chicago	IL	151
Northwestern University	IL	155
Rosalind Franklin University of Medicine & Science	IL	157
Rush University	IL	157
Southern Illinois University Carbondale	IL	159
University of Chicago	IL	161
University of Illinois at Chicago	IL	161
Indiana University-Purdue University Indianapolis	IN	168
University of Iowa	IA	175
University of Kentucky	KY	200
University of Louisville	KY	200
Louisiana State University Health Sciences Center at Shreveport	LA	205
Louisiana State University Health Sciences Center-New Orleans	LA	205
Tulane University	LA	207
Johns Hopkins University	MD	215
Uniformed Services University of the Health Sciences	MD	545
University of Maryland Baltimore	MD	219
Harvard University	MA	227
Tufts University	MA	237
University of Massachusetts Medical School	MA	229
#Central Michigan University	MI	240
Michigan State University	MI	246
#Oakland University	MI	248
University of Michigan-Ann Arbor	MI	251
Wayne State University	MI	252
#Western Michigan University	MI	252
Mayo Medical School	MN	254
University of Minnesota-Twin Cities	MN	264
University of Mississippi Medical Center	MS	270
Saint Louis University	MO	281
University of Missouri - Columbia	MO	283
University of Missouri - Kansas City	MO	283
Washington University in St. Louis	MO	284
Creighton University	NE	289
University of Nebraska Medical Center	NE	292
University of Nevada, Reno	NV	294
Dartmouth College	NH	296
#Rowan University	NJ	305
University of New Mexico Main Campus	NM	312
Albany Medical College	NY	313
Columbia University in the City of New York	NY	321
#Hofstra University	NY	326
Icahn School of Medicine at Mount Sinai	NY	327
New York Medical College	NY	334
New York University	NY	334
State University of New York at Stony Brook	NY	342
State University of New York Health Science Center at Brooklyn	NY	342
State University of New York Upstate Medical University	NY	342
University at Buffalo-SUNY	NY	341
University of Rochester	NY	349
Yeshiva University	NY	351
Duke University	NC	354
East Carolina University	NC	367
University of North Carolina at Chapel Hill	NC	368
Wake Forest University	NC	370
University of North Dakota Main Campus	ND	371
Case Western Reserve University	OH	375
Northeast Ohio Medical University	OH	385
Ohio State University Main Campus, The	OH	386
University of Cincinnati Main Campus	OH	390
University of Toledo	OH	392
Wright State University Main Campus	OH	393
Oregon Health & Science University	OR	405
#Commonwealth Medical College, The	PA	413
Drexel University	PA	415
Temple University	PA	433
Thomas Jefferson University	PA	434
University of Pennsylvania	PA	435
University of Pittsburgh	PA	435
Ponce School of Medicine & Health Sciences	PR	552
#San Juan Bautista School of Medicine	PR	552
Universidad Central Del Caribe	PR	553
University of Puerto Rico-Medical Sciences Campus	PR	554
Brown University	RI	438
Medical University of South Carolina	SC	445
University of South Carolina Columbia	SC	447
#University of South Carolina School of Medicine-Greenville	SC	448
University of South Dakota, The	SD	451
East Tennessee State University	TN	459
Meharry Medical College	TN	456
Vanderbilt University	TN	463
Baylor College of Medicine	TX	467
Texas A & M University	TX	483
Texas Tech University	TX	487
Texas Tech University Health Sciences Center	TX	487
University of Texas Health Science Center at Houston (UTHealth), The	TX	492
#University of Texas Health Science Center at San Antonio	TX	493
University of Texas Medical Branch, The	TX	493
University of Texas Southwestern Medical Center	TX	493
University of Utah, The	UT	496
University of Vermont	VT	500
Eastern Virginia Medical School	VA	504
University of Virginia	VA	511
Virginia Commonwealth University	VA	511
#Virginia Tech Carilion School of Medicine	VA	515
University of Washington	WA	524
#Marshall University	WV	529
West Virginia University	WV	530
Medical College of Wisconsin	WI	534
University of Wisconsin-Madison	WI	536

MFCD: American Association for Marriage and Family Therapy: marriage and family therapy (M,D)

Institution	State	Page
Auburn University	AL	1
Northcentral University	AZ	16
Alliant International University-San Diego	CA	26
Chapman University	CA	38
Hope International University	CA	47
Loma Linda University	CA	51
San Diego State University	CA	35
University of San Diego	CA	73
Colorado State University	CO	80
Regis University	CO	84
Central Connecticut State University	CT	87
Fairfield University	CT	89
Southern Connecticut State University	CT	88
University of Connecticut	CT	92
University of Saint Joseph	CT	92
Florida State University	FL	115
Nova Southeastern University	FL	109
Mercer University	GA	128
University of Georgia	GA	133
Valdosta State University	GA	134
Northern Illinois University	IL	154
Northwestern University	IL	155
Christian Theological Seminary	IN	165
Purdue University Calumet	IN	171
Purdue University Main Campus	IN	171
Friends University	KS	186
Kansas State University	KS	188
Louisville Presbyterian Theological Seminary	KY	197
University of Kentucky	KY	200
University of Louisville	KY	200

University of Louisiana at Monroe ... LA ... 208
University of Maryland College Park ... MD .. 219
University of Massachusetts Boston ... MA .. 228
Michigan State University ... MI ... 246
Bethel University ... MN .. 253
Capella University ... MN .. 254
St. Cloud State University ... MN .. 261
Saint Mary's University of Minnesota ... MN .. 264
University of Minnesota-Twin Cities ... MN .. 264
Reformed Theological Seminary ... MS .. 269
University of Southern Mississippi ... MS .. 270
Saint Louis University ... MO .. 281
School of Professional Psychology at Forest Institute, The ... MO .. 281
University of Nebraska - Lincoln ... NE ... 292
University of Nevada, Las Vegas ... NV ... 294
University of New Hampshire ... NH ... 298
Seton Hall University ... NJ ... 307
Iona College ... NY ... 327
Syracuse University Main Campus ... NY ... 347
University of Rochester ... NY ... 349
Appalachian State University ... NC .. 367
East Carolina University ... NC .. 367
Pfeiffer University ... NC .. 365
North Dakota State University Main Campus ... ND .. 371
Ohio State University Main Campus, The . OH .. 386
University of Akron, Main Campus, The ... OH .. 390
Oklahoma State University ... OK .. 397
Lewis and Clark College ... OR .. 403
University of Oregon ... OR .. 406
Drexel University ... PA ... 415
Evangelical Theological Seminary ... PA ... 416
La Salle University ... PA ... 420
Seton Hill University ... PA ... 433
University of Rhode Island ... RI ... 440
Converse College ... SC ... 443
Abilene Christian University ... TX ... 464
St. Mary's University ... TX ... 479
Texas Tech University ... TX ... 487
#University of Houston - Clear Lake ... TX ... 489
Brigham Young University ... UT ... 495
Utah State University ... UT ... 497
Virginia Polytechnic Institute and State University ... VA ... 515
Pacific Lutheran University ... WA .. 521
Seattle Pacific University ... WA .. 523
Edgewood College ... WI ... 532
University of Wisconsin-Stout ... WI ... 538

MIDWF: Accreditation Commission for Midwifery Education: nurse midwifery (C,M,D)

California State University-Fullerton ... CA ... 33
San Diego State University ... CA ... 35
University of California-San Francisco ... CA ... 72
University of Colorado Denver|Anschutz Medical Campus ... CO ... 86
Yale University ... CT ... 93
Georgetown University ... DC ... 95
University of Florida ... FL ... 116
University of Miami ... FL ... 118
Emory University ... GA .. 124
University of Illinois at Chicago ... IL ... 161
University of Indianapolis ... IN ... 173
Frontier Nursing University ... KY ... 194
University of Michigan-Ann Arbor ... MI ... 251
Wayne State University ... MI ... 252
University of Minnesota-Twin Cities ... MN .. 264
University of New Mexico Main Campus .. NM .. 312
Columbia University in the City of New York ... NY ... 321
New York University ... NY ... 334
State University of New York at Stony Brook ... NY ... 342
State University of New York Health Science Center at Brooklyn ... NY ... 342
East Carolina University ... NC .. 367
Case Western Reserve University ... OH ... 375
Ohio State University Main Campus, The . OH .. 386
University of Cincinnati Main Campus ... OH .. 390
Oregon Health & Science University ... OR .. 405
Philadelphia University ... PA ... 430
University of Pennsylvania ... PA ... 435
University of Puerto Rico-Medical Sciences Campus ... PR ... 554
Vanderbilt University ... TN ... 463
Baylor University ... TX ... 467
Texas Tech University ... TX ... 487
University of Utah, The ... UT ... 496
Shenandoah University ... VA ... 509
Seattle University ... WA .. 523
University of Washington ... WA .. 524
Marquette University ... WI ... 534

MIL: Commission on Accreditation of Allied Health Education Programs: medical illustrator (M)

Georgia Regents University ... GA .. 126
University of Illinois at Chicago ... IL ... 161
Johns Hopkins University ... MD .. 215

MLTAB: Accrediting Bureau of Health Education Schools: medical laboratory technician (C,A)

Spencerian College ... KY ... 199

MLTAD: National Accrediting Agency for Clinical Laboratory Sciences: medical laboratory technician (C,A)

Calhoun Community College ... AL ... 2
Gadsden State Community College ... AL ... 3
Jefferson State Community College ... AL ... 5
Wallace State Community College - Hanceville ... AL ... 9
Brookline College ... AZ ... 12
Phoenix College ... AZ ... 15
Pima Community College ... AZ ... 17
Arkansas State University-Beebe ... AR ... 19
Arkansas State University-Jonesboro ... AR ... 19
National Park Community College ... AR ... 22
North Arkansas College ... AR ... 22
Phillips Community College of the University of Arkansas ... AR ... 24
South Arkansas Community College ... AR ... 23
De Anza College ... CA ... 44
Southwestern College ... CA ... 68
Arapahoe Community College ... CO ... 78
Delaware Technical Community College, Owens Campus ... DE ... 93
Eastern Florida State College ... FL ... 101
Florida State College at Jacksonville ... FL ... 105
Indian River State College ... FL ... 106
Keiser University ... FL ... 108
Miami Dade College ... FL ... 109
Central Georgia Technical College ... GA .. 122
College of Coastal Georgia ... GA .. 123
Dalton State College ... GA .. 123
Darton State College ... GA .. 124
Georgia Piedmont Technical College ... GA .. 126
North Georgia Technical College ... GA .. 129
Okefenokee Technical College ... GA .. 130
Southeastern Technical College ... GA .. 132
Southwest Georgia Technical College ... GA .. 132
West Georgia Technical College ... GA .. 134
Wiregrass Georgia Technical College ... GA .. 134
Kapiolani Community College ... HI ... 136
Elgin Community College ... IL ... 144
Illinois Central College ... IL ... 146
John A. Logan College ... IL ... 148
Kankakee Community College ... IL ... 149
Kaskaskia College ... IL ... 149
Oakton Community College ... IL ... 155
Rend Lake College ... IL ... 156
Shawnee Community College ... IL ... 158
Southeastern Illinois College ... IL ... 159
Southern Illinois University Carbondale ... IL ... 159
Southern Illinois University Edwardsville ... IL ... 159
Southwestern Illinois College ... IL ... 160
MedTech College ... IN ... 171
Des Moines Area Community College ... IA ... 177
Hawkeye Community College ... IA ... 178
Indian Hills Community College ... IA ... 179
Iowa Central Community College ... IA ... 179
Barton County Community College ... KS ... 184
Seward County Community College/Area Technical School ... KS ... 190
Eastern Kentucky University ... KY ... 193
Henderson Community College ... KY ... 195
Madisonville Community College ... KY ... 196
Somerset Community College ... KY ... 196
Southeast Kentucky Community and Technical College ... KY ... 196
West Kentucky Community and Technical College ... KY ... 196
Delgado Community College ... LA ... 203
Fortis College ... LA ... 202
Louisiana State University at Alexandria .. LA ... 205
South Louisiana Community College Ardoin Campus ... LA ... 203
Southern University at Shreveport-Louisiana ... LA ... 207
University of Maine at Augusta ... ME .. 212
University of Maine at Presque Isle ... ME .. 212
Allegany College of Maryland ... MD .. 213
Anne Arundel Community College ... MD .. 213
Community College of Baltimore County, The ... MD .. 214
Bristol Community College ... MA .. 231
Bunker Hill Community College ... MA .. 231
Mount Wachusett Community College ... MA .. 232
Quincy College ... MA .. 235
Springfield Technical Community College ... MA .. 233
Ferris State University ... MI ... 242
Kellogg Community College ... MI ... 244
Macomb Community College ... MI ... 246
Northern Michigan University ... MI ... 248
Alexandria Technical & Community College ... MN .. 257
Hibbing Community College, A Technical and Community College ... MN .. 258
Lake Superior College ... MN .. 259
Minnesota State Community and Technical College ... MN .. 259
Minnesota West Community and Technical College ... MN .. 260
North Hennepin Community College ... MN .. 260
Rasmussen College - St. Cloud ... MN .. 263
Saint Paul College-A Community & Technical College ... MN .. 261
South Central College ... MN .. 261
Copiah-Lincoln Community College ... MS .. 266
Hinds Community College ... MS .. 267
Meridian Community College ... MS .. 267
Mississippi Delta Community College ... MS .. 268
Mississippi Gulf Coast Community College ... MS .. 268
Northeast Mississippi Community College ... MS .. 269
Pearl River Community College ... MS .. 269
Moberly Area Community College ... MO .. 279
Ozarks Technical Community College ... MO .. 279
Saint Louis Community College at Forest Park ... MO .. 281
Three Rivers Community College ... MO .. 282
Central Community College ... NE ... 288
Mid-Plains Community College ... NE ... 290
Southeast Community College ... NE ... 292
College of Southern Nevada ... NV ... 294
River Valley Community College ... NH ... 296
Brookdale Community College ... NJ ... 299
Camden County College ... NJ ... 300
Mercer County Community College ... NJ ... 302
Middlesex County College ... NJ ... 303
Central New Mexico Community College . NM .. 309
San Juan College ... NM .. 311
Broome Community College ... NY ... 315
Dutchess Community College ... NY ... 323
Farmingdale State College ... NY ... 346
Nassau Community College ... NY ... 332
Orange County Community College ... NY ... 335
Alamance Community College ... NC .. 357
Asheville - Buncombe Technical Community College ... NC .. 357
Beaufort County Community College ... NC .. 358
Central Piedmont Community College ... NC .. 359
Coastal Carolina Community College ... NC .. 359
College of the Albemarle ... NC .. 359
Davidson County Community College ... NC .. 360
Halifax Community College ... NC .. 361
Sandhills Community College ... NC .. 363
Southeastern Community College ... NC .. 364
Southwestern Community College ... NC .. 364
Stanly Community College ... NC .. 364
Wake Technical Community College ... NC .. 364
Western Piedmont Community College ... NC .. 365
Bismarck State College ... ND .. 372
Cincinnati State Technical and Community College ... OH .. 376
Clark State Community College ... OH .. 377
Columbus State Community College ... OH .. 378
Cuyahoga Community College ... OH .. 378
Eastern Gateway Community College - Jefferson County Campus ... OH .. 379
Edison State Community College ... OH .. 379
Lakeland Community College ... OH .. 382
Lorain County Community College ... OH .. 383
Marion Technical College ... OH .. 383
Shawnee State University ... OH .. 388
Stark State College ... OH .. 389
Washington State Community College ... OH .. 392
Youngstown State University ... OH .. 394
Zane State College ... OH .. 394
Eastern Oklahoma State College ... OK .. 395
Northeastern Oklahoma Agricultural and Mechanical College ... OK .. 396
Rose State College ... OK .. 399
Seminole State College ... OK .. 399
Tulsa Community College ... OK .. 400
Portland Community College ... OR .. 407
Community College of Allegheny County . PA ... 413
Community College of Philadelphia ... PA ... 413
Harcum College ... PA ... 417
Harrisburg Area Community College ... PA ... 417
Laurel Business Institute ... PA ... 421
Montgomery County Community College . PA ... 424
Mount Aloysius College ... PA ... 424
Reading Area Community College ... PA ... 431
Community College of Rhode Island ... RI ... 439
Florence - Darlington Technical College ... SC ... 443
Greenville Technical College ... SC ... 444
Midlands Technical College ... SC ... 445
Spartanburg Community College ... SC ... 447
Tri-County Technical College ... SC ... 447
Trident Technical College ... SC ... 447
York Technical College ... SC ... 449
Lake Area Technical Institute ... SD ... 450
Mitchell Technical Institute ... SD ... 450
Fortis Institute ... TN ... 454
Jackson State Community College ... TN ... 460
Northeast State Community College ... TN ... 461
Southwest Tennessee Community College ... TN ... 461
Volunteer State Community College ... TN ... 461
Amarillo College ... TX ... 465
Austin Community College District ... TX ... 466
Central Texas College ... TX ... 468
Del Mar College ... TX ... 471
El Centro College ... TX ... 470
El Paso Community College ... TX ... 472
Grayson College ... TX ... 472
Houston Community College ... TX ... 473
McLennan Community College ... TX ... 476
Navarro College ... TX ... 477
Northeast Texas Community College ... TX ... 477
St. Philip's College ... TX ... 465
San Jacinto College Central ... TX ... 479
Tarleton State University ... TX ... 483
Tyler Junior College ... TX ... 488
University of Texas at Brownsville and Texas Southmost College, The ... TX ... 491
Victoria College ... TX ... 493
Weber State University ... UT ... 497
J. Sargeant Reynolds Community College VA ... 512
Northern Virginia Community College ... VA ... 513
Wytheville Community College ... VA ... 514
Clover Park Technical College ... WA .. 518
Shoreline Community College ... WA .. 523
Wenatchee Valley College ... WA .. 525
Marshall University ... WV .. 529
Pierpont Community & Technical College WV .. 528
Southern West Virginia Community and Technical College ... WV .. 528
Blackhawk Technical College ... WI ... 539
Chippewa Valley Technical College ... WI ... 539
Madison Area Technical College ... WI ... 540
Milwaukee Area Technical College ... WI ... 540
Moraine Park Technical College ... WI ... 540
Northcentral Technical College ... WI ... 541
Northeast Wisconsin Technical College ... WI ... 541
Southwest Wisconsin Technical College .. WI ... 541
Western Technical College ... WI ... 541
Casper College ... WY .. 542

MT: National Accrediting Agency for Clinical Laboratory Sciences: medical technology/laboratory scientist (C,B)

Auburn University at Montgomery ... AL ... 2
Tuskegee University ... AL ... 8
University of Alabama at Birmingham ... AL ... 8
University of Alaska Anchorage ... AK ... 10
Arizona State University ... AZ ... 11
Arkansas State University-Jonesboro ... AR ... 19
University of Arkansas for Medical Sciences ... AR ... 24
California State University-Dominguez Hills ... CA ... 33
Loma Linda University ... CA ... 51
San Francisco State University ... CA ... 35
San Jose State University ... CA ... 36
University of California-Davis ... CA ... 70
University of California-Irvine ... CA ... 71
University of California-San Diego ... CA ... 71
Metropolitan State University of Denver ... CO ... 83
University of Hartford ... CT ... 92
University of Delaware ... DE ... 94
George Washington University ... DC ... 95
Howard University ... DC ... 95
Florida Gulf Coast University ... FL ... 115
University of Central Florida ... FL ... 115
University of West Florida ... FL ... 117
Armstrong Atlantic State University ... GA .. 120
Georgia Regents University ... GA .. 126
Thomas University ... GA .. 132
University of Hawaii at Manoa ... HI ... 136
Idaho State University ... ID ... 138
Illinois State University ... IL ... 147
Northern Illinois University ... IL ... 154
Rush University ... IL ... 157
University of Illinois at Springfield ... IL ... 161
Indiana University-Purdue University Indianapolis ... IN ... 168
Allen College ... IA ... 175
Mercy College of Health Sciences ... IA ... 181
St. Luke's College ... IA ... 182
Wichita State University ... KS ... 191
Bellarmine University ... KY ... 192
Eastern Kentucky University ... KY ... 193
University of Kentucky ... KY ... 200
Louisiana State University Health Sciences Center at Shreveport ... LA ... 205
Louisiana State University Health Sciences Center-New Orleans ... LA ... 205
McNeese State University ... LA ... 207
Our Lady of the Lake College ... LA ... 206
University of Louisiana at Monroe ... LA ... 208
Morgan State University ... MD .. 217
Salisbury University ... MD .. 220
Stevenson University ... MD .. 218
University of Maryland Baltimore ... MD .. 219
University of Massachusetts Dartmouth ... MA .. 229
University of Massachusetts Lowell ... MA .. 229
Andrews University ... MI ... 239
Eastern Michigan University ... MI ... 242
Ferris State University ... MI ... 242
Grand Valley State University ... MI ... 243
Michigan State University ... MI ... 246
Northern Michigan University ... MI ... 248
Saginaw Valley State University ... MI ... 249
Wayne State University ... MI ... 252

St. Cloud State University .... MN .. 261
University of Minnesota-Twin Cities .... MN .. 264
University of Mississippi Medical Center ... MS .. 270
University of Southern Mississippi .... MS .. 270
Saint Louis University .... MO .. 281
Southeast Missouri Hospital College of Nursing and Health Sciences .... MO .. 282
Montana State University .... MT .. 287
University of Nebraska Medical Center .... NE .. 292
University of New Hampshire .... NH .. 298
University of New Mexico Main Campus .. NM .. 312
Albany College of Pharmacy and Health Sciences .... NY ... 313
City University of New York College of Staten Island .... NY ... 317
City University of New York York College .... NY ... 319
Long Island University - Post Campus .... NY ... 329
Marist College .... NY ... 330
St. John's University .... NY ... 339
State University of New York at Stony Brook .... NY ... 342
State University of New York Upstate Medical University .... NY ... 342
University at Buffalo-SUNY .... NY ... 341
Carolinas College of Health Sciences .... NC .. 353
East Carolina University .... NC .. 367
University of North Carolina at Chapel Hill NC .. 368
Wake Forest University .... NC .. 370
Winston-Salem State University .... NC .. 370
University of North Dakota Main Campus . ND .. 371
Bowling Green State University .... OH .. 374
Ohio Northern University .... OH .. 386
Ohio State University Main Campus, The . OH .. 386
University of Cincinnati Main Campus .... OH .. 390
Wright State University Main Campus .... OH .. 393
Northeastern State University .... OK .. 396
Oregon Health & Science University .... OR .. 405
Oregon Institute of Technology .... OR .. 405
Lancaster General College of Nursing and Health Sciences .... PA ... 421
Neumann University .... PA ... 424
Thomas Jefferson University .... PA ... 434
Inter American University of Puerto Rico Metropolitan Campus .... PR ... 550
Inter American University of Puerto Rico San German Campus .... PR ... 551
Pontifical Catholic University of Puerto Rico, The .... PR ... 552
University of Puerto Rico-Medical Sciences Campus .... PR ... 554
South Dakota State University .... SD ... 452
Austin Peay State University .... TN ... 459
Lincoln Memorial University .... TN ... 456
University of Tennessee, Knoxville .... TN ... 463
Vanderbilt University .... TN ... 463
Tarleton State University .... TX ... 483
Texas A & M University - Corpus Christi .. TX ... 483
Texas Southern University .... TX ... 485
Texas State University-San Marcos .... TX ... 487
Texas Tech University Health Sciences Center .... TX ... 487
University of Texas at El Paso .... TX ... 492
University of Texas Health Science Center at San Antonio .... TX ... 493
University of Texas M.D. Anderson Cancer Center, The .... TX ... 493
University of Texas Medical Branch, The . TX ... 493
University of Texas - Pan American .... TX ... 492
Brigham Young University .... UT ... 495
University of Utah, The .... UT ... 496
Weber State University .... UT ... 497
University of Vermont .... VT ... 500
Jefferson College of Health Sciences .... VA ... 506
Norfolk State University .... VA ... 507
Old Dominion University .... VA ... 507
Virginia Commonwealth University .... VA ... 511
Heritage University .... WA ... 520
University of Washington .... WA ... 524
Marshall University .... WV ... 529
West Liberty University .... WV ... 530
West Virginia University .... WV ... 530
Marquette University .... WI ... 534
University of Wisconsin-Milwaukee .... WI ... 537
University of Wisconsin-Stevens Point .... WI ... 538

MUS: National Association of Schools of Music: music (C,A,B,M,D)

Alabama State University .... AL 1
Auburn University .... AL 1
Birmingham-Southern College .... AL 2
Huntingdon College .... AL 4
Jacksonville State University .... AL 4
Judson College .... AL 5
Samford University .... AL 6
Stillman College .... AL 7
Troy University .... AL 7
University of Alabama at Birmingham .... AL 8
University of Alabama in Huntsville .... AL 8
University of Alabama, The .... AL 8
University of Mobile .... AL 9
University of Montevallo .... AL 9
University of North Alabama .... AL 9
University of South Alabama .... AL 9
University of Alaska Anchorage .... AK 10
University of Alaska Fairbanks .... AK 10
Arizona State University .... AZ 11
Northern Arizona University .... AZ 16
University of Arizona .... AZ 18
Arkansas State University-Jonesboro .... AR 19
Arkansas Tech University .... AR 20
Harding University Main Campus .... AR 21
Henderson State University .... AR 21
Hendrix College .... AR 21
Ouachita Baptist University .... AR 22
Southern Arkansas University .... AR 23
University of Arkansas at Fort Smith .... AR 24
University of Arkansas at Little Rock .... AR 24
University of Arkansas at Monticello .... AR 24
University of Arkansas at Pine Bluff .... AR 24
University of Arkansas Main Campus .... AR 23
University of Central Arkansas .... AR 25
Azusa Pacific University .... CA 29
Biola University .... CA 29
California Baptist University .... CA 30
California Institute of the Arts .... CA 31
California Polytechnic State University-San Luis Obispo .... CA 32
California State Polytechnic University-Pomona .... CA 32
California State University-Chico .... CA 33
California State University-Dominguez Hills .... CA 33
California State University-East Bay .... CA 33
California State University-Fresno .... CA 33
California State University-Fullerton .... CA 33
California State University-Long Beach .... CA 33
California State University-Los Angeles .... CA 34
California State University-Northridge .... CA 34
California State University-Sacramento .... CA 34
California State University-San Bernardino CA 34
California State University-Stanislaus .... CA 35
Chapman University .... CA 38
Colburn School, The .... CA 40
Humboldt State University .... CA 35
La Sierra University .... CA 50
LAMA .... CA 50
Loyola Marymount University .... CA 53
Master's College and Seminary, The .... CA 53
Musicians Institute .... CA 55
Pacific Union College .... CA 57
Pepperdine University .... CA 58
Point Loma Nazarene University .... CA 59
San Francisco Conservatory of Music .... CA 62
San Francisco State University .... CA 35
San Jose State University .... CA 36
Sonoma State University .... CA 36
University of Redlands .... CA 73
University of Southern California .... CA 74
University of the Pacific .... CA 73
Westmont College .... CA 76
Adams State University .... CO 78
Colorado Christian University .... CO 79
Colorado Mesa University .... CO 79
Colorado State University .... CO 80
Colorado State University-Pueblo .... CO 80
Fort Lewis College .... CO 81
Metropolitan State University of Denver .... CO 83
University of Colorado Boulder .... CO 85
University of Colorado DenverlAnschutz Medical Campus .... CO 86
University of Denver .... CO 86
University of Northern Colorado .... CO 86
Western State Colorado University .... CO 86
Central Connecticut State University .... CT 87
University of Connecticut .... CT 92
University of Hartford .... CT 92
Western Connecticut State University .... CT 88
Yale University .... CT 93
University of Delaware .... DE 94
American University .... DC 94
Catholic University of America, The .... DC 94
George Washington University .... DC 95
Howard University .... DC 95
Baptist College of Florida, The .... FL 98
Broward College .... FL 99
Florida Atlantic University .... FL ... 114
Florida College .... FL ... 104
Florida International University .... FL ... 115
Florida Memorial University .... FL ... 104
Florida Southern College .... FL ... 105
Florida State University .... FL ... 115
Hillsborough Community College .... FL ... 106
Jacksonville University .... FL ... 107
Lynn University .... FL ... 108
Miami Dade College .... FL ... 109
Palm Beach Atlantic University .... FL ... 110
Rollins College .... FL ... 111
Stetson University .... FL ... 117
University of Central Florida .... FL ... 115
University of Florida .... FL ... 116
University of Miami .... FL ... 118
University of North Florida .... FL ... 116
University of South Florida .... FL ... 116
University of Tampa .... FL ... 118
University of West Florida .... FL ... 117
Armstrong Atlantic State University .... GA .. 120
Berry College .... GA .. 121
Clayton State University .... GA .. 123
Columbus State University .... GA .. 123
Georgia College & State University .... GA .. 125
Georgia Regents University .... GA .. 126
Georgia Southern University .... GA .. 126
Georgia State University .... GA .. 126
Kennesaw State University .... GA .. 127
Mercer University .... GA .. 128
Morehouse College .... GA .. 129
Reinhardt University .... GA .. 130
Shorter University .... GA .. 131
Spelman College .... GA .. 132
Toccoa Falls College .... GA .. 133
Truett McConnell College .... GA .. 133
University of Georgia .... GA .. 133
University of West Georgia .... GA .. 133
Valdosta State University .... GA .. 134
Wesleyan College .... GA .. 134
Young Harris College .... GA .. 134
University of Hawaii at Manoa .... HI .. 136
Boise State University .... ID .. 137
Brigham Young University-Idaho .... ID .. 137
Idaho State University .... ID .. 138
Northwest Nazarene University .... ID .. 139
University of Idaho .... ID .. 139
Augustana College .... IL .. 139
Bradley University .... IL .. 140
Chicago State University .... IL .. 141
Concordia University Chicago .... IL .. 143
DePaul University .... IL .. 143
Eastern Illinois University .... IL .. 144
Harper College .... IL .. 145
Illinois Central College .... IL .. 146
Illinois State University .... IL .. 147
Illinois Wesleyan University .... IL .. 148
Joliet Junior College .... IL .. 149
Millikin University .... IL .. 153
Moody Bible Institute .... IL .. 153
North Park University .... IL .. 154
Northeastern Illinois University .... IL .. 154
Northern Illinois University .... IL .. 154
Northwestern University .... IL .. 155
Olivet Nazarene University .... IL .. 155
Roosevelt University .... IL .. 157
Saint Xavier University .... IL .. 158
Southern Illinois University Carbondale .... IL .. 159
Southern Illinois University Edwardsville ... IL .. 159
University of Illinois at Urbana-Champaign IL .. 162
VanderCook College of Music .... IL .. 162
Western Illinois University .... IL .. 162
Wheaton College .... IL .. 163
Anderson University .... IN .. 163
Ball State University .... IN .. 164
Bethel College .... IN .. 164
Butler University .... IN .. 164
DePauw University .... IN .. 165
Indiana State University .... IN .. 167
Indiana University Bloomington .... IN .. 167
Indiana University-Purdue University Fort Wayne .... IN .. 168
Indiana University-Purdue University Indianapolis .... IN .. 168
Indiana Wesleyan University .... IN .. 169
Saint Mary-of-the-Woods College .... IN .. 172
Saint Mary's College .... IN .. 172
Taylor University .... IN .. 173
University of Evansville .... IN .. 173
University of Indianapolis .... IN .. 173
Valparaiso University .... IN .. 174
Central College .... IA .. 176
Clarke University .... IA .. 176
Coe College .... IA .. 176
Drake University .... IA .. 177
Iowa State University .... IA .. 175
Luther College .... IA .. 180
Morningside College .... IA .. 181
Simpson College .... IA .. 182
University of Iowa .... IA .. 175
University of Northern Iowa .... IA .. 176
Wartburg College .... IA .. 183
Baker University .... KS .. 184
Benedictine College .... KS .. 184
Bethany College .... KS .. 184
Emporia State University .... KS .. 186
Fort Hays State University .... KS .. 186
Friends University .... KS .. 186
Kansas State University .... KS .. 188
MidAmerica Nazarene University .... KS .. 188
Pittsburg State University .... KS .. 189
Southwestern College .... KS .. 190
Tabor College .... KS .. 190
University of Kansas Main Campus .... KS .. 190
Washburn University .... KS .. 191
Wichita State University .... KS .. 191
Asbury University .... KY ... 192
Campbellsville University .... KY ... 193
Eastern Kentucky University .... KY ... 193
Kentucky State University .... KY ... 197
Morehead State University .... KY ... 198
Murray State University .... KY ... 198
Northern Kentucky University .... KY ... 198
Southern Baptist Theological Seminary, The .... KY ... 199
University of Kentucky .... KY ... 200
University of Louisville .... KY ... 200
Western Kentucky University .... KY ... 200
Centenary College of Louisiana .... LA ... 201
Grambling State University .... LA ... 207
Louisiana College .... LA ... 202
Louisiana State University and Agricultural and Mechanical College .... LA ... 204
Louisiana Tech University .... LA ... 207
Loyola University New Orleans .... LA ... 205
McNeese State University .... LA ... 207
New Orleans Baptist Theological Seminary .... LA ... 206
Nicholls State University .... LA ... 208
Northwestern State University .... LA ... 208
Southeastern Louisiana University .... LA ... 208
Southern University and A&M College .... LA ... 206
University of Louisiana at Lafayette .... LA ... 208
University of Louisiana at Monroe .... LA ... 208
University of New Orleans .... LA ... 205
Xavier University of Louisiana .... LA ... 209
University of Maine .... ME ... 212
University of Southern Maine .... ME ... 212
Community College of Baltimore County, The .... MD ... 214
Howard Community College .... MD ... 215
Johns Hopkins University .... MD ... 215
Montgomery College .... MD ... 216
Morgan State University .... MD ... 217
Salisbury University .... MD ... 220
Towson University .... MD ... 220
University of Maryland College Park .... MD ... 219
Anna Maria College .... MA ... 222
Boston Conservatory, The .... MA ... 224
Boston University .... MA ... 224
Bridgewater State University .... MA ... 229
Gordon College .... MA ... 226
Holyoke Community College .... MA ... 231
New England Conservatory of Music .... MA ... 234
Salem State University .... MA ... 230
University of Massachusetts .... MA ... 228
University of Massachusetts Lowell .... MA ... 229
Westfield State University .... MA ... 230
Albion College .... MI 239
Alma College .... MI 239
Andrews University .... MI 239
Calvin College .... MI 240
Central Michigan University .... MI 240
Cornerstone University .... MI 241
Eastern Michigan University .... MI 242
Grand Rapids Community College .... MI 243
Grand Valley State University .... MI 243
Hope College .... MI 244
Michigan State University .... MI 246
Northern Michigan University .... MI 248
Oakland University .... MI 248
Saginaw Valley State University .... MI 249
Spring Arbor University .... MI 250
University of Michigan-Ann Arbor .... MI 251
University of Michigan-Flint .... MI 251
Wayne State University .... MI 252
Western Michigan University .... MI 252
Anoka-Ramsey Community College .... MN .. 257
Augsburg College .... MN .. 253
Bemidji State University .... MN .. 258
College of Saint Benedict .... MN .. 254
Concordia College .... MN .. 255
Gustavus Adolphus College .... MN .. 255
Hamline University .... MN .. 256
McNally Smith College of Music .... MN .. 256
Minnesota State University Moorhead .... MN .. 259
Minnesota State University, Mankato .... MN .. 259
Normandale Community College .... MN .. 260
Northwestern College .... MN .. 263
St. Cloud State University .... MN .. 261
Saint John's University .... MN .. 263
Saint Mary's University of Minnesota .... MN .. 264
St. Olaf College .... MN .. 264
Southwest Minnesota State University .... MN .. 261
University of Minnesota Duluth .... MN .. 264
University of Minnesota-Twin Cities .... MN .. 264
University of Saint Thomas .... MN .. 265
Winona State University .... MN .. 262
Alcorn State University .... MS .. 265
Belhaven University .... MS .. 266
Delta State University .... MS .. 266
Jackson State University .... MS .. 267
Mississippi College .... MS .. 268
Mississippi State University .... MS .. 268
Mississippi University for Women .... MS .. 268
Mississippi Valley State University .... MS .. 269
University of Mississippi .... MS .. 270
University of Southern Mississippi .... MS .. 270
William Carey University .... MS .. 270
Central Methodist University .... MO .. 272
Cottey College .... MO .. 273
Culver-Stockton College .... MO .. 273
Drury University .... MO .. 273
Evangel University .... MO .. 274
Lincoln University .... MO .. 276
Maryville University of Saint Louis .... MO .. 276
Missouri Baptist University .... MO .. 278
Missouri State University .... MO .. 278
Missouri Western State University .... MO .. 279
Northwest Missouri State University .... MO .. 279

Southeast Missouri State University ... MO .. 282
Southwest Baptist University ... MO .. 282
Truman State University ... MO .. 282
University of Central Missouri ... MO .. 283
University of Missouri - Columbia ... MO .. 283
University of Missouri - Kansas City ... MO .. 283
University of Missouri - Saint Louis ... MO .. 283
Webster University ... MO .. 284
William Jewell College ... MO .. 285
Montana State University ... MT .. 287
Montana State University - Billings ... MT .. 287
University of Montana - Missoula, The ... MT .. 286
Concordia University ... NE ... 289
Hastings College ... NE ... 289
Nebraska Wesleyan University ... NE ... 291
University of Nebraska at Kearney ... NE ... 292
University of Nebraska at Omaha ... NE ... 293
University of Nebraska - Lincoln ... NE ... 292
Wayne State College ... NE ... 291
University of Nevada, Las Vegas ... NV ... 294
University of Nevada, Reno ... NV ... 294
Keene State College ... NH ... 298
University of New Hampshire ... NH ... 298
College of New Jersey, The ... NJ ... 300
Kean University ... NJ ... 302
Montclair State University ... NJ ... 303
New Jersey City University ... NJ ... 303
Rider University ... NJ ... 305
Rowan University ... NJ ... 305
Rutgers the State University of New Jersey New Brunswick Campus ... NJ ... 306
William Paterson University of New Jersey ... NJ ... 308
Eastern New Mexico University Main Campus ... NM .. 309
New Mexico State University Main Campus ... NM .. 310
University of New Mexico Main Campus .. NM .. 312
College of Saint Rose, The ... NY ... 321
Hartwick College ... NY ... 325
Houghton College ... NY ... 326
Ithaca College ... NY ... 327
Molloy College ... NY ... 331
Nassau Community College ... NY ... 332
Nazareth College of Rochester ... NY ... 332
Nyack College ... NY ... 335
Roberts Wesleyan College ... NY ... 337
Schenectady County Community College . NY ... 340
State University of New York at Binghamton ... NY ... 341
State University of New York at Fredonia . NY ... 342
State University of New York at New Paltz NY ... 342
State University of New York College at Buffalo ... NY ... 343
State University of New York College at Oneonta ... NY ... 343
State University of New York College at Oswego ... NY ... 344
State University of New York College at Potsdam ... NY ... 344
Syracuse University Main Campus ... NY ... 347
University of Rochester ... NY ... 349
Villa Maria College of Buffalo ... NY ... 350
Appalachian State University ... NC .. 367
Brevard College ... NC .. 352
Chowan University ... NC .. 353
East Carolina University ... NC .. 367
Elizabeth City State University ... NC .. 367
Fayetteville State University ... NC .. 367
Gardner-Webb University ... NC .. 354
Greensboro College ... NC .. 354
Mars Hill College ... NC .. 356
Meredith College ... NC .. 356
North Carolina Agricultural and Technical State University ... NC .. 367
Pfeiffer University ... NC .. 365
Queens University of Charlotte ... NC .. 365
Salem College ... NC .. 366
University of North Carolina at Greensboro ... NC .. 369
University of North Carolina at Pembroke NC .. 369
University of North Carolina Wilmington ... NC .. 369
Western Carolina University ... NC .. 369
Wingate University ... NC .. 370
Winston-Salem State University ... NC .. 370
Dickinson State University ... ND .. 371
Minot State University ... ND .. 371
North Dakota State University Main Campus ... ND .. 371
University of Mary ... ND .. 373
University of North Dakota Main Campus . ND .. 371
Valley City State University ... ND .. 372
Ashland University ... OH .. 374
Baldwin Wallace University ... OH .. 374
Bluffton University ... OH .. 374
Bowling Green State University ... OH .. 374
Capital University ... OH .. 375
Case Western Reserve University ... OH .. 375
Cedarville University ... OH .. 375
Central State University ... OH .. 376
Cincinnati Christian University ... OH .. 376
Cleveland Institute of Music ... OH .. 377
Cleveland State University ... OH .. 377
College of Mount St. Joseph ... OH .. 377
College of Wooster, The ... OH .. 377
Heidelberg University ... OH .. 380
Hiram College ... OH .. 380
Kent State University Main Campus ... OH .. 382
Marietta College ... OH .. 383
Miami University ... OH .. 384
Mount Vernon Nazarene University ... OH .. 384
Muskingum University ... OH .. 384
Oberlin College ... OH .. 385
Ohio Northern University ... OH .. 386
Ohio State University Main Campus, The . OH .. 386
Ohio University Main Campus ... OH .. 387
Ohio Wesleyan University ... OH .. 387
Otterbein University ... OH .. 387
Sinclair Community College ... OH .. 388
University of Akron, Main Campus, The ... OH .. 390
University of Cincinnati Main Campus ... OH .. 390
University of Dayton ... OH .. 391
University of Mount Union ... OH .. 391
University of Toledo ... OH .. 392
Wittenberg University ... OH .. 393
Wright State University Main Campus ... OH .. 393
Xavier University ... OH .. 393
Youngstown State University ... OH .. 394
Cameron University ... OK .. 394
East Central University ... OK .. 395
Northeastern State University ... OK .. 396
Oklahoma Baptist University ... OK .. 397
Oklahoma Christian University ... OK .. 397
Oklahoma City University ... OK .. 397
Oklahoma State University ... OK .. 397
Oral Roberts University ... OK .. 398
Southeastern Oklahoma State University . OK .. 399
Southern Nazarene University ... OK .. 399
Southwestern Oklahoma State University . OK .. 400
University of Central Oklahoma ... OK .. 400
University of Oklahoma Norman Campus . OK .. 401
University of Science and Arts of Oklahoma ... OK .. 401
University of Tulsa ... OK .. 401
George Fox University ... OR .. 403
Linfield College ... OR .. 404
Marylhurst University ... OR .. 404
Pacific University ... OR .. 407
Portland State University ... OR .. 406
Southern Oregon University ... OR .. 406
University of Oregon ... OR .. 406
University of Portland ... OR .. 408
Western Oregon University ... OR .. 406
Willamette University ... OR .. 408
Bloomsburg University of Pennsylvania ... PA ... 427
Bucknell University ... PA ... 411
Bucks County Community College ... PA ... 411
Cairn University ... PA ... 411
Carnegie Mellon University ... PA ... 412
Clarion University of Pennsylvania ... PA ... 428
Curtis Institute of Music ... PA ... 414
Duquesne University ... PA ... 415
Edinboro University of Pennsylvania ... PA ... 428
Elizabethtown College ... PA ... 415
Gettysburg College ... PA ... 417
Immaculata University ... PA ... 418
Indiana University of Pennsylvania ... PA ... 428
Kutztown University of Pennsylvania ... PA ... 429
Lebanon Valley College ... PA ... 421
Mansfield University of Pennsylvania ... PA ... 429
Marywood University ... PA ... 423
Mercyhurst University ... PA ... 423
Messiah College ... PA ... 423
Millersville University of Pennsylvania ... PA ... 429
Moravian College ... PA ... 424
Penn State University Park ... PA ... 426
Seton Hill University ... PA ... 433
Slippery Rock University of Pennsylvania . PA ... 429
Susquehanna University ... PA ... 433
Temple University ... PA ... 433
University of the Arts, The ... PA ... 435
West Chester University of Pennsylvania . PA ... 430
Westminster College ... PA ... 437
York College of Pennsylvania ... PA ... 438
Community College of Rhode Island ... RI ... 439
Providence College ... RI ... 439
Rhode Island College ... RI ... 439
University of Rhode Island ... RI ... 440
Anderson University ... SC ... 441
Charleston Southern University ... SC ... 441
Claflin University ... SC ... 442
Coastal Carolina University ... SC ... 442
Coker College ... SC ... 442
College of Charleston ... SC ... 443
Columbia College ... SC ... 443
Converse College ... SC ... 443
Furman University ... SC ... 444
Lander University ... SC ... 444
Limestone College ... SC ... 444
Newberry College ... SC ... 445
North Greenville University ... SC ... 445
Presbyterian College ... SC ... 446
South Carolina State University ... SC ... 446
Southern Wesleyan University ... SC ... 446
University of South Carolina Aiken ... SC ... 448
University of South Carolina Columbia ... SC ... 447
Winthrop University ... SC ... 449
Augustana College ... SD ... 449
Black Hills State University ... SD ... 451
Northern State University ... SD ... 451
South Dakota State University ... SD ... 452
University of South Dakota, The ... SD ... 451
Austin Peay State University ... TN ... 459
Belmont University ... TN ... 453
Carson-Newman University ... TN ... 453
East Tennessee State University ... TN ... 459
Fisk University ... TN ... 454
Lee University ... TN ... 455
Lipscomb University ... TN ... 456
Maryville College ... TN ... 456
Middle Tennessee State University ... TN ... 459
Rhodes College ... TN ... 458
Southern Adventist University ... TN ... 458
Tennessee State University ... TN ... 459
Tennessee Technological University ... TN ... 460
Trevecca Nazarene University ... TN ... 462
Union University ... TN ... 462
University of Memphis, The ... TN ... 460
University of Tennessee at Chattanooga .. TN ... 463
University of Tennessee at Martin ... TN ... 463
University of Tennessee, Knoxville ... TN ... 463
Vanderbilt University ... TN ... 463
Abilene Christian University ... TX ... 464
Amarillo College ... TX ... 465
Angelo State University ... TX ... 465
Baylor University ... TX ... 467
Dallas Baptist University ... TX ... 470
Del Mar College ... TX ... 471
East Texas Baptist University ... TX ... 471
Hardin-Simmons University ... TX ... 472
Howard Payne University ... TX ... 473
Lamar University ... TX ... 486
Midwestern State University ... TX ... 476
Odessa College ... TX ... 477
Prairie View A & M University ... TX ... 482
St. Mary's University ... TX ... 479
Sam Houston State University ... TX ... 487
Southern Methodist University ... TX ... 481
Southwestern Baptist Theological Seminary ... TX ... 481
Southwestern University ... TX ... 481
Stephen F. Austin State University ... TX ... 482
Tarleton State University ... TX ... 483
Texas A & M University - Commerce ... TX ... 483
Texas A & M University - Corpus Christi .. TX ... 483
Texas A & M University - Kingsville ... TX ... 484
Texas Christian University ... TX ... 484
Texas Lutheran University ... TX ... 485
Texas State University-San Marcos ... TX ... 487
Texas Tech University ... TX ... 487
Texas Wesleyan University ... TX ... 488
Texas Woman's University ... TX ... 488
University of Houston ... TX ... 489
University of Mary Hardin-Baylor ... TX ... 490
University of North Texas ... TX ... 490
University of Texas at Arlington, The ... TX ... 491
University of Texas at Austin ... TX ... 491
University of Texas at Brownsville and Texas Southmost College, The ... TX ... 491
University of Texas at El Paso ... TX ... 492
University of Texas at San Antonio ... TX ... 492
University of Texas - Pan American ... TX ... 492
Wayland Baptist University ... TX ... 494
West Texas A & M University ... TX ... 484
Brigham Young University ... UT ... 495
Snow College ... UT ... 498
Southern Utah University ... UT ... 497
University of Utah, The ... UT ... 496
Utah State University ... UT ... 497
Weber State University ... UT ... 497
Christopher Newport University ... VA ... 503
George Mason University ... VA ... 505
Hampton University ... VA ... 505
James Madison University ... VA ... 506
Longwood University ... VA ... 506
Norfolk State University ... VA ... 507
Old Dominion University ... VA ... 507
Radford University ... VA ... 508
Shenandoah University ... VA ... 509
University of Mary Washington ... VA ... 510
Virginia Commonwealth University ... VA ... 511
Virginia Polytechnic Institute and State University ... VA ... 515
Virginia State University ... VA ... 515
Central Washington University ... WA .. 517
Eastern Washington University ... WA .. 519
Gonzaga University ... WA .. 520
Pacific Lutheran University ... WA .. 521
Seattle Pacific University ... WA .. 523
University of Puget Sound ... WA .. 524
Walla Walla University ... WA .. 524
Washington State University ... WA .. 525
Western Washington University ... WA .. 525
Whitworth University ... WA .. 525
Marshall University ... WV .. 529
Shepherd University ... WV .. 529
West Liberty University ... WV .. 530
West Virginia University ... WV .. 530
West Virginia Wesleyan College ... WV .. 531
Alverno College ... WI ... 531
Carthage College ... WI ... 532
Lawrence University ... WI ... 533
Silver Lake College of the Holy Family ... WI ... 536
University of Wisconsin-Eau Claire ... WI ... 536
University of Wisconsin-Green Bay ... WI ... 536
University of Wisconsin-La Crosse ... WI ... 536
University of Wisconsin-Madison ... WI ... 536
University of Wisconsin-Milwaukee ... WI ... 537
University of Wisconsin-Oshkosh ... WI ... 537
University of Wisconsin-Platteville ... WI ... 537
University of Wisconsin-River Falls ... WI ... 537
University of Wisconsin-Stevens Point ... WI ... 538
University of Wisconsin-Superior ... WI ... 538
University of Wisconsin-Whitewater ... WI ... 538
Viterbo University ... WI ... 539
Casper College ... WY .. 542
Northwest College ... WY .. 543
University of Wyoming ... WY .. 543

NAIT: The Association of Technology, Management, and Applied Engineering: technology, applied technology, engineering technology and technology-related programs (A, B,M)

Jacksonville State University ... AL ... 4
University of Arkansas at Fort Smith ... AR ... 24
University of Arkansas at Pine Bluff ... AR ... 24
California Polytechnic State University-San Luis Obispo ... CA ... 32
California State University-Chico ... CA ... 33
College of the Redwoods Community College District ... CA ... 40
San Jose State University ... CA ... 36
Central Connecticut State University ... CT ... 87
Idaho State University ... ID ... 138
Eastern Illinois University ... IL ... 144
Illinois State University ... IL ... 147
Northern Illinois University ... IL ... 154
Southern Illinois University Carbondale ... IL ... 159
Western Illinois University ... IL ... 162
Indiana State University ... IN ... 167
Ivy Tech Community College-Central Indiana ... IN ... 169
Purdue University Calumet ... IN ... 171
Purdue University Main Campus ... IN ... 171
Iowa State University ... IA ... 175
University of Northern Iowa ... IA ... 176
Eastern Kentucky University ... KY ... 193
Morehead State University ... KY ... 198
Western Kentucky University ... KY ... 200
Baton Rouge Community College ... LA ... 202
Bossier Parish Community College ... LA ... 202
Delgado Community College ... LA ... 203
L.E. Fletcher Technical Community College ... LA ... 203
Nicholls State University ... LA ... 208
Nunez Community College ... LA ... 203
River Parishes Community College ... LA ... 203
South Louisiana Community College ... LA ... 203
South Louisiana Community College Ardoin Campus ... LA ... 203
Southeastern Louisiana University ... LA ... 208
Sowela Technical Community College ... LA ... 204
University of Louisiana at Lafayette ... LA ... 208
University of Southern Maine ... ME .. 212
Central Michigan University ... MI ... 240
Bemidji State University ... MN .. 258
Minnesota State University Moorhead ... MN .. 259
St. Cloud State University ... MN .. 261
Alcorn State University ... MS .. 265
Holmes Community College ... MS .. 267
Jackson State University ... MS .. 267
East Central College ... MO .. 273
Linn State Technical College ... MO .. 276
Southeast Missouri State University ... MO .. 282
University of Central Missouri ... MO .. 283
University of Nebraska at Kearney ... NE ... 292
Farmingdale State College ... NY ... 346
State University of New York College at Buffalo ... NY ... 343
East Carolina University ... NC .. 367
Elizabeth City State University ... NC .. 367
North Carolina Agricultural and Technical State University ... NC .. 367
University of North Dakota Main Campus . ND .. 371
Bowling Green State University ... OH .. 374
Kent State University Main Campus ... OH .. 382
Ohio Northern University ... OH .. 386
Ohio University Main Campus ... OH .. 387
Owens Community College ... OH .. 387
Southwestern Oklahoma State University . OK .. 400
California University of Pennsylvania ... PA ... 428
Millersville University of Pennsylvania ... PA ... 429
Pennsylvania College of Technology ... PA ... 427
Cleveland State Community College ... TN ... 460
Jackson State Community College ... TN ... 460
Middle Tennessee State University ... TN ... 459
Nashville State Community College ... TN ... 461
Northeast State Community College ... TN ... 461
Tennessee State University ... TN ... 459
Tennessee Technological University ... TN ... 460
Walters State Community College ... TN ... 462
Texas A & M University - Kingsville ... TX ... 484

Texas Southern University ... TX ... 485
University of Texas at Tyler ... TX ... 492
Norfolk State University ... VA ... 507
Virginia State University ... VA ... 515
Pierpont Community & Technical College ... WV ... 528
University of Wisconsin-Platteville ... WI ... 537

NATUR: Council on Naturopathic Medical Education: naturopathic medical education (FP,D)

Southwest College of Naturopathic Medicine & Health Sciences ... AZ ... 17
University of Bridgeport ... CT ... 91
National University of Health Sciences ... IL ... 154
National College of Natural Medicine ... OR ... 404
Bastyr University ... WA ... 516

NDT: Commission on Accreditation of Allied Health Education Programs: neurodiagnostic technology (C,A)

Gateway Community College ... AZ ... 14
Orange Coast College ... CA ... 39
Lincoln Land Community College ... IL ... 151
Indiana University-Purdue University Indianapolis ... IN ... 168
Kirkwood Community College ... IA ... 180
Scott Community College ... IA ... 178
Laboure College ... MA ... 227
Minneapolis Community and Technical College ... MN ... 259
Catawba Valley Community College ... NC ... 359
Pamlico Community College ... NC ... 362
Cuyahoga Community College ... OH ... 378
Southeast Technical Institute ... SD ... 452
Vanderbilt University ... TN ... 463
Alvin Community College ... TX ... 465
Bellevue College ... WA ... 517

NH: Higher Learning Commission, North Central Association

American Indian College of the Assemblies of God ... AZ ... 11
Arizona Christian University (formerly Southwestern College) ... AZ ... 11
Arizona State University ... AZ ... 11
Arizona Western College ... AZ ... 11
Central Arizona College ... AZ ... 12
Chandler-Gilbert Community College ... AZ ... 14
Cochise College ... AZ ... 12
Coconino Community College ... AZ ... 13
Diné College ... AZ ... 13
Eastern Arizona College ... AZ ... 13
Estrella Mountain Community College ... AZ ... 14
Everest College Phoenix ... AZ ... 13
Frank Lloyd Wright School of Architecture. AZ ... 13
Gateway Community College ... AZ ... 14
Glendale Community College ... AZ ... 14
Grand Canyon University ... AZ ... 13
Mesa Community College ... AZ ... 15
Mohave Community College ... AZ ... 15
Northcentral University ... AZ ... 16
Northern Arizona University ... AZ ... 16
Northland Pioneer College ... AZ ... 16
Paradise Valley Community College ... AZ ... 15
Phoenix College ... AZ ... 15
Phoenix Seminary ... AZ ... 16
#Pima Community College ... AZ ... 17
Prescott College ... AZ ... 17
Rio Salado College ... AZ ... 15
Scottsdale Community College ... AZ ... 15
South Mountain Community College ... AZ ... 15
Southwest College of Naturopathic Medicine & Health Sciences ... AZ ... 17
Southwest University of Visual Arts ... AZ ... 17
Thunderbird School of Global Management ... AZ ... 18
Tohono O'odham Community College ... AZ ... 18
University of Advancing Technology ... AZ ... 18
University of Arizona ... AZ ... 18
University of Phoenix ... AZ ... 18
Western International University ... AZ ... 19
Yavapai College ... AZ ... 19
Arkansas Baptist College ... AR ... 19
Arkansas Northeastern College ... AR ... 19
Arkansas State University-Beebe ... AR ... 19
Arkansas State University-Jonesboro ... AR ... 19
Arkansas State University-Mountain Home AR ... 20
Arkansas State University-Newport ... AR ... 20
Arkansas Tech University ... AR ... 20
Black River Technical College ... AR ... 20
Central Baptist College ... AR ... 20
College of the Ouachitas ... AR ... 20
Cossatot Community College of the University of Arkansas ... AR ... 24
Crowley's Ridge College ... AR ... 20
East Arkansas Community College ... AR ... 21
Harding University Main Campus ... AR ... 21
Henderson State University ... AR ... 21
Hendrix College ... AR ... 21
John Brown University ... AR ... 21
Lyon College ... AR ... 21
Mid-South Community College ... AR ... 21
National Park Community College ... AR ... 22
North Arkansas College ... AR ... 22
NorthWest Arkansas Community College . AR ... 22
Ouachita Baptist University ... AR ... 22
Ozarka College ... AR ... 22
Philander Smith College ... AR ... 22
Phillips Community College of the University of Arkansas ... AR ... 24
Pulaski Technical College ... AR ... 22
Rich Mountain Community College ... AR ... 23
South Arkansas Community College ... AR ... 23
Southeast Arkansas College ... AR ... 23
Southern Arkansas University ... AR ... 23
Southern Arkansas University Tech ... AR ... 23
University of Arkansas at Fort Smith ... AR ... 24
University of Arkansas at Little Rock ... AR ... 24
University of Arkansas at Monticello ... AR ... 24
University of Arkansas at Pine Bluff ... AR ... 24
University of Arkansas Community College at Batesville ... AR ... 25
University of Arkansas Community College at Hope ... AR ... 25
University of Arkansas Community College at Morrilton ... AR ... 25
University of Arkansas for Medical Sciences ... AR ... 24
University of Arkansas Main Campus ... AR ... 23
University of Central Arkansas ... AR ... 25
University of the Ozarks ... AR ... 25
Williams Baptist College ... AR ... 25
Adams State University ... CO ... 78
Aims Community College ... CO ... 78
Arapahoe Community College ... CO ... 78
Art Institute of Colorado, The ... CO ... 78
College for Financial Planning ... CO ... 78
Colorado Christian University ... CO ... 79
Colorado College ... CO ... 79
Colorado Mesa University ... CO ... 79
Colorado Mountain College ... CO ... 79
Colorado Northwestern Community College ... CO ... 80
Colorado School of Mines ... CO ... 80
Colorado State University ... CO ... 80
Colorado State University-Global Campus. CO ... 80
Colorado State University-Pueblo ... CO ... 80
Colorado Technical University ... CO ... 81
Community College of Aurora ... CO ... 81
Community College of Denver ... CO ... 81
@Denver School of Nursing ... CO ... 81
Denver Seminary ... CO ... 81
Fort Lewis College ... CO ... 81
Front Range Community College ... CO ... 81
Iliff School of Theology ... CO ... 82
Jones International University ... CO ... 82
Lamar Community College ... CO ... 82
Metropolitan State University of Denver ... CO ... 83
Morgan Community College ... CO ... 83
Naropa University ... CO ... 83
Nazarene Bible College ... CO ... 83
Northeastern Junior College ... CO ... 83
Otero Junior College ... CO ... 83
Pikes Peak Community College ... CO ... 84
Pueblo Community College ... CO ... 84
Red Rocks Community College ... CO ... 84
Regis University ... CO ... 84
Rocky Mountain College of Art & Design . CO ... 85
@Rocky Vista University ... CO ... 85
Trinidad State Junior College ... CO ... 85
United States Air Force Academy ... CO ... 545
University of Colorado Boulder ... CO ... 85
University of Colorado Colorado Springs .. CO ... 85
University of Colorado Denver|Anschutz Medical Campus ... CO ... 86
University of Denver ... CO ... 86
University of Northern Colorado ... CO ... 86
University of the Rockies ... CO ... 86
Western State Colorado University ... CO ... 86
Adler School of Professional Psychology . IL ... 139
American Academy of Art ... IL ... 139
American InterContinental University ... IL ... 139
Augustana College ... IL ... 139
Aurora University ... IL ... 140
Benedictine University ... IL ... 140
Black Hawk College ... IL ... 140
Blackburn College ... IL ... 140
Blessing-Rieman College of Nursing ... IL ... 140
Bradley University ... IL ... 140
Carl Sandburg College ... IL ... 141
Chamberlain College of Nursing - Addison IL ... 141
Chicago State University ... IL ... 141
Chicago Theological Seminary ... IL ... 141
City Colleges of Chicago Harold Washington College ... IL ... 141
City Colleges of Chicago Harry S Truman College ... IL ... 142
City Colleges of Chicago Kennedy-King College ... IL ... 142
City Colleges of Chicago Malcolm X College ... IL ... 142
City Colleges of Chicago Olive-Harvey College ... IL ... 142
City Colleges of Chicago Richard J. Daley College ... IL ... 142
City Colleges of Chicago Wilbur Wright College ... IL ... 142
College of DuPage ... IL ... 142
College of Lake County ... IL ... 143
Columbia College Chicago ... IL ... 143
Concordia University Chicago ... IL ... 143
Danville Area Community College ... IL ... 143
DePaul University ... IL ... 143
DeVry University - Chicago Campus ... IL ... 144
Dominican University ... IL ... 144
East-West University ... IL ... 144
Eastern Illinois University ... IL ... 144
Elgin Community College ... IL ... 144
Elmhurst College ... IL ... 145
Erikson Institute ... IL ... 145
Eureka College ... IL ... 145
Fox College ... IL ... 145
Garrett-Evangelical Theological Seminary IL ... 145
Governors State University ... IL ... 145
Greenville College ... IL ... 145
Harper College ... IL ... 145
Harrington College of Design ... IL ... 146
Heartland Community College ... IL ... 146
Hebrew Theological College ... IL ... 146
Highland Community College ... IL ... 146
Illinois Central College ... IL ... 146
Illinois College ... IL ... 146
Illinois College of Optometry ... IL ... 146
&Illinois Eastern Community Colleges Frontier Community College ... IL ... 146
&Illinois Eastern Community Colleges Lincoln Trail College ... IL ... 147
&Illinois Eastern Community Colleges Olney Central College ... IL ... 147
&Illinois Eastern Community Colleges Wabash Valley College ... IL ... 147
Illinois Institute of Art, The ... IL ... 147
Illinois Institute of Technology ... IL ... 147
Illinois State University ... IL ... 147
Illinois Valley Community College ... IL ... 148
Illinois Wesleyan University ... IL ... 148
Institute for Clinical Social Work ... IL ... 148
John A. Logan College ... IL ... 148
John Marshall Law School ... IL ... 148
John Wood Community College ... IL ... 148
Joliet Junior College ... IL ... 149
Judson University ... IL ... 149
Kankakee Community College ... IL ... 149
Kaskaskia College ... IL ... 149
Kendall College ... IL ... 149
Kishwaukee College ... IL ... 149
Knowledge Systems Institute ... IL ... 149
Knox College ... IL ... 150
Lake Forest College ... IL ... 150
Lake Forest Graduate School of Management ... IL ... 150
Lake Land College ... IL ... 150
Lakeview College of Nursing ... IL ... 150
Le Cordon Bleu College of Culinary Arts in Chicago ... IL ... 150
Lewis and Clark Community College ... IL ... 150
Lewis University ... IL ... 150
Lexington College ... IL ... 151
Lincoln Christian University ... IL ... 151
Lincoln College ... IL ... 151
Lincoln Land Community College ... IL ... 151
Loyola University Chicago ... IL ... 151
Lutheran School of Theology at Chicago .. IL ... 152
MacCormac College ... IL ... 152
MacMurray College ... IL ... 152
McCormick Theological Seminary ... IL ... 152
McHenry County College ... IL ... 152
McKendree University ... IL ... 152
Methodist College ... IL ... 152
Midstate College ... IL ... 152
Midwestern University ... IL ... 153
Millikin University ... IL ... 153
Monmouth College ... IL ... 153
Moody Bible Institute ... IL ... 153
Moraine Valley Community College ... IL ... 153
Morton College ... IL ... 153
National-Louis University ... IL ... 153
National University of Health Sciences ... IL ... 154
North Central College ... IL ... 154
North Park University ... IL ... 154
Northeastern Illinois University ... IL ... 154
Northern Illinois University ... IL ... 154
Northern Seminary ... IL ... 155
Northwestern College ... IL ... 155
Northwestern University ... IL ... 155
Oakton Community College ... IL ... 155
Olivet Nazarene University ... IL ... 155
Parkland College ... IL ... 155
Prairie State College ... IL ... 156
Principia College ... IL ... 156
Quincy University ... IL ... 156
Rend Lake College ... IL ... 156
Resurrection University ... IL ... 156
Richland Community College ... IL ... 156
Robert Morris University ... IL ... 156
Rock Valley College ... IL ... 157
Rockford University ... IL ... 157
Roosevelt University ... IL ... 157
Rosalind Franklin University of Medicine & Science ... IL ... 157
Rush University ... IL ... 157
Saint Anthony College of Nursing ... IL ... 158
St. Augustine College ... IL ... 158
Saint Francis Medical Center College of Nursing ... IL ... 158
St. John's College ... IL ... 158
Saint Xavier University ... IL ... 158
Sauk Valley Community College ... IL ... 158
School of the Art Institute of Chicago ... IL ... 158
Shawnee Community College ... IL ... 158
Shimer College ... IL ... 159
South Suburban College of Cook County . IL ... 159
Southeastern Illinois College ... IL ... 159
Southern Illinois University Carbondale ... IL ... 159
Southern Illinois University Edwardsville ... IL ... 159
Southwestern Illinois College ... IL ... 160
Spertus Institute for Jewish Learning and Leadership ... IL ... 160
Spoon River College ... IL ... 160
@Taylor Business Institute ... IL ... 160
Toyota Technological Institute at Chicago IL ... 160
Trinity Christian College ... IL ... 160
Trinity College of Nursing & Health Sciences ... IL ... 160
Trinity International University ... IL ... 160
Triton College ... IL ... 161
University of Chicago ... IL ... 161
University of Illinois at Chicago ... IL ... 161
University of Illinois at Springfield ... IL ... 161
University of Illinois at Urbana-Champaign IL ... 162
University of St. Francis ... IL ... 162
VanderCook College of Music ... IL ... 162
Waubonsee Community College ... IL ... 162
Western Illinois University ... IL ... 162
Wheaton College ... IL ... 163
American College of Education ... IN ... 163
Anabaptist Mennonite Biblical Seminary ... IN ... 163
Ancilla College ... IN ... 163
Anderson University ... IN ... 163
Ball State University ... IN ... 164
Bethany Theological Seminary ... IN ... 164
Bethel College ... IN ... 164
Butler University ... IN ... 164
Calumet College of Saint Joseph ... IN ... 164
Christian Theological Seminary ... IN ... 165
Concordia Theological Seminary ... IN ... 165
DePauw University ... IN ... 165
Earlham College and Earlham School of Religion ... IN ... 165
Franklin College of Indiana ... IN ... 165
Goshen College ... IN ... 166
Grace College and Seminary ... IN ... 166
Hanover College ... IN ... 166
@Harrison College - Indianapolis Downtown Campus ... IN ... 166
Holy Cross College ... IN ... 166
Huntington University ... IN ... 166
Indiana State University ... IN ... 167
Indiana Tech ... IN ... 167
Indiana University Bloomington ... IN ... 167
Indiana University East ... IN ... 167
Indiana University Kokomo ... IN ... 168
Indiana University Northwest ... IN ... 168
Indiana University-Purdue University Fort Wayne ... IN ... 168
Indiana University-Purdue University Indianapolis ... IN ... 168
Indiana University South Bend ... IN ... 168
Indiana University Southeast ... IN ... 168
Indiana Wesleyan University ... IN ... 169
Ivy Tech Community College-Central Indiana ... IN ... 169
Manchester University ... IN ... 170
Marian University ... IN ... 170
Martin University ... IN ... 171
Oakland City University ... IN ... 171
Purdue University Calumet ... IN ... 171
Purdue University Main Campus ... IN ... 171
Purdue University North Central Campus . IN ... 172
Rose-Hulman Institute of Technology ... IN ... 172
Saint Joseph's College ... IN ... 172
Saint Mary-of-the-Woods College ... IN ... 172
Saint Mary's College ... IN ... 172
Saint Meinrad School of Theology ... IN ... 173
Taylor University ... IN ... 173
TCM International Institute ... IN ... 173
Trine University ... IN ... 173
University of Evansville ... IN ... 173
University of Indianapolis ... IN ... 173
University of Notre Dame ... IN ... 174
University of Saint Francis ... IN ... 174
University of Southern Indiana ... IN ... 174
Valparaiso University ... IN ... 174
Vincennes University ... IN ... 174
Wabash College ... IN ... 175
AIB College of Business ... IA ... 175
Allen College ... IA ... 175
Ashford University ... IA ... 175
Briar Cliff University ... IA ... 176
Buena Vista University ... IA ... 176
Central College ... IA ... 176
Clarke University ... IA ... 176

&Clinton Community College ... IA ... 178
Coe College ... IA ... 176
Cornell College ... IA ... 177
Des Moines Area Community College ... IA ... 177
Des Moines University ... IA ... 177
Divine Word College ... IA ... 177
Dordt College ... IA ... 177
Drake University ... IA ... 177
&Ellsworth Community College ... IA ... 179
Emmaus Bible College ... IA ... 178
Faith Baptist Bible College and Seminary IA ... 178
Graceland University ... IA ... 178
Grand View University ... IA ... 178
Grinnell College ... IA ... 178
Hawkeye Community College ... IA ... 178
Indian Hills Community College ... IA ... 179
Iowa Central Community College ... IA ... 179
Iowa Lakes Community College ... IA ... 179
Iowa State University ... IA ... 175
Iowa Wesleyan College ... IA ... 179
Iowa Western Community College ... IA ... 179
Kaplan University ... IA ... 180
Kirkwood Community College ... IA ... 180
Loras College ... IA ... 180
Luther College ... IA ... 180
Maharishi University of Management ... IA ... 180
&Marshalltown Community College ... IA ... 179
Mercy College of Health Sciences ... IA ... 181
Morningside College ... IA ... 181
Mount Mercy University ... IA ... 181
&Muscatine Community College ... IA ... 178
North Iowa Area Community College ... IA ... 181
Northeast Iowa Community College ... IA ... 181
Northwest Iowa Community College ... IA ... 181
Northwestern College ... IA ... 181
Palmer College of Chiropractic ... IA ... 182
St. Ambrose University ... IA ... 182
St. Luke's College ... IA ... 182
&Scott Community College ... IA ... 178
Simpson College ... IA ... 182
Southeastern Community College ... IA ... 182
Southwestern Community College ... IA ... 182
University of Dubuque ... IA ... 182
University of Iowa ... IA ... 175
University of Northern Iowa ... IA ... 176
Upper Iowa University ... IA ... 183
Waldorf College ... IA ... 183
Wartburg College ... IA ... 183
Wartburg Theological Seminary ... IA ... 183
Western Iowa Tech Community College ... IA ... 183
William Penn University ... IA ... 183
Allen County Community College ... KS ... 183
Baker University ... KS ... 184
Barton County Community College ... KS ... 184
Benedictine College ... KS ... 184
Bethany College ... KS ... 184
Bethel College ... KS ... 184
Brown Mackie College-Salina ... KS ... 185
Butler Community College ... KS ... 185
Central Baptist Theological Seminary ... KS ... 185
Central Christian College of Kansas ... KS ... 185
Cleveland University - Kansas City ... KS ... 185
Cloud County Community College ... KS ... 185
Coffeyville Community College ... KS ... 185
Colby Community College ... KS ... 185
Cowley County Community College ... KS ... 186
Dodge City Community College ... KS ... 186
Donnelly College ... KS ... 186
Emporia State University ... KS ... 186
Flint Hills Technical College ... KS ... 186
Fort Hays State University ... KS ... 186
Fort Scott Community College ... KS ... 186
Friends University ... KS ... 186
Garden City Community College ... KS ... 187
Haskell Indian Nations University ... KS ... 187
Hesston College ... KS ... 187
Highland Community College ... KS ... 187
Hutchinson Community College and Area Vocational School ... KS ... 187
Independence Community College ... KS ... 187
Johnson County Community College ... KS ... 187
Kansas City Kansas Community College . KS ... 187
Kansas State University ... KS ... 188
Kansas Wesleyan University ... KS ... 188
Labette Community College ... KS ... 188
Manhattan Area Technical College ... KS ... 188
Manhattan Christian College ... KS ... 188
McPherson College ... KS ... 188
MidAmerica Nazarene University ... KS ... 188
Neosho County Community College ... KS ... 189
Newman University ... KS ... 189
North Central Kansas Technical College .. KS ... 189
Northwest Kansas Technical College ... KS ... 189
Ottawa University ... KS ... 189
Pittsburg State University ... KS ... 189
Pratt Community College ... KS ... 190
Saint Paul School of Theology ... KS ... 190
@Salina Area Technical College ... KS ... 190
Seward County Community College/Area Technical School ... KS ... 190
Southwestern College ... KS ... 190
Sterling College ... KS ... 190
Tabor College ... KS ... 190
United States Army Command and General Staff College ... KS ... 545
University of Kansas Main Campus ... KS ... 190
University of Saint Mary ... KS ... 191
Washburn University ... KS ... 191
Wichita Area Technical College ... KS ... 191
Wichita State University ... KS ... 191
Adrian College ... MI ... 238
Albion College ... MI ... 239
Alma College ... MI ... 239
Alpena Community College ... MI ... 239
Andrews University ... MI ... 239
Aquinas College ... MI ... 239
Baker College of Flint ... MI ... 239
Bay Mills Community College ... MI ... 240
Bay Noc Community College ... MI ... 240
Calvin College ... MI ... 240
Central Michigan University ... MI ... 240
Cleary University ... MI ... 241
College for Creative Studies ... MI ... 241
Concordia University ... MI ... 241
Cornerstone University ... MI ... 241
Cranbrook Academy of Art ... MI ... 241
Davenport University ... MI ... 241
Delta College ... MI ... 242
Eastern Michigan University ... MI ... 242
Ferris State University ... MI ... 242
Finlandia University ... MI ... 242
Glen Oaks Community College ... MI ... 242
Gogebic Community College ... MI ... 242
Grace Bible College ... MI ... 243
Grand Rapids Community College ... MI ... 243
Grand Valley State University ... MI ... 243
Great Lakes Christian College ... MI ... 243
Henry Ford Community College ... MI ... 243
Hillsdale College ... MI ... 243
Hope College ... MI ... 244
Jackson College ... MI ... 244
Kalamazoo College ... MI ... 244
Kalamazoo Valley Community College ... MI ... 244
Kellogg Community College ... MI ... 244
Kettering University ... MI ... 244
Keweenaw Bay Ojibwa Community College ... MI ... 245
Kirtland Community College ... MI ... 245
Kuyper College ... MI ... 245
Lake Michigan College ... MI ... 245
Lake Superior State University ... MI ... 245
Lansing Community College ... MI ... 245
Lawrence Technological University ... MI ... 245
Macomb Community College ... MI ... 246
Madonna University ... MI ... 246
Marygrove College ... MI ... 246
Michigan School of Professional Psychology ... MI ... 246
Michigan State University ... MI ... 246
Michigan Technological University ... MI ... 247
Mid Michigan Community College ... MI ... 247
Monroe County Community College ... MI ... 247
Montcalm Community College ... MI ... 247
Mott Community College ... MI ... 247
Muskegon Community College ... MI ... 247
North Central Michigan College ... MI ... 247
Northern Michigan University ... MI ... 248
Northwestern Michigan College ... MI ... 248
Northwood University ... MI ... 248
Oakland Community College ... MI ... 248
Oakland University ... MI ... 248
Olivet College ... MI ... 249
Robert B. Miller College ... MI ... 249
Rochester College ... MI ... 249
Sacred Heart Major Seminary ... MI ... 249
Saginaw Chippewa Tribal College ... MI ... 249
Saginaw Valley State University ... MI ... 249
St. Clair County Community College ... MI ... 249
Schoolcraft College ... MI ... 250
Siena Heights University ... MI ... 250
Southwestern Michigan College ... MI ... 250
Spring Arbor University ... MI ... 250
Thomas M. Cooley Law School ... MI ... 250
University of Detroit Mercy ... MI ... 250
University of Michigan-Ann Arbor ... MI ... 251
University of Michigan-Dearborn ... MI ... 251
University of Michigan-Flint ... MI ... 251
@Van Andel Institute Graduate School ... MI ... 251
Walsh College of Accountancy and Business Administration ... MI ... 251
Washtenaw Community College ... MI ... 252
Wayne County Community College District ... MI ... 252
Wayne State University ... MI ... 252
West Shore Community College ... MI ... 252
Western Michigan University ... MI ... 252
Adler Graduate School ... MN .. 253
Alexandria Technical & Community College ... MN .. 257
Anoka-Ramsey Community College ... MN .. 257
Anoka Technical College ... MN .. 257
Augsburg College ... MN .. 253
Bemidji State University ... MN .. 258
Bethany Lutheran College ... MN .. 253
Bethel University ... MN .. 253
Capella University ... MN .. 254
Carleton College ... MN .. 254
Central Lakes College ... MN .. 258
Century College ... MN .. 258
College of Saint Benedict ... MN .. 254
College of Saint Scholastica, The ... MN .. 254
Concordia College ... MN .. 255
Concordia University, St. Paul ... MN .. 255
Crown College ... MN .. 255
Dakota County Technical College ... MN .. 258
Dunwoody College of Technology ... MN .. 255
Fond du Lac Tribal and Community College ... MN .. 258
Gustavus Adolphus College ... MN .. 255
Hamline University ... MN .. 256
Hazelden Graduate School of Addiction Studies ... MN .. 256
Hennepin Technical College ... MN .. 258
Hibbing Community College, A Technical and Community College ... MN .. 258
Inver Hills Community College ... MN .. 258
Itasca Community College ... MN .. 258
Lake Superior College ... MN .. 259
Leech Lake Tribal College ... MN .. 256
Luther Seminary ... MN .. 256
Macalester College ... MN .. 256
Martin Luther College ... MN .. 256
Mayo Medical School ... MN .. 254
@McNally Smith College of Music ... MN .. 256
Mesabi Range Community & Technical College ... MN .. 259
Metropolitan State University ... MN .. 259
Minneapolis College of Art Design ... MN .. 257
Minneapolis Community and Technical College ... MN .. 259
Minnesota State College - Southeast Technical ... MN .. 259
Minnesota State Community and Technical College ... MN .. 259
Minnesota State University Moorhead ... MN .. 259
Minnesota State University, Mankato ... MN .. 259
Minnesota West Community and Technical College ... MN .. 260
Normandale Community College ... MN .. 260
North Central University ... MN .. 262
North Hennepin Community College ... MN .. 260
Northland Community and Technical College ... MN .. 260
Northwest Technical College ... MN .. 260
Northwestern College ... MN .. 263
Northwestern Health Sciences University . MN .. 263
Pine Technical College ... MN .. 260
Rainy River Community College ... MN .. 260
Rasmussen College - St. Cloud ... MN .. 263
Ridgewater College ... MN .. 260
Riverland Community College ... MN .. 260
Rochester Community and Technical College ... MN .. 261
St. Catherine University ... MN .. 263
St. Cloud State University ... MN .. 261
Saint Cloud Technical and Community College ... MN .. 261
Saint John's University ... MN .. 263
Saint Mary's University of Minnesota ... MN .. 264
St. Olaf College ... MN .. 264
Saint Paul College-A Community & Technical College ... MN .. 261
South Central College ... MN .. 261
Southwest Minnesota State University ... MN .. 261
United Theological Seminary of the Twin Cities ... MN .. 264
University of Minnesota-Crookston ... MN .. 264
University of Minnesota Duluth ... MN .. 264
University of Minnesota-Morris ... MN .. 264
University of Minnesota-Twin Cities ... MN .. 264
University of Saint Thomas ... MN .. 265
Vermilion Community College ... MN .. 261
Walden University ... MN .. 265
#White Earth Tribal and Community College ... MN .. 265
Winona State University ... MN .. 262
A. T. Still University of Health Sciences ... MO .. 271
Aquinas Institute of Theology ... MO .. 271
Avila University ... MO .. 271
Baptist Bible College ... MO .. 271
Calvary Bible College and Theological Seminary ... MO .. 271
@Central Christian College of the Bible ... MO .. 272
Central Methodist University ... MO .. 272
College of the Ozarks ... MO .. 272
Columbia College ... MO .. 272
Conception Seminary College ... MO .. 272
Concordia Seminary ... MO .. 272
Cottey College ... MO .. 273
Covenant Theological Seminary ... MO .. 273
Cox College ... MO .. 273
Crowder College ... MO .. 273
Culver-Stockton College ... MO .. 273
Drury University ... MO .. 273
East Central College ... MO .. 273
Eden Theological Seminary ... MO .. 274
Evangel University ... MO .. 274
Fontbonne University ... MO .. 274
Global University ... MO .. 274
Goldfarb School of Nursing at Barnes-Jewish College ... MO .. 274
Hannibal-La Grange University ... MO .. 274
Harris-Stowe State University ... MO .. 275
Jefferson College ... MO .. 275
Kansas City Art Institute ... MO .. 275
Kansas City University of Medicine & Biosciences ... MO .. 275
Kenrick-Glennon Seminary-Kenrick School of Theology ... MO .. 275
Lincoln University ... MO .. 276
Lindenwood University ... MO .. 276
Linn State Technical College ... MO .. 276
Logan College of Chiropractic ... MO .. 276
Maryville University of Saint Louis ... MO .. 276
&Metropolitan Community College - Blue River ... MO .. 277
&Metropolitan Community College - Business and Technology ... MO .. 277
&Metropolitan Community College - Longview ... MO .. 277
&Metropolitan Community College - Maple Woods ... MO .. 277
&Metropolitan Community College - Penn Valley ... MO .. 277
Midwestern Baptist Theological Seminary MO .. 277
Mineral Area College ... MO .. 278
Missouri Baptist University ... MO .. 278
Missouri Southern State University ... MO .. 278
Missouri State University ... MO .. 278
Missouri State University - West Plains ... MO .. 278
Missouri University of Science & Technology ... MO .. 284
Missouri Valley College ... MO .. 278
Missouri Western State University ... MO .. 279
Moberly Area Community College ... MO .. 279
North Central Missouri College ... MO .. 279
Northwest Missouri State University ... MO .. 279
Ozarks Technical Community College ... MO .. 279
Park University ... MO .. 280
Ranken Technical College ... MO .. 280
Research College of Nursing ... MO .. 280
Rockhurst University ... MO .. 280
St. Charles Community College ... MO .. 280
St. Louis College of Pharmacy ... MO .. 281
Saint Louis Community College at Forest Park ... MO .. 281
Saint Louis University ... MO .. 281
Saint Luke's College of Health Sciences .. MO .. 281
School of Professional Psychology at Forest Institute, The ... MO .. 281
Southeast Missouri Hospital College of Nursing and Health Sciences ... MO .. 282
Southeast Missouri State University ... MO .. 282
Southwest Baptist University ... MO .. 282
State Fair Community College ... MO .. 282
Stephens College ... MO .. 282
Three Rivers Community College ... MO .. 282
Truman State University ... MO .. 282
University of Central Missouri ... MO .. 283
University of Missouri - Columbia ... MO .. 283
University of Missouri - Kansas City ... MO .. 283
University of Missouri - Saint Louis ... MO .. 283
Washington University in St. Louis ... MO .. 284
Webster University ... MO .. 284
Wentworth Military Academy and Junior College ... MO .. 285
Westminster College ... MO .. 285
William Jewell College ... MO .. 285
William Woods University ... MO .. 285
Bellevue University ... NE ... 288
Bryan College of Health Sciences ... NE ... 288
Central Community College ... NE ... 288
Chadron State College ... NE ... 291
Clarkson College ... NE ... 288
College of Saint Mary ... NE ... 289
Concordia University ... NE ... 289
Creighton University ... NE ... 289
Doane College ... NE ... 289
Grace University ... NE ... 289
Hastings College ... NE ... 289
Little Priest Tribal College ... NE ... 290
Metropolitan Community College ... NE ... 290
Mid-Plains Community College ... NE ... 290
Midland University ... NE ... 290
Nebraska Indian Community College ... NE ... 290
Nebraska Methodist College ... NE ... 291
Nebraska Wesleyan University ... NE ... 291
Northeast Community College ... NE ... 291
Peru State College ... NE ... 291
Saint Gregory the Great Seminary ... NE ... 292
Southeast Community College ... NE ... 292
Union College ... NE ... 292
University of Nebraska at Kearney ... NE ... 292
University of Nebraska at Omaha ... NE ... 293
University of Nebraska - Lincoln ... NE ... 292
University of Nebraska Medical Center ... NE ... 292
University of Nebraska - Nebraska College of Technical Agriculture ... NE ... 293
Wayne State College ... NE ... 291
Western Nebraska Community College ... NE ... 293
York College ... NE ... 293
Central New Mexico Community College . NM .. 309
Clovis Community College ... NM .. 309
Eastern New Mexico University Main Campus ... NM .. 309

Eastern New Mexico University-Roswell ... NM .. 309
Institute of American Indian Arts ... NM .. 309
Luna Community College ... NM .. 309
Mesalands Community College ... NM .. 309
Navajo Technical College ... NM .. 310
New Mexico Highlands University ... NM .. 310
New Mexico Institute of Mining and Technology ... NM .. 310
New Mexico Junior College ... NM .. 310
New Mexico Military Institute ... NM .. 310
New Mexico State University at Alamogordo ... NM .. 310
New Mexico State University at Carlsbad . NM .. 311
New Mexico State University Dona Ana Community College ... NM .. 311
New Mexico State University Main Campus ... NM .. 310
Northern New Mexico College ... NM .. 311
St. John's College ... NM .. 311
San Juan College ... NM .. 311
Santa Fe Community College ... NM .. 311
Santa Fe University of Art and Design ... NM .. 311
Southwestern College ... NM .. 312
@Southwestern Indian Polytechnic Institute NM .. 312
University of New Mexico Main Campus .. NM .. 312
University of the Southwest ... NM .. 312
Western New Mexico University ... NM .. 312
Bismarck State College ... ND .. 372
Cankdeska Cikana Community College ... ND .. 370
Dakota College at Bottineau ... ND .. 372
Dickinson State University ... ND .. 371
Ft. Berthold Community College ... ND .. 371
Lake Region State College ... ND .. 372
Mayville State University ... ND .. 371
Minot State University ... ND .. 371
North Dakota State College of Science ... ND .. 372
North Dakota State University Main Campus ... ND .. 371
Sanford College of Nursing ... ND .. 372
Sitting Bull College ... ND .. 372
Turtle Mountain Community College ... ND .. 373
United Tribes Technical College ... ND .. 373
University of Jamestown ... ND .. 373
University of Mary ... ND .. 373
University of North Dakota Main Campus . ND .. 371
Valley City State University ... ND .. 372
Williston State College ... ND .. 372
Air Force Institute of Technology ... OH .. 544
Antioch University Midwest ... OH .. 373
Art Academy of Cincinnati ... OH .. 373
Ashland University ... OH .. 374
Athenaeum of Ohio ... OH .. 374
Aultman College of Nursing and Health Sciences ... OH .. 374
Baldwin Wallace University ... OH .. 374
Belmont College ... OH .. 374
Bluffton University ... OH .. 374
Bowling Green State University ... OH .. 374
Capital University ... OH .. 375
Case Western Reserve University ... OH .. 375
Cedarville University ... OH .. 375
Central Ohio Technical College ... OH .. 376
Central State University ... OH .. 376
Chatfield College ... OH .. 376
Christ College of Nursing and Health Sciences, The ... OH .. 376
Cincinnati Christian University ... OH .. 376
Cincinnati College of Mortuary Science ... OH .. 376
Cincinnati State Technical and Community College ... OH .. 376
Clark State Community College ... OH .. 377
Cleveland Institute of Art ... OH .. 377
Cleveland Institute of Music ... OH .. 377
Cleveland State University ... OH .. 377
College of Mount St. Joseph ... OH .. 377
College of Wooster, The ... OH .. 377
Columbus College of Art & Design ... OH .. 378
Columbus State Community College ... OH .. 378
Cuyahoga Community College ... OH .. 378
Davis College ... OH .. 378
Defiance College, The ... OH .. 379
Denison University ... OH .. 379
Eastern Gateway Community College - Jefferson County Campus ... OH .. 379
Edison State Community College ... OH .. 379
Franciscan University of Steubenville ... OH .. 379
Franklin University ... OH .. 380
God's Bible School and College ... OH .. 380
Good Samaritan College of Nursing and Health Science ... OH .. 380
Heidelberg University ... OH .. 380
Hiram College ... OH .. 380
Hocking College ... OH .. 380
James A. Rhodes State College ... OH .. 381
John Carroll University ... OH .. 381
Kent State University Main Campus ... OH .. 382
Kenyon College ... OH .. 382
Kettering College ... OH .. 382
Lake Erie College ... OH .. 382
Lakeland Community College ... OH .. 382
Lorain County Community College ... OH .. 383
Lourdes University ... OH .. 383
Malone University ... OH .. 383
Marietta College ... OH .. 383
Marion Technical College ... OH .. 383
Mercy College of Ohio ... OH .. 383
Methodist Theological School in Ohio ... OH .. 383
Miami University ... OH .. 384
Mount Carmel College of Nursing ... OH .. 384
Mount Vernon Nazarene University ... OH .. 384
Muskingum University ... OH .. 384
North Central State College ... OH .. 385
Northeast Ohio Medical University ... OH .. 385
Northwest State Community College ... OH .. 385
Notre Dame College ... OH .. 385
Oberlin College ... OH .. 385
Ohio Christian University ... OH .. 385
Ohio Dominican University ... OH .. 386
Ohio Northern University ... OH .. 386
Ohio State University Agricultural Technical Institute, The ... OH .. 386
Ohio State University Main Campus, The . OH .. 386
Ohio University Main Campus ... OH .. 387
Ohio Wesleyan University ... OH .. 387
Otterbein University ... OH .. 387
Owens Community College ... OH .. 387
Pontifical College Josephinum ... OH .. 388
Saint Mary Seminary and Graduate School of Theology ... OH .. 388
Shawnee State University ... OH .. 388
Sinclair Community College ... OH .. 388
Southern State Community College ... OH .. 389
Stark State College ... OH .. 389
Terra State Community College ... OH .. 389
Tiffin University ... OH .. 389
Trinity Lutheran Seminary ... OH .. 390
Union Institute & University ... OH .. 390
United Theological Seminary ... OH .. 390
University of Akron-Wayne College, The .. OH .. 390
University of Akron, Main Campus, The ... OH .. 390
University of Cincinnati-Blue Ash College . OH .. 391
University of Cincinnati-Clermont College . OH .. 391
University of Cincinnati Main Campus ... OH .. 390
University of Dayton ... OH .. 391
University of Findlay, The ... OH .. 391
University of Mount Union ... OH .. 391
University of Northwestern Ohio ... OH .. 391
University of Rio Grande ... OH .. 392
University of Toledo ... OH .. 392
Urbana University ... OH .. 392
Ursuline College ... OH .. 392
Walsh University ... OH .. 392
Washington State Community College ... OH .. 392
Wilberforce University ... OH .. 393
Wilmington College ... OH .. 393
Winebrenner Theological Seminary ... OH .. 393
Wittenberg University ... OH .. 393
Wright State University Main Campus ... OH .. 393
Xavier University ... OH .. 393
Youngstown State University ... OH .. 394
Zane State College ... OH .. 394
Bacone College ... OK .. 394
Cameron University ... OK .. 394
Carl Albert State College ... OK .. 394
@College of the Muscogee Nation ... OK .. 395
@Comanche Nation College ... OK .. 395
Connors State College ... OK .. 395
East Central University ... OK .. 395
Eastern Oklahoma State College ... OK .. 395
Langston University ... OK .. 395
Mid-America Christian University ... OK .. 396
Murray State College ... OK .. 396
Northeastern Oklahoma Agricultural and Mechanical College ... OK .. 396
Northeastern State University ... OK .. 396
Northern Oklahoma College ... OK .. 396
Northwestern Oklahoma State University . OK .. 396
Oklahoma Baptist University ... OK .. 397
Oklahoma Christian University ... OK .. 397
Oklahoma City Community College ... OK .. 397
Oklahoma City University ... OK .. 397
Oklahoma Panhandle State University ... OK .. 397
Oklahoma State University ... OK .. 397
Oklahoma State University Institute of Technology-Okmulgee ... OK .. 398
Oklahoma State University - Oklahoma City ... OK .. 398
Oklahoma Wesleyan University ... OK .. 398
Oral Roberts University ... OK .. 398
Phillips Theological Seminary ... OK .. 398
Redlands Community College ... OK .. 399
Rogers State University ... OK .. 399
Rose State College ... OK .. 399
St. Gregory's University ... OK .. 399
Seminole State College ... OK .. 399
Southeastern Oklahoma State University . OK .. 399
Southern Nazarene University ... OK .. 399
Southwestern Christian University ... OK .. 400
Southwestern Oklahoma State University . OK .. 400
Tulsa Community College ... OK .. 400
University of Central Oklahoma ... OK .. 400
University of Oklahoma Norman Campus . OK .. 401
University of Science and Arts of Oklahoma ... OK .. 401
University of Tulsa ... OK .. 401
#Western Oklahoma State College ... OK .. 401
Augustana College ... SD ... 449
Black Hills State University ... SD ... 451
Dakota State University ... SD ... 451
Dakota Wesleyan University ... SD ... 450
Kilian Community College ... SD ... 450
Lake Area Technical Institute ... SD ... 450
Mitchell Technical Institute ... SD ... 450
Mount Marty College ... SD ... 450
National American University ... SD ... 450
Northern State University ... SD ... 451
Oglala Lakota College ... SD ... 450
Presentation College ... SD ... 450
Sinte Gleska University ... SD ... 451
Sioux Falls Seminary ... SD ... 451
Sisseton-Wahpeton College ... SD ... 451
South Dakota School of Mines and Technology ... SD ... 452
South Dakota State University ... SD ... 452
Southeast Technical Institute ... SD ... 452
University of Sioux Falls ... SD ... 452
University of South Dakota, The ... SD ... 451
Western Dakota Technical Institute ... SD ... 452
Alderson Broaddus University ... WV .. 526
American Public University System ... WV .. 526
Appalachian Bible College ... WV .. 526
Bethany College ... WV .. 526
Blue Ridge Community and Technical College ... WV .. 527
Bluefield State College ... WV .. 529
Bridgemont Community and Technical College ... WV .. 527
Concord University ... WV .. 529
Davis & Elkins College ... WV .. 526
Eastern West Virginia Community and Technical College ... WV .. 528
Fairmont State University ... WV .. 529
Future Generations Graduate School ... WV .. 526
Glenville State College ... WV .. 529
Huntington Junior College ... WV .. 526
Kanawha Valley Community & Technical College ... WV .. 528
Marshall University ... WV .. 529
Mountwest Community and Technical College ... WV .. 528
New River Community and Technical College ... WV .. 528
#Ohio Valley University ... WV .. 527
Pierpont Community & Technical College WV .. 528
Salem International University ... WV .. 527
Shepherd University ... WV .. 529
Southern West Virginia Community and Technical College ... WV .. 528
University of Charleston ... WV .. 527
West Liberty University ... WV .. 530
West Virginia Northern Community College ... WV .. 528
@West Virginia School of Osteopathic Medicine ... WV .. 530
West Virginia State University ... WV .. 530
West Virginia University ... WV .. 530
West Virginia University at Parkersburg ... WV .. 530
West Virginia Wesleyan College ... WV .. 531
Wheeling Jesuit University ... WV .. 531
Alverno College ... WI ... 531
Bellin College, Inc. ... WI ... 531
Beloit College ... WI ... 531
Blackhawk Technical College ... WI ... 539
Cardinal Stritch University ... WI ... 532
Carroll University ... WI ... 532
Carthage College ... WI ... 532
Chippewa Valley Technical College ... WI ... 539
College of Menominee Nation ... WI ... 532
Columbia College of Nursing ... WI ... 532
Concordia University Wisconsin ... WI ... 532
Edgewood College ... WI ... 532
Fox Valley Technical College ... WI ... 539
Gateway Technical College ... WI ... 540
Herzing University ... WI ... 533
Lac Courte Oreilles Ojibwa Community College ... WI ... 533
Lakeland College ... WI ... 533
Lakeshore Technical College ... WI ... 540
Lawrence University ... WI ... 533
Madison Area Technical College ... WI ... 540
Maranatha Baptist Bible College & Seminary ... WI ... 533
Marian University ... WI ... 534
Marquette University ... WI ... 534
Medical College of Wisconsin ... WI ... 534
Mid-State Technical College ... WI ... 540
Milwaukee Area Technical College ... WI ... 540
Milwaukee Institute of Art & Design ... WI ... 534
Milwaukee School of Engineering ... WI ... 534
Moraine Park Technical College ... WI ... 540
Mount Mary University ... WI ... 535
Nicolet Area Technical College ... WI ... 540
Northcentral Technical College ... WI ... 541
Northeast Wisconsin Technical College ... WI ... 541
Northland College ... WI ... 535
Ripon College ... WI ... 535
Sacred Heart School of Theology ... WI ... 535
Saint Norbert College ... WI ... 535
Silver Lake College of the Holy Family ... WI ... 536
Southwest Wisconsin Technical College .. WI ... 541
University of Wisconsin Colleges ... WI ... 538
University of Wisconsin-Eau Claire ... WI ... 536
University of Wisconsin-Green Bay ... WI ... 536
University of Wisconsin-La Crosse ... WI ... 536
University of Wisconsin-Madison ... WI ... 536
University of Wisconsin-Milwaukee ... WI ... 537
University of Wisconsin-Oshkosh ... WI ... 537
University of Wisconsin-Parkside ... WI ... 537
University of Wisconsin-Platteville ... WI ... 537
University of Wisconsin-River Falls ... WI ... 537
University of Wisconsin-Stevens Point ... WI ... 538
University of Wisconsin-Stout ... WI ... 538
University of Wisconsin-Superior ... WI ... 538
University of Wisconsin-Whitewater ... WI ... 538
Viterbo University ... WI ... 539
Waukesha County Technical College ... WI ... 541
Western Technical College ... WI ... 541
Wisconsin Indianhead Technical College . WI ... 541
Wisconsin Lutheran College ... WI ... 539
Wisconsin School of Professional Psychology ... WI ... 539
Casper College ... WY .. 542
Central Wyoming College ... WY .. 542
Eastern Wyoming College ... WY .. 542
Laramie County Community College ... WY .. 543
Northern Wyoming Community College District ... WY .. 543
Northwest College ... WY .. 543
University of Wyoming ... WY .. 543
Western Wyoming Community College ... WY .. 543

NMT: Joint Review Committee on Education Programs in Nuclear Medicine Technology: nuclear medicine technology (C,A,B)

University of Alabama at Birmingham ... AL ... 8
Gateway Community College ... AZ ... 14
University of Arkansas for Medical Sciences ... AR ... 24
Kaiser Permanente School of Allied Health Sciences ... CA ... 49
Gateway Community College ... CT ... 88
Lincoln College of New England ... CT ... 90
Delaware Technical Community College, Stanton-Wilmington Campus ... DE ... 93
Adventist University of Health Sciences ... FL ... 97
Hillsborough Community College ... FL ... 106
Santa Fe College ... FL ... 113
Armstrong Atlantic State University ... GA .. 120
Georgia Regents University ... GA .. 126
College of DuPage ... IL ... 142
Triton College ... IL ... 161
Indiana University-Purdue University Indianapolis ... IN ... 168
Allen College ... IA ... 175
Mercy College of Health Sciences ... IA ... 181
University of Iowa ... IA ... 175
Bluegrass Community and Technical College ... KY ... 194
Delgado Community College ... LA ... 203
Central Maine Medical Center College of Nursing and Health Professions ... ME .. 209
Frederick Community College ... MD .. 214
Johns Hopkins University ... MD .. 215
Prince George's Community College ... MD .. 217
MCPHS University ... MA .. 233
Regis College ... MA .. 236
Salem State University ... MA .. 230
#Springfield Technical Community College MA .. 233
University of Massachusetts Medical School ... MA .. 229
Worcester State University ... MA .. 230
Ferris State University ... MI ... 242
Saint Mary's University of Minnesota ... MN .. 264
University of Mississippi Medical Center ... MS .. 270
Saint Louis University ... MO .. 281
University of Missouri - Columbia ... MO .. 283
University of Nebraska Medical Center ... NE .. 292
University of Nevada, Las Vegas ... NV .. 294
Gloucester County College ... NJ .. 302
City University of New York Bronx Community College ... NY ... 317
Molloy College ... NY ... 331
University at Buffalo-SUNY ... NY ... 341
Caldwell Community College and Technical Institute ... NC .. 358
Forsyth Technical Community College ... NC .. 360
University of North Carolina at Chapel Hill NC .. 368
Cuyahoga Community College ... OH .. 378
Ohio State University Main Campus, The . OH .. 386
University of Cincinnati Main Campus ... OH .. 390
University of Findlay, The ... OH .. 391
Community College of Allegheny County . PA ... 413
Lancaster General College of Nursing and Health Sciences ... PA ... 421
Misericordia University ... PA ... 424
Robert Morris University ... PA ... 431
#Thomas Jefferson University ... PA ... 434
University of Puerto Rico-Medical Sciences Campus ... PR ... 554
Midlands Technical College ... SC ... 445
Southeast Technical Institute ... SD ... 452
Baptist College of Health Sciences ... TN ... 453
Chattanooga State Community College ... TN ... 460

South College ... TN ... 458
Vanderbilt University ... TN ... 463
Amarillo College ... TX ... 465
Del Mar College ... TX ... 471
Galveston College ... TX ... 472
Houston Community College ... TX ... 473
University of the Incarnate Word ... TX ... 490
University of Utah, The ... UT ... 496
University of Vermont ... VT ... 500
Old Dominion University ... VA ... 507
Virginia Commonwealth University ... VA ... 511
Bellevue College ... WA .. 517
Kanawha Valley Community & Technical College ... WV .. 528
West Virginia University ... WV .. 530
Wheeling Jesuit University ... WV .. 531

NRPA: National Recreation and Park Association: recreation, park resources, and leisure studies (B)

Arizona State University ... AZ ... 11
Northern Arizona University ... AZ ... 16
Arkansas Tech University ... AR ... 20
California Polytechnic State University-San Luis Obispo ... CA ... 32
California State University-Chico ... CA ... 33
California State University-Fresno ... CA ... 33
California State University-Long Beach ... CA ... 33
California State University-Sacramento ... CA ... 34
San Francisco State University ... CA ... 35
San Jose State University ... CA ... 36
Metropolitan State University of Denver ... CO ... 83
Georgia Southern University ... GA .. 126
University of Georgia ... GA .. 133
University of Idaho ... ID ... 139
Chicago State University ... IL ... 141
Eastern Illinois University ... IL ... 144
Illinois State University ... IL ... 147
University of Illinois at Urbana-Champaign IL ... 162
University of St. Francis ... IL ... 162
Western Illinois University ... IL ... 162
Indiana University Bloomington ... IN ... 167
University of Northern Iowa ... IA ... 176
Kansas State University ... KS ... 188
Pittsburg State University ... KS ... 189
Eastern Kentucky University ... KY ... 193
Western Kentucky University ... KY ... 200
Grambling State University ... LA ... 207
University of Maine at Machias ... ME .. 212
Frostburg State University ... MD .. 220
Springfield College ... MA .. 236
Central Michigan University ... MI ... 240
Ferris State University ... MI ... 242
Minnesota State University, Mankato ... MN .. 259
University of Mississippi ... MS .. 270
University of Southern Mississippi ... MS .. 270
Missouri State University ... MO .. 278
Northwest Missouri State University ... MO .. 279
Southeast Missouri State University ... MO .. 282
University of Missouri - Columbia ... MO .. 283
University of New Hampshire ... NH .. 298
Ithaca College ... NY ... 327
State University of New York College at Cortland ... NY ... 343
State University of New York, The College at Brockport ... NY ... 342
Appalachian State University ... NC .. 367
East Carolina University ... NC .. 367
North Carolina Central University ... NC .. 368
North Carolina State University ... NC .. 368
University of North Carolina at Greensboro ... NC .. 369
University of North Carolina Wilmington ... NC .. 369
Winston-Salem State University ... NC .. 370
Bowling Green State University ... OH .. 374
Kent State University Main Campus ... OH .. 382
Ohio University Main Campus ... OH .. 387
University of Toledo ... OH .. 392
Oklahoma State University ... OK .. 397
California University of Pennsylvania ... PA ... 428
East Stroudsburg University of Pennsylvania ... PA ... 428
Lock Haven University ... PA ... 429
Slippery Rock University of Pennsylvania . PA ... 429
Temple University ... PA ... 433
York College of Pennsylvania ... PA ... 438
Benedict College ... SC ... 441
Clemson University ... SC ... 442
Middle Tennessee State University ... TN ... 459
University of Tennessee, Knoxville ... TN ... 463
Texas A & M University ... TX ... 483
Texas State University-San Marcos ... TX ... 487
University of North Texas ... TX ... 490
Brigham Young University ... UT ... 495
University of Utah, The ... UT ... 496
Utah State University ... UT ... 497
George Mason University ... VA ... 505
Longwood University ... VA ... 506
Old Dominion University ... VA ... 507
Radford University ... VA ... 508
Virginia Wesleyan College ... VA ... 515
Eastern Washington University ... WA .. 519
Western Washington University ... WA .. 525

University of Wisconsin-La Crosse ... WI ... 536

NUR: Accreditation Commission for Education in Nursing: nursing (B,M,D)

Oakwood University ... AL ... 6
Troy University ... AL ... 7
Tuskegee University ... AL ... 8
University of Alaska Anchorage ... AK ... 10
Brookline College ... AZ ... 12
Arkansas State University-Jonesboro ... AR ... 19
Arkansas Tech University ... AR ... 20
Harding University Main Campus ... AR ... 21
Southern Arkansas University ... AR ... 23
University of Arkansas at Fort Smith ... AR ... 24
University of Arkansas at Little Rock ... AR ... 24
University of Arkansas at Monticello ... AR ... 24
Charles R. Drew University of Medicine & Science ... CA ... 38
Pacific Union College ... CA ... 57
Sonoma State University ... CA ... 36
Colorado State University-Pueblo ... CO ... 80
Denver School of Nursing ... CO ... 81
Metropolitan State University of Denver ... CO ... 83
Platt College ... CO ... 84
Quinnipiac University ... CT ... 91
St. Vincent's College ... CT ... 91
Delaware State University ... DE ... 93
Wesley College ... DE ... 94
University of the District of Columbia ... DC ... 97
Adventist University of Health Sciences ... FL ... 97
Bethune Cookman University ... FL ... 99
Broward College ... FL ... 99
Edison State College ... FL ... 101
Florida Agricultural and Mechanical University ... FL ... 114
Florida State College at Jacksonville ... FL ... 105
Indian River State College ... FL ... 106
Miami Dade College ... FL ... 109
Polk State College ... FL ... 110
State College of Florida, Manatee-Sarasota ... FL ... 114
University of Tampa ... FL ... 118
Albany State University ... GA .. 119
College of Coastal Georgia ... GA .. 123
Georgia College & State University ... GA .. 125
Georgia Regents University ... GA .. 126
Georgia Southwestern State University ... GA .. 126
Gordon State College ... GA .. 127
LaGrange College ... GA .. 128
Middle Georgia State College ... GA .. 128
Piedmont College ... GA .. 130
Thomas University ... GA .. 132
University of North Georgia ... GA .. 133
University of Guam ... GU .. 546
University of Hawaii at Hilo ... HI ... 136
Boise State University ... ID ... 137
Brigham Young University-Idaho ... ID ... 137
Bradley University ... IL ... 140
Chicago State University ... IL ... 141
Governors State University ... IL ... 145
Methodist College ... IL ... 152
Rockford University ... IL ... 157
Saint Francis Medical Center College of Nursing ... IL ... 158
St. John's College ... IL ... 158
Bethel College ... IN ... 164
Indiana State University ... IN ... 167
Indiana University East ... IN ... 167
Indiana University Northwest ... IN ... 168
Indiana University-Purdue University Fort Wayne ... IN ... 168
Indiana University-Purdue University Indianapolis ... IN ... 168
Purdue University Calumet ... IN ... 171
Purdue University North Central Campus . IN ... 172
University of Evansville ... IN ... 173
Vincennes University ... IN ... 174
Emporia State University ... KS ... 186
Kansas Wesleyan University ... KS ... 188
Frontier Nursing University ... KY ... 194
Kentucky State University ... KY ... 197
Midway College ... KY ... 197
Northern Kentucky University ... KY ... 198
Thomas More College ... KY ... 199
University of Pikeville ... KY ... 200
Dillard University ... LA ... 201
Grambling State University ... LA ... 207
Louisiana State University at Alexandria .. LA ... 205
Loyola University New Orleans ... LA ... 205
Our Lady of Holy Cross College ... LA ... 206
Our Lady of the Lake College ... LA ... 206
University of New England ... ME .. 213
Bowie State University ... MD .. 220
Coppin State University ... MD .. 220
Notre Dame of Maryland University ... MD .. 217
Washington Adventist University ... MD .. 221
Anna Maria College ... MA .. 222
Becker College-Worcester ... MA .. 223
Endicott College ... MA .. 226
Regis College ... MA .. 236
University of Massachusetts Dartmouth ... MA .. 229
Andrews University ... MI ... 239
Davenport University ... MI ... 241
Ferris State University ... MI ... 242
Lake Superior State University ... MI ... 245
St. Catherine University ... MN .. 263
Alcorn State University ... MS .. 265
Lincoln University ... MO .. 276
Missouri Southern State University ... MO .. 278
Southwest Baptist University ... MO .. 282
Webster University ... MO .. 284
Montana State University - Northern ... MT .. 287
Salish Kootenai College ... MT .. 288
Bryan College of Health Sciences ... NE .. 288
Clarkson College ... NE .. 288
College of Saint Mary ... NE .. 289
Midland University ... NE .. 290
Nebraska Wesleyan University ... NE .. 291
Great Basin College ... NV .. 294
Roseman University of Health Sciences ... NV .. 295
Franklin Pierce University ... NH .. 296
Rivier University ... NH .. 297
College of Saint Elizabeth ... NJ ... 300
Kean University ... NJ ... 302
New Jersey City University ... NJ ... 303
Ramapo College of New Jersey ... NJ ... 305
Thomas Edison State College ... NJ ... 308
Eastern New Mexico University Main Campus ... NM .. 309
City University of New York College of Staten Island ... NY ... 317
City University of New York Medgar Evers College ... NY ... 319
City University of New York York College NY ... 319
Daemen College ... NY ... 322
Elmira College ... NY ... 323
Excelsior College ... NY ... 324
Farmingdale State College ... NY ... 346
Maria College of Albany ... NY ... 330
New York City College of Technology/City University of New York ... NY ... 319
Saint Joseph's College, New York ... NY ... 339
State University of New York College of Technology at Delhi ... NY ... 345
Trocaire College ... NY ... 348
Wagner College ... NY ... 350
Barton College ... NC .. 352
Gardner-Webb University ... NC .. 354
North Carolina Agricultural and Technical State University ... NC .. 367
North Carolina Central University ... NC .. 368
University of North Carolina at Chapel Hill NC .. 368
University of North Carolina at Greensboro ... NC .. 369
Dickinson State University ... ND .. 371
Minot State University ... ND .. 371
University of Jamestown ... ND .. 373
Case Western Reserve University ... OH .. 375
Franciscan University of Steubenville ... OH .. 379
Kettering College ... OH .. 382
Mercy College of Ohio ... OH .. 383
Shawnee State University ... OH .. 388
University of Rio Grande ... OH .. 392
Walsh University ... OH .. 392
Youngstown State University ... OH .. 394
Bacone College ... OK .. 394
East Central University ... OK .. 395
Langston University ... OK .. 395
Northeastern State University ... OK .. 396
Northwestern Oklahoma State University . OK .. 396
Oklahoma City University ... OK .. 397
Oklahoma Panhandle State University ... OK .. 397
Rogers State University ... OK .. 399
Southwestern Oklahoma State University . OK .. 400
University of Central Oklahoma ... OK .. 400
University of Tulsa ... OK .. 401
Cedar Crest College ... PA ... 412
Clarion University of Pennsylvania ... PA ... 428
DeSales University ... PA ... 414
East Stroudsburg University of Pennsylvania ... PA ... 428
Gwynedd-Mercy University ... PA ... 417
La Roche College ... PA ... 420
Lock Haven University ... PA ... 429
Mansfield University of Pennsylvania ... PA ... 429
Marywood University ... PA ... 423
Millersville University of Pennsylvania ... PA ... 429
Mount Aloysius College ... PA ... 424
Neumann University ... PA ... 424
Penn State University Park ... PA ... 426
Pennsylvania College of Technology ... PA ... 427
Slippery Rock University of Pennsylvania . PA ... 429
Inter American University of Puerto Rico Aguadilla Campus ... PR ... 549
Inter American University of Puerto Rico Arecibo Campus ... PR ... 549
Inter American University of Puerto Rico Metropolitan Campus ... PR ... 550
Pontifical Catholic University of Puerto Rico, The ... PR ... 552
Universidad Adventista de las Antillas ... PR ... 553
Universidad Metropolitana ... PR ... 552
University of Puerto Rico at Arecibo ... PR ... 553
University of Puerto Rico-Humacao ... PR ... 554
University of Puerto Rico-Mayaguez Campus ... PR ... 554
University of the Sacred Heart ... PR ... 555

Charleston Southern University ... SC ... 441
Coastal Carolina University ... SC ... 442
Francis Marion University ... SC ... 444
Presentation College ... SD ... 450
Aquinas College ... TN ... 452
Austin Peay State University ... TN ... 459
Cumberland University ... TN ... 454
Lincoln Memorial University ... TN ... 456
Lipscomb University ... TN ... 456
South College ... TN ... 458
Southern Adventist University ... TN ... 458
Tennessee State University ... TN ... 459
University of Tennessee at Martin ... TN ... 463
Vanderbilt University ... TN ... 463
Angelo State University ... TX ... 465
Houston Baptist University ... TX ... 473
Lamar University ... TX ... 486
Lubbock Christian University ... TX ... 476
Prairie View A & M University ... TX ... 482
Sam Houston State University ... TX ... 487
Stephen F. Austin State University ... TX ... 482
Texas A & M International University ... TX ... 483
University of Texas at Brownsville and Texas Southmost College, The ... TX ... 491
Wayland Baptist University ... TX ... 494
Dixie State College of Utah ... UT ... 497
Utah Valley University ... UT ... 497
Weber State University ... UT ... 497
University of the Virgin Islands ... VI ... 555
ECPI College of Technology ... VA ... 504
Norfolk State University ... VA ... 507
Virginia Commonwealth University ... VA ... 511
Walla Walla University ... WA ... 524
Alderson Broaddus University ... WV .. 526
Marshall University ... WV .. 529
University of Charleston ... WV .. 527
West Virginia Wesleyan College ... WV .. 531
Cardinal Stritch University ... WI ... 532

NURSE: Commission on Collegiate Nursing Education: nursing (B,M,D)

Auburn University ... AL ... 1
Auburn University at Montgomery ... AL ... 2
Jacksonville State University ... AL ... 4
Samford University ... AL ... 6
Spring Hill College ... AL ... 7
University of Alabama at Birmingham ... AL ... 8
University of Alabama in Huntsville ... AL ... 8
University of Alabama, The ... AL ... 8
University of Mobile ... AL ... 9
University of North Alabama ... AL ... 9
University of South Alabama ... AL ... 9
Arizona State University ... AZ ... 11
Grand Canyon University ... AZ ... 13
Northern Arizona University ... AZ ... 16
University of Arizona ... AZ ... 18
University of Phoenix ... AZ ... 18
Henderson State University ... AR ... 21
University of Arkansas for Medical Sciences ... AR ... 24
University of Arkansas Main Campus ... AR ... 23
University of Central Arkansas ... AR ... 25
American University of Health Sciences ... CA ... 28
Azusa Pacific University ... CA ... 29
Biola University ... CA ... 29
Brandman University ... CA ... 29
California Baptist University ... CA ... 30
California State University-Bakersfield ... CA ... 32
California State University-Channel Islands ... CA ... 32
California State University-Chico ... CA ... 33
California State University-Dominguez Hills ... CA ... 33
California State University-East Bay ... CA ... 33
California State University-Fresno ... CA ... 33
California State University-Fullerton ... CA ... 33
California State University-Long Beach ... CA ... 33
California State University-Los Angeles ... CA ... 34
California State University-Northridge ... CA ... 34
California State University-Sacramento ... CA ... 34
California State University-San Bernardino CA ... 34
California State University-San Marcos ... CA ... 35
California State University-Stanislaus ... CA ... 35
Charles R. Drew University of Medicine & Science ... CA ... 38
Concordia University ... CA ... 41
Dominican University of California ... CA ... 42
Fresno Pacific University ... CA ... 45
Holy Names University ... CA ... 47
Loma Linda University ... CA ... 51
Mount St. Mary's College ... CA ... 54
National University ... CA ... 55
Point Loma Nazarene University ... CA ... 59
Samuel Merritt University ... CA ... 61
San Diego State University ... CA ... 35
San Francisco State University ... CA ... 35
San Jose State University ... CA ... 36
University of California-Davis ... CA ... 70
University of California-Irvine ... CA ... 71
University of California-Los Angeles ... CA ... 71
University of California-San Francisco ... CA ... 72
University of San Diego ... CA ... 73
University of San Francisco ... CA ... 73

Vanguard University of Southern California ... CA ... 74
West Coast University ... CA ... 75
Western University of Health Sciences ... CA ... 76
Adams State University ... CO ... 78
American Sentinel University ... CO ... 78
Aspen University ... CO ... 78
Colorado Christian University ... CO ... 79
Colorado Mesa University ... CO ... 79
Regis University ... CO ... 84
University of Colorado Colorado Springs .. CO ... 85
University of Colorado DenverlAnschutz Medical Campus ... CO ... 86
University of Northern Colorado ... CO ... 86
Central Connecticut State University ... CT ... 87
Fairfield University ... CT ... 89
Sacred Heart University ... CT ... 91
Southern Connecticut State University ... CT ... 88
University of Connecticut ... CT ... 92
University of Hartford ... CT ... 92
University of Saint Joseph ... CT ... 92
Western Connecticut State University ... CT ... 88
Yale University ... CT ... 93
University of Delaware ... DE ... 94
Wilmington University ... DE ... 94
Catholic University of America, The ... DC ... 94
George Washington University ... DC ... 95
Georgetown University ... DC ... 95
Howard University ... DC ... 95
Trinity Washington University ... DC ... 96
Barry University ... FL ... 98
Florida Atlantic University ... FL ... 114
Florida Gulf Coast University ... FL ... 115
Florida International University ... FL ... 115
Florida Southern College ... FL ... 105
Florida State University ... FL ... 115
Jacksonville University ... FL ... 107
Keiser University ... FL ... 108
Northwest Florida State College ... FL ... 109
Nova Southeastern University ... FL ... 109
Palm Beach Atlantic University ... FL ... 110
Remington College-Tampa Campus ... FL ... 111
St. Petersburg College ... FL ... 112
University of Central Florida ... FL ... 115
University of Florida ... FL ... 116
University of Miami ... FL ... 118
University of North Florida ... FL ... 116
University of South Florida ... FL ... 116
University of West Florida ... FL ... 117
Armstrong Atlantic State University ... GA ... 120
Brenau University ... GA ... 122
Clayton State University ... GA ... 123
Columbus State University ... GA ... 123
Emory University ... GA ... 124
Georgia Regents University ... GA ... 126
Georgia Southern University ... GA ... 126
Georgia State University ... GA ... 126
Kennesaw State University ... GA ... 127
Mercer University ... GA ... 128
Shorter University ... GA ... 131
South University ... GA ... 131
University of West Georgia ... GA ... 133
Valdosta State University ... GA ... 134
Chaminade University of Honolulu ... HI ... 135
Hawaii Pacific University ... HI ... 135
University of Hawaii at Manoa ... HI ... 136
Idaho State University ... ID ... 138
Lewis-Clark State College ... ID ... 138
Northwest Nazarene University ... ID ... 139
Aurora University ... IL ... 140
Benedictine University ... IL ... 140
Blessing-Rieman College of Nursing ... IL ... 140
Chamberlain College of Nursing - Addison IL ... 141
DePaul University ... IL ... 143
Eastern Illinois University ... IL ... 144
Elmhurst College ... IL ... 145
Illinois State University ... IL ... 147
Illinois Wesleyan University ... IL ... 148
Lakeview College of Nursing ... IL ... 150
Lewis University ... IL ... 150
Loyola University Chicago ... IL ... 151
MacMurray College ... IL ... 152
McKendree University ... IL ... 152
Methodist College ... IL ... 152
Millikin University ... IL ... 153
North Park University ... IL ... 154
Northern Illinois University ... IL ... 154
Olivet Nazarene University ... IL ... 155
Resurrection University ... IL ... 156
Rush University ... IL ... 157
Saint Anthony College of Nursing ... IL ... 158
Saint Xavier University ... IL ... 158
Southern Illinois University Edwardsville ... IL ... 159
Trinity Christian College ... IL ... 160
Trinity College of Nursing & Health Sciences ... IL ... 160
University of Illinois at Chicago ... IL ... 161
University of St. Francis ... IL ... 162
Western Illinois University ... IL ... 162
Anderson University ... IN ... 163
Ball State University ... IN ... 164
Goshen College ... IN ... 166
Huntington University ... IN ... 166
Indiana University Kokomo ... IN ... 168
Indiana University-Purdue University Indianapolis ... IN ... 168
Indiana University South Bend ... IN ... 168
Indiana University Southeast ... IN ... 168
Indiana Wesleyan University ... IN ... 169
Marian University ... IN ... 170
Purdue University Main Campus ... IN ... 171
Saint Joseph's College ... IN ... 172
Saint Mary's College ... IN ... 172
University of Indianapolis ... IN ... 173
University of Saint Francis ... IN ... 174
University of Southern Indiana ... IN ... 174
Valparaiso University ... IN ... 174
Allen College ... IA ... 175
Briar Cliff University ... IA ... 176
Clarke University ... IA ... 176
Coe College ... IA ... 176
Dordt College ... IA ... 177
Grand View University ... IA ... 178
Kaplan University ... IA ... 180
Luther College ... IA ... 180
Mercy College of Health Sciences ... IA ... 181
Morningside College ... IA ... 181
Mount Mercy University ... IA ... 181
Northwestern College ... IA ... 181
St. Ambrose University ... IA ... 182
University of Dubuque ... IA ... 182
University of Iowa ... IA ... 175
Upper Iowa University ... IA ... 183
Baker University ... KS ... 184
Benedictine College ... KS ... 184
Bethel College ... KS ... 184
Fort Hays State University ... KS ... 186
MidAmerica Nazarene University ... KS ... 188
Newman University ... KS ... 189
Pittsburg State University ... KS ... 189
Southwestern College ... KS ... 190
Tabor College ... KS ... 190
University of Saint Mary ... KS ... 191
Washburn University ... KS ... 191
Wichita State University ... KS ... 191
Bellarmine University ... KY ... 192
Berea College ... KY ... 192
Eastern Kentucky University ... KY ... 193
Kentucky Christian University ... KY ... 194
Morehead State University ... KY ... 198
Murray State University ... KY ... 198
Spalding University ... KY ... 199
Union College ... KY ... 200
University of Kentucky ... KY ... 200
University of Louisville ... KY ... 200
Western Kentucky University ... KY ... 200
Louisiana College ... LA ... 202
Louisiana State University Health Sciences Center-New Orleans ... LA ... 205
Loyola University New Orleans ... LA ... 205
McNeese State University ... LA ... 207
Nicholls State University ... LA ... 208
Northwestern State University ... LA ... 208
Southeastern Louisiana University ... LA ... 208
Southern University and A&M College ... LA ... 206
University of Louisiana at Lafayette ... LA ... 208
University of Louisiana at Monroe ... LA ... 208
Husson University ... ME ... 210
Saint Joseph's College of Maine ... ME ... 211
University of Maine ... ME ... 212
University of Maine at Fort Kent ... ME ... 212
University of Southern Maine ... ME ... 212
Coppin State University ... MD ... 220
Frostburg State University ... MD ... 220
Johns Hopkins University ... MD ... 215
Salisbury University ... MD ... 220
Stevenson University ... MD ... 218
Towson University ... MD ... 220
Uniformed Services University of the Health Sciences ... MD ... 545
University of Maryland Baltimore ... MD ... 219
American International College ... MA ... 221
Boston College ... MA ... 224
College of Our Lady of the Elms ... MA ... 225
Curry College ... MA ... 225
Emmanuel College ... MA ... 226
Fitchburg State University ... MA ... 229
Framingham State University ... MA ... 230
Laboure College ... MA ... 227
MCPHS University ... MA ... 233
MGH Institute of Health Professions ... MA ... 234
Northeastern University ... MA ... 235
Salem State University ... MA ... 230
Simmons College ... MA ... 236
University of Massachusetts ... MA ... 228
University of Massachusetts Boston ... MA ... 228
University of Massachusetts Lowell ... MA ... 229
University of Massachusetts Medical School ... MA ... 229
Worcester State University ... MA ... 230
Baker College of Flint ... MI ... 239
Calvin College ... MI ... 240
Eastern Michigan University ... MI ... 242
Finlandia University ... MI ... 242
Grand Valley State University ... MI ... 243
Hope College ... MI ... 244
Madonna University ... MI ... 246
Michigan State University ... MI ... 246
Northern Michigan University ... MI ... 248
Oakland University ... MI ... 248
Robert B. Miller College ... MI ... 249
Rochester College ... MI ... 249
Saginaw Valley State University ... MI ... 249
Siena Heights University ... MI ... 250
Spring Arbor University ... MI ... 250
University of Detroit Mercy ... MI ... 250
University of Michigan-Ann Arbor ... MI ... 251
University of Michigan-Flint ... MI ... 251
Wayne State University ... MI ... 252
Western Michigan University ... MI ... 252
Augsburg College ... MN ... 253
Bemidji State University ... MN ... 258
Bethel University ... MN ... 253
Capella University ... MN ... 254
College of Saint Benedict ... MN ... 254
College of Saint Scholastica, The ... MN ... 254
Concordia College ... MN ... 255
Crown College ... MN ... 255
Gustavus Adolphus College ... MN ... 255
Metropolitan State University ... MN ... 259
Minnesota School of Business ... MN ... 257
Minnesota State University Moorhead ... MN ... 259
Minnesota State University, Mankato ... MN ... 259
St. Cloud State University ... MN ... 261
Saint John's University ... MN ... 263
Saint Mary's University of Minnesota ... MN ... 264
St. Olaf College ... MN ... 264
University of Minnesota-Twin Cities ... MN ... 264
Walden University ... MN ... 265
Winona State University ... MN ... 262
Alcorn State University ... MS ... 265
Delta State University ... MS ... 266
Mississippi College ... MS ... 268
Mississippi University for Women ... MS ... 268
University of Mississippi Medical Center ... MS ... 270
University of Southern Mississippi ... MS ... 270
William Carey University ... MS ... 270
Avila University ... MO ... 271
Central Methodist University ... MO ... 272
College of the Ozarks ... MO ... 272
Cox College ... MO ... 273
Goldfarb School of Nursing at Barnes-Jewish College ... MO ... 274
Maryville University of Saint Louis ... MO ... 276
Missouri Southern State University ... MO ... 278
Missouri State University ... MO ... 278
Missouri Western State University ... MO ... 279
Research College of Nursing ... MO ... 280
Saint Louis University ... MO ... 281
Saint Luke's College of Health Sciences .. MO ... 281
Southeast Missouri State University ... MO ... 282
Truman State University ... MO ... 282
University of Central Missouri ... MO ... 283
University of Missouri - Columbia ... MO ... 283
University of Missouri - Kansas City ... MO ... 283
University of Missouri - Saint Louis ... MO ... 283
William Jewell College ... MO ... 285
Carroll College ... MT ... 285
Montana State University ... MT ... 287
University of Great Falls ... MT ... 288
Creighton University ... NE ... 289
Nebraska Methodist College ... NE ... 291
Union College ... NE ... 292
University of Nebraska Medical Center ... NE ... 292
Nevada State College ... NV ... 294
University of Nevada, Las Vegas ... NV ... 294
University of Nevada, Reno ... NV ... 294
Colby-Sawyer College ... NH ... 295
Saint Anselm College ... NH ... 297
University of New Hampshire ... NH ... 298
Bloomfield College ... NJ ... 299
Caldwell College ... NJ ... 300
College of New Jersey, The ... NJ ... 300
Fairleigh Dickinson University ... NJ ... 301
Felician College ... NJ ... 302
Georgian Court University ... NJ ... 302
Monmouth University ... NJ ... 303
Richard Stockton College of New Jersey, The ... NJ ... 305
Rowan University ... NJ ... 305
Rutgers the State University of New Jersey Camden Campus ... NJ ... 306
Rutgers the State University of New Jersey Newark Campus ... NJ ... 306
Saint Peter's University ... NJ ... 306
Seton Hall University ... NJ ... 307
Thomas Edison State College ... NJ ... 308
William Paterson University of New Jersey ... NJ ... 308
New Mexico Highlands University ... NM ... 310
New Mexico State University Main Campus ... NM ... 310
Northern New Mexico College ... NM ... 311
University of New Mexico Main Campus .. NM ... 312
Western New Mexico University ... NM ... 312
Adelphi University ... NY ... 313
Alfred State College ... NY ... 345
City University of New York Herbert H. Lehman College ... NY ... 318
City University of New York Hunter College ... NY ... 318
College of Mount Saint Vincent ... NY ... 320
College of New Rochelle, The ... NY ... 320
Columbia University in the City of New York ... NY ... 321
Concordia College ... NY ... 321
Dominican College of Blauvelt ... NY ... 322
D'Youville College ... NY ... 323
Hartwick College ... NY ... 325
Keuka College ... NY ... 328
Le Moyne College ... NY ... 328
Long Island University - Post Campus ... NY ... 329
Mercy College ... NY ... 330
Molloy College ... NY ... 331
Mount Saint Mary College ... NY ... 332
Nazareth College of Rochester ... NY ... 332
New York Institute of Technology ... NY ... 333
New York University ... NY ... 334
Niagara University ... NY ... 334
Pace University ... NY ... 335
Roberts Wesleyan College ... NY ... 337
Sage Colleges, The ... NY ... 338
St. Francis College ... NY ... 338
St. John Fisher College ... NY ... 338
State University of New York at Binghamton ... NY ... 341
State University of New York at Stony Brook ... NY ... 342
State University of New York College at Plattsburgh ... NY ... 344
State University of New York Empire State College ... NY ... 346
State University of New York Health Science Center at Brooklyn ... NY ... 342
State University of New York Institute of Technology at Utica-Rome ... NY ... 346
State University of New York Upstate Medical University ... NY ... 342
State University of New York, The College at Brockport ... NY ... 342
University at Buffalo-SUNY ... NY ... 341
University of Rochester ... NY ... 349
Utica College ... NY ... 349
Appalachian State University ... NC ... 367
Cabarrus College of Health Sciences ... NC ... 352
Duke University ... NC ... 354
East Carolina University ... NC ... 367
Fayetteville State University ... NC ... 367
Lees-McRae College ... NC ... 356
Lenoir-Rhyne University ... NC ... 356
Queens University of Charlotte ... NC ... 365
University of North Carolina at Chapel Hill NC ... 368
University of North Carolina at Charlotte .. NC ... 368
University of North Carolina at Greensboro ... NC ... 369
University of North Carolina at Pembroke NC ... 369
University of North Carolina Wilmington ... NC ... 369
Western Carolina University ... NC ... 369
Winston-Salem State University ... NC ... 370
North Dakota State University Main Campus ... ND ... 371
Sanford College of Nursing ... ND ... 372
University of Mary ... ND ... 373
University of North Dakota Main Campus . ND ... 371
Ashland University ... OH ... 374
Bowling Green State University ... OH ... 374
Capital University ... OH ... 375
Case Western Reserve University ... OH ... 375
Cedarville University ... OH ... 375
Cleveland State University ... OH ... 377
College of Mount St. Joseph ... OH ... 377
Defiance College, The ... OH ... 379
Franklin University ... OH ... 380
Hiram College ... OH ... 380
Hondros College ... OH ... 381
Kent State University Main Campus ... OH ... 382
Lourdes University ... OH ... 383
Malone University ... OH ... 383
Mercy College of Ohio ... OH ... 383
Miami University ... OH ... 384
Mount Carmel College of Nursing ... OH ... 384
Mount Vernon Nazarene University ... OH ... 384
Muskingum University ... OH ... 384
Notre Dame College ... OH ... 385
Ohio Northern University ... OH ... 386
Ohio State University Main Campus, The . OH ... 386
Ohio University Main Campus ... OH ... 387
Otterbein University ... OH ... 387
University of Akron, Main Campus, The ... OH ... 390
University of Cincinnati Main Campus ... OH ... 390
University of Toledo ... OH ... 392
Urbana University ... OH ... 392
Ursuline College ... OH ... 392
Wright State University Main Campus ... OH ... 393
Xavier University ... OH ... 393
Oklahoma Baptist University ... OK ... 397
Oklahoma Christian University ... OK ... 397
Oklahoma Wesleyan University ... OK ... 398
Oral Roberts University ... OK ... 398
Southern Nazarene University ... OK ... 399
George Fox University ... OR ... 403
Linfield College ... OR ... 404
Oregon Health & Science University ... OR ... 405
University of Portland ... OR ... 408
Alvernia University ... PA ... 409
Bloomsburg University of Pennsylvania ... PA ... 427

California University of Pennsylvania ... PA ... 428
Carlow University ... PA ... 412
Chatham University ... PA ... 412
Drexel University ... PA ... 415
Duquesne University ... PA ... 415
Eastern University ... PA ... 415
Edinboro University of Pennsylvania ... PA ... 428
Gannon University ... PA ... 416
Holy Family University ... PA ... 418
Immaculata University ... PA ... 418
Indiana University of Pennsylvania ... PA ... 428
La Salle University ... PA ... 420
Lancaster General College of Nursing and Health Sciences ... PA ... 421
Messiah College ... PA ... 423
Misericordia University ... PA ... 424
Moravian College ... PA ... 424
Penn State University Park ... PA ... 426
Robert Morris University ... PA ... 431
Saint Francis University ... PA ... 432
Temple University ... PA ... 433
Thomas Jefferson University ... PA ... 434
University of Pennsylvania ... PA ... 435
University of Pittsburgh ... PA ... 435
University of Scranton, The ... PA ... 436
Villanova University ... PA ... 436
Waynesburg University ... PA ... 437
West Chester University of Pennsylvania ... PA ... 430
Widener University ... PA ... 437
Wilkes University ... PA ... 437
York College of Pennsylvania ... PA ... 438
Universidad Del Turabo ... PR ... 552
University of Puerto Rico-Medical Sciences Campus ... PR ... 554
Rhode Island College ... RI ... 439
Salve Regina University ... RI ... 440
University of Rhode Island ... RI ... 440
Clemson University ... SC ... 442
Lander University ... SC ... 444
Medical University of South Carolina ... SC ... 445
Newberry College ... SC ... 445
South Carolina State University ... SC ... 446
University of South Carolina Aiken ... SC ... 448
University of South Carolina Beaufort ... SC ... 448
University of South Carolina Columbia ... SC ... 447
University of South Carolina Upstate ... SC ... 448
Augustana College ... SD ... 449
Mount Marty College ... SD ... 450
National American University ... SD ... 450
South Dakota State University ... SD ... 452
University of Sioux Falls ... SD ... 452
University of South Dakota, The ... SD ... 451
Baptist College of Health Sciences ... TN ... 453
Belmont University ... TN ... 453
Bethel University ... TN ... 453
Carson-Newman University ... TN ... 453
Christian Brothers University ... TN ... 453
East Tennessee State University ... TN ... 459
King University ... TN ... 455
Martin Methodist College ... TN ... 456
Middle Tennessee State University ... TN ... 459
Milligan College ... TN ... 457
Tennessee Technological University ... TN ... 460
Tennessee Wesleyan College ... TN ... 462
Trevecca Nazarene University ... TN ... 462
Union University ... TN ... 462
University of Memphis, The ... TN ... 460
University of Tennessee at Chattanooga ... TN ... 463
University of Tennessee, Knoxville ... TN ... 463
Abilene Christian University ... TX ... 464
Baylor University ... TX ... 467
Concordia University Texas ... TX ... 469
East Texas Baptist University ... TX ... 471
Hardin-Simmons University ... TX ... 472
McMurry University ... TX ... 476
Midwestern State University ... TX ... 476
Prairie View A & M University ... TX ... 482
Southwestern Adventist University ... TX ... 481
Tarleton State University ... TX ... 483
Texas A & M University ... TX ... 483
Texas A & M University - Corpus Christi ... TX ... 483
Texas A & M University - Texarkana ... TX ... 484
Texas Christian University ... TX ... 484
Texas State University-San Marcos ... TX ... 487
Texas Tech University Health Sciences Center ... TX ... 487
Texas Woman's University ... TX ... 488
University of Houston - Victoria ... TX ... 489
University of Mary Hardin-Baylor ... TX ... 490
University of Texas at Arlington, The ... TX ... 491
University of Texas at Austin ... TX ... 491
University of Texas at El Paso ... TX ... 492
University of Texas at Tyler ... TX ... 492
University of Texas Health Science Center at Houston (UTHealth), The ... TX ... 492
University of Texas Health Science Center at San Antonio ... TX ... 493
University of Texas Medical Branch, The ... TX ... 493
University of Texas - Pan American ... TX ... 492
University of the Incarnate Word ... TX ... 490
West Texas A & M University ... TX ... 484
Brigham Young University ... UT ... 495
Southern Utah University ... UT ... 497
University of Utah, The ... UT ... 496
Western Governors University ... UT ... 498
Westminster College ... UT ... 498
Norwich University ... VT ... 500
University of Vermont ... VT ... 500
Bon Secours Memorial College of Nursing ... VA ... 502
Eastern Mennonite University ... VA ... 504
George Mason University ... VA ... 505
Hampton University ... VA ... 505
James Madison University ... VA ... 506
Jefferson College of Health Sciences ... VA ... 506
Liberty University ... VA ... 506
Longwood University ... VA ... 506
Lynchburg College ... VA ... 506
Marymount University ... VA ... 507
Old Dominion University ... VA ... 507
Radford University ... VA ... 508
Sentara College of Health Sciences ... VA ... 509
Shenandoah University ... VA ... 509
Stratford University ... VA ... 510
University of Virginia ... VA ... 511
University of Virginia's College at Wise, The ... VA ... 511
Gonzaga University ... WA ... 520
Northwest University ... WA ... 521
Olympic College ... WA ... 521
Pacific Lutheran University ... WA ... 521
Seattle Pacific University ... WA ... 523
Seattle University ... WA ... 523
University of Washington ... WA ... 524
Washington State University ... WA ... 525
Whitworth University ... WA ... 525
American Public University System ... WV ... 526
Bluefield State College ... WV ... 529
Fairmont State University ... WV ... 529
Shepherd University ... WV ... 529
West Liberty University ... WV ... 530
West Virginia University ... WV ... 530
Wheeling Jesuit University ... WV ... 531
Alverno College ... WI ... 531
Bellin College, Inc. ... WI ... 531
Cardinal Stritch University ... WI ... 532
Carroll University ... WI ... 532
Columbia College of Nursing ... WI ... 532
Concordia University Wisconsin ... WI ... 532
Edgewood College ... WI ... 532
Herzing University ... WI ... 533
Maranatha Baptist Bible College & Seminary ... WI ... 533
Marian University ... WI ... 534
Marquette University ... WI ... 534
Milwaukee School of Engineering ... WI ... 534
Silver Lake College of the Holy Family ... WI ... 536
University of Wisconsin-Eau Claire ... WI ... 536
University of Wisconsin-Green Bay ... WI ... 536
University of Wisconsin-Madison ... WI ... 536
University of Wisconsin-Milwaukee ... WI ... 537
University of Wisconsin-Oshkosh ... WI ... 537
Viterbo University ... WI ... 539
Wisconsin Lutheran College ... WI ... 539
University of Wyoming ... WY ... 543

NW: Northwest Commission on Colleges and Universities

Alaska Pacific University ... AK ... 10
Ilisagvik College ... AK ... 10
Prince William Sound Community College ... AK ... 11
University of Alaska Anchorage ... AK ... 10
University of Alaska Fairbanks ... AK ... 10
University of Alaska Southeast ... AK ... 11
Boise State University ... ID ... 137
Brigham Young University-Idaho ... ID ... 137
College of Idaho, The ... ID ... 138
College of Southern Idaho ... ID ... 138
@College of Western Idaho ... ID ... 138
Eastern Idaho Technical College ... ID ... 138
Idaho State University ... ID ... 138
Lewis-Clark State College ... ID ... 138
North Idaho College ... ID ... 138
Northwest Nazarene University ... ID ... 139
University of Idaho ... ID ... 139
Aaniiih Nakoda College ... MT ... 285
Blackfeet Community College ... MT ... 285
Carroll College ... MT ... 285
Chief Dull Knife College ... MT ... 285
Dawson Community College ... MT ... 286
Flathead Valley Community College ... MT ... 286
Fort Peck Community College ... MT ... 286
Great Falls College Montana State University ... MT ... 287
Little Big Horn College ... MT ... 286
Miles Community College ... MT ... 286
Montana State University ... MT ... 287
Montana State University - Billings ... MT ... 287
Montana State University - Northern ... MT ... 287
Montana Tech of The University of Montana ... MT ... 287
Rocky Mountain College ... MT ... 288
Salish Kootenai College ... MT ... 288
Stone Child College ... MT ... 288
University of Great Falls ... MT ... 288
University of Montana - Helena College of Technology, The ... MT ... 287
University of Montana - Missoula, The ... MT ... 286
University of Montana Western, The ... MT ... 286
College of Southern Nevada ... NV ... 294
Great Basin College ... NV ... 294
Nevada State College ... NV ... 294
Roseman University of Health Sciences ... NV ... 295
Sierra Nevada College ... NV ... 295
Truckee Meadows Community College ... NV ... 294
University of Nevada, Las Vegas ... NV ... 294
University of Nevada, Reno ... NV ... 294
Western Nevada College ... NV ... 295
Art Institute of Portland, The ... OR ... 402
Blue Mountain Community College ... OR ... 402
Central Oregon Community College ... OR ... 402
Chemeketa Community College ... OR ... 402
Clackamas Community College ... OR ... 402
Clatsop Community College ... OR ... 402
Columbia Gorge Community College ... OR ... 402
Concordia University ... OR ... 402
Corban University ... OR ... 403
Eastern Oregon University ... OR ... 405
George Fox University ... OR ... 403
Klamath Community College ... OR ... 403
Lane Community College ... OR ... 403
Lewis and Clark College ... OR ... 403
Linfield College ... OR ... 404
Linn-Benton Community College ... OR ... 404
Marylhurst University ... OR ... 404
Mount Angel Seminary ... OR ... 404
Mt. Hood Community College ... OR ... 404
Multnomah University ... OR ... 404
National College of Natural Medicine ... OR ... 404
Northwest Christian University ... OR ... 405
Oregon College of Art and Craft ... OR ... 405
@Oregon College of Oriental Medicine ... OR ... 405
Oregon Health & Science University ... OR ... 405
Oregon Institute of Technology ... OR ... 405
Oregon State University ... OR ... 406
Pacific Northwest College of Art ... OR ... 406
Pacific University ... OR ... 407
Portland Community College ... OR ... 407
Portland State University ... OR ... 406
Reed College ... OR ... 407
Rogue Community College ... OR ... 407
Southern Oregon University ... OR ... 406
Southwestern Oregon Community College ... OR ... 407
@Tillamook Bay Community College ... OR ... 408
Treasure Valley Community College ... OR ... 408
Umpqua Community College ... OR ... 408
University of Oregon ... OR ... 406
University of Portland ... OR ... 408
University of Western States ... OR ... 408
Warner Pacific College ... OR ... 408
Western Oregon University ... OR ... 406
Western Seminary ... OR ... 408
Willamette University ... OR ... 408
Brigham Young University ... UT ... 495
Dixie State College of Utah ... UT ... 497
LDS Business College ... UT ... 495
Rocky Mountain University of Health Professions ... UT ... 496
Salt Lake Community College ... UT ... 498
Snow College ... UT ... 498
Southern Utah University ... UT ... 497
University of Utah, The ... UT ... 496
Utah State University ... UT ... 497
Utah Valley University ... UT ... 497
Weber State University ... UT ... 497
Western Governors University ... UT ... 498
Westminster College ... UT ... 498
Art Institute of Seattle, The ... WA ... 516
Bastyr University ... WA ... 516
Bates Technical College ... WA ... 516
Bellevue College ... WA ... 517
Bellingham Technical College ... WA ... 517
Big Bend Community College ... WA ... 517
Cascadia Community College ... WA ... 517
Central Washington University ... WA ... 517
Centralia College ... WA ... 517
City University of Seattle ... WA ... 517
Clark College ... WA ... 518
Clover Park Technical College ... WA ... 518
Columbia Basin College ... WA ... 518
Cornish College of the Arts ... WA ... 518
Eastern Washington University ... WA ... 519
Edmonds Community College ... WA ... 519
Everett Community College ... WA ... 519
Evergreen State College, The ... WA ... 519
Gonzaga University ... WA ... 520
Grays Harbor College ... WA ... 520
Green River Community College ... WA ... 520
Heritage University ... WA ... 520
Highline Community College ... WA ... 520
Lake Washington Institute of Technology ... WA ... 520
Lower Columbia College ... WA ... 521
North Seattle Community College ... WA ... 522
Northwest Indian College ... WA ... 521
Northwest University ... WA ... 521
Olympic College ... WA ... 521
Pacific Lutheran University ... WA ... 521
Peninsula College ... WA ... 522
Pierce College District ... WA ... 522
Renton Technical College ... WA ... 522
Saint Martin's University ... WA ... 522
Seattle Central Community College ... WA ... 522
Seattle Pacific University ... WA ... 523
Seattle University ... WA ... 523
Shoreline Community College ... WA ... 523
Skagit Valley College ... WA ... 523
South Puget Sound Community College ... WA ... 524
South Seattle Community College ... WA ... 523
Spokane Community College ... WA ... 518
Spokane Falls Community College ... WA ... 518
Tacoma Community College ... WA ... 524
Trinity Lutheran College ... WA ... 524
University of Puget Sound ... WA ... 524
University of Washington ... WA ... 524
Walla Walla Community College ... WA ... 524
Walla Walla University ... WA ... 524
Washington State University ... WA ... 525
Wenatchee Valley College ... WA ... 525
Western Washington University ... WA ... 525
Whatcom Community College ... WA ... 525
Whitman College ... WA ... 525
Whitworth University ... WA ... 525
Yakima Valley Community College ... WA ... 525

NY: New York State Board of Regents

Bramson O R T College ... NY ... 315
Christie's Education, Inc. ... NY ... 316
City University of New York Stella and Charles Guttman Community College ... NY ... 319
Cold Spring Harbor Laboratory/Watson School of Biological Sciences ... NY ... 320
Elmezzi Graduate School of Molecular Medicine, The ... NY ... 323
Globe Institute of Technology ... NY ... 325
Holy Trinity Orthodox Seminary ... NY ... 326
Institute of Design and Construction ... NY ... 327
Louis V. Gerstner Jr. Graduate School of Biomedical Sciences, Memorial Sloa n-Kettering Cancer Ctr ... NY ... 329
Memorial Hospital School of Nursing ... NY ... 330
New York Academy of Art ... NY ... 333
New York Career Institute ... NY ... 333
New York College of Health Professions ... NY ... 333
Northeastern Seminary ... NY ... 335
Phillips Beth Israel School of Nursing ... NY ... 336
Rabbi Isaac Elchanan Theological Seminary ... NY ... 336
Richard Gilder Graduate School at the American Museum of Natural History ... NY ... 337
Rockefeller University ... NY ... 338
Salvation Army College for Officer Training ... NY ... 340
Samaritan Hospital School of Nursing ... NY ... 340
Technical Career Institutes ... NY ... 347
Union Graduate College ... NY ... 348
USC The Business College ... NY ... 349
Wood Tobé-Coburn School ... NY ... 350

OPD: Commission on Opticianry Accreditation: opticianry (A)

Middlesex Community College ... CT ... 89
Broward College ... FL ... 99
Hillsborough Community College ... FL ... 106
Miami Dade College ... FL ... 109
Ogeechee Technical College ... GA ... 129
Indiana University Bloomington ... IN ... 167
Benjamin Franklin Institute of Technology ... MA ... 223
College of Southern Nevada ... NV ... 294
Camden County College ... NJ ... 300
Essex County College ... NJ ... 301
Raritan Valley Community College ... NJ ... 305
New York City College of Technology/City University of New York ... NY ... 319
Technical Career Institutes ... NY ... 347
Durham Technical Community College ... NC ... 360
Roane State Community College ... TN ... 461
Tyler Junior College ... TX ... 488
J. Sargeant Reynolds Community College ... VA ... 512
Seattle Central Community College ... WA ... 522

OPE: Commission on Accreditation of Allied Health Education Programs: orthotics and prosthetics (C,B,M)

California State University-Dominguez Hills ... CA ... 33
University of Hartford ... CT ... 92
St. Petersburg College ... FL ... 112
Georgia Institute of Technology ... GA ... 125
Northwestern University ... IL ... 155
Eastern Michigan University ... MI ... 242
Century College ... MN ... 258
University of Pittsburgh ... PA ... 435
University of Texas Southwestern Medical Center ... TX ... 493
University of Washington ... WA ... 524

OPT: American Optometric Association: optometry (FP,D)

University of Alabama at Birmingham ... AL ... 8
Southern California College of Optometry ... CA ... 67
University of California-Berkeley ... CA ... 70
Western University of Health Sciences ... CA ... 76
Nova Southeastern University ... FL ... 109

Illinois College of Optometry ... IL ... 146
Indiana University Bloomington ... IN ... 167
@MCPHS University ... MA .. 233
New England College of Optometry, The . MA .. 234
Ferris State University ... MI ... 242
University of Missouri - Saint Louis ... MO .. 283
State University of New York College of Optometry ... NY ... 345
Ohio State University Main Campus, The . OH .. 386
Northeastern State University ... OK .. 396
Pacific University ... OR .. 407
Salus University ... PA ... 433
Inter American University of Puerto Rico School of Optometry ... PR ... 551
Southern College of Optometry ... TN ... 458
University of Houston ... TX ... 489
University of the Incarnate Word ... TX ... 490

OPTR: American Optometric Association: optometric residency programs

University of Alabama at Birmingham ... AL ... 8
Southern California College of Optometry CA ... 67
University of California-Berkeley ... CA ... 70
Nova Southeastern University ... FL ... 109
Illinois College of Optometry ... IL ... 146
Indiana University Bloomington ... IN ... 167
New England College of Optometry, The . MA .. 234
Ferris State University ... MI ... 242
University of Missouri - Saint Louis ... MO .. 283
State University of New York College of Optometry ... NY ... 345
Ohio State University Main Campus, The . OH .. 386
Northeastern State University ... OK .. 396
Pacific University ... OR .. 407
Salus University ... PA ... 433
Inter American University of Puerto Rico Bayamon Campus ... PR ... 550
Southern College of Optometry ... TN ... 458
University of Houston ... TX ... 489

OPTT: American Optometric Association: optometric technician (C,A)

Indiana University Bloomington ... IN ... 167
Madison Area Technical College ... WI ... 540

OSTEO: American Osteopathic Association, Office of Osteopathic Education: osteopathic medicine (FP,D)

@Alabama College of Osteopathic Medicine AL ... 1
Touro University California ... CA ... 69
Western University of Health Sciences ... CA ... 76
Rocky Vista University ... CO ... 85
Nova Southeastern University ... FL ... 109
Midwestern University ... IL ... 153
@Marian University ... IN ... 170
Des Moines University ... IA ... 177
University of Pikeville ... KY ... 200
University of New England ... ME .. 213
Michigan State University ... MI ... 246
@William Carey University ... MS .. 270
A. T. Still University of Health Sciences ... MO .. 271
Kansas City University of Medicine & Biosciences ... MO .. 275
Rowan University ... NJ ... 305
New York Institute of Technology ... NY ... 333
Touro College ... NY ... 348
@Campbell University ... NC .. 352
Ohio University Main Campus ... OH .. 387
Lake Erie College of Osteopathic Medicine ... PA ... 420
Philadelphia College of Osteopathic Medicine ... PA ... 430
Lincoln Memorial University ... TN ... 456
University of North Texas Health Science Center at Fort Worth ... TX ... 490
Edward Via College of Osteopathic Medicine ... VA ... 504
Pacific Northwest University of Health Sciences ... WA .. 521
West Virginia School of Osteopathic Medicine ... WV .. 530

OT: American Occupational Therapy Association: occupational therapy (M,D)

Alabama State University ... AL ... 1
#Tuskegee University ... AL ... 8
University of Alabama at Birmingham ... AL ... 8
University of South Alabama ... AL ... 9
University of Central Arkansas ... AR ... 25
California State University-Dominguez Hills ... CA ... 33
Dominican University of California ... CA ... 42
Loma Linda University ... CA ... 51
Samuel Merritt University ... CA ... 61
San Jose State University ... CA ... 36
University of Southern California ... CA ... 74
Colorado State University ... CO ... 80
Quinnipiac University ... CT ... 91
Sacred Heart University ... CT ... 91
Howard University ... DC ... 95
Barry University ... FL ... 98
Florida Agricultural and Mechanical University ... FL ... 114
Florida Gulf Coast University ... FL ... 115
Florida International University ... FL ... 115
Nova Southeastern University ... FL ... 109
University of Florida ... FL ... 116
University of St. Augustine for Health Sciences ... FL ... 118
Brenau University ... GA .. 122
Georgia Regents University ... GA .. 126
Idaho State University ... ID ... 138
Chicago State University ... IL ... 141
Governors State University ... IL ... 145
Midwestern University ... IL ... 153
Rush University ... IL ... 157
University of Illinois at Chicago ... IL ... 161
Indiana University-Purdue University Indianapolis ... IN ... 168
University of Indianapolis ... IN ... 173
University of Southern Indiana ... IN ... 174
St. Ambrose University ... IA ... 182
Eastern Kentucky University ... KY ... 193
Spalding University ... KY ... 199
Louisiana State University Health Sciences Center at Shreveport ... LA ... 205
Louisiana State University Health Sciences Center-New Orleans ... LA ... 205
Husson University ... ME .. 210
University of New England ... ME .. 213
University of Southern Maine ... ME .. 212
Towson University ... MD .. 220
American International College ... MA .. 221
Bay Path College ... MA .. 222
Boston University ... MA .. 224
Salem State University ... MA .. 230
Springfield College ... MA .. 236
Tufts University ... MA .. 237
Worcester State University ... MA .. 230
Baker College of Flint ... MI ... 239
Eastern Michigan University ... MI ... 242
Grand Valley State University ... MI ... 243
Saginaw Valley State University ... MI ... 249
Wayne State University ... MI ... 252
Western Michigan University ... MI ... 252
College of Saint Scholastica, The ... MN .. 254
St. Catherine University ... MN .. 263
University of Minnesota-Twin Cities ... MN .. 264
University of Mississippi Medical Center ... MS .. 270
Maryville University of Saint Louis ... MO .. 276
Rockhurst University ... MO .. 280
Saint Louis University ... MO .. 281
University of Missouri - Columbia ... MO .. 283
Washington University in St. Louis ... MO .. 284
College of Saint Mary ... NE ... 289
Creighton University ... NE ... 289
University of New Hampshire ... NH ... 298
Kean University ... NJ ... 302
Richard Stockton College of New Jersey, The ... NJ ... 305
Seton Hall University ... NJ ... 307
University of New Mexico Main Campus .. NM .. 312
Western New Mexico University ... NM .. 312
City University of New York York College NY ... 319
Columbia University in the City of New York ... NY ... 321
Dominican College of Blauvelt ... NY ... 322
D'Youville College ... NY ... 323
Ithaca College ... NY ... 327
Keuka College ... NY ... 328
Mercy College ... NY ... 330
New York Institute of Technology ... NY ... 333
New York University ... NY ... 334
Sage Colleges, The ... NY ... 338
State University of New York at Stony Brook ... NY ... 342
State University of New York Health Science Center at Brooklyn ... NY ... 342
Touro College ... NY ... 348
University at Buffalo-SUNY ... NY ... 341
Utica College ... NY ... 349
East Carolina University ... NC .. 367
Lenoir-Rhyne University ... NC .. 356
University of North Carolina at Chapel Hill NC .. 368
Winston-Salem State University ... NC .. 370
University of Mary ... ND .. 373
University of North Dakota Main Campus . ND .. 371
Cleveland State University ... OH .. 377
Ohio State University Main Campus, The . OH .. 386
Shawnee State University ... OH .. 388
University of Findlay, The ... OH .. 391
University of Toledo ... OH .. 392
Xavier University ... OH .. 393
Pacific University ... OR .. 407
Alvernia University ... PA ... 409
Chatham University ... PA ... 412
Duquesne University ... PA ... 415
Elizabethtown College ... PA ... 415
Gannon University ... PA ... 416
Misericordia University ... PA ... 424
Philadelphia University ... PA ... 430
Saint Francis University ... PA ... 432
Temple University ... PA ... 433
Thomas Jefferson University ... PA ... 434
University of Pittsburgh ... PA ... 435
University of Scranton, The ... PA ... 436
University of the Sciences in Philadelphia PA ... 435
University of Puerto Rico-Medical Sciences Campus ... PR ... 554
New England Institute of Technology ... RI ... 439
Medical University of South Carolina ... SC ... 445
University of South Dakota, The ... SD ... 451
Belmont University ... TN ... 453
Milligan College ... TN ... 457
Tennessee State University ... TN ... 459
Texas Tech University Health Sciences Center ... TX ... 487
Texas Woman's University ... TX ... 488
University of Texas at El Paso ... TX ... 492
University of Texas Health Science Center at San Antonio ... TX ... 493
University of Texas Medical Branch, The . TX ... 493
University of Texas - Pan American ... TX ... 492
University of Utah, The ... UT ... 496
James Madison University ... VA ... 506
Jefferson College of Health Sciences ... VA ... 506
Radford University ... VA ... 508
Shenandoah University ... VA ... 509
Virginia Commonwealth University ... VA ... 511
Eastern Washington University ... WA .. 519
University of Puget Sound ... WA .. 524
University of Washington ... WA .. 524
West Virginia University ... WV .. 530
Concordia University Wisconsin ... WI ... 532
Mount Mary University ... WI ... 535
University of Wisconsin-La Crosse ... WI ... 536
University of Wisconsin-Madison ... WI ... 536
University of Wisconsin-Milwaukee ... WI ... 537

OTA: American Occupational Therapy Association: occupational therapy assistant (C,A)

Wallace State Community College - Hanceville ... AL ... 9
Pima Medical Institute-Tucson ... AZ ... 17
Pulaski Technical College ... AR ... 22
South Arkansas Community College ... AR ... 23
Grossmont College ... CA ... 46
Sacramento City College ... CA ... 53
Santa Ana College ... CA ... 60
Stanbridge College ... CA ... 68
Pueblo Community College ... CO ... 84
Goodwin College ... CT ... 90
Housatonic Community College ... CT ... 88
Lincoln College of New England ... CT ... 90
Manchester Community College ... CT ... 88
Delaware Technical Community College, Owens Campus ... DE ... 93
Delaware Technical Community College, Stanton-Wilmington Campus ... DE ... 93
Adventist University of Health Sciences ... FL ... 97
Concorde Career Institute ... FL ... 100
Daytona State College ... FL ... 101
Florida State College at Jacksonville ... FL ... 105
Keiser University ... FL ... 108
Polk State College ... FL ... 110
State College of Florida, Manatee-Sarasota ... FL ... 114
Augusta Technical College ... GA .. 121
Chattahoochee Technical College ... GA .. 122
Darton State College ... GA .. 124
Georgia Northwestern Technical College . GA .. 125
Middle Georgia State College ... GA .. 128
Kapiolani Community College ... HI ... 136
City Colleges of Chicago Wilbur Wright College ... IL ... 142
Illinois Central College ... IL ... 146
John A. Logan College ... IL ... 148
Kaskaskia College ... IL ... 149
Lewis and Clark Community College ... IL ... 150
Lincoln Land Community College ... IL ... 151
McHenry County College ... IL ... 152
Parkland College ... IL ... 155
Rend Lake College ... IL ... 156
Shawnee Community College ... IL ... 158
South Suburban College of Cook County . IL ... 159
Southeastern Illinois College ... IL ... 159
University of Southern Indiana ... IN ... 174
Hawkeye Community College ... IA ... 178
Indian Hills Community College ... IA ... 179
Kirkwood Community College ... IA ... 180
Brown Mackie College-Salina ... KS ... 185
Neosho County Community College ... KS ... 189
Newman University ... KS ... 189
Washburn University ... KS ... 191
Jefferson Community and Technical College ... KY ... 195
Madisonville Community College ... KY ... 196
Bossier Parish Community College ... LA ... 202
Delgado Community College ... LA ... 203
University of Louisiana at Monroe ... LA ... 208
Kennebec Valley Community College ... ME .. 210
Allegany College of Maryland ... MD .. 213
Community College of Baltimore County, The ... MD .. 214
Bristol Community College ... MA .. 231
North Shore Community College ... MA .. 232
Quinsigamond Community College ... MA .. 232
Springfield Technical Community College MA .. 233
Grand Rapids Community College ... MI ... 243
Macomb Community College ... MI ... 246
Mott Community College ... MI ... 247
Anoka Technical College ... MN .. 257
Northland Community and Technical College ... MN .. 260
St. Catherine University ... MN .. 263
Holmes Community College ... MS .. 267
Itawamba Community College ... MS .. 267
Pearl River Community College ... MS .. 269
East Central College ... MO .. 273
Jefferson College ... MO .. 275
Metropolitan Community College - Penn Valley ... MO .. 277
Moberly Area Community College ... MO .. 279
North Central Missouri College ... MO .. 279
Ozarks Technical Community College ... MO .. 279
St. Charles Community College ... MO .. 280
State Fair Community College ... MO .. 282
Three Rivers Community College ... MO .. 282
University of Missouri - Kansas City ... MO .. 283
Central Community College ... NE ... 288
#College of Southern Nevada ... NV .. 294
River Valley Community College ... NH .. 296
Eastern New Mexico University-Roswell ... NM .. 309
Western New Mexico University ... NM .. 312
Jamestown Community College ... NY ... 327
La Guardia Community College/City University of New York ... NY ... 318
Maria College of Albany ... NY ... 330
Mercy College ... NY ... 330
Orange County Community College ... NY ... 335
Rockland Community College ... NY ... 338
#Touro College ... NY ... 348
Cabarrus College of Health Sciences ... NC .. 352
Cape Fear Community College ... NC .. 358
Durham Technical Community College ... NC .. 360
Pitt Community College ... NC .. 362
North Dakota State College of Science ... ND .. 372
Cincinnati State Technical and Community College ... OH .. 376
Cuyahoga Community College ... OH .. 378
James A. Rhodes State College ... OH .. 381
Lorain County Community College ... OH .. 383
Marion Technical College ... OH .. 383
North Central State College ... OH .. 385
Northwest State Community College ... OH .. 385
Owens Community College ... OH .. 387
Shawnee State University ... OH .. 388
Sinclair Community College ... OH .. 388
Stark State College ... OH .. 389
Zane State College ... OH .. 394
Murray State College ... OK .. 396
Oklahoma City Community College ... OK .. 397
Southwestern Oklahoma State University . OK .. 400
Tulsa Community College ... OK .. 400
Linn-Benton Community College ... OR .. 404
Community College of Allegheny County . PA ... 413
Harcum College ... PA ... 417
Kaplan Career Institute - ICM Campus ... PA ... 419
Lehigh Carbon Community College ... PA ... 421
Mercyhurst University ... PA ... 423
Pennsylvania College of Technology ... PA ... 427
Philadelphia University ... PA ... 430
Inter American University of Puerto Rico Ponce Campus ... PR ... 550
Community College of Rhode Island ... RI ... 439
New England Institute of Technology ... RI ... 439
Greenville Technical College ... SC ... 444
Trident Technical College ... SC ... 447
Lake Area Technical Institute ... SD ... 450
Chattanooga State Community College ... TN ... 460
Cleveland State Community College ... TN ... 460
Concorde Career College ... TN ... 453
Nashville State Community College ... TN ... 461
Roane State Community College ... TN ... 461
Amarillo College ... TX ... 465
Anamarc College ... TX ... 465
Austin Community College District ... TX ... 466
Del Mar College ... TX ... 471
Houston Community College ... TX ... 473
Laredo Community College ... TX ... 475
Lone Star College System ... TX ... 476
Navarro College ... TX ... 477
Panola College ... TX ... 478
St. Philip's College ... TX ... 465
South Texas College ... TX ... 480
Salt Lake Community College ... UT ... 498
Jefferson College of Health Sciences ... VA ... 506
Southwest Virginia Community College ... VA ... 514
Tidewater Community College ... VA ... 514
Virginia Highlands Community College ... VA ... 514
Bates Technical College ... WA .. 516
Green River Community College ... WA .. 520
Lake Washington Institute of Technology . WA .. 520
University of Charleston ... WV .. 527
Fox Valley Technical College ... WI ... 539
Madison Area Technical College ... WI ... 540

Milwaukee Area Technical College ... WI ... 540
Western Technical College ... WI ... 541
Wisconsin Indianhead Technical College . WI ... 541
Casper College ... WY .. 542

PA: National Accrediting Agency for Clinical Laboratory Sciences: pathologist's assistant (C,M)

Harding University Main Campus ... AR ... 21
Quinnipiac University ... CT ... 91
Rosalind Franklin University of Medicine & Science ... IL ... 157
Indiana University-Purdue University Indianapolis ... IN ... 168
University of Maryland Baltimore ... MD .. 219
Wayne State University ... MI .. 252
Duke University ... NC .. 354
Drexel University ... PA ... 415
West Virginia University ... WV .. 530

PAST: Association for Clinical Pastoral Education: clinical pastoral education

Eastern Mennonite University ... VA ... 504

PCSAS: Psychological Clinical Science Accreditation System: psychological clinical science (D)

Arizona State University ... AZ ... 11
University of Arizona ... AZ ... 18
University of California-Berkeley ... CA ... 70
University of California-Los Angeles ... CA ... 71
University of Southern California ... CA ... 74
University of Delaware ... DE ... 94
University of South Florida ... FL ... 116
Northwestern University ... IL ... 155
University of Illinois at Urbana-Champaign IL ... 162
University of Iowa ... IA ... 175
University of Kentucky ... KY .. 200
Harvard University ... MA .. 227
University of Minnesota-Twin Cities ... MN .. 264
University of Missouri - Columbia ... MO .. 283
Washington University in St. Louis ... MO .. 284
State University of New York at Stony Brook ... NY ... 342
University of Oregon ... OR .. 406
University of Pennsylvania ... PA ... 435
University of Pittsburgh ... PA ... 435
University of Virginia ... VA ... 511

PDPSY: American Psychological Association: post-doctoral residency in professional psychology

Stanford University ... CA ... 68
University of California-Los Angeles ... CA ... 71
University of California-San Diego ... CA ... 71
University of Southern California ... CA ... 74
Johns Hopkins University ... MD .. 215
University of Massachusetts Medical School ... MA .. 229
University of Michigan-Ann Arbor ... MI ... 251
University of Rochester ... NY ... 349
Brown University ... RI ... 438
University of Washington ... WA .. 524
Medical College of Wisconsin ... WI ... 534

PERF: Commission on Accreditation of Allied Health Education Programs: perfusionist (C,B,M)

University of Arizona ... AZ ... 18
Quinnipiac University ... CT ... 91
Barry University ... FL ... 98
Rush University ... IL ... 157
University of Iowa ... IA ... 175
University of Nebraska Medical Center ... NE ... 292
Long Island University - Post Campus ... NY ... 329
State University of New York Upstate Medical University ... NY ... 342
University of Pittsburgh ... PA ... 435
Medical University of South Carolina ... SC ... 445
Vanderbilt University ... TN ... 463
Milwaukee School of Engineering ... WI ... 534

PH: Council on Education for Public Health: public health (B,M,D)

University of Alabama at Birmingham ... AL ... 8
University of Alaska Anchorage ... AK ... 10
University of Arizona ... AZ ... 18
University of Arkansas for Medical Sciences ... AR ... 24
#California State University-Fresno ... CA ... 33
California State University-Fullerton ... CA ... 33
California State University-Long Beach ... CA ... 33
California State University-Northridge . CA ... 34
Charles R. Drew University of Medicine & Science ... CA ... 38
Claremont Graduate University ... CA ... 39
Loma Linda University ... CA ... 51
National University ... CA ... 55
San Diego State University ... CA ... 35
San Francisco State University ... CA ... 35
San Jose State University ... CA ... 36
Touro University California ... CA ... 69
University of California-Berkeley ... CA ... 70
University of California-Davis ... CA ... 70
University of California-Irvine ... CA ... 71
University of California-Los Angeles ... CA ... 71
University of Southern California ... CA ... 74
Colorado State University ... CO ... 80
University of Colorado DenverIAnschutz Medical Campus ... CO ... 86
University of Northern Colorado ... CO ... 86
Southern Connecticut State University ... CT ... 88
Yale University ... CT ... 93
George Washington University ... DC ... 95
Florida Agricultural and Mechanical University ... FL ... 114
Florida International University ... FL ... 115
Nova Southeastern University ... FL ... 109
University of Florida ... FL ... 116
University of Miami ... FL ... 118
University of North Florida ... FL ... 116
University of South Florida ... FL ... 116
University of West Florida ... FL ... 117
Armstrong Atlantic State University ... GA .. 120
Emory University ... GA .. 124
Georgia Regents University ... GA .. 126
Georgia Southern University ... GA .. 126
Georgia State University ... GA .. 126
Mercer University ... GA .. 128
Morehouse School of Medicine ... GA .. 129
University of Georgia ... GA .. 133
University of Hawaii at Manoa ... HI ... 136
Idaho State University ... ID ... 138
DePaul University ... IL ... 143
Northern Illinois University ... IL ... 154
Northwestern University ... IL ... 155
Southern Illinois University Carbondale ... IL ... 159
University of Illinois at Chicago ... IL ... 161
University of Illinois at Urbana-Champaign IL ... 162
Indiana University Bloomington ... IN ... 167
Indiana University-Purdue University Indianapolis ... IN ... 168
Des Moines University ... IA ... 177
University of Iowa ... IA ... 175
University of Kansas Main Campus ... KS ... 190
Eastern Kentucky University ... KY ... 193
University of Kentucky ... KY ... 200
University of Louisville ... KY ... 200
Western Kentucky University ... KY ... 200
Tulane University ... LA ... 207
University of New England ... ME .. 213
Johns Hopkins University ... MD .. 215
Morgan State University ... MD .. 217
Uniformed Services University of the Health Sciences ... MD .. 545
University of Maryland Baltimore ... MD .. 219
University of Maryland College Park ... MD .. 219
Harvard University ... MA .. 227
Northeastern University ... MA .. 235
Tufts University ... MA .. 237
University of Massachusetts ... MA .. 228
University of Michigan-Ann Arbor ... MI ... 251
Wayne State University ... MI ... 252
University of Minnesota-Twin Cities ... MN .. 264
Jackson State University ... MS .. 267
University of Southern Mississippi ... MS .. 270
Missouri State University ... MO .. 278
Saint Louis University ... MO .. 281
University of Missouri - Columbia ... MO .. 283
Washington University in St. Louis ... MO .. 284
University of Montana - Missoula, The ... MT .. 286
University of Nebraska Medical Center ... NE ... 292
University of Nevada, Las Vegas ... NV ... 294
University of Nevada, Reno ... NV ... 294
Dartmouth College ... NH ... 296
University of New Hampshire ... NH ... 298
New Jersey Institute of Technology ... NJ ... 303
Rutgers the State University of New Jersey New Brunswick Campus ... NJ ... 306
New Mexico State University Main Campus ... NM .. 310
University of New Mexico Main Campus .. NM .. 312
City University of New York Brooklyn College ... NY ... 317
City University of New York Graduate Center ... NY ... 317
City University of New York Herbert H. Lehman College ... NY ... 318
City University of New York Hunter College ... NY ... 318
Columbia University in the City of New York ... NY ... 321
Icahn School of Medicine at Mount Sinai . NY ... 327
New York Medical College ... NY ... 334
New York University ... NY ... 334
State University of New York at Stony Brook ... NY ... 342
State University of New York Health Science Center at Brooklyn ... NY ... 342
University at Albany, SUNY ... NY ... 341
University at Buffalo-SUNY ... NY ... 341
University of Rochester ... NY ... 349
East Carolina University ... NC .. 367
University of North Carolina at Chapel Hill NC .. 368
University of North Carolina at Charlotte .. NC .. 368
University of North Carolina at Greensboro ... NC .. 369
Bowling Green State University ... OH .. 374
Case Western Reserve University ... OH .. 375
Cleveland State University ... OH .. 377
Northeast Ohio Medical University ... OH .. 385
Ohio State University Main Campus, The . OH .. 386
Ohio University Main Campus ... OH .. 387
University of Akron, Main Campus, The ... OH .. 390
University of Cincinnati Main Campus ... OH .. 390
University of Toledo ... OH .. 392
Wright State University Main Campus ... OH .. 393
Youngstown State University ... OH .. 394
Oregon Health & Science University ... OR .. 405
Oregon State University ... OR .. 406
Portland State University ... OR .. 406
Arcadia University ... PA ... 409
Drexel University ... PA ... 415
East Stroudsburg University of Pennsylvania ... PA ... 428
Temple University ... PA ... 433
Thomas Jefferson University ... PA ... 434
University of Pennsylvania ... PA ... 435
University of Pittsburgh ... PA ... 435
West Chester University of Pennsylvania . PA ... 430
Ponce School of Medicine & Health Sciences ... PR ... 552
University of Puerto Rico-Medical Sciences Campus ... PR ... 554
Brown University ... RI ... 438
University of South Carolina Columbia ... SC ... 447
East Tennessee State University ... TN ... 459
Meharry Medical College ... TN ... 456
University of Tennessee, Knoxville ... TN ... 463
Vanderbilt University ... TN ... 463
Texas A & M University ... TX ... 483
University of North Texas Health Science Center at Fort Worth ... TX ... 490
University of Texas at El Paso ... TX ... 492
University of Texas Health Science Center at Houston (UTHealth), The ... TX ... 492
University of Texas Medical Branch, The . TX ... 493
Brigham Young University ... UT ... 495
University of Utah, The ... UT ... 496
Westminster College ... UT ... 498
Eastern Virginia Medical School ... VA ... 504
George Mason University ... VA ... 505
Old Dominion University ... VA ... 507
University of Virginia ... VA ... 511
Virginia Commonwealth University ... VA ... 511
Virginia Polytechnic Institute and State University ... VA ... 515
University of Washington ... WA .. 524
West Virginia University ... WV .. 530
Medical College of Wisconsin ... WI ... 534
University of Wisconsin-La Crosse ... WI ... 536
University of Wisconsin-Madison ... WI ... 536

PHAR: Accreditation Council for Pharmaceutical Education: pharmacy (FP,D)

Auburn University ... AL ... 1
Samford University ... AL ... 6
University of Arizona ... AZ ... 18
Harding University Main Campus ... AR ... 21
University of Arkansas for Medical Sciences ... AR ... 24
California Northstate College of Pharmacy CA ... 32
Loma Linda University ... CA ... 51
Touro University California ... CA ... 69
#University of California-San Diego ... CA ... 71
University of California-San Francisco ... CA ... 72
University of Southern California ... CA ... 74
University of the Pacific ... CA ... 73
Western University of Health Sciences ... CA ... 76
Regis University ... CO ... 84
University of Colorado DenverIAnschutz Medical Campus ... CO ... 86
University of Connecticut ... CT ... 92
@University of Saint Joseph ... CT ... 92
Howard University ... DC ... 95
Florida Agricultural and Mechanical University ... FL ... 114
Nova Southeastern University ... FL ... 109
Palm Beach Atlantic University ... FL ... 110
University of Florida ... FL ... 116
@University of South Florida ... FL ... 116
Mercer University ... GA .. 128
South University ... GA .. 131
University of Georgia ... GA .. 133
University of Hawaii at Hilo ... HI ... 136
Idaho State University ... ID ... 138
Chicago State University ... IL ... 141
Midwestern University ... IL ... 153
@Roosevelt University ... IL ... 157
@Rosalind Franklin University of Medicine & Science ... IL ... 157
Southern Illinois University Edwardsville ... IL ... 159
University of Illinois at Chicago ... IL ... 161
Butler University ... IN ... 164
@Manchester University ... IN ... 170
Purdue University Main Campus ... IN ... 171
Drake University ... IA ... 177
University of Iowa ... IA ... 175
University of Kansas Main Campus ... KS ... 190
Sullivan University ... KY ... 199
University of Kentucky ... KY ... 200
University of Louisiana at Monroe ... LA ... 208
Xavier University of Louisiana ... LA ... 209
@Husson University ... ME .. 210
University of New England ... ME .. 213
Notre Dame of Maryland University ... MD .. 217
University of Maryland Baltimore ... MD .. 219
University of Maryland Eastern Shore ... MD .. 219
MCPHS University ... MA .. 233
Northeastern University ... MA .. 235
@Western New England University ... MA .. 238
Ferris State University ... MI ... 242
University of Michigan-Ann Arbor ... MI ... 251
Wayne State University ... MI ... 252
University of Minnesota-Twin Cities ... MN .. 264
University of Mississippi ... MS .. 270
St. Louis College of Pharmacy ... MO .. 281
University of Missouri - Kansas City ... MO .. 283
University of Montana - Missoula, The ... MT .. 286
Creighton University ... NE .. 289
University of Nebraska Medical Center ... NE .. 292
Roseman University of Health Sciences ... NV .. 295
@Fairleigh Dickinson University ... NJ ... 301
Rutgers the State University of New Jersey New Brunswick Campus ... NJ ... 306
University of New Mexico Main Campus .. NM .. 312
Albany College of Pharmacy and Health Sciences ... NY ... 313
@D'Youville College ... NY ... 323
St. John Fisher College ... NY ... 338
St. John's University ... NY ... 339
Touro College ... NY ... 348
University at Buffalo-SUNY ... NY ... 341
Campbell University ... NC .. 352
University of North Carolina at Chapel Hill NC .. 368
Wingate University ... NC .. 370
North Dakota State University Main Campus ... ND ... 371
@Cedarville University ... OH .. 375
Northeast Ohio Medical University ... OH .. 385
Ohio Northern University ... OH .. 386
Ohio State University Main Campus, The . OH .. 386
University of Cincinnati Main Campus ... OH .. 390
University of Findlay, The ... OH .. 391
University of Toledo ... OH .. 392
Southwestern Oklahoma State University . OK .. 400
Oregon State University ... OR .. 406
Pacific University ... OR .. 407
Duquesne University ... PA ... 415
Lake Erie College of Osteopathic Medicine ... PA ... 420
Temple University ... PA ... 433
Thomas Jefferson University ... PA ... 434
University of Pittsburgh ... PA ... 435
University of the Sciences in Philadelphia PA ... 435
Wilkes University ... PA ... 437
University of Puerto Rico-Medical Sciences Campus ... PR ... 554
University of Rhode Island ... RI ... 440
Medical University of South Carolina ... SC ... 445
@Presbyterian College ... SC ... 446
University of South Carolina Columbia ... SC ... 447
South Dakota State University ... SD ... 452
Belmont University ... TN ... 453
East Tennessee State University ... TN ... 459
Lipscomb University ... TN ... 456
@South College ... TN ... 458
Union University ... TN ... 462
Texas A & M University - Kingsville ... TX ... 484
Texas Southern University ... TX ... 485
Texas Tech University Health Sciences Center ... TX ... 487
University of Houston ... TX ... 489
@University of North Texas Health Science Center at Fort Worth ... TX ... 490
University of Texas at Austin ... TX ... 491
University of the Incarnate Word ... TX ... 490
University of Utah, The ... UT ... 496
Appalachian College of Pharmacy ... VA ... 501
Hampton University ... VA ... 505
Shenandoah University ... VA ... 509
Virginia Commonwealth University ... VA ... 511
University of Washington ... WA .. 524
Washington State University ... WA .. 525
@Marshall University ... WV .. 529
University of Charleston ... WV .. 527
West Virginia University ... WV .. 530
@Concordia University Wisconsin ... WI ... 532
University of Wisconsin-Madison ... WI ... 536
University of Wyoming ... WY ... 543

PHLEB: National Accrediting Agency for Clinical Laboratory Sciences: phlebotomist (C)

Phillips Community College of the University of Arkansas ... AR ... 24
South Arkansas Community College ... AR ... 23

Southeast Arkansas College ... AR ... 23
Dalton State College ... GA .. 123
Kapiolani Community College ... HI ... 136
College of Lake County ... IL ... 143
Kankakee Community College ... IL ... 149
Moraine Valley Community College ... IL ... 153
South Suburban College of Cook County . IL ... 159
Bossier Parish Community College ... LA ... 202
Delgado Community College ... LA ... 203
L.E. Fletcher Technical Community College ... LA ... 203
Southern University at Shreveport-Louisiana ... LA ... 207
Mid Michigan Community College ... MI ... 247
Minneapolis Community and Technical College ... MN .. 259
St. Catherine University ... MN .. 263
University of Southern Mississippi ... MS .. 270
Miles Community College ... MT .. 286
Orange County Community College ... NY ... 335
Trocaire College ... NY ... 348
Asheville - Buncombe Technical Community College ... NC .. 357
Brunswick Community College ... NC .. 358
Cape Fear Community College ... NC .. 358
Carolinas College of Health Sciences ... NC .. 353
Halifax Community College ... NC .. 361
Nash Community College ... NC .. 362
Rockingham Community College ... NC .. 363
Southeastern Community College ... NC .. 364
Southwestern Community College ... NC .. 364
Wake Technical Community College ... NC .. 364
Bismarck State College ... ND .. 372
Turtle Mountain Community College ... ND .. 373
Columbus State Community College ... OH .. 378
Edison State Community College ... OH .. 379
Lorain County Community College ... OH .. 383
Zane State College ... OH .. 394
Seminole State College ... OK .. 399
Tulsa Community College ... OK .. 400
Community College of Beaver County ... PA ... 413
Community College of Philadelphia ... PA ... 413
Montgomery County Community College . PA ... 424
Southwest Tennessee Community College ... TN ... 461
Austin Community College District ... TX ... 466
Weatherford College ... TX ... 494
Mid-State Technical College ... WI ... 540
Milwaukee Area Technical College ... WI ... 540
Northcentral Technical College ... WI ... 541

PLNG: Planning Accreditation Board: certified planning (B,M)

Alabama Agricultural and Mechanical University ... AL ... 1
#Auburn University ... AL ... 1
Arizona State University ... AZ ... 11
University of Arizona ... AZ ... 18
California Polytechnic State University-San Luis Obispo ... CA ... 32
California State Polytechnic University-Pomona ... CA ... 32
San Jose State University ... CA ... 36
University of California-Berkeley ... CA ... 70
University of California-Irvine ... CA ... 71
University of California-Los Angeles ... CA ... 71
University of Southern California ... CA ... 74
University of Colorado Denver|Anschutz Medical Campus ... CO ... 86
Florida Atlantic University ... FL ... 114
Florida State University ... FL ... 115
University of Florida ... FL ... 116
Georgia Institute of Technology ... GA .. 125
University of Hawaii at Manoa ... HI ... 136
University of Illinois at Chicago ... IL ... 161
University of Illinois at Urbana-Champaign IL ... 162
Ball State University ... IN ... 164
Iowa State University ... IA ... 175
University of Iowa ... IA ... 175
Kansas State University ... KS ... 188
University of Kansas Main Campus ... KS ... 190
University of Louisville ... KY ... 200
University of New Orleans ... LA ... 205
Morgan State University ... MD .. 217
University of Maryland College Park ... MD .. 219
Harvard University ... MA .. 227
Massachusetts Institute of Technology ... MA .. 233
Tufts University ... MA .. 237
#University of Massachusetts ... MA .. 228
Eastern Michigan University ... MI ... 242
#Michigan State University ... MI ... 246
University of Michigan-Ann Arbor ... MI ... 251
Wayne State University ... MI ... 252
University of Minnesota-Twin Cities ... MN .. 264
Jackson State University ... MS .. 267
Missouri State University ... MO .. 278
University of Nebraska - Lincoln ... NE ... 292
Rutgers the State University of New Jersey New Brunswick Campus ... NJ ... 306
University of New Mexico Main Campus .. NM .. 312
City University of New York Hunter College ... NY ... 318
Columbia University in the City of New York ... NY ... 321
Cornell University ... NY ... 322
New York University ... NY ... 334
Pratt Institute ... NY ... 336
University at Albany, SUNY ... NY ... 341
University at Buffalo-SUNY ... NY ... 341
East Carolina University ... NC .. 367
University of North Carolina at Chapel Hill NC .. 368
Cleveland State University ... OH .. 377
Ohio State University Main Campus, The . OH .. 386
University of Cincinnati Main Campus ... OH .. 390
Portland State University ... OR .. 406
University of Oregon ... OR .. 406
Indiana University of Pennsylvania ... PA ... 428
Temple University ... PA ... 433
University of Pennsylvania ... PA ... 435
University of Puerto Rico-Rio Piedras Campus ... PR ... 555
Clemson University ... SC ... 442
University of Memphis, The ... TN ... 460
Texas A & M University ... TX ... 483
Texas Southern University ... TX ... 485
University of Texas at Arlington, The ... TX ... 491
University of Texas at Austin ... TX ... 491
University of Utah, The ... UT ... 496
University of Virginia ... VA ... 511
Virginia Commonwealth University ... VA ... 511
Virginia Polytechnic Institute and State University ... VA ... 515
Eastern Washington University ... WA .. 519
University of Washington ... WA .. 524
University of Wisconsin-Madison ... WI ... 536
University of Wisconsin-Milwaukee ... WI ... 537

PNUR: Accreditation Commission for Education in Nursing: practical nursing (C)

Bevill State Community College ... AL ... 2
Bishop State Community College ... AL ... 2
Calhoun Community College ... AL ... 2
Chattahoochee Valley Community College AL ... 2
Gadsden State Community College ... AL ... 3
George C. Wallace Community College - Dothan ... AL ... 3
George Corley Wallace State Community College - Selma ... AL ... 4
James H. Faulkner State Community College ... AL ... 4
Lawson State Community College ... AL ... 5
Northeast Alabama Community College ... AL ... 5
Shelton State Community College ... AL ... 6
Trenholm State Technical College ... AL ... 7
Wallace State Community College - Hanceville ... AL ... 9
Front Range Community College ... CO ... 81
Northeastern Junior College ... CO ... 83
Pueblo Community College ... CO ... 84
Delaware Technical Community College, Terry Campus ... DE ... 93
Santa Fe College ... FL ... 113
Augusta Technical College ... GA .. 121
Columbus Technical College ... GA .. 123
Savannah Technical College ... GA .. 131
Carrington College - Boise ... ID ... 137
Carl Sandburg College ... IL ... 141
College of DuPage ... IL ... 142
Lake Land College ... IL ... 150
Ivy Tech Community College-Central Indiana ... IN ... 169
MedTech College ... IN ... 171
Vincennes University ... IN ... 174
Western Iowa Tech Community College ... IA ... 183
Dodge City Community College ... KS ... 186
Hutchinson Community College and Area Vocational School ... KS ... 187
Wichita Area Technical College ... KS ... 191
Southeast Kentucky Community and Technical College ... KY ... 196
L.E. Fletcher Technical Community College ... LA ... 203
College of Southern Maryland ... MD .. 214
Hagerstown Community College ... MD .. 215
Howard Community College ... MD .. 215
Mount Wachusett Community College ... MA .. 232
Northern Essex Community College ... MA .. 232
Quincy College ... MA .. 235
Quinsigamond Community College ... MA .. 232
Davenport University ... MI ... 241
Grand Rapids Community College ... MI ... 243
Minneapolis Community and Technical College ... MN .. 259
Rochester Community and Technical College ... MN .. 261
Saint Paul College-A Community & Technical College ... MN .. 261
Meridian Community College ... MS .. 267
Mississippi Delta Community College ... MS .. 268
Mississippi Gulf Coast Community College ... MS .. 268
Metropolitan Community College - Penn Valley ... MO .. 277
Southeast Community College ... NE ... 292
Western Nebraska Community College ... NE ... 293
College of Southern Nevada ... NV ... 294
Kaplan College ... NV ... 294
NHTI-Concord's Community College ... NH .. 296
St. Joseph School of Nursing ... NH .. 297
Salem Community College ... NJ ... 307
Union County College ... NJ ... 308
Central New Mexico Community College . NM .. 309
Farmingdale State College ... NY ... 346
Suffolk County Community College Ammerman Campus ... NY ... 346
Trocaire College ... NY ... 348
Durham Technical Community College ... NC .. 360
Gaston College ... NC .. 360
Rowan-Cabarrus Community College ... NC .. 363
Sampson Community College ... NC .. 363
Wayne Community College ... NC .. 364
Dickinson State University ... ND .. 371
North Dakota State College of Science ... ND .. 372
United Tribes Technical College ... ND .. 373
Hocking College ... OH .. 380
Lorain County Community College ... OH .. 383
Treasure Valley Community College ... OR .. 408
Harrisburg Area Community College ... PA ... 417
Lehigh Carbon Community College ... PA ... 421
Northampton Community College ... PA ... 425
Pennsylvania College of Technology ... PA ... 427
Reading Area Community College ... PA ... 431
Community College of Rhode Island ... RI ... 439
Central Carolina Technical College ... SC ... 441
Greenville Technical College ... SC ... 444
Horry-Georgetown Technical College ... SC ... 444
Midlands Technical College ... SC ... 445
Orangeburg-Calhoun Technical College ... SC ... 446
Technical College of the Lowcountry ... SC ... 447
Tri-County Technical College ... SC ... 447
Trident Technical College ... SC ... 447
York Technical College ... SC ... 449
Lake Area Technical Institute ... SD ... 450
Austin Community College District ... TX ... 466
El Centro College ... TX ... 470
Ogden-Weber Applied Technology College ... UT ... 496
Snow College ... UT ... 498
Uintah Basin Applied Technology College UT ... 496
Vermont Technical College ... VT ... 501
Centra College of Nursing ... VA ... 503
Riverside School of Health Careers ... VA ... 509
Chippewa Valley Technical College ... WI ... 539
Milwaukee Area Technical College ... WI ... 540

POD: American Podiatric Medical Association: podiatry (FP,D)

Samuel Merritt University ... CA ... 61
Western University of Health Sciences ... CA ... 76
Barry University ... FL ... 98
Rosalind Franklin University of Medicine & Science ... IL ... 157
Des Moines University ... IA ... 177
New York College of Podiatric Medicine ... NY ... 333
Kent State University Main Campus ... OH .. 382
Temple University ... PA ... 433

POLYT: Commission on Accreditation of Allied Health Education Programs: polysomnographic technologist education (C,A)

Wallace State Community College - Hanceville ... AL ... 9
Gateway Community College ... AZ ... 14
Orange Coast College ... CA ... 39
Pueblo Community College ... CO ... 84
Central Florida Institute ... FL ... 99
Santa Fe College ... FL ... 113
Moraine Valley Community College ... IL ... 153
Mercy College of Health Sciences ... IA ... 181
Johnson County Community College ... KS ... 187
Bluegrass Community and Technical College ... KY ... 194
Southcentral Kentucky Community and Technical College ... KY ... 196
West Kentucky Community and Technical College ... KY ... 196
Community College of Baltimore County, The ... MD .. 214
Montgomery College ... MD .. 216
Northern Essex Community College ... MA .. 232
Baker College of Flint ... MI ... 239
Minneapolis Community and Technical College ... MN .. 259
Coahoma Community College ... MS .. 266
Sanford-Brown College ... MO .. 281
Southeast Community College ... NE ... 292
Thomas Edison State College ... NJ ... 308
Genesee Community College ... NY ... 325
Hudson Valley Community College ... NY ... 326
State University of New York at Stony Brook ... NY ... 342
Catawba Valley Community College ... NC .. 359
Central Carolina Community College ... NC .. 359
Lenoir Community College ... NC .. 361
Pitt Community College ... NC .. 362
Sandhills Community College ... NC .. 363
Cuyahoga Community College ... OH .. 378
Mercy College of Ohio ... OH .. 383
Linn-Benton Community College ... OR .. 404
Oregon Institute of Technology ... OR .. 405
East Tennessee State University ... TN ... 459
Miller-Motte Technical College ... TN ... 457
Roane State Community College ... TN ... 461
Volunteer State Community College ... TN ... 461
Alvin Community College ... TX ... 465
Collin County Community College District TX ... 469
J. Sargeant Reynolds Community College VA ... 512
Highline Community College ... WA .. 520

PSPSY: American Psychological Association: combined professional-scientific psychology (D)

University of California-Santa Barbara ... CA ... 72
Florida State University ... FL ... 115
Northeastern University ... MA .. 235
Pace University ... NY ... 335
University at Buffalo-SUNY ... NY ... 341
Yeshiva University ... NY ... 351
Utah State University ... UT ... 497
James Madison University ... VA ... 506

PTA: American Physical Therapy Association: physical therapy (M,D)

Alabama State University ... AL ... 1
University of Alabama at Birmingham ... AL ... 8
University of South Alabama ... AL ... 9
Northern Arizona University ... AZ ... 16
Arkansas State University-Jonesboro ... AR ... 19
@Harding University Main Campus ... AR ... 21
University of Central Arkansas ... AR ... 25
Azusa Pacific University ... CA ... 29
California State University-Fresno ... CA ... 33
California State University-Long Beach ... CA ... 33
California State University-Northridge ... CA ... 34
California State University-Sacramento ... CA ... 34
Chapman University ... CA ... 38
Loma Linda University ... CA ... 51
Mount St. Mary's College ... CA ... 54
Samuel Merritt University ... CA ... 61
@San Diego State University ... CA ... 35
San Francisco State University ... CA ... 35
University of California-San Francisco ... CA ... 72
University of Southern California ... CA ... 74
University of the Pacific ... CA ... 73
Western University of Health Sciences ... CA ... 76
Regis University ... CO ... 84
University of Colorado Denver|Anschutz Medical Campus ... CO ... 86
Quinnipiac University ... CT ... 91
Sacred Heart University ... CT ... 91
University of Connecticut ... CT ... 92
University of Hartford ... CT ... 92
University of Delaware ... DE ... 94
George Washington University ... DC ... 95
Howard University ... DC ... 95
Florida Agricultural and Mechanical University ... FL ... 114
Florida Gulf Coast University ... FL ... 115
Florida International University ... FL ... 115
Nova Southeastern University ... FL ... 109
University of Central Florida ... FL ... 115
University of Florida ... FL ... 116
University of Miami ... FL ... 118
University of North Florida ... FL ... 116
University of St. Augustine for Health Sciences ... FL ... 118
University of South Florida ... FL ... 116
Armstrong Atlantic State University ... GA .. 120
Emory University ... GA .. 124
Georgia Regents University ... GA .. 126
Georgia State University ... GA .. 126
Mercer University ... GA .. 128
University of North Georgia ... GA .. 133
Idaho State University ... ID ... 138
Bradley University ... IL ... 140
Governors State University ... IL ... 145
Midwestern University ... IL ... 153
Northern Illinois University ... IL ... 154
Northwestern University ... IL ... 155
Rosalind Franklin University of Medicine & Science ... IL ... 157
University of Illinois at Chicago ... IL ... 161
Indiana University-Purdue University Indianapolis ... IN ... 168
University of Evansville ... IN ... 173
University of Indianapolis ... IN ... 173
Clarke University ... IA ... 176
Des Moines University ... IA ... 177
St. Ambrose University ... IA ... 182
University of Iowa ... IA ... 175
@University of Saint Mary ... KS ... 191
#Wichita State University ... KS ... 191
Bellarmine University ... KY ... 192
University of Kentucky ... KY ... 200
@Western Kentucky University ... KY ... 200
Louisiana State University Health Sciences Center at Shreveport ... LA ... 205

Louisiana State University Health Sciences Center-New Orleans ... LA ... 205
Husson University ... ME .. 210
University of New England ... ME .. 213
University of Maryland Baltimore ... MD .. 219
University of Maryland Eastern Shore ... MD .. 219
American International College ... MA .. 221
Boston University ... MA .. 224
@MCPHS University ... MA .. 233
MGH Institute of Health Professions ... MA .. 234
Northeastern University ... MA .. 235
Simmons College ... MA .. 236
Springfield College ... MA .. 236
University of Massachusetts Lowell ... MA .. 229
Andrews University ... MI ... 239
Central Michigan University ... MI ... 240
Grand Valley State University ... MI ... 243
Oakland University ... MI ... 248
University of Michigan-Flint ... MI ... 251
Wayne State University ... MI ... 252
College of Saint Scholastica, The ... MN .. 254
St. Catherine University ... MN .. 263
University of Minnesota-Twin Cities ... MN .. 264
University of Mississippi Medical Center ... MS .. 270
Maryville University of Saint Louis ... MO .. 276
Missouri State University ... MO .. 278
Rockhurst University ... MO .. 280
Saint Louis University ... MO .. 281
Southwest Baptist University ... MO .. 282
University of Missouri - Columbia ... MO .. 283
Washington University in St. Louis ... MO .. 284
University of Montana - Missoula, The ... MT .. 286
Creighton University ... NE ... 289
University of Nebraska Medical Center ... NE ... 292
University of Nevada, Las Vegas ... NV ... 294
Franklin Pierce University ... NH .. 296
Richard Stockton College of New Jersey, The ... NJ ... 305
Rutgers the State University of New Jersey Camden Campus ... NJ ... 306
Seton Hall University ... NJ ... 307
University of New Mexico Main Campus .. NM .. 312
City University of New York College of Staten Island ... NY ... 317
City University of New York Hunter College ... NY ... 318
Clarkson University ... NY ... 320
Columbia University in the City of New York ... NY ... 321
Daemen College ... NY ... 322
Dominican College of Blauvelt ... NY ... 322
D'Youville College ... NY ... 323
Ithaca College ... NY ... 327
Mercy College ... NY ... 330
Nazareth College of Rochester ... NY ... 332
New York Institute of Technology ... NY ... 333
New York Medical College ... NY ... 334
New York University ... NY ... 334
Sage Colleges, The ... NY ... 338
State University of New York at Stony Brook ... NY ... 342
State University of New York Health Science Center at Brooklyn ... NY ... 342
State University of New York Upstate Medical University ... NY ... 342
Touro College ... NY ... 348
University at Buffalo-SUNY ... NY ... 341
Utica College ... NY ... 349
Duke University ... NC .. 354
East Carolina University ... NC .. 367
Elon University ... NC .. 354
University of North Carolina at Chapel Hill NC .. 368
Western Carolina University ... NC .. 369
Winston-Salem State University ... NC .. 370
@University of Jamestown ... ND .. 373
University of Mary ... ND .. 373
University of North Dakota Main Campus . ND .. 371
Cleveland State University ... OH .. 377
College of Mount St. Joseph ... OH .. 377
Ohio State University Main Campus, The . OH .. 386
Ohio University Main Campus ... OH .. 387
University of Cincinnati Main Campus ... OH .. 390
University of Dayton ... OH .. 391
University of Findlay, The ... OH .. 391
University of Toledo ... OH .. 392
Walsh University ... OH .. 392
Youngstown State University ... OH .. 394
Langston University ... OK .. 395
@George Fox University ... OR .. 403
Pacific University ... OR .. 407
Arcadia University ... PA ... 409
Chatham University ... PA ... 412
Drexel University ... PA ... 415
Duquesne University ... PA ... 415
Gannon University ... PA ... 416
Lebanon Valley College ... PA ... 421
Misericordia University ... PA ... 424
Neumann University ... PA ... 424
Saint Francis University ... PA ... 432
Slippery Rock University of Pennsylvania . PA ... 429
Temple University ... PA ... 433
Thomas Jefferson University ... PA ... 434
University of Pittsburgh ... PA ... 435
University of Scranton, The ... PA ... 436
University of the Sciences in Philadelphia PA ... 435
Widener University ... PA ... 437
University of Puerto Rico-Medical Sciences Campus ... PR ... 554
University of Rhode Island ... RI ... 440
Medical University of South Carolina ... SC ... 445
University of South Carolina Columbia ... SC ... 447
University of South Dakota, The ... SD ... 451
Belmont University ... TN ... 453
East Tennessee State University ... TN ... 459
Tennessee State University ... TN ... 459
University of Tennessee at Chattanooga .. TN ... 463
Angelo State University ... TX ... 465
Baylor University ... TX ... 467
Hardin-Simmons University ... TX ... 472
Texas State University-San Marcos ... TX ... 487
Texas Tech University Health Sciences Center ... TX ... 487
Texas Woman's University ... TX ... 488
University of North Texas Health Science Center at Fort Worth ... TX ... 490
University of Texas at El Paso ... TX ... 492
University of Texas Health Science Center at San Antonio ... TX ... 493
University of Texas Medical Branch, The . TX ... 493
University of Texas Southwestern Medical Center ... TX ... 493
@University of the Incarnate Word ... TX ... 490
Rocky Mountain University of Health Professions ... UT ... 496
University of Utah, The ... UT ... 496
University of Vermont ... VT ... 500
Hampton University ... VA ... 505
Lynchburg College ... VA ... 506
Marymount University ... VA ... 507
Old Dominion University ... VA ... 507
@Radford University ... VA ... 508
Shenandoah University ... VA ... 509
Virginia Commonwealth University ... VA ... 511
Eastern Washington University ... WA .. 519
University of Puget Sound ... WA .. 524
University of Washington ... WA .. 524
@Marshall University ... WV .. 529
West Virginia University ... WV .. 530
Wheeling Jesuit University ... WV .. 531
Carroll University ... WI ... 532
Concordia University Wisconsin ... WI ... 532
Marquette University ... WI ... 534
University of Wisconsin-La Crosse ... WI ... 536
University of Wisconsin-Madison ... WI ... 536
University of Wisconsin-Milwaukee ... WI ... 537

PTAA: American Physical Therapy Association: physical therapy assistant (A)

Bishop State Community College ... AL ... 2
Calhoun Community College ... AL ... 2
George C. Wallace Community College - Dothan ... AL ... 3
Jefferson State Community College ... AL ... 5
Wallace State Community College - Hanceville ... AL ... 9
Brookline College ... AZ ... 12
Gateway Community College ... AZ ... 14
#Mohave Community College ... AZ ... 15
Pima Medical Institute-Tucson ... AZ ... 17
Arkansas State University-Jonesboro ... AR ... 19
Arkansas Tech University ... AR ... 20
NorthWest Arkansas Community College . AR ... 22
South Arkansas Community College ... AR ... 23
@Casa Loma College-Van Nuys ... CA ... 37
Cerritos College ... CA ... 37
College of the Sequoias ... CA ... 40
Concorde Career College ... CA ... 41
#Concorde Career College ... CA ... 41
Concorde Career College ... CA ... 41
@Gurnick Academy of Medical Arts ... CA ... 46
Loma Linda University ... CA ... 51
#Ohlone College ... CA ... 57
Sacramento City College ... CA ... 53
San Diego Mesa College ... CA ... 62
@Stanbridge College ... CA ... 68
Arapahoe Community College ... CO ... 78
Concorde Career College ... CO ... 81
Morgan Community College ... CO ... 83
#Pueblo Community College ... CO ... 84
#Capital Community College ... CT ... 88
#Housatonic Community College ... CT ... 88
#Manchester Community College ... CT ... 88
#Naugatuck Valley Community College ... CT ... 89
#Northwestern Connecticut Community-Technical College ... CT ... 89
Norwalk Community College ... CT ... 89
#Tunxis Community College ... CT ... 89
Delaware Technical Community College, Owens Campus ... DE ... 93
Delaware Technical Community College, Stanton-Wilmington Campus ... DE ... 93
Broward College ... FL ... 99
College of Central Florida ... FL ... 100
#Concorde Career Institute ... FL ... 100
@Concorde Career Institute ... FL ... 100
Daytona State College ... FL ... 101
Florida Gateway College ... FL ... 104
Florida State College at Jacksonville ... FL ... 105
Gulf Coast State College ... FL ... 106
@Hodges University ... FL ... 106
Indian River State College ... FL ... 106
Keiser University ... FL ... 108
Miami Dade College ... FL ... 109
Pensacola State College ... FL ... 110
Polk State College ... FL ... 110
Praxis Institute, The ... FL ... 111
St. Petersburg College ... FL ... 112
Seminole State College of Florida ... FL ... 113
State College of Florida, Manatee-Sarasota ... FL ... 114
Athens Technical College ... GA .. 120
@Atlanta Technical College ... GA .. 121
Chattahoochee Technical College ... GA .. 122
Darton State College ... GA .. 124
South University ... GA .. 131
Kapiolani Community College ... HI ... 136
Carrington College - Boise ... ID ... 137
Idaho State University ... ID ... 138
Black Hawk College ... IL ... 140
College of DuPage ... IL ... 142
Elgin Community College ... IL ... 144
Fox College ... IL ... 145
Illinois Central College ... IL ... 146
Kankakee Community College ... IL ... 149
Kaskaskia College ... IL ... 149
Lake Land College ... IL ... 150
Morton College ... IL ... 153
Oakton Community College ... IL ... 155
@SOLEX College ... IL ... 159
Southern Illinois University Carbondale ... IL ... 159
Southwestern Illinois College ... IL ... 160
University of Evansville ... IN ... 173
University of Indianapolis ... IN ... 173
University of Saint Francis ... IN ... 174
Vincennes University ... IN ... 174
Hawkeye Community College ... IA ... 178
Indian Hills Community College ... IA ... 179
Kirkwood Community College ... IA ... 180
Mercy College of Health Sciences ... IA ... 181
North Iowa Area Community College ... IA ... 181
Western Iowa Tech Community College ... IA ... 183
Colby Community College ... KS ... 185
Hutchinson Community College and Area Vocational School ... KS ... 187
Kansas City Kansas Community College . KS ... 187
Labette Community College ... KS ... 188
Washburn University ... KS ... 191
Hazard Community and Technical College KY ... 195
Jefferson Community and Technical College ... KY ... 195
Madisonville Community College ... KY ... 196
Somerset Community College ... KY ... 196
Southeast Kentucky Community and Technical College ... KY ... 196
West Kentucky Community and Technical College ... KY ... 196
Bossier Parish Community College ... LA ... 202
Delgado Community College ... LA ... 203
Louisiana College ... LA ... 202
Our Lady of the Lake College ... LA ... 206
Kennebec Valley Community College ... ME .. 210
@University of Maine at Presque Isle ... ME .. 212
Allegany College of Maryland ... MD .. 213
Anne Arundel Community College ... MD .. 213
Baltimore City Community College ... MD .. 213
Carroll Community College ... MD .. 214
Chesapeake College ... MD .. 214
College of Southern Maryland ... MD .. 214
@Howard Community College ... MD .. 215
Montgomery College ... MD .. 216
Bay State College ... MA .. 222
Berkshire Community College ... MA .. 231
Mount Wachusett Community College ... MA .. 232
North Shore Community College ... MA .. 232
Springfield Technical Community College MA .. 233
Baker College of Flint ... MI ... 239
Delta College ... MI ... 242
Finlandia University ... MI ... 242
Henry Ford Community College ... MI ... 243
Kellogg Community College ... MI ... 244
Macomb Community College ... MI ... 246
Mid Michigan Community College ... MI ... 247
Mott Community College ... MI ... 247
Washtenaw Community College ... MI ... 252
Anoka-Ramsey Community College ... MN .. 257
Lake Superior College ... MN .. 259
Northland Community and Technical College ... MN ... 260
St. Catherine University ... MN ... 263
Hinds Community College ... MS ... 267
Itawamba Community College ... MS ... 267
Meridian Community College ... MS ... 267
Pearl River Community College ... MS ... 269
Concorde Career College ... MO .. 272
@Jefferson College ... MO ... 275
Linn State Technical College ... MO .. 276
Metropolitan Community College - Penn Valley ... MO ... 277
Mineral Area College ... MO .. 278
Missouri Western State University ... MO .. 279
Ozarks Technical Community College ... MO .. 279
@Flathead Valley Community College ... MT .. 286
Great Falls College Montana State University ... MT .. 287
Clarkson College ... NE ... 288
Nebraska Methodist College ... NE ... 291
Northeast Community College ... NE ... 291
Southeast Community College ... NE ... 292
College of Southern Nevada ... NV ... 294
Mount Washington College ... NH ... 297
River Valley Community College ... NH .. 296
Essex County College ... NJ ... 301
Mercer County Community College ... NJ ... 302
Union County College ... NJ ... 308
San Juan College ... NM .. 311
Broome Community College ... NY ... 315
City University of New York Kingsborough Community College ... NY ... 318
Genesee Community College ... NY ... 325
Herkimer County Community College ... NY ... 326
La Guardia Community College/City University of New York ... NY ... 318
Nassau Community College ... NY ... 332
Niagara County Community College ... NY ... 334
Onondaga Community College ... NY ... 335
Orange County Community College ... NY ... 335
Suffolk County Community College Ammerman Campus ... NY ... 346
SUNY Canton-College of Technology ... NY ... 345
Villa Maria College of Buffalo ... NY ... 350
Caldwell Community College and Technical Institute ... NC .. 358
Central Piedmont Community College ... NC .. 359
Craven Community College ... NC .. 359
Fayetteville Technical Community College NC .. 360
Guilford Technical Community College ... NC .. 360
Martin Community College ... NC .. 361
Nash Community College ... NC .. 362
South College-Asheville ... NC .. 366
Southwestern Community College ... NC .. 364
Surry Community College ... NC .. 364
@Bradford School ... OH .. 375
Clark State Community College ... OH .. 377
Cuyahoga Community College ... OH .. 378
Edison State Community College ... OH .. 379
Hocking College ... OH .. 380
James A. Rhodes State College ... OH .. 381
Lorain County Community College ... OH .. 383
Marion Technical College ... OH .. 383
North Central State College ... OH .. 385
Owens Community College ... OH .. 387
Professional Skills Institute ... OH .. 388
Shawnee State University ... OH .. 388
Sinclair Community College ... OH .. 388
Stark State College ... OH .. 389
@Terra State Community College ... OH .. 389
University of Cincinnati Main Campus ... OH .. 390
Washington State Community College ... OH .. 392
Zane State College ... OH .. 394
Carl Albert State College ... OK .. 394
Murray State College ... OK .. 396
Northeastern Oklahoma Agricultural and Mechanical College ... OK .. 396
Oklahoma City Community College ... OK .. 397
Southwestern Oklahoma State University . OK .. 400
Tulsa Community College ... OK .. 400
Lane Community College ... OR .. 403
Mt. Hood Community College ... OR .. 404
Butler County Community College ... PA ... 411
California University of Pennsylvania ... PA ... 428
Central Penn College ... PA ... 412
Community College of Allegheny County . PA ... 413
Harcum College ... PA ... 417
Lackawanna College ... PA ... 420
Lehigh Carbon Community College ... PA ... 421
Mercyhurst University ... PA ... 423
Mount Aloysius College ... PA ... 424
@Huertas Junior College ... PR ... 549
@Inter American University of Puerto Rico Ponce Campus ... PR ... 550
University of Puerto Rico at Ponce ... PR ... 555
University of Puerto Rico-Humacao ... PR ... 554
Community College of Rhode Island ... RI ... 439
New England Institute of Technology ... RI ... 439
Greenville Technical College ... SC ... 444
Horry-Georgetown Technical College ... SC ... 444
Midlands Technical College ... SC ... 445
Technical College of the Lowcountry ... SC ... 447
Trident Technical College ... SC ... 447
Lake Area Technical Institute ... SD ... 450
Chattanooga State Community College ... TN ... 460
Concorde Career College ... TN ... 453
Jackson State Community College ... TN ... 460
Roane State Community College ... TN ... 461
South College ... TN ... 458
Southwest Tennessee Community College ... TN ... 461
Volunteer State Community College ... TN ... 461
Walters State Community College ... TN ... 462
Amarillo College ... TX ... 465
Austin Community College District ... TX ... 466
Blinn College ... TX ... 467
Del Mar College ... TX ... 471
El Paso Community College ... TX ... 472

Houston Community College ... TX ... 473
@Kaplan College ... TX ... 474
Kilgore College ... TX ... 475
Laredo Community College ... TX ... 475
Lone Star College System ... TX ... 476
McLennan Community College ... TX ... 476
Northeast Texas Community College ... TX ... 477
Odessa College ... TX ... 477
St. Philip's College ... TX ... 465
San Jacinto College South ... TX ... 479
South Plains College ... TX ... 480
South Texas College ... TX ... 480
Tarrant County College District ... TX ... 482
Victoria College ... TX ... 493
@Weatherford College ... TX ... 494
Western Technical College ... TX ... 494
Wharton County Junior College ... TX ... 494
Dixie State College of Utah ... UT ... 497
Provo College ... UT ... 496
Salt Lake Community College ... UT ... 498
Jefferson College of Health Sciences ... VA ... 506
Northern Virginia Community College ... VA ... 513
Tidewater Community College ... VA ... 514
Wytheville Community College ... VA ... 514
Green River Community College ... WA .. 520
Lake Washington Institute of Technology . WA .. 520
Olympic College ... WA .. 521
Spokane Falls Community College ... WA .. 518
Whatcom Community College ... WA .. 525
Blue Ridge Community and Technical College ... WV .. 527
Mountwest Community and Technical College ... WV .. 528
Pierpont Community & Technical College WV .. 528
Blackhawk Technical College ... WI ... 539
Chippewa Valley Technical College ... WI ... 539
Gateway Technical College ... WI ... 540
Madison Area Technical College ... WI ... 540
Milwaukee Area Technical College ... WI ... 540
Northeast Wisconsin Technical College ... WI ... 541
Southwest Wisconsin Technical College .. WI ... 541
Western Technical College ... WI ... 541
Laramie County Community College ... WY .. 543

RABN: Association of Advanced Rabbinical and Talmudic Schools: rabbinical and Talmudic education (B, M,D)

Yeshiva Ohr Elchonon Chabad/West Coast Talmudical Seminary ... CA ... 77
Yeshiva Toras Chaim Talmudical Seminary of Denver ... CO ... 87
Beth Benjamin Academy of Connecticut ... CT ... 87
Talmudic College of Florida ... FL ... 117
@Yeshiva Gedolah Rabbinical College ... FL ... 119
Telshe Yeshiva-Chicago ... IL ... 160
Bais HaMedrash & Mesivta of Baltimore .. MD .. 213
Ner Israel Rabbinical College ... MD .. 217
Yeshiva College of the Nation's Capital ... MD .. 221
Yeshiva Beth Yehuda - Yeshiva Gedolah of Greater Detroit ... MI ... 253
Bais Medrash Toras Chesed ... NJ ... 299
Beth Medrash Govoha ... NJ ... 299
Mesivta Keser Torah ... NJ ... 303
@Rabbi Jacob Joseph School ... NJ ... 304
Rabbinical College of America ... NJ ... 304
Talmudical Academy of New Jersey ... NJ ... 307
Yeshiva Gedolah Zichron Leyma ... NJ ... 308
Yeshiva Toras Chaim ... NJ ... 308
Yeshiva Yesodei Hatorah ... NJ ... 308
Yeshivas Be'er Yitzchok ... NJ ... 308
Be'er Yaakov Talmudic Seminary ... NY ... 314
Beis Medrash Heichal Dovid ... NY ... 314
@Bet Medrash Gadol Ateret Torah ... NY ... 315
Beth Hamedrash Shaarei Yosher Institute NY ... 315
Beth Hatalmud Rabbinical College ... NY ... 315
Beth Medrash Meor Yitzchok ... NY ... 315
Central Yeshiva Tomchei Tmimim Lubavitch America ... NY ... 316
Kehilath Yakov Rabbinical Seminary ... NY ... 328
Machzikei Hadath Rabbinical College ... NY ... 329
Mesivta of Eastern Parkway Rabbinical Seminary ... NY ... 331
Mesivta Tifereth Jerusalem of America ... NY ... 331
Mesivta Torah Vodaath Seminary ... NY ... 331
Mirrer Yeshiva Central Institute ... NY ... 331
Ohr Hameir Theological Seminary ... NY ... 335
Ohr Somayach Tanenbaum Educational Center ... NY ... 335
Rabbinical Academy Mesivta Rabbi Chaim Berlin ... NY ... 336
Rabbinical College Beth Shraga ... NY ... 336
Rabbinical College Bobover Yeshiva B'nei Zion ... NY ... 337
Rabbinical College Ch'san Sofer ... NY ... 337
Rabbinical College of Long Island ... NY ... 337
@Rabbinical College Ohr Shimon Yisroel ... NY ... 337
@Rabbinical College Ohr Yisroel ... NY ... 337
Rabbinical Seminary M'kor Chaim ... NY ... 337
Rabbinical Seminary of America ... NY ... 337
Sh'or Yoshuv Rabbinical College ... NY ... 340
Talmudical Institute of Upstate New York . NY ... 347
Talmudical Seminary of Bobov ... NY ... 347
Talmudical Seminary Oholei Torah ... NY ... 347
Torah Temimah Talmudical Seminary ... NY ... 348
United Talmudical Seminary ... NY ... 349
U.T.A. Mesivta of Kiryas Joel ... NY ... 349
@Yeshiva and Kolel Bais Medrash Elyon .... NY ... 351
@Yeshiva and Kollel Harbotzas Torah ... NY ... 351
Yeshiva Derech Chaim ... NY ... 350
Yeshiva D'Monsey Rabbinical College ... NY ... 350
@Yeshiva Gedolah Imrei Yosef D'Spinka .... NY ... 350
Yeshiva Gedolah Kesser Torah ... NY ... 351
Yeshiva Gedolah Ohr Yisrael ... NY ... 351
Yeshiva Karlin Stolin Beth Aaron V'Israel Rabbinical Institute ... NY ... 351
Yeshiva Mikdash Melech ... NY ... 351
Yeshiva of Far Rockaway ... NY ... 350
Yeshiva of Machzikai Hadas ... NY ... 351
Yeshiva of Nitra Rabbinical College ... NY ... 351
Yeshiva of the Telshe Alumni ... NY ... 351
Yeshiva Shaar HaTorah-Grodno ... NY ... 351
Yeshiva Shaarei Torah of Rockland ... NY ... 351
@Yeshiva Sholom Shachna ... NY ... 351
Yeshiva Zichron Aryeh ... NY ... 351
Yeshivas Novominsk ... NY ... 351
Yeshivath Viznitz ... NY ... 352
Yeshivath Zichron Moshe ... NY ... 352
Rabbinical College of Telshe ... OH ... 388
Talmudical Yeshiva of Philadelphia ... PA ... 433
Yeshiva Beth Moshe ... PA ... 438

RAD: Joint Review Committee on Education in Radiologic Technology: radiography (C,A,B)

Gadsden State Community College ... AL ... 3
George C. Wallace Community College - Dothan ... AL ... 3
Jefferson State Community College ... AL ... 5
Southern Union State Community College AL ... 7
Trenholm State Technical College ... AL ... 7
University of South Alabama ... AL ... 9
Wallace State Community College - Hanceville ... AL ... 9
Arizona Western College ... AZ ... 11
Central Arizona College ... AZ ... 12
Gateway Community College ... AZ ... 14
Pima Community College ... AZ ... 17
Pima Medical Institute-Tucson ... AZ ... 17
Yavapai College ... AZ ... 19
Arkansas State University-Jonesboro ... AR ... 19
National Park Community College ... AR ... 22
North Arkansas College ... AR ... 22
South Arkansas Community College ... AR ... 23
Southeast Arkansas College ... AR ... 23
University of Arkansas at Fort Smith ... AR ... 24
University of Arkansas for Medical Sciences ... AR ... 24
Antelope Valley College ... CA ... 28
Bakersfield College ... CA ... 29
Cabrillo College ... CA ... 30
California State University-Northridge ... CA ... 34
Cañada College ... CA ... 64
Chaffey College ... CA ... 37
Charles R. Drew University of Medicine & Science ... CA ... 38
City College of San Francisco ... CA ... 38
Cypress College ... CA ... 56
El Camino College ... CA ... 43
Foothill College ... CA ... 44
Fresno City College ... CA ... 68
Kaiser Permanente School of Allied Health Sciences ... CA ... 49
Loma Linda University ... CA ... 51
#Los Angeles City College ... CA ... 51
Merced College ... CA ... 54
Merritt College ... CA ... 59
Moorpark College ... CA ... 74
Mt. San Antonio College ... CA ... 55
Orange Coast College ... CA ... 39
Pasadena City College ... CA ... 58
San Diego Mesa College ... CA ... 62
Santa Barbara City College ... CA ... 64
Santa Rosa Junior College ... CA ... 65
University of California-Los Angeles ... CA ... 71
#Yuba College ... CA ... 77
Colorado Mesa University ... CO ... 79
Community College of Denver ... CO ... 81
Concorde Career College ... CO ... 81
Red Rocks Community College ... CO ... 84
UCH Memorial Hospital School Of Radiologic Technology ... CO ... 85
Capital Community College ... CT ... 88
Gateway Community College ... CT ... 88
Middlesex Community College ... CT ... 89
Naugatuck Valley Community College ... CT ... 89
Quinnipiac University ... CT ... 91
St. Vincent's College ... CT ... 91
University of Hartford ... CT ... 92
Delaware Technical Community College, Owens Campus ... DE ... 93
Delaware Technical Community College, Stanton-Wilmington Campus ... DE ... 93
Adventist University of Health Sciences ... FL ... 97
#Cambridge Institute of Allied Health & Technology ... FL ... 99
Dade Medical College ... FL ... 100
Eastern Florida State College ... FL ... 101
Edison State College ... FL ... 101
Gulf Coast State College ... FL ... 106
Hillsborough Community College ... FL ... 106
Indian River State College ... FL ... 106
Keiser University ... FL ... 108
Miami Dade College ... FL ... 109
Palm Beach State College ... FL ... 110
Pensacola State College ... FL ... 110
Polk State College ... FL ... 110
Professional Training Center ... FL ... 111
St. Petersburg College ... FL ... 112
Santa Fe College ... FL ... 113
South Florida State College ... FL ... 113
State College of Florida, Manatee-Sarasota ... FL ... 114
Valencia College ... FL ... 118
Albany Technical College ... GA .. 120
Armstrong Atlantic State University ... GA .. 120
Athens Technical College ... GA .. 120
Central Georgia Technical College ... GA .. 122
Chattahoochee Technical College ... GA .. 122
College of Coastal Georgia ... GA .. 123
Columbus Technical College ... GA .. 123
Dalton State College ... GA .. 123
Emory University ... GA .. 124
Georgia Northwestern Technical College . GA .. 125
Gwinnett Technical College ... GA .. 127
Lanier Technical College ... GA .. 128
Moultrie Technical College ... GA .. 129
Oconee Fall Line Technical College-South Campus ... GA .. 129
Ogeechee Technical College ... GA .. 129
Okefenokee Technical College ... GA .. 130
Southeastern Technical College ... GA .. 132
West Georgia Technical College ... GA .. 134
Kapiolani Community College ... HI ... 136
Boise State University ... ID ... 137
College of Southern Idaho ... ID ... 138
Idaho State University ... ID ... 138
Lewis-Clark State College ... ID ... 138
North Idaho College ... ID ... 138
City Colleges of Chicago Malcolm X College ... IL ... 142
City Colleges of Chicago Wilbur Wright College ... IL ... 142
College of DuPage ... IL ... 142
College of Lake County ... IL ... 143
Danville Area Community College ... IL ... 143
Elgin Community College ... IL ... 144
Harper College ... IL ... 145
Heartland Community College ... IL ... 146
Illinois Central College ... IL ... 146
Illinois Eastern Community Colleges Olney Central College ... IL ... 147
Kaskaskia College ... IL ... 149
Kishwaukee College ... IL ... 149
Lincoln Land Community College ... IL ... 151
Moraine Valley Community College ... IL ... 153
Northwestern College ... IL ... 155
Parkland College ... IL ... 155
Rend Lake College ... IL ... 156
Sauk Valley Community College ... IL ... 158
Southwestern Illinois College ... IL ... 160
Trinity College of Nursing & Health Sciences ... IL ... 160
Triton College ... IL ... 161
Ball State University ... IN ... 164
Indiana University Kokomo ... IN ... 168
Indiana University Northwest ... IN ... 168
Indiana University-Purdue University Fort Wayne ... IN ... 168
Indiana University-Purdue University Indianapolis ... IN ... 168
Indiana University South Bend ... IN ... 168
Ivy Tech Community College-Central Indiana ... IN ... 169
University of Saint Francis ... IN ... 174
University of Southern Indiana ... IN ... 174
Allen College ... IA ... 175
Indian Hills Community College ... IA ... 179
Iowa Central Community College ... IA ... 179
Mercy College of Health Sciences ... IA ... 181
Northeast Iowa Community College ... IA ... 181
St. Luke's College ... IA ... 182
Scott Community College ... IA ... 178
University of Iowa ... IA ... 175
Fort Hays State University ... KS ... 186
Hutchinson Community College and Area Vocational School ... KS ... 187
Labette Community College ... KS ... 188
Newman University ... KS ... 189
Washburn University ... KS ... 191
Bluegrass Community and Technical College ... KY ... 194
Elizabethtown Community and Technical College ... KY ... 195
Hazard Community and Technical College KY ... 195
Jefferson Community and Technical College ... KY ... 195
Madisonville Community College ... KY ... 196
Morehead State University ... KY ... 198
Northern Kentucky University ... KY ... 198
Owensboro Community and Technical College ... KY ... 196
St. Catharine College ... KY ... 198
Somerset Community College ... KY ... 196
Southcentral Kentucky Community and Technical College ... KY ... 196
Southeast Kentucky Community and Technical College ... KY ... 196
Spencerian College ... KY ... 199
West Kentucky Community and Technical College ... KY ... 196
Career Technical College ... LA ... 201
Delgado Community College ... LA ... 203
Fortis College ... LA ... 202
Louisiana State University at Alexandria .. LA ... 205
Louisiana State University at Eunice ... LA ... 205
McNeese State University ... LA ... 207
Northwestern State University ... LA ... 208
Our Lady of Holy Cross College ... LA ... 206
Our Lady of the Lake College ... LA ... 206
Southern University at Shreveport-Louisiana ... LA ... 207
University of Louisiana at Monroe ... LA ... 208
Central Maine Medical Center College of Nursing and Health Professions ... ME .. 209
Eastern Maine Community College ... ME .. 210
Kennebec Valley Community College ... ME .. 210
Southern Maine Community College ... ME .. 211
Allegany College of Maryland ... MD .. 213
Anne Arundel Community College ... MD .. 213
Chesapeake College ... MD .. 214
Community College of Baltimore County, The ... MD .. 214
Hagerstown Community College ... MD .. 215
Howard Community College ... MD .. 215
Montgomery College ... MD .. 216
Prince George's Community College ... MD .. 217
Wor-Wic Community College ... MD .. 221
Bunker Hill Community College ... MA .. 231
Holyoke Community College ... MA .. 231
Massachusetts Bay Community College ... MA .. 231
Massasoit Community College ... MA .. 232
MCPHS University ... MA .. 233
Middlesex Community College ... MA .. 232
North Shore Community College ... MA .. 232
Northern Essex Community College ... MA .. 232
Quinsigamond Community College ... MA .. 232
Regis College ... MA .. 236
Roxbury Community College ... MA .. 232
Springfield Technical Community College MA .. 233
Delta College ... MI ... 242
Ferris State University ... MI ... 242
Grand Rapids Community College ... MI ... 243
Henry Ford Community College ... MI ... 243
Jackson College ... MI ... 244
Kellogg Community College ... MI ... 244
Lake Michigan College ... MI ... 245
Lansing Community College ... MI ... 245
Mid Michigan Community College ... MI ... 247
Northern Michigan University ... MI ... 248
Oakland Community College ... MI ... 248
St. Clair County Community College ... MI ... 249
Washtenaw Community College ... MI ... 252
Wayne State University ... MI ... 252
Century College ... MN .. 258
Dunwoody College of Technology ... MN .. 255
Lake Superior College ... MN .. 259
Minnesota State College - Southeast Technical ... MN .. 259
Minnesota State Community and Technical College ... MN .. 259
Minnesota West Community and Technical College ... MN .. 260
Northland Community and Technical College ... MN .. 260
Riverland Community College ... MN .. 260
St. Catherine University ... MN .. 263
Copiah-Lincoln Community College ... MS .. 266
Hinds Community College ... MS .. 267
Itawamba Community College ... MS .. 267
Jones County Junior College ... MS .. 267
Meridian Community College ... MS .. 267
Mississippi Delta Community College ... MS .. 268
Mississippi Gulf Coast Community College ... MS .. 268
Northeast Mississippi Community College MS .. 269
Pearl River Community College ... MS .. 269
University of Mississippi Medical Center ... MS .. 270
Avila University ... MO .. 271
Cox College ... MO .. 273
Linn State Technical College ... MO .. 276
Metropolitan Community College - Penn Valley ... MO .. 277
Mineral Area College ... MO .. 278
Missouri Southern State University ... MO .. 278
Saint Louis Community College at Forest Park ... MO .. 281
Sanford-Brown College ... MO .. 281
Southeast Missouri Hospital College of Nursing and Health Sciences ... MO .. 282
State Fair Community College ... MO .. 282
University of Missouri - Columbia ... MO .. 283

Alegent Health School of Radiologic Technology ... NE ... 288
Clarkson College ... NE ... 288
Mary Lanning Healthcare School of Radiology ... NE ... 290
Nebraska Methodist College ... NE ... 291
Southeast Community College ... NE ... 292
University of Nebraska Medical Center ... NE ... 292
Great Basin College ... NV ... 294
University of Nevada, Las Vegas ... NV ... 294
Lebanon College ... NH .. 297
NHTI-Concord's Community College ... NH .. 296
Bergen Community College ... NJ ... 299
Brookdale Community College ... NJ ... 299
Burlington County College ... NJ ... 299
County College of Morris ... NJ ... 300
Cumberland County College ... NJ ... 301
Essex County College ... NJ ... 301
Mercer County Community College ... NJ ... 302
Middlesex County College ... NJ ... 303
Passaic County Community College ... NJ ... 304
Clovis Community College ... NM .. 309
New Mexico State University Dona Ana Community College ... NM .. 311
#Northern New Mexico College ... NM .. 311
Broome Community College ... NY ... 315
City University of New York Bronx Community College ... NY ... 317
Fulton-Montgomery Community College ... NY ... 325
Hostos Community College-City University of New York ... NY ... 318
Long Island University - Post Campus ... NY ... 329
Monroe Community College ... NY ... 332
New York City College of Technology/City University of New York ... NY ... 319
Niagara County Community College ... NY ... 334
North Country Community College ... NY ... 335
Orange County Community College ... NY ... 335
St. John's University ... NY ... 339
State University of New York Health Science Center at Brooklyn ... NY ... 342
State University of New York Upstate Medical University ... NY ... 342
Trocaire College ... NY ... 348
Westchester Community College ... NY ... 350
Asheville - Buncombe Technical Community College ... NC .. 357
Caldwell Community College and Technical Institute ... NC .. 358
Cape Fear Community College ... NC .. 358
Carolinas College of Health Sciences ... NC .. 353
Carteret Community College ... NC .. 358
Catawba Valley Community College ... NC .. 359
Cleveland Community College ... NC .. 359
Edgecombe Community College ... NC .. 360
Fayetteville Technical Community College ... NC .. 360
Forsyth Technical Community College ... NC .. 360
Guilford Technical Community College ... NC .. 360
Johnston Community College ... NC .. 361
Lenoir Community College ... NC .. 361
Pitt Community College ... NC .. 362
Rowan-Cabarrus Community College ... NC .. 363
Sandhills Community College ... NC .. 363
South College-Asheville ... NC .. 366
Southwestern Community College ... NC .. 364
University of North Carolina at Chapel Hill ... NC .. 368
Vance-Granville Community College ... NC .. 364
Wake Technical Community College ... NC .. 364
Sanford College of Nursing ... ND .. 372
Aultman College of Nursing and Health Sciences ... OH .. 374
Central Ohio Technical College ... OH .. 376
Columbus State Community College ... OH .. 378
Cuyahoga Community College ... OH .. 378
Eastern Gateway Community College - Jefferson County Campus ... OH .. 379
Fortis College ... OH .. 379
James A. Rhodes State College ... OH .. 381
Kettering College ... OH .. 382
Lakeland Community College ... OH .. 382
Lorain County Community College ... OH .. 383
Marion Technical College ... OH .. 383
Mercy College of Ohio ... OH .. 383
North Central State College ... OH .. 385
Owens Community College ... OH .. 387
Shawnee State University ... OH .. 388
Sinclair Community College ... OH .. 388
University of Cincinnati-Blue Ash College . OH .. 391
University of Rio Grande ... OH .. 392
Xavier University ... OH .. 393
Zane State College ... OH .. 394
Bacone College ... OK .. 394
Carl Albert State College ... OK .. 394
Rose State College ... OK .. 399
Tulsa Community College ... OK .. 400
Western Oklahoma State College ... OK .. 401
Portland Community College ... OR .. 407
Bucks County Community College ... PA ... 411
Community College of Allegheny County . PA ... 413
Community College of Philadelphia ... PA ... 413
Drexel University ... PA ... 415
Fortis Institute ... PA ... 416
Gannon University ... PA ... 416
Harcum College ... PA ... 417
Harrisburg Area Community College ... PA ... 417
Holy Family University ... PA ... 418
Johnson College ... PA ... 419
Lancaster General College of Nursing and Health Sciences ... PA ... 421
Mansfield University of Pennsylvania ... PA ... 429
Misericordia University ... PA ... 424
Montgomery County Community College . PA ... 424
Northampton Community College ... PA ... 425
Pennsylvania College of Technology ... PA ... 427
Sanford-Brown Institute-Pittsburgh ... PA ... 433
Thomas Jefferson University ... PA ... 434
Inter American University of Puerto Rico Ponce Campus ... PR ... 550
Inter American University of Puerto Rico San German Campus ... PR ... 551
Universidad Central Del Caribe ... PR ... 553
University of Puerto Rico-Medical Sciences Campus ... PR ... 554
Community College of Rhode Island ... RI 439
Aiken Technical College ... SC ... 440
Florence - Darlington Technical College ... SC ... 443
Greenville Technical College ... SC ... 444
Horry-Georgetown Technical College ... SC ... 444
Midlands Technical College ... SC ... 445
Orangeburg-Calhoun Technical College ... SC ... 446
Piedmont Technical College ... SC ... 446
Spartanburg Community College ... SC ... 447
Technical College of the Lowcountry ... SC ... 447
Trident Technical College ... SC ... 447
York Technical College ... SC ... 449
Mitchell Technical Institute ... SD ... 450
Presentation College ... SD ... 450
Austin Peay State University ... TN ... 459
Baptist College of Health Sciences ... TN ... 453
Chattanooga State Community College ... TN ... 460
Columbia State Community College ... TN ... 460
Concorde Career College ... TN ... 453
East Tennessee State University ... TN ... 459
Fortis Institute ... TN ... 454
Jackson State Community College ... TN ... 460
Roane State Community College ... TN ... 461
South College ... TN ... 458
Southwest Tennessee Community College ... TN ... 461
University of Tennessee, Knoxville ... TN ... 463
Volunteer State Community College ... TN ... 461
Amarillo College ... TX ... 465
Angelina College ... TX ... 465
Austin Community College District ... TX ... 466
Baptist Health System School of Health Professions ... TX ... 467
Baptist Hospitals of Southeast Texas School of Radiologic Technology ... TX ... 467
Blinn College ... TX ... 467
Brookhaven College ... TX ... 470
Coastal Bend College ... TX ... 468
Del Mar College ... TX ... 471
El Centro College ... TX ... 470
El Paso Community College ... TX ... 472
Galveston College ... TX ... 472
Houston Community College ... TX ... 473
Howard College ... TX ... 473
Lamar Institute of Technology ... TX ... 486
Laredo Community College ... TX ... 475
Lone Star College System ... TX ... 476
McLennan Community College ... TX ... 476
Midwestern State University ... TX ... 476
Odessa College ... TX ... 477
Paris Junior College ... TX ... 478
St. Philip's College ... TX ... 465
San Jacinto College Central ... TX ... 479
Tarrant County College District ... TX ... 482
Tyler Junior College ... TX ... 488
University of Texas M.D. Anderson Cancer Center, The ... TX ... 493
Weatherford College ... TX ... 494
Wharton County Junior College ... TX ... 494
Dixie State College of Utah ... UT ... 497
Salt Lake Community College ... UT ... 498
Champlain College ... VT ... 499
Southern Vermont College ... VT ... 500
Central Virginia Community College ... VA ... 512
Piedmont Virginia Community College ... VA ... 513
Riverside School of Health Careers ... VA ... 509
Southside Regional Medical Center Professional Schools ... VA ... 509
Southwest Virginia Community College ... VA ... 514
Tidewater Community College ... VA ... 514
Virginia Commonwealth University ... VA ... 511
Virginia Western Community College ... VA ... 514
Carrington College - Spokane ... WA .. 517
Spokane Community College ... WA .. 518
Tacoma Community College ... WA .. 524
Bluefield State College ... WV .. 529
Southern West Virginia Community and Technical College ... WV .. 528
University of Charleston ... WV .. 527
West Virginia Northern Community College ... WV .. 528
West Virginia University ... WV .. 530
Bellin College, Inc. ... WI ... 531
Blackhawk Technical College ... WI ... 539
Chippewa Valley Technical College ... WI ... 539
Lakeshore Technical College ... WI ... 540
Madison Area Technical College ... WI ... 540
Marian University ... WI ... 534
Milwaukee Area Technical College ... WI ... 540
Moraine Park Technical College ... WI ... 540
Northcentral Technical College ... WI ... 541
Northeast Wisconsin Technical College ... WI ... 541
University of Wisconsin-Madison ... WI ... 536
Western Technical College ... WI ... 541
Casper College ... WY .. 542
Laramie County Community College ... WY .. 543

RADDOS: Joint Review Committee on Education in Radiologic Technology: medical dosimetry (C,B,M)

University of Arkansas at Little Rock ... AR 24
Loma Linda University ... CA 51
Southern Illinois University Carbondale ... IL 159
Indiana University-Purdue University Indianapolis ... IN 168
University of Maryland Baltimore ... MD .. 219
Suffolk University ... MA .. 237
State University of New York at Stony Brook ... NY ... 342
Pitt Community College ... NC .. 362
University of North Carolina at Chapel Hill NC .. 368
Thomas Jefferson University ... PA ... 434
University of Texas Health Science Center at San Antonio ... TX ... 493
University of Texas M.D. Anderson Cancer Center, The ... TX ... 493
Bellevue College ... WA .. 517
University of Wisconsin-La Crosse ... WI ... 536

RADMAG: Joint Review Committee on Education in Radiologic Technology: magnetic resonance (C,B)

Arkansas State University-Jonesboro ... AR 19
Morehead State University ... KY ... 198
University of Nebraska Medical Center ... NE ... 292
Thomas Jefferson University ... PA ... 434
Southwest University at El Paso ... TX ... 481
West Virginia University ... WV .. 530

RTT: Joint Review Committee on Education in Radiologic Technology: radiation therapist/technologist (C,A,B)

University of South Alabama ... AL 9
Gateway Community College ... AZ 14
Arkansas State University-Jonesboro ... AR 19
City College of San Francisco ... CA 38
Kaiser Permanente School of Allied Health Sciences ... CA 49
Loma Linda University ... CA 51
Gateway Community College ... CT 88
#Howard University ... DC 95
#Cambridge Institute of Allied Health & Technology ... FL 99
Hillsborough Community College ... FL ... 106
Armstrong Atlantic State University ... GA .. 120
Georgia Northwestern Technical College . GA .. 125
Georgia Regents University ... GA .. 126
Southern Illinois University Carbondale ... IL 159
University of St. Francis ... IL 162
Indiana University Northwest ... IN 168
Indiana University-Purdue University Indianapolis ... IN 168
University of Iowa ... IA 175
St. Catharine College ... KY ... 198
Delgado Community College ... LA ... 203
Southern Maine Community College ... ME .. 211
Community College of Baltimore County, The ... MD .. 214
Laboure College ... MA .. 227
MCPHS University ... MA .. 233
Suffolk University ... MA .. 237
University of Massachusetts Medical School ... MA .. 229
Grand Valley State University ... MI 243
University of Michigan-Flint ... MI 251
Wayne State University ... MI 252
University of Minnesota-Twin Cities ... MN .. 264
Saint Louis University ... MO .. 281
University of Nebraska Medical Center ... NE ... 292
NHTI-Concord's Community College ... NH .. 296
Bergen Community College ... NJ ... 299
Erie Community College City Campus ... NY ... 323
Nassau Community College ... NY ... 332
State University of New York Upstate Medical University ... NY ... 342
Forsyth Technical Community College ... NC .. 360
Pitt Community College ... NC .. 362
University of North Carolina at Chapel Hill NC .. 368
Ohio State University Main Campus, The . OH .. 386
University of Cincinnati-Blue Ash College . OH .. 391
Oregon Health & Science University ... OR .. 405
Community College of Allegheny County . PA ... 413
Gwynedd-Mercy University ... PA ... 417
Thomas Jefferson University ... PA ... 434
Baptist College of Health Sciences ... TN ... 453
Chattanooga State Community College ... TN ... 460
Amarillo College ... TX ... 465
Galveston College ... TX ... 472
Texas State University-San Marcos ... TX ... 487
University of Texas M.D. Anderson Cancer Center, The ... TX ... 493
University of Texas Southwestern Medical Center ... TX ... 493
University of Vermont ... VT ... 500
University of Virginia ... VA ... 511
Virginia Commonwealth University ... VA ... 511
Virginia Western Community College ... VA ... 514
Bellevue College ... WA .. 517
West Virginia University ... WV .. 530
University of Wisconsin-La Crosse ... WI ... 536

SC: Southern Association of Colleges and Schools, Commission on Colleges

Air University ... AL ... 544
Alabama Agricultural and Mechanical University ... AL 1
Alabama Southern Community College ... AL 1
Alabama State University ... AL 1
Amridge University ... AL 1
Athens State University ... AL 1
Auburn University ... AL 1
Auburn University at Montgomery ... AL 2
Bevill State Community College ... AL 2
Birmingham-Southern College ... AL 2
Bishop State Community College ... AL 2
Calhoun Community College ... AL 2
Central Alabama Community College ... AL 2
Chattahoochee Valley Community College AL 2
Concordia College Alabama ... AL 3
Enterprise State Community College ... AL 3
Faulkner University ... AL 3
Gadsden State Community College ... AL 3
George C. Wallace Community College - Dothan ... AL 3
George Corley Wallace State Community College - Selma ... AL 4
Huntingdon College ... AL 4
Jacksonville State University ... AL 4
James H. Faulkner State Community College ... AL 4
Jefferson Davis Community College ... AL 5
Jefferson State Community College ... AL 5
J.F. Drake State Technical College ... AL 4
Judson College ... AL 5
Lawson State Community College ... AL 5
Lurleen B. Wallace Community College ... AL 5
Marion Military Institute ... AL 5
Miles College ... AL 5
Northeast Alabama Community College ... AL 5
Northwest - Shoals Community College ... AL 6
Oakwood University ... AL 6
Samford University ... AL 6
Shelton State Community College ... AL 6
Snead State Community College ... AL 6
Southern Union State Community College AL 7
Spring Hill College ... AL 7
Stillman College ... AL 7
Talladega College ... AL 7
@Trenholm State Technical College ... AL 7
Troy University ... AL 7
Tuskegee University ... AL 8
United States Sports Academy ... AL 8
University of Alabama at Birmingham ... AL 8
University of Alabama in Huntsville ... AL 8
University of Alabama, The ... AL 8
University of Mobile ... AL 9
University of Montevallo ... AL 9
University of North Alabama ... AL 9
University of South Alabama ... AL 9
University of West Alabama, The ... AL 9
Wallace State Community College - Hanceville ... AL 9
Adventist University of Health Sciences ... FL 97
Ave Maria University ... FL 98
Baptist College of Florida, The ... FL 98
Barry University ... FL 98
Beacon College ... FL 99
Bethune Cookman University ... FL 99
Broward College ... FL 99
Chipola College ... FL 99
Clearwater Christian College ... FL ... 100
College of Central Florida ... FL ... 100
Daytona State College ... FL ... 101
Eastern Florida State College ... FL ... 101
Eckerd College ... FL ... 101
Edison State College ... FL ... 101
Edward Waters College ... FL ... 102
Embry-Riddle Aeronautical University ... FL ... 102
Everglades University ... FL ... 103
Flagler College ... FL ... 103
#Florida Agricultural and Mechanical University ... FL ... 114
Florida Atlantic University ... FL ... 114
Florida College ... FL ... 104
Florida Gateway College ... FL ... 104
Florida Gulf Coast University ... FL ... 115
Florida Institute of Technology ... FL ... 104
Florida International University ... FL ... 115
Florida Keys Community College ... FL ... 104

Florida Memorial University ... FL ... 104
Florida National University Hialeah Campus ... FL ... 105
Florida Southern College ... FL ... 105
Florida State College at Jacksonville ... FL ... 105
Florida State University ... FL ... 115
Gulf Coast State College ... FL ... 106
Hillsborough Community College ... FL ... 106
Hodges University ... FL ... 106
Indian River State College ... FL ... 106
Jacksonville University ... FL ... 107
Keiser University ... FL ... 108
Lake-Sumter State College ... FL ... 108
Lynn University ... FL ... 108
Miami Dade College ... FL ... 109
Miami International University of Art & Design ... FL ... 109
New College of Florida ... FL ... 115
North Florida Community College ... FL ... 109
Northwest Florida State College ... FL ... 109
Nova Southeastern University ... FL ... 109
Palm Beach Atlantic University ... FL ... 110
Palm Beach State College ... FL ... 110
Pasco-Hernando Community College ... FL ... 110
Pensacola State College ... FL ... 110
Polk State College ... FL ... 110
Ringling College of Art and Design ... FL ... 111
Rollins College ... FL ... 111
St. John Vianney College Seminary ... FL ... 112
St. Johns River State College ... FL ... 112
Saint Leo University ... FL ... 112
St. Petersburg College ... FL ... 112
St. Thomas University ... FL ... 112
#St. Vincent De Paul Regional Seminary ... FL ... 112
Santa Fe College ... FL ... 113
Seminole State College of Florida ... FL ... 113
South Florida State College ... FL ... 113
Southeastern University ... FL ... 113
State College of Florida, Manatee-Sarasota ... FL ... 114
Stetson University ... FL ... 117
Tallahassee Community College ... FL ... 117
University of Central Florida ... FL ... 115
University of Florida ... FL ... 116
University of Miami ... FL ... 118
University of North Florida ... FL ... 116
University of South Florida ... FL ... 116
University of South Florida St. Petersburg FL ... 116
University of South Florida Sarasota-Manatee ... FL ... 117
University of Tampa ... FL ... 118
University of West Florida ... FL ... 117
Valencia College ... FL ... 118
Warner University ... FL ... 119
Webber International University ... FL ... 119
Abraham Baldwin Agricultural College ... GA ... 119
Agnes Scott College ... GA ... 119
Albany State University ... GA ... 119
Albany Technical College ... GA ... 120
Altamaha Technical College ... GA ... 120
Andrew College ... GA ... 120
Armstrong Atlantic State University ... GA ... 120
Art Institute of Atlanta, The ... GA ... 120
Athens Technical College ... GA ... 120
Atlanta Metropolitan State College ... GA ... 121
Atlanta Technical College ... GA ... 121
Augusta Technical College ... GA ... 121
Bainbridge College ... GA ... 121
Bauder College ... GA ... 121
Berry College ... GA ... 121
Brenau University ... GA ... 122
#Brewton-Parker College ... GA ... 122
Central Georgia Technical College ... GA ... 122
Chattahoochee Technical College ... GA ... 122
Clark Atlanta University ... GA ... 122
Clayton State University ... GA ... 123
College of Coastal Georgia ... GA ... 123
Columbia Theological Seminary ... GA ... 123
Columbus State University ... GA ... 123
Columbus Technical College ... GA ... 123
Covenant College ... GA ... 123
Dalton State College ... GA ... 123
Darton State College ... GA ... 124
East Georgia State College ... GA ... 124
Emmanuel College ... GA ... 124
Emory University ... GA ... 124
Fort Valley State University ... GA ... 124
Georgia College & State University ... GA ... 125
Georgia Gwinnett College ... GA ... 125
Georgia Highlands College ... GA ... 125
Georgia Institute of Technology ... GA ... 125
Georgia Military College ... GA ... 125
Georgia Northwestern Technical College ... GA ... 125
Georgia Perimeter College ... GA ... 125
Georgia Piedmont Technical College ... GA ... 126
Georgia Regents University ... GA ... 126
Georgia Southern University ... GA ... 126
Georgia Southwestern State University ... GA ... 126
Georgia State University ... GA ... 126
Gordon State College ... GA ... 127
Gwinnett Technical College ... GA ... 127
Interdenominational Theological Center ... GA ... 127
Kennesaw State University ... GA ... 127
LaGrange College ... GA ... 128
Lanier Technical College ... GA ... 128
Life University ... GA ... 128
Mercer University ... GA ... 128
Middle Georgia State College ... GA ... 128
Morehouse College ... GA ... 129
Morehouse School of Medicine ... GA ... 129
@Moultrie Technical College ... GA ... 129
North Georgia Technical College ... GA ... 129
Oglethorpe University ... GA ... 130
Okefenokee Technical College ... GA ... 130
Paine College ... GA ... 130
Piedmont College ... GA ... 130
Point University ... GA ... 130
Reinhardt University ... GA ... 130
Savannah College of Art and Design ... GA ... 131
Savannah State University ... GA ... 131
Savannah Technical College ... GA ... 131
Shorter University ... GA ... 131
South Georgia State College ... GA ... 131
South Georgia Technical College ... GA ... 131
South University ... GA ... 131
Southeastern Technical College ... GA ... 132
Southern Crescent Technical College ... GA ... 132
Southern Polytechnic State University ... GA ... 132
Southwest Georgia Technical College ... GA ... 132
Spelman College ... GA ... 132
Thomas University ... GA ... 132
Toccoa Falls College ... GA ... 133
Truett McConnell College ... GA ... 133
University of Georgia ... GA ... 133
University of North Georgia ... GA ... 133
University of West Georgia ... GA ... 133
Valdosta State University ... GA ... 134
Wesleyan College ... GA ... 134
West Georgia Technical College ... GA ... 134
Wiregrass Georgia Technical College ... GA ... 134
Young Harris College ... GA ... 134
Alice Lloyd College ... KY ... 191
Asbury Theological Seminary ... KY ... 192
Asbury University ... KY ... 192
Ashland Community and Technical College ... KY ... 194
Bellarmine University ... KY ... 192
Berea College ... KY ... 192
Big Sandy Community and Technical College ... KY ... 194
Bluegrass Community and Technical College ... KY ... 194
Brescia University ... KY ... 192
Campbellsville University ... KY ... 193
Centre College ... KY ... 193
Clear Creek Baptist Bible College ... KY ... 193
Eastern Kentucky University ... KY ... 193
Elizabethtown Community and Technical College ... KY ... 195
Frontier Nursing University ... KY ... 194
Galen College of Nursing ... KY ... 194
Gateway Community and Technical College ... KY ... 195
Georgetown College ... KY ... 194
Hazard Community and Technical College KY ... 195
Henderson Community College ... KY ... 195
Hopkinsville Community College ... KY ... 195
Jefferson Community and Technical College ... KY ... 195
Kentucky Christian University ... KY ... 194
Kentucky State University ... KY ... 197
Kentucky Wesleyan College ... KY ... 197
Lindsey Wilson College ... KY ... 197
Louisville Presbyterian Theological Seminary ... KY ... 197
Madisonville Community College ... KY ... 196
Maysville Community and Technical College ... KY ... 196
Mid-Continent University ... KY ... 197
Midway College ... KY ... 197
Morehead State University ... KY ... 198
Murray State University ... KY ... 198
Northern Kentucky University ... KY ... 198
Owensboro Community and Technical College ... KY ... 196
St. Catharine College ... KY ... 198
Somerset Community College ... KY ... 196
Southcentral Kentucky Community and Technical College ... KY ... 196
Southeast Kentucky Community and Technical College ... KY ... 196
Southern Baptist Theological Seminary, The ... KY ... 199
Spalding University ... KY ... 199
Sullivan University ... KY ... 199
Thomas More College ... KY ... 199
Transylvania University ... KY ... 199
Union College ... KY ... 200
University of Kentucky ... KY ... 200
University of Louisville ... KY ... 200
University of Pikeville ... KY ... 200
University of the Cumberlands ... KY ... 200
West Kentucky Community and Technical College ... KY ... 196
Western Kentucky University ... KY ... 200
Baton Rouge Community College ... LA ... 202
Bossier Parish Community College ... LA ... 202
Centenary College of Louisiana ... LA ... 201
Delgado Community College ... LA ... 203
Dillard University ... LA ... 201
Grambling State University ... LA ... 207
L.E. Fletcher Technical Community College ... LA ... 203
Louisiana College ... LA ... 202
Louisiana Delta Community College ... LA ... 203
Louisiana State University and Agricultural and Mechanical College ... LA ... 204
Louisiana State University at Alexandria ... LA ... 205
Louisiana State University at Eunice ... LA ... 205
Louisiana State University Health Sciences Center at Shreveport ... LA ... 205
Louisiana State University Health Sciences Center-New Orleans ... LA ... 205
Louisiana State University in Shreveport ... LA ... 205
Louisiana State University Paul M. Hebert Law Center ... LA ... 205
Louisiana Tech University ... LA ... 207
Loyola University New Orleans ... LA ... 205
McNeese State University ... LA ... 207
New Orleans Baptist Theological Seminary ... LA ... 206
Nicholls State University ... LA ... 208
Northwestern State University ... LA ... 208
Notre Dame Seminary, Graduate School of Theology ... LA ... 206
Nunez Community College ... LA ... 203
Our Lady of Holy Cross College ... LA ... 206
Our Lady of the Lake College ... LA ... 206
River Parishes Community College ... LA ... 203
Saint Joseph Seminary College ... LA ... 206
South Louisiana Community College ... LA ... 203
Southeastern Louisiana University ... LA ... 208
Southern University and A&M College ... LA ... 206
Southern University at New Orleans ... LA ... 206
Southern University at Shreveport-Louisiana ... LA ... 207
@Sowela Technical Community College ... LA ... 204
Tulane University ... LA ... 207
University of Louisiana at Lafayette ... LA ... 208
University of Louisiana at Monroe ... LA ... 208
University of New Orleans ... LA ... 205
Xavier University of Louisiana ... LA ... 209
Alcorn State University ... MS ... 265
Belhaven University ... MS ... 266
Blue Mountain College ... MS ... 266
Coahoma Community College ... MS ... 266
Copiah-Lincoln Community College ... MS ... 266
Delta State University ... MS ... 266
East Central Community College ... MS ... 266
East Mississippi Community College ... MS ... 266
Hinds Community College ... MS ... 267
Holmes Community College ... MS ... 267
Itawamba Community College ... MS ... 267
Jackson State University ... MS ... 267
Jones County Junior College ... MS ... 267
Meridian Community College ... MS ... 267
Millsaps College ... MS ... 267
Mississippi College ... MS ... 268
Mississippi Delta Community College ... MS ... 268
Mississippi Gulf Coast Community College ... MS ... 268
Mississippi State University ... MS ... 268
Mississippi University for Women ... MS ... 268
Mississippi Valley State University ... MS ... 269
Northeast Mississippi Community College MS ... 269
Northwest Mississippi Community College MS ... 269
Pearl River Community College ... MS ... 269
Reformed Theological Seminary ... MS ... 269
Rust College ... MS ... 269
Southwest Mississippi Community College MS ... 269
Tougaloo College ... MS ... 270
University of Mississippi ... MS ... 270
University of Mississippi Medical Center ... MS ... 270
University of Southern Mississippi ... MS ... 270
William Carey University ... MS ... 270
Alamance Community College ... NC ... 357
Appalachian State University ... NC ... 367
Asheville - Buncombe Technical Community College ... NC ... 357
Barton College ... NC ... 352
Beaufort County Community College ... NC ... 358
Belmont Abbey College ... NC ... 352
Bennett College ... NC ... 352
Bladen Community College ... NC ... 358
Blue Ridge Community College ... NC ... 358
#Brevard College ... NC ... 352
Brunswick Community College ... NC ... 358
Cabarrus College of Health Sciences ... NC ... 352
Caldwell Community College and Technical Institute ... NC ... 358
Campbell University ... NC ... 352
Cape Fear Community College ... NC ... 358
Carolinas College of Health Sciences ... NC ... 353
Carteret Community College ... NC ... 358
Catawba College ... NC ... 353
Catawba Valley Community College ... NC ... 359
Central Carolina Community College ... NC ... 359
Central Piedmont Community College ... NC ... 359
Chowan University ... NC ... 353
Cleveland Community College ... NC ... 359
Coastal Carolina Community College ... NC ... 359
College of the Albemarle ... NC ... 359
Craven Community College ... NC ... 359
Davidson College ... NC ... 353
Davidson County Community College ... NC ... 360
Duke University ... NC ... 354
Durham Technical Community College ... NC ... 360
East Carolina University ... NC ... 367
Edgecombe Community College ... NC ... 360
Elizabeth City State University ... NC ... 367
Elon University ... NC ... 354
Fayetteville State University ... NC ... 367
Fayetteville Technical Community College NC ... 360
Forsyth Technical Community College ... NC ... 360
Gardner-Webb University ... NC ... 354
Gaston College ... NC ... 360
#Greensboro College ... NC ... 354
Guilford College ... NC ... 355
Guilford Technical Community College ... NC ... 360
Halifax Community College ... NC ... 361
Haywood Community College ... NC ... 361
High Point University ... NC ... 355
Isothermal Community College ... NC ... 361
James Sprunt Community College ... NC ... 361
Johnson C. Smith University ... NC ... 355
Johnston Community College ... NC ... 361
Lees-McRae College ... NC ... 356
Lenoir Community College ... NC ... 361
Lenoir-Rhyne University ... NC ... 356
Livingstone College ... NC ... 356
Louisburg College ... NC ... 356
Mars Hill College ... NC ... 356
Martin Community College ... NC ... 361
Mayland Community College ... NC ... 361
McDowell Technical Community College ... NC ... 362
Meredith College ... NC ... 356
Methodist University ... NC ... 356
Mid-Atlantic Christian University ... NC ... 357
Mitchell Community College ... NC ... 362
Montgomery Community College ... NC ... 362
Montreat College ... NC ... 357
Mount Olive College ... NC ... 357
Nash Community College ... NC ... 362
North Carolina Agricultural and Technical State University ... NC ... 367
North Carolina Central University ... NC ... 368
North Carolina State University ... NC ... 368
North Carolina Wesleyan College ... NC ... 365
Pamlico Community College ... NC ... 362
Pfeiffer University ... NC ... 365
Piedmont Community College ... NC ... 362
Pitt Community College ... NC ... 362
Queens University of Charlotte ... NC ... 365
Randolph Community College ... NC ... 362
Richmond Community College ... NC ... 362
Roanoke-Chowan Community College ... NC ... 363
Robeson Community College ... NC ... 363
Rockingham Community College ... NC ... 363
Rowan-Cabarrus Community College ... NC ... 363
Saint Augustine's University ... NC ... 366
Salem College ... NC ... 366
Sampson Community College ... NC ... 363
Sandhills Community College ... NC ... 363
Shaw University ... NC ... 366
South Piedmont Community College ... NC ... 363
Southeastern Baptist Theological Seminary ... NC ... 366
Southeastern Community College ... NC ... 364
Southwestern Community College ... NC ... 364
Stanly Community College ... NC ... 364
Surry Community College ... NC ... 364
Tri-County Community College ... NC ... 364
University of North Carolina at Asheville ... NC ... 368
University of North Carolina at Chapel Hill NC ... 368
University of North Carolina at Charlotte ... NC ... 368
University of North Carolina at Greensboro ... NC ... 369
University of North Carolina at Pembroke NC ... 369
University of North Carolina School of the Arts ... NC ... 369
University of North Carolina Wilmington ... NC ... 369
Vance-Granville Community College ... NC ... 364
Wake Forest University ... NC ... 370
Wake Technical Community College ... NC ... 364
Warren Wilson College ... NC ... 370
Wayne Community College ... NC ... 364
Western Carolina University ... NC ... 369
Western Piedmont Community College ... NC ... 365
Wilkes Community College ... NC ... 365
William Peace University (formerly Peace College) ... NC ... 370
Wilson Community College ... NC ... 365
Wingate University ... NC ... 370
Winston-Salem State University ... NC ... 370
Aiken Technical College ... SC ... 440
Allen University ... SC ... 441
Anderson University ... SC ... 441
#Benedict College ... SC ... 441
Central Carolina Technical College ... SC ... 441
Charleston Southern University ... SC ... 441
Citadel, The Military College of South Carolina, The ... SC ... 442
Claflin University ... SC ... 442
Clemson University ... SC ... 442
Coastal Carolina University ... SC ... 442
Coker College ... SC ... 442

College of Charleston ... SC ... 443
Columbia College ... SC ... 443
Columbia International University ... SC ... 443
Converse College ... SC ... 443
Denmark Technical College ... SC ... 443
Erskine College ... SC ... 443
Florence - Darlington Technical College ... SC ... 443
Francis Marion University ... SC ... 444
Furman University ... SC ... 444
Greenville Technical College ... SC ... 444
Horry-Georgetown Technical College ... SC ... 444
Lander University ... SC ... 444
Limestone College ... SC ... 444
Medical University of South Carolina ... SC ... 445
Midlands Technical College ... SC ... 445
Morris College ... SC ... 445
Newberry College ... SC ... 445
North Greenville University ... SC ... 445
Northeastern Technical College ... SC ... 446
Orangeburg-Calhoun Technical College ... SC ... 446
Piedmont Technical College ... SC ... 446
Presbyterian College ... SC ... 446
Sherman College of Chiropractic ... SC ... 446
South Carolina State University ... SC ... 446
Southern Wesleyan University ... SC ... 446
Spartanburg Community College ... SC ... 447
Spartanburg Methodist College ... SC ... 447
Technical College of the Lowcountry ... SC ... 447
Tri-County Technical College ... SC ... 447
Trident Technical College ... SC ... 447
University of South Carolina Aiken ... SC ... 448
University of South Carolina Beaufort ... SC ... 448
University of South Carolina Columbia ... SC ... 447
&University of South Carolina Salkehatchie SC ... 448
&University of South Carolina Sumter ... SC ... 448
&University of South Carolina Union ... SC ... 448
University of South Carolina Upstate ... SC ... 448
Voorhees College ... SC ... 449
Williamsburg Technical College ... SC ... 449
Winthrop University ... SC ... 449
Wofford College ... SC ... 449
York Technical College ... SC ... 449
Aquinas College ... TN ... 452
Austin Peay State University ... TN ... 459
Baptist College of Health Sciences ... TN ... 453
Belmont University ... TN ... 453
Bethel University ... TN ... 453
Bryan College ... TN ... 453
Carson-Newman University ... TN ... 453
Chattanooga State Community College ... TN ... 460
Christian Brothers University ... TN ... 453
Cleveland State Community College ... TN ... 460
Columbia State Community College ... TN ... 460
Cumberland University ... TN ... 454
Dyersburg State Community College ... TN ... 460
East Tennessee State University ... TN ... 459
Emmanuel Christian Seminary ... TN ... 454
#Fisk University ... TN ... 454
Freed-Hardeman University ... TN ... 454
Jackson State Community College ... TN ... 460
John A. Gupton College ... TN ... 455
Johnson University ... TN ... 455
King University ... TN ... 455
Lane College ... TN ... 455
Lee University ... TN ... 455
LeMoyne-Owen College ... TN ... 455
Lincoln Memorial University ... TN ... 456
Lipscomb University ... TN ... 456
Martin Methodist College ... TN ... 456
Maryville College ... TN ... 456
Meharry Medical College ... TN ... 456
Memphis College of Art ... TN ... 456
Memphis Theological Seminary ... TN ... 457
Mid-America Baptist Theological Seminary TN ... 457
Middle Tennessee School of Anesthesia .. TN ... 457
Middle Tennessee State University ... TN ... 459
Milligan College ... TN ... 457
Motlow State Community College ... TN ... 461
Nashville State Community College ... TN ... 461
Northeast State Community College ... TN ... 461
Pellissippi State Community College ... TN ... 461
Pentecostal Theological Seminary ... TN ... 458
Rhodes College ... TN ... 458
Richmont Graduate University ... TN ... 458
Roane State Community College ... TN ... 461
Sewanee: The University of the South ... TN ... 458
South College ... TN ... 458
Southern Adventist University ... TN ... 458
Southern College of Optometry ... TN ... 458
Southwest Tennessee Community College ... TN ... 461
Tennessee State University ... TN ... 459
Tennessee Technological University ... TN ... 460
Tennessee Wesleyan College ... TN ... 462
Trevecca Nazarene University ... TN ... 462
Tusculum College ... TN ... 462
Union University ... TN ... 462
University of Memphis, The ... TN ... 460
University of Tennessee at Chattanooga .. TN ... 463
University of Tennessee at Martin ... TN ... 463
University of Tennessee, Knoxville ... TN ... 463
Vanderbilt University ... TN ... 463
Victory University (formerly Crichton College) ... TN ... 463
Volunteer State Community College ... TN ... 461
Walters State Community College ... TN ... 462
Watkins College of Art, Design & Film ... TN ... 464
Welch College ... TN ... 464
Abilene Christian University ... TX ... 464
Alvin Community College ... TX ... 465
Amarillo College ... TX ... 465
Amberton University ... TX ... 465
American College of Acupuncture and Oriental Medicine ... TX ... 465
Angelina College ... TX ... 465
Angelo State University ... TX ... 465
AOMA Graduate School of Integrative Medicine ... TX ... 466
Art Institute of Houston, The ... TX ... 466
Austin College ... TX ... 466
Austin Community College District ... TX ... 466
Austin Graduate School of Theology ... TX ... 466
Austin Presbyterian Theological Seminary. TX ... 467
Baptist Missionary Association Theological Seminary ... TX ... 467
Baylor College of Medicine ... TX ... 467
Baylor University ... TX ... 467
Blinn College ... TX ... 467
Brazosport College ... TX ... 468
Brite Divinity School ... TX ... 468
Brookhaven College ... TX ... 470
Cedar Valley College ... TX ... 470
Central Texas College ... TX ... 468
Cisco College ... TX ... 468
Clarendon College ... TX ... 468
Coastal Bend College ... TX ... 468
@College of Biblical Studies-Houston ... TX ... 468
College of Saints John Fisher & Thomas More, The ... TX ... 469
College of the Mainland ... TX ... 469
Collin County Community College District TX ... 469
Concordia University Texas ... TX ... 469
Criswell College ... TX ... 470
Dallas Baptist University ... TX ... 470
Dallas Theological Seminary ... TX ... 471
Del Mar College ... TX ... 471
East Texas Baptist University ... TX ... 471
Eastfield College ... TX ... 470
El Centro College ... TX ... 470
El Paso Community College ... TX ... 472
Frank Phillips College ... TX ... 472
Galveston College ... TX ... 472
Graduate Institute of Applied Linguistics ... TX ... 472
Grayson College ... TX ... 472
Hardin-Simmons University ... TX ... 472
Hill College ... TX ... 473
Houston Baptist University ... TX ... 473
Houston Community College ... TX ... 473
Howard College ... TX ... 473
Howard Payne University ... TX ... 473
Huston-Tillotson University ... TX ... 473
Jacksonville College ... TX ... 474
#Jarvis Christian College ... TX ... 474
Kilgore College ... TX ... 475
Lamar Institute of Technology ... TX ... 486
Lamar State College-Orange ... TX ... 486
Lamar State College-Port Arthur ... TX ... 486
Lamar University ... TX ... 486
Laredo Community College ... TX ... 475
Lee College ... TX ... 475
LeTourneau University ... TX ... 475
Lone Star College System ... TX ... 476
Lubbock Christian University ... TX ... 476
McLennan Community College ... TX ... 476
McMurry University ... TX ... 476
Midland College ... TX ... 476
Midwestern State University ... TX ... 476
Mountain View College ... TX ... 471
Navarro College ... TX ... 477
North Central Texas College ... TX ... 477
North Lake College ... TX ... 471
Northeast Texas Community College ... TX ... 477
Northwest Vista College ... TX ... 464
Oblate School of Theology ... TX ... 477
Odessa College ... TX ... 477
Our Lady of the Lake University ... TX ... 477
Palo Alto College ... TX ... 465
Panola College ... TX ... 478
Paris Junior College ... TX ... 478
Parker University ... TX ... 478
Prairie View A & M University ... TX ... 482
Ranger College ... TX ... 478
Rice University ... TX ... 479
Richland College ... TX ... 471
St. Edward's University ... TX ... 479
St. Mary's University ... TX ... 479
St. Philip's College ... TX ... 465
Sam Houston State University ... TX ... 487
San Antonio College ... TX ... 465
&San Jacinto College Central ... TX ... 479
&San Jacinto College North ... TX ... 479
&San Jacinto College South ... TX ... 479
Schreiner University ... TX ... 480
Seminary of the Southwest ... TX ... 480
South Plains College ... TX ... 480
South Texas College ... TX ... 480
Southern Methodist University ... TX ... 481
Southwest Texas Junior College ... TX ... 481
Southwestern Adventist University ... TX ... 481
Southwestern Assemblies of God University ... TX ... 481
Southwestern Baptist Theological Seminary ... TX ... 481
Southwestern Christian College ... TX ... 481
Southwestern University ... TX ... 481
Stephen F. Austin State University ... TX ... 482
Sul Ross State University ... TX ... 487
Tarleton State University ... TX ... 483
Tarrant County College District ... TX ... 482
Temple College ... TX ... 482
Texarkana College ... TX ... 482
Texas A & M International University ... TX ... 483
Texas A & M University ... TX ... 483
Texas A & M University - Central Texas ... TX ... 483
Texas A & M University - Commerce ... TX ... 483
Texas A & M University - Corpus Christi .. TX ... 483
Texas A & M University - Kingsville ... TX ... 484
Texas A & M University System Health Science Center ... TX ... 484
Texas A & M University - Texarkana ... TX ... 484
Texas Chiropractic College ... TX ... 484
Texas Christian University ... TX ... 484
Texas College ... TX ... 485
Texas Lutheran University ... TX ... 485
Texas Southern University ... TX ... 485
Texas State Technical College Harlingen . TX ... 485
Texas State Technical College Marshall ... TX ... 486
Texas State Technical College Waco ... TX ... 486
Texas State Technical College West Texas ... TX ... 486
Texas State University-San Marcos ... TX ... 487
Texas Tech University ... TX ... 487
Texas Tech University Health Sciences Center ... TX ... 487
Texas Wesleyan University ... TX ... 488
Texas Woman's University ... TX ... 488
Trinity University ... TX ... 488
Trinity Valley Community College ... TX ... 488
Tyler Junior College ... TX ... 488
University of Dallas ... TX ... 488
University of Houston ... TX ... 489
University of Houston - Clear Lake ... TX ... 489
University of Houston - Downtown ... TX ... 489
University of Houston - Victoria ... TX ... 489
University of Mary Hardin-Baylor ... TX ... 490
University of North Texas ... TX ... 490
University of North Texas at Dallas ... TX ... 490
University of North Texas Health Science Center at Fort Worth ... TX ... 490
University of St. Thomas ... TX ... 490
University of Texas at Arlington, The ... TX ... 491
University of Texas at Austin ... TX ... 491
University of Texas at Brownsville and Texas Southmost College, The ... TX ... 491
University of Texas at Dallas, The ... TX ... 491
University of Texas at El Paso ... TX ... 492
University of Texas at San Antonio ... TX ... 492
University of Texas at Tyler ... TX ... 492
University of Texas Health Science Center at Houston (UTHealth), The ... TX ... 492
University of Texas Health Science Center at San Antonio ... TX ... 493
University of Texas M.D. Anderson Cancer Center, The ... TX ... 493
University of Texas Medical Branch, The . TX ... 493
University of Texas of the Permian Basin . TX ... 493
University of Texas - Pan American ... TX ... 492
University of Texas Southwestern Medical Center ... TX ... 493
University of the Incarnate Word ... TX ... 490
Vernon College ... TX ... 493
Victoria College ... TX ... 493
Wade College Infomart ... TX ... 494
Wayland Baptist University ... TX ... 494
Weatherford College ... TX ... 494
West Texas A & M University ... TX ... 484
Western Texas College ... TX ... 494
Wharton County Junior College ... TX ... 494
Wiley College ... TX ... 495
Appalachian College of Pharmacy ... VA ... 501
Averett University ... VA ... 502
Blue Ridge Community College ... VA ... 511
Bluefield College ... VA ... 502
Bridgewater College ... VA ... 502
Central Virginia Community College ... VA ... 512
Christendom College ... VA ... 503
Christopher Newport University ... VA ... 503
College of William & Mary ... VA ... 503
Dabney S. Lancaster Community College VA ... 512
Danville Community College ... VA ... 512
Eastern Mennonite University ... VA ... 504
Eastern Shore Community College ... VA ... 512
Eastern Virginia Medical School ... VA ... 504
ECPI College of Technology ... VA ... 504
Emory & Henry College ... VA ... 504
Ferrum College ... VA ... 504
George Mason University ... VA ... 505
Germanna Community College ... VA ... 512
Hampden-Sydney College ... VA ... 505
Hampton University ... VA ... 505
Hollins University ... VA ... 505
Institute for the Psychological Sciences ... VA ... 505
J. Sargeant Reynolds Community College VA ... 512
James Madison University ... VA ... 506
Jefferson College of Health Sciences ... VA ... 506
John Tyler Community College ... VA ... 512
Liberty University ... VA ... 506
Longwood University ... VA ... 506
Lord Fairfax Community College ... VA ... 512
Lynchburg College ... VA ... 506
Marine Corps University ... VA ... 544
Mary Baldwin College ... VA ... 507
Marymount University ... VA ... 507
Mountain Empire Community College ... VA ... 513
New River Community College ... VA ... 513
Norfolk State University ... VA ... 507
Northern Virginia Community College ... VA ... 513
Old Dominion University ... VA ... 507
Patrick Henry Community College ... VA ... 513
Paul D. Camp Community College ... VA ... 513
Piedmont Virginia Community College ... VA ... 513
Radford University ... VA ... 508
Randolph College ... VA ... 508
Randolph-Macon College ... VA ... 508
Rappahannock Community College ... VA ... 513
Regent University ... VA ... 508
Richard Bland College ... VA ... 508
Roanoke College ... VA ... 509
Shenandoah University ... VA ... 509
Southern Virginia University ... VA ... 509
Southside Virginia Community College ... VA ... 513
Southwest Virginia Community College ... VA ... 514
Sweet Briar College ... VA ... 510
Thomas Nelson Community College ... VA ... 514
Tidewater Community College ... VA ... 514
Union Presbyterian Seminary ... VA ... 510
University of Mary Washington ... VA ... 510
University of Richmond ... VA ... 510
University of Virginia ... VA ... 511
University of Virginia's College at Wise, The ... VA ... 511
Virginia Commonwealth University ... VA ... 511
Virginia Highlands Community College ... VA ... 514
#Virginia Intermont College ... VA ... 514
Virginia Military Institute ... VA ... 515
Virginia Polytechnic Institute and State University ... VA ... 515
Virginia State University ... VA ... 515
@Virginia Tech Carilion School of Medicine VA ... 515
Virginia Union University ... VA ... 515
Virginia Wesleyan College ... VA ... 515
Virginia Western Community College ... VA ... 514
Washington and Lee University ... VA ... 516
Wytheville Community College ... VA ... 514

SCPSY: American Psychological Association: school psychology (D)

Arizona State University ... AZ ... 11
University of Arizona ... AZ ... 18
University of Central Arkansas ... AR ... 25
University of California-Berkeley ... CA ... 70
University of California-Riverside ... CA ... 71
#University of Northern Colorado ... CO ... 86
University of Connecticut ... CT ... 92
University of Florida ... FL ... 116
University of South Florida ... FL ... 116
Georgia State University ... GA .. 126
University of Georgia ... GA .. 133
Illinois State University ... IL ... 147
Loyola University Chicago ... IL ... 151
Northern Illinois University ... IL ... 154
Ball State University ... IN ... 164
Indiana State University ... IN ... 167
Indiana University Bloomington ... IN ... 167
University of Iowa ... IA ... 175
University of Kansas Main Campus ... KS ... 190
#University of Kentucky ... KY ... 200
Louisiana State University and Agricultural and Mechanical College ... LA ... 204
Tulane University ... LA ... 207
University of Maryland College Park ... MD .. 219
University of Massachusetts ... MA .. 228
Central Michigan University ... MI .. 240
Michigan State University ... MI .. 246
#University of Minnesota-Twin Cities ... MN .. 264
Mississippi State University ... MS .. 268
University of Southern Mississippi ... MS .. 270
#University of Missouri - Columbia ... MO .. 283
University of Nebraska - Lincoln ... NE .. 292
Rutgers the State University of New Jersey New Brunswick Campus ... NJ ... 306
Alfred University ... NY ... 313
City University of New York Graduate Center ... NY ... 317
Fordham University ... NY ... 324
Hofstra University ... NY ... 326
New York University ... NY ... 334
St. John's University ... NY ... 339
Syracuse University Main Campus ... NY ... 347
Teachers College, Columbia University ... NY ... 347
University at Albany, SUNY ... NY ... 341
North Carolina State University ... NC .. 368
University of North Carolina at Chapel Hill NC .. 368
Kent State University Main Campus ... OH .. 382
Oklahoma State University ... OK .. 397

University of Oregon ... OR ... 406
Duquesne University ... PA ... 415
Lehigh University ... PA ... 422
Penn State University Park ... PA ... 426
Temple University ... PA ... 433
University of Rhode Island ... RI ... 440
University of South Carolina Columbia ... SC ... 447
University of Tennessee, Knoxville ... TN ... 463
Texas A & M University ... TX ... 483
Texas Woman's University ... TX ... 488
University of Houston ... TX ... 489
University of Texas at Austin ... TX ... 491
University of Utah, The ... UT ... 496
University of Washington ... WA ... 524
University of Wisconsin-Madison ... WI ... 536
University of Wisconsin-Milwaukee ... WI ... 537

SP: American Speech-Language-Hearing Association: speech-language pathology (M)

Alabama Agricultural and Mechanical University ... AL ... 1
Auburn University ... AL ... 1
University of Alabama, The ... AL ... 8
University of Montevallo ... AL ... 9
University of South Alabama ... AL ... 9
Arizona State University ... AZ ... 11
Northern Arizona University ... AZ ... 16
University of Arizona ... AZ ... 18
Arkansas State University-Jonesboro ... AR ... 19
Harding University Main Campus ... AR ... 21
University of Arkansas at Little Rock ... AR ... 24
University of Arkansas Main Campus ... AR ... 23
University of Central Arkansas ... AR ... 25
California State University-Chico ... CA ... 33
California State University-East Bay ... CA ... 33
California State University-Fresno ... CA ... 33
California State University-Fullerton ... CA ... 33
California State University-Long Beach ... CA ... 33
California State University-Los Angeles ... CA ... 34
California State University-Northridge ... CA ... 34
California State University-Sacramento ... CA ... 34
@California State University-San Marcos ... CA ... 35
Chapman University ... CA ... 38
Loma Linda University ... CA ... 51
San Diego State University ... CA ... 35
San Francisco State University ... CA ... 35
San Jose State University ... CA ... 36
University of Redlands ... CA ... 73
University of the Pacific ... CA ... 73
University of Colorado Boulder ... CO ... 85
University of Northern Colorado ... CO ... 86
Southern Connecticut State University ... CT ... 88
University of Connecticut ... CT ... 92
Gallaudet University ... DC ... 95
George Washington University ... DC ... 95
Howard University ... DC ... 95
#University of the District of Columbia ... DC ... 97
Florida Atlantic University ... FL ... 114
Florida International University ... FL ... 115
Florida State University ... FL ... 115
Nova Southeastern University ... FL ... 109
University of Central Florida ... FL ... 115
University of Florida ... FL ... 116
University of South Florida ... FL ... 116
Armstrong Atlantic State University ... GA ... 120
Georgia State University ... GA ... 126
University of Georgia ... GA ... 133
University of West Georgia ... GA ... 133
Valdosta State University ... GA ... 134
#University of Hawaii at Manoa ... HI ... 136
Idaho State University ... ID ... 138
Eastern Illinois University ... IL ... 144
@Elmhurst College ... IL ... 145
Governors State University ... IL ... 145
Illinois State University ... IL ... 147
@Midwestern University ... IL ... 153
Northern Illinois University ... IL ... 154
Northwestern University ... IL ... 155
Rush University ... IL ... 157
Saint Xavier University ... IL ... 158
Southern Illinois University Carbondale ... IL ... 159
Southern Illinois University Edwardsville ... IL ... 159
University of Illinois at Urbana-Champaign ... IL ... 162
Western Illinois University ... IL ... 162
Ball State University ... IN ... 164
Indiana State University ... IN ... 167
Indiana University Bloomington ... IN ... 167
Purdue University Main Campus ... IN ... 171
@St. Ambrose University ... IA ... 182
University of Iowa ... IA ... 175
University of Northern Iowa ... IA ... 176
Fort Hays State University ... KS ... 186
Kansas State University ... KS ... 188
University of Kansas Main Campus ... KS ... 190
Wichita State University ... KS ... 191
Eastern Kentucky University ... KY ... 193
Murray State University ... KY ... 198
University of Kentucky ... KY ... 200
University of Louisville ... KY ... 200
Western Kentucky University ... KY ... 200
Louisiana State University and Agricultural and Mechanical College ... LA ... 204
Louisiana State University Health Sciences Center at Shreveport ... LA ... 205
Louisiana State University Health Sciences Center-New Orleans ... LA ... 205
Louisiana Tech University ... LA ... 207
Southeastern Louisiana University ... LA ... 208
Southern University and A&M College ... LA ... 206
University of Louisiana at Lafayette ... LA ... 208
University of Louisiana at Monroe ... LA ... 208
University of Maine ... ME ... 212
Loyola University Maryland ... MD ... 216
Towson University ... MD ... 220
University of Maryland College Park ... MD ... 219
Boston University ... MA ... 224
Emerson College ... MA ... 226
MGH Institute of Health Professions ... MA ... 234
Northeastern University ... MA ... 235
University of Massachusetts ... MA ... 228
Worcester State University ... MA ... 230
@Calvin College ... MI ... 240
Central Michigan University ... MI ... 240
Eastern Michigan University ... MI ... 242
@Grand Valley State University ... MI ... 243
Michigan State University ... MI ... 246
Wayne State University ... MI ... 252
Western Michigan University ... MI ... 252
Minnesota State University Moorhead ... MN ... 259
Minnesota State University, Mankato ... MN ... 259
St. Cloud State University ... MN ... 261
University of Minnesota Duluth ... MN ... 264
University of Minnesota-Twin Cities ... MN ... 264
Jackson State University ... MS ... 267
Mississippi University for Women ... MS ... 268
University of Mississippi ... MS ... 270
University of Southern Mississippi ... MS ... 270
Fontbonne University ... MO ... 274
Missouri State University ... MO ... 278
Rockhurst University ... MO ... 280
Saint Louis University ... MO ... 281
Southeast Missouri State University ... MO ... 282
Truman State University ... MO ... 282
University of Central Missouri ... MO ... 283
University of Missouri - Columbia ... MO ... 283
@University of Montana - Missoula, The ... MT ... 286
University of Nebraska at Kearney ... NE ... 292
University of Nebraska at Omaha ... NE ... 293
University of Nebraska - Lincoln ... NE ... 292
University of Nevada, Reno ... NV ... 294
University of New Hampshire ... NH ... 298
Kean University ... NJ ... 302
Montclair State University ... NJ ... 303
@Richard Stockton College of New Jersey, The ... NJ ... 305
Seton Hall University ... NJ ... 307
William Paterson University of New Jersey ... NJ ... 308
Eastern New Mexico University Main Campus ... NM ... 309
New Mexico State University Main Campus ... NM ... 310
University of New Mexico Main Campus ... NM ... 312
Adelphi University ... NY ... 313
City University of New York Brooklyn College ... NY ... 317
City University of New York Herbert H. Lehman College ... NY ... 318
City University of New York Hunter College ... NY ... 318
City University of New York Queens College ... NY ... 319
College of Saint Rose, The ... NY ... 321
Hofstra University ... NY ... 326
Ithaca College ... NY ... 327
Long Island University - Post Campus ... NY ... 329
Mercy College ... NY ... 330
@Molloy College ... NY ... 331
Nazareth College of Rochester ... NY ... 332
New York Medical College ... NY ... 334
New York University ... NY ... 334
St. John's University ... NY ... 339
State University of New York at Fredonia ... NY ... 342
State University of New York at New Paltz ... NY ... 342
State University of New York College at Buffalo ... NY ... 343
@State University of New York College at Cortland ... NY ... 343
State University of New York College at Plattsburgh ... NY ... 344
Syracuse University Main Campus ... NY ... 347
Teachers College, Columbia University ... NY ... 347
Touro College ... NY ... 348
University at Buffalo-SUNY ... NY ... 341
Appalachian State University ... NC ... 367
East Carolina University ... NC ... 367
North Carolina Central University ... NC ... 368
University of North Carolina at Chapel Hill ... NC ... 368
University of North Carolina at Greensboro ... NC ... 369
Western Carolina University ... NC ... 369
Minot State University ... ND ... 371
University of North Dakota Main Campus ... ND ... 371
Bowling Green State University ... OH ... 374
Case Western Reserve University ... OH ... 375
Cleveland State University ... OH ... 377
Kent State University Main Campus ... OH ... 382
Miami University ... OH ... 384
Ohio State University Main Campus, The ... OH ... 386
Ohio University Main Campus ... OH ... 387
University of Akron, Main Campus, The ... OH ... 390
University of Cincinnati Main Campus ... OH ... 390
University of Toledo ... OH ... 392
Northeastern State University ... OK ... 396
Oklahoma State University ... OK ... 397
University of Central Oklahoma ... OK ... 400
University of Tulsa ... OK ... 401
@Pacific University ... OR ... 407
Portland State University ... OR ... 406
University of Oregon ... OR ... 406
Bloomsburg University of Pennsylvania ... PA ... 427
California University of Pennsylvania ... PA ... 428
Clarion University of Pennsylvania ... PA ... 428
Duquesne University ... PA ... 415
East Stroudsburg University of Pennsylvania ... PA ... 428
Edinboro University of Pennsylvania ... PA ... 428
Indiana University of Pennsylvania ... PA ... 428
La Salle University ... PA ... 420
Marywood University ... PA ... 423
Misericordia University ... PA ... 424
Penn State University Park ... PA ... 426
Temple University ... PA ... 433
University of Pittsburgh ... PA ... 435
West Chester University of Pennsylvania ... PA ... 430
Carlos Albizu University ... PR ... 547
Universidad Del Turabo ... PR ... 552
University of Puerto Rico-Medical Sciences Campus ... PR ... 554
University of Rhode Island ... RI ... 440
South Carolina State University ... SC ... 446
University of South Carolina Columbia ... SC ... 447
University of South Dakota, The ... SD ... 451
East Tennessee State University ... TN ... 459
Tennessee State University ... TN ... 459
University of Memphis, The ... TN ... 460
University of Tennessee, Knoxville ... TN ... 463
Vanderbilt University ... TN ... 463
Abilene Christian University ... TX ... 464
Baylor University ... TX ... 467
Lamar University ... TX ... 486
Our Lady of the Lake University ... TX ... 477
Stephen F. Austin State University ... TX ... 482
#Texas A & M University - Kingsville ... TX ... 484
Texas Christian University ... TX ... 484
Texas State University-San Marcos ... TX ... 487
Texas Tech University Health Sciences Center ... TX ... 487
Texas Woman's University ... TX ... 488
University of Houston ... TX ... 489
University of North Texas ... TX ... 490
University of Texas at Austin ... TX ... 491
University of Texas at Dallas, The ... TX ... 491
University of Texas at El Paso ... TX ... 492
University of Texas - Pan American ... TX ... 492
West Texas A & M University ... TX ... 484
Brigham Young University ... UT ... 495
University of Utah, The ... UT ... 496
Utah State University ... UT ... 497
University of Vermont ... VT ... 500
Hampton University ... VA ... 505
James Madison University ... VA ... 506
Longwood University ... VA ... 506
Old Dominion University ... VA ... 507
Radford University ... VA ... 508
University of Virginia ... VA ... 511
Eastern Washington University ... WA ... 519
University of Washington ... WA ... 524
Washington State University ... WA ... 525
Western Washington University ... WA ... 525
Marshall University ... WV ... 529
West Virginia University ... WV ... 530
Marquette University ... WI ... 534
University of Wisconsin-Eau Claire ... WI ... 536
University of Wisconsin-Madison ... WI ... 536
University of Wisconsin-Milwaukee ... WI ... 537
University of Wisconsin-River Falls ... WI ... 537
University of Wisconsin-Stevens Point ... WI ... 538
University of Wisconsin-Whitewater ... WI ... 538
University of Wyoming ... WY ... 543

SPAA: Network of Schools of Public Policy, Affairs and Administration: public affairs and administration (M)

Auburn University ... AL ... 1
Auburn University at Montgomery ... AL ... 2
Jacksonville State University ... AL ... 4
Troy University ... AL ... 7
University of Alabama at Birmingham ... AL ... 8
Arizona State University ... AZ ... 11
University of Arizona ... AZ ... 18
Arkansas State University-Jonesboro ... AR ... 19
University of Arkansas at Little Rock ... AR ... 24
California State Polytechnic University-Pomona ... CA ... 32
California State University-Bakersfield ... CA ... 32
California State University-Chico ... CA ... 33
California State University-Dominguez Hills ... CA ... 33
California State University-Fresno ... CA ... 33
California State University-Fullerton ... CA ... 33
California State University-Long Beach ... CA ... 33
California State University-Los Angeles ... CA ... 34
California State University-San Bernardino ... CA ... 34
California State University-Stanislaus ... CA ... 35
Naval Postgraduate School ... CA ... 544
San Diego State University ... CA ... 35
San Francisco State University ... CA ... 35
San Jose State University ... CA ... 36
University of LaVerne ... CA ... 72
University of San Francisco ... CA ... 73
University of Southern California ... CA ... 74
University of Colorado Denver|Anschutz Medical Campus ... CO ... 86
University of Connecticut ... CT ... 92
University of Delaware ... DE ... 94
American University ... DC ... 94
George Washington University ... DC ... 95
Florida Atlantic University ... FL ... 114
Florida Gulf Coast University ... FL ... 115
Florida International University ... FL ... 115
Florida State University ... FL ... 115
University of Central Florida ... FL ... 115
University of North Florida ... FL ... 116
University of South Florida ... FL ... 116
Albany State University ... GA ... 119
Clark Atlanta University ... GA ... 122
Georgia College & State University ... GA ... 125
Georgia Regents University ... GA ... 126
Georgia Southern University ... GA ... 126
Georgia State University ... GA ... 126
Kennesaw State University ... GA ... 127
Savannah State University ... GA ... 131
University of Georgia ... GA ... 133
University of West Georgia ... GA ... 133
Valdosta State University ... GA ... 134
Boise State University ... ID ... 137
DePaul University ... IL ... 143
Governors State University ... IL ... 145
Northern Illinois University ... IL ... 154
Southern Illinois University Carbondale ... IL ... 159
Southern Illinois University Edwardsville ... IL ... 159
University of Illinois at Chicago ... IL ... 161
University of Illinois at Springfield ... IL ... 161
Indiana University Bloomington ... IN ... 167
Indiana University Northwest ... IN ... 168
Indiana University-Purdue University Fort Wayne ... IN ... 168
Indiana University-Purdue University Indianapolis ... IN ... 168
Indiana University South Bend ... IN ... 168
Kansas State University ... KS ... 188
University of Kansas Main Campus ... KS ... 190
Wichita State University ... KS ... 191
Eastern Kentucky University ... KY ... 193
Kentucky State University ... KY ... 197
Morehead State University ... KY ... 198
Northern Kentucky University ... KY ... 198
University of Kentucky ... KY ... 200
University of Louisville ... KY ... 200
Western Kentucky University ... KY ... 200
Grambling State University ... LA ... 207
Louisiana State University and Agricultural and Mechanical College ... LA ... 204
Southern University and A&M College ... LA ... 206
University of New Orleans ... LA ... 205
Bowie State University ... MD ... 220
University of Baltimore ... MD ... 221
University of Maryland Baltimore County ... MD ... 219
University of Maryland College Park ... MD ... 219
Bridgewater State University ... MA ... 229
Northeastern University ... MA ... 235
Suffolk University ... MA ... 237
Central Michigan University ... MI ... 240
Eastern Michigan University ... MI ... 242
Grand Valley State University ... MI ... 243
Oakland University ... MI ... 248
Wayne State University ... MI ... 252
Western Michigan University ... MI ... 252
University of Minnesota-Twin Cities ... MN ... 264
Jackson State University ... MS ... 267
Mississippi State University ... MS ... 268
Missouri State University ... MO ... 278
Saint Louis University ... MO ... 281
University of Missouri - Columbia ... MO ... 283
University of Missouri - Kansas City ... MO ... 283
University of Missouri - Saint Louis ... MO ... 283
University of Nebraska at Omaha ... NE ... 293
University of Nevada, Las Vegas ... NV ... 294
Kean University ... NJ ... 302
Rutgers the State University of New Jersey Camden Campus ... NJ ... 306
Rutgers the State University of New Jersey New Brunswick Campus ... NJ ... 306
Rutgers the State University of New Jersey Newark Campus ... NJ ... 306
Seton Hall University ... NJ ... 307
New Mexico State University Main Campus ... NM ... 310
University of New Mexico Main Campus ... NM ... 312
Baruch College/City University of New York ... NY ... 316

City University of New York John Jay College of Criminal Justice ... NY ... 318
Columbia University in the City of New York ... NY ... 321
Long Island University - Post Campus ... NY ... 329
New School, The ... NY ... 332
New York University ... NY ... 334
State University of New York at Binghamton ... NY ... 341
State University of New York, The College at Brockport ... NY ... 342
Syracuse University Main Campus ... NY ... 347
University at Albany, SUNY ... NY ... 341
Appalachian State University ... NC .. 367
East Carolina University ... NC .. 367
North Carolina State University ... NC .. 368
University of North Carolina at Chapel Hill ... NC .. 368
University of North Carolina at Charlotte .. NC .. 368
University of North Carolina at Greensboro ... NC .. 369
University of North Carolina Wilmington ... NC .. 369
University of North Dakota Main Campus . ND .. 371
Cleveland State University ... OH .. 377
Kent State University Main Campus ... OH .. 382
Ohio State University Main Campus, The . OH .. 386
University of Dayton ... OH .. 391
University of Toledo ... OH .. 392
Wright State University Main Campus ... OH .. 393
Portland State University ... OR .. 406
University of Oregon ... OR .. 406
Willamette University ... OR .. 408
Carnegie Mellon University ... PA ... 412
University of Pittsburgh ... PA ... 435
Villanova University ... PA ... 436
University of Puerto Rico-Rio Piedras Campus ... PR ... 555
College of Charleston ... SC ... 443
University of South Carolina Columbia ... SC ... 447
University of South Dakota, The ... SD ... 451
Tennessee State University ... TN ... 459
University of Memphis, The ... TN ... 460
University of Tennessee at Chattanooga .. TN ... 463
Texas A & M International University ... TX ... 483
Texas A & M University ... TX ... 483
Texas Southern University ... TX ... 485
Texas State University-San Marcos ... TX ... 487
Texas Tech University ... TX ... 487
University of North Texas ... TX ... 490
University of Texas at Arlington, The ... TX ... 491
University of Texas at Austin ... TX ... 491
University of Texas at Dallas, The ... TX ... 491
University of Texas at El Paso ... TX ... 492
University of Texas at San Antonio ... TX ... 492
Brigham Young University ... UT ... 495
University of Utah, The ... UT ... 496
University of Vermont ... VT ... 500
George Mason University ... VA ... 505
James Madison University ... VA ... 506
Old Dominion University ... VA ... 507
Virginia Commonwealth University ... VA ... 511
Virginia Polytechnic Institute and State University ... VA ... 515
Seattle University ... WA ... 523
University of Washington ... WA ... 524
West Virginia University ... WV .. 530

SURGA: Commission on Accreditation of Allied Health Education Programs: surgical assistant (C,A)

Gulf Coast State College ... FL ... 106
College of Southern Idaho ... ID ... 138
Madisonville Community College ... KY ... 196
Wayne County Community College District ... MI ... 252
University of Cincinnati Main Campus ... OH .. 390
Eastern Virginia Medical School ... VA ... 504

SURGT: Commission on Accreditation of Allied Health Education Programs: surgical technology (C,A)

Bevill State Community College ... AL ... 2
Calhoun Community College ... AL ... 2
James H. Faulkner State Community College ... AL ... 4
Lurleen B. Wallace Community College ... AL ... 5
Southern Union State Community College AL ... 7
Virginia College ... AL ... 3
Gateway Community College ... AZ ... 14
Mohave Community College ... AZ ... 15
Pima Community College ... AZ ... 17
Arkansas State University-Newport ... AR ... 20
North Arkansas College ... AR ... 22
South Arkansas Community College ... AR ... 23
Southeast Arkansas College ... AR ... 23
University of Arkansas at Fort Smith ... AR ... 24
University of Arkansas for Medical Sciences ... AR ... 24
American Career College-Los Angeles ... CA ... 27
CNI College ... CA ... 39
Concorde Career College ... CA ... 41
Everest College-Reseda ... CA ... 43
Fresno City College ... CA ... 68
Las Positas College ... CA ... 37
MiraCosta Community College District ... CA ... 54
Skyline College ... CA ... 64
Southwestern College ... CA ... 68
Aims Community College ... CO ... 78
Concorde Career College ... CO ... 81
Everest College ... CO ... 81
Manchester Community College ... CT ... 88
Central Florida Institute ... FL ... 99
College of Central Florida ... FL ... 100
Concorde Career Institute ... FL ... 100
Daytona State College ... FL ... 101
Eastern Florida State College ... FL ... 101
Everest Institute ... FL ... 102
Florida State College at Jacksonville ... FL ... 105
Fortis College ... FL ... 105
Gulf Coast State College ... FL ... 106
Indian River State College ... FL ... 106
Palm Beach State College ... FL ... 110
Pensacola State College ... FL ... 110
Santa Fe College ... FL ... 113
Southeastern College ... FL ... 113
Albany Technical College ... GA .. 120
Athens Technical College ... GA .. 120
Augusta Technical College ... GA .. 121
Central Georgia Technical College ... GA .. 122
Columbus Technical College ... GA .. 123
Georgia Northwestern Technical College . GA .. 125
Gwinnett Technical College ... GA .. 127
Lanier Technical College ... GA .. 128
Moultrie Technical College ... GA .. 129
Ogeechee Technical College ... GA .. 129
Okefenokee Technical College ... GA .. 130
Savannah Technical College ... GA .. 131
Southeastern Technical College ... GA .. 132
Southern Crescent Technical College ... GA .. 132
Southwest Georgia Technical College ... GA .. 132
West Georgia Technical College ... GA .. 134
Wiregrass Georgia Technical College ... GA .. 134
College of Southern Idaho ... ID ... 138
College of Western Idaho ... ID ... 138
Eastern Idaho Technical College ... ID ... 138
City Colleges of Chicago Malcolm X College ... IL ... 142
College of DuPage ... IL ... 142
College of Lake County ... IL ... 143
Elgin Community College ... IL ... 144
Illinois Central College ... IL ... 146
John A. Logan College ... IL ... 148
John Wood Community College ... IL ... 148
Kaskaskia College ... IL ... 149
Lincoln Land Community College ... IL ... 151
Parkland College ... IL ... 155
Prairie State College ... IL ... 156
Rend Lake College ... IL ... 156
Richland Community College ... IL ... 156
Robert Morris University ... IL ... 156
Rock Valley College ... IL ... 157
Shawnee Community College ... IL ... 158
Southeastern Illinois College ... IL ... 159
Triton College ... IL ... 161
Waubonsee Community College ... IL ... 162
Ivy Tech Community College-Central Indiana ... IN ... 169
National College ... IN ... 171
University of Saint Francis ... IN ... 174
Vincennes University ... IN ... 174
Des Moines Area Community College ... IA ... 177
Iowa Lakes Community College ... IA ... 179
Iowa Western Community College ... IA ... 179
Kirkwood Community College ... IA ... 180
Mercy College of Health Sciences ... IA ... 181
Scott Community College ... IA ... 178
Western Iowa Tech Community College ... IA ... 183
Hutchinson Community College and Area Vocational School ... KS ... 187
Neosho County Community College ... KS ... 189
Seward County Community College/Area Technical School ... KS ... 190
Wichita Area Technical College ... KS ... 191
Ashland Community and Technical College ... KY ... 194
Bluegrass Community and Technical College ... KY ... 194
Hazard Community and Technical College KY ... 195
Jefferson Community and Technical College ... KY ... 195
Madisonville Community College ... KY ... 196
National College ... KY ... 198
Owensboro Community and Technical College ... KY ... 196
St. Catharine College ... KY ... 198
Somerset Community College ... KY ... 196
Southcentral Kentucky Community and Technical College ... KY ... 196
Southeast Kentucky Community and Technical College ... KY ... 196
Spencerian College ... KY ... 199
West Kentucky Community and Technical College ... KY ... 196
Bossier Parish Community College ... LA ... 202
Career Technical College ... LA ... 201
Delgado Community College ... LA ... 203
Fortis College ... LA ... 202
Our Lady of the Lake College ... LA ... 206
South Louisiana Community College Ardoin Campus ... LA ... 203
Southern University at Shreveport-Louisiana ... LA ... 207
Eastern Maine Community College ... ME .. 210
Anne Arundel Community College ... MD .. 213
Baltimore City Community College ... MD .. 213
Chesapeake College ... MD .. 214
Community College of Baltimore County, The ... MD .. 214
Frederick Community College ... MD .. 214
Montgomery College ... MD .. 216
Bunker Hill Community College ... MA .. 231
Massachusetts Bay Community College ... MA .. 231
North Shore Community College ... MA .. 232
Quincy College ... MA .. 235
Quinsigamond Community College ... MA .. 232
Springfield Technical Community College MA .. 233
Baker College of Flint ... MI ... 239
Delta College ... MI ... 242
Henry Ford Community College ... MI ... 243
Lansing Community College ... MI ... 245
Macomb Community College ... MI ... 246
Northern Michigan University ... MI ... 248
Oakland Community College ... MI ... 248
Wayne County Community College District ... MI ... 252
Anoka Technical College ... MN .. 257
Lake Superior College ... MN .. 259
Minnesota West Community and Technical College ... MN .. 260
Northland Community and Technical College ... MN .. 260
Rasmussen College - St. Cloud ... MN .. 263
Rochester Community and Technical College ... MN .. 261
Saint Cloud Technical and Community College ... MN .. 261
Saint Mary's University of Minnesota ... MN .. 264
East Central Community College ... MS .. 266
Hinds Community College ... MS .. 267
Holmes Community College ... MS .. 267
Itawamba Community College ... MS .. 267
Meridian Community College ... MS .. 267
Mississippi Gulf Coast Community College ... MS .. 268
Pearl River Community College ... MS .. 269
Lincoln University ... MO .. 276
Metropolitan Community College - Penn Valley ... MO .. 277
Ozarks Technical Community College ... MO .. 279
Saint Louis Community College at Forest Park ... MO .. 281
Southeast Missouri Hospital College of Nursing and Health Sciences ... MO .. 282
Flathead Valley Community College ... MT .. 286
Great Falls College Montana State University ... MT .. 287
Nebraska Methodist College ... NE ... 291
Southeast Community College ... NE ... 292
College of Southern Nevada ... NV ... 294
Great Bay Community College ... NH ... 295
Atlantic Cape Community College ... NJ ... 299
Bergen Community College ... NJ ... 299
Berkeley College ... NJ ... 299
Eastwick College ... NJ ... 301
Sussex County Community College ... NJ ... 307
Central New Mexico Community College . NM .. 309
San Juan College ... NM .. 311
City University of New York Kingsborough Community College ... NY ... 318
Nassau Community College ... NY ... 332
New York University ... NY ... 334
Niagara County Community College ... NY ... 334
Onondaga Community College ... NY ... 335
Trocaire College ... NY ... 348
Asheville - Buncombe Technical Community College ... NC ... 357
Blue Ridge Community College ... NC ... 358
Cabarrus College of Health Sciences ... NC ... 352
Cape Fear Community College ... NC ... 358
Carolinas College of Health Sciences ... NC ... 353
Catawba Valley Community College ... NC ... 359
Central Piedmont Community College ... NC ... 359
Cleveland Community College ... NC ... 359
Coastal Carolina Community College ... NC ... 359
College of the Albemarle ... NC ... 359
Durham Technical Community College ... NC ... 360
Edgecombe Community College ... NC ... 360
Fayetteville Technical Community College NC ... 360
Guilford Technical Community College ... NC ... 360
Lenoir Community College ... NC ... 361
Robeson Community College ... NC ... 363
Rockingham Community College ... NC ... 363
Sandhills Community College ... NC ... 363
South College-Asheville ... NC ... 366
South Piedmont Community College ... NC ... 363
Wake Technical Community College ... NC ... 364
Wilson Community College ... NC ... 365
Bismarck State College ... ND ... 372
Central Ohio Technical College ... OH ... 376
Cincinnati State Technical and Community College ... OH .. 376
Columbus State Community College ... OH .. 378
Cuyahoga Community College ... OH .. 378
Fortis College ... OH .. 379
Lakeland Community College ... OH .. 382
Lorain County Community College ... OH .. 383
Owens Community College ... OH .. 387
Sinclair Community College ... OH .. 388
University of Akron, Main Campus, The ... OH .. 390
University of Cincinnati-Clermont College . OH .. 391
Community Care College ... OK .. 395
Concorde Career College ... OR .. 402
Mt. Hood Community College ... OR .. 404
Community College of Allegheny County . PA ... 413
Delaware County Community College ... PA ... 414
Great Lakes Institute of Technology ... PA ... 417
Harrisburg Area Community College ... PA ... 417
Lackawanna College ... PA ... 420
Lancaster General College of Nursing and Health Sciences ... PA ... 421
Luzerne County Community College ... PA ... 422
Montgomery County Community College . PA ... 424
Mount Aloysius College ... PA ... 424
Pennsylvania College of Technology ... PA ... 427
Pittsburgh Technical Institute ... PA ... 430
New England Institute of Technology ... RI ... 439
Aiken Technical College ... SC ... 440
Central Carolina Technical College ... SC ... 441
Florence - Darlington Technical College ... SC ... 443
Greenville Technical College ... SC ... 444
Horry-Georgetown Technical College ... SC ... 444
Midlands Technical College ... SC ... 445
Piedmont Technical College ... SC ... 446
Spartanburg Community College ... SC ... 447
Technical College of the Lowcountry ... SC ... 447
Tri-County Technical College ... SC ... 447
York Technical College ... SC ... 449
Presentation College ... SD ... 450
Southeast Technical Institute ... SD ... 452
Western Dakota Technical Institute ... SD ... 452
Chattanooga State Community College ... TN ... 460
Concorde Career College ... TN ... 453
Fortis Institute ... TN ... 454
Miller-Motte Technical College ... TN ... 457
Nashville State Community College ... TN ... 461
Northeast State Community College ... TN ... 461
Amarillo College ... TX ... 465
Angelina College ... TX ... 465
Austin Community College District ... TX ... 466
Baptist Health System School of Health Professions ... TX ... 467
Cisco College ... TX ... 468
College of Health Care Professions, The . TX ... 469
Collin County Community College District TX ... 469
Del Mar College ... TX ... 471
El Centro College ... TX ... 470
El Paso Community College ... TX ... 472
Houston Community College ... TX ... 473
Howard College ... TX ... 473
Kilgore College ... TX ... 475
Lamar State College-Port Arthur ... TX ... 486
Lone Star College System ... TX ... 476
McLennan Community College ... TX ... 476
North Central Texas College ... TX ... 477
Paris Junior College ... TX ... 478
St. Philip's College ... TX ... 465
San Jacinto College Central ... TX ... 479
South Plains College ... TX ... 480
Tarrant County College District ... TX ... 482
Temple College ... TX ... 482
Texas State Technical College Harlingen . TX ... 485
Trinity Valley Community College ... TX ... 488
Tyler Junior College ... TX ... 488
Vernon College ... TX ... 493
Wharton County Junior College ... TX ... 494
Dixie State College of Utah ... UT ... 497
Everest College ... UT ... 495
Salt Lake Community College ... UT ... 498
Stevens-Henager College ... UT ... 496
Miller-Motte Technical College ... VA ... 507
Piedmont Virginia Community College ... VA ... 513
Riverside School of Health Careers ... VA ... 509
Sentara College of Health Sciences ... VA ... 509
Bellingham Technical College ... WA ... 517
Clover Park Technical College ... WA .. 518
Columbia Basin College ... WA .. 518
Renton Technical College ... WA .. 522
#Seattle Central Community College ... WA .. 522
Spokane Community College ... WA .. 518
Yakima Valley Community College ... WA .. 525
Southern West Virginia Community and Technical College ... WV .. 528
West Virginia Northern Community College ... WV .. 528
West Virginia University at Parkersburg ... WV .. 530
Chippewa Valley Technical College ... WI ... 539
Gateway Technical College ... WI ... 540
Madison Area Technical College ... WI ... 540
Mid-State Technical College ... WI ... 540
Milwaukee Area Technical College ... WI ... 540
Moraine Park Technical College ... WI ... 540
Northcentral Technical College ... WI ... 541
Northeast Wisconsin Technical College ... WI ... 541
Waukesha County Technical College ... WI ... 541
Western Technical College ... WI ... 541

Laramie County Community College ... WY .. 543

SURTEC: Accrediting Bureau of Health Education Schools: surgical technologist (C,A)

American Career College-Los Angeles ... CA ... 27
American Career College-Ontario ... CA ... 27
CBD College ... CA ... 37
CNI College ... CA ... 39
Central Florida Institute ... FL ... 99
City College ... FL ... 100
Lincoln Tech Fern Park Orlando Campus FL ... 108
Southeastern College ... FL ... 113
Southwest Florida College ... FL ... 114
Fortis College ... LA ... 202
Anthem College ... MO .. 271
Mandl School ... NY .. 329
Heritage College ... OK .. 395
Baptist Health System School of Health Professions ... TX ... 467
College of Health Care Professions, The . TX ... 469
Concorde Career Institute ... TX ... 469
Sanford-Brown College ... TX ... 480

SW: Council on Social Work Education: social work (B,M)

Alabama Agricultural and Mechanical University ... AL ... 1
Alabama State University ... AL ... 1
Auburn University ... AL ... 1
Jacksonville State University ... AL ... 4
@Judson College ... AL ... 5
Miles College ... AL ... 5
Oakwood University ... AL ... 6
Talladega College ... AL ... 7
Troy University ... AL ... 7
Tuskegee University ... AL ... 8
University of Alabama at Birmingham ... AL ... 8
University of Alabama, The ... AL ... 8
University of Montevallo ... AL ... 9
University of North Alabama ... AL ... 9
University of South Alabama ... AL ... 9
University of Alaska Anchorage ... AK ... 10
University of Alaska Fairbanks ... AK ... 10
Arizona State University ... AZ ... 11
Northern Arizona University ... AZ ... 16
Arkansas State University-Jonesboro ... AR ... 19
Harding University Main Campus ... AR ... 21
Philander Smith College ... AR ... 22
Southern Arkansas University ... AR ... 23
University of Arkansas at Little Rock ... AR ... 24
University of Arkansas at Monticello ... AR ... 24
University of Arkansas at Pine Bluff ... AR ... 24
University of Arkansas Main Campus ... AR ... 23
Azusa Pacific University ... CA ... 29
California State University-Bakersfield ... CA ... 32
California State University-Chico ... CA ... 33
California State University-Dominguez Hills ... CA ... 33
California State University-East Bay ... CA ... 33
California State University-Fresno ... CA ... 33
California State University-Fullerton ... CA ... 33
California State University-Long Beach ... CA ... 33
California State University-Los Angeles ... CA ... 34
@California State University-Monterey Bay . CA ... 34
California State University-Northridge ... CA ... 34
California State University-Sacramento ... CA ... 34
California State University-San Bernardino CA ... 34
California State University-Stanislaus ... CA ... 35
Humboldt State University ... CA ... 35
La Sierra University ... CA ... 50
Loma Linda University ... CA ... 51
Pacific Union College ... CA ... 57
Point Loma Nazarene University ... CA ... 59
San Diego State University ... CA ... 35
San Francisco State University ... CA ... 35
San Jose State University ... CA ... 36
University of California-Berkeley ... CA ... 70
University of California-Los Angeles ... CA ... 71
University of Southern California ... CA ... 74
Whittier College ... CA ... 76
Colorado State University ... CO ... 80
Colorado State University-Pueblo ... CO ... 80
Metropolitan State University of Denver ... CO ... 83
University of Denver ... CO ... 86
Central Connecticut State University ... CT ... 87
Eastern Connecticut State University ... CT ... 87
Sacred Heart University ... CT ... 91
Southern Connecticut State University ... CT ... 88
University of Connecticut ... CT ... 92
University of Saint Joseph ... CT ... 92
Western Connecticut State University ... CT ... 88
Delaware State University ... DE ... 93
Catholic University of America, The ... DC ... 94
Gallaudet University ... DC ... 95
Howard University ... DC ... 95
University of the District of Columbia ... DC ... 97
Barry University ... FL ... 98
Florida Agricultural and Mechanical University ... FL ... 114
Florida Atlantic University ... FL ... 114
Florida Gulf Coast University ... FL ... 115
Florida International University ... FL ... 115
Florida Memorial University ... FL ... 104
Florida State University ... FL ... 115
Saint Leo University ... FL ... 112
Southeastern University ... FL ... 113
University of Central Florida ... FL ... 115
@University of North Florida ... FL ... 116
University of South Florida ... FL ... 116
University of West Florida ... FL ... 117
Warner University ... FL ... 119
Albany State University ... GA .. 119
Clark Atlanta University ... GA .. 122
Dalton State College ... GA .. 123
Georgia Regents University ... GA .. 126
Georgia State University ... GA .. 126
Kennesaw State University ... GA .. 127
Savannah State University ... GA .. 131
Thomas University ... GA .. 132
University of Georgia ... GA .. 133
Valdosta State University ... GA .. 134
University of Guam ... GU .. 546
Brigham Young University Hawaii ... HI ... 135
Hawaii Pacific University ... HI ... 135
University of Hawaii at Manoa ... HI ... 136
Boise State University ... ID ... 137
Brigham Young University-Idaho ... ID ... 137
Idaho State University ... ID ... 138
Lewis-Clark State College ... ID ... 138
Northwest Nazarene University ... ID ... 139
Aurora University ... IL ... 140
Bradley University ... IL ... 140
Chicago State University ... IL ... 141
DePaul University ... IL ... 143
Dominican University ... IL ... 144
Governors State University ... IL ... 145
Illinois State University ... IL ... 147
Lewis University ... IL ... 150
Loyola University Chicago ... IL ... 151
MacMurray College ... IL ... 152
Northeastern Illinois University ... IL ... 154
Olivet Nazarene University ... IL ... 155
St. Augustine College ... IL ... 158
Southern Illinois University Carbondale ... IL ... 159
Southern Illinois University Edwardsville ... IL ... 159
Trinity Christian College ... IL ... 160
University of Chicago ... IL ... 161
University of Illinois at Chicago ... IL ... 161
University of Illinois at Springfield ... IL ... 161
University of Illinois at Urbana-Champaign IL ... 162
University of St. Francis ... IL ... 162
Western Illinois University ... IL ... 162
Anderson University ... IN ... 163
Ball State University ... IN ... 164
Goshen College ... IN ... 166
Huntington University ... IN ... 166
Indiana State University ... IN ... 167
Indiana University-Purdue University Indianapolis ... IN ... 168
Indiana Wesleyan University ... IN ... 169
Manchester University ... IN ... 170
Saint Mary's College ... IN ... 172
Taylor University ... IN ... 173
University of Indianapolis ... IN ... 173
University of Saint Francis ... IN ... 174
University of Southern Indiana ... IN ... 174
Valparaiso University ... IN ... 174
Briar Cliff University ... IA ... 176
Buena Vista University ... IA ... 176
Clarke University ... IA ... 176
Dordt College ... IA ... 177
Loras College ... IA ... 180
Luther College ... IA ... 180
Mount Mercy University ... IA ... 181
Northwestern College ... IA ... 181
St. Ambrose University ... IA ... 182
University of Iowa ... IA ... 175
University of Northern Iowa ... IA ... 176
Wartburg College ... IA ... 183
Bethel College ... KS ... 184
Fort Hays State University ... KS ... 186
Kansas State University ... KS ... 188
Newman University ... KS ... 189
Pittsburg State University ... KS ... 189
University of Kansas Main Campus ... KS ... 190
Washburn University ... KS ... 191
Wichita State University ... KS ... 191
Asbury University ... KY ... 192
Brescia University ... KY ... 192
Campbellsville University ... KY ... 193
Eastern Kentucky University ... KY ... 193
Kentucky Christian University ... KY ... 194
Kentucky State University ... KY ... 197
Morehead State University ... KY ... 198
Murray State University ... KY ... 198
Northern Kentucky University ... KY ... 198
Spalding University ... KY ... 199
Union College ... KY ... 200
University of Kentucky ... KY ... 200
University of Louisville ... KY ... 200
University of Pikeville ... KY ... 200
Western Kentucky University ... KY ... 200
Grambling State University ... LA ... 207
Louisiana College ... LA ... 202
Louisiana State University and Agricultural and Mechanical College ... LA ... 204
Northwestern State University ... LA ... 208
Southeastern Louisiana University ... LA ... 208
Southern University and A&M College ... LA ... 206
Southern University at New Orleans ... LA ... 206
Tulane University ... LA ... 207
University of Louisiana at Monroe ... LA ... 208
University of Maine ... ME .. 212
University of Maine at Presque Isle ... ME .. 212
University of New England ... ME .. 213
University of Southern Maine ... ME .. 212
Bowie State University ... MD .. 220
Coppin State University ... MD .. 220
Frostburg State University ... MD .. 220
Hood College ... MD .. 215
McDaniel College ... MD .. 216
Morgan State University ... MD .. 217
Salisbury University ... MD .. 220
@Sojourner-Douglass College ... MD .. 218
University of Maryland Baltimore ... MD .. 219
University of Maryland Baltimore County .. MD .. 219
Anna Maria College ... MA .. 222
Boston College ... MA .. 224
Boston University ... MA .. 224
Bridgewater State University ... MA .. 229
College of Our Lady of the Elms ... MA .. 225
Eastern Nazarene College ... MA .. 225
Gordon College ... MA .. 226
Regis College ... MA .. 236
Salem State University ... MA .. 230
Simmons College ... MA .. 236
Smith College ... MA .. 236
Springfield College ... MA .. 236
Western New England University ... MA .. 238
Westfield State University ... MA .. 230
Wheelock College ... MA .. 238
Adrian College ... MI ... 238
Andrews University ... MI ... 239
Calvin College ... MI ... 240
Central Michigan University ... MI ... 240
Cornerstone University ... MI ... 241
Eastern Michigan University ... MI ... 242
Ferris State University ... MI ... 242
Grand Valley State University ... MI ... 243
Hope College ... MI ... 244
Kuyper College ... MI ... 245
Madonna University ... MI ... 246
Marygrove College ... MI ... 246
Michigan State University ... MI ... 246
Northern Michigan University ... MI ... 248
Oakland University ... MI ... 248
Saginaw Valley State University ... MI ... 249
Siena Heights University ... MI ... 250
Spring Arbor University ... MI ... 250
University of Detroit Mercy ... MI ... 250
University of Michigan-Ann Arbor ... MI ... 251
University of Michigan-Flint ... MI ... 251
Wayne State University ... MI ... 252
Western Michigan University ... MI ... 252
Augsburg College ... MN .. 253
Bemidji State University ... MN .. 258
Bethel University ... MN .. 253
College of Saint Scholastica, The ... MN .. 254
Concordia College ... MN .. 255
Metropolitan State University ... MN .. 259
Minnesota State University Moorhead ... MN .. 259
Minnesota State University, Mankato ... MN .. 259
@North Central University ... MN .. 262
St. Catherine University ... MN .. 263
St. Cloud State University ... MN .. 261
St. Olaf College ... MN .. 264
Southwest Minnesota State University ... MN .. 261
University of Minnesota Duluth ... MN .. 264
University of Minnesota-Twin Cities ... MN .. 264
University of Saint Thomas ... MN .. 265
Winona State University ... MN .. 262
Alcorn State University ... MS .. 265
Delta State University ... MS .. 266
Jackson State University ... MS .. 267
Mississippi College ... MS .. 268
Mississippi State University ... MS .. 268
Mississippi Valley State University ... MS .. 269
Rust College ... MS .. 269
University of Mississippi ... MS .. 270
University of Southern Mississippi ... MS .. 270
Avila University ... MO .. 271
Evangel University ... MO .. 274
Fontbonne University ... MO .. 274
@Lincoln University ... MO .. 276
Lindenwood University ... MO .. 276
Missouri State University ... MO .. 278
Missouri Western State University ... MO .. 279
Park University ... MO .. 280
Saint Louis University ... MO .. 281
Southeast Missouri State University ... MO .. 282
@Southwest Baptist University ... MO .. 282
University of Central Missouri ... MO .. 283
University of Missouri - Columbia ... MO .. 283
University of Missouri - Kansas City ... MO .. 283
University of Missouri - Saint Louis ... MO .. 283
Washington University in St. Louis ... MO .. 284
William Woods University ... MO .. 285
Salish Kootenai College ... MT .. 288
University of Montana - Missoula, The ... MT .. 286
Chadron State College ... NE .. 291
Creighton University ... NE .. 289
Nebraska Wesleyan University ... NE .. 291
Union College ... NE .. 292
University of Nebraska at Kearney ... NE .. 292
University of Nebraska at Omaha ... NE .. 293
University of Nevada, Las Vegas ... NV .. 294
University of Nevada, Reno ... NV .. 294
Plymouth State University ... NH .. 298
University of New Hampshire ... NH .. 298
Centenary College ... NJ .. 300
Georgian Court University ... NJ .. 302
Kean University ... NJ .. 302
Monmouth University ... NJ .. 303
Ramapo College of New Jersey ... NJ .. 305
Richard Stockton College of New Jersey, The ... NJ .. 305
Rutgers the State University of New Jersey New Brunswick Campus ... NJ .. 306
Rutgers the State University of New Jersey Newark Campus ... NJ .. 306
Seton Hall University ... NJ .. 307
Eastern New Mexico University Main Campus ... NM .. 309
New Mexico Highlands University ... NM .. 310
New Mexico State University Main Campus ... NM .. 310
Western New Mexico University ... NM .. 312
Adelphi University ... NY .. 313
@City University of New York College of Staten Island ... NY .. 317
City University of New York Herbert H. Lehman College ... NY .. 318
City University of New York Hunter College ... NY .. 318
City University of New York Medgar Evers College ... NY .. 319
City University of New York York College NY .. 319
College of New Rochelle, The ... NY .. 320
College of Saint Rose, The ... NY .. 321
Columbia University in the City of New York ... NY .. 321
Concordia College ... NY .. 321
Daemen College ... NY .. 322
Dominican College of Blauvelt ... NY .. 322
Fordham University ... NY .. 324
Iona College ... NY .. 327
Keuka College ... NY .. 328
Long Island University - Post Campus ... NY .. 329
Marist College ... NY .. 330
Mercy College ... NY .. 330
Molloy College ... NY .. 331
Nazareth College of Rochester ... NY .. 332
New York University ... NY .. 334
Niagara University ... NY .. 334
Nyack College ... NY .. 335
Roberts Wesleyan College ... NY .. 337
Siena College ... NY .. 340
Skidmore College ... NY .. 341
State University of New York at Binghamton ... NY .. 341
State University of New York at Fredonia . NY .. 342
State University of New York at Stony Brook ... NY .. 342
State University of New York College at Buffalo ... NY .. 343
State University of New York College at Plattsburgh ... NY .. 344
State University of New York, The College at Brockport ... NY .. 342
Syracuse University Main Campus ... NY .. 347
Touro College ... NY .. 348
University at Albany, SUNY ... NY .. 341
University at Buffalo-SUNY ... NY .. 341
Yeshiva University ... NY .. 351
Appalachian State University ... NC .. 367
Barton College ... NC .. 352
Bennett College ... NC .. 352
Campbell University ... NC .. 352
East Carolina University ... NC .. 367
Elizabeth City State University ... NC .. 367
Fayetteville State University ... NC .. 367
Johnson C. Smith University ... NC .. 355
Livingstone College ... NC .. 356
Mars Hill College ... NC .. 356
Meredith College ... NC .. 356
Methodist University ... NC .. 356
North Carolina Agricultural and Technical State University ... NC .. 367
North Carolina Central University ... NC .. 368
North Carolina State University ... NC .. 368
Shaw University ... NC .. 366
University of North Carolina at Chapel Hill NC .. 368
University of North Carolina at Charlotte .. NC .. 368
University of North Carolina at Greensboro ... NC .. 369
University of North Carolina at Pembroke NC .. 369
University of North Carolina Wilmington ... NC .. 369
Warren Wilson College ... NC .. 370
Western Carolina University ... NC .. 369
Winston-Salem State University ... NC .. 370
Minot State University ... ND .. 371
University of Mary ... ND .. 373

University of North Dakota Main Campus . ND .. 371
Ashland University ... OH .. 374
Bluffton University ... OH .. 374
Bowling Green State University ... OH .. 374
Capital University ... OH .. 375
Case Western Reserve University ... OH .. 375
Cedarville University ... OH .. 375
Cleveland State University ... OH .. 377
College of Mount St. Joseph ... OH .. 377
Defiance College, The ... OH .. 379
Franciscan University of Steubenville ... OH .. 379
Lourdes University ... OH .. 383
Malone University ... OH .. 383
Miami University ... OH .. 384
Mount Vernon Nazarene University ... OH .. 384
Ohio Dominican University ... OH .. 386
Ohio State University Main Campus, The . OH .. 386
Ohio University Main Campus ... OH .. 387
@Union Institute & University ... OH .. 390
University of Akron, Main Campus, The ... OH .. 390
University of Cincinnati Main Campus ... OH .. 390
University of Findlay, The ... OH .. 391
University of Rio Grande ... OH .. 392
University of Toledo ... OH .. 392
Ursuline College ... OH .. 392
Wright State University Main Campus ... OH .. 393
Xavier University ... OH .. 393
Youngstown State University ... OH .. 394
East Central University ... OK .. 395
Northeastern State University ... OK .. 396
Northwestern Oklahoma State University . OK .. 396
Oral Roberts University ... OK .. 398
University of Oklahoma Norman Campus . OK .. 401
Concordia University ... OR .. 402
George Fox University ... OR .. 403
Pacific University ... OR .. 407
Portland State University ... OR .. 406
University of Portland ... OR .. 408
Alvernia University ... PA ... 409
Bloomsburg University of Pennsylvania ... PA ... 427
Bryn Mawr College ... PA ... 410
Cabrini College ... PA ... 411
Cairn University ... PA ... 411
California University of Pennsylvania ... PA ... 428
Carlow University ... PA ... 412
Cedar Crest College ... PA ... 412
Chatham University ... PA ... 412
@East Stroudsburg University of Pennsylvania ... PA ... 428
Eastern University ... PA ... 415
Edinboro University of Pennsylvania ... PA ... 428
Elizabethtown College ... PA ... 415
Gannon University ... PA ... 416
Juniata College ... PA ... 419
Kutztown University of Pennsylvania ... PA ... 429
La Salle University ... PA ... 420
Lock Haven University ... PA ... 429
Mansfield University of Pennsylvania ... PA ... 429
Marywood University ... PA ... 423
Mercyhurst University ... PA ... 423
Messiah College ... PA ... 423
Millersville University of Pennsylvania ... PA ... 429
Misericordia University ... PA ... 424
Saint Francis University ... PA ... 432
Seton Hill University ... PA ... 433
Shippensburg University of Pennsylvania . PA ... 429
Slippery Rock University of Pennsylvania . PA ... 429
Temple University ... PA ... 433
University of Pennsylvania ... PA ... 435
University of Pittsburgh ... PA ... 435
Valley Forge Christian College ... PA ... 436
West Chester University of Pennsylvania . PA ... 430
Widener University ... PA ... 437
Inter American University of Puerto Rico Arecibo Campus ... PR ... 549
Inter American University of Puerto Rico Fajardo Campus ... PR ... 550
Inter American University of Puerto Rico Metropolitan Campus ... PR ... 550
Pontifical Catholic University of Puerto Rico, The ... PR ... 552
@Universidad del Este ... PR ... 552
@Universidad Del Turabo ... PR ... 552
University of Puerto Rico-Humacao ... PR ... 554
University of Puerto Rico-Rio Piedras Campus ... PR ... 555
University of the Sacred Heart ... PR ... 555
Providence College ... RI ... 439
Rhode Island College ... RI ... 439
Salve Regina University ... RI ... 440
Benedict College ... SC ... 441
Coker College ... SC ... 442
Columbia College ... SC ... 443
Limestone College ... SC ... 444
South Carolina State University ... SC ... 446
University of South Carolina Columbia ... SC ... 447
Winthrop University ... SC ... 449
Oglala Lakota College ... SD ... 450
Presentation College ... SD ... 450
University of Sioux Falls ... SD ... 452
University of South Dakota, The ... SD ... 451
Austin Peay State University ... TN ... 459
Belmont University ... TN ... 453
East Tennessee State University ... TN ... 459
Freed-Hardeman University ... TN ... 454
Lincoln Memorial University ... TN ... 456
Lipscomb University ... TN ... 456
Middle Tennessee State University ... TN ... 459
Southern Adventist University ... TN ... 458
Tennessee State University ... TN ... 459
@Trevecca Nazarene University ... TN ... 462
Union University ... TN ... 462
University of Memphis, The ... TN ... 460
University of Tennessee at Chattanooga .. TN ... 463
University of Tennessee at Martin ... TN ... 463
University of Tennessee, Knoxville ... TN ... 463
Abilene Christian University ... TX ... 464
@Angelo State University ... TX ... 465
Baylor University ... TX ... 467
Hardin-Simmons University ... TX ... 472
Howard Payne University ... TX ... 473
Lamar University ... TX ... 486
Lubbock Christian University ... TX ... 476
Midwestern State University ... TX ... 476
Our Lady of the Lake University ... TX ... 477
Prairie View A & M University ... TX ... 482
St. Edward's University ... TX ... 479
Stephen F. Austin State University ... TX ... 482
Tarleton State University ... TX ... 483
Texas A & M University - Commerce ... TX ... 483
Texas A & M University - Kingsville ... TX ... 484
Texas Christian University ... TX ... 484
Texas Southern University ... TX ... 485
Texas State University-San Marcos ... TX ... 487
Texas Tech University ... TX ... 487
Texas Woman's University ... TX ... 488
University of Houston ... TX ... 489
University of Houston - Clear Lake ... TX ... 489
University of Houston - Downtown ... TX ... 489
University of Mary Hardin-Baylor ... TX ... 490
University of North Texas ... TX ... 490
University of Texas at Arlington, The ... TX ... 491
University of Texas at Austin ... TX ... 491
University of Texas at El Paso ... TX ... 492
University of Texas at San Antonio ... TX ... 492
University of Texas of the Permian Basin . TX ... 493
University of Texas - Pan American ... TX ... 492
West Texas A & M University ... TX ... 484
Brigham Young University ... UT ... 495
University of Utah, The ... UT ... 496
Utah State University ... UT ... 497
@Utah Valley University ... UT ... 497
Weber State University ... UT ... 497
Castleton State College ... VT ... 501
Champlain College ... VT ... 499
University of Vermont ... VT ... 500
Christopher Newport University ... VA ... 503
Eastern Mennonite University ... VA ... 504
Ferrum College ... VA ... 504
George Mason University ... VA ... 505
James Madison University ... VA ... 506
Longwood University ... VA ... 506
Mary Baldwin College ... VA ... 507
Norfolk State University ... VA ... 507
Radford University ... VA ... 508
Virginia Commonwealth University ... VA ... 511
Virginia Intermont College ... VA ... 514
@Virginia State University ... VA ... 515
Virginia Union University ... VA ... 515
@Virginia Wesleyan College ... VA ... 515
Eastern Washington University ... WA ... 519
Heritage University ... WA ... 520
Pacific Lutheran University ... WA ... 521
Seattle University ... WA ... 523
University of Washington ... WA ... 524
Walla Walla University ... WA ... 524
Bethany College ... WV .. 526
Concord University ... WV .. 529
Marshall University ... WV .. 529
Shepherd University ... WV .. 529
University of Charleston ... WV .. 527
@West Liberty University ... WV .. 530
West Virginia State University ... WV .. 530
West Virginia University ... WV .. 530
Carthage College ... WI ... 532
Concordia University Wisconsin ... WI ... 532
Marian University ... WI ... 534
Mount Mary University ... WI ... 535
University of Wisconsin-Eau Claire ... WI ... 536
University of Wisconsin-Green Bay ... WI ... 536
University of Wisconsin-Madison ... WI ... 536
University of Wisconsin-Milwaukee ... WI ... 537
University of Wisconsin-Oshkosh ... WI ... 537
University of Wisconsin-River Falls ... WI ... 537
@University of Wisconsin-Stevens Point ... WI ... 538
University of Wisconsin-Superior ... WI ... 538
University of Wisconsin-Whitewater ... WI ... 538
Viterbo University ... WI ... 539
University of Wyoming ... WY .. 543

TEAC: Teacher Education Accreditation Council: teacher education (B,M,D)

@Northcentral University ... AZ 16
University of Phoenix ... AZ 18
Chapman University ... CA ... 38
Adams State University ... CO 78
Colorado State University ... CO 80
Colorado State University-Pueblo ... CO 80
Fort Lewis College ... CO 81
Regis University ... CO 84
@Western State Colorado University ... CO 86
@Strayer University ... DC 96
@Flagler College ... FL ... 103
@Jose Maria Vargas University ... FL ... 107
@University of Miami ... FL ... 118
@Hawaii Pacific University ... HI 135
@University of Hawaii at Hilo ... HI 136
@American InterContinental University ... IL 139
@Greenville College ... IL 145
@Knox College ... IL 150
American College of Education ... IN ... 163
@Buena Vista University ... IA ... 176
St. Ambrose University ... IA ... 182
@Centenary College of Louisiana ... LA ... 201
@Louisiana College ... LA ... 202
Tulane University ... LA ... 207
University of Southern Maine ... ME .. 212
Boston College ... MA .. 224
@Cambridge College ... MA .. 224
Lesley University ... MA .. 228
@University of Massachusetts Boston ... MA .. 228
@Worcester State University ... MA .. 230
Adrian College ... MI 238
Albion College ... MI 239
Alma College ... MI 239
Aquinas College ... MI 239
@Baker College of Flint ... MI 239
Calvin College ... MI 240
Central Michigan University ... MI 240
@Cornerstone University ... MI 241
@Ferris State University ... MI 242
Hope College ... MI 244
@Lake Superior State University ... MI 245
Marygrove College ... MI 246
Michigan State University ... MI 246
Michigan Technological University ... MI 247
Northern Michigan University ... MI 248
Oakland University ... MI 248
Olivet College ... MI 249
@Robert B. Miller College ... MI 249
@Rochester College ... MI 249
Siena Heights University ... MI 250
Spring Arbor University ... MI 250
University of Detroit Mercy ... MI 250
University of Michigan-Ann Arbor ... MI 251
University of Michigan-Dearborn ... MI 251
Wayne State University ... MI 252
Bethel University ... MN .. 253
College of Saint Scholastica, The ... MN .. 254
@Concordia College ... MN .. 255
@Rust College ... MS ... 269
@Lindenwood University ... MO .. 276
Rockhurst University ... MO .. 280
@University of Missouri - Columbia ... MO .. 283
William Woods University ... MO .. 285
Montana State University ... MT ... 287
University of Nebraska - Lincoln ... NE ... 292
@Southern New Hampshire University ... NH .. 297
University of New Hampshire ... NH .. 298
Bloomfield College ... NJ ... 299
Caldwell College ... NJ ... 300
Centenary College ... NJ ... 300
College of Saint Elizabeth ... NJ ... 300
@Drew University ... NJ ... 301
Fairleigh Dickinson University ... NJ ... 301
Felician College ... NJ ... 302
Georgian Court University ... NJ ... 302
New Jersey City University ... NJ ... 303
Princeton University ... NJ ... 304
Ramapo College of New Jersey ... NJ ... 305
Richard Stockton College of New Jersey, The ... NJ ... 305
Rutgers the State University of New Jersey Camden Campus ... NJ ... 306
Rutgers the State University of New Jersey New Brunswick Campus ... NJ ... 306
Rutgers the State University of New Jersey Newark Campus ... NJ ... 306
Saint Peter's University ... NJ ... 306
Thomas Edison State College ... NJ ... 308
Alfred University ... NY ... 313
Bard College ... NY ... 314
@Barnard College ... NY ... 314
@Boricua College ... NY ... 315
@Cazenovia College ... NY ... 316
Colgate University ... NY ... 320
College of Mount Saint Vincent ... NY ... 320
@College of New Rochelle, The ... NY ... 320
@Cornell University ... NY ... 322
Daemen College ... NY ... 322
Dominican College of Blauvelt ... NY ... 322
@Elmira College ... NY ... 323
Hartwick College ... NY ... 325
@Hobart and William Smith Colleges ... NY ... 326
Hofstra University ... NY ... 326
Houghton College ... NY ... 326
@Keuka College ... NY ... 328
Le Moyne College ... NY ... 328
Long Island University - Post Campus ... NY ... 329
Manhattan College ... NY ... 329
Medaille College ... NY ... 330
Nazareth College of Rochester ... NY ... 332
New York University ... NY ... 334
@Pratt Institute ... NY ... 336
@Roberts Wesleyan College ... NY ... 337
Rochester Institute of Technology ... NY ... 337
St. Francis College ... NY ... 338
St. John's University ... NY ... 339
@Saint Joseph's College, New York ... NY ... 339
St. Lawrence University ... NY ... 339
@Sarah Lawrence College ... NY ... 340
@Skidmore College ... NY ... 341
State University of New York at Binghamton ... NY ... 341
State University of New York College at Plattsburgh ... NY ... 344
State University of New York Empire State College ... NY ... 346
@Touro College ... NY ... 348
Union Graduate College ... NY ... 348
University at Albany, SUNY ... NY ... 341
University at Buffalo-SUNY ... NY ... 341
Utica College ... NY ... 349
@Vassar College ... NY ... 349
@Wells College ... NY ... 350
@Yeshiva University ... NY ... 351
Brevard College ... NC .. 352
@Lees-McRae College ... NC .. 356
Case Western Reserve University ... OH .. 375
Cincinnati Christian University ... OH .. 376
College of Mount St. Joseph ... OH .. 377
@Lake Erie College ... OH .. 382
Lourdes University ... OH .. 383
Ohio Christian University ... OH .. 385
Wilmington College ... OH .. 393
Xavier University ... OH .. 393
University of Tulsa ... OK .. 401
@Holy Family University ... PA ... 418
Robert Morris University ... PA ... 431
@Saint Francis University ... PA ... 432
Temple University ... PA ... 433
@University of Pittsburgh ... PA ... 435
University of Scranton, The ... PA ... 436
@Bayamon Central University ... PR ... 547
@Caribbean University ... PR ... 547
@Inter American University of Puerto Rico Aguadilla Campus ... PR ... 549
@Inter American University of Puerto Rico Arecibo Campus ... PR ... 549
Inter American University of Puerto Rico Barranquitas Campus ... PR ... 550
Inter American University of Puerto Rico Fajardo Campus ... PR ... 550
Inter American University of Puerto Rico Guayama Campus ... PR ... 550
Inter American University of Puerto Rico Metropolitan Campus ... PR ... 550
Inter American University of Puerto Rico Ponce Campus ... PR ... 550
Inter American University of Puerto Rico San German Campus ... PR ... 551
@National University College ... PR ... 551
@Pontifical Catholic University of Puerto Rico, The ... PR ... 552
@Universidad Adventista de las Antillas ... PR ... 553
@Universidad del Este ... PR ... 552
Universidad Del Turabo ... PR ... 552
@Universidad Metropolitana ... PR ... 552
@Lane College ... TN ... 455
Abilene Christian University ... TX ... 464
@Rice University ... TX ... 479
Texas Lutheran University ... TX ... 485
Texas State University-San Marcos ... TX ... 487
@University of Houston - Victoria ... TX ... 489
University of St. Thomas ... TX ... 490
University of Texas at Tyler ... TX ... 492
Brigham Young University ... UT ... 495
Dixie State College of Utah ... UT ... 497
Southern Utah University ... UT ... 497
University of Utah, The ... UT ... 496
Utah State University ... UT ... 497
Utah Valley University ... UT ... 497
@Weber State University ... UT ... 497
Westminster College ... UT ... 498
Bluefield College ... VA ... 502
Emory & Henry College ... VA ... 504
Hollins University ... VA ... 505
Mary Baldwin College ... VA ... 507
Randolph College ... VA ... 508
Randolph-Macon College ... VA ... 508
Regent University ... VA ... 508
Roanoke College ... VA ... 509
Shenandoah University ... VA ... 509
University of Richmond ... VA ... 510
University of Virginia ... VA ... 511
University of Virginia's College at Wise, The ... VA ... 511
Washington and Lee University ... VA ... 516
Saint Martin's University ... WA ... 522
Alderson Broaddus University ... WV .. 526
Davis & Elkins College ... WV .. 526
@Ohio Valley University ... WV .. 527
University of Charleston ... WV .. 527
Wheeling Jesuit University ... WV .. 531

Lakeland College ... WI ... 533

TED: National Council for Accreditation of Teacher Education: teacher education (B,M,S,D)

Alabama Agricultural and Mechanical University ... AL ... 1
Alabama State University ... AL ... 1
Athens State University ... AL ... 1
Auburn University ... AL ... 1
Auburn University at Montgomery ... AL ... 2
Birmingham-Southern College ... AL ... 2
Faulkner University ... AL ... 3
Jacksonville State University ... AL ... 4
Miles College ... AL ... 5
Oakwood University ... AL ... 6
Samford University ... AL ... 6
Stillman College ... AL ... 7
Troy University ... AL ... 7
Tuskegee University ... AL ... 8
University of Alabama at Birmingham ... AL ... 8
University of Alabama in Huntsville ... AL ... 8
University of Alabama, The ... AL ... 8
University of Montevallo ... AL ... 9
University of North Alabama ... AL ... 9
University of South Alabama ... AL ... 9
University of West Alabama, The ... AL ... 9
Alaska Pacific University ... AK ... 10
University of Alaska Anchorage ... AK ... 10
University of Alaska Fairbanks ... AK ... 10
University of Alaska Southeast ... AK ... 11
Northern Arizona University ... AZ ... 16
Arkansas State University-Jonesboro ... AR ... 19
Arkansas Tech University ... AR ... 20
Harding University Main Campus ... AR ... 21
Henderson State University ... AR ... 21
Hendrix College ... AR ... 21
John Brown University ... AR ... 21
Lyon College ... AR ... 21
Ouachita Baptist University ... AR ... 22
Philander Smith College ... AR ... 22
Southern Arkansas University ... AR ... 23
University of Arkansas at Fort Smith ... AR ... 24
University of Arkansas at Little Rock ... AR ... 24
University of Arkansas at Monticello ... AR ... 24
University of Arkansas at Pine Bluff ... AR ... 24
University of Arkansas Main Campus ... AR ... 23
University of Central Arkansas ... AR ... 25
University of the Ozarks ... AR ... 25
Williams Baptist College ... AR ... 25
Azusa Pacific University ... CA ... 29
California Lutheran University ... CA ... 31
California Polytechnic State University-San Luis Obispo ... CA ... 32
California State University-Bakersfield ... CA ... 32
California State University-Chico ... CA ... 33
California State University-Dominguez Hills ... CA ... 33
California State University-East Bay ... CA ... 33
California State University-Fresno ... CA ... 33
California State University-Fullerton ... CA ... 33
California State University-Long Beach ... CA ... 33
California State University-Los Angeles ... CA ... 34
California State University-Monterey Bay ... CA ... 34
California State University-Northridge ... CA ... 34
California State University-San Bernardino CA ... 34
California State University-San Marcos ... CA ... 35
California State University-Stanislaus ... CA ... 35
Loyola Marymount University ... CA ... 53
Point Loma Nazarene University ... CA ... 59
San Diego State University ... CA ... 35
San Jose State University ... CA ... 36
Sonoma State University ... CA ... 36
Stanford University ... CA ... 68
University of LaVerne ... CA ... 72
University of San Diego ... CA ... 73
University of the Pacific ... CA ... 73
Metropolitan State University of Denver ... CO ... 83
University of Colorado Boulder ... CO ... 85
University of Colorado Colorado Springs .. CO ... 85
University of Colorado DenverlAnschutz Medical Campus ... CO ... 86
University of Northern Colorado ... CO ... 86
Central Connecticut State University ... CT ... 87
Eastern Connecticut State University ... CT ... 87
Fairfield University ... CT ... 89
Quinnipiac University ... CT ... 91
Sacred Heart University ... CT ... 91
Southern Connecticut State University ... CT ... 88
University of Connecticut ... CT ... 92
University of Hartford ... CT ... 92
University of New Haven ... CT ... 92
University of Saint Joseph ... CT ... 92
Western Connecticut State University ... CT ... 88
Delaware State University ... DE ... 93
University of Delaware ... DE ... 94
Wesley College ... DE ... 94
Wilmington University ... DE ... 94
American University ... DC ... 94
Catholic University of America, The ... DC ... 94
Gallaudet University ... DC ... 95
George Washington University ... DC ... 95
Howard University ... DC ... 95
Trinity Washington University ... DC ... 96
University of the District of Columbia ... DC ... 97
Bethune Cookman University ... FL ... 99
Florida Agricultural and Mechanical University ... FL ... 114
Florida Atlantic University ... FL ... 114
Florida Gulf Coast University ... FL ... 115
Florida International University ... FL ... 115
Florida State University ... FL ... 115
Nova Southeastern University ... FL ... 109
Stetson University ... FL ... 117
University of Central Florida ... FL ... 115
University of Florida ... FL ... 116
University of North Florida ... FL ... 116
University of South Florida ... FL ... 116
University of South Florida St. Petersburg FL ... 116
University of West Florida ... FL ... 117
Albany State University ... GA ... 119
Armstrong Atlantic State University ... GA .. 120
Berry College ... GA .. 121
Brenau University ... GA .. 122
Brewton-Parker College ... GA .. 122
Clark Atlanta University ... GA .. 122
Clayton State University ... GA .. 123
Columbus State University ... GA .. 123
Dalton State College ... GA .. 123
Emory University ... GA .. 124
Fort Valley State University ... GA .. 124
Georgia College & State University ... GA .. 125
Georgia Regents University ... GA .. 126
Georgia Southern University ... GA .. 126
Georgia Southwestern State University ... GA .. 126
Georgia State University ... GA .. 126
Kennesaw State University ... GA .. 127
Mercer University ... GA .. 128
Middle Georgia State College ... GA .. 128
Paine College ... GA .. 130
Point University ... GA .. 130
University of Georgia ... GA .. 133
University of North Georgia ... GA .. 133
University of West Georgia ... GA .. 133
Valdosta State University ... GA .. 134
University of Guam ... GU .. 546
University of Hawaii at Manoa ... HI ... 136
University of Hawaii - West Oahu ... HI ... 136
Boise State University ... ID ... 137
Idaho State University ... ID ... 138
Lewis-Clark State College ... ID ... 138
Northwest Nazarene University ... ID ... 139
University of Idaho ... ID ... 139
Augustana College ... IL ... 139
Aurora University ... IL ... 140
Bradley University ... IL ... 140
Chicago State University ... IL ... 141
Concordia University Chicago ... IL ... 143
Dominican University ... IL ... 144
Eastern Illinois University ... IL ... 144
Governors State University ... IL ... 145
Illinois State University ... IL ... 147
Lewis University ... IL ... 150
Loyola University Chicago ... IL ... 151
Millikin University ... IL ... 153
National-Louis University ... IL ... 153
Northeastern Illinois University ... IL ... 154
Northern Illinois University ... IL ... 154
Olivet Nazarene University ... IL ... 155
Roosevelt University ... IL ... 157
Saint Xavier University ... IL ... 158
Southern Illinois University Carbondale ... IL ... 159
Southern Illinois University Edwardsville ... IL ... 159
University of St. Francis ... IL ... 162
Western Illinois University ... IL ... 162
Wheaton College ... IL ... 163
Anderson University ... IN ... 163
Ball State University ... IN ... 164
Bethel College ... IN ... 164
Butler University ... IN ... 164
Calumet College of Saint Joseph ... IN ... 164
Franklin College of Indiana ... IN ... 165
Goshen College ... IN ... 166
Grace College and Seminary ... IN ... 166
Hanover College ... IN ... 166
Huntington University ... IN ... 166
Indiana State University ... IN ... 167
Indiana University Bloomington ... IN ... 167
Indiana University East ... IN ... 167
Indiana University Kokomo ... IN ... 168
Indiana University Northwest ... IN ... 168
Indiana University-Purdue University Fort Wayne ... IN ... 168
Indiana University South Bend ... IN ... 168
Indiana University Southeast ... IN ... 168
Indiana Wesleyan University ... IN ... 169
Manchester University ... IN ... 170
Marian University ... IN ... 170
Oakland City University ... IN ... 171
Purdue University Calumet ... IN ... 171
Purdue University Main Campus ... IN ... 171
Purdue University North Central Campus . IN ... 172
Saint Joseph's College ... IN ... 172
Saint Mary-of-the-Woods College ... IN ... 172
Saint Mary's College ... IN ... 172
Taylor University ... IN ... 173
Trine University ... IN ... 173
University of Evansville ... IN ... 173
University of Indianapolis ... IN ... 173
University of Saint Francis ... IN ... 174
University of Southern Indiana ... IN ... 174
Valparaiso University ... IN ... 174
Vincennes University ... IN ... 174
Graceland University ... IA ... 178
Luther College ... IA ... 180
Northwestern College ... IA ... 181
Wartburg College ... IA ... 183
Baker University ... KS ... 184
Benedictine College ... KS ... 184
Bethany College ... KS ... 184
Bethel College ... KS ... 184
Emporia State University ... KS ... 186
Fort Hays State University ... KS ... 186
Friends University ... KS ... 186
Haskell Indian Nations University ... KS ... 187
Kansas State University ... KS ... 188
Kansas Wesleyan University ... KS ... 188
McPherson College ... KS ... 188
MidAmerica Nazarene University ... KS ... 188
Newman University ... KS ... 189
Ottawa University ... KS ... 189
Pittsburg State University ... KS ... 189
Southwestern College ... KS ... 190
Sterling College ... KS ... 190
Tabor College ... KS ... 190
University of Kansas Main Campus ... KS ... 190
University of Saint Mary ... KS ... 191
Washburn University ... KS ... 191
Wichita State University ... KS ... 191
Asbury University ... KY ... 192
Bellarmine University ... KY ... 192
Berea College ... KY ... 192
Campbellsville University ... KY ... 193
Eastern Kentucky University ... KY ... 193
Georgetown College ... KY ... 194
Kentucky State University ... KY ... 197
Morehead State University ... KY ... 198
Murray State University ... KY ... 198
Northern Kentucky University ... KY ... 198
Spalding University ... KY ... 199
Thomas More College ... KY ... 199
Transylvania University ... KY ... 199
University of Kentucky ... KY ... 200
University of Louisville ... KY ... 200
Western Kentucky University ... KY ... 200
Grambling State University ... LA ... 207
Louisiana College ... LA ... 202
Louisiana State University and Agricultural and Mechanical College ... LA ... 204
Louisiana State University at Alexandria .. LA ... 205
Louisiana State University in Shreveport .. LA ... 205
Louisiana Tech University ... LA ... 207
McNeese State University ... LA ... 207
Nicholls State University ... LA ... 208
Northwestern State University ... LA ... 208
Our Lady of Holy Cross College ... LA ... 206
Southeastern Louisiana University ... LA ... 208
Southern University and A&M College ... LA ... 206
Southern University at New Orleans ... LA ... 206
University of Louisiana at Lafayette ... LA ... 208
University of Louisiana at Monroe ... LA ... 208
University of New Orleans ... LA ... 205
Xavier University of Louisiana ... LA ... 209
University of Maine ... ME .. 212
University of Maine at Farmington ... ME .. 212
Bowie State University ... MD ... 220
Coppin State University ... MD ... 220
Frostburg State University ... MD ... 220
Hood College ... MD ... 215
Johns Hopkins University ... MD ... 215
Loyola University Maryland ... MD ... 216
McDaniel College ... MD ... 216
Morgan State University ... MD ... 217
Mount St. Mary's University ... MD ... 217
Notre Dame of Maryland University ... MD ... 217
Salisbury University ... MD ... 220
Stevenson University ... MD ... 218
Towson University ... MD ... 220
University of Maryland Baltimore County .. MD ... 219
University of Maryland College Park ... MD ... 219
University of Maryland Eastern Shore ... MD ... 219
Bridgewater State University ... MA ... 229
Fitchburg State University ... MA ... 229
Salem State University ... MA ... 230
University of Massachusetts ... MA ... 228
University of Massachusetts Lowell ... MA ... 229
Westfield State University ... MA ... 230
Wheelock College ... MA ... 238
Andrews University ... MI ... 239
Concordia University ... MI ... 241
Eastern Michigan University ... MI ... 242
Grand Valley State University ... MI ... 243
Madonna University ... MI ... 246
Saginaw Valley State University ... MI ... 249
Western Michigan University ... MI ... 252
Augsburg College ... MN ... 253
Capella University ... MN ... 254
College of Saint Benedict ... MN ... 254
Concordia University, St. Paul ... MN ... 255
Gustavus Adolphus College ... MN ... 255
Hamline University ... MN ... 256
Minnesota State University Moorhead ... MN .. 259
Minnesota State University, Mankato ... MN .. 259
St. Cloud State University ... MN .. 261
Saint John's University ... MN .. 263
St. Olaf College ... MN .. 264
University of Minnesota Duluth ... MN .. 264
University of Minnesota-Morris ... MN .. 264
University of Minnesota-Twin Cities ... MN .. 264
University of Saint Thomas ... MN .. 265
Walden University ... MN .. 265
Winona State University ... MN .. 262
Alcorn State University ... MS .. 265
Delta State University ... MS .. 266
Jackson State University ... MS .. 267
Millsaps College ... MS .. 267
Mississippi College ... MS .. 268
Mississippi State University ... MS .. 268
Mississippi University for Women ... MS .. 268
Mississippi Valley State University ... MS .. 269
University of Mississippi ... MS .. 270
University of Southern Mississippi ... MS .. 270
William Carey University ... MS .. 270
Drury University ... MO .. 273
Evangel University ... MO .. 274
Fontbonne University ... MO .. 274
Harris-Stowe State University ... MO .. 275
Lincoln University ... MO .. 276
Maryville University of Saint Louis ... MO .. 276
Missouri Baptist University ... MO .. 278
Missouri Southern State University ... MO .. 278
Missouri State University ... MO .. 278
Missouri Western State University ... MO .. 279
Northwest Missouri State University ... MO .. 279
Saint Louis University ... MO .. 281
Southeast Missouri State University ... MO .. 282
Truman State University ... MO .. 282
University of Central Missouri ... MO .. 283
University of Missouri - Kansas City ... MO .. 283
University of Missouri - Saint Louis ... MO .. 283
Webster University ... MO .. 284
Montana State University - Billings ... MT .. 287
University of Montana - Missoula, The ... MT .. 286
University of Montana Western, The ... MT .. 286
Chadron State College ... NE ... 291
Concordia University ... NE ... 289
Creighton University ... NE ... 289
Doane College ... NE ... 289
Hastings College ... NE ... 289
Nebraska Wesleyan University ... NE ... 291
Peru State College ... NE ... 291
Union College ... NE ... 292
University of Nebraska at Kearney ... NE ... 292
University of Nebraska at Omaha ... NE ... 293
Wayne State College ... NE ... 291
York College ... NE ... 293
University of Nevada, Reno ... NV ... 294
Keene State College ... NH ... 298
Plymouth State University ... NH ... 298
College of New Jersey, The ... NJ ... 300
Kean University ... NJ ... 302
Monmouth University ... NJ ... 303
Montclair State University ... NJ ... 303
New Jersey City University ... NJ ... 303
Rider University ... NJ ... 305
Rowan University ... NJ ... 305
Seton Hall University ... NJ ... 307
William Paterson University of New Jersey ... NJ ... 308
Eastern New Mexico University Main Campus ... NM .. 309
New Mexico Highlands University ... NM .. 310
New Mexico State University Main Campus ... NM ... 310
University of New Mexico Main Campus .. NM .. 312
Western New Mexico University ... NM .. 312
Adelphi University ... NY ... 313
Canisius College ... NY ... 316
City University of New York Brooklyn College ... NY ... 317
City University of New York College of Staten Island ... NY ... 317
City University of New York Herbert H. Lehman College ... NY ... 318
City University of New York Hunter College ... NY ... 318
City University of New York Medgar Evers College ... NY ... 319
City University of New York Queens College ... NY ... 319
City University of New York The City College ... NY ... 317
City University of New York York College NY ... 319
College of Saint Rose, The ... NY ... 321
Concordia College ... NY ... 321
Dowling College ... NY ... 323
Five Towns College ... NY ... 324
Fordham University ... NY ... 324
Iona College ... NY ... 327
Manhattanville College ... NY ... 330
Metropolitan College of New York ... NY ... 331
Molloy College ... NY ... 331
Mount Saint Mary College ... NY ... 332
New York City College of Technology/City University of New York ... NY .. 319

New York Institute of Technology ... NY ... 333
Niagara University ... NY ... 334
Nyack College ... NY ... 335
Pace University ... NY ... 335
Relay Graduate School of Education ... NY ... 337
Sage Colleges, The ... NY ... 338
St. Bonaventure University ... NY ... 338
St. John Fisher College ... NY ... 338
St. Thomas Aquinas College ... NY ... 340
Siena College ... NY ... 340
State University of New York at Fredonia ... NY ... 342
State University of New York at New Paltz ... NY ... 342
State University of New York at Stony Brook ... NY ... 342
State University of New York College at Buffalo ... NY ... 343
State University of New York College at Cortland ... NY ... 343
State University of New York College at Geneseo ... NY ... 343
State University of New York College at Old Westbury ... NY ... 343
State University of New York College at Oneonta ... NY ... 343
State University of New York College at Oswego ... NY ... 344
State University of New York College at Potsdam ... NY ... 344
State University of New York, The College at Brockport ... NY ... 342
Syracuse University Main Campus ... NY ... 347
Teachers College, Columbia University ... NY ... 347
University of Rochester ... NY ... 349
Wagner College ... NY ... 350
Appalachian State University ... NC ... 367
Barton College ... NC ... 352
Bennett College ... NC ... 352
Campbell University ... NC ... 352
Catawba College ... NC ... 353
Chowan University ... NC ... 353
Duke University ... NC ... 354
East Carolina University ... NC ... 367
Elizabeth City State University ... NC ... 367
Elon University ... NC ... 354
Fayetteville State University ... NC ... 367
Gardner-Webb University ... NC ... 354
Greensboro College ... NC ... 354
High Point University ... NC ... 355
Lenoir-Rhyne University ... NC ... 356
Livingstone College ... NC ... 356
Mars Hill College ... NC ... 356
Meredith College ... NC ... 356
Methodist University ... NC ... 356
Montreat College ... NC ... 357
North Carolina Agricultural and Technical State University ... NC ... 367
North Carolina Central University ... NC ... 368
North Carolina State University ... NC ... 368
North Carolina Wesleyan College ... NC ... 365
Pfeiffer University ... NC ... 365
Queens University of Charlotte ... NC ... 365
Salem College ... NC ... 366
Shaw University ... NC ... 366
University of North Carolina at Asheville ... NC ... 368
University of North Carolina at Chapel Hill ... NC ... 368
University of North Carolina at Charlotte ... NC ... 368
University of North Carolina at Greensboro ... NC ... 369
University of North Carolina at Pembroke ... NC ... 369
University of North Carolina Wilmington ... NC ... 369
Wake Forest University ... NC ... 370
Western Carolina University ... NC ... 369
Wingate University ... NC ... 370
Winston-Salem State University ... NC ... 370
Dickinson State University ... ND ... 371
Mayville State University ... ND ... 371
Minot State University ... ND ... 371
North Dakota State University Main Campus ... ND ... 371
University of North Dakota Main Campus ... ND ... 371
Valley City State University ... ND ... 372
Antioch University Midwest ... OH ... 373
Ashland University ... OH ... 374
Baldwin Wallace University ... OH ... 374
Bluffton University ... OH ... 374
Bowling Green State University ... OH ... 374
Capital University ... OH ... 375
Cedarville University ... OH ... 375
Central State University ... OH ... 376
Cleveland State University ... OH ... 377
College of Wooster, The ... OH ... 377
Defiance College, The ... OH ... 379
Franciscan University of Steubenville ... OH ... 379
Heidelberg University ... OH ... 380
Hiram College ... OH ... 380
John Carroll University ... OH ... 381
Kent State University Main Campus ... OH ... 382
Malone University ... OH ... 383
Marietta College ... OH ... 383
Miami University ... OH ... 384
Mount Vernon Nazarene University ... OH ... 384
Muskingum University ... OH ... 384
Notre Dame College ... OH ... 385
Ohio Dominican University ... OH ... 386
Ohio Northern University ... OH ... 386
Ohio State University Main Campus, The ... OH ... 386
Ohio University Main Campus ... OH ... 387
Ohio Wesleyan University ... OH ... 387
Otterbein University ... OH ... 387
Shawnee State University ... OH ... 388
University of Akron, Main Campus, The ... OH ... 390
University of Cincinnati Main Campus ... OH ... 390
University of Dayton ... OH ... 391
University of Findlay, The ... OH ... 391
University of Mount Union ... OH ... 391
University of Rio Grande ... OH ... 392
University of Toledo ... OH ... 392
Ursuline College ... OH ... 392
Walsh University ... OH ... 392
Wittenberg University ... OH ... 393
Wright State University Main Campus ... OH ... 393
Youngstown State University ... OH ... 394
Cameron University ... OK ... 394
East Central University ... OK ... 395
Langston University ... OK ... 395
Northeastern State University ... OK ... 396
Northwestern Oklahoma State University ... OK ... 396
Oklahoma Baptist University ... OK ... 397
Oklahoma Christian University ... OK ... 397
Oklahoma City University ... OK ... 397
Oklahoma Panhandle State University ... OK ... 397
Oklahoma State University ... OK ... 397
Oklahoma Wesleyan University ... OK ... 398
Oral Roberts University ... OK ... 398
Southeastern Oklahoma State University ... OK ... 399
Southern Nazarene University ... OK ... 399
Southwestern Oklahoma State University ... OK ... 400
University of Central Oklahoma ... OK ... 400
University of Oklahoma Norman Campus ... OK ... 401
University of Science and Arts of Oklahoma ... OK ... 401
George Fox University ... OR ... 403
Lewis and Clark College ... OR ... 403
Oregon State University ... OR ... 406
Pacific University ... OR ... 407
Portland State University ... OR ... 406
University of Portland ... OR ... 408
Western Oregon University ... OR ... 406
Willamette University ... OR ... 408
Bloomsburg University of Pennsylvania ... PA ... 427
California University of Pennsylvania ... PA ... 428
Clarion University of Pennsylvania ... PA ... 428
Duquesne University ... PA ... 415
East Stroudsburg University of Pennsylvania ... PA ... 428
Edinboro University of Pennsylvania ... PA ... 428
Indiana University of Pennsylvania ... PA ... 428
King's College ... PA ... 419
Kutztown University of Pennsylvania ... PA ... 429
Lock Haven University ... PA ... 429
Mansfield University of Pennsylvania ... PA ... 429
Marywood University ... PA ... 423
Millersville University of Pennsylvania ... PA ... 429
Penn State University Park ... PA ... 426
Shippensburg University of Pennsylvania ... PA ... 429
Slippery Rock University of Pennsylvania ... PA ... 429
University of Scranton, The ... PA ... 436
West Chester University of Pennsylvania ... PA ... 430
Widener University ... PA ... 437
University of Puerto Rico-Aguadilla ... PR ... 553
University of Puerto Rico at Arecibo ... PR ... 553
University of Puerto Rico at Bayamon ... PR ... 554
University of Puerto Rico at Cayey ... PR ... 554
University of Puerto Rico at Ponce ... PR ... 555
University of Puerto Rico at Utuado ... PR ... 555
University of Puerto Rico-Humacao ... PR ... 554
University of Puerto Rico-Mayaguez Campus ... PR ... 554
University of Puerto Rico-Rio Piedras Campus ... PR ... 555
Rhode Island College ... RI ... 439
University of Rhode Island ... RI ... 440
Anderson University ... SC ... 441
Benedict College ... SC ... 441
Charleston Southern University ... SC ... 441
Citadel, The Military College of South Carolina, The ... SC ... 442
Claflin University ... SC ... 442
Clemson University ... SC ... 442
Coastal Carolina University ... SC ... 442
Coker College ... SC ... 442
College of Charleston ... SC ... 443
Columbia College ... SC ... 443
Converse College ... SC ... 443
Erskine College ... SC ... 443
Francis Marion University ... SC ... 444
Furman University ... SC ... 444
Lander University ... SC ... 444
Limestone College ... SC ... 444
Morris College ... SC ... 445
Newberry College ... SC ... 445
North Greenville University ... SC ... 445
Presbyterian College ... SC ... 446
South Carolina State University ... SC ... 446
Southern Wesleyan University ... SC ... 446
University of South Carolina Aiken ... SC ... 448
University of South Carolina Beaufort ... SC ... 448
University of South Carolina Columbia ... SC ... 447
University of South Carolina Upstate ... SC ... 448
Winthrop University ... SC ... 449
Augustana College ... SD ... 449
Black Hills State University ... SD ... 451
Dakota State University ... SD ... 451
Northern State University ... SD ... 451
South Dakota State University ... SD ... 452
University of Sioux Falls ... SD ... 452
University of South Dakota, The ... SD ... 451
Austin Peay State University ... TN ... 459
Belmont University ... TN ... 453
Carson-Newman University ... TN ... 453
Christian Brothers University ... TN ... 453
Cumberland University ... TN ... 454
East Tennessee State University ... TN ... 459
Freed-Hardeman University ... TN ... 454
Lee University ... TN ... 455
LeMoyne-Owen College ... TN ... 455
Lipscomb University ... TN ... 456
Middle Tennessee State University ... TN ... 459
Milligan College ... TN ... 457
Southern Adventist University ... TN ... 458
Tennessee State University ... TN ... 459
Tennessee Technological University ... TN ... 460
Trevecca Nazarene University ... TN ... 462
Union University ... TN ... 462
University of Memphis, The ... TN ... 460
University of Tennessee at Chattanooga ... TN ... 463
University of Tennessee at Martin ... TN ... 463
Vanderbilt University ... TN ... 463
Angelo State University ... TX ... 465
Baylor University ... TX ... 467
Lamar University ... TX ... 486
Midwestern State University ... TX ... 476
Prairie View A & M University ... TX ... 482
Sam Houston State University ... TX ... 487
Stephen F. Austin State University ... TX ... 482
Texas Tech University ... TX ... 487
Trinity University ... TX ... 488
University of Houston ... TX ... 489
University of Houston - Clear Lake ... TX ... 489
University of North Texas ... TX ... 490
University of Texas at Arlington, The ... TX ... 491
University of Texas of the Permian Basin ... TX ... 493
Weber State University ... UT ... 497
Western Governors University ... UT ... 498
University of Vermont ... VT ... 500
College of William & Mary ... VA ... 503
Eastern Mennonite University ... VA ... 504
George Mason University ... VA ... 505
Hampton University ... VA ... 505
James Madison University ... VA ... 506
Liberty University ... VA ... 506
Longwood University ... VA ... 506
Marymount University ... VA ... 507
Norfolk State University ... VA ... 507
Old Dominion University ... VA ... 507
Radford University ... VA ... 508
Virginia Commonwealth University ... VA ... 511
Virginia Polytechnic Institute and State University ... VA ... 515
Virginia State University ... VA ... 515
Virginia Union University ... VA ... 515
Gonzaga University ... WA ... 520
Pacific Lutheran University ... WA ... 521
Seattle Pacific University ... WA ... 523
Seattle University ... WA ... 523
Western Washington University ... WA ... 525
Whitworth University ... WA ... 525
Bethany College ... WV ... 526
Bluefield State College ... WV ... 529
Concord University ... WV ... 529
Fairmont State University ... WV ... 529
Glenville State College ... WV ... 529
Marshall University ... WV ... 529
Shepherd University ... WV ... 529
West Liberty University ... WV ... 530
West Virginia State University ... WV ... 530
West Virginia University ... WV ... 530
West Virginia University at Parkersburg ... WV ... 530
West Virginia Wesleyan College ... WV ... 531
Alverno College ... WI ... 531
Cardinal Stritch University ... WI ... 532
Edgewood College ... WI ... 532
Marian University ... WI ... 534
Marquette University ... WI ... 534
University of Wisconsin-Platteville ... WI ... 537
University of Wisconsin-Stout ... WI ... 538
University of Wisconsin-Whitewater ... WI ... 538
Viterbo University ... WI ... 539
University of Wyoming ... WY ... 543

THEA: National Association of Schools of Theatre: theatre (C,A,B,M,D)

Alabama State University ... AL ... 1
Auburn University ... AL ... 1
Jacksonville State University ... AL ... 4
University of Alabama at Birmingham ... AL ... 8
University of Alabama, The ... AL ... 8
University of Arizona ... AZ ... 18
University of Arkansas at Little Rock ... AR ... 24
University of Central Arkansas ... AR ... 25
AMDA College and Conservatory of the Performing Arts ... CA ... 27
California Institute of the Arts ... CA ... 31
California State University-Chico ... CA ... 33
California State University-Dominguez Hills ... CA ... 33
California State University-Fresno ... CA ... 33
California State University-Fullerton ... CA ... 33
California State University-Long Beach ... CA ... 33
California State University-Northridge ... CA ... 34
California State University-San Bernardino ... CA ... 34
California State University-Stanislaus ... CA ... 35
Chapman University ... CA ... 38
Dell'Arte International School of Physical Theatre ... CA ... 42
Loyola Marymount University ... CA ... 53
San Diego State University ... CA ... 35
San Francisco State University ... CA ... 35
San Jose State University ... CA ... 36
Theatre of Arts ... CA ... 69
University of California-Los Angeles ... CA ... 71
Vanguard University of Southern California ... CA ... 74
Metropolitan State University of Denver ... CO ... 83
University of Northern Colorado ... CO ... 86
University of Hartford ... CT ... 92
Howard University ... DC ... 95
Florida International University ... FL ... 115
Florida State University ... FL ... 115
Miami Dade College ... FL ... 109
University of Florida ... FL ... 116
University of South Florida ... FL ... 116
Columbus State University ... GA ... 123
Georgia Southern University ... GA ... 126
Kennesaw State University ... GA ... 127
University of Georgia ... GA ... 133
University of West Georgia ... GA ... 133
Valdosta State University ... GA ... 134
Boise State University ... ID ... 137
Idaho State University ... ID ... 138
Bradley University ... IL ... 140
Eastern Illinois University ... IL ... 144
Illinois State University ... IL ... 147
Loyola University Chicago ... IL ... 151
Northern Illinois University ... IL ... 154
Southern Illinois University Carbondale ... IL ... 159
Southern Illinois University Edwardsville ... IL ... 159
University of Illinois at Urbana-Champaign ... IL ... 162
Western Illinois University ... IL ... 162
Ball State University ... IN ... 164
Butler University ... IN ... 164
Indiana University Bloomington ... IN ... 167
Indiana University-Purdue University Fort Wayne ... IN ... 168
Purdue University Main Campus ... IN ... 171
Vincennes University ... IN ... 174
University of Iowa ... IA ... 175
Kansas State University ... KS ... 188
Morehead State University ... KY ... 198
Murray State University ... KY ... 198
University of Kentucky ... KY ... 200
University of Louisville ... KY ... 200
Western Kentucky University ... KY ... 200
Grambling State University ... LA ... 207
Louisiana State University and Agricultural and Mechanical College ... LA ... 204
Northwestern State University ... LA ... 208
University of New Orleans ... LA ... 205
Community College of Baltimore County, The ... MD ... 214
Towson University ... MD ... 220
College of the Holy Cross ... MA ... 225
Salem State University ... MA ... 230
Hope College ... MI ... 244
Oakland University ... MI ... 248
Wayne State University ... MI ... 252
Western Michigan University ... MI ... 252
Normandale Community College ... MN ... 260
St. Cloud State University ... MN ... 261
St. Olaf College ... MN ... 264
University of Minnesota-Twin Cities ... MN ... 264
Winona State University ... MN ... 262
Belhaven University ... MS ... 266
University of Mississippi ... MS ... 270
University of Southern Mississippi ... MS ... 270
Missouri State University ... MO ... 278
University of Central Missouri ... MO ... 283
University of Missouri - Kansas City ... MO ... 283
University of Montana - Missoula, The ... MT ... 286
University of Nebraska - Lincoln ... NE ... 292
University of Nevada, Las Vegas ... NV ... 294
Kean University ... NJ ... 302
Montclair State University ... NJ ... 303
Rowan University ... NJ ... 305
University of New Mexico Main Campus ... NM ... 312
AMDA College and Conservatory of the Performing Arts ... NY ... 313
American Academy of Dramatic Arts ... NY ... 313
Ithaca College ... NY ... 327
State University of New York at Fredonia ... NY ... 342
State University of New York at New Paltz ... NY ... 342
State University of New York College at Buffalo ... NY ... 343

State University of New York College at Oswego ... NY ... 344
State University of New York College at Potsdam ... NY ... 344
State University of New York, The College at Brockport ... NY ... 342
Appalachian State University ... NC .. 367
East Carolina University ... NC .. 367
Mars Hill College ... NC .. 356
North Carolina Agricultural and Technical State University ... NC .. 367
North Carolina Central University ... NC .. 368
University of North Carolina at Greensboro ... NC .. 369
Western Carolina University ... NC .. 369
North Dakota State University Main Campus ... ND .. 371
University of North Dakota Main Campus . ND .. 371
Bowling Green State University ... OH .. 374
Kent State University Main Campus ... OH .. 382
Miami University ... OH .. 384
Ohio State University Main Campus, The . OH .. 386
Ohio University Main Campus ... OH .. 387
Otterbein University ... OH .. 387
Sinclair Community College ... OH .. 388
University of Cincinnati Main Campus ... OH .. 390
Youngstown State University ... OH .. 394
Oklahoma State University ... OK .. 397
University of Oklahoma Norman Campus . OK .. 401
Portland State University ... OR .. 406
University of Portland ... OR .. 408
Bloomsburg University of Pennsylvania ... PA .. 427
California University of Pennsylvania ... PA .. 428
Indiana University of Pennsylvania ... PA .. 428
Lehigh University ... PA .. 422
Messiah College ... PA .. 423
Penn State University Park ... PA .. 426
Slippery Rock University of Pennsylvania . PA .. 429
Temple University ... PA .. 433
University of Pittsburgh ... PA .. 435
West Chester University of Pennsylvania . PA .. 430
Coastal Carolina University ... SC .. 442
College of Charleston ... SC .. 443
Francis Marion University ... SC .. 444
University of South Carolina Columbia ... SC .. 447
Winthrop University ... SC .. 449
University of South Dakota, The ... SD .. 451
University of Memphis, The ... TN .. 460
University of Tennessee at Chattanooga .. TN .. 463
Baylor University ... TX .. 467
Del Mar College ... TX .. 471
KD Studio-Actors Conservatory ... TX .. 475
Midwestern State University ... TX .. 476
Southern Methodist University ... TX .. 481
Stephen F. Austin State University ... TX .. 482
Texas Tech University ... TX .. 487
University of Texas - Pan American ... TX .. 492
University of the Incarnate Word ... TX .. 490
Brigham Young University ... UT .. 495
Snow College ... UT .. 498
Christopher Newport University ... VA .. 503
James Madison University ... VA .. 506
Longwood University ... VA .. 506
Old Dominion University ... VA .. 507
Radford University ... VA .. 508
Virginia Commonwealth University ... VA .. 511
Virginia Polytechnic Institute and State University ... VA .. 515
Davis & Elkins College ... WV .. 526
West Virginia University ... WV .. 530
Marquette University ... WI .. 534
University of Wisconsin-Madison ... WI .. 536
University of Wisconsin-Stevens Point ... WI .. 538
University of Wisconsin-Whitewater ... WI .. 538
Casper College ... WY .. 542

THEOL: Association of Theological Schools: theology (M,FP,D)

Samford University ... AL ... 6
Phoenix Seminary ... AZ ... 16
American Baptist Seminary of the West ... CA ... 27
Azusa Pacific University ... CA ... 29
Biola University ... CA ... 29
Church Divinity School of the Pacific ... CA ... 38
Claremont School of Theology ... CA ... 39
Dominican School of Philosophy and Theology ... CA ... 42
Franciscan School of Theology ... CA ... 45
Fresno Pacific University ... CA ... 45
Fuller Theological Seminary ... CA ... 45
Golden Gate Baptist Theological Seminary ... CA ... 45
Graduate Theological Union ... CA ... 46
International Theological Seminary ... CA ... 48
La Sierra University ... CA ... 50
Logos Evangelical Seminary ... CA ... 51
Loyola Marymount University ... CA ... 53
Pacific Lutheran Theological Seminary ... CA ... 57
Pacific School of Religion ... CA ... 57
Saint John's Seminary ... CA ... 61
Saint Patrick's Seminary & University ... CA ... 61
San Francisco Theological Seminary ... CA ... 63
Santa Clara University ... CA ... 64
@Shepherd University School of Theology .. CA ... 66
Starr King School for the Ministry ... CA ... 68
Westminster Theological Seminary in California ... CA ... 76
@World Mission University ... CA ... 77
Denver Seminary ... CO ... 81
Iliff School of Theology ... CO ... 82
St. John Vianney Theological Seminary ... CO ... 85
Hartford Seminary ... CT ... 90
Yale University ... CT ... 93
Catholic University of America, The ... DC ... 94
Howard University ... DC ... 95
Pontifical Faculty of the Immaculate Conception at the Dominican House of S tudies ... DC ... 96
Wesley Theological Seminary ... DC ... 97
Barry University ... FL ... 98
Knox Theological Seminary ... FL ... 108
St. Vincent De Paul Regional Seminary ... FL ... 112
Columbia Theological Seminary ... GA .. 123
Emory University ... GA .. 124
Interdenominational Theological Center ... GA .. 127
Mercer University ... GA .. 128
Bexley Seabury ... IL ... 140
Catholic Theological Union ... IL ... 141
Chicago Theological Seminary ... IL ... 141
Garrett-Evangelical Theological Seminary IL ... 145
Lincoln Christian University ... IL ... 151
Lutheran School of Theology at Chicago .. IL ... 152
McCormick Theological Seminary ... IL ... 152
Meadville Lombard Theological School ... IL ... 152
Moody Bible Institute ... IL ... 153
North Park University ... IL ... 154
Northern Seminary ... IL ... 155
Trinity International University ... IL ... 160
University of Chicago ... IL ... 161
University of Saint Mary of the Lake-Mundelein Seminary ... IL ... 162
Anabaptist Mennonite Biblical Seminary ... IN ... 163
Anderson University ... IN ... 163
Bethany Theological Seminary ... IN ... 164
Christian Theological Seminary ... IN ... 165
Concordia Theological Seminary ... IN ... 165
Earlham College and Earlham School of Religion ... IN ... 165
Grace College and Seminary ... IN ... 166
@Indiana Wesleyan University ... IN ... 169
Mid-America Reformed Seminary ... IN ... 171
Oakland City University ... IN ... 171
Saint Meinrad School of Theology ... IN ... 173
University of Notre Dame ... IN ... 174
University of Dubuque ... IA ... 182
Wartburg Theological Seminary ... IA ... 183
Central Baptist Theological Seminary ... KS ... 185
Saint Paul School of Theology ... KS ... 190
Asbury Theological Seminary ... KY ... 192
Lexington Theological Seminary ... KY ... 197
Louisville Presbyterian Theological Seminary ... KY ... 197
Southern Baptist Theological Seminary, The ... KY ... 199
New Orleans Baptist Theological Seminary ... LA ... 206
Notre Dame Seminary, Graduate School of Theology ... LA ... 206
Mount St. Mary's University ... MD .. 217
Saint Mary's Seminary and University ... MD .. 218
Andover Newton Theological School ... MA .. 222
Blessed John XXIII National Seminary ... MA .. 223
Boston College ... MA .. 224
Boston University ... MA .. 224
Episcopal Divinity School ... MA .. 226
Gordon-Conwell Theological Seminary ... MA .. 227
Harvard University ... MA .. 227
Hellenic College-Holy Cross Greek Orthodox School of Theology ... MA .. 227
Saint John's Seminary ... MA .. 236
Andrews University ... MI ... 239
Calvin Theological Seminary ... MI ... 240
Cornerstone University ... MI ... 241
Ecumenical Theological Seminary ... MI ... 242
@Puritan Reformed Theological Seminary .. MI ... 249
Sacred Heart Major Seminary ... MI ... 249
SS. Cyril and Methodius Seminary ... MI ... 250
Western Theological Seminary ... MI ... 252
Bethel University ... MN .. 253
Luther Seminary ... MN .. 256
Saint John's University ... MN .. 263
United Theological Seminary of the Twin Cities ... MN .. 264
University of Saint Thomas ... MN .. 265
Reformed Theological Seminary ... MS .. 269
Wesley Biblical Seminary ... MS .. 270
Aquinas Institute of Theology ... MO .. 271
Concordia Seminary ... MO .. 272
Covenant Theological Seminary ... MO .. 273
Eden Theological Seminary ... MO .. 274
Kenrick-Glennon Seminary-Kenrick School of Theology ... MO .. 275
Midwestern Baptist Theological Seminary MO .. 277
Nazarene Theological Seminary ... MO .. 279
Urshan Graduate School of Theology ... MO .. 284
Drew University ... NJ ... 301
New Brunswick Theological Seminary ... NJ ... 303
Princeton Theological Seminary ... NJ ... 304
Seton Hall University ... NJ ... 307
Christ the King Seminary ... NY ... 316
Colgate Rochester Crozer Divinity School NY ... 320
General Theological Seminary ... NY ... 325
New York Theological Seminary ... NY ... 334
Northeastern Seminary ... NY ... 335
Nyack College ... NY ... 335
Saint Bernard's School of Theology & Ministry ... NY ... 338
Saint Joseph's Seminary ... NY ... 339
Saint Vladimir's Orthodox Theological Seminary ... NY ... 340
Union Theological Seminary ... NY ... 349
Campbell University ... NC .. 352
Carolina Graduate School of Divinity ... NC .. 353
Duke University ... NC .. 354
Gardner-Webb University ... NC .. 354
Hood Theological Seminary ... NC .. 355
Shaw University ... NC .. 366
Southeastern Baptist Theological Seminary ... NC .. 366
Wake Forest University ... NC .. 370
Ashland University ... OH .. 374
Athenaeum of Ohio ... OH .. 374
Bexley Seabury ... OH .. 374
Cincinnati Christian University ... OH .. 376
Methodist Theological School in Ohio ... OH .. 383
Payne Theological Seminary ... OH .. 388
Pontifical College Josephinum ... OH .. 388
Saint Mary Seminary and Graduate School of Theology ... OH .. 388
Trinity Lutheran Seminary ... OH .. 390
United Theological Seminary ... OH .. 390
Winebrenner Theological Seminary ... OH .. 393
Oral Roberts University ... OK .. 398
Phillips Theological Seminary ... OK .. 398
George Fox University ... OR .. 403
Mount Angel Seminary ... OR .. 404
Multnomah University ... OR .. 404
Western Seminary ... OR .. 408
Biblical Theological Seminary ... PA ... 410
Byzantine Catholic Seminary of SS. Cyril and Methodius ... PA ... 411
Evangelical Theological Seminary ... PA ... 416
Lancaster Theological Seminary ... PA ... 421
Lutheran Theological Seminary at Gettysburg ... PA ... 422
Lutheran Theological Seminary at Philadelphia ... PA ... 422
Moravian College ... PA ... 424
Palmer Theological Seminary of Eastern University ... PA ... 425
Pittsburgh Theological Seminary ... PA ... 431
@Reformed Episcopal Seminary ... PA ... 431
Reformed Presbyterian Theological Seminary ... PA ... 431
Saint Charles Borromeo Seminary ... PA ... 432
St. Tikhon's Orthodox Theological Seminary ... PA ... 432
Saint Vincent Seminary ... PA ... 432
Trinity Episcopal School for Ministry ... PA ... 434
Westminster Theological Seminary ... PA ... 437
Dominican Study Center of the Caribbean PR ... 548
Evangelical Seminary of Puerto Rico ... PR ... 549
Columbia International University ... SC ... 443
Erskine College ... SC ... 443
Lutheran Theological Southern Seminary of Lenoir-Rhyne University ... SC ... 445
Sioux Falls Seminary ... SD ... 451
Emmanuel Christian Seminary ... TN ... 454
Lipscomb University ... TN ... 456
Memphis Theological Seminary ... TN ... 457
Pentecostal Theological Seminary ... TN ... 458
Sewanee: The University of the South ... TN ... 458
Vanderbilt University ... TN ... 463
Abilene Christian University ... TX ... 464
Austin Presbyterian Theological Seminary. TX ... 467
Baptist Missionary Association Theological Seminary ... TX ... 467
Baylor University ... TX ... 467
Brite Divinity School ... TX ... 468
Dallas Theological Seminary ... TX ... 471
Hardin-Simmons University ... TX ... 472
Houston Graduate School of Theology ... TX ... 473
Oblate School of Theology ... TX ... 477
@Redeemer Theological Seminary ... TX ... 478
Seminary of the Southwest ... TX ... 480
Southern Methodist University ... TX ... 481
Southwestern Baptist Theological Seminary ... TX ... 481
University of St. Thomas ... TX ... 490
Baptist Theological Seminary at Richmond ... VA ... 502
Eastern Mennonite University ... VA ... 504
John Leland Center for Theological Studies, The ... VA ... 506
Protestant Episcopal Theological Seminary in Virginia ... VA ... 508
Regent University ... VA ... 508
Union Presbyterian Seminary ... VA ... 510
Virginia Union University ... VA ... 515
@Seattle School of Theology and Psychology, The ... WA .. 523
Seattle University ... WA .. 523
Nashotah House ... WI ... 535
Sacred Heart School of Theology ... WI ... 535

TRACS: Transnational Association of Christian Colleges and Schools: christian studies education (C,A,B,M,D)

International Baptist College ... AZ ... 14
@Shorter College ... AR ... 23
Bethesda University of California ... CA ... 29
California Christian College ... CA ... 30
Community Christian College ... CA ... 41
Epic Bible College ... CA ... 43
Evangelia University ... CA ... 43
Grace Mission University ... CA ... 46
King's University, The ... CA ... 50
Shasta Bible College and Graduate School ... CA ... 65
Southern California Seminary ... CA ... 67
@Veritas Evangelical Seminary ... CA ... 75
World Mission University ... CA ... 77
@Pensacola Christian College ... FL ... 110
Trinity Baptist College ... FL ... 117
University of Fort Lauderdale ... FL ... 118
Beulah Heights University ... GA .. 121
Georgia Christian University ... GA .. 124
Luther Rice University ... GA .. 128
Pacific Islands University ... GU .. 546
New Saint Andrews College ... ID ... 138
Christian Life College ... IL ... 141
Mid-America Reformed Seminary ... IN ... 171
@Faith Theological Seminary ... MD .. 214
Maple Springs Baptist Bible College & Seminary ... MD .. 216
Boston Baptist College ... MA .. 223
@Manthano Christian College ... MI ... 246
Central Baptist Theological Seminary of Minneapolis ... MN .. 254
Lutheran Brethren Seminary ... MN .. 256
Apex School of Theology ... NC .. 352
Heritage Bible College ... NC .. 355
New Life Theological Seminary ... NC .. 357
Piedmont International University ... NC .. 365
Shepherds Theological Seminary ... NC .. 366
Southern Evangelical Seminary ... NC .. 366
Ohio Mid Western College (Formerly Temple Baptist College) ... OH .. 386
Hillsdale Free Will Baptist College ... OK .. 395
#Gutenberg College ... OR .. 403
Bob Jones University ... SC ... 441
Clinton College ... SC ... 442
@Crown College of the Bible, The ... TN ... 453
@Hiwassee College ... TN ... 454
Oxford Graduate School ... TN ... 458
Tennessee Temple University ... TN ... 462
Visible Music College ... TN ... 464
Grace School of Theology ... TX ... 472
Messenger College ... TX ... 476
Paul Quinn College ... TX ... 478
Central Baptist Theological Seminary ... VA ... 503
Patrick Henry College ... VA ... 508
Virginia Baptist College ... VA ... 511
Virginia University of Lynchburg ... VA ... 515
Bakke Graduate University ... WA .. 516
Faith Evangelical College & Seminary ... WA .. 519
Seattle School of Theology and Psychology, The ... WA .. 523
@Tacoma Bible College ... WA .. 524
Northland International University ... WI ... 535

VET: American Veterinary Medical Association: veterinary medicine (FP,D)

Auburn University ... AL ... 1
Tuskegee University ... AL ... 8
University of California-Davis ... CA ... 70
Western University of Health Sciences ... CA ... 76
Colorado State University ... CO ... 80
University of Florida ... FL ... 116
University of Georgia ... GA .. 133
University of Illinois at Urbana-Champaign IL ... 162
Purdue University Main Campus ... IN ... 171
Iowa State University ... IA ... 175
Kansas State University ... KS ... 188
Louisiana State University and Agricultural and Mechanical College ... LA ... 204
Tufts University ... MA .. 237
Michigan State University ... MI ... 246
University of Minnesota-Twin Cities ... MN .. 264
Mississippi State University ... MS .. 268
University of Missouri - Columbia ... MO .. 283
Cornell University ... NY ... 322
North Carolina State University ... NC .. 368
Ohio State University Main Campus, The : OH .. 386
Oklahoma State University ... OK .. 397
Oregon State University ... OR .. 406
University of Pennsylvania ... PA ... 435
@Lincoln Memorial University ... TN ... 456
University of Tennessee, Knoxville ... TN ... 463
Texas A & M University ... TX ... 483

Virginia Polytechnic Institute and State University ... VA ... 515
Washington State University ... WA .. 525
University of Wisconsin-Madison ... WI ... 536

WC: Western Association of Schools and Colleges, Accrediting Commission for Senior Colleges and Universities

American Samoa Community College ... AS ... 546
Academy for Jewish Religion ... CA ... 26
Academy of Art University ... CA ... 26
Alliant International University-San Diego . CA ... 26
@Allied American University ... CA ... 27
American Conservatory Theater ... CA ... 27
American Film Institute Conservatory ... CA ... 27
American Jewish University ... CA ... 27
American University of Armenia ... CA ... 28
Argosy University, Orange County ... CA ... 28
Art Center College of Design ... CA ... 28
Azusa Pacific University ... CA ... 29
Biola University ... CA ... 29
Brandman University ... CA ... 29
@Brooks Institute ... CA ... 30
California Baptist University ... CA ... 30
California College of the Arts ... CA ... 30
California Institute of Integral Studies ... CA ... 31
California Institute of Technology ... CA ... 31
California Institute of the Arts ... CA ... 31
California Lutheran University ... CA ... 31
California Maritime Academy ... CA ... 31
California Northstate College of Pharmacy CA ... 32
California Polytechnic State University-San Luis Obispo ... CA ... 32
California State Polytechnic University-Pomona ... CA ... 32
California State University-Bakersfield ... CA ... 32
California State University-Channel Islands ... CA ... 32
California State University-Chico ... CA ... 33
California State University-Dominguez Hills ... CA ... 33
California State University-East Bay ... CA ... 33
California State University-Fresno ... CA ... 33
California State University-Fullerton ... CA ... 33
California State University-Long Beach ... CA ... 33
California State University-Los Angeles ... CA ... 34
California State University-Monterey Bay . CA ... 34
California State University-Northridge ... CA ... 34
California State University-Sacramento ... CA ... 34
California State University-San Bernardino CA ... 34
California State University-San Marcos ... CA ... 35
California State University-Stanislaus ... CA ... 35
Cedars-Sinai Medical Center Graduate Program in Biomedical Sciences and Tra nslational Medicine ... CA ... 37
Chapman University ... CA ... 38
Charles R. Drew University of Medicine & Science ... CA ... 38
Chicago School of Professional Psychology Los Angeles Campus ... CA ... 38
City of Hope ... CA ... 39
Claremont Graduate University ... CA ... 39
Claremont McKenna College ... CA ... 39
Claremont School of Theology ... CA ... 39
Cogswell Polytechnical College ... CA ... 40
@Columbia College Hollywood ... CA ... 41
Concordia University ... CA ... 41
Dominican School of Philosophy and Theology ... CA ... 42
Dominican University of California ... CA ... 42
Fashion Institute of Design and Merchandising-Los Angeles ... CA ... 44
Fielding Graduate University ... CA ... 44
Franciscan School of Theology ... CA ... 45
Fresno Pacific University ... CA ... 45
Fuller Theological Seminary ... CA ... 45
Golden Gate Baptist Theological Seminary ... CA ... 45
Golden Gate University ... CA ... 45
Graduate Theological Union ... CA ... 46
Harvey Mudd College ... CA ... 46
&Heald College, Concord ... CA ... 46
&Heald College, Fresno ... CA ... 46
&Heald College, Hayward ... CA ... 46
&Heald College, Milpitas ... CA ... 47
&Heald College, Rancho Cordova ... CA ... 47
&Heald College, Roseville ... CA ... 47
&Heald College, Salinas ... CA ... 47
&Heald College, San Francisco ... CA ... 47
&Heald College, Stockton ... CA ... 47
@High Tech High Graduate School of Education ... CA ... 47
Holy Names University ... CA ... 47
Hope International University ... CA ... 47
Humboldt State University ... CA ... 35
Humphreys College ... CA ... 47
International Technological University ... CA ... 48
John F. Kennedy University ... CA ... 49
@John Paul the Great Catholic University ... CA ... 49
Keck Graduate Institute ... CA ... 39
La Sierra University ... CA ... 50
Laguna College of Art & Design ... CA ... 50
#Life Pacific College ... CA ... 50
Logos Evangelical Seminary ... CA ... 51
Loma Linda University ... CA ... 51
Loyola Marymount University ... CA ... 53
Marymount California University ... CA ... 53
Master's College and Seminary, The ... CA ... 53
Menlo College ... CA ... 54
Mills College ... CA ... 54
Mount St. Mary's College ... CA ... 54
National Hispanic University, The ... CA ... 55
National University ... CA ... 55
Naval Postgraduate School ... CA ... 544
@NewSchool of Architecture and Design ... CA ... 56
Notre Dame de Namur University ... CA ... 56
Occidental College ... CA ... 56
Otis College of Art and Design ... CA ... 57
@Pacific College of Oriental Medicine ... CA ... 57
Pacific Oaks College ... CA ... 57
Pacific School of Religion ... CA ... 57
Pacific Union College ... CA ... 57
Pacifica Graduate Institute ... CA ... 57
Palo Alto University ... CA ... 58
Pardee RAND Graduate School of Policy Studies ... CA ... 58
Patten University ... CA ... 58
Pepperdine University ... CA ... 58
Phillips Graduate Institute ... CA ... 59
Pitzer College ... CA ... 59
Point Loma Nazarene University ... CA ... 59
Pomona College ... CA ... 60
@Presidio Graduate School ... CA ... 60
Providence Christian College ... CA ... 60
@Rudolf Steiner College ... CA ... 61
Saint John's Seminary ... CA ... 61
Saint Mary's College of California ... CA ... 61
Saint Patrick's Seminary & University ... CA ... 61
Samuel Merritt University ... CA ... 61
San Diego Christian College ... CA ... 62
San Diego State University ... CA ... 35
San Francisco Art Institute ... CA ... 62
San Francisco Conservatory of Music ... CA ... 62
San Francisco State University ... CA ... 35
San Francisco Theological Seminary ... CA ... 63
San Joaquin College of Law ... CA ... 63
San Jose State University ... CA ... 36
@Sanford-Burnham Graduate School of Biomedical Sciences ... CA ... 64
Santa Clara University ... CA ... 64
Saybrook University ... CA ... 65
Scripps College ... CA ... 65
Scripps Research Institute, The ... CA ... 65
Simpson University ... CA ... 66
Sofia University (formerly Institute of Transpersonal Psychology) ... CA ... 66
Soka University of America ... CA ... 66
Sonoma State University ... CA ... 36
Southern California College of Optometry CA ... 67
Southern California Institute of Architecture ... CA ... 67
Southern California University of Health Sciences ... CA ... 67
Stanford University ... CA ... 68
Teachers College of San Joaquin ... CA ... 69
Thomas Aquinas College ... CA ... 69
Touro College Los Angeles ... CA ... 69
Touro University California ... CA ... 69
Trident University International ... CA ... 70
#United States University ... CA ... 70
University of California-Berkeley ... CA ... 70
University of California-Davis ... CA ... 70
University of California-Hastings College of the Law ... CA ... 71
University of California-Irvine ... CA ... 71
University of California-Los Angeles ... CA ... 71
University of California-Merced ... CA ... 71
University of California-Riverside ... CA ... 71
University of California-San Diego ... CA ... 71
University of California-San Francisco ... CA ... 72
University of California-Santa Barbara ... CA ... 72
University of California-Santa Cruz ... CA ... 72
University of LaVerne ... CA ... 72
University of Redlands ... CA ... 73
University of San Diego ... CA ... 73
University of San Francisco ... CA ... 73
University of Southern California ... CA ... 74
University of the Pacific ... CA ... 73
University of the West ... CA ... 74
Vanguard University of Southern California ... CA ... 74
West Coast University ... CA ... 75
Western University of Health Sciences ... CA ... 76
Westminster Theological Seminary in California ... CA ... 76
Westmont College ... CA ... 76
Whittier College ... CA ... 76
William Jessup University ... CA ... 76
Woodbury University ... CA ... 76
Wright Institute, The ... CA ... 77
University of Guam ... GU .. 546
Brigham Young University Hawaii ... HI ... 135
Chaminade University of Honolulu ... HI ... 135
Hawaii Pacific University ... HI ... 135
University of Hawaii at Hilo ... HI ... 136
University of Hawaii at Manoa ... HI ... 136
University of Hawaii Maui College ... HI ... 137
University of Hawaii - West Oahu ... HI ... 136
Ashford University ... IA ... 175
Northern Marianas College ... MP .. 547

WJ: Western Association of Schools and Colleges, Accrediting Commission for Community and Junior Colleges

American Samoa Community College ... AS ... 546
Allan Hancock College ... CA ... 26
American River College ... CA ... 53
Antelope Valley College ... CA ... 28
Bakersfield College ... CA ... 49
Barstow Community College District ... CA ... 29
Berkeley City College ... CA ... 59
Butte College ... CA ... 30
Cabrillo College ... CA ... 30
Cañada College ... CA ... 64
Carrington College California - Sacramento ... CA ... 36
Cerritos College ... CA ... 37
Cerro Coso Community College ... CA ... 49
Chabot College ... CA ... 37
Chaffey College ... CA ... 37
Citrus College ... CA ... 38
City College of San Francisco ... CA ... 38
Coastline Community College ... CA ... 39
College of Alameda ... CA ... 59
College of Marin ... CA ... 40
College of San Mateo ... CA ... 64
College of the Canyons ... CA ... 40
College of the Desert ... CA ... 40
#College of the Redwoods Community College District ... CA ... 40
College of the Sequoias ... CA ... 40
College of the Siskiyous ... CA ... 41
Columbia College ... CA ... 77
Contra Costa College ... CA ... 41
Copper Mountain College ... CA ... 42
Cosumnes River College ... CA ... 53
Crafton Hills College ... CA ... 61
Cuesta College ... CA ... 42
Cuyamaca College ... CA ... 46
Cypress College ... CA ... 56
De Anza College ... CA ... 44
Deep Springs College ... CA ... 42
Defense Language Institute ... CA ... 544
Diablo Valley College ... CA ... 41
East Los Angeles College ... CA ... 51
El Camino College ... CA ... 43
Evergreen Valley College ... CA ... 63
Fashion Institute of Design and Merchandising-Los Angeles ... CA ... 44
Feather River College ... CA ... 44
Folsom Lake College ... CA ... 53
Foothill College ... CA ... 44
Fresno City College ... CA ... 68
Fullerton College ... CA ... 56
Gavilan College ... CA ... 45
Glendale Community College ... CA ... 45
Golden West College ... CA ... 39
Grossmont College ... CA ... 46
#Hartnell College ... CA ... 46
Imperial Valley College ... CA ... 48
Irvine Valley College ... CA ... 67
Lake Tahoe Community College ... CA ... 50
Laney College ... CA ... 59
Las Positas College ... CA ... 37
Lassen Community College ... CA ... 50
Long Beach City College ... CA ... 51
Los Angeles City College ... CA ... 51
Los Angeles County College of Nursing and Allied Health ... CA ... 52
Los Angeles Harbor College ... CA ... 51
Los Angeles Mission College ... CA ... 52
Los Angeles Pierce College ... CA ... 52
Los Angeles Southwest College ... CA ... 52
Los Angeles Trade-Technical College ... CA ... 52
Los Angeles Valley College ... CA ... 52
Los Medanos College ... CA ... 42
Mendocino College ... CA ... 54
Merced College ... CA ... 54
Merritt College ... CA ... 59
MiraCosta Community College District ... CA ... 54
Mission College ... CA ... 75
#Modesto Junior College ... CA ... 77
Monterey Peninsula College ... CA ... 54
Moorpark College ... CA ... 74
Moreno Valley College ... CA ... 60
Mt. San Antonio College ... CA ... 55
Mt. San Jacinto College ... CA ... 55
MTI College ... CA ... 55
Napa Valley College ... CA ... 55
Norco College ... CA ... 60
Ohlone College ... CA ... 57
Orange Coast College ... CA ... 39
Oxnard College ... CA ... 74
Palo Verde College ... CA ... 58
Palomar College ... CA ... 58
Pasadena City College ... CA ... 58
Porterville College ... CA ... 49
Reedley College ... CA ... 69
Rio Hondo College ... CA ... 60
Riverside City College ... CA ... 61
Sacramento City College ... CA ... 53
Saddleback College ... CA ... 67
Salvation Army College for Officer Training at Crestmont, The ... CA ... 61
San Bernardino Valley College ... CA ... 62
San Diego City College ... CA ... 62
San Diego Mesa College ... CA ... 62
San Diego Miramar College ... CA ... 62
San Joaquin Delta College ... CA ... 63
San Joaquin Valley College, Inc. - Visalia CA ... 63
San Jose City College ... CA ... 63
Santa Ana College ... CA ... 60
Santa Barbara City College ... CA ... 64
Santa Monica College ... CA ... 65
Santa Rosa Junior College ... CA ... 65
Santiago Canyon College ... CA ... 60
Shasta College ... CA ... 65
Sierra College ... CA ... 66
Skyline College ... CA ... 64
Solano Community College ... CA ... 66
Southwestern College ... CA ... 68
Taft College ... CA ... 69
Ventura College ... CA ... 74
#Victor Valley College ... CA ... 75
West Hills College Coalinga ... CA ... 75
West Hills College Lemoore ... CA ... 75
West Los Angeles College ... CA ... 52
West Valley College ... CA ... 75
@Willow International Community College Center ... CA ... 69
Woodland Community College ... CA ... 77
#Yuba College ... CA ... 77
College of Micronesia-FSM ... FM .. 546
Guam Community College ... GU .. 546
Hawaii Tokai International College ... HI ... 135
Kapiolani Community College ... HI ... 136
University of Hawaii Hawaii Community College ... HI ... 136
University of Hawaii Honolulu Community College ... HI ... 136
University of Hawaii Kauai Community College ... HI ... 136
University of Hawaii Leeward Community College ... HI ... 137
University of Hawaii Windward Community College ... HI ... 137
College of the Marshall Islands ... MH .. 546
Northern Marianas College ... MP .. 547
Palau Community College ... PW .. 547

Index of FICE Numbers

001001 .... Air University .... AL 544
001002 .... Alabama A & M University .... AL 1
001003 .... Faulkner University .... AL 3
001004 .... University of Montevallo .... AL 9
001005 .... Alabama State University .... AL 1
001007 .... Central Alabama Community College .... AL 2
001008 .... Athens State University .... AL 1
001009 .... Auburn University .... AL 1
001012 .... Birmingham-Southern College .... AL 2
001013 .... Calhoun Community College .... AL 2
001015 .... Enterprise State Community College .... AL 3
001016 .... University of North Alabama .... AL 9
001017 .... Gadsden State Community College .... AL 3
001018 .... George C. Wallace Cmty Col-Dothan .... AL 3
001019 .... Huntingdon College .... AL 4
001020 .... Jacksonville State University .... AL 4
001021 .... Jefferson Davis Community College .... AL 5
001022 .... Jefferson State Community College .... AL 5
001023 .... Judson College .... AL 5
001024 .... The University of West Alabama .... AL 9
001026 .... Marion Military Institute .... AL 5
001028 .... Miles College .... AL 5
001029 .... University of Mobile .... AL 9
001030 .... Bishop State Community College .... AL 2
001031 .... Northeast Alabama Community College .... AL 5
001033 .... Oakwood University .... AL 6
001034 .... Alabama Southern Community College .... AL 1
001036 .... Samford University .... AL 6
001037 .... Selma University .... AL 6
001038 .... Snead State Community College .... AL 6
001040 .... Southern Union State Cmty College .... AL 7
001041 .... Spring Hill College .... AL 7
001044 .... Stillman College .... AL 7
001046 .... Talladega College .... AL 7
001047 .... Troy University .... AL 7
001050 .... Tuskegee University .... AL 8
001051 .... The University of Alabama .... AL 8
001052 .... University of Alabama at Birmingham .... AL 8
001055 .... University of Alabama in Huntsville .... AL 8
001057 .... University of South Alabama .... AL 9
001059 .... Lawson State Community College .... AL 5
001060 .... James Faulkner State Cmty College .... AL 4
001061 .... Alaska Pacific University .... AK 10
001063 .... University of Alaska Fairbanks .... AK 10
001065 .... University of Alaska Southeast .... AK 11
001070 .... Thunderbird Sch of Global Mgmt .... AZ 18
001071 .... Arizona Western College .... AZ 11
001072 .... Cochise College .... AZ 12
001073 .... Eastern Arizona College .... AZ 13
001074 .... Grand Canyon University .... AZ 13
001075 .... Maricopa Cty Cmty Col District Ofc .... AZ 14
001076 .... Glendale Community College .... AZ 14
001077 .... Mesa Community College .... AZ 15
001078 .... Phoenix College .... AZ 15
001079 .... Yavapai College .... AZ 19
001081 .... Arizona State University .... AZ 11
001082 .... Northern Arizona University .... AZ 16
001083 .... University of Arizona .... AZ 18
001085 .... Univ of Arkansas at Monticello .... AR 24
001086 .... Univ of Arkansas at Pine Bluff .... AR 24
001087 .... Arkansas Baptist College .... AR 19
001088 .... Lyon College .... AR 21
001089 .... Arkansas Tech University .... AR 20
001090 .... Arkansas State University-Jonesboro .... AR 19
001091 .... Arkansas State University-Beebe .... AR 19
001092 .... University of Central Arkansas .... AR 25
001093 .... Central Baptist College .... AR 20
001094 .... University of the Ozarks .... AR 25
001095 .... Crowley's Ridge College .... AR 20
001097 .... Harding University Main Campus .... AR 21
001098 .... Henderson State University .... AR 21
001099 .... Hendrix College .... AR 21
001100 .... John Brown University .... AR 21
001101 .... Univ of Arkansas Little Rock .... AR 24
001102 .... Ouachita Baptist University .... AR 22
001103 .... Philander Smith College .... AR 22
001104 .... Phillips Cmty Col-Univ of Arkansas .... AR 24
001105 .... Shorter College .... AR 23
001106 .... Williams Baptist College .... AR 25
001107 .... Southern Arkansas University .... AR 23
001108 .... University of Arkansas Main Campus .... AR 23
001109 .... Univ of Arkansas for Medical Sci .... AR 24
001110 .... Univ of Arkansas at Fort Smith .... AR 24
001111 .... Allan Hancock College .... CA 26
001113 .... Antelope Valley College .... CA 28
001116 .... Art Center College of Design .... CA 28
001117 .... Azusa Pacific University .... CA 29
001118 .... Bakersfield College .... CA 49
001119 .... Barstow Community College District .... CA 29
001120 .... American Baptist Seminary of West .... CA 27
001122 .... Biola University .... CA 29
001123 .... Brooks Institute .... CA 30
001124 .... Cabrillo College .... CA 30
001125 .... California Baptist University .... CA 30
001127 .... California College of the Arts .... CA 30
001131 .... California Institute of Technology .... CA 31
001132 .... California Institute of the Arts .... CA 31
001133 .... California Lutheran University .... CA 31
001134 .... California Maritime Academy .... CA 31
001136 .... California State Univ System Office .... CA 32
001137 .... California State Univ-Fullerton .... CA 33
001138 .... California State U-East Bay .... CA 33
001139 .... California State Univ-Long Beach .... CA 33
001140 .... California State Univ-Los Angeles .... CA 34
001141 .... Calif State Univ-Dominguez Hills .... CA 33
001142 .... Calif State Univ-San Bernardino .... CA 34
001143 .... Calif Poly State Un-San Luis Obispo .... CA 32
001144 .... California State Poly Univ-Pomona .... CA 32
001146 .... California State University-Chico .... CA 33
001147 .... California State University-Fresno .... CA 33
001149 .... Humboldt State University .... CA 35
001150 .... California State Univ-Sacramento .... CA 34
001151 .... San Diego State University .... CA 35
001153 .... California State Univ-Northridge .... CA 34
001154 .... San Francisco State University .... CA 35
001155 .... San Jose State University .... CA 36
001156 .... Sonoma State University .... CA 36
001157 .... California State Univ-Stanislaus .... CA 35
001161 .... Cerritos College .... CA 37
001162 .... Chabot College .... CA 37
001163 .... Chaffey College .... CA 37
001164 .... Chapman University .... CA 38
001165 .... Church Divinity School of Pacific .... CA 38
001166 .... Citrus College .... CA 38
001167 .... City College of San Francisco .... CA 38
001169 .... Claremont Graduate University .... CA 39
001170 .... Claremont McKenna College .... CA 39
001171 .... Harvey Mudd College .... CA 46
001172 .... Pitzer College .... CA 59
001173 .... Pomona College .... CA 60
001174 .... Scripps College .... CA 65
001176 .... West Hills College Coalinga .... CA 75
001177 .... Cogswell Polytechnical College .... CA 40
001178 .... College of Marin .... CA 40
001179 .... Notre Dame de Namur University .... CA 56
001181 .... College of San Mateo .... CA 64
001182 .... College of the Desert .... CA 40
001183 .... Holy Names University .... CA 47
001185 .... College of the Redwoods CC District .... CA 40
001186 .... College of the Sequoias .... CA 40
001187 .... College of the Siskiyous .... CA 41
001189 .... Contra Costa Cmty Coll District Ofc .... CA 41
001190 .... Contra Costa College .... CA 41
001191 .... Diablo Valley College .... CA 41
001192 .... Cuesta College .... CA 42
001193 .... Cypress College .... CA 56
001194 .... Deep Springs College .... CA 42
001195 .... Defense Language Institute .... CA 544
001196 .... Dominican University of California .... CA 42
001197 .... El Camino College .... CA 43
001199 .... Foothill College .... CA 44
001200 .... Fuller Theological Seminary .... CA 45
001201 .... Fullerton College .... CA 56
001202 .... Gavilan College .... CA 45
001203 .... Glendale Community College .... CA 45
001204 .... Golden Gate Baptist Theol Seminary .... CA 45
001205 .... Golden Gate University .... CA 45
001206 .... Golden West College .... CA 39
001207 .... Graduate Theological Union .... CA 46
001208 .... Grossmont College .... CA 46
001209 .... Hartnell College .... CA 46
001212 .... Humphreys College .... CA 47
001214 .... Imperial Valley College .... CA 48
001215 .... La Sierra University .... CA 50
001216 .... University of LaVerne .... CA 72
001217 .... Lassen Community College .... CA 50
001218 .... Loma Linda University .... CA 51
001219 .... Long Beach City College .... CA 51
001220 .... The Master's College and Seminary .... CA 53
001221 .... Los Angeles Cmty Coll District Ofc .... CA 51
001223 .... Los Angeles City College .... CA 51
001224 .... Los Angeles Harbor College .... CA 51
001226 .... Los Angeles Pierce College .... CA 52
001227 .... Los Angeles Trade-Technical College .... CA 52
001228 .... Los Angeles Valley College .... CA 52
001229 .... Southern Calif Univ of Health Sci .... CA 67
001230 .... Southern Calif College of Optometry .... CA 67
001231 .... Los Rios Cmty College District Ofc .... CA 52
001232 .... American River College .... CA 53
001233 .... Sacramento City College .... CA 53
001236 .... Menlo College .... CA 54
001237 .... Merced College .... CA 54
001238 .... Mills College .... CA 54
001239 .... MiraCosta Community College Dist .... CA 54
001240 .... Modesto Junior College .... CA 77
001242 .... Monterey Peninsula College .... CA 54
001243 .... Mount St. Mary's College .... CA 54
001245 .... Mt. San Antonio College .... CA 55
001246 .... Mt. San Jacinto College .... CA 55
001247 .... Napa Valley College .... CA 55
001249 .... Occidental College .... CA 56
001250 .... Orange Coast College .... CA 39
001251 .... Otis College of Art and Design .... CA 57
001252 .... Hope International University .... CA 47
001253 .... Fresno Pacific University .... CA 45
001254 .... Pacific Lutheran Theol Seminary .... CA 57
001255 .... Pacific Oaks College .... CA 57
001256 .... Pacific School of Religion .... CA 57
001258 .... Pacific Union College .... CA 57
001259 .... Palo Verde College .... CA 58
001260 .... Palomar College .... CA 58
001261 .... Pasadena City College .... CA 58
001262 .... Point Loma Nazarene University .... CA 59
001265 .... Peralta Cmty Colleges District Ofc .... CA 58
001266 .... Laney College .... CA 59
001267 .... Merritt College .... CA 59
001268 .... Porterville College .... CA 49
001269 .... Rio Hondo College .... CA 60
001270 .... Riverside City College .... CA 61
001272 .... San Bernardino Valley College .... CA 62
001273 .... San Diego City College .... CA 62
001275 .... San Diego Mesa College .... CA 62
001278 .... San Francisco Conservatory of Music .... CA 62
001279 .... San Francisco Theological Seminary .... CA 63
001280 .... San Joaquin Delta College .... CA 63
001281 .... William Jessup University .... CA 76
001282 .... San Jose City College .... CA 63
001284 .... Santa Ana College .... CA 60
001285 .... Santa Barbara City College .... CA 64
001286 .... Santa Monica College .... CA 65
001287 .... Santa Rosa Junior College .... CA 65
001288 .... Claremont School of Theology .... CA 39
001289 .... Shasta College .... CA 65
001290 .... Sierra College .... CA 66
001291 .... Simpson University .... CA 66
001292 .... Solano Community College .... CA 66
001293 .... Vanguard Univ of South California .... CA 74
001294 .... Southwestern College .... CA 68
001295 .... Southwestern Law School .... CA 68
001296 .... Dominican Sch Philosophy & Theology .... CA 42
001299 .... Saint John's Seminary .... CA 61
001302 .... Saint Mary's College of California .... CA 61
001305 .... Stanford University .... CA 68
001306 .... State Center Cmty College District .... CA 68
001307 .... Fresno City College .... CA 68
001308 .... Reedley College .... CA 69
001309 .... Taft College .... CA 69
001310 .... Naval Postgraduate School .... CA 544
001311 .... Univ of California Ofc of President .... CA 70
001312 .... University of California-Berkeley .... CA 70
001313 .... University of California-Davis .... CA 70
001314 .... University of California-Irvine .... CA 71
001315 .... Univ of California-Los Angeles .... CA 71
001316 .... University of California-Riverside .... CA 71
001317 .... University of California-San Diego .... CA 71
001319 .... Univ of California-San Francisco .... CA 72
001320 .... Univ of California-Santa Barbara .... CA 72
001321 .... University of California-Santa Cruz .... CA 72
001322 .... University of Redlands .... CA 73
001325 .... University of San Francisco .... CA 73
001326 .... Santa Clara University .... CA 64
001328 .... University of Southern California .... CA 74
001329 .... University of the Pacific .... CA 73
001334 .... Ventura College .... CA 74
001335 .... Victor Valley College .... CA 75
001338 .... West Valley College .... CA 75
001339 .... Corban University .... OR 403
001341 .... Westmont College .... CA 76
001342 .... Whittier College .... CA 76
001343 .... Woodbury University .... CA 76
001344 .... Yuba College .... CA 77
001345 .... Adams State University .... CO 78
001346 .... Arapahoe Community College .... CO 78
001347 .... Colorado College .... CO 79
001348 .... Colorado School of Mines .... CO 80
001349 .... University of Northern Colorado .... CO 86
001350 .... Colorado State University .... CO 80

Code	Institution	State	Page
001352	Denver Seminary	CO	81
001353	Fort Lewis College	CO	81
001354	Iliff School of Theology	CO	82
001355	Lamar Community College	CO	82
001358	Colorado Mesa University	CO	79
001359	Colorado Northwestern Cmty College	CO	80
001360	Metropolitan State Univ Denver	CO	83
001361	Northeastern Junior College	CO	83
001362	Otero Junior College	CO	83
001363	Regis University	CO	84
001365	Colorado State University-Pueblo	CO	80
001368	Trinidad State Junior College	CO	85
001369	United States Air Force Academy	CO	545
001370	University of Colorado Boulder	CO	85
001371	University of Denver	CO	86
001372	Western State Colorado University	CO	86
001374	Albertus Magnus College	CT	87
001378	Central Connecticut State Univ	CT	87
001379	Connecticut College	CT	89
001380	Western Connecticut State Univ	CT	88
001385	Fairfield University	CT	89
001387	Hartford Seminary	CT	90
001389	Holy Apostles College and Seminary	CT	90
001392	Manchester Community College	CT	88
001393	Mitchell College	CT	90
001397	University of New Haven	CT	92
001398	Northwestern CT Cmty-Tech College	CT	89
001399	Norwalk Community College	CT	89
001401	Post University	CT	90
001402	Quinnipiac University	CT	91
001403	Sacred Heart University	CT	91
001406	Southern Connecticut State Univ	CT	88
001409	University of Saint Joseph	CT	92
001414	Trinity College	CT	91
001415	United States Coast Guard Academy	CT	545
001416	University of Bridgeport	CT	91
001417	University of Connecticut	CT	92
001422	University of Hartford	CT	92
001424	Wesleyan University	CT	92
001425	Eastern Connecticut State Univ	CT	87
001426	Yale University	CT	93
001428	Delaware State University	DE	93
001429	Goldey-Beacom College	DE	93
001431	University of Delaware	DE	94
001433	Wesley College	DE	94
001434	American University	DC	94
001436	Capitol College	MD	213
001437	The Catholic University of America	DC	94
001441	Univ of the District of Columbia	DC	97
001443	Gallaudet University	DC	95
001444	George Washington University	DC	95
001445	Georgetown University	DC	95
001448	Howard University	DC	95
001459	Strayer University	DC	96
001460	Trinity Washington University	DC	96
001464	Wesley Theological Seminary	DC	97
001466	Barry University	FL	98
001467	Bethune Cookman University	FL	99
001468	St. Thomas University	FL	112
001469	Florida Institute of Technology	FL	104
001470	Eastern Florida State College	FL	101
001471	College of Central Florida	FL	100
001472	Chipola College	FL	99
001473	Clearwater Christian College	FL	100
001475	Daytona State College	FL	101
001477	Edison State College	FL	101
001478	Edward Waters College	FL	102
001479	Embry-Riddle Aeronautical Univ	FL	102
001480	Florida A and M University	FL	114
001481	Florida Atlantic University	FL	114
001482	Florida College	FL	104
001484	Florida State College Jacksonville	FL	105
001485	Florida Keys Community College	FL	104
001486	Florida Memorial University	FL	104
001487	Eckerd College	FL	101
001488	Florida Southern College	FL	105
001489	Florida State University	FL	115
001490	Gulf Coast State College	FL	106
001493	Indian River State College	FL	106
001495	Jacksonville University	FL	107
001497	Jones College	FL	107
001499	Everest Univ-North Orlando Campus	FL	102
001500	Broward College	FL	99
001501	Florida Gateway College	FL	104
001502	Lake-Sumter State College	FL	108
001504	State Col of FL, Manatee-Sarasota	FL	114
001505	Lynn University	FL	108
001506	Miami Dade College	FL	109
001507	New College of Florida	FL	115
001508	North Florida Community College	FL	109
001509	Nova Southeastern University	FL	109
001510	Northwest Florida State College	FL	109
001512	Palm Beach State College	FL	110
001513	Pensacola State College	FL	110
001514	Polk State College	FL	110
001515	Rollins College	FL	111
001519	Santa Fe College	FL	113
001520	Seminole State College of Florida	FL	113
001521	Southeastern University	FL	113
001522	South Florida State College	FL	113
001523	St. Johns River State College	FL	112
001526	Saint Leo University	FL	112
001528	St. Petersburg College	FL	112
001531	Stetson University	FL	117
001533	Tallahassee Community College	FL	117
001534	Everest University-Tampa Campus	FL	103
001535	University of Florida	FL	116
001536	University of Miami	FL	118
001537	University of South Florida	FL	116
001538	University of Tampa	FL	118
001540	Webber International University	FL	119
001541	Abraham Baldwin Agricultural Coll	GA	119
001542	Agnes Scott College	GA	119
001543	Darton State College	GA	124
001544	Albany State University	GA	119
001545	Andrew College	GA	120
001546	Armstrong Atlantic State University	GA	120
001547	Point University	GA	130
001554	Berry College	GA	121
001555	Thomas University	GA	132
001556	Brenau University	GA	122
001557	Brewton-Parker College	GA	122
001558	College of Coastal Georgia	GA	123
001559	Clark Atlanta University	GA	122
001560	Columbia Theological Seminary	GA	123
001561	Columbus State University	GA	123
001562	Georgia Perimeter College	GA	125
001563	Emmanuel College	GA	124
001564	Emory University	GA	124
001566	Fort Valley State University	GA	124
001568	Interdenominational Theol Center	GA	127
001569	Georgia Institute of Technology	GA	125
001570	Southern Polytechnic State Univ	GA	132
001571	Georgia Military College	GA	125
001572	Georgia Southern University	GA	126
001573	Georgia Southwestern State Univ	GA	126
001574	Georgia State University	GA	126
001575	Gordon State College	GA	127
001577	Kennesaw State University	GA	127
001578	LaGrange College	GA	128
001579	Georgia Regents University	GA	126
001580	Mercer University	GA	128
001582	Morehouse College	GA	129
001585	University of North Georgia	GA	133
001586	Oglethorpe University	GA	130
001587	Paine College	GA	130
001588	Piedmont College	GA	130
001589	Reinhardt University	GA	130
001590	Savannah State University	GA	131
001591	Shorter University	GA	131
001592	South Georgia State College	GA	131
001594	Spelman College	GA	132
001596	Toccoa Falls College	GA	133
001597	Truett McConnell College	GA	133
001598	University of Georgia	GA	133
001599	Valdosta State University	GA	134
001600	Wesleyan College	GA	134
001601	University of West Georgia	GA	133
001602	Georgia College & State University	GA	125
001604	Young Harris College	GA	134
001605	Chaminade University of Honolulu	HI	135
001606	Brigham Young University Hawaii	HI	135
001610	University of Hawaii at Manoa	HI	136
001611	University of Hawaii at Hilo	HI	136
001612	Univ of Hawaii Honolulu Cmty Col	HI	136
001613	Kapiolani Community College	HI	136
001614	Univ of Hawaii Kauai Cmty College	HI	136
001615	Univ of Hawaii Maui College	HI	137
001616	Boise State University	ID	137
001617	The College of Idaho	ID	138
001619	College of Southern Idaho	ID	138
001620	Idaho State University	ID	138
001621	Lewis-Clark State College	ID	138
001623	North Idaho College	ID	138
001624	Northwest Nazarene University	ID	139
001625	Brigham Young University-Idaho	ID	137
001626	University of Idaho	ID	139
001628	American Academy of Art	IL	139
001632	Aquinas Institute of Theology	MO	271
001633	Augustana College	IL	139
001634	Aurora University	IL	140
001636	Southwestern Illinois College	IL	160
001637	Bethany Theological Seminary	IN	164
001638	Black Hawk College	IL	140
001639	Blackburn College	IL	140
001640	Prairie State College	IL	156
001641	Bradley University	IL	140
001643	Spoon River College	IL	160
001647	City Colleges of Chicago	IL	141
001648	City Cols of Chicago Harry Truman	IL	142
001649	City Cols of Chicago RJ Daley Col	IL	142
001650	City Cols of Chicago Malcolm X	IL	142
001652	City Cols of Chicago Washington Col	IL	141
001654	City Cols of Chicago Kennedy-King	IL	142
001655	City Cols of Chicago W Wright Col	IL	142
001657	Midwestern University	IL	153
001659	Rosalind Franklin U of Med/Science	IL	157
001661	Chicago Theological Seminary	IL	141
001663	Spertus Inst for Jewish Lrng & Ldrs	IL	160
001664	University of St. Francis	IL	162
001665	Columbia College Chicago	IL	143
001666	Concordia University Chicago	IL	143
001669	Danville Area Community College	IL	143
001671	DePaul University	IL	143
001672	DeVry University - Home Office	IL	144
001674	Eastern Illinois University	IL	144
001675	Elgin Community College	IL	144
001676	Elmhurst College	IL	145
001678	Eureka College	IL	145
001681	Highland Community College	IL	146
001682	Garrett-Evangelical Theol Seminary	IL	145
001684	Greenville College	IL	145
001685	Hebrew Theological College	IL	146
001688	Illinois College	IL	146
001689	Illinois College of Optometry	IL	146
001691	Illinois Institute of Technology	IL	147
001692	Illinois State University	IL	147
001693	Northeastern Illinois University	IL	154
001694	Chicago State University	IL	141
001696	Illinois Wesleyan University	IL	148
001698	John Marshall Law School	IL	148
001699	Joliet Junior College	IL	149
001700	Judson University	IL	149
001701	Kaskaskia College	IL	149
001703	Kendall College	IL	149
001704	Knox College	IL	150
001705	Illinois Valley Community College	IL	148
001706	Lake Forest College	IL	150
001707	Lewis University	IL	150
001708	Lincoln Christian University	IL	151
001709	Lincoln College	IL	151
001710	Loyola University Chicago	IL	151
001712	Lutheran School of Theology Chicago	IL	152
001716	MacCormac College	IL	152
001717	MacMurray College	IL	152
001721	McCormick Theological Seminary	IL	152
001722	McKendree University	IL	152
001723	Meadville Lombard Theol School	IL	152
001724	Millikin University	IL	153
001725	Monmouth College	IL	153
001727	Moody Bible Institute	IL	153
001728	Morton College	IL	153
001732	National Univ of Health Sciences	IL	154
001733	National-Louis University	IL	153
001734	North Central College	IL	154
001735	North Park University	IL	154
001736	Northern Seminary	IL	155
001737	Northern Illinois University	IL	154
001739	Northwestern University	IL	155
001741	Olivet Nazarene University	IL	155
001742	Illinois Eastern CC Olney Central	IL	147
001744	Principia College	IL	156
001745	Quincy University	IL	156
001746	Robert Morris University	IL	156
001747	Rock Valley College	IL	157
001748	Rockford University	IL	157
001749	Roosevelt University	IL	157
001750	Dominican University	IL	144
001752	Sauk Valley Community College	IL	158
001753	School of the Art Institute Chicago	IL	158
001754	Bexley Seabury	IL	140
001756	Shimer College	IL	159
001757	Southeastern Illinois College	IL	159
001758	Southern Illinois Univ Carbondale	IL	159
001759	Southern Illinois Univ Edwardsville	IL	159
001765	Univ of Saint Mary Lake-Mundelein	IL	162
001767	Benedictine University	IL	140
001768	Saint Xavier University	IL	158
001769	South Suburban Col of Cook County	IL	159
001771	Trinity Christian College	IL	160
001772	Trinity International University	IL	160
001773	Triton College	IL	161
001774	University of Chicago	IL	161
001775	Univ of Illinois Urbana-Champaign	IL	162
001776	University of Illinois at Chicago	IL	161
001778	VanderCook College of Music	IL	162
001779	Illinois Eastern CC Wabash Valley	IL	147
001780	Western Illinois University	IL	162
001781	Wheaton College	IL	163
001783	Worsham College of Mortuary Science	IL	163
001784	Ancilla College	IN	163
001785	Anderson University	IN	163
001786	Ball State University	IN	164
001787	Bethel College	IN	164
001788	Butler University	IN	164
001789	Christian Theological Seminary	IN	165
001792	DePauw University	IN	165
001793	Earlham Col/Earlham Sch of Rel	IN	165
001795	University of Evansville	IN	173
001798	Franklin College of Indiana	IN	165
001799	Goshen College	IN	166
001800	Grace College and Seminary	IN	166
001801	Hanover College	IN	166
001803	Huntington University	IN	166
001804	University of Indianapolis	IN	173
001805	Indiana Tech	IN	167
001807	Indiana State University	IN	167
001808	University of Southern Indiana	IN	174
001809	Indiana University Bloomington	IN	167
001811	Indiana University East	IN	167
001813	Indiana Univ-Purdue Un Indianapolis	IN	168
001814	Indiana University Kokomo	IN	168
001815	Indiana University Northwest	IN	168
001816	Indiana University South Bend	IN	168
001817	Indiana University Southeast	IN	168
001820	Manchester University	IN	170

001821 .... Marian University .... IN 170
001822 .... Indiana Wesleyan University .... IN 169
001823 .... Anabaptist Mennonite Biblical Sem .... IN 163
001824 .... Oakland City University .... IN 171
001825 .... Purdue University Main Campus .... IN 171
001826 .... Purdue Univ North Central Campus .... IN 172
001827 .... Purdue University Calumet .... IN 171
001828 .... Indiana Univ-Purdue Univ Fort Wayne .... IN 168
001830 .... Rose-Hulman Institute of Technology .... IN 172
001832 .... University of Saint Francis .... IN 174
001833 .... Saint Joseph's College .... IN 172
001834 .... Calumet College of Saint Joseph .... IN 164
001835 .... Saint Mary-of-the-Woods College .... IN 172
001836 .... Saint Mary's College .... IN 172
001838 .... Taylor University .... IN 173
001839 .... Trine University .... IN 173
001840 .... University of Notre Dame .... IN 174
001842 .... Valparaiso University .... IN 174
001843 .... Vincennes University .... IN 174
001844 .... Wabash College .... IN 175
001846 .... Briar Cliff University .... IA 176
001847 .... Buena Vista University .... IA 176
001848 .... Southeastern Community College .... IA 182
001850 .... Central College .... IA 176
001852 .... Clarke University .... IA 176
001853 .... Clinton Community College .... IA 178
001854 .... Coe College .... IA 176
001855 .... Des Moines University .... IA 177
001856 .... Cornell College .... IA 177
001857 .... Southwestern Community College .... IA 182
001858 .... Divine Word College .... IA 177
001859 .... Dordt College .... IA 177
001860 .... Drake University .... IA 177
001862 .... Ellsworth Community College .... IA 179
001864 .... Iowa Lakes Community College .... IA 179
001865 .... Iowa Central Community College .... IA 179
001866 .... Graceland University .... IA 178
001867 .... Grand View University .... IA 178
001868 .... Grinnell College .... IA 178
001869 .... Iowa State University .... IA 175
001871 .... Iowa Wesleyan College .... IA 179
001873 .... Loras College .... IA 180
001874 .... Luther College .... IA 180
001875 .... Marshalltown Community College .... IA 179
001877 .... North Iowa Area Community College .... IA 181
001879 .... Morningside College .... IA 181
001880 .... Mount Mercy University .... IA 181
001881 .... Ashford University .... IA 175
001882 .... Muscatine Community College .... IA 178
001883 .... Northwestern College .... IA 181
001885 .... Scott Community College .... IA 178
001887 .... Simpson College .... IA 182
001889 .... St. Ambrose University .... IA 182
001890 .... University of Northern Iowa .... IA 176
001891 .... University of Dubuque .... IA 182
001892 .... University of Iowa .... IA 175
001893 .... Upper Iowa University .... IA 183
001895 .... Waldorf College .... IA 183
001896 .... Wartburg College .... IA 183
001897 .... Wartburg Theological Seminary .... IA 183
001900 .... William Penn University .... IA 183
001901 .... Allen County Community College .... KS 183
001902 .... Cowley County Community College .... KS 186
001903 .... Baker University .... KS 184
001904 .... Bethany College .... KS 184
001905 .... Bethel College .... KS 184
001906 .... Butler Community College .... KS 185
001907 .... Central Baptist Theol Seminary .... KS 185
001908 .... Central Christian College of Kansas .... KS 185
001909 .... Cloud County Community College .... KS 185
001910 .... Coffeyville Community College .... KS 185
001911 .... Colby Community College .... KS 185
001913 .... Dodge City Community College .... KS 186
001914 .... Donnelly College .... KS 186
001915 .... Fort Hays State University .... KS 186
001916 .... Fort Scott Community College .... KS 186
001917 .... Barclay College .... KS 184
001918 .... Friends University .... KS 186
001919 .... Garden City Community College .... KS 187
001920 .... Hesston College .... KS 187
001921 .... Highland Community College .... KS 187
001923 .... Hutchinson Cmty Col & Area Voc Sch .... KS 187
001924 .... Independence Community College .... KS 187
001925 .... Kansas City Kansas Community Col .... KS 187
001926 .... Pittsburg State University .... KS 189
001927 .... Emporia State University .... KS 186
001928 .... Kansas State University .... KS 188
001929 .... Kansas Wesleyan University .... KS 188
001930 .... Labette Community College .... KS 188
001931 .... Manhattan Christian College .... KS 188
001933 .... McPherson College .... KS 188
001936 .... Neosho County Community College .... KS 189
001937 .... Ottawa University .... KS 189
001938 .... Pratt Community College .... KS 190
001939 .... Newman University .... KS 189
001940 .... Southwestern College .... KS 190
001943 .... University of Saint Mary .... KS 191
001945 .... Sterling College .... KS 190
001946 .... Tabor College .... KS 190
001947 .... US Army Command & Gen Staff Col .... KS 545
001948 .... University of Kansas Main Campus .... KS 190
001949 .... Washburn University .... KS 191
001950 .... Wichita State University .... KS 191
001951 .... Alice Lloyd College .... KY 191
001952 .... Asbury University .... KY 192
001953 .... Asbury Theological Seminary .... KY 192
001954 .... Bellarmine University .... KY 192
001955 .... Berea College .... KY 192
001958 .... Brescia University .... KY 192
001959 .... Campbellsville University .... KY 193
001960 .... Spalding University .... KY 199
001961 .... Centre College .... KY 193
001962 .... University of the Cumberlands .... KY 200
001963 .... Eastern Kentucky University .... KY 193
001964 .... Georgetown College .... KY 194
001965 .... Kentucky Christian University .... KY 194
001968 .... Kentucky State University .... KY 197
001969 .... Kentucky Wesleyan College .... KY 197
001971 .... Lexington Theological Seminary .... KY 197
001972 .... Lindsey Wilson College .... KY 197
001974 .... Louisville Presbyterian Theol Semin .... KY 197
001975 .... Midway College .... KY 197
001976 .... Morehead State University .... KY 198
001977 .... Murray State University .... KY 198
001979 .... West Kentucky Cmty & Tech Col .... KY 196
001980 .... University of Pikeville .... KY 200
001982 .... Southern Baptist Theol Seminary .... KY 199
001983 .... St. Catharine College .... KY 198
001987 .... Transylvania University .... KY 199
001988 .... Union College .... KY 200
001989 .... University of Kentucky .... KY 200
001990 .... Ashland Cmty & Technical College .... KY 194
001991 .... Elizabethtown Cmty & Tech Col .... KY 195
001993 .... Henderson Community College .... KY 195
001994 .... Hopkinsville Community College .... KY 195
001996 .... Big Sandy Community & Tech Col .... KY 194
001997 .... Somerset Community College .... KY 196
001998 .... Southeast Kentucky Cmty/Tech Co .... KY 196
001999 .... University of Louisville .... KY 200
002001 .... Thomas More College .... KY 199
002002 .... Western Kentucky University .... KY 200
002003 .... Centenary College of Louisiana .... LA 201
002004 .... Dillard University .... LA 201
002005 .... Nicholls State University .... LA 208
002006 .... Grambling State University .... LA 207
002007 .... Louisiana College .... LA 202
002008 .... Louisiana Tech University .... LA 207
002009 .... LA State University System Office .... LA 204
002010 .... Louisiana State Univ & A&M College .... LA 204
002011 .... Louisiana State Univ at Alexandria .... LA 205
002012 .... Louisiana State Univ at Eunice .... LA 205
002013 .... Louisiana State Univ in Shreveport .... LA 205
002014 .... LA State Univ Hlth Sci Ctr-New Orln .... LA 205
002015 .... University of New Orleans .... LA 205
002016 .... Loyola University New Orleans .... LA 205
002017 .... McNeese State University .... LA 207
002019 .... New Orleans Baptist Theol Seminary .... LA 206
002020 .... University of Louisiana at Monroe .... LA 208
002021 .... Northwestern State University .... LA 208
002022 .... Notre Dame Seminary Grad Sch Theol .... LA 206
002023 .... Our Lady of Holy Cross College .... LA 206
002024 .... Southeastern Louisiana University .... LA 208
002025 .... Southern University and A&M College .... LA 206
002026 .... Southern University at New Orleans .... LA 206
002027 .... Saint Joseph Seminary College .... LA 206
002029 .... Tulane University .... LA 207
002031 .... University of Louisiana Lafayette .... LA 208
002032 .... Xavier University of Louisiana .... LA 209
002033 .... University of Maine at Presque Isle .... ME 212
002035 .... Bangor Theological Seminary .... ME 209
002036 .... Bates College .... ME 209
002038 .... Bowdoin College .... ME 209
002039 .... Colby College .... ME 209
002040 .... University of Maine at Farmington .... ME 212
002041 .... University of Maine at Fort Kent .... ME 212
002043 .... Husson University .... ME 210
002044 .... Maine Maritime Academy .... ME 211
002050 .... University of New England .... ME 213
002051 .... Saint Joseph's College of Maine .... ME 211
002052 .... Thomas College .... ME 211
002053 .... University of Maine .... ME 212
002054 .... University of Southern Maine .... ME 212
002055 .... University of Maine at Machias .... ME 212
002057 .... Allegany College of Maryland .... MD 213
002058 .... Anne Arundel Community College .... MD 213
002061 .... Baltimore City Community College .... MD 213
002062 .... Bowie State University .... MD 220
002063 .... Cmty College of Baltimore County .... MD 214
002064 .... College of Southern Maryland .... MD 214
002065 .... Notre Dame of Maryland University .... MD 217
002067 .... Washington Adventist University .... MD 221
002068 .... Coppin State University .... MD 220
002071 .... Frederick Community College .... MD 214
002072 .... Frostburg State University .... MD 220
002073 .... Goucher College .... MD 215
002074 .... Hagerstown Community College .... MD 215
002075 .... Harford Community College .... MD 215
002076 .... Hood College .... MD 215
002077 .... Johns Hopkins University .... MD 215
002078 .... Loyola University Maryland .... MD 216
002080 .... Maryland Institute College of Art .... MD 216
002083 .... Morgan State University .... MD 217
002086 .... Mount St. Mary's University .... MD 217
002087 .... Ner Israel Rabbinical College .... MD 217
002089 .... Prince George's Community College .... MD 217
002091 .... Salisbury University .... MD 220
002092 .... St. John's College .... MD 217
002093 .... St. John's College .... NM 311
002095 .... St. Mary's College of Maryland .... MD 218
002096 .... Saint Mary's Seminary & University .... MD 218
002099 .... Towson University .... MD 220
002102 .... University of Baltimore .... MD 221
002103 .... University of Maryland College Park .... MD 219
002104 .... University of Maryland Baltimore .... MD 219
002105 .... Univ of Maryland Baltimore County .... MD 219
002106 .... Univ of Maryland Eastern Shore .... MD 219
002107 .... Stevenson University .... MD 218
002108 .... Washington College .... MD 221
002109 .... McDaniel College .... MD 216
002114 .... American International College .... MA 221
002115 .... Amherst College .... MA 221
002116 .... Andover Newton Theological School .... MA 222
002117 .... Anna Maria College .... MA 222
002118 .... Assumption College .... MA 222
002120 .... Merrimack College .... MA 234
002121 .... Babson College .... MA 222
002122 .... Bay Path College .... MA 222
002123 .... Becker College-Worcester .... MA 223
002124 .... Bentley University .... MA 223
002126 .... Berklee College of Music .... MA 223
002128 .... Boston College .... MA 224
002129 .... The Boston Conservatory .... MA 224
002130 .... Boston University .... MA 224
002133 .... Brandeis University .... MA 224
002139 .... Clark University .... MA 225
002140 .... College of Our Lady of the Elms .... MA 225
002141 .... College of the Holy Cross .... MA 225
002143 .... Curry College .... MA 225
002144 .... Dean College .... MA 225
002145 .... Eastern Nazarene College .... MA 225
002146 .... Emerson College .... MA 226
002147 .... Emmanuel College .... MA 226
002148 .... Endicott College .... MA 226
002149 .... Episcopal Divinity School .... MA 226
002150 .... Fisher College .... MA 226
002151 .... Benjamin Franklin Inst of Tech .... MA 223
002153 .... Gordon College .... MA 226
002154 .... Hellenic Coll-Holy Cross Greek Orth .... MA 227
002155 .... Harvard University .... MA 227
002157 .... Hebrew College .... MA 227
002158 .... Lasell College .... MA 227
002160 .... Lesley University .... MA 228
002161 .... University of Massachusetts Lowell .... MA 229
002164 .... The New England Coll of Optometry .... MA 234
002165 .... MCPHS University .... MA 233
002167 .... Berkshire Community College .... MA 231
002168 .... Cape Cod Community College .... MA 231
002169 .... Greenfield Community College .... MA 231
002170 .... Holyoke Community College .... MA 231
002171 .... Massachusetts Bay Community College .... MA 231
002172 .... Mount Wachusett Community College .... MA 232
002173 .... North Shore Community College .... MA 232
002174 .... Northern Essex Community College .... MA 232
002175 .... Quinsigamond Community College .... MA 232
002176 .... Bristol Community College .... MA 231
002177 .... Massasoit Community College .... MA 232
002178 .... Massachusetts Institute of Tech .... MA 233
002180 .... Massachusetts College of Art/Design .... MA 230
002181 .... Massachusetts Maritime Academy .... MA 230
002183 .... Bridgewater State University .... MA 229
002184 .... Fitchburg State University .... MA 229
002185 .... Framingham State University .... MA 230
002187 .... Massachusetts Col of Liberal Arts .... MA 230
002188 .... Salem State University .... MA 230
002189 .... Westfield State University .... MA 230
002190 .... Worcester State University .... MA 230
002192 .... Mount Holyoke College .... MA 234
002193 .... Mount Ida College .... MA 234
002194 .... New England Conservatory of Music .... MA 234
002197 .... Nichols College .... MA 235
002199 .... Northeastern University .... MA 235
002201 .... Pine Manor College .... MA 235
002202 .... Blessed John XXIII Natl Seminary .... MA 223
002205 .... Quincy College .... MA 235
002206 .... Regis College .... MA 236
002208 .... Simmons College .... MA 236
002209 .... Smith College .... MA 236
002210 .... Univ of Massachusetts Dartmouth .... MA 229
002211 .... Springfield College .... MA 236
002214 .... Saint John's Seminary .... MA 236
002217 .... Stonehill College .... MA 237
002218 .... Suffolk University .... MA 237
002219 .... Tufts University .... MA 237
002221 .... University of Massachusetts .... MA 228
002222 .... University of Massachusetts Boston .... MA 228
002224 .... Wellesley College .... MA 237
002225 .... Wentworth Institute of Technology .... MA 237
002226 .... Western New England University .... MA 238
002227 .... Wheaton College .... MA 238
002228 .... Wheelock College .... MA 238
002229 .... Williams College .... MA 238
002230 .... Woods Hole Oceanographic Inst .... MA 238
002233 .... Worcester Polytechnic Institute .... MA 238
002234 .... Adrian College .... MI 238
002235 .... Albion College .... MI 239
002236 .... Alma College .... MI 239

Code	Institution	State	Page
002237	Alpena Community College	MI	239
002238	Andrews University	MI	239
002239	Aquinas College	MI	239
002240	Bay Noc Community College	MI	240
002241	Calvin College	MI	240
002242	Calvin Theological Seminary	MI	240
002243	Central Michigan University	MI	240
002246	Cleary University	MI	241
002247	Concordia University	MI	241
002248	Cranbrook Academy of Art	MI	241
002249	Davenport University	MI	241
002251	Delta College	MI	242
002259	Eastern Michigan University	MI	242
002260	Ferris State University	MI	242
002261	Mott Community College	MI	247
002262	Kettering University	MI	244
002263	Glen Oaks Community College	MI	242
002264	Gogebic Community College	MI	242
002265	Grace Bible College	MI	243
002266	Cornerstone University	MI	241
002267	Grand Rapids Community College	MI	243
002268	Grand Valley State University	MI	243
002269	Great Lakes Christian College	MI	243
002270	Henry Ford Community College	MI	243
002272	Hillsdale College	MI	243
002273	Hope College	MI	244
002274	Jackson College	MI	244
002275	Kalamazoo College	MI	244
002276	Kellogg Community College	MI	244
002277	Lake Michigan College	MI	245
002278	Lansing Community College	MI	245
002279	Lawrence Technological University	MI	245
002282	Madonna University	MI	246
002284	Marygrove College	MI	246
002288	Rochester College	MI	249
002290	Michigan State University	MI	246
002292	Michigan Technological University	MI	247
002293	Lake Superior State University	MI	245
002294	Monroe County Community College	MI	247
002295	Montcalm Community College	MI	247
002297	Muskegon Community College	MI	247
002299	North Central Michigan College	MI	247
002301	Northern Michigan University	MI	248
002302	Northwestern Michigan College	MI	248
002303	Oakland Community College	MI	248
002307	Oakland University	MI	248
002308	Olivet College	MI	249
002310	St. Clair County Community College	MI	249
002311	Kuyper College	MI	245
002313	Sacred Heart Major Seminary	MI	249
002314	Saginaw Valley State University	MI	249
002315	Schoolcraft College	MI	250
002316	Siena Heights University	MI	250
002317	Southwestern Michigan College	MI	250
002318	Spring Arbor University	MI	250
002322	Finlandia University	MI	242
002323	University of Detroit Mercy	MI	250
002325	University of Michigan-Ann Arbor	MI	251
002326	University of Michigan-Dearborn	MI	251
002327	University of Michigan-Flint	MI	251
002328	Washtenaw Community College	MI	252
002329	Wayne State University	MI	252
002330	Western Michigan University	MI	252
002331	Western Theological Seminary	MI	252
002332	Anoka-Ramsey Community College	MN	257
002334	Augsburg College	MN	253
002335	Riverland Community College	MN	260
002336	Bemidji State University	MN	258
002337	Bethany Lutheran College	MN	253
002339	Central Lakes College	MN	258
002340	Carleton College	MN	254
002341	College of Saint Benedict	MN	254
002342	St. Catherine University	MN	263
002343	The College of Saint Scholastica	MN	254
002345	University of Saint Thomas	MN	265
002346	Concordia College	MN	255
002347	Concordia University, St. Paul	MN	255
002350	Vermilion Community College	MN	261
002353	Gustavus Adolphus College	MN	255
002354	Hamline University	MN	256
002355	Hibbing Community College	MN	258
002356	Itasca Community College	MN	258
002357	Luther Seminary	MN	256
002358	Macalester College	MN	256
002360	Minnesota State University, Mankato	MN	259
002361	Martin Luther College	MN	256
002362	Minneapolis Cmty & Tech College	MN	259
002365	Minneapolis College of Art Design	MN	257
002366	Crossroads College	MN	255
002367	Minnesota State University Moorhead	MN	259
002369	North Central University	MN	262
002370	North Hennepin Community College	MN	260
002371	Northwestern College	MN	263
002373	Rochester Community & Tech College	MN	261
002375	Southwest Minnesota State Univ	MN	261
002377	St. Cloud State University	MN	261
002379	Saint John's University	MN	263
002380	St Mary's University of Minnesota	MN	264
002382	St. Olaf College	MN	264
002383	Crown College	MN	255
002385	Northland Community & Tech College	MN	260
002386	United Theol Seminary-Twin Cities	MN	264
002388	University of Minnesota Duluth	MN	264
002389	University of Minnesota-Morris	MN	264
002391	William Mitchell College of Law	MN	265
002393	Minnesota State Col-Southeast Tech	MN	259
002394	Winona State University	MN	262
002396	Alcorn State University	MS	265
002397	Belhaven University	MS	266
002398	Blue Mountain College	MS	266
002401	Coahoma Community College	MS	266
002402	Copiah-Lincoln Community College	MS	266
002403	Delta State University	MS	266
002404	East Central Community College	MS	266
002405	East Mississippi Community College	MS	266
002407	Hinds Community College	MS	267
002408	Holmes Community College	MS	267
002409	Itawamba Community College	MS	267
002410	Jackson State University	MS	267
002411	Jones County Junior College	MS	267
002413	Meridian Community College	MS	267
002414	Millsaps College	MS	267
002415	Mississippi College	MS	268
002416	Mississippi Delta Community College	MS	268
002417	Mississippi Gulf Coast Cmty College	MS	268
002422	Mississippi University for Women	MS	268
002423	Mississippi State University	MS	268
002424	Mississippi Valley State University	MS	269
002426	Northeast Mississippi Cmty College	MS	269
002427	Northwest Mississippi Cmty College	MS	269
002430	Pearl River Community College	MS	269
002433	Rust College	MS	269
002435	Southeastern Baptist College	MS	269
002436	Southwest Mississippi Cmty College	MS	269
002439	Tougaloo College	MS	270
002440	University of Mississippi	MS	270
002441	University of Southern Mississippi	MS	270
002447	William Carey University	MS	270
002449	Avila University	MO	271
002450	Calvary Bible Col & Theol Seminary	MO	271
002453	Central Methodist University	MO	272
002454	University of Central Missouri	MO	283
002456	Columbia College	MO	272
002457	Concordia Seminary	MO	272
002458	Cottey College	MO	273
002459	Crowder College	MO	273
002460	Culver-Stockton College	MO	273
002461	Drury University	MO	273
002462	Eden Theological Seminary	MO	274
002463	Evangel University	MO	274
002464	Fontbonne University	MO	274
002466	Harris-Stowe State University	MO	275
002467	Conception Seminary College	MO	272
002468	Jefferson College	MO	275
002469	St Louis Cmty Col Center	MO	281
002471	St Louis Cmty Col Forest Park	MO	281
002473	Kansas City Art Institute	MO	275
002474	Kansas City Univ of Med & BioSci	MO	275
002476	Kenrick-Glennon Seminary	MO	275
002477	A. T. Still Univ of Health Sciences	MO	271
002479	Lincoln University	MO	276
002480	Lindenwood University	MO	276
002482	Maryville University of Saint Louis	MO	276
002484	Metropolitan Cmty Col-Penn Valley	MO	277
002485	Midwestern Baptist Theol Seminary	MO	277
002486	Mineral Area College	MO	278
002488	Missouri Southern State University	MO	278
002489	Missouri Valley College	MO	278
002490	Missouri Western State University	MO	279
002491	Moberly Area Community College	MO	279
002494	Nazarene Theological Seminary	MO	279
002495	Truman State University	MO	282
002496	Northwest Missouri State University	MO	279
002498	Park University	MO	280
002499	Rockhurst University	MO	280
002500	College of the Ozarks	MO	272
002501	Southeast Missouri State University	MO	282
002502	Southwest Baptist University	MO	282
002503	Missouri State University	MO	278
002504	St. Louis College of Pharmacy	MO	281
002506	Saint Louis University	MO	281
002509	Saint Paul School of Theology	KS	190
002512	Stephens College	MO	282
002514	North Central Missouri College	MO	279
002515	Univ of Missouri System Admin	MO	283
002516	University of Missouri - Columbia	MO	283
002517	Missouri Univ of Science Tech	MO	284
002518	Univ of Missouri - Kansas City	MO	283
002519	Univ of Missouri - Saint Louis	MO	283
002520	Washington University in St. Louis	MO	284
002521	Webster University	MO	284
002522	Wentworth Military Academy/Jr Col	MO	285
002523	Westminster College	MO	285
002524	William Jewell College	MO	285
002525	William Woods University	MO	285
002526	Carroll College	MT	285
002527	University of Great Falls	MT	288
002528	Miles Community College	MT	286
002529	Dawson Community College	MT	286
002530	Montana State University - Billings	MT	287
002531	Montana Tech of the Univ of Montana	MT	287
002532	Montana State University	MT	287
002533	Montana State University - Northern	MT	287
002534	Rocky Mountain College	MT	288
002536	The University of Montana-Missoula	MT	286
002537	The University of Montana Western	MT	286
002539	Chadron State College	NE	291
002540	College of Saint Mary	NE	289
002541	Concordia University	NE	289
002542	Creighton University	NE	289
002544	Doane College	NE	289
002547	Grace University	NE	289
002548	Hastings College	NE	289
002551	University of Nebraska at Kearney	NE	292
002553	Midland University	NE	290
002554	University of Nebraska at Omaha	NE	293
002555	Nebraska Wesleyan University	NE	291
002557	Mid-Plains Community College	NE	290
002559	Peru State College	NE	291
002560	Western Nebraska Community College	NE	293
002563	Union College	NE	292
002565	University of Nebraska - Lincoln	NE	292
002566	Wayne State College	NE	291
002567	York College	NE	293
002568	University of Nevada, Reno	NV	294
002569	University of Nevada, Las Vegas	NV	294
002572	Colby-Sawyer College	NH	295
002573	Dartmouth College	NH	296
002575	Franklin Pierce University	NH	296
002579	New England College	NH	297
002580	Southern New Hampshire University	NH	297
002581	NHTI-Concord's Community College	NH	296
002582	Manchester Community College	NH	296
002583	Great Bay Community College	NH	295
002586	Rivier University	NH	297
002587	Saint Anselm College	NH	297
002589	University of New Hampshire	NH	298
002590	Keene State College	NH	298
002591	Plymouth State University	NH	298
002595	Assumption College for Sisters	NJ	298
002596	Atlantic Cape Community College	NJ	299
002597	Bloomfield College	NJ	299
002598	Caldwell College	NJ	300
002599	Centenary College	NJ	300
002600	College of Saint Elizabeth	NJ	300
002601	Cumberland County College	NJ	301
002603	Drew University	NJ	301
002607	Fairleigh Dickinson University	NJ	301
002608	Georgian Court University	NJ	302
002609	Rowan University	NJ	305
002610	Felician College	NJ	302
002613	New Jersey City University	NJ	303
002615	Middlesex County College	NJ	303
002616	Monmouth University	NJ	303
002617	Montclair State University	NJ	303
002619	New Brunswick Theological Seminary	NJ	303
002621	New Jersey Institute of Technology	NJ	303
002622	Kean University	NJ	302
002624	Ocean County College	NJ	304
002625	William Paterson University of NJ	NJ	308
002626	Princeton Theological Seminary	NJ	304
002627	Princeton University	NJ	304
002628	Rider University	NJ	305
002629	Rutgers State Univ Central Office	NJ	306
002631	Rutgers State Univ - Newark	NJ	306
002632	Seton Hall University	NJ	307
002638	Saint Peter's University	NJ	306
002639	Stevens Institute of Technology	NJ	307
002642	The College of New Jersey	NJ	300
002643	Union County College	NJ	308
002649	Santa Fe Univ of Art and Design	NM	311
002650	University of the Southwest	NM	312
002651	Eastern New Mexico University	NM	309
002653	New Mexico Highlands University	NM	310
002654	New Mexico Inst of Mining & Tech	NM	310
002655	New Mexico Junior College	NM	310
002656	New Mexico Military Institute	NM	310
002657	NM State University-Main Campus	NM	310
002658	NM State University-Alamogordo	NM	310
002659	NM State University-Carlsbad	NM	311
002660	San Juan College	NM	311
002661	Eastern New Mexico Univ - Roswell	NM	309
002663	Univ of New Mexico Main Campus	NM	312
002664	Western New Mexico University	NM	312
002665	Vaughn Col of Aeronautics & Tech	NY	349
002666	Adelphi University	NY	313
002667	Dowling College	NY	323
002668	Alfred University	NY	313
002669	Bank Street College of Education	NY	314
002670	Baptist Bible College and Seminary	PA	410
002671	Bard College	NY	314
002674	New York Theological Seminary	NY	334
002677	Brooklyn Law School	NY	315
002678	Bryant & Stratton College	NY	315
002681	Canisius College	NY	316
002685	Cazenovia College	NY	316
002687	CUNY Brooklyn College	NY	317
002688	CUNY City College	NY	317
002689	CUNY Hunter College	NY	318
002690	CUNY Queens College	NY	319
002691	CUNY Borough of Manhattan CC	NY	317
002692	CUNY Bronx Community College	NY	317
002693	CUNY John Jay Col Criminal Justice	NY	318
002694	CUNY Kingsborough Cmty College	NY	318
002696	NYC Col of Tech/City Univ of NY	NY	319
002697	CUNY Queensborough Cmty Col	NY	319

002698 .... CUNY College of Staten Island .... NY 317
002699 .... Clarkson University .... NY 320
002700 .... Colgate Roch Crozer Divinity School .... NY 320
002701 .... Colgate University .... NY 320
002703 .... College of Mount Saint Vincent .... NY 320
002704 .... The College of New Rochelle .... NY 320
002705 .... College of Saint Rose .... NY 321
002707 .... Columbia University in City of NY .... NY 321
002708 .... Barnard College .... NY 314
002709 .... Concordia College .... NY 321
002710 .... Cooper Union .... NY 321
002711 .... Cornell University .... NY 322
002712 .... D'Youville College .... NY 323
002713 .... Dominican College of Blauvelt .... NY 322
002718 .... Elmira College .... NY 323
002722 .... Fordham University .... NY 324
002726 .... General Theological Seminary .... NY 325
002728 .... Hamilton College .... NY 325
002729 .... Hartwick College .... NY 325
002731 .... Hobart and William Smith Colleges .... NY 326
002732 .... Hofstra University .... NY 326
002733 .... Holy Trinity Orthodox Seminary .... NY 326
002734 .... Houghton College .... NY 326
002735 .... Hilbert College .... NY 326
002737 .... Iona College .... NY 327
002739 .... Ithaca College .... NY 327
002740 .... Jewish Theol Seminary of America .... NY 328
002741 .... American Jewish University .... CA 27
002742 .... The Juilliard School .... NY 328
002744 .... Keuka College .... NY 328
002748 .... Le Moyne College .... NY 328
002749 .... New York Col of Podiatric Medicine .... NY 333
002751 .... Long Island University .... NY 329
002754 .... Long Island Univ - Post Campus .... NY 329
002758 .... Manhattan College .... NY 329
002759 .... Manhattan School of Music .... NY 330
002760 .... Manhattanville College .... NY 330
002763 .... Maria College of Albany .... NY 330
002765 .... Marist College .... NY 330
002769 .... Marymount Manhattan College .... NY 330
002772 .... Mercy College .... NY 330
002775 .... Molloy College .... NY 331
002777 .... Medaille College .... NY 330
002778 .... Mount Saint Mary College .... NY 332
002779 .... Nazareth College of Rochester .... NY 332
002783 .... New York Law School .... NY 333
002784 .... New York Medical College .... NY 334
002785 .... New York University .... NY 334
002788 .... Niagara University .... NY 334
002790 .... Nyack College .... NY 335
002791 .... Pace University .... NY 335
002795 .... Paul Smith's College .... NY 336
002796 .... Polytechnic Institute of NY Univ .... NY 336
002798 .... Pratt Institute .... NY 336
002803 .... Rensselaer Polytechnic Institute .... NY 337
002805 .... Roberts Wesleyan College .... NY 337
002806 .... Rochester Institute of Technology .... NY 337
002807 .... Rockefeller University .... NY 338
002808 .... Daemen College .... NY 322
002810 .... The Sage Colleges .... NY 338
002812 .... Trocaire College .... NY 348
002813 .... Sarah Lawrence College .... NY 340
002814 .... Skidmore College .... NY 341
002815 .... St. Bernard's Sch of Theol/Ministry .... NY 338
002816 .... Siena College .... NY 340
002817 .... St. Bonaventure University .... NY 338
002820 .... St. Francis College .... NY 338
002821 .... St. John Fisher College .... NY 338
002822 .... Christ the King Seminary .... NY 316
002823 .... St. John's University .... NY 339
002825 .... Saint Joseph's College, New York .... NY 339
002826 .... Saint Joseph's Seminary .... NY 339
002829 .... St. Lawrence University .... NY 339
002832 .... St. Thomas Aquinas College .... NY 340
002833 .... St Vladimir Orthodox Theol Seminary .... NY 340
002834 .... Excelsior College .... NY 324
002835 .... University at Albany, SUNY .... NY 341
002836 .... SUNY at Binghamton .... NY 341
002837 .... University at Buffalo-SUNY .... NY 341
002838 .... SUNY at Stony Brook .... NY 342
002839 .... SUNY Health Science Ctr at Brooklyn .... NY 342
002840 .... SUNY Upstate Medical University .... NY 342
002841 .... SUNY The College at Brockport .... NY 342
002842 .... SUNY College at Buffalo .... NY 343
002843 .... SUNY College at Cortland .... NY 343
002844 .... SUNY at Fredonia .... NY 342
002845 .... SUNY College at Geneseo .... NY 343
002846 .... SUNY at New Paltz .... NY 342
002847 .... SUNY College at Oneonta .... NY 343
002848 .... SUNY College at Oswego .... NY 344
002849 .... SUNY College at Plattsburgh .... NY 344
002850 .... SUNY College at Potsdam .... NY 344
002851 .... SUNY Col Envrnmtl Sci & Forestry .... NY 345
002853 .... SUNY Maritime College .... NY 346
002854 .... Alfred State College .... NY 345
002855 .... SUNY Canton-College of Technology .... NY 345
002856 .... SUNY College of A&T Cobleskill .... NY 344
002857 .... SUNY College of Tech at Delhi .... NY 345
002858 .... Farmingdale State College .... NY 346
002859 .... SUNY College A&T Morrisville .... NY 345
002860 .... SUNY Adirondack .... NY 345
002861 .... Cayuga Community College .... NY 316
002862 .... Broome Community College .... NY 315
002863 .... Corning Community College .... NY 322
002864 .... Dutchess Community College .... NY 323
002866 .... Fashion Institute of Technology .... NY 324
002867 .... Fulton-Montgomery Community College .... NY 325
002868 .... Hudson Valley Community College .... NY 326
002869 .... Jamestown Community College .... NY 327
002870 .... Jefferson Community College .... NY 327
002871 .... Mohawk Valley Community College .... NY 331
002872 .... Monroe Community College .... NY 332
002873 .... Nassau Community College .... NY 332
002874 .... Niagara County Community College .... NY 334
002875 .... Onondaga Community College .... NY 335
002876 .... Orange County Community College .... NY 335
002877 .... Rockland Community College .... NY 338
002878 .... Suffolk Cty Cmty Col Ammerman .... NY 346
002879 .... Sullivan County Community College .... NY 347
002880 .... Ulster County Community College .... NY 348
002881 .... Westchester Community College .... NY 350
002882 .... Syracuse University Main Campus .... NY 347
002883 .... Utica College .... NY 349
002885 .... Albny Col Pharmacy & Health Sci .... NY 313
002886 .... Albany Law School .... NY 313
002887 .... Albany Medical College .... NY 313
002889 .... Union College .... NY 348
002890 .... Union Theological Seminary .... NY 349
002892 .... US Merchant Marine Academy .... NY 545
002893 .... United States Military Academy .... NY 545
002894 .... University of Rochester .... NY 349
002895 .... Vassar College .... NY 349
002896 .... Villa Maria College of Buffalo .... NY 350
002899 .... Wagner College .... NY 350
002900 .... Webb Institute .... NY 350
002901 .... Wells College .... NY 350
002903 .... Yeshiva University .... NY 351
002905 .... North Carolina A&T State University .... NC 367
002906 .... Appalachian State University .... NC 367
002907 .... Univ of North Carolina Asheville .... NC 368
002908 .... Barton College .... NC 352
002910 .... Belmont Abbey College .... NC 352
002911 .... Bennett College .... NC 352
002912 .... Brevard College .... NC 352
002913 .... Campbell University .... NC 352
002914 .... Catawba College .... NC 353
002915 .... Central Piedmont Community College .... NC 359
002916 .... Chowan University .... NC 353
002917 .... College of the Albemarle .... NC 359
002918 .... Davidson College .... NC 353
002919 .... Davidson County Community College .... NC 360
002920 .... Duke University .... NC 354
002923 .... East Carolina University .... NC 367
002926 .... Elizabeth City State University .... NC 367
002927 .... Elon University .... NC 354
002928 .... Fayetteville State University .... NC 367
002929 .... Gardner-Webb University .... NC 354
002930 .... Greensboro College .... NC 354
002931 .... Guilford College .... NC 355
002933 .... High Point University .... NC 355
002934 .... Isothermal Community College .... NC 361
002935 .... Laurel University .... NC 355
002936 .... Johnson C. Smith University .... NC 355
002937 .... King's College .... NC 355
002939 .... Lees-McRae College .... NC 356
002940 .... Lenoir Community College .... NC 361
002941 .... Lenoir-Rhyne University .... NC 356
002942 .... Livingstone College .... NC 356
002943 .... Louisburg College .... NC 356
002944 .... Mars Hill College .... NC 356
002945 .... Meredith College .... NC 356
002946 .... Methodist University .... NC 356
002947 .... Mitchell Community College .... NC 362
002948 .... Montreat College .... NC 357
002949 .... Mount Olive College .... NC 357
002950 .... North Carolina Central University .... NC 368
002951 .... North Carolina Wesleyan College .... NC 365
002953 .... William Peace University .... NC 370
002954 .... Univ of North Carolina Pembroke .... NC 369
002955 .... Pfeiffer University .... NC 365
002956 .... Piedmont International University .... NC 365
002957 .... Queens University of Charlotte .... NC 365
002958 .... Rockingham Community College .... NC 363
002960 .... Salem College .... NC 366
002961 .... Sandhills Community College .... NC 363
002962 .... Shaw University .... NC 366
002963 .... Southeastern Baptist Theol Seminary .... NC 366
002964 .... Southeastern Community College .... NC 364
002968 .... Saint Augustine's University .... NC 366
002970 .... Surry Community College .... NC 364
002971 .... Univ of NC General Administration .... NC 366
002972 .... North Carolina State University .... NC 368
002973 .... Gaston College .... NC 360
002974 .... Univ of North Carolina Chapel Hill .... NC 368
002975 .... Univ of North Carolina Charlotte .... NC 368
002976 .... Univ of North Carolina Greensboro .... NC 369
002978 .... Wake Forest University .... NC 370
002979 .... Warren Wilson College .... NC 370
002980 .... Wayne Community College .... NC 364
002981 .... Western Carolina University .... NC 369
002982 .... Western Piedmont Community College .... NC 365
002983 .... Wilkes Community College .... NC 365
002984 .... Univ of North Carolina Wilmington .... NC 369
002985 .... Wingate University .... NC 370
002986 .... Winston-Salem State University .... NC 370
002988 .... Bismarck State College .... ND 372
002989 .... Dickinson State University .... ND 371
002990 .... University of Jamestown .... ND 373
002991 .... Lake Region State College .... ND 372
002992 .... University of Mary .... ND 373
002993 .... Mayville State University .... ND 371
002994 .... Minot State University .... ND 371
002995 .... Dakota College at Bottineau .... ND 372
002996 .... North Dakota State Col of Science .... ND 372
002997 .... North Dakota State Univ Main Campus .... ND 371
003005 .... Univ of North Dakota Main Campus .... ND 371
003007 .... Williston State College .... ND 372
003008 .... Valley City State University .... ND 372
003009 .... Air Force Institute of Technology .... OH 544
003010 .... Antioch University .... OH 373
003011 .... Art Academy of Cincinnati .... OH 373
003012 .... Ashland University .... OH 374
003013 .... Athenaeum of Ohio .... OH 374
003014 .... Baldwin Wallace University .... OH 374
003016 .... Bluffton University .... OH 374
003018 .... Bowling Green State University .... OH 374
003023 .... Capital University .... OH 375
003024 .... Case Western Reserve University .... OH 375
003025 .... Cedarville University .... OH 375
003026 .... Central State University .... OH 376
003029 .... Cincinnati Christian University .... OH 376
003030 .... Ohio Christian University .... OH 385
003031 .... Cleveland Institute of Music .... OH 377
003032 .... Cleveland State University .... OH 377
003033 .... College of Mount St. Joseph .... OH 377
003035 .... Ohio Dominican University .... OH 386
003036 .... Franciscan Univ of Steubenville .... OH 379
003037 .... The College of Wooster .... OH 377
003039 .... Columbus College of Art & Design .... OH 378
003040 .... Cuyahoga Community College .... OH 378
003041 .... The Defiance College .... OH 379
003042 .... Denison University .... OH 379
003044 .... Trinity Lutheran Seminary .... OH 390
003045 .... The University of Findlay .... OH 391
003046 .... Franklin University .... OH 380
003048 .... Heidelberg University .... OH 380
003049 .... Hiram College .... OH 380
003050 .... John Carroll University .... OH 381
003051 .... Kent State University Main Campus .... OH 382
003065 .... Kenyon College .... OH 382
003066 .... Lake Erie College .... OH 382
003068 .... Lorain County Community College .... OH 383
003069 .... Lourdes University .... OH 383
003072 .... Malone University .... OH 383
003073 .... Marietta College .... OH 383
003075 .... Methodist Theological School Ohio .... OH 383
003077 .... Miami University .... OH 384
003078 .... Wright State University Main Campus .... OH 393
003083 .... University of Mount Union .... OH 391
003084 .... Muskingum University .... OH 384
003085 .... Notre Dame College .... OH 385
003086 .... Oberlin College .... OH 385
003089 .... Ohio Northern University .... OH 386
003090 .... The Ohio State Univ Main Campus .... OH 386
003100 .... Ohio University Main Campus .... OH 387
003109 .... Ohio Wesleyan University .... OH 387
003110 .... Otterbein University .... OH 387
003113 .... Pontifical College Josephinum .... OH 388
003115 .... Rabbinical College of Telshe .... OH 388
003116 .... University of Rio Grande .... OH 392
003119 .... Sinclair Community College .... OH 388
003121 .... Tiffin University .... OH 389
003122 .... United Theological Seminary .... OH 390
003123 .... The Univ of Akron, Main Campus .... OH 390
003125 .... University of Cincinnati Main .... OH 390
003127 .... University of Dayton .... OH 391
003131 .... University of Toledo .... OH 392
003133 .... Urbana University .... OH 392
003134 .... Ursuline College .... OH 392
003135 .... Walsh University .... OH 392
003141 .... Wilberforce University .... OH 393
003142 .... Wilmington College .... OH 393
003143 .... Wittenberg University .... OH 393
003144 .... Xavier University .... OH 393
003145 .... Youngstown State University .... OH 394
003146 .... Western Oklahoma State College .... OK 401
003147 .... Bacone College .... OK 394
003149 .... Southern Nazarene University .... OK 399
003150 .... Cameron University .... OK 394
003151 .... Oklahoma Wesleyan University .... OK 398
003152 .... University of Central Oklahoma .... OK 400
003153 .... Connors State College .... OK 395
003154 .... East Central University .... OK 395
003155 .... Eastern Oklahoma State College .... OK 395
003156 .... Redlands Community College .... OK 399
003157 .... Langston University .... OK 395
003158 .... Murray State College .... OK 396
003160 .... Northeastern Oklahoma A&M College .... OK 396
003161 .... Northeastern State University .... OK 396
003162 .... Northern Oklahoma College .... OK 396
003163 .... Northwestern Oklahoma State Univ .... OK 396
003164 .... Oklahoma Baptist University .... OK 397
003165 .... Oklahoma Christian University .... OK 397
003166 .... Oklahoma City University .... OK 397
003167 .... Univ of Science & Arts of Oklahoma .... OK 401
003168 .... Rogers State University .... OK 399

Code	Institution	State	Page
003170	Oklahoma State University	OK	397
003172	Oklahoma State Univ - Okmulgee	OK	398
003174	Oklahoma Panhandle State University	OK	397
003176	Carl Albert State College	OK	394
003178	Seminole State College	OK	399
003179	Southeastern Oklahoma State Univ	OK	399
003180	Southwestern Christian University	OK	400
003181	Southwestern Oklahoma State Univ	OK	400
003183	St. Gregory's University	OK	399
003184	University of Oklahoma Norman	OK	401
003185	University of Tulsa	OK	401
003186	Blue Mountain Community College	OR	402
003188	Central Oregon Community College	OR	402
003189	Clatsop Community College	OR	402
003191	Concordia University	OR	402
003193	Eastern Oregon University	OR	405
003194	George Fox University	OR	403
003196	Lane Community College	OR	403
003197	Lewis and Clark College	OR	403
003198	Linfield College	OR	404
003199	Marylhurst University	OR	404
003203	Mount Angel Seminary	OR	404
003204	Mt. Hood Community College	OR	404
003206	Multnomah University	OR	404
003207	Pacific Northwest College of Art	OR	406
003208	Northwest Christian University	OR	405
003209	Western Oregon University	OR	406
003210	Oregon State University	OR	406
003211	Oregon Institute of Technology	OR	405
003212	Pacific University	OR	407
003213	Portland Community College	OR	407
003216	Portland State University	OR	406
003217	Reed College	OR	407
003218	Chemeketa Community College	OR	402
003219	Southern Oregon University	OR	406
003220	Southwestern Oregon Community Col	OR	407
003221	Treasure Valley Community College	OR	408
003222	Umpqua Community College	OR	408
003223	University of Oregon	OR	406
003224	University of Portland	OR	408
003225	Warner Pacific College	OR	408
003227	Willamette University	OR	408
003228	Bryn Athyn Col of the New Church	PA	410
003229	Albright College	PA	409
003230	Allegheny College	PA	409
003231	Community College of Allegheny Cty	PA	413
003233	Alvernia University	PA	409
003235	Arcadia University	PA	409
003237	Bryn Mawr College	PA	410
003238	Bucknell University	PA	411
003239	Bucks County Community College	PA	411
003240	Butler County Community College	PA	411
003241	Cabrini College	PA	411
003242	Carnegie Mellon University	PA	412
003243	Cedar Crest College	PA	412
003244	Chatham University	PA	412
003245	Chestnut Hill College	PA	413
003247	Misericordia University	PA	424
003249	Community College of Philadelphia	PA	413
003251	Curtis Institute of Music	PA	414
003252	Delaware Valley College	PA	414
003253	Dickinson College	PA	414
003256	Drexel University	PA	415
003258	Duquesne University	PA	415
003259	Eastern University	PA	415
003260	Palmer Theol Sem of Eastern Univ	PA	425
003262	Elizabethtown College	PA	415
003263	Evangelical Theological Seminary	PA	416
003265	Franklin & Marshall College	PA	416
003266	Gannon University	PA	416
003267	Geneva College	PA	417
003268	Gettysburg College	PA	417
003269	Grove City College	PA	417
003270	Gwynedd-Mercy University	PA	417
003272	Harcum College	PA	417
003273	Harrisburg Area Community College	PA	417
003274	Haverford College	PA	418
003275	Holy Family University	PA	418
003276	Immaculata University	PA	418
003277	Indiana University of Pennsylvania	PA	428
003279	Juniata College	PA	419
003280	Keystone College	PA	419
003282	King's College	PA	419
003283	Lackawanna College	PA	420
003284	Lafayette College	PA	420
003285	Lancaster Bible College	PA	421
003286	Lancaster Theological Seminary	PA	421
003287	La Salle University	PA	420
003288	Lebanon Valley College	PA	421
003289	Lehigh University	PA	422
003290	Lincoln University	PA	422
003291	Lutheran Theol Seminary Gettysburg	PA	422
003292	Lutheran Theol Seminary at Phila	PA	422
003293	Lycoming College	PA	422
003294	Manor College	PA	423
003296	Marywood University	PA	423
003297	Mercyhurst University	PA	423
003298	Messiah College	PA	423
003300	Moore College of Art and Design	PA	424
003301	Moravian College	PA	424
003302	Mount Aloysius College	PA	424
003303	Carlow University	PA	412
003304	Muhlenberg College	PA	424
003306	Valley Forge Christian College	PA	436
003309	Peirce College	PA	425
003311	Salus University	PA	433
003313	Widener University	PA	437
003315	Bloomsburg Univ of Pennsylvania	PA	427
003316	California University of PA	PA	428
003317	Cheyney University of Pennsylvania	PA	428
003318	Clarion University of Pennsylvania	PA	428
003320	East Stroudsburg University of PA	PA	428
003321	Edinboro University of Pennsylvania	PA	428
003322	Kutztown University of Pennsylvania	PA	429
003323	Lock Haven University	PA	429
003324	Mansfield University of PA	PA	429
003325	Millersville University of PA	PA	429
003326	Shippensburg University of PA	PA	429
003327	Slippery Rock University of PA	PA	429
003328	West Chester University of PA	PA	430
003329	Penn State University Park	PA	426
003350	The University of the Arts	PA	435
003351	Cairn University	PA	411
003352	Philadelphia Col of Osteopathic Med	PA	430
003353	Univ of Sciences in Philadelphia	PA	435
003354	Philadelphia University	PA	430
003356	Pittsburgh Theological Seminary	PA	431
003357	Point Park University	PA	431
003358	Reformed Presbyterian Theo Seminary	PA	431
003359	Robert Morris University	PA	431
003360	Rosemont College	PA	432
003362	Seton Hill University	PA	433
003364	Saint Charles Borromeo Seminary	PA	432
003366	Saint Francis University	PA	432
003367	Saint Joseph's University	PA	432
003368	Saint Vincent College	PA	432
003369	Susquehanna University	PA	433
003370	Swarthmore College	PA	433
003371	Temple University	PA	433
003376	Thiel College	PA	434
003378	University of Pennsylvania	PA	435
003379	University of Pittsburgh	PA	435
003384	The University of Scranton	PA	436
003385	Ursinus College	PA	436
003386	Valley Forge Military College	PA	436
003388	Villanova University	PA	436
003389	Washington & Jefferson College	PA	436
003391	Waynesburg University	PA	437
003392	Westminster College	PA	437
003393	Westminster Theological Seminary	PA	437
003394	Wilkes University	PA	437
003395	Pennsylvania College of Technology	PA	427
003396	Wilson College	PA	437
003399	York College of Pennsylvania	PA	438
003401	Brown University	RI	438
003402	Bryant University	RI	438
003404	Johnson & Wales University	RI	439
003406	Providence College	RI	439
003407	Rhode Island College	RI	439
003408	Community College of Rhode Island	RI	439
003409	Rhode Island School of Design	RI	440
003410	Roger Williams University	RI	440
003411	Salve Regina University	RI	440
003413	Naval War College	RI	545
003414	University of Rhode Island	RI	440
003417	Allen University	SC	441
003418	Anderson University	SC	441
003419	Charleston Southern University	SC	441
003420	Benedict College	SC	441
003421	Bob Jones University	SC	441
003422	Southern Wesleyan University	SC	446
003423	The Citadel Military College of SC	SC	442
003424	Claflin University	SC	442
003425	Clemson University	SC	442
003426	University of South Carolina Sumter	SC	448
003427	Coker College	SC	442
003428	College of Charleston	SC	443
003429	Columbia International University	SC	443
003430	Columbia College	SC	443
003431	Converse College	SC	443
003432	Erskine College	SC	443
003434	Furman University	SC	444
003435	Lander University	SC	444
003436	Limestone College	SC	444
003437	Lutheran Theol Southern Seminary	SC	445
003438	Medical Univ of South Carolina	SC	445
003439	Morris College	SC	445
003440	Newberry College	SC	445
003441	North Greenville University	SC	445
003445	Presbyterian College	SC	446
003446	South Carolina State University	SC	446
003447	Spartanburg Methodist College	SC	447
003448	Univ of South Carolina-Columbia	SC	447
003449	University of South Carolina Aiken	SC	448
003450	Univ of South Carolina Beaufort	SC	448
003451	Coastal Carolina University	SC	442
003454	Univ of South Carolina Salkehatchie	SC	448
003455	Voorhees College	SC	449
003456	Winthrop University	SC	449
003457	Wofford College	SC	449
003458	Augustana College	SD	449
003459	Black Hills State University	SD	451
003461	Dakota Wesleyan University	SD	450
003463	Dakota State University	SD	451
003465	Mount Marty College	SD	450
003466	Northern State University	SD	451
003467	Presentation College	SD	450
003469	University of Sioux Falls	SD	452
003470	South Dakota Sch of Mines & Tech	SD	452
003471	South Dakota State University	SD	452
003474	The University of South Dakota	SD	451
003477	Aquinas College	TN	452
003478	Austin Peay State University	TN	459
003479	Belmont University	TN	453
003480	Bethel University	TN	453
003481	Carson-Newman University	TN	453
003482	Christian Brothers University	TN	453
003483	Columbia State Community College	TN	460
003484	Covenant College	GA	123
003485	Cumberland University	TN	454
003486	Lipscomb University	TN	456
003487	East Tennessee State University	TN	459
003490	Fisk University	TN	454
003492	Freed-Hardeman University	TN	454
003494	Hiwassee College	TN	454
003495	Johnson University	TN	455
003496	King University	TN	455
003499	Lane College	TN	455
003500	Lee University	TN	455
003501	LeMoyne-Owen College	TN	455
003502	Lincoln Memorial University	TN	456
003504	Martin Methodist College	TN	456
003505	Maryville College	TN	456
003506	Meharry Medical College	TN	456
003507	Memphis College of Art	TN	456
003509	The University of Memphis	TN	460
003510	Middle Tennessee State University	TN	459
003511	Milligan College	TN	457
003517	Southern College of Optometry	TN	458
003518	Southern Adventist University	TN	458
003519	Rhodes College	TN	458
003522	Tennessee State University	TN	459
003523	Tennessee Technological University	TN	460
003524	Tennessee Temple University	TN	462
003525	Tennessee Wesleyan College	TN	462
003526	Trevecca Nazarene University	TN	462
003527	Tusculum College	TN	462
003528	Union University	TN	462
003529	Univ of Tennessee Chattanooga	TN	463
003530	University of Tennessee, Knoxville	TN	463
003531	University of Tennessee at Martin	TN	463
003534	Sewanne:The University of the South	TN	458
003535	Vanderbilt University	TN	463
003536	Bryan College	TN	453
003537	Abilene Christian University	TX	464
003539	Alvin Community College	TX	465
003540	Amarillo College	TX	465
003541	Angelo State University	TX	465
003543	Austin College	TX	466
003544	Austin Presbyterian Theol Seminary	TX	467
003545	Baylor University	TX	467
003546	Coastal Bend College	TX	468
003549	Blinn College	TX	467
003553	Cisco College	TX	468
003554	Clarendon College	TX	468
003556	Commonwealth Inst Funeral Service	TX	469
003557	Concordia University Texas	TX	469
003558	North Central Texas College	TX	477
003560	Dallas Baptist University	TX	470
003561	Cedar Valley College	TX	470
003562	Dallas Theological Seminary	TX	471
003563	Del Mar College	TX	471
003564	East Texas Baptist University	TX	471
003565	Texas A & M University - Commerce	TX	483
003566	Seminary of the Southwest	TX	480
003568	Frank Phillips College	TX	472
003570	Grayson College	TX	472
003571	Hardin-Simmons University	TX	472
003572	Trinity Valley Community College	TX	488
003573	Hill College	TX	473
003574	Howard College	TX	473
003575	Howard Payne University	TX	473
003576	Houston Baptist University	TX	473
003577	Huston-Tillotson University	TX	473
003578	University of the Incarnate Word	TX	490
003579	Jacksonville College	TX	474
003580	Kilgore College	TX	475
003581	Lamar University	TX	486
003582	Laredo Community College	TX	475
003583	Lee College	TX	475
003584	LeTourneau University	TX	475
003586	Lubbock Christian University	TX	476
003588	University of Mary Hardin-Baylor	TX	490
003590	McLennan Community College	TX	476
003591	McMurry University	TX	476
003592	Midwestern State University	TX	476
003593	Navarro College	TX	477
003594	University of North Texas	TX	490
003595	Oblate School of Theology	TX	477
003596	Odessa College	TX	477
003598	Our Lady of the Lake University	TX	477
003599	University of Texas - Pan American	TX	492
003600	Panola College	TX	478
003601	Paris Junior College	TX	478
003602	Paul Quinn College	TX	478
003603	Ranger College	TX	478

003604 .... Rice University .... TX 479
003606 .... Sam Houston State University .... TX 487
003607 .... Alamo Cmty Coll Dist Central Office .... TX 464
003608 .... St. Philip's College .... TX 465
003609 .... San Jacinto College Central .... TX 479
003610 .... Schreiner University .... TX 480
003611 .... South Plains College .... TX 480
003612 .... University of Houston - Downtown .... TX 489
003613 .... Southern Methodist University .... TX 481
003614 .... Southwest Texas Junior College .... TX 481
003615 .... Texas State University-San Marcos .... TX 487
003616 .... Southwestern Assemblies of God Univ .... TX 481
003617 .... Southwestern Baptist Theol Seminary .... TX 481
003618 .... Southwestern Christian College .... TX 481
003619 .... Southwestern Adventist University .... TX 481
003620 .... Southwestern University .... TX 481
003621 .... St. Edward's University .... TX 479
003623 .... St. Mary's University .... TX 479
003624 .... Stephen F. Austin State University .... TX 482
003625 .... Sul Ross State University .... TX 487
003626 .... Tarrant County College District .... TX 482
003627 .... Temple College .... TX 482
003628 .... Texarkana College .... TX 482
003629 .... The Texas A&M Univ System Office .... TX 482
003630 .... Prairie View A & M University .... TX 482
003631 .... Tarleton State University .... TX 483
003632 .... Texas A & M University .... TX 483
003634 .... Texas State Technical College Waco .... TX 486
003635 .... Texas Chiropractic College .... TX 484
003636 .... Texas Christian University .... TX 484
003637 .... Jarvis Christian College .... TX 474
003638 .... Texas College .... TX 485
003639 .... Texas A & M University - Kingsville .... TX 484
003641 .... Texas Lutheran University .... TX 485
003642 .... Texas Southern University .... TX 485
003644 .... Texas Tech University .... TX 487
003645 .... Texas Wesleyan University .... TX 488
003646 .... Texas Woman's University .... TX 488
003647 .... Trinity University .... TX 488
003648 .... Tyler Junior College .... TX 488
003651 .... University of Dallas .... TX 488
003652 .... University of Houston .... TX 489
003654 .... University of St. Thomas .... TX 490
003655 .... Univ of Texas System Administration .... TX 491
003656 .... The Univ of Texas at Arlington .... TX 491
003658 .... University of Texas at Austin .... TX 491
003659 .... University of Texas HSC San Antonio .... TX 493
003661 .... University of Texas at El Paso .... TX 492
003662 .... Victoria College .... TX 493
003663 .... Wayland Baptist University .... TX 494
003664 .... Weatherford College .... TX 494
003665 .... West Texas A & M University .... TX 484
003668 .... Wharton County Junior College .... TX 494
003669 .... Wiley College .... TX 495
003670 .... Brigham Young University .... UT 495
003671 .... Dixie State College of Utah .... UT 497
003672 .... LDS Business College .... UT 495
003674 .... Stevens-Henager College .... UT 496
003675 .... The University of Utah .... UT 496
003677 .... Utah State University .... UT 497
003678 .... Southern Utah University .... UT 497
003679 .... Snow College .... UT 498
003680 .... Weber State University .... UT 497
003681 .... Westminster College .... UT 498
003682 .... Bennington College .... VT 498
003683 .... Castleton State College .... VT 501
003684 .... Champlain College .... VT 499
003685 .... College of St. Joseph .... VT 499
003686 .... Goddard College .... VT 499
003687 .... Green Mountain College .... VT 499
003688 .... Johnson State College .... VT 501
003689 .... Lyndon State College .... VT 501
003690 .... Marlboro College .... VT 499
003691 .... Middlebury College .... VT 499
003692 .... Norwich University .... VT 500
003693 .... Southern Vermont College .... VT 500
003694 .... Saint Michael's College .... VT 500
003696 .... University of Vermont .... VT 500
003697 .... Vermont College of Fine Arts .... VT 500
003698 .... Vermont Technical College .... VT 501
003702 .... Averett University .... VA 502
003703 .... Bluefield College .... VA 502
003704 .... Bridgewater College .... VA 502
003705 .... College of William and Mary .... VA 503
003706 .... Christopher Newport University .... VA 503
003707 .... Richard Bland College .... VA 508
003708 .... Eastern Mennonite University .... VA 504
003709 .... Emory & Henry College .... VA 504
003711 .... Ferrum College .... VA 504
003712 .... Tidewater Community College .... VA 514
003713 .... Hampden-Sydney College .... VA 505
003714 .... Hampton University .... VA 505
003715 .... Hollins University .... VA 505
003719 .... Longwood University .... VA 506
003720 .... Lynchburg College .... VA 506
003721 .... James Madison University .... VA 506
003723 .... Mary Baldwin College .... VA 507
003724 .... Marymount University .... VA 507
003726 .... American National University .... VA 501
003727 .... Northern Virginia Community College .... VA 513
003728 .... Old Dominion University .... VA 507
003731 .... Protestant Episcopal Theol Seminary .... VA 508
003732 .... Radford University .... VA 508
003733 .... Randolph-Macon College .... VA 508
003734 .... Randolph College .... VA 508
003735 .... Virginia Commonwealth University .... VA 511
003736 .... Roanoke College .... VA 509
003737 .... Shenandoah University .... VA 509
003738 .... Southern Virginia University .... VA 509
003742 .... Sweet Briar College .... VA 510
003743 .... Union Presbyterian Seminary .... VA 510
003744 .... University of Richmond .... VA 510
003745 .... University of Virginia .... VA 511
003746 .... University of Mary Washington .... VA 510
003747 .... University of Virginia Col at Wise .... VA 511
003748 .... Eastern Shore Community College .... VA 512
003749 .... George Mason University .... VA 505
003751 .... Patrick Henry Community College .... VA 513
003752 .... Virginia Intermont College .... VA 514
003753 .... Virginia Military Institute .... VA 515
003754 .... Virginia Poly Inst & State Univ .... VA 515
003758 .... Danville Community College .... VA 512
003759 .... J. Sargeant Reynolds Community Col .... VA 512
003760 .... Virginia Western Community College .... VA 514
003761 .... Wytheville Community College .... VA 514
003762 .... Virginia University of Lynchburg .... VA 515
003764 .... Virginia State University .... VA 515
003765 .... Norfolk State University .... VA 507
003766 .... Virginia Union University .... VA 515
003767 .... Virginia Wesleyan College .... VA 515
003768 .... Washington and Lee University .... VA 516
003769 .... Bellevue College .... WA 517
003770 .... Big Bend Community College .... WA 517
003771 .... Central Washington University .... WA 517
003772 .... Centralia College .... WA 517
003773 .... Clark College .... WA 518
003774 .... Columbia Basin College .... WA 518
003775 .... Eastern Washington University .... WA 519
003776 .... Everett Community College .... WA 519
003777 .... Heritage University .... WA 520
003778 .... Gonzaga University .... WA 520
003779 .... Grays Harbor College .... WA 520
003780 .... Green River Community College .... WA 520
003781 .... Highline Community College .... WA 520
003782 .... Lower Columbia College .... WA 521
003783 .... Northwest University .... WA 521
003784 .... Olympic College .... WA 521
003785 .... Pacific Lutheran University .... WA 521
003786 .... Peninsula College .... WA 522
003787 .... Seattle Central Community College .... WA 522
003788 .... Seattle Pacific University .... WA 523
003790 .... Seattle University .... WA 523
003791 .... Shoreline Community College .... WA 523
003792 .... Skagit Valley College .... WA 523
003793 .... Spokane Community College .... WA 518
003794 .... Saint Martin's University .... WA 522
003796 .... Tacoma Community College .... WA 524
003797 .... University of Puget Sound .... WA 524
003798 .... University of Washington .... WA 524
003799 .... Walla Walla University .... WA 524
003800 .... Washington State University .... WA 525
003801 .... Wenatchee Valley College .... WA 525
003802 .... Western Washington University .... WA 525
003803 .... Whitman College .... WA 525
003804 .... Whitworth University .... WA 525
003805 .... Yakima Valley Community College .... WA 525
003806 .... Alderson Broaddus University .... WV 526
003808 .... Bethany College .... WV 526
003809 .... Bluefield State College .... WV 529
003810 .... Concord University .... WV 529
003811 .... Davis & Elkins College .... WV 526
003812 .... Fairmont State University .... WV 529
003813 .... Glenville State College .... WV 529
003815 .... Marshall University .... WV 529
003816 .... So West Virginia Cmty/Tech College .... WV 528
003818 .... University of Charleston .... WV 527
003819 .... Ohio Valley University .... WV 527
003820 .... Salem International University .... WV 527
003822 .... Shepherd University .... WV 529
003823 .... West Liberty University .... WV 530
003826 .... West Virginia State University .... WV 530
003827 .... West Virginia University .... WV 530
003828 .... West Virginia Univ at Parkersburg .... WV 530
003830 .... West Virginia Wesleyan College .... WV 531
003831 .... Wheeling Jesuit University .... WV 531
003832 .... Alverno College .... WI 531
003835 .... Beloit College .... WI 531
003837 .... Cardinal Stritch University .... WI 532
003838 .... Carroll University .... WI 532
003839 .... Carthage College .... WI 532
003840 .... Western Technical College .... WI 541
003842 .... Concordia University Wisconsin .... WI 532
003848 .... Edgewood College .... WI 532
003850 .... Silver Lake College of Holy Family .... WI 536
003854 .... Lakeland College .... WI 533
003856 .... Lawrence University .... WI 533
003861 .... Marian University .... WI 534
003863 .... Marquette University .... WI 534
003866 .... Milwaukee Area Technical College .... WI 540
003868 .... Milwaukee School of Engineering .... WI 534
003869 .... Mount Mary University .... WI 535
003874 .... Nashotah House .... WI 535
003875 .... Northland College .... WI 535
003884 .... Ripon College .... WI 535
003892 .... Saint Norbert College .... WI 535
003894 .... University of Wisconsin System .... WI 536
003895 .... University of Wisconsin-Madison .... WI 536
003896 .... University of Wisconsin-Milwaukee .... WI 537
003897 .... University of Wisconsin Colleges .... WI 538
003899 .... University of Wisconsin-Green Bay .... WI 536
003911 .... Viterbo University .... WI 539
003915 .... University of Wisconsin-Stout .... WI 538
003917 .... University of Wisconsin-Eau Claire .... WI 536
003919 .... University of Wisconsin-La Crosse .... WI 536
003920 .... University of Wisconsin-Oshkosh .... WI 537
003921 .... University of Wisconsin-Platteville .... WI 537
003923 .... University of Wisconsin-River Falls .... WI 537
003924 .... University of Wisconsin-Stevens Pt .... WI 538
003925 .... University of Wisconsin-Superior .... WI 538
003926 .... University of Wisconsin-Whitewater .... WI 538
003928 .... Casper College .... WY 542
003929 .... Eastern Wyoming College .... WY 542
003930 .... North Wyoming Cmty College District .... WY 543
003931 .... Northwest College .... WY 543
003932 .... University of Wyoming .... WY 543
003933 .... Western Wyoming Community College .... WY 543
003935 .... University of Guam .... GU 546
003936 .... Pontifical Catholic Univ of PR .... PR 552
003937 .... University of the Sacred Heart .... PR 555
003938 .... Inter Amer Univ of PR San German .... PR 551
003939 .... Inter Amer Univ of PR Aguadilla .... PR 549
003940 .... Inter Amer Univ of PR Metropolitan .... PR 550
003941 .... Universidad del Este .... PR 552
003942 .... Univ of Puerto Rico-Central Admin .... PR 553
003943 .... University of Puerto Rico-Humacao .... PR 554
003944 .... Univ of Puerto Rico-Mayaguez .... PR 554
003946 .... University of the Virgin Islands .... VI 555
003947 .... Univ of California-Hastings Col Law .... CA 71
003948 .... San Francisco Art Institute .... CA 62
003954 .... University of Central Florida .... FL 115
003955 .... University of West Florida .... FL 117
003956 .... Dalton State College .... GA 123
003961 .... Harper College .... IL 145
003963 .... AIB College of Business .... IA 175
003965 .... Bay State College .... MA 222
003966 .... Boston Architectural College .... MA 223
003969 .... University of Minnesota-Twin Cities .... MN 264
003974 .... Mesivta Tifereth Jerusalem of Amer .... NY 331
003976 .... Rabbin Academy Mesivta Rabbi Berlin .... NY 336
003977 .... Rabbinical College Ch'san Sofer .... NY 337
003978 .... Rabbinical Seminary of America .... NY 337
003979 .... Teachers College, Columbia Univ .... NY 347
003981 .... Univ of NC School of the Arts .... NC 369
003982 .... Cleveland Institute of Art .... OH 377
003985 .... Oral Roberts University .... OK 398
003986 .... DeSales University .... PA 414
003987 .... La Roche College .... PA 420
003988 .... Neumann University .... PA 424
003990 .... Florence-Darlington Tech College .... SC 443
003991 .... Greenville Technical College .... SC 444
003992 .... Piedmont Technical College .... SC 446
003993 .... Midlands Technical College .... SC 445
003994 .... Spartanburg Community College .... SC 447
003995 .... Central Carolina Technical College .... SC 441
003996 .... York Technical College .... SC 449
003998 .... Chattanooga State Community College .... TN 460
003999 .... Cleveland State Community College .... TN 460
004003 .... Central Texas College .... TX 468
004004 .... John Tyler Community College .... VA 512
004007 .... Madison Area Technical College .... WI 540
004027 .... Utah Valley University .... UT 497
004033 .... Asheville-Buncombe Tech Cmty Col .... NC 357
004049 .... Penn Foster College .... AZ 16
004054 .... Hebrew Union Col-Jewish Inst of Rel .... NY 325
004056 .... Sioux Falls Seminary .... SD 451
004057 .... National American University .... SD 450
004058 .... Gratz College .... PA 417
004060 .... Winebrenner Theological Seminary .... OH 393
004061 .... St Mary Seminary & Graduate School .... OH 388
004062 .... Pitt Community College .... NC 362
004069 .... University of Minnesota-Crookston .... MN 264
004071 .... Walsh Col of Accountacy & Bus Admn .... MI 251
004072 .... Northwood University .... MI 248
004075 .... Eastern Iowa Cmty College District .... IA 177
004076 .... Kirkwood Community College .... IA 180
004080 .... Starr King School for the Ministry .... CA 68
004283 .... Grantham University .... MO 274
004431 .... M Lanning Healthcare Sch Radiology .... NE 290
004452 .... Montgomery County Community College .... PA 424
004453 .... El Centro College .... TX 470
004480 .... De Anza College .... CA 44
004481 .... Ohlone College .... CA 57
004484 .... John F. Kennedy University .... CA 49
004490 .... Patten University .... CA 58
004494 .... Everest College-San Bernardino .... CA 43
004503 .... Everest College .... CO 81
004506 .... Colorado Mountain College .... CO 79
004507 .... Everest College .... CO 81
004508 .... Univ of CO Denver/Anschultz Med Cam .... CO 86
004509 .... Univ of Colorado at Colorado Spring .... CO 85
004513 .... Housatonic Community College .... CT 88
004549 .... Univ of Hawaii Leeward Cmty Col .... HI 137
004568 .... Midstate College .... IL 152
004579 .... International Business College .... IN 169
004586 .... Kaplan University .... IA 180
004587 .... Northeast Iowa Community College .... IA 181

Code	Institution	State	Page
004595	Hawkeye Community College	IA	178
004598	Iowa Western Community College	IA	179
004600	Northwest Iowa Community College	IA	181
004608	Barton County Community College	KS	184
004617	Natl College of Business & Tech	TN	457
004618	Spencerian College	KY	199
004619	Sullivan University	KY	199
004625	Delgado Community College	LA	203
004641	Dunwoody College of Technology	MN	255
004642	Globe University	MN	255
004645	Minneapolis Business College	MN	257
004646	Minnesota School of Business	MN	257
004650	Chesapeake College	MD	214
004661	Hampshire College	MA	227
004666	Salter College	MA	236
004667	Sch of the Museum Fine Arts-Boston	MA	236
004673	Baker College of Flint	MI	239
004688	Univ of Mississippi Medical Center	MS	270
004697	San Mateo County CC District Office	CA	64
004703	Logan College of Chiropractic	MO	276
004707	Covenant Theological Seminary	MO	273
004711	Linn State Technical College	MO	276
004713	Three Rivers Community College	MO	282
004729	Mount Washington College	NH	297
004731	Daniel Webster College	NH	296
004736	Bergen Community College	NJ	299
004740	Mercer County Community College	NJ	302
004741	Rutgers State Univ - Camden	NJ	306
004742	Central New Mexico Cmty College	NM	309
004743	Clovis Community College	NM	309
004759	CUNY York College	NY	319
004765	CUNY Graduate Center	NY	317
004776	Central Yeshiva Tomchei Tmimim	NY	316
004788	Herkimer County Community College	NY	326
004798	Mirrer Yeshiva Central Institute	NY	331
004799	Monroe College	NY	331
004804	New York Institute of Technology	NY	333
004811	Everest Institute	NY	324
004835	Caldwell Cmty College & Tech Inst	NC	358
004838	Guilford Technical Community Col	NC	360
004844	Wake Technical Community College	NC	364
004845	Wilson Community College	NC	365
004852	Clark State Community College	OH	377
004853	Bradford School	OH	375
004855	Davis College	OH	378
004861	University of Northwestern Ohio	OH	391
004866	Stautzenberger College	OH	389
004868	Univ of Cincinnati-Blue Ash College	OH	391
004878	Clackamas Community College	OR	402
004882	Oregon Health & Science University	OR	405
004889	Cambria-Rowe Business College	PA	412
004890	Central Penn College	PA	412
004893	DuBois Business College	PA	415
004894	Erie Business Center, Main	PA	416
004898	McCann School of Business & Tech	PA	423
004901	Newport Business Institute	PA	425
004902	Penn Commercial Business/Tech Sch	PA	425
004910	Kaplan Career Institute	PA	419
004914	Newport Business Institute	PA	425
004920	Trident Technical College	SC	447
004923	Clinton College	SC	442
004924	Forrest College	SC	444
004925	Horry-Georgetown Technical College	SC	444
004926	Tri-County Technical College	SC	447
004927	University of South Carolina Union	SC	448
004934	Daymar Institute	TN	454
004937	Jackson State Community College	TN	460
004938	South College	TN	458
004947	West Tennessee Business College	TN	464
004948	Texas A&M System Health Sci Center	TX	484
004949	Baylor College of Medicine	TX	467
004951	University of Texas HSC at Houston	TX	492
004952	The Univ of Texas Medical Branch	TX	493
004972	Galveston College	TX	472
004977	South Texas College of Law	TX	480
004988	Central Virginia Community College	VA	512
004992	Miller-Motte Technical College	VA	507
004996	Dabney S. Lancaster Community Col	VA	512
004999	Bellingham Technical College	WA	517
005000	Pierce College District	WA	522
005001	Edmonds Community College	WA	519
005006	Walla Walla Community College	WA	524
005007	West Virginia Junior College	WV	531
005008	Mountain State College	WV	527
005015	University of Wisconsin-Parkside	WI	537
005019	Univ Adventista de las Antillas	PR	553
005022	Bayamon Central University	PR	547
005026	Inter Amer Univ of PR Arecibo	PR	549
005027	Inter Amer Univ of PR Barranquitas	PR	550
005028	Inter Amer Univ of PR Bayamon	PR	550
005029	Inter Amer Univ of PR Ponce	PR	550
005204	Beal College	ME	209
005208	The College of Westchester	NY	321
005210	Cleveland Institute of Electronics	OH	377
005220	Salt Lake Community College	UT	498
005223	New River Community College	VA	513
005245	Univ of Arkansas Cmty Col/Morrilton	AR	25
005252	Ridgewater College	MN	260
005254	Lanier Technical College	GA	128
005255	Moultrie Technical College	GA	129
005256	Wiregrass Georgia Tech College	GA	134
005257	GA Northwestern Technical College	GA	125
005258	Univ of Hawaii Cmty College	HI	136
005260	J.F. Drake State Technical College	AL	4
005263	Minnesota West Cmty & Tech College	MN	260
005264	Flint Hills Technical College	KS	186
005265	North Central Kansas Tech College	KS	189
005267	Northwest Kansas Technical College	KS	189
005271	Southcentral KY Cmty & Tech Col	KY	196
005273	Gateway Cmty & Technical College	KY	195
005276	Central Maine Community College	ME	210
005277	Eastern Maine Community College	ME	210
005291	White Mountains Community College	NH	296
005294	Waukesha County Technical College	WI	541
005301	NE Wisconsin Technical College	WI	541
005304	Chippewa Valley Technical College	WI	539
005306	Bates Technical College	WA	516
005309	Lake Area Technical Institute	SD	450
005310	Pittsburgh Institute of Aeronautics	PA	430
005313	North Central State College	OH	385
005316	Coastal Carolina Community College	NC	359
005317	Forsyth Technical Community College	NC	360
005318	Catawba Valley Community College	NC	359
005320	Cape Fear Community College	NC	358
005363	Denmark Technical College	SC	443
005372	South Puget Sound Community College	WA	524
005373	Lake Washington Inst of Technology	WA	520
005378	Northeast State Community College	TN	461
005380	Mid-State Technical College	WI	540
005384	Nicolet Area Technical College	WI	540
005387	Northcentral Technical College	WI	541
005389	Gateway Technical College	WI	540
005390	Blackhawk Technical College	WI	539
005447	Randolph Community College	NC	362
005448	Durham Technical Community College	NC	360
005449	Central Carolina Community College	NC	359
005461	Salem Community College	NJ	307
005463	Alamance Community College	NC	357
005464	Richmond Community College	NC	362
005466	So LA Cmty Col T.H. Harris Campus	LA	204
005467	Sowela Technical Community College	LA	204
005480	Centl LA Tech Col Huey P Long Camp	LA	202
005482	South LA Cmty Col Gulf Area Campus	LA	204
005489	Central LA Tech Community College	LA	202
005498	Wichita Area Technical College	KS	191
005499	Salina Area Technical College	KS	190
005500	Manhattan Area Technical College	KS	188
005511	Okefenokee Technical College	GA	130
005525	Southern Maine Community College	ME	211
005526	S Central LA Tech Col Young Mem Cam	LA	203
005528	South LA Cmty Col Teche Area Campus	LA	204
005533	St Paul Col A Cmty & Tech College	MN	261
005534	Saint Cloud Technical & Cmty Coll	MN	261
005535	Pine Technical College	MN	260
005537	South Central College	MN	261
005541	Minnesota State Cmty & Tech College	MN	259
005544	Alexandria Technical & Cmty Col	MN	257
005599	Augusta Technical College	GA	121
005600	Athens Technical College	GA	120
005601	Albany Technical College	GA	120
005615	Southwest Georgia Technical College	GA	132
005617	South Georgia Technical College	GA	131
005618	Savannah Technical College	GA	131
005619	North Georgia Technical College	GA	129
005621	Southern Crescent Technical College	GA	132
005622	Georgia Piedmont Technical College	GA	126
005624	Columbus Technical College	GA	123
005691	Shelton State Community College	AL	6
005692	Reid State Technical College	AL	6
005697	Northwest-Shoals Community College	AL	6
005699	George Wallace St Cmty Col-Selma	AL	4
005707	Southeast Arkansas College	AR	23
005732	Univ of Arkansas CC at Hope	AR	25
005733	Bevill State Community College	AL	2
005734	Trenholm State Technical College	AL	7
005739	Mesabi Range Cmty & Tech College	MN	259
005752	Clover Park Technical College	WA	518
005753	Owens Community College	OH	387
005754	Rowan-Cabarrus Community College	NC	363
005757	Lake Superior College	MN	259
005759	Northwest Technical College	MN	260
005760	Northern Maine Community College	ME	210
005761	L.E. Fletcher Technical Cmty Coll	LA	203
005763	Central Georgia Technical College	GA	122
006165	Los Angeles County Col of Nursing	CA	52
006191	St. Vincent's College	CT	91
006214	Blessing-Rieman College of Nursing	IL	140
006225	Trinity Col Nursing/Hlth Sci	IL	160
006228	Methodist College	IL	152
006240	St Francis Med Ctr Col of Nursing	IL	158
006250	Resurrection University	IL	156
006273	Mercy College of Health Sciences	IA	181
006305	Central ME Med Ctr Col Nur/Hlth Prf	ME	209
006324	Laboure College	MA	227
006385	Chamberlain Col of Nursing-Addison	IL	141
006389	Goldfarb School of Nursing	MO	274
006392	Research College of Nursing	MO	280
006399	Bryan College of Health Sciences	NE	288
006404	Nebraska Methodist College	NE	291
006438	Phillip Beth Israel Sch of Nursing	NY	336
006443	Cochran School of Nursing	NY	320
006445	Crouse Hospital College of Nursing	NY	322
006448	The Belanger School of Nursing	NY	314
006461	St. Elizabeth College of Nursing	NY	338
006467	St. Joseph's College of Nursing	NY	339
006477	Cabarrus College of Health Sciences	NC	352
006487	Aultman College Nursing/Health Sci	OH	374
006489	Christ Col of Nursing & Health Sci	OH	376
006494	Good Samaritan Col Nursing/Hlth Sci	OH	380
006606	Baptist Hlth Sys Sch Hlth Profess	TX	467
006622	Jefferson Col of Health Sciences	VA	506
006639	Bellin College, Inc.	WI	531
006640	Columbia College of Nursing	WI	532
006656	College of DuPage	IL	142
006661	Angelina College	TX	465
006720	College of Alameda	CA	59
006724	KY Community & Technical Col System	KY	194
006731	Casa Loma College-Van Nuys	CA	37
006750	Valencia College	FL	118
006751	Univ of Hawaii Community Colleges	HI	136
006753	Illinois Central College	IL	146
006755	Brown Mackie College-Salina	KS	185
006756	Northshore Technical Community Col	LA	203
006760	University of Maine at Augusta	ME	212
006768	Mid Michigan Community College	MI	247
006771	College for Creative Studies	MI	241
006775	Rainy River Community College	MN	260
006777	Flathead Valley Community College	MT	286
006782	Genesee Community College	NY	325
006785	Schenectady County Cmty College	NY	340
006787	Clinton Community College	NY	320
006788	Tompkins Cortland Community College	NY	347
006789	Columbia-Greene Community College	NY	321
006791	Purchase College, SUNY	NY	344
006799	Craven Community College	NC	359
006804	Lakeland Community College	OH	382
006807	Community College of Beaver County	PA	413
006810	Lehigh Carbon Community College	PA	421
006811	Luzerne County Community College	PA	422
006815	Orangeburg-Calhoun Technical Col	SC	446
006819	Blue Ridge Community College	VA	511
006823	Evangelical Seminary of Puerto Rico	PR	549
006835	Dyersburg State Community College	TN	460
006836	Motlow State Community College	TN	461
006858	Unity College	ME	211
006863	Ventura County Cmty College Dist	CA	74
006865	Camden County College	NJ	300
006867	Columbus State Community College	OH	378
006871	Thomas Nelson Community College	VA	514
006873	Marian Court College	MA	228
006895	University of Nebraska Medical Ctr	NE	292
006901	Gloucester County College	NJ	302
006911	Montgomery College	MD	216
006931	Waubonsee Community College	IL	162
006938	Linn-Benton Community College	OR	404
006941	Dallas Christian College	TX	470
006942	Mid-America Christian University	OK	396
006949	Kalamazoo Valley Community College	MI	244
006951	Univ of South Carolina Upstate	SC	448
006960	Maysville Cmty & Technical College	KY	196
006961	Jefferson Cmty & Tech Col	KY	195
006962	Hazard Community & Technical Coll	KY	195
006964	Rutgers State Univ - New Brunswick	NJ	306
006973	Canada College	CA	64
006975	Lincoln University	CA	51
006977	Great Basin College	NV	294
006982	Naugatuck Valley Community College	CT	89
006991	Rancho Santiago Cmty Col District	CA	60
006994	Kern Community College District	CA	49
007006	Grossmont-Cuyamaca C C District	CA	46
007012	Samuel Merritt University	CA	61
007022	CUNY Herbert H. Lehman College	NY	318
007025	Lebanon College	NH	297
007026	Icahn Sch of Medicine at Mt Sinai	NY	327
007031	Pamlico Community College	NC	362
007032	MidAmerica Nazarene University	KS	188
007035	Kettering College	OH	382
007047	Los Angeles Southwest College	CA	52
007053	DE Tech Cmty College, Owens Campus	DE	93
007085	Mount Vernon Nazarene University	OH	384
007091	Everest Institute	PA	416
007096	College of the Mainland	TX	469
007099	Virginia Highlands Community Col	VA	514
007107	Essex County College	NJ	301
007108	Univ of Puerto Rico-Rio Piedras	PR	555
007109	SUNY College at Old Westbury	NY	343
007110	Delaware County Community College	PA	414
007111	North Country Community College	NY	335
007113	Arizona Christian University	AZ	11
007115	Moorpark College	CA	74
007118	Parkland College	IL	155
007119	Rend Lake College	IL	156
007120	Des Moines Area Community College	IA	177
007121	Faith Baptist Bible Col & Seminary	IA	178
007164	Bryan College	CA	30
007170	Lincoln Land Community College	IL	151
007171	Kirtland Community College	MI	245
007178	Wyo Seminary	OR	408
007190	WyoTech-Fremont	CA	77
007191	Northampton Community College	PA	425
007206	University of Puerto Rico at Cayey	PR	554
007228	Univ of Puerto Rico at Arecibo	PR	553
007234	Heald College, San Francisco	CA	47
007260	Southwest Virginia Community Col	VA	514
007263	Holy Cross College	IN	166
007264	Mesivta Torah Vodaath Seminary	NY	331

007265 .... Carl Sandburg College .... IL 141
007266 .... Pima Community College .... AZ 17
007273 .... Baruch College/CUNY .... NY 316
007275 .... Eastern Gateway CC - Jefferson Co. .... OH 379
007276 .... Saint Meinrad School of Theology .... IN 173
007279 .... Hawaii Pacific University .... HI 135
007283 .... Central Arizona College .... AZ 12
007287 .... Brazosport College .... TX 468
007289 .... Central Wyoming College .... WY 542
007291 .... St. Luke's College .... IA 182
007296 .... Coleman University .... CA 40
007297 .... Redstone College .... CO 84
007304 .... Culinary Institute of America .... NY 322
007316 .... Western Iowa Tech Community College .... IA 183
007329 .... ITT Technical Institute .... IN 169
007350 .... Anoka Technical College .... MN 257
007351 .... Brown College .... MN 254
007358 .... Univ of NE-NE Col of Tech Agricult .... NE 293
007362 .... MedTech College .... IN 171
007375 .... Island Drafting and Technical Inst .... NY 327
007394 .... Berkeley College .... NY 314
007401 .... Mandl School .... NY 329
007405 .... Wood Tobe-Coburn School .... NY 350
007430 .... Antonelli Inst of Art & Photography .... PA 409
007436 .... Kaplan Career Inst - ICM Campus .... PA 419
007437 .... Pittsburgh Technical Institute .... PA 430
007439 .... Fountainhead College of Technology .... TN 454
007440 .... Lincoln Col of Technology Nashville .... TN 455
007459 .... Paier College of Art .... CT 90
007465 .... American Academy of Dramatic Arts .... NY 313
007466 .... LIM College .... NY 328
007468 .... School of Visual Arts .... NY 340
007469 .... Hussian School of Art .... PA 418
007470 .... Art Institute of Pittsburgh .... PA 410
007477 .... Heald College, Rancho Cordova .... CA 47
007481 .... Sanford-Brown College of Boston Inc .... MA 236
007484 .... Newbury College .... MA 235
007486 .... The New England Institute of Art .... MA 235
007491 .... TESST College of Technology .... MD 218
007501 .... Vatterott College-Omaha .... NE 293
007502 .... Berkeley College .... NJ 299
007531 .... Academy of Art University .... CA 26
007532 .... Finger Lakes Community College .... NY 324
007536 .... Cosumnes River College .... CA 53
007540 .... Missouri Baptist University .... MO 278
007544 .... Appalachian Bible College .... WV 526
007547 .... Lincoln College of Technology .... CO 83
007548 .... Westwood College-Denver North .... CO 87
007549 .... Coyne College .... IL 143
007555 .... Lakes Region Community College .... NH 295
007560 .... River Valley Community College .... NH 296
007570 .... Univ of Montana-Helena Col of Tech .... MT 287
007572 .... AMDA Col & Conservatory Perf Arts .... NY 313
007582 .... Aims Community College .... CO 78
007586 .... Remington College-Tampa Campus .... FL 111
007598 .... Hocking College .... OH 380
007602 .... Northeastern Technical College .... SC 446
007606 .... Bryman College-LA Wilshire .... CA 30
007607 .... Concorde Career College .... CA 41
007635 .... Capital Community College .... CT 88
007640 .... Fayetteville Tech Community College .... NC 360
007644 .... Lake Land College .... IL 150
007649 .... Rocky Mountain Col of Art & Design .... CO 85
007669 .... SW Wisconsin Technical College .... WI 541
007678 .... Spartan Col Aeronautics/Technology .... OK 400
007684 .... Kishwaukee College .... IL 149
007686 .... Southern Un at Shreveport-Louisiana .... LA 207
007687 .... James Sprunt Community College .... NC 361
007690 .... Kankakee Community College .... IL 149
007691 .... McHenry County College .... IL 152
007692 .... Moraine Valley Community College .... IL 153
007693 .... Shawnee Community College .... IL 158
007694 .... College of Lake County .... IL 143
007707 .... Columbia College .... CA 77
007713 .... Skyline College .... CA 64
007728 .... Middle Georgia State College .... GA 128
007729 .... County College of Morris .... NJ 300
007730 .... Burlington County College .... NJ 299
007731 .... Raritan Valley Community College .... NJ 305
007738 .... Southern Arkansas University Tech .... AR 23
007759 .... Lincoln Technical Institute .... PA 422
007764 .... Southeast Technical Institute .... SD 452
007777 .... Remington College Cleveland Campus .... OH 388
007779 .... Lansdale School of Business .... PA 421
007780 .... New Castle School of Trades .... PA 425
007781 .... Kaplan Career Inst/Broomall Campus .... PA 419
007783 .... Middle TN School of Anesthesia .... TN 457
007819 .... The Art Institute of Portland .... OR 402
007832 .... Lincoln Technical Institute .... PA 422
007839 .... Triangle Tech, Pittsburgh .... PA 434
007845 .... New England Institute of Technology .... RI 439
007870 .... Hillsborough Community College .... FL 106
007871 .... Wallace State Cmty Coll-Hanceville .... AL 9
007885 .... University of Hawaii System Office .... HI 135
007892 .... Sampson Community College .... NC 363
007893 .... Flagler College .... FL 103
007912 .... Thaddeus Stevens Col of Technology .... PA 434
007930 .... Concorde Career College .... CA 41
007933 .... Front Range Community College .... CO 81
007936 .... Lincoln College of Technology .... MD 215
007938 .... Lincoln College of Technology .... IN 170
007947 .... Beth Medrash Govoha .... NJ 299
007948 .... Wilmington University .... DE 94
007950 .... West Shore Community College .... MI 252
007954 .... Normandale Community College .... MN 260
007959 .... The Univ System of Maryland Office .... MD 219
007985 .... South Piedmont Community College .... NC 363
007986 .... Halifax Community College .... NC 361
007987 .... Bladen Community College .... NC 358
007988 .... Martin Community College .... NC 361
007993 .... California State Univ-Bakersfield .... CA 32
007996 .... Univ of Colorado System Office .... CO 85
008001 .... Univ of Illinois University Admin .... IL 161
008002 .... Indiana University .... IN 167
008004 .... University of Alabama System Office .... AL 8
008005 .... Univ of Alaska System .... AK 10
008008 .... University of Arkansas System Ofc .... AR 23
008012 .... University of Maine System Office .... ME 212
008017 .... Univ of Massachusetts Central Ofc .... MA 228
008025 .... Univ of Nebraska Central Admin .... NE 292
008026 .... Nevada System of Higher Education .... NV 294
008027 .... University System of New Hampshire .... NH 298
008037 .... Gateway Community College .... CT 88
008038 .... Middlesex Community College .... CT 89
008051 .... Univ of Tennessee System Office .... TN 463
008067 .... LSU Health Sci Ctr Shreveport .... LA 205
008068 .... State Univ Sys FL, Bd of Governors .... FL 114
008071 .... Concorde Career College .... CA 41
008073 .... Butte College .... CA 30
008074 .... DE Tech & Cmty College Ofc of Pres .... DE 93
008075 .... St. John Vianney College Seminary .... FL 112
008076 .... John A. Logan College .... IL 148
008078 .... Springfield Technical Community Col .... MA 233
008080 .... State Fair Community College .... MO 282
008081 .... Carteret Community College .... NC 358
008082 .... Cleveland Community College .... NC 359
008083 .... Haywood Community College .... NC 361
008085 .... McDowell Tech Community College .... NC 362
008087 .... Montgomery Community College .... NC 362
008093 .... Heald College, Fresno .... CA 46
008133 .... Zane State College .... OH 394
008145 .... Nashville State Community College .... TN 461
008146 .... Everest Univ-Pompano Beach Campus .... FL 102
008155 .... The Evergreen State College .... WA 519
008175 .... Howard Community College .... MD 215
008221 .... Universal Technical Institute .... AZ 18
008223 .... St. Vincent De Paul Reg Seminary .... FL 112
008228 .... Seward County Cmty Col/Area Tech Sc .... KS 190
008237 .... Southern Illinois University .... IL 159
008242 .... Inter Amer Univ of PR Central Ofc .... PR 549
008244 .... Johnson County Community College .... KS 187
008246 .... Dine College .... AZ 13
008278 .... Terra State Community College .... OH 389
008284 .... Mitchell Technical Institute .... SD 450
008290 .... University System of Georgia Office .... GA 134
008303 .... Gateway Community College .... AZ 14
008304 .... Scottsdale Community College .... AZ 15
008308 .... Cecil College .... MD 214
008310 .... Auburn University at Montgomery .... AL 2
008317 .... Central LA Tech Col Avoyelles Camp .... LA 202
008350 .... Art Institute of Philadelphia .... PA 410
008353 .... Lincoln College of Technology .... TX 475
008403 .... Indian Hills Community College .... IA 179
008404 .... Brookdale Community College .... NJ 299
008425 .... Daymar College-Paducah .... KY 193
008466 .... Southwestern Community College .... NC 364
008492 .... Alegent Hlth Sch of Radiologic Tech .... NE 288
008495 .... Jamestown Business College .... NY 327
008503 .... Mountain View College .... TX 471
008504 .... Richland College .... TX 471
008510 .... Eastfield College .... TX 470
008537 .... Concorde Career College .... CA 41
008543 .... Atlanta Technical College .... GA 121
008545 .... Rockford Career College .... IL 157
008546 .... Ivy Tech Cmty Coll of IN-Cnt Office .... IN 169
008552 .... Stevens Inst of Bus & Arts .... MO 282
008557 .... Nash Community College .... NC 362
008558 .... Beaufort County Community College .... NC 358
008568 .... Vet Tech Institute .... PA 436
008596 .... West Los Angeles College .... CA 52
008597 .... Feather River College .... CA 44
008609 .... Rabbinical College of America .... NJ 304
008611 .... Hostos Cmty College-CUNY .... NY 318
008612 .... Robeson Community College .... NC 363
008613 .... Roanoke-Chowan Community College .... NC 363
008614 .... Rab Col Bobover Yesh B'nei Zion .... NY 337
008617 .... Rabbinical Seminary M'kor Chaim .... NY 337
008635 .... IntelliTec Medical Institute .... CO 82
008659 .... Lord Fairfax Community College .... VA 512
008660 .... Germanna Community College .... VA 512
008661 .... Southside Virginia Community Col .... VA 513
008677 .... Northwest State Community College .... OH 385
008694 .... Rasmussen College - St. Cloud .... MN 263
008711 .... Coast Cmty College Dist Admin Ofc .... CA 39
008788 .... SUNY System Office .... NY 341
008843 .... Alaska Bible College .... AK 10
008844 .... California Christian College .... CA 30
008846 .... The Wright Institute .... CA 77
008848 .... Warner University .... FL 119
008849 .... Palm Beach Atlantic University .... FL 110
008855 .... Edgecombe Community College .... NC 360
008859 .... John A. Gupton College .... TN 455
008860 .... SIT .... VT 500
008862 .... East Central College .... MO 273
008863 .... Walters State Community College .... TN 462
008871 .... Concorde Career College .... CO 81
008878 .... Miami Int'l Univ of Art & Design .... FL 109
008880 .... Morrison Institute of Technology .... IL 153
008887 .... Concorde Career College .... OR 402
008895 .... San Diego CC Dist Admin Offices .... CA 62
008896 .... Pikes Peak Community College .... CO 84
008902 .... Columbia Centro Universitario .... PR 548
008903 .... College of the Canyons .... CA 40
008904 .... Virginia Cmty College System Office .... VA 511
008906 .... Macomb Community College .... MI 246
008916 .... New England Law | Boston .... MA 235
008918 .... Saddleback College .... CA 67
008976 .... Clayton State University .... GA 123
008988 .... Lurleen B. Wallace Cmty College .... AL 5
009010 .... Madisonville Community College .... KY 196
009016 .... Univ of So Florida St. Petersburg .... FL 116
009020 .... Foothill-De Anza Cmty Coll District .... CA 44
009032 .... Empire College School of Business .... CA 43
009043 .... Elmira Business Institute .... NY 323
009047 .... Huntington Junior College .... WV 526
009054 .... WV Northern Community College .... WV 528
009058 .... Bethel University .... MN 253
009077 .... USC The Business College .... NY 349
009079 .... Everest College .... OR 403
009082 .... International Business College .... TX 474
009089 .... Hannibal-La Grange University .... MO 274
009135 .... Illinois Eastern CC System Office .... IL 146
009137 .... Metro CC-Kansas City Admin Ctr .... MO 277
009139 .... Metropolitan Cmty Col-Maple Woods .... MO 277
009140 .... Metropolitan Community Col-Longview .... MO 277
009145 .... Governors State University .... IL 145
009146 .... Yosemite Community College District .... CA 77
009157 .... WyoTech .... WY 544
009159 .... Paul D. Camp Community College .... VA 513
009160 .... Rappahannock Community College .... VA 513
009163 .... San Antonio College .... TX 465
009185 .... Rose State College .... OK 399
009186 .... Dean Institute of Technology .... PA 414
009190 .... Oregon University System .... OR 405
009192 .... Sierra Nevada College .... NV 295
009193 .... Reformed Theological Seminary .... MS 269
009194 .... Lakeshore Technical College .... WI 540
009225 .... Texas State Tech College Harlingen .... TX 485
009226 .... Francis Marion University .... SC 444
009230 .... Wayne County Community College Dist .... MI 252
009231 .... Washington County Community College .... ME 211
009232 .... Catholic Theological Union .... IL 141
009236 .... Nashua Community College .... NH 296
009248 .... Samaritan Hospital Sch of Nursing .... NY 340
009256 .... Moraine Park Technical College .... WI 540
009259 .... Laramie County Community College .... WY 543
009267 .... Everest College .... VA 504
009270 .... The Art Institute of Atlanta .... GA 120
009272 .... Crafton Hills College .... CA 61
009275 .... Northern Kentucky University .... KY 198
009313 .... Daymar College-Owensboro .... KY 193
009314 .... Great Falls Col Montana State Univ .... MT 287
009322 .... Williamsburg Technical College .... SC 449
009331 .... Dallas County Cmty Coll Dist Office .... TX 470
009333 .... Univ of Illinois at Springfield .... IL 161
009335 .... Mestiva Eastern Pkwy Rabbinical Sem .... NY 331
009336 .... Johnston Community College .... NC 361
009339 .... Utah System of Higher Education .... UT 496
009344 .... Ramapo College of New Jersey .... NJ 305
009345 .... The Richard Stockton College of NJ .... NJ 305
009346 .... Minnesota State Coll & Univ Sys Ofc .... MN 257
009354 .... Sanford College of Nursing .... ND 372
009387 .... Perry Technical Institute .... WA 522
009401 .... Colorado Christian University .... CO 79
009407 .... Lincoln College of New England .... CT 90
009412 .... Fortis College .... OH 379
009420 .... Sanford-Brown College-Tysons Corner .... VA 509
009430 .... Tri-County Community College .... NC 364
009449 .... Pennco Tech .... PA 426
009454 .... Griggs University .... MI 243
009466 .... Kaplan College .... TX 475
009479 .... St Paul's Sch of Nurs-Staten Island .... NY 339
009507 .... Georgia Highlands College .... GA 125
009542 .... Community College of Denver .... CO 81
009543 .... Red Rocks Community College .... CO 84
009544 .... Spokane Falls Community College .... WA 518
009549 .... Western Texas College .... TX 494
009618 .... Tulsa Welding School .... OK 400
009621 .... Herzing University .... WI 533
009629 .... Mountain Empire Community College .... VA 513
009635 .... Florida International University .... FL 115
009637 .... Southern Univ & A&M Col Sys Ofc .... LA 206
009642 .... Texas State Tech College System .... TX 485
009645 .... Bard College at Simon's Rock .... MA 222
009646 .... Piedmont Community College .... NC 362
009647 .... Oklahoma State Univ - Oklahoma City .... OK 398
009651 .... Texas A&M International University .... TX 483
009652 .... University of Puerto Rico at Ponce .... PR 555
009684 .... Blue Ridge Community College .... NC 358
009704 .... North Seattle Community College .... WA 522
009706 .... South Seattle Community College .... WA 523
009707 .... Bluegrass Cmty & Tech Col .... KY 194
009721 .... Bradford School .... PA 410
009740 .... Inver Hills Community College .... MN 258
009741 .... The University of Texas at Dallas .... TX 491
009742 .... North Orange Cty Cmty Col District .... CA 56

Code	Institution	State	Page
009743	Bellevue University	NE	288
009744	Fox Valley Technical College	WI	539
009747	Gordon-Conwell Theological Seminary	MA	227
009748	Carrington College CA-Sacramento	CA	36
009756	Univ of Massachusetts Worcester	MA	229
009763	Tulsa Community College	OK	400
009764	Tunxis Community College	CT	89
009765	Three Rivers Community College	CT	89
009767	City Cols of Chicago Olive-Harvey	IL	142
009768	University of North Texas H.S.C.	TX	490
009769	Metropolitan College of New York	NY	331
009777	Kaplan College	IN	170
009782	Saint Luke's College of Health Sci	MO	281
009786	Illinois Eastern CC Lincoln Trail	IL	147
009795	Missouri College	MO	278
009797	Midland College	TX	476
009800	Rush University	IL	157
009826	Kennebec Valley Community College	ME	210
009841	University of North Florida	FL	116
009862	Clarkson College	NE	288
009863	Lancaster Genl Col Nursing/Hlth Sci	PA	421
009892	Duluth Business University, Inc.	MN	255
009896	Oakton Community College	IL	155
009903	Vance-Granville Community College	NC	364
009910	Technical College of the Lowcountry	SC	447
009912	Volunteer State Community College	TN	461
009914	Roane State Community College	TN	461
009917	Ivy Tech Cmty Col-Central Indiana	IN	169
009928	Piedmont Virginia Community College	VA	513
009929	SUNY College of Optometry	NY	345
009930	Univ of Texas of the Permian Basin	TX	493
009932	Texas State Technical Col W. Texas	TX	486
009936	Middlesex Community College	MA	232
009941	Belmont College	OH	374
009942	Shawnee State University	OH	388
009962	Luna Community College	NM	309
009975	NW LA Tech Col Northwest Campus	LA	203
009976	College of the Ouachitas	AR	20
009981	Morgan Community College	CO	83
009982	Victory University	TN	463
009986	Seton Hall University School of Law	NJ	307
009987	Saint Anthony College of Nursing	IL	158
009989	Santa Barbara Business College	CA	64
009992	Oak Hills Christian College	MN	263
009994	Passaic County Community College	NJ	304
010010	American Samoa Community College	AS	546
010014	Garrett College	MD	214
010017	Payne Theological Seminary	OH	388
010019	University Texas SW Medical Center	TX	493
010020	Lewis and Clark Community College	IL	150
010027	James A. Rhodes State College	OH	381
010043	Bon Secours Memorial Col of Nursing	VA	502
010051	La Guardia Community College/CUNY	NY	318
010056	Aiken Technical College	SC	440
010060	Vernon College	TX	493
010074	St Patrick's Seminary & University	CA	61
010097	CUNY Medgar Evers College	NY	319
010098	Neumont University	UT	496
010106	Seattle Community Colleges	WA	522
010111	Cerro Coso Community College	CA	49
010115	University of Texas at San Antonio	TX	492
010130	Wade College Infomart	TX	494
010142	Touro College	NY	348
010148	Colorado Technical University	CO	81
010149	Pepperdine University	CA	58
010153	Helene Fuld College of Nursing	NY	325
010170	Western Dakota Technical Institute	SD	452
010176	Westmoreland County Community Col	PA	437
010182	Rogue Community College	OR	407
010195	Art Institute of Fort Lauderdale	FL	98
010198	ECPI College of Technology	VA	504
010248	The Art Institutes International MN	MN	253
010256	Benedictine College	KS	184
010264	South College-Asheville	NC	366
010266	Hillsdale Free Will Baptist College	OK	395
010279	Hickey College	MO	275
010286	SUNY Empire State College	NY	346
010316	Lincoln College of Technology	IL	151
010338	Eastern Virginia Medical School	VA	504
010340	Los Medanos College	CA	42
010343	College of Micronesia-FSM	FM	546
010345	Cincinnati State Tech & Cmty Col	OH	376
010356	Everest Institute	WV	526
010362	College of Southern Nevada	NV	294
010363	Western Nevada College	NV	295
010364	Whatcom Community College	WA	525
010365	Charles Drew Univ of Med & Science	CA	38
010374	Metropolitan State University	MN	259
010378	Rabbinical College of Long Island	NY	337
010387	El Paso Community College	TX	472
010388	Reading Area Community College	PA	431
010391	Oklahoma City Community College	OK	397
010395	University of San Diego	CA	73
010402	Dakota County Technical College	MN	258
010405	Pinnacle Career Institute	MO	280
010410	TESST College of Technology	MD	218
010434	Renton Technical College	WA	522
010438	Haskell Indian Nations University	KS	187
010439	Southwest Tennessee Community Coll	TN	461
010441	Pardee RAND Grad Sch of Policy Stds	CA	58
010453	Washington State Community College	OH	392
010460	American Baptist College	TN	452
010474	Marymount California University	CA	53
010487	West Georgia Technical College	GA	134
010489	National College	IN	171
010491	Hennepin Technical College	MN	258
010501	Lakeview College of Nursing	IL	150
010503	Wichita Technical Institute	KS	191
010509	Hallmark College of Technology	TX	472
010529	Memphis Theological Seminary	TN	457
010530	Quinebaug Valley Community College	CT	89
010546	Century College	MN	258
010549	Kehilath Yakov Rabbinical Seminary	NY	328
010554	Concordia College Alabama	AL	3
010567	Colegio Universitario de San Juan	PR	548
010573	West Virginia Junior College	WV	531
010618	Mid-America College of Funeral Svc	IN	171
010633	Houston Community College	TX	473
010652	Pasco-Hernando Community College	FL	110
010674	Texas Tech University Health Sci Ct	TX	487
010684	Erie Community College City Campus	NY	323
010687	The Ohio State University AT Inst	OH	386
010724	Carlos Albizu University	PR	547
010727	DeVry University - Chicago Campus	IL	144
010736	Marion Technical College	OH	383
010761	Dallas Institute of Funeral Service	TX	471
010771	Gupton Jones Coll of Funeral Svc	GA	127
010784	Cmty Colleges of Spokane Dist 17	WA	518
010805	University of Cincinnati-Clermont	OH	391
010813	Amer Acad McAllister Inst Funeral	NY	313
010814	Pittsburgh Inst of Mortuary Science	PA	430
010818	The University of Akron-Wayne Col	OH	390
010819	Conservatory of Music Puerto Rico	PR	548
010854	Thomas Jefferson School of Law	CA	69
010861	West Virginia Business College	WV	527
010879	Richland Community College	IL	156
010880	Chatfield College	OH	376
010881	Stark State College	OH	389
010906	Cincinnati Col of Mortuary Science	OH	376
010913	Madison Media Inst-Col Media Arts	WI	533
010923	Union Institute & University	OH	390
010943	Rabbinical College Beth Shraga	NY	336
010975	Univ of Puerto Rico at Bayamon	PR	554
010997	East Georgia State College	GA	124
010998	Pennsylvania Institute of Tech	PA	427
011009	Palau Community College	PW	547
011031	Technical Career Institutes	NY	347
011046	Central Ohio Technical College	OH	376
011074	Bainbridge College	GA	121
011107	Everest College-Anaheim	CA	43
011109	Everest College-Reseda	CA	43
011112	Fashion Inst Design & Merchandising	CA	44
011113	Maharishi University of Management	IA	180
011117	Alliant International Univ-SanDiego	CA	26
011123	Everest College-Gardena	CA	43
011127	Bay Medical Center	FL	99
011133	Eastern Idaho Technical College	ID	138
011145	Lone Star College System	TX	476
011150	Asnuntuck Community College	CT	88
011161	Texas A&M University-Corpus Christi	TX	483
011163	University of Texas at Tyler	TX	492
011165	Uintah Basin Applied Tech Coll	UT	496
011166	Broadview University	UT	495
011167	Community College of Vermont	VT	501
011189	United Talmudical Seminary	NY	349
011192	Beth Hamedrash Shaarei Yosher Inst	NY	315
011194	Stanly Community College	NC	364
011197	Mayland Community College	NC	361
011210	Bunker Hill Community College	MA	231
011220	Univ of Hawaii Windward Cmty Col	HI	137
011245	West Virginia School of Osteo Med	WV	530
011385	College of the Atlantic	ME	210
011460	National University	CA	55
011462	University of Alaska Anchorage	AK	10
011572	Colorado School of Trades	CO	80
011574	Bauder College	GA	121
011626	Westwood College-South Bay	CA	76
011644	Univ of Maryland University College	MD	219
011647	SBI Campus-Affil of Sanford-Brown	NY	340
011649	Loyola Marymount University	CA	53
011667	Northeast Community College	NE	291
011670	Yeshiva of Nitra Rabbinical College	NY	351
011672	Mendocino College	CA	54
011673	Maine College of Art	ME	210
011678	SUNY Inst of Tech at Utica-Rome	NY	346
011689	The Refrigeration School	AZ	17
011711	University of Houston - Clear Lake	TX	489
011719	Universidad Del Turabo	PR	552
011721	University of Houston System	TX	489
011727	DE Tech Cmty College, Terry Campus	DE	93
011732	Mayo Medical School	MN	254
011745	Ohio Technical College	OH	387
011792	Franciscan School of Theology	CA	45
011810	Taylor Business Institute	IL	160
011820	San Diego Miramar College	CA	62
011821	Yeshivath Zichron Moshe	NY	352
011824	Wisconsin Indianhead Tech College	WI	541
011862	Northland Pioneer College	AZ	16
011864	Mohave Community College	AZ	15
011922	Beth Hatalmud Rabbinical College	NY	315
011930	Roxbury Community College	MA	232
011934	Vermont Law School	VT	500
011940	ICPR Junior College	PR	549
011941	American University of Puerto Rico	PR	547
011950	Corcoran College of Art and Design	DC	95
011984	Ohr Hameir Theological Seminary	NY	335
011989	Talmudical Academy of New Jersey	NJ	307
012011	Talmudical Seminary Oholei Torah	NY	347
012015	Austin Community College District	TX	466
012031	San Diego Christian College	CA	62
012050	Rosedale Technical Institute	PA	432
012059	Trinity Bible College	ND	373
012064	Hamilton Technical College	IA	178
012088	Sullivan Col of Technology & Design	KY	199
012105	National Park Community College	AR	22
012107	Institute of Design & Construction	NY	327
012123	University of Puerto Rico-Aguadilla	PR	553
012154	California Inst of Integral Studies	CA	31
012165	Atlanta Metropolitan State College	GA	121
012182	Chattahoochee Valley Community Coll	AL	2
012183	Burlington College	VT	498
012203	Memorial Hospital School of Nursing	NY	330
012260	East Arkansas Community College	AR	21
012261	North Arkansas College	AR	22
012277	New York Chiropractic College	NY	333
012300	Palmer College of Chiropractic	IA	182
012309	University of Western States	OR	408
012315	Cornish College of the Arts	WA	518
012328	Northwestern Health Sciences Univ	MN	263
012358	Plaza College	NY	336
012362	Northwestern College	IL	155
012364	St. Paul's School of Nursing	NY	339
012393	Thomas Jefferson University	PA	434
012452	Evergreen Valley College	CA	63
012500	Ranken Technical College	MO	280
012523	Talmudical Yeshiva of Philadelphia	PA	433
012525	Caribbean University	PR	547
012547	Emmanuel Christian Seminary	TN	454
012550	Los Angeles Mission College	CA	52
012561	Five Towns College	NY	324
012574	Ringling College of Art and Design	FL	111
012580	Saint Louis Christian College	MO	280
012584	The Illinois Institute of Art	IL	147
012586	Metropolitan Community College	NE	290
012627	Thomas M. Cooley Law School	MI	250
012670	Bel-Rea Inst of Animal Technology	CO	78
012693	Pellissippi State Community College	TN	461
012744	Southside Reg Med Ctr Prof Schs	VA	509
012750	Edison State Community College	OH	379
012803	PFIC at Dominican House of Studies	DC	96
012813	John Wood Community College	IL	148
012842	Oxnard College	CA	74
012860	Arkansas Northeastern College	AR	19
012870	Southern State Community College	OH	389
012873	WyoTech-Long Beach	CA	77
012877	Sanford-Brown Col-Farmington	CT	91
012891	Antonelli College	OH	373
012896	Virginia Marti Col of Art & Design	OH	392
012907	Lake Tahoe Community College	CA	50
012912	MTI College	CA	55
012954	Hudson County Community College	NJ	302
012976	Nebraska Christian College	NE	290
013007	Nazarene Bible College	CO	83
013022	City University of Seattle	WA	517
013026	Machzikei Hadath Rabbinical College	NY	329
013027	Yeshivath Viznitz	NY	352
013029	Boricua College	NY	315
013039	South University	GA	131
013103	California Western School of Law	CA	36
013132	International Col of Broadcasting	OH	381
013134	Yeshiva Beth Moshe	PA	438
013208	Baptist Bible College	MO	271
013231	University of Houston - Victoria	TX	489
013263	South Hills School of Bus & Tech	PA	433
014659	Oglala Lakota College	SD	450
015361	Guam Community College	GU	546
020503	Academy College	MN	253
020520	Kaplan College	OH	382
020522	Black River Technical College	AR	20
020530	Liberty University	VA	506
020537	Eastwick College	NJ	301
020543	Trumbull Business College	OH	390
020552	Harrington College of Design	IL	146
020554	Bossier Parish Community College	LA	202
020555	Delta Sch of Business & Technology	LA	201
020568	Daymar College-Chillicothe	OH	378
020603	MIAT College of Technology	MI	246
020609	Brown College of Court Reporting	GA	122
020630	Montserrat College of Art	MA	234
020635	Coastline Community College	CA	39
020637	Sherman College of Chiropractic	SC	446
020653	Prescott College	AZ	17
020662	The New School	NY	332
020681	Adler School of Prof Psychology	IL	139
020682	Cox College	MO	273
020683	Douglas Education Center	PA	415
020690	New York School of Interior Design	NY	334
020693	Vatterott College-Quincy	IL	162
020705	Concordia University	CA	41
020712	Kaplan College	AZ	14
020732	Telshe Yeshiva-Chicago	IL	160
020735	Univ of Arkansas CC at Batesville	AR	25
020739	Wor-Wic Community College	MD	221
020744	Illinois Eastern CC Frontier CC	IL	146
020746	South Arkansas Community College	AR	23
020748	Life University	GA	128

020753 .... Pulaski Technical College .... AR 22
020757 .... Briarcliffe College .... NY 315
020758 .... Southern Calif Inst of Architecture .... CA 67
020771 .... Milwaukee Institute of Art & Design .... WI 534
020774 .... North Lake College .... TX 471
020780 .... Sacred Heart School of Theology .... WI 535
020789 .... The Art Institute of Colorado .... CO 78
020798 .... Heald College, Concord .... CA 46
020814 .... Arlington Baptist College .... TX 466
020836 .... TESST College of Technology .... MD 218
020839 .... Northern New Mexico College .... NM 311
020870 .... Ozarka College .... AR 22
020876 .... Concordia Theological Seminary .... IN 165
020896 .... Concorde Career Institute .... FL 100
020902 .... Triangle Tech, Erie .... PA 434
020907 .... Cleveland University - Kansas City .... KS 185
020917 .... Kaplan College .... CA 49
020925 .... Laurel Technical Institute .... PA 421
020936 .... Southwest Institute of Technology .... TX 481
020937 .... Long Island Business Institute .... NY 329
020961 .... Fielding Graduate University .... CA 44
020979 .... Univ NH School of Law .... NH 298
020983 .... Western Technical College .... TX 494
020988 .... University of Phoenix .... AZ 18
020992 .... American Conservatory Theater .... CA 27
020995 .... Central Community College .... NE 288
021000 .... Universidad Politecnica De PR .... PR 553
021002 .... Brookhaven College .... TX 470
021006 .... Carrington College - Phoenix .... AZ 12
021049 .... Sumner College .... OR 408
021064 .... O'More College of Design .... TN 457
021067 .... Trinity Lutheran College .... WA 524
021068 .... Bramson O R T College .... NY 315
021073 .... Pennsylvania Academy of Fine Arts .... PA 426
021077 .... Truckee Meadows Community College .... NV 294
021078 .... University of Hawaii - West Oahu .... HI 136
021102 .... Columbia College Hollywood .... CA 41
021108 .... California College San Diego .... CA 31
021111 .... Rich Mountain Community College .... AR 23
021113 .... Cuyamaca College .... CA 46
021122 .... Great Lakes Institute of Technology .... PA 417
021136 .... American InterContinental Univ .... IL 139
021142 .... Johnson College .... PA 419
021160 .... Sanford-Brown College .... GA 131
021163 .... Pueblo Community College .... CO 84
021171 .... The Art Institute of Houston .... TX 466
021175 .... Naropa University .... CO 83
021191 .... Mission College .... CA 75
021192 .... Court Reporting Institute of Dallas .... TX 469
021206 .... Saybrook University .... CA 65
021207 .... San Joaquin Valley Col Inc-Visalia .... CA 63
021208 .... Yorktowne Business Institute .... PA 438
021211 .... Midwest Institute .... MO 277
021218 .... Everest Institute .... FL 102
021274 .... YTI Career Institute .... PA 438
021279 .... Sojourner-Douglass College .... MD 218
021286 .... The Art Institute of Cincinnati .... OH 374
021290 .... Triangle Tech, Greensburg .... PA 434
021366 .... Wisconsin Lutheran College .... WI 539
021383 .... Palo Alto University .... CA 58
021400 .... Riverside School of Health Careers .... VA 509
021404 .... St. Joseph School of Nursing .... NH 297
021408 .... Martin University .... IN 171
021415 .... Savannah College of Art and Design .... GA 131
021434 .... Salish Kootenai College .... MT 288
021435 .... Sterling College .... VT 500
021437 .... Sinte Gleska University .... SD 451
021446 .... Kilian Community College .... SD 450
021448 .... Vet Tech Institute of Houston .... TX 493
021449 .... DE Tech Cmty Col, Stanton-Wilmingtn .... DE 93
021464 .... Institute of American Indian Arts .... NM 309
021466 .... South Mountain Community College .... AZ 15
021519 .... Keiser University .... FL 108
021520 .... Yeshiva Shaar HaTorah-Grodno .... NY 351
021535 .... Oakbridge Academy of Arts .... PA 425
021553 .... Chicago Sch Prof Psych-LA Campus .... CA 38
021571 .... Concorde Career College .... TN 453
021584 .... Harrison College-Indianapolis Dwntn .... IN 166
021585 .... Ohio Business College Lorain Branch .... OH 385
021596 .... The Baptist College of Florida .... FL 98
021597 .... New Hope Christian College .... OR 405
021603 .... Internatl Academy of Design & Tech .... IL 148
021610 .... Uniformed Svcs Univ of Health Sci .... MD 545
021618 .... Musicians Institute .... CA 55
021633 .... Universidad Central Del Caribe .... PR 553
021634 .... New York Career Institute .... NY 333
021636 .... Massachusetts School of Prof Psyc .... MA 233
021642 .... Sch of Prof Psych at Forest Inst .... MO 281
021651 .... EDP University of Puerto Rico .... PR 548
021660 .... Ctr Advanced Studies PR & Caribbean .... PR 548
021661 .... Nunez Community College .... LA 203
021662 .... ITI Technical College .... LA 202
021686 .... East-West University .... IL 144
021691 .... Davis College .... NY 322
021700 .... Swedish Inst College of Health Sci .... NY 347
021706 .... United States Sports Academy .... AL 8
021707 .... Brunswick Community College .... NC 358
021715 .... Western International University .... AZ 19
021727 .... Condorde Career Institute .... FL 100
021744 .... Triangle Tech, Dubois .... PA 434
021758 .... Centra College of Nursing .... VA 503
021775 .... Rio Salado College .... AZ 15
021785 .... Eagle Gate College .... UT 495
021799 .... Argosy University, Orange County .... CA 28
021800 .... Northwest Indian College .... WA 521
021802 .... Metro Business College .... MO 276
021829 .... Cambridge College .... MA 224
021830 .... Orleans Technical Institute .... PA 425
021854 .... St. Augustine College .... IL 158
021882 .... Sitting Bull College .... ND 372
021883 .... Pentecostal Theological Seminary .... TN 458
021887 .... Prince Institute-Rocky Mountains .... CO 84
021889 .... Hobe Sound Bible College .... FL 106
021891 .... Centro de Estuds Multidiciplinarios .... PR 548
021907 .... Fortis College .... OH 379
021916 .... Torah Temimah Talmudical Seminary .... NY 348
021922 .... Thomas Edison State College .... NJ 308
021928 .... Restaurant School/Walnut Hill Col .... PA 431
021975 .... Baton Rouge School of Computers .... LA 201
021989 .... Michigan Sch Professnl Psychology .... MI 246
021997 .... Heritage Christian University .... AL 4
021999 .... American Indian Col of Assem of God .... AZ 11
022018 .... Kaplan College .... IN 170
022023 .... Sanford-Brown Institute-Pittsburgh .... PA 433
022027 .... Ozark Christian College .... MO 279
022039 .... Erie Institute of Technology .... PA 416
022042 .... Chattanooga College .... TN 453
022052 .... Sanford-Brown College .... MO 281
022061 .... Independence University .... UT 495
022148 .... South LA Cmty College Ardoin Campus .... LA 203
022171 .... Pima Medical Institute-Tucson .... AZ 17
022178 .... Hopfer Sch of Nurs-Mt Vernon Hosp .... NY 323
022180 .... Carrington College - Boise .... ID 137
022187 .... Florida Technical College .... FL 105
022188 .... Brookline College .... AZ 12
022195 .... Mildred Elley .... NY 331
022202 .... Le Cordon Bleu Col of Culinary Arts .... CA 50
022205 .... God's Bible School and College .... OH 380
022209 .... Cossatot Cmty Coll Univ of Arkansas .... AR 24
022220 .... Amer Film Institute Conservatory .... CA 27
022260 .... East Los Angeles College .... CA 51
022285 .... Life Chiropractic College West .... CA 50
022316 .... MGH Institute of Health Professions .... MA 234
022340 .... Cameron College .... LA 201
022342 .... Keystone Technical Institute .... PA 419
022345 .... Boise Bible College .... ID 137
022365 .... Cankdeska Cikana Community College .... ND 370
022372 .... Phillips Graduate Institute .... CA 59
022375 .... Everest College .... NV 293
022392 .... Anthem College .... MO 271
022402 .... So LA Cmty Col Charles Coreil Camp .... LA 204
022418 .... American Career College-Los Angeles .... CA 27
022425 .... Bastyr University .... WA 516
022427 .... Berkeley City College .... CA 59
022429 .... United Tribes Technical College .... ND 373
022449 .... Goodwin College .... CT 90
022455 .... Fortis College .... FL 105
022506 .... Everest College .... MO 274
022537 .... IntelliTec College .... CO 82
022539 .... Berks Technical Institute .... PA 410
022540 .... New England Culinary Institute .... VT 499
022552 .... Pennsylvania School of Business .... PA 427
022594 .... Amberton University .... TX 465
022606 .... National University College .... PR 551
022608 .... Huertas Junior College .... PR 549
022624 .... Yeshiva Ohr Elchonon Chabad .... CA 77
022631 .... Anthem College .... AZ 11
022651 .... Yeshiva Derech Chaim .... NY 350
022664 .... Central Christian College of Bible .... MO 272
022676 .... Sofia University .... CA 66
022699 .... Pennsylvania Col of Art & Design .... PA 427
022704 .... Southeastern Bible College .... AL 7
022706 .... Life Pacific College .... CA 50
022713 .... Wisc Sch of Professional Psychology .... WI 539
022734 .... Reconstructionist Rabbinical Col .... PA 431
022743 .... Conway School of Landscape Design .... MA 225
022751 .... Concorde Career Institute .... FL 100
022768 .... Westminster Theological Seminary .... CA 76
022769 .... Community College of Aurora .... CO 81
022773 .... Sisseton-Wahpeton College .... SD 451
022774 .... South Coast College .... CA 66
022781 .... Santa Fe Community College .... NM 311
022788 .... Southwest Florida College .... FL 114
022795 .... Oconee Fall Line Tech Col-South .... GA 129
022808 .... Lincoln College of Technology .... FL 108
022809 .... Mid-Atlantic Christian University .... NC 357
022827 .... Inter Amer Univ of PR Guayama .... PR 550
022828 .... Inter Amer Univ of PR Fajardo .... PR 550
022843 .... Interactive College of Technology .... GA 127
022866 .... Little Big Horn College .... MT 286
022884 .... Gwinnett Technical College .... GA 127
022895 .... Pace Institute .... PA 425
022896 .... Consolidated School of Business .... PA 414
022898 .... Kaplan Career Institute .... PA 419
022913 .... The Art Institute of Seattle .... WA 516
022950 .... Everest College Phoenix .... AZ 13
022960 .... Prince Institute - Southeast .... AL 6
022980 .... Design Institute of San Diego .... CA 42
022985 .... Everest College .... UT 495
022993 .... Trinity Episcopal School Ministry .... PA 434
023001 .... Everest College .... WA 519
023011 .... Turtle Mountain Community College .... ND 373
023013 .... Prism Career Inst-Upr Darby Campus .... PA 431
023014 .... Ohio Valley College of Technology .... OH 387
023040 .... Missouri Tech .... MO 278
023043 .... Platt College .... CA 59
023044 .... YTI Career Institute-Capital Region .... PA 438
023053 .... Parker University .... TX 478
023057 .... Fortis College .... FL 105
023058 .... Florida Career College .... FL 103
023063 .... Kaplan College .... CA 49
023065 .... Professional Business College .... NY 336
023068 .... Platt College .... OK 398
023108 .... Lancaster County Career & Tech Ctr .... PA 421
023122 .... Texas School of Business .... TX 485
023139 .... Westwood College-O'Hare Airport .... IL 163
023141 .... Schiller International University .... FL 113
023154 .... Northeast Texas Community College .... TX 477
023172 .... Maranatha Baptist Bible Col & Sem .... WI 533
023182 .... KD Studio-Actors Conservatory .... TX 475
023192 .... Lake Forest Graduate School of Mgmt .... IL 150
023201 .... Ohr Somayach Tanenbaum Educ Ctr .... NY 335
023202 .... Houston Graduate School of Theology .... TX 473
023230 .... Biblical Theological Seminary .... PA 410
023251 .... Key College .... FL 108
023262 .... Kaplan Career Institute .... TN 455
023263 .... Fortis Institute .... TN 454
023265 .... Interface College .... WA 520
023268 .... Meridian College .... FL 109
023289 .... Emmaus Bible College .... IA 178
023301 .... Pioneer Pacific College .... OR 407
023305 .... Laguna College of Art & Design .... CA 50
023312 .... Baptist Missionary Assn Theol Sem .... TX 467
023344 .... Centura College .... VA 503
023355 .... Universidad Teologica Del Caribe .... PR 553
023377 .... Professional Skills Institute .... OH 388
023405 .... St Louis Col Hlth Careers-S Taylor .... MO 281
023406 .... Humacao Community College .... PR 549
023410 .... Fortis College .... AL 3
023413 .... Palo Alto College .... TX 465
023427 .... Fortis College .... VA 505
023430 .... Fort Peck Community College .... MT 286
023462 .... WyoTech .... FL 119
023465 .... Ogden-Weber Applied Tech College .... UT 496
023471 .... New England Sch of Communications .... ME 211
023482 .... Mid-South Community College .... AR 21
023485 .... Lamar State College-Port Arthur .... TX 486
023506 .... Yeshiva and Kollel Harbotzas Torah .... NY 351
023519 .... Kaplan College .... CA 49
023522 .... Le Cordon Bleu Col of Culinary Arts .... IL 150
023576 .... Navajo Technical College .... NM 310
023580 .... Thomas Aquinas College .... CA 69
023582 .... Lamar State College-Orange .... TX 486
023593 .... Shasta Bible Col & Graduate School .... CA 65
023608 .... Provo College .... UT 496
023613 .... The Landing School .... ME 210
023614 .... Collin County Cmty College District .... TX 469
023616 .... Concorde Career College .... MO 272
023621 .... Full Sail University .... FL 106
023628 .... Austin Graduate School of Theology .... TX 466
023638 .... Yeshiva Beth Yehuda .... MI 253
024535 .... Medical College of Wisconsin .... WI 534
024544 .... Northeast Ohio Medical University .... OH 385
024600 .... Univ of Puerto Rico-Medical Sci .... PR 554
024821 .... Morehouse School of Medicine .... GA 129
024824 .... Ponce Sch Medicine & Hlth Sciences .... PR 552
024827 .... Western Univ of Health Sciences .... CA 76
024911 .... Beckfield College .... KY 192
024915 .... Southwest University of Visual Arts .... AZ 17
025000 .... San Joaquin College of Law .... CA 63
025034 .... Amridge University .... AL 1
025039 .... Warren County Community College .... NJ 308
025042 .... Walden University .... MN 265
025054 .... Atlantic University College .... PR 547
025058 .... Yesh Karlin Stolin Beth Aaron Inst .... NY 351
025059 .... Sh'or Yoshuv Rabbinical College .... NY 340
025061 .... City University of New York .... NY 316
025068 .... Yeshiva Mikdash Melech .... NY 351
025083 .... Southeast Community College .... NE 292
025086 .... Central Georgia Technical College .... GA 122
025089 .... Talmudic College of Florida .... FL 117
025106 .... Blackfeet Community College .... MT 285
025110 .... SW Indian Polytechnic Institute .... NM 312
025154 .... City College .... FL 100
025162 .... Wesley Biblical Seminary .... MS 270
025175 .... Aaniiih Nakoda College .... MT 285
025184 .... The National Hispanic University .... CA 55
025203 .... Interior Designers Institute .... CA 48
025228 .... Fox College .... IL 145
025256 .... The Art Institute of New York City .... NY 314
025276 .... Lexington College .... IL 151
025306 .... St. Charles Community College .... MO 280
025322 .... Lac Courte Oreilles Ojibwa Cmty Col .... WI 533
025326 .... Landmark College .... VT 499
025332 .... Frank Lloyd Wright School of Arch .... AZ 13
025340 .... National Col of Natural Medicine .... OR 404
025349 .... Ponce Paramedical College .... PR 551
025356 .... Clear Creek Baptist Bible College .... KY 193
025366 .... Commonwealth Technical Inst at HGAC .... PA 413
025383 .... Delta College of Arts & Technology .... LA 201
025395 .... Irvine Valley College .... CA 67
025408 .... Globe Institute of Technology .... NY 325
025410 .... Alaska Career College .... AK 10
025412 .... Stratford University .... VA 510
025452 .... Chief Dull Knife College .... MT 285
025460 .... Tri-State College of Acupuncture .... NY 348

025462 .... Laurel Business Institute .... PA 421
025463 .... Yeshiva of the Telshe Alumni .... NY 351
025476 .... Florida National University Hialeah .... FL 105
025490 .... Kaplan College .... CA 49
025506 .... Talmudic Institute Upstate New York .... NY 347
025508 .... Nebraska Indian Community College .... NE 290
025530 .... School of Advertising Art .... OH 388
025537 .... Ft. Berthold Community College .... ND 371
025554 .... University of Texas MD Anderson .... TX 493
025578 .... The Art Institute of York - PA .... PA 410
025590 .... University of Advancing Technology .... AZ 18
025593 .... United Education Institute .... CA 70
025602 .... Phillips Theological Seminary .... OK 398
025688 .... Sussex County Community College .... NJ 307
025693 .... Le Cordon Bleu Col of Culinary Arts .... TX 475
025694 .... Escuela de Artes Plasticas de PR .... PR 548
025703 .... Los Angeles ORT College .... CA 52
025720 .... Vista College .... TX 494
025728 .... Vista College .... UT 498
025729 .... Business Informatics Center, Inc. .... NY 316
025737 .... Institute for Clinical Social Work .... IL 148
025762 .... Mid-Continent University .... KY 197
025769 .... Charter College .... AK 10
025779 .... Santa Barbara Business College .... CA 64
025780 .... Santa Barbara Business College .... CA 64
025782 .... Nossi College of Art .... TN 457
025784 .... Maryland Univ of Integrative Health .... MD 216
025798 .... New England School of Acupuncture .... MA 235
025829 .... Kaplan Career Institute .... OH 381
025830 .... Gwinnett College .... GA 127
025875 .... Universidad Metropolitana .... PR 552
025889 .... Medtech College .... VA 507
025909 .... Wright Career College .... KS 191
025911 .... Career Point College .... TX 468
025919 .... Kaplan College .... TX 474
025929 .... Heald College, Hayward .... CA 46
025931 .... Heald College, Roseville .... CA 47
025932 .... Heald College, Milpitas .... CA 47
025933 .... Heald College, Stockton .... CA 47
025943 .... CollegeAmerica Denver .... CO 78
025971 .... Heritage Institute-Fort Myers .... FL 106
025973 .... South Baylo University .... CA 66
025982 .... University of Southernmost Florida .... FL 118
025994 .... New York Coll of Health Professions .... NY 333
025997 .... Vatterott College-NorthPark .... MO 284
025998 .... Everest University-Largo .... FL 102
026001 .... New York Academy of Art .... NY 333
026021 .... Northwest College of Art & Design .... WA 521
026037 .... Oregon College of Oriental Medicine .... OR 405
026047 .... Center for Advanced Legal Studies .... TX 468
026055 .... Remington College, Mobile Campus .... AL 6
026068 .... Career Technical College .... LA 201
026090 .... Emperor's Coll of Trad Oriental Med .... CA 43
026092 .... Vatterott College-Des Moines .... IA 183
026094 .... Valley College - Martinsburg Campus .... WV 527
026095 .... Career Training Academy .... PA 412
026109 .... Stone Child College .... MT 288
026110 .... Heritage College .... CO 82
026130 .... Pinnacle Career Institute .... KS 189
026142 .... Miller-Motte Technical College .... TN 457
026150 .... Sanford-Brown College .... TX 480
026158 .... College of Court Reporting, Inc. .... IN 165
026164 .... Sanford-Brown Institute .... FL 112
026167 .... Le Cordon Bleu Col Cul Arts Scottsd .... AZ 14
026215 .... Career College of Northern Nevada .... NV 293
026220 .... Southwest Acupuncture College .... NM 312
026227 .... Knowledge Systems Institute .... IL 149
026236 .... Paradise Valley Community College .... AZ 15
029031 .... Tennessee Board of Regents Office .... TN 459
029042 .... San Jose/Evergreen Cmty Col Dist .... CA 63
029072 .... Montana University System Office .... MT 286
029078 .... Sistema Universitario Ana G. Mendez .... PR 552
029120 .... Beth Benjamin Academy of CT .... CT 87
029137 .... San Jacinto College District .... TX 479
029139 .... West Valley-Mission C C District .... CA 75
029162 .... Vermont State College System Office .... VT 501
029171 .... Charter Oak State College .... CT 87
029172 .... Mid-America Baptist Theol Seminary .... TN 457
029283 .... Massachusetts Board of Higher Educ .... MA 228
029371 .... PA State Sys Higher Ed Off of Chanc .... PA 427
029384 .... University of Puerto Rico at Utuado .... PR 555
030001 .... Yeshiva Gedolah Imrei Yosef .... NY 350
030012 .... McNally Smith College of Music .... MN 256
030018 .... Welch College .... TN 464
030021 .... Kentucky Mountain Bible College .... KY 196
030025 .... J.F. Ingram State Technical College .... AL 4
030026 .... Central LA Tech Col Oakdale Campus .... LA 202
030032 .... Everest Institute .... FL 102
030063 .... Inst of Business & Medical Careers .... CO 82
030070 .... Frontier Nursing University .... KY 194
030073 .... Oregon College of Art and Craft .... OR 405
030079 .... Gallipolis Career College .... OH 380
030086 .... Florida College of Natural Health .... FL 104
030106 .... Virginia College .... AL 3
030108 .... Fortis Institute .... PA 416
030113 .... California State Univ-San Marcos .... CA 35
030115 .... Fortis Institute .... PA 416
030116 .... Fortis Institute .... PA 416
030121 .... Remington College-Colorado Springs .... CO 85
030149 .... Platt College .... CO 84
030160 .... Univ of Puerto Rico-Carolina .... PR 554
030219 .... EDIC College .... PR 548
030224 .... College of the Marshall Islands .... MH 546
030226 .... Le Cordon Bleu Col Cul Arts Prtlnd .... OR 403
030255 .... Mech-Tech College .... PR 551
030256 .... Dell'Arte Intl Sch Phys Theatre .... CA 42
030265 .... Remington College .... TX 478
030277 .... Pacific Col of Oriental Medicine .... CA 57
030282 .... Trinity College of Florida .... FL 117
030290 .... Chattahoochee Technical College .... GA 122
030297 .... Universal Technology College of PR .... PR 553
030299 .... Consolidated School of Business .... PA 413
030300 .... Ogeechee Technical College .... GA 129
030314 .... Internatl Academy of Design & Tech .... FL 107
030321 .... Altamaha Technical College .... GA 120
030330 .... Northern Marianas College .... MP 547
030340 .... Heald College, Salinas .... CA 47
030345 .... Owensboro Cmty & Technical College .... KY 196
030357 .... Las Positas College .... CA 37
030358 .... Heritage Institute-Jacksonville .... FL 106
030375 .... Hodges University .... FL 106
030399 .... Fremont College .... CA 45
030426 .... Everest College-City of Industry .... CA 43
030430 .... United States Naval Academy .... MD 545
030431 .... Thomas More College of Liberal Arts .... NH 298
030432 .... Kaplan College .... NV 294
030439 .... NewSchool of Arch & Design .... CA 56
030519 .... Adler Graduate School .... MN 253
030542 .... Fortis College .... FL 105
030612 .... Midwest Col of Oriental Medicine .... WI 534
030627 .... Platt College .... CA 59
030633 .... NW Arkansas Community College .... AR 22
030646 .... Univ of TX Brownsville/TX Southmost .... TX 491
030662 .... Bryan University .... KS 185
030663 .... Bryan University .... MO 271
030665 .... Southeastern Technical College .... GA 132
030666 .... Bay Mills Community College .... MI 240
030669 .... IntelliTec College .... CO 82
030675 .... Institute of Technology .... CA 48
030691 .... Allen College .... IA 175
030695 .... Sage College .... CA 61
030709 .... SE MO Hosp Coll Nurs & Health Sci .... MO 282
030716 .... College of Business and Technology .... FL 100
030718 .... ITT Technical Institute .... WA 520
030719 .... Mount Carmel College of Nursing .... OH 384
030722 .... Chandler-Gilbert Community College .... AZ 14
030725 .... World Medicine Institute .... HI 137
030727 .... Westwood College-Los Angeles Campus .... CA 76
030737 .... The Paralegal Institute .... AZ 16
030761 .... Southwestern College .... NM 312
030763 .... Beulah Heights University .... GA 121
030764 .... The Bryman School .... AZ 12
030775 .... Rabbi Jacob Joseph School .... NJ 304
030782 .... Amer College Trad Chinese Medicine .... CA 27
030790 .... ETI Technical College of Niles .... OH 379
030791 .... North Central Institute .... TN 457
030792 .... Westwood College-DuPage .... IL 163
030794 .... Lyme Academy College of Fine Arts .... CT 90
030799 .... City College .... FL 99
030819 .... YTI Career Institute .... PA 438
030830 .... Ozarks Technical Community College .... MO 279
030837 .... Galen College of Nursing .... KY 194
030838 .... Heartland Community College .... IL 146
030844 .... Valley College - Beckley Campus .... WV 527
030888 .... Watkins College of Art & Design .... TN 464
030893 .... Heritage Bible College .... NC 355
030908 .... Lake Erie College of Osteo Medicine .... PA 420
030913 .... Regent University .... VA 508
030926 .... Messenger College .... TX 476
030927 .... Skyline College .... VA 509
030955 .... ASA Inst of Bus & Computer Tech .... NY 314
030964 .... Leech Lake Tribal College .... MN 256
030970 .... Mercy College of Ohio .... OH 383
030980 .... St. John's College .... IL 158
030982 .... Yo San Univ of Trad Chinese Med .... CA 77
031004 .... Coconino Community College .... AZ 13
031007 .... Carroll Community College .... MD 214
031009 .... Luther Rice University .... GA 128
031013 .... Granite State College .... NH 298
031015 .... Bidwell Training Center .... PA 410
031019 .... Trinity Baptist College .... FL 117
031033 .... JNA Institute of Culinary Arts .... PA 419
031034 .... South Texas College .... TX 480
031042 .... Carolinas Col of Health Sciences .... NC 353
031060 .... Missouri State Univ-West Plains .... MO 278
031062 .... Our Lady of the Lake College .... LA 206
031065 .... Sentara College of Health Sciences .... VA 509
031070 .... SW Col of Naturopathic Med/Hlth Sci .... AZ 17
031085 .... Everglades University .... FL 103
031090 .... Living Arts Col @ Sch of Commun Art .... NC 356
031091 .... MCC Computer Technology Institute .... PA 423
031095 .... Dongguk University .... CA 42
031108 .... Bakke Graduate University .... WA 516
031121 .... John Dewey College .... PR 551
031136 .... Southern Calif Institute of Tech .... CA 67
031147 .... The Praxis Institute .... FL 111
031150 .... Arizona College .... AZ 11
031151 .... Heritage College .... OK 395
031155 .... Adventist University of Health Sci .... FL 97
031158 .... Kaplan College .... TX 475
031163 .... Ohio College of Massotherapy .... OH 386
031166 .... E San Gabriel Vly Reg Occ Pgm Tech .... CA 43
031169 .... Baptist Theol Seminary Richmond .... VA 502
031203 .... CollegeAmerica-Flagstaff .... AZ 13
031226 .... Eastern International College .... NJ 301
031229 .... York County Community College .... ME 211
031239 .... Southeastern College .... FL 113
031251 .... College of Menominee Nation .... WI 532
031256 .... Miami Ad School .... FL 109
031264 .... Centura College .... VA 503
031268 .... Pacifica Graduate Institute .... CA 57
031271 .... Yeshivas Novominsk .... NY 351
031275 .... Advanced Technology Institute .... VA 501
031281 .... The Col of Health Care Professions .... TX 469
031287 .... Mount Sierra College .... CA 55
031291 .... Fond du Lac Tribal & Cmty College .... MN 258
031292 .... Rabbinical College Ohr Shimon Yisr .... NY 337
031305 .... Urban College of Boston .... MA 237
031313 .... Five Brn Univ Grad Sch Trad Chn Med .... CA 44
031473 .... Yeshiva D'Monsey Rabbinical College .... NY 350
031533 .... Amer Col Acupuncture & Oriental Med .... TX 465
031555 .... Oconee Fall Line Tech Col-North .... GA 129
031563 .... Estrella Mountain Community College .... AZ 14
031564 .... AOMA Grad Sch Integrative Medicine .... TX 466
031576 .... Colegio de Ciencias Artes y Televis .... PR 548
031633 .... Pacific States University .... CA 57
031643 .... Creative Center .... NE 289
031703 .... Texas A & M University - Texarkana .... TX 484
031713 .... Univ of St Augustine for Health Sci .... FL 118
031733 .... Atlanta's John Marshall Law School .... GA 121
031773 .... San Juan Bautista Sch of Medicine .... PR 552
031795 .... Texas Health and Science University .... TX 485
031804 .... Pennsylvania Highlands Cmty Col .... PA 427
031823 .... New Hampshire Institute of Art .... NH 297
031893 .... National Defense University .... DC 544
031894 .... The Col of Saints J Fisher & T More .... TX 469
031943 .... Boston Grad Sch of Psychoanalysis .... MA 224
031983 .... Universidad Pentecostal Mizpa .... PR 553
031993 .... Christian Life College .... IL 141
032063 .... Mesalands Community College .... NM 309
032103 .... Le Cordon Bleu Col of Culinary Arts .... CA 50
032163 .... Unification Theological Seminary .... NY 348
032183 .... University of the Potomac .... DC 97
032253 .... American Univ of Health Sciences .... CA 28
032353 .... MA School of Law at Andover .... MA 233
032383 .... Florida College of Integrative Med .... FL 104
032423 .... CNI College .... CA 39
032483 .... Boston Baptist College .... MA 223
032503 .... CBD College .... CA 37
032553 .... Florida Gulf Coast University .... FL 115
032563 .... Yeshiva Gedolah Rabbinical College .... FL 119
032603 .... California State Univ-Monterey Bay .... CA 34
032613 .... Metropolitan Cmty Col-Blue River .... MO 277
032643 .... South Florida Bible College .... FL 113
032663 .... Bethesda University of California .... CA 29
032673 .... Capella University .... MN 254
032723 .... Kaplan College .... TX 474
032783 .... Charter College-Canyon Country .... CA 38
032793 .... Myotherapy Institute .... NE 290
032803 .... Seattle Inst of Oriental Medicine .... WA 523
032843 .... Michigan Jewish Institute .... MI 246
032883 .... Academy of Chinese Culture & Health .... CA 26
032893 .... Colorado Heights University .... CO 79
032943 .... Blue Cliff College .... LA 201
032993 .... Pacific College .... CA 57
033083 .... Bristol University .... CA 29
033104 .... Rabbi Isaac Elchanan Theol Seminary .... NY 336
033164 .... FINE Mortuary College .... MA 226
033173 .... The American College .... PA 409
033213 .... The Scripps Research Institute .... CA 65
033233 .... Little Priest Tribal College .... NE 290
033274 .... Acupnct & Integrat Med Col-Berkeley .... CA 26
033323 .... Southern California Seminary .... CA 67
033394 .... Western Governors University .... UT 498
033433 .... South Orange County Cmty Col Dist .... CA 67
033434 .... North Dakota Univ System Office .... ND 371
033436 .... Iowa Valley Cmty College District .... IA 179
033437 .... Colorado State Univ System Office .... CO 80
033438 .... SD State Board of Regents Sys Ofc .... SD 451
033440 .... WV Higher Educ Policy Commission .... WV 529
033441 .... Nebraska State College System .... NE 291
033442 .... The Texas State University System .... TX 486
033443 .... Board of Regents, State of Iowa .... IA 175
033444 .... University of Louisiana System Ofc .... LA 207
033445 .... NC Community College System .... NC 357
033463 .... Acad for Nurs & Health Occupations .... FL 97
033473 .... International Baptist College .... AZ 14
033484 .... Professional Training Center .... FL 111
033554 .... Richmont Graduate University .... TN 458
033673 .... Professional Golfers Career College .... CA 60
033674 .... Community Care College .... OK 395
033723 .... Northwest Vista College .... TX 464
033733 .... Beacon College .... FL 99
033743 .... Florida Coastal School of Law .... FL 103
033903 .... Lincoln Tech Fern Park Orlando Camp .... FL 108
033965 .... Texas State Tech Coll Marshall .... TX 486
033993 .... Bryan College .... CA 30
034003 .... Quest College .... TX 478
034033 .... Epic Bible College .... CA 43
034095 .... Chester Career College .... VA 503
034145 .... Acupuncture & Massage College .... FL 97
034165 .... Dallas Nursing Institute .... TX 471
034194 .... Northeastern Seminary .... NY 335
034224 .... College of Biblical Studies-Houston .... TX 468
034225 .... Blue Cliff College .... LA 201
034226 .... Blue Cliff College .... LA 201

FICE	Institution	State	Page
034253	Rosedale Bible College	OH	388
034254	Central Florida Institute	FL	99
034263	The Col of Health Care Professions	TX	469
034275	University of Antelope Valley	CA	70
034283	Klamath Community College	OR	403
034296	Atlantic Inst of Oriental Medicine	FL	98
034297	East West College of Natural Med	FL	101
034343	Fortis College	FL	105
034383	Pacific Islands University	GU	546
034403	Baptist College of Health Sciences	TN	453
034433	New York Coll of Trad Chinese Med	NY	333
034555	National Labor College	MD	217
034563	Cld Sprg Hrbr Lab/Watson Sc Bio Sci	NY	320
034567	Crossroads Bible College	IN	165
034573	Allegheny Wesleyan College	OH	373
034613	Ilisagvik College	AK	10
034633	UT Col Dental Hygiene Careers Unltd	UT	496
034664	The Seattle Sch of Theology & Psych	WA	523
034684	National Institute of Massotherapy	OH	385
034754	Tri-State Bible College	OH	389
034784	Phoenix Seminary	AZ	16
034803	Fortis College	LA	202
034835	Cascadia Community College	WA	517
034963	Yeshiva Shaarei Torah of Rockland	NY	351
035043	National Grad Sch of Quality Mgmt	MA	234
035103	Erikson Institute	IL	145
035134	Apex School of Theology	NC	352
035135	Williamson Christian College	TN	464
035163	The King's University	CA	50
035243	Academy Five Element Acupuncture	FL	97
035253	Blue Cliff College	MS	266
035283	Midwest University	MO	277
035324	Advanced Training Associates	CA	26
035343	Jones International University	CO	82
035344	American Inst Alternative Medicine	OH	373
035393	American Public University System	WV	526
035423	Concorde Career Institute	TX	469
035424	Copper Mountain College	CA	42
035443	Atenas College	PR	547
035453	University of the Rockies	CO	86
035493	Ultimate Medical Acad-Clearwater	FL	118
035533	Southeastern College	FL	113
035593	Appalachian School of Law	VA	502
035703	Carolina Christian College	NC	353
035705	Northpoint Bible College	MA	235
035793	Texas County Technical College	MO	282
035844	Colorado School of Healing Arts	CO	80
035924	City of Hope	CA	39
035933	Southwest Institute of Healing Arts	AZ	17
036115	Southern Evangelical Seminary	NC	366
036175	Phoenix Inst of Herbal Med/Acup	AZ	16
036183	Institute of Technical Arts	FL	107
036273	Lamar Institute of Technology	TX	486
036353	Carver College	GA	122
036393	West Coast Ultrasound Institute	CA	75
036543	Career Training Solutions	VA	502
036633	Hood Theological Seminary	NC	355
036653	Christendom College	VA	503
036654	Christie's Education, Inc.	NY	316
036663	Pillar College	NJ	304
036683	Birthingway College of Midwifery	OR	402
036763	Family of Faith College	OK	395
036863	Colorado Sch of Trad Chinese Med	CO	80
036894	Faith Evangelical Col & Seminary	WA	519
036914	Ave Maria School of Law	FL	98
036954	The Salvation Army Ofr Trng Crestmt	CA	61
036955	Arizona Sch of Acup/Oriental Med	AZ	11
036957	Santiago Canyon College	CA	60
036963	University of the West	CA	74
036964	Saber College	FL	112
036983	West Coast University	CA	75
037093	Edward Via Col of Osteo Med	VA	504
037133	Beis Medrash Heichal Dovid	NY	314
037233	Culinary Institute LeNotre	TX	470
037243	DigiPen Institute of Technology	WA	519
037263	Ohio Mid-Western College	OH	386
037303	Baton Rouge Community College	LA	202
037333	Baptist University of the Americas	TX	467
037353	Inst Clin Acupuncture/Oriental Med	HI	135
037384	SS. Cyril and Methodius Seminary	MI	250
037473	Bexley Seabury	OH	374
037524	SUM Bible Col & Theol Seminary	CA	69
037563	Anamarc College	TX	465
037603	Hawaii Tokai International College	HI	135
037723	Saginaw Chippewa Tribal College	MI	249
037844	Tohono O'odham Community College	AZ	18
037863	Advanced College	CA	26
037894	River Parishes Community College	LA	203
038023	U.T.A. Mesivta of Kiryas Joel	NY	349
038044	Medtech College	GA	128
038103	Silicon Valley University	CA	66
038133	Northcentral University	AZ	16
038144	Soka University of America	CA	66
038214	Universal College of Healing Arts	NE	292
038224	Maple Springs Baptist Bible College	MD	216
038273	New Life Theological Seminary	NC	357
038303	SAE Inst of Technology Nashville	TN	458
038323	Dade Medical College	FL	100
038333	American Acad Acupunct/Oriental Med	MN	253
038383	Nightingale College	UT	496
038385	Northwest Career College	NV	295
038403	Oxford Graduate School	TN	458
038513	Graduate Inst Applied Linguistics	TX	472
038533	Keck Graduate Institute	CA	39
038553	Ecclesia College	AR	21
038564	W.L. Bonner College	SC	449
038626	Virginia Baptist College	VA	511
038683	World Mission University	CA	77
038684	LAMA	CA	50
038713	Folsom Lake College	CA	53
038724	Institute Psychological Sciences	VA	505
038725	Northland International University	WI	535
038743	Cambridge Junior College	CA	36
038744	Community Christian College	CA	41
038813	Union Graduate College	NY	348
038834	Aviation Institute of Maintenance	VA	502
038883	Dragon Rises Col of Oriental Med	FL	101
038893	Stanbridge College	CA	68
038943	Huntsville Bible College	AL	4
038993	Calvary Baptist Theol Seminary	PA	412
039035	Southern Technical College	FL	114
039193	St Tikhon's Orthodox Theol Seminary	PA	432
039214	White Earth Tribal/Community Col	MN	265
039324	Gutenberg College	OR	403
039373	Yeshiva Col of the Nation's Capital	MD	221
039393	Wolford College	FL	119
039394	Centura College	FL	99
039395	Carolina Graduate Sch of Divinity	NC	353
039396	Daytona College	FL	101
039413	Ave Maria University	FL	98
039454	Logos Evangelical Seminary	CA	51
039463	Franklin W. Olin Col of Engineering	MA	226
039483	Harrisburg Univ Science/Technology	PA	418
039493	Won Institute of Graduate Studies	PA	438
039513	Patrick Henry College	VA	508
039563	South Louisiana Community College	LA	203
039573	Blue Ridge Cmty & Technical College	WV	527
039603	New River Community/Technical Col	WV	528
039653	New England Col Business & Finance	MA	234
039663	Central Baptist Theol Seminary	VA	503
039713	American Career College-Ontario	CA	27
039733	Expression College for Digital Arts	CA	44
039803	California State U-Channel Islands	CA	32
039823	Visible Music College	TN	464
039863	Aviator Col of Aeronaut Sci & Tech	FL	98
039893	Mid-America Reformed Seminary	IN	171
039923	Knox Theological Seminary	FL	108
039953	University of East-West Medicine	CA	72
039994	Hawaii College of Oriental Medicine	HI	135
040024	Ecumenical Theological Seminary	MI	242
040053	United States University	CA	70
040373	Los Angeles Film School	CA	52
040383	ATA College	KY	192
040385	Pierpont Community/Technical Col	WV	528
040386	Kanawha Valley Cmty/Tech College	WV	528
040414	Mountwest Cmty & Technical College	WV	528
040443	Hazelden Grad Sch of Addiction Stds	MN	256
040473	Bridgemont Cmty & Tech College	WV	527
040513	The Art Institute of Phoenix	AZ	12
040653	Roseman Univ of Health Sciences	NV	295
040743	Hondros College	OH	381
040803	Aspen University	CO	78
040813	Bais Medrash Toras Chesed	NJ	299
040834	Cambridge Inst Allied Health & Tech	FL	99
040933	Academy of Natural Therapy	CO	78
040943	Robert B. Miller College	MI	249
040953	The King's College	NY	328
040963	Charleston School of Law	SC	441
041004	William Howard Taft University	CO	87
041103	University of Management & Tech	VA	510
041113	West Hills College Lemoore	CA	75
041123	Louisiana Culinary Institute	LA	204
041143	Nevada State College	NV	294
041144	The Institute of World Politics	DC	96
041145	Valley College of Medical Careers	CA	74
041155	Talmudical Seminary of Bobov	NY	347
041156	Mayfield College	CA	54
041174	Milwaukee Career College	WI	534
041180	Byzantine Catholic Seminary	PA	411
041184	Zarem/Golde ORT Tech Institute	IL	163
041187	American College of Technology	MO	271
041188	New York Film Academy, Los Angeles	CA	56
041190	Eastern WV Community & Tech College	WV	528
041191	City Vision College	MO	272
041193	Han Univ of Traditional Medicine	AZ	13
041196	Yeshiva of Far Rockaway	NY	350
041212	Inst of Taoist Educ/Acupuncture	CO	82
041215	Columbia Southern University	AL	2
041218	Criswell College	TX	470
041228	Presbyterian Theol Sem in America	CA	60
041234	Yeshivas Be'er Yitzchok	NJ	308
041238	Williamson Free Sch of Mech Trades	PA	437
041242	The Catholic Distance University	VA	503
041247	Ambria College of Nursing	IL	139
041271	University of California-Merced	CA	71
041273	Columbia College	VA	504
041274	Digital Media Arts College	FL	101
041276	California Coast University	CA	30
041277	American Sentinel University	CO	78
041279	Trident University International	CA	70
041292	New Charter University	CA	56
041301	Louisiana Delta Community College	LA	203
041302	Inst of Production and Recording	MN	256
041305	Pacific NW Univ of Health Sciences	WA	521
041311	Yeshiva Toras Chaim	NJ	308
041314	Phoenix School of Law	AZ	16
041317	Southwest University at El Paso	TX	481
041331	California Univ Management/Sciences	CA	36
041338	Southeast Culinary/Hospitality Coll	VA	509
041347	Intl Professional Sch of Bodywork	CA	48
041359	Allied Health Institute	FL	97
041361	World College	VA	516
041381	Yeshiva of Machzikai Hadas	NY	351
041398	Delaware College of Art and Design	DE	93
041400	Global Health College	VA	505
041403	Montana Bible College	MT	286
041405	Horizon University	CA	47
041418	Louisville Bible College	KY	197
041425	Touro College Los Angeles	CA	69
041426	Touro University California	CA	69
041427	Pontifical JP II Inst for Stds M&F	DC	96
041429	Georgia Gwinnett College	GA	125
041432	Hult International Business School	MA	227
041433	John Hancock University	IL	148
041435	Charlotte School of Law	NC	353
041438	Woodland Community College	CA	77
041440	Virginia International University	VA	515
041449	Mater Ecclesiae College	RI	439
041460	National Career College	CA	55
041461	Urshan Graduate School of Theology	MO	284
041464	Daoist Trad Col of Chinese Med Arts	NC	353
041483	Denver School of Nursing	CO	81
041519	Columbia Gorge Community College	OR	402
041538	Bethel College	VA	502
041539	Providence Christian College	CA	60
041542	Carolina Col of Biblical Studies	NC	353
041550	NW School of Wooden Boatbuilding	WA	521
041555	Academy for Jewish Religion	CA	26
041563	University of Fort Lauderdale	FL	118
041565	Georgia Christian University	GA	124
041574	National Paralegal College	AZ	16
041604	Angeles College	CA	28
041612	Bainbridge Graduate Institute	WA	516
041618	Brandman University	CA	29
041620	Jose Maria Vargas University	FL	107
041633	Compass College of Cinematic Arts	MI	241
041647	Keweenaw Bay Ojibwa Cmty Col	MI	245
041672	The Commonwealth Medical College	PA	413
041697	Unitek College	CA	70
041698	Gurnick Academy of Medical Arts	CA	46
041720	S California Univ Sch Oriental Med	CA	67
041730	Shepherds Theological Seminary	NC	366
041735	Moreno Valley College	CA	60
041737	Grace College of Divinity	NC	354
041761	Norco College	CA	60
041763	Bergin University of Canine Studies	CA	29
041771	Pima Medical Institute	CO	84
041780	Simmons College of Kentucky	KY	199
041789	Ashdown College of Health Sciences	CA	29
041795	North American College	TX	477
041803	Mesivta Keser Torah	NJ	303
041806	Appalachian College of Pharmacy	VA	501
041825	Millennia Atlantic University	FL	109
041850	Colorado Academy of Veterinary Tech	CO	79
041855	Academy of Couture Art	CA	26
041884	Bais HaMedrash & Mesivta Baltimore	MD	213
041888	Inst Doctoral Stds in Visual Arts	ME	210
041889	Northwest Institute Literary Arts	WA	521
041893	Allied American University	CA	27
041921	American Medical Academy	FL	97
041924	Yeshiva Gedolah Zichron Leyma	NJ	308
041928	Be'er Yaakov Talmudic Seminary	NY	314
041932	Rocky Mountain Univ Health Prof	UT	496
041937	John Paul the Great Catholic Univ	CA	49
041944	American Col of Healthcare Sciences	OR	401
042061	International Inst Restorative Prac	PA	418
042066	SAE Institute Atlanta	GA	130
042087	Colorado State Univ-Global Campus	CO	80
042118	College of Western Idaho	ID	138
042176	Sessions College for Prof Design	AZ	17
045816	SOLEX College	IL	159
666003	Claremont University Consortium	CA	39
666006	Education Corporation of America	AL	3
666013	American University of Armenia	CA	28
666018	Saint Vincent Seminary	PA	432
666020	Salvation Army Col Ofcr Training	NY	340
666050	Central Baptist Theol Sem of Mnpls	MN	254
666086	Carrington College CA-Admin Office	CA	36
666092	Maine Community College System	ME	210
666106	Ashworth College	GA	120
666120	Henley-Putnam University	CA	47
666127	St. John Vianney Theol Seminary	CO	85
666132	Alliant Internatl Univ Pres Ofc	CA	26
666153	Arkansas State University-Newport	AR	20
666166	New Saint Andrews College	ID	138
666169	Harrison Middleton University	AZ	14
666176	Olivet University	CA	57
666185	Wisconsin Technical College System	WI	539
666187	Arkansas State University System	AR	19
666188	Louisiana Cmty & Tech Coll System	LA	202
666228	Brite Divinity School	TX	468
666233	The Colburn School	CA	40
666234	Washington Baptist University	VA	516
666235	United States Army War College	PA	545
666237	McKinley College	CO	83
666242	American College of Education	IN	163

666245 .... APT College .... CA 28
666251 .... National College of Midwifery .... NM 310
666255 .... Holmes Inst Consciousness Studies .... CO 82
666281 .... Midwives College of Utah .... UT 496
666295 .... Metropolitan Cmty Col-Business/Tech .... MO 277
666310 .... Southwest University .... LA 207
666311 .... Arkansas State Univ-Mountain Home .... AR 20
666315 .... Dunlap-Stone University .... AZ 13
666333 .... TCM International Institute .... IN 173
666337 .... Dominican Study Center of Caribbean .... PR 548
666340 .... John Leland Ctr Theological Studies .... VA 506
666350 .... Babel Univ Prof Sch of Translation .... HI 135
666360 .... International Theological Seminary .... CA 48
666367 .... Toyota Technological Inst Chicago .... IL 160
666373 .... University Philosophical Research .... CA 73
666385 .... Carrington College - Spokane .... WA 517
666393 .... National Intelligence University .... DC 544
666395 .... Rio Grande Bible Institute .... TX 479
666398 .... Taft Law School .... CA 69
666461 .... Inste Bible College .... IA 179
666462 .... Community Col System New Hampshire .... NH 295
666478 .... Yuba Community College District .... CA 77
666601 .... Inter Amer Univ of PR Sch Optometry .... PR 551
666602 .... Fortis College .... OH 379
666616 .... Robert E. Webber Inst Worship Stds .... FL 111
666640 .... Evangelia University .... CA 43
666642 .... Grace Mission University .... CA 46
666643 .... Gerstner Grad Sch of Biomedical Sci .... NY 329
666644 .... Lutheran Brethren Seminary .... MN 256
666647 .... Tillamook Bay Community College .... OR 408
666649 .... NM State Univ Dona Ana Cmty College .... NM 311
666651 .... Anaheim University .... CA 28
666653 .... Atlantic University .... VA 502
666656 .... Connecticut Bd of Regents Higher Ed .... CT 87
666658 .... Suffolk Cty Cmty Coll Central Admin .... NY 346
666659 .... Prince William Sound Cmty College .... AK 11
666670 .... California Intercontinental Univ .... CA 31
666671 .... Elmezzi Grad Sch of Molecular Med .... NY 323
666687 .... Global University .... MO 274
666707 .... Yeshiva & Kolel Bais Medrash Elyon .... NY 351
666710 .... Brighton College .... AZ 12
666711 .... California Intrntl Business Univ .... CA 31
666712 .... Heald College, Central Office .... CA 46
666713 .... California Miramar University .... CA 32
666714 .... Future Generations Graduate School .... WV 526
666715 .... Lakewood College .... OH 383
666719 .... College of Medicine, Mayo Clinic .... MN 254
666721 .... AMDA Col & Conservatory of Perf Art .... CA 27
666745 .... Marine Corps University .... VA 544
666747 .... San Jacinto College North .... TX 479
666748 .... San Jacinto College South .... TX 479
666759 .... Northwestern Polytechnic University .... CA 56
666770 .... California Southern University .... CA 32
666776 .... U.S. Career Institute .... CO 86
666786 .... CA Natl Univ for Advanced Studies .... CA 32
666809 .... College for Financial Planning .... CO 78
666811 .... Antioch University Midwest .... OH 373
666813 .... Inter Amer Univ of PR School of Law .... PR 551
666828 .... Bryant & Stratton College Sys Ofc .... NY 315
666923 .... Baker College System .... MI 239
666925 .... Chabot-Las Positas CC District .... CA 37
666971 .... Huntington Col of Health Sciences .... TN 454
666974 .... The JAG Legal Center & School .... VA 544
666982 .... American Graduate University .... CA 27
666993 .... WV Council Cmty/Tech Col Educ .... WV 527
667002 .... Rocky Vista University .... CO 85
667003 .... Rich Gilder Grad Sch @ Am Mus Nat H .... NY 337
667005 .... Radians College .... DC 96
667006 .... The SANS Technology Institute .... MD 218
667007 .... Sotheby's Institute of Art .... NY 341
667008 .... Five Br Univ, Grad Sch Trad Ch Med .... CA 44
667009 .... National Test Pilot School .... CA 55
667014 .... All Saints Bible College .... TN 452
667016 .... Faith Theological Seminary .... MD 214
667017 .... Acacia University .... AZ 11
667020 .... CA Northstate College of Pharmacy .... CA 32
667026 .... Antioch Sch Ch Plnt/Ldrship Dev .... IA 175
667027 .... Saint Gregory the Great Seminary .... NE 292
667028 .... LSU Paul M. Hebert Law Center .... LA 205
667029 .... Westwood College .... CO 87
667034 .... Rasmussen College Corporate Office .... MN 263
667035 .... Martinsburg College .... WV 527
667039 .... Riverside Community College Distric .... CA 60
667040 .... San Bernardino Community Col Dist .... CA 61
667041 .... West Hills Community College Dist .... CA 75
667045 .... Eternity Bible College .... CA 43
667046 .... Mid-South Christian College .... TN 457
667049 .... Abraham Lincoln University .... CA 26
667050 .... Reformed Episcopal Seminary .... PA 431
667052 .... Alhambra Medical University .... CA 26
667053 .... Stanton University .... CA 68
667055 .... Redeemer Theological Seminary .... TX 478
667056 .... Shepherd Univ Sch of Theology .... CA 66
667057 .... Sonoran Desert Institute .... AZ 17
667058 .... Univ of So Florida Sarasota-Manatee .... FL 117
667069 .... Sanford-Burnham Grad Sch Biomed Sci .... CA 64
667070 .... International Technological Univ .... CA 48
667071 .... Cedars-Sinai Med Grad Pgm Biomed Sc .... CA 37
667074 .... Midwest Institute-Earth City .... MO 277
667077 .... Yeshiva Gedolah Ohr Yisrael .... NY 351
667083 .... Tribeca Flashpoint Media Arts Acad .... IL 160
667085 .... Van Andel Institute Graduate School .... MI 251
667086 .... Texas A & M Univ - Central Texas .... TX 483
667087 .... Teachers College of San Joaquin .... CA 69
667088 .... Rudolf Steiner College .... CA 61
667089 .... B.H. Carroll Theological Institute .... TX 467
667090 .... American Evangelical University .... CA 27
667091 .... Heartland Christian College .... MO 275
667092 .... Native American Bible College .... NC 357
667093 .... Valor Christian College .... OH 392
667094 .... University of Fairfax .... VA 510
667095 .... Shiloh University .... IA 182
667096 .... Apollos University .... CA 28
667097 .... UCH Memorial Hosp Sch Radiolgc Tech .... CO 85
667098 .... Theatre of Arts .... CA 69
667099 .... Puritan Reformed Theological Sem .... MI 249
667100 .... Grace School of Theology .... TX 472
667101 .... Pensacola Christian College .... FL 110
667103 .... Veritas Evangelical Seminary .... CA 75
667104 .... Health Career Institute .... FL 106
667105 .... iGlobal University .... VA 505
667106 .... Lighthouse College .... TX 475
667107 .... Instituto de Banca y Comercio .... PR 549
667108 .... Southern States University .... CA 68
667109 .... Yeshiva Yesodei Hatorah .... NJ 308
667110 .... Yeshiva Zichron Aryeh .... NY 351
667111 .... Beth Medrash Meor Yitzchok .... NY 315
667112 .... Yeshiva Gedolah Kesser Torah .... NY 351
667113 .... Yeshiva Toras Chaim Talmudical Sem .... CO 87
667114 .... Univ of SC Sch of Med-Greenville .... SC 448
667115 .... Grace Communion Seminary .... CA 45
667116 .... Azure College .... FL 98
667117 .... Relay Graduate School of Education .... NY 337
667118 .... High Tech High Grad Sch of Educ .... CA 47
667119 .... St. Anthony Sch of Echocardiography .... IN 172
667120 .... Irish American University .... DE 94
667121 .... Graduate School USA .... DC 95
667122 .... College of the Muscogee Nation .... OK 395
667123 .... Comanche Nation College .... OK 395
667124 .... University of North Texas at Dallas .... TX 490
667125 .... Willow International Cmty Col Ctr .... CA 69
667126 .... CUNY Guttman Community College .... NY 319
667127 .... Orlando Medical Institute .... FL 110
667128 .... NCTI-College of Emergency Svcs .... OR 405
667129 .... Standard Healthcare Svcs Col of Nur .... VA 510
667130 .... San Ignacio College .... FL 112
667131 .... Eastwick College .... NJ 301
667132 .... Intl Reformed Univ & Seminary .... CA 48
667133 .... Methodist Theol Seminary in America .... CA 54
667134 .... Kansas City College & Bible School .... KS 187
667135 .... New England Bible College .... ME 211
667136 .... Bethany College of Missions .... MN 253
667137 .... Brookes Bible Institute .... MO 271
667138 .... Alabama Col of Osteopathic Medicine .... AL 1
667139 .... Tacoma Bible College .... WA 524
667140 .... Manthano Christian College .... MI 246
667141 .... The Crown College of the Bible .... TN 453
667142 .... Advanced Computing Institute .... CA 26
667143 .... Los Angeles Pacific College .... CA 52
667145 .... Rabbinical College Ohr Yisroel .... NY 337
667146 .... Bet Medrash Gadol Ateret Torah .... NY 315
667147 .... Yeshiva Sholom Shachna .... NY 351
667148 .... Virginia Tech Carilion Sch of Med .... VA 515
667149 .... Chamberlain College of Nursing .... IL 141
667150 .... Presidio Graduate School .... CA 60
667151 .... Rockbridge Seminary .... MO 280
667152 .... KP Sch of Allied Health Sciences .... CA 49
667153 .... Bapt Hosp SE TX Sch of Rad Tech .... TX 467
667154 .... Finger Lakes Health Col of Nursing .... NY 324
667155 .... Unilatina International College .... FL 118
667156 .... Radiological Technologies Univ-VT .... IN 172
667202 .... National College .... KY 198

Index of Universities, Colleges and Schools

Institution	State	Page
59th Dental Training Squadron	US SERVICE SCHOOLS	544
A. T. Still University of Health Sciences	MISSOURI	271
Aaniiih Nakoda College	MONTANA	285
Abilene Christian University	TEXAS	464
Abraham Baldwin Agricultural College	GEORGIA	119
Abraham Lincoln University	CALIFORNIA	26
Acacia University	ARIZONA	11
Academy College	MINNESOTA	253
Academy for Five Element Acupuncture	FLORIDA	97
Academy for Jewish Religion	CALIFORNIA	26
Academy for Nursing and Health Occupations	FLORIDA	97
Academy of Art University	CALIFORNIA	26
Academy of Chinese Culture and Health Sciences	CALIFORNIA	26
Academy of Couture Art	CALIFORNIA	26
Academy of Natural Therapy	COLORADO	78
Acupuncture & Massage College	FLORIDA	97
Acupuncture and Integrative Medicine College-Berkeley	CALIFORNIA	26
Adams State University	COLORADO	78
Adelphi University	NEW YORK	313
Adler Graduate School	MINNESOTA	253
Adler School of Professional Psychology	ILLINOIS	139
Adrian College	MICHIGAN	238
Advanced College	CALIFORNIA	26
Advanced Computing Institute	CALIFORNIA	26
Advanced Technology Institute	VIRGINIA	501
Advanced Training Associates	CALIFORNIA	26
Adventist University of Health Sciences	FLORIDA	97
Agnes Scott College	GEORGIA	119
AIB College of Business	IOWA	175
Aiken Technical College	SOUTH CAROLINA	440
Aims Community College	COLORADO	78
Air Force Institute of Technology	US SERVICE SCHOOLS	544
Air University	US SERVICE SCHOOLS	544
Alabama Agricultural and Mechanical University	ALABAMA	1
Alabama College of Osteopathic Medicine	ALABAMA	1
Alabama Southern Community College	ALABAMA	1
Alabama State University	ALABAMA	1
Alamance Community College	NORTH CAROLINA	357
Alamo Community College District Central Office	TEXAS	464
Alaska Bible College	ALASKA	10
Alaska Career College	ALASKA	10
Alaska Pacific University	ALASKA	10
Albany College of Pharmacy and Health Sciences	NEW YORK	313
Albany Law School	NEW YORK	313
Albany Medical College	NEW YORK	313
Albany State University	GEORGIA	119
Albany Technical College	GEORGIA	120
Albertus Magnus College	CONNECTICUT	87
Albion College	MICHIGAN	239
Albright College	PENNSYLVANIA	409
Alcorn State University	MISSISSIPPI	265
Alderson Broaddus University	WEST VIRGINIA	526
Alegent Health School of Radiologic Technology	NEBRASKA	288
Alexandria Technical & Community College	MINNESOTA	257
Alfred State College	NEW YORK	345
Alfred University	NEW YORK	313
Alhambra Medical University	CALIFORNIA	26
Alice Lloyd College	KENTUCKY	191
All Saints Bible College	TENNESSEE	452
Allan Hancock College	CALIFORNIA	26
Allegany College of Maryland	MARYLAND	213
Allegany College of Maryland Bedford County Campus	PENNSYLVANIA	409
Allegany College of Maryland Somerset County Campus	PENNSYLVANIA	409
Allegheny College	PENNSYLVANIA	409
Allegheny Wesleyan College	OHIO	373
Allen College	IOWA	175
Allen County Community College	KANSAS	183
Allen County Community College Burlingame Campus	KANSAS	184
Allen University	SOUTH CAROLINA	441
Alliant International University-Fresno	CALIFORNIA	27
Alliant International University-Irvine	CALIFORNIA	27
Alliant International University-Los Angeles	CALIFORNIA	27
Alliant International University President's Office	CALIFORNIA	26
Alliant International University-San Diego	CALIFORNIA	26
Alliant International University-San Francisco	CALIFORNIA	27
Allied American University	CALIFORNIA	27
Allied Health Institute	FLORIDA	97
Alma College	MICHIGAN	239
Alpena Community College	MICHIGAN	239
Altamaha Technical College	GEORGIA	120
Alvernia University	PENNSYLVANIA	409
Alverno College	WISCONSIN	531
Alvin Community College	TEXAS	465
Amarillo College	TEXAS	465
Amberton University	TEXAS	465
Ambria College of Nursing	ILLINOIS	139
AMDA College and Conservatory of the Performing Arts	CALIFORNIA	27
AMDA College and Conservatory of the Performing Arts	NEW YORK	313
American Academy McAllister Institute of Funeral Service	NEW YORK	313
American Academy of Acupuncture and Oriental Medicine	MINNESOTA	253
American Academy of Art	ILLINOIS	139
American Academy of Dramatic Arts	NEW YORK	313
American Academy of Dramatic Arts, Los Angeles Campus	CALIFORNIA	27
American Baptist College	TENNESSEE	452
American Baptist Seminary of the West	CALIFORNIA	27
American Career College-Los Angeles	CALIFORNIA	27
American Career College-Ontario	CALIFORNIA	27
American Career College-Orange County	CALIFORNIA	27
American College of Acupuncture and Oriental Medicine	TEXAS	465
American College of Education	INDIANA	163
American College of Healthcare Sciences	OREGON	401
American College of Technology	MISSOURI	271
American College of Traditional Chinese Medicine	CALIFORNIA	27
American College, The	PENNSYLVANIA	409
American Conservatory Theater	CALIFORNIA	27
American Evangelical University	CALIFORNIA	27
American Film Institute Conservatory	CALIFORNIA	27
American Graduate University	CALIFORNIA	27
American Indian College of the Assemblies of God	ARIZONA	11
American Institute College of Health Professions	FLORIDA	97
American Institute of Alternative Medicine	OHIO	373
American InterContinental University	FLORIDA	97
American InterContinental University	GEORGIA	120
American InterContinental University	ILLINOIS	139
American InterContinental University-Houston Campus	TEXAS	465
American International College	MASSACHUSETTS	221
American Jewish University	CALIFORNIA	27
American Medical Academy	FLORIDA	97
American National University	VIRGINIA	501
American Public University System	WEST VIRGINIA	526
American River College	CALIFORNIA	53
American Samoa Community College	AMERICAN SAMOA	546
American Sentinel University	COLORADO	78
American University	DISTRICT OF COLUMBIA	94
American University of Armenia	CALIFORNIA	28
American University of Health Sciences	CALIFORNIA	28
American University of Puerto Rico	PUERTO RICO	547
Amherst College	MASSACHUSETTS	221
Amridge University	ALABAMA	1
Ana G. Mendez University System Capital Area Campus	MARYLAND	213
Ana G. Mendez University System Metro Orlando Campus	FLORIDA	98
Ana G. Mendez University System South Florida Campus	FLORIDA	98
Ana G. Mendez University System Tampa Bay Campus	FLORIDA	98
Anabaptist Mennonite Biblical Seminary	INDIANA	163
Anaheim University	CALIFORNIA	28
Anamarc College	NEW MEXICO	309
Anamarc College	TEXAS	465
Ancilla College	INDIANA	163
Anderson University	INDIANA	163
Anderson University	SOUTH CAROLINA	441
Andover Newton Theological School	MASSACHUSETTS	222
Andrew College	GEORGIA	120
Andrews University	MICHIGAN	239
Angeles College	CALIFORNIA	28
Angeles College-Garden Grove	CALIFORNIA	28
Angelina College	TEXAS	465
Angelo State University	TEXAS	465
Anna Maria College	MASSACHUSETTS	222
Anne Arundel Community College	MARYLAND	213
Anoka-Ramsey Community College	MINNESOTA	257
Anoka-Ramsey Community College Cambridge Campus	MINNESOTA	262
Anoka Technical College	MINNESOTA	257
Antelope Valley College	CALIFORNIA	28
Anthem Career College	TENNESSEE	452
Anthem College	ARIZONA	11
Anthem College	COLORADO	78
Anthem College	FLORIDA	98
Anthem College	GEORGIA	120
Anthem College	MINNESOTA	253
Anthem College	MISSOURI	271
Anthem College	TENNESSEE	452
Anthem College	TEXAS	466
Anthem College-Fenton	MISSOURI	271
Anthem College-Milwaukee	WISCONSIN	531
Antioch School of Church Planting and Leadership Development	IOWA	175
Antioch University	OHIO	373
Antioch University Los Angeles	CALIFORNIA	28
Antioch University Midwest	OHIO	373
Antioch University New England	NEW HAMPSHIRE	295
Antioch University Santa Barbara	CALIFORNIA	28
Antioch University Seattle	WASHINGTON	516
Antonelli College	MISSISSIPPI	265
Antonelli College	OHIO	373
Antonelli Institute of Art and Photography	PENNSYLVANIA	409
AOMA Graduate School of Integrative Medicine	TEXAS	466
Apex School of Theology	NORTH CAROLINA	352
Apollos University	CALIFORNIA	28

Institution	State	Page
Appalachian Bible College	WEST VIRGINIA	526
Appalachian College of Pharmacy	VIRGINIA	501
Appalachian School of Law	VIRGINIA	502
Appalachian State University	NORTH CAROLINA	367
APT College	CALIFORNIA	28
Aquinas College	MICHIGAN	239
Aquinas College	TENNESSEE	452
Aquinas Institute of Theology	MISSOURI	271
Arapahoe Community College	COLORADO	78
Arcadia University	PENNSYLVANIA	409
Argosy University, Atlanta	GEORGIA	120
Argosy University, Chicago	ILLINOIS	139
Argosy University, Dallas	TEXAS	466
Argosy University, Denver	COLORADO	78
Argosy University, Hawaii	HAWAII	135
Argosy University, Inland Empire	CALIFORNIA	28
Argosy University, Los Angeles	CALIFORNIA	28
Argosy University, Nashville	TENNESSEE	453
Argosy University, Orange County	CALIFORNIA	28
Argosy University, Phoenix	ARIZONA	11
Argosy University, Salt Lake City	UTAH	495
Argosy University, San Diego	CALIFORNIA	28
Argosy University, San Francisco Bay Area	CALIFORNIA	28
Argosy University, Sarasota	FLORIDA	98
Argosy University, Schaumburg	ILLINOIS	139
Argosy University, Seattle	WASHINGTON	516
Argosy University, Tampa	FLORIDA	98
Argosy University, Twin Cities	MINNESOTA	253
Argosy University, Washington DC	VIRGINIA	502
Arizona Christian University (formerly Southwestern College)	ARIZONA	11
Arizona College	ARIZONA	11
Arizona College-Mesa	ARIZONA	11
Arizona School of Acupuncture and Oriental Medicine	ARIZONA	11
Arizona State University	ARIZONA	11
Arizona Western College	ARIZONA	11
Arkansas Baptist College	ARKANSAS	19
Arkansas Northeastern College	ARKANSAS	19
Arkansas State University-Beebe	ARKANSAS	19
Arkansas State University-Heber Springs	ARKANSAS	20
Arkansas State University-Jonesboro	ARKANSAS	19
Arkansas State University-Mountain Home	ARKANSAS	20
Arkansas State University-Newport	ARKANSAS	20
Arkansas State University-Searcy	ARKANSAS	20
Arkansas State University System	ARKANSAS	19
Arkansas Tech University	ARKANSAS	20
Arkansas Tech University-Ozark Campus	ARKANSAS	20
Arlington Baptist College	TEXAS	466
Armstrong Atlantic State University	GEORGIA	120
Art Academy of Cincinnati	OHIO	373
Art Center College of Design	CALIFORNIA	28
Art Institute of Atlanta, The	GEORGIA	120
Art Institute of California, A College of Argosy University - Hollywood, Th	EALIFORNIA	28
Art Institute of California, A College of Argosy University - Inland Em pire, The	CALIFORNIA	28
Art Institute of California, A College of Argosy University - Los Angel es, The	CALIFORNIA	29
Art Institute of California, A College of Argosy University - Orange Co unty, The	CALIFORNIA	29
Art Institute of California, A College of Argosy University - Sacrament o, The	CALIFORNIA	29
Art Institute of California, A College of Argosy University - San Diego, Th	EALIFORNIA	29
Art Institute of California, A College of Argosy University - San Franc isco, The	CALIFORNIA	29
Art Institute of California, A College of Argosy University - Sunnyvale, Th	EALIFORNIA	29
Art Institute of Charlotte, The	NORTH CAROLINA	352
Art Institute of Cincinnati, The	OHIO	374
Art Institute of Colorado, The	COLORADO	78
Art Institute of Dallas	TEXAS	466
Art Institute of Fort Lauderdale, The	FLORIDA	98
Art Institute of Fort Worth, The	TEXAS	466
Art Institute of Houston, The	TEXAS	466
Art Institute of Indianapolis, The	INDIANA	164
Art Institute of Las Vegas, The	NEVADA	293
Art Institute of Michigan, The	MICHIGAN	239
Art Institute of New York City, The	NEW YORK	314
Art Institute of Ohio-Cincinnati, The	OHIO	374
Art Institute of Philadelphia	PENNSYLVANIA	410
Art Institute of Phoenix, The	ARIZONA	12
Art Institute of Pittsburgh	PENNSYLVANIA	410
Art Institute of Portland, The	OREGON	402
Art Institute of Raleigh-Durham, The	NORTH CAROLINA	352
Art Institute of St. Louis, The	MISSOURI	271
Art Institute of Salt Lake City, The	UTAH	495
Art Institute of Seattle, The	WASHINGTON	516
Art Institute of Tucson, The	ARIZONA	12
Art Institute of Wisconsin, The	WISCONSIN	531
Art Institute of York - Pennsylvania, The	PENNSYLVANIA	410
Art Institutes International - Kansas City, The	KANSAS	184
Art Institutes International Minnesota, The	MINNESOTA	253
ASA Institute of Business & Computer Technology	NEW YORK	314
Asbury Theological Seminary	KENTUCKY	192
Asbury University	KENTUCKY	192
Ashdown College of Health Sciences	CALIFORNIA	29
Asheville - Buncombe Technical Community College	NORTH CAROLINA	357
Ashford University	IOWA	175
Ashland Community and Technical College	KENTUCKY	194
Ashland University	OHIO	374
Ashworth College	GEORGIA	120
Asnuntuck Community College	CONNECTICUT	88
Aspen University	COLORADO	78
Assumption College	MASSACHUSETTS	222
Assumption College for Sisters	NEW JERSEY	298
ATA Career Education-Spring Hill	FLORIDA	98
ATA College	KENTUCKY	192
Atenas College	PUERTO RICO	547
Athenaeum of Ohio	OHIO	374
Athens State University	ALABAMA	1
Athens Technical College	GEORGIA	120
Atlanta Metropolitan State College	GEORGIA	121
Atlanta Technical College	GEORGIA	121
Atlanta's John Marshall Law School	GEORGIA	121
Atlantic Cape Community College	NEW JERSEY	299
Atlantic Institute of Oriental Medicine	FLORIDA	98
Atlantic University	VIRGINIA	502
Atlantic University College	PUERTO RICO	547
Auburn University	ALABAMA	1
Auburn University at Montgomery	ALABAMA	2
Augsburg College	MINNESOTA	253
Augusta Technical College	GEORGIA	121
Augustana College	ILLINOIS	139
Augustana College	SOUTH DAKOTA	449
Aultman College of Nursing and Health Sciences	OHIO	374
Aurora University	ILLINOIS	140
Austin College	TEXAS	466
Austin Community College District	TEXAS	466
Austin Graduate School of Theology	TEXAS	466
Austin Peay State University	TENNESSEE	459
Austin Presbyterian Theological Seminary	TEXAS	467
Ave Maria School of Law	FLORIDA	98
Ave Maria University	FLORIDA	98
Averett University	VIRGINIA	502
Aviation Institute of Maintenance	VIRGINIA	502
Aviator College of Aeronautical Science & Technology	FLORIDA	98
Avila University	MISSOURI	271
Azure College	FLORIDA	98
Azusa Pacific University	CALIFORNIA	29
Babel University Professional School of Translation	HAWAII	135
Babson College	MASSACHUSETTS	222
Bacone College	OKLAHOMA	394
Bainbridge College	GEORGIA	121
Bainbridge Graduate Institute	WASHINGTON	516
Bais HaMedrash & Mesivta of Baltimore	MARYLAND	213
Bais Medrash Toras Chesed	NEW JERSEY	299
Baker College of Allen Park	MICHIGAN	240
Baker College of Auburn Hills	MICHIGAN	240
Baker College of Cadillac	MICHIGAN	240
Baker College of Clinton Township	MICHIGAN	240
Baker College of Flint	MICHIGAN	239
Baker College of Jackson	MICHIGAN	240
Baker College of Muskegon	MICHIGAN	240
Baker College of Owosso	MICHIGAN	240
Baker College of Port Huron	MICHIGAN	240
Baker College System	MICHIGAN	239
Baker University	KANSAS	184
Baker University School of Professional and Graduate Studies	KANSAS	184
Bakersfield College	CALIFORNIA	49
Bakke Graduate University	WASHINGTON	516
Baldwin Wallace University	OHIO	374
Ball State University	INDIANA	164
Baltimore City Community College	MARYLAND	213
Bangor Theological Seminary	MAINE	209
Bank Street College of Education	NEW YORK	314
Baptist Bible College	MISSOURI	271
Baptist Bible College and Seminary	PENNSYLVANIA	410
Baptist College of Florida, The	FLORIDA	98
Baptist College of Health Sciences	TENNESSEE	453
Baptist Health System School of Health Professions	TEXAS	467
Baptist Hospitals of Southeast Texas School of Radiologic Technology	TEXAS	467
Baptist Missionary Association Theological Seminary	TEXAS	467
Baptist Theological Seminary at Richmond	VIRGINIA	502
Baptist University of the Americas	TEXAS	467
Barclay College	KANSAS	184
Bard College	NEW YORK	314
Dard College at Simon's Rock	MASSACHUSETTS	222
Bard High School Early College Manhattan	NEW YORK	314
Bard High School Early College Queens	NEW YORK	314
Barnard College	NEW YORK	314
Barry University	FLORIDA	98
Barstow Community College District	CALIFORNIA	29
Barton College	NORTH CAROLINA	352
Barton County Community College	KANSAS	184
Barton County Community College Fort Riley Campus	KANSAS	184
Baruch College/City University of New York	NEW YORK	316
Bastyr University	WASHINGTON	516
Bates College	MAINE	209
Bates Technical College	WASHINGTON	516
Baton Rouge Community College	LOUISIANA	202
Baton Rouge Community College, Acadian Branch	LOUISIANA	204
Baton Rouge Community College, Jackson Branch	LOUISIANA	204
Baton Rouge Community College, New Roads Branch	LOUISIANA	204
Baton Rouge School of Computers	LOUISIANA	201
Bauder College	GEORGIA	121
Bay College West Campus	MICHIGAN	240
Bay Medical Center	FLORIDA	99
Bay Mills Community College	MICHIGAN	240
Bay Noc Community College	MICHIGAN	240
Bay Path College	MASSACHUSETTS	222
Bay State College	MASSACHUSETTS	222
Bayamon Central University	PUERTO RICO	547
Baylor College of Medicine	TEXAS	467
Baylor University	TEXAS	467

Institution	State	Page
Beacon College	FLORIDA	99
Beal College	MAINE	209
Beaufort County Community College	NORTH CAROLINA	358
Becker College-Worcester	MASSACHUSETTS	223
Beckfield College	KENTUCKY	192
Beckfield College	OHIO	374
Be'er Yaakov Talmudic Seminary	NEW YORK	314
Beis Medrash Heichal Dovid	NEW YORK	314
Bel-Rea Institute of Animal Technology	COLORADO	78
Belanger School of Nursing, The	NEW YORK	314
Belhaven University	MISSISSIPPI	266
Bellarmine University	KENTUCKY	192
Bellevue College	WASHINGTON	517
Bellevue University	NEBRASKA	288
Bellin College, Inc.	WISCONSIN	531
Bellingham Technical College	WASHINGTON	517
Belmont Abbey College	NORTH CAROLINA	352
Belmont College	OHIO	374
Belmont University	TENNESSEE	453
Beloit College	WISCONSIN	531
Bemidji State University	MINNESOTA	258
Benedict College	SOUTH CAROLINA	441
Benedictine College	KANSAS	184
Benedictine University	ILLINOIS	140
Benedictine University at Mesa	ARIZONA	12
Benedictine University at Springfield	ILLINOIS	140
Benjamin Franklin Institute of Technology	MASSACHUSETTS	223
Bennett College	NORTH CAROLINA	352
Bennington College	VERMONT	498
Bentley University	MASSACHUSETTS	223
Berea College	KENTUCKY	192
Bergen Community College	NEW JERSEY	299
Bergin University of Canine Studies	CALIFORNIA	29
Berkeley City College	CALIFORNIA	59
Berkeley College	NEW JERSEY	299
Berkeley College	NEW YORK	314
Berklee College of Music	MASSACHUSETTS	223
Berks Technical Institute	PENNSYLVANIA	410
Berkshire Community College	MASSACHUSETTS	231
Berry College	GEORGIA	121
Bet Medrash Gadol Ateret Torah	NEW YORK	315
Beth Benjamin Academy of Connecticut	CONNECTICUT	87
Beth Hamedrash Shaarei Yosher Institute	NEW YORK	315
Beth Hatalmud Rabbinical College	NEW YORK	315
Beth Medrash Govoha	NEW JERSEY	299
Beth Medrash Meor Yitzchok	NEW YORK	315
Bethany College	KANSAS	184
Bethany College	WEST VIRGINIA	526
Bethany College of Missions	MINNESOTA	253
Bethany Lutheran College	MINNESOTA	253
Bethany Theological Seminary	INDIANA	164
Bethel College	INDIANA	164
Bethel College	KANSAS	184
Bethel College	VIRGINIA	502
Bethel University	MINNESOTA	253
Bethel University	TENNESSEE	453
Bethesda University of California	CALIFORNIA	29
Bethune Cookman University	FLORIDA	99
Beulah Heights University	GEORGIA	121
Bevill State Community College	ALABAMA	2
Bexley Seabury	ILLINOIS	140
Bexley Seabury	OHIO	374
B.H. Carroll Theological Institute	TEXAS	467
Biblical Theological Seminary	PENNSYLVANIA	410
Bidwell Training Center	PENNSYLVANIA	410
Big Bend Community College	WASHINGTON	517
Big Sandy Community and Technical College	KENTUCKY	194
Biola University	CALIFORNIA	29
Birmingham-Southern College	ALABAMA	2
Birthingway College of Midwifery	OREGON	402
Bishop State Community College	ALABAMA	2
Bismarck State College	NORTH DAKOTA	372
Black Hawk College	ILLINOIS	140
Black Hawk College East Campus	ILLINOIS	140
Black Hills State University	SOUTH DAKOTA	451
Black River Technical College	ARKANSAS	20
Blackburn College	ILLINOIS	140
Blackfeet Community College	MONTANA	285
Blackhawk Technical College	WISCONSIN	539
Bladen Community College	NORTH CAROLINA	358
Blessed John XXIII National Seminary	MASSACHUSETTS	223
Blessing-Rieman College of Nursing	ILLINOIS	140
Blinn College	TEXAS	467
Bloomfield College	NEW JERSEY	299
Bloomsburg University of Pennsylvania	PENNSYLVANIA	427
Blue Cliff College	LOUISIANA	201
Blue Cliff College	MISSISSIPPI	266
Blue Mountain College	MISSISSIPPI	266
Blue Mountain Community College	OREGON	402
Blue Ridge Community and Technical College	WEST VIRGINIA	527
Blue Ridge Community College	NORTH CAROLINA	358
Blue Ridge Community College	VIRGINIA	511
Bluefield College	VIRGINIA	502
Bluefield State College	WEST VIRGINIA	529
Bluegrass Community and Technical College	KENTUCKY	194
Bluffton University	OHIO	374
Board of Regents, State of Iowa	IOWA	175
Bob Jones University	SOUTH CAROLINA	441
Boise Bible College	IDAHO	137
Boise State University	IDAHO	137
Bolivar Technical College	MISSOURI	271
Bon Secours Memorial College of Nursing	VIRGINIA	502
Boricua College	NEW YORK	315
Bossier Parish Community College	LOUISIANA	202
Boston Architectural College	MASSACHUSETTS	223
Boston Baptist College	MASSACHUSETTS	223
Boston College	MASSACHUSETTS	224
Boston Conservatory, The	MASSACHUSETTS	224
Boston Graduate School of Psychoanalysis	MASSACHUSETTS	224
Boston University	MASSACHUSETTS	224
Boston University Medical Campus	MASSACHUSETTS	224
Bowdoin College	MAINE	209
Bowie State University	MARYLAND	220
Bowling Green State University	OHIO	374
Bowling Green State University Firelands College	OHIO	375
Bradford School	OHIO	375
Bradford School	PENNSYLVANIA	410
Bradley University	ILLINOIS	140
Bramson O R T College	NEW YORK	315
Brandeis University	MASSACHUSETTS	224
Brandman University	CALIFORNIA	29
Brazosport College	TEXAS	468
Bread Loaf School of English in Vermont	VERMONT	498
Brenau University	GEORGIA	122
Brescia University	KENTUCKY	192
Brevard College	NORTH CAROLINA	352
Brewton-Parker College	GEORGIA	122
Briar Cliff University	IOWA	176
Briarcliffe College	NEW YORK	315
Bridgemont Community and Technical College	WEST VIRGINIA	527
Bridgewater College	VIRGINIA	502
Bridgewater State University	MASSACHUSETTS	229
Brigham Young University	UTAH	495
Brigham Young University Hawaii	HAWAII	135
Brigham Young University-Idaho	IDAHO	137
Brighton College	ARIZONA	12
Bristol Community College	MASSACHUSETTS	231
Bristol University	CALIFORNIA	29
Brite Divinity School	TEXAS	468
Broadview Entertainment Arts University	UTAH	495
Broadview University	IDAHO	137
Broadview University	UTAH	495
Brookdale Community College	NEW JERSEY	299
Brookdale Community College Western Monmouth Branch Campus	NEW JERSEY	299
Brookes Bible Institute	MISSOURI	271
Brookhaven College	TEXAS	470
Brookline College	ARIZONA	12
Brookline College	NEW MEXICO	309
Brooklyn Law School	NEW YORK	315
Brooks Institute	CALIFORNIA	30
Broome Community College	NEW YORK	315
Broward College	FLORIDA	99
Brown College	MINNESOTA	254
Brown College of Court Reporting	GEORGIA	122
Brown Mackie College	ALABAMA	2
Brown Mackie College	NEW MEXICO	309
Brown Mackie College	TEXAS	468
Brown Mackie College-Akron	OHIO	375
Brown Mackie College-Atlanta	GEORGIA	122
Brown Mackie College-Boise	IDAHO	137
Brown Mackie College-Cincinnati	OHIO	375
Brown Mackie College-Findlay	OHIO	375
Brown Mackie College-Fort Wayne	INDIANA	164
Brown Mackie College-Greenville	SOUTH CAROLINA	441
Brown Mackie College-Hopkinsville	KENTUCKY	193
Brown Mackie College-Indianapolis	INDIANA	164
Brown Mackie College-Kansas City	KANSAS	185
Brown Mackie College-Louisville	KENTUCKY	193
Brown Mackie College-Merrillville	INDIANA	164
Brown Mackie College-Miami	FLORIDA	99
Brown Mackie College-Michigan City	INDIANA	164
Brown Mackie College-North Canton	OHIO	375
Brown Mackie College-Northern Kentucky	KENTUCKY	193
Brown Mackie College-Oklahoma City	OKLAHOMA	394
Brown Mackie College-Phoenix	ARIZONA	12
Brown Mackie College-Quad Cities	IOWA	176
Brown Mackie College-St. Louis	MISSOURI	271
Brown Mackie College-Salina	KANSAS	185
Brown Mackie College-South Bend	INDIANA	164
Brown Mackie College-Tucson	ARIZONA	12
Brown Mackie College-Tulsa	OKLAHOMA	394
Brown University	RHODE ISLAND	438
Brunswick Community College	NORTH CAROLINA	358
Bryan College	CALIFORNIA	30
Bryan College	TENNESSEE	453
Bryan College of Health Sciences	NEBRASKA	288
Bryan University	ARKANSAS	20
Bryan University	KANSAS	185
Bryan University	MISSOURI	271
Bryan University Online	ARIZONA	12
Bryant & Stratton College	NEW YORK	315
Bryant & Stratton College	NEW YORK	316
Bryant & Stratton College	OHIO	375
Bryant & Stratton College	VIRGINIA	502
Bryant & Stratton College	WISCONSIN	532
Bryant & Stratton College System Office	NEW YORK	315
Bryant University	RHODE ISLAND	438
Bryman College-LA Wilshire	CALIFORNIA	30
Bryman School, The	ARIZONA	12
Bryn Athyn College of the New Church	PENNSYLVANIA	410
Bryn Mawr College	PENNSYLVANIA	410
Bucknell University	PENNSYLVANIA	411
Bucks County Community College	PENNSYLVANIA	411
Buena Vista University	IOWA	176
Bunker Hill Community College	MASSACHUSETTS	231
Burlington College	VERMONT	498
Burlington County College	NEW JERSEY	299

Business Informatics Center, Inc.	NEW YORK	316
Butler Community College	KANSAS	185
Butler County Community College	PENNSYLVANIA	411
Butler of Andover	KANSAS	185
Butler of Council Grove	KANSAS	185
Butler of Marion	KANSAS	185
Butler of McConnell	KANSAS	185
Butler of Rose Hill	KANSAS	185
Butler University	INDIANA	164
Butte College	CALIFORNIA	30
Byzantine Catholic Seminary of SS. Cyril and Methodius	PENNSYLVANIA	411
Cabarrus College of Health Sciences	NORTH CAROLINA	352
Cabrillo College	CALIFORNIA	30
Cabrini College	PENNSYLVANIA	411
Cairn University	PENNSYLVANIA	411
Caldwell College	NEW JERSEY	300
Caldwell Community College and Technical Institute	NORTH CAROLINA	358
Calhoun Community College	ALABAMA	2
California Baptist University	CALIFORNIA	30
California Christian College	CALIFORNIA	30
California Coast University	CALIFORNIA	30
California College of the Arts	CALIFORNIA	30
California College San Diego	CALIFORNIA	31
California Institute of Integral Studies	CALIFORNIA	31
California Institute of Technology	CALIFORNIA	31
California Institute of the Arts	CALIFORNIA	31
California Intercontinental University	CALIFORNIA	31
California International Business University	CALIFORNIA	31
California Lutheran University	CALIFORNIA	31
California Maritime Academy	CALIFORNIA	31
California Miramar University	CALIFORNIA	32
California National University for Advanced Studies	CALIFORNIA	32
California Northstate College of Pharmacy	CALIFORNIA	32
California Polytechnic State University-San Luis Obispo	CALIFORNIA	32
California Southern University	CALIFORNIA	32
California State Polytechnic University-Pomona	CALIFORNIA	32
California State University-Bakersfield	CALIFORNIA	32
California State University-Channel Islands	CALIFORNIA	32
California State University-Chico	CALIFORNIA	33
California State University-Dominguez Hills	CALIFORNIA	33
California State University-East Bay	CALIFORNIA	33
California State University-Fresno	CALIFORNIA	33
California State University-Fullerton	CALIFORNIA	33
California State University-Long Beach	CALIFORNIA	33
California State University-Los Angeles	CALIFORNIA	34
California State University-Monterey Bay	CALIFORNIA	34
California State University-Northridge	CALIFORNIA	34
California State University-Sacramento	CALIFORNIA	34
California State University-San Bernardino	CALIFORNIA	34
California State University-San Marcos	CALIFORNIA	35
California State University-Stanislaus	CALIFORNIA	35
California State University System Office, The	CALIFORNIA	32
California University of Management and Sciences	CALIFORNIA	36
California University of Management and Sciences Virginia	VIRGINIA	502
California University of Pennsylvania	PENNSYLVANIA	428
California Western School of Law	CALIFORNIA	36
Calumet College of Saint Joseph	INDIANA	164
Calvary Baptist Theological Seminary	PENNSYLVANIA	412
Calvary Bible College and Theological Seminary	MISSOURI	271
Calvin College	MICHIGAN	240
Calvin Theological Seminary	MICHIGAN	240
Cambria-Rowe Business College	PENNSYLVANIA	412
Cambridge College	MASSACHUSETTS	224
Cambridge Institute of Allied Health & Technology	FLORIDA	99
Cambridge Junior College	CALIFORNIA	36
Camden County College	NEW JERSEY	300
Camden County College Camden City Campus	NEW JERSEY	300
Cameron College	LOUISIANA	201
Cameron University	OKLAHOMA	394
Campbell University	NORTH CAROLINA	352
Campbellsville University	KENTUCKY	193
Cañada College	CALIFORNIA	64
Canisius College	NEW YORK	316
Cankdeska Cikana Community College	NORTH DAKOTA	370
Cape Cod Community College	MASSACHUSETTS	231
Cape Fear Community College	NORTH CAROLINA	358
Capella University	MINNESOTA	254
Capital Community College	CONNECTICUT	88
Capital University	OHIO	375
Capital University Law School	OHIO	375
Capitol College	MARYLAND	213
Carbon County Higher Education Center/Rawlins	WYOMING	542
Cardinal Stritch University	WISCONSIN	532
Career College of Northern Nevada	NEVADA	293
Career Point College	OKLAHOMA	394
Career Point College	TEXAS	468
Career Technical College	LOUISIANA	201
Career Training Academy	PENNSYLVANIA	412
Career Training Solutions	VIRGINIA	502
Caribbean University	PUERTO RICO	547
Carl Albert State College	OKLAHOMA	394
Carl Albert State College Sallisaw Campus	OKLAHOMA	394
Carl Sandburg College	ILLINOIS	141
Carl Sandburg College The Branch Campus	ILLINOIS	141
Carl Sandburg College The Extension Center	ILLINOIS	141
Carleton College	MINNESOTA	254
Carlos Albizu University	PUERTO RICO	547
Carlos Albizu University Miami Campus	FLORIDA	99
Carlow University	PENNSYLVANIA	412
Carnegie Mellon University	PENNSYLVANIA	412
Carnegie Mellon University Silicon Valley Campus	CALIFORNIA	36
Carolina Christian College	NORTH CAROLINA	353
Carolina College of Biblical Studies	NORTH CAROLINA	353
Carolina Graduate School of Divinity	NORTH CAROLINA	353
Carolinas College of Health Sciences	NORTH CAROLINA	353
Carrington College	NEVADA	293
Carrington College - Albuquerque	NEW MEXICO	309
Carrington College - Boise	IDAHO	137
Carrington College California - Administrative Office	CALIFORNIA	36
Carrington College California - Citrus Heights	CALIFORNIA	36
Carrington College California - Pleasant Hill	CALIFORNIA	36
Carrington College California - Pomona	CALIFORNIA	36
Carrington College California - Sacramento	CALIFORNIA	36
Carrington College California - San Jose	CALIFORNIA	37
Carrington College California - San Leandro	CALIFORNIA	37
Carrington College California - Stockton	CALIFORNIA	37
Carrington College - Mesa	ARIZONA	12
Carrington College - Phoenix	ARIZONA	12
Carrington College - Spokane	WASHINGTON	517
Carrington College - Tucson	ARIZONA	12
Carrington College - Westside	ARIZONA	12
Carroll College	MONTANA	285
Carroll Community College	MARYLAND	214
Carroll University	WISCONSIN	532
Carson-Newman University	TENNESSEE	453
Carteret Community College	NORTH CAROLINA	358
Carthage College	WISCONSIN	532
Carver College	GEORGIA	122
Casa Loma College-Anaheim	CALIFORNIA	37
Casa Loma College-Hawthorne	CALIFORNIA	37
Casa Loma College-Van Nuys	CALIFORNIA	37
Cascadia Community College	WASHINGTON	517
Case Western Reserve University	OHIO	375
Casper College	WYOMING	542
Castleton State College	VERMONT	501
Catawba College	NORTH CAROLINA	353
Catawba Valley Community College	NORTH CAROLINA	359
Catholic Distance University, The	VIRGINIA	503
Catholic Theological Union	ILLINOIS	141
Catholic University of America, The	DISTRICT OF COLUMBIA	94
Cayuga Community College	NEW YORK	316
Cazenovia College	NEW YORK	316
CBD College	CALIFORNIA	37
Cecil College	MARYLAND	214
Cedar Crest College	PENNSYLVANIA	412
Cedar Valley College	TEXAS	470
Cedars-Sinai Medical Center Graduate Program in Biomedical Sciences and Tra nslational Medicine	CALIFORNIA	37
Cedarville University	OHIO	375
Centenary College	NEW JERSEY	300
Centenary College of Louisiana	LOUISIANA	201
Center for Advanced Legal Studies	TEXAS	468
Center for Advanced Studies On Puerto Rico and the Caribbean	PUERTO RICO	548
Center of Cinematography, Art & Television	FLORIDA	99
Centra College of Nursing	VIRGINIA	503
Central Alabama Community College	ALABAMA	2
Central Arizona College	ARIZONA	12
Central Baptist College	ARKANSAS	20
Central Baptist Theological Seminary	KANSAS	185
Central Baptist Theological Seminary	VIRGINIA	503
Central Baptist Theological Seminary of Minneapolis	MINNESOTA	254
Central Carolina Community College	NORTH CAROLINA	359
Central Carolina Technical College	SOUTH CAROLINA	441
Central Christian College of Kansas	KANSAS	185
Central Christian College of the Bible	MISSOURI	272
Central College	IOWA	176
Central Community College	NEBRASKA	288
Central Community College Columbus Campus	NEBRASKA	288
Central Community College Hastings Campus	NEBRASKA	288
Central Connecticut State University	CONNECTICUT	87
Central Florida Institute	FLORIDA	99
Central Georgia Technical College	GEORGIA	122
Central Lakes College	MINNESOTA	258
Central Louisiana Technical College Avoyelles Campus	LOUISIANA	202
Central Louisiana Technical College Huey P. Long Campus	LOUISIANA	202
Central Louisiana Technical College Oakdale Campus	LOUISIANA	202
Central Louisiana Technical Community College	LOUISIANA	202
Central Maine Community College	MAINE	210
Central Maine Medical Center College of Nursing and Health Professions	MAINE	209
Central Methodist University	MISSOURI	272
Central Michigan University	MICHIGAN	240
Central New Mexico Community College	NEW MEXICO	309
Central Ohio Technical College	OHIO	376
Central Ohio Technical College Coshoctin Campus	OHIO	376
Central Ohio Technical College Knox Campus	OHIO	376
Central Ohio Technical College Pataskala Campus	OHIO	376
Central Oregon Community College	OREGON	402
Central Penn College	PENNSYLVANIA	412
Central Piedmont Community College	NORTH CAROLINA	359
Central State University	OHIO	376
Central Texas College	TEXAS	468
Central Virginia Community College	VIRGINIA	512
Central Washington University	WASHINGTON	517
Central Wyoming College	WYOMING	542
Central Yeshiva Tomchei Tmimim Lubavitch America	NEW YORK	316
Centralia College	WASHINGTON	517
Centre College	KENTUCKY	193
Centro de Estudios Multidisciplinarios	PUERTO RICO	548
Centura College	FLORIDA	99
Centura College	VIRGINIA	503
Century College	MINNESOTA	258
Cerritos College	CALIFORNIA	37
Cerro Coso Community College	CALIFORNIA	49
Chabot College	CALIFORNIA	37

Chabot-Las Positas Community College District ... CALIFORNIA ... 37
Chadron State College ... NEBRASKA ... 291
Chaffey College ... CALIFORNIA ... 37
Chamberlain College of Nursing ... FLORIDA ... 99
Chamberlain College of Nursing ... ILLINOIS ... 141
Chamberlain College of Nursing ... VIRGINIA ... 503
Chamberlain College of Nursing - Addison ... ILLINOIS ... 141
Chamberlain College of Nursing-Atlanta ... GEORGIA ... 122
Chamberlain College of Nursing-Cleveland ... OHIO ... 376
Chamberlain College of Nursing-Columbus Campus ... OHIO ... 376
Chamberlain College of Nursing-Houston ... TEXAS ... 468
Chamberlain College of Nursing Indianapolis Campus ... INDIANA ... 165
Chamberlain College of Nursing-Jacksonville Campus ... FLORIDA ... 99
Chamberlain College of Nursing-Phoenix Campus ... ARIZONA ... 12
Chamberlain College of Nursing-St. Louis ... MISSOURI ... 272
Chamberlain College of Nursing Tinley Park ... ILLINOIS ... 141
Chaminade University of Honolulu ... HAWAII ... 135
Champlain College ... VERMONT ... 499
Chandler-Gilbert Community College ... ARIZONA ... 14
Chandler-Gilbert Community College-Williams Campus ... ARIZONA ... 15
Chapman University ... CALIFORNIA ... 38
Charles R. Drew University of Medicine & Science ... CALIFORNIA ... 38
Charleston School of Law ... SOUTH CAROLINA ... 441
Charleston Southern University ... SOUTH CAROLINA ... 441
Charlotte School of Law ... NORTH CAROLINA ... 353
Charter College ... ALASKA ... 10
Charter College ... WASHINGTON ... 517
Charter College-Canyon Country ... CALIFORNIA ... 38
Charter College-Fife ... WASHINGTON ... 517
Charter College-Lancaster Campus ... CALIFORNIA ... 38
Charter College-Long Beach ... CALIFORNIA ... 38
Charter College-Lynnwood ... WASHINGTON ... 517
Charter College-Oxnard ... CALIFORNIA ... 38
Charter Oak State College ... CONNECTICUT ... 87
Chatfield College ... OHIO ... 376
Chatham University ... PENNSYLVANIA ... 412
Chattahoochee Technical College ... GEORGIA ... 122
Chattahoochee Valley Community College ... ALABAMA ... 2
Chattanooga College ... TENNESSEE ... 453
Chattanooga State Community College ... TENNESSEE ... 460
Chef's Academy, The ... NORTH CAROLINA ... 353
Chemeketa Community College ... OREGON ... 402
Chesapeake College ... MARYLAND ... 214
Chester Career College ... VIRGINIA ... 503
Chestnut Hill College ... PENNSYLVANIA ... 413
Cheyney University of Pennsylvania ... PENNSYLVANIA ... 428
Chicago School of Professional Psychology-Chicago ... ILLINOIS ... 141
Chicago School of Professional Psychology-Irvine Campus CALIFORNIA ... 38
Chicago School of Professional Psychology Los Angeles Campus ... CALIFORNIA ... 38
Chicago School of Professional Psychology-Washington DC ... DISTRICT OF COLUMBIA ... 95
Chicago School of Professional Psychology-Westwood Campus ... CALIFORNIA ... 38
Chicago State University ... ILLINOIS ... 141
Chicago Theological Seminary ... ILLINOIS ... 141
Chief Dull Knife College ... MONTANA ... 285
Chipola College ... FLORIDA ... 99
Chippewa Valley Technical College ... WISCONSIN ... 539
Chippewa Valley Technical College-Chippewa Falls Campus ... WISCONSIN ... 541
Chippewa Valley Technical College-Gateway ... WISCONSIN ... 541
Chippewa Valley Technical College Menomonie Campus .. WISCONSIN ... 541
Chippewa Valley Technical College River Falls Campus ... WISCONSIN ... 541
Chippewa Valley Technical College-West ... WISCONSIN ... 541
Chowan University ... NORTH CAROLINA ... 353
Christ College of Nursing and Health Sciences, The ... OHIO ... 376
Christ the King Seminary ... NEW YORK ... 316
Christendom College ... VIRGINIA ... 503
Christian Brothers University ... TENNESSEE ... 453
Christian Life College ... ILLINOIS ... 141
Christian Theological Seminary ... INDIANA ... 165
Christie's Education, Inc. ... NEW YORK ... 316
Christopher Newport University ... VIRGINIA ... 503
Church Divinity School of the Pacific ... CALIFORNIA ... 38
Cincinnati Christian University ... OHIO ... 376
Cincinnati College of Mortuary Science ... OHIO ... 376
Cincinnati State Technical and Community College ... OHIO ... 376
Cisco College ... TEXAS ... 468
Citadel, The Military College of South Carolina, The ... SOUTH CAROLINA ... 442
Citrus College ... CALIFORNIA ... 38
City College ... FLORIDA ... 99
City College ... FLORIDA ... 100
City College at Montana State University Billings ... MONTANA ... 287
City College of San Francisco ... CALIFORNIA ... 38
City Colleges of Chicago ... ILLINOIS ... 141
City Colleges of Chicago Harold Washington College ... ILLINOIS ... 141
City Colleges of Chicago Harry S Truman College ... ILLINOIS ... 142
City Colleges of Chicago Kennedy-King College ... ILLINOIS ... 142
City Colleges of Chicago Malcolm X College ... ILLINOIS ... 142
City Colleges of Chicago Olive-Harvey College ... ILLINOIS ... 142
City Colleges of Chicago Richard J. Daley College ... ILLINOIS ... 142
City Colleges of Chicago Wilbur Wright College ... ILLINOIS ... 142
City of Hope ... CALIFORNIA ... 39
City University of New York ... NEW YORK ... 316
City University of New York Borough of Manhattan Community College ... NEW YORK ... 317
City University of New York Bronx Community College ... NEW YORK ... 317
City University of New York Brooklyn College ... NEW YORK ... 317
City University of New York College of Staten Island ... NEW YORK ... 317
City University of New York Graduate Center ... NEW YORK ... 317
City University of New York Herbert H. Lehman College ... NEW YORK ... 318
City University of New York Hunter College ... NEW YORK ... 318
City University of New York John Jay College of Criminal Justice ... NEW YORK ... 318
City University of New York Kingsborough Community College ... NEW YORK ... 318
City University of New York Medgar Evers College ... NEW YORK ... 319
City University of New York Queens College ... NEW YORK ... 319
City University of New York Queensborough Community College ... NEW YORK ... 319
City University of New York Stella and Charles Guttman Community College ... NEW YORK ... 319
City University of New York The City College ... NEW YORK ... 317
City University of New York York College ... NEW YORK ... 319
City University of Seattle ... WASHINGTON ... 517
City Vision College ... MISSOURI ... 272
Clackamas Community College ... OREGON ... 402
Claflin University ... SOUTH CAROLINA ... 442
Claremont Graduate University ... CALIFORNIA ... 39
Claremont McKenna College ... CALIFORNIA ... 39
Claremont School of Theology ... CALIFORNIA ... 39
Claremont University Consortium ... CALIFORNIA ... 39
Clarendon College ... TEXAS ... 468
Clarion University of Pennsylvania ... PENNSYLVANIA ... 428
Clark Atlanta University ... GEORGIA ... 122
Clark College ... WASHINGTON ... 518
Clark State Community College ... OHIO ... 377
Clark State Community College Greene Center ... OHIO ... 377
Clark University ... MASSACHUSETTS ... 225
Clarke University ... IOWA ... 176
Clarkson College ... NEBRASKA ... 288
Clarkson University ... NEW YORK ... 320
Clary Sage College ... OKLAHOMA ... 394
Clatsop Community College ... OREGON ... 402
Clayton State University ... GEORGIA ... 123
Clear Creek Baptist Bible College ... KENTUCKY ... 193
Clearwater Christian College ... FLORIDA ... 100
Cleary University ... MICHIGAN ... 241
Cleary University-Livingston Campus ... MICHIGAN ... 241
Clemson University ... SOUTH CAROLINA ... 442
Cleveland Community College ... NORTH CAROLINA ... 359
Cleveland Institute of Art ... OHIO ... 377
Cleveland Institute of Electronics ... OHIO ... 377
Cleveland Institute of Music ... OHIO ... 377
Cleveland State Community College ... TENNESSEE ... 460
Cleveland State University ... OHIO ... 377
Cleveland University - Kansas City ... KANSAS ... 185
Clinton College ... SOUTH CAROLINA ... 442
Clinton Community College ... IOWA ... 178
Clinton Community College ... NEW YORK ... 320
Cloud County Community College ... KANSAS ... 185
Cloud County Community College Geary County Campus KANSAS ... 185
Clover Park Technical College ... WASHINGTON ... 518
Clovis Community College ... NEW MEXICO ... 309
CNI College ... CALIFORNIA ... 39
Coahoma Community College ... MISSISSIPPI ... 266
Coast Community College District Administration Offices .. CALIFORNIA ... 39
Coastal Bend College ... TEXAS ... 468
Coastal Carolina Community College ... NORTH CAROLINA ... 359
Coastal Carolina University ... SOUTH CAROLINA ... 442
Coastline Community College ... CALIFORNIA ... 39
Cochise College ... ARIZONA ... 12
Cochise College Sierra Vista Campus ... ARIZONA ... 13
Cochran School of Nursing ... NEW YORK ... 320
Coconino Community College ... ARIZONA ... 13
Coconino County Community College Flagstaff Fourth Street Campus ... ARIZONA ... 13
Coconino County Community College Page/Lake Powell Campus ... ARIZONA ... 13
Coe College ... IOWA ... 176
Coffeyville Community College ... KANSAS ... 185
Cogswell Polytechnical College ... CALIFORNIA ... 40
Coker College ... SOUTH CAROLINA ... 442
Colburn School, The ... CALIFORNIA ... 40
Colby College ... MAINE ... 209
Colby Community College ... KANSAS ... 185
Colby-Sawyer College ... NEW HAMPSHIRE ... 295
Cold Spring Harbor Laboratory/Watson School of Biological Sciences ... NEW YORK ... 320
Colegio de Cinematografia, Artes y Television ... PUERTO RICO ... 548
Colegio Universitario de San Juan ... PUERTO RICO ... 548
Coleman University ... CALIFORNIA ... 40
Colgate Rochester Crozer Divinity School ... NEW YORK ... 320
Colgate University ... NEW YORK ... 320
College for Creative Studies ... MICHIGAN ... 241
College for Financial Planning ... COLORADO ... 78
College of Alameda ... CALIFORNIA ... 59
College of Biblical Studies-Houston ... TEXAS ... 468
College of Business and Technology ... FLORIDA ... 100
College of Central Florida ... FLORIDA ... 100
College of Charleston ... SOUTH CAROLINA ... 443
College of Coastal Georgia ... GEORGIA ... 123
College of Court Reporting, Inc. ... INDIANA ... 165
College of DuPage ... ILLINOIS ... 142
College of Health Care Professions-Dallas, The ... TEXAS ... 469
College of Health Care Professions-Fort Worth, The ... TEXAS ... 469
College of Health Care Professions, The ... TEXAS ... 469
College of Idaho, The ... IDAHO ... 138
College of Lake County ... ILLINOIS ... 143
College of Lake County Lakeshore Campus ... ILLINOIS ... 143
College of Lake County Southlake Campus ... ILLINOIS ... 143
College of Marin ... CALIFORNIA ... 40
College of Medicine, Mayo Clinic ... MINNESOTA ... 254
College of Menominee Nation ... WISCONSIN ... 532
College of Menominee Nation Oneida Campus ... WISCONSIN ... 532
College of Micronesia-FSM ... FED ST OF MICRONESIA ... 546

Institution	State	Page
College of Mount St. Joseph	OHIO	377
College of Mount Saint Vincent	NEW YORK	320
College of New Jersey, The	NEW JERSEY	300
College of New Rochelle, The	NEW YORK	320
College of Our Lady of the Elms	MASSACHUSETTS	225
College of Saint Benedict	MINNESOTA	254
College of Saint Elizabeth	NEW JERSEY	300
College of St. Joseph	VERMONT	499
College of Saint Mary	NEBRASKA	289
College of Saint Rose, The	NEW YORK	321
College of Saint Scholastica, The	MINNESOTA	254
College of Saints John Fisher & Thomas More, The	TEXAS	469
College of San Mateo	CALIFORNIA	64
College of Southern Idaho	IDAHO	138
College of Southern Maryland	MARYLAND	214
College of Southern Nevada	NEVADA	294
College of the Albemarle	NORTH CAROLINA	359
College of the Atlantic	MAINE	210
College of the Canyons	CALIFORNIA	40
College of the Desert	CALIFORNIA	40
College of the Holy Cross	MASSACHUSETTS	225
College of the Mainland	TEXAS	469
College of the Marshall Islands	MARSHALL ISLANDS	546
College of the Muscogee Nation	OKLAHOMA	395
College of the Ouachitas	ARKANSAS	20
College of the Ozarks	MISSOURI	272
College of the Redwoods Community College District	CALIFORNIA	40
College of the Sequoias	CALIFORNIA	40
College of the Siskiyous	CALIFORNIA	41
College of Westchester, The	NEW YORK	321
College of Western Idaho	IDAHO	138
College of William & Mary	VIRGINIA	503
College of Wooster, The	OHIO	377
CollegeAmerica Cheyenne	WYOMING	542
CollegeAmerica Colorado Springs	COLORADO	78
CollegeAmerica Denver	COLORADO	78
CollegeAmerica-Flagstaff	ARIZONA	13
CollegeAmerica Fort Collins	COLORADO	79
CollegeAmerica-Phoenix	ARIZONA	13
Collin County Community College District	TEXAS	469
Colorado Academy of Veterinary Technology	COLORADO	79
Colorado Christian University	COLORADO	79
Colorado College	COLORADO	79
Colorado Heights University	COLORADO	79
Colorado Mesa University	COLORADO	79
Colorado Mountain College	COLORADO	79
Colorado Mountain College Alpine Campus	COLORADO	79
Colorado Mountain College Aspen Campus	COLORADO	79
Colorado Mountain College Roaring Fork Campus-Spring Valley	COLORADO	79
Colorado Mountain College Summit Campus-Breckinridge Campus	COLORADO	79
Colorado Mountain College-Timberline Campus	COLORADO	79
Colorado Mountain College Vail/Eagle Valley Campus	COLORADO	79
Colorado Mountain College West Garfield Campus	COLORADO	80
Colorado Northwestern Community College	COLORADO	80
Colorado Northwestern Community College Craig	COLORADO	80
Colorado School of Healing Arts	COLORADO	80
Colorado School of Mines	COLORADO	80
Colorado School of Trades	COLORADO	80
Colorado School of Traditional Chinese Medicine	COLORADO	80
Colorado State University	COLORADO	80
Colorado State University-Global Campus	COLORADO	80
Colorado State University-Pueblo	COLORADO	80
Colorado State University System Office	COLORADO	80
Colorado Technical University	COLORADO	81
Colorado Technical University	SOUTH DAKOTA	449
Colorado Technical University, Kansas City	MISSOURI	272
Columbia Basin College	WASHINGTON	518
Columbia Centro Universitario	PUERTO RICO	548
Columbia College	CALIFORNIA	77
Columbia College	MISSOURI	272
Columbia College	SOUTH CAROLINA	443
Columbia College	VIRGINIA	504
Columbia College Chicago	ILLINOIS	143
Columbia College Hollywood	CALIFORNIA	41
Columbia College of Nursing	WISCONSIN	532
Columbia Gorge Community College	OREGON	402
Columbia-Greene Community College	NEW YORK	321
Columbia International University	SOUTH CAROLINA	443
Columbia Southern University	ALABAMA	2
Columbia State Community College	TENNESSEE	460
Columbia Theological Seminary	GEORGIA	123
Columbia University in the City of New York	NEW YORK	321
Columbus College of Art & Design	OHIO	378
Columbus State Community College	OHIO	378
Columbus State Community College-Delaware	OHIO	378
Columbus State University	GEORGIA	123
Columbus Technical College	GEORGIA	123
Comanche Nation College	OKLAHOMA	395
Commonwealth Institute of Funeral Service	TEXAS	469
Commonwealth Medical College, The	PENNSYLVANIA	413
Commonwealth Technical Institute at the Hiram G. Andrews Center	PENNSYLVANIA	413
Community Care College	OKLAHOMA	395
Community Christian College	CALIFORNIA	41
Community College of Allegheny County	PENNSYLVANIA	413
Community College of Allegheny County Boyce Campus	PENNSYLVANIA	413
Community College of Allegheny County North Campus	PENNSYLVANIA	413
Community College of Allegheny County South Campus	PENNSYLVANIA	413
Community College of Aurora	COLORADO	81
Community College of Baltimore County, The	MARYLAND	214
Community College of Beaver County	PENNSYLVANIA	413
Community College of Denver	COLORADO	81
Community College of Philadelphia	PENNSYLVANIA	413
Community College of Rhode Island	RHODE ISLAND	439
Community College of the Air Force	US SERVICE SCHOOLS	544
Community College of Vermont	VERMONT	501
Community College System of New Hampshire	NEW HAMPSHIRE	295
Community Colleges of Spokane District 17	WASHINGTON	518
Compass College of Cinematic Arts	MICHIGAN	241
Conception Seminary College	MISSOURI	272
Concord Law School of Kaplan University	CALIFORNIA	41
Concord University	WEST VIRGINIA	529
Concorde Career College	CALIFORNIA	41
Concorde Career College	COLORADO	81
Concorde Career College	MISSISSIPPI	266
Concorde Career College	MISSOURI	272
Concorde Career College	OREGON	402
Concorde Career College	TENNESSEE	453
Concorde Career College	TEXAS	469
Concorde Career Institute	FLORIDA	100
Concorde Career Institute	TEXAS	469
Concordia College	MINNESOTA	255
Concordia College	NEW YORK	321
Concordia College Alabama	ALABAMA	3
Concordia Seminary	MISSOURI	272
Concordia Theological Seminary	INDIANA	165
Concordia University	CALIFORNIA	41
Concordia University	MICHIGAN	241
Concordia University	NEBRASKA	289
Concordia University	OREGON	402
Concordia University Chicago	ILLINOIS	143
Concordia University Texas	TEXAS	469
Concordia University Wisconsin	WISCONSIN	532
Concordia University, St. Paul	MINNESOTA	255
Connecticut Board of Regents for Higher Education	CONNECTICUT	87
Connecticut College	CONNECTICUT	89
Connors State College	OKLAHOMA	395
Connors State College Muskogee Port Branch Campus	OKLAHOMA	395
Conservatory of Music of Puerto Rico	PUERTO RICO	548
Consolidated School of Business	PENNSYLVANIA	414
Consolidated School of Business	PENNSYLVANIA	413
Contra Costa College	CALIFORNIA	41
Contra Costa Community College District Office	CALIFORNIA	41
Converse College	SOUTH CAROLINA	443
Conway School of Landscape Design	MASSACHUSETTS	225
Cooper Union	NEW YORK	321
Copiah-Lincoln Community College	MISSISSIPPI	266
Copper Mountain College	CALIFORNIA	42
Coppin State University	MARYLAND	220
Corban University	OREGON	403
Corcoran College of Art and Design	DISTRICT OF COLUMBIA	95
Cornell College	IOWA	177
Cornell University	NEW YORK	322
Cornerstone University	MICHIGAN	241
Corning Community College	NEW YORK	322
Cornish College of the Arts	WASHINGTON	518
Cossatot Community College of the University of Arkansas	ARKANSAS	24
Cosumnes River College	CALIFORNIA	53
Cottey College	MISSOURI	273
County College of Morris	NEW JERSEY	300
Court Reporting Institute of Arlington	VIRGINIA	504
Court Reporting Institute of Dallas	TEXAS	469
Court Reporting Institute of St. Louis	MISSOURI	273
Covenant College	GEORGIA	123
Covenant Theological Seminary	MISSOURI	273
Cowley County Community College	KANSAS	186
Cox College	MISSOURI	273
Coyne College	ILLINOIS	143
Crafton Hills College	CALIFORNIA	61
Cranbrook Academy of Art	MICHIGAN	241
Craven Community College	NORTH CAROLINA	359
Creative Center	NEBRASKA	289
Creighton University	NEBRASKA	289
Criswell College	TEXAS	470
Crossroads Bible College	INDIANA	165
Crossroads College	MINNESOTA	255
Crouse Hospital College of Nursing	NEW YORK	322
Crowder College	MISSOURI	273
Crowley's Ridge College	ARKANSAS	20
Crown College	MINNESOTA	255
Crown College of the Bible, The	TENNESSEE	453
Cuesta College	CALIFORNIA	42
Culinary Institute LeNotre	TEXAS	470
Culinary Institute of America	NEW YORK	322
Culinary Institute of America at Greystone, The	CALIFORNIA	42
Culinary Institute of America San Antonio	TEXAS	470
Culver-Stockton College	MISSOURI	273
Cumberland County College	NEW JERSEY	301
Cumberland University	TENNESSEE	454
Curry College	MASSACHUSETTS	225
Curtis Institute of Music	PENNSYLVANIA	414
Cuyahoga Community College	OHIO	378
Cuyahoga Community College Eastern Campus	OHIO	378
Cuyahoga Community College Metropolitan Campus	OHIO	378
Cuyahoga Community College Western Campus	OHIO	378
Cuyahoga Community College Westshore	OHIO	378
Cuyamaca College	CALIFORNIA	46
Cypress College	CALIFORNIA	56
Dabney S. Lancaster Community College	VIRGINIA	512
Dade Medical College	FLORIDA	100
Dade Medical College-Hollywood	FLORIDA	101
Dade Medical College-Homestead	FLORIDA	101
Dade Medical College-Jacksonville	FLORIDA	101
Dade Medical College-Miami	FLORIDA	101
Dade Medical College-West Palm Beach	FLORIDA	101

Daemen College ..... NEW YORK 322
Dakota College at Bottineau ..... NORTH DAKOTA 372
Dakota County Technical College ..... MINNESOTA 258
Dakota State University ..... SOUTH DAKOTA 451
Dakota Wesleyan University ..... SOUTH DAKOTA 450
Dallas Baptist University ..... TEXAS 470
Dallas Christian College ..... TEXAS 470
Dallas County Community College District Office ..... TEXAS 470
Dallas Institute of Funeral Service ..... TEXAS 471
Dallas Nursing Institute ..... TEXAS 471
Dallas Theological Seminary ..... TEXAS 471
Dalton State College ..... GEORGIA 123
Daniel Webster College ..... NEW HAMPSHIRE 296
Danville Area Community College ..... ILLINOIS 143
Danville Community College ..... VIRGINIA 512
Daoist Traditions College of Chinese Medical Arts ..... NORTH CAROLINA 353
Dartmouth College ..... NEW HAMPSHIRE 296
Darton State College ..... GEORGIA 124
Davenport University ..... MICHIGAN 241
Davenport University Battle Creek ..... MICHIGAN 241
Davenport University Flint ..... MICHIGAN 241
Davenport University Holland ..... MICHIGAN 241
Davenport University Kalamazoo ..... MICHIGAN 241
Davenport University Lansing ..... MICHIGAN 241
Davenport University Livonia ..... MICHIGAN 241
Davenport University Midland ..... MICHIGAN 241
Davenport University Saginaw ..... MICHIGAN 242
Davenport University Warren ..... MICHIGAN 242
Davidson College ..... NORTH CAROLINA 353
Davidson County Community College ..... NORTH CAROLINA 360
Davis & Elkins College ..... WEST VIRGINIA 526
Davis College ..... NEW YORK 322
Davis College ..... OHIO 378
Dawson Community College ..... MONTANA 286
Daymar College-Bellevue ..... KENTUCKY 193
Daymar College-Bowling Green ..... KENTUCKY 193
Daymar College-Chillicothe ..... OHIO 378
Daymar College-Jackson ..... OHIO 378
Daymar College-Lancaster ..... OHIO 379
Daymar College-Louisville ..... KENTUCKY 193
Daymar College-Louisville East ..... KENTUCKY 193
Daymar College-Madisonville ..... KENTUCKY 193
Daymar College-New Boston ..... OHIO 379
Daymar College Online ..... KENTUCKY 193
Daymar College-Owensboro ..... KENTUCKY 193
Daymar College-Paducah ..... KENTUCKY 193
Daymar College-Scottsville ..... KENTUCKY 193
Daymar Institute ..... TENNESSEE 454
Daytona College ..... FLORIDA 101
Daytona State College ..... FLORIDA 101
De Anza College ..... CALIFORNIA 44
Dean College ..... MASSACHUSETTS 225
Dean Institute of Technology ..... PENNSYLVANIA 414
Deep Springs College ..... CALIFORNIA 42
Defense Language Institute ..... US SERVICE SCHOOLS 544
Defiance College, The ..... OHIO 379
Del Mar College ..... TEXAS 471
Delaware College of Art and Design ..... DELAWARE 93
Delaware County Community College ..... PENNSYLVANIA 414
Delaware State University ..... DELAWARE 93
Delaware Technical Community College, Office of the President ..... DELAWARE 93
Delaware Technical Community College, Owens Campus . DELAWARE 93
Delaware Technical Community College, Stanton-Wilmington Campus ..... DELAWARE 93
Delaware Technical Community College, Terry Campus ... DELAWARE 93
Delaware Valley College ..... PENNSYLVANIA 414
Delgado Community College ..... LOUISIANA 203
Dell'Arte International School of Physical Theatre ..... CALIFORNIA 42
Delta College ..... MICHIGAN 242
Delta College of Arts & Technology ..... LOUISIANA 201
Delta School of Business & Technology, DBA Delta Tech . LOUISIANA 201
Delta State University ..... MISSISSIPPI 266
Denison University ..... OHIO 379
Denmark Technical College ..... SOUTH CAROLINA 443
Denver School of Nursing ..... COLORADO 81
Denver Seminary ..... COLORADO 81
DePaul University ..... ILLINOIS 143
DePauw University ..... INDIANA 165
Des Moines Area Community College ..... IOWA 177
Des Moines Area Community College Boone Campus ..... IOWA 177
Des Moines Area Community College Carroll Campus ..... IOWA 177
Des Moines Area Community College Newton Campus ..... IOWA 177
Des Moines Area Community College Urban Campus ..... IOWA 177
Des Moines Area Community College West Des Moines Campus ..... IOWA 177
Des Moines University ..... IOWA 177
DeSales University ..... PENNSYLVANIA 414
Design Institute of San Diego ..... CALIFORNIA 42
DeVry University - Arlington Campus ..... VIRGINIA 504
DeVry University - Chicago Campus ..... ILLINOIS 144
DeVry University - Columbus Campus ..... OHIO 379
DeVry University - Decatur Campus ..... GEORGIA 124
DeVry University - Federal Way Campus ..... WASHINGTON 519
DeVry University - Fort Washington Campus ..... PENNSYLVANIA 414
DeVry University - Home Office ..... ILLINOIS 144
DeVry University - Houston Campus ..... TEXAS 471
DeVry University - Irving Campus ..... TEXAS 471
DeVry University - Kansas City Campus ..... MISSOURI 273
DeVry University - Miramar Campus ..... FLORIDA 101
DeVry University - North Brunswick Campus ..... NEW JERSEY 301
DeVry University - Orlando Campus ..... FLORIDA 101
DeVry University - Phoenix Campus ..... ARIZONA 13
DeVry University - Pomona Campus ..... CALIFORNIA 42
DeVry University - Westminster Campus ..... COLORADO 81
Diablo Valley College ..... CALIFORNIA 41
Dickinson College ..... PENNSYLVANIA 414
Dickinson State University ..... NORTH DAKOTA 371
DigiPen Institute of Technology ..... WASHINGTON 519
Digital Media Arts College ..... FLORIDA 101
Dillard University ..... LOUISIANA 201
Diné College ..... ARIZONA 13
Dine College Shiprock Branch ..... NEW MEXICO 309
Divine Word College ..... IOWA 177
Dixie State College of Utah ..... UTAH 497
Doane College ..... NEBRASKA 289
Dodge City Community College ..... KANSAS 186
Dominican College of Blauvelt ..... NEW YORK 322
Dominican School of Philosophy and Theology ..... CALIFORNIA 42
Dominican Study Center of the Caribbean ..... PUERTO RICO 548
Dominican University ..... ILLINOIS 144
Dominican University of California ..... CALIFORNIA 42
Dongguk University ..... CALIFORNIA 42
Donnelly College ..... KANSAS 186
Dordt College ..... IOWA 177
Dorothea Hopfer School of Nursing at Mount Vernon Hospital ..... NEW YORK 323
Douglas Education Center ..... PENNSYLVANIA 415
Dowling College ..... NEW YORK 323
Dragon Rises College of Oriental Medicine ..... FLORIDA 101
Drake University ..... IOWA 177
Drew University ..... NEW JERSEY 301
Drexel University ..... PENNSYLVANIA 415
Drury University ..... MISSOURI 273
Drury University Cabool Campus ..... MISSOURI 273
Drury University Ft. Leonard Wood Campus ..... MISSOURI 273
Drury University Lebanon Campus ..... MISSOURI 273
Drury University Rolla Campus ..... MISSOURI 273
DuBois Business College ..... PENNSYLVANIA 415
Duke University ..... NORTH CAROLINA 354
Duluth Business University, Inc. ..... MINNESOTA 255
Dunlap-Stone University ..... ARIZONA 13
Dunwoody College of Technology ..... MINNESOTA 255
Duquesne University ..... PENNSYLVANIA 415
Durham Technical Community College ..... NORTH CAROLINA 360
Dutchess Community College ..... NEW YORK 323
Dyersburg State Community College ..... TENNESSEE 460
D'Youville College ..... NEW YORK 323

Eagle Gate College ..... UTAH 495
Earlham College and Earlham School of Religion ..... INDIANA 165
East Arkansas Community College ..... ARKANSAS 21
East Carolina University ..... NORTH CAROLINA 367
East Central College ..... MISSOURI 273
East Central Community College ..... MISSISSIPPI 266
East Central University ..... OKLAHOMA 395
East Georgia State College ..... GEORGIA 124
East Los Angeles College ..... CALIFORNIA 51
East Mississippi Community College ..... MISSISSIPPI 266
East San Gabriel Valley Regional Occupational Program and Technical Center ..... CALIFORNIA 43
East Stroudsburg University of Pennsylvania ..... PENNSYLVANIA 428
East Tennessee State University ..... TENNESSEE 459
East Texas Baptist University ..... TEXAS 471
East West College of Natural Medicine ..... FLORIDA 101
East-West University ..... ILLINOIS 144
Eastern Arizona College ..... ARIZONA 13
Eastern Arizona College Gila Pueblo Campus ..... ARIZONA 13
Eastern Arizona College Payson Campus ..... ARIZONA 13
Eastern Connecticut State University ..... CONNECTICUT 87
Eastern Florida State College ..... FLORIDA 101
Eastern Gateway Community College - Jefferson County Campus ..... OHIO 379
Eastern Idaho Technical College ..... IDAHO 138
Eastern Illinois University ..... ILLINOIS 144
Eastern International College ..... NEW JERSEY 301
Eastern Iowa Community College District ..... IOWA 177
Eastern Kentucky University ..... KENTUCKY 193
Eastern Maine Community College ..... MAINE 210
Eastern Mennonite University ..... VIRGINIA 504
Eastern Michigan University ..... MICHIGAN 242
Eastern Nazarene College ..... MASSACHUSETTS 225
Eastern New Mexico University Main Campus ..... NEW MEXICO 309
Eastern New Mexico University-Roswell ..... NEW MEXICO 309
Eastern Oklahoma State College ..... OKLAHOMA 395
Eastern Oklahoma State College McAlester Campus ..... OKLAHOMA 395
Eastern Oregon University ..... OREGON 405
Eastern Shore Community College ..... VIRGINIA 512
Eastern University ..... PENNSYLVANIA 415
Eastern Virginia Medical School ..... VIRGINIA 504
Eastern Washington University ..... WASHINGTON 519
Eastern West Virginia Community and Technical College .. WEST VIRGINIA 528
Eastern Wyoming College ..... WYOMING 542
Eastern Wyoming College-Douglas Campus ..... WYOMING 543
Eastfield College ..... TEXAS 470
Eastwick College ..... NEW JERSEY 301
Ecclesia College ..... ARKANSAS 21
Eckerd College ..... FLORIDA 101
Ecotech Institute ..... COLORADO 81
Ecotech Institute ..... TEXAS 472
ECPI College of Technology ..... VIRGINIA 504
Ecumenical Theological Seminary ..... MICHIGAN 242
Eden Theological Seminary ..... MISSOURI 274
Edgecombe Community College ..... NORTH CAROLINA 360
Edgewood College ..... WISCONSIN 532
EDIC College ..... PUERTO RICO 548
Edinboro University of Pennsylvania ..... PENNSYLVANIA 428
Edison State College ..... FLORIDA 101

Institution	State	Page
Edison State Community College	OHIO	379
Edison State Community College Darke County Campus	OHIO	379
Edmonds Community College	WASHINGTON	519
EDP University of Puerto Rico	PUERTO RICO	548
Education Corporation of America	ALABAMA	3
Edward Via College of Osteopathic Medicine	VIRGINIA	504
Edward Waters College	FLORIDA	102
El Camino College	CALIFORNIA	43
El Camino College Compton Center	CALIFORNIA	43
El Centro College	TEXAS	470
El Paso Community College	TEXAS	472
Elgin Community College	ILLINOIS	144
Elizabeth City State University	NORTH CAROLINA	367
Elizabethtown College	PENNSYLVANIA	415
Elizabethtown Community and Technical College	KENTUCKY	195
Ellsworth Community College	IOWA	179
Elmezzi Graduate School of Molecular Medicine, The	NEW YORK	323
Elmhurst College	ILLINOIS	145
Elmira Business Institute	NEW YORK	323
Elmira College	NEW YORK	323
Elon University	NORTH CAROLINA	354
Embry-Riddle Aeronautical University	FLORIDA	102
Embry-Riddle Aeronautical University-Prescott Campus	ARIZONA	13
Embry-Riddle Aeronautical University-Worldwide	FLORIDA	102
Emerson College	MASSACHUSETTS	226
Emmanuel Christian Seminary	TENNESSEE	454
Emmanuel College	GEORGIA	124
Emmanuel College	MASSACHUSETTS	226
Emmaus Bible College	IOWA	178
Emory & Henry College	VIRGINIA	504
Emory University	GEORGIA	124
Emperor's College of Traditional Oriental Medicine	CALIFORNIA	43
Empire College School of Business	CALIFORNIA	43
Emporia State University	KANSAS	186
Endicott College	MASSACHUSETTS	226
Enterprise State Community College	ALABAMA	3
Epic Bible College	CALIFORNIA	43
Episcopal Divinity School	MASSACHUSETTS	226
Erie Business Center South	PENNSYLVANIA	416
Erie Business Center, Main	PENNSYLVANIA	416
Erie Community College City Campus	NEW YORK	323
Erie Community College North Campus	NEW YORK	323
Erie Community College-South Campus	NEW YORK	323
Erie Institute of Technology	PENNSYLVANIA	416
Erikson Institute	ILLINOIS	145
Erskine College	SOUTH CAROLINA	443
Escuela de Artes Plasticas de Puerto Rico	PUERTO RICO	548
Esperanza College	PENNSYLVANIA	416
Essex County College	NEW JERSEY	301
Essex County College-West Essex Branch Campus	NEW JERSEY	301
Estrella Mountain Community College	ARIZONA	14
Eternity Bible College	CALIFORNIA	43
ETI Technical College of Niles	OHIO	379
Eureka College	ILLINOIS	145
Evangel University	MISSOURI	274
Evangelia University	CALIFORNIA	43
Evangelical Seminary of Puerto Rico	PUERTO RICO	549
Evangelical Theological Seminary	PENNSYLVANIA	416
Everest College	COLORADO	81
Everest College	GEORGIA	124
Everest College	MISSOURI	274
Everest College	NEVADA	293
Everest College	OREGON	403
Everest College	TEXAS	472
Everest College	UTAH	495
Everest College	VIRGINIA	504
Everest College	WASHINGTON	519
Everest College-Anaheim	CALIFORNIA	43
Everest College-City of Industry	CALIFORNIA	43
Everest College-Gardena	CALIFORNIA	43
Everest College-Ontario Metro	CALIFORNIA	43
Everest College Phoenix	ARIZONA	13
Everest College Phoenix-Mesa	ARIZONA	13
Everest College-Reseda	CALIFORNIA	43
Everest College-San Bernardino	CALIFORNIA	43
Everest College-Santa Ana	CALIFORNIA	43
Everest College-West LA	CALIFORNIA	44
Everest Institute	FLORIDA	102
Everest Institute	GEORGIA	124
Everest Institute	NEW YORK	324
Everest Institute	PENNSYLVANIA	416
Everest Institute	WEST VIRGINIA	526
Everest University-Brandon Campus	FLORIDA	102
Everest University-Jacksonville Campus	FLORIDA	102
Everest University-Lakeland Campus	FLORIDA	102
Everest University-Largo	FLORIDA	102
Everest University-Melbourne Campus	FLORIDA	102
Everest University-North Orlando Campus	FLORIDA	102
Everest University-Orange Park	FLORIDA	102
Everest University-Pompano Beach Campus	FLORIDA	102
Everest University-South Orlando Campus	FLORIDA	103
Everest University-Tampa Campus	FLORIDA	103
Everett Community College	WASHINGTON	519
Everglades University	FLORIDA	103
Evergreen State College, The	WASHINGTON	519
Evergreen Valley College	CALIFORNIA	63
Excelsior College	NEW YORK	324
Ex'pression College for Digital Arts	CALIFORNIA	44
Ex'pression College for Digital Arts-San Jose	CALIFORNIA	44
Fairfield University	CONNECTICUT	89
Fairleigh Dickinson University	NEW JERSEY	301
Fairmont State University	WEST VIRGINIA	529
Faith Baptist Bible College and Seminary	IOWA	178
Faith Evangelical College & Seminary	WASHINGTON	519
Faith Theological Seminary	MARYLAND	214
Family of Faith College	OKLAHOMA	395
Farmingdale State College	NEW YORK	346
Fashion Institute of Design and Merchandising-Los Angeles	CALIFORNIA	44
Fashion Institute of Design and Merchandising-Orange County	CALIFORNIA	44
Fashion Institute of Design and Merchandising-San Diego	CALIFORNIA	44
Fashion Institute of Design and Merchandising-San Francisco	CALIFORNIA	44
Fashion Institute of Technology	NEW YORK	324
Faulkner University	ALABAMA	3
Fayetteville State University	NORTH CAROLINA	367
Fayetteville Technical Community College	NORTH CAROLINA	360
FCC-Anthem College	FLORIDA	103
Feather River College	CALIFORNIA	44
Felician College	NEW JERSEY	302
Ferris State University	MICHIGAN	242
Ferrum College	VIRGINIA	504
Fielding Graduate University	CALIFORNIA	44
FINE Mortuary College	MASSACHUSETTS	226
Finger Lakes Community College	NEW YORK	324
Finger Lakes Health College of Nursing	NEW YORK	324
Finlandia University	MICHIGAN	242
Fisher College	MASSACHUSETTS	226
Fisk University	TENNESSEE	454
Fitchburg State University	MASSACHUSETTS	229
Five Branches University, Graduate School of Traditional Chinese Medicine	CALIFORNIA	44
Five Towns College	NEW YORK	324
Flagler College	FLORIDA	103
Flathead Valley Community College	MONTANA	286
Flint Hills Technical College	KANSAS	186
Florence - Darlington Technical College	SOUTH CAROLINA	443
Florida Agricultural and Mechanical University	FLORIDA	114
Florida Atlantic University	FLORIDA	114
Florida Career College	FLORIDA	103
Florida Coastal School of Law	FLORIDA	103
Florida College	FLORIDA	104
Florida College of Integrative Medicine	FLORIDA	104
Florida College of Natural Health	FLORIDA	104
Florida Gateway College	FLORIDA	104
Florida Gulf Coast University	FLORIDA	115
Florida Institute of Technology	FLORIDA	104
Florida International University	FLORIDA	115
Florida Keys Community College	FLORIDA	104
Florida Memorial University	FLORIDA	104
Florida National University Hialeah Campus	FLORIDA	105
Florida National University South Campus	FLORIDA	105
Florida National University Training Center	FLORIDA	105
Florida Southern College	FLORIDA	105
Florida State College at Jacksonville	FLORIDA	105
Florida State University	FLORIDA	115
Florida Technical College	FLORIDA	105
Folsom Lake College	CALIFORNIA	53
Fond du Lac Tribal and Community College	MINNESOTA	258
Fontbonne University	MISSOURI	274
Foothill College	CALIFORNIA	44
Foothill-De Anza Community College District System Office	CALIFORNIA	44
Fordham University	NEW YORK	324
Forrest College	SOUTH CAROLINA	444
Forsyth Technical Community College	NORTH CAROLINA	360
Fort Hays State University	KANSAS	186
Fort Lewis College	COLORADO	81
Fort Peck Community College	MONTANA	286
Fort Scott Community College	KANSAS	186
Fort Valley State University	GEORGIA	124
Fortis College	ALABAMA	3
Fortis College	FLORIDA	105
Fortis College	INDIANA	165
Fortis College	LOUISIANA	202
Fortis College	MARYLAND	214
Fortis College	OHIO	379
Fortis College	UTAH	495
Fortis College	VIRGINIA	505
Fortis College-Montgomery (Atlanta Highway)	ALABAMA	3
Fortis College-Montgomery (Eastdale Circle)	ALABAMA	3
Fortis College, Phoenix	ARIZONA	13
Fortis Institute	ALABAMA	3
Fortis Institute	FLORIDA	106
Fortis Institute	FLORIDA	105
Fortis Institute	PENNSYLVANIA	416
Fortis Institute	TENNESSEE	454
Fortis Institute-Nashville	TENNESSEE	454
Fortis Institute-Pensacola	FLORIDA	106
Fortis Institute-Port St. Lucie	FLORIDA	106
Fountainhead College of Technology	TENNESSEE	454
Fox College	ILLINOIS	145
Fox Valley Technical College	WISCONSIN	539
Fox Valley Technical College	WISCONSIN	541
Framingham State University	MASSACHUSETTS	230
Francis Marion University	SOUTH CAROLINA	444
Franciscan School of Theology	CALIFORNIA	45
Franciscan University of Steubenville	OHIO	379
Frank Lloyd Wright School of Architecture	ARIZONA	13
Frank Phillips College	TEXAS	472
Franklin & Marshall College	PENNSYLVANIA	416
Franklin College of Indiana	INDIANA	165
Franklin Pierce University	NEW HAMPSHIRE	296
Franklin University	OHIO	380
Franklin W. Olin College of Engineering	MASSACHUSETTS	226
Frederick Community College	MARYLAND	214

Institution	State	Page
Freed-Hardeman University	TENNESSEE	454
Fremont College	CALIFORNIA	45
Fresno City College	CALIFORNIA	68
Fresno Pacific University	CALIFORNIA	45
Friends University	KANSAS	186
Front Range Community College	COLORADO	81
Front Range Community College Boulder County Campus.	COLORADO	82
Front Range Community College Larimer Campus	COLORADO	82
Frontier Nursing University	KENTUCKY	194
Frostburg State University	MARYLAND	220
Ft. Berthold Community College	NORTH DAKOTA	371
Full Sail University	FLORIDA	106
Fuller Theological Seminary	CALIFORNIA	45
Fullerton College	CALIFORNIA	56
Fulton-Montgomery Community College	NEW YORK	325
Furman University	SOUTH CAROLINA	444
Future Generations Graduate School	WEST VIRGINIA	526
Gadsden State Community College	ALABAMA	3
Galen College of Nursing	FLORIDA	106
Galen College of Nursing	KENTUCKY	194
Galen College of Nursing	OHIO	380
Galen College of Nursing	TEXAS	472
Gallaudet University	DISTRICT OF COLUMBIA	95
Gallipolis Career College	OHIO	380
Galveston College	TEXAS	472
Gannon University	PENNSYLVANIA	416
Garden City Community College	KANSAS	187
Gardner-Webb University	NORTH CAROLINA	354
Garrett College	MARYLAND	214
Garrett-Evangelical Theological Seminary	ILLINOIS	145
Gaston College	NORTH CAROLINA	360
Gateway Community and Technical College	KENTUCKY	195
Gateway Community College	ARIZONA	14
Gateway Community College	CONNECTICUT	88
Gateway Technical College	WISCONSIN	540
Gateway Technical College Burlington Center	WISCONSIN	542
Gateway Technical College Elkhorn Campus	WISCONSIN	542
Gateway Technical College Racine Campus	WISCONSIN	542
Gavilan College	CALIFORNIA	45
General Theological Seminary	NEW YORK	325
Genesee Community College	NEW YORK	325
Geneva College	PENNSYLVANIA	417
George C. Wallace Community College - Dothan	ALABAMA	3
George Corley Wallace State Community College - Selma.	ALABAMA	4
George Fox University	OREGON	403
George Mason University	VIRGINIA	505
George Washington University	DISTRICT OF COLUMBIA	95
George Williams College of Aurora University	WISCONSIN	533
Georgetown College	KENTUCKY	194
Georgetown University	DISTRICT OF COLUMBIA	95
Georgia Christian University	GEORGIA	124
Georgia College & State University	GEORGIA	125
Georgia Gwinnett College	GEORGIA	125
Georgia Highlands College	GEORGIA	125
Georgia Institute of Technology	GEORGIA	125
Georgia Military College	GEORGIA	125
Georgia Northwestern Technical College	GEORGIA	125
Georgia Perimeter College	GEORGIA	125
Georgia Piedmont Technical College	GEORGIA	126
Georgia Regents University	GEORGIA	126
Georgia Southern University	GEORGIA	126
Georgia Southwestern State University	GEORGIA	126
Georgia State University	GEORGIA	126
Georgian Court University	NEW JERSEY	302
Germanna Community College	VIRGINIA	512
Gettysburg College	PENNSYLVANIA	417
Gillette College	WYOMING	543
Glen Oaks Community College	MICHIGAN	242
Glendale Community College	ARIZONA	14
Glendale Community College	CALIFORNIA	45
Glendale Community College North	ARIZONA	15
Glenville State College	WEST VIRGINIA	529
Global Health College	VIRGINIA	505
Global University	MISSOURI	274
Globe Institute of Technology	NEW YORK	325
Globe University	MINNESOTA	255
Globe University	SOUTH DAKOTA	450
Globe University-Appleton	WISCONSIN	533
Globe University-Eau Claire	WISCONSIN	533
Globe University-Green Bay	WISCONSIN	533
Globe University-La Crosse	WISCONSIN	533
Globe University-Madison East	WISCONSIN	533
Globe University-Middleton	WISCONSIN	533
Globe University-Wausau	WISCONSIN	533
Gloucester County College	NEW JERSEY	302
Goddard College	VERMONT	499
God's Bible School and College	OHIO	380
Gogebic Community College	MICHIGAN	242
Golden Gate Baptist Theological Seminary	CALIFORNIA	45
Golden Gate University	CALIFORNIA	45
Golden West College	CALIFORNIA	39
Goldey-Beacom College	DELAWARE	93
Goldfarb School of Nursing at Barnes-Jewish College	MISSOURI	274
Golf Academy of America	ARIZONA	13
Golf Academy of America	CALIFORNIA	45
Golf Academy of America	FLORIDA	106
Golf Academy of America	SOUTH CAROLINA	444
Golf Academy of America	TEXAS	472
Gonzaga University	WASHINGTON	520
Good Samaritan College of Nursing and Health Science	OHIO	380
Goodwin College	CONNECTICUT	90
Gordon College	MASSACHUSETTS	226
Gordon-Conwell Theological Seminary	MASSACHUSETTS	227
Gordon-Conwell Theological Seminary-Jacksonville	FLORIDA	106
Gordon State College	GEORGIA	127
Goshen College	INDIANA	166
Goucher College	MARYLAND	215
Governors State University	ILLINOIS	145
Grace Bible College	MICHIGAN	243
Grace College and Seminary	INDIANA	166
Grace College of Divinity	NORTH CAROLINA	354
Grace Communion Seminary	CALIFORNIA	45
Grace Mission University	CALIFORNIA	46
Grace School of Theology	TEXAS	472
Grace University	NEBRASKA	289
Graceland University	IOWA	178
Graceland University	MISSOURI	274
Graduate Institute of Applied Linguistics	TEXAS	472
Graduate School USA	DISTRICT OF COLUMBIA	95
Graduate Theological Union	CALIFORNIA	46
Grambling State University	LOUISIANA	207
Grand Canyon University	ARIZONA	13
Grand Rapids Community College	MICHIGAN	243
Grand Valley State University	MICHIGAN	243
Grand Valley State University Meijer Campus	MICHIGAN	243
Grand Valley State University Pew Campus	MICHIGAN	243
Grand View University	IOWA	178
Granite State College	NEW HAMPSHIRE	298
Grantham University	MISSOURI	274
Gratz College	PENNSYLVANIA	417
Grays Harbor College	WASHINGTON	520
Grayson College	TEXAS	472
Great Basin College	NEVADA	294
Great Bay Community College	NEW HAMPSHIRE	295
Great Falls College Montana State University	MONTANA	287
Great Lakes Christian College	MICHIGAN	243
Great Lakes Institute of Technology	PENNSYLVANIA	417
Green Mountain College	VERMONT	499
Green River Community College	WASHINGTON	520
Greenfield Community College	MASSACHUSETTS	231
Greensboro College	NORTH CAROLINA	354
Greenville College	ILLINOIS	145
Greenville Technical College	SOUTH CAROLINA	444
Griggs University	MICHIGAN	243
Grinnell College	IOWA	178
Grossmont College	CALIFORNIA	46
Grossmont-Cuyamaca Community College District	CALIFORNIA	46
Grove City College	PENNSYLVANIA	417
Guam Community College	GUAM	546
Guilford College	NORTH CAROLINA	355
Guilford Technical Community College	NORTH CAROLINA	360
Gulf Coast State College	FLORIDA	106
Gupton Jones College of Funeral Service	GEORGIA	127
Gurnick Academy of Medical Arts	CALIFORNIA	46
Gustavus Adolphus College	MINNESOTA	255
Gutenberg College	OREGON	403
Gwinnett College	GEORGIA	127
Gwinnett Technical College	GEORGIA	127
Gwynedd-Mercy University	PENNSYLVANIA	417
Gwynedd-Mercy University Plymouth Meeting at East Norriton	PENNSYLVANIA	417
Hagerstown Community College	MARYLAND	215
Halifax Community College	NORTH CAROLINA	361
Hallmark College of Technology	TEXAS	472
Hamilton College	NEW YORK	325
Hamilton Technical College	IOWA	178
Hamline University	MINNESOTA	256
Hampden-Sydney College	VIRGINIA	505
Hampshire College	MASSACHUSETTS	227
Hampton University	VIRGINIA	505
Han University of Traditional Medicine	ARIZONA	13
Hannibal-La Grange University	MISSOURI	274
Hanover College	INDIANA	166
Harcum College	PENNSYLVANIA	417
Hardin-Simmons University	TEXAS	472
Harding School of Theology	TENNESSEE	454
Harding University Main Campus	ARKANSAS	21
Harford Community College	MARYLAND	215
Harper College	ILLINOIS	145
Harrington College of Design	ILLINOIS	146
Harris-Stowe State University	MISSOURI	275
Harrisburg Area Community College	PENNSYLVANIA	417
Harrisburg Area Community College Gettysburg Campus	PENNSYLVANIA	418
Harrisburg Area Community College Lancaster Campus	PENNSYLVANIA	418
Harrisburg Area Community College Lebanon Campus	PENNSYLVANIA	418
Harrisburg Area Community College York Campus	PENNSYLVANIA	418
Harrisburg University of Science and Technology	PENNSYLVANIA	418
Harrison College	OHIO	380
Harrison College - Anderson Campus	INDIANA	166
Harrison College - Columbus Indiana Campus	INDIANA	166
Harrison College - Elkhart Campus	INDIANA	166
Harrison College - Evansville Campus	INDIANA	166
Harrison College - Fort Wayne Campus	INDIANA	166
Harrison College - Indianapolis Downtown Campus	INDIANA	166
Harrison College - Indianapolis East Campus	INDIANA	166
Harrison College - Indianapolis Northwest Campus	INDIANA	166
Harrison College - Lafayette Campus	INDIANA	166
Harrison College - Terre Haute Campus	INDIANA	166
Harrison Middleton University	ARIZONA	14
Hartford Seminary	CONNECTICUT	90
Hartnell College	CALIFORNIA	46
Hartwick College	NEW YORK	325
Harvard University	MASSACHUSETTS	227
Harvey Mudd College	CALIFORNIA	46
Haskell Indian Nations University	KANSAS	187
Hastings College	NEBRASKA	289

Institution	State	Page
Haverford College	PENNSYLVANIA	418
Hawaii College of Oriental Medicine	HAWAII	135
Hawaii Pacific University	HAWAII	135
Hawaii Tokai International College	HAWAII	135
Hawkeye Community College	IOWA	178
Haywood Community College	NORTH CAROLINA	361
Hazard Community and Technical College	KENTUCKY	195
Hazelden Graduate School of Addiction Studies	MINNESOTA	256
Heald College, Central Office	CALIFORNIA	46
Heald College, Concord	CALIFORNIA	46
Heald College, Fresno	CALIFORNIA	46
Heald College, Hayward	CALIFORNIA	46
Heald College, Honolulu	HAWAII	135
Heald College, Milpitas	CALIFORNIA	47
Heald College, Modesto	CALIFORNIA	47
Heald College, Portland	OREGON	403
Heald College, Rancho Cordova	CALIFORNIA	47
Heald College, Roseville	CALIFORNIA	47
Heald College, Salinas	CALIFORNIA	47
Heald College, San Francisco	CALIFORNIA	47
Heald College, Stockton	CALIFORNIA	47
Health Career Institute	FLORIDA	106
Heartland Christian College	MISSOURI	275
Heartland Community College	ILLINOIS	146
Hebrew College	MASSACHUSETTS	227
Hebrew Theological College	ILLINOIS	146
Hebrew Union College-Jewish Institute of Religion	NEW YORK	325
Heidelberg University	OHIO	380
Helene Fuld College of Nursing	NEW YORK	325
Hellenic College-Holy Cross Greek Orthodox School of Theology	MASSACHUSETTS	227
Henderson Community College	KENTUCKY	195
Henderson State University	ARKANSAS	21
Hendrix College	ARKANSAS	21
Henley-Putnam University	CALIFORNIA	47
Hennepin Technical College	MINNESOTA	258
Hennepin Technical College	MINNESOTA	256
Henry Ford Community College	MICHIGAN	243
Heritage Bible College	NORTH CAROLINA	355
Heritage Christian University	ALABAMA	4
Heritage College	COLORADO	82
Heritage College	MISSOURI	275
Heritage College	OKLAHOMA	395
Heritage College-Wichita	KANSAS	187
Heritage Institute-Fort Myers	FLORIDA	106
Heritage Institute-Jacksonville	FLORIDA	106
Heritage University	WASHINGTON	520
Herkimer County Community College	NEW YORK	326
Herzing University	ALABAMA	4
Herzing University	FLORIDA	106
Herzing University	GEORGIA	127
Herzing University	LOUISIANA	202
Herzing University	MINNESOTA	256
Herzing University	WISCONSIN	533
Herzing University-Akron	OHIO	380
Herzing University Brookfield Campus	WISCONSIN	533
Herzing University Kenosha Campus	WISCONSIN	533
Herzing University Online Campus	WISCONSIN	533
Herzing University Toledo Campus	OHIO	380
Hesston College	KANSAS	187
Hibbing Community College, A Technical and Community College	MINNESOTA	258
Hickey College	MISSOURI	275
High Point University	NORTH CAROLINA	355
High Tech High Graduate School of Education	CALIFORNIA	47
Highland Community College	ILLINOIS	146
Highland Community College	KANSAS	187
Highlands College of Montana Tech	MONTANA	287
Highline Community College	WASHINGTON	520
Hilbert College	NEW YORK	326
Hill College	TEXAS	473
Hillsborough Community College	FLORIDA	106
Hillsdale College	MICHIGAN	243
Hillsdale Free Will Baptist College	OKLAHOMA	395
Hinds Community College	MISSISSIPPI	267
Hiram College	OHIO	380
Hiwassee College	TENNESSEE	454
Hobart and William Smith Colleges	NEW YORK	326
Hobe Sound Bible College	FLORIDA	106
Hocking College	OHIO	380
Hocking College Perry Campus	OHIO	381
Hodges University	FLORIDA	106
Hofstra University	NEW YORK	326
Hollins University	VIRGINIA	505
Holmes Community College	MISSISSIPPI	267
Holmes Institute of Consciousness Studies	COLORADO	82
Holy Apostles College and Seminary	CONNECTICUT	90
Holy Cross College	INDIANA	166
Holy Family University	PENNSYLVANIA	418
Holy Names University	CALIFORNIA	47
Holy Trinity Orthodox Seminary	NEW YORK	326
Holyoke Community College	MASSACHUSETTS	231
Hondros College	OHIO	381
Hood College	MARYLAND	215
Hood Theological Seminary	NORTH CAROLINA	355
Hope College	MICHIGAN	244
Hope International University	CALIFORNIA	47
Hopkinsville Community College	KENTUCKY	195
Horizon University	CALIFORNIA	47
Horry-Georgetown Technical College	SOUTH CAROLINA	444
Hostos Community College-City University of New York	NEW YORK	318
Houghton College	NEW YORK	326
Housatonic Community College	CONNECTICUT	88
Houston Baptist University	TEXAS	473
Houston Community College	TEXAS	473
Houston Graduate School of Theology	TEXAS	473
Howard College	TEXAS	473
Howard Community College	MARYLAND	215
Howard Payne University	TEXAS	473
Howard University	DISTRICT OF COLUMBIA	95
Hudson County Community College	NEW JERSEY	302
Hudson Valley Community College	NEW YORK	326
Huertas Junior College	PUERTO RICO	549
Hult International Business School	MASSACHUSETTS	227
Humacao Community College	PUERTO RICO	549
Humboldt State University	CALIFORNIA	35
Humphreys College	CALIFORNIA	47
Huntingdon College	ALABAMA	4
Huntington College of Health Sciences	TENNESSEE	454
Huntington Junior College	WEST VIRGINIA	526
Huntington University	INDIANA	166
Huntsville Bible College	ALABAMA	4
Hussian School of Art	PENNSYLVANIA	418
Husson University	MAINE	210
Huston-Tillotson University	TEXAS	473
Hutchinson Community College and Area Vocational School	KANSAS	187
Icahn School of Medicine at Mount Sinai	NEW YORK	327
ICPR Junior College	PUERTO RICO	549
ICPR Junior College-Arecibo Campus	PUERTO RICO	549
ICPR Junior College-Manati Branch Campus	PUERTO RICO	549
ICPR Junior College-Mayaguez Campus	PUERTO RICO	549
Idaho State University	IDAHO	138
iGlobal University	VIRGINIA	505
Iliff School of Theology	COLORADO	82
Ilisagvik College	ALASKA	10
Illinois Central College	ILLINOIS	146
Illinois College	ILLINOIS	146
Illinois College of Optometry	ILLINOIS	146
Illinois Eastern Community Colleges Frontier Community College	ILLINOIS	146
Illinois Eastern Community Colleges Lincoln Trail College	ILLINOIS	147
Illinois Eastern Community Colleges Olney Central College	ILLINOIS	147
Illinois Eastern Community Colleges System Office	ILLINOIS	146
Illinois Eastern Community Colleges Wabash Valley College	ILLINOIS	147
Illinois Institute of Art-Schaumburg, The	ILLINOIS	147
Illinois Institute of Art, The	ILLINOIS	147
Illinois Institute of Technology	ILLINOIS	147
Illinois Institute of Technology Downtown Campus	ILLINOIS	147
Illinois Institute of Technology Institute of Design	ILLINOIS	147
Illinois Institute of Technology Rice Campus	ILLINOIS	147
Illinois State University	ILLINOIS	147
Illinois Valley Community College	ILLINOIS	148
Illinois Wesleyan University	ILLINOIS	148
Immaculata University	PENNSYLVANIA	418
Imperial Valley College	CALIFORNIA	48
Independence Community College	KANSAS	187
Independence University	UTAH	495
Indian Hills Community College	IOWA	179
Indian Hills Community College Centerville	IOWA	179
Indian River State College	FLORIDA	106
Indiana State University	INDIANA	167
Indiana Tech	INDIANA	167
Indiana Tech-Elkhart	INDIANA	167
Indiana Tech-Indianapolis	INDIANA	167
Indiana Tech-Louisville	KENTUCKY	194
Indiana University	INDIANA	167
Indiana University Bloomington	INDIANA	167
Indiana University East	INDIANA	167
Indiana University Kokomo	INDIANA	168
Indiana University Northwest	INDIANA	168
Indiana University of Pennsylvania	PENNSYLVANIA	428
Indiana University-Purdue University Columbus	INDIANA	169
Indiana University-Purdue University Fort Wayne	INDIANA	168
Indiana University-Purdue University Indianapolis	INDIANA	168
Indiana University South Bend	INDIANA	168
Indiana University Southeast	INDIANA	168
Indiana Wesleyan University	INDIANA	169
Inste Bible College	IOWA	179
Institute for Clinical Social Work	ILLINOIS	148
Institute for Doctoral Studies in the Visual Arts	MAINE	210
Institute for the Psychological Sciences	VIRGINIA	505
Institute of American Indian Arts	NEW MEXICO	309
Institute of Business and Medical Careers	COLORADO	82
Institute of Business and Medical Careers	WYOMING	543
Institute of Clinical Acupuncture and Oriental Medicine	HAWAII	135
Institute of Design and Construction	NEW YORK	327
Institute of Production and Recording	MINNESOTA	256
Institute of Taoist Education and Acupuncture	COLORADO	82
Institute of Technical Arts	FLORIDA	107
Institute of Technology	CALIFORNIA	48
Institute of World Politics, The	DISTRICT OF COLUMBIA	96
Instituto de Banca y Comercio	PUERTO RICO	549
IntelliTec College	COLORADO	82
IntelliTec Medical Institute	COLORADO	82
Inter American University of Puerto Rico Aguadilla Campus	PUERTO RICO	549
Inter American University of Puerto Rico Arecibo Campus	PUERTO RICO	549
Inter American University of Puerto Rico Barranquitas Campus	PUERTO RICO	550
Inter American University of Puerto Rico Bayamon Campus	PUERTO RICO	550
Inter American University of Puerto Rico Central Office	PUERTO RICO	549
Inter American University of Puerto Rico Fajardo Campus	PUERTO RICO	550

Institution	State	Page
Inter American University of Puerto Rico Guayama Campus	PUERTO RICO	550
Inter American University of Puerto Rico Metropolitan Campus	PUERTO RICO	550
Inter American University of Puerto Rico Ponce Campus	PUERTO RICO	550
Inter American University of Puerto Rico San German Campus	PUERTO RICO	551
Inter American University of Puerto Rico School of Law	PUERTO RICO	551
Inter American University of Puerto Rico School of Optometry	PUERTO RICO	551
Interactive College of Technology	GEORGIA	127
Interactive College of Technology	KENTUCKY	194
Interdenominational Theological Center	GEORGIA	127
Interface College	WASHINGTON	520
Interior Designers Institute	CALIFORNIA	48
International Academy of Design and Technology	CALIFORNIA	48
International Academy of Design and Technology	FLORIDA	107
International Academy of Design and Technology	ILLINOIS	148
International Academy of Design and Technology	MICHIGAN	244
International Academy of Design and Technology	NEVADA	293
International Academy of Design and Technology	TENNESSEE	454
International Academy of Design and Technology	TEXAS	474
International Academy of Design and Technology	WASHINGTON	520
International Academy of Design and Technology-Schaumburg	ILLINOIS	148
International Baptist College	ARIZONA	14
International Business College	INDIANA	169
International Business College	TEXAS	474
International Business College-East Campus	TEXAS	474
International College of Broadcasting	OHIO	381
International Institute for Restorative Practices	PENNSYLVANIA	418
International Professional School of Bodywork	CALIFORNIA	48
International Reformed University and Seminary	CALIFORNIA	48
International Technological University	CALIFORNIA	48
International Theological Seminary	CALIFORNIA	48
Inver Hills Community College	MINNESOTA	258
Iona College	NEW YORK	327
Iowa Central Community College	IOWA	179
Iowa Lakes Community College	IOWA	179
Iowa Lakes Community College Emmetsburg Campus	IOWA	179
Iowa Lakes Community College Spencer Campus	IOWA	179
Iowa State University	IOWA	175
Iowa Valley Community College District	IOWA	179
Iowa Wesleyan College	IOWA	179
Iowa Western Community College	IOWA	179
Iowa Western Community College Clarinda Center	IOWA	180
Irish American University	DELAWARE	94
Irvine Valley College	CALIFORNIA	67
Island Drafting and Technical Institute	NEW YORK	327
Isothermal Community College	NORTH CAROLINA	361
Itasca Community College	MINNESOTA	258
Itawamba Community College	MISSISSIPPI	267
Ithaca College	NEW YORK	327
ITI Technical College	LOUISIANA	202
ITT Technical Institute	ALABAMA	4
ITT Technical Institute	ARIZONA	14
ITT Technical Institute	ARKANSAS	21
ITT Technical Institute	CALIFORNIA	48
ITT Technical Institute	CALIFORNIA	49
ITT Technical Institute	CALIFORNIA	48
ITT Technical Institute	COLORADO	82
ITT Technical Institute	FLORIDA	107
ITT Technical Institute	GEORGIA	127
ITT Technical Institute	IDAHO	138
ITT Technical Institute	ILLINOIS	148
ITT Technical Institute	INDIANA	169
ITT Technical Institute	IOWA	180
ITT Technical Institute	KANSAS	187
ITT Technical Institute	KENTUCKY	194
ITT Technical Institute	LOUISIANA	202
ITT Technical Institute	MARYLAND	215
ITT Technical Institute	MASSACHUSETTS	227
ITT Technical Institute	MICHIGAN	244
ITT Technical Institute	MINNESOTA	256
ITT Technical Institute	MISSISSIPPI	267
ITT Technical Institute	MISSOURI	275
ITT Technical Institute	NEBRASKA	290
ITT Technical Institute	NEVADA	293
ITT Technical Institute	NEVADA	294
ITT Technical Institute	NEW JERSEY	302
ITT Technical Institute	NEW MEXICO	309
ITT Technical Institute	NEW YORK	327
ITT Technical Institute	NORTH CAROLINA	355
ITT Technical Institute	OHIO	381
ITT Technical Institute	OKLAHOMA	395
ITT Technical Institute	OREGON	403
ITT Technical Institute	PENNSYLVANIA	419
ITT Technical Institute	PENNSYLVANIA	418
ITT Technical Institute	PENNSYLVANIA	419
ITT Technical Institute	PENNSYLVANIA	418
ITT Technical Institute	PENNSYLVANIA	419
ITT Technical Institute	SOUTH CAROLINA	444
ITT Technical Institute	TENNESSEE	455
ITT Technical Institute	TEXAS	474
ITT Technical Institute	UTAH	495
ITT Technical Institute	VIRGINIA	506
ITT Technical Institute	WASHINGTON	520
ITT Technical Institute	WEST VIRGINIA	527
ITT Technical Institute	WISCONSIN	533
Ivy Tech Community College-Central Indiana	INDIANA	169
Ivy Tech Community College of Indiana- North Central	INDIANA	170
Ivy Tech Community College of Indiana-Anderson	INDIANA	169
Ivy Tech Community College of Indiana-Bloomington	INDIANA	169
Ivy Tech Community College of Indiana-Central Office	INDIANA	169
Ivy Tech Community College of Indiana-Columbus	INDIANA	169
Ivy Tech Community College of Indiana-East Central	INDIANA	169
Ivy Tech Community College of Indiana-East Chicago	INDIANA	169
Ivy Tech Community College of Indiana-Elkhart	INDIANA	169
Ivy Tech Community College of Indiana-Kokomo	INDIANA	169
Ivy Tech Community College of Indiana-Lafayette	INDIANA	170
Ivy Tech Community College of Indiana-Lawrenceburg-Riverfront	INDIANA	170
Ivy Tech Community College of Indiana-Logansport	INDIANA	170
Ivy Tech Community College of Indiana-Marion	INDIANA	170
Ivy Tech Community College of Indiana-Michigan City	INDIANA	170
Ivy Tech Community College of Indiana-Northeast	INDIANA	170
Ivy Tech Community College of Indiana-Northwest	INDIANA	170
Ivy Tech Community College of Indiana-Richmond	INDIANA	170
Ivy Tech Community College of Indiana-Southeast	INDIANA	170
Ivy Tech Community College of Indiana-Southern Indiana	INDIANA	170
Ivy Tech Community College of Indiana-Southwest	INDIANA	170
Ivy Tech Community College of Indiana-Valparaiso	INDIANA	170
Ivy Tech Community College of Indiana-Wabash	INDIANA	170
Ivy Tech Community College of Indiana-Wabash Valley	INDIANA	170
Ivy Tech Community College of Indiana-Warsaw	INDIANA	170
J. Sargeant Reynolds Community College	VIRGINIA	512
Jackson College	MICHIGAN	244
Jackson State Community College	TENNESSEE	460
Jackson State University	MISSISSIPPI	267
Jacksonville College	TEXAS	474
Jacksonville State University	ALABAMA	4
Jacksonville University	FLORIDA	107
James A. Rhodes State College	OHIO	381
James H. Faulkner State Community College	ALABAMA	4
James Madison University	VIRGINIA	506
James Sprunt Community College	NORTH CAROLINA	361
Jamestown Business College	NEW YORK	327
Jamestown Community College	NEW YORK	327
Jamestown Community College Cattaraugus County Campus	NEW YORK	327
Jarvis Christian College	TEXAS	474
Jefferson College	MISSOURI	275
Jefferson College of Health Sciences	VIRGINIA	506
Jefferson Community and Technical College	KENTUCKY	195
Jefferson Community College	NEW YORK	327
Jefferson Davis Community College	ALABAMA	5
Jefferson State Community College	ALABAMA	5
Jewish Theological Seminary of America	NEW YORK	328
J.F. Drake State Technical College	ALABAMA	4
J.F. Ingram State Technical College	ALABAMA	4
JNA Institute of Culinary Arts	PENNSYLVANIA	419
John A. Gupton College	TENNESSEE	455
John A. Logan College	ILLINOIS	148
John Brown University	ARKANSAS	21
John Carroll University	OHIO	381
John Dewey College	PUERTO RICO	551
John Dewey College-Bayamon	PUERTO RICO	551
John Dewey College-Carolina	PUERTO RICO	551
John Dewey College-Fajardo	PUERTO RICO	551
John Dewey College-Juana Diaz	PUERTO RICO	551
John Dewey College-Manati	PUERTO RICO	551
John F. Kennedy University	CALIFORNIA	49
John Hancock University	ILLINOIS	148
John Leland Center for Theological Studies, The	VIRGINIA	506
John Marshall Law School	ILLINOIS	148
John Paul the Great Catholic University	CALIFORNIA	49
John Tyler Community College	VIRGINIA	512
John Wood Community College	ILLINOIS	148
Johns Hopkins University	MARYLAND	215
Johnson & Wales University	FLORIDA	107
Johnson & Wales University	RHODE ISLAND	439
Johnson & Wales University-Charlotte	NORTH CAROLINA	355
Johnson & Wales University - Denver Campus	COLORADO	82
Johnson C. Smith University	NORTH CAROLINA	355
Johnson College	PENNSYLVANIA	419
Johnson County Community College	KANSAS	187
Johnson State College	VERMONT	501
Johnson University	TENNESSEE	455
Johnson University Florida	FLORIDA	107
Johnston Community College	NORTH CAROLINA	361
Joint Forces Staff College	US SERVICE SCHOOLS	544
Joliet Junior College	ILLINOIS	149
Jones College	FLORIDA	107
Jones County Junior College	MISSISSIPPI	267
Jones International University	COLORADO	82
Jose Maria Vargas University	FLORIDA	107
Judge Advocate General's Legal Center & School, The	US SERVICE SCHOOLS	544
Judson College	ALABAMA	5
Judson University	ILLINOIS	149
Juilliard School, The	NEW YORK	328
Juniata College	PENNSYLVANIA	419
Kaiser Permanente School of Allied Health Sciences	CALIFORNIA	49
Kalamazoo College	MICHIGAN	244
Kalamazoo Valley Community College	MICHIGAN	244
Kalamazoo Valley Community College Arcadia Commons Campus	MICHIGAN	244
Kanawha Valley Community & Technical College	WEST VIRGINIA	528
Kankakee Community College	ILLINOIS	149
Kansas City Art Institute	MISSOURI	275
Kansas City College and Bible School	KANSAS	187
Kansas City Kansas Community College	KANSAS	187
Kansas City University of Medicine & Biosciences	MISSOURI	275
Kansas State University	KANSAS	188
Kansas State University-Salina, College of Technology and Aviation	KANSAS	188
Kansas Wesleyan University	KANSAS	188

Institution	State	Page
Kapiolani Community College	HAWAII	136
Kaplan Career Institute	MICHIGAN	244
Kaplan Career Institute	OHIO	381
Kaplan Career Institute	PENNSYLVANIA	419
Kaplan Career Institute	TENNESSEE	455
Kaplan Career Institute/Broomall Campus	PENNSYLVANIA	419
Kaplan Career Institute - ICM Campus	PENNSYLVANIA	419
Kaplan College	ARIZONA	14
Kaplan College	CALIFORNIA	49
Kaplan College	FLORIDA	108
Kaplan College	INDIANA	170
Kaplan College	NEVADA	294
Kaplan College	NORTH CAROLINA	355
Kaplan College	OHIO	381
Kaplan College	OHIO	382
Kaplan College	TEXAS	474
Kaplan College	TEXAS	475
Kaplan College	TEXAS	474
Kaplan College	TEXAS	475
Kaplan University	IOWA	180
Kaplan University	MARYLAND	215
Kaplan University	NEBRASKA	290
Kaplan University-Augusta	MAINE	210
Kaplan University-Cedar Falls	IOWA	180
Kaplan University-Council Bluffs	IOWA	180
Kaplan University-Lewiston	MAINE	210
Kaplan University-Maine	MAINE	210
Kaskaskia College	ILLINOIS	149
KD Studio-Actors Conservatory	TEXAS	475
Kean University	NEW JERSEY	302
Keck Graduate Institute	CALIFORNIA	39
Keene State College	NEW HAMPSHIRE	298
Kehilath Yakov Rabbinical Seminary	NEW YORK	328
Keiser University	FLORIDA	108
Kellogg Community College	MICHIGAN	244
Kendall College	ILLINOIS	149
Kendall College of Art & Design	MICHIGAN	244
Kennebec Valley Community College	MAINE	210
Kennesaw State University	GEORGIA	127
Kenrick-Glennon Seminary-Kenrick School of Theology	MISSOURI	275
Kent State University at Ashtabula	OHIO	382
Kent State University East Liverpool Campus	OHIO	382
Kent State University Geauga Campus	OHIO	382
Kent State University Main Campus	OHIO	382
Kent State University Salem Campus	OHIO	382
Kent State University Stark Campus	OHIO	382
Kent State University Trumbull Campus	OHIO	382
Kent State University Tuscarawas Campus	OHIO	382
Kentucky Christian University	KENTUCKY	194
Kentucky Community and Technical College System	KENTUCKY	194
Kentucky Mountain Bible College	KENTUCKY	196
Kentucky State University	KENTUCKY	197
Kentucky Wesleyan College	KENTUCKY	197
Kenyon College	OHIO	382
Kern Community College District	CALIFORNIA	49
Kettering College	OHIO	382
Kettering University	MICHIGAN	244
Keuka College	NEW YORK	328
Keweenaw Bay Ojibwa Community College	MICHIGAN	245
Key College	FLORIDA	108
Keystone College	PENNSYLVANIA	419
Keystone Technical Institute	PENNSYLVANIA	419
Kilgore College	TEXAS	475
Kilian Community College	SOUTH DAKOTA	450
King University	TENNESSEE	455
King's College	NORTH CAROLINA	355
King's College	PENNSYLVANIA	419
King's College, The	NEW YORK	328
King's University, The	CALIFORNIA	50
Kirkwood Community College	IOWA	180
Kirkwood Community College-Iowa City	IOWA	180
Kirtland Community College	MICHIGAN	245
Kishwaukee College	ILLINOIS	149
Klamath Community College	OREGON	403
Knowledge Systems Institute	ILLINOIS	149
Knox College	ILLINOIS	150
Knox Theological Seminary	FLORIDA	108
Kutztown University of Pennsylvania	PENNSYLVANIA	429
Kuyper College	MICHIGAN	245
La Guardia Community College/City University of New York	NEW YORK	318
La Roche College	PENNSYLVANIA	420
La Salle University	PENNSYLVANIA	420
La Sierra University	CALIFORNIA	50
Labette Community College	KANSAS	188
Laboure College	MASSACHUSETTS	227
Lac Courte Oreilles Ojibwa Community College	WISCONSIN	533
Lackawanna College	PENNSYLVANIA	420
Lafayette College	PENNSYLVANIA	420
LaGrange College	GEORGIA	128
Laguna College of Art & Design	CALIFORNIA	50
Lake Area Technical Institute	SOUTH DAKOTA	450
Lake Erie College	OHIO	382
Lake Erie College of Osteopathic Medicine	PENNSYLVANIA	420
Lake Erie College of Osteopathic Medicine Bradenton	FLORIDA	108
Lake Forest College	ILLINOIS	150
Lake Forest Graduate School of Management	ILLINOIS	150
Lake Land College	ILLINOIS	150
Lake Michigan College	MICHIGAN	245
Lake Michigan College Bertrand Crossing	MICHIGAN	245
Lake Michigan College South Haven	MICHIGAN	245
Lake Region State College	NORTH DAKOTA	372
Lake-Sumter State College	FLORIDA	108
Lake Superior College	MINNESOTA	259
Lake Superior State University	MICHIGAN	245
Lake Tahoe Community College	CALIFORNIA	50
Lake Washington Institute of Technology	WASHINGTON	520
Lakeland College	WISCONSIN	533
Lakeland Community College	OHIO	382
Lakes Region Community College	NEW HAMPSHIRE	295
Lakeshore Technical College	WISCONSIN	540
Lakeview College of Nursing	ILLINOIS	150
Lakewood College	OHIO	383
LAMA	CALIFORNIA	50
Lamar Community College	COLORADO	82
Lamar Institute of Technology	TEXAS	486
Lamar State College-Orange	TEXAS	486
Lamar State College-Port Arthur	TEXAS	486
Lamar University	TEXAS	486
Lancaster Bible College	PENNSYLVANIA	421
Lancaster County Career and Technology Center	PENNSYLVANIA	421
Lancaster General College of Nursing and Health Sciences	PENNSYLVANIA	421
Lancaster Theological Seminary	PENNSYLVANIA	421
Lander University	SOUTH CAROLINA	444
Landing School, The	MAINE	210
Landmark College	VERMONT	499
Lane College	TENNESSEE	455
Lane Community College	OREGON	403
Laney College	CALIFORNIA	59
Langley School of Music of Bard College	MASSACHUSETTS	227
Langston University	OKLAHOMA	395
Langston University Oklahoma City Campus	OKLAHOMA	396
Langston University Tulsa Campus	OKLAHOMA	396
Lanier Technical College	GEORGIA	128
Lansdale School of Business	PENNSYLVANIA	421
Lansing Community College	MICHIGAN	245
Laramie County Community College	WYOMING	543
Laramie County Community College Albany County Campus	WYOMING	543
Laredo Community College	TEXAS	475
Las Positas College	CALIFORNIA	37
Lasell College	MASSACHUSETTS	227
Lassen Community College	CALIFORNIA	50
Laurel Business Institute	PENNSYLVANIA	421
Laurel Technical Institute	PENNSYLVANIA	421
Laurel University	NORTH CAROLINA	355
Lawrence Technological University	MICHIGAN	245
Lawrence University	WISCONSIN	533
Lawson State Community College	ALABAMA	5
LDS Business College	UTAH	495
Le Cordon Bleu College of Culinary Arts	CALIFORNIA	50
Le Cordon Bleu College of Culinary Arts in Atlanta	GEORGIA	128
Le Cordon Bleu College of Culinary Arts in Austin	TEXAS	475
Le Cordon Bleu College of Culinary Arts in Cambridge	MASSACHUSETTS	228
Le Cordon Bleu College of Culinary Arts in Chicago	ILLINOIS	150
Le Cordon Bleu College of Culinary Arts in Dallas	TEXAS	475
Le Cordon Bleu College of Culinary Arts in Las Vegas	NEVADA	294
Le Cordon Bleu College of Culinary Arts in Los Angeles	CALIFORNIA	50
Le Cordon Bleu College of Culinary Arts in Miami	FLORIDA	108
Le Cordon Bleu College of Culinary Arts in Minneapolis/St Paul	MINNESOTA	256
Le Cordon Bleu College of Culinary Arts in Orlando	FLORIDA	108
Le Cordon Bleu College of Culinary Arts in Portland	OREGON	403
Le Cordon Bleu College of Culinary Arts in Scottsdale	ARIZONA	14
L.E. Fletcher Technical Community College	LOUISIANA	203
Le Moyne College	NEW YORK	328
Lebanon College	NEW HAMPSHIRE	297
Lebanon Valley College	PENNSYLVANIA	421
L'Ecole Culinaire	MISSOURI	276
L'Ecole Culinaire Kansas City	MISSOURI	276
L'Ecole Culinaire Memphis	TENNESSEE	455
Lee College	TEXAS	475
Lee University	TENNESSEE	455
Leech Lake Tribal College	MINNESOTA	256
Lees-McRae College	NORTH CAROLINA	356
Lehigh Carbon Community College	PENNSYLVANIA	421
Lehigh University	PENNSYLVANIA	422
LeMoyne-Owen College	TENNESSEE	455
Lenoir Community College	NORTH CAROLINA	361
Lenoir-Rhyne University	NORTH CAROLINA	356
Lesley University	MASSACHUSETTS	228
LeTourneau University	TEXAS	475
Lewis and Clark College	OREGON	403
Lewis and Clark Community College	ILLINOIS	150
Lewis-Clark State College	IDAHO	138
Lewis University	ILLINOIS	150
Lexington College	ILLINOIS	151
Lexington Theological Seminary	KENTUCKY	197
Liberty University	VIRGINIA	506
Life Chiropractic College West	CALIFORNIA	50
Life Pacific College	CALIFORNIA	50
Life University	GEORGIA	128
Lighthouse College	TEXAS	475
LIM College	NEW YORK	328
Limestone College	SOUTH CAROLINA	444
Lincoln Christian University	ILLINOIS	151
Lincoln College	ILLINOIS	151
Lincoln College- Normal	ILLINOIS	151
Lincoln College of New England	CONNECTICUT	90
Lincoln College of New England Hartford College Campus	CONNECTICUT	90
Lincoln College of Technology	COLORADO	83
Lincoln College of Technology	FLORIDA	108
Lincoln College of Technology	ILLINOIS	151
Lincoln College of Technology	INDIANA	170
Lincoln College of Technology	MARYLAND	215
Lincoln College of Technology	TEXAS	475

Lincoln College of Technology Nashville .... TENNESSEE 455
Lincoln Land Community College .... ILLINOIS 151
Lincoln Memorial University .... TENNESSEE 456
Lincoln Tech Fern Park Orlando Campus .... FLORIDA 108
Lincoln Technical Institute .... PENNSYLVANIA 422
Lincoln University .... CALIFORNIA 51
Lincoln University .... MISSOURI 276
Lincoln University .... PENNSYLVANIA 422
Lindenwood University .... MISSOURI 276
Lindenwood University Belleville Campus .... ILLINOIS 151
Lindsey Wilson College .... KENTUCKY 197
Linfield College .... OREGON 404
Linn-Benton Community College .... OREGON 404
Linn State Technical College .... MISSOURI 276
Lipscomb University .... TENNESSEE 456
Little Big Horn College .... MONTANA 286
Little Priest Tribal College .... NEBRASKA 290
LIU Riverhead .... NEW YORK 329
Living Arts College @ School of Communication Arts .... NORTH CAROLINA 356
Livingstone College .... NORTH CAROLINA 356
Lock Haven University .... PENNSYLVANIA 429
Lock Haven University Clearfield Branch Campus .... PENNSYLVANIA 430
Logan College of Chiropractic .... MISSOURI 276
Logos Evangelical Seminary .... CALIFORNIA 51
Loma Linda University .... CALIFORNIA 51
Lone Star College System .... TEXAS 476
Long Beach City College .... CALIFORNIA 51
Long Island Business Institute .... NEW YORK 329
Long Island University .... NEW YORK 329
Long Island University Brentwood Campus .... NEW YORK 329
Long Island University Brooklyn Campus .... NEW YORK 329
Long Island University Hudson Graduate Center at Rockland .... NEW YORK 329
Long Island University Hudson Graduate Center at Westchester .... NEW YORK 329
Long Island University - Post Campus .... NEW YORK 329
Longwood University .... VIRGINIA 506
Lorain County Community College .... OHIO 383
Loras College .... IOWA 180
Lord Fairfax Community College .... VIRGINIA 512
Los Angeles City College .... CALIFORNIA 51
Los Angeles Community College District Office .... CALIFORNIA 51
Los Angeles County College of Nursing and Allied Health . CALIFORNIA 52
Los Angeles Film School .... CALIFORNIA 52
Los Angeles Harbor College .... CALIFORNIA 51
Los Angeles Mission College .... CALIFORNIA 52
Los Angeles ORT College .... CALIFORNIA 52
Los Angeles Pacific College .... CALIFORNIA 52
Los Angeles Pierce College .... CALIFORNIA 52
Los Angeles Southwest College .... CALIFORNIA 52
Los Angeles Trade-Technical College .... CALIFORNIA 52
Los Angeles Valley College .... CALIFORNIA 52
Los Medanos College .... CALIFORNIA 42
Los Rios Community College District Office .... CALIFORNIA 52
Louis V. Gerstner Jr. Graduate School of Biomedical Sciences, Memorial Sloa n-Kettering Cancer Ctr .... NEW YORK 329
Louisburg College .... NORTH CAROLINA 356
Louisiana College .... LOUISIANA 202
Louisiana Community & Technical College System .... LOUISIANA 202
Louisiana Culinary Institute .... LOUISIANA 204
Louisiana Delta Community College .... LOUISIANA 203
Louisiana State University and Agricultural and Mechanical College .... LOUISIANA 204
Louisiana State University at Alexandria .... LOUISIANA 205
Louisiana State University at Eunice .... LOUISIANA 205
Louisiana State University Health Sciences Center at Shreveport .... LOUISIANA 205
Louisiana State University Health Sciences Center-New Orleans .... LOUISIANA 205
Louisiana State University in Shreveport .... LOUISIANA 205
Louisiana State University Paul M. Hebert Law Center .... LOUISIANA 205
Louisiana State University System Office .... LOUISIANA 204
Louisiana Tech University .... LOUISIANA 207
Louisville Bible College .... KENTUCKY 197
Louisville Presbyterian Theological Seminary .... KENTUCKY 197
Lourdes University .... OHIO 383
Lower Columbia College .... WASHINGTON 521
Loyola Marymount University .... CALIFORNIA 53
Loyola University Chicago .... ILLINOIS 151
Loyola University Health Sciences Campus .... ILLINOIS 151
Loyola University Maryland .... MARYLAND 216
Loyola University New Orleans .... LOUISIANA 205
Loyola University Water Town Campus .... ILLINOIS 152
Lubbock Christian University .... TEXAS 476
Luna Community College .... NEW MEXICO 309
Lurleen B. Wallace Community College .... ALABAMA 5
Luther College .... IOWA 180
Luther Rice University .... GEORGIA 128
Luther Seminary .... MINNESOTA 256
Lutheran Brethren Seminary .... MINNESOTA 256
Lutheran School of Theology at Chicago .... ILLINOIS 152
Lutheran Seminary Program of the Southwest .... TEXAS 476
Lutheran Theological Seminary at Gettysburg .... PENNSYLVANIA 422
Lutheran Theological Seminary at Philadelphia .... PENNSYLVANIA 422
Lutheran Theological Southern Seminary of Lenoir-Rhyne University .... SOUTH CAROLINA 445
Luzerne County Community College .... PENNSYLVANIA 422
Lycoming College .... PENNSYLVANIA 422
Lyme Academy College of Fine Arts .... CONNECTICUT 90
Lynchburg College .... VIRGINIA 506
Lyndon State College .... VERMONT 501
Lynn University .... FLORIDA 108
Lyon College .... ARKANSAS 21
Macalester College .... MINNESOTA 256
MacCormac College .... ILLINOIS 152
Machzikei Hadath Rabbinical College .... NEW YORK 329
MacMurray College .... ILLINOIS 152
Macomb Community College .... MICHIGAN 246
Madison Area Technical College .... WISCONSIN 540
Madison Area Technical College Commercial Avenue Education Center .... WISCONSIN 542
Madison Area Technical College Downtown Education Center .... WISCONSIN 542
Madison Area Technical College Fort Atkinson .... WISCONSIN 542
Madison Area Technical College Portage .... WISCONSIN 542
Madison Area Technical College Reedsburg .... WISCONSIN 542
Madison Area Technical College Watertown .... WISCONSIN 542
Madison Media Institute-College of Media Arts .... WISCONSIN 533
Madisonville Community College .... KENTUCKY 196
Madonna University .... MICHIGAN 246
Maharishi University of Management .... IOWA 180
Maine College of Art .... MAINE 210
Maine Community College System .... MAINE 210
Maine Maritime Academy .... MAINE 211
Malone University .... OHIO 383
Manchester Community College .... CONNECTICUT 88
Manchester Community College .... NEW HAMPSHIRE 296
Manchester University .... INDIANA 170
Mandl School .... NEW YORK 329
Manhattan Area Technical College .... KANSAS 188
Manhattan Christian College .... KANSAS 188
Manhattan College .... NEW YORK 329
Manhattan School of Music .... NEW YORK 330
Manhattanville College .... NEW YORK 330
Manor College .... PENNSYLVANIA 423
Mansfield University of Pennsylvania .... PENNSYLVANIA 429
Manthano Christian College .... MICHIGAN 246
Maple Springs Baptist Bible College & Seminary .... MARYLAND 216
Maranatha Baptist Bible College & Seminary .... WISCONSIN 533
Maria College of Albany .... NEW YORK 330
Marian Court College .... MASSACHUSETTS 228
Marian University .... INDIANA 170
Marian University .... WISCONSIN 534
Maricopa County Community College District Office .... ARIZONA 14
Marietta College .... OHIO 383
Marine Corps University .... US SERVICE SCHOOLS 544
Marion Military Institute .... ALABAMA 5
Marion Technical College .... OHIO 383
Marist College .... NEW YORK 330
Marlboro College .... VERMONT 499
Marlboro College Graduate School .... VERMONT 499
Marquette University .... WISCONSIN 534
Mars Hill College .... NORTH CAROLINA 356
Marshall University .... WEST VIRGINIA 529
Marshall University-South Charleston Campus .... WEST VIRGINIA 531
Marshalltown Community College .... IOWA 179
Martin Community College .... NORTH CAROLINA 361
Martin Luther College .... MINNESOTA 256
Martin Methodist College .... TENNESSEE 456
Martin University .... INDIANA 171
Martinsburg College .... WEST VIRGINIA 527
Mary Baldwin College .... VIRGINIA 507
Mary Lanning Healthcare School of Radiology .... NEBRASKA 290
Marygrove College .... MICHIGAN 246
Maryland Institute College of Art .... MARYLAND 216
Maryland University of Integrative Health .... MARYLAND 216
Marylhurst University .... OREGON 404
Marymount California University .... CALIFORNIA 53
Marymount Manhattan College .... NEW YORK 330
Marymount University .... VIRGINIA 507
Maryville College .... TENNESSEE 456
Maryville University of Saint Louis .... MISSOURI 276
Marywood University .... PENNSYLVANIA 423
Massachusetts Bay Community College .... MASSACHUSETTS 231
Massachusetts Board of Higher Education .... MASSACHUSETTS 228
Massachusetts College of Art and Design .... MASSACHUSETTS 230
Massachusetts College of Liberal Arts .... MASSACHUSETTS 230
Massachusetts Institute of Technology .... MASSACHUSETTS 233
Massachusetts Maritime Academy .... MASSACHUSETTS 230
Massachusetts School of Law at Andover .... MASSACHUSETTS 233
Massachusetts School of Professional Psychology .... MASSACHUSETTS 233
Massasoit Community College .... MASSACHUSETTS 232
Master's College and Seminary, The .... CALIFORNIA 53
Mater Ecclesiae College .... RHODE ISLAND 439
Mayfield College .... CALIFORNIA 54
Mayland Community College .... NORTH CAROLINA 361
Mayo Clinic College of Medicine-Mayo Graduate School .... MINNESOTA 254
Mayo Medical School .... MINNESOTA 254
Mayo School of Health Sciences .... MINNESOTA 254
Maysville Community and Technical College .... KENTUCKY 196
Mayville State University .... NORTH DAKOTA 371
McCann School of Business & Technology .... PENNSYLVANIA 423
McCook Community College .... NEBRASKA 290
McCormick Theological Seminary .... ILLINOIS 152
McCurtain County Higher Education Center .... OKLAHOMA 396
McDaniel College .... MARYLAND 216
McDowell Technical Community College .... NORTH CAROLINA 362
McHenry County College .... ILLINOIS 152
McKendree University .... ILLINOIS 152
McKinley College .... COLORADO 83
McLennan Community College .... TEXAS 476
McMurry University .... TEXAS 476
McNally Smith College of Music .... MINNESOTA 256
McNeese State University .... LOUISIANA 207
McPherson College .... KANSAS 188
MCPHS-Manchester Campus .... NEW HAMPSHIRE 297
MCPHS University .... MASSACHUSETTS 233

Institution	State	Page
MCPHS-Worcester Campus	MASSACHUSETTS	233
Meadville Lombard Theological School	ILLINOIS	152
Mech-Tech College	PUERTO RICO	551
Medaille College	NEW YORK	330
Medaille College Amherst Branch Campus	NEW YORK	330
Medaille College Rochester Branch Campus	NEW YORK	330
Medical Careers Institute	VIRGINIA	507
Medical College of Wisconsin	WISCONSIN	534
Medical University of South Carolina	SOUTH CAROLINA	445
Medtech College	DISTRICT OF COLUMBIA	96
Medtech College	GEORGIA	128
MedTech College	INDIANA	171
Medtech College	VIRGINIA	507
MedTech College-Lexington	KENTUCKY	197
MedVance Institute of Fort Lauderdale	FLORIDA	109
Meharry Medical College	TENNESSEE	456
Memorial Hospital School of Nursing	NEW YORK	330
Memphis College of Art	TENNESSEE	456
Memphis Theological Seminary	TENNESSEE	457
Mendocino College	CALIFORNIA	54
Menlo College	CALIFORNIA	54
Merced College	CALIFORNIA	54
Mercer County Community College	NEW JERSEY	302
Mercer University	GEORGIA	128
Mercy College	NEW YORK	330
Mercy College of Health Sciences	IOWA	181
Mercy College of Ohio	OHIO	383
Mercyhurst University	PENNSYLVANIA	423
Mercyhurst University Northeast	PENNSYLVANIA	423
Meredith College	NORTH CAROLINA	356
Meridian College	FLORIDA	109
Meridian Community College	MISSISSIPPI	267
Merrimack College	MASSACHUSETTS	234
Merritt College	CALIFORNIA	59
Mesa Center for Higher Education	ARIZONA	15
Mesa Community College	ARIZONA	15
Mesa Community College at Red Mountain	ARIZONA	15
Mesa State College-Montrose Campus	COLORADO	83
Mesabi Range Community & Technical College	MINNESOTA	259
Mesabi Range Community & Technical College-Eveleth	MINNESOTA	262
Mesalands Community College	NEW MEXICO	309
Mesivta Keser Torah	NEW JERSEY	303
Mesivta of Eastern Parkway Rabbinical Seminary	NEW YORK	331
Mesivta Tifereth Jerusalem of America	NEW YORK	331
Mesivta Torah Vodaath Seminary	NEW YORK	331
Messenger College	TEXAS	476
Messiah College	PENNSYLVANIA	423
Methodist College	ILLINOIS	152
Methodist Theological School in Ohio	OHIO	383
Methodist Theological Seminary in America	CALIFORNIA	54
Methodist University	NORTH CAROLINA	356
Metro Business College	MISSOURI	276
Metro Business College	MISSOURI	277
Metro Business College	MISSOURI	276
Metro Business College	MISSOURI	277
Metropolitan Career Center Computer Technology Institute	PENNSYLVANIA	423
Metropolitan College of New York	NEW YORK	331
Metropolitan Community College	NEBRASKA	290
Metropolitan Community College - Blue River	MISSOURI	277
Metropolitan Community College - Business and Technology	MISSOURI	277
Metropolitan Community College Elkhorn Valley Campus	NEBRASKA	290
Metropolitan Community College - Kansas City Administrative Center	MISSOURI	277
Metropolitan Community College - Longview	MISSOURI	277
Metropolitan Community College - Maple Woods	MISSOURI	277
Metropolitan Community College - Penn Valley	MISSOURI	277
Metropolitan Community College South Omaha Campus	NEBRASKA	290
Metropolitan State University	MINNESOTA	259
Metropolitan State University	MINNESOTA	262
Metropolitan State University of Denver	COLORADO	83
MGH Institute of Health Professions	MASSACHUSETTS	234
Miami Ad School	FLORIDA	109
Miami Dade College	FLORIDA	109
Miami International University of Art & Design	FLORIDA	109
Miami-Jacobs Career College	OHIO	384
Miami University	OHIO	384
Miami University Hamilton Campus	OHIO	384
Miami University Middletown	OHIO	384
MIAT College of Technology	MICHIGAN	246
Michigan Jewish Institute	MICHIGAN	246
Michigan School of Professional Psychology	MICHIGAN	246
Michigan State University	MICHIGAN	246
Michigan Technological University	MICHIGAN	247
Mid-America Baptist Theological Seminary	TENNESSEE	457
Mid-America Christian University	OKLAHOMA	396
Mid-America College of Funeral Service	INDIANA	171
Mid-America Reformed Seminary	INDIANA	171
Mid-Atlantic Christian University	NORTH CAROLINA	357
Mid-Continent University	KENTUCKY	197
Mid Michigan Community College	MICHIGAN	247
Mid-Plains Community College	NEBRASKA	290
Mid-South Christian College	TENNESSEE	457
Mid-South Community College	ARKANSAS	21
Mid-State Technical College	WISCONSIN	540
Mid-State Technical College Marshfield Campus	WISCONSIN	542
Mid-State Technical College Stevens Point Campus	WISCONSIN	542
MidAmerica Nazarene University	KANSAS	188
Middle Georgia State College	GEORGIA	128
Middle Tennessee School of Anesthesia	TENNESSEE	457
Middle Tennessee State University	TENNESSEE	459
Middlebury College	VERMONT	499
Middlesex Community College	CONNECTICUT	89
Middlesex Community College	MASSACHUSETTS	232
Middlesex County College	NEW JERSEY	303
Midland College	TEXAS	476
Midland University	NEBRASKA	290
Midlands Technical College	SOUTH CAROLINA	445
Midstate College	ILLINOIS	152
Midway College	KENTUCKY	197
Midwest College of Oriental Medicine	ILLINOIS	153
Midwest College of Oriental Medicine	WISCONSIN	534
Midwest Institute	MISSOURI	277
Midwest Institute-Earth City	MISSOURI	277
Midwest University	MISSOURI	277
Midwestern Baptist Theological Seminary	MISSOURI	277
Midwestern State University	TEXAS	476
Midwestern University	ARIZONA	15
Midwestern University	ILLINOIS	153
Midwives College of Utah	UTAH	496
Mildred Elley	NEW YORK	331
Mildred Elley-New York City	NEW YORK	331
Miles College	ALABAMA	5
Miles Community College	MONTANA	286
Millennia Atlantic University	FLORIDA	109
Miller-Motte College	NORTH CAROLINA	357
Miller-Motte Technical College	GEORGIA	129
Miller-Motte Technical College	MISSISSIPPI	267
Miller-Motte Technical College	NORTH CAROLINA	357
Miller-Motte Technical College	SOUTH CAROLINA	445
Miller-Motte Technical College	TENNESSEE	457
Miller-Motte Technical College	VIRGINIA	507
Millersville University of Pennsylvania	PENNSYLVANIA	429
Milligan College	TENNESSEE	457
Millikin University	ILLINOIS	153
Mills College	CALIFORNIA	54
Millsaps College	MISSISSIPPI	267
Milwaukee Area Technical College	WISCONSIN	542
Milwaukee Area Technical College	WISCONSIN	540
Milwaukee Area Technical College	WISCONSIN	542
Milwaukee Career College	WISCONSIN	534
Milwaukee Institute of Art & Design	WISCONSIN	534
Milwaukee School of Engineering	WISCONSIN	534
Mineral Area College	MISSOURI	278
Minneapolis Business College	MINNESOTA	257
Minneapolis College of Art Design	MINNESOTA	257
Minneapolis Community and Technical College	MINNESOTA	259
Minneapolis Media Institute	MINNESOTA	257
Minnesota School of Business	MINNESOTA	257
Minnesota State College - Southeast Technical	MINNESOTA	259
Minnesota State College Southeast Technical Red Wing Campus	MINNESOTA	262
Minnesota State Colleges and Universities System Office	MINNESOTA	257
Minnesota State Community and Technical College	MINNESOTA	259
Minnesota State Community and Technical College Detroit Lakes	MINNESOTA	262
Minnesota State Community and Technical College Moorhead	MINNESOTA	262
Minnesota State Community and Technical College Wadena	MINNESOTA	262
Minnesota State University Moorhead	MINNESOTA	259
Minnesota State University, Mankato	MINNESOTA	259
Minnesota West Community and Technical College	MINNESOTA	260
Minnesota West Community and Technical College Canby Campus	MINNESOTA	262
Minnesota West Community and Technical College Granite Falls Campus	MINNESOTA	262
Minnesota West Community and Technical College Jackson Campus	MINNESOTA	262
Minnesota West Community and Technical College Pipestone Campus	MINNESOTA	262
Minnesota West Community and Technical College Worthington Campus	MINNESOTA	262
Minot State University	NORTH DAKOTA	371
MiraCosta Community College District	CALIFORNIA	54
Mirrer Yeshiva Central Institute	NEW YORK	331
Misericordia University	PENNSYLVANIA	424
Mission College	CALIFORNIA	75
Mississippi College	MISSISSIPPI	268
Mississippi Delta Community College	MISSISSIPPI	268
Mississippi Gulf Coast Community College	MISSISSIPPI	268
Mississippi State University	MISSISSIPPI	268
Mississippi University for Women	MISSISSIPPI	268
Mississippi Valley State University	MISSISSIPPI	269
Missouri Baptist University	MISSOURI	278
Missouri College	MISSOURI	278
Missouri Southern State University	MISSOURI	278
Missouri State University	MISSOURI	278
Missouri State University - West Plains	MISSOURI	278
Missouri Tech	MISSOURI	278
Missouri University of Science & Technology	MISSOURI	284
Missouri University of Science & Technology Engineering Education Center	MISSOURI	278
Missouri Valley College	MISSOURI	278
Missouri Western State University	MISSOURI	279
Mitchell College	CONNECTICUT	90
Mitchell Community College	NORTH CAROLINA	362
Mitchell Technical Institute	SOUTH DAKOTA	450
Moberly Area Community College	MISSOURI	279
Modesto Junior College	CALIFORNIA	77
Mohave Community College	ARIZONA	15
Mohawk Valley Community College	NEW YORK	331
Molloy College	NEW YORK	331
Monmouth College	ILLINOIS	153
Monmouth University	NEW JERSEY	303
Monroe College	NEW YORK	331
Monroe Community College	NEW YORK	332
Monroe County Community College	MICHIGAN	247

Montana Bible College ..... MONTANA 286
Montana State University ..... MONTANA 287
Montana State University - Billings ..... MONTANA 287
Montana State University - Northern ..... MONTANA 287
Montana Tech of The University of Montana ..... MONTANA 287
Montana University System Office ..... MONTANA 286
Montcalm Community College ..... MICHIGAN 247
Montclair State University ..... NEW JERSEY 303
Monterey Institute of International Studies ..... CALIFORNIA 54
Monterey Peninsula College ..... CALIFORNIA 54
Montgomery College ..... MARYLAND 216
Montgomery Community College ..... NORTH CAROLINA 362
Montgomery County Community College ..... PENNSYLVANIA 424
Montgomery County Community College West Campus ..... PENNSYLVANIA 424
Montreat College ..... NORTH CAROLINA 357
Montserrat College of Art ..... MASSACHUSETTS 234
Moody Bible Institute ..... ILLINOIS 153
Moody Bible Institute-Spokane ..... WASHINGTON 521
Moody Theological Seminary-Michigan ..... MICHIGAN 247
Moore College of Art and Design ..... PENNSYLVANIA 424
Moorpark College ..... CALIFORNIA 74
Moraine Park Technical College ..... WISCONSIN 542
Moraine Park Technical College ..... WISCONSIN 540
Moraine Valley Community College ..... ILLINOIS 153
Moravian College ..... PENNSYLVANIA 424
Moravian Theological Seminary ..... PENNSYLVANIA 424
Morehead State University ..... KENTUCKY 198
Morehouse College ..... GEORGIA 129
Morehouse School of Medicine ..... GEORGIA 129
Moreno Valley College ..... CALIFORNIA 60
Morgan Community College ..... COLORADO 83
Morgan State University ..... MARYLAND 217
Morningside College ..... IOWA 181
Morris College ..... SOUTH CAROLINA 445
Morrison Institute of Technology ..... ILLINOIS 153
Morton College ..... ILLINOIS 153
Motlow State Community College ..... TENNESSEE 461
Mott Community College ..... MICHIGAN 247
Moultrie Technical College ..... GEORGIA 129
Mount Aloysius College ..... PENNSYLVANIA 424
Mount Angel Seminary ..... OREGON 404
Mount Carmel College of Nursing ..... OHIO 384
Mount Holyoke College ..... MASSACHUSETTS 234
Mount Ida College ..... MASSACHUSETTS 234
Mount Marty College ..... SOUTH DAKOTA 450
Mount Mary University ..... WISCONSIN 535
Mount Mercy University ..... IOWA 181
Mount Olive College ..... NORTH CAROLINA 357
Mount Saint Mary College ..... NEW YORK 332
Mount St. Mary's College ..... CALIFORNIA 54
Mount St. Mary's University ..... MARYLAND 217
Mount Sierra College ..... CALIFORNIA 55
Mount Vernon Nazarene University ..... OHIO 384
Mount Wachusett Community College ..... MASSACHUSETTS 232
Mount Washington College ..... NEW HAMPSHIRE 297
Mountain Empire Community College ..... VIRGINIA 513
Mountain State College ..... WEST VIRGINIA 527
Mountain View College ..... TEXAS 471
Mountwest Community and Technical College ..... WEST VIRGINIA 528
Mt. Hood Community College ..... OREGON 404
Mt. San Antonio College ..... CALIFORNIA 55
Mt. San Jacinto College ..... CALIFORNIA 55
MTI College ..... CALIFORNIA 55
Muhlenberg College ..... PENNSYLVANIA 424
Multnomah University ..... OREGON 404
Murray State College ..... OKLAHOMA 396
Murray State University ..... KENTUCKY 198
Muscatine Community College ..... IOWA 178
Musicians Institute ..... CALIFORNIA 55
Muskegon Community College ..... MICHIGAN 247
Muskingum University ..... OHIO 384
Myotherapy Institute ..... NEBRASKA 290

Napa Valley College ..... CALIFORNIA 55
Naropa University ..... COLORADO 83
Nash Community College ..... NORTH CAROLINA 362
Nashotah House ..... WISCONSIN 535
Nashua Community College ..... NEW HAMPSHIRE 296
Nashville State Community College ..... TENNESSEE 461
Nassau Community College ..... NEW YORK 332
National American University ..... SOUTH DAKOTA 450
National American University-Albuquerque ..... NEW MEXICO 310
National American University-Albuquerque West ..... NEW MEXICO 310
National American University-Austin ..... TEXAS 477
National American University-Bellevue ..... NEBRASKA 290
National American University-Bloomington ..... MINNESOTA 262
National American University-Brooklyn Center ..... MINNESOTA 262
National American University-Burnsville ..... MINNESOTA 262
National American University-Centennial ..... COLORADO 83
National American University-Colorado Springs ..... COLORADO 83
National American University-Colorado Springs South ..... COLORADO 83
National American University-Denver ..... COLORADO 83
National American University-Georgetown ..... TEXAS 477
National American University-Independence ..... MISSOURI 279
National American University-Indianapolis ..... INDIANA 171
National American University-Lee's Summit ..... MISSOURI 279
National American University-Lewisville ..... TEXAS 477
National American University-Mesquite ..... TEXAS 477
National American University-Overland Park ..... KANSAS 189
National American University-Richardson ..... TEXAS 477
National American University-Rochester ..... MINNESOTA 262
National American University-Roseville ..... MINNESOTA 262
National American University-Sioux Falls ..... SOUTH DAKOTA 450
National American University-South Austin ..... TEXAS 477
National American University-Tigard ..... OREGON 404
National American University-Tulsa ..... OKLAHOMA 396
National American University-Weldon Spring ..... MISSOURI 279
National American University-Wichita ..... KANSAS 189
National American University-Wichita West ..... KANSAS 189
National American University-Zona Rosa ..... MISSOURI 279
National Career College ..... CALIFORNIA 55
National College ..... INDIANA 171
National College ..... KENTUCKY 198
National College ..... OHIO 384
National College ..... OHIO 385
National College ..... OHIO 384
National College ..... OHIO 385
National College ..... OHIO 384
National College ..... VIRGINIA 507
National College ..... WEST VIRGINIA 527
National College of Business and Technology ..... TENNESSEE 457
National College of Midwifery ..... NEW MEXICO 310
National College of Natural Medicine ..... OREGON 404
National College of Technical Instruction-College of Emergency Services ..... OREGON 405
National Defense University ..... US SERVICE SCHOOLS 544
National Graduate School of Quality Systems Management, The ..... MASSACHUSETTS 234
National Hispanic University, The ..... CALIFORNIA 55
National Institute of Massotherapy ..... OHIO 385
National Intelligence University ..... US SERVICE SCHOOLS 544
National Labor College ..... MARYLAND 217
National-Louis University ..... ILLINOIS 153
National-Louis University Elgin Campus ..... ILLINOIS 154
National-Louis University Florida Regional Campus ..... FLORIDA 109
National-Louis University Lisle Campus ..... ILLINOIS 154
National-Louis University Milwaukee/Beloit Campus ..... WISCONSIN 535
National-Louis University North Shore Campus ..... ILLINOIS 154
National-Louis University Wheeling Campus ..... ILLINOIS 154
National Paralegal College ..... ARIZONA 16
National Park Community College ..... ARKANSAS 22
National Test Pilot School ..... CALIFORNIA 55
National University ..... CALIFORNIA 55
National University College ..... PUERTO RICO 551
National University College Ponce Campus ..... PUERTO RICO 551
National University College Rio Grande Campus ..... PUERTO RICO 551
National University of Health Sciences ..... ILLINOIS 154
Native American Bible College ..... NORTH CAROLINA 357
Naugatuck Valley Community College ..... CONNECTICUT 89
Navajo Technical College ..... NEW MEXICO 310
Naval Postgraduate School ..... US SERVICE SCHOOLS 544
Naval War College ..... US SERVICE SCHOOLS 545
Navarro College ..... TEXAS 477
Nazarene Bible College ..... COLORADO 83
Nazarene Theological Seminary ..... MISSOURI 279
Nazareth College of Rochester ..... NEW YORK 332
Nebraska Christian College ..... NEBRASKA 290
Nebraska Indian Community College ..... NEBRASKA 290
Nebraska Indian Community College-Santee ..... NEBRASKA 290
Nebraska Indian Community College-South Sioux City ..... NEBRASKA 291
Nebraska Methodist College ..... NEBRASKA 291
Nebraska State College System ..... NEBRASKA 291
Nebraska Wesleyan University ..... NEBRASKA 291
Neosho County Community College ..... KANSAS 189
Ner Israel Rabbinical College ..... MARYLAND 217
Neumann University ..... PENNSYLVANIA 424
Neumont University ..... UTAH 496
Nevada State College ..... NEVADA 294
Nevada System of Higher Education ..... NEVADA 294
New Brunswick Theological Seminary ..... NEW JERSEY 303
New Castle School of Trades ..... PENNSYLVANIA 425
New Charter University ..... CALIFORNIA 56
New College of Florida ..... FLORIDA 115
New England Bible College ..... MAINE 211
New England College ..... NEW HAMPSHIRE 297
New England College of Business and Finance ..... MASSACHUSETTS 234
New England College of Optometry, The ..... MASSACHUSETTS 234
New England Conservatory of Music ..... MASSACHUSETTS 234
New England Culinary Institute ..... VERMONT 499
New England Institute of Art, The ..... MASSACHUSETTS 235
New England Institute of Technology ..... RHODE ISLAND 439
New England Law | Boston ..... MASSACHUSETTS 235
New England School of Acupuncture ..... MASSACHUSETTS 235
New England School of Communications ..... MAINE 211
New Hampshire Institute of Art ..... NEW HAMPSHIRE 297
New Hope Christian College ..... OREGON 405
New Hope Christian College-Hawaii ..... HAWAII 135
New Jersey City University ..... NEW JERSEY 303
New Jersey Institute of Technology ..... NEW JERSEY 303
New Life Theological Seminary ..... NORTH CAROLINA 357
New Mexico Highlands University ..... NEW MEXICO 310
New Mexico Institute of Mining and Technology ..... NEW MEXICO 310
New Mexico Junior College ..... NEW MEXICO 310
New Mexico Military Institute ..... NEW MEXICO 310
New Mexico State University at Alamogordo ..... NEW MEXICO 310
New Mexico State University at Carlsbad ..... NEW MEXICO 311
New Mexico State University Dona Ana Community College ..... NEW MEXICO 311
New Mexico State University Dona Ana Community College East Mesa Campus ..... NEW MEXICO 311
New Mexico State University Grants ..... NEW MEXICO 311
New Mexico State University Main Campus ..... NEW MEXICO 310
New Orleans Baptist Theological Seminary ..... LOUISIANA 206
New River Community and Technical College ..... WEST VIRGINIA 528
New River Community College ..... VIRGINIA 513
New River Technical College Greenbrier Valley Campus ..... WEST VIRGINIA 528
New River Technical College Mercer County Campus ..... WEST VIRGINIA 528
New River Technical College Nicholas County Campus ..... WEST VIRGINIA 528

Institution	State	Page
New Saint Andrews College	IDAHO	138
New School, The	NEW YORK	332
New York Academy of Art	NEW YORK	333
New York Career Institute	NEW YORK	333
New York Chiropractic College	NEW YORK	333
New York City College of Technology/City University of New York	NEW YORK	319
New York College of Health Professions	NEW YORK	333
New York College of Podiatric Medicine	NEW YORK	333
New York College of Traditional Chinese Medicine	NEW YORK	333
New York Film Academy, Los Angeles	CALIFORNIA	56
New York Graduate School of Psychoanalysis	NEW YORK	333
New York Institute of Technology	NEW YORK	333
New York Law School	NEW YORK	333
New York Medical College	NEW YORK	334
New York School of Interior Design	NEW YORK	334
New York Theological Seminary	NEW YORK	334
New York University	NEW YORK	334
Newberry College	SOUTH CAROLINA	445
Newbury College	MASSACHUSETTS	235
Newman University	KANSAS	189
Newport Business Institute	PENNSYLVANIA	425
NewSchool of Architecture and Design	CALIFORNIA	56
NHTI-Concord's Community College	NEW HAMPSHIRE	296
Niagara County Community College	NEW YORK	334
Niagara University	NEW YORK	334
Nicholls State University	LOUISIANA	208
Nichols College	MASSACHUSETTS	235
Nicolet Area Technical College	WISCONSIN	540
Nightingale College	UTAH	496
Norco College	CALIFORNIA	60
Norfolk State University	VIRGINIA	507
Normandale Community College	MINNESOTA	260
North American College	TEXAS	477
North Arkansas College	ARKANSAS	22
North Carolina Agricultural and Technical State University	NORTH CAROLINA	367
North Carolina Central University	NORTH CAROLINA	368
North Carolina Community College System	NORTH CAROLINA	357
North Carolina State University	NORTH CAROLINA	368
North Carolina Wesleyan College	NORTH CAROLINA	365
North Central College	ILLINOIS	154
North Central Institute	TENNESSEE	457
North Central Kansas Technical College	KANSAS	189
North Central Michigan College	MICHIGAN	247
North Central Missouri College	MISSOURI	279
North Central State College	OHIO	385
North Central Texas College	TEXAS	477
North Central University	MINNESOTA	262
North Country Community College	NEW YORK	335
North Dakota State College of Science	NORTH DAKOTA	372
North Dakota State University Main Campus	NORTH DAKOTA	371
North Dakota University System Office	NORTH DAKOTA	371
North Florida Community College	FLORIDA	109
North Georgia Technical College	GEORGIA	129
North Greenville University	SOUTH CAROLINA	445
North Hennepin Community College	MINNESOTA	260
North Idaho College	IDAHO	138
North Iowa Area Community College	IOWA	181
North Lake College	TEXAS	471
North Orange County Community College District	CALIFORNIA	56
North Park University	ILLINOIS	154
North Platte Community College-North Campus	NEBRASKA	291
North Seattle Community College	WASHINGTON	522
North Shore Community College	MASSACHUSETTS	232
Northampton Community College	PENNSYLVANIA	425
Northampton Community College Monroe County Branch Campus	PENNSYLVANIA	425
Northcentral Technical College	WISCONSIN	541
Northcentral University	ARIZONA	16
Northeast Alabama Community College	ALABAMA	5
Northeast Community College	NEBRASKA	291
Northeast Iowa Community College	IOWA	181
Northeast Iowa Community College Peosta Campus	IOWA	181
Northeast Mississippi Community College	MISSISSIPPI	269
Northeast Ohio Medical University	OHIO	385
Northeast State Community College	TENNESSEE	461
Northeast Texas Community College	TEXAS	477
Northeast Wisconsin Technical College	WISCONSIN	541
Northeast Wisconsin Technical College-Marinette Campus	WISCONSIN	542
Northeast Wisconsin Technical College-Sturgeon Bay Campus	WISCONSIN	542
Northeastern Illinois University	ILLINOIS	154
Northeastern Junior College	COLORADO	83
Northeastern Oklahoma Agricultural and Mechanical College	OKLAHOMA	396
Northeastern Seminary	NEW YORK	335
Northeastern State University	OKLAHOMA	396
Northeastern State University at Broken Arrow	OKLAHOMA	396
Northeastern State University at Muskogee	OKLAHOMA	396
Northeastern Technical College	SOUTH CAROLINA	446
Northeastern University	MASSACHUSETTS	235
Northern Arizona University	ARIZONA	16
Northern Arizona University Yuma Branch Campus	ARIZONA	16
Northern Essex Community College	MASSACHUSETTS	232
Northern Illinois University	ILLINOIS	154
Northern Kentucky University	KENTUCKY	198
Northern Maine Community College	MAINE	210
Northern Marianas College	NORTHERN MARIANAS	547
Northern Michigan University	MICHIGAN	248
Northern New Mexico College	NEW MEXICO	311
Northern Oklahoma College	OKLAHOMA	396
Northern Seminary	ILLINOIS	155
Northern State University	SOUTH DAKOTA	451
Northern Virginia Community College	VIRGINIA	513
Northern Wyoming Community College District	WYOMING	543
Northland College	WISCONSIN	535
Northland Community and Technical College	MINNESOTA	260
Northland Community and Technical College East Grand Forks	MINNESOTA	262
Northland International University	WISCONSIN	535
Northland Pioneer College	ARIZONA	16
Northland Pioneer College Little Colorado Campus	ARIZONA	16
Northland Pioneer College Painted Desert Campus	ARIZONA	16
Northland Pioneer College Silver Creek Campus	ARIZONA	16
Northland Pioneer College White Mountain Campus	ARIZONA	16
Northpoint Bible College	MASSACHUSETTS	235
Northshore Technical Community College	LOUISIANA	203
NorthWest Arkansas Community College	ARKANSAS	22
Northwest Career College	NEVADA	295
Northwest Christian University	OREGON	405
Northwest College	WYOMING	543
Northwest College of Art & Design (NCAD)	WASHINGTON	521
Northwest Florida State College	FLORIDA	109
Northwest Indian College	WASHINGTON	521
Northwest Institute of Literary Arts	WASHINGTON	521
Northwest Iowa Community College	IOWA	181
Northwest Kansas Technical College	KANSAS	189
Northwest Louisiana Technical College Natchitoches Campus	LOUISIANA	204
Northwest Louisiana Technical College Northwest Campus	LOUISIANA	203
Northwest Louisiana Technical College Shreveport Campus	LOUISIANA	204
Northwest Mississippi Community College	MISSISSIPPI	269
Northwest Missouri State University	MISSOURI	279
Northwest Nazarene University	IDAHO	139
Northwest School of Wooden Boatbuilding	WASHINGTON	521
Northwest - Shoals Community College	ALABAMA	6
Northwest State Community College	OHIO	385
Northwest Technical College	MINNESOTA	260
Northwest University	WASHINGTON	521
Northwest Vista College	TEXAS	464
Northwestern College	ILLINOIS	155
Northwestern College	IOWA	181
Northwestern College	MINNESOTA	263
Northwestern College-SW Campus	ILLINOIS	155
Northwestern Connecticut Community-Technical College	CONNECTICUT	89
Northwestern Health Sciences University	MINNESOTA	263
Northwestern Michigan College	MICHIGAN	248
Northwestern Oklahoma State University	OKLAHOMA	397
Northwestern Oklahoma State University	OKLAHOMA	396
Northwestern Oklahoma State University	OKLAHOMA	397
Northwestern Polytechnic University	CALIFORNIA	56
Northwestern State University	LOUISIANA	208
Northwestern University	ILLINOIS	155
Northwestern University Chicago Downtown Campus	ILLINOIS	155
Northwood University	FLORIDA	109
Northwood University	MICHIGAN	248
Northwood University	TEXAS	477
Norwalk Community College	CONNECTICUT	89
Norwich University	VERMONT	500
Nossi College of Art	TENNESSEE	457
Notre Dame College	OHIO	385
Notre Dame de Namur University	CALIFORNIA	56
Notre Dame of Maryland University	MARYLAND	217
Notre Dame Seminary, Graduate School of Theology	LOUISIANA	206
Nova Southeastern University	FLORIDA	109
Nunez Community College	LOUISIANA	203
Nyack College	NEW YORK	335
Nyack College Manhattan Center	NEW YORK	335
Oak Hills Christian College	MINNESOTA	263
Oakbridge Academy of Arts	PENNSYLVANIA	425
Oakland City University	INDIANA	171
Oakland Community College	MICHIGAN	248
Oakland Community College Auburn Hills	MICHIGAN	248
Oakland Community College High Lakes	MICHIGAN	248
Oakland Community College Orchard Ridge	MICHIGAN	248
Oakland Community College Royal Oak	MICHIGAN	248
Oakland Community College Southfield	MICHIGAN	248
Oakland University	MICHIGAN	248
Oakton Community College	ILLINOIS	155
Oakton Community College Ray Hartstein Campus	ILLINOIS	155
Oakwood University	ALABAMA	6
Oberlin College	OHIO	385
Oblate School of Theology	TEXAS	477
Occidental College	CALIFORNIA	56
Ocean County College	NEW JERSEY	304
Oconee Fall Line Technical College-North Campus	GEORGIA	129
Oconee Fall Line Technical College-South Campus	GEORGIA	129
Odessa College	TEXAS	477
Ogden-Weber Applied Technology College	UTAH	496
Ogeechee Technical College	GEORGIA	129
Oglala Lakota College	SOUTH DAKOTA	450
Oglethorpe University	GEORGIA	130
Ohio Business College	OHIO	385
Ohio Business College, Lorain Branch	OHIO	385
Ohio Christian University	OHIO	385
Ohio College of Massotherapy	OHIO	386
Ohio Dominican University	OHIO	386
Ohio Mid-Western College (Formerly Temple Baptist College)	OHIO	386
Ohio Northern University	OHIO	386
Ohio State University Agricultural Technical Institute, The	OHIO	386
Ohio State University at Lima Campus, The	OHIO	386
Ohio State University at Marion, The	OHIO	386
Ohio State University Main Campus, The	OHIO	386
Ohio State University Mansfield Campus, The	OHIO	386
Ohio State University Newark Campus, The	OHIO	387

Ohio Technical College ... OHIO ... 387
Ohio University Chillicothe Campus ... OHIO ... 387
Ohio University Eastern Campus ... OHIO ... 387
Ohio University Lancaster Campus ... OHIO ... 387
Ohio University Main Campus ... OHIO ... 387
Ohio University Southern Campus ... OHIO ... 387
Ohio University Zanesville Branch ... OHIO ... 387
Ohio Valley College of Technology ... OHIO ... 387
Ohio Valley University ... WEST VIRGINIA ... 527
Ohio Wesleyan University ... OHIO ... 387
Ohlone College ... CALIFORNIA ... 57
Ohr Hameir Theological Seminary ... NEW YORK ... 335
Ohr Somayach Tanenbaum Educational Center ... NEW YORK ... 335
Okefenokee Technical College ... GEORGIA ... 130
Oklahoma Baptist University ... OKLAHOMA ... 397
Oklahoma Christian University ... OKLAHOMA ... 397
Oklahoma City Community College ... OKLAHOMA ... 397
Oklahoma City University ... OKLAHOMA ... 397
Oklahoma Panhandle State University ... OKLAHOMA ... 397
Oklahoma State University ... OKLAHOMA ... 397
Oklahoma State University Center for Health Sciences College of Osteopathic Medicine ... OKLAHOMA ... 398
Oklahoma State University Institute of Technology-Okmulgee ... OKLAHOMA ... 398
Oklahoma State University - Oklahoma City ... OKLAHOMA ... 398
Oklahoma State University - Tulsa ... OKLAHOMA ... 398
Oklahoma Technical College ... OKLAHOMA ... 398
Oklahoma Wesleyan University ... OKLAHOMA ... 398
Old Dominion University ... VIRGINIA ... 507
Olivet College ... MICHIGAN ... 249
Olivet Nazarene University ... ILLINOIS ... 155
Olivet University ... CALIFORNIA ... 57
Olympic College ... WASHINGTON ... 521
Omaha School of Massage and Healthcare of Herzing University ... NEBRASKA ... 291
O'More College of Design ... TENNESSEE ... 457
Onondaga Community College ... NEW YORK ... 335
Oral Roberts University ... OKLAHOMA ... 398
Orange Coast College ... CALIFORNIA ... 39
Orange County Community College ... NEW YORK ... 335
Orange County Community College Newburgh Branch Campus ... NEW YORK ... 335
Orangeburg-Calhoun Technical College ... SOUTH CAROLINA ... 446
Oregon College of Art and Craft ... OREGON ... 405
Oregon College of Oriental Medicine ... OREGON ... 405
Oregon Culinary Institute ... OREGON ... 405
Oregon Health & Science University ... OREGON ... 405
Oregon Institute of Technology ... OREGON ... 405
Oregon State University ... OREGON ... 406
Oregon University System ... OREGON ... 405
Orlando Medical Institute ... FLORIDA ... 110
Orleans Technical Institute ... PENNSYLVANIA ... 425
Otero Junior College ... COLORADO ... 83
Otis College of Art and Design ... CALIFORNIA ... 57
Ottawa University ... KANSAS ... 189
Ottawa University Arizona ... ARIZONA ... 16
Ottawa University Jeffersonville ... INDIANA ... 171
Ottawa University Kansas City ... KANSAS ... 189
Ottawa University Wisconsin ... WISCONSIN ... 535
Otterbein University ... OHIO ... 387
Ouachita Baptist University ... ARKANSAS ... 22
Our Lady of Holy Cross College ... LOUISIANA ... 206
Our Lady of the Lake College ... LOUISIANA ... 206
Our Lady of the Lake University ... TEXAS ... 477
Owens Community College ... OHIO ... 387
Owens Community College Findlay Campus ... OHIO ... 388
Owensboro Community and Technical College ... KENTUCKY ... 196
Oxford Graduate School ... TENNESSEE ... 458
Oxnard College ... CALIFORNIA ... 74
Oyster Ridger Higher Education/Kemmerer ... WYOMING ... 543
Ozark Christian College ... MISSOURI ... 279
Ozarka College ... ARKANSAS ... 22
Ozarks Technical Community College ... MISSOURI ... 279
Ozarks Technical Community College Richwood Valley ... MISSOURI ... 280
Ozarks Technical Community College Table Rock Campus ... MISSOURI ... 280

Pace Institute ... PENNSYLVANIA ... 425
Pace University ... NEW YORK ... 335
Pacific College ... CALIFORNIA ... 57
Pacific College of Oriental Medicine ... CALIFORNIA ... 57
Pacific College of Oriental Medicine ... ILLINOIS ... 155
Pacific College of Oriental Medicine ... NEW YORK ... 336
Pacific Islands University ... GUAM ... 546
Pacific Lutheran Theological Seminary ... CALIFORNIA ... 57
Pacific Lutheran University ... WASHINGTON ... 521
Pacific Northwest College of Art ... OREGON ... 406
Pacific Northwest University of Health Sciences ... WASHINGTON ... 521
Pacific Oaks College ... CALIFORNIA ... 57
Pacific School of Religion ... CALIFORNIA ... 57
Pacific States University ... CALIFORNIA ... 57
Pacific Union College ... CALIFORNIA ... 57
Pacific University ... OREGON ... 407
Pacifica Graduate Institute ... CALIFORNIA ... 57
Paier College of Art ... CONNECTICUT ... 90
Paine College ... GEORGIA ... 130
Palau Community College ... PALAU ... 547
Palm Beach Atlantic University ... FLORIDA ... 110
Palm Beach State College ... FLORIDA ... 110
Palmer College of Chiropractic ... IOWA ... 182
Palmer College of Chiropractic, Florida Campus ... FLORIDA ... 110
Palmer College of Chiropractic, West Campus ... CALIFORNIA ... 58
Palmer Theological Seminary of Eastern University ... PENNSYLVANIA ... 425
Palo Alto College ... TEXAS ... 465
Palo Alto University ... CALIFORNIA ... 58
Palo Verde College ... CALIFORNIA ... 58
Palomar College ... CALIFORNIA ... 58
Pamlico Community College ... NORTH CAROLINA ... 362
Panola College ... TEXAS ... 478
Paradise Valley Community College ... ARIZONA ... 15
Paralegal Institute, The ... ARIZONA ... 16
Pardee RAND Graduate School of Policy Studies ... CALIFORNIA ... 58
Paris Junior College ... TEXAS ... 478
Park University ... MISSOURI ... 280
Parker University ... TEXAS ... 478
Parkland College ... ILLINOIS ... 155
Pasadena City College ... CALIFORNIA ... 58
Pasco-Hernando Community College ... FLORIDA ... 110
Passaic County Community College ... NEW JERSEY ... 304
Patrick Henry College ... VIRGINIA ... 508
Patrick Henry Community College ... VIRGINIA ... 513
Patten University ... CALIFORNIA ... 58
Paul D. Camp Community College ... VIRGINIA ... 513
Paul Quinn College ... TEXAS ... 478
Paul Smith's College ... NEW YORK ... 336
Payne Theological Seminary ... OHIO ... 388
Pearl River Community College ... MISSISSIPPI ... 269
Peirce College ... PENNSYLVANIA ... 425
Pellissippi State Community College ... TENNESSEE ... 461
Peninsula College ... WASHINGTON ... 522
Penn Commercial Business/Technical School ... PENNSYLVANIA ... 425
Penn Foster College ... ARIZONA ... 16
Penn State Abington ... PENNSYLVANIA ... 426
Penn State Altoona ... PENNSYLVANIA ... 426
Penn State Beaver ... PENNSYLVANIA ... 426
Penn State Berks ... PENNSYLVANIA ... 426
Penn State Brandywine ... PENNSYLVANIA ... 426
Penn State Dickinson School of Law, The ... PENNSYLVANIA ... 426
Penn State DuBois ... PENNSYLVANIA ... 426
Penn State Erie, The Behrend College ... PENNSYLVANIA ... 426
Penn State Fayette, The Eberly Campus ... PENNSYLVANIA ... 426
Penn State Great Valley School of Graduate Professional Studies ... PENNSYLVANIA ... 426
Penn State Greater Allegheny ... PENNSYLVANIA ... 426
Penn State Harrisburg ... PENNSYLVANIA ... 426
Penn State Hazleton ... PENNSYLVANIA ... 426
Penn State Lehigh Valley ... PENNSYLVANIA ... 426
Penn State Milton S. Hershey Medical Center College of Medicine ... PENNSYLVANIA ... 426
Penn State Mont Alto ... PENNSYLVANIA ... 426
Penn State New Kensington ... PENNSYLVANIA ... 426
Penn State Schuylkill ... PENNSYLVANIA ... 426
Penn State Shenango ... PENNSYLVANIA ... 426
Penn State University Park ... PENNSYLVANIA ... 426
Penn State Wilkes-Barre ... PENNSYLVANIA ... 426
Penn State Worthington-Scranton ... PENNSYLVANIA ... 426
Penn State York ... PENNSYLVANIA ... 426
Pennco Tech ... PENNSYLVANIA ... 426
Pennsylvania Academy of the Fine Arts ... PENNSYLVANIA ... 426
Pennsylvania College of Art & Design ... PENNSYLVANIA ... 427
Pennsylvania College of Technology ... PENNSYLVANIA ... 427
Pennsylvania Highlands Community College ... PENNSYLVANIA ... 427
Pennsylvania Institute of Health and Technology ... PENNSYLVANIA ... 427
Pennsylvania Institute of Technology ... PENNSYLVANIA ... 427
Pennsylvania School of Business ... PENNSYLVANIA ... 427
Pennsylvania State System of Higher Education, Office of the Chancellor ... PENNSYLVANIA ... 427
Pensacola Christian College ... FLORIDA ... 110
Pensacola State College ... FLORIDA ... 110
Pentecostal Theological Seminary ... TENNESSEE ... 458
Pepperdine University ... CALIFORNIA ... 58
Peralta Community Colleges District Office ... CALIFORNIA ... 58
Perry Technical Institute ... WASHINGTON ... 522
Peru State College ... NEBRASKA ... 291
Pfeiffer University ... NORTH CAROLINA ... 365
Philadelphia College of Osteopathic Medicine ... PENNSYLVANIA ... 430
Philadelphia College of Osteopathic Medicine Georgia Campus ... GEORGIA ... 130
Philadelphia University ... PENNSYLVANIA ... 430
Philander Smith College ... ARKANSAS ... 22
Phillips Beth Israel School of Nursing ... NEW YORK ... 336
Phillips Community College of the University of Arkansas ... ARKANSAS ... 24
Phillips Community College of the University of Arkansas-DeWitt ... ARKANSAS ... 25
Phillips Community College of the University of Arkansas-Stuttgart ... ARKANSAS ... 25
Phillips Graduate Institute ... CALIFORNIA ... 59
Phillips Theological Seminary ... OKLAHOMA ... 398
Phoenix College ... ARIZONA ... 15
Phoenix Institute of Herbal Medicine and Acupuncture ... ARIZONA ... 16
Phoenix School of Law ... ARIZONA ... 16
Phoenix Seminary ... ARIZONA ... 16
Piedmont College ... GEORGIA ... 130
Piedmont Community College ... NORTH CAROLINA ... 362
Piedmont International University ... NORTH CAROLINA ... 365
Piedmont Technical College ... SOUTH CAROLINA ... 446
Piedmont Virginia Community College ... VIRGINIA ... 513
Pierce College District ... WASHINGTON ... 522
Pierpont Community & Technical College ... WEST VIRGINIA ... 528
Pikes Peak Community College ... COLORADO ... 84
Pillar College ... NEW JERSEY ... 304
Pima Community College ... ARIZONA ... 17
Pima Community College Community Campus ... ARIZONA ... 17
Pima Community College Desert Vista Campus ... ARIZONA ... 17
Pima Community College Downtown Campus ... ARIZONA ... 17
Pima Community College East Campus ... ARIZONA ... 17
Pima Community College Northwest Campus ... ARIZONA ... 17
Pima Community College West Campus ... ARIZONA ... 17

Pima Medical Institute — COLORADO — 84
Pima Medical Institute-Albuquerque — NEW MEXICO — 311
Pima Medical Institute-Chula Vista — CALIFORNIA — 59
Pima Medical Institute-Colorado Springs — COLORADO — 84
Pima Medical Institute-Denver — COLORADO — 84
Pima Medical Institute-East Valley — ARIZONA — 17
Pima Medical Institute-Houston — TEXAS — 478
Pima Medical Institute-Las Vegas — NEVADA — 295
Pima Medical Institute-Mesa — ARIZONA — 17
Pima Medical Institute-Renton — WASHINGTON — 522
Pima Medical Institute-Seattle — WASHINGTON — 522
Pima Medical Institute-Tucson — ARIZONA — 17
Pine Manor College — MASSACHUSETTS — 235
Pine Technical College — MINNESOTA — 260
Pinnacle Career Institute — KANSAS — 189
Pinnacle Career Institute — MISSOURI — 280
Pioneer Pacific College — OREGON — 407
Pioneer Pacific College-Eugene Branch — OREGON — 407
Pitt Community College — NORTH CAROLINA — 362
Pittsburg State University — KANSAS — 189
Pittsburgh Institute of Aeronautics — PENNSYLVANIA — 430
Pittsburgh Institute of Mortuary Science — PENNSYLVANIA — 430
Pittsburgh Technical Institute — PENNSYLVANIA — 430
Pittsburgh Theological Seminary — PENNSYLVANIA — 431
Pitzer College — CALIFORNIA — 59
Platt College — CALIFORNIA — 59
Platt College — COLORADO — 84
Platt College — OKLAHOMA — 398
Platt College — TEXAS — 478
Platt College-OKC Central — OKLAHOMA — 399
Plaza College — NEW YORK — 336
Plymouth State University — NEW HAMPSHIRE — 298
Point Loma Nazarene University — CALIFORNIA — 59
Point Park University — PENNSYLVANIA — 431
Point University — GEORGIA — 130
Polk State College — FLORIDA — 110
Polytechnic Institute of New York University — NEW YORK — 336
Polytechnic University of Puerto Rico — FLORIDA — 111
Polytechnic University of Puerto Rico-Orlando Campus — FLORIDA — 111
Pomona College — CALIFORNIA — 60
Ponce Paramedical College — PUERTO RICO — 551
Ponce School of Medicine & Health Sciences — PUERTO RICO — 552
Pontifical Catholic University of Puerto Rico-Arecibo Campus — PUERTO RICO — 552
Pontifical Catholic University of Puerto Rico-Mayaguez Campus — PUERTO RICO — 552
Pontifical Catholic University of Puerto Rico, The — PUERTO RICO — 552
Pontifical College Josephinum — OHIO — 388
Pontifical Faculty of the Immaculate Conception at the Dominican House of S tudies — DISTRICT OF COLUMBIA — 96
Pontifical John Paul II Institute for Studies on Marriage and Family — DISTRICT OF COLUMBIA — 96
Porterville College — CALIFORNIA — 49
Portland Community College — OREGON — 407
Portland State University — OREGON — 406
Post University — CONNECTICUT — 90
Potomac State College of West Virginia University — WEST VIRGINIA — 531
PowerSport Institute — OHIO — 388
Prairie State College — ILLINOIS — 156
Prairie View A & M University — TEXAS — 482
Pratt Community College — KANSAS — 190
Pratt Institute — NEW YORK — 336
Praxis Institute, The — FLORIDA — 111
Presbyterian College — SOUTH CAROLINA — 446
Presbyterian Theological Seminary in America — CALIFORNIA — 60
Prescott College — ARIZONA — 17
Presentation College — SOUTH DAKOTA — 450
Presentation College Fairmont — MINNESOTA — 263
Presentation College Lakota — SOUTH DAKOTA — 451
Presidio Graduate School — CALIFORNIA — 60
Prince George's Community College — MARYLAND — 217
Prince Institute-Rocky Mountains — COLORADO — 84
Prince Institute - Southeast — ALABAMA — 6
Prince William Sound Community College — ALASKA — 11
Princeton Theological Seminary — NEW JERSEY — 304
Princeton University — NEW JERSEY — 304
Principia College — ILLINOIS — 156
Prism Career Institute-Upper Darby Campus — PENNSYLVANIA — 431
Professional Business College — NEW YORK — 336
Professional Golfers Career College — CALIFORNIA — 60
Professional Golfers Career College — FLORIDA — 111
Professional Golfers Career College — SOUTH CAROLINA — 446
Professional Skills Institute — OHIO — 388
Professional Training Center — FLORIDA — 111
Protestant Episcopal Theological Seminary in Virginia — VIRGINIA — 508
Providence Christian College — CALIFORNIA — 60
Providence College — RHODE ISLAND — 439
Provo College — UTAH — 496
Pueblo Community College — COLORADO — 84
Pueblo Community College Fremont Campus — COLORADO — 84
Pulaski Technical College — ARKANSAS — 22
Purchase College, State University of New York — NEW YORK — 344
Purdue University Calumet — INDIANA — 171
Purdue University Main Campus — INDIANA — 171
Purdue University North Central Campus — INDIANA — 172
Puritan Reformed Theological Seminary — MICHIGAN — 249

Queens University of Charlotte — NORTH CAROLINA — 365
Quest College — TEXAS — 478
Quincy College — MASSACHUSETTS — 235
Quincy University — ILLINOIS — 156
Quinebaug Valley Community College — CONNECTICUT — 89
Quinnipiac University — CONNECTICUT — 91
Quinsigamond Community College — MASSACHUSETTS — 232
Rabbi Isaac Elchanan Theological Seminary — NEW YORK — 336
Rabbi Jacob Joseph School — NEW JERSEY — 304
Rabbinical Academy Mesivta Rabbi Chaim Berlin — NEW YORK — 336
Rabbinical College Beth Shraga — NEW YORK — 336
Rabbinical College Bobover Yeshiva B'nei Zion — NEW YORK — 337
Rabbinical College Ch'san Sofer — NEW YORK — 337
Rabbinical College of America — NEW JERSEY — 304
Rabbinical College of Long Island — NEW YORK — 337
Rabbinical College of Telshe — OHIO — 388
Rabbinical College Ohr Shimon Yisroel — NEW YORK — 337
Rabbinical College Ohr Yisroel — NEW YORK — 337
Rabbinical Seminary M'kor Chaim — NEW YORK — 337
Rabbinical Seminary of America — NEW YORK — 337
Radford University — VIRGINIA — 508
Radians College — DISTRICT OF COLUMBIA — 96
Radiological Technologies University-VT — INDIANA — 172
Rainy River Community College — MINNESOTA — 260
Ramapo College of New Jersey — NEW JERSEY — 305
Rancho Santiago Community College District — CALIFORNIA — 60
Randolph College — VIRGINIA — 508
Randolph Community College — NORTH CAROLINA — 362
Randolph-Macon College — VIRGINIA — 508
Ranger College — TEXAS — 478
Ranken Technical College — MISSOURI — 280
Rappahannock Community College — VIRGINIA — 513
Raritan Valley Community College — NEW JERSEY — 305
Rasmussen College - Appleton — WISCONSIN — 535
Rasmussen College - Aurora — ILLINOIS — 156
Rasmussen College - Bismarck — NORTH DAKOTA — 372
Rasmussen College - Blaine — MINNESOTA — 263
Rasmussen College - Bloomington — MINNESOTA — 263
Rasmussen College - Brooklyn Park — MINNESOTA — 263
Rasmussen College Corporate Office — MINNESOTA — 263
Rasmussen College - Eagan — MINNESOTA — 263
Rasmussen College - Fargo/Moorhead — NORTH DAKOTA — 372
Rasmussen College - Fort Myers — FLORIDA — 111
Rasmussen College - Green Bay — WISCONSIN — 535
Rasmussen College-Kansas City/Overland Park — KANSAS — 190
Rasmussen College - Lake Elmo/Woodbury — MINNESOTA — 263
Rasmussen College - Land O'Lakes — FLORIDA — 111
Rasmussen College - Mankato — MINNESOTA — 263
Rasmussen College - Mokena/Tinley Park — ILLINOIS — 156
Rasmussen College - Moorhead Park — MINNESOTA — 263
Rasmussen College - New Port Richey — FLORIDA — 111
Rasmussen College - Ocala — FLORIDA — 111
Rasmussen College - Rockford — ILLINOIS — 156
Rasmussen College - Romeoville/Joliet — ILLINOIS — 156
Rasmussen College - St. Cloud — MINNESOTA — 263
Rasmussen College - Tampa/Brandon — FLORIDA — 111
Rasmussen College Topeka — KANSAS — 190
Rasmussen College - Wausau — WISCONSIN — 535
Reading Area Community College — PENNSYLVANIA — 431
Reconstructionist Rabbinical College — PENNSYLVANIA — 431
Red Rocks Community College — COLORADO — 84
Red Rocks Community College Arvada Campus — COLORADO — 84
Redeemer Theological Seminary — TEXAS — 478
Redlands Community College — OKLAHOMA — 399
Redstone College — COLORADO — 84
Redstone College-Denver East — COLORADO — 84
Reed College — OREGON — 407
Reedley College — CALIFORNIA — 69
Reformed Episcopal Seminary — PENNSYLVANIA — 431
Reformed Presbyterian Theological Seminary — PENNSYLVANIA — 431
Reformed Theological Seminary — FLORIDA — 111
Reformed Theological Seminary — MISSISSIPPI — 269
Reformed Theological Seminary — NORTH CAROLINA — 366
Reformed Theological Seminary — VIRGINIA — 508
Refrigeration School, The — ARIZONA — 17
Regent University — VIRGINIA — 508
Regis College — MASSACHUSETTS — 236
Regis University — COLORADO — 84
Regis University Las Vegas Campus — NEVADA — 295
Reid State Technical College — ALABAMA — 6
Reinhardt University — GEORGIA — 130
Relay Graduate School of Education — NEW YORK — 337
Remington College — TENNESSEE — 458
Remington College — TEXAS — 478
Remington College-Baton Rouge Campus — LOUISIANA — 206
Remington College Cleveland Campus — OHIO — 388
Remington College-Cleveland West Campus — OHIO — 388
Remington College-Colorado Springs — COLORADO — 85
Remington College-Dallas Campus — TEXAS — 478
Remington College-Fort Worth Campus — TEXAS — 478
Remington College-Honolulu Campus — HAWAII — 135
Remington College-Houston Southeast Campus — TEXAS — 478
Remington College-Lafayette Campus — LOUISIANA — 206
Remington College-Little Rock — ARKANSAS — 23
Remington College-North Houston Campus — TEXAS — 478
Remington College of Nursing — FLORIDA — 111
Remington College Online — FLORIDA — 111
Remington College-Shreveport — LOUISIANA — 206
Remington College-Tampa Campus — FLORIDA — 111
Remington College, Mobile Campus — ALABAMA — 6
Rend Lake College — ILLINOIS — 156
Rensselaer at Hartford — CONNECTICUT — 91
Rensselaer Polytechnic Institute — NEW YORK — 337
Renton Technical College — WASHINGTON — 522
Research College of Nursing — MISSOURI — 280
Restaurant School at Walnut Hill College, The — PENNSYLVANIA — 431
Resurrection University — ILLINOIS — 156
Rhode Island College — RHODE ISLAND — 439
Rhode Island School of Design — RHODE ISLAND — 440
Rhodes College — TENNESSEE — 458
Rice University — TEXAS — 479

Institution	State	Page
Rich Mountain Community College	ARKANSAS	23
Richard Bland College	VIRGINIA	508
Richard Gilder Graduate School at the American Museum of Natural History	NEW YORK	337
Richard Stockton College of New Jersey, The	NEW JERSEY	305
Richland College	TEXAS	471
Richland Community College	ILLINOIS	156
Richmond Community College	NORTH CAROLINA	362
Richmont Graduate University	TENNESSEE	458
Rider University	NEW JERSEY	305
Ridgewater College	MINNESOTA	260
Ridgewater College Hutchinson Campus	MINNESOTA	262
Ringling College of Art and Design	FLORIDA	111
Rio Grande Bible Institute	TEXAS	479
Rio Hondo College	CALIFORNIA	60
Rio Salado College	ARIZONA	15
Ripon College	WISCONSIN	535
River Parishes Community College	LOUISIANA	203
River Valley Community College	NEW HAMPSHIRE	296
Riverland Community College	MINNESOTA	260
Riverland Community College Albert Lea Campus	MINNESOTA	262
Riverside City College	CALIFORNIA	61
Riverside Community College District	CALIFORNIA	60
Riverside School of Health Careers	VIRGINIA	509
Rivier University	NEW HAMPSHIRE	297
Roane State Community College	TENNESSEE	461
Roanoke-Chowan Community College	NORTH CAROLINA	363
Roanoke College	VIRGINIA	509
Robert B. Miller College	MICHIGAN	249
Robert E. Webber Institute for Worship Studies, The	FLORIDA	111
Robert Morris University	ILLINOIS	156
Robert Morris University	PENNSYLVANIA	431
Roberts Wesleyan College	NEW YORK	337
Robeson Community College	NORTH CAROLINA	363
Rochester College	MICHIGAN	249
Rochester Community and Technical College	MINNESOTA	261
Rochester Institute of Technology	NEW YORK	337
Rock Valley College	ILLINOIS	157
Rockbridge Seminary	MISSOURI	280
Rockefeller University	NEW YORK	338
Rockford Career College	ILLINOIS	157
Rockford University	ILLINOIS	157
Rockhurst University	MISSOURI	280
Rockingham Community College	NORTH CAROLINA	363
Rockland Community College	NEW YORK	338
Rocky Mountain College	MONTANA	288
Rocky Mountain College of Art & Design	COLORADO	85
Rocky Mountain University of Health Professions	UTAH	496
Rocky Vista University	COLORADO	85
Roger Williams University	RHODE ISLAND	440
Rogers State University	OKLAHOMA	399
Rogers State University-Bartlesville	OKLAHOMA	399
Rogers State University-Pryor	OKLAHOMA	399
Rogue Community College	OREGON	407
Rollins College	FLORIDA	111
Roosevelt University	ILLINOIS	157
Roosevelt University Albert A. Robin Campus	ILLINOIS	157
Rosalind Franklin University of Medicine & Science	ILLINOIS	157
Rose-Hulman Institute of Technology	INDIANA	172
Rose State College	OKLAHOMA	399
Rosedale Bible College	OHIO	388
Rosedale Technical Institute	PENNSYLVANIA	432
Roseman University of Health Sciences	NEVADA	295
Rosemont College	PENNSYLVANIA	432
Rowan-Cabarrus Community College	NORTH CAROLINA	363
Rowan University	NEW JERSEY	305
Rowan University at Camden	NEW JERSEY	305
Roxbury Community College	MASSACHUSETTS	232
Rudolf Steiner College	CALIFORNIA	61
Ruidoso Branch Community College	NEW MEXICO	311
Rush University	ILLINOIS	157
Rust College	MISSISSIPPI	269
Rutgers Graduate School of Biomedical Sciences	NEW JERSEY	306
Rutgers-New Jersey Medical School	NEW JERSEY	306
Rutgers - Robert Wood Johnson Medical School	NEW JERSEY	306
Rutgers School of Dental Medicine	NEW JERSEY	306
Rutgers School of Health Related Professions	NEW JERSEY	306
Rutgers School of Nursing	NEW JERSEY	306
Rutgers-School of Public Health	NEW JERSEY	306
Rutgers the State University of New Jersey Camden Campus	NEW JERSEY	306
Rutgers the State University of New Jersey Central Office	NEW JERSEY	306
Rutgers the State University of New Jersey New Brunswick Campus	NEW JERSEY	306
Rutgers the State University of New Jersey Newark Campus	NEW JERSEY	306
Saber College	FLORIDA	112
Sacramento City College	CALIFORNIA	53
Sacred Heart Major Seminary	MICHIGAN	249
Sacred Heart School of Theology	WISCONSIN	535
Sacred Heart University	CONNECTICUT	91
Saddleback College	CALIFORNIA	67
SAE Institute Atlanta	GEORGIA	130
SAE Institute of Technology Nashville	TENNESSEE	458
Sage College	CALIFORNIA	61
Sage Colleges, The	NEW YORK	338
Saginaw Chippewa Tribal College	MICHIGAN	249
Saginaw Valley State University	MICHIGAN	249
St. Ambrose University	IOWA	182
St. Andrews University	NORTH CAROLINA	366
Saint Anselm College	NEW HAMPSHIRE	297
Saint Anthony College of Nursing	ILLINOIS	158
St. Anthony School of Echocardiography	INDIANA	172
St. Augustine College	ILLINOIS	158
Saint Augustine's University	NORTH CAROLINA	366
St. Bernard's School of Theology & Ministry	NEW YORK	338
St. Bonaventure University	NEW YORK	338
St. Catharine College	KENTUCKY	198
St. Catherine University	MINNESOTA	263
Saint Charles Borromeo Seminary	PENNSYLVANIA	432
St. Charles Community College	MISSOURI	280
St. Clair County Community College	MICHIGAN	249
St. Cloud State University	MINNESOTA	261
Saint Cloud Technical and Community College	MINNESOTA	261
St. Edward's University	TEXAS	479
St. Elizabeth College of Nursing	NEW YORK	338
St. Francis College	NEW YORK	338
Saint Francis Medical Center College of Nursing	ILLINOIS	158
Saint Francis University	PENNSYLVANIA	432
Saint Gregory the Great Seminary	NEBRASKA	292
St. Gregory's University	OKLAHOMA	399
St. Gregory's University Tulsa Campus	OKLAHOMA	399
St. John Fisher College	NEW YORK	338
St. John Vianney College Seminary	FLORIDA	112
St. John Vianney Theological Seminary	COLORADO	85
St. John's College	ILLINOIS	158
St. John's College	MARYLAND	217
St. John's College	NEW MEXICO	311
St. Johns River State College	FLORIDA	112
Saint John's Seminary	CALIFORNIA	61
Saint John's Seminary	MASSACHUSETTS	236
Saint John's University	MINNESOTA	263
St. John's University	NEW YORK	339
St. Joseph School of Nursing	NEW HAMPSHIRE	297
Saint Joseph Seminary College	LOUISIANA	206
Saint Joseph's College	INDIANA	172
Saint Joseph's College of Maine	MAINE	211
St. Joseph's College of Nursing	NEW YORK	339
Saint Joseph's College, New York	NEW YORK	339
Saint Joseph's College, New York - Suffolk Campus	NEW YORK	339
Saint Joseph's Seminary	NEW YORK	339
Saint Joseph's University	PENNSYLVANIA	432
St. Lawrence University	NEW YORK	339
Saint Leo University	FLORIDA	112
Saint Louis Christian College	MISSOURI	280
Saint Louis College of Health Careers-Fenton Campus	MISSOURI	281
Saint Louis College of Health Careers-South Taylor	MISSOURI	281
St. Louis College of Pharmacy	MISSOURI	281
Saint Louis Community College at Florissant Valley	MISSOURI	281
Saint Louis Community College at Forest Park	MISSOURI	281
Saint Louis Community College at Meramec	MISSOURI	281
Saint Louis Community College at Wildwood	MISSOURI	281
Saint Louis Community College Center	MISSOURI	281
Saint Louis University	MISSOURI	281
St. Luke's College	IOWA	182
Saint Luke's College of Health Sciences	MISSOURI	281
Saint Martin's University	WASHINGTON	522
Saint Mary-of-the-Woods College	INDIANA	172
Saint Mary Seminary and Graduate School of Theology	OHIO	388
Saint Mary's College	INDIANA	172
Saint Mary's College of California	CALIFORNIA	61
St. Mary's College of Maryland	MARYLAND	218
Saint Mary's Seminary and University	MARYLAND	218
St. Mary's University	TEXAS	479
Saint Mary's University of Minnesota	MINNESOTA	264
Saint Meinrad School of Theology	INDIANA	173
Saint Michael's College	VERMONT	500
Saint Norbert College	WISCONSIN	535
St. Olaf College	MINNESOTA	264
Saint Patrick's Seminary & University	CALIFORNIA	61
Saint Paul College-A Community & Technical College	MINNESOTA	261
Saint Paul School of Theology	KANSAS	190
St. Paul's School of Nursing	NEW YORK	339
Saint Paul's School of Nursing-Staten Island	NEW YORK	339
Saint Peter's University	NEW JERSEY	306
Saint Peter's University Englewood Cliffs Campus	NEW JERSEY	307
St. Petersburg College	FLORIDA	112
St. Philip's College	TEXAS	465
St. Thomas Aquinas College	NEW YORK	340
St. Thomas University	FLORIDA	112
St. Tikhon's Orthodox Theological Seminary	PENNSYLVANIA	432
Saint Vincent College	PENNSYLVANIA	432
St. Vincent De Paul Regional Seminary	FLORIDA	112
Saint Vincent Seminary	PENNSYLVANIA	432
St. Vincent's College	CONNECTICUT	91
Saint Vladimir's Orthodox Theological Seminary	NEW YORK	340
Saint Xavier University	ILLINOIS	158
Saint Xavier University Orland Park Campus	ILLINOIS	158
Salem College	NORTH CAROLINA	366
Salem Community College	NEW JERSEY	307
Salem International University	WEST VIRGINIA	527
Salem State University	MASSACHUSETTS	230
Salina Area Technical College	KANSAS	190
Salisbury University	MARYLAND	220
Salish Kootenai College	MONTANA	288
Salt Lake Community College	UTAH	498
Salter College	MASSACHUSETTS	236
Salus University	PENNSYLVANIA	433
Salvation Army College for Officer Training	NEW YORK	340
Salvation Army College for Officer Training at Crestmont, The	CALIFORNIA	61
Salve Regina University	RHODE ISLAND	440
Sam Houston State University	TEXAS	487
Samaritan Hospital School of Nursing	NEW YORK	340
Samford University	ALABAMA	6
Sampson Community College	NORTH CAROLINA	363
Samuel Merritt University	CALIFORNIA	61

Institution	State	Page
San Antonio College	TEXAS	465
San Bernardino Community College District	CALIFORNIA	61
San Bernardino Valley College	CALIFORNIA	62
San Diego Christian College	CALIFORNIA	62
San Diego City College	CALIFORNIA	62
San Diego Community College District Administrative Offices	CALIFORNIA	62
San Diego Mesa College	CALIFORNIA	62
San Diego Miramar College	CALIFORNIA	62
San Diego State University	CALIFORNIA	35
San Francisco Art Institute	CALIFORNIA	62
San Francisco Conservatory of Music	CALIFORNIA	62
San Francisco State University	CALIFORNIA	35
San Francisco Theological Seminary	CALIFORNIA	63
San Ignacio College	FLORIDA	112
San Jacinto College Central	TEXAS	479
San Jacinto College District	TEXAS	479
San Jacinto College North	TEXAS	479
San Jacinto College South	TEXAS	479
San Joaquin College of Law	CALIFORNIA	63
San Joaquin Delta College	CALIFORNIA	63
San Joaquin Valley College-Bakersfield	CALIFORNIA	63
San Joaquin Valley College-Fresno	CALIFORNIA	63
San Joaquin Valley College-Fresno Aviation Campus	CALIFORNIA	63
San Joaquin Valley College-Hanford	CALIFORNIA	63
San Joaquin Valley College-Modesto	CALIFORNIA	63
San Joaquin Valley College-Rancho Cordova	CALIFORNIA	63
San Joaquin Valley College-Rancho Cucamonga	CALIFORNIA	63
San Joaquin Valley College-Temecula	CALIFORNIA	63
San Joaquin Valley College-Victor Valley (Hesperia)	CALIFORNIA	63
San Joaquin Valley College, Inc. - Visalia	CALIFORNIA	63
San Jose City College	CALIFORNIA	63
San Jose/Evergreen Community College District	CALIFORNIA	63
San Jose State University	CALIFORNIA	36
San Juan Bautista School of Medicine	PUERTO RICO	552
San Juan College	NEW MEXICO	311
San Mateo County Community College District Office	CALIFORNIA	64
Sandford-Brown College	OHIO	388
Sandhills Community College	NORTH CAROLINA	363
Sanford-Brown College	ARIZONA	17
Sanford-Brown College	GEORGIA	131
Sanford-Brown College	ILLINOIS	158
Sanford-Brown College	INDIANA	173
Sanford-Brown College	MICHIGAN	249
Sanford-Brown College	MISSOURI	281
Sanford-Brown College	OREGON	407
Sanford-Brown College	TEXAS	480
Sanford-Brown College-Farmington	CONNECTICUT	91
Sanford-Brown College-Houston	TEXAS	480
Sanford-Brown College of Boston, Inc.	MASSACHUSETTS	236
Sanford-Brown College-Tysons Corner	VIRGINIA	509
Sanford-Brown Institute	FLORIDA	112
Sanford-Brown Institute	FLORIDA	113
Sanford-Brown Institute	FLORIDA	112
Sanford-Brown Institute	FLORIDA	113
Sanford-Brown Institute	PENNSYLVANIA	433
Sanford-Brown Institute-Pittsburgh	PENNSYLVANIA	433
Sanford-Brown Institute-Wilkins Township	PENNSYLVANIA	433
Sanford-Burnham Graduate School of Biomedical Sciences	CALIFORNIA	64
Sanford College of Nursing	NORTH DAKOTA	372
SANS Technology Institute, The	MARYLAND	218
Santa Ana College	CALIFORNIA	60
Santa Barbara Business College	CALIFORNIA	64
Santa Barbara Business College-Online	CALIFORNIA	64
Santa Barbara City College	CALIFORNIA	64
Santa Clara University	CALIFORNIA	64
Santa Fe College	FLORIDA	113
Santa Fe Community College	NEW MEXICO	311
Santa Fe University of Art and Design	NEW MEXICO	311
Santa Monica College	CALIFORNIA	65
Santa Rosa Junior College	CALIFORNIA	65
Santiago Canyon College	CALIFORNIA	60
Sarah Lawrence College	NEW YORK	340
Sauk Valley Community College	ILLINOIS	158
Savannah College of Art and Design	GEORGIA	131
Savannah State University	GEORGIA	131
Savannah Technical College	GEORGIA	131
Saybrook University	CALIFORNIA	65
SBI Campus-An Affiliate of Sanford-Brown	NEW YORK	340
Schenectady County Community College	NEW YORK	340
Schiller International University	FLORIDA	113
School of Advanced Air and Space Studies	US SERVICE SCHOOLS	545
School of Advertising Art	OHIO	388
School of Professional Psychology at Forest Institute, The	MISSOURI	281
School of the Art Institute of Chicago	ILLINOIS	158
School of the Museum of Fine Arts-Boston	MASSACHUSETTS	236
School of Visual Arts	NEW YORK	340
Schoolcraft College	MICHIGAN	250
Schreiner University	TEXAS	480
Scott Community College	IOWA	178
Scottsdale Community College	ARIZONA	15
Scripps College	CALIFORNIA	65
Scripps Research Institute, The	CALIFORNIA	65
Seattle Central Community College	WASHINGTON	522
Seattle Community Colleges	WASHINGTON	522
Seattle Institute of Oriental Medicine	WASHINGTON	523
Seattle Pacific University	WASHINGTON	523
Seattle School of Theology and Psychology, The	WASHINGTON	523
Seattle University	WASHINGTON	523
Selma University	ALABAMA	6
Seminario Teologico de Puerto Rico	PUERTO RICO	552
Seminary of the Southwest	TEXAS	480
Seminole State College	OKLAHOMA	399
Seminole State College of Florida	FLORIDA	113
Sentara College of Health Sciences	VIRGINIA	509
Sessions College for Professional Design	ARIZONA	17
Seton Hall University	NEW JERSEY	307
Seton Hall University School of Law	NEW JERSEY	307
Seton Hill University	PENNSYLVANIA	433
Sewanee: The University of the South	TENNESSEE	458
Seward County Community College/Area Technical School	KANSAS	190
Shasta Bible College and Graduate School	CALIFORNIA	65
Shasta College	CALIFORNIA	65
Shaw University	NORTH CAROLINA	366
Shawnee Community College	ILLINOIS	158
Shawnee State University	OHIO	388
Shelton State Community College	ALABAMA	6
Shenandoah University	VIRGINIA	509
Shepherd University	WEST VIRGINIA	529
Shepherd University School of Theology	CALIFORNIA	66
Shepherds Theological Seminary	NORTH CAROLINA	366
Sherman College of Chiropractic	SOUTH CAROLINA	446
Shiloh University	IOWA	182
Shimer College	ILLINOIS	159
Shippensburg University of Pennsylvania	PENNSYLVANIA	429
Sh'or Yoshuv Rabbinical College	NEW YORK	340
Shoreline Community College	WASHINGTON	523
Shorter College	ARKANSAS	23
Shorter University	GEORGIA	131
Siena College	NEW YORK	340
Siena Heights University	MICHIGAN	250
Sierra College	CALIFORNIA	66
Sierra Nevada College	NEVADA	295
Silicon Valley University	CALIFORNIA	66
Silver Lake College of the Holy Family	WISCONSIN	536
Simmons College	MASSACHUSETTS	236
Simmons College of Kentucky	KENTUCKY	199
Simpson College	IOWA	182
Simpson College West Des Moines	IOWA	182
Simpson University	CALIFORNIA	66
Sinclair Community College	OHIO	388
Sinte Gleska University	SOUTH DAKOTA	451
Sioux Falls Seminary	SOUTH DAKOTA	451
Sisseton-Wahpeton College	SOUTH DAKOTA	451
Sistema Universitario Ana G. Mendez	PUERTO RICO	552
SIT	VERMONT	500
Sitting Bull College	NORTH DAKOTA	372
Skagit Valley College	WASHINGTON	523
Skidmore College	NEW YORK	341
Skyline College	CALIFORNIA	64
Skyline College	VIRGINIA	509
Slippery Rock University of Pennsylvania	PENNSYLVANIA	429
Smith College	MASSACHUSETTS	236
Snead State Community College	ALABAMA	6
Snow College	UTAH	498
Sofia University (formerly Institute of Transpersonal Psychology)	CALIFORNIA	66
Sojourner-Douglass College	MARYLAND	218
Soka University of America	CALIFORNIA	66
Solano Community College	CALIFORNIA	66
SOLEX College	ILLINOIS	159
Somerset Community College	KENTUCKY	196
Sonoma State University	CALIFORNIA	36
Sonoran Desert Institute	ARIZONA	17
Sotheby's Institute of Art	NEW YORK	341
South Arkansas Community College	ARKANSAS	23
South Baylo University	CALIFORNIA	66
South Baylo University	VIRGINIA	509
South Carolina State University	SOUTH CAROLINA	446
South Central College	MINNESOTA	261
South Central College Faribault Campus	MINNESOTA	262
South Central Louisiana Technical College Lafourche Campus	LOUISIANA	204
South Central Louisiana Technical College River Parishes Campus	LOUISIANA	204
South Central Louisiana Technical College Young Memorial Campus	LOUISIANA	203
South Coast College	CALIFORNIA	66
South College	TENNESSEE	458
South College-Asheville	NORTH CAROLINA	366
South Dakota School of Mines and Technology	SOUTH DAKOTA	452
South Dakota State Board of Regents System Office	SOUTH DAKOTA	451
South Dakota State University	SOUTH DAKOTA	452
South Florida Bible College	FLORIDA	113
South Florida State College	FLORIDA	113
South Georgia State College	GEORGIA	131
South Georgia Technical College	GEORGIA	131
South Hills School of Business and Technology	PENNSYLVANIA	433
South Louisiana Community College	LOUISIANA	203
South Louisiana Community College Ardoin Campus	LOUISIANA	203
South Louisiana Community College Charles B Coreil Campus	LOUISIANA	204
South Louisiana Community College Gulf Area Campus	LOUISIANA	204
South Louisiana Community College Teche Area Campus	LOUISIANA	204
South Louisiana Community College T.H. Harris Campus	LOUISIANA	204
South Mountain Community College	ARIZONA	15
South Orange County Community College District	CALIFORNIA	67
South Piedmont Community College	NORTH CAROLINA	363
South Plains College	TEXAS	480
South Puget Sound Community College	WASHINGTON	524
South Seattle Community College	WASHINGTON	523
South Suburban College of Cook County	ILLINOIS	159
South Suburban College of Cook County University and College Center	ILLINOIS	159
South Texas College	TEXAS	480
South Texas College of Law	TEXAS	480

Institution	State	Page
South University	ALABAMA	7
South University	FLORIDA	113
South University	GEORGIA	131
South University	MICHIGAN	249
South University	NORTH CAROLINA	366
South University	OHIO	389
South University	TEXAS	480
South University	VIRGINIA	509
South University Columbia Campus	SOUTH CAROLINA	446
Southcentral Kentucky Community and Technical College	KENTUCKY	196
Southeast Arkansas College	ARKANSAS	23
Southeast Community College	NEBRASKA	292
Southeast Culinary and Hospitality College	VIRGINIA	509
Southeast Kentucky Community and Technical College	KENTUCKY	196
Southeast Missouri Hospital College of Nursing and Health Sciences	MISSOURI	282
Southeast Missouri State University	MISSOURI	282
Southeast Technical Institute	SOUTH DAKOTA	452
Southeastern Baptist College	MISSISSIPPI	269
Southeastern Baptist Theological Seminary	NORTH CAROLINA	366
Southeastern Bible College	ALABAMA	7
Southeastern College	FLORIDA	113
Southeastern Community College	IOWA	182
Southeastern Community College	NORTH CAROLINA	364
Southeastern Community College Keokuk Campus	IOWA	182
Southeastern Illinois College	ILLINOIS	159
Southeastern Louisiana University	LOUISIANA	208
Southeastern Oklahoma State University	OKLAHOMA	399
Southeastern Technical College	GEORGIA	132
Southeastern University	FLORIDA	113
Southern Adventist University	TENNESSEE	458
Southern Arkansas University	ARKANSAS	23
Southern Arkansas University Tech	ARKANSAS	23
Southern Baptist Theological Seminary, The	KENTUCKY	199
Southern California College of Optometry	CALIFORNIA	67
Southern California Institute of Architecture	CALIFORNIA	67
Southern California Institute of Technology	CALIFORNIA	67
Southern California Seminary	CALIFORNIA	67
Southern California University of Health Sciences	CALIFORNIA	67
Southern California University School of Oriental Medicine and Acupuncture	CALIFORNIA	67
Southern College of Optometry	TENNESSEE	458
Southern Connecticut State University	CONNECTICUT	88
Southern Crescent Technical College	GEORGIA	132
Southern Evangelical Seminary	NORTH CAROLINA	366
Southern Illinois University	ILLINOIS	159
Southern Illinois University Carbondale	ILLINOIS	159
Southern Illinois University Carbondale School of Medicine	ILLINOIS	159
Southern Illinois University Edwardsville	ILLINOIS	159
Southern Maine Community College	MAINE	211
Southern Methodist University	TEXAS	481
Southern Nazarene University	OKLAHOMA	399
Southern New Hampshire University	NEW HAMPSHIRE	297
Southern Oregon University	OREGON	406
Southern Polytechnic State University	GEORGIA	132
Southern State Community College	OHIO	389
Southern State Community College Fayette Campus	OHIO	389
Southern State Community College North Campus	OHIO	389
Southern State Community College South Campus	OHIO	389
Southern States University	CALIFORNIA	67
Southern States University	CALIFORNIA	68
Southern Technical College	FLORIDA	114
Southern Technical College-Auburndale	FLORIDA	114
Southern Technical College-Brandon	FLORIDA	114
Southern Technical College-Mount Dora	FLORIDA	114
Southern Technical College-Orlando	FLORIDA	114
Southern Union State Community College	ALABAMA	7
Southern University and A&M College	LOUISIANA	206
Southern University and Agricultural & Mechanical College System Office	LOUISIANA	206
Southern University at New Orleans	LOUISIANA	206
Southern University at Shreveport-Louisiana	LOUISIANA	207
Southern Utah University	UTAH	497
Southern Vermont College	VERMONT	500
Southern Virginia University	VIRGINIA	509
Southern Wesleyan University	SOUTH CAROLINA	446
Southern West Virginia Community and Technical College.	WEST VIRGINIA	528
Southern West Virginia Community and Technical College-Boone/Lincoln Campus	WEST VIRGINIA	528
Southern West Virginia Community and Technical College-Williamson Campus	WEST VIRGINIA	528
Southern West Virginia Community and Technical College-Wyoming/McDowell Cam pus	WEST VIRGINIA	528
Southside Regional Medical Center Professional Schools	VIRGINIA	509
Southside Virginia Community College	VIRGINIA	513
Southwest Acupuncture College	COLORADO	85
Southwest Acupuncture College	NEW MEXICO	312
Southwest Acupuncture College-Albuquerque	NEW MEXICO	312
Southwest Baptist University	MISSOURI	282
Southwest Baptist University Mountain View Center	MISSOURI	282
Southwest Baptist University Salem Center	MISSOURI	282
Southwest Baptist University Springfield Center	MISSOURI	282
Southwest College of Naturopathic Medicine & Health Sciences	ARIZONA	17
Southwest Colorado Community College-East	COLORADO	85
Southwest Colorado Community College-West	COLORADO	85
Southwest Florida College	FLORIDA	114
Southwest Georgia Technical College	GEORGIA	132
Southwest Institute of Healing Arts	ARIZONA	17
Southwest Institute of Technology	TEXAS	481
Southwest Minnesota State University	MINNESOTA	261
Southwest Mississippi Community College	MISSISSIPPI	269
Southwest Tennessee Community College	TENNESSEE	461
Southwest Texas Junior College	TEXAS	481
Southwest University	LOUISIANA	207
Southwest University at El Paso	TEXAS	481
Southwest University of Visual Arts	ARIZONA	17
Southwest University of Visual Arts	NEW MEXICO	312
Southwest Virginia Community College	VIRGINIA	514
Southwest Wisconsin Technical College	WISCONSIN	541
Southwestern Adventist University	TEXAS	481
Southwestern Assemblies of God University	TEXAS	481
Southwestern Baptist Theological Seminary	TEXAS	481
Southwestern Christian College	TEXAS	481
Southwestern Christian University	OKLAHOMA	400
Southwestern College	CALIFORNIA	68
Southwestern College	KANSAS	190
Southwestern College	NEW MEXICO	312
Southwestern College Wichita East	KANSAS	190
Southwestern Community College	IOWA	182
Southwestern Community College	NORTH CAROLINA	364
Southwestern Illinois College	ILLINOIS	160
Southwestern Illinois College Granite City Campus	ILLINOIS	160
Southwestern Illinois College Red Bud Campus	ILLINOIS	160
Southwestern Indian Polytechnic Institute	NEW MEXICO	312
Southwestern Law School	CALIFORNIA	68
Southwestern Michigan College	MICHIGAN	250
Southwestern Michigan College Niles Area Campus	MICHIGAN	250
Southwestern Oklahoma State University	OKLAHOMA	400
Southwestern Oklahoma State University-Sayre	OKLAHOMA	400
Southwestern Oregon Community College	OREGON	407
Southwestern University	TEXAS	481
Sowela Technical Community College	LOUISIANA	204
Spalding University	KENTUCKY	199
Spartan College of Aeronautics and Technology	OKLAHOMA	400
Spartanburg Community College	SOUTH CAROLINA	447
Spartanburg Methodist College	SOUTH CAROLINA	447
Spelman College	GEORGIA	132
Spencerian College	KENTUCKY	199
Spertus Institute for Jewish Learning and Leadership	ILLINOIS	160
Spokane Community College	WASHINGTON	518
Spokane Falls Community College	WASHINGTON	518
Spoon River College	ILLINOIS	160
Spoon River College-Macomb Campus	ILLINOIS	160
Spring Arbor University	MICHIGAN	250
Spring Hill College	ALABAMA	7
Springfield College	MASSACHUSETTS	236
Springfield Technical Community College	MASSACHUSETTS	233
SS. Cyril and Methodius Seminary	MICHIGAN	250
Stanbridge College	CALIFORNIA	68
Standard Healthcare Services College of Nursing	VIRGINIA	510
Stanford University	CALIFORNIA	68
Stanly Community College	NORTH CAROLINA	364
Stanton University	CALIFORNIA	68
Stark State College	OHIO	389
Starr King School for the Ministry	CALIFORNIA	68
State Center Community College District	CALIFORNIA	68
State College of Florida, Manatee-Sarasota	FLORIDA	114
State Fair Community College	MISSOURI	282
State University of New York at Binghamton	NEW YORK	341
State University of New York at Fredonia	NEW YORK	342
State University of New York at New Paltz	NEW YORK	342
State University of New York at Stony Brook	NEW YORK	342
State University of New York College at Buffalo	NEW YORK	343
State University of New York College at Cortland	NEW YORK	343
State University of New York College at Geneseo	NEW YORK	343
State University of New York College at Old Westbury	NEW YORK	343
State University of New York College at Oneonta	NEW YORK	343
State University of New York College at Oswego	NEW YORK	344
State University of New York College at Plattsburgh	NEW YORK	344
State University of New York College at Potsdam	NEW YORK	344
State University of New York College of Agriculture and Technology at Coble skill	NEW YORK	344
State University of New York College of Agriculture and Technology at Morri sville	NEW YORK	345
State University of New York College of Environmental Science and Forestry	NEW YORK	345
State University of New York College of Optometry	NEW YORK	345
State University of New York College of Technology at Delhi	NEW YORK	345
State University of New York Empire State College	NEW YORK	346
State University of New York Health Science Center at Brooklyn	NEW YORK	342
State University of New York Institute of Technology at Utica-Rome	NEW YORK	346
State University of New York Maritime College	NEW YORK	346
State University of New York System Office	NEW YORK	341
State University of New York Upstate Medical University	NEW YORK	342
State University of New York, The College at Brockport	NEW YORK	342
State University System of Florida, Board of Governors	FLORIDA	114
Stautzenberger College	OHIO	389
Stephen F. Austin State University	TEXAS	482
Stephens College	MISSOURI	282
Sterling College	KANSAS	190
Sterling College	VERMONT	500
Stetson University	FLORIDA	117
Stevens-Henager College	IDAHO	139
Stevens-Henager College	UTAH	496
Stevens-Henager College-Boise	IDAHO	139
Stevens Institute of Business & Arts	MISSOURI	282
Stevens Institute of Technology	NEW JERSEY	307
Stevenson University	MARYLAND	218
Stillman College	ALABAMA	7
Stone Child College	MONTANA	288
Stonehill College	MASSACHUSETTS	237
Stratford University	VIRGINIA	510
Stratford University Baltimore Campus	MARYLAND	218
Strayer University	DISTRICT OF COLUMBIA	96

Institution	State	Page
Suffolk County Community College Ammerman Campus	NEW YORK	346
Suffolk County Community College Central Administration	NEW YORK	346
Suffolk County Community College Eastern Campus	NEW YORK	346
Suffolk County Community College Grant Campus	NEW YORK	346
Suffolk University	MASSACHUSETTS	237
Sul Ross State University	TEXAS	487
Sullivan College of Technology and Design	KENTUCKY	199
Sullivan County Community College	NEW YORK	347
Sullivan University	KENTUCKY	199
SUM Bible College and Theological Seminary	CALIFORNIA	69
Sumner College	OREGON	408
SUNY Adirondack	NEW YORK	345
SUNY Canton-College of Technology	NEW YORK	345
Surry Community College	NORTH CAROLINA	364
Susquehanna University	PENNSYLVANIA	433
Sussex County Community College	NEW JERSEY	307
Swarthmore College	PENNSYLVANIA	433
Swedish Institute--College of Health Sciences	NEW YORK	347
Sweet Briar College	VIRGINIA	510
Syracuse University Main Campus	NEW YORK	347
Tabor College	KANSAS	190
Tacoma Bible College	WASHINGTON	524
Tacoma Community College	WASHINGTON	524
Taft College	CALIFORNIA	69
Taft Law School	CALIFORNIA	69
Talladega College	ALABAMA	7
Tallahassee Community College	FLORIDA	117
Talmudic College of Florida	FLORIDA	117
Talmudical Academy of New Jersey	NEW JERSEY	307
Talmudical Institute of Upstate New York	NEW YORK	347
Talmudical Seminary of Bobov	NEW YORK	347
Talmudical Seminary Oholei Torah	NEW YORK	347
Talmudical Yeshiva of Philadelphia	PENNSYLVANIA	433
Tarleton State University	TEXAS	483
Tarrant County College District	TEXAS	482
Taylor Business Institute	ILLINOIS	160
Taylor University	INDIANA	173
TCM International Institute	INDIANA	173
Teachers College of San Joaquin	CALIFORNIA	69
Teachers College, Columbia University	NEW YORK	347
Technical Career Institutes	NEW YORK	347
Technical College of the Lowcountry	SOUTH CAROLINA	447
Telshe Yeshiva-Chicago	ILLINOIS	160
Temple College	TEXAS	482
Temple University	PENNSYLVANIA	433
Tennessee Board of Regents Office	TENNESSEE	459
Tennessee State University	TENNESSEE	459
Tennessee Technological University	TENNESSEE	460
Tennessee Temple University	TENNESSEE	462
Tennessee Wesleyan College	TENNESSEE	462
Terra State Community College	OHIO	389
TESST College of Technology	MARYLAND	218
Texarkana College	TEXAS	482
Texas A & M International University	TEXAS	483
Texas A & M University	TEXAS	483
Texas A & M University at Galveston	TEXAS	484
Texas A & M University Baylor College of Dentistry	TEXAS	484
Texas A & M University - Central Texas	TEXAS	483
Texas A & M University - Commerce	TEXAS	483
Texas A & M University - Corpus Christi	TEXAS	483
Texas A & M University - Kingsville	TEXAS	484
Texas A & M University-San Antonio	TEXAS	484
Texas A & M University System Health Science Center	TEXAS	484
Texas A & M University System Office, The	TEXAS	482
Texas A & M University - Texarkana	TEXAS	484
Texas Chiropractic College	TEXAS	484
Texas Christian University	TEXAS	484
Texas College	TEXAS	485
Texas County Technical College	MISSOURI	282
Texas Health and Science University	TEXAS	485
Texas Lutheran University	TEXAS	485
Texas School of Business	TEXAS	485
Texas School of Business-Friendswood	TEXAS	485
Texas Southern University	TEXAS	485
Texas State Technical College Harlingen	TEXAS	485
Texas State Technical College Marshall	TEXAS	486
Texas State Technical College System	TEXAS	485
Texas State Technical College Waco	TEXAS	486
Texas State Technical College West Texas	TEXAS	486
Texas State University-San Marcos	TEXAS	487
Texas State University System, The	TEXAS	486
Texas Tech University	TEXAS	487
Texas Tech University Health Sciences Center	TEXAS	487
Texas Wesleyan University	TEXAS	488
Texas Woman's University	TEXAS	488
Thaddeus Stevens College of Technology	PENNSYLVANIA	434
Theatre of Arts	CALIFORNIA	69
Thiel College	PENNSYLVANIA	434
Thomas Aquinas College	CALIFORNIA	69
Thomas College	MAINE	211
Thomas Edison State College	NEW JERSEY	308
Thomas Jefferson School of Law	CALIFORNIA	69
Thomas Jefferson University	PENNSYLVANIA	434
Thomas M. Cooley Law School	MICHIGAN	250
Thomas M. Cooley Law School Ann Arbor Campus	MICHIGAN	250
Thomas M. Cooley Law School Auburn Hills Campus	MICHIGAN	250
Thomas M. Cooley Law School Grand Rapids Campus	MICHIGAN	250
Thomas M. Cooley Law School Tampa Bay Campus	FLORIDA	117
Thomas More College	KENTUCKY	199
Thomas More College of Liberal Arts, The	NEW HAMPSHIRE	298
Thomas Nelson Community College	VIRGINIA	514
Thomas University	GEORGIA	132
Three Rivers Community College	CONNECTICUT	89
Three Rivers Community College	MISSOURI	282
Thunderbird School of Global Management	ARIZONA	18
Tidewater Community College	VIRGINIA	514
Tiffin University	OHIO	389
Tillamook Bay Community College	OREGON	408
Toccoa Falls College	GEORGIA	133
Tohono O'odham Community College	ARIZONA	18
Tohono O'odham Community College West Campus	ARIZONA	18
Tompkins Cortland Community College	NEW YORK	347
Torah Temimah Talmudical Seminary	NEW YORK	348
Tougaloo College	MISSISSIPPI	270
Touro College	NEW YORK	348
Touro College Bay Shore	NEW YORK	348
Touro College Flatbush	NEW YORK	348
Touro College Los Angeles	CALIFORNIA	69
Touro College South	FLORIDA	117
Touro Law School	NEW YORK	348
Touro University California	CALIFORNIA	69
Towson University	MARYLAND	220
Toyota Technological Institute at Chicago	ILLINOIS	160
Transylvania University	KENTUCKY	199
Treasure Valley Community College	OREGON	408
Trenholm State Technical College	ALABAMA	7
Trevecca Nazarene University	TENNESSEE	462
Tri-County Community College	NORTH CAROLINA	364
Tri-County Technical College	SOUTH CAROLINA	447
Tri-State Bible College	OHIO	389
Tri-State College of Acupuncture	NEW YORK	348
Triangle Tech	PENNSYLVANIA	434
Triangle Tech, Bethlehem	PENNSYLVANIA	434
Triangle Tech, Dubois	PENNSYLVANIA	434
Triangle Tech, Erie	PENNSYLVANIA	434
Triangle Tech, Greensburg	PENNSYLVANIA	434
Triangle Tech, Pittsburgh	PENNSYLVANIA	434
Tribeca Flashpoint Media Arts Academy	ILLINOIS	160
Trident Technical College	SOUTH CAROLINA	447
Trident University International	CALIFORNIA	70
Trine University	INDIANA	173
Trine University-Fort Wayne Regional Campus	INDIANA	173
Trine University-South Bend Regional Campus	INDIANA	173
Trinidad State Junior College	COLORADO	85
Trinidad State Junior College San Luis Valley Campus	COLORADO	85
Trinity Baptist College	FLORIDA	117
Trinity Bible College	NORTH DAKOTA	373
Trinity Christian College	ILLINOIS	160
Trinity College	CONNECTICUT	91
Trinity College of Florida	FLORIDA	117
Trinity College of Nursing & Health Sciences	ILLINOIS	160
Trinity Episcopal School for Ministry	PENNSYLVANIA	434
Trinity International University	ILLINOIS	160
Trinity International University, Florida Regional Center	FLORIDA	118
Trinity Law School	CALIFORNIA	70
Trinity Lutheran College	WASHINGTON	524
Trinity Lutheran Seminary	OHIO	390
Trinity University	TEXAS	488
Trinity Valley Community College	TEXAS	488
Trinity Washington University	DISTRICT OF COLUMBIA	96
Triton College	ILLINOIS	161
Trocaire College	NEW YORK	348
Troy University	ALABAMA	7
Truckee Meadows Community College	NEVADA	294
Truett McConnell College	GEORGIA	133
Truman State University	MISSOURI	282
Trumbull Business College	OHIO	390
Tufts University	MASSACHUSETTS	237
Tulane University	LOUISIANA	207
Tulsa Community College	OKLAHOMA	400
Tulsa Community College Metro Campus	OKLAHOMA	400
Tulsa Community College Northeast Campus	OKLAHOMA	400
Tulsa Community College Southeast Campus	OKLAHOMA	400
Tulsa Community College West Campus	OKLAHOMA	400
Tulsa Welding School	OKLAHOMA	400
Tunxis Community College	CONNECTICUT	89
Turtle Mountain Community College	NORTH DAKOTA	373
Tusculum College	TENNESSEE	462
Tuskegee University	ALABAMA	8
Tyler Junior College	TEXAS	488
UCH Memorial Hospital School Of Radiologic Technology	COLORADO	85
Uintah Basin Applied Technology College	UTAH	496
Ulster County Community College	NEW YORK	348
Ultimate Medical Academy-Clearwater	FLORIDA	118
Ultimate Medical Academy Online-Tampa	FLORIDA	118
Umpqua Community College	OREGON	408
Unification Theological Seminary	NEW YORK	348
Uniformed Services University of the Health Sciences	US SERVICE SCHOOLS	545
Unilatina International College	FLORIDA	118
Union College	KENTUCKY	200
Union College	NEBRASKA	292
Union College	NEW YORK	348
Union County College	NEW JERSEY	308
Union County College Elizabeth Campus	NEW JERSEY	308
Union County College Plainfield Campus	NEW JERSEY	308
Union County College Scotch Plains	NEW JERSEY	308
Union Graduate College	NEW YORK	348
Union Institute & University	OHIO	390
Union Presbyterian Seminary	VIRGINIA	510
Union Theological Seminary	NEW YORK	349
Union University	TENNESSEE	462
United Education Institute	CALIFORNIA	70
United States Air Force Academy	US SERVICE SCHOOLS	545
United States Army Command and General Staff College	US SERVICE SCHOOLS	545
United States Army War College	US SERVICE SCHOOLS	545
United States Coast Guard Academy	US SERVICE SCHOOLS	545

United States Merchant Marine Academy .... US SERVICE SCHOOLS 545
United States Military Academy .... US SERVICE SCHOOLS 545
United States Naval Academy .... US SERVICE SCHOOLS 545
United States Sports Academy .... ALABAMA 8
United States University .... CALIFORNIA 70
United Talmudical Seminary .... NEW YORK 349
United Theological Seminary .... OHIO 390
United Theological Seminary of the Twin Cities .... MINNESOTA 264
United Tribes Technical College .... NORTH DAKOTA 373
Unitek College .... CALIFORNIA 70
Unity College .... MAINE 211
Universal College of Healing Arts .... NEBRASKA 292
Universal Technical Institute .... ARIZONA 18
Universal Technology College of Puerto Rico .... PUERTO RICO 553
Universidad Adventista de las Antillas .... PUERTO RICO 553
Universidad Central Del Caribe .... PUERTO RICO 553
Universidad del Este .... PUERTO RICO 552
Universidad Del Turabo .... PUERTO RICO 552
Universidad Metropolitana .... PUERTO RICO 552
Universidad Pentecostal Mizpa .... PUERTO RICO 553
Universidad Politecnica De Puerto Rico .... PUERTO RICO 553
Universidad Teologica Del Caribe .... PUERTO RICO 553
University at Albany, SUNY .... NEW YORK 341
University at Buffalo-SUNY .... NEW YORK 341
University of Advancing Technology .... ARIZONA 18
University of Akron-Wayne College, The .... OHIO 390
University of Akron, Main Campus, The .... OHIO 390
University of Alabama at Birmingham .... ALABAMA 8
University of Alabama in Huntsville .... ALABAMA 8
University of Alabama System Office .... ALABAMA 8
University of Alabama, The .... ALABAMA 8
University of Alaska Anchorage .... ALASKA 10
University of Alaska Fairbanks .... ALASKA 10
University of Alaska Southeast .... ALASKA 11
University of Alaska System .... ALASKA 10
University of Antelope Valley .... CALIFORNIA 70
University of Arizona .... ARIZONA 18
University of Arizona Phoenix Biomedical Campus .... ARIZONA 18
University of Arizona South .... ARIZONA 18
University of Arkansas at Fort Smith .... ARKANSAS 24
University of Arkansas at Little Rock .... ARKANSAS 24
University of Arkansas at Monticello .... ARKANSAS 24
University of Arkansas at Monticello College of Technology-Crussett .... ARKANSAS 25
University of Arkansas at Monticello College of Technology-McGehee .... ARKANSAS 25
University of Arkansas at Pine Bluff .... ARKANSAS 24
University of Arkansas Community College at Batesville .... ARKANSAS 25
University of Arkansas Community College at Hope .... ARKANSAS 25
University of Arkansas Community College at Morrilton .... ARKANSAS 25
University of Arkansas for Medical Sciences .... ARKANSAS 24
University of Arkansas Main Campus .... ARKANSAS 23
University of Arkansas System Office .... ARKANSAS 23
University of Baltimore .... MARYLAND 221
University of Bridgeport .... CONNECTICUT 91
University of California-Berkeley .... CALIFORNIA 70
University of California-Davis .... CALIFORNIA 70
University of California-Hastings College of the Law .... CALIFORNIA 71
University of California-Irvine .... CALIFORNIA 71
University of California-Los Angeles .... CALIFORNIA 71
University of California-Merced .... CALIFORNIA 71
University of California Office of the President .... CALIFORNIA 70
University of California-Riverside .... CALIFORNIA 71
University of California-San Diego .... CALIFORNIA 71
University of California-San Francisco .... CALIFORNIA 72
University of California-Santa Barbara .... CALIFORNIA 72
University of California-Santa Cruz .... CALIFORNIA 72
University of Central Arkansas .... ARKANSAS 25
University of Central Florida .... FLORIDA 115
University of Central Missouri .... MISSOURI 283
University of Central Oklahoma .... OKLAHOMA 400
University of Charleston .... WEST VIRGINIA 527
University of Chicago .... ILLINOIS 161
University of Cincinnati-Blue Ash College .... OHIO 391
University of Cincinnati-Clermont College .... OHIO 391
University of Cincinnati Main Campus .... OHIO 390
University of Colorado Boulder .... COLORADO 85
University of Colorado Colorado Springs .... COLORADO 85
University of Colorado DenverlAnschutz Medical Campus .... COLORADO 86
University of Colorado System Office .... COLORADO 85
University of Connecticut .... CONNECTICUT 92
University of Connecticut Health Center .... CONNECTICUT 92
University of Connecticut School of Law .... CONNECTICUT 92
University of Dallas .... TEXAS 488
University of Dayton .... OHIO 391
University of Delaware .... DELAWARE 94
University of Denver .... COLORADO 86
University of Detroit Mercy .... MICHIGAN 250
University of Detroit Mercy Corktown Campus .... MICHIGAN 251
University of Detroit Mercy Riverfront Campus .... MICHIGAN 251
University of Dubuque .... IOWA 182
University of East-West Medicine .... CALIFORNIA 72
University of Evansville .... INDIANA 173
University of Fairfax .... VIRGINIA 510
University of Findlay, The .... OHIO 391
University of Florida .... FLORIDA 116
University of Fort Lauderdale .... FLORIDA 118
University of Georgia .... GEORGIA 133
University of Great Falls .... MONTANA 288
University of Guam .... GUAM 546
University of Hartford .... CONNECTICUT 92
University of Hawaii at Hilo .... HAWAII 136
University of Hawaii at Manoa .... HAWAII 136
University of Hawaii Community Colleges .... HAWAII 136
University of Hawaii Hawaii Community College .... HAWAII 136
University of Hawaii Honolulu Community College .... HAWAII 136
University of Hawaii Kauai Community College .... HAWAII 136
University of Hawaii Leeward Community College .... HAWAII 137
University of Hawaii Maui College .... HAWAII 137
University of Hawaii System Office .... HAWAII 135
University of Hawaii - West Oahu .... HAWAII 136
University of Hawaii Windward Community College .... HAWAII 137
University of Houston .... TEXAS 489
University of Houston - Clear Lake .... TEXAS 489
University of Houston - Downtown .... TEXAS 489
University of Houston System .... TEXAS 489
University of Houston - Victoria .... TEXAS 489
University of Idaho .... IDAHO 139
University of Illinois at Chicago .... ILLINOIS 161
University of Illinois at Chicago College of Medicine at Peoria .... ILLINOIS 162
University of Illinois at Chicago College of Medicine at Rockford .... ILLINOIS 162
University of Illinois at Chicago College of Medicine at Urbana .... ILLINOIS 162
University of Illinois at Springfield .... ILLINOIS 161
University of Illinois at Urbana-Champaign .... ILLINOIS 162
University of Illinois University Administration .... ILLINOIS 161
University of Indianapolis .... INDIANA 173
University of Iowa .... IOWA 175
University of Jamestown .... NORTH DAKOTA 373
University of Kansas Edwards Campus .... KANSAS 190
University of Kansas Main Campus .... KANSAS 190
University of Kansas Medical Center .... KANSAS 191
University of Kentucky .... KENTUCKY 200
University of LaVerne .... CALIFORNIA 72
University of Louisiana at Lafayette .... LOUISIANA 208
University of Louisiana at Monroe .... LOUISIANA 208
University of Louisiana System Office .... LOUISIANA 207
University of Louisville .... KENTUCKY 200
University of Maine .... MAINE 212
University of Maine at Augusta .... MAINE 212
University of Maine at Farmington .... MAINE 212
University of Maine at Fort Kent .... MAINE 212
University of Maine at Machias .... MAINE 212
University of Maine at Presque Isle .... MAINE 212
University of Maine System Office .... MAINE 212
University of Management & Technology .... VIRGINIA 510
University of Mary .... NORTH DAKOTA 373
University of Mary Hardin-Baylor .... TEXAS 490
University of Mary Washington .... VIRGINIA 510
University of Maryland Baltimore .... MARYLAND 219
University of Maryland Baltimore County .... MARYLAND 219
University of Maryland College Park .... MARYLAND 219
University of Maryland Eastern Shore .... MARYLAND 219
University of Maryland University College .... MARYLAND 219
University of Massachusetts .... MASSACHUSETTS 228
University of Massachusetts Boston .... MASSACHUSETTS 228
University of Massachusetts Central Office .... MASSACHUSETTS 228
University of Massachusetts Dartmouth .... MASSACHUSETTS 229
University of Massachusetts Lowell .... MASSACHUSETTS 229
University of Massachusetts Medical School .... MASSACHUSETTS 229
University of Memphis, The .... TENNESSEE 460
University of Miami .... FLORIDA 118
University of Michigan-Ann Arbor .... MICHIGAN 251
University of Michigan-Dearborn .... MICHIGAN 251
University of Michigan-Flint .... MICHIGAN 251
University of Minnesota-Crookston .... MINNESOTA 264
University of Minnesota Duluth .... MINNESOTA 264
University of Minnesota-Morris .... MINNESOTA 264
University of Minnesota-Twin Cities .... MINNESOTA 264
University of Minnesota-Twin Cities Rochester Campus .... MINNESOTA 265
University of Mississippi .... MISSISSIPPI 270
University of Mississippi Medical Center .... MISSISSIPPI 270
University of Missouri - Columbia .... MISSOURI 283
University of Missouri - Kansas City .... MISSOURI 283
University of Missouri - Saint Louis .... MISSOURI 283
University of Missouri System Administration .... MISSOURI 283
University of Mobile .... ALABAMA 9
University of Montana - Helena College of Technology, The .... MONTANA 287
University of Montana - Missoula College, The .... MONTANA 288
University of Montana - Missoula, The .... MONTANA 286
University of Montana Western, The .... MONTANA 286
University of Montevallo .... ALABAMA 9
University of Mount Union .... OHIO 391
University of Nebraska at Kearney .... NEBRASKA 292
University of Nebraska at Omaha .... NEBRASKA 293
University of Nebraska Central Administration .... NEBRASKA 292
University of Nebraska - Lincoln .... NEBRASKA 292
University of Nebraska Medical Center .... NEBRASKA 292
University of Nebraska - Nebraska College of Technical Agriculture .... NEBRASKA 293
University of Nevada, Las Vegas .... NEVADA 294
University of Nevada, Reno .... NEVADA 294
University of New England .... MAINE 213
University of New Hampshire .... NEW HAMPSHIRE 298
University of New Hampshire at Manchester .... NEW HAMPSHIRE 298
University of New Hampshire School of Law .... NEW HAMPSHIRE 298
University of New Haven .... CONNECTICUT 92
University of New Mexico-Gallup .... NEW MEXICO 312
University of New Mexico-Los Alamos .... NEW MEXICO 312
University of New Mexico Main Campus .... NEW MEXICO 312
University of New Mexico-Taos .... NEW MEXICO 312
University of New Mexico-Valencia .... NEW MEXICO 312
University of New Orleans .... LOUISIANA 205
University of North Alabama .... ALABAMA 9
University of North Carolina at Asheville .... NORTH CAROLINA 368

University of North Carolina at Chapel Hill ..... NORTH CAROLINA 368
University of North Carolina at Charlotte ..... NORTH CAROLINA 368
University of North Carolina at Greensboro ..... NORTH CAROLINA 369
University of North Carolina at Pembroke ..... NORTH CAROLINA 369
University of North Carolina General Administration ..... NORTH CAROLINA 366
University of North Carolina School of the Arts ..... NORTH CAROLINA 369
University of North Carolina Wilmington ..... NORTH CAROLINA 369
University of North Dakota Main Campus ..... NORTH DAKOTA 371
University of North Florida ..... FLORIDA 116
University of North Georgia ..... GEORGIA 133
University of North Texas ..... TEXAS 490
University of North Texas at Dallas ..... TEXAS 490
University of North Texas Health Science Center at Fort Worth ..... TEXAS 490
University of Northern Colorado ..... COLORADO 86
University of Northern Iowa ..... IOWA 176
University of Northwestern Ohio ..... OHIO 391
University of Notre Dame ..... INDIANA 174
University of Oklahoma Health Sciences Center ..... OKLAHOMA 401
University of Oklahoma Norman Campus ..... OKLAHOMA 401
University of Oklahoma Schusterman Center ..... OKLAHOMA 401
University of Oregon ..... OREGON 406
University of Pennsylvania ..... PENNSYLVANIA 435
University of Philosophical Research ..... CALIFORNIA 73
University of Phoenix ..... ARIZONA 18
University of Phoenix Atlanta Campus ..... GEORGIA 133
University of Phoenix Augusta Campus ..... GEORGIA 133
University of Phoenix Austin Campus ..... TEXAS 490
University of Phoenix Baton Rouge Campus ..... LOUISIANA 209
University of Phoenix Bay Area Campus ..... CALIFORNIA 73
University of Phoenix Birmingham Campus ..... ALABAMA 9
University of Phoenix Boston Campus ..... MASSACHUSETTS 237
University of Phoenix Central Valley Campus ..... CALIFORNIA 73
University of Phoenix Charlotte Campus ..... NORTH CAROLINA 370
University of Phoenix Chicago Campus ..... ILLINOIS 162
University of Phoenix Cleveland Main Campus ..... OHIO 391
University of Phoenix Colorado Main Campus ..... COLORADO 86
University of Phoenix Colorado Springs Main Campus ..... COLORADO 86
University of Phoenix Columbia SC Campus ..... SOUTH CAROLINA 447
University of Phoenix Columbus GA Campus ..... GEORGIA 133
University of Phoenix Dallas Campus ..... TEXAS 490
University of Phoenix Des Moines Campus ..... IOWA 183
University of Phoenix Detroit Main Campus ..... MICHIGAN 251
University of Phoenix El Paso Campus ..... TEXAS 490
University of Phoenix Hawaii Campus ..... HAWAII 137
University of Phoenix Houston Campus ..... TEXAS 490
University of Phoenix Idaho Campus ..... IDAHO 139
University of Phoenix Indianapolis Campus ..... INDIANA 174
University of Phoenix Jackson Campus ..... MISSISSIPPI 270
University of Phoenix Jersey City Campus ..... NEW JERSEY 308
University of Phoenix Kansas City Campus ..... MISSOURI 284
University of Phoenix Las Vegas Campus ..... NEVADA 295
University of Phoenix Little Rock Campus ..... ARKANSAS 25
University of Phoenix Louisville Campus ..... KENTUCKY 200
University of Phoenix Maryland Campus ..... MARYLAND 218
University of Phoenix McAllen Campus ..... TEXAS 490
University of Phoenix Memphis Campus ..... TENNESSEE 462
University of Phoenix Milwaukee Main Campus ..... WISCONSIN 536
University of Phoenix Minneapolis/St. Paul Campus ..... MINNESOTA 265
University of Phoenix Nashville Campus ..... TENNESSEE 463
University of Phoenix New Mexico Campus ..... NEW MEXICO 312
University of Phoenix North Florida Campus ..... FLORIDA 118
University of Phoenix Oklahoma City Campus ..... OKLAHOMA 401
University of Phoenix Omaha Campus ..... NEBRASKA 293
University of Phoenix Oregon Campus ..... OREGON 408
University of Phoenix Richmond-Virginia Beach Campus ..... VIRGINIA 510
University of Phoenix Sacramento Valley Campus ..... CALIFORNIA 73
University of Phoenix St. Louis Campus ..... MISSOURI 284
University of Phoenix San Antonio Campus ..... TEXAS 490
University of Phoenix San Diego Campus ..... CALIFORNIA 73
University of Phoenix Savannah Campus ..... GEORGIA 133
University of Phoenix South Florida Main Campus ..... FLORIDA 118
University of Phoenix Southern Arizona Campus ..... ARIZONA 19
University of Phoenix Southern California Campus ..... CALIFORNIA 73
University of Phoenix Utah Campus ..... UTAH 496
University of Phoenix Washington DC Campus ..... DISTRICT OF COLUMBIA 97
University of Phoenix Western Washington Campus ..... WASHINGTON 524
University of Pikeville ..... KENTUCKY 200
University of Pittsburgh ..... PENNSYLVANIA 435
University of Pittsburgh at Bradford ..... PENNSYLVANIA 435
University of Pittsburgh at Greensburg ..... PENNSYLVANIA 435
University of Pittsburgh at Johnstown ..... PENNSYLVANIA 435
University of Pittsburgh at Titusville ..... PENNSYLVANIA 435
University of Portland ..... OREGON 408
University of Puerto Rico-Aguadilla ..... PUERTO RICO 553
University of Puerto Rico at Arecibo ..... PUERTO RICO 553
University of Puerto Rico at Bayamon ..... PUERTO RICO 554
University of Puerto Rico at Cayey ..... PUERTO RICO 554
University of Puerto Rico at Ponce ..... PUERTO RICO 555
University of Puerto Rico at Utuado ..... PUERTO RICO 555
University of Puerto Rico-Carolina ..... PUERTO RICO 554
University of Puerto Rico-Central Administration ..... PUERTO RICO 553
University of Puerto Rico-Humacao ..... PUERTO RICO 554
University of Puerto Rico-Mayaguez Campus ..... PUERTO RICO 554
University of Puerto Rico-Medical Sciences Campus ..... PUERTO RICO 554
University of Puerto Rico-Rio Piedras Campus ..... PUERTO RICO 555
University of Puget Sound ..... WASHINGTON 524
University of Redlands ..... CALIFORNIA 73
University of Rhode Island ..... RHODE ISLAND 440
University of Rhode Island Feinstein Providence Campus ..... RHODE ISLAND 440
University of Rhode Island Narragansett Bay Campus ..... RHODE ISLAND 440
University of Richmond ..... VIRGINIA 510
University of Rio Grande ..... OHIO 392
University of Rochester ..... NEW YORK 349
University of St. Augustine for Health Sciences ..... FLORIDA 118
University of St. Francis ..... ILLINOIS 162
University of Saint Francis ..... INDIANA 174
University of St. Francis ..... NEW MEXICO 312
University of Saint Joseph ..... CONNECTICUT 92
University of Saint Joseph School of Pharmacy ..... CONNECTICUT 92
University of Saint Mary ..... KANSAS 191
University of Saint Mary of the Lake-Mundelein Seminary ..... ILLINOIS 162
University of Saint Thomas ..... MINNESOTA 265
University of St. Thomas ..... TEXAS 490
University of San Diego ..... CALIFORNIA 73
University of San Francisco ..... CALIFORNIA 73
University of Science and Arts of Oklahoma ..... OKLAHOMA 401
University of Scranton, The ..... PENNSYLVANIA 436
University of Sioux Falls ..... SOUTH DAKOTA 452
University of South Alabama ..... ALABAMA 9
University of South Carolina Aiken ..... SOUTH CAROLINA 448
University of South Carolina Beaufort ..... SOUTH CAROLINA 448
University of South Carolina Columbia ..... SOUTH CAROLINA 447
University of South Carolina Lancaster ..... SOUTH CAROLINA 448
University of South Carolina Salkehatchie ..... SOUTH CAROLINA 448
University of South Carolina School of Medicine-Greenville ..... SOUTH CAROLINA 448
University of South Carolina Sumter ..... SOUTH CAROLINA 448
University of South Carolina Union ..... SOUTH CAROLINA 448
University of South Carolina Upstate ..... SOUTH CAROLINA 448
University of South Dakota, The ..... SOUTH DAKOTA 451
University of South Florida ..... FLORIDA 116
University of South Florida St. Petersburg ..... FLORIDA 116
University of South Florida Sarasota-Manatee ..... FLORIDA 117
University of Southern California ..... CALIFORNIA 74
University of Southern Indiana ..... INDIANA 174
University of Southern Maine ..... MAINE 212
University of Southern Mississippi ..... MISSISSIPPI 270
University of Southernmost Florida ..... FLORIDA 118
University of Southernmost Florida-Coral Gables Campus ..... FLORIDA 118
University of Tampa ..... FLORIDA 118
University of Tennessee at Chattanooga ..... TENNESSEE 463
University of Tennessee at Martin ..... TENNESSEE 463
University of Tennessee Health Science Center ..... TENNESSEE 463
University of Tennessee System Office ..... TENNESSEE 463
University of Tennessee, Knoxville ..... TENNESSEE 463
University of Texas at Arlington, The ..... TEXAS 491
University of Texas at Austin ..... TEXAS 491
University of Texas at Brownsville and Texas Southmost College, The ..... TEXAS 491
University of Texas at Dallas, The ..... TEXAS 491
University of Texas at El Paso ..... TEXAS 492
University of Texas at San Antonio ..... TEXAS 492
University of Texas at Tyler ..... TEXAS 492
University of Texas Health Science Center at Houston (UTHealth), The ..... TEXAS 492
University of Texas Health Science Center at San Antonio. ..... TEXAS 493
University of Texas M.D. Anderson Cancer Center, The ..... TEXAS 493
University of Texas Medical Branch, The ..... TEXAS 493
University of Texas of the Permian Basin ..... TEXAS 493
University of Texas - Pan American ..... TEXAS 492
University of Texas Southwestern Medical Center ..... TEXAS 493
University of Texas System Administration ..... TEXAS 491
University of the Arts, The ..... PENNSYLVANIA 435
University of the Cumberlands ..... KENTUCKY 200
University of the District of Columbia ..... DISTRICT OF COLUMBIA 97
University of the Incarnate Word ..... TEXAS 490
University of the Ozarks ..... ARKANSAS 25
University of the Pacific ..... CALIFORNIA 73
University of the Potomac ..... DISTRICT OF COLUMBIA 97
University of the Potomac ..... VIRGINIA 511
University of the Rockies ..... COLORADO 86
University of the Sacred Heart ..... PUERTO RICO 555
University of the Sciences in Philadelphia ..... PENNSYLVANIA 435
University of the Southwest ..... NEW MEXICO 312
University of the Virgin Islands ..... VIRGIN ISLANDS 555
University of the Virgin Islands-St. Croix ..... VIRGIN ISLANDS 555
University of the West ..... CALIFORNIA 74
University of Toledo ..... OHIO 392
University of Tulsa ..... OKLAHOMA 401
University of Utah, The ..... UTAH 496
University of Vermont ..... VERMONT 500
University of Virginia ..... VIRGINIA 511
University of Virginia's College at Wise, The ..... VIRGINIA 511
University of Washington ..... WASHINGTON 524
University of West Alabama, The ..... ALABAMA 9
University of West Florida ..... FLORIDA 117
University of West Georgia ..... GEORGIA 133
University of Western States ..... OREGON 408
University of Wisconsin Baraboo/Sauk County ..... WISCONSIN 538
University of Wisconsin Barron County ..... WISCONSIN 538
University of Wisconsin Colleges ..... WISCONSIN 538
University of Wisconsin-Eau Claire ..... WISCONSIN 536
University of Wisconsin Fond du Lac ..... WISCONSIN 538
University of Wisconsin Fox Valley ..... WISCONSIN 538
University of Wisconsin-Green Bay ..... WISCONSIN 536
University of Wisconsin-La Crosse ..... WISCONSIN 536
University of Wisconsin-Madison ..... WISCONSIN 536
University of Wisconsin Manitowoc ..... WISCONSIN 538
University of Wisconsin Marathon County ..... WISCONSIN 538
University of Wisconsin Marinette ..... WISCONSIN 538
University of Wisconsin Marshfield/Wood County ..... WISCONSIN 538
University of Wisconsin-Milwaukee ..... WISCONSIN 537
University of Wisconsin-Oshkosh ..... WISCONSIN 537
University of Wisconsin-Parkside ..... WISCONSIN 537
University of Wisconsin-Platteville ..... WISCONSIN 537
University of Wisconsin Richland ..... WISCONSIN 538
University of Wisconsin-River Falls ..... WISCONSIN 537
University of Wisconsin Rock County ..... WISCONSIN 539

Institution	State	Page
University of Wisconsin Sheboygan	WISCONSIN	539
University of Wisconsin-Stevens Point	WISCONSIN	538
University of Wisconsin-Stout	WISCONSIN	538
University of Wisconsin-Superior	WISCONSIN	538
University of Wisconsin System	WISCONSIN	536
University of Wisconsin Washington County	WISCONSIN	539
University of Wisconsin Waukesha	WISCONSIN	539
University of Wisconsin-Whitewater	WISCONSIN	538
University of Wyoming	WYOMING	543
University System of Georgia Office	GEORGIA	134
University System of Maryland Office, The	MARYLAND	219
University System of New Hampshire	NEW HAMPSHIRE	298
Upper Iowa University	IOWA	183
Urban College of Boston	MASSACHUSETTS	237
Urbana University	OHIO	392
Urshan Graduate School of Theology	MISSOURI	284
Ursinus College	PENNSYLVANIA	436
Ursuline College	OHIO	392
U.S. Career Institute	COLORADO	86
USC The Business College	NEW YORK	349
U.T.A. Mesivta of Kiryas Joel	NEW YORK	349
Utah College of Dental Hygiene at Careers Unlimited, The	UTAH	496
Utah State University	UTAH	497
Utah State University Eastern	UTAH	498
Utah System of Higher Education	UTAH	496
Utah Valley University	UTAH	497
Utica College	NEW YORK	349
Valdosta State University	GEORGIA	134
Valencia College	FLORIDA	118
Valley City State University	NORTH DAKOTA	372
Valley College - Beckley Campus	WEST VIRGINIA	527
Valley College - Martinsburg Campus	WEST VIRGINIA	527
Valley College of Medical Careers	CALIFORNIA	74
Valley Forge Christian College	PENNSYLVANIA	436
Valley Forge Military College	PENNSYLVANIA	436
Valor Christian College	OHIO	392
Valparaiso University	INDIANA	174
Van Andel Institute Graduate School	MICHIGAN	251
Vance-Granville Community College	NORTH CAROLINA	364
Vanderbilt University	TENNESSEE	463
VanderCook College of Music	ILLINOIS	162
Vanguard University of Southern California	CALIFORNIA	74
Vassar College	NEW YORK	349
Vatterott Career College	TENNESSEE	463
Vatterott College-Cleveland	OHIO	392
Vatterott College-Des Moines	IOWA	183
Vatterott College-Joplin	MISSOURI	284
Vatterott College-Kansas City	MISSOURI	284
Vatterott College-Memphis	TENNESSEE	463
Vatterott College-NorthPark	MISSOURI	284
Vatterott College-Oklahoma City	OKLAHOMA	401
Vatterott College-Omaha	NEBRASKA	293
Vatterott College-Quincy	ILLINOIS	162
Vatterott College-St. Charles	MISSOURI	284
Vatterott College-Saint Joseph	MISSOURI	284
Vatterott College-Springfield	MISSOURI	284
Vatterott College-Sunset Hills	MISSOURI	284
Vatterott College-Tulsa	OKLAHOMA	401
Vatterott College - Wichita	KANSAS	191
Vaughn College of Aeronautics and Technology	NEW YORK	349
Venango College of Clarion University	PENNSYLVANIA	430
Ventura College	CALIFORNIA	74
Ventura County Community College District	CALIFORNIA	74
Veritas Evangelical Seminary	CALIFORNIA	75
Vermilion Community College	MINNESOTA	261
Vermont College of Fine Arts	VERMONT	500
Vermont Law School	VERMONT	500
Vermont State Colleges System Office	VERMONT	501
Vermont Technical College	VERMONT	501
Vernon College	TEXAS	493
Vet Tech Institute	PENNSYLVANIA	436
Vet Tech Institute of Houston	TEXAS	493
Victor Valley College	CALIFORNIA	75
Victoria College	TEXAS	493
Victory University (formerly Crichton College)	TENNESSEE	463
Villa Maria College of Buffalo	NEW YORK	350
Villanova University	PENNSYLVANIA	436
Vincennes University	INDIANA	174
Vincennes University-Jasper Center	INDIANA	175
Virginia Baptist College	VIRGINIA	511
Virginia College	ALABAMA	3
Virginia College	FLORIDA	119
Virginia College	GEORGIA	134
Virginia College	LOUISIANA	209
Virginia College	MISSISSIPPI	270
Virginia College	NORTH CAROLINA	370
Virginia College	OKLAHOMA	401
Virginia College	SOUTH CAROLINA	448
Virginia College	SOUTH CAROLINA	449
Virginia College	VIRGINIA	511
Virginia College Austin	TEXAS	494
Virginia College School of Business and Health	TENNESSEE	464
Virginia Commonwealth University	VIRGINIA	511
Virginia Community College System Office	VIRGINIA	511
Virginia Highlands Community College	VIRGINIA	514
Virginia Intermont College	VIRGINIA	514
Virginia International University	VIRGINIA	515
Virginia Marti College of Art & Design	OHIO	392
Virginia Military Institute	VIRGINIA	515
Virginia Polytechnic Institute and State University	VIRGINIA	515
Virginia State University	VIRGINIA	515
Virginia Tech Carilion School of Medicine	VIRGINIA	515
Virginia Union University	VIRGINIA	515
Virginia University of Lynchburg	VIRGINIA	515
Virginia Wesleyan College	VIRGINIA	515
Virginia Western Community College	VIRGINIA	514
Visible Music College	TENNESSEE	464
Vista College	TEXAS	494
Vista College	UTAH	498
Viterbo University	WISCONSIN	539
Volunteer State Community College	TENNESSEE	461
Voorhees College	SOUTH CAROLINA	449
Wabash College	INDIANA	175
Wade College Infomart	TEXAS	494
Wagner College	NEW YORK	350
Wake Forest University	NORTH CAROLINA	370
Wake Technical Community College	NORTH CAROLINA	364
Walden University	MINNESOTA	265
Waldorf College	IOWA	183
Walla Walla Community College	WASHINGTON	524
Walla Walla University	WASHINGTON	524
Wallace State Community College - Hanceville	ALABAMA	9
Walsh College Novi Campus	MICHIGAN	251
Walsh College of Accountancy and Business Administration	MICHIGAN	251
Walsh University	OHIO	392
Walters State Community College	TENNESSEE	462
Warner Pacific College	OREGON	408
Warner University	FLORIDA	119
Warren County Community College	NEW JERSEY	308
Warren Wilson College	NORTH CAROLINA	370
Wartburg College	IOWA	183
Wartburg Theological Seminary	IOWA	183
Washburn University	KANSAS	191
Washington & Jefferson College	PENNSYLVANIA	436
Washington Adventist University	MARYLAND	221
Washington and Lee University	VIRGINIA	516
Washington Baptist University	VIRGINIA	516
Washington College	MARYLAND	221
Washington County Community College	MAINE	211
Washington State Community College	OHIO	392
Washington State University	WASHINGTON	525
Washington University in St. Louis	MISSOURI	284
Washington University in St. Louis-School of Medicine	MISSOURI	284
Washtenaw Community College	MICHIGAN	252
Watkins College of Art, Design & Film	TENNESSEE	464
Waubonsee Community College	ILLINOIS	162
Waukesha County Technical College	WISCONSIN	541
Wayland Baptist University	TEXAS	494
Wayne Community College	NORTH CAROLINA	364
Wayne County Community College District	MICHIGAN	252
Wayne County Community College District Downriver Campus	MICHIGAN	252
Wayne County Community College District Eastern Campus	MICHIGAN	252
Wayne County Community College District Northwest Campus	MICHIGAN	252
Wayne County Community College District Western Campus	MICHIGAN	252
Wayne State College	NEBRASKA	291
Wayne State University	MICHIGAN	252
Waynesburg University	PENNSYLVANIA	437
Weatherford College	TEXAS	494
Webb Institute	NEW YORK	350
Webber International University	FLORIDA	119
Weber State University	UTAH	497
Webster University	MISSOURI	284
Weill Cornell Medical College	NEW YORK	350
Welch College	TENNESSEE	464
Wellesley College	MASSACHUSETTS	237
Wells College	NEW YORK	350
Wenatchee Valley College	WASHINGTON	525
Wentworth Institute of Technology	MASSACHUSETTS	237
Wentworth Military Academy and Junior College	MISSOURI	285
Wesley Biblical Seminary	MISSISSIPPI	270
Wesley College	DELAWARE	94
Wesley Theological Seminary	DISTRICT OF COLUMBIA	97
Wesleyan College	GEORGIA	134
Wesleyan University	CONNECTICUT	92
West Chester University of Pennsylvania	PENNSYLVANIA	430
West Coast Ultrasound Institute	ARIZONA	19
West Coast Ultrasound Institute	CALIFORNIA	75
West Coast University	CALIFORNIA	75
West Coast University	TEXAS	494
West Georgia Technical College	GEORGIA	134
West Hills College Coalinga	CALIFORNIA	75
West Hills College Lemoore	CALIFORNIA	75
West Hills Community College District	CALIFORNIA	75
West Kentucky Community and Technical College	KENTUCKY	196
West Liberty University	WEST VIRGINIA	530
West Los Angeles College	CALIFORNIA	52
West Shore Community College	MICHIGAN	252
West Tennessee Business College	TENNESSEE	464
West Texas A & M University	TEXAS	484
West Valley College	CALIFORNIA	75
West Valley-Mission Community College District	CALIFORNIA	75
West Virginia Business College	WEST VIRGINIA	527
West Virginia Council for Community & Technical College Education	WEST VIRGINIA	527
West Virginia Higher Education Policy Commission	WEST VIRGINIA	529
West Virginia Junior College	WEST VIRGINIA	531
West Virginia Northern Community College	WEST VIRGINIA	529
West Virginia Northern Community College	WEST VIRGINIA	528
West Virginia Northern Community College	WEST VIRGINIA	529
West Virginia School of Osteopathic Medicine	WEST VIRGINIA	530
West Virginia State University	WEST VIRGINIA	530

Institution	State	Page
West Virginia University	WEST VIRGINIA	530
West Virginia University at Parkersburg	WEST VIRGINIA	530
West Virginia University Institute of Technology	WEST VIRGINIA	531
West Virginia Wesleyan College	WEST VIRGINIA	531
Westchester Community College	NEW YORK	350
Western Carolina University	NORTH CAROLINA	369
Western Colorado Community College-Tilman M. Bishop Campus	COLORADO	86
Western Connecticut State University	CONNECTICUT	88
Western Dakota Technical Institute	SOUTH DAKOTA	452
Western Governors University	UTAH	498
Western Illinois University	ILLINOIS	162
Western Illinois University Quad Cities	ILLINOIS	163
Western International University	ARIZONA	19
Western International University East Valley Campus	ARIZONA	19
Western International University Ft. Huachuca Campus	ARIZONA	19
Western International University Peoria Campus	ARIZONA	19
Western International University Scottsdale Campus	ARIZONA	19
Western Iowa Tech Community College	IOWA	183
Western Kentucky University	KENTUCKY	200
Western Michigan University	MICHIGAN	252
Western Nebraska Community College	NEBRASKA	293
Western Nebraska Community College Alliance Campus	NEBRASKA	293
Western Nebraska Community College Sidney Campus	NEBRASKA	293
Western Nevada College	NEVADA	295
Western New England University	MASSACHUSETTS	238
Western New Mexico University	NEW MEXICO	312
Western Oklahoma State College	OKLAHOMA	401
Western Oregon University	OREGON	406
Western Piedmont Community College	NORTH CAROLINA	365
Western Seminary	OREGON	408
Western State Colorado University	COLORADO	86
Western State University College of Law	CALIFORNIA	76
Western Technical College	TEXAS	494
Western Technical College	WISCONSIN	541
Western Texas College	TEXAS	494
Western Theological Seminary	MICHIGAN	252
Western University of Health Sciences	CALIFORNIA	76
Western Washington University	WASHINGTON	525
Western Wyoming Community College	WYOMING	543
Western Wyoming Community College Outreach Afton/Star Valley	WYOMING	543
Western Wyoming Community College Outreach Evanston	WYOMING	544
Westfield State University	MASSACHUSETTS	230
Westminster Choir College	NEW JERSEY	308
Westminster College	MISSOURI	285
Westminster College	PENNSYLVANIA	437
Westminster College	UTAH	498
Westminster Theological Seminary	PENNSYLVANIA	437
Westminster Theological Seminary in California	CALIFORNIA	76
Westmont College	CALIFORNIA	76
Westmoreland County Community College	PENNSYLVANIA	437
Westwood College	COLORADO	87
Westwood College-Anaheim	CALIFORNIA	76
Westwood College-Annandale	VIRGINIA	516
Westwood College-Arlington Ballston	VIRGINIA	516
Westwood College-Atlanta Midtown	GEORGIA	134
Westwood College-Atlanta Northlake	GEORGIA	134
Westwood College-Chicago Loop	ILLINOIS	163
Westwood College-Denver North	COLORADO	87
Westwood College-Denver South	COLORADO	87
Westwood College-DuPage	ILLINOIS	163
Westwood College-Inland Empire	CALIFORNIA	76
Westwood College - Los Angeles Campus	CALIFORNIA	76
Westwood College-O'Hare Airport	ILLINOIS	163
Westwood College-Online	COLORADO	87
Westwood College-River Oaks	ILLINOIS	163
Westwood College-South Bay	CALIFORNIA	76
Wharton County Junior College	TEXAS	494
Whatcom Community College	WASHINGTON	525
Wheaton College	ILLINOIS	163
Wheaton College	MASSACHUSETTS	238
Wheeling Jesuit University	WEST VIRGINIA	531
Wheelock College	MASSACHUSETTS	238
White Earth Tribal and Community College	MINNESOTA	265
White Mountains Community College	NEW HAMPSHIRE	296
Whitman College	WASHINGTON	525
Whittier College	CALIFORNIA	76
Whitworth University	WASHINGTON	525
Wichita Area Technical College	KANSAS	191
Wichita State University	KANSAS	191
Wichita Technical Institute	KANSAS	191
Widener University	PENNSYLVANIA	437
Widener University School of Law	DELAWARE	94
Wilberforce University	OHIO	393
Wiley College	TEXAS	495
Wilkes Community College	NORTH CAROLINA	365
Wilkes University	PENNSYLVANIA	437
Willamette University	OREGON	408
William Carey University	MISSISSIPPI	270
William Howard Taft University	COLORADO	87
William Jessup University	CALIFORNIA	76
William Jewell College	MISSOURI	285
William Mitchell College of Law	MINNESOTA	265
William Paterson University of New Jersey	NEW JERSEY	308
William Peace University (formerly Peace College)	NORTH CAROLINA	370
William Penn University	IOWA	183
William Woods University	MISSOURI	285
Williams Baptist College	ARKANSAS	25
Williams College	MASSACHUSETTS	238
Williamsburg Technical College	SOUTH CAROLINA	449
Williamson Christian College	TENNESSEE	464
Williamson Free School of Mechanical Trades	PENNSYLVANIA	437
Williston State College	NORTH DAKOTA	372
Willow International Community College Center	CALIFORNIA	69
Wilmington College	OHIO	393
Wilmington College Blue Ash Branch	OHIO	393
Wilmington University	DELAWARE	94
Wilson College	PENNSYLVANIA	437
Wilson Community College	NORTH CAROLINA	365
Winebrenner Theological Seminary	OHIO	393
Wingate University	NORTH CAROLINA	370
Winona State University	MINNESOTA	262
Winona State University-Rochester	MINNESOTA	262
Winston-Salem State University	NORTH CAROLINA	370
Winthrop University	SOUTH CAROLINA	449
Wiregrass Georgia Technical College	GEORGIA	134
Wisconsin Indianhead Technical College	WISCONSIN	541
Wisconsin Indianhead Technical College-Ashland Campus	WISCONSIN	542
Wisconsin Indianhead Technical College-New Richmond Campus	WISCONSIN	542
Wisconsin Indianhead Technical College-Rice Lake Campus	WISCONSIN	542
Wisconsin Indianhead Technical College-Superior Campus	WISCONSIN	542
Wisconsin Lutheran College	WISCONSIN	539
Wisconsin School of Professional Psychology	WISCONSIN	539
Wisconsin Technical College System	WISCONSIN	539
Wittenberg University	OHIO	393
W.L. Bonner College	SOUTH CAROLINA	449
Wofford College	SOUTH CAROLINA	449
Wolford College	FLORIDA	119
Won Institute of Graduate Studies	PENNSYLVANIA	438
Wood Tobé-Coburn School	NEW YORK	350
Woodbury University	CALIFORNIA	76
Woodland Community College	CALIFORNIA	77
Woods Hole Oceanographic Institution	MASSACHUSETTS	238
Wor-Wic Community College	MARYLAND	221
Worcester Polytechnic Institute	MASSACHUSETTS	238
Worcester State University	MASSACHUSETTS	230
World College	VIRGINIA	516
World Medicine Institute	HAWAII	137
World Mission University	CALIFORNIA	77
Worsham College of Mortuary Science	ILLINOIS	163
Wright Career College	KANSAS	191
Wright Career College	NEBRASKA	293
Wright Career College	OKLAHOMA	401
Wright Institute, The	CALIFORNIA	77
Wright State University Lake Campus	OHIO	393
Wright State University Main Campus	OHIO	393
WyoTech	FLORIDA	119
WyoTech	WYOMING	544
WyoTech-Blairsville	PENNSYLVANIA	438
WyoTech-Fremont	CALIFORNIA	77
WyoTech-Long Beach	CALIFORNIA	77
WyoTech-Sacramento	CALIFORNIA	77
Wytheville Community College	VIRGINIA	514
Xavier University	OHIO	393
Xavier University of Louisiana	LOUISIANA	209
Yakima Valley Community College	WASHINGTON	525
Yale University	CONNECTICUT	93
Yavapai College	ARIZONA	19
Yavapai College Verde Valley Campus	ARIZONA	19
Yeshiva and Kolel Bais Medrash Elyon	NEW YORK	351
Yeshiva and Kollel Harbotzas Torah	NEW YORK	351
Yeshiva Beth Moshe	PENNSYLVANIA	438
Yeshiva Beth Yehuda - Yeshiva Gedolah of Greater Detroit	MICHIGAN	253
Yeshiva College of the Nation's Capital	MARYLAND	221
Yeshiva Derech Chaim	NEW YORK	350
Yeshiva D'Monsey Rabbinical College	NEW YORK	350
Yeshiva Gedolah Imrei Yosef D'Spinka	NEW YORK	350
Yeshiva Gedolah Kesser Torah	NEW YORK	351
Yeshiva Gedolah Ohr Yisrael	NEW YORK	351
Yeshiva Gedolah Rabbinical College	FLORIDA	119
Yeshiva Gedolah Zichron Leyma	NEW JERSEY	308
Yeshiva Karlin Stolin Beth Aaron V'Israel Rabbinical Institute	NEW YORK	351
Yeshiva Mikdash Melech	NEW YORK	351
Yeshiva of Far Rockaway	NEW YORK	350
Yeshiva of Machzikai Hadas	NEW YORK	351
Yeshiva of Nitra Rabbinical College	NEW YORK	351
Yeshiva of the Telshe Alumni	NEW YORK	351
Yeshiva Ohr Elchonon Chabad/West Coast Talmudical Seminary	CALIFORNIA	77
Yeshiva Shaar HaTorah-Grodno	NEW YORK	351
Yeshiva Shaarei Torah of Rockland	NEW YORK	351
Yeshiva Sholom Shachna	NEW YORK	351
Yeshiva Toras Chaim	NEW JERSEY	308
Yeshiva Toras Chaim Talmudical Seminary of Denver	COLORADO	87
Yeshiva University	NEW YORK	351
Yeshiva Yesodei Hatorah	NEW JERSEY	308
Yeshiva Zichron Aryeh	NEW YORK	351
Yeshivas Be'er Yitzchok	NEW JERSEY	308
Yeshivas Novominsk	NEW YORK	351
Yeshivath Viznitz	NEW YORK	352
Yeshivath Zichron Moshe	NEW YORK	352
Yo San University of Traditional Chinese Medicine	CALIFORNIA	77
York College	NEBRASKA	293
York College of Pennsylvania	PENNSYLVANIA	438
York County Community College	MAINE	211
York Technical College	SOUTH CAROLINA	449
Yorktowne Business Institute	PENNSYLVANIA	438
Yosemite Community College District	CALIFORNIA	77
Young Harris College	GEORGIA	134
Youngstown State University	OHIO	394
YTI Career Institute	PENNSYLVANIA	438

YTI Career Institute-Capital Region .... PENNSYLVANIA 438
Yuba College .... CALIFORNIA 77
Yuba Community College District .... CALIFORNIA 77

Zane State College .... OHIO 394
Zarem/Golde ORT Technical Institute .... ILLINOIS 163